THE
CONCISE DICTIONARY
OF
NATIONAL BIOGRAPHY

The Index and Epitome to the Main Work and its Supplement, printed by Spottiswoode & Co., published by Smith, Elder & Co., 1903; second edition from plates, 1906; reprinted at the Oxford University Press, 1920, 1924, 1925, and 1930.

Index and Epitome 1901–1911, printed by Spottiswoode & Co. and published by Smith, Elder & Co., 1913; reprinted at the Oxford University Press, 1920, 1924, and 1925.

Epitome of 1901–1911, combined with Epitome of 1912–1921 in one alphabet, 1930.

PREFACE

(BY SIR SIDNEY LEE)

THIS Volume was designed by the late Mr. George Smith, the proprietor and publisher of the 'Dictionary of National Biography,' in consultation with the present Editor, when the great work was nearing completion. It is intended to form a summary guide to the vast and varied contents of the Dictionary and its Supplement. Every name, about which substantive biographic information is given in the sixty-three volumes of the Dictionary or in the three Supplementary Volumes, finds mention here in due alphabetical order. An Epitome is given of the leading facts and dates that have been already recorded at length in the pages of the original work, and there is added a precise reference to the volume and page where the full article appears.

Generally speaking, each entry in the Index and Epitome consists of one-fourteenth of the number of words that appear in the text of the original memoir. At times this proportion varies to a small extent. Condensation of a very brief article on the estimated scale became hardly possible if any intelligible fragment of it were to be preserved. In such instances the Epitome bears to the original article a higher proportion than one-fourteenth. On the other hand, in the case of the longer articles, it has often been found possible to reduce them to a smaller space than the stipulated proportion required. But the aggregate divergence from the projected ratio of one-fourteenth proves to be very slight.

The exclusive aim of the Index and Epitome is to make bare facts and dates as ready of rapid reference as possible. The condensation has been attempted with the sole object of serving the practical purposes of utility. No endeavour has been made to satisfy the requirements of literary form. With a view to economising space, and in harmony with the simple objects of the Index, the lists of authorities which are appended to each article of the Dictionary, and form one of its most distinctive features, have been ignored. The plan of the Epitome has compelled, too, the systematic suppression of other particulars which are invariably accorded a place in the articles of the Dictionary. Years of birth and death are alone admitted to the Index; the day of the month is suffered to pass unnoticed. Precise details of parentage are only introduced in cases where the parents form the subjects of separate entries and it has been found desirable to define the relationship subsisting between one entry and another. Places of birth or death are omitted unless they belong to a foreign country; in such instances it is usually essential to the intelligibility of the memoir to state where the career described in it began or ended. On the other hand, room has been found for all memorable achievements with the dates of their accomplishment, for titles of an author's chief books with dates of publication, for notices of scientific inventions, for dates of institution to offices, and for detailed particulars of education.

A few errors of fact and date which figure in the original work have been corrected in the Index. But, with that reservation, the Index literally reflects in brief and bald outline the results embodied in the Dictionary and Supplement.

The labour involved in condensing so massive a work as the 'Dictionary of National Biography' and Supplement has been great. No one without practical experience of similar undertakings is likely to realise the vast amount of time and trouble which the preparation of this Volume has entailed on all engaged in its production. The separate articles which it supplies amount to 30,378; the cross-references number 3,474. The risks of error in handling the million facts and dates which are embodied in the book are obvious, but the Editor feels justified in assuring those into whose hands this Volume comes that his assistants and himself have done all in their power to reduce the chances of error to the lowest possible limit.

The Editor tenders his best thanks to those who have co-operated with him in the laborious undertaking. The work of epitomising the Dictionary and Supplement has been distributed thus:

DICTIONARY OF NATIONAL BIOGRAPHY:

Volumes I.—VI.	Mr. C. E. HUGHES.
VII.—XII.	The Rev. ANDREW CLARK, M.A.
XIII.—XVIII.	Mr. RICHARD GREENTREE, B.A.
XIX.—XXX.	Mr. G. LE GRYS NORGATE, B.A.
XXXI.—XXXV.	Miss ELIZABETH LEE.
XXXVI.	Mr. P. C. YORKE, M.A.
XXXVII.—XLI.	Mr. A. F. POLLARD, M.A.
XLII.	Mr. G. LE GRYS NORGATE, B.A.
XLIII.—XLVIII.	Mr. E. I. CARLYLE, M.A.
XLIX.—LI.	Mr. C. E. HUGHES.
LII.	Mr. G. LE GRYS NORGATE, B.A.
LIII.	Mr. THOMAS SECCOMBE, M.A.
LIV.	Mr. G. LE GRYS NORGATE, B.A.
LV.—LVII.	Mr. P. C. YORKE, M.A.
LVIII.—LX.	The Rev. ANDREW CLARK, M.A.
LXI.—LXIII.	Mr. C. E. HUGHES.

SUPPLEMENT TO DICTIONARY OF NATIONAL BIOGRAPHY:

Volumes I.—III.	Mr. C. E. HUGHES.

In revising both the manuscripts and the proofs of the Index and Epitome, which have been very voluminous, the Editor has had the advantage of the assistance of Mr. RICHARD GREENTREE, B.A., formerly scholar of Balliol College, Oxford, and Craven Scholar of the University.

January 21, 1903.

CONTENTS

NOTE ON THE DICTIONARY

The *Dictionary of National Biography* comprises the following distinct works:

The D.N.B. from the earliest times to 1900, 22 volumes, in alphabetical order throughout the series except that Vol. 22 is supplementary. (Volumes not sold separately except to complete sets.)

The Twentieth Century D.N.B., which is in all respects an independent work of reference:

    (*a*) 1901–1911;

    (*b*) 1912–1921, with a cumulative index 1901–1921.

The Concise D.N.B., being an epitome of both the above works, in one volume, but arranged in two alphabets:

    (*a*) to 1900;

    (*b*) 1901–1921.

THE Epitome of 1901–1911 was made under the supervision of Sir Sidney Lee, and was published in 1913. It has now been reset and combined with the Epitome of 1912–1921.

When referring from the *Concise D.N.B.* to the main *Dictionary*, it is important to note that the latter now comprises four alphabetical series:

1. *The D.N.B. original issue*, containing obituaries from the earliest times to the dates of publication (1885–1900).

2. *Supplement* containing additional obituaries, mostly 1885–1900.

3. *The Twentieth Century D.N.B.* Obituaries 1901–1911.

4. *The Twentieth Century D.N.B.* Obituaries 1912–1921.

The *year of death* is therefore the necessary clue to the whereabouts of a memoir in the Dictionary.

DICTIONARY OF NATIONAL BIOGRAPHY

INDEX AND EPITOME

ABBADIE, JACQUES (or JAMES) (1654?–1727), dean of Killaloe; educated at Puylaurens, Saumur, and Sedan, where he graduated D.D.; appointed minister of the French church at Berlin by Frederick William, elector of Brandenburg, c. 1680; accompanied Marshal Schomberg to Holland, England, and Ireland, 1688-9; after battle of the Boyne proceeded to London, and became minister of the French church in the Savoy; appointed dean of Killaloe, 1699; finally retired to Marylebone, London, where he died. He published several religious and political works, of which the most important are 'Traité de la Vérité de la Religion chrétienne,' 1684; 'Traité de la Divinité de Nôtre Seigneur Jésus-Christ,' 1689; and 'L'Art de se connoître soi-même,' 1692, translated into English in 1694, 1719, and 1694 respectively. [i. 1]

ABBOT, CHARLES (d. 1817), botanist; D.D., New College, Oxford, 1802; chaplain to Marquis of Tweeddale; published 'Flora Bedfordiensis,' 1798. [i. 3]

ABBOT, CHARLES, first BARON COLCHESTER (1757–1829), speaker of House of Commons; educated at Westminster and Christ Church, Oxford, where he distinguished himself in classics; studied at the Middle Temple, 1779; clerk of the rules in court of king's bench, 1794; M.P. for Helston, Cornwall, 1795; introduced first Census Act, 1800; chief secretary for Ireland, 1801; speaker of House of Commons, 1802; retired as Lord Colchester, 1816; travelled in France and Italy, 1819–22, and on his return again took an active part in politics. [i. 3]

ABBOT, GEORGE (1562–1633), archbishop of Canterbury; born at Guildford, and educated at the free grammar school; B.A., Balliol College, Oxford, 1582; probationer-fellow, 1583; M.A., and took holy orders, 1585; during the eight succeeding years studied theology, did tutorial work, and as a vehement supporter of the puritans won great academical fame for his preaching; appointed private chaplain to Thomas Sackville, lord Buckhurst, chancellor of the university, 1592; B.D., 1593; D.D. and master of University College, 1597; dean of Winchester, 1600; vice-chancellor of the university, 1600, 1603, and 1605; came into conflict, in 1603, with Laud, then proctor of the university, who asserted the perpetual visibility of the church of Christ in the papacy before the Reformation; began, 1604, with seven other Oxford graduates, revision of the four gospels, Acts, and Apocalypse, for Authorised Version; became chaplain to the Earl of Dunbar and visited Scotland to aid in re-establishing episcopacy there, 1608; bishop of Coventry and Lichfield, 1609; translated to bishopric of London, 1610; archbishop of Canterbury, 1611; largely responsible for marriage of Princess Elizabeth with Elector Palatine of Germany, 1613; opposed the divorce of the Countess of Essex, 1613; introduced at court George Villiers, 1615; attacked the scheme for marriage between Prince Charles and the Infanta of Spain, 1617–1622; opposed the king's 'declaration of sports' permitting Sunday amusements, 1618; endowed a hospital

erected at his expense at Guildford, 1619; accidentally shot a keeper while hunting in Bramshill Park, Hampshire, and was formally pardoned by the king, 1621; reluctantly consented to the Spanish marriage, 1623; opposed Charles I's arbitrary government and was ordered to withdraw to Canterbury, his archiepiscopal authority being given to a commission of five bishops, 1627; restored to favour, 1628, but thenceforth lived chiefly in retirement; died at Croydon. Wrote religious works, principally controversial. [i. 5]

ABBOT, GEORGE (1603–1649), religious writer; fought on parliamentary side in civil war. Published religious works, including 'Book of Job Paraphrased,' 1640. [i. 20]

ABBOT, JOHN (fl. 1623), poet; educated at Sidney-Sussex College, Cambridge; B.D. 1617; wrote poem entitled 'Jesus Præfigured,' 1623. [i. 21]

ABBOT, SIR MAURICE or MORRIS (1565–1642), merchant; brother of George Abbot, archbishop of Canterbury [q. v.]; educated at Guildford Grammar School; one of the original directors of the East India Company, 1600; governor, 1624; member of Levant Company before 1607; on commissions for settlement of trade disputes with Holland, 1615, 1619, and 1620; M.P. for Kingston-upon-Hull, 1621 and 1624; member of council for establishing Virginia, 1624; knighted and returned M.P. for London, 1625; lord mayor of London 1638, when Thomas Heywood wrote the description of the pageant. [i. 21]

ABBOT, ROBERT (1560–1617), bishop of Salisbury; elder brother of George Abbot, archbishop of Canterbury [q. v.]; educated at Guildford free school; fellow of Balliol College, Oxford, 1581; M.A., 1582; D.D., 1597; gained a reputation for preaching which was increased by the publication of several religious works; one of chaplains in ordinary to James I, 1603; master of Balliol, 1609–15; fellow of Chelsea College, founded by King James, 1610; regius professor of divinity at Oxford, 1612; bishop of Salisbury, 1615. [i. 24]

ABBOT, ROBERT (1588?–1662?), divine; M.A. Cambridge; presented to living of Cranbrook by Archbishop Abbot, of whom he was no relation, 1616; vicar of Southwick, Hampshire, 1643, and, later, of St. Austin's London. Published religious works. [i. 25]

ABBOT, WILLIAM (1789–1843), actor and dramatist; first appeared at Bath, 1806; engaged at Covent Garden, 1812; stage-manager to a company visiting Paris, 1827; unsuccessful in subsequent tour in the French provinces; played Romeo to Miss Fanny Kemble's Juliet, 1830; died in America in distressed circumstances. [i. 26]

ABBOTSHALL, LORD (1620?–1688). [See RAMSAY, SIR ANDREW.]

ABBOTT, AUGUSTUS (1804–1867), major-general royal artillery, brother of Sir James Abbot [q. v.];

B

educated at Winchester College ; second lieutenant, Bengal artillery, 1819 ; captain, 1835 ; major, 1845 ; colonel, 1858 ; colonel commandant Bengal artillery, 1858 ; major-general, 1859 ; served in march to Kandahar 1839, at Jalalabad 1842, at Tutamdara, Jalgah and Parwandara 1840, and in march to and occupation of Jalalabad 1841–2 ; C.B., 1842 ; inspector-general of ordnance, 1855.
[Suppl. i. 1]

ABBOTT, CHARLES, first BARON TENTERDEN (1762–1832), lord chief justice ; educated at Canterbury Grammar School and Corpus Christi College, Oxford, 1781 ; chancellor's medallist for Latin composition, 1784, and for English composition, 1786 ; B.A., and fellow, 1785 ; student at Middle Temple, 1787 ; practised several years as a special pleader under the bar ; called to bar and joined Oxford circuit, 1796 ; junior counsel to the treasury ; recorder of Oxford, 1801 ; published successful work on mercantile law, 1802 ; puisne judge in court of common pleas, 1816 ; moved to king's bench, 1816 ; chief justice, 1818 ; raised to peerage, 1827. [i. 26]

ABBOTT, CHARLES STUART AUBREY, third BARON TENTERDEN (1834–1882), under-secretary for foreign affairs ; educated at Eton ; entered Foreign Office, 1854 ; permanent under-secretary for foreign affairs, 1873 ; K.C.B., 1878. [i. 30]

ABBOTT, EDWIN (1808–1882), educational writer ; head master of Philological School, Marylebone ; compiled Concordance to Pope's works, 1875. [i. 30]

ABBOTT, SIR FREDERICK (1805–1892), major-general royal engineers ; brother of Sir James Abbott [q. v.] ; received commission in Bengal engineers, 1823 ; major, 1843 ; colonel, 1854 ; major-general, 1858 ; served in Burmese war, 1824–6 ; garrison-engineer at Calcutta, 1841 ; chief engineer at relief of Jalalabad, 1842 ; C.B., 1846 ; lieutenant-governor of Addiscombe College, 1851–61 ; knighted, 1854. [Suppl. i. 3]

ABBOTT, SIR JAMES (1807–1896), general ; brother of Sir Frederick Abbott [q. v.] ; educated at East India Company's College, Addiscombe ; second lieutenant Bengal artillery, 1823 ; first lieutenant, 1827 ; captain, 1841 ; colonel, 1861 ; major-general, 1866 ; lieutenant-general and colonel-commandant royal artillery, 1877 ; general, 1877 ; served in march to Kandahar, 1838–9 ; assistant to Major Elliott D'Arcy Todd [q. v.] in mission to Herat, 1839, and carried to Russian court Hazrat's offer to liberate Russian captives, 1839–40 ; commissioner of Hazara, 1845–53 ; served in second Sikh war, 1848 ; K.C.B., 1894 ; published poetical and other writings. [Suppl. i. 4]

ABBOTT, SIR JOHN JOSEPH CALDWELL (1821–1893), premier of Canada ; son of Joseph Abbott [q. v.] ; educated at McGill University, Montreal ; B.C.L., 1847 ; dean in faculty of law ; hon. D.C.L. ; Q.C., 1862 ; solicitor for Canadian Pacific Railway Company, 1880, and director, 1887 ; signed Annexation Manifesto, 1849 ; raised 'Argenteuil Rangers' for government, 1861 ; M.P. for Argenteuil, 1859–74 and 1881–7 ; solicitor-general east in (Sandfield) Macdonald-Sicotte government, 1862–3 ; joined conservatives, 1865 ; confidential adviser to Sir Hugh Allen at time of 'Pacific Scandal'; delegate to England in connection with dismissal of Letellier de St.-Just ; Canadian privy councillor, 1887 ; premier of Canada, 1891–2 ; K.C.M.G., 1892. [Suppl. i. 5]

ABBOTT, JOSEPH (1789–1863), missionary in Canada, 1818 ; first Anglican incumbent of St. Andrew's. Published 'Philip Musgrave,' 1846. [Suppl. i. 5]

ABBOTT, KEITH EDWARD (d. 1873), consul-general successively at Tabriz and Odessa ; brother of Sir James Abbott (1807–1896) [q. v.] ; died at Odessa. [Suppl. i. 1]

ABBOTT, LEMUEL (d. 1776), poetical writer ; vicar of Thornton, Leicestershire, 1773. [i. 30]

ABBOTT, LEMUEL (1760–1803), portrait-painter ; pupil of Frank Hayman ; exhibited at Royal Academy between 1788 and 1800 ; painted celebrated portraits of Nelson and Cowper. [i. 30]

ABBOTT, SAUNDERS ALEXIUS (d. 1894), major-general ; brother of Sir James Abbott [q. v.] ; major-general in Bengal army ; agent at Lahore for Sind, Punjáb and Delhi railway, 1863 ; subsequently home director. [Suppl. i. 1]

ABBOTT, THOMAS EASTOE (1779–1854), poetical writer ; published poetical works, 1814–39. [i. 30]

ABDY, EDWARD STRUTT (1791–1846), writer on America ; fellow of Jesus College, Cambridge ; B.A., 1813 ; M.A., 1817 ; published work on United States of America, 1835. [i. 30]

ABDY, MARIA (d. 1867), poetess, niece of James and Horace Smith [q. v.] ; published poems, 1830–62. [i. 31]

À BECKETT, GILBERT ABBOTT (1811–1856), comic writer ; educated at Westminster School ; called to bar at Gray's Inn ; first editor of 'Figaro in London'; on original staff of 'Punch'; for many years leader-writer for 'Times' and 'Morning Herald,' and contributor to 'Illustrated London News'; metropolitan police magistrate, 1849 ; died at Boulogne-sur-Mer. He wrote over fifty plays and several humorous works. [i. 31]

À BECKETT, GILBERT ARTHUR (1837–1891), comic writer ; son of Gilbert Abbott à Beckett [q. v.] ; entered Westminster School, 1849 ; B.A. Christ Church, Oxford, 1860 ; entered Lincoln's Inn, 1857 ; clerk in office of examiners of criminal law accounts, 1862 ; journalist and author of plays and libretti ; regular member of staff of 'Punch,' 1879. His dramatic work includes, in collaboration with Mr. W. S. Gilbert, 'The Happy Land' (1873). [Suppl. i. 7]

À BECKETT, SIR WILLIAM (1806–1869), chief justice of Victoria ; brother of Gilbert Abbott à Beckett [q. v.] ; educated at Westminster School ; called to bar, 1829 ; solicitor-general of New South Wales, 1841, and subsequently attorney-general ; judge, 1846 ; chief justice of Victoria and knighted, 1851 ; retired to England, 1863 ; wrote several biographical, poetical, and legal works. [i. 32]

ABEL (d. 764), archbishop of Rheims ; aided Boniface in missionary work in Germany ; held office in abbey of Lobbes ; elected archbishop of Rheims, 744, but Pope Zacharias refused to confirm election, and he retired to Lobbes ; became abbot of the monastery, and died there ; left several works in manuscript. [i. 32]

ABEL, CLARKE (1780–1826), botanist ; educated for medical profession ; naturalist to Lord Macartney on his mission to China ; published description of journey, 1818 ; afterwards physician to Lord Amherst, governor-general of India. [i. 32]

ABEL, JOHN (1577–1674), architect of timber houses ; built old town-halls of Hereford and Leominster ; at the siege of Hereford, 1645, he constructed corn-mills for the use of the besieged. [i. 33]

ABEL, KARL FRIEDRICH (1725–1787), player on the viol-di-gamba ; member of Dresden court band, 1748–1758 ; journeyed to England and became one of queen's chamber musicians, 1759 ; joined John Christian Bach in giving concerts in England, 1765 ; toured on continent ; died in London. His portrait was twice painted by Gainsborough. [i. 33]

ABELL, JOHN (1660?–1716?), lutenist and singer ; 'gentleman of his majesty's chapel,' 1679 ; sent by Charles II to cultivate his voice in Italy, 1681–82 ; at the Revolution went to continent and performed before king of Poland ; intendant at Cassel ; performed in England, 1700 ; published two collections of songs, 1701. [i. 34]

ABELL, THOMAS (a. 1540), Roman catholic martyr ; M.A. Oxford, 1516 ; chaplain, c. 1528, to Catherine of Arragon, who entrusted him with secret commission to Emperor Charles V respecting divorce from Henry VIII ; rector of Bradwell-by-the-Sea, Essex, 1530 ; imprisoned in the Tower for opposition to the divorce, 1532 ; included in act of attainder against Catherine's accomplices, 1534 ; beheaded, 1540. [i. 34]

ABELL, WILLIAM (fl. 1640), alderman of London, 1636 ; sheriff of London and master of the Vintners' Company, 1637 ; licenser of tavern-keepers, 1639 ; gained great unpopularity by his efforts to induce vintners to agree to Charles I's demand of tax on wine, and was imprisoned by order of Commons, 1640–2 ; under surveillance at Hatfield for debt and treasonable utterances, 1652 ; given a passport to Holland, 1655. His actions were severely condemned in many broadsides and pamphlets. [i. 35]

ABERCORN, first DUKE OF (1811–1885). [See HAMILTON, JAMES.]

ABERCORN, EARLS OF. [See HAMILTON, JAMES, first EARL, *d.* 1617; HAMILTON, JAMES, sixth EARL, 1656–1734; HAMILTON, JAMES, seventh EARL, *d.* 1744; HAMILTON, JAMES, eighth EARL, 1712–1789.]

ABERCROMBIE, JOHN (1726–1806), writer on horticulture; employed in Kew Gardens; market gardener at Hackney, and later at Tottenham; published 'Every Man his own Gardener,' 1767 (said to have been submitted to Goldsmith for revision and returned without alteration), and other works on gardening. [i. 36]

ABERCROMBIE, JOHN (1780–1844), physician; educated at Marischal College, Aberdeen; M.D. Edinburgh, 1803; studied at St. George's Hospital, London; practised in Edinburgh, where he did much for the poor; L.R.C.P., 1823, F.R.C.P., and physician in ordinary to the king in Scotland, 1824; M.D. Oxford, 1835; lord-rector of Marischal College, 1836; published pathological works. [i. 37]

ABERCROMBY, ALEXANDER, LORD ABERCROMBY (1745–1795), judge and essayist; studied at Edinburgh; sheriff-depute of Clackmannanshire, 1766–80; sat on court of session bench as Lord Abercromby, 1792; one of the lords-commissioners of justiciary; contributed to the 'Mirror' (1779) and 'Lounger' (1785–6). [i. 38]

ABERCROMBY, ALEXANDER (1784–1853), colonel, son of Sir Ralph Abercromby [q. v.]; entered the army as volunteer, 1799; aide-de-camp to Sir John Moore in Sicily, 1806; lieutenant-colonel 28th regiment, 1808; after 1809 served in Peninsular and Waterloo campaigns; M.P. for Clackmannanshire, 1817. [i. 39]

ABERCROMBY, DAVID (*d.* 1701–2?), Scottish physician; educated as a Roman catholic; lived for eighteen years with jesuit order in France, and gained reputation as scholar; returned to Scotland, and wrote against M. Menzies, a protestant divine of Aberdeen; after two years, renounced Romanism and went to London, whence he retired to Amsterdam, and practised as physician; published medical and metaphysical works. [i. 39]

ABERCROMBY, JAMES, first BARON DUNFERMLINE (1776–1858), son of Sir Ralph Abercromby [q.v.]; called to bar at Lincoln's Inn, 1801; M.P. for Midhurst, 1807, Calne, 1812–30, and Edinburgh, 1832; judge-advocate-general, 1827; master of the mint, 1834; speaker of House of Commons, 1835–9; raised to the peerage on retirement, 1839. [i. 40]

ABERCROMBY, JOHN (*d.* 1561?), Scottish Benedictine; executed for opposing the Reformation. [i. 41]

ABERCROMBY, SIR JOHN (1772–1817), general; son of Sir Ralph Abercromby [q.v.]; ensign, 75th regiment, 1786; captain, 1792; aide-de-camp to his father in Flanders, 1793 and 1794; major, 94th regiment, 1794; lieutenant-colonel, 112th regiment, 1794; military secretary to his father, 1796–9; colonel, 1800; distinguished himself under General Hutchinson in Egypt; major-general, 1805; colonel, 53rd regiment, 1807; captured Mauritius, 1809; lieutenant-general and temporary governor of Madras, 1812; G.C.B., 1816; died at Marseilles. [i. 41]

ABERCROMBY, PATRICK (1656–1716?), antiquary and historian; graduated at St. Andrews University, 1685; practised as physician in Edinburgh; physician to James II, 1685. Published pamphlets opposing the Scottish union, 1707, 'Martial Atchievements of the Scots Nation' (1711–16), and other writings. [i. 42]

ABERCROMBY, SIR RALPH (1734–1801), general; educated at Rugby; studied law at Edinburgh and Leipzig; cornet, 3rd dragoon guards, 1756; aide-de-camp to General Sir William Pitt in Germany, 1758; captain, 1762; major, 1770; lieutenant-colonel, 1773; for a short time M.P. for Clackmannanshire; returned to the army and distinguished himself as major-general in Flanders; K.B., 1795; commanded expedition against the French in West Indies, 1795–6, and reduced St. Lucia and Trinidad; took command of troops successively in Ireland and Scotland, 1797–9; co-operated with the British fleet in capturing the Dutch fleet, and assisting the Archduke Charles against France, 1799; commanded troops in Mediterranean, 1800; proceeded to Egypt and defeated French at Alexandria, where he died of wounds. [i. 43]

ABERCROMBY, ROBERT (1534–1613), Scottish jesuit, said, on insufficient evidence, to have converted Anne of Denmark to the Roman catholic faith. [i. 46]

ABERCROMBY, SIR ROBERT (1740–1827), military commander; brother of Sir Ralph Abercromby [q. v.]; ensign, 1758, and lieutenant, 1759, 44th regiment; captain, 1761; major 62nd regiment, 1772; lieutenant-colonel 37th regiment, 1773; served throughout American war; colonel and aide-de-camp to the king, 1781; colonel 75th regiment, 1787; in India, 1788; governor and commander-in-chief of Bombay, 1790; reduced Tippoo Sultan, 1792; knighted and commander of the Indian forces; conducted the second Rohilla war; returned to England, 1797; M.P. for Clackmannanshire, 1798; governor of Edinburgh Castle, 1801; general, 1802. [i. 47]

ABERCROMBY, ROBERT WILLIAM DUFF (1835–1895). [See DUFF, SIR ROBERT WILLIAM.]

ABERDARE, BARON. [See BRUCE, HENRY AUSTIN, 1815–1895.]

ABERDEEN, EARLS OF. [See GORDON, GEORGE, first EARL, 1637–1720; GORDON, GEORGE HAMILTON, fourth EARL, 1784–1860.]

ABERGAVENNY, BARONS. [See NEVILLE, EDWARD, first BARON, *d.* 1476; NEVILLE, GEORGE, third BARON, 1471?–1535.]

ABERNETHY, JOHN (1680–1740), Irish dissenter; M.A. Glasgow; studied divinity at Edinburgh and Dublin, where his preaching was soon in great demand; ordained, as presbyterian, at Antrim, 1703, where he remained for over nine years; removed by synod to Dublin, 1717, but after three months returned to Antrim; gave rise, by his opposition to the synod, to a division (ultimately permanent) of the presbyterians into two parties (subscribers and non-subscribers); accepted a 'call' to Dublin, 1730; strongly opposed the Test Act, 1731; wrote several religious works. [i. 48]

ABERNETHY, JOHN (1764–1831), surgeon; studied at St. Bartholomew's Hospital, where he was assistant-surgeon 1787, and surgeon 1815–27; F.R.S. 1796; lecturer on anatomy and physiology at College of Surgeons, 1814; attracted a large class by his lectures on anatomy at his house in Bartholomew Close; gained distinction by extending John Hunter's operation for the cure of aneurism, 1797. Published medical works, but his reputation rests rather on his power of exposition than on his learning. [i. 49]

ABERSHAW, or **AVERSHAWE**, LOUIS JEREMIAH or JERRY (1773?–1795), highwayman; for some years the terror of the roads between London, Kingston, and Wimbledon; hanged on Kennington Common. [i. 52]

ABINGDON, fourth EARL OF (1740–1799). [See BERTIE, WILLOUGHBY.]

ABINGER, first BARON. [See SCARLETT, JAMES, 1769–1844.]

ABINGTON. [See HABINGTON.]

ABINGTON, FRANCES (1737–1815), actress; in girlhood successively a flower-seller, street-singer, domestic servant, and cook-maid (under Robert Baddeley [q. v.]); appeared first at the Haymarket as Miranda in 'The Busybody,' 1755; acted at Bath, Richmond, and Drury Lane with small success; went to Dublin and drew crowded houses as Lady Townley; returned to Drury Lane on Garrick's invitation, 1764; transferred her services to Covent Garden, 1782; absent from the stage, 1790–7; last appeared, 1799; her Shakespearean rôles include Portia, Beatrice, Desdemona, Olivia, and Ophelia; original representative of Lady Teazle, 1777. [i. 52]

ABNEY, SIR THOMAS (1640–1722), lord mayor of London; alderman of Vintry ward 1692, and of Bridge Without, 1716; sheriff of London and Middlesex, 1693–1694, when he was one of the original promoters and directors of the bank of England; knighted by William III; president and benefactor of St. Thomas's Hospital; lord mayor, 1700–1; M.P. for the city of London, 1702. [i. 54]

ABNEY, SIR THOMAS (*d.* 1750), justice of the common pleas, 1743; died of gaol distemper at the 'Black Sessions.' [i. 55]

ABOYNE, EARLS OF. [See GORDON, CHARLES, first EARL, *d.* 1681; GORDON, CHARLES, second EARL, *d.* 1702.]

ABOYNE, second VISCOUNT (*d.* 1649). [See GORDON, JAMES.]

ABRAHAM, ROBERT (1773–1850), architect; executed works at Arundel Castle, the synagogue near the Haymarket, and the Westminster Bridewell.   [i. 56]

ABYNDON, RICHARD DE (d. 1327 ?). [See RICHARD.]

ACCA (d. 740), fifth bishop of Hexham; educated in household of Bosa, who superseded Wilfred as bishop of York, 678; accompanied Wilfred in various missionary journeys in England and on continent; abbot of Hexham and friend of Bede; bishop of Hexham, 709; expelled, 732; buried at Hexham.   [i. 56]

ACCUM, FRIEDRICH CHRISTIAN (1769–1838), chemist; scientific lecturer at Surrey Institute, 1803; advocated introduction of gas for lighting; engineer to London Gaslight Company, 1810; librarian of the Royal Institution, but, being dismissed, went to Berlin, 1822; wrote several scientific works.   [i. 57]

ACHEDUN. [See ACTON.]

ACHERLEY, ROGER (1665 ?–1740), lawyer; called to bar at Inner Temple, 1691; worked actively for the house of Hanover without substantial reward; author of many legal and constitutional treatises, including 'The Britannic Constitution,' 1727.   [i. 57]

ACHESON, SIR ARCHIBALD, second EARL OF GOSFORD in Irish peerage and first BARON WORLINGHAM in peerage of United Kingdom (1776–1849), governor-in-chief of Canada; honorary M.A., Christ Church, Oxford, 1797; became member for co. Armagh in Irish parliament, 1798, and member of House of Commons in first parliament of United Kingdom, 1801; re-elected 1802 and 1806; succeeded to earldom, 1807; representative peer for Ireland, 1811; lord lieutenant and *custos rotulorum* of Armagh, 1832 till death; privy councillor and captain of yeoman of guard, 1834; supported whig policy of 'conciliation' in Ireland, 1835; governor-in-chief of British North America, Newfoundland excepted, 1835–8; created Baron Worlingham, 1835; adopted policy of conciliation towards the rebel leader Louis Joseph Papineau [q. v.] and his party; his action resented by the legislature; resigned, 1837; knight grand cross (civil side), 1838; vice-admiral of coast of Ulster.   [Suppl. i. 8]

ACKERMANN, RUDOLPH (1764–1834), art publisher and bookseller; educated at Schneeberg, and apprenticed as coachbuilder; settled in London as coach-designer; opened print-shop in Strand; patented method for making articles waterproof, 1801; established art lithography in England, 1817; worked extensively for relief of sufferers after the war, 1814; published numerous illustrated books.   [i. 58]

ACKLAND, THOMAS GILBANK (1791–1844), divine; published poems.   [i. 59]

ACLAND, LADY CHRISTIAN HENRIETTA CAROLINE, generally called LADY HARRIET (1750–1815), daughter of Stephen, first Earl of Ilchester; accompanied her husband, John Dyke Acland [q. v.], to America, 1776, and followed him throughout the campaign.   [i. 59]

ACLAND, SIR HENRY WENTWORTH (1815–1900), physician; son of Sir Thomas Dyke Acland [q. v.]; educated at Harrow; M.A., Christ Church, Oxford, 1842; M.D., 1848; lifelong friend of John Ruskin; fellow, All Souls' College, Oxford, 1840; studied medicine at St. George's Hospital and Edinburgh; gold medallist for medical jurisprudence, 1844; L.R.C.P., 1846; F.R.C.P., 1850; Harveian orator, 1865; 'conciliarius,' 1882–3–4; F.R.S., 1847; Radcliffe librarian and Aldrichian professor of clinical medicine, Oxford, 1851; regius professor of medicine, 1858–94, and master of Ewelme Hospital, Oxford; president of the General Medical Council, 1874–87; honorary physician to King Edward VII, when Prince of Wales, whom he accompanied to America, 1860; K.C.B., 1884; honorary M.D. and LL.D., Dublin; published writings dealing with sanitation and medical education.   [Suppl. i. 10]

ACLAND, SIR JOHN (d. 1620), benefactor of Exeter College, Oxford; knighted by James I, 1604; knight of shire for Devon, 1607; contributed largely towards building new hall at Exeter College, Oxford, where he founded two scholarships.   [i. 60]

ACLAND, JOHN (*fl.* 1753–1796), poor law reformer; rector of Broad Clyst, 1753; published a pamphlet, 'A Plan for rendering the Poor independent of Public Contributions,' 1786.   [i. 60]

ACLAND, JOHN DYKE (d. 1778), soldier and politician; M.P. for Callington, Cornwall, 1774; opposed government's measures for peace; served, as major, on General Burgoyne's expedition to America, 1776, accompanied by wife, Lady Christian Henrietta Acland [q. v.]; died from effects of exposure in a duel.   [i. 61]

ACLAND, SIR THOMAS DYKE (1787–1871), politician and philanthropist; educated at Harrow; B.A., Christ Church, Oxford, 1808; M.A., 1814; hon. D.C.L., 1831; M.P. for county of Devon, 1812–18, 1820–30, and North Devon, 1837–57; much interested in religious movements.   [i. 62]

ACLAND, SIR THOMAS DYKE (1809–1898), politician; son of Sir Thomas Dyke Acland (1787–1871) [q.v.]; M.A., Christ Church, Oxford, 1835; fellow of All Souls', 1831–9; M.P. for West Somerset, 1837–41; took leading part in establishing Oxford local examinations, 1857–8; D.C.L., Oxford, 1858; M.P. for North Devonshire, 1865–85, and for West Somerset, 1885–6; eleventh baronet, 1871; privy councillor, 1883; published speeches and pamphlets, mainly on agriculture and education.   [Suppl. i. 12]

ACLAND, SIR WROTH PALMER (1770–1816), soldier; ensign 17th regiment, 1787; after successive promotions was colonel 1803, and brigadier-general under Sir Arthur Wellesley, afterwards Duke of Wellington, 1808; lieutenant-general and K.C.B., 1814; died of fever.   [i. 62]

ACONTIUS, JACOBUS (1500?–1566?), philosopher and engineer; born in the Tyrol; came to England *c.* 1559, having studied law and published a work, 'De Methodo,' at Bâle; discovered many new mechanical contrivances and received a pension of 60*l.* from Elizabeth; attached himself to nonconformist Dutch church in Austin Friars, and took active part in controversies with conformists; undertook with some success to reclaim land inundated by the Thames, 1562–66; enjoyed patronage of the Earl of Leicester; published 'Stratagema Satanæ' (1565), and other works, principally theological.   [i. 63]

A'COURT, WILLIAM, first BARON HEYTESBURY (1779–1860), diplomatist; secretary of Naples Legation, 1801; to special Vienna mission, 1807; envoy to Barbary 1813, Naples 1814, Spain 1822; ambassador to Portugal 1824, Russia 1828–32; P.C. 1817; G.C.B. 1819; created a peer 1828; viceroy of Ireland, 1844–6.   [xxvi. 328]

ACTON, CHARLES JANUARIUS EDWARD (1803–1847), cardinal; born at Naples; educated at Westminster, and Magdalene College, Cambridge; entered college of the Academia Ecclesiastica, Rome, which he left with rank of prelate; received successive appointments from pope; brought about division of England into eight catholic vicariates, 1840; cardinal, 1842.   [i. 65]

ACTON, EDWARD (d. 1707), captain in navy; took part in capture of Gibraltar, 1704; killed in engagement with French off Dungeness.   [i. 66]

ACTON, ELIZA (1799–1859), authoress; published from 1826 poems and other writings on various subjects. Her 'Modern Cookery' appeared in 1845, and 'The English Bread Book,' 1857.   [i. 66]

ACTON, HENRY (1797–1843), unitarian divine; apprenticed as printer; became pupil of Dr. Morell at Brighton; minister at Walthamstow, 1821, Exeter, 1823; published many sermons and pamphlets.   [i. 67]

ACTON, JOHN (d. 1350), writer on canon law; possibly educated at Oxford; canon of Lincoln, *c.* 1329; prebendary of Welton Royal, *c.* 1343; wrote commentary on ecclesiastical 'constitutions' of Otho and Ottobone.   [i. 67]

ACTON, SIR JOHN FRANCIS EDWARD, sixth Baronet (1736–1811), prime minister of Naples under Ferdinand IV; son of physician at Besançon, where he was born; entered Tuscan naval service, and, having distinguished himself, was entrusted with the reorganisation of the Neapolitan navy, 1779; became minister of war, generalissimo of sea and land forces, and minister of finance; during the French wars was alternatively in hiding or enjoying almost absolute power ; took refuge in Sicily on entry of French into Naples, 1806 ; died at Palermo. [i. 67]

ACTON, RALPH (14th cent.), theologian ; probably graduated in philosophy and theology at Oxford ; wrote several scripture commentaries. [i. 68]

ACWORTH, GEORGE (d. 1578 ?), divine ; M.A., Cambridge, 1555 ; public orator of Cambridge University, 1559 ; advocate, 1562 ; LL.D., 1563 ; chancellor and vicar-general to bishop of Winchester ; judge of prerogative court, Ireland, 1577 ; received patent to exercise ecclesiastical jurisdiction in Ireland, 1578. [i. 69]

ADAIR, JAMES (fl. 1775), historian of the American Indians ; traded among Indians of Georgia and the Carolinas, 1735–75 ; published 1775, 'History of American Indians,' arguing that the Indians are descended from the lost ten tribes. [Suppl. i. 13]

ADAIR, JAMES (d. 1798), serjeant-at-law ; M.A., Peterhouse, Cambridge, 1767 ; assisted Wilkes in his quarrel with Horne Tooke, 1770 ; counsel in trial of printers of 'Junius's Letters,' 1771 ; recorder of London, 1779-89 ; whig M.P. for Cockermouth and, subsequently, Higham Ferrars, 1780 till death ; reputed author of some constitutional works. [i. 69]

ADAIR, JAMES MAKITTRICK (1728–1802), originally JAMES MAKITTRICK ; M.D. Edinburgh, 1766 ; practised as physician in Antigua, and afterwards in Andover, Guildford, and Bath ; published medical writings.
[i. 70]

ADAIR, JOHN (d. 1722), surveyor and map-maker ; F.R.S., 1688 ; commissioned by the privy council to survey the Scottish shires, 1683, and acts of tonnage to raise the funds for his work were passed 1686, 1695, and 1705 ; published charts of the Scottish coasts, 1703, but the work was not completed ; left, in print or manuscript, many maps and charts of Scotland. [i. 70]

ADAIR PATRICK (1625 ?–1694), presbyterian minister ; studied divinity at Glasgow, 1644 ; ordained at Cairncastle, co. Antrim, 1646 ; protested with ministers of Antrim and Down against execution of Charles I, 1649 ; forced to hide from parliamentary generals, but subsequently took an active part in presbyterian church matters in Ireland ; headed a deputation to congratulate William III, 1689, and was appointed a trustee for distributing the *regium donum* ; published work on history of presbyterianism in Ireland. [i. 72]

ADAIR, SIR ROBERT (1763–1855), diplomatist ; close friend of Charles James Fox ; after 1788, travelled to study effects of French Revolution ; M.P. for Appleby and Camelford ; employed by Fox on diplomatic business in Vienna, 1806, and subsequently in Constantinople and the Low Countries ; K.C.B., 1809. [i. 73]

ADALBERT LEVITA or DIACONUS (fl. 700), English saint ; said to have been the first archdeacon of Utrecht, and to have preached the gospel in Western Germany and in Kennemaria, 702, where he built a church at Egmont, in North Holland. [i. 73]

ADALBERT OF SPALDING (fl. 1160 ?), said to have been a Cluniac monk of the abbey of Spalding, Lincolnshire. [i. 74]

ADAM ANGLICUS, possibly identical with Adam Angligena [q. v.], or with Adam Goddam [q. v.] ; wrote a commentary on the sentences of Peter Lombard. [i. 75]

ADAM ANGLIGENA (d. 1181 ?), theologian ; possibly identical with Adam, bishop of St. Asaph, 1175, or with Adam de Parvo-Ponte, canon of Paris, 1147 ; distinguished teacher in Paris, c. 1150. [i. 75]

ADAM OF BARKING (fl. 1217 ?), Benedictine monk of Sherborne Abbey, Dorset ; wrote scriptural treatises. [i. 76]

ADAM OF BUCKFIELD (fl. 1300 ?), commentator on Aristotle ; possibly a Franciscan. [i. 77]

ADAM OF CAITHNESS (d. 1222), Scottish bishop ; prior and, 1207, abbot of the Cistercians at Melrose ; bishop of Caithness, 1213 ; murdered, 1222. [i. 77]

ADAM THE CARTHUSIAN (fl. 1340), doctor of theology. [i. 77]

ADAM OF DOMERHAM (d. after 1291), monk of Glastonbury ; cellarer and afterwards sacristan to the abbey ; wrote a history of the abbey. [i. 77]

ADAM OF EVESHAM (d. 1191), prior of Bermondsey, 1157 ; abbot of Evesham, 1161. [i. 78]

ADAM GODDAMUS (d. 1358). [See GODDAM.]

ADAM DE MARISCO (d. 1257?), Franciscan of Worcester ; educated at Oxford ; adviser and friend of Robert Grosseteste and Simon de Montfort. [i. 79]

ADAM MURIMUTHENSIS (1275 ?–1347). [See MURIMUTH.]

ADAM OF ORLTON (d. 1345), bishop of Hereford 1317, of Worcester 1327, and of Winchester 1333 ; employed on several embassies by Edward II ; took active part in the various risings against the king, 1321–2 ; charged before parliament with treason and deprived of lands and revenues, 1322 ; joined Queen Isabella's party on her landing, 1326 ; largely responsible for the king's resignation, 1327 ; made treasurer and restored to possessions under Edward III ; entrusted frequently with diplomatic commissions. [i. 79]

ADAM SCOTUS or ANGLICUS (fl. 1180), theological writer ; Præmonstratensian canon ; perhaps abbot and bishop of Casa Candida (Whithorn), Galloway ; renowned throughout Europe for his sermons and treatises, which were first published at Paris, 1518. [i. 81]

ADAM DE STRATTON (fl. 1265–1290). [See STRATTON.]

ADAM OF USK (fl. 1400), lawyer, and writer of a Latin chronicle of English history, 1377–1404 ; educated at Oxford and entered the church ; pleaded in the archbishop of Canterbury's court, 1390–7 ; joined Henry IV's party in the revolution, 1399 ; banished to Rome for criticism of Henry IV's government, 1402. [i. 83]

ADAM, ALEXANDER (1741–1809), writer on Roman antiquities ; educated at Edinburgh ; LL.D., 1780 ; headmaster of Watson's Hospital, 1759 ; rector of Edinburgh High School, 1768 ; published educational works. [i. 84]

ADAM, SIR CHARLES (1780–1853), admiral ; brother of Sir Frederick Adam [q. v.] ; captain, 1799 ; served in French and Spanish wars, 1801–13 ; captain of the royal yacht ; K.C.B. 1835 ; M.P. for Clackmannan and Kinross, 1833–41 ; governor of Greenwich Hospital, 1847 ; admiral, 1848. [i. 85]

ADAM, SIR FREDERICK (1781–1853), soldier, brother of Sir Charles Adam [q. v.] ; ensign 1795, and after rapid promotion purchased command of 21st regiment, 1805 ; served in Sicily till 1813, when he went as colonel to Spain ; distinguished himself in the Castalla campaign ; major-general, 1814 ; at Waterloo ; K.C.B., 1815 ; G.C.B., 1840 ; general, 1846. [i. 85]

ADAM, JAMES (d. 1794), for some years architect to George III ; associated with his brother Robert Adam [q. v.] [i. 86]

ADAM, JEAN (1710–1765), Scottish poetess ; published poems by subscription, 1734, and soon afterwards opened girls' school at Crawford Bridge ; met with pecuniary troubles and died in Glasgow poorhouse ; said, with small foundation, to have written the song 'There's nae luck aboot the house.' [i. 86]

ADAM, JOHN (1779–1825), Anglo-Indian statesman ; son of William Adam (1751–1839) [q. v.] ; educated at Charterhouse and Edinburgh University ; private and political secretary to Marquis of Hastings in India ; acting governor-general of India for seven months, 1823. [i. 87]

ADAM, ROBERT (1728–1792), architect ; brother of John, James, and William Adam ; educated at Edinburgh University ; visited Italy and studied architecture, 1754 ; F.R.S. and F.S.A. ; architect to King George III, 1762–8 ; M.P. for Kinross-shire ; with his brothers built the Adelphi, London, 1769–71 ; with his brother James designed a number of important mansions in various parts of the country and much improved street architecture of London ; published works on architecture ; buried in Westminster Abbey. [i. 88]

ADAM, THOMAS (1701–1784), divine ; B.A., Hart Hall, Oxford ; held living of Wintringham, Lincolnshire,

1724 till death; wrote several religious works, including 'Private Thoughts on Religion,' published posthumously. [i. 89]

ADAM, WILLIAM (*d.* 1748), architect; assisted his brother Robert Adam [q. v.] in building the Adelphi, London, 1769–1771. [i. 89]

ADAM, WILLIAM (1751–1839), politician; called to Scottish bar, 1773; M.P. for Gatton, Surrey; supporter of Lord North, 1774, and successively M.P. for five Scottish constituencies; wounded Fox in a duel, after quarrel over a speech by Fox in the house, but later became his firm ally; treasurer of ordnance, 1780; called to English bar, 1782; took a leading part in impeachment of Warren Hastings, 1788; K.C., 1796; attorney-general to Prince of Wales; privy councillor, 1815; lord chief commissioner of Scottish jury court, 1816; intimate friend of Sir Walter Scott. [i. 90]

ADAM, WILLIAM PATRICK (1823–1881), liberal whip, 1874–80; educated at Rugby and Trinity College, Cambridge; called to bar, 1849; secretary to Lord Elphinstone in India, 1853–8; M.P. for Clackmannan and Kinross, 1859–80; during different periods lord of the treasury and commissioner of public works; privy councillor, 1873; governor of Madras, 1880. [i. 91]

ADAMNAN or **ADOMNAN** (625 ?–704), abbot of Iona, 679; advocated adoption of regulations of Romish church; stated to have taken part in synods and conventions in Ireland. The biography of Columba is generally ascribed to him. [i. 92]

ADAMS, ANDREW LEITH (*d.* 1882), zoologist, son of Francis Adams [q. v.]; army surgeon, 1848–73; professor of zoology at Dublin, 1873–8, and of natural history at Cork, 1878–82. Published zoological writings and accounts of travels in India. [i. 94]

ADAMS, CLEMENT (1519 ?–1587), schoolmaster and author; M.A., King's College, Cambridge, 1544; schoolmaster to the royal henchmen at Greenwich from 1552; wrote in Latin an account of Hugh Willoughby and Richard Chancellor's voyage to Russia of 1553 (printed with an English translation in Hakluyt's 'Collections,' 1589); engraved before 1584 the 'mappe-monde' by Sebastian Cabot, but no copy of Adams's engraving is now known. [i. 94]

ADAMS, FRANCIS (1796–1861), physician and classical scholar; M.A., Aberdeen; M.C.S., London, 1815; practised medicine at Banchory Ternan; expert in Greek philology; hon. M.D., Aberdeen, 1856; translated and edited the Greek medical writers Paulus Ægineta, 1844–7, Hippocrates, 1849, and Aretæus, 1856. [i. 95]

ADAMS, FRANCIS WILLIAM LAUDERDALE (1862–1893), author; son of Andrew Leith Adams [q.v.]; went to Australia and worked on staff of 'Sydney Bulletin'; died by his own hand at Alexandria; chief works 'Leicester,' an autobiographical novel, 1884, and 'Tiberius,' a powerful drama, 1894. [Suppl. i. 14]

ADAMS, GEORGE (1698 ?–1768 ?), poet and translator; fellow of St. John's College, Cambridge; took holy orders; translated into English prose the tragedies of Sophocles, 1729; wrote 'Life of Socrates,' 1746, and theological works. [i. 96]

ADAMS, GEORGE, the elder (*d.* 1773), mathematical instrument maker to George III; obtained wide reputation as maker of celestial and terrestrial globes. [i. 97]

ADAMS, GEORGE, the younger (1750–1795), mathematical instrument maker to George III, son of George Adams the elder [q. v.]; published scientific essays. [i. 97]

ADAMS, JAMES (1737–1802), philologist; professor of languages at Jesuit College of St. Omer; settled after French revolution in Edinburgh; published 'Pronunciation of the English Language,' 1799. [i. 97]

ADAMS, JOHN (*fl.* 1680), topographer; barrister of Inner Temple; published a map of England, 1677 (revised 1693), and an index to English towns. [i. 97]

ADAMS, JOHN (1662–1720), provost of King's College, Cambridge, 1712; graduated M.A. 1686; chaplain to William III and Anne. [i. 98]

ADAMS, JOHN (1750 ?–1814), compiler of books for young readers; graduated at Aberdeen, and subsequently opened a school at Putney. [i. 98]

ADAMS, JOHN, *alias* ALEXANDER SMITH (1760 ?–1829), seaman; took part in mutiny and, 1789, seizure of H.M.S. Bounty, in which he subsequently sailed to Pitcairn's Island, where he founded and successfully governed an English-speaking settlement. [i. 98]

ADAMS, JOHN COUCH (1819–1892), discoverer of planet 'Neptune'; sizar, St. John's College, Cambridge, 1839; senior wrangler and first Smith's prizeman, 1843; fellow (till 1852) and tutor; fellow of Pembroke College, 1853 till death; made observations determining particulars of 'Neptune,' 1841–5, and deposited results at Royal Observatory, Greenwich, 1845, but the publication of his discovery was anticipated by Leverrier, July, 1846; refused knighthood 1847, and Adams prize was founded at Cambridge; F.R.S., 1849; Copley medallist, 1848; professor of mathematics, St. Andrews, 1858–9; Lowndean professor of astronomy and geometry, Cambridge, 1858; director of Cambridge observatory, 1861; president of Royal Astronomical Society, 1851–3, and 1874–6, and received gold medal, 1866, for researches in connection with theory of secular acceleration of the moon's mean motion. His 'Scientific Papers' were published 1896–1901. [Suppl. i. 15]

ADAMS, JOSEPH (1756–1818), originally an apothecary; M.D. Aberdeen, 1796; practised in Madeira; physician to Small-pox Hospital, 1805; published medical treatises. [i. 99]

ADAMS, RICHARD (1619–1661), collector of verse; fellow-commoner of Catharine Hall, Cambridge, 1635; left a small manuscript volume of poems, of some of which he was probably author. [i. 100]

ADAMS, RICHARD (1626 ?–1698), ejected minister; graduated at Cambridge and Oxford; rector of St. Mildred's, Bread Street, 1655; retired as nonconformist, 1662. [i. 100]

ADAMS, ROBERT (*d.* 1595), architect; author of a plan of Middleburgh, 1588, and other drawings. [i. 100]

ADAMS, ROBERT (1791–1875), surgeon; M.D. Dublin, 1842; F.R.C.S., Ireland, 1818, and was three times president; practised in Dublin and lectured on surgery at the hospitals; surgeon to the queen in Ireland, 1861. [i. 100]

ADAMS, SARAH FLOWER (1805–1848), poetess; wife of William Bridges Adams [q. v.]; contributed to 'Monthly Repository'; her principal work, 'Vivia Perpetua,' a dramatic poem, 1841; wrote several hymns, including 'Nearer to Thee.' [i. 101]

ADAMS, THOMAS (*d.* 1620 ?), printer; freeman of Stationers' Company, 1590; liveryman, 1598; warden, 1614. His books were of all classes, including music. [i. 101]

ADAMS, THOMAS (*fl.* 1612–1653), divine; 'the prose Shakespeare of puritan theologians'; preacher at Willington, Bedfordshire, 1612; vicar of Wingrave, Bucks, 1614–36; held preachership of St. Gregory's under St. Paul's Cathedral, 1618–23; chaplain to Sir Henry Montague, lord chief justice; published sermons and theological treatises. [i. 102]

ADAMS, SIR THOMAS (1586–1668), lord mayor of London, 1645; educated at Cambridge; draper; alderman, sheriff, and master of Drapers' Company, 1639; imprisoned in Tower for loyalty; created baronet after Restoration; founded Arabic lecture at Cambridge. [i. 102]

ADAMS, THOMAS (1633 ?–1670), divine; B.A. and fellow, Brasenose College, Oxford, 1652; M.A. and lecturer-dean, 1655; ejected from fellowship for nonconformity, 1662; wrote religious works. [i. 103]

ADAMS, THOMAS (1730 ?–1764), soldier; volunteered for service in Netherlands under Duke of Cumberland, 1747; ensign, 37th foot, 1747; captain, 1756; major, 84th foot; as commander of crown and E.I.C. forces in Bengal conducted glorious campaign, including battles of Gheriah and Andwanala, 1762–3; brigadier-general, 1764. [i. 103]

ADAMS, WILLIAM (*d.* 1620), navigator; apprenticed as sailor at age of twelve; served Company of Barbary Merchants; joined as pilot-major fleet of five ships from Rotterdam bound for India; in spite of the ships being carried through the straits of Magellan and scattered, ultimately reached Japan, where, after some weeks' imprisonment, having found favour with Iyéyasu, the ruler, he settled; obtained trading privileges for Dutch merchants, 1611. Later three English ships came to open trade with Japan; a settlement was founded, of which Adams was second in command, 1613. He subsequently engaged in trading voyages to Loochoo Islands, Siam, and Cochin China, 1613–18. Iyéyasu died in 1616, and English and Dutch privileges being curtailed, the English venture failed, and war broke out between English and Dutch. Adams was buried on the hill overlooking harbour of Yokosuka, 1620. [i. 104]

ADAMS, WILLIAM (1706–1789), divine; master of Pembroke College, Oxford, from 1775; lifelong friend of Dr. Johnson, whose acquaintance he made when both were at Oxford; D.D. Oxford, 1756. [i. 106]

ADAMS, WILLIAM (*fl.* 1790), potter; pupil of Josiah Wedgwood, and subsequently in business at Tunstall as Adams & Co. [i. 107]

ADAMS, SIR WILLIAM (1783–1827). [See RAWSON.]

ADAMS, WILLIAM (1814–1848), author of 'Sacred Allegories'; educated at Eton; postmaster at Merton College, Oxford; fellow and tutor, 1837; vicar of St. Peter's-in-the-East, 1840; published ethical works. [i. 107]

ADAMS, WILLIAM (1772–1851), lawyer; fellow of Trinity Hall, Cambridge; LL.D. and member of College of Advocates, 1799; prepared, 1814, as one of three commissioners, despatches relating to maritime law in negotiations for treaty with U.S.A. after capture of Washington; one of three plenipotentiaries sent to conclude convention of commerce with U.S.A., 1815. [i. 108]

ADAMS, WILLIAM BRIDGES (1797–1872), inventor of 'fish-joint' for uniting ends of rails, 1847; made numerous improvements in machinery; wrote scientific and technical works. [i. 108]

ADAMS, WILLIAM HENRY DAVENPORT (1828–1891), miscellaneous writer; edited provincial newspaper in Isle of Wight; founded 'Scottish Guardian,' 1870, and was editor, 1870–8; projected and edited 'Whitehall Library of Wit and Humour.' His works include 'Memorable Battles in English History,' 1862, and a Concordance to Shakespeare's plays, 1886. [Suppl. i. 17]

ADAMSON, HENRY (*d.* 1639), poetical writer; published 'The Muses Threnodie,' 1638. [i. 109]

ADAMSON, JOHN (*d.* 1653), principal of Edinburgh University, 1625 till death; professor of philosophy at St. Andrews; professor at Edinburgh, 1589–1604; vicar of North Berwick, and, later, of Libberton; published several theses and poems, and edited 'Muses Welcome' and probably the poems of Andrew Melville, his friend. [i. 109]

ADAMSON, JOHN (1787–1855), antiquary and Portuguese scholar; in counting-house of his brother, a Lisbon merchant, 1803; left England and studied Portuguese at Lisbon, 1807; articled as solicitor in Newcastle; undersheriff of Newcastle, 1811; a founder of the Antiquarian Society of Newcastle, 1813; F.S.A.; published translations from Portuguese and original works in verse and prose, including 'Memoirs of Camoens,' 1820, and edited several books for the Typographical Society of Newcastle. [i. 110]

ADAMSON, PATRICK (1537–1592), Scottish prelate; M.A. St. Andrews, 1558; minister of Ceres in Fife, 1563; travelled in France, 1566; presented to living at Paisley, *c.* 1572; one of deputies chosen by general assembly to discuss jurisdiction of kirk, 1575; chaplain to regent; archbishop of St. Andrews, 1576; repeatedly charged with offences against the church, 1577–9; escaped to St. Andrews Castle, where he fell dangerously ill; cured by a 'wise woman,' who was ultimately burned for witchcraft; James VI's ambassador to Elizabeth, 1583; earned unpopularity by his strong parliamentary measures against presbyterians; charged with heresy and other offences and excommunicated by synod, 1585; his sentence remitted as illegal; again assailed by the assembly and excommunicated, 1588; said to have signed a 'Recantation' of the episcopal system which is probably spurious, 1590; wrote religious works in verse and prose. [i. 111]

ADAMSON, THOMAS (*fl.* 1680), master-gunner; published 'England's Defence, a Treatise concerning Invasion,' 1680. [i. 115]

ADDA (*d.* 565), king of Bernicia; succeeded his father Ida, 559; reigned about eight years. [i. 115]

ADDENBROOKE, JOHN (1680–1719), founder of hospital at Cambridge; educated at Catharine Hall, Cambridge; M.D., 1712; published an 'Essay on Freethinking,' 1714. [i. 115]

ADDINGTON, first BARON (1805–1889). [See HUBBARD, JOHN GELLIBRAND.]

ADDINGTON, ANTHONY (1713–1790), physician; educated at Winchester and Trinity College, Oxford; B.A., 1739; M.A., 1740; M.B., 1741; M.D., 1744; practised at Reading; F.C.P., 1756; censor, 1757; practised in London; attended Lord Chatham in his severe illness, 1767, and Prince of Wales, 1788. [i. 116]

ADDINGTON, HENRY, first VISCOUNT SIDMOUTH (1757–1844), son of Anthony Addington [q. v.]; educated at Winchester; admitted to Lincoln's Inn, 1771; commoner of Brasenose College, Oxford, 1774; B.A., 1778; won chancellor's gold medal for English essay, 1779; intimate with William Pitt from childhood; M.P. for Devizes, 1783; speaker of the House of Commons, 1789–1801; much occupied with the proceedings against Warren Hastings, 1795; first lord of the treasury and chancellor of exchequer, 1801; quarrelled with Pitt, 1803; his actions severely satirised by Canning; resigned, 1804; created Viscount Sidmouth and entered cabinet as president of council, 1805, but left it after a few months; president of council in Perceval's ministry, and later home secretary, 1812; dealt severely with the Luddites in the north; sought to check liberty of press in hope of quieting disorders among labouring classes, 1817; Manchester massacre, 1819, partly due to his coercive measures; retired from office, 1821, and from cabinet, 1824; voted against the Reform Bill, 1832. [i. 117]

ADDINGTON, HENRY UNWIN (1790–1870), permanent under-secretary for foreign affairs, 1842–54. [i. 121]

ADDINGTON, STEPHEN (1729–1796), independent minister at Spaldwick, Huntingdonshire; published educational works; D.D. [i. 121]

ADDISON, CHARLES GREENSTREET (*d.* 1866), legal writer; barrister, 1842; published legal and historical works. [i. 121]

ADDISON, JOHN (*fl.* 1538), divine; D.D. Pembroke Hall, Cambridge, 1523; deprived of his spiritual promotions for concealment of revelations of Elizabeth Barton [q. v.] [i. 121]

ADDISON, JOHN (1766?–1844), composer and performer on double-bass; composed and performed in operas given at Covent Garden and Lyceum. [i. 122]

ADDISON, JOSEPH (1672–1719), essayist, poet, and statesman, son of Lancelot Addison [q. v.]; educated at Charterhouse with Steele, and at Queen's College, Oxford; obtained demyship at Magdalen, 1689; M.A., 1693; probationer-fellow, 1697; fellow, 1698–1711; distinguished as a classical scholar; his Latin poems favourably noticed by Dryden, 1693; granted pension 300*l.* a year to qualify him for diplomatic service by foreign travel, 1697; travelled on the continent, 1699–1703; member of Kitcat Club; wrote on commission 'The Campaign,' a poem in honour of Blenheim, 1704; under-secretary of state, 1706; secretary to Wharton, when lord lieutenant of Ireland, 1709; formed close friendship with Swift, Steele, and other well-known writers; M.P. for Lostwithiel, 1708, and for Malmesbury, 1709 till death; defended whigs in the 'Whig Examiner' periodical, 1710; lost office on fall of whigs, 1711; contributed to Steele's 'Tatler,' 1709–11, and produced with Steele 'Spectator,' 1711–12; his 'Cato' acted with great success at Drury Lane, 1713; contributed to 'Guardian,' edited by Steele, 1713, and to a revived 'Spectator,' 1714; produced unsuccessfully 'The Drummer,' a prose comedy, 1715; regained his old secretaryship and produced the 'Freeholder,' 1715–16; one of lords commissioners of trade; married Countess of Warwick, 1716; retired from office with pension of 1,500*l.* a year, 1718; several papers in the 'Old Whig' by Addison, and in 'The Plebeian' by Steele, 1719, deal with a quarrel between the two. [i. 122]

ADDISON, LANCELOT (1632–1703), divine; B.A. Queen's College, Oxford, 1655; M.A., 1657; in capacity of Terræ filius delivered an attack on puritanism, and, being compelled to retract, left Oxford, 1657 ; chaplain of Dunston, 1660, and of Tangier, 1662 ; received the living of Milkirk, Wiltshire, 1671 ; B.D. and D.D., Oxford, 1675 ; dean of Lichfield, 1683 ; wrote theological and devotional works. [i. 131]

ADDISON, LAURA (d. 1852), actress ; first appeared 1843, at Worcester ; played Desdemona to Macready's Othello c. 1843, and Juliet, Portia, Isabella, Imogen, Miranda, and Lady Macbeth under Phelps at Sadler's Wells, 1846 seq. ; with Kean at Haymarket, 1849. [i. 133]

ADDISON, THOMAS (1793–1860), physician ; M.D. Edinburgh, 1815 ; surgeon at Lock Hospital ; assistant physician at Guy's Hospital, 1824 ; physician, 1837 ; discovered ' Addison's disease ' ; wrote medical works of some importance. [i. 133]

ADDY, WILLIAM (fl. 1685), author of a system of shorthand, in which the bible was printed, 1687. [i. 134]

ADEL- [See ETHEL-]

ADELA (1062 ?–1137), mother of Stephen, king of England ; daughter of William the Conqueror and Matilda of Flanders ; married, 1080, Stephen, earl of Meaux and Brie, who succeeded to Blois and Chartres, 1090 ; ruled with great thoroughness during her husband's absence on the first crusade, 1095–9 ; regent on her husband's death, 1101, till majority of her eldest son Theobald, 1109 ; took the veil ; effected an alliance between Theobald and Henry I of England, 1118. [i. 134]

ADELAIDE, QUEEN OF WILLIAM IV (1792–1849), eldest daughter of George, duke of Saxe-Coburg Meiningen ; married William, duke of Clarence, 1818 ; resided principally at Bushey Park until accession of William, 1830 ; unpopular owing to her supposed interference with politics during the reform agitation. [i. 136]

ADELARD OF BATH, or ÆTHELHARD (12th cent.), philosophical writer ; seems to have travelled largely in Europe, Asia, and Africa ; wrote a work on Arabic science, which was published after 1472, and one on ' Identity and Difference.' [i. 137]

ADELIZA (d. 1066 ?), daughter of William I ; possibly betrothed to Harold, 1062. [i. 137]

ADELIZA OF LOUVAIN (d. 1151), second queen of Henry I, daughter of Godfrey of Louvain, descendant of Charles the Great ; married Henry I, 1121 ; patronised literature ; on Henry's death retired probably to Arundel Castle ; afterwards married William de Albini. [i. 137]

ADKINS, ROBERT (1626–1685), ejected minister ; fellow of Wadham College, Oxford, where his preaching attracted much attention ; chaplain to Cromwell ; minister of Theydon (1653–7) ; removed successively to two churches at Exeter, whence he was ejected, 1660, 1662. [i. 138]

ADLER, NATHAN MARCUS (1803–1890), chief rabbi ; educated in Germany ; ordained, 1828 ; Ph.D., Erlangen, 1828 ; chief rabbi of Oldenburg, 1829, of Hanover, 1830, of London, 1844 ; took chief part in founding Jews' College, London, 1855 ; made proposal which resulted in United Synagogues bill, 1870 ; annotated Onkelos' paraphrase of the Pentateuch. [Suppl. i. 18]

ADOLPH, JOSEPH ANTONY (1729–1762), painter ; in England, 1745–55 ; painted portrait of George III when Prince of Wales. [i. 139]

ADOLPHUS FREDERICK, DUKE OF CAMBRIDGE (1774–1850), seventh son of George III ; K.G., 1786 ; colonel in Hanoverian army, 1793 ; served as colonel and major-general in campaign of 1794–5 ; lieutenant-general in Hanoverian service, 1798, and in British army, 1803 ; created Duke of Cambridge, 1801 ; privy councillor, 1802 ; field marshal, 1813 ; viceroy of Hanover, 1816–37 ; chancellor of St. Andrews University, 1811–14 ; married Princess Augusta, third daughter of Frederick of Hesse-Cassel, 1818. [i. 139]

ADOLPHUS, JOHN (1768–1845), barrister and historical writer ; admitted attorney 1790 ; published ' Biographical Memoirs of the French Revolution,' 1799, and ' History of England from 1760–1783,' 1802 ; called to the bar, 1807 ; defended Thistlewood and the Cato Street conspirators, 1820 ; wrote historical, biographical, and miscellaneous works. [i. 140]

ADOLPHUS, JOHN LEYCESTER (1795–1862), barrister and author ; educated at Merchant Taylors' and St. John's College, Oxford ; published criticisms on ' Waverley Novels,' assigning their authorship to Scott, 1821 ; called to bar, 1822. [i. 142]

ADRAIN, ROBERT (1775–1843), mathematician ; engaged in rebellion in Ireland, 1798, and fled to America ; professor of mathematics at various colleges, including Columbia College, New York ; published mathematical works. [i. 142]

ADRIAN IV (d. 1159), pope ; whose name is said to have been NICHOLAS BREAKSPEAR ; of humble origin ; studied at Arles, and after serving in menial offices was admitted to, and subsequently became abbot of, the order of St. Rufus, near Valence ; cardinal of Albano, 1146 ; elected pope on death of Anastasius IV, 1154 ; his pontificate a period of constant struggles with the Emperor Frederick, who set forth imperial claims over North Italy, and in a lesser degree with William, the Norman king of Sicily. His object was to maintain the claims of the Roman church as defined by Gregory VII. He granted Ireland to Henry II. [i. 143]

ADRIAN DE CASTELLO (1460 ?–1521 ?), statesman and reviver of learning ; sent by pope Innocent VIII as nuncio to Scotland, 1488 ; collector of Peter's pence in England, 1489 ; prebendary of St. Paul's Cathedral, and rector of St. Dunstan-in-the-East, 1492 ; English ambassador at Rome and clerk to the papal treasury, 1492 ; made, in his absence, bishop of Hereford 1502, and of Bath and Wells 1504 ; left Rome on the death of pope Alexander VI, 1503 ; returned 1511, on accession of Leo X, and though implicated in the attempt to murder him, was dealt with leniently ; deprived of collectorship and of the bishopric of Bath, 1518 ; published classical and philosophical works. [i. 146]

ADY, JOSEPH (1770–1852), notorious circular-letter impostor. [i. 147]

ADYE, SIR JOHN MILLER (1819–1900), general ; cadet at Woolwich, 1834 ; second lieutenant royal artillery, 1836 ; captain, 1852 ; brigade major of artillery in Turkey, 1854 ; served at defence of Cawnpore, 1857 ; lieutenant-colonel, 1857 ; deputy adjutant-general of artillery in India, 1863–6 ; colonel, 1867 ; K.O.B. 1873 ; major-general, 1875 ; governor of military academy, Woolwich, 1875 ; chief of staff under Lord Wolseley in Egypt, 1882 ; G.C.B., 1882 ; governor of Gibraltar, 1882–6 ; colonel commandant, 1881 ; general, 1884 ; opposed rectification of Afghan frontier ; published autobiographical and other writings. [Suppl. i. 18]

ADYE, STEPHEN PAYNE (d. 1794), soldier ; served as brigade-major of artillery in North America ; published a work on courts-martial. [i. 148]

ÆLFGAR, EARL (d. 1062 ?), son of Leofric of Mercia and Godgifu (Lady Godiva) ; supported King Eadward the Confessor against Godwine at Gloucester, 1051 ; earl of East-Anglia ; outlawed for treason, 1055 ; invaded Herefordshire, but was defeated by Harold ; made peace and was restored to his earldom ; earl of Mercia, 1057 ; outlawed 1058 ; regained his earldom with help of Northmen ; left two sons, Eadwine and Morkere. [i. 148]

ÆLFGIFU [Lat. ELGIVA] (fl. 956), was the wife of King Eadwig, from whom she was parted by Archbishop Oda on account of kinship. She and her mother Æthelgifu from their hostility to Dunstan, have been made the victims of monastic legend. Later legends confound her and her mother, and give an untrustworthy account of various cruelties perpetrated on her by Oda and the monks. [i. 149]

ÆLFGIFU (fl. 1030), ' of Northampton,' perhaps the mistress of Olaf, ' the Saint,' and certainly of Cnut, to whom she bore Harold and Swend. In 1030 Cnut sent her with Swend to rule over Norway. [i. 150]

ÆLFHEAH, known as ST. ALPHEGE, and also called GODWINE (954–1012), archbishop of Canterbury ; monk at Deerhurst ; anchorite at Bath ; bishop of Winchester, 984 ; archbishop of Canterbury, 1006 ; promoted council of Enham, which made enactments against heathenism and sale of slaves ; incurred hatred of Northmen by confirming Olaf Tryggwesson in his Christianity, and obtaining from him promise, 994, not again to invade England ; captured in invasion of Danes 1011, and, on refusing to ransom himself, was put to death. Cnut translated his body to Canterbury, and Anselm in 1078 induced Lanfranc to recognise his canonisation. [i. 150]

ÆLFHERE (d. 983), ealdorman of the Mercians. [i. 152]

ÆLFRED (849–901), king of the West-Saxons, the son of Ethelwulf [q. v.] ; born at Wantage ; sent to Rome, where Leo IV hallowed him to king, 853, returning to England in 856 ; no attempt was made to set him on the throne on his father's death, though he perhaps bore the title of secundarius during his brothers' reigns ; assisted his brother, Ethelred I, against the Danes, and fought at Æscesdún, Basing, and Merton (871) ; succeeded his brother, defeated the Danes at Wilton, and obtained a respite by concluding a treaty, 871 ; the legendary account of the harshness of his early rule and of his three years' sojourn in hiding at Glastonbury untrustworthy in its particulars and largely mythical ; called to meet, according to authentic history, the second great invasion of the Danes in December 878, headed by Guthrum, who overran Somerset without opposition ; gathered a small company, with which he took post at Athelney ; seven weeks later defeated the Danes at Ethandún (seemingly Edington in Wiltshire), on which peace followed (Guthrum being baptised and assigned a dominion in the north and east of England—roughly speaking, the part beyond Watling Street—under the nominal overlordship of Ælfred) ; war with Guthrum renewed in 884 by Ælfred ; acquired London, which he fortified and about the same time received the submission of the Angles and Saxons throughout Britain, as well as of several princes of Wales ; assailed, after a few years of comparative quiet, by another great host of Northmen, who were joined by the Danes of East-Anglia in 894. War raged in all parts of England until 897, when the invaders withdrew, and Ælfred, by improving his ships, put an end to the ravagings of the smaller vikings. Ælfred died on 28 Oct. 901, and was buried at New Minster (afterwards Hyde Abbey) at Winchester. His wife Ealhswith survived him. Ælfred not only saved Wessex from the perils of the Scandinavian invasions, but made his kingdom a centre for the deliverance and union of the whole country. The stress of the times naturally strengthened the royal authority. Much of the fame of Ælfred's institutions is legendary. His legislation consisted simply in selecting the best of the laws of the earlier kings, but the account of his division of England into hundreds and shires may have some basis in a reorganisation of southern Mercia. Ælfred's promotion of learning is perhaps the most distinctive feature of his rule. His foundation of schools at Oxford is fabulous, but he brought to Wessex the best scholars of the time, including Plegmund, Werfrith, Grimbold, John the Old-Saxon, Asser, and John Scotus Erigena. Men of eminence in any useful art, like the seafaring Othhere, were also encouraged. The time of his own greatest literary activity lay between 886 and 893. His chief writings were his translations of Boethius' 'Consolation of Philosophy,' of the histories of Bæda and 'Orosius,' and of the 'Pastoral Care' of Gregory the Great. His Boethius was edited by Samuel Fox in 1864 ; his Bæda is printed in Smith's edition of 1722 ; his Orosius was edited by Dr. Bosworth in 1851, and his Gregory's 'Pastoral' by Henry Sweet for the Early-English Text Society in 1871–2. These works were not merely translations ; they were carefully recast in a thoroughly English spirit, so that they form a part of the country's earliest literature. [i. 153]

ÆLFRED (d. 1036), ætheling ; younger son of Ethelred II and Emma [q. v.] ; fled to Normandy with his brother Eadward on conquest of England by Sweyn, 1013 ; after death of Cnut (1035) landed at Dover, and was captured at Guildford by Godwin. While being conveyed to Ely he was blinded by his captors, and died there of his wounds. [i. 152]

ÆLFRIC (d. 1005), archbishop of Canterbury, possibly seventh abbot of St. Albans, was bishop of Ramsbury and Wilton, and was elected to Canterbury in 995. His body was buried at Abingdon and translated to Canterbury in Cnut's reign. His will is extant. [i. 162]

ÆLFRIC, called BATA (fl. 1005), a monk and a disciple of Ælfric (fl. 1006) [q. v.] [i. 164]

ÆLFRIC, called GRAMMATICUS (fl. 1006), erroneously identified with Ælfric (d. 1005) [q. v.] and Ælfric (d.

1051) [q. v.] ; pupil of Ethelwold [q. v.] ; monk at Winchester ; successively abbot of Cerne and Ensham ; author of two books of 'Homilies,' translations from Latin writers. The Paschal homily against transubstantiation was published in 1566 under ecclesiastical patronage as ' A Testimonie of Antiquitie,' and re-edited in 1877. The 'Homilies' were published in 1844–6. Ten other works of his survive. Ælfric is a most prominent figure in Anglo-Saxon literature, and his writings are important from their illustration of the belief and practice of the early English church. [i. 164]

ÆLFRIC (fl. 950 ?–1016 ?), ealdorman of the East-Mercians, son of Ælfhere [q. v.] ; succeeded his father in 983, and was banished in 986, but restored to favour before 991 ; attempted to betray an English fleet to the Danes, 992, and in 1003 would not fight against Swend ; perhaps identical with ealdorman Ælfric who fell at Assandún in 1016. [i. 163]

ÆLFRIC (fl. 1045), abbot of St. Albans, possibly eleventh abbot. Matthew Paris, whose account is full of errors, says that Ælfric was chancellor of King Ethelred before he became monk, that he composed and set to music a life of St. Alban, and that he died during a dispute with monks of Ely occasioned by his own duplicity. [i. 163]

ÆLFRIC (fl. 1050), archbishop-elect of Canterbury ; rejected by Eadward for Robert of London. [i. 164]

ÆLFRIC, called PUTTOC (d. 1051), archbishop of York, and provost of Winchester ; consecrated to York in 1023 ; held Worcester temporarily (1040–1), and was accused of persuading Harthacnut to lay waste the shire because the men of Worcester would not receive him as bishop. [i. 166]

ÆLFSIGE (d. 959), bishop of Winchester, 951 ; elected to Canterbury, 958, but died on his way to Rome to receive the pall. [i. 167]

ÆLFTHRYTH [Lat. ELTRUDIS] (d. 929), daughter of King Ælfred ; wife of Baldwin II of Flanders ; ancestress of Matilda, William the Conqueror's wife. [i. 167]

ÆLFTHRYTH [Lat. ELFRIDA] (945 ?–1000), daughter of Ordgar [q. v.] ; mother of Ethelred II ; slew her stepson Eadward. William of Malmesbury's romantic account of her life is mainly fabulous. [i. 167]

ÆLFWEARD (d. 1044), bishop of London ; monk of Ramsey ; abbot of Evesham, 1014 ; bishop of London, 1035. Smitten with leprosy at close of life, he retired to Ramsey, which he enriched with numerous relics. [i. 168]

ÆLFWIG (d. 1066), abbot of New Minster (1063) ; uncle of Harold ; fell at the battle of Hastings. [i. 168]

ÆLFWINE (d. 1047), bishop of Winchester, 1032 ; chaplain of Cnut and (in legend and ballad) the lover of Cnut's widow, Emma ; bishop, 1032. [i. 169]

ÆLLA (d. 514 ?), Saxon ealdorman ; landed in Britain, 477 ; captured Anderida, 491 ; became king of South-Saxons and 'first Bretwalda.' [i. 169]

ÆLLA (d. 588), first king of the Deirans, 559 ; son of Iffa and grandfather of Oswald [q. v.] ; threw off Bernician yoke. [i. 169]

ÆLLA (d. 867), king of the Northumbrians ; slain by the Danes in a great battle near York. [i. 169]

ÆLNOTH (fl. 1085–1109), monkish biographer ; native of Canterbury ; wrote a Latin life of St. Canute the Martyr (printed Copenhagen, 1602). [i. 170]

ÆLSINUS (10th cent.), a Winchester monk, illuminator and miniaturist. [i. 170]

ÆSC or **OISC** [ASH] (d. 512 ?), king of Kent ; son of Hengist the Jute : landed at Ebbsfleet, 449 ; shared his father's victories at Crayford (457) and Wippedsfleet ; reigned in Kent, 488–512. [i. 170]

ÆTHEL- [See ETHEL-]

ÆTHELSTAN. [See ATHELSTAN.]

AFFLECK, SIR EDMUND (1723 ?–1788), admiral ; lieutenant, 1745 ; captain, 1757 ; sailed with Rodney to relieve Gibraltar, 1779 ; served in N. America, and distinguished himself in repulse of French at St. Christopher's, and leeward of Dominica, 1782. [i. 171]

AFFLECK, PHILIP (1726–1799), admiral, brother of Sir Edmund Affleck [q. v.]; lieutenant, 1755; distinguished himself under Boscawen at Louisbourg, 1758; served under Rodney in West Indies, 1780; admiralty lord, 1793–9. [i. 171]

AGARD or **AGARDE**, ARTHUR (1540–1615), antiquary; appointed 1570 deputy chamberlain of the exchequer; drew up catalogues of state papers and records, and also a Latin treatise elucidating ' Domesday Book'; one of the earliest members of a society of antiquaries founded by Archbishop Parker, 1572. His essays for this society on the antiquity of shires, and of parliament, on old land measures, heralds, the Inns of Court, and similar topics, were printed by T. Hearne in his 'Collections' (1720 and 1775). His scholarly acumen enabled him to fix the authorship of the 'Dialogus de Scaccario' [see FITZNEALE or FITZNIGEL, RICHARD]. He was buried in Westminster Abbey cloisters. Many of his manuscripts are in the British Museum. [i. 172]

AGAS, RADULPH or RALPH (1540 ?–1621), land surveyor and maker of maps; practised as a surveyor in his native Suffolk, but is known for his three celebrated maps or rather bird's-eye views of Oxford (1578, Bodleian Libr.), Cambridge (1592, ib.), and London (1592 ?, Pepysian and Guildhall Libraries). His admirable view of London was reissued with spurious alterations by G. Vertue in 1737, and accurately by W. H. Overall in 1874 (' Civitas Londinum '). [i. 173]

AGASSE, JAMES LAURENT (d. 1846 ?), artist; born at Geneva; studied at Paris, and practised in England, 1801–45, as a painter of horses and dogs. [i. 175]

AGELNOTH. [See ETHELNOTH.]

AGGAS, EDWARD (fl. 1564–1601), apprentice to H. Toy [q. v.], and afterwards bookseller and printer in St. Paul's Churchyard; a number of his publications are translations, possibly his own. [i. 175]

AGGAS or **ANGUS**, ROBERT (d. 1679), scene-painter to Dorset Garden Theatre, temp. Charles II. [i. 176]

AGLIO, AUGUSTINE (1777–1857), artist; born at Cremona; studied at Milan; decorated London interiors and theatre ceilings; sent landscapes to Royal Academy, and executed much lithographic work. [i. 176]

AGLIONBY, EDWARD (1520–1587 ?), recorder of Warwick, 1572, and M.P. for that town; made an oration to Elizabeth on her visit ther ; rendered from Latin the 'Epistle of Dr. Mathewe Gribalde,' 1550. [i. 176]

AGLIONBY, JOHN (d. 1611), royal chaplain and principal of St. Edmund Hall, Oxford. [i. 177]

AGNEW, SIR ANDREW, BART. (1687–1771), general, of Wigtonshire; fought at Ramillies, Oudenarde, and Malplaquet; promoted lieutenant-colonel, 1740; distinguished himself at Dettingen, and against Jacobites at Blair Castle (1746); as 'sheriff' of Tynemouth Castle was known to Walter Scott. [i. 177]

AGNEW, SIR ANDREW, BART. (1793–1849), Sabbatarian promoter; took charge in 1832 of abortive parliamentary movement to ' protect the Lord's Day.' [i. 178]

AGNEW, PATRICK ALEXANDER VANS (1822–1848), Indian official; assistant to resident at Lahore, 1848; despatched on administrative mission to Multan; was there murdered by natives (April), an outrage which led to second Sikh war and annexation of Punjáb. [i. 178]

AGUILAR, GRACE (1816–1847), novelist; of (Spanish) Jewish parentage; after some girlish dramas and poems, produced in 1842 'Spirit of Judaism' and similar essays. Better known are her novels 'Home Influence,' 1847, ' A Mother's Recompense,' 1850, and the pathetic fifteenth-century Spanish story, 'The Vale of Cedars,' 1850 (last two translated into German). [i. 179]

AGUS or **AGAS**, BENJAMIN (fl. 1662), divine, of Wymondham, Norfolk; published a ' Vindication of Nonconformity.' [i. 180]

AGUTTER, WILLIAM (1758–1835), preacher; M.A. Magdalen College, Oxford, 1784; noted for his sermons, especially one contrasting deathbeds of Dr. Johnson and David Hume (1786). [i. 180]

AICKIN or **AIKIN**, FRANCIS (d. 1805), actor; Dublin weaver's son; played at Smock Alley, Dublin; appeared at Drury Lane as Dick in ' Confederacy,' 1765; later in tragic parts, and managed Liverpool and Edinburgh theatres. [i. 181]

AICKIN or **AIKIN**, JAMES (d. 1803), actor; brother of Francis Aikin [q. v.]; appeared at Canongate, Edinburgh, 1766, Drury Lane, 1767, in heavy parts; fought duel with John Kemble over a theatre quarrel, 1792. [i. 181]

AIDAN (d. 606), West Scottish king (of Dalriada). [i. 181]

AIDAN, SAINT (d. 651), first bishop of Lindisfarne; set out from Iona, 635, to evangelise Northumbria; was befriended by King Oswald, whose people flocked to hear the monks of Lindisfarne; on Oswald's death worked chiefly in Deira, winning the heart of King Oswini, whose death at Bamborough (August 651) he survived but a few days; buried at Lindisfarne. [i. 182]

AIKENHEAD, MARY (1787–1858), founder of the Irish sisters of charity; bred a protestant; opened the first (Roman catholic) convent of sisters of charity, Dublin, 1816. [i. 183]

AIKENHEAD, THOMAS (1678 ?–1697), Edinburgh apothecary's son; hanged for ridiculing the bible. [i. 183]

AIKIN, ANNA LETITIA (1743–1825). [See BARBAULD.]

AIKIN, ARTHUR (1773–1854), chemist; son of John Aikin [q. v.]; educated by Barbauld at Palgrave; a pioneer of Geological Society, 1807 ; a fellow of Linnean Society; secretary of Society of Arts; treasurer of Chemical Society, 1841 ; published manuals of mineralogy and chemistry, a 'Dictionary' of these sciences (1807–14), and translated Denon's 'Travels' (1801). [i. 184]

AIKIN, CHARLES ROCHEMONT (1775–1847), doctor; M.R.C.S.; wrote on 'Cowpox' (1800), and collaborated in the 'Chemical Dictionary' of his elder brother, Arthur Aikin [q. v.] [i. 184]

AIKIN, EDMUND (1780–1820), architect; brother of Arthur and Charles Aikin [q. v.]; contributed architectural articles to Rees's 'Encyclopædia.' [i. 185]

AIKIN, JOHN (1713–1780), scholar and theological tutor; born in Scotland; studied at Aberdeen with distinction; became divinity tutor at (dissenting) Warrington Academy (1761–78); D.D. Aberdeen. [i. 185]

AIKIN, JOHN (1747–1822), author; son of preceding; studied at Edinburgh, London, and Leyden (M.D.); practised at Yarmouth; removed to Stoke Newington, 1798; his house a resort of liberal thinkers, Priestley, Darwin, Howard, and others; compiled 'Memoirs of Medicine in Great Britain,' the lion's share of the ten-vol. 'General Biography,' and wrote biographical and critical essays and prefaces. [i. 185]

AIKIN, LUCY (1781–1864), daughter of preceding; lived chiefly at Hampstead, where she compiled her 'historical memoirs' of the courts of Elizabeth (1818), of James I (1822), of Charles I (1833), her lives of Addison and Mrs. Barbauld (her aunt), and minor pieces. Her correspondence with Channing (1826–1842) is a valuable illustration of the unitarian circle to which the Aikins belonged. [i. 186]

AIKMAN, WILLIAM (1682–1731), portraitist; studied under Sir J. Medina; practised at Edinburgh; painted portraits of Allan Ramsay and Thomson (whom he assisted), Gay, Somervile, and Argyll; modelled his style on Kneller. [i. 187]

AILESBURY, EARLS OF. [See BRUCE, ROBERT, first EARL, d. 1685; BRUCE, THOMAS, second EARL, 1655 ?–1741.]

AILMER (d. 1137). [See ETHELMÆR.]

AILRED OF RIEVAULX (1109 ?–1166). [See ETHELRED.]

AINGER, THOMAS (1799–1863), honorary prebendary of St. Paul's. [i. 188]

AINSLIE, GEORGE ROBERT (1776–1839), general; ensign 19th regiment, 1793, captain, 1794, major, 1799; lieutenant-colonel in a fencible regiment, 1800; lieutenant-colonel 25th regiment, 1807 ; brevet-colonel, 1810 ; governor of Eustatius, 1812, of Dominica, 1813–14 ; major-general, 1814 ; collector of Anglo-Norman coins ; author of ' Anglo-French Coinage,' 1830. [i. 188]

AINSLIE, HENRY (1760–1834), senior wrangler, second Smith's prizeman, and fellow of Pembroke Hall, Cambridge, 1781 ; physician to Addenbrook's Hospital, 1787 ; M.D. 1793, F.R.C.P. 1795 ; physician to St. Thomas's Hospital, 1795–1800 ; Harveian orator, 1802.: [i. 188]

AINSLIE, HEW (1792–1878), amanuensis to Dugald Stewart ; attracted to Robert Owen's settlement at New Harmony, Indiana, 1822 ; afterwards a brewer ; his collected songs and ballads, published New York, 1855. [i. 188]

AINSLIE, SIR ROBERT (1730 ?–1812), ambassador and numismatist ; knighted 1775 ; ambassador to Constantinople, 1776–92 ; pensioned, 1796 ; M.P. for Milborne Port, Somerset, 1796–1802 ; created baronet, 1804 ; formed collection of ancient Eastern and north African coins, descriptions of which were published by l'Abbate Domenico Sestini in eleven volumes, 1789–1806 ; also of illustrations of Eastern life, drawings of which by Luigi Mayer were engraved by Thomas Milton and published in three volumes 1801–4. [i. 188]

AINSLIE, ROBERT (1766–1838), writer to the signet, 1789 ; brother of Sir Whitelaw [q. v.] ; correspondent of Burns, and author of two small religious works. [i. 190]

AINSLIE, SIR WHITELAW (1767–1837), surgeon in East India Company's service, 1788–1815 ; published ' Materia Medica of Hindoostan ' (1813) and similar works. [i. 190]

AINSWORTH, HENRY (1571–1623 ?), leader of the separatist congregation at Amsterdam ; scholar of Caius College, Cambridge, 1587–91 ; became a Brownist and bookseller's porter at Amsterdam in 1593, and then ' teacher ' at Francis Johnson's church ; with Johnson founded an independent congregation there ; sole or part author of ' Confession of Faith of the People called Brownists,' 1596 ; finally separated from Johnson in 1610 ; died at Amsterdam. In rabbinical and oriental scholarship he was equalled by few in Europe, writing numerous controversial and exegetical works, many of them now rare. [i. 191]

AINSWORTH, ROBERT (1660–1743), lexicographer ; was educated at Bolton, and kept schools there and, after 1698, at Bethnal Green, Hackney, and other places near London ; collected coins, and was elected F.S.A. in 1724 ; wrote an important treatise on education, 1698, and compiled a Latin-English dictionary, 1736. [i. 194]

AINSWORTH, WILLIAM FRANCIS (1807–1896), geologist ; cousin of William Harrison Ainsworth [q. v.] ; L.R.C.S., Edinburgh, 1827 ; studied geology in London, Paris, and Brussels ; founded, 1830, ' Edinburgh Journal of Natural and Geographical Science ' (1830–1) ; surgeon and geologist to expedition to Euphrates, under Francis Rawdon Chesney [q. v.], 1835 ; took charge of expedition to Christians of Chaldæa, 1838–40 ; published accounts of both expeditions ; editor of ' New Monthly Magazine,' 1871 ; original fellow of Royal Geographical Society, 1830 ; F.S.A., 1830. His works include ' Travels in the Track of the Ten Thousand Greeks,' 1844. [Suppl. i. 20]

AINSWORTH, WILLIAM HARRISON (1805–1882), novelist ; educated at Manchester Grammar School, and articled to a solicitor there in 1821 ; went to London to finish his legal education in 1824, and was in business as a publisher, 1826–8, Scott writing ' Bonnets of Bonnie Dundee ' for one of his annuals ; his first novel, ' Rookwood,' published 1834, immediately successful ; edited ' Bentley's Miscellany,' 1840–2, and ' Ainsworth's Magazine,' 1842–53, when he acquired ' New Monthly Magazine ' ; lived at Kensal Green, where Dickens, Thackeray, Landseer, Clarkson Stanfield, Talfourd, Jerrold, and Cruikshank were among his guests. He wrote thirty-nine novels, chiefly historical, of which the best known are ' Jack Sheppard,' 1839, ' Tower of London,' 1840, ' Old St. Paul's,' 1841, ' The Miser's Daughter,' 1842, and ' Windsor Castle,' 1843. [i. 197]

AIO (d. 974), historian ; a fabulous monk of Croyland Abbey, whose supposititious work is quoted in Ingulf's forged ' Chronicle.' [i. 199]

AIRAY, CHRISTOPHER (1601–1670), pioneer in English logic ; fellow of Queen's College, Oxford,

1627, and subsequently incumbent of Milford, Hampshire ; published ' Fasciculus Præceptorum Logicorum,' 1628. [i. 199]

AIRAY, HENRY (1560 ?–1616), puritan divine ; fellow of Queen's College, Oxford, 1586 ; provost, 1598 ; as vice-chancellor in 1606 he came into conflict with Laud ; rector of Bletchingdon, 1616 ; an evangelical Calvinist, he preached fierce sermons against Rome. [i. 199]

AIRD, THOMAS (1802–1876), Scottish poet ; educated at Edinburgh, where he became acquainted with Carlyle, James Hogg, and De Quincey ; published his first work, ' Martzoufle,' 1826 ; contributed to ' Blackwood's Magazine ' ; edited ' Dumfriesshire and Galloway Herald,' 1835–63 ; published collected poems, 1848. [i. 201]

AIREY, SIR GEORGE (1761–1833), general ; ensign, 71st regiment, 1779 ; accompanied 48th regiment to West, Indies as lieutenant, 1781 ; captain 1788 ; assisted Sir Charles Grey in reducing French West India Islands, 1793 ; lieutenant-colonel 8th regiment, 1798 ; held offices in Minorca, Ireland, Sicily, and the Ionian Islands ; lieutenant-general, 1821 ; received command of 39th regiment, 1823 ; K.C.H. [i. 201]

AIREY, SIR JAMES TALBOT (1812–1898), general ; son of Sir George Airey [q. v.] ; enr'gn, 1830 ; extra aide-de-camp to Major-general Elphinstone, 1841 ; served at Cabul and in Gwalior campaign ; major, 1851 ; served in Crimea ; lieutenant-general and K.C.B., 1877 ; general, 1881. [Suppl. i. 21]

AIREY, RICHARD, LORD AIREY (1803–1881), general ; son of Sir George Airey [q. v.] ; educated at Sandhurst, and was successively ensign, lieutenant, captain, major, and lieutenant-colonel, 34th regiment, 1821–38 ; colonel and military secretary to Lord Hardinge, 1852 ; quartermaster-general to Crimean army, 1854–5 ; major-general and K.C.B., 1854 ; quartermaster-general, 1855–65 ; exonerated himself of charges of inefficiency in Crimea, 1856 ; governor of Gibraltar, 1865–70 ; G.C.B., 1867 ; general, 1871 ; created peer, 1876 ; president of the commission on the short service system, 1879. [i. 202]

AIRTH, first EARL (1591–1661). [See GRAHAM, WILLIAM.]

AIRY, SIR GEORGE BIDDELL (1801–1892), astronomer royal ; sizar of Trinity College, Cambridge, 1819 ; senior wrangler, and first Smith's prizeman, 1823 ; fellow, 1824 ; member of Astronomical Society, 1828, and of Geological Society, 1829 ; Lucasian professor of mathematics at Cambridge, 1826 ; Plumian professor of astronomy and director of Cambridge observatory, 1828 ; astronomer royal, 1835–81 ; F.R.S., 1836 ; equipped Royal Observatory with instruments designed by himself ; created at Greenwich magnetic and meteorological department, 1838 ; reduced all planetary and lunar observations made at Greenwich from 1750 to 1830 ; gold medallist, Royal Astronomical Society, 1846 ; controlled British expeditions to observe transit of Venus, 1874, and subsequently reduced collected data ; D.C.L., Oxford, 1844 ; LL.D., Cambridge, 1862, and Edinburgh ; K.C.B., 1872 ; published voluminous writings on astronomical subjects. [Suppl. i. 22]

AISLABIE, JOHN (1670–1742), statesman ; M.P. for Ripon, 1695–1702 and 1705–21, and for Northallerton, 1702 ; one of commissioners for executing office of lord high admiral, 1712 ; successively treasurer of navy, and chancellor of exchequer, 1714–18 ; supported South Sea Company's scheme for paying off national debt, 1719, and on its failure was expelled the house, 1721. [i. 203]

AITCHISON, SIR CHARLES UMPHERSTON (1832–1896), lieutenant-governor of the Punjáb ; educated at Edinburgh (M.A., 1853, LL.D., 1877), and at Halle ; entered Indian civil service, 1855 ; under-secretary in political department, India, 1859–65 ; commissioner of Lahore ; foreign secretary, 1868–78 ; chief commissioner of British Burma, 1878–81 ; lieutenant-governor of the Punjáb, 1882 ; member of governor-general's council, 1887–8 ; K.C.S.I., 1881 ; C.I.E., 1882 ; published ' Collection of Treaties . . . relating to India ' (1862–92, 11 vols.), and other works. [Suppl. i. 25]

AITKEN, JAMES (1752–1777), incendiary, known as JOHN THE PAINTER ; apprenticed as house-painter in Edinburgh ; came to London and took to highway-robbery on Finchley Common ; fled to America and took part in tea-duty riots at Boston; returned, 1775, and, being imbued with anti-monarchical principles, planned destruction of British navy when about to sail against America; succeeded in firing some storehouses at Portsmouth and Bristol, and was ultimately executed at Portsmouth. [i. 205]

AITKEN, JOHN (1793-1833), editor of 'Constable's Miscellany'; employed in a bank, but in 1822 became bookseller in Edinburgh; wrote occasional verse and prose. [i. 206]

AITKEN, ROBERT (1800-1873), preacher; ordained, 1823; withdrew from English church; preached in Wesleyan and other chapels, and returned to English church, 1840; beneficed in Cornish parishes; directed building of a fine church at Pendeen. [i. 206]

AITKEN, Sir WILLIAM (1825-1892), pathologist; M.D. Edinburgh, 1848; assistant pathologist to medical commission in Crimea, 1855; professor of pathology at army medical school, Fort Pitt, Chatham (afterwards at Netley), 1860-92; F.R.S, 1873; knighted, 1887; published medical writings. [Suppl. i. 26]

AITKIN, JOHN (d. 1790), surgeon; M.R.C.S. Edinburgh, 1770; surgeon and lecturer at Edinburgh, 1779; made some practical improvements in surgery and wrote medical works. [i. 206]

AITON, JOHN (1797-1863), religious writer; son of William Aiton (1760-1848) [q. v.]; published a refutation of Robert Owen, 1824. [i. 207]

AITON, WILLIAM (1731-1793), botanist; assistant gardener at Botanic Garden, Chelsea, 1754; manager of Kew Botanic Gardens, 1759; manager of royal forcing and pleasure gardens at Kew and Richmond, 1783; published 'Hortus Kewensis,' 1789. [i. 207]

AITON, WILLIAM (1760-1848), sheriff-substitute of Lanark; authority on Scottish husbandry; wrote historical and agricultural works. [i. 207]

AITON, WILLIAM TOWNSEND (1766-1849), botanist; son of William Aiton (1731-1793) [q. v.], whom he assisted and succeeded at Kew, 1793; edited his father's 'Hortus Kewensis,' 1810-13; a founder and fellow of the Royal Horticultural Society. [i. 208]

AKENSIDE, MARK (1721-1770), poet and physician; after 1737 contributed frequently to the 'Gentleman's Magazine'; sent to Edinburgh to study theology, 1739, but abandoned it for medicine, 1740; member of the Medical Society of Edinburgh, 1740; practised in Newcastle, 1741-3; went to London and published 'Pleasures of the Imagination,' a didactic poem, 1744; toured in Holland, and graduated doctor of physic at Leyden; practised at Northampton, 1744, and at Hampstead, 1745-7; becoming embarrassed, he was relieved and provided for by Jeremiah Dyson, and ultimately rose to eminence in his profession; doctor (by mandamus) of Cambridge University and F.R.S., 1753; F.C.P., 1754; physician to Christ's Hospital, 1759; physician to the queen, 1761; collected poems published, 1772. [i. 208]

AKERMAN, JOHN YONGE (1806-1873), numismatist and antiquary; secretary to William Cobbett, and later, to Lord Albert Conyngham; F.S.A., 1834; joint secretary, 1848, and sole secretary, 1853-60; started and contributed largely to 'Numismatic Journal'; helped to found Numismatic Society of London, 1836. [i. 211]

ALABASTER, WILLIAM (1567-1640), Latin poet and divine; nephew by marriage of John Still, author of 'Gammer Gurton's Needle'; educated at Westminster and Trinity College, Cambridge; began a Latin epic to Elizabeth, preserved in manuscript; wrote 'Roxana' before 1592; accompanied Earl of Essex as chaplain to Cadiz, 1596; converted to Romanism; after publishing several religious works and suffering imprisonment was reconverted to protestantism; D.D., prebendary of St. Paul's and rector of Therfield, Hertfordshire. [i. 211]

ALAIN DE LILLE or DE L'ISLE (1114-1203), scholar; has been identified with Alain de Flandre, bishop of Auxerre, c. 1152; nationality uncertain; probably spent much time in England with Cistercians; wrote 'Commentary on Merlin's Prophecies,' and in prose and verse on other subjects; possibly rector of the ecclesiastical school, Paris; retired to abbey of Citeaux, where he died. [i. 212]

ALAN OF BECCLES (d. 1240), official secretary to Archbishops Pandulph and Thomas de Blundeville of Norwich, 1218-36; archdeacon of Sudbury, 1225; one of the arbitrators between Bishop Grosseteste and his chapter, 1239. [i. 214]

ALAN OF LYNN (fl. 1424?), Carmelite monk and scholastic. [i. 214]

ALAN OF TEWKESBURY (12th century), writer; probably for some years canon of Benevento, Italy, where he became interested in Henry II's struggle with Becket; entered monastery of Christ Church, Canterbury, 1174; incurred Henry II's displeasure by procuring authority to collect Peter's pence; subsequently Abbot of Tewkesbury till death; wrote life of Becket. [i. 214]

ALAN OF WALSINGHAM (d. 1364?), architect; junior monk at Ely, 1314; sub-prior, 1321; designed St. Mary's Chapel, now Trinity Church, Ely; sacristan 1321; rebuilt tower of the cathedral and made other additions, constructing the unique 'lantern'; prior, 1341; bishop-elect of Ely, 1344 and 1361, but election set aside by the pope. [i. 215]

ALAN, WILLIAM (1532-1594). [See ALLEN, WILLIAM.]

ALAND, Sir JOHN FORTESCUE, first BARON FORTESCUE OF CREDAN (1670-1746), justice of common pleas, 1728-46; solicitor-general to Prince of Wales, 1714, and to king, 1715; baron of exchequer, 1717; justice of king's bench, 1728. [i. 216]

ALANE, ALEXANDER (1500-1565). [See ALESIUS, ALEXANDER.]

ALASCO, JOHN (1499-1560). [See LASKI, JOHN.]

ALBAN, St. (d. 304?), called 'protomartyr of Britain'; said by Bede to have suffered (22 June, c. 304), on site of future abbey of St. Albans, martyrdom for sheltering a Christian cleric who converted him; Offa (d. 796) [q. v.] is believed to have discovered the martyr's body. [Suppl. i. 27]

ALBANY, LOUISA, COUNTESS OF (1753-1824), wife of Prince Charles Edward, the Young Pretender; daughter of Gustavus Adolphus, prince of Stolberg-Gedern; on death of her father became pensioner of Empress Maria Theresa; canoness of Mons, 1770; secretly married Charles Edward, 1772; left him after eight years, and lived with Alfieri the poet; on outbreak of French revolution came to England and was received at court; on death of Alfieri (1803) lived with Fabre, a French artist; died at Florence. [i. 216]

ALBANY, DUKE OF (1853-1884). [See LEOPOLD.]

ALBANY, DUKES OF. [See STEWART, ROBERT, first DUKE, 1340?-1420; STEWART, MURDAC or MURDOCH, second DUKE, d. 1425; STEWART, ALEXANDER, DUKE OF ALBANY, 1454?-1485; STEWART, JOHN, DUKE OF ALBANY, 1481-1536.]

ALBEMARLE, DUKES OF. [See MONCK, GEORGE, first DUKE, 1608-1670; MONCK, CHRISTOPHER, second DUKE, 1653-1688.]

ALBEMARLE, EARLS OF. [See WILLIAM DE FORS, d. 1242; WILLIAM DE FORS d. 1260; KEPPEL, ARNOLD JOOST VAN, first EARL of the Keppel family, 1669-1718; KEPPEL, WILLIAM ANNE, second EARL, 1702-1754; KEPPEL, GEORGE, third EARL, 1724-1772; KEPPEL, GEORGE THOMAS, sixth EARL, 1799-1891; KEPPEL, WILLIAM COUTTS, seventh EARL, 1832-1894.]

ALBERT FRANCIS CHARLES AUGUSTUS EMMANUEL PRINCE-CONSORT OF ENGLAND (1819-1861), second son of Ernest, duke of Saxe-Coburg-Gotha, and of Louise, daughter of Augustus, duke of Saxe-Gotha-Altenburg; educated under private tutor; visited England with Duke of Coburg, 1836, when the Princess Victoria expressed her willingness to accept Albert as consort; continued his education at Brussels and Bonn, 1836-8; travelled through Italy with Baron Stockmar; came to England and became betrothed to Queen Victoria, 1839; married 1840; his annuity, proposed at 50,000l., was fixed at 30,000l., largely through influence of Peel; counselled by Stockmar; became a director of the Ancient Concerts and assisted Philharmonic Society; appointed regent in case of queen's death, 1840; placed by Peel at head of royal commission on rebuilding of Houses of Parliament,

1841 ; LL.D., Cambridge, 1843 ; chancellor of Cambridge University, 1847 ; largely aided the queen in the performance of her political duties, and offered advice to ministers ; created favourable impression by sympathy with condition of working-classes, 1848 ; advocated successfully alterations in system of study at Cambridge ; projected idea of International Exhibition (carried out, 1851) ; on his suggestion a camp for training troops formed at Chobham, 1853 ; gave advice of value throughout the Crimean war ; suggested in regard to Trent affair a conciliatory attitude which averted war with United States, November 1861 ; showed signs of serious illness early in 1861 ; typhoid fever developed late in the year ; he died 14 Dec. [i. 217]

ALBERT VICTOR CHRISTIAN EDWARD, DUKE OF CLARENCE AND AVONDALE and EARL OF ATHLONE (1864–1892), eldest son of the Prince of Wales (afterwards Edward VII) ; joined training ship Britannia at Portsmouth, 1877 ; entered Trinity College, Cambridge, 1883 ; hon. LL.D., 1888 ; captain and aide-de-camp to Queen Victoria, 1889 ; betrothed to Princess Mary of Teck (afterwards Duchess of Cornwall and York and Princess of Wales), 1891, but died before marriage. [Suppl. i. 28]

ALBERTAZZI, EMMA (1813–1847), vocalist ; pupil of Sir Michael Costa, 1827 ; studied in Italy under Professor Celli ; sang with great success in Milan, Madrid, Paris, and London ; died of consumption. [i. 231]

ALBERTI, GEORGE WILLIAM (1723–1758), essayist ; born at Osterode-am-Harz ; graduated at Göttingen, 1745 ; spent some years in England ; protestant minister of Tundern, Hanover ; published philosophical and theological works. [i. 232]

ALBERY, JAMES (1838–1889), dramatist ; became playwright, and in 1866 his ' Dr. Davy ' was produced at the Lyceum. His most successful play was ' Two Roses,' produced at the Vaudeville, 1870, with (Sir) Henry Irving as Digby Grant. [Suppl. i. 29]

ALBIN, ELEAZAR (*fl.* 1713–1759), naturalist and teacher of water-colour drawing ; published works on natural history, with coloured illustrations. [i. 232]

ALBIN, HENRY (1624–1696), ejected minister ; educated at Glastonbury and Oxford ; ordained ; ejected for nonconformity from West Cammel, 1660, and from Donyatt, Somerset ; ' stated preacher ' at Frome Selwood, Shepton Mallet, Bruton, and Wincanton in rotation, 1687. [i. 233]

ALBINI (BRITO), WILLIAM DE (*d.* 1156), justiciar ; son of Robert de Todeni, lord of Belvoir, itinerant justice, 1130 ; lands forfeited by Stephen, but afterwards restored. [i. 233]

ALBINI (PINCERNA), WILLIAM DE, EARL OF ARUNDEL (*d.* 1176), son of William de Albini Pincerna (the Butler), by Maud, daughter of Roger le Bigod [q. v.] ; married Adeliza [q. v.], widow of Henry I, adherent of Stephen ; confirmed by Henry II in his earldom, and served under him against Prince Henry, 1173. [i. 233]

ALBINI, WILLIAM DE, EARL OF ARUNDEL, also EARL OF SUSSEX (*d.* 1221), grandson of preceding ; favourite of King John, but in the barons' revolt adhered to their side ; justiciar, 1217. [i. 234]

ALBINI or **AUBENEY,** WILLIAM DE (*d.* 1236), grandson of preceding ; sheriff and itinerant justice under Richard I, John, and Henry III ; of the moderate party in the barons' revolt ; finally fought against John ; high in Henry III's favour. [i. 234]

ALBINUS (*d.* 732), abbot of St. Peter's, Canterbury ; assisted Bede in his ' Historia Ecclesiastica.' [i. 234]

ALBIS or **ALBIUS** (1593–1676). [See WHITE, THOMAS.]

ALCESTER, BARON. [See SEYMOUR, FREDERICK BEAUCHAMP PAGET, 1821–1895.]

ALCHFRITH (*fl.* 655), under-king of the Deirans ; son of Oswiu, king of Northumbria, and Eanflæd, daughter of Eadwine ; married Cyneburh, daughter of Penda, king of Mercia ; with Oswiu defeated Mercians, 655 ; took part in struggle between Celtic and Roman churches, and finally joined Roman party. [i. 235]

ALCHIN, WILLIAM TURNER (1790–1865), antiquary ; librarian of Guildhall Library ; compiled indexes to Winchester and Salisbury ecclesiastical registers. [i. 235]

ALCHMUND (*d.* 781), bishop of Hexham, 767 ; regarded as a saint. [i. 236]

ALCOCK, JOHN (1430–1500), bishop of Rochester, 1472, Worcester, 1476, Ely, 1486 ; LL.D., Cambridge, *c.* 1461 ; rector, St. Margaret's, Fish Street ; dean, St. Stephen's, Westminster ; master of rolls, 1462 ; prebendary of St. Paul's and Salisbury, 1468 ; privy councillor, 1470–1 ; on several royal commissions under Richard III and Henry VII ; lord chancellor, 1474 (conjointly with Rotherham, bishop of Lincoln) and 1485 ; tutor to Edward V ; comptroller of royal buildings, 1485 ; published religious works. [i. 236]

ALCOCK, JOHN (1740?–1791), doctor of music, son of John Alcock (1715–1806) [q. v.], Mus. Bac., Oxford, 1766 ; organist at Walsall, 1773 till death ; published vocal and instrumental music. [i. 237]

ALCOCK or **ALLCOCK,** JOHN (1715–1806), doctor of music ; organist at Lichfield Cathedral, 1749–60 ; Mus. Doc., Oxford, 1761 ; won Catch Club prizes, 1770, 1771, and 1772 ; published musical compositions. [i. 237]

ALCOCK, NATHAN (1707–1779), physician ; studied at Edinburgh and Leyden, where he graduated M.D., 1737 ; lectured on chemistry at Oxford, though unauthorised by the university ; M.A. and incorporated of Jesus College, 1741 ; M.D., 1749 ; F.R.S. ; F.R.C.P., 1754 ; afterwards practised at Runcorn. [i. 237]

ALCOCK, SIR RUTHERFORD (1809–1897), diplomatist ; served as army surgeon in Portugal, 1832–6, and Spain, 1836 ; nominated consul at Fuchow, China, 1844, and at Shanghai, 1846 ; first consul-general in Japan, 1858–65 ; K.C.B., 1862 ; honorary D.C.L., Oxford, 1863 ; minister-plenipotentiary at Peking, 1865–7 ; president of Geographical Society, 1876–8 ; published numerous works relating to Japan. [Suppl. i. 29]

ALCOCK, SIMON (*d.* 1459 ?), scholastic writer ; M.A. and D.D. Oxford ; held livings in Essex ; prebendary of Hereford, 1436 ; probably canon of Lincoln ; his writings never published. [i. 238]

ALCOCK, THOMAS (*d.* 1564), traveller in employ of Muscovy Company, 1558–63 ; journeyed in Russia and Poland, and crossing the Caspian Sea entered Persia, where he was murdered. [i. 238]

ALCOCK, THOMAS (1709–1798), miscellaneous writer, younger brother of Dr. Nathan Alcock [q. v.] ; M.A. Oxford, 1741 ; held livings of Runcorn and, later, St. Budrock's, Plymouth. [i. 238]

ALCOCK, THOMAS (1784–1833), surgeon to St. James's workhouse, 1813–28 ; contributed largely to medical journals. [i. 239]

ALCUIN or **ALBINUS** (English name EALWHINE) (735–804), theologian, man of letters, and coadjutor of Charlemagne in educational reforms ; born at York and educated in cloister school under Archbishop Egbert and Ethelbert, afterwards archbishop ; assisted in conduct of the school at York, and became master, 778 ; met Charlemagne at Parma, 781, and settled on the continent ; endowed with abbeys of Ferrières, Troyes, and St. Martin at Tours ; took important part in council of Frankfort ; retired as abbot of Tours, 796 ; wrote metrical annals, hagiological and philosophical works. [i. 239]

ALDAM, THOMAS (*d.* 1660), quaker ; early disciple of George Fox ; imprisoned at York, 1652. [i. 241]

ALDAY, JOHN (*fl.* 1570), translator from French ; chiefly known by his English version, published *c.* 1567, of two French pamphlets, entitled ' Theatrum Mundi ' ; translated also ' Praise and Dispraise of Women,' 1579, and possibly a French summary of Pliny, 1566. [i. 241]

ALDBOROUGH, second EARL OF. [See STRATFORD, EDWARD.]

ALDER, JOSHUA (1792–1867), zoologist ; friend of Thomas Bewick ; member of Newcastle Literary and Scientific Society, 1815 ; devoted himself to conchology and zoophytology ; received civil list pension of 70*l.*, 1857 ; published with Albany Hancock a work on British Mollusca, 1845–55. [i. 241]

ALDERSEY, LAURENCE (*fl.* 1581-1586), traveller; went to Jerusalem, journeying overland to Venice, 1581, and to Alexandria, visiting Tunis, Cyprus, and Syria, 1586; his accounts of his travels are in Hakluyt's 'Voyages.' [i. 242]

ALDERSON, AMELIA (1769-1853). [See OPIE.]

ALDERSON, SIR EDWARD HALL (1787-1857), judge; educated at Charterhouse and Caius College, Cambridge; Browne's medallist, 1807; senior wrangler, first Smith's prizeman, and first chancellor's medallist, 1809; called to bar, Inner Temple, 1811; reporter to king's bench, 1817-22; judge of court of common pleas, 1830; baron of exchequer, 1834. [i. 242]

ALDERSON, SIR JAMES (1794-1882), physician; son of John Alderson [q. v.]; M.A., Pembroke College, Cambridge, 1825; M.D., Magdalen College, Oxford, 1829; F.R.C.P., 1830; practised in Hull, and later in London; connected with St. Mary's hospital; president, College of Physicians, 1867; knighted, 1869; physician-extraordinary to queen, 1874. [i. 243]

ALDERSON, JOHN (1757-1829), physician; practised in Hull; published essays on fever (1788) and paralysis (1792); physician to Hull infirmary, where a statue of him (1833) was erected. [i. 243]

ALDFRITH, **EALDFRITH** or **EAHFRITH** (*d.* 705), king of Northumbria; illegitimate son of Oswiu; succeeded his brother Ecgfrith, 685; renowned for his learning and piety; resisted the Romish party. [i. 244]

ALDGYTH (*fl.* 1063), daughter of Ælfgar, earl of Mercia; married Gruffydd, king of Wales, and later, probably, Harold, who had conquered Gruffydd, and was already pledged to a daughter of William I. [i. 245]

ALDHELM (640?-709), bishop of Sherborne, related to King Ine; educated under Theodore and Hadrian at Canterbury, and was foremost in the intellectual movement led by them; abbot of Malmesbury; built churches at Malmesbury, Bruton, and Wareham, and monasteries at Frome and Bradford; wrote works in verse and prose. [i. 245]

ALDHUN or **EALDHUN** (*d.* 1018), bishop of Durham; appointed to Bernician see of Chester-le-Street, Durham, 990; to escape ravages of Danes left Chester with his monks, and carried the body of St. Cuthbert to Ripon, 995; returned and built church at Durham; consecrated to the see, 998. [i. 247]

ALDIS, SIR CHARLES (1775?-1863), surgeon; studied at Guy's and St. Bartholomew's hospitals, 1794; surgeon to Norman Cross barracks, *c.* 1798; introduced vaccination in Hertford; founded Cancer hospital, Clifford Street, London. [i. 247]

ALDIS, CHARLES JAMES BERRIDGE (1808-1872), physician; son of Sir Charles Aldis [q. v.]; educated at St. Paul's School and Trinity College, Cambridge; M.D., 1837; F.R.C.P., 1838; physician successively to several London dispensaries; effected improvements in sanitation, and did much to ameliorate condition of workshop hands; published medical works. [i. 248]

ALDRED THE GLOSSATOR (10th century), writer of the glosses in Northumbrian dialect inserted in the 'Lindisfarne Gospels,' *c.* 700. [i. 248]

ALDRED (*d.* 1069), archbishop of York; monk of Winchester; abbot of Tavistock, 1027; bishop of Worcester, 1044; ambassador from King Eadward the Confessor to Emperor Henry III, 1054; took charge of sees of Hereford and Ramsbury; journeyed to Jerusalem, 1058; archbishop of York, 1060; went to Rome to receive the pall, which was refused; was degraded from episcopate for various offences; robbed by brigands, whereat the pope was intimidated by Tostig and granted the pall; spent lavishly in cause of the church; after battle of Hastings upheld rights of Eadgar; submitted to William the Conqueror, whom and Matilda he crowned. [i. 249]

ALDRICH, HENRY (1647-1710), divine and scholar; educated at Westminster and Christ Church, Oxford; M.A., 1669; D.D., 1682; dean of Christ Church, 1689 till death; said to have designed chapel of Trinity College and All Saints' church, Oxford; left large musical library to his college; composed or adapted several anthems and songs; entrusted, with Spratt, with publication of Clarendon's 'Memoirs.' [i. 251]

ALDRICH or **ALDRIDGE**, ROBERT, (*d.* 1556), scholar and divine; educated at Eton and King's College, Cambridge; B.A., 1512; M.A. and schoolmaster of Eton, 1515; corresponded with and worked for Erasmus; prebendary of Lincoln, 1528; D.D., 1530; archdeacon of Colchester, 1531; canon of Windsor, 1534; registrar of order of Garter; provost of Eton, 1536; bishop of Carlisle, 1537; signed act of Six Articles, 1539, and the opinion on the king's marriage with Anne of Cleves, 1540; under Edward VI protested against church reforms. [i. 252]

ALDRIDGE, WILLIAM (1737-1797), nonconformist minister; having idled away his youth, entered the Countess of Huntingdon's college at Trevecca; preached at Margate, Dover, and Wapping; left the countess's connexion and occupied the Jewry Street chapel for nearly twenty years. [i. 253]

ALDULF, king of Northumbria (*d.* 810). [See EARDWULF.]

ALDULF or **EALDULF** (*d.* 1002), archbishop of York; possibly chancellor to King Eadgar; monk and later abbot of Peterborough; elected to see of York, 992. [i. 253]

ALED, TUDUR (*fl.* 1480-1525), Welsh poet; Franciscan; pupil of Dafydd ab Edmwnd, and teacher of Gruffydd Hiraethog. [i. 254]

ALEFOUNDER, JOHN (*d.* 1795), portrait and miniature painter; silver medallist (Royal Academy), 1782; died in India. [i. 254]

ALEMOOR, LORD (*d.* 1776). [See PRINGLE, ANDREW.]

ALESIUS, ALEXANDER (1500-1565), Lutheran divine; born and educated at Edinburgh; canon of St. Andrews; gained applause by confuting Luther's arguments, and was chosen to reclaim Patrick Hamilton [q. v.], abbot of Fern, from Lutheran opinions, but was himself converted; imprisoned by provost of St. Andrews; fled to Germany, 1532; met Luther and Melanchthon; went to England as bearer of a letter from Melanchthon to Henry VIII, 1535; warmly welcomed by Cranmer and Latimer; divinity lecturer at Cambridge; practised as physician in London, where his religious views met with opposition, 1537; returned to Germany, 1540; professor of theology at Frankfort-on-the-Oder; attached as theologian to an unsuccessful embassy to Luther to induce him to sanction less extreme views than he himself professed, 1541; dean of theological faculty, Leipzig, 1543; visited Naumburg, 1554 and 1561, Nürnberg, 1555, and Dresden, 1561; engaged in arranging disputes among protestant parties; revisited England and translated into Latin Edward VI's first liturgy; twice rector of university of Leipzig, where he died; published many exegetical, dogmatic, and controversial works. [i. 254]

ALEXANDER I (1078?-1124), king of Scotland; fourth son of Malcolm Canmore and Margaret, grandniece of Edward the Confessor; on his father's death, 1093, was protected by Edgar Atheling; on death of his brother Edgar, who reigned 1097-1107, succeeded to the kingdom north of Forth and Clyde; married Sibylla, a natural daughter of Henry I; earned title of 'Fierce' by his defeat of the men of Moray and Mearns, *c.* 1115, and founded a church at Scone in honour of the victory; entered into dispute concerning filling of see of St. Andrews, maintaining that right of investiture lay with pope or archbishop of Canterbury and not with archbishop of York, but died before its final settlement. [i. 259]

ALEXANDER II (1198-1249), king of Scotland; son of William the Lion and Ermengarde, daughter of Richard, viscount of Beaumont; knighted by King John of England, 1212; succeeded William the Lion, king of Scotland, 1214, and took part with barons against John; besieged Norham 1215; after invasions of Scotland by John and of England by Alexander, the latter did homage to Louis, the dauphin, at Dover; invaded England again, 1217, but, on defeat of Louis, made peace with Henry III, confirmed by treaty, 1219; married Joan, elder daughter of John, 1221; reduced Argyle and Caithness, 1222, and subdued insurrections, 1224 and 1228; repelled Norse invasion, 1230; married, secondly, Mary, daughter of Ingelram de Couci, 1239; quarrelled with Henry III over an alleged intended alliance with France; dispute settled by treaty at Newcastle, 1244; died of fever while attempting to wrest the Hebrides from Norway. [i. 261]

ALEXANDER III (1241–1285), king of Scotland; son of Alexander II [q. v.] and Mary de Couci; succeeded his father as a child, 1249; married Margaret, daughter of Henry III; knighted by Henry, who demanded homage, 1251; detected a plot to obtain papal legitimation of Marjory, a natural daughter of Alexander II, whereby her children might be heirs; removed chief conspirators from office; acted through regents—the Earl of Menteith and the Comyns, 1251–5, and, from 1255, fifteen nobles chosen by Henry III; was in hands of a new regency, combining two parties of nobility, 1258. Alexander successfully re-sumed his father's project of uniting the Hebrides to his kingdom, 1261; assisted Henry III against the barons, 1264, and did homage to Edward I, 1278.   [i. 264]

ALEXANDER (d. 1148), bishop of Lincoln; nephew of Roger, bishop of Salisbury, by whom he was adopted; archdeacon of Sarum, 1121; bishop of Lincoln, 1123; accompanied archbishops William of Canterbury and Thurstan of York to Rome, 1125; took part in councils directed against marriage of clergy; built castles at Slea-ford, Newark, and Banbury, and religious houses at Haver-holme, Thame, Dorchester-on-Thames; supported King Stephen, although he had previously sworn to receive Henry's daughter, Empress Maud, as queen; his loyalty being suspected, he and his uncle were arrested at Oxford, 1139; his castles surrendered; took part in reception of Maud by Bishop Henry of Blois at Winchester, 1141; revisited Rome, 1145; probably crowned Stephen at Lin-coln, 1146.   [i. 267]

ALEXANDER OF CANTERBURY (*fl.* 1120?), monk of Christchurch, Canterbury; author of 'Dicta Anselmi Archiepiscopi.'   [i. 271]

ALEXANDER OF ASHBY (*fl.* 1220), prior of the Austin priory, Ashby, Northampton; wrote theological tracts, chronicles, and Latin poems.   [i. 271]

ALEXANDER OF HALES (d. 1245), philosopher; trained for the church; held successively various ecclesias-tical appointments, and was finally archdeacon; retired to France; studied theology and metaphysics in Paris, where he lectured; lecturer to the Franciscan order, 1222–38; student of Aristotle and his Arab commentators; wrote 'Summa Theologiæ' (printed, 1475).   [i. 271]

ALEXANDER, Mrs. CECIL FRANCES (1818–1895), poetess, née Humphreys; with a friend, Lady Harriet Howard, wrote tracts in connection with Oxford move-ment from 1842; married, 1850, William Alexander, bishop of Derry (afterwards archbishop of Armagh). Her poetical works comprise many hymns, including 'There is a green hill far away.'   [Suppl. i. 30]

ALEXANDER, DANIEL ASHER (1768–1846), archi-tect; educated at St. Paul's school; silver medallist, Royal Academy; surveyor to London Dock Company (1796–1831) and to Trinity House; designed lighthouses at Harwich and Lundy Island, and prisons at Dartmoor and Maidstone.   [i. 272]

ALEXANDER, HELEN (1654–1729), heroine of Scot-tish covenanters; avowed adherence to presbyterianism and the covenant; assisted many fugitives, including John Welsh and James Renwick. Her experiences were published from her dictation.   [i. 272]

ALEXANDER, Sir JAMES EDWARD (1803–1885), general; lieutenant, 1825; in Balkans during Russo-Turkish war, 1829; captain, 1830; aide-de-camp to Sir Benjamin D'Urban [q. v.] in Kaffir war, 1835; knighted, 1838; aide-de-camp successively to D'Urban and Sir Wil-liam Rowan in Canada, 1847–55; in Crimea, 1855–6; colonel, 1858; in Maori war, 1860–2; major-general, 1868; C.B., 1873; general, 1881; published works relating to his service, and other writings. He was responsible for the preservation of Cleopatra's Needle.   [Suppl. i. 31]

ALEXANDER, JOHN (d. 1743), presbyterian minister at Stratford-on-Avon and at Dublin; moderator of general synod of Ulster, 1734.   [i. 273]

ALEXANDER, JOHN (1736–1765), commentator; son of John Alexander (d. 1743) [q. v.]; educated at Daventry, with Priestley, 1751; studied biblical criticism under Dr. George Benson; wrote several scriptural paraphrases.   [i. 273]

ALEXANDER, MICHAEL SOLOMON (1799–1845), first Anglican bishop of Jerusalem; born and educated in Germany in Jewish faith; private tutor in England; converted, 1825; taught Hebrew in Dublin and was ordained, 1827; worked at Danzig in connection with Society for Promoting Christianity among Jews, 1827–30; professor of Hebrew, King's College, London, 1832–41; assisted in revising New Testament in Hebrew, 1835; bishop of united church of England and Ireland in Jerusalem, 1841; died in Egypt on journey to England; published religious works.   [i. 273]

ALEXANDER, Sir WILLIAM, EARL OF STIRLING (1567?–1640), poet and statesman; perhaps educated at Stirling, Glasgow, and Leyden; travelled as tutor to Archi-bald, earl of Argyle, to France, Spain, and Italy; tutor to Prince Henry, son of James VI; gentleman of bed-chamber to Prince Henry, 1603; knighted, 1609; on death of Prince Henry, 1612, appointed to same position in household of Prince Charles; formed friendship with Drum-mond of Hawthornden, c. 1613; master of requests, 1614; assisted the king in a metrical version of the Psalms (published 1631), and received patent for sole printing rights for thirty-one years; granted jurisdiction over Nova Scotia and Canada, 1621; published 'Encouragement to Colonies,' 1625; secretary of state for Scotland, 1626 till death; raised to peerage, 1630; extraordinary judge of court of session, 1631; Earl of Stirling, 1633; died insolvent in London; published many volumes of poetry.   [i. 275]

ALEXANDER, WILLIAM (1726–1783), American general; son of James Alexander, who had fled to America after the rebellion of 1715; clerk in his mother's provision business at New York; joined army commissariat; aide-de-camp and secretary to General Shirley; claimed unsuc-cessfully the earldom of Stirling, 1762; surveyor-general, New York; governor of Columbia College; commanded American militia regiment in war of independence, and served throughout the war; major-general, 1777. [i. 280]

ALEXANDER, WILLIAM (1767–1816), artist, and first keeper of prints and drawings in British Museum, 1808; student at Royal Academy, 1784; junior draughtsman with Lord Macartney's embassy to China, 1792; professor of drawing at Military College, Great Marlow, 1802; published several volumes of engravings.   [i. 281]

ALEXANDER, WILLIAM LINDSAY (1808–1884), congregational divine; educated at Leith High School, Edinburgh and St. Andrews; D.D., 1846; classical tutor in Blackburn Theological Academy, 1827–31; pastor, 1835–1877, of North College Street Congregational Church (which removed, 1861, to Augustine Church, George IV Bridge, Edinburgh); reviser of Old Testament, 1870; pro-fessor of theology at Theological Hall, Edinburgh, 1854, and principal, 1877; LL.D. Edinburgh, 1884; published religious and other writings.   [Suppl. i. 32]

ALEYN, CHARLES (d. 1640), poet; educated at Sidney Sussex College, Cambridge; private tutor to Sir Edward Sherburne.   [i. 281]

ALF- [See ÆLF-]

ALFIELD or **AUFIELD**, THOMAS, *alias* BADGER (d. 1585), seminary priest; educated at Eton and Cam-bridge; became catholic; recanted under torture; tor-tured and hanged for disseminating Roman catholic lite-rature.   [i. 282]

ALFORD, HENRY (1810–1871), dean of Canterbury, 1857–71; educated at Trinity College, Cambridge; Bell scholar; graduated 1832; ordained curate at Ampton, 1833; fellow of Trinity, 1834; vicar of Wymeswold, 1835–53; studied German at Bonn, 1847; minister of Quebec Chapel, Marylebone, 1853; edited Greek Testa-ment, 1849–61; published sermons and poems, including translation of the 'Odyssey' in blank verse, and took part in revising the New Testament; first editor of 'Contem-porary Review.'   [i. 282]

ALFORD, MARIANNE MARGARET, VISCOUNTESS ALFORD, known as LADY MARIAN ALFORD (1817–1888), artist, daughter of Spencer Compton, second Marquis of Northampton [q. v.]; married, 1841, John Hume Cust, viscount Alford (son of Earl Brownlow); friend of the leading artists of the day; assisted in founding Royal School of Art Needlework, Kensington; published 'Needle-work as Art,' 1886.   [Suppl. i. 33]

ALFORD, MICHAEL (1587–1652), jesuit and ecclesiastical historian; studied philosophy at Seville; English penitentiary at Rome, 1615; pursued missionary labours in Leicestershire. [i. 284]

ALFRED, KING (849–901). [See ÆLFRED.]

ALFRED OF BEVERLEY (*fl.* 1143), chronicler; treasurer of church of Beverley; compiled history up to 1129. [i. 285]

ALFRED, surnamed ANGLICUS and PHILOSOPHICUS (12th–13th cent.), writer; possibly translator of Aristotle, and author of 'De Motu Cordis,' 1220. [i. 285]

ALFRED ERNEST ALBERT, DUKE OF EDINBURGH and DUKE OF SAXE-COBURG AND GOTHA (1844–1900), second son of Queen Victoria and Prince Albert; educated for navy; served in Channel, North America, West Indies, and Mediterranean; elected by suffrage king of Greece, 1862, but was compelled on political grounds to refuse crown; captain, 1866; created Duke of Edinburgh and Earl of Ulster and Kent, and elected Master of Trinity House, 1866; commissioned H.M.S. Galatea, 1867, and visited many parts of the world, 1867–71; served in the Mediterranean fleet; rear-admiral, 1878; vice-admiral, 1882; commanded Channel squadron, 1883–4; commander-in-chief in Mediterranean, 1886–9; admiral, 1887; commander-in-chief at Devonport, 1890–3; admiral of the fleet, 1893; succeeded, 1893, his father's brother as reigning Duke of Saxe-Coburg and Gotha, in virtue of renunciation in 1863 by his brother, Prince of Wales, of title to duchy; relinquished privileges as English peer; died at Rosenau, near Coburg. He married, 1874, Grand Duchess Marie Alexandrovna, only daughter of Alexander II, tsar of Russia. [Suppl. i. 34]

ALICE MAUD MARY, PRINCESS OF GREAT BRITAIN AND IRELAND, DUCHESS OF SAXONY, GRAND DUCHESS OF HESSE-DARMSTADT (1843–1878), third child of Queen Victoria and Prince Albert; married, 1862, Frederick of Hesse, nephew of Louis III, grand duke of Hesse-Darmstadt; foundress of Women's Union for Nursing Sick and Wounded in War. [i. 285]

ALISON, ARCHIBALD (1757–1839), writer of an essay on 'Taste' (1790); of Balliol College, Oxford, 1784; took holy orders; studied natural history as disciple of Gilbert White; prebendary of Salisbury, 1791; minister of episcopal chapel, Cowgate, Edinburgh, 1800 till death; adherent of the Scottish 'common-sense' philosophy; published sermons. [i. 286]

ALISON, SIR ARCHIBALD (1792–1867), historian; younger son of Archibald Alison [q. v.]; educated at Edinburgh; called to bar, 1814; travelled on the continent; advocate depute, 1822; published work on Scottish criminal law, 1832–3; sheriff of Lanarkshire, 1834; successfully suppressed distress riots and strikes, 1837; published his 'History of Europe,' 1833–42, and a continuation, 1852–9; elected lord rector of Marischal College, Aberdeen, against Macaulay, 1845, and of Glasgow against Palmerston, 1851; created baronet, 1852; published autobiography besides historical works. [i. 287]

ALISON, WILLIAM PULTENEY (1790–1859), physician; elder son of Archibald Alison [q. v.]; educated at Edinburgh; M.D., 1811; physician to New Town dispensary, 1815; professor of medical jurisprudence, Edinburgh, 1820–2; professor of 'institutes of medicine,' first jointly, afterwards solely, for twenty years; published 'Outlines of Physiology,' 1831, in which the leading idea was that of a life-force distinct from the physical forces of dead matter; professor of practice of medicine, 1842–56; appointed first physician to her majesty for Scotland; hon. D.C.L., Oxford, 1850; successfully advocated legal relief of the destitute in Scotland. [i. 290]

ALKEN, HENRY (*fl.* 1816–1831), draughtsman and engraver; said to have been stud-groom to the Duke of Beaufort; published many etchings of sporting subjects, mostly coloured. [i. 292]

ALKEN, SAMUEL (*fl.* 1780–1796), draughtsman; engraved plates after Morland and others, and published sets of original etchings. [i. 292]

ALLAM, ANDREW (1655–1685), antiquary; graduated at St. Edmund's Hall, Oxford, and was made tutor and subsequently vice-principal; took holy orders, 1680; assisted Anthony à Wood in his 'Athenæ Oxonienses,' and produced other works, chiefly historical. [i. 293]

ALLAN, DAVID (1744–1796), Scottish painter; apprenticed to Robert Foulis, the Glasgow printer; went to Rome, where he met Gavin Hamilton, 1764; probably exhibited at Royal Academy, 1771 and 1773; gained gold medal of St. Luke's for historical composition, 1773; earned title of the 'Scottish Hogarth' by pictures of Venetian Carnival exhibited at Royal Academy, 1779; painted portraits in London, 1777–80; director and master of Trustees' Academy at Edinburgh, 1786; illustrated poems by Burns, Allan Ramsay, and others. [i. 293]

ALLAN, GEORGE (1736–1800), antiquary and topographer; practised as an attorney at Darlington, Durham; acquired numerous collections of manuscripts, charters, and genealogical records relating chiefly to Durham, many of which he printed at a private press erected at Darlington, c. 1768. His library was open to antiquaries, and was of great assistance to several well-known historical works, notably Hutchinson's 'History of Durham.' [i. 294]

ALLAN, SIR HENRY MARSHMAN HAVELOCK (1830–1897). [See HAVELOCK-ALLAN.]

ALLAN, PETER (1798–1849), coloniser of the 'Marsden Rock'; successively valet, gamekeeper to Marquis of Londonderry, landlord of a tavern at Whitburn, and superintendent of quarries near Durham; excavated cavern on the coast near Sunderland in bay of Marsden; lived in it from 1828 till his death. The cavern was destroyed by fall of cliff, 1865. [i. 295]

ALLAN, PETER JOHN (1825–1848), poet; lived mostly in Nova Scotia and New Brunswick. His poems, published posthumously, show traces of Byron's influence. [i. 296]

ALLAN, ROBERT (1774–1841), Scottish poet; by trade a muslin-weaver; died at New York. His poems, though melodious, achieved little success. [i. 296]

ALLAN, THOMAS (1777–1833), mineralogist; amassed a large collection of minerals; contributed the article on 'Diamond' to the 'Encyclopædia Britannica'; F.R.S. and member of the Edinburgh Royal Society; published geological works. [i. 297]

ALLAN, SIR WILLIAM (1782–1850), painter of Russian scenery and life; educated in Edinburgh; apprenticed to a coachmaker; studied at the Trustees' Academy and Royal Academy schools; exhibited first in Royal Academy, 1803; went to Russia, 1805, and spent some years travelling in the interior; returned to Edinburgh, 1814; master of the Trustees' School, 1826; travelled on continent and in Asia Minor; R.A., London, 1835; president of Royal Scottish Academy, 1838; limner to queen in Scotland, 1841; knighted 1842. [i. 297]

ALLARDICE, ROBERT BARCLAY (1779–1854), pedestrian, commonly known as CAPTAIN BARCLAY; entered 23rd regiment 1805; served in Walcheren expedition as aide-de-camp to the Marquis of Huntly, 1809; claimed unsuccessfully earldoms of Airth, Strathern, and Monteith, 1839–40; noted for his walking feats, which included walking one mile in each of one thousand successive hours. [i. 298]

ALLARDYCE, ALEXANDER (1846–1896), author; educated at Aberdeen; engaged in journalism in India, 1868–75; subsequently reader to Messrs. William Blackwood & Sons at Edinburgh; published novels and edited John Ramsay's 'Scotland and Scotsmen in Eighteenth Century,' and 'Letters from and to Charles Kirkpatrick Sharpe' [q. v.] [Suppl. i. 36]

ALLDE, **ALDEE** or **ALDEY**, EDWARD (*fl.* 1583–1634), printer; freeman of Stationers' Company, 1584; his name appears in the registers down to 1623. [i. 299]

ALLDE, **ALDAYE**, **ALDE** or **ALDYE**, JOHN (*fl.* 1555–1592), printer; first freeman of Stationers' Company, 1555; mentioned in the original charter of the company, 1557. [i. 299]

ALLECTUS (250 ?–296), Roman emperor in Britain; minister of Carausius [q. v.]; assassinated Carausius, proclaimed himself emperor, 293; struck numerous coins at London and Colchester; fell in battle in Hampshire. [ix. 35]

ALLEINE, JOSEPH (1634–1668), author of 'An Alarm to the Unconverted'; entered Lincoln College, Oxford, 1649; scholar of Corpus Christi, 1651; B.D. and tutor, 1653 ; ordained as associate of George Newton at Taunton, 1654 ; ejected, 1662 ; imprisoned for evangelical preaching ; wrote religious works. [i. 299]

ALLEINE, RICHARD (1611–1681), author of ' Vindiciæ Pietatis ' and other religious works ; graduated B.A., St. Alban Hall, and M.A. New Inn Hall, Oxford ; ordained ; rector of Batcombe, Somerset, 1641–61 ; appointed assistant to the commissioners for ' ejecting scandalous ministers,' 1654 ; ejected under Act of Uniformity and preached semi-privately in neighbourhood of Frome Selwood. [i. 300]

ALLEINE, WILLIAM (1614–1677), divine ; younger brother of Richard Alleine [q. v.] ; B.A. and M.A. St. Alban Hall, Oxford ; private chaplain in London ; vicar of Blandford, Bristol, c. 1653 ; ejected from living 1662 ; preached in private ; later, held livings at Bristol and Yeovil. [i. 301]

ALLEN. [See also ALLAN, ALLEIN, ALLEINE, ALLEYN, ALLIN.]

ALLEN, ALEXANDER (1814–1842), philologist ; son of John Allen (1771–1839) [q. v.] ; educated at his father's school, Hackney, and at London University ; carried on his father's school on his death ; doctor of philosophy, Leipzig, 1840 ; published works principally philological. [i. 302]

ALLEN, ANTHONY (d. 1754), barrister and antiquary ; educated at Eton and King's College, Cambridge ; master in chancery ; wrote unpublished biographical account of members of Eton College. [i. 302]

ALLEN, BENNET (fl. 1761–1782), miscellaneous writer ; B.A. Wadham College, Oxford, 1757 ; M.A., 1760 ; took holy orders and settled in London ; published pamphlet entitled ' Modern Chastity,' by way of defence of Lord Baltimore, who was charged with rape, 1768 ; subsequently contributed to ' Morning Post,' and was imprisoned for killing in a duel one whom he had slandered in an anonymous article, 1782. [i. 302]

ALLEN, EDMUND (1519 ?–1559), bishop-elect of Rochester, 1559 ; M.A. Corpus Christi College, Cambridge, 1537 ; studied abroad, where, probably, he graduated B.D. ; chaplain to Princess Elizabeth, 1549, and to her when queen ; acted as ambassador ; published several religious works. [i. 303]

ALLEN, GRANT (1848–1899), author, whose full name was CHARLES GRANT BLAIRFINDIE ALLEN ; born in Canada ; educated at King Edward's school, Birmingham ; B.A. Merton College, Oxford, 1871 ; professor of mental and moral philosophy in college at Spanish Town, Jamaica, for education of negroes, 1873–6 ; returned to England, 1876, and adopted literature as profession ; published ' Physiological Æsthetics,' 1877 ; assisted Sir William Wilson Hunter [q. v.] in compilation of ' Imperial Gazetteer of India ' ; published, 1884, his first novel, 'Philistia,' which had appeared serially in ' Gentleman's Magazine,' and subsequently produced under his own name and pseudonyms more than thirty works of fiction, including 'The Woman who did' (1895) and 'The British Barbarians' (1896). [Suppl. i. 36]

ALLEN, JAMES BAYLIS (1803–1876), line-engraver ; articled as general engraver ; studied drawing under J. V. Barber ; employed by the Findens in London, 1824 ; engraved plates (including ' Rivers of France ') after Turner and other artists. [i. 304]

ALLEN, JAMES C. (d. 1831), line-engraver ; pupil of W. B. Cooke, in conjunction with whom, after 1821, he engraved series of plates, including ' Views of the Colosseum,' after drawings by Major-general Cockburn. [i. 305]

ALLEN, JAMES MOUNTFORD (1809–1883), architect ; practised in London, and later as a church-architect at Crewkerne, Somerset. [i. 305]

ALLEN, JOHN (1476–1534), archbishop of Dublin ; studied at Oxford and Cambridge ; in Italy on ecclesiastical business for Archbishop Warham ; took holy orders, 1499 ; vicar of Chislet, 1503 ; presented to livings of Sundridge (1508) and Aldington (1511) ; rural dean of Risebergh, Buckingham, 1512 ; rector of South Ockendon, Essex, and prebendary of Lincoln Cathedral, 1516 ; rector of Gaulsby, 1523 ; acted as Wolsey's agent in suppressing minor monasteries, 1524–5 ; prebendary of Nottingham, 1526, and of St. Paul's Cathedral, 1527 ; accom-

panied Wolsey to France ; archbishop of Dublin, 1528, when he resigned his prebends ; chancellor of Ireland, 1528–32 ; fined under statutes of provisors and *præmunire*, 1531 ; murdered by followers of Lord Thomas Fitzgerald, 1534. [i. 305]

ALLEN or ALLIN, JOHN (1596–1671), New England puritan colonist ; left living at Ipswich to avoid persecutions of Bishop Wren ; went to New England with band of puritans, 1638 ; pastor of church at Dedham, Massachusetts, 1639 ; resisted attempts to subject colonists to British government, 1646 ; took part in dispute with English divines on baptism, 1662. [i. 307]

ALLEN or ALLEYN, JOHN (1660 ?–1741), physician and inventor ; M.D. ; extra-licentiate, College of Physicians, 1692 ; practised at Bridgewater, Somerset ; published 'Synopsis Medicinæ,' 1719, and 'Specimina Ichnographica,' 1730, a book describing several inventions, including a new method of navigating vessels. [i. 307]

ALLEN, JOHN (fl. 1764), nonconformist divine ; minister successively of baptist churches in Petticoat Lane (now Middlesex Street), London, and Broadstairs, Newcastle ; dismissed for misconduct ; died in New York ; published popular tracts. [i. 308]

ALLEN, JOHN, the younger (d. 1831), bookseller and antiquary of Hereford ; made a large collection of antiquities, books, prints, &c., relating to Herefordshire, of which county he left an unpublished and unfinished history. [i. 308]

ALLEN, JOHN (1771–1839), dissenting layman ; author of 'Modern Judaism,' 1816, and other works of religious history ; kept academy at Hackney. [i. 309]

ALLEN, JOHN (1771–1843), political and historical writer ; M.D. Edinburgh, 1791 ; in the confidence of Jeffrey and his coadjutors on the 'Edinburgh Review' ; accompanied Lord Holland to Spain, 1801–5 and 1808 ; warden of Dulwich College, 1811–20, and master, 1820 till death ; published ' Inquiry into Rise and Growth of Royal Prerogative in England,' 1830, and contributed historical and political articles to 'Edinburgh Review,' ' Annual Register,' and 'Encyclopædia Britannica.' [i. 309]

ALLEN, JOHN (d. 1855), revolutionist ; tried for high treason with Arthur O'Connor, 1798 ; concerned in Robert Emmet's rising, 1803 ; fled to France and served in French army in Peninsula ; colonel in French army, 1810. [i. 310]

ALLEN, JOSEPH WILLIAM (1803–1852), landscape painter ; originally a tutor ; worked as scene-painter for the Olympic ; took an active part in establishing Society of British Artists. [i. 310]

ALLEN, RALPH (1694–1764), philanthropist ; employed in Bath post office ; obtained patronage of General Wade by detecting a Jacobite plot ; raised and equipped one hundred volunteers at Bath, 1745 ; deputy postmaster, Bath ; devised and managed a system of cross-posts for England and Wales by which he amassed a large fortune ; became intimate with Pope, Fielding (who drew from him Squire Allworthy in 'Tom Jones'), the elder Pitt, and other eminent people ; gave large sums in charity, principally in Bath. [i. 311]

ALLEN, THOMAS (1542–1632), mathematician ; educated at Trinity College, Oxford ; B.A., 1563 ; fellow, 1565 ; M.A., 1567 ; obtained patronage of Earl of Northumberland, and came in contact with most mathematicians and scholars of his day ; refused offer of a bishopric from Earl of Leicester ; left historical, antiquarian, astronomical, philosophical, and mathematical manuscripts, some of which are preserved in Bodleian Library. [i. 312]

ALLEN, THOMAS (1608–1673), nonconformist divine ; graduated at Caius College, Cambridge ; held living of St. Edmund's, Norwich ; 'silenced' by Bishop Wren for disagreement with 'Book of Sports,' 1636 ; fled to Charlestown, New England, 1638 ; returned to Norwich, 1652 ; ejected, 1662 ; published religious works. [i. 313]

ALLEN, THOMAS (1681–1755), divine ; B.A. New College, Oxford, and ordained, 1705 ; successively clerk in Lincoln's Inn, and schoolmaster ; vicar of Irchester, Northamptonshire, 1706, and of Kettering, 1715 ; wrote various religious works. [i. 313]

ALLEN, THOMAS (1803–1833), topographer; produced from 1827 illustrated volumes relating to Lambeth, Westminster, Southwark, Yorkshire, Surrey, Sussex, and Lincolnshire. [i. 314]

ALLEN, WILLIAM (1532–1594), cardinal; B.A. and fellow, Oriel College, Oxford, 1550; M.A., 1554; principal of St. Mary's Hall, 1556; proctor, 1556–7; his zeal for the catholic faith making it impossible for him to remain in Oxford, he took up residence at university of Louvain, 1561; owing to ill-health, returned to England in disguise, 1562; stayed in Lancashire (where he rigorously opposed occasional conformity), Oxford, and Norfolk; finally returned to Low Countries, 1565; ordained at Mechlin; lectured on theology; went on pilgrimage to Rome, 1567; opened, with the assistance of several eminent divines, a catholic seminary at Douay, 1568; B.D.; regius professor of divinity at Douay, 1570; D.D., 1571; canon of church of Our Lady at Cambray, 1575; his seminary, to escape persecutions of Calvinists, removed to Rheims, 1578; arranged for foundation of an English jesuit college at Rome, 1579; his efforts consistently opposed by the protestants; resided at the English hospital, Rome, after 1585; as supporter of Philip II of Spain's claim to English throne made cardinal, 1587, so that, in the event of Philip's success, he might reconcile the realm to the church; received from the pope an abbey in Calabria and the revenues of the archbishopric of Palermo; nominated archbishop of Mechlin, 1589, but did not obtain the see; apostolic librarian; entrusted, with Cardinal Colonna, with revision of the Vulgate; published many religious writings. [i. 314]

ALLEN, WILLIAM (1770–1843), quaker, scientist, and philanthropist; entered Bevan's chemical establishment at Plough Court, which, from 1795, he carried on; fellow Linnean Society, 1801; F.R.S., 1807; lecturer at Guy's Hospital, 1802–26; intimate with Clarkson, Wilberforce, and James Mill; active opposer of slavery; engaged in schemes of social improvement, and made several journeys on the continent, examining prisons and other public institutions, 1816–33; helped to found an agricultural colony at Lindfield, Sussex. [i. 322]

ALLEN, WILLIAM (1793–1864), naval officer; lieutenant, 1815; commander, 1836; captain, 1842; took part in the Niger expeditions of 1832 and 1841–2; rear-admiral, 1862; published books of travel. [i. 322]

ALLENSON, JOHN (*fl.* 1616), puritan divine; pupil at Cambridge of Dr. Whitaker; B.D., 1590; fellow of St. John's, 1584; senior dean and sacrist, 1603; senior bursar, 1604; suspended for puritan opinions successively from curacies of Barnwell and Horningsea, Cambridgeshire; edited works by Dr. Whitaker. [i. 323]

ALLESTREE, RICHARD (1619–1681), royalist divine; B.A. and moderator in philosophy, Christ Church College, Oxford, where his tutor was Richard Busby, 1640; took arms for the king and served under Sir John Biron, 1641, and was present at Kineton Field; twice captured, but was released; M.A., 1643; entered holy orders and became censor of his college; expelled from Oxford by parliamentarians, 1648; frequently employed in carrying messages to and from the king; in prison several weeks and released on account of ill-health, 1659; canon of Christ Church and D.D., 1660; chaplain in ordinary to the king, 1663; regius professor of divinity, 1663–79; provost of Eton College, 1665; author of 'The Whole Duty of Man' and tracts and sermons. [i. 324]

ALLESTRY, JACOB (1653–1686), poetical writer; educated at Westminster and Christ Church, Oxford; music reader, 1679; terræ filius, 1682; contributed to 'Examen Poeticum,' published 1693. [i. 325]

ALLEY, WILLIAM (1510?–1570), bishop of Exeter, 1560; educated at Eton and King's College, Cambridge; B.A., 1533; during Mary's reign travelled in north of England, gaining a precarious livelihood by practising physic and teaching; divinity reader and, in 1559, penetentiary and prebendary of St. Paul's; D.D. Oxford, 1561; wrote religious works. [i. 326]

ALLEYN, EDWARD (1566–1626), actor and founder of Dulwich College; one of Earl of Worcester's players, 1586; married a step-daughter of Philip Henslowe [q. v.], 1592, whose partner he became; attached to Lord Ad-

miral's company; toured with Lord Strange's company, 1593; acted in London, 1594–7; acquired interest in bear-baiting house, Paris Garden, 1594; built, with Henslowe, Fortune theatre, Cripplegate, 1600, where he acted at head of Lord Admiral's company; purchased with Henslowe office of master of Royal Game of bears, bulls, and mastiff dogs, 1604; retired soon after the accession of James I, when the Lord Admiral's company was taken over by Prince Henry; last recorded appearance, 1604; played hero in Marlowe's 'Tamburlaine,' 'Jew of Malta,' and 'Faustus'; acquired great wealth and landed property; bought manor of Dulwich, 1605; built and endowed the college, 1613–16, and received patent for its incorporation, 1619; personally managed its affairs, 1617–22, and possibly till death; lost his wife and afterwards married a daughter of Dr. Donne; on terms of friendship with many persons of note, and patron of Dekker, John Taylor, and other writers. [i. 327]

ALLIBOND, JOHN (1597–1658), son of Peter Allibond [q. v.]; schoolmaster; M.A. Magdalen College, Oxford, 1619; D.D., 1643; master of Magdalen College School, 1625–32, and lecturer on music; held successively three church livings in Gloucestershire after 1634; wrote Latin poems. [i. 330]

ALLIBOND, PETER (1560–1629), translator; B.A. Magdalen Hall, Oxford, 1581; M.A., 1585; travelled abroad and subsequently became rector of Chenies, Buckinghamshire; translated theological works from Latin and French. [i. 330]

ALLIBOND or **ALLIBONE**, SIR RICHARD (1636–1688), judge; grandson of Peter Allibond [q. v.]; Roman catholic; educated at Douay; entered Gray's Inn, 1663; king's counsel and knighted, 1686; serjeant-at-law and justice of king's bench, 1687; incurred unpopularity by opposing the seven bishops, 1688. [i. 330]

ALLIES, JABEZ (1787–1856), antiquary and writer on folklore; practised as solicitor in London; F.S.A., c. 1840; retired to Worcester; published works on antiquities of Worcestershire and Herefordshire, and on Shakespeare's fairy mythology. [i. 331]

ALLIN, SIR THOMAS (1612–1685), naval commander; originally merchant and shipowner in Lowestoft; supported royalists during civil war; captain, 1660; commander-in-chief in the Downs, 1663; fought against Dutch in Mediterranean, 1664, and at Lowestoft, 1665; knighted and appointed admiral; defeated Dutch off Isle of Wight and French off Dungeness, 1666; engaged against Barbary pirates, 1668–70; comptroller of navy, 1670–8; commander-in-chief in the Narrow Seas against French, 1778. [i. 332]

ALLINGHAM, JOHN TILL (*fl.* 1799–1810), dramatist; educated for the law; wrote many popular plays, much of the success of which was due to the actor, Charles Mathews. [i. 333]

ALLINGHAM, WILLIAM (1824–1889), poet; born at Ballyshannon, Donegal, where, c. 1837, he entered the bank managed by his father; received appointment in customs, c. 1846; became acquainted with Leigh Hunt in London; published 'Poems,' 1850, and 'Day and Night Songs' (a second series of which contained illustrations by pre-Raphaelite artists), 1854; edited 'The Ballad Book' for 'Golden Treasury Series,' 1864; published 'Laurence Bloomfield in Ireland,' his most ambitious work, 1864; his poetical works were collected in six volumes, 1888–93; editor of 'Fraser's Magazine,' 1874–9. A collection entitled 'Varieties in Prose' appeared posthumously, 1893. [Suppl. i. 38]

ALLISON, THOMAS (*fl.* 1697), Arctic voyager; published, 1699, an account of his voyage in 1697–8 from Archangel to the neighbourhood of North Cape. [i. 333]

ALLIX, PETER (1641–1717), protestant preacher; born at Alençon; educated at Saumur and Sedan; worked with Claude on French translation of the bible; pastor of St. Agobile, Champagne; translated to Charenton, Paris, 1670; moderator of synod at Lisy, 1683; on revocation of edict of Nantes came to England, 1685, and founded in London a church for protestant refugees; D.D. of Oxford and Cambridge; treasurer of Salisbury Cathedral, 1690; published many theological works in Latin, French, and English. [i. 334]

ALLMAN, GEORGE JAMES (1812–1898), botanist and zoologist; educated at Belfast; B.A. Trinity College, Dublin, 1839; M.D., 1847; F.R.C.S. Ireland, 1844; M.D. Oxford, 1847; professor of botany, Dublin University, 1844; F.R.S., 1854; regius professor of natural history, Edinburgh University, 1855–70; president of Linnean Society, 1874–83, and gold medallist, 1896. His most important work was his investigation into the morphology of the cœlenterata and polyzoa. [Suppl. i. 40]

ALLMAN, WILLIAM (1776–1846), botanist; B.A. Trinity College, Dublin, 1796; M.A., 1801; M.D., 1804; practised medicine in Clonmel till 1809; professor of botany, Dublin, 1809–44; published botanical works. [i. 335]

ALLOM, THOMAS (1804–1872), architect; furnished drawings for series of illustrated works on 'Cumberland and Westmoreland,' 'Scotland,' 'Constantinople,' and other places; exhibited frequently at Royal Academy. [i. 335]

ALLON, HENRY (1818–1892), congregational divine; studied theology at Cheshunt College; sole pastor, 1852, at Union Chapel, Islington; honorary secretary of Cheshunt College, 1862, and trustee of Countess of Huntingdon's connexion; honorary D.D. Yale University, 1871, and St. Andrews, 1885; president of congregational union, 1864 and 1881; editor of 'British Quarterly Review,' 1877–86; edited volumes of hymns and wrote religious publications. [Suppl. i. 41]

ALLON, HENRY ERSKINE (1864–1897), composer; son of Henry Allon (1818–1892) [q. v.]; educated at University College, London, and Trinity College, Cambridge; wrote sonatas and assisted in founding 'New Musical Quarterly Review.' [Suppl. i. 42]

ALLOTT, ROBERT (*fl.* 1600), editor of 'England's Parnassus,' 1600, and of 'Wits Theater of the Little World,' 1599. [i. 336]

ALLOTT, WILLIAM (*d.* 1590?), catholic divine; educated at Cambridge; retired to Louvain on Elizabeth's accession; in high favour with Mary Queen of Scots; returned and preached in England, but was imprisoned and banished; canon of St. Quintin, Picardy. [i. 337]

ALLOWAY, LORD (*d.* 1829). [See CATHCART, DAVID.]

ALLPORT, SIR JAMES JOSEPH (1811–1892), railway manager; chief clerk, then traffic manager and manager, Birmingham and Derby railway; manager of Newcastle and Darlington line, 1844–50, and of Manchester, Sheffield and Lincolnshire, 1850–3; general manager of Midland railway, 1853–7, director, 1857, and again general manager, 1860–80; managing director of Palmer's Shipbuilding Company, Jarrow, 1857–60; knighted, 1884. Under his management the Midland railway grew into one of the chief English railway systems. [Suppl. i. 42]

ALLSOP, THOMAS (1795–1880), stockbroker and author; entered silk mercery trade in London, 1812; joined Stock Exchange; made the acquaintance of Coleridge, 1818; on the poet's death published his 'Letters, Conversations, and Recollections'; intimate with Lamb, Hazlitt, Barry Cornwall, and other eminent men; provided Feargus O'Connor with his property qualification as representative of chartism on his election as M.P. for Nottingham; was in sympathy with Orsini, the conspirator against Napoleon III. A reward was offered for his apprehension as accessory in the 'attempt of Orsini,' but the overtness of his actions disarmed suspicion. [i. 337]

ALMACK, WILLIAM (*d.* 1781), founder of Almack's Assembly Rooms; apparently came to London as valet of Duke of Hamilton; proprietor of a tavern in St. James's Street; opened a gaming club in Pall Mall, known as Almack's Club (now Brooks's), before 1763; erected his assembly rooms in King Street, 1764. [i. 339]

ALMEIDA or **MEADE**, JOHN (1572–1653), jesuit missionary; taken without his parents' consent to Viana, Portugal, at age of ten; admitted member of Society of Jesus, 1592; ordained, 1602; spent many years travelling on foot through Brazil as missionary. [i. 340]

ALMON, JOHN (1737–1805), bookseller and journalist; apprenticed to printer at Liverpool; travelled on continent, 1758–9; employed in London as printer; contributed to the 'Gazetteer,' and attracted attention of Lord Temple, Burke, and other members of the opposition; formed acquaintance with Wilkes, 1761, which lasted till Wilkes's death; established himself in Piccadilly as book and pamphlet seller; imprisoned and fined for supporting Wilkes; 1770; proprietor and editor of 'General Advertiser,' 1784; tried for libel, 1786, and retired in financial difficulties to France; died in England; wrote and edited miscellaneous works. [i. 340]

ALMOND, MRS. EMMA (1814–1868). [See ROMER.]

ALMS, JAMES (1728–1791), captain in navy; of humble origin; served as midshipman at battles of Namur and Finisterre and in East Indies, 1744–9; as lieutenant at capture of Gheriah, 1756, and blockade of Brest, 1759, and as captain at reduction of Martinique and Havana; in actions at Praya Bay, 1781, Sadras, Providien, Negapatam, and Trincomalee, 1782; retired, 1784. [i. 342]

ALNWICK, MARTIN OF (*d.* 1336). [See MARTIN.]

ALNWICK, WILLIAM (*d.* 1449), bishop of Norwich and of Lincoln; LL.D. Cambridge; monk of St. Albans; first confessor of the Brigetine nuns at Syon, 1414; prior of Wymondham, and archdeacon of Sarum, 1420; received stall of Knaresborough-cum-Bickhill in York Cathedral, 1421; bishop of Norwich, 1426; confessor to Henry VI; translated to see of Lincoln, 1436; settled disputes between dean and chapter, and published (1440) a new code of statutes for regulation of the cathedral, which originated a contest between him and the dean, still undecided at his death; took part in founding Eton School and King's College, Cambridge. [i. 343]

ALPHAGE or **ALPHEGE**, ST. [See ÆLFHEAH.]

ALPHERY, NIKEPHOR (*fl.* 1618–1660), divine; rector of Woolley, Huntingdonshire, 1618; ejected, *c.* 1643; reinstated, 1660. [i. 345]

ALSOP, ANTHONY (*d.* 1726), poetical writer; M.A. Christ Church, Oxford, 1696; B.D., 1706; censor and tutor; published selections from Æsop, 1698; prebendary of Winchester and rector of Brightwell, Berkshire; left England on losing an action for breach of promise of marriage; returned and met death by drowning. [i. 345]

ALSOP, VINCENT (*d.* 1703), nonconformist divine; M.A. St. John's College, Cambridge; took holy orders as conformist, and became tutor at Oakham; afterwards received presbyterian ordination; 'presented' to Wilby, Northamptonshire; ejected, 1662; preached semi-privately and suffered imprisonment; published 'Antisozzo,' a witty attack on Bishop Sherlock, 1675; minister of a congregation at Westminster; said to have drawn up the presbyterians' address to James II for general indulgence. [i. 345]

ALSTON, CHARLES (1683–1760), scientific writer; studied medicine under Boerhaave at Leyden; lecturer in botany and materia medica at Edinburgh, and superintendent of botanical gardens, 1710 till death. [i. 346]

ALSTON, SIR EDWARD (1595–1669), president of College of Physicians, 1635–66; M.D. St. John's College, Cambridge, 1626; elected fellow of the College of Physicians, 1631; knighted, 1660. [i. 347]

ALSTON, EDWARD RICHARD (1845–1881), zoologist; wrote papers on mammalia and birds; zoological secretary, Linnean Society, 1880-1. [i. 347]

ALTEN, SIR CHARLES, COUNT VON (1764–1840), general; of protestant Hanoverian family; served in Hanoverian army, 1781–1803, and on its disbandment (1803) joined British army and held command (1805–1815); in Hanover, 1805, at Copenhagen, 1807, in Sweden and Spain, 1808, Walcheren, 1809, the Peninsula and at Waterloo; major-general, 1816; became field-marshal in reorganised Hanoverian army. [i. 347]

ALTHAM, SIR JAMES (*d.* 1617), judge; M.P. Bramber, Sussex, 1589; reader at Gray's inn, 1600; double reader and serjeant-at-law, 1603; baron of exchequer and knighted, 1606; decided against the king's superiority over the law, 1610 and later, but admitted error in deciding that the crown had no right to grant commendams. [i. 348]

ALTHAUS, JULIUS (1833–1900), physician; born in Lippe-Detmold, Germany; M.D. Berlin, 1855; assisted in founding hospital for epilepsy and paralysis, Regent's Park, of which he was physician, 1866–94; published writings mainly on therapeutic effects of electricity. [Suppl. i. 43]

ALTHORP, VISCOUNT. [See SPENCER, JOHN CHARLES, 1782–1845.]

ALVANLEY, BARON. [See ARDEN.]

ALVES, ROBERT (1745–1794), poet and prose writer; educated at Aberdeen; head-master, Banff grammar school, 1773–9; taught classics and modern languages in Edinburgh; published poems and literary history. [i. 349]

ALVEY, RICHARD (d. 1584), master of the Temple, 1560; fellow, St. John's College, Cambridge, 1537; B.D., 1543; successively rector of Thorington, Grinstead, and Sandon, 1540–52; canon of Westminster, 1552; deprived of preferments under Mary, but under Elizabeth restored to Thorington; again canon of Westminster, 1560–75; rector of Bursted Parva, Essex, 1571–6. [i. 349]

ALVEY, THOMAS (1645–1704), physician; M.D. Merton College, Oxford, 1671; F.R.C.P., 1676; Harveian orator, 1684. [i. 350]

AMBERLEY, VISCOUNT (1842–1876.) [See RUSSELL, JOHN.]

AMBROSE, ISAAC (1604–1663), divine; B.A. Brasenose, Oxford, 1624; presented to cure of Castleton, Derbyshire, 1627; one of king's four preachers in Lancashire, 1631; twice imprisoned by commissioners of array; worked for establishment of presbyterianism; successively at Leeds, Preston, and Garstang, whence he was ejected for nonconformity, 1662; published religious works. [i. 350]

AMBROSE, JOHN (d. 1771), captain in navy; served in Channel and Mediterranean, 1734–44; court-martialled for neglect of duty at Toulon (1744) and cashiered; restored to rank and half-pay, 1748; retired rear-admiral, 1750. [i. 351]

AMBROSE, MISS (1720 ? – 1818). [See PALMER, ELEANOR, LADY.]

AMBROSIUS AURELIANUS, called EMRYS (fl. 440), British leader; probably descended from Constantine; opposed Saxon invaders and confined them to limits of isle of Thanet. [i. 351]

AMELIA (1783–1810), princess; youngest child of George III; delicate in health; died of erysipelas, having been a confirmed invalid for two years. [i. 352]

AMES, JOSEPH (1619–1695), naval commander under the Commonwealth; transported many royalists to colonies. [i. 352]

AMES, JOSEPH (1689–1759), bibliographer and antiquary, grandson of preceding; apprenticed to plane maker in London; entered business at Wapping as either shipchandler, ironmonger, or patten maker, and continued successfully till death; became acquainted with Rev. J. Lewis of Margate, and other antiquaries, on whose suggestion he prepared his 'Typographical Antiquities,' 1749; F.S.A., 1736; F.R.S., 1743; published also an illustrated catalogue of English engraved portraits, and memoirs of the Wren family. [i. 353]

AMES, WILLIAM (1576–1633), puritan divine and casuist; educated at Christ's College, Cambridge, where his religious zeal resulted in his suspension by the vice-chancellor 'from all degrees taken or to be taken'; being prevented by the Bishop of London from settling as a preacher at Colchester, he went to Leyden; worsted in a controversy with Grevinchovius, the Arminian minister at Rotterdam, 1613; chaplain to Sir Horace Vere, English governor of Brill, Holland, whose daughter he married; employed by Calvinists at synod of Dort, 1619; professor of theology, Franeker, 1622; owing to ill-health removed to Rotterdam, where he died; wrote theological works. [i. 355]

AMES, WILLIAM (d. 1662), baptist minister and quaker; joined quakers, 1655; officer in parliamentary army settled in Amsterdam, 1657; returned to England and was imprisoned for attending quaker meeting, 1662. [i. 355]

AMESBURY, BARON (1751–1832). [See DUNDAS, CHARLES.]

AMHERST, FRANCIS KERRIL (1819–1883), Roman catholic prelate; educated at St. Mary's College, Oscott, where, after ordination, he became professor; missionary rector of St. Augustin's church, Stafford, 1856; bishop of Northampton, 1858–79; preconised to titular see of Sozusa, 1880. [i. 357]

AMHERST, JEFFREY, BARON AMHERST (1717–1797), field-marshal; ensign in guards, 1731; aide-de-camp to General Ligonier in Germany; successively on staff of Ligonier and Duke of Cumberland; lieutenant-colonel, 15th regiment, 1756; major-general, commanding expedition to North America, 1758; took Louisburg, Cape Breton Isle, succeeded James Abercromby as commander-in-chief, and took Fort Du Quesne, 1758; took Ticonderoga and Crown Point, and shared in capture of Montreal, 1759; governor-general of British North America and knighted, 1761; took strong but unsuccessful measures against Indian chief Pontiac; returned to England, 1763; governor of Virginia, 1763, and of Guernsey, 1770; privy councillor, 1772; created Baron Amherst, 1776; held various military offices; field-marshal, 1796. [i. 357]

AMHERST, JOHN (1718 ?–1778), admiral, younger brother of Jeffrey Amherst [q. v.]; captain, 1744; flag-captain in East Indies and in North America, 1755, in Mediterranean, 1756; at Louisbourg, Belle-Isle, and Gibraltar, 1761–2; commander-in-chief at Plymouth, 1776. [i. 359]

AMHERST, WILLIAM PITT, EARL AMHERST OF ARRACAN (1773–1857), statesman; nephew of Jeffrey Amherst [q. v.]; envoy to Pekin to represent to the emperor wrongs suffered under his rule by British subjects, 1816; repelled by his discourteous reception, he returned, 1817; governor-general of India, 1823–8; declared war on king of Burmah, 1824; peace made after capture of Rangoon, Martaban, and Prome, and cession of Tenasserim, Arracan, and Assam; created Earl Amherst, 1826; returned to England, 1828, and retired from public affairs. [i. 360]

AMHURST, NICHOLAS (1697–1742), poet and political writer; educated at Merchant Taylors' and St. John's College, Oxford; expelled from university perhaps on account of his whig principles, 1719; settled in London; started bi-weekly periodical, 'Terræ Filius,' in which Oxford was severely satirised, 1721; suffered short imprisonment, 1737, for libel of Colley Cibber in 'Craftsman,' which he started, 1726; published occasional poems. [i. 361]

AMMONIO, ANDREA (1477–1517), Latin secretary to Henry VIII; born at Lucca; educated at Rome; sent to England as collector for the pope; held ecclesiastical offices at Westminster and Salisbury; accompanied Henry VIII in French campaign as Latin secretary, and celebrated his victories in a Latin poem, 1513. [i. 363]

AMNER, JOHN (d. 1641), organist of Ely Cathedral, 1610; Mus. Bac. Oxford, 1613; published sacred music. [i. 363]

AMNER, RALPH (d. 1664), minor canon; lay clerk of Ely Cathedral, 1604–9; minor canon, St. George's, Windsor; gentleman of Chapel Royal, 1623. [i. 363]

AMNER, RICHARD (1736–1803), unitarian divine; studied at Daventry, 1755–62; minister at Yarmouth, 1762–4, and at Hampstead, 1765; published theological works; his name unwarrantably appended to indelicate notes by George Steevens in his edition of Shakespeare. [i. 364]

AMORY, THOMAS (1701–1774), dissenting tutor; studied divinity at Taunton academy, where he was assistant, 1725, and principal, 1738; ordained, 1730; successively minister in Hull Bishops, Taunton, and London (1759); one of Dr. Williams's trustees, 1767; D.D. Edinburgh, 1768; strenuously supported agitation against subscription to Toleration Act, 1772. [i. 364]

AMORY, THOMAS (1691 ?–1788), eccentric writer; of Irish descent, though not born in Ireland; probably lived in Dublin, where he knew Swift; lived at Westminster, c. 1757, with a country house near Hounslow; published, 1755, 'Memoirs, containing Lives of several Ladies of Great Britain,' and, 1756–66, 'Life of John Buncle, Esq.,' virtually a continuation of 'Memoirs.' [i. 365]

AMOS, ANDREW (1791–1860), lawyer; born in India; educated at Eton and Trinity College, Cambridge; fifth wrangler and fellow, 1813; called to bar and joined middle circuit; recorder of Oxford; sat on criminal law commissions, 1834–43; first professor of law, University College, London, 1829; succeeded Macaulay as fourth member of governor-general's council in India, 1837–43; county court judge for Marylebone, Brentford, and Brompton, 1843; Downing professor of law, Cambridge, 1848 till death; published legal, constitutional, and literary works. [i. 366]

AMOS, SHELDON (1835–1886), jurist, son of Andrew Amos [q. v.]; B.A. Clare College, Cambridge, 1859; barrister at Inner Temple, 1862; reader till 1869; professor of jurisprudence, University College, London, 1869–79; judge of court of appeal (native tribunals) in Egypt, c. 1882; advocated higher education and political emancipation of women. His publications include a 'Systematic View of the Science of Jurisprudence,' 1872. [Suppl. i. 44]

AMPHLETT, SIR RICHARD PAUL (1809–1883), judge; sixth wrangler, St. Peter's College, Cambridge, 1831; called to bar, Lincoln's Inn, 1834; joined Oxford circuit; took silk, 1858; M.P., East Worcestershire, 1868; president Legal Education Association, 1873; baron of exchequer, 1874; promoted to court of appeal, 1876; retired, 1877. [i. 367]

AMPTHILL, first BARON (1829–1884). [See RUSSELL, ODO WILLIAM LEOPOLD.]

AMYOT, THOMAS (1775–1850), antiquary; of Huguenot origin; articled to a Norwich attorney; election agent (1802) and private secretary (1806) to Mr. Windham, whose speeches he published, 1812; held several appointments in colonial department; connected with Royal, Percy, and Shakespeare societies, and Society of Antiquaries. [i. 368]

AMYRAUT or **AMAROTT,** PAUL (fl. 1636–1662), divine; of German birth; vicar of Ermington; suspended for puritanism, 1636; held living of Munsley, Norfolk, and was ejected 1662. [i. 369]

ANARAWD (d. 915?), Welsh prince; succeeded his father, Rhodri, as king of all Wales, 877; defeated Saxons at Cymryd, 880; 'cum Anglis' devastated Cardigan, c. 893. [i. 370]

ANCELL, SAMUEL (d. 1802), military writer; served with 58th regiment; besieged at Gibraltar, 1779–83; published account of siege, 1784. [i. 370]

ANCRUM, first EARL OF (1578–1654). [See KER, ROBERT.]

ANDERDON, JOHN LAVICOUNT (1792–1874), angler; educated at Harrow; became partner in a London business firm, 1816; published devotional works and a book on angling. [i. 370]

ANDERDON, WILLIAM HENRY (1816–1890), jesuit, son of John Lavicount Anderdon [q. v.]; B.A. University College, Oxford, 1839; M.A., 1842; entered Roman catholic church, 1850; ordained priest at Oscott, 1853; secretary to (Cardinal) Manning in London, 1863; on mission in America, 1868–70; D.D. Rome, 1869; joined Society of Jesus, 1872; engaged in missionary work in England; published religious and other works. [Suppl. i. 45]

ANDERSON, ADAM (1692?–1765), historian of commerce; for forty years clerk in the South Sea House, ultimately becoming chief clerk of stock and new annuities; published (1764) history of commercial enterprise from earliest times to 1762. [i. 371]

ANDERSON, ADAM (d. 1846), physicist; rector of Perth academy, and afterwards professor of natural philosophy at St. Andrews; published articles on physics. [i. 371]

ANDERSON, ALEXANDER (1582–1619?), mathematician; taught mathematics in Paris early in seventeenth century; friend of Vieta, whose writings he edited, 1615–17; published mathematical works. [i. 371]

ANDERSON, ALEXANDER (d. 1811), botanist; superintendent of botanic garden, St. Vincent; went on botanising expedition to Guiana, 1791. [i. 372]

ANDERSON, ANDREW (d. 1861), champion Scottish draught-player; stocking-weaver; published book on 'Draughts,' 1848. [i. 372]

ANDERSON, ANTHONY (d. 1593), theological writer and preacher; rector of Medbourne, Leicestershire, 1573–93; vicar of Stepney, and rector of Denge, Essex, 1587; sub-dean of Chapel Royal, 1592; published theological works of puritanic character. [i. 372]

ANDERSON, CHRISTOPHER (1782–1852), theological writer and preacher; originally in insurance office, but became baptist minister in Edinburgh; founded Gaelic School and Edinburgh Bible societies; supported Indian missions; published 'Annals of English Bible,' 1835, and other works. [i. 373]

ANDERSON, SIR EDMUND (1530–1605), judge; educated at Lincoln College, Oxford; studied at Inner Temple, 1550; reader at his inn of court, 1567; double reader at Inner Temple, 1574; serjeant-at-law, 1577; serjeant-at-law to queen, 1579; knighted and made lord chief justice of common pleas, 1582; took part in trial of Babington, of Secretary Davison, and of Mary Queen of Scots, 1586, and in the trials of Perrot, 1590, Earl of Essex, 1601, and Raleigh, 1603; showed great severity towards puritans, and notably John Udall. [i. 373]

ANDERSON, GEORGE (fl. 1740), mathematician; friend of the mathematician William Jones, whose letters to him were published, 1841. [i. 376]

ANDERSON, GEORGE (1760–1796), accountant; of humble origin; educated and sent by friends to Wadham College, Oxford; M.A., 1784; took deacon's orders, but obtained post in board of control, to which he ultimately became accountant-general; translated Archimedes's 'Arenarius,' 1784. [i. 376]

ANDERSON, SIR GEORGE WILLIAM (1791–1857), Indian civil servant; employed chiefly on judicial duties in Bombay civil service, 1806–31; framed 'Bombay Code of 1827'; principal collector and political agent of Southern Mahratta districts, 1831; Bombay member of Indian law commission, 1835–8; member of council of governor of Bombay, 1838; governor of Bombay, 1841–2; knighted and made C.B.; governor of Mauritius, 1849; K.C.B. and (1850–5) governor of Ceylon. [i. 377]

ANDERSON, JAMES (1662–1728), genealogist and antiquary; M.A. Edinburgh, 1680; writer to the signet, 1691; published, 1705, 'An Historical Essay showing that the Crown and Kingdom of Scotland is Imperial and Independent,' in which documents, cited in a pamphlet by William Atwood on the supremacy of the crown of England over that of Scotland, were shown to be forgeries; rewarded by Scottish parliament; devoted himself to collecting facsimiles of Scottish charters and other muniments, for which work money was voted by the Scottish parliament, but never paid, the parliament terminating it at the union; postmaster-general for Scotland, 1715; retained office for only eighteen months, but continued to draw salary; his facsimiles, published 1729 under title of 'Diplomata'; also published 'Collections relating to Mary Queen of Scots.' [i. 378]

ANDERSON, JAMES (1680?–1739), preacher; brother of Adam Anderson [q. v.]; educated at Aberdeen; minister of presbyterian churches in Swallow Street, London, 1710, and Lisle Street, Leicester Fields, 1734. Published sermons, works on history, freemasonry, and other subjects. [i. 380]

ANDERSON, JAMES (1739–1808), economist; after age of fifteen managed farms near Edinburgh and in Aberdeenshire; published essays on agriculture; LL.D. Aberdeen, 1780; advocated protection of Scottish fisheries, provoking remonstrance from Bentham, 1783; employed by Pitt to survey fisheries, 1784; retired to Isleworth, 1797; published many economic works. [i. 381]

ANDERSON, JAMES (d. 1809), botanist; physician-general of East India Company, Madras, where he attempted to introduce silk cultivation and interested himself in plants of commercial value. [i. 382]

ANDERSON, JAMES (1760–1835), navy captain; served in American and first French revolutionary wars; commander, 1806; post-captain, 1812; sent to Quebec, but returned, mistrusting the capabilities of his ship; court-martialled and acquitted. [i. 382]

ANDERSON, Sir JAMES CALEB (1792–1861), inventor; son of John Anderson (*fl.* 1816) [q. v.]; created baronet, 1813, in appreciation of his father's services to Ireland; patented inventions in machinery. [i. 382]

ANDERSON, JAMES ROBERTSON (1811–1895), actor; appeared with Macready at Covent Garden as Florizel ('Winter's Tale'), 1837, and subsequently played Biron ('Love's Labour's Lost'), Romeo, Iago, and Cassio; seen as Othello, Orlando, Faulconbridge, Posthumus, Antony ('Julius Cæsar' and 'Antony and Cleopatra'), Richard I, and Mercutio, at Drury Lane, which theatre he managed, 1849–51; joint-manager of the Surrey, 1863; wrote a few dramas. [Suppl. i. 46]

ANDERSON, JOHN (1668 ?–1721) ,theologian; minister of Dumbarton, and (1720) of Ramshorn (now St. David's) Church, Glasgow; took active part in controversy between episcopacy and presbyterianism, and published works in the presbyterian interest. [i. 382]

ANDERSON, JOHN (1726–1796), natural philosopher; officer in corps raised to resist Jacobite rebellion, 1745; studied at Glasgow; professor of oriental languages, 1756, and of natural philosophy, 1760; interested in practical applications of science. [i. 383]

ANDERSON, JOHN (*fl.* 1799), wood-engraver; pupil of Thomas Bewick; engraved blocks for George Samuel's illustrations of 'Grove Hill,' a poem. [i. 384]

ANDERSON, JOHN (*d.* 1804), physician to General Sea-bathing Infirmary, Margate; M.D. Edinburgh; F.S.A. [i. 384]

ANDERSON, JOHN (*fl.* 1816), founder of Fermoy; of humble origin; established himself as provision exporter, Cork, 1780; purchased land on estate of Fermoy, Munster; built town of Fermoy and opened and improved roads in Ireland; refused baronetcy, which was, however, conferred on his son, James Caleb Anderson [q. v.], 1813. [i. 384]

ANDERSON, JOHN (*fl.* 1825), genealogist; writer to the signet; secretary to Scottish Society of Antiquaries; wrote history of family of Frisel or Fraser, 1825. [i. 385]

ANDERSON, JOHN (1789–1832), genealogist; L.R.C.S. Edinburgh; surgeon to Lanarkshire militia, and to Duke of Hamilton, the history of whose family he published, 1825–7. [i. 385]

ANDERSON, JOHN (1795–1845), diplomatic agent; entered service of East India Company, 1813; after holding various appointments was 'senior merchant,' secretary to government, and Malay translator, 1827; agent to governor of Pulo Penang, 1823; engaged in mercantile duties in London, where he died; published works relating to Eastern policy and commerce. [i. 385]

ANDERSON, JOHN (1805–1855), missionary; educated at Edinburgh; prizeman in Latin and moral philosophy; ordained minister of Scottish church and sent as missionary to Madras, 1836; established Madras Christian College; on disruption of Church of Scotland joined Free Church and carried on mission in connection with that church, 1843; especially successful in regard to female education; died at Madras. [i. 386]

ANDERSON, JOHN (1833–1900), naturalist; M.D. Edinburgh, 1862; assisted in founding Royal Physical Society, Edinburgh; professor of natural history in Free Church College, Edinburgh; curator of Indian museum, Calcutta, 1865; accompanied scientific expeditions to Yunnan, 1867, Burmah, 1875–6, and the Mergui archipelago, 1881–2, and published accounts of journeys; F.R.S., 1879; honorary LL.D. Edinburgh, 1885; F.L.S.; F.S.A.; professor of comparative anatomy, medical school, Calcutta; returned to London, 1886; contributed to 'Proceedings' of various learned societies, and published several works. [Suppl. i. 46]

ANDERSON, JOHN HENRY (1815–1874), conjurer and actor; known as 'Wizard of the North,' occupied Covent Garden theatre when it was burnt down, 1856. [i. 387]

ANDERSON, JOSEPH (1789–1877), lieutenant-colonel; ensign, 1805; lieutenant-colonel, 1812; served in Australia and India; military commander and civil governor of penal settlement, Norfolk Island; squatter, 1848, and member of legislative council, Victoria, 1852. [i. 387]

ANDERSON, LIONEL, *alias* MUNSON (*d.* 1680), Roman catholic priest; tried, with seven others, on unsubstantiated charge of receiving orders from see of Rome; condemned, hanged, drawn, and quartered. [i. 387]

ANDERSON, LUCY (1790–1878), pianist; played regularly at principal concerts after 1818; introduced into England many great works by Beethoven, Hummel, and other composers. [i. 388]

ANDERSON, PATRICK (1575–1624), Scottish jesuit; educated in Scotland; entered Society of Jesus, Rome, 1597; missionary to Scotland, 1609; first jesuit rector of Scots College, Rome, 1615; was betrayed and imprisoned in Edinburgh when revisiting Scotland; liberated; wrote theological works. [i. 389]

ANDERSON, PATRICK (*fl.* 1618–1635), physician; author of a history of Scotland and several medical works. [i. 389]

ANDERSON, ROBERT (*fl.* 1668–1696), mathematician and silk-weaver; experimented with view of improving gunnery, after 1671; wrote scientific works chiefly relating to firearms. [i. 390]

ANDERSON, ROBERT (1750–1830), editor and biographer of British poets; intended for ministry, but took to medicine; M.D. Edinburgh; devoted himself to literature; edited 'Complete Edition of Poets of Great Britain,' 1792–5, and separate editions of various authors; for a time edited 'Edinburgh Magazine'; among first to recognise genius of the poet Campbell. [i. 390]

ANDERSON, ROBERT (1770–1833), Cumbrian poet; educated at charity and quaker schools; apprenticed to pattern drawer in Carlisle; his first poem, entitled 'Lucy Gray,' probably suggested Wordsworth's 'She dwelt among the untrodden ways'; published ballads in Cumbrian dialect, 1805; fell into habits of intemperance, and died in extreme poverty. [i. 391]

ANDERSON, THOMAS (1832–1870), botanist; M.D. Edinburgh, 1853; entered Bengal medical service, Calcutta, 1854; director of Calcutta botanic garden; organised and superintended Bengal forest department, 1864; left an incomplete work on Indian flora. [i. 392]

ANDERSON, THOMAS (1819–1874), chemist; Hope prizeman, 1839–40, and M.D. Edinburgh, 1841; studied on continent; F.R.S. Edinburgh, 1845; regius professor of chemistry, Glasgow, 1852; gained high honours from English and Scottish scientific societies; conducted experiments in organic and agricultural chemistry. [i. 392]

ANDERSON, WALTER (*d.* 1800), historian; for fifty years minister of Chirnside, Berwickshire; wrote historical works. [i. 393]

ANDERSON, WILLIAM (*d.* 1778), surgeon and naturalist; accompanied Captain Cook as surgeon's mate, 1772–5, and later as naturalist; contributed observations to Cook's 'Voyages.' [i. 393]

ANDERSON, WILLIAM (1757–1837), Scottish painter; exhibited pictures, chiefly of marine subjects, at Royal Academy, 1787 to 1814. [i. 393]

ANDERSON, WILLIAM (1766–1846), gardener at Edinburgh; curator of botanic gardens of Society of Apothecaries, Chelsea; F.L.S., 1815. [i. 393]

ANDERSON, WILLIAM (1805–1866), miscellaneous writer; brother of John Anderson (1789–1832) [q. v.]; entered lawyer's office, Edinburgh; took to journalism; published volumes of verse and prose; in London, 1836–42; produced 'Gift of All Nations,' an annual; chief sub-editor of 'Glasgow Daily Mail,' 1845; compiled various works, including 'Scottish Nation,' 1859–63. [i. 394]

ANDERSON, WILLIAM (1799–1873), Scottish preacher; pastor of congregation in John Street, Glasgow, 1822 till death; LL.D. Glasgow, 1850; advocated separation of church and state, and political and social reforms; published pamphlets and theological books. [i. 394]

ANDERSON, Sir WILLIAM (1835–1898), director-general of ordnance; born in St. Petersburg, where, and at King's College, London, he was educated; president of Institution of Civil Engineers, Ireland, 1863; designed gun and turret mountings of the Moncrieff type for British and Russian governments; designed machinery for manufacture of cordite, *c.* 1888; director-general of ordnance factories, 1889 ; M.I.C.E., 1869, vice-president, 1896 ; F.R.S., 1891 ; K.C.B., 1897 ; honorary D.C.L. Durham, 1889 ; published scientific writings. [Suppl. i. 47]

ANDERSON, WILLIAM (1842-1900), anatomist ; educated at City of London School ; F.R.C.S., 1869 ; surgical registrar and assistant demonstrator of anatomy, St. Thomas's Hospital, 1871 ; professor of anatomy and surgery at Imperial Naval Medical College, Tōkio, 1873-80 ; joined surgical staff of St. Thomas's, 1880, and was surgeon, 1891 ; professor of anatomy at Royal Academy, 1891. Published works on Japanese and Chinese art, his collections of which were made over to the British Museum, 1882. [Suppl. i. 48]

ANDERTON, HENRY (1630-1665 ?), painter ; pupil of Streater ; executed portraits of Charles II and many of his courtiers. [i. 395]

ANDERTON, JAMES (*fl.* 1624), Roman catholic controversialist ; probably a priest ; published between 1608 and 1624, under name of ' John Brereley, Priest,' learned works, including ' The Protestants Apologie for the Roman Church,' in which he quoted passages from protestant writers admitting claims of the Roman church. [i. 395]

ANDERTON, LAURENCE, *alias* SCROOP (1577-1643), jesuit ; B.A. Christ's College, Cambridge, 1597 ; entered Society of Jesus, Rome, 1604, and worked as missioner in England ; published theological works. [i. 396]

ANDRE, JOHN (1751-1780), major ; born and educated at Geneva ; came to England ; was befriended by Miss Seward at Lichfield ; entered army, served in America, and was captured at St. John's, 1775 ; on release was aide-de-camp successively to General Grey and Sir Henry Clinton ; adjutant-general ; entrusted with secret negotiations with Benedict Arnold, who was plotting betrayal of West Point to British ; captured by Americans and hanged as spy. A monument was erected to his memory in Westminster Abbey. [i. 397]

ANDREAS or ANDRÉ, BERNARD (*fl.* 1500), poet and historian ; Augustinian friar ; Frenchman by birth ; came to England with or shortly before Henry VII ; poet laureate ; tutor to Prince Arthur ; presented to parish of Guisnes, near Calais, 1500 ; received benefice of Higham, 1501 ; wrote an incomplete life of Henry VII, also other works in verse and prose. [i. 398]

ANDREE, JOHN (1699 ?-1785), physician ; M.D. Rheims, 1739 ; L.C.P., 1741 ; a founder of London Hospital, of which he was first physician, 1740-64 ; wrote medical works. [i. 399]

ANDREE, JOHN, the younger (*fl.* 1790), surgeon ; son of John Andree (1699 ?-1785) [q. v.] ; surgeon to Magdalen hospital, 1766, to Finsbury dispensary, 1781, and to St. Clement Danes workhouse, 1784 ; M.D., *c.* 1798 ; one of first to operate successfully for croup of the larynx ; published medical works. [i. 399]

ANDREW, JAMES, LL.D. (1774 ?-1833), schoolmaster ; established military academy at Addiscombe, and on its purchase by East India Company was appointed headmaster and professor of mathematics, 1809. [i. 400]

ANDREWE, LAURENCE (*fl.* 1510-1537), translator and printer ; native of Calais ; practised as printer in London, and produced scientific works translated by himself. [i. 400]

ANDREWE, THOMAS (*fl.* 1604), poetical writer ; served as soldier in Low Countries ; wrote ' The Unmasking of a Female Machiavell,' 1604. [i. 400]

ANDREWES, GERRARD (1750-1825), divine ; educated at Westminster and Trinity College, Cambridge ; M.A., 1779 ; D.D., 1809 ; held living of St. James's, Piccadilly, 1802 ; dean of Canterbury, 1809. [i. 401]

ANDREWES, LANCELOT (1555-1626), bishop of Winchester ; educated at Merchant Taylors' and Pembroke Hall, Cambridge ; fellow of Pembroke and of Jesus College, Oxford ; received holy orders, 1580 ; chaplain to Earl of Huntingdon ; obtained living of St. Giles's, Cripplegate, 1589 ; prebendary of St. Paul's ; master of Pembroke till 1605 ; chaplain to Whitgift and chaplain in ordinary to the queen ; dean of Westminster, 1601 ; bishop of Chichester, 1605, of Ely, 1609, and of Win-

chester, 1619 ; dean of Chapel Royal, 1619 ; privy councillor for England, 1609, and for Scotland, 1617 ; took part in Hampton Court conference, 1604 ; first on list of divines appointed to make ' authorised version ' of bible, 1611 ; renowned for his patristic learning ; wrote theological works. [i. 401]

ANDREWS, EUSEBIUS (*d.* 1650), royalist ; secretary to Lord Capel ; barrister ; joined king's army, and after surrender of Worcester, 1645, returned to his legal practice ; became involved in a bogus plot arranged by Barnard, a parliamentary spy ; condemned after sixteen weeks' imprisonment, and beheaded on Tower Hill. [i. 405]

ANDREWS, GEORGE (*fl.* 1776), barrister ; called to bar, 1740 ; published, 1754, reports of king's bench cases, 1737-40. [i. 406]

ANDREWS, HENRY (1743-1820), astronomical calculator to ' Nautical,' ' Moore's ' and other almanacs ; successively domestic servant at Sleaford and Lincoln, usher at Stilton, and bookseller and schoolmaster at Royston. [i. 406]

ANDREWS, HENRY C. (*fl.* 1799-1828), botanical artist ; published botanical works, for which he engraved illustrations, 1799-1828. [i. 406]

ANDREWS, JAMES PETTIT (1737 ?-1797), antiquary and historian ; served in Berkshire militia ; entered legal profession ; police court magistrate, Queen Square, Westminster, 1792, till death ; published translations and works, principally historical. [i. 407]

ANDREWS, JOHN (*fl.* 1615), poet ; M.A. Trinity College, Oxford ; probably curate of Beswick Bassett, Wiltshire ; published the underrated poem, ' Anatomie of Basenesse,' 1615, and several religious works. [i. 407]

ANDREWS, JOHN (1736-1809), author ; published, 1774-1806, ' History of the War with America, France, Spain, and Holland, 1775-83 ' (1785-6), and other historical writings. [i. 408]

ANDREWS, MILES PETER (*d.* 1814), dramatist ; son of a drysalter of Watling Street ; owned powder magazine at Dartford ; M.P. for Bewdley ; occupied mansion in Green park ; wrote several plays, produced at Drury Lane, Haymarket, and Covent Garden, 1774-95. [i. 408]

ANDREWS, ROBERT (*d.* 1766 ?), translator of ' Virgil ' into blank verse, 1766 ; successively minister of presbyterian or protestant dissenting congregations at Lydgate, Rusholme, and Bridgnorth. [i. 409]

ANDREWS, THOMAS (1813-1885), professor of chemistry ; educated at Belfast academy and Glasgow University ; studied chemistry under Dumas at Paris ; received diploma of Royal College of Surgeons, Edinburgh ; M.D., 1835 ; vice-president of Northern (now Queen's) College, Belfast, 1845 ; professor of chemistry, Queen's College, Belfast, 1849-79 ; F.R.S., 1849 ; honorary F.R.S. Edinburgh, 1870 ; LL.D. Edinburgh, 1871, Trinity College, Dublin, 1873, and Glasgow, 1877 ; D.Sc., 1879, Queen's University of Ireland, where an Andrews studentship was established in his memory. He discovered the existence of a critical temperature above which gas cannot be converted into a liquid by pressure. [Suppl. i. 49]

ANDREWS, WILLIAM (*fl.* 1656-1683), author of astrological works, including ' Annus Prodigiosus,' 1672. [i. 409]

ANDREWS, WILLIAM (1802-1880), secretary and subsequently president of Dublin Natural History Society ; devoted his attention chiefly to botany and marine ichthyology. [i. 409]

ANDREWS, WILLIAM EUSEBIUS (1773-1837), journalist and author ; of humble parents, who were converts to Roman catholic faith ; apprenticed to printers of ' Norfolk Chronicle,' which he subsequently managed ; went to London and started, to vindicate Roman catholic principles, various journals, of which the ' Orthodox Journal and Catholic Monthly Intelligencer ' appeared at intervals and in different forms for many years. His published works are chiefly connected with religious controversies. [i. 409]

ANDROS, SIR EDMUND (1637-1714), colonial governor ; gentleman in ordinary to queen of Bohemia, 1660 ; major in Rupert's dragoons, 1672 ; bailiff of Guernsey, 1674 ;

knighted, 1678; governor of province of New York, 1674–1681, of New England, 1685–9, of Virginia 1692–8 (recalled in each case owing to disputes arising from severity of his rule), and of Jersey, 1704–6; died in London.   [i. 411]

ANEURIN (*fl.* 603 ?), Welsh poet; identified by some with Gildas the historian; son of Caw ab Geraint, lord of Cwm Cawlwyd; educated at St. Cadoc's College, Llancarvan; probably present as bard and priest at battle of Cattraeth, when he was captured; on being released returned to Wales, and probably made acquaintance of Taliesin; murdered by Eidyn ab Einygan; wrote 'Gododin,' an epic poem on defeat of Britons by Saxons at Cattraeth.   [i. 411]

ANGAS, CALEB (1782–1860), Yorkshire agriculturist; contributed important letters to the 'Sun,' advocating free trade.   [i. 413]

ANGAS, GEORGE FIFE (1789–1879), merchant and shipowner till 1833; commissioner for formation of colony of South Australia, 1834; having suffered losses, emigrated to Adelaide, 1851, where he died; founded National and Provincial and other banks.   [i. 413]

ANGAS, GEORGE FRENCH (1822–1886), artist and zoologist; joined several of (Sir) George Grey's expeditions, and subsequently published sketches and accounts of travels in Australia, New Zealand, and South Africa; director and secretary of government museum, Sydney; contributed in England tales of adventure to various journals; fellow of the Linnean, Zoological, and Royal Geographical societies.   [Suppl. i. 51]

ANGAS, WILLIAM HENRY (1781–1832), sailor missionary; spent early years at sea; became baptist minister, 1817, and sailor missionary, 1822.   [i. 413]

ANGEL, JOHN (*fl.* 1555), chaplain to King Philip and Queen Mary.   [i. 413]

ANGEL or **ANGELL**, JOHN (*d.* 1655), preacher; graduated at Magdalen Hall, Oxford; was ordained and became evangelical preacher; town preacher and lecturer, Leicester, *c.* 1630; suspended for preaching without licence, 1634; lecturer at Grantham, 1650–5.   [i. 413]

ANGELIS, PETER (1685–1734), painter of landscapes and conversation pieces; born at Dunkirk; having worked at Antwerp, where he became member of Painters Guild of St. Luke, was in London, *c.* 1719–28; went to Rome, and finally settled at Rennes, Brittany.   [i. 414]

ANGELL, JOHN (*fl.* 1758), stenographer, of Dublin; published system of shorthand, being a variation of Mason's system, 1758.   [i. 414]

ANGELO, DOMENICO (1716–1802), fencing-master, named originally DOMENICO ANGELO MALEVOLTI TREMAMONDO; born at Leghorn; studied horsemanship at Paris; migrated to England, *c.* 1755; patronised by English noblemen; opened in Soho a fencing-school, which became very fashionable; published, in 1763, 'L'Ecole d'Armes'; later retired to Eton.   [lvii. 183]

ANGELO, HENRY (1760–1839 ?), fencing-master; son of Domenico Angelo [q. v.]; became, *c.* 1785, head of his father's fencing-school; published 'Reminiscences' (1830) and 'Angelo's Pic-Nic' (1834).   [lvii. 183]

ANGELO, HENRY, the younger (1780–1852), fencing-master and superintendent of sword-exercise in the army; son of Henry Angelo [q. v.]   [lvii. 183]

ANGELUS À SANCTO FRANCISCO (1601–1678) (religious pseudonym of RICHARD MASON, D.D.), Franciscan; priest of restored English province, 1628; successively filled various offices in his order; was provincial 1659–62; retired to St. Bonaventure's convent, Douay, 1675; wrote several theological works.   [i. 415]

ANGELUS, CHRISTOPHER (*d.* 1638), Greek scholar; native of Peloponnesus; came to England to escape persecution, 1608; studied at Cambridge and Balliol College, Oxford; published works in Greek, Latin, and English.   [i. 415]

ANGERSTEIN, JOHN JULIUS (1735–1823), merchant, philanthropist, and amateur of fine art; underwriter in Lloyds, 1756; through his influence 'Old Lloyd's' coffee house was abandoned for the present establishment; devised systems of state lotteries; at various times head of largest trading firms in city; besides other

philanthropic works, re-established Veterinary College; acquired collection of pictures, which formed nucleus of National Gallery.   [i. 416]

ANGERVILLE, RICHARD (1281–1345). [See BURY, RICHARD DE.]

ANGIER, JOHN (1605–1677), nonconformist divine; B.A. Emmanuel College, Cambridge; came under influence of puritans; made pastor of Ringley, 1630; ordained by bishop of Bangor, but without subscription; suspended from Ringley; pastor of Denton, 1632 till death; twice excommunicated; signed the 'Harmonious Consent,' 1648; imprisoned for opposition to Commonwealth; escaped persecution under Act of Uniformity, owing to esteem in which he was held; published sermons.   [i. 417]

ANGIERS or **ANGIER**, PAUL (*fl.* 1749), engraver; pupil of John Tinney.   [i. 419]

ANGLESEY, first MARQUIS OF (1768–1854). [See PAGET, HENRY WILLIAM.]

ANGLESEY, EARLS OF. [See VILLIERS, CHRISTOPHER, first EARL, 1593 ?–1630; ANNESLEY, ARTHUR, first EARL of the second creation, 1614–1686; ANNESLEY, RICHARD, sixth EARL, 1694–1761.]

ANGLUS, THOMAS (1593–1676). [See WHITE, THOMAS.]

ANGUS, EARLS OF. [See UMFRAVILLE, GILBERT DE, 1244 ?–1307; DOUGLAS, GEORGE, first EARL, 1380 ?–1403; DOUGLAS, WILLIAM, second EARL, 1398 ?–1437; DOUGLAS, GEORGE, fourth EARL, 1412 ?–1462; DOUGLAS, ARCHIBALD, fifth EARL, 1449 ?–1514; DOUGLAS, ARCHIBALD, sixth EARL, 1489 ?–1557; DOUGLAS, ARCHIBALD, eighth EARL, 1555–1588; DOUGLAS, WILLIAM, ninth EARL, 1533–1591; DOUGLAS, WILLIAM, tenth EARL, 1554–1611; DOUGLAS, WILLIAM, eleventh EARL, 1589–1660.]

ANGUS, LORD (1609–1665). [See DOUGLAS, ARCHIBALD, EARL OF ORMOND.]

ANGUS, JOHN (1724–1801), independent minister at Bishop's Stortford, Hertfordshire, 1748–1801.   [i. 419]

ANLABY, WILLIAM (1552 ?–1597), Roman catholic missionary; educated as protestant, but was converted, and entered college of Douay, 1574; ordained, 1577; missionary in Yorkshire; hanged as seminary priest.   [i. 419]

ANNALY, BARON (1718–1784). [See GORE, JOHN.]

ANNAND, WILLIAM (1633–1689), dean of Edinburgh; B.A. University College, Oxford, 1655; ordained by an Irish bishop, and M.A., 1656; Anglican minister at Weston-in-the-Green; vicar of Leighton Buzzard, 1661; chaplain to Earl of Middleton; minister of Tolbooth church, 1663, and, later, of Tron church, Edinburgh; dean of Edinburgh, 1676; published religious works.   [i. 419]

ANNANDALE, first MARQUIS OF (*d.* 1721). [See JOHNSTONE, WILLIAM.]

ANNE OF BOHEMIA (1366–1394), first queen of Richard II; eldest daughter of Emperor Charles II, by fourth wife, Elizabeth of Pomerania; arrangements for her marriage made by Earl of Kent and two others, 1379, but her arrival was delayed by Wat Tyler's rebellion; she eventually reached London and was married, 1382; Richard II was devoted to her, but the expenses of the household, largely increased by her Bohemian retinue, had much to do with the struggles between Richard and parliament; in 1392 she acted as mediatrix between king and city of London, which had refused the king a loan; died childless at Sheen, of the pestilence.   [i. 420]

ANNE (1456–1485), queen of Richard III; daughter of Richard Nevill, earl of Warwick, 'the king-maker,' and of Anne, heiress of the former earls of the Beauchamp family; betrothed at Angers, 1470, to Edward, prince of Wales, son of Henry VI, to be married in the event of Warwick's expedition to restore Henry VI being successful, an arrangement which the death of Warwick and Prince Edward prevented; married Richard, duke of Gloucester, 1474, and when he usurped the throne, 1483, became queen; survived but less than a year her only son, who was born *c.* 1476, and died 1484.   [i. 423]

ANNE (1507–1536), second queen of Henry VIII; daughter of Sir Thomas Boleyn, afterwards Earl of Wiltshire and Ormonde; 'one of the French queen's women,' *c.* 1519–22, having, probably, gone to France with her father when he was ambassador ; returned to England, 1522 ; corresponded with Henry VIII, who had become attached to her ; became Henry VIII's mistress after 1527, the king having instituted proceedings with a view to his divorce from Catherine of Arragon ; secretly married in January 1533. Catherine's marriage being declared null, Anne was crowned on Whit Sunday, and her daughter, Princess Elizabeth, was born in September. In 1536 Henry, whose passion had gradually died, charged her with criminal intercourse with several persons, including her own brother, and she was condemned to death ; whereupon her marriage being declared invalid she was executed. [i. 425]

ANNE OF CLEVES (1515–1557), fourth queen of Henry VIII ; daughter of John, duke of Cleves, and Mary, only daughter of William, duke of Juliers ; her father being the most powerful supporter of protestantism in west of Germany, she was selected by Cromwell as wife for Henry on death of Jane Seymour ; arrangements for the match made in 1539 ; married at Greenwich, 1540. The king soon wearied of her, and a catholic reaction gave him an excuse a few months later for having the marriage annulled by parliament ; Anne was pensioned on condition of remaining in England, and on her death was buried in Westminster Abbey. [i. 429]

ANNE OF DENMARK (1574–1619), queen of James I ; daughter of Frederick II of Denmark and Norway, and Sophia, daughter of Ulric III, duke of Mecklenburg ; was born at Skanderborg, Jutland ; negotiations concerning her marriage begun in 1585, but Elizabeth, who was keeping James's mother, Mary Queen of Scots, in confinement, refused to sanction it ; on the execution of Mary, the Scottish nobility decided that the match should be concluded, 1587, and after some delay Anne was married by proxy at Copenhagen, 20 Aug..1589, and to James in person 23 Nov. following at Opsloe, Norway ; she arrived with him at Leith, 1 May 1590 ; crowned with James at Windsor, 1603, and took up residence in London, 1604 ; took great interest in the court entertainments, and personally appeared in masks by Jonson and Dekker ; fond of progresses through the country, that to Bath in 1613 being most notable. She largely indulged a taste for building, and consequently, in spite of many parliamentary grants, died heavily in debt. Her inclination towards the Roman church occasioned, 1604, a proclamation banishing jesuits and seminary priests from the kingdom, but, though she is said to have declared herself a catholic, she died professing protestantism. [i. 431]

ANNE (1665–1714), queen of Great Britain and Ireland ; born at St. James's Palace, London ; second daughter of James II, by his first wife, Anne Hyde, daughter of Earl of Clarendon ; educated in protestant faith ; confirmed by Dr. Lake, 1676, together with her elder sister, Mary (who married Prince of Orange, 1677); proposals for her marriage with Prince George of Hanover entertained but abandoned, 1681 ; married George, prince of Denmark, 1683 ; several children were born to them, but all died young ; joined William of Orange on the deposition of James, and by the Declaration of Right, 1688, had the crown settled on her and her posterity after that of William's wife, Mary ; ascended the throne, 8 March 1702, and gave the Duchess of Marlborough, with whom she had been intimate from an early age, high appointments in the royal household, which the duchess held till 1711, when she was superseded by Mrs. Masham, her cousin ; Anne's husband, Prince George, died 1708. Throughout her reign the queen favoured tory and high church principles, regarding it as her right to appoint her ministers according to her own choice ; and the final estrangement of the Duchess of Marlborough was largely due to the duke's persistent advice to replace tory ministers by whigs, on the ground that the tory ministry was unfavourable to the war of the Spanish succession. She evinced particular interest in the church, and endeavoured to take the ecclesiastical patronage of the crown into her own hands. In 1704 she granted the crown revenues from tenths and first-fruits to form, for the benefit of the church, a fund known as 'Queen Anne's Bounty,' and, in 1711, an act was passed on her recommendation for the building of fifty churches in London. In 1703 Anne recognised Charles III, second son of Emperor Leopold I, as king of Spain, and in the following years the English armies fighting in defence of his claim won several glorious victories ; the war was closed by the treaty of Utrecht, 1713. The most important constitutional feature of Anne's reign was the Act of Union with Scotland, passed 1707. She was interred in Henry VII's chapel, Westminster. Her portrait, painted by Kneller, is at Windsor. [i. 441]

ANNESLEY, ALEXANDER (*d.* 1813), London solicitor and member of Middle Temple ; wrote legal and political works. [ii. 1]

ANNESLEY, ARTHUR, first EARL OF ANGLESEY (1614–1686), son of Sir Francis Annesley [q. v.] ; graduated at Magdalen College, Oxford, 1634 ; entered Lincoln's Inn ; made the grand tour ; sent to Ireland by parliament to defeat Ormond's negotiations with the Scots in Ulster, 1645 and 1647 ; member for Dublin in Richard Cromwell's parliament, 1658 ; commissioned by Charles II to treat with parliament ; made Earl of Anglesey 1661 ; president of council of state, February 1660 ; M.P. for Carmarthen in Convention parliament, and after the Restoration, privy councillor ; vice-treasurer and receiver-general for Ireland, 1660–7 ; treasurer of navy, 1667 ; lord privy seal, 1672 ; dismissed for adverse criticism of the king's government, 1682 ; wrote historical and other works. [ii. 1]

ANNESLEY, SIR FRANCIS, bart., BARON MOUNT-NORRIS and first VISCOUNT VALENTIA (1585–1660) ; held several small offices of state in Dublin, 1606 ; took leading part in colonisation of Ulster, 1608 ; member for county Armagh in Irish parliament, 1613 ; knighted, 1616 ; principal secretary of state for Ireland, 1618 ; baronet, 1620 ; vice-treasurer and receiver-general of Ireland, 1625 ; raised to Irish peerage, 1628 ; 'treasurer-at-war' in addition to other offices, 1632 ; quarrelled with Sir Thomas Wentworth, afterwards Earl of Strafford, who became lord-deputy, 1633 ; charged (1634 and 1635) with malversion and other offences, and sentenced to death ; deprived of offices and imprisoned ; his sentence declared unjust by the commons, 1641 ; became Viscount Valentia by reversion, 1642 ; clerk of signet in Ireland, 1648 ; secretary of state at Dublin under Henry Cromwell. [ii. 3]

ANNESLEY, JAMES (1715–1760), claimant ; son of Lord Altham, by his wife, or by a woman called Juggy Landy ; lived with his father as legitimate son for some years, but afterwards shifted for himself. On death of Lord Altham (1727) his brother, afterwards Earl of Anglesey, succeeded to title, and contrived to get his nephew sent to America as a slave. Annesley entered navy (1740), returned to England, and taking legal action against his uncle (1743) was declared legitimate, but being without funds died before the case could be prosecuted further. [ii. 5]

ANNESLEY, RICHARD, sixth EARL OF ANGLESEY (1694–1761), succeeded his brother as fifth Baron Altham, 1727, and his cousin as sixth Earl of Anglesey, seventh Viscount Valentia, seventh Baron Mountnorris, and Baron Newport-Pagnell, 1737 ; married (1715) Anne Prest or Prust, who died without issue, 1741 ; lived with Ann Simpson (1737–40), and *c.* 1741, till death, with Juliana Donnovan (whom he married, 1752) ; both wives on his death (1761) claimed the titles of Valentia and Mountnorris for their children. The Countess Juliana won her case, and her son Arthur succeeded, but was unable to substantiate his claim to the titles of Anglesey and Newport-Pagnell. James Annesley [q. v.] unsuccessfully laid claim to title of Altham in 1743. [ii. 6]

ANNESLEY, SAMUEL (1620 ?–1696), puritan nonconformist ; graduated B.A. and M.A. Queen's College, Oxford ; ordained ; chaplain in Globe man-of-war to Earl of Warwick's fleet, 1644 ; obtained living of Cliffe ; preached before the House of Commons, 1648 ; LL.D. Oxford ; lecturer of St. Paul's, 1657 ; vicar of St. Giles, Cripplegate, 1658 ; ejected, 1662 ; preached semi-privately, and kept a meeting-house in Little St. Helen's. [ii. 7]

ANNET, PETER (1693–1769), deistical writer ; schoolmaster ; lost his employment through bitter attacks on the apologetic writings of Bishop Sherlock and others, *c.* 1744 ; perhaps author of 'History of the Man after God's own Heart,' 1761 ; attacked Old Testament in 'Free Enquirer,' 1761 ; tried for blasphemous libel, and was condemned to imprisonment, pillory, and hard labour, 1763 ; his writings form a link between the deism of the early eighteenth century and that of the revolutionary period. [ii. 9]

ANNING, MARY (1799–1847), discoverer of the ichthyosaurus; daughter of a carpenter and vendor of natural curiosities; discovered, 1811, skeleton of ichthyosaurus in cliff near Lyme, and subsequently the first specimens of plesiosaurus and pterodactylus. [Suppl. i. 51]

ANSDELL, RICHARD (1815–1885), animal painter; exhibited at Royal Academy from 1840; R.A., 1870; he three times gained the Heywood medal at Manchester exhibitions. [Suppl. i. 52]

ANSELL, CHARLES (1794–1881), actuary; employed in Atlas Assurance Company, 1808–64; consulting actuary to several companies; gave expert evidence before select parliamentary committees, 1841–53; published a work dealing with friendly societies from a scientific standpoint. [ii. 10]

ANSELL, GEORGE FREDERICK (1826–1880), inventor; studied medicine and chemistry, and became assistant to Dr. Hofmann at School of Mines; held post in mint, 1856–66; experimented, with valuable results, on dangers of fire-damp in mines. [ii. 10]

ANSELM, SAINT (1033–1109), archbishop of Canterbury; born at Aosta; educated in Abbey of St. Leger, near Aosta; travelled in Burgundy, France, and Normandy, and resided at Avranches, c. 1059; entered monastic order at Bec, 1060; prior, successor to Lanfranc, 1063–78; abbot, 1078–93; visited England soon after 1063, and was admitted by monks of Christ Church a member of their house, where he became acquainted with Eadmer, his biographer; called to deathbed of William the Conqueror at Rouen, but fell ill and did not recover before the king's death; reluctantly accepted the archbishopric of Canterbury from William II, who was lying ill at Gloucester; enthroned at Canterbury, 1093; consecrated, assisted by seven bishops, the church of the abbey erected by William I on field on which he had defeated Harold, 1094; applied for permission to go to Rome and receive his pallium from the pope, 1095; there being two rivals for the papacy, Urban and Clement, neither of whom William II had recognised, had, as abbot of Bec, recognised Urban and refused to withdraw his allegiance; a council, at which no definite decision was reached, held at Rockingham to decide between the claims of the king and the pope on his obedience; his deposition aimed at in the king's subsequent (unsuccessful) acknowledgment of Urban as pope; a form of reconciliation made by William with him, on which he received the pallium from the papal legate; obtained leave, with difficulty, to go to Rome in order to interest the pope in the condition of England, 1097; his estates seized by the king; received by the pope with honour, and promised assistance in his episcopal work, but not materially assisted, since delegates from William succeeded in influencing Urban; returned to England on death of William, 1100; obeying a papal decree, refused to consecrate prelates invested by Henry I; revisited Rome; thence went to Lyons, and remained there till the point in dispute with the king should be decided. The matter was finally settled, 1107, when the king ceded the right of investiture and Anselm promised that elected prelates should not be debarred from consecration on account of having done homage to the king. Anselm wrote many theological and philosophical works, including the famous 'Monologion,' 'Proslogion,' and 'Cur Deus Homo.' [ii. 10]

ANSLAY, BRIAN (fl. 1521), yeoman of wine-cellar to Henry VIII; published 'Boke of the Cyte of Ladies,' 1521. [ii. 31]

ANSON, GEORGE, BARON ANSON (1697–1762), admiral; volunteer under Captain Chamberlen, 1712; midshipman and lieutenant under Sir John Norris in Baltic, 1716; second lieutenant under Sir George Byng, 1718–19; commanded sloop against Dutch smugglers, 1722; captain of frigate protecting commerce on Carolina coast, 1724; commander 1731; on Carolina coast, 1732–5; protected trade on west African coast and West Indies against French, 1737–9; commanded squadron in Pacific, 1740, and in spite of damage from storms inflicted considerable injuries on Spaniards; returned with rich prizes, having sailed round the world, 1744; went on half-pay as captain; rear-admiral, 1745; vice-admiral of Channel fleet, 1746; defeated French off Finisterre, 1747; raised to peerage; married Lady Elizabeth Yorke, daughter of lord chancellor, 1748; occupied with reforms connected with naval administration and dockyards; first lord of admiralty, 1751–6, and 1757–62;

last served at sea in blockade of Brest, 1758; admiral of fleet, 1761; died without issue. [ii. 31]

ANSON, GEORGE (1797–1857), general; served with 3rd guards at Waterloo; M.P., 1818; successively principal storekeeper and clerk of ordnance; held military commands in India, where he was commander-in-chief, 1856; died of cholera. [ii. 36]

ANSPACH, ELIZABETH, MARGRAVINE OF (1750–1828), dramatist; married William, afterwards sixth Earl of Craven, 1767; separated from him, 1783; travelled on continent, and subsequently lived with the margrave of Anspach, whom she married on the death of her husband, 1791; settled in England, 1792; died at Naples; wrote several plays produced at Drury Lane, Covent Garden, and elsewhere. [ii. 36]

ANSTED, DAVID THOMAS (1814–1880), geologist; fellow of Jesus College, Cambridge; professor of geology at King's College, London; assistant secretary to Geological Society, 1844–7; wrote works on geology and travel. [ii. 37]

ANSTER, JOHN (1793–1867), regius professor of civil law, Dublin; scholar of Trinity College, Dublin, 1814; published poems with translations from German, 1819; called to Irish bar, 1824; LL.D., 1825; published translation of first part of Goethe's 'Faust,' 1835; registrar to court of admiralty, Ireland, 1837; regius professor of civil law, Dublin, 1850; published second part of 'Faust,' 1864. [ii. 38]

ANSTEY, CHRISTOPHER (1724–1805), poet; educated at Eton; scholar and fellow of King's College, Cambridge, where he distinguished himself by his verses; in conjunction with Dr. Roberts, translated Gray's 'Elegy' into Latin, 1762; published 'New Bath Guide,' 1766; resided at Bath, 1770–1805; published occasional verses. [ii. 38]

ANSTEY, JOHN (d. 1819), poet; second son of Christopher Anstey [q. v.]; barrister of Lincoln's Inn; published humorous poem entitled 'The Pleader's Guide,' 1796. [ii. 39]

ANSTEY, THOMAS CHISHOLM (1816–1873), lawyer; educated at Wellington and University College, London; called to bar, 1839; became interested in the Oxford movement, and was converted to Roman catholicism; professor of law at Roman catholic college, Prior Park, Bath; took to politics as supporter of extreme section of O'Connell's followers; M.P. for Youghal, 1847–52; attorney-general of Hong Kong, 1854; his radical policy led to his suspension and recall, 1859; practised, except from 1866–8, at Bombay bar, till death; published many legal and political tracts. [ii. 40]

ANSTICE, JOSEPH (1808–1836), classical scholar; educated at Westminster and Christ Church, Oxford; professor of classical literature, King's College, London, 1831–5. [ii. 41]

ANSTIE, FRANCIS EDMUND (1833–1874), physician; educated at King's College, London; M.R.C.S. and L.S.A., 1856; M.B. London, 1857; M.D., 1859; F.C.P., 1865; assistant-physician, Westminster Hospital, 1860, and full physician, 1873; first dean of Medical School for Women, 1874; for some years on editorial staff of 'Lancet'; influential in bringing about reforms in poor laws; contributed largely to medical journals and published several scientific works. [ii. 41]

ANSTIS, JOHN, the elder (1669–1744), Garter king of arms; educated at Exeter College, Oxford; entered Inner Temple, 1688; M.P. for St. Germans, 1702; deputy general to auditors of imprest and commissioner of prizes, 1703; M.P. for St. Maw's, 1711–13, and for Launceston or Dunheved, 1714; received reversionary patent for office of Garter, 1714; imprisoned for supposed intrigue with Pretender, 1715, and during his confinement the office of Garter, having become vacant, was given to Sir John Vanbrugh; cleared himself of charge of treason, and with great difficulty obtained post of Garter, 1718; published several heraldic works, and left large collections of manuscripts relating chiefly to heraldry. [ii. 43]

ANSTIS, JOHN, the younger (1708–1754), joint Garter king of arms; son of John Anstis [q. v.]; gentleman commoner, Corpus Christi College, Oxford, 1725; joined his father in office of Garter, 1727; F.S.A., 1736; LL.D., 1749. [ii. 44]

ANSTRUTHER, SIR ALEXANDER (1769–1819), Anglo-Indian judge; called to bar at Lincoln's Inn; advocate-general, Madras, 1803; recorder of Bombay, and knighted, 1812; published reports of exchequer cases. [ii. 45]

ANSTRUTHER, SIR JOHN (1753–1811), politician, and Anglo-Indian judge; called to bar at Lincoln's Inn, 1779; M.P. for Cockermouth, 1790–6; took part in impeachment of Warren Hastings; chief-justice of Bengal, and baronet, 1797; returned to England, 1806; privy councillor; M.P. for Kilkenny. [ii. 45]

ANSTRUTHER, ROBERT (1768–1809), general; educated at Westminster; ensign, 1788, lieutenant and captain, 1792, in Scots guards; served in Flanders, 1793–4; major and lieutenant-colonel in 68th regiment in West Indies, 1797; served as captain and lieutenant-colonel in guards in Helder expedition, 1799; quartermaster-general to Sir Ralph Abercromby in Mediterranean, 1800; colonel and deputy quartermaster-general in England; adjutant-general, Ireland; brigadier-general in Portugal, 1807; fought at Vimeiro and in the retreat from Toro, and died day before battle of Corunna. [ii. 45]

ANSTRUTHER, SIR WILLIAM, LORD (d. 1711), judge; M.P. for Fifeshire, 1681 and 1689–1707; sided with Prince of Orange; lord of session and privy councillor; baronet of Nova Scotia, 1694; lord of justiciary, 1704; published a volume of essays. [ii. 46]

ANTHONY, FRANCIS (1550–1623), empiric and chemical physician; M.A. Cambridge, 1574; perhaps M.D.; after 1600 was repeatedly fined and imprisoned for practising in London without license from College of Physicians, but finally succeeded in defying the college with the aid of friends at court; the efficacy of his chief remedy, *aurum potabile*, he defended in several pamphlets. [ii. 47]

ANTHONY, JOHN (1585–1655), physician; son of Francis Anthony [q. v.]; M.D., 1619, Pembroke College, Cambridge; L.C.P., 1625; succeeded to his father's practice; wrote 'Comfort of the Soul,' published 1654. [ii. 48]

ANTON, ROBERT (fl. 1616), poetical writer; B.A. Magdalene College, Cambridge, 1610; published 'Philosophers Satyrs,' in verse, 1616. [ii. 48]

ANTRIM, MARQUIS OF (1609–1683). See MACDONNELL, RANDAL.]

ANTRIM, EARLS OF. [See MACDONNELL, SIR RANDAL, first EARL, d. 1636; MACDONNELL, RANDAL, second EARL, 1609–1683; MACDONNELL, ALEXANDER, third EARL, d. 1696?.]

APLIN, PETER (1753–1817), admiral; served in American war under Hyde Parker and Cornwallis; admiral. [ii. 48]

APPERLEY, CHARLES JAMES (1779–1843), sporting writer, known as 'Nimrod'; entered Rugby, 1790; cornet in Sir Watkin Wynn's ancient light British dragoons, 1798; having lost money in farming experiments, he became contributor to the 'Sporting Magazine,' 1822; member of staff of 'Sporting Review'; published a series of sporting memoirs and reminiscences. [Suppl. i. 53]

APPLETON, CHARLES EDWARD CUTTS BIRCH (1841–1879), man of letters; educated at Reading and St. John's College, Oxford; B.A., 1863; D.C.L., 1871; studied in Germany; founded 'The Academy,' 1869, and edited it till his death; visited America, 1875, and took up the question of international copyright; travelled for his health to Egypt, where he died. [ii. 48]

APPLETON, HENRY (fl. 1650–1654), captain in navy, and commodore; served in Mediterranean, in Dutch war (1652), in conjunction with Badiley; caused Badiley's defeat off Elba by neglecting to send reinforcements; defeated and captured by Dutch off Leghorn, 1653; ransomed, and deprived of his command. [ii. 49]

APPLEYARD, SIR MATHEW (1606–1669), royalist military commander; knighted after taking of Leicester; M.P. for Headon. [ii. 50]

APPOLD, JOHN GEORGE (1800–1865), mechanician; in business at Finsbury as fur-skin dyer; brought out many scientific and mechanical inventions. [ii. 50]

APSLEY, first BARON (1714–1794). [See BATHURST, HENRY.]

APSLEY, SIR ALLEN (1569?–1630), lieutenant of the Tower; having been ruined at court by gambling, sailed with Essex to Cadiz, 1596; went to Ireland; became victualler of Munster, 1605, and to navy, 1610; lieutenant of Tower, 1617. [ii. 51]

APSLEY, SIR ALLEN (1616–1683), royalist leader; son of Sir Allen Apsley [q. v.]; educated at Merchant Taylors' and Trinity College, Oxford; M.A., 1663; commanded company of horse, 1642; royalist governor of Exeter and later of Barnstaple, which he surrendered to the parliamentarians, 1646; engaged with Sir John Berkeley in negotiations between king and army, 1647; appointed to various offices in royal household after 1660; colonel in Duke of York's army, 1667; M.P. for Thetford, 1661–1678; buried in Westminster Abbey; published a long poem, 'Order and Disorder,' 1679. [ii. 51]

AQUEPONTANUS (1532?–1596?). [See BRIDGE-WATER, JOHN.]

ARABELLA STUART (1575–1615), daughter of Charles Stuart, earl of Lennox, younger brother of Lord Darnley; next heir to English throne after James I; became engaged to William Seymour, who was also of royal descent; and the marriage was celebrated secretly, 1610; died in Tower. [ii. 53]

ARAM, EUGENE (1704–1759), criminal; with slight assistance educated himself till able to open a small school at Ramsgill, where he married; being suspected of complicity in a fraud practised by one Daniel Clark, he disappeared for some years, during which he continually prosecuted his studies; while school usher at Lyme Regis, 1758, was arrested on information of Houseman, an accomplice, on a charge of murdering Clark; condemned and executed, Houseman being sole witness; left philological writings of considerable value. [ii. 53]

ARBLAY, FRANCES (BURNEY), MADAME D' (1752–1840), novelist, daughter of Dr. Burney; self-educated; published her first novel, 'Evelina,' anonymously (though her father soon divulged the secret), 1778; brought by its success to the notice of most of the literary personages of the day; published 'Cecilia,' with similar success, 1782; made the acquaintance of Mrs. Delaney, who procured her the appointment of second keeper of the queen's robes, 1786; being broken in health, obtained with difficulty permission to retire, 1790; married General d'Arblay, a French refugee in England, 1793; published 'Camilla,' 1796; joined her husband, who had endeavoured to obtain employment in Paris, 1802; returned to England, 1812; published her last novel, 'The Wanderer,' 1814; rejoined her husband in Paris, and retired to Belgium; passed the rest of her life in England, after the Waterloo campaign; edited her father's 'Memoirs,' 1832; published 'Diary and Letters,' 1842–6. [ii. 55]

ARBUCKLE, JAMES (1700–1734?), poet and essayist; published between 1719 and 1727 verses, letters, and essays, many of which had appeared in periodicals. [ii. 58]

ARBUTHNOT, ALEXANDER (1538–1583), Scottish divine and poet; educated at St. Andrews; studied civil law at Bourges; licensed minister, and appointed to living at Logie Buchan, 1568; principal of King's College, Aberdeen, 1569; received living of Arbuthnot, Kincardineshire; incurred King James VI's displeasure; being a zealous presbyterian, and having been appointed minister of St. Andrews, in 1583, was ordered to return to King's College, where he died, and was buried; published and left in manuscript, verse and prose works. [ii. 59]

ARBUTHNOT or **ARBUTHNET**, ALEXANDER (d. 1585), printer, of Edinburgh; with Thomas Bassandyne obtained permission to print first bible issued in Scotland, 1575, and in 1576 was, with his associate, granted exclusive rights of printing and selling for ten years; brought out the work (a reprint of the Genevan version of 1561), 1579; made king's printer, 1579, when he was licensed to print, sell, and import psalm-books, prayers, and catechisms for seven years. [ii. 60]

ARBUTHNOT, CHARLES (1767–1850), diplomatist; précis writer in foreign office, 1793; M.P. for East Looe, 1795; under foreign secretary; ambassador extraordinary, Constantinople, 1804; privy councillor; held various government offices, and from 1809 was M.P. successively for Eye and Orford (Suffolk), and St. Germans and St Ives (Cornwall). [ii. 61]

ARBUTHNOT, SIR CHARLES GEORGE (1824–1899), general; educated at Rugby and Royal Military Academy; lieutenant, royal artillery, 1845; captain, 1855; in Crimea; lieutenant-colonel, 1864; in India, 1868–80, was deputy adjutant-general, 1873–7, and inspector-general of artillery, 1877–80, except while serving in Afghan campaigns; colonel, 1874; inspector-general of artillery in England, 1883; president ordnance committee, 1885; succeeded Lord Roberts chief of army in Burma, 1887; general, 1890; G.C.B., 1894. [Suppl. i. 54]

ARBUTHNOT, GEORGE (1802–1865), civilian; appointed junior clerk in treasury, 1820; served in that department till death, when he was auditor of civil list and secretary to ecclesiastical commissioners; acted as private secretary to Sir Charles Wood, chancellor of exchequer, Sir Robert Peel, and to six successive secretaries and two assistant secretaries of the treasury; regarded as an authority on currency questions. [ii. 61]

ARBUTHNOT, JOHN (1667–1735), physician and wit; M.D. St. Andrews, 1696; settled in London and taught mathematics; F.R.S., 1704; attended Prince George of Denmark for a sudden illness at Epsom; physician in ordinary to Queen Anne, 1709; F.R.C.P., 1710, censor, 1723, Harveian orator, 1727; formed close friendship with Swift, and was acquainted with Pope and most literary men of the day; published 'History of John Bull' (1712) and several witty political pamphlets; contributed largely to 'Memoirs of Martinus Scriblerus,' published with Pope's 'Works,' 1741; attended Anne in her last illness; suffered much in health during his later years; died at Hampstead; published, besides his poetical writings, medical and scientific works. [ii. 62]

ARBUTHNOT, MARRIOT (1711?–1794), admiral; lieutenant, 1739; commander, 1746; captain, 1747; commanded the Portland at Quiberon Bay, 1759; commanded guardship, Portsmouth, 1771–3; commissioner of navy, Halifax, 1775–8; admiral, 1778; commander of North American station, 1779–81 (with the exception of a short period, when Sir George Rodney took the command), and took part in the action off mouth of Chesapeake and Cape Henry; admiral of the blue, 1793. [ii. 65]

ARBUTHNOT, SIR ROBERT (1773–1853), soldier; cornet 23rd light dragoons, 1797; served in Irish rebellion, 1798, and at capture of Cape of Good Hope, 1806; aide-de-camp to Beresford in South America, and, as captain in 20th light dragoons, aide-de-camp and afterwards military secretary to that general throughout greater part of peninsular campaign; K.T.S.; K.C.B., 1815; major-general, 1830; commanded in Ceylon and Bengal, 1838–41; lieutenant-general, 1841; colonel, 76th foot, 1843. [ii. 66]

ARBUTHNOT, SIR THOMAS (1776–1849), lieutenant-general; brother of Sir Robert Arbuthnot [q. v.]; ensign, 29th foot, 1794; joined staff corps under Moore, 1803; quartermaster-general, Cape of Good Hope; served in Peninsula and West Indies; K.C.B., 1815; lieutenant-general, 1838. [ii. 67]

ARCHANGEL, FATHER (1571–1606). [See FORBES, JOHN.]

ARCHBOLD, JOHN FREDERICK (1785–1870), legal writer; entered Lincoln's Inn, 1809; barrister, 1814. He published a number of legal treatises, which include: 'Summary of Law relative to Pleading and Evidence in Criminal Cases,' 1824; 'Practice of Court of Common Pleas,' 1829; and several works on parish laws. [Suppl. i. 54]

ARCHDALE, JOHN (fl. 1664–1707), governor of North Carolina; accompanied to New England his brother-in-law, Ferdinando Gorges, who became governor of Maine, 1664; returned to England, 1674; joined quakers; visited North Carolina, 1686, and subsequently became one of the proprietors of the colony; commissioner for Gorges in government of Maine, 1687–88; governor of North Carolina, 1695–7; M.P. for Chipping Wycombe, Buckinghamshire, 1698; refused oath and was deprived of seat, 1699; published 'Description of Carolina,' 1707. [Suppl. i. 56]

ARCHDALL, MERVYN (1723–1791), antiquary; educated at Dublin University; domestic chaplain to Pocock, bishop of Ossory, who presented him to living of Attanagh and prebend of Cloneamery, 1762; prebendary of Mayne,

1764; member of Royal Irish Academy; published historical and topographical works. [ii. 67]

ARCHDEKIN or **ARSDEKIN**, RICHARD (1618–1693), Irish jesuit; studied classics, philosophy, and (at Louvain) theology; entered Society of Jesus at Mechlin, 1642; taught humanities, 1650, and later studied at Antwerp and Lille; professor of philosophy and theology at Louvain and Antwerp, where he died; published theological works in English, Irish, and Latin. [ii. 68]

ARCHER, EDWARD (1718–1789), physician; studied medicine at Edinburgh and Leyden, where he graduated M.D. 1746; physician to the newly founded smallpox hospital, 1747, to which institution he devoted most of his energies. [ii. 69]

ARCHER, FREDERICK (1857–1886), jockey; apprenticed to Matthew Dawson [q. v.], the trainer at Newmarket, 1867; won Two Thousand Guineas upon Lord Falmouth's Atlantic, 1874; won the Two Thousand Guineas, Oaks, Derby, St. Leger, and Grand Prix, 1885. He died by his own hand when ill. [Suppl. i. 57]

ARCHER, FREDERICK SCOTT (1813–1857), inventor of collodion process; son of a butcher; started business as sculptor; first successfully used collodion process in photography, 1850; practised as photographer in Bloomsbury. [ii. 69]

ARCHER, JAMES (1551?–1624?), Irish jesuit; first rector of Irish College, Salamanca. [ii. 70]

ARCHER, JAMES (fl. 1822), catholic preacher; began preaching at a public-house in Lincoln's Inn Fields; chaplain to the Bavarian minister in London, 1791; created D.D. by Pope Pius VII, 1821; published sermons. [ii. 70]

ARCHER, JOHN (1598–1682), judge; B.A. Queens' College, Cambridge, 1619; M.A., 1622; called to bar at Gray's Inn, 1620; M.P., 1656; serjeant, 1658; justice of common bench and knighted, 1663. The King, Charles II, attempted to remove him from office (1672), but he refused to surrender the patent without due legal procedure, and though relieved by royal prohibition from his duties, he continued to receive his salary till death. [ii. 70]

ARCHER, JOHN (fl. 1660–1684), physician; practised in Dublin, 1660; court physician to Charles II, 1671; published a self-advertising work called 'Every Man his own Doctor,' 1671. [ii. 71]

ARCHER, JOHN WYKEHAM (1808–1864), artist and antiquary; apprenticed to an animal engraver in Clerkenwell; returned to London, 1831, after publishing several engravings in his native town, and was employed by various publishers in steel and wood engraving and watercolour painting. His works include a series of drawings of old London. [ii. 72]

ARCHER, SIR SYMON (1581–1662), antiquary; knighted, 1624; sheriff of Warwickshire, 1628; M.P., 1640; amassed much of the material used in Dugdale's 'History of Warwickshire' and other valuable antiquarian information. [ii. 73]

ARCHER, THOMAS (1554–1630?), divine; M.A. (1582) and fellow Trinity College, Cambridge; held livings in Bedfordshire; chaplain to Whitgift, 1599, and to the king, 1605; left manuscript obituaries of eminent contemporaries. [ii. 73]

ARCHER, THOMAS (d. 1743), architect; pupil of Sir John Vanbrugh; 'groom porter' to Anne, George I, and George II; built Cliefden House and St. John's Church, Westminster (1728). [ii. 73]

ARCHER, THOMAS (d. 1848), actor and dramatist; took Shakespearean rôles at Drury Lane, 1823; visited United States and Paris, and led a Shakespearean company in Belgium and Germany; wrote many successful dramas. [ii. 73]

ARCHER, WILLIAM (1830–1897), naturalist and librarian; secretary of Dublin Microscopical Club; contributed to 'Proceedings' of Royal Society, and other learned bodies; F.R.S., 1875; secretary for foreign correspondence to the Royal Irish Academy, 1875–80; librarian (1876) to Royal Dublin Society, and (1877–95) to National Library of Ireland, of which he compiled a catalogue. [Suppl. i. 57]

ARCHIBALD, SIR ADAMS GEORGE (1814–1892), Canadian statesman; born at Truro, Nova Scotia; educated at Picton College; attorney of Prince Edward Island and Nova Scotia, 1838; called to bar of Nova Scotia, 1839; member for Colchester in Nova Scotia House of Assembly, 1851; Q.C., 1855; attorney-general, 1860; advocate-general in vice-admiralty court at Halifax, 1862–3; took part in consultations in London which led to Canadian federation, 1866; secretary of state under new dominion government, 1867–8; member for Colchester in dominion parliament, 1869–70; first lieutenant-governor of Manitoba, 1870–2; judge in equity in Nova Scotia, 1873, and lieutenant-governor, 1873–83; M.P. for Colchester in Canadian House of Commons, 1888–91; K.C.M.G., 1886. [Suppl. i. 58]

ARCHIBALD, SIR THOMAS DICKSON (1817–1876), judge; born at Truro, Nova Scotia; educated at Picton College; qualified as attorney and barrister-at-law in Nova Scotia, 1837; called to bar at Middle Temple, 1852; junior counsel to treasury, 1868; appointed justice of queen's bench and invested with coif, 1872; knighted, 1873; transferred to common pleas, 1875. [Suppl. i. 59]

ARDBRECAIN (d. 656). [See ULTAN.]

ARDEN, EDWARD (1542?–1583), high sheriff of Warwickshire, 1575; accused of complicity, though probably innocent, in an attempt by his son-in-law to assassinate the queen, and hanged at Tyburn, 1583. Has been erroneously connected with Mary Arden, Shakespeare's mother. [ii. 74]

ARDEN, RICHARD PEPPER, BARON ALVANLEY (1745–1804), judge; educated at Manchester grammar school and Trinity College, Cambridge; distinguished in classics; twelfth wrangler; M.A., fellow, and called to bar, 1769; judge on South Wales circuit, 1776; took silk, 1780; M.P. for Newton, and solicitor-general, 1782–3; attorney-general and chief-justice of Chester, 1784; master of rolls, 1788; sat successively for Aldborough, Hastings, and Bath; lord chief-justice of common pleas, 1801. [ii. 74]

ARDERNE, JAMES (1636–1691), dean of Chester; graduated B.A., 1656, and M.A. Christ's College, Cambridge; M.A. Oxford, 1658; curate of St. Botolph, Aldersgate, 1666–82; fellow commoner of Brasenose; D.D., 1673; chaplain to Charles II; rector of Davenham, 1681; dean of Chester, 1682; published religious works. [ii. 75]

ARDERNE, JOHN (fl. 1370), first great English surgeon; lived at Newark, 1349–70; practised surgery in London after 1370; cured many distinguished persons, and probably enjoyed patronage of Black Prince. Left manuscripts which show, for the period, a remarkable knowledge of surgery. [ii. 76]

ARDERON, WILLIAM (1703–1767), naturalist; officer of excise and, later, managing clerk at the New Mills, Norwich; F.R.S., 1745; wrote largely on natural history and microscopical science. [ii. 77]

ARDMILLAN, LORD (1805–1876). [See CRAWFURD, JAMES.]

ARGALL, JOHN (fl. 1604), divine; M.A. Christ Church, Oxford, 1565; held living of Halesworth, Suffolk. [ii. 78]

ARGALL, RICHARD (fl. 1621), poet; educated at Oxford; perhaps author of a volume of religious poems (1621) containing 'The Bride's Ornament,' republished in 1654 in name of Richard Aylett. [ii. 78]

ARGALL, SIR SAMUEL (d. 1626), adventurer; went as trader in 1609 to Virginia, whither he subsequently made frequent voyages; visited the Potomac and Chesapeake Bay, 1612–13; reduced French settlements in Maine, St. Croix, and Nova Scotia, 1613; deputy-governor of Virginia and admiral of the adjacent seas, 1617; served in expedition against Algiers, under Sir R. Mansell, 1620; knighted, 1622; admiral of squadron of English and Dutch ships operating on French and Spanish coasts, 1625–6; died at sea. [ii. 78]

ARGENTINE, GILES DE (d. 1284), justiciar in Normandy, 1247; itinerant justice, 1253; constable of Windsor, 1263; on council of nine after battle of Lewes. [ii. 80]

ARGENTINE, JOHN (d. 1508), provost of King's, Cambridge; M.D. King's College, Cambridge; provost, 1501; D.D., 1504; physician and dean of chapel to Prince of Wales; master of hospital of St. John Baptist, Dorchester, 1499. [ii. 80]

ARGENTINE, alias SEXTEN, RICHARD (d. 1568), physician and divine; M.D. Cambridge, 1541; physician, schoolmaster, and lecturer in divinity at Ipswich; held livings successively at Ipswich and Exeter, repeatedly changing his religious views in accordance with prevailing opinions. [ii. 80]

ARGYLE or **ARGYLL**, DUKES OF. [See CAMPBELL, ARCHIBALD, first DUKE, d. 1703; CAMPBELL, JOHN, second DUKE, 1678–1743; CAMPBELL, ARCHIBALD, third DUKE, 1682–1761.]

ARGYLE or **ARGYLL**, MARQUIS OF (1598–1661). [See CAMPBELL, ARCHIBALD.]

ARGYLE or **ARGYLL**, EARLS OF. [See CAMPBELL, COLIN, first EARL, d. 1493; CAMPBELL, ARCHIBALD, second EARL, d. 1513; CAMPBELL, COLIN, third EARL, d. 1530; CAMPBELL, ARCHIBALD, fourth EARL, d. 1588; CAMPBELL, ARCHIBALD, fifth EARL, 1530–1573; CAMPBELL, COLIN, sixth EARL, d. 1584; CAMPBELL, ARCHIBALD, seventh EARL, 1576?–1638; CAMPBELL, ARCHIBALD, eighth EARL, 1598–1661; CAMPBELL, ARCHIBALD, ninth EARL, d. 1685; CAMPBELL, ARCHIBALD, tenth EARL, d. 1703.]

ARGYLE or **ARGYLL**, COUNTESS OF (1621?–1706?). [See CAMPBELL, ANNA MACKENZIE.]

ARGYLL, eighth DUKE OF. [See CAMPBELL, GEORGE DOUGLAS, 1823–1900.]

ARKISDEN, THOMAS (fl. 1633), stenographer; M.A. Emmanuel College, Cambridge, 1633; invented a shorthand alphabet. [ii. 81]

ARKWRIGHT, SIR RICHARD (1732–1792), engineer; apprenticed to a barber; established himself at Bolton, before 1755, as a barber, and gradually formed a large business; gave up business at Bolton and turned his attention to mechanical inventions, c. 1767; invented and erected near Hockley a spinning-mill, 1769; went into partnership with two manufacturers of ribbed stockings and erected machinery at Cromford, Derbyshire, 1771; applied the mill to manufacture of calicoes, 1773; patented a series of adaptations and inventions for performing in one machine the whole process of yarn manufacture, 1775; one of his mills (at Chorley) sacked by rioters, 1779; his repeated complaints against infringements of his patent during the following years were met by a combination of manufacturers, who obtained a verdict against Arkwright on the questions: (1) Is the invention new? (2) Is it invented by the defendant? (3) Was it sufficiently described in the specification? His letters patent cancelled, 1785; visited Scotland and assisted in erection of New Lanark mills, c. 1784; built several mills in Derbyshire and Lancashire; introduced Boulton & Watt's steam-engine into his mill at Nottingham, 1790; knighted, 1786; high sheriff of Derbyshire, 1787. [ii. 81]

ARKWRIGHT, RICHARD (1755–1843), mill-owner, son of Sir Richard Arkwright [q. v.]; inherited his father's business and amassed a large fortune. [ii. 86]

ARLINGTON, first EARL OF (1618–1685). [See BENNET, HENRY.]

ARMIN, ROBERT (fl. 1610), actor and dramatist; apprenticed to a goldsmith in Lombard Street; perhaps one of the lord chamberlain's players, 1598; seems to have succeeded Kemp in the rôle of Dogberry; in company of actors licensed by James I, 1603; probably member of Lord Chandos's company. [ii. 86]

ARMINE or **ARMYNE**, MARY, LADY (d. 1676), philanthropist, née Talbot; second wife of Sir William Armine [q. v.]; took practical interest in missionaries among North American Indians; founded three hospitals in England. [ii. 87]

ARMINE, RICHARD DE (d. 1340?). [See AYREMINNE, RICHARD DE.]

ARMINE, WILLIAM DE (d. 1336). [See AYREMINNE, WILLIAM DE.]

ARMINE or **ARMYNE**, SIR WILLIAM (1593-1651), parliamentarian; baronet, 1619; M.P. for Boston, 1621 and 1624, for Grantham, 1625, and for Lincolnshire, 1626, 1628, and 1641; assistant to managers of Buckingham's impeachment, 1626; imprisoned for refusing to collect arbitrary loan in Lincolnshire, 1627-8; sheriff of Lincolnshire, 1630, of Huntingdonshire, 1639; accompanied Charles to Scotland, 1641; discussed terms with king at Oxford in behalf of parliament, 1643; member of council of state, 1649, 1650, and 1651. [ii. 87]

ARMITAGE, EDWARD (1817-1896), historical painter; studied under Paul Delaroche in Paris; gained premiums in cartoon competitions for decoration of new houses of parliament, 1843, 1845, and 1847; commissioned to execute two frescoes for House of Lords; exhibited at Royal Academy from 1848, generally biblical subjects; R.A., 1872; member of committee of artists employed in decoration of Westminster Hall who made report on fresco-painting, 1871; professor and lecturer on painting to Royal Academy, 1875; published lectures, 1883.
[Suppl. i. 60]

ARMITAGE, TIMOTHY (d. 1655), pastor of first nonconformist church in Norwich, 1647; superintendent of numerous congregations of Norfolk and Suffolk.
[ii. 88]

ARMSTRONG, SIR ALEXANDER (1818-1899), naval medical officer; studied medicine at Trinity College, Dublin, and at Edinburgh; graduated, 1841; assistant-surgeon in navy, 1842; in medical charge of party for exploration of Xanthus, 1843; appointed to royal yacht, 1846; surgeon, 1849; surgeon and naturalist in Arctic expedition under (Sir) Robert John Le Mesurier Maclure [q. v.], 1849-54; medical superintendent of Malta hospital, 1859-64; director-general of medical department of navy, 1869-71; K.C.B., 1871; F.R.S., 1873. [Suppl. i. 61]

ARMSTRONG, ARCHIBALD (d. 1672), known as 'Archie'; jester to James I and Charles I; gained wide reputation as sheep-stealer at Eskdale; was attached to household of James VI of Scotland, and accompanied him to England, where he gained great social distinction, and amassed a large fortune; accompanied Charles and Buckingham to Spain, 1623; expelled from court for insulting Archbishop Laud, 1637; remained in London and spent his time in distraining mercilessly on his debtors; retired to Arthuret, Cumberland; credited with the authorship of 'A Banquet of Jests,' 1630. [ii. 89]

ARMSTRONG, COSMO (fl. 1800-1836), governor of Society of Engravers; exhibited with Associated Engravers, 1821; pupil of Thomas Milton; engraved plates for Cooke's 'British Poets' and other works. [ii. 91]

ARMSTRONG, EDMUND JOHN (1841-1865), poet; entered Trinity College, Dublin, 1859; suffered seriously from over-work, 1860, and subsequently spent much time in Jersey and Brittany; president of Undergraduate Philosophical Society, Trinity College, 1864; published poems, 1865, and prose works, 1877. [ii. 91]

ARMSTRONG, GEORGE (fl. 1767), physician; brother of John Armstrong (1709-1779) [q. v.]; established dispensary in London for relief of poor children, 1769; published a work on diseases of children. [ii. 92]

ARMSTRONG, JAMES (1780-1839), Irish unitarian minister; trained at Rademon academy; classical assistant in Belfast academy; graduated at Trinity College, Dublin; ordained minister of Strand Street chapel, Dublin, 1806; one of founders of Irish Unitarian Society, 1830; D.D. Geneva, 1834. [ii. 92]

ARMSTRONG, JOHN or JOHNIE (d. 1528), border freebooter; lived near Langholm, whence he made excursions at head of twenty-four horsemen; hanged with his followers at Carlenrigg Chapel. [ii. 93]

ARMSTRONG, JOHN (1674-1742), major-general and quartermaster-general in Ireland; surveyor-general of ordnance and chief engineer; F.R.S., 1723. [ii. 94]

ARMSTRONG, JOHN (1709-1779), poet, physician, and essayist; M.D. Edinburgh, 1732; physician to hospital for wounded soldiers, London, 1746; physician to the army in Germany, 1760, and on return of troops received half-pay for remainder of his life; intimately acquainted for many years with Wilkes, with whom he quarrelled over the publication of some verses. His works include essays on various subjects, and a didactic poem called 'The Art of Preserving Health,' 1744. [ii. 94]

ARMSTRONG, JOHN (1771-1797), journalist; M.A. Edinburgh; private tutor; wrote for London press, 1790; published poetical and prose works. [ii. 96]

ARMSTRONG, JOHN, the elder (1784-1829), physician; M.D. Edinburgh, 1807; physician to Sunderland Infirmary; removed to London, 1818; physician to London Fever Institution, 1819-24; L.C.P., 1820; lectured on anatomy and medicine; published medical works. [ii. 97]

ARMSTRONG, JOHN, the younger (1813-1856), bishop of Grahamstown; son of John Armstrong (1784-1829) [q. v.]; educated at Charterhouse; scholar of Lincoln College, Oxford; B.A., 1836; ordained, 1837; after holding three curacies, became priest-vicar of Exeter Cathedral, 1841; rector of St. Paul's, Exeter, 1843; vicar of Tidenham, Gloucestershire, 1845; strongly advocated in magazine articles a scheme of female penitentiaries which ultimately took definite shape; accepted new bishopric of Grahamstown, Cape of Good Hope, 1853; published many sermons and tracts. [ii. 97]

ARMSTRONG, ROBERT ARCHIBALD (1788-1867), Gaelic lexicographer; educated at Edinburgh and St. Andrews University; kept successively several schools in London; published a Gaelic dictionary, 1825; established and kept a grammar school at South Lambeth; received civil list pension of 60l., 1852. [ii. 99]

ARMSTRONG, SIR THOMAS (1624?-1684), royalist; born at Nimeguen; served under Charles I, and during the Commonwealth was three times imprisoned for fidelity to the royal cause; knighted, 1660; lieutenant of first troop of guards, and subsequently captain of the horse; fell into disfavour at court and joined English regiment in Flanders, 1679; implicated in Rye House plot, 1682; escaped to Leyden, but was arrested and executed in London, Judge Jeffreys giving him unfair trial. [ii. 100]

ARMSTRONG, WILLIAM (fl. 1596), border moss-trooper, known as KINMONT WILLIE, from his castle of Morton Tower or Kinmont in Canobie, Dumfriesshire; captured, but escaped, 1587; imprisoned at Carlisle, 1596, where the Scotch warden demanded his release, and on being refused succeeded in carrying him off. His fate is unknown. [ii. 101]

ARMSTRONG, WILLIAM (1602?-1658?), known as CHRISTIE'S WILL, border freebooter; imprisoned in Jedburgh tolbooth, and released through interposition of Earl of Traquair, whose devoted servant he afterwards became. [ii. 102]

ARMSTRONG, WILLIAM (1778-1857), mayor of Newcastle-on-Tyne, 1850; corn-merchant; prominent in municipal affairs; much interested in mathematics; active member of local literary societies. [Suppl. i. 62]

ARMSTRONG, SIR WILLIAM GEORGE, BARON ARMSTRONG OF CRAGSIDE (1810-1900), inventor; son of William Armstrong (1778-1857) [q. v.], of Newcastle-on-Tyne; educated at grammar school, Bishop Auckland; subsequently studied law in London; partner in legal firm of Donkin, Stable & Armstrong, Newcastle, 1833; constructed 'water-pressure wheel,' 1839, and hydro-electric machine, c. 1844; secretary, 1845, and chairman, 1855-67, to Whittle Dean (afterwards Newcastle and Gateshead) Water Company; patented hydraulic crane, 1846; F.R.S., 1846; first manager of Elswick-on-Tyne engineering works, 1847; invented hydraulic pressure accumulator, 1850; designed submarine mines for use in Crimean war, 1854; invented rifled-bore breechloading gun, with cylinder constructed on scientific principles, which was favourably reported upon by General Peel's committee on rifled cannon, 1858; patented inventions and presented patents to nation; Elswick Ordnance Company established for purpose of making Armstrong guns for British government, under his supervision, 1859; appointed engineer of rifled ordnance at Woolwich, and knighted and made C.B., 1859; resigned appointment at Woolwich, 1863, when government returned largely to muzzle-loaders; finished a 6-inch breechloading gun with wire-wound cylinder, 1880; government once more adopting breechloading guns; established, in conjunction with firm of Messrs. Mitchell & Swan, new shipyard at Elswick for construction of warships, 1882; incorporated with his own business the works of Sir Joseph Whitworth [q. v.] at Openshaw, near Manchester, for manufacture of Whitworth guns, 1897; conducted important electrical experiments at his residence at Cragside, near Rothbury; Telford medallist of the Institution of Civil Engineers; honorary LL.D. Cambridge, 1862; D.C.L. Oxford, 1870; received Albert medal from Society of Arts, 1878; D.C.L. Durham, 1882; president of Institute of Civil Engineers, 1882; raised to peerage, 1887; master of engineering, Dublin, 1892; Bessemer medallist, 1891. He was a liberal benefactor of Newcastle. Published writings on engineering subjects, as well as 'Electric Movement in Air and Water,' 1897-99.   [Suppl. i. 62]

ARNALD, RICHARD (1700-1756), divine; B.A. Corpus Christi College; fellow and M.A. Emmanuel College, Cambridge; presented to living of Thurcaston, Leicestershire, 1733; prebendary of Lincoln; published sermons and commentary on Apocrypha.   [ii. 103]

ARNALL, WILLIAM (1715 ?-1741 ?), political writer; in pay of Walpole; wrote 'Free Briton' and succeeded Concanen in the 'British Journal.'   [ii. 103]

ARNE, CECILIA (1711-1789), singer; pupil of Geminiani; first appeared at Drury Lane, 1730; married Thomas Augustine Arne [q. v.], 1736; in Dublin, 1742; engaged at Vauxhall Gardens, 1745.   [ii. 103]

ARNE, MICHAEL (1741 ?-1786), musician; son of Dr. Thomas Augustine Arne [q. v.]; appeared in Otway's 'Orphan' when very young; took to the harpsichord; member of Madrigal Society; died in great destitution; produced many songs and musical scores.   [ii. 104]

ARNE, THOMAS AUGUSTINE (1710-1778), musical composer; educated at Eton; privately studied music; gave up his legal studies and wrote music for Addison's 'Rosamond,' 1733, Fielding's 'Tom Thumb,' altered into 'The Opera of Operas,' 1733, Milton's 'Comus,' 1738, Congreve's 'Judgment of Paris,' and Thomson and Mallet's 'Alfred' (which included 'Rule Britannia,' 1740), 'As you like it' and 'Twelfth Night'; appointed composer to Drury Lane Theatre, 1744, and later, leader of the band; wrote songs for 'The Tempest,' 1746; produced two oratorios: 'Abel,' 1755, and 'Judith,' 1764; Mus. Doc. Oxford, 1759; transferred his services to Covent Garden, 1760; set to music the ode by Garrick performed at the Shakespeare jubilee at Stratford-on-Avon, 1769; produced numerous light operas and incidental music.   [ii. 104]

ARNISTON, BARONS. [See DUNDAS, SIR JAMES, d. 1679; DUNDAS, ROBERT, d. 1726; DUNDAS, ROBERT, 1685-1753; DUNDAS, ROBERT, 1713-1787.]

ARNOLD, BENEDICT (1741-1801), general; born at Norwich, Connecticut; bookseller and druggist; took American side in war between England and the American colonies; after battle of Lexington served as volunteer, obtained a command and was severely wounded at Quebec, 1775; subsequently commanded at Montreal and was conspicuous at Saratoga, 1777; governor of Philadelphia; accused of peculation; partially acquitted and reprimanded by Washington, 1780; obtained command of West Point, which he arranged to surrender to British commander Clinton; joined British and was made brigadier-general; came to England, 1782; afterwards distinguished himself at Guadaloupe.   [ii. 107]

ARNOLD, CORNELIUS (1711-1757 ?), poetical writer; educated at Merchant Taylors' School; published poetical works, 1757.   [ii. 109]

ARNOLD, JOHN (1736 ?-1799), mechanician; apprenticed to watchmaking trade in Bodmin; went to Holland, and subsequently set up in business in London; introduced at court; made several improvements in the manufacture of chronometers.   [ii. 109]

ARNOLD, JOSEPH (1782-1818), naturalist; M.D. Edinburgh, 1807; surgeon in navy, 1808; made several voyages, and collected scientific specimens; died at Padang, Sumatra; F.L.S., 1815.   [ii. 110]

ARNOLD, MATTHEW (1822-1888), poet and critic; son of Dr. Thomas Arnold [q. v.]; educated at Rugby, Winchester, and Balliol College, Oxford; Newdigate prizeman, 1843; graduated, 1844; fellow of Oriel College, 1845; master at Rugby; private secretary to Marquis of Lansdowne, 1847; inspector of schools, 1851; published

'The Strayed Reveller and other Poems,' 1849, 'Empedocles on Etna,' 1852, 'Poems' (containing 'Sohrab and Rustum,' 'Scholar-Gipsy,' and 'Requiescat'), 1853, and 'Poems, second series,' 1855; professor of poetry at Oxford, 1857-67; published 'On Translating Homer,' 1861 (second volume, 1862), 'On Study of Celtic Literature,' 1867, 'Essays in Criticism,' 1865 (second series, 1888), 'Culture and Anarchy,' 1869, 'Friendship's Garland,' 1871, 'Literature and Dogma,' 1873; lectured in America, 1883-4 and 1886, and issued 'Discourses in America,' 1885; published also works on educational subjects. He adopted from Swift the phrase 'sweetness and light' to explain his literary and social creed. His most permanent work is in his poetry (3 vols. 1885). His letters appeared in 1895. His portrait by Mr. G. F. Watts, R.A., is in the National Portrait Gallery.   [Suppl. i. 70]

ARNOLD, SIR NICHOLAS (1507 ?-1580), gentleman pensioner of Henry VIII in 1526; employed by Cromwell in connection with dissolution of monasteries; knight of shire for Gloucester, 1545; commander of garrison, Queenborough, 1545, Boulogneberg, 1546-9; knighted by Edward VI; imprisoned in Tower on suspicion of complicity in Wyatt's rebellion, 1554-5, and for his connection with Sir Henry Dudley [q. v.] and Richard Uvedale [q. v.] in plot to drive Spaniards from England, 1556; sheriff of Gloucestershire, 1559; sent to Ireland to inquire into complaints against Sussex's administration, 1562; lord justice in Ireland, 1564-5; M.P. for Gloucester, 1563, and for Gloucestershire, 1572. He did much to improve the breed of English horses.   [Suppl. i. 75]

ARNOLD, RICHARD (d. 1521 ?), antiquary; haberdasher in London, 1473; arrested as spy while on business visit to Flanders, 1488, and imprisoned at Sluys. Published a work on the customs of London (1502).   [ii. 110]

ARNOLD, SAMUEL (1740-1802), musical composer; educated in Chapel Royal; composer to Covent Garden, before 1763; brought out his first opera, 'Maid of the Mill,' 1765; member Royal Society of Musicians, 1764; set Browne's ode, the 'Cure of Saul,' as an oratorio, 1767; leased Marylebone Gardens, 1769, where he produced many operas and burlettas; Mus. Doc. Oxford, 1773; organist to Chapels Royal, 1783, and of Westminster Abbey, 1793. Published collection of cathedral music, 1790.   [ii. 111]

ARNOLD, SAMUEL JAMES (1774-1852), dramatist; son of Samuel Arnold (1740-1802) [q. v.]; produced at the Haymarket, Drury Lane, the English Opera, and the Lyceum many original musical plays (including 'The Prior Claim,' written in conjunction with Pye, the poet laureate, whose daughter he married) and several notable foreign operas; F.R.S.   [ii. 112]

ARNOLD, THOMAS (1679-1737), sailor; made commander for bravery in battle off Cape Passaro; captain, 1727; served on Carolina coast.   [ii. 113]

ARNOLD, THOMAS (1742-1816), physician; M.D., F.R.C.P.; owned and conducted a lunatic asylum in Leicester; published works on insanity.   [ii. 113]

ARNOLD, THOMAS (1795-1842), headmaster of Rugby; educated at Winchester and Corpus Christi College, Oxford; first class classics, 1814; fellow of Oriel, 1815; won chancellor's Latin and English essay prizes, 1815 and 1817; ordained, 1818; headmaster of Rugby, 1828-42; B.D. and D.D., 1828; added mathematics, modern history, and modern languages to the ordinary school course; published, 1829, a pamphlet on the 'Christian Duty of Conceding the Roman Catholic Claims'; published 'Principles of Church Reform,' 1833; regius professor of history at Oxford, 1841; published sermons, an edition of Thucydides, and works on Roman and modern history.   [ii. 113]

ARNOLD, THOMAS (1823-1900), professor of English literature, younger son of Dr. Thomas Arnold [q. v.]; B.A. University College, Oxford, 1845; M.A., 1865; entered Lincoln's Inn, 1846; clerk in colonial office, 1847; went to New Zealand, 1847; started school at Fort Hill, near Nelson, 1849; inspector of schools in Tasmania, 1850-6; entered Roman catholic church, 1856; professor of English literature at catholic university, Dublin, 1856-62; left church of Rome, 1865, but rejoined it, 1876; fellow of Royal University of Ireland, and professor of English language and literature, University College, St. Stephen's Green, 1882-1900; published a 'Manual of English Literature,' 1862, and other works.   [Suppl. i. 76]

ARNOLD, THOMAS JAMES (1804?-1877), barrister; called, 1829; police magistrate, 1847-77; published legal manuals and translations of Goethe's 'Reineke Fuchs' (1860), of 'Faust' (1877), and of Anacreon (1869). [ii. 117]

ARNOLD, THOMAS KERCHEVER (1800-1853), educationalist; B.A. Trinity College, Cambridge, 1821; fellow; M.A., 1824; rector of Lyndon, Rutland, 1830-53; published many classical works, educational adaptations from American and German authors, sermons and other theological writings. [ii. 118]

ARNOLD, WILLIAM DELAFIELD (1828-1859), Anglo-Indian official and novelist; younger son of Dr. Thomas Arnold [q. v.]; educated at Christ Church, Oxford; went to India as ensign in 58th native infantry; assistant-commissioner of Punjáb; director of public instruction, 1856; invalided home and died at Gibraltar; published 'Oakfield,' a novel, 1853. [ii. 119]

ARNOT, HUGO (1749-1786), historical writer; advocate, 1772; published 'History of Edinburgh,' 1779, and 'Criminal Trials in Scotland,' 1785. [ii. 119]

ARNOT, WILLIAM (1808-1875), preacher; apprenticed as gardener; studied for ministry at Glasgow; minister of St. Peter's Church, Glasgow, 1838, and of one of the leading free church congregations in Edinburgh, 1863-75; thrice visited America on ministerial work; published religious and biographical works. [ii. 119]

ARNOTT, GEORGE ARNOTT WALKER (1799-1868), botanist; M.A. Edinburgh, 1818; studied law, but abandoned the profession for botany; travelled on continent; botanical lecturer, 1839, and professor, 1845, Glasgow; associated with Sir William Hooker in botanical publications. [ii. 120]

ARNOTT, NEIL (1788-1874), physician and natural philosopher; M.A. Marischal College, Aberdeen, 1805; went to London and became a student at St. George's Hospital, 1806; visited China as surgeon in East India Company's service, 1807 and 1809; practised in London, 1811-1855; lectured on natural science at Philomathic Institution; M.D. Aberdeen, 1814; physician successively to French (1816) and Spanish embassies; a founder and original member of senate of university of London, 1836; physician extraordinary to Queen Victoria, 1837; F.R.S., 1838; member of Medical Council, 1854; published 'Elements of Physics,' 1827-9. [ii. 121]

ARNOUL or **ARNULF** (1040-1124). [See ERNULF.]

ARNOULD, SIR JOSEPH (1814-1886), Indian judge and author; educated at Charterhouse and Wadham College, Oxford; Newdigate prizeman, 1834; B.A., 1836; probationer fellow, 1838-41; moderator of philosophy, 1840; called to the bar at the Middle Temple, 1841; contributed to Douglas Jerrold's 'Weekly Newspaper' and wrote leaders for 'Daily News'; knighted and appointed to seat on bench of supreme court (afterwards high court of judicature) of Bombay, 1859; published legal and other writings. [Suppl. i. 78]

ARNULF, EARL OF PEMBROKE (fl. 1110), fifth son of Roger de Montgomery [see ROGER DE MONTGOMERIE, EARL OF SHREWSBURY, d. 1093]; built Pembroke Castle about 1090; rebelled against Henry I, and marrying, after much negotiation, the daughter of Murchadh, king of Leinster, died next day. [xlix. 103]

ARNWAY, JOHN (1601-1653), royalist divine; rector of Hodnet and Ightfield, 1635; archdeacon of Lichfield and Coventry and prebendary of Woolvey; exiled during protectorate; died in Virginia. [ii. 122]

ARRAN, EARLS OF. [See HAMILTON, JAMES, first EARL, 1477?-1529; HAMILTON, JAMES, second EARL, d. 1575; HAMILTON, JAMES, third EARL, 1530-1609; STEWART, JAMES, d. 1596.]

ARROWSMITH, AARON (1750-1823), geographer; left practically destitute in early life; found employment with a map-maker in London, 1770; published several maps, including a chart of the world (Mercator's projection), now rare, 1790, 'Map of Scotland,' 1807, and 'Atlas of Southern India,' 1822. [ii. 123]

ARROWSMITH, EDMUND (1585-1628), jesuit; known sometimes as BRADSHAW and RIGBY; educated at Douay; ordained, 1612; returned to England on English mission, 1613; entered Society of Jesus, 1624; executed

for taking order of priesthood beyond the seas. His hand is preserved as a relic at Ashton, Newton-le-Willows. [ii. 124]

ARROWSMITH, JOHN (1602-1659), puritan divine; graduated at Cambridge, 1623; incumbent of St. Nicholas' Chapel, King's Lynn, 1631; D.D. and regius professor of divinity, 1644; rector of St. Martin's, Ironmonger Lane, 1645; vice-chancellor of Cambridge, 1647; master of Trinity, 1649; published sermons. [ii. 124]

ARROWSMITH, JOHN (1790-1873), map-maker; nephew of Aaron Arrowsmith [q. v.], whom he assisted, 1810-23; began business alone, 1823, and ultimately became head of his uncle's house; an original fellow of Royal Geographical Society, 1830; published many maps and charts. [ii. 125]

ARSDEKIN, RICHARD (1618-1693). [See ARCHDEKIN, RICHARD.]

ARTAUD, WILLIAM (fl. 1776-1822), portrait painter; exhibited in the Royal Academy between 1784 and 1822. [ii. 125]

ARTHUR, real or fabulous King of Britain; born probably towards end of the 5th century; perhaps son of Uther Pendragon, brother of Ambrosius Aurelianus [q. v.], and leader of the Roman party in Britain; obtained command of British army, c. 516, and is credited by Nennius with twelve victories over the invading Saxons, of which probably only that at Badon Hill (c. 520) is historical; said to have died at battle of Camlan. [ii. 126]

ARTHUR, DUKE or COUNT OF BRITTANY (1187-1203), posthumous son of Geoffrey, third son of King Henry II and Constance, daughter and heiress of Conan le Petit, count of Brittany; declared his heir by his uncle, Richard I, 1190; supported by Philip of France on the accession of his next uncle John; captured by King John at Mirabel, 1202; murdered at Rouen, probably by John's orders. [ii. 129]

ARTHUR (1486-1502), eldest son of Henry VII and Elizabeth of York, eldest daughter of Edward IV; K.B., 1489; married Katharine of Arragon, 1501. [ii. 131]

ARTHUR, ARCHIBALD (1744-1797), professor of moral philosophy, Glasgow; M.A. Glasgow; received preacher's licence, 1767; chaplain and librarian, Glasgow University; professor of moral philosophy, 1796; compiled catalogue of Glasgow University Library, published 1791; published theological and literary discourses, 1803. [ii. 131]

ARTHUR, SIR GEORGE (1784-1854), lieutenant-general; joined 91st Argyllshire Highlanders, 1804; lieutenant in Italy, 1806, and in Egypt, 1807; captain in Sicily, 1808, and in Walcheren, 1809; deputy assistant adjutant-general; military secretary to Sir George Don, governor of Jersey; major 7th West India regiment, and assistant quartermaster-general, Jamaica, 1812; lieutenant-governor, British Honduras, 1814-22, Van Diemen's Land, 1823-37, and Upper Canada, 1837-41; baronet, 1841; governor of Bombay, 1842; elected provisional governor-general, but compelled by ill-health to return home, 1846; privy councillor and hon. D.C.L. Oxford; colonel 50th Queen's Own regiment, 1853. [ii. 132]

ARTHUR, JAMES (d. 1670?), divine; professor of divinity, Salamanca University; subsequently retired to convent of St. Dominic, Lisbon; published and left in manuscript commentaries on Aquinas's 'Summa.' [ii. 135]

ARTHUR, THOMAS (d. 1532), divine; fellow, St. John's College, Cambridge, and principal, St. Mary's Hostel, 1518; charged with heresy, 1526 and 1527, and recanted to Romanism; wrote tragedies. [ii. 136]

ARTHUR, THOMAS (1593-1666?), Irish catholic physician; educated at Bordeaux; studied medicine at Paris; practised in Limerick, 1619, and in Dublin, 1624; wrote Latin elegiacs. [ii. 136]

ARTLETT, RICHARD AUSTIN (1807-1873), engraver; pupil of Robert Cooper and James Thomson; produced several portraits; remembered chiefly for engravings of sculpture. [ii. 136]

ARUNDALE, FRANCIS (1807-1853), architect; pupil of Augustus Pugin; travelled on the continent and in Egypt and Palestine; published several illustrated works on architectural subjects. [ii. 136]

ARUNDEL, EARLS OF. [See ALBINI, WILLIAM DE, first EARL, *d.* 1176 ; ALBINI, WILLIAM DE, third EARL, *d.* 1221 ; FITZALAN, RICHARD, first EARL of the second creation, 1267–1302 ; FITZALAN, EDMUND, second EARL, 1285–1326 ; FITZALAN, RICHARD, third EARL, 1307 ?–1376 ; FITZALAN, RICHARD, fourth EARL, 1346–1397 ; FITZALAN, THOMAS, fifth EARL, 1381–1415 ; FITZALAN, JOHN, seventh EARL, 1408–1435 ; FITZALAN, HENRY, twelfth EARL, 1511 ?–1580 ; HOWARD, PHILIP, thirteenth EARL, 1557–1595 ; HOWARD, THOMAS, fourteenth EARL, 1586–1646 ; HOWARD, HENRY FREDERICK, fifteenth EARL, 1608–1652.]

ARUNDEL, THOMAS (1353–1414), archbishop of Canterbury ; bishop of Ely, 1374 ; chancellor, 1386–9 ; archbishop of York, 1388 ; again chancellor, 1391–6 ; archbishop of Canterbury, 1396 ; was perhaps implicated in a conspiracy of his brother, Earl of Arundel, the Duke of Gloucester, and Earl of Warwick against King Richard II ; impeached by House of Commons and banished, 1397, for assisting the commission of regency eleven years before, in derogation of the king's authority ; went to Rome and sought intercession of Boniface IX, who at Richard II's request translated him to St. Andrews, a see which acknowledged the rival pope ; returned to England with Henry IV, whom he crowned, 1399 ; again chancellor, 1399, 1407, and 1412 ; strenuously resisted lollardy. [ii. 137]

ARUNDELL OF CORNWALL. The three principal branches of the Cornish family of Arundell were the Arundells of Lanherne, Trerice, and Tolverne.

The ARUNDELLS OF LANHERNE settled at Lanherne about the middle of the thirteenth century. The more important members of this branch not noticed elsewhere are Roger, marshal of England ; William de Arundell, canon of Exeter Cathedral (*d.* 1246) ; Sir Ralph Arundell, sheriff of Cornwall, 1260 ; Sir John Arundell, K.B., ' the Magnificent,' M.P. and sheriff of Cornwall, died *c.* 1433 ; John Arundell, sheriff and admiral of Cornwall, attainted, 1483 ; and Sir John Arundell, who was made knight banneret at Therouenne, and died in 1545.

The ARUNDELLS OF TRERICE include Sir John Arundell, vice-admiral of Cornwall early in fifteenth century (*d.* 1471), and the Hon. Richard Arundell, M.P. (*d.* 1759).

The ARUNDELLS OF TOLVERNE include Sir Thomas Arundell (*d.* 1443), Sir Thomas Arundell (*d.* 1652), knighted by James I, and his son, John Arundell, colonel of horse for Charles II (*d.* 1671).

The ARUNDELLS OF MENADARVA appear to have been founded by one Robert Arundell, a natural son of Sir John Arundell of Trerice [q. v.] [ii. 141]

ARUNDELL, BLANCHE, LADY (1583–1649), defender of Wardour Castle ; daughter of Edward, earl of Worcester ; married Thomas Arundell of Wardour, Wiltshire ; defended Wardour Castle for nine days against parliamentarians, 1643. [ii. 143]

ARUNDELL, FRANCIS VYVYAN JAGO (1780–1846), antiquary ; M.A. Exeter College, Oxford, 1809 ; rector of Landulph, 1805 ; chaplain to British factory, Smyrna, 1822–36 ; journeyed in Asia Minor, 1826–35, and published descriptions of his travels and discoveries, 1834 ; made large collections of antiquities, coins, and manuscripts. [ii. 143]

ARUNDELL, HENRY, third BARON ARUNDELL OF WARDOUR (1606 ?–1694), fought for Charles I in civil wars ; dislodged parliamentarians, 1644, from Wardour Castle, which had been taken from his mother, Lady Blanche Arundell [q. v.] ; master of horse to Henrietta Maria, 1663 ; one of the ambassadors sent by Charles II to Louis XIV to arrange secret treaty of Dover, 1669 ; accused by Titus Oates of complicity in a popish plot against Charles, and arrested, 1678 ; imprisoned in Tower, but not tried ; released 1684 ; privy councillor, 1686 ; keeper of privy seal, 1687 ; published religious and courtly poems. [ii. 144]

ARUNDELL, HUMPHRY, OF LANHERNE (1513–1550), rebel ; leader of an insurrection due to enclosure of common lands, 1549 ; unsuccessfully besieged Exeter ; ultimately captured and executed at Tyburn. [ii. 145]

ARUNDELL, SIR JOHN, OF LANHERNE (*d.* 1379), naval commander ; repulsed French off Cornwall, 1379, but was caught in storm and drowned. [ii. 146]

ARUNDELL, JOHN (*d.* 1477), bishop of Chichester ; fellow, Exeter College, Oxford, 1421–30 ; chaplain to Henry VI ; bishop of Chichester, 1458. [ii. 146]

ARUNDELL, JOHN, OF LANHERNE (*d.* 1504), divine ; M.A. Exeter College, Oxford ; dean of Exeter, 1483–96 ; bishop of Lichfield and Coventry, 1496, and Exeter, 1502. [ii. 146]

ARUNDELL, SIR JOHN, OF TRERICE (1495–1561), vice-admiral of the west, called ' Jack of Tilbury' ; knighted at battle of Spurs, 1513 ; twice sheriff of Cornwall ; esquire of the body to Henry VIII. [ii. 146]

ARUNDELL, SIR JOHN, OF TRERICE (1576–1656 ?), royalist, nicknamed ' Jack for the King' ; grandson of Sir John Arundell (1495–1561) [q. v.] ; at various times M.P. for Cornwall, Bodmin, Tregony, and Michell ; governor, 1643, of Pendennis Castle, which he was compelled to surrender to Fairfax, 1646. [ii. 147]

ARUNDELL, MARY, OF LANHERNE (*d.* 1691), translator ; left manuscript translations from Latin. [ii. 147]

ARUNDELL, RICHARD, first BARON ARUNDELL OF TRERICE (*d.* 1687), M.P. for Lostwithiel ; colonel in king's army ; governor, Pendennis Castle, 1662. [ii. 148]

ARUNDELL, SIR THOMAS, OF LANHERNE (*d.* 1552), alleged conspirator ; sheriff of Dorset, 1531–2 ; gentleman of privy chamber to Wolsey ; knighted, 1533 ; a commissioner for suppression of religious houses, 1535 ; imprisoned in Tower for alleged implication in Cornish rising, 1550–1 ; executed for share in Somerset's conspiracy. [ii. 148]

ARUNDELL, THOMAS, first BARON ARUNDELL OF WARDOUR (1560–1639), soldier of fortune ; made count of Holy Roman Empire by Emperor Rudolph II for services against the Turks, 1595. [ii. 148]

ARUNDELL, THOMAS, second BARON ARUNDELL OF WARDOUR (1584–1643), fought for royalists in civil war. [ii. 149]

ASAPH (*d. c.* 596), Welsh saint ; known also as ASAAF, ASSA, or ASA ; grandson of Pabo [q. v.] ; succeeded St. Kentigern [q. v.], *c.* 570, in the monastery at confluence of rivers Clwyd and Elwy ; the monastery, perhaps in Asaph's time, elevated into a cathedral foundation ; possibly first bishop of the see of Llanelwy (known since *c.* 1100 as St. Asaph) ; his anniversary formerly celebrated at St. Asaph on 1 May. [Suppl. i. 78]

ASBURY, FRANCIS (1745–1816), Wesleyan bishop ; went as preacher to America, 1771 ; made joint superintendent, and, later, bishop of the Methodist Episcopal Church, United States of America, 1784. [ii. 149]

ASCHAM, ANTHONY (*fl.* 1553), astrologer ; M.B. Cambridge, 1540 ; vicar of Burneston, Yorkshire, 1553 ; published astronomical and astrological works. [ii. 149]

ASCHAM, ANTONY (*d.* 1650), parliamentarian ambassador ; educated at Eton and King's College, Cambridge ; tutor to James, duke of York ; Hamburg agent of the republic, 1649 ; ambassador to Madrid, 1650, where he was murdered on his arrival. [ii. 150]

ASCHAM, ROGER (1515–1568), author ; educated at St. John's College, Cambridge, where he distinguished himself in classics ; B.A. and fellow, 1534 ; M.A., 1537 ; Greek reader at St. John's, 1538 ; visited Yorkshire ; returned to Cambridge, 1542 ; published ' Toxophilus,' a treatise on archery, in which accomplishment he had considerable skill, 1545 ; public orator, Cambridge University, 1546 ; succeeded Grindal as tutor to Princess Elizabeth, 1548 ; resigned this post and returned to his duties at Cambridge, 1550 ; secretary to Sir Richard Morysin, English ambassador to Charles V, 1550–3, during which period he travelled largely on the continent ; Latin secretary to Queen Mary, 1553 ; was specially permitted to continue in his profession of protestantism ; married and resigned his offices at Cambridge, 1554 ; private tutor to Queen Elizabeth, 1558 ; prebendary of York, 1559 ; troubled with ill-health during latter years of his life. His ' Scholemaster,' a treatise on practical education, which he left unfinished, was published in 1570. [ii. 150]

ASGILL, SIR CHARLES (1763 ?–1823), general ; ensign 1st foot guards, 1778 ; lieutenant with captain's rank, 1781 ; captured at the capitulation of York Town

C

1781 ; chosen to suffer death in retaliation for the execution of an American prisoner, but released ; lieutenant-colonel in guards, 1790 ; served in Flanders ; colonel, 1795 ; staff-brigadier in Ireland, 1797 ; major-general, 1798 ; colonel 46th foot, and commander of Dublin, 1800 ; general, 1814. [ii. 159]

ASGILL, JOHN (1659–1738), eccentric writer ; student of Middle Temple, 1686 ; called to the bar, 1692 ; published a pamphlet to prove that death was not obligatory upon Christians, 1699 ; went to Ireland ; member for Enniscorthy in Irish House of Commons, 1703 ; expelled and his pamphlet ordered to be burned ; returned to England ; M.P. for Bramber in parliament of 1705–7 ; expelled after his book had again been ordered to be burned ; became involved in financial difficulties, and passed the rest of his life in Fleet or within rules of King's Bench ; published several pamphlets. [ii. 159]

ASH, JOHN (1724 ?–1779), baptist pastor at Loughwood, Dorset, and later at Pershore, Worcestershire ; published an English dictionary, 1775. [ii. 161]

ASH, JOHN (1723–1798), physician ; M.D. Trinity College, Oxford, 1754 ; first physician of General Hospital, Birmingham, at which town he practised ; F.C.P., 1787 ; practised in London after 1787, and held various posts in the College of Physicians. [ii. 161]

ASH, SIMON OF (*fl.* 1200). [See SIMON.]

ASHBEE, HENRY SPENCER (1834–1900), bibliographer ; founder and senior partner of London mercantile firm of Charles Lavy & Co., whose parent house was in Hamburg ; organised branch at Paris, 1868 ; subsequently devoted his leisure to travel and book-collecting ; formed the finest Cervantic library out of Spain ; published 'Notes on Curious and Uncommon Books' (privately, 1877–85) and other bibliographical writings ; he bequeathed many valuable books to the British Museum. [Suppl. i. 79]

ASHBORNE, THOMAS OF (*fl.* 1382). [See THOMAS.]

ASHBURNHAM, JOHN (1603–1671), royalist ; protégé of Duke of Buckingham ; groom of bedchamber, 1628 ; M.P. for Hastings, 1640 ; 'discharged and disabled ' by the commons for contempt, being prevented by his attendance on the king from attending in the house, 1643 ; treasurer and paymaster of royalist army ; attended king at Hampton Court, 1647 ; lost the confidence of the royalists owing to his connection with an unsuccessful attempt to effect Charles's escape, 1647 ; suffered many hardships, but, at the Restoration, again became groom of the bedchamber. [ii. 162]

ASHBURNHAM, WILLIAM (*d.* 1679), royalist ; brother of John Asburnham [q. v.] ; M.P. for Ludgershall, 1640 ; governor of Weymouth, 1644 ; cofferer of the household after the Restoration. [ii. 164]

ASHBURTON, BARONS. [See DUNNING, JOHN, first BARON, 1731–1785 ; BARING, ALEXANDER, first BARON of the second creation, 1774–1848 ; BARING, WILLIAM BINGHAM, second BARON, 1799–1864.]

ASHBURY, JOSEPH (1638–1720), actor ; served in army in Ireland ; lieutenant of foot, Dublin, after the Restoration ; master of revels and patentee to the Duke of Ormonde, lord-lieutenant of Ireland, 1682 ; gained reputation for the Irish stage and for himself as actor and manager. [ii. 164]

ASHBY, GEORGE (*d.* 1475), poetical writer ; clerk of signet to Henry VI, and afterwards to Margaret of Anjou ; perhaps confined in the Fleet, *c.* 1461 ; tutor to Henry VI's son Edward ; left verses in manuscript. [ii. 164]

ASHBY, GEORGE (1724–1808), antiquary ; educated at Westminster, Eton, and St. John's College, Cambridge ; M.A., 1748 ; fellow and B.D., 1756 ; rector of Hungerton, 1754–67, and of Twyford, Leicestershire, 1759–69 ; president, St. John's College, 1769–75 ; F.S.A., 1775 ; accepted living of Barrow, Suffolk, and also in 1780 that of Stansfield ; wrote largely on antiquarian subjects. [ii. 165]

ASHBY, HARRY (1744–1818), writing engraver ; apprenticed at Wotton-under-Edge, Gloucestershire, to a clockmaker ; employed later in London as writing engraver ; executed plates for several works on penmanship. [ii. 165]

ASHBY, SIR JOHN (*d.* 1693), admiral ; lieutenant, 1665 ; captain, 1668 ; fought at Bantry Bay ; knighted ; made second rear-admiral of the blue, 1689 ; admiral of the blue at Barfleur, 1692. [ii. 166]

ASHBY, RICHARD (1614–1680), jesuit, whose real name was THIMELBY ; entered Society of Jesus, 1632 ; professor at Liège ; joined English mission, *c.* 1648 ; rector of St. Omer's College ; wrote theological works. [ii. 166]

ASHDOWNE, WILLIAM (1723–1810), unitarian preacher ; preacher at general baptist church, Dover, from 1759 to 1781, when he was elected pastor ; published religious works. [ii. 167]

ASHE, JOHN (1671–1735), religious writer ; dissenting minister at Ashford. [ii. 167]

ASHE, JONATHAN (*fl.* 1813), masonic writer ; D.D. Trinity College, Dublin, 1808 ; published a work on freemasonry, 1813. [ii. 167]

ASHE, ROBERT HOADLEY (1751–1826), divine ; D.D. Pembroke College, Oxford, 1794 ; held living of Crewkerne, Somerset, 1775–1826. [ii. 167]

ASHE, ST. GEORGE (1658 ?–1718), Irish bishop ; fellow, Trinity College, Dublin, 1679 ; provost, 1692 ; bishop of Cloyne, 1695, of Clogher, 1697, and of Derry, 1717 ; known chiefly for his intimacy with Dean Swift, who was his pupil at Trinity College. [ii. 168]

ASHE, SIMEON (*d.* 1662), nonconformist divine ; educated at Emmanuel College, Cambridge ; ejected for nonconformity from a living which he held in Staffordshire ; chaplain to Earl of Manchester ; after civil war received living of St. Austin ; wrote several pamphlets and sermons. [ii. 168]

ASHE or **ASH**, THOMAS (*fl.* 1600–1618), legal writer ; called to bar at Gray's Inn, 1574 ; pensioner, 1597 ; published legal works. [ii. 169]

ASHE, THOMAS (1770–1835), novelist ; held commission in 83rd foot regiment ; entered a counting-house at Bordeaux ; did secretarial work in Dublin and subsequently spent some years in foreign travel ; wrote novels and miscellaneous works. [ii. 169]

ASHE, THOMAS (1836–1889), poet ; B.A. St. John's College, Cambridge, 1859 ; curate of Silverstone, Northamptonshire, 1860 ; mathematical and modern form master at Leamington college, 1865, and subsequently at Queen Elizabeth's school, Ipswich ; wrote several volumes of poetry (collected, 1885). [Suppl. i. 80]

ASHFIELD, EDMUND (*fl.* 1680–1700), artist ; pupil of John Michael Wright [q. v.] ; executed crayon and oil portraits. [ii. 169]

ASHFORD, WILLIAM (1746 ?–1824), landscape painter ; settled in Dublin, 1764 ; abandoned a situation in Dublin ordnance department in the interests of art ; first president, Royal Hibernian Academy, 1823. [ii. 169]

ASHHURST. [See ASHURST.]

ASHLEY, first BARON (1621–1683). [See COOPER, ANTHONY ASHLEY.]

ASHLEY, SIR ANTHONY (1551–1627), clerk of the privy council ; probably educated at Oxford ; clerk of the council before 1588 ; journeyed with Norris and Drake to Spain, 1589 ; M.A. Oxford, 1592 ; secretary for war in the 'honourable voyage unto Cadiz' and knighted, 1596 ; made baronet, 1622 ; author of 'The Mariners Mirrour of Navigation,' 1588. [ii. 170]

ASHLEY, CHARLES JANE (1773–1843), performer on violoncello ; son of John Ashley (1734 ?–1805) [q. v.] ; secretary of Royal Society of Musicians. [ii. 171]

ASHLEY, GENERAL CHARLES (1770 ?–1818), violinist ; son of John Ashley (1734 ?–1805) [q. v.] ; pupil of Giardini and Barthelemon ; took part in Handel commemoration, 1784 ; member Royal Society of Musicians, 1791. [ii. 171]

ASHLEY, JOHN (1734 ?–1805), musician ; member of Royal Society of Musicians, 1765 ; assistant conductor at Handel commemoration, 1784 ; manager of oratorio concerts, Covent Garden, 1795. [ii. 171]

ASHLEY, JOHN JAMES (1772–1815), singing master; son of John Ashley (1734?–1805) [q. v.]; pupil of Schroeter; member of Royal Society of Musicians, 1792. [ii. 171]

ASHLEY, RICHARD (1775–1836), violinist; son of John Ashley (1734?–1805) [q. v.]; member of Royal Society of Musicians, 1796. [ii. 171]

ASHLEY, ROBERT (1565–1641), miscellaneous writer; educated at Oxford; fellow commoner, Hart Hall, 1580; called to bar at Middle Temple; proficient linguist in European tongues and author of miscellaneous works. [ii. 172]

ASHMOLE, ELIAS (1617–1692), antiquary and astrologer; educated at Lichfield; solicitor, 1638; joined royalists, and in 1644 was appointed commissioner of excise at Lichfield; studied physics and mathematics at Brasenose College, Oxford; commissioner of excise, captain of horse and comptroller of ordnance, Worcester; Windsor Herald, 1660; held successively several government appointments; presented, 1677, his collection of curiosities to Oxford University, to which he subsequently bequeathed his library; M.D. Oxford, 1690; wrote or edited antiquarian and Rosicrucian works. [ii. 172]

ASHMORE, JOHN (*fl.* 1621), translator; published the first translation into English of selected Odes of Horace. [ii. 174]

ASHPITEL, ARTHUR (1807–1869), architect; practised 1842–54; spent some time in Rome, of which city he bequeathed two drawings to the nation; published verse and political pamphlets. [ii. 174]

ASHPITEL, WILLIAM HURST (1776–1852), architect; concerned as assistant in building of London docks and Kennet and Avon canal. [ii. 175]

ASHTON, CHARLES (1665–1752), divine; B.A. Queens' College, Cambridge; fellow, 1687; chaplain to Bishop Patrick; held living of Rattenden, Essex, 1699; chaplain to Chelsea hospital; prebendary of Ely, master of Jesus College, Cambridge, and D.D., 1701; vice-chancellor, Cambridge, 1702; published works on classical subjects and made textual emendations. [ii. 175]

ASHTON, EDWARD (*d.* 1658), colonel in army; executed for complicity in Ormonde's plot against lord protector, 1658. [ii. 175]

ASHTON, HENRY (1801–1872), architect; pupil of Sir Robert Smirke; executed designs for many London street improvements, notably Victoria Street. [ii. 176]

ASHTON, HUGH (*d.* 1522), archdeacon of York; M.A. Oxford, 1507; canon and prebendary in St. Stephen's, Westminster, 1509; prebendary of Strensall, York, 1515; archdeacon of Winchester, 1511–19, of Cornwall, 1515, and of West Riding, York, 1516; rector of Grasmere, Ambleside (before 1511), of Barnake, Lichfield, and (1522) of Burton Latimer, Northamptonshire. [ii. 176]

ASHTON, SIR JOHN DE (*fl.* 1370), military commander; distinguished himself at siege of Noyon by English, 1370; knight of shire, 1389. [ii. 177]

ASHTON, SIR JOHN DE (*d.* 1428), son of Sir John de Ashton (*fl.* 1370) [q. v.]; knight of shire for Lancashire, 1413; seneschal of Bayeux, 1416. [ii. 177]

ASHTON, JOHN (*d.* 1691), Jacobite conspirator; clerk of closet to Mary of Modena, wife of James II; probably held commission in army; arrested in 1690 for conspiring to restore James II; hanged at Tyburn. [ii. 177]

ASHTON, PETER (*fl.* 1546), English translator of Paulus Jovius's 'Turcicarum rerum Commentarius,' 1546. [ii. 178]

ASHTON, SIR RALPH DE (*fl.* 1460–1483), officer of state; in his seventeenth year page of honour to Henry VI; held various offices under Edward IV; vice-constable of England and lieutenant of the Tower, 1483; perhaps murdered at Ashton-under-Lyne. [ii. 178]

ASHTON, SIR ROBERT DE (*d.* 1385), officer; M.P., 1324; lord treasurer (1362 and 1373); admiral of the Narrow Seas, 1369; king's chamberlain, 1373; constable of Dover and warden of Cinque ports, 1380. [ii. 179]

ASHTON, THOMAS DE (*fl.* 1346), warrior; fought with great valour under Neville at Neville's Cross, 1346; accompanied John of Gaunt to Spain, 1385. [ii. 179]

ASHTON or **ASSHETON**, SIR THOMAS DE (*fl.* 1446), alchemist; specially licensed by Henry VI to pursue his experiments, 1446. [ii. 180]

ASHTON, THOMAS (*d.* 1578), schoolmaster; M.A. Cambridge, 1563; and fellow, Trinity College; entered orders; first headmaster of Shrewsbury school from 1562 to *c.* 1568; subsequently employed by Earl of Essex in communications between Elizabeth and privy council. [ii. 180]

ASHTON, THOMAS (1716–1775), divine; educated at Eton and King's College, Cambridge, where he made the acquaintance of Horace Walpole; rector of Sturminster Marshall, Dorsetshire, 1749, and of St. Botolph, Bishopsgate, 1752; D.D., 1759; preacher at Lincoln's Inn, 1762–4. [ii. 180]

ASHURST, HENRY (1614?–1680), merchant; apprenticed to draper in London; entered common council, and subsequently became an alderman; treasurer to Society for the Propagation of the Gospel; gave large sums in charity, particularly in Lancashire. [ii. 181]

ASHURST, JAMES (*d.* 1679), divine; vicar of Arlesey, *c.* 1631; left the living under Act of Uniformity, but continued to conduct services there as nonconformist. [ii. 181]

ASHURST or **ASHHURST**, WILLIAM HENRY (1725–1807), judge; educated at Charterhouse; entered Inner Temple, 1750; practised as special pleader; called to the bar, 1754; serjeant, 1770; judge of king's bench, 1770–99; one of the commissioners entrusted with great seal, 1783 and 1792–3. [ii. 182]

ASHURST, WILLIAM HENRY (1792–1855), solicitor; an enthusiastic radical, refusing to pay taxes till the Reform Bill should be passed, 1832; member of common council of London; under-sheriff of London; supplied funds and procured evidence to support Rowland Hill's postal scheme; a founder of the Society of Friends of Italy and of the People's International League, 1851 and 1852. [ii. 182]

ASHWARDBY, JOHN (*fl.* 1392), follower of Wycliffe; fellow of Oriel College, Oxford; vicar of St. Mary's; vice-chancellor of the university, 1392. [ii. 183]

ASHWELL, ARTHUR RAWSON (1824–1879), principal of Chichester Theological College; entered Trinity College, Cambridge, 1843; foundation scholar, Caius College, 1846; fifteenth wrangler, 1847; took orders; curate of Speldhurst, 1848, and of St. Mary-the-Less, Cambridge, 1849; vice-principal, St. Mark's College, Chelsea, 1851–3; principal, Oxford Diocesan Training College, Culham, 1853; minister, Holy Trinity Church, Conduit Street, London, 1862; principal, Training College, Durham, 1865; canon-residentiary and principal Theological College, Chichester, 1870; wrote extensively for literary magazines. [ii. 183]

ASHWELL, GEORGE (1612–1695), controversialist; scholar, Wadham College, Oxford, 1627; M.A. and fellow, 1635; B.D., 1646; chaplain to Sir Anthony Cope of Hanwell, Oxfordshire; rector of Hanwell, 1658; published Anglo-catholic controversial works. [ii. 184]

ASHWELL, JOHN (*d.* 1541?), prior of Newnham; B.D. Cambridge; held benefices of Mistley, Littlebury, and Halstead; chaplain to Lord Abergavenny's troops in France, 1515; prebendary of St. Paul's, 1521; prior, Newnham Abbey, *c.* 1527; opposed principles of Reformation, but took oath of supremacy to Henry VIII, 1534. [ii. 185]

ASHWOOD, BARTHOLOMEW (1622–1680), puritan divine; graduated at Oxford; held benefice of Bickleigh, Devonshire, and later that of Axminster, whence he was ejected, 1662; published religious works. [ii. 185]

ASHWOOD, JOHN (1657–1706), nonconformist minister; tutor at Axminster and later at Chard; minister at Exeter; lecturer at Spitalfields; minister at Peckham. His 'Life,' by Thomas Reynolds, was published 1707.

ASHWORTH, CALEB (1722–1775), diss[enting] originally carpenter; studied for the ind[...] under Doddridge, 1739, and became [...] academy, which he removed to [...] Scotland, 1759; published [...] works.

ASHWORTH, SIR CHARLES (d. 1832), major-general; ensign 68th foot, 1798; after successive promotions served in Peninsula as brigadier-general; major-general, 1825; K.C.B., 1831. [ii. 187]

ASHWORTH, HENRY (1785–1811), navy lieutenant; prisoner, 1804; escaped, 1808; died of wounds received at Tarragona. [ii. 187]

ASHWORTH, HENRY (1794–1880), opponent of corn-laws; of quaker parentage; educated at Ackworth; a founder of Anti-Corn Law League; friend and strenuous supporter of Cobden from 1837; published 'Recollections of Richard Cobden,' 1876, and other works. [ii. 187]

ASHWORTH, JOHN (1813–1875), preacher, manufacturer, and author; his parents poor woollen weavers; educated at Sunday school; founded a chapel for the destitute of Rochdale, and became its minister, 1858; visited United States and Palestine; published tracts, which achieved vast popularity. [ii. 188]

ASKE, ROBERT (d. 1537), leader of the 'Pilgrimage of Grace'; attorney and fellow of Gray's Inn; led Yorkshire insurrection called 'Pilgrimage of Grace,' which was a protest against the suppression of the smaller monasteries, and other oppressive legislative measures, 1536; came to London at request of Henry VIII to declare causes of complaint, and although apparently pardoned, was ultimately executed at York. [ii. 189]

ASKEW, ANNE (1521–1546), protestant martyr; married Thomas Kyme, on death of her sister, who was to have married him; turned out of doors by her husband; came to London; underwent examinations for heresy, 1545, but was befriended by Bishop Bonner; set at liberty, but again arraigned for heresy; refused to recant, and was burned at Smithfield. [ii. 190]

ASKEW, ANTHONY (1722–1774), classical scholar; M.B. Emmanuel College, Cambridge, 1745; studied at Leyden and travelled abroad; M.D., 1750; physician to St. Bartholomew's and Christ's hospitals; registrar of College of Physicians; left extensive library of books and manuscripts, chiefly classical; author of a manuscript volume of Greek inscriptions. [ii. 192]

ASKEW, EGEON (b. 1576), divine; B.A. Oxford, 1597; chaplain, Queen's College, 1598; M.A., 1600; minister of Greenwich, Kent, c. 1603; published a volume of sermons. [ii. 193]

ASKHAM, JOHN (1825–1894), poet; shoemaker at Wellingborough; librarian of literary institute, Wellingborough; member of first school board there, 1871; school attendance officer and sanitary inspector, 1874; published five volumes of poems (1863–93). [Suppl. i. 81]

ASPINALL, JAMES (d. 1861), divine; successively curate of Rochdale, incumbent of St. Luke's, Liverpool (1831), and rector of Althorpe, 1844–61; published sermons and miscellaneous writings. [ii. 193]

ASPINWALL, EDWARD (d. 1732), divine; educated at Cambridge; chaplain to Earl of Radnor; sub-dean of Chapel Royal; prebendary of Westminster, 1729; published theological works. [ii. 194]

ASPINWALL, WILLIAM (fl. 1648–1662), nonconformist minister; B.A. Magdalene College, Cambridge; held livings of Maghull, Lancashire, and Mattersey, Nottinghamshire, whence he was rejected under Act of Uniformity, 1662; formed meeting-house at Thurnsco, Yorkshire, and, later, was perhaps congregational minister at Cockermouth; published religious works. [ii. 194]

ASPLAND, ROBERT (1782–1845), unitarian minister; Ward scholar at Bristol academy, where he studied for baptist ministry; proceeded to Marischal College, Aberdeen, but left, 1800, his views being considered 'unsound'; secretary, South Unitarian Society, 1803; minister, Gravel Pit chapel, Hackney, 1805–45; established several unitarian periodicals, including the 'Monthly Repository,' which he [edit]ed 1806–26; formed Christian Tract Society, 1809; [...] Hackney academy for training unitarian ministers, [helped] to found and was secretary to Unitarian [...] secretary to British and Foreign Unitarian [...] 1835–41; published many religious [works]. [ii. 195]

[ASPLAND, [...] BROOK (1805–1869), unitarian [...]nd [q. v.]; M.A. Glasgow,

1822; unitarian minister successively at Chester, Bristol, Dukinfield, and Hackney; secretary of Manchester College, York, 1846–57, and of British and Foreign Unitarian Association, 1859. [ii. 196]

ASPLEY, WILLIAM (fl. 1588–1637), stationer and printer; freeman of Stationers' Company, 1597; warden, 1637; with Andrew Wise obtained license for publishing 'Much Ado about Nothing,' and '2 Henry IV,' 1600. [ii. 197]

ASPLIN, WILLIAM (1687–1758), theologian; B.A. Trinity College, Oxford, 1707; vice-principal, St. Albans Hall; military chaplain; successively vicar of Banbury, Horley, and Burthorpe, Gloucestershire; published theological writings. [ii. 197]

ASPULL, GEORGE (1813–1832), musician; displayed extraordinary musical genius at very early age; played piano before George IV, 1824; having performed in Paris, undertook concert tours in Great Britain and Ireland; wrote songs and pianoforte music. [ii. 197]

ASSER (d. 909?), bishop of Sherborne, c. 900; monk of St. David's, perhaps bishop of St. David's; entered household of King Ælfred, with whom he studied six months each year, c. 885; received monasteries of Amesbury and Banwell, and, later, Exeter and its district; wrote life of Ælfred, and a chronicle of English history between 849 and 887. [ii. 198]

ASSHETON. [See ASHTON.]

ASSHETON, NICHOLAS (1590–1625), diarist; wrote a journal extending from May 1617 to March 1619. [ii. 199]

ASSHETON, WILLIAM (1641–1711), divine; B.A. and fellow, Brasenose College, Oxford, 1663; M.A., and took holy orders; chaplain to Duke of Ormonde, chancellor of the university; D.D.; prebendary of York, 1673; obtained livings of St. Antholin's, London, and Beckenham, Kent; originated a scheme for providing pensions to widows of clergy and others, which was adopted unsuccessfully by the Mercers' Company; published theological works, including 'The Possibility of Apparitions' (1706), occasioned by Defoe's fabricated story of the appearance of the ghost of Mrs. Veal. [ii. 199]

ASSIGNY. [See D'ASSIGNY, MARIUS.]

ASTBURY, JOHN (1688?–1743), potter at Shelton, Staffordshire; introduced use of Bideford pipeclay, and was first to use calcined flint in the pottery manufacture (1720). [ii. 201]

ASTELL, MARY (1668–1731), authoress; settled in London, c. 1688, and afterwards at Chelsea; published anonymously in 1694 'Serious Proposal to Ladies,' in which she advocated a scheme of religious retirement for women in an establishment 'rather academic than monastic,' which should be conducted on Church of England principles. The project elicited much comment, favourable and unfavourable, but ultimately fell to the ground. Published other works of a religious and controversial nature. [ii. 201]

ASTELL, WILLIAM (1774–1847), director of East India Company, 1800–47; several times chairman and deputy-chairman; M.P. for Bridgewater, 1800, and, later, for Bedfordshire, of which county he was deputy-lieutenant. [ii. 202]

ASTLE, THOMAS (1735–1803), antiquary and palæographer; articled as attorney, but abandoned the profession for antiquarian work and came to London; F.S.A., 1763; gained notice of Hon. George Grenville, who obtained him post of commissioner for regulating public records at Westminster; royal commissioner for methodising state papers at Whitehall, 1764; F.R.S., 1766; chief clerk of record office in the Tower, 1775, and keeper of the records, 1783; published 'Origin and Progress of Writing' (1784), and other archæological works; conducted 'The Antiquarian Repository,' and contributed largely to 'Archæologia.' His collection of manuscripts (the 'Stowe') is now in the British Museum. [ii. 203]

ASTLEY, SIR JACOB, BARON ASTLEY (1579–1652), royalist; served in the Netherlands; governor of Plymouth and isle of St. Nicholas, 1638; sent as sergeant-major to Newcastle to provide against expected Scottish invasion, 1639; on council of war, 1640; joined king at Nottingham as major-general, 1642, and served with distinction during the civil war; made baron, 1644; his force routed, 1646, and himself imprisoned at Warwick; released on surrender of Oxford. [ii. 205]

ASTLEY, JOHN (d. 1595), master of the jewel house; held a confidential position in household of Princess Elizabeth; in Frankfort during Mary's reign; master of jewel house on Elizabeth's accession, 1558; M.P. for Maidstone, 1586 and 1589; published 'Art of Riding' (1584). [ii. 206]

ASTLEY, JOHN (1730?-1787), portrait painter; pupil of Hudson; visited Rome, where he was a companion of (Sir) Joshua Reynolds; on his return obtained patronage of Horace Walpole; acquired great wealth by his art and by judicious marriages. [ii. 207]

ASTLEY, SIR JOHN DUGDALE (1828-1894), the sporting baronet; educated at Winchester, Eton, and Christ Church, Oxford; served in Crimea, 1854-5; brevet-major, 1855; promoted sport throughout armies at Balaclava; retired as lieutenant-colonel, 1859; raced under name of Mr. S. Thellusson, 1869; succeeded to baronetcy, 1873; conservative M.P. for North Lincolnshire, 1874-80; published 'Fifty Years of my Life,' 1894. [Suppl. i. 81]

ASTLEY, PHILIP (1742-1814), equestrian performer; trained as cabinet maker; joined General Elliott's light horse, 1759; became breaker-in, and rose to rank of sergeant-major; opened an exhibition of horsemanship at Lambeth, and in 1770 a wooden circus at Westminster; subsequently, with partial success, established in all nineteen equestrian theatres, including buildings at Paris and Dublin; opened Astley's Royal Amphitheatre, London, 1798 (destroyed by fire, 1803, and rebuilt, 1804); died in Paris. [ii. 207]

ASTON, ANTHONY (fl. 1712-1731), dramatist and actor; educated as attorney; said to have played in London theatres, but principally toured in England and Ireland; delivered a ludicrous speech to House of Commons against restriction of number of theatres, 1735. [ii. 208]

ASTON, SIR ARTHUR (d. 1649), royalist general; in Russia with letters of recommendation from James I, c. 1613-18, and in camp of king of Poland during his war against Turks, 1618-31; attended Gustavus Adolphus in the Lützen campaign; sergeant-major-general at beginning of Scottish rebellion, 1640; knighted, 1641; colonel-general of royalist dragoons on outbreak of civil war, 1642; governor of Reading, during the siege of which town he was wounded; governor of Oxford, 1643, and having met with an accident, 1644, was pensioned; in Ireland, 1646; killed at capture of Drogheda by Cromwell. [ii. 208]

ASTON or ASHTON, JOHN (fl. 1382), follower of Wycliffe; M.A. Merton College, Oxford; one of the Oxford Wycliffites prosecuted by Archbishop Courtney, 1382; expelled from the university, recanted and was readmitted, 1382; prohibited from preaching, 1387. [ii. 210]

ASTON, JOSEPH (1762-1844), miscellaneous writer; stationer, 1803, in Manchester; where, and later at Rochdale, he published and edited newspapers; published verses, plays, and other works. [ii. 211]

ASTON, SIR RICHARD (d. 1778), judge; practised as barrister; king's counsel, 1759; lord chief-justice of common pleas, Ireland, 1761; knighted and transferred to king's bench, England, 1765; member of the court which declared faulty the writ of outlawry against Wilkes, 1768; one of the commissioners entrusted with the great seal, 1770-1. [ii. 211]

ASTON, SIR THOMAS (1600-1645), royalist; educated at Brasenose College, Oxford; made baronet, 1628; high sheriff of Cheshire, 1635; commanded royalist forces at Middlewich, 1643, when he was defeated and captured, but rejoined king's army; was afterwards captured in a skirmish in Staffordshire, and died of wounds while attempting to escape from prison at Stafford; published 'Remonstrance against Presbytery,' 1641. [ii. 212]

ASTON, WALTER, BARON ASTON OF FORFAR (1584-1639), ambassador; K.B., 1603; ambassador to Spain, 1620-5 and 1635-8; raised to Scottish peerage, 1627. Patron of the poet Drayton. [ii. 213]

ASTON, WILLIAM (1735-1800), jesuit; educated at St. Omer; joined Society of Jesus at Watten, 1751; professor of poetry, St. Omer, 1761; president, Little College, Bruges; canon, St. John's church, Liège. [ii. 213]

ASTRY, RICHARD (1632?-1714), antiquary; B.A. Queens' College, Cambridge, 1651; M.A., 1654; left in manuscript historical collections relating to Huntingdonshire (Lansd. MS. 921). [ii. 214]

ASTY, JOHN (1672?-1730), dissenting clergyman; minister in family of the Fleetwoods, Stoke Newington; pastor to congregation at Moorfields, 1713-30. [ii. 214]

ATHELARD OF BATH (12th century). [See ADELARD.]

ATHELM (d. 923), probably monk of Glastonbury; first bishop of Wells, 909; archbishop of Canterbury, 914. [ii. 215]

ATHELSTAN or ÆTHELSTAN (895-940), king of West-Saxons and Mercians, and afterwards of all the English; son of Eadward the Elder, probably by a mistress of noble birth; crowned at Kingston, Surrey, 925; crushed a coalition of minor kings formed to resist his imperial policy, and was acknowledged as overlord at Emmet, 926; obtained homage of Welsh princes; conquered Western Devonshire, and conciliated Welsh in Wessex; invaded Scotland, 933 or 934; at the battle of Brunanburh practically established unity of England by routing subject princes and Danish pirate kings, who had united to overthrow the West-Saxon supremacy, 937; buried at Malmesbury Abbey. [ii. 215]

ATHERSTONE, EDWIN (1788-1872), writer in verse and prose; published 'The Fall of Nineveh' in instalments, 1828, 1847, and 1868; wrote historical romances. [ii. 217]

ATHERTON, JOHN (1598-1640), Irish bishop; educated at Gloucester Hall (Worcester College) and Lincoln College, Oxford; rector of Huish Comb Flower, Somerset; prebendary of St. John's, Dublin, 1630; chancellor of Killaloe, 1634; chancellor of Christ Church and rector of Killaban and Ballintubride, 1635; bishop of Waterford and Lismore, 1636; found guilty of unnatural crime, degraded and hanged at Dublin, 1640. [ii. 217]

ATHERTON, WILLIAM (1775-1850), Wesleyan minister; president of Wesleyan conference, 1846; superintendent of Wakefield district, and chairman of Leeds district, 1849. [ii. 218]

ATHERTON, SIR WILLIAM (1806-1864), lawyer; special pleader, 1832-9; called to bar, 1839; advanced liberal M.P., Durham, 1852, 1857, and 1859; Q.C., 1852; standing counsel to admiralty, 1855-9; solicitor-general and knighted, 1859; attorney-general, 1861. [ii. 218]

ATHLONE, EARLS OF. [See GINKEL, GODERT DE, first EARL, 1630-1703; GINKEL, FREDERICK CHRISTIAN, second EARL, 1668-1719.]

ATHLUMNEY, first BARON (1802-1873). [See SOMERVILLE, SIR WILLIAM MEREDYTH.]

ATHOLE or ATHOLL, DUKES OF. [See MURRAY, JOHN, first DUKE, 1659-1724; MURRAY, JAMES, second DUKE, 1690?-1764; MURRAY, JOHN, third DUKE, 1729-1774.]

ATHOLE or ATHOLL, MARQUISES OF. [See MURRAY, JOHN, first MARQUIS, 1635?-1703; MURRAY, JOHN, second MARQUIS, 1659-1724.]

ATHOLE or ATHOLL, EARLS OF. [See DURWARD, ALAN, d. 1268; STEWART, WALTER, d. 1437; STEWART, JOHN, first EARL of a new creation, 1440?-1512; STEWART, JOHN, third EARL, d. 1542; STEWART, JOHN, fourth EARL, d. 1578.]

ATHONE, JOHN (d. 1350). [See ACTON, JOHN.]

ATKINE, ATKINS, or ETKINS, JAMES (1613?-1687), Scottish bishop; M.A. Edinburgh, 1636; at Oxford; beneficed successively Birsay (Orkney) and Winifrith (Dorset); bishop of Moray, 1676, of Galloway, 1680. [ii. 219]

ATKINS. [See ATKYNS.]

ATKINS, HENRY, M.D. (1558-1635), physician; graduated at Oxford; M.D. Nantes; president College Physicians six times between 1607 and 1625; attended Henry, prince of Wales, in his last illness, 1612. [ii. 219]

ATKINS, JOHN (1685–1757), naval surgeon; in actions at Malaga (1703) and Vaia Bay (1710); sailed to Guinea, Brazil, and West Indies with expedition to put down piracy, 1721–3; published 'Navy Surgeon' (1732) and an account of his voyage. [ii. 220]

ATKINS, RICHARD (1559?–1581), protestant martyr; a catholic till nineteen years of age; in Rome, 1581, where his denunciations against the church issued in his torture and death at the hands of the inquisition. [ii. 220]

ATKINS, SAMUEL (*fl.* 1787–1808), marine painter; contributed to Royal Academy, 1787–96; in East Indies, 1796–1804; exhibited till 1808. [ii. 221]

ATKINS, WILLIAM (1601–1681), jesuit; entered Society of Jesus, 1635; rector of 'College of St. Aloysius,' 1653; died, a victim of Oates's plot, in Stafford gaol. [ii. 221]

ATKINSON, SIR HARRY (1831–1892), prime minister of New Zealand; educated at Rochester and Blackheath; emigrated to New Zealand, 1855; captain in Waitara war, 1860–4; minister of defence in cabinet of Sir Frederick Aloysius Weld [q. v.], 1864–5; took prominent part in struggle between centralism and provincialism, 1874–6; prime minister of New Zealand, 1876–7, 1883–4, and 1887–91, and colonial treasurer, 1875–6, 1876–7, 1879–83, and 1887–1891; K.C.M.G., 1888; speaker of legislative council, 1891. [Suppl. i. 83]

ATKINSON, HENRY (1781–1829), mathematician; assisted his father and sister in management of schools at Great Bavington (Northumberland), West Woodburn, West Belsay, Stamfordham, and Hawkwell; settled in Newcastle-on-Tyne, 1808; contributed to the Newcastle Literary and Philosophical Society many remarkable papers on scientific topics. [ii. 221]

ATKINSON, JAMES (1759–1839), surgeon, bibliographer, and portraitist; senior surgeon to York County hospital and to the York dispensary; surgeon to Duke of York; published 'Medical Bibliography,' 1834. [ii. 222]

ATKINSON, JAMES (1780–1852), Persian scholar; studied medicine in Edinburgh and London; medical officer on an East Indiaman; assistant surgeon in Bengal service, 1805; assistant assay master, Calcutta mint, 1813–28; superintendent of 'Government Gazette,' 1817, and of 'Press,' 1823; surgeon to 55th regiment native infantry, 1833; superintending surgeon to army of Indus, 1838–41; member of medical board, 1845; published translations from Persian. [ii. 223]

ATKINSON, JOHN AUGUSTUS (*b.* 1775), painter; taken at age of nine to St. Petersburg, where he gained patronage of Empress Catherine and Emperor Paul; returned to England, 1801; exhibited in Royal Academy between 1802 and 1829; prepared plates for several volumes published in Russia or England. Notable among his pictures are 'Battle of Waterloo' (1819) and 'Seven Ages' (1812). [ii. 223]

ATKINSON, JOHN CHRISTOPHER (1814–1900), antiquary; B.A. St. John's College, Cambridge, 1838; vicar of Danby, Yorkshire, 1847–1900; honorary D.C.L. Durham, 1887; prebendary of York, 1891; published 'Forty Years in a Moorland Parish' (a collection of local legends and traditions), 1891, and other antiquarian works, besides books for children. [Suppl. i. 83]

ATKINSON, JOSEPH (1743–1818), dramatist; served in army; wrote and adapted several plays which were produced in Dublin, 1785–1800. [ii. 224]

ATKINSON, MILES (1741–1811), divine; B.A. Peterhouse, Cambridge, 1763; headmaster of Drighlington school, near Leeds; minister in Leeds and neighbourhood, 1763 till death. [ii. 224]

ATKINSON, PAUL (1656–1729), Franciscan friar; definitor of English province; condemned on account of his priestly character to perpetual imprisonment in Hurst Castle, Hampshire, where he died. [ii. 225]

ATKINSON, PETER (1725–1805), architect at York; assistant to John Carr, to whose practice he succeeded. [ii. 225]

ATKINSON, PETER (1776–1822), architect; son of Peter Atkinson (1725–1805) [q. v.]; built bridge over Ouse, York, 1810. [ii. 225]

ATKINSON, STEPHEN (*fl.* 1619), metallurgist; 'finer' in Tower of London, 1586; silver refiner in Devonshire; obtained leave to search for gold and silver in Crawford Muir, 1616, but was unsuccessful. [ii. 225]

ATKINSON, THOMAS (1600–1639), divine; scholar, St. John's College, Oxford, 1615; B.D., 1630; senior proctor of the university; rector of Islip, 1638; wrote Latin poems and a Latin tragedy. [ii. 225]

ATKINSON, THOMAS (1801?–1833), poet and miscellaneous writer; bookseller at Glasgow. [ii. 226]

ATKINSON, THOMAS WITLAM (1799–1861), architect; worked successively as bricklayer's labourer, quarryman, and stonemason; taught drawing at Ashton-under-Lyne; studied Gothic architecture, and in 1827 established himself as architect in London; built St. Luke's Church, Cheetham Hill, Manchester; abandoned architecture for art and travel, in the course of which he visited oriental Russia, 1848–53; published, 1858 and 1860, volumes containing journals and topographical drawings; F.R.G.S., 1858; fellow of Geological Society, 1859. [Suppl. i. 84]

ATKINSON, WILLIAM (*d.* 1509), translator; D.D. Pembroke Hall, Cambridge, 1498; canon of Lincoln, 1504, and of Windsor, 1507; translated from French three books (1502) of the 'Imitation of Christ.' [ii. 226]

ATKINSON, WILLIAM (1773?–1839), architect; began life as a carpenter; pupil of James Wyatt; academy gold medallist, 1795. [ii. 226]

ATKINSON, WILLIAM (1757–1846), poetical writer; B.A. and fellow, Jesus College, Cambridge, 1780; M.A., 1783; rector of Warham All Saints, Norfolk; published 'Poetical Essays,' 1786. [ii. 226]

ATKYNS, SIR EDWARD (1587–1669), judge; student of Lincoln's Inn, 1601; called to bar, 1614; governor of the society, 1630; 'autumn reader,' 1632; defended Prynne when charged before Star Chamber with libels appearing in 'Histriomastix'; serjeant, 1640; created by the Commons baron of exchequer, 1645; removed by the Lords to court of common pleas, 1648; nominated one of the judges to try disturbers of peace in eastern counties, 1650; renominated judge, 1659; created anew baron of exchequer and knighted, 1660. [ii. 227]

ATKYNS, SIR EDWARD (1630–1698), judge; son of Sir Edward Atkyns (1587–1669) [q. v.]; called to bar at Lincoln's Inn, 1653; autumn reader, 1675; serjeant, baron of exchequer, and knighted, 1679; lord chief baron, 1686; refused allegiance to William III and resigned, 1688. [ii. 228]

ATKYNS, JOHN TRACY (*d.* 1773), judge; called to bar at Lincoln's Inn, 1732; cursitor baron of exchequer, 1755; published (1765–8) notes of chancery cases, 1736–54. [ii. 228]

ATKYNS, RICHARD (1615–1677), writer on typography; educated at Balliol College, Oxford; travelled abroad with Lord Arundell of Wardour's son for three years; raised troop of horse for king, 1642; after Restoration made deputy-lieutenant for Gloucestershire; published, 1660, a broadside by which he hoped to prove that the right to printing belonged to the crown alone, and to secure for himself the office of patentee for printing law books; committed for debt, 1677, to the Marshalsea, where he died. [ii. 228]

ATKYNS, SIR ROBERT (1621–1709), judge; son of Sir Edward Atkyns (1587–1669) [q. v.]; M.A. Oxford; called to bar at Lincoln's Inn, 1645; M.P. for Evesham, 1659; made K.B. at Charles II's coronation; M.P. for Eastlow, bencher of his inn, and recorder of Bristol, 1661; judge of court of common pleas, 1672; retired from bench, probably on account of disaffection to Charles II's government, 1679; resigned his recordership; succeeded his brother as chief baron, 1689; speaker of House of Lords (the great seal being in commission), 1689–93; retired from bench, 1694; published legal treatises. [ii. 230]

ATKYNS, SIR ROBERT (1647–1711), topographer; son of Sir Robert Atkyns (1621–1709) [q. v.]; knighted, 1663; M.P. for Cirencester, 1681, and Gloucestershire, 1685; published topographical work on Gloucestershire, 1712. [ii. 232]

ATLAY, JAMES (1817–1894), bishop of Hereford; educated at Grantham and Oakham; B.A. St. John's College, Cambridge, 1840; fellow, 1842; M.A., 1843; B.D.,

1850 ; D.D., 1859 ; tutor, 1846-59 ; vicar of Madingley, 1847-52 ; Whitehall preacher, 1856 ; select preacher at Cambridge, 1858 and 1859 ; vicar of Leeds, 1859-68 ; canon residentiary at Ripon, 1861 ; bishop of Hereford, 1868-94. [Suppl. i. 85]

ATMORE, CHARLES (1759-1826), Wesleyan minister ; sent out by Wesley as itinerant evangelist, 1781 ; successively minister in many English towns ; president, Wesleyan conference, 1811. [ii. 233]

ATSLOWE, EDWARD (*d.* 1594), physician ; fellow and M.D. New College, Oxford, 1566 ; F.C.P. ; physician to Earl of Essex ; twice imprisoned (1579 and 1585) for supposed connection with conspiracies in behalf of Mary Queen of Scots. [ii. 233]

ATTAWELL, HUGH (*d.* 1621). [See ATWELL.]

ATTERBURY, FRANCIS (1662-1732), bishop of Rochester ; son of Lewis Atterbury (*d.* 1693) [q. v.] ; educated at Westminster and Christ Church, Oxford ; tutor at Christ Church ; took part as protestant in the controversy resulting from James II's attempts to force his religion on the university, *c.* 1687 ; took holy orders, 1687 ; lecturer of St. Bride's, London, 1691 ; chaplain to William and Mary, and preacher at Bridewell Hospital ; gained considerable repute by his opposition to Erastianism in church and state, and was appointed archdeacon of Totnes, prebendary of Exeter Cathedral, and D.D., 1701 ; chaplain in ordinary to Anne ; dean of Carlisle, 1704 ; preacher at Rolls Chapel, 1709 ; dean of Christ Church, 1712 ; bishop of Rochester and dean of Westminster, 1713 ; took part in coronation of George I ; leant towards the Jacobite cause ; held direct communications with the Jacobites, 1717 ; imprisoned in the Tower for alleged connection with an attempt to restore the Stuarts, 1720 ; deprived of his offices and banished ; went to Brussels, 1723, and thence to France ; entered the service of James II's son, the old Pretender ; died in France ; was buried privately in Westminster Abbey. [ii. 233]

ATTERBURY, LEWIS the elder (*d.* 1693), divine ; D.D. Christ Church, Oxford, 1660 ; rector of Great or Broad Risington, Gloucestershire, 1654 ; received living of Middleton-Keynes, Buckinghamshire, 1657 ; chaplain to Duke of Gloucester, 1660. [ii. 238]

ATTERBURY, LEWIS, LL.D., the younger (1656-1731), divine ; son of Lewis Atterbury (*d.* 1693) [q. v.] ; educated at Westminster and Christ Church, Oxford ; B.A., 1679 ; M.A., 1680 ; chaplain to lord mayor of London, 1683 ; rector of Sywell, Northamptonshire, 1684 ; LL.D., 1687 ; one of six chaplains to Princess Anne of Denmark, at Whitehall ; preacher at Highgate chapel, 1695 ; successively rector of Shepperton and Hornsey ; published religious works. [ii. 238]

ATTERBURY, LUFFMAN (*d.* 1796), musician ; trained as carpenter and builder, but devoted his leisure to music ; musician in ordinary to George III ; member of the Madrigal Society, 1765. [ii. 239]

ATTERSOLL, WILLIAM (*d.* 1640), puritan divine ; B.A. Clare Hall, Cambridge, 1582 ; M.A. Peterhouse, 1586 ; occupied living of Isfield, Sussex, 1600-40 ; published biblical commentaries and religious treatises. [ii. 239]

ATTERSOLL, WILLIAM (*fl.* 1662), puritan divine ; probably son of William Attersoll [q. v.] ; ejected from living of Hoadley, Sussex, 1662. [ii. 240]

ATTWOOD, THOMAS (1765-1838), musician ; as chorister of Chapel Royal attracted attention of Prince of Wales (George IV), who sent him to study music at Naples, 1783 ; studied under Mozart at Vienna, 1785 ; music master to Duchess of York ; organist of St. Paul's and composer to Chapel Royal, 1796. [ii. 240]

ATTWOOD, THOMAS (1783-1856), political reformer ; son of a Birmingham banker ; entered his father's bank, *c.* 1800 ; captain in volunteer infantry, 1803-5 ; high bailiff of Birmingham, 1811 ; agitated successfully for repeal of orders in council restricting British trade with continent and United States, 1812-13 ; opposed in several pamphlets policy of reducing paper currency when specie was scarce, *c.* 1816 ; founded, 1830, 'Birmingham Political Union for Protection of Public Rights,' which supported Earl Grey's government during passage of Reform Bill ; returned to parliament as one of two members for Birmingham, 1832 ; supported Daniel O'Connell,

1833 ; allied himself with the chartists, and presented (1839) their 'national petition' to House of Commons. [Suppl. i. 86]

ATWATER, WILLIAM (1440-1521), bishop of Lincoln ; probably fellow of Magdalen College, Oxford, 1480 ; D.D., 1493 ; vice-chancellor of the university, 1497 and 1500 ; temporarily chancellor, 1500 ; dean of Chapel Royal, 1502 ; canon of Windsor and registrar of order of Garter, 1504 ; prebendary, Salisbury Cathedral, 1509 ; chancellor of Lincoln, 1506-12, and prebendary, 1512 ; archdeacon of Lewes, 1509-12, and of Huntingdon, 1514 ; bishop of Lincoln, 1514. [ii. 241]

ATWELL, ATTAWEL, or **ATTEWELL,** HUGH (*d.* 1621), actor ; played in first representation of Jonson's 'Epicœne,' 1609 ; member of Alleyn's company. [ii. 241]

ATWOOD, GEORGE (1746-1807), mathematician ; educated at Westminster and Trinity College, Cambridge ; third wrangler and first Smith's prizeman, 1769 ; fellow and tutor ; M.A., 1772 ; F.R.S., 1776 ; occupied a post in connection with the revenue after 1784 ; published mathematical works. [ii. 242]

ATWOOD, PETER (1643-1712), Dominican friar ; several times imprisoned, and finally executed on account of his sacerdotal character. [ii. 242]

ATWOOD, THOMAS (*d.* 1793), chief judge of Dominica, and, later, of the Bahamas ; probably author of 'History of Dominica,' 1791. [ii. 242]

ATWOOD, WILLIAM (*d.* 1705 ?), English barrister ; chief-justice and judge of court of admiralty, New York, 1701 ; suspended on charges of corruption and maladministration, 1702, and returned to England ; published statement of his 'Case' (1703), and many political books and pamphlets. [ii. 242]

AUBERT, ALEXANDER (1730-1805), astronomer ; educated for mercantile career in Geneva, Leghorn, and Genoa ; director and governor, London Assurance Company, 1753 ; F.R.S., 1772 ; F.S.A., 1784 ; built private observatory at Loampit Hill, near Deptford, 1786, and at Islington, 1788. [ii. 243]

AUBIGNY, SEIGNEURS OF. [See STUART, SIR JOHN, first SEIGNEUR, 1365 ?-1429 ; STUART, BERNARD, third SEIGNEUR, 1447 ?-1508 ; STUART, ESMÉ, sixth SEIGNEUR, 1542 ?-1583 ; STUART, CHARLES, tenth SEIGNEUR, 1640-1672.]

AUBREY, JOHN (1626-1697), antiquary ; grandson of William Aubrey [q. v.] ; educated at Trinity College, Oxford ; entered Middle Temple, 1646 ; brought to light megalithic remains at Avebury, 1649 ; F.R.S., 1663 ; lost most of his property through litigation and extravagance, 1662-77 ; empowered by patent, 1671, to make antiquarian surveys under the crown ; formed large topographical collections in Wiltshire and Surrey ; left in manuscript much antiquarian and historical material, including 'Minutes of Lives,' which was used largely by Anthony à Wood. [ii. 244]

AUBREY, WILLIAM (1529-1595), civilian ; B.C.L. Oxford, 1549 ; fellow of All Souls' ; New Inn Hall, 1550 ; professor of civil law, 1553-9 ; D.C.L., 1554 ; advocate in court of arches ; chancellor to Archbishop Whitgift ; master in chancery. [ii. 245]

AUCHER, JOHN (1619-1700), royalist divine ; educated at Cambridge ; fellow of Peterhouse, but ejected for loyalty ; D.D., 1660 ; rector of All Hallows, Lombard Street, London, 1662-85 ; published religious works. [ii. 246]

AUCHINLECK, LORD (1706-1782). [See BOSWELL, ALEXANDER.]

AUCHINOUL, LORD (1553 ?-1591). [See BELLENDEN, SIR LEWIS.]

AUCHMUTY, SIR SAMUEL (1756-1822), general ; born in New York ; volunteer with 45th regiment on outbreak of American war, 1775 ; ensign, 1777 ; lieutenant, 1778 ; came to England ; adjutant of 52nd regiment in India, 1783 ; captain, 1788 ; brigade-major, 1790 ; served against Tippoo Sultan and at Seringapatam, 1790-2 ; deputy-quartermaster-general, Calcutta, and brevet-major, 1794 ; brevet lieutenant-colonel, 1795 ; military secretary to Sir Robert Abercromby, 1795-7 ; returned to England, 1797 ; lieutenant-colonel, 10th regiment, 1800 ; adjutant-general to Abercromby in Egypt ; K.B., 1803 ; commandant in

Isle of Thanet, and colonel, 103rd regiment, 1806 ; in Buenos Ayres, 1806–8 ; major-general, 1808 ; and commander-in-chief at Madras, 1810 ; colonel, 78th regiment, 1811 ; returned to England, 1813 ; lieutenant-general ; commander-in-chief in Ireland and Irish privy councillor, 1821. [ii. 246]

AUCKLAND, EARL OF (1784–1849). [See EDEN, GEORGE.]

AUCKLAND, BARONS. [See EDEN, WILLIAM, first BARON, 1744–1814 ; EDEN, GEORGE, second BARON, 1784–1849 ; EDEN, ROBERT JOHN, third BARON, 1799–1870.]

AUDELAY. [See AWDELAY.]

AUDINET, PHILIP (1766–1837), line-engraver ; apprenticed to John Hall ; engraved portraits for Harrison's 'Biographical Magazine' and other works. [ii. 248]

AUDLEY, BARONS. [See TOUCHET, JAMES, seventh BARON, first creation, 1465 ?–1497 ; TOUCHET, JAMES, first BARON, third creation, 1617 ?–1684.]

AUDLEY, EDMUND (d. 1524), bishop of Salisbury ; B.A. Lincoln College, Oxford, 1463 ; prebendary of Hereford, 1464, of Salisbury, 1467, of Lincoln, 1472, of Wells, 1475, and of York, 1478 ; canon of Windsor, 1472 ; archdeacon of East Riding of Yorkshire, 1475, and of Essex, 1479 ; bishop of Rochester, 1480 ; translated to Hereford, 1492, and to Salisbury, 1502 ; chancellor of order of Garter. [ii. 248]

AUDLEY, ALDITHEL, or ALDITHELEY, HENRY DE (d. 1246), royalist baron ; lord-marcher and constable on Welsh borders, 1223. [ii. 249]

AUDLEY, HUGH (d. 1662), moneylender ; held a post in court of wards ; amassed great wealth between 1605 and 1662. [ii. 249]

AUDLEY, ALDITHEL, or ALDITHELEY, JAMES DE, knight (d. 1272), royalist baron ; son of Henry Audley [q. v.] ; lord-marcher : defeated, along with Prince Edward, by Llewelyn and some English barons at Hereford, 1263 : opposed Simon de Montfort's government, 1264 ; joined Gloucester in royalist cause, 1265 ; justiciary of Ireland, 1270. [ii. 249]

AUDLEY or AUDELEY, JAMES DE (1316 ?–1386), a 'first founder' of order of Garter, 1344 ; served with Black Prince in France, 1346 ; took part in the naval battle off Sluys, 1350 ; again with Black Prince in France, 1354–6 ; one of commanders of French expedition, 1359 ; governor of Aquitaine, 1362 ; grand seneschal of Poitou, 1369. [ii. 250]

AUDLEY, THOMAS, BARON AUDLEY OF WALDEN (1488–1544), lord chancellor ; the founder of Magdalene College, Cambridge ; town clerk of Colchester, 1516 ; M.P., 1523 ; entered Middle Temple ; autumn reader, 1526 ; member of Princess Mary's council, 1525 ; attorney of duchy of Lancaster ; groom of the chamber, 1527 ; member of Wolsey's household ; chancellor of duchy of Lancaster and speaker of House of Commons, 1529 ; serjeant-at-law and king's serjeant, 1531 ; knight and keeper of great seal, 1532 ; lord chancellor, 1533 ; sanctioned Henry's divorce from Catherine of Arragon, 1533 ; presided at trials of Bishop Fisher and More, 1535 ; created peer, 1538 ; K.G., 1540 ; carried through parliament acts for attainder of Earl of Essex and for dissolution of Henry's marriage with Anne of Cleves, 1540 ; passed judgment on Catherine Howard, 1542 ; resigned great seal, 1544. [ii. 251]

AUFRERE, ANTHONY (1756–1833), antiquary : edited the 'Lockhart Letters,' 1817, and published, among other works, translations from the German and Italian. [ii. 254]

AUGUSTA SOPHIA (1768–1840), princess, daughter of George III ; born at Buckingham House, London ; on death of her father, received a residence at Frogmore and Clarence House, St. James's, where she died. Buried at Windsor. [ii. 255]

AUGUSTINE, ST. (d. 604), first archbishop of Canterbury ; prior of Pope Gregory I's monastery of St. Andrew, Rome ; sent as missionary to England with forty monks ; received with tolerance by King Ethelbert, who was afterwards converted ; consecrated 'bishop of the English' at Arles ; founded monastery of Christchurch, Canterbury ; organised missions into Western Kent and the East-Saxon kingdom. [ii. 255]

AUGUSTUS FREDERICK, DUKE OF SUSSEX (1773–1843), sixth son of George III and Queen Charlotte ; born at Buckingham Palace, London ; educated at Göttingen University ; married, 1793, Lady Augusta Murray, subsequently created Duchess of Inverness ; marriage declared void under Royal Marriage Act, 1794 ; raised to peerage as Baron Arklow, Earl of Inverness, and Duke of Sussex, 1801 ; strongly supported progressive political policy ; grand master of freemasons, 1811 ; president of Society of Arts, 1816, and of Royal Society, 1830–9. [ii. 257]

AULDBON, LORD (d. 1608). [See LYON, SIR THOMAS.]

AUNGERVILLE, RICHARD (1281–1345). [See BURY, RICHARD DE.]

AURELIUS, ABRAHAM (1575–1632), pastor of French protestant church, London ; graduated at Leyden, 1596 ; published Latin verses. [ii. 258]

AUST, SARAH (1744–1811), known, as authoress, by name of 'Hon. Mrs. Murray' ; published, 1799, a topographical work on Scotland and Northern England. [ii. 258]

AUSTEN, SIR FRANCIS WILLIAM (1774–1865), admiral ; brother of Jane Austen [q. v.] ; served in East Indies, 1788–1800, and in North Sea and Baltic, 1811–14 ; rear-admiral, 1830 ; vice-admiral, 1838 ; admiral, 1848 ; admiral of the fleet, 1863. [ii. 258]

AUSTEN, JANE (1775–1817), novelist ; lived successively at Steventon, near Basingstoke (where she was born), Bath, Southampton, Chawton, near Alton, and Winchester (where she died and is buried). Of her novels, 'Sense and Sensibility' appeared in 1811, 'Pride and Prejudice' in 1813, 'Mansfield Park' in 1814, 'Emma' in 1816, 'Northanger Abbey' and 'Persuasion' posthumously in 1818. [ii. 259]

AUSTEN, RALPH (d. 1676), writer on gardening ; studied at Magdalen College, Oxford ; proctor, 1630 ; deputy-registrary to visitors, 1647, subsequently registrary ; published books on gardening. [ii. 260]

AUSTIN, CHARLES (1799–1874), lawyer ; educated at Jesus College, Cambridge ; gained Hulsean prize for an essay on Christian evidences, 1822 ; B.A., 1824 ; barrister, Middle Temple, 1827 ; joined Norfolk circuit ; Q.C., 1841 ; abandoned practice, 1848, and lived in retirement, having achieved unprecedented success at the parliamentary bar. [ii. 261]

AUSTIN, HENRY (fl. 1613), author of a poem called 'The Scourge of Venus, or the Wanton Lady. With the Rare Birth of Adonis,' 1613. [ii. 262]

AUSTIN, JOHN (1613–1669), catholic writer, under pseudonym, WILLIAM BIRCHLEY ; pensioner, St. John's College, Cambridge ; entered Lincoln's Inn, but was prevented by his religious convictions from practising as a lawyer ; private tutor in Staffordshire during civil war ; published religious works. [ii. 263]

AUSTIN, JOHN (1717–1784), Irish jesuit ; entered Society of Jesus in Champagne, 1735 ; prefect of Irish college, Poitiers ; preacher in Dublin, 1750. [ii. 264]

AUSTIN, JOHN (fl. 1820), Scottish inventor ; published works on systems of stenography and stenographic music, devised by himself. [ii. 264]

AUSTIN, JOHN (1790–1859), jurist ; entered army and served in Sicily, but sold his commission and studied law ; called to bar at Inner Temple, 1818 ; abandoned practice, 1825 ; professor of jurisprudence, London University (now University College), 1826 ; studied law in Germany, 1826–8 ; resigned his chair, 1832 ; member of criminal law commission, 1833 ; commissioned with Sir G. C. Lewis to inquire into state of government of Malta, 1836 ; lived, 1841–3, in Germany, and, 1844–8, in Paris ; was made corresponding member of the French institute of moral and political sciences ; published 'The Province of Jurisprudence determined,' 1832. [ii. 265]

AUSTIN, ROBERT (fl. 1644), puritan divine ; published a tract defending parliament's action against the king, 1644 ; D.D. [ii. 268]

AUSTIN, SAMUEL, the elder (fl. 1629), religious poet ; M.A. Exeter College, Oxford, 1630 ; received benefice in Cornwall ; published 'Austin's Urania, or the Heavenly Muse,' 1629. [ii. 269]

AUSTIN, SAMUEL, the younger (*fl.* 1658), poetical writer; son of Samuel Austin (*fl.* 1629) [q. v.]; B.A., 1656, Wadham College, Oxford, where his self-conceit made him the laughing-stock of the university wits; published 'Panegyrick' on the Restoration, 1661.
[ii. 269]

AUSTIN, SAMUEL (*d.* 1834), painter; exhibited water-colour drawings at Society of British Artists, 1824-6, and at Society of Painters in Water-colours, of which he became associate (1827). [ii. 270]

AUSTIN, SARAH (1793-1867), translator; *née* Taylor; wife of John Austin (1790-1350) [q. v.]; translated from German and French and edited several works, chiefly historical, including 'Germany from 1760-1814' (1854), Ranke's 'History of the Popes' (1840), and 'History of Reformation in Germany' (1845). [ii. 270]

AUSTIN, WILLIAM (1587-1634), miscellaneous writer; barrister of Lincoln's Inn; his works (prose and verse), which were all published posthumously (1635-71), show a wide knowledge of patristic literature. [ii. 271]

AUSTIN, WILLIAM (*fl.* 1662), classical scholar; son of William Austin (1587-1634) [q. v.]; barrister of Gray's Inn; wrote poems to celebrate marriage of Charles II, 1662, and a description, in verse, of the plague of London, 1666. [ii. 272]

AUSTIN, WILLIAM (1754-1793), physician; B.A. Wadham College, Oxford, 1776; lectured on Arabic; studied medicine at St.Bartholomew's Hospital; M.A.,1780, and M.D., 1783; practised at Oxford; professor of chemistry and physician to Radcliffe Infirmary, 1785; physician to St. Bartholomew's, 1786; F.C.P., 1787; delivered (1790) Gulstonian Lectures, which were published 1791.
[ii. 272]

AUSTIN, WILLIAM (1721-1820), engraver and draughtsman; his plates, chiefly landscapes, of small merit; during latter years of life taught drawing in London and Brighton. [ii. 273]

AUVERQUERQUE, COUNT OF (1641-1708). [See NASSAU, HENRY.]

AVANDALE, first BARON (*d.* 1488). [See STEWART, ANDREW.]

AVELING, THOMAS WILLIAM BAXTER (*d.*1884), minister of Kingsland congregational church, 1838-84; chairman of Congregational Union, 1876. [ii. 274]

AVERELL, ADAM (1754-1847), Irish primitive Wesleyan minister; educated at Trinity College, Dublin; ordained by Bishop Cope, 1777; adopted evangelical views under the influence of Wesley; curate to Dr. Ledwich at Aghaboe, 1789-91; president of primitive Wesleyan methodist conference, 1818-41. [ii. 274]

AVERY, BENJAMIN (*d.* 1764), presbyterian minister; abandoned ministry in consequence of Salters' Hall controversy on subscription (1719), and became physician; treasurer, Guy's hospital; trustee, Dr. Williams's Library, 1728-64; LL.D. [ii. 274]

AVERY, JOHN? (*fl.* 1695), pirate; established himself at Perim and levied a toll on all ships passing through Red Sea; disbanded his crew in West Indies, and possibly lived in hiding in England. [ii. 275]

AVESBURY, ROBERT OF (*fl.* 1350). [See ROBERT.]

AVERSHAWE, LOUIS JEREMIAH (1773 ?-1795). [See ABERSHAW.]

AVISON, CHARLES (1710 ?-1770), musician; studied in Italy; organist of St. Nicholas, Newcastle, 1736-70; published music and an 'Essay on Musical Expression,' 1752. [ii. 275]

AVONMORE, VISCOUNTS. [See YELVERTON, BARRY, first VISCOUNT,1736-1805; YELVERTON,WILLIAM CHARLES, fourth VISCOUNT, 1824-1883.]

AWDELAY, JOHN (*fl.* 1426), canon of monastery of Haghmon, Shropshire; wrote verses, chiefly devotional.
[ii. 275]

AWDELAY or **AWDELEY,** JOHN, otherwise called JOHN SAMPSON or SAMPSON AWDELAY (*fl.* 1559-1577), London printer and miscellaneous writer; freeman of Stationers' Company, 1559; printed, 1561-77, ballads, news-sheets, and religious tracts, many, including 'Fraternitye of Vacabondes' (1565), being of his own composition. [ii. 276]

AXTEL, DANIEL (*d.* 1600), parliamentarian; of good family, but a grocer's apprentice; entered parliamentary army and rose to rank of lieutenant-colonel; commanded soldiers at king's trial at Westminster; accompanied Cromwell to Ireland; returned to England before the Restoration; executed for being concerned in king's death. [ii. 276]

AYLESBURY, SIR THOMAS (1576-1657), patron of mathematical learning; M.A. Christ Church, Oxford, 1605; secretary to the Earl of Nottingham, lord high admiral of England; baronet and master of mint, 1627; cashiered as a royalist, 1642; retired to continent, 1652.
[ii. 277]

AYLESBURY, THOMAS (*fl.* 1622-1659), theologian; M.A. and B.D. Cambridge and Oxford; published several Calvinistic works. [ii. 278]

AYLESBURY, WILLIAM (1615-1656), translator; son of Sir Thomas Aylesbury [q. v.]; B.A. Christ Church, Oxford, 1631; travelled in France and Italy, as tutor to Duke of Buckingham and his brother, in whose service he continued till defeat of royalists; retired to continent on fall of Charles; returned to England, 1650; secretary to governor of Jamaica, 1656; published, at Charles I's request, translation of Davila's 'History of French Civil Wars.' [ii. 278]

AYLESFORD, first EARL OF (1647 ?-1719). [See FINCH, HENEAGE.]

AYLETT, ROBERT (1583-1655 ?), religious poet; LL.D. Trinity Hall, Cambridge, 1614; published religious verse, including a volume entitled 'Divine and Moral Speculations,' 1654. [ii. 279]

AYLIFFE, JOHN (1676-1732), jurist; educated at Winchester and New College, Oxford; M.A., 1703; LL.B. and LL.D. 1710; proctor in chancellor's court; published 'Ancient and Present State of University of Oxford,' 1714, and, in consequence of certain allegations contained in it, was expelled from the university and deprived of his privileges and degrees: published (1726 and 1732) two treatises on 'Canon Law' and 'Civil Law.' His 'New Pandect of Roman Civil Law' appeared posthumously, 1734. [ii. 279]

AYLMER, CHARLES (1786-1847), Irish jesuit; entered Society of Jesus, Stonyhurst College, Lancashire; rector, Clongowes College, Ireland, 1817; superior of Dublin Residence, 1816, 1822, and 1829; D.D. [ii. 281]

AYLMER, JOHN (1521-1594), bishop of London; B.A. Queens' College, Cambridge, 1541; chaplain to Henry Grey, marquis of Dorset; tutor to Lady Jane Grey; archdeacon of Stow, 1553; deprived of preferments for opposing in convocation doctrine of transubstantiation, and fled to continent; returned to England, 1558; archdeacon of Lincoln, 1562; D.D. Oxford, 1573; bishop of London, 1577; became very unpopular owing to his arbitrary and unconciliatory disposition; his published writings are chiefly sermons and devotional works. [ii. 281]

AYLMER, MATTHEW, BARON AYLMER (*d.* 1720), naval commander-in-chief; lieutenant, 1678; captain in the Mediterranean, 1679-89; commander in battle off Beachy Head, 1690; commander-in-chief at Barfleur, 1692; rear-admiral, 1693; vice-admiral, 1693, and commander-in-chief, 1698, 'in Mediterranean; commander-in-chief of fleet, 1709-11 and 1714-20. [ii. 283]

AYLOFFE, JOHN (*d.* 1685), satirist; wrote 'Marvell's Ghost,' a satire against the Stuarts; possibly executed for complicity in Rye House plot. [ii. 284]

AYLOFFE, SIR JOSEPH (1709-1781), baronet; antiquary; educated at Westminster, Lincoln's Inn, and St. John's College, Oxford; F.S.A. and F.R.S., 1732; member of 'Gentlemen's Society at Spalding,' 1739; secretary for commission superintending erection of Westminster Bridge, 1736-7; one of the three keepers of state papers, 1763; for many years vice-president of Society of Antiquaries, to whose journal, 'Archæologia,' he contributed largely; published 'Calendars of the Ancient Charters,' 1772, and projected topographical and other works which met with little support. [ii. 284]

AYLOFFE, WILLIAM (*d.* 1585), lawyer; called to bar at Lincoln's Inn, 1560; 'reader' at his inn, 1571; serjeant-at-law, 1577; was judge of queen's bench in 1579. [ii. 285]

AYLWARD, THEODORE (1730–1801), musician; member Royal Society of Musicians, 1763; professor of music, Gresham College, 1771; organist, St. George's Chapel, Windsor, 1788; Mus. Doc. Oxford, 1791 [ii. 286]

AYLWORTH, WILLIAM (1625–1679). [See HARCOURT.]

AYMER or **ÆTHELMÆR** (ETHELMAR) DE VALENCE, or DE LUSIGNAN (d. 1260), bishop of Winchester; son of Isabella, widow of King John, by Hugh X, Count of La Marche; came to England, 1247; received several livings from Henry III; elected bishop of Winchester, 1250; election confirmed by Innocent IV, 1251; incurred Henry III's anger by refusing to be bound by the grant to the king of a tenth of the clergy's income for three years; made himself generally unpopular by his violent behaviour; sent on an embassy to France, 1257; nominated by Henry on committee created by parliament of Oxford for redress of grievances, 1258; his property seized on his refusing to swear to provisions there drawn up; retired to France and died in Paris. [ii. 286]

AYMER DE VALENCE, EARL OF PEMBROKE (d. 1324), nephew of Bishop Aymer (d. 1260) [q. v.]; succeeded to earldom, 1296; served in Flanders, 1297, and in Scotland, 1298; guardian of Scotland, 1306–7; led van of Edward II's army against Bruce, 1306; defeated Scots at Ruthven, 1306, and was defeated at Loudon Hill, 1307; sided with Lancaster against Edward II, but went over to the court party, 1312; lieutenant of Scotland; shared in king's defeat at Bannockburn, 1314; largely responsible for formal peace between Thomas, earl of Lancaster, and Edward II, 1318; accompanied expedition to Scotland, 1323; died at Paris on embassy to Charles IV. [ii. 288]

AYREMINNE or **AYERMIN**, RICHARD DE (d. 1340?), diocesan chancellor; keeper of rolls, 1324; chancellor of diocese of Norwich, 1325, and of Salisbury, 1339; clerk of privy seal, 1327. [ii. 290]

AYREMINNE or **AYERMIN**, WILLIAM DE (d. 1336), bishop of Norwich; elder brother of Richard de Ayreminne [q. v.]; master of rolls, 1316–24; made guardian for life of Jewish converts' house, 1317; captured by Scottish invaders, 1319, but released a few months later; papal nominee to the bishopric of Norwich, and consecrated against King Edward II's wish, in France, 1325; treasurer to Edward III, 1331. [ii. 290]

AYRES, JOHN (fl. 1680–1700), penman; footman to William Ashurst, lord mayor of London (1693–4), who paid for his education; became teacher of writing and accounts, St. Paul's Churchyard; introduced the Italian hand into England between 1680 and 1700; he executed and published many caligraphic works, including 'A Tutor to Penmanship,' 1698. [ii. 291]

AYRES, PHILIP (1638–1712), pamphleteer and writer; educated at Westminster and St. John's College, Oxford; private tutor in Buckinghamshire; published many translations and original works in verse and prose. [ii. 292]

AYRTON, ACTON SMEE (1816–1886), politician; practised as solicitor at Bombay; called to bar at Middle Temple, 1853; liberal M.P. for Tower Hamlets, 1857–74; parliamentary secretary to treasury, 1868–9; privy councillor, 1869; first commissioner of works, 1869–73; judge-advocate-general, 1873–4. [Suppl. i. 89]

AYRTON, EDMUND (1734–1808), musician; organist of Southwell Minster, 1754; gentleman of Chapel Royal, vicar choral of St. Paul's Cathedral, and lay vicar of Westminster, 1764; member Royal Society of Musicians, 1765; master of children of Chapel Royal, 1780–1805; Mus. Doc. [ii. 292]

AYRTON, MATILDA CHAPLIN (1846–1883), medical student; née Chaplin; studied at London Medical College for Women; took high honours at extramural examinations at Surgeons' Hall, Edinburgh, 1870 and 1871; B. ès. Sc. and B. ès. L. Paris, 1871; opened and lectured in a school for native midwives in Japan, 1873; M.D. Paris, 1879; licentiate, King and Queen's College of Physicians, Ireland; worked at Royal Free Hospital, London, and at Algiers and Montpellier. [ii. 292]

AYRTON, WILLIAM (1777–1858), musical writer; F.R.S., F.S.A.; son of Edmund Ayrton [q. v.]; musical director of the King's Theatre, 1817 and 1821; edited the 'Harmonicon,' 1823–33; published 'Musical Library,' 1834–6. [ii. 293]

AYSCOUGH, ANNE (1521–1546). [See ASKEW, ANNE.]

AYSCOUGH, FRANCIS (1700–1763), divine; M.A. Corpus Christi College, Oxford, 1723; took orders; fellow, 1729; D.D., 1735; clerk of closet to Prince Frederick, 1740; preceptor to Prince George (George III); dean of Bristol, 1761. [ii. 294]

AYSCOUGH, GEORGE EDWARD (d. 1779), dramatist and traveller; son of Francis Ayscough [q. v.]; produced version of Voltaire's 'Semiramis,' Drury Lane, 1776; published account of travels in Italy. [ii. 294]

AYSCOUGH, SAMUEL (1745–1804), librarian and index-maker; once working miller; overseer of street paviors, 1770; bookseller's assistant and assistant in cataloguing department of British Museum; published catalogue of undescribed manuscripts in British Museum, 1782; assistant librarian, c. 1785; ordained curate of Normanton-on-Soar, Nottinghamshire; assistant curate, St. Giles's-in-the-Fields; compiled index to 'Monthly Review,' 1786 (continued, 1796); joint compiler of catalogue of books in British Museum, 1787; F.S.A., 1789; published 'Index to Shakespeare,' 1790; delivered the annual Fairfield Lectures, 1790–1804; prepared catalogues (still unpublished) of ancient rolls and charters in British Museum, 1787–92; vicar of Cudham, Kent, c. 1803. [ii. 294]

AYSCOUGH, WILLIAM (d. 1450), bishop of Salisbury; prebendary of Lincoln Cathedral, 1436–8; bishop of Salisbury, 1438; Henry VI's confessor; lived continually at court, and thus caused such discontent in his diocese that on visiting it he was murdered at Edington, Wiltshire, after saying mass; LL.D. [ii. 297]

AYSCU or **AYSCOUGH,** EDWARD (fl. 1633), historian; B.A. Christ's College, Cambridge, 1590; published, 1607, history of relations between England and Scotland from William I to the Union. [ii. 298]

AYSCUE, SIR GEORGE (fl. 1646–1671), admiral; knighted by Charles I; was a captain in 1646; appointed admiral of Irish seas under parliament, 1649; actively engaged in relief of Dublin when besieged by Ormonde, 1649; assisted in reduction of Scilly, 1651; reduced Barbados and Virginian settlements, 1651–2; defeated Dutch in the Downs, and engaged them off Plymouth, the result being indecisive, 1652; superseded in his command but pensioned, 1652; commanded Swedish fleet, 1658; appointed a commissioner of the navy at Restoration; in second Dutch war (1664–6) successively rear-admiral, admiral of the blue, and admiral of the white; prisoner in Holland, 1666–7; probably did not serve again after return to England, 1667. [ii. 298]

AYTON, RICHARD (1786–1823), miscellaneous writer; educated for bar, but did not enter the profession; wrote and adapted plays, some of which were produced with moderate success; his essays published 1825. [ii. 299]

AYTON or **AYTOUN,** SIR ROBERT (1570–1638), poet; M.A. St. Andrews, 1588; travelled on continent; studied civil law at Paris; returned to England, 1603; gentleman of bedchamber and private secretary to the queen; knighted, 1612; ambassador to Germany to deliver the king's 'Apology'; competed for provostship of Eton, which fell to Wotton, 1623; master of the royal hospital of St. Katherine, 1636; buried in Westminster Abbey; wrote poems, of no extraordinary merit, in Latin, Greek, French, and English. [ii. 300]

AYTOUN, WILLIAM EDMONDSTOUNE (1813–1865), poet; educated at Edinburgh Academy and University; studied German literature in Aschaffenburg; admitted writer of the signet, 1835; called to Scottish bar, 1840; collaborated with (Sir) Theodore Martin in 'Bon Gaultier Ballads,' published 1845; joined staff of 'Blackwood's Magazine,' to which he contributed largely, 1844; professor of rhetoric and belles-lettres, Edinburgh, 1845; sheriff of Orkney, 1852; hon. D.C.L. Oxford, 1853; published 'Firmilian,' a dramatic poem, 1854, his annotated collection of 'Ballads of Scotland,' 1858, and (jointly with (Sir) Theodore Martin) 'Poems and Ballads of Goethe,' 1858. [ii. 302]

B

BAALUN or BALUN, JOHN DE (*d.* 1235), justice itinerant for Gloucestershire, 1225 ; accompanied John to Ireland, 1210 ; lost his lands for taking part in barons' war. [ii. 303]

BAALUN or BALUN, ROGER DE (*d.* 1226), justice itinerant appointed by Henry III. [ii. 303]

BAAN. [See DE BAAN.]

BABBAGE, CHARLES (1792–1871), mathematician and scientific mechanician ; M.A. Peterhouse, Cambridge, 1817 ; F.R.S., 1816 ; took part in foundation of Astronomical Society, 1820 ; secretary till 1824, and, later, successively vice-president, foreign secretary, and member of council ; obtained government grant for making a calculating machine based on 'method of differences,' 1823, but the work of construction ceased, owing to disagreements with the engineer ; offered the government (1834) an improved design, which was refused (1842) on grounds of expense ; devoted thirty-seven years of his life and a large share of his fortune to the perfecting of this machine ; Lucasian professor of mathematics, Cambridge, 1828–39, but delivered no lectures : principal founder of Statistical Society, 1834 ; published several scientific works, including 'Economy of Manufactures,' 1832, and 'Table of Logarithms,' 1827. [ii. 304]

BABELL or BABEL, WILLIAM (1690 ?–1723), private musician to George I ; pupil of Dr. Pepusch ; organist, All Hallows, Bread Street ; arranged many popular airs for the harpsichord. [ii. 307]

BABER, EDWARD COLBORNE (1843–1890), Chinese scholar ; educated at Christ's Hospital and Magdalene College, Cambridge ; B.A., 1867 ; student interpreter at Peking, 1866 ; first-class assistant, 1872 ; vice-consul at Tamsuy, Formosa, 1872 ; Chinese secretary of legation at Peking, 1879 ; consul-general in Korea, 1885–6 ; political resident at Bhamô. He made and described three journeys into the interior of China. [Suppl. i. 89]

BABER, HENRY HERVEY (1775–1869), philologist ; M.A. Oxford, 1805 ; keeper of printed books at British Museum, 1812–37 ; rector of Stretham, Cambridgeshire, 1827–69. [ii. 307]

BABER, SIR JOHN (1625–1704), physician to Charles II ; M.B. Christ's College, Oxford, 1646 ; M.D. Leyden, 1648, and Oxford, 1650 ; F.C.P., 1657 ; knight and physician to the king, 1660. [ii. 307]

BABINGTON, ANTHONY (1561–1586), catholic conspirator ; page to Mary Queen of Scots, *c.* 1579 ; came to London and made many friends of his own creed at court ; assisted in forming a secret society for protection of jesuits in England, 1580 ; travelled on continent, where he made acquaintance of Mary Stuart's emissaries ; induced by Ballard, a catholic priest, to organise a catholic conspiracy to murder Elizabeth and release Mary, 1586 ; detected by Walsingham's spies, and after attempting to save himself by giving information, fled in disguise, and was finally captured and taken to the Tower ; executed with Ballard and other conspirators. Mary's complicity in this conspiracy brought about her own execution. [ii. 308]

BABINGTON, BENJAMIN GUY (1794–1866), physician and linguist ; midshipman, but left navy for Indian civil service ; appointed to Madras presidency ; returned from India owing to weak health ; studied medicine at Guy's Hospital and Cambridge ; M.D., 1830 ; F.C.P., 1831 ; physician at Guy's Hospital, 1840–58 ; F.R.S. ; president Royal Medical and Chirurgical Society, 1861 ; member of medical council of general board of health ; published medical works, and works on and translations from German and oriental languages. [ii. 311]

BABINGTON, BRUTE (*d.* 1610), bishop ; B.A. and fellow, Christ's College, Cambridge, 1576 ; incorporated at Oxford, 1578 ; prebendary of Lichfield, 1592 ; bishop of Derry, 1610. [ii. 312]

BABINGTON, CHARLES CARDALE (1808–1895), botanist and archæologist ; educated at Charterhouse ; B.A. St. John's College, Cambridge, 1830 ; M.A., 1833 ; fellow, 1882 ; one of the founders of Entomological Society, 1833 ; after many botanical excursions in British Isles he published a 'Manual of British Botany,' 1843 ; founder, 1836, and for fifty-five years secretary of the Ray Club ; assisted in founding Cambridge Antiquarian Society, 1840 ; edited 'Annals and Magazine of Natural History' from 1842 ; professor of botany at Cambridge, 1861 ; fellow of Linnean and Geological Societies ; F.S.A., 1859 ; F.R.S., 1851 ; his works include 'Flora of Cambridgeshire,' 1860, and 'The British Rubi,' 1869. [Suppl. i. 90]

BABINGTON, CHURCHILL (1821–1889), archæologist ; B.A. St. John's College, Cambridge, 1843 ; elected fellow and ordained, 1846 ; M.A., 1846 ; B.D., 1853 ; D.D., 1879 ; honorary fellow, 1880 ; Disney professor of archæology at Cambridge, 1865 ; rector of Cockfield, Suffolk, 1866 ; published works on numismatics, botany, and ornithology, and edited 'Orations of Hyperides,' 1850–3. [Suppl. i. 92]

BABINGTON, FRANCIS (*d.* 1569), divine ; M.A. Cambridge, 1552 ; fellow, All Souls, Oxford, and proctor, 1557 ; master of Balliol, 1559 ; rector of Lincoln College, 1560 ; vice-chancellor, 1560–2 ; Lady Margaret reader in divinity, 1561 ; chaplain to Earl of Leicester ; resigned rectorship of Lincoln, being suspected of clandestine Roman catholicism, and fled the country, 1563. [ii. 312]

BABINGTON, GERVASE (1550 ?–1610), bishop ; fellow, Trinity College, Cambridge ; M.A. Oxford, 1578 ; prebendary of Hereford ; treasurer of Llandaff, 1590 ; bishop of Llandaff, 1591, of Exeter, 1595, and of Worcester, 1597 ; queen's counsel for marches of Wales ; summoned to Hampton Court conference, 1604 ; published several religious works. [ii. 313]

BABINGTON, HUMFREY (1615–1691), divine ; D.D. (1669) and vice-master, Trinity College, Cambridge ; rector of Boothby Painel, Lincolnshire. [ii. 314]

BABINGTON, JOHN (*fl.* 1635), author of a volume dealing with geometry and the use of fireworks for military purposes, published in 1635. [ii. 314]

BABINGTON, SIR WILLIAM (*d.* 1455), judge ; king's attorney, 1414 ; serjeant-at-law, 1415, but neglected to appear to writ until compelled by parliamentary order, 1417 ; chief baron of exchequer, 1419 ; justice, 1420, and chief-justice, 1423, of common bench ; retired, 1436. [ii. 315]

BABINGTON, WILLIAM (1756–1833), physician and mineralogist ; apprenticed to practitioner in Londonderry, and subsequently studied at Guy's Hospital, London ; assistant surgeon, Haslar Naval Hospital, 1777 ; apothecary, 1781, and physician, 1795–1811, to Guy's Hospital ; M.D. Aberdeen, 1795 ; hon. M.D. Dublin, 1831 ; one of the founders and, in 1822, president of Geological Society ; F.R.S. ; published geological and chemical works. [ii. 315]

BABYON, or BABYO, or BABION, PETER (*fl.*1317–1366), divine ; renowned as writer of elegant verse and prose in Edward II's reign ; wrote also religious works. [ii. 316]

BACHE, FRANCIS EDWARD (1833–1858), musician ; son of Samuel Bache [q. v.] ; played violin at Birmingham festival, 1846 and 1847 ; organist of All Saints' Church, Gordon Square, 1850 ; visited Leipzig, Paris, Algiers, and Rome, 1853–7 ; composed numerous pianoforte pieces. [ii. 317]

BACHE, SAMUEL (1804–1876), unitarian minister ; minister at Old Meeting, Dudley, 1829–32 ; joint-minister in Birmingham at New Meeting, 1832–62, and at Church of the Messiah, 1862–8 ; took part in establishing Hospital Sunday, 1859 ; published religious works. [ii. 317]

BACHE, SARAH (1771 ?–1844), hymn-writer ; kept Islington school at Birmingham ; author of the hymn 'See how he loved.' [ii. 318]

BACHHOFFNER, GEORGE HENRY (1810–1879), one of the founders (1837) of London Polytechnic Institution, where he lectured on scientific subjects. [ii. 318]

BACK, SIR GEORGE (1796–1878), admiral and Arctic navigator ; midshipman, 1808 ; captured by French at Deba, 1809 ; returned to England, 1814 ; served against French on North American station ; admiralty mate,

1817; accompanied Franklin on voyage of discovery to Spitzbergen seas, 1818, and in expeditions to Coppermine river, 1819-22, and Mackenzie river, 1824-7; lieutenant, 1822; commander, 1827; led exploring expedition to Great Fish river, 1833-5; captain, and gold medallist, Geographical Society, 1835; commanded an expedition to complete coast-line between Regent's Inlet and Cape Turnagain, 1836; received in 1837 both medals of Geographical Society, of which he was subsequently vice-president and member of council; knighted, 1839; admiral, 1857; F.R.S.; published accounts of his voyages.   [ii. 318]

BACKHOUSE, EDWARD (1808-1879), quaker; wrote 'Early Church History,' published posthumously, 1884.   [ii. 320]

BACKHOUSE, WILLIAM (1593-1662), Rosicrucian philosopher; educated at Christ Church, Oxford; adopted Elias Ashmole as his son; left in manuscript (Ashmol. MSS.) translations in verse and prose of French works on occult philosophy.   [ii. 320]

BACKWELL, EDWARD (d. 1683), London goldsmith and banker at Unicorn, Lombard Street; probably chief; originator of system of banknotes; had financial dealings with Cromwell; alderman for Bishopsgate ward, 1657; sent to Paris to receive money for sale of Dunkirk to French, 1662; after treaty at Dover, 1670, was a frequent intermediary in money transactions between Charles II and Louis; sued by several creditors, a large sum being due to him from the exchequer, which Charles II had just closed, 1672; took refuge temporarily in Holland after judgment had been given against him; M.P. for Wendover, 1679 and 1680.   [ii. 321]

BACON, ANN, LADY (1528-1610), mother of Francis Bacon [q. v.]; associated with her father, Sir Anthony Cooke, as governess when he was tutor to Edward VI; married Sir Nicholas Bacon [q. v.] c. 1557; won great repute for her learning; translated Bishop Jewel's 'Apologie for the Church of England,' 1564.   [ii. 323]

BACON, ANTHONY (1558-1601), diplomatist, elder son of Sir Nicholas and Ann Bacon [q. v.]; educated at Trinity College, Cambridge, 1573-5; 'ancient' of Gray's Inn, 1576; at Burghley's suggestion toured on continent in search of political intelligence, 1579-92; M.P. for Wallingford, 1593; entered service of Earl of Essex, 1593, and became his private 'under-secretary of state for foreign affairs,' in which capacity he was in communication with spies and ambassadors in all parts of Europe; lived with Essex at Essex House, by the Strand, 1595-1600; M.P. for Oxford, 1597; he was generous beyond his means, and frequently in embarrassed circumstances.   [ii. 324]

BACON, EDWARD (d. 1618), sheriff of Suffolk; third son of Sir Nicholas Bacon [q. v.], 'ancient' of Gray's Inn, 1576; M.P. successively for Yarmouth, Tavistock, Weymouth, and Suffolk; sheriff of Suffolk, 1601; knighted 1603.   [ii. 371]

BACON, FRANCIS, first BARON VERULAM and VISCOUNT ST. ALBANS (1561-1626), lord chancellor; younger son of Sir Nicholas Bacon (1509-1579) [q. v.]; educated at Trinity College, Cambridge, 1573-5; admitted to Gray's Inn, 1576; attached to embassy of Sir Amias Paulet to France, 1576-9; utter barrister, 1582; M.P., Melcombe Regis, 1584; wrote 'Letter of Advice to Queen Elizabeth,' urging strong measures against catholics, c. 1584; M.P., Taunton, and bencher of Gray's Inn, 1586; M.P., Liverpool, 1589; made acquaintance of Earl of Essex, who subsequently treated him with great generosity, c. 1591; M.P., Middlesex, 1593; queen's counsel, 1596; published 'Essays,' 1597; M.P., Southampton, 1597; appointed, among others, to investigate causes of Essex's revolt, 1601; nominated king's counsel and knighted by James I, 1603; one of the commissioners for arrangement of union with Scotland, and confirmed as king's counsel, 1604; published 'Advancement of Learning,' 1605; married Alice Barnham, 1606; solicitor-general, 1607; published 'De Sapientia Veterum,' 1609; supported James's claims in connection with the 'great contract,' by which the king was to receive a fixed income in exchange for that derived from feudal tenures and other sources, 1610; attorney-general, 1613; chief prosecutor at trial of Somerset, 1616; privy councillor, 1616; lord-keeper, 1617; wrote 'New Atlantis' between 1614 and 1618; lord-chancellor and raised to peerage as Baron Verulam, 1618; took court side in prosecution of Raleigh (1618), of Suffolk (1619), and of

Yelverton (1620); published 'Novum Organum,' 1620; made Viscount St. Albans, 1621; charged before House of Lords with bribery; confessed that he was guilty of 'corruption and neglect'; deprived of great seal, fined, condemned to confinement during the king's pleasure, and disabled from sitting in parliament; remained in Tower only a few days, the fine being subsequently assigned by the king to trustees for Bacon's own use; published 'Life of Henry VII,' 1622, 'De Augmentis Scientiarum' (the 'Advancement of Learning' completed and translated into Latin), 1623, and an enlarged edition of the 'Essays,' 1625; engaged on 'Sylva Sylvarum' at the time of his death.

Bacon's works may be divided into three classes, the philosophical (which form by far the greatest portion), the literary, and the professional works. The principal and best known of the philosophical works are: (1) the 'Advancement of Learning,' published in English in 1605; (2) the 'Novum Organum,' published in Latin in 1620, under the general title 'Francisci de Verulamio . . . Instauratio Magna,' with a second title (after the preface) 'Pars secunda operis, quæ dicitur Novum Organum sive indicia vera de interpretatione naturæ'; and (3) the 'De Augmentis,' published in Latin in 1623 with the title 'Opera F. Baconis de Verulamio . . . Tomus primus, qui continet de Dignitate et Augmentis Scientiarum libros ix.' It was Bacon's ambition to create a new system of philosophy, based on a right interpretation of nature, to replace that of Aristotle; the 'Novum Organum' describes the method by which the renovation of knowledge was to be achieved, and is thus the keystone to the whole system. The 'Advancement of Learning,' of which the 'De Augmentis' may be regarded as an enlarged edition, was included in the 'Great Instauration' as a preliminary review of the present state of knowledge. Of Bacon's literary works, the most important are the 'Essays,' first published in 1597, and issued in final form, 1625; 'De Sapientia Veterum,' published in 1609; 'Apophthegms New and Old,' published in 1624; and the 'History of Henry the Seventh,' 1622. The largest and most important of his professional works are the treatises entitled 'Maxims of the Law' and 'Reading on the Statute of Uses.'   [ii. 328]

BACON, SIR FRANCIS (1587-1657), judge; studied at Barnard's Inn and Gray's Inn; called to bar at Gray's Inn, 1615; autumn reader, 1634; serjeant at law, 1640; knighted and appointed judge of king's bench, 1642; sole judge at trial of Lord Macguire, 1645; retired after Charles's execution.   [ii. 360]

BACON, SIR JAMES (1798-1895), judge; called to the bar at Gray's Inn, 1827; member, 1833, and barrister, 1845, of Lincoln's Inn; bencher, 1846; treasurer, 1869; took silk, 1846; under-secretary and secretary of causes to master of rolls, 1859; commissioner in bankruptcy for London district, 1868; chief judge under Bankruptcy Act, 1869-83; vice-chancellor, 1870-86; knighted, 1871; privy councillor, 1886.   [Suppl. i. 93]

BACON, JOHN (d. 1321), judge; attorney to Queen Eleanor, 1279; guardian of Ledes Castle, Kent, 1291; justice of common pleas, 1313; served on several legal commissions.   [ii. 361]

BACON, JOHN (d. 1346). [See BACONTHORPE.]

BACON, JOHN, R.A. (1740-1799), sculptor; apprenticed as modeller in china factory, 1754-62; later in an artificial stone factory; student at Royal Academy, on its foundation, 1768, and received the first gold medal awarded for sculpture, 1769; gold medallist, Society of Arts, and A.R.A., 1770. Among his works may be mentioned the monuments to Pitt in Westminster Abbey and to Dr. Johnson in St. Paul's Cathedral.   [ii. 361]

BACON, JOHN (1738-1816), junior, and afterwards senior, clerk in first-fruits department of Queen Anne's Bounty office; published improved edition of Ecton's 'Thesaurus rerum ecclesiasticarum.'   [ii. 362]

BACON, JOHN (1777-1859), sculptor; son of John Bacon, R.A. [q. v.]; gold medallist, Royal Academy, 1794; executed monuments in Westminster Abbey and St. Paul's Cathedral.   [ii. 362]

BACON, MONTAGU (1688-1749), scholar and critic; fellow-commoner Trinity College, Cambridge, 1705; M.A. per literas regias, 1734; rector of Newbold Verdun, 1743; wrote 'Critical, Historical, and Explanatory Notes upon Hudibras,' published 1752.   [ii. 363]

BACON, NATHANIEL (*d.* 1622), sheriff of Norfolk; second son of Sir Nicholas Bacon [q. v.]; 'ancient' of Gray's Inn, 1576; M.P. successively for Tavistock, Norfolk, and Lynn; sheriff of Norfolk, 1599; knighted, 1604. [ii. 371]

BACON, SIR NATHANIEL (*fl.* 1640), painter; grandson of Sir Nicholas Bacon [q. v.]; M.A. Corpus Christi College, Cambridge, 1628; studied painting in Italy; K.B., 1625. [ii. 364]

BACON, NATHANIEL (1593–1660), puritan; half-brother of Francis Bacon and son of Sir Nicholas Bacon [q. v.]; entered Gray's Inn, 1611; bencher; called to bar, 1617; J.P. for Essex; recorder of Ipswich, and perhaps of Bury St. Edmunds; member of Suffolk committee for defence against royalists; M.P. for Cambridge University, 1645, and for Ipswich, 1658 and 1660; master of requests during Richard Cromwell's protectorate. Published 'Historical Discovery of the Uniformity of the Government of England from Edward III to Elizabeth,' 1647 and 1651, and was possibly author of 'A Relation of the fearful Estate of Francis Spira,' 1638. [ii. 364]

BACON, *alias* SOUTHWELL, NATHANIEL (1598–1676). [See SOUTHWELL.]

BACON, NATHANIEL (1642?–1676), Virginian patriot; entered Gray's Inn, 1664; emigrated to Virginia and settled at Curles; member of governor's council; chosen general of colonist volunteers, but marched against Indians before receiving his commission and was declared rebel; arrested, but set at liberty; subsequently sat in assembly, which passed 'Bacon's Laws.' [ii. 365]

BACON, SIR NICHOLAS (1509–1579), lord-keeper; entered Corpus Christi College, Cambridge, 1523; bible-clerk; B.A., 1527; journeyed to Paris; called to bar at Gray's Inn, 1533; 'ancient,' 1536; bencher, 1550; treasurer, 1552; solicitor of court of augmentations, 1537; solicitor of Cambridge University; attorney of court of wards and liveries, 1546; high steward of St. Albans; lord-keeper of great seal, 1558; privy councillor and knight; received patent to exercise jurisdiction of lord chancellor, 1559; advocated stringent measures against Mary Stuart, though as president of conferences held in 1568 and 1570 to consider her relations with England and Scotland he was judicially impartial; opposed her marriage to Duke of Norfolk, 1569, and her proposed restoration, 1570; supported bill for expulsion of all French denizens from England, 1572; buried in St. Paul's Cathedral. [ii. 366]

BACON, NICHOLAS (*d.* 1624), high sheriff of Suffolk; eldest son of Sir Nicholas Bacon [q. v.]; 'ancient,' Gray's Inn, 1576; knighted, 1578; high sheriff of Suffolk, 1581; M.P., Suffolk, 1572–83; created premier baronet of England, 1611. [ii. 371]

BACON, PHANUEL (1700–1783), divine and dramatist; M.A. Magdalen College, Oxford, 1722; B.D., 1731; D.D., 1735; vicar of Bramber, Sussex, and rector of Balden, Oxfordshire; wrote humorous verse, and five plays. [ii. 371]

BACON, PHILEMON (*d.* 1666), naval captain; fought in actions with Dutch off Lowestoft and North Foreland, in the second of which he was killed. [ii. 372]

BACON, RICHARD MACKENZIE (1775–1844), musician and journalist; edited 'Norwich Mercury' from 1816 till death; obtained with Bryan Donkin a patent for improvements in printing, 1813; proprietor and editor of 'Quarterly Musical Magazine,' 1818–28; published many biographical, musical, and miscellaneous works. [ii. 372]

BACON, ROBERT (*d.* 1248), first Dominican writer in England; brother or uncle of Roger Bacon; studied at Oxford and Paris; perhaps treasurer of Salisbury Cathedral, 1233, being a member of the Dominican order and lecturer in its schools at Oxford; publicly rebuked Henry III for his fondness for foreign favourites, notably Peter de Roches, 1233; wrote among other works a life of Edmund Rich. [ii. 373]

BACON, ROGER (1214?–1294), philosopher; studied at Oxford and Paris, where he probably graduated doctor; returned to England *c.* 1250; and probably remained at Oxford till *c.* 1257, when he incurred the suspicion of the Franciscan order, to which he belonged, and was sent under superveillance to Paris, where he remained in confinement ten years; produced at request of Pope Clement IV treatises on the sciences (grammar, logic, mathematics,

physics, and modern philosophy)—'Opus Majus,' and, perhaps, 'Opus Secundum' and 'Opus Tertium'; again in confinement for his heretical propositions, *c.* 1278–92; said to have died and to have been buried at Oxford; wrote also on chemistry and alchemy. [ii. 374]

BACON, THOMAS (*fl.* 1336), justice of common pleas; raised to king's bench, 1332. [ii. 378]

BACON, *alias* SOUTHWELL, THOMAS (1592–1637), jesuit. [See SOUTHWELL.]

BACON, THOMAS (*fl.* 1795), sculptor; brother of John Bacon (1777–1859) [q. v.]; exhibited at the Royal Academy, 1793, 1794, and 1795. [ii. 363]

BACONTHORPE, BACON, or BACHO, JOHN (*d.* 1346), the 'Resolute Doctor'; grandnephew of Roger Bacon [q. v.]; brought up at a Carmelite monastery near Walsingham; graduated at Paris; returned to Oxford, where, *c.* 1321, he preached the doctrine afterwards inculcated by Wycliffe, that priestly power was subordinate to the kingly; head of Carmelite order in England, 1329–33; went to Rome, 1333; returned to England, 1346; wrote commentaries on the bible, on Aristotle's works and treatises, and other subjects. [ii. 379]

BADBY, JOHN (*d.* 1410), lollard; blacksmith or tailor in Worcestershire; condemned before Worcester diocesan court for denial of transubstantiation, and burned at Smithfield. [ii. 381]

BADBY, WILLIAM (*d.* 1380), Carmelite; doctor of theology at Carmelite school, Oxford; confessor of John of Gaunt; appointed bishop of Worcester shortly before his death; wrote theological works. [ii. 381]

BADCOCK, JOHN (*fl.* 1816–1830), sporting writer; published under pseudonyms 'Jon Bee' and 'John Hinds,' many works on pugilism and the turf, including a dictionary of slang; edited also Samuel Foote's works. [ii. 381]

BADCOCK, SAMUEL (1747–1788), theological and literary critic; trained for dissenting ministry; minister at South Molton, Devonshire, his native town, 1778–86; joined established church; curate of Broad Clyst, and ordained deacon and priest, 1787; contributed largely to literary magazines, particularly the 'Monthly Review.' [ii. 382]

BADDELEY, ROBERT (1733–1794), comedian; cook to Foote; valet to a gentleman on 'the grand tour'; went on stage, and in 1763 joined Drury Lane company, winning reputation as exponent of foreign footmen; the original Moses in 'School for Scandal.' [ii. 383]

BADDELEY, SOPHIA (1745–1786), actress and vocalist; *née* Snow; wife of Robert Baddeley [q. v.], who introduced her to the stage; played Ophelia at Drury Lane, 1765; a popular singer at Ranelagh and Vauxhall; played in Edinburgh, 1783–5. [ii. 383]

BADDELEY, THOMAS (*fl.* 1822), Roman catholic priest; author of a tract defending Roman catholic principles. [ii. 384]

BADELEY, EDWARD LOWTH (*d.* 1868), ecclesiastical lawyer; M.A. Brasenose College, Oxford, 1828; called to bar at Inner Temple, 1841; published several tracts dealing with legal proceedings in church matters. [ii. 384]

BADENOCH, LORD OF. [See STEWART, ALEXANDER, 1343?–1405?]

BADEN-POWELL, SIR GEORGE (1847–1898). [See POWELL.]

BADEW, RICHARD (*fl.* 1320–1330), founder of University Hall, Cambridge; chancellor of Cambridge, 1326. [ii. 385]

BADGER, GEORGE PERCY (1815–1888), Arabic scholar; printer; spent youth at Malta; travelled in Arabia; studied at Church Missionary Society's Institution, Islington; priest, 1842; sent as delegate to Eastern churches, 1842–44 and 1850; published 'Nestorians and their Rituals,' 1852; government chaplain on Bombay establishment, 1845; chief chaplain to force under Sir James Outram [q. v.] in Persian expedition, 1856–7; returned to England, 1861; secretary to Sir Henry Bartle Edward Frere [q. v.] on mission to Zanzibar, 1872; created D.C.L. by archbishop of Canterbury, 1873. His works include an 'English-Arabic Lexicon,' 1881. [Suppl. i. 94]

BADHAM, CHARLES (1780–1845), medical and poetical writer; M.D. Edinburgh, 1802; L.R.C.P. London, 1803; M.A. Pembroke College, Oxford, 1812; M.D., 1817; F.R.S., and F.R.C.P., 1818; censor of College of Physicians, 1821; physician to Duke of Sussex and to Westminster general dispensary; travelled extensively in Europe; professor of physic, Glasgow, 1827; wrote Harveian oration, delivered 1840; published medical works and a verse translation of Juvenal. [ii. 385]

BADHAM, CHARLES (1813–1884), classical scholar; son of Charles Badham (1780–1845) [q. v.]; educated at Eton and Wadham College, Oxford; M.A., 1839; studied in Germany and Italy; M.A. St. Peter's College, Cambridge; ordained priest, 1848; D.D., 1852; headmaster, Louth grammar school, 1851, and of Edgbaston proprietary school, 1854; hon. Litt.D. Leyden, 1860; examiner in classics, London University, 1863; professor of classics and logic, Sydney University, 1867; died at Sydney. He published editions with notes of Plato, and some plays of Euripides, also critical essays on Shakespeare. [ii. 386]

BADHAM, CHARLES DAVID (1806–1857), naturalist; educated at Eton and Oxford; F.R.C.P.; successively held curacies in Norfolk and Suffolk; published works on natural history. [ii. 387]

BADILEY, RICHARD (d. 1657), admiral; parliamentary captain and commander-in-chief in Downs and North Sea, 1649–51; in Mediterranean, 1652; engaged the Dutch off Elba with partial success, and again, in conjunction with Appleton, off Leghorn, with disastrous results; returned home, 1653, was acquitted of blame and made rear-admiral; served on the northern coast of Africa, 1654–5; vice-admiral of fleet in Downs, 1656. [ii. 388]

BÆDA (673–735). [See BEDE.]

BAFFIN, WILLIAM (d. 1622), navigator and discoverer; probably native of London; sailed in expedition to Greenland, 1612; entered service of Muscovy company, and was chief pilot in expeditions to protect Spitzbergen fisheries, 1613 and 1614; pilot in North-West passage expedition, 1615, and on his return gave it as his opinion that a passage existed up Davis Strait; made charts of waters north of Davis Strait on a subsequent voyage, 1616, and declared that there was no North-West passage in that direction; joined service of East India Company, 1617; master's mate in Red Sea and Persian Gulf, 1617–1619; master in Persian Gulf, 1620, where he was in an engagement with Dutch and Portuguese; killed at siege of Kishm in an expedition, arranged by the Persian government, to expel Portuguese from Ormuz; wrote accounts of most of his voyages. [ii. 389]

BAGARD or **BAGGARD**, THOMAS (d. 1544), civilian; canon of his college (afterwards Christ Church), Oxford, 1525; admitted to College of Advocates, London, 1528; chancellor of diocese of Worcester, 1532; canon of Worcester, 1541. [ii. 391]

BAGE, ROBERT (1728–1801), novelist; educated at Derby, and attained proficiency in Latin; trained as paper-maker; founded paper manufactory at Elford, which he carried on till his death; continued his education and gained considerable knowledge of modern languages; he published six novels between 1781 and 1796, several of which were translated into German. [ii. 391]

BAGEHOT, WALTER (1826–1877), economist and journalist; educated at Bristol and at University College, London, under Professors Long and De Morgan; B.A. (London) with mathematical scholarship, 1846; M.A. and gold medallist in intellectual and moral philosophy and political economy, 1848; called to the bar, 1852; spent some months in Paris; entered his father's shipowning and banking business, 1852; contributed essays to 'Prospective Review,' and, after 1855, to 'National Review,' of which he was an editor; editor of 'Economist,' 1860, till death; published 'The English Constitution,' 'Physics and Politics,' and works on economical questions. [ii. 393]

BAGFORD, JOHN (1650–1716), shoemaker in London and professional collector of books; formed collection of broadsides known as the 'Bagford Ballads,' and brought together a number of title-pages and engravings, to obtain which he mutilated many rare volumes. [ii. 396]

BAGGALLAY, SIR RICHARD (1816–1888), judge; M.A. Gonville and Caius College, Cambridge, 1842; Frankland fellow, 1845–7; honorary fellow, 1880; called to the bar at Lincoln's Inn, 1843; bencher, 1861; treasurer, 1875; took silk, 1861; counsel to Cambridge University, 1869; M.P. for Hereford, 1865–8, and for Mid-Surrey, 1870–75; solicitor-general, 1868 and 1874; knighted, 1868; attorney-general, 1874; justice (afterwards lord-justice) of appeal, and privy councillor, 1875; retired from bench, 1885. [Suppl. i. 95]

BAGGERLEY, HUMPHREY (fl. 1654), royalist captain in service of James, seventh earl of Derby, of whose final hours he wrote a narrative. [ii. 396]

BAGGS, CHARLES MICHAEL (1806–1845), catholic bishop and antiquary; educated at Sedgeley Park, at St. Edmund's College, Hertfordshire, and at the English college, Rome; remained at Rome, 1824–44; won many academic honours; D.D. and ordained, 1830; teacher at English college; rector, 1840; 'cameriere d'onore' and later, monsignore to Pope Gregory XVI; bishop of Pella, 1844; vicar-apostolic of western district in England, where he arrived 1844; acquired great reputation as a controversialist at Rome; published works on ecclesiastical archæology, and dissertations on points of religious controversy. [ii. 396]

BAGNAL, SIR HENRY (1556?–1598), marshal of army in Ireland, son of Sir Nicholas Bagnal [q. v.]; educated at Jesus College, Oxford; knighted 1578; held command under Arthur Grey, baron Grey de Wilton, 1580; member for Anglesey in English parliament, 1586; marshal of the army in Ireland, and privy councillor, 1590; chief commissioner for government of Ulster, 1591; quarrelled with Hugh O'Neill, earl of Tyrone [q. v.], who had married Bagnal's sister Mabel against his wish; slain in action with Tyrone's men on Blackwater. [Suppl. i. 95]

BAGNAL, SIR NICHOLAS (1510?–1590?), marshal of army in Ireland; gentleman pensioner of Henry VIII; served in Ireland, 1539–44, and in France, 1544; marshal of army in Ireland, 1547–53; with lord-deputy, Sir Edward Bellingham [q. v.], defeated Irish, 1548; knighted, 1551; M.P. for Stoke-on-Trent, 1559; reappointed marshal, 1565, with Sir Henry Sidney [q. v.], as deputy; chief commissioner for government of Ulster, 1584; member for co. Down in Irish parliament, 1585; resigned office of marshal to his son, 1590. [Suppl. i. 96]

BAGNALL, GIBBONS (1719–1800), poetical writer; graduate of Oxford and Cambridge; vicar of Holm Lacy, Herefordshire; prebendary of Hereford, 1760; rector of Upton Bishop; vicar of Sellack, 1783; published poetical writings. [ii. 398]

BAGOT, SIR CHARLES (1781–1843), governor-general of Canada; brother of William Bagot, second baron Bagot [q. v.]; educated at Rugby and Christ Church, Oxford; M.A., 1804; entered Lincoln's Inn, 1801; M.P. for Castle Riding, 1807; parliamentary under-secretary for foreign affairs, 1807; minister plenipotentiary to France, 1814, and to United States, 1815–20; privy councillor, 1815; G.C.B., 1820; ambassador to St. Petersburg, 1820, and to the Hague, 1824; governor-general of Canada, 1841; inaugurated representative government, for which he was censured by Lord Stanley; requested recall, and died in Canada soon after arrival of his successor, Sir Charles Theophilus (afterwards baron) Metcalfe [q. v.] [Suppl. i. 98]

BAGOT, LEWIS (1740–1802), bishop; educated at Westminster and Christ Church, Oxford; M.A., 1764; canon of Christ Church, 1771; held livings in Sussex; D.C.L., 1772; bishop of Bristol, 1782; translated to Norwich, 1783, and to St. Asaph, 1790. [ii. 399]

BAGOT, RICHARD (1782–1854), bishop; educated at Rugby and Christ Church, Oxford; M.A., 1806; D.D., 1829; fellow of All Souls'; rector of Leigh, Staffordshire, 1806, and of Blithfield, 1807; canon of Windsor, 1807, and of Worcester, 1817; dean of Canterbury, 1827–45; bishop of Oxford, 1829–45, during which period he reluctantly played a part in the Oxford movement; bishop of Bath and Wells, 1845; published charges. [ii. 399]

BAGOT, SIR WILLIAM (fl. 1397), minister of Richard II; one of the 'souuerains conseillers' left in charge of the kingdom on Richard's departure for Ireland, 1399; committed to Tower after Richard's resignation. [ii. 400]

BAGOT, WILLIAM, second BARON BAGOT (1773–1856), educated at Westminster and Magdalen College, Oxford ; D.C.L., 1834 ; fellow of Society of Antiquaries and of Linnean, Horticultural, and Zoological societies. [ii. 400]

BAGSHAW, CHRISTOPHER (d. 1625 ?), priest ; B.A. and probationer fellow, Balliol College, Oxford, 1572 ; M.A., 1575 ; principal, Gloucester Hall, 1579 ; went to France, 1582 ; converted to Romanism and made priest ; D.D. Paris ; came to England to make converts ; imprisoned in Tower, 1587 ; after liberation resided abroad ; published controversial works. [ii. 400]

BAGSHAW, EDWARD, the elder (d. 1662), royalist ; B.A. Brasenose College, Oxford, 1608 ; entered Middle Temple ; as Lent reader, 1639, delivered lectures in favour of puritan principles ; M.P., Southwark, 1640 ; joined the king when he retired to Oxford ; imprisoned at Southwark by parliamentarians, 1644–6 ; published works dealing with political and religious questions. [ii. 401]

BAGSHAW, EDWARD, the younger (1629–1671), divine ; son of Edward Bagshaw (d. 1662) [q. v.] ; educated at Westminster and Christ Church, Oxford ; M.A. and Senior of the Act, 1651 ; M.A. Cambridge, 1654 ; appointed second master at Westminster, 1656 ; ordained 1659 ; vicar of Ambrosden, Oxford ; ejected for nonconformity, 1662 ; chaplain to Earl of Anglesey ; imprisoned for sedition, 1663–5, and again, later, for refusing to take oath of supremacy and allegiance ; a prisoner on parole when he died ; published controversial and other religious works. [ii. 402]

BAGSHAW, HENRY (1632–1709), divine ; brother of Edward Bagshaw (1629–1671) [q. v.] ; educated at Westminster and Christ Church, Oxford ; M.A., 1657 ; D.D., 1671 ; chaplain to Sir Richard Fanshaw, 1663, to archbishop of York, 1666, and to Lord-chancellor Danby, 1672 ; successively prebendary of York and Durham ; published sermons. [ii. 403]

BAGSHAW, WILLIAM (1628–1702), divine ; known as the 'Apostle of the Peak' ; born at Litton ; educated at Corpus Christi College, Cambridge ; assistant minister and private chaplain at Sheffield ; held living of Glossop ; ejected for nonconformity, 1662 ; continued to preach and lecture, in spite of the issue of several warrants against him, till his death ; published religious works. [ii. 403]

BAGSTER, SAMUEL, the younger (1800–1835), printer and author ; son of Samuel Bagster, the elder [q. v.] ; entered his father's business, 1815, and started printing business for himself, 1824 ; subsequently produced many learned publications, including some of the polyglot bibles issued by Bagster & Sons ; wrote 'Treasury of Scripture Knowledge,' and a book on management of bees. [ii. 404]

BAGSTER, SAMUEL, the elder (1772–1851), founder of publishing firm of Bagster & Sons ; bookseller in Strand, 1794–1816, and in Paternoster Row after 1816. His principal productions were polyglot editions of the bible (including the 'Biblia Sacra Polyglotta Bagsteriana,' 1817–28), an octoglot edition of the church of England liturgy, 1821, 'The English Hexapla,' giving the six most important versions in English of the New Testament, and an extensively annotated 'Comprehensive Bible,' edited by William Greenfield, 1827. [ii. 405]

BAGWELL, WILLIAM (fl. 1655), a London merchant who, owing to losses in trade, was almost constantly in prison for debt, 1634–50, during which time he wrote an elaborate astronomical treatise, published in simplified form as the 'Mystery of Astronomy made Plain,' 1655 ; published also two poems. [ii. 406]

BAIKIE, WILLIAM BALFOUR (1825–1864), naturalist and philologist ; M.D. Edinburgh ; entered navy ; assistant surgeon ; served in Mediterranean and at Haslar Hospital, 1851–4 ; surgeon and naturalist to Niger expedition, 1854, and again in 1857, when, being left by the other explorers, he collected and governed a native settlement at Lukoja ; published works relating to natural history of Orkney and to the Hausa and Fulfulde languages. [ii. 406]

BAILEY. [See also BAILLIE, BAILY, BAYLEY, and BAYLY.]

BAILEY. JAMES (d. 1864), classical scholar ; M.A. Trinity College, Cambridge, 1823 ; Browne medallist for Greek ode and epigrams ; members' prizeman, 1815 and 1816 ; master of Perse grammar school, Cambridge ; received pension from the queen, 1850 ; published classical works. [ii. 407]

BAILEY or **BAILY**, JOHN (1643–1697), protestant dissenting minister ; began to preach in his twenty-second year ; ordained, 1670 ; imprisoned in Lancaster for nonconformity, and on being released went to Ireland, where he was again imprisoned ; liberated on condition of leaving the country ; emigrated to New England, 1683 ; minister in Boston, 1684, Watertown, 1686, and again in Boston, 1693. [ii. 407]

BAILEY, JOHN (1750–1819), agriculturist and engraver ; tutor, land surveyor, and subsequently land agent to Lord Tankerville at Chillingham. Having cultivated a taste for engraving, he executed several topographical plates for Hutchinson's works on Cumberland, Durham, and Northumberland. [ii. 408]

BAILEY, JOHN EGLINGTON (1840–1888), antiquary ; in the firm of Ralli Brothers, Manchester, till 1886 ; admitted to Society of Antiquaries, 1874 ; honorary secretary of Chetham Society, Manchester. He contributed to the 'Dictionary of National Biography' and published antiquarian and other writings. [Suppl. i. 99]

BAILEY, NATHAN or NATHANIEL (d. 1742), lexicographer ; kept a boarding-school at Stepney ; published an etymological English dictionary, 1721, and other philological works. [ii. 409]

BAILEY, SAMUEL (1791–1870), philosophical writer ; entered office of his father, a master cutler of Sheffield, but gradually turned his attention to literary and political pursuits ; elected a town trustee, 1828 ; stood unsuccessfully as candidate for Sheffield in parliamentary elections, 1832 and 1834 ; several times president of Sheffield Literary and Philosophical Society ; chairman of Sheffield Banking Company, which he helped to found, 1831 ; published many works on political economy and philosophy, including 'Letters on the Philosophy of the Human Mind,' 1855–63. [ii. 409]

BAILEY, THOMAS (1785–1856), miscellaneous writer ; silk hosier at Nottingham ; member of town council, 1836–43 ; proprietor and editor of 'Nottingham Mercury,' 1845–52 ; published works relating to topography of Nottinghamshire, besides political and poetical writings. [ii. 411]

BAILLIE or **BAILLY**, CHARLES (1542–1625), member of Queen Mary's household ; probably a Fleming, though by descent a Scot ; arrested at Dover with letters relating to a proposed rising in Mary's behalf, 1571 ; imprisoned in Marshalsea and afterwards in Tower ; released probably in 1573 ; died in Belgium. [ii. 411]

BAILLIE, CHARLES, LORD JERVISWOODE (1804–1879), lord justiciary ; admitted advocate at Scottish bar, 1830 ; advocate depute, 1844–6 and 1852 ; sheriff of Stirlingshire, 1853–8 ; lord-advocate for Scotland, 1858 ; M.P., Linlithgow, 1859 ; raised to rank and precedence of earl's son, 1859 ; judge of court of session, 1859 ; lord of justiciary, 1862 ; retired, 1874. [ii. 412]

BAILLIE, CUTHBERT (d. 1514), lord high treasurer of Scotland ; successively incumbent of Thankerton, commendator of Glenluce, prebendary of Cumnock and Sanquhar, and (1512) lord high treasurer of Scotland. [ii. 413]

BAILLIE, LADY GRIZEL (1665–1746), poetess ; distinguished herself in childhood by heroic services to her father, Sir Patrick Hume, and his friend the patriot Robert Baillie [q. v.] ; lived with her father in retirement at Utrecht, and returned to Scotland at Restoration ; left poems in manuscript. [ii. 413]

BAILLIE, JOANNA (1762–1851), Scottish dramatist and poetess ; educated at Glasgow ; published 'Fugitive Verses,' 1790 ; issued first volume of 'Plays on the Passions,' 1798, second volume, 1802, third, 1812 ; of these 'De Montfort' was produced by Kemble and Mrs. Siddons at Drury Lane, 1800 ; the series was completed by three dramas contained in 'Miscellaneous Plays,' 1836 ; her most successful play, 'The Family Legend,' was produced, at Drury Lane, 1810. In addition to her plays she published several poems, songs, and dramatic ballads. [ii. 414]

BAILLIE, JOHN (1741-1806), divine; united secessionist minister in Newcastle-upon-Tyne, 1767-83, where his irregular habits brought about a secession from his congregation; assistant schoolmaster and subsequently lecturer in Newcastle; published historical and religious works. [ii. 417]

BAILLIE, JOHN (1772-1833), colonel; entered service of East India Company, 1790; director, 1823; ensign in India, 1793; lieutenant, 1794; professor of Arabic and Persian and of Mohammedan law, Fort William College, 1801-7; captain and political agent during Mahratta war; resident at Lucknow, 1807-15; retired and returned to England; M.P., Hedon, 1820-30, Inverness, 1830-2; published text of 'The Five Books upon Arabic Grammar,' 1801. [ii. 418]

BAILLIE, MARIANNE (1795?-1830), traveller and verse-writer, *née* Wather; published impressions of a continental tour made in 1818, and of a visit to Portugal, 1821-3, as well as several poetical pieces. [ii. 418]

BAILLIE, MATTHEW (1761-1823), morbid anatomist; brother of Joanna Baillie [q. v.]; entered Balliol College, Oxford, and during vacation studied medicine in London under Dr. William Hunter; M.B., 1787; physician to St. George's Hospital, 1787-99; M.D. and F.C.P., 1789; F.R.S.; published 'Morbid Anatomy of some of the most important Parts of the Human Body' (thoracic and abdominal organs and the brain), 1795; physician extraordinary to George III. He is commemorated in Westminster Abbey by a bust and inscription. [ii. 419]

BAILLIE, ROBERT (1599-1662), presbyterian divine; M.A. Glasgow; received episcopal ordination; regent of philosophy, Glasgow University.; presented to presbyterian parish of Kilwinning, Ayrshire; member of general assembly at Glasgow, 1638; chaplain to Lord Eglinton's regiment, 1639; sent by covenanting lords to London to draw up accusations against Laud, 1640; with covenanters' army at Dunse Law, 1639, and in 1640; professor of divinity, Glasgow, 1642; waited on Charles II at the Hague on his being proclaimed in Scotland, 1649; D.D.; principal, Glasgow University, 1660; published controversial and other theological works. [ii. 420]

BAILLIE, ROBERT (*d.* 1684), patriot; an object of suspicion to the ruling episcopal party in Scotland, and imprisoned and fined, 1676; came to London and associated with Sydney, Russell, and Monmouth to obtain, if possible, mitigation of government measures; arrested, though innocent, for alleged complicity in Rye House plot; imprisoned, and ultimately hanged in Edinburgh. [ii. 422]

BAILLIE, THOMAS (*d.* 1802), navy captain; lieutenant, 1745; served at Minorca, 1756; commander with post rank, 1757; engaged on convoy service, 1757-60; appointed to Greenwich Hospital, 1761; lieutenant-governor, 1774; having published charges against the internal government of the hospital, was deprived of his office and brought to trial for libel, 1778; defended by Erskine, afterwards lord chancellor, and acquitted; remained unemployed till 1782, when he was made clerk of deliveries. [ii. 423]

BAILLIE, WILLIAM, LORD PROVAND (*d.* 1593), Scottish judge of court of session; president of the court, 1556-7, and 1568-93. [ii. 424]

BAILLIE, WILLIAM (*fl.* 1648), Scottish general; went to Sweden in early life, and served under Gustavus Adolphus as colonel of regiment of Dutch foot, 1632; returned to Scotland, 1638; served with covenanters; under Leslie at Dunse Law, 1639, and at Marston Moor, 1644; commanded force against Montrose, and was worsted at Alford and Kilsyth, 1645; lieutenant-general of foot under Duke of Hamilton at Preston, 1648. [ii. 424]

BAILLIE, WILLIAM (*d.* 1782), lieutenant-colonel under East India Company; entered East India Company's army, 1759, as lieutenant in infantry at Madras; brevet-captain, 1763; substantive captain, 1764; major, 1772; lieutenant-colonel, 1775; commanded at Pondicherry during destruction of French works, 1779; while attempting to join forces with Munro, was defeated by Hyder Ali and taken prisoner, 1780; died in captivity at Seringapatam. [ii. 425]

BAILLIE, WILLIAM (1723-1810), amateur engraver and etcher; educated at Dublin; entered Middle Temple, but received commission in army and fought at Culloden and Minden; retired with captain's rank, 1761; commissioner of stamps, 1773-95; etched many plates, chiefly after Dutch and Flemish masters, which he published himself. [ii. 425]

BAILLIE, WILLIAM, LORD POLKEMMET (*d.* 1816), Scottish judge, 1793-1811; advocate, 1758. [ii. 425]

BAILLIE-COCHRANE, ALEXANDER D. R. W. C., first BARON LAMINGTON (1816-1890). [See COCHRANE-BAILLIE.]

BAILY, CHARLES (1815-1878), architect; for some years principal assistant to the city architect, London; F.S.A., 1844; contributed to publications of Surrey Archæological Society. [ii. 426]

BAILY, EDWARD HODGES (1788-1867), sculptor; entered merchant's office at Bristol; forsook commerce and became pupil of Flaxman, 1807; A.R.A., 1817; R.A., 1821; executed the statue of 'Eve at the Fountain' for British Literary Institution, 1818, and many other celebrated portrait statues and groups. [ii. 427]

BAILY, FRANCIS (1774-1844), astronomer; apprenticed in a London mercantile house, 1788-95; travelled in America, 1795-8; entered into partnership with a London stockbroker, 1799; published successful works on annuities and assurances, 1808 and 1810; turned his attention to astronomy, and, 1820, was one of the founders of the Astronomical Society, of which he was four times president; retired from business, 1825; greatly advanced astronomy by his revision of star catalogues, including those of Flamsteed, Lalande, and Lacaille, his simplified tables for reduction of aberration, nutation, &c., and his reform of the 'Nautical Almanac'; received the Astronomical Society's gold medal, 1843, for a successful repetition of 'Cavendish's experiment' for measuring the earth's density; hon. D.C.L. Dublin, 1835, and Oxford, 1844; permanent trustee of British Association, 1839; vice-president Geographical Society, 1830; long vice-president and treasurer of the Royal Society. [ii. 432]

BAILY, JOHN WALKER (1809-1873), archæologist; brother of Charles Baily [q. v.]; master of Ironmongers' Company, 1862-3; formed collection of Romano-British and mediæval remains excavated in city of London. [ii. 432]

BAILY, THOMAS (*d.* 1591), catholic divine; fellow and M.A. Clare Hall, Cambridge, 1549; master, *c.* 1557; on Elizabeth's accession removed to Louvain and thence to Douay, where, and at Rheims, he was employed in government of the English College; D.D. Louvain. [ii. 432]

BAIN. [See also BAINE and BAYNE.]

BAIN, ALEXANDER (1810-1877), telegraphic inventor; apprenticed as clockmaker at Wick; came as journeyman to London, 1837; applied electricity to working of clocks; invented electric fire-alarms, and, in 1843, the automatic chemical telegraph. [ii. 432]

BAINBRIDGE, CHRISTOPHER (1464?-1514), archbishop of York, and cardinal; provost of Queen's College, Oxford, in 1495; prebendary of Salisbury and, later, of Lincoln, till 1500; treasurer of St. Paul's, 1497; archdeacon of Surrey, 1501; prebendary and dean of York, 1503; dean of Windsor, 1505; master of rolls, 1504-7; bishop of Durham, 1507; archbishop of York, 1508; ambassador from Henry VIII to pope, 1509; cardinal, 1511; LL.D. [ii. 433]

BAINBRIDGE, JOHN (1582-1643), physician and astronomer; M.A. Emmanuel College, Cambridge, 1607; M.D., 1614; L.C.P., 1618; first Savilian professor, Oxford, 1619; M.D., Oxford, 1620; junior (1631) and senior (1635) reader of Linacre's lecture. He published astronomical works and left many mathematical collections in manuscript. [ii. 434]

BAINBRIGG, REGINALD (1489?-1555?), probably uncle of Reginald Bainbrigg (1545-1606) [q. v.]; M.A. Cambridge, 1509; B.D., 1526; proctor of university, 1517; master of Catherine Hall, *c.* 1527; prebendary of Wells, 1537. [ii. 435]

BAINBRIGG or **BAYNBRIDGE**, REGINALD (1545-1606), antiquary; B.A. Peterhouse, Cambridge, 1577;

headmaster of Appleby Grammar School, 1574–1606. Collected stones bearing ancient inscriptions in Northumberland, Cumberland, and Westmoreland, while several papers relating to these counties in the Cottonian MSS. are attributed to him. [ii. 434]

BAINBRIGG, THOMAS (*d.* 1646), master of Christ's College, Cambridge; master, 1620; vice-chancellor of the university, 1627; perhaps authorised Milton's rustication or expulsion from his college. [ii. 435]

BAINBRIGG, BAMBRIDGE, or **BEMBRIDGE,** THOMAS (1636–1703), protestant controversialist; M.A. Cambridge, 1661; proctor, 1678; D.D., 1684; fellow and vice-master of Trinity College; M.A. Oxford, 1669; vicar of Chesterton; rector of Orwell; published protestant controversial pamphlets. [ii. 435]

BAINBRIGGE, SIR PHILIP (1786–1862), lieutenant-general; entered navy as midshipman, but in 1800 received an ensigncy in 20th regiment; lieutenant, 1800; studied at Deptford; gazetted to company in 18th royal Irish in West Indies, 1805; inspector of fortifications, Curaçoa, 1807; entered Royal Military College, High Wycombe, 1809; deputy assistant quartermaster-general in Portugal, 1811; rendered important services at several engagements in Peninsular war; major; served in France, 1815; brevet lieutenant-colonel, 1817; C.B., 1838; deputy quartermaster-general, Dublin, 1841; major-general, and commander of Belfast district, 1846; commander of forces in Ceylon, 1852–4; lieutenant-general, and K.C.B., 1854. [ii. 436]

BAINE, JAMES (1710–1790), Scottish divine; M.A. Glasgow; successively minister at Killearn and Paisley; resigned living of Paisley; being an ardent supporter of evangelical doctrine, joined Gillespie, founder of the Relief church, and became minister of the first Relief congregation in Edinburgh, 1766; published a history of modern church reformation. [ii. 437]

BAINES, EDWARD (1774–1848), journalist; apprenticed as printer in Preston, Lancashire, and in Leeds; started as printer on his own account; became proprietor of 'Leeds Mercury,' 1801, and entered largely into the whig agitations of the day; M.P. for Leeds, 1834–41; published works relating to history of George III's reign, and topography of Yorkshire and Lancashire. [ii. 438]

BAINES, SIR EDWARD (1800–1890), journalist and economist; son of Edward Baines [q. v.]; educated at the New College, Manchester; entered office of 'Leeds Mercury,' 1815, and was editor, 1818; studied sociology and economics, and advocated repeal of corn laws; supported catholic emancipation, 1829; published 'History of Cotton Manufacture in Great Britain,' 1835; advocated public education independent of state; served on schools inquiry commission, 1865; M.P. for Leeds, 1859–74; chairman of Yorkshire College, Leeds, 1880–7; knighted, 1880; published writings on political and social subjects. [Suppl. i. 100]

BAINES, FRANCIS (1648–1710). [See SANDERS.]

BAINES, JOHN (1787–1838), mathematician; contributed largely to 'Ladies' Diary,' 'Gentleman's Diary,' 'York Miscellany,' and similar periodicals. [ii. 439]

BAINES, MATTHEW TALBOT (1799–1860), politician; son of Edward Baines [q. v.]; graduated at Trinity College, Cambridge; called to bar, 1825; Q.C., 1841; M.P. for Hull, 1847, and Leeds, 1852; president of poor-law board, 1849; chancellor of duchy of Lancaster, 1855. [ii. 439]

BAINES, PAUL (*d.* 1617). [See BAYNES.]

BAINES, PETER AUGUSTINE (1786–1843), Roman catholic bishop; studied for the church at the English Benedictine abbey of Lambspring, Hanover, which was seized by the Prussians in 1803, when the students came to England, and inaugurated the Benedictine College of St. Lawrence, Ampleforth; entered Benedictine order, 1804; ordained subdeacon, 1807, and priest, 1810; teacher at Ampleforth till 1817, when he undertook charge of mission at Bath; appointed coadjutor-bishop to Bishop Collingridge, and, later, bishop of Siga, 1823; toured for his health on the continent; preached frequently in Rome, 1827–9; returned to England, and succeeded Bishop Collingridge as vicar-apostolic of western district, 1829; purchased Prior Park, where he founded ecclesiastical and

lay colleges; author of numerous controversial writings, sermons, lectures, and pastoral charges. [ii. 439]

BAINES, ROGER (1546–1623). [See BAYNES.]

BAINES, SIR THOMAS (1622–1680), physician; friend of Sir John Finch, M.D.; M.A. Christ's College, Cambridge, 1649; M.D. Padua and Cambridge; Gresham professor of music; knighted, 1672; accompanied Finch on embassies to Florence, Tuscany, and Constantinople, where he died. [ii. 441]

BAINES, THOMAS (1822–1875), artist and explorer; artist with British army in Kafir war, 1848–51; accompanied exploring expeditions to North-west Australia, Zambesi (under Livingstone), Victoria Falls, the Tati goldfields, and the Kafir country. [ii. 441]

BAINES, THOMAS (1806–1881), journalist; son of Edward Baines [q. v.]; editor of 'Liverpool Times,' 1829; published histories of Lancashire, Cheshire, and Yorkshire. [ii. 442]

BAINHAM, JAMES (*d.* 1532), martyr; member of Middle Temple; practised as lawyer; accused of protestant heresy, 1531; imprisoned and tortured in Tower; recanted, but withdrew recantation, and was burned at Smithfield. [ii. 442]

BAIOCIS, JOHN DE (*d.* 1249). [See BAYEUX.]

BAIRD, SIR DAVID (1757–1829), general; ensign, 1772; served at Gibraltar, 1773–6; lieutenant, 1778; captain of 73rd (afterwards 71st) Highland light infantry in India, under Monro, 1780; joined Colonel Baillie's force, and, after its defeat by Hyder Ali, was captured; released, 1784; major, 1787; in England, 1789–91; commanded sepoy brigade against Tippoo; took Pondicherry, 1793; colonel, 1795; at the Cape, 1795–8; major-general in second war against Tippoo, 1798; stormed Seringapatam, 1799; commanded Indian force in Egypt against French, 1801–2; returned to India, and received command of northern division of Madras army, 1802; resigned, and returned to England; knighted; lieutenant-general in expedition to recapture Cape of Good Hope, 1805; commanded first division in expedition invading Denmark, 1807; second in command under Moore in Spain, 1808; wounded at Coruña; K.B., 1809; created baronet, 1810; general, 1814; governor of Kinsale, 1819, and of Fort George, 1829; commander of Irish forces and privy councillor, 1820. [ii. 442]

BAIRD, GEORGE HUSBAND (1761–1840), principal of Edinburgh University; educated at Edinburgh; private tutor, 1784; licensed as presbyterian preacher, 1787; presented to parish of Dunkeld, 1787, and to New Greyfriars church, Edinburgh, 1792; professor of oriental languages, Edinburgh; principal of Edinburgh University, 1793; translated to North parish church, 1799, and to the high parish church, 1801; did much for education of poor in Scottish highlands and islands. [ii. 445]

BAIRD, JAMES (1802–1876), ironmaster; with his father and brothers leased coalfields of Sunnyside, Hollandhirst, and New Gartsherrie, 1826, and the ironstone in lands of Cairnhill, 1828; assumed, 1830, active management of the business, which was subsequently enlarged and included coalmines and ironworks in Ayr, Stirling, Dumbarton, and Cumberland; M.P. for Falkirk burghs, 1851–7; deputy-lieutenant for counties of Ayr and Inverness. He was a liberal benefactor to the church of Scotland. [ii. 446]

BAIRD, SIR JOHN (1620–1698), Scottish judge; admitted advocate, 1647; knighted, 1651; lord of session, with title of Lord Newbyth, 1664–81, and 1689 till death; M.P. for Aberdeenshire in Scottish parliaments, 1665 and 1667; commissioner for negotiation of treaty of union, 1670. [ii. 447]

BAIRD, JOHN (*d.* 1804), Irish divine; presbyterian minister in Dublin, 1767–77; D.D.; conformed, and was rector of Cloghran, near Dublin, 1782; published 'Dissertation on the Old Testament,' 1778. [ii. 448]

BAIRD, JOHN (1799–1861), Scottish divine; successively minister of Legertwood, Eccles, and Swinton, Berwickshire; founded Plinian Society, Edinburgh, 1823; evangelical preacher in Ireland, 1825; minister of Yetholm, Roxburghshire, 1829–61; worked extensively for education of Scottish gipsies. [ii. 448]

BAIRD, WILLIAM (1803–1872), Scottish physician; practised in London; employed in zoological department of British Museum, 1841–72; published 'Natural History of British Entomostraca,' 1850, and 'Cyclopædia of Natural Sciences,' 1858.   [ii. 448]

BAKER, ALEXANDER (1582–1638), jesuit; entered Society of Jesus, 1610; twice visited India as missionary.   [iii. 1]

BAKER, ANNE ELIZABETH (1786–1881), philologist; assisted her brother, George Baker [q. v.], in his 'History of Northamptonshire,' and published 'Glossary of Northamptonshire Words,' 1854.   [iii. 1]

BAKER, ANSELM (1834–1885), artist; Cistercian monk at Mount St. Bernard's Abbey, Leicestershire, 1857; executed mural paintings and designed heraldic and other illustrations for several publications.   [iii. 1]

BAKER, AUGUSTINE (1575–1641). [See BAKER, DAVID.]

BAKER, CHARLES (1617–1679), jesuit; real name DAVID LEWIS; entered English college at Rome, 1638; priest, 1642; joined Society of Jesus, 1644; professed father, 1655; missioner in South Wales; victim of Titus Oates's plot and executed at Usk.   [iii. 1]

BAKER, CHARLES (1803–1874), deaf and dumb instructor; assistant instructor successively at deaf and dumb institutions at Edgbaston, Birmingham, and Doncaster; wrote works relating to teaching of deaf and dumb.   [iii. 2]

BAKER, DAVID, in religion AUGUSTINE (1575–1641), Benedictine monk; educated at Christ's Hospital, London, and Broadgates Hall (now Pembroke College), Oxford; member of Lincoln's Inn, and, 1596, of Inner Temple; entered Benedictine monastery at Padua, 1605; ordained priest; spiritual director of English Benedictine nuns at Cambrai, 1624; conventual at Douay, 1633; joined English mission; left collections for ecclesiastical history.
[iii. 2]

BAKER, DAVID BRISTOW (1803–1852), religious writer; M.A. St. John's College, Cambridge, 1832; incumbent of Claygate, Surrey.   [iii. 5]

BAKER, DAVID ERSKINE (1730–1767), writer on the drama; grandson of Daniel Defoe; educated in the Tower as a royal engineer; joined a company of strolling players; published 'Companion to Playhouse,' 1764; wrote and translated dramatic pieces.   [iii. 5]

BAKER, FRANKLIN (1800–1867), unitarian divine; M.A. Glasgow, 1823; minister of Bank Street Chapel, Bolton, 1823–64. His works include a history of nonconformity in Bolton (1854).   [iii. 6]

BAKER, GEOFFREY (fl. 1350), chronicler; less correctly known as WALTER OF SWINBROKE; wrote two chronicles, of which the earlier and shorter extends from the first day of creation to 1326, and the second from 1303 to 1356.   [iii. 6]

BAKER, GEORGE (1540–1600), surgeon; member of Barber Surgeons' Company; master, 1597; attached to household of Earl of Oxford; wrote and translated several works on surgery and medicine, 1574–97. [iii. 7]

BAKER, SIR GEORGE (1722–1809), physician; educated at Eton and King's College, Cambridge; graduate and fellow, 1745; M.D., 1756; F.C.P., 1757; F.R.S., baronet, and physician to king and queen, 1776; published medical works, including a demonstration that the Devonshire colic epidemic was a form of lead-poisoning.   [iii. 7]

BAKER, GEORGE (1773?–1847), musician; studied music in London, and performed in public; Mus. Bac. Oxford, c. 1797; organist at Derby, 1810, and at Rugeley, 1824–47; his best work probably 'The Storm.'   [iii. 8]

BAKER, GEORGE (1781–1851), topographer; published in parts, between 1822 and 1841, an elaborate history of Northamptonshire, which, from want of subscribers, remained unfinished.   [iii. 9]

BAKER, HENRY (1734–1766), author and lawyer; grandson of Daniel Defoe; left legal writings in manuscript.   [iii. 9]

BAKER, HENRY (1698–1774), naturalist and poet; made a large fortune as a teacher of the deaf and dumb by an original system; married Daniel Defoe's youngest daughter, Sophia, 1729; conducted with Defoe the 'Universal Spectator and Weekly Journal,' 1728–33; F.S.A. and F.R.S., 1740; took part in establishing Society of Arts, 1754; published poems, translations, and works on natural science.   [iii. 9]

BAKER, HENRY AARON (1753–1836), Irish architect; secretary to Royal Hibernian Academy; teacher of architecture in Dublin Society's school, 1787. [iii. 10]

BAKER, SIR HENRY WILLIAMS, BART. (1821–1877), hymn writer; M.A. Trinity College, Cambridge, 1847; vicar of Monkland, near Leominster, 1851; promoted and edited 'Hymns Ancient and Modern,' 1861, to which collection he contributed many original hymns besides translations from the Latin.   [iii. 11]

BAKER, HUMPHREY (fl. 1562–1587), arithmetician and astrologer; published 'The Wellspring of Sciences,' 1562, and other mathematical writings.   [iii. 11]

BAKER, SIR JOHN (d. 1558), lawyer; joint ambassador to Denmark, 1526; speaker of House of Commons, attorney-general, and privy-councillor; chancellor of exchequer, 1545–58.   [iii 12]

BAKER, JOHN (1661–1716), admiral; lieutenant, 1688; captain, 1691; served against French in Mediterranean, 1691–1707; rear-admiral of white, 1708; vice-admiral of blue and second in command in Mediterranean, 1709–13, and 1714 till his death at Port Mahon. [iii. 12]

BAKER, JOHN (d. 1745), vice-master of Trinity, Cambridge; M.A. Trinity College, Cambridge, 1702; D.D., 1717; vice-master, 1722; rector of Dickleburgh, Norfolk, 1731; firm supporter of Dr. Richard Bentley. [iii. 13]

BAKER, JOHN (d. 1771), flower-painter; an original member of Royal Academy.   [iii. 13]

BAKER, JOHN WYNN (d. 1775), agricultural and rural economist; F.R.S., 1771; promoted agriculture in Ireland; published works on rural and agricultural economy.   [iii. 13]

BAKER, PACIFICUS (1695–1774), Franciscan friar; provincial of the English province, 1761 and 1770; published religious works.   [iii. 13]

BAKER, PHILIP (fl. 1558–1601), divine; educated at Eton; M.A. King's College, Cambridge, 1548; D.D., 1562; provost, 1558; vice-chancellor of Cambridge University, 1562; compelled to fly to Louvain owing to his Roman catholic leanings, 1570.   [iii. 14]

BAKER, SIR RICHARD (1568–1645), religious and historical writer; probably grandson of Sir John Baker [q. v.]; shared rooms with (Sir) Henry Wotton at Hart Hall, Oxford; studied law in London; travelled abroad; M.A., 1594; knighted, 1603; high sheriff of Oxfordshire, 1620; died in Fleet prison where he was confined for debt, 1635–45; during residence in Fleet he published religious writings and (1643) a chronicle of the kings of England from the Roman period to 1625.   [iii. 14]

BAKER, RICHARD (1741–1818), theological writer; M.A. Pembroke College, Cambridge, 1765; D.D., 1788; fellow; rector of Cawston-with-Portland, Norfolk, 1772; published religious works.   [iii. 16]

BAKER, ROBERT (fl. 1563), voyager; made two voyages to Guinea, of which he wrote accounts in verse, printed in Hakluyt's 'Voyages,' 1589.   [iii. 16]

BAKER, SAMUEL (d. 1660?), divine; M.A. and fellow, Christ's College, Cambridge, 1619; D.D., 1639; prebendary of St. Paul's, 1636; canon of Windsor, 1638, and of Canterbury, 1639; sequestered from preferments by Long parliament.   [iii. 17]

BAKER, SIR SAMUEL WHITE (1821–1893), traveller and sportsman; brother of Valentine Baker [q. v.]; visited Ceylon, 1846 and 1848, and successfully established English colony at Newera Eliya; superintended construction of railway connecting Danube with Black Sea, 1859; travelled in Asia Minor, 1860–1; explored Nile tributaries of Abyssinia, 1861–2, and rested at Khartoum, 1862; started up Nile, and reached Gondokoro, 1863; met John Hanning Speke [q. v.] and James Augustus Grant [q. v.] returning from Upper Nile, and, travelling through the Latuka country and Kamrasi's country, arrived at White Nile and Karuma falls, January 1864, and at Mbakovia on lake, which he named Albert Nyanza, March 1864 ; explored the river from Magungo to Island of Patooan, returning to Khartoum, May 1865 ; received gold medal of Royal Geographical Society ; knighted, 1866 ; honorary M.A. Cambridge, 1866 ; F.R.S., 1869 ; published account of expedition, 1806 ; accompanied Prince of Wales to Egypt and Nile, 1869 ; appointed for four years governor-general of Equatorial Nile basin with rank of pacha, and major-general in Ottoman army, 1869 ; arrived at Gondokoro, his seat of government, 1871, established system of administration and vigorously opposed slave trade ; published ‘ Ismailia,’ 1874 ; continued to travel occasionally in many parts of the world for purpose of hunting big game.   [Suppl. i. 101]

BAKER, THOMAS (1625 ?–1689), mathematician ; educated at Magdalen Hall, Oxford ; vicar of Bishop's Nympton, Devonshire, 1681 ; published a work on the solution of biquadratic equations, 1684.   [iii. 17]

BAKER (*fl.* 1700–1709), dramatist ; probably educated at Oxford ; published several comedies, which were played at Drury Lane.   [iii. 17]

BAKER, THOMAS (1656–1740), antiquary ; educated at Durham ; fellow of St. John's College, Cambridge, 1680 ; received living of Long Newton, which he resigned as a nonjuror, 1690 ; resigned fellowship owing to non-compliance with abjuration oath, 1717, but resided in college as commoner master till death ; left in manuscript a very complete and accurate history of Cambridge, with other antiquarian writings.   [iii. 18]

BAKER, Sir THOMAS (1771 ?–1845), vice-admiral ; entered navy, 1781 ; lieutenant, 1792 ; commander, 1795 ; captain, 1797 ; captured (neutral) Danish merchant vessels convoyed by frigate on suspicion that they carried contraband, and occasioned coalition of Russia and Denmark in armed neutrality, 1800 ; attached to channel fleet, 1803 ; effected important capture of French frigate Didon, 1805 ; flag-captain to Rear-admiral (Sir) Thomas Bertie [q. v.] in Baltic, 1808 ; C.B., 1815 ; colonel of marines, 1819 ; rear-admiral, 1821 ; commander-in-chief off South America, 1829–33 ; K.C.B., 1831 ; vice-admiral, 1837.   [Suppl. i. 105]

BAKER, THOMAS BARWICK LLOYD (1807–1886), one of the founders of reformatory school system ; educated at Eton and Christ Church, Oxford ; entered Lincoln's Inn, 1828 ; magistrate for Gloucestershire, 1833 ; deputy-lieutenant of Gloucestershire, and high sheriff, 1847–1848 ; founded, 1852, with George Henry Bengough (1829–1865), Hardwicke reformatory school, and subsequently did much work in connection with prevention of crime.   [Suppl. i. 106]

BAKER, Sir THOMAS DURAND (1837–1893), lieutenant-general ; ensign, 18th royal Irish foot, 1854 ; captain, 1858 ; major, 1873 ; lieutenant-colonel, 1881 ; major-general, 1886 ; served in Crimea, 1854–6 ; in India, 1857–63 ; New Zealand, 1863–7 ; quartermaster-general in Ashanti expedition, 1873–4 ; chief of staff, 1874 ; C.B., 1874 ; deputy assistant quartermaster-general on headquarters staff in London, 1874 ; assistant adjutant-general, 1875 ; aide-de-camp to the queen, 1877 ; attached to Russian army during Russo-Turkish war, 1877 ; military secretary to Lord Lytton in India, 1878 ; accompanied Sir Frederick (afterwards earl) Roberts in Kabul campaign, 1879–80 ; K.C.B., 1881 ; quartermaster-general to forces, 1890 ; temporary lieutenant-general, 1891.   [Suppl. i. 107]

BAKER, VALENTINE, afterwards known as BAKER PACHA (1827–1887), cavalry officer ; brother of Sir Samuel Baker [q. v.] ; ensign, 12th lancers, 1852 ; served in Kaffir war, 1852–3, and in Crimea, 1854–6 ; major, 10th hussars, 1859 ; assistant quartermaster-general, Aldershot, 1874 ; convicted of criminal offence and dismissed from army, 1875 ; took service under sultan during Russo-Turkish war, 1877–8 ; defended position at Tashkessan, and was promoted ferik or lieutenant-general, 1877 ; entered Egyptian service and commanded police, 1882–7 ; on intelligence staff of force under Sir Gerald Graham [q. v.] in Egypt, 1884 ; published works on military subjects.   [Suppl. i. 109]

BAKER, WILLIAM (1668–1732), bishop of Norwich ; fellow, and afterwards warden, Wadham College, Oxford ; bishop of Bangor, 1723, and of Norwich, 1727.   [iii. 20]

BAKER, WILLIAM (1742–1785), printer ; apprenticed and subsequently in business in London ; linguist and classical scholar ; published essays and (1783) a volume of extracts from classical authors.   [iii. 21]

BAKER, Sir WILLIAM ERSKINE (1808–1881), general ; lieutenant in Bengal engineers, 1826 ; captain, 1840 ; served in Sikh war, and was subsequently employed in the public works department ; returned to England as colonel, 1857 ; military secretary to India Office ; K.C.B., 1870 ; general, 1877.   [iii. 21]

BAKEWELL, ROBERT (1725–1795), grazier ; greatly improved breed of oxen and sheep, produced Dishley or ‘ Leicestershire long-horn’ cattle, and was first to carry on trade of ram-letting on large scale.   [iii. 22]

BAKEWELL, ROBERT (1768–1843), geologist : made extensive mineralogical surveys in England and Ireland ; published ‘ Introduction to Geology,’ 1813 ; established himself in London as geological instructor, and subsequently extended his surveys to the Alps, publishing an account of his travels, 1823.   [iii. 23]

BALAM, RICHARD (*fl.* 1653), mathematician : author of a work on ‘ Algebra,’ published 1653.   [iii. 24]

BALATINE, ALAN (*fl.* 1560), scientist ; probably of Scottish origin ; his ‘ Chronicon Universale’ used by Edward Hall in his ‘ Chronicle.’   [iii. 24]

BALCANQUHALL, WALTER (1548–1616), presbyterian divine ; minister of St. Giles, Edinburgh, 1574 ; chaplain of the ‘ Altar called Jesus,’ 1579 ; compelled to fly from Scotland to escape arrest for preaching against the government, 1584 and 1596 ; publicly rebuked in St. Giles by the king, 1586 ; minister of Trinity College Church, 1598.   [iii. 24]

BALCANQUHALL, WALTER (1586 ?–1645), royalist ; son of Walter Balcanquhall [q. v.] ; M.A. Edinburgh, 1609 ; B.D. and fellow, Pembroke College, Oxford, 1611 ; chaplain to king ; master of Savoy, London, 1617 ; D.D. Oxford, 1618 ; sent by James to synod of Dort ; dean of Rochester 1624, and of Durham, 1639.   [iii. 25]

BALCARRES, EARLS OF. [See LINDSAY, ALEXANDER, first EARL, 1618–1659 ; LINDSAY, COLIN, third EARL, 1654 ?–1722 ; LINDSAY, ALEXANDER, sixth EARL, 1752–1825.]

BALCARRES, COUNTESS OF (1621 ?–1706 ?) [See CAMPBELL, ANNA MACKENZIE.]

BALCHEN, Sir JOHN (1670–1744), admiral ; attached, after holding a commission in Rooke's fleet on Spanish coast, 1701–2 ; served in the Channel and North Sea, 1705, and on coast of Guinea, 1705 ; twice captured by French in the Channel, 1708 and 1709 ; engaged in suppressing piracy in West Indies, 1715–16 ; second in command to Byng in Mediterranean, 1718 ; in Baltic, 1719, 1720, 1721, 1726, and 1727 ; rear-admiral, 1728 ; second in command in Mediterranean, 1731 ; vice-admiral, 1734 ; admiral of the white, 1743 ; governor of Greenwich Hospital and knighted, 1744 ; went down with his ship in the Channel.   [iii. 26]

BALD, ALEXANDER (1783–1859), poetical writer ; regularly contributed to ‘ Scots Magazine’ ; among the first to acknowledge the merits of James Hogg, the Ettrick Shepherd.   [iii. 28]

BALDOCK, RALPH DE (*d.* 1313), bishop of London ; held prebendal stall of Holborn, 1271 ; dean of St. Paul's, 1294 ; bishop of London, 1304 ; lord chancellor, 1307 ; wrote a history of England.   [iii. 28]

BALDOCK, ROBERT DE (*d.* 1327), lord chancellor ; prebendary of St. Paul's ; privy seal, 1320 ; lord chancellor, *c.* 1324 ; died from injuries received in riots attending Queen Isabella's invasion of England, 1326.   [iii. 28]

BALDOCK, Sir ROBERT (*d.* 1691), judge ; called to bar at Gray's Inn, 1651 ; recorder of Great Yarmouth, 1671 ; knighted ; serjeant and autumn reader at Gray's Inn, 1677 ; counsel for king in trial of the seven bishops, 1688 ; king's bench judge, 1688.   [iii. 29]

BALDRED or **BALTHERE** (*d.* 608 ?), saint ; a Northumbrian anchorite who lived alone on the Bass Rock in Firth of Forth ; feast-day, 6 March.   [iii. 30]

BALDRED (*fl.* 823–825), king of Kent ; deposed by Ecgberht, and fled ‘ northwards over the Thames.’   [iii. 30]

BALDREY, JOSHUA KIRBY (1754-1828), engraver and draughtsman; exhibited portraits at Royal Academy, 1793-4; executed engravings after Salvator Rosa, Reynolds, and other artists. [iii. 30]

BALDUCHIE, LORD (*d.* 1608). [See LYON, SIR THOMAS.]

BALDWIN (*d.* 1098), abbot and physician; monk of St. Denys; prior of Liberau, Alsace; physician to Edward the Confessor; abbot of St. Edmund's, 1065; subsequently became a favourite physician of the Conqueror; entered into a dispute with Herfast, bishop of Elmham, who asserted his authority over the abbey, and was finally successful in obtaining a confirmation of its independence. [iii. 30]

BALDWIN OF MOELES (*d.* 1100 ?), son of Gilbert, count of Eu, who was grandson of Richard the Fearless; received at the Conquest large estates in Devon, of which county he became sheriff. [iii. 31]

BALDWIN OF CLARE (*fl.* 1141), warrior; grandson of Richard the Fearless; fought at battle of Lincoln (1141) under Stephen, with whom he was captured. [iii. 34]

BALDWIN OF REDVERS (*d.* 1155), warrior, grandson of Baldwin of Moeles [q. v.]; earl of Devon and lord of Okehampton and perhaps of Isle of Wight; raised revolts against King Stephen in Devonshire and subsequently in Normandy; held Corfe Castle against king, 1139. [iii. 34]

BALDWIN (*d.* 1190), archbishop of Canterbury; a Cistercian monk of Ford in Devonshire; became abbot; bishop of Worcester, 1180; archbishop of Canterbury, 1180; employed by King Henry II in negotiations with Rhys ap Gruffydd, prince of South Wales; entered into dispute with dissolute monks of Christ Church, who were supported by the pope and various European princes against the archbishop's authority, but a compromise was effected in 1189; made a legatine visitation to Wales, 1187, and preached there in favour of the crusades, 1188; officiated at Richard I's coronation, 1189; died, a crusader, in the Holy Land; wrote religious works. [iii. 32]

BALDWIN, GEORGE (*d.* 1826), mystical writer; travelled in Cyprus and the East Indies; in Egypt, 1773; succeeded, 1775, in establishing direct commerce from England to Egypt; consul-general in Egypt, 1786-98; joined, after adventurous travels in Europe, the English commander in the Malta campaign of 1801; studied magnetic cures in Egypt, considering himself possessed of magnetic gifts. On this and on political subjects he wrote several works and pamphlets. [iii. 35]

BALDWIN, JOHN (*d.* 1545), judge; member of Inner Temple; M.P. for Hindon, Wiltshire, 1529-36; attorney-general for Wales and the marches, 1530-2; serjeant-at-law, 1531; knighted, 1534; chief-justice of common pleas, 1535; judge at trials of Bishop Fisher, Sir Thomas More, Anne Boleyn, and Lord Darcy. [iii. 37]

BALDWIN, RICHARD, D.D. (1672 ?-1758), provost of Trinity College, Dublin, 1717. [iii. 37]

BALDWIN, ROBERT (1804-1858), Canadian statesman; admitted attorney and called to bar of Upper Canada, 1825; honorary head of Upper Canada bar, 1847-1848 and 1850-8; represented York (now Toronto) in legislative assembly, 1830; member of executive council of Upper Canada, 1836; advocated establishment of parliamentary government; solicitor-general for Upper Canada, 1840; member of Lord Sydenham's executive council on union with Lower Canada, 1841; member of united legislative assembly, 1841; submitted resolutions, which were passed unanimously, to secure that in local affairs local ministers should be answerable to the local houses for all acts of the executive authority, 1841; attorney-general for Upper Canada, in first period of cabinet government in Canada, 1842-3; member for Rimouski in Lower Canada, 1842; again attorney-general of Upper Canada, 1848, under Lord Elgin, and introduced many reforms in administration; resigned, 1851; C.B., 1854. [Suppl. i. 110]

BALDWIN, THOMAS (1750-1820), architect; city architect, *c.* 1775-1800, at Bath; where he designed many public and private buildings. [iii. 38]

BALDWIN, SIR TIMOTHY (1620-1696), lawyer; B.A. Balliol College, Oxford, 1638; D.C.L., 1652; principal of Hart Hall (now Hertford College); knighted, 1670; master in chancery, 1670-82; clerk in House of Lords, 1680; wrote legal works. [iii. 38]

BALDWIN, WILLIAM (*fl.* 1547), author; studied at Oxford; corrector of press to Edward Whitchurch, printer; employed in preparing theatrical exhibitions for courts of Edward VI and Mary; clergyman and schoolmaster; superintended publication of and contributed to 'Mirror for Magistrates,' 1559; published poetical and other works. [iii. 38]

BALDWIN or **BAWDEN**, WILLIAM (1563-1632), jesuit; studied at Oxford; joined Society of Jesus in Belgium, 1590; professed father, 1602; in Spain, 1595; captured by English fleet at Dunkirk; vice-prefect of English mission, Brussels, *c.* 1600-10; accused of complicity in Gunpowder plot; arrested and imprisoned in England, 1610-18; died at St. Omer. [iii. 39]

BALDWULF, **BEADWULF**, or **BADULF** (*d.* 803 ?), probably last Anglian bishop of Whithern or Candida Casa, Galloway, 791, till death. [iii. 40]

BALDWYN, EDWARD (1746-1817), pamphleteer; M.A. St. John's College, Oxford, 1784; rector of Abdon, Shropshire. [iii. 40]

BALE, JOHN (1495-1563), bishop of Ossory; educated at Carmelite convent, Norwich, and Jesus College, Oxford; converted to protestantism; held living of Thornden, Suffolk; lived in Germany, 1540-7, on fall of Cromwell, who had protected him; vicar of Swaffham, Norfolk, 1551; bishop of Ossory, 1553; fled to continent, 1553; subsequently prebendary of Canterbury; wrote several religious plays, a history of English writers, and numerous controversial works of great bitterness. [iii. 41]

BALE, ROBERT (*fl.* 1461), chronicler; notary of London and judge of civil courts; wrote a chronicle of London, and other historical works. [iii. 42]

BALE, ROBERT (*d.* 1503), prior of Carmelite monastery, Burnham; wrote historical works. [iii. 42]

BALES or **BAYLES**, *alias* EVERS, CHRISTOPHER (*d.* 1590), priest; sent on English mission from Rheims, 1588; executed, 1590, as priest of foreign ordination exercising sacerdotal functions in England. [iii. 43]

BALES, PETER, or BALESIUS (1547-1610 ?), calligraphist; educated at Gloucester Hall, Oxford; resided in the Old Bailey, working as a writing-master, and was frequently employed in connection with state correspondence and intercepted letters; published 'The Writing Schoolemaster,' 1590. [iii. 43]

BALFE, MICHAEL WILLIAM (1808-1870), musical composer; first appeared in public as a violinist, 1817; articled to Charles Edward Horn the singer, 1823; violinist in Drury Lane orchestras and at oratorio concerts; went to Italy under patronage of Count Mazzara; studied singing and composition at Milan and Paris, and appeared with great success as Figaro in Rossini's 'Barbiere,' 1827; produced his first opera, 'I Rivali di se stessi,' at Palermo, 1830; returned to England, 1833; his 'Siege of Rochelle' produced at Drury Lane, 1835; produced other compositions, including 'Falstaff,' at short intervals; toured in Ireland and west of England; produced 'Le Puits d'Amour' in Paris and his highly successful 'Bohemian Girl'; in London, 1843; conductor of the Italian Opera, Her Majesty's Theatre, 1846; produced the 'Sicilian Bride,' 1852; wrote several works for the Pyne-Harrison company at Covent Garden, 1857-63. [iii. 44.]

BALFE, VICTOIRE (1837-1871). [See CRAMPTON.]

BALFOUR, ALEXANDER (1767-1829), Scottish novelist; apprenticed as weaver; clerk in Arbroath, 1793; began at an early age to contribute verse and prose to newspapers, and finally devoted himself to literature. His novels include: 'Campbell,' 1819, and 'The Foundling of Glenthorn,' 1823. [iii. 48]

BALFOUR, SIR ANDREW (1630-1694), botanist; educated at St. Andrews and Oxford; M.D. Caen, 1661; practised as physician successively in London, St. Andrews, and Edinburgh; founded botanic gardens, Edinburgh; left botanical writings. [iii. 48]

BALFOUR, CLARA LUCAS (1808–1878), lecturer and authoress; *née* Liddell; lectured and wrote on temperance and questions relating to women's influence, from 1841; wrote, with a subsidiary theological aim, in support of temperance. [iii. 49]

BALFOUR, EDWARD GREEN (1813–1889), surgeon-general and writer on India; L.R.C.S. Edinburgh. 1833; entered medical department of Indian army, 1834; assistant-surgeon, 1836; full surgeon, 1852; formed Government Central Museum, Madras, 1850, and was superintendent till 1859; published 'Encyclopædia of India,' 1857; political agent at court of nawab of Carnatic; surgeon-general and head of Madras medical department, 1871–6; returned to England, 1876; largely responsible for the opening of the Madras Medical College to women, 1875; published works chiefly relating to India. [Suppl. i. 113]

BALFOUR, FRANCIS (*fl.* 1812), Anglo-Indian: probably M.D. of Edinburgh; surgeon in East India Company's service, 1777; retired, 1807; intimate with Warren Hastings; published works on medicine and oriental languages. [iii. 50]

BALFOUR, FRANCIS MAITLAND (1851–1882), naturalist; educated at Harrow and Trinity College, Cambridge; B.A., 1873; fellow; lecturer on animal morphology at Cambridge, 1876; published a monograph on the embryonic history of the elasmobranch fishes, 1878, and a complete treatise on embryology, 1880–1; F.R.S., 1878; 'royal medallist,' 1881; obtained a special professorship of animal morphology at Cambridge, 1882; killed while climbing in Switzerland. [iii. 50]

BALFOUR, SIR GEORGE (1809–1894), general and politician; brother of Edward Green Balfour [q. v.]; educated at Military Academy, Addiscombe; entered royal artillery, 1826; served with Malacca field force, 1832–3, and with Madras forces in China, 1840–2; consul at Shanghai, 1843–66; captain, 1844; C.B., 1854; member of military finance commission, 1859–60; chief of military finance department, 1860–2; assistant to controller-in-chief at war office, London, 1868–71; K.C.B., 1870; major-general, 1865; general, 1877; liberal M.P. for Kincardineshire, 1872–92. [Suppl. i. 114]

BALFOUR, SIR JAMES, LORD PITTENDREICH (*d.* 1583), Scottish judge; educated for the priesthood; served in galleys for complicity in plot for assassination of Cardinal Beaton, 1547–9; chief judge of consistorial court of archbishop of St. Andrews, and, on its abolition, one of the commissaries of the court appointed in its stead; probably connected with murder of Darnley; governor of Edinburgh Castle; president of court of session till 1568; gained the reputation of having served, deserted, and profited by all parties; probably author of part of 'Balfour's Practicks' (published 1774), the earliest text-book of Scottish law. [iii. 52]

BALFOUR, SIR JAMES (1600–1657), historian; devoted himself to study of Scottish history and antiquities; studied heraldry in London, and, on his return to Scotland, 1630, was knighted and made Lyon king-of-arms and king's commissioner; created baronet, 1633. Most of his historical, heraldic, and other manuscripts are preserved in the Advocates' Library. His 'Annals of Scotland from Malcolm III to Charles II' was printed, 1837. [iii. 53]

BALFOUR, JAMES (1705–1795), philosopher; studied at Edinburgh and Leyden; called to Scottish bar; treasurer to faculty of advocates; professor of moral philosophy, Edinburgh, 1754, and of law of nature and nations, 1764; published philosophical works. [iii. 55]

BALFOUR, JOHN, third BARON BALFOUR OF BURLEIGH (*d.* 1688); educated in France; has been traditionally and erroneously styled 'Covenanter,' John Balfour the 'Covenanter' being 'of Kinloch.' [iii. 55]

BALFOUR, JOHN HUTTON (1808–1884), botanist; M.A. Edinburgh; M.D., 1832; F.R.C.S., Edinburgh, 1833; professor of botany at Glasgow, 1841, and at Edinburgh, 1845; retired as emeritus professor of botany, 1879; assisted in establishing Botanical Society and Botanical Club, Edinburgh; F.R.S. (Edinburgh and London); LL.D.; wrote botanical text-books. [iii. 56]

BALFOUR, NISBET (1743–1823), general; lieutenant, 1765; captain, 1770; served in American war; lieutenant-colonel, 1778; commandant at Charleston, 1779; colonel and king's aide-de-camp; served in Flanders, 1794; general, 1803; M.P. for Wigton Burghs and Arundel between 1790 and 1802. [iii. 56]

BALFOUR, ROBERT (1550 ?–1625 ?), Scottish philosopher and philologist; educated at St. Andrews and Paris; professor of Greek at, and, *c.* 1586, principal of, college of Guienne, Bordeaux; published commentary on Aristotle (1618), and other works. [iii. 57]

BALFOUR, ROBERT, second BARON BALFOUR OF BURLEIGH (*d.* 1663), by royal patent having married the heiress of the title; president of the 'estates' of Scottish parliament, 1640; served against Montrose; commissioner of treasury and exchequer, 1649. [iii. 58]

BALFOUR, ROBERT, fifth BARON BALFOUR OF BURLEIGH (*d.* 1757): Jacobite; condemned to death for shooting his former sweetheart's husband, but escaped, 1710; estates forfeited for his share in rebellion, 1715. [iii. 58]

BALFOUR, THOMAS GRAHAM (1813–1891), physician; M.D. Edinburgh, 1834; assistant surgeon in grenadier guards, 1840–8; inspector-general in charge of new statistical branch of army, 1859–73; F.R.S., 1858; F.R.C.P., 1860; surgeon-general, 1876. [Suppl. i. 115]

BALFOUR, SIR WILLIAM (*d.* 1660), parliamentary general; in Dutch service till 1627; lieutenant-colonel; governor of Tower, 1630; employed by king on mission in Netherlands, 1631; lieutenant-general of parliamentary horse at Edgehill, 1642, and other engagements in civil war. [iii. 59]

BALFOUR, WILLIAM (1785–1838), lieutenant-colonel; served in Mediterranean, at Copenhagen, and in Peninsular war. [iii. 60]

BALGUY, CHARLES (1708–1767), physician; M.D. St. John's College, Cambridge, 1750; published, besides medical treatises, a translation of Boccaccio's 'Decameron.' [iii. 60]

BALGUY, JOHN (1686–1748), divine; M.A. St. John's College, Cambridge, 1726; incumbent of Lamesby and Tanfield, 1711; took part in the Bangorian controversy, 1718; prebendary of Salisbury, 1727; published tracts defending Dr. Clarke's metaphysical and ethical principles. [iii. 60]

BALGUY, THOMAS (1716–1795), divine; son of John Balguy [q. v.]; M.A. St. John's College, Cambridge, 1741; D.D., 1758; vicar of Alton, Hampshire, 1771; prebendary of Winchester, 1758; archdeacon of Winchester, 1759; published and edited religious works, in which he followed the principles of Warburton. [iii. 61]

BALIOL, ALEXANDER DE, LORD OF CAVERS (*fl.* 1246 ?–1309 ?); perhaps son of Henry de Baliol (*d.* 1246); served in Edward's Welsh wars, 1277; one of the Scottish barons who bound themselves to receive Margaret of Norway as queen in the event of failure of male issue of Alexander III, 1284; chamberlain of Scotland, 1287–96; fought on English side in wars with Scotland. [iii. 61]

BALIOL, BERNARD DE, the elder (*fl.* 1135–1167), did homage with David I of Scotland to the Empress Matilda, daughter of Henry I, 1135, but joined King Stephen's party, 1138; taken prisoner at Lincoln, 1141. [iii. 62]

BALIOL, BERNARD DE, the younger (*fl.* 1167), has been identified with Bernard de Baliol (*fl.* 1135–1167) [q. v.]; joined the northern barons who captured William the Lion, 1174. [iii. 63]

BALIOL, EDWARD DE (*d.* 1363), king of Scotland; eldest son of John de Baliol, king of Scotland [q. v.], and Mabel, daughter of John de Warenne, earl of Surrey; succeeded to his French fiefs, 1314; invaded Scotland at head of barons displaced by Bruce, 1332; crowned at Scone; did homage to Edward III, to whom he subsequently surrendered ancient Lothian; compelled to take refuge in England from Scottish patriots under Sir Andrew Murray and Earl of Moray, 1334; restored by Edward III's aid, 1335; left almost entirely in Edward's hands the wars which followed; retired to England, 1338; surrendered kingdom of Scotland to Edward III, 1356, in return for pension of 2,000*l.* [iii. 63]

BALIOL, HENRY DE (*d.* 1246), chamberlain of Scotland, 1219–*c.* 1231; probably supported barons against John; attended Henry III in Gascon war, 1241. [iii. 65]

BALIOL, JOHN DE (*d.* 1269), founder of Balliol College, Oxford; one of the regents of Scotland during Alexander III's minority till 1255, when he was deprived for treason; founded Balliol College, Oxford, 1263; sided with Henry III in barons' war, 1258-65. [iii. 66]

BALIOL, JOHN DE (1249-1315), king of Scotland; third son of John de Baliol (*d.* 1269) [q. v.]; on death, in 1290, of Margaret, the Maid of Norway, grandchild of Alexander III, claimed throne of Scotland in right of his maternal grandmother, Margaret, eldest daughter of David, brother of William the Lion; his only serious rivals were Robert Bruce and John Hastings, thcugh there were thirteen claimants in all; settlement of the dispute entrusted to Edward I, who obtained recognition as superior lord of Scotland and selected Baliol; crowned at Scone, 1292; condemned for contumacy on declining to appear in Scottish suit before judges at Westminster, 1293, but yielded and attended parliament held in London, 1294; determined, on being treated with haughtiness, to brave Edward's displeasure, and, on his return to Scotland, refused to send men to the French war; allied himself with Philip of France, 1295; invaded England, 1296; formally renounced homage and fealty; brought to submission by Edward and taken captive to England; liberated, 1299; died in retirement at Castle Galliard, Normandy. [iii. 66]

BALL, SIR ALEXANDER JOHN (1757-1809), rear-admiral; lieutenant, 1778; commander, 1783; on home station, 1790-3, and Newfoundland station, 1793-6; served in Mediterranean under Nelson, with whom he formed a close friendship, 1798; at Aboukir Bay, 1798; reduced Malta, 1798-1800; commissioner of navy at Gibraltar; made baronet and governor of Malta; rear-admiral, 1805. [iii. 70]

BALL, ANDREW (*d.* 1653), navy captain; captain, 1648; served with Captain Penn in Mediterranean, 1650-1652; commanded squadron at Copenhagen, but being caught in a storm returned, 1652; as captain of the fleet encountered Dutch off Portland and was killed. [iii. 72]

BALL, FRANCES (1794-1861), founder of convents; called Mother Frances Mary Theresa; joined institute of Blessed Virgin Mary at Micklegate Bar convent, York, and in 1821 introduced the institute into Ireland, whence it spread to various parts of the world. [iii. 72]

BALL, HANNAH (1734-1792), Wesleyan methodist attracted at High Wycombe by methodist preachers, including Wesley, with whom she corresponded; opened a Sunday school, 1769; extracts from her diary (begun in 1766) and letters have been published. [iii. 73]

BALL, JOHN (*d.* 1381), priest; probably attached to abbey of St. Mary's, York; frequently reprimanded and imprisoned for preaching at Colchester doctrines which were in great part those of Wycliffe, and which in 1381 brought about Tyler's rebellion; released by rebels from the archbishop's prison, Maidstone, where he was confined; captured at Coventry; executed at St. Albans. [iii. 73]

BALL, JOHN (1585-1640), puritan divine; M.A. St. Mary's Hall, Oxford; obtained ordination without subscription, 1610; presented to living of Whitmore, Staffordshire; 'deprived,' and more than once imprisoned for nonconformity; published religious works. [iii. 74]

BALL, JOHN (1665?-1745), presbyterian; son of Nathanael Ball [q. v.]; minister at Honiton, 1705-45; opened seminary which, on account of his learning, was not suppressed under Toleration Act; published religious works. [iii. 75]

BALL, JOHN (1818-1889), man of science and politician; son of Nicholas Ball [q. v.]; educated at Christ's College, Cambridge; honorary fellow, 1888; travelled on continent and made series of observations of glaciers; called to Irish bar, 1845; assistant poor law commissioner, 1846-7, 1849-51; M.P. for co. Carlow, 1852; under-secretary for colonies, 1855-7; first president of Alpine Club, 1857; published 'The Alpine Guide,' 1863-8; joined bot anical expedition to Morocco, 1871; F.R.S., 1868; fellow of Linnean, Geographical, and Antiquarian societies. His publications include treatises on physical and geographical science, and the botany of the Alps. [Suppl. i. 115]

BALL, JOHN THOMAS (1815-1898), lord chancellor of Ireland; educated at Trinty College, Dublin; LL.D., 1844; called to Irish bar, 1840, and to inner bar, 1854; vicar-general of province of Armagh, 1862; bencher of King's Inns, 1863; queen's advocate in Ireland, 1865; solicitor-general for Ireland, 1868; attorney-general, 1868 and 1874; M.P. for Dublin University, 1868; opposed Irish Church Act; honorary D.C.L. Oxford, 1870; assisted in framing future constitution of disestablished Church of Ireland; opposed Gladstone's Irish land bill, 1870, and Irish university bill, 1873; lord chancellor of Ireland, 1875-80; vice-chancellor of Dublin University, 1880; published 'Reformed Church of Ireland,' 1886, and 'Historical Review of Legislative Systems operative in Ireland,' 1888. [Suppl. i. 118]

BALL, NATHANAEL (1623-1681), divine; M.A. King's College, Cambridge; vicar of Barley, Hertfordshire; ejected, 1659; minister at Royston; resigned under Act of Uniformity; licensed as 'general presbyterian preacher in any allowed place,' 1672; assisted Walton in his great Polyglot,' and left religious writings. [iii. 75]

BALL, NICHOLAS (1791-1865), Irish judge; educated at Trinity College, Dublin; called to Irish bar, 1814; bencher of King's Inn, 1836; M.P. for Clonmel, 1835; attorney-general and privy councillor for Ireland, 1837; judge of common pleas (Ireland), 1839. [iii. 76]

BALL or **BALLE**, PETER (*d.* 1675), physician; doctor of philosophy and physic, Padua, 1660; hon. F.R.C.P., 1664; original F.R.S. [iii. 77]

BALL, ROBERT (1802-1857), naturalist; in under-secretary's office, Dublin, 1827-52; president of Geological Society of Ireland; director of Trinity College Museum, 1844; hon. LL.D. Trinity College, 1850; secretary of the Queen's University, Ireland, 1851. [iii. 77]

BALL, THOMAS (1590-1659), divine; M.A. Queens' College, Cambridge, 1625; fellow; weekly lecturer at Northampton from c. 1630; published a religious treatise called 'Pastorum Propugnaculum,' 1656, and was joint editor of Dr. John Preston's works. [iii. 78]

BALL or **BALLE**, WILLIAM (*d.* 1690), astronomer; joined meetings of the 'Oxonian Society' at Gresham College, 1659; joint founder and first treasurer of Royal Society, 1660; acquired some celebrity for his observations of the planet Saturn. [iii. 78]

BALLANCE, JOHN (1839-1893), prime minister of New Zealand; born in Ireland; emigrated to New Zealand, where he founded 'Wanganui Herald'; served in Maori war, 1867; entered House of Representatives, 1875; treasurer, 1878-9; minister for lands and native affairs, 1884; leader of liberal opposition, 1889; prime minister, 1891, adopting a bold and successful progressive policy. [Suppl. i. 120]

BALLANDEN. [See BELLENDEN.]

BALLANTINE, JAMES (1808-1877), artist and author; originally a house-painter in Edinburgh; one of the first to revive art of glass-painting, on which he published a treatise; executed stained-glass windows for House of Lords; published poetical and other works. [iii. 79]

BALLANTINE, WILLIAM (1812-1887), serjeant-at-law; educated at St. Paul's School; called to bar at Inner Temple, 1834; honorary bencher, 1878; serjeant-at-law, 1856; conducted prosecution at trial of Franz Müller, 1864; appeared for the Tichborne claimant at the first stage of legal proceedings, 1871 [see ORTON, ARTHUR]; successfully defended Mulhar Rao, Gaekwar of Baroda, on a charge of attempted murder, 1875; published reminiscences. [Suppl. i. 120]

BALLANTYNE, JAMES (1772-1833), printer of Sir Walter Scott's works; attended with Scott Kelso grammar school; solicitor in Kelso, 1795; undertook printing and editing of 'Kelso Mail,' 1796; printed Scott's 'Minstrelsy of Scottish Border,' 1802, and thenceforth continued to print Scott's works; received loan from Scott for establishment of a printing business in Edinburgh, 1802, and took with his brother John [q. v.] half share in bookselling business (started, 1808); proprietor, with his brother, of 'Weekly Journal,' 1817; ruined by bankruptcy of Constable & Co., 1826; thenceforth employed in editing 'Weekly Journal,' and in literary management of the printing-house for the creditors' trustees. [iii. 80]

BALLANTYNE, JAMES ROBERT (*d.* 1864), orientalist; superintended reorganisation of government Sanskrit college at Benares, 1845; librarian to India Office, London, 1861; published oriental works with object of making Indian philosophies accessible to Europeans. [iii. 81]

BALLANTYNE, JOHN (1774–1821), publisher; brother of James Ballantyne (1772–1833) [q. v.]; partner in his father's business as general merchant, Kelso, 1795; clerk in his brother's printing establishment, 1806; manager of publishing firm established by Scott, 1808; auctioneer, 1813; the 'Novelist's Library' edited gratuitously for his benefit by Scott, 1820. [iii. 82]

BALLANTYNE, JOHN (1778–1830), divine; educated at Edinburgh; secessionist minister at Stonehaven, Kincardineshire, 1805; published controversial pamphlets. [iii. 83]

BALLANTYNE, ROBERT MICHAEL (1825–1894), author; brother of James Robert Ballantyne [q. v.]; apprenticed as clerk in service of Hudson Bay Fur Company, and spent some time in trading with Indians; in printing and publishing firm of Thomas Constable, Edinburgh, 1848–55; published, from 1856, many novels for boys; exhibited watercolour paintings at Royal Scottish Academy. [Suppl. i. 122]

BALLANTYNE, THOMAS (1806–1871), journalist; successively editor of 'Bolton Free Press,' 'Manchester Guardian,' 'Liverpool Journal,' and 'Mercury'; associated with Cobden and Bright in corn-law agitation; edited 'Leader,' 'Old St. James's Chronicle,' and 'Statesman' (which he started), and was connected with 'Illustrated London News'; published selections from Carlyle and other writers. [iii. 83]

BALLANTYNE, WILLIAM (1616–1661). [See BALLENDEN.]

BALLARD, EDWARD GEORGE (1791–1860), miscellaneous writer; employed in the stamp office, 1809, and, later, in excise office till 1817. [iii. 83]

BALLARD, GEORGE (1706–1755), antiquary; apprenticed as staymaker; studied Anglo-Saxon and proceeded to Oxford, 1750, having received an annuity from various gentlemen interested in his work; clerk at Magdalen College, and, later, one of the university bedells; assisted Ames in his 'History of Printing'; left archæological writings. [iii. 84]

BALLARD, JOHN (*d.* 1586), Roman catholic priest; probably educated at Rheims; joined English mission, 1581; travelled to Rome, 1584, with Anthony Tyrrell, and obtained pope's sanction for plot to assassinate Elizabeth; instigated Anthony Babington [q. v.] to organise the plot, 1586, and on its discovery was racked and executed. [iii. 84]

BALLARD, JOHN ARCHIBALD (1829–1880), general: joined Bombay engineers, 1850; went to Constantinople, being ordered to Europe on medical certificate, and received rank of lieutenant-colonel in Turkish army; distinguished himself at sieges of Silistria and Giurgevo; commanded under Omar Pasha in campaign to relieve Kars; returned to India as C.B., 1856; assistant-quartermaster-general in Persian campaign and Indian mutiny; lieutenant-general, 1879. [iii. 85]

BALLARD, SAMUEL JAMES (1764?–1829), vice-admiral; entered navy, 1776; commander, 1794; postcaptain, 1795; employed in convoying trade for Baltic, Newfoundland and Quebec, 1796–8; attached to Mediterranean fleet, 1799–1801; at reduction of Guadeloupe, 1810; rear-admiral, 1814; vice-admiral, 1825. [iii. 86]

BALLARD, VOLANT VASHON (1774?–1832), rear-admiral; lieutenant, 1795; captain, 1798; in West Indies, 1809–10; rear-admiral, 1825. [iii. 87]

BALLENDEN or **BALLANTYNE**, WILLIAM (1616–1661), Roman catholic divine; educated at Edinburgh; converted to catholicism at Paris; became priest at Rome; returned to Scotland on catholic mission, 1649; first prefect-apostolic of the mission, 1653. [iii. 87]

BALLINGALL, SIR GEORGE (1780–1855), surgeon; studied at St. Andrews; military surgeon in India, 1806–18; professor of military surgery, Edinburgh, 1825; knighted, 1830; F.R.S. London and Edinburgh; published medical works. [iii. 88]

BALLIOL. [See BALIOL.]

BALLOW or **BELLEWE**, HENRY (1707–1782), lawyer; held post in the exchequer; friend of Akenside the poet; left legal manuscripts. [iii. 88]

BALLYANN, BARON OF (*d.* 1554). [See KAVANAGH, CAHIR MACART.]

BALMER, GEORGE (*d.* 1846), painter; son of a house-painter; attracted attention by his pictures at Newcastle; painted continental scenes during a tour in Europe. [iii. 89]

BALMER, ROBERT (1787–1844), minister; educated at Edinburgh and Selkirk; licensed preacher by secession church, 1812; minister at Berwick-on-Tweed, 1814–44; professor of pastoral, and, later, of systematic, theology in secession church; D.D., Glasgow, 1840. [iii. 89]

BALMERINO, BARONS. [See ELPHINSTONE, JAMES, first BARON, 1553?–1612; ELPHINSTONE, JOHN, second BARON, *d.* 1649; ELPHINSTONE, JOHN, third BARON, 1623–1704; ELPHINSTONE, JOHN, fourth BARON, 1682–1736; ELPHINSTONE, ARTHUR, sixth BARON, 1688–1746.]

BALMFORD, JAMES (*b.* 1556), divine; published religious works, including a 'Dialogue concerning the unlawfulness of playing at Cards,' 1594. [iii. 89]

BALMFORD, SAMUEL (*d.* 1659?), puritan divine. [iii. 90]

BALMUTO, LORD (1742–1824). [See BOSWELL, CLAUD IRVINE.]

BALMYLE or **BALMULE**, NICHOLAS DE (*d.* 1320?), chancellor of Scotland; educated as clerk in monastery of Arbroath; temporarily executed functions of archbishop of St. Andrews, 1297; chancellor of Scotland, 1301–7; bishop of Dunblane, *c.* 1307. [iii. 90]

BALNAVES, HENRY (*d.* 1579), Scottish reformer; educated at St. Andrews and Cologne; became acquainted with Swiss and German reformers; lord of session, 1538; secretary of state to the regent; depute-keeper of privy seal, 1542; deprived of offices, 1543; confined in Blackness Castle; transported to Rouen, 1546; reinstated lord of session, 1563; took prominent part in behalf of protestant reformers. [iii. 91]

BALNEA, HENRY DE (*fl.* 1400?), English Carthusian monk; author of 'Speculum Spiritualium.' [iii. 92]

BALSHAM, HUGH DE (*d.* 1286), bishop of Ely and founder of Peterhouse, Cambridge; subprior of monastery of Ely; elected by the monks bishop of Ely on death of William de Kilkenny, 1256; his election displeasing to Henry III, who allowed John de Waleran, to whom he had committed the temporalities of the see, to do much harm to the diocese; confirmed as bishop by the pope, 1257; obtained charter to introduce 'studious scholars' into his hospital of St. John, Cambridge, in lieu of the secular brethren already residing there, 1280; obtained charter to separate his scholars from the brethren of the hospital, 1284, and founded and endowed Peterhouse for them. [iii. 92]

BALTHER (*d.* 756), saint; presbyter of Lindisfarne; probably lived as an anchorite at Tyningham in Scotland. [iii. 98]

BALTIMORE, EARLS OF. [See CALVERT, GEORGE, first EARL, 1590?–1642; CALVERT, FREDERICK, seventh EARL, 1731–1771.]

BALTINGLAS, third VISCOUNT (*d.* 1585). [See EUSTACE, JAMES.]

BALTRODDI, WALTER DE (*d.* 1270), bishop of Caithness, 1261; doctor of the canon law. [iii. 98]

BALTZAR, THOMAS (1630?–1663), violinist; born at Lübeck; settled, 1656, in England, where he became famous; one of the king's musicians. [iii. 98]

BALUN, JOHN DE (*d.* 1235). [See BAALUN.]

BALVAIRD, first BARON (1597?–1644). [See MURRAY, SIR ANDREW.]

BALWEARIE, LORD (*d.* 1532). [See SCOTT, SIR WILLIAM.]

BALY, WILLIAM (1814–1861), physician; studied at University College, London, St. Bartholomew's Hospital, Paris, Heidelberg, and Berlin; M.D. Berlin, 1836;

physician to Millbank Penitentiary, 1841 ; physician to the queen, 1859 ; F.R.C.P., 1846 ; F.R.S., 1847 ; published works on the hygiene of prisons and other medical subjects. [iii. 99]

BAMBRIDGE, CHRISTOPHER (1464 ?-1514). [See BAINBRIDGE.]

BAMBRIDGE, THOMAS (*fl.* 1729), attorney and warden of the Fleet ; joint-warden to Fleet prison, 1728 ; taken into custody for cruelty, 1729 ; twice tried for murder of a prisoner and acquitted ; was latterly himself imprisoned in the Fleet. [iii. 99]

BAMFORD, SAMUEL (1788-1872), poet and weaver ; actively interested in welfare of labouring classes ; unjustly imprisoned for connection with the gatherings dispersed by the Peterloo massacre, 1819 ; obtained post as messenger at Somerset House, but subsequently returned to trade as weaver ; published poems and other writings. [iii. 100]

BAMPFIELD, SIR COPLESTONE (1636-1691), justice ; educated at Corpus Christi College, Oxford ; active in promoting Charles II's restoration ; M.P. for Tiverton, 1659, and for Devonshire, 1671-9 and 1685-7. [iii. 101]

BAMPFIELD, FRANCIS (*d.* 1683), divine ; M.A. Wadham College, Oxford, 1638 ; prebendary of Exeter ; held living of Sherborne ; ejected from preferments, 1662 ; repeatedly imprisoned for preaching ; died in Newgate ; published religious works. [iii. 101]

BAMPFIELD, JOSEPH (*fl.* 1639-1685), royalist colonel ; ensign under Lord Ashley, 1639, in Scottish war ; colonel during civil war, in west of England ; frequently employed by Charles I in secret negotiations ; dismissed as untrustworthy by Charles II ; acted as Cromwell's agent in Paris after 1654 ; commanded English regiment in Holland after Restoration. [iii. 101]

BAMPFIELD, THOMAS (*d.* 1693), speaker of House of Commons, 1658-9 ; recorder of Exeter ; M.P. for Exeter, 1654, 1656, and 1660. [iii. 103]

BAMPFYLDE, COPLESTONE WARRE (*d.* 1791), landscape painter ; exhibited at Society of Artists, Free Society of Artists, and Royal Academy, 1763-83. [iii. 103]

BAMPFYLDE, JOHN CODRINGTON (1754-1796), poet ; educated at Cambridge ; published sonnets, 1778 ; led a dissipated life, and was confined in private asylum. [iii. 103]

BAMPTON, JOHN (*fl.* 1340), Carmelite at Cambridge ; D.D. ; wrote theological treatises. [iii. 103]

BAMPTON, JOHN (*d.* 1751), founder of Bampton lectures ; M.A. Trinity College, Oxford, 1712 ; prebendary of Salisbury, 1718 ; left legacy for foundation of the Bampton divinity lectures at Oxford. [iii. 104]

BANASTRE, ALARD (*fl.* 1174), sheriff of Oxfordshire, with judicial powers, 1174-5. [iii. 104]

BANBURY, first EARL OF. [See KNOLLYS, WILLIAM, 1547-1632.]

BANCHINUS (*fl.* 1382). [See BANKYN, JOHN.]

BANCK, JOHN VAN DER (1694 ?-1739). [See VANDERBANK.]

BANCK, PETER VAN DER (1649-1697). [See VANDERBANK.]

BANCKS, JOHN (1709-1751). [See BANKS.]

BANCROFT, EDWARD (1744-1821), naturalist and chemist ; frequently visited America, and published Natural History of Guiana,' 1769 ; made important discoveries in dyeing and calico-printing. [iii. 105]

BANCROFT, EDWARD NATHANIEL (1772-1842), physician ; son of Edward Bancroft [q. v.] ; M.B. St. John's College, Cambridge, 1794 ; physician to forces in the Windward Islands, Portugal, Mediterranean, and Egypt ; M.D., 1804 ; fellow and Gulstonian lecturer, 1806, and censor, 1808, College of Physicians; physician to St. George's Hospital, 1808-11 ; physician, 1811, to forces in Jamaica, where he remained till death, being ultimately deputy inspector-general of army hospitals ; identified yellow with malarial fever in his 'Essay,' 1811. [iii. 106]

BANCROFT, GEORGE (*fl.* 1548), translator ; published 'Answere that Preachers at Basile made for defence of the Lord's Supper,' 1548, a heated attack on the catholics, translated from Latin. [iii. 107]

BANCROFT, JOHN (1574-1640), seventh bishop of Oxford ; nephew of Archbishop Bancroft ; educated at Westminster ; M.A. Christ Church, Oxford, 1599 ; rector of Finchley, 1601-8 ; B.D., 1607 ; D.D. and prebendary of St. Paul's, 1609 ; master of University College, Oxford, 1610-32 ; bishop of Oxford, 1632 ; built an episcopal residence at Cuddesdon, Oxfordshire, 1635. [iii. 107]

BANCROFT, JOHN (*d.* 1696), dramatist and surgeon ; published several plays, 1679-91. [iii. 108]

BANCROFT, RICHARD (1544-1610), archbishop of Canterbury ; B.A. Christ's College, Cambridge, 1567 ; prebendary of St. Patrick's, Dublin ; D.D., 1585 ; treasurer of St. Paul's, 1585 ; ecclesiastical commissioner ; canon of Westminster, 1587 ; prebendary of St. Paul's, 1590 ; largely responsible for detection of printers of the Marprelate tracts ; chaplain to Archbishop Whitgift, 1592 ; bishop of London, 1597 ; archbishop of Canterbury, 1604 ; laid before the privy council his 'Articles of Abuses,' in which he protested, in name of the clergy, against 'prohibitions' by civil judges of proceedings in ecclesiastical courts, 1605 ; supported scheme of new translation of bible ; D.D. and chancellor of university of Oxford, 1608 ; his works chiefly directed against puritans. [iii. 108]

BANCROFT, THOMAS (*fl.* 1633-1658), poet ; educated at Catherine Hall, Cambridge. His publications include 'Two Bookes of Epigrammes and Epitaphs' (1633), which celebrated many men of letters of the time ; contributed to Brome's 'Lachrymæ Musarum' (1649). [iii. 112]

BANCROFT, THOMAS (1756-1811), divine ; B.A. Brasenose College, Oxford, 1781 ; Craven scholar, 1780 ; head-master, Henry VIII's school, Chester ; vicar of Bolton-le-Moors, 1793 ; one of the four ' king's preachers' of Lancashire ; published sermons. [iii. 113]

BANDINEL, BULKELEY (1781-1861), librarian of Bodleian ; educated at Winchester and New College, Oxford ; chaplain to Sir James Saumarez in Baltic ; Bodley's librarian, 1813-60 ; honorary curator, 1860 ; published catalogue, 1843. [iii. 113]

BANDINEL, DAVID (*d.* 1645), dean of Jersey, 1623 ; took the side of the parliament during the civil war, chiefly owing to his animosity to Sir Philip de Carteret, lieutenant-governor of Jersey. Carteret died from the rigours of a siege directed by Bandinel ; and his son, Sir George Carteret, arrested and imprisoned Bandinel and his son, who died after attempting to escape. [iii. 114]

BANDINEL, JAMES (1783-1849), clerk in foreign office ; brother of Bulkeley Bandinel [q. v.] ; published a work on the African slave trade, 1842. [iii. 115]

BANIM, JOHN (1798-1842), novelist, dramatist, and poet, the 'Scott of Ireland' ; studied at drawing academy of Royal Dublin Society ; teacher of drawing at Kilkenny ; removed to Dublin and took up literature ; wrote 'The Celt's Paradise,' a poem ; produced 'Damon and Pythias,' performed at Covent Garden Theatre, with Macready and Kemble in principal parts, 1821 ; settled in London, contributed largely to periodicals, and wrote, in conjunction with his brother Michael [q. v.], several successful novels in a series called 'O'Hara Tales' ; went abroad for his health, and soon found himself in straitened circumstances, but was relieved by public subscription. The 'O'Hara Tales' (first series), 1825, to some extent fulfilled the author's object of doing for the Irish what the 'Waverley Novels' had done for the Scottish people. [iii. 115]

BANIM, MICHAEL (1796-1874), novelist ; brother of John Banim [q. v.] ; studied for bar, but abandoned the law for commerce ; began to assist his brother in the 'O'Hara Tales,' 1822, several of which he wrote ; met with serious financial misfortunes, c. 1840 ; postmaster of Kilkenny, c. 1852-73. [iii. 117]

BANISTER or **BANESTER,** JOHN (1540-1610), surgeon to Earl of Warwick's forces at Havre, 1563 ; studied at Oxford ; served in Leicester's expedition to Low Countries, 1585 ; wrote, compiled, and edited medical works. [iii. 118]

BANISTER, JOHN (1630–1679), musician; sent by Charles II to study in France, having attracted his attention by his violin playing, and on his return made leader of the king's band, 1663; produced several compositions, including music for the 'Tempest' (written in conjunction with Pelham Humphrey). [iii. 119]

BANISTER, JOHN (d. 1692 ?), naturalist; travelled in East Indies and Virginia as missionary, and wrote on natural history of those countries. [iii. 119]

BANISTER, RICHARD (d. 1626), oculist; published, 1622, a second edition, with additions, of Guilleman's treatise on diseases of the eyes (Paris, 1585). [iii. 120]

BANISTER, SIR WILLIAM (d. 1721), one of the judges of South Wales; baron of exchequer and knighted, 1713; removed, 1714. [iii. 120]

BANKE, RICHARD (fl. 1410), judge; baron of exchequer, 1410; reappointed, 1414. [iii. 120]

BANKES, GEORGE (1788–1856), last of cursitor barons of exchequer; appointed, 1824; educated at Westminster and Trinity Hall, Cambridge; called to bar, 1815; chief secretary of board of control, 1829; junior lord of treasury, 1830; M.P. for Corfe Castle, 1816–23 and 1826–32, and for Dorset, 1841–56; judge-advocate-general and privy councillor, 1852. [iii. 120]

BANKES, HENRY (1757–1834), politician and author; M.A. Trinity College, Cambridge, 1781; M.P. for Corfe Castle, 1780–1826; published a history of Rome. [iii. 121]

BANKES, SIR JOHN (1589–1644), chief justice of common pleas, 1641; educated at Queen's College, Oxford; called to bar at Gray's Inn, 1614; bencher, 1629; treasurer, 1632; M.P. for Morpeth, 1628; attorney-general, 1634; represented crown against John Hampden, 1637; privy councillor, 1641; impeached by parliament and his property confiscated; continued to perform duties of his office at Oxford. [iii. 121]

BANKES, MARY, LADY (d. 1661), heroine of Corfe Castle; wife of Sir John Bankes [q. v.]; occupied the family residence of Corfe Castle for royalists at outbreak of civil war; besieged in 1643 by Sir Walter Earle, who was unsuccessful, and again, 1645–6, when the castle was betrayed by an officer of the garrison. [iii. 123]

BANKES, WILLIAM JOHN (d. 1855), traveller; M.A. Trinity College, Cambridge, 1811; M.P. successively for Truro, Cambridge University, Marlborough, and Dorsetshire; travelled widely in the East. [iii. 124]

BANKHEAD, JOHN (1738–1833), Irish presbyterian minister; minister at Ballycarry, co. Antrim, 1763–1833; moderator of synod, 1800; published catechism, based on Westminster Shorter Catechism, 1786. [iii. 124]

BANKS, —— (fl. 1588–1637), Scottish showman, for whose 'dancing horse,' Morocco, allusion is made by all the best authors of his day; originally served the Earl of Essex; went to Paris, 1601, where he was imprisoned on suspicion that the horse's tricks were performed by magic; returned to England, 1608; probably became a vintner in Cheapside. [iii. 125]

BANKS, BENJAMIN (1750–1795), violin maker; pupil of Peter Walmsley; subsequently copied the instruments of Nicholas Amati. [iii. 126]

BANKS, SIR EDWARD (1769?–1835), builder, of humble origin; knighted, 1822. His works include Waterloo, Southwark, and London bridges. [iii. 126]

BANKS, GEORGE LINNÆUS (1821–1881), miscellaneous writer; apprenticed as cabinet maker; advocated social advancement of the people; between 1848 and 1864 edited successively several journals in England and Ireland. His writings include poems and dramatic pieces. [iii. 127]

BANKS, ISABELLA, known as MRS. LINNÆUS BANKS (1821–1897), novelist; née Varley; schoolmistress at Cheetham, near Manchester; married, 1846, George Linnæus Banks [q. v.], whom she assisted in his journalistic work; published poetical works and novels, including the 'Manchester Man,' 1876. [Suppl. i. 123]

BANKS, JOHN (fl. 1696), dramatist; studied law, and was a member of the Society of New Inn; wrote, 1677–96, seven plays, in verse, chiefly on historical subjects, of which the 'Unhappy Favourite' and 'Virtue Betrayed,' were very successfully produced. [iii. 127]

BANKS or **BANCKS**, JOHN (1709–1751), miscellaneous writer; weaver's apprentice; came to London and entered service of a bookseller and bookbinder; published poems (2 vols. 1738) and other works, including a 'Life of Christ' and an account of Oliver Cromwell. [iii. 128]

BANKS, JOHN SHERBROOKE (1811–1857), major; cadet in Bengal native infantry, 1829; quartermaster and interpreter, 1833; served at Cabul, 1842; military secretary to Lord Dalhousie; succeeded Sir Henry Lawrence as chief commissioner of Lucknow, 1857. [iii. 128]

BANKS, SIR JOSEPH (1743–1820), president of the Royal Society, 1778–1820; educated at Harrow, Eton, and Christ Church, Oxford; studied natural history; F.R.S., 1766; travelled in Newfoundland; accompanied Cook in his expedition round the world in the Endeavour, 1768–1771, making valuable natural history collections; on his return created hon. D.C.L. of Oxford; visited Iceland, 1772; baronet, 1781; C.B., 1795; P.C., 1797. His collections and library are preserved in the British Museum. [iii. 129]

BANKS, SARAH SOPHIA (1744–1818), virtuoso; sister of Sir Joseph Banks [q. v.]; collected objects of natural history, books, and coins, which were presented to the British Museum. [iii. 133]

BANKS, THOMAS (1735–1805), sculptor; apprenticed as ornament carver; studied under Scheemakers; obtained medals from Society of Arts for classic bas-reliefs and statues, 1763–9; Royal Academy gold medallist, 1770; obtained a travelling studentship and studied in Italy, 1772–9; executed several works at St. Petersburg, 1781; exhibited at Royal Academy, 1780–1803; R.A., 1785; friend of Horne Tooke, and arrested on the charge of high treason about the same time as Tooke. Works by him are in Westminster Abbey, St. Paul's Cathedral, and the Royal Academy. [iii. 133]

BANKS, THOMAS CHRISTOPHER (1765–1854), genealogist; educated for the law; practised largely in cases of disputed inheritance; published many genealogical books, including the 'Dormant and Extinct Baronage of England' (1807–9), a similar work on the peerage (1812), and pamphlets in support of spurious claims to peerages, among which were the dukedom of Norfolk, 1812, and the earldoms of Stirling and Salisbury, 1830. [iii. 134]

BANKS, WILLIAM STOTT (1820–1872), antiquary; attorney, 1851; clerk to Wakefield justices, 1870; published 'Walks in Yorkshire' (1866–72). [iii. 136]

BANKTON, LORD (1685–1760). [See MACDOWELL, ANDREW.]

BANKWELL, **BAKWELL**, **BACQWELL**, or **BANQUELLE**, JOHN DE (d. 1308), judge; justice itinerant for Kent, 1299; baron of exchequer, 1307. [iii. 136]

BANKWELL, ROGER DE (fl. 1340), judge; appointed justice of king's bench, 1341. [iii. 136]

BANKYN or **BANEKYNE**, JOHN (fl. 1382), friar of Augustinian monastery, London; D.D. Oxford; opposed Wycliffe at Blackfriars council, 1382. [iii. 136]

BANNARD, JOHN (fl. 1412), Augustinian friar at Oxford; according to Wood, professor of theology, and afterwards chancellor of the university. [iii. 137]

BANNATYNE, GEORGE (1545–1608 ?), collector of Scottish poems; burgess of Edinburgh, 1587; made, in 1568, a manuscript collection of poems by fifteenth and sixteenth century poets. The 'Bannatyne MS.' has been printed by the Hunterian Club. [iii. 137]

BANNATYNE, RICHARD (d. 1605), secretary to John Knox; subsequently clerk to the advocate Samuel Cockburn; wrote 'Memorials of Transactions in Scotland from 1569 to 1573.' [iii. 138]

BANNATYNE, SIR WILLIAM MACLEOD (1743–1833), Scottish judge; admitted advocate, 1765; promoted to bench as Lord Bannatyne, 1799; knighted, 1823; original member of Highland Society and Bannatyne Club, and a projector of and contributor to the 'Lounger' and 'Mirror.' [iii. 138]

BANNERMAN, ANNE (*d.* 1829), Scottish poetical writer; published 'Poems,' 1800, and 'Tales of Superstition and Chivalry,' 1802. [iii. 139]

BANNERMAN, JAMES (1807–1868), theologian; educated at Edinburgh; professor of apologetics and pastoral theology, New College (Free church), Edinburgh, 1849–68; published theological works. [iii. 139]

BANNERMANN, ALEXANDER (*fl.* 1766), engraver; member of Incorporated Society of Artists, 1766; executed several portraits for Walpole's 'Anecdotes of Painters.' [iii. 139]

BANNISTER, CHARLES (1738?–1804), actor and vocalist; performed first in London at Haymarket Theatre, 1762; appeared at Ranelagh as imitator of popular vocalists; acted or sang at the Haymarket, the Royalty, Covent Garden, and Drury Lane. [iii. 140]

BANNISTER, JOHN (1760–1836), comedian; son of Charles Bannister [q. v.]; student at Royal Academy; appeared at Haymarket as Dick in Murphy's 'Apprentice,' 1778; engaged as stock actor at Drury Lane, 1778–9; created Don Whiskerandos in the 'Critic,' Drury-Lane, 1779, and subsequently numbered among his parts Charles Surface, Parolles, George Barnwell, Brisk (Congreve's 'Double Dealer'), Speed ('Two Gentlemen of Verona'), Sir Anthony Absolute, Bob Acres, and Tony Lumpkin; acting-manager of Drury Lane, 1802–3; retired, 1815. [iii. 140]

BANNISTER, JOHN (1816–1873), philologist; M.A. Trinity College, Dublin, 1853; LL.D., 1866; perpetual curate of Bridgehill, Derbyshire, 1846–57, and of St. Day, Cornwall, 1857–73; published works on Cornish language. [iii. 141]

BANNISTER, SAXE (1790–1877), miscellaneous writer; M.A. Queen's College, Oxford, 1815; called to bar at Lincoln's Inn; attorney-general of New South Wales, 1823–6; bedel to Royal College of Physicians, 1848; published pamphlets and legal and historical works. [iii. 142]

BANSLEY, CHARLES (*fl.* 1548), poet; published a rhyming satire on feminine love of dress, 1540. [iii. 143]

BANTING, WILLIAM (1797–1878), writer on corpulence; undertaker in London; published 'A Letter on Corpulence,' 1863. [iii. 143]

BANYER, HENRY (*fl.* 1739), medical writer; physician at Wisbeach; extraordinary L.C.S., 1736; published medical works. [iii. 143]

BAPTIST, JOHN GASPARS (*d.* 1691), portrait and tapestry painter; pupil of Bossaert. [iii. 144]

BARBAR, THOMAS (*fl.* 1587), divine; M.A. St. John's College, Cambridge, 1567; B.D., 1576; preacher at St. Mary-le-Bow, *c.* 1576; suspended for refusing to take the ex-officio oath, 1584. [iii. 144]

BARBAULD, ANNA LETITIA (1743–1825), miscellaneous writer; *née* Aikin; acquired considerable learning at an early age; published poems, 1773, and, with her brother, prose essays; married Rev. Rochemont Barbauld, 1774; established boys' school at Palgrave, Suffolk, where were written her 'Hymns in Prose for Children'; gave up the school, 1785; published selection of English prose and poetry, entitled 'The Female Speaker,' and 'Eighteen Hundred and Eleven,' a poem, 1811 (original of Macaulay's 'New Zealander'). [iii. 144]

BARBER, CHARLES (*d.* 1854), landscape painter; teacher of drawing at the Royal Institution, Liverpool, where he helped to found the Architectural and Archæological Association. [iii. 146]

BARBER, CHARLES CHAPMAN (*d.* 1882), barrister; B.A. St. John's College, Cambridge, 1833; called to bar at Lincoln's Inn; acted for defendants in Tichborne trials, 1867 and 1872, and for crown in subsequent prosecution for perjury. [iii. 146]

BARBER, CHRISTOPHER (1736–1810), miniaturist; exhibited at Royal Academy from 1770. [iii. 146]

BARBER, EDWARD (*d.* 1674?), baptist minister in the Spital, Bishopsgate Street, London; originally clergyman of established church; wrote controversial and other religious works. [iii. 146]

BARBER, JOHN (*d.* 1549), clergyman and civilian; D.C.L. All Souls' College, Oxford, and member of College of Advocates, 1532; joined a plot against Cranmer, 1543; probably identical with John Barbour, proctor for Anne Boleyn on occasion of her divorce. [iii. 147]

BARBER, JOHN VINCENT (*fl.* 1830), painter; son of Joseph Barber [q. v.]; exhibited at the Royal Academy, 1812, 1821, 1829, and 1830. [iii. 148]

BARBER, JOSEPH (1757–1811), landscape painter; established drawing-school at Birmingham. [iii. 148]

BARBER, MARY (1690?–1757), poetess; wife of a tailor in Dublin; attracted by her poems the attention of Swift, who provided her with introductions in England, where she published with some success, by subscription (1734), 'Poems on Several Occasions.' Being in pecuniary distress she obtained from Swift his unpublished 'Polite Conversations,' the publication (1738) and sale of which placed her in comfortable circumstances. [iii. 148]

BARBER, SAMUEL (1738?–1811), Irish presbyterian minister at Rathfriland, co. Down, 1763–1811; licensed, 1761; colonel of Rathfriland volunteers, 1782; urged sweeping civil and ecclesiastical reforms in volunteer conventions, 1782, 1783, and 1793; moderator of general synod, 1790; imprisoned on charge of high treason, 1798; published, 1786, vigorous 'Remarks' on the bishop of Cloyne's 'Present State of the Church of Ireland.' [iii. 149]

BARBON, NICHOLAS (*d.* 1698), writer on money; probably son of Praisegod Barbon [q. v.]; M.D. Utrecht, 1661; hon F.C.P., 1664; M.P. for Bramber, 1690 and 1695; erected many buildings in London after fire of 1666; first instituted fire insurance in England; wrote two treatises on raising value of coinage. [iii. 150]

BARBON or **BAREBONE** or **BAREBONES**, PRAISE-GOD (1596?–1679), anabaptist and politician; leather-seller in Fleet Street; freeman of Leathersellers' Company, 1623; warder of yeomanry, 1630; third warder, 1648; chosen minister by pædo-baptist members of a divided congregation in Fleet Street, 1630; published defence of pædo-baptism, 1642; M.P. for City of London, 1653; opposed restoration of Charles II by circulating an account of Charles's life in Holland and petitioning parliament, 1660; confined, after the Restoration, for some time in the Tower. [iii. 151]

BARBOUR, JOHN (1316?–1395), Scottish poet; archdeacon of Aberdeen; probably studied and taught at Oxford and Paris; one of auditors of exchequer, 1372, 1382, and 1384; clerk for audit of king's household, 1373; composed his poem 'Brus,' celebrating the war of independence and deeds of King Robert and James Douglas, 1375. Other poems which have with reasonable certainty been ascribed to him are the 'Legend of Troy,' and 'Legends of the Saints,' being translations from Guido da Colonna's 'Historia Destructionis Troiæ' and the 'Legenda Aurea.' [iii. 153]

BARCAPLE, LORD (1803–1870). [See MAITLAND, EDWARD FRANCIS.]

BARCHAM, JOHN (1572?–1642). [See BARKHAM.]

BARCLAY, ALEXANDER (1475?–1552), poet, scholar, and divine; probably of Scottish birth; travelled on the continent; priest in college of Ottery St. Mary, Devonshire; translated Brant's 'Narrenschiff' into English verse as 'The Shyp of Folys,' 1508; became a Benedictine monk at Ely, where he wrote his 'Eclogues' and translated a 'Life of St. George' from Baptist Mantuan; left Ely before dissolution of the monasteries and joined Franciscan order at Canterbury; rector of All Hallows, Lombard Street, London, 1552. His works include a translation of Sallust's 'Bellum Jugurthinum.' [iii. 156]

BARCLAY, ANDREW WHYTE (1817–1884), physician; M.D. Edinburgh, 1839, and Cambridge, 1852; physician, St. George's Hospital, 1862–82; wrote medical works. [iii. 161]

BARCLAY, DAVID (1610–1686), Scottish soldier and politician; served under Gustavus Adolphus; commanded with Middleton before Inverness, 1646; member of Scottish and (1654–6) Cromwell's parliaments; arrested, 1665; released; quaker, 1666. [iii. 167]

BARCLAY, SIR GEORGE (*fl.* 1696), principal agent in assassination plot against William III, 1696 ; of Scottish descent ; commanded under M'Donald at Killiecrankie ; lieutenant in James's horse-guards ; commissioned, 1696, to stir up a rising in James's favour in England, but detected. [iii. 161]

BARCLAY, HUGH (1799–1884), Scottish lawyer ; member of Glasgow faculty of law, 1821 ; sheriff substitute of western Perthshire, 1829, and of Perthshire, 1833 ; published legal works, including 'Digest of Law of Scotland' (1852-3). [iii. 162]

BARCLAY, JOHN (1582–1621), author of the 'Argenis,' born at Pont-à-Mousson ; perhaps educated by jesuits ; lived in London, 1606-16, and in Rome, 1616–21 ; published 'Satyricon,' 1603-7, 'Sylvæ' (Latin poems), 1606, 'Icon Animorum,' 1614, and 'Argenis,' a Latin satire on political faction and conspiracy, 1621. [iii. 162]

BARCLAY, JOHN (1734-1798), minister of church of Scotland ; M.A. St. Andrews ; assistant minister at Errol, whence he was dismissed for inculcating obnoxious doctrines ; assistant minister at Fettercairn, Kincardineshire, 1763 ; published religious treatises, including 'Without Faith, without God' (1769), and was inhibited from preaching at Fettercairn, 1772 ; appealed unsuccessfully to synod ; formed with his disciples (who designated themselves Bereans) congregations at Sauchyburn and Edinburgh, teaching in the main the doctrines of Calvin ; subsequently founded a church of Bereans in London. [iii. 164]

BARCLAY, JOHN (1741-1823), general ; lieutenant in marines, 1756 ; served throughout seven years' war and American war ; captain, 1762 ; brevet-major, 1777 ; brevet-lieutenant-colonel, 1783 ; employed on staff in England ; general, 1813 ; retired, 1814. [iii. 166]

BARCLAY, JOHN (1758-1826), anatomist ; nephew of John Barclay (1734-1798) [q. v.] ; educated at St. Andrews ; licensed minister ; M.D. Edinburgh, 1796 ; lectured on anatomy in Edinburgh, 1797-1825 ; F.C.P. Edinburgh, 1806 ; published works on anatomy. [iii. 166]

BARCLAY, JOSEPH (1831-1881), bishop of Jerusalem, 1881 ; M.A. Trinity College, Dublin, 1857 ; missionary at Constantinople for Society for Promoting Christianity among Jews, 1858 ; incumbent of Christ Church, Jerusalem, 1861-70 ; returned to England and received living of Stapleford ; D.D. Dublin, 1880 ; published translations from Talmud. [iii. 167]

BARCLAY, ROBERT (1648-1690), quaker apologist ; son of David Barclay [q. v.] ; educated at Scottish college, Paris ; joined quakers, 1667 ; published 'Catechism and Confession of Faith,' 1673, and 'The Apology,' 1676, upholding quaker doctrines ; travelled in Holland and Germany, and made acquaintance of Elizabeth, princess Palatine ; several times imprisoned, but by 1679 was enjoying favour at court ; received, with Penn and other quakers, proprietorship of East New Jersey, 1683, of which he was appointed nominal governor ; died at Ury, where he had resided for many years. 'The Apology' is the standard exposition of the tenets of his sect, of which the essential principle is that all true knowledge comes from divine revelation to the heart of the individual. [iii. 167]

BARCLAY, ROBERT (1774-1811), lieutenant-colonel ; served with distinction in East Indies, 1789-95 ; with Moore in Sweden and Portugal as lieutenant-colonel, 1806 ; died from effects of wound received at Busaco. [iii. 170]

BARCLAY, CAPTAIN ROBERT (1779-1854). [See ALLARDICE, ROBERT BARCLAY.]

BARCLAY, ROBERT (1833-1876), ecclesiastical historiographer ; educated at Friends' schools ; opened stationery manufacturing business, London, 1855 ; frequently preached at quaker meetings and missions, though not a minister ; published 'Inner Life of Religious Societies of Commonwealth,' 1876. [iii. 170]

BARCLAY, THOMAS (*fl.* 1620), scholar ; studied at Bordeaux ; professor of ancient and modern law, Toulouse, at Poitiers, and finally again at Toulouse. [iii. 171]

BARCLAY, THOMAS (1792-1873), principal of Glasgow University ; M.A. King's College, Aberdeen, 1812 ; reporter for 'Times,' London, 1818-22 ; minister of Dunrossness, Shetland, 1822, and of Lerwick, 1827 ; clerk of

synod of Shetland, 1831 ; D.D. Aberdeen, 1849 ; principal of Glasgow University, 1858-73. [iii. 172]

BARCLAY, WILLIAM (1546 or 1547-1608), Scottish jurist ; educated at Aberdeen ; emigrated to France, 1571 ; studied at Paris and Bourges, where he taught law ; professor of civil law at Pont-à-Mousson University, councillor of state, and master of requests ; LL.D. ; resigned chair and came to England, 1603 ; returned to France, 1604, and became professor of civil law and dean of faculty of law at Angers, 1605 ; died at Angers ; his most important work, 'De Regno et Regali Potestate,' 1600. [iii. 173]

BARCLAY, WILLIAM (1570 ?-1630 ?), Scottish miscellaneous writer M.A. and M.D. Louvain ; professor of humanity, Paris University ; practised medicine in Scotland, and subsequently settled at Nantes ; his works include 'Nepenthes, or the Vertues of Tobacco,' 1614. [iii. 174]

BARCLAY, WILLIAM (1797-1859), miniature painter ; exhibited at Royal Academy and at the Salon. [iii. 174]

BARCROFT, GEORGE (*d.* 1610), musician ; B.A. Trinity College, Cambridge, 1574 ; minor canon and organist at Ely Cathedral, 1579-1610. [iii. 175]

BARD, HENRY, VISCOUNT BELLAMONT (1604 ?-1660), soldier and diplomatist ; educated at Eton and King's College, Cambridge ; D.C.L. Oxford, 1643 ; fought for king during civil war ; captured by parliamentarians and exiled, 1647 ; killed in sandstorm while on embassy from Charles II to Persia. [iii. 175]

BARDELBY, ROBERT DE (*fl.* 1323), judge ; one of keepers of great seal, 1302-21 ; canon of Chichester ; justice, 1323. [iii. 175]

BARDNEY, RICHARD OF (*fl.* 1503), Benedictine of Bardney, Lincolnshire ; B.D. Oxford ; wrote a metrical life of Grosstête, 1503. [iii. 176]

BARDOLF, HUGH (*d.* 1203), justiciar of curia regis ; itinerant justice, 1184-9 ; associated in the charge of the kingdom in Henry's absence, 1188 ; justiciar with Puiset and Longchamp, 1189. [iii. 176]

BARDOLF or **BARDOLPH**, THOMAS, fifth BARON BARDOLF (1368-1408), warrior ; succeeded to barony, 1386 ; supported the Percies during Richard II's reign ; accompanied Henry IV on invasion of Scotland, 1400 ; implicated in Hotspur's rebellion, 1403 ; joined Northumberland, 1405, and suffered confiscation of lands ; assisted Owen Glendower [q. v.] in Wales, 1405-6 ; invaded north of England with Northumberland, and was defeated by Sir Thomas Rokeby [q. v.] at Bramham Moor, where he died of wounds. Lord Bardolf figures in Shakespeare's 'Henry IV.' [Suppl. i. 123]

BARDOLF, WILLIAM (*d.* 1276), baronial leader ; made constable of Nottingham by provisions of Oxford ; surrendered Nottingham to the king, 1264 ; joined Henry III and was captured at Lewes. [iii. 176]

BARDSLEY, SIR JAMES LOMAX(1801-1876), physician ; M.D. Edinburgh, 1823 ; president, Royal Medical Society ; physician to Manchester Infirmary, 1823-43 ; knighted, 1853 ; published medical writings. [iii. 176]

BARDSLEY, SAMUEL ARGENT (1764-1851), physician ; educated at London, Edinburgh, and Leyden ; M.D., 1789 ; physician to Manchester Infirmary, 1790-1823 ; published medical and other writings. [iii. 177]

BARDWELL, THOMAS (*d.* 1780 ?), portrait painter ; well-known copyist ; published 'Practice of Painting and Perspective made easy,' 1756. [iii. 177]

BAREBONES, PRAISEGOD (1596 ?-1679). [See BARBON.]

BARENGER, JAMES (1780-1831), animal painter ; exhibited at Royal Academy, 1807-1831. [iii. 177]

BARET or **BARRET**, JOHN (*d.* 1580 ?), lexicographer ; M.A. Trinity College, Cambridge, 1558 ; fellow ; M.D., 1577 ; published 'An Alvearie, or Triple Dictionarie in English, Latin, and French,' 1574. [iii. 177]

BARETTI, GIUSEPPE MARC' ANTONIO (1719-1789), miscellaneous writer ; born at Turin ; keeper of stores of new fortifications, Cuneo, 1743-5 ; at Turin 1747-51 ; led by his impetuous disposition into literary controversy with Bartoli, professor of literature at Turin, who appealed to the authorities ; came to England, obtained an engagement in Italian Opera House and opened school for teaching Italian, 1751; made acquaintance of Dr. Johnson and Thrale; published 'Italian and English Dictionary,' 1760; returned to Italy after visiting Portugal and Spain, 1760, and at Johnson's suggestion published account of his travels, 1762; undertook publication of 'La Frusta Letteraria' ('The Literary Scourge'), which Italian writers resented, 1765; returned to London, 1766; F.S.A.; travelled with Thrale in France and Flanders; tried at Old Bailey for killing ruffian who attacked him in Haymarket, and acquitted, 1769; accompanied the Thrales and Johnson to France, 1775; published in French a 'Discourse on Shakespeare,' 1777. His portrait was painted by Sir Joshua Reynolds. [iii. 178]

BARFF, SAMUEL (1793 ?-1880), phil-hellene; born presumably in England; banker and merchant at Zante, 1816, where he took part with Byron in Greek struggle for independence. [iii. 182]

BARFORD, WILLIAM, D.D. (d. 1792), scholar and divine; educated at Eton; D.D. King's College, Cambridge, 1771; public orator, 1761-8; chaplain to House of Commons, 1769; prebendary of Canterbury, 1770; vicar of All Hallows, Lombard Street, 1773-92; published poems and dissertations in Latin and Greek. [iii. 182]

BARGENY, BARONS. [See HAMILTON, JOHN, first BARON, d. 1658; HAMILTON, JOHN, second BARON, d. 1693.]

BARGRAVE, ISAAC (1586-1643), dean of Canterbury; M.A. Clare Hall, Cambridge; M.A. Oxford, and rector of Eythorne, 1611; 'taxor' at Cambridge, 1612; chaplain to Wotton at Venice; D.D. Cambridge, and prebendary of Canterbury, 1622; received living of St. Margaret's, Westminster; chaplain to Prince Charles; dean of Canterbury, 1625; became very unpopular among clergy, and at beginning of civil war was arrested and confined three weeks in the Fleet, 1642; published sermons. [iii. 183]

BARGRAVE, JOHN (1610-1680), divine; nephew of Isaac Bargrave [q. v.]; fellow of St. Peter's College, Cambridge; ejected, 1643; travelled on continent till Restoration; canon of Canterbury, 1662; went on mission to ransom English captives at Algiers. [iii. 184]

BARHAM, CHARLES FOSTER (1804-1884), physician; M.B. Cambridge, 1827; M.D., 1860; successively senior physician and consulting physician at Royal Cornwall Infirmary; wrote scientific papers. [iii. 184]

BARHAM, CHARLES MIDDLETON, first BARON (1726-1813). [See MIDDLETON, CHARLES.]

BARHAM, FRANCIS FOSTER (1808-1871), the 'Alist'; son of T. F. Barham (1766-1844) [q. v.]; enrolled attorney, 1831; joint editor and proprietor of 'New Monthly Magazine,' 1839-40; originated 'Alism,' a system which 'included and reconciled all divine truths' wheresoever found; formed society of Alists. His publications include a revised version of the bible (1848) and an edition of Jeremy Collier's 'Ecclesiastical History of Great Britain' (1840). [iii. 185]

BARHAM, HENRY (1670?-1726), naturalist; apprenticed as surgeon; master-surgeon in navy; visited Spain, Madras, and Jamaica, where he became surgeon-major of the military forces; published treatise on silk manufacture, 1719; F.R.S., 1717; returned to Jamaica, 1720, and died there. His works include a 'History of Jamaica,' and a treatise entitled 'Hortus Americanus,' containing much information on natural history. [iii. 186]

BARHAM, NICHOLAS (d. 1577), lawyer; called to bar at Gray's Inn, 1542; 'ancient,' 1552; Lent reader, 1558; serjeant-at-law, 1567; M.P. for Maidstone, 1563; conducted prosecution of Duke of Norfolk for conspiring with Mary Queen of Scots against Elizabeth, 1572, and of the duke's secretary, Higford; died of gaol fever contracted at trial of Jencks, a malcontent Roman catholic. [iii. 187]

BARHAM, RICHARD HARRIS (1788-1845), author of 'Ingoldsby Legends'; educated at St. Paul's School and Brasenose College, Oxford; incumbent of Snargate, 1817; minor canon of St. Paul's, 1821; appointed priest-in-ordinary of chapels royal, 1824; divinity lecturer at St. Paul's and vicar of St. Faith's, 1842. The 'Ingoldsby Legends' were printed in 'Bentley's Miscellany' and the 'New Monthly Magazine' and were published collectively, 1840; second and third series appeared, 1847. [iii. 188]

BARHAM, THOMAS FOSTER (1766-1844), musician; B.A. St. John's College, Cambridge, 1792; engaged in mercantile pursuits; published original musical compositions and miscellaneous works. [iii. 189]

BARHAM, THOMAS FOSTER (1794-1869), physician and classical scholar; son of Thomas Foster Barham [q. v.]; M.B. Queens' College, Cambridge, 1820; practised at Penzance; physician to Exeter dispensary and institution for blind, 1830; actively supported unitarian congregations at Exeter; published theological and classical works. [iii. 190]

BARHAM, WILLIAM FOSTER (1802-1847 ?), poet; son of Thomas Foster Barham (1766-1844) [q. v.]; B.A. Trinity College, Cambridge, 1824; Porson prizeman, 1821 and 1822; M.A., 1827; author of an unpublished poem on 'Moskow.' [iii. 190]

BARING, ALEXANDER, first BARON ASHBURTON (1774-1848), financier and statesman; son of Sir Francis Baring [q. v.], whose financial house he entered; spent some time in United States; M.P. for Taunton, 1806-26, Callington, 1826-31, Thetford, 1831-2, and North Essex, 1833-5; opposed measures against American commerce; president of board of trade and master of mint, 1834; raised to peerage, 1835; commissioner at Washington for settlement of boundary dispute, 1842; published political and economic pamphlets. [iii. 190]

BARING, CHARLES THOMAS (1807-1879), bishop of Durham; grandson of Sir Francis Baring [q. v.]; graduated at Christ Church, Oxford, first-class classics and mathematics, 1829; incumbent of All Saints, Marylebone, 1847; chaplain in ordinary to the queen and select preacher at Oxford, 1850; bishop of Gloucester and Bristol, 1856, of Durham, 1861. [iii. 191]

BARING, SIR FRANCIS (1740-1810), London merchant; founder of financial house of Baring Brothers & Co.; a director of East India Company, 1779, chairman, 1792-3; baronet, 1793; M.P., 1784-90 and 1794-1806; published financial treatises. [iii. 192]

BARING, SIR FRANCIS THORNHILL, BARON NORTHBROOK (1796-1866), statesman; grandson of Sir Francis Baring [q. v.]; M.P. for Portsmouth, 1826-65; lord of treasury, 1830-4, and joint secretary, 1834 and 1835-9; chancellor of exchequer, 1839-41; first lord of admiralty, 1849-52; peer, 1866. [iii. 193]

BARING, HARRIET, LADY ASHBURTON (d. 1857), née Montagu; daughter of sixth Earl of Sandwich; married William Bingham Baring, second baron Ashburton [q. v.], 1823; of literary tastes; friend of Carlyle. [iii. 193]

BARING, THOMAS (1799-1873), financier; grandson of Sir Francis Baring [q. v.]; M.P. for Great Yarmouth, 1835-7, and Huntingdon, 1844-73; chancellor of exchequer, 1852 and 1858. [iii. 193]

BARING, WILLIAM BINGHAM, second BARON ASHBURTON (1799-1864), statesman; son of Alexander Baring, first baron [q. v.]; M.P. from 1826 to 1848; secretary to board of control, 1841-5; paymaster, 1845-6; president of Geographical Society, 1860-4. [iii. 193]

BARKER, ANDREW (d. 1577), merchant of Bristol; engaged in trade with Spanish settlements; fitted out expedition, 1576, and was killed by Spaniards. [iii. 194]

BARKER, BENJAMIN (1776-1838), landscape painter; brother of Thomas Barker (1769-1847) [q. v.]; exhibited at Royal Academy, 1800-21. [iii. 194]

BARKER, SIR CHRISTOPHER (d. 1549), Garter king-of-arms; Lysley pursuivant and, later, Suffolk herald in Duke of Suffolk's service; successively Calais pursuivant extraordinary, Rougedragon pursuivant, Richmond herald (1522), Norroy king-of-arms and Garter king-of-arms (1536); knighted, 1548. [iii. 194]

BARKER or **BARKAR**, CHRISTOPHER (1529?-1599), queen's printer; originally member of Drapers' Company; Genevan bible first printed in England by him, 1575; printed two different versions of bible, 1576; purchased patent including right to print Old and New Testament in English, thereby becoming queen's printer, 1577; warden of Stationers' Company, 1582; obtained exclusive patent for all state printing and for religious books,

1589. He produced thirty-eight editions of the bible or parts thereof between 1575 and 1588, and his deputies produced thirty-four between 1588 and 1599. [iii. 195]

BARKER, COLLET (1784-1831), explorer ; captain in 39th regiment in Peninsula and in Ireland ; sailed for Australia, 1828 ; successively commandant of settlements at Raffles Bay and King George's Sound ; lost his life while exploring neighbourhood of St. Vincent's Gulf. [iii. 197]

BARKER, EDMOND (1721-1780 ?), physician ; M.D. Leyden, 1747 ; member of Ivy Lane Club, founded by Dr. Johnson ; librarian to College of Physicians, 1760.
[iii. 197]

BARKER, EDMUND HENRY (1788-1839), classical scholar ; educated at Trinity College, Cambridge ; imprisoned in Fleet owing to financial losses arising from an unsuccessful lawsuit to prove his father's legitimacy ; edited many editions of Greek and Latin authors and compiled with Professor Dunbar of Edinburgh a Greek and English lexicon. [iii. 198]

BARKER, FRANCIS (d. 1859 ?), Irish physician ; established first fever hospital in Ireland, at Waterford ; professor of chemistry, Dublin ; M.D., 1810 ; secretary to Irish board of health, 1820-52. [iii. 199]

BARKER, FREDERICK (1808-1882), Australian bishop ; M.A. Jesus College, Cambridge, 1839 ; bishop of Sydney and metropolitan of Australia, 1854 ; D.D., 1854 ; formed general synod with authority over church in Australia and Tasmania ; died at San Remo. [iii. 199]

BARKER, GEORGE (1776-1845), solicitor of Birmingham, where he founded Philosophical Society, and greatly improved general hospital ; member of Royal Society, 1839. [iii. 200]

BARKER, Sir GEORGE ROBERT (1817-1861), colonel royal artillery : served as captain in Crimean war, and as colonel during Indian mutiny ; K.C.B. [iii. 200]

BARKER, HENRY ASTON (1774-1856), panorama painter ; son of Robert Barker (1739-1806) [q. v.] ; pupil at Royal Academy, 1788 ; between 1802 and 1822 prepared and exhibited panoramas including Constantinople, Malta, Venice, and battle of Waterloo. [iii. 201]

BARKER, HUGH (d. 1632), lawyer ; master of school attended by Selden at Chichester ; D.L. Oxford, 1605 ; dean of court of arches. [iii. 201]

BARKER, JAMES (1772-1838), navy captain ; lieutenant, 1795 ; at battles of L'Orient, St. Vincent, and the Nile ; commander, 1798 ; post captain, 1812. [iii. 201]

BARKER, JOHN (fl. 1464), scholar ; educated at Eton and King's College, Cambridge ; wrote 'Scutum Inexpugnabile,' a work on logic. [iii. 202]

BARKER, JOHN (d. 1653), navy captain ; London ship-owner ; obtained, with others, letters of marque for vessel, which he commanded in Mediterranean ; captain of one of his own ships in Dutch war, 1652 ; confirmed as captain in navy, 1653 ; killed in fight off Portland.
[iii. 202]

BARKER, JOHN (1708-1748), medical writer ; M.D. Wadham College, Oxford, 1743 ; M.C.P., 1746 ; physician to his majesty's forces in Low Countries, 1747 ; published works on epidemic fever of 1740-2. [iii. 203]

BARKER, JOHN (1682-1762), presbyterian divine ; minister to congregation at Mare Street, Hackney, 1714-1738 ; pastor of Salters' Hall congregation, 1741-62 ; published sermons. [iii. 202]

BARKER, JOHN (1771-1849), British consul-general in Egypt, 1829-33 ; born in Smyrna ; entered London banking house ; private secretary to John Spencer Smith, British ambassador to the Porte, 1797-9 ; British consul at Alexandria, 1825 ; retired to Suediah, near Antioch, 1833.
[iii. 204]

BARKER, JOSEPH (1806-1875), preacher and controversialist ; wool-spinner at Bramley, near Leeds, and Wesleyan preacher and home missionary ; joined Methodist New Connexion ; travelling preacher successively on Hanley, Halifax, Newcastle-on-Tyne, and Sunderland circuits, 1829-33 ; preacher on Chester circuit, 1835-7 ; expelled from Methodist New Connexion for denying the 'divine appointment of baptism,' 1841 ; pastor at Newcastle-on-Tyne ; imprisoned for connection with Chartist agitation, 1848 ; went to Central Ohio, 1851 ; made

lecturing tours, 1857-8 ; returned to England, 1860 ; joined primitive methodists at Bilston and Tunstall, and was local preacher, 1863-8 ; died at Omaha. Published controversial and religious works ; conducted printing business, issued 'Barker's Library,' a cheap series of theological, philosophical, and ethical works, and founded several periodicals, including 'The People,' to propagate his extreme opinions. [iii. 204]

BARKER, MATTHEW (1619-1698), nonconformist divine ; M.A. Trinity College, Cambridge ; conducted school at Banbury till 1641 ; incumbent of St. Leonard's, Eastcheap, 1650 ; ejected, 1662 ; preached at meeting-house in Miles Lane, 1666 ; published religious works.
[iii. 207]

BARKER, MATTHEW HENRY (1790-1846), writer of sea tales ; served on East Indiaman and in navy ; naval editor of 'United Service Gazette.' [iii. 207]

BARKER, ROBERT (d. 1645), king's printer ; son of Christopher Barker [q. v.] : freeman of Stationers' Company, 1589 ; liveryman, 1592 ; received reversion of his father's patent for English bibles, prayer-books, statutes, and proclamations, 1589 ; specially licensed 'to print all statutes and libels for life,' 1603, and 'all books in Latin, Greek, and Hebrew, Trimelius's Latin bible, and all charts and maps, 1604 ; his most important publication was the first edition of the authorised version of the English bible, 1611, and the 'Wicked' bible, 1631. [iii. 207]

BARKER, Sir ROBERT (1729 ?-1789), officer of East India Company in India, 1749 ; captain of artillery at Chandernagore and Plassey, 1758 ; major in Draper's expedition from Madras to Philippine islands, 1762 ; K.B., 1763 ; provincial commander-in-chief in Bengal, 1770 ; concluded treaty with the Rohillas, 1772 ; quarrelled with Warren Hastings and returned to England ; M.P. for Wallingford ; published scientific treatises.
[iii. 208]

BARKER, ROBERT (1739-1806), reputed inventor of panoramas ; portrait painter and teacher of drawing in Edinburgh ; exhibited panorama at Edinburgh, Holyrood, and Glasgow, and in London, 1789 ; subsequently exhibited in London other panoramas, including a view of fleet at Spithead, 1794. [iii. 209]

BARKER, SAMUEL (1686-1759), hebraist ; wrote a Hebrew grammar, published 1761. [iii. 210]

BARKER, THOMAS (fl. 1651), author of 'The Art of Angling,' 1651 ; probably gained a living by accompanying gentlemen on fishing expeditions. [iii. 210]

BARKER, THOMAS (1722-1809), scientist and miscellaneous writer ; published 'An Account of Discoveries concerning Comets,' 1757, and other works. [iii. 211]

BARKER, THOMAS (1769-1847), painter ; attracted attention of a wealthy coachmaker of Bath, who provided him with means of studying in Rome ; painted chiefly landscapes and rustic scenes ; exhibited occasionally at Royal Academy, 1791-1829, and at British Institution, 1807-47 ; 'The Woodman' and 'Old Tom' are two of his best-known pictures. [iii. 211]

BARKER, THOMAS JONES (1815-1882), painter ; son of Thomas Barker (1769-1847) [q. v.] ; studied in Paris, 1834-45, and exhibited frequently at the Salon ; returned to England, 1845, and became known as painter of portraits and military subjects ; made many sketches at seat of hostilities during Franco-German war, 1870 ; his works include 'Meeting of Wellington and Blucher' and 'Nelson on board the San Josef.' [iii. 212]

BARKER, THOMAS RICHARD (1799-1870), independent minister ; educated at Christ's Hospital ; pastor at Alresford, Hampshire, 1822, Harpenden, 1824, and Uxbridge, 1833-8 ; tutor in classics and Hebrew, Spring Hill College, Birmingham, 1838-70. [iii. 213]

BARKER, WILLIAM (fl. 1572), translator ; M.P. for Great Yarmouth ; secretary to Duke of Norfolk, for complicity in whose plots he was confined in Tower, 1571 ; probably author of translations from Italian and Greek, including Xenophon's 'Cyropædia.' [iii. 213]

BARKER, WILLIAM BURCKHARDT (1810 ?-1856), orientalist, son of John Barker (1771-1849) [q. v.] ; born at Aleppo ; in England, 1819 ; journeyed to sources of the Orontes, Syria ; for many years official resident at Tarsus, and subsequently professor of Arabic, Turkish, Russian, and Hindustani, Eton College; during the Crimean war, chief superintendent of land transport at Sinope, where he died; published oriental works. [iii. 213]

BARKER, WILLIAM HIGGS (1744–1815), hebraist; B.A. Trinity College, Cambridge, 1765; Perry exhibitioner, 1764–7; master of Carmarthen grammar school, 1767; published Hebrew grammar (1774) and lexicon (1812). [iii. 214]

BARKHAM or **BARCHAM,** JOHN (1572?–1642), antiquary and historian; M.A. Corpus Christi College, 1594; B.D., 1603; chaplain to Bancroft and Abbot, archbishops of Canterbury; prebendary of St. Paul's, 1610, assisted Speed in 'History of Britain,' and left in manuscript a treatise on coins. [iii. 214]

BARKING, RICHARD DE (d. 1246), judge; prior and, 1222, abbot of Westminster; successively privy councillor, baron of exchequer, and treasurer; lord justice during king's absence in Welsh wars, 1245. [iii. 215]

BARKLY, ARTHUR CECIL STUART (1843–1890), colonial governor; son of Sir Henry Barkly [q. v.]; lieutenant-governor of Falkland Islands, 1886–7, and of Heligoland, 1888–90. [Suppl. i. 126]

BARKLY, SIR HENRY (1815–1898), colonial governor; M.P. for Leominster, 1845–8; governor and commander-in-chief of British Guiana, 1848–53; K.C.B., 1853; governor of Jamaica, 1853–6, Victoria, 1856–63, Mauritius, 1863–70, and Cape Colony, 1870–7; high commissioner for settling affairs of territories adjacent to eastern frontier of Cape Colony, 1870; proclaimed Griqualand West a British dependency, 1871; G.C.M.G., 1874; opposed Lord Carnarvon's attempt to force federation on Cape Colony, though considering it ultimately desirable; commissioner on defence of British possessions and commerce abroad, 1879; F.R.S., 1864; F.R.G.S., 1870. [Suppl. i. 124]

BARKSDALE, CLEMENT (1609–1687), author; educated at Merton College and Gloucester Hall (afterwards Worcester College), Oxford; chaplain of Lincoln College; vicar of Hereford and master of the free school, 1637; chaplain to Chandos family during civil war; published works chiefly of religious character. [iii. 215]

BARKSTEAD, JOHN (d. 1662), regicide; goldsmith in London; captain of parliamentary infantry under Colonel Venn; governor of Reading, 1645; commanded regiment at siege of Colchester; one of the king's judges, 1648; governor of Yarmouth, 1649, and of the Tower, 1652; M.P. for Colchester, 1654, and Middlesex, 1656; knighted, 1656; escaped to continent, 1660; arrested, 1661; brought to England and executed. [iii. 216]

BARKSTED, WILLIAM (fl. 1611), actor and poet; one of the company known as 'children of the chapel' and later as 'children of the queen's revels'; author of the poems, 'Mirrha, the Mother of Venus' (1607), and 'Hiren, or the Faire Greeke,' 1611. [iii. 217]

BARKWORTH or LAMBERT, MARK (d. 1601), Benedictine monk; laboured on English mission; hanged at Tyburn, as catholic priest unlawfully abiding in England. [iii. 218]

BARLING, JOHN (1804–1883), dissenting minister, joined unitarians, and was minister in Halifax, 1854–8; published religious treatises. [iii. 218]

BARLOW, EDWARD, known as AMBROSE (1587–1641), Benedictine monk; worked on English mission in Lancashire; executed at Lancaster as catholic priest unlawfully abiding in England. [iii. 218]

BARLOW, alias BOOTH, EDWARD (1639–1719), priest and mechanician; educated at Lisbon; worked on English mission in Yorkshire and Lancashire; invented repeating clocks, c. 1676, and, later, repeating watches; wrote works on meteorology, published posthumously. [iii. 219]

BARLOW, FRANCIS (1626?–1702), animal painter and engraver; executed plates for Æsop's fables, published with Mrs. Behn's translation, 1666. [iii. 219]

BARLOW, SIR GEORGE HILARO (1762–1846), governor-general; appointed to Bengal civil service, 1778; sub-secretary in revenue department, 1788; chief secretary to government, 1796; member of supreme council, 1801; baronet, 1803; governor-general, 1805–7;

governor of Madras, 1807; caused great discontent by his economical reforms in the army, an unsuccessful mutiny being the result; recalled, 1812. [iii. 220]

BARLOW, HENRY CLARK (1806–1876), writer on Dante; educated as architect; student at Royal Academy; relinquished the profession in consequence of an accident, 1827; studied medicine at Edinburgh; M.D., 1837; devoted himself to scientific pursuits and artistic criticism in Paris; studied Italian; in Italy, 1841–6; spent many years in research and in collation of manuscripts relating to Dante, in various countries of Europe; published 'Critical, Historical, and Philosophical Contributions to Study of "Divina Commedia,"' 1864; author of many works relating to Dante and Italy. [iii. 221]

BARLOW, PETER (1776–1862), mathematician, physicist, and optician; began life in obscure mercantile position; schoolmaster; assistant mathematical master (1801), and subsequently, till 1847, professor in Royal Military Academy; honorary M.I.C.E., 1820; received Society of Arts' gold medal for scheme for correcting ships' compasses, 1821; F.R.S., 1823; published 'Mathematical and Philosophical Dictionary,' 1814, and 'Essay on Strength of Timber,' 1817. [iii. 222]

BARLOW, PETER WILLIAM (1809–1885), civil engineer; associate M.I.C.E., 1827; resident engineer under Sir William Cubitt [q. v.] of various sections of London and Dover railway, 1836–40, and of the whole line, 1840; engineer-in-chief; F.R.S., 1845; employed in connection with several railways in Ireland from 1850; investigated construction of bridges of great span, 1858; engineer for Lambeth bridge, 1860–2; constructed Tower subway, 1869–1870. [Suppl. i. 126]

BARLOW, SIR ROBERT (1757–1843), admiral; lieutenant, 1778; captain, 1793; attached to fleet under Lord Howe; knighted, 1801; flag-captain to Lord Keith in Downs, 1805–6; commissioner of Chatham dockyard, 1808; K.C.B., 1820; rear-admiral, 1823; admiral, 1840; G.C.B., 1842. [Suppl. i. 127]

BARLOW, RUDESIND (1585–1656), Benedictine monk; superior of St. Gregory's at Douay. [iii. 224]

BARLOW, THOMAS (1607–1691), bishop of Lincoln; M.A. Queen's College, Oxford, 1633; metaphysical reader to university, 1635; strongly supported views then considered orthodox at Oxford, but on its surrender to Fairfax, and again at the Restoration, accommodated himself to circumstances and escaped ejection; provost of Queen's, 1657; librarian of Bodleian, 1642–60; D.D., Lady Margaret professor of divinity, and prebendary of Worcester, 1660; bishop of Lincoln, 1675; displayed strong anti-popish principles in publication of controversial and other tracts; he was one of first to declare his loyalty to James II, and turned whig at William III's accession. In addition to published works, which were chiefly religious, he left many learned treatises in manuscript. [iii. 224]

BARLOW, THOMAS OLDHAM (1824–1889), mezzotint engraver; articled as engraver at Manchester, where he studied designing; established himself independently in London, 1847; executed plates after John Phillips, Millais, Turner, Landseer, and others; R.A., 1881; director of etching class at South Kensington, 1886. [Suppl. i. 127]

BARLOW, THOMAS WORTHINGTON (1823?–1856), antiquary and naturalist; F.L.S., 1848; called to bar at Gray's Inn, 1848; practised at Manchester; queen's advocate, Sierra Leone, 1856; published work so unnatural history and the antiquities of Cheshire. [iii. 229]

BARLOW, WILLIAM (d. 1568), bishop of Chichester; D.D. Oxford; canon of St. Osyth's, Essex; prior of Blackmore, Tiptree, 1509, Lees, 1515, Bromehill, c. 1524; wrote, on suppression of Bromehill by Wolsey, a series of heretical pamphlets which were prohibited, 1529, the author subsequently recanting; attached to embassy to France and Rome, 1530; successively prior of Haverfordwest and Bisham; bishop of St. Asaph and, later, of St. David's, 1536; founded Christ College and grammar school, Brecon, 1542; bishop of Bath and Wells, 1548; resigned see on Mary's accession; imprisoned in Tower, but having recanted succeeded in reaching Germany; bishop of Chichester, 1559, and prebendary of Westminster, 1560. [iii. 229]

BARLOW, WILLIAM (d. 1613), bishop of Lincoln; M.A., St. John's College, Cambridge, 1587; fellow of Trinity Hall, 1590; D.D., 1599; chaplain to Whitgift;

prebendary of St. Paul's, 1597, Westminster, 1601-13, and Canterbury, 1606-8 ; dean of Chester, 1602-5 : chaplain to Elizabeth : took part in and drew up report of Hampton Court ,conference, 1604 ; bishop of Rochester, 1605 : one of the preachers of the controversial sermons commanded by James at Hampton Court, 1606 ; bishop of Lincoln, 1608 ; published biography of Richard Cosin (1598) and other works. [iii. 231]

BARLOW or **BARLOWE**, WILLIAM (d. 1625). divine ; B.A. Balliol College, Oxford, 1564 ; prebendary of Winchester, 1581 ; prebendary and, later, treasurer of Lichfield, 1588 ; chaplain to Prince Henry, son of James I ; published works relating to ships' compasses and the loadstone. [iii. 233]

BARMBY, JOHN GOODWYN (1820-1881), Christian socialist ; joined group of revolutionists in London, 1837 ; visited Paris, 1840 ; founded Communist Propaganda Society, 1841 ; unitarian minister successively at Southampton, Topsham, Lympstone, Lancaster, and Wakefield ; published religious works, and contributed to communist journals. [iii. 234]

BARNARD, Sir ANDREW FRANCIS (1773-1855), general ; ensign, 1794 ; captain, 1794 ; served at St. Domingo, 1795, and subsequently in West Indies, under Sir Ralph Abercromby ; accompanied expedition to Helder, 1799 ; lieutenant-colonel, and inspecting field officer of militia in Canada, 1808-9 ; served in Peninsula, 1810-14 ; colonel and K.C.B., 1813 ; present at Quatre Bras and wounded at Waterloo : lieutenant-governor of Chelsea Hospital, 1849 ; general, 1851. [iii. 235]

BARNARD, ANNE, LADY (1750-1825), authoress of 'Auld Robin Gray' ; daughter of James Lindsay, fifth earl of Balcarres ; wrote, 1771, ballad, 'Auld Robin Gray' (published anonymously) ; married Andrew Barnard (1793), with whom, when appointed colonial secretary to Macartney, she went to the Cape of Good Hope ; returned to England, 1807, and lived in Berkeley Square, where her house became a literary centre. [iii. 236]

BARNARD, CHARLOTTE ALINGTON (1830-1869), ballad-writer ; between 1858 and 1869, under pseudonym of CLARIBEL, wrote about one hundred ballads. [iii. 237]

BARNARD, EDWARD (1717-1781), provost of Eton ; educated at Eton : M.A. St. John's College, Cambridge, 1742 ; D.D., 1756 ; fellow, 1744-56 ; headmaster of Eton, 1754 ; provost, 1764 : canon of Windsor, 1761. [iii. 237]

BARNARD, EDWARD WILLIAM (1791-1828), divine and poet ; educated at Harrow ; M.A. Trinity College, Cambridge, 1817 ; held living of Brantingthorp, Yorkshire ; published imitations of Meleager (1817) and translations from Marc-Antonio Flaminio (posthumously), 1829. [iii. 237]

BARNARD, FREDERICK (1846-1896), humorous artist ; executed many cuts for household edition of Dickens's works, 1871-9, and issued series of 'Character Sketches from Dickens,' 1879-84 ; exhibited at Royal Academy ; contributed to many periodicals, including ' Punch ' and Mr. Harry Furniss's ' Lika Joko,' 1894-5. [Suppl. i. 128]

BARNARD, Sir HENRY WILLIAM (1799-1857), lieutenant-general ; nephew of Sir A. F. Barnard [q. v.] ; educated at Sandhurst ; obtained commission in grenadier guards, 1814 ; served on his uncle's staff at Paris, and on Keane's staff in Jamaica ; major-general in Crimea, 1854-5 ; Simpson's chief of staff, 1855 ; on staff in Bengal during Indian mutiny, 1857 ; died of pestilence at Delhi. [iii. 238]

BARNARD, JOHN (fl. 1641), musician ; minor canon of St. Paul's ; published collections of church music, 1641. [iii. 238]

BARNARD or **BERNARD**, JOHN (d. 1683), biographer ; B.A. and fellow, Lincoln College, Oxford, 1648 ; M.A., 1651 ; prebendary of Lincoln, 1672 ; D.D., 1669 ; published life of Dr. Heylyn, 1683. [iii. 239]

BARNARD, JOHN (fl. 1685-1693), supporter of James II : B.A. and fellow, Brasenose College, Oxford, 1682 ; took orders in church of England, but afterwards declared himself papist, and supported James II ; lecturer in moral philosophy, Queen's College, 1687-8 ; corrected and enlarged Bohun's ' Geographical Dictionary.' [iii. 239]

BARNARD, Sir JOHN (1685-1764), merchant and politician ; alderman of London, 1728-56 ; sheriff, 1735 ; lord mayor, 1737 ; knighted, 1732 ; M.P. for city of London, 1722-61 ; recognised as a high authority on financial questions ; a statue to him was erected on the Royal Exchange by his fellow citizens, 1747 ; his publications include ' A Present for an Apprentice,' 1740. [iii. 240]

BARNARD, THOMAS (1728-1806), bishop ; educated at Westminster ; M.A. Cambridge, 1749 ; archdeacon of Derry and D.D. Dublin, 1761 ; dean of Derry, 1769 ; bishop of Killaloe and Kilfenora, 1780, and of Limerick, Ardfert, and Aghadoe, 1794 ; F.R.S., 1783 ; member of the Literary Club, to which Johnson and his friends belonged. [iii. 241]

BARNARD, WILLIAM (1697-1768), bishop of Derry ; D.D. Trinity College, Cambridge, 1740 ; vicar of St. Bride's, Fleet Street, 1729 ; prebendary of Westminster, 1732 ; dean of Rochester, 1743 ; bishop of Raphoe, 1744, and of Derry, 1747. [iii. 241]

BARNARD, WILLIAM (1774-1849), mezzotint engraver ; for some years keeper of British Institution. [iii. 242]

BARNARDISTON, Sir NATHANIEL (1588-1653), puritan ; knighted, 1618 ; M.P. for Sudbury, Suffolk, 1625-6 ; refused to act as commissioner for collection of loan enforced without parliamentary consent, 1625, and was imprisoned, 1627-8 ; M.P. for Suffolk, 1628, and in 1640 in both Long and Short parliaments : took covenant and became parliamentary assessor for Suffolk, 1643 ; apparently took no active part in Great Rebellion. [iii. 242]

BARNARDISTON, Sir SAMUEL (1620-1707), whig politician ; son of preceding : knighted, 1660 ; baronet, 1663 ; deputy-governor of East India Company, 1668 ; fined and imprisoned for protesting against ruling of House of Lords in trading dispute, 1668 ; stood as whig M.P. for Suffolk, 1672, and, though gaining more votes, his opponent was returned with him by Sir William Soame, the sheriff ; declared duly elected by the Commons ; brought an action for malice against Soame in the king's bench, and recovered damages ; verdict reversed by the exchequer chamber on appeal, and reversal confirmed against Barnardiston's suit by the House of Lords ; M.P. for Suffolk, 1678-1702 ; fined and imprisoned for expressing openly dissatisfaction at proceedings following discovery of Rye House plot, 1684-8 ; judgment against him reversed, 1689. [iii. 244]

BARNARDISTON, Sir THOMAS (d. 1669), parliamentarian ; son of Sir Nathaniel Barnardiston [q. v.] ; knighted, 1641 ; M.P. for Bury St. Edmunds, 1645 ; fought on side of parliament ; M.P. for Suffolk, 1654, 1656, and 1659 ; supported Restoration ; created baronet, 1663. [iii. 246]

BARNARDISTON, THOMAS (d. 1752), legal reporter ; serjeant-at-law, 1735 ; published reports of chancery and king's bench cases. [iii. 247]

BARNATO, BARNETT ISAACS (1852-1897), financier ; real name ISAACS ; went to South Africa, 1873 ; assumed name of Barnato and traded as diamond dealer at Kimberley ; established in London firm of Barnato Brothers, 1880 ; floated Barnato Diamond Mining Company, Kimberley, 1881 ; amalgamated with De Beers company, controlled by Mr. Cecil Rhodes, 1888 ; member of Kimberley divisional council from 1880 ; member for Kimberley in Cape Assembly, 1888 and 1894 ; invested in mining and other property in Rand ; chief manipulator of ' Kaffir boom ' in London, 1895, suffering heavy losses ; drowned himself during voyage from Cape Town. [Suppl. i. 129]

BARNBARROCH, LORD (d. 1597). [See VANS, SIR PATRICK.]

BARNBY, Sir JOSEPH (1838-1896), composer and conductor ; chorister in York minster ; studied at Royal Academy of Music ; organist and choirmaster at St. Andrew's, Wells Street, London, 1863-71, and at St. Anne's, Soho, 1871-86 ; musical adviser to Messrs. Novello, 1861-76 ; formed, 1867, and conducted ' Mr. Joseph Barnby's Choir,' which gave many successful 'oratorio concerts' till 1872, when it was amalgamated with M. Gounod's choir as Royal Albert Hall Choral Society (now Royal Choral Society) ; precentor of Eton, 1875-92 ; second principal of Guildhall School of Music, 1892-6 ; knighted, 1892 ; composed chiefly sacred vocal music. [Suppl. i. 130]

BARNES, AMBROSE (1627–1710), nonconformist; merchant-adventurer, 1655; mayor of Newcastle, 1661; did much to alleviate sufferings of nonconformists in Charles II's reign; wrote social and political treatises. [iii. 247]

BARNES, BARNABE (1569 ?–1609), poet; educated at Brasenose College, Oxford; accompanied Earl of Essex to join French against Parma, 1591; issued (perhaps privately) Parthenophil and Parthenophe, Sonnettes, Madrigals, Elegies, and Odes,' 1593, and 'A Divine Centurie of Spirituall Sonnets,' 1595. In his play 'The Devil's Charter,' parallels have been found to passages in 'The Tempest' and 'Cymbeline.' [iii. 247]

BARNES, SIR EDWARD (1776–1838), lieutenant-general; ensign, 1792; colonel, 1810; on staff in Peninsula, 1812–14, and as adjutant-general in campaign of 1815, being wounded at Waterloo; K.C.B.; lieutenant-general, 1825; governor of Ceylon, 1824–31; commander-in-chief in India, and G.C.B., 1831; M.P. for Sudbury, 1837. [iii. 249]

BARNES, JOHN (d. 1661), Benedictine monk; educated at Oxford, and, being converted to catholicism, at Salamanca, entered Benedictine monastery at Valladolid, and was professed, 1604; ordained priest, 1608; assistant of English mission, 1613; banished from England; divinity lecturer at Douay; raised suspicions of his order, and was imprisoned by inquisition at Rome, where he died; published religious works. [iii. 249]

BARNES, JOSHUA (1654–1712), Greek scholar and antiquary; educated at Christ's Hospital and Emmanuel College, Cambridge; fellow, 1678; M.A., 1679; B.D., 1686; professor of Greek, 1695. His works include 'Sacred Poems,' dramatic pieces in English and Latin, a 'Life of Edward III' (1688), an edition of Homer (1710), and various religious treatises. [iii. 250]

BARNES, JULIANA (b. 1388 ?). [See BERNERS.]

BARNES, RICHARD (1532–1587), bishop of Durham; fellow of Brasenose College, Oxford, 1552; M.A., 1557; D.D., 1579; chancellor, 1561, and, later, canon-residentiary and prebendary of York; suffragan-bishop of Nottingham, 1567; bishop of Carlisle, 1570, and of Durham, 1577. [iii. 252]

BARNES, ROBERT (1495–1540), protestant divine and martyr; joined convent of Austin friars, Cambridge, and subsequently became prior of the house; D.D., 1523; brought before vice-chancellor of Clare Hall for preaching sermon of puritanical character, and, having been examined by Wolsey and four bishops, was called upon (1526) to abjure or burn; abjured; committed to the Fleet, and afterwards to the custody of the Austin friars; escaped to Antwerp, 1528; became acquainted with Luther and other reformers; returned to London on Cromwell's invitation, 1531; sent to Germany to procure from Lutheran divines approval of King Henry's divorce and second marriage, 1535, and was also employed in negotiating marriage with Anne of Cleves, 1539; attacked Gardiner with much scurrilous abuse at St. Paul's Cross; subsequently asked and received the bishop's pardon, but, returning to his old doctrines, was imprisoned under bill of attainder and ultimately burned; published religious tracts in German and English. [iii. 253]

BARNES, THOMAS (1747–1810), unitarian divine and educational reformer; minister at Cockey Moor, 1768, and at Cross Street chapel, Manchester, 1780–1810; mainly instrumental in establishing College of Arts and Sciences; hon. D.D. Edinburgh, 1784; principal of Manchester College, c. 1784–98. [iii. 257]

BARNES, THOMAS (1785–1841), editor of the 'Times,' 1817–41; educated at Christ's Hospital and Pembroke College, Cambridge; acquainted with Hunt, Lamb, and Hazlitt. [iii. 257]

BARNES, WILLIAM (1801–1886) the Dorsetshire poet; son of a farmer in Vale of Blackmore; entered solicitor's office at Dorchester, 1818; master of a school at Mere, Wiltshire, 1823; executed woodcuts for several publications; contributed to 'County Chronicle,' 1833, 'Poems in Dorset Dialect,' published, 1844; removed school to Dorchester, 1835; entered at St. John's College, Cambridge, as ten years' man, 1838; B.D., 1850; pastor of Whitcombe, 1847–52; published 'Philological Grammar,' 1854, and 'Hwomely Rhymes,' 1858; rector of Came,

1862–86. His works include 'Se Gefylsta: an Anglo-Saxon Delectus,' 1849; 'Tiw: or a View of Roots and Stems of English as a Teutonic Tongue,' 1862; and 'Grammar and Glossary of Dorset Dialect,' 1863. His poems in Dorset dialect were collected, 1879. [Suppl. i. 131]

BARNESTAPOLIUS, OBERTUS (d. 1599). [See TURNER ROBERT.]

BARNET, JOHN (d. 1373), bishop; prebendary of St. Paul's, 1347, and of Lichfield, 1354; bishop of Worcester, 1362, Bath and Wells, 1363, and Ely, 1366; treasurer of England, 1363–70. [iii. 258]

BARNETT, CURTIS (d. 1746), commodore; flag-lieutenant to Sir Charles Wager in Baltic, 1726; served as commander on Irish coast, 1730; in Mediterranean, 1731–4, and during Spanish war, 1740–2; commodore of squadron in East Indies in French war, 1744; died at Fort St. David's. [iii. 258]

BARNETT, JOHN (1802–1890), singer and musical composer; of German origin; articled to Samuel James Arnold [q. v.]; first appeared in public at Lyceum, 1813, and continued to sing till 1817; musical director at Olympic, 1832; composed 'Mountain Sylph,' opera, produced at Lyceum, 1834, and 'Fair Rosamund' (Drury Lane), 1837; opened St. James's Theatre for English opera, but achieved small success; devoted himself to teaching singing; published 'School for the Voice,' 1844. [Suppl. i. 133]

BARNETT, MORRIS (1800–1856), actor and dramatist; played with great success Tom Drops in the 'Schoolfellows' (Douglas Jerrold) at Drury Lane, 1833; wrote several popular dramas including 'Monsieur Jacques' and 'The Serious Family'; on staff of 'Morning Post' and 'Era.' [iii. 260]

BARNEWALL, ANTHONY (1721–1739), officer in the German army; son of John, eleventh lord Trimleston; served in Germany with Hamilton's cuirassiers; killed at Krotzka. [iii. 260]

BARNEWALL, JOHN, third BARON TRIMLESTON (1470–1538), high chancellor of Ireland; second justice of king's bench 1509; high treasurer of Ireland, 1524; high chancellor, 1534–8. [iii. 260]

BARNEWALL, NICHOLAS, first VISCOUNT KINGS-LAND (1592–1663), M.P. for co. Dublin in Irish parliaments, 1634 and 1639; fled on outbreak of Irish rebellion, 1643; created Viscount Kingsland, 1645. [iii. 261]

BARNEWALL, NICHOLAS, third VISCOUNT KINGS-LAND (1668–1725), captain in James's Irish army, 1688; outlawed; subscribed Irish catholic petition against infraction of treaty of Limerick, 1703. [iii. 261]

BARNEWALL or **BARNWALL**, SIR PATRICK (d. 1622), statesman; imprisoned in Dublin and afterwards in Tower for supporting petition in favour of those who refused to attend protestant church on Sundays, 1605; opposed creation of new boroughs in Ireland, 1613. [iii. 261]

BARNEWALL, RICHARD VAUGHAN (1780–1842), lawyer; called to bar at Inner Temple, 1806; reported in court of king's bench, 1817–1834. [iii. 262]

BARNEY, JOSEPH (1751–1827), fruit and flower painter; studied under Zucchi and Angelica Kauffmann; drawing master at Royal Military Academy. [iii. 262]

BARNFIELD, RICHARD (1574–1627), poet; B.A. Brasenose College, Oxford, 1592; published 'Affectionate Shepherd' (1594), 'Cynthia, with certain Sonnets' (1595), and other poems (1598), including two pieces, which appeared in the 'Passionate Pilgrim,' 1599, and were long attributed to Shakespeare. [iii. 262]

BARNHAM, BENEDICT (1559–1598), merchant and benefactor of St. Alban's Hall, Oxford, where he was educated; liveryman of Drapers' Company; alderman of London, 1591; member, Society of Antiquaries, 1572. [iii. 263]

BARNHAM, SIR FRANCIS (d. 1646 ?), parliamentarian; knighted, 1603; M.P. for Grampound, 1603 and 1614, and Maidstone, 1621, 1624, 1629, and 1640; supported parliamentarians in civil war. [iii. 264]

BARNINGHAM, JOHN (d. 1448), theologian; educated at Oxford and Paris; prior of White Carmelites at Ipswich; wrote religious treatises. [iii. 264]

BARNS, LORD (d. 1594). [See SETON, SIR JOHN.]

BARNSTON, JOHN (d. 1645), divine; fellow, Brasenose College, Oxford, where he endowed, 1628, a lectureship in Hebrew; prebendary of Salisbury, 1600; D.D., 1615. [iii. 264]

BARO, PETER (1534–1599), controversialist; born at Etampes; bachelor of civil law, Bourges, 1556; admitted advocate at Paris, 1557; entered ministry at Geneva, 1560; lecturer in divinity and Hebrew, King's College, Cambridge; Lady Margaret professor of divinity, 1574; D.D., 1576; reprimanded by the vice-chancellor for preaching Arminian doctrine and criticising the Lambeth Articles, 1595; published controversial and other religious works. He was almost the first divine in England who combated the endeavours to impart a definitely ultra-Calvinistic character to the church of England. [iii. 265]

BARON or **BARRON**, BARTHOLOMEW or BONAVENTURA (d. 1696), Irish Franciscan and miscellaneous writer; entered Franciscan order in Italy, c. 1636; lived at college of St. Isidore, Rome: successively provincial commissary of Franciscans and custos of Scotland; spent close of his life at Rome. His publications include several poems, a treatise on Boethius, and an exposition of the works of Duns Scotus. [iii. 267]

BARON, BERNARD (d. 1762), engraver; reproduced works by Vandyck, Kneller, Hogarth, Rubens, Titian, Watteau, Teniers, and other artists. [iii. 267]

BARON or **BARRON**, GEOFFREY (d. 1651), Irish rebel; elder brother of Bartholomew Baron [q. v.]; delegate of Irish confederates to court of France, 1642; executed on taking of Limerick. [iii. 268]

BARON, JOHN (1786–1851), physician; M.D. Edinburgh, 1805; practised at Gloucester; physician to General Infirmary; admitted to the Royal Society, 1823; retired to Cheltenham, 1832; founder of Medical Benevolent Fund, and active supporter of Medical Missionary Society of Edinburgh. His publications include a 'Life of Edward Jenner' and three works on tubercle. [iii. 269]

BARON or **BARRON**, RICHARD (d. 1766), republican; educated at Glasgow, 1737–40; edited Milton's prose works, Algernon Sidney's 'Discourse concerning Government,' and collections of republican tracts and other works. [iii. 270]

BARON, ROBERT (1593?–1639), divine; successively professor of divinity at St. Salvator's College, St. Andrews, and at Marischal College, Aberdeen; minister of Greyfriars, Aberdeen, 1624; D.D., 1627; published controversial and other religious writings. [iii. 270]

BARON, ROBERT (fl. 1645), poet and dramatist; educated at Cambridge. His publications include 'Cyprian Academy,' 1647, which, with other of his works, contains whole passages from Milton's minor poems (1645), 'Mirza,' a tragedy, resembling Denham's 'Sophy' (1642); and 'Apologie for Paris,' 1649, many passages of which are possibly imitated from Jonson's 'Catiline.' He was a skilful plagiarist, but was detected after the lapse of a century. [iii. 270]

BARON, STEPHEN (d. 1520?), Franciscan friar of the Strict Observance; confessor to Henry VIII and provincial of his order in England. [iii. 272]

BARONS or **BARNES**, WILLIAM (d. 1505), bishop of London; LL.D. Oxford; commissary of chapter and of prerogative court, Canterbury; deputed to reply in St. Paul's to objections to banns of Prince Arthur and Katharine of Arragon, 1501; master of rolls, 1502; bishop of London, 1504. [iii. 272]

BARONSDALE, WILLIAM (d. 1608), physician; M.D. St. John's College, Cambridge, 1568; Linacre lecturer on medicine; F.C.P.; president College of Physicians, 1589–1600. [iii. 272]

BAROWE or **BARROW**, THOMAS (d. 1497?), divine and judge; prebendary of Westminster and master of rolls, 1483; master in chancery; keeper of great seal, 1484. [iii. 272]

BARRA, LORD (d. 1654). [See HAY, SIR JOHN.]

BARRALET, JOHN JAMES (d. 1812), water-colour painter; member of London Society of Artists; emigrated to Philadelphia, 1795. [iii. 273]

BARRALLIER, FRANCIS LOUIS or FRANCIS (1773?–1853), soldier and explorer; ensign in New South Wales corps, 1800; surveyor to expedition to Bass's Straits (of which he prepared charts) and Hunter's River, 1800–3; lieutenant, 1805; served at Martinique, 1809, and Guadaloupe, 1810; surveyed Barbados, 1812–17; brevet lieutenant-colonel, 1840. [iii. 273]

BARRATT, ALFRED (1844–1881), philosophical writer; educated at Rugby; B.A. Balliol College, Oxford, 1866; fellow of Brasenose College, 1869; called to the bar, 1872; secretary of Oxford University commission, 1880; published 'Physical Ethics,' 1869, and left unfinished a work on 'Physical Metempiric.' [iii. 274]

BARRAUD, HENRY (1811–1874), painter; exhibited chiefly portraits at Royal Academy, 1833–59. [iii. 275]

BARRAUD, WILLIAM (1810–1850), animal painter; exhibited at Royal Academy and other exhibitions, 1828–1850; brother of Henry Barraud [q. v.] [iii. 275]

BARRÉ, ISAAC (1726–1802), colonel and politician; graduated at Trinity College, Dublin, 1745; served under Wolfe against Rochefort, 1757; M.P. for Chipping Wycombe, 1761–74, and Calne, 1774–90; adjutant-general and governor of Stirling, 1763–4; vice-treasurer of Ireland and privy councillor; treasurer of navy, 1782. [iii. 275]

BARRE, RICHARD (fl. 1170–1202), ecclesiastic and judge; envoy to papal court at time of Becket's murder; keeper of great seal, 1170; archdeacon of Ely, 1184?–96; justice of king's court, 1196. [iii. 276]

BARRÉ, WILLIAM VINCENT (1760?–1829), author; born in Germany of Huguenot parents; served in Russian navy; interpreter to Bonaparte, against whom he wrote satiric verses and was compelled to fly to England, 1803; published 'History of French Consulate under Napoleon Buonaparte,' whom he scurrilously attacked. [iii. 276]

BARRET, GEORGE, the elder (1728?–1784), painter; apprenticed as staymaker in Dublin, where he studied and subsequently taught drawing; came to England, 1762, and quickly achieved success as landscape painter; master painter to Chelsea Hospital. [iii. 277]

BARRET, GEORGE, the younger (d. 1842), painter; son of George Barret (1728?–1784) [q. v.]; exhibited chiefly landscapes at Royal Academy, from 1795, and at Society of Painters in Watercolours, 1805–42. [iii. 278]

BARRET, JOHN (d. 1563), Carmelite friar of King's Lynn; D.D. Cambridge, 1533; vicar of Bishop's Thorpe, 1558, and prebendary of Norwich; published religious works. [iii. 278]

BARRET, JOHN (d. 1580?). [See BARET.]

BARRET, JOHN (1631–1713), nonconformist divine; M.A. Emmanuel College, Cambridge; presbyterian minister at Nottingham, 1656, where, being ejected in 1662, he held conventicles; published religious works. [iii. 278]

BARRET, JOSEPH (1665–1699), religious writer; son of John Barret (1631–1713) [q. v.]; in business at Nottingham; his 'Remains' appeared, 1700. [iii. 279]

BARRET, PATRICK (d. 1415), bishop of Ferns, Wexford, 1400; chancellor of Ireland, 1410–12; compiled catalogue of bishops of Ferns. [iii. 279]

BARRET, RICHARD (d. 1599), catholic divine; educated at Douay and Rome; D.D. Rome, 1582; superintendent, 1582, and president, 1588, of English college at Rheims and, on its removal thence, at Douay. [iii. 279]

BARRET, ROBERT (fl. 1600), military and poetical writer; saw service among French, Dutch, Italians, and Spaniards; published in London, 1598, 'Theorike and Practike of Modern Warres,' and left in manuscript an epic poem entitled 'The Sacred War.' [iii. 279]

BARRET, WILLIAM (d. 1584), British consul at Aleppo, 1584; wrote treatise on 'Money and Measures of Babylon, Balsara, and the Indies.' [iii. 280]

BARRET, WILLIAM (fl. 1595), divine; M.A. Trinity College, Cambridge, 1588; summoned before Archbishop Whitgift for preaching anti-Calvinistic sermon at Cambridge, 1595; fled to continent and embraced catholicism, 1597; subsequently lived as layman in England. [iii. 280]

D

BARRETT, EATON STANNARD (1786–1820), poetical writer; studied at Middle Temple, London; published 'Woman, and other Poems,' 1810, and several political satires. [iii. 281]

BARRETT, ELIZABETH (1809–1861). [See BROWNING.]

BARRETT, GEORGE (1752–1821), actuary to Hope Life Office, 1813. He prepared a series of life tables, portions of which only were published. [iii. 281]

BARRETT, JOHN (d. 1810), navy captain; lieutenant in navy, 1793; made post-captain after capture of St. Lucia, 1795; served against Danes, 1808; wrecked and drowned while convoying Baltic trade. [iii. 282]

BARRETT, JOHN (1753–1821), divine; fellow and M.A. Trinity College, Dublin, 1778; D.D., 1790; vice-provost, 1807. His publications include an astrological work on the Zodiac; he edited the 'Codex Z Dublinensis Rescriptus,' discovered while examining manuscripts in Trinity College, 1787. [iii. 282]

BARRETT, LUCAS (1837–1862), geologist and naturalist; educated at University College School; studied at Ebersdorf; made voyages to Shetland, Norway, Greenland, and Spain, studying marine fauna; curator of Woodwardian Museum, Cambridge, and fellow Geological Society, 1855; director of geological survey of Jamaica, 1859; lost his life off Port Royal while diving to investigate Jamaican coral reefs. [iii. 283]

BARRETT, STEPHEN (17,18–1801), classical teacher; M.A. University College, Oxford, 1744; master at free school, Ashford; held living of Hothfield, Kent, 1773–1801. His works include a Latin translation of Pope's 'Pastorals,' 1746. [iii. 284]

BARRETT, WILLIAM (1733–1789), surgeon and antiquary; qualified as surgeon, 1755; collected materials for history of Bristol (published, 1789), accepting from Thomas Chatterton [q. v.] as authentic the forged 'Rowley' manuscripts, 1789; F.S.A., 1775. [iii. 284]

BARRI, GIRALDUS DE (1146?–1220?). [See GIRALDUS CAMBRENSIS.]

BARRINGTON, DAINES (1727–1800), lawyer, antiquary, and naturalist; son of John Shute, first viscount Barrington [q. v.]; called to bar at Inner Temple; marshal of high court of admiralty, 1751; justice of counties of Merioneth, Carnarvon, and Anglesey, 1757; recorder of Bristol, 1764; K.C., and bencher of his inn; second justice of Chester, 1778–85; vice-president of the Society of Antiquaries; commissary-general of stores at Gibraltar till death; said to have induced White to write his 'Natural History of Selborne.' His writings include 'Observations on the Statutes,' 1766, and a translation of King Alfred's 'Orosius,' 1773. [iii. 286]

BARRINGTON, GEORGE (b. 1755), pickpocket and author; real name WALDRON; ran away from school and joined a company of strolling players, assuming name George Barrington; turned pickpocket; came to London, and having been twice sentenced to hard labour, was ultimately transported for seven years to Botany Bay, 1790; released in consideration of good behaviour, 1792; became superintendent of convicts and high constable of Paramatta, New South Wales; published description of voyage to Botany Bay (1801–3) and historical works relating to Australia. [iii. 288]

BARRINGTON, JOHN SHUTE, first VISCOUNT BARRINGTON (1678–1734), lawyer, polemic, and Christian apologist; originally named SHUTE; Ph.D. and L.A.M. Utrecht; called to bar at Inner Temple; sent to Scotland to win presbyterian support for the union; inherited estates in Essex and assumed name of Barrington, 1709; published 'Dissuasive from Jacobitism,' 1713; M.P. for Berwick-upon-Tweed, 1715 and 1722; raised to peerage, 1720; expelled from House of Commons for connection with Harburg lottery, which was patronised by the king and Prince of Wales, 1723; published a 'History of the Apostles' and (1701–5) works relating to rights of protestant dissenters. [iii. 289]

BARRINGTON, SIR JONAH (1760–1834), lawyer; educated at Trinity College, Dublin; called to bar; judge in admiralty, 1798; member for Tuam in Irish House of Commons, 1792–8, and for Bannagher, 1799–1800; deprived of office for appropriating money paid into his court, 1830; died at Versailles; wrote works relating to history of Ireland. [iii. 291]

BARRINGTON, SAMUEL (1729–1800), admiral; son of John Shute, first viscount Barrington [q. v.]; lieutenant, 1745; served under Hawke in Basque Roads expedition, 1757; under Rodney at destruction of shipping at Havre-de-Grâce, 1759; with Hon. J. Byron at Louisbourg, 1760, and with Keppel at Belle Isle, 1761; flag-captain under Duke of Cumberland, 1768; attached to Channel fleet, 1771–4; commander-in-chief in West Indies, 1778; took St. Lucia; superseded by Byron; served as second in command at Grenada; second in command of Channel fleet, 1779 and 1782; admiral, 1787. [iii. 291]

BARRINGTON, SHUTE (1734–1826), divine; brother of Samuel Barrington [q. v.]; educated at Eton; M.A. Merton College, Oxford, 1757; chaplain-in-ordinary to George III, 1760; canon of Christ Church, 1761; D.C.L., 1762; held a stall at Windsor, 1776; bishop of Llandaff, 1769, Salisbury, 1782, and Durham, 1791 till his death, when he was count palatine and custos rotulorum of Durham; published religious works. [iii. 294]

BARRINGTON, WILLIAM WILDMAN, second VISCOUNT BARRINGTON (1717–1793), statesman; brother of Shute Barrington [q. v.]; M.P. for Berwick-upon-Tweed, 1740, and Plymouth, 1754 and 1755; introduced plan for formation of militia, 1745; lord commissioner of admiralty, and member of committee for impeachment of Lovat, 1746; privy councillor, 1755; chancellor of exchequer, 1761; treasurer of navy, 1762; secretary at war, 1765–78; joint postmaster-general, 1782. [iii. 295]

BARRITT, THOMAS (1743–1820), antiquary; collected and investigated antiquities in neighbourhood of Manchester. [iii. 295]

BARRON, HUGH (d. 1791), portrait-painter; pupil of Reynolds; worked in Lisbon and Rome; exhibited at Royal Academy, 1783 and 1786. [iii. 296]

BARRON, WILLIAM AUGUSTUS (fl. 1777), landscape painter; brother of Hugh Barron [q. v.]; held position in exchequer. [iii. 296]

BARROUGH, PHILIP (fl. 1590). [See BARROW.]

BARROW, SIR GEORGE (1806–1876), author; son of Sir John Barrow [q. v.]; clerk in colonial office, 1825; secretary to order of St. Michael and St. George, 1870. His works include 'The Valley of Tears,' a volume of poems. [iii. 296]

BARROW or **BARROWE**, HENRY (d. 1593), church reformer; B.A. Clare Hall, Cambridge, 1570; entered Gray's Inn, 1576; led a profligate life, but subsequently gave himself up to study of the bible; made the acquaintance of Greenwood, and largely adopted 'Brownist' tenets; arrested at instance of Whitgift, and examined by legal and ecclesiastical authorities, 1586; imprisoned in Fleet for denying their authority; published with two fellow-prisoners an account of the examination and other works, for which they were arraigned, and ultimately hanged at Tyburn. His principles required the admission of the supreme authority of Jesus Christ and of Holy Scripture. [iii. 297]

BARROW, ISAAC (1630–1677), divine and mathematical and classical scholar; educated at Charterhouse, Felstead, and Peterhouse, Cambridge; B.A. Trinity College, Cambridge, 1648; fellow, 1649; M.A., 1652; incorporated M.A. Oxford, 1653; travelled abroad, 1655–9; took holy orders, 1659; professor of Greek at Cambridge, 1660, and, later, of geometry at Gresham College; first Lucasian professor of mathematics at Cambridge, 1663; resigned in favour of his pupil, Isaac Newton, 1669, having previously resigned the Gresham professorship; wrote 'Exposition of the Creed, Decalogue, and Sacraments,' 1669; D.D. by royal mandate, 1670; master of Trinity, where he founded the library, 1672; published 'Euclidis Elementa,' 1655, and 'Archimedis Opera,' 1675. As a mathematician he was considered by his contemporaries second only to Newton, while no more perfect piece of controversial writing than his treatise on the 'Pope's Supremacy' (1680) is extant. His sermons now rank among the finest. [iii. 299]

BARROW, ISAAC (1614–1680), divine; fellow of Peterhouse, Cambridge; ejected from fellowship as royalist, 1643; chaplain of New College, Oxford, 1643–5; returned to fellowship, 1660; bishop of Sodor and Man, 1663, and governor of Isle of Man, 1664; translated to St. Asaph, 1669. [iii. 298]

BARROW, JOHN (*fl.* 1756), geographical compiler; compiled history of the discoveries made by Europeans in different parts of the world, 1756. [iii. 305]

BARROW, Sir JOHN (1764–1848), secretary of the admiralty; born of humble parents; timekeeper and subsequently partner in a Liverpool ironfoundry; comptroller of household in suite of Lord Macartney; private secretary to Macartney at Cape of Good Hope, whither he was sent on mission to reconcile Boers and Kaffirs, and to obtain topographical information; auditor-general of public records; lived near Table Mountain, 1800–2; returned to England, 1803; second secretary of the admiralty, 1804–6 and 1807–45; hon. D.C.L. Edinburgh, 1821; created baronet, 1835; founder of Royal Geographical Society; contributed to the 'Encyclopædia Britannica.' His works include ' Voyages of Discovery and Research in the Arctic Regions,' an ' Autobiography,' and volumes descriptive of his travels. [iii. 305]

BARROW or **BARROUGH**, PHILIP (*fl.* 1590), medical writer; licensed by Cambridge University to practise chirurgery and physic; published 'Method of Phisicke,' 1590. [iii. 308]

BARROW, THOMAS (*d.* 1497 ?). [See BAROWE.]

BARROW, THOMAS (1747–1813), learned jesuit; rendered great services to English academy at Liège and to Stonyhurst College; published verses in Hebrew and Greek. [iii. 308]

BARROW, WILLIAM (1610–1679). [See WARING.]

BARROW, WILLIAM (1754–1836), divine; gained at Queen's College, Oxford, 1778, chancellor's prize for essay on ' Education ' (enlarged and published, 1802); D.C.L., and Bampton lecturer, 1799; prebendary, 1815, and vicar-general, 1821, of collegiate church of Eaton; archdeacon of Nottingham, 1830–2; F.S.A. [iii. 308]

BARROWBY, WILLIAM (1682–1751), physician; M.D. Emmanuel College, Cambridge, 1713; F.C.P., 1718; F.R.S., 1721; joint physician to St. Bartholomew's, 1750; published work on anatomy. [iii. 309]

BARRY, Mrs. ANN SPRANGER (1734–1801), actress; *née* Street; married an actor named Dancer, and played in Portsmouth and York, *c.* 1756; played Cordelia (to Lear of Spranger Barry [q. v.], whom she married), Juliet, Desdemona, and other parts at Dublin, 1758–67; at Haymarket, 1767, where she soon gained great reputation. Her last appearance was at Covent Garden as Lady Randolph, her great character, 1798. [iii. 309]

BARRY, Sir CHARLES (1795–1860), architect; articled as surveyor in Lambeth, 1810–16; regularly exhibited at Royal Academy; travelled in France, Italy, Greece, Turkey, and Egypt, 1817–20; built houses of Travellers' Club (1829–31), Reform Club, Pall Mall (1837); and Bridgewater House (1847); R.A.; queen's gold medallist for architecture; gained first premium in Houses of Parliament competition, 1836, and was occupied in building them, 1840–60. They were finished by his son, Edward M. Barry [q. v.] [iii. 310]

BARRY, Sir DAVID (1780–1835), physician and physiologist; surgeon in army in Peninsula; published works on influence of atmospheric pressure on bodily functions; M.D.; F.R.S. [iii. 313]

BARRY, DAVID FITZ-DAVID, first EARL OF BARRYMORE (1605–1642), soldier; served against Scots, 1639, and supported royal cause in Ireland, 1641–2; probably died from wounds received at battle of Liscarrol. [iii. 313]

BARRY, DAVID FITZJAMES DE, VISCOUNT BUTTE-VANT (1550–1617), soldier; second son of James Barry Roe, viscount Buttevant; succeeded to title, 1581, during life of his elder brother, who was deaf and dumb; supported Desmond's rebellion, 1579–83, but during Hugh O'Neill's rebellion, 1594–1603, served against the rebels. [iii. 313]

BARRY, Sir EDWARD (1696–1776), physician; M.D. Leyden, 1719, and Trinity College, Dublin, 1740; F.R.S.

1733; fellow of King and Queen's College of Physicians (Ireland), 1740; president, 1749; F.C.P. London, 1762; created baronet, 1775; professor of physic, Dublin; published medical works. [iii. 314]

BARRY, EDWARD (1759–1822), religious and medical writer; M.D. St. Andrews; curate of St. Marylebone, London; grand chaplain to the freemasons; published medical and theological works. [iii. 314]

BARRY, EDWARD MIDDLETON (1830–1880), architect; son of Sir Charles Barry [q. v.]; educated at King's College, London; rebuilt Covent Garden Theatre, 1857, and Floral Hall, 1858; R.A., 1869; professor of architecture at Royal Academy, 1873–80; treasurer of the Academy, 1874; competed for Albert Memorial, 1862, and for Law Courts, 1867. Among his works are the New Palace, Westminster, 1866–8, new picture galleries added to the National Gallery, 1871–5, and Inner Temple Buildings, 1875–9. [iii. 315]

BARRY, ELIZABETH (1658–1713), actress; owed her entrance on the stage to patronage of Earl of Rochester; first appeared at Dorset Garden as Isabella, queen of Hungary in ' Mustapha,' 1673; ' created ' more than one hundred rôles, including Monimia (the ' Orphan '), Cordelia (Tate's version of ' King Lear '), Belvidera (' Venice Preserved '), Cassandra (Dryden's ' Cleomenes '), and Zara (Congreve's ' Mourning Bride '); retired, 1710. [iii. 317]

BARRY, GEORGE (1748–1805), topographical writer; minister at Kirkwall, 1782, and Shapinshay, 1793; D.D. Edinburgh, 1804; published ' History of Orkney Islands,' 1805. [iii. 319]

BARRY, GERAT or GERALD (*fl.* 1624–1642), colonel in the Spanish army; served in Spanish army in Low Countries and Germany; distinguished himself at siege of Breda, 1625 (of which he published an account, 1628), and subsequently as colonel in Ireland during rising of 1641, for assisting which he was outlawed, 1642; published ' Military Discipline,' 1634. [iii. 319]

BARRY, HENRY (1750–1822), colonel; ensign, 1768; aide-de-camp and private secretary to Lord Rawdon during American war; served in India; colonel, 1793. [iii. 320]

BARRY, JAMES, BARON SANTRY (1603–1673), lawyer; recorder of Dublin; prime serjeant-at-law, 1629; second baron of exchequer and knighted, 1634; chairman of Dublin convention which voted unconditional restoration of Charles II, 1659; appointed chief-justice of king's bench and created Baron Santry, 1660. [iii. 320]

BARRY, JAMES (1741–1806), painter; studied under West at Dublin; exhibited at Dublin, and secured friendship of Burke, who brought him to London, 1763, and introduced him to Reynolds and others; visited Paris and Rome; R.A., 1773; published ' Inquiry into Obstructions to Arts in England,' 1775; exhibited at Royal Academy, 1771–6; decorated the walls of the Society of Arts with six pictures on subject of ' Human Culture,' 1777–83; received Society of Arts gold medal; professor of painting at Royal Academy, 1782; expelled from the academy in consequence of continued quarrels with his fellow academicians, 1799; published several engravings. [iii. 321]

BARRY, JAMES (1795–1865), woman who lived as a man; hospital assistant in the army, 1813; assistant surgeon, 1815; surgeon-major, 1827; deputy inspector-general, 1851; inspector-general, 1858; served at Malta and Cape of Good Hope. [iii. 324]

BARRY, JOHN (1745–1803), commodore, U.S.A.; went to sea at early age, and settled at Philadelphia, *c.* 1760; joined United States navy at outbreak of revolution, 1776; as commander of the Lexington captured the Edward, the first ship taken by America; subsequently suffered defeat and lost his ship; served in army, 1778–80; commodore, 1794. [iii. 325]

BARRY, JOHN MILNER (1768–1822), physician; M.D. Edinburgh, 1792; founded, and was first physician of, Cork Fever Hospital; introduced into Ireland vaccination, on which and other subjects he wrote papers. [iii. 325]

BARRY, JOHN O'BRIEN MILNER (1815–1881), medical writer; son of John Milner Barry [q. v.]; M.D. Edinburgh, 1837; F.R.C.P.; published medical treatises. [iii. 325]

BARRY or **BARREY**, LODOWICK (17th cent.), dramatist; published 'Ram Alley or Merry Tricks,' a comedy in verse, 1611.   [iii. 326]

BARRY, MARTIN (1802–1855), physician; M.D. Edinburgh, 1833; studied at Heidelberg; F.R.S., 1840; discovered presence of spermatozoa in ovum, 1843.
[iii. 326]

BARRY, PHILIP DE (*fl.* 1183), warrior, nephew of Robert Fitz-Stephen; held possessions in Cork. [iii. 327]

BARRY, SIR REDMOND (1813–1880), lawyer; B.A. Trinity College, Dublin, 1833; called to the bar, 1838; commissioner of court of requests, Melbourne, 1839; solicitor-general of Victoria, 1850; judge, 1851; first chancellor, Melbourne University, 1855; knighted, 1860.
[iii. 327]

BARRY, ROBERT DE (*fl.* 1175), warrior; brother of Philip de Barry [q. v.]; wounded at siege of Wexford, 1169.   [iii. 327]

BARRY, SPRANGER (1719–1777), actor; originally Dublin silversmith, but became bankrupt; played successfully Lear, Henry V, Hotspur, and other characters at Dublin, and Othello, under management of Garrick and Lacey, at Drury Lane, 1746; appeared alternately with Garrick in 'Hamlet' and 'Macbeth'; played Romeo to Mrs. Cibber's Juliet at Covent Garden, 1750; in partnership with Woodward built new theatre at Dublin (1758), and Cork (1761); reappeared at Drury Lane (as Othello), 1767, and Covent Garden, 1774.   [iii. 327]

BARRY, THOMAS DE (*fl.* 1560), canon of Glasgow and chief magistrate of Bothwell; wrote poem on Otterburn.   [iii. 329]

BARRYMORE, first EARL OF (1605–1642). [See BARRY, DAVID FITZ-DAVID.]

BARTER, RICHARD, M.D. (1802–1870), physician; qualified at London College of Physicians; established St. Anne's water-cure establishment at Blarney, 1842; set up first hot-air baths in British dominions, and subsequently instituted Turkish baths.   [iii. 329]

BARTHÉLEMON, FRANÇOIS HIPPOLITE (1741–1808), violinist; born at Bordeaux; served as officer in Irish brigade; adopted profession of music; composed and produced several operas in London and Paris; leader at Vauxhall Gardens, 1770.   [iii. 329]

BARTHLET or **BARTLETT**, JOHN (*fl.* 1566), theological writer; minister of church of England with strong Calvinistic opinions; divinity lecturer at St. Giles', Cripplegate; published 'Pedegrewe of Heretiques,' 1566.
[iii. 329]

BARTHOLOMEW (*d.* 1184), divine; native of Brittany; bishop of Exeter, 1161; consented to Constitutions of Clarendon, 1164; one of five bishops sent with Henry II's appeal to Alexander III at Sens; took part in coronation of the young Henry, 1170, and was the only bishop who escaped excommunication for his share in that ceremony; left religious manuscripts.   [iii. 330]

BARTHOLOMEW, SAINT (*d.* 1193), Northumbrian hermit; ordained in Norway; joined monks at Durham; became hermit at Farne.   [iii. 331]

BARTHOLOMEW ANGLICUS (*fl.* 1230–1250). [See BARTHOLOMEW DE GLANVILLE.]

BARTHOLOMEW, ALFRED (1801–1845), architect; articled in London; one of earliest members of a society of Freemasons of the Church for furtherance of true principles of architecture; editor of 'Builder,' and author of several practical works on architecture.   [iii. 332]

BARTHOLOMEW, ANN CHARLOTTE (*d.* 1862), authoress and miniaturist; published plays and poems; married Walter Turnbull, and afterwards Valentine Bartholomew [q. v.], 1840; exhibited flower and fruit pieces in watercolour.   [iii. 332]

BARTHOLOMEW, DAVID EWEN (*d.* 1821), navy captain; pressed out of merchant ship, 1794; lieutenant, 1805; commander, 1812; engaged on coast of Georgia and up St. Mary's river, 1815; captain and C.B., 1815; died in St. Iago.   [iii. 333]

BARTHOLOMEW, VALENTINE (1799–1879), flower painter in ordinary to Queen Victoria and Duchess of Kent; member of Watercolour Society, 1835–79.
[iii. 333]

BARTLEMAN, JAMES (1769–1821), vocalist; chorister at Westminster; bass singer at the 'Ancient Concerts,' 1788, and, excepting from 1791–5, was permanently connected with that institution.   [iii. 333]

BARTLET, JOHN (*fl.* 1662), nonconformist divine; held livings in Exeter; ejected, 1662; published religious works.   [iii. 334]

BARTLET, WILLIAM (*d.* 1682), independent minister; lecturer at Bideford, 1649; ejected, 1662; published two learned religious treatises.   [iii. 334]

BARTLETT, BENJAMIN (1714–1787), apothecary; formed collection of English coins and seals; F.S.A., 1764; published memoir on 'Episcopal Coins of Durham and Monastic Coins of Reading,' and left in manuscript 'History of Manchester,' published in Nichols's 'Topographical Antiquities.'   [iii. 334]

BARTLETT, THOMAS (1789–1864), divine; M.A. St. Edmund Hall, Oxford, 1816; published works maintaining evangelical principles.   [iii. 335]

BARTLETT, WILLIAM HENRY (1809–1854), topographical draughtsman; employed by John Britton, the architect, to make sketches in England for architectural publications; subsequently visited Europe, the East, and America, and published illustrated topographical works.
[iii. 335]

BARTLEY, GEORGE (1782?–1858), comedian; employed at Bath theatre; appeared at Cheltenham as Orlando in 'As you like it,' 1800; engaged as Orlando by Sheridan at Drury Lane, 1802; reappeared at Drury Lane as Falstaff, 1815; stage-manager of Covent Garden, 1829; last appeared at Princess's, 1852.   [iii. 335]

BARTLEY, SARAH (1783–1850), actress; wife of George Bartley [q. v.]; engaged as Lady Townley in the 'Provoked Husband' at Covent Garden, 1805; created Teresa in Coleridge's 'Remorse' at Drury Lane, 1813; toured with her husband in America, 1818–20; last appeared as Lady Macbeth.   [iii. 336]

BARTLOT, RICHARD (1471–1557), physician; M.D. All Souls' College, Oxford, 1508; president, College of Physicians, 1527, 1528, 1531, and 1548.   [iii. 337]

BARTOLOZZI, FRANCESCO (1727–1815), engraver; born in Florence, where he studied art; apprenticed to John Wagner, an engraver, at Venice; came to England, 1764, as 'engraver to the king,' and was also engaged by Richard Dalton [q. v.], librarian to George III; joined incorporated Society of Arts, 1765; original member of Royal Academy, 1769; took charge of National Academy at Lisbon, 1802, and there died. Among his best works are engravings after Italian masters and Holbein.
[iii. 337]

BARTOLOZZI, GAETANO STEFANO (1757–1821), engraver; son of Francesco Bartolozzi [q. v.]; opened a musical and fencing academy in Paris, becoming involved in difficulties owing to his indolence.   [iii. 339]

BARTON, ANDREW (*d.* 1511), Scottish naval commander; merchant seaman; gained favour of James IV by exploits against Portuguese ships; cleared Scottish coasts of Flemish pirates, 1506; sent to assist Denmark against Lubeck, 1508; shot in encounter with Sir Thomas and Sir Edward Howard, who had been dispatched by Henry VIII to capture him.   [iii. 340]

BARTON, BERNARD (1784–1849), poet; of quaker parentage; coal and corn merchant at Woodbridge, 1807; banking clerk at Woodbridge, 1809–49; he formed a close friendship with Lamb, and was intimately acquainted with Southey and other literary men of his time; published 'The Convict's Appeal,' 1818, 'Household Verses,' 1845, and other volumes of poems.   [iii. 340]

BARTON, CHARLES (1768–1843), conveyancer; called to bar, 1795; published legal writings. [iii. 342]

BARTON, EDWARD (1562?–1597), second English ambassador to Constantinople; appointed, 1590; served in Turkish army against Maximilian, 1595; died of plague at Halke.   [iii. 342]

BARTON, ELIZABETH (1506?–1534), NUN or MAID OF KENT; domestic servant at Aldington, Kent, c. 1525, when she was attacked by some internal disease, fell into nervous derangement which issued in religious mania; subject to trances, during which her utterances had such

effect on her hearers that on recovery she determined to feign divine inspiration; Edward Bocking [q. v.] and William Hadley, monks of Canterbury, directed by Archbishop Warham to observe her; induced by Bocking to anathematise all opponents of the Roman catholic church; removed to priory of St. Sepulchre, Canterbury, where a cell was assigned her; inveighed against Henry's divorce from Catherine of Aragon, prophesying that he would die in month succeeding his marriage with Anne Boleyn, and subsequently saying that he was no longer king in the sight of God—an utterance which Cromwell regarded as incitement to rebellion; repeatedly examined, and ultimately executed with her accomplices at Tyburn.
[iii. 343]

BARTON, FRANCES (1737-1815). [See ABINGTON.]

BARTON, JOHN DE (*fl.* 1304), judge; otherwise called DE RYTON and DE FRYTON; member of itinerary court constituted for Yorkshire, 1304.   [iii. 346]

BARTON, JOHN (15th cent.), physician; author of 'Confutatio Lollardorum,' of which a manuscript copy is preserved at All Souls' College, Oxford.   [iii. 346]

BARTON, MATTHEW (1715 ?-1795), admiral; entered navy, 1730; lieutenant, 1739; with Boscawen in North America, 1755; senior officer on Guinea coast, 1757-8; started under Keppel for Goree, but was wrecked on African shore and captured by emperor of Morocco; ransomed, 1760; served in Belle-Isle expedition, 1761, at Martinique, 1762, and at Jamaica and Havana, 1763; admiral, 1779.   [iii. 346]

BARTON, RICHARD (1601-1669), jesuit; entered Society of Jesus, 1625; rector of English college, Liège, 1642; provincial of English province, 1656-60; rector of English college, St. Omer, 1660-9.   [iii. 347]

BARTON, SIR ROBERT (1770-1853), general; served as volunteer in French national guard, 1790, and subsequently held commission in English army in Holland and the Peninsula; general, 1819; knighted, 1837. [iii. 348]

BARTON, THOMAS (*d.* 1683), royalist divine; graduated at Magdalen Hall, Oxford; rector of Eynesbury, 1629, of Westmeston, *c.* 1631 till 1642 (when he was deprived) and 1660-83; D.D., 1663; wrote theological works.   [iii. 348]

BARTON, THOMAS (1730 ?-1780), divine; graduated at Dublin; opened school at Norriston, Pennsylvania; tutor at Philadelphia academy; missionary of Society for Propagation of Gospel, 1754-9, and subsequently rector at Lancaster, Pennsylvania.   [iii. 348]

BARTON, WILLIAM (1598 ?-1678), hymnologist; probably vicar of Mayfield, Staffordshire; published verse-translation of the psalms, 1644, and 'Century of Select Hymns,' 1659.   [iii. 348]

BARTTELOT, EDMUND MUSGRAVE (1859-1888), major; son of Sir Walter Barttelot Barttelot [q. v.]; educated at Rugby and Sandhurst; joined 7th fusiliers, 1879; served in Afghanistan, 1880, and in Egypt, 1882 and 1883; in expedition for relief of Gordon; brevet major, 1883; accompanied Mr. (now Sir) H. M. Stanley's expedition to relieve Emin Pasha, 1887-8; remained with stores at Yambuya, where he was shot by an Arab.
[Suppl. i. 135]

BARTTELOT, SIR WALTER BARTTELOT (1820-1893), politician; educated at Rugby; served with 1st royal dragoons, 1839-53, retired as captain; M.P. for West Sussex, 1860-85, and for Horsham division, 1885-93; opposed Irish land bill, 1881; created baronet, 1875; C.B., 1880; privy councillor, 1892.   [Suppl. i. 134]

BARVITUS (*fl.* 545), Scottish saint; perhaps disciple and companion of St. Brandan, whose life he is said to have written.   [iii. 349]

BARWELL, LOUISA MARY (1800-1885), musician; daughter of Richard Mackenzie Bacon [q. v.], with whom she was associated in editorship of 'Quarterly Musical Magazine'; married John Barwell of Norwich; wrote educational works and contributed to 'Quarterly Journal of Education.'   [iii. 349]

BARWELL, RICHARD (1741-1804), Anglo-Indian; born at Calcutta; writer on Bengal establishment of East India Company, 1756; member of council in Bengal under Warren Hastings (whom he supported) as governor-general, 1773; retired with an immense fortune, 1780; M.P. for St. Ives, 1784, and Winchelsea, 1790 and 1796.
[iii. 350]

BARWICK, JOHN (*fl.* 1340), doctor of theology at Oxford, where he studied at Franciscan schools; his works include a commentary on Peter Lombard.   [iii. 351]

BARWICK, JOHN (1612-1664), divine; B.A. St. John's College, Cambridge, 1635; fellow; M.A., 1638; opposed parliament at outbreak of war, 1642, and was compelled to leave Cambridge; made chaplain to Bishop Morton, and received stall at Durham and two rectories; settled in London, whence, assisted by his brother, he communicated to Charles I, and later to Charles II, the designs of the rebels; charged with high treason and at length committed to Tower, 1650; released without trial, 1652; renewed his management of king's correspondence; sent by the bishops to Charles at Breda, 1659; royal chaplain; refused a bishopric and was made dean of Durham, 1660; dean of St. Paul's, 1661; prolocutor of lower house of convocation of province of Canterbury.   [iii. 351]

BARWICK, PETER (1619-1705), physician, brother of John Barwick (1612-1664) [q.v.]; M.A. St. John's College, Cambridge, 1647; fellow; M.D., 1655; supported his brother in his efforts to assist royal cause during civil war; physician in ordinary to Charles II, 1660; F.C.P., 1665; wrote 'Vita Johannis Barwick,' a life of his brother, published 1721.   [iii. 353]

BASEVI, GEORGE (1794-1845), architect; pupil of Sir John Soane; his works include the Fitzwilliam Museum, Cambridge, begun 1837, and, with Sydney Smith, the Conservative Club House, 1843-5.   [iii. 354]

BASHAM, WILLIAM RICHARD (1804-1877), physician; M.D. Edinburgh, 1834; physician to Westminster Hospital, 1843; published works on dropsy and the renal diseases.   [iii. 354]

BASING, BARON (1826-1894). [See SCLATER-BOOTH, GEORGE.]

BASING or BASINGSTOKE, JOHN (*d.* 1252), divine; probably studied at Oxford, Paris, and Athens; had returned to England and was archdeacon of Leicester by 1235; friend of Grosseteste; did much to encourage the study of Greek, and his writings include 'Donatus Græcorum,' a translation into Latin of a Greek grammar.
[iii. 354]

BASIRE, ISAAC (1607-1676), divine and traveller; studied at Rotterdam, 1623, and at Leyden, 1625; settled in England, 1628; became chaplain to Morton, then bishop of Lichfield and Coventry, 1629; B.D. Cambridge; by royal mandate university preacher through England and Ireland, and rector of Egglescliff, 1636; D.D., 1640; chaplain extraordinary to Charles I, 1641; collated to stall in Durham Cathedral, 1643; archdeacon of Northumberland, 1644; received living of Stanhope, 1645; seized by parliamentarians and compelled to go abroad, 1646; arrived in 1649 at Rome, whence he set out to the East to disseminate the Anglo-catholic faith; returned to England after successful missionary work, 1661, and was restored to his former offices; among his works are a 'History of the English and Scottish Presbytery,' 1659, and a life of Cosin, bishop of Durham; he also left in manuscript notes of several of his journeys.   [iii. 356]

BASIRE, ISAAC (1704-1768), map engraver; executed frontispiece to edition of Bailey's dictionary, 1755.
[iii. 360]

BASIRE, JAMES (1730-1802), engraver; son of Isaac Basire (1704-1768) [q.v.]; accompanied to Italy Richard Dalton [q. v.], keeper of royal drawings; engraver to Society of Antiquaries, *c.* 1763-1802; William Blake was his apprentice, 1771-8; his views of Oxford after Turner, and his 'Pylades and Orestes' after West, are among the best known of his works.   [iii. 358]

BASIRE, JAMES (1769-1822), engraver; son of James Basire (1730-1802) [q.v.]; engraver to Society of Antiquaries, by which Society much of his work was published; probably executed or assisted in more than one of the Oxford plates after Turner.   [iii. 360]

BASIRE, JAMES (1796-1869), engraver; son of James Basire (1769-1822) [q.v.]; executed plates of Sussex country houses.   [iii. 360]

BASKERVILLE, HANNIBAL (1597–1668), antiquary; son of Sir Thomas Baskerville [q. v.]; born at Saint Valery, Picardy; educated at Brasenose College, Oxford; left in manuscript antiquarian notes. [iii. 360]

BASKERVILLE, JOHN (1706–1775), printer; taught writing and book-keeping and carved monumental inscriptions at Birmingham, where he kept a school in the Bull Ring, 1737; started business at Moor Street as japanner, 1740; began to occupy himself with typefounding, 1750, and after experimenting several years produced a type with which he was satisfied; his first work a quarto edition of Virgil, which appeared 1757; produced his 'Milton,' 1758; elected printer to Cambridge University for ten years, 1758; first printed his editions of the prayer-book, 1760, and of the bible, one of the finest ever published, 1763; brought out a Greek New Testament (quarto and octavo), 1763, a quarto Horace, 1770, and in 1772–3 a famous series of quarto editions of Latin authors; his printing plant purchased after his death, in 1779, by Beaumarchais; he has the reputation of being the finest printer of modern times, though the opinion of contemporary experts was somewhat unfavourable to his type. [iii. 361]

BASKERVILLE, SIR SIMON (1574–1641), physician; fellow of Exeter College, Oxford; M.A.; M.B., 1611; M.D.; F.C.P., 1615; physician successively to James I and Charles I; knighted, 1636. [iii. 368]

BASKERVILLE, SIR THOMAS (d. 1597), general; served at Porto Rico, in France, 1589, Brittany, 1594, and Picardy, 1596. [iii. 369]

BASKERVILLE, THOMAS (1630–1720), topographer; son of Hannibal Baskerville [q. v.]; wrote account of a journey (1677–8) through various English counties. [iii. 369]

BASKERVILLE, THOMAS (1812–1840 ?), physician; M.C.S., 1835; published a botanical work. [iii. 369]

BASKETT, JOHN (d. 1742), king's printer; joint purchaser of bible patent and queen's printer, 1709, for term of thirty years, after which, having bought the reversion, he obtained renewal for sixty years; printed editions of Book of Common Prayer, 1713; master of Stationers' Company, 1714 and 1715; produced at Oxford 'The Vinegar Bible,' in two volumes, 1716–17; obtained right to print bibles in Scotland; bankrupt, 1731; his last volume a New Testament, 1742. [iii. 369]

BASS, GEORGE (d. 1812 ?), explorer; apprenticed to a surgeon at Boston, Lincolnshire; surgeon in navy; sailed to Sydney, 1795; explored coast of New South Wales and circumnavigated Tasmania; gave name to Bass's Strait. [iii. 371]

BASS, MICHAEL THOMAS (1799–1884), brewer; entered as traveller his father's brewery business, which rapidly increased after Great Exhibition (1851) and opening of Trent and Mersey Canal; liberal M.P. for Derby, 1848–83; exhibited lively concern in questions relating to welfare of working classes, and improved social conditions in Burton and Derby by numerous charities. [iii. 371]

BASSANTIN, JAMES (d. 1568), Scottish astronomer; educated at Glasgow University; taught mathematics at Paris; returned to Scotland, 1562; principal work, 'Astronomique Discours,' Lyons, 1557. [iii. 372]

BASSE or **BAS**, WILLIAM (d. 1653 ?), poet; retainer to Sir Richard (afterwards Lord) Wenman of Thame Park; probably attached to household of Lord Norreys at Ricot or Rycote, Oxfordshire; published 'Sword and Buckler,' 1602, and 'Great Brittaines Sunnes-set,' 1613, but he is best known by his occasional verses and an 'Epitaph on Shakespeare'; his 'Angler's Song,' quoted in Walton's 'Compleat Angler,' possesses distinction. [iii. 373]

BASSENDYNE or **BASSINDEN**, THOMAS (d. 1577), printer, bookbinder, and bookseller at the Nether Bow, Edinburgh; king's printer; produced an edition of Sir David Lindsay's works, 1574; printed earliest translation of New Testament published in Scotland, 1576. [iii. 374]

BASSET OF CORNWALL. This family was among the early Norman settlers in England, at first residing in Oxfordshire and other midland counties, and subsequently migrating to Cornwall. Members of it intermarried with prominent Cornish families; during the reigns of Henries VI, VII, and VIII were frequently sheriffs of Cornwall; they were staunch royalists during the civil wars. [iii. 375]

BASSET, ALAN, BARON OF WYCOMBE (d. 1233); younger son of Thomas Basset [q. v.]; close attendant and supporter of John; sent on political mission to France, 1220; sheriff of Rutland, 1217–29. [iii. 376]

BASSET, SIR FRANCIS (d. 1645), recorder and M.P. for St. Ives, 1640; sheriff of Cornwall, 1642–4; actively supported royalist cause in Cornwall, 1643; knighted after battle of Braddock Down, near Lostwithiel. [iii. 376.]

BASSET, FRANCIS, BARON DE DUNSTANVILLE OF TEHIDY and BARON BASSET OF STRATTON (1757–1835), patriot and political writer; at Harrow and Eton; M.A. King's College, Cambridge, 1786; recorder of Penryn, 1778; actively assisted defences of Cornwall when Spanish and French fleets threatened Plymouth, 1779; baronet and M.P. for Penryn, 1779; strongly opposed peace with America; raised to peerage, 1796; expended large sums in developing mining interests of Cornwall and was a liberal patron of the fine arts; wrote political and agricultural treatises. [iii. 377]

BASSET, FULK (d. 1259), bishop of London; son of Alan Basset, baron of Wycombe [q. v.]; provost of Beverley; dean of York, 1239; succeeded to Basset estates, 1241; elected bishop of London by canons of St. Paul's in opposition to wishes of Henry III, 1241; led opposition to Pope Innocent IV's demand on incomes of beneficed clergy, 1246; probably suspended with other bishops for refusal to pay first year's income of all vacant livings to archbishopric of Canterbury, 1247; supported Grosseteste's opposition to tenth of church revenues granted to Henry III by pope, 1252; took king's side after meeting of barons at Oxford, 1258; died of pestilence. [iii. 378]

BASSET, FULK DE (d. 1271). [See SANDFORD.]

BASSET, GILBERT (d. 1241), baronial leader; son of Alan Basset [q. v.]; succeeded his father in barony of Wycombe, 1233; joined barons' opposition to Henry III's foreign relations; outlawed for refusing to meet Henry III at Gloucester, 1233; was reconciled to Henry, 1234, and became one of his familiar councillors. [iii. 380]

BASSET, JOHN (1791–1843), writer on mining; sheriff of Cornwall, 1837; M.P. for Helston, 1840; published treatises on subjects connected with mining. [iii. 381]

BASSET, JOSHUA (1641 ?–1720), master of Sidney Sussex College, Cambridge; M.A. Gonville and Caius College, Cambridge, 1665; B.D., 1671; senior fellow, 1673; master of Sidney Sussex College, 1686; by mandate from James II, 1687, declared himself a papist; left college on James's revocation of all mandamuses, 1688. His name appears on the title-page of 'Ecclesiæ Theoria Nova Dodwelliana exposita' (1713) only, but he is credited with authorship of 'Reason and Authority, or the Motives of a late Protestant's Reconciliation to the Catholick Church' (1687), and another eirenicon. [iii. 381]

BASSET, PETER (fl. 1421), chamberlain and intimate friend of Henry V, whose life he is stated by Bale to have written under title of 'Acta Regis Henrici Quinti'; other historical writings attributed to him. [iii. 383]

BASSET, SIR PHILIP (d. 1271), justiciar and royalist baron; son of Alan Basset, baron of Wycombe [q. v.]; joined opposition to king under earl marshal, 1233, and was outlawed; made peace with king, 1234; chosen by barons, deputy to protest against papal policy in England, 1244; associated with justiciar in regency when Henry left for France, 1259; joined royal party, 1260; justiciar of England, 1261–3; fought for king at Dover, 1263, Northampton, and Lewes, where he was made prisoner, 1264; released, 1265; sheriff of Somerset and Dorset; member of king's council, 1270. [iii. 384]

BASSET, RALPH (d. 1127 ?), justiciar; one of five arbitrators between archbishop of York and abbot of Ripon, 1106. [iii. 385]

BASSET, RALPH (d. 1265), baron of Drayton, Staffordshire; fell at Evesham by De Montfort's side, 1265. [iii. 385]

BASSET, RALPH (*d*. 1282 ?), baron of Sapcote, Leicestershire ; constable of Northampton, 1258 ; custos pacis for Leicestershire, 1264 ; fought for barons at Evesham, 1265. [iii. 385]

BASSET, RICHARD (*d*. 1144 ?), justiciary of all England under Henry I ; son of Ralph Basset (*d*. 1127 ?) [q. v.] [iii. 385]

BASSET, THOMAS, BARON OF HEDENDON (*d*. 1182 ?), itinerant justice for Essex and Hertfordshire ; baron of exchequer, *c.* 1169 ; and sheriff of Oxfordshire, 1164. [iii. 386]

BASSET, WILLIAM (*d*. 1185 ?), judge ; son of Richard Basset [q. v.] ; sheriff of Warwickshire and Leicestershire, 1163–70 ; and of Lincolnshire, 1177–84. [iii. 386]

BASSET, WILLIAM (*d*. 1249 ?), judge ; justiciar, 1225 ; justice itinerant for Derbyshire and Northamptonshire, 1226, 1227, and 1232. [iii. 386]

BASSET, WILLIAM (*fl*. 1341), justice of common pleas, *c.* 1337–41, and of king's bench, 1341–*c*. 1350. [iii. 386]

BASSET, WILLIAM (1644–1695), divine ; M.A. Magdalen College, Oxford ; rector of St. Swithin's, London, 1683 ; published theological works. [iii. 386]

BASSINGBOURNE, HUMPHREY DE (*fl*. 1206), itinerant justice ; perhaps archdeacon of Salisbury between 1188 and 1222. [iii. 386]

BASSNETT, CHRISTOPHER (1677 ?–1744), nonconformist minister at Liverpool, where he assisted in establishing a free school for poor children, 1716. [iii. 387]

BASTARD, JOHN POLLEXFEN (1756–1816), colonel of East Devonshire militia, 1782 ; prevented destruction of Plymouth dockyards in workmen's revolt, 1799 ; M.P. for Devonshire, 1784–1816. [iii. 387]

BASTARD, THOMAS (1566–1618), satirist and divine ; educated at Winchester ; admitted perpetual fellow, New College, Oxford, 1588 ; M.A. ; chaplain to Thomas, earl of Suffolk ; held two Dorsetshire livings ; published 'Chrestoleros : Seuen Bookes of Epigrames,' 1598. [iii. 387]

BASTON or **BOSTON**, PHILIP (*d*. 1320 ?), Carmelite of Nottingham ; gained considerable reputation in rhetoric and poetry at Oxford. [iii. 388]

BASTON, ROBERT (*fl*. 1300), Carmelite ; brother of Philip Baston [q. v.] ; Carmelite monk and prior of abbey of Scarborough ; crowned with laurel as rhetorician and poet at Oxford ; accompanied Edward II to sing his praises on expedition to relieve Stirling, and was captured by Bruce, who forced him to sing his countrymen's defeat ; wrote poems on second Scottish war and on miscellaneous subjects. [iii. 388]

BASTWICK, JOHN (1593–1654), physician and controversialist ; educated at Emmanuel College, Cambridge ; M.D. Padua ; published puritanical controversial treatises, for which he was fined and subsequently imprisoned ; released by Long parliament, 1640 ; captain of Leicester trained bands, 1642 ; published tractates against ' Independents,' 1648. [iii. 389]

BATE, CHARLES SPENCE (1819–1889), scientific writer ; practised as dentist ; L.R.C.S., 1860 ; member of Odontological Society, 1856, vice-president, 1860–2, and president, 1885 ; president, British Dental Association, 1883 ; closely connected with Plymouth Institution from 1852 ; F.L.S., 1854 ; F.R.S., 1861 ; published writings on crustacea, dentistry, and other subjects. [Suppl. i. 136]

BATE, GEORGE (1608–1669), court physician ; M.D. St. Edmund Hall, Oxford, 1637 ; physician to Charles I at Oxford ; F.C.P., 1640 ; physician to Oliver Cromwell, and subsequently to Charles II ; F.R.S. ; published medical and political writings. [iii. 390]

BATE, HENRY (1745–1824). [See DUDLEY, SIR HENRY BATE.]

BATE, JAMES (1703–1775), scholar, brother of Julius Bate [q. v.] ; B.A. Corpus Christi College, Cambridge, 1723 ; fellow of St. John's College ; M.A., 1727 ; chaplain to Horace Walpole when ambassador in Paris ; received living at Deptford, 1731 ; published religious works. [iii. 390]

BATE, JOHN (*d*. 1429), theologian ; educated at Carmelite monastery, York, and at Oxford : deacon, 1415 ;

prior of Carmelites at York. His works include treatises on Aristotle. [iii. 391]

BATE, JULIUS (1711–1771), divine ; M.A. St. John's College, Cambridge, 1740 ; rector of Sutton ; Hutchinsonian mystic, and connected with publication of Hutchinson's works ; published Hebrew-English dictionary, 1767. [iii. 391]

BATECUMBE or **BADECUMBE**, WILLIAM (*d*. 1487 ?), mathematician ; perhaps professor of mathematics at Oxford in Henry V's reign ; left manuscript treatises from which Chaucer compiled his 'Astrolabe.' [iii. 392]

BATEMAN, HEZEKIAH LINTHICUM (1812–1875), actor ; born in United States ; entered firm of mechanical engineers, but subsequently joined the elder Booth and Ellen Tree (Mrs. Charles Kean) ; manager of St. Louis Theatre, 1855, and of Lyceum, London, 1870–5. Under his management (Sir) Henry Irving gained his first success in the ' Bells.' [iii. 392]

BATEMAN, JAMES (1811–1897), horticulturist ; M.A. Magdalen College, Oxford, 1845 ; took great interest in collecting and cultivating tropical plants ; F.L.S., 1833 ; F.R.S., 1838 ; fellow of Royal Horticultural Society ; published writings on orchids and other horticultural subjects. [Suppl. i. 137]

BATEMAN, JOHN FREDERIC LA TROBE-, formerly styled JOHN FREDERIC BATEMAN (1810–1889), civil engineer ; began business, 1833 ; associated with (Sir) William Fairbairn [q. v.] in laying out reservoirs on river Bann, Ireland, 1835 ; engaged on Longdendale works for Manchester water supply, 1846–77, and on Lake Thirlmere works, 1879 ; published ' History of Manchester Waterworks,' 1884 : superintended supply of water to Glasgow from Loch Katrine, 1856–60 ; constructed waterworks for many other towns in British Islands and abroad : designed scheme to supply London with water from river Severn, 1865 ; M.I.C.E., 1840, and was president, 1878 and 1879 ; F.R.S., 1860. [Suppl. i. 138]

BATEMAN, SIDNEY FRANCES (1823–1881), actress ; *née* Cowell : married Hezekiah Bateman [q. v.], 1839 ; wrote several plays produced in England and America ; managed Lyceum, 1875–8, and Sadler's Wells, 1878–81. [iii. 392]

BATEMAN, STEPHEN (*d*. 1584). [See BATMAN.]

BATEMAN, THOMAS (1778–1821), physician ; studied at St. George's Hospital ; M.D. Edinburgh, 1801 ; pupil of Dr. Willan and subsequently physician to public dispensary and to fever hospital, London, 1804 ; L.C.P., 1805 ; connected with ' Edinburgh Medical and Surgical Journal ' ; became principal authority in London on skin diseases ; published ' Synopsis of Cutaneous Diseases,' 1813, in which he followed and established the reputation of Willan. [iii. 393]

BATEMAN, THOMAS (1821–1861), archæologist, son of William Bateman (1787–1835) [q. v.] ; country gentleman in neighbourhood of the Peak ; formed large archæological and ethnological collections, of which the foundations were laid by his father and grandfather ; published accounts of his investigations. [iii. 394]

BATEMAN, WILLIAM (1298 ?–1355), bishop of Norwich, called WILLIAM OF NORWICH ; D.C.L. Cambridge ; archdeacon of Norwich, 1328 ; took up residence at court of Pope John XXII at Avignon and was subsequently appointed auditor of the palace ; dean of Lincoln, 1340 ; twice despatched by Pope Benedict XII to reconcile French king and Edward III ; bishop of Norwich, 1344 ; repeatedly employed by Edward III in political negotiations, 1348–54. Founded Trinity Hall, Cambridge, 1350, for students of canon and civil law to recruit ranks of clergy thinned by pestilence of 1349, and completed (1351) scheme for founding college originated by Edmund Gonville, who died before it was fully established ; died, perhaps from poison, at Avignon. [iii. 395]

BATEMAN, WILLIAM (1787–1835), archæologist ; excavated several barrows of Peak district and communicated results to ' Archæologia.' [iii. 395]

BATEMAN-CHAMPAIN, SIR JOHN UNDERWOOD (1835–1887), colonel ; educated at Addiscombe ; second lieutenant, Bengal engineers, 1853 ; captain, 1863 ; major, 1872 ; colonel, 1882 ; assistant principal at Thomason College, Rurki, India, 1857 ; served at Delhi, Agra, Cawnpore, and Lucknow, 1857-8; engaged on construction of electric telegraph to India through Russia, Turkey, and Persia, 1862-87; chief director of government Indo-European telegraph, 1870; K.C.M.G.; member of council of Royal Geographical Society and Society of Telegraph Engineers. [Suppl. i. 139]

BATES, HARRY (1850-1899), sculptor; studied under Jules Dalou at Lambeth, at Royal Academy, and under Rodin in Paris; A.R.A., 1892; executed much decorative work for metropolitan buildings. Among the most notable of his productions is the statue of Queen Victoria at Dundee. [Suppl. i. 140]

BATES, HENRY WALTER (1825-1892), naturalist; clerk in Allsopp's offices, Burton-on-Trent, 1845; went with Alfred Russel Wallace to Pará, 1848, and journeyed to the Tapajos and Upper Amazons, 1851-9, fixing his headquarters at Ega, 1854-9, and reaching St. Paulo, 1857; revealed by his researches in natural history over eight thousand species new to science; published 'Naturalist on the Amazons,' 1863; assistant secretary to Royal Geographical Society, 1864-92; F.L.S., 1871; F.R.S., 1881; president of Entomological Society, 1869 and 1878; edited several works on natural history and topography. [Suppl. i. 141]

BATES, JOAH (1741-1799), musician; scholar of Eton, 1756, and King's College, Cambridge, 1760; M.A., 1767; fellow and college tutor; private secretary to Lord Sandwich, first lord of admiralty; conductor to concerts of Ancient Music and, 1784, to Handel commemoration at Westminster; commissioner of customs; published 'Treatise on Harmony.' [iii. 397]

BATES, JOSHUA (1788-1864), financier; entered counting-house of W. R. Gray, merchant, of Boston, United States, America; began business, but became bankrupt on declaration of war with England, 1812; employed by Gray as general European agent; admitted partner in Baring Brothers, and ultimately became senior partner; appellant arbitrator, 1854, to joint commission for consideration of claims arising from peace of 1815. He was a great benefactor to city of Boston. [iii. 398]

BATES, SARAH (d. 1811), singer; wife of Joah Bates [q. v.]; studied singing in London under her husband and Sacchini, and was a successful concert singer, chiefly of sacred music. [iii. 399]

BATES, THOMAS (fl. 1704-1719), naval surgeon in Mediterranean; distinguished himself during cattle plague (1714), of which he wrote an account; F.R.S., 1719. [iii. 399]

BATES, THOMAS (1775-1849), stockbreeder; farmed at Wark Eals, North Tyne, and Halton Castle, where he achieved renown as breeder of shorthorns; won many prizes at the Royal Agricultural Society's shows from 1839; contributed to newspapers letters chiefly on politics of agriculture. [Suppl. i. 144]

BATES, WILLIAM (1625-1699), presbyterian divine; B.A. King's College, Cambridge, 1647; held living of St. Dunstan's-in-the-West, London; ejected, 1662; royal chaplain and commissioner for Savoy conference, 1660; D.D. by royal mandate, 1661; made repeated unsuccessful efforts to obtain relief for nonconformists; published theological writings. [iii. 399]

BATESFORD, JOHN DE (d. 1319), judge; acted as justice of assize in several counties, 1293-1311; regularly summoned to parliament, 1295-1318. [iii. 400]

BATESON, THOMAS (1580?-1620?), musical composer; organist of Chester Cathedral, 1599; vicar-choral of cathedral of the Trinity, Dublin, 1609; Mus. Bac. Dublin; published two volumes of madrigals. [iii. 401]

BATESON, WILLIAM HENRY (1812-1881), divine; educated at Shrewsbury; B.A. St. John's College, Cambridge, 1836; fellow, 1837; senior bursar, 1846, and master, 1857; public orator, 1848; vice-chancellor, 1858. [iii. 401]

BATH, MARQUISES OF. [See THYNNE, THOMAS, first MARQUIS, 1734-1796; THYNNE, JOHN ALEXANDER, fourth MARQUIS, 1831-1896.]

BATH, EARLS OF. [See GRENVILLE, JOHN, 1628-1701; and PULTENEY, WILLIAM, 1684-1764.]

BATHE or **BATHONIA, HENRY** DE (d. 1260), judge of common pleas, 1238-50; served on commissions of assize for various counties, 1240-60; fined for corrupt practices, 1251; restored to favour, 1253. [iii. 402]

BATHE, JOHN (1610-1649), jesuit; studied at English college, Seville; entered Society of Jesus at Dublin, 1638; 'missioner' in residence at Drogheda, where he was shot by Cromwell's soldiers. [iii. 402]

BATHE, WILLIAM (1564-1614), jesuit; brought up in protestant religion, but subsequently became Romanist; educated at Oxford; entered jesuit novitiate of Tournai, c. 1596; after studying at Louvain and Padua, was appointed rector of Irish College at Salamanca; died at Madrid. His works include 'Introduction to Art of Music,' 1584, and 'Janua Linguarum,' 1611, a system for teaching languages. [iii. 402]

BATHER, EDWARD (1779-1847), divine; M.A. Oriel College, Oxford, 1808; vicar of Meol-Brace, 1804; archdeacon of Salop, and prebendary of Lichfield, 1828; published religious works. [iii. 403]

BATHER, LUCY ELIZABETH (1836-1864), writer for children, known as AUNT LUCY; daughter of Dr. Blomfield, bishop of London. [iii. 404]

BATHILDA, BALTECHILDIS, BALDECHILD, or **BALDHILD** (d. 678?), queen; wife of Clovis II, king of the Franks; of Saxon birth; carried off by pirates when young, and sold to Erchinwald, mayor of palace (640-c. 658), in times of Dagobert and his son, Clovis II; married, 649; became regent during last two years of her husband's reign, during which he was afflicted with madness, and during minority of her son; credited with procuring the murder of one Dalphinus, said to have been archbishop of Lyons. She gave generously to many ecclesiastical institutions. Her most cherished work was the reconstruction of nunnery of Chelles, to which she retired, c. 664. Three of her sons became Frankish kings. [iii. 404]

BATHURST, ALLEN, first EARL BATHURST (1684-1775); educated at Trinity College, Oxford; tory M.P. for Cirencester, 1705-12; raised to peerage, 1712; privy councillor, 1742; captain of band of pensioners, 1742-4; earl, 1772. [iii. 406]

BATHURST, BENJAMIN (1784-1809), diplomatist; son of Henry Bathurst (1744-1837) [q. v.]; secretary of legation at Leghorn; mysteriously disappeared while on mission from Vienna to England. [iii. 407]

BATHURST, HENRY, second EARL BATHURST (1714-1794); son of first earl; lawyer; B.A. Balliol College, Oxford, 1733; called to bar at Lincoln's Inn, 1736; M.P. for Cirencester, 1735-54, solicitor-general and attorney-general to Frederick, prince of Wales, 1745; judge of common pleas, 1754; created Baron Apsley, 1771; lord chancellor, 1771-8; lord president of council, 1779-82. [iii. 407]

BATHURST, HENRY (fl. 1814), archdeacon of Norwich, 1814; son of Henry Bathurst (1744-1837) [q. v.]; chancellor of church of Norwich, 1805. [iii. 409]

BATHURST, HENRY, third EARL BATHURST (1762-1834); son of second earl; tory statesman; master of mint, 1804; held seals of foreign office, 1809; president of board of trade; secretary for war and colonies; lord president of council, 1828-30. [iii. 408]

BATHURST, HENRY (1744-1837), bishop of Norwich; educated at Winchester and New College, Oxford; canon of Christ Church, Oxford, 1775; prebendary of Durham, 1795; bishop of Norwich, 1805. [iii. 408]

BATHURST, JOHN (1607-1659), physician to Oliver Cromwell; M.A. Pembroke College, Cambridge, 1621; M.D. and F.R.C.P., 1637; M.P. for Richmond, Yorkshire, 1656 and 1658. [iii. 409]

BATHURST, RALPH (1620-1704), divine; scholar of Trinity College, Oxford, 1637; B.A., 1638; fellow, 1640; ordained priest, 1644; M.D., 1654; though a royalist, was employed by state as physician to navy; among the originators of the Royal Society; abandoned medicine on Restoration; chaplain to king, 1663; president of Trinity, 1664; F.R.S., 1663; dean of Wells, 1670; he gave both pecuniary and personal help to the rebuilding of Trinity College; left miscellaneous writings in English and Latin. [iii. 409]

BATHURST, RICHARD (*d.* 1762), essayist; born in Jamaica; M.B. Peterhouse, Cambridge, 1745; subsequently army physician in West Indies; friend of Dr. Johnson, and member of the club at the King's Head; contributor to the 'Adventurer'; died at Havannah. [iii. 411]

BATHURST, THEODORE (*d.* 1651), Latin poet; nephew of Ralph Bathurst [q. v.]; educated at Pembroke College, Cambridge; translated Spenser's 'Shepherd's Calendar' into Latin verse (published 1653). [iii. 411]

BATHURST, WALTER (1764?-1827), navy captain; served under Rodney in West Indies, 1782; under Lord St. Vincent at Cadiz, 1793; captain, 1798; held commands in East Indies, Baltic, and Mediterranean; killed at Navarino. [iii. 412]

BATMAN, JOHN (1800-1840), reputed founder of colony of Victoria; born at Paramatta, New South Wales; formed company (1835) for colonising Port Phillip, whither he proceeded secretly to report on the district; made treaty with aboriginal chiefs for assignment of six hundred thousand acres, including site of Melbourne. The Sydney authorities refused to recognise the treaty, but several of Batman's party settled at Port Phillip, and, in 1837, Melbourne was founded. [iii. 412]

BATMAN, STEPHEN (*d.* 1584), translator and author; educated at Cambridge; domestic chaplain to Archbishop Parker; employed by Parker to collect library, now in Corpus Christi College, Cambridge; rector of Merstham, Surrey, 1573; published religious and historical works and translations. [iii. 414]

BATMANSON, JOHN (*d.* 1531), prior of Charterhouse; studied theology at Oxford; employed by Edward Lee in connection with his critical attack on Erasmus; prior of London Charterhouse, 1529; published religious works. [iii. 414]

BATT, ANTHONY (*d.* 1651), Benedictine monk at English monastery of Dieulouard, Lorraine; published devotional works. [iii. 415]

BATT, WILLIAM (1744-1812), scientist and medical writer; studied at Oxford, Montpellier (M.D., 1770), and Leyden; practised medicine at Genoa; professor of chemistry, Genoa, 1774-87; wrote medical treatises. [iii. 415]

BATTEL, ANDREW (*fl.* 1589-1614), traveller; sailed with Captain Cocke for Rio de la Plata, 1539; driven by storm to St. Sebastian; captured by Indians and delivered to Portuguese; imprisoned at St. Paul-de-Loanda, and subsequently employed as trader at Longo and along coast; returned to England, 1605. [iii. 415]

BATTELEY, JOHN (1646-1708), divine; fellow of Trinity College, Cambridge; domestic chaplain successively to Archbishops Sancroft and Tillotson; chancellor of Brecknock, 1684; archdeacon of Canterbury, 1687, and prebendary, 1688; master of King's Bridge hospital, 1688; wrote work on ancient state of Isle of Thanet (published, 1711), and other treatises. [iii. 416]

BATTELEY, NICHOLAS (1648-1704), antiquary; brother of John Batteley [q. v.]; B.A. Trinity College, Cambridge, 1668; M.A. Peterhouse, 1672; held livings in Kent, 1680-5; published 'Antiquities of Canterbury,' 1703. [iii. 417]

BATTELEY, OLIVER (1697-1766), divine; son of Nicholas Batteley [q. v.]; B.D. Christ Church, Oxford, 1734; prebendary of Llandaff, 1757; edited John Batteley's works. [iii. 417]

BATTELL, RALPH (1649-1713), divine; D.D. *comitiis regiis*, Peterhouse, Cambridge, 1705; sub-dean of Chapel Royal; sub-almoner to Queen Anne; prebendary of Worcester, 1685; published religious works. [iii. 417]

BATTEN, ADRIAN (*fl.* 1630), musician; educated in choir, Winchester Cathedral; vicar-choral, Westminster, 1614; organist and vicar-choral, St. Paul's, 1624; composed church music. [iii. 418]

BATTEN, SIR WILLIAM (*d.* 1667), admiral; obtained letters of marque for the Salutation, 1626; surveyor of the navy, 1638; second in command of Warwick's fleet, 1642; engaged in preventing assistance from reaching king by sea, 1643; resigned command, 1647, but resumed it on personal invitation of officers; joined Prince of Wales in Holland, where he was knighted; declined to serve against parliament and returned; reinstated surveyor of navy, 1660; M.P. for Rochester, 1661; master of Trinity House, 1663-7. [iii. 418]

BATTENBERG, PRINCE HENRY OF (1858-1896). [See HENRY MAURICE.]

BATTIE, WILLIAM (1704-1776), physician; educated at King's College, Cambridge; founded Battie scholarship, 1747; Craven scholar, 1725; M.A., 1730; M.D., 1737; F.C.P., 1738, Harveian orator, 1746; president, 1764; Lumleian orator, 1749-54; published editions of Aristotle and Isocrates, and several medical lectures. [iii. 420]

BATTINE, WILLIAM (1765-1836), lawyer and poet; fellow, Trinity Hall, Cambridge; LL.D. and fellow of College of Doctors of Law, London, 1785; advocate-general in high court of admiralty; chancellor of diocese of Lincoln; F.R.S., 1797; published 'Another Cain' (1822), a dramatic poem. [iii. 421]

BATTISHILL, JONATHAN (1738-1801), composer; chorister at St. Paul's; conductor of band at Covent Garden; member of Madrigal Society, 1758, and of Royal Society of Musicians, 1761; engaged in theatrical composition; set music to hymns by Charles Wesley; published church music and glees; buried in St. Paul's. [iii. 421]

BATTLEY, RICHARD (1770-1856), chemist; medical attendant to Newcastle collieries; assistant surgeon in navy; apothecary in city of London. Introduced improvements in pharmaceutical operations. [iii. 422]

BATTY, ROBERT (*d.* 1848), topographical writer; son of Robert Batty (1763?-1849) [q. v.]; M.B. Caius College, Cambridge, 1813; served in Western Pyrenees and Waterloo campaign; exhibited at Royal Academy, 1825-32; published topographical works illustrated by himself. [iii. 422]

BATTY, ROBERT (1763?-1849), obstetric physician; M.D. St. Andrews, 1797; L.C.P., 1806; physician to lying-in hospital, Brownlow Street; edited 'Medical and Physical Journal.' [iii. 422]

BATY, RICHARD (*d.* 1758), divine; M.A. Glasgow, 1725; vicar of Kirkandrew-upon-Esk, 1732; had local fame as oculist; published religious works. [iii. 423]

BAUMBURGH, THOMAS DE (*fl.* 1332), keeper of the great seal; held living of Emildon, Northumberland, 1328; joint-keeper of the great seal, 1332, 1334, 1338, and 1339-40. [iii. 423]

BAUME, PIERRE HENRI JOSEPH (1797-1875), socialist; born at Marseilles; educated at Naples; private secretary to King Ferdinand, *c.* 1815-25; acquired considerable wealth in England, which he bequeathed to philanthropic institutions in Isle of Man; gained repute during Owenite socialistic agitation. [iii. 423]

BAVAND, WILLIAM (*fl.* 1559), student of Middle Temple; published translation from Ferrarius Montanus. [iii. 424]

BAVANT, JOHN (*fl.* 1552-1586), Roman catholic divine; M.A. Oxford, 1552; D.D. Rome; joined English mission, 1581; imprisoned in Wisbech Castle. [iii. 424]

BAWDEN, WILLIAM (1563-1632). [See BALDWIN.]

BAWDWEN, WILLIAM (1762-1816), antiquary; vicar of Hooton Pagnel; translated part of Domesday Book (two volumes published, 1809-12). [iii. 424]

BAXENDELL, JOSEPH (1815-1887), meteorologist and astronomer; joint-secretary and editor to Manchester Literary and Philosophical Society, 1861; astronomer to Manchester Corporation from 1859; meteorologist to Southport Corporation; made important meteorological and terrestrial-magnetical researches; F.R.A.S., 1858; F.R.S., 1884. [Suppl. i. 145]

BAXTER, ANDREW (1686-1750), philosophical writer; educated at King's College, Aberdeen; travelled on continent, 1741-7, and made acquaintance of Wilkes, with whom he corresponded till death; published 'Enquiry into the Nature of the Human Soul' (1733). [iii. 425]

BAXTER, CHARLES (1809-1879), portrait and subject painter; exhibited at Royal Academy from 1834; member of Society of British Artists, 1842. [iii. 425]

BAXTER, SIR DAVID (1793–1872), manager of Sugar Refining Company, Dundee; became, on failure of this business (1826), partner with his father and brothers in a linen manufactory; successfully introduced power-loom weaving, 1836; created baronet, 1863. He was a generous benefactor of Dundee, and established several foundations in Edinburgh University. [iii. 426]

BAXTER, EVAN BUCHANAN (1844–1885), physician; born at St. Petersburg; studied at King's College, London, and Lincoln College, Oxford; M.D. London, 1870; professor of materia medica and therapeutics, King's College, London, 1874; F.R.C.P., 1877; wrote, edited, and translated medical works. [iii. 427]

BAXTER, JOHN (1781–1858), printer and publisher; first printer to use the inking roller, an appliance made under his superintendence at Lewes; his publications include 'Baxter's Bible.' [iii. 427]

BAXTER, NATHANIEL (*fl.* 1606), poet and preacher; probably educated at Magdalen College, Oxford; tutor in Greek to Sir Philip Sidney; warden of St. Mary's College, Youghal, Ireland, 1592–9; vicar of Troy, Monmouthshire, 1602; published 'Sir Philip Sidney's "Ourania"' (1606) and puritanical controversial works. [iii. 428]

BAXTER, RICHARD (1615–1691), presbyterian divine; taught by Richard Wickstead, chaplain to council at Ludlow; after brief experience of court-life, studied for ministry at Wroxeter; was ordained and became head-master of a school at Dudley, 1638; assistant minister at Bridgnorth, Shropshire; lecturer at Kidderminster, 1641; sided with parliament and recommended the 'protestation,' 1642; retired to Gloucester and thence to Coventry, where he officiated as chaplain to garrison; chaplain to Colonel Whalley's regiment after 1645, and present at several sieges; returned to Kidderminster after living in retirement, where he wrote 'Aphorisms of Justification' (1649) and the 'Saint's Everlasting Rest' (1650); came to London, 1660; one of the king's chaplains; prepared the 'Reformed Liturgy' for Savoy conference; retired from church of England on passing of Act of Uniformity; suffered much ill-treatment under Charles II and James II; imprisoned, 1685–6, and fined by Judge Jeffreys on charge of libelling the church in his 'Paraphrase of New Testament' (1685); complied with Toleration Act. His numerous writings include 'Reliquiæ Baxterianæ,' an autobiography. [iii. 429]

BAXTER, ROBERT DUDLEY (1827–1875), political writer; B.A. Trinity College, Cambridge, 1849; entered his father's firm, Baxter & Co., parliamentary lawyers, 1860; published political works. [iii. 437]

BAXTER, ROGER (1784–1827), jesuit; entered Society of Jesus, 1810; missionary in Maryland and Pennsylvania, where he died; published religious works. [iii. 437]

BAXTER, THOMAS (*fl.* 1732), pseudo-mathematician; published 'The Circle Squared,' 1732. [iii. 437]

BAXTER, THOMAS (1782–1821), china painter; studied at Royal Academy; established a school of china painting in London, 1814. [iii. 437]

BAXTER, WILLIAM (1650–1723), scholar; nephew of Richard Baxter [q. v.]; educated at Harrow; schoolmaster at Mercers' School, London. Works include 'Anacreon,' 1695, an edition of 'Horace,' 1701, and a dictionary of British antiquities, 1719. [iii. 438]

BAXTER, WILLIAM (*d.* 1871), botanist; curator of Oxford botanic garden, 1813–54; associate of Linnean Society, 1817; published 'British Phænogamous Botany,' 1834–43. [iii. 438]

BAXTER, WILLIAM EDWARD (1825–1890), traveller; educated at Edinburgh University; partner in his father's mercantile firm of Edward Baxter & Co. (afterwards W. E. Baxter & Co.); liberal M.P. for Montrose burghs, 1855–85; secretary to admiralty, 1868–71; joint secretary of the treasury, 1871–3; privy councillor, 1873; published works on foreign travel. [Suppl. i. 146]

BAYARD, NICHOLAS (*fl.* 1300?), according to Bale and Pits a Dominican theologian at Oxford; D.D.; said by Quétif to have been a Frenchman of the thirteenth century. Merton College possesses a manuscript of his 'Distinctiones Theologicæ.' [iii. 439]

BAYES, JOSHUA (1671–1746), nonconformist divine; itinerant preacher to churches around London; minister at Leather Lane, 1723; lecturer at Salters' Hall, 1732. Completed 'Epistle to Galatians' in Matthew Henry's unfinished 'Commentary.' [iii. 439]

BAYEUX, JOHN DE, or DE BAIOCIS (*d.* 1249), justice itinerant for Cornwall, Devon, Somerset, and Dorset, 1218, and for Dorset, 1225. [iii. 440]

BAYEUX, THOMAS OF (*d.* 1100). [See THOMAS.]

BAYFIELD, RICHARD, *alias* SOMERSAM (*d.* 1531), martyr; Benedictine of abbey of Bury St. Edmunds, 1514; priest, 1515; chamberlain of the abbey, *c.* 1525; burnt at Smithfield for assisting Tyndall to import forbidden books. [iii. 440]

BAYFIELD, ROBERT (*fl.* 1668), physician, of Norwich; wrote religious and medical works, 1655–62. [iii. 440]

BAYLEE, JOSEPH (1808–1883), theological writer; M.A. Trinity College, Dublin, 1848; D.D., 1852; founded and was first principal, 1856–71, of St. Aidan's Theological College, Birkenhead; vicar of Shepscombe, Gloucestershire, 1871–83; published controversial and other theological works. [iii. 441]

BAYLEY, CORNELIUS (1751–1812), divine; methodist preacher; took orders, and was incumbent of St. James's Church, Manchester; D.D. Cambridge, 1800; published a Hebrew grammar. [iii. 441]

BAYLEY, SIR EDWARD CLIVE (1821–1884), Indian statesman; under foreign secretary to Indian government and deputy-commissioner of Gujarat, 1849, and of Kangra district, 1851; returned to England; called to bar, 1857; held several posts in Allahabad, 1857–8; Indian judge, 1859; temporary foreign secretary, 1861; home secretary, 1862–72; member of supreme council, 1873–8; K.C.S.I., 1877; published writings on Indian history and antiquities. [iii. 441]

BAYLEY, F. W. N. (1808–1853), first editor of 'Illustrated London News,' 1842; published miscellaneous works in verse and prose. [iii. 442]

BAYLEY, HENRY VINCENT (1777–1844), divine; educated at Eton; B.A. Trinity College, Cambridge, 1800; fellow, 1802; chaplain to Bishop Majendie of Chester, 1803; sub-dean of Lincoln, 1805–28; archdeacon of Stow and prebendary of Liddington, 1823; D.D., 1824; appointed to stall in Westminster Abbey, 1828. [iii. 442]

BAYLEY, SIR JOHN (1763–1841), judge; educated at Eton; called to bar at Gray's Inn, 1792; judge of king's bench, 1808; judge of exchequer court, 1830–4; made baronet and privy councillor, 1834; published legal and religious works. [iii. 443]

BAYLEY, JOHN [WHITCOMB] (*d.* 1869), antiquary; junior clerk in Tower Record Office; chief clerk, 1819, and, later, sub-commissioner on the Public Records. Wrote and edited historical works, including 'History and Antiquities of Tower of London,' and an unfinished 'Parliamentary History of England.' [iii. 443]

BAYLEY, PETER (1778?–1823), miscellaneous writer; educated at Rugby and Merton College, Oxford; called to bar at Temple; published writings in verse and prose. [iii. 444]

BAYLEY, ROBERT S. (*d.* 1859), independent minister; pastor successively in Louth, Sheffield, and London; assisted in founding People's College, Sheffield; published miscellaneous writings. [iii. 444]

BAYLEY, THOMAS (1582–1663). [See BAYLIE.]

BAYLEY, THOMAS BUTTERWORTH (1744–1802), agriculturist and philanthropist; educated at Edinburgh; J.P. for county palatine of Lancaster; introduced many improvements in prison construction, sanitation, and agricultural methods. [iii. 445]

BAYLEY, WALTER (1529–1593), physician; educated at Winchester; fellow of New College, Oxford, 1550; M.D., 1563; canon of Wells; regius professor of physic, Oxford, 1561; physician to Elizabeth; F.C.P., 1581; published treatise on preservation of the eyesight. [iii. 445]

BAYLEY, WILLIAM BUTTERWORTH (1782–1860), Anglo-Indian; educated at Eton; entered Bengal civil service, 1799; registrar of Sudder court; judge at Burdwan, 1813 ; secretary in judicial and revenue department, 1814 ; chief secretary to government, 1819 ; member of supreme council, 1825 ; governor-general, 1828–30 ; returned to England ; director, East India Company, 1833 ; chairman of court, 1840. [iii. 446]

BAYLIE, THOMAS (1582–1663), puritan divine ; M.A., and fellow, Magdalen College, Oxford, 1611 ; B.D., 1621 ; rector successively of Manningford Bruce and Mildenhall, Wiltshire ; ejected, 1660 ; set up conventicle at Marlborough. [iii. 446]

BAYLIES, WILLIAM (1724–1787), physician ; M.D. Aberdeen, 1748 ; F.C.P. Edinburgh, 1757 ; practised at Dresden and Berlin ; L.C.P. London, 1765 ; published remarks on waters at Stratford-on-Avon and Bath. [iii. 447]

BAYLIS, EDWARD (1791–1861), founder between 1838 and 1854 of several insurance offices, of which the English and Scottish Law alone still survives. [iii. 447]

BAYLIS, THOMAS HUTCHINSON (1823–1876), promoter of insurance offices ; son of Edward Baylis [q. v.] ; clerk in Anchor, and, in 1850, manager of Trafalgar insurance offices ; founded several offices with varying success. [iii. 447]

BAYLY, ANSELM (d. 1794), critic and theologian ; B.C.L. Christ Church, Oxford, 1749 ; minor canon of St. Paul's and Westminster, and sub-dean of Chapel Royal ; published critical and theological works. [iii. 448]

BAYLY, BENJAMIN (1671–1720), divine ; M.A. Oxford, 1695 ; rector of St. James's, Bristol, 1697–1720 ; published 'Essay on Inspiration ' (1707). [iii. 448]

BAYLY, JOHN (d. 1633), chaplain to Charles I ; son of Lewis Bayly [q. v.] ; guardian of Christ's Hospital, Ruthin. [iii. 448]

BAYLY, LEWIS (d. 1631), bishop of Bangor : D.D. probably of Exeter College, Oxford, 1613 ; vicar of Evesham ; chaplain to Henry, prince of Wales ; bishop of Bangor, 1616 ; brought into disfavour by his puritanism ; published at beginning of seventeenth century 'Practice of Piety,' which won and retained extraordinary popularity. [iii. 448]

BAYLY, THOMAS (d. 1657 ?), royalist divine ; son of Lewis Bayly [q. v.] ; M.A. Magdalene College, Cambridge, 1631 ; sub-dean of Wells, 1638 ; incorporated M.A. Oxford, 1644 ; D.D. ; assisted as commissioned officer in defence of Raglan Castle, 1646 ; converted to Roman catholicism in France ; imprisoned for writings offensive to authorities of Commonwealth ; subsequently settled at Douay and finally went to Italy ; published religious works. [iii. 449]

BAYLY, THOMAS HAYNES (1797–1839), miscellaneous writer ; educated at Winchester and St. Mary Hall, Oxford ; abandoned original idea of entering church ; produced songs, ballads, and dramatic pieces, including 'I'd be a butterfly,' 'She wore a wreath of roses,' and 'Perfection,' a successful farce ; became involved in financial difficulties, 1831, and in a short time wrote thirty-six pieces for stage ; published five novels. [iii. 451]

BAYLY, WILLIAM (1737–1810), astronomer : assistant at Royal Observatory ; accompanied astronomical expedition sent by Royal Society to North Cape, 1769, and Cook's voyages, 1772 and 1776 ; head-master of Royal Academy, Portsmouth, 1785–1807 ; published observations made during his voyages. [iii. 452]

BAYNARD, ANN (1672–1697), daughter of Dr. Edward Baynard [q. v.] ; noted for her learning and piety. [iii. 452]

BAYNARD, EDWARD (b. 1641), physician ; studied at Leyden ; honorary F.C.P. London, 1687 ; published 'Health, a Poem,' 1719. [iii. 453]

BAYNARD, FULK (fl. 1226), itinerant justice in Norfolk. [iii. 453]

BAYNARD, ROBERT (d. 1331), justice ; son of Fulk Baynard [q. v.] ; frequently knight of shire for Norfolk, 1289–1327 ; justice of king's bench, 1327. [iii. 453]

BAYNBRIGG, CHRISTOPHER (1464 ?–1514). [See BAINBRIDGE.]

BAYNE, ALEXANDER, of Rires (d. 1737), Scottish lawyer ; advocate, 1714 ; curator of Advocates' Library,

and first professor of Scots law, Edinburgh University, 1722 ; published legal writings. [iii. 453]

BAYNE, PETER (1830–1896), journalist and author ; M.A. Marischal College, Aberdeen, 1850 ; studied for ministry at Edinburgh ; editor of 'Glasgow Commonwealth,' and, 1856, of ' Witness ' (Edinburgh) ; editor of ' Dial,' 1860–2, and of ' Weekly Review,' the organ of English presbyterian church, 1862–5 ; leader-writer for ' Christian World,' and contributor to London periodicals and reviews ; published essays and biographical, historical, and other works. [Suppl. i. 146]

BAYNE, WILLIAM (d. 1782), navy lieutenant, 1749 ; captain, 1760 ; at reduction of Martinique, 1762 ; served at Fort Royal, and off Chesapeake, 1781 ; killed in action with French. [iii. 454]

BAYNES, ADAM (1622–1670), captain in parliamentary army, and successively commissioner of excise and of customs ; member of army and admiralty committees ; several times M.P. for Leeds, and, 1659, for Appleby ; imprisoned in Tower for treasonable practices, 1666. [iii. 454]

BAYNES, JAMES (1766–1837), watercolour painter ; pupil of Romney ; exhibited at Royal Academy, 1796–1837. [iii. 455]

BAYNES, JOHN (1758–1787), lawyer ; B.A. Trinity College, Cambridge, 1777 ; fellow, 1779 ; M.A., 1780 ; studied law at Gray's Inn ; became a zealous whig ; published political writings in verse and prose. [iii. 455]

BAYNES, PAUL (d. 1617), puritan divine ; fellow, Christ's College, Cambridge ; refused absolute subscription and was compelled to leave university ; successfully replied to charge of conducting conventicles ; his religious writings were all published posthumously. [iii. 455]

BAYNES, RALPH (d. 1559), bishop ; M.A. St. John's College, Cambridge, 1521 ; university preacher ; opposed Latimer ; professor of Hebrew at Paris ; bishop of Lichfield and Coventry, 1554 ; D.D., 1555 ; deprived of bishopric, 1559 ; published a Hebrew grammar. [iii. 456]

BAYNES, ROGER (1546–1623), secretary to Cardinal Allen ; abjured protestantism, c. 1579 ; secretary to Cardinal Allen at Rome ; published 'Praise of Solitarinesse,' 1577, and 'The Baynes of Aqvisgrane,' 1617. [iii. 456]

BAYNES, THOMAS SPENCER (1823–1887), philosopher ; educated at Edinburgh, where he studied logic under Sir William Hamilton [q. v.] ; graduate of London, 1850 ; teacher of philosophy at Philosophical Institution, Edinburgh, and assistant to Hamilton, 1850 ; editor of ' Edinburgh Guardian,' 1850–4 ; introduced to Carlyle by G. H. Lewes ; assistant editor of 'Daily News,' 1858–64 ; professor of logic, metaphysics, and English literature, St. Andrews, 1864 ; wrote articles on Shakespeare's obscure and unfamiliar words and on his school-learning, which were collected as ' Shakespeare Studies,' 1894 ; superintended ninth edition of 'Encyclopædia Britannica,' 1873–1887, being associated with Professor William Robertson Smith [q. v.] from 1880. [Suppl. i. 147]

BAYNHAM, JAMES (d. 1552). [See BAINHAM.]

BAYNING, first BARON (1728–1810). [See TOWNSHEND, CHARLES.]

BAYNTON, SIR ANDREW (fl. 1540), scholar ; attended Knyvett on embassy from Henry VIII to the emperor ; several times M.P. [iii. 457]

BAYNTON, THOMAS (d. 1820), surgeon at Bristol Published works on ulcer and spinal diseases. [iii. 457]

BAYNTUN, SIR HENRY WILLIAM (1766–1840), admiral ; captain, 1794 ; served in West Indies, Mediterranean, and at Buenos Ayres, 1794–1807 ; at Trafalgar, 1805 ; rear-admiral, 1812 ; vice-admiral, 1821 ; admiral, 1837 ; K.C.B., 1815 ; G.C.B., 1839. [iii. 457]

BAZALGETTE, SIR JOSEPH WILLIAM (1819–1891), civil engineer ; pupil of Sir John Benjamin McNeill [q. v.] ; engineer at Westminster, 1842 ; chief engineer to metropolitan board of works, 1855–89 ; carried out construction of metropolitan drainage system, 1858–75, and Thames embankment, 1862–74 ; M.I.C.E., 1838, president, 1884 ; C.B., 1871 ; knighted, 1874. He did much work in connection with metropolitan bridges, and published many valuable professional reports. [Suppl. i. 149]

BAZLEY, SIR THOMAS (1797–1885), manufacturer and politician; cotton-spinner and merchant in Manchester, 1826–62; member of council of Anti-Cornlaw League; chairman of Manchester Chamber of Commerce, 1845–59; M.P. for Manchester, 1858–80; created baronet, 1869; published pamphlets. [Suppl. i. 151]

BEACH or **BECHE**, JOHN (d. 1539), abbot; educated at Oxford; abbot of St. John's, Colchester, 1538, opposing its dissolution, 1539; subsequently attainted of treason, and perhaps hanged at Colchester. [iii. 458]

BEACH, THOMAS (d. 1737), poet; wine merchant at Wrexham; published 'Eugenio, or the Virtuous and Happy Life,' 1737. [iii. 458]

BEACH, THOMAS (1738–1806), portrait-painter; pupil of Reynolds; exhibited at Royal Academy, 1785–1797. [iii. 458]

BEACH, THOMAS MILLER, (1841–1894), government spy, known as 'MAJOR LE CARON'; apprenticed as draper at Colchester; went to New York, 1861, and served with federalists under name of Henry le Caron; major, 1865; joined Fenian organisation; furnished English government with information about intended Fenian invasion of Canada, 1866; paid spy in United States, 1867–1889; military organiser of Irish republican army; reported to English government second Fenian invasion of Canada, 1868; betrayed to Canadian government plans of John O'Neill, the Fenian leader, and Louis Riel [q. v.], 1871; M.D. Detroit; practised medicine successively at Detroit and Braidwood; retained confidence of Fenians; closely connected with Irish Land League agitation and Fenian movement in England, 1879, and communicated plans of the Clan-na-Gael to Mr. Robert Anderson, chief of criminal detective department in London; finally left America, 1888; gave evidence against Irish agitators at Parnell commission, 1889; published 'Twenty-five Years in Secret Service,' 1892. [Suppl. i. 151]

BEACON. [See BECON.]

BEACONSFIELD, EARL OF (1804–1881). [See DISRAELI, BENJAMIN.]

BEADLE, JOHN (d. 1667), divine; educated at Cambridge; rector of Little Leighs and (1632) of Barnstone (1656); signed 'Essex Testimony'; published 'Journal of a Thankful Christian.' [iii. 459]

BEADON, SIR CECIL (1816–1881), Indian statesman; educated at Eton and Shrewsbury; entered Bengal civil service, 1836; under-secretary to Bengal government, 1843; represented Bengal presidency on commission on Indian postal system, 1850; successively secretary to Bengal government, home and foreign secretary to Indian government, member of governor-general's council and lieutenant-governor of Bengal; his deservedly brilliant reputation marred by unfortunate measures in regard to tea-planting in Assam, the disastrous mission to Bhutan, and failure (partly due to ill-health) in relieving the Orissa famine; returned to England, 1866; K.C.S.I. [iii. 459]

BEADON, FREDERICK (1777–1879), divine; son of Richard Beadon (1737–1824) [q. v.]; educated at Charterhouse and Trinity College, Oxford; presented to living of Weston-super-Mare; rector of North Stoneham, 1811; canon residentiary of Wells, 1812–75. [iii. 461]

BEADON, RICHARD (1737–1824), bishop; B.A. St. John's College, Cambridge, 1758; fellow and tutor; public orator, 1768; master of Jesus College, Cambridge, 1781; bishop of Gloucester, 1789, and of Bath and Wells, 1802. [iii. 462]

BEAL, SAMUEL (1825–1889), Chinese scholar; B.A. Trinity College, Cambridge, 1847; ordained priest, 1852; naval chaplain on China station; naval interpreter, 1856–8; professor of Chinese, University College, London, 1877; D.C.L. Durham, 1885; published translations from Chinese, and other writings. [Suppl. i. 153]

BEAL, WILLIAM (1815–1870), religious writer; educated at King's College, London, and Trinity College, Cambridge; B.A., 1847; LL.D. Aberdeen; vicar of Brooke, Norfolk, 1847; published religious works. [iv. 1]

BEALE, BARTHOLOMEW (fl. 1680), portraitist and physician; son of Mary Beale [q. v.] [iv. 3]

BEALE, CHARLES (fl. 1689), portrait-painter, son of Mary Beale [q. v.]; retired from profession, 1689. [iv. 3]

BEALE, FRANCIS (fl. 1656), author of 'Royall Game of Chesse Play,' 1656. [iv. 1]

BEALE, JOHN (1603–1683?), scientific writer; educated at Eton and King's College, Cambridge; M.A., 1636; rector of Yeovil, Somerset, 1660–83; F.R.S., 1663; chaplain to Charles II, 1665; wrote on Herefordshire orchards. [iv. 1]

BEALE, MARY (1632–1697), portrait-painter, née Cradock; perhaps a pupil of Sir Peter Lely, but more probably of Robert Walker; copied many of Lely's pictures. Her works include portraits of Charles II, Cowley, James, duke of Monmouth, and Milton. [iv. 2]

BEALE, ROBERT (1541–1601), diplomatist and antiquary; compelled to leave England during Mary's reign, owing to his religious opinions; connected with English embassy in Paris, 1564; secretary to Walsingham, when ambassador resident there, 1570; M.P., Totnes, 1572; clerk to the council; sent by Elizabeth to Lutheran princes of Germany, to plead for toleration of Cryptocalvinists, who denied doctrine of ubiquity of the body of Jesus, 1577–8; acted as secretary of state during Walsingham's absence, 1578, 1581, and 1583; deputy to Walsingham when governor of Mines Royal, 1581; engaged in negotiating with Mary Queen of Scots between 1581 and 1584; M.P. for Dorchester, 1585, 1586, and 1588; notified Mary of sentence of death passed on her, 1586, and read warrant before her execution, 1587; served under Leicester in attempt to relieve Sluys, 1587; employed in negotiation with the States, 1589; banished from court and parliament for his attitude in debate upon supply and towards inquisitorial practices of bishops, 1592; M.P., Lostwithiel, Cornwall, 1592; envoy to treat for peace with Spain at Boulogne, 1600; wrote legal, historical, political, and other works; member of Elizabethan Society of Antiquaries. [iv. 3]

BEALE, THOMAS WILLERT (1828–1894), miscellaneous writer; called to bar at Lincoln's Inn, 1863; studied music under Edward Roeckel; managed operas in London and provinces; originated national music meetings at Crystal Palace; published songs, and pianoforte and dramatic pieces. [Suppl. i. 154]

BEALE, WILLIAM (d. 1651), royalist divine; educated at Westminster and Trinity College, Cambridge; B.A., 1610; fellow of Jesus College, 1611; M.A., 1613; archdeacon of Carmarthen, 1623; D.D., 1627; master of Jesus College, 1632, and of St. John's College, 1634; vice-chancellor of university, 1634; rendered considerable assistance to the king at outbreak of war, 1642; captured and imprisoned by Cromwell, 1642–5; ultimately went into exile in Spain, where he died. [iv. 7]

BEALE, WILLIAM (1784–1854), musician; chorister at Westminster Abbey; gentleman of Chapel Royal, 1816; organist to Trinity College, Cambridge, 1820, and to two London churches, 1821; composed glees and madrigals. [iv. 8]

BEALES, EDMOND (1803–1881), political agitator; educated at Eton and Trinity College, Cambridge; M.A., 1828; called to bar at Middle Temple, 1830; equity draughtsman and conveyancer; achieved celebrity by his connection with Polish Exiles' Friends Society, Circassian Committee, Emancipation Society, Garibaldi Committee, and the Reform League, of which he was president at the time of the Hyde Park riots, July 1866; county court circuit judge, 1870. [iv. 9]

BEALKNAP or **BELKNAP**, SIR ROBERT DE (d. 1400?), judge; king's sergeant and justice of assize, 1366; commissioner for defence of Kentish coast; chief justice of common pleas; unsuccessful in quelling Wat Tyler's rebellion, 1381; knighted, 1385; exiled to Ireland for giving opinion unfavourable to parliament's action towards Michael de la Pole; recalled, 1397. [iv. 9]

BEAMISH, NORTH LUDLOW (1797–1872), military writer; obtained commission in 4th Irish dragoons, 1816; subsequently attached to the vice-regal suite in Hanover. His works include translations of Count von Bismarck's military writings. [iv. 10]

BEAMONT, WILLIAM JOHN (1828–1868), divine; B.A. Trinity College, Cambridge, 1850; fellow, 1852; M.A., 1853; ordained, 1854; missionary in Palestine; chaplain in British army during Crimean war; published religious, oriental, and other works. [iv. 11]

BEAN or **BEYN**, SAINT (*fl.* 1011). first bishop of Murthlach; perhaps identical with the Irish Mophiog, the day of each (16 Dec.) being the same. [iv. 12]

BEARBLOCK or **BEREBLOCK**, JOHN (*fl.* 1566), draughtsman; educated at Oxford; M.A., 1565; senior proctor of the university, 1579; executed drawings of the Oxford colleges, which have been several times reproduced. [iv. 12]

BEARCROFT, PHILIP (1697-1761), antiquary; B.A. Magdalen Hall, Oxford, 1716; fellow, Merton College, and M.A., 1719; B.D. and D.D., 1730; took orders: chaplain to the king, 1738; master of Charterhouse, 1753; prebendary of Wells, 1755; published antiquarian writings. [iv. 12]

BEARD, CHARLES (1827-1888), unitarian divine; son of John Relly Beard [q. v.]; B.A. London University, 1847; assistant at Hyde chapel, Gee Cross, Cheshire, 1850, and sole pastor, 1854-66; minister at Renshaw Street chapel, Liverpool, 1867-88; vice-president of University College, Liverpool; Hibbert lecturer, 1883; LL.D. St. Andrews, 1888; published religious writings. [Suppl. i. 154]

BEARD, JOHN (1716?-1791), actor and vocalist; trained in the King's chapel; appeared at Drury Lane as Sir John Loverule in 'The Devil to pay,' 1737; at Covent Garden in the 'Beggar's Opera,' as Macheath, which became his favourite character, 1743; manager of Covent Garden Theatre, 1761; retired, 1767. [iv. 13]

BEARD, JOHN RELLY (1800-1876), unitarian minister; took charge of congregations at Salford, 1825, at Strangeways, Manchester, 1848-64, and at Sale, 1865-73; hon. D.D. Giessen University, 1838; first principal of Unitarian Home Missionary Board, Manchester; published religious and other works, which did much for the cause of popular education. [iv. 14]

BEARD, RICHARD (*fl.* 1553-1574). [See BEEARD.]

BEARD, THOMAS (*d.* 1632), puritan divine; educated at Cambridge; rector of Hengrave, 1598; master of Huntingdon hospital and grammar school, where Oliver Cromwell was educated under his care; J.P. for Huntingdonshire, 1630; D.D. Cambridge; wrote religious works, including the 'Theatre of Gods Judgements,' 1597. [iv. 14]

BEARD, WILLIAM (1772-1868), collector of bones, which he found in excavations in the neighbourhood of Hutton, Bleadon, and Sandford. His collection, containing many bones of great rarity, is now in the museum at Taunton Castle. [iv. 15]

BEARDMORE, NATHANIEL (1816-1872), engineer to works for draining and navigating river Lee, 1850; published writings on hydraulic engineering. [iv. 16]

BEARDSLEY, AUBREY VINCENT (1872-1898), artist in black and white; worked in architect's office, and later as clerk in office of Guardian Insurance Company; illustrated 'Morte d'Arthur'; contributed drawings to 'Pall Mall Budget'; art editor of 'Yellow Book,' 1894; joined Mr. Arthur Symons in production of 'The Savoy' magazine, 1896. His work included designs for Oscar Wilde's 'Salome,' the 'Rape of the Lock,' 'Mademoiselle de Maupin,' and Ernest Dowson's 'Pierrot of the Minute.' [Suppl. i. 155]

BEATNIFFE, RICHARD (1740-1818), bookseller and topographer; journeyman bookbinder at Norwich, where he subsequently kept a secondhand bookshop; published 'Norfolk Tour,' 1772. [iv. 16]

BEATON or **BETHUNE**, DAVID (1494-1546), archbishop of St. Andrews; educated at St. Andrews, Glasgow, and Paris; abbot of Arbroath, 1523; bishop of Mirepoix in Foix, 1537; cardinal of San Stefano on Monte Celio; archbishop of St. Andrews, 1539; at an early age resident for Scotland at court of France; lord privy seal, 1528; chancellor, 1543; protonotary apostolic and legate *a latere*, 1543; murdered by John Leslie, in revenge for his condemnation of Wishart, one of the most popular preachers of Reformation. [iv. 17]

BEATON or **BETHUNE**, JAMES (*d.* 1539), archbishop of St. Andrews; M.A. St. Andrews, 1493; prior of Whithorn and abbot of Dunfermline, 1504; bishop of Galloway; archbishop of Glasgow, 1509; archbishop of St. Andrews and primate, 1522; lord treasurer, 1505-6; chancellor, 1513-26; one of the regents during James V's minority. [iv. 18]

BEATON or **BETHUNE**, JAMES (1517-1603), archbishop of Glasgow; brother of David Beaton [q. v.]; educated in Paris; abbot of Arbroath; counsellor of queen regent during struggles with lords of congregation; on death of regent went to Paris, where he remained till death as Scottish ambassador; last Roman catholic archbishop of Glasgow, 1552. [iv. 19]

BEATSON, ALEXANDER (1759-1833), governor of St. Helena; ensign, Madras infantry, 1776; engineer and field officer; colonel, 1801; governor of St. Helena, 1808-1813; major-general, 1810; lieutenant-general, 1814; introduced in St. Helena improved system of agriculture and wrote miscellaneous works. [iv. 20]

BEATSON, BENJAMIN WRIGGLESWORTH (1803-1874), classical scholar; educated at Merchant Taylors' School and Pembroke College, Cambridge; M.A., 1828; fellow; published classical works. [iv. 20]

BEATSON, GEORGE STEWARD (*d.* 1874), surgeon-general; M.D. Glasgow, 1836; on army medical staff in Ceylon, 1839-51, and subsequently in Burmah and Turkey; surgeon-general and principal medical officer of European troops in India, 1863-8 and 1871; in charge of Netley Hospital, 1868; C.B., 1869. [iv. 21]

BEATSON, ROBERT (1742-1818), miscellaneous writer; educated for military profession; accompanied royal engineers against Rochefort, 1757, and to West Indies, 1759; retired, 1766; devoted himself to practical agriculture in Fifeshire, on which, and on military and political subjects, he published works, including 'Political Index to the Histories of Great Britain and Ireland' (1786). [iv. 21]

BEATTIE, GEORGE (1786-1823), Scottish poet; son of a Kincardineshire crofter; established himself successfully as an attorney at Montrose; committed suicide from disappointment in love. His principal poems were contributed to the 'Montrose Review.' [iv. 22]

BEATTIE, JAMES (1735-1803), Scottish poet; son of a shopkeeper and small farmer; M.A. Marischal College, Aberdeen, 1753; schoolmaster and parish clerk at Fardoun, Kincardine; studied divinity at Aberdeen; master at Aberdeen grammar school, 1758; professor of moral philosophy and logic at Marischal College, 1760; published 'Original Poems and Translations,' 1761; formed acquaintance with Gray, 1765; published 'Essay on Truth,' 1770, and, anonymously, first book of the 'Minstrel,' 1771; met Dr. Johnson and members of his circle, 1771; hon. LL.D. Oxford, 1773; published second book of 'Minstrel,' 1774, 'Evidences of the Christian Religion,' 1786, and 'Elements of Moral Science,' 1790-93. [iv. 22]

BEATTIE, JAMES HAY (1768-1790), son of James Beattie [q.v.]; educated at Marischal College; M.A., 1786; appointed assistant and successor to his father in chair of moral philosophy and logic, Aberdeen, 1787. [iv. 25]

BEATTIE, WILLIAM (1793-1875), physician; studied medicine at Edinburgh; M.D., 1818; practised in Edinburgh, and subsequently in Cumberland; attended Duke of Clarence (afterwards William IV) on visits to Germany, 1822, 1825, and 1826; studied at Paris; L.R.C.P. London, 1827; practised at Hampstead, 1827-45. He was on terms of the closest friendship with Thomas Campbell, while the Countess of Blessington and Lady Byron were among his intimate acquaintances. His writings include several poems, a series of descriptive and historical works, illustrated by W. H. Bartlett [q. v.], and 'The Life and Letters of Thomas Campbell' (1849). [iv. 25]

BEATTY, SIR WILLIAM (*d.* 1842), surgeon; physician to Greenwich Hospital, 1806-40. Published, 1807, 'Narrative of Death of Lord Nelson,' whom he attended at Trafalgar; M.D. St. Andrews, and L.C.P., 1817; F.R.S., 1818; knighted, 1831. [iv. 27]

BEAUCHAMP, EARLS. [See LYGON, WILLIAM, first EARL, 1747-1816; LYGON, FREDERICK, sixth EARL, 1830-1891.]

BEAUCHAMP, GUY DE, EARL OF WARWICK (*d.* 1315), lord ordainer; one of seven earls who signed letter rejecting pope's authority in Scottish questions, 1301; attended Edward II in his last campaign, 1307; took part in procuring Gaveston's banishment, 1308; chosen one of the ordainers, 1310; assisted Lancaster in capture of Gaveston, 1312, but took no part in his execution. [iv. 28]

BEAUCHAMP, HENRY DE, DUKE OF WARWICK (1425–1445), succeeded his father, Richard, earl of Warwick [q. v.], 1439 ; created duke, 1444. [iv. 28]

BEAUCHAMP, SIR JOHN DE, BARON BEAUCHAMP (*d.* 1388), steward of household to Richard II ; beheaded for treason. [iv. 29]

BEAUCHAMP, RICHARD DE, EARL OF WARWICK (1382–1439), son of Thomas, earl of Warwick [q. v.] ; K.B., 1399 ; succeeded his father, 1401 ; admitted to order of Garter between 1403 and 1420 ; visited Jerusalem and several European countries, 1408–10 ; lord high steward at Henry V's coronation, 1413 ; instrumental in suppressing lollard rising, 1414 ; deputy of Calais ; accompanied English embassy to council of Constance, 1414 ; went with Henry V to France, 1415, and held important commands in the war ; arranged truce preparatory to treaty of Troyes ; charged with care of educating infant Henry VI, 1428 ; arranged truce with Scotland, 1430 ; lieutenant of France and Normandy, 1437 ; died at Rouen. [iv. 29]

BEAUCHAMP, RICHARD DE (1430?–1481), divine ; son of Sir Walter de Beauchamp [q. v.] ; bishop of Hereford, 1448 ; translated to Salisbury, 1450 ; chancellor of order of Garter, 1475 ; dean of Windsor, 1478. [iv. 31]

BEAUCHAMP, ROBERT DE (*d.* 1252), constable of Oxford and sheriff of the county, 1215 ; judge, 1234 ; justice itinerant, 1234 and 1238. [iv. 31]

BEAUCHAMP, THOMAS DE, EARL OF WARWICK (*d.* 1401), statesman ; accompanied John of Gaunt in French campaign, 1373, and Richard in Scottish campaign, 1385 ; joined Gloucester and Arundel in opposing Richard, 1387 ; imprisoned for treason in Tower (the Beauchamp Tower being named after him), 1397 ; sentenced to forfeiture and imprisonment in Isle of Man ; liberated on triumph of Henry IV, 1399. [iv. 32]

BEAUCHAMP, WALTER DE (*d.* 1236), castellan of Worcester and sheriff of Worcestershire, 1216 ; declared for Louis of France, 1216 ; excommunicated, but restored to offices by Henry III ; itinerant justice, 1226 and 1227. [iv. 32]

BEAUCHAMP, SIR WALTER DE (*fl.* 1415), lawyer ; fought in French wars of Henry IV and Henry V ; knight of shire for Wiltshire, 1415 ; speaker of House of Commons, 1416. [iv. 33]

BEAUCHAMP, WILLIAM DE (*d.* 1260), judge ; accompanied John's expedition to Poitou, 1214, and subsequently assisted baronial party ; sheriff of Bedfordshire and Buckinghamshire, 1234–7 ; baron of exchequer, 1234. [iv. 33]

BEAUCLERK, LORD AMELIUS (1771–1846), admiral ; lieutenant, 1792 ; commander, 1793 ; at blockade of Toulon, 1794 ; on Irish coast, 1796 ; rear admiral, 1811 ; vice-admiral, 1819 ; commander-in-chief at Lisbon and on Portuguese coast, 1824–7, and at Plymouth, 1836–9 ; admiral, 1830 ; F.R.S. ; K.C.B., 1815 ; G.C.H., 1831 ; G.C.B., 1835. [iv. 33]

BEAUCLERK, LORD AUBREY (1710?–1741), postcaptain ; in Leeward Islands, 1731 ; in Mediterranean, 1734–5 and 1737–9 ; killed in attack on Boca Chica. [iv. 34]

BEAUCLERK, CHARLES, first DUKE OF ST. ALBANS (1670–1726), son of Charles II by Nell Gwynn ; created Duke of St. Albans, 1684 ; served in imperial army against Turks, 1688, and under William III in Landen campaign, 1693 ; captain of band of pensioners ; volunteer in Flanders, 1694 and 1697 ; dismissed from captaincy of pensioners by tory ministry, 1712, but restored by George I ; K.G., 1718. [iv. 34]

BEAUCLERK, LADY DIANA (1734–1808), amateur artist ; eldest daughter of Charles Spencer, second duke of Marlborough ; married second Viscount Bolingbroke, 1757 ; was divorced, and married Topham Beauclerk [q. v.], 1768. Her works include illustrations for Dryden's 'Fables.' [iv. 35]

BEAUCLERK, TOPHAM (1739–1780), friend of Dr. Johnson ; grandson of Charles Beauclerk, first duke of St. Albans ; educated at Trinity College, Oxford ; enjoyed friendship of Dr. Johnson after 1757 ; married Lady Diana Spencer, 1768. [iv. 36]

BEAUFEU, BELLOFAGO, or BELLOFOCO, ROBERT DE (*fl.* 1190), secular canon of Salisbury ; reputed author of 'Encomium Topographiæ' and other works. [iv. 36]

BEAUFEU or BELLO FAGO, ROGER DE (*fl.* 1305), judge ; on commission of trailbaston for western circuit, 1305 ; summoned to attend Edward I at Berwick-on-Tweed on invasion of Scotland, 1301. [iv. 36]

BEAUFEU, WILLIAM, otherwise DE BELLAFAGO, BELLOFAGO, BELFOU, GALSAGUS, VELSON (*d.* 1091), bishop of Thetford ; consecrated by Lanfranc, 1086. [iv. 37]

BEAUFORT, DUKES OF. [See SOMERSET, HENRY, first DUKE, 1629–1700 ; SOMERSET, HENRY, second DUKE, 1684–1714 ; SOMERSET, HENRY, seventh DUKE, 1792–1853.]

BEAUFORT, DANIEL AUGUSTUS (1739–1821), geographer ; son of Daniel Cornelis de Beaufort [q. v.] ; M.A. Trinity College, Dublin, 1764 ; hon. LL.D., 1789 ; vicar of Collon, co. Louth, 1790–1821 ; published map of Ireland, 1792. [iv. 38]

BEAUFORT, DANIEL CORNELIS DE (1700–1788), provost and archdeacon of Tuam ; French refugee. [iv. 38]

BEAUFORT, EDMUND, second DUKE OF SOMERSET (*d.* 1455) ; younger brother of Duke John ; held command in France, 1431 ; recaptured Harfleur from French, 1440 ; relieved Calais, and obtained earldom of Dorset, 1442 ; succeeded to earldom of Somerset, 1444, and to dukedom, 1448 ; lieutenant of France ; during his term of rule most of the English ascendency in France lost ; returned, and, with Henry's support, carried on government ; imprisoned in Tower on appointment of York as protector, 1453 ; killed at first battle of St. Albans. [iv. 38]

BEAUFORT, EDMUND, styled fourth DUKE OF SOMERSET (1438?–1471), son of Edmund Beaufort, second duke of Somerset [q. v.] ; styled fourth duke after death of his brother, Henry Beaufort, third duke [q. v.], whose attainder, however, was not reversed, and whose titles consequently remained forfeit ; fought for Lancastrians at Tewkesbury, and was taken prisoner and executed. [Suppl. i. 156]

BEAUFORT, SIR FRANCIS (1774–1857), rear-admiral and hydrographer ; son of Daniel Augustus Beaufort [q. v.] ; navy lieutenant, 1796 ; commander, 1800 ; surveyed entrance to Rio de la Plata, 1807 ; post-captain, 1810 ; surveyed coast of Karamania, 1811–12, and published results, 1817 ; hydrographer to navy, 1829–55 ; rear-admiral on retired list, 1846 ; K.C.B., 1848 ; prepared atlas used by Society for Diffusion of Useful Knowledge ; F.R.S. and F.R.A.S. [iv. 39]

BEAUFORT, FRANCIS LESTOCK (1815–1879), son of Sir Francis Beaufort [q. v.] ; author of the 'Digest of Criminal Law Procedure in Bengal' (1850). [iv. 41]

BEAUFORT, HENRY (*d.* 1447), bishop of Winchester ; second and illegitimate son of John of Gaunt, by Catherine Swynford ; declared legitimate by Richard II, 1397 ; read law at Aachen ; received prebendal stalls at Lincoln, 1389 and 1391 ; dean of Wells, 1397 ; bishop of Lincoln, 1398 ; chancellor of Oxford University, 1399 ; chancellor, 1403–4 ; member of king's council, 1403 ; bishop of Winchester, 1404 ; exercised considerable influence over Prince of Wales, and thus came into conflict with Archbishop Arundel [q. v.], who in great measure guided the king's actions ; chancellor on accession of Henry V, 1413 ; accompanied unsuccessful embassy to France with terms of peace, 1414 ; attended council at Constance, 1417, and effected change in the policy by which Henry V, in alliance with the Emperor Sigismund, had previously opposed the election of a pope until measures had been taken to reform church ; nominated cardinal by Cardinal Colonna, the new pope (Martin V) elected after the council had pledged itself to reformation ; forbidden by Henry V to accept the cardinalate ; named guardian of the infant prince by Henry V on his deathbed, 1422 ; member of council, 1422 ; chancellor, 1424–6 ; nominated cardinal-priest of St. Eusebius, 1426 ; legate in Germany, Hungary, and Bohemia ; assisted pope in Hussite war ; employed in affairs of French kingdom, 1430–1 ; crowned Henry VI king of France, at Paris, 1431 ; defeated, with support of parliament, an attempt by Duke of Gloucester and his party to deprive him of his see on ground that a cardinal could not hold an English see, 1432 ; attempted unsuccessfully to arrange peace with France,

1439 and 1440, but did not discourage efforts to prosecute the war with vigour, lending large sums for equipment of expeditions. Buried in Winchester Cathedral, the building of which he completed. [iv. 41]

BEAUFORT, HENRY, third DUKE OF SOMERSET (1436–1464), son of Edmund Beaufort, second duke [q. v.]; succeeded to dukedom, 1455; lieutenant of Isle of Wight, 1457; nominated by Margaret captain of Calais in place of Earl of Warwick, 1459; was refused admission by Warwick and defeated at Newnham bridge (Neullay), 1460; defeated Yorkists at Wakefield, 1460, and at second battle of St. Albans, 1461; attainted, 1461; submitted to Edward, 1462; pardoned, 1463; returned to Margaret, 1464; captured and executed at Hexham, the act restoring his dignities being annulled. [Suppl. i. 157]

BEAUFORT, JOHN, first EARL OF SOMERSET and MARQUIS OF DORSET and of SOMERSET (1373 ?–1410), eldest son of John of Gaunt, by his mistress, Catherine Swynford [q. v.]; legitimated, 1397; served against Barbary, 1390; knighted, c. 1391; served with Teutonic knights in Lithuania, 1394; created Earl of Somerset and Marquis of Dorset and Somerset, and elected K.G., 1397; lieutenant of Aquitaine, 1397; admiral of the Irish fleet, 1398, and later of northern fleet; deprived of marquisates on Richard II's fall, 1399; great chamberlain, 1399; privy councillor and captain of Calais, 1401; lieutenant of South Wales, 1403; deputy - constable of England, 1404. [Suppl. i. 158]

BEAUFORT, JOHN, first DUKE OF SOMERSET (1403–1444), son of John Beaufort, son of John of Gaunt, by Catherine Swynford [q. v.]; earl of Somerset, 1419; duke, 1443; captain-general in Aquitaine and Normandy, 1443. [iv. 48]

BEAUFORT, MARGARET, COUNTESS OF RICHMOND AND DERBY (1443–1509), daughter and heiress of John, first duke of Somerset [q. v.]; married, 1455, Edmund Tudor, earl of Richmond (d. 1456); on outbreak of Wars of Roses retired to Pembroke, where she was detained in honourable confinement after triumph of Yorkists, 1461; married Henry Stafford, and subsequently Lord Stanley (afterwards Earl of Derby); took an active part in planning marriage of Henry with Elizabeth of York, and insurrections of 1484 and 1485, after which she lived chiefly in retirement: she instituted, on advice of John Fisher, the foundations bearing the name of 'Lady Margaret' at both universities, and Christ's (1505) and St. John's colleges, Cambridge (1508); she was an early patron of Caxton and Wynkyn de Worde. [iv. 48]

BEAUFORT, SIR THOMAS, DUKE OF EXETER (d. 1427), son of John of Gaunt, by Catherine Swynford [q. v.]; legitimated, 1397; admiral of fleet for northern parts, 1403; commanded royal forces in rebellion, 1405; captain of Calais, 1407; admiral of northern and western seas, 1409; chancellor, 1410–12; took prominent part in French wars, 1412–27; lieutenant of Normandy and K.G., 1416; created Duke of Exeter for life, 1416; relieved Roxburgh, 1417; negotiated treaty of Troyes, 1420; on council under Gloucester's protectorate. [iv. 49]

BEAUFOY, HENRY (d. 1795), whig politician; M.P. for Minehead, 1780, and Great Yarmouth, 1784 and 1790; advocated repeal of test and corporation acts, 1787–90; published political works. [iv. 50]

BEAUFOY, MARK (1764–1827), astronomer and physicist; principal founder of Society for Improvement of Naval Architecture, 1791; made valuable observations to determine laws of diurnal variation and on eclipses of Jupiter's satellites; received Astronomical Society's silver medal, 1827; colonel, Tower Hamlets militia, 1797; member of Royal Society (1815), and of Astronomical Society, and fellow of Linnean Society. [iv. 51]

BEAULIEU, LUKE DE (d. 1723), divine: native of France; educated at Saumur; took refuge in England on account of his religion, 1667; chaplain to Judge Jeffreys, 1683–8; B.D. Christ Church, Oxford, and rector of Whitchurch, near Reading, 1685; published 'Claustrum Animæ,' 1677–78, and other religious works. [iv. 52]

BEAUMONT, SIR ALBANIS (d. 1810 ?), engraver and landscape painter; born in Piedmont; published between 1787 and 1806 many views in South of France, the Alps, and Italy, some of which were coloured by Bernard Long the elder. [iv. 52]

BEAUMONT, BASIL (1669–1703), rear-admiral; lieutenant, 1688; captain, 1689; commanded squadron off Dunkirk, 1696; senior officer at Spithead, 1699; commanded squadron in the Downs and North Sea, 1689–1703; rear-admiral, 1703; drowned in wreck on Goodwin Sands. [iv. 53]

BEAUMONT, FRANCIS (d. 1598), judge; educated at Peterhouse, Cambridge: called to the bar at Middle Temple; autumn reader, 1581; serjeant-at-law, 1589; M.P. for Aldborough, 1572; judge of common pleas, 1593. [iv. 54]

BEAUMONT, FRANCIS (1584–1616), dramatist; son of Francis Beaumont (d. 1598) [q. v.]; educated at Broadgates Hall (afterwards Pembroke College), Oxford; entered Inner Temple, 1600; made acquaintance of Drayton and Jonson, for several of whose plays he wrote commendatory verses; wrote conjointly with John Fletcher from about 1606 to 1616; the first collected edition of Beaumont and Fletcher's plays appeared in 1647. [iv. 54]

BEAUMONT, SIR GEORGE HOWLAND (1753–1827), art patron and landscape painter; educated at Eton and New College, Oxford; M.P. for Beeralston, 1790–6; acquainted with Dr. Johnson, Reynolds, Scott, Wordsworth, Byron, and Coleridge; presented several valuable pictures to the National Gallery, the foundation of which owed much to his endeavours. His own paintings do not rise above mediocrity. [iv. 56]

BEAUMONT, HENRY (1612–1673). [See HARCOURT.]

BEAUMONT, JOHN (fl. 1550), legal adviser to corporation of Leicester, 1530; on commission for ecclesiastical survey of Leicestershire, 1534; reader, 1537, double reader, 1543, and treasurer, 1547, of Inner Temple; recorder of Leicester and master of rolls, 1550; deprived of his offices and fined for grossly abusing his position for his own advantage, 1552. [iv. 57]

BEAUMONT, SIR JOHN (1583–1627), poet; son of Francis Beaumont (d. 1598) [q. v.]; educated at Broadgates Hall (now Pembroke College), Oxford; entered Inner Temple, 1600; published 'Metamorphosis of Tobacco,' 1602; made baronet on his introduction to the king by Buckingham, 1626. His poems were published by his son under the title 'Bosworth Field, with other poems,' 1629. The work on which he probably spent most labour, a poem entitled 'The Crown of Thorns,' has disappeared. [iv. 58]

BEAUMONT, JOHN (d. 1701), colonel; attended Charles II in exile, and was employed at James II's court; as lieutenant-colonel cashiered by court-martial for opposing admission of Irishmen into his regiment, 1688; accompanied Prince of Orange at his landing; fought as colonel at battle of Boyne, in Flanders, and in Holland. [iv. 59]

BEAUMONT, JOHN (d. 1731), geologist and writer on spiritualism; surgeon at Stone-Easton, Somerset; wrote letters to Royal Society on 'Rock-plants in Lead Mines of Mendip Hills,' 1676 and 1683; F.R.S., 1685; published 'Treatise of Spirits and Magical Practices,' 1705. [iv. 60]

BEAUMONT, JOHN THOMAS BARBER (1774–1841), founder of insurance offices; founded County Fire and Provident Life offices, 1807; in early life secured medals for historic painting from Royal Academy and Society of Arts. [iv. 60]

BEAUMONT, JOSEPH (1616–1699), master of Peterhouse; B.A. Peterhouse, Cambridge, 1634; fellow, 1636; M.A., 1638; ejected from Cambridge, as royalist, 1644; published 'Psyche,' an epic poem, 1648; canon of Ely, 1646; domestic chaplain to Wren, bishop of Ely, 1650; D.D. and chaplain to king, 1660; master of Jesus College, 1662, and of Peterhouse, 1663; regius professor of divinity, 1674. [iv. 61]

BEAUMONT, JOSEPH (1794–1855), Wesleyan minister; became widely known as an eloquent preacher on circuit; minister successively at Edinburgh (where he graduated M.D.), Hull, Liverpool, London, Nottingham, and Bristol. [iv. 62]

BEAUMONT, LOUIS DE (d. 1333), bishop of Durham; said to have been related to kings of France, Sicily, and England; born in France; treasurer of Salisbury Cathedral, c. 1291; prebendary of Auckland; consecrated bishop of Durham, 1318; the remainder of his life was principally occupied with bickerings with the prior and chapter of St. Mary's, Durham, and Archbishop Melton of York. [iv. 62.]

BEAUMONT, PHILIP (1563-1635). [See TESIMOND, OSWALD.]

BEAUMONT, ROBERT DE (d. 1118), count of Meulan; distinguished himself at Senlac, 1066, and was rewarded with land in Warwickshire; became one of the most prominent laymen under William II, whom he assisted in his struggle in Normandy with Robert, 1096, and in invasion of France, 1097; became Henry I's 'trusted counsellor'; despatched on mission to Normandy, 1103; fought at Tenchebrai, 1106. [iv. 64]

BEAUMONT, ROBERT DE, EARL OF LEICESTER (1104-1168), justiciary of England; son of Robert de Beaumont (d. 1118) [q. v.]; Stephen's chief adviser with his twin-brother, 1137; took active part in civil war, 1139; secured interest with Angevin party on Stephen's defeat, 1141; founded abbey of St. Mary de Pré, Leicester; chief justiciar under Henry II, 1155 and 1156; regent during Henry's absence, 1158-63, and 1165. [iv. 66]

BEAUMONT, ROBERT DE, EARL OF LEICESTER (d. 1190), son of Robert de Beaumont (1104-1168) [q. v.]; joined Prince Henry in rebellion against Henry II, 1173; his English fiefs confiscated and Leicester burned; imprisoned at Falaise, 1173-4; restored in blood and honours, 1177; went on pilgrimage to Palestine, 1189, and died in Greece on his return journey. [iv. 67]

BEAUMONT, ROBERT (d. 1567), divine; educated at Westminster and Peterhouse, Cambridge; B.A. and fellow, 1544; M.A., 1550; during Mary's reign fled to Zurich; Margaret professor of divinity, Cambridge, 1559; master of Trinity College, 1561; D.D., 1564; vice-chancellor of university, 1565 and 1566; canon of Ely, 1564; he was a prominent figure in the Calvinist opposition at Cambridge to ordinances of Elizabeth and Parker. [iv. 68]

BEAUMONT, ROBERT (fl. 1639), essayist; author of 'Love's Missives to Virtue,' published 1660. [iv. 69]

BEAUMONT, THOMAS WENTWORTH (1792-1848), politician; educated at Eton and St. John's College, Cambridge; B.A., 1813; M.P. for Northumberland, 1818-1826, and South Northumberland 1830-7; joint-founder of 'Westminster Review.' [iv. 69]

BEAUMONT, WALERAN DE, COUNT OF MEULAN (1104-1166), warrior; brother of Robert de Beaumont, earl of Leicester (1104-1168) [q. v.]; joined movement in favour of William 'Clito' and Anjou, 1112, and was imprisoned for five years; espoused Stephen's cause, 1135, and became his chief adviser; joined Geoffrey of Anjou, 1143; went on pilgrimage to Jerusalem, 1145; assisted Matilda against Stephen, 1150. [iv. 69]

BEAUVALE, BARON (1782-1853). [See LAMB, FREDERICK JAMES.]

BEAVER, PHILIP (1766-1813), navy captain; lieutenant, 1783; accompanied unsuccessful expedition for colonising island of Bulama, near Sierra Leone, 1792-4; took part in conquest of Cape of Good Hope, 1795, and in reduction of Ceylon; commander, and, later, assistant-captain of fleet under Lord Keith, 1799; commanded at bombardments of Genoa, 1800; post-captain in Egypt, 1800-1; placed in charge of Essex sea fencibles, 1803; in West Indies, 1806-9; assisted in reduction of Mauritius, 1810; served in Mozambique and on Madagascar coast, 1811-12; died at Table Bay. [iv. 70]

BEAVOR, EDMOND (d. 1745), navy captain; lieutenant, 1734; served in West Indies; captain, 1743; lost in a storm while engaged against Scottish rebels, 1745. [iv. 72]

BEAZLEY, SAMUEL (1786-1851), architect and playwright; served as volunteer in Peninsula; designed several London theatres; wrote upwards of a hundred dramatic pieces. [iv. 72]

BECHE, SIR HENRY THOMAS DE LA (1796-1855), geologist; entered military school at Marlow, 1810, but left army at peace of 1815; studied geology in Dorset, France, Switzerland (1824), Jamaica, publishing papers embodying results of his investigations; began at his own expense geological map of England; was appointed, 1832, by government to conduct geological survey, and ultimately secured the erection of the Jermyn Street museum, opened 1851; president of Geological Society, 1847; knighted,

1848; received Wollaston medal, 1855; published geological works. [iv. 73]

BECHER, ELIZA, LADY (1791-1872), actress, née O'Neill; first appeared at Drogheda Theatre and subsequently made her mark as Juliet at Dublin; played Juliet at Covent Garden, 1814, and soon achieved success in tragic characters; married, 1819, William Becher, M.P., afterwards baronet, and retired from stage. [iv. 74]

BECHER, HENRY (fl. 1561), translator; vicar of Mayfield; translated into English two books of 'St. Ambrose de Vocatione Gentium.' [iv. 75]

BECHER, JOHN THOMAS (1770-1848), divine and social economist; educated at Westminster and Oxford; M.A., 1795; successively vicar of Rumpton and of Midsomer Norton; prebendary, 1818, and subsequently vicar-general of Southwell; rector of Barnborough, 1830; wrote on questions relating to social economy. [iv. 75]

BECK. [See also BEK.]

BECK, CAVE (1623-1706?), writer on pasigraphy; M.A. St. John's College, Cambridge; incorporated M.A. Oxford, 1643; master of free grammar school, Ipswich, 1655-7; rector of St. Helen's and perpetual curate of St. Margaret's, Ipswich, 1662; published 'The Universal Character' (1657), a system for universal language both for writing and speaking. [iv. 76]

BECK, DAVID (d. 1656), portrait-painter; born at Delft; pupil of Vandyck; worked at courts of England, France, and Denmark, and subsequently entered service of queen of Sweden. [iv. 77]

BECK, THOMAS ALCOCK (1795-1846), author of 'Annales Furnesienses' (1844), an exhaustive history of Furness abbey. [iv. 77]

BECKE, EDMUND (fl. 1550), divine; ordained, 1551; supervised editions of the bible with annotations, 1549 and 1551. [iv. 77]

BECKER, LYDIA ERNESTINE (1827-1890), advocate of women's suffrage; secretary, 1867, of Manchester women's suffrage committee, which was merged in the same year in Manchester National Society for Women's Suffrage, Miss Becker continuing as secretary; editor of 'Women's Suffrage Journal,' 1870-90; member of Manchester school board from 1870; published pamphlets on women's suffrage. [Suppl. i. 159]

BECKET, THOMAS (1118?-1170), archbishop of Canterbury. [See THOMAS.]

BECKET, WILLIAM (1684-1738), surgeon and antiquary; F.R.S., 1718; original member of Society of Antiquaries, 1717; surgeon to St. Thomas's Hospital, Southwark; published historical and practical works on surgery. [iv. 78]

BECKETT, GILBERT ARTHUR À. (1837-1891). [See À BECKETT.]

BECKETT, ISAAC (1653-1719), mezzotint engraver; associated with Lutterel as mezzotint engraver; executed, between 1681 and 1688, subject plates and portraits of celebrities. [iv. 78]

BECKFORD, PETER (1740-1811), sportsman and master of foxhounds; published 'Thoughts upon Hare and Fox Hunting,' 'Essays on Hunting,' 1781, and 'Familiar Letters from Italy,' 1805; M.P. for Morpeth, 1768. [iv. 79]

BECKFORD, WILLIAM (1709-1770), lord mayor of London; born in Jamaica, of which colony his father was governor; educated at Westminster; attained considerable eminence as merchant in London; alderman of Billingsgate ward, 1752; M.P. for city of London, 1754, 1761, and 1768; sheriff of the city, 1755; lord mayor, 1762 and 1769; strongly supported Wilkes when charged with libel in the 'North Briton,' 1763; presented an address to the king complaining of a false return made at the Middlesex election, 1770, and replied to the king's curt answer with an impromptu speech, which was subsequently inscribed on a monument erected in his honour in Guildhall; laid first stone of Newgate, 1770; master of the Ironmongers' Company, 1753. [iv. 80]

BECKFORD, WILLIAM (d. 1799), historian; published works relating to Jamaica, where he lived many years, and a history of France (1794). [iv. 82]

BECKFORD, WILLIAM (1759–1844), author of 'Vathek'; son of William Beckford (1709–1770) [q. v.]; travelled in Europe with a private tutor; wrote 'Vathek' in French, 1781 or 1782, of which an anonymous translation in English (perhaps by Rev. S. Henley) was published, 1784, and the first French edition, 1787; spent some time in Paris, Lausanne, and Cintra; M.P. successively for Wells and Hindon, from which constituency he retired in 1794, but again represented it, 1806–20; lived in almost complete seclusion at his family mansion of Fonthill Giffard, where he spent large sums in fantastic decoration and in collecting works of art and curios; compelled by extravagance to dispose of Fonthill, 1822. His publications include letters written in various parts of Europe and a translation of the oriental tale 'Al Raoui.' [iv. 82]

BECKINGHAM, CHARLES (1699–1731), dramatist; educated at Merchant Taylors' School; wrote poems and two plays, 'Scipio Africanus' (1718) and 'Henry IV of France' (1719), which were produced at Lincoln's Inn Fields theatre. [iv. 85]

BECKINGHAM, ELIAS DE (d. 1305 ?), king's serjeant and justice for Middlesex, 1274; justice of common pleas, 1285–1305. [iv. 85]

BECKINGTON, THOMAS (1390 ?–1465), bishop and statesman; educated at Winchester and New College, Oxford; fellow, 1408–20; entered service of Humphrey, duke of Gloucester, 1420; prebendary of York, 1423; canon of Wells, 1439; master of St. Katherine's Hospital, London; dean of arches, 1423; prolocutor of convocation, c. 1433–8; accompanied embassies to France and to the court of John, count of Armagnac, between 1432 and 1442; king's secretary, c. 1439; lord privy seal, c. 1443; bishop of Bath and Wells, 1443. He adorned the city of Wells with many fine buildings. [iv. 86]

BECKINSALL, JOHN (1496 ?–1559). [See BEKINSAU.]

BECKLEY, WILLIAM (d. 1438), Carmelite; probably graduated D.D. at Cambridge, where he spent many years; head of Carmelite friary at Sandwich; wrote theological works. [iv. 87]

BECKMAN, SIR MARTIN (d. 1702), colonel, chief engineer and master gunner of England; Swedish captain of artillery; entered service of Charles II as engineer, 1660; accompanied Lord Sandwich's expedition to Algiers and Tangiers, 1661–2; third engineer of Great Britain, 1670, second engineer, 1681, and chief engineer, 1685; accompanied Prince Rupert to Holland, 1673; on commission for strengthening fortifications of Portsmouth, 1678; major; served with Lord Dartmouth at Tangiers, 1683; knighted, 1685; head of royal laboratory at Woolwich, 1688; served under Major-general Thomas Tollemache [q. v.] in Ireland and France, 1691–4, and as colonel commanding ordnance train for sea expedition, 1692; commanded ordnance trains in expeditions against Gibraltar and France, 1695–6. [Suppl. i. 160]

BECKWITH, SIR GEORGE (1753–1823), lieutenant-general; ensign, 37th regiment, 1771; lieutenant, 1775; major, 1781; took prominent part in American war, 1776–82; lieutenant-colonel, 1790; colonel, 1795; lieutenant-general, 1805; governor of Bermuda and commandant, 1797; governor of St. Vincent, 1804, and of Barbados, 1808; completed conquest of Martinique, 1809, and Guadaloupe, 1810; K.B., 1809; commanded forces in Ireland, 1816–20. [iv. 88]

BECKWITH, JOHN CHARLES (1789–1862), major-general; nephew of Sir George Beckwith [q. v.]; ensign, 1803; lieutenant, 1805; served in Hanover and, under Moore, in Peninsula; captain, 1808; accompanied Walcheren expedition; with Wellington in Portugal, 1810; deputy assistant quartermaster-general; lost his leg at Waterloo, and was made lieutenant-colonel and C.B., 1815; settled in Piedmont among the Waldenses and devoted his life to educating them and reawakening in them the evangelical faith; major-general, 1846. [iv. 89]

BECKWITH, JOHN CHRISTMAS (1759–1809), organist; organist of St. Peter Mancroft's, Norwich, 1794, and of Norwich Cathedral, 1808–9; Mus. Doc. Oxford, 1803; published chants adapted to the Psalms (1808). [iv. 90]

BECKWITH, JOSIAH (fl. 1784), antiquary; educated as attorney; produced enlarged edition of Blount's 'Fragmenta Antiquitatis,' 1784. [iv. 90]

BECKWITH, SIR THOMAS SYDNEY (1772–1831), lieutenant-general; brother of Sir George Beckwith [q. v.]; lieutenant, 71st regiment in India, 1791; captain, 1794; major in Manningham's rifle brigade (the 95th) at Copenhagen, 1802; lieutenant-colonel, 1803; accompanied expedition to Hanover, 1806; served in Denmark, 1807, and Peninsula, 1808–11; assistant quartermaster-general in Canada, 1812; major-general and K.C.B., 1814; colonel of rifle brigade, 1827; commander-in-chief at Bombay, 1829; lieutenant-general, 1830. [iv. 90]

BECON, JOHN (d. 1587), divine; M.A. St. John's College, Cambridge, 1564; university orator, 1571–3; proctor, 1571–2; canon (1574) and chancellor (1575) of Norwich; LL.D., 1576; precentor of Chichester, 1579; prebendary of Lichfield, 1581; joint-chancellor of Lichfield and Coventry, 1582. [iv. 92]

BECON or **BEACON**, RICHARD (fl. 1594), Irish administrator and author; M.A. St. John's College, Cambridge, 1575; called to bar at Gray's Inn, 1585; attorney for province of Munster, 1586–91; published political pamphlet on Ireland, 1594. [iv. 92]

BECON, THOMAS (1512–1567), protestant divine; B.A. St. John's College, Cambridge, 1530; vicar of Brenzett, Kent; manifested sympathy with Reformation, and was compelled to recant, 1541 and 1543; supported himself by teaching; rector of St. Stephen, Walbrook, 1548; chaplain to Cranmer and Protector Somerset, and preacher in Canterbury Cathedral; on Edward's death committed to Tower as 'seditious preacher,' 1553–4, and ejected from his living as married priest; on release, retired to Strasburg; returned to England, 1558, and was restored to his benefice and preachership; D.D. Cambridge; published religious works, most of which were 'proclaimed' as 'heretical' by Roman catholic authorities. [iv. 92]

BEDDOES, THOMAS (1760–1808), physician; M.D. Pembroke College, Oxford; studied medicine at London and Edinburgh; reader in chemistry at Oxford, 1788–92; succeeded in establishing at Clifton a 'Pneumatic Institute' for the treatment of disease by inhalation, 1798; married Anna, sister of Maria Edgeworth; wrote and edited several medical and other works. [iv. 94]

BEDDOES, THOMAS LOVELL (1803–1849), poet and physiologist; son of Thomas Beddoes [q. v.]; educated at Charterhouse and Pembroke College, Oxford; published 'The Bride's Tragedy' (written in 1819), which enjoyed considerable success, 1822; graduated B.A., and began 'Death's Jest Book,' 1825; studied physiology under Blumenbach at Göttingen; M.A. Oxford, 1828; M.D. Würzburg University, 1832; settled at Zurich, 1835; took great interest in cause of liberal politics, and was compelled to fly to Berlin from the anti-liberal insurgents at Zurich, 1841; from 1842 to 1848 lived much on continent; died at Bâle. 'Death's Jest Book' was published in 1850, and a volume of his poems and fragments in 1851. [iv. 95]

BEDDOME, BENJAMIN (1717–1795), hymn-writer; baptist minister at Bourton-on-the-Water, Gloucestershire, 1740–95. Wrote hymns, a volume of which was published in 1818. [iv. 97]

BEDE or **BÆDA** (673–735), historian and scholar; placed under charge of Benedict Biscop, abbot of Wearmouth, and of Ceolfrith, abbot of Jarrow; ordained deacon, 692, and priest, 703; spent his life mainly at Jarrow from the time when Ceolfrith was appointed abbot; being a diligent teacher and Latin, Greek, and Hebrew scholar, found many pupils among the monks of Wearmouth and Jarrow; buried at Jarrow, but his bones were taken to Durham during the first half of the eleventh century. The epithet 'Venerable' was first added to his name in the century following his death. His 'Historia Ecclesiastica' was brought to an end in 731, and by that year he had written nearly forty works, chiefly biblical commentaries. The treatise 'De Natura Rerum,' one of his earliest works, contains such physical science as was then known, and has the merit of referring phenomena to natural causes. Collective editions of his works were printed at Paris, 1544 and 1554, Basle, 1563, Cologne, 1612, London, 1843–4, and in J. P. Migne's 'Patrologiæ Cursus Completus,' Paris, 1844. [iv. 98]

BEDEL, HENRY (*fl.* 1571), divine ; probably M.A. Corpus Christi College, Oxford, 1566 ; vicar of Christ Church, London, 1567–76. [iv. 105]

BEDELL, WILLIAM (1571–1642), bishop ; scholar of Emmanuel College, Cambridge, 1585 ; M.A., 1592 ; fellow, 1593 ; ordained priest, 1597 ; B.D., 1599 ; appointed to church of St. Mary's, Bury St. Edmund's, 1602–7 ; chaplain to Sir Henry Wotton at Venice, 1607–10 ; rector of Horningsheath, 1616 ; provost of Trinity College, Dublin, 1627 ; bishop of Kilmore and Ardagh (co. Longford), 1629 ; resigned see of Ardagh, 1633 ; died from hardships endured during rebellion of 1641. [iv. 105]

BEDEMAN or **STEVINE**, LAWRENCE (*fl.* 1372–1410), scholar ; fellow, and rector (1379–80) of Stapeldon Hall (now Exeter College), Oxford ; suspended from preaching as advocate of Wycliffe's doctrines, 1382 ; rector of Lifton, Devonshire, 1382–1410. [iv. 108]

BEDERIC or **DE BURY**, HENRY (*fl.* 1380), theologian : entered Augustinian monastery at Clare, Suffolk ; studied probably at Oxford and Cambridge and at Paris, where he graduated D.D. ; provincial in England ; wrote theological works. [iv. 109]

BEDFORD, DUKES OF. [See JOHN OF LANCASTER, 1389–1435 ; TUDOR, JASPER, 1431 ?–1495 ; RUSSELL, WILLIAM, first DUKE of the RUSSELL family, 1613–1700 ; RUSSELL, JOHN, fourth DUKE, 1710–1771 ; RUSSELL, FRANCIS, fifth DUKE, 1765–1805 ; RUSSELL, JOHN, sixth DUKE, 1766–1839 ; RUSSELL, FRANCIS CHARLES HASTINGS, ninth DUKE, 1819–1891.]

BEDFORD, EARLS OF. [See RUSSELL, JOHN, first EARL, 1486 ?–1555 ; RUSSELL, FRANCIS, second EARL, 1527 ?–1585 ; RUSSELL, FRANCIS, fourth EARL, 1593–1641.]

BEDFORD, COUNTESS OF (*d.* 1627). [See RUSSELL, LUCY.]

BEDFORD, ARTHUR (1668–1745), miscellaneous writer ; M.A. Brasenose College, Oxford, 1691 ; incumbent of Temple Church, Bristol, 1692, and Newton St. Loe, Somerset, 1700 ; joined Collier in crusade against the stage, and issued several tracts ; chaplain to Haberdashers' Company's hospital at Hoxton, 1724 ; chaplain to Frederick, prince of Wales ; published works on music, chronology, and other subjects. [iv. 109]

BEDFORD, FRANCIS (1799–1883), bookbinder ; entered workshop of Charles Lewis [q. v.] ; in partnership with John Clarke of Frith Street, Soho, 1841–50 ; went to Cape of Good Hope, 1851, and subsequently established himself in Blue Anchor Yard, Westminster. [Suppl. i. 162]

BEDFORD, HILKIAH (1663–1724), nonconformist divine ; educated at St. John's College, Cambridge ; fellow ; rector of Wittering ; ejected at the revolution ; chaplain to Dr. Ken ; fined and imprisoned unjustly on suspicion of having written 'The Hereditary Right of the Crown of England asserted' (1713) ; became a bishop among nonjurors ; published religious and other works. [iv. 110]

BEDFORD, JOHN (1810–1879), Wesleyan ; educated as solicitor at Wakefield ; Wesleyan minister at Glasgow, 1831, and subsequently in Manchester, Birmingham, West Bromwich, and Derby ; president of conference, 1867. [iv. 110]

BEDFORD, PAUL (1792 ?–1871), comedian ; first appeared on stage at Swansea ; in Drury Lane opera company, 1824–33 ; joined Macready's company as singer at Covent Garden, 1833 ; subsequently played second low-comedy parts at Adelphi ; last appeared, 1868, at Queen's Theatre. [iv. 111]

BEDFORD, THOMAS (*fl.* 1650), theologian ; B.D. Queens' College, Cambridge ; rector of St. Martin Outwich, London, before 1649 ; published theological works and (1620–50) took prominent part in religious controversy. [iv. 112]

BEDFORD, THOMAS (*d.* 1773), nonjuror ; son of Hilkiah Bedford [q. v.] ; educated at Westminster and St. John's College, Cambridge ; minister to nonjurors at Compton, Derbyshire ; published edition of Symeon of Durham's history of Durham Cathedral (1732) and other works of ecclesiastical history. [iv. 112]

BEDFORD, WILLIAM (1764 ?–1827), vice-admiral ; captain in navy, 1794 ; served in North Sea, 1801, at blockade of Brest, 1805, and as flag-captain in expedition to Basque roads, 1809 ; vice-admiral, 1821. [iv. 113]

BEDINGFELD, THOMAS (1760–1789), poet : educated at Liège : studied conveyancing at Newcastle and Lincoln's Inn ; began practice as chamber counsel, 1787. A volume of his poems was published in 1800. [iv. 113]

BEDINGFIELD or **BENIFIELD**, SIR HENRY (1511–1583), supporter of Queen Mary ; privy councillor, 1553 ; constable of Tower, 1555, when the Princess Elizabeth was committed to his charge for complicity in Wyatt's rebellion ; knight of shire for Norfolk, 1553, 1554, and 1557 ; retired from public life on Elizabeth's accession. [iv. 113]

BEDINGFIELD, SIR HENRY (1633–1687), chief-justice of common pleas ; called to bar at Lincoln's Inn, 1657 ; received the coif, 1683 ; king's serjeant and knighted ; sub-steward of Great Yarmouth, 1684 ; judge, 1686 ; chief-justice common pleas, 1686. [iv. 115]

BEDINGFIELD, THOMAS (*d.* 1613), son of Sir Henry Bedingfield (*d.* 1583) [q. v.] ; gentleman pensioner to Queen Elizabeth ; published miscellaneous works. [iv. 115]

BEDINGFIELD, SIR THOMAS (1593 ?–1661), lawyer ; called to bar at Gray's Inn, 1615 ; Lent reader, 1636 ; attorney-general of duchy of Lancaster and knighted ; committed for contempt of House of Lords in refusing to defend Sir Edward Herbert, who was impeached by the Commons for sharing in the attempt to arrest the five members, 1642 ; serjeant-at-law and justice of common pleas, 1648 ; retired at interregnum ; reappointed serjeant, 1660. [iv. 115]

BEDLAY, LORD (1590 ?–1664). [See ROBERTSON, JAMES.]

BEDLOE, WILLIAM (1650–1680), adventurer ; worked as clockmaker and cobbler ; educated by David Lewis, a jesuit ; came to London, 1670, and lived by sharping ; claimed to have been anticipated by Oates in making revelations of the popish plot, 1678–9 ; in receipt of 10*l.* weekly from the royal funds, 1679 ; public confidence in his statements diminished, *c.* 1680. He published several works on his 'Revelations,' the chief being 'A Narrative and Impartial Discovery of the Horrid Popish Plot . . . by Captain William Bedloe, lately engaged in that horrid design,' &c., 1679. [iv. 116]

BEDWELL, THOMAS (*d.* 1595), mathematician ; B.A. Trinity College, Cambridge, 1567 ; fellow ; M.A., 1570 ; keeper of ordnance stores in Tower ; military engineer at Tilbury and Gravesend at time of Spanish Armada. [iv. 118]

BEDWELL, WILLIAM (*d.* 1632), Arabic scholar ; nephew of Thomas Bedwell [q. v.] ; M.A. Cambridge, 1588 ; rector of St. Ethelburgh's, Bishopsgate Street, 1601 ; one of the Westminster translators of the bible, 1604 ; published at Leyden Epistles of John in English and Arabic, 1612 ; published Arabic and mathematical works (including treatise explaining use of carpenter's square), and left a manuscript Arabic lexicon. [iv. 119]

BEDYLL, THOMAS (*d.* 1537) ; divine ; clerk of privy council ; B.C.L. New College, Oxford, 1508 ; secretary to archbishop Warham, 1520–32 ; royal chaplain and clerk of council, 1532 ; employed by Henry VIII in business relating to his divorce and the royal supremacy. [iv. 120]

BEE, ST. (*d.* 660 ?). [See BEGHA.]

BEEARD, **BEARD**, or **BERDE**, RICHARD (*fl.* 1553–1574), author ; rector of St. Mary Hill, London, 1560–74 ; published poetical pieces. [iv. 121]

BEECHAM, JOHN (1787–1856), methodist ; general secretary to Wesleyan Missionary Society, 1831 ; president Wesleyan conference, 1850 ; published historical and other works. [iv. 121]

BEECHEY, FREDERICK WILLIAM (1796–1856), rear-admiral and geographer ; son of Sir William Beechey [q. v.] ; entered navy, 1806 ; lieutenant, 1815 ; accompanied Franklin's Arctic expedition, 1818, an account of which he published, 1843 ; employed in survey of coasts of North Africa, 1821–3, South America, 1835, and Ireland, 1837 ; captain, 1827 ; rear-admiral ; president, Royal Geographical Society, 1855 ; published geographical works. [iv. 121]

BEECHEY, GEORGE D. (*fl.* 1817–1855), portrait painter; brother of Sir William Beechey [q. v.]; exhibited at Royal Academy, 1817–32; became court painter to king of Oudh. [iv. 122]

BEECHEY, HENRY WILLIAM (*d.* 1870?), painter and explorer; brother of George D. Beechey [q. v.]; secretary (*c.* 1816) to consul-general in Egypt, where he accompanied exploring expeditions on the Nile; surveyed, with his brother, coast-line from Tripoli to Derna, 1821–2; F.S.A., 1825; probably died in New Zealand. [iv. 122]

BEECHEY, SIR WILLIAM (1753–1839), painter; worked in a London lawyer's office; first exhibited, 1775; A.R.A., portrait painter to Queen Charlotte, knight, and R.A., 1793. [iv. 123]

BEECHING, JAMES (1788–1858), inventor of 'self-righting' lifeboat; boatbuilders' apprentice; invented at Great Yarmouth the 'self-righting' lifeboat, 1851. [iv. 123]

BEEDOME, THOMAS (*d.* 1641?), author of 'Poems Divine and Humane,' published 1641, and edited by Henry Glapthorne. [iv. 124]

BEEKE, HENRY (1751–1837), divine; M.A. Corpus Christi College, Oxford, 1776; D.D., 1800; fellow of Oriel, 1775; professor of modern history, 1801; vicar of St. Mary the Virgin, Oxford, 1782; dean of Bristol, 1814. Gained wide reputation as financial authority; published a work on the income tax. [iv. 124]

BEESLEY, ALFRED (1800–1847), author of 'History of Banbury,' 1841. [iv. 125]

BEESLEY or **BISLEY**, GEORGE (*d.* 1591), catholic missioner; educated at Douay; ordained priest, 1587; joined English mission, 1588; executed. [iv. 125]

BEESTON, SIR WILLIAM (*fl.* 1702), lieutenant-governor of Jamaica; went to Jamaica, 1660; member for Port Royal in first house of assembly and judge of court of common pleas, Jamaica, 1664; speaker of house of assembly, 1677–9; knighted, 1692; lieutenant-governor, 1693; resisted, as commander-in-chief, French invasion, 1694; superseded, 1702, on refusing to account for money which he was accused of appropriating; left topographical and other manuscripts. [iv. 125]

BEGA (8th cent.?), saint; perhaps founded monasteries in Cumberland and Northumbria. Her history has been confused with that of St. Hein and St. Begu. [iv. 126]

BEGBIE, JAMES (1798–1869), physician; M.D., 1821, F.R.C.S., 1822, and F.R.C.P., 1847, Edinburgh; physician in ordinary to queen in Scotland; published medical essays. [iv. 126]

BEGBIE, JAMES WARBURTON (1826–1876), physician; son of James Begbie [q.v.]; M.D., 1847, and F.R.C.P., 1852, Edinburgh; studied in Paris; physician to Royal Infirmary, Edinburgh, 1855–65; hon. LL.D. Edinburgh, 1875; published medical works. [iv. 127]

BEGG, JAMES (1808–1883), free church minister; M.A. Glasgow; licensed as preacher, 1829; ordained, 1830; minister at Paisley, 1831, Liberton, 1835–43, and Newington, 1843–83; supported measures of evangelical party in Scotland, and took keen interest in cause of protestantism; moderator of general assembly of free church, 1865. [iv. 127]

BEGHA (*d.* 660?), saint; Irish virgin of royal birth; fled to Scotland to avoid marriage; founded monasteries in England and at Strathclyde (*c.* 656). [iv. 128]

BEHN, AFRA, APHRA, or AYFARA (1640–1689), dramatist and novelist, *née* Johnson; lived as child in Surinam, West Indies; returned to England, 1658; married Behn, a city merchant, and gained entrance to the court; employed by Charles II as spy in Antwerp on outbreak of Dutch war; returned to London and became a professional writer; made friends among playwrights, and in 1671 brought out her 'Forc'd Marriage' at the Duke's Theatre; achieved popularity as a dramatist, some of her plays continuing to hold the stage in the eighteenth century; wrote poems, novels (including 'Oroonoko'), and many ephemeral pamphlets. [iv. 129]

BEHNES or **BURLOWE**, HENRY (*d.* 1837), sculptor; worked under name of Burlowe; exhibited at Royal Academy, 1831–3; subsequently employed in Rome as bust modeller. [iv. 131]

BEHNES, WILLIAM (*d.* 1864), sculptor; brother of Henry Behnes [q. v.]; trained as a piano manufacturer; student of Royal Academy, 1819; gained high reputation, chiefly for portrait busts, between 1820 and 1840; bankrupt, 1861; was picked up from the street and died in Middlesex Hospital. [iv. 131]

BEIGHTON, HENRY (*d.* 1743), surveyor; surveyed Warwickshire, 1725–9, and illustrated Dr. Thomas's edition of Dugdale's 'Warwickshire'; prepared map of Warwickshire (published 1750); editor of 'Ladies' Diary,' 1713–34; F.R.S., 1720; published and left in manuscript scientific writings. [iv. 132]

BEIGHTON, THOMAS (1790–1844), missionary; sent by London Missionary Society to Malacca; established printing press, from which he issued works translated by himself into Malay language. [iv. 132]

BEILBY, RALPH (1744–1817), engraver; in partnership, 1777–97, as engraver with Thomas Bewick, who was his pupil; engaged with Bewick on engravings for Osterwald's bible, 1806, and other works. [iv. 133]

BEILBY, WILLIAM (1783–1849), physician; M.D., 1816, Edinburgh; practised at Edinburgh; philanthropist and interested in religious matters. [iv. 133]

BEITH, ALEXANDER (1799–1891), divine; educated at Glasgow University; minister successively at Oban, Glasgow, Kilbrandon, Glenelg, and Stirling (1839–76); among founders of free church of Scotland, 1843; D.D. Princetown University, U.S.A., 1850; moderator of general assembly of free church, 1858; published pamphlets and religious works. [Suppl. i. 163]

BEITH or **BEETH**, WILLIAM (15th cent.), Dominican; probably provincial of his order in England, *c.* 1480; author of learned works. [iv. 133]

BEK, name of Lincolnshire family descended from Walter Bek, who came over with William the Conqueror. From his three sons sprang three great Lincolnshire families: (1) Bek of Eresby; (2) Bek of Luceby; (3) Bek of Botheby. [iv. 133]

BEK, ANTONY I (*d.* 1310), bishop of Durham; son of Walter Bek, baron of Eresby, Lincolnshire; held five benefices in see of Canterbury; bishop of Durham, 1283; one of royal commissioners to arrange marriage of Prince Edward with Margaret of Scotland, 1290; one of Edward I's chief advisers during negotiations respecting Baliol; substantially assisted Edward in Scottish expeditions, 1296 and 1298; entered into dispute with Richard de Hoton, prior of convent of Durham, concerning visitation of the convent, 1300; refused to accept Edward's decision as mediator, and was deprived of his temporalities, but regained them on application to the pope; granted sovereignty of Isle of Man by Edward II, 1307. [iv. 134]

BEK, ANTONY II (1279–1343), divine; son of Walter Bek of Luceby, constable of Lincoln Castle; educated at Oxford; prebendary of Lincoln; chancellor of the cathedral, 1316; appointed bishop of Lincoln, 1320, but election was annulled by the pope; dean of Lincoln, 1329; chaplain to the pope and clerk of Roman curia; bishop of Norwich, 1337; perhaps poisoned by monks of his cathedral. [iv. 136]

BEK, THOMAS I (*d.* 1293), divine; elder brother of Antony Bek I [q. v.]; chancellor of Oxford University, 1269; keeper of wardrobe to Edward I, 1274; lord-treasurer and temporary keeper of great seal, 1279; prebendary of Lincoln, and, later, bishop of St. David's, 1280; unsuccessfully opposed, as a protest in behalf of the independence of the Welsh church, archbishop Peckham's visitation of the Welsh diocese, 1284; perhaps went on pilgrimage to Holy Land, 1290. [iv. 137]

BEK, THOMAS II (1282–1347), divine; youngest brother of Antony Bek II [q. v.]; doctor of canon law; prebendary of Lincoln, 1335; bishop of Lincoln, 1340. [iv. 138]

BEKE, CHARLES TILSTONE (1800–1874), Abyssinian explorer; entered on business career in London, 1820, but subsequently studied law at Lincoln's Inn; published 'Origines Biblicæ,' 1834, and papers on oriental subjects, 1834–5; fellow of Society of Antiquaries, Royal Geographical Society, and other learned institutions; journeyed in Abyssinia, making many valuable discoveries, 1840–3; published 'The Sources of the Nile,' 1860; travelled in Syria and Palestine, 1861–2, for purpose of exploring localities mentioned in Genesis; undertook mission to King Theodore of Abyssinia to urge him to release British prisoners, 1864, and on outbreak of war, following Theodore's non-compliance, supplied British government with valuable information; explored alleged situation of Mount Sinai, 1873–4. His 'Discoveries of Sinai in Arabia and of Midian' was published posthumously.   [iv. 138]

BEKINSAU, JOHN (1496?–1559), divine; fellow of New College, Oxford, 1520; M.A., 1526; Greek lecturer at Paris University; published a treatise, 'De supremo et absoluto Regis imperio,' 1546.   [iv. 141]

BEKYNTON, THOMAS (1390?–1465). [See BECKINGTON.]

BELASYSE, ANTHONY (d. 1552), civilian; B.C.L. Cambridge, 1520; LL.D., probably of a foreign university; advocate, 1528; held benefices; prebendary of Auckland (1540), Lincoln (1544), Wells (1546), and York (1549); canon of Westminster (1540); master in chancery, 1544; master of Sherburn Hospital, co. Durham, c. 1545.   [iv. 141]

BELASYSE, JOHN, BARON BELASYSE (1614–1689), royalist; created baron, 1645; fought for Charles I in many engagements; after Restoration, appointed lord-lieutenant of East Riding, governor of Hull, and subsequently governor of Tangier; first lord commissioner of treasury, 1687.   [iv. 142]

BELASYSE, THOMAS, EARL FAUCONBERG (1627–1700), supporter of Cromwell; married Mary, Cromwell's daughter, 1657; privy councillor of Charles II. [iv. 142]

BELCHER, SIR EDWARD (1799–1877), admiral; entered navy, 1812; lieutenant, 1818; commander, 1829; employed successively on survey of coasts of Northern and Western Africa, Ireland, Western America, China, Borneo, Philippine Islands, and Formosa, 1830–47; captain and C.B., 1841; knighted, 1843; commanded expedition to Arctic in search of Sir John Franklin, 1852; vice-admiral, 1866; admiral, 1872; published accounts of voyages, and other works.   [iv. 142]

BELCHER, JAMES (1781–1811), prize-fighter; fought Bill Warr at Covent Garden; beat successively Tom Jones of Paddington, 1799, Jack Bartholomew, 1800, Andrew Gamble, 1800, Joe Berks, 1801 and 1802, and John Firby, 1803; lost an eye, 1803, and became publican; was subsequently many times beaten, his last fight being with Tom Cribb, 1809.   [Suppl. i. 164]

BELCHER, TOM (1783–1854), pugilist; brother of James Belcher [q. v.]; defeated Dogherty and Firby, but was beaten by Dutch Sam (Samuel Elias, 1775–1816).   [Suppl. i. 165]

BELCHIAM, THOMAS (1508–1537), Franciscan friar of convent of Greenwich; imprisoned for refusing to take oath of royal supremacy; died in Newgate.   [iv. 143]

BELCHIER, DAUBRIDGCOURT or DAWBRIDGECOURT (1580?–1621), dramatist; B.A. Christ Church, Oxford, 1600; settled in the Low Countries; wrote dramatic and other works.   [iv. 144]

BELCHIER, JOHN (1706–1785), surgeon; educated at Eton; surgeon to Guy's Hospital, 1736; F.R.S., 1732; contributed to 'Philosophical Transactions.'   [iv. 144]

BELER, ROGER DE (d. 1326), judge; supporter of Earl of Lancaster and included in the amnesty, 1318; baron of exchequer, 1322; murdered near Reresby.   [iv. 144]

BELESME, ROBERT DE (fl. 1098). [See BELLÊME.]

BELET, MICHAEL (fl. 1182), judge; sheriff of Worcestershire, 1176–81 and 1184, of Leicestershire and Warwickshire, 1185–7 and 1189–90; justice itinerant for Warwickshire and Leicestershire, 1177, and for Lincolnshire, 1178.   [iv. 145]

BELET, MICHAEL (fl. 1238), judge; son of Michael Belet (fl. 1182) [q. v.]; incumbent of Hinclesham, 1201, and Setburgham (now Serbergham), 1204; receiver of rents of see of Coventry, 1223; founded priory at Wroxton for Augustinian canons regular, c. 1230.   [iv. 145]

BELETH, JOHN (fl. 1182?), author of 'Rationale divinorum officiorum'; perhaps rector of a theological school at Paris.   [iv. 146]

BELFAST, EARL OF (by courtesy) (1827–1853). [See CHICHESTER, FREDERICK RICHARD.]

BELFORD, WILLIAM (1709–1780), general; entered royal artillery on its formation, 1726; fireworker, 1729; first lieutenant, 1740; adjutant at Carthagena, 1741; served in Flanders, 1742–5; lieutenant-colonel, 1749; major-general, 1758; commander of Woolwich district, with charge of arsenal, 1758; general, 1777.   [iv. 146]

BELFOUR, HUGO JOHN (1802–1827), author of poems signed ST. JOHN DORSET; curate, 1826, in Jamaica, where he died.   [iv. 147]

BELFOUR, JOHN (1768–1842), orientalist and miscellaneous writer; member of Royal Society of Literature. His works include a Coptic version, with literal translation, of the Psalms.   [iv. 147]

BELFRAGE, HENRY (1774–1835), divine of secession church; educated at Edinburgh; entered theological hall of his church, Selkirk, 1789; ordained, 1794; appointed to Falkirk congregation; hon. D.D. St. Andrews, 1824; published religious works, 1814–33.   [iv. 147]

BELHAVEN, VISCOUNT (1574?–1639). [See DOUGLAS, ROBERT.]

BELHAVEN, second BARON (1656–1708). [See HAMILTON, JOHN.]

BELING, RICHARD. [See BELLINGS.]

BELKNAP, SIR ROBERT DE (d. 1400?). [See BEALKNAP.]

BELL, ALEXANDER MONTGOMERIE (1808–1866), writer on law; educated at Glasgow; member of Society of Writers to Signet, 1835; professor of conveyancing, Edinburgh, 1856. His lectures (published posthumously) form a standard treatise on conveyancing.   [iv. 148]

BELL, ANDREW (1726–1809), engraver; half-proprietor, and subsequently sole proprietor, of the 'Encyclopædia Britannica' (first published in three volumes, 1771), for which he furnished plates.   [iv. 149]

BELL, ANDREW (1753–1832), founder of Madras system of education; educated at St. Andrews; tutor in Virginia, 1774–81; sailed for India, 1787, and in two years held simultaneously eight army chaplainships; superintendent of Madras Male Orphan Asylum, 1789, where he successfully introduced a system of mutual instruction by the scholars; returned to England, 1796; received pension from East India Company; published, 1797, a work on his educational system, which was adopted in many schools, including Christ's Hospital; rector of Swanage 1801; master of Sherburn Hospital, Durham, 1809; superintendent of National Society for Promoting Education of Poor in Principles of Established Church, with full powers to carry out Madras system, 1811; journeyed abroad to spread his ideas, but with small success, 1816; prebendary of Westminster, 1819; buried in Westminster Abbey. His system was found applicable to certain parts, and certain parts alone, of school-work.   [iv. 149]

BELL, ARCHIBALD (1755–1854), miscellaneous writer; member of faculty of advocates, Edinburgh, 1795; sheriff-depute of Ayrshire.   [iv. 152]

BELL, BEAUPRÉ (1704–1745), antiquary; M.A. Trinity College, Cambridge, 1729; became active member of Spalding Society; assisted Blomefield in history of Norfolk, and Hearne in many antiquarian works; left books, medals, and manuscripts to Trinity College.   [iv. 153]

BELL, BENJAMIN (1749–1806), surgeon; apprenticed as surgeon at Dumfries; studied medicine at Edinburgh and Paris; surgeon to Royal Infirmary, Edinburgh, 1772, and Watson's Hospital, 1778; published works on agriculture and medical subjects.   [iv. 153]

BELL, SIR CHARLES (1774–1842), discoverer of distinct functions of the nerves; educated at Edinburgh; published a 'System of Dissections,' illustrated by his own drawings, 1798; F.C.S. Edinburgh, 1799; published in London, 'Anatomy of Expression,' 1806, and 'New Idea of the Anatomy of the Brain,' 1811, formulating his nerve theory; his discovery complete in its modern form in 1826, and his investigations published in the 'Nervous System of the Human Body,' 1830; knighted; medallist, Royal Society, 1829; professor of surgery, Edinburgh, 1836; wrote on surgery, and (1836) joined Brougham in annotating Paley's 'Natural Theology.'   [iv. 154]

BELL, FRANOIS (1590–1643), Franciscan friar; educated at jesuit colleges of St. Omer and Valladolid; ordained: entered convent of Douay; successively confessor to the Poor Clares, Gravelines, and to Franciscan nuns at Brussels; superior of St. Bonaventure's convent, Douay, 1630; English missioner, 1634–43; executed as jesuit; linguist and author of religious works and translations. [iv. 157]

BELL, SIR GEORGE (1794–1877), colonel; ensign, 1811; captain, 1828; in Canada, 1836–8; brevet-major, 1839; served in Gibraltar, Nova Scotia, West Indies, Mediterranean, Turkey, and the Crimea; C.B., 1855; colonel, 1863; K.C.B., 1867. [iv. 157]

BELL, GEORGE JOSEPH (1770–1843), lawyer, brother of Sir Charles Bell [q. v.]; studied at Edinburgh; advocate, 1791; published works on Scottish bankruptcy law, 1804 and 1810; professor of conveyancing to Society of Writers to Signet, 1816–18; professor of Scots law, Edinburgh, 1822; on commission, 1823, which resulted in Scottish Judicature Act (1825), and chairman, 1833, of commission which resulted in Scottish Bankruptcy Act (1839); clerk of session, 1832. [iv. 158]

BELL, HENRY (1767–1830), builder of Comet steamship; apprenticed as millwright; worked under Rennie in London; conceived idea of applying steam to navigation, and made engine for first practical steamboat that appeared on any European river—the Comet, which plied (1812–20) on the Clyde. [iv. 159]

BELL, HENRY GLASSFORD (1803–1874), sheriff; studied law at Edinburgh; started and conducted 'Edinburgh Literary Journal,' 1828; published a defence of Mary Queen of Scots, 1830; advocate, 1832; sheriff-substitute of Lanarkshire, 1839–67; sheriff-principal, 1867–1874; one of the originators of the Royal Scotch Academy; published miscellaneous works in verse and prose. [iv. 160]

BELL, HENRY NUGENT (1792–1822), genealogist; registered at Inner Temple, 1818; successfully advocated claim of Mr. Hastings to earldom of Huntingdon. [iv. 161]

BELL, JACOB (1810–1859), founder of Pharmaceutical Society; in business as pharmaceutical chemist; founded, 1841, Pharmaceutical Society of Great Britain (incorporated 1843); established and superintended for eighteen years 'Pharmaceutical Journal'; M.P. for St. Albans, 1850; brought forward bill to regulate qualifications of pharmaceutical chemists, 1851; fellow of Chemical, Linnean, and Zoological societies, and of Society of Arts; published works relating to pharmacy. [iv. 162]

BELL, JAMES (1524–1584), Roman catholic priest; educated at Oxford; adopted protestantism, c. 1563, but became reconciled to Roman church, 1581, and was executed at Lancaster as a heretic. [iv. 163]

BELL, JAMES (*fl.* 1551–1596), reformer; B.A. Corpus Christi College, Oxford, 1551; fellow of Trinity College and lecturer in rhetoric, 1556; published religious works. [iv. 164]

BELL, JAMES (1769–1833), geographical author; gave up his business as a weaver and became classical tutor to university students, c. 1806; edited and annotated Rollin's 'Ancient History,' 1828; published 'System of Geography,' 1830. His 'Gazetteer of England and Wales' appeared in 1836. [iv. 164]

BELL, JOHN (*d.* 1556), bishop; educated at Balliol College, Oxford; LL.B. Cambridge, 1504; LL.D. Oxford, 1531; vicar-general and chancellor of diocese of Worcester, 1518; prebendary of Lichfield, St. Paul's, Lincoln, and Southwell; one of Henry VIII's chaplains; employed by Henry in matters relating to his divorce; bishop of Worcester, 1537; undertook revision of Epistles to Thessalonians in Testament of 1542; resigned bishopric, 1543; benefactor of Balliol College. [iv. 165]

BELL, JOHN (1691–1780), traveller; sent by Russian emperor on embassy to Persia, 1715–18, and to China, 1717–22; merchant at Constantinople; published account of journey to China, 1763. [iv. 166]

BELL, JOHN (1747–1798), artillerist; served in artillery in Gibraltar and England; invented military and nautical contrivances; first lieutenant, 1794. [iv. 167]

BELL, JOHN (1763–1820), surgeon, brother of Sir Charles Bell ([q. v.]; educated at Edinburgh; F.R.C.S. Edinburgh, 1786; held appointment at Royal Infirmary, but was excluded on limitation of number of surgeons, 1800; travelled to Italy for his health, 1817; died in Italy. His works include 'Anatomy of Human Body' and 'Principles of Surgery' (1801–8), 'Observations on Italy' appearing posthumously in 1825. [iv. 167]

BELL, JOHN (1745–1831), publisher; refused to join the combination of publishing firms which issued 'Johnson's Poets'; brought out 'Bell's British Poets,' 109 vols., 1777–82, and similar editions of 'Shakespeare' and the 'British Theatre'; first printer to discard long f (s). [iv. 168]

BELL, JOHN (1764–1836), lawyer; B.A. Trinity College, Cambridge, 1786; senior wrangler; fellow; M.A., 1789; studied at Middle Temple and Gray's Inn; called to bar, 1792; king's counsel, 1816. [iv. 169]

BELL, SIR JOHN (1782–1876), general; ensign, 1805; served in Peninsular war; C.B., 1815; chief secretary to Cape of Good Hope government, 1828–41; lieutenant-governor of Guernsey, 1848–54; colonel, 1850; G.C.B. and general, 1860. [iv. 170]

BELL, JOHN (1811–1895), sculptor; studied at Royal Academy, where he exhibited between 1832 and 1879. His works include the Wellington monument at the Guildhall, 1855–6, and the Guards' Memorial in Waterloo Place, 1858–60; published writings on subjects connected with his art. [Suppl. i. 165]

BELL, JOHN GRAY (1823–1866), bookseller; son of Thomas Bell (*d.* 1860) [q. v.]; bookseller in London, 1848, and in Manchester, 1854–66; issued antiquarian works. [iv. 170]

BELL, JOHN MONTGOMERIE (1804–1862), Scottish advocate; called to Edinburgh bar, 1825; advocate-depute, 1847; sheriff of Kincardine, 1851; published treatise on Scottish law of arbitration, 1861. [iv. 170]

BELL, JONATHAN ANDERSON (*d.* 1865), architect; educated at Edinburgh; studied art in Rome, 1829–30; executed drawings for architectural publications, including Le Keux's 'Memorials of Cambridge.' [iv. 170]

BELL, MARIA, LADY (*d.* 1825), amateur painter; pupil of William Hamilton, R.A. (her brother), and Reynolds; exhibited at Royal Academy, 1809–24. [iv. 171]

BELL, PATRICK (1799–1869), inventor of reaping machine; studied at St. Andrews; constructed machine for reaping, 1828; minister of Carmylie, Arbroath, 1843; hon. LL.D. St. Andrews. [iv. 171]

BELL, SIR ROBERT (*d.* 1577), judge; educated at Cambridge; autumn reader at Middle Temple, 1565; M.P. for Lyme Regis, 1562; speaker, 1572–6; knighted; serjeant-at-law; chief baron of exchequer, 1577. [iv. 172]

BELL, ROBERT (1800–1867), journalist; educated at Trinity College, Dublin; settled in London, 1828; editor of the 'Atlas' weekly journal; indicted for libelling Lord Lyndhurst; found guilty, but escaped punishment; contributed to Lardner's 'Cabinet Cyclopædia,' 1830 seq.; began an edition of English poets, of which 24 vols. appeared, 1854–7, and produced several dramatic pieces, novels, and other writings. [iv. 173]

BELL, ROBERT CHARLES (1806–1872), line-engraver; practised at Edinburgh; engraved 'Preston Pans' (completed 1872), after Sir William Allen, for Royal Scottish Association. [iv. 174]

BELL, THOMAS (*fl.* 1573–1610), anti-Romanist writer; perhaps held benefice in Lancashire; became Roman catholic, studied at Douay and Rome, and was priest, 1581; sent to England, 1582; arrested, c. 1592; recanted; wrote polemics against Romanism. [Suppl. i. 166]

BELL, THOMAS (1733–1802), divine; educated at Edinburgh; minister of Relief congregation at Jedburgh, 1767, and at Glasgow, 1777; translated religious works from Dutch and Latin. [iv. 174]

BELL, THOMAS (1785–1860), antiquary; land valuer and surveyor; promoter of Newcastle Literary and Philosophical Society, and a founder of Newcastle Society of Antiquaries. [iv. 174]

BELL, THOMAS (1792–1880), dental surgeon ; studied at Guy's and St. Thomas's Hospitals ; F.R.C.S., 1844 ; dental surgeon at Guy's, 1817–61 ; lecturer on comparative anatomy ; professor of zoology, King's College, London, 1836 ; F.R.S., 1828 ; vice-president, Zoological Society ; secretary of Royal Society, 1848–53 ; president of Linnean Society, 1853–61 ; published zoological works and an edition of White's ' Selborne.' [iv. 175]

BELL, WILLIAM (*fl.* 1599), lawyer ; educated at Balliol College, Oxford ; studied at Clement's Inn ; clerk of peace for Hampshire. [iv. 175]

BELL, WILLIAM (1625–1683), divine ; B.A. St. John's College, Oxford, 1647 ; fellow ; ejected from benefice in Norfolk by parliamentary visitors ; B.D., 1661 ; prebendary of St. Paul's, 1665 ; chaplain to king, 1667. [iv. 175]

BELL, WILLIAM (1740 ?–1804 ?), portrait painter ; gained Royal Academy gold medal, 1771. [iv. 176]

BELL, WILLIAM (1731–1816), divine ; M.A. Magdalene College, Cambridge, 1756 ; domestic chaplain and secretary to Princess Amelia, daughter of George III ; prebendary of Westminster, 1765 ; D.D., 1767 ; rector of Christ Church, London, 1780–99 ; treasurer of St. Paul's ; published sermons and other religious works. [iv. 176]

BELLAMONT, EARL OF (1636–1701). [See COOTE, RICHARD.]

BELLAMONT, VISCOUNT (1604 ?–1660). [See BARD, HENRY.]

BELLAMY, DANIEL, the elder (*b.* 1687), miscellaneous writer ; educated at St. John's College, Oxford ; published religious, dramatic, and other works. [iv. 177]

BELLAMY, DANIEL, the younger (*d.* 1788), divine ; M.A. Trinity College, Cambridge, 1759 ; vicar of St. Stephen's, near St. Albans, 1749 ; published miscellaneous, religious, and dramatic works. [iv. 178]

BELLAMY, GEORGE ANNE (1731 ?–1788), actress ; illegitimate daughter of Lord Tyrawley ; educated in a convent at Boulogne ; on returning to England became acquainted with Garrick and went on stage ; first appeared in ' Love for Love,' at Covent Garden, 1742 ; successfully played Juliet to Garrick's Romeo in the rivalry with Barry and Mrs. Cibber, 1750 ; died in reduced circumstances ; published her ' Apology,' 1785. [iv. 178]

BELLAMY, RICHARD (1743 ?–1813), bass singer ; Mus. Bac. ; gentleman of Chapel Royal, 1771 ; vicar choral of St. Paul's, 1777 ; almoner and master of choristers, 1793–1800. [iv. 179]

BELLAMY, THOMAS (1745–1800), miscellaneous writer ; hosier and subsequently bookseller's clerk ; started ' General Magazine and Impartial Review,' 1787, and other unsuccessful periodicals ; published poetical, dramatic, and other works. [iv. 179]

BELLAMY, THOMAS LUDFORD (1770–1843), singer ; son of Richard Bellamy [q. v.] ; sang at Handel commemoration, Westminster, 1784 ; stage-manager, Dublin theatre, 1797 ; embarked unsuccessfully in various theatrical enterprises ; engaged at Covent Garden, and later at Drury Lane ; choirmaster of Spanish chapel, 1819. [iv. 180]

BELLASIS. [See BELASYSE.]

BELLASIS, EDWARD (1800–1873), lawyer ; educated at Christ's Hospital ; called to bar at Inner Temple, 1824 ; practised in court of chancery and in county palatine of Lancaster ; engaged as barrister in parliamentary business, 1836–66 ; serjeant-at-law, 1844 ; one of commissioners to examine working of Heralds' College, 1869 ; evinced great interest in Tractarian movement, 1833–45, and took part in discussion produced by Pius IX's bull in 1850 ; entered the Roman catholic communion, 1850 ; magistrate of Middlesex and Westminster ; published religious writings, and left an autobiography and manuscript verses. [iv. 180]

BELLEMAN or **BELMAIN**, JOHN (*fl.* 1553), French tutor of Edward VI ; left manuscript translation into French of Edward VI's second Prayer-book. [iv. 182]

BELLÊME, ROBERT OF, EARL OF SHREWSBURY (*fl.* 1098), a magnate of Normandy ; knighted, 1073 ; supported Duke Robert in the revolt against William I,

1077 ; pardoned, but on the death of the Conqueror again joined Duke Robert against William Rufus ; took part in defence of Rochester, and on surrender was reconciled to the king, 1088 ; captured and imprisoned by Duke Robert, but was soon released ; engaged in war with his neighbours in Normandy ; joined Henry of Coutances (Henry I) in suppressing revolt of citizens of Rouen, 1090 ; captain of king's forces in Rufus's abortive invasion of France, 1097 ; engaged in war with Helias of Maine, 1098 ; captured Helias and delivered him to Rufus, who continued the war ; earl of Shrewsbury, 1098 ; did homage to Henry I, 1100, but with his brothers and Duke Robert conspired against him, 1101 ; outlawed, 1102 ; fortified himself in Shrewsbury ; forced to surrender ; returned to Normandy ; after several attempts to obtain allies against Henry, made peace with him, 1106 ; soon afterwards he joined Fulk of Anjou against Henry ; sent, 1112, by Louis of France as ambassador to Henry, who seized and kept him in close confinement until his death. [iv. 182]

BELLENDEN, ADAM (*d.* 1639 ?), bishop ; son of Sir John Bellenden [q. v.] ; M.A. Edinburgh, 1590 ; minister at Falkirk, 1608 ; ' suspended,' 1614 ; released, 1615 ; left presbyterian church, and was made bishop of Dunblane, 1616, and of Aberdeen, 1635 ; deprived of see on abolition of episcopacy in Scotland, 1638. [iv. 186]

BELLENDEN, SIR JOHN, of Auchnoul or Auchinoul (*d.* 1577) ; Scottish lawyer ; justice-clerk, 1547 ; privy councillor to Mary Queen of Scots, 1561 ; implicated in murder of Rizzio, but soon restored to favour ; joined nobles against Mary at Bothwell ; privy councillor to Regent Murray ; employed in framing pacification of Perth, 1573. [iv. 187]

BELLENDEN, **BALLENDEN**, or **BALLENTYNE**, JOHN (*fl.* 1533–1587), poet ; educated at St. Andrews and Paris ; D.D. Sorbonne ; translated, by command of James V of Scotland, into Scottish vernacular, Boece's ' Historia Scotorum ' (1536) and Livy, first published in 1822 ; archdeacon of Moray and canon of Ross ; opposed Reformation and withdrew to the continent. [iv. 186]

BELLENDEN, SIR LEWIS, LORD AUCHINOL (1553 ?–1591), Scottish judge ; eldest son of Sir John Bellenden [q. v.] ; justice-clerk, 1578 ; privy councillor, 1579 ; judge, 1584 ; instrumental in Earl of Arran's downfall, 1585 ; accompanied James VI in his matrimonial excursion to Norway and Denmark, 1589–90. [iv. 188]

BELLENDEN, WILLIAM (*d.* 1633 ?), Scottish professor ; employed in diplomatic service by James VI and Mary Queen of Scots ; professor at university of Paris ; produced works illustrating Roman history by extracts from Roman authors. [iv. 189]

BELLENDEN, WILLIAM, BARON BELLENDEN (*d.* 1671), created Lord Bellenden, 1661, and treasurer-depute and privy councillor of Scotland, 1661 ; supported Lauderdale against Middleton's faction. [iv. 189]

BELLERS, FETTIPLACE (1687–1750 ?), dramatist and philosophical writer ; F.R.S., 1711 ; produced a tragedy which was acted at Drury Lane, 1732, and philosophical works, including ' A Delineation of Universal Law,' 1750. [iv. 190]

BELLERS, JOHN (1654–1725), philanthropist ; member of Society of Friends ; devised schemes for the abolition of war, education of poor children, improvement of prisons, and establishment of hospitals. He wrote many short works, the most important being ' Proposals for Raising a Colledge of Industry of all useful Trades and Husbandry,' 1695. [iv. 190]

BELLERS, WILLIAM (*fl.* 1761–1774), landscape-painter ; contributed to exhibitions of Free Society of Artists, 1761–73. [iv. 191]

BELLEW, HENRY WALTER (1834–1892), surgeon-general ; studied at St. George's Hospital, London ; M.R.C.P., 1855 ; served in Crimea, 1854–5 ; assistant surgeon, Bengal medical service, 1855 ; surgeon, 1867 ; deputy surgeon-general, 1881 ; served with Major (Sir) Henry Lumsden [q. v.] on Candahar mission ; C.S.I., 1873 ; chief political officer at Cabul ; retired as surgeon-general, 1886 ; published journals, works on oriental languages, and other writings. [Suppl. i. 167]

BELLEW, JOHN CHIPPENDALL MONTESQUIEU (1823–1874), author, preacher, and public reader; son of Captain Robert Higgins; educated at St. Mary's Hall, Oxford; assumed his mother's maiden name, Bellew, 1844; after holding two curacies in England, he was chaplain of St. John's Cathedral, Calcutta, 1851–5; successively minister at several London churches; was converted to Roman catholicism, 1868, and devoted himself to literature and public readings; published miscellaneous works. [iv. 192]

BELLEW, RICHARD (*fl.* 1585), legal reporter; published reports in Norman-French of cases in time of Richard II. [iv. 193]

BELLIN, SAMUEL (1799–1893), engraver; practised in England, *c.* 1834–70. His plates are all from popular English painters of his day. [Suppl. i. 168]

BELLINGER, FRANCIS (*d.* 1721), physician; L.C.P., 1708; published medical works. [iv. 193]

BELLINGHAM, SIR EDWARD (*d.* 1549), lord deputy of Ireland; served in Hungary with Sir Thomas Seymour, and with Earl of Surrey in Boulogne and Isle of Wight (1545); privy councillor of Edward VI; lord deputy of Ireland, 1548; suppressed rebellion in King's and Queen's counties. [iv. 193]

BELLINGHAM, RICHARD (1592?–1672), governor of Massachusetts; recorder of Boston, Lincolnshire, 1625–1633; deputy-governor of Massachusetts, 1635; governor, 1641; held the office uninterruptedly, 1665–72; assistant major-general, 1664. [iv. 194]

BELLINGS, RICHARD (*d.* 1677), Irish historian; studied at Lincoln's Inn; composed a sixth book to Sidney's 'Arcadia,' 1628; Irish M.P.; secretary to supreme council of Irish confederation, 1642; royalist, 1645–9, retiring to France till Restoration; wrote a history of contemporary Irish affairs (part printed 1882). [iv. 194]

BELLOFAGO or **BELLAFAGO**. [See BEAUFEU.]

BELLOMONT. [See BEAUMONT.]

BELLOMONT, CHARLES HENRY, EARL OF (*d.* 1683). [See KIRKHOVEN, CHARLES HENRY.]

BELLOT, HUGH (1542–1596), bishop; B.A. Christ's College, Cambridge, 1564; M.A. and fellow of Jesus College, 1567; D.D., 1579; bishop of Bangor, 1585; member of council of Wales; bishop of Chester, 1595; assisted William Morgan in translating bible into Welsh. [iv. 195]

BELLOT, THOMAS (1806–1857), surgeon and philologist; M.R.C.S., 1828; surgeon in navy, 1831; F.R.C.S., 1844; in charge of naval hospital of Therapia on Bosphorus, 1854–5; published 'Sanscrit Derivations of English Words' (1856), and some classical translations. [iv. 195]

BELMEIS or **BELESMAINS**, JOHN, JOHN OF THE FAIR HANDS (*d.* 1203?), divine; brought up in household of archbishop Theobald; treasurer of York, *c.* 1158; friend and adviser of Becket during controversy with Henry II; bishop of Poitiers, 1162; papal legate, *c.* 1177; one of five chief ecclesiastics sent to convert Toulouse, 1178; elected archbishop of Narbonne, 1181, but transferred by pope to see of Lyons; resigned, 1193; came to England to perform vows at Becket's tomb; retired to St. Bernard's abbey of Clairvaux, *c.* 1194; said to have written a history and other learned works, now lost. [iv. 196]

BELMEIS or **BEAUMEIS**, RICHARD DE, surnamed RUFUS (*d.* 1128), bishop; follower of Roger of Montgomery and Earl Hugh; but afterwards adherent of Henry I; royal agent, till 1123, in Shropshire, the forfeited palatinate of Robert of Bellême; bishop of London, 1108; devoted revenue of bishopric to carrying out the rebuilding of St. Paul's; founded St. Osyth's Priory, Essex, where he died. [iv. 198]

BELMEIS or **BEAUMEIS**, RICHARD DE (*d.* 1162), bishop; nephew of Richard de Belmeis [q. v.]; at an early age prebendary of St. Paul's and prebendary of St. Alkmund's, Shrewsbury; converted estates of secular canons of St. Alkmund to foundation of college at Lilleshall of canons regular of the Arroasian branch of Augustinian order; bishop of London, 1152. [iv. 200]

BELOE, WILLIAM (1756–1817), divine; educated at Bene't College, Cambridge; for three years assistant master under Parr at Norwich grammar school; rector of All Hallows, London Wall, 1796; keeper of printed books at British Museum, 1803–6; contributed to Tooke's 'Biographical Dictionary,' and established with Archdeacon Nares the 'British Critic,' 1793. Works include 'Anecdotes of Literature and Scarce Books,' 1806–12, the 'Sexagenarian,' consisting of personal recollections, and several classical translations. [iv. 201]

BELPER, first BARON (1801–1880). [See STRUTT, EDWARD.]

BELSHAM, THOMAS (1750–1829), unitarian divine; minister of independent congregation at Worcester, 1778; professor of divinity at Daventry, 1781–9, and, having adopted unitarianism, at Hackney College, 1789–96; minister of Gravel Pit chapel, Hackney, 1794, and Essex Street chapel, 1805; published theological works. [iv. 202]

BELSHAM, WILLIAM (1752–1827), political writer and historian; brother of Thomas Belsham [q. v.]; published philosophical and historical works in support of whig principles. [iv. 203]

BELSON, JOHN (*fl.* 1688), catholic gentleman; renowned for knowledge of history and controversial matters. [iv. 203]

BELSON, THOMAS (*d.* 1589), catholic gentleman; executed for assisting catholic priests. [iv. 204]

BELT, THOMAS (1832–1878), geologist; made geological investigations in Australian gold-diggings, 1852–62; superintendent of Nova Scotia Gold Company's mines, 1862; conducted gold-mining operations of Chontales Company, Nicaragua, 1868–72; fellow, Geological Society; died at Denver, Colorado; published works chiefly relating to glacial period. [iv. 204]

BELTZ, GEORGE FREDERICK (1777–1841), Lancaster herald; gentleman usher of scarlet rod of order of the Bath, and Brunswick herald, 1814; portcullis pursuivant, 1817–22; Lancaster herald, 1822; published genealogical writings. [iv. 204]

BELZONI, GIOVANNI BAPTISTA (1778–1823), actor, engineer, and traveller; born at Padua; came to London, 1803, and exhibited feats of strength at Astley's Amphitheatre; toured in Spain and Portugal, and introduced improved hydraulic machines in Egypt, 1815; engaged in archæological exploration in Egypt, and published an account of his discoveries, 1820; died of dysentery at Gato, Benin, while on journey of exploration to Timbuktu. [iv. 205]

BEN, BANE, BENE, BENNET, or **BIORT,** JAMES (*d.* 1332), bishop; archdeacon and, 1328, bishop of St. Andrews; chamberlain of Scotland, *c.* 1331, on Baliol's invasion fled to Bruges, where he died. [iv. 206]

BENAZECH, CHARLES (1767?–1794), painter; son of Peter Paul Benazech [q. v.]; studied under Greuze in Paris. His best-known pictures are of incidents in French Revolution. [iv. 207]

BENAZECH, PETER PAUL (1744?–1783?), line-engraver; pupil of Francis Vivarès. [iv. 207]

BENBOW, JOHN (1653–1702), vice-admiral; served as master's mate in Mediterranean, 1678; master, 1679; probably in merchant service, 1681–9; captain, 1689; successively master attendant of Chatham and Deptford dockyards, 1690–6; master of the fleet in battle off Beachy Head, 1690, and Barfleur and La Hogue, 1692; commanded bombarding flotilla at St. Malo, 1693 and 1695, and at Dunkirk, 1694; commander-in-chief of squadron before Dunkirk, and, later, that in the Soundings, 1696; commander-in-chief in West Indies, 1698–1700, and in Downs, 1700–1; vice-admiral of the blue, 1701; again in West Indies, 1701–2; encountered French under Du Casse off Santa Marta, and followed them for several days, but gave up the pursuit because his captains protested against his plan; died of wounds at Port Royal. [iv. 207]

BENBOW, JOHN (1681?–1708), traveller, son of John Benbow (1653–1702) [q. v.]; volunteer in navy, 1695; joined merchant service; served in East Indies as fourth mate, and subsequently second mate, 1701; wrecked off Madagascar, captured by natives, but escaped and returned to England. [iv. 211]

BENDIGO (1811–1889). [See THOMPSON, WILLIAM.]

BENDINGS, WILLIAM (*fl.* 1180), judge; one of Henry II's envoys to Ireland to fetch Reimund Fitzgerald, 1176; appointed to northern circuit, 1179; sheriff of Dorset and Somerset, 1184. [iv. 212]

BENDISH, BRIDGET (1650-1726), daughter of General Henry Ireton, by Bridget, Oliver Cromwell's eldest daughter; married Thomas Bendish, 1670; said to have compromised herself in Rye House plot, 1683. [iv. 212]

BENDLOWES, EDWARD (1603?-1676). [See BENLOWES.]

BENDLOWES, WILLIAM (1516-1584), lawyer; educated at St. John's College, Cambridge: called to bar at Lincoln's Inn; serjeant-at-law, 1555; M.P. successively for Helston, Penrhyn, and Dunheved, 1553-4; a governor of Lincoln's Inn, 1576; some of his reports published posthumously. [iv. 213]

BENEDICT (*d.* 1193), chancellor to archbishop of Canterbury, 1174; prior of Christ Church, Canterbury, 1175; abbot of Peterborough, 1177-93; built a large portion of his church; wrote histories of the passion and Thomas Becket's miracles. [iv. 213]

BENEDICT BISCOP (628?-690), founder of monasteries; thegn of Oswiu, king of Northumbria; monk of monastery of Lerins, 665-7; conducted Theodore of Tarsus from Rome to Canterbury, 669; abbot of St. Peter's, Canterbury, 669; built, 674, at mouth of river Wear, monastery of St. Peter, which by papal letter was exempted from external control, 678; established sister monastery of St. Paul at Jarrow; collected an extensive library. [iv. 214]

BENEDICT CHELYDONIUS or CALEDONIUS (*fl.* 1519), abbot of Scottish monastery at Vienna; opponent of Luther. [iv. 216]

BENEDICT OF GLOUCESTER (*fl.* 1120), monk of St. Peter's, Gloucester; compiled a life of St. Dubricius. [iv. 216]

BENEDICT OF NORWICH (*fl.* 1340), abbot of Austin friars at Norwich; suffragan of Norwich; linguist, scientist, and theologian. [iv. 216]

BENEDICT, SIR JULIUS (1804-1885), musician; born at Stuttgart; pupil of J. C. L. Abeille, Hummel, and Weber; conductor at Kärnthnerthor Theatre, Vienna, 1823-5, and at San Carlo and Fondo theatres, Naples, 1825-35; conducted series of Italian comic operas at Lyceum, 1836; conductor of English opera, Drury Lane; accompanied Jenny Lind on American tour, 1850; conductor of Italian opera, 1852; for many years conducted Norwich festival; knighted, 1871; in 1862 was performed his well-known 'Lily of Killarney.' [iv. 216]

BENEFACTA, RICHARD (*d.* 1090?). [See CLARE, RICHARD DE.]

BENEFIELD, SEBASTIAN (1559-1630), divine; B.A. and M.A. Corpus Christi College, Oxford; D.D., 1608; Margaret professor of divinity, 1613; rector of Meysey-Hampton, Gloucestershire; published scholarly religious works. [iv. 217]

BENESE, RICHARD (*d.* 1546), divine; B.C.L. Oxford, 1519; canon of Augustinian priory of Merton, which he surrendered to Henry VIII, 1538; published a work on land surveying. [iv. 218]

BENET, FATHER (1563-1611). [See CANFIELD, BENEDICT.]

BENET or **BENEDICTUS,** MAGISTER (*d.* 1226), bishop of Rochester; keeper of great seal on deposition of Longchamp, 1191; bishop of Rochester, 1215. [iv. 218]

BENET, WILLIAM (*d.* 1533), ambassador; LL.D.; canon of Leighlin, 1522; occasionally acted as Cardinal Wolsey's commissary; accompanied embassy to Rome, 1528, on business connected with Henry VIII's divorce; ambassador at Rome, 1529-33; died at Susa in Piedmont. [iv. 218]

BENEZET, ANTHONY (1713-1784), philanthropist; born at St. Quentin, France, whence his family came to England on account of their protestant opinions; joined Society of Friends; emigrated to America, 1731; schoolmaster in Friends' school, Philadelphia, 1742; founded school for females, 1755; interested himself in cause of negroes and Indians; published pamphlets embodying his religious and social opinions. [iv. 219]

BENFIELD, PAUL (*d.* 1810), Indian trader; civil servant of East India Company, 1764; acquired large fortune by trade contracts, and moneylending; ordered home and resigned the service, the character of a transaction between him and nawáb of the Carnatic being called in question, 1777; M.P. for Cricklade, 1780; subsequently restored to his position; finally returned to England, 1793; lost fortune in unfortunate speculations; died in Paris in indigent circumstances. [iv. 220]

BENGER, ELIZABETH OGILVY (1778-1827), author; came to London, 1800; made acquaintance of the Lambs, Mrs. Inchbald, Campbell, Smirke the painter, and others; published poem 'On the Slave Trade,' illustrated with engravings after Smirke, 1809; wrote two novels, several historical works, and translated one volume of Klopstock's letters. [iv. 221]

BENHYEM or **BENHAM,** HUGO DE (*d.* 1282), bishop of Aberdeen, 1272; wrote theological works. [iv. 222]

BENISCH, ABRAHAM (1811-1878), hebraist; born of Jewish parents at Drosau, Bohemia; studied medicine at Vienna; settled in England, 1841; edited 'Jewish Chronicle,' 1854-69, and 1875-8; zealously promoted cause of his co-religionists; published works on Hebrew literature. [iv. 222]

BEN ISRAEL, MANASSEH (1604-1657). [See MANASSEH.]

BENJAMIN, JUDAH PHILIP (1811-1884), lawyer; born of Jewish parents of English nationality in St. Croix, West Indies; educated at Yale; called to the bar, New Orleans, 1832; counsellor of supreme court, New Orleans, 1848; senator for Louisiana, 1852 and 1857; on secession of South Carolina cast in his lot with the South and was attorney-general, and, later, acting secretary of war, in cabinet of Davis's provisional government for the Southern confederacy, 1861; secretary of state, 1864; on fall of confederacy came to England; studied English law at Lincoln's Inn; called to the bar, 1866; joined northern circuit; published a work on contract of sale (1868), which was immediately successful; 'Palatine silk' for county of Lancaster; obtained large practice, chiefly in colonial appeals before the privy council; retired, 1883; several of his speeches published. [iv. 222]

BENLOWES, EDWARD (1603?-1676), poet, educated at St. John's College, Cambridge; inherited estate of Brent Hall, but squandered his money on friends, among whom were many distinguished men; his chief work, 'Theophila, or Love's Sacrifice' (1652), was illustrated by Hollar and others. [iv. 226]

BENN, GEORGE (1801-1882), historian; educated under Sheridan Knowles at Belfast; engaged in distilling near Downpatrick; subsequently discovered the presence of iron ore in Glenravel hills, which were successfully worked; published writings relating to history of Belfast. [iv. 227]

BENN or **BEN,** WILLIAM (1600-1680), divine; educated at Queen's College, Oxford; chaplain to Marchioness of Northampton; preacher at All Saints, Dorchester, 1629-62; ejected under Act of Uniformity; a volume of his sermons was published posthumously. [iv. 228]

BENNET, BENJAMIN (1674-1726), nonconformist divine; ordained, 1699; colleague with Richard Gilpin [q. v.] at Newcastle-on-Tyne, 1703; published hymns and religious and historical works including 'Memorial of Reformation in England,' 1717. [iv. 228]

BENNET, CHRISTOPHER (1617-1655), physician; M.A. Lincoln College, Oxford, 1639; incorporated M.A. Cambridge, where he graduated M.D., 1646; F.C.P., 1649; and censor, 1654; published treatise on consumption, 1654. [iv. 229]

BENNET, GEORGE (1750-1835), hebraist; presbyterian minister at Carlisle, and subsequently of Strathmiglo, Fife; devoted much time to study of Hebrew; one of principal contributors to 'British Critic'; published 'Olam Hanashamoth, a View of the Intermediate State,' 1800. [iv. 229]

BENNET, HENRY (*fl.* 1561), of Calais; translator; published, 1561, a volume of translations from German reformers. [iv. 230]

BENNET, HENRY, first EARL OF ARLINGTON (1618-1685), member of Cabal ministry ; grandson of Sir John Bennet [q. v.] ; educated at Westminster and Christ Church, Oxford ; joined royal forces as volunteer ; travelled in France and Italy ; agent of Prince Charles at Madrid, 1658 ; keeper of privy purse after Restoration ; secretary of state, 1662–74 ; M.P. ; centre of opposition to Clarendon, 1663 ; created Lord Arlington, 1663 ; probably ultimately responsible for outbreak of first Dutch war ; arranged conclusion of triple alliance, 1668 ; member of Cabal ; arranged secret treaty of Dover, 1670 ; peer and K.G., 1672 ; unsuccessfully impeached in House of Commons as instrument of the king's evil measures, 1674 ; lord chamberlain, 1674 ; spent his last years in retirement. [iv. 230]

BENNET, JOHN (fl. 1600), musician ; composed and published many excellent madrigals, 1599–1614. [iv. 233]

BENNET, SIR JOHN (d. 1627), ecclesiastic and civilian ; educated at Christ Church, Oxford ; junior proctor, 1585 ; LL.D., 1589 ; prebendary of York, 1591 ; vicar-general in spirituals to Archbishop of York ; chancellor of the diocese ; M.P. for Ripon, 1597 and 1603, and York, 1601 ; member of council of the north, 1599 ; knighted, 1603 ; judge of prerogative court of Canterbury ; chancellor to Queen Anne of Denmark ; M.P. for Oxford University, 1614 and 1620 ; impeached, 1621, for administering estates of intestates in consonance with wishes of highest bidder ; trial discontinued by the Lords owing to his illness, but resumed in Star-chamber, 1622 ; sentenced to fine, imprisonment, and permanent disability from holding office ; sentence remitted, with exception of fine, 1624. [iv. 233]

BENNET, JOHN (d. 1686), controversial writer ; M.A. Christ Church, Oxford, 1683 ; published (1683) a pamphlet in reply to Samuel Johnson's 'Julian the Apostate.' [iv. 235]

BENNET, JOSEPH (1629–1707), nonconformist divine ; B.A. St. John's College, Cambridge, 1650 ; obtained living of Brightling, 1658 ; ejected under Act of Uniformity, 1662 ; subsequently took charge of nonconformist congregations at Hellingly and Hastings. [iv. 235]

BENNET, ROBERT (d. 1617), bishop ; B.A. Trinity College, Cambridge, 1569 ; incorporated at Oxford, 1572 ; master of hospital of St. Cross, Winchester, 1583 ; dean of Windsor, 1595 ; registrar of order of Garter, 1596 ; bishop of Hereford, 1603. [iv. 236]

BENNET, ROBERT (1605–1683), parliamentary colonel during civil war ; member of council of state, 1653 ; M.P. for Cornwall, 1653, for Launceston and Looe, 1654, and Launceston, 1659. [iv. 236]

BENNET or BENNETT, ROBERT (d. 1687), author ; B.D. Oxford ; rector of Waddesden, 1648 ; ejected, 1662 ; subsequently preached to small congregation at Aylesbury ; published 'Theological Concordance of Synonymous Terms in Holy Scriptures,' 1657. [iv. 237]

BENNET, SIR THOMAS (1592–1670), judge ; LL.D. All Souls' College, Oxford, 1624 ; member of Gray's Inn ; admitted to College of Advocates, 1626 ; master in chancery, 1635–70 ; knighted, 1661. [iv. 237]

BENNET, THOMAS (1645?–1681), grammarian ; M.A. Christ Church, Oxford, 1669 ; corrector of University Press ; obtained livings of Steventon by Abingdon and Hungerford ; published work known as ' Oxford [Latin] Grammar,' 1673. [iv. 237]

BENNET, THOMAS (1673–1728), divine ; M.A. St. John's College, Cambridge, 1694 ; fellow ; lecturer at St. Olave's, Southwark, deputy chaplain to Chelsea Hospital, and morning preacher at St. Lawrence Jewry, c. 1711 ; presented to St. Giles, Cripplegate ; D.D., 1711 ; published works, including controversial treatises directed against dissenters and quakers, a paraphrase of the 'Book of Common Prayer, with Annotations' (1708), and a Hebrew grammar (1726). [iv. 238]

BENNET, WILLIAM (1746–1820), bishop of Cloyne ; educated at Harrow and Emmanuel College, Cambridge ; M.A., 1770 ; fellow, 1773 ; D.D., 1790 ; bishop of Cork and Ross, 1790–4, and of Cloyne, 1794–1820 ; F.S.A., 1790 ; published archæological writings. [iv. 239]

BENNET or BENNETT, WILLIAM (1767?–1833 ?), musician ; studied under J. C. Bach and Schroeter ; organist of St. Andrew's, Plymouth, 1793 ; published musical compositions. [iv. 240]

BENNETT, AGNES MARIA (d. 1808), novelist ; wrote seven novels, published between 1785 and 1816, several of which were translated into French. [iv. 240]

BENNETT, CHARLES HENRY (1829–1867), draughtsman on wood ; worked on staff of 'Punch.' [iv. 241]

BENNETT, EDWARD TURNER (1797–1836), zoologist ; surgeon in London ; promoted establishment of entomological society, 1832, which ultimately developed into London Zoological Society ; published zoological works. [iv. 241]

BENNETT, GEORGE JOHN (1800–1879), actor ; served in navy, 1813–17 ; appeared at Covent Garden as Richard III and Hotspur, 1823 ; in Covent Garden company 1830–41 ; with Macready at Drury Lane, 1841–3, and with Phelps at Sadler's Wells, 1844–62. [iv. 241]

BENNETT, JAMES (1785–1856), printer and bookseller at Tewkesbury, 1810–52 ; published 'History of Tewkesbury,' 1830. [iv. 242]

BENNETT, JAMES (1774–1862), congregational minister ; minister at Romsey, 1797–1813 ; tutor and pastor at Rotherham, 1813 ; transferred to London, 1828 ; secretary to London Missionary Society ; published works, chiefly theological. [iv. 242]

BENNETT, JAMES GORDON (1800–1872), journalist ; went to America, 1819 ; obtained employment in printing and publishing offices at Boston ; successively on staff of 'Charleston Courier,' 'National Advocate,' and 'Enquirer' ; started the short-lived 'New York Globe' ; contributed to 'New York Mirror' ; founded 'New York Herald,' of which for some time he prepared the entire contents, 1835 ; subsidised Stanley's expedition to find Livingstone, 1871–2. He made great improvements in the system of obtaining news, and regularly employed men of literary attainments. [iv. 243]

BENNETT, SIR JAMES RISDON (1809–1891), physician ; son of Rev. James Bennett [q. v.] ; M.D. Edinburgh, 1833 ; physician to Aldersgate Street dispensary, 1837 ; assistant physician to St. Thomas's Hospital, 1843, and physician, 1849 ; physician to City of London Hospital for Diseases of Chest, 1848 ; F.R.S., 1875 ; knighted and made president Royal College Physicians, 1876 ; published medical treatises. [Suppl. i. 168]

BENNETT, SIR JOHN (1814–1897), sheriff of London and Middlesex ; brother of William Cox Bennett [q. v.] ; watchmaker in Cheapside, 1846–89 ; sheriff of London and Middlesex, 1872 ; knighted ; common councillor for ward of Cheap, 1862–89 ; thrice elected alderman, but each election annulled. [Suppl. i. 169]

BENNETT, JOHN HUGHES (1812–1875), physician and physiologist ; apprenticed as surgeon at Maidstone, 1829 ; one of presidents of Royal Medical Society ; M.D. Edinburgh, 1837 ; proceeded to Paris ; founded, and was first president of, Parisian Medical Society ; studied in Germany ; lectured on histology at Edinburgh, 1841 ; F.R.S. and F.C.P. Edinburgh ; physician to Royal Dispensary, and pathologist to Royal Infirmary ; editor of 'London and Edinburgh Monthly Journal of Medical Science,' 1846 ; professor of Institutes of Medicine, Edinburgh, 1848–74 ; LL.D. Edinburgh, 1875. His works include important treatises on clinical medicine, physiology, pathology, pneumonia, cancerous and cancroid growths, and leucocythæmia. [iv. 244]

BENNETT, JOHN JOSEPH (1801–1876), botanist ; studied at Middlesex Hospital ; was, till 1870, keeper of Banksian herbarium and library on its transfer to British Museum in 1827 ; F.R.S., 1841 ; F.L.S., 1828, and secretary, 1840–60 ; published botanical papers. [iv. 246]

BENNETT, WILLIAM COX (1820–1895), miscellaneous writer ; watchmaker at Greenwich ; on staff of 'Weekly Dispatch,' 1869–70 ; member of London council of the Education League ; published songs and other writings. [Suppl. i. 168]

BENNETT, WILLIAM JAMES EARLY (1804–1886), ritualist divine ; born at Halifax, Nova Scotia ; educated at Westminster and Christ Church, Oxford ; M.A., 1829 ;

usher at Westminster School, 1826–8 ; minister of Portman Chapel, 1836–43, and of St. Paul's, Knightsbridge, 1840 ; attracted hostile notice owing to his ritualistic innovations and, in consequence, resigned incumbency, 1850 ; vicar of Frome Selwood, Somerset, 1852–86 ; published sermons and controversial and other religious writings. [Suppl. i. 169]

BENNETT, WILLIAM MINEARD (1778–1858), miniaturist ; pupil of Sir Thomas Lawrence ; exhibited at Royal Academy, 1812–16 and 1834–5. [iv. 247]

BENNETT, SIR WILLIAM STERNDALE (1816–1875), musical composer ; in choir of King's College, Cambridge, 1824–6 ; studied violin under Oury and Spagnoletti, and piano under Cipriani Potter, and Crotch at Royal Academy of Music, 1826–36 ; attracted Mendelssohn's attention by his first concerto (1832), which was the occasion of a long intimacy ; organist at Wandsworth church, 1834 ; attended the Lower Rhine Festival conducted by Mendelssohn, 1836, and visited the Rhine, where he conceived the idea of the 'Naiads,' which was produced at the Society of Musicians, 1837 ; conducted performance of the 'Naiads' at the Gewandhaus, Leipzig, 1837 ; took prominent part in forming Bach Society, 1849 ; appointed permanent conductor at Philharmonic Society's concerts, 1855, and professor of music at Cambridge, 1856 ; Mus. Doc., 1856 ; composed the 'May Queen,' 1858 ; principal of Academy of Music, 1866 ; received Beethoven gold medal from Philharmonic Society, 1867 ; hon. M.A. Cambridge, 1867 ; D.C.L. Oxford, 1870 ; knighted, 1871. His works include overtures to the 'Tempest' (1832) and 'Merry Wives of Windsor' (1833) ; 'Paradise and the Peri' (1862), symphony in G minor (1864), 'Woman of Samaria' (1867), and 'Ajax' (1872). [iv. 247]

BENNIS, GEORGE GEARY (1790–1866), author ; for some years grocer in Limerick ; director of a *librairie des étrangers,* Paris, 1830–6 ; librarian to British embassy ; editor of 'Galignani's Messenger' ; published miscellaneous works. [iv. 251]

BENOIST, ANTOINE (1721–1770), draughtsman and engraver ; born at Soissons ; teacher of drawing in England. [iv. 252]

BENOLT, THOMAS (d. 1534), herald ; Berwick pursuivant in Edward IV's reign ; Rougecroix pursuivant in Richard III's reign ; Windsor herald under Henry VII ; Norroy king-at-arms, 1510 ; Clarencieux king-at-arms, 1511 ; issued the challenges for tournaments at Field of Cloth of Gold, 1520. [iv. 252]

BENSLEY, ROBERT (1738 ?–1817 ?), actor ; appeared at Drury Lane as Pierre ('Venice Preserved'), 1765, subsequently playing Edmund ('King Lear'), Buckingham ('Richard III'), and Merlin ('Cymon') ; at Covent Garden, 1767–75 ; alternated between Drury Lane and Haymarket, 1775 to 1796, when he retired from stage with a benefit performance of the 'Grecian Daughter,' in which he took Evander to Mrs. Siddons's Euphrasia. [iv. 253]

BENSLEY, THOMAS (d. 1833), printer ; produced Macklin's folio bible (1800), Hume's 'History of England,' and an octavo Shakespeare ; originated some mechanical adjustments adopted by the 'Times,' 1814. [iv. 254]

BENSLY, ROBERT LUBBOCK (1831–1893), orientalist ; educated at King's College, London, and Gonville and Caius College, Cambridge ; B.A., 1855 ; lecturer in Hebrew, 1861–89 ; fellow, 1876–93 ; under-librarian of the university, 1864–76 ; Lord Almoner's professor of Arabic, 1887–93 ; member of Old Testament revision committee, 1870 ; published translations and works connected with oriental research. [Suppl. i. 171]

BENSON, CHRISTOPHER (1789–1868), divine ; M.A. Trinity College, Cambridge, 1815 ; first Hulsean lecturer, Cambridge, 1820 ; canon of Worcester, 1825 ; for several years master of the Temple ; published religious works, including 'Chronology of our Saviour's Life' (1819). [iv. 255]

BENSON, EDWARD WHITE (1829–1896), archbishop of Canterbury ; educated at King Edward's School, Birmingham, and Trinity College, Cambridge ; B.A., 1852 ; senior chancellor's medallist ; master at Rugby, 1852 ; fellow of Trinity, 1853 ; ordained deacon, 1853 ; first master of Wellington College, 1859–72 ; examining chaplain of Wordsworth, bishop of Lincoln, 1868 ; prebendary of Lincoln, 1869 ; chancellor of Lincoln Minster, 1872 ; first

bishop of Truro, 1877 ; formed divinity school at Truro ; served on royal commission upon ecclesiastical courts, 1881 ; archbishop of Canterbury, 1882 ; advocated Parish Councils Bill in House of Lords, 1893 ; member of 'sweating' committee of House of Lords ; introduced Clergy Discipline Bill, passed, 1892 ; obtained appointment of royal commission to inquire into working of Education Acts, 1886 ; created house of laymen to sit in connection with convocation of his province, 1886 ; vigorously opposed disestablishment of Welsh church, and organised Central Church Committee for Church Defence and Instruction, 1893 ; presided and delivered judgment at trial of Dr. Edward King, bishop of Lincoln, for alleged ritual offences, 1889–90 ; made preaching tour in Ireland, 1896 ; published sermons and other works, including 'Cyprian ; his Life, his Times, his Work' (posthumously, 1897), and 'The Apocalypse' (posthumously, 1900). [Suppl. i. 171]

BENSON, GEORGE (1699–1762), divine ; educated at Glasgow ; pastor of congregation of protestant dissenters at Abingdon, 1723 ; embraced Arminian doctrines ; joint pastor of presbyterian congregation at Birmingham, c. 1742 ; D.D. Aberdeen, 1744 ; pastor of congregation of protestant dissenters in Poor Jewry Lane, Crutchedfriars, 1749–62 ; published theological works, including paraphrases of St. Paul's Epistles and the Seven Catholic Epistles, and, in 1738, a 'History of the First Planting of the Christian Religion.' [iv. 255]

BENSON, SIR JOHN (1812–1874), architect and engineer ; county surveyor to East Riding of Cork, 1846 ; engineer to Cork harbour commissioners, 1850 ; architect of Great Industrial Exhibition, Dublin, 1853 ; knighted, 1853. [iv. 257]

BENSON, JOSEPH (1749–1821), Scottish divine ; educated under presbyterian minister, but subsequently joined methodists ; opened school in Cumberland, c. 1765 ; went to London, 1766 ; appointed by Wesley classical master of Kingswood school ; entered St. Edmund Hall, Oxford, 1769 ; presented to parish of Rowley, near West Bromwich ; became famous as a preacher ; published controversial and other religious works. [iv. 257]

BENSON, MARTIN (1689–1752), bishop ; educated at Charterhouse and Christ Church, Oxford ; prebendary of Durham, 1724 ; chaplain to Prince of Wales, 1726 ; rector of Bletchley, 1727 ; D.D. Cambridge, 1728 ; bishop of Gloucester, 1735. [iv. 258]

BENSON, ROBERT, BARON BINGLEY (1676–1731), politician ; M.P. for Thetford, 1702–5, and York, 1705–13 ; treasury lord, 1710 ; chancellor, under-treasurer of exchequer, and privy councillor, 1711 ; raised to peerage, 1713 ; ambassador-extraordinary to Spain, 1713 ; treasurer of household, 1730. [iv. 259]

BENSON, ROBERT (1797–1844), lawyer ; M.A. Trinity College, Cambridge, 1821 ; called to bar at Middle Temple, 1821 ; practised in equity courts ; recorder of Salisbury, 1836. His works include, 'Memoirs of Rev. Arthur Collier' (1837). [iv. 259]

BENSON or **BOSTON,** WILLIAM (d. 1549), divine ; member of Benedictine house at Boston, Lincolnshire ; B.D. Cambridge, 1521 ; D.D., 1528 ; abbot of Benedictine monastery of St. Mary and St. Modwen, Burton-on-Trent, 1531 ; abbot of monastery of Westminster, 1533 ; surrendered monastery to the king, and was dean of Westminster, 1540. [iv. 259]

BENSON, WILLIAM (1682–1754), critic and politician ; sheriff of Wiltshire, 1710 ; published 'Letter to Sir Jacob Bankes . . . concerning the late Minehead Doctrine,' 1711 ; M.P. for Shaftesbury, 1715 ; surveyor-general of works in place of Sir Christopher Wren ; auditor of the imprest ; a generous patron of literature ; erected monument to Milton in Westminster Abbey. [iv. 261]

BENSTEDE, SIR JOHN DE (d. 1323 ?), judge ; keeper of great seal, 1297, 1298, and 1304–5 ; chancellor of exchequer, 1305–7 ; keeper of wardrobe, 1308 ; one of commission of trailbaston on northern circuit, 1306 ; justice of common bench, 1307, and of common pleas, 1309. [iv. 261]

BENT, JAMES THEODORE (1852–1897), explorer and archæologist ; educated at Repton school and Wadham College, Oxford ; B.A., 1875 ; entered Lincoln's Inn, 1874 ; travelled abroad ; studied local traditions and customs in Karpathos, Samos, and Thasos, 1885–7, and engaged in archæological research on coast of Asia Minor, 1888–9, Bahrein Islands, 1889, Cilicia Tracheia, 1890, Mashonaland, 1891, Abyssinia, 1893, and the Arabian peninsula, 1893–7 ; published works relating to his travels. [Suppl. i. 179]

BENTHAM, EDWARD (1707–1776), divine ; entered Corpus Christi College, Oxford, 1724 ; vice-principal, Magdalen Hall 1730 ; fellow of Oriel, 1731 ; M.A., 1732 ; prebendary of Hereford, 1743 ; D.D., 1749 ; canon of Christ Church, Oxford, 1754 ; regius professor of divinity, 1763 ; published philosophical, religious, and other works.
[iv. 262]

BENTHAM GEORGE (1800–1884), botanist ; son of Sir Samuel Bentham [q. v.], and nephew of Jeremy Bentham [q. v.]; lived in France, 1814–27 ; studied at Montauban ; published translations in French from works of Jeremy Bentham (Paris, 1823), and 'Catalogue des Plantes indigènes des Pyrénées,' &c. (1826) ; studied at Lincoln's Inn, 1826 ; published, 1827, 'Outlines of a new System of Logic,' in which the doctrine of qualification of predicate was first clearly set forth ; F.L.S., 1828 ; honorary secretary of Horticultural Society, 1829–40 ; published memoirs of *genera* and natural orders of Indian plants, 1832–6 ; published 'Handbook of British Flora,' 1858 ; worked on descriptive botany at Kew after 1861, and produced works on flora of Hongkong and Australia, 'Genera Plantarum' (7 vols., 1863–78), and 'Outlines of Botany' ; vice-president, Linnean Society, 1858 ; president, 1861–74 ; member of Royal Society, 1862 ; received royal medal, 1859 ; C.M.G., 1878. [iv. 263]

BENTHAM, JAMES (1708–1794), divine ; M.A. Trinity College, Cambridge, 1738 ; vicar of Stapleford, Cambridgeshire, 1733–7 ; minor canon of Ely, 1737 ; rector of Feltwell St. Nicholas, Norfolk, 1768–74, and of Northwold, 1774–9 ; prebendary of Ely, 1779 ; published 'History of Ely Cathedral,' 1771, and two works embodying suggestions for improvement of the fen country.
[iv. 267]

BENTHAM, JEREMY (1748–1832), writer on jurisprudence ; educated at Westminster and Queen's College, Oxford ; M.A., 1766 ; called to bar at Lincoln's Inn, of which society he became a member in 1817 ; made very little effort to succeed as a barrister, but turned his mind to physical science and speculations on politics and jurisprudence ; produced, between 1776 and 1780, work printed in 1780 as 'Introduction to Principles of Morals and Legislation' ; published anonymously, 1776, 'Fragment on Government,' a masterly criticism on Blackstone's 'Commentaries,' which obtained for him the friendship of Lord Shelburne ; wrote, in Russia, 'Defence of Usury,' and a series of letters on a 'Panopticon,' or house for inspection of industries, by which he hoped to improve the condition of prison discipline, the scheme meeting with considerable favour, though a partial failure ; published 'Protest against Law Taxes' and 'Supply without Burden, or Escheat vice Taxation,' 1795 ; directed his attention to defects of poor laws, 1797–8 ; completed criticism on working of English libel law, 1809 ; wrote, at Ford Abbey, 'Chrestomathia,' 'The Church of England and its Catechism,' and 'Not Paul, but Christ' ; published 'A Catechism of Parliamentary Reform,' 1817 ; aided in establishing 'Westminster Review,' 1823 ; published 'Petition for Justice,' 1829, letters advocating sale of public offices, 1830, and 'Pannomial Fragments,' 1831. In his numerous works Bentham sought to compass the whole field of ethics, jurisprudence, logic, and political economy. To the last science his contributions are of small account, and to the literature of logic he made no very valuable additions ; his nephew, George Bentham's 'Outlines of a New System of Logic' contains his ideas on the subject. His influence on jurisprudence and ethics can scarcely be over-estimated. His 'Introduction to Principles of Morals and Legislation' expounded many schemes which since his time have been applied to the amendment of the administration of justice. In the history of ethics he stands out as one of the ablest champions of utilitarianism. [iv. 268]

BENTHAM, JOSEPH (1594 ?–1671), divine ; rector of Broughton and, later, of Neather Wickenden, Buckinghamshire ; sequestered by order of parliament, 1643 ; restored to parish of Broughton, 1660 ; published sermons and religious treatises. [iv. 280]

BENTHAM, SIR SAMUEL (1757–1831), naval architect and engineer ; brother of Jeremy Bentham [q. v.];

educated at Westminster ; apprenticed as shipwright ; travelled in Russia and Siberia, studying methods of working metals, 1780–2 ; received rank of lieutenant-colonel from Prince Potemkin, who made him superintendent of his shipbuilding yard at Kritchev ; directed equipment of flotilla at Cherson for service against Turks, 1787 ; commanded flotilla in the Liman, 1788, and received military cross of St. George, rank of brigadier-general, and sword of honour ; returned to England, 1791 ; assisted Jeremy Bentham in fitting up his Panopticon ; inspector-general of navy works, 1795–1807 ; introduced numerous improvements in machinery of dockyard and build of ships ; commissioner of the navy, 1807–12 ; published papers on professional subjects. [iv. 281]

BENTHAM, THOMAS (1513–1578), bishop ; perpetual fellow, Magdalen College, Oxford, 1546 ; M.A., 1547 ; ejected from fellowship, 1553 ; bishop of Lichfield and Coventry, 1559 ; D.D., 1565 ; translated Ezekiel and Daniel (1568) in the Bishops' Bible. [iv. 284]

BENTINCK, LORD GEORGE, whose full christian names were WILLIAM GEORGE FREDERIC CAVENDISH (1802–1848), statesman ; fifth child and second surviving son of fourth Duke of Portland ; cornet, 10th hussars, 1819 ; private secretary to Canning (who married Bentinck's mother's sister) when Canning was foreign secretary and leader of House of Commons ; major, 2nd life guards, 1825 ; M.P. for King's Lynn, 1826–48 ; devoted himself to horse-racing ; rode his first public match at Goodwood, 1824 ; introduced many improvements in management of racecourse ; strongly opposed Sir Robert Peel's measures for suspension of restrictions on imported corn to meet failure of potato crop in Ireland and insufficient supply of corn in England ; accepted leadership of protectionists, 1846 ; sold his racing stud, 1846 ; proposed a scheme, which was rejected, for employment of distressed Irish on construction of railways in Ireland, 1847 ; resigned leadership, December 1847 ; chairman of committee to inquire into interests of sugar and coffee planters, 1848 ; advocated unsuccessfully maintenance of protective duty on foreign sugar. [iv. 297]

BENTINCK, SIR HENRY JOHN WILLIAM (1796–1878), general ; ensign, Coldstream guards, 1813 ; lieutenant-colonel, 1851 ; served in Crimea ; colonel, 1854 ; K.C.B., 1855 ; general, 1867. [iv. 284]

BENTINCK, JOHN ALBERT (1737–1775), captain ; grandson of William Bentinck, first earl of Portland [q. v.]; midshipman, 1753 ; commander, under Lord Anson at St. Malo, 1758 ; captain, 1758 ; employed in cruising, 1760–2 ; held various commands at Portsmouth, 1766–73 ; count of the empire. [iv. 285]

BENTINCK, WILLIAM, first EARL OF PORTLAND (1649–1709), son of Henry Bentinck of Diepenheim ; page of honour in William of Orange's household ; gentleman of prince's bedchamber ; accompanied William to England, 1670 ; D.C.L. Oxford, 1670 ; sent by William on mission to Charles II to negotiate the marriage with Princess Mary, which took place in 1677 ; took large share in preparations for William's invasion of England, 1688 ; created Baron Cirencester, Viscount Woodstock, and Earl of Portland, and appointed groom of the stole, first gentleman of the bedchamber and privy councillor, on coronation of William and Mary ; obtained command of regiment of Dutch guards, and subsequently held rank of lieutenant-general in English army ; became the most trusted agent of William's foreign policy ; accompanied king on his Irish campaign, 1690, at Landen, 1693, and in Dutch campaign, 1694 ; K.G., 1697 ; conducted negotiations for peace of Ryswyk, 1697 ; went on an embassy to France to treat concerning Spanish succession, 1698 ; signed first partition treaty, 1698 ; resigned places in royal household from jealousy of Albemarle, 1699 ; took active part in direction of Scottish affairs, and incurred much odium by collapse of Darien scheme ; signed second partition treaty, 1700 ; his impeachment in House of Lords after debates on partition treaties dismissed, 1701.
[iv. 285]

BENTINCK, LORD WILLIAM CAVENDISH (1774–1839), governor-general of India ; second son of William Henry, third duke of Portland [q. v.]; captain, 1792 ; lieutenant-colonel, 24th light dragoons, 1794 ; on Duke of York's staff in Netherlands, 1794 ; attached to head-quarters staff of Marshal Suwarrof's army in Italy and served in campaigns of 1799 ; with Austrian forces, 1801 ;

governor of Madras, 1803; major-general; recalled after mutiny at Velore, for which he was held mainly responsible, 1807; commanded brigade at Coruña; lieutenant-general; commander-in-chief of British forces in Sicily, 1811; served in Spain, 1813; commanded successful expedition against Genoa, 1814; governor-general of Bengal, 1827; effected important financial reforms, and greatly improved condition of revenue, reorganised judicial department, and extended system of employment of natives in official positions; first governor-general of India, 1833; met Macaulay, with whom he contracted a warm friendship; returned to England, 1835; liberal M.P. for Glasgow, 1837. [iv. 292]

BENTINCK, WILLIAM HENRY CAVENDISH, third DUKE OF PORTLAND (1738–1809), statesman; educated at Eton and Christ Church, Oxford; M.P. for Weobly, Herefordshire, 1760; succeeded to dukedom, 1762; lord chamberlain of household and privy councillor, 1765; married Lady Dorothy Cavendish, daughter of William, fourth duke of Devonshire, 1766; lord lieutenant of Ireland, 1782; prime minister, 1783; chancellor of Oxford University, 1792; allied with Pitt at time of French revolution; home secretary, 1794–1801; K.G. and lord lieutenant of Nottinghamshire, 1794; greatly assisted passing of Act of Union with Ireland, 1798; lord president of the council in Addington's and Pitt's cabinets; retired on death of Pitt, but returned to public life when Pitt's friends came again into power, 1807; prime minister, 1807; resigned, 1809. [iv. 302]

BENTINCK-SCOTT, WILLIAM JOHN CAVENDISH, fifth DUKE OF PORTLAND (1800–1879), succeeded to his brother's title of Marquis of Titchfield, 1824; M.P. for King's Lynn, 1824–6; succeeded to dukedom, 1854; deputy lieutenant of Nottinghamshire, 1859–79; lived life of a recluse. [iv. 304]

BENTLEY, CHARLES (1806–1854), painter; member of old Water-Colour Society, 1844; painted chiefly coast and river scenes. [iv. 305]

BENTLEY, GEORGE (1828–1895), publisher and author; son of Richard Bentley (1794–1871) [q. v.]; educated at King's College, London; entered his father's office, c. 1845; edited 'Temple Bar Magazine,' 1866–95; succeeded his father as publisher in ordinary to the queen; member of Stationers' Company and F.R.G.S. Among the more notable novelists whom he introduced to the public are Wilkie Collins, Mrs. Henry Wood, Miss Rhoda Broughton, Miss 'Marie Corelli,' Mr. 'Maarten Maartens,' and Mrs. Riddell. [Suppl. i. 180]

BENTLEY, SIR JOHN (d. 1772), vice-admiral; entered navy, c. 1720; lieutenant, 1734; commander after battle of Toulon, 1744; served at Finisterre and in Bay of Biscay, 1747, and at blockade of Brest, 1759; knighted, 1759; commissioner of navy, 1761; promoted to flag, 1763; vice-admiral, 1770. [iv. 305]

BENTLEY, JOSEPH CLAYTON (1809–1851), landscape painter and line-engraver; exhibited paintings at London and provincial exhibitions from 1833. Some of his best engravings are in Vernon Gallery. [iv. 306]

BENTLEY, NATHANIEL (1735?–1809), beau; called DIRTY DICK; known for many years as the 'Beau of Leadenhall Street' (where he kept a warehouse); frequently presented himself at court, but in later life developed habits of squalor, the filth of his premises becoming proverbial. [iv. 306]

BENTLEY, RICHARD (1662–1742), scholar and critic; B.A. St. John's College, Cambridge, 1680; master of Spalding school, Lincolnshire, 1682; appointed chaplain to Stillingfleet, bishop of Worcester, 1690; brought into great repute as a minute and accurate scholar by his critical letter to Mill in Mill's edition of the 'Chronicle of Malelas,' 1691; delivered the first course of Boyle lectures, taking as his subject 'A Confutation of Atheism,' 1692; prebendary of Worcester, 1692; keeper of royal libraries and F.R.S., 1694; chaplain in ordinary to king, 1695; contributed to second edition of William Wotton's 'Reflections on Ancient and Modern Learning' (1697), an essay in which he proved the 'Letters of Phalaris' to be forgeries, and reviewed an edition of them edited, in 1695, by the Hon. Charles Boyle, who had printed in his preface an insolent reference to Bentley; answered by Boyle and his friends in 'Dr. Bentley's Dissertations on the Epistles

of Phalaris,' &c., 1698; retaliated in 1699, with his 'Dissertation on the Letters of Phalaris,' which effectually crushed his aggressors and takes rank as a permanent masterpiece of literature; master of Trinity College, Cambridge, 1700–42; having committed a number of petty encroachments on the privileges of the fellows, he was, 1714, brought to trial before the bishop of Ely (Moore), who died before delivering sentence, leaving judgment against Bentley among his papers; ruled with practically despotic power, and in 1733 was again brought before bishop of Ely (Dr. Greene) and deprived of his mastership, but retained it because the successive vice-masters, who alone could execute the sentence, refused to act against him. His works include valuable editions of many classical authors, including a daring Horace, 1711, and a somewhat unsympathetic edition of 'Paradise Lost,' 1732. Among his numerous contributions to classical scholarship may be mentioned his discovery and restoration of the 'digamma' to certain words in the Homeric poems. [iv. 306]

BENTLEY, RICHARD (1708–1782), miscellaneous writer; youngest son of Richard Bentley (1662–1742) [q. v.]; entered Trinity College, Cambridge, 1718; fellow, 1723; lived many years in south of France and in Jersey; constant correspondent of Horace Walpole until 1761, when there was a rupture between them; executed drawings for editions of Gray's poems printed by Walpole, 1753; wrote, after 1761, some unsuccessful plays. [iv. 314]

BENTLEY, RICHARD (1794–1871), publisher; educated at St. Paul's School; joined his brother Samuel [q. v.] in printing business, 1819; in partnership (1829) with Henry Colburn; started 'Bentley's Miscellany,' with Dickens as editor, 1837; published 'Young England' newspaper, 1845, and 'Bentley's Quarterly Review,' 1859; one of his successful ventures was the issue of 127 volumes of 'Standard Novels.' [iv. 316]

BENTLEY, ROBERT (1821–1893), botanist; studied medicine at King's College, London; M.R.C.S., 1847; F.L.S., 1849; lectured on botany, London Hospital; professor of botany at London Institution and King's College, and of botany and materia medica to Pharmaceutical Society; edited 'Pharmaceutical Journal'; published botanical writings. [Suppl. i. 181]

BENTLEY, SAMUEL (1785–1868), printer and antiquary; brother of Richard Bentley (1794–1871) [q. v.]; educated at St. Paul's School; in partnership with John Nichols, his brother Richard [q. v.], 1819, and, later, with his nephew, John Bentley, Wilson, and Fley. He prepared and published several antiquarian works, including 'Excerpta Historica' (1831). [iv. 317]

BENTLEY, THOMAS (1693?–1742), classical scholar; grandson of Thomas Bentley, half-brother of Dr. Richard Bentley (1662–1742) [q. v.]; educated at St. Paul's School and Trinity College, Cambridge; M.A., 1715; fellow; librarian of Trinity; LL.D., 1724; published annotated editions of classical authors, including Horace (1713), and Callimachus (1741). [iv. 318]

BENTLEY, THOMAS (1731–1780), manufacturer of porcelain; apprenticed to woollen and cotton trades in Manchester; removed to Liverpool, 1754, where he was a prominent member of the body of dissenters called Octagonians; entered into partnership with Josiah Wedgwood for manufacture and sale of ornamental pottery, 1768; came to London, 1769. [iv. 317]

BENWELL, JOHN HODGES (1764–1785), genre painter; studied at Royal Academy; executed drawings in water-colours combined with crayons. [iv. 319]

BENWELL, MARY (fl. 1761–1800), portrait painter; exhibited crayon portraits and miniatures at Incorporated Society of Artists and Royal Academy, 1761–91. [iv. 319]

BENWELL, WILLIAM (1765–1796), classical scholar; M.A. Trinity College, Oxford, 1789; rector of Chilton, Suffolk. He edited Xenophon's 'Memorabilia,' 1804. [iv. 319]

BENYNG or DE BININ WILLIAM (fl. 1250), biographer; prior of Cistercian abbey of Newbattle until 1243; abbot of Cupar, 1243–58; wrote life of John Scot, bishop of Dunkeld. [iv. 320]

BEORHTRIC or BRIHTRIC, king of the West-Saxons (d. 802), succeeded Cynewulf, 785; married Eadburh, daughter of Offa, king of the Mercians, 787; died from the effects of poison prepared by Eadburh for her husband's favourite. During his reign the Northmen first landed (787) in England. [iv. 320]

BEORHTWULF or **BERTULF**, king of the Mercians (*d.* 852), succeeded Wiglaf, 839; defeated by invading Danes, 851. [iv. 320]

BEORN, Earl of the Middle Angles (*d.* 1049), son of Ulf and Estrith, Cnut's sister; received earldom, *c.* 1045; murdered by order of Godwine's eldest son, Sweyn, who had been banished, 1046, and whose lands had been divided between Beorn and Harold. [iv. 320]

BEORNWULF, king of the Mercians (*d.* 826), deposed Ceolwulf and succeeded to kingdom, 823; settled, at councils held at Clevesho, 824 and 825, the long dispute between see of Canterbury and Mercian crown; defeated at Ellandune by Ecgberht, king of Wessex, 825; killed in fight against East Anglians. [iv. 321]

BERANGER, GABRIEL (*d.* 1817), artist; born in Rotterdam; opened print shop and artist's warehouse, Dublin, 1750; antiquarian draughtsman in Dublin exchequer office; executed drawings of antiquities in many parts of Ireland. [iv. 321]

BERCHET, PETER (1659-1720), painter; born in France; worked on decorations of William III's palace at Loo; executed paintings in several important buildings in England. [iv. 322]

BERCHTHUN, SAINT (*d.* 733), abbot; first abbot of Beverley, 700. [iv. 322]

BERDMORE, SAMUEL (1740-1802), master of Charterhouse; B.A. Jesus College, Cambridge, 1759; fellow; M.A., 1762; master of Charterhouse School, 1769-1791; D.D., 1773; published works of criticism on poetry. [iv. 323]

BERE, RICHARD (*d.* 1524), scholar; abbot of Glastonbury, 1493; accompanied an embassy to Rome, 1503; engaged with archbishop Warham in dispute concerning genuineness of relics of St. Dunstan at Glastonbury, which was still unsettled when he died. [iv. 323]

BEREBLOCK, JOHN (*fl.* 1566). [See BEARBLOCK.]

BEREFORD, RALPH DE (*fl.* 1329), judge; served on commissions of oyer and terminer in various counties, 1314-24; justice itinerant, *c.* 1330. [iv. 324]

BEREFORD, RICHARD DE (*fl.* 1283-1317), judge; treasurer of Irish exchequer, 1300; justice of assize for six English counties, 1310; chancellor of Ireland, 1314. [iv. 324]

BEREFORD, WILLIAM DE (*d.* 1326), judge; probably justice itinerant, *c.* 1292; appointed justice of common bench, 1294 and 1307; one of twenty-one English members of parliament appointed to confer on Scottish affairs with Scottish representatives, 1305; chief-justice of common bench, 1309. [iv. 324]

BERENGARIA (*d.* after 1230), queen of Richard I; daughter of Sancho VI of Navarre; married and crowned at Limasol, Cyprus, 1191; proceeded to Acre and remained there till 1192, when she travelled to Sicily, Rome, Pisa, Genoa, Marseilles, and Poitou; was perhaps with Richard at Chaluz when he received his death wound; founded, 1230, Cistercian monastery at Espan, in Maine, where she was buried. [iv. 325]

BERENGER, RICHARD (*d.* 1782), for many years gentleman of horse to George III; famous for his charming manner in social life; published works on horsemanship and some poems and essays. [iv. 326]

BERESFORD, JAMES (1764-1840), miscellaneous writer; M.A. Merton College, Oxford, 1798; fellow; rector of Kibworth Beauchamp, Leicestershire; author of 'Miseries of Human Life,' 1867. [iv. 327]

BERESFORD, JOHN (1738-1805), Irish statesman; second son of Marcus, earl of Tyrone; B.A. Trinity College, Dublin, 1757; called to bar, 1760, but never practised; M.P. for Waterford, 1760-1805; privy councillor, 1768; first commissioner of revenue, 1780; introduced reforms in methods of revenue collection and greatly improved architecture and street communication of Dublin; principal adviser of Pitt in his Irish policy; privy councillor of England, 1786; dismissed from office by Lord Fitzwilliam, 1795, but reinstated on Fitzwilliam's recall; helped to bring about the union, 1801; retired from office, 1802. [iv. 327]

BERESFORD, LORD JOHN GEORGE DE LA POER (1773-1862), primate of Ireland; educated at Eton and Christ Church, Oxford; M.A., 1796; D.D., 1805; priest, 1797; dean of St. Macartin's, Clogher, 1799; bishop of Cork and Ross, 1805, of Raphoe, 1807, and of Clogher, 1819; archbishop of Dublin and privy councillor in Ireland, 1820; archbishop of Armagh and primate of Ireland, 1822; vice-chancellor of Dublin University, 1829, and chancellor, 1851; published speeches and sermons. [iv. 328]

BERESFORD, SIR JOHN POO (1766-1844), admiral; natural son of Lord de la Poer (afterwards Marquis of Waterford); entered navy, 1782; captain, 1795; successfully engaged French in Hampton roads, 1795; commanded in North Sea, 1803, and on North American station, 1806; commanded blockade of Lorient, 1808-9; senior officer off Brest, 1810, in North Sea, 1811, and on American coast. 1812-14; commanded Royal Sovereign yacht, 1814; baronet and rear-admiral, 1814; K.C.B., 1819; commanded at Leith, 1820-3, and at Nore, 1830-3; vice-admiral, 1821; admiral, 1838; represented various constituencies in parliament between 1812 and 1835. [iv. 329]

BERESFORD, MARCUS GERVAIS (1801-1885), archbishop of Armagh; M.A. Trinity College, Cambridge, 1828; D.D., 1840; rector of Kildallon, co. Cavan, 1824; vicar of Drung and Larah, *c.* 1827; archdeacon of Ardagh, 1839; bishop of Kilmore and Ardagh, 1854; bishop of Clogher and archbishop of Armagh, 1862; Irish privy councillor; honorary D.C.L. Oxford, 1864. [Suppl. i. 182]

BERESFORD, WILLIAM CARR, VISCOUNT BERESFORD (1768-1854), general; illegitimate son of George de la Poer Beresford, marquis of Waterford; entered military school, Strasburg, 1785; ensign, 1785; served in Nova Scotia, 1786; captain, 1791; at Toulon, 1791-3; in Corsica, at captures of Martello, Bastia, Calvi, and San Fiorenzo, 1794; brevet-major; lieutenant-colonel, 1794; commanded Connaught rangers in reconquest of West Indies, 1795, in Jersey, 1797-9, India, 1800, and Egypt, 1801-3; brevet-colonel, 1803; commanded first brigade at capture of the Cape, 1805; in conjunction with Sir Home Popham captured Buenos Ayres, but being compelled subsequently to capitulate, was there imprisoned for six months; returned to England, 1807; occupied Madeira as governor and commander-in-chief, in name of king of Portugal, 1807-8; major-general and commandant of Lisbon, 1808; fought at Coruña, 1809; marshal in Portuguese army; local lieutenant-general in Portugal, 1809; reorganised Portuguese army; K.B. and Conde de Trancoso in Portuguese peerage, 1810; with valuable assistance from Colonel Hardinge, quartermaster-general of Portuguese army, won battle of Albuera, 1811; wounded at Badajoz; present at Vittoria and battles of Pyrenees, 1813; commanded centre of army at battles of Nivelle, the Nive, and Orthez, 1814; created Lord Beresford of Albuera and Cappoquin, co. Carlow, after battle of Toulouse; resumed command of Portuguese army at Lisbon; lieutenant-general, 1812; governor of Jersey, 1814; returned to England, 1822; lieutenant-general of ordnance and colonel of 16th regiment, 1822; Viscount Beresford, 1823; general, 1825; master-general of ordnance, 1828-30; published pamphlets defending his conduct at Albuera against attacks by Colonel Napier. [iv. 330]

BEREWYK, JOHN DE (*d.* 1312), judge; entrusted with charge of vacant abbey of St. Edmund, 1279, and of see of Lincoln 1279-81; treasurer of Queen Eleanor, 1284; justice itinerant, 1292. [iv. 335]

BERGENROTH, GUSTAV ADOLPH (1813-1869), historical student; born at Oletzko, East Prussia; educated at Königsberg University; manifested advanced democratic opinions in outbreak of 1848; emigrated to California, 1850; came to London with view of studying Tudor period of history, 1857; after research in Spanish archives at Simancas, published (1862-8) calendar of Simancas documents relating to English affairs between 1485 and 1525; died at Madrid. [iv. 335]

BERGNE, JOHN BRODRIBB (1800-1873), numismatist and antiquary; entered foreign office, 1817, and was superintendent of treaty department, 1854-73; member of commission to revise slave trade instructions, 1865; a founder and treasurer (1843-57) of the Numismatic Society; F.S.A.; contributed to 'Numismatic Chronicle.' [iv. 336]

BERINGTON, CHARLES (1748–1798), catholic divine; educated at Douay and in English seminary, Paris; D.D., 1776; member of catholic committee, 1788; vicar-apostolic of midland district, 1795; renounced, under compulsion of the holy see, the committee's doctrines, 1797. [iv. 337]

BERINGTON, JOSEPH (1746–1827), catholic divine; educated at St. Omer; ordained priest in France; leader of fifteen priests known as 'Staffordshire Clergy'; priest at Oscott, 1786, and subsequently in London district, from which he was twice suspended for opinions expressed in certain of his works; priest at Buckland, Berkshire, 1814–27; published philosophical, historical, and theological works. [iv. 337]

BERKELEY, FAMILY OF. Roger, first tenant of Berkeley, 1086, was succeeded by his nephew William, and by William's son. Part of Berkeley, with the castle, passed in Henry II's reign to Robert Fitz-Harding, whose family intermarried with the Berkeleys, and has held the property for seven hundred years. From one of Fitz-Harding's descendants sprang the Berkeley family of Beverston Castle, important in fifteenth and sixteenth centuries; while from another came the Berkeleys of Stoke Gifford, Gloucestershire, of Bruton and Pylle, Somerset (now represented by Edward Berkeley-Portman, Baron, 1837, and Viscount Portman, 1873), and of Boycourt, Kent. Berkeley Castle ultimately passed to James Berkeley, who was summoned to parliament, 1421–61, in right of his possession of the castle. From James's youngest son was descended Chief Baron Sir Robert Berkeley (d. 1656) [q. v.], of Spetchley. James's eldest son, William, died childless, after which the castle passed into the family of his nephew Maurice. Maurice's descendant, George (d. 1698) [q. v.], was created Viscount Dursley and Earl of Berkeley, 1679, after whom the earldom descended to Frederick Augustus, fifth earl. The fifth earl alleged that he secretly married, in 1785, a lady whom he publicly married in 1796. His secret marriage not being proved, the title of sixth earl went to Thomas Moreton Fitzhardinge Berkeley, the eldest of his sons born after the public marriage. [iv. 339]

BERKELEY, CRAVEN FITZHARDINGE (1805–1855), member of parliament; son of Frederick Augustus, fifth earl of Berkeley; officer in 1st life guards; M.P. for Cheltenham, 1832; re-elected, 1835, 1837, 1841, 1848, and 1852; defeated, 1847, and his election in 1848 declared void. [iv. 343]

BERKELEY, ELIZA (1734–1800), authoress, née Frinsham; married George Berkeley (1733–1795), the bishop's son, 1761; published with prefaces 'Sermons' by her husband, 1799, and 'Poems,' 1797, by her eldest son, George Monck Berkeley [q. v.] [iv. 344]

BERKELEY, FRANCIS HENRY FITZHARDINGE (1794–1870), politician; fourth son of Frederick Augustus, fifth earl of Berkeley; born before his parents' marriage in 1796; educated at Christ Church, Oxford; M.P. for Bristol, 1837, and 1841–70; repeatedly advocated ballot, but without success, 1848–70. [iv. 345]

BERKELEY, GEORGE, BARON BERKELEY (1601–1658), succeeded to family honours, 1613; K.B., 1616; canon-commoner, Christ Church, Oxford, 1619; M.A., 1623; spent much time in foreign travel. [iv. 346]

BERKELEY, GEORGE, first EARL OF BERKELEY (1628–1698), statesman; younger son of George Berkeley (1601–1658) [q. v.]; succeeded as Baron Berkeley, 1658; educated at Christ Church, Oxford; one of commissioners to invite Charles to England from The Hague, 1660; on council for foreign plantations, 1661; original member of Royal African Company, and F.R.S., 1663; created Viscount Dursley and Earl of Berkeley, 1679; governor of Levant Company, 1680; a master of Trinity House, 1681; member of East India Company; privy councillor, 1685; member of provisional government after flight of James II, 1688. [iv. 347]

BERKELEY, GEORGE (1693?–1746), politician, fourth son of Charles, second earl of Berkeley; educated at Westminster and Trinity College, Cambridge; M.A., 1713; M.P. for Dover, 1718, and for Heydon, Yorkshire, 1734–46; master-keeper and governor of St. Katharine's, near the Tower, 1723. [iv. 348]

BERKELEY, GEORGE (1685–1753), bishop of Cloyne; educated at Kilkenny, and Trinity College, Dublin; M.A.

and fellow, 1707; studied philosophy and published 'Essay towards a New Theory of Vision,' 1709, 'Treatise concerning Human Knowledge,' 1710, and 'Dialogues between Hylas and Philonous,' 1713; junior dean, 1710–11; junior Greek lecturer, 1712; came to England, 1713, and became associated with Steele, Addison, Pope, Swift, and others; chaplain to Lord Peterborough while ambassador to king of Sicily, 1713–14; travelled as tutor to son of Bishop St. George Ashe [q. v.], 1716–20; dean of Derry, 1724; circulated proposals for founding, in the Bermudas, college for training of missionaries, 1725; senior fellow, Dublin, 1717; divinity lecturer and senior Greek lecturer, 1721; D.D., 1721; Hebrew lecturer and senior proctor, 1722; came to England, 1724, and obtained charter for proposed college, 1725; went to America, 1728, and returned on failure to receive from government money for furthering his scheme, 1732; published 'Alciphron,' 1732; bishop of Cloyne, 1734; published 'Querist,' 1735–7, in which he made a number of suggestions upon uses of money; retired to Oxford, 1752, and there died. As a philosopher he aimed at discrediting materialism. He formed a link between Locke and Hume. [iv. 348]

BERKELEY, GEORGE CHARLES GRANTLEY FITZHARDINGE (1800–1881), writer; sixth son of Frederick Augustus, fifth earl of Berkeley; educated at Corpus Christi College and Sandhurst; joined Coldstream guards, 1816, and subsequently entered 82nd foot; M.P. for West Gloucestershire, 1832–52; his romance, 'Berkeley Castle,' savagely reviewed in 'Fraser's Magazine,' 1836; Berkeley, in consequence, publicly assaulted Fraser, the publisher (who brought an action against him and obtained damages), and fought a duel with Dr. Maginn, the author; proposed, 1836, and obtained, 1841, admission of ladies to gallery of House of Commons; devoted himself largely to field-sports after 1852; published autobiographical, sporting, and other works. [iv. 356]

BERKELEY, GEORGE CRANFIELD, seventeenth BARON BERKELEY (1753–1818), admiral; entered navy, 1766; accompanied Caroline Matilda to Denmark; with Captain Cook during survey of coast of Newfoundland and Gulf of St. Lawrence; lieutenant, 1772; on Victory at Ushant, 1778; surveyor-general of ordnance, 1786; wounded at victory of 1 June 1794; rear-admiral, 1799; vice-admiral, on Halifax station, 1805; held chief command on Portuguese coast and in Tagus, 1808–12; admiral, 1810; M.P. for Gloucester, 1781–1812; G.C.B., 1814. [iv. 358]

BERKELEY, GEORGE MONCK (1763–1793), miscellaneous writer; son of Eliza Berkeley [q. v.], educated at Eton, St. Andrews, Magdalen Hall, Oxford, and Inner Temple; LL.B. Dublin, 1789; his works include two dramatic pieces, and 'Poems' edited by his mother (1797). [iv. 359]

BERKELEY, GILBERT (1501–1581), bishop; B.D. Oxford, c. 1539; bishop of Bath and Wells, 1560; chancellor of Wells, 1560–2; D.D., 1563; opposed attempt of burgesses of Wells to obtain renewal of their ancient corporation, 1574. [iv. 359]

BERKELEY, JAMES, third EARL OF BERKELEY (1680–1736), admiral; captain of frigate in Channel, 1701; served in Mediterranean with Sir George Rooke and Sir Clowdisley Shovell, 1704–7; raised to flag-rank, 1708; with Byng in the Forth, 1708; lord-lieutenant of Gloucestershire, 1710–11 and 1714; first lord commissioner of admiralty, 1717–27; lord high admiral and commander-in-chief in channel, 1719; K.G., 1718. [iv. 360]

BERKELEY, JOHN, first BARON BERKELEY OF STRATTON (d. 1678), soldier; ambassador from Charles I to Christina of Sweden to propose alliance to help elector palatine, 1637; knighted, 1638; held commission in army raised to coerce Scots; M.P. for Heytesbury, 1640; imprisoned in Tower on accusation of conspiring to corrupt army in interest of king; received bail; royalist commander-in-chief in Devonshire; took Exeter, 1643; defeated at Alresford, 1644; lieutenant-colonel of Devonshire and Cornwall, 1645; surrendered Exeter to Fairfax, 1646; unsuccessfully attempted to mediate between king and parliamentary leaders, 1647; accompanied Charles in his flight until the king went to Carisbrooke; retired to France; governor to Duke of York, 1652; accompanied Duke of York under Turenne in Flanders, 1652–5, and in Netherlands, 1656; raised to peerage, 1658; on admiralty staff, 1660; lord-president of Connaught for life, 1661;

privy councillor, 1663 ; one of masters of ordnance, 1663 ; on committee of Tangier, 1665 ; lord-lieutenant of Ireland, 1670–2 ; one of the ambassadors extraordinary at congress of Nimeguen, 1676–7 ; published an apology for his share in proceedings connected with Charles I's flight from Hampton Court. [iv. 361]

BERKELEY, JOHN, third BARON BERKELEY OF STRATTON (1663–1697), admiral; second son of John Berkeley (d. 1678) [q. v.], lieutenant, 1685 ; rear-admiral of fleet under Lord Dartmouth, 1688 ; vice-admiral of red squadron under Admiral Herbert, 1689 ; successively vice-admiral of blue, and admiral of blue under Killigrew, Delavall, and Shovell, 1693 ; took part in attack on Brest, 1694 ; bombarded Dieppe and Havre, 1694 ; combined with Dutch in ineffectual bombardment of St. Malo, 1695 ; engaged in harassing French coast, 1695–7. [iv. 364]

BERKELEY, MAURICE FREDERICK FITZ-HARDINGE, first BARON FITZHARDINGE (1788–1867), admiral, son of fifth Earl of Berkeley ; entered navy, 1802 ; flag-lieutenant, 1810 : commanded flagship at Cork, 1828–1831 ; in Mediterranean, 1841 ; admiral, 1862 ; with brief intervals M.P. for Gloucester, 1831–57, and held seat at admiralty, 1833–57 ; raised to peerage, 1861 ; privy councillor and K.C.B., 1855 ; G.C.B., 1861. [iv. 365]

BERKELEY, MILES JOSEPH (1803–1889), botanist; educated at Rugby and Christ's College, Cambridge ; M.A., 1828 ; honorary fellow, 1883 ; curate of St. John's, Margate, 1829 ; perpetual curate of Apethorpe and Wood Newton, 1833 ; rural dean of Rothwell ; vicar of Sibbertoft, Northamptonshire, 1868 ; F.L.S., 1836 ; F.R.S., 1879. His works include 'Introduction to Cryptogamic Botany,' 1857, 'Outlines of British Fungology,' 1860, and the volume on fungi in Smith's 'English Flora,' 1836. [Suppl. i. 183]

BERKELEY, ROBERT (d. 1219), justiciar; eldest son of Maurice Berkeley (d. 1190) ; succeeded to manor of Berkeley, 1190 ; justiciar at Derby, 1208 ; sided with barons against John, and Berkeley Castle being forfeited, he died still dispossessed. [iv. 366]

BERKELEY, SIR ROBERT (1584–1656), judge ; called to bar at Middle Temple, 1608 ; high sheriff of Worcestershire, 1613 ; called to degree of coif, 1627 ; king's serjeant and justice of court of king's bench, 1632 ; supported king in imposition of ship-money, 1635–7, and was impeached in House of Lords, 1641 ; fined, and incapacitated from holding office, 1642. [iv. 366]

BERKELEY, ROBERT (1713–1804), author of 'Considerations on Oath of Supremacy,' and 'Considerations on Declaration against Transubstantiation.' [iv. 367]

BERKELEY, SIR WILLIAM (1639–1666), vice-admiral ; lieutenant, 1661 ; commander, 1662 ; rear-admiral of red squadron under Duke of York, 1664 ; in Channel, 1664–5 ; lieutenant-governor of Portsmouth, 1665 ; killed in battle with Dutch off North Foreland. [iv. 368]

BERKELEY, SIR WILLIAM (d. 1677), governor of Virginia ; brother of John, first baron Berkeley of Stratton [q. v.] ; M.A. Merton College, Oxford, 1629 ; one of commissioners of Canada, 1632 ; gentleman of privy chamber to Charles I ; governor of Virginia, 1641 ; deprived of office by parliament, but reappointed at Restoration ; returned to England, 1677 ; published 'The Lost Lady,' a tragedy, 1638. [iv. 368]

BERKENHOUT, JOHN (1730?–1791), physician ; studied in Germany ; entered Prussian army ; captain ; obtained commission in English army, 1756 ; studied medicine at Edinburgh and at Leyden, where he graduated doctor of physic, 1765 ; accompanied government commissioners to America, 1778–80 ; published 'Outlines of Natural History of Great Britain,' 1769–71, 3 vols. ; 'Biographia Literaria,' 1771, and several medical and other works. [iv. 369]

BERKLEY, JAMES JOHN (1819–1862), engineer ; educated at King's College, London ; pupil of Robert Stephenson, 1839 ; chief resident engineer, Great Indian Peninsula Railway, 1849 ; completed line from Bombay to Tanna (twenty miles), initiating Indian railway system, 1853 ; completed line from Bombay to Calcutta, Madras, and Nagpore (1,237 miles), 1856 ; held several municipal appointments in Bombay ; M.I.C.E., 1855. [iv. 370]

BERKSHIRE, EARL OF (1579–1623). [See NORRIS, FRANCIS.]

BERKSTED, BIRKSTED, or BURGHSTED, STEPHEN (d. 1287), bishop of Chichester, 1262 ; one of those chosen after the battle of Lewes to nominate council of nine to exercise royal power, 1264 ; suspended by cardinal-legate, 1266, and summoned to Rome, where he remained till 1272. [iv. 371]

BERLIOZ, HARRIET CONSTANCE (1800–1854). [See SMITHSON.]

BERMINGHAM, SIR JOHN, EARL OF LOUTH (d. 1328), lord justice of Ireland ; knighted, 1312 ; commander-in-chief of English forces in Ireland, 1318 ; defeated Edward Bruce near Dundalk ; created Earl of Louth, 1318 ; lord justice of Ireland, 1321 ; slain in quarrel between Anglo-Irish families of Oriel. [iv. 371]

BERMINGHAM, MICHEL (b. 1685), surgeon ; member of Academy of Surgery, Paris ; published medical writings (1720–50). [iv. 372]

BERMINGHAM, PATRICK (d. 1532), judge ; chief justice of king's bench in Ireland, 1513–32 ; chancellor of green wax of exchequer, Ireland, 1521. [iv. 372]

BERMINGHAM, WILLIAM (d. 1312), archbishop of Tuam, 1289 ; litigated on visitatorial powers with Dominican friars of Athenry, who obtained judgment against him from lord chancellor, 1297 ; attempted unsuccessfully to unite sees of Annadown and Tuam. [iv. 372]

BERNAL, RALPH (d. 1854), politician ; M.A. Christ's College, Cambridge, 1809 ; barrister, 1810 ; M.P. for Lincoln, 1818–20, Rochester, 1820–41, and 1847–52, and Weymouth, 1841–7 ; chairman of committees, c. 1830–1850 ; president British Archæological Society, 1853. His collection of works of art sold for 71,000l., 1855. [iv. 373]

BERNAL OSBORNE, RALPH (1808–1882), politician ; eldest son of Ralph Bernal [q. v.] ; educated at Charterhouse and Trinity College, Cambridge ; ensign, 71st regiment, 1831 ; liberal M.P. for Chipping Wycombe, 1841 ; married daughter of Sir Thomas Osborne, whose name he assumed, 1844 ; secretary of admiralty, 1852–8 ; M.P. for Middlesex, 1847, 1852, Dover, 1857–59, Liskeard, 1859–65, Nottingham, 1866–8, and Waterford, 1869–74. [iv. 373]

BERNARD. [See also BARNARD.]

BERNARD (fl. 865), traveller in Palestine : called SAPIENS ; erroneously identified with Bernard, a Scottish monk, and with another native of Scotland who, according to Dempster, preached the crusade in Scotland, 1095–1105 ; set out from Rome between 863 and 867, and on return from Palestine proceeded to monastery of Mont St. Michel, Brittany ; wrote a description of his journey in Palestine. A 'History of Jerusalem' and other works have also been attributed to him. [iv. 374]

BERNARD (fl. 1093), warrior ; of Neufmarché or 'of Newmarch' ; came to England with Conqueror ; joined Norman lords against Rufus, 1088, and was defeated at Worcester ; invaded and settled in Brecheiniog ; founded and endowed priory of St. John at Brecknock. [iv. 376]

BERNARD (d. 1333?), bishop ; chancellor of Scotland, c. 1307 ; abbot of Arbroath, c. 1311 ; probably drew up letter from Scottish nation to John XXII, claiming right to choose its own king ; bishop of Sodor, 1324 ; wrote Latin poem on victory of Bannockburn. [iv. 376]

BERNARD A SANCTO FRANCISCO (1628–1709). [See EYSTON.]

BERNARD, CHARLES (1650–1711), surgeon ; surgeon to St. Bartholomew's Hospital, 1686 ; serjeant-surgeon to Queen Anne, 1702 ; master of Barber Surgeons' Company, 1703. [iv. 377]

BERNARD, DANIEL (d. 1588), brother of John Bernard (d. 1567) [q. v.] ; D.D. Christ Church, Oxford, 1585 ; canon of Christ Church, 1577 ; vice-chancellor of Oxford, 1586. [iv. 382]

BERNARD, EDWARD (1638–1696), critic and astronomer ; educated at Merchant Taylors' School and St. John's College, Oxford ; fellow, 1658 ; M.A., 1662 ; D.D.,1684 ; studied oriental mathematical manuscripts at Leyden, 1668 ; chaplain to Dr. Mews, bishop of Bath and Wells ;

1673; Savilian professor, Oxford, 1673–91; F.R.S., 1673; tutor at Paris to Dukes of Grafton and Northumberland, sons of Charles II by Duchess of Cleveland, 1676; returned to Oxford, 1677; obtained living of Brightwell, Berkshire, 1691; left works in manuscript which were purchased by the Bodleian. His writings include 'De mensuris et ponderibus antiquis libri tres' (1688), 'Etymologicon Britannicum' (1689), 'Chronologiæ Samaritanæ Synopsis' (1691), and some astronomical works. [iv. 378]

BERNARD, FRANCIS (1627–1698), physician; M.D. Cambridge, 1678; F.C.P., 1687; assistant physician to St. Bartholomew's Hospital, 1678; physician in ordinary to James II, 1698. His library of medical books was reputed to be the largest ever made in England. [iv. 380]

BERNARD, SIR FRANCIS (1711?–1779), governor of Massachusetts Bay; educated at Westminster and Christ Church, Oxford; M.A., 1736; called to bar at Middle Temple; bencher; practised on midland circuit; governor of province of New Jersey, 1758, and of Massachusetts Bay, 1760; his thorough administration of the home government's policy, for which he was as a reward created baronet in 1769, undoubtedly hastened the war; recalled, 1769; D.C.L. Oxford, 1772. He published political writings. [iv. 380]

BERNARD, HERMAN HEDWIG (1785–1857), hebraist; for many years Hebrew teacher at Cambridge; published works relating to Hebrew literature and history. [iv. 381]

BERNARD, JOHN (d. 1567?), author; B.A. Queen's College, Cambridge, 1544; Trotter's priest, 1544; fellow, c. 1545; M.A., 1547; bursar, 1551–2; wrote protestant religious tract in Latin, published (1568) by his brother Thomas Bernard [q. v.]. [iv. 381]

BERNARD, JOHN (1756–1828), actor; light comedian on Norwich circuit, 1774; member of Bath company, 1777; in Ireland, 1780–4; played Archer in 'Beaux' Stratagem' at Covent Garden, 1787; again at Covent Garden, 1793–6; played in New York, 1797, Philadelphia, 1797–1803, Boston, 1803; joint manager of Federal theatre, Boston, 1806–10; travelled in United States and Canada, 1810–17; made last appearance, Boston, 1819; selections from his 'Reminiscences' appeared after his death. [iv. 382]

BERNARD, JOHN PETER (d. 1750), biographer; graduate of Leyden; taught literature and mathematics in London after 1733; contributed largely to 'General Dictionary, Historical and Critical,' 1734–41. [iv. 383]

BERNARD, MOUNTAGUE (1820–1882), international lawyer, B.C.L. Trinity College, Oxford; Vinerian scholar and fellow; called to the bar at Lincoln's Inn, 1846; one of founders of 'Guardian,' 1846; first professor of international law, Oxford, 1859–74; judge of chancellor's court; on commission of naturalisation and allegiance, 1868; fellow of All Souls' College, c. 1870; one of high commissioners who signed treaty of Washington, 1871; privy councillor; member of judicial committee of council; D.C.L.; member of University of Oxford Commission, 1877; original member of Institut de Droit International (founded, 1873); published works relating to international law. [iv. 383]

BERNARD, NICHOLAS (d. 1661), divine; educated at Cambridge; chaplain and librarian to archbishop Ussher; dean of Kilmore, 1627; incorporated M.A. Oxford, 1628; prebendary of Dromore and dean of Ardagh, 1637; preacher of Gray's Inn, 1651; chaplain and almoner to Oliver Cromwell; published religious, historical, and other works, including a life of archbishop Ussher, 1656. [iv. 384]

BERNARD, RICHARD (1568–1641), puritan divine; M.A. Christ's College, Cambridge, 1598; vicar of Worksop, 1601 presented to Batcombe, 1613. His numerous publications include an edition, with translations, of 'Terence' (1598), 'Bible Battels, or the Sacred Art Military' (1629), works directed against the separatists, and various religious and other treatises, some of which enunciated benevolent schemes which have since been generally adopted. [iv. 386]

BERNARD, THOMAS (d. 1582), divine; brother of John Bernard (d. 1567?) [q. v.]; M.A. King's College, Cambridge, 1533; B.D. Oxford, 1567; canon of Christ Church, Oxford, 1546; Cranmer's chaplain, 1547. [iv. 381]

BERNARD, SIR THOMAS (1750–1818), philanthropist; son of Sir Francis Bernard [q. v.]; educated at Harvard; secretary to his father in America; came to England; called to bar at Middle Temple, 1780; conveyancer; with bishop of Durham, Wilberforce, and others, founded Society for Bettering Condition of Poor, 1796; set on foot plan of Royal Institution, Piccadilly, 1799; established British Institution for Promotion of Fine Arts, 1805; chancellor of diocese of Durham; M.A. Lambeth and LL.D. Edinburgh, 1801. He was connected with foundation of many societies for relief of poor, and was a liberal benefactor of the Foundling Hospital. [iv. 387]

BERNARD, WILLIAM BAYLE (1807–1875), dramatist; born at Boston, America, of English parents; came to England, 1820; clerk in army accounts office, 1826–30; wrote many dramatic pieces of considerable merit, the greater number being still unprinted. [iv. 389]

BERNARDI, JOHN (1657–1736), major; son of Genoese nobleman living in Worcestershire; ran away, and subsequently went to Holland with his uncle, Colonel Anseline, and enlisted in States army, afterwards exchanging into an English independent regiment; received English commission under Fenwick, 1674; captain, 1685; accompanied James II on Irish expedition from St. Germains; served in Scotland, and was captured after James's defeat at the Boyne, 1690; died in Newgate, after nearly forty years' imprisonment. [iv. 389]

BERNAYS, ALBERT JAMES (1823–1892), chemist; educated at King's College school; Ph.D. Giessen; analyst and lecturer on chemistry at Derby, 1845; lecturer on chemistry at St. Mary's Hospital, London, 1855–60, and at St. Thomas's Hospital, 1860–92; fellow of Chemical Society and of Institute of Chemistry; published popular works on chemistry. [Suppl. i, 183]

BERNERS, second BARON (1467–1533). [See BOURCHIER, JOHN.]

BERNERS, BERNES, or **BARNES,** JULIANA (b. 1388?), writer; said to have been daughter of Sir James Berners (whose son was created Baron Berners, temp. Henry IV) prioress of Sopwell nunnery, Hertfordshire; probably spent youth at court and shared in the woodland sports then fashionable; published work on field-sports and heraldry, 'The Boke of St. Albans' (1486). The 'Boke' contained treatises on 'Hawking,' 'Hunting,' 'Lynage of Coote Armiris,' and the 'Blasyng of Armys.' An edition printed by Wynkyn de Worde, 1496, contained also a 'Treatyse on Fysshynge with an Angle.' [iv. 390]

BERNHER, AUGUSTINE (fl. 1554), servant of Latimer; of Swiss or Belgian origin; minister of congregation in London during Mary's reign; attended Latimer while imprisoned in Tower, 1553, and with other bishops at Oxford, 1554; a constant friend of the martyrs during Marian persecution; rector of Sutton in Elizabeth's reign; wrote religious works. [iv. 392]

BERNICIA, kings of. [See IDA, d. 559; ADDA, d. 565; ETHELFRID, d. 617; OSWALD, 605?–642; OSWY, 612?–670.]

BERNINGHAM, RICHARD DE (fl. 1313), justice itinerant; frequently summoned to parliament, 1313–1324; included in judicial commissions; collector of scutages in Yorkshire, 1314–15; knight of Yorkshire, 1323. [iv. 393]

BERRIDGE, JOHN (1716–1793), evangelical clergyman; M.A. Clare Hall, Cambridge, 1742; fellow; inducted to college of Everton, Bedfordshire, 1755, where he remained till death; became acquainted with Wesley and Whitefield, 1758; began preaching tours in neighbouring counties, 1759; at first an Arminian and afterwards a Calvinist; published religious works. [iv. 393]

BERRIMAN, JOHN (1691–1768), divine; M.A. St. Edmund Hall, Oxford, 1720; rector of St. Olave's and St. Alban's; published religious works and edited his brother William's 'Christian Doctrines' (1751). [iv. 394]

BERRIMAN, WILLIAM (1688–1750), divine; brother of John Berriman [q. v.]; educated at Merchant Taylors' School and Oriel College, Oxford; M.A., 1711; D.D., 1722; domestic chaplain to Dr. Robinson, bishop of London, 1720; fellow of Eton College, 1727; Boyle lecturer, 1730–1; published theological works. [iv. 594]

BERROW, CAPEL (1715–1782), divine; educated at Merchant Taylors' School and Christ's College, Cambridge; M.A., 1758; successively lecturer of St. Benedict and Paul's Wharf, rector of Rossington, and chaplain to Honourable Society of Judges and Serjeants in Serjeants' Inn; published theological works.   [iv. 395]

BERRY, CHARLES (1783–1877), unitarian minister; educated for independent ministry, but subsequently developed heretical views; minister of Great Meeting, Leicester, 1803–59; opened (1808) a school, which he conducted for over thirty years; one of founders of Literary and Philosophical Society, and town museum, Leicester.   [iv. 395]

BERRY, SIR EDWARD (1768–1831), rear-admiral; volunteer in East Indies, 1779–83; lieutenant, 1794; distinguished himself under Nelson at Porto Ferrajo, 1796, and at Cape St. Vincent, 1797; commander, 1796; Nelson's flag-captain at battle of Nile, of which he wrote an account, 1798; captured by French while carrying despatches; returned to England, and was knighted, 1798; served at blockade of Malta, 1800, Trafalgar, 1805, and St. Domingo, 1806; baronet, 1806; K.C.B., 1815; rear-admiral, 1821.   [iv. 396]

BERRY, JAMES (*fl.* 1655), major-general; clerk in ironworks, Shropshire, *c.* 1642; took service under Cromwell; captain-lieutenant at battle of Gainsborough, 1643; president of council of adjutators, 1647; employed in suppressing attempted rising in Nottinghamshire, 1655; major-general of Hereford, Shropshire, and Wales, 1655; member of Cromwell's House of Lords; member of council of state and of committee who nominated to office, 1659; imprisoned (1660) by council of state in Scarborough Castle.   [iv. 397]

BERRY, SIR JOHN (1635–1690), admiral; entered navy, 1663; served as boatswain in West Indies; captain, 1665; commanded squadron against French and Dutch at St. Nevis and St. Kitts, 1667; knighted for services at battle of Solebay, 1672; conducted Duke of York to Scotland in the Gloucester, which was wrecked off Yorkshire coast with considerable loss of life, 1682; vice-admiral of squadron sent against Tangier, 1683; commissioner of navy, 1683.   [iv. 398]

BERRY, MARY (1763–1852), authoress; travelled in Holland, Switzerland, Italy, and France, 1783–5; began at Florence, 1783, 'Journals and Correspondence,' which she completed, 1852; made acquaintance of Horace Walpole, 1788, who addressed many letters to her and her sister Agnes in most affectionate terms, and wrote for their amusement his 'Reminiscences of Courts of George I and II'; removed, 1791, to Little Strawberry Hill, a house of Walpole's, which, on his death, he left to the sisters. To Mary and Agnes, and their father, Robert Berry, Walpole entrusted his literary remains, and in 1798 the 'Works of Horace Walpole' appeared, nominally edited by Robert Berry, but in reality by Mary. She published Mme. du Deffand's letters from the originals at Strawberry Hill, 1810. Her works include 'Life of Rachel Wriothesley' (1819), 'Social Life of England and France from 1660 to 1830' (1828–31).   [iv. 399]

BERRY, WILLIAM (1774–1851), genealogist; clerk in College of Arms, 1793–1809; published: 'History of Guernsey,' 1815; genealogical peerage of England, Scotland, and Ireland, begun in 1832 and never completed; 'Encyclopædia Heraldica,' 1828–40, and several county genealogies.   [iv. 401]

BERSTEDE or **BURGSTED**, WALTER DE (*fl.* 1257), justice itinerant; sub-sheriff of Kent, 1257; sheriff, 1257–8; constable of Dover Castle; justice itinerant in Leicestershire, 1262, and in Norfolk, Suffolk, and Lincolnshire, 1263.   [iv. 401]

BERTHA, BERCTA, or ADILBERGA (*d.* before 616), daughter of Haribert, king of Franks; married Æthelberht, king of Kent; came to England with Liudhard, bishop of Senlis, and introduced Christianity at St. Martin's Church, Canterbury, where Augustine and his companions afterwards preached.   [iv. 402]

BERTHEAU, CHARLES (1660–1732), pastor of church of Charenton, Paris, and, after edict of Nantes (1685), of French church, Threadneedle Street, London.   [iv. 402]

BERTHON, EDWARD LYON (1813–1899), inventor; studied surgery in Liverpool and Dublin; travelled on continent; invented screw-propeller for ships, which he abandoned on its rejection by admiralty, 1835; studied at Magdalene College, Cambridge; M.A., 1849; curate of Lymington, 1845; held living of Holy Trinity, Fareham, 1847–55; invented a nautical log, which was condemned by admiralty; designed collapsible boat, which was tried and adversely reported upon by admiralty; held living of Romsey; recurred to design of collapsible boats, which at length were approved by admiralty; published reminiscences.   [Suppl. i. 184]

BERTIE, SIR ALBEMARLE (1755–1824), admiral: lieutenant, 1777; captain, 1782; in action of First of June, 1794; rear-admiral, 1804; vice-admiral, 1808; commander-in-chief at Cape of Good Hope; commanded at capture of Mauritius, 1810; baronet, 1812; admiral, 1814; K.C.B., 1815.   [iv. 402]

BERTIE, CATHARINE, DUCHESS (DOWAGER) OF SUFFOLK (1520–1580), only child of William Willoughby, eighth baron Willoughby of Eresby; married, 1536, Charles Brandon, duke of Suffolk (*d.* 1545), and *c.* 1552, Richard Bertie; distinguished for her zeal for the Reformation.   [iv. 403]

BERTIE, MONTAGUE, second EARL OF LINDSEY (1608?–1666), royalist; served in Low Countries; raised regiment of cavalry for king, 1642; prisoner after Edgehill; after being exchanged, fought at Naseby; as privy councillor and gentleman of bedchamber, accompanied Charles in his flight, in Isle of Wight; privy councillor, and one of judges for trial of regicides, 1660; K.G., 1661.   [iv. 403]

BERTIE, PEREGRINE, LORD WILLOUGHBY DE ERESBY (1555–1601), soldier; son of Richard and Catharine Bertie [q. v.], who were fleeing from Marian persecution when he was born, at Lower Wesel, Cleves; naturalised in England, 1559; succeeded to barony of Eresby, 1580; sent to Denmark to discuss commercial relations with England, 1582, and petition to Frederick II to help Henry of Navarre, 1585; governor of Bergen-op-Zoom, 1586; helped to surprise Axel, 1586; succeeded Norris in command of cavalry, 1587; assisted Leicester in attempt to relieve Sluys, and succeeded him as commander of English forces in Low Countries, 1587; defended Bergen against Spaniards, 1588; returned to England, 1589; nominated to command of army sent to aid Henry of Navarre at Dieppe, 1589; took part in capture of Vendôme, Mons, Alençon, and Falaise; returned home, 1590; governor of Berwick and warden of East March, 1598–1601. [iv. 404]

BERTIE, RICHARD (1517–1582), husband of the Duchess Dowager of Suffolk; B.A. Corpus Christi College, Oxford, 1537; joined household of Thomas Wriothesley, lord chancellor (afterwards Earl of Southampton); fled from Marian persecution to Wesel, Cleves, 1555, removed thence successively to Strasburg and Weinheim, and ultimately to Poland, where the king placed him in earldom of Kroze, Samogitia; returned to England after Mary's death; knight for county of Lincoln, 1563; M.A. Cambridge, 1564.   [iv. 407]

BERTIE, ROBERT, first EARL OF LINDSEY (1582–1642), admiral; eldest son of Peregrine Bertie [q. v.]; accompanied expedition against Spain, 1597; at siege of Amiens, 1598; retired to Lincolnshire; drained and reclaimed fens lying between Kyme Eau and the Glen, 1635–8; lord high chamberlain, 1626; served in Low Countries, 1624, and in Buckingham's naval expeditions; Earl of Lindsey, 1626; admiral of fleet for relief of Rochelle, 1628; K.B., and privy councillor, 1630; lord high admiral of England, 1636; governor of Berwick, 1639; raised counties of Lincoln and Nottingham for king, 1642; died from wounds received at Edgehill.   [iv. 408]

BERTIE, SIR THOMAS (1758–1825), admiral; entered navy, 1773; lieutenant, 1780; commander, 1782; married daughter of Peregrine Bertie, esq., whose name he assumed, 1788; post-captain, 1790; with Nelson at Copenhagen, 1801; at blockade of Cadiz, 1802; vice-admiral and knight, 1813; admiral, 1825.   [iv. 409]

BERTIE, VERE (*d.* 1680), judge; son of Montague Bertie [q. v.]; called to bar at Middle Temple, 1659; master of benchers, 1674; serjeant-at-law, before 1665; baron of exchequer, 1675; justice of common pleas, 1678; discharged from office in 1679.   [iv. 410]

E

BERTIE, WILLOUGHBY, fourth EARL OF ABINGDON (1740–1799), politician, succeeded to earldom, 1760; educated at Westminster and Magdalen College, Oxford; M.A., 1761; adopted democratic principles and became a friend and supporter of Wilkes; published 'Thoughts on Burke's Letter on Affairs of America,' 1777, and a eulogy on French revolution, 1798, both of which pamphlets gained considerable popularity. [iv. 410]

BERTON, WILLIAM OF (*fl.* 1376), chancellor of Oxford; B.D. Merton College, Oxford, 1376; D.D., and chancellor of the university, *c.* 1380; issued decree condemning Wycliffe's sacramental doctrine; signed condemnation of Wycliffe's 'conclusions,' 1382. [iv. 411]

BERTRAM. [See RATRAMNUS.]

BERTRAM, CHARLES (1723–1765), sometimes self-styled CHARLES JULIUS; literary forger; English teacher in school for naval cadets, Copenhagen; produced between 1747 and 1757 an alleged transcript of a manuscript work on Roman antiquities by Richard of Cirencester, a fourteenth-century chronicler and an inmate of Westminster, together with a copy of an ancient itinerary of Britain, at many points supplementing and correcting the itinerary of Antoninus; imposed on Dr. William Stukeley and most English antiquaries; published works of Gildas and Nennius, with the text of his forgery and a commentary on it, at Copenhagen, 1757, and several philological works. His imposture was finally exposed by B. B. Woodward in 'Gentleman's Magazine,' 1866–7. [iv. 412]

BERTRAM, ROGER (*d.* 1242), judge and baronial leader; deprived of castle and barony of Mitford for share in barons' rebellion, 1215; justice itinerant for Northumberland, Cumberland, and Lancashire, between 1225 and 1237. [iv. 413]

BERTRAM, ROGER (*fl.* 1264), baronial leader; son of Roger Bertram (*d.* 1242) [q. v.]; captured by Henry III at Northampton, 1264; freed by victory at Lewes; summoned to De Montfort's parliament, 1264. [iv. 414]

BERTRIC (*d.* 802). [See BEORHTRIC.]

BERTULF (*d.* 852). [See BEORHTWULF.]

BERWICK, DUKE OF (1670–1734). [See FITZJAMES, JAMES.]

BERWICK, third BARON (*d.* 1842). [See HILL, WILLIAM NOEL.]

BERWICK, EDWARD (*b.* 1750), Irish divine; scholar of Trinity College, Dublin; rector of Clongish, and domestic chaplain to Earl of Moira; published classical and theological works. [iv. 414]

BESSBOROUGH, fourth EARL OF (1781–1847). [See PONSONBY, JOHN WILLIAM.]

BESSE, JOSEPH (1683?–1757), quaker convert from Anglican church; writing master at Colchester; published controversial and other works, including 'Sufferings of the Quakers from 1650 to 1689,' 1753. [iv. 414]

BESSEMER, SIR HENRY (1813–1898), engineer and inventor; engaged at Charlton in his father's business as manufacturer of gold chains and type-founder; came to London, 1830, and traded in art work in white metal; invented perforated die for impressing date on stamps affixed to deeds, 1833, and soon afterwards produced plumbago pencils; invented type-composing machine, *c.* 1838; engaged in manufacture of bronze powder and gold paint by an original process, 1840; made experiments with view to obtaining stronger material for gun manufacture than that in use; patented combination of cast iron and steel, 1855, and in the same and following years obtained patents for the manufacture of steel by new process from melted pig-iron through which air under pressure or steam was blown with object of abstracting carbon; described process in paper read at Cheltenham meeting of British Association for Advancement of Science, 1856; established, 1859, steel works at Sheffield, where he made a speciality of gun-making, and subsequently was extensively occupied in manufacture of steel rails; invented swinging saloon for sea-going vessels, which was tried with small success, 1875; received Albert gold medal from Society of Arts, 1872; one of founders, 1868, and president, 1871–3, of Iron and Steel Institute; M.I.C.E., 1877; F.R.S., 1879; knighted, 1879. The Bessemer steel manufacture was introduced into the United States and developed by Alexander L. Holley (1867–70), and at present it is probably equal to that of the rest of the world collectively. [Suppl. i. 185]

BEST, CHARLES (*fl.* 1602), poet; contributed to Francis Davidson's 'Poetical Rapsodie.' [iv. 415]

BEST, GEORGE (*d.* 1584?), navigator; accompanied Frobisher in voyages to discover North-west Passage, 1576, 1577, and 1578, of which he published an account, 1578. [iv. 415]

BEST, afterwards **BESTE**, HENRY DIGBY (1768–1836), author; M.A., and fellow, Magdalen College, Oxford, 1791; curate of St. Martin's, Lincoln; published 'Christian Religion Defended against Philosophers and Republicans of France,' 1793; entered Roman catholic church, 1799; lived some years in France and Italy after 1818, and published accounts of his residence there, 1826 and 1828. His 'Personal and Literary Memorials' appeared in 1829. [iv. 416]

BEST, PAUL (1590?–1657), controversialist; M.A. Jesus College, Cambridge; fellow of Catharine Hall, 1617; served under Gustavus Adolphus; studied unitarian theology in Germany; returned to England; submitted his conclusions on doctrine of the Trinity to Roger Ley, a fellow-student at Cambridge, who appears to have made them public, with result that Best was imprisoned in the Gatehouse, 1645; released, 1647, having addressed three petitions to House of Commons. [iv. 417]

BEST, SAMUEL (1738–1825), pretended prophet; according to various accounts a servant in London and a Spitalfields weaver; inmate of Shoreditch workhouse, 1787, where, under name of 'Poor-help,' he received visitors and professed to foretell their future; gained considerable reputation, and subsequently removed to Kingsland Road. [iv. 418]

BEST, THOMAS (1570?–1638?), navy captain; perhaps son of George Best [q. v.]; went to sea, 1583; inflicted on Portuguese at Surat defeats which effected recognition of English trading rights as equal to those of Portugal, 1612; opened trade with Siam, 1613; appointed chief commander at Bantam, but, owing to disagreement with East India Company, was dismissed, 1617; senior officer in Downs, 1623; commanded expedition against Dutch, who had blockaded a Dunkirk privateer at Aberdeen; served in disastrous expedition to Rhé, 1627; master of Trinity House, 1634, probably till death. [iv. 418]

BEST, WILLIAM DRAPER, first BARON WYNFORD (1767–1845), judge; educated at Wadham College, Oxford; barrister, Middle Temple, 1789; joined home circuit; serjeant-at-law, 1799; whig M.P. for Petersfield, 1802; recorder of Guildford, 1809; tory M.P. for Bridport, 1812; solicitor-general, 1813, and attorney-general, 1816, to Prince of Wales; chief-justice of Chester, 1818; elevated to king's bench, 1818; knighted, 1819; chief-justice of common pleas and privy councillor, 1824; raised to peerage, 1829; a deputy speaker of the House of Lords; D.C.L. Oxford, 1834. [iv. 420]

BEST, WILLIAM THOMAS (1826–1897), musician; studied engineering at Liverpool, where he became organist of baptist chapel, Pembroke Road, and subsequently adopted musical profession; organist at church for the blind, 1847, and to Liverpool Philharmonic Society, 1849; organist at Royal Panopticon (now the Alhambra), *c.* 1853, and at St. Martin's-in-the-Fields, and Lincoln's Inn; organist to Liverpool corporation, 1855–94; inaugurated organ at Albert Hall, 1871; for some years organist of West Derby church. He published 'The Art of Organ Playing,' 1869, besides pianoforte and vocal pieces and organ compositions, including 'Benedicite,' 1864, and a service in F, also editing much of the music of Handel and Bach. [Suppl. i. 191]

BESTON, JOHN (*d.* 1428), prior of Carmelite convent, Bishop's Lynn; doctor in theology, Cambridge and Paris; wrote theological works. [iv. 421]

BETAGH, THOMAS (1739–1811), jesuit; professor of languages at seminary of Society of Jesus, Pont-à-Mousson; schoolmaster at Dublin, where he became parish priest and vicar-general of diocese. [iv. 421]

BETHAM, EDWARD (1707–1783), divine; fellow, 1731, and bursar, King's College, Cambridge; held living of Greenford, Middlesex, where he founded and endowed charity schools (1780); one of preachers at Whitehall; fellow of Eton, 1771. [iv. 422]

BETHAM, JOHN (*d.* 1709), catholic priest; educated and ordained at Douay; studied at Paris; doctor of the Sorbonne, 1677; chaplain to James II in England, and later at St. Germains; opened and presided over St. Gregory's Seminary, Paris, 1701; published sermons. [iv. 422]

BETHAM, MARY MATILDA (1776–1852), miniaturist and woman of letters; eldest daughter of William Betham [q. v.]; published 'Biographical Dictionary of Celebrated Women,' 1804; gave Shakespearean readings in London; exhibited miniature portraits at Royal Academy; formed friendships with the Lambs, Coleridge, Southey, and others; published three volumes of verse. [iv. 423]

BETHAM, WILLIAM (1749–1839), antiquary; headmaster of endowed school at Stonham Aspel, Suffolk, 1784–1833; rector of Stoke Lacy, 1833; published 'Genealogical Tables of Sovereigns of the World,' 1795, and 'Baronetage of England,' 1801–5. [iv. 423]

BETHAM, Sir WILLIAM (1779–1853), Ulster king-of-arms; son of William Betham (1749–1839) [q. v.]; deputy-keeper of records in 'the tower,' Dublin Castle, 1805; sub-commissioner under record commission, 1811–1812; knighted, 1812; Ulster king-of-arms, 1820; member of Royal Irish Academy, 1826. Published: 'Irish Antiquarian Researches,' 1827; 'The Gael and Cymbri,' 1834; and 'Etruria Celtica,' 1842. [iv. 424]

BETHEL, SLINGSBY (1617–1697), republican; in business in Hamburg, 1637–49; M.P., Knaresborough, 1659; member of council of state, 1660; chosen sheriff of London and Middlesex, 1680, though unable to serve in consequence of not having taken oaths commanded by Corporation Act; subsequently qualified and elected, the election and taking of the oaths being the subject of several pamphlets; in Hamburg, 1682–9. His chief work is 'The World's Mistake in Oliver Cromwell,' 1668. [iv. 425]

BETHELL, CHRISTOPHER (1773–1859), bishop of Bangor; M.A. King's College, Cambridge, 1799; D.D., 1817; dean of Chichester, 1814–24; prebendary of Exeter, 1830; bishop of Gloucester, 1824, of Exeter, 1830, and of Bangor, 1830–59; published theological works. [iv. 426]

BETHELL, RICHARD, first BARON WESTBURY (1800–1873), lord chancellor; B.A. Wadham College, Oxford, 1818; fellow; called to bar at Middle Temple, 1823; practised in equity courts; Q.C., 1840; liberal M.P. for Aylesbury, 1851, and for Wolverhampton, 1852; vice-chancellor of duchy of Lancaster, 1851; solicitor-general in 'government of all the talents,' 1852; attorney-general, 1856; supported Succession Duty Bill, Oxford University Bill (1854), Probate and Administration Bill (1857), and other important measures; first of the Statute Law Revision Acts passed under his guidance, 1861; introduced the second of these acts, 1863; lord chancellor, with title of Baron Westbury of Westbury in Wiltshire, 1861; passed an unsuccessful act to facilitate the proof of title to and the conveyance of real estate, 1862; sat as member of judicial committee of privy council to hear appeals on 'Essays and Reviews' cases, 1864, and acquitted defendants on all counts; resigned office on passing of vote of censure on him in House of Commons as being inattentive to public interests, 1865; retired to Italy, but soon returned to sit on appeals in House of Lords and privy council; arbitrator in winding-up of affairs of European Assurance Society, a work which his death interrupted. He had extraordinary power of sarcastic speech and an unequalled mastery of luminous exposition. [iv. 426]

BETHUNE, ALEXANDER (1804–1843), Scottish poet; employed as a labourer; published 'Tales and Sketches of Scottish Peasantry,' which were immediately successful, 1838; produced, with his brother John, 'Lectures on Practical Economy,' 1839; turnkey in Glasgow prison; brought out his 'Scottish Peasants' Fireside,' 1842; prevented by his last illness from undertaking editorship of 'Dumfries Standard.' [iv. 431]

BETHUNE, Sir HENRY LINDESAY (1787–1851), major-general; appointed to Madras artillery, 1804; as subaltern accompanied Sir John Malcolm to Persia, 1810; employed in disciplining Persian army; returned to England, 1821; went back to Persia, 1834; served in war of succession, 1835, and in 1836–9 as major-general in Asia; died at Tabriz. [iv. 432]

BETHUNE, JOHN (1812–1839), poet; brother of Alexander Bethune [q. v.]; apprenticed as carver; set up weaving looms with his brother, 1825, but failed in the business; overseer of estate of Inchtyre, 1835; contributed to his brother's 'Tales of Scottish Peasantry,' and various Scottish periodicals. [iv. 432]

BETHUNE, JOHN DRINKWATER (1762–1844), historian of the siege of Gibraltar; son of one John Drinkwater; ensign in royal Manchester volunteers, *c.* 1777; stationed at Gibraltar during siege by Spanish, 1779–83, of which he published an account, *c.* 1785; captain; stationed at Gibraltar, 1787; military secretary and deputy judge-advocate during English occupation of Corsica; published 'Narrative of Battle of St. Vincent'; lieutenant-colonel, 1796; placed on half-pay as colonel; commissary general of Helder force, 1799; member and subsequently chairman of parliamentary commission of military inquiry, 1805; comptroller of army accounts, 1811–25; assumed surname of Bethune. [iv. 433]

BETHUNE, JOHN ELLIOT DRINKWATER (1801–1851), Indian legislator; son of John Drinkwater Bethune [q. v.]; educated at Trinity College, Cambridge; called to bar, 1827; counsel to home office; legislative member of supreme council of India, 1848; effected several important legislative reforms, and established school for native girls at Calcutta. [iv. 434]

BETHUNE, ROBERT DE (*d.* 1148). [See ROBERT.]

BETTERTON, THOMAS (1635?–1710), actor and dramatist; probably first acted in company licensed to Rhodes, a bookseller, 1659, his chief successes being in 'Pericles,' the 'Mad Lover,' the 'Loyal Subject,' the 'Bondman,' and the 'Changeling'; joined Sir John Davenant's company at Lincoln's Inn Fields Theatre, 1661; visited Paris by royal command, with view of introducing in England improvements in dramatic representation; played Hamlet, 1661, and Mercutio, Sir Toby Belch, Macbeth, and Bosola ('Duchess of Malfi'), 1662–6; associated after Davenant's death (1668) with Harris and Davenant's son Charles in management of Dorset Garden Theatre, 1671; played Orestes in Charles Davenant's 'Circe,' Œdipus in Dryden and Lee's 'Œdipus,' Timon of Athens, King Lear, Troilus, and other characters in adaptations of Shakespeare by Dryden, Shadwell, and Tate; amalgamated with the rival company of Drury Lane, 1682; opened 'theatre in Little Lincoln's Inn Fields,' 1695; produced successfully Congreve's 'Love for Love,' Congreve undertaking to provide a play each year, a promise which was not kept; opened theatre erected by Sir John Vanbrugh in Haymarket, 1705, but resigned management to Congreve and Vanbrugh; performances of 'Love for Love' (1709) and the 'Maid's Tragedy' (1710) given for his benefit at Haymarket; highly esteemed as an actor by most of his contemporaries. His dramas include the 'Roman Virgin,' acted 1670, adapted from Webster's 'Appius and Virginia,' the 'Prophetess,' 1690, an opera from the 'Prophetess' of Beaumont and Fletcher, 'King Henry IV,' 1700 (in which he played Falstaff), from Shakespeare, the 'Amorous Widow,' *c.* 1670, from Molière's 'Georges Dandin,' and the 'Bondman,' 1719, from Massinger. [iv. 434]

BETTES, JOHN (*d.* 1570?), miniature painter; executed oil-painting of Queen Elizabeth and engravings for Hall's 'Chronicle.' [iv. 441]

BETTESWORTH, GEORGE EDMUND BYRON (1780–1808), naval captain; lieutenant, 1804; served in West Indies; carried Nelson's despatches from Antigua to England, and was promoted post-captain, 1805; killed in engagement off Bergen. [iv. 441]

BETTS, JOHN (*d.* 1695), physician; B.A. Corpus Christi College, Oxford, 1647; M.D., 1654; physician to Charles II; F.C.P., 1664; censor, College of Physicians, 1671, 1673, 1685, and 1686; 'elect,' 1685; published medical works. [iv. 442]

BETTY, WILLIAM HENRY WEST (1791–1874), actor, called the 'Young Roscius'; played Romeo at Belfast, and Hamlet and Prince Arthur, at Dublin 1803; played at Cork, Waterford, Glasgow, Edinburgh

Birmingham, and at Covent Garden and Drury Lane, 1804; appeared on alternate nights at Drury Lane and Covent Garden, 1805, adding Richard III and Macbeth to his Shakespearean repertoire; last appeared as boy actor at Bath, 1808; fellow-commoner of Christ's College, Cambridge, 1809; returned to stage, 1812, and finally retired, 1824. [iv. 442]

BEULAN, a priest to whom the author of 'Historia Britonum' (perhaps 'Nennius') dedicated his work. Some historical writings have been attributed to him. [iv. 443]

BEUNO or **BEINO**, St. (d. 660?), monk; related to St. Cadoc the Wise of Llancarfan and to St. Kentigern; became a monk; established religious society at Clynnog Fawr, Carnarvonshire, 616; founded several churches. [iv. 444]

BEVAN, EDWARD (1770–1860), physician and apiarian; studied at St. Bartholomew's Hospital; M.D. St. Andrews, 1818; after some years' practice retired to Bridstow, near Ross, Herefordshire, where he developed an apiary; one of founders of Entomological Society, 1833; published 'The Honey-Bee: its Natural History, Physiology, and Management,' 1827. [iv. 444]

BEVAN, JOSEPH GURNEY (1753–1814), quaker; entered his father's business of chemist and druggist, 1776; retired, 1794; able quaker apologist. His works include 'Refutation of Misrepresentations of Quakers,' 1800, 'Thoughts on Reason and Revelation,' 1805, 'The Life of St. Paul,' 1807, and memoirs of Robert Barclay, Isaac Penington, and Sarah Stephenson. [iv. 445]

BEVER, JOHN (d. 1311), chronicler. [See JOHN OF LONDON.]

BEVER, THOMAS (1725–1791), scholar and civilian; LL.D. All Souls' College, Oxford, 1758; admitted to Doctors' Commons, 1758; judge of Cinque Ports and chancellor of Lincoln and Bangor; lectured on civil law, Oxford, 1762; published a 'History of Legal Polity of the Roman State,' 1781. [iv. 446]

BEVERIDGE, WILLIAM (1637–1708), bishop; M.A. St. John's College, Cambridge, 1660; vicar of Ealing, 1661–72; published 'Collection of Canons received by Greek Church,' 1672; vicar of St. Peter's, Cornhill, 1672; prebendary of St. Paul's, 1674; D.D., 1679; prebendary of Canterbury, 1684; bishop of St. Asaph, 1704. Several religious works by him were published posthumously. [iv. 447]

BEVERLEY, CHARLES JAMES (1788–1868), naturalist; assistant-surgeon in navy, 1810; accompanied Polar expeditions under Ross (1818) and Parry (1819–20); and assisted in preparation of examples of Arctic zoology; full surgeon and F.R.S., 1821. [iv. 448]

BEVERLEY, HENRY ROXBY (1796–1863), actor; played low comedy parts at Adelphi, 1838; manager of Victoria Theatre, 1839, and later of the Sunderland theatre and other houses, principally in north of England. [iv. 449]

BEVERLEY, St. JOHN OF (d. 721). [See JOHN.]

BEVERLEY, JOHN OF (d. 1414), Carmelite; doctor and professor of divinity at Oxford; B.D., 1393; canon of St. John's Church, Beverley; probably same with John of Beverley the lollard, who was drawn and hanged at St. Giles's Fields; left works in manuscript. [iv. 449]

BEVERLEY, JOHN (1743–1827), esquire bedell of Cambridge University; M.A. Christ's College, Cambridge, 1770; esquire bedell, 1770–1827; held office under the admiralty. His works include an account of Cambridge University customs. [iv. 450]

BEVERLEY or **INGLEBERD**, PHILIP (fl. 1290), Oxford benefactor; rector of Kayingham, Yorkshire; endowed University College, Oxford. [iv. 450]

BEVERLEY, THOMAS OF (fl. 1174). [See THOMAS.]

BEVERLEY, WILLIAM ROXBY (1814?–1889), scene-painter; employed (1830) at Theatre Royal, Manchester, managed by his father, William Roxby (1765–1842), who had taken the name of Beverley; subsequently accompanied his father on tour, and was with his brother, Henry Beverley [q. v.], at Victoria Theatre, London, 1839; principal artist at Princess's Theatre, 1846; painted scenes for Vestris and Mathews at Lyceum, 1847–55; executed dioramic views for 'Ascent of Mont Blanc,' exhibited by Albert Smith at Egyptian Hall, Piccadilly, 1852; scenic

director at Covent Garden, 1853; began (1854) connection with Drury Lane, which lasted till 1884, and worked exclusively for that theatre, 1868–79; painted panorama of Lakes of Killarney for Grand Theatre, Islington, 1884; exhibited pictures at Royal Academy between 1865 and 1880. [Suppl. i. 192]

BEVILLE, ROBERT (d. 1824), barrister-at-law; called to bar at Inner Temple; practised on Norfolk circuit; registrar to Bedford Level corporation, 1812–24; published treatise on law of homicide. [iv. 450]

BEVIN, ELWAY (fl. 1605–1631), composer; of Welsh origin; gentleman-extraordinary of Chapel Royal, 1605; according to Wood organist of Bristol, 1589 till 1637, when, as Roman catholic, he was dismissed from appointments; published 'Brief Instruction of Art of Musicke,' 1631, and composed some church music. [iv. 451]

BEVIS or **BEVANS**, JOHN (1693–1771), astronomer; M.A. Christ Church, Oxford, 1718; physician in London before 1730; fitted up an observatory at Stoke Newington, c. 1738; compiled 'Uranographia Britannica,' 1745–50, which was not published, the intending publisher becoming bankrupt; fellow, 1765, and foreign secretary, 1766–71, of Royal Society. He was a diligent observer, and published astronomical and medical works. [iv. 451]

BEWICK, JANE (1787–1881), writer of memoirs; daughter of Thomas Bewick [q. v.], a memoir of whom, written by himself, she edited and issued, 1862. [iv. 452]

BEWICK, JOHN (1760–1795), wood-engraver; younger brother of Thomas Bewick [q. v.], to whom he was apprenticed at Newcastle, 1777; obtained employment in London on blocks for children's books, 1782; executed illustrations for 'Gay's Fables' (1788), 'Emblems of Mortality,' a copy of Holbein's 'Icones' (1789), 'Proverbs Exemplified' (1790), 'Progress of Man and Society' (1791), 'Looking-Glass for the Mind' (1792), and other works. As an engraver he falls far below his brother. [iv. 453]

BEWICK, ROBERT ELLIOT (1788–1849), wood-engraver, son of Thomas Bewick [q. v.], whose partner he became, 1812; assisted in 'Fables of Æsop' (1818) and 'History of British Fishes.' [iv. 454]

BEWICK, THOMAS (1753–1828), wood-engraver; apprenticed to Ralph Beilby [q. v.], 1767, and was soon entrusted with most of Beilby's wood-engraving business; executed cuts for several children's books, 1771–4; came to London, 1776, and shortly afterwards went again to Newcastle and entered into partnership with Beilby; engraved blocks for 'Gay's Fables' (1779), 'Select Fables' (1784), 'General History of Quadrupeds' (1790), for which Beilby supplied the letterpress, 'History of British Birds' (1797 and 1804), the text being by the Rev. Mr. Cotes, and 'Fables of Æsop' (1818), in which he was assisted by his son, R. E. Bewick [q. v.], and two of his pupils; left unfinished illustrations for a 'History of British Fishes.' The 'Chillingham Bull' (1789) was one of his most ambitious works. [iv. 455]

BEWICK, WILLIAM (1795–1866), portrait and historical painter; pupil of Haydon, 1817–20; copied Michael Angelo's Prophets and Sibyls in Sistine Chapel, 1826–9; exhibited copies, 1840; took part in Westminster Hall competition, 1843. He excelled in reproducing Rembrandt. [iv. 460]

BEWLEY, WILLIAM (d. 1783), friend of Dr. Burney; practised medicine at Massingham, Norfolk; contributed largely to 'Monthly Review.' [iv. 460]

BEXFIELD, WILLIAM RICHARD (1824–1853), composer; articled to Dr. Buck, organist of Norwich Cathedral; Mus. Bac. Oxford, 1846; organist at Boston, Lincolnshire, and, 1848, of St. Helen's, Bishopsgate; Mus. Doc. Cambridge, 1849; wrote oratorio, 'Israel Restored,' 1851. [iv. 461]

BEXLEY, first BARON (1766–1821). [See VANSITTART, NICHOLAS.]

BIANCONI, CHARLES (1786–1875), promoter of the Irish car system in Ireland; born at Tregolo, Lombardy; itinerant vendor of prints in Ireland; opened as carver and gilder a shop in Carrick-on-Suir, 1806; instituted car to carry passengers, goods, and mail-bags between Clonmel and Cahir (8 miles), 1815, the result of which was that a car system was formed and rapidly extended; deputy-lieutenant, 1863; friend and adherent of O'Connell. [iv. 461]

BIBBY, THOMAS (1799–1863), Irish poetical writer; educated at Kilkenny and Trinity College, Dublin; one of the best Greek scholars of his day; lived latterly in eccentric retirement; published two dramatic poems 'Gerald of Kildare,' 1854, and 'Silken Thomas,' 1859. [iv. 462]

BIBELESWORTH or **BIBBESWORTH**, WALTER DE (*fl.* 1270), poet; accompanied Prince Edward to Holy Land, 1270; wrote two French poems. [iv. 463]

BIBER, GEORGE EDWARD (1801–1874), miscellaneous writer; born at Ludwigsburg, Würtemberg, and studied at lyceum there: Ph.D. Tübingen; LL.D. Göttingen; took part in agitation for German unity, and retired successively to Italy and the Grisons: master in Pestalozzi institution, Yverdun; head of classical school at Hampstead, and later at Coombe Wood; became naturalised; vicar of Holy Trinity, Roehampton, 1842–74; member of council of English Church Union, 1863–4; published works dealing with theological questions; edited 'John Bull,' 1848–56. [iv. 463]

BICHENO, JAMES EBENEZER (1785–1851), statesman; called to bar at Middle Temple, 1822; joined Oxford circuit; F.L.S., 1812, and secretary, 1824–32; published 'Ireland and its Economy,' 1830; member of commission to investigate condition of poor in Ireland, *c.* 1833; colonial secretary in Van Diemen's Land, 1842, where he died; wrote works on economic and scientific subjects. [v. 1]

BICKERSTAFF, WILLIAM (1728–1789), antiquary; under-master of Lower Free grammar school, Leicester, 1750; held successively various curacies in Leicestershire; contributed papers on antiquarian subjects to 'Gentleman's Magazine.' [v. 2]

BICKERSTAFFE, ISAAC (*d.* 1812?), dramatic writer; page to Lord Chesterfield, when lord lieutenant of Ireland; produced between 1756 and 1771 many successful dramatic pieces, including 'Love in a Village' (1762); fled abroad, being suspected of a capital crime, 1772; died abroad in degraded circumstances. [v. 2]

BICKERSTETH, EDWARD (1786–1850), evangelical divine; received appointment in General Post Office, *c.* 1800; in partnership with his brother-in-law, a solicitor at Norwich, 1812; abandoned practice of law, and was ordained; one of secretaries of Church Missionary Society, 1816–30, during which time he travelled as 'deputation'; assistant minister of Wheler Episcopal Chapel, Spitalfields; rector of Watton, Hertfordshire, 1830. Took an active part in opposing the Tractarian movement; one of the founders of the Parker Society and of the Irish Church Missions Society; frequently acted as 'deputation' for Society for Conversion of Jews, and other religious associations. His works include 'Help to Studying the Scriptures' and 'Christian Psalmody,' a collection of over seven hundred hymns. [v. 3]

BICKERSTETH, EDWARD (1814–1892), dean of Lichfield; M.A. Sidney Sussex College, Cambridge, 1839; D.D., 1864; vicar of Aylesbury and archdeacon of Buckinghamshire, 1853; honorary canon of Christ Church, Oxford, 1866; dean of Lichfield, 1875; during several years prolocutor over lower house of convocation of Canterbury; published religious writings [Suppl. i. 194]

BICKERSTETH, EDWARD (1850–1897), bishop of South Tokyo, Japan; B.A. Pembroke College, Cambridge, 1873; fellow, 1875; M.A., 1876; ordained deacon, 1873; priest, 1874; head of Cambridge mission to Delhi, 1877–1882; rector of Framlingham, 1882; bishop of South Tokyo, Japan, 1886. [Suppl. i. 194]

BICKERSTETH, HENRY, BARON LANGDALE (1783–1851), master of rolls, brother of Edward Bickersteth (1786–1850) [q.v.]; studied medicine in London and Edinburgh; Hewitt scholar, Caius College, Cambridge, 1802; senior wrangler and senior Smith's mathematical prizeman, 1808; B.A. and fellow; called to bar at Inner Temple, 1811; bencher, 1827; M.A., 1811; gave valuable evidence before commission on procedure of court of chancery, 1824; K.C., 1827; sworn privy councillor, appointed master of rolls, and created Baron Langdale of Langdale, Westmoreland, 1836; temporarily speaker of House of Lords, 1850; head of commission entrusted with seal, 1850. [v. 4]

BICKERSTETH, ROBERT (1816–1884), bishop of Ripon; graduated at Queens' College, Cambridge, 1841; hon. secretary of Irish Church Missions, 1850; canon residentiary and treasurer, Salisbury Cathedral, 1854; bishop of Ripon, 1857; gained considerable reputation as evangelical preacher. [v. 6]

BICKERTON, SIR RICHARD (1727–1792), vice-admiral; entered navy, 1739; lieutenant in West Indies, 1746–1748; post-captain in Mediterranean, 1759, West Indies, and Channel, 1761; knighted, 1773; baronet, 1778; assisted in second relief of Gibraltar, 1781; commodore of first class in East Indies, 1782–4; commander-in-chief at Leeward Islands, 1786–7; rear-admiral, 1787; vice-admiral, 1790; port-admiral at Plymouth till death. [v. 6]

BICKERTON, SIR RICHARD HUSSEY (1759–1832), admiral; son of Sir Richard Bickerton [q.v.]; entered navy, 1771; lieutenant, 1777; commander, 1779; in Channel, 1779–80, West Indies, 1781 and 1787–90, and Channel, 1793–4, West Indies and Newfoundland, 1794, North Sea, 1795, and Channel, 1797–9; rear-admiral, 1799; served at Cadiz and on Egyptian coast; commander-in-chief in Mediterranean; second in command under Nelson, 1804–5; admiral, 1810; commander-in-chief at Portsmouth, 1812; K.C.B., 1815; general of marines, 1830. [v. 7]

BICKHAM, GEORGE, the younger (*d.* 1758), engraver; son of George Bickham (*d.* 1769) [q.v.]; published essay on drawing, also humorous and other engravings. [v. 8]

BICKHAM, GEORGE, the elder (*d.* 1769), writing master and engraver; published portraits, engravings, and (1743) 'The Universal Penman.' [v. 8]

BICKLEY, THOMAS (1518–1596), bishop of Chichester; chorister in free school of Magdalen College, Oxford; fellow, 1541; one of Edward VI's chaplains at Windsor; retired to France during Mary's reign; chancellor in Lichfield Cathedral and warden of Merton College, Oxford, after Elizabeth's accession; bishop of Chichester, 1585. [v. 8]

BICKNELL, ALEXANDER (*d.* 1796), author; published works, including fiction and histories, between 1777 and 1785. [v. 9]

BICKNELL, ELHANAN (1788–1861), patron of art; collected, between 1838 and 1850, at his residence at Herne Hill, Surrey, many valuable pictures by masters of the modern British school. [v. 9]

BICKNELL, HERMAN (1830–1875), author, orientalist, and traveller; son of Elhanan Bicknell [q.v.]; educated at Paris, Hanover, University College, and St. Bartholomew's Hospital; graduated at College of Surgeons, 1854; military surgeon in Hong Kong, 1855, India, 1856–60, and at Aldershot; resigned commission, and devoted himself to languages and to travelling in all parts of the world. Translations from Háfiz by him were published posthumously. [v. 10]

BICKNELL, M—— (1695?–1723), actress; first heard of as playing at the Haymarket in Cibber's 'Careless Husband,' 1706; at Drury Lane, from 1708 to 1721, when she was the original Lady Wrangle in Cibber's 'Refusal'; last appeared, 1723. [v. 11]

BICKNOR or **BYKENORE**, ALEXANDER (*d.* 1349), archbishop of Dublin; prebendary of Maynooth and treasurer of Ireland; elected archbishop of Dublin, 1310, but his election set aside by Edward II; consecrated, 1317; lord justice of Ireland, 1318; went on embassies to France, 1323 and 1324; joined conspiracy formed in France to overthrow the Despensers; sided with Queen Isabella against Edward II, 1326; papal collector, 1330; during last years of his life, engaged in dispute with archbishop of Armagh concerning primacy of Ireland; founded college in St. Patrick's Church, 1320. [v. 11]

BIDDER, GEORGE PARKER (1806–1878), engineer; exhibited, when very young, by his father as a 'calculating phenomenon'; educated at Edinburgh; took to engineering, and became associated with Robert Stephenson in London and Birmingham railway, 1834; obtained work in connection with parliamentary committees; a founder of the Electric Telegraph Company. His constructive works include the Victoria Docks, London. [v. 12]

BIDDLE, JOHN (1615–1662), unitarian; M.A. Magdalen Hall, Oxford, 1641; master of free school of St. Maryle-Crypt, Gloucester; imprisoned in Gloucester by parliamentary commissioners, his religious views being called in question, but released on bail, 1645; brought before parliamentary commission at Westminster, and, having published works refuting Godhead of Holy Spirit, was remanded to prison, 1647; liberated on bail, but soon afterwards again confined in Newgate; released by decree of oblivion, 1652; published 'A Two-fold Catechism,' 1654, and was imprisoned in Gatehouse, 1654–5; became entangled in dispute with a baptist pastor, and was exiled to Scilly Islands, 1655–8; released, but rearrested; subsequently died from disease contracted in prison. His controversial writings attracted considerable attention. [v. 13]

BIDDLECOMBE, SIR GEORGE (1807–1878), captain and author; midshipman in mercantile marine, 1823; second master in royal navy, 1833; in active service, and engaged in naval surveys, c. 1828–54; master attendant at Woolwich yard, 1864–8; staff-captain and C.B., 1867; knighted, 1873; published works relating to naval matters. [v. 16]

BIDDULPH, SIR THOMAS MYDDLETON (1809–1878), general; lieutenant, 1829; master of Queen Victoria's household, 1851; colonel, 1854; K.C.B., 1863; keeper of Queen Victoria's privy purse, 1867; lieutenant-general, 1873; brevet-general and privy councillor, 1877. [v. 17]

BIDDULPH, THOMAS TREGENNA (1763–1838), evangelical divine; M.A. Queen's College, Oxford, 1787; incumbent of Bengeworth, near Evesham, 1793–1803, and of St. James's, Bristol, 1799–1838; published theological works. [v. 17]

BIDGOOD, JOHN (1624–1690), physician; educated at Exeter College, Oxford; Petreian fellow, 1642; bachelor of physic, 1648; excluded from fellowship by parliamentarian visitors, 1649–60; M.D. Padua; practised at Chard and subsequently at Exeter; incorporated M.D. Oxford, 1660; F.C.P., 1686. [v. 18]

BIDLAKE, JOHN (1755–1814), divine and poet; M.A. and D.D. Christ Church, Oxford, 1808; minister at Stonehouse; chaplain to prince regent and Duke of Clarence; Bampton lecturer, 1811; afflicted with blindness, 1811; published religious and poetical works. [v. 18]

BIDWILL, JOHN CARNE (1815–1853), botanist and traveller; became merchant at Sydney, New South Wales; accompanied exploring expeditions in New Zealand and made several botanical discoveries; contributed to the 'Gardener's Chronicle.' [v. 18]

BIFFIN or **BEFFIN**, SARAH (1784–1850), miniature painter; born without arms or legs. but contrived to use pencil and paintbrush with her mouth; travelled about the country exhibiting her powers, 1812; received medal from Society of Artists, 1821. [v. 19]

BIFIELD, NICHOLAS (1579–1622). [See BYFIELD.]

BIGG, JOHN STANYAN (1828–1865), poet and journalist; published 'The Sea King,' a metrical romance, 1848; edited in Ireland 'Downshire Protestant'; returned and became editor and proprietor of 'Ulverston Advertiser,' 1860–5. His most important poem, 'Night and the Soul' (1854), shows that his sympathies were with the 'Spasmodic School.' [v. 19]

BIGG, WILLIAM REDMORE (1755–1828), painter; pupil of Edward Penny, R.A.; entered Academy schools, 1778; R.A., 1814. [v. 20]

BIGGAR, JOSEPH GILLIS (1828–1890), Irish politician; provision merchant at Belfast, 1861–80; town councillor, 1871; chairman of Belfast water commission; joined Isaac Butt's Home Rule Association, 1870; M.P. for co. Cavan, 1874 till death; joined Irish Republican Brotherhood (the Fenians), 1875, and became member of supreme council, but was expelled from the body, 1877, for refusing to sever his connection with the parliamentary movement; treasurer of land league, 1879; opposed Gladstone's Irish policy, 1880–1; suspended for disorderly conduct, 1881; he was one of the Irish politicians whose conduct was investigated during the Parnell commission, 1887; he adopted, with considerable success, from 1875, a policy of parliamentary 'obstruction.' [Suppl. i. 195]

BIGLAND, JOHN (1750–1832), schoolmaster and author; village schoolmaster; published 'Reflections on Resurrection and Ascension of Christ,' 1803; adopted literary profession and published series of popular works connected chiefly with geography and history. [v. 20]

BIGLAND, RALPH (1711–1784), Garter king-of-arms; blue mantle, College of Arms, 1757; Somerset and registrar, 1763; Norroy king-of-arms, 1773; Clarenceux, 1774; Garter king-of-arms, 1780; made collections for history of Gloucestershire. [v. 21]

BIGNELL, HENRY (1611–1660?), divine; B.A. St. Mary's Hall, Oxford; rector, 1645, of St. Peter-le-Bayly, Oxford, whence he was ejected for scandalous conduct. [v. 21]

BIGNELL, MRS. (1695?–1723). [See BICKNELL, M——.]

BIGOD or **BYGOD**, SIR FRANCIS (1508–1537), rebel; knighted, c. 1529; educated at Oxford; in Cardinal Wolsey's service, 1527; employed under Thomas Cromwell in advancing Henry VIII's reforms in Yorkshire; hanged for heading insurrection at Beverley in connection with Pilgrimage of Grace. [v. 21]

BIGOD, HUGH, first EARL OF NORFOLK (d. 1176 or 1177), second son of Roger Bigod (d. 1107); governor of Norwich till 1122; king's dapifer, 1123; took active part in rebellions against Henry I; Earl of Norfolk on Stephen's accession; held Norwich against Stephen, 1136; surrendered and was pardoned; fought under Stephen at Lincoln, 1141; joined Henry of Anjou's party and held Ipswich against Stephen, 1153, but escaped punishment on its fall; showed signs of hostility to Henry II, but gave in his submission, 1157; assisted prince Henry's rebellion against his father, 1173; submitted to Henry II, 1174; probably died in Holy Land, whither he had accompanied Philip of Flanders on pilgrimage. [v. 22]

BIGOD, HUGH (d. 1266), justiciar; chief ranger of Farndale forest, Yorkshire, 1255; chief justiciar, 1258–60; keeper of Tower of London, 1258; governor of Dover Castle, 1258–61. [v. 24]

BIGOD, ROGER, second EARL OF NORFOLK (d. 1221), son of Hugh, first earl [q. v.]; steward of royal household under Richard I; ambassador to Philip of France to arrange crusade; justiciar after Richard's return; justice itinerant in Norfolk; enjoyed John's favour until 1213, when he was imprisoned; released and restored to favour; joined barons against John, 1215. [v. 24]

BIGOD, ROGER, fourth EARL OF NORFOLK (d. 1270), marshal of England; grandson of Roger Bigod, second earl [q. v.]; knighted, 1233; head of commission of justices itinerant in Essex and Hertfordshire, 1234; accompanied unsuccessful embassy to Lyons to protest against papal exactions, 1245; earl marshal, 1246; played prominent part in bringing forward Provisions of Oxford, 1258; supported Henry III against Simon de Montfort, 1259, but subsequently joined de Montfort's party. [v. 25]

BIGOD, ROGER, fifth EARL OF NORFOLK (1245–1306), marshal of England; son of Hugh Bigod (d. 1266) [q. v.]; refused, with Earl of Hereford, to serve in Gascony unaccompanied by Edward I, 1297, and, on the king's departure to Flanders, protested in arms against taxation without national consent, Edward renouncing the right at Ghent, 1298; gave up marshal's rod, 1301. [v. 26]

BIGSBY, JOHN JEREMIAH (1792–1881), geologist; M.D. Edinburgh, 1814; army medical officer at Cape, 1817; commissioned to report on geology of Upper Canada, 1819; British secretary and medical officer of Canadian boundary commission, 1822; fellow, Geological Society, 1823; F.R.S., 1869; practised medicine at Newark, 1827–1846, and in London, 1846–81; published scientific and other writings. [v. 27]

BIGSBY, ROBERT (1806–1873), antiquary; educated for legal profession, but abandoned it and turned his attention to study and accumulation of antiquities, acquiring several curious relics of Sir Francis Drake; published historical, antiquarian, and other works. [v. 27]

BILFRITH (fl. 750), anchorite of Lindisfarne; adorned with gold and gems the 'Durham Book,' a manuscript of the gospels now in Cottonian Library. [v. 28]

BILL, ROBERT (1754–1827), inventor; educated for the army, but occupied himself with literary and scientific pursuits; originated improvements in domestic and other contrivances. [v. 28]

BILL, WILLIAM (*d.* 1561), dean of Westminster; B.A. St. John's College, Cambridge, 1533; fellow, 1535; M.A., 1536; D.D. and master of his college, 1547; Linacre lecturer, 1547–9; vice-chancellor, 1549; master of Trinity and itinerary chaplain to the king, 1551; deprived of mastership by Mary, but reinstated, 1558; chief almoner, 1554; fellow and provost of Eton College, 1559; prebendary of Lincoln, 1559; on commission for revision of prayer-book, 1560; dean of Westminster, 1560. [v. 29]

BILLING, ARCHIBALD (1791–1881), physician; A.B. Trinity College, Dublin, 1811; M.D., 1818; incorporated M.D. Oxford, 1818; F.C.P., 1819, censor, College of Physicians, 1823, and councillor, 1852–5; physician to London Hospital, 1822–45; instituted clinical lectures in London, 1823; member of senate of London University, 1836; F.R.S.; published medical works and a text-book on engraved gems, coins, and similar objects. [v. 30]

BILLING, SIR THOMAS (*d.* 1481?), lawyer; member of Gray's Inn; M.P. for London, 1448; recorder, 1451; serjeant-at-law, 1454; king's serjeant, 1458; knighted, *c.* 1458; took part against the Lancastrians; judge of king's bench, 1464; chief-justice of king's bench, 1469 till death. [v. 31]

BILLINGHAM or **BULLINGHAM**, RICHARD (*fl.* 1350), schoolman; educated at Merton College, Oxford; concerned in riot occasioned by election to chancellorship of university, 1349. [v. 32]

BILLINGS, JOSEPH (*b.* 1758?), explorer; sailed as A.B. under Captain Cook on his last voyage; lieutenant in Russian navy; commanded Russian exploring expedition to north-eastern parts of Asia, 1785, and was promoted successively captain-lieutenant, and captain of second and first class. [v. 32]

BILLINGS, ROBERT WILLIAM (1813–1874), architect; employed in illustrating architectural works; published on his own account 'Architectural Antiquities of County of Durham' (1846), 'Baronial and Ecclesiastical Antiquities of Scotland' (1845–52), and other works; restored many important old buildings in England and Scotland. [v. 33]

BILLINGSLEY, SIR HENRY (*d.* 1606), lord mayor of London and first translator of Euclid into English; scholar of St. John's College, Cambridge, 1551; studied at Oxford; apprenticed to London haberdasher; sheriff of London, 1584; lord mayor, 1596; knighted, *c.* 1597; M.P. for London, 1604; published, 1570, the first translation of Euclid into English. [v. 33]

BILLINGSLEY, JOHN, the elder (1625–1684), non-conformist divine; educated at St. John's College, Cambridge; fellow of Corpus Christi College, Oxford, 1648; incorporated B.A., 1649; minister at Chesterfield; ejected, 1662, but continued to preach in private; published controversial and other religious works. [v. 34]

BILLINGSLEY, JOHN, the younger (1657–1722), nonconformist divine; son of John Billingsley (1625–1684) [q. v.]; educated at Trinity College, Cambridge; ministered successively at Chesterfield, Sheffield, Selston, Kingston-upon-Hull, and at Crutched Friars (1706); sided with opponents of subscription, 1719; published religious tracts. [v. 35]

BILLINGSLEY, MARTIN (*fl.* 1618–1637), writing-master, probably to Prince Charles; published 'The Pens Excellencie, or the Secretarys Delight,' 1618. [v. 35]

BILLINGSLEY, NICHOLAS (1633–1709), poet and divine; educated at Eton and Merton College, Oxford; held living of Weobley; ejected, 1662; kept school at Abergavenny; received living of Blakeney in parish of Awre, Gloucestershire, from which he was subsequently suspended; published religious poems. [v. 36]

BILLINGTON, ELIZABETH (1768–1818), singer; daughter of Carl Weichsel, a native of Freiberg, Saxony, principal oboist at the King's Theatre; studied music under her father and Schroeter; appeared at concert at Oxford, 1782; married James Billington, double bass player at Drury Lane, 1783; engaged at Covent Garden, 1786; received lessons from Sacchini at Paris, 1786, and later from Morelli, Paer, and Himmel; sang at Covent Garden, the concerts of ancient music, the oratorios, and Handel commemorations, till 1793; travelled on continent, where, on her husband's death, she married M.

Felissent, a Frenchman, 1799; appeared, on alternate nights, at Covent Garden and Drury Lane, 1801; sang at King's Theatre in Italian opera, 1802 till 1811, when she retired; one of England's greatest singers. [v. 37]

BILLINGTON, THOMAS (*d.* 1832), harpsichord and singing master; brother-in-law of Elizabeth Billington [q. v.]; member of Royal Society of Musicians, 1777; published instrumental and other musical compositions. [v. 39]

BILLINGTON, WILLIAM (1827–1884), dialect writer; employed in cotton mills at Blackburn; published verse and prose writings in Lancashire dialect. [v. 40]

BILNEY or **BYLNEY**, THOMAS (*d.* 1531), martyr; educated at Trinity Hall, Cambridge; LL.B.; gained friendship of Matthew Parker and Latimer; licensed to preach throughout diocese of Ely, 1525, and delivered many sermons against prayers to saints and image worship; arrested at instance of Wolsey and confined in Tower, 1527; persuaded to recant and released, 1529; preached in Norfolk, 1531; apprehended and subsequently burned at Bishopsgate. He maintained a consistent orthodoxy, after mediæval standards, on the power of the pope and of the church, the sacrifice of the mass, and the doctrine of transubstantiation. [v. 40]

BILSON, THOMAS (1547–1616), bishop of Winchester; educated at Winchester and New College, Oxford; M.A., 1570; D.D., 1581; prebendary of Winchester, and warden of Winchester College, 1576; bishop of Worcester, 1596, and of Winchester, 1597; published religious works. [v. 43]

BINCKES, WILLIAM (*d.* 1712), dean of Lichfield; B.A. St. John's College, Cambridge, 1674; fellow of Peterhouse; M.A., 1678; prebendary of Lincoln, 1683, and of Lichfield, 1697; D.D., 1699; dean of Lichfield, 1703. [v. 44]

BINDLEY, CHARLES, known as HARRY HIEOVER (1795–1859), sporting writer; published works on sporting subjects, including a revised and corrected edition of Delabere Blaine's 'Encyclopædia of Rural Sports,' 1852. [v. 45]

BINDLEY, JAMES (1737–1818), book collector; educated at Charterhouse and Peterhouse, Cambridge; M.A., 1762; commissioner of stamp duties, 1765; senior commissioner, 1781–1818; F.S.A., 1765; formed valuable collection of rare books, engravings, and medals. [v. 45]

BINDON, FRANCIS (*d.* 1765), painter and architect; executed portraits of Swift, Richard Baldwin [q. v.], and other eminent Irishmen; retired, *c.* 1750. [v. 46]

BINGHAM, GEORGE (1715–1800), divine; educated at Westminster and Christ Church, Oxford; fellow of All Souls; M.A., 1739; B.D., 1748; proctor, 1745–6; rector of Pimperne, Dorsetshire, 1748; proctor for diocese of Salisbury in convocations of 1761, 1768, 1774, and 1780. He assisted the Rev. John Hutchins in compiling his 'History of Dorsetshire,' and published religious works. [v. 46]

BINGHAM, GEORGE CHARLES, third EARL OF LUCAN (1800–1888), field-marshal; educated at Westminster; ensign, 1816; lieutenant, 1820; major, 1825; and lieutenant-colonel, 1826–37, 17th lancers; M.P. for co. Mayo, 1826–30; succeeded to earldom, 1839; elected representative peer of Ireland, 1840; lord-lieutenant of Mayo, 1845; major-general, 1851; commanded cavalry division in army in Turkey, 1854; directed charge of heavy brigade at Balaclava, and followed light brigade with two regiments of the heavy brigade to cover its retirement; censured by Lord Raglan and recalled, 1855; K.C.B. and colonel of 8th hussars, 1855; lieutenant-general, 1858; general, 1865; colonel of 1st life guards, 1865; G.C.B., 1869; field-marshal, 1887. [Suppl. i. 196]

BINGHAM, SIR GEORGE RIDOUT (1777–1833), major-general; ensign in Corsica, 1793; served in Cape and in Kaffir war, 1800; major, 1801; lieutenant-colonel of 2nd battalion 53rd foot in Ireland, 1805; in Peninsula, 1809–14; knighted; brigadier-general in St. Helena till 1819; commanded Cork district, 1827–32. [v. 47]

BINGHAM, JOHN (1607–1689), nonconformist divine; educated at St. John's College, Cambridge; head-master in free school, Derby; vicar of Marston-upon-Dove, Derbyshire; ejected, 1662, subsequently suffering considerable persecution; assisted Walton with his great polyglot bible. [v. 47]

BINGHAM, JOSEPH (1668–1723), divine; B.A. University College, Oxford, 1688; fellow, 1689; withdrew from university, being unjustly charged with preaching impious and heretical doctrines, 1695; collated to living of Havant, 1712; lost money in South Sea Bubble; published 'Origines Ecclesiasticæ,' or 'Antiquities of the Christian Church,' 10 vols., 1708–22, and other works relating to ecclesiastical history and doctrine.   [v. 48]

BINGHAM, MARGARET, COUNTESS OF LUCAN (*d.* 1814), amateur painter; married, 1760, Sir Charles Bingham (created Earl of Lucan, 1795); spent many years in embellishment of Shakespeare's historical plays. Her miniatures were extravagantly praised by Horace Walpole.   [v. 50]

BINGHAM, PEREGRINE, the elder (1754–1826), biographer and poet; B.C.L. New College, Oxford, 1780; rector of Berwick St. John, Wiltshire, 1817; published memoirs of his father, George Bingham [q. v.]   [v. 51]

BINGHAM, PEREGRINE, the younger (1788–1864), legal writer; son of Peregrine Bingham (1754–1826) [q. v.]; B.A. Magdalen College, Oxford, 1810; called to bar at Middle Temple, 1818; for many years legal reporter; published legal works.   [v. 51]

BINGHAM or **BYNGHAM**, SIR RICHARD (1528–1599), governor of Connaught; served in Scotland under Somerset, 1547, at St. Quentin, 1557, in expedition against Out-isles of Scotland, 1558, under Don John of Austria against Turks, in conquest of Cyprus, 1572, in Low Countries, 1573, and under Dutch flag against Spaniards, 1578; knighted and appointed governor of Connaught, 1584; rigorously suppressed Connaught rebellion, 1586; temporarily recalled to take part in war in Netherlands, 1587–8; repressed O'Rourke's revolt, 1590–1; imprisoned in Fleet on charge of exercising undue severity, 1596; returned to Ireland as marshal, 1598.   [v. 52]

BINGHAM, RICHARD, the elder (1765–1858), divine; educated at Winchester and New College, Oxford; B.A., 1787; D.C.L., 1801; prebendary of Chichester, 1807; imprisoned at Winchester for fraud, 1813, and published vehement protestation of innocence; issued, 1829, third edition of 'Origines Ecclesiasticæ,' published by his ancestor, Joseph Bingham [q. v.]   [v. 53]

BINGHAM, RICHARD, the younger (1798–1872), divine; son of Richard Bingham (1765–1858) [q. v.]; M.A. Magdalen Hall, Oxford, 1827; vicar of Queenborough, isle of Sheppey, 1856–70; published writings relating to liturgical revision, and an edition of works of Joseph Bingham [q. v.]   [v. 54]

BINGLEY, BARON (1676–1731). [See BENSON, ROBERT.]

BINGLEY, WILLIAM (1774–1823), miscellaneous writer; M.A. St. Peter's College, Cambridge, 1803; minister of Fitzroy chapel, Charlotte Street, London, 1816–23; F.L.S.; published works on various subjects, including topography and natural history.   [v. 55]

BINHAM or **BYNHAM**, SIMON (*fl.* 1335), chronicler; monk of priory of Binham, Norfolk; assisted in opposing exactions of Hugh, abbot (1308–26) of St. Albans; said to have contributed to 'Chronicle of Rishanger.'   [v. 56]

BINHAM or **BYNHAM**, WILLIAM (*fl.* 1370), prior of Wallingford; D.D. Oxford, where he was for a time intimate with Wycliffe, against whom he afterwards wrote 'Contra Positiones Wiclevi.'   [v. 56]

BINNEMAN, HENRY (*d.* 1583). [See BYNNEMAN, HENRY.]

BINNEY, EDWARD WILLIAM (1812–1881), geologist; practised as solicitor in Manchester from 1836; a founder and first honorary secretary of Manchester Geological Society; president, 1857–9 and 1865–7; member of London Geological Society, 1853; F.R.S., 1856; wrote many papers on geological subjects, of which Sigillaria was among the most important.   [v. 56]

BINNEY, THOMAS (1798–1874), nonconformist divine; apprenticed to a Newcastle bookseller; studied at theological seminary at Wymondley, Hertfordshire; pastor of St. James's Street chapel, Newport, Isle of Wight, 1824, and congregation at Weigh House, London, 1829–69;

acquired high reputation as preacher; visited Australia, 1857; LL.D. Aberdeen, 1852; on two occasions he was elected chairman of the Congregational Union of England and Wales; wrote polemical works and verse of a religious character.   [v. 57]

BINNING, LORD (1697–1733). [See HAMILTON, CHARLES.]

BINNING, HUGH (1627–1653), Scottish divine; M.A. Glasgow; professor of philosophy, 1647–51; licensed minister; called to parish of Govan, near Glasgow, 1649; ordained, 1650; sided with protesters against resolutioners, and took prominent part in dispute before Cromwell at Glasgow, 1651; published religious works.   [v. 59]

BINNS, SIR HENRY (1837–1899), prime minister of Natal; went to Natal, 1858; conducted sugar estate at Riet River, 1860, and floated, 1868, Umhlanga Valley Sugar Estate Company, of which he was general manager till 1892; nominee member of legislative council, 1879, and was member for Victoria county, 1883–99; prime minister of Natal, 1897; colonial secretary and minister of agriculture, 1897, but soon resigned latter portfolio; advocated and (1898) brought about entrance of Natal into South African customs union; K.C.M.G., 1898.   [Suppl. i. 198]

BINNS, JOHN (1772–1860), journalist and politician; engaged as plumber in London, 1794; member of London Corresponding Company; connected with schemes of United Irishmen; in prison, 1798–1801; went to America, 1801; edited successively 'Republican Argus' and 'Democratic Press.'   [v. 60]

BINYON, EDWARD (1830?–1876), landscape painter; contributed to exhibitions of Royal Academy and Dudley Gallery, 1857–76.   [v. 61]

BIONDI, SIR GIOVANNI FRANCESCO (1572–1644), historian; born at Lesina, in Gulf of Venice; secretary to Venetian ambassador at Paris; came to England, 1609; represented James I at Calvinist assembly, Grenoble, 1615; knighted, 1622; gentleman of king's privy chamber; died at Aubonne, Switzerland; published in Italian at Venice three romances and a work on the Wars of the Roses, which all appeared in English translations.   [v. 61]

BIRCH, CHARLES BELL (1832–1893), sculptor, son of Jonathan Birch [q. v.]; studied at school of design, Somerset House, and at Royal academies, Berlin and London; assistant to John Henry Foley [q v.]; won premium from Art Union of London for 'Wood Nymph,' 1864; exhibited at Burlington House from 1864; A.R.A., 1880; produced bronze 'Griffin' on Temple Bar memorial, Fleet Street, 1880; his works include a statue of Lord Beaconsfield at Liverpool, and statues of Queen Victoria at Aberdeen and Oodeypore, India.   [Suppl. i. 199]

BIRCH, JAMES (*fl.* 1759–1795), heresiarch; watchmotion maker in London; joined Muggletonians, *c.* 1759, but rejected part of their doctrine, 1772; began to claim personal inspiration, 1778; published theological works.   [v. 62]

BIRCH, JOHN (1616–1691), presbyterian colonel; merchant in Bristol; after surrender of Bristol to royalists, levied regiment in London and served as colonel under Sir William Waller; wounded at Arundel; present at battle of Alresford, blockade of Oxford, and skirmish at Cropredy Bridge; entrusted with care of Bath; assisted in assault on Bristol, 1645, which, later, was given into his charge; took Hereford and became its governor; M.P. for Leominster; opposed extreme measures of Cromwellians; imprisoned at Hereford, 1654–5; took prominent part in Restoration; member of council of state, 1660; auditor of excise; M.P. for Leominster in Convention parliament, Penrhyn, 1671–8, and for Weobly, 1678–91.   [v. 62]

BIRCH, JOHN (1745?–1815), surgeon; served as surgeon in army, and afterwards settled in London; surgeon to St. Thomas's Hospital, 1784–1815; surgeon extraordinary to prince regent; advocated use of electricity as a remedial agent, and opposed introduction of vaccination; published medical works.   [v. 64]

BIRCH, JONATHAN (1783–1847), translator of 'Faust'; in office of John Argelander, a timber merchant at Memel (with whom, in 1807, the three eldest sons of Frederick William III of Prussia took refuge), 1803–12;

returned to England, 1812 ; on terms of close intimacy with Frederick William IV of Prussia ; published several works, including translations of Goethe's 'Faust,' 1839–43, and the 'Nibelungen Lied,' 1848.   [v. 65]

BIRCH, PETER (1652 ?–1710), divine ; educated at Cambridge and Christ Church, Oxford ; M.A., 1674 ; D.D., 1688 ; successively curate of St. Thomas's, Oxford, rector of St. Ebbe's Church and lecturer at Carfax ; chaplain to James, duke of Ormonde ; chaplain to House of Commons and prebendary of Westminster, 1689 ; rector of St. James's, Westminster, 1692, but was removed owing, probably, to his high church principles, which were offensive to the court ; vicar of St. Bride's, Fleet Street, 1695 ; published sermons.   [v. 66]

BIRCH, SIR RICHARD JAMES HOLWELL (1803–1875), general ; ensign, Bengal infantry, 1821 ; judge-advocate-general to Bengal forces, 1841 ; C.B., 1849 ; secretary to Indian military department, 1852 ; colonel, 1854 ; major-general, 1858 ; K.C.B., 1860 ; lieutenant-general, 1862.   [v. 67]

BIRCH, SAMUEL (1757–1841), dramatist ; pastry-cook in Cornhill ; common councillor, 1781 ; alderman of Candlewick ward, 1807–40 ; sheriff, 1811 ; lord mayor, 1814 ; wrote poems and musical dramas, of which the 'Adopted Child' (1795) was the most successful. [v. 67]

BIRCH, SAMUEL (1813–1885), egyptologist ; grandson of Samuel Birch [q. v.] ; educated at Merchant Taylors' School, where he studied Chinese ; entered service of commissioners of public records, 1834 ; assistant in department of antiquities in British Museum, 1836, and was assistant-keeper, 1844–61 ; studied egyptology, and quickly established importance of Champollion's system of decipherment of Egyptian ; keeper of oriental, British, and mediæval antiquities at British Museum, 1861, and, from 1866 till death, of oriental antiquities alone ; founded Society of Biblical Archæology, 1870, and was president, 1870–85 ; LL.D. Aberdeen, 1862, and Cambridge, 1875 ; D.C.L. Oxford, 1876 ; honorary fellow of Queen's College, Oxford ; Rede lecturer at Cambridge, 1875 ; he published translations from oriental writings and archæological, egyptological, and other treatises, besides popular educational works on Egyptian language and history.   [Suppl. i. 199]

BIRCH, THOMAS (1705–1766), divine ; rector of Ulting, Essex, 1732, Llandewi-Velfrey, Pembroke (a sinecure), 1743, Siddington, near Cirencester, 1744, St. Michael, Wood Street, London, 1744, St. Margaret Pattens, London, 1746–66, and Depden, Suffolk, 1761–6 ; D.D. Marischal College, Aberdeen, and of Lambeth, 1753 ; F.R.S. and F.S.A., 1735 ; secretary of Royal Society, 1752–65 ; bequeathed historical and biographical manuscripts to the British Museum ; published historical works and contributed to 'General Dictionary, Historical and Critical' (1734–41).   [v. 68]

BIRCH, THOMAS LEDLIE (d. 1808), Irish presbyterian divine ; minister of Saintfield, 1776 ; went to America after insurrection of 1798, with which he was connected ; published religious works.   [v. 70]

BIRCH, WILLIAM (1755–1834), enamel painter and engraver ; practised after 1794 in Philadelphia ; received Society of Arts medal, 1785.   [v. 70]

BIRCHENSHA, JOHN (fl. 1664–1672), musician ; lived in family of Earl of Kildare, and afterwards taught the viol in London ; prepared notes for a work on the mathematical basis of music.   [v. 70]

BIRCHINGTON, STEPHEN (fl. 1382), historical writer ; monk of Christ Church, Canterbury, 1382 ; treasurer and warden of manors of the monastery ; wrote historical works.   [v. 71]

BIRCHLEY, WILLIAM (1613–1669). [See AUSTIN, JOHN.]

BIRCKBEK, SIMON (1584–1656), divine ; B.A. Queen's College, Oxford, 1604 ; B.D., 1616 ; vicar of Gilling, and of Forcet, near Richmond, Yorkshire, 1617 ; published religious works.   [v. 71]

BIRD, CHARLES SMITH (1795–1862), divine ; articled as conveyancing solicitor, Liverpool, 1812 ; scholar of Trinity College, Cambridge, 1818 ; fellow, 1820 ; took pupils, among whom was Lord Macaulay ; vicar of

Gainsborough, and prebendary of Lincoln, 1843 ; chancellor of Lincoln Cathedral, 1859 ; F.L.S., 1828 ; published poems and theological works.   [v. 71]

BIRD, EDWARD (1772–1819), painter ; conducted a drawing school at Bristol ; first exhibited at Royal Academy, 1809 ; awarded premium by British Institution for 'Death of Eli' ; R.A., 1815 ; court painter to Queen Charlotte. 'The Field of Chevy Chace' is considered his greatest work.   [v. 72]

BIRD, FRANCIS (1667–1731), sculptor ; studied at Brussels and Rome, and under Gibbons and Cibber, to whose practice he succeeded ; employed in decorations of St. Paul's Cathedral ; his best work is the statue of Dr. Busby in Westminster Abbey.   [v. 73]

BIRD, GOLDING (1814–1854), physician ; studied at Guy's Hospital, 1832 ; licensed, without examination, to practise as apothecary, 1836 ; M.D. St. Andrews, 1838 ; M.A., 1840 ; L.C.P., London, 1840 ; F.C.P., 1845 ; lecturer on natural philosophy at Guy's Hospital, 1836–53 ; physician to Finsbury dispensary ; assistant physician to Guy's, 1843–53 ; lecturer on materia medica, College of Physicians, 1847 ; F.R.S., and member of Linnean and Geological societies ; published 'Elements of Natural Philosophy,' 1839, and medical works.   [v. 74]

BIRD, JAMES (1788–1839), dramatist and poetical writer ; apprenticed as miller but abandoned the trade for that of stationer, 1820 ; wrote two plays which were produced with some success, and some narrative poems.   [v. 75]

BIRD, JOHN (d. 1558), bishop ; Carmelite friar ; B.D. Oxford, 1510 ; D.D., 1513 ; provincial of his order, 1516–19, and 1522–5 ; suffragan to bishop of Llandaff, with title of bishop of Penrith, 1537 ; accompanied Wotton on embassy to Germany, 1539 ; bishop of Bangor, 1539, and of Chester, 1541 ; deprived of his bishopric on account of his being married, 1554 ; suffragan to Bonner, bishop of London, 1554 ; left religious writings in manuscript.   [v. 76]

BIRD, JOHN (1709–1776), mathematical instrument maker ; employed by Sisson, in London, in making mathematical instruments, 1740 ; carried on business independently in Strand, 1745 ; acquired considerable fame by making instruments of improved accuracy for the astronomer Bradley ; constructed brass mural quadrant for Greenwich Observatory, 1750, and for several continental observatories ; published treatises describing his methods of working.   [v. 77]

BIRD, RICHARD (d. 1609), canon of Canterbury ; B.D. Trinity College, Cambridge, 1569 ; fellow ; M.A., 1572 ; D.D., 1608 ; archdeacon of Cleveland, 1589 ; canon of Canterbury, 1590.   [v. 77]

BIRD, ROBERT MERTTINS (1788–1853), Bengal civil servant ; commissioner of revenue and circuit for Gorakhpur division, 1829 ; member of board of revenue, 1832 ; successfully conducted settlement of revenue of north-west provinces, 1833–41 ; returned to England, 1842.   [v. 78]

BIRD, SAMUEL (fl. 1600), divine ; M.A. Queens' College, Cambridge, 1573 ; fellow, Corpus Christi College, 1573–6 ; minister of St. Peter's, Ipswich, c. 1580–1604 ; incorporated M.A. Oxford, 1605 ; published religious works.   [v. 79]

BIRD, WILLIAM (1538 ?–1623). [See BYRD.]

BIRDSALL, JOHN AUGUSTINE (1775–1837), Benedictine ; joined Benedictines at Lamspringe, Hanover, 1795 ; priest, 1801 ; came to England on suppression of abbey, 1803 ; established catholic mission at Cheltenham, 1810, and at Broadway, Worcestershire, 1828 ; provincial of Canterbury, 1822 ; re-elected, 1826 ; president-general of Benedictines in England, and cathedral prior of Winchester, 1826 ; abbot of Westminster, 1830.   [iv. 79]

BIRINUS, SAINT (d. 650), first bishop of Dorchester ; Benedictine monk of Rome ; landed in Wessex, 634 ; made many converts to Christianity ; bishop of Dorchester, 635.   [v. 80]

BIRKBECK, GEORGE (1776–1841), founder of mechanics' institutions ; M.D. Edinburgh, 1799 ; professor of natural philosophy, Andersonian University, Glasgow, 1799 ; established, 1800, for working men at Glasgow, cheap courses of lectures on science, which developed into the 'Glasgow Mechanics' Institution,' 1823 ; practised as physician in London ; founder and first president of Birk-beck Mechanics' Institution, London, 1824 ; founder and councillor of University College, London, 1827.　[v. 80]

BIRKENHEAD or **BERKENHEAD**, SIR JOHN (1616–1679), author of 'Mercurius Aulicus'; M.A. Oriel College, Oxford, 1639 ; probationer-fellow, All Souls' College, 1640 ; devised and mostly wrote 'Mercurius Aulicus,' the weekly journal of royalists at Oxford, 1642–5 ; in exile with Prince Charles, 1648 ; probably knighted at St. Germains, 1649 ; D.C.L., 1661 ; M.P. for Wilton ; member of Royal Society ; one of masters of requests ; published satirical poems.　[iv. 81]

BIRKENSHAW, JOHN (*fl.* 1664–1672). [See BIRCHENSHA.]

BIRKHEAD or **BIRKET**, GEORGE (*d.* 1614), arch-priest ; educated at Douay and Rome ; ordained, 1577 ; joined English mission, 1580 ; archpriest of England, 1608–14.　[v. 83]

BIRKHEAD, HENRY (1617 ?–1696), Latin poet ; scholar, Trinity College, Oxford, 1635 ; studied at St. Omer ; B.A. : fellow of All Souls', 1638–57 ; M.A., 1641 ; registrar of diocese of Norwich, 1660–81 ; published poems in Latin and left in manuscript an allegorical play ; professorship of poetry at Oxford founded in 1708 from funds left by him.　[v. 83]

BIRKS, THOMAS RAWSON (1810–1883), divine and philosopher ; second wrangler and second Smith's prize-man, Trinity College, Cambridge, 1834 ; fellow ; vicar of Trinity Church, Cambridge, 1866–77 ; honorary canon of Ely, 1871 ; professor of moral philosophy, Cambridge, 1872. His works include 'The Bible and Modern Thought,' 1861, and 'Modern Utilitarianism,' 1874.　[v. 84]

BIRMINGHAM, JOHN (1816–1884), astronomer ; re-vised Schjellerup's 'Catalogue of Red Stars,' 1872 ; dis-covered a deep red star in Cygnus, which became known by his name, 1881 ; inspector under board of works.　[v. 85]

BIRNIE, ALEXANDER (1826–1862), poet and jour-nalist ; baptist minister at Preston ; painter at Falkirk ; joined staff of 'Falkirk Advertiser' ; started 'Falkirk Liberal,' which was unsuccessful ; made his way on foot to Edinburgh and thence to Newcastle, and died of starva-tion at Morpeth.　[v. 86]

BIRNIE, SIR RICHARD (1760 ?–1832), police magis-trate ; partner in an extensive saddler and harness-maker's business in Haymarket, London ; police magis-trate at Union Hall and subsequently at Bow Street ; knighted, 1821.　[v. 86]

BIRNIE, WILLIAM (1563–1619), Scottish divine ; M.A. St. Leonard's College, St. Andrews, 1588 ; became shipmaster merchant ; vicar of Lanark, 1597 ; master and economus of St. Leonard's hospital and almshouse, 1603 ; dean of Chapel Royal, 1612 ; constant moderator of presbytery, 1606 ; member of high commission court, 1610 and 1615.　[v. 87]

BIRNSTAN (*d.* 933). [See BYRNSTAN.]

BIRREL, ROBERT (*fl.* 1567–1605), diarist ; burgess of Edinburgh ; wrote a diary, 1532–1605, published in 'Fragments of Scottish History,' 1798.　[v. 88]

BISBY or **BISBIE**, NATHANIEL (1635–1695), divine ; M.A. Christ Church, Oxford, 1660 ; D.D., 1668 ; rector of Long Melford, 1660 ; deprived as nonjuror, 1690 ; wrote against nonconformists.　[v. 88]

BISCHOFF, JAMES (1776–1845), author of works on the wool trade ; connected with woollen trade in Leeds, and subsequently carried on business as merchant and insurance broker in London ; published works aiming at reform in laws relating to wool.　[v. 88]

BISCOE, JOHN (*d.* 1679), puritan divine ; B.A. New Inn Hall, Oxford, 1627 ; minister of St. Thomas's, South-wark ; ejected, 1660 ; published religious works. [v. 89]

BISCOE, RICHARD (*d.* 1748), divine ; dissenting minister of meeting-house in Old Jewry, 1716 ; conformed and became rector of St. Martin Outwich, London, 1727 ; chaplain to George II ; Boyle lecturer, 1736–8 ; published lectures, 1742.　[v. 89]

BISHOP, ANN (1814–1884), soprano singer ; *née* Rivière ; student of Royal Academy of Music, 1824–31 ; married Sir Henry Rowley Bishop [q. v.], 1831 ; took prominent place at Vauxhall ; eloped with Bochsa, the harp-player, 1839 ; travelled and sang in European towns, 1839–46, in England, 1846–7, America, 1847, and Aus-tralia, 1855 ; died at New York.　[v. 89]

BISHOP, GEORGE (1785–1861), astronomer ; pro-prietor of a wine-making business in London ; admitted to Royal Astronomical Society, 1830 ; secretary, 1833–9 ; treasurer, 1840–57 : president, 1857 and 1858 ; F.R.S., 1848 ; fellow of Society of Arts ; on council of University College, London ; erected, 1836, an observatory near his residence at South Villa, Regent's Park, where Rev. William Dawes and John Russell Hind conducted many important investigations.　[v. 90]

BISHOP, SIR HENRY ROWLEY (1786–1855), musi-cal composer ; his first opera, 'The Circassian Bride,' produced at Drury Lane, 1809 ; composer and director at Covent Garden, 1810 ; produced 'Knight of Snowdoun' (founded on Scott's 'Lady of the Lake'), 1811, which was followed, in rapid succession, by other pieces, including 'Midsummer Night's Dream,' 1816, 'Comedy of Errors,' 1819, 'Antiquary,' 1820, 'Twelfth Night,' 1820, 'Henry IV Part II,' 1821, 'Two Gentlemen of Verona,' 1821, and 'As you like it,' 1824 ; original member of Philharmonic So-ciety, 1813 ; musical director of King's Theatre, Hay-market, 1816–17 ; sole manager, 1820, of the 'oratorios' given during Lent ; engaged, 1825, at Drury Lane, where he produced 'Aladdin' as counter-attraction to Weber's 'Oberon' at Covent Garden, 1826 ; wrote music for 'Faustus' in collaboration with Cooke and Horn, 1825, 'Hamlet,' 1830, 'Kenilworth' and 'Waverley,' 1832, and 'Love's Labour's Lost,' 1839, and 'Fortunate Isles' to cele-brate Queen Victoria's marriage, 1840 ; musical director at Vauxhall Gardens, 1830–3 ; Mus. Bac. Oxford, 1839 ; professor of harmony, Royal Academy of Music ; Reid Professor at Edinburgh, 1841–3 ; conducted Antient Con-certs, 1840–8 ; knighted, 1842 ; professor of music, Ox-ford, 1848 ; Mus. Doc., 1853. His fame rests almost en-tirely on his glees.　[v. 91]

BISHOP, JOHN (1665–1737), musical composer ; teacher of choristers at King's College, Cambridge, 1688 ; organist of Winchester College, 1695 ; lay-vicar, 1696, and organist and master of choristers, 1729, Winchester Cathedral ; published psalm-tunes and anthems and left compositions in manuscript.　[v. 94]

BISHOP, JOHN (1797–1873), surgeon ; studied at St. George's Hospital ; obtained diploma of Royal College of Surgeons, 1824 ; senior surgeon, Islington dispensary, and surgeon Northern and St. Pancras dispensaries ; F.R.S., *c.* 1844 ; wrote surgical works.　[v. 95]

BISHOP, SAMUEL (1731–1795), poet ; educated at Merchant Taylors' School and St. John's College, Oxford ; fellow, 1753 ; M.A., 1758 ; head-master of Merchant Taylors' School, 1783 ; rector of Ditton, Kent, and St. Martin Outwich, London ; published essays and poems.　[v. 95]

BISHOP, WILLIAM (1554–1624), catholic divine ; educated at Oxford and at English college, Rheims ; or-dained priest, 1583 ; joined English mission ; imprisoned in Marshalsea, 1583–4 ; studied at Paris ; returned to English mission, 1591 ; D.D. Paris ; sent to Rome to remonstrate against maladministration of George Black-well [q. v.], archpriest ; confined in English college ; imprisoned for refusing oath of allegiance to James I, 1611 ; on release went to Arras College, Paris ; vicar-apostolic and bishop of Chalcedon, 1623 ; came to Eng-land, 1623 ; published theological works.　[v. 96]

BISLEY, GEORGE (*d.* 1591). [See BEESLEY.]

BISSAIT or **BISSET**, BALDRED (*fl.* 1303), divine ; rector of Kinghorn ; commissioner to pope in dispute be-tween Boniface VIII, Edward I, and Scottish government. His 'Progressus contra figmenta regis Angliæ' contains earliest mention of Scottish coronation stone.　[v. 97]

BISSE, PHILIP (1667–1721), bishop of Hereford ; educated at Winchester and New College, Oxford ; M.A., 1693 ; D.D., 1705 ; F.R.S., 1706 ; bishop of St. David's, 1710, and Hereford, 1713 ; published sermons.　[v. 98]

BISSE, THOMAS (*d.* 1731), divine; younger brother of Philip Bisse [q. v.]; M.A. Corpus Christi College, Oxford, 1698; D.D., 1712; preacher at Rolls chapel, 1715; chancellor of Hereford, 1716; prebendary of Hereford, 1731; published religious works. [v. 98]

BISSET, CHARLES (1717–1791), physician and military engineer; studied medicine at Edinburgh; second surgeon of military hospital, Jamaica, 1740; served in Admiral Vernon's fleet; returned to England, 1745; ensign in 42nd Highlanders, 1746; prepared reports of progress of siege of Bergen-op-Zoom; engineer-extraordinary in engineer brigade; practised medicine at Skelton, Yorkshire; published works on fortification and on medical subjects. [v. 99]

BISSET, JAMES (1762?–1832), artist, publisher, and verse writer; established museum and curiosity shop at Birmingham; coined medals and practised as miniature and fancy painter; opened museum, news-room, and picture gallery at Leamington, 1812. His publications include 'Poetic Survey round Birmingham' (1800) and several volumes of verse. [v. 100]

BISSET, JAMES (1795–1872), scholar; educated at Marischal College and University, Aberdeen; D.D., 1851; assumed control of private school kept by his father, and developed remarkable teaching ability, 1812; minister at Bourtrie, Aberdeenshire, 1826; moderator of general assembly of church of Scotland, 1862. [v. 100]

BISSET, SIR JOHN (1777–1854), commissary-general; commissary-general in Spain, 1811; knight commander of Guelphic order, 1830; K.C.B., 1850; published a work on commissariat duties. [v. 101]

BISSET, BISSAT, or **BISSART,** PETER (*d.* 1568), professor of canon law; studied at St. Andrews, Paris, and Bologna; LL.D., and subsequently professor of canon law, Bologna; wrote two works in Latin. [v. 101]

BISSET, ROBERT (1759–1805), historian; LL.D.; master of an academy in Sloane Street, Chelsea. His works include a life of Burke (1798) and a 'History of George III' (1804). [v. 101]

BISSET, WILLIAM (*d.* 1747), divine; educated at Westminster and Trinity College, Cambridge; B.A., 1690; rector of Whiston, 1697; elder brother of St. Catherine's Collegiate Church, 1699; published, 1710, reply to Dr. Sacheverell's sermon of 5 Nov. 1709, occasioning pamphlet war to which he largely contributed; chaplain to Queen Caroline. [v. 102]

BISSET, WILLIAM (1758–1834), Irish bishop; educated at Westminster and Christ Church, Oxford; B.A., 1779; M.A., 1782; D.D.; rector of Dunbin, co. Louth, 1784; prebendary of Armagh, 1791–1807; archdeacon of Ross, 1804; chancellor of Armagh, 1817; bishop of Raphoe, 1822. [v. 102]

BIX, ANGEL (*d.* 1695), Franciscan friar; chaplain to Spanish ambassador in London in James II's reign; published sermons. [v. 103]

BIZARI, PIETRO (1530?–1586?), Italian historian and poet; adopted reformed faith and came to England; fellow, St. John's College, Cambridge, 1549; prebendary of Salisbury, 1567; published historical, poetical, and other works in Italian and Latin, and left manuscripts, which include a 'Universal History.' [v. 103]

BLAAUW, WILLIAM HENRY (1793–1870), antiquary; educated at Eton and Christ Church, Oxford; M.A., 1815; F.S.A., 1850; treasurer of Camden Society; published, 1844, history of barons' war of Henry III's reign. [v. 105]

BLACADER or **BLACKADER,** ROBERT (*d.* 1508), Scottish archbishop; prebendary of Glasgow and rector of Cardross; bishop of Aberdeen, 1480, and of Glasgow, before 1484; archbishop of Glasgow, 1492; frequently employed in public transactions with English; died in Holy Land on pilgrimage to Jerusalem. [v. 105]

BLACATER, ADAM (*fl.* 1319), born in Scotland; professor of philosophy successively in Poland and at Bologna and rector of a college in Paris University. [v. 105]

BLACHFORD, BARON (1811–1889). [See ROGERS, FREDERIC.]

BLACK, ADAM (1784–1874), politician and publisher; carried on bookselling business at Edinburgh, at first alone, and subsequently in partnership with his nephew Charles; twice lord-provost of and, 1856–65, liberal M.P. for Edinburgh. His firm acquired copyrights of 'Encyclopædia Britannica,' 1827, and Scott's novels, 1851. [v. 105]

BLACK, ALEXANDER (1789–1864), Scottish theologian; studied medicine at Aberdeen; ordained minister of Tarves, 1818; professor of divinity, Marischal College, 1832–43; accompanied expedition to the East in connection with proposed formation of mission to Jews, 1839; joined Free church, 1843; D.D. [v. 106]

BLACK, JAMES (1788?–1867), physician; L.C.S. Edinburgh, 1808; served in navy; practised successively at Manchester, 1839–48, Bolton, 1848–56, and Edinburgh; M.D. Glasgow, 1820; L.R.C.S., 1823; F.R.C.P., 1860; published medical works and papers on geological subjects. [v. 106]

BLACK, JOHN (1783–1855), journalist; employed as clerk at Dunse; in accountant's office at Edinburgh, where he studied at the university; contributed to 'Universal Magazine'; went to London, 1810; translator of foreign correspondence and reporter to 'Morning Chronicle'; became editor, 1817, and maintained the journal's position as the most uncompromising of opposition papers till 1843, when a decline of energy in its management occasioned a request for his resignation; retired to Snodland, near Maidstone; published translations from Leopold von Buch, Schlegel, and others. [v. 107]

BLACK, JOSEPH (1728–1799), chemist; studied medicine at Glasgow and at Edinburgh, where he graduated M.D. with an important thesis, 'De humore acido a cibis orto, et Magnesia alba,' which laid the foundations of quantitative analysis and pneumatic chemistry, 1754; professor of medicine, Glasgow, 1756–66; practised as physician; made investigations into the question of 'latent heat,' which formed the basis of modern thermal science, and gave the first impulse to Watt's improvements in the steam engine, 1756–62; experimented with object of testing validity of thermometrical indications, and originated theory of 'specific heat,' 1760; professor of medicine and chemistry, Edinburgh, 1766–97. He was first physician to George III for Scotland and a member of Royal Society, Edinburgh, and Royal College of Physicians. [v. 109]

BLACK, PATRICK (1813–1879), physician; educated at Eton and Christ Church, Oxford; M.D., 1836; physician to St. Bartholomew's Hospital, 1860; lecturer on medicine; F.C.P.; published medical treatises. [v. 112]

BLACK, ROBERT (1752–1817), Irish presbyterian divine; educated at Glasgow; ordained minister of Dromore, 1777; captain of Irish volunteers, 1782; joint-minister at Derry, 1784; synod agent for *regium donum*, 1788–1817; D.D.; strongly advocated catholic emancipation and parliamentary reform, and was the friend and correspondent of Castlereagh; committed suicide from disappointment at lack of success of his opposition to establishment of Belfast Academical Institution (opened 1814). [v. 112]

BLACK, WILLIAM (1749–1829), physician; M.D. Leyden, 1772; L.C.P., 1787; practised in London; one of the first Englishman who published (1788) statistics of diseases and mortality. [v. 113]

BLACK, WILLIAM (1841–1898), novelist; studied art at Glasgow; became contributor to 'Glasgow Citizen'; came to London, 1864, and was connected, 1865, with 'Morning Star,' for which paper he was war correspondent during Franco-Prussian war, 1866; subsequently sub-editor of 'Daily News.' His novels include 'A Daughter of Heth,' 1871, 'The Strange Adventures of a Phaeton,' 1872, and 'A Princess of Thule,' 1874.
[Suppl. i. 202]

BLACK, WILLIAM HENRY (1808–1872), antiquary; assistant keeper in Public Record Office. He was a prolific writer on antiquarian subjects. [v. 114]

BLACKADDER, ADAM (*fl.* 1674–1696), covenanter, son of John Blackadder the elder [q. v.]; apprenticed as merchant at Stirling; repeatedly imprisoned for Calvinistic principles; retired to Sweden, and subsequently settled in Edinburgh; wrote narrative of his father's sufferings. [v. 114]

BLACKADDER, JOHN, the elder (1615–1686), Scottish divine; M.A. Glasgow, 1650; called to parish of Troqueer, 1652; ordained, 1653; ejected by episcopal party and imprisoned at Edinburgh, 1662; preached in conventicles and was outlawed, 1674; fled to Rotterdam, 1678; returned to Edinburgh, 1679; arrested, 1681, and imprisoned on Bass Rock, where he died. [v. 115]

BLACKADDER, JOHN, the younger (1664–1729), lieutenant-colonel; son of John Blackadder (1615–1686) [q. v.]; educated at Edinburgh; served in Cameronian regiment against highlanders at Dunkeld, under Prince of Orange in Flanders, and in Marlborough's campaigns; promoted to command of regiment, 1709; sold commission; fought at Stirling, 1715; deputy governor of Stirling Castle, 1717. [v. 115]

BLACKADDER, WILLIAM (1647–1704), physician; brother of John Blackadder (1664–1729) [q. v.]; educated at Edinburgh; M.D. Leyden, 1680; accompanied Earl of Argyle in expedition to Scotland, 1685; apprehended and imprisoned; on liberation retired to Holland; conducted secret negotiations for Prince of Orange in Edinburgh, 1688; physician to William III. [v. 116]

BLACKADER, CUTHBERT, or more correctly ROBERT (d. 1485), Scottish border chieftain; fought for Lancastrians in Wars of the Roses; killed at Bosworth. [v. 116]

BLACKADER, ROBERT (d. 1508). [See BLACADER.]

BLACKALL, JOHN (1771–1860), physician; M.A. Balliol College, Oxford, 1796; M.D., 1801; studied at St. Bartholomew's Hospital; physician to Devon and Exeter Hospital, 1797; resigned, 1801; reappointed, 1807; physician to St. Thomas's lunatic asylum, 1812; published 'Observations on Nature and Cure of Dropsies,' 1813; F.C.P., 1815. [v. 117]

BLACKALL or **BLACKHALL**, OFFSPRING (1654–1716), bishop of Exeter; educated at St. Catharine Hall, Cambridge; rector of St. Mary, Aldermary, London, 1694; chaplain to William III; Boyle lecturer, 1700; bishop of Exeter, 1708; renowned as a preacher; published sermons and controversial pamphlets. [v. 117]

BLACKALL, SAMUEL (d. 1792), divine; grandson of Offspring Blackall [q. v.]; M.A. Emmanuel College, Cambridge, 1763; B.D., 1770; fellow and tutor; rector of Loughborough, 1786–92; published sermons and controversial pamphlets. [v. 118]

BLACKBOURNE, JOHN (1683–1741), nonjuror; M.A. Trinity College, Cambridge, 1705; consecrated by 'King James III' bishop of nonjurors, 1725; member of the section of nonjurors known as 'nonusagers.' His publications include an edition of Bacon's works (1730). [v. 119]

BLACKBURN, COLIN, BARON BLACKBURN (1813–1896), judge; educated at Eton and Trinity College, Cambridge; M.A., 1838; honorary LL.D. Edinburgh, 1870; called to bar at Inner Temple, 1838; honorary bencher, 1877; joined northern circuit; appointed justice of queen's bench, and invested with coif, 1859; knighted, 1860; justice of high court, 1875; raised to peerage, 1876; privy councillor, 1876; retired, 1886; served on several royal commissions; published legal writings. [Suppl. i. 203]

BLACKBURN, WILLIAM (1750–1790), surveyor and architect; studied at Royal Academy; obtained highest premium in competition for penitentiary houses, 1782, and subsequently executed designs for prisons and other structures throughout the country. [v. 120]

BLACKBURNE, ANNA (d. 1794), botanist; friend and correspondent of Linnæus. [v. 121]

BLACKBURNE, FRANCIS (1705–1787), divine; educated at St. Catharine Hall, Cambridge; rector of Richmond, Yorkshire, 1739–87; prebendary of York; published 'The Confessional,' 1766, controversial works, and memoirs of Thomas Hollis [q. v.] [v. 121]

BLACKBURNE, FRANCIS (1782–1867), Irish lawyer; educated at Trinity College, Dublin; studied at King's Inn, Dublin, and Lincoln's Inn, London; called to bar, 1805; joined home circuit; administered Insurrection Act on its renewal, 1822, in Limerick; serjeant, 1826; attorney-general for Ireland, 1830–4 and 1841; master of rolls in Ireland, 1842; chief-justice of queen's bench, 1846; lord chancellor of Ireland, 1852, and resigned the same year; commissioner of national education, 1852; lord justice of appeal in Ireland, 1856; reappointed lord chancellor, but resigned, 1866; vice-chancellor of Dublin University. [v. 122]

BLACKBURNE, JOHN (1690–1786), botanist; maintained extensive garden at Orford. [v. 123]

BLACKBURNE, LANCELOT (1658–1743), archbishop of York; educated at Westminster and Christ Church, Oxford; ordained, 1681; M.A., 1683; prebendary of Exeter, 1691, and sub-dean, 1695; rector of Calstock, Cornwall, 1696; resigned sub-deanery, 1702; reinstated, 1704; dean of Exeter, 1705; bishop of Exeter, 1717–24; archbishop of York, 1724–43. [v. 123]

BLACKBURNE, RICHARD (b. 1652), physician; B.A. Trinity College, Cambridge, 1669; M.D. Leyden, 1676; F.R.C.P., 1687; censor, College of Physicians, 1688; probably wrote 'Thomæ Hobbes Angli Malmesburiensis Philosophi Vita,' sometimes attributed to Hobbes himself, and certainly wrote a supplement to it. [v. 124]

BLACKBURNE, SIR WILLIAM (1764–1839), major-general; infantry cadet in Madras army, 1782; Mahratta interpreter at Tanjore, 1787; captain, 1801; resident at Tanjore, 1801–23; major-general; knighted, 1838. [v. 125]

BLACKER, GEORGE (1791–1871), antiquary; M.A. Trinity College, Dublin, 1858; vicar of Maynooth, 1840; prebendary in St. Patrick's Cathedral; published (privately) antiquarian works. [v. 125]

BLACKER, VALENTINE (1778–1823), lieutenant-colonel; obtained commission in Madras cavalry, 1798; cornet, 1799; aide-de-camp to Colonel Stevenson in Wainâd, 1800; quartermaster-general, 1810; served in Deccan, 1817; lieutenant-colonel; surveyor-general of India; C.B., 1818; published history of Mahratta war. [v. 125]

BLACKERBY, RICHARD (1574–1648), puritan; M.A. Trinity College, Cambridge; minister at Feltwell, Norfolk; taught classics and theology to private pupils at Ashdon, Essex; minister at Great Thurlow. [v. 126]

BLACKET, JOSEPH (1786–1810), poet; apprenticed to his brother, a shoemaker, in London, 1797; suffered much from poverty, but gained patrons and achieved some reputation as a poet. A volume of his poetry was published in 1809, and his 'Remains,' containing poems and dramatic sketches, in 1811. [v. 126]

BLACKHALL, GILBERT (fl. 1667), Scottish catholic; entered Scots College, Rome, 1626; ordained; returned to Scotland, 1630; fled from jesuit opposition to Paris; missionary in Scotland, 1637–43; wrote autobiography in Paris, c. 1666. [v. 127]

BLACKHALL, OFFSPRING (1654–1716). [See BLACKALL.]

BLACKIE, JOHN STUART (1809–1895), Scottish professor and man of letters; educated at Marischal College, Aberdeen, Edinburgh University, Göttingen, and Berlin; studied for Scottish bar; advocate, 1834; appointed first regius professor of humanity (Latin) at Marischal College, Aberdeen, 1839, and installed, 1841; instituted 'Hellenic Society,' Aberdeen, 1850; professor of Greek at Edinburgh, 1852–82; founded and endowed Celtic chair at Edinburgh, 1882. His publications include 'Faust... translated into English Verse,' 1834; 'Lyrical Dramas of Æschylus... translated into English Verse,' 1850, 'Lays and Legends of Ancient Greece,' 1857, and many other works in verse and prose. [Suppl. i. 204]

BLACKLOCK, THOMAS (1721–1791), poet; born of humble parents; lost his sight when six months old; began to write poetry when twelve years old, and was noticed by Dr. Stevenson, a physician of Edinburgh, where he studied at the university; made the acquaintance of David Hume, who exerted himself in his behalf; minister at Kirkcudbright, c. 1762–4; took private pupils in Edinburgh; D.D. Marischal College, Aberdeen, 1767; published poems, religious works, and translations. [v. 127]

BLACKLOCK, WILLIAM JAMES (1815?–1858), landscape painter; apprenticed as bookseller at Carlisle; adopted art as profession, and exhibited at Royal Academy and other exhibitions, 1836–55. [v. 129]

BLACKLOE, THOMAS (1593-1676). [See WHITE, THOMAS.]

BLACKMAN, JOHN (*fl.* 1436-1448). [See BLAKMAN.]

BLACKMORE, CHEWNING (1663-1737), minister; son of William Blackmore [q. v.] ; minister at Worcester, 1688-1737. [v. 131]

BLACKMORE, SIR RICHARD (*d.* 1729), physician and writer; educated at Westminster and St. Edmund Hall, Oxford; M.A., 1676 ; M.D. Padua ; F.R.C.P., 1687 ; censor, College of Physicians, 1716 ; elect, 1716-22 ; physician in ordinary to William III, and knighted, 1697 ; physician to Queen Anne. He produced religious and medical treatises and some indifferent poems, including 'Creation,' 1712, which was warmly praised by Dr. Johnson. [v. 129]

BLACKMORE, RICHARD DODDRIDGE (1825-1900), novelist and barrister; educated at Blundell's school, Tiverton, and Exeter College, Oxford; M.A., 1852 ; engaged as private tutor; called to bar at Middle Temple, 1852 ; practised as conveyancer; classical master at Wellesley House school, Twickenham Common, 1853 ; published 'Poems by Melanter,' 1853, and, later, 'Epullia,' and other volumes of verse, including 'The Farm and Fruit of Old,' 1862 ; established himself, *c.* 1858, at Gomer House, Teddington, where he remained till death; produced 'Clara Vaughan,' 1864, 'Cradock Nowell,' 1866, 'Lorna Doone,' 1869, and twelve other novels.
[Suppl. i. 207]

BLACKMORE, THOMAS (1740 ?-1780 ?), mezzotint engraver; practised in London, 1769-71. His works include plates after pictures by Reynolds and Vandyck. [v. 131]

BLACKMORE, WILLIAM (*d.* 1684), nonconformist divine; M.A. Lincoln College, Oxford; rector of Pentloe, Essex, 1645 ; presbyter, 1647 ; rector of St. Peter's, Cornhill, 1656 ; arrested on charge of complicity in Christopher Love's plot, but released, 1651 ; seceded with nonconformists, 1662. [v. 131]

BLACKNER, JOHN (1770-1816), historian of Nottingham ; apprenticed as stocking-maker in Nottingham ; edited successively the 'Statesman' (a London radical daily paper), 1812, and 'Nottingham Review'; published 'History of Nottingham' (1815). [v. 132]

BLACKRIE, ALEXANDER (*d.* 1772), apothecary; published work exposing secret of Dr. Chittick's cure for gravel, 1766. [v. 132]

BLACKSTONE, JOHN (*d.* 1753), botanist; apothecary in London ; published botanical works. [v. 132]

BLACKSTONE or BLAXTON, WILLIAM (*d.* 1675), one of the earliest episcopal clergymen in Massachusetts; lived successively on peninsula of Shawmut (where Boston now stands), in colony of Roger Williams, 1631, and at Blaxton river, near Providence. [v. 132]

BLACKSTONE, SIR WILLIAM (1723-1780), judge; educated at Charterhouse School and Pembroke College, Oxford; entered Middle Temple, 1741; fellow of All Souls,' 1744; B.C.L., 1745 ; called to bar; recorder of Wallingford; first professor of English law, Oxford, 1758-66 ; published 'Considerations on Copyholders,' 1758, and his edition of the Great Charter, 1759 ; M.P. for Hindon, Wiltshire, and principal of New Inn Hall, 1761-6 ; solicitor-general to the queen, 1763 ; published lectures as 'Commentaries on the Laws of England,' 4 vols., 1765-9, which met with a considerable amount of more or less hostile criticism, but still remains the best general history of English law; M.P. for Westbury, Wiltshire, 1768 ; gave it as his opinion that Wilkes was disqualified from sitting in parliament, and was answered by Grenville's quoting from the 'Commentaries' the causes of disqualification, none of which applied to Wilkes; retired from parliament ; appointed justice of common pleas, 1770, but exchanged into court of king's bench ; returned to common pleas in same year. The 'Commentaries' have passed through numerous editions, and have been translated into French, German, Italian, and Russian. [v. 133]

BLACKWALL, ANTHONY (1674-1730), classical scholar; M.A. Emmanuel College, Cambridge, 1698 ; headmaster of Derby school and lecturer of All Saints, Derby; headmaster of Market Bosworth grammar school, 1722-6 and 1729-30, where Dr. Johnson was perhaps his assistant for a few months : rector of Clapham, 1726-9. His most important work is the 'Sacred Classics Defended,' 1725. [v. 140]

BLACKWALL, JOHN (1790-1881), zoologist; engaged in importation of Irish linen at Manchester; retired to Llanrwst, North Wales, 1833; contributed to scientific publications ; published 'History of Spiders of Great Britain and Ireland,' 1861-4. [v. 142]

BLACKWELL, ALEXANDER (*d.* 1747), adventurer; probably brother of Dr. Thomas Blackwell [q. v.] ; practised as printer in London, 1730 ; became bankrupt; studied medicine and agriculture; inspector of Duke of Chandos's improvements at Cannons ; physician in ordinary to king of Sweden ; suspected of quackery; arrested for his connection with a political intrigue, the true nature and object of which remain a mystery; condemned without public trial and executed; published works on agriculture. [v. 142]

BLACKWELL, ELIZABETH (*fl.* 1737), botanical delineator ; wife of Alexander Blackwell [q. v.] ; relieved her husband when in embarrassed circumstances by publishing 'A Curious Herbal,' 1737, containing illustrations of medicinal plants, which she executed, engraved, and coloured. [v. 144]

BLACKWELL, GEORGE (1545 ?-1613), archpriest; B.A. Trinity College, Oxford, 1562 ; perpetual fellow, 1566 ; M.A., 1567 ; left fellowship and retired to Gloucester Hall : entered English College at Douay, 1574 ; ordained priest, 1575 ; B.D., 1575 ; joined English mission, 1576 ; imprisoned 1578, and, after release, lived in continual fear of arrest; appointed archpriest over secular clergy, 1598 ; incurred great unpopularity by his stern fulfilment of his duties ; deprived of office, 1608, for subscribing to an oath which was imposed on catholics in 1606, to test their civil allegiance, and which was twice condemned by the pope ; published theological works. [v. 144]

BLACKWELL, JOHN (1797-1840), Welsh poet; shoemaker at Mold, Flintshire ; educated by friends' liberality; B.A. Jesus College, Oxford, 1828 ; presented to living of Manor Deivy, Pembrokeshire; edited a Welsh illustrated magazine, 'Y Cylchgrawn.' His poems and essays were published in 1851. [v. 146]

BLACKWELL, THOMAS, the elder (1660 ?-1728), Scottish divine; presbyterian minister at Paisley, Renfrewshire, 1694, and Aberdeen, 1700 ; professor of divinity, Marischal College, 1710-28, principal, 1717-28 ; published theological writings. [v. 147]

BLACKWELL, THOMAS, the younger (1701-1757), classical scholar; son of Thomas Blackwell (1660 ?-1728) [q. v.]; studied at Marischal College, Aberdeen ; M.A., 1718 ; professor of Greek, 1723-57 ; principal, 1748-57 ; LL.D., 1752. His works include 'An Enquiry into Life and Writings of Homer,' 1735, and 'Memoirs of the Court of Augustus,' 1753-5, a third and incomplete volume being published posthumously, 1764. [v. 147]

BLACKWOOD, ADAM (1539-1613), Scottish writer; educated at university of Paris; studied civil law at Toulouse; taught philosophy at Paris; published 'De Vinculo,' 1575, and another work condemning heretics as rebels against divinely constituted authority; counsellor or judge of parliament of Poictiers ; entered into controversy with George Buchanan ; published, in French, account of sufferings of Mary Queen of Scots, 1587.
[v. 149]

BLACKWOOD, GEORGE FREDERICK (1838-1880), major; educated at Edinburgh Academy and at Addiscombe; second lieutenant, Bengal artillery, 1857 ; captain, 1867 ; commanded artillery in Looshai expedition, 1872 ; major, 1875 ; served in second Afghan campaign; killed at Maiwand. [v. 150]

BLACKWOOD, HELEN SELINA (1807-1867). [See SHERIDAN.]

BLACKWOOD, HENRY (*d.* 1614), physician ; M.D. Paris ; M.C.P. Paris, and subsequently dean of the faculty; left philosophical and medical manuscripts. [v. 150]

BLACKWOOD, SIR HENRY (1770-1832), vice-admiral; entered navy as volunteer, 1781 ; lieutenant, 1790 ; studied in Paris, 1792 ; captain, 1795 ; attached to North Sea fleet, 1796-8 ; on Newfoundland station, 1798-9 ; in

Channel, 1799 ; rendered distinguished service at blockade of Malta, 1800 ; commanded inshore squadron at Trafalgar, 1805 ; took part in ceremonies at Nelson's funeral ; commanded inshore squadron at blockade of Toulon, 1810 ; baronet and rear-admiral, 1814 ; K.C.B., 1819 ; commander-in-chief in East Indies, 1819–22 ; vice-admiral, 1821 ; commander-in-chief at Nore, 1827–30.   [v. 150]

BLACKWOOD, JOHN (1818–1879), publisher ; son of William Blackwood [q. v.] ; educated at Edinburgh University ; entered London publishing firm, 1839 ; superintendent of London branch of Blackwood's Edinburgh firm, 1840–5 ; editor of 'Blackwood's Magazine' on death of eldest brother, 1845 ; became, by death of another brother, head of publishing business, 1852 ; published nearly all George Eliot's works.   [v. 152]

BLACKWOOD, WILLIAM (1776–1834), publisher ; apprenticed as bookseller at Edinburgh ; manager of publishing business, Glasgow ; employed by bookseller in London ; began business independently in Edinburgh, 1804 ; principal founder of 'Edinburgh Encyclopædia,' 1810 ; combined, as Edinburgh agent, with John Murray, in publication of Scott's 'Tales of my Landlord' ; established, 1817, 'Edinburgh Monthly Magazine,' which became 'Blackwood's Edinburgh Magazine.' His publications include 'Edinburgh Encyclopædia,' 1810 (completed 1830), and 'New Statistical Account of Scotland.'
[v. 153]

BLADEN, MARTIN (1680–1746), soldier and politician ; educated at Westminster ; served in Low Countries and Spain ; aide-de-camp to Henri de Ruvigny [q. v.] ; lieutenant-colonel ; M.P. for Stockbridge, 1715–34, Maldon, Essex, 1734–41, and Portsmouth, 1741–6 ; comptroller of the mint, 1714 ; commissioner of trade and plantations, 1717–46 ; a steady supporter of Sir Robert Walpole.
[v. 154]

BLADES, WILLIAM (1824–1890), printer and bibliographer ; apprenticed to his father's printing firm of Blades & East, London, 1840, and subsequently became partner ; wrote 'Life of Caxton' (2 volumes, 1861–3), for which he carefully collated many works from Caxton's press ; liveryman of Scriveners' Company ; published works chiefly relating to early history of printing, and edited facsimiles and other reprints.   [Suppl. i. 210]

BLAGDEN, SIR CHARLES (1748–1820), physician ; M.D. Edinburgh, 1768 ; medical officer in army till 1814 ; F.R.S., 1772, and secretary, 1784 ; contributed to 'Philosophical Transactions.'   [v. 155]

BLAGDON, FRANCIS WILLIAM (1778–1819), journalist and author ; engaged successively as newspaper seller, amanuensis, and probably teacher of Spanish and Italian ; undertook various literary works, including series of 'Modern Discoveries,' 1802–3, and 'Flowers of Literature' (with Rev. F. Prevost), 1803–9 ; assistant editor of 'Morning Post,' c. 1806 ; came into conflict with William Cobbett [q. v.], 1809. His works include 'Authentic Memoirs of George Morland,' 1806, and 'Letters of Princess of Wales,' 1813.   [Suppl. i. 211]

BLAGGE or **BLAGE,** ROBERT (d. 1522 ?), judge ; appointed for life king's remembrancer in exchequer, 1502 ; third baron of exchequer, 1511 ; repeatedly justice of the peace for Kent and Middlesex ; joint-surveyor of crown lands, 1515 ; one of general purveyors of king's revenue, 1515 ; successively commissioner of sewers in several counties, 1515–17.   [v. 156]

BLAGRAVE, DANIEL (1603–1668), regicide ; nephew of John Blagrave [q. v.] ; educated for the bar ; M.P. for Reading, 1640 ; recorder of Reading, 1645–56 and 1658 ; signed Charles I's death warrant ; sat in Convention parliament, 1658 ; settled at Aachen, 1660, and there died.   [v. 156]

BLAGRAVE, JOHN (d. 1611), mathematician ; educated at St. John's College, Oxford ; published works describing instruments of his own invention, and other mathematical treatises.   [v. 157]

BLAGRAVE, JOSEPH (1610–1682), astrologer ; lived at Swallowfield, near Reading. His works include : 'Ephemerides, with Rules for Husbandry,' 1658, 1659, 1660, and 1665 ; 'Astrological Practice of Physick,' 1671, and 'Introduction to Astrology,' published posthumously, 1682.   [v. 157]

BLAGRAVE, THOMAS (d. 1688), musician ; gentleman of the chapel, 1661 ; clerk of the cheque, 1662 ; member of Charles II's private band ; author of some songs published in contemporary collections.   [v. 158]

BLAGROVE, HENRY GAMBLE (1811–1872), musician ; studied with Spagnoletti, 1821, and at Royal Academy of Music under Dr. Crotch and F. Cramer ; solo-violinist in royal private band, 1830–7 ; studied with Spohr at Cassel, 1832–4 ; played with success on continent ; connected with state band, 1837–72 ; published violin exercises and studies.   [v. 158]

BLAGUE or **BLAGE,** THOMAS (d. 1611), divine ; B.A. Queens' College, Cambridge ; non-resident rector of Braxted Magna, Essex, 1570 ; held livings of St. Vedast, Foster Lane, London, 1571, and Ewelme, Oxfordshire, 1580–96 ; D.D. Oxford ; dean of Rochester, 1591 ; non-resident rector of Bangor, 1604 ; author of 'A Schoole of wise Conceytes,' 1572.   [v. 159]

BLAIKIE, WILLIAM GARDEN (1820–1899), Scottish divine ; educated at Marischal College, Aberdeen, and Edinburgh ; licensed by Aberdeen presbytery, 1841 ; minister of Drumblade, 1842 ; joined free church of Scotland, 1843 ; minister of Pilrig, 1844–68 ; edited 'Free Church Magazine,' 1849–53, 'North British Review, 1860–1863, 'Sunday Magazine,' 1873–4, and 'Catholic Presbyterian,' 1879–83 ; professor of apologetics and pastoral theology, New College, Edinburgh, 1868–97 ; Cunningham lecturer, 1888 ; moderator to general assembly, 1892 ; honorary D.D. Edinburgh, 1864, and LL.D. Aberdeen, 1872 ; published religious, biographical, and other works.
[Suppl. i. 212]

BLAIR, HUGH (1718–1800), divine ; M.A. Edinburgh, 1739 ; licensed preacher, 1741 ; ordained minister of Colessie, Fife, 1742 ; minister to Lady Yester's church, Edinburgh, 1754, and to High church, 1758–1800 ; professor of rhetoric, 1760 ; regius professor of rhetoric and belles-lettres, 1762. Published 'Critical Dissertation on Poems of Ossian,' 1763, and Sermons, 5 vols. 1777–1801. He belonged to the distinguished literary circle that included Hume, A. Carlyle, Adam Ferguson, Adam Smith, and Robertson.   [v. 160]

BLAIR, JAMES (1656–1743), Scottish episcopalian divine ; held a benefice in revived episcopal church in Scotland till c. 1679 ; sent as missionary to Virginia, 1685 ; commissary under Sir Francis Nicholson when lieutenant-governor, 1689 ; obtained charter, 1692, for a college in Virginia, of which he became president, 1729 ; president of council of Virginia ; published commentary on Sermon on the Mount.   [v. 161]

BLAIR, SIR JAMES HUNTER (1741–1787), lord-provost of Edinburgh ; one of head partners in Coutts's banking house, Edinburgh ; married, 1770, and took wife's name of Blair, 1777 ; M.P. for Edinburgh, 1781 and 1784 ; lord-provost, 1784. Burns wrote an elegy on his death.
[v. 162]

BLAIR, JOHN (fl. 1300), chaplain to Sir William Wallace ; educated at Dundee and university of Paris ; joined Benedictines at Dunfermline ; chaplain to Sir William Wallace when governor of Scotland ; wrote life of Wallace.   [v. 162]

BLAIR, JOHN (d. 1782), chronologist ; educated at Edinburgh ; schoolmaster near London ; published 'Chronology of World from Creation to 1753,' 1754 ; F.R.S., 1755 ; chaplain to Princess-dowager of Wales ; prebendary of Westminster, 1761 ; rector of St. John the Evangelist, Westminster, 1776.   [v. 162]

BLAIR, PATRICK, M.D. (fl. 1728), physician ; practised as doctor successively at Dundee, London, and Boston, Lincolnshire ; published medical and botanical works.
[v. 163]

BLAIR, ROBERT (1593–1666), divine ; M.A. Glasgow ; professor at Glasgow University, c. 1615–22 ; licensed presbyterian preacher, 1616 ; minister of Bangor, Ireland, 1623 ; suspended, 1631, and deposed for nonconformity, 1632 ; restored, again ejected and excommunicated, 1634 ; minister at Burntisland, 1638, and at St. Andrews, 1639 ; moderator of general assembly, 1646 ; chaplain in ordinary to king ; joined party of 'resolutioners,' 1650 ; resigned as covenanter, 1661, and continued to preach at hazard of his life ; left political and theological manuscripts.
[v. 163]

BLAIR, ROBERT (1699-1746), poetical writer; educated at Edinburgh and in Holland; ordained minister of Athelstaneford, East Lothian, 1731; published, 1743, the 'Grave,' a poem in blank verse, which enjoyed instant success. Blair forms, as a poet, a connecting link between Otway and Crabbe. [v. 164]

BLAIR,' ROBERT, of Avontoun (1741-1811), judge; son of Robert Blair (1699-1746); educated at Edinburgh; advocate depute and solicitor-general for Scotland, 1789-1806; dean of Faculty of Advocates, 1801; president of College of Justice, 1808. [v. 166]

BLAIR, ROBERT (d. 1828), inventor of the 'aplanatic' telescope; appointed to chair of practical astronomy erected for his benefit, Edinburgh, 1785; invented fluid lenses of media, consisting of metallic solutions, with object of removing the 'secondary spectrum'; fellow of Royal Society of Edinburgh (1786), in whose 'Transactions' appeared, 1794, an abridgment of his 'Experiments on Refrangibility of Light.' [v. 166]

BLAIR, WILLIAM (1741-1782), captain, royal navy; commander, 1777; captain, 1778; fought at Doggerbank, 1781; killed in battle off Dominica. [v. 167]

BLAIR, WILLIAM (1766-1822), surgeon; surgeon to Lock Hospital, the Asylum, Finsbury and Bloomsbury dispensaries, female penitentiary, Pentonville, and New Rupture Society; M.R.C.S.; edited 'London Medical Review and Magazine'; published works on surgical and miscellaneous subjects, including stenography and cipher writing. [v. 168]

BLAK or **BLACK,** JOHN (d. 1563), Dominican friar of Aberdeen; stoned to death by protestants; wrote religious treatises. [v. 169]

BLAKE, CHARLES (1664-1730), divine and poet; educated at Merchant Taylors' School and St. John's College, Oxford; M.A., 1688; D.D., 1696; successively prebendary of Chester and (1716) of York; archdeacon of York, 1720; published Latin verses. [v. 169]

BLAKE, SIR FRANCIS (1708-1780), mathematician; assisted government in Durham during rebellion, 1745; baronet, 1774; F.R.S., 1746. [v. 169]

BLAKE, SIR FRANCIS (1738?-1818), political writer; son of Sir Francis Blake (1708-1780) [q. v.]; educated at Westminster and Trinity Hall, Cambridge; LL.B., 1763; published political tracts. [v. 169]

BLAKE, JAMES (1649-1728), jesuit, known as JAMES CROSS; professed father of Society of Jesus, 1675; provincial in England, 1701. [v. 170]

BLAKE, JOHN BRADBY (1745-1773), naturalist; supercargo in East India Company, Canton; collected Chinese plants and seeds, which were successfully propagated in Great Britain and the colonies. [v. 170]

BLAKE, MALACHI (1687-1760), dissenting minister; presbyterian minister of Blandford; published, 1735, account of fire at Blandford (1731). [v. 170]

BLAKE, ROBERT (1599-1657), admiral and general at sea; entered St. Alban Hall, Oxford, 1615; removed to Wadham College; graduated; engaged in business of merchant; M.P. for Bridgwater, 1640 and 1645; took part in defence of Bristol against royalists, 1643; lieutenant-colonel of Popham's regiment; held Lyme against royalists, 1643-4; took, and held, Taunton, 1644-5; governor of Taunton, 1645; appointed admiral and general at sea, 1649; unsuccessfully blockaded Prince Rupert at Kinsale, 1649, and pursued him to Portugal, 1650; blockaded mouth of Tagus, 1650, and subsequently followed Rupert to Mediterranean and destroyed many of his ships; commanded squadron in Irish Sea, and reduced Scilly Islands, which were held by royalist privateers, 1651; assisted in reduction of Jersey, 1651; member of council of state, 1651-2; with Rear-admiral Bourne, defeated Dutch under Tromp in Downs, 1652; defeated De Witt and De Ruyter off mouth of Thames, and, later, was defeated by Tromp off Dungeness, 1652; in company with Deane, Monck, and Penn, fought indecisive battle with Tromp off Portsmouth, 1653, the advantage being slightly with the English; took part in battle of 3 June, 1653; engaged in admiralty business at London, and executive duties at Portsmouth; destroyed Turkish pirate fleet at Porto Farina, 1655; destroyed Spanish West Indian fleet at Santa Cruz, 1657; died of fever while returning to England. His body was buried in Westminster Abbey, but removed after Restoration. [v. 170]

BLAKE, THOMAS (1597?-1657), puritan; M.A. Christ Church, Oxford; took holy orders; joined covenanters, 1648; pastor successively at Shrewsbury and Tamworth; assistant to Cromwell's commissioners for ejecting ministers; published works on puritan theology. [v. 179]

BLAKE, WILLIAM (1773-1821), dissenting minister; educated at Northampton under Horsey; presbyterian minister at Crewkerne, 1798-1821; published religious works. [v. 180]

BLAKE, WILLIAM (1757-1827), poet and painter; apprenticed to James Basire, engraver to Society of Antiquaries, 1771-8; executed plates for Gough's 'Sepulchral Monuments'; student at Royal Academy, 1778; engraved plates for Harrison's 'Novelists' Magazine'; kept, in partnership, printseller's shop in Broad Street, 1784-7; engraved and published 'Songs of Innocence,' 1789, and 'Songs of Experience,' 1794; employed by Johnson, the bookseller, on engravings for Mary Wollstonecraft's works, 1791; illustrated Young's 'Night Thoughts'; (Edwards's edition), 1793-1800; made designs for Blair's 'Grave,' which were subsequently engraved by Schiavonetti; executed series of 'Spiritual Portraits,' c. 1818; executed and engraved 'Inventions to Book of Job,' his finest work, from 1820, and produced designs for 'Divina Commedia,' of which only seven were published, 1827; exhibited at Royal Academy, 1780-1808, his 'Prophetic Books' (1793-1804), and most of his other works, engraved and coloured by hand. His favourite tenet, which he translated into art, was that 'all things exist in the human imagination alone.' [v. 180]

BLAKELEY, WILLIAM (1830-1897), actor; accompanied Sothern on tour; appeared first in London at Prince of Wales's Theatre, 1867; at Olympic, 1871; with Sothern in America, 1880; at Criterion, with which his name is chiefly associated, 1881. Among his best parts was Hardcastle in 'She stoops to conquer.' [Suppl. i. 213]

BLAKELY, FLETCHER (1783-1862), Irish remonstrant minister; graduated at Glasgow; presbyterian minister of Moneyrea, co. Down, 1809-57; adopted unitarian principles; joined remonstrant secession from synod of Ulster, 1829; joint-editor of 'Bible Christian,' 1830-3; published tracts and sermons. [v. 184]

BLAKELY, JOHNSTON (1781-1814), commander in United States navy; born in Dublin; entered United States navy, 1800; lieutenant, 1812; commanded sloop in Channel, and captured English brig, 1814; lost in the Atlantic. [v. 185]

BLAKENEY, SIR EDWARD (1778-1868), field-marshal; commanded 7th foot in Peninsular campaign, 1811-1814; in Belgium and at Paris, 1815; colonel, 1810, foot, 1832-54; commander-in-chief in Ireland, 1838-55; colonel of 1st foot, 1854-68; governor of Chelsea Hospital, 1856; general, 1854; field-marshal, 1862. [v. 186]

BLAKENEY, RICHARD PAUL (1820-1884), divine; B.A. Dublin, 1842; LL.D.; rural dean of Bridlington, 1876; canon of York, 1882; D.D. Edinburgh, 1868; published controversial works. [v. 186]

BLAKENEY, WILLIAM, BARON BLAKENEY (1672-1761), defender of Minorca; volunteered with army in Flanders; ensign, 1702; adjutant in Marlborough's campaigns; colonel, 1737; brigadier-general in expedition to Cartagena, 1741; major-general, and lieutenant-governor of Stirling Castle, 1744; defended Stirling against highlanders, 1745; lieutenant-general and lieutenant-governor of Minorca, 1747; gallantly defended Minorca against French, but, from want of reinforcements, was compelled to surrender, 1756; made K.B., colonel of Enniskillen regiment, and a peer of Ireland. [v. 186]

BLAKESLEY, JOSEPH WILLIAMS (1808-1885), dean of Lincoln; educated at St. Paul's School and Corpus Christi and Trinity College, Cambridge, when he became a friend of Tennyson; M.A., 1834; B.D., 1849; fellow of Trinity, 1831; tutor, 1839-45; vicar of Ware, 1845-72; canon of Canterbury, 1863; proctor in convocation for his chapter; dean of Lincoln, 1872; wrote extensively for the 'Times.' His chief work was an edition of Herodotus, 1852-4. [v. 187]

BLAKEWAY, JOHN BRICKDALE (1765–1826), topographer; educated at Westminster and Oriel College, Oxford; M.A., 1795; called to bar at Lincoln's Inn, 1789; joined Oxford circuit; ordained, 1793; minister, 1794, and, subsequently, official of Royal Peculiar of St. Mary's, Shrewsbury; published history of Shrewsbury, 1825. [v. 189]

BLAKEY, NICHOLAS (*fl.* 1753), Irish engraver; lived chiefly in Paris; associated with Francis Hayman, R.A., in producing set of English historical prints. [v. 189]

BLAKEY, ROBERT (1795–1878), miscellaneous writer; of humble parentage; received private tuition; contributed to 'Newcastle Magazine' and other periodicals; published philosophical works, 1831 and 1833; produced, 1838, 'Newcastle Liberator,' and, 1840, 'Northern Liberator and Champion' newspapers; studied philosophy in France and Belgium; published 'History of Philosophy of Mind,' 1848; professor of logic and metaphysics, Queen's College, Belfast, 1849. His works include books on angling. [v. 189]

BLAKISTON, JOHN (1603–1649), regicide; mercer in Newcastle; excommunicated for puritanical principles; M.P. for Newcastle, 1641; one of Charles I's judges, signing his death-warrant. [v. 190]

BLAKISTON, JOHN (1785–1867), major; served at Assaye, at capture of Bourbon, Mauritius, and Java, and in Peninsular war; published reminiscences. [Suppl. i. 214]

BLAKISTON, THOMAS WRIGHT (1832–1891), explorer and ornithologist; son of preceding; educated at Royal Military Academy, Woolwich; commissioned in royal artillery, 1851; served in Crimea; member of scientific expedition under John Palliser [q. v.] for exploration of British North America between Canada and Rocky Mountains, 1857; served in Chinese war, 1859, and organised exploration of middle and upper course of Yangtsze-Kiang, 1861; resigned commission, 1862; settled as merchant in Hakodate, Japan, and engaged in ornithological and other investigations, on which he published various writings; died at San Diego, California; published 'Five Months on the Yang-tsze,' 1862. [Suppl. i. 214]

BLAKMAN, BLAKEMAN, or **BLACKMAN**, JOHN (*fl.* 1436–1448), biographer; fellow of Merton College, Oxford, 1436, and, later, was fellow of Eton; said to have been B.D. and monk of Charterhouse; wrote, in Latin, a memoir of Henry VI, published, 1732, by Thomas Hearne [q. v.] [Suppl. i. 215]

BLAMIRE, SUSANNA (1747–1794), poetess; the 'Muse of Cumberland'; was associated with Catherine Gilpin. Some of her poems, which depict with admirable truth the Cumbrian folk, appeared in magazines, but no collection of them was published until 1842. She wrote several songs of high merit in Scottish dialect, including 'The Traveller's Return' and 'What ails this heart o' mine?' [v. 191]

BLAMIRE, WILLIAM (1790–1862), tithe commissioner; nephew of Susanna Blamire [q. v.]; educated at Westminster and Christ Church, Oxford; B.A., 1811; farmer at Thackwood Nook, Cumberland; high sheriff of Cumberland, 1828; whig M.P. for Carlisle, 1831; chief commissioner, 1836–51, for carrying into effect Tithe Commutation Bill of 1834; commissioner for carrying out Copyhold Enfranchisement Act, 1841; enclosure commissioner. [v. 192]

BLANCHARD, EDWARD LITT LAMAN (1820–1889), miscellaneous writer; son of William Blanchard [q. v.], whom he accompanied to New York, 1831; edited Chambers's 'London Journal,' 1841, and 'New London Magazine,' 1845. He produced pantomimes for Drury Lane for thirty-seven years, besides many other dramatic pieces, and contributed extensively to newspapers and periodicals. [Suppl. i. 216]

BLANCHARD, SAMUEL LAMAN (1804–1845), author; clerk to a proctor in Doctors' Commons; made acquaintance of Douglas Jerrold; joined travelling troop of actors; contributed to 'Monthly Magazine'; secretary to Zoological Society, 1827–30; published 'Lyric Offerings'; acting editor of 'Monthly Magazine'; edited 'True Sun,' 1832–6, 'Constitutional,' 1836, and 'Courier,' 1837–9 (all liberal papers), and 'Court Journal,' 1837; connected with 'Examiner,' 1841–5; edited 'George Cruikshank's Omnibus,' 1842; published L. E. Landon's

'Life and Literary Remains,' 1841. Three volumes of his essays appeared in 1846. [v. 194]

BLANCHARD, WILLIAM (1769–1835), comedian; in office of his uncle, William Blanchard, proprietor of 'York Chronicle,' 1782; joined Welsh's travelling company of actors, 1785; became manager of several provincial theatres; played, 1800, Bob Acres at Covent Garden, where he remained almost continuously till death. His characters include Sir Hugh Evans, Fluellen, Menenius, and Polonius. [v. 195]

BLANCHARD, WILLIAM ISAAC (*d.* 1796), stenographer; practised as shorthand-writer in Westminster Hall, 1767–96; published two original systems of stenography. [v. 196]

BLAND, ELIZABETH (*fl.* 1681–1712), hebraist; *née* Fisher; married, 1681; wrote in Hebrew a phylactery for Thoresby's 'Musæum Thoresbianum.' [v. 196]

BLAND, HUMPHREY (1686?–1763), general and military writer; obtained commission, 1704; served as lieutenant and captain in Marlborough's campaigns; at battle of Almanara, 1710; successively lieutenant-colonel and colonel of dragoons, and colonel of foot; quartermaster-general at headquarters, 1742; served in Flanders; major-general in Culloden campaign; governor of Gibraltar, 1749, and of Edinburgh, 1752–63; commander-in-chief of forces in Scotland, 1753; published 'Treatise on Discipline,' 1727. [v. 196]

BLAND, JOHN (*d.* 1555), Marian martyr; educated at Eton and Cambridge; M.A.; schoolmaster; rector of Adisham, Kent; opposed celebration of mass, 1553; burned at Canterbury. [v. 197]

BLAND, JOHN (1702–1750), writing-master; educated at Westminster; clerk in custom-house, 1717; writing-master at academy in Little Tower Street, and subsequently established himself independently; published 'Essay on Writing,' 1730. [v. 198]

BLAND, JOHN (*d.* 1788), dramatist; author of drama, 'Song of Solomon,' 1750. [v. 198]

BLAND, MARIA THERESA (1769–1838), vocalist; daughter of Italian Jews named Romanzini; first sang at Drury Lane, 1786; married the actor Bland, 1790; attached to Drury Lane almost continuously from 1789 to 1824, but sang also at Haymarket and Vauxhall; developed melancholia after 1824. [v. 198]

BLAND, MILES (1786–1867), mathematician; B.A., second wrangler, and Smith's prizeman, St. John's College, Cambridge, 1808; fellow, 1808; public mathematical examiner, 1817–18; prebendary of Wells and D.D., 1826; F.R.S.; F.S.A.; published mathematical works. [v. 199]

BLAND, NATHANIEL (1803–1865), Persian scholar; educated at Eton and Christ Church, Oxford; B.A., 1825; contributed valuable papers to Royal Asiatic Society's 'Journal,' 1843–53; committed suicide. [Suppl. i. 216]

BLAND, ROBERT, the elder (1730–1816), physician; M.D. St. Andrews, 1778; L.C.P., 1786; published works on midwifery. [v. 199]

BLAND, ROBERT, the younger (1779?–1825), divine; son of Robert Bland (1730–1816) [q. v.]; educated at Harrow and Pembroke College, Cambridge; B.A., 1802; assistant master, Harrow; minister to English church, Amsterdam; held two English curacies; published works relating to Greek classics. [v. 199]

BLAND, TOBIAS (1563?–1604), divine; B.A. Pembroke Hall, Cambridge, 1581; expelled from Corpus Christi College for libelling the master; M.A., 1584; B.D., 1591; sub-almoner to Elizabeth, 1594; canon of Peterborough, 1602. [v. 200]

BLAND, WILLIAM (1789–1868), Australian statesman; son of Robert Bland the elder [q. v.]; passed naval surgeon, fifth rate, 1809; exiled to Sydney for duelling, 1814; pardoned; practised surgery; imprisoned twelve months for libel; passed naval surgeon, 1826; member of elective legislature for Sydney, 1843. [v. 200]

BLANDFORD, WALTER (1619–1675), bishop; fellow, Wadham College, Oxford, 1644; warden, 1659; prebendary of Gloucester; chaplain in ordinary to the king; vice-chancellor of the university, 1663; bishop of Oxford, 1665; dean of Chapel Royal; bishop of Worcester, 1671. [v. 201]

BLANDIE or BLANDY, WILLIAM (*fl.* 1580), author; educated at Winchester and New College, Oxford; B.A., 1566; 'fellow' of Middle Temple; served with English army in Low Countries, 1580; published works relating to political and civil customs.   [v. 201]

BLANDY, MARY (*d.* 1752), murderess; at the instance of her lover, William Henry, son of fifth Lord Cranstoun, poisoned her father, who objected to her engagement; was convicted and hanged at Oxford.
[v. 202]

BLANE, SIR GILBERT (1749–1834), physician; M.D. Glasgow, 1778; private physician to Admiral Rodney, whom he accompanied to West Indies, 1779; physician to fleet, 1779–83; came to England with Rodney, 1781, but returned, 1782; L.C.P., 1781; did much to improve sanitary condition of navy; published work on means for preserving health of seamen, 1780; physician at St. Thomas's Hospital on return to England, 1783, till 1795; physician extraordinary, and later physician in ordinary to Prince of Wales, 1785; commissioner for sick and wounded seamen, 1795–1802; assisted in framing rules forming basis of Quarantine Act, 1799; sent to report on condition of army in Walcheren expedition, and arranged for transport of sick and wounded; created baronet, 1812; physician in ordinary to George IV; F.R.S.; published dissertations on medical subjects.   [v. 202]

BLANEFORDE, HENRY (*fl.* 1330), chronicler; monk of St. Albans; wrote chronicle for years 1323–4 (Cotton MSS. Claudius D. vi.)   [v. 204]

BLANFORD, HENRY FRANCIS (1834–1893), meteorologist and geologist; studied at Royal School of Mines; appointed to geological survey of India, 1855; professor at Presidency College, Calcutta, 1862–72; meteorological reporter to government of Bengal, 1872, and later to government of India; retired and returned to England, 1888; published scientific writings.   [Suppl. i. 217]

BLANKETT, JOHN (*d.* 1801), admiral; volunteer and midshipman at reduction of Louisbourg, 1758, and Quebec, 1759; lieutenant, 1761; commander, 1779; served in East Indies; captain, 1780; in Mediterranean, 1783; commanded convoy to China, 1790; commodore of squadron sent to Cape of Good Hope, serving at reduction of that settlement; served in Egyptian operations; rear-admiral, 1799.   [v. 205]

BLANTYRE, BARONS. [See STEWART, WALTER, first BARON, *d.* 1437; STEWART, ALEXANDER, fifth BARON, *d.* 1704.]

BLAQUIERE, JOHN, BARON DE BLAQUIERE (1732–1812), politician; son of a French emigrant; under Lord Harcourt as secretary of legation in France, 1771–2, and chief secretary in Ireland, 1772–7; M.P. successively for several Irish and English constituencies; privy councillor, 1774; baronet, 1784; raised to Irish peerage, 1800.   [v. 205]

BLATHWAYT, WILLIAM (1649?–1717), politician; secretary to Sir William Temple at the Hague, 1668; engaged in public business successively at Rome, Stockholm, and Copenhagen; secretary-at-war, 1683–1704; clerk of privy council, 1689; secretary of state with William III in Flanders; commissioner of trade, 1696–1706; M.P. for Newtown, Isle of Wight, 1685–8, and Bath, 1693–1710.
[v. 206]

BLAYNEY, ANDREW THOMAS, eleventh BARON BLAYNEY (1770–1834), lieutenant-general; ensign, 1789; captain, 1792; major in 89th regiment, part of which he raised in Ireland, 1794; served under Duke of York in Flanders, 1794–5; lieutenant-colonel of 89th regiment in Ireland, 1798; assisted in reduction of Malta; major-general in Peninsula, 1810; captured at Malaga; imprisoned in France, 1810–14; lieutenant-general, 1819; published account of his captivity, 1814.   [v. 206]

BLAYNEY, BENJAMIN (1728–1801), Hebrew scholar; M.A. Worcester College, Oxford, 1753; fellow, and afterwards vice-principal, Hertford College; B.D., 1768; prepared for Clarendon Press edition of authorised version of bible, 1769; regius professor of Hebrew, canon of Christ Church, and D.D., 1787; published dissertations on and translations of Old Testament Scriptures.   [v. 208]

BLEDRI, surnamed DDOETH, or the Wise (*d.* 1022?), perhaps bishop of Llandaff between 995 and 1005.   [v. 208]

BLEECK, ARTHUR HENRY (1827?–1877), orientalist; successively employed in British Museum and in land transport corps at Sinope during Crimean war; published works on oriental languages and a translation of the 'Avesta.'   [v. 209]

BLEEK, WILHELM HEINRICH IMMANUEL (1827–1875), philologist; born at Berlin; educated at Bonn and Berlin; set out with W. B. Blaikie [q. v.] in expedition up Niger, 1854; interpreter to Sir George Grey at Capetown, 1857, and subsequently librarian to Grey's library; published works on South African languages.
[v. 209]

BLEGBOROUGH, RALPH (1769–1827), physician; educated at Edinburgh and Guy's and St. Thomas's hospitals; M.D. Aberdeen, 1804; L.C.P., 1805; devoted himself exclusively to midwifery.   [v. 210]

BLENCOW or BLINCOW, JOHN (*fl.* 1640), divine; fellow, St. John's College, Oxford, 1627; B.C.L., 1633; probably expelled from fellowship, 1648.   [v. 210]

BLENCOWE, SIR JOHN (1642–1726), judge; called to bar at Inner Temple, 1673; master of the bench, 1687; serjeant-at-law, 1689; M.P. for Brackley, Northamptonshire, 1690–5; baron of exchequer, 1696; probably removed to king's bench, 1697, and to common pleas, 1714; knighted, 1714; retired, 1722.   [v. 210]

BLENCOWE, WILLIAM (1683–1712), decipherer; son of Sir John Blencowe [q. v.]; B.A. Magdalen College, Oxford, 1701; fellow of All Souls, 1702; M.A., 1704; decipherer to government, 1703; shot himself during temporary insanity.   [v. 211]

BLENERHASSET, THOMAS (1550?–1625?), poet; educated at Cambridge; entered army; captain at Guernsey Castle; one of 'undertakers' for plantation of Ulster, 1610. His publications include an expansion (1578) of the 'Mirrour for Magistrates' and a work on 'Plantation in Ulster.'   [v. 211]

BLENKINSOP, JOHN (1783–1831), one of pioneers of the locomotive; engaged in Middleton collieries, near Leeds; obtained, 1811, patent for double cylinder locomotive worked by means of racked rail and toothed wheel, which was successfully tested, 1812. Locomotives made upon the Blenkinsop pattern were employed regularly from 1812.   [Suppl. i. 217]

BLENKIRON, WILLIAM (1807?–1871), breeder of racehorses; farmer in Yorkshire; manufacturer of stocks and collars, 1845; kept racehorses at Dalston, and subsequently at Middle Park, Kent, Waltham Cross, and Esher, his stud becoming the most celebrated in Europe.
[v. 212]

BLENNERHASSET, HARMAN (1764?–1831), lawyer; educated at Westminster and Dublin; B.A., and LL.B., 1790; travelled on continent, adopted republican principles, and settled, 1798, near Parkersburg on the Ohio; became implicated in schemes of Aaron Burr; arrested, but released, 1807; lawyer in Montreal, 1819; retired to Guernsey.   [v. 213]

BLESSINGTON, MARGUERITE, COUNTESS OF (1789–1849), authoress; *née* Power; married, 1804, captain Maurice Farmer (*d.* 1817), from whom she separated almost immediately; married, 1818, Charles John Gardiner, first earl of Blessington; travelled on continent with her husband and Alfred, count d'Orsay, 1822; made acquaintance of Byron; settled in Paris, 1828; removed to London, 1831; published her first novel, 'Cassidy,' 1833; edited 'Book of Beauty' from 1834, and 'The Keepsake,' 1841–1849; contributed to 'Daily News' on its foundation, 1846; became bankrupt, 1849, and fled to Paris to Count d'Orsay, who had lived with her for some years; died in Paris. Her first book, 'The Magic Lantern,' was published anonymously, 1822, and between 1833 and 1847 she produced numerous works of fiction and personal reminiscence. 'Country Quarters,' a novel, appeared posthumously in 1850.   [v. 213]

BLETHYN, WILLIAM (*d.* 1590), divine; educated at Oxford; bishop of Llandaff, 1575.   [v. 215]

BLEW, WILLIAM JOHN (1808–1894), liturgiologist; M.A. Wadham College, Oxford, 1832; curate of Nuthurst, 1832–40, and of St. Anne's, Soho, 1840–2; incumbent of St. John's, Milton-next-Gravesend, 1842–50; published edition of 'Aberdeen Breviary,' 1854, translations from Greek, and other works.   [Suppl. i. 218]

BLEWITT, JONAS (*d.* 1805), organist in city of London; published a 'Treatise on the Organ,' and musical compositions. [v. 215]

BLEWITT, JONATHAN (1780?-1853), composer; son of Jonas Blewitt [q. v.]; organist successively in London, Haverhill, Brecon, Sheffield, and at St. Andrew's, Dublin; in London, 1826; produced numerous pantomime compositions; at different times musical director at Theatre Royal, Dublin, Sadler's Wells, and Vauxhall. [v. 216]

BLEWITT, OCTAVIAN (1810-1884), secretary, Royal Literary Fund; studied medicine at infirmary of St. George's, Hanover Square, London; secretary of Royal Literary Fund, 1839-84; knight of the order of Leopold, 1872; published topographical and other works. [v. 216]

BLICKE, SIR CHARLES (1745-1815), surgeon; surgeon of St. Bartholomew's Hospital, 1787; governor of College of Surgeons, 1801; knighted, 1803; edited 'Essay on Yellow Fever of Jamaica,' 1772, anonymous. [v. 217]

BLIGH, RICHARD (1780-1838?), chancery barrister; educated at Westminster and Trinity College, Cambridge; M.A., 1806; published legal works. [v. 218]

BLIGH, SIR RICHARD RODNEY (1737-1821), admiral; entered navy, 1751; commander under Rodney in West Indies, 1762; captured by French, 1793; rear-admiral, 1794; released, 1795; second in command in Jamaica, 1796-9; vice-admiral, 1799; commander-in-chief at Leith, 1803-4; admiral, 1804; G.C.B. 1820. [v. 218]

BLIGH, THOMAS (*not* EDWARD) (1685-1775), lieutenant-general; Irish M.P. for Athboy, co. Meath, 1715; captain, 1717; lieutenant-colonel, 6th horse; colonel of 20th foot, 1740; brigadier-general, 1745; major-general, 1747; colonel, 6th horse, 1747; lieutenant-general, 1754; commanded unsuccessful expedition against French to create diversion in favour of Ferdinand of Brunswick, 1758; retired, 1759. [v. 217]

BLIGH, WILLIAM (1754-1817), vice-admiral; entered navy and accompanied Cook as sailing-master in second voyage round world, 1772-4, and discovered bread-fruit at Otaheite; lieutenant; commanded vessel sailing to Otaheite to obtain bread-fruit plants, 1787; cast adrift in open boat by his mutinous crew; landed at Timor, 1789; reached England, 1790; post-captain; sailed to Society Islands, 1791; received Society of Arts' medal, 1794; F.R.S., 1801; captain-general and governor of New South Wales, 1805; forcibly deposed, 1808, and imprisoned till 1810; returned to England, 1811; rear-admiral, 1811, and vice-admiral of blue, 1814. [v. 219]

BLIGHT, WILLIAM (1785-1862), rear-admiral; lieutenant, 1803; at Trafalgar, 1805; agent for transports, Palermo, 1812-14; commander, 1821; post-captain, 1830; retired as rear-admiral, 1855. [v. 220]

BLIND, MATHILDE (1841-1896), poetess; born at Mannheim; daughter of a banker named Cohen; adopted name of Blind; came to London, *c.* 1849; published 'Poems by Claude Lake,' 1867, 'The Prophecy of St. Oran,' 1881, 'The Heather on Fire,' 1886, 'Ascent of Man,' 1888, 'Dramas in Miniature,' 1891, 'Songs and Sonnets,' 1893, and 'Birds of Passage,' 1895. She translated Strauss's 'Old Faith and New,' 1873-4, and 'Journal of Marie Bashkirtseff,' 1890. [Suppl. i. 219]

BLISS, NATHANIEL (1700-1764), astronomer; M.A. Pembroke College, Oxford, 1723; rector of St. Ebbe's, Oxford, 1736; Savilian professor of geometry and F.R.S., 1742; assisted Bradley at Royal Observatory; astronomer-royal, 1762-4. Observations made under his supervision were published in 1805. [v. 220]

BLISS, PHILIP (1787-1857), antiquary: educated at Merchant Taylors' School and St. John's College, Oxford; fellow, 1809; D.C.L., 1820; ordained priest, 1818; under-librarian of Bodleian, 1822-8; university registrar, 1824-1853; keeper of archives, 1826-57; registrar of university court, 1831; principal of St. Mary Hall, 1848-57; deputy professor of civil law; compiled and edited many anti-quarian works, including editions of Wood's 'Athenæ Oxonienses,' 1813-20, and 'Reliquiæ Hearnianæ,' 1857. [v. 221]

BLITH, WALTER (*fl.* 1649), agricultural writer; published, 1649, 'The English Improver, or a new Survey of Husbandry,' reissued, 1652, as 'The English Improver Improved.' He was probably a captain in parliamentary army. [Suppl. i. 220]

BLITHEMAN or **BLYTHEMAN**, WILLIAM (*d.* 1591), organist and gentleman of the chapel under Elizabeth; left musical compositions in manuscript. Dr. John Bull [q. v.] was perhaps his pupil. [v. 222]

BLIZARD, THOMAS (1772-1838), surgeon; nephew of Sir William Blizard [q. v.]; surgeon to London Hospital; published surgical writings. [v. 222]

BLIZARD, SIR WILLIAM (1743-1835), surgeon; studied at London and St. Bartholomew's hospitals; surgeon, 1780, to London Hospital, where, with Dr. Maclaurin, he founded medical school, 1785; F.R.S., 1787; twice president of College of Surgeons; published medical writings. [v. 223]

BLOCHMANN, HENRY FERDINAND (1838-1878), orientalist; born at Dresden; studied oriental languages at Leipzig and Paris; came to England and enlisted in British army, 1858; went as private soldier to India, obtained employment in office at Fort William, received discharge, and entered service of Peninsular and Oriental Company as interpreter; assistant professor of Arabic and Persian, in Calcutta Madrasa, 1860-2; M.A. and LL.D. Calcutta, 1861; professor of mathematics, Doveton College, 1862-5; returned to the Madrasa, 1865, and ultimately became principal; published oriental works, including translation of first volume of 'Ain-i-Akbari' of Abúl-Fazl. [Suppl. i. 220]

BLOET, **BLUET**, or **BLOETT**, ROBERT (*d.* 1123), Norman divine; chancellor successively to William the Conqueror and William II; consecrated bishop of Lincoln, 1094; justiciary under Henry I; besieged Tickhill, Robert of Belesme's castle, for the king, 1102. [v. 223]

BLOIS, PETER DE (*fl.* 1190). [See PETER.]

BLOMBERG, WILLIAM NICHOLAS (1702?-1750), divine; M.A. Merton College, Oxford, 1726; fellow; held livings in Middlesex and Kent; published life of his grandfather, Edmund Dickinson, M.D. [v. 224]

BLOME, RICHARD (*d.* 1705), publisher and compiler; issued many splendid works by the aid of subscriptions adroitly levied. His publications include editions of Guillim's 'Display of Heraldrie,' 1660 and 1679; 'Geographical Description of . . . the World,' 1670; and 'Britannia,' 1673. [v. 225]

BLOMEFIELD, FRANCIS (1705-1752), topographer; B.A. Gonville and Caius College, Cambridge, 1727; rector of Hargham, 1729-30; held living of Fersfield, 1730; set up private press, 1736, and began to issue in numbers his 'History of Norfolk,' 1739; died leaving the third volume unfinished. The published volumes, chiefly based on Le Neve's collections, contained accounts of Thetford and Norwich. His work was continued by the Rev. Charles Parkin, and ultimately finished by a hack writer, the whole being republished, 1805-10. [v. 226]

BLOMEFIELD, LEONARD, formerly LEONARD JENYNS (1800-1893), naturalist; educated at Eton and St. John's College, Cambridge; B.A., 1822; curate, 1823, and vicar, 1828-49, of Swaffham Bulbeck, Cambridgeshire; published 'Manual of British Vertebrate Animals,' 1835; removed successively to South Stoke, near Bath, 1850, Swainswick, 1852, and Bath, 1860; founder, 1855, and first president of Bath Natural History and Antiquarian Field Club; presented to the town of Bath the 'Jenyns Library'; member of Linnean Society and of Cambridge Philosophical Society, 1822; original member of Zoological (1826), Entomological (1834), and Ray (1844) societies; adopted name of Blomefield, 1871; published writings relating to natural history and an autobiography (privately printed, 1889). [Suppl. i. 221]

BLOMEFIELD, MILES (1525-1574?), alchemist; licensed physician by Cambridge University; practised at Bury St. Edmunds; published works on alchemy. [v. 228]

BLOMEFIELD, SIR THOMAS (1744-1822), major-general; joined navy, but entered as cadet military academy, Woolwich, 1758; lieutenant fire-worker, *c.* 1759; commanded bomb-ketch at bombardment of Havre; joined Hawke's fleet at Quiberon; personal aide-de-camp successively to General Conway and Lord Townshend, master-general of ordnance, 1771; brigade-major to Brigadier Phillips in American war; wounded at Saratoga; captain, inspector of artillery, and superintendent of Royal Brass Foundry, 1780; entrusted with reorganisation of ordnance department, 1783; lieutenant-colonel, 1793; colonel, 1800; major-general, 1803; colonel-commandant of battalion, 1806; commanded artillery in Copenhagen expedition, 1807; created baronet. [v. 228]

BLOMFIELD, SIR ARTHUR WILLIAM (1829–1899), architect; son of Charles James Blomfield [q. v.]; educated at Rugby and Trinity College, Cambridge; M.A., 1853; articled to Philip Charles Hardwick (1822–1892), son of Philip Hardwick [q. v.]; opened office in Adelphi Terrace, 1856; president of Architectural Association, 1861; F.R.I.B.A., 1867, and vice-president, 1886; architect to Bank of England, 1883; associated with Arthur Edmund Street, son of George Edmund Street [q. v.], in erection of Law Courts in London, 1881; A.R.A., 1888; knighted, 1889. His works include Sion College Library on Thames Embankment, Queen's School at Eton College, the scheme for Church House, Dean's Yard, Westminster, and many churches in England and abroad. He made important restorations in the cathedrals of Salisbury, Canterbury, Lincoln, and Chichester. [Suppl. i. 223]

BLOMFIELD, CHARLES JAMES (1786–1857), bishop of London; B.A. Trinity College, Cambridge, 1808; fellow; presented to St. Botolph, Bishopsgate; bishop of Chester, 1824; translated to see of London, 1828; instituted, 1836, for building and endowing churches in metropolis a fund which, 1854, was merged in London Diocesan Church Building Society; in the Tractarian movement (c. 1842) upheld definitely the views of neither party while agreeing on some points with both; edited five plays of Æschylus, with notes and glossaries, three Greek lyric poets for Gaisford's 'Poetæ Minores Græci' (1823), and contributed on classical subjects to magazines. [v. 229]

BLOMFIELD, EDWARD VALENTINE (1788–1816), classical scholar; brother of Charles James Blomfield [q. v.]; B.A. Caius College, Cambridge, 1811; first chancellor's classical medallist; classical lecturer and fellow, Emmanuel College, till death. His chief work, a translation of Matthiæ's 'Greek Grammar,' appeared posthumously edited by his brother. [v. 230]

BLOMFIELD, EZEKIEL (1778–1818). nonconformist divine; minister at Wymondham; founded Norfolk and Norwich Auxiliary British and Foreign Bible Society; partner of Brightley, printer, of Bungay; published various compilations. [v. 231]

BLON, JACQUES CRISTOPHE, LE (1670–1741). [See LE BLON.]

BLONDEL, JAMES AUGUSTUS (d. 1734), physician; born in Paris; M.D. Leyden, 1692; practised in London; L.C.P., 1711; published medical writings. [v. 232]

BLOOD, HOLCROFT (1660?–1707), general; son of Thomas Blood [q. v.]; served at sea in Dutch war, 1672, and in Irish campaigns after 1688; rendered signal service as engineer, Namur, 1695, and Hochstädt, c. 1703; subsequently promoted brigadier-general. [v. 232]

BLOOD, THOMAS (1618?–1680), adventurer; obtained estates in Ireland which were forfeited at Restoration; headed unsuccessful attempt to take Dublin Castle from royalists, 1663; escaped arrest, and subsequently fled to Holland; returned to England, associated with Fifth-monarchy men, and later with covenanters till 1666; attempted, perhaps at Buckingham's instigation, to assassinate Duke of Ormonde, who, however, escaped, 1670; formed an elaborate plan, 1671, to steal the crown jewels, and actually with an accomplice made off with the crown and globe, but was arrested; obtained admission to Charles II's presence, gained his favour, and received back his Irish estates; committed by court of king's bench for slander of Buckingham, 1680, but received bail. [v. 232]

BLOMFIELD, BENJAMIN, first BARON BLOOMFIELD (1768–1846), lieutenant-general; second lieutenant, royal artillery, 1781; chief equerry to Prince of Wales, c. 1806; major-general, 1814; knighted, 1815; keeper of privy purse and receiver of duchy of Lancaster, 1817; minister plenipotentiary at Stockholm, 1824; raised to Irish peerage, 1825; commanded garrison at Woolwich. [v. 235]

BLOOMFIELD, JOHN ARTHUR DOUGLAS, second BARON BLOOMFIELD (1802–1879), diplomatist: son of Benjamin Bloomfield [q. v.]; joined diplomatic service, 1818; envoy extraordinary and minister plenipotentiary at St. Petersburg, 1844, and Berlin, 1851; envoy extraordinary and plenipotentiary to emperor of Austria, 1860–71; created peer of United Kingdom, 1871. [v. 235]

BLOOMFIELD, ROBERT (1766–1823), poet; worked as shoemaker under his brother George, in London; endured extreme poverty; wrote his 'Farmer's Boy,' c. 1798 (published 1800); under-sealer in seal office, 1802; manufactured Æolian harps; embarked unsuccessfully in book-trade; visited Wales and wrote 'Banks of the Wye,' 1811. A collected edition of his works appeared in 1824. [v. 236]

BLOOR, JOSEPH (d. 1846), assistant at Robert Bloor's Old Derby China Works. [v. 237]

BLOOR, ROBERT (d. 1846), ceramist, brother of Joseph Bloor [q. v.]; worked in and, c. 1811, bought Old Derby China Works. [v. 237]

BLORE, EDWARD (1787–1879), architect and artist; son of Thomas Blore [q. v.]; employed on illustrations for his father's 'History of Rutland,' Britton's 'English Cathedrals,' and Surtees's 'Antiquities of Durham'; built Sir Walter Scott's house at Abbotsford, c. 1816; managed production of Scott's 'Provincial Antiquities of Scotland'; architect to William IV and Queen Victoria, and to Westminster Abbey; F.R.S.; F.S.A.; hon. D.C.L. Oxford, 1834; published 'Monumental Remains of Eminent Persons,' 1824. [v. 37]

BLORE, ROBERT (d. 1866?), manufacturer of porcelain 'biscuit' figures in Bridge Gate, Derby; apprenticed at Old Derby China Works. [v. 238]

BLORE, THOMAS (1764–1818), topographer; solicitor at Derby, and, later, at Hopton; entered Middle Temple, 1795; published topographical writings and left manuscript collections for history of Hertfordshire. [v. 238]

BLOUNT, CHARLES, fifth BARON MOUNTJOY (d. 1545), son of William Blount, fourth baron [q. v.]; page to Queen Catherine; served with Henry VIII in France, 1544; patron of learning. [v. 239]

BLOUNT, CHARLES, EARL OF DEVONSHIRE and eighth BARON MOUNTJOY (1563–1606), grandson of Charles Blount, fifth baron [q. v.]; M.A. Oxford, 1589; entered Inner Temple; came to court, c. 1583; M.P. for Beeralston, 1584, 1586, and 1593; knighted, 1586; served in Netherlands, in pursuit of Armada, and in Brittany, 1586–93; captain of town and island of Portsmouth, 1594; lieutenant of land forces in Essex's expedition to Azores, 1597; K.G., 1597; implicated in Essex's conspiracy, but escaped punishment; lord deputy of Ireland, 1601; put down Tyrone's rebellion; reinstated deputy by James I; styled lord-lieutenant, 1603; suppressed disaffection resulting from military occupation; returned to England, and was created Earl of Devonshire, 1603; master of ordnance, 1603; keeper of Portsmouth Castle, 1604; commissioner to discharge office of earl marshal, 1605; married, 1605, Lord Rich's divorced wife, Essex's sister, Penelope, with whom he had contracted a liaison in early life. [v. 240]

BLOUNT, CHARLES (1654–1693), deist; son of Sir Henry Blount [q. v.]; author of freethinking books which have caused him to be considered as a link between Herbert of Cherbury and Toland. These include 'Anima Mundi'; an attack on priestcraft entitled 'Great is Diana of the Ephesians,' 1680; and a translation with notes of 'The Two First Books of Apollonius Tyaneus,' 1680. He published also political papers of whig tendency, and a 'Vindication of Liberties of the Press.' [v. 243]

BLOUNT, SIR CHRISTOPHER (1565?–1601), soldier; probably younger brother of Charles, earl of Devonshire [q. v.]; gentleman of horse to Elizabeth; served in Netherlands; knighted, 1588; married, c. 1589, widow of first Earl of Essex (d. 1576); colonel of land force, and, later, camp master in Essex's expedition to Cadiz, 1596; joined attempt on Azores, 1597; M.P. for Staffordshire, 1597; marshal of Essex's army in Ireland, 1599; assisted in Essex's conspiracy against government, and was executed on Tower Hill. [v. 245]

BLOUNT or **BLUNT**, EDWARD (*fl.* 1588-1632), stationer; freeman of Stationers' Company, 1588; published Florio's 'Italian and English Dictionary,' 1596, and translation of 'Montaigne's Essays,' 1607, Marlowe's 'Hero and Leander,' 1598, Shelton's 'Don Quixote,' 1620, the first folio of Shakespeare's 'Works,' with Isaac Jaggard and others, 1623, and Lyly's 'Sixe Court Comedies,' 1632, besides 'Ars Aulica,' 1607, and other translations by himself. [v. 246]

BLOUNT, Sir HENRY (1602-1682), traveller; B.A. Trinity College, Oxford, 1618; entered Gray's Inn; travelled on continent and in Egypt; published 'Voyage to the Levant,' 1636; knighted, 1640; sided with royalists in civil war. [v. 247]

BLOUNT, Sir JAMES (*d.* 1493), lieutenant of Hammes, 1476; son of Walter Blount, first baron Montjoy (*d.* 1474) [q. v.]; knighted, 1485. [v. 258]

BLOUNT, Sir JOHN (*fl.* 1413), governor of Calais; son of Sir Walter Blount [q. v.]; K.G., 1413; at siege of Rouen, 1418. [v. 258]

BLOUNT, Sir JOHN, third BARON MOUNTJOY (*d.* 1485), second son of Walter Blount, first baron [q. v.]; captain of Guisnes and Hammes, 1477. [v. 258]

BLOUNT, MARTHA (1690-1762), friend of Pope; educated at Hammersmith and in Paris; made acquaintance of Pope as early as 1705; Pope dedicated to her his 'Epistle on Women,' 1735, and at his death bequeathed her considerable property. [v. 248]

BLOUNT, MOUNTJOY, BARON MOUNTJOY and EARL OF NEWPORT (1597 ?-1666), natural son of Charles Blount, earl of Devonshire [q. v.], by Penelope, lady Rich; created Baron Mountjoy, in Irish peerage, 1618, and in English peerage, 1627; served in Low Countries, 1622; created Earl of Newport, Isle of Wight, 1628; rear-admiral of fleet in Rochelle expedition, 1628; accompanied Charles I to Scotland, 1639; joined opposition in the Lords to Charles I in Long parliament; constable of Tower, 1641; fought with king's forces in Yorkshire, 1642; lieutenant-general under Duke of Newcastle; quarrelled with Newcastle and was imprisoned in Pomfret Castle, and subsequently committed to custody of gentleman usher of House of Lords, 1643; released, 1644; fought for king at Newbury, 1644; taken prisoner at Dartmouth, 1646; released on bail; committed to Tower on suspicion of treason, 1655; pensioned as gentleman of bedchamber, 1662. [v. 249]

BLOUNT, RICHARD (1565-1638), jesuit; educated at Oxford, English College, Douay (temporarily removed to Rheims), and Rome; ordained priest, 1589; went to Spain and came thence to England, 1591, in disguise; entered Society of Jesus in England, 1596; professed of four vows, 1608; superior of English missions, 1617; provincial, 1623; lived in hiding in London. [v. 252]

BLOUNT, Sir THOMAS (*d.* 1400), supporter of Richard II; deputy king's 'naperer,' 1377; joined barons' insurrection against Henry IV, 1399; captured and executed near Oxford. [v. 253]

BLOUNT, Sir THOMAS (*fl.* 1422), treasurer of Calais in Henry VI's reign; son of Sir Walter Blount [q. v.]; founded chantry at Newark, 1422. [v. 258]

BLOUNT or **BLUNT**, THOMAS (*fl.* 1668), parliamentarian colonel; on committee of Kent, 1643; imprisoned, 1660; member of Royal Society, 1665; noted for several ingenious inventions. [v. 253]

BLOUNT, THOMAS (1618-1679), miscellaneous writer; entered Inner Temple; compelled, being Roman catholic, to flee from his home during agitation due to popish plot, 1678; published historical, legal, and other works, including 'Academie of Eloquence,' 1654, 'Glossographia,' 1656, 'A Law Dictionary,' 1670, 'Fragmenta Antiquitatis, Ancient Tenures of Land,' 1679, and 'Boscobel,' 1660, a history of Charles II's escape after battle of Worcester. He left in manuscript a 'History of Hereford,' now lost. [v. 254]

BLOUNT, Sir THOMAS POPE (1649-1697), politician; son of Sir Henry Blount [q. v.]; created baronet, 1679; M.P. for St. Albans; knight of shire for Hertford; commissioner of accounts in House of Commons; published 'Censura celebriorum Authorum,' 1690, 'A Natural History,' 1693, 'Remarks on Poetry,' 1694, and 'Essays on several Subjects,' 1692. [v. 256]

BLOUNT, Sir WALTER (*d.* 1403), soldier; accompanied Black Prince to Spain, 1367; probably went with John of Gaunt to Castile, 1386; one of Gaunt's executors, 1399; M.P. for Derbyshire, 1399; killed at battle of Shrewsbury. He figures as Blunt in Shakespeare's '1 Henry IV.' [v. 257]

BLOUNT, WALTER, first BARON MONTJOY or MOUNTJOY (*d.* 1474), lord high treasurer of England; grandson of Sir Walter Blount [q. v.]; fought for Yorkists at Towton, 1461; knighted; governor of Calais; high treasurer of England, and raised to peerage, 1465; K.G. [v. 258]

BLOUNT, WILLIAM (*d.* 1471), son of Walter Blount (*d.* 1474) [q. v.]; killed fighting for Edward IV at Barnet. [v. 258]

BLOUNT, WILLIAM, fourth BARON MOUNTJOY (*d.* 1534), statesman and patron of learning; grandson of Walter Blount (*d.* 1474) [q. v.]; privy councillor; studied in Paris, *c.* 1496, under Erasmus, whom he brought to England, 1498; became intimate with Prince Henry, afterwards Henry VIII; served against Perkin Warbeck, 1497; lieutenant of marches of Calais, 1509; bailiff of Tournai, 1514-17; attended Henry VIII at Field of Cloth of Gold, 1520, and at meeting with Charles V at Dover, 1522; master of mint; K.G. Among the scholars whom he befriended were Erasmus, Leland, Richard Whytforde, Battus, and Richard Sampson. [v. 259]

BLOW, JAMES (*d.* 1759), printer; apprenticed to Patrick Neill [q. v.], at Glasgow, and was subsequently his assistant in Belfast; printed works for the presbyterians, 'Church Catechism in Irish and English,' 1722, and some editions of the bible, after *c.* 1726. [v. 260]

BLOW, JOHN (1648-1708), composer; one of children of Chapel Royal, 1660; organist of Westminster Abbey, 1669-80; master of the children of Chapel Royal, 1674; organist of Chapel Royal, 1676; composer in ordinary to James II, 1685; almoner and master of choristers at St. Paul's Cathedral, 1687-93; composer to Chapel Royal, 1699; buried in Westminster Abbey. His compositions include anthems for 'Divine Services and Anthems,' 1663, the 'Club Anthem' 'I will always give thanks,' 1663, duet to Herrick's 'Goe, perjur'd man,' 'Venus and Adonis' (a masque never printed), and a collection of part-songs. [v. 261]

BLOWER, SAMUEL (*d.* 1701), nonconformist divine; ejected from fellowship at Magdalen and, 1662, from Woodstock, Oxfordshire; subsequently founded Castle Hill meeting-house, Northampton. [v. 263]

BLOXAM, ANDREW (1801-1878), divine; educated at Rugby and Worcester College, Oxford, fellow; made collection of natural-history specimens on voyage to Sandwich Islands, 1824; wrote works relating to natural history. [v. 264]

BLOXAM, JOHN ROUSE (1807-1891), historian of Magdalen College; educated at Rugby and Worcester and Magdalen Colleges, Oxford; M.A., 1835; D.D., 1847; fellow of Magdalen College, 1836-63; pro-proctor of university, 1841; held various offices at his college till 1862; he was in full sympathy with the Tractarians; vicar of Upper Beeding, Sussex, 1862-91; published and left in manuscript valuable collections relating to the history of Magdalen College. [Suppl. i. 224]

BLOXAM, MATTHEW HOLBECHE (1805-1888), antiquary; brother of John Rouse Bloxam [q. v.]; educated at Rugby, where he was articled as solicitor; clerk to magistrates for Rugby division, 1832-72; F.S.A., 1863; published, 1829, 'Principles of Gothic Architecture' (issued in an enlarged form, 1882), and other architectural and antiquarian works. [Suppl. i. 226]

BLOXHAM, JOHN (*d.* 1334 ?), Carmelite of Chester; educated at Oxford; provincial of his order in England; wrote religious works. [v. 264]

BLOXHAM, JOHN (*d.* 1387), warden of Merton College, Oxford; bachelor of theology, Oxford; seventh warden of Merton, 1375. [v. 264]

BLUND or **BLUNT**, JOHN LE (*d.* 1248), divine; educated at Oxford and Paris; canon of Chichester; chancellor of York; nominated archbishop of Canterbury by Peter des Roches and elected, 1232, but the pope refused assent and the election was annulled. [v. 264]

BLUNDELL, HENRY (1724–1810), art collector; made at Ince-Blundell Hall, Lancashire, valuable collection of pictures, statuary, and other works of art; published works relating to his collection. [v. 265]

BLUNDELL, JAMES (1790–1877), physician; M.D. Edinburgh, 1813; lectured on midwifery at Guy's Hospital; L.C.P., 1818; F.C.P., 1838; published medical works. [v. 266]

BLUNDELL, PETER (1520–1601), merchant; of humble origin; accumulated great wealth as merchant and manufacturer in kersey trade; endowed Blundell's school (erected 1604), Tiverton, and left considerable sums for charitable purposes. [v. 266]

BLUNDELL, WILLIAM (1620–1698), topographer; captain of dragoons in royalist army, 1642; wounded at Lancaster. He left a topographical manuscript relating to Isle of Man (published 1876–7), and other writings. [v. 267]

BLUNDEVILL, RANDULPH DE, EARL OF CHESTER (d. 1232), warrior and statesman; succeeded as earl of Chester, 1180; married Constance, widow of Geoffrey, son of Henry II, 1187; joined, in Richard's interest, in siege of Nottingham, 1194; accompanied Richard to Normandy; quarrelled with Constance and imprisoned her in castle of St. Jean Beveron, 1196; married Clemence, sister of Geoffrey, c. 1200; accompanied John abroad, 1199; led armies engaged in Welsh wars, 1210 seq.; accompanied John to Poitou, 1214; took John's and, later, Henry III's side against barons, 1215; with Fulk de Bréauté stormed and plundered Worcester, 1216; laid siege unsuccessfully to Mountsorrel, Leicestershire, and shared in royalist victory at Lincoln, 1217; received earldom of Lincoln; went to Holy Land, 1218; joined in siege of Damietta, 1219; deserted royal party and plotted ineffectually with Aumâle and De Bréauté to surprise the Tower and obtain dismissal of Hubert de Burgh, but ultimately submitted; took part with Henry in siege of Nantes, 1230, and was left in Brittany with Aumâle and William Marshall in charge of the army; returned to England, 1231. [v. 267]

BLUNDEVILLE or **BLUNVILLE**, THOMAS DE (d. 1236), bishop of Norwich; nephew of Hubert de Burgh; clerk in exchequer; bishop of Norwich, 1226. [v. 272]

BLUNDEVILLE, THOMAS (fl. 1561), writer on horsemanship; inherited and lived on estate at Newton Flotman; published 'The fower chiefyst offices belonging to Horsemanshippe,' 1565–6, and works on horses, government, education of young gentlemen, logic, and astronomy. [v. 271]

BLUNT. [See also BLOUNT.]

BLUNT, ARTHUR CECIL (1844–1896). [See CECIL, ARTHUR.]

BLUNT, HENRY (1794–1843), divine; educated at Merchant Taylors' School and Pembroke College, Cambridge; B.A., 1817; fellow; vicar of Clare, Suffolk, 1820; incumbent, 1830, and rector, 1832, Trinity Church, Sloane Street; rector of Streatham, 1835–43; published religious works, including lectures on the life of Christ. [v. 272]

BLUNT, JOHN LE (d. 1248). [See BLUND.]

BLUNT, JOHN HENRY (1823–1884), divine; engaged in business as manufacturing chemist; entered University College, Durham, 1850; M.A., 1855; vicar of Kennington, near Oxford, 1868; held crown living of Beverston, Gloucestershire, 1873–84; D.D., 1882; published works of theology and ecclesiastical history. [v. 273]

BLUNT, JOHN JAMES (1794–1855), divine; B.A. and fellow, St. John's College, Cambridge, 1816; M.A., 1819; B.D., 1826; appointed a Wort's travelling bachelor, 1818; travelled in Italy and Sicily, and published results of observations; preached (and afterwards published) Hulsean Lectures, 1831 and 1832; rector of Great Oakley, Essex, 1834–9; Lady Margaret professor of divinity, 1839; author of sermons, lectures, and other theological works, some of which were published posthumously. [v. 274]

BLYKE, RICHARD (d. 1775), antiquary; F.R.S.; F.S.A.; deputy-auditor of office of imprest; clerk of journals, 1764; left manuscript collections for topographical history of Herefordshire. [v. 276]

BLYSSE, JOHN (d. 1530), physician; B.A. Oxford, 1507; M.C.P., 1525; left 'astronomical tables' at Merton College, Oxford, now lost. [v. 276]

BLYTH, SIR ARTHUR (1823–1891), premier of South Australia; born and educated at Birmingham; went to South Australia, 1839; engaged in business as ironmonger in Adelaide; member of Adelaide chamber of commerce; member for Yatala district in legislative council, 1855; member for Gumeracha in first elected council, 1857, and 1870; commissioner of works, 1857 and 1858–60; treasurer, 1860–1, 1862, and 1865; commissioner of lands and immigration, 1864–5 and 1870–1; chief secretary and premier, 1866–7; premier and treasurer, 1871–2; premier, 1873–5; member for North Adelaide, 1875; treasurer, 1876; agent-general for the colony in England, 1877; K.C.M.G., 1877; C.B., 1886. [Suppl. i. 226]

BLYTH, EDWARD (1810–1873), zoologist; druggist at Tooting; curator of museum of Asiatic Society of Bengal, Calcutta, 1841; returned to England with pension, 1862; published catalogues of the museum and other zoological works. [v. 276]

BLYTHE, GEOFFREY (d. 1530), bishop of Lichfield and Coventry; educated at Eton and King's College, Cambridge; prebendary of York, and archdeacon of Cleveland, 1493; treasurer of church of Sarum, 1494; prebendary of St. Paul's, c. 1496; dean of York, 1496; master of King's Hall, 1499–1528; prebendary and archdeacon of Sarum, 1499; bishop of Lichfield and Coventry, 1503; LL.D.; lord-president of Wales, 1512–1524. [v. 277]

BLYTHE, GEOFFREY (d. 1542), divine; M.A. King's College, Cambridge, 1523; LL.D., 1529; master of King's Hall, Cambridge, 1528. [v. 278]

BLYTHE, JOHN (d. 1499), bishop of Salisbury; warden of King's Hall, Cambridge, 1488; master of rolls, 1492; bishop of Salisbury, 1494; chancellor of Cambridge University, 1493–5. [v. 278]

BLYTHE, JOHN DEAN (1842–1869), miscellaneous writer; successively factory hand, newspaper reporter at Ashton-under-Lyne, and assistant in a Manchester firm; left miscellaneous writings, selections from which were published posthumously. [v. 278]

BOADEN, JAMES (1762–1839), journalist; editor of 'Oracle' newspaper, 1789; studied at Middle Temple; wrote several successful plays and published an exposure (1796) of the Ireland Shakespearean forgeries, a work (1837) on Shakespeare's 'Sonnets,' identifying Mr. W. H. with William Herbert (afterwards Earl of Pembroke), and biographies of actors and actresses. [v. 278]

BOADEN, JOHN (d. 1839), portrait painter; son of James Boaden [q. v.]; exhibited at Royal Academy, 1810–1833. [v. 279]

BOADICEA (d. 62), wife of Prasutagus, king (d. c. 60), of Iceni of Norfolk and Suffolk, who revolted ineffectually against Ostorius, c. 50; headed revolt of Iceni and Trinobantes, destroyed Camulodunum and Londinium, and, being at length defeated by Suetonius Paullinus, took poison. [v. 279]

BOAG, JOHN (1775–1863), compiler of the 'Imperial Lexicon'; educated at Glasgow; joined congregationalists and acted for many years as evangelist; pastor and schoolmaster at Blackburn, Linlithgowshire; published 'Imperial Lexicon' (c. 1847–8), which held its own until publication of Ogilvie's 'Dictionary.' [v. 280]

BOARDMAN, **BORDMAN**, **BOURDMAN**, or **BOURMAN**, ANDREW (1550?–1639), divine; M.A. St. John's College, Cambridge, 1575; D.D., 1594; Lady Margaret fellow, 1573; Greek lecturer, 1580; junior bursar, 1582; held livings at Allchurch, Warwickshire, 1586–1639. [v. 281]

BOASE, CHARLES WILLIAM (1828–1895), historian; B.A. Exeter College, Oxford, 1850; fellow, 1850; M.A., 1853; ordained deacon, 1855; tutor, 1855–84; lecturer in Hebrew, 1859–69, and in modern history, 1884–94; university reader in modern history, 1884–94; honorary secretary of Oxford Historical Society, 1884; published historical works relating to Oxford and other writings, including a translation (with Dr. G. W. Kitchin) of Ranke's 'History of England.' [Suppl. i. 227]

BOASE, GEORGE CLEMENT (1829–1897), bibliographer, brother of Charles William Boase [q. v.]; engaged in banking and insurance offices successively in Penzance and London; in Australia, 1854–64; manager of provision business of Whitehead & Co, 1865–74: retired and occupied himself with literary pursuits; published bibliographical and antiquarian writings. [Suppl. i. 228]

BOASE, HENRY (1763–1827), banker and author; chief clerk in Messrs. Ransom, Morland, and Hammersley's London banking house, 1792, and managing partner, *c.* 1799; became partner in Penzance Union Bank; fellow of Royal Society of Literature, 1821; published works on finance, [v. 281]

BOASE, HENRY SAMUEL (1799–1883), geologist, son of Henry Boase [q. v.]; studied chemistry at Dublin; M.D. Edinburgh, 1821; physician at Penzance; removed to London; F.R.S., 1837; managing partner to Turnbull Brothers, bleachers, of Claverhouse Bleachfield; published scientific works. [v. 282]

BOAST, JOHN (1543?–1594). [See BOSTE.]

BOATE, DE BOOT, BOOTIUS, or **BOTIUS**, ARNOLD (1600?–1653?), hebraist; M.D. Leyden; studied Hebrew rabbinical writings; practised medicine at Dublin; physician-general of English forces in Ireland; removed to Paris; published 'Animadversiones sacræ ad textum Hebraicum Veteris Testamenti,' 1644, also medical and other works. [v. 283]

BOATE, DE BOOT, BOOTIUS, or **BOTIUS**, GERARD (1604–1650), physician; brother of Arnold Boate [q. v.]; born at Gorcum, Holland; M.D. Leyden, 1628; settled in London; physician to the king; produced, in conjunction with his brother, a treatise depreciatory of the Aristotelian philosophy, 1641; L.C.P., 1646; doctor to hospital at Dublin, 1649; wrote 'Ireland's Naturall History,' which was published posthumously in 1652 by Samuel Hartlib, Milton's friend. [v. 284]

BOBART or **BOBERT**, JACOB, the elder (1599–1680), botanist; born at Brunswick; superintendent, 1632, of Oxford Physic Garden, of which he published a catalogue. [v. 285]

BOBART, JACOB, the younger (1641–1719), botanist; son of Jacob Bobart (1599–1680) [q. v.]; succeeded his father as superintendent of Oxford Physic Garden; botanical professor, Oxford, 1683–*c.* 1719; brought out the third part of Morison's 'Historia Plantarum,' 1699, and left manuscripts relating to botanical subjects. [v. 286]

BOBBIN, TIM (1708–1786). [See COLLIER, JOHN.]

BOCFELD, ADAM (*fl.* 1350), Franciscan; wrote commentaries on Aristotle. [v. 286]

BOCHER, BOUCHER, or **BUTCHER**, JOAN (*d.* 1550), anabaptist martyr; sometimes called JOAN OF KENT; friend of Anne Askew [q. v.]; asserted, 1548, that Christ did not 'take flesh of the virgin'; examined by Cranmer, imprisoned, and subsequently burned at Smithfield. [v. 286]

BOCK, EBERHARDT OTTO GEORGE VON (*d.* 1814), baron; entered Hanoverian cavalry, *c.* 1781; captain, 1800; came to England; raised, and was made colonel of 1st dragoons, king's German legion, 1804; major-general, 1810; served in Peninsula; wrecked in transport on Tulbest rocks. [v. 287]

BOCKING, EDWARD (*d.* 1534), Benedictine; leading supporter of Elizabeth Barton [q. v.]; D.D. Canterbury College, Oxford, 1518; warden; entered Benedictine priory of Christ Church, Canterbury, *c.* 1526; sent to report on Elizabeth Barton's alleged revelations, and induced her to feign her manifestations; hanged as one of her supporters. [v. 287]

BOCKING, RALPH (*d.* 1270), Dominican; private confessor to Richard Wych, bishop of Chichester, whose life he wrote. [v. 288]

BOCKMAN, R. (*fl.* 1750), portrait painter and mezzotint engraver in Amsterdam and later in England; produced engravings after Vandyck and others. [v. 288]

BOCLAND, GEOFFREY DE (*fl.* 1195–1224), justice; justiciar, 1195–7, 1201–4, and 1218; justice itinerant in Herefordshire, 1220; dean of St. Martin's-le-Grand; concerned in barons' revolt, 1216; died before 1231. [v. 289]

BOCLAND, HUGH DE, or HUGH OF BUCKLAND (*d.* 1119?), sheriff of Berkshire before 1100, and subsequently sheriff of Middlesex and other counties. [v. 289]

BODDINGTON, HENRY JOHN (1811–1865), artist; son of Edward Williams; took his wife's name, Boddington, to prevent confusion with relations who were artists; from 1837 exhibited scenes of country life at Royal Academy and Society of British Artists. [v. 290]

BODE, JOHN ERNEST (1816–1874), divine; educated at Eton, Charterhouse, and Christ Church, Oxford; M.A., 1840; censor, 1844; examiner in classics, 1846–8; Bampton lecturer, 1855; rector of Westwell, 1847, and of Castle Camps, 1860; published poetical and other works. [v. 290]

BODEN, JOSEPH (*d.* 1811), lieutenant-colonel; lieutenant in Bombay native infantry, 1781; major, 1802; lieutenant-colonel, 1806; judge-advocate; member of military board, Bombay; left money to found Boden professorship of Sanscrit, Oxford. [v. 291]

BODENHAM, JOHN (*fl.* 1600), reputed editor of Elizabethan miscellanies; planned publication of the Elizabethan miscellanies; 'Wits Commonwealth,' 1597, 'Wits Theater,' 1598, 'Belvedere, or the Garden of the Muses,' 1600, and 'Englands Helicon,' 1600. [v. 291]

BODICHON, BARBARA LEIGH SMITH (1827–1891), benefactress of Girton College; daughter of Benjamin Smith [q. v.]; studied water-colour drawing under William Henry Hunt [q. v.]; married Dr. Eugène Bodichon, 1857; proposed plan of and endowed Girton College. [Suppl. i. 229]

BODKIN, SIR WILLIAM HENRY (1791–1874), legal writer; hon. secretary of Society for Suppression of Mendicity, 1821; called to bar at Gray's Inn, 1826; joined home circuit; recorder of Dover, 1832; M.P. for Rochester, 1841–7; assistant judge of Middlesex sessions, 1859; knighted, 1867; counsel to treasury; wrote work relating to poor laws. [v. 292]

BODLEY, SIR JOSIAS (1550?–1618), military engineer; educated at Merton College, Oxford; served in Netherlands; captain in Leinster against Tyrone, 1598; governor of Newry; trenchmaster at sieges of Kinsale, 1601, Waterford, 1603, and other garrisons; superintendent of Irish castles, 1607; assisted in survey of Ulster plantations, 1609; appointed for life director-general of fortifications in Ireland, 1612; left manuscripts relating to his life and duties in Ireland. [v. 293]

BODLEY, LAURENCE (*d.* 1615), canon of Exeter; elder brother of Sir Josias Bodley [q. v.]; M.A. Christ Church, Oxford, 1568; D.D.; canon of Exeter before 1588. [v. 294]

BODLEY, SIR THOMAS (1545–1613), diplomatist and scholar; eldest brother of Josias and Laurence Bodley [q. v.]; educated at Geneva, whither his parents had fled from protestant persecution, and at Magdalen College, Oxford; M.A., 1566; lecturer in natural philosophy; university proctor, and deputy public orator, 1569; usher to the queen; engaged in missions to Denmark, 1585, and to Henry III of France, 1588; queen's permanent resident in United Provinces, 1589–96; began, 1598, formation of Bodleian Library, Oxford, which was opened 1603 and endowed by Bodley in 1611; knighted, 1604. A portrait of him is in the Bodleian Library. [v. 294]

BOECE or **BOETHIUS**, HECTOR (1465?–1536), historian; educated at Dundee and Paris, in which university he was regent or professor, *c.* 1492–8; Erasmus being one of his contemporaries; assisted William Elphinstone, bishop of Aberdeen, in founding (1505) university of Aberdeen; first principal; published lives of bishops of Mortlach and Aberdeen, 1522, and history of Scotland to accession of James III, 1527 (both printed in Paris): the history was translated into Scottish prose by John Bellenden, 1530–3 (printed 1536), and into English for Holinshed's chronicles by William Harrison, 1577; chaplain of St. Andrew's altar in church of St. Nicholas, Aberdeen; vicar of Tullynessle, 1528. [v. 297]

BOEHM, ANTHONY WILLIAM (1673–1722), divine; born at Pyrmont, Germany; came to London, 1701; opened school, 1702; assistant chaplain to Prince George, and subsequently to George I; published and left in manuscript many works and translations in German and English. [v. 300]

BOEHM, SIR JOSEPH EDGAR, first BARONET (1834–1890), sculptor; born at Vienna; studied sculpture in London, Italy, Paris, and Vienna; exhibited at Royal Academy from 1862, and soon obtained extensive practice as portrait sculptor; R.A., 1880; lecturer on sculpture at Royal Academy; sculptor in ordinary to Queen Victoria; created baronet, 1889. [Suppl. i. 229]

BOGAN, ZACHARY (1625–1659), author; M.A. Corpus Christi College, Oxford, 1650; fellow, 1647; tutor; published religious and learned works. [v. 301]

BOGDANI or **BOGDANE**, JAMES (d. 1720), painter of still-life and birds; born in Hungary; patronised in England by Queen Anne. [v. 301]

BOGLE GEORGE (1746–1781), diplomatist; educated at Edinburgh University; entered service of East India Company, 1769; assistant secretary to revenue board, 1772; envoy to and subsequently personal friend of Lama of Tibet, 1774–5; superintended renewal of leases of company's provinces, 1776; commissioner of lawsuits; collector of Rangpúr, 1779; left manuscript journal. [v. 302]

BOGUE, DAVID (1750–1825), divine; educated at Edinburgh; licensed as preacher; usher in academies at Edmonton, Hampstead, and Camberwell; congregational minister at Gosport; tutor in institution for training for ministry, Gosport, 1780; a founder of the London Missionary Society, British and Foreign Bible Society, and Religious Tract Society; published religious works, including 'History of Dissenters,' 1809. [v. 302]

BOGUE, RICHARD (1783–1813), captain royal artillery; second lieutenant royal artillery, 1798; second captain, 1806; killed at Leipzig. [v. 303]

BOHEMUS, MAURITIUS (fl. 1647–1662), nonconformist divine; born at Colberg; rector of Hallaton, Leicestershire; ejected, 1662; published religious works. [v. 303]

BOHLER, JOHN (1797–1872), botanist; became collector of medicinal plants for doctors, and subsequently published botanical writings. [v. 304]

BOHN, HENRY GEORGE (1796–1884), bookseller and publisher; entered his father's business of bookbinder and second-hand bookseller; began business independently, 1831; published 'guinea catalogue' of old books, 1841; took up the 'remainder' trade; published 'Standard Library,' 1846, 'Scientific' and 'Antiquarian,' 1847, 'Classical,' 1848, 'Illustrated,' 1849, 'Shilling Series,' 1850, 'Ecclesiastical,' 1851, 'Philological,' 1852, 'British Classics,' 1853, the series numbering in all over 600 volumes; he made some translations for his 'Classical Library,' and produced works and compilations, including reprint of Lowndes's 'Bibliographer's Manual.' [v. 304]

BOHN, JAMES STUART BURGES (1803–1880), bookseller; educated at Winchester and Göttingen; opened bookselling business in London, 1834; republished Dugdale's 'Monasticon' and compiled catalogues. [v. 306]

BOHUN, EDMUND (1645–1699), chief-justice of Carolina; fellow-commoner Queens' College, Cambridge, 1663; on commission of peace; licenser of publications, 1692; imprisoned, 1693, for sanctioning publication of tract by Charles Blount [q. v.] defending doctrine of conquest by William III; chief-justice of Carolina, 1698; published tracts, compilations, and translations. [v. 306]

BOHUN, HENRY DE, first EARL OF HEREFORD (1176–1220), created earl, 1199; grandson of Humphrey III de Bohun [q. v.]; constable of England; joined barons against John, 1215; died on pilgrimage to Holy Land. [v. 307]

BOHUN, HUMPHREY III DE (d. 1187), baron; sewer to Stephen, 1140; taken prisoner at Winchester while fighting for Matilda, 1141; attended council at Clarendon, 1164; took Henry II's side in rebellion of Prince Henry, 1173. [v. 307]

BOHUN, HUMPHREY V DE, second EARL OF HEREFORD and first EARL OF ESSEX (d. 1274), constable of England; joined Richard of Cornwall against the king, 1227; marshal of the household, 1236; sheriff of Kent, 1239–41; took part in Henry's French expedition, 1242; joined federation of barons, 1258; justice itinerant, 1260; served with king against de Montfort, 1263; taken prisoner at Lewes, 1264. [v. 308]

BOHUN, HUMPHREY VII DE, third EARL OF HEREFORD and second EARL OF ESSEX (d. 1298), constable of England; served with Welsh army of occupation, 1286; joined Roger Bigod, earl of Norfolk [q. v.], in opposing Edward I's reforms; refused to serve in Gascony, and was deprived of office of constable, 1297. [v. 309]

BOHUN, HUMPHREY VIII DE, fourth EARL OF HEREFORD and third EARL OF ESSEX (1276–1322), constable of England; sent to oppose Robert Bruce, 1308; among barons who besieged Gaveston at Scarborough, 1312; taken prisoner at Bannockburn, 1314, and exchanged for Bruce's wife, then captive in England; quelled rising in Wales, 1315; served in expedition against Scotland, 1318–19; took lead in denouncing the Despensers; defeated by king and slain at Boroughbridge, Yorkshire, 1322. [v. 309]

BOHUN, WILLIAM DE, EARL OF NORTHAMPTON (d. 1360), earl, 1337; son of Humphrey de Bohun VIII [q. v.]; king's lieutenant and captain-general in Brittany, 1342 and 1345–6; fought at Cressy; warden of Scottish marches, 1350; in France, 1355, and Gascony, 1357–9. [v. 310]

BOILEAU, SIR JOHN PETER (1794–1869), archæologist; second lieutenant of Rifle Corps, 1813; created baronet, 1838; F.R.S., 1843; F.S.A., 1852; vice-president Society of Antiquaries, 1858–62, and 1863–7, and of other scientific societies; sheriff in Norfolk, 1844; published archæological papers. [v. 311]

BOIS, JOHN (1561–1644), translator of the bible; educated at St. John's and Magdalene Colleges, Cambridge; fellow of St. John's, 1580; Greek lecturer at Cambridge, 1584–95; appointed one of Cambridge translators for King James's bible, 1604, and member of board of revision; translated portions of Apocrypha and of the section from Chronicles to Canticles; assisted in Sir Henry Savile's edition of 'St. Chrysostom' (printed in 1610–13); prebendary of Ely, 1615; published treatise on Greek accents, 1630. His critical notes on passages in Greek Testament appeared posthumously, 1655. [v. 311]

BOISIL, SAINT (d. 664), superior of the monastery at Melrose; gives name to St. Boswell's, Roxburghshire; several religious writings are attributed to him. [v. 313]

BOISSIER, GEORGE RICHARD (1791–1851), ecclesiologist; B.A. Magdalene College, Cambridge, 1828; incumbent of Oakfield, Kent; published 'Notes on Cambridgeshire Churches,' 1827. [v. 313]

BOIT, CHARLES (d. 1726?), enamel painter; born at Stockholm; worked with success as enamel painter in London; ran into debt and fled to Paris, where he prospered; died in Paris. [v. 313]

BOITARD, LOUIS PETER (fl. 1750), engraver; born in France; pupil of La Farge; executed in England portraits and plates for publications. [v. 314]

BOKENHAM or **BOKENAM**, OSBERN (1393–1447?), poet; professed member of Augustinian convent of Stoke Clare, Suffolk. His writings include poems in Suffolk dialect commemorating lives of twelve holy women and of the 11,000 virgins (Arundel MSS. Brit. Mus. No. 327, printed for Roxburghe Club, 1835). [v. 314]

BOKYNGHAM or **BUCKINGHAM**, JOHN (d. 1398), bishop; prebendary and, 1349, dean of Lichfield; prebendary of Lincoln, 1352; keeper of privy seal to Edward III; elected bishop of Ely, but election quashed by pope, 1361; bishop of Lincoln, 1363–97, and retired to Christ Church monastery, Canterbury; opponent of the Wycliffites. [v. 315]

BÖLCKOW, HENRY WILLIAM FERDINAND (1806–1878), ironmaster; born at Sulten, Mecklenburg; came to England, 1827; entered partnership, 1841, as manufacturer of iron at Middlesbrough, to which town he was an extensive benefactor, and (1853) first mayor; M.P., 1868. [v. 316]

BOLD, HENRY (d. 1677), divine; educated at Christ Church, Oxford; chaplain to Earl of Arlington. [v. 317]

BOLD, HENRY (1627–1683), poetical writer; educated at Winchester and New College, Oxford; probationer-fellow; dislodged, 1648; employed in the examiner's office in Chancery; published several volumes of poems in English and Latin and translations from Latin. [v. 316]

BOLD, JOHN (1679–1751), divine; B.A. St. John's College, Cambridge, 1698; curate of Stoney Stanton, 1702–1751; wrote religious works. [v. 317]

BOLD, SAMUEL (1649–1737), controversialist; vicar of Shapwick, Dorsetshire, 1674; resigned or was ejected, 1688; rector of Steeple, Isle of Purbeck (1682–1737), to which Tyneham was united in 1721; preached against persecution, and published 'Plea for Moderation towards Dissenters,' 1682, for which he was fined and imprisoned. His works include tracts defending John Locke's philosophy. [v. 317]

BOLDERO, EDMUND (1608–1679), divine; M.A. and fellow of Pembroke Hall, Cambridge, 1631; ejected from fellowship under Commonwealth and imprisoned; D.D., 1660; held rectories in Suffolk; master of Jesus College, Cambridge, 1663; vice-chancellor of university, 1668 and 1674. [v. 318]

BOLEYN, ANNE (1507–1536). [See ANNE.]

BOLEYN, GEORGE, VISCOUNT ROCHFORD (d. 1536), son of Sir Thomas Boleyn, earl of Wiltshire [q. v.] and brother of Anne Boleyn; chief steward of honour of Beaulieu, 1529; governor of Bethlehem Hospital, 1529; knighted and created Viscount Rochford, c. 1530; warden of Cinque ports, 1534; arraigned for incest and high treason, and executed, 17 May, two days before his sister. [v. 319]

BOLEYN, GEORGE (d. 1603), divine; perhaps son of George Boleyn, viscount Rochford [q. v.]; sizar, Trinity Hall, Cambridge, 1544; M.A., 1560; prebendary of York, 1560; prebendary of Chichester; canon of Canterbury, 1566; D.D., and dean of Lichfield, 1576; prebendary of Dasset Parva, 1577–9. [v. 320]

BOLEYN, SIR THOMAS, EARL OF WILTSHIRE (1477–1539), lord privy seal; keeper of exchange at Calais and of foreign exchange in England, 1509; joint-constable of Norwich Castle, 1512; accompanied Sir Edward Poynings on embassy to Low Countries; took part in invasion of France, 1513; sheriff of Kent, 1517; went on embassy to Francis I, 1519–20, and negotiated arrangements for Field of Cloth of Gold; Wolsey's agent in conferences at Calais, 1521; joint-ambassador to Spain, 1522–3; treasurer of household, 1522; created Viscount Rochford, 1525; ambassador with Sir Anthony Browne to France, 1527; created Earl of Wiltshire and Ormonde, 1529; lord privy seal; ambassador to Charles V, 1530, and to France on business of Henry VIII's divorce; father of Queen Anne Boleyn. [v. 321]

BOLINGBROKE, EARL OF (1580?–1646). [See ST. JOHN, OLIVER.]

BOLINGBROKE, VISCOUNT (1678–1751). [See ST. JOHN, HENRY.]

BOLINGBROKE, HENRY (1785–1855), writer on Demerara, whither he made a voyage in 1798. [v. 323]

BOLLAND, SIR WILLIAM (1772–1840), judge; M.A. Trinity College, Cambridge, 1797; called to bar at Middle Temple, 1801; practised at Old Bailey; recorder of Reading, 1817–29; baron of exchequer, 1829–39; one of originators of Roxburghe Club. [v. 323]

BOLLARD, NICHOLAS (fl. 1500?), naturalist; author of a manuscript work on cultivation of trees. [v. 324]

BOLRON, ROBERT (fl. 1674–1680), informer; successively jeweller's apprentice, foot-soldier, and manager of Sir Thomas Gascoigne's collieries, Barmbow, Yorkshire; became party to popish plot against James II, and informed against Gascoigne, who was tried and acquitted. [v. 324]

BOLTON, DUKES OF. [See PAULET, CHARLES, first DUKE, 1625?–1699; PAULET, CHARLES, second DUKE, 1661–1722; PAULET, CHARLES, third DUKE, 1685–1754; PAULET, HARRY, sixth DUKE, 1719–1794.]

BOLTON, DUCHESS OF (1708–1760). [See FENTON, LAVINIA.]

BOLTON, first BARON (1746–1807). [See ORDE, THOMAS.]

BOLTON or **BOULTON**, EDMUND (1575?–1633?), historian and poet; free commoner, Trinity Hall, Cambridge; studied at Inner Temple; contributed to 'England's Helicon,' 1600; formulated a scheme, 1617, for a royal academy of letters and science, which was favourably received by James I, who died before it was carried out; subsequently imprisoned successively in Fleet and Marshalsea. Among his writings are 'The Roman Histories of Lucius Iulius Florus' (translated), 1618, 'Nero Cæsar,' 1624, and a life of Henry II. [v. 325]

BOLTON, SIR FRANCIS JOHN (1831–1887), soldier and electrician; enlisted in royal artillery; ensign in Gold Coast artillery corps, 1857; served at Crobboe Heights, 1858; captain, 12th foot, 1860; engaged, with Captain (afterwards Rear-admiral) Philip Howard Colomb [q. v.], in developing system of visual signalling; invented oxy-calcium light for night signalling; brevetmajor, 1868; assisted in founding Society of Telegraph Engineers and Electricians, 1871; lieutenant-colonel, 1877 honorary colonel, 1881; designed and controlled coloured fountains and electric lights for exhibitions at South Kensington, 1883–6; knighted, 1884. [Suppl. i. 230]

BOLTON, SIR GEORGE (d. 1807?), preceptor to royal princesses; knighted; wrote on firearms. [v. 327]

BOLTON, JAMES (fl. 1775–1795), naturalist; of humble birth; published works on natural history. [v. 327]

BOLTON, JAMES JAY (1824–1863), evangelical divine; educated in America and at Corpus Christi College, Cambridge; B.A., 1848; incumbent of St. Paul's Episcopal Chapel, Kilburn; published religious works. [v. 328]

BOLTON, SIR RICHARD (1570?–1648), lawyer; practised at English bar; recorder of Dublin, 1604; member of Society of King's Inn, Dublin, 1610–13; M.P. for Dublin, 1613; knighted, 1618; solicitor-general for Ireland, 1619; attorney-general to court of wards, Dublin, 1622; chief baron of Irish exchequer, 1625; chancellor of Ireland, 1639; chief adviser of Strafford in his attempts to introduce arbitrary government; impeached of high treason by Irish House of Commons, but the impeachment abandoned, 1641–2; one of principal counsellors of Ormonde in negotiating with Irish confederation concerning peace, 1644; published 'Statutes of Ireland,' 1621, and other legal writings. [v. 328]

BOLTON, ROBERT (1572–1631), puritan; educated at Blackburn and Lincoln and Brasenose colleges, Oxford; B.A., 1596; fellow of Brasenose and M.A., 1602; lecturer in logic and moral and natural philosophy; B.D., 1609; rector of Broughton, Northamptonshire, 1610–31; published religious works. [v. 330]

BOLTON, ROBERT (1697–1763), divine; M.A. Wadham College, Oxford, 1718; LL.D.; transferred to Hart Hall, 1719; fellow of Dulwich College, 1722–5; preacher at Rolls Chapel, London, 1729; dean of Carlisle, 1735, and vicar of St. Mary's, Reading, 1738–63; published religious works. [v. 332]

BOLTON, SAMUEL (1606–1654), divine; educated at Christ's College, Cambridge; member of Westminster assembly of divines, 1643; D.D.; master of Christ's College, 1645; vice-chancellor of Cambridge University, 1651; published religious works. [v. 333]

BOLTON, WILLIAM (d. 1532), architect; prior of monastery of St. Bartholomew's, Smithfield, c. 1506; said to have designed Henry VII's chapel in Westminster Abbey. [v. 333]

BOLTS, WILLEM or WILLIAM (1740?–1808), Dutch adventurer; merchant in Lisbon; entered Bengal civil service, 1759; second in council at Benares, 1764; resigned the service, being reprimanded for using the East India Company's authority for private trading scheme, 1766; deported to England, 1768; published work attacking government in Bengal; became colonel in Austrian service, 1778, and founded establishments in India for an Austrian East India Company; died in Paris. [v. 333]

BOMELIUS, ELISEUS or LICIUS (d. 1574?), physician and astrologer; born at Wesel; M.D. Cambridge; physician and astrologer in London; arrested for practising without license of College of Physicians, 1567; 'open prisoner,' 1570; settled in Russia, 1570, and, as magician, gained favour of Ivan IV; arrested, c. 1574, on charges of intriguing with kings of Poland and Sweden against the tsar, and subsequently died in prison; published astrological works. [v. 334]

BONAR, ANDREW ALEXANDER (1810–1892), Scottish divine; brother of Horatius Bonar [q. v.]; educated at Edinburgh; licensed preacher, 1835; ordained minister of Collace, Perthshire, 1838; joined Free church, 1843; minister of Finnieston, Glasgow, 1856–92; published religious writings. [Suppl. i. 232]

BONAR, ARCHIBALD (1753–1816), divine; son of John Bonar the elder [q. v.]; educated at Edinburgh; minister successively at Newburn, Glasgow, and Cramond; published religious works. [v. 335]

BONAR, HORATIUS (1808–1889), Scottish divine; educated at Edinburgh University; engaged in mission work at Leith; minister of new North Church, Kelso, 1837; joined Free church, 1843; honorary D.D. Aberdeen, 1853; minister of Chalmers Memorial Church, Edinburgh, 1866; moderator of general assembly of Free church, 1883; edited several religious periodicals, and published hymns (including ' I heard the voice of Jesus say ') and other religious writings. [Suppl. i. 231]

BONAR, JAMES (1757–1821), brother of Archibald Bonar [q. v.]; educated at Edinburgh; solicitor in excise office; treasurer of Royal Society, Edinburgh; promoter of Astronomical Institution; contributed to ' Encyclopædia Britannica ' and ' Edinburgh Encyclopædia.' [v. 335]

BONAR, JOHN, the elder (1722–1761), Scottish divine; educated at Edinburgh University; minister of Cockpen, near Dalkeith, 1746; called to collegiate church of Perth, 1756; published sermons and other religious works. [v. 336]

BONAR, JOHN, the younger (1747–1807), first solicitor of excise in Scotland; son of John Bonar (1722–1761) [q. v.]; educated at Edinburgh; joint-editor of ' Miscellaneous Pieces of Poetry,' 1765. [v. 336]

BONAR, JOHN JAMES (1803–1891), Scottish divine; brother of Horatius Bonar [q. v.]; educated at Edinburgh; D.D., 1883; licensed preacher, 1827; minister of St. Andrew's, Greenock, 1835; joined Free church, 1843; published religious handbooks. [Suppl. i. 232]

BONAVENTURA, THOMASINE (d. 1510 ?), Cornish benefactress; Cornish peasant girl; married successively three rich London merchants, the last being Sir John Percyvall, lord mayor, 1498; worked for the improvement of social conditions in Cornwall. [v. 336]

BOND, DANIEL (1725–1803), painter; exhibited landscapes at Society of Arts, 1762–3, and received premiums from the society, 1764 and 1765. [v. 337]

BOND, DENNIS (d. 1658), politician; woollen draper at Dorchester; bailiff, 1630; mayor, 1635; M.P., 1640; one of commissioners to try Charles I, 1649; member of council of state, 1649–53; president of council, 1652 and 1653; member of council's committee for trade, 1655; M.P. for Weymouth and Melcombe Regis, 1654 and 1656; buried in Westminster Abbey, but body exhumed, 1661. [v. 337]

BOND, Sir EDWARD AUGUSTUS (1815–1898), principal librarian of British Museum; educated at Merchant Taylors' School; assistant in Record Office, 1833, and in British Museum, 1838; Egerton librarian, 1850; keeper of manuscripts, 1866!; principal librarian, 1878–88; substituted printed for manuscript catalogue in printed book department, and adopted sliding press for books; founded, with Sir E. Maunde Thompson, Palæographical Society, 1873; C.B., 1885; K.C.B., 1898; honorary LL.D. Cambridge. He edited historical and other works. [Suppl. i. 232]

BOND, GEORGE (1750–1796), lawyer; barrister of Middle Temple; serjeant, 1786; practised at Surrey sessions. [v. 338]

BOND, HENRY JOHN HALES (1801–1883), physician; M.B. Corpus Christi College, Cambridge, 1825; M.D., 1831; studied at London, Edinburgh, and Paris; regius professor of physic, Cambridge, 1851–72. [v. 338]

BOND, JOHN (1550–1612), physician and classical scholar; M.A. Oxford, 1579; master of free school, Taunton; practised as physician; probably chief secretary to lord chancellor Egerton; M.P. for Taunton, 1601 and 1603; published commentaries on Horace (1606), and left notes on Persius (published posthumously, 1614). [v. 339]

BOND, JOHN (1612–1676), puritan divine; son of Dennis Bond [q. v.]; B.A. St. Catharine's College, Cambridge, 1631; fellow; M.A., 1635; LL.D., 1645; minister, 1645, and master of the Savoy; master of Trinity Hall, 1646; vice-chancellor of Cambridge University, 1658; professor of law, Gresham College, London, 1649; lost preferments at Restoration. [v. 340]

BOND, JOHN JAMES (1819–1883), chronologist; senior assistant keeper in public record office; compiled chronological tables. [v. 340]

BOND, JOHN LINNELL (1766 – 1837), architect, gold medallist, Royal Academy, 1786; prepared design for Waterloo Bridge. [v. 340]

BOND, MARTIN (1558–1643), merchant adventurer; son of William Bond (d. 1576) [q. v.]; chief captain of train-bands, 1588–1643; treasurer of St. Bartholomew's Hospital, 1619–36. [v. 340]

BOND, NATHANIEL (1634–1707), king's serjeant; son of Dennis Bond [q. v.]; B.C.L. All Souls' College, Oxford, 1654; called to bar at Inner Temple, 1661; M.P.; recorder of Weymouth, 1683; serjeant-at-law, 1689; king's serjeant and knighted, 1693. [v. 338]

BOND, NICHOLAS (1540–1608), president of Magdalen College, Oxford; B.A. St. John's College, Cambridge, 1564; fellow of Magdalen College, Oxford, 1565–75; M.A. Oxford, 1574; D.D., 1580; canon of Westminster, 1582; chaplain of Savoy and chaplain in ordinary to queen; vice-chancellor of Oxford University, 1590–1 and 1592–3; president of Magdalen College, 1590. [v. 341]

BOND, OLIVER (1760 ?–1798), republican; wool merchant in Dublin; original member of ' Society of United Irishmen,' 1791; tried and imprisoned in Newgate as secretary of society for publication of resolutions condemning government's policy towards Ireland and catholics, 1793; directed organisation to establish independent Irish republic, 1798; found guilty of high treason; died in prison. [v. 341]

BOND, THOMAS (1765–1837), topographer; town clerk of East Looe and West Looe, Cornwall, on which places he published a topographical work (1823). [v. 342]

BOND, WILLIAM (d. 1576), sheriff of London in 1567. [v. 340]

BOND, WILLIAM (d. 1735), dramatist; wrote ' Tuscan Treaty ' (acted at Covent Garden, 1733), and other works, including contributions to ' Plain Dealer,' 1724. [v. 342]

BONE, HENRY (1755–1834), painter; employed in London as enameller; exhibited portraits in Royal Academy from 1780; enamel painter to Prince of Wales, 1800, and to the king 1801, till death; A.R.A., 1801; R.A., 1811. [v. 343]

BONE, HENRY PIERCE (1779–1855), painter; son of Henry Bone [q. v.]; painted classical subjects in oils, 1806–33, and subsequently in enamels. [v. 344]

BONE, ROBERT TREWICK (1790–1840), painter; brother of Henry Pierce Bone [q. v.]; painter of sacred, classic, and domestic subjects. [v. 344]

BONER, CHARLES (1815–1870), author; lived with Baron August Doernberg and, later, with Prince Thurn and Taxis in Germany and Ratisbon; special correspondent of ' Daily News' in Vienna, 1865; published poetical and other works. [v. 344]

BONHAM, Sir SAMUEL GEORGE (1803–1863), politician; employed under East India Company; governor of Penang, Singapore, and Malacca, 1837–47; governor of Hongkong and plenipotentiary and superintendent of trade in China, 1847; K.C.B., 1851; returned to England and was made baronet, 1853. [v. 345]

BONHAM, THOMAS (d. 1629 ?), physician; M.D. St. John's College, Cambridge, and incorporated at Oxford, 1611; his medical writings were published posthumously. [v. 345]

BONHOTE, ELIZABETH (1744–1818), authoress; published novels, essays, and other works, 1773–1810. [v. 345]

BONIFACE, SAINT (680–755), the apostle of Germany; born at Kirton or Crediton, Devonshire; his original name Winfrid or Winfrith ; educated in monastery at Exeter, and at Nursling, near Winchester ; ordained priest, *c.* 710 ; went to Frisia, 716, but being refused by Radbod, the pagan chief, permission to preach, returned to Nursling ; went to Rome, 718, and obtaining letters of authority from Gregory II proceeded to Bavaria and Thuringia ; on death of Radbod laboured successfully among Frisians and Hessians, 719–22 ; bishop, 723 ; instituted ecclesiastical organisation in Hessia and Thuringia ; archbishop, 732 ; organised Bavarian church, 739 ; appointed legate to Pope Zacharias, and entrusted with reformation of Frankish church, 741 ; took possession of see of Mentz, with jurisdiction over sees of Worms, Cologne, Utrecht, and others established by him in Germany, 746 ; established monasteries at Fritzlar, Utrecht, Fulda, Amanaburg, and Ordorf or Ohrdruf ; slain with his followers by pagans at Dokkum on the Bordau. He left a set of ecclesiastical statutes, fifteen sermons, and other religious works. [v. 346]

BONIFACE OF SAVOY (*d.* 1270), archbishop ; son of Thomas I, count of Savoy ; entered Carthusian order ; bishop of Belley, near Chambery, 1234 ; undertook administration of bishopric of Valence, 1241 ; related to Henry III by the marriage of his sister Beatrix's daughter Eleanor ; elected archbishop of Canterbury, 1241 ; came to England, 1244 ; reformed financial management of archbishopric ; attended council of Lyons, 1244 ; returned to England, 1249 ; instituted visitation of province of Canterbury, which was strongly resisted ; retired to Rome, 1250–2 ; made expedition to relieve his brother Thomas when imprisoned for tyranny by people of Turin, 1255 ; took part at first with bishops against king and pope, 1256, but joined papal legate in excommunicating rebellious barons (1263) at Boulogne ; returned to England, 1265 ; died at St. Helena, Savoy, while accompanying Edward I on crusade. [v. 350]

BONINGTON, RICHARD PARKES (1801–1828), painter ; studied water-colour painting under Louis Francia at Calais and at the Louvre and Institute, and under Baron Gros in Paris ; first exhibited at Salon, 1822 ; made drawings for Baron Taylor's 'Voyages Pittoresques dans l'ancienne France' and other works ; began to paint in oil-colours, *c.* 1824 ; visited England (1825), where he first exhibited, 1826 ; painted, in England, 'Deux femmes au milieu d'un paysage' (engraved for the 'Anniversary,' 1828) : died during visit to England. [v. 352]

BONNAR, GEORGE WILLIAM (1796–1836), wood-engraver ; executed wood-engravings for Douce's edition of 'The Dance of Death,' 1833, and other works. [v. 354]

BONNAR, WILLIAM (1800–1853), painter ; foreman of decorative business ; member of Royal Scottish Academy soon after its foundation. His pictures include portraits and historical, rural, and humorous pieces.
[v. 354]

BONNEAU, JACOB (*d.* 1786), painter : teacher of drawing and perspective ; member of the Society of British Artists, exhibiting landscapes, 1765–78. [v. 355]

BONNELL, JAMES (1653–1699), accountant-general of Ireland ; born of English parents at Genoa ; came to England, his father (and himself in reversion) having been appointed accountant-general of Ireland in return for services to Charles II while in exile ; educated at St. Catharine's Hall, Cambridge ; undertook, *c.* 1684, duties of accountant-general of Ireland. He translated parts of Synesius into English. [v. 355]

BONNER or **BONER**, EDMUND (1500 ?–1569), bishop of London ; educated at Pembroke College, Oxford ; was ordained and took degrees of bachelor of canon and civil law, 1519 ; D.C.L., 1525 ; chaplain to Cardinal Wolsey, 1529 ; sent to Rome to protest against Henry VIII's being cited thither on the question of his divorce, 1532 ; received benefice of Cherry Burton, 1532 ; appealed in person to Clement VII against Henry's excommunication after marriage with Anne Boleyn, 1533 ; received living of East Dereham, Norfolk, 1534 ; bishop of Hereford and ambassador to French court, 1538 ; bishop of London, 1539 ; ambassador to the emperor, 1542–3 ; imprisoned in Fleet for non-acceptance of Edward VI's injunctions and the Book of Homilies, 1547 ; reprimanded for neglecting to enforce use of new prayer-book, and imprisoned in Marshalsea, 1549–53 ; deprived of bishopric for omission to set forth in a sermon at Paul's Cross that Edward's authority in his minority was not less than if he were of

mature years ; restored to his see, 1553 ; joined in judicial capacity with great severity in Marian persecution ; refused oath of supremacy and was deprived of bishopric, 1559 ; died in the Marshalsea. [v. 356]

BONNER, RICHARD (*fl.* 1548), author of a treatise on the sacrament. [v. 360]

BONNEY, HENRY KAYE (1780–1862), divine ; educated at Charterhouse, Emmanuel and Christ's colleges, Cambridge ; M.A., 1805 ; D.D., 1824 ; prebendary of Lincoln, 1807 ; examining chaplain to Dr. Pelham, bishop of Lincoln, 1820 ; dean of Stamford, 1827. His published works include a life of Jeremy Taylor, 1815. [v. 360]

BONNOR, CHARLES (*fl.* 1777–1829 ?), actor ; apprenticed as coachmaker ; appeared successfully on stage at Bath, 1777, and played at Covent Garden, 1783 ; endeavoured ineffectually to establish an English theatre in Paris, 1784 ; appointed deputy-comptroller of the post-office and retired from stage, *c.* 1785 ; comptroller-general, 1788 ; comptroller of inland department, 1792–4. [v. 361]

BONNOR, THOMAS (*fl.* 1763–1807), topographical draughtsman ; engraved plates for several county histories. [v. 362]

BONNYCASTLE, JOHN (1750 ?–1821), mathematical writer ; kept an academy at Hackney ; professor of mathematics, Royal Military Academy, Woolwich, *c.* 1782 ; wrote works on elementary mathematics. [v. 362]

BONNYCASTLE, SIR RICHARD HENRY (1791–1847), lieutenant-colonel royal engineers ; first lieutenant, royal engineers, 1809 ; in American campaigns, 1812–14, and with army of occupation in France ; served during Canadian rebellion of 1837–9 ; knighted, 1838 ; commanding engineer in Newfoundland ; lieutenant-colonel, 1840 ; retired, 1847 ; published topographical works relating to America. [v. 363]

BONOMI, JOSEPH, the elder (1739–1808), architect ; born at Rome ; came to England, 1767 ; settled in practice in London, 1784 ; A.R.A., 1789 ; exhibited drawings at Royal Academy, 1783–1806. His works, which are chiefly in Grecian renaissance style, include several country mansions. [v. 363]

BONOMI, JOSEPH, the younger (1796–1878), sculptor and draughtsman ; son of Joseph Bonomi (1739–1808) [q. v.] ; student at Royal Academy ; studied sculpture under Nollekens ; visited Egypt with Lepsius, 1842 ; made drawings for Warren and Fahey's panorama of Nile ; curator of Soane's Museum, Lincoln's Inn Fields, 1861–78 ; illustrated egyptological works. [v. 363]

BONVILLE, ANTHONY, *alias* TERILL (1621–1676), jesuit ; born at Canford ; educated at St. Omer and English college, Rome ; ordained priest, 1647 ; entered Society of Jesus, 1647 ; successively professor of philosophy at Florence and Parma, and of theology and mathematics at Liège ; published philosophical and religious treatises. [v. 364]

BONVISI, ANTONIO (*d.* 1558), merchant ; of Italian descent ; probably born in London ; dealt in wool, jewels, and foreign articles, and acted as banker to government ; fled to continent at beginning of Edward VI's reign, being a catholic ; died at Louvain. [v. 365]

BONWICKE, AMBROSE, the younger (1692–1714), nonjuror ; son of Ambrose Bonwicke (1652–1722) [q. v.] ; educated at Merchant Taylors' School and St. John's College, Cambridge, having been, as nonjuror, disqualified at Oxford. [v. 366]

BONWICKE, AMBROSE, the elder (1652–1722), nonjuror ; educated at Merchant Taylors' School and St. John's College, Oxford ; fellow ; M.A., 1675 ; B.D., 1682 ; ordained priest, 1680 ; head-master of Merchant Taylors' School, 1686 ; refused oath of allegiance to William III, and was dismissed from head-mastership, 1691. [v. 366]

BONYTHON, CHARLES (*d.* 1705), lawyer ; called to bar at Gray's Inn, 1678 ; steward of courts of Westminster, 1683–1705 ; M.P. for Westminster, 1685–7 ; serjeant-at-law, 1692 ; committed suicide. [v. 367]

BONYTHON, RICHARD (1580–1650 ?), American settler ; settled in Maine, America, 1631 ; commissioner for government of Maine, 1636 ; member of council, 1640–7. [v. 367]

BOOKER, JOHN (1603–1667), astrologer ; apprenticed as haberdasher in London, and was subsequently writing-master at Hadley and clerk in the city ; became professional astrologer ; licenser of mathematical works ; published 'Telescopium Uranium,' an almanack, from 1631, 'Bloody Irish Almanack,' and other works.   [v. 368]

BOOKER, LUKE (1762–1835), divine and poet ; rector of Tedstone-de-la-Mere, Herefordshire, 1806, and, in addition, vicar of Dudley, 1812 ; published history of Dudley Castle, 1825, and poetical and religious works.   [v. 368]

BOOLDE, WILLIAM (*fl.* 1455), monk and 'notarius' of Christ Church, Canterbury ; wrote historical and topographical works.   [v. 369]

BOOLE, GEORGE (1815–1864), mathematician ; opened a school in Lincolnshire, *c.* 1835 ; professor of mathematics, Queen's College, Cork, 1849–64 ; public examiner, Queen's University ; Royal Society medallist, 1844 ; Keith medallist, Royal Society, Edinburgh, 1857 ; LL.D. Dublin ; D.C.L. Oxford ; published, besides text-books on 'Differential Equations,' 'Finite Differences,' and other mathematical treatises, 'Laws of Thought' (1854), in which he employed symbolic language and notation in a generalisation of logical processes, the fundamental principle being that of continued dichotomy.   [v. 369]

BOONE, JAMES SHERGOLD (1799–1859), author ; educated at Charterhouse and Christ Church, Oxford ; M.A., 1823 ; master at Charterhouse ; incumbent of St. John's, Paddington, 1832–59 ; edited 'The Council of Ten,' 1822–3 ; published sermons, essays, and poems. [v. 370]

BOORDE or **BORDE**, ANDREW (1490 ?–1549), physician and traveller ; educated at Oxford ; joined Carthusians ; suffragan bishop of Chichester, *c.* 1521 ; studied medicine abroad ; took oath of conformity at London Charterhouse, 1534 ; sent abroad by Cromwell to report on state of feeling about Henry VIII, 1535 ; practised medicine at Glasgow, 1536 ; journeyed to Jerusalem, 1538 ; settled at Montpellier, *c.* 1538–42 ; imprisoned in Fleet, 1549 ; published accounts of his travels and treatises on medical subjects.   [v. 371]

BOOT, ARNOLD (1600 ?–1653 ?). [See BOATE.]

BOOTH, ABRAHAM (1734–1806), dissenting minister ; superintendent of Kirby-Woodhouse baptist congregation, 1760 ; ordained pastor of Particular baptist church, Little Prescot Street, Goodman's Fields, 1769 ; published works vindicating baptist doctrine. [v. 373]

BOOTH, BARTON (1681–1733), actor ; educated at Westminster ; appeared as Oroonoko at Smock Alley Theatre, Dublin, 1698 ; engaged by Betterton at Lincoln's Inn Fields, 1700–4, and accompanied him to newly erected Haymarket Theatre, 1705 ; played Ghost to Wilks's Hamlet at Drury Lane, 1708 ; gained great reputation by his performance of Pyrrhus in Philips's 'Distressed Mother,' 1712, and Cato in Addison's tragedy, 1713 ; became by command of Queen Anne joint-manager with Colley Cibber, Doggett, and Wilks, of Drury Lane, *c.* 1713 ; retired, 1727 ; published 'Death of Dido, a Masque,' 1716. Among his best impersonations were Brutus, Lear, Henry VIII, and Hotspur.   [v. 374]

BOOTH, BENJAMIN (*fl.* 1789), writer on bookkeeping ; merchant in New York and afterwards in London ; published a system of bookkeeping, 1789.
          [v. 376]

BOOTH, MRS. CATHERINE (1829–1890), 'mother of the Salvation Army' ; daughter of John Mumford, a coachbuilder ; came to London, 1844, and joined Wesleyan church in Brixton ; excommunicated with 're-formers' from Wesleyan church, 1848 ; married, 1855, William Booth, pastor of reformers, who held, 1858–61, a ministry at Gateshead, where Mrs. Booth first appeared as preacher, 1860 ; founded at Whitechapel with her husband, 1865, 'Christian Revival Association' ; which by 1877 had developed into the 'Salvation Army' ; published many religious papers and addresses.   [Suppl. i. 233]

BOOTH, DAVID (1766–1846), lexicographer ; brewer near Newburgh, Fifeshire, and, later, schoolmaster at Newburgh ; came to London and superintended for press publications of Society for Diffusion of Useful Knowledge, *c.* 1820 ; published first volume of an 'Analytical Dictionary of English Language' (1835), and other works.
          [v. 376]

BOOTH, EDWARD (1639–1719). [See BARLOW.]

BOOTH, SIR FELIX (1775–1850), promoter of Arctic exploration ; head of firm of Booth & Co., distillers ; sheriff of London and Middlesex, 1828 ; provided funds for Captain Ross's voyage of discovery in north-eastern America, 1828 ; baronet, 1835.   [v. 377]

BOOTH, GEORGE, first BARON DELAMER or DELAMERE (1622–1684), took parliamentarian side in civil war ; military commissioner for Cheshire and treasurer-at-war, 1655 ; M.P. for Cheshire, 1645, 1654, and 1656 ; joined 'New Royalists' ; entered plot for restoring Charles, and commanded king's forces in Cheshire, Lancashire, and North Wales, 1659 ; seized Chester, but was defeated by Lambert at Nantwich ; apprehended, but released on bail ; raised to peerage at Charles II's coronation ; *custos rotulorum* in county of Chester, 1660–73.   [v. 377]

BOOTH, GEORGE, second EARL OF WARRINGTON (1675–1758), lord-lieutenant of Chester, 1694 ; published pamphlet in defence of divorce for incompatibility of temper, 1739.   [v. 379]

BOOTH, GEORGE (1791–1859), divine ; M.A. Lincoln College, Oxford, 1816 ; B.D., 1823 ; fellow, Magdalen College, Oxford, 1816–34, vice-president, 1830, and dean of divinity, 1832 ; vicar of Findon, 1833 ; published Latin verses.   [v. 380]

BOOTH, HENRY, second BARON DELAMERE and first EARL OF WARRINGTON (1652–1694), custos rotulorum of county of Chester, 1673–*c.* 1683 ; committed to Tower on suspicion of being concerned in Rye House plot, 1683, but released on bail ; charged with complicity in Monmouth's rebellion, and acquitted, 1685 ; took up arms for Prince of Orange, 1688 ; one of those deputed to advise James to retire from the metropolis ; privy councillor, 1689 ; chancellor of exchequer, 1689–90 ; lord-lieutenant of city and county of Chester ; reappointed custos rotulorum of the county ; created Earl of Warrington, 1690 ; mayor of Chester, 1691.   [v. 380]

BOOTH, HENRY (1788–1869), railway projector ; corn merchant at Liverpool ; honorary secretary to committee for promoting railway between Liverpool and Manchester, 1822, and secretary and treasurer to company, 1826 ; secretary to northern section of London and North-Western Railway company, 1846 ; director, 1848–1849 ; published writings on questions relating to railways and other subjects, and invented many mechanical contrivances still in use on railways.   [v. 382]

BOOTH, JAMES (*d.* 1778), lawyer ; licensed and practised as conveyancer, being disabled as Roman catholic from practising at bar.   [v. 384]

BOOTH, JAMES (1806–1878), mathematician ; M.A., 1840, Trinity College, Dublin ; LL.D., 1842 ; principal of Bristol College, 1840–3 ; ordained, 1842 ; vice-principal of Liverpool Collegiate Institution, 1843–8 ; vicar of Stone, near Aylesbury, 1859 ; F.R.S., 1846 ; F.R.A.S., 1859 ; published works on mathematics and education.   [v. 384]

BOOTH, JAMES (1796–1880), legal writer ; educated at St. John's College, Cambridge ; called to bar at Lincoln's Inn, 1824 ; practised in chancery courts ; counsel to speaker of House of Commons, 1839 ; secretary to board of trade, 1850–65 ; C.B., 1866. He prepared the Clauses Consolidation Acts, and published legal writings.   [v. 385]

BOOTH, JOHN (1584–1659), genealogist ; made researches into Cheshire pedigrees.   [v. 385]

BOOTH, JOHN (1779–1857), cattle breeder ; son of Thomas Booth (*d.* 1835) [q. v.]   [v. 390]

BOOTH, JUNIUS BRUTUS (1796–1852), actor ; first appeared on stage at a theatre in Pancras Street, London, 1813, and subsequently played in Belgium and Holland ; at Covent Garden as Sylvius ('As you like it'), 1815 ; acting manager at Worthing ; played Richard III at Covent Garden, Iago to Kean's Othello at Drury Lane, and, returning to Covent Garden, gave Richard III amid general disapproval, 1817 ; in America from 1821 till 1852, except from 1825–6, when he played Brutus at Drury Lane and travelled on continent, and 1836–7, when he appeared at several London theatres.   [v. 386]

BOOTH or **BOTHE**, LAWRENCE (*d.* 1480), archbishop of York ; licentiate in civil and canon law ; Pembroke Hall, Cambridge ; master, 1450 ; chancellor of university; prebendary and, 1456, dean of St. Paul's; provost of Beverley, 1453; prebendary of York and of Lichfield; chancellor to Queen Margaret; keeper of privy seal, c. 1456; tutor to Prince of Wales; bishop of Durham, 1457; suspended, 1462–4; keeper of great seal, 1473–4; archbishop of York, 1476. [v. 387]

BOOTH, PENISTON (1681–1765), dean of Windsor, 1729; chancellor of London, 1733; D.D. [v. 388]

BOOTH, RICHARD (1788–1864), cattle breeder at Studley and, 1835, at Warlaby; son of Thomas Booth (d. 1835) [q. v.] [v. 390]

BOOTH, ROBERT (d. 1657), puritan divine; M.A. Trinity College, Cambridge, 1610; minister of Halifax, 1650–7; left philosophical manuscript. [v. 389]

BOOTH, Sir ROBERT (1626–1681), chief-justice of king's bench in Ireland; son of Robert Booth [q. v.]; educated at St. John's College, Cambridge; called to bar at Gray's Inn, 1649; judge of common pleas, Ireland, 1660; knighted, 1668; chief-justice of common pleas (1669) and of king's bench (1679) in Ireland. [v. 389]

BOOTH, SARAH (1793–1867), actress; at Surrey Theatre, 1810, and Covent Garden, where, later, she played Cordelia to Junius Brutus Booth's Lear. [v. 389]

BOOTH, THOMAS (fl. 1611), divine; B.D. Trinity College, Cambridge, 1609. [v. 390]

BOOTH, THOMAS (d. 1835), cattle breeder, at Killerby, Yorkshire, and, 1819, at Warlaby; raised a greatly improved breed of shorthorns. [v. 390]

BOOTH or BOTHE, WILLIAM (1390?–1464), archbishop of York; half-brother of Lawrence Booth [q. v.]; studied at Gray's Inn and Pembroke Hall, Cambridge; prebendary of Southwell, 1416; sub-dean of St. Paul's Cathedral, c. 1420, and chancellor, 1421; prebendary of Lincoln, 1420, and of St. Paul's, 1421; bishop of Coventry and Lichfield, 1447; archbishop of York, 1452. [Suppl. i. 235]

BOOTH, Sir WILLIAM (d. 1703), captain in the navy; captain, 1673; served against Algerine pirates in Mediterranean; knighted and appointed commissioner of navy, 1689; engaged in unsuccessful plot to assist James II., and fled to France. [v. 391]

BOOTHBY, Sir BROOKE (1743–1824), baronet and poet; friend of the Edgeworths and the Lichfield literary circle; published poems and works on political questions of the day. [v. 391]

BOOTHBY, Miss HILL (1708–1756), friend of Dr. Johnson, her letters to whom were published in 1805. [v. 391]

BOOTHBY, LOUISA CRANSTOUN, LADY (1812?–1858). [See NISBETT.]

BOOTHROYD, BENJAMIN (1768–1836), independent minister and Hebrew scholar; ordained minister, 1790, at Pontefract, where he opened a shop as bookseller and printer; co-pastor at Highfield chapel, Huddersfield, 1818; LL.D.; D.D. Glasgow, 1824; published at his own press a Hebrew bible, 1810–13, a 'Family Bible,' 1818, and other works. [v. 392]

BOOTT, FRANCIS (1792–1863), physician; born in Boston, United States; educated at Harvard; made several journeys to England; M.D. Edinburgh, 1824; practised in London; F.L.S., 1819, secretary, 1832–9, and treasurer, 1856–61; published botanical and medical works. [v. 393]

BORDE, ANDREW (1490?–1549). [See BOORDE.]

BORDWINE, JOSEPH (d. 1835), professor at Addiscombe; born in America; served under General Whitlock; professor of fortification at East India Company's College, Addiscombe; published work on fortification. [v. 393]

BOREMAN or BOURMAN, ROBERT (d. 1675), royalist divine; educated at Westminster and Trinity College, Cambridge; B.A., 1631; fellow, 1634; M.A., 1635; deprived of fellowship; restored, 1660; D.D., 1660; prebendary of Westminster, 1667; published religious works, including a pamphlet directed against Richard Baxter. [v. 394]

BORGARD, ALBERT (1659–1751), lieutenant-general; born at Holbech; served in Danish army against Sweden, 1675–9; fire-worker, 1679; served in Polish and Prussian armies; lieutenant-colonel under Lord Galway in Spain and Portugal; chief fire master in England, 1712; formed, and became colonel-commandant of, regiment of royal artillery, 1722; lieutenant-general, 1739. [v. 395]

BORGARUCCI, GIULIO (fl. 1564–1579), physician; came to England as protestant refugee; M.C.P.; M.D. Cambridge, 1572; successfully treated plague in London (1563) by bleeding; physician to royal household for life, 1573. [v. 396]

BORINGDON, JOHN, second BARON (1772–1840). [See PARKER, JOHN.]

BORLAND, JAMES (1774–1863), inspector-general of army hospitals; surgeon's mate, 42nd highlanders, 1792; served in Flanders, West Indies, and Helder expedition, 1793–9; inspector-general of army hospitals, 1807; reported, with Dr. Lemprière and Sir Gilbert Blane [q. v.] on state of health at Walcheren; M.D.; principal medical officer in Mediterranean, 1810–16; honorary physician to H.R.H. Duke of Kent. [v. 396]

BORLASE or BURLACE, EDMUND (d. 1682), historical writer; educated at Dublin; doctor of physic, Leyden, 1650; practised at Chester; M.D. Oxford, 1660; published works on Irish history. [v. 397]

BORLASE, HENRY (1806–1835), separatist clergyman; B.A. Trinity College, Cambridge, 1828; took orders in established church, but subsequently joined 'Plymouth Brethren'; published religious writings. [v. 398]

BORLASE, Sir JOHN (1576–1648), soldier; master of ordnance in Ireland, 1633–49; lord justice in Ireland, 1640–4. [v. 398]

BORLASE, WILLIAM (1695–1772), antiquary; M.A. Exeter College, Oxford; presented, 1722, to living of Ludgvan, near Penzance, to which the vicarage of St. Just was added, 1732; published, in 'Philosophical Transactions,' essay on Cornish diamonds, and was made F.R.S., 1750; subsequently produced several works, including 'Cornish Antiquities,' 1754; LL.D., 1766; presented collections to Ashmolean Museum. [v. 398]

BOROUGH, CHRISTOPHER (fl. 1579–1587), traveller; son of Stephen Borough [q. v.]; acted as Russian interpreter to Muscovy Company's expedition into Persia and Media, 1579. His account of the journey appears in Hakluyt. [v. 399]

BOROUGH, BURGH, or DE BURGO, JOHN (d. 1386), divine; D.D. Cambridge; chancellor of the university, 1384; rector of Collingham, Nottinghamshire; wrote theological works. [v. 400]

BOROUGH, Sir JOHN (d. 1643), Garter king-of-arms; studied at Gray's Inn; keeper of Tower records, 1623; Norroy king-of-arms, 1623; knighted, 1624; Garter king-of-arms, 1634; attended Charles I during civil war; clerk to conferences between royalists and parliamentarians at York, Ripon, and London; D.C.L. Oxford, 1643; wrote historical works, some of which were printed posthumously. [v. 401]

BOROUGH, STEPHEN (1525–1584), navigator; served as master in the only successful ship of three which attempted the first voyage of the English to Russia, 1553; discovered Russia and named North Cape; discovered entrance to Kara Sea, 1556; took charge of fleet of three ships of merchant adventurers on voyage to Muscovy, 1560, and probably again in 1561; chief pilot and one of four masters of queen's ships in Medway, 1563–84; wrote records of his voyages, some of which were published in Hakluyt. [v. 402]

BOROUGH, WILLIAM (1536–1599), navigator and author; brother of Stephen Borough [q. v.], with whom, as common seaman, he sailed to Russia, 1553, 1556, and 1557; engaged in voyages to St. Nicholas, 1558–68; accompanied voyage to discover passage to Cathay, 1568; dispersed pirates in Gulf of Finland, 1570; agent to merchant adventurers journeying between St. Nicholas, Moscow, and Narva, 1574–5; comptroller of queen's navy; probably commanded fleet at Flushing, 1585; vice-admiral under Drake in expedition to Cadiz, 1587, when he was put under arrest for questioning Drake on wisdom of an attack on Lagos; commanded a vessel against Armada, 1588. His works include a treatise on variation of compass, several charts, and accounts of his voyages (printed in Hakluyt). [v. 404]

BORRELL, H. P. (d. 1851), numismatist; engaged in trade at Smyrna; published writings on numismatics. [v. 406]

BORRER, WILLIAM (1781–1862), botanist; fellow of Royal, Linnean, and Wernerian societies; contributed to botanical publications. [v. 406]

BORROW, GEORGE (1803–1881), author; educated at Edinburgh High School; articled to solicitor at Norwich; adopted literature as profession; assisted in compiling 'Newgate Calendar'; toured through England and journeyed in France, Germany, Russia, Spain, and the East, studying the language of each country he visited; agent for British and Foreign Bible Society; settled at Oulton Broad, where he became celebrated for his promiscuous hospitality; published translations and several volumes, including 'Bible in Spain' (1843), 'Gypsies in Spain' (1841), 'Lavengro' (1851), and 'Romany Rye' (1857), relating to his travels, and marked by their idealisation of an open air and vagrant life. [v. 407]

BORSTALE, THOMAS (d. 1290?), theologian; Augustinian friar at Norwich; D.D. Sorbonne, Paris. [v. 408]

BORTHWICK, DAVID (d. 1581), lord advocate of Scotland; educated at St. Leonard's College, St. Andrews; called to bar, 1549; legal adviser to Bothwell; king's advocate and lord of session, 1573. [v. 408]

BORTHWICK, PETER (1804–1852), editor of the 'Morning Post'; educated at Edinburgh University and Jesus College, Cambridge; fellow-commoner, Downing College; spoke against abolition of slavery; M.P. for Evesham, 1835–47; called to bar at Gray's Inn, 1847; editor of 'Morning Post,' 1850–2; published speeches. [v. 409]

BORTHWICK, WILLIAM, fourth BARON BORTHWICK (d. 1542), guardian of James V, 1513. [v. 410]

BORTHWICK, WILLIAM (1760–1820), general; served in royal artillery in Flanders; prepared siege trains for Ciudad Rodrigo and Badajoz, 1812; major-general, 1812. [v. 410]

BORTON, SIR ARTHUR (1814–1893), general and governor of Malta; educated at Eton; ensign, 9th foot, 1832; colonel, 1854; major-general, 1864; lieutenant-general, 1875; general, 1877; colonel of Norfolk regiment, 1889; served in Afghanistan campaign, 1842, Satlaj campaign, 1845–6, Crimea, 1854–6, and Canada, 1856; commanded Maisur division of Madras army, 1870–5; K.C.B., 1877; governor and commander-in-chief of Malta, 1878–1884; G.C.M.G., 1880; G.C.B., 1884. [Suppl. i. 235]

BORUWLASKI or **BORUSLAWSKI,** JOSEPH (1739–1837), dwarf; born at Halicz, Polish Galicia; enjoyed, until his marriage, the patronage of Countess Humiecka, with whom he travelled in France, Holland, and Germany; came to England, where he lived chiefly on proceeds of concerts; published 'Memoirs' in French and English (the English a translation by M. des Carrières), 1788. [v. 410]

BOSA (d. 705), bishop; monk of Hilda's monastery at Streoneshalch (Whitby); bishop of York, 678, on division of Wilfrid's diocese by Ecgfrith and Archbishop Theodore; superseded by Wilfrid, 686, but probably reinstated, 691. [v. 411]

BOSANQUET, CHARLES (1769–1850), city merchant; governor of South Sea Company; high sheriff of Northumberland, 1828, and J.P. and D.L. for that county; lieutenant-colonel, 1819, and later colonel of light horse volunteers; published economic treatises. [v. 412]

BOSANQUET, JAMES WHATMAN (1804–1877), chronologist; educated at Westminster; became partner in banking-house of Bosanquet, Salt & Co.; published works embodying researches into biblical and Assyrian chronology. [v. 412]

BOSANQUET, SIR JOHN BERNARD (1773–1847), judge; educated at Eton and Christ Church, Oxford; M.A., 1800; called to bar at Lincoln's Inn, 1800; counsel to East India Company and to Bank of England; serjeant-at-law, 1814; king's serjeant, 1827; presided over commission to inquire into practice of common law courts, 1828–30; judge of common pleas and knighted, 1830; privy councillor, 1833; lord commissioner of great seal, 1835–6. [v. 413]

BOSANQUET, SAMUEL RICHARD (1800–1882), author; educated at Eton and Christ Church, Oxford; M.A., 1829; called to bar at Inner Temple; one of revising barristers appointed on passing of Reform Act, 1832; chairman of Monmouthshire quarter sessions; published miscellaneous works, including 'Hindoo Chronology and Antediluvian History.' [v. 413]

BOSCAWEN, FAMILY OF. The first member of importance, Hugh (d. 1641), recorder of Truro, whose son Edward was father of Hugh, first viscount Falmouth [q. v.], from whom was descended Edward [q. v.], the admiral, whose youngest son, George Evelyn, was third viscount; George Evelyn's son, Edward [q. v.], became first Earl of Falmouth. [v. 414.]

BOSCAWEN, EDWARD (1711–1761), admiral, third son of Hugh, first viscount Falmouth [q. v.]; lieutenant, 1732; served at Porto Bello, 1739–40, at Cartagena, 1741; commanded small squadron in Soundings, 1746; wounded off Finisterre, 1747; appointed commander-in-chief by land and sea in East Indies, 1747; unsuccessfully attempted to reduce Pondicherry; nominally M.P. for Truro after 1741; lord commissioner of admiralty, 1751–61; vice-admiral, 1755; commanded on North American station, in Channel, off Brest, and in Bay of Biscay at intervals between 1755 and 1757; second in command under Hawke, 1757; admiral of the blue, 1758; commander-in-chief of fleet at siege of Louisburg, 1758; privy councillor, 1759; commanded squadron in Mediterranean, and defeated French in Lagos Bay, 1759; general of marines; commanded fleet in Quiberon Bay, 1760; his portrait was painted by Reynolds. [v. 415]

BOSCAWEN, EDWARD, first EARL OF FALMOUTH (1787–1841), son of George Evelyn, third viscount Falmouth; ensign in Coldstream guards; recorder of Truro; created earl, 1820. [v. 419]

BOSCAWEN, HUGH, first VISCOUNT FALMOUTH (d. 1734), M.P. for Tregony, 1702–5, county of Cornwall, 1705–10, Truro, 1710–13, and Penryn, 1713–1720; steward of duchy of Lancaster and lord warden of the Stannaries, 1708; comptroller of household, 1714–20; joint vice-treasurer of Ireland, 1717–34; raised to peerage, 1720. [v. 420]

BOSCAWEN, WILLIAM (1752–1811), author; nephew of Edward Boscawen (1711–1761) [q. v.]; educated at Eton and Exeter College, Oxford; commissioner of victualling office, 1785; published translations of Horace and other works. [v. 420]

BOSGRAVE, JAMES (1547?–1623), jesuit; entered Society of Jesus at Rome, 1564; ordained priest, 1572; came to England, 1580; suffered much persecution, and was sent into exile, 1585; died in Poland. [v. 420]

BOSHAM, HERBERT DE (fl. 1162–1186). [See HERBERT.]

BOSO (d. 1181?), third English cardinal; nephew of Nicholas Breakspear, pope Adrian IV [q. v.]; monk of St. Albans; joined Adrian at Rome; cardinal-priest, 1155; wrote in verse lives of female saints. [v. 421]

BOSSAM, JOHN (fl. 1550), painter and draughtsman in black and white. [v. 422]

BOSSEWELL, JOHN (fl. 1572), antiquary and public notary; published writings on heraldry. [v. 422]

BOSTE or **BOAST,** JOHN (1543?–1594), catholic priest; M.A. Oxford; entered English College, Douay (temporarily removed to Rheims); ordained priest; joined English mission, 1581; executed. [v. 422]

BOSTOCK, JOHN (d. 1465). [See WHETHAMSTEDE.]

BOSTOCK, JOHN, the elder (1740–1774), physician; M.D. Edinburgh, 1769; extra licentiate, College of Physicians, London, 1770; practised in Liverpool; physician to Royal Infirmary. [v. 422]

BOSTOCK, JOHN, the younger (1773–1846), physician, son of John Bostock (1740–1774) [q. v.]; M.D. Edinburgh, 1798; practised in Liverpool; removed (1817) to London, where he abandoned medicine for general science; lectured on chemistry at Guy's Hospital; F.R.S.; president, Geological Society, 1826; vice-president, Royal Society, 1832; chief work, 'System of Physiology,' 1824. [v. 422]

BOSTON BURIENSIS (*fl.* 1410), or JOHN BOSTON OF BURY, bibliographer; Augustinian monk of Bury St. Edmund's; wrote 'Catalogus Scriptorum Ecclesiæ,' a list, with authors' names, of books, in libraries of English monasteries and elsewhere; and 'Speculum Cœnobitarum,' an account of origin of monastic life. [v. 423]

BOSTON, THOMAS, the elder (1677–1732), Scottish divine; employed in office of Alexander Cockburn, writer to signet, 1689; M.A. Edinburgh, 1694; studied theology, 1690–1701; parish schoolmaster at Glencairn, 1696; ordained minister at Simprin, Berwickshire, 1699; clerk of synod, 1701; minister at Ettrick, 1707–32; basing his views on a work entitled 'Marrow of Modern Divinity,' he, with eleven others, opposed act of assembly (1720) condemning the book, the twelve being nicknamed 'the twelve apostles' and 'Marrow-men'; published religious works, a treatise on Hebrew accents appearing posthumously. [v. 424]

BOSTON, THOMAS, the younger (1713–1767), Scottish relief minister; son of Thomas Boston (1677–1732) [q. v.]; educated at Edinburgh University; ordained, 1733; minister at Oxnam, Roxburghshire, 1749; prohibited by presbytery, 1758, from employment in any office; continued in his ministry at Jedburgh in independent capacity, and with Thomas Gillespie and another minister formed, 1761, new ecclesiastical body called 'presbytery of relief,' of which Boston was first moderator. [v. 426]

BOSVILLE, WILLIAM (1745–1813), *bon vivant*; lieutenant, 1769; served in American war; retired from army, 1777; travelled in France, Italy, and Morocco, and subsequently settled in Welbeck Street, London, where he became renowned for his hospitality. [v. 427]

BOSWELL, ALEXANDER, LORD AUCHINLECK (1706–1782), Scottish judge; graduated at Leyden, 1727; member of Faculty of Advocates, 1729; sheriff-depute of Wigtownshire, 1748–50; lord of session, 1754; lord justiciary, 1755–80. [v. 428]

BOSWELL, SIR ALEXANDER (1775–1822), antiquary and poet; eldest son of James Boswell the elder [q. v.]; educated at Westminster and Oxford; settled at Auchinleck, where he established a private press, 1815, and issued a series of reprints of old poems under title of 'Frondes Caducæ,' 1816–18; member of Roxburghe Club, 1819; conservative M.P. for Plympton, Devonshire, 1818 and 1820; accepted Chiltern Hundreds, 1821; created baronet, 1821; died from effects of duel with James Stuart of Dunearn, whom he had attacked in the 'Glasgow Sentinel'; originated the idea of erecting on banks of the Doon the monument to Burns; published poetical and antiquarian writings, and edited several reprints of old works. [v. 428]

BOSWELL, CLAUD IRVINE, LORD BALMUTO (1742–1824), Scottish judge; nephew of James Boswell, the elder [q. v.]; educated at Edinburgh University; member of Faculty of Advocates, 1766; lord of session, 1799–1822. [v. 430]

BOSWELL, EDWARD (1760–1842), solicitor; published antiquarian works. [v. 430]

BOSWELL, JAMES, the elder (1740–1795), biographer of Johnson; son of Alexander Boswell, lord Auchinleck [q. v.]; educated at Edinburgh High School and university; studied law at Glasgow under Adam Smith, and at Edinburgh; made acquaintance of Johnson in London, 1763; studied civil law at Utrecht, 1765, and travelled thence to Berlin and Geneva, meeting Voltaire and Rousseau; made acquaintance of Wilkes in Italy, and was introduced to General Paoli in Corsica; returned to England, 1766; advocate, 1766; published 'Account of Corsica,' 1768, and 'Essays in Favour of the Brave Corsicans,' 1769; took part in Shakespearean jubilee celebration at Stratford, 1769; made frequent visits to Johnson in London between 1772 and 1784; toured with Johnson in Hebrides, August to November, 1773; elected member of Literary Club, 1773; began to keep terms at Inner Temple, 1775; succeeded to his father's estate, 1782; published 'Letter to People of Scotland on Present State of the Nation,' hoping to gain political influence, 1783; published 'Journal of Tour to Hebrides,' the work being revised by Malone, 1786; called to English bar, 1786; recorder of Carlisle, 1788–90; came to reside in London, 1789; published 'Life of Johnson' (also previously revised by Malone), 1791; secretary of foreign correspondence to Royal Academy, 1791. His portrait was painted by Reynolds. [v. 431]

BOSWELL, JAMES, the younger (1778–1822), lawyer; second surviving son of James Boswell the elder [q. v.]; educated at Westminster and Brasenose College, Oxford; M.A., 1806; Vinerian fellow; called to bar at Inner Temple, 1805; commissioner of bankrupts; completed second edition of Malone's Shakespeare; member of Roxburghe Club; edited third variorum Shakespeare, 1821. [v. 438]

BOSWELL, JOHN (1698–1757), author; B.A. Balliol College, Oxford, 1720; tutor; M.A. St. John's College, Cambridge; prebendary of Wells, 1736; published miscellaneous works. [v. 439]

BOSWELL, ROBERT (1746–1804), psalmist; writer to signet; teaching elder in church of 'Sandemanians,' Edinburgh; published metrical version of Psalms. [v. 440]

BOSWELL, SIR WILLIAM (*d.* 1649), diplomatist; fellow, Jesus College, Cambridge, 1606; secretary to Sir Dudley Carleton, when ambassador at the Hague, succeeding him in the post; knighted, 1633; continued Carleton's policy at the Hague, and supported Gomarists against Barneveldt and the 'remonstrants.' [v. 440]

BOSWORTH, JOSEPH (1789–1876), Anglo-Saxon scholar; M.A. and LL.D. Aberdeen; member of Trinity College, Cambridge; vicar of Little Horwood, Buckinghamshire, 1817–29; chaplain at Amsterdam, 1829, and afterwards at Rotterdam; D.D. Cambridge, 1839; incorporated member of Christ Church, Oxford; Rawlinson professor of Anglo-Saxon, Oxford, 1858; F.R.S.; published 'Anglo-Saxon Dictionary,' 1838, and translated Ælfred's 'Orosius,' 1855. [v. 440]

BOSWORTH, WILLIAM (1607–1650 ?), poetical writer. A volume of his poems was published posthumously in 1651. [v. 442]

BOTELER. [See BUTLER.]

BOTELER, EDWARD (*d.* 1670), divine; fellow of Magdalene College, Cambridge; ejected, 1644; king's chaplain, 1660; prebendary of Lincoln, 1665. [v. 442]

BOTELER, NATHANIEL (*fl.* 1625–1627), navy captain; served in expeditions to Cadiz and Isle of Ré; wrote an account of naval customs (published, 1685). [v. 442]

BOTELER, WILLIAM FULLER (1777–1845), commissioner of bankruptcy; educated at Charterhouse and St. John's College, Cambridge; senior wrangler, 1799; fellow of St. Peter's College; M.A., 1802; called to bar at Lincoln's Inn, 1804; K.C., 1831; senior commissioner of district court of bankruptcy, Leeds, 1844. [v. 442]

BOTEVILLE, FRANCIS (1545 ?–1608). [See THYNNE.]

BOTEVILLE, WILLIAM (*d.* 1546). [See THYNNE.]

BOTFIELD, BERIAH (1807–1863), bibliographer; educated at Harrow and Christ Church, Oxford; B.A., 1828; sheriff of Northamptonshire, 1831; M.P. for Ludlow, 1840–7, and 1857–63; established private press at Norton Hall, Northamptonshire. His publications include 'Notes on Cathedral Libraries of England,' 1849, and editions for the Roxburghe, Maitland, Abbotsford, and Bannatyne clubs, and Surtees Society. [v. 443]

BOTHWELL, EARLS OF. [See HEPBURN, PATRICK, third EARL, 1512 ?–1556; HEPBURN, JAMES, fourth EARL, 1536 ?–1578; HEPBURN, FRANCIS STEWART, fifth EARL, *d.* 1624.]

BOTHWELL, ADAM (1527 ?–1593), divine; bishop of Orkney, 1559; on commission for revising Book of Discipline, 1563; lord of session, 1565; performed, after protestant form, marriage ceremony of Mary Queen of Scots and James Hepburn, earl of Bothwell, at Holyrood House, and crowned and anointed Mary's son, Charles James, at Stirling, 1567; suspended from ministry for solemnising the marriage, 1567–8; exchanged greater part of temporalities of Orkney, while retaining title of bishop, for abbacy of Holyrood House, 1570; on commission to frame revised ecclesiastical settlement, 1572; one of council of twelve forming provisional government overthrown on 10 June, 1578; one of lords of articles at parliament, 1584. [v. 444]

BOTLEY, SAMUEL (1642–1696 ?), writer on stenography. [v. 446]

BOTOLPH or **BOTULF** (d. 630), saint; studied in Germany, where he became a Benedictine monk; founded monastery at Ikanho (perhaps near present town of Boston), 654; commemorated on 17 June. [v. 446]

BOTONER, WILLIAM (1415–1482 ?). [See WORCESTER.]

BOTT, THOMAS (1688–1754), divine; held various livings in Norfolk; published 'Answer to Warburton's Divine Legation,' 1743. [v. 446]

BOTT, THOMAS (1829–1870), china painter; artist in Royal Porcelain Works, Worcester, where his work in ' Worcester enamel' gained considerable reputation. [v. 447]

BOTTETOURT, JOHN DE (d. 1324), baron and admiral; governor of St. Briavel's Castle, and warden of Forest of Dean; commanded fleet at burning of Cherbourg, 1295; served under Edward I in Gascony and Scotland; joined Warwick against Piers Gaveston. [v. 447]

BOTTISHAM or **BOTTLESHAM**, WILLIAM OF (d. 1400), bishop; Dominican; D.D., and fellow, Pembroke College, Cambridge; bishop of Bethlehem, c. 1385, Llandaff, 1386, and Rochester, 1389. [v. 447]

BOTTOMLEY, JOSEPH (fl. 1820), musician; organist at Bradford, 1807, and Sheffield, 1820; published dictionary of music (1816) and other musical works. [vi. 1]

BOUCH, SIR THOMAS (1822–1880), civil engineer; resident engineer on Stockton and Darlington railway; manager and engineer of Edinburgh and Northern railway, 1849; instituted steam ferries over Forth and Tay; constructed Tay bridge, 1870–7; knighted, 1879; died from mental shock resulting from destruction of Tay bridge by hurricane; M.I.C.E., 1858. [vi. 1]

BOUCHER, JOHN (1777–1818), divine; fellow, Magdalen College, Oxford, 1799; M.A., 1802; vicar of Kirk Newton, Northumberland, 1804–18; his sermons were published posthumously. [vi. 2]

BOUCHER, JOHN (1819–1878), divine; unitarian minister successively at Southport, Glasgow, and Hackney; studied for Anglican orders at St. John's College, Cambridge; B.A., 1857. [vi. 2]

BOUCHER, JONATHAN (1738–1804), divine; engaged in tuition in America, c. 1754–62; held successively several ecclesiastical charges in America, where until the war of independence he was intimate with George Washington; returned to England, 1775; vicar of Epsom, 1785–1804; published sermons and writings relating to Cumberland, and left incomplete a supplement to Johnson's 'Dictionary.' [vi. 3]

BOUCHERY, WEYMAN (1683–1712), Latin poet; M.A. Jesus College, Cambridge, 1706; rector of Little Blakenham, 1709; published a Latin poem. [vi. 4]

BOUCHIER, BARTON (1794–1865), religious writer; son of Jonathan Boucher [q. v.]; changed his name to Bouchier after 1822; M.A. Balliol College, Oxford, 1827; published hymns and religious works. [vi. 4]

BOUCHIER or **BOURCHIER**, GEORGE (d. 1643), royalist; merchant of Bristol; hanged for conspiring to deliver Bristol to Prince Rupert, 1643. [vi. 4]

BOUCICAULT, DION (1820 ?–1890), originally called BOURCICAULT, actor and dramatist; educated at London University; produced his 'London Assurance' at Covent Garden theatre, 1841; sometimes wrote in conjunction with Benjamin Webster [q. v.]; manager of Astley's, 1863; produced 'Arrah-na-Pogue' at Princess's, 1865, himself playing Shaun; retired, 1876, to America, where he died. His plays, invariably adapted from some previous play or novel by another hand, include 'Faust and Marguerite,' 1852, and the 'Colleen Bawn,' 1860. [Suppl. i. 237]

BOUGH, SAMUEL (1822–1878), landscape-painter; successively shoemaker and lawyer's clerk in Carlisle; wandered about England making sketches; scene-painter in Manchester and Glasgow; took to landscape-painting, member of Royal Scottish Academy, 1875. [vi. 4]

BOUGHEN, EDWARD (1587–1660 ?), royalist divine; educated at Westminster and Christ Church, Oxford;

M.A., 1612; rector of Woodchurch, 1633–40; D.D., 1646; published sermons and religious works. [vi. 5]

BOUGHTON, JOAN (d. 1494), martyr; burnt at Smithfield, at the age of eighty or more, for supporting Wycliffe's doctrines. [vi. 6]

BOULT, SWINTON (1809–1876), agent for insurance offices in Liverpool; founded, 1836, and became managing director of, Liverpool Fire Office (afterwards Liverpool, London, and Globe Insurance Company). [vi. 6]

BOULTBEE, THOMAS POWNALL (1818–1884), divine; M.A. St. John's College, Cambridge, 1844; theological tutor and chaplain of Cheltenham College, 1852–63; principal of London College of Divinity, 1863; LL.D., 1872; prebendary of St. Paul's, 1883; published religious works. [vi. 6]

BOULTER, HUGH (1672–1742), archbishop of Armagh; educated at Merchant Taylors' School and Christ Church, Oxford; M.A., 1693; D.D., 1708; fellow of Magdalen College; chaplain to Archbishop Tenison; chaplain to George I in Hanover, bishop of Bristol, and dean of Christ Church, Oxford, 1719; protestant archbishop of Armagh, 1724; frequently acted as lord justice in Ireland, displaying prejudice against the Irish. [vi. 7]

BOULTON, MATTHEW (1728–1809), engineer; entered partnership with Watt, whom he greatly assisted in completion and introduction of the steam-engine; made coins for Great Britain and other countries, and supplied new mint with machinery (1805); F.R.S. [vi. 8]

BOULTON, RICHARD (fl. 1697–1724), physician; educated at Brasenose College, Oxford; published medical works. [vi. 9]

BOUND, NICHOLAS (d. 1613). [See BOWNDE.]

BOUQUET, HENRY (1719–1765), general; born at Rolle, Switzerland; served in armies of States-General of Holland, king of Sardinia, and Prince of Orange; captain-commandant of Swiss guards at Hague, 1748; lieutenant-colonel in America, 1754; brigadier-general and commandant in southern British America. [vi. 9]

BOUQUETT, PHILIP (1669–1748), Hebrew professor; educated at Westminster and Trinity College, Cambridge; fellow; M.A., 1696; D.D., 1711; professor of Hebrew, 1712. [vi. 10]

BOURCHIER, GEORGE (d. 1643). [See BOUCHIER.]

BOURCHIER, HENRY, first EARL OF ESSEX (d. 1483), great-grandson of Robert Bourchier [q. v.]; lieutenant-general under Duke of York in France, 1440; captain of Crotoy, Picardy, 1443; married Isabel, aunt of Edward IV; treasurer of England, 1455–6 and 1471–83; with March and Warwick at battle of Northampton, 1460; created Earl of Essex, 1461. [vi. 10]

BOURCHIER, HENRY, second EARL OF ESSEX (d. 1539), grandson of Henry Bourchier, first earl [q. v.]; member of Henry VII's privy council; captain of Henry VIII's bodyguard; served at Terouenne and Tournay, 1513; chief captain of king's forces, 1514; attended Henry at Guisnes, 1520. [vi. 11]

BOURCHIER or **BOUSSIER**, JOHN DE (d. 1330 ?) judge; justice of assize for Kent, Surrey, and Sussex, 1315; justice of common bench, 1321 till death. [vi. 11]

BOURCHIER, JOHN, second BARON BERNERS (1467–1533), statesman and author; great-nephew of Henry Bourchier, first earl of Essex [q. v.]; marshal of Surrey's army in Scotland, 1513; chancellor of exchequer, 1516; accompanied John Kite, archbishop of Armagh, to Spain to negotiate alliance between Henry VIII and Charles V, 1518; attended Henry at Field of Cloth of Gold, 1520; deputy of Calais, 1520–33; published translation of Froissart's 'Chronicles,' 1523–5; and translated 'Huon of Burdeux' (probably printed in 1534), 'Castell of Love' (printed 1540), and, under title of 'Golden Boke of Marcus Aurelius' (1534), a French version of Guevara's 'El redox de Principes.' [vi. 12]

BOURCHIER, SIR JOHN (d. 1660), regicide; M.P. for Ripon, 1645; one of Charles I's judges, 1648; signed death-warrant; member of council of state, 1651 and 1652; surrendered as regicide, 1660, but died before settlement of exceptions to act of indemnity. [vi. 14]

BOURCHIER or **BOUSSIER**, ROBERT (d. 1349), chancellor; son of John de Bourchier [q. v.]; M.P. for Essex, 1330, 1332, 1338, and 1339; chancellor, 1340–1; fought at Crecy, 1346. [vi. 14]

BOURCHIER, THOMAS (1404?–1486), cardinal; brother of Henry Bourchier, first earl of Essex [q. v.]; educated at Oxford; prebendary of Lichfield, 1424; chancellor of Oxford University, 1434; bishop of Worcester, 1434, and of Ely, 1443; archbishop of Canterbury, 1454; lord-chancellor, 1455–6; Lancastrian, drawing up with Waynflete terms of agreement between Lancastrians and Yorkists, 1458; crowned Edward IV, 1461, and his queen, Elizabeth Woodville, 1465; nominated cardinal, 1467, and installed, 1473; raised troops for restoration of Edward IV to throne, 1471; one of four arbitrators to whom difficulties between England and France were referred by peace of Amiens, 1475; headed deputation which persuaded the queen-dowager to entrust her second son, Richard, to his uncle, the Protector; officiated at coronation of Richard III, 1483; married Henry VII to Elizabeth of York, 1486. [vi. 15]

BOURCHIER, THOMAS (d. 1586?), friar of Observant order of Franciscans; probably educated at Magdalen Hall, Oxford; doctor of theology, Sorbonne, Paris; joined Reformed Franciscans at Rome; penitentiary in the Lateran; wrote a history of Franciscan martyrs (1582). [vi. 18]

BOURDIEU, ISAAC DU (1597?–1692?). [See DU BOURDIEU.]

BOURDIEU, JEAN DU (1642?–1720). [See DU BORDIEU.]

BOURDILLON, JAMES DEWAR (1811–1883), Madras civil servant; went to Madras, 1829; secretary to government in revenue and public works departments, 1854–61; did much for improvement of irrigation and system of land revenue. [vi. 19]

BOURGEOIS, SIR PETER FRANCIS (1756–1811), painter; studied under De Loutherbourg; exhibited at Royal Academy and British Institution between 1779 and 1810; R.A., 1793; landscape-painter to George III, 1794; painter to Stanislaus, king of Poland, and knighted, 1791; bequeathed 371 pictures to Dulwich College. [vi. 19]

BOURKE, SIR RICHARD (1777–1855), colonial governor; educated for bar; ensign in grenadier guards, 1798; captain, 1799; assistant quartermaster-general to army in Portugal, 1808–9; in Galicia, 1812; colonel and C.B.; major-general, 1821; lieutenant-governor of eastern Cape of Good Hope, 1825–8; governor of New South Wales, 1831–7; established regular scheme of emigration; K.C.B., 1835; general, 1851. [vi. 20]

BOURKE, RICHARD SOUTHWELL, sixth EARL OF MAYO (1822–1872), viceroy and governor-general of India; graduated at Trinity College, Dublin; M.P. for Kildare, 1847–52, Coleraine, 1852–7, and Cockermouth, after 1857; chief secretary for Ireland, under conservative governments, 1852, 1858, and 1866; viceroy and governor-general of India, 1869; assassinated at Port Blair. His policy was to endeavour, while insisting on the superior power of Britain, to maintain intimate relations of friendship with neighbouring states, opposing their neutralisation in the European sense. In finance he adopted a policy of 'decentralisation.' [vi. 21]

BOURMAN, ROBERT (d. 1675). [See BOREMAN.]

BOURN, NICOL (fl. 1581). [See BURNE.]

BOURN, SAMUEL, the elder (1648–1719), dissenting minister; educated at Emmanuel College, Cambridge; presbyterian minister at Calne, 1679, and Bolton, 1695–1719. A volume of his sermons appeared, 1722. [vi. 24]

BOURN, SAMUEL, the younger (1689–1754), dissenting minister; second son of Samuel Bourn (1648–1719) [q. v.]; joint-pastor at New Meeting, Birmingham, and at Coseley, 1732; published controversial and religious works. [vi. 25]

BOURN, SAMUEL (1714–1796), dissenting minister; second son of Samuel Bourn (1689–1754) [q. v.]; educated at Glasgow University; joint-minister of presbyterian congregation at Norwich, 1754; published controversial and religious works. [vi. 27]

BOURN, THOMAS (1771–1832), school teacher; compiled 'Gazetteer of the World,' 1807. [vi. 28]

BOURN, WILLIAM (d. 1583). [See BOURNE.]

BOURNE, GILBERT (d. 1569), bishop of Bath and Wells; fellow, All Souls' College, Oxford, 1531; B.A., 1532; prebendary of Worcester, 1541, of St. Paul's, 1545; proctor for clergy of diocese of London, 1547; chaplain to Bishop Bonner; bishop of Bath and Wells, 1554; warden of Welsh marches; refused oaths of allegiance to Elizabeth, and was committed to Tower, 1559; subsequently detained in private custody. [vi. 28]

BOURNE, HENRY (1696–1733), divine and antiquary; M.A. Christ College, Cambridge, 1724; published 'Antiquitates Vulgares,' 1725, and left unfinished a history of Newcastle (published, 1736). [vi. 29]

BOURNE, HUGH (1772–1852), founder of the primitive methodists; local preacher among Wesleyan methodists; revived camp meetings for preaching and fellowship, 1807, and accordingly was expelled from Wesleyan Methodist Society, 1808; founded primitive methodists, 1810, and subsequently travelled in Scotland, Ireland, and America, enrolling recruits; published work relating to his sect. [vi. 29]

BOURNE, IMMANUEL (1590–1679), divine; M.A. Christ Church, Oxford, 1616; rector of Waltham-on-the-Wolds, 1656; conformed at Restoration; rector of Aylestone, 1670–9; published religious works. [vi. 30]

BOURNE, NEHEMIAH (fl. 1649–1662), major in parliamentary army; captain in navy on remodelling of fleet, c. 1649; rear-admiral of fleet, 1652; commissioner for equipment of fleets, 1652; emigrated to America on Restoration. [vi. 31]

BOURNE, REUBEN (fl. 1692), dramatist; member of Middle Temple; published 'The Contented Cuckold,' a comedy, 1692. [vi. 31]

BOURNE, ROBERT (1761–1829), physician; M.D. Worcester College, Oxford, 1787; F.R.C.P., 1790; professor of physic, 1803, and clinical medicine, 1824, Oxford. [vi. 32]

BOURNE, VINCENT (1695–1747), Latin poet; educated at Westminster and Trinity College, Cambridge; fellow, 1720; M.A., 1721; master at Westminster School, Cowper being one of his pupils; housekeeper and deputy serjeant-at-arms to House of Commons, 1734; published 'Poemata, Latine partim reddita, partim scripta' (1734), some of which were translated by Cowper and Lamb. [vi. 32]

BOURNE or **BOURN**, WILLIAM (d. 1583), mathematician; self-taught; probably employed at Gravesend as gunner and ship-carpenter; published almanacks and works on gunnery and navigation, leaving manuscripts on similar subjects. [vi. 33]

BOURNE, WILLIAM STURGES- (1769–1845), politician; educated with Canning at Winchester and Christ Church, Oxford; M.A., 1793; D.C.L., 1831; called to bar at Lincoln's Inn, 1793; M.P., 1798–1831; joint-secretary of treasury, 1804–6; lord of treasury, 1807–9; privy councillor, 1814; home secretary, 1827; commissioner of woods and forests, 1827; lord warden of New Forest, 1828–1831. [vi. 34]

BOUTEL, MRS. (fl. 1663–1696), actress; member of Theatre Royal company; her first recorded character, Estifania in 'Rule a Wife, and Have a Wife,' c. 1664, and her last, Thomyris, in 'Cyrus the Great,' 1696. [vi. 35]

BOUTELL, CHARLES (1812–1877), archæologist; B.A. St. John's College, Cambridge, 1834; incorporated at Trinity College, Oxford, and M.A., 1836; rector of Norwood, Surrey; published works on archæology and heraldry. [vi. 35]

BOUTFLOWER, HENRY CREWE (1796–1863). Hulsean essayist; M.A. St. John's College, Cambridge, 1822; Hulsean prizeman, 1816; head-master, Bury school, Lancashire, 1823; rector of Elmdon, 1857–63; published Hulsean essay. [vi. 36]

BOUVERIE, EDWARD PLEYDELL- (1818–1889), politician; second son of William Pleydell-Bouverie, third earl of Radnor [q. v.]; M.A. Trinity College, Cambridge, 1838; barrister, Inner Temple, 1843; liberal M.P., Kilmarnock, 1844–74; president of poor-law board, 1855–8; opposed Gladstone's Irish University Bill, 1873; wrote numerous letters to the 'Times' signed E. P. B. [xlv. 423]

BOUVERIE, SIR HENRY FREDERICK (1783–1852), general; ensign, 1799; aide-de-camp to Rosslyn, 1807, and Wellesley, 1809; on staff, 1810; colonel, 1814; K.C.B., 1815; governor and commander-in-chief of Malta, 1836–1843; lieutenant-general, 1838; G.C.B., 1852. [vi. 36]

BOUVERIE, WILLIAM PLEYDELL-, third EARL OF RADNOR (1779–1869), whig politician; M.P. for Downton, 1801, and Salisbury, 1802–28; actively supported social measures; friend of William Cobbett. [vi. 36]

BOUYER, REYNOLD GIDEON (d. 1826), divine; LL.B. Jesus College, Cambridge, 1769; prebendary of Sarum, 1785; established parochial libraries throughout Northumberland. [vi. 37]

BOVEY or **BOEVEY**, CATHARINA (1669–1726), philanthropist; née Riches; married, 1684; associated with a Mrs. Mary Pope in many charitable works. [vi. 37]

BOVILL, SIR WILLIAM (1814–1873), judge; barrister of Middle Temple, 1841; Q.C., 1855; conservative M.P. for Guildford, 1857, solicitor-general and chief-justice of common pleas, 1866; hon. D.C.L. Oxford, 1870; F.R.S.; presided at first Tichborne trial. [vi. 38]

BOVILLUS (d. 1526). [See BULLOCK, HENRY.]

BOWACK, JOHN (fl. 1737), writing-master at Westminster School; clerk to turnpike commissioners, 1732; assistant secretary to Westminster Bridge commissioners, 1737; began publication of 'Antiquities of Middlesex,' 1706. [vi. 39]

BOWATER, SIR EDWARD (1787–1861), lieutenant-general; educated at Harrow; ensign, 1804; served in Peninsula and Waterloo campaigns, 1808–15; groom-in-waiting in ordinary to the queen, 1846; lieutenant-general and colonel 49th foot. [vi. 39]

BOWDEN, JOHN (d. 1750), presbyterian divine; minister at Frome, 1707–50; published sermons and contributed to 'Divine Hymns and Poems' (1704). [vi. 40]

BOWDEN, JOHN WILLIAM (1798–1844), ecclesiastical writer; educated at Harrow and Trinity College, Oxford; M.A., 1823; commissioner of stamps, 1826–40; intimate friend of John Henry Newman, and a zealous partisan in the Tractarian movement. His works include a 'Life of Gregory VII' (1840). [vi. 41]

BOWDEN, SAMUEL (fl. 1733–1761). physician; published poems, 1733–5. [vi. 41]

BOWDICH, THOMAS EDWARD (1791–1824), African traveller; obtained writership in service of African Company, and went to Cape Coast Castle, 1814; formed treaty with king of Ashantee, granting peace to British settlements on Gold Coast, 1815; returned to England, 1818; studied science in Paris; published works and translations relating to Ashantee and African exploration. [vi. 41]

BOWDLER, HENRIETTA MARIA (1754–1830), religious writer; sister of John Bowdler the elder [q. v.]; published religious poems and essays. [vi. 43]

BOWDLER, JANE (1743–1784), authoress; sister of Henrietta Maria Bowdler [q. v.]; a selection of her poems and essays appeared, 1786. [vi. 43]

BOWDLER, JOHN, the younger (1783–1815), author; younger son of John Bowdler (1746–1823) [q. v.]; barrister of Lincoln's Inn, 1807; selections from his verse and prose appeared, 1816. [vi. 44]

BOWDLER, JOHN, the elder (1746–1823), author; chamber conveyancer, 1770–80; one of founders of Church Building Society; published political and religious pamphlets. [vi. 43]

BOWDLER, THOMAS (1754–1825), editor of Shakespeare; brother of John Bowdler the elder [q. v.]; M.D. Edinburgh, 1776; F.R.S. and L.C.P., 1781; F.S.A., 1784; visited Low Countries, 1787, and wrote narrative of their political disunion; published 'Family Shakespeare' (10 vols. 1818), an expurgated version of the text; prepared, on similar lines, edition of Gibbon's 'History.' His works gave rise to the term 'bowdlerise.' [vi. 44]

BOWDLER, THOMAS, the younger (1782–1856), divine; son of John Bowdler the elder [q. v.]; M.A. St. John's College, Cambridge, 1806; prebendary of St. Paul's, 1849; edited (1826) his uncle's 'Gibbon.' [vi. 46]

BOWEN, CHARLES SYNGE CHRISTOPHER, BARON BOWEN (1835–1894), judge; educated at Rugby and Balliol College, Oxford; fellow, 1857; M.A., 1872; D.C.L., 1883; called to bar at Lincoln's Inn, 1861; bencher, 1879; joined western circuit; junior counsel against 'Claimant' in 'Tichborne case,' 1871–4; appointed judge of queen's bench and knighted, 1879; lord of appeal in ordinary, receiving life peerage, 1893; published translations from Virgil, and other writings. [Suppl. i. 238]

BOWEN, EMANUEL (fl. 1752). map-engraver to George II and Louis XV. [vi. 48]

BOWEN, SIR GEORGE FERGUSON (1821–1899), colonial governor; educated at Charterhouse and Trinity College, Oxford; B.A. and fellow of Brasenose, 1844; M.A., 1847; entered Lincoln's Inn, 1844; president of university of Corfu, 1847–51; chief secretary to government in Ionian Islands, 1854; K.C.M.G., 1856; first governor of Queensland, 1859; G.C.M.G., 1860; appointed governor of New Zealand, 1867; successfully pursued policy of conciliation towards Maoris and settlers; governor of Victoria, 1872; honorary D.C.L. Oxford, 1875; appointed to Mauritius, 1879, and Hongkong, 1882; reconstructed colonial legislature and established friendly foreign policy; retired from office, 1887; privy councillor, 1886; honorary LL.D. Cambridge, 1886; chief of royal commission on new constitution of Malta, 1887; published 'Mount Athos, Thessaly, and Epirus' (1852), and other works. [Suppl. i. 240]

BOWEN, JAMES (d. 1774), painter and topographer; made collections for history of Shropshire. [vi. 46]

BOWEN, JAMES (1751–1835), rear-admiral; commanded ship in African and West India trade; master in navy, 1781–9; inspecting agent of transports in Thames, 1789; master of Howe's flagship in battle of 1 June 1794; captain, 1795; commissioner of transport board, c. 1803, and of navy, 1816–25; rear-admiral, 1825. [vi. 46]

BOWEN, JOHN (1756–1832), painter and genealogist; son of James Bowen (d. 1774) [q. v]; made antiquarian collections relating to Shropshire. [vi. 47]

BOWEN, JOHN (1815–1859), colonial bishop; emigrated to Canada, 1835; returned home and entered Trinity College, Dublin, 1843; LL.D., 1857; visited many foreign stations of Church Missionary Society, 1848–51 and 1854–6; bishop of Sierra Leone, 1857. [vi. 47]

BOWEN, THOMAS (d. 1790), map-engraver; son of Emanuel Bowen [q. v.]; his works include maps and charts of West Indies from Captain James Speer's surveys. [vi. 48]

BOWER, ALEXANDER (fl. 1804–1830), assistant-librarian at Edinburgh University; published biographical and historical works. [vi. 48]

BOWER, ARCHIBALD (1686–1766), historian; educated at Scots college at Douay; entered Society of Jesus, 1706; studied divinity at Rome, 1717–21; professed of four vows, c. 1723; came to England, 1726; conformed to church of England; classical tutor to Lord Aylmer; contributed history of Rome to 'Universal History,' 1735–44; readmitted jesuit, 1745, but again left the society, 1747; published 'History of the Popes,' 7 vols. 1748–66; accused, in pamphlets, by Rev. Alban Butler and Rev. John Douglas (afterwards bishop of Salisbury), and proved guilty of being secretly a member of catholic church. [vi. 48]

BOWER or **BOWERS**, GEORGE (d. 1690), engraver to the mint, 1664–90. [vi. 51]

BOWER or **BOWMAKER**, WALTER (d. 1449), abbot of Inchcolm; probably member of Augustinian priory of St. Andrews; B.C.L.; commissioner to collect ransom money of James I (of Scotland), 1423 and 1424; present at council held at Perth, 1432; reputed continuator (1440–7) of Fordun's 'Chronica Gentis Scotorum,' as it appears in the 'Scotichronicon,' of which he wrote an abridgment called 'Book of Cupar.' A complete edition of the 'Scotichronicon' was published in 1759. [vi. 52]

BOWERBANK, JAMES SCOTT (1797–1877), geologist; partner in London distillery; lectured on botany, 1822–4, and human osteology, 1831; one of founders of 'London Clay Club,' 1836, and of Palæontographical Society, 1847; F.R.S., 1842; most important work, 'Fossil Fruits of the London Clay' (1840). [vi. 53]

F

BOWERS, GEORGE HULL (1794–1872), divine; D.D. Clare College, Cambridge, 1849; dean of Manchester, 1847–71; joint founder of Marlborough School; published works on ecclesiastical matters. [vi. 54]

BOWES, ELIZABETH (1502 ?–1568), disciple of John Knox; *née* Aske; married Richard, son of Sir Ralph Bowes; fell under influence of John Knox, who adopted her as a relative and married her daughter, Marjory; lived chiefly with Knox, from 1556. [vi. 55]

BOWES, SIR GEORGE (1517–1556), commander in border wars; accompanied Hertford in his raid, 1544, and was knighted. [vi. 55]

BOWES, SIR GEORGE (1527–1580), soldier; son of Elizabeth Bowes [q. v.]; marshal of Berwick, 1560; knighted, 1560; provost marshal of Earl of Sussex's army; M.P. for Knaresborough, 1571, and Morpeth, 1572; high sheriff of county palatine, 1576. [vi. 56]

BOWES, SIR JEROME (d. 1616), ambassador; temporarily banished from court for slandering Earl of Leicester, 1577; ambassador to Russia, 1583; dismissed after death of the Czar Ivanvasilovitch; translated from French an 'Apology for Christians of France,' 1579. [vi. 57]

BOWES, JOHN (1690–1767), lord chancellor of Ireland; called to bar in England, 1718, and in Ireland, 1725; solicitor-general, 1730; M.P. for Taghmon, 1731; attorney-general for Ireland, 1739, chief baron of exchequer, 1741, and chancellor, 1757; received title of Baron of Clonlyon, 1758; lord justice in Ireland, 1765 and 1766. [vi. 58]

BOWES, JOHN (1804–1874), preacher; preached among Wesleyans; became primitive methodist minister; renounced all party appellations and started mission at Dundee, 1830; open-air preacher; published pamphlets. [vi. 58]

BOWES, MARMADUKE (d. 1585), catholic martyr; executed at York for harbouring catholic priests. [vi. 59]

BOWES, SIR MARTIN (1500 ?–1566), lord mayor of London; deputy 'keeper of exchange,' 1530; sub-treasurer of mint; sheriff of London, 1540; lord mayor, 1545. [vi. 59]

BOWES, MARY ELEANOR, COUNTESS OF STRATHMORE (1749–1800); *née* Bowes; married, 1767, John Lyon, ninth earl of Strathmore (d. 1776); married Lieutenant Andrew Stoney; left Stoney and, 1789, obtained divorce for cruelty; published 'Confessions' and other writings. [vi. 60]

BOWES, PAUL (d. 1702), editor of D'Ewes's 'Journals'; pensioner of St. John's College, Cambridge, 1650; called to bar at Middle Temple, 1661; bencher, 1679; F.R.S., 1699; edited 'Journals' of his uncle, Sir Simonds D'Ewes, 1682. [vi. 61]

BOWES, SIR ROBERT (1495 ?–1554), commander and lawyer; warden of east and middle marches, 1550, and drew up 'Book of State of Frontiers and Marches betwixt England and Scotland'; privy councillor, 1551; master of rolls, 1552. [vi. 61]

BOWES, ROBERT (1535 ?–1597), English ambassador to Scotland; son of Elizabeth Bowes [q. v.]; sheriff of county palatine of Durham, 1569; M.P. for Carlisle, 1571; treasurer of Berwick, 1575–97; ambassador in Scotland, 1577–83. [vi. 62]

BOWES, THOMAS (*fl.* 1586), translator; translated first and second parts of Peter de Primaudaye's 'French Academy,' 1586–94. [vi. 62]

BOWES, SIR WILLIAM (1389–1460 ?), military commander; served in French wars, 1415–32; knighted at Verneuil; governor of Berwick. [vi. 63]

BOWET, HENRY (d. 1423), archbishop of York; chaplain to Urban VI at Rome; enjoyed confidence of Richard II; prebendary of Lincoln before 1386; banished as abettor of Bolingbroke, 1399; prebendary of London; one of four regents of king's possessions in southern France; bishop of Bath and Wells, 1401; treasurer, 1402; archbishop of York, 1407; accompanied army against Scottish invaders, 1417. [vi. 63]

BOWIE, JAMES (d. 1853), botanist; travelled in Brazil, 1814, and the Cape, 1817 and 1827; collector for Kew Gardens, 1814–23. [vi. 65]

BOWLBY, THOMAS WILLIAM (1817–1860), 'Times' correspondent; solicitor in London; correspondent of the 'Times' in Berlin, 1848, and China, 1860; captured by Tartar general San-ko-lin-sin; died from effects of ill-treatment. [vi. 65]

BOWLE or **BOWLES**, JOHN (d. 1637), bishop of Rochester; fellow, Trinity College, Cambridge; D.D., 1613; incorporated D.D. Oxford, 1615; dean of Salisbury, 1620; bishop of Rochester, 1629; published religious works. [vi. 66]

BOWLE, JOHN (1725–1788), writer on Spanish literature; M.A. Oriel College, Oxford, 1750; F.S.A., 1776; vicar of Idmiston; member of Johnson's Essex Head Club; earliest discoverer of Lauder's forgeries; published, 1781, a life of Cervantes in Spanish. [vi. 66]

BOWLER, THOMAS WILLIAM (d. 1869), landscape painter; assistant-astronomer at the Cape; published views of South African scenery. [vi. 67]

BOWLES, CAROLINE ANNE (1786–1854). [See SOUTHEY.]

BOWLES, EDWARD (1613–1662), presbyterian minister; educated at Catharine Hall, Cambridge; parliamentary minister in York, 1644; actively supported Restoration, 1660; published religious works. [vi. 67]

BOWLES, SIR GEORGE (1787–1876), general; served in Peninsular and Waterloo campaigns; in Canada, 1818–20; deputy adjutant-general in West Indies, 1820–5; lieutenant-colonel in Canada, 1838; master of queen's household, 1845; major-general, 1846; K.C.B. and lieutenant of Tower, 1851. [vi. 68]

BOWLES, JOHN (d. 1637). [See BOWLE.]

BOWLES, PHINEAS (d. 1722), major-general; colonel of foot regiment in Ireland, 1705; served at Barcelona, Almanza, Saragossa (1710), and was captured in Castile; raised corps of dragoons (now 12th lancers), 1715. [vi. 68]

BOWLES, PHINEAS (d. 1749), lieutenant-general; son of Phineas Bowles (d. 1722) [q. v.]; succeeded his father as colonel of 12th dragoons; lieutenant-general, 1745, and governor of Londonderry. [vi. 68]

BOWLES, WILLIAM (1705–1780), naturalist; studied science in Paris; superintendent of state mines in Spanish service, 752; published work in Spanish on natural history and geography of Spain, 1775. [vi. 69]

BOWLES, WILLIAM LISLE (1762–1850), divine, poet, and antiquary; educated at Winchester and Trinity College, Oxford; B.A., 1792; vicar of Bremhill, Wiltshire, 1804–50; prebendary of Salisbury, 1804, and canon residentiary, 1828; chaplain to prince regent, 1818; published poems, his sonnets being especially graceful, 1789–1837, an edition of Pope, 1806, and various ecclesiastical and antiquarian works. [vi. 69]

BOWLEY, ROBERT KANZOW (1813–1870), amateur musician; conductor of Benevolent Society of Musical Amateurs; connected with Sacred Harmonic Society, 1834–70; originated plan of Handel festivals, 1856. [vi. 71]

BOWLY, SAMUEL (1802–1884), quaker; cheese factor at Gloucester; took active part in the anti-slavery agitation, and was a strong advocate of total abstinence. [vi. 71]

BOWMAN, EDDOWES (1810–1869), dissenting tutor; son of John Eddowes Bowman (1785–1841) [q. v.]; sub-manager of Varteg ironworks, near Pontypool, 1835–40; M.A. Glasgow; professor of classical literature and history at Manchester, New College, 1846–53; published theological and other works. [vi. 71]

BOWMAN, HENRY (*fl.* 1677), musician: organist of Trinity College, Cambridge; published songs and other musical compositions. [vi. 72]

BOWMAN, HENRY (1814–1883), architect; son of John Eddowes Bowman (1785–1841) [q. v.]; joint author of 'Ecclesiastical Architecture of Great Britain,' 1845. [vi. 73]

BOWMAN, JOHN EDDOWES, the elder (1785–1841), banker and naturalist; managing partner of a bank at Wrexham; fellow of Linnean and Geological Societies; published writings on natural history. [vi. 72]

BOWMAN, JOHN EDDOWES, the younger (1819–1854), chemist; son of John Eddowes Bowman (1785–1841) [q. v.]; professor of chemistry, King's College, London, 1851; published scientific works. [vi. 73]

BOWMAN, WALTER (d. 1782), antiquary; comptroller of port of Bristol; F.S.A., 1735; F.R.S., 1742. [vi. 73]

BOWMAN, SIR WILLIAM (1816–1892), ophthalmic surgeon; surgeon, King's College Hospital, 1856; professor of physiology and general and morbid anatomy, 1848; member of council, 1879; surgeon to Royal Ophthalmic Hospital, Moorfields, 1851–76; F.R.S., 1841; F.R.C.S., 1844; first president of Ophthalmological Society of United Kingdom, 1880; created baronet, 1884; established, with Robert Bentley Todd (1809–1860) [q. v.], St. John's House and sisterhood; published surgical writings. [Suppl. i. 242]

BOWNAS, SAMUEL (1676–1753), quaker minister; came under influence of Anne Wilson, a quakeress, and subsequently travelled as missionary in Great Britain and Ireland; went to America, 1702, and was imprisoned in Long Island for preaching, 1702–3; returned to England, 1706; revisited America, 1726–8; wrote autobiographical and other works. [vi. 73]

BOWNDE or **BOUND**, NICHOLAS (d. 1613), divine; fellow of Peterhouse, Cambridge, 1570; M.A., 1575; D.D., 1594; incorporated M.A. Oxford, 1577; minister of church of St. Andrew the Apostle, Norwich, 1611–13; published religious works, including 'The Doctrine of the Sabbath,' 1595, which gave rise to the first disagreement between high church party and puritans on point of doctrine. [vi. 74]

BOWNE, PETER (1575–1624?), physician; fellow, Corpus Christi College, Oxford; D.M., 1614; F.C.P., 1617; published 'Pseudo-Medicorum Anatomia,' 1624. [vi. 75]

BOWNESS, WILLIAM (1809–1867), painter of domestic and figure subjects: self-taught; exhibited at Royal Academy, 1836–67; wrote pieces in Westmoreland dialect. [vi. 75]

BOWRING, SIR JOHN (1792–1872), linguist, writer, and traveller; acquired many languages in a mercantile house at Exeter, clerk in London house of Milford & Co., who sent him to Peninsula, 1811; began business independently; editor of 'Westminster Review,' 1824; LL.D. Groningen, 1829; made journeys to examine system of keeping public accounts in European countries; appointed (1831) secretary to commission for inspecting accounts of United Kingdom; sent by government on commercial mission to Belgium, 1833, and Egypt, Syria, and Turkey, 1837–8; M.P. for Clyde burghs, 1835–7; assisted in forming Anti-Cornlaw League, 1838; M.P. for Bolton, 1841; obtained issue of florin as first step towards introduction of decimal system of currency; consul at Canton, 1847; plenipotentiary to China, governor, commander-in-chief and vice-admiral of Hong-Kong, 1854; knighted, 1854; established diplomatic and commercial relations with Siam, 1855; went on commercial mission to Philippine Islands, 1858; returned to England, 1860; investigated British commercial relations with Italy, 1860; F.R.S. His publications include accounts of his missions, works connected with European and eastern poetry, hymns, and political and economical treatises. [vi. 76]

BOWTELL, JOHN (1753–1813), topographer; bookbinder and stationer at Cambridge; left manuscript history of Cambridge. [vi. 80]

BOWYER, SIR GEORGE (1740?–1800), admiral; lieutenant, 1758; captain, 1762; served in West Indies under Byng and Rodney, 1778–81; M.P., Queenborough, 1784; rear-admiral, 1793; wounded in engagement off Ushant, 1794; created baronet, 1794; admiral 1799. [vi. 81]

BOWYER, SIR GEORGE (1811–1883), seventh baronet; lawyer; cadet at Royal Military College, Woolwich; called to bar at Middle Temple, and created hon. M.A. Oxford, 1839; equity draughtsman and conveyancer; D.C.L. Oxford, 1844; reader in law at Middle Temple, 1850; M.P. for Dundalk, 1852–68, and for Wexford county, 1874–80; magistrate and deputy-lieutenant of Berkshire; published a series of valuable text-books on constitutional jurisprudence. [vi. 81]

BOWYER, ROBERT (1758–1834), painter; exhibited miniatures at Royal Academy, 1783–1828; produced, with assistance of other artists, an illustrated edition of Hume's 'History of England.' [vi. 82]

BOWYER, WILLIAM, the elder (1663–1737), printer; apprenticed to Miles Flesher, 1679; freeman of Stationers' Company, 1686; liveryman, and one of twenty printers allowed by Star-chamber, 1700. [vi. 82]

BOWYER, WILLIAM, the younger (1699–1777), 'the learned printer'; son of William Bowyer (1663–1737) [q. v.]; educated under Ambrose Bonwicke the elder [q. v.], and at St. John's College, Cambridge; partner with, and corrector of the press for, his father, 1722; printer of votes of House of Commons, 1729; printer to Society of Antiquaries, and F.S.A., 1736; liveryman of Stationers' Company, 1738; master, 1771; in partnership with James Emonson, 1754–7; printer to Royal Society, 1761; appointed printer of rules of parliament and journal of House of Lords, 1767; published 'Origin of Printing,' 1774. He supplied notes and prefaces to many of his publications, and wrote (1763) 'Conjectural Emendations' of the Greek Testament. [vi. 83]

BOXALL, JOHN (d. 1571), secretary of state; educated at Winchester, and graduated at New College, Oxford; dean of Ely, prebendary of Winchester, and secretary of state to Mary, 1553–8; warden of Winchester College, 1554; privy councillor, and master and councillor of court of requests, 1556; registrar of order of Garter; D.D., and prebendary of York and Salisbury, 1558; deprived of ecclesiastical preferments, 1560; committed to Tower and subsequently to 'free custody' of the archbishop. [vi. 86]

BOXALL, SIR WILLIAM (1800–1879), portrait-painter; studied at Royal Academy and in Italy; first exhibited at Royal Academy, 1823; R.A., 1863; director of National Gallery, 1865–74; knighted, 1867. [vi. 87]

BOXER, EDWARD (1784–1855), rear-admiral; entered navy, 1798; commander, 1815; took part in siege of Acre, and was made C.B., 1840; harbour-master at Quebec, 1843–53; rear-admiral, 1853; second in command in Mediterranean, and superintendent at Balaclava, 1854; died of cholera. [vi. 87]

BOYCE, SAMUEL (d. 1775), author of a dramatic pastoral, and several poems. [vi. 88]

BOYCE, THOMAS (d. 1793), dramatist; rector of Worlingham, Suffolk; author of 'Harold,' a tragedy (1786). [vi. 88]

BOYCE, WILLIAM (1710–1779), musician; chorister at St. Paul's Cathedral; composer and joint-organist to Chapel Royal, 1736; member of Royal Society of Musicians; produced 'Solomon,' his best work, 1743; Mus.Doc. Cambridge, 1749; organist of Allhallows the Great and Less, Thames Street, 1749–69; master of the king's band of musicians, and conductor of festivals of Sons of the Clergy, 1755; organist of Chapel Royal, 1758; composed birthday and new year odes, settings to masques and plays (including 'Tempest,' 'Cymbeline' and 'Winter's Tale'), songs (including 'Hearts of Oak'), and church music, editing also the collection entitled 'Cathedral Music.' [vi. 88]

BOYCOTT, CHARLES CUNNINGHAM (1832–1897), land agent, from whose name the word 'boycott' is derived; educated at Woolwich; obtained commission in 39th foot, 1850; retired as captain; agent for Lord Erne's estates in county Mayo, 1873; came into conflict with Land League agitators, 1879, and suffered annoyances which in 1880 gave rise to word 'boycott.' [Suppl. i. 243]

BOYD, ANDREW KENNEDY HUTCHINSON (1825–1899), Scottish divine; studied at King's College and Middle Temple, London, and at Glasgow; B.A., 1846; minister of St. Bernard's, Edinburgh, 1859; honorary D.D. Edinburgh, 1864; minister of first charge, St. Andrews, 1865; LL.D. St. Andrews, 1889; moderator of general assembly, 1890. His publications include 'Recreations of a Country Parson,' three series, 1859–61–78. [Suppl. i. 244]

BOYD, ARCHIBALD (1803–1883), divine; M.A. Trinity College, Dublin; D.D., 1868; honorary canon of Gloucester, 1857–67; dean of Exeter, 1867; published 'History of Book of Common Prayer' (1850) and other works. [vi. 90]

BOYD, BENJAMIN (1796-1851), Australian squatter ; stockbroker in London, 1824-39 ; went to Sydney to organise branches of Royal Australian Banking Company ; engaged in whaling and sheep farming.   [vi. 91]

BOYD, HENRY (d. 1832), translator of Dante ; probably educated at Dublin University ; published translations in English verse of Dante's 'Inferno,' 1785, and 'Divina Commedia,' 1802, also other translations and original poems.   [vi. 91]

BOYD, HUGH (1746-1794), essayist ; M.A. Trinity College, Dublin, 1765 ; studied law in London ; became acquainted with Goldsmith, Garrick, Burke, and Reynolds ; secretary to Lord Macartney, governor of Madras, 1781, and subsequently master-attendant at Madras ; conducted 'Madras Courier' and other papers in India ; his writings were collected and published after his death. The 'Letters of Junius' have been attributed to him.   [vi. 92]

BOYD, HUGH STUART (1781-1848), Greek scholar ; educated at Pembroke Hall, Cambridge ; taught Greek when blind (1828-48) to Elizabeth Barrett Browning ; published classical translations and other works.   [vi. 92]

BOYD, JAMES (1795-1856), author ; M.A. Glasgow : studied medicine ; licensed preacher by presbytery of Dumbarton, 1822 ; house governor in George Heriot's Hospital, Edinburgh, 1825 ; classical master, high school, Edinburgh, 1829-56 ; edited school-books.   [vi. 93]

BOYD, MARK (1805 ?-1879), author ; engaged in business in London ; promoted colonisation of Australia and New Zealand ; published 'Reminiscences.' [vi. 93]

BOYD, MARK ALEXANDER (1563-1601), Latin scholar ; educated at Glasgow ; served in troop of horse under Henri III, 1587 ; subsequently travelled in France and Low Countries, meeting with many adventures ; published letters and Latin and Greek poems, 1592, leaving also manuscripts in prose and verse.   [vi. 94]

BOYD, ROBERT, LORD BOYD (d. 1469 ?), Scottish statesman ; created Lord Boyd, 1454 ; one of regents during minority of James III, 1460 ; conspired with his brother, Sir Alexander, obtained possession of king's person, and was made by act of parliament sole governor of realm ; negotiated marriage between James and Margaret of Norway, 1468 ; appointed great chamberlain for life, 1467 ; found guilty of treason, 1469 ; fled to Alnwick, Northumberland, where he died.   [vi. 95]

BOYD, ROBERT, fourth LORD BOYD (d. 1590), statesman ; assisted the regent Arran in quelling Lennox's rebellion, 1544 ; took part with lords of congregation in war against queen regent, 1559 ; signed treaty of Berwick and joined English army at Prestonpans, 1560 ; subscribed to 'Book of Discipline of Kirk,' 1561 ; perhaps privy to murder of Darnley ; member of jury which acquitted Bothwell, 1567, but joined confederacy of nobles to protect the young prince against Bothwell after his marriage to Mary ; subsequently again took Bothwell's part against his calumniators ; made a permanent member of privy council, 1567 ; with Mary's forces at Langside, 1568 ; member of Mary's council, 1569 ; suspected of complicity in murder of Murray, 1570 ; joined regent's party (perhaps at Mary's suggestion), and was made privy councillor, 1570 ; appointed by Morton extraordinary lord of session, 1573 ; party to 'Raid of Ruthven' and banished, 1583 ; restored to place on bench, 1586 ; one of wardens of marches, 1587.   [vi. 96]

BOYD, ROBERT, of Trochrig (1578-1627), divine ; educated at Edinburgh and on continent ; professor in university of Saumur, 1606 ; principal of Glasgow University, 1615-21, and of Edinburgh University, 1622, but was deprived for nonconformity with 'five articles of Perth' ; minister of Paisley, 1627 ; wrote 'Commentary on Epistle to Ephesians' (published posthumously) and other works.   [vi. 98]

BOYD, SIR ROBERT (1710-1794), general ; storekeeper (civilian) of ordnance at Port Mahon, Minorca, till 1756 ; distinguished himself at siege, 1756, and was made lieutenant-colonel, 1758 ; colonel of 39th foot, 1766 ; lieutenant-governor of Malta, 1768 ; lieutenant-general, 1777 ; second in command at defence of Gibraltar, 1779-83 ; K.B. ; general, 1793.   [vi. 99]

BOYD, ROBERT (d. 1883), alienist ; M.R.C.S., 1830 ; M.D. Edinburgh, 1831 ; F.R.C.P., 1852 ; proprietor of a private lunatic asylum, Southall Park ; published treatises relating to insanity.   [vi. 100]

BOYD, THOMAS, EARL OF ARRAN (fl. 1469), son of Robert, first lord Boyd [q. v.] ; created Earl of Arran and Baron Kilmarnock, 1467 ; married Lady Mary, sister of James III of Scotland, 1467 ; escorted Margaret of Norway from Denmark to Scotland, 1469 ; fled on hearing of his father's trial, and died at Antwerp.   [vi. 95]

BOYD, WALTER (1754 ?-1837), financier ; banker in Paris ; fled from revolution and established business with Paul Benfield [q. v.] in London, 1793 ; contracted for large government loans ; M.P. for Shaftesbury, 1796-1802 ; bankrupt, 1799 ; visited France, c. 1802, and was detained until 1814 ; M.P. for Lymington, 1823-30 ; wrote pamphlets on financial subjects.   [vi. 100]

BOYD, WILLIAM, fourth EARL OF KILMARNOCK (1704-1746), general ; educated at Glasgow ; joined Young Pretender in hope of advancement, 1745 ; made privy councillor to Prince Charles, colonel of guards, and subsequently general ; fought at Falkirk, 1746 ; captured at Culloden ; executed on Tower Hill.   [vi. 101]

BOYD, WILLIAM (d. 1772), Irish presbyterian divine ; ordained minister of Macosquin, co. Derry, 1710 ; carried commission signed by many presbyterians to Colonel Suitte, governor of New England, proposing emigration to that colony, 1718 ; signed Westminster confession, 1721 ; elected moderator at Dungannon, 1730 ; one of the divines who drew up 'Serious Warning,' 1747 ; published religious works.   [vi. 102]

BOYD, ZACHARY (1585 ?-1653), Scottish divine ; M.A. St. Andrews, 1607 ; minister of Barony parish, Glasgow, 1623 ; dean of faculty, rector, and vice-chancellor of Glasgow University ; published works in verse and prose, and left various manuscripts.   [vi. 103]

BOYDELL, JOHN (1719-1804), engraver ; studied at St. Martin's Lane academy ; published small sets of land cape engravings and views of London, Oxford, and other towns ; set up as printseller and publisher of engravings, c. 1751, and rapidly established extensive trade ; sheriff of London, 1785 ; lord mayor, 1790 ; commissioned well-known artists to paint pictures illustrative of Shakespeare (engravings from which were contained in an edition of Shakespeare published in 1802) and built Shakespeare Gallery in Pall Mall for their exhibition ; compelled by financial difficulties to dispose of his property by lottery, but died before lottery was drawn.   [vi. 104]

BOYDELL, JOSIAH (1752-1817), painter and engraver ; nephew of John Boydell [q. v.], and partner and successor in his engraving business : painted pictures for the Shakespeare Gallery ; exhibited at Royal Academy, 1772-99 ; master of Stationers' Company and alderman of Cheap ward.   [vi. 106]

BOYER, ABEL (1667-1729), miscellaneous writer ; born in Upper Languedoc ; came to England, 1689 ; French teacher to William, duke of Gloucester ; published yearly register of political and other occurrences, 1703-13, and 'Political State of Great Britain,' a monthly periodical, 1711-29.   [vi. 107]

BOYES, JOHN FREDERICK (1811-1879), classical scholar ; educated at Merchant Taylors' School and St. John's College, Oxford ; M.A. ; head-master, Walthamstow proprietary school ; published works relating to classical and English poetry.   [vi. 108]

BOYLE, CHARLES, fourth EARL OF ORRERY and first BARON MARSTON (1676-1731), antagonist of Bentley ; educated at Christ Church, Oxford ; edited epistles of Phalaris, which led to controversy with Richard Bentley [q. v.], and to Swift's 'Battle of the Books' ; fought at Malplaquet ; major-general, 1709 ; took part in negotiations preceding treaty of Utrecht ; privy councillor ; lord of bedchamber, 1714-16 ; imprisoned for connection with Layer's Jacobite plot, 1721.   [vi. 109]

BOYLE, DAVID, LORD BOYLE (1772-1853), president of session ; called to Scottish bar, 1793 ; solicitor-general for Scotland, 1807 ; M.P. for Ayrshire, 1807-11 ; justiciary and lord justice clerk, 1811 ; privy councillor, 1820 ; lord justice general and president of Scottish court of session, c. 1840-52.   [vi. 109]

BOYLE, HENRY, BARON CARLETON (*d.* 1725), politician ; M.P. for Tamworth, 1689–90, Cambridge University, 1692–1705, Westminster, 1705–10 ; chancellor of exchequer, 1701 ; lord treasurer of Ireland, 1704–10 ; principal secretary of state, 1708–10 ; raised to peerage, 1714 ; lord president of council, 1721–5 ; patron of Addison. [vi. 110]

BOYLE, HENRY, EARL OF SHANNON (1682–1764), whig politician ; privy councillor, chancellor of exchequer, commissioner of revenue, and speaker of Irish House of Commons, 1733 ; created Earl of Shannon, 1756 ; frequently acted as lord justice of Ireland. [vi. 110]

BOYLE, JOHN (1563 ?–1620), Irish bishop, brother of Richard, first earl of Cork [q. v.] ; D.D. Oxford ; bishop of Roscarberry, Cork, and Cloyne, 1617. [vi. 112]

BOYLE, JOHN, fifth EARL OF CORK, fifth EARL OF ORRERY, and second BARON MARSTON (1707–1762), author; son of Charles Boyle [q. v.] ; educated at Christ Church, Oxford ; D.C.L., 1743 ; F.R.S., 1750 ; friend of Swift, Pope, and Johnson ; his works include 'Remarks on Swift,' 1751, and a 'Translation of Letters of Pliny the Younger,' 1751. [vi. 111]

BOYLE, MICHAEL, the elder (1580 ?–1635), Irish bishop : educated at Merchant Taylors' School and St. John's College, Oxford ; M.A., 1601 ; D.D., 1611 ; bishop of Waterford and Lismore, 1619. [vi. 112]

BOYLE, MICHAEL, the younger (1609 ?–1702), archbishop of Armagh, nephew of Michael Boyle (1580 ?–1635) [q. v.] ; M.A. Trinity College, Dublin ; incorporated M.A. Oxford, 1637 ; D.D., 1637 ; chaplain-general to English army in Munster ; privy councillor in Ireland and bishop of Cork, Cloyne, and Ross, 1660 ; bishop of Dublin, 1663 ; chancellor of Ireland, 1665 ; archbishop of Armagh, 1675. [vi. 112]

BOYLE, MURRAGH, VISCOUNT BLESSINGTON (*d.*1712), son of Michael Boyle (1609 ?–1702) [q. v.] ; wrote 'The Lost Princess,' a tragedy. [vi. 113]

BOYLE, RICHARD, first EARL OF CORK (1566–1643), Irish statesman ; called the 'great earl' ; educated at Bennet's (Corpus Christi) College, Cambridge ; entered Middle Temple ; went to Ireland, 1588 ; escheator to John Crofton, escheator general, 1590 ; imprisoned on charge of embezzling records, 1592 ; again accused of embezzling records, but obtained acquittal ; clerk of council of Munster ; conveyed news to Elizabeth of victory near Kinsale, 1601 ; purchased for 1,000*l.* Sir Walter Raleigh's Irish possessions, out of which he rapidly acquired a large fortune ; knighted, 1603 ; privy councillor for Munster, 1606, and for Ireland, 1612 ; created Lord Boyle, baron of Youghal, 1616, and Viscount Dungarvan and Earl of Cork, 1620 ; appointed one of lords justices of Ireland, 1629 ; lord high treasurer, 1631 ; he worked skilfully and with persistent secrecy to undermine Wentworth's authority from 1633, and was probably largely responsible for his impeachment, 1641. [vi. 113]

BOYLE, RICHARD (*d.* 1644), divine ; brother of Michael Boyle the elder [q. v.] ; dean of Waterford, 1603 ; bishop of Cork, Cloyne, and Ross, 1620 ; archbishop of Tuam, 1638. [vi. 116]

BOYLE, RICHARD, first EARL OF BURLINGTON and second EARL OF CORK (1612–1697), statesman ; son of Richard Boyle, first earl of Cork [q. v.] ; knighted, 1624 ; assisted his father in Irish rebellion, 1642 ; supported king during war ; created Baron Clifford of Lanesborough, Yorkshire, 1643 ; lord-lieutenant of West Riding of Yorkshire, and custos rotulorum, *c.* 1663 ; created Earl of Burlington, 1663 ; promoted cause of William and Mary. [vi. 116]

BOYLE, RICHARD, third EARL OF BURLINGTON and fourth EARL OF CORK (1695–1753), statesman ; privy councillor, 1714 ; lord-lieutenant of West Riding of Yorkshire, custos rotulorum of North and West Ridings, and lord high treasurer of Ireland, 1715 ; K.C.G., 1730 ; he was a patron of literature and art, and spent large sums of money in gratifying a taste for architecture, altering and partly reconstructing Burlington House, London, 1716. [vi. 117]

BOYLE, HON. ROBERT (1627–1691), natural philosopher and chemist ; son of Richard Boyle, first earl of Cork [q. v.] ; educated at Eton and by private tutors ; studied on continent ; returned to England, 1644 ; settled at Oxford, 1654, erected laboratory, and in 1660 published ' New Experiments Physico-Mechanical,' to second edition of which (1662) was appended his ' Defence against Linus,' containing experimental proof of proportional relation between elasticity and pressure, known as ' Boyle's Law ' ; published moral and religious essays, and studied Hebrew, Greek, Chaldee, and Syriac ; governor of Corporation for the Spread of the Gospel in New England, 1661–89, and a director of the East India Company ; took leading part in founding Royal Society, on first council of which he sat, declining office of president from a scruple about the oaths. His voluminous writings (published between 1660 and 1691), while embodying no great discovery, exhibit vividly the fruitfulness of the experimental method ; the first complete edition of them was published by Birch in 1744, 5 vols. Boyle bequeathed his mineralogical collections to the Royal Society, and by his will founded and endowed the 'Boyle Lectures.' [vi. 118]

BOYLE, ROGER, BARON BROGHILL and first EARL OF ORRERY (1621–1679), statesman, soldier, and dramatist ; son of Richard Boyle, first earl of Cork [q. v.] ; created Baron Broghill, 1627 ; educated at Trinity College, Dublin, and at Oxford ; travelled in France and Italy ; commanded troops in Scotland, and (1641–2) Ireland ; served under parliamentarians, 1647–8 ; accepted from Cromwell general's command in Ireland, 1650 ; M.P. for Cork, 1654, and for Cork and Edinburgh, 1656, being sent, as lord president of council, to Scotland ; member of Cromwell's council ; obtained command in Munster, being convinced that Richard Cromwell's cause was hopeless, and, with Sir Charles Coote, secured Ireland for the king ; M.P. for Arundel in Convention parliament ; one of lords justices of Ireland, and created Earl of Orrery, 1660 ; impeached for raising money by his own authority from the king's subjects, but proceedings stopped by the king's proroguing parliament ; his publications include a ' Treatise on the Art of War ' (1677), and rhymed tragedies, some of which were produced with success. [vi. 123]

BOYLE, ROGER (1617 ?–1687), bishop ; educated at Trinity College, Dublin ; dean of Cork ; bishop of Down and Connor, 1667, and of Clogher, 1672 ; wrote religious works. [vi. 126]

BOYNE, first VISCOUNT (1639–1723). [See HAMILTON, GUSTAVUS.]

BOYNE, JOHN (*d.* 1810), water-colour painter and engraver ; drawing master in London ; his works include heads from Shakespeare's plays. [vi. 127]

BOYS or **BOSCHUS**, DAVID (*d.* 1451), Carmelite; lecturer in theology at Oxford ; head of Carmelite community at Gloucester. [vi. 127]

BOYS, EDWARD (1599–1667), divine ; educated at Eton and Corpus Christi College, Oxford ; M.A., 1627 ; B.D., 1634 ; rector of Mautboy, Norfolk, 1639–67. [vi. 127]

BOYS, EDWARD (1785–1866), captain ; son of John Boys (1749–1824) [q. v.] ; entered navy, 1796 ; prisoner in France, 1803–9 ; commander, 1814 ; superintendent of Deal dockyard, 1837–41 ; published account of his captivity, 1827. [vi. 128]

BOYS, JOHN (1571–1625), divine ; M.A. Corpus Christi College, Cambridge ; fellow of Clare Hall ; master of Eastbridge Hospital ; D.D., 1605 ; dean of Canterbury, 1619 ; member of high commission court, 1620 ; chief works, ' Expositions ' of the Dominical epistles and gospels and of the proper psalms. [vi. 128]

BOYS, JOHN (1561–1644). [See BOIS.]

BOYS, JOHN (1614 ?–1661), translator of Virgil ; nephew of Edward Boys (1599–1667) [q. v.] ; presented to mayor of Canterbury declaration in favour of the assembly of a free parliament, and narrowly escaped imprisonment, 1660 ; published verse translations from Virgil. [vi. 129]

BOYS, SIR JOHN (1607–1664), royalist ; captain in royal army and governor of Donnington Castle, Berkshire, which he three times successfully defended, 1644 ; knighted, and appointed colonel, 1644 ; imprisoned for petitioning for free parliament, 1659 ; receiver of customs at Dover under Charles II. [vi. 130]

BOYS, JOHN (1749–1824), Kentish agriculturist; famous for his breed of Southdown sheep; published works on agricultural subjects.   [vi. 131]

BOYS, THOMAS (1792–1880), theologian and antiquary; M.A. Trinity College, Cambridge, 1817; attached to military chest in Peninsula, 1813; ordained, 1822; incumbent of Holy Trinity, Hoxton; professor of Hebrew at Missionary College, Islington, 1836; published translation of bible into Portuguese.   [vi. 131]

BOYS, THOMAS SHOTTER (1803–1874), water-colour painter and lithographer; studied painting in Paris; exhibited at Royal Academy from 1824; executed, lithographed, and engraved illustrations for several publications, including Ruskin's 'Stones of Venice.'   [vi. 132]

BOYS, WILLIAM (1735–1803), surgeon; mayor of Sandwich, 1767 and 1782; F.S.A., 1776; surgeon to sick and wounded seamen at Deal, 1789; published archæological and topographical writings.   [v. 132]

BOYSE, JOSEPH (1660–1728), presbyterian minister; ministered at Brownist church at Amsterdam, 1682; minister at Dublin, 1683–1728; published controversial tracts in behalf of the presbyterian dissent.   [vi. 133]

BOYSE, SAMUEL (1708–1749), poet; son of Joseph Boyse [q. v.]; educated at Glasgow University; adopted no profession, and during the latter part of his life experienced great poverty. His writings include 'The Deity,' a poem (1739), and 'An Historical Review of the Transactions of Europe, 1739–45' (1747).   [vi. 135]

BRABAZON, ROGER LE (d. 1317), judge; justice itinerant of pleas of forest in Lancashire, 1287; justice of king's bench, 1289; prepared proofs of legality of Edward I's claim to suzerainty over Scotland, 1291; justice itinerant in west of England, 1291; chief-justice, 1295–1316; member of Prince Edward's council, 1297; sat on trial of Earl of Atholl and convicted him, 1307; commissioner of various royal forests, 1300–16.   [vi. 137]

BRABAZON, SIR WILLIAM (d. 1552), lord justice of Ireland; knighted and appointed vice-treasurer and general receiver of Ireland, 1534; lord justice of Ireland, 1543, 1546, and 1549; Irish privy councillor, 1547.   [vi. 138]

BRABOURNE, BARON (1829–1893). [See KNATCHBULL-HUGESSEN, EDWARD HUGESSEN.]

BRABOURNE, THEOPHILUS (b. 1590), divine; ordained before 1628; minister at Norwich; published 'Discourse upon Sabbath Day,' maintaining that Saturday was the sabbath, 1628, and 'Defence of Sabbath Day,' 1632; imprisoned and ultimately recanted to the satisfaction of the high commission court.   [vi. 139]

BRACEGIRDLE, ANNE (1663?–1748), actress; appeared at Theatre Royal, 1688, as Lucia in Shadwell's 'Squire of Alsatia'; with Betterton at Lincoln's Inn Fields Theatre as Angelica in 'Love for Love,' 1695; created Belinda in Vanbrugh's 'Provoked Wife,' and Almeria in Congreve's 'Mourning Bride,' 1697; played Isabella, Portia, Desdemona, Ophelia, Cordelia, and Mrs. Ford, in Shakespearean adaptations; eclipsed by Mrs. Oldfield, 1707, retiring from the stage in consequence.   [vi. 141]

BRACEGIRDLE, JOHN (d. 1614), poet; B.D. Queens' College, Cambridge, 1602; vicar of Rye, 1602–14; author of a poetical translation from Boethius.   [vi. 142]

BRACKEN, HENRY (1697–1764), physician; studied in London, Paris, and Leyden; M.D. Leyden; mayor of Lancaster, 1747–8, and 1757–8; groundlessly imprisoned for abetting Jacobite rebellion, 1746; published works on farriery.   [vi. 142]

BRACKENBURY, CHARLES BOOTH (1831–1890), major-general; second lieutenant, royal artillery, 1850; served in Crimea; captain, 1865; military correspondent of the 'Times' with Austrian army, 1866, in Le Mans campaign, 1870–1, and Turkish war, 1877; colonel, 1882; director of artillery studies at Woolwich, 1887; received temporary rank of major-general, 1889; wrote on military subjects.   [Suppl. i. 245]

BRACKENBURY, SIR EDWARD (1785–1864), lieutenant-colonel; lieutenant, 1803; served in Peninsula; attached to Portuguese and Spanish army, 1814–16; knighted, 1836; lieutenant-colonel, 1837.   [vi. 143]

BRACKENBURY, JOSEPH (1788–1864), poet; graduated at Corpus Christi College, Cambridge; chaplain to Madras establishment, 1812; published poems.   [vi. 144]

BRACKENBURY or **BRAKENBURY,** SIR ROBERT (d. 1485), constable of the Tower; appointed master and worker of moneys and keeper of king's exchange at Tower of London, and constable for life of Tower, 1483; served against rebels headed by Henry Stafford, second duke of Buckingham [q. v.]; 'esquire of royal body'; keeper of lions in Tower, 1484; vice-admiral and commissioner of admiralty, 1484; knighted; sheriff of Kent, 1485; refused to obey command of Richard III to make away with princes in Tower and delivered keys to Sir James Tyrrell [q. v.]; held command under Richard at Bosworth and was killed.   [Suppl. i. 246]

BRACKLEY, VISCOUNTS. [See EGERTON, SIR THOMAS, first VISCOUNT, 1540?–1617; EGERTON, JOHN, second VISCOUNT, 1579–1649.]

BRACTON, BRATTON, or **BRETTON,** HENRY DE (d. 1268), ecclesiastic and judge; justice itinerant for Nottinghamshire and Derbyshire, 1245, Northumberland, Westmoreland, Cumberland, and Lancashire, 1246, and western counties between 1260 and 1267; chancellor of Exeter Cathedral, 1264; prebendary of Exeter and of Bosham, and perhaps chief-justice; wrote, between 1235 and 1259, 'De Legibus et Consuetudinibus Angliæ' (first complete edition, Richard Tottell's, 1569), the earliest attempt to treat the whole extent of the law in a manner at once systematic and practical.   [vi. 144]

BRADBERRY, sometimes called **BRADBURY,** DAVID (1736–1803), nonconformist divine; minister of baptist congregations in London, Ramsgate, and Manchester; published religious works.   [vi. 147]

BRADBRIDGE or **BRODEBRIDGE,** WILLIAM (1501–1578), bishop of Exeter; B.A. Magdalen College, Oxford, 1528; fellow, 1529; M.A., 1532; B.D., 1539; espoused reformed religion and fled from England, 1553; prebendary of Sarum, 1555; canon of Chichester; subscribed to articles of 1562 and 1571; chancellor of Chichester, 1562; dean of Salisbury, 1563; bishop of Exeter, 1571.   [vi. 147]

BRADBURN, SAMUEL (1751–1816), methodist preacher; itinerant minister, c. 1772, and one of the greatest preachers of his day.   [vi. 149]

BRADBURY, GEORGE (d. 1696), judge; M.A. Oxford, 1663; called to bar at Middle Temple, 1667; one of chiefs of bar summoned to consult with peers on political crisis, 1688; judge in exchequer court, 1689.   [vi. 149]

BRADBURY, HENRY (1831–1860), writer on printing; studied nature-printing in Vienna.   [vi. 150]

BRADBURY, THOMAS (1677–1759), congregational minister; pastor of independent congregations in New Street, Fetter Lane, 1707, and at New Court, Lincoln's Inn Fields, 1728; published religious works and sermons, many of which were political.   [vi. 150]

BRADDOCK, EDWARD (1695–1755), major-general; ensign, 1710; captain and lieutenant-colonel, grenadier company, 1735; second major, Coldstreams, 1743; accompanied Admiral Lestock's expedition to L'Orient, 1746; served under Prince of Orange in Holland, 1746–8; colonel of 14th foot at Gibraltar, 1753; major-general, 1754; general and commander-in-chief in North America, 1755; commanded expedition against Fort Duquesne, 1755, when he was mortally wounded.   [vi. 153]

BRADDOCKE, JOHN (1656–1719), divine; M.A. St. Catharine's Hall, Cambridge, 1678; chaplain to Bishop of Exeter, 1707; master of Eastbridge Hospital, Kent, 1709.   [vi. 155]

BRADDON, LAURENCE (d. 1724), politician; called to bar at Middle Temple; imprisoned, 1683–9, for disseminating rumours that Earl of Essex (who died in Tower, 1683) was murdered; solicitor to wine licence office, 1695; published works relating to Essex's death, and other writings.   [vi. 155]

BRADE, JAMES (1795?–1860). [See BRAID.]

BRADE, WILLIAM (fl. 1615), English musician; violinist to Duke of Holstein-Gottorp and to town of Hamburg; capellmeister to margrave of Brandenburg, 1619; perhaps died at Frankfurt, 1647; published musical compositions.   [vi. 156]

BRADFIELD, HENRY JOSEPH STEELE (1805–1852), surgeon and author; stipendiary magistrate in Tobago, 1835, and Trinidad, 1836; colonial secretary in Barbados, 1842; dismissed; published poetical and other works. [vi. 156]

BRADFORD, first EARL OF (1619–1708). [See NEWPORT, FRANCIS.]

BRADFORD, BARONS OF. [See NEWPORT, RICHARD, first BARON, 1587–1651; NEWPORT, FRANCIS, second BARON, 1619–1708.]

BRADFORD, JOHN (1510 ?–1555), protestant martyr; studied at Inner Temple, 1547; entered St. Catharine's Hall, Cambridge, 1548; M.A., 1549; fellow of Pembroke Hall; chaplain to Bishop Ridley; prebendary of St. Paul's, 1551; one of king's chaplains in ordinary; imprisoned on charge of preaching seditious sermons, 1553–5; condemned and burnt at Smithfield; wrote sermons and other religious works and translations. [vi. 157]

BRADFORD, JOHN (d. 1780), Welsh poet, presided in bardic chair of Glamorgan, 1750. [vi. 159]

BRADFORD, JOHN (1750–1805), dissenting minister; B.A. Wadham College, Oxford; curate at Frelsham, Berkshire; joined Countess of Huntingdon's connexion; preached at City Chapel, Grub Street, London, 1797–1805; published religious works. [vi. 160]

BRADFORD, SAMUEL (1652–1731), bishop of Rochester; educated at St. Paul's School, Charterhouse, and Corpus Christi College, Cambridge; M.A., 1680; D.D., 1705; incorporated M.A. Oxford, 1697; rector of St. Mary-le-Bow, 1693; chaplain in ordinary to William III, 1698; prebendary of Westminster, 1708; Boyle lecturer, 1699; master of Corpus Christi College, 1716–24; bishop of Carlisle, 1718; bishop of Rochester and dean of Westminster, 1723; dean of order of Bath, 1725. [vi. 160]

BRADFORD, SIR THOMAS (1777–1853), general; ensign, 1793; assistant adjutant-general in Scotland, 1801; served in Peninsula, 1808; colonel, 1810; commanded Portuguese division at Vittoria; held command in France, 1815–17, and in Scotland, 1819–25; commander-in-chief at Bombay, 1825–9; G.C.B., 1838; general, 1841. [vi. 161]

BRADFORD WILLIAM (1590–1657), second governor of Plymouth, New England; joined Brownists, 1606, and followed them to Amsterdam, 1607; accompanied the community to Leyden, 1609, and, in the Mayflower, to Plymouth, New England, 1620; succeeded Carver as governor of Plymouth, 1621, and was re-elected every year (with exception of two intervals of three years and two years respectively at his own request); joint author of 'A Diary of Occurrences,' 1622, leaving in manuscript a 'History of the Plymouth Plantation' (published 1856). [vi. 161]

BRADFORD, WILLIAM (1663–1752), first printer in Pennsylvania; accompanied William Penn on his first voyage to Pennsylvania, 1682; established first American paper mill, near Philadelphia, 1686; appointed royal printer for New York and New Jersey; projected first book printed in America, 1688; began publication of 'New York Gazette,' the first New York newspaper, 1725. [vi. 164]

BRADICK, WALTER (1706–1794), merchant at Lisbon; published poetical and other writings. [vi. 165]

BRADLAUGH, CHARLES (1833–1891), freethought advocate and politician; private soldier in army, 1850–3; clerk in solicitor's office in London, 1853; entered into freethought and radical propaganda under name of 'Iconoclast'; proprietor of 'National Reformer' from 1862; member of parliamentary reform league, 1866; elected M.P. for Northampton, 1880; was refused right to affirm instead of swearing on bible; unseated; re-elected, 1881, and was ejected from house by force; expelled, 1882; re-elected, 1882, and excluded, 1883; re-elected, 1884, excluded, 1885; again elected, 1885, and allowed to take his seat, 1886, remaining M.P. for Northampton till death. He engaged in several lawsuits to maintain freedom of press, published pamphlets, and from 1874 to 1885 was associated with Mrs. Besant's work. [Suppl. i. 248]

BRADLEY, CHARLES (1789–1871), preacher; educated at St. Edmund Hall, Oxford; vicar of Glasbury, Brecknockshire, 1825–71; incumbent of St. James's Chapel, Clapham, 1829–52; published sermons. [vi. 165]

BRADLEY, EDWARD (1827–1889), author of 'Verdant Green'; B.A. University College, Durham, 1848; licentiate in theology, 1849; rector of Stretton, Rutland, 1871; published 'Adventures of Mr. Verdant Green, an Oxford Freshman,' 1853–6; vicar of Lenton with Hanby, 1883; contributed extensively (as E. B. or 'Cuthbert Bede') to periodicals, and published works in verse and prose, some illustrated by himself. [Suppl. i. 250]

BRADLEY, GEORGE (1816–1863), editor of 'Newcastle Guardian,' 1848; published system of shorthand. [vi. 166]

BRADLEY, JAMES (1693–1762), divine and astronomer; M.A. Balliol College, Oxford, 1717; made observations on Jovian system and had his 'Corrected Tables' printed in Halley's 'Planetary Tables,' 1719; F.R.S., 1718; presented to vicarage of Bridstow, 1719; chaplain to bishop of Hereford; elected Savilian professor of astronomy at Oxford, and resigned preferments, 1721; announced discovery of 'aberration of light' in paper read to Royal Society, 1729; lecturer on experimental philosophy at Oxford, 1729–60; astronomer-royal, and D.D. by diploma, Oxford, 1742; published discovery of nutation of earth's axis in paper read to Royal Society, 1748, and was awarded Copley medal; member of council of Royal Society, 1752–62. His observations were published in two volumes (1798 and 1805). [vi. 166]

BRADLEY, RALPH (1717–1788), lawyer; called to bar at Gray's Inn; conveyancing barrister at Stockton-on-Tees; published works on conveyancing. [vi. 171]

BRADLEY, RICHARD (d. 1732), botanist; F.R.S., 1720; appointed professor of botany at Cambridge, 1724; lectured on 'Materia Medica,' 1729; published horticultural works. [vi. 172]

BRADLEY, THOMAS (1597–1670), divine; B.A. Exeter College, Oxford, 1620; accompanied Buckingham to Isle of Rhé and Rochelle as chaplain, 1627; chaplain to Charles I, 1628; D.D. Oxford, 1642; temporarily deprived of his livings in Yorkshire by parliamentary committee; prebendary of York, 1666; published sermons. [vi. 172]

BRADLEY, THOMAS (1751–1813), physician; M.D. Edinburgh, and L.C.P., 1791; physician to Westminster Hospital, 1794–1811; published revised edition of Fox's 'Medical Dictionary,' 1803. [vi. 173]

BRADLEY, WILLIAM (1801–1857), portrait painter; exhibited at Royal Academy and other institutions between 1823 and 1846. [vi. 173]

BRADOCK, THOMAS (fl. 1576–1604), translator; M.A. Christ's College, Cambridge, 1580; incorporated M.A. Oxford, 1584; head-master, Reading grammar school, 1588; translated into Latin Jewell's confutation of Harding's attack on Jewell's 'Apologia.' [vi. 173]

BRADSHAIGH, RICHARD (1601–1669). [See BARTON.]

BRADSHAW, ANN MARIA (1801–1862), actress and vocalist; née Tree; appeared, after 1819, as Ariel, Viola, Imogen, Julia ('Two Gentlemen of Verona'), Ophelia, and Rosalind at Covent Garden; retired, 1825. [vi. 174]

BRADSHAW, GEORGE (1801–1853), originator of railway guides; engraver and printer at Belfast and afterwards at Manchester; first produced, 1839, 'Railway Time Tables,' which developed into 'Bradshaw's Monthly Railway Guide' (first published 1841); associate of Institution of Civil Engineers, 1842. [vi. 174]

BRADSHAW, HENRY (d. 1513), Benedictine monk of Chester; studied theology at Gloucester College, Oxford. Wrote 'De Antiquitate et Magnificentia Urbis Cestriæ' and 'Chronicon and a Life of St. Werburgh' in English verse (published 1521). [vi. 175]

BRADSHAW, HENRY (d. 1661), parliamentarian; elder brother of John Bradshaw (1602–1659) [q. v.]; served in parliamentary army; sat on court-martial which tried Earl of Derby and other royalists at Chester, 1652; imprisoned for this act, 1660–1; pardoned, 1661. [vi. 181]

BRADSHAW, HENRY (1831–1886), scholar, antiquary, and librarian; educated at Eton and King's College, Cambridge; fellow, 1853; B.A., 1854; assistant in Cambridge University Library, 1856–8; appointed to supervise and arrange manuscripts and early printed books at Cambridge, 1859; took prominent part in exposing pretences of forger Simonides, 1863; librarian of the university, 1867-86; published treatises on typographical and antiquarian subjects, some containing original discoveries. The 'Henry Bradshaw Society,' for editing rare liturgical texts, was founded in his memory, 1890.   [Suppl. i. 251]

BRADSHAW, JAMES (1636?-1702), nonconformist divine; educated at Corpus Christi College, Oxford; ordained minister of Hindley Lancashire: concerned in Sir George Booth's royalist rising; ejected, 1662; minister at Rainford chapel, Prescot, 1672; published religious works.   [vi. 176]

BRADSHAW, JAMES (1717-1746), Jacobite rebel; merchant in Manchester; joined cause of Young Pretender, 1745; captured at Culloden and subsequently executed.   [vi. 176]

BRADSHAW, JOHN (1576-1618). [See WHITE.]

BRADSHAW, JOHN (1602-1659), regicide; called to bar at Gray's Inn, 1627; judge of sheriffs' court, London, 1643; chief-justice of Chester and judge in Wales, 1647; serjeant-at-law, 1648; lord president of parliamentary commission for trial of Charles I, 1649; presided at Charles's trial and pronounced sentence, and subsequently at trials of leading royalists; president of council of state, 1649-52; attorney-general of Cheshire and North Wales, 1649; chancellor of duchy of Lancaster, 1649-53; opposed Cromwell's gradual assumption of arbitrary power, and temporarily retired from political life; member of council of state and commissioner of great seal, 1659; buried in Westminster Abbey. In 1660 Bradshaw, Cromwell, Ireton, and Pride, though dead, were attainted, and their bodies exhumed, hanged, and reburied at Tyburn.   [vi. 176]

BRADSHAW, JOHN (*fl.* 1679), political writer; condemned to death for violence at Corpus Christi College, Oxford, but pardoned; subsequently turned quaker and, later, papist.   [vi. 181]

BRADSHAW, LUCRETIA (*fl.* 1714), actress; married Martin Folkes [q. v.], 1714; played Sylvia in the 'Double Dealer.'   [xix. 362]

BRADSHAW, RICHARD (*fl.* 1650), parliamentarian; quartermaster-general under Sir William Brereton [q. v.] in civil war; employed by parliament on diplomatic missions, 1650-9; commissioner of navy, 1660.   [vi. 181]

BRADSHAW, THOMAS (*fl.* 1591), poet; M.A. Oxford, 1549; published 'The Shepherd's Starre,' 1591, a Theocritean paraphrase in prose and verse.   [vi. 182]

BRADSHAW, WILLIAM (1571-1618), puritan divine; M.A. Emmanuel College, Cambridge; came under influence of Thomas Cartwright [q. v.]; fellow of Sidney Sussex College, Cambridge, 1599; lecturer at Chatham, 1601, but suspended for heretical teaching; lecturer at Christ Church, Newgate, c. 1605; published 'English Puritanisme,' 1605, basing a scheme of church polity on complete autonomy of individual congregations, while advocating strongly duty of submission to civil authority.   [vi. 182]

BRADSHAW, WILLIAM (*fl.* 1700), hack writer, employed by the eccentric bookseller John Dunton, whom he robbed.   [vi. 185]

BRADSHAW, WILLIAM (1671-1732), bishop of Bristol; M.A. New College, Oxford, 1700; prebendary of Canterbury, 1717; D.D., 1723; dean of Christ Church, Oxford, and bishop of Bristol, 1724.   [vi. 185]

BRADSHAWE, NICHOLAS (*fl.* 1635), author of 'Canticvm Evangelicvm Summam Sacri Evangelii continens,' 1635.   [vi. 186]

BRADSTREET, ANNE (1612-1672), poetess; *née* Dudley; settled at Charlestown, New England, 1630, at Ipswich, 1634, and Merrimac, 1638; published 'The Tenth Muse' (1650), and left in manuscript 'Meditations.'   [vi. 186]

BRADSTREET, DUDLEY (1711-1763), adventurer; employed as spy by government officials and the Dukes of Newcastle and Cumberland during Jacobite rising, 1745; wrote an acting play entitled the 'Magician, or Bottle Conjurer,' printed with his 'Life' (1755).   [vi. 187]

BRADSTREET, ROBERT (1766-1836), poet; M.A. St. John's College, Cambridge, 1789; published 'The Sabine Farm,' a poem, 1810.   [vi. 187]

BRADSTREET, SIR SAMUEL (1735?-1791), baronet; called to Irish bar, 1758; recorder of Dublin, 1766; M.P. for city of Dublin in Irish parliament, 1776 and 1783; judge, 1784; commissioner of great seal, 1788.   [vi. 188]

BRADWARDINE, THOMAS (1290?-1349), archbishop of Canterbury; educated at Merton College, Oxford; university proctor, 1325; expanded his lectures on theology into a treatise which earned for him the title of Doctor Profundus; chaplain to Richard of Bury, bishop of Durham, 1335; chancellor and prebendary of St. Paul's, 1337; prebendary of Lincoln; royal chaplain and confessor, 1338; one of commissioners to treat of peace with King Philip after battles of Cressy and Neville's Cross; consecrated archbishop of Canterbury at Avignon, 1349; wrote religious treatises.   [vi. 188]

BRADY, SIR ANTONIO (1811-1881), admiralty official; second-class clerk in accountant-general's office, Somerset House, 1844; registrar of contracts, 1864; first superintendent of admiralty new contract department, 1869-70; knighted, 1870; devoted himself to social, educational, and religious reforms.   [vi. 190]

BRADY, HENRY BOWMAN (1835-1891), naturalist and pharmacist; carried on business as pharmaceutical chemist at Newcastle, 1855-76; on council of pharmaceutical Society; F.L.S., 1859-87; F.R.S., 1874; honorary LL.D. Aberdeen, 1888; published 'Report on Foraminifera, collected by H.M.S. Challenger,' 1884, and other works.   [Suppl. i. 254]

BRADY, HUGH (*d.* 1584), Irish bishop; bishop of Meath and Irish privy councillor, 1563; bishop of united see of Meath and Clonmacnoise from 1568. [Suppl. i. 254]

BRADY, JOHN (*d.* 1814), clerk in victualling office; published 'Clavis Calendaria,' 1812.   [vi. 191]

BRADY, SIR MAZIERE (1796-1871), Irish lawyer; M.A. Trinity College, Dublin, 1819; called to Irish bar, 1819; solicitor-general for Ireland, 1837; attorney-general, 1839; chief baron of exchequer, 1840; judge of Irish court of chancery, 1846; lord chancellor in Ireland, 1847-52, 1853-8 and 1859-66; first vice-chancellor of the Queen's University, 1850; created baronet, 1869.   [vi. 191]

BRADY, NICHOLAS (1659-1726), divine and poet; educated at Westminster and Christ Church, Oxford; B.A., 1682; B.A. Dublin, 1685; M.A., 1686; D.D., 1699; prebendary of Cork, 1688; upheld cause of Prince of Orange during revolution: held living of Richmond, Surrey, 1696-1726, rectory of Stratford-on-Avon, 1702-5, and rectory of Clapham, 1705-6; chaplain to William III, Mary, and Anne, and to Duke of Ormonde's regiment of horse; wrote, with Nahum Tate, metrical version of Psalms.   [vi. 192]

BRADY, ROBERT (*d.* 1700), historian and physician; M.D. and master of Caius College, Cambridge, 1660; F.C.P., 1680; physician in ordinary to Charles II and James II; regius professor of physic at Cambridge; M.P. for the university, 1681 and 1685; published works on English history.   [vi. 193]

BRADY, THOMAS (1752?-1827), general; major-general, 1796, and lieutenant-general, 1801, in Austrian service; governor of Dalmatia, 1804; privy councillor, 1807; general, 1809.   [vi. 193]

BRAGG, PHILIP (*d.* 1759), lieutenant-general; served in Marlborough's campaigns; captain in Ireland, 1713; master of Royal Hospital, Kilmainham, 1732; lieutenant-general, 1747; M.P. for Armagh.   [vi. 194]

BRAGGE, WILLIAM (1823-1884), engineer and antiquary; engineer on railway from Chester to Holyhead; engaged in railway engineering in Brazil; managing director of firm of Sir John Brown & Co., Sheffield, 1858-72; developed organisation for manufacture of watches by machinery at Birmingham, 1876; collected books and curios; F.S.A.; F.R.G.S. [vi. 194]

BRAHAM, FRANCES ELIZABETH ANNE, afterwards COUNTESS WALDEGRAVE (1821-1879). [See WALDEGRAVE.]

BRAHAM, JOHN (1774?–1856), tenor singer; first appeared at Covent Garden, 1787; engaged at Royalty Theatre, Wellclose Square, 1787–9; at Bath, 1794–6; achieved great success at Drury Lane, 1796; toured on continent with Nancy Storace, 1797–1801; associated with Storace at Drury Lane from 1805 until her retirement, 1808; continued attached to Drury Lane, but appeared also at other theatres, in Italian opera, and in most provincial festivals and important concerts and oratorios; made provincial tour with Mrs. Billington, 1810; joined Yates in buying the Colosseum, Regent's Park, 1831, and built St. James's Theatre, 1835, both speculations proving disastrous; toured unsuccessfully in America, 1840; retired, 1852. The duet 'All's Well' is one of the best-remembered of his works. [vi. 195]

BRAHAM, ROBERT (*fl.* 1555), editor of Lydgate's 'Auncient Historie of Warres betwixte Grecians and Troyans' (1555). [vi. 197]

BRAID, JAMES (1795?–1860), writer on hypnotism; educated at Edinburgh University; M.R.C.S.E.; surgeon to miners at Earl Hopetoun's works in Lanarkshire; made experiments relating to mesmerism, and proved the personal nature of the mesmeric influence; published works on hypnotism, which term he originated. [vi. 198]

BRAIDLEY, BENJAMIN (1792–1845), writer on Sunday schools; constable of Manchester, 1831, and boroughreeve, 1832; high constable of hundred of Salford; published a work on 'Sunday Schools.' [vi. 199]

BRAIDWOOD, JAMES (1800–1861), superintendent of London fire-brigade; builder, and afterwards superintendent of fire-engines in Edinburgh; superintendent of London fire-engine establishment, 1832; killed in a fire near London Bridge; published pamphlet relating to fire-brigades. [vi. 199]

BRAIDWOOD, THOMAS (1715–1806), teacher of the deaf and dumb; educated at Edinburgh University; kept mathematical school at Edinburgh, and subsequently school for teaching the deaf and dumb, which he removed, in 1783, to Hackney. [vi. 199]

BRAILSFORD, JOHN, the elder (*fl.* 1712–1739), poetical writer; M.A. St. John's College, Cambridge, 1717; rector of Kirby, Nottinghamshire. [vi. 200]

BRAILSFORD, JOHN, the younger (*d.* 1775), divine; M.A. Emmanuel College, Cambridge, 1766; head-master of free school, Birmingham, 1766–75. [vi. 200]

BRAITHWAITE, JOHN (*fl.* 1660), quaker; follower of George Fox, writing in support of his doctrines. [vi. 200]

BRAITHWAITE, JOHN (1700?–1768?), historian; served under African Company, in fleet in Anne's reign, and, later, in army; published 'History of Morocco,' 1727–8' (1729). [vi. 201]

BRAITHWAITE, JOHN, the elder (*d.* 1818), engineer; constructed one of the earliest successful diving bells, c. 1783. [vi. 201]

BRAITHWAITE, JOHN, the younger (1797–1870), engineer; son of John Braithwaite (*d.* 1818) [q. v.]; arranged ventilation of House of Lords by means of air-pumps, 1820; constructed donkey-engine, 1822; manufactured first practical steam fire-engine, c. 1829; built with Ericsson caloric engine, 1833; engineer-in-chief to Eastern Counties railway, 1836–43; F.S.A., 1819; M.I.C.E., 1838; M.S.A., 1819; joint-founder and editor of 'Railway Times,' 1837. [vi. 201]

BRAITHWAITE, RICHARD (1588?–1673). [See BRATHWAITE.]

BRAKELONDE, JOCELIN DE (*fl.* 1200). [See JOCELIN.]

BRAMAH, JOSEPH (1748–1814), inventor; worked as cabinet-maker in London; invented Bramah locks; patented the 'Bramah' hydraulic press, 1795. [vi. 202]

BRAMHALL, JOHN (1594–1663), archbishop of Armagh; M.A. Sidney Sussex College, Cambridge, 1616; D.D., 1630; sub-dean of Ripon; chaplain to Wentworth in Ireland, 1633; bishop of Derry, 1634; impeached by Irish Commons for rigorous opposition to covenanters, and imprisoned, but liberated through influence of Ussher, 1641; came to England and assisted royalists, 1644;

retired to continent, 1644; in Ireland, 1648–9, but again retired to continent; archbishop of Armagh, 1661; speaker of Irish House of Lords, 1661; enforced conformity, though with comparative moderation. His religious writings were collected and published 1677. [vi. 203]

BRAMIS or **BROMIS**, JOHN (14th cent.), writer; monk of Thetford; translated 'Romance of Waldef' from French metre into Latin prose. [vi. 206]

BRAMLEY-MOORE, JOHN (1800–1886), chairman of the Liverpool docks; in trade in the Brazils; alderman of Liverpool, 1841; chairman of dockyard committee, 1842; mayor, 1848; conservative M.P. for Maldon, 1854–9, and for Lincoln, 1862–5; chairman of Brazilian chamber of commerce in Liverpool. [Suppl. i. 255]

BRAMSTON, FRANCIS (*d.* 1683), judge; son of Sir John Bramston the elder [q. v.]; M.A. Queens' College, Cambridge, 1640; fellow, c. 1642; called to bar at Middle Temple, 1642; steward of king's courts in Essex, 1660; bencher and reader of Middle Temple, 1668; serjeant-at-law and steward of court of common pleas, Whitechapel, 1669; baron of exchequer, 1678–9. [vi. 206]

BRAMSTON, JAMES (1694?–1744), poet; educated at Westminster and Christ Church, Oxford; M.A., 1720; vicar of two Sussex parishes; published 'Art of Politicks,' 1729, and 'Man of Taste,' and other poems. [vi. 207]

BRAMSTON, JAMES YORKE (1763–1836), catholic bishop; educated at Trinity College, Cambridge; studied at Lincoln's Inn; theological student at English college, Lisbon, 1792; engaged in missionary work at Lisbon; entrusted with catholic mission in St. George's-in-the-Fields; vicar-general of London district, under Bishop Poynter, 1812; vicar-apostolic, 1827; bishop of Usulæ *in partibus infidelium*, 1823. [vi. 207]

BRAMSTON, Sir JOHN, the elder (1577–1654), judge; educated at Jesus College, Cambridge; studied at Middle Temple; reader, 1623; counsel to Cambridge University, 1607; serjeant-at-law, 1623; queen's serjeant, 1632; king's serjeant, 1634; chief-justice of king's bench, 1635; presided temporarily in House of Lords, 1640; impeached by Commons for subscribing opinion on ship-money, 1640; removed from office in king's bench, 1642, but restored, 1643, having been made serjeant-at-law. [vi. 208]

BRAMSTON, Sir JOHN, the younger (1611–1700), lawyer; son of Sir John Bramston (1577–1654) [q. v.]; educated at Wadham College, Oxford; called to bar at Middle Temple, 1635; K.B., 1660; frequently acted as chairman of committees of whole House of Commons; M.P. for Maldon, 1685, and, later, for Chelmsford; left autobiography (published 1845). [vi. 210]

BRAMWELL, GEORGE WILLIAM WILSHERE, BARON BRAMWELL (1808–1892), judge; studied law under Fitzroy Kelly [q. v.]; called to bar at Inner Temple, 1838; joined home circuit; Q.C., 1851; served, 1853, on commission resulting in Companies Act (1862); appointed judge of exchequer and knighted, 1856; lord justice, 1876–81; raised to peerage, 1882. [Suppl. i. 256]

BRANCASTRE or **BRAMCESTRE**, JOHN DE (*d.* 1218), clerk in exchequer; vicar of Brancaster, Norfolk; prebendary of Lincoln, 1208. [vi. 211]

BRANCH, THOMAS (*fl.* 1753), author of 'Thoughts on Dreaming' (1738) and 'Principia Legis et Æquitatis' (1753). [vi. 211]

BRANCKER or **BRANKER**, THOMAS (1633–1676), mathematician; B.A. Exeter College, Oxford, 1655; fellow, 1656; M.A., 1658; rector of Tilston, near Malpas, 1668; head-master of Macclesfield grammar school; published translation of introduction to algebra from High Dutch of Rhonius. [vi. 211]

BRAND, BARBARINA, LADY DACRE (1768–1854), poet and dramatist; daughter of Admiral Sir Chaloner Ogle; married, first, Valentine Wilmot, and, secondly, 1819, Thomas Brand, twenty-first lord Dacre; wrote dramas, translations, and poems. [vi. 212]

BRAND, HANNAH (*d.* 1821), actress and dramatist; schoolmistress at Norwich; appeared at King's Theatre, Haymarket, in her own tragedy of 'Huniades,' 1792; played Lady Townly in 'Provoked Husband' at York Theatre, 1794; again became governess; published 'Dramatic and Poetical Works,' 1798. [vi. 212]

BRAND, Sir HENRY BOUVERIE WILLIAM, first
Viscount Hampden and twenty-third Baron Dacre
(1814–1892), speaker; educated at Eton; private secretary
to Sir George Grey [q. v.], 1846; liberal M.P. for Lewes,
1852, 1857, 1859, and 1865, and for Cambridgeshire, 1868–
1884; parliamentary secretary to treasury, 1859–66;
speaker of House of Commons, 1872–84; G.C.B., 1881;
created Viscount Hampden of Glynde, 1884; succeeded to
title of Dacre, 1890. [Suppl. i. 257]

BRAND, Sir JOHANNES HENRICUS (JAN HEN-
DRIK) (1823–1888), president of the Orange Free State;
born at Cape Town; educated at South African College,
Cape Town, and Leyden: LL.D. Leyden, 1845; called to
bar at Inner Temple, 1849; practised in supreme court of
Cape Colony; member for Clanwilliam in first House of
Assembly, 1854; professor of law, South African College,
1858; elected president of Orange Free State, 1863; engaged in war with Basutos, 1865–6 and 1867; re-elected
president, 1869, 1874, and 1879; remained neutral during
Transvaal war, 1881; G.C.M.G., 1886; resigned, 1887, in
consequence of vote of censure of Raad on his negotiations with President Kruger of Transvaal, who unsuccessfully sought his alliance against British on railway
question; withdrew resignation. [Suppl. i. 258]

BRAND, JOHN (1668?–1738), Scottish minister;
M.A. Edinburgh, 1688; minister of Borrowstouness, Linlithgowshire, 1695; journeyed to Orkney, 1701, and published 'A Brief Description of Orkney.' [vi. 213]

BRAND, JOHN (1744–1806), antiquary; apprenticed
as cordwainer at Newcastle, 1758; B.A. Lincoln College,
Oxford, 1775; received perpetual curacy of Cramlington,
near Newcastle, 1774; F.S.A., 1777; rector of St. Mary-
at-Hill and St. Mary Hubbard, London, 1784; resident
secretary to Society of Antiquaries, 1784–1806; published
'History of Newcastle-upon-Tyne' and other works, leaving in manuscript antiquarian collections. [vi. 213]

BRAND, JOHN (d. 1808), divine; M.A. Caius College, Cambridge, 1772; rector of St. George's, Southwark, 1797–1808; published in tory interest pamphlets
on politics and political economy. [vi. 214]

BRAND, THOMAS (1635–1691), nonconformist
divine; educated at Merton College, Oxford; studied law
at the Temple; ordained minister of Staplehurst, whence
he was driven by persecution. He built many meeting-
houses, and devoted large sums to charitable purposes.
[vi. 215]

BRANDARD, ROBERT (1805–1862), engraver;
studied under Edward Goodall; exhibited oil and water-
colour paintings between 1831 and 1858. [vi. 216]

BRANDE, WILLIAM THOMAS (1788–1866), chemist; apprenticed as apothecary; delivered lectures in
London on physics, chemistry, and materia medica, 1808;
F.R.S., 1809; professor of chemistry, 1812, and, later, of
materia medica, to Apothecaries' Company; succeeded
Sir Humphry Davy as professor of chemistry at Royal
Institution, 1813; chief officer of coinage department of
mint, 1854; joint-editor of 'Quarterly Journal of Science
and Art,' 1825; one of secretaries of Royal Society, 1816–
1826; fellow and member of Senate of London University,
and examiner in chemistry, 1846–58; hon. D.C.L. Oxford;
F.R.S. Edinburgh; published 'Manual of Chemistry' and
'Dictionary of Pharmacy and Materia Medica,' besides
editing 'Dictionary of Science and Art,' 1842. [vi. 216]

BRANDER, GUSTAVUS (1720–1787), merchant and
antiquary; trader in London; director of Bank of England; F.R.S.; curator of British Museum; collected antiquarian curiosities, pictures, and books. [vi. 218]

BRANDON, first Viscount (d. 1694). [See Gerard,
Charles.]

BRANDON, CHARLES, first Duke of Suffolk (d.
1545), soldier and statesman; squire of the royal body to
Henry VIII, and chamberlain of principality of North
Wales, 1509; marshal of king's bench, 1510; ranger of
New Forest, 1512; created Viscount Lisle, 1513; marshal
of army invading France, 1513; created Duke of Suffolk,
1514; went on royal mission to France, 1514, and, although
he had already a wife living, secretly married Henry's
sister, Mary, at Paris, 1515, the validity of the marriage
being secured by a papal bull; accompanied Henry to
Field of Cloth of Gold, 1520; commanded unsuccessful
invasion of France, 1523; supported Henry in efforts to

obtain divorce from Catherine of Arragon; warden of
marches against Scotland, 1542; commanded army invading France and captured Boulogne, 1544; steward of
king's household. [vi. 218]

BRANDON, HENRY (1535–1551), and CHARLES
(1537?–1551), Dukes of Suffolk; sons of Charles Brandon, first duke of Suffolk [q. v.]; educated under Thomas
(afterwards Sir Thomas) Wilson, and at St. John's College, Cambridge, where they caught the sweating sickness,
which proved fatal. [vi. 222]

BRANDON, JOHN (fl. 1687), divine; B.A. Oriel College, Oxford, 1665; rector of Finchamstead; published
religious works. [vi. 222]

BRANDON, JOHN RAPHAEL (1817–1877), architect; carried on business with his brother, Joshua Arthur
Brandon [q. v.], whom he assisted in writing 'Parish
Churches,' 1848, 'Analysis of Gothic Architecture,' 1847,
and 'Open Timber Roofs of Middle Ages,' 1849; committed suicide. [vi. 222]

BRANDON, JOSHUA ARTHUR (1802–1847), architect; joint-author with his brother, John Raphael Brandon [q. v.], in architectural publications. [vi. 222]

BRANDON, RICHARD (d. 1649), executioner of
Charles I and various distinguished royalists; son of
Gregory Brandon, common hangman of London.
[vi. 223]

BRANDON, SAMUEL (16th cent.), author of 'The
Tragi-comœdi of the Virtuous Octavia,' 1598. [vi. 224]

BRANDON, Sir THOMAS (d. 1509), diplomatist;
uncle to Charles Brandon, duke of Suffolk [q. v.]; Lancastrian; accompanied embassies to conclude peace with
France, 1492, and a treaty with Emperor Maximilian at
Antwerp, 1503; held offices in royal household; K.G.
[vi. 224]

BRANDRAM, SAMUEL (1824–1892), reciter; educated at Merchant Taylors' and King's College schools
and Trinity College, Oxford; M.A., 1849; called to bar
at Lincoln's Inn, 1850; practised as barrister till 1876;
became professional reciter, gaining wide popularity;
published selections for recitation. [Suppl. i. 260]

BRANDRETH, JEREMIAH, called Jeremiah Coke
(d. 1817), rebel; served in army; headed, as tool of one
Oliver, a rising in midland counties; executed at Derby.
[vi. 224]

BRANDRETH, JOSEPH (1746–1815), physician;
M.D. Edinburgh, 1770; established the Dispensary at
Liverpool; published medical treatises. [vi. 225]

BRANDRETH, THOMAS SHAW (1788–1873), scholar and mathematician; educated at Eton and Trinity
College, Cambridge; second wrangler, second Smith's
prizeman, and chancellor's medallist, 1810; M.A., 1813;
fellow; called to bar; practised at Liverpool; F.R.S.,
1821; invented several mechanical devices connected with
locomotion; published a treatise on the digamma, and a
verse translation of the 'Iliad.' [vi. 225]

BRANDT, FRANCIS FREDERICK (1819–1874), legal
writer; called to bar at Inner Temple, 1847; published
treatises, relating chiefly to the law as affecting sport.
[vi. 226]

BRANDWOOD, JAMES (1739–1826), quaker; joined
quakers, 1761, and became itinerant preacher. A selection from his letters and papers was published posthumously, 1828. [vi. 226]

BRANKER, THOMAS (1633–1676). [See Brancker.]

BRANSBY, JAMES HEWS (1783–1847), unitarian
divine; minister of presbyterian congregation at Moreton
Hampstead, Devonshire, 1803; kept a school at Dudley;
developed tendency to kleptomania, and subsequently
committed forgery, and was permitted to retire to Wales,
1828; published historical and other works. [vi. 227]

BRANSTON, ALLEN ROBERT (1778–1827), wood-
engraver; apprenticed to his father as copper-plate engraver; came to London, 1799; illustrated Bloomfield's
'Wild Flowers,' 1806, and other works. [vi. 227]

BRANTHWAITE, WILLIAM (d. 1620), translator
of the bible; B.A. Clare Hall, Cambridge, 1582; fellow
of Emmanuel College, 1584; M.A., 1586; D.D., 1598;
member of one of two Cambridge committees appointed
to revise translation of bible, 1607–11, his share being the
Apocrypha. [vi. 228]

BRANTINGHAM, THOMAS DE (d. 1394), lord treasurer and bishop of Exeter ; canon and prebendary of St. Paul's, 1361 ; treasurer of Calais and Guisnes, 1361–8 ; prebendary of Hereford, 1363 ; treasurer of Bath and Wells Cathedral, 1367 ; lord treasurer, 1369–71, 1377–81, and 1389 ; bishop of Exeter, 1370 ; one of lords appointed to reform and regulate realm and king's household, 1386. [Suppl. i. 260]

BRANWHITE, CHARLES (1817–1880), landscape painter ; son of Nathan Branwhite [q. v.] ; practised as landscape painter in water-colour ; exhibited pictures from 1849. [vi. 228]

BRANWHITE, NATHAN (fl. 1825), miniature painter and engraver ; son of Peregrine Branwhite [q. v.] ; exhibited at Royal Academy between 1802 and 1825 [vi. 228]

BRANWHITE, PEREGRINE (1745–1795 ?), minor poet ; conducted a school at Lavenham, Suffolk ; published poetical writings. [vi. 229]

BRAOSE, PHILIP DE (fl. 1172), soldier ; uncle of William de Braose [q.v.] ; held command in Henry II's military operations at Wexford, 1172. [vi. 229]

BRAOSE, WILLIAM DE (d. 1211), rebel baron ; sheriff of Herefordshire, 1192–9 ; justice itinerant in Staffordshire, 1196 ; with Richard in Normandy, 1195 ; granted, by John, all the lands he could conquer from Welsh ; sheriff of Herefordshire, 1206–7 ; obtained honour of Limerick (without the city), 1201 ; attended John at Rouen, 1203 ; received grant of city of Limerick at ferm, 1203 ; lost favour, and subsequently (1210) raised a rebellion in Wales ; died an outlaw in France. [vi. 229]

BRASBRIDGE, JOSEPH (1743–1832), autobiographer ; silversmith in London ; became bankrupt ; published 'Fruits of Experience,' an autobiography, 1824. [vi. 231]

BRASBRIDGE, THOMAS (fl. 1590), divine ; fellow of Magdalen College, Oxford, 1562 ; M.A., 1564 ; obtained living at Banbury, where he opened a school and practised medicine ; published miscellaneous writings. [vi. 231]

BRASBRIGG or BRACEBRIGGE, JOHN (fl. 1428), priest of convent of Syon. Reputed author of manuscript entitled 'Catholicon continens quatuor partes grammaticæ.' [vi. 231]

BRASS or BRASSE, JOHN (1790–1833), educational writer ; fellow, Trinity College, Cambridge, 1811 ; M.A., 1814 ; D.D., 1829 ; held living of Stotfold, Bedfordshire, 1824–33 ; published educational works. [vi. 231]

BRASSEY, ANNA or ANNIE, BARONESS BRASSEY (1839–1887), traveller and authoress ; née Allnutt ; married, 1860, Mr. Thomas Brassey (created Baron Brassey, 1886) ; published 'Voyage of the Sunbeam,' 1878, and other descriptions of long sea-voyages ; dame chevalière of order of St. John of Jerusalem, 1881 ; died at sea near Brisbane. [Suppl. i. 261]

BRASSEY, THOMAS (1805–1870), railway contractor ; originally articled to a land surveyor ; contracted for various works on London and Southampton railway, and subsequently for many large railway undertakings, including English Great Northern (1847–51), Canadian Grand Trunk (1852–9), Crimean (1854), Australian (1859–1863), Argentine (1864), and Indian (1858–65). [vi. 232]

BRATHWAITE, RICHARD (1588?–1673), poet ; educated at Oriel College, Oxford ; possibly served on royalist side in civil war ; produced between 1611 and 1665 a number of works of varying merit, of which the most famous is 'Barnabæ Itinerarium, or Barnabee's Journal,' a record of English travel in doggerel verse (1638). [vi. 233]

BRAVONIUS (d. 1207). [See SENATUS.]

BRAXFIELD, LORD (1722–1799). [See MACQUEEN, ROBERT.]

BRAY, ANNA ELIZA (1790–1883), novelist ; née Kempe ; married Charles Alfred Stothard [q. v.], an artist, 1818 ; he died, 1821, while engaged on a work, 'Monumental Effigies of Great Britain,' which was completed by his widow and published 1832 ; she married, secondly, the Rev. Edward Atkyns Bray [q. v.] ; published several novels of historical character between 1826 and 1874, besides other writings, including letters to Southey on legends of the Tamar and the Tavy. [vi. 234]

BRAY, CHARLES (1811–1884), philosophical writer ; ribbon manufacturer at Coventry, 1835 till 1856 ; engaged in numerous enterprises for amelioration of condition of working classes ; published philosophical writings, based chiefly on phrenology and the docrine of necessity. [vi. 235]

BRAY, EDWARD ATKYNS (1778–1857), miscellaneous writer ; called to the bar at Middle Temple, 1806 ; joined western circuit, but abandoned law for the church ; vicar of Tavistock and perpetual curate of Brent Tor, 1812 : B.D. Trinity College, Cambridge, 1822 ; published selections of sermons by eminent divines. His 'Poetical Remains' appeared, 1859. [vi. 236]

BRAY, JOHN (fl. 1377), physician : author of a manuscript list of herbs in Latin, French, and English. [vi. 237]

BRAY, SIR REGINALD (d. 1503), statesman and architect ; receiver-general and steward of household to Sir Henry Stafford, second husband of Margaret, countess of Richmond, mother of Earl of Richmond, afterwards Henry VII ; actively engaged in bringing about marriage of Earl of Richmond with the Princess Elizabeth ; created K.B. at Henry VII's coronation ; K.G. ; privy councillor and joint chief-justice of forests south of Trent ; high treasurer and chancellor of duchy of Lancaster ; paymaster of forces in Brittany, 1492 ; high steward of Oxford (and perhaps of Cambridge) university, 1494 ; knight-banneret, after Blackheath, 1497 ; conducted improvements in St. George's Chapel, Windsor, and probably designed Henry VII's Chapel, Westminster. [vi. 237]

BRAY, THOMAS (1656–1730), divine ; B.A. All Souls' College, Oxford, 1678 ; M.A. Hart Hall, 1693 ; rector of Sheldon, 1690 ; published 'Catechetical Lectures,' which brought him immediate popularity ; selected by the bishop of London as his commissary in Maryland, which province had lately been divided into parishes ; projected a scheme for establishing parochial libraries in England, which was successful, and developed into the Society for Promoting Christian Knowledge ; D.D. Magdalen College, Oxford, 1696 ; arrived in Maryland, 1700, but returned at once, finding that he could serve the Maryland church better in England ; obtained charter incorporating society for propagating gospel throughout British plantations, 1701 ; received living of St. Botolph-Without, Aldgate, 1706 ; negrophile ; published religious works and writings relating to his various projects. [vi. 239]

BRAY, THOMAS (1759–1820), archbishop of Cashel ; author of a work in Latin and English (privately printed, 1813), containing a papal bull against freemasonry, and a decree of Council of Trent against duellists ; D.D. [vi. 241]

BRAY, WILLIAM (d. 1644), divine ; M.A. Christ's College, Cambridge, 1620 ; B.D., 1631 ; chaplain to Archbishop Laud ; prebendary of St. Paul's, 1632 ; vicar of St. Martin's-in-the-Fields, 1633 ; sequestered, 1643. [vi. 241]

BRAY, WILLIAM (1736–1832), antiquary ; educated at Rugby ; held position in board of green cloth for nearly fifty years ; F.S.A., 1771, treasurer, 1803. He completed the Rev. Owen Manning's 'History of Surrey' (1804–14), and published antiquarian writings of his own. [vi. 242]

BRAYBROC, HENRY DE (d. 1234 ?), judge ; sheriff of Rutlandshire, Buckinghamshire, Northamptonshire, and Bedfordshire ; joined barons against John, and was excommunicated, 1215 ; reinstated in his lands after battle of Lincoln, 1217 ; justice of assize in Bedfordshire and Buckinghamshire, 1224 ; imprisoned by Falkes de Breauté [q. v.] ; justice itinerant for Bedfordshire and Buckinghamshire, 1225 ; justice of bench, 1227. [vi. 242]

BRAYBROKE, ROBERT DE (d. 1404), ecclesiastic and judge ; licentiate in civil law at Oxford ; prebendary of York, 1366, Lincoln, 1378, and Lichfield, 1379 ; dean of Salisbury, 1380 ; bishop of London and chancellor of Bristol, 1381 ; tried, unsuccessfully, to mediate between Richard II and barons, 1387 ; reformed chapter of St. Paul's, 1398 ; privy councillor under Henry IV. [vi. 243]

BRAYBROOKE, BARONS OF. [See GRIFFIN, JOHN GRIFFIN, first BARON, 1719–1797 ; NEVILLE, RICHARD ALDWORTH GRIFFIN-, second BARON, 1750–1825 ; NEVILLE, RICHARD GRIFFIN, third BARON, 1783–1858 ; NEVILLE, RICHARD CORNWALLIS, fourth BARON, 1820–1861.]

BRAYLEY, EDWARD WEDLAKE, the elder (1773–1854), topographer and archæologist; associated with John Britton (1771–1857) [q. v.] in several publications, including 'Beauties of England and Wales,' to which he contributed; F.S.A., 1823; librarian and secretary of Russell Institution, Great Coram Street, 1825–54; published topographical and archæological works. [vi. 244]

BRAYLEY, EDWARD WILLIAM, the younger (1802–1870), writer on science; son of Edward Wedlake Brayley [q. v.]; studied science in London and Royal Institutions; joint-librarian of London Institution, Finsbury Circus; joint-editor of 'Annals of Philosophy,' 'Zoological Journal,' and 'Philosophical Magazine,' 1822–1845; an original member of the Chemical and Zoological societies; wrote and edited several scientific works, and contributed to 'English Cyclopædia' and other works; F.R.S., 1854. [vi. 246]

BRAYNE, WILLIAM (d. 1657), governor of Jamaica; lieutenant-colonel of foot in Scotland, 1653; governor of Inverlochy; governor of Jamaica, 1656–7. [Suppl. i. 262]

BREADALBANE, second MARQUIS (1796–1862). [See CAMPBELL, JOHN.]

BREADALBANE, EARLS. [See CAMPBELL, JOHN, first EARL, 1635–1716; CAMPBELL, JOHN, third EARL, 1696–1782; CAMPBELL, JOHN, fifth EARL, 1796–1862.]

BREAKSPEAR, NICHOLAS (d. 1159). [See ADRIAN IV.]

BREARCLIFFE, JOHN (1609?–1682). [See BRIERCLIFFE.]

BREAUTÉ, FALKES DE (d. 1226), military adventurer; a Norman of mean birth; sheriff of Glamorgan, 1211; became one of John's evil counsellors; held command in royal army against barons, 1215–17; conducted his operations with considerable success, and contributed largely to the victory over the dauphin Louis at Lincoln which virtually ended the war; abetted Albemarle's revolt, 1220; assisted Hubert de Burgh in quelling insurrection in favour of Louis at Oxford, 1222; joined Earl of Chester and other lords in scheme for seizing the Tower, 1223; surrendered to king at Northampton on threats of excommunication; found guilty of more than thirty acts of wrongful disseisin, 1224, and heavily fined; ordered his garrison at Bedford to seize the justices, one of them, Henry de Braybroc [q. v.], being in consequence captured and imprisoned at Bedford Castle, which was commanded by Falkes's brother William, and was surrendered to the king after a stubborn resistance; captured soon afterwards, and, his possessions being forfeited, was committed to keeping of bishop of London; banished, 1225; enlisted the sympathies of the pope, who appealed unsuccessfully to Henry III in his behalf. [vi. 247]

BRECHIN, SIR DAVID (d. 1321), Scottish warrior; gained title of 'The Flower of Chivalry' for feats of arms probably in crusades; supported English cause in Scotland; warden of Dundee, 1312; captured at Bannockburn, 1314, and gained favour of King Robert; executed for complicity in Lord Soulis's conspiracy against Robert. [vi. 251]

BREE, ROBERT (1759–1839), physician; B.A. University College, Oxford, 1778; studied medicine at Edinburgh; M.A., 1781; M.D., 1791; F.R.C.S., 1807; censor, College of Physicians, 1810, 1819, and 1830; elect, 1830; Harveian lecturer, 1827; F.R.S.; vice-president, 1811; published medical writings. [vi. 252]

BREEKS, JAMES WILKINSON (1830–1872), Indian civil servant; entered Madras civil service, 1849; commissioner of the Nilagiris, c. 1867; died from illness contracted while collecting tribal utensils, arms, &c., for Indian Museum, Calcutta; wrote 'Account of Tribes and Monuments of the Nilagiris,' published posthumously by government. [vi. 252]

BREEN, JAMES (1826–1866), astronomer; calculator at Greenwich, c. 1842; assistant in Cambridge observatory, 1846; spent some years in study abroad; F.R.A.S., 1862; published astronomical writings. [vi. 253]

BREGWIN or **BREGOWINE** (d. 765), archbishop of Canterbury; born in the old Saxon land; came to England to study; archbishop, 759; buried at Canterbury. [vi. 253]

BREKELL, JOHN (1697–1769), presbyterian divine; sole pastor at Kaye Street, Liverpool, 1744–69; published religious works. [vi. 254]

BREMBRE, SIR NICHOLAS (d. 1388), lord mayor of London; alderman of Bread Street ward, 1376; lord mayor, 1377 and 1378; one of collectors of customs for port of London, c. 1379–86, his comptroller being Geoffrey Chaucer; accompanied king to Smithfield on rising of Commons, 1381, and was knighted; M.P. for city of London, 1383; obtained by force his election as lord mayor, 1383; supported Richard II's struggle for absolute power, 1387, and was executed. [vi. 255]

BREMER, SIR JAMES JOHN GORDON (1786–1850), rear-admiral; lieutenant in navy, 1805; captain, 1814; C.B., 1815; took part in Burmese war; K.C.H., 1836; commanded expedition to China, 1840–1; K.C.B., 1841; second in command of Channel squadron, 1846; commodore superintendent of Woolwich dockyard, 1846; rear-admiral, 1849. [vi. 256]

BREMNER, DAVID (d. 1852), engineer for Clyde trustees; son of James Bremner [q. v.]. [vi. 257]

BREMNER, JAMES (1784–1856), engineer; settled as shipbuilder at Pulteney Town, and was engaged in designing harbours and piers on northern coast of Scotland; published professional writings. [vi. 257]

BREMNER, ROBERT (d. 1789), music printer and publisher; produced several collections of songs and works of musical instruction, including 'Rudiments of Music' (1756). [vi. 257]

BRENAN, — (fl. 1756), painter in Dublin; published 'Painter's Breakfast,' a dramatic satire, 1756. [vi. 258]

BRENAN, JOHN (1768?–1830), physician; M.D. Glasgow; practised at Dublin from 1801; started 'Milesian Magazine' (1812), in which he attacked College of Physicians and ventilated grievances in satirical verse of considerable poignancy; discovered remedy for puerperal fever and internal inflammation. [vi. 258]

BRENCHLEY, JULIUS LUCIUS (1816–1873), traveller and author; M.A. St. John's College, Cambridge, 1843; ordained curate of Holy Trinity, Maidstone, 1843; made (1847–67) journeys to Utah, New Mexico, Panama, Ecuador, Peru and Chili, India, China and Mongolia, and Japan, Australia and New Zealand, Siberia and Poland; bequeathed large miscellaneous collections to Maidstone; published writings on his travels. [Suppl. i. 263]

BRENDAN or **BRENAINN**, SAINT (490?–573), of Birr, now Parsonstown, King's County; of second order of Irish saints; a disciple of St. Finnian of Clonard. His day is 29 Nov. [vi. 259]

BRENDAN or **BRENAINN**, S.'NT (484–577), of Clonfert; of second order of Irish sai.ts; studied under St. Ita, Bishop Erc, and St. Jarlath of Tuam; presbyter; perhaps made journey to western and northern islands, which formed basis of mediæval legend of 'Navigation of St. Brendan,' in the original form of which two journeys are described; visited Brittany between 520 and 530; founded monastery of Cluain Fearta, 553. His day is 16 May. [vi. 259]

BRENT, CHARLOTTE (d. 1802), singer; pupil of Dr. Arne; first appeared in public, 1758; engaged at Covent Garden, 1759–70, creating principal parts in several operas; married Thomas Pinto, 1766; toured with her husband in Scotland and Ireland, 1770–80; last appeared in 'Comus' at Covent Garden, 1784. [vi. 261]

BRENT, JOHN (1808–1882), antiquary and novelist; held offices in Canterbury corporation; F.S.A., 1853; member of British Archæological Association and other societies; published poetical works and novels, and contributed to archæological publications. [vi. 261]

BRENT, SIR NATHANIEL (1573?–1652), warden of Merton College, Oxford; M.A. Merton College, Oxford, 1598; university proctor, 1607; bachelor of law, 1623; warden of Merton, 1622; commissary of diocese of Canterbury and vicar-general to the archbishop; judge of prerogative court; knighted, 1629; successfully opposed Laud, who on a visitation to Merton, 1638, insisted on many radical reforms; sided with parliament on outbreak of civil war; was made judge-marshal, and signed the covenant; deposed from wardenship by Charles I,

1645 ; resumed office, 1646 ; president of parliamentary commission for visitation of universities, 1647–51 ; published translation into English of Pietro Sarpi's 'History of Council of Trent,' 1620, and other works.   [vi. 262]

BRENTFORD, EARL OF (1573 ?–1651). [See RUTH-VEN, PATRICK.]

BRENTON, EDWARD PELHAM (1774–1839), navy captain ; entered navy, 1788 ; lieutenant, 1795 ; captain, 1808 ; served in American war, 1811 ; flag-captain to Sir Benjamin Hallowell, 1815 ; published 'Naval History of Great Britain, 1783–1822,' 1823.   [vi. 264]

BRENTON, SIR JAHLEEL (1770–1844), vice-admiral ; born in Rhode Island ; served in royalist navy at outbreak of war of independence ; accepted commission in Swedish navy, and was promoted lieutenant in English navy, 1790 ; post-captain, 1800 ; flag-captain to Sir James Saumarez, 1801 ; prisoner of war in French hands, 1803–6 ; served in Mediterranean, 1807 till 1810, when he was wounded in action off Naples ; baronet, 1812 ; K.C.B., 1815 ; commissioner of dockyard of Port Mahon, 1813, and, later, of Cape of Good Hope till 1822 ; rear-admiral, 1830 ; lieutenant-governor, Greenwich Hospital, 1831 ; vice-admiral, 1840 ; published religious writings. [vi. 265]

BRERELEY, JOHN (*fl.* 1624). [See ANDERTON, JAMES.]

BRERELEY or BRIERLEY, ROGER (1586–1637), divine and poet : perpetual curate of Grindleton Chapel, Mitton-in-Craven, where his followers became known as Grindletonians ; probably charged (before 1628) at York by high commissioners with holding doctrines of antinomian tendency, but acquitted ; received living of Burnley, Lancashire, 1631. Volumes of his literary remains appeared posthumously.   [vi. 266]

BRERETON, JOHN (*fl.* 1603), voyager to New England ; accompanied first party of English who landed in New England with intention of settling, 1603, but returned almost immediately ; published 'Description of Elizabeth's Ile, and some others towards North Part of Virginie, 1602.'   [vi. 267]

BRERETON, OWEN SALUSBURY (1715–1798), antiquary ; educated at Westminster and Trinity College, Cambridge ; called to bar, 1738 ; recorder of Liverpool, 1742–98 ; vice-president, Society of Arts, 1765–98 ; M.R.S. ; bencher of Lincoln's Inn ; treasurer and keeper of Black Book ; M.P. for Ilchester, 1775–80 ; contributed to 'Archæologia' and 'Philosophical Transactions.'   [vi. 268]

BRERETON, THOMAS (1691–1722), dramatist ; B.A. Brasenose College, Oxford, 1712 ; held government office connected with customs at Chester ; drowned while attempting to escape prosecution for libel ; published two English adaptations from plays by Racine and Corneille, and some poetical writings.   [vi. 269]

BRERETON, THOMAS (1782–1832), lieutenant-colonel ; volunteered in West Indies, 1797 ; ensign, 1798 ; captain, 1804 ; invalided home, 1813 ; lieutenant-governor of Senegal and Goree, 1814 ; lieutenant-colonel royal African corps, 1815 ; commanded Cape Town garrison, 1819–23 ; commanded troops quartered near Bristol at outbreak of the Reform riots, 1831 ; court-martialled for negligence, inaction, and neglect of civil authority ; committed suicide before trial was concluded.   [vi. 269]

BRERETON, SIR WILLIAM (*d.* 1541), lord justice in Ireland ; knighted, 1523 ; deputy chamberlain of Chester ; marshal of army in Ireland and Irish privy councillor, 1539 ; temporarily lord justice of Ireland, 1540.   [Suppl. i. 264]

BRERETON, SIR WILLIAM (1604–1661), parliamentary commander ; created baronet, 1627 ; travelled in Great Britain, Ireland, and on continent, 1634–5 (his 'Diary' published by Chetham Society, 1844) ; M.P. for Cheshire, 1628 and 1640 ; headed parliamentary movement in Cheshire, *c.* 1642 ; commander-in-chief of forces in Cheshire and neighbouring southern counties ; defeated Sir Thomas Aston at Nantwich and at Middlewich, 1643 ; defeated Rupert at Tarvin and captured Liverpool and Shrewsbury, 1644 ; captured Lichfield and Dudley Castle and defeated Lord Ashley near Stow-in-the-Wold, 1646 ; chief forester of Macclesfield forest and seneschal of hundred of Macclesfield on conclusion of war. [vi. 271]

BRERETON, SIR WILLIAM (1789–1864), lieutenant-general ; second lieutenant, royal artillery, 1805 ; served in Peninsular and Waterloo campaigns, 1809–15 ; after varied service, he was second in command in Bocca Tigris expedition, and at capture of Canton, 1848 ; at siege of Sevastopol, 1854 ; K.C.B., 1861 ; lieutenant-general, 1864.   [vi. 272]

BRERE WOOD or BRYER WOOD, EDWARD (1565 ?–1613), antiquary and mathematician ; M.A. Brasenose College, Oxford, 1590 ; first professor of astronomy, Gresham College, London, 1596 ; member of Old Society of Antiquaries ; left mathematical, religious, and antiquarian manuscripts, which were published posthumously.   [vi. 273]

BRERE WOOD, SIR ROBERT (1588–1654), judge ; educated at Brasenose College, Oxford ; called to bar at Middle Temple, 1615 ; judge of North Wales, 1637 ; recorder of Chester, 1639 ; reader at Middle Temple, 1638 ; serjeant-at-law, 1640 ; king's serjeant, 1641 ; knighted, 1643 ; judge, 1644.   [vi. 274]

BRERE WOOD, THOMAS (*d.* 1748), poetical writer ; grandson of Sir Robert Brerewood [q. v.] His 'Galfred and Juetta' appeared in 1772.   [vi. 274]

BRETLAND, JOSEPH (1742–1819), dissenting minister ; minister of Mint Chapel, Exeter, 1770–2 and 1789–1793, and at George's meeting house, Exeter, 1794–7, where he kept a classical school, 1772–90 ; tutor at academy in west of England for educating protestant dissenters, 1799–1805.   [vi. 274]

BRETNOR, THOMAS (*fl.* 1607–1618), almanac maker ; published two almanacs, 1607 and 1615, and a work (translated from French) on opium.   [vi. 275]

BRETON, JOHN LE (*d.* 1275), bishop of Hereford ; canon, and, *c.* 1268, bishop of Hereford. He was believed at beginning of 14th century to have been author of the work known as 'Britton' (mainly Bracton's treatise on English law condensed), probably written *c.* 1290.   [vi. 275]

BRETON, NICHOLAS (1545 ?–1626 ?), poet ; probably educated at Oxford, perhaps at Oriel College ; produced between 1577 and 1626, satirical, religious, romantic and pastoral writings, in verse and prose, which include (in verse) 'The Countess of Penbrook's (Pembroke's) Passion' (first privately printed) (1853), 'Pasquil's Mad-cappe' (earliest known copy) (1626), 'The Soules Heavenly Exercise' (1601), 'The Passionate Shepheard' (1604), 'The Honour of Valour' (1605), and (in prose) an angling idyll entitled 'Wits Trenchmour' (1597), 'The Wil of Wit, Wit's Will or Wil's Wit' (1599), 'Crossing of Proverbs,' 1616, 'The Figvre of Foure' (first published *c.* 1597), and 'A Mad World, my Masters' (1603), a dialogue.   [vi. 275]

BRETON, WILLIAM (*d.* 1356). [See BRITON.]

BRETT, ARTHUR (*d.* 1677 ?), poet ; educated at Westminster and Christ Church, Oxford ; M.A., 1659 ; vicar of Market Lavington, Wiltshire ; subsequently subsisted by begging in London ; published poetical writings.   [vi. 281]

BRETT, GEORGE (1630–1659). [See KEYNES.]

BRETT, HENRY (*d.* 1724), colonel ; studied at Oxford and the Temple ; M.P. for borough of Bishop's Castle, Shropshire, *c.* 1700 ; lieutenant-colonel of foot regiment raised by Sir Charles Hotham, 1705 ; member of Addison's circle.   [vi. 282]

BRETT, JOHN (*d.* 1785), navy captain ; lieutenant, 1734 ; captain, 1741 ; served on North American coast, 1755 ; published translations from Spanish of Feyjoo.   [vi. 282]

BRETT, JOHN WATKINS (1805–1863), telegraphic engineer ; originated scheme of submarine telegraphy ; established telegraphic communication between England and France, 1850.   [vi. 283]

BRETT, SIR PEIRCY (1709–1781), admiral ; second lieutenant under Commodore Anson at Paita, 1741 ; engaged and disabled the Elisabeth, which, with munitions of war, was convoying Young Pretender's vessel to Scotland, 1745 ; served at Finisterre, 1747 ; knighted, 1753 ; commodore in Downs, 1758–61 ; second in command in Mediterranean, 1762 ; lord commissioner of admiralty, 1766–70 ; vice-admiral, 1770 ; admiral, 1778.   [vi. 283]

BRETT, RICHARD (1560?-1637), divine; B.A. Hart Hall, Oxford; fellow of Lincoln College; D.D., 1605; rector of Quainton, 1595; appointed by James I one of translators of bible into English; published translations from Greek into Latin. [vi. 284]

BRETT, ROBERT (1808-1874), surgeon; studied at St. George's Hospital, London; M.R.C.S.E., and L.S.A.L., 1830; practised at Stoke Newington; took active part in Tractarian movement, Dr. Pusey being among his friends; vice-president of English Church Union. [vi. 284]

BRETT, THOMAS (1667-1744), nonjuring divine; LL.B. Corpus Christi College, Cambridge, 1689; LL.D., 1697; rector of Ruckinge, 1705, and soon afterwards adopted nonjuring principles; resigned living, 1714; consecrated bishop by nonjuring bishops Collier, Spinckes, and Howes, 1716; published religious and other works. [vi. 285]

BRETT, WILLIAM BALIOL, VISCOUNT ESHER (1815-1899), judge; educated at Westminster and Caius College, Cambridge; M.A., 1845; called to bar at Lincoln's Inn, 1846; bencher, 1861; joined northern circuit; Q.C., 1861; conservative M.P. for Helston, Cornwall, 1866-8; solicitor-general, 1868; additional justice of common pleas, 1868; justice in high court, 1875; privy councillor, 1876; lord justice of appeal, 1877; master of rolls, 1883; created Baron Esher of Esher, 1885; retired, and was created Viscount Esher, 1897. [Suppl. i. 264]

BRETTARGH, KATHARINE (1579-1601), puritan; sister of John Bruen [q. v.]; married William Brettargh, c. 1599; persecuted for her religious opinions. [vi. 286]

BRETTELL, JACOB (1793-1862), unitarian divine; educated at Manchester College, York; minister of Rotherham, 1816; took part in anti-corn law agitation. [vi. 287]

BRETTELL, JACOB CHARLES CATES (1817-1867), lawyer; son of Jacob Brettell [q. v.]; educated for unitarian ministry; became Roman catholic and went to America, where he was successively tutor, minister of a German church, and barrister; published poetical, religious, and other works. [vi. 287]

BRETTINGHAM, MATTHEW, the elder (1699-1769), architect; pupil of William Kent, designer of Holkham, the Earl of Leicester's seat in Norfolk, on which Brettingham worked; designed mansions in Palladian style; published 'Remarks' on places visited in Continental tours. [vi. 287]

BRETTINGHAM, MATTHEW, the younger (1725-1803), architect; son of Matthew Brettingham (1699-1769) [q. v.]; worked in Palladian style. [vi. 288]

BRETTINGHAM, ROBERT FURZE (1750-1806?), architect; nephew of Matthew Brettingham the elder [q.v.]; studied in Italy; erected many mansions throughout the country, and, after 1790, obtained extensive practice as prison architect; resident clerk of board of works, c. 1771-1805. [vi. 288]

BREVAL, JOHN DURANT (1680?-1738), miscellaneous writer; educated at Westminster and Trinity College, Cambridge; fellow, 1702; M.A., 1704; expelled for alleged misconduct, 1708; volunteer in army in Flanders; became successively ensign and captain; employed by Marlborough in diplomatic missions; subsequently engaged in dramatic and other writing in London; noticed at some length in the 'Dunciad' in retaliation for his merciless ridicule of Pope. [vi. 289]

BREVINT or **BREVIN**, DANIEL (1616-1695), divine; educated at protestant university at Saumur; M.A., 1624; fellow of Jesus College, Oxford, 1637; incorporated M.A. Oxford, 1638; deprived of fellowship by parliamentary commissioners; retired to Jersey, his birthplace, and thence to France; chaplain to Turenne; returned to England, 1660; received stall in Durham Cathedral, 1660; D.D. Oxford, 1663; dean and prebendary of Lincoln, 1682; published protestant polemics, and devotional works, including 'The Christian Sacrament and Sacrifice,' 1673. [vi. 290]

BREWER, ANTONY (fl. 1655), dramatic writer; wrote 'The Love-sick King.' [vi. 292]

BREWER, EBENEZER COBHAM (1810-1897), miscellaneous writer; son of John Sherren Brewer [q. v.]; B.C.L. Trinity Hall, Cambridge, 1835; ordained priest, 1836; LL.D., 1840. His works include 'Dictionary of Phrase and Fable,' 1870. [Suppl. i. 266]

BREWER, GEORGE (b. 1766), miscellaneous writer; served as midshipman in navy; lieutenant in Swedish navy, 1791; attorney in London; contributed to the 'European Magazine,' and published dramas, novels, and miscellaneous writings. [vi. 292]

BREWER, JAMES NORRIS (fl. 1799-1829), author of many novels and topographical compilations, including contributions to series called 'Beauties of England and Wales.' [vi. 293]

BREWER, JEHOIADA (1752?-1817), dissenting minister; published religious writings. [vi. 293]

BREWER, JOHN (1744-1822), English Benedictine monk; appointed to mission at Bath, where a new chapel built by him was destroyed by rioters, 1780. [vi. 294]

BREWER, JOHN SHERREN (1810-1879), historical writer; graduated at Queen's College, Oxford, 1832; lecturer in classical literature, King's College, London, 1839, and professor of English language and literature and lecturer in modern history, 1855-77; commissioned, 1856, by master of rolls, Sir John Romilly, to prepare calendar of state papers of Henry VIII; principal of Working Men's College; received crown living of Toppesfield, 1877; published historical works, including 'Student's Hume.' [vi. 294]

BREWER, SAMUEL (d. 1743?), botanist; engaged in woollen manufacture at Trowbridge, Wiltshire; having met with misfortune became head-gardener to Duke of Beaufort at Badminton. He rendered valuable assistance to Dillenius in his botanical work. [vi. 295]

BREWER, THOMAS (fl. 1624), author of tracts in verse and prose, including 'The Life and Death of the Merry Deuill of Edmonton' (prose), 1631, 'A Knot of Fooles' (satirical verses), 1624; and poems descriptive of the plague. [vi. 296]

BREWER, THOMAS (b. 1611), musician; educated at Christ's Hospital; a celebrated performer on viol; published musical compositions. [vi. 297]

BREWER, BRIWERE, or BRUER, WILLIAM (d. 1226), baron and judge: sheriff of Devon; justice itinerant, 1187; one of four justices left by Richard in charge of the kingdom, 1189; assisted Richard, then in captivity, at interview with Emperor Henry VI, and, later, with other envoys, arranged peace of Nantes, 1193; one of John's evil advisers; signed charter surrendering crown and kingdom of England to Innocent III, 1213; joined barons after their entry into London, 1215; signed Great Charter; leader in John's army on outbreak of baronial war; assisted Henry III against French, c. 1216; baron of exchequer, 1221. [vi. 297]

BREWSTER, ABRAHAM (1796-1874), Irish lawyer; M.A. Dublin, 1847; called to Irish bar, 1819; took silk, 1835; solicitor-general of Ireland, 1846; privy councillor in Ireland, 1853; attorney-general, 1853-5; lord justice of appeal in Ireland, 1866; lord-chancellor of Ireland, 1867. [vi. 299]

BREWSTER, SIR DAVID (1781-1868), natural philosopher; educated at Edinburgh University; editor of 'Edinburgh Magazine' (afterwards called successively, 'Edinburgh Philosophical Journal' and 'Edinburgh Journal of Science'), 1802; licensed preacher, 1804, but subsequently abandoned clerical profession; LL.D. St. Andrews, 1807; M.A. Cambridge; editor of 'Edinburgh Encyclopædia,' 1807-29; F.R.S., and Copley medallist, 1815; Rumford medallist, 1818, and subsequently Royal medallist for discoveries in relation to polarisation of light; invented kaleidoscope, 1816; M.I.C.E. London, 1820; first director of Royal Scottish Society of Arts, 1821; assisted in organising British Association for Advancement of Science, 1831; knighted, 1831; principal of united colleges of St. Salvator and St. Leonard in university of St. Andrews, 1838; aided Scottish Free church movement, 1844; vice-chancellor, Edinburgh University, 1860; president, Royal Society of Edinburgh, 1864. His works relate chiefly to optical investigations. [vi. 299]

BREWSTER, SIR FRANCIS (d. 1704), writer on trade; lord mayor of Dublin, 1674; published writings on trade and navigation. [vi. 303]

BREWSTER, JOHN (1753–1842), author; M.A. Lincoln College, Oxford, 1778; rector of Redmarshall, 1805, Boldon, 1809, and Egglescliffe, 1814; published 'History of Stockton-on-Tees,' and religious works. [vi. 303]

BREWSTER, PATRICK (1788–1859), Scottish divine; brother of Sir David Brewster [q. v.]; held second charge of Abbey Church, Paisley, 1818–59; published sermons. [vi. 304]

BREWSTER, THOMAS (*b.* 1705), translator; M.D. St. John's College, Oxford, 1738; fellow; published verse translations from Persius, 1733–84. [vi. 304]

BREWSTER, WILLIAM (1560?–1644), a founder of Plymouth, New England; educated at Peterhouse, Cambridge; entered, *c.* 1584, service of William Davison [q. v.], whom he accompanied on embassy to Low Countries, 1585–7; keeper of 'post office' at Scrooby, 1594–1607; interested himself in separatist movement, and after suffering considerable persecution went to Amsterdam, 1608; set up printing press at Leyden; sailed for Virginia in Mayflower, 1620, and founded New Plymouth, where he worked as teacher and preacher. [vi. 304]

BRIAN (926–1014), king of Ireland; known as Brian mac Kennedy (or Cennedigh); son of Cenneide; with his brother Mathgamhain, chief of the Dal Cais; defeated Danes at Sulcoit, Tipperary, *c.* 968; chief of Dal Cais, 976; defeated and slew Maelmuadh, king of Cashel, 978, and succeeded him; defeated Gillapatric, king of Ossory, and was acknowledged king of Leinster, 984; allied with Maelsechlainn mac Domhnaill, chief king of Ireland, and defeated Danes at Glenmama, Wicklow, 1000; defeated Maelsechlainn and became chief king of Ireland, 1001; received submission of Connaughtmen; made charter acknowledging ecclesiastical supremacy of Armagh, 1004; made circuit of Ireland, receiving hostages of all territories through which he passed, joined Maelsechlainn and besieged Danes near Dublin, without success, 1013; defeated Danes at Cluantarbh; after the battle was murdered by a Dane in his tent, 1014. [vi. 306]

BRIANT. [See BRYAN.]

BRIANT, ALEXANDER (1553–1581), jesuit; educated at Hart Hall, Oxford, and at Douay and Rheims; ordained priest, 1578; joined English mission, 1579; imprisoned in Compter, tortured, and executed for high treason at Tyburn, having been admitted while in prison to the Society of Jesus. [vi. 309]

BRICE, ANDREW (1690–1773), printer; apprenticed in Exeter; carried on a printing business in spite of financial difficulties for many years after 1714; issued a weekly newspaper, *c.* 1715–73. His works include a 'Grand Gazetteer, or Topographic Dictionary,' 1759. [vi. 310]

BRICE or **BRYCE**, EDWARD (1569?–1636), first presbyterian minister in Ireland; entered Edinburgh University, *c.* 1589; minister of Bothkenner, 1595, and Drymen, 1602; deposed on charge of adultery; received cure of Templecorran, co. Antrim, *c.* 1614; prebendary of Kilroot, 1619; silenced for non-subscription to the canons, 1636. [vi. 310]

BRICE, THOMAS (*d.* 1570), martyrologist; ordained deacon and priest, 1560; published 'A Compendious Register in Metre' (1559), containing names of martyrs in England, 4 Feb. 1555 to 17 Nov. 1558. [vi. 311]

BRICIE, BRICIUS, or **BRIXIUS** (*d.* 1222), bishop; second prior of Lesmahagow; bishop of Moray, 1203; founded college of canons at Spynie. [vi. 312]

BRICMORE, BRICHEMORE, or **BRYGEMOORE**, H— (14th cent.), surnamed SOPHISTA; scholastic; said to have studied at Oxford, to have been canon of Holy Rood, Edinburgh, and to have written commentaries on Aristotle; perhaps identical with BRICHEMON. [vi. 312]

BRIDE, SAINT (453–523). [See BRIGIT.]

BRIDELL, FREDERICK LEE (1831–1863), landscape painter; apprenticed to a picture dealer, who arranged for his education abroad; exhibited at Royal Academy from 1851. 'The Temple of Venus,' 1858, and 'Sunset on the Atlantic,' 1857, are among his best-known works. [vi. 312]

BRIDEOAKE, RALPH (1613–1678), bishop of Chichester; M.A. Brasenose College, Oxford, 1636; master of Manchester free grammar school, 1638, and feoffee,

1663; lost mastership on outbreak of civil war; preacher of the rolls; vicar of Witney, Oxfordshire, 1654–63; commissioner for approbation and admission of presbyterian ministers, 1659; chaplain to Charles II, canon of Windsor, and D.D., 1660; dean of Salisbury, 1667; bishop of Chichester, 1675. [vi. 313]

BRIDFERTH (*fl.* 1000). [See BYRHTFERTH.]

BRIDGE, BEWICK (1767–1833), mathematician and senior wrangler; B.A. St. Peter's College, Cambridge, 1790; M.A., 1793; B.D., 1811; fellow; professor of mathematics at East India Company's College, Haileybury; vicar of Cherryhinton, 1816–33; F.R.S.; published mathematical works. [vi. 314]

BRIDGE, SIR JOHN (1824–1900), police magistrate; M.A. Trinity College, Oxford, 1849; called to bar at Inner Temple, 1850; practised on home circuit; police magistrate in London; chief metropolitan magistrate, 1890; knighted, 1890. [Suppl. i. 267]

BRIDGE or **BRIDGES**, RICHARD (*fl.* 1750), organ-builder; constructed organ for Christ Church, Spitalfields, and other churches. [vi. 315]

BRIDGE, WILLIAM (1600?–1670), puritan divine; M.A. Emmanuel College, Cambridge, 1626; fellow; lecturer at Colchester, 1631; rector of St. Peter's Hungate, Norwich, 1636; excommunicated; high pastor at Rotterdam; frequently preached before Long parliament; ejected from living at Great Yarmouth, 1662; one of the writers of the 'Apologetical Narration,' 1643. [vi. 315]

BRIDGEMAN, HENRY (1615–1682), bishop of Sodor and Man; son of John Bridgeman [q. v.]; B.A. Oriel College, Oxford, 1632; fellow of Brasenose College, 1633–9; M.A., 1635; rector of Barrow, Cheshire, 1639 (sequestered, 1643), and of Bangor-is-coed, Flintshire, 1640 (sequestered, 1646); regained rectories on Restoration; dean of Chester, D.D., and prebendary of York, 1660; bishop of Sodor and Man, 1671. [vi. 316]

BRIDGEMAN, JOHN (1577–1652), bishop of Chester; B.D. Peterhouse, Cambridge, 1596; foundation fellow of Magdalene College, 1599; M.A., and incorporated M.A. Oxford, 1600; D.D., 1612; canon residentiary of Exeter; prebendary of Peterborough; chaplain to James I; bishop of Chester, 1619; opposed nonconformity; lived in retirement after temporary overthrow of episcopacy. [vi. 317]

BRIDGEMAN, SIR ORLANDO (1606?–1674), lord keeper; son of John Bridgeman [q. v.]; B.A. Queens' College, Cambridge, and fellow of Magdalene College, 1624; called to bar at Inner Temple, 1632; bencher, *c.* 1660; chief-justice of Chester, 1638; attorney of court of wards, and solicitor-general to Prince of Wales, 1640; M.P. for Wigan in Long parliament and knighted, 1640; sat in Oxford parliament, 1644; serjeant-at-arms, chief-baron of exchequer, and baronet, 1660; presided at trial of regicides; lord chief-justice of common pleas, 1660–8; lord keeper of great seal, 1667–72. [vi. 318]

BRIDGES. [See also BRYDGES.]

BRIDGES, CHARLES (1794–1869), evangelical divine; M.A. Queens' College, Cambridge, 1831; vicar of Weymouth, 1849; published religious writings. [vi. 320]

BRIDGES, JOHN (*d.* 1618), bishop of Oxford, 1604; M.A. Pembroke Hall, Cambridge, 1560; fellow, 1556; D.D. Canterbury, 1575; dean of Salisbury, 1577; took part in Hampton Court conference, 1603; published religious works, of which the most important, being the immediate cause of the Martin Marprelate tracts, is 'A Defence of the Government established in the Church of Englande for Ecclesiasticall Matters,' 1587, replying to Cartwright's 'Discourse on Ecclesiastical Government' (1574), and Theodore Beza's 'Judgment.' [vi. 320]

BRIDGES, JOHN (1666–1724), topographer; bencher of Lincoln's Inn; solicitor to customs, 1695; governor of Bridewell and Bethlehem hospitals; F.S.A., 1718. Left manuscript collections for history of Northamptonshire (published 1762–91). [vi. 321]

BRIDGES, NOAH (*fl.* 1661), stenographer and mathematician; educated at Balliol College, Oxford; B.C.L., 1646; clerk of parliaments at Oxford, 1643 and 1644; kept a school at Putney; published works on arithmetic, stenography, and cryptography. [vi. 322]

BRIDGES, THOMAS (*fl.* 1759-1775), dramatist and parodist; published comic operas (produced at Haymarket, 1771 and 1775) and parodies of Homer and other poets. [vi. 323]

BRIDGET, SAINT (453-523). [See BRIGIT.]

BRIDGETOWER, GEORGE AUGUSTUS POLGREEN (1779-1840 ?), violinist; studied under Barthelemon; first appeared at Drury Lane at an oratorio concert, 1790; became member of the Prince of Wales's private band at Brighton; at Vienna met Beethoven, who composed for him his Kreutzer Sonata; Mus.Bac. Cambridge, 1811. [vi. 323]

BRIDGETT, THOMAS EDWARD (1829-1899), Roman catholic priest; pensioner of St. John's College, Cambridge, 1847; entered Roman catholic church, 1850; joined Redemptorist order; priest, 1856; founded Confraternity of Holy Family, Limerick, 1868; wrote mainly on history of Reformation. [Suppl. i. 267]

BRIDGEWATER, third DUKE OF (1736-1803). [See EGERTON, FRANCIS.]

BRIDGEWATER, EARLS OF. [See EGERTON, JOHN, first EARL, 1579-1649; EGERTON, JOHN, second EARL, 1622-1686; EGERTON, JOHN, third EARL, 1646-1701; EGERTON, FRANCIS, sixth EARL, 1736-1803; EGERTON, FRANCIS HENRY, eighth EARL, 1756-1829.]

BRIDGEWATER, JOHN (1532 ?-1596 ?), latinised form AQUEPONTANUS, catholic divine; M.A. Hart Hall, Oxford, 1556; rector of Lincoln College, Oxford, 1563-74; canon residentiary of Wells; domestic chaplain to Robert Dudley, earl of Leicester; master of Hospital of St. Katharine, near Bedminster, 1570; prebendary of Wells, 1572; visited English college at Douay, 1574; published theological and historical works in Latin. [vi. 324]

BRIDGMAN or **BRIDGEMAN**, CHARLES (*d.* 1738), gardener to George I and George II; king's gardener before 1729; laid out Serpentine and gardens between it and Kensington Palace, 1730-3; probably designed royal gardens at Richmond. He did much towards abolishing formal methods of landscape gardening. [Suppl. i. 268]

BRIDGMAN, RICHARD WHALLEY (1761 ?-1820), legal writer; attorney and one of clerks to Grocers' Company; published legal works. [vi. 325]

BRIDLINGTON, JOHN OF, SAINT (*d.* 1379). [See JOHN.]

BRIDPORT, VISCOUNT (1727-1814). [See HOOD, ALEXANDER.]

BRIDPORT or **BRIDLESFORD**, GILES OF (*d.* 1262), bishop of Salisbury; dean of Wells, 1253; went on embassy from Henry III to Alexander IV, 1256; bishop of Salisbury, 1257; nominated by Henry III one of arbitrators between king and barons, 1261; founded College of Vaux, Salisbury, 1260. [vi. 325]

BRIERCLIFFE or **BREARCLIFFE**, JOHN (1609 ?-1682), antiquary; made collections for history of Halifax. [vi. 325]

BRIERLEY, BENJAMIN (1825-1896), Lancashire dialect writer; son of a hand-loom weaver; worked as hand-loom weaver and, later, as silk-warper; became (1863) sub-editor of 'Oldham Times'; assisted in founding Manchester Literary Club, 1864; edited 'Ben Brierley's Journal,' 1869-91. He published works written largely in dialect of South Lancashire. A collected edition appeared, 1882-6. [Suppl. i. 269]

BRIERLEY, ROGER (1586-1637). [See BRERELEY.]

BRIERLY, SIR OSWALD WALTERS (1817-1894), marine painter; studied at academy of Henry Sass [q. v.] at Bloomsbury; first exhibited at Royal Academy, 1839; settled in Auckland, 1841-51; F.R.G.S., 1853; accompanied Hon. Henry Keppel during operations in Baltic, 1854, and in Black Sea and Sea of Azov, 1855, publishing drawings of incidents in war; with Duke of Edinburgh in voyage round world, 1867-8, and with Prince and Princess of Wales in tour to Nile and Crimea, 1868; associate, 1872, and member, 1880, of Royal Water-colour Society, to whose exhibitions he contributed scenes from naval history; marine painter to Queen Victoria, 1874; knighted, 1885. [Suppl. i. 270]

BRIGGS, HENRY (1561-1630), mathematician; M.A. St. John's College, Cambridge, 1585; fellow, 1588; first professor of geometry, Gresham College, London, 1596-1620; Savilian professor of astronomy, fellow-commoner of Merton College, and incorporated M.A., Oxford, 1619; published and left in manuscript works on mathematics and navigation. [vi. 326]

BRIGGS, HENRY PERRONET (1791 ?-1844), subject and portrait painter; exhibited at Royal Academy from 1814; R.A., 1832. [vi. 327]

BRIGGS, JOHN (1788-1861), catholic divine; educated at St. Cuthbert's College, Ushaw; received tonsure and four minor orders, 1804; professor at St. Cuthbert's, and, in 1832, president; bishop of Trachis in Thessalia, 1833; vicar-apostol.c of northern district, 1836; bishop of Beverley, 1850-60. [vi. 327]

BRIGGS, JOHN (1785-1875), Indian officer; served in Mahratta wars, and became resident at Sattára; senior commissioner for government of Mysore, 1831; resident at Nágpur, 1832; left India, 1835; major-general, 1838; member of court of proprietors of East India Company; F.R.S.; translated Persian works into English. [vi. 328]

BRIGGS, JOHN JOSEPH (1819-1876), naturalist and topographer; contributed writings on natural history and archæology to the 'Field' and other newspapers; fellow, Royal Society of Literature; member of British Archæological Association. His works include a 'History of Melbourne, Derbyshire.' [vi. 328]

BRIGGS, SIR JOHN THOMAS (1781-1865), accountant-general of the navy; secretary to commission on civil affairs of navy, 1806-9; commissioner and accountant-general of victualling board; accountant-general of navy, 1832; knighted, 1851. [vi. 329]

BRIGGS, WILLIAM (1642-1704), physician and oculist; fellow, Corpus Christi College, Cambridge, 1668; M.A., 1670; studied under Vieussens at Montpellier; M.D. Cambridge, 1677; F.C.P., 1682; censor, 1685, 1686, and 1692; physician in ordinary to William III from 1696; published 'Theory of Vision,' 1682-3. [vi. 329]

BRIGHAM, NICHOLAS (*d.* 1558), antiquary; appointed by Mary general receiver of subsidies, fifteenths, and benevolences, 1558; wrote epitaph on Chaucer, for whose bones he built tomb in Westminster Abbey, 1555. [vi. 330]

BRIGHT, SIR CHARLES TILSTON (1832-1888), telegraph engineer; educated at Merchant Taylors' school; entered employ of Electric Telegraph Company, 1847; consulting engineer of Magnetic Company, 1860-70; patented the acoustic telegraph known as 'Bright's Bells,' 1855; engineer to Atlantic Cable Company, 1856; on board the Niagara, which, with the Agamemnon, under Professor W. Thomson (Lord Kelvin), laid the first cable from Valentia to Newfoundland, 1858; knighted, 1858; engaged in cable-laying work in Mediterranean, Persian Gulf, and West Indian Islands; liberal M.P. for Greenwich, 1865; M.I.C.E., 1862; president of Institute of Electrical Engineers, 1886-7. [Suppl. i. 271]

BRIGHT, HENRY (1814-1873), water-colour painter; dispenser at Norwich Hospital; studied art and exhibited at Royal Academy, 1845-50; member of Institute of Painters in Water-colours. [vi. 331]

BRIGHT, HENRY ARTHUR (1830-1884), merchant and author; educated at Rugby; B.A. Trinity College, Cambridge, 1857; M.A., 1860; partner in shipping firm of Gibbs, Bright & Co.; on commission of peace for London, 1865, and for Middlesex, 1870; member of Roxburghe Club and Philobiblon Society, for each of which he edited a publication. [vi. 331]

BRIGHT, JACOB (1821-1899), radical politician, brother of John Bright (1811-1889) [q. v.]; M.P. for Manchester, 1867-74 and 1876-85, and southern division, Manchester, 1886-95; privy councillor, 1895. [Suppl. i. 291]

BRIGHT, SIR JOHN (1619-1688), parliamentarian; raised companies for parliament; captain, 1643; governor of Sheffield, 1644; served under Cromwell in Scotland; high sheriff of Yorkshire, and governor of Hull and York, 1654 and 1655; probably joined royalist party before Restoration; created baronet, 1660. [vi. 333]

BRIGHT, JOHN (1783-1870), physician; M.D. Wadham College, Oxford, 1808; physician to General Hospital, Birmingham, 1810; F.C.P., 1809; Harveian orator, 1830; lord chancellor's adviser in lunacy, 1836. [vi. 333]

BRIGHT, JOHN (1811-1889), orator and statesman; son of a Rochdale miller; worked in his father's mill; made first public speech, 1830, in defence of temperance movement; gained reputation as orator by his opposition of principle of church rates, 1834-41; advocated abolition of capital punishment; formed friendship with Cobden, c. 1835; treasurer of Rochdale branch of Anti-Cornlaw League, 1840; began agitation in London against corn laws, 1842, and subsequently carried on campaign in midlands and Scotland; M.P. for Durham, 1843; opposed Maynooth grant, 1845; spoke against Lord Ashley's ten hours factories bill, 1846; M.P. for Manchester, 1847 and 1852; introduced bill for repeal of game laws, 1848; advocated facilitation of sale of encumbered estates in Ireland, provision of occupation for peasantry by increased partition of landed property, and disestablishment; chairman, 1848, of select committee (for which he had moved, 1847) to inquire into obstacles to cultivation of cotton in India; subsequently assisted in rais'ng funds for private commission of inquiry in India; joined Cobden in forming 'The Commons' League,' for financial and parliamentary reform, 1849; opposed Russell's resolution excluding Sir David Salomons [q. v.] from House of Commons as a Jew, 1851; recommended that government of India should be made a department of the British government, 1853; opposed war with Russia, 1853-4; opposed Russell's Oxford University reform bill, and grant to dissenting ministers in Ireland, 1854; defeated in election at Manchester and elected for Birmingham, 1857, 1858, 1865, 1868, 1873, 1874, 1880-5; advocated de-centralisation in India, 1858 and 1879; opposed government reform bill, in speech in which he insisted on need for redistribution, 1859; negotiated preliminary treaty of commerce with France, 1860; member of committee to inquire into precedents for power of Lords to deal with tax bills, 1860; supported northern cause in American war, 1861; member of Jamaica committee for trial of Governor Eyre for execution of Gordon, 1865; supported, 1866, Gladstone's government reform bill, which was defeated; advocated Irish disestablishment, 1868; president of board of trade in Gladstone's first ministry, 1868-1870; member of cabinet and of privy council, 1868; temporarily withdrew from politics owing to ill-health, 1870-2; chancellor of duchy of Lancaster, 1873; opposed Beaconsfield's Turkish policy, 1876, and advocated neutrality; chancellor of duchy of Lancaster with seat in cabinet in Gladstone's ministry, 1880; supported Bradlaugh's request for permission to affirm, 1880; lord rector of Glasgow University, 1880; approved of re-establishment of autonomy of Transvaal, 1881; resigned chancellorship of the duchy of Lancaster on British intervention in Egyptian affairs, 1882; M.P. for central division of Birmingham, 1885; made in 1887 last public speech (an attack on Gladstone's home rule bill of 1886); honorary D.C.L. Oxford, 1886. Bright and Cobden were the two leading representatives of the emergence of the manufacturing class as a force in English politics after the Reform Act of 1832. Volumes of his speeches and addresses were published, 1868 and 1879. Bright's portrait, by Mr. W. W. Ouless, R.A., is in the National Portrait Gallery. [Suppl. i. 273]

BRIGHT, MYNORS (1818-1883), decipherer of Pepys; son of John Bright (1783-1870) [q. v.]: M.A. Magdalene College, Cambridge, 1843; fellow and president of the college; afterwards proctor, 1853; deciphered and published Pepys's 'Diary,' 1875-9. [vi. 333]

BRIGHT, RICHARD (1789-1858), physician; studied at Edinburgh and Guy's Hospital, London; M.D. Edinburgh, 1812; studied at Peterhouse, Cambridge; travelled on continent, 1818-20; physician, Guy's Hospital, 1824-43; consulting physician, 1843; assisted Addison in 'Elements of Practice of Medicine' (1839); published first volume of 'Reports of Medical Cases,' 1827, containing his discovery of 'Bright's Disease,' and second volume, 1831; contributed to 'Guy's Hospital Reports,' first published, 1836; F.C.P., 1832, Gulstonian lecturer, 1833, censor, 1836 and 1839, Lumleian lecturer, 1837, and member of council, 1838 and 1843; F.R.S., 1821; physician extraordinary to Queen Victoria, 1837; published accounts of travels, medical treatises, and other writings. [vi. 334]

BRIGHT, TIMOTHY (1551?-1615), inventor of modern shorthand; M.D. Trinity College, Cambridge, 1579; studied medicine in Paris; physician to St. Bartholomew's Hospital, 1586-90; abandoned medical profession; rector of Methley, 1591, and of Berwick-in-Elmet, Yorkshire, 1594; published 'A Treatise of Melancholie,' 1586 (said to have suggested to Burton his 'Anatomy of Melancholy'), and 'Characterie,' 1588, a work on the lost art of shorthand, which Bright re-invented. [vi. 337]

BRIGHTMAN, THOMAS (1562-1607), puritan divine; M.A. and fellow, Queens' College, Cambridge, 1584; B.D., 1591; rector of Hawnes, Bedfordshire, 1592; wrote biblical commentaries (including a treatise on the Apocalypse, which he believed himself to have written under divine inspiration), published posthumously. [vi. 339]

BRIGHTWELL, CECILIA LUCY (1811-1875), etcher and authoress; drew and lithographed figures for her father Thomas Brightwell's work on 'Fauna of East Norfolk,' 1848; produced some original etchings and others after old and modern artists; published works for the young, mainly biographical. [vi. 340]

BRIGIT, SAINT, of Kildare (453-523), Irish saint; born at Faugher, near Dundalk; daughter of Dubhthach (grandson of Tuathal Teachtmhar, monarch of Erinn), by his bondmaid and concubine Brotsech; lived, when grown up, with her father, who, disliking her generous bestowal of his property on the poor, gave her her freedom; took the veil and was probably invested with rank corresponding with that of bishop; founded the church of Kildare. Her day is 1 Feb. [vi. 340]

BRIGSTOCKE, THOMAS (1809-1881), portrait-painter; exhibited at Royal Academy, 1843-65. [vi. 342]

BRIHTNOTH (d. 991), earldorman of East-Saxons; died of wounds received in battle against Norwegian fleet near Maldon. [vi. 342]

BRIHTRIC (d. 802). [See BEORHTRIC.]

BRIHTWALD (650?-731), archbishop of Canterbury; abbot of Reculver, c. 670; elected archbishop of Canterbury, 692, and consecrated by archbishop of Lyons, 693; presided at council of Estrefeld (near Ripon?), in which Wilfrith, archbishop of York, was excommunicated, 702; an energetic and tactful ecclesiastic. [vi. 343]

BRIHTWOLD (d. 1045), monk of Glastonbury; eighth bishop of Ramsbury, 1005-45. [vi. 344]

BRIMLEY, GEORGE (1819-1857), essayist; B.A. Trinity College, Cambridge; college librarian, 1845; contributed to 'Spectator' and 'Fraser's Magazine,' essays, of which a selection was published, 1858. [vi. 344]

BRIND, SIR JAMES (1808-1888), general; educated at East India Company's College Addiscombe; second lieutenant, Bengal artillery, 1827; captain, 1845; major, 1856; colonel, 1861; major-general, 1867; general, and colonel-commandant, royal artillery, 1877; distinguished himself at siege of Delhi, 1857; C.B., 1858; commanded Sirhind division, Bengal army, 1873-8; G.C.B., 1884. [Suppl. i. 291]

BRIND, RICHARD (d. 1718), chorister and, 1707-18, organist of St. Paul's Cathedral. [vi. 344]

BRINDLEY, JAMES (1716-1772), engineer; began business, 1742, as repairer of old machinery at Leek, and introduced many important improvements in machinery; designed canal from Worsley coal mines to Manchester, 1759, and subsequently constructed over 365 miles of canals, including Bridgewater (Manchester and Liverpool) and Grand Trunk (Trent and Mersey). [vi. 345]

BRINE, JOHN (1703-1765), baptist minister; born of poor parents; joined baptists when young; pastor of congregation at Curriers' Hall, Cripplegate, London, 1730; published religious works. [vi. 345]

BRINKELOW, HENRY (d. 1546), satirist; left order of St. Francis and became citizen and mercer of London; adopted opinions of reforming party and, under pseudonym of Roderigo Mors, published satires on social and religious subjects; perhaps banished from England. [vi. 346]

BRINKLEY, JOHN (1763-1835), bishop and astronomer; senior wrangler, and first Smith's prizeman, Caius College, Cambridge, 1788; M.A., 1791; D.D., 1806;

Andrews professor of astronomy, Dublin University, and first astronomer royal for Ireland, 1792; F.R.S., 1803; claimed to have discovered an annual (double) parallax for α Lyræ of 2″ 52, 1810, and, though he was mistaken, Greenwich observations failed to disprove his statements; Copley medallist, 1824; president, Royal Irish Academy, 1822-35; president Royal Astronomical Society, 1831-3; prebendary of Kilgoghlin and rector of Derrybrush, 1806; bishop of Cloyne, 1826; published 'Elements of Astronomy' (1808). [vi. 347]

BRINKNELL or BRYNKNELL, THOMAS (d.1539 ?), divine; D.D. University College, Oxford, 1508; prebendary of Lincoln, and master of St. John's Hospital, Banbury, 1511; professor of divinity, Oxford, 1521. [vi. 348]

BRINSLEY, JOHN, the elder (fl. 1663), puritan divine; M.A. Christ's College, Cambridge, 1588; took orders; master of school at Ashby-de-la-Zouch; ejected from mastership, c. 1620, for his religious opinions; published translations and educational works. [vi. 348]

BRINSLEY, JOHN, the younger (1600-1665), puritan divine; son of John Brinsley (fl. 1663) [q. v.]; M.A. Emmanuel College, Cambridge, 1623; appointed minister to corporation of Great Yarmouth, 1625, but dismissed by court of high commission, 1627; again town preacher of Yarmouth, 1644; ejected, 1660; published religious treatises. [vi. 349]

BRINTON or BRUNTON, THOMAS (d. 1389), bishop of Rochester: Benedictine monk at Norwich; 'doctor decretorum,' Oxford; penitentiary of holy see; bishop of Rochester, 1373; confessor to the king. [vi. 350]

BRINTON, WILLIAM (1823-1867), physician; studied at King's College, London; M.D. London, 1848; F.C.P., 1854; lecturer on forensic medicine, St. Thomas's Hospital, and subsequently physician and lecturer on physiology; published treatises relating chiefly to diseases of the stomach. [vi. 350]

BRIOT, NICHOLAS (1579-1646), medallist and coin-engraver; engraver-general of coins of France, 1605-25; endeavoured, but without success, to introduce improved methods of coining in France; chief engraver to English mint, 1633; master of Scottish mint, 1635. [vi. 351]

BRISBANE, SIR CHARLES (1769 ?-1829), rear-admiral; entered navy, 1779; lieutenant, 1790; in Mediterranean under Captain Nelson and Lord Hood, 1793-4; commander, 1794; promoted captain for his capture of Dutch ships in Saldana Bay, 1796; knighted for success against Dutch off Curaçao, 1807; governor of St. Vincent, 1808-29; K.C.B., 1815; rear-admiral, 1819. [iv. 352]

BRISBANE, SIR JAMES (1774-1826), commodore; brother of Sir Charles Brisbane [q. v.]; lieutenant in navy, 1794; commander, 1797; commanded squadron blockading Corfu, 1808; engaged in reduction of Ionian Islands; in Channel, 1812, and Mediterranean, 1815; C.B., 1815; knighted, 1816; commander-in-chief in East Indies, 1825; died at Penang. [vf. 353]

BRISBANE, JOHN (d. 1776 ?), physician; M.D. Edinburgh, 1750; L.C.P., 1766; physician to Middlesex Hospital, 1758-73; published 'Anatomy of Painting,' 1769. [vi. 353]

BRISBANE, SIR THOMAS MAKDOUGALL- (1773-1860), soldier and astronomer: educated at Edinburgh University; ensign, 1789; major, 1795; with Sir Ralph Abercromby in West Indies, 1795-8; lieutenant-colonel, 1800; in Jamaica, 1800-3; devoted himself to astronomy at his observatory at Brisbane, Scotland: colonel and assistant adjutant-general, 1810; brigadier-general under Wellington in Peninsula, 1812; major-general, 1813; in Canada, 1813; K.C.B., 1814; governor of New South Wales, 1821-5; encouraged emigration but lacked energy as governor; erected observatory at Paramatta, near Sydney, 1822; returned to England, 1825: colonel of 34th regiment, 1826; M.R.S. Edinburgh, 1811, and president, 1833-60; gold medallist, Royal Astronomical Society, 1828; built and equipped observatory, and, 1841, magnetic observatory, Makerstoun, Scotland; Keith medallist, 1818; M.R.S., 1810; created baronet, 1836; G.C.B., 1837; general, 1841. [vi. 353]

BRISTOL, EARLS OF. [See DIGBY, JOHN, first EARL, 1580-1654; DIGBY, GEORGE, second EARL, 1612-1677; HERVEY, JOHN, first EARL of the second creation,

1655-1751; HERVEY, AUGUSTUS JOHN, third EARL, 1724-1779; HERVEY, FREDERICK AUGUSTUS, fourth EARL, 1730-1803.]

BRISTOL, RALPH DE (d. 1232), bishop of Cashel; first treasurer of St. Patrick's Cathedral, Dublin, 1219; bishop of Cashel, 1223. [vi. 356]

BRISTOW, EDMUND (1787-1876), painter; exhibited at Royal Academy and other exhibitions, 1809-1838. [vi. 357]

BRISTOW, HENRY WILLIAM (1817-1889), geologist; educated at King's College, London; director of Geographical Survey for England and Wales, 1872-88: F.G.S., 1843; F.R.S., 1862; published geological works. [Suppl. i. 292]

BRISTOW, RICHARD (1538-1581), Roman catholic divine; M.A. Christ Church, Oxford, 1562; fellow of Exeter, 1567; appointed by Dr. Allen first moderator of studies at Douay; priest, 1573; D.D. Douay, 1575; had care of the seminary on removal to Rheims, 1578; returned to England for his health, 1581; published theological works, and assisted Allen in revising 'Douay Bible.' [vi. 357]

BRISTOWE, JOHN SYER (1827-1895), physician; educated at King's College school; studied at St. Thomas's Hospital; M.R.C.S. and L.S.A., 1849; M.D. London, 1852; physician, St. Thomas's Hospital, 1860; lecturer on medicine, 1876-92; F.R.C.P., 1858; Croonian lecturer, 1872, and Lumleian lecturer, 1879; F.R.S., 1881; honorary LL.D. Edinburgh, 1884; president of Medical Society of London, 1893; published 'Theory and Practice of Medicine,' 1876, and other medical writings. [Suppl. i. 293]

BRIT, BRYTTE, or BRITHUS, WALTER (fl. 1390), mathematician; fellow of Merton College, Oxford, and reputed author of a treatise on surgery and astronomical and mathematical works. [vi. 358]

BRITHWALD (650 ?-731). [See BRIHTWALD.]

BRITHWOLD (d. 1045). [See BRIHTWOLD.]

BRITO or LE BRETON, RANULPH (d. 1246), canon of St. Paul's; king's treasurer; displaced and fined on charge of misapplying revenues, 1232; canon of St. Paul's: imprisoned on false charge of treason, 1239, but released at instance of prelates. [vi. 358]

BRITON or BRETON, WILLIAM (d. 1356), theologian; Franciscan or Cistercian; wrote 'Vocabularium Bibliæ,' a treatise explaining obscure biblical words. [vi. 359]

BRITTAIN, THOMAS (1806-1884), naturalist; professional accountant; one of promoters of Manchester Microscopical Society, 1858; wrote on various subjects, including natural history. [vi. 359]

BRITTON, JOHN (d. 1275). [See BRETON.]

BRITTON, JOHN (1771-1857), antiquary and topographer; cellarman in Smithfield and subsequently attorney's clerk; published 'Adventures of Pizarro,' 1799, and received commission to prepare 'Beauties of Wiltshire,' 1801; first edited with E. W. Brayley [q. v.], and subsequently contributed to 'Beauties of England and Wales,' 1801-14; published 'Architectural Beauties of Great Britain,' 1805-14, with supplement, 1818-26, and other writings, including an 'Autobiography,' 1850. [vi. 360]

BRITTON, THOMAS (1654 ?-1714), the 'musical small-coal man'; vendor of small-coal in Clerkenwell; established over his shop a musical club, where concerts of vocal and instrumental music were given every Thursday, 1678, the greatest performers of the day taking part. He also interested himself in chemistry and the occult sciences, of works relating to which he formed a large collection. His portrait by Woolaston is in National Portrait Gallery. [vi. 361]

BRIWER, WILLIAM (d. 1226). [See BREWER.]

BRIXIUS (d. 1222). [See BRICIE.]

BROADBENT, THOMAS BIGGIN (1793-1817), tutor; son of William Broadbent [q. v.]; graduated at Glasgow, 1813; classical tutor in unitarian academy, Hackney, 1813-16. [vi. 363]

BROADBENT, WILLIAM (1755–1827), unitarian divine; educated at Daventry academy, where he became tutor in classics, 1782, and in mathematics, natural philosophy, and logic, 1784; minister at Warrington, 1792–1822; joined unitarians of Belsham school. [vi. 363]

BROADFOOT, GEORGE (1807–1845), major; ensign 34th regiment Madras native infantry, 1826; commanded sappers in Sir Robert Sale's march from Cabul to Jellálabád, 1841; distinguished himself in Pollock's Cabul campaign; C.B. and commissioner of Moulmein, and later governor-general of Sikh frontier; died of wounds received at Ferozshah. [vi. 364]

BROADHEAD, WILLIAM (1815–1879), instigator of trades-union outrages; worked as saw-grinder successively at Sheffield and Loxley Valley; became secretary of saw-grinders' union, c. 1848, and instigated numerous outrages against employers and anti-union workmen; coming under suspicion (1866) made as witness an avowal of his practices in a government examination of the union's organisation; emigrated to America, 1869; subsequently grocer in Sheffield. He figures as Grotait in Charles Reade's novel, 'Put Yourself in his Place.' [Suppl. i. 294]

BROADWOOD, JOHN (1732–1812), pianoforte manufacturer; entered partnership with Burkhardt Tschudi, a Swiss harpsichord maker, who retired in favour of Broadwood, 1769; his first patent for a 'new constructed pianoforte,' was dated 1783, and the firm rapidly acquired a European reputation. [vi. 364]

BROCAS, SIR BERNARD (1330?–1395), warrior; fought at Poitiers, and probably at Crécy and Najara; constable of Aquitaine; captain of Calais after Edward III's death; M.P. for Hampshire in ten parliaments, 1367–95; chamberlain to Richard II's queen, Anne of Bohemia. [vi. 365]

BROCHMAEL, YSGYTHRAWG (*fl.* 584), king of Powis; probably lord of Uriconium and Severn Valley, and leader of Britons against West-Saxons at Fethan-leag; mentioned in Llywarch Hen's elegy. [vi. 366]

BROCK, DANIEL DE LISLE (1762–1842), bailiff of Guernsey; jurat of royal court of Guernsey, 1798; several times represented Guernsey in London in respect of measures relating to the island; bailiff of Guernsey, 1821–1842. [vi. 366]

BROCK, SIR ISAAC (1769–1812), major-general; brother of Daniel de Lisle Brock [q. v.]; ensign in 8th (king's) regiment, 1785; raised men for an independent company, and was gazetted captain; served in West Indies, 1791–3; major, 1795; served in North Holland, 1799, and in Baltic operations, 1801, in Canada, 1802–5, and from 1806; commanded at Quebec, and (1810) in Upper Canada; major-general, 1811; received surrender of General Hull's forces at Detroit, and was made extra knight of Bath, 1812; killed in engagement with General Van Rennselaer at Queenstown, where a monument to him now stands. [vi. 367]

BROCK, WILLIAM (1807–1875), dissenting divine; studied at Stepney College; advocated abolition of West Indian slavery, 1834; pastor of Bloomsbury Chapel, London, 1848–72; toured in United States, 1866; first president of London Association of Baptist Churches; president of Baptist Union of Great Britain and Ireland, 1869; published controversial works. [vi. 368]

BROCK, WILLIAM JOHN (1817?–1863), divine; B.A.; incumbent of living of Hayfield, 1853–63; published poems and sermons. [vi. 369]

BROCKEDON, WILLIAM (1787–1854), painter, author, and inventor; student at Royal Academy, 1809; contributed regularly to exhibitions of Royal Academy and British Institution, 1812–37, several of his pictures (on biblical subjects) becoming famous; member of academies of Rome and Florence; made many journeys in the Alps, and published 'Illustrations of Passes of the Alps' (1827–9), and 'Journals of Excursions in the Alps' (1833); published 'Italy, Classical, Historical, and Picturesque,' 1842–4, with illustrations by himself and other artists; took out patents for inventions, including a substitute for corks, made with vulcanised india-rubber, and an artificial plumbago for lead-pencils; assisted in founding Royal Geographical Society, 1830, and was member of its first council; F.R.S., 1834. [vi. 369]

BROCKETT, JOHN TROTTER (1788–1842), antiquary; attorney at Newcastle; made collections of books, coins, and medals; originated Newcastle Typographical Society, and contributed to its series of private publications. His own publications include a 'Glossary of North Country Words in Use,' 1825. [vi. 372]

BROCKIE, MARIANUS (1687–1755), Benedictine monk; born in Edinburgh; joined Scottish Benedictines at Ratisbon, 1708; professor of philosophy and divinity at Scottish monastery, Erfurt; on catholic mission in Scotland, 1727–39; prior of St. James's, Ratisbon; wrote 'Monasticon Scoticon'; D.D. [vi. 373]

BROCKLESBY, RICHARD (1636–1714), non-abjuring divine; M.A. Sidney Sussex College, Cambridge, 1660; rector of Folkingham, Lincolnshire; declined to abjure and retired to Stamford; published 'Explication of Gospel Theism,' 1706. [vi. 373]

BROCKLESBY, RICHARD (1722–1797), physician; educated with Burke at school at Ballitore, co. Kildare; studied at Edinburgh; M.D. Leyden, 1745; L.C.P., 1751; incorporated M.D. Cambridge, 1754; F.C.P., 1756; appointed physician to army, 1758, and served in Germany; enjoyed friendship of Burke and Johnson, attending the latter in his last illness; Harveian orator, College of Physicians, 1760; F.R.S.; published 'Œconomical and Medical Observations,' 1764, and other medical works, including an essay on therapeutic application of music. [vi. 374]

BROCKY, CHARLES (1807–1855), portrait and subject painter; born at Temeswar, Hungary; studied in Vienna and Paris; settled in London, c. 1838; exhibited at Royal Academy, 1839–54. [vi. 375]

BRODERIC, ALAN, LORD MIDLETON (1660?–1728). [See BRODRICK.]

BRODERIP, FRANCES FREELING (1830–1878), authoress; *née* Hood; married Rev. John Somerville Broderip, 1849; published works, mainly for the young, in some of which Thomas Hood the younger assisted. [vi. 375]

BRODERIP, JOHN (*d.* 1771?), organist; organist of Wells Cathedral, 1741; sub-treasurer, 1769; published religious musical compositions. [vi. 376]

BRODERIP, ROBERT (*d.* 1808), organist and composer; composed a volume of musical instruction and several collections of psalms, glees, &c. [vi. 376]

BRODERIP, WILLIAM (1683–1726), organist; sub-treasurer of Wells Cathedral, 1706; received cathedral stall, 1708; organist, 1712–26; composed an anthem (in Tudway collection). [vi. 376]

BRODERIP, WILLIAM JOHN (1789–1859), lawyer and naturalist; B.A. Oriel College, Oxford, 1812; called to bar at Lincoln's Inn, 1817; magistrate at Thames police-court, 1822–46, and at Westminster, 1846–56; bencher of Gray's Inn, 1850; treasurer, 1851; F.L.S., 1824; F.R.S., 1828; a founder and original fellow of Zoological Society, 1826; published zoological writings. [vi. 377]

BRODIE, ALEXANDER (1617–1680), Scottish lawyer; educated at King's College, Aberdeen; M.P. for co. Elgin, 1643; representative to general assembly of Scottish church; lord of session and commissioner to meet Charles II at Hague, 1649; retired till 1658; superseded at Restoration. [vi. 377]

BRODIE, ALEXANDER (1830–1867), sculptor; brother of William Brodie (1815–1881) [q. v.]; studied at Royal Scottish Academy; committed suicide. [vi. 378]

BRODIE, SIR BENJAMIN COLLINS, the elder (1783–1862), surgeon; studied anatomy in London under Abernethy and Wilson; entered St. George's Hospital, 1803, as pupil of Sir Everard Home, and was surgeon, 1822; F.R.S., 1810; Copley medallist, 1811, for papers on 'Influence of Brain on Action of the Heart' and 'Effects produced by certain Vegetable Poisons'; published 'Diseases of the Joints,' 1818; professor of comparative anatomy and physiology, Royal College of Surgeons, 1816; attended George IV; sergeant-surgeon to William IV, 1832, and subsequently to Queen Victoria; created baronet, 1834; president of Royal Society, 1858–61, of Royal College of Surgeons, 1844; D.C.L. Oxford; contributed to scientific publications. [vi. 378]

BRODIE, Sir BENJAMIN COLLINS, the younger (1817–1880), chemist; son of Sir Benjamin Collins Brodie (1783–1862) [q. v.]; educated at Harrow and Balliol College, Oxford; B.A., 1838; professor of chemistry at Oxford, 1855; president of Chemical Society, 1859 and 1860; F.R.S.; hon. D.C.L. Oxford, 1872. His most important discovery was that of graphitic acid. [vi. 380]

BRODIE, DAVID (1709?–1787), captain royal navy; lieutenant in navy, 1736; captain, 1748; served at capture of Port Louis, in unsuccessful attempt on Santiago, and in battle off Havanna, 1748; pensioned, 1753. [vi. 380]

BRODIE, GEORGE (1786?–1867), historian; educated at Edinburgh University; member of Faculty of Advocates, 1811; attacked Stuarts in 'History of British Empire from Accession of Charles I to Restoration'; historiographer of Scotland, 1836. [vi. 381]

BRODIE, PETER BELLINGER (1778–1854), conveyancer; pupil of Charles Butler; called to bar at Inner Temple, 1815; member of real property commission, 1828, assisting largely in drawing up its reports; published 'Treatise on a Tax on Successions to Real and Personal Property,' 1850. [vi. 381]

BRODIE, WILLIAM (d. 1788), burglar; cabinet-maker in Edinburgh, and one of ordinary deacon councillors of the city; assumed leadership of a gang of burglars, who (1788) broke into the excise office, Canongate; hanged, one of his confederates turning king's evidence. [vi. 382]

BRODIE, WILLIAM (1815–1881), sculptor; showed talent for modelling, and was enabled by friends to study at Trustees' School of Design, Edinburgh; member of Royal Scottish Academy, 1859, and secretary, 1876; executed portrait busts of contemporary celebrities. [vi. 383]

BRODRICK, ALAN, Viscount Midleton (1660?–1728), Irish statesman; attainted by Irish parliament of James II as a supporter of William of Orange; king's serjeant, 1691; solicitor-general for Ireland, 1695–1703; member for city of Cork in Irish parliament, 1692; speaker, 1703; attorney-general for Ireland, 1707; chief-justice of queen's bench, 1710; dismissed for revolutionary principles, 1711; again member for city of Cork and speaker, 1713; lord chancellor of Ireland, 1714–25; made Baron Brodrick of Midleton, 1715, and Viscount Midleton, 1717. [vi. 383]

BRODRICK, THOMAS (d. 1769), vice-admiral; entered navy, c. 1723; lieutenant, 1739; served at Porto Bello, 1731, and, as commander, at Cartagena, 1741; in Leeward Islands, 1744–8; rear-admiral in Mediterranean, 1756; vice-admiral (1759) at blockades of Toulon and Cadiz. [vi. 384]

BROGHILL, Baron (1621–1679). [See Boyle, Roger.]

BROGRAVE, Sir JOHN (d. 1613), lawyer; autumn reader at Gray's Inn, 1576; treasurer, 1580 and 1584; attorney for duchy of Lancaster, 1580; counsel to Cambridge University, 1581; knighted by James I; left legal writings. [vi. 385]

BROKE. [See also Brook and Brooke.]

BROKE or **BROOKE,** ARTHUR (d. 1563), translator; author of 'The Tragicall Historye of Romeus and Iulieth,' 1562, a free translation from the French version of Bandello's Italian story, in the 'Histoires Tragiques' (Paris, 1559) of Pierre Boaistuau de Launay and Belle-Forest. The volume is the source whence Shakespeare drew the plot of 'Romeo and Juliet.' [vi. 385]

BROKE, Sir PHILIP BOWES VERE (1776–1841), rear-admiral; educated at Royal Naval Academy, Portsmouth dockyard; entered navy, 1792; served in Mediterranean; captain, 1801; commanded Shannon on coast of Spitzbergen, 1807, and at reduction of Madeira; engaged in cruising on outbreak of American war, 1812, bringing his crew to high state of proficiency; captured American frigate Chesapeake; received severe wound and returned to England, 1813; created baronet, 1813; K.C.B., 1815; rear-admiral, 1830. [vi. 386]

BROKE or **BROOKE,** Sir RICHARD (d. 1529), chief baron of exchequer; double reader at Middle Temple, and serjeant-at-law, 1510; under sheriff and (1511–20) recorder of London, representing city in several parliaments;

judge of common pleas and knight, 1520; chief baron of exchequer, 1526. [vi. 388]

BROKE or **BROOKE,** Sir ROBERT (d. 1558), speaker; B.A. Oxford, 1521; autumn reader at Middle Temple, 1542; double reader, 1551; common serjeant and (1545) recorder of London, representing city in several parliaments; serjeant-at-law, 1552; speaker of House of Commons, 1554; chief-justice of common pleas, 1554; knighted, 1555; left legal works (including 'Abridgement' of year books down to his time) published posthumously. [vi. 389]

BROKE or **BROOK,** THOMAS (fl. 1550), translator; alderman, chief clerk of exchequer and customer of Calais; adopted 'reformed' opinions and endured much persecution; imprisoned in the Fleet, 1539 and 1540–2; M.P., 1539; paymaster of Dover, 1549; published translations of religious works, including the preface to John Calvin's Geneva Book of Common Prayer. [vi. 390]

BROKESBY or **BROOKESBUY,** FRANCIS (1637–1714), nonjuring divine; fellow of Trinity College, Cambridge; B.D., 1666; rector of Rowley, Yorkshire, 1670; deprived for refusing oath to William and Mary, 1690; chaplain to nonjurors of St. John's College, Oxford, 1706; refused oath of abjuration on death of James II; published religious, antiquarian, and other works. [vi. 391]

BROME, ADAM DE (d. 1332), founder (1324) and first provost (1325) of Oriel College, Oxford; chancellor of Durham, 1316. [vi. 392]

BROME, ALEXANDER (1620–1666), poet; attorney; royalist in civil war; published dramatic and poetical works, and edited plays by Richard Brome [q. v.], and variorum translation of Horace, 1666. [vi. 392]

BROME, JAMES (d. 1719), writer of travels; vicar of Newington, 1677; chaplain to Cinque ports; published books of English and continental travel. [vi. 393]

BROME, RICHARD (d. 1652?), dramatist; servant to Ben Jonson, whose friendship he afterwards enjoyed; wrote in conjunction with Jonson's eldest son, Benjamin, 'A Fault in Friendship,' a comedy, 1623; subsequently wrote plays for the Globe and Blackfriars (King's players), and the Cockpit in Drury Lane and Salisbury Court in Fleet Street (Queen's players), and other theatres; associated with Thomas Heywood in authorship of 'Late Lancashire Witches,' printed 1634. His works (twenty-four in number) include: 'A Jovial Crew,' acted 1641, printed 1652; 'The Northern Lass,' printed 1632; 'Queen and Concubine,' printed 1659, and 'Queen's Exchange,' printed 1657, hints for which were probably taken from Shakespeare's 'Winter's Tale,' 'Henry VIII,' 'King Lear,' and 'Macbeth.' Some of his plays may be described as comedies of actual life after the model of Jonson, others as romantic comedies. The two species, however, are not strictly kept asunder. Ten plays were published under the care of Alexander Brome (no relation) [q. v.] [vi. 393]

BROME, THOMAS (d. 1380), Carmelite divine; D.D. Oxford; prior of Carmelite monastery in London; provincial in England, 1362–79; wrote religious works. [vi. 397]

BROMFIELD, EDMUND DE (d. 1393), bishop of Llandaff; monk of Benedictine monastery, Bury St. Edmunds; sent to Rome as public procurator for Benedictine order; appointed by pope, abbot of Bury St. Edmunds, and, on arrival in England, imprisoned ten years under statute of Provisors; bishop of Llandaff, 1389. [vi. 397]

BROMFIELD, WILLIAM (1712–1792), surgeon; surgeon to Lock Hospital (the plan of which he formed with Martin Madan), to St. George's Hospital, and to George III's queen; published surgical works. [vi. 398]

BROMFIELD, WILLIAM ARNOLD (1801–1851), botanist; M.B. Glasgow, 1823; travelled in many parts of the world, and died at Damascus; made collections for flora of Isle of Wight, published 1856. [vi. 398]

BROMHALL, ANDREW (fl. 1659), divine; rector of Maiden Newton, Dorsetshire; one of 'triers' for Dorsetshire, commissioned to eject immoral and inefficient ministers, 1653–4. [vi. 399]

BROMLEY, HENRY (pseudonym) (fl. 1793). [See Wilson, Anthony.]

BROMLEY, JAMES (1800–1838), mezzotint-engraver; son of William Bromley (1769–1842) [q. v.]; exhibited at Suffolk Street Gallery, 1829–33.   [vi. 399]

BROMLEY, JOHN (*d.* 1717), translator; probably M.A. Christ Church, Oxford, 1688; curate of St. Giles's-in-the-Fields; joined Roman catholic church; corrector of press in king's printing house; probably translator of 'Canons and Decrees of the Council of Trent,' 1687.
                                                   [vi. 399]

BROMLEY, SIR RICHARD MADOX (1813–1865), civil servant; entered admiralty department of civil service, 1829; secretary to commission for auditing public accounts, 1848; civil C.B., 1854; accountant-general of navy during Russian war; K.C.B., 1858; commissioner of Greenwich Hospital, 1863.   [vi. 399]

BROMLEY, SIR THOMAS (*d.* 1555 ?), judge; reader at Inner Temple, 1532 and 1539; king's serjeant, 1540; judge of king's bench, 1544; on Edward VI's council of regency; implicated in Northumberland's plot, but escaped punishment; chief-justice of common pleas, 1553–5.   [vi. 400]

BROMLEY, SIR THOMAS (1530–1587), lord chancellor; B.C.L. Oxford, 1560; autumn reader at Middle Temple, 1566; recorder of London, 1566–9; solicitor-general, 1569; treasurer of Inner Temple, 1574; lord chancellor, 1579; took his seat in House of Lords, 1582; presided over trial of Mary Queen of Scots, 1586.
                                                   [vi. 400]

BROMLEY, VALENTINE WALTER (1848–1877), painter; associate of Institute of Painters in Water-Colours; contributed to 'Illustrated London News.'
                                                   [vi. 403]

BROMLEY, WILLIAM (1664–1732), secretary of state; B.A. Christ Church, Oxford, 1681; travelled on continent and published, 1692 and 1702, accounts of his tours; knight for Warwickshire, 1689; refused allegiance to William III; M.P. for Oxford University, 1702–32; D.C.L., 1702; speaker of House of Commons, 1710; secretary of state, 1713–4.   [vi. 403]

BROMLEY, WILLIAM (1699 ?–1737), politician; son of William Bromley (1664–1732) [q. v.]; D.C.L. Oriel College, Oxford, 1732; M.P. for borough of Warwick, 1727, and for Oxford University, 1737.   [vi. 404]

BROMLEY, WILLIAM (1769–1842), line-engraver; associate engraver, 1819, of Royal Academy, where he exhibited between 1786 and 1842; engraved G. J. Corbould's drawings of Elgin marbles.   [vi. 404]

BROMPTON, JOHN (*fl.* 1436), supposed chronicler; abbot of Jorvaux, 1436; possibly author of chronicle from coming of St. Augustine to death of Richard I. [vi. 405]

BROMPTON, RICHARD (*d.* 1782), portrait-painter; studied under Benjamin Wilson and Raphael Mengs; portrait-painter to Empress of Russia. William Pitt, first earl of Chatham, sat to him.   [vi. 405]

BROMSGROVE, RICHARD (*d.* 1435), successively monk, infirmarer, and, 1418, abbot of Benedictine abbey of Evesham.   [vi. 405]

BROMYARDE, JOHN DE (*fl.* 1390), Dominican friar; studied at Oxford; lectured on theology at Cambridge; opposed Wycliffe's doctrines; wrote 'Summa Predicantium' (Nuremberg, 1485).   [vi. 405]

BRONTË, ANNE (1820–1849), authoress; sister of Charlotte Brontë [q. v.]; governess, 1839, and after; wrote verse, and, under the pseudonym of Acton Bell, assisted her sisters in 'Poems by Currer, Ellis, and Acton Bell,' 1846; published 'Tenant of Wildfell Hall' and 'Agnes Grey,' 1848.   [vi. 406]

BRONTË, CHARLOTTE, afterwards NICHOLLS (1816–1855), novelist; daughter of Patrick Brontë [q. v.], sister of Emily Jane Brontë [q. v.], and Anne Brontë [q. v.]; educated at a school for clergymen's daughters at Cowan's Bridge, and, 1831–2, at Roehead, where she taught, 1835–8; governess, 1839 and 1841; went, in 1842, with Emily Brontë to study languages at a school at Brussels, where, during 1843, she was retained as teacher; much distressed by the vicious habits of her brother; wrote, her sisters co-operating, a volume of verse entitled 'Poems by Currer, Ellis, and Acton Bell,' 1846; her 'Professor' refused by Messrs. Smith & Elder, while Emily's 'Wuthering Heights' and

Anne's 'Agnes Grey' were accepted in 1847 by J. Cautley Newby, and published in 1848; her 'Jane Eyre,' accepted with enthusiasm by Smith & Elder, 1847, achieved immediate success. Miss Brontë then produced 'Shirley,' 1849, and 'Villette,' 1853, both under the pseudonym of Currer Bell. The secret of authorship, which by 1849 had become transparent, was in that year openly abandoned. She married, in 1854, her father's curate, the Rev. A. B. Nicholls. Her 'Professor' appeared posthumously in 1857, and 'Emma,' a fragment, in the 'Cornhill Magazine,' 1860.   [vi. 406]

BRONTË, EMILY JANE (1818–1848), authoress; sister of Charlotte Brontë [q. v.]; assisted her sisters in 'Poems by Currer, Ellis, and Acton Bell,' 1846, using pseudonym of Ellis Bell; regarded by some as the ablest of the sisters; published 'Wuthering Heights,' 1848. [vi. 406]

BRONTË, PATRICK (1777–1861), author and perpetual curate of Haworth, Yorkshire, from 1820 till death; born in co. Down of parents named Prunty; B.A. St. John's College, Cambridge, 1806; was father of Anne, Charlotte, Emily Jane Brontë, and four other children, all of whom he survived.   [vi. 406]

BRONTË, PATRICK BRANWELL (1817–1848), brother of Charlotte Brontë [q. v.]; clerk on the Leeds and Manchester railroad; dismissed for culpable negligence, 1842; private tutor, 1843–5; took to opium and died of consumption.   [vi. 406]

BROOK. [See also BROKE and BROOKE.]

BROOK, ABRAHAM (*fl.* 1789), bookseller of Norwich; published work on physics, 1789.   [vi. 413]

BROOK, SIR BASIL (1576–1646 ?), royalist; knighted, 1604; committed to Tower by House of Commons, 1644; imprisoned in King's Bench, 1645; translated from French 'Entertainments for Lent.'   [vi. 413]

BROOK, BENJAMIN (1776–1848), nonconformist divine; studied at Rotherham College; congregationalist minister at Tutbury, Staffordshire, 1801–30; member of educational board of Springhill College, opened 1838; wrote on history of religious liberty.   [vi. 414]

BROOK, CHARLES (1814–1872), philanthropist; partner in banking and cotton-spinning firm of Jonas Brook Brothers, at Melton; spent large sums of money in promoting welfare of his workpeople.   [vi. 414]

BROOK, DAVID (*d.* 1558), judge; reader at Inner Temple, 1534 and 1540; treasurer, 1540; serjeant-at-law, c. 1547; received coif, 1547; king's serjeant, 1551; lord chief baron of exchequer, 1553.   [vi. 414]

BROOKBANK, BROOKSBANK, or BROOKES-BANKE, JOSEPH (*b.* 1612), minister and schoolmaster; B.A. Brasenose College, Oxford; minister at West Wycombe, Buckinghamshire, c. 1648; minister and schoolmaster in Jerusalem Court, Fleet Street, 1654; published educational and religious works.   [vi. 415]

BROOKE. [See also BROKE and BROOK.]

BROOKE, BARONS. [See GREVILLE, SIR FULKE, first BARON, 1554–1628; GREVILLE, ROBERT, second BARON, 1608–1643.]

BROOKE, SIR ARTHUR (1772–1843), lieutenant-general; ensign, 44th regiment, 1792; in West Indies, 1795–8; lieutenant-colonel, 1804; commanded 44th in garrison at Malta, 1804–12; colonel, 1813; in Spain, 1813; C.B.; served in United States; governor of Yarmouth; colonel of 86th regiment and K.C.B., 1833; lieutenant-general, 1837.   [vi. 416]

BROOKE, SIR ARTHUR DE CAPELL (1791–1858), baronet; M.A. Magdalen College, Oxford, 1816; entered army and (1846) became major; spent many years in foreign travel; originated and was president of Raleigh Club, which became merged in Royal Geographical Society; M.R.S.; published works of travel.   [vi. 417]

BROOKE, CHARLES (1777–1852), jesuit from 1818; provincial, 1826–32; superior of Stonyhurst College; collected materials for history of English province.
                                                   [vi. 417]

BROOKE, CHARLES (1804–1879), surgeon and inventor; educated at Rugby and St. John's College, Cambridge; B.M., 1828; M.A., 1853; studied medicine at St. Bartholomew's Hospital; M.C.S., 1834; F.C.S., 1844;

on surgical staff of Metropolitan Free Hospital and Westminster Hospital; F.R.S., 1847; invented self-recording meteorological instruments, and published religious and scientific works. [vi. 417]

BROOKE, CHARLOTTE (*d.* 1793), authoress; daughter of Henry Brooke (1703?–1783) [q. v.]; published 'Reliques of Irish Poetry' (consisting of Irish poems in original character with translations in English verse), 1789, and other works. [vi. 418]

BROOKE, CHRISTOPHER (*d.* 1628), poet; studied law at Lincoln's Inn; bencher and summer reader, 1614; became acquainted with Selden, Jonson, Drayton, and John Davies of Hereford. His works include 'The Ghost of Richard the Third,' 1614, and an eclogue appended to William Browne's 'Shepheard's Pipe,' 1614. [vi. 419]

BROOKE, ELIZABETH, LADY (1601–1683), religious writer; *née* Colepeper; married Sir Robert Brooke, 1620. Selections from her religious writings appeared posthumously. [vi. 420]

BROOKE, MRS. FRANCES (1724–1789), authoress; *née* Moore; conducted weekly periodical called 'The Old Maid,' 1755; married, *c.* 1756, Rev. John Brooke, D.D., rector of Colney, Norfolk, and chaplain to garrison of Quebec, whither the pair went soon after marriage; published 'Virginia,' a tragedy, 1756; produced several novels, and a tragedy 'The Siege of Sinope' (played at Covent Garden, 1781), and in 1783 'Rosina,' a highly successful musical entertainment. [vi. 420]

BROOKE, GEORGE (1568–1603), conspirator; M.A. King's College, Cambridge, 1586; prebendary of York; disappointed of mastership of hospital of St. Cross, near Winchester, promised him by Elizabeth, in consequence of which he formed, 1603, with Sir Griffin Markham, scheme to obtain possession of James I's person, from which sprang the 'Bye' plot; sent to Tower and subsequently executed at Winchester. [vi. 421]

BROOKE, GUSTAVUS VAUGHAN (1818–1866), actor; first appeared at Dublin, 1833; with Macready at Drury Lane, 1840; played Othello with success at Olympic, 1848, and having appeared as Richard III, Shylock, Virginius, Hamlet, and Brutus, successfully in United States and Australia, experienced misfortune as manager of Astor Place Opera House, New York, 1852, and, later, in Melbourne; drowned at sea. [vi. 422]

BROOKE, HENRY, eighth BARON COBHAM (*d.* 1619), conspirator; brother of George Brooke [q. v.]; friend and political ally of Sir Robert Cecil, who married his sister Elizabeth; warden of Cinque ports, 1597; K.G., 1599; arrested (1603) for complicity in 'Main' plot to place Arabella Stuart on throne; declared that he had been instigated to communicate with the ambassador of the Spanish archduke by Sir Walter Ralegh, who was accordingly also arrested; condemned to death, but confined in Tower till 1619. [vi. 423]

BROOKE, HENRY (1694–1757), divine; M.A. Oriel College, Oxford, 1720; D.C.L., 1727; fellow; head-master of Manchester grammar school (where he was educated), 1727–49; fellow of collegiate church, 1728; held living of Tortworth, Gloucestershire, 1730–57; published 'Essay concerning Christian Peaceableness' (1741) and other writings. [vi. 424]

BROOKE, HENRY (1703?–1783), author; educated at Trinity College, Dublin; studied at Temple, London; published, 1735, a poem called 'Universal Beauty,' said to have furnished foundation for Darwin's 'Botanic Garden'; published tragedy entitled 'Gustavus Vasa,' which was prohibited by lord chamberlain, but was subsequently acted in Dublin, where other dramatic pieces by him were produced; settled in Dublin, *c.* 1740; contributed to Edward Moore's 'Fables for Female Sex,' published 1744; barrack-master at Dublin, *c.* 1745; employed by Irish Roman catholics to advocate publicly their claims for relaxation of penal laws, and published 'Tryal of Cause of Roman Catholics,' 1761; published 'Juliet Grenville,' a novel, 1774. An edition of his works was issued by his daughter, Charlotte Brooke [q. v.], 1792. [vi. 424]

BROOKE, HENRY (1738–1806), painter; historical painter in London, 1761–7; subsequently met with pecuniary embarrassments. [vi. 427]

BROOKE, HENRY JAMES (1771–1857), crystallographer; studied for bar, but subsequently engaged in various businesses; collected minerals; F.G.S., 1815; F.L.S., 1818; F.R.S., 1819; published 'Introduction to Crystallography,' 1823. [vi. 427]

BROOKE, HUMPHREY (1617–1693), physician; M.D. St. John's College, Oxford, 1659; F.C.P., 1674; censor; published medical and other writings. [vi. 427]

BROOKE, SIR JAMES (1803–1868), rájá of Saráwak; born at Benares; educated at Norwich; ran away from school and was made cadet of infantry in Bengal, *c.* 1819; served in Burma war, wounded and invalided home; resigned East India Company's service, 1830; made voyage in private schooner to Borneo, 1838, and, proceeding to Saráwak, was received courteously by Muda Hassim, uncle of the Malay sultan of Brunei, the nominal ruler of the whole island; revisited Saráwak, 1840, took part in suppressing rebellion then in progress, and at invitation of Muda Hassim assumed government of the country, 1841; substituted simple scheme of taxation for unpopular system of forced trade; put down piracy among Malays, Dayáks, and other tribes in Bornean seas; charges of cruelty and illegal conduct brought against him, but found by a government commission of inquiry at Singapore impossible to establish; revisited England, 1847; hon. D.C.L. Oxford; K.C.B.; British commissioner and consul-general of Borneo, and governor of Labuan; finally left Saráwak, 1863. [vi. 428]

BROOKE, JOHN (*d.* 1582), translator; B.A. Trinity College, Cambridge, 1554; translated religious works from the French. [vi. 430]

BROOKE, JOHN CHARLES (1748–1794), Somerset herald; Rouge Croix pursuivant, 1773; Somerset herald, 1777; F.S.A., 1775; killed in accident at Haymarket Theatre; left manuscript collections, chiefly relating to Yorkshire. [vi. 430]

BROOKE, RALPH (1553–1625), herald; educated at Merchant Taylors' School; Rouge Croix pursuivant in College of Arms, 1580; York herald, 1593; published, 1597, 'A Discoverie of certaine Errrours' in Camden's 'Britannia' (1594), which occasioned a bitter controversy with Camden and Vincent. Brooke's 'Catalogue of English kings, princes, and peers,' appeared in 1619. [vi. 431]

BROOKE, RICHARD (1791–1861), antiquary; solicitor at Liverpool; member of Society of Antiquaries and of council of Liverpool Literary and Philosophical Society; published antiquarian writings chiefly relating to English battlefields of the fifteenth century. [vi. 432]

BROOKE, ROBERT (*d.* 1802?), governor of St. Helena; ensign on Bengal establishment of East India Company, 1764; substantive captain, 1767; served against Cossim Ali, Soojah Dowlah, and Hyder Ali (1768–1769); collector of Corah; served in Rohilla war; erected industrial village of Prosperous, co. Kildare, with object of developing cotton manufacture, the undertaking, however, failing commercially, 1787; governor of St. Helena, *c.* 1787. [vi. 432]

BROOKE, SAMUEL (*d.* 1631), master of Trinity College, Cambridge; brother of Christopher Brooke [q. v.]; M.A. Trinity College, Cambridge, 1604; D.D., 1615; chaplain to Henry, prince of Wales, and subsequently to James I and Charles I; professor of divinity, Gresham College, 1612–29; rector of St. Margaret's, Lothbury, London, 1618; incorporated D.D. Oxford, 1621; master of Trinity College, Cambridge, 1629; wrote Latin plays and religious treatises. [vi. 433]

BROOKE, WILLIAM HENRY (*d.* 1860), satirical draughtsman; portrait-painter in London; contributed drawings to 'Satirist,' a monthly periodical, 1812–14; exhibited at Royal Academy, 1810–26. [vi. 434]

BROOKE, ZACHARY (1716–1788), divine; fellow, St. John's College, Cambridge; M.A., 1741; D.D., 1753; Margaret professor of divinity, Cambridge, 1765; chaplain to the king; published controversial writings. [vi. 434]

BROOKES, JOSHUA (1754–1821), eccentric divine; of humble origin; educated with friends' assistance at Brasenose College, Oxford; M.A., 1781; chaplain of collegiate church, Manchester, 1790–1821; assistant-master at Manchester grammar school, where his eccentric manners and deficiency as teacher, though not as scholar, made him unpopular. [vi. 434]

BROOKES, JOSHUA (1761–1833), anatomist ; studied in London and Paris ; successfully taught anatomy in London, and formed large private museum ; F.R.S. ; published writings, mainly anatomical. [vi. 435]

BROOKES, RICHARD (*fl.* 1750), physician ; published compilations and translations on medicine and other subjects, including a ' General Gazetteer,' 1762. [vi. 436]

BROOKFIELD, WILLIAM HENRY (1809–1874), divine ; M.A. Trinity College, Cambridge, 1836 ; curate of St. Luke's, Berwick Street, 1841 ; inspector of schools, 1848 ; chaplain in ordinary to Queen Victoria. [vi. 436]

BROOKING, CHARLES (1723–1759), marine painter ; originally ship painter at Deptford ; became noted as painter of sea-pieces. [vi. 436]

BROOKS, CHARLES WILLIAM SHIRLEY (1816–1874), editor of ' Punch ' ; articled as solicitor ; passed Incorporated Law Society's examination, 1838 ; parliamentary reporter to ' Morning Chronicle,' which journal sent him (1853), as special commissioner to inquire into subject of labour and the poor in Russia, Syria, and Egypt ; leader-writer on ' Illustrated London News ' ; conducted ' Literary Gazette,' 1858–9 ; joined staff of ' Punch,' 1851, contributing under signature ' Epicurus Rotundus ' ; editor, 1870 ; F.S.A., 1872 ; published several novels, dramatic pieces, and volumes of humorous verse. [vi. 437]

BROOKS, FERDINAND (1584?–1642). [See GREEN, HUGH.]

BROOKS, GABRIEL (1704–1741), calligrapher ; contributed plates to ' Universal Penman ' (1741). [vi. 438]

BROOKS, JAMES (1512–1560), bishop of Gloucester ; fellow, Corpus Christi College, Oxford, 1532 ; B.A., 1532 ; D.D., 1546 ; master of Balliol College, 1547 ; chaplain and almoner to Bishop Gardiner ; bishop of Gloucester, 1554 ; delegated by the pope to examine Cranmer, Ridley, and Latimer, 1555 ; commissioned by Cardinal Pole to visit Oxford University, 1558 ; refused oath of supremacy to Elizabeth, and died in prison. [vi. 438]

BROOKS, JOHN (*fl.* 1755), engraver : enameller of china in Dublin and London. [vi. 439]

BROOKS, THOMAS (1608–1680), puritan divine ; educated at Emmanuel College, Cambridge ; chaplain to Rainsborough, admiral of Parliamentary fleet ; minister at St. Margaret's, Fish Street Hill, 1653 ; ejected, 1662 ; continued ministry in a building in Moorfields ; published religious works. [vi. 439]

BROOKSHAW, RICHARD (*fl.* 1804), mezzotint-engraver : worked in England and subsequently in Paris, where his plates gained him a high reputation. [vi. 440]

BROOM, HERBERT (1815–1882), legal writer ; graduated at Trinity College, Cambridge, 1837 ; LL.D., 1864 ; called to bar at Inner Temple, 1840 ; published legal works and two novels. [vi. 440]

BROOME, SIR FREDERICK NAPIER (1842–1896), colonial governor ; engaged in sheep-farming in New Zealand, 1857–69 ; contributor to ' Times ' ; colonial secretary of Natal, 1875, and of Mauritius, 1877 ; lieutenant-governor of Mauritius, 1880 ; governor of Western Australia, 1882–90, Barbados, 1890, and later of Trinidad. [Suppl. i. 295]

BROOME, WILLIAM (1689–1745), translator of Homer ; educated at Eton and St. John's College, Cambridge ; assisted Ozell and Oldisworth in prose translation of ' Iliad ' (published, 1712) ; employed by Pope in condensing Eustathius's notes on Homer ; collaborated with Pope and Fenton in translation of ' Odyssey,' 1722–6 ; LL.D., 1728 ; rector of Oakley Magna and vicar of Eye, Suffolk ; chaplain to Lord Cornwallis ; published sermons and poems and contributed translations of the pseudo-Anacreon to ' Gentleman's Magazine.' [vi. 441]

BROOMFIELD, MATTHEW (*fl.* 1550), Welsh poet ; left works in manuscript. [vi. 442]

BROTHERS, RICHARD (1757–1824), enthusiast ; born at Placentia, Newfoundland ; studied at Woolwich ; midshipman, *c.* 1771 ; served as master's mate at Ushant ;

in West Indies, 1781 : travelled in France, Spain, and Italy ; came to London, 1787, and, *c.* 1792, gave himself out to be a descendant of David, declaring that he was to be ' revealed ' as prince of the Hebrews and ruler of the world, and that King George must deliver up his crown to him ; arrested on charge of treasonable practices, 1795, and confined as criminal lunatic, but subsequently removed to private asylum at Islington ; released (1806), warrant for high treason being withdrawn ; published ' A Revealed Knowledge of the Prophecies and Times, wrote under the direction of the Lord God,' 2 vols. 1794, and other works of similar tendency. [vi. 442]

BROTHERTON, EDWARD (1814–1866), Swedenborgian ; engaged in silk trade at Manchester, and on retiring interested himself in popular education, his letters to Manchester newspapers leading to formation of Education Aid Society ; published writings on mormonism, spiritualism, and popular education. [vi. 445]

BROTHERTON, JOSEPH (1783–1857), parliamentary reformer : engaged in cotton manufacture at Manchester till 1819 ; joined Bible Christian Church, 1805, becoming pastor, 1818 ; M.P. for Salford, 1832–57 ; chairman of private bills committee, free-trader and reformer ; contributed essays to ' Letters on Religious Subjects ' (*c.* 1819). [vi. 446]

BROTHERTON, THOMAS OF (1300–1338). [See THOMAS.]

BROTHERTON, SIR THOMAS WILLIAM (1785–1868), general ; ensign, 1800 ; captain, 1801 ; in Egypt, 1801, Hanover, 1805, and Peninsula, 1808–14 ; major, 1812 ; C.B., 1814 ; lieutenant-colonel, 1817 ; colonel and aide-de-camp to king, 1830 ; general, 1860 ; G.C.B., 1861. [vi. 446]

BROUGH, ROBERT BARNABAS (1828–1860), writer ; said to have practised as portrait-painter in Manchester ; set on foot ' Liverpool Lion,' weekly satirical journal ; wrote alone, or in conjunction with his brother, William Brough (1826–1870) [q. v.], series of burlesques, played with some success at London theatres. [vi. 447]

BROUGH, WILLIAM (*d.* 1671), dean of Gloucester ; B.D. Christ's College, Cambridge, 1627 ; D.D., 1636 ; chaplain to the king ; canon of Windsor, 1638 ; ejected by parliamentary commissioners : dean of Gloucester, 1644 ; D.D. Oxford, 1645 ; published religious works. [vi. 448]

BROUGH, WILLIAM (1826–1870), journalist and author ; brother of Robert Barnabas Brough [q. v.], with whom he was associated in dramatic pieces. [vi. 448]

BROUGHAM, HENRY (1665–1698), divine ; M.A. Queen's College, Oxford, 1689 ; prebendary of Lincoln, 1691 ; published, 1694, work proving spuriousness of ' Genuine Remains ' of Dr. Barlow, late bishop of Lincoln, published by Sir Peter Pett, 1692, Barlow having left his remains to Brougham and William Offley, on condition of their not making them public. [vi. 448]

BROUGHAM, HENRY PETER, BARON BROUGHAM AND VAUX (1778–1868), lord chancellor ; educated at high school and university, Edinburgh ; passed advocate, 1800 ; went on southern circuit ; joined, 1802, founders of ' Edinburgh Review,' contributing three articles to the first number ; admitted member of Lincoln's Inn, 1803 ; supported himself in London mainly by writing for ' Edinburgh Review ' ; secretary to Lords Rosslyn and St. Vincent on mission to Lisbon, 1806 ; secured good opinion of Wilberforce by his sympathy with anti-slavery movement : called to bar, 1808 ; M.P. for Camelford, 1810, for Winchelsea, 1815 ; advocated retrenchment and a sound commercial policy, drew attention to importance of popular education, and instituted inquiry into charity abuses, which he extended to Eton, Winchester, and the universities ; was constantly consulted by the Princess of Wales, who, on becoming queen, appointed him her attorney-general ; called within the bar, 1820 ; defended Queen Caroline during her trial, 1820 ; urged government to resist the dictation of the Holy Alliance in Europe, 1824 ; proposed vote of censure on government of Demerara, 1824 ; lord rector of Glasgow University, 1825 ; brought forward, 1828, scheme of law reform, which was occasion of vast improvement in system of common law procedure ; M.P. for Knaresborough, and later for Yorkshire, 1830 ; received great seal, and was elevated to peerage as Baron Brougham and Vaux, 1830 ; effected

considerable improvements in court of chancery, the
abolition of court of delegates, the substitution for it of
judicial committee of privy council, and institution of
the central criminal court; brought in a bankruptcy
bill which eventually became basis of a statute; published
'Observations on Education of the People,' 1825; formed
Society for Diffusion of Useful Knowledge, 1825; founded
London University, 1828; made celebrated speech on
second reading of Reform Bill, 1831; lost office on dismissal of Lord Melbourne's government, 1834; advocated
immediate abolition of slavery, 1838; sat constantly in
supreme court of appeal and in judicial committee of
privy council; strenuously opposed repeal of navigation
acts, 1849; president of Social Science Association, 1857
and 1860-5; chancellor of Edinburgh University, 1860;
received second patent of peerage, with remainder to
his brother William and his heirs male, 1860, in recognition of services in cause of education and suppression of
slavery; hon. D.C.L. Oxford; F.R.S. His critical, historical, and miscellaneous writings were published under
his own direction in a collected edition, 11 vols., 1855-61.
His works include 'An Enquiry into the Colonial Policy of
European Powers,' 2 vols. 1803, 'Historical Sketches of
Statesmen in time of George III,' 1839-43, 'Demosthenes
upon the Crown, translated,' 1840, and 'Life and Times
of Lord Brougham,' written by himself, published posthumously, 3 vols., 1871.   [vi. 448]

BROUGHAM, JOHN (1814-1880), actor and dramatist; educated at Trinity College, Dublin; studied surgery at Peter Street Hospital; appeared at Tottenham
Street Theatre, 1830, and at the Olympic, 1831; manager
of Lyceum, 1840; went to New York and managed successively Park Theatre, Niblo's Garden, Brougham's
Lyceum, and Bowery Theatre; in England, 1860-5;
returned to America; acted at Winter Garden Theatre,
1865; manager of Brougham's, 1869; subsequently connected with several stock companies; died at New York;
wrote many dramatic pieces.   [vi. 458]

BROUGHAM, WILLIAM, second BARON BROUGHAM
AND VAUX (1795-1886), brother of Henry Peter, first baron
[q. v.]; B.A. Jesus College, Cambridge, 1819; M.P. for
Southwark, 1831-5; master in chancery, 1835-40.
                                               [vi. 457]

BROUGHTON, BARON (1786-1869). [See HOBHOUSE,
JOHN CAM.]

BROUGHTON, ARTHUR (d. 1796), botanist; M.D.
Edinburgh, 1779; settled in Jamaica, where he died;
published medical and botanical works.   [vi. 459]

BROUGHTON, HUGH (1549-1612), divine and rabbinical scholar; B.A. Magdalene College, Cambridge, 1570;
successively fellow of St. John's and Christ's colleges;
prebendary and reader in divinity at Durham; published
'A Concent of Scripture,' 1588, in which he attempted to
settle the scripture chronology; in Germany, c. 1590-1 and
1592-1603; published at Middleburg 'An Epistle to the
learned Nobilitie of England,' touching translating the
Bible from the Original,' 1597; published, 1599, 'Explication' of article respecting Christ's descent into hell, maintaining that hades was place not of torment but of departed souls; in England, 1603; preacher to English congregation, Middleburg, 1604-11; satirised by Ben Jonson.
His works, which include versions of the prophets, were
collected by Dr. John Lightfoot and published, 1662.
                                               [vi. 459]

BROUGHTON, JOHN (1705-1789), pugilist; attached
himself as 'public bruiser' to George Taylor's booth in
Tottenham Court Road; joined yeoman of guard; established theatre for boxing in Hanway Street, 1742; beaten
by Slack, 1750.   [vi. 462]

BROUGHTON, RICHARD (d. 1634), Roman catholic
historian; studied at Oxford and at English college,
Rheims; priest, 1593; joined catholic mission in England;
vicar-general to Dr. Smith, bishop of Calcedon. His works
include 'The Ecclesiastical Historie of Great Brittaine'
(Douay, 1633).   [vi. 462]

BROUGHTON, SAMUEL DANIEL (1787-1837), army
surgeon; studied at St. George's Hospital; assistant-surgeon, 2nd life guards, 1812; served as additional surgeon,
with temporary rank, in Peninsula, and South of France,
and at Waterloo; surgeon, 1821; F.R.S.; F.G.S.; published
letters relating to campaigning experiences.   [vi. 463]

BROUGHTON, THOMAS (1704-1774), divine; educated at Eton and Gonville and Caius College, Cambridge;
M.A.; vicar of Bedminster, near Bristol, 1744; prebendary
of Salisbury; published biographical and miscellaneous
works, including 'Dictionary of Religions,' 1742, and a
translation of 'Don Quixote,' with the name of Jarvis,
who had been unable to bring the work to a successful
issue, prefixed.   [vi. 464]

BROUGHTON, THOMAS (1712-1777), divine; fellow,
Exeter College, Oxford, 1734; B.A., 1737; joined methodists;
curate at Tower of London, 1736; lecturer at St. Helen's,
Bishopsgate Within, and (1741) at Allhallows, Lombard Street; secretary of Society for Promoting Christian
Knowledge, 1743-77; held living of Wotton, Surrey,
1752-77; published sermons.   [vi. 464]

BROUGHTON, THOMAS DUER (1778-1835), writer
on India; cadet on Bengal establishment, 1795; lieutenant on Madras establishment, 1797; colonel, 1829;
published writings on India and selections from Hindoo
poetry.   [vi. 465]

BROUGHTON, WILLIAM GRANT (1788-1853),
divine; clerk in East India House, 1807-12; entered
Pembroke Hall, Cambridge, 1814; M.A., 1823; D.D.,
1836; chaplain to Tower of London, 1828, and, later,
archdeacon of New South Wales; bishop of Australia,
1836; bishop of Sydney and metropolitan of Australasia, on subdivision of diocese of Australia, 1847; published writings relating to authorship of 'Εἰκὼν Βασιλική,'
and other works.   [vi. 465]

BROUGHTON, WILLIAM ROBERT (1762-1821), navy
captain; employed on survey of Columbia river, c. 1790;
on north-west coast of America, c. 1794; made survey of
coast of Asia, 1794-8; captain, 1797; held command in
Lord Gambier's expedition, 1809; at reduction of Mauritius, 1810; took charge of expedition to Java, 1811;
C.B.; died at Florence; published accounts of his voyages
and surveys.   [vi. 466]

BROUN. [See BROWN and BROWNE.]

BROUN, JOHN ALLAN (1817-1879), magnetician
and meteorologist; educated at Edinburgh University;
director of magnetic observatory at Makerstoun, 1842-9,
the results of his observations forming vols. xvii-xix.
of 'Transactions of Royal Society of Edinburgh' (1845-
1850); director of Trevandrum Magnetic Observatory,
1852; built observatory on Agustia Malley, the highest
peak of Travancore Ghats; left India, 1865; lived successively at Lausanne and Stuttgart, and came to
London, 1873; aided by grant from Royal Society, undertook to complete reduction of magnetic observations
made at colonial stations; M.R.S., 1853. Published reports on Makerstoun and Trevandrum observatories. He
discovered that the earth loses or gains magnetic intensity not locally, but as a whole, and that great magnetic
disturbances proceed from particular solar meridians.
                                               [vi. 467]

BROUN, SIR RICHARD (1801-1858), miscellaneous
writer; succeeded to the baronetcy, 1844; wrote pamphlets, articles, and letters regarding many schemes, of
which 'The London Necropolis and National Mausoleum
at Woking,' 1849, is the most notable.   [vi. 469]

BROUNCKER, HENRY, third VISCOUNT BROUNCKER
(d. 1688), courtier; brother of William Brouncker, second
viscount Brouncker [q. v.]; M.D. Oxford, 1646; commissioner of trade and plantations, 1671.   [vi. 470]

BROUNCKER or BROUNKER, WILLIAM, second
VISCOUNT BROUNCKER of Castle Lyons in Irish peerage
(1620 ?-1684), first president of the Royal Society; M.D.
Oxford, 1647; first to introduce continued fractions and
to give a series for quadrature of a portion of the equi-
lateral hyperbola; original member of Royal Society, 1662,
and first president, 1662-77; president of Gresham College, 1664-7; chancellor of Queen Catherine, 1662; commissioner for executing office of lord high admiral, 1664;
master of St. Catherine's Hospital, 1681.   [vi. 469]

BROWELL, WILLIAM (1759-1831), navy captain;
lieutenant, 1778; served at Toulon, 1794; captain, 1794;
flag-captain under Lord Hugh Seymour at battle off
Lorient, 1795; one of captains of Greenwich Hospital,
1805, and lieutenant-governor, 1809-31.   [vi. 471]

BROWN, CHARLES (*d.* 1753), naval officer ; entered the navy about 1693 ; received his first command, 1709 ; served in the Baltic and the Mediterranean ; distinguished himself at Portobello, 1739 ; commissioner of the navy at Chatham, 1741. [vii. 1]

BROWN, CHARLES ARMITAGE (1786–1842), friend of Keats ; in business at St. Petersburg till 1810 ; inherited a competency, and devoted himself to literature ; met Keats before September, 1817 ; travelled with him in Scotland, 1818, and made him an inmate of his house at Hampstead till 1820 ; in Italy, 1822–35 ; lectured on Keats and Shakespeare ; went to New Zealand, 1841. From him Keats learned Ariosto. His papers about Keats were of service to Lord Houghton in his life of the poet. He published a work on the personal interpretation of Shakespeare's sonnets, 1838. [vii. 1]

BROWN, CHARLES PHILIP (1798–1884), Telugu scholar ; son of David Brown (1763–1812) [q. v.] ; entered Madras civil service, 1817 ; postmaster-general and Telugu translator to the Madras government, 1846–55 ; professor of Telugu in University College, London ; published Telugu grammar, dictionary, and reader, and other linguistic works. [vii. 2]

BROWN, DAVID (*fl.* 1795), landscape-painter ; painted copies of George Morland's works ; exhibited at the Royal Academy, 1792–7 ; taught drawing in the country. [vii. 3]

BROWN, DAVID (1763–1812), Bengal chaplain ; educated at Cambridge ; went to Calcutta, 1786 ; zealous in the cause of missions. [vii. 3]

BROWN, FORD MADOX (1821–1893), painter ; born at Calais ; studied art at Bruges, Ghent, and Antwerp ; exhibited 'The Giaour's Confession' at English Royal Academy, 1841 ; studied in Paris, 1843–4 ; exhibited cartoon, 'Bringing Body of Harold to the Conqueror,' at Westminster Hall, 1844 ; studied in Rome, 1845 ; accepted Dante Gabriel Rossetti as pupil, 1848, and thus came into contact with pre-Raphaelites, by whom his work was gradually influenced ; executed panels for town-hall, Manchester, illustrating history of that city, 1878 ; one of the founders of Hogarth Club ; a leading member, 1861–74, of firm of Morris, Marshall, Faulkner & Co., manufacturers of artistic furniture, founded by William Morris [q. v.] [Suppl. i. 296]

BROWN, GEORGE, or GREGORY in religion (*d.* 1628), an English Benedictine ; died in France. [vii. 4]

BROWN, GEORGE (1650–1730), arithmetician ; minister of Stranraer, and 1680, of Kilmaurs, Ayrshire : invented a method of teaching the simple rules of arithmetic, which he explained in his 'Rotula Arithmetica,' 1700 ; wrote other arithmetical works. [vii. 4]

BROWN, SIR GEORGE (1790–1865), general : ensign, 1806 ; served with distinction in the Peninsula ; lieutenant-colonel, 1814 ; after many staff appointments, became lieutenant-general, 1851 ; K.C.B., 1852 ; commanded the light division in the Crimea, and the English contingent against Kertch, 1855 ; commander-in-chief in Ireland, 1860–5. [vii. 4]

BROWN, GEORGE (1818–1880), Canadian politician ; son of Peter Brown [q. v.] ; publisher and business manager of 'British Chronicle' in New York ; founded 'Globe,' political journal at Toronto, in support of reform party ; abandoned reform party and became extreme radical member for county of Kent in Canadian legislative assembly, 1851 ; member for Lambton county, 1854, Toronto, 1857–61, and South Oxford, 1863–7 ; formed (1858) ministry, which lasted for four days ; president of council, 1864 ; member of senate, 1873 , refused the honour of K.C.M.G., 1879 ; died from effects of shot fired by discharged employé at 'Globe' office. [Suppl. i. 299]

BROWN, GEORGE HILARY (1786–1856), Roman catholic prelate ; professor of theology at Ushaw ; missioner at Lancaster ; vicar-apostolic of the Lancashire district, titular bishop of Tloa, 1840 ; Roman catholic bishop of Liverpool, 1850 ; D.D. [vii. 5]

BROWN, GILBERT (*d.* 1612), Scottish catholic divine ; a Cistercian ; abbot of New Abbey, Kirkcudbright ; an influential opponent of the Reformation in the southwest of Scotland, 1578–94 ; imprisoned, 1605 ; died in exile at Paris ; published controversial tracts. [vii. 5]

BROWN, HUGH STOWELL (1823–1886), baptist minister ; son of Robert Brown (*d.* 1846) [q. v.] ; employed in ordnance surveys in Cheshire, Shrewsbury, and York ; entered London and Birmingham Railway Company's works, 1840 ; baptist minister at Stony Stratford, 1847–86 ; president of Baptist Union, 1878 ; published lectures. [Suppl. i. 300.]

BROWN, IGNATIUS (1630–1679), Roman catholic writer ; of Irish parentage ; educated in Spain ; rector of jesuit college at Poitiers, 1676 ; confessor to queen of Spain ; died at Valladolid ; published controversial tracts. [vii. 6]

BROWN, JAMES (1709–1788), orientalist ; educated at Westminster School ; resident in the Levant, 1722–5, acquiring Turkish and modern Greek ; projected a trade directory for London, 1732, afterwards carried out by Henry Kent ; in 1741 travelled through Russia to Reshd in Persia, where he established a factory ; returned to London, 1746 ; compiled a Persian dictionary and grammar, never published. [vii. 6]

BROWN, JAMES (1812–1881), Roman catholic prelate ; professor at Oscott ; president of Sedgeley Park academy ; bishop of Shrewsbury, 1851 ; showed great energy in his diocese ; D.D. [vii. 7]

BROWN, JAMES BALDWIN, the elder (1785–1843), miscellaneous writer : called to bar at Inner Temple, 1816 ; judge of requests at Oldham, 1840 ; wrote memoir of Howard the philanthropist, and works on the penal laws. [vii. 7]

BROWN, JAMES BALDWIN, the younger (1820–1884), congregational divine : eldest son of James Baldwin Brown the elder [q. v.] ; one of the first graduates of London University ; congregational minister at Derby, 1843, and in London, 1846 ; famous for his liberal theological views both in the pulpit and in the press ; published theological treatises. [vii. 7]

BROWN, JOHN (*d.* 1532), sergeant painter to Henry VIII ; employed chiefly as an heraldic painter ; alderman of London, 1522–5 ; gave his house to be a hall for the company of Painter Stainers. [vii. 8]

BROWN, JOHN (1610 ?–1679), of Wamphray, Scottish ecclesiastic ; educated at Edinburgh ; minister of Wamphray, Dumfries, 1655 ; ejected, 1662, and banished ; minister of the Scottish church at Rotterdam ; published doctrinal and historical treatises. [vii. 9]

BROWN, JOHN (1627 ?–1685), the 'Christian carrier' ; one of the most famous of the covenanter martyrs ; a small farmer and carrier at Priestfield, Ayrshire ; shot by order of Claverhouse at his own door and in his wife's presence. [vii. 9]

BROWN, JOHN (*d.* 1736), chemist ; F.R.S., 1722 ; published discoveries in chemistry. [vii. 10]

BROWN, JOHN (1715–1766), author of the 'Estimate' ; educated at Wigton and St. John's College, Cambridge ; B.A., 1735 ; minor canon of Carlisle and a whig preacher ; rector of Great Horkesley, Essex, 1756, and of St. Nicholas, Newcastle, 1761 ; gained the friendship of Warburton by an 'Essay upon Satire,' published in Dodsley's miscellanies ; wrote an essay (1751) on Shaftesbury's 'Characteristics,' which is memorable for its clear statement of utilitarianism : brought into repute by his 'Estimate of the Manners and Principles of the Times,' 1757 ; committed suicide on being forbidden by the doctors to go to St. Petersburg, where he hoped for a high educational post ; published numerous tragedies, epics, odes, sermons, essays. [vii. 10]

BROWN, JOHN (1722–1787), of Haddington, biblical commentator ; as a herd-boy taught himself Latin, Greek, and Hebrew ; at one time a pedlar ; served as a soldier in the Edinburgh garrison, 1745 ; taught school in Kinross-shire and Midlothian : joined the Burgher church, 1747 ; minister to the Burgher congregation at Haddington, 1750–87 ; acted as professor of divinity to Burgher students after 1768 ; published an explanation of the Westminster Confession of Faith, 1758. His 'Self-interpreting Bible,' 1778, a plain commentary for the people, became immensely popular. [vii. 12]

BROWN, JOHN (1735–1788), medical reformer ; son of a Berwickshire labourer ; educated at Dunse school ; became a private tutor at Edinburgh ; enabled to complete his medical course by the liberality of the Edinburgh medical professors, Monro and Cullen ; vigorously attacked their system in his tutorial lectures, alleging that most diseases were due to weakness, and that their practice of blood-letting was erroneous ; incurred the hostility of the faculty in Edinburgh ; compelled to take his M.D. degree from St. Andrews, 1779 ; in consequence of debt and other troubles left Edinburgh for London in 1786. His 'Elementa Medicinæ,' 1780, setting forth his views, had made him famous, and he was gaining a good practice in London, when he was cut off by apoplexy. His ideas have since been generally adopted.   [vii. 14]

BROWN, JOHN (d. 1829), miscellaneous writer ; published a 'History of Bolton,' 1825 ; went to London to advocate the claims of his friend, Samuel Crompton, the inventor ; committed suicide in despair at his want of success in life.   [vii. 17]

BROWN, JOHN (1754–1832), of Whitburn, Scottish divine ; eldest son of John Brown (1722–1787) [q. v.] ; educated at Edinburgh ; minister of the Burgher church at Whitburn, Linlithgowshire, 1776–1832 ; wrote memoirs of James Hervey, 1806, and many religious treatises.   [vii. 17]

BROWN, JOHN (1778–1848), of Langton, theologian ; minister of Langton, Berwickshire, 1810 ; D.D. Glasgow, 1815 ; joined the Free church in 1843 ; wrote in defence of presbyterian orders and church government.   [vii. 18]

BROWN, JOHN (1784–1858), of Edinburgh, divine ; eldest son of John Brown (1754–1832) [q. v.] ; educated at Edinburgh ; taught school in Fife ; minister of the Burgher church at Biggar, 1806, and of the Relief church at Edinburgh, 1822 ; D.D., 1830 ; professor of exegetics in the Relief college, 1834, and in the United Presbyterian College, 1847 ; wrote expositions of several epistles, and many religious treatises.   [vii. 18]

BROWN, JOHN (1780–1859), geologist ; apprenticed as stonemason ; abandoned his trade (1830) for geological study ; contributed to scientific journals.
          [Suppl. i. 301]

BROWN, JOHN (1797–1861), geographer ; midshipman in the East India Company's service till 1819 ; afterwards a wealthy diamond merchant ; advocated Arctic exploration and the search for Sir John Franklin.
          [vii. 20]

BROWN, JOHN (1810–1882), essayist ; son of John Brown (1784–1858) [q. v.] ; educated at Edinburgh High School and University ; M.D., 1833 ; practised in Edinburgh with success till his death ; published ' Horæ Subsecivæ,' three volumes of essays, 1858–82, and 'Rab and his Friends,' 1859.   [vii. 20]

BROWN, Sir JOHN (1816–1896), pioneer of armour-plate manufacture ; apprenticed to factor at Fargate ; manager of business, 1831 ; invented conical steel spring buffer for railway wagons, 1848 ; opened Atlas Steel Works, Sheffield, 1856 ; originated use of rolled steel armour plating for war vessels, 1860, and his method was approved by royal commission, 1863 ; knighted, 1867.
          [Suppl. i. 301]

BROWN, JOHN CRAWFORD (1805–1867), landscape-painter ; travelled in Holland and Spain.   [vii. 21]

BROWN, JOHN WRIGHT (1836–1863), botanist ; of Edinburgh ; student of Scottish flora.   [vii. 21]

BROWN, JOSEPH (1784–1868), physician ; army surgeon in Wellington's campaigns ; M.D. Edinburgh, 1819 ; practised in Sunderland ; wrote on medical subjects.   [vii. 21]

BROWN, LANCELOT (1715–1783), reviver of the natural style of landscape-gardening ; laid out gardens at Kew and Blenheim ; architect of many country houses ; high sheriff of Huntingdon, 1770 ; known as 'Capability Brown.'   [vii. 22]

BROWN, LEVINIUS (1671–1764), jesuit ; educated at St. Omer and Rome ; resided at Ladyholt, Sussex, 1700, where he was a friend of Alexander Pope ; rector of the English college at Rome, 1723–31 ; provincial, 1733 ; rector of Liège College, 1737 ; spent his last years at St. Omer.
          [vii. 22]

BROWN, OLIVER MADOX (1855–1874), novelist and painter in water-colours ; son of Ford Madox Brown [q. v.] ; first exhibited, 1869 ; published 'Gabriel Denver,'

his first novel, 1873. Other novels are contained in his ' Literary Remains,' 1876.   [vii. 22]

BROWN, PETER (1784–1863), Canadian journalist ; went to New York, 1838, and founded 'British Chronicle ' newspaper ; removed to Toronto, 1843, and renamed paper ' The Banner,' which became organ of Free church of Scotland in Canada.   [Suppl. i. 299]

BROWN, PHILIP (d. 1779), botanist ; medical practitioner in Manchester ; collected foreign plants.
          [vii. 23]

BROWN, RAWDON LUBBOCK (1803–1883), historical student ; resided in Venice, 1833–83, making careful researches among the Venetian archives, especially among the reports sent home by the Venetian ambassadors in London. His 'Calendar of State Papers . . . in the Archives of Venice ' is indispensable for the study of English history from 1202 to 1558. In addition he wrote historical works in English and Italian.   [vii. 24]

BROWN, Sir RICHARD (d. 1669). [See Browne.]

BROWN, ROBERT (d. 1753), painter ; assisted Sir James Thornhill in painting the cupola of St. Paul's ; painted altar-pieces in several London churches. Some of his pictures have been engraved.   [vii. 24]

BROWN, Sir ROBERT (d. 1760), diplomatist ; merchant in Venice and British resident till 1734 ; created baronet, 1732 ; M.P. for Ilchester, 1734 ; a noted miser.
          [vii. 25]

BROWN, ROBERT (1757–1831), writer on agriculture ; a Haddington farmer ; published 'Treatise on Rural Affairs,' 1811, and other works.   [vii. 25]

BROWN, ROBERT (d. 1846), divine ; chaplain of St. Matthew's chapel, Douglas, 1817 ; vicar of Kirk Braddan, 1836–46.   [Suppl. i. 300]

BROWN, ROBERT (1773–1858), botanist ; educated at Aberdeen and Edinburgh ; studied flora of Scotland, 1791 ; army official in Ireland, 1795, and London, 1798 ; naturalist to Captain Flinders's Australasian expedition, 1801–5 ; librarian to the Linnean Society, and to Sir Joseph Banks ; published ' Prodromus Floræ Novæ Hollandiæ et insulæ Van-Diemen,' 1810 ; D.C.L. Oxford, 1832 ; eminent for his investigations into the impregnation of plants.   [vii. 25]

BROWN, ROBERT (1842–1895), geographical compiler ; B.A. Edinburgh, 1860 ; studied at Leyden, Copenhagen, and Rostock ; Ph.D. Rostock ; botanist to British Columbia expedition, and commander of Vancouver expedition, 1864 ; travelled widely, 1861–9 ; lecturer in natural history in high school and Heriot-Watt College, Edinburgh, 1869–76 ; removed to London, 1876 ; compiled several popular geographical works and published scientific and other volumes. He was F.L.S., and on council of Royal Geographical Society.   [Suppl. i. 302]

BROWN, SAMUEL (fl. 1700), surgeon at Madras ; collector of Indian plants.   [vii. 27]

BROWN, Sir SAMUEL (1776–1852), engineer ; naval officer, 1795 ; commander, 1811 ; captain, 1842 ; knighted, 1838 ; devised an improved method of chain-links for ship-cables and suspension bridges.   [vii. 27]

BROWN, SAMUEL (1817–1856), chemist ; M.D. Edinburgh, 1839 ; devoted himself to chemical research ; wrote on the atomic theory.   [vii. 28]

BROWN, SAMUEL (1810–1875), statist ; an actuary by profession ; advocated uniformity of coinage and weights and measures ; joint-editor of the ' Journal of the Institute of Actuaries.'   [vii. 28]

BROWN, STEPHEN (fl. 1340 ?), theologian ; supposed to have been born at Aberdeen ; a Carmelite monk, and reputed author of several theological pieces. His identity is doubtful. Stephen Brown, bishop of Ross in Ireland, 1399, was a different person.   [vii. 28]

BROWN, THOMAS (fl. 1170). [See Thomas.]

BROWN or BROUNS, THOMAS (d. 1445), ecclesiastic ; LL.D. ; sub-dean of Lincoln, 1414 ; dean of Salisbury, 1431 ; bishop of Rochester, 1435, and of Norwich, 1436 ; ambassador to France, 1439.   [vii. 29]

BROWN, THOMAS (fl. 1570), translator ; of Lincoln's Inn ; translated the ' Nobilitas Literata ' of Sturmius.   [vii. 29]

BROWN, THOMAS (1663–1704), satirist; entered Christ Church, Oxford, 1678, where he wrote the famous 'I do not love thee, Dr. Fell,' and other verses, Latin and English; taught school at Kingston-on-Thames; afterwards settled in London as a hack writer and translator; fertile in satirical verses; wrote against Dryden, Durfey, Titus Oates, Sir Richard Blackmore. His collected works appeared in 1707. [vii. 29]

BROWN, THOMAS (1778–1820), the last of the Scottish school of metaphysicians; educated in London and at Edinburgh University; a disciple of Dugald Stewart; criticised Erasmus Darwin's 'Zoonomia,' 1798; studied medicine at Edinburgh, 1798–1803, and practised there, 1806; wrote philosophical tracts, and tried to obtain a chair in the university; elected professor of moral philosophy, 1810; became an extremely popular lecturer; published poetry and essays. His 'Lectures' were once highly esteemed, but were severely criticised by Sir William Hamilton. [vii. 31]

BROWN, THOMAS EDWARD (1830–1897), Manx poet; son of Robert Brown (d. 1846) [q. v.]; educated at King William's College, Isle of Man, and Christ Church, Oxford; B.A., 1853; fellow of Oriel, 1854–8; M.A., 1856; master of King William's College and vice-principal, 1858–61; head-master of Crypt School, Gloucester, 1861–4; second master at Clifton, 1864–93; curate of St. Barnabas, Bristol, 1884–93. He published 'Fo'c'sle Yarns,' 1881, and other tales in verse in Manx dialect appeared in subsequent years. A collected edition of his poems was issued, 1900. [Suppl. i. 303]

BROWN, THOMAS JOSEPH (1798–1880), Roman catholic prelate; Benedictine monk, 1813; professor of theology at Downside, 1823–41; took prominent part in controversies both in the press and on the platform, 1830; D.D., 1834; titular bishop of Apollonia, 1840, and in charge of the Welsh district; bishop of Newport and Menevia, 1850. [vii. 33]

BROWN or **BROWNE**, ULYSSES MAXIMILIAN VON (1705–1757), count, baron de Camus and Mountany; Austrian general; of Irish extraction; entered the Austrian service early and rose rapidly; colonel of infantry, 1734; distinguished himself at the battle of Piacenza and the operations round Genoa, and advanced as far as Toulon, 1743–8; field-marshal, 1753; accepted second command in Bohemia, and died of wounds received before Prague. [vii. 35]

BROWN, WILLIAM (d. 1814), rear-admiral; lieutenant R.N., 1788; commander, 1792; captain, 1793; commanded the Ajax in the action off Cape Finisterre, 22 July 1805, and was partly to blame for its indecisive character; commissioner of dockyards; rear-admiral, 1812; appointed to the Jamaica station, 1813. [vii. 35]

BROWN, WILLIAM (1766–1835), historical writer; D.D. Aberdeen, 1816; minister of Eskdalemuir, Dumfries, 1792–1835; wrote 'Antiquities of the Jews,' 1826. [vii. 36]

BROWN, WILLIAM (1777–1857), admiral in the Argentina service; born in Ireland; taken to America as a boy; went to sea, and was pressed into the English navy, 1796; captain of a merchantman; settled at Buenos Ayres, 1812; accepted naval command, 1814, and defeated two Spanish squadrons; privateer against the Spaniards; defeated a Brazilian fleet in the La Plata, 1826 and 1827, but was then overpowered by superior force; blockaded Monte Video, 1842–5. [vii. 36]

BROWN, SIR WILLIAM (1784–1864), benefactor to Liverpool; engaged in the linen-trade at Baltimore, and opened a branch office in Liverpool, 1809; afterwards an Anglo-American banker; alderman of Liverpool, 1831; advocate of free trade and the volunteer movement; M.P. for South Lancashire, 1846–59; erected free public library and Derby museum at Liverpool, 1860; created baronet, 1863. [vii. 37]

BROWN, WILLIAM LAURENCE (1755–1830), theological writer; educated at St. Andrews and Utrecht; minister of the English church, Utrecht, 1778, and professor of philosophy and church history there, 1788; D.D. St. Andrews, 1784; professor of divinity, Aberdeen; principal of Aberdeen University, 1796; wrote theological treatises. [vii. 37]

BROWNBILL, THOMAS ROBSON (1822?–1864). [See ROBSON.]

BROWNE. [See also BROUN and BROWN.]

BROWNE, ALEXANDER (fl. 1660), miniature-painter, engraver, and printseller; published 'Ars Pictoria,' 1675. [vii. 38]

BROWNE, SIR ANTHONY (d. 1548), politican; knighted, 1523; esquire of the body to Henry VIII, 1524; ambassador to France, 1528 and 1533; master of the horse, 1539; K.G., 1540; justice in eyre, 1545; named guardian to Prince Edward and Princess Elizabeth. He received Battle Abbey, 1538, and other large grants of church lands and manors, and was a great builder. Cowdray, Sussex, and other large estates, he inherited from his half-brother, the Earl of Southampton, 1543. [vii. 38]

BROWNE, ANTHONY (1510?–1567), judge; reader of the Middle Temple, 1553; active in prosecution of puritans in Essex, 1554; serjeant-at-law, 1555; chief-justice of the common pleas, 1558; reduced to the place of puisne justice, 1559, for refusing to cede his official patronage to Queen Elizabeth; knighted, 1566. [vii. 39]

BROWNE, ANTHONY, first VISCOUNT MONTAGUE (1526–1592), eldest son of Sir Anthony Browne (d. 1548) [q. v.]; a staunch Roman catholic, but of unquestioned loyalty both to Edward VI and to Elizabeth, though stoutly opposing in parliament the acts of supremacy and allegiance, 1559 and 1562; knighted, 1547; imprisoned for recusancy, 1551; entertained Edward VI at Cowdray, Sussex, 1552; created Viscount Montague, 1554; made master of the horse, and sent on an embassy to the pope; lieutenant-general at St. Quentin, 1557; ambassador to Spain, 1561; on the commission which tried Mary Queen of Scots, 1587; entertained Elizabeth at Cowdray, 1591. [vii. 40]

BROWNE, ARTHUR (1756?–1805), Irish lawyer; born in New England; of Irish parentage; educated at Harvard and Trinity College, Dublin, where he was elected junior fellow, 1777; LL.D., 1784; senior fellow, 1795–1805; became regius professor of law in Dublin, 1785; several times professor of Greek; practised at the Irish bar; last 'prime serjeant,' 1802; M.P. for Dublin University in the Irish parliament, 1783–1800; advocated the union; wrote on legal and miscellaneous subjects. [vii. 41]

BROWNE, DAVID (fl. 1638), writer on penmanship; published at St. Andrews 'The New Invention, intituled Calligraphia,' 1622. [vii. 41]

BROWNE, EDWARD (1644–1708), physician and traveller; eldest son of Sir Thomas Browne (1605–1682) [q. v.]; educated at Norwich grammar school and Trinity College, Cambridge; M.B., 1663; attended lectures in London; travelled in Italy, Holland, Austria, Hungary, North Greece, and the Low Countries, 1668–73; settled as a practitioner in London, 1675; president, Royal College of Physicians, 1704. His collected travels appeared in 1685. [vii. 42]

BROWNE, EDWARD (d. 1730), quaker; native of Cork, and subsequently a wealthy merchant in Sunderland. [vii. 43]

BROWNE, EDWARD HAROLD (1811–1891), bishop of Ely and of Winchester; educated at Eton and Emmanuel College, Cambridge; M.A., 1836; D.D., 1864; fellow, 1837–40; accepted charge of Holy Trinity, Stroud, 1840; vice-principal of St. David's College, Lampeter, 1843–9; prebendary of Exeter, 1849; vicar of Heavitree, Exeter, and canon of Exeter, 1857; bishop of Ely, 1864–73, and of Winchester, 1873–90; published religious writings. [Suppl. i. 304]

BROWNE, FELICIA DOROTHEA (1793–1835). [See HEMANS.]

BROWNE, GEORGE (d. 1556), archbishop of Dublin; the chief instrument of Henry VIII in the Irish reformation; provincial of the Austin Friars, 1534; archbishop of Dublin, 1536; spoke in the Irish parliament in favour of Henry VIII's ecclesiastical supremacy, and obtained for the king a grant of the first-fruits of the Irish abbeys; travelled widely, publishing the royal injunctions and collecting first-fruits; hated by the clergy and by most of the Irish council; in disfavour; took a leading part in introducing the first English prayer-book in Ireland, 1550; made by patent primate of Ireland; at Mary's accession deprived of the primacy and deposed from his archbishopric as being a married man; D.D. [vii. 43]

BROWNE, GEORGE, COUNT DE (1698–1792), soldier of fortune; educated at Limerick; took service with the elector palatine; transferred himself to the Russian service, 1730; taken prisoner and enslaved by the Turks; served in Finland and against the Swedes; contributed materially to the victories of Kollin, 1757, and Zorndorf, 1758; field-marshal; governor of Livonia. [vii. 45]

BROWNE, HABLOT KNIGHT (1815–1882), water-colour painter and book-illustrator; known as PHIZ; apprenticed to an engraver, and subsequently opened a studio; illustrated Charles Dickens's 'Sunday as it is by Timothy Sparks,' 1836, and the 'Pickwick Papers,' taking the pseudonym Phiz to match the author's pseudonym Boz; fond of horses, hunting, and water-colour painting; a prolific illustrator, especially of novels by Dickens, Lever, and Ainsworth. [vii. 45]

BROWNE, HENRY (1804–1875), classical and biblical scholar; M.A. Cambridge, 1830; principal of Chichester Theological College, 1842–7; rector of Pevensey, Sussex, 1854–75; published classical text-books and treatises on biblical chronology. [vii. 47]

BROWNE, ISAAC HAWKINS, the elder (1705–1760), wit and poet; educated at Westminster School and Trinity College, Cambridge; barrister of Lincoln's Inn; M.P. for Wenlock, 1744–54; his conversational powers praised by Samuel Johnson; wrote poems, some of which are distinguished by their sprightly humour. [vii. 47]

BROWNE, ISAAC HAWKINS, the younger (1745–1818), essayist; son of Isaac Hawkins Browne the elder [q. v.]; educated at Westminster and Hertford College, Oxford; D.C.L., 1773; M.P. for Bridgnorth, 1784–1812; published essays on moral and religious subjects. [vii. 48]

BROWNE or **BROWN**, JAMES (1616–1685), theologian; B.A. Oriel College, Oxford, 1638; chaplain in the army of the parliament; his 'Antichrist in Spirit' answered by George Fox. [vii. 49]

BROWNE, JAMES (1793–1841), journalist and historian; educated at St. Andrews University; minister of the church of Scotland; Scottish advocate; finally settled in Edinburgh as a journalist; LL.D. St. Andrews. His works include a 'History of the Highlands,' 1835. [vii. 49]

BROWNE, JOHN (1642–1700 ?), surgeon; served as naval surgeon; surgeon to St. Thomas's Hospital, 1683–91, and to Charles II and William III; author of anatomical and surgical treatises. [vii. 49]

BROWNE, JOHN (1741–1801), engraver of land-scapes; pupil of John Tinney and William Woollett. [vii. 50]

BROWNE, JOHN (1823–1886), nonconformist historian; B.A. London, 1843; minister at Lowestoft, 1844–6, and Wrentham, Suffolk, 1848–86; published 'History of Congregationalism,' 1877, and other works. [Suppl. i. 304]

BROWNE, JOSEPH (*fl.* 1706), physician; libelled Queen Anne's administration, 1706; wrote and lectured against Harvey's theory of the circulation of the blood. [vii. 51]

BROWNE, JOSEPH (1700–1767), provost of Queen's College, Oxford, 1756; rector of Bramshot, Hampshire, and professor of natural philosophy at Oxford, 1746–67. [vii. 51]

BROWNE, LANCELOT (*d.* 1605), physician; educated at Cambridge; M.D., 1576; F.R.C.P., 1584; physician to Queen Elizabeth and James I. [vii. 51]

BROWNE, LYDE, the elder (*d.* 1787), virtuoso; director of the Bank of England; possessed a famous cabinet of Greek and Roman art treasures at Wimbledon. [vii. 52]

BROWNE, LYDE, the younger (*d.* 1803), lieutenant-colonel; entered the army, 1777; lieutenant-colonel, 1800; shot by Emmet's mob in Dublin. [vii. 52]

BROWNE, MOSES (1704–1787), chief poetical contributor to the 'Gentleman's Magazine'; pen-cutter; and subsequently vicar of Olney, 1753; wrote poems, including 'Piscatory Eclogues,' 1729, and sermons. [vii. 52]

BROWNE, PATRICK (1720 ?–1790), naturalist; visited Antigua, 1737; studied science in Paris, and at Leyden; M.D., 1743; settled in Jamaica; published 'Civil

and Natural History of Jamaica,' 1756, and other zoological works. [vii. 53]

BROWNE, PETER (*d.* 1735), divine; fellow of Trinity College, Dublin, 1692; provost, 1699; bishop of Cork and Ross, 1710; published theological tractates. [vii. 53]

BROWNE, SIR RICHARD (*d.* 1669), parliamentary general and a leader of the presbyterian party; officer of the London trained bands; sent to disarm the Kentish royalists, 1642; present at the siege of Winchester; suppressed Kentish rising, 1643; fought at Alresford, 1644; major-general with task of reducing the Oxford district, 1644; present at the surrender of Oxford, 1646; a commissioner to receive Charles from the Scots, 1647; present at the seizure of Charles at Holmby, and afterwards favourable to the king; M.P. for Wycombe, but expelled by the influence of the army, 1648, and imprisoned for five years; excluded from parliament for refusing the 'engagement,' 1656; M.P. for London in Richard Cromwell's parliament; privy to Sir George Booth's rising, 1659; intrigued for the recall of Charles II; knighted; lord mayor of London, 1660, and made a baronet for suppressing Venner's rising. [vii. 54]

BROWNE, SIR RICHARD (1605–1683), diplomatist; educated at Merton College, Oxford; travelled in France; clerk of the council, 1641–72; resident at the French court for Charles I and Charles II, 1641–60; provided in Paris a chapel for Anglican services, a home for Anglican divines, and a cemetery for protestants; created baronet, 1649; returned to England, 1660. [vii. 55]

BROWNE or **BROWN**, RICHARD (*fl.* 1674–1694), physician; educated at Queen's College, Oxford; M.D. Leyden, 1675; published medical treatises. [vii. 55]

BROWNE, ROBERT (1550 ?–1633 ?), separatist; regarded as the founder of congregationalism; was connected with several families of influence, particularly with Cecil, lord Burghley; B.A. Corpus Christi College, Cambridge, 1572, that college being then notoriously puritan in sympathies; probably ordained about 1573; taught school in London, and preached at Islington without episcopal licence; preached constantly in villages near Cambridge, and in Cambridge itself, c. 1578, denouncing the parochial system and ordination, whether by bishops or by presbytery; destroyed a licence to preach which his brother had obtained for him from the bishop of Ely, and was then inhibited; went to Norwich c. 1580, and, with Robert Harrison, collected a congregation, which they called 'the church,' but which was popularly known as 'the Brownists'; imprisoned by the bishop of Norwich for seditious preaching at Bury St. Edmunds, 1581, but set free by Burghley, who also delivered him from the primate; emigrated to Middleburg with his followers, 1581, whence he issued books, the circulation of which in England was punished by death; quarrelled with Harrison, 1583, and was followed by four families to Scotland, where he was again imprisoned; imprisoned on his return to England, 1584; began preaching at Northampton, 1586; excommunicated by the bishop of Peterborough for ignoring a citation; submitted to the bishop, and became master of Stamford grammar school, 1586; rector of Achurch, Northamptonshire, 1591–1631; died in Northampton gaol, to which he had been sent for an assault committed in a characteristic outbreak of temper. [vii. 57]

BROWNE, SAMUEL (1575 ?–1632), divine; M.A. All Souls, Oxford, 1605; minister of St. Mary's, Shrewsbury; published tracts. [vii. 61]

BROWNE, SAMUEL (*d.* 1668), judge; called to bar at Lincoln's Inn, 1623; M.P. for Clifton, Devonshire, 1640; an active member of the Commons committee for the impeachment of Laud, 1644; one of the commissioners to treat with Charles in the Isle of Wight, 1648; serjeant-at-law, 1648; justice of the common pleas and knighted, 1660. [vii. 61]

BROWNE, SIMON (1680–1732), congregationalist; pastor at Portsmouth, and (1716–23) in the Old Jewry, London; published hymns and sermons. [vii. 62]

BROWNE, THEOPHILUS (1763–1835), unitarian; fellow of Peterhouse, Cambridge, 1785; vicar of Cherry-Hinton, Cambridgeshire, 1793, but resigned on adopting unitarianism; unitarian minister at Warminster, 1800, Norwich, 1809, Congleton, 1812, and Gloucester, 1815–23; published theological treatises. [vii. 62]

BROWNE, THOMAS (*d.* 1585), head-master of West-minster School, 1564–70; educated at Eton and King's, Cambridge; B.D., 1559; rector of Dunton-Waylett, Essex, 1564, of St. Leonard's, Foster Lane, London, 1567, and of Chelsea, 1574; author of occasional poems. [vii. 63]

BROWNE or **BROWN**, THOMAS (1604?–1673), divine; student of Christ Church, Oxford, 1620; B.D.; domestic chaplain to Archbishop Laud, 1637; canon of Windsor, 1639; rector of St. Mary Aldermary, London, and of Oddington, Oxfordshire; took refuge in Holland; recovered his benefices, 1660; published sermons. [vii. 64]

BROWNE, SIR THOMAS (1605–1682), physician and author; educated at Winchester and Broadgates Hall, Oxford; M.A., 1629; practised medicine in Oxfordshire; studied medicine at Montpellier and Padua; M.D. Leyden, 1633; incorporated M.D. at Oxford, 1637; settled in Norwich, 1637, and practised physic; expressed his belief in witchcraft at a trial of witches at Bury St. Edmunds, 1664; knighted in 1671, on occasion of a royal visit to Norwich. His 'Religio Medici' appeared without his sanction in 1642, but was reissued with his approval in 1643, and was afterwards published on the continent in Latin, Dutch, French, and German translations. 'Pseudodoxia Epidemica: Enquiries into Vulgar Errors,' appeared in 1646, and 'Hydriotaphia: Urn Burial,' and a mystical treatise entitled 'The Garden of Cyrus,' in 1658. Communications from him are to be found in the works of John Evelyn, William Dugdale, Christopher Merrett, John Ray, and Anthony à Wood. The best edition of his collected works is by Simon Wilkin, 1835. [vii. 64]

BROWNE, THOMAS (1672–1710), physician; son of Edward Browne (1644–1708) [q. v.]; of Trinity College, Cambridge; M.D., 1700; fellow of the College of Physicians, 1707. [vii. 72]

BROWNE, THOMAS (1708?–1780), herald and land-surveyor; called 'Sense Browne,' to distinguish him from Lancelot Brown [q. v.]; Garter king-of-arms, 1774. [vii. 72]

BROWNE, SIR THOMAS GORE (1807–1887), colonel and colonial governor; ensign 28th foot, 1824; captain, 1829; major, 1834; served in first Afghan war; C.B., 1843; lieutenant-colonel, 1845; governor of St. Helena, 1851, New Zealand, 1855, and Tasmania, 1862–8; K.C.M.G., 1869; temporarily governor of Bermuda, 1870–1. [Suppl. i. 305]

BROWNE, WILLIAM (1591–1643?), poet; educated at Tavistock and Exeter College, Oxford; entered the Inner Temple, 1611; published 'Britannia's Pastorals,' book i., 1613, book ii., 1616, but book iii. remained in manuscript till 1852; contributed eclogues to 'The Shepheards Pipe,' 1614; superintended the Inner Temple masque on the story of Ulysses and Circe, 1615; returned to Oxford as tutor to the Hon. Robert Dormer, 1624, and then graduated M.A.; in the retinue of the Earl of Pembroke at Wilton. His poetry, which closely resembles Spenser, greatly influenced Milton, Keats, and Mrs. Browning. Works collected by W. Carew Hazlitt, 1868. [vii. 72]

BROWNE, WILLIAM (1628–1678), botanist; fellow of Magdalen College, Oxford; B.D., 1665. [vii. 75]

BROWNE, SIR WILLIAM (1692–1774), physician; M.A. Peterhouse, Cambridge, 1714; M.D., 1721; practised medicine at Lynn, 1716–49; knighted, 1748; removed to London, 1749; president of the College of Physicians, 1765; founded the Browne medals at Cambridge; published verses and orations. [vii. 75]

BROWNE, WILLIAM (1748–1825), gem and seal engraver; exhibited at the Royal Academy, 1770–1823; chiefly employed by the courts of Russia and France. [vii. 76]

BROWNE, WILLIAM GEORGE (1768–1813), oriental traveller; B.A. Oxford, 1789; went to Egypt in 1792, and to Darfur, 1793–6; returned to England, 1798, by way of Syria and Constantinople; published narrative of his travels, 1800; travelled in Turkey and the Levant, 1800–2; set out for Tartary, 1812, travelling through Asia Minor and Armenia, but was murdered near Tabriz in Persia, 1813. [vii. 76]

BROWNING, ELIZABETH BARRETT (1806–1861), poetess; the name of Barrett adopted by her father, originally named Moulton, on succeeding to an estate;

read Homer in Greek and wrote verses at the age of eight; her spine injured by a fall at the age of fifteen, in consequence of which for many years she was compelled to lie on her back; published her 'Essay on Mind,' 1826, and in 1833, 'Prometheus Bound,' her first volume of poems; constantly wrote prose and verse from this time onwards; met Robert Browning, 1845; married him, 1846, and went with him through France to Florence, where they mainly resided till her death. She took a keen interest in Italy and the Italian struggle for freedom. [vii. 78]

BROWNING, JOHN (*fl.* 1584), divine; fellow of Trinity College, Cambridge; B.D., 1577; censured for heretical preaching, 1572; D.D. Oxford, 1580, and incorporated D.D. at Cambridge, 1581; as vice-master of Trinity, tried to eject the master for marrying, 1584, but was by him expelled from his fellowship. [vii. 82]

BROWNING, JOHN (*fl.* 1634), divine and author. [vii. 82]

BROWNING, ROBERT (1812–1889), poet; son of Robert Browning, a clerk in the Bank of England; educated at a school at Peckham, and by a private tutor; studied Greek at University College, London, 1829–30; displayed in early years some power of musical composition and wrote settings for a number of songs; published 'Pauline,' 1832; first visited Italy, 1834; produced (1835) 'Paracelsus,' which attracted the friendly notice of Carlyle, Leigh Hunt, Wordsworth, Dickens, and other men of letters; published a tragedy, 'Strafford,' which was played at Covent Garden by Macready and Helen Faucit, 1837; published 'Sordello,' 1840; 'Bells and Pomegranates' (comprising 'Pippa Passes,' 1841, 'A Blot in the 'Scutcheon,' performed at Drury Lane, 1843, by Phelps and Helen Faucit, 'Luria,' and 'A Soul's Tragedy,' 1846, and other pieces, eight in all), 1841–6; made acquaintance, 1845, of Elizabeth Barrett Moulton Barrett [see BROWNING, ELIZABETH BARRETT], whom he married, 1846; lived at Pisa, 1846–7; and at Florence, 1847–51, and returned to England, 1851; in Paris, 1851–2; lived in Italy, staying chiefly at Florence, from 1852 till 1855; returned (1856) to Italy, living for the most part at Rome and Florence, where Mrs. Browning died, 1861; in 1861 Browning settled in London, but frequently revisited Italy in later life; published 'Dramatis Personæ,' 1864; honorary M.A. Oxford, 1868; made acquaintance, 1868, of George Smith, who became his publisher and intimate friend; published, in four successive instalments, 1868–9, 'The Ring and the Book,' the rewriting of which had occupied him since 1862; published 'Balaustion's Adventure,' and 'Prince Hohenstiel-Schwangau,' 1871. Fifine at the Fair,' 1872, 'Red Cotton Nightcap Country,' 1873, 'The Inn Album,' 1875, 'Pacchiarotto,' 1876; translation of 'Agamemnon,' 1877, 'La Saisiaz,' and 'Two Poets of Croisic' (one volume), 1878, and 'Dramatic Idylls,' first series, 1879, and second series, 1880; honorary LL.D. Edinburgh, 1884; foreign correspondent to Royal Academy, 1886; died at Venice, 16 Dec. 1889; buried in Westminster Abbey; his last volume of poems, 'Asolando,' appeared on the day of his death. Portraits of him by Field, Talfourd, Mr. G. F. Watts, R.A., and Mr. Rudolf Lehmann, are in the National Portrait Gallery. His poems were collected in two volumes, 1896; several volumes of his correspondence with Mrs. Browning have been published. Browning was at his best in psychological monologue; his poems everywhere attest unflinching optimism. [Suppl. i. 306]

BROWNLOW, RICHARD (1553–1638), chief prothonotary of court of common pleas, 1591–1638; entered the Inner Temple, 1583; left in manuscript law reports. [vii. 82]

BROWNRIG, RALPH (1592–1659), bishop of Exeter; educated at Ipswich and Pembroke Hall, Cambridge; M.A., 1617; D.D., 1626; rector of Barley, Hertfordshire, 1621; master of St. Catharine's Hall, Cambridge; deprived of the mastership, 1645; canon of Durham, 1641; bishop of Exeter, 1641; lived in retirement during the Commonwealth, ordaining privately; chaplain of the Inner and Middle Temples, 1658; a strict Calvinist; left sermons in manuscript. [vii. 83]

BROWNRIGG, ELIZABETH (*d.* 1767), murderess; wife of a London house-painter; practised as midwife; barbarously murdered her apprentice; hanged at Tyburn. [vii. 84]

BROWNRIGG, SIR ROBERT (1759–1833), general; ensign, 1775; captain, 1784; served in the Netherlands,

1793; colonel, 1796; quartermaster-general, 1803; lieutenant-general, 1808; governor of Ceylon, 1811; took Kandy and annexed the kingdom, 1815; created baronet, 1816; general, 1819; returned to England, 1820. [vii. 85]

BROWNRIGG, WILLIAM (1711–1800), chemist; studied medicine at London and at Leyden; M.D., 1737; practised at Whitehaven for many years; made valuable researches into the phenomena of fire-damp, mineral waters, and platina. [vii. 85]

BROWN-SÉQUARD, CHARLES EDWARD (1817–1894), physiologist; born in Mauritius; studied medicine at Paris; M.D., 1846; secretary of Société de Biologie, 1848; subdued epidemic of cholera in Mauritius, 1854–5; professor at Virginia Medical College, Richmond, Virginia, 1855; engaged in scientific teaching in Paris, 1855–1857; established, 1858, and published till 1864, 'Journal de Physiologie'; lectured in England on physiology and pathology; fellow of Faculty of Physicians and Surgeons at Glasgow, 1859; F.R.S. and F.R.C.P., 1860; professor of physiology and pathology of nervous system at Harvard, U.S.A., 1863–8; founded, with Vulpian and Charcot, 'Archives de Physiologie,' Paris; sole editor, 1889; professor of pathology at Paris, 1869–72, of physiology at Geneva, 1877, and of experimental medicine at College of France, 1878–94; honorary LL.D. of Cambridge, 1881; contributed to scientific publications. [Suppl. i. 319]

BROWNSWERD, JOHN (1540?–1589), master of Macclesfield grammar school; published Latin poems. [vii. 86]

BROXHOLME, NOEL (1689?–1748), physician; educated at Westminster; student of Christ Church, Oxford, 1705; M.A., 1711; Radcliffe travelling fellow, 1715; M.D., 1723; F.R.C.P., 1725; practised in London. [vii. 87]

BRUCE, ALEXANDER, second EARL OF KINCARDINE (d. 1681), resided in North Germany and Holland, 1657–60; succeeded his brother in title and estates at Culross, Fifeshire, 1663, where he managed his coal, salt, stone, and marble works; privy councillor in Scotland; extraordinary lord of session, 1667; continued to support Lauderdale till 1674; dismissed from the privy council for trying to protect the covenanters, 1676. [vii. 87]

BRUCE, ALEXANDER BALMAIN (1831–1899), Scottish divine; educated at Edinburgh University; minister at Cardross, 1859, and Broughty Ferry, 1868; Cunningham lecturer, 1874; professor of apologetics and New Testament exegesis at Free Church Hall, Glasgow, 1875–99; Gifford lecturer, Glasgow University, 1896–7; published sermons and other religious works, and assisted in compilation of hymn-books. [Suppl. i. 321]

BRUCE, ARCHIBALD (1746–1816), Scottish divine; educated at Glasgow; minister of the Anti-burgher congregation at Whitburn, Linlithgow, 1768; divinity professor to the Anti-burgher ('Associate') church, 1786–1806; with three other clergymen formed a secession church; author of poems, chiefly satirical. [vii. 89]

BRUCE, DAVID (1324–1371), DAVID II, king of Scotland; only son of Robert de Bruce VIII [q. v.], by his second wife; born at Dunfermline, 5 March 1324; succeeded, 9 June 1329; was crowned, 24 Nov. 1331; his supporters, led by the regent Archibald Douglas, defeated at Halidon Hill, 1333, by Edward Baliol, who was actively assisted in his claim to the Scottish crown by Edward III; retired to Dumbarton, and thence to France, 1334; for seven years he was royally entertained by the French king; returned to Scotland in May 1341, and took the administration of affairs into his own hands, 1342; invaded England at the request of Philip of France, and was taken prisoner at Neville's Cross, 17 Oct. 1346; remained in captivity for eleven years; set free by the treaty of Berwick, 1357, on the severe terms of paying a ransom of 100,000 merks in ten years; began to intrigue for the remission of the ransom on condition of bequeathing his crown to a son of Edward III, proposals to this effect being brought before the estates in 1363.

David was married to Joanna, sister of Edward III, 12 July 1328; she accompanied him in his exiles, and died near London, 14 Aug. 1362. Next year he married Margaret Drummond, widow of Sir John Logie, and divorced her in 1369. He had no child. [vii. 89]

BRUCE, DAVID (fl. 1660), physician; M.A. St. Andrews; studied physic in France; M.D. Valence, 1657; incorporated M.D. at Oxford, 1660; physician to the Duke of York; subsequently practised at Edinburgh. [vii. 94]

BRUCE, EDWARD (d. 1318), king of Ireland; younger brother of Robert de Bruce VIII [q. v.], king of Scotland; took part in the Ayrshire campaign, 1307; subdued Galloway, 1308; reduced Dundee, 1313; besieged Stirling Castle, and granted the governor a year's truce, June 1313; commanded the right wing at Bannockburn, 1314; recognised as heir presumptive, May 1315; accepted an invitation from the Ulster chieftains, took Carrickfergus, and was crowned king of Ireland, 1315; opposed by the clergy; being joined by his brother, pushed on to Limerick, but when left alone, fell back on Carrickfergus, 1317; killed in battle at Dundalk. [vii. 94]

BRUCE, EDWARD, first BARON BRUCE OF KINLOSS (1549?–1611), judge; judge of the commissary court, Edinburgh, before 1583; granted Kinloss Abbey, Ayrshire, in commendam, 1583; envoy to Queen Elizabeth, 1594; lord of session, 1597; envoy to Queen Elizabeth, 1598 and 1601; created Baron Bruce of Kinloss, 1603; accompanied James I to England, 1603, and was appointed master of the rolls. [vii. 96]

BRUCE, SIR FREDERICK WILLIAM ADOLPHUS (1814–1867), diplomatist; youngest son of Thomas Bruce, seventh earl of Elgin [q. v.]; attached to Lord Ashburton's mission to Washington, 1842; colonial secretary at Hongkong, 1844; lieutenant-governor of Newfoundland, 1846; chargé d'affaires to Bolivia, 1848, and to Uruguay, 1851; consul-general in Egypt, 1853; secretary to the embassy to China, 1857; envoy to China, 1858; K.C.B., 1862; envoy to Washington, 1865; died at Boston. [vii. 97]

BRUCE, GEORGE WYNDHAM HAMILTON KNIGHT- (1852–1896), first bishop of Mashonaland; educated at Eton and Merton College, Oxford; M.A., 1881; D.D., 1886; curate of St. Andrew, Bethnal Green, 1884–6; bishop of Bloemfontein, 1886, and of Mashonaland, 1891–1894; vicar of Bovey Tracey, 1895–6; published personal memoirs. [Suppl. i. 322]

BRUCE, HENRY AUSTIN, first BARON ABERDARE (1815–1895), statesman; called to bar at Lincoln's Inn, 1837; stipendiary magistrate for Merthyr Tydvil and Aberdare, 1847–52; liberal M.P. for Merthyr Tydvil, 1852–68; under-secretary of state for home department, 1862–4; privy councillor and vice-president of committee of council on education, 1864; M.P. for Renfrewshire, 1869; home secretary, 1869–73; conducted reform in licensing laws; lord president of council, 1873–4; created Baron Aberdare, 1873; F.R.S., 1876; president of Royal Geographical Society, 1881, and of Royal Historical Society, 1878–92; chairman of National African (afterwards Royal Niger) Company, 1882–95; first president of University College, Cardiff, 1883; first chancellor of university of Wales, 1894; G.C.B., 1885. [Suppl. i. 322]

BRUCE, JAMES (1660?–1730), Irish presbyterian; eldest son of Michael Bruce (1635–1693) [q. v.]; minister of Killeleagh, co. Down, 1684; fled to Scotland, 1689; returned to Killeleagh, 1692; founded a presbyterian college there, 1697; joined the 'subscribers' to the Westminster Confession, 1721, but was tolerant to the 'non-subscribers.' [vii. 97]

BRUCE, JAMES (1730–1794), African traveller; educated at Harrow; engaged in the Portuguese wine trade, 1753; visited Spain and Portugal, 1754; studied Arabic and Ethiopic; studied antiquities in Italy, especially at the Pæstum; consul at Algiers, 1763, with a mission to study antiquities; made an archæological tour in Barbary, 1765; shipwrecked near Crete; visited Palmyra and Baalbec; reached Egypt, 1768; sailed up the Nile to Assouan; crossed the desert to the Red Sea; landed at Masuah, the port of Abyssinia, September 1769; reached Gondar, the capital, February 1770; explored the sources of the Blue Nile; left Gondar, 1771; travelled to Sennaar in Nubia; reached Assouan, November 1772, and England, 1774; published his travels, 1790; died of a fall. [vii. 98]

BRUCE, JAMES (1765?–1806), essayist; educated at St. Andrews and Cambridge; episcopalian clergyman in Scotland; tory journalist in London. 1803. [vii. 102]

BRUCE, JAMES (1808–1861), author; journalist at Aberdeen, at Cupar-Fife, 1845, and at Belfast, 1850 (?) till death; published 'Letters on the . . . Condition of the Highlands,' 1847, biographies and travels. [vii. 103]

BRUCE, JAMES, eighth EARL OF ELGIN and twelfth EARL OF KINCARDINE (1811–1863), diplomatist; second son of Thomas Bruce, seventh earl of Elgin [q. v.]; educated at Eton and Oxford; fellow of Merton, 1832; M.P. Southampton, 1841; succeeded to the peerage, 1841; governor of Jamaica, 1842; governor-general of Canada, 1847–54, during a period of distress and unrest; envoy to China, 1857; negotiated the treaty of Tientsin, 1858; visited Japan and concluded a treaty, 1858; post-master-general, 1859; envoy to China, 1860–1, punishing the emperor's treachery by destroying the summer palace at Pekin; viceroy of India, 1862. [vii. 104]

BRUCE, SIR JAMES LEWIS KNIGHT- (1791–1866), judge; known as J. L. Knight till September 1837; edu-cated at Sherborne school; solicitor; called to bar at Lincoln's Inn, 1817; practised in the equity courts; M.P. for Bishop's Castle, 1831; vice-chancellor and knighted, 1841; chief judge in bankruptcy, 1842; lord justice of appeal, 1851. [vii. 106]

BRUCE, JOHN (1745–1826), historian; educated at Edinburgh, where he was professor of logic; keeper of the state paper office; historiographer to the East India Company; M.P. for Michael, Cornwall, 1809–14; joint king's printer for Scotland; published philosophical and historical works. [vii. 107]

BRUCE, JOHN (1802–1869), antiquary; educated partly at Aberdeen; lawyer; devoted himself to historical research from 1840; edited the Calendars of Domestic State Papers for 1625–39; published numerous historical tracts. [vii. 108]

BRUCE, JOHN COLLINGWOOD (1805–1892), anti-quary; M.A. Glasgow, 1826; LL.D., 1853; proprietor of Percy Street academy, Newcastle, 1834–63; F.S.A., 1852; secretary and vice-president of Society of Antiquaries of Newcastle, 1846; published antiquarian works.
[Suppl. i. 325]

BRUCE, SIR JOHN HOPE (1684?–1766), baronet of Kinross; reputed author of the ballad 'Hardyknute'; governor of Bermuda, 1721; lieutenant-general, 1758; M.P. for Kinross-shire. [vii. 109]

BRUCE, MICHAEL (1635–1693), Irish presbyterian; M.A. Edinburgh, 1654; minister of Killinchy, co. Down, 1657; continued to preach, in defiance of the bishop, 1660; outlawed, 1664; returned to Scotland, 1666; sen-tenced to transportation for field-preaching, July 1668; imprisoned in London; allowed to return to Killinchy, 1670; driven out by the rebellion, 1688; minister of Anwoth, Wigtonshire, 1689 till death. [vii. 109]

BRUCE, MICHAEL (1686–1735), Irish presbyterian; eldest son of James Bruce (1660?–1730) [q. v.]; minister of Holywood, co. Down, 1711; held liberal opinions in theology; a leader of the 'non-subscribers' (to the West-minster Confession), 1720. [vii. 111]

BRUCE, MICHAEL (1746–1767), poet; son of a poor weaver in Kinross-shire; at one time a herd-boy; edu-cated at Edinburgh University, 1762–5; taught school in Kinross-shire and Clackmannanshire, 1765–6; died of consumption; his poems published posthumously, 1770. The 'Ode to the Cuckoo' is variously attributed to him and to John Logan. [vii. 111]

BRUCE, PETER HENRY (1692–1757), military engi-neer; born in Westphalia; of Scottish descent; educated in Scotland, 1698; studied fortification in Germany, 1704; entered the Prussian service, 1706; entered the Russian service and visited Constantinople, 1711; attended Peter the Great at court and in the field, 1711–24; settled in Scotland, 1724; superintended fortifications at the Bahamas, 1740–4, and in Scotland, 1745; published 'Memoirs.' [vii. 113]

BRUCE, ROBERT DE I (d. 1094?), founder of the family in England and Scotland. He came from Bruis, a castle near Cherbourg, with William the Conqueror, 1066, and received large grants of land in Cleveland, York-shire. [vii. 114]

BRUCE, ROBERT DE II (1078?–1141), son of Robert de Bruce I [q. v.]; a companion of David I of Scotland

at the court of Henry I; received the lordship of Annan-dale, in Dumfriesshire, 1124; benefactor to the church in Yorkshire; forfeited Annandale by fighting on the English side, 1138. [vii. 114]

BRUCE, ROBERT DE III (fl. 1138–1189?), second son of Robert de Bruce II [q. v.]; received the lordship of Annandale, possibly in 1138; confirmed in it, 1166.
[vii. 114]

BRUCE, ROBERT DE IV, son of Robert de Bruce III [q. v.]; died before 1191, possibly during his father's life-time. [vii. 115]

BRUCE, ROBERT DE V (d. 1245), son of William de Bruce (d. 1215), son and heir of Robert de Bruce III [q. v.] His marriage with Isabel, second daughter of David, earl of Huntingdon, younger brother of William the Lion, founded the claim of his descendants to the crown. [vii. 115]

BRUCE, ROBERT DE VI (1210–1295), called the COMPETITOR, from his claim to the crown; son of Robert de Bruce V [q. v.]; recognised as heir-presumptive, 1238–41; married Isabel, daughter of Gilbert de Clare, earl of Gloucester, 1244; succeeded his father as Lord of Annandale, 1245; a justiciary in England, 1250; suc-ceeded to his mother's English estates, 1251; one of the regents in Scotland, 1255; frequently a justiciary in Eng-land from 1257; sheriff of Cumberland and warden of Carlisle Castle; fought for Henry III in the barons' wars; chief-justice of the king's bench, 1268; returned to Scot-land, 1272; recognised the right of Princess Margaret to the crown, 1284; entered a league to assert his own claim, 1286; assented to the marriage of Princess Margaret with Edward, prince of Wales, and the union of Scotland and England, 1290; accepted arbitration of Edward I on his claim to the crown, 1291; prepared to resist an unfavour-able decision, June 1292; prevented by his great age from further action, when Edward I decided in favour of John de Baliol [q. v.], November 1292. [vii. 115]

BRUCE, ROBERT DE VII (1253–1304), son of the Competitor, Robert de Bruce VI [q. v.]; styled EARL OF CARRICK (jure uxoris), 1274?–92; afterwards styled LORD OF ANNANDALE; accompanied Edward, prince of Wales, on the crusade, 1269; married Marjory, countess of Carrick, c. 1274; envoy of Alexander III, 1278; privy to his father's designs on the crown, 1286–92; absent in Norway, 1293; paid homage to Edward I for his English fiefs, became warden of Carlisle Castle, and joined Ed-ward I in his war with John de Baliol [q. v.], 1295; paid homage to Edw-rd I, as king of Scotland, 24 Aug. 1296, and thenceforward lived in England. [vii. 116]

BRUCE, ROBERT DE VIII (1274–1329), king and liberator of Scotland; son of Robert de Bruce VII [q. v.]; Earl of Carrick on his mother's death, 1292; paid homage to Edward I, as king of Scotland, 24 Aug. 1296; refused, with other Scottish nobles, to accompany Edward I to Flanders, 1297, and ravaged the lands of Edward's adhe-rents; was still in arms against Edward in 1298; co-regent of Scotland, 1299; during Edward's invasion of Scotland, 1302–4, apparently favoured Edward, but was really in treaty with the patriotic party; murdered John Comyn, at Dumfries, 10 Feb. 1306; crowned king at Scone, 27 March; defeated at Methven, 19 June; wan-dered in the central and western highlands, and sought shelter on the island of Rachrine, on north coast of Antrim; excommunicated and outlawed; returned to Arran, and thence to Carrick; won the battle of Loudon Hill, 10 May 1307, but had to fall back for a time; harried the lands of his chief opponents, Buchan and Lorne, 1308; recognised as king by the Scottish clergy, 1310; the Hebrides ceded to him by the king of Norway, 1312; raided the north of England, 1312, 1313; defeated Edward II at Bannockburn, 24 June 1314; subdued the Hebrides, 1316; joined his brother, Edward Bruce (d. 1318) [q. v.], in a campaign in Ireland, 1317; took Ber-wick, 1318; initiated legislation for the defence and ad-ministration of the kingdom; conspiracy of Sir William Soulis against him detected, 1320; baffled an invasion by Edward II, and ravaged Yorkshire, 1322; recognised by the pope as king of Scotland, 1323; settled the succession, 1326; concluded peace with Edward III, April 1328; died of leprosy; his body buried at Dunfermline, his heart (which had been destined for Jerusalem) at Mel-rose. He married, first, Isabella, daughter of Donald, earl of Mar, and had by her a daughter, Marjory, through whom the crown descended to the Stuarts; secondly, Elizabeth de Burgh, daughter of the Earl of Ulster, by whom he had a son, David Bruce [q. v.], his successor. [vii. 117]

BRUCE, ROBERT (d. 1602), political agent and spy; in service of James Beaton, archbishop of Glasgow, and of Mary Stuart; studied at Scottish College, Pont-à-Mousson, 1581–5; sent by Duke of Guise and Prince of Parma as envoy to James VI of Scotland, 1587, and tried, unsuccessfully, to win him to Roman catholic cause; imprisoned at Brussels on charge of misappropriating funds and betraying plans, 1599–1600; in Scotland, 1601; died in Paris; left unfinished a work against the jesuits. [Suppl. i. 326]

BRUCE, ROBERT (1554–1631), Scottish presbyterian; studied law at Paris and theology at St. Andrews; presbyterian minister in Edinburgh, 1587; moderator of the general assembly, 1588 and 1592; anointed Anne of Denmark at her coronation, 1590; resisted the attempt to introduce episcopacy into Scotland, 1596; ordered to leave Edinburgh, 1600; confined to Inverness, 1605–9, and again 1620–4; resided chiefly on his estate of Kinnaird, Stirlingshire, 1624 till death; published sermons in the Scottish dialect. [vii. 128]

BRUCE, ROBERT (d. 1685), succeeded as second EARL OF ELGIN, 1663, and created EARL OF AILESBURY, 1664; joint lord-lieutenant of Bedfordshire, 1660, and lord-lieutenant, 1667; privy councillor, 1678; lord chamberlain, 1685. [vii. 129]

BRUCE, THOMAS, third EARL OF ELGIN and second EARL OF AILESBURY (1655?–1741), eldest surviving son of Robert Bruce (d. 1685), second earl [q. v.]; succeeded to the earldom, 1685; courtier of James II, 1688; imprisoned as a Jacobite, 1690, 1696; resided in Brussels, 1696–1741. [vii. 130]

BRUCE, THOMAS, seventh EARL OF ELGIN and eleventh EARL OF KINCARDINE (1766–1841), succeeded in 1771; educated at Harrow and in Paris; entered the army, 1785; envoy to the emperor, 1790; to Brussels, 1792; to Berlin, 1795; and to the Porte, 1799–1803; detained in France, 1803–6; major-general, 1837. He employed artists to make drawings of sculptures, &c., at Athens, 1800–3, and arranged for the conveyance of the Parthenon frieze, &c., to England, 1803–12. He sold these 'Elgin marbles' to the nation, 1816. [vii. 130]

BRUCE, SIR WILLIAM (d. 1710), architect, of Kinross; designed Holyrood House, 1671–9, and several mansions in Scotland; intrigued for the Restoration; clerk to the bills, 1660; created baronet, 1668; king's surveyor in Scotland, 1671; M.P. for Kinross-shire, 1681. [vii. 131]

BRUCE, WILLIAM (1702–1755), a publisher in Dublin; published pamphlets. [vii. 132]

BRUCE, WILLIAM (1757–1841), theologian; educated at Trinity College, Dublin, and Warrington academy; presbyterian minister at Lisburn, 1779, in Dublin, 1782, and in Belfast, 1789–1831?; principal of Belfast academy, 1790–1822; D.D. Glasgow, 1786; a founder of the Unitarian Society, 1831; resident in Dublin, 1836; published exegetical works. [vii. 133]

BRUCE, WILLIAM (1790–1868), Irish presbyterian; second son of William Bruce (1757–1841) [q. v]; B.A. Trinity College, Dublin, 1809; presbyterian minister in Belfast, 1812–67; professor of classics and Hebrew, 1821–1825, and of Hebrew, 1825–49, in Belfast academy; inclined to unitarianism; a leader of the 'non-subscribers,' 1862; published controversial works. [vii. 135]

BRUCKNER, JOHN (1726–1804), Lutheran divine; born in Zeeland; educated at Franeker; Lutheran pastor at Leyden; pastor of the Walloon church at Norwich, 1753–1804, and of the Dutch church there, 1766–1804; taught French; committed suicide. [vii. 135]

BRUDENELL, JAMES THOMAS, seventh EARL OF CARDIGAN (1797–1868), lieutenant-general; involved by his domineering temper in constant wrangles with his brother officers; M.P. for Marlborough, 1818–29; cornet, 1824; lieutenant-colonel by purchase, 1830; M.P. for North Northamptonshire, 1832; commanded the 15th hussars, 1832–3, and the 11th hussars, 1836–47; succeeded to the earldom, 1837; major-general, 1847; commanded the light cavalry brigade in the Crimea, and destroyed it

in the famous 'charge,' 1854; colonel of the 5th dragoon guards, 1859, and of the 11th hussars, 1860; lieutenant-general, 1861. [vii. 136]

BRUDENELL, ROBERT (1461–1531), judge; educated at Cambridge; barrister before 1490; M.P., 1503; serjeant-at-law, 1504; justice of the king's bench, 1507; justice of the common pleas, 1509, and chief-justice, 1521–1531. [vii. 138]

BRUEN, JOHN (1560–1625), a typical puritan layman; sent to St. Alban Hall, Oxford, 1577; married and became a hunting squire, 1580; began to practise great strictness in religious observances, 1587; his house frequented by puritans; lived latterly in Chester. [vii. 139]

BRUERNE, RICHARD (1519?–1565), ecclesiastic; obnoxious to the reformers; fellow of Lincoln College, Oxford, 1538, and of Eton, 1545; B.D., 1547; professor of Hebrew, Oxford, 1548–59; canon of Christ Church, 1553, and of Windsor, 1557; elected provost of Eton, 1561, but his election annulled. [vii. 140]

BRUGIS, THOMAS (fl. 1640?), army surgeon during the civil war, afterwards in practice at Rickmansworth, Hertfordshire; published medical handbooks. [vii. 140]

BRÜHL, JOHN MAURICE, COUNT OF (1736–1809), diplomatist and astronomer; born in Saxony; studied at Leipzig; employed in the Saxon diplomatic service at Paris, 1755, and Warsaw, 1759; ambassador to London, 1764–1809; published astronomical works. [vii. 141]

BRUMMELL, GEORGE BRYAN (1778–1840), generally called BEAU BRUMMELL; educated at Eton; cornet in the 10th hussars, 1794; captain, 1796; retired, 1798; friend of the prince regent, and leader of fashion in London; retired to Calais in debt, 1816; removed to Caen, 1830; died in the asylum there. [vii. 141]

BRUNÆUS, THOMAS (d. 1380). [See BROME, THOMAS.]

BRUNDISH, JOHN JELLIAND (d. 1786), poetical writer; fellow of Caius College, Cambridge; author of 'An Elegy on a Family Tomb,' 1783. [vii. 142]

BRUNEL, ISAMBARD KINGDOM (1806–1859), civil engineer; only son of Sir Marc I. Brunel [q. v.]; educated privately and in Paris; clerk to his father, 1823; resident engineer of the Thames tunnel, 1826; designed Clifton suspension bridge, 1831; engineer to the Great Western railway, 1833; applied the screw propeller to steamships, 1845; designed the Great Eastern steamship, 1852–8; designed numerous docks and bridges, both iron and masonry; an advocate of broad-gauge railways and of very large steamers; invented improvements in artillery. [vii. 143]

BRUNEL, SIR MARC ISAMBARD (1769–1849), civil engineer; born in Normandy; educated for the church at Gisors and Rouen; served for six years in French navy; emigrated to America, 1793; practised as surveyor, architect, and civil engineer; planned the defences of New York; came to England, 1799, to patent his machinery for making ships' blocks; erected saw-mills with improved machinery, 1805–12; improved dockyard machinery at Chatham, 1812; experimented in steam navigation, 1812; imprisoned for debt, 1821; improved docks at Liverpool, 1823–6; engineer of Thames tunnel, 1825–1843; knighted, 1841. [vii. 144]

BRUNING, ANTHONY (1716–1776), jesuit, 1733; served in the English mission; professor at Liège; left in manuscript theological treatises. [vii. 147]

BRUNING, GEORGE (1738–1802), jesuit, 1756; served in the English mission; lived at East Hendred, Berkshire, and at Isleworth; published theological tracts. [vii. 147]

BRUNLEES, SIR JAMES (1816–1892), civil engineer; engaged in gardening and farm work; studied at Edinburgh University; assistant to (Sir) John Hawkshaw [q. v.] on Lancashire and Yorkshire railway; prepared plans for several railways in Brazil from 1856, and assisted in Mersey railway; knighted, 1886; constructed Avonmouth dock, Bristol, 1868–77; M.I.C.E., 1852, and president, 1882–3; wrote on engineering subjects. [Suppl. i. 328]

BRUNNE, ROBERT DE, or MANNYNG (fl. 1288–1338). [See MANNYNG.]

BRUNNING, BENJAMIN (*fl.* 1664), nonconformist; fellow of Jesus College, Cambridge, 1645; ejected, 1662; subsequently nonconformist minister at Ipswich; author of sermons. [vii. 147]

BRUNTON, ALEXANDER (1772–1854), minister and professor of oriental languages in Edinburgh. His works include a biography of his wife, Mary Brunton [q. v.], 1819, and a 'Persian Grammar,' 1822. [vii. 148]

BRUNTON, ELIZABETH (1799–1860). [See YATES.]

BRUNTON, GEORGE (1799–1836), Scottish lawyer and journalist; educated in Edinburgh; solicitor, 1831; wrote a collection of short biographies entitled ' An Historical Account of the Senators of the College of Justice from MDXXXII.' [vii. 147]

BRUNTON, LOUISA (1785 ?–1860). [See CRAVEN.]

BRUNTON, MARY (1778–1818), novelist; born in Orkney; married Alexander Brunton [q. v.]; settled in Edinburgh, 1803; wrote novels. [vii. 148]

BRUNTON, WILLIAM (1777–1851), engineer and inventor; working engineer, 1790; employed in Boulton and Watt's works. Soho, 1796–1818; had works of his own in Birmingham, 1815–25; a civil engineer in London, 1825–35; ruined by mining and brewery speculations in Wales; maker of the first marine steam engines. [vii. 148]

BRUNYARD, WILLIAM (*fl.* 1350), reputed author of theological treatises; probably identical with John de Bromyarde [q. v.] [vii. 149]

BRUODINE, ANTHONY (*fl.* 1672), Irish Franciscan; lecturer in a convent at Prague; wrote theological and historical treatises. [vii. 149]

BRUTTON, NICHOLAS (1780–1843), lieutenant-colonel; ensign of foot, 1795; served in India, 1799–1805; exchanged into the hussars, and served in India, 1809–17; major, 1821; in command of the 11th hussars in England, 1830–7; retired to Bordeaux. [vii. 149]

BRWYNLLYS, BEDO (*fl.* 1450–1480), Welsh poet. [vii. 150]

BRYAN, AUGUSTINE (*d.* 1726), classical scholar; B.A. Trinity College, Cambridge, 1711; rector of Piddlehinton, Dorset, 1722; edited Plutarch's ' Lives' (1723–9), completed after his death by Moses du Soul. [vii. 150]

BRYAN, SIR FRANCIS (*d.* 1550), courtier and diplomatist; captain of a ship-of-war, 1513; in high favour at Henry VIII's court, 1515; knighted for service in the field, 1522; employed in several missions to France, 1523–1525; sent to Rome to obtain the pope's sanction for Queen Catherine's divorce, 1528, and displayed great energy in forwarding the cause of his cousin, Anne Boleyn; cited Catherine to appear before Cranmer, 1533; turned against Anne Boleyn, 1536; married the widow of the Earl of Ormonde, and went to Ireland as lord marshal, 1548; appointed lord justice, 1549; published verses and translations. [vii. 150]

BRYAN, JOHN (*d.* 1545), logician; educated at Eton and King's College, Cambridge; rector of Shellow-Bowells, Essex, 1523. [vii. 152]

BRYAN, JOHN (*d.* 1676), nonconformist; educated at Emmanuel College, Cambridge; vicar of Holy Trinity, Coventry, 1644; ejected, 1662; continued to preach and to educate nonconformists; D.D.; founded presbyterian congregation in Coventry, 1672; published sermons and poems. [vii. 153]

BRYAN, MARGARET (*fl.* 1815), proprietress of a girls' school at Blackheath; published treatises on astronomy and physics. [vii. 154]

BRYAN, MATTHEW (*d.* 1699), Jacobite preacher; educated at Oxford; D.C.L. Oxford, 1685; incumbent of St. Mary's, Newington, and lecturer at St. Michael's, Crooked Lane; nonjuror and minister of a Jacobite congregation in Fleet Street; published sermons. [vii. 154]

BRYAN, MICHAEL (1757–1821), connoisseur; resided in Flanders, 1782–90; agent for the purchase of important pictures, 1798–1804; published 'Biographical . . . Dictionary of Painters and Engravers,' 1813–16. [vii. 155]

BRYANT, HENRY (1721–1799), botanist; B.A. St. John's College, Cambridge, 1749; rector of Colby. [vii. 155]

BRYANT, JACOB (1715–1804), classical scholar; educated at Eton, 1730–6; fellow of King's College, Cambridge; tutor to the Marquis of Blandford; secretary to the Duke of Marlborough, 1756; held lucrative office in the ordnance; resided for several years at Blenheim, and published description of the Marlborough collection of antique gems, 1783; resided latterly at Farnham Royal, Buckinghamshire; published treatises on ancient mythology and Homeric questions, in one of which he denied that such a city as Troy ever existed, and wrote on theological subjects. [vii. 155]

BRYCE, SIR ALEXANDER (*d.* 1832), military engineer; educated at Woolwich, 1782; commissioned in the artillery, 1787; transferred to the engineers, 1789; captain, 1794; served in America, Egypt (under Sir Ralph Abercromby), and Italy; major-general, 1825; inspector-general of fortifications, 1829. [vii. 157]

BRYCE, DAVID (1803–1876), architect in Edinburgh; apprentice and partner to William Burn [q. v.]; in business as an architect, 1844–76; revived the 'Scottish Baronial' style; architect of Fettes College. [vii. 158]

BRYCE, JAMES, the elder (1767–1857), divine; educated at Glasgow; minister of the Anti-burgher church, 1795; removed to Ireland; minister of the Anti-burgher church at Killaig, Londonderry, 1805–57; founder of the Associate Presbytery of Ireland. [vii. 158]

BRYCE, JAMES, the younger (1806–1877), geologist; third son of James Bryce the elder [q. v.]; educated at Glasgow; schoolmaster at Belfast, 1828, at Glasgow, 1846–74; published various mathematical treatises and papers on the geology of the north of Ireland and of Scotland. [vii. 159]

BRYDALL, JOHN (*b.* 1635 ?), law-writer; of Queen's College, Oxford, and Lincoln's Inn; secretary to the master of the rolls. [vii. 159]

BRYDGES, EDMUND, second BARON CHANDOS (*d.* 1573), eldest surviving son of Sir John Brydges [q. v.], served in France; succeeded to the barony, 1556. [vii. 163]

BRYDGES, GEORGE, sixth BARON CHANDOS (*d.* 1655), succeeded to the barony, 1621; fought in the civil war. [vii. 161]

BRYDGES, GILES, third BARON CHANDOS (1547–1594), son of Edmund Brydges, baron Chandos [q.v.], M.P. Gloucestershire, 1572; succeeded to the barony, 1573. [vii. 163]

BRYDGES, GREY, fifth BARON CHANDOS (1579 ?–1621), imprisoned in connection with the insurrection of the Earl of Essex, 1601; succeeded to the barony, 1602; a favourite courtier of James I, 1605; on service in the Low Countries, 1610; kept great state at Sudeley Castle; reputed author of ' Horæ Subsecivæ,' 1620. [vii. 160]

BRYDGES, SIR HARFORD JONES (1764–1847), diplomatist; originally in the East India Company's service; as Harford Jones, created baronet in 1807; envoy to Persia, 1807–11; took the name of Brydges, 1826; published travels and pamphlets. [vii. 161]

BRYDGES, JAMES, first DUKE OF CHANDOS (1673–1744), M.P. for Hereford city, 1698–1714; paymaster of the forces abroad, 1707–12; succeeded as ninth Baron Chandos, and was created Earl of Carnarvon, 1714; created Duke of Chandos, 1719; lord lieutenant of Hereford and Radnor shires, 1721; chancellor of St. Andrews University; built the great house at Canons, near Edgware; patron of Handel; satirised by Pope. [vii. 162]

BRYDGES, SIR JOHN, first BARON CHANDOS (1490 ?–1556); Roman catholic; knighted, 1513; servant and companion of Henry VIII, 1532; constable of Sudeley Castle, 1538; served in France, 1549; lieutenant of the Tower, 1553 to June 1554; suppressed Wyatt's rebellion, and was created Baron Chandos of Sudeley, 1554; ordered to superintend the execution of Bishop Hooper at Gloucester, 1555. [vii. 163]

BRYDGES, SIR RICHARD (*d.* 1558), son of Sir John Brydges [q. v.]. knighted, 1553. [vii. 164]

BRYDGES, SIR SAMUEL EGERTON (1762–1837), bibliographer and genealogist; educated at Queens' College, Cambridge, 1780; barrister of the Middle Temple,

G

1787; urged his elder brother to claim the barony of Chandos, 1790–1803; issued bibliographical and genealogical works; resided at Lee Priory, near Canterbury, 1810–18, issuing from his private press reprints of rare English pieces; M.P. for Maidstone, 1812–18; created baronet, 1814; lived chiefly at Geneva after 1818. His bibliographical books are numerous and valuable; his poems and novels mediocre. [vii. 164]

BRYDGES, SIR THOMAS (*d.* 1559), son of Sir John Brydges [q. v.], lieutenant of Tower, 1554. [vii. 164]

BRYDON, WILLIAM (1811–1873), army surgeon; went to India, 1835; sole survivor of the retreat from Cabul, 1842; in the sieges of Jellalabad, 1842, and of Lucknow, 1857; settled in Scotland, 1859. [vii. 166]

BRYDONE, PATRICK (1736–1818), traveller; travelled partly as a tutor, in Switzerland, Italy, Sicily, and Malta, 1765–71; lived latterly in Berwickshire; published travels and papers on electricity. [vii. 166]

BRYDSON, THOMAS (1806–1855), poet; educated at Glasgow and Edinburgh; minister of Kilmalcolm, Renfrewshire, 1842–55. [vii. 167]

BRYER, HENRY (*d.* 1799), engraver and printseller in London. [vii. 167]

BRYERWOOD, EDWARD (1565?–1613). [See BREREWOOD.]

BRYGHTWELL or **BRYTHWELL**, THOMAS (*d.* 1390), fellow of Merton College, Oxford: a Wycliffite; submitted to the church, 1382; prebendary of St. Paul's, 1386, and of Lincoln; chancellor of Oxford University, 1388; D.D. [vii. 167]

BRYNE, ALBERTUS (1621?–1677?), composer; organist of St. Paul's, *c.* 1638, of Westminster Abbey, and of Dulwich College, 1671–7. [vii. 168]

BRYNKNELL, THOMAS (*d.* 1539?). [See BRINKNELL.]

BRYSKETT, LODOWICK or LEWIS (*fl.* 1571–1611), translator; of Italian origin; educated at Trinity College, Cambridge, 1559; official in Ireland, 1571; accompanied Philip Sidney on his continental tour, 1572–5; held offices under government in Ireland, 1577–1600; friend of Edmund Spenser, 1582; Irish landowner, 1606; published translations and poems, contributing two elegies to Spenser's 'Astrophel,' 1586. [vii. 168]

BRYSON, ALEXANDER (1802–1869), medical writer; educated at Edinburgh and Glasgow; naval surgeon, 1827; director-general of the naval medical department, 1864. [vii. 169]

BRYSON, JAMES (1730?–1796), Irish presbyterian; minister at Lisburn, 1764, and at Belfast, 1773; an originator of the Orange Society, 1795; published sermons. [vii. 169]

BRYSON, WILLIAM (1730–1815), Irish presbyterian; minister of the 'non-subscribers' at Antrim, 1764–1810; published sermons. [vii. 170]

BUC or **BUCK**, SIR GEORGE (*d.* 1623), poet; went on the expedition to Cadiz, 1596; knighted, 1603; master of the revels and licenser of plays, 1608–22; author of poems and works on English history. [vii. 170]

BUCCLEUCH, DUKES OF. [See SCOTT, HENRY, third DUKE, 1746–1812; SCOTT, WALTER FRANCIS, fifth DUKE, 1806–1884.]

BUCER or **BUTZER**, MARTIN (1491–1551), protestant divine; entered Dominican monastery at Schlettstadt, his native town, 1508; studied at Heidelberg, where he heard Luther dispute, April 1518; corresponded with Luther, and became a protestant: obtained papal dispensation from his monastic vow, 1521; became pastor at Landstuhl, in the Palatinate, 1522; travelled in order to propagate reformed doctrines; preached at Weissenburg, in Lower Alsace, 1522 or 1523, and was excommunicated; took refuge in Strassburg, 1523, where he became representative reformer; lived mainly at Strassburg till 1549; favoured the tenets of Zwingli in the great eucharistic controversy, 1525–30, and was consequently involved in controversy both with Luther and his followers and with Erasmus; consulted by Henry VIII about his divorce from Catherine of Arragon;

laboured after Zwingli's death to find a common statement of belief which would unite the Lutherans, the reformed churches of South Germany, and the Swiss church, 1531–8; censured Servetus, 1531; approved of Calvin's views on church discipline, 1538; consulted by the promoters of the attempt to reconcile protestants and catholics, 1540–6, and by the archbishop of Cologne in the effort to protestantise his diocese, 1541–3; caused Strassburg to resist to the last the interim imposed by Charles V, 1548; but was forced to withdraw to England, April 1549; kindly received in London by Cranmer, Edward VI. and the Protector Somerset; was appointed regius professor of divinity at Cambridge, 1549, where his views excited much controversy; consulted as to the Book of Common Prayer, 1550; buried in the university church, 1551; his body exhumed by Queen Mary's commissioners, 1557; produced ninety-six separate treatises. [vii. 172]

BUCHAN, EARLS OF. [See COMYN, ALEXANDER, second EARL, *d.* 1289; COMYN, JOHN, third EARL, *d.* 1313?; STEWART, ALEXANDER, first EARL of the second creation, 1343?–1405?; STEWART, JOHN, first EARL of the third creation, 1381?–1424; ERSKINE, JAMES, sixth EARL of the fourth creation, *d.* 1640; ERSKINE, DAVID STEUART, eleventh EARL, 1742–1829.]

BUCHAN, ALEXANDER PETER (1764–1824), physician; son of William Buchan [q. v.]; studied in London, Edinburgh, and Leyden (M.D., 1793); practised in London; published medical tracts. [vii. 178]

BUCHAN, ANDREW OF (*d.* 1309?), bishop of Caithness, 1296; Cistercian; abbot of Cupar-Angus, 1272. [vii. 178]

BUCHAN or **SIMPSON**, ELSPETH (1738–1791), foundress of the 'Buchanite' sect (extinct 1848); wife of a potter; separated from him, 1781; persuaded Hugh White, Relief minister of Irvine, that she was inspired, 1783; on being expelled from Irvine, settled in Closeburn, Dumfries, 1784. [vii. 178]

BUCHAN, PETER (1790–1854), collector of Scottish ballads; by the help of his kinsman, the Earl of Buchan, set up a press in Peterhead, 1816, where he printed his own works and collections; published poems and historical tracts. [vii. 179]

BUCHAN, THOMAS (*d.* 1720), Jacobite general; a highlander by birth; served abroad; commanded a foot-regiment in Scotland, 1682; employed against the covenanters, 1684; colonel, 1686; appointed major-general by James II in Ireland, 1689, and sent to command his forces in Scotland; surprised at Cromdale, 1690; retired to Lochaber; retired to France, 1692; Jacobite agent in Scotland, 1707. [vii. 180]

BUCHAN, WILLIAM (1729–1805), author of the popular 'Domestic Medicine,' 1769; studied medicine at Edinburgh; practised in Yorkshire; settled in Edinburgh, 1766; removed to London, 1778; published medical tracts. [vii. 180]

BUCHANAN, ANDREW (1690–1759), Virginia merchant in Glasgow; bought Drumpellier, Lanarkshire, 1735; lord provost of Glasgow, 1740; strenuously opposed the insurgents, 1745. [vii. 181]

BUCHANAN, SIR ANDREW (1807–1882), diplomatist; entered the diplomatic service, 1825; was resident at nearly every court, first as attaché, afterwards as minister; retired, 1878; created baronet, 1878. [vii. 181]

BUCHANAN, CLAUDIUS (1766–1815), Indian traveller; educated at Glasgow University, 1782; clerk in London, 1787; of Queens' College, Cambridge, 1791; chaplain in Bengal, 1797; vice-provost of college at Fort William, 1799–1807; D.D. Glasgow and Cambridge; made two tours in south and west of India, 1806–7; returned to England, 1808; advocate of missions; issued translations of the scriptures into various oriental languages. [vii. 182]

BUCHANAN, DAVID (1595?–1652?), Scottish historian; resided in Paris, 1636; back in Scotland before 1644; published and left in manuscript treatises on Scottish history, biography, and topography. [vii. 184]

BUCHANAN, DAVID, the elder (1745–1812), printer and publisher at Montrose; published miniature editions of English classics. [vii. 185]

BUCHANAN, DAVID, the younger (1779-1848), journalist in Edinburgh; son of David Buchanan the elder [q. v.]; editor of the ' Caledonian Mercury,' 1810-27, and of the ' Edinburgh Courant,' 1827-48; wrote on political economy and statistics. [vii. 185]

BUCHANAN, DUGALD (1716-1768), Gaelic poet, ' the Cowper of the highlands '; native of Balquhidder; catechist at Kinloch Rannoch, 1755. [vii. 185]

BUCHANAN, FRANCIS HAMILTON (1762-1829), writer on Indian subjects; M.D. Edinburgh, 1783; naval surgeon; Bengal surgeon, 1794; travelled in Burma, 1795, in Mysore and Malabar, 1800, and in Nepál, 1802; compiled a statistical survey of Bengal, 1807-15; settled in Scotland, 1816; published travels. [vii. 186]

BUCHANAN, GEORGE (1506-1582), historian and scholar; studied at Paris, 1520-2; served at the siege of Werk, 1523; studied at St. Andrews under John Major, 1524; B.A., 1525; went to Paris, 1526; graduated M.A. in the Scots college, Paris, March 1528; taught grammar in the college of St. Barbe; tutor to Gilbert, earl of Cassilis, at Paris, 1529-34; returned to Scotland, 1536; tutor to a natural son of James V, 1536; urged by the king to satirise the morals of the clergy, and so provoked Cardinal Beaton; escaped from prison at St. Andrews, and fled to London, 1539; taught Latin at Bordeaux, 1540-3; taught in the college of Cardinal le Moine at Paris, 1544-7; invited to teach in the college at Coimbra, 1547, and imprisoned there by the inquisition, 1549-51; came to England, 1552; returned to Paris, and taught in the college of Boncourt, 1553; tutor to Timoléon de Cossé, comte de Brissac (killed in action, 1569), 1554-9, in France and Italy; returned to Scotland and professed himself a protestant before 1563; lay member of the general assembly, 1563-8, and moderator, 1567; principal of St. Leonard's College, St. Andrews, 1566-70; assigned a pension out of the revenues of Crossraguel Abbey; lived in England, October 1568, to January 1569, as secretary of Regent Moray's commissioners, and vouched that the casket letters were in Queen Mary's handwriting; published, in Scottish dialect (1570), pamphlets attacking the Hamiltons on account of Moray's assassination, and ridiculing Maitland of Lethington, the queen's advocate; resided at Stirling as tutor to James VI, 1570-8; keeper of the privy seal, 1570-8; published ' Detectio Mariæ Reginæ,' a venomous attack on Queen Mary, 1571, in Latin and, 1572, in French and Scottish; wrote Latin poems. His ' De Jure Regni apud Scotos,' 1579, was long a text-book of the opponents of absolutism. His ' Ierum Scoticarum historia,' 1582, was the chief source from which foreigners derived their knowledge of Scotland. [vii. 186]

BUCHANAN, GEORGE (1790 ?-1852), civil engineer; third son of David Buchanan the elder [q. v.]; educated at Edinburgh; constructed harbours and bridges; an authority on salmon-fishery disputes; published scientific treatises. [vii. 193]

BUCHANAN, SIR GEORGE (1831-1895), physician; B.A. London, 1851; studied medicine at University College; M.D. London, 1855; physician at London Fever Hospital, 1861-8, and, later, consulting physician; F.R.C.P., 1866, censor, 1892-4, and Lettsomian lecturer, 1867; F.R.S., 1882; permanent inspector in the medical department of privy council, 1869; principal medical officer, 1879-92, of local government board; knighted, 1892; honorary LL.D. Edinburgh, 1893; fellow of University College, 1864; chairman of royal commission on tuberculosis. His reports have become classical works in sanitary literature. [Suppl. i. 328]

BUCHANAN, JAMES (1804-1870),Free church leader; educated at Glasgow; minister of North Leith, 1828, and of St. Giles, Edinburgh, 1840; joined the Free church, 1843; minister of Free St. Stephen's, Edinburgh; D.D. Princeton; LL.D. Glasgow; professor in the Free church college, 1845-68; published theological works. [vii. 194]

BUCHANAN, JOHN LANNE (fl. 1780-1816), author; educated at Glasgow; assistant minister at Comrie; missioner in the Hebrides, 1780; subsequently resided in London; published works on the Hebrides and highlands. [vii. 195]

BUCHANAN, ROBERT (1813-1866), socialist; taught school; lecturer in Manchester before 1839; journalist in Glasgow; published controversial writings. [vii. 195]

BUCHANAN, ROBERT (1785-1873), benefactor of Glasgow University; educated at Glasgow; minister of Peebles, 1813-24; assistant professor of logic in Glasgow, 1824, and professor, 1827-64; author of tragedies and poems. [vii. 195]

BUCHANAN, ROBERT (1802-1875), Free church leader; educated at Glasgow; minister of Gargunnock, 1826, of Salton, Haddingtonshire, 1829, and of the Tron church, Glasgow, 1833-43; took leading part in anti-patronage agitation, 1838, and joined the Free church, 1843; D.D. Glasgow, 1840; died at Rome; wrote on church history, also a narrative of travels in Palestine. [vii. 196]

BUCHANAN, ROBERTSON (1770-1816), civil engineer of Glasgow; published treatises on machinery. [vii. 197]

BUCHANAN, WILLIAM (1781-1863), Scottish advocate; son of David Buchanan the elder [q. v.]; educated at Edinburgh; advocate, 1806; solicitor of teinds, 1856; author of law reports, &c. [vii. 197]

BUCK, ADAM (1759-1833), portrait-painter; exhibited at Royal Academy from 1795; published ' Paintings on Greek Vases,' 1811. [Suppl. i. 330]

BUCK, CHARLES (1771-1815), author of 'A Theological Dictionary,' 1802, and other pieces; congregational minister at Sheerness and in London. [vii. 198]

BUCK, SIR GEORGE (d. 1623). [See BUC, SIR GEORGE.]

BUCK, JOHN WILLIAM (d. 1821), of Lincoln's Inn, 1813; barrister; published law reports. [vii. 198]

BUCK, SAMUEL (1696-1779), draughtsman and engraver; issued series of views of towns, ruined abbeys, and castles, &c., in England and Wales; worked in conjunction with his brother Nathaniel, 1727-53. [vii. 198]

BUCK, ZACHARIAH (1798-1879), composer; chorister at Norwich; organist of St. Peter Mancroft, 1818-1821, and of Norwich Cathedral, 1819-77; Mus.Doc. Lambeth, 1847. [vii. 199]

BUCKE, CHARLES (1781-1846), dramatist and miscellaneous writer. [vii. 199]

BUCKENHAM, ROBERT (fl. 1530), prior of the Black Friars, Cambridge; B.D., 1524; D.D., 1531; preached against Latimer at Cambridge, 1529; withdrew to Edinburgh, 1534; went to Louvain to take part in the proceedings against William Tyndale, 1535. [vii. 199]

BUCKERIDGE or **BUCKRIDGE**, JOHN (1562 ?-1631), bishop of Rochester and Ely; educated at Merchant Taylors' School; fellow of St. John's College, Oxford, 1578; B.A., 1583; D.D., 1597; tutor to William Laud; prebendary of Rochester, 1587; chaplain to Archbishop Whitgift, 1596; rector of North Fambridge, Essex, 1596-9, and of North Kilworth, Leicestershire, 1599-1608; vicar of St. Giles, Cripplegate, 1604; president of St John's, Oxford, 1605-11; preached at Hampton Court, 1606; canon of Windsor, 1606; bishop of Rochester, 1611; voted in favour of the Earl of Essex's divorce, 1613; defended Dr. Richard Montague, 1626; bishop of Ely, 1628; edited Bishop Andrewes's sermons, 1629; published sermons. [vii. 200]

BUCKHURST, first BARON (1536-1608). [See SACKVILLE, THOMAS.]

BUCKINGHAM, DUKES OF. [See STAFFORD, HUMPHREY, first DUKE, 1402-1460; STAFFORD, HENRY, second DUKE, 1454 ?-1483; STAFFORD, EDWARD, third DUKE, 1478-1521; VILLIERS, GEORGE, first DUKE of the second creation, 1592-1628; VILLIERS, GEORGE, second DUKE, 1628-1687.]

BUCKINGHAM, first MARQUIS OF (1753-1813). [See GRENVILLE, GEORGE NUGENT-TEMPLE-.]

BUCKINGHAM, EARL OF. [See THOMAS OF WOODSTOCK, 1355-1397.]

BUCKINGHAM AND CHANDOS, DUKES OF. [See GRENVILLE, RICHARD TEMPLE NUGENT BRYDGES CHANDOS, first DUKE, 1776-1839; GRENVILLE, RICHARD PLANTAGENET TEMPLE NUGENT BRYDGES CHANDOS, second DUKE, 1797-1861; GRENVILLE, RICHARD PLANTAGENET CAMPBELL TEMPLE NUGENT BRYDGES CHANDOS, third DUKE, 1823-1889.]

BUCKINGHAM, JAMES SILK (1786–1855), author and traveller; at sea for several years from 1796; journalist at Calcutta, 1818; expelled from India for attacks on the government, 1823; travelled in Syria and Palestine, 1823; journalist in London, 1824–30; M.P. for Sheffield, 1832–7; travelled in America, 1837–40, and on the continent, 1847; received a pension, 1851; travelled as a lecturer; author of an autobiography, travels, and temperance pamphlets. [vii. 202]

BUCKINGHAM, LEICESTER SILK (1825–1867), dramatist; youngest son of James Silk Buckingham [q. v.]; travelled with his father; a popular lecturer, 1854; his first pieces put on the stage, 1856; produced historical treatises, comedies, and farces. [vii. 203]

BUCKINGHAM, OSBERN (1393–1447 ?). [See BOKENHAM.]

BUCKINGHAMSHIRE, first DUKE OF (1648–1721). [See SHEFFIELD, JOHN.]

BUCKINGHAMSHIRE, EARLS OF. [See HOBART, JOHN, first EARL, 1694?–1756; HOBART, JOHN, second EARL, 1723–1793; HOBART, GEORGE, third EARL, 1732–1804; HOBART, ROBERT, fourth EARL, 1760–1815.]

BUCKLAND, FRANCIS TREVELYAN (1826–1880), naturalist; son of William Buckland [q. v.]; educated at Winchester, 1839–44; B.A. Christ Church, Oxford, 1848; studied surgery at St. George's Hospital, London, 1848–51; army surgeon in London, 1854; contributor to the 'Field,' 1856–65; started 'Land and Water' in 1866; inspector of salmon fisheries, 1867–80; published 'Curiosities of Natural History,' and kindred works. [vii. 204]

BUCKLAND, RALPH (1564–1611), Roman catholic divine; educated at Merchant Taylors' School, 1571, and Magdalen College, Oxford, 1579; law-student in London; studied at Rheims and Rome, 1586; ordained priest, 1588; sent on the English mission; banished, 1606; author of theological works. [vii. 205]

BUCKLAND, WILLIAM (1784–1856), geologist; educated at Winchester, 1798, and Corpus Christi, Oxford, 1801, fellow, 1808–25; made geological tour in the south-west of England, 1808–12; professor of mineralogy at Oxford, 1813, and reader in geology, 1819; canon of Christ Church, Oxford, 1825; dean of Westminster, 1845–56; president of the Geological Society, 1824 and 1840; upheld the Mosaic account of the flood; wrote geological papers. [vii. 206]

BUCKLE, SIR CLAUDE HENRY MASON (1803–1894), admiral; entered Royal Naval College, Portsmouth, 1817; lieutenant, 1827; captain, 1845; flag-captain to Commodore Arthur Fanshawe on west coast of Africa, 1849–50; in Black Sea, 1854; C.B., 1855; superintendent Deptford dockyard, 1857–63; commander-in-chief at Queenstown, 1867–70; K.C.B., 1875; admiral, 1877. [Suppl. i. 330]

BUCKLE, HENRY THOMAS (1821–1862), historian of civilisation; son of a wealthy London shipowner; received no school or college training; being left independent at his father's death, devoted himself to travelling on the continent, where he acquired the principal languages, 1840 and 1843; settled in London, 1842; bought and read thousands of books, making careful notes; had settled the plan of his 'History of Civilisation in England' by 1853; published the first volume, 1857, the second, 1861; died at Damascus on an Eastern tour; inclined to freethought in religion. Miscellaneous works by him appeared posthumously. [vii. 208]

BUCKLER, BENJAMIN (1718–1780), antiquary; of Oriel College, Oxford, 1732; fellow of All Souls', 1739; D.D., 1759; vicar of Cumnor, 1755; keeper of archives, Oxford, 1777–80; published 'Stemmata Chicheleana,' 1765. [vii. 211]

BUCKLER, JOHN (1770–1851), topographical artist; practised as architect in London till 1826; issued aquatint engravings of colleges, cathedrals, &c., 1797–1815; exhibited in water-colours at the Royal Academy, 1796–1849; F.S.A., 1810. [vii. 212]

BUCKLER, WILLIAM (1814–1884), entomologist; exhibited water-colours at the Academy, 1836–56; a student of larvæ. [vii. 213]

BUCKLEY, CECIL WILLIAM (1828–1872), naval officer, 1845–72; received the Victoria cross for services in the Black Sea, 1855; captain R.N., 1862. [vii. 213]

BUCKLEY, JOHN (d. 1598). [See JONES, JOHN.]

BUCKLEY, MRS. OLIVIA (1799–1847), organist; daughter of Sophia Dussek [q. v.]; married a Mr. Buckley; wrote pianoforte music and songs, and published (1843) 'Musical Truths.' [xvi. 268]

BUCKLEY, ROBERT or SIGEBERT (1517–1610), English Benedictine; professed at Westminster during the Marian revival, c. 1557; imprisoned as a recusant, 1560–1603, latterly at Framlingham; imprisoned in London, 1605–10. He was the last of the old English Benedictine congregation, and surrendered his authority for perpetuating the succession to Thomas Preston, 1609. [vii. 213]

BUCKLEY, THEODORE WILLIAM ALOIS (1825–1856), translator from the classics; servitor of Christ Church, Oxford, 1845; chaplain; M.A., 1853; became a literary hack; author of classical translations and miscellaneous works. [vii. 214]

BUCKLEY, WILLIAM (d. 1570 ?), mathematician; educated at Eton and King's College, Cambridge; M.A., 1545; tutor to the royal henchmen, 1550; taught mathematics at King's, Cambridge, c. 1552; published an arithmetical tract. [vii. 215]

BUCKLEY, WILLIAM (1780–1856), colonist; enlisted, 1799; transported for a plot to shoot the Duke of Kent, 1802; escaped from Port Phillip, December 1803; lived with native tribes till July 1835; pardoned, and employed as interpreter; settled in Tasmania, 1837. [vii. 215]

BUCKMAN, JAMES (1816–1884), geologist; studied natural science in London; professor at Cirencester Agricultural College, 1848–63; farmed land in Dorset, 1863–84; wrote botanical, geological, and agricultural papers. [vii. 216]

BUCKMASTER, THOMAS (fl. 1566), almanack-maker. [vii. 216]

BUCKMASTER, WILLIAM (d. 1545), divine; fellow of Peterhouse, Cambridge, 1517; D.D., 1528; carried to court as vice-chancellor the university's reply to Henry VIII's questions concerning his divorce, 1530; signed the articles of religion, 1536; prebendary of St. Paul's, 1539. [vii. 216]

BUCKNILL, SIR JOHN CHARLES (1817–1897), physician; educated at Rugby and University College, London; L.S.A., M.R.C.S., and M.B. London, 1840; M.D., 1852; first medical superintendent, Devon County Asylum, 1844–62; chancellor's medical visitor of lunatics, 1862–76; F.R.C.P., 1859; censor, 1879–80; Lumleian lecturer, 1878; F.R.S., 1866; knighted, 1894; published 'Manual of Psychological Medicine,' 1858, and other works. [Suppl. i. 331]

BUCKSHORN, JOSEPH (fl. 1670), Dutch painter; employed by Sir Peter Lely to fill in his canvases, 1670; painted portraits in Lely's manner. [vii. 217]

BUCKSTONE, JOHN BALDWIN (1802–1879), comedian; solicitor's clerk; went on the provincial stage, c. 1820; performed at the Surrey Theatre, 1823; his first piece played, 1826; manager of the Haymarket, 1853–76; composed numerous farces. [vii. 217]

BUDD, GEORGE (fl. 1756), painter; London hosier; painted portraits and landscapes. [vii. 218]

BUDD, GEORGE (1808–1882), professor of medicine in King's College, London, 1846–63; fellow of Caius College, Cambridge, 1831; M.D., 1840; studied also in London and Paris; physician to the hospital ship at Greenwich, 1837; practised in London, 1840–67; retired to Barnstaple; wrote medical tracts. [vii. 219]

BUDD, HENRY (1774–1853), theologian; son of Richard Budd [q. v.]; M.A. St. John's College, Cambridge, 1801; chaplain of Bridewell Hospital, London, 1801–31; rector of White Roothing, Essex, 1808–53; published tracts. [vii. 219]

BUDD, RICHARD (1746–1821), physician; M.D. Jesus College, Cambridge, 1775; practised at Newbury, Berkshire; physician to St. Bartholomew's Hospital, 1780–1801, and an active official of the Royal College of Physicians. [vii. 220]

BUDD, WILLIAM (1811–1880), physician; studied medicine at London, Edinburgh, Paris; M.D. Edinburgh,

1838 : practised at North Tawton, Devonshire, 1839, and
in Bristol, 1842-73 ; made important researches into the
conditions of zymotic diseases ; published numerous
medical papers. [vii. 220]

BUDDEN, JOHN (1566-1620), professor of civil law at
Oxford, 1611-20 ; scholar of Trinity College, Oxford, 1583 ;
M.A. Gloucester Hall, 1589 ; philosophy reader of Magda-
len College, and D.C.L., 1602 ; principal of New Inn Hall.
1609-18, and of Broadgates Hall, 1618-20 ; wrote two
Latin biographies, 1602 and 1607. [vii. 221]

BUDDLE, ADAM (d. 1715), botanist ; M.A. Cambridge, 1685 ; nonjuror, 1689 ; possessed a fine collection
of mosses and grasses ; rector of North Fambridge, Essex,
1703 ; left an English flora in manuscript. [vii. 222]

BUDDLE, JOHN (1773-1843), mining engineer ; taught
by his father, a practical miner ; manager of Wallsend
colliery, 1806 ; made experiments on ventilation in mines
and introduced an improved method of coal-working.
[vii. 222]

BUDGE, EDWARD (1800-1865), theological writer ;
B.A. Cambridge, 1824 ; vicar of Manaccan, Cornwall,
1839 ; rector of Bratton Clovelly, Devon, 1846-65 ; published sermons. [vii. 223]

BUDGELL, EUSTACE (1686-1737), miscellaneous
writer ; cousin of Addison ; educated at Trinity College,
Oxford, 1705 ; barrister of the Inner Temple ; contributed
to the ' Spectator ' ; held official posts in Ireland, 1714-18 ;
travelled ; ruined by the South Sea scheme, 1721 ; lost
his reason ; wrote against Walpole, 1728 ; journalist,
1733-5 ; accused of embezzlement ; drowned himself.
[vii. 224]

BUDGET, SAMUEL (1794-1851), a successful
Bristol merchant. [vii. 226]

BUDWORTH, JOSEPH. afterwards PALMER (d. 1815).
[See PALMER.]

BUDWORTH, WILLIAM (d. 1745), schoolmaster ;
M.A. Cambridge, 1726 ; vicar of Brewood, Staffordshire,
and master of the school there ; declined the services of
Samuel Johnson as usher, 1736. [vii. 226]

BUFTON, ELEANOR, afterwards MRS. ARTHUR
SWANBOROUGH (1840 ?-1893), actress ; appeared at St.
James's, 1854 ; with Charles Kean at the Princess's,
1856-7 ; last appeared (1872) at Drury Lane. Her parts
include Regan (' Lear '), Hermia (' Midsummer Night's
Dream '), Ferdinand (' Tempest '), and Hero (' Much
Ado '). [Suppl. i. 332]

BUGG, FRANCIS (1640-1724 ?), writer against
quakerism ; wool-comber at Mildenhall, Suffolk, and,
from boyhood, a quaker ; suspected of informing against
a quaker meeting, 1675 ; left the society after a long
quarrel, 1680 ; issued virulent pamphlets against the
quakers, 1682-1724. [vii. 226]

BUGGA or **BUGGE**, SAINT (d. 751). [See EAD-
BURGA.]

BUISSIÈRE or **BUSSIÈRE**, PAUL (d. 1739), anatomical writer ; surgeon of Orange, France ; Huguenot
exile ; settled in Copenhagen ; naturalised in England,
1688 ; practised as surgeon in London. [vii. 228]

BUIST, GEORGE (1805-1860), journalist and man of
science ; studied at St. Andrews and Edinburgh ; licentiate of the church of Scotland, 1826 ; newspaper editor
in Dundee, Perth, and Cupar-Fife, 1832-8 ; LL.D. ; edited
the ' Bombay Times,' 1839-59 ; inspector of the Bombay
observatories, 1842-59 ; published scientific and other
papers. [vii. 228]

BUITE, SAINT (d. 521), born near Mellifont, Louth ;
visited Wales and Italy ; returned through Germany and
Scotland to Antrim, and thence to Louth, where he built
Monasterboice, i.e. the Monastery of Buite. [vii. 229]

BULKELEY or **BOKELEY**, ARTHUR (d. 1553),
bishop of Bangor ; doctor of canon law, Oxford, 1525 ;
rector of Llanddeusant, Anglesey, and canon of St. Asaph,
1525 ; rector of St. James, Garlick Hythe, London, 1531 ;
prebendary of Clynnoc Vechan, 1537 ; bishop of Bangor,
1541 ; resident in his diocese ; involved in lawsuits.
[vii. 231]

BULKELEY, LAUNCELOT (1568 ?-1650), archbishop
of Dublin ; M.A. Oxford, 1593 ; beneficed in Wales, 1593-
1620 ; archdeacon of Dublin, 1613-19 ; archbishop of

Dublin, 1619 ; claimed the primacy unsuccessfully ; imprisoned, 1647 ; his see sequestered by the Commonwealth,
1649. [vii. 231]

BULKELEY, SIR RICHARD (1533-1621), knight ;
constable of Beaumaris, 1561 ; M.P. for Anglesey, 1570-
1614 ; knighted, 1576 ; a favourite courtier of Queen
Elizabeth. [vii. 231]

BULKELEY, RICHARD (d. 1650), royalist general ;
lost Anglesey, 1648. [vii. 232]

BULKELEY, SIR RICHARD (1644-1710), enthusiast ;
M.A., and fellow of Trinity College, Dublin, 1681 ; succeeded to baronetcy of Dunlavan, 1685 ; took up with the
so-called ' prophets of the Cevennes,' c. 1708 ; published
pamphlets. [vii. 233]

BULKELEY, LADY or MRS. SOPHIA (fl. 1688), a
court beauty, 1668 ; married Henry Bulkeley. master of
the household ; lady of the bedchamber to James II's
queen, and present at the birth of the Prince of Wales,
1688. [vii. 233]

BULKLEY, CHARLES (1719-1797), baptist minister ;
educated at Northampton academy, 1736 ; presbyterian
minister at Welford, Northamptonshire, and Colchester ;
joined the general baptists ; minister of that denomination
in London, 1743-97 ; published philosophical tracts and
sermons. [vii. 234]

BULKLEY, PETER (1583-1659), puritan divine ;
fellow of St. John's College, Cambridge ; M.A., 1608 ; rector
of Odell, Bedfordshire, 1620 ; ejected for contempt of church
ceremonies, 1634 ? ; emigrated to New England, 1635 ;
founded Concord, 1636 ; pastor of Concord till death ;
published sermons. [vii. 235]

BULL, DANIEL (fl. 1657-1681), nonconformist
divine ; intruded minister of Stoke Newington, 1657-60 ;
ejected, 1662 ; afterwards presbyterian minister in London ; published sermons. [vii. 236]

BULL, GEORGE (1634-1710), Anglican theologian ;
bishop of St. David's ; left Exeter College, Oxford, 1649,
to avoid taking ' the Engagement' ; educated privately ;
ordained secretly by Bishop Skinner, 1655 ; minister of
St. George's, near Bristol ; rector of Suddington St.
Mary's, 1658-85 ; vicar of Suddington St. Peter's, Gloucestershire, 1662-85 ; published ' Harmonia Apostolica,' 1670 ;
prebendary of Gloucester, 1678 ; published ' Defensio
Fidei Nicaenae,' 1685 ; rector of Avening, Gloucestershire,
1685 ; D.D. Oxford, 1686 ; published ' Judicium Ecclesiæ Catholicæ,' 1694 ; bishop of St. David's, 1705 ; published theological works and sermons. [vii. 236]

BULL, HENRY (d. 1575 ?), theologian ; fellow of
Magdalen College, Oxford ; B.A., 1539 ; ejected from his
fellowship by Queen Mary's commissioners, 1553 ; published theological works and (1577) translated Luther's
' Psalmi Graduum.' [vii. 239]

BULL, JOHN (1563 ?-1628), composer ; Mus.Bac.
Oxford, 1586 ; Mus.Doc., 1592 ; chorister of the Chapel
Royal, c. 1572 ; organist of Hereford Cathedral, 1582 ;
singing-man of the Chapel Royal, 1585, and organist,
1591-1613 ; professor of music at Gresham College, 1597-
1607 ; travelled in France and Germany, 1601 ; conductor
at the entertainment of James I and Prince Henry by the
Merchant Taylors' Company, 1607 ; musician to Prince
Henry, 1611 ; left England, 1613 ; an organist of the
Chapel Royal, Brussels, c. 1614 ; organist of Antwerp
Cathedral, 1617-28. [vii. 239]

BULL, JOHN (d. 1642), a London weaver ; imprisoned
for pretending to inspiration, 1636. [vii. 242]

BULL, WILLIAM (1738-1814), congregationalist
minister ; studied at Daventry academy, 1759 ; pastor at
Newport Pagnel, 1764, and conducted school on a large
scale from 1783 onwards ; friend of Rev. John Newton of
Olney, and of the poet Cowper. [vii. 243]

BULLAKER. [See also BULLOKAR.]

BULLAKER, THOMAS, in religion JOHN BAPTIST
(1604 ?-1642), catholic martyr ; educated at St. Omer and
Valladolid, where he became a Franciscan ; studied theology at Segovia ; worked in the English mission ; executed
for celebrating mass. [vii. 244]

BULLEIN, RICHARD (d. 1563), physician.
[vii. 246]

BULLEIN, WILLIAM (*d.* 1576), physician; rector of Blaxhall, Suffolk, 1550–3; studied medicine abroad; resided in London from 1561. His 'Booke of Simples' (part of his 'Bulwarke against Sicknes,' 1562) is one of the earliest English herbals. 'A Dialogue against the Fever Pestilence' appeared 1564. [vii. 244]

BULLEN, SIR CHARLES (1769–1853), naval officer; served in Mediterranean and, after 1801, on west coast of Africa; commanded the Britannia at Trafalgar, 1805; rear-admiral, 1837; K.C.B., 1839; admiral, 1852. [vii. 246]

BULLEN, GEORGE (1816–1894), keeper of printed books at British Museum; supernumerary assistant in department of printed books in British Museum, 1838; senior assistant, 1850; superintendent of reading room, 1866; keeper of printed books, 1875–90; assisted in compiling printed catalogue; F.S.A., 1877; hon. LL.D. Glasgow, 1889; C.B., 1890. [Suppl. i. 332]

BULLER, CHARLES (1806–1848), liberal politician; taught by Thomas Carlyle, 1822–5; B.A. Trinity College, Cambridge, 1828; M.P. for West Looe, Cornwall, 1830–1; called to bar at Lincoln's Inn, 1831; M.P. for Liskeard, 1832–48; secretary to the governor-general of Canada, 1838; judge-advocate-general, 1846; chief poor law commissioner, 1847; published pamphlets. [vii. 246]

BULLER, SIR FRANCIS (1746–1800), judge; special pleader, 1765; barrister of the Inner Temple, 1772; judge of the county palatine of Chester, 1777; justice of the king's bench, 1778; created baronet, 1790; justice of the common pleas, 1794–1800. [vii. 248]

BULLER, SIR GEORGE (1802–1884), general; entered the army, 1820; colonel, 1841; commanded brigade, and afterwards division, in the Kaffir and Boer wars, 1847–8 and 1852–3; commanded brigade in the Crimea, 1854; wounded at Inkerman; K.C.B., 1855; lieutenant-general, 1862; general, 1871. [vii. 249]

BULLINGHAM, JOHN (*d.* 1598), bishop of Gloucester; fellow of Magdalen College, Oxford, 1550; a catholic; withdrew to Rouen; was restored to his fellowship, and graduated M.A., 1554; chaplain to Bishop Gardiner; rector of Boxwell, Gloucestershire, 1554; prebendary of St. Paul's, 1565; rector of St. Mary Magdalene, Milk Street, 1566; D.D., 1568; prebendary of Lincoln, 1568; canon of Worcester, 1570; rector of Withington, Gloucestershire, of Burton-by-Lincoln, and of Brington, Huntingdon, 1571; bishop of Gloucester, 1581–98, holding also the see of Bristol *in commendam*, 1581–9; scurrilously attacked by Martin Marprelate. [vii. 250]

BULLINGHAM, NICHOLAS (1512?–1576), bishop of Lincoln and Worcester; fellow of All Souls' College, Oxford, 1536; B.C.L., 1541; studied canon law; chaplain to Archbishop Cranmer; prebendary of Lincoln, 1547; rector of Thimbleby, Lincolnshire, 1552; deprived of his preferments, as being married, 1553; withdrew to Emden; restored to his preferments, 1558; chaplain to Archbishop Parker; LL.D. Cambridge, 1559; bishop of Lincoln, 1560; purged King's College, Cambridge, of Romanism, 1566; translated to Worcester, 1571. [vii. 251]

BULLINGHAM, RICHARD (*fl.* 1350). [See BILLINGHAM.]

BULLOCH, JOHN (1805–1882), author of 'Studies of the Text of Shakespeare,' 1878; worked at Aberdeen as mechanic. [vii. 253]

BULLOCK, CHRISTOPHER (1690?–1724), comedian; son of William Bullock (1657?–1740?) [q. v.]; first appeared in 1708 at Drury Lane; attached to the Lincoln's Inn Fields Theatre, 1715–24; produced seven plays, some possibly written by other hands. [vii. 253]

BULLOCK, GEORGE (1521?–1580?), Roman catholic divine; fellow of St. John's College, Cambridge; B.A., 1539; witness at Bishop Gardiner's trial, 1551; withdrew to Nevers in France; canon of Durham, 1554; B.D., 1554; master of St. John's College, Cambridge, 1554, and Lady Margaret professor of divinity, 1556; vicar of St. Sepulchre, London, 1555–6; rector of Much Munden, Hertfordshire, 1556; deprived of his preferments for recusancy, 1559; divinity lecturer at Antwerp, 1567; died at Antwerp; author of 'Œconomia Concordantiarum Scripturæ sacræ,' 1567. [vii. 254]

BULLOCK, HENRY, latinised BOVILLUS (*d.* 1526), divine; B.A. Cambridge, 1504, and fellow of Queens' College, 1506; D.D., 1520; studied Greek and lectured on St. Matthew; friend of Erasmus; rector of St. Martin's, Ludgate, 1522–6; published Latin orations and epistles. [vii. 254]

BULLOCK, WILLIAM (1657?–1740?), comedian; first mentioned in 1696; attached to Lincoln's Inn Fields Theatre, 1716 till death. [vii. 255]

BULLOCK, WILLIAM (*fl.* 1827), antiquary and naturalist; Liverpool goldsmith; exhibited a museum of curiosities, 1808; exhibited his collections in London, 1812–19; sold them, 1819; travelled in Mexico, 1822, and on his return exhibited his Mexican collections; travelled in the States and Mexico, 1826–7; perhaps settled in Cincinnati; published narrative of his travels. [vii. 256]

BULLOCK, WILLIAM THOMAS (1818–1879), theological writer; B.A. Oxford, 1847; assistant secretary, 1850, and secretary, 1865–79, of the Society for the Propagation of the Gospel; published biblical papers and sermons. [vii. 256]

BULLOKAR, JOHN (*fl.* 1622), lexicographer; physician at Chichester; published 'An English Expositor,' 1616 (3rd edit. 1641), and a metrical life of Christ, 1618. [vii. 257]

BULLOKAR, WILLIAM (*fl.* 1586), phonetist; engaged in tuition, 1550; served in the army, 1557; again employed in teaching, 1573; advocated spelling reform in a pamphlet, 1575, and in a book, 1580; translated 'Æsop's Fables,' 1585; issued an English grammar, 1586. [vii. 257]

BULMER, AGNES (1775–1836), poetess; wrote 'Messiah's Kingdom,' 1833. [vii. 258]

BULMER, WILLIAM (1757–1830), printer; apprenticed at Newcastle-on-Tyne; friend of Thomas Bewick; printed under his own name in London, 1791–1819. [vii. 258]

BULSTRODE, EDWARD (1588–1659), lawyer; barrister of the Inner Temple, 1613; a justice of North Wales, 1649, and in Warwickshire, 1653; published law reports. [vii. 259]

BULSTRODE, SIR RICHARD (1610–1711), diplomatist; second son of Edward Bulstrode [q. v.]; educated at Pembroke College, Cambridge; entered the Inner Temple, 1633; served in the king's army, 1642, ultimately becoming quartermaster-general; agent at Brussels, 1673; knighted, 1675; envoy at Brussels, 1676–88; followed James II to St. Germains; author of 'Life of James II.' [vii. 259]

BULSTRODE, WHITELOCKE (1650–1724), essayist; second son of Sir Richard Bulstrode [q. v.]; entered the Inner Temple, 1664; commissioner of excise; bought Hounslow manor, Middlesex, 1705; published controversial tracts and essays. [vii. 260]

BULTEEL, HENRY BELLENDEN (1800–1866), theologian; fellow of Exeter College, Oxford, 1823–9; M.A., 1824; curate in Oxford, 1826; preached in dissenting chapels; left the Anglican church and built a chapel in Oxford, 1831; adopted some of Edward Irving's ideas, 1832; published controversial tracts. [vii. 261]

BULTEEL, JOHN (*fl.* 1683), miscellaneous writer; issued pamphlets, romances, and translations between 1656 and 1683. [vii. 261]

BULWER, EDWARD GEORGE EARLE LYTTON, BARON LYTTON (1803–1873). [See LYTTON.]

BULWER, JOHN (*fl.* 1654), physician; published 'Philocophus, or the Deafe and Dumbe Man's Friend,' 1648, advocating the instruction of deaf-mutes, partly by gestures, partly by reading the lips (an idea borrowed from the Spanish); published medical and rhetorical treatises. [vii. 262]

BULWER, ROSINA BOYLE, LADY LYTTON (1804–1882). [See LYTTON.]

BULWER, WILLIAM HENRY LYTTON EARLE, BARON DALLING AND BULWER (1801–1872), diplomatist, better known as SIR HENRY BULWER; educated at Harrow and at Trinity and Downing colleges, Cambridge; published poems, 1822; in Greece, acting for the revolutionary committee, 1824; army officer, 1825–9; attaché at Berlin, 1827, Vienna, 1829, and the Hague, 1830; in

Belgium during the revolution, 1830; M.P. for Wilton, 1830, for Coventry, 1831, and for Marylebone, 1835; chargé d'affaires at Brussels, 1835; secretary of embassy at Constantinople, 1837; chargé d'affaires at Paris, 1839; ambassador at Madrid, 1843–8; K.C.B., 1848; ambassador at Washington, 1849; concluded the Bulwer-Clayton treaty; minister at Florence, 1852; commissioner in the Danubian principalities, 1856; ambassador at Constantinople, 1858–65; M.P. for Tamworth, 1868; created Baron Dalling and Bulwer, 1871; published historical works. [vii. 263]

BUNBURY, SIR HENRY EDWARD (1778–1860), seventh baronet (succeeded, 1820), of Mildenhall, Suffolk, soldier and historian; son of Henry William Bunbury [q. v.]; educated at Westminster; served in the army, 1795–1809; distinguished himself at the battle of Maida, 1806; under-secretary of state for war, 1809–16; major-general and K.C.B., 1815; conveyed to Napoleon sentence of deportation to St. Helena, 1815; M.P. for Suffolk, 1830; a pioneer of the volunteer movement, 1859; author of military narratives. [vii. 265]

BUNBURY, HENRY WILLIAM (1750–1811), artist and caricaturist; educated at Westminster and St. Catharine's' Hall, Cambridge; travelled in France and Italy before 1771; chiefly drew in pencil and chalk, and had his designs reproduced by engravers; executed numerous drawings, especially burlesque. [vii. 267]

BUNDY, RICHARD (d. 1739), divine; B.A. Oxford, 1713; chaplain in ordinary to George II; D.D. Lambeth, vicar of St. Bride's, Fleet Street, and prebendary of Westminster, 1732–3; published sermons and translations. [vii. 268]

BUNGAY, THOMAS (fl. 1290), Franciscan; studied at Paris; divinity lecturer of his order in Oxford and Cambridge; provincial minister in England; vulgarly accounted a magician. [vii. 268]

BUNN, ALFRED (1796 ?–1860), theatrical manager; nicknamed 'Poet Bunn'; stage-manager of Drury Lane, 1823; manager of Birmingham Theatre, 1826; manager of Drury Lane and Covent Garden theatres, 1833–48; brought out English operas; published verses. [vii. 269]

BUNN, MARGARET AGNES (1799–1883), actress; née Somerville; first appeared at Drury Lane, 1816, at Covent Garden, 1818; married Alfred Bunn [q. v.], 1819; acted at Drury Lane, 1823; retired while still young. [vii. 269]

BUNNING, JAMES BUNSTONE (1802–1863), architect; entered his father's office, 1815; surveyor to several public bodies and companies, 1825 onwards; architect to the city of London, 1843–1863. [vii. 270]

BUNNY, EDMUND (1540–1618), theological writer; B.A. and fellow of Magdalen College, Oxford, 1560; entered Gray's Inn, 1561; prebendary of St. Paul's, 1564; fellow of Merton, 1565; B.D., 1570; chaplain to Archbishop Grindal, 1570; sub-dean of York, 1570–9; prebendary of York, 1575; rector of Bolton Percy, Yorkshire, 1575–1600, prebendary of Carlisle, 1585; travelled over England, preaching; wrote doctrinal and devotional tracts. [vii. 271]

BUNNY, FRANCIS (1543–1617), theological writer; fellow of Magdalen College, Oxford, 1561–72; M.A., 1567; prebendary of Durham, 1572; archdeacon of Northumberland, 1573–8; rector of Ryton, Durham, 1578 till death; author of devotional tracts. [vii. 272]

BUNSEN, FRANCES (1791–1876), née Waddington; Welsh heiress; married at Rome, 1817, Baron Christian Bunsen (German ambassador, 1841–54); at Carlsruhe, 1855–76; published 'Memoir of Baron Bunsen,' 1868. [vii. 272]

BUNTING, EDWARD (1773–1843), musician; organist and music-teacher in Belfast, 1784; travelled in Ireland, collecting old Irish airs, 1792; published two series of these, 1796 and 1809; settled in Dublin, 1819; published a third collection, 1840. [vii. 273]

BUNTING, JABEZ (1779–1858), Wesleyan methodist; studied medicine, c. 1793; admitted a Wesleyan minister, 1799; served at many centres; stationed at head quarters in London, 1833; president of the theological institute, 1835; organised the connexion, and completed its severance from the Anglican church; published sermons. [vii. 273]

BUNTING, WILLIAM MACLARDIE (1805–1866), Wesleyan; eldest son of Jabez Bunting [q. v.]; minister at various centres, 1828–49; published sermons and hymns. [vii. 275]

BUNYAN, JOHN (1628–1688), author of 'Pilgrim's Progress'; son of Thomas Bunyan (d. 1676), tinsmith, of Elstow, near Bedford; learned reading and writing; was early set to his father's trade; lost his mother, June 1644; enlisted that year, in anger at his father's re-marriage, possibly in the parliamentary forces (stationed at Newport Pagnel, 1644–6); deeply moved by the death of a comrade, shot while serving in his place; profited by two devotional books belonging to his wife; gave up amusements and a bad habit of swearing; read the bible narratives; attended church services; overheard a religious conversation of certain poor women in Bedford, and in 1653 joined their society, which then met in St. John's Church, under 'Mr. Gifford' (d. c. 1656), an ex-royalist officer; removed from Elstow to Bedford, 1655; chosen deacon in his church; began to preach; lost his wife, c. 1656, and was left with four young children, one of them blind; his first publications 'Some Gospel Truths opened,' 1656, and 'A Vindication' of it, 1657, both directed against the quakers; being set apart as a preacher, 1657, preached throughout the district, still working at his craft; indicted at the assizes in consequence of the opposition of the settled presbyterian clergy, 1658; married, c. 1659, his second wife. Elizabeth (d. 1691); arrested for preaching, 12 Nov. 1660, and imprisoned, the laws against unlicensed preaching being rigorously enforced; allowed out of prison, pending trial, to preach at his meeting-house; sentenced to a short term of imprisonment at the Bedford assizes, January 1661, but, refusing to discontinue public preaching, was kept in prison (with an interval of a few weeks in 1666) till the spring of 1672, when he was released by Charles II's Declaration of Indulgence; allowed much freedom in prison, making tagged laces for a living, preaching to the prisoners, and writing numerous pieces, prose and verse. He is supposed to have undergone a short imprisonment in 1675, and to have then written his 'Pilgrim's Progress,' published in 1678. Otherwise he was unmolested, and from 1672 till death preached in many places, especially in London, and wrote largely. He was buried in Bunhill Fields, London. His collected works were published in 1736. [vii. 275]

BURBAGE, JAMES (d. 1597), actor; a joiner by trade; one of the Earl of Leicester's players, 1574; leased land in Finsbury Fields (1576), on which he erected, of wood, the first building in England specially intended for plays; acquired a house in Blackfriars, and converted it into 'Blackfriars Theatre,' 1596; lived in Holywell Street, Shoreditch, 1576–97. The first English playhouse is mentioned in an order of council, August 1577, and was known as 'The Theatre'; the fabric was removed, c. December 1598, to the Bankside and set up as the Globe Theatre. [vii. 284]

BURBAGE, RICHARD (1567 ?–1619), actor; son of James Burbage [q. v.], from whom he inherited a share in Blackfriars Theatre, and an interest in the Globe Theatre (burnt down 1613); acted as a boy at the theatre in Shoreditch; was an actor of repute by 1588; an actor of chief parts, 1595–1618, in plays by Shakespeare, Ben Jonson, and Beaumont and Fletcher; excelled in tragedy; lived in Holywell Street, Shoreditch, 1603–19; known also as a painter in oil-colours. [vii. 285]

BURCH, EDWARD (fl. 1771), artist; art-student, 1769; R.A., 1771; exhibited at the Academy, 1771–1808; miniature-painter; librarian of the Royal Academy, 1780. [vii. 289]

BURCHARD, SAINT (d. 754), first bishop of Würzburg; reputed of English origin; evangelised the district of the Main; consecrated bishop of Würzburg, 741; resigned, 751; retired to a monastery at Homburg; canonised, 984; some manuscript sermons ascribed to him. [vii. 289]

BURCHELL, WILLIAM JOHN (1782 ?–1863), explorer and naturalist; botanist at St. Helena, 1805–10; studied Cape-Dutch at Cape Town, 1810; travelled extensively in South Africa, 1811–15, making scientific observations, and collecting natural history specimens; published account of his travels, 1822; at Lisbon, 1825; at Rio Janeiro, 1825–6; travelled in the Brazilian forests, 1826–9, collecting plants and insects; hon. D.C.L. Oxford, 1834. Botanical manuscripts by him are at Kew. [vii. 290]

BURCHETT, JOSIAH (1666 ?–1746), secretary of the admiralty; clerk to Samuel Pepys, 1680–7; secretary to Admiral Edward Russell, 1694, and perhaps earlier; joint-secretary, 1695, and sole secretary, 1698–1742, of the admiralty; M.P. for Sandwich, 1703–13, 1721–41; published a naval history, 1720. [vii. 291]

BURCHETT, RICHARD (1815–1875), historical painter; student at the School of Design at Somerset House, 1841; headed agitation against the management; assistant-master, and, 1851, head-master of the art school, South Kensington; exhibited at the Academy, 1847–73; published treatises on drawing. [vii. 292]

BURCKHARDT, JOHN LEWIS (1784–1817), traveller in the East; educated at Leipzig, 1800, and Göttingen, 1804; came to England, 1806; studied Arabic at Cambridge and Malta, 1809; travelled, disguised as a Mohammedan trader of Hindustan, from the coast to Aleppo; resided at Aleppo two years, studying Arabic and Mohammedan law; made a tour to Palmyra, Damascus, Baalbek, 1810; journeyed through Palestine and Arabia to Egypt, 1812; travelled along the Nile above Assouan, 1813; journeyed through Abyssinia to Suakim, 1814; crossed to Jeddah; went, in the train of the viceroy of Egypt, to Mekka and Medina, 1815; journeyed to Suez and Sinai, 1816; died at Cairo; published travels. [vii. 292]

BURDER, GEORGE (1752–1832), congregationalist theologian; engraver, 1773; took to preaching, 1776; pastor at Lancaster, 1778; travelling preacher in England and Wales; pastor at Coventry, 1784; pastor of the Fetter Lane, London, congregation, 1803–32; secretary of the London Missionary Society, 1803–27; a founder of the London Missionary Society, 1795, of the Religious Tract Society, 1799, and of the British and Foreign Bible Society, 1804; edited devotional books. [vii. 294]

BURDER, HENRY FORSTER (1783–1864), congregationalist; eldest son of George Burder [q. v.]; a merchant's clerk; studied at Hoxton Academy and Glasgow University; M.A. Glasgow, 1807; professor of philosophy and mathematics, Hoxton College, 1810–30; pastor in Hackney, 1814–52; published sermons and devotional books; D.D. Glasgow. [vii. 295]

BURDER, SAMUEL (1773–1837), divine; congregational minister at St. Albans; ordained in the Anglican church, c. 1809; preacher in various London churches; published theological works. [vii. 296]

BURDER, THOMAS HARRISON (1789–1843), physician; son of George Burder [q. v.]; M.D. Edinburgh, 1815; practitioner in London, 1815–34; retired to Tunbridge Wells. [vii. 296]

BURDETT, SIR FRANCIS (1770–1844), politician; educated at Westminster and Oxford; travelled on the continent; was in Paris during the early part of the French revolution; returned to England and married Sophia Coutts, 1793; M.P. for Boroughbridge, 1796; advocated parliamentary reform, and denounced the war with France; suffered heavy expenses over the disputed election for Middlesex, 1802–6; M.P. for Westminster, 1807–37; denounced flogging in the army and corruption in parliament; imprisoned on political charges, 1810, and again, 1820; after Reform Bill inclined to the conservatives; conservative M.P. for North Wilts, 1837–44. [vii. 296]

BURDON, WILLIAM (1764–1818), miscellaneous writer; wealthy coal-owner; educated at Newcastle-on-Tyne; fellow of Emmanuel College, Cambridge, 1788–96; M.A., 1788; lived near Morpeth; published political pamphlets. [vii. 299]

BURDY, SAMUEL (1760 ?–1820), historian; B.A. Trinity College, Dublin, 1781; curate of Ardglass, 1783, and incumbent of Kilclief, co. Down, c. 1800–20; published 'History of Ireland,' memoirs, and poems. [vii. 299]

BURELL, JOHN (*fl.* 1590). [See BURREL.]

BURFORD, first EARL OF (1670–1726). [See BEAU-CLERK, CHARLES.]

BURFORD, ROBERT (1791–1861), artist; exhibited panoramas in Leicester Square, praised by Ruskin; exhibited at the Academy from 1812. [vii. 300]

BURFORD, THOMAS (*fl.* 1740–1765), mezzotint engraver, chiefly of portraits. [vii. 301]

BURGES or **BURGESS**, CORNELIUS (1589 ?–1665), puritan divine; B.A. Wadham College, Oxford, 1615; M.A. Lincoln College, 1618; D.D., 1627; rector of St. Magnus, London Bridge, 1626–41; chaplain in ordinary to Charles I, c. 1626; brought before the court of high commission, 1635, for charging the bishops with favouring Arminianism and Romanism; conveyed to Charles I at York the petition of the London clergy against 'the etcetera oath,' 1640; of great influence with the House of Commons; put forward as spokesman of the proposal to suppress cathedrals, 1641; chaplain to Essex's regiment of horse, 1642; a vice-president of the Westminster assembly, 1643; opposed imposition of 'covenant,' 1643; lecturer at St. Paul's and resident in the deanery, 1644; agitated against the execution of Charles I, 1649; preacher at Wells Cathedral, 1650–60; bought the deanery and part of the cathedral estates; ruined by their forfeiture, 1660; sold his library; published sermons and controversial tracts. [vii. 301]

BURGES, GEORGE (1786 ?–1864), classical scholar; educated at Charterhouse and Trinity College, Cambridge; M.A., 1810; long a private tutor in Cambridge; attacked Blomfield in Valpy's 'Classical Journal'; published classical texts and translations, including 'Greek Anthology' for Bohn's classical library. [vii. 304]

BURGES, SIR JAMES BLAND (1752–1824), politician; known as SIR JAMES LAMB after 1821, by royal license; educated at Westminster and University College, Oxford; travelled on the continent, 1773; barrister of Lincoln's Inn, 1777; commissioner in bankruptcy, 1777; M.P. for Helston, Cornwall, 1787–90; supported Warren Hastings when impeached; advocated abolition of slavery and amelioration of conditions of imprisonment for debt; under-secretary for foreign affairs, 1789–95; created baronet, 1795; wrote poems, plays, and epigrams. [vii. 305]

BURGES, JOHN (1745–1807), physician; educated at Westminster; M.D. Christ Church, Oxford, 1774; physician to St. George's Hospital, London, 1774–87; made collections for 'Materia Medica.' [vii. 306]

BURGES, MARY ANNE (1763–1813), authoress, linguist, and naturalist. [vii. 307]

BURGES, WILLIAM (1827–1881), architect; trained by Edward Blore [q. v.], 1844, and Digby Wyatt, 1849; studied mediæval architecture on the continent; employed, 1856 onwards, in important buildings and restorations; designed Brisbane Cathedral, 1859, and Cork Cathedral, 1862; restored Cardiff Castle, 1865; wrote architectural papers. [vii. 307]

BURGESS, ANTHONY (*fl.* 1652), nonconformist; entered St. John's College, Cambridge, 1623; fellow of Emmanuel College; chaplain to the parliamentary garrison, Coventry; member of the Westminster Assembly; rector of Sutton Coldfield, Warwickshire; ejected, 1662; author of sermons and doctrinal treatises. [vii. 308]

BURGESS, DANIEL (1645–1713), nonconformist; educated at Westminster; entered Magdalen Hall, Oxford, 1660; acted as domestic chaplain to nonconformist gentry; master of Charleville school, co. Cork; ordained by the presbytery of Dublin; imprisoned at Marlborough for preaching, 1674; pastor to a congregation in London, 1685–1713; his meeting-house sacked by the Sacheverell mob, 1710; published sermons and devotional pieces. [vii. 308]

BURGESS, DANIEL (*d.* 1747), secretary to Princess Sophia, 1714, at Hanover, and afterwards to the Princess of Wales; son of Daniel Burgess (1645–1713) [q. v.]; in the government service, 1702; obtained the government grant (*regium donum*) for English dissenting ministers, 1723. [vii. 309]

BURGESS, HENRY (1808–1886), divine; educated at Stepney dissenting college; nonconformist minister; ordained in the Anglican church, 1850; LL.D. Glasgow, 1851; Ph.D. Göttingen, 1852; incumbent of Clifton Reynes, Buckinghamshire, 1854–61; vicar of Whittlesea, Cambridgeshire, 1861–86; published essays and translations from the Syriac. [vii. 309]

BURGESS, JOHN (1563–1635), puritan; B.A. St. John's College, Cambridge, 1586; rector of St. Peter Hungate, Norwich, 1590; resigned in consequence of the surplice question, c. 1591; beneficed in Lincoln diocese, c. 1596; imprisoned for sermon preached at Greenwich before James I, 1604 ; led the opposition to the 1603 canons ; ejected from his benefice ; retired to Leyden, where he studied medicine and graduated M.D. ; incorporated M.D. at Cambridge ; returned to England, c. 1612 ; forbidden to practise in London ; practised medicine at Isleworth, Middlesex ; preacher at Bishopsgate ; rector of Sutton Coldfield, Warwick, 1617–35 ; chaplain to Sir Horatio Vere abroad, 1620 ; prebendary of Lichfield, 1625 ; published controversial tracts. [vii. 310]

BURGESS, JOHN (d. 1671), nonconformist ; intruded rector of Ashprington, Devonshire ; ejected, 1662 ; retired to Dartmouth ; afterwards pastor at Hackney ; kept a boarding-school at Islington. [vii. 312]

BURGESS, JOHN BAGNOLD (1829–1897), painter ; grandson of William Burgess (1749 ?–1812) [q. v.] ; studied at Royal Academy ; exhibited at Academy first in 1850, and regularly, 1852–97 ; visited Spain, 1858, and after, the majority of his pictures being studies of Spanish life and character ; R.A., 1889. [Suppl. i. 333]

BURGESS, JOHN CART (1798–1863), painter of flowers in water-colours ; teacher of painting ; exhibited at the Royal Academy, 1812 ; published treatises on painting and perspective. [vii. 312]

BURGESS, JOSEPH TOM (1828–1886), antiquary ; wood engraver at Northampton, c. 1844 ; went with Dr. David Alfred Doudney [q. v.] to Ireland, and became editor of ' Clare Journal ' ; edited various local newspapers in England and published miscellaneous works, including ' Historic Warwickshire,' 1876. [Suppl. i. 335]

BURGESS, RICHARD (1796–1881), divine ; of St. John's College, Cambridge ; priest, 1823 ; Anglican chaplain at Geneva, 1828, and Rome, 1831 ; rector of Upper Chelsea, 1836–61 ; prebendary of St. Paul's, 1850 ; rector of Horningsheath, Suffolk, 1869. [vii. 312]

BURGESS, THOMAS (fl. 1786), historical painter ; exhibited in London, 1766 ; exhibited at the Academy, 1778–86 ; taught drawing in London. [vii. 313]

BURGESS, THOMAS (1784 ?–1807), painter : son of William Burgess (1749 ?–1812) [q. v.] ; exhibited at the Academy, 1802–6. [vii. 313]

BURGESS, THOMAS (1756–1837), bishop of St. David's and Salisbury ; educated at Winchester and Corpus Christi College, Oxford ; B.A., 1778 ; fellow, 1783 ; resided in Oxford till 1791 ; prebendary of Durham, 1794 ; rector of Winston, Durham, 1795 ; bishop of St. David's, 1803 ; worked hard for his diocese : founded St. David's College, Lampeter, for education of Welsh clergy, 1822 ; translated to Salisbury, 1825 ; author of charges, sermons, and pamphlets ; D.D. [vii. 313]

BURGESS, THOMAS (1791–1854), catholic prelate ; educated at Ampleforth : Benedictine monk, 1807 ; secular priest, 1830 ; priest of Portland Chapel, Bath, 1832 ; bishop of Clifton, 1851 ; D.D. [vii. 314]

BURGESS, WILLIAM (1749 ?–1812), painter ; son of Thomas Burgess (fl. 1786) [q. v.] ; exhibited in London, 1769 ; exhibited at the Academy, 1774–99 ; teacher of drawing. [vii. 314]

BURGESS, WILLIAM (1755 ?–1813), engraver ; issued prints of Lincolnshire churches ; baptist minister at Fleet, Lincolnshire. [vii. 315]

BURGESS, WILLIAM OAKLEY (1818–1844), mezzotint engraver ; pupil of Thomas Goff Lupton ; engraved pictures by Sir Thomas Lawrence. [vii. 315]

BURGH, BENEDICT (fl. 1472), translator of Cato's precepts, printed by Caxton, 1483 ; rector of Sandon, Essex, 1440 ; prebendary of St. Paul's, 1472. [vii. 315]

BURGH, HUBERT DE (d. 1243), chief justiciar ; of Norman-Irish birth ; employed by Richard I ; envoy from King John to Portugal, 1200 ; chamberlain to King John, 1201 ; perhaps gaoler of John's nephew, Arthur, at Falaise, 1202 ; envoy to Philip of France, 1203 ; defended Chinon, 1204 ; seneschal of Niort and Poitou, 1214 ; named a conservator of Magna Charta, and appointed justiciar, 1215 ; defended Dover Castle against French, 1216 ; continued in the justiciarship after John's death ; destroyed the French fleet off North Foreland, August, 1217 ; head of the national party against the foreigners and the bishop of Winchester, 1219 ; married (his fourth wife) Margaret, sister of Alexander II of Scotland, 1221 ; demanded the surrender of the royal castles held by nobles, 1221 ; defeated the nobles' plot to seize the king, 1223 ; advised Henry III to declare himself of full age and banish the bishop of Winchester, 1227 ; created Earl of Kent, 1227 ; violently attacked by Henry III in consequence of the lack of money in the treasury, 1229 ; deprived of power by combination of the church, the nobles, and the Londoners, 1231 ; granted justiciarship of Ireland, June 1232 ; dismissed from office, July 1232, and accused of many crimes ; imprisoned in the tower, 1232, and in Devizes Castle, February 1233 ; escaped to Chepstow, November 1233, to Richard, earl of Pembroke ; his outlawry reversed and earldom restored, 1234 ; reconciled to the bishop of Winchester, 1237 ; acquitted after a renewal of the old charges, 1239. [vii. 315]

BURGH, JAMES (1714–1775), political writer ; educated at St. Andrews ; press corrector, afterwards usher, in London ; kept private school at Stoke Newington, 1747–71 ; author of ' Political Disquisitions,' 1774–5, and pamphlets. [vii. 322]

BURGH, SIR JOHN (1562–1594), military and naval commander ; took troops from Lincolnshire to serve in Netherlands, 1585 ; knighted ; governor of Doesburg ; governor of the Briel, 1588 ; commanded one of the English regiments which helped Henry IV of France, 1589–90 ; knighted on the field at Ivry, 1590 ; commanded the squadron which captured the great Spanish treasure-ship off the Azores, 1592 ; killed in a duel respecting the plunder. [vii. 322]

BURGH, RICHARD DE (d. 1243), Irish settler ; dispossessed by King John of his lands in Connaught ; pilgrim to Compostella, 1222 ; restored by Henry III, 1222 ; fought against Aedh O'Conor of Connaught, 1230 ; invaded the Irish estates of Richard, the earl marshal, and contributed to his death, 1234 ; sailed to join Henry III in France ; died in France. [vii. 323]

BURGH, RICHARD DE, second EARL OF ULSTER and fourth EARL OF CONNAUGHT (1259 ?–1326), eldest son of Walter de Burgh, earl of Ulster [q. v.] ; succeeded to earldom, 1271 ; made war on his late guardian, 1282 ; ravaged Connaught, 1286 ; deposed Brian O'Neill and made Niall Culanach O'Neill, king of Ireland, 1286 ; ceded Isle of Man to Edward I, 1290 ; conquered Magnus O'Conor of Connaught, 1292 ; summoned by Edward to serve in France, 1294 ; imprisoned by Fitzgerald, his feudal enemy, 1294–5 ; made Aedh O'Conor chief in Connaught, 1296 ; joined Edward I in Scotland, 1296 ; summoned to serve in France, 1297 ; served in Scotland, 1304 ; built Sligo Castle, 1310 ; at war with other Irish nobles, 1311 ; made Felim O'Conor chief in Connaught, 1315 ; fought against Edward Bruce, 1315 ; imprisoned at Dublin, 1317, in order that he might not join his son-in-law, Robert Bruce ; frequently summoned to serve with Edward II in Scotland till 1322. [vii. 324]

BURGH, ULICK DE, fifth EARL and MARQUIS OF CLANRICARDE (1604–1657), succeeded to earldom, 1635 ; served with Charles I against Scots, 1639 ; of suspected loyalty, 1641 ; Charles I's commissioner to meet the Irish confederates, 1643 ; commander of the forces in Connaught, 1644 ; created marquis, 1645 ; tried to reconcile the Irish to Charles I, 1646 ; reduced Galway, 1648 ; deputy in Ireland for Ormonde, December 1650 ; distrusted by the Irish ; capitulated to the parliament, 1652. [vii. 325]

BURGH, SIR ULYSSES BAGENAL, second BARON DOWNES (1788–1863), general ; ensign, 1804 ; captain, 1806 ; aide-de-camp to Wellington in Peninsula, 1809–14 ; lieutenant-colonel, 1812 ; K.C.B., 1814 ; colonel, 1825 ; succeeded to barony, 1826 ; clerk of the ordnance, 1828–1830 ; general, 1854. [vii. 327]

BURGH, WALTER DE, called EARL OF ULSTER (d. 1271), second son of Richard de Burgh (d. 1243) [q. v.] ; succeeded his brother in the estates, 1248 ; granted possession, 1250 ; came of age, 1253 ; at war with the Irish of Connaught, 1256–70 ; at war with Fitzgerald, 1264–5. [vii. 328]

BURGH, WALTER HUSSEY (1742–1783), Irish lawyer ; known as Walter Hussey till 1762 ; B.A. Dublin, 1762 ; married, 1767 ; Irish barrister, 1769 ; M.P. in the Irish parliament for Athy, 1769, and for Dublin University, 1776 ; prime serjeant, 1777 ; advocated free trade ; opposed the union , chief baron of the Irish exchequer, 1782 ; celebrated orator. [vii. 329]

BURGH, WILLIAM DE (*d.* 1204), Anglo-Norman baron of Ireland; from 1200 harried the Connaught Irish, supporting the attempts of the pretender, Cathal Carrach, to dispossess Cathal Crobhderg of the throne of Connaught.   [xix. 105]

BURGH, WILLIAM DE, sixth LORD OF CONNAUGHT and third EARL OF ULSTER (1312–1332), succeeded as a minor, 1326; knighted, and obtained possession of his estates, 1328; at war with the O'Brians, 1328–30; attended parliament in Dublin, 1329; at war with Fitzgerald, 1330; imprisoned; in England, 1331; at war with Sir Walter de Burgh, 1332.   [vii. 331]

BURGH, WILLIAM (1741–1808), controversialist; an Irish landowner; with Walter Hussey Burgh [q. v.] M.P. for Athy, 1769–76; advocated abolition of slavery: opposed the union; hon. D.C.L. Oxford, 1788; wrote against unitarianism.   [vii. 331]

BURGHALL, EDWARD (*d.* 1665), puritan; schoolmaster at Bunbury, Cheshire, 1632; plundered by royalist troops, 1643; intruded vicar of Acton, Cheshire, 1646–62; taught school, 1663; left diary in manuscript. [vii. 332]

BURGHERS, MICHAEL (1653?–1727), engraver; born in Amsterdam; settled in Oxford, 1673; engraved for the university press, 1676–1720; engraver to the university, 1692; principally engraved portraits.
                                              [vii. 333]

BURGHERSH, BARON. [See FANE.]

BURGHERSH, BARTHOLOMEW, BARON BURGHERSH, the elder (*d.* 1355), succeeded to barony, 1310; served in Scotland, 1317: imprisoned in the Tower, 1321; constable of Dover Castle frequently from 1327; chamberlain of Edward III and his attendant in France and Scotland; envoy to Philip of France, 1329; admiral of Channel fleet, 1337; served in Gascony, 1349. [vii. 333]

BURGHERSH, BARTHOLOMEW, BARON BURGHERSH, the younger (*d.* 1369), son of Bartholomew, baron Burghersh, the elder [q. v.]; served in Flanders, 1339, in Brittany, 1342–3, at Crecy, 1346, at Calais, 1347, in Gascony, 1349; K.G., 1350; pilgrim to Palestine, 1354; succeeded his father, 1355; served in France, 1355–6, and 1359–60; commissioner on the state of Ireland, 1362, and to Pope Urban V, 1366.   [vii. 334]

BURGHERSH, HENRY (1292–1340), bishop of Lincoln; educated abroad; proposed for the see of Winchester by his family, 1319; intruded into the see of Lincoln, 1320; his temporalities seized by Edward II, 1322, but restored, 1324?; supported Queen Isabella, 1326; commissioner to obtain Edward II's abdication, 1327; lord treasurer, 1327; lord chancellor, 1328–30; candidate for see of Canterbury, 1328; accompanied Edward III to France, 1329; baptised the Prince of Wales, 1330; imprisoned in Tower, 1330; lord treasurer, 1334–7; employed by Edward III in Flanders, 1338, in the southern counties, 1340, and again in Flanders, 1340, where he died.   [vii. 335]

BURGHLEY, BARONS. [See CECIL, WILLIAM, first BARON, 1520–1598; CECIL, THOMAS, second BARON, 1542–1622.]

BURGIS EDWARD (1673?–1747), in religion AMBROSE; Dominican friar; wrote on ecclesiastical history.
                                              [vii. 338]

BURGO, DR. (1710?–1776). [See BURKE, THOMAS.]

BURGON, JOHN WILLIAM (1813–1888), dean of Chichester; son of Thomas Burgon [q. v.]; studied at University College, London; published 'Life of Sir Thomas Gresham,' 1839; entered Worcester College, Oxford, 1841; fellow of Oriel, 1846; M.A., 1848; vicar of St. Mary's, Oxford, 1864; Gresham professor of divinity, 1867; dean of Chichester, 1876; published 'Lives of Twelve Good Men,' 1888, sermons, and works of religious controversy; 'a high churchman of the old school.'   [Suppl. i. 335]

BURGON, THOMAS (1787–1858), Turkey merchant and member of court of assistants of Levant Company; employed in coin department of British Museum, 1841.
                                              [Suppl. i. 335]

BURGOYNE, HUGH TALBOT (1833–1870), captain royal navy, only son of Sir John Fox Burgoyne [q. v.]; entered navy, 1847; gained Victoria cross for service in Black Sea, 1855; drowned in the turret-ship Captain off Cape Finisterre.   [vii. 338]

BURGOYNE, SIR JOHN (1739–1785), general; seventh baronet of Sutton, Bedfordshire; entered the army when young; rapidly promoted; raised a regiment of light dragoons for India, 1781; served in India, 1782–1785; major-general, 1783.   [vii. 339]

BURGOYNE, JOHN (1722–1792), dramatist and general; educated at Westminster; lieutenant, 1741; eloped with Lady Charlotte Stanley, daughter of the Earl of Derby, 1743; captain, *c.* 1743; resided in France to escape his creditors, 1749–55; lieutenant-colonel, 1758; raised dragoon regiment, 1759; M.P. for Midhurst, 1761; brigadier-general in Portugal, 1762; governor of Fort William, 1768–78; M.P. for Preston, 1768; major-general, 1772; attacked Clive in parliament, 1773; wrote plays, 1774–86; served in New England, 1775, and censured his brother-officers; second in command in Canada, 1776, and censured his superior officer; lieutenant-general, 1777; given supreme command in Canada, but capitulated at Saratoga, October 1777; made commander-in-chief in Ireland by the whigs, 1782; manager of the impeachment of Warren Hastings; wrote plays, including the 'Heiress,' 1786.   [vii. 340]

BURGOYNE, SIR JOHN FOX (1782–1871), engineer officer; illegitimate son of John Burgoyne (1722–1792) [q. v.]; educated at Eton and Woolwich; entered royal engineers, 1798; served in Malta, Sicily, Egypt, 1800–7; engineer in Sir John Moore's expedition, 1808–9; engineer with Wellington throughout the Peninsular war; engineer in American campaign, 1814–15; commander of the engineers in France, 1815–18, and in Portugal, 1826; chairman of public works board, Ireland, 1831–45; major-general and K.C.B., 1838; inspector-general of fortifications, 1845–68; lieutenant-general, 1850; present in the Crimean campaign, 1853–5; general, 1855; created baronet, 1856; constable of the Tower of London, 1865; field-marshal, 1868.   [vii. 342]

BURGOYNE, MONTAGU (1750–1836), politician; educated at Trinity Hall, Cambridge; held sinecure office in the exchequer; published pamphlets.   [vii. 344]

BURGOYNE, SIR MONTAGUE ROGER (*d.* 1817), eighth baronet of Sutton, Bedfordshire; eldest son of Sir John Burgoyne [q. v.]; cornet Scots Greys, 1789; lieutenant-colonel 32nd light dragoons, 1795; major-general, 1810.   [vii. 339]

BURGSTED, WALTER DE (*fl.* 1257). [See BERSTEDE.]

BURGUNDY, DUCHESS OF (1446–1503). [See MARGARET.]

BURHILL or **BURGHILL**, ROBERT (1572–1641), divine; fellow of Corpus Christi College, Oxford, 1585; M.A., 1594; D.D., 1632; rector of Northwold, Norfolk, and of Snailwell, Cambridgeshire, and prebendary of Hereford, 1604; assisted Sir Walter Ralegh in his 'History of the World'; wrote works on controversial divinity.
                                              [vii. 344]

BURHRED or **BURGRÆD** (reigned 852–874), king of Mercia; succeeded Beorhtwulf [q. v.]; subdued the revolt of North Wales and Anglesey, by help of Æthelwulf of the West-Saxons, 853; married Æthelswyth, Æthelwulf's daughter, 854; solicited West-Saxon help against the Danes, 868; vainly besieged the Danes in Nottingham; accepted Danish supremacy; received the expelled Northumbrian king, 872; conquered by the Danes, 874; fled to Rome, and died there.   [vii. 344]

BURKE, EDMUND (1729–1797), statesman; second son of Richard Burke, attorney, of Dublin; brought up as a protestant by his father; entered Trinity College, Dublin, 1743; B.A., 1748; entered the Middle Temple, London, 1750; troubled by weak health; travelled in the west of England and in France; punished for neglect of his legal studies by discontinuance of the allowance from his father, 1755; first published works, 'Vindication of Natural Society,' and 'On the Sublime and Beautiful,' 1756; married a catholic, who afterwards turned protestant, Jane Nugent, daughter of his physician, 1756, and was for some time dependent on his father-in-law; unsuccessfully applied for the consulship at Madrid, 1759; started the 'Annual Register,' 1759, and contributed to it till 1788; private secretary to William Gerard Hamilton, 1759–64, accompanying him to Ireland, 1761–2, and again 1763–4; resigned a pension which Hamilton had obtained for him, 1764; private secretary to the Marquis of Rockingham, July 1765, who from time to

time helped him by advances of money and destroyed his bonds at his death; inherited a small Irish estate from a brother, 1765, which he sold in 1790; elected M.P. for Wendover, 1765–74, through the influence of Ralph, second earl Verney; first spoke in parliament, 27 Jan. 1766, on the American question; acknowledged as an orator of the highest class, but out of touch with the house; visited Ireland, 1766; vehemently attacked the administration of Chatham and Grafton, especially in regard to their dealing with East Indian, 1766, and American questions, 1767; participated in the stockjobbing operations of a brother, a kinsman, and Lord Verney; was partly involved in their ruin, 1769, and remained for the rest of his life in continuous financial difficulties; bought his estate at Beaconsfield, 1768, before the crash came; vigorously attacked the foreign and domestic policy of the tory government, 1769; issued 'Thoughts on the Present Discontents,' 23 April 1770, accusing the government of strangling public opinion; carried the day in favour of giving publicity to proceedings in parliament, 1771; agent for New York province, 1771; violently assailed by pamphleteers under the impression that he was author of the 'Letters of Junius,' 1772; voted for removal of disabilities of protestant dissenters and advocated taxing absentee Irish landlords, 1773; visited Paris, February–March 1773, and returned with a pronounced aversion to French democracy; joined by Charles James Fox in his violent attacks on North's conduct of affairs, 1774–5; M.P. for Bristol, 1774–80, on the invitation of the citizens, who afterwards took offence at his championship of Irish trade and catholic emancipation; strongly advocated peace with America, 1775–6; delivered his great speech against employing Indians in the American war, February 1778; helped Admiral Keppel in his successful defence before a court-martial, 1779; advocated economical reform in the public service and restrictions on the slave-trade, 1780; became M.P. for Malton, Yorkshire, 1781–94, through Lord Rockingham's influence; again advocated economical reform, and, by his attacks on the conduct of the American war, forced North to resign, 1781–2; kept out of the cabinet by the whigs on their coming into office, but made paymaster of the forces, March–July 1782; urged economical reform with partial success, and the conferring of self-government on Ireland, 1782; retired from the ministry with Fox, July 1782; acquiesced in the coalition government of Fox and North under the Duke of Portland, and accepted paymastership of the forces, 1783; active member of the committee which investigated the affairs of the East India Company, wrote the 'Ninth Report,' on the trade of Bengal and the system pursued by Warren Hastings, and the 'Eleventh Report,' on the system of presents, and drafted the government's East India bill, 1783; lord rector of Glasgow University, 1784 and 1785; personally unpopular in the House of Commons; continued his attack on Warren Hastings, 1785; travelled in Scotland, 1785; joined by Philip Francis in urging the impeachment of Hastings, 1786, which was accomplished, 10 May 1787; opened the case for the impeachment in Westminster Hall, February 1788; again passed over by Fox in forming a cabinet, 1788; joined Fox in upholding right of Prince of Wales to regency, 1788; supported Wilberforce in advocating abolition of the slave-trade, 1788–9; spoke in parliament against the French democracy, February 1790, and issued his 'Reflections on the French Revolution,' November 1790; estranged in consequence from Fox and Sheridan; prevailed on the new parliament to continue the impeachment of Hastings, 1790; LL.D. Dublin, 1791; finally quarrelled with Fox and the whigs, 1791; voted against removal of disabilities from unitarians, and against parliamentary reform, advised his friends to support Pitt and the tories, pleaded for war with France, and openly joined the ministerial party, 1792; continued his quarrel with Fox and Sheridan, 1794; delivered his nine-days' speech for the impeachment of Hastings in reply to the defence, 1794; retired from parliament, July; pensioned by the ministry, 1794; encouraged the foundation of Maynooth College, 1795; present at the acquittal of Hastings, 1795; established a school for sons of French refugees at Penn, Buckinghamshire, and wrote 'Letters on a Regicide Peace,' 1796. His collected works were published, 1792–1827.
[vii 345]

BURKE, EDMUND PLUNKETT (1802–1835), judge; educated at Caen, Normandy, and Cambridge; called to bar at the Inner Temple; judge in St. Lucia, West Indies, 1832; wrote on civil law. [vii. 365]

BURKE, JOHN (1787–1848), genealogical and heraldic writer; issued 'Peerage and Baronetage,' 1826, 'Extinct Peerage,' 1831, 'Commoners,' 1833–8 (in later editions called 'Landed Gentry '), 'Extinct Baronetcies,' 1838, and 'Knightage,' 1841, also works on the royal family and on heraldry. [vii. 365]

BURKE, Sir JOHN BERNARD (1814–1892), Ulster king-of-arms, son of John Burke [q. v.]; educated at Caen College, Normandy; called to bar at Middle Temple, 1839; Ulster king-of-arms in Ireland, 1853; knighted, 1854; keeper of state papers in Ireland, 1855; honorary LL.D. Dublin, 1862; C.B., 1868; appointed a governor of National Gallery of Ireland, 1874. He annually re-edited his father's works, including 'Peerage,' 1847–92, publishing also 'Vicissitudes of Families,' 1859–63, and other genealogical works. [Suppl. i. 338]

BURKE, PETER (1811–1881), legal writer; eldest son of John Burke [q. v.]; educated at Caen, Normandy; barrister of the Inner Temple, 1839; serjeant-at-law, 1859; wrote on legal subjects and remarkable trials. [vii. 366]

BURKE, ROBERT O'HARA (1820–1861), Australian explorer; educated in Belgium; captain in the Austrian service; entered the Irish constabulary, 1848; inspector of police in Victoria, 1853; leader of expedition to cross Australia from south to north, 1860; reached estuary of Flinders river, 1861; starved to death at Cooper's Creek, June 1861; buried at Melbourne. [vii. 366]

BURKE, THOMAS (1710?–1776), latinised DE BURGO, church historian; native of Dublin; joined Dominicans at Rome, 1726; compiled 'Officia propria Sanctorum Hiberniæ,' 1751 (revised edition, 1769); began the history of the Dominicans in Ireland, 1753 (published, 1762, 'Hibernia Dominicana,' and a supplement, 1772); bishop of Ossory, 1759; wrote theological works. [vii. 367]

BURKE, THOMAS (1749–1815), engraver, chiefly of works by Angelica Kauffmann. [vii. 368]

BURKE, THOMAS HENRY (1829–1882), under-secretary for Ireland, 1869–82; began official life at Dublin Castle, 1847; murdered in Phœnix Park. [vii. 368]

BURKE, THOMAS NICHOLAS (1830–1883), Dominican preacher and lecturer; at Rome, 1847; joined Dominicans at Perugia; studied theology at Rome; priest on the English mission, 1853; founded the convent at Tallaght, Dublin; prior of convent in Rome; lectured in the United States, 1872; published lectures and sermons.
[vii. 368]

BURKE, ULICK RALPH (1845–1895), Spanish scholar; B.A. Trinity College, Dublin, 1867; called to bar at Middle Temple, 1870; travelled in Spain, and subsequently studied Spanish literature and history; barrister at high court of North-West Provinces, India, 1873–8, and in Cyprus, 1885–9; registrar of quarter-sessions, 1889; published 'History of Spain,' 1895, and other works.
[Suppl. i. 338]

BURKE, WILLIAM (d. 1798), supposed author of the 'Letters of Junius'; entered Westminster School, 1743, and Christ Church, Oxford, 1747; B.C.L., 1755; under-secretary of state, 1755–8; M.P. for Great Bedwin, 1766–74; stock-jobber; bankrupt, 1769; in India, 1777–1792; lived with his kinsman, Edmund Burke [q. v.], at Beaconsfield, 1793. [vii. 369]

BURKE, WILLIAM (1792–1829), murderer; navvy in Scotland, 1818; lodged with William Hare in Edinburgh, 1827, and sold a dead body to the surgeons; smothered people for the purpose of selling their bodies, 1828; hanged at Edinburgh. [vii. 370]

BURKHEAD, HENRY (fl. 1645), author; published at Kilkenny, 1646, 'Cola's Fury, or Lirenda's Misery,' a tragedy on the Irish troubles. [vii. 371]

BURKITT, WILLIAM (1650–1703), divine and commentator; educated at Cambridge grammar school and at Pembroke Hall, Cambridge; M.A., 1672; rector of Milden, Suffolk; vicar of Dedham, Essex, 1692–1703; author of sermons and expository works. [vii. 371]

BURLEIGH, BARONS OF. [See BALFOUR, ROBERT, second BARON, d. 1663; BALFOUR, JOHN, third BARON, d. 1688; BALFOUR, ROBERT, fifth BARON, d. 1757.]

BURLEY, JOHN (d. 1333), Carmelite of Stamford.
[vii. 372]

BURLEY or **BURLEIGH**, JOHN (*d.* 1648), royalist officer; captain of a ship-of-war, 1642; served in Charles I's army, becoming a general of ordnance; executed for a quixotic attempt to release Charles at Newport, 1648. [vii. 372]

BURLEY, SIR SIMON (1336–1388), soldier and courtier; served at sea, 1350, and in France, 1355; attended the Black Prince in Aquitaine, 1364; envoy to Pedro of Castile, 1366–7; taken prisoner by the French, 1369; exchanged, 1370; made guardian to Prince Richard; accompanied Richard II to London, 1377; governor of Windsor Castle, 1377–88; tutor of Richard II, 1380; negotiated the king's marriage with Anne of Bohemia, and escorted her to London, 1381; K.G., 1381; constable of Dover Castle, 1384–7; served in Scotland, 1385; impeached by Richard's opponents and beheaded, 1388. [vii. 373]

BURLEY, WALTER (1275–1345 ?), Aristotelian commentator; probably a secular priest; reputed fellow of Merton College, Oxford; studied at Paris under Duns Scotus; almoner to Philippa, consort of Edward III, 1327; envoy to the pope, 1327 and 1330; possibly prebendary of Wells, 1332; reputed tutor to the Black Prince, *c.* 1342; possibly identical with a petitioner for the archdeaconry of Richmond, 1345. His 'De Vita et Moribus Philosophorum' was printed 1467. Several other treatises by him were issued in the fifteenth and early part of the sixteenth century, and many survive in manuscript. [vii. 374]

BURLEY, WILLIAM (*fl.* 1436), speaker of the House of Commons, 1436 and 1444; M.P. for Shropshire at intervals from 1417 to 1455; sheriff of Shropshire, 1426. [vii. 376]

BURLINGTON, EARLS OF. [See BOYLE, RICHARD, first EARL, 1612–1697; BOYLE, RICHARD, third EARL, 1695–1753.]

BURLOWE, HENRY (*d.* 1837). [See BEHNES.]

BURLY, JOHN (*d.* 1333). [See BURLEY.]

BURMAN, THOMAS (*d.* 1674), sculptor. [vii. 376]

BURN, EDWARD (1762–1837), writer against Dr. Joseph Priestley [q. v.]; educated at Trevecca College, Wales; entered St. Edmund Hall, Oxford, 1784; M.A., 1791; lecturer of St. Mary's Chapel, Birmingham, 1785–1837; rector of Smethcott, Shropshire; published sermons and tracts. [vii. 376]

BURN, JOHN (1744 ?–1802), lawyer; a Westmoreland squire; son of Richard Burn [q. v.]; issued revised editions of his father's manuals. [vii. 377]

BURN, JOHN SOUTHERDEN (1799 ?–1870), antiquary; solicitor, 1819; registrar of marriages at chapels prior to 1754, 1831; secretary to commission for inquiry into non-parochial registers, 1836–41; published 'History of . . . foreign Refugees settled in England,' 1846, and other antiquarian works. [Suppl. i. 339]

BURN, RICHARD (1709–1785), legal writer; B.A. Queen's College, Oxford, 1734; vicar of Orton, Westmoreland, 1736–85; D.C.L., 1762; chancellor of Carlisle, 1765. His works include 'Justice of the Peace,' 1755, 'Ecclesiastical Law,' 1760, 'History of Westmoreland and Cumberland,' 1771. [vii. 377]

BURN, WILLIAM (1789–1870), architect of numerous mansions in Great Britain and Ireland; in business in Edinburgh, *c.* 1814; removed to London, 1844. [vii. 378]

BURNABY, ANDREW (1734 ?–1812), traveller; at Westminster School, 1748; M.A. Queens' College, Cambridge, 1757; travelled in North America, 1759–60; chaplain at Leghorn, 1762–7, travelling in Italy and Corsica; vicar of Greenwich, 1769; archdeacon of Leicester, 1786; author of travels, sermons, and charges. [vii. 379]

BURNABY, CHARLES (?) (*fl.* 1700), reputed author of four comedies, printed 1700–2. It is possible that they were really written by William Burnaby of Merton College, Oxford, 1691, and the Middle Temple, 1693, translator of Petronius, 1694. [vii. 379]

BURNABY, FREDERICK GUSTAVUS (1842–1885), cavalry officer and traveller; educated at Harrow and in Germany; a facile linguist; cornet, 1859; lieutenant-colonel, 1880; commanded the 3rd household cavalry, 1881–5; travelled in Central and Southern America, *c.* 1862, in Spain and Morocco, 1868, in South Russia, 1870,

in Spain, 1874, and in the Soudan, 1875; rode from Kazala to Khiva, 1875; rode from Scutari into Armenia, and thence to Batoum, 1876; attended Valentine Baker's operations in the Russo-Turkish war, 1877; contested Birmingham, 1880; attached himself to the Egyptian expedition, 1884; killed in action in the attempt to relieve Khartoum; student of military ballooning, and author of narratives of his travels. [vii. 380]

BURNARD, NEVILL NORTHEY (1818–1878), sculptor, chiefly of portrait-busts; native of Cornwall; carver of marble to London sculptors; exhibited at the Academy, 1855–67. [vii. 382]

BURNE or **BOURN**, NICOL (*fl.* 1581), controversialist; Calvinist; professor at St. Andrews; adopted catholicism; imprisoned at St. Andrews and Edinburgh, 1580; banished, 1581; published, at Paris, 1581, a virulent attack on Knox and Luther. [vii. 383]

BURNE, ROBERT (1755 ?–1825), general; ensign, 1773; served in India, 1784–98; lieutenant-colonel of the 36th foot, 1799; served in Hanover, 1805, and at Buenos Ayres, 1807; colonel, 1808; served at Vimeiro and Coruña, 1808; and at Flushing, 1809; major-general, 1811; invalided from Spain, 1811; held home commands, 1812–14; lieutenant-general, 1821. [vii. 383]

BURNE-JONES, SIR EDWARD COLEY (1833–1898), painter; educated at King Edward's School, Birmingham, and Exeter College, Oxford, where he made acquaintance of William Morris [q. v.] and others, who formed 'the Brotherhood'; became friend of Rossetti, and studied art; executed St. Frideswide's window in Christ Church Cathedral, Oxford, 1859; came to London; associate of the 'Old Society,' 1863; comparatively little known until, in 1877, he exhibited 'Chant d'Amour,' 'Days of Creation,' and 'Beguiling of Merlin' at the Grosvenor Gallery; exhibited also at the New Gallery; elected A.R.A., 1885; exhibited at Royal Academy 'The Depths of the Sea' (1886); exhibited frequently at Paris from 1878; honorary D.C.L. Oxford, 1881; honorary fellow, Exeter College, 1882; created baronet, 1894. He did much decorative work. Among the best-known of his pictures are the 'Pygmalion' series (1879), the 'Golden Stairs' (1880), 'King Cophetua' (1884), and the 'Garden of Pan' (1887). [Suppl. i. 340]

BURNELL, ARTHUR COKE (1840–1882), an authority on Sanscrit and the languages of Southern India; of King's College, London; entered the Indian Civil Service, 1857; served in Madras, 1860–8; tour through Arabia, Egypt, Nubia, 1868; magistrate at Mangalore and Tanjore, 1869–80; published treatises on Hindu law, translations from the Sanscrit, and linguistic and historical tracts; collector of Sanscrit manuscripts now at the India Office; hon. Ph.D. Strasburg. [vii. 384]

BURNELL, EDWARD (*fl.* 1542), professor of Greek at Rostock. [vii. 386]

BURNELL, HENRY (*fl.* 1641), published at Dublin, 1641, 'Landgartha,' a burlesque tragedy, performed there in 1639. [vii. 386]

BURNELL, ROBERT (*d.* 1292), bishop of Bath and Wells; accompanied Prince Edward to France, 1260, and in Wales, 1263; began to acquire estates in Shropshire 1263; employed on a mission in South Wales, 1265; licensed to impark his land, 1266, and to have a weekly market and two fairs at Acton Burnell, 1269; befriended by Prince Edward, who tried to obtain Canterbury for him, 1270; trusted minister of Edward I, and in constant attendance on him at home and abroad; co-regent during Edward's absence on crusade, 1272; lord chancellor, 1274 till death; bishop of Bath and Wells, 1275; one of Prince Llewelyn's judges, 1276; employed on a mission in France and Gascony, 1278; postulated for archbishop of Canterbury at the request of Edward I, 1278, and elected to see of Winchester, 1280, but set aside by the pope; settled the court of chancery in London, 1280, instead of following the court; employed on the Welsh border, 1282–3; framed the statute of Rhuddlan, 1282; parliament met in his hall at Acton, 1283; with Edward I in France, 1286–9; conducted an inquiry into the conduct of the judges during the king's absence, 1290; lived a covetous and ambitious life, owning estates in nineteen counties (eighty-two manors); built the episcopal hall at Wells; procured franchises and liberties for Wells Cathedral; defended the rights of the crown against Peckham, the Franciscan primate. [vii. 386]

BURNES, SIR ALEXANDER (1805–1841), Indian political officer; officer in the Bombay native infantry, 1821; studied native languages; assistant resident in Cutch, 1829; visited Sind and the Punjáb, 1830; visited Afghanistan, Bokhára, the Turkoman country, Persia, 1832; in England, 1833–5; envoy to Dost Mahomed, 1836; advised alliance with him; knighted, 1839; political officer with the army at Cabul, 1839–41; slain in the massacre. [vii. 389]

BURNES, JAMES (1801–1862), physician in India; studied medicine in Edinburgh and London; in the medical service at Bombay, 1821; surgeon at Cutch; accompanied the Sind expedition, 1825; published his 'Narrative,' 1830; in England, 1834–6; LL.D. Glasgow, 1834; garrison-surgeon, 1837, and afterwards physician-general at Bombay; returned to England, 1849. [vii. 391]

BURNESTON or **BORASTON**, SIMON (fl. 1338), preacher and theological writer; reputed D.D. Cambridge; member of the Dominican convent, Oxford; provincial. [vii. 391]

BURNET, ALEXANDER (1614–1684), archbishop in Scotland; a relative of the Earls of Traquair and Teviot; chaplain to the Earl of Traquair; refugee in England, c. 1639; took Anglican orders; beneficed in Kent; ejected 1650; crossed the Channel, and held correspondence for Charles II; chaplain to Dunkirk garrison, c. 1660; bishop of Aberdeen, 1663; archbishop of Glasgow, 1664; a strong high churchman, opposed to terms with the presbyterians, provoking the covenanter rising by his severity, 1666; strongly opposed to Lauderdale's conciliatory policy, 1669; compelled to resign his see, 1669, but restored, 1674; archbishop of St. Andrews, 1679–84. [vii. 392]

BURNET, ELIZABETH (1661–1709), authoress of 'A Method of Devotion,' 1709; née Blake; married, 1678, Robert Berkeley (d. 1693) of Spetchley, Worcestershire; resided at the Hague, 1684–9; married (third wife) Gilbert Burnet (1643–1715) [q. v.], 1699. [vii. 393]

BURNET, GILBERT (1643–1715), bishop of Salisbury; of an Aberdeenshire family; son of a well-to-do Edinburgh lawyer, three times exiled for refusing the covenant; his mother a strict presbyterian; educated at Marischal College, Aberdeen; M.A.; studied law; afterwards studied divinity and history; probationer of the Scottish church, 1661; practised extemporary preaching; thought ill of the oppressive policy of the Scottish bishops, 1663; visited Cambridge, Oxford, and London, and refused the parish of Saltoun, Haddingtonshire, 1663; studied Hebrew at Amsterdam, visited Paris and the court at London, 1664; F.R.S., 1664; minister of Saltoun, 1665–9; wrote against the Scottish bishops and in favour of Lauderdale's milder policy, 1666; clerk of Haddington presbytery, 1667; sounded as to a proposal to divorce Charles II's queen for barrenness; in Lauderdale's confidence, 1667; employed by Archbishop Leighton to negotiate with the presbyterians, 1669; employed by the Duchess of Hamilton to obtain the king's sanction for placing presbyterian ministers in certain parishes; professor of divinity at Glasgow, 1669; advised the privy council to send a commission into the west to inquire into the growing discontent; employed by Leighton to urge the moderate presbyterians to accept the offers of the court, 1670, and by the Duchess of Hamilton to arrange her family papers (published 'Memoirs of the Dukes of Hamilton,' 1676); persuaded the Duke of Hamilton to accept the court measures, 1671; summoned to London to advise Lauderdale, and offered the bishopric of Edinburgh, 1671; married his first wife [see BURNET, MARGARET], 1671; joined the Duke of Hamilton in reprobating Lauderdale's new policy of violence, 1672; wrote in favour of obedience to episcopacy, and against popery, 1673; visited London; as king's chaplain remonstrated with Charles II on his profligacy, 1673; incurred the hatred of Lauderdale, 1673; went to London, June 1674; dismissed by the king from his chaplaincy; preached in London churches; chaplain of the Rolls Chapel and lecturer of St. Clement's, 1675–84; witness against Lauderdale before the House of Commons, 1675; offered the see of Chichester, 1678; deprecated persecution of Roman catholics during the popish plot, 1678–80, incurring the dislike both of the court and of the extreme anti-popery party; published his 'History of the Reformation in England,' vol. i. 1679 [vol. ii. 1681, vol. iii. 1714]; remonstrated with Charles II on his evil life, 1680; attended the deathbed of the Earl of Rochester, 1680; intimate with William, lord Russell, 1681; asked, but was refused, the mastership of the Temple; obtained places in England for dispossessed Scottish clergy, 1682; wrote against popery; attended Lord Russell on the scaffold; withdrew to Paris, 1683; returned to England; ejected from his chaplaincy at the Rolls and his lectureship by Charles II, 1684; visited Paris, Rome, Geneva, Strasburg, Frankfort, Heidelberg, and Utrecht, 1685–6 [publishing a narrative of his tour, 1687]; visited the Hague on invitation of the Prince of Orange, 1686; outlawed by James II, 1687; married his second wife, Mary Scott (d. 1698), 1687; obtained from Mary, consort of the Prince of Orange, a promise to place power in William's hands; advised Sophia of Hanover of the intended invasion of England; drafted William's 'declaration'; accompanied William to Torbay and London, 1688; bishop of Salisbury, 1689; advocated toleration in the House of Lords; preached the coronation sermon; carried the bill to attaint Sir John Fenwick, 1697; appointed to attend Peter the Great, 1698; married his third wife [see BURNET, ELIZABETH]; published 'Exposition of the xxxix Articles,' 1699 (censured by the lower house of convocation, 1701); had charge of the succession bill, 1701; attended William on his deathbed, 1702; opposed the occasional conformity bill, 1703; obtained first-fruits and tenths for church purposes ('Queen Anne's Bounty'), 1704; spoke against Sacheverell, 1710; remonstrated with Anne for countenancing the Pretender, James Edward; lived latterly in Clerkenwell; wrote a 'History of his own Times' (published, 1723–34), sermons, controversial treatises, and political pamphlets. [vii. 394]

BURNET, GILBERT (1690–1726), pamphleteer; son of Gilbert Burnet (1643–1715) [q. v.]; educated at Leyden and Merton College, Oxford; B.A., 1706; chaplain to George I, 1718; rector of East Barnet, 1719–26. [vii. 404]

BURNET, JAMES M. (1788–1816), landscape-painter; came to London, 1810; exhibited at the Academy, 1812–1814. [vii. 405]

BURNET, JOHN (1784–1868), painter and engraver; trained in Edinburgh; came to London, 1806; engraved pictures by David Wilkie; exhibited at the Academy, 1808–23, and at the British Institution; pensioned, 1860; wrote treatises on drawing and painting. [vii. 406]

BURNET, MARGARET (1630?–1685?), eldest daughter of John Kennedy, sixth earl of Cassilis; a determined presbyterian; long in the confidence of Lauderdale; married Bishop Gilbert Burnet (1643–1715) [q. v.], 1671. [vii. 407]

BURNET, SIR THOMAS (1632?–1715?), physician; studied medicine at Montpellier; M.D., 1659; practised in Edinburgh; published 'Thesaurus Medicinæ practicæ,' 1672; original fellow of the Edinburgh College of Physicians, 1681; knighted before 1691; published medical works. [vii. 408]

BURNET, THOMAS (1635?–1715), master of the Charterhouse, 1685–1715; educated at Northallerton school and Cambridge; fellow of Christ's College, 1657; M.A., 1658; withstood James II's attempt to appoint a catholic pensioner of the Charterhouse, 1687; chaplain and clerk of the closet to William III, 1689–92; published works on theology and cosmogony, which excited much contemporary criticism. [vii. 408]

BURNET, THOMAS (d. 1750), divine; rector of West Kington, Wiltshire, 1706–50; D.D. New College, Oxford, 1720; wrote works of doctrinal theology. [vii. 410]

BURNET, SIR THOMAS (1694–1753), judge; youngest son of Gilbert Burnet (1643–1715) [q. v.]; at Leyden, 1706–7; travelled in Germany, Switzerland, and Italy; entered the Middle Temple, 1709; barrister, 1715; consul at Lisbon, 1719; serjeant-at-law, 1736; justice of the common pleas, 1741; knighted, 1745; published pamphlets, chiefly political. [vii. 410]

BURNET, WILLIAM (d. 1729), colonial governor; son of Gilbert Burnet (1643–1715) [q. v.]; educated at Cambridge and Leyden; governor of New York and of Massachusetts, 1728. [vii. 404]

BURNETT, GEORGE (1776?–1811), compiler of 'Specimens of English Prose,' 1807; entered Balliol College, Oxford, and subsequently the dissenting college at

Manchester; pastor at Yarmouth; studied medicine at Edinburgh; surgeon in a militia regiment; tutor in Poland, of which country he printed a 'View,' 1807. [vii. 411]

BURNETT, GEORGE (1822–1890), historian and heraldic author; called to Scottish bar, 1845; Lyon depute, 1864; Lyon king-of-arms, 1866; LL.D. Edinburgh, 1884; chief work, an edition of 'Exchequer Rolls, 1264-1507' (1881–90). [Suppl. i. 344]

BURNETT, GILBERT THOMAS (1800–1835), professor of botany at King's College, London, 1831–5; practised medicine in London; published botanical text-books. [vii. 412]

BURNETT, JAMES, LORD MONBODDO (1714–1799), Scottish judge; educated at Aberdeen, Edinburgh, and Gröningen; advocate, 1737; sheriff of Kincardine, 1764; lord of session, taking his title from his estate, 1767; visited at Monboddo by Samuel Johnson, 1773; published 'Origin . . . of Language,' 1773–92, 'Antient Metaphysics,' 1779–99, and law reports. [vii. 412]

BURNETT, JOHN (1729–1784), Aberdeen merchant; founder of the Burnett prize. [vii. 414]

BURNETT, JOHN (1764?–1810), advocate, 1785; sheriff of Haddington, 1803; judge-admiral of Scotland, 1810; wrote 'Criminal Law of Scotland.' [vii. 414]

BURNETT, SIR WILLIAM (1779–1861), apprentice to a Montrose surgeon; naval surgeon at St. Vincent, the Nile, Trafalgar; physician to the Mediterranean fleet, 1810–13, and at Chatham, 1814; practised at Chichester, 1816?–22; physician-general of the navy, 1824?–41; knighted, 1831; patented a disinfecting fluid; published medical tracts. [vii. 414]

BURNEY, CHARLES (1726–1814), musician and author; educated at Chester; taught music by his brother at Shrewsbury, 1741, and by Thomas Augustus Arne in London, 1744–7; published his first compositions, 1745–7; organist and conductor of concerts in London, 1749; organist at Lynn Regis, 1751–60; Mus. Doc. Oxford, 1769; travelled in France, Switzerland, Italy, 1770 (publishing an account of his tour, 1771); travelled in Belgium, Holland, Germany, Austria, 1772, and published a narrative of his tour, 1773; organist at Chelsea hospital, 1783–1814; pensioned, 1806; author of musical compositions, biographies of musicians, and a 'History of Music,' 1776–89. [vii. 415]

BURNEY, CHARLES (1757–1817), classical scholar; son of Charles Burney (1726–1814) [q. v.]; educated at Charterhouse, Caius College, Cambridge, and Aberdeen; M.A., 1781; D.D. Lambeth, 1812; kept private school at Hammersmith, 1786–93, and at Greenwich, 1793–1813; rector of Cliffe, Kent, and of St. Paul's, Deptford; prebendary of Lincoln, 1817; published tracts and papers, chiefly of Greek lexicography and tragic metres. His library was bought for the British Museum. [vii. 418]

BURNEY, FRANCES (1752–1840). [See ARBLAY, MADAME D'.]

BURNEY, JAMES (1750–1821), rear-admiral R.N.; son of Charles Burney (1726–1814) [q. v.]; entered the navy, 1764; sailed with Captain Cook on his second (1772–4) and third voyages (1775–80); captain, 1782; in the action off Cuddalore, 1783; retired; wrote 'Discoveries in the Pacific,' 1803–17; 'North-eastern Voyages of Discovery,' 1819, and some pamphlets. [vii. 419]

BURNEY, SARAH HARRIET (1770?–1844), novelist; published 'Clarentine,' 1796, and other novels later; youngest daughter of Charles Burney (1726–1814) [q. v.]; resided in Florence, 1816–39. [vii. 419]

BURNEYEAT, JOHN (1631–1690), quaker; a Cumberland farmer; joined the quakers, 1653; began to interrupt church services and was imprisoned, 1657; in Scotland, 1658; in Ireland, 1659; again imprisoned at Carlisle, 1660; went on circuit to Barbados, Virginia, New England, 1664–7, and travelled over the greater part of England, Wales, and Ireland, 1668–70; imprisoned in London, 1670; went to America, 1670; returned to England, 1673; went finally to Ireland, c. 1676; imprisoned at Dublin, 1683; afterwards lived unmolested; published pamphlets. [vii. 420]

BURNHAM, RICHARD (1711–1752), clergyman, possibly a congregationalist; compiler of 'Pious Memorials,' published 1753. [vii. 421]

BURNHAM, RICHARD (1749?–1810), baptist and hymn-writer; a Wesleyan at High Wycombe; baptist pastor at Staines; preacher in London, 1780 till death. [vii. 422]

BURNS, ALLAN (1781–1813), lecturer on surgery and anatomy at Glasgow; studied medicine in Glasgow, 1795; visited Russia, 1804; published anatomical treatises. [vii. 422]

BURNS, SIR GEORGE, first baronet (1795–1890), ship-owner; brother of John Burns [q. v.]; entered partnership with his brother James as general merchant at Glasgow, c. 1818; founded, 1839, with Samuel Cunard [q. v.], Robert Napier (1791–1876) [q. v.], and others Cunard Company, which obtained admiralty contract for carrying North American mails; created baronet, 1889. [Suppl. i. 344]

BURNS, ISLAY (1817–1872), theologian; educated at Aberdeen and Glasgow; D.D. Aberdeen, 1863; minister of Free St. Peter's, Dundee, 1843–64; professor in the Free Church College, Glasgow, 1864–72; wrote memoirs and works on church history. [vii. 422]

BURNS, JABEZ (1805–1876), temperance lecturer; a methodist; in business in Yorkshire; came to London, 1826; joined the general baptists; published his first book, 1828; pastor in Edinburgh, 1829; at Perth, 1830–5; advocate of total abstinence; pastor in Marylebone, 1835; D.D. Middletown, 1846; baptist delegate to America, 1847; wrote sermons, devotional books, and travels. [vii. 423]

BURNS, JAMES (17th cent.), merchant; baillie of Glasgow. His 'Memoirs of the Civil War . . . 1644 to 1661' are preserved in the mutilated transcript of George Crawford. [vii. 424]

BURNS, JAMES (1789–1871), shipowner; employed steam-power, 1824; a founder of the Cunard Company, 1839. [vii. 424]

BURNS, JAMES DRUMMOND (1823–1864), divine; educated at Heriot's Hospital, the University, 1837, and the Free Church College, Edinburgh, 1843; Free church minister at Dunblane, 1845, at Funchal, Madeira, 1847–1853, and at Hampstead, 1855–64; author of hymns and sermons. [vii. 424]

BURNS, JOHN (1774–1850), author of 'Principles of Midwifery,' 1809; studied medicine at Glasgow; surgeon's clerk in Glasgow Infirmary, 1792; M.D.; lectured on anatomy, and afterwards on midwifery; professor of surgery in Glasgow University, 1815; drowned at sea; author of medical works. [vii. 425]

BURNS, ROBERT (1759–1796), poet; son of a cottar (d. 1784); born at Alloway; educated by his father; worked as a farm-labourer, 1772; read the 'Spectator,' Pope's 'Homer,' Allan Ramsay, and pedlar's slip-songs; composed his first verses, 1775; learnt surveying, 1777, and associated with tippling smugglers at Kirkoswald; wrote 'Death of Poor Mailie,' 'John Barleycorn,' and occasional poems; read Thomson, Shenstone, Sterne, and Ossian; member of convivial, debating, and masonic clubs at Tarbolton, 1780–1; courted Ellison Begbie ('Mary Morison' of the song), who rejected him; worked in a flax-dresser's shop at Irvine, June-December 1781; began a common-place book, 1783; farmed 118 acres in partnership with his brother Gilbert at Mossgiel, 1784–8; wrote some of his best work—'Cottar's Saturday Night,' 'The Twa Dogs,' 'Halloween,' 'The Jolly Beggars,' the addresses 'To a Mouse' and 'To a Mountain Daisy'—and some of his sharpest satires—'Death and Dr. Hornbook' (against a village grocer-druggist) and 'Holy Willie's Prayer' (against a Mauchline elder)—in 1785 and 1786; conceived the idea of sending to a magazine his 'Epistle to Davie' (Sillar), 1785; discovered that 'The Twa Herds,' a satire against two Calvinists, had a lively circulation in manuscript; gave Jean Armour, daughter of a Mauchline mason, a written declaration of marriage, which her father destroyed, April 1786, preferring his daughter's loss of reputation to the proposed match; obtained the post of overseer on a Jamaica plantation, 1786, and, to provide passage-money, arranged with John Wilson, printer, Kilmarnock, for an edition of his poems; trysted with Mary Campbell, a sailor's daughter from Argyllshire, to go with him as his wife, 1786; composed after her death, in memory of her, 'Will ye go to the Indies, my Mary?' 'To Mary in Heaven' (October 1789), and 'Highland Mary' (November 1792) ; his poems favourably mentioned in Edinburgh reviews and praised personally to Burns ; gained access to the literary circles by his reputation as 'a heaven-taught ploughman,' and by his convivial powers to the masonic and drinking clubs of the capital ; the second (1787) edition of his poems undertaken by William Creech, who about 1788 completed his payment of 500*l.*, Burns parting with the copyright ; met James Johnson, projector of the 'Scots Musical Museum,' to the six volumes (1787-1803) of which he contributed songs ; erected a memorial-stone to the poet Fergusson, February 1787 ; travelled through the border counties and Argyllshire, 1787 ; spent July at Mossgiel, renewing his relations with Jean Armour ; returned to Edinburgh in August 1787 ; travelled through the central highlands and the eastern counties in September, and Stirling, Clackmannan, and Kinross in October ; began in Edinburgh a tender correspondence with Margaret Chalmers ('Peggy'), and also with Agnes M'Lehose ('Clarinda'), whose husband was abroad ; decided to marry Jean Armour, an intention effected in August 1788 ; gave up his share in the farm at Mossgiel, lending his brother Gilbert 180*l*. to carry it on, and engaged Ellisland, a farm six miles from Dumfries, March 1788 ; lived at Ellisland, June 1788 to December1791 his wife Jean (to whom he addressed 'O' a' the airts the wind can blaw') living for the time at Mauchline ; turned his holding into a dairy-farm, to be managed by his wife, while he took an exciseman's place, about August 1789, at a salary of 40*l*. ; wrote 'Auld Lang Syne' and 'Tam o' Shanter,' *c*. 1789 ; gave up Ellisland and settled in Dumfries, December 1791, as exciseman on a salary of 70*l*. ; suspected by the government on account of the Jacobite sentiment of his songs and his freeman's sympathy with the French democracy, coming within an ace of dismissal, December 1792 ; gladly accepted an invitation by George Thomson, then projecting a new collection of Scottish songs, to supply words for old melodies, 1792, 'Scots wha hae' (1793) being written for this purpose ; his reputation prejudiced and health shattered by his association with the hard-drinking gentry of the district ; fell asleep by the roads'de after a carouse, a mischance followed by rheumatic fever ; died at Dumfries. A subscription and a memorial edition of his works (1800), edited by James Currie, provided for the immediate wants of his family. His children shared their father's independent spirit, his wife resigning a pension of 50*l*. as soon as they were able to support her (1818). [vii. 426]

BURNS, ROBERT (1789-1869), theologian ; educated at Edinburgh ; minister at Paisley, 1811 ; joined the Free church, 1843 ; delegate to America, 1844 ; minister of Knox's church, Toronto, 1845-56 ; professor in Knox's (presbyterian) College, Toronto, 1856 till death ; D.D. ; wrote tracts on points of church history. [vii. 438]

BURNS, WILLIAM CHALMERS (1815-1868), missionary ; educated at Aberdeen ; licentiate of the church of Scotland, 1839 ; revivalist preacher in Scotland, north of England, and Canada ; missionary in China, 1846 till death ; translated the 'Pilgrim's Progress' into Chinese. [vii. 439]

BURNSIDE, ROBERT (1759-1826), baptist ; educated at Merchant Taylors' School and Aberdeen University ; preacher and pastor in London, 1780-1826 ; teacher of languages ; wrote religious tracts. [vii. 439]

BURRANT, ROBERT (*fl*. 1553), editor of Sir David Lindsay's 'Tragical Death of David Beaton' ; translated 'Precepts of Cato,' 1553. [vii. 439]

BURRARD, SIR HARRY (1755-1813), general ; entered the army, 1772 ; M.P. for Lymington, 1780 ; served in America, 1778-9, 1781-2, in Flanders, 1793-5, and at Copenhagen, 1807 ; lieutenant-general, 1805 ; created baronet, 1807 ; sent to take command in Portugal, 1808 ; allowed Arthur Wellesley, whom he had been selected to supersede, to command against the French at Vimiera (21 Aug.), but forbade pursuit after their rout ; acquitted by court-martial ; commanded the guards brigade in London, 1810. [vii. 440]

BURREL or **BUREL**, JOHN (*fl*. 1590), poet ; author of a description of James VI's queen's entry into Edinburgh, 1590 ; supposed to be the same with John Burrel, a goldsmith of Edinburgh, whose name occurs in a title-deed of 1628. [vii. 440]

BURRELL, LITELLUS (1753-1827), major-general ; served in the Bengal army, 1770-1821, rising from the rank of volunteer-private to major-general ; returned to England, 1821. [vii. 441]

BURRELL, SOPHIA, LADY (1750 ?-1802), dramatist ; published poems and tragedies, 1773-1800 ; *née* Raymond ; married (1) Sir William Burrell [q. v.], 1773 ; (2) the Rev. William Clay, 1797. [vii. 442]

BURRELL, SIR WILLIAM (1732-1796), antiquary ; educated at St. John's College, Cambridge ; LL.D., 1760 ; advocate at Doctors' Commons, 1760 ; practised in the admiralty court ; chancellor of Worcester, 1764, and of Rochester ; M.P. for Haslemere, 1768 ; married, 1773 [see BURRELL, SOPHIA, LADY] ; baronet by reversion, 1789 ; collected materials for a history of Sussex ; lived at Deepdene, Sussex, 1787-96 ; wrote law reports. [vii. 442]

BURROUGH, CHRISTOPHER. [See BOROUGH.]

BURROUGH, EDWARD (1634-1663), quaker ; became a presbyterian ; joined the quakers, 1652 ; travelling minister in Scotland and north of England ; wrote tracts while in prison. 1653 ; preached in London and Bristol, 1654 ; expelled from Ireland, 1656 ; imprisoned for refusing oath of abjuration, 1656 ; vindicated the quakers against John Bunyan, 1657 ; pleaded for toleration with Oliver Cromwell, 1657, and Richard Cromwell, 1658 ; at Dunkirk, 1659 ; begged Charles II to protect the persecuted quakers in New England, 1660 ; visited Bristol, 1662 ; died in Newgate prison ; published pamphlets. [vii. 443]

BURROUGH, SIR JAMES (1691-1764), amateur architect ; educated at Bury St. Edmunds and Caius College, Cambridge ; B.A., 1711 ; fellow, 1738 ; master, 1754-64 ; esquire bedell, 1727 ; knighted, 1754 : consulted or employed on most Cambridge buildings of his day ; an advocate of the classical style in architecture. [vii. 444]

BURROUGH, SIR JAMES (1750-1839), judge ; barrister of the Inner Temple, 1773 ; recorder of Portsmouth ; knighted, 1816 : justice of the common pleas, 1816-29. [vii. 445]

BURROUGH, STEPHEN (1525-1584). [See BOROUGH.]

BURROUGH, WILLIAM (1536-1599). [See BOROUGH.]

BURROUGHES or **BURROUGHS**, JEREMIAH (1599-1646), congregational divine ; M.A. Emmanuel College, Cambridge, 1624 ; puritan rector of Tivetshall, Norfolk, 1631-6 ; minister at Rotterdam, 1637-41 ; preacher at Stepney and Cripplegate, 1641 till death ; member of Westminster Assembly, 1643 ; presented the congregationalist case to parliament, 1644 ; wrote devotional and controversial treatises. [vii. 445]

BURROUGHS, SIR JOHN (*d*. 1643). [See BOROUGH.]

BURROUGHS, JOSEPH (1685-1761), baptist minister ; educated at Leyden ; preacher and pastor in London, 1714-61 ; published sermons. [vii. 447]

BURROW, EDWARD JOHN (1785-1861), miscellaneous writer ; M.A. Magdalene College, Cambridge, 1808 ; D.D. Trinity College, Oxford, 1820 ; incumbent of Bempton, Yorkshire, 1810-16, and of Hampstead chapel-of-ease, 1816-23 ; civil chaplain at Gibraltar, 1835 ; archdeacon of Gibraltar, 1842 ; resided latterly in Devonshire ; published treatises on shells, art (including the 'Elgin Marbles,' 1817 and 1837), and theology. [vii. 447]

BURROW, SIR JAMES (1701-1782), editor of law reports, 1756-80 ; master of the crown office ; barrister of the Inner Temple, 1725 ; knighted, 1773. [vii. 448]

BURROW, REUBEN (1747-1792), mathematician ; a small farmer's son ; clerk and, subsequently, usher in London ; kept school at Portsmouth ; assistant at Greenwich Observatory, 1770 ; opened a school in Greenwich ; mathematical teacher at the Tower, 1775 ? ; edited Carnan's 'Ladies' . . . Almanack,' 1775-82 ; employed in teaching and survey work in Bengal, 1782-92 ; published 'A Restitution of . . . Apollonius Pergæus on Inclinations,' 1779. [vii. 448]

BURROWES, JOHN FRECKLETON (1787-1852), composer ; organist of St. James's, Piccadilly ; published text-books on music. [vii. 449]

BURROWES, PETER (1753-1841), Irish politician ; educated at Trinity College, Dublin ; barrister of the

Middle Temple, 1785 ; M.P. for Enniscorthy in the Irish parliament ; opposed the union : counsel for Robert Emmet, 1803 ; judge of insolvent debtors' court, 1821. [vii. 450]

BURROWS, SIR GEORGE, first baronet (1801–1887), physician ; studied at St. Bartholomew's Hospital ; B.A. Caius College, Cambridge, 1825 ; M.D., 1831 ; D.C.L., 1872 ; junior fellow and mathematical lecturer, 1825–35 ; studied medicine on continent ; lecturer on medical jurisprudence at St. Bartholomew's, 1834 ; lecturer on medicine, 1841 ; physician, 1841–63 ; F.R.C.P., 1832, and president, 1871–1875 ; F.R.S., 1846 ; LL.D. Cambridge, 1881 ; physician in ordinary to Queen Victoria, 1873 ; created baronet, 1874 ; honorary fellow of Caius College, 1880 ; published medical writings. [Suppl. i. 345]

BURROWS, GEORGE MAN (1771–1846), physician ; studied medicine and practised in London ; kept a private asylum after 1816 ; M.D. St. Andrews, 1824 ; agitated for improving medical education ; wrote on insanity. [vii. 450]

BURROWS, SIR JOHN CORDY (1813–1876), surgeon ; apprenticed in Suffolk ; studied in London ; practised in Brighton, 1837 ; knighted, 1873 ; promoted public improvements in Brighton. [vii. 451]

BURSTOUGH, ROBERT (1651–1709), divine ; M.A. Queen's College, Oxford, 1682 ; prebendary of Exeter, 1701 ; archdeacon of Barnstaple, 1703 ; author of works of controversial divinity. [vii. 451]

BURT, ALBIN R. (d. 1842), engraver and portrait-painter ; exhibited at the Royal Academy, 1830. [vii. 452]

BURT, EDWARD (d. 1755), author of 'Letters from a Gentleman in the North of Scotland' (printed, 1754) ; employed by General Wade in Scotland, 1724–8. [vii. 452]

BURT, WILLIAM (1778–1826), miscellaneous writer ; educated at Exeter ; solicitor's apprentice at Bridgwater ; solicitor and journalist at Plymouth ; wrote on various topics, including banking and politics. [vii. 452]

BURTHOGGE, RICHARD (1638 ?–1694 ?), theologian ; educated at Exeter grammar school ; B.A. Oxford, 1658 ; M.D. Leyden, 1662 ; practised medicine at Bowden ; published philosophical and theological treatises, in one of which he anticipated Hamilton's doctrine of the 'relativity of knowledge.' [vii. 453]

BURTON, first BARON (d. 1743). [See PAGET, HENRY.]

BURTON, CASSIBELAN (1609–1682), translator ; only son of William Burton (1575–1645) [q. v.] ; translated Martial (not published) ; gave his father's collections to Walter Chetwynd [q. v.] [viii. 1]

BURTON, CATHARINE (1668–1714), Carmelite nun at Antwerp, 1694. [viii. 1]

BURTON, CHARLES (1793–1866), theologian ; educated at Glasgow and St. John's College, Cambridge ; LL.B., 1822 ; D.C.L. Magdalen College, Oxford, 1829 ; originally Wesleyan minister ; rector of All Saints', Manchester (built by himself), 1820 ; published hymns, poems, sermons, and controversial tracts. [viii. 1]

BURTON, CHARLES EDWARD (1846–1882), astronomer ; B.A. Dublin ; assistant in Lord Rosse's observatory, 1868 ; observed the eclipse in Sicily, 1870, the transit of Venus at Rodriguez, 1874, and the opposition of Mars, near Dublin, 1879 ; wrote astronomical papers. [viii. 2]

BURTON, DECIMUS (1800–1881), architect ; designed Horner's Colosseum, 1823 ; laid out Hyde Park, 1825 ; architect of a building estate at Tunbridge Wells, 1828–1848 ; designed many country houses ; travelled in Italy, Greece, and North America. [viii. 3]

BURTON, EDWARD (1584 ?–1624 ?). [See CATCHER, EDWARD.]

BURTON, EDWARD (1794–1836), theologian ; educated at Westminster ; student of Christ Church, Oxford, 1813 ; M.A., 1818 ; travelled ; Bampton lecturer, 1828 ; regius professor of divinity, Oxford, 1829–36 ; D.D., 1829 ; wrote classical and theological works. [viii. 4]

BURTON, SIR FREDERIC WILLIAM (1816–1900), painter in water-colours, and director of National Portrait Gallery ; member of Royal Hibernian Academy, 1839 ;

practised with success as portrait-painter in Dublin ; lived in Munich, 1851–8, and studied German masters ; member of 'Old' (now Royal) Water-Colour Society, 1856 ; F.S.A., 1863 ; director of National Gallery, London, 1874–1894 ; LL.D. Trinity College, Dublin, 1896. A portrait by him of 'George Eliot' is in the National Portrait Gallery. Among his best pictures are 'Peasantry of Franconia waiting for Confession,' and 'The Meeting on the Turret Stairs.' [Suppl. i. 346]

BURTON, GEORGE (1717–1791), chronologer ; published treatises on biblical chronology, 1766–87 ; M.A. Cambridge, 1740 ; rector of Elveden, 1740, and of Heringswell, Suffolk, 1751. [viii. 4]

BURTON, HENRY (1578–1648), independent ; M.A. St. John's College, Cambridge, 1602 ; tutor to Sir Robert Carey's sons ; clerk of the closet to Prince Henry, and to Prince Charles, 1612–25 ; offended Charles I by accusing Laud of popery, April 1625 ; rector of St. Matthew's, Friday Street, 1625 ; prosecuted for attacks on the bishops, 1627 ; imprisoned, 1629 ; tried in the Star-chamber for 'seditious' preaching, and sentenced to deprivation, degradation, fine, pillory, loss of ears, and perpetual imprisonment, 1636 ; his removal to Lancaster Castle witnessed by sympathetic crowds, 1636 ; removed to Castle Cornet, Guernsey, 1636 . freed by parliament, November 1640 ; made a triumphal progress from Dartmouth to London ; his sentence reversed, 1641 ; ministered to an independent congregation in St. Matthew's, Friday Street, 1642 ; Tuesday lecturer at St. Mary's, Aldermanbury, till 1645 ; wrote polemical tracts. [viii. 5]

BURTON, HEZEKIAH (d. 1681), divine ; fellow of Magdalene College, Cambridge, 1651 ; B.D., 1661 ; D.D., 1669 ; prebendary of Norwich, 1667 ; rector of St. George's, Southwark, 1668, and of Barnes, Surrey, 1680 ; his sermons published posthumously. [viii. 7]

BURTON, ISABEL, LADY (1831–1896), wife of Sir Richard Francis Burton [q. v.], whom she married, 1861 ; daughter of Henry Raymond Arundell ; shared, as far as possible, her husband's life in travel and literature, and after his death prepared his biography and a memorial edition of his works ; published 'Inner Life of Syria' (1875) and 'Arabia, Egypt, and India,' 1879. [Suppl. i. 348]

BURTON, JAMES (1788–1862). [See HALIBURTON, JAMES.]

BURTON, JAMES DANIEL (1784–1817), methodist ; itinerant preacher, 1805, chiefly in Lancashire ; published a devotional tract. [viii. 8]

BURTON, JOHN (1696–1771), classical scholar ; scholar of Corpus Christi College, Oxford, 1713, tutor, 1717, fellow, 1721 ; M.A., 1721 ; D.D., 1752 ; fellow of Eton, 1733 ; vicar of Mapledurham, Oxfordshire, 1734–66 ; rector of Worplesdon, Surrey, 1766–71 ; wrote tracts, sermons, Latin verses, and Greek text-books. [viii. 8]

BURTON, JOHN (1710–1771), antiquary ; educated at Merchant Taylors' School and St. John's College, Cambridge ; M.B., 1733 ; studied medicine at Leyden ; M.D. Rheims ; practised medicine in York ; wrote on midwifery and on the antiquities of Yorkshire. [viii. 10]

BURTON, JOHN HILL (1809–1881), Scottish historian ; educated at Aberdeen ; articled to a solicitor ; read for the bar in Edinburgh ; advocate, but had little practice ; wrote much for Edinburgh booksellers, reviews, and newspapers ; made his mark by a life of David Hume, 1846 ; secretary to the prison board, 1854–81 ; published 'History of Scotland,' 1853, 'The Bookhunter,' 1860, 'The Scot Abroad,' 1864, and many other treatises and editions, chiefly historical. [viii. 10]

BURTON, SIR RICHARD FRANCIS (1821–1890), explorer and scholar ; taken abroad at an early age by his parents ; matriculated at Trinity College, Oxford, 1840, but did not graduate ; cadet in Indian army, 1842 ; ensign 18th regiment Bombay native infantry, 1842 ; captain ; studied oriental languages ; assistant in Sind survey ; lived a wandering life among natives and gained intimate knowledge of Muhammadan manners and customs ; returned to England, 1849 ; published three philological works relating to Asiatic languages, 1849, and other volumes on India, 1851–3 ; made pilgrimage to Mecca, adopting various disguises and assuming name of Al-Haj (the pilgrim) Abdullah, 1853, and published 'Personal Narrative,' 1855 ;

explored Somaliland, 1854 ; served in Crimea, 1855 ; went on expedition with Speke, as second in command, to discover sources of Nile, 1856–9 ; reached Lake Tanganyika, 1858 (Speke, on the return journey, left the party and alone discovered Victoria Nyanza) ; travelled in North America, 1860 ; married Isabel Arundell [see BURTON, ISABEL, LADY], 1861 ; British consul at Fernando Po, 1861–5, and at Santos, 1865–9, during both of which periods he made numerous journeys of discovery ; consul at Damascus, 1869–71 ; consul at Trieste (1872), whence he made many tours into neighbouring unexplored territories ; went to the Gold Coast for gold in company with Captain Verney Lovett Cameron [q. v.], 1881–2 ; nominated K.C.M.G., 1885 ; in his later years devoted himself to literature, publishing translations of Camoens, 1880 and 1884, 'Book of the Sword,' 1884, and complete translation of 'The Arabian Nights,' 1885–8. His translations of the ' Pentamerone ' of Basile and of 'Catullus' appeared posthumously. [Suppl. i. 349]

BURTON, ROBERT (1577–1640), author of the ' Anatomy of Melancholy,' 1621 ; called ' Democritus Junior ' ; educated at Nuneaton and Sutton Coldfield schools ; entered Brasenose College, Oxford, 1593 ; student of Christ Church, 1599 ; B.D., 1614 ; vicar of St. Thomas's, Oxford, 1616, and rector of Segrave, Leicestershire, 1630–40. [viii. 12]

BURTON, ROBERT or RICHARD (1632 ?–1725 ?), reputed to be a miscellaneous writer. [See CROUCH, NATHANIEL.]

BURTON, SIMON (1690 ?–1744), physician ; educated at Rugby and New College, Oxford ; M.D., 1720 ; began practice at Warwick ; removed to Savile Row, London, 1732. [viii. 16]

BURTON, THOMAS (fl. 1656–1659), diarist ; M.P. for Westmoreland, 1656 ; reputed author of a diary (printed, 1828), containing reports of proceedings in parliament, 3 Dec. 1656–22 April 1659. [viii. 17]

BURTON, WILLIAM (d. 1616), puritan ; educated at Winchester ; fellow of New College, Oxford, 1561–5 ; B.A., 1565 ; perhaps usher in Norwich school, 1576 ; minister in Norwich, 1584 ?–9 ; received into household of Thomas, baron Wentworth ; preached in Bristol, 1590 ; vicar of St. Giles's, Reading, 1591 ; resided in London from about 1608 : published catechism and sermons ; translated seven dialogues of Erasmus, 1606. [viii. 17]

BURTON, WILLIAM (1575–1645), antiquary ; B.A. Brasenose College, Oxford, 1594 ; barrister of the Inner Temple, 1603 ; retired to his estate at Falde, Staffordshire ; published his ' Description of Leicestershire,' 1622 ; finished revision of it, 1638 ; gave John Leland's manuscripts to the Bodleian, 1631. [viii. 18]

BURTON, WILLIAM (1609–1657), author of 'A Commentary on Antoninus his Itinerary . . . (for) Britain,' 1658 ; educated at St. Paul's School, London ; member of Queen's College, and Gloucester Hall, Oxford ; B.C.L., 1630 ; usher in Thomas Farnaby's school ; master of Kingston-on-Thames school ; published Latin orations and translations from Latin. [viii. 19]

BURTON, WILLIAM EVANS (1802–1860), actor and dramatist ; educated at St. Paul's School, London ; went on the provincial stage, 1823 ; first acted in London, 1831 ; went to the United States, 1834 ; managed National and Burton's theatres, New York, 1841–58 ; afterwards head of a travelling company : wrote plays, humorous books, and magazine articles. [viii. 20]

BURTON, WILLIAM PATON (1828–1883), landscape painter in water-colours ; educated at Edinburgh ; exhibited in London, 1862–80. [viii. 21]

BURTT, JOSEPH (1818–1876), archæologist ; employed in calendaring records at Westminster chapterhouse, 1832 ; assistant-keeper of the Record Office, 1859–1876 ; arranged muniments at Westminster Abbey and Lincoln Cathedral ; wrote archæological papers. [viii. 21]

BURY, VISCOUNT (1832 – 1894). [See KEPPEL, WILLIAM COUTTS, seventh EARL OF ALBEMARLE.]

BURY, ARTHUR (1624–1713), theologian ; son of John Bury (1580–1667) [q. v.] ; entered Exeter College, Oxford, 1639 ; fellow, 1643 (ejected, 1648 ; restored, 1662) ; canon of Exeter, 1661 ; rector of Exeter College, 1666–89, expelled by the visitor for disobedience ; his

expulsion confirmed by the House of Lords, 1694 ; **D.D.**, 1666 ; part vicar of Bampton, Oxfordshire, 1671–1707 ; published ' The Naked Gospel,' 1690, an attempt to set aside later dogmatic accretions ; his book burnt by Oxford University, 1690 ; published other theological treatises, and sermons. [viii. 21]

BURY, LADY CHARLOTTE SUSAN MARIA (1775–1861), novelist ; youngest daughter of the fifth Duke of Argyll ; married (1) in 1796, Colonel John Campbell (d. 1809) ; (2) in 1818, Rev. Edward John Bury (d. 1832) ; lady-in-waiting to Caroline, princess of Wales, 1809 ; published numerous novels, 1826–64, poems, and a ' Diary Illustrative of the Times of George IV,' 1838. [viii. 22]

BURY, EDWARD (1616–1700), nonconformist ; a presbyterian minister ; intruded rector of Great Bolas, Shropshire, before 1654 ; ejected, 1662 ; resided at Great Bolas till 1680 ; suffered for nonconformity, 1681, and for a time moved from place to place ; became blind ; published devotional tracts. [viii. 23]

BURY, EDWARD (1794–1858), engineer ; at one time manufacturing engineer at Liverpool ; constructed railway engines, 1830, and steamship engines, 1840 ; manager of rolling stock of London and Birmingham railway, 1838, and of Great Northern railway. [viii. 24]

BURY, MRS. ELIZABETH (1644–1720), nonconformist ; née Lawrence ; married (1) in 1667, Griffith Lloyd (d. 1682) ; (2) in 1697, Samuel Bury [q. v.] ; wrote ' Diary,' beginning 1664. [viii. 24]

BURY, HENRY DE (fl. 1380). [See BEDERIC.]

BURY, JOHN OF (fl. 1460). [See JOHN.]

BURY, JOHN (fl. 1557), translator ; M.A. Cambridge, 1555 ; published a translation from Isocrates, 1557. [viii. 25]

BURY or **BERRY**, JOHN (1580–1667), divine ; scholar of Corpus Christi College, Oxford, 1597 ; Blundell fellow of Balliol College, 1603 ; M.A., 1605 ; vicar of Heavitree, Devonshire, 1626, and rector of Widworthy ; canon of Exeter, 1627 ; rector of St. Mary Major, Exeter, 1662–7 ; published sermons. [viii. 25]

BURY, RICHARD DE (1281–1345), bishop of Durham, patron of learning and collector of books ; named from his birthplace, Bury St. Edmunds ; son of Sir Richard Aungerville ; studied at Oxford ; entered Benedictine monastery at Durham ; tutor to Edward III when Prince of Wales ; treasurer of Guienne ; of the household of Edward III ; dean of Wells, 1333 ; bishop of Durham, 1333 ; lord chancellor, September 1334 to July 1335 ; lord high treasurer, 1337 ; employed by Edward III in Paris, Hainault, Germany, 1336, and in Scotland, 1337 and 1342 ; founded a library in Durham College, Oxford ; wrote ' Philobiblon ' (first printed, 1473). [viii. 25]

BURY, SAMUEL (1663–1730), presbyterian ; son of Edward Bury (1616–1700) [q. v.] ; studied at Doolittle's academy, Islington ; presbyterian minister at Bury St. Edmunds from before 1689 to 1719 ; minister at Bristol, 1720–30 ; published sermons and hymns. [viii. 27]

BURY, THOMAS (1655–1722), judge ; B.A. Lincoln College, Oxford, 1668 ; barrister of Gray's Inn, 1676 ; serjeant-at-law, 1700 ; baron of the exchequer, 1701, and chief baron, 1716–22. [viii. 28]

BURY, THOMAS TALBOT (1811–1877), architect ; pupil of Augustus Pugin, 1824 ; started business, 1830 ; exhibited at the Academy, 1846–72 ; designed many churches and schools ; wrote on architectural subjects. [viii. 29]

BUSBY, RICHARD (1606–1695), head-master of Westminster School ; educated at Westminster ; student of Christ Church, Oxford, 1624 ; M.A., 1631 ; D.D., 1660 ; head-master of Westminster, 1638–95 ; rector of Cudworth, Somerset, 1639 (ejected, c. 1648) ; prebendary of Westminster and canon of Wells, 1660 : a famous schoolmaster and a zealous churchman ; published classical schoolbooks. [viii. 29]

BUSBY, THOMAS (1755–1838), composer ; taught by various masters in London ; sang at Vauxhall, 1769 ; articled to Battishill, 1777 ; journalist and parliamentary reporter ; organist at St. Mary's, Newington, 1785 ; taught music and French ; joint-editor of a 'Musical

Dictionary,' 1786; edited two collections of music; organist at St. Mary Woolnoth, 1798; produced his first oratorio, 'The Prophecy,' 1799; Mus. Doc. Cambridge, 1801; composed music for stage; published treatises on musical subjects. [viii. 31]

BUSH, PAUL (1490–1558), first bishop of Bristol; B.A. Oxford, 1518; afterwards D.D.; a Bonhomme friar; provost of house of Bonhommes at Edington, Wiltshire; prebendary of Salisbury, 1539, and canon; chaplain to Henry VIII; bishop of Bristol, 1542; resigned 1554, to avoid deprivation for marriage; rector of Winterbourne, Gloucestershire, 1555–8; published devotional tracts and verses. [viii. 32]

BUSHE, CHARLES KENDAL (1767–1843), Irish judge; entered Trinity College, Dublin, 1782; Irish barrister, 1790, subsequently acquiring an extensive practice; M.P. for Callan in the Irish parliament, 1797; opposed the union; serjeant-at-law, 1805; solicitor-general for Ireland, 1805–22; chief-justice of king's bench, 1822–1841. [viii. 34]

BUSHELL, BROWN (d. 1651), sea-captain: in the parliamentary garrison at Scarborough; seized the castle there for the parliament, when the commander surrendered to the royalists, 1643; surrendered to royalists, 1644?; sent to London under suspicion, 1645; given command of ship-of-war; delivered his ship to the Prince of Wales, 1648; imprisoned in Windsor Castle, 1649–50; executed. [viii. 34]

BUSHELL, SETH (1621–1684), divine; educated at St. Mary Hall, Oxford, 1639–44; M.A., 1655; D.D., 1672; minister of Whitley, Yorkshire, and of Euxton, Lancashire, under the Commonwealth; vicar of Preston, 1664–82, and of Lancaster, 1682–4; published sermons. [viii. 35]

BUSHELL, THOMAS (1594–1674), speculator and mining engineer; page to Francis Bacon, who taught him what was then known of mineralogy; seal-bearer to Bacon; lay hid in the Isle of Wight for a few years from 1621; lived in hiding on the Calf of Man, 1626–9; his walks and fountains at Enstone, Oxford, visited by Charles I, and by the queen, 1636; farmed royal mines in Wales, 1636–7; master of the mint at Aberystwith, 1637, at Shrewsbury, 1642, and at Oxford, 1643; held Lundy for Charles I till 1647, and then lived in concealment; gave security for good behaviour, 1652; leased crown mines from Protector; wrote pamphlets respecting his schemes. [viii. 35]

BUSHER, LEONARD (fl. 1614), pioneer of religious toleration; member of Brownist congregation of Thomas Helwys [q. v.]; published 'Religious Peace,' 1614, probably the earliest publication in which liberty of conscience is openly advocated. [Suppl. i. 356]

BUSHNAN, JOHN STEVENSON (1808?–1884), writer on medical subjects; M.D. Heidelberg; qualified as practitioner at Edinburgh, 1830; editor, in London, of 'The Medical Times and Gazette,' 1849–52; lost his sight; pensioner of the Charterhouse. [viii. 37]

BUSHNELL, MRS. CATHERINE (1825–1861). [See HAYES, CATHERINE.]

BUSHNELL, JOHN (d. 1701), sculptor; pupil of Thomas Burman [q. v.], in London; then studied in France, Rome, Venice; executed many statues for public buildings in London; died insane. [viii. 38]

BUSHNELL, WALTER (1609–1667), divine; M.A. Magdalen Hall, Oxford, 1634; vicar of Box, Wiltshire, 1644; ejected, 1656; restored, 1660, and held the living till death; published narrative of the proceedings against him. [viii. 38]

BUSK, GEORGE (1807–1886), man of science; born at St. Petersburg; student at College of Surgeons and St. Thomas's and St. Bartholomew's hospitals; served as surgeon in navy; settled in London, 1855; F.R.C.S., 1843, and president, 1871; treasurer of Royal Institution; Hunterian professor and trustee of Hunterian Museum; F.R.S., 1850; F.L.S., 1846; F.Z.S., 1856; president of Anthropological Institute, 1873–4; published scientific treatises. [Suppl. i. 357]

BUSK, HANS, the elder (1772–1862), a Radnorshire squire; published poems, 1814–34. [viii. 39]

BUSK, HANS, the younger (1815–1882), a pioneer of the volunteer movement, son of Hans Busk the elder

[q. v.]; educated at King's College, London; M.A. Trinity College, Cambridge, 1844; called to bar at Middle Temple, 1841; high sheriff of Radnorshire, 1847; wrote on military and naval topics. [viii. 39]

BUSS, ROBERT WILLIAM (1804–1875), painter of theatrical portraits, and of historical and humorous subjects; exhibited at Royal Academy and other institutions, 1826–59; illustrated books; wrote on art topics. [viii. 40]

BUSSY, SIR JOHN (d. 1399), sheriff of Lincoln, 1379, 1381, 1391; M.P. for Lincolnshire, 1388–98; speaker of the House of Commons, 1394, 1397, 1398; subservient to Richard II; executed at Bristol by the Lancastrians. [viii. 40]

BUTCHELL, MARTIN VAN (1735–1812?), eccentric; pupil of John Hunter; practised as dentist, truss-maker, and fistula specialist; advertised largely; kept mummified body of his first wife in his parlour for years from 1775. [viii. 40]

BUTCHER, EDMUND (1757–1822), unitarian; apprenticed to a London linendraper; wrote for periodicals; presbyterian student at Daventry academy, 1783; minister at Sowerby, Yorkshire; in London, 1789–97, and at Sidmouth, 1798–1820; withdrew to Bath, 1821; published hymns, sermons, and devotional books. [viii. 41]

BUTCHER, RICHARL (1583–1665?), compiler of 'The Survey and Antiquitie of . . . Stamforde,' 1646; town clerk of Stamford. [viii. 42]

BUTCHER, SAMUEL (1811–1876), bishop of Meath; entered Trinity College, Dublin, 1829; fellow, 1837–52, and lecturer; D.D., 1849; professor of ecclesiastical history, 1850, and of divinity, 1852–66; incumbent of Ballymoney, Cork, 1854–66; bishop of Meath, 1866; published sermons and charges. [viii. 42]

BUTE, third EARL OF (1713–1792). [See STUART, JOHN.]

BUTE, third MARQUIS OF (1847–1900). [See STUART, JOHN PATRICK CRICHTON.]

BUTLER, ALBAN (1711–1773), hagiographer; compiler of 'The Lives of the . . . Principal Saints,' 1756–9; educated at Douay; professor of philosophy and divinity at Douay; ordained priest, 1735; sent into England, 1746; chaplain to the Duke of Norfolk, and tutor to his heir (d. 1767); president of the English College at St. Omer, 1768–73; published also travels, sermons, and biographies. [viii. 43]

BUTLER, CHARLES (d. 1647), author of 'The Feminine Monarchie, or a Treatise concerning Bees,' 1609; chorister of Magdalen College, Oxford, 1579–85; M.A., 1587; master of Basingstoke school, and rector of Nately-Scures, Hampshire, 1593–1600; vicar of Wootton St. Lawrence, 1600–47; published also treatises on rhetoric, English grammar (advocating spelling-reform), music, and affinity as a bar to marriage. [viii. 44]

BUTLER, CHARLES (1750–1832), Roman catholic lawyer; educated at Douay, 1759–66; studied conveyancing in London, 1769; entered Lincoln's Inn, 1775; an eminent conveyancer, 1775–1826; secretary of committees for repeal of penal laws, 1782–91; first catholic barrister since James II, 1791; published several legal, historical, biographical, and theological works. [viii. 45]

BUTLER, EDMUND (d. 1551), archbishop of Cashel; studied at Oxford; prior of canons regular at Athassel, Tipperary; archbishop of Cashel, 1527; held synod at Limerick, 1529; surrendered Athassel Abbey to the crown, 1537; present in parliament at Dublin, 1541; one of the king's commissioners at Limerick, 1550. [viii. 47]

BUTLER, SIR EDWARD GERARD (1770–1825), soldier; cornet, 1792; served in Flanders, 1793; knighted for saving the emperor's life at Villiers-en-Couche, 1794; major, 1796, lieutenant-colonel, 1804; served in the West Indies, 1797–1806, and at the La Plata, 1806; major-general, 1814. [viii. 48]

BUTLER, ELEANOR, LADY (1745?–1829), recluse; sister of the seventeenth Earl of Ormonde; one of 'the ladies of the vale' of Llangollen, 1779–1829. [viii. 48]

BUTLER, GEORGE (1774–1853), head-master of Harrow; second son of Weeden Butler the elder [q. v.]; fellow of Sidney Sussex College, Cambridge; senior wrangler, 1794; M.A., 1797; D.D., 1805; head-master of

Harrow, 1805-29; rector of Gayton, Northamptonshire, 1814; chancellor of Peterborough, 1836; dean of Peterborough, 1842; published sermons and Harrow notes.
[viii. 49]

BUTLER, GEORGE (1819-1890), canon of Winchester; son of George Butler [q. v.]; educated at Harrow, Trinity College, Cambridge, and Exeter College, Oxford; Petrean fellow, 1842; M.A., 1846; tutor at Durham University, 1848; examiner at Oxford, 1850-2; curate, 1854; principal of Butler's Hall, Oxford, 1856-8; vice-principal of Cheltenham College, 1857-65; principal of Liverpool College, 1866-82; canon of Winchester, 1882; published sermons and other writings. [Suppl. i. 358]

BUTLER, GEORGE SLADE (1821-1882), writer on antiquities of Sussex; solicitor, 1843; town clerk of Rye, Sussex; F.S.A., 1862. [viii. 50]

BUTLER, JAMES, second EARL OF ORMONDE (1331-1382), styled 'the noble earl' in virtue of his being son of a granddaughter of Edward I; succeeded to earldom, 1338; a favourite with Edward III and Richard II; lord justice of Ireland, April 1359, and again, March 1360; held command under the Duke of Clarence in the war, 1361-2; lord deputy, 1364; lord justice, 1376-8.
[viii. 50]

BUTLER, JAMES, fourth EARL OF ORMONDE (d. 1452), styled 'the white earl'; succeeded, 1405; lord deputy of Ireland, 1407; went with Thomas of Lancaster to France, 1412; served in Henry V's French wars; lord-lieutenant of Ireland, 1420; made war on the O'Mores, 1422; lord-lieutenant, 1424; lord justice, 1426; lord deputy, 1440; lord-lieutenant, 1443-6. [viii. 50]

BUTLER, JAMES, fifth EARL OF ORMONDE and EARL OF WILTSHIRE (1420-1461), eldest son of James Butler, fourth earl [q. v.]; attended Richard, duke of York, to France, 1439; a zealous Lancastrian; created Earl of Wiltshire in the English peerage, 1449; lord deputy of Ireland, 1450-1; succeeded to the Ormonde peerage, 1452; lord-lieutenant, 1453-5; made lord high treasurer of England, 1455; fought at St. Albans, 22 May 1455; again made lord high treasurer, 1458; K.G., 1459; fought at Wakefield, December 1460, Mortimer's Cross, February 1461, Towton, March 1461; beheaded at Newcastle-on-Tyne; attainted and his estates forfeited. [viii. 51]

BUTLER, JAMES (d. 1546), created VISCOUNT THURLES, 1535; restored as ninth EARL OF ORMONDE, 1541; poisoned in London, 1546. [viii. 73]

BUTLER, JAMES (fl. 1631-1634), Irishman in the imperialist service; raised regiment in Poland, called 'the Irish regiment,' from its officers; brought this regiment to Frankfort-on-Oder to reinforce Tiefenbach in spring of 1631; sent to Tilly to ask further help; present at the storming of Magdeburg, 20 May 1631; defeated the Saxons at Nimburg-on-Elbe, November 1631; fought in the Polish service against Russia, 1632-4. [viii. 51]

BUTLER, JAMES, twelfth EARL and first DUKE OF ORMONDE (1610-1688), son of Thomas, viscount Thurles (d. 1619); grandson of Walter Butler, eleventh earl of Ormonde [q. v.]; styled Viscount Thurles, 1619; succeeded to the earldom, 1633; created marquis, 1642; created Earl of Brecknock in the English peerage, 1660; created Duke of Ormonde in the Irish peerage, 1661, and in the English peerage, 1682; placed by his mother under a catholic tutor at Finchley, 1619; made king's ward and brought up in the protestant religion at Lambeth under Archbishop Abbot; entrusted to Richard Preston, earl of Desmond, 1624-8; lived with his grandfather at Drury Lane, 1625-7, and at Carrickfergus, 1630; came to England, 1631; returned to Ireland, 1633; opposed Wentworth in the Irish parliament, but urged granting supplies to Charles I, 1634; raised troop of cuirassiers, 1638; supported Wentworth (now Earl of Strafford), 1640; assembled troops at Carrickfergus, July 1640; defended Strafford in the Irish parliament, 1641; commander against the Irish rebels, but kept inactive by the lords justices, 1641; defeated rebels, January-March 1642; quieted Connaught, 1642; again obstructed by the lords justices, 1642; commissioned by Charles I to ascertain the demands of the Irish rebels, 1643; defeated them at Ross, 18 March 1643; ordered in April to conclude truce; concluded truce for a year in September; sent five thousand troops into Cheshire, November 1643; lord-

lieutenant of Ireland, January 1644; sent Irish troops into Scotland to help Montrose; opposed both by the catholic rebels and by the protestant parliamentarians, April 1644-April 1645; negotiated peace with the rebels; superseded in August 1645 by Glamorgan; arranged terms of peace between the king's forces and the catholic rebels, March 1646; asked parliament for help against the rebels, October-November 1646; induced by the rebels' rejection of his terms (February 1647) to approach parliament, with which he concluded peace, June 1647; conferred with Charles I at Hampton Court, August 1647; withdrew to Paris, 1648; royalist commander in Ireland, October 1648; concluded peace with rebels, January 1649; proclaimed Charles II; attacked Dublin; defeated at Rathmines, August 1649; his garrisons crushed by Cromwell, September-December 1649; left Ireland, December 1650; employed in personal attendance on Charles II or on embassies in his interest, 1651-9; royalist spy in England, January-March 1658; negotiated with Monck, 1659; received back his estates, and also his grandfather's county palatine of Tipperary; appointed lord steward of the household, 1660; lord high steward at the coronation, 1661; restored the protestant episcopate in Ireland; appointed lord-lieutenant of Ireland, 4 Nov. 1661; resided in Ireland, July 1662-June 1664; in London, July 1664-May 1665; again in Ireland, 1665-8; returned to London, 1668; dismissed from the lord-lieutenancy, March 1669; chancellor of Oxford University, 1669; his life attempted by Thomas Blood, 1669, at Buckingham's instigation; opposed attempts to repeal Act of Settlement, 1671-3; in Ireland on private affairs, July 1671-April 1675; recalled to London, 1675; lord-lieutenant of Ireland, 1677-82; at court in London, 1682, returned to Ireland, 1684; removed from the lord-lieutenancy, October 1684; proclaimed James II before he left Dublin, February 1685; lord high steward at James II's coronation; continued to be lord steward of the household; withdrew, as much as he could, from public life, 1685, broken by the deaths of his wife and children; resisted some of James II's arbitrary acts, 1687. [viii. 52]

BUTLER, JAMES (d. 1709), Irishman in the French service; killed at Malplaquet. [viii. 73]

BUTLER, JAMES, second DUKE OF ORMONDE (1665-1745), eldest surviving son of Thomas Butler, earl of Ossory [q. v.]; educated in France, 1675, and at Oxford, 1679; resided in Ireland, 1680-2; styled Earl of Ossory, 1680; married Lady Anne Hyde (d. 1684), 1682; at the siege of Luxemburg, April-June 1684; served against Monmouth, 1685; married Lady Mary Somerset (d. 1733), 1685; succeeded to the dukedom, 1688; elected chancellor of Oxford University, 23 July 1688; K.G., 1688; signed petition for a free parliament, 17 Nov. 1688; joined Prince of Orange, 25 Nov. 1688; lord high constable at coronation of William and Mary, 1689; attainted, and his estates forfeited, by James II, May 1689; fought at the Boyne, secured Dublin, and took Kilkenny Castle, July 1690; went with William III to Holland, 1691; fought at Steinkirk, 1692; taken prisone at Landen, 1693, but exchanged; present at William III's deathbed, March 1702; commanded troops sent against Cadiz and Vigo, August-October 1702; in Ireland as lord-lieutenant, September 1703-June 1705, and again 1710-11; appointed commander-in-chief and captain-general, 1712; sent to command in Flanders, April 1712, but directed to remain inactive; lord-warden of the Cinque ports, 1713-14; lord-lieutenant of Ireland, 1713; deprived of the captain-generalship, 1714; a recognised leader of the Jacobites in London; impeached, 21 June 1715; withdrew to France, 8 Aug.; attainted and his estates forfeited, 20 Aug. 1715; sailed to Plymouth to head an expected rising, 1715; accepted command of Spanish fleet intended to restore Stuarts, 1719; was living at Madrid, 1721; resided chiefly at Avignon; visited Madrid, 1740, to suggest an invasion of England; buried in Westminster Abbey. [viii. 60]

BUTLER, JAMES ARMAR (1827-1854), captain in the army; educated abroad and at Sandhurst; ensign, 1843; served in the Kaffir war, 1846-7; captain, 1853; defended Silistria against the Russians, 1854. [viii. 65]

BUTLER, JOHN, sixth EARL OF ORMONDE (d. 1478), knighted before 1460; attainted, 1461, with his brother, James Butler, fifth earl [q. v.]; soon pardoned and recovered his estates; died in Palestine on a pilgrimage.
[viii. 66]

BUTLER, JOHN (*d.* 1800), Roman catholic bishop of Cork, 1763-86; succeeded to barony of Dunboyne (under attainder), December 1785; was refused dispensation to resign his see and marry; embraced protestantism, 1787; reconciled to catholicism, 1800; bequeathed the Dunboyne estate to Maynooth College; D.D. [viii. 66]

BUTLER, JOHN (1717-1802), bishop of Hereford; born at Hamburg; entered University College, Oxford, 1733; D.C.L., 1752; chaplain to the Princess-dowager of Wales, 1754; a popular London preacher; minister of Great Yarmouth, 1758; prebendary of Winchester, 1760; rector of Everley, Wiltshire; chaplain to George III; bishop of Oxford, 1777; translated to see of Hereford, 1788; published political tracts, sermons, and charges. [viii. 67]

BUTLER, JOSEPH (1692-1752), bishop of Durham; son of a retired draper at Wantage, a presbyterian; educated at Samuel Jones's dissenting school, Gloucestershire; sent Samuel Clarke criticisms on his Boyle lectures, 1713; conformed to the Anglican church; entered Oriel College, Oxford, 1715; B.A., 1718; B.C.L., 1721; D.C.L., 1733; ordained priest, 1718; preacher at the Rolls, 1719-1726; prebendary of Salisbury, 1721-38; rector of Houghton-le-Skerne, Durham, 1722-5; rector of Stanhope, 1725-1740; published 'Fifteen Sermons,' 1726, and the 'Analogy of Religion,' maintaining that the frame of nature shows a moral governor revealed through conscience, 1736; prebendary of Rochester, 1736-40; clerk of the closet to the queen, 1736; bishop of Bristol, 1738; asked John Wesley to cease preaching in his diocese, 1739; dean of St. Paul's, 1740; clerk of the closet to the king, 1746; said to have refused see of Canterbury, 1747; suggested plan for establishing bishops in American colonies, 1750; translated to Durham, 1750; suspected by some to have died a Roman catholic. His collected works were published in 1804. [viii. 67]

BUTLER, SIR PIERCE or PIERS, eighth EARL OF ORMONDE and first EARL OF OSSORY (*d.* 1539), succeeded to the Ormonde earldom, 1515; active in suppressing Irish rebellions; lord deputy, 1521-4; lord treasurer of Ireland, 1524; forced by Henry VIII to surrender the Ormonde title to Sir Thomas Boleyn, 1527; created, in compensation, Earl of Ossory, February 1528; lord justice, 1528; given large grants of land for helping to suppress Sir Thomas Fitzgerald's rising, 1534-5; suppressed the Earl of Desmond's rising. [viii. 72]

BUTLER, PIERCE, third VISCOUNT GALMOY (1652-1740), colonel in the French service; hon. D.C.L. Oxford, 1677; lord-lieutenant of Kilkenny; colonel of horse besieging Londonderry, 1689; fought at the Boyne, 1690, and Aughrim, 1691; outlawed, but given the benefit of the treaty of Limerick, 1691; withdrew to France; created Earl of Newcastle by James II; attainted, and his estates confiscated, 1697; served with distinction as colonel of Irish horse in the French service. [viii. 73]

BUTLER, RICHARD, first VISCOUNT MOUNTGARRET (*d.* 1571), created 1550. [viii. 73]

BUTLER, RICHARD, third VISCOUNT MOUNTGARRET (1578-1651), joined in the rebellion of his father-in-law, Hugh, earl of Tyrone, 1597-8; succeeded, and had his estates confirmed, 1605; sat in the Irish parliament, 1613, 1615, 1634; took castles in Kilkenny, Waterford, and Tipperary, and was chosen general of the Irish rebels, 1641; defeated at Kilrush, 1642; fought at Ross, 1643; excepted, though dead, from pardon in the act of 1652. [viii. 73]

BUTLER, RICHARD (*d.* 1791), officer in the American army; by birth an Irishman; emigrated before 1760; lieutenant-colonel, 1775; major-general, 1791; killed while fighting in St. Clair's expedition against the Indians. [viii. 74]

BUTLER, SAMUEL (1612-1680), satirist; son of a Worcestershire farmer; educated at Worcester free school; for some years page to Elizabeth, countess of Kent, at Wrest, Bedfordshire, *c.* 1628; clerk to various puritan justices of the peace, including Sir Samuel Luke of Bedfordshire, and Sir Henry Rosewell of Devonshire, from whom he derived traits for 'Hudibras'; sojourned in France and Holland; published an anonymous pamphlet in favour of the Stuarts, 1659; secretary to the lord president of Wales, 1660; steward of Ludlow Castle; married a widow with a jointure, and came to London;

published 'Hudibras,' part i. 1663, part ii. 1664, and part iii. 1668; was neglected by the court, and, according to the most authentic accounts, died in poverty. Some manuscript pieces were first printed in 1754. [viii. 74]

BUTLER, SAMUEL (1774-1839), bishop of Lichfield; educated at Rugby and St. John's College, Cambridge; B.A., 1796; fellow, 1797; D.D., 1811; head-master of Shrewsbury, 1798-1836; vicar of Kenilworth, 1802; prebendary of Lichfield, 1807; edited 'Æschylus' (four volumes), 1809-26; bishop of Lichfield and Coventry, 1836; published atlases and text-books of ancient and modern geography. [viii. 76]

BUTLER, SIMON (1757-1797), Irish politician; called to the Irish bar, 1778; presided at the first meeting of the Dublin 'United Irishmen,' 1791; issued digest of the laws against catholics, 1792; political prisoner for six months in Newgate, 1793; subsequently withdrew to Edinburgh. [viii. 77]

BUTLER, THEOBALD (*d.* 1205-6), first 'butler' of Ireland, 'Pincerna Hiberniæ'; named WALTER, WALTERI, and FITZWALTER from his father; BUTLER and LE BOTILLER from his office; elder brother of Hubert Walter [q. v.], the primate and justiciar; met with as owner of Amounderness, Lancashire, *c.* 1166; went with Prince John to Ireland, 1185; granted lands in Limerick, and fought with the Irish, 1185; granted Arklow, co. Wicklow, before 1189; in England, 1188; in France, 1189; in constant attendance on John, who (as Dominus Hiberniæ, 1177) made him 'butler'; first used the title, May 1192; governor of Lancaster Castle for Prince John, 1192; surrendered it to the justiciar, 1194; sheriff of Lancashire, 1194-1200; justice itinerant, 1198; deprived, by King John, of Amounderness and Limerick, 1201; made his peace and got back Amounderness, 1202; retired to Ireland, 1203; founded monasteries in Ireland. [viii. 77]

BUTLER, THOMAS (*fl.* 1570), translator; published a catholic 'Treatise of . . . the Masse,' translated from the Italian, 1570; B.A. Cambridge, 1548; LL.D. of some foreign university. [viii. 79]

BUTLER, THOMAS, tenth EARL OF ORMONDE (1532-1614), called 'the black earl'; son of James Butler, ninth earl [q. v.]; brought up at Henry VIII's court as a protestant; knighted, 1547; sent to Ireland to allay disaffection among his Irish tenantry, 1554; tried to reconcile the Irish and their English rulers; privy councillor and lord treasurer of Ireland, 1559; deprived of Clonmel and other manors by the Earl of Desmond, 1560; his lands ravaged by Desmond, 1561-7; persuaded Shan O'Neill, king of Ulster, to acknowledge Elizabeth's supremacy, 1561; made war on O'Neill to protect the MacDonnells, 1563; fought with Desmond at Affone, 1565; at Elizabeth's court, 1565-9; returned to Ireland, where his brother had revolted, July 1569; suppressed the Earl of Thomond's rebellion, 1570; repressed risings in Munster, 1571; visited London, 1572, and again 1579; crushed the Desmonds in Kerry, 1580-3; helped to capture and kill the Spanish refugees who had escaped the wreck of the Armada, 1588; helped to suppress the Earl of Tyrone's rebellion, 1598-9; lord treasurer, 1599; granted confiscated lands in Munster, 1602; vice-admiral of Ireland, 1612. [viii. 79]

BUTLER, THOMAS, EARL OF OSSORY (1634-1680), eldest son of James Butler, first duke of Ormonde [q. v.]; lived in Kilkenny Castle from birth till 1647; taken to France, 1648; educated in a French protestant school at Caen, 1648-52; in London, 1652-5; imprisoned for some months in the Tower as a political suspect, 1655; went to Holland, 1656; married Emilia, a relative of the Prince of Orange, 1659; gambled; in favour with Charles II and the Duke of York, 1660; lieutenant-general of horse, 1661, and of the army in Ireland, 1665; M.P. for Bristol, 1661; called to the Irish House of Peers, 1662; lord deputy of Ireland, 1664-5; a volunteer in the sea-fight in the Downs, 1 and 2 June 1666; created Baron Butler of Moore Park in the English peerage, 1666; quarrelled with Buckingham, 1666; lord deputy in Ireland, 1668-9; attended the Prince of Orange on his visit, 1670-1; took part in the attack on the Dutch merchant fleet, 1672; commanded a ship at Southwold Bay, May 1672; K.G., 1672; envoy to Paris, November 1672; rear-admiral, 1673; in the sea fight, 11 Aug. 1673; sent to offer the Prince of Orange marriage with Princess Mary, November 1674; made a campaign in Flanders, 1677; commanded

British contingent at Mons, 1678 ; defended his father in the House of Lords against Shaftesbury, 1679 ; ordered to take command at Tangier, 1680. [viii. 81]

BUTLER, THOMAS HAMLY (1762?–1823), composer ; chorister of the Chapel Royal ; studied in Italy ; wrote music to Cumberland's 'Widow of Delphi,' produced 1780 ; music-master in Edinburgh, 1780–1823. [viii. 85]

BUTLER, WALTER, of Kilcash, eleventh EARL OF ORMONDE (1569–1633), served under his uncle, Thomas Butler, tenth earl of Ormonde [q. v.], 1599–1600 ; succeeded to earldom, 1614 ; refused to accept James I's award of the estates to Sir Richard Preston, baron Dingwall, and was imprisoned in the Fleet, 1617–25 ; deprived of the county palatine of Tipperary ; recovered part of his estates, 1625 ; lived in Drury Lane, 1625–7 ; retired to Ireland, 1627 ? ; acknowledged heir to the estates of his uncle, Thomas, tenth earl of Ormonde, 1630. [viii. 86]

BUTLER, WALTER, COUNT (d. 1634), of Irish extraction ; fought at the battle of Prague, 1620 ; lieutenant-colonel of, and in temporary command of, his kinsman's [see BUTLER, JAMES, fl. 1631–1634] Irish regiment at Frankfort-on-Oder, 1631 ; prisoner in the hands of the Swedes under Gustavus Adolphus, 1631 ; collected recruits in Poland ; sent by Wallenstein to defend Sagan against Saxons, 1632 ; ordered by Wallenstein to bring his dragoons to Prague, February 1634 ; went with Wallenstein to Eger, but sent his chaplain, 23 Feb., to receive instructions from Piccolomini ; arranged murder of Wallenstein and his officers, 25 Feb. 1634 ; rewarded by the grant of the estate of Friedberg ; fought at Nördlingen, September 1634 ; reduced Aurach and Schorndorf in Würtemberg, 1634. [viii. 86]

BUTLER, WEEDEN, the elder (1742–1823), miscellaneous writer ; solicitor's clerk ; amanuensis to Dr. William Dodd, 1764–77 ; preacher at Pimlico chapel, 1776–1814 ; kept a private school at Chelsea ; published biographies and dramatic pieces. [viii. 89]

BUTLER, WEEDEN, the younger (1773–1831), author ; eldest son of Weeden Butler the elder [q. v.] ; M.A. Sidney Sussex College, Cambridge, 1797 ; preacher in London ; rector of Great Woolston, Buckinghamshire, 1816 ; usher in, afterwards master of, his father's school in Chelsea ; published pamphlets and verses. [viii. 89]

BUTLER or **BOTELER**, WILLIAM (d. 1410 ?), writer against Wycliffism ; provincial of the Franciscans in England ; member of Franciscan convent at Oxford ; wrote against English translations of the bible, 1401 ; afterwards lived in the convent at Reading. [viii. 89]

BUTLER, WILLIAM (1535–1618), physician ; M.A. Clare Hall, Cambridge, 1566 ; licensed to practise medicine, 1572 ; attended Prince Henry, 1612 ; an eccentric. [viii. 90]

BUTLER, WILLIAM ARCHER (1814?–1848), professor of moral philosophy at Dublin, 1837–48 ; brought up as a Roman catholic ; embraced protestantism ; B.A. Trinity College, Dublin ; prebendary of Raphoe, 1837 ; rector of Raymoghy, Donegal, 1842 ; visited Wordsworth, 1844 ; active in alleviating distress in the Irish famine, 1846–7 ; contributed to the 'Dublin University Review.' His professorial 'Lectures' were published, 1856, and sermons, 1855–6. [viii. 91]

BUTLER, WILLIAM JOHN (1818–1894), dean of Lincoln ; educated at Westminster and Trinity College, Cambridge ; M.A., 1844 ; M.A. Oxford, 1847 ; honorary canon of Christ Church, 1872 ; vicar of Wantage, 1846 ; founder, 1850, and warden till death of sisterhood of St. Mary's, Wantage ; elected proctor for clergy of Oxford, 1874 ; canon of Worcester, 1880 ; appointed dean of Lincoln, 1885. His 'Life and Letters' appeared, 1897. [Suppl. i. 359]

BUTT, CHARLES PARKER (1830–1892), judge ; called to bar at Lincoln's Inn, 1854 ; bencher, 1869 ; practised in consular courts at Constantinople ; Q.C., 1868 ; liberal M.P. for Southampton, 1880 ; appointed justice of high court, probate, divorce, and admiralty division, and knighted, 1883 ; president of the division, 1891. [Suppl. i. 360]

BUTT, GEORGE (1741–1795), divine ; educated at Westminster and Christ Church, Oxford ; M.A., 1768 ; D.D., 1793 ; rector of Stanford and vicar of Clifton, Worcestershire, 1771 ; vicar of Newchurch, Isle of Wight,

1778–83 ; rector of Notgrove, Gloucestershire, 1783 ; chaplain to George III, 1783 ; vicar of Kidderminster, 1787 ; published sermons and verses. [viii. 92]

BUTT, ISAAC (1813–1879), founder of the Irish home rule party ; scholar of Trinity College, Dublin ; LL.D., 1840 ; edited the 'Dublin University Magazine,' 1834–8 ; professor of political economy, 1836–41 ; Irish barrister, 1838 ; opposed O'Connell ; M.P. for Harwich, 1852 ; M.P. for Youghal, 1852–65 ; barrister of the Inner Temple, 1859 ; defended Fenian prisoners, 1865–9 ; M.P. for Limerick, 1871 ; published translation of Virgil's 'Georgics' and historical and political tracts. [viii. 93]

BUTTER, JOHN (1791–1877), ophthalmic surgeon ; studied in Devonshire hospitals ; M.D. Edinburgh, 1820 ; practised as an oculist in Plymouth ; became blind, 1856 ; wrote medical treatises. [viii. 94]

BUTTER, NATHANIEL (d. 1664), printer and journalist ; son of a London stationer ; freeman of Stationers' Company, 1604 ; issued books in his own name, 1604–11 ; issued pamphlets describing murders and plays, 1605–39 ; issued weekly redactions of foreign newsletters, 1622–39 ; issued half-yearly volumes of foreign news, 1630–40. [viii. 94]

BUTTER, WILLIAM (1726–1805), physician ; M.D. Edinburgh, 1761 ; practised successively in Derby and London ; wrote on medical subjects. [viii. 95]

BUTTERFIELD, ROBERT (fl. 1629), Anglican controversialist ; M.A. St. John's College, Cambridge, 1626 ; published ' Maschil,' 1629. [viii. 95]

BUTTERFIELD, SWITHUN (d. 1611), author of religious and legal tracts ; possibly of Pembroke Hall, Cambridge, 1608. [viii. 96]

BUTTERFIELD, WILLIAM (1814–1900), architect ; articled at Worcester ; established himself in London ; erected missionary college of St. Augustine's, Canterbury, 1845, chapel of Balliol College, Oxford, 1856–7, All Saints', Margaret Street, London, 1859, new buildings at Merton College, Oxford, 1864, school buildings at Rugby, 1875, and Keble College, Oxford, 1876 ; executed designs for several colonial cathedrals ; made a careful study of Gothic architecture. [Suppl. i. 360]

BUTTERWORTH, EDWIN (1812–1848), publisher of historical and biographical works on Lancashire, 1829–47 ; youngest son of James Butterworth [q. v.] ; collected materials for history of Lancashire ; registrar of births and deaths at Chadderton. Some of his collections are preserved at Oldham. [viii. 96]

BUTTERWORTH, HENRY (1786–1860), London law publisher ; apprentice to his uncle, Joseph Butterworth [q. v.] ; began business on his own account, 1818. [viii. 97]

BUTTERWORTH, JAMES (1771–1837), author of poems in the Lancashire dialect and of contributions to Lancashire county history, 1800–30 ; son of a Lancashire weaver ; taught school ; postmaster of Oldham. [viii. 97]

BUTTERWORTH, JOHN (1727–1803), baptist minister at Coventry, 1753–1803 ; published ' A New Concordance,' 1767. [viii. 98]

BUTTERWORTH, JOSEPH (1770–1826), law bookseller, Fleet Street, London ; son of John Butterworth [q. v.] ; M.P. for Dover ; Wesleyan philanthropist ; published a priced 'Catalogue of Law Books.' [viii. 98]

BUTTEVANT, VISCOUNT (1550–1617). [See BARRY, DAVID FITZJAMES DE.]

BUTTON, RALPH (d. 1680), puritan ; B.A. Exeter College, Oxford, 1630 ; fellow of Merton, 1633 ; M.A., 1640 ; withdrew to London, 1642 ; professor of geometry in Gresham College, 1643–8 ; a delegate to visit Oxford University, 1647 ; intruded canon of Christ Church, and public orator, 1648–60 ; left Oxford, 1660 ; kept a school at Brentford ; and at Islington, 1672–80. [viii. 98]

BUTTON, SIR THOMAS (d. 1634), admiral ; entered the navy, c. 1589 ; served in the West Indies ; present at the siege of Kinsale, 1601 ; explored Hudson's Bay, 1612–1613 ; admiral in charge of Irish coasts, 1614–34 ; knighted, 1616 ; served against Algiers, 1620 ; served on commission for inquiring into state of navy, 1625 ; quarrelled with the navy board, 1628. [viii. 99]

BUTTON or **BITTON**, WILLIAM I (*d.* 1264), bishop of Bath and Wells ; named from Bitton, Gloucestershire ; rector of Sowy ; sub-dean, and afterwards archdeacon, of Wells ; bishop of Bath and Wells, 1247 ; went to Rome to protest against the primate's claims, 1251 ; present in parliament, 1253 ; ambassador to Castile ; with Henry III in Gascony, 1254 ; quarrelled with the abbot of Glastonbury over certain possessions and rights which the abbey had lost to the bishopric ; present at the dedication of Salisbury Cathedral, 1258. [viii. 100]

BUTTON or **BITTON**, WILLIAM II (*d.* 1274), bishop of Bath and Wells ; nephew of William Button I [q. v.] ; dean of Wells ; bishop of Bath and Wells, 1267 ; reverenced locally as a saint. [viii. 1υ1]

BUTTON, SIR WILLIAM (*d.* 1655), royalist, second baronet ; plundered by the parliamentary troops, 1643–4 ; fined for 'delinquency,' 1646. [viii. 101]

BUTTS, JOHN (*d.* 1764), self-taught Irish landscape-painter. [viii. 101]

BUTTS, ROBERT (1684–1748), bishop of Ely ; educated at Bury St. Edmunds and Trinity College, Cambridge ; M.A., 1711 ; D.D., 1728 ; preacher at Bury, 1703 ; political agent ; rector of Ickworth, Suffolk, 1717–33 ; chaplain to George II, 1728 ; dean of Norwich, 1731 ; bishop of Norwich, 1733 ; translated to Ely, 1738 ; published sermons and charges. [viii. 102]

BUTTS, SIR WILLIAM (*d.* 1545), physician to Henry VIII and his court ; owned lands in Norfolk ; B.A. Gonville Hall, Cambridge, 1506 ; M.D., 1518. [viii. 103]

BUXHULL, SIR ALAN (1323–1381), constable of the Tower of London, 1365–81 ; inherited his father's lands in Sussex and Dorset, 1325 ; served with Edward III in France, 1355 ; chamberlain to Edward III, 1369 ; castellan in Normandy, 1370 ; K.G., 1372. [viii. 104]

BUXTON, BERTHA H. (1844–1881), novelist ; *née* Leopold ; published novels and books for children, 1874 ?–1881 ; travelled with her parents, who were German musicians ; married a London club-manager. [viii. 105]

BUXTON, CHARLES (1823–1871), liberal politician ; third son of Sir Thomas Fowell Buxton [q. v.] ; B.A. Trinity College, Cambridge, 1845 ; partner in Truman, Hanbury, Buxton & Co.'s brewery, Spitalfields, 1845 ; bought an estate in Kerry, 1852 ; M.P. for Newport, 1857, for Maidstone, 1859, and for East Surrey, 1865–71 ; published biography of his father and political pamphlets, 1853–69. [viii. 105]

BUXTON, JEDIDIAH (1707–1772), calculating prodigy ; farm-labourer at Elmton, Derbyshire ; exhibited in London, 1754. [viii. 106]

BUXTON, RICHARD (1786–1865), botanist ; a Lancashire shoemaker and self-taught botanist ; published ' Botanical Guide' to Manchester district, 1849. [viii. 106]

BUXTON, SIR THOMAS FOWELL (1786–1845), philanthropist ; educated at private schools ; entered Trinity College, Dublin, 1803 ; partner in Truman, Hanbury & Co.'s brewery, 1808 ; advocated prison reform, 1816–20 ; M.P. for Weymouth, 1818–37 ; advocated abolition of slavery in British dominions, 1822–33 ; advocated repression of African slave-trade and the Niger expedition, 1839–40 ; created baronet, 1840 ; accorded a monument in Westminster Abbey. [viii. 107]

BY, JOHN (1781–1836), lieutenant-colonel royal engineers ; studied at Royal Military Academy, Woolwich ; second lieutenant royal engineers, 1799 ; lieutenant, 1801 ; first captain, 1809 ; lieutenant-colonel, 1824 ; served in Canada, 1802–11, and Portugal, 1811 ; in charge of royal gunpowder mills at Faversham, Purfleet, and Waltham Abbey, 1812–21 ; constructed Rideau canal from the St. Lawrence to the Canadian lakes, 1826–32, Bytown (now Ottawa) being named after him. [Suppl. i. 363]

BYAM, EDWARD (1585–1639), divine ; brother of Henry Byam [q. v.] ; demy of Magdalen College, Oxford, 1601–10 ; M.A., 1607 ; vicar of Dulverton, Somerset, 1612–1625 ; precentor of Cloyne, 1637, and prebendary of Lismore, 1639, holding also other Irish preferments. [viii. 110]

BYAM, HENRY (1580–1669), divine ; brother of Edward Byam [q. v.] ; student of Christ Church, Oxford,

1599 ; M.A., 1605 ; B.D., 1612 ; D.D.. 1643 ; rector of Luccombe and of Selworthy, Somerset, 1614 ; sequestered, 1656 ; prebendary of Exeter, 1632 ; chaplain to the royalist garrison in Jersey, 1646–51 ; prebendary of Wells, 1660 ; published sermons. [viii. 109]

BYAM, JOHN (1583 ?–1653), divine ; brother of Edward Byam [q. v.] ; M.A. Exeter College, Oxford, 1606 ; rector of Clotworthy, Somerset, 1609 ; vicar of Dulverton, 16ż5 ; sequestered and imprisoned for royalist correspondence. [viii. 109]

BYER, NICHOLAS (*d.* 1681), portrait-painter ; of Norwegian birth ; protégé of Sir William Temple. [viii. 110]

BYERLEY, KATHARINE (1797–1862). [See THOMSON.]

BYERLEY, THOMAS (*d.* 1826), London journalist ; published under the pseudonyms of Stephen Collet and of Reuben Percy ' Relics of Literature,' 1823, ' The Percy Anecdotes,' 1821–3, and ' London . . . Memorials,' 1823. [viii. 110]

BYERS or **BYRES**, JAMES (1733–1817), virtuoso ; resided in Rome, 1750–90, collecting antique art treasures ; studied Etruscan architecture. [viii. 110]

BYFIELD, ADONIRAM (*d.* 1660), puritan, third son of Nicholas Byfield [q. v.] ; educated at Emmanuel College, Cambridge ; chaplain to a parliamentary regiment ; a clerk of the Westminster Assembly, of which he took minutes (printed 1874) ; rector, till 1645, and vicar, till 1657, of Fulham ; rector of Collingbourn Ducis, Wiltshire, before 1654 ; on Wiltshire committee for ejecting clergy, 1654. [viii. 111]

BYFIELD, JOHN (*fl.* 1830), wood engraver. [viii. 111]

BYFIELD, NICHOLAS (1579–1622), puritan ; studied at Exeter College, Oxford, 1597–1601 ; preacher at Chester before 1611 ; vicar of Isleworth, 1615–22 ; published theological works. [viii. 112]

BYFIELD, RICHARD (1598 ?–1664), puritan ; entered Queen's College, Oxford, 1615 ; M.A., 1622 ; rector of Long Ditton, Surrey, before 1630 ; elected into the Westminster Assembly, 1645 ; on the Surrey committee for ejecting clergy, 1654 ; ejected from Long Ditton, 1662 ; published theological treatises. [viii. 113]

BYLES, SIR JOHN BARNARD (1801–1884), judge ; barrister of the Inner Temple, 1831 ; recorder of Buckingham, 1840–55 ; serjeant-at-law, 1843 ; one of the last queen's serjeants, 1857 ; knighted, 1858 ; justice of the common pleas, 1858–73 ; published legal treatises. [viii. 113]

BYLOT or **BILOT**, ROBERT (*fl.* 1610–1616), explorer of the north-west passage ; sailed with Henry Hudson [q. v.], 1610–11, and Sir Thomas Button [q. v.], 1612–13, and Gibbons, 1614 ; commanded the attempt of 1615 with William Baffin [q. v.] as mate. [viii. 114]

BYNG, ANDREW (1574–1651), professor of Hebrew, Cambridge, 1608 ; educated at Peterhouse, Cambridge ; one of the translators of the authorised version, 1605 ; D.D. [viii. 115]

BYNG, GEORGE, VISCOUNT TORRINGTON (1663–1733), admiral ; served in the navy, 1678–81 ; officer of Tangier garrison, 1681–3 ; lieutenant in the army, 1684–1690 ; naval lieutenant, 1684 ; at Bombay, 1685–7 ; canvassed ship-commanders to join the Prince of Orange, 1688 ; served under Admiral Herbert, 1689 ; at Beachy Head, 1690 ; served in Mediterranean, 1693–5 ; served under Sir Clowdisley Shovell, 1702–3 ; rear-admiral, 1703 ; present at taking of Gibraltar and the battle off Malaga, 1704 ; knighted, 1704 ; vice-admiral, 1705 ; served in Mediterranean, 1706–7 ; repulsed James Edward the Pretender's fleet, 1708 ; commanded in Mediterranean, 1709 ; commissioner of the admiralty, 1709–18 ; prevented supplies reaching the Jacobite insurgents, 1715 ; created baronet, 1715 ; sent to the Baltic, 1717 ; admiral of the fleet, 1718 ; held command in Mediterranean, 1718–20, destroying Spanish fleet off Cape Passaro, 31 July 1718 ; treasurer of the navy, 1721–4 ; created Viscount Torrington, 1721 ; first lord of the admiralty, 1727–33. [viii. 115]

BYNG, JOHN (1704–1757), admiral ; fourth son of George Byng, viscount Torrington [q. v.] ; entered the navy, 1718 ; commanded a frigate in the Mediterranean, 1727–36, selecting the easy post of guardship at Port

Mahon, Minorca; rear-admiral, 1745; commanded in Mediterranean, 1747–8; sent to prevent the French taking Minorca, 1756; reached Port Mahon, 19 May, handled his ships unskilfully, and was defeated, 20 May; sailed back, in accordance with the resolutions of his council of war, 25 May; recalled; sentenced by court-martial to death for neglect of duty, 27 Jan. 1757; shot at Portsmouth.
[viii. 118]

BYNG, SIR JOHN, EARL OF STRAFFORD (1772–1860), general; served in Flanders, 1793–5, in the Irish rebellion, 1798, and at Walcheren, 1809; colonel, 1810; commanded brigade in Peninsula and south of France, 1811–14; major-general, 1813; commanded brigade at Waterloo and in France, 1815; lieutenant-general, 1825; commander-in-chief in Ireland, 1828–31; M.P. for Poole, 1831; created Baron Strafford, 1835; general, 1841; created Earl of Strafford, 1847; field-marshal, 1855.
[viii. 121]

BYNG, THOMAS (d. 1599), civilian; fellow of Peterhouse, Cambridge, 1558; M.A., 1559; LL.D., 1570; public orator, 1565; prebendary of York, 1567; master of Clare Hall, Cambridge, 1571; regius professor of civil law, 1574; dean of arches, 1595; wrote official letters, orations, and verses.
[viii. 122]

BYNHAM, SIMON (*fl.* 1335). [See BINHAM.]

BYNNEMAN, HENRY (d. 1583), London printer; apprenticed, 1560; liveryman of the Stationers' Company, 1578; imprinted books under his own name, 1566–83.
[viii. 122]

BYRD, WILLIAM (1538?–1623), composer; pupil of Tallis; organist of Lincoln, 1563; joint-organist of the Chapel Royal, 1569; granted monopoly of issuing printed music and music-paper, 1575; published 'Cantiones . . . sacræ,' 1575; lived obscurely, as a catholic recusant, at Harlington, Middlesex, 1578–88; composed the first English madrigals, 1588; published 'Psalmes, Sonets, and Songs,' 1588; published 'Songs of Sundrie Natures,' and 'Liber primus Sacrarum Cantionum,' 1589, 'Liber secundus,' 1591, 'Gradualia,' 1607, and 'Psalmes, Songs, and Sonnets,' 1611; composed numerous pieces, many still in manuscript.
[viii. 123]

BYRHTFERTH or **BRIDFERTH**, (*fl.* 1000), mathematician; possibly at first monk of Thorney; monk of Ramsey after 970; pupil of Abbo of Fleury (d. 1004); travelled in France; wrote commentaries on treatises of Bæda (printed 1612), and a mathematical treatise (Ashmole MS., 328).
[viii. 126]

BYRNE, ANNE FRANCES (1775–1837), flower and fruit painter; eldest daughter of William Byrne [q. v.]; exhibited at the Royal Academy and elsewhere in London, 1796–1832.
[viii. 127]

BYRNE, CHARLES (1761–1783), Irish giant; exhibited in various towns; measured eight feet two inches, 1782; his skeleton 92¾ inches in length.
[viii. 127]

BYRNE, JULIA CLARA (1819–1894), author; daughter of Hans Busk (1772–1862) [q. v.]; married William Pitt Byrne, 1842. She published a number of books, some of which she illustrated herself, dealing with her own experiences, social questions, and the customs of various countries.
[Suppl. i. 364]

BYRNE, LETITIA (1779–1849), engraver; third daughter of William Byrne [q. v.]; book-illustrator; exhibited landscapes at the Royal Academy, 1799–1848.
[viii. 127]

BYRNE, MILES (1780–1862), United Irishman; a leader of the 1798 insurrection; clerk in a Dublin timber-yard, 1799–1803; a leader in Robert Emmet's sedition, 1803; sent to solicit Napoleon's help, 1803; served in Napoleon's Irish legion, 1804–15; captain, 1810; chef-de-bataillon, 1830–5; lived latterly in Paris.
[viii. 127]

BYRNE, OSCAR (1795?–1867), ballet-master; first appeared on stage, 1803; abroad or in Ireland for several years; employed in London, 1850–67.
[viii. 128]

BYRNE, WILLIAM (1743–1805), landscape engraver; trained in Birmingham and Paris; exhibited in London, 1760–80.
[viii. 128]

BYRNES, THOMAS JOSEPH (1860–1898), premier of Queensland; born in Queensland; B.A. and LL.B. Melbourne University; called to the bar in Victoria, 1884; practised at supreme court bar, Queensland; member of legislative council, and solicitor general, 1890; prime minister of Queensland, 1898.
[Suppl. i. 365]

BYRNSTAN, BIRNSTAN, or BEORNSTAN (d.933), bishop of Winchester; attendant on King Edward the Elder as thegn, 900–2; priest, 902–10; perhaps monk at Winchester; bishop of Winchester, 931; afterwards reputed saint; translated to a new tomb, 1150.
[viii. 129]

BYROM, JOHN (1692–1763), teacher of shorthand; entered Merchant Taylors' School, 1707; fellow of Trinity College, Cambridge, 1714; M.A., 1715; studied medicine at Montpellier, 1716; taught shorthand in Manchester (where he chiefly lived), London, and Cambridge; succeeded to estates, 1740; copyrighted his system, 1742; a Jacobite; his shorthand system printed, 1767; his verses collected and published, 1773, and his diary printed, 1854–7.
[viii. 129]

BYRON, GEORGE GORDON, sixth BARON (1788–1824), poet; son of a profligate, called 'mad Jack' Byron (1756–1791), late of the guards, by his second wife (m. at Bath, 1785), Catherine Gordon (d. 1811), of Gicht, Aberdeen, an hysterical Scotch heiress; born in London, after his father had dissipated his mother's fortune in France; hopelessly lame in both feet; removed to Aberdeen, where his mother took lodgings, having an income (under trust) of 135l., afterwards of 190l. a year; lost his father in August 1791, who, having fled from his creditors to France, died at Valenciennes; alternately petted and abused by his mother; taught the bible by his nurse, May Gray; educated at Aberdeen grammar school, 1794–8; unexpectedly became heir-presumptive to the barony in consequence of the fifth baron's grandson falling in action in Corsica, 1794; succeeded to title and encumbered estates, 1798; taken to the family seat of Newstead Abbey, Nottinghamshire, 1798; put under the guardianship of the fifth Earl of Carlisle, a distant relative; sent to private schools, Newstead Abbey being let, 1799; wrote lampoons, 1799, and love verses, 1800; at Harrow, 1801–5, where he proved himself a poor scholar, a considerable reader, and a good boxer and batsman; proposed to Mary Anne Chaworth, heiress of Annesley Hall, Nottinghamshire, who rejected him, 1803; at Trinity College, Cambridge, October 1805–May 1806, May 1807–May 1808; M.A. July 1808; at Cambridge read much history and fiction, and practised boxing and swimming, but kept low company and lived extravagantly; got deeply in debt, the income (500l.) allowed him by the court of chancery being inadequate for his position and expectations; his chief college friend, John Cam Hobhouse, printed privately at Newark, October 1806, a small volume of poems by Byron entitled 'Fugitive Pieces,' which Byron reprinted with changes in January 1807, and published, with further changes, in the summer of 1807, as 'Hours of Idleness'; his book denounced by the 'Edinburgh Review,' January 1808; settled at Newstead, July 1808, where he entertained company in theatrical imitation of Medmenham; took his seat in the House of Lords, March 1809; issued 'English Bards and Scotch Reviewers' (1809), which soon ran into its fifth edition; sailed with Hobhouse from Falmouth, July 1809; rode from Lisbon to Cadiz; sailed from Cadiz, visiting Gibraltar and Malta on the way, to North Greece; rode through Acarnania to Athens, 24 Dec.; addressed 'Maid of Athens' to Theresa Macri, his hostess's daughter; sailed, 5 March 1810, from Athens to Smyrna, Ephesus, the Troad, swimming the Hellespont (3 May), and Constantinople; parted company with Hobhouse; sailed, 14 July, for Athens; travelled in the Morea; wintered in Athens; reached Portsmouth, July 1811; took London lodgings, October 1811; spoke twice in the House of Lords, February and April 1812; published 'Childe Harold,' cantos i. and ii., March 1812; made the acquaintance of Thomas Moore; proposed to Anne Isabella, daughter of Sir Robert Milbanke, but was rejected, 1812; tried to sell Newstead, September 1812; injured his constitution by devices to avoid corpulency; published a succession of poems, 1813–16; annoyed by the attentions of Lady Caroline Lamb, 1813; proposed again to Miss Milbanke, September 1814; married her 2 Jan. 1815; took the additional name of Noel, April; made his will, July; much importuned by his creditors; sold his library, November; frequented the theatre and theatrical suppers; accused, 8 Jan. 1816, of insanity by his wife, who left him, 15 Jan.; signed a deed of separation and withdrew to the continent, April; travelled through Belgium and the Rhine country to Geneva; travelled in

Switzerland with Shelley in June, and with Hobhouse in September; wrote 'Childe Harold,' canto iii.; travelled with Hobhouse to Italy, October; wintered in Venice; father of a child by Jane Clairmont, January 1817; visited Rome, April-May 1817; settled in a house on the Grand Canal, Venice, and abandoned himself to degrading excesses; wrote canto iv. of 'Childe Harold,' July 1817; received large sums for his copyrights; sold Newstead, November 1817; wrote the first five cantos of 'Don Juan,' 1818-20; met Teresa, countess Guiccioli (1803-1873), April 1819, whom he followed to Ravenna and Bologna, and took from her husband to live with him in Venice; visited by Thomas Moore, to whom he entrusted his autobiography (burnt, May 1824); followed to Ravenna the Countess Guiccioli, who had returned to her husband, 1819; wrote much while at Ravenna, the bulk of his work consisting of dramas (beginning with 'Marino Faliero,' April-July 1820); lived with Countess Guiccioli at Pisa, October 1821-July 1822, and wrote later cantos of 'Don Juan'; started a short-lived newspaper, 'The Liberal,' with Leigh Hunt as editor, in which he printed his 'Vision of Judgment,' a poem satirising Southey's apotheosis of George III; present at the cremation of Shelley, 1822; lived at Genoa with Countess Guiccioli, August 1822-July 1823; offered to join the Greek insurgents, May 1823; sailed from Genoa, July; lingered in Cephalonia, August-December; landed at Missolonghi, January 1824; enlisted a regiment of Suliotes, which he disbanded, in consequence of their mutinous temper, in February; tried to raise another corps to garrison Missolonghi; died of marsh-fever, 19 April; buried in England, at Hucknall Torkard; his collected 'Life [by Tom Moore] and Works,' published, 1832-5.   [viii. 132]

BYRON, HENRY JAMES (1834-1884), dramatist; medical student in London and Buxton; appeared on the stage; began to write for the stage, c. 1856; entered the Middle Temple, 1858; joint-manager of the Princess of Wales's Theatre, London, 1865-7; manager of theatres in Liverpool, 1867; acted, in his own pieces, in London, 1869-81; manager of Criterion Theatre, London, 1874; editor of 'Fun'; wrote 'Paid in Full,' a novel, 1865; produced a number of farces, comedies, and extravaganzas, between 1857 and 1882.   [viii. 155]

BYRON, JOHN, first BARON BYRON (d. 1652), M.P. for Nottingham, 1624-5; K.B. at Charles I's coronation, 1625; M.P. for Nottinghamshire, 1628-9; served in the Low Countries; served against the Scots, 1640; lieutenant of the Tower, December 1641-February 1642; joined Charles I at York; sent from Coventry to Oxford; held Oxford, 28 Aug.-10 Sept. 1642; victorious at Powick

Bridge, 22 Sept.; fought at Edgehill, 23 Oct. 1642; served in Buckinghamshire and Oxfordshire, December 1642-May 1643; fought at Roundway Down and Newbury, 1643; created Baron Byron of Rochdale, October 1643; given command in Lancashire; defeated at Nantwich, 1644; fought at Marston Moor, Ormskirk, and Montgomery, 1644; besieged in Chester, 1645-6; surrendered Carnarvon Castle, 1646; went to Paris; sent to seize Anglesey, 1648; sent by Ormonde to invite Charles II to Ireland, January 1649; proscribed by the parliament; tutor to the Duke of York.   [viii. 157]

BYRON, JOHN (1723-1786), navigator; midshipman of the Wager, 1740; wrecked on the Chili coast, 1741; sailed from Valparaiso, 1744, reaching England, February 1746; captain, 1746; cruised off the coast of Guinea, 1749, and of France, 1757-63; commanded the Dolphin in the voyage round the world, 2 July 1764 to 9 May 1766; published a 'Narrative' of his shipwreck, 1768; governor of Newfoundland, 1769-72; rear-admiral, 1775; commanded the West Indies fleet, 1778-9; worsted off Grenada, 1779.   [viii. 161]

BYRON, SIR THOMAS (d. 1644), commander of the Prince of Wales's regiment; severely wounded at Hopton Heath, 1643; wounded in a scuffle at Oxford, 7 Dec. 1643, and died of the wound.   [viii. 163]

BYRTH, THOMAS (1793-1849), divine; quaker; druggist's apprentice, 1809-14; taught school; entered Magdalen Hall, Oxford, 1818; joined the Anglican church, 1819; curate in Devonshire, 1823-5; M.A., 1826; vicar of Latchford, Cheshire, 1827; rector of Wallasey, 1834-49; D.D., 1839; published sermons.   [viii. 164]

BYSSHE, SIR EDWARD (1615?-1679), herald; entered Trinity College, Oxford, 1633; barrister of Lincoln's Inn; M.P. for Bletchingley, 1640; appointed Garter king-of-arms by parliament, 1646-60; M.P. for Reigate, 1654, and for Gatton, Surrey, 1659; Clarenceux king-of-arms, 1661; knighted, 1661; M.P. for Bletchingley, 1661; edited heraldic treatises and (1665) Palladius, 'de Gentibus Indiæ et Bragmanibus.'   [viii. 164]

BYSSHE, EDWARD (fl. 1712), miscellaneous writer; published 'The Art of English Poetry,' 1702; translated Xenophon's 'Memorabilia,' 1712.   [viii. 165]

BYTHNER, VICTORINUS (1605?-1670?), hebraist; native of Poland; taught Hebrew at Oxford, 1635-43; at Cambridge, 1643; in London; again in Oxford, 1651; practised medicine in Cornwall, 1664; published treatises on Hebrew grammar.   [viii. 165]

C

CABANEL, RUDOLPH (1762-1839), architect; born at Aix-la-Chapelle; came to England early in life; constructed theatres in London; invented the 'Cabanel' roof.   [viii. 166]

CABBELL, BENJAMIN BOND (1781-1874), patron of art; educated at Westminster and Oxford, 1800-3; barrister of the Middle Temple, 1816; F.R.S., 1837; M.P. for St. Albans, 1846, and for Boston, 1847-57; a freemason.   [viii. 166]

CABOT, SEBASTIAN (1474-1557), navigator and map-maker; born in Bristol; son of a Venetian, John Cabot, or Caboto, trading at Bristol; taken to Venice, 1476; brought back to England, 1493; named with his father and brothers in Henry VII's licence to make a voyage of discovery, March 1496; sailed with them, 1497, discovering Nova Scotia; not mentioned in the similar licence obtained by his father, February 1498; probably did not accompany his father in the American voyages of 1498 and 1499; made for Henry VIII a map of Gascony and Guienne, 1512; employed at Seville as map-maker for Ferdinand the Catholic, 1512-16; returned to England, 1516; according to Eden, was designed to sail with Sir Thomas Perte (1517) on a voyage of discovery, which did not take place; returned to Spain, 1519; pilot-major to the emperor Charles V, 1519-26; investigated the variation of the compass needle; made proposals to the Venetians to send him to seek a north-east passage to

China, 1522; commanded unsuccessful expedition to the La Plata, 1526-30; imprisoned and banished to Oran in Africa, 1530; recalled to Seville, 1533; reinstated in his office of pilot-major, 1533-44; published an engraved map of the world, 1544; returned to Bristol, 1547; pensioned by Edward VI, 1548; his return in vain demanded by Charles V, 1550 and 1553; settled dispute between Hanseatic League and merchants of London, 1551; again approached the Venetians with the project of seeking north-east passage to China, 1551; suggested the formation of the Company of Merchant Adventurers of London to seek for the passage, 1551; supervised the north-east expeditions to Russia, 1553 and 1556; his pension confirmed by Queen Mary, 1555; deprived of half his pension, perhaps at the instance of Philip II, 1557.   [viii. 166]

CADDICK, RICHARD (1740-1819), hebraist; B.A. Christ Church, Oxford, 1776; M.A., 1799; resided near London, 1780-1819; published a Hebrew grammar, a Hebrew New Testament, and sermons.   [viii. 171]

CADE, JOHN (d. 1450), rebel; said to have been a young Irishman of the household of Sir Thomas Dacre in Sussex; banished for murder, 1449; served in France; soon returned, under the name of Aylmer, a physician; leader of the Kentish rebellion, May 1450; given out to be a nobleman, Mortimer, cousin of the Duke of York; encamped on Blackheath; demanded the dismissal of certain ministers of Henry VI; defeated the king's troops at Sevenoaks, 27 June ; entered Southwark, 1 July ; and London, 2 July : beheaded Baron Say and William Crowmer, sheriff of Kent, 4 July ; repulsed at London Bridge ; amnestied, 6 July ; withdrew to Rochester ; repulsed at Queenborough ; mortally wounded at Heathfield, 12 July. [viii. 171]

CADE, JOHN (1734–1806), antiquary ; educated at Darlington school; linendraper in London and Dublin ; retired and studied English antiquities. [viii. 174]

CADE or CADDY, LAURENCE (*fl.* 1583), Roman catholic seminarist; educated at Trinity College, Cambridge ; became a catholic ; entered Douay College, 1578 ; imprisoned in the Tower ; publicly renounced catholicism, 1581 ; Carmelite friar at Paris, 1583. [viii. 174]

CADE, SALUSBURY (1660 ?–1720), physician ; M.D. Trinity College, Oxford, 1691 ; physician to St. Bartholomew's Hospital, London, 1708–20. [viii. 175]

CADELL (*d.* 909), Welsh prince ; son of Rhodri Mawr ; began to reign over Ceredigion, 877 ; said to have conquered Powys ; ravaged Dyved and Brecheiniog ; submitted to King Alfred, 885 ? ; his territory ravaged by Anarawd, king of Gwynedd 894 ; harassed by the Irish Danes. [viii. 175]

CADELL (*d.* 943), Welsh prince ; son of Arthvael ; lord of Morganwg and part of Gwent; rebelled against the West-Saxons, 940 ; killed by the Saxons. [viii. 175]

CADELL (*d.* 1175), Welsh prince ; son of Gruffudd, the son of Rhys ; ruled over part of Ceredigion and the vale of Towy, 1137 ; captured the Norman castles on the Towy, including Carmarthen, 1145–7 ; wasted Kidwelly, 1152 ; won back Ceredigion from Owain Gwynedd ; severely handled by the Flemings of Tenby in an ambuscade ; made pilgrimage to Rome ; became a monk at Strata Florida. [viii. 176]

CADELL, FRANCIS (1822–1879), Australian explorer ; midshipman in the East India Company's service ; served in the Chinese war, 1840–1 ; captain of a vessel, 1844 ; studied steamboat building ; examined the mouth of the Murray river, 1848 ; explored the Murray and its tributaries in steamers, 1853–9 ; squatter on the Darling ; murdered by his crew at sea. [viii. 176]

CADELL, JESSIE (1844–1884), Persian scholar ; wife of an army officer ; long resident at Peshawur ; published 'Ida Craven,' a novel, 1876 ; wrote on Omar Khayyam, 1879 ; died at Florence. [viii. 177]

CADELL, ROBERT (1788–1849), Edinburgh publisher ; entered the house of Archibald Constable & Co., 1807 ; partner, 1811 ; dissolved partnership, 1826 ; secured copyright of Sir Walter Scott's novels, 1827, of which he issued several editions. [viii. 178]

CADELL, THOMAS, the elder (1742–1802), London publisher ; apprenticed to Andrew Millar in the Strand, 1758 ; partner, 1765 ; took over the business, 1767 ; retired, 1793 ; alderman of London, 1798, and sheriff, 1800–1. [viii. 179]

CADELL, THOMAS, the younger (1773–1836), publisher ; son of Thomas Cadell the elder [q. v.]; took over his father's business, 1793, and carried it on till death. [viii. 179]

CADELL, WILLIAM ARCHIBALD (1775–1855), traveller ; educated at Edinburgh ; Scottish advocate, 1798 ; F.R.S., 1810 ; published narrative of his continental ' Journey, 1817–18,' 1820 ; author of mathematical papers. [viii. 179]

CADEMAN or CADYMAN, SIR THOMAS (1590 ?–1651), physician to Queen Henrietta Maria ; M.A. Trinity College, Cambridge, 1609 ; M.D. Padua, 1620 ; catholic recusant, 1626 ; F.R.C.P., 1630 ; held patent for distilling strong waters and vinegar ; wrote medical tracts. [viii. 180]

CADOC the WISE, in Welsh CATTWG DDOETH (*d.* 570 ?), Welsh saint ; son of Gwynllyw Filwr, lord of Gwynllwg in Glamorganshire ; taught by Irish ascetics ; visited Rome, Jerusalem, Ireland, and Scotland ; founded abbey and school of Llancarvan, Glamorganshire ; suffered martyrdom at Beneventum ; commemorated on 14 Jan. ; reputed composer of proverbs, triads, and fables. [viii. 181]

CADOGAN. [See also CADWGAN.]

CADOGAN, CHARLES, second BARON CADOGAN (1691–1776), general ; entered the army, 1706 ; served in Marlborough's later campaigns, and in Scotland, 1715 ; M.P. for Reading, and for Newport, Isle of Wight ; succeeded to barony, 1726 ; general, 1761. [viii. 186]

CADOGAN, HENRY (1780–1813), colonel ; educated at Eton ; entered the army, 1797 ; gained rapid promotion by purchase ; lieutenant-colonel, 1805 ; aide-de-camp to Wellesley in the Peninsula, 1808–10 ; commanded the 71st Highlanders, 1810–11 ; commanded brigade, 1811–13 ; killed at Vittoria ; honoured with a monument in St. Paul's. [viii. 181]

CADOGAN, WILLIAM (1601–1661), parliamentarian ; went to Ireland, 1633 ; captain of horse there before 1641 ; major of horse in Cromwell's Irish army, 1649 ; governor of Trim, 1649–61. [viii. 182]

CADOGAN, WILLIAM, first EARL CADOGAN (1675–1726), general ; cornet at the Boyne, 1690 ; served in the dragoons under William III in Ireland and Flanders ; quartermaster-general to Marlborough, 1701–11, and present in all his great battles ; colonel of the dragoon regiment, called 'Cadogan's horse,' 1703–12 ; brigadier-general, 1704 ; M.P. for Woodstock from 1705 ; major-general, 1706 ; envoy to the Spanish Netherlands, 1707–10 ; lieutenant-general, 1709–12 ; lieutenant of the Tower, 1709–1715 ; took Bouchain, 1711 ; quartermaster-general to Ormonde, 1712 ; withdrew to Holland ; ejected by the Jacobite party from his offices, 1712 ; returned to London, 1714 ; restored to his lieutenant-generalship, 1714 ; lieutenant of ordnance, 1714–18 ; colonel of Coldstream guards, 1714 ; M.P. for Woodstock, 1714 ; envoy at the Hague, 1714–18 ; second in command against Scotch insurgents, 1715–16 ; created Baron Cadogan, 1716 ; governor of the Isle of Wight, 1716 ; general, 1717 ; created Earl Cadogan, 1718 ; negotiated the quadruple alliance, 1720 ; commander-in-chief, 1722. [viii. 182]

CADOGAN, WILLIAM (1711–1797), physician ; B.A. Oriel College, Oxford, 1731 ; M.D. Leyden, 1737 ; army physician ; practised medicine in Bristol ; physician to the London Foundling Hospital, 1754 ; M.D. Oxford, 1755 ; wrote on medical topics. [viii. 187]

CADROE, SAINT (*d.* 976 ?), abbot in Lorraine ; born in Scotland of noble parents ; brought up by a clerical kinsman, Beanus, at Iona ; studied at Armagh ; taught in Scotland ; travelled from Abernethy, 940 ?, through Strathclyde to Winchester, 942 ?, thence to Peronne, 943 ; anchorite in ' Sylva Theorascensis ' ; monk at Fleury, 944 ; abbot of Wassor, near Dinant, 946, and of St. Felix and (948) of St. Symphorien, both near Metz. [viii. 187]

CADVAN (6th cent.), Welsh saint ; fled from Brittany from the Franks early in the sixth century ; built churches in Wales ; abbot of a monastery on Bardsey Isle. [viii. 190]

CADVAN (*d.* 617 ? or 634?), semi-mythical king of Gwynedd (or North Wales) ; fought against the Angles of Northumbria. [viii. 190]

CADWALADER. [See CÆDWALLA.]

CADWALADR (*d.* 1172), Welsh prince ; son of Gruffudd ap Cynan, king of Gwynedd ; with his brother, Owain, conquered Meirionydd, 1121, and the north of Ceredigion, 1135–6 ; granted lordship of these when Owain succeeded to Gwynedd, 1137 ; expelled by Owain for slaying (1143) Anarawd, son of Gruffudd of South Wales ; to avenge himself, brought over Danes from Ireland, who, suspecting treachery, blinded him ; ransomed ; driven from Meirionydd by his nephews, 1146–8, from Ceredigion by the brothers of Anarawd, and from Anglesey by Owain ; fled to the English ; restored by Henry II, 1157 ; invaded South Wales, 1158 ; resisted Henry II's third invasion, 1165 ; buried at Bangor. [viii. 190]

CADWALADR CASAIL (*fl.* 1590), Welsh poet. [viii. 191]

CADWALADR VENDIGAID, i.e. the BLESSED (*d.* 664 ?), semi-mythical king of the Britons ; led the North and Strathclyde Welsh in their struggle against the Angles under Oswiu and Penda ; died of the plague. [viii. 191]

CADWALLADOR, ROGER (1568-1610), Roman catholic martyr; educated at Rheims and Valladolid; catholic priest in Herefordshire, 1594; arrested and executed, 1610. [viii. 192]

CADWALLON. [See CÆDWALLA.]

CADWGAN (d. 1112), Welsh prince; son of Bleddyn ap Cynvyn, king of part of Gwynedd; attacked Rhys ap Tewdwr, king of South Wales, 1087, but was defeated at Llechryd; ravaged Dyved, 1093, but was driven out by the Normans; joined Gruffudd ap Cynan, king of Gwynedd, in recovering Ceredigion and Dyved and ravaging the English border; ravaged Pembrokeshire; repulsed William Rufus's invasion, 1097; defeated in Anglesey by the Earl of Shrewsbury, 1099; accepted Ceredigion and part of Powys as a fief from the earl, 1100; joined him in making war on Henry I, 1102; restored to his territories by Iorwerth, 1110, from Ceredigion by his nephews, who had been incited to attack his son Owain for carrying off Nest, wife of Gerald of Windsor; deposed by Henry I; granted Powys, 1111; murdered by his nephew. [viii. 192]

CADWGAN, also called MARTIN (d. 1241), bishop of Bangor; styled 'of Llandyvai'; abbot of Whitland, Carmarthenshire; named bishop of Bangor by King John, 1215; resigned, 1236, and entered Dore Abbey, Herefordshire. [viii. 194]

CADYMAN, SIR THOMAS (1590?-1651). [See CADEMAN.]

CÆDMON (corruptly CEDMON), SAINT (fl. 670), poet; entered the monastery of Streaneshalch (Whitby), when already an elderly man, between 658 and 680; said by Bæda to have been an unlearned man, who received suddenly, in a vision, the power of putting into English verse passages translated to him from the scriptures; generally recognised as a saint; commemorated on 11 or 12 Feb. The name Cædmon cannot be explained in English, and has been conjectured to be Celtic (an adaptation of the British Catumanus). In 1655 François Dujon (Franciscus Junius) published at Amsterdam from the unique Bodleian manuscript long scriptural poems, which he took to be those of Cædmon. It is now generally admitted that these poems are of at least two dates, the first portion (containing versions of Genesis, Exodus, Daniel) being earlier than the second portion (1. the fall of man; 2. the descent into hell, ascension, and second advent; 3. the temptation), and all of them later than Cædmon. Three pieces are by some still claimed for Cædmon himself: 1. a Northumbrian version of Bæda's Latin paraphrase of Cædmon's first song, found in a Cambridge manuscript of Bæda, in a hand possibly of the eighth century; 2. 'The Dream of the Holy Rood,' of which a fragment is found in runes on the Ruthwell cross, Dumfriesshire, and the whole in a West-Saxon manuscript at Vercelli; 3. the fragment on the temptation and fall of man, interpolated in the version of Genesis in the Bodleian manuscript, published in 1655. [viii. 195]

CÆDWALLA (d. 634), also spelt CADWALADER and CADWALLON, king of Gwynedd or North Wales; son of Cadvan (d. 617? or 634?) [q. v.]; invaded Northumbria, 629; defeated by the Anglian king, Eadwine, and driven to Ireland; in alliance with Penda of Mercia, defeated and slew Eadwine at Hatfield, near Doncaster, 633; mercilessly ravaged Northumbria; killed Osric and Eanfrith, Northumbrian princes, who tried to recover the kingdom, 634; defeated and slain near Hexham by Oswald, nephew of Eadwine. [viii. 201]

CÆDWALLA (659?-689), king of Wessex; expelled from Wessex by King Centwine; lived as an outlaw in the forest of Anderida; met Wilfrith, c. 681; ravaged Sussex, and killed King Æthelwealh, 685; acknowledged king of Wessex, 686; subdued Sussex, ravaged Kent, and conquered the Isle of Wight; resigned, 688; baptised at Rome by Pope Sergius I, 689; died at Rome. [viii. 201]

CAERLEON, LEWIS OF (15th cent.), mathematician, theologian, and medical writer of Oxford. [x. 128]

CAERNARVON. [See CARNARVON.]

CÆSAR, ADELMARE (d. 1569), physician; originally known as CESARE ADELMARE; graduate of Padua; censor of the College of Physicians, London, 1555; medical adviser to Queen Mary in 1558, and subsequently to Queen Elizabeth. [viii. 204]

CÆSAR, SIR CHARLES (1590-1642), judge; third son of Sir Julius Cæsar [q. v.]; entered Magdalen College Oxford, 1602; fellow of All Souls', 1605-11, by king's mandate; M.A., 1608; entered the Inner Temple, 1611; D.C.L., 1612; knighted, 1613; M.P. for Bletchingley, Surrey, 1614; master of chancery, 1615-39; judge of court of audience and master of the faculties from before 1626 till death; paid James I 15,000l. for the mastership of the rolls, 1639; died of small-pox. [viii. 202]

CÆSAR, HENRY (1562?-1636), dean of Ely; educated at Oxford and Cambridge; withdrew to the continent as a Roman catholic; returned and recanted, 1583; vicar of Lostwithiel, Cornwall; prosecuted as a suspected papist, 1584, 1589; D.D. Oxford, 1595; rector of St. Christopher-le-Stocks, London, 1596-7, and of Somersham, Huntingdonshire, 1597; prebendary of Westminster, 1609-25; dean of Ely, 1614-36. [viii. 203]

CÆSAR, SIR JULIUS (1558-1636), judge; son of an Italian, Cesare Adelmare, physician to Queen Mary and Elizabeth [see CÆSAR, ADELMARE]; M.A. Magdalen Hall, Oxford, 1578; entered the Inner Temple, 1580; LL.D. Paris, 1581; D.C.L. Oxford, 1584; judge of the admiralty, 1584; a master of chancery, 1588-91; M.P., Reigate, 1589, Bletchingley, 1593, Windsor, 1596 and 1601, Westminster, 1607-11, Middlesex, 1614, and Maldon, 1620-2; master of requests, 1591 (senior master, 1600); master of St. Katharine's Hospital, London, 1596; knighted, 1603; chancellor of the exchequer, 1606; master of the rolls, 1614-36; wrote on legal topics. [viii. 204]

CÆSAR, JULIUS (1656?-1712?), physician, of Rochester; composed catches. [viii. 207]

CÆSAR, SIR THOMAS (1561-1610), judge; brother of Sir Julius Cæsar [q. v.]; left Merchant Taylors' School, 1578; entered the Inner Temple, 1580; cursitor baron of the exchequer and knighted, 1610. [viii. 207]

CAFFIN, SIR JAMES CRAWFORD (1812-1883), admiral; entered the navy, 1824; commander, 1842; on the commission which adopted screw-propeller for navy, 1845; captain, 1847; served in the Baltic, 1854-5; director of stores, 1858-68; rear-admiral, 1865; K.C.B., 1868; admiral, 1877. [viii. 208]

CAFFYN, MATTHEW (1628-1714), general (or Arminian) baptist; claimed to have been expelled from Oxford for nonconformity; farmer and baptist minister at and near Horsham, Sussex, his native place; several times imprisoned for unlicensed preaching; engaged in platform and pamphlet war with quakers, 1655-62; first accused of Arianism, 1673; local churches and the baptist assembly greatly agitated by his doctrinal position, 1691-1701, the result being a schism in the connexion, 1701-4; wrote polemical tracts. [viii. 208]

CAHILL, DANIEL WILLIAM (1796-1864), Roman catholic lecturer; educated at Carlow College and Maynooth, 1816; ordained; teacher of mathematical sciences at Carlow College, 1825; created D.D. by the pope; kept school at Williamstown, 1835-41, and at Blackrock, Dublin, 1841-6; journalist in Dublin till 1859; lectured and preached in the United States on behalf of Roman catholic institutions, 1860-4; remains removed to Glasnevin, 1885. [viii. 210]

CAILLAUD, JOHN (d. 1810), Indian officer; arrived in India, 1753; in constant service till his retirement, 1775; brigadier-general, 1763; settled at Aston-Rowant, Oxfordshire; hon. D.C.L. Oxford, 1773. [viii. 210]

CAILLIN (fl. 560), Irish saint; educated at Rome; recalled to stay feuds among his kindred, the Conmaicne, of Dunmor (Connaught); obtained for them lands in Roscommon, Mayo, and other counties: at Dunbaile converted to Christianity Aedh dubh (afterwards called Aedh finn), son of Fergna, king of Breifney; received Dunbaile (now Fenagh, in Leitrim) from Aedh dubh, and built a monastery there; commemorated on 13 Nov. [viii. 211]

CAIMIN or CAMIN, SAINT (d. 653); of the race of Cathaoir Mór of Leinster; son of Dima, a noble, and Cumman; an ascetic; lived on Keltra island in Lough Derg; reputed author of glosses on the 119th Psalm. [viii. 212]

CAIN, RHYS (16th cent.), Welsh poet; named from his birth near the river Cain, Merionethshire; wrote complimentary poems, 1570-1600. [viii. 213]

CAINNECH or **CANNICUS**, SAINT (*d.* 598 ?), Irish saint, after whom Kilkenny (Cill-cainneth) and Cambuskenneth, in Scotland, were named ; studied in Wales and Italy ; lived at Clonard Abbey, Meath, *c.* 543, and subsequently at Glasnevin, Dublin ; visited Columba at Iona ; founded Aghaboe (Achadh-bo) Abbey, Queen's County, some time before 577. [viii. 213]

CAIRD, SIR JAMES (1816–1892), agriculturist and author ; educated at high school and university, Edinburgh ; managed a farm near Stranraer ; occupied farm of Baldoon, near Wigtown, 1841-60 ; took part in free trade controversy ; commissioned by Peel to report to government on agricultural state of Ireland, 1846 ; special commissioner of ' Times ' to inquire into distressed state of agriculture since adoption of free trade, 1850 ; liberal conservative M.P. for Dartmouth, 1857-9 ; toured in Canada and United States, 1858-9, and published ' Prairie Farming in America,' 1859 ; M.P. for Stirling burghs, 1859-65 ; chairman of royal commission on condition of sea fisheries, 1863-6 ; advocated increased importation of cotton from India, 1863 ; enclosure commissioner, 1865-82 ; senior member of land commission, 1882 ; C.B., 1869 ; F.R.S., 1865 ; on commission to inquire into Indian famine, 1878-1879 ; president of Statistical Society, 1880 and 1881 ; K.C.B., 1882 ; honorary LL.D. Edinburgh, 1884 ; privy councillor, 1889 ; director of land department of board of agriculture, 1889-91. He published numerous writings on agricultural questions. [Suppl. i. 365]

CAIRD, JOHN (1820–1898), principal of Glasgow University ; studied at Glasgow University ; M.A., 1845 ; honorary D.D., 1860 ; minister of Lady Yester's, Edinburgh, 1847-9, Errol, Perthshire, 1849-57, and Park Church, Glasgow, 1857 ; professor of theology, Glasgow, 1862 ; principal, 1873 ; honorary LL.D. Edinburgh, 1884 ; Gifford lecturer at Glasgow, 1890-1 and 1896 ; published works, including ' Introduction to the Philosophy of Religion ' (1880). [Suppl. i. 368]

CAIRNCROSS, ALEXANDER (*d.* 1701), archbishop of Glasgow ; a dyer in Edinburgh ; parson of Dumfries ; bishop of Brechin, 1684 ; archbishop of Glasgow, 1684-7 ; bishop of Raphoe, 1693-1701. [viii. 215]

CAIRNCROSS, ROBERT (*d.* 1544), bishop of Ross ; provost of Corstorphine ; abbot of Holyrood ; bishop of Ross, 1539, holding *in commendam* the abbacy of Fern ; lord high treasurer of Scotland, 1528-9 and 1537-9. [viii. 215]

CAIRNECH, SAINT (*d.* 539 ?), son of ' Sarran, king of Britain ' ; harassed in his monastery by his brother, King Luirig ; delivered by his cousin, Mucertach MacErca ; attended a synod at Tours ; bishop of Temhar (Tara) and the clan O'Neil, *c.* 504. [viii. 215]

CAIRNES, DAVID (1645–1722), defender of Londonderry ; a lawyer ; advised defence of town, December 1688 ; sent to William III to ask help ; commanded regiment during the siege, April-August 1689 ; afterwards recorder and M.P. for Londonderry. [viii. 216]

CAIRNES, JOHN ELLIOT (1823–1875), economist ; educated at private schools ; employed in a brewery at Drogheda ; M.A. Trinity Col ege, Dublin, 1854 ; professor of political economy, 1856-61, and at Galway, 1859-65 ; Irish barrister, 1857 ; professor of political economy, University College, London, 1866 ; invalided, 1872 ; hon. LL.D. Dublin, 1874 ; published anti-slavery tracts, economic treatises, and pamphlets on university education in Ireland. [viii. 216]

CAIRNS, HUGH McCALMONT, first EARL CAIRNS, (1819–1885), lord chancellor; educated at Belfast academy and Trinity College, Dublin ; B.A., 1838 ; barrister of the Middle Temple, 1844 ; migrated to Lincoln's Inn and soon acquired a large practice ; M.P. for Belfast, 1852 ; Q.C., 1856 ; made his mark as a speaker in parliament, 1858 ; attorney-general and lord justice of appeal, 1866 ; created Baron Cairns, 1867 ; lord chancellor, 1868 ; leader of the conservative opposition in the lords, 1869-74 ; strongly opposed disestablishment of Irish church ; lord chancellor, 1874-80 ; created Earl Cairns, 1878 ; a lucid lawyer ; philanthropist. [viii. 217]

CAIRNS, JOHN (1818–1892), presbyterian divine ; son of a shepherd ; studied at Edinburgh University ; M.A., 1841 ; honorary D.D., 1858 ; honorary LL.D., 1884 ; entered Presbyterian Secession Hall, 1840 ; studied at

Berlin, 1843-4 ; licensed preacher, 1845 ; minister of Golden Square Church, Berwick-on-Tweed, 1845-76 ; professor of apologetics in United Presbyterian Theological Hall, 1867, and joint professor of systematic theology and apologetics, 1876 ; principal, 1879 ; Cunningham lecturer at Free Church, 1877 and 1880 ; preached in America and in many Continental towns ; published religious works and translations and contributed largely to periodicals ; he wrote the article on Kant in the ' Encyclopædia Britannica,' 8th edition. [Suppl. i. 369]

CAIRNS, WILLIAM (*d.* 1848), philosophical writer ; educated at Glasgow ; divinity student at the Anti-burgher College, 1800 ; minister of the secession church, Johnshaven, Kincardineshire, 1808-15 ; professor of logic in Belfast Institution, 1815-48 ; published ' Treatise on Moral Freedom,' 1844. [viii. 220]

CAISTOR, RICHARD (*d.* 1420), theologian : vicar of St. Stephen's, Norwich, 1402 ; his tomb in Norwich subsequently a place of pilgrimage. [viii. 220]

CAITHNESS, EARLS OF. [See SINCLAIR, SIR WILLIAM, first EARL, 1404 ?-1480 ; SINCLAIR, GEORGE, fourth EARL, *d.* 1582 ; SINCLAIR, GEORGE, fifth EARL, 1566 ?-1643 ; SINCLAIR, JAMES, fourteenth EARL, 1821-1881.]

CAIUS or **KAY**, JOHN, called the elder (*fl.* 1480), translator into English of a Latin poem on the defence of Rhodes (1480), printed in London, 1506. [viii. 221]

CAIUS, JOHN (1510–1573), scholar and physician, called John Caius, junior ; educated at Norwich, and Gonville Hall, Cambridge (fellow, 1533 ; M.A., 1535) ; studied Greek ; went to Padua, 1539 ; lectured there on Aristotle, studied medicine under Giambattista Montano and anatomy under André Vesale ; M.D. Padua, 1541 ; visited the great libraries of Italy, France, and Germany ; lectured on anatomy in London, 1544-64 ; resided at Shrewsbury (where he observed the ' sweating sickness '), and Norwich ; F.C.P., 1547 ; physician to Edward VI and Mary ; refounded Gonville Hall, Cambridge, 1557, and was master, 1559-73 ; dismissed from attendance on Queen Elizabeth as a Roman catholic, 1568 ; published under the name ' Londinensis ' a tract claiming for Cambridge priority over Oxford, 1568 ; edited and translated Galen, and wrote on medical subjects and Greek pronunciation. [viii. 221]

CAIUS or **KEY**, THOMAS (*d.* 1572), author ; fellow of All Souls' College, Oxford, 1525 ; M.A., 1530 ; registrar of the university, 1535-52 ; prebendary of Salisbury, 1559 ; master of University College, Oxford, 1561-72 ; rector of Tredington, Worcestershire, 1563-72 ; defended the priority of Oxford against John Caius (1510-1573) [q. v.] ; author of translations into English and Latin. [viii. 225]

CALAH, JOHN (1758–1798), composer of church music ; organist of Newark-on-Trent, 1781-5, and of Peterborough Cathedral, 1785-98. [viii. 226]

CALAMY, BENJAMIN (1642–1686), divine ; second son of Edmund Calamy the elder [q. v.] ; educated at St. Paul's School ; entered Catharine Hall, Cambridge, before 1660 ; M.A., 1668 and fellow ; D.D., 1680 ; incumbent of St. Mary, Aldermanbury, 1677 ; vicar of St. Lawrence Jewry, 1683 ; prebendary of St. Paul's, 1685 ; tried to obtain pardon for Alderman Henry Cornish [q. v.], 1685 ; published sermons. [viii. 226]

CALAMY, EDMUND, the elder (1600–1666), puritan ; B.A. Pembroke Hall, Cambridge, 1619 ; known as a Calvinist ; B.D., 1632 ; vicar of St. Mary's, Swaffham, Cambridge ; lecturer at Bury St. Edmunds, 1627 ?-36, retiring when the bishop insisted on observance of church ceremonies ; lecturer at Rochford, Essex ; incumbent of St. Mary's, Aldermanbury, 1639-62 ; one of the authors of ' Smectymnuus,' written against Bishop Joseph Hall's claim of divine right for episcopacy ; member of Westminster Assembly, 1643 ; presbyterian and intolerant of congregationalism ; opposed Charles I's trial and execution ; advocated the Restoration ; compelled by his wife to refuse the see of Lichfield and Coventry ; member of Savoy conference, 1661 ; ejected, 1662 ; imprisoned for unlicensed preaching, 1663 ; published sermons. [viii. 227]

CALAMY, EDMUND, the younger (1635 ?-1685), puritan ; eldest son of Edmund Calamy the elder [q. v.] ; educated at Sidney Sussex College, Cambridge, 1652-6, and at Pembroke Hall, Cambridge, 1656; M.A., 1658; ordained presbyterian minister, 1653; intruded rector of Moreton, Essex, 1659–62; withdrew to London; preached in private houses; opened meeting-house, 1672. [viii. 230]

CALAMY, EDMUND (1671–1732), nonconformist biographer; only son of Edmund Calamy the younger [q. v.]; educated in private schools kept by ejected puritan ministers; studied at Utrecht, 1688–91; resided in Oxford, 1691–2, reading in the Bodleian and preaching in meeting-houses in the district; assistant minister to presbyterian congregation at Blackfriars, 1692–5, and at Bishopsgate, 1695–1703; brought about a public presbyterian ordination, 1694; presbyterian minister at Westminster and lecturer at Salters' Hall, 1703–32; visited Scotland, 1709, and was made D.D. of Edinburgh, Aberdeen, and Glasgow; visited the west of England, 1713; published sermons and biographies, including an 'Account of the Ministers . . . ejected by the Act for Uniformity,' 1702, and 'A Continuation of the Account,' 1727; wrote an autobiography (printed, 1829). [viii. 231]

CALAMY, EDMUND (1697 ?–1755), presbyterian; eldest son of Edmund Calamy (1671–1732) [q. v.]; educated at Westminster School, Edinburgh University (M.A., 1717), and Leyden; assistant presbyterian minister in London, 1726–49. [viii. 235]

CALCOTT. [See also CALLCOTT.]

CALCOTT, WELLINS (*fl.* 1756–1769), author of essays (published 1756), and a treatise on freemasonry, 1769. [viii. 235]

CALCRAFT, SIR GRANBY THOMAS (1770–1820), cavalry officer; younger son of John Calcraft the elder [q. v.]; cornet, 1788; served in Flanders, 1793–5; knighted for protecting the Emperor Leopold at Villiers-en-Couche, 1794; aide-de-camp to General Lord Paget, 1799; in command of the 3rd dragoon guards, 1800–13; M.P. for Wareham, 1807–8; served through the Peninsular war, partly in command of cavalry brigades, 1809–13; major-general, 1813. [viii. 235]

CALCRAFT, JOHN, the elder (1726–1772), politician; son of the Duke of Rutland's election agent at Grantham; placed by the Rutland influence in the pay office; made agent for several regiments by Henry Fox, lord Holland, paymaster-general, 1757; deputy commissary-general, 1757–63; made a fortune as army contractor; deserted Fox for Pitt, 1763; M.P. for Rochester, 1768; agitated for parliamentary reform; bought Rempston, Isle of Purbeck, 1757, and Wareham, Dorset, 1767. [viii. 236]

CALCRAFT, JOHN, the younger (1765–1831), politician; eldest son of John Calcraft the elder [q. v.]; M.P. for Wareham. 1786–90, 1800–6, and 1818–31, for Rochester, 1806–18, and for Dorset, 1831; clerk of ordnance, 1806–7; paymaster-general, 1828–30; a whig; joined tories, 1828; voted for the Reform bill, 1831; committed suicide. [viii. 237]

CALCRAFT, WILLIAM (1800–1879), hangman; successively shoemaker, watchman, butler, and hawker; employed to flog boys at Newgate; first acted as hangman, 1828; appointed hangman, 1829; last public execution, 26 May, and first private, 3 Aug. 1868; pensioned, 1874. [viii. 238]

CALDECOTT, JOHN (1800–1849), astronomer; commercial agent for the rajah of Travancore at Allepey, 1832–6; director of the rajah's observatory at Trevandrum, 1837–49; author of meteorological and other papers. [viii. 238]

CALDECOTT, RANDOLPH (1846–1886), artist; educated at Chester school; early showed drawing talent; bank official at Whitchurch and Manchester; settled in London, 1872; drew for periodicals; made his mark as a book-illustrator, 1875; designed in colour children's books, 1878–85; worked for the 'Graphic'; exhibited at various galleries. [viii. 239]

CALDECOTT, THOMAS (1744–1833), bibliophile; educated at Winchester; fellow of New College, Oxford; B.C.L., 1770; barrister of the Middle Temple; collected a fine library of English sixteenth-century literature; printed privately Shakespearean commentaries. [viii. 240]

CALDER, JAMES TAIT (1794 ?–1864), author; educated at Edinburgh; parish schoolmaster of Canisbay,

Caithness; published poems, 1842–6, and a meritorious 'Sketch of the . . . History of Caithness,' 1861. [viii. 241]

CALDER, JOHN (1733–1815), author; educated at Aberdeen; secretary to the Duke of Northumberland; librarian of Dr. Daniel Williams's Library, London; nonconformist minister in London; helped in Thomas Percy's edition of the 'Spectator.' [viii. 241]

CALDER, ROBERT (1650 ?–1723), Scottish episcopalian; educated at Aberdeen; minister of Neuthorn, Berwickshire, 1689, but ejected as a Jacobite; in prison at Edinburgh, 1693; conducted a private episcopalian chapel at Aberdeen till 1707; prevented from settling in Elgin; conducted chapel in Edinburgh; published treatises in defence of episcopalian positions; reputed compiler of the caustic 'Scottish Presbyterian Eloquence displayed,' 1693. [viii. 241]

CALDER, SIR ROBERT (1745–1818), admiral; entered the navy, 1759; shared in the prize-money for the Spanish Hermione, the richest prize on record, 1762; commanded ships on the home station, 1780–3; fought at the battle of St. Vincent; knighted for bringing home the despatches, 1797; created baronet, 1798; rear-admiral, 1799; allowed a French squadron to outmanoeuvre him, 1801; came upon Villeneuve's fleet off Finisterre, 22 July 1805; neglected to engage it, 23 July; dispersed his ships, and had to fall back before Villeneuve, 9 Aug., leaving English coast exposed to attack; recalled, and censured for error of judgment, 1805; admiral, 1810. [viii. 242]

CALDERBANK, JAMES (1769–1821), Benedictine monk; priest; stationed at Weston, Somerset; at Bath, 1809–17, and afterwards at Liverpool; published controversial letters. [viii. 243]

CALDERBANK, LEONARD (1809–1864), Roman catholic priest and canon of Clifton; educated at Ampleforth, at Prior Park, Bath, 1829, and in Rome; priest, 1832; missioner in west of England from 1833; vice-president and professor at Prior Park, 1849–50. [viii. 244]

CALDERON, PHILIP HERMOGENES (1833–1898), painter; born at Poitiers; articled to civil engineer in England; studied in Paris under François Edouard Picot; first exhibited Royal Academy, 1853; R.A., 1867; keeper of Royal Academy, 1887. He was regarded as the leader of the 'St. John's Wood school' of painters. Among his most important works are 'After the Battle,' 1862, 'Her Most High, Noble, and Puissant Grace,' 1866 (gold medal, Paris, 1867), and 'The Renunciation of St. Elizabeth of Hungary,' 1891. [Suppl. i. 371]

CALDERWOOD, DAVID (1575–1650), presbyterian apologist; educated at Edinburgh; minister of Crailing, Roxburghshire, 1604; confined to his parish for opposing Bishop James Law, 1608; one of the protesters against James I's church measures, 1617; personally scolded by the king; banished; in Holland, 1619–25; published 'The Altar of Damascus,' 1621, a defence of presbyterianism; and an expanded Latin version of it, 1623; minister of Pencaitland, East Lothian, 1640; one of the compilers of the official 'Directory for Public Worship'; wrote 'History of the Kirk of Scotland' (first printed, in an abridgment, 1678); published controversial tracts. [viii. 244]

CALDERWOOD, HENRY (1830–1897), philosopher; educated at Edinburgh University and Theological Hall of United Presbyterian Church; licensed preacher, 1856; published, 1854, 'Philosophy of the Infinite,' a criticism of the agnostic tendencies of Sir William Hamilton's philosophy; ordained minister of Greyfriars Church, Glasgow, 1856–68; examiner in philosophy, Glasgow, 1861; LL.D. Glasgow, 1865; professor of moral philosophy, Edinburgh, 1868; F.R.S. Edinburgh, 1869; moderator of synod, 1880; edited 'United Presbyterian Magazine'; first chairman of Edinburgh school board, 1873–7; published philosophical works, including 'Evolution and Man's Place in Nature,' 1893. [Suppl. i. 373]

CALDERWOOD, MARGARET (1715–1774), diarist; née Steuart; married, 1735; withdrew to Brussels, 1756; wrote from that date a diary and narrative of events in Scotland (printed 1842). [viii. 246]

CALDERWOOD, SIR WILLIAM, LORD POLTON (1660 ?–1733), Scottish advocate, 1687; knighted before 1707; lord of session, 1711. [viii. 246]

CALDICOTT, ALFRED JAMES (1842–1897), musician; chorister at Worcester Cathedral; articled as organist; studied music at Leipzig; organist at St. Stephen's, Worcester, 1865–82; composed operettas for Thomas German Reed [q. v.]; conducted at Prince of Wales's Theatre, 1889–90; conductor to Miss Agnes Huntingdon's light opera company in America, 1890; professor at Royal College of Music and Guildhall School of Music, 1890–2; principal of London College of Music; conductor at Comedy Theatre, 1893. He composed many part-songs, operettas, and glees. [Suppl. i. 374]

CALDWALL, JAMES (b. 1739), portrait-engraver; exhibited, 1768–80. [viii. 246]

CALDWALL, RICHARD (1505 ?–1584), physician; B.A. Brasenose College, Oxford, 1533; student of Christ Church, 1547; M.D., 1555; practised in London.
[viii. 246]

CALDWELL, SIR ALEXANDER (1763–1839), artillery officer; educated at Woolwich; served in Bengal, 1783–1806; at the storming of Seringapatam, 1799; major, 1807; served in Java, 1811; lieutenant-colonel, 1812; retired, 1821; major-general and K.C.B., 1837.
[viii. 247]

CALDWELL, ANDREW, the elder (1733–1808), Irish barrister; studied law in London; Irish barrister, 1760; published pamphlets. [viii. 247]

CALDWELL, SIR BENJAMIN (1737 ?–1820), admiral; entered the navy, 1756; commanded frigate, 1765; commander of the Agamemnon in the Bay of Biscay, 1781, and in the West Indies, 1782–3; rear-admiral, 1793; commanded the Impregnable in the action of 1 June 1794; in command on Leeward Islands station, 1794–5; admiral, 1799; G.C.B., 1820. [viii. 248]

CALDWELL, HUME (1733–1762), Irishman; colonel in the Austrian service; served through the seven years' war; led the storming party at Schweidnitz, 1761; died of wounds. [viii. 248]

CALDWELL, SIR JAMES LILLYMAN (1770–1863), general; cadet in East India Company's service, 1788; ensign, Madras engineers, 1789; captain-lieutenant, 1796; captain, 1802; colonel, 1825; major-general, 1846; general, 1854; served in campaigns against Tippu, 1791–2 and 1799; engineer in charge of central division of Madras army, 1811; special surveyor of fortresses, 1813; C.B., 1815; acting chief engineer of Madras, 1816; lieutenant-colonel-commandant of his corps, 1824; retired and was made K.C.B., 1837; G.C.B., 1848. [Suppl. i. 375]

CALDWELL, JOHN (1628–1679). [See FENWICK.]

CALDWELL, ROBERT (1814–1891), coadjutor bishop of Madras; B.A. Glasgow, 1837; LL.D., 1857; sent by London Missionary Society to Madras; joined English church and associated himself with Society for Propagation of Gospel, 1841; established himself at Tinnevelly, 1841; consecrated bishop of Tinnevelly as coadjutor to bishop of Madras, 1877; assisted in Tamil versions of Prayer-book, 1842 and 1872, and bible, 1858–69; D.D. Durham, 1874; published 'Comparative Grammar of South Indian Family of Languages,' 1856, and works relating to history of Tinnevelly mission, and other writings. [Suppl. i. 376]

CALENIUS, WALTER (d. 1151), archdeacon of Oxford; name used by John Bale for an undefined 'Walter,' who was archdeacon of Oxford from 1115 to 1138, and before and after these dates; king's justiciar, 1118 ? and 1125. This Walter, according to Geoffrey of Monmouth, brought from Brittany the Celtic original of the Chronicle which Geoffrey professed to translate. 'Calena,' a misreading for Calleva (i.e. Silchester), being, in the bastard-Latin of the sixteenth century, used for Oxford, Bale, by 'Calenius,' meant only 'Walter of Oxford.' White Kennett, following the later but equally erroneous identification of Calena, styles him 'Walter of Wallingford.' He is sometimes confused with later archdeacons of Oxford, Walter of Coutances, 1183, and Walter Map, 1196. [viii. 249]

CALETO or **CAUX,** JOHN DE (d. 1263), minister of Henry III; so called probably from his birthplace, the Pays de Caux, Normandy; monk of St. Swithun's, Winchester, and (1247) chosen prior; abbot of Peterborough, by royal mandate, 1250–63; justice itinerant, 1254–8; treasurer of England, 1260. [viii. 250]

CALEY, JOHN (d. 1834), government official; employed in the Record Office; keeper of records in the Augmentation Office, 1787, and (concurrently) in the treasury at Westminster, 1818, and (jointly with both offices) special sub-commissioner of records; secretary to the first record commission, 1801–31; accused of incompetence, indolence, and dishonesty in his offices; F.S.A., 1786; wrote on archæological subjects. [viii. 251]

CALFHILL or **CALFIELD,** JAMES (1530 ?–1570), divine; at Eton, 1540; at King's College, Cambridge, 1545; student of Christ Church, Oxford, 1548; M.A., 1552; canon of Christ Church and B.D., 1561; rector of St. Andrew Wardrobe, London, and prebendary of St. Paul's, 1562; Lady Margaret professor of divinity, Oxford, 1564; rector and dean of Bocking, and archdeacon of Colchester, 1565–70; D.D., 1566; nominated bishop of Worcester, but died before consecration; Calvinist; wrote Latin verses and a polemical tract. [viii. 252]

CALGACUS (fl. 84 ?). [See GALGACUS.]

CALHOUN, PATRICK (1727–1796), American settler; emigrated from Ireland, 1733; settled successively in Pennsylvania, Virginia, and South Carolina; fought against the Indians and against the British. [viii. 253]

CALKIN, JAMES (1786–1862), composer; music-master in London; organist of Regent Square Church, Gray's Inn Road, London. [viii. 253]

CALL, SIR JOHN (1732–1801), military engineer; went to Bengal with Benjamin Robins (d. 1751), chief engineer to the East India Company, 1750; employed in fortifying Fort St. David, Carnatic, 1751; served with Clive, 1752; chief engineer at Fort St. David, 1752–7; chief engineer of the Coromandel coast, 1758; at siege of Pondicherry, 1761, and Vellore, 1762; returned to England, 1769; high sheriff of Cornwall, 1771; served on commission on crown lands from 1782; M.P. for Callington, 1784–90; created baronet, 1791; became blind, 1795.
[viii. 253]

CALLACHAN, KING OF IRELAND (d. 954). [See CEALLACHAN.]

CALLANAN, JEREMIAH JOHN (1795–1829), poet; native of Cork; Erse scholar; at Maynooth and Trinity College, Dublin; taught school; wandered in south-west Ireland, collecting legends and songs (never published); died at Lisbon; wrote verses, and translated largely from the Irish and Portuguese; his poems printed, 1830.
[viii. 254]

CALLANDER, EARL OF (d. 1674). [See LIVINGSTONE, JAMES.]

CALLANDER, JAMES (1745–1832). [See CAMPBELL, SIR JAMES.]

CALLANDER, JOHN (d. 1789), Scottish advocate; wrote notes on Milton and the Greek poets; published redaction of Australian voyages, 1766–8, and other works.
[viii. 255]

CALLAWAY, HENRY (1817–1890), missionary bishop of St. John's, Kaffraria; schoolmaster at Heavitree, 1833; studied surgery at St. Bartholomew's Hospital; L.R.C.S., 1842; L.A.S., 1844; M.D. Aberdeen, 1853; joined Society for Propagation of Gospel, 1854, and proceeded to Durban; in charge of mission church of Ekukanyeni, near Pietermaritzburg, 1854; minister of St. Andrew's Church, 1855; settled at Spring Vale on the Insunguze, 1868, and studied native traditions; consecrated at Edinburgh missionary bishop of St. John's, Kaffraria, 1873; honorary D.D. Oxford, 1874; resigned bishopric, 1886; chief work, 'Religious System of the Amazulu,' 1868–70. [Suppl. i. 378]

CALLCOTT, SIR AUGUSTUS WALL (1779–1844), painter; chorister of Westminster Abbey; art student of the Royal Academy; R.A., 1810; married, 1827 [see CALLCOTT, MARIA, LADY]; knighted, 1837; exhibited at the Academy, 1799; exhibited in the main English landscapes, 1804–24, foreign landscapes, 1830–6, and figure-paintings, 1837–40. [viii. 256]

CALLCOTT, JOHN WALL (1766–1821), composer; brother of preceding; learned the organ, 1778, clarinet, 1780, and oboe, 1781; sang in the chorus of operas; assistant-organist of St. George-the-Martyr, Bloomsbury, 1783–5; Mus. Bac. Oxford, 1784; organist of the Female Orphans Asylum, 1793–1802; Mus. Doc. Oxford, 1800; lecturer on music at the Royal Institution, 1806;

latterly insane; published 'Musical Grammar,' 1806; his glees and catches published, 1824; some of his manuscripts preserved in British Museum. [viii. 256]

CALLCOTT, MARIA, LADY (1785–1842), author; *née* Dundas; married (1) in India, Thomas Graham (*d.* 1822), captain R.N., in 1809; and (2) Sir Augustus Wall Callcott [q. v.]; published descriptions of her surroundings in India, Brazil, Chili, Italy, also 'Little Arthur's History of England,' 1835. [viii. 258]

CALLCOTT, WILLIAM HUTCHINS (1807–1882), composer; son of John Wall Callcott [q. v.]; organist of Ely Place Chapel; composed songs, glees, and arrangements for the piano. [viii. 258]

CALLENDER, GEORGE WILLIAM (1830–1878), surgeon; student of St. Bartholomew's Hospital, London, 1849, and surgeon, 1871; lectured there on anatomy, 1865, and surgery, 1873; published anatomical treatises. [viii. 259]

CALLENDER, JAMES THOMSON (*d.* 1803), journalist; prosecuted for a pamphlet, 1793; withdrew to America, 1794; journalist at Philadelphia, 1794–8, and Richmond; wrote bitterly against the first three presidents of the United States. [viii. 259]

CALLIS, ROBERT (*fl.* 1634), serjeant-at-law; of Gray's Inn; serjeant-at-law, 1627; published law tracts. [viii. 260]

CALLOW, JOHN (1822–1878), painter of landscapes and sea-pieces in water-colours; studied in Paris, 1835–1844; an esteemed teacher of drawing and painting in London; taught drawing at the military academies of Addiscombe, 1851–60, and Woolwich. [viii. 260]

CALTHORPE, SIR HENRY (1586–1637), lawyer; of the Middle Temple; counsel in political cases, 1627 and 1630; recorder of London, 1635–6, by king's mandate; attorney of court of wards, 1636; knighted. [viii. 260]

CALTHROPE, SIR CHARLES (*d.* 1616), Irish lawyer; attorney-general for Ireland, 1583–1606, employed in safeguarding crown claims on forfeited estates; knighted, 1604; justice of common pleas in Ireland, 1606. [viii. 261]

CALVELEY, SIR HUGH (*d.* 1393), soldier; commander of free-lances in the war in Brittany, 1341–64; fought at Auray, 1364; served with Henry of Trastamare, 1366, but left him and joined the Black Prince, 1367; wasted the county of Armagnac; governor of the Channel islands, 1376–88; deputy of Calais, and fighting the French, 1377–9; governor of Brest; a commander in Buckingham's futile invasion of France, 1380; founded college at Bunbury, Cheshire, 1385. [viii. 262]

CALVER, EDWARD (*fl.* 1649), puritan; published metrical pieces, 1641–9. [viii. 263]

CALVERLEY, CHARLES STUART (1831–1884) poet and parodist; son of the Rev. Henry Blayds, who assumed the name Calverley, 1852; at Harrow, 1846–9; athlete and writer of Latin verse; scholar of Balliol College, Oxford, 1850–2; migrated to Christ's College, Cambridge, 1852, fellow, 1858, M.A., 1859; barrister of the Inner Temple, 1865; published 'Verses and Translations,' 1862; translated Theocritus, 1869. [viii. 264]

CALVERLEY, HENRY (1604–1661), royalist; heir of Walter Calverley [q. v.]; fined for delinquency. [viii. 265]

CALVERLEY, WALTER (*d.* 1605), murderer, whose tragic history was widely celebrated; squire of Calverley Hall, Yorkshire; studied at Cambridge, 1579; forced by his guardian to marry Philippa Brooke; by gambling and drink brought himself to bankruptcy; murdered two of his young sons, 1605; pressed to death at York; subject of 'Miseries of Enforced Marriage,' 1607, and 'Yorkshire Tragedy,' 1608. [viii. 265]

CALVERT, CAROLINE LOUISA WARING (1834–1872), author of descriptions of Australian scenery and Australian tales, published under her maiden name, LOUISA ATKINSON; daughter of a settler in New South Wales; lived on the rivers Hawkesbury and Kurrajong; collected specimens for the government botanist; the genus *Atkinsonia* and the species (*Epacris*) *Calvertiana* named after her; married (1870) James Snowden Calvert [q. v.] [viii. 265]

CALVERT, CHARLES, the elder (1754–1797), estate agent and amateur painter. [viii. 266]

CALVERT, CHARLES, the younger (1785–1852), landscape-painter; cotton merchant, then art-teacher, in Manchester. [viii. 266]

CALVERT, CHARLES ALEXANDER (1828–1879), actor; educated at King's College School, London; clerk in the city; appeared on the provincial stage, 1852; appeared in London, 1855; stage-manager at Manchester, 1859; staged Shakespearean plays, 1864–77. [viii. 266]

CALVERT, EDWARD (1799–1883), artist; midshipman in the navy; art student at Plymouth and London; friend of William Blake; exhibited at the Royal Academy, 1825–36; engraver. [viii. 267]

CALVERT, FREDERICK, sixth BARON BALTIMORE (1731–1771), a rake; lived much abroad; the title extinct on his death; published journal of a 'Tour in the East ... 1763–4,' and Latin verses. [viii. 268]

CALVERT, FREDERICK BALTIMORE (1793–1877), actor and lecturer; son of Charles Calvert the elder [q. v.]; educated for Roman catholic priesthood; went on the stage; published 'A Defence of the Drama,' 1824; travelled as a lecturer on elocution in Great Britain and America, 1829–46; lecturer in Edinburgh and Glasgow, 1846–77; published treatises on elocution. [viii. 268]

CALVERT, FREDERICK CRACE (1819–1873), chemist; resided in France studying and practising chemistry, 1835–46, chiefly under Michel Eugène Chevreul; chemical teacher, specialist, and manufacturer in Manchester, 1846–73; died at the Vienna exhibition; published scientific papers. [viii. 269]

CALVERT, GEORGE, first BARON BALTIMORE (1580?–1632), statesman; entered Trinity College, Oxford, 1594; B.A., 1597; travelled; secretary to Sir Robert Cecil; clerk of council in Ireland, 1608; M.P. for Bossiney, 1609–11; temporary secretary of state, 1612–13; a commissioner to investigate Irish grievances, 1613; knighted, 1617; secretary of state, 1619–25; a pensioner of the king, 1620; M.P. for Yorkshire, 1621; received large grants of land in Longford county; planted a colony (Avalon) in Newfoundland, 1621–3; professed Roman catholic, 1625; created baron, 1625; wintered at Avalon, 1628–9; prevented by the Virginia Company from planting a colony south of the James river, 1629–31; obtained a grant of land for a colony (Maryland) north of the Potomac, 1632. [viii. 269]

CALVERT, GEORGE (1795–1825), surgeon. [viii. 272]

CALVERT, SIR HARRY (1763?–1826), general; entered the army, 1778; served in America, 1779–81; prisoner-of-war, 1781–3; captain, 1785; aide-de-camp to the Duke of York in Holland, 1793–4; adjutant-general of the forces, 1799–1818; major-general, 1803; G.C.B., 1815; created baronet, 1818; lieutenant-governor of Chelsea Hospital, 1820; general, 1821; his journals published, 1853. [viii. 272]

CALVERT, JAMES SNOWDEN (1825–1884), Australian explorer; emigrated, 1840; joined Ludwig Leichhardt's exploring party, 1844–5. [viii. 273]

CALVERT, LEONARD (*d.* 1647), governor of Maryland; second son of George Calvert, baron Baltimore [q. v.]; planted Maryland, 1634; fought with Captain Clayborne, a prior settler, 1635; sent out to Maryland with a new commission, 1644; finally defeated Clayborne, 1646–7. [viii. 273]

CALVERT, MICHAEL (1770–1862), author of a 'History of Knaresborough,' 1844; druggist. [viii. 274]

CALVERT, RAISLEY (*d.* 1794), sculptor. [viii. 266]

CALVERT, THOMAS (1606–1679), puritan; educated at Cambridge; preacher in York minster and incumbent of two churches in York; ejected, 1662; published sermons. [viii. 274]

CALVERT, THOMAS (1775–1840), divine; called Thomas Jackson till 1819, when he inherited property; B.A. St. John's College, Cambridge, 1797; fellow, 1798; tutor, 1814; D.D., 1823; Norrisian professor of divinity, 1814–24; vicar of Holme, Yorkshire, 1822; warden of Manchester, 1823; published sermons. [viii. 275]

CAMBELL or **CAMPBELL**, SIR JAMES (1570–1642), ironmonger, of London; alderman, 1620; lord mayor, 1629; knighted, 1630. [viii. 275]

CAMBRENSIS, GIRALDUS (1146?–1220?). [See GIRALDUS.]

CAMBRIDGE, DUKE OF (1774–1850). [See ADOLPHUS FREDERICK.]

CAMBRIDGE, EARLS OF. [See LANGLEY, EDWARD DE, 1341–1402; RICHARD, d. 1415; HAMILTON, JAMES, first EARL, 1589–1625; HAMILTON, JAMES, second EARL, 1606–1649; HAMILTON, WILLIAM, third EARL, 1616–1651.]

CAMBRIDGE, JOHN (d. 1335). [See CANTEBRIG, JOHN DE.]

CAMBRIDGE, RICHARD OWEN (1717–1802), author; educated at Eton and St. John's College, Oxford, 1734; entered Lincoln's Inn, 1737; published satirical verses, 1752–6, and a 'History of the War upon the Coast of Coromandel,' 1761. [viii. 276]

CAMDEN, MARQUIS OF (1759–1840), [See PRATT, JOHN JEFFREYS.]

CAMDEN, EARL OF (1713–1793). [See PRATT, CHARLES.]

CAMDEN, WILLIAM (1551–1623), antiquary and historian; educated at Christ's Hospital and (1564–6) at St. Paul's School; servitor (apparently to Thomas Cooper, schoolmaster) at Magdalen College, Oxford, 1566; migrated to Broadgates Hall, and afterwards to Christ Church (perhaps as servitor); asked grace for B.A., 1570; left Oxford, 1571, having been excluded from an All Souls' fellowship by the catholic fellows; began to travel up and down England, probably subsidised by Gabriel Goodman (d. 1601), dean of Westminster, collecting archæological material; usher of Westminster School, 1575–93; appointed head-master, 1593; continued in vacations, 1578–1600, his personal tours of antiquarian investigation; published 'Britannia,' 1586; asked grace for M.A., June 1588; prebendary of Salisbury (though a layman), 1589–1623; published a Greek grammar, 1597; Clarenceux king-of-arms, 1597–1623; answered in his fifth edition of 'Britannia,' 1600, the criticisms (printed, 1599) of Ralph Brooke (or Brookesmouth) [q. v.]; printed the epitaphs in Westminster Abbey, 1600; published certain chronicles (being some of his early collections for the 'Britannia'), 'Anglica . . . a veteribus scripta,' Frankfort, 1603, containing in the text of Asser [q. v.] the interpolation about King Alfred's foundations in Oxford, and, 1605, 'Remains concerning Britain'; issued the sixth (greatly enlarged) edition of 'Britannia,' and printed the official account of the Gunpowder plot trials, 1607; named a foundation fellow of Matthew Sutcliffe's projected college at Chelsea, 1610; offered M.A. by Oxford University, 1613; communicated to Thuanus (Jacques Auguste de Thou) his manuscript history of Elizabeth's reign, c. 1607; published 'Annales . . . regnante Elizabetha . . . ad annum 1589,' 1615 [the second part was printed posthumously, 1628]; wrote a skeleton life of James I (printed, 1691); founded a chair of history in Oxford University, 1622; memorial verses, 'Camdeni Insignia,' printed after his death by Oxford University, 1624; his correspondence printed by Thomas Smith, 1691. [viii. 277]

CAMELEAC (d. 927). [See CIMELLIAUC.]

CAMELFORD, first BARON (1737–1793). [See PITT, THOMAS.]

CAMERON, SIR ALAN (1753–1828), of Errach, general; volunteer officer in America, 1775–82; prisoner of war, 1782; returned to Scotland, 1784; raised the Cameron Highlanders (79th regiment), 1794; commanded it in Flanders, 1795, and the West Indies, 1796; lieutenant-colonel, 1796; recruited his regiment, 1798; commanded it in Holland, 1799, and Egypt, 1801; raised a second battalion, 1804; colonel, 1804; commanded the 79th in Denmark, 1807; brigadier-general, 1808; collected the stragglers of Sir John Moore's army, 1809; commanded brigade at Talavera, 1809, and Busaco, 1810; major-general and invalided home, 1810; K.C.B., 1815; lieutenant-general, 1819. [viii. 285]

CAMERON, ALEXANDER (1747–1828), Roman catholic prelate; educated at Rome; missioner at Strathaven, 1772; rector of the Scots college, Valladolid, 1780; titular bishop of Maximianopolis, 1798; coadjutor-bishop in Scotland, 1802, and vicar-apostolic of the Lowlands, 1806–25. [viii. 286]

CAMERON, SIR ALEXANDER (1781–1850), of Inverailort, general; ensign, 1797; lieutenant, 1800; served in Holland, 1799, Denmark, 1800, and Egypt, 1801; captain, 1805; served with distinction in Peninsula, 1808–13; brevet major, 1811; brevet lieutenant-colonel, 1812; served in Flanders, 1813, and at Quatre Bras and Waterloo, 1815; major-general and K.C.B., 1838. [viii. 286]

CAMERON, ARCHIBALD (1707–1753), Jacobite; a younger son of Lochiel; studied medicine at Edinburgh and Paris; practised in Lochaber; acted as physician to the insurgents, 1745; effected the escape of Prince Charles, 1746; became physician to a regiment in the French service; arrested, 1753, while collecting money in Scotland; executed at London. [viii. 287]

CAMERON, CHARLES DUNCAN (d. 1870), British consul; army officer, 1846–51; served in South Africa, 1846–7 and 1851–2; political agent in Zululand and magistrate in Natal; officer in the Turkish service at Kars, 1855; British vice-consul in Asia Minor, 1858; consul at Massowah, 1862; imprisoned by King Theodore at Gondar, 1864, an act which occasioned the Abyssinian war; released, 1868. [viii. 288]

CAMERON, CHARLES HAY (1795–1880), jurist; barrister, Lincoln's Inn, 1820; commissioner on law administration in Ceylon, 1831, and on the poor laws, 1833; law member of the Supreme Council of India, 1835; employed in codifying the Indian penal laws; returned to England, 1848; retired to Ceylon, 1875. [viii. 288]

CAMERON, DONALD (1695?–1748), the GENTLE LOCHIEL; succeeded to chieftaincy of the clan Cameron, 1719; reluctantly joined Prince Charles, 1745; accompanied him to Edinburgh and Derby; wounded at Falkirk, 1745, and Culloden, 1746; attainted; escaped with Prince Charles to France, 1746; commanded regiment in the French service. [viii. 289]

CAMERON, SIR DUNCAN ALEXANDER (1808–1888), general; ensign, 42nd royal highlanders, 1825; captain, 1833; lieutenant-colonel, 1843; served in Crimea, with local rank in Turkey of brigadier; C.B., 1855; major-general, 1859; commander of forces in New Zealand, 1861; K.C.B., 1864; resigned commission and returned to England, 1865; colonel, 1863; general, 1874; governor of Sandhurst, 1868–75; G.C.B., 1873. [Suppl. i. 379]

CAMERON, SIR EWEN or EVAN (1629–1719), of Lochiel; a hostage in the hands of the Marquis of Argyll, 1641–7; resided in Lochaber, 1647, hunting wolves and fighting the Macdonalds; raised his clan to fight the Commonwealth forces, 1652; submitted on honourable terms to Monck, 1658; accompanied Monck to London; received at Charles II's court, 1660, but his claims disregarded; at feud with the Macintoshes; knighted, 1681; raised his clan to join Viscount Dundee, 1690; retired to Lochaber after Killiecrankie; submitted to William III, 1692; sent his clan to join the Earl of Mar's rising, 1714. [viii. 290]

CAMERON, GEORGE POULETT (1806–1882), colonel; cadet in the Madras army, 1821; served against the Mahrattas, 1824–5; served with Don Pedro in Portugal, 1832–3; in the Persian service, 1836–8; in the East India Company's service, 1842–58; published travels and memoirs. [viii. 293]

CAMERON, HUGH (1705–1817), millwright; introduced spinning-wheel into the highlands; designed the first barley-mill north of the Forth; built numerous lint-mills in the highlands. [viii. 293]

CAMERON, JOHN (d. 1446), bishop of Glasgow; probably of a Midlothian family; official of Lothian, 1422; rector of Cambuslang, Lanarkshire, 1424; secretary to James I of Scotland; provost of Lincluden, 1425; keeper of the privy seal; keeper of the great seal, 1426; chancellor of Scotland, 1426–39; bishop of Glasgow, 1428; supported the royal authority against the ecclesiastical courts; envoy to the council of Basle, 1433, to Italy, 1436, and to England, 1437. [viii. 293]

CAMERON, JOHN (1579?-1625), theologian; educated at Glasgow; taught Greek and Latin at Bordeaux, 1600, and Sedan, 1602; sent by the protestant church at Bordeaux to study divinity at Paris, Geneva, and Heidelberg, 1604-8; protestant minister at Bordeaux, 1608-17; professor of divinity at Saumur, 1618; withdrew to London, 1620; principal of Glasgow University, 1622; hated for his subserviency to James I; returned to Saumur, 1623; professor of divinity at Montauban, 1624; wrote theological treatises. [viii. 295]

CAMERON, JOHN (1724-1799), presbyterian; bookseller's apprentice at Edinburgh; graduated M.A. there; minister of the reformed presbyterian church; itinerant preacher in Ulster, 1750; presbyterian minister at Dunluce, 1755-99; published, mainly anonymously, treatises of a unitarian tendency. [viii. 296]

CAMERON, JOHN (1771-1815), of Fassiefern, colonel; educated at Aberdeen; ensign, 1793; lieutenant, 1794; served in Holland, 1799, and Egypt, 1801; major, 1801; lieutenant-colonel, 1808; commanded Gordon Highlanders (92nd regiment) in Holland, 1809, and throughout the Peninsular war, 1810-14; killed at Quatre Bras. [viii. 297]

CAMERON, SIR JOHN (1773-1844), general; educated at Eton; ensign, 1787; served in West Indies, 1793; captain, 1794; prisoner of war, 1794-7; served in West Indies, 1797-1800; lieutenant-colonel, 1807; commanded battalion of 9th regiment in Portugal, 1808, Holland, 1809, and the Peninsula, 1810-13; colonel, 1814; held command in Canada, 1814, and France, 1815; K.C.B., 1815; major-general, 1821; lieutenant-general, 1837. [viii. 298]

CAMERON, JOHN ALEXANDER (d. 1885), war correspondent; bank clerk in Inverness; merchant's clerk in Bombay; war correspondent in Afghanistan, 1878-80, Natal, 1880-1, Egypt, 1882, Madagascar, Tonquin, and Egypt, 1884; killed in action. [viii. 299]

CAMERON, JULIA MARGARET (1815-1879), photographer of Charles Darwin, Alfred Tennyson, and Robert Browning; née Pattle; born at Calcutta; married, 1838, Charles Hay Cameron [q. v.]; came to England, 1848; took up photography, c. 1865; retired to Ceylon, 1875. [viii. 300]

CAMERON, LUCY LYTTELTON (1781-1858), writer of religious tales for children; daughter of George Butt [q. v.]; married, 1806, the Rev. Charles Richard Cameron. [viii. 300]

CAMERON, RICHARD (d. 1680), covenanter; schoolmaster and precentor at Falkland, Fife; tutor in the family of Scott of Harden; field preacher in Dumfries and Lanark shires; went to Holland, 1678; returned, 1680; joined in the act of deposing Charles II at Sanquhar; outlawed; killed in a skirmish at Aird's Moss, Ayrshire. The 'Reformed Presbyterians' are from him popularly termed 'Cameronians.' [viii. 301]

CAMERON, VERNEY LOVETT (1844-1894), African explorer; entered navy, 1857; midshipman, 1860; lieutenant, 1865; in Abyssinian campaign, 1868; employed in suppression of slave trade in East Africa; leader of Royal Geographical Society's expedition to aid Livingstone, 1873; journeyed from Bahenneko to Unyanyembe, where he heard of Livingstone's death; proceeded to Lake Tanganyika, and the sources of the Zambesi and Bihé, and arrived at Katombela, 1875; commander and C.B., 1876; received R.G.S. gold medal; honorary D.C.L. Oxford; travelled in Asiatic Turkey, 1878; accompanied Sir Richard Francis Burton [q v.] to west coast of Africa, 1882; retired from navy, 1883; published tales of adventure and accounts of his travels. [Suppl. i. 379]

CAMERON, WILLIAM (1751-1811), Scottish poet; educated at Aberdeen; minister of Kirknewton, Midlothian, 1786; joint-editor of the Scots 'Paraphrases'; wrote chiefly didactic verse. [viii. 302]

CAMIDGE, JOHN, the elder (1735-1803), organist; chorister of York Minster; partly taught by Handel; organist of York Minster, 1756-99. [viii. 302]

CAMIDGE, JOHN, the younger (1790-1859), organist; taught by his father, Matthew Camidge [q. v.]; Mus.Bac., 1812, and Mus. Doc. Cambridge, 1819; assistant organist at York Minster, and organist, 1842-59; published church music. [viii. 303]

CAMIDGE, MATTHEW (1758-1844), organist; son of John Camidge the elder [q. v.]; chorister of the Chapel Royal; assistant organist at York Minster; organist, 1799-1842; published musical compositions. [viii. 303]

CAMM, ANNE (1627-1705), quakeress; née Newby; educated in puritan surroundings in London, 1640-7; married, at Kendal, 1650, John Audland (d. 1663); joined the quakers, 1652, and preached for the rest of her life, especially in Oxfordshire; imprisoned at Banbury, 1653; married Thomas Camm [q. v.], c. 1665. [viii. 303]

CAMM, JOHN (1604?-1656), quaker minister; joined the quakers, 1652; came to London to interview Cromwell, 1654; visited Bristol and London, 1656; published tracts. [viii. 304]

CAMM, THOMAS (1641-1707), quaker minister; son of John Camm [q. v.]; imprisoned for not paying tithes, 1674; fined for unlicensed preaching, 1678; imprisoned, probably for preaching, 1680-6; published tracts. [viii. 304]

CAMMIN, SAINT (d. 653). [See CAIMIN.]

CAMOCKE, GEORGE (1666?-1722?), naval officer; of an Essex family; born in Ireland; entered the navy, 1682; lieutenant, 1690; served in the Channel, the Mediterranean, and off Spain, 1690-7; served, chiefly on the Irish coast, 1699-1712; captain, 1702; served in Mediterranean, 1713-14; convoyed the Spanish army from Sicily to Spain on his own responsibility, 1714, and was cashiered in consequence, 1715; rear-admiral in the Spanish service; tried to bribe English naval officers to join the Jacobite party, 1718; defeated off Cape Passaro, 1718; banished by Spain to Ceuta, 1719. [viii. 305]

CAMOYS, THOMAS DE, fifth BARON (d. 1420), succeeded to the barony, 1372; served in France, c. 1377, Scotland, 1385, and Spain, 1386; removed, by Gloucester's influence, from the court of Richard II, 1388; served against the Welsh, 1401; envoy to Flanders, 1405, and France, 1406; commanded left wing at Agincourt, 1415; K.G., 1416. [viii. 306]

CAMPBELL, ALEXANDER (d. 1608), bishop of Brechin, 1566-1608; made bishop by the Earl of Argyll, solely that that nobleman might get hold of the estates of the see; never consecrated, though he sat in parliament; studied at Geneva, 1573; acted as minister at Brechin after his return in 1574, and was frequently prosecuted in the church courts for neglect of duty. [viii. 307]

CAMPBELL, ALEXANDER, second EARL OF MARCHMONT (1675-1740), younger son of Patrick Hume, first earl; took the name Campbell on his marriage with the heiress of Campbell of Cessnock, Ayrshire, 1697; studied law at Utrecht; Scottish advocate, 1696; lord of session with style of Lord Cessnock, 1704-14; M.P. for Berwickshire in the Scottish parliament, 1706; advocated the union; lord-lieutenant of Berwickshire, 1715; envoy to Denmark, 1715-21; lord clerk register of Scotland, 1716-33; envoy to the congress at Cambray, 1722; succeeded to the earldom, 1724; a representative Scottish peer; opposed Walpole's excise scheme, 1733. [viii. 308]

CAMPBELL, ALEXANDER (1764-1824), miscellaneous writer; organist and music-master in Edinburgh, Sir Walter Scott being one of his pupils; studied medicine; published tours in Scotland, collections of Scottish songs, musical compositions, and verses. [viii. 308]

CAMPBELL, ALEXANDER (1788-1866), founder of the 'Campbellites'; native of Antrim; studied at Glasgow, 1808; followed his father, a secession church minister, to the United States, 1809; ordained minister in his father's sect, 1811; prospered as a farmer; allied himself to the baptists, 1812; quarrelled with the baptists, 1826, and founded a new church, called 'the Church of the Disciples' (popularly 'the Campbellites'); founded for it Bethany College, West Virginia, 1841; wrote theological tracts. [viii. 310]

CAMPBELL, SIR ALEXANDER (1822-1892), Canadian politician; taken to Canada at early age; admitted attorney, and called to bar, 1842; Q.C. and bencher of Law Society, 1856; dean of faculty of law, Queen's University, Kingston; member for Cataraqui of legislative council, 1858, and speaker, 1863; commissioner of crown lands, 1863-4; privy councillor of Canada, 1867; postmaster-general, 1867-73, 1879, 1880, and 1885-7;

senator, 1867; leader of conservative opposition in senate, 1873-8; receiver-general, 1878; minister of militia, 1879; minister of justice, 1881; K.C.M.G., 1879; lieutenant-governor of Ontario, 1887-92. [Suppl. i. 381]

CAMPBELL, ANNA MACKENZIE, COUNTESS OF BALCARRES, and afterwards of ARGYLL (1621?-1706?), daughter of Colin Mackenzie, earl of Seaforth; married, 1640, Alexander Lindsay, afterwards earl of Balcarres (d. 1659), an ardent royalist; joined her husband in the highlands, 1651; sold her jewels to meet debts incurred by her husband in the king's cause, 1651; accompanied her husband to France, 1654; governess to the Prince of Orange at the Hague, 1657-9; returned to France, 1660; was living in England in distressed circumstances, 1661; returned to Scotland, 1662; received a pension from the crown, 1664; laboured to clear the Balcarres estates of debt; married, 1670, Archibald Campbell, marquis and eighth earl of Argyll [q. v.]; impoverished by his forfeiture, 1681; imprisoned at Stirling, 1685, but released after Argyll's execution. [viii. 311]

CAMPBELL, ARCHIBALD, second EARL OF ARGYLL (d. 1513), eldest son of Colin Campbell, first earl [q. v.]; succeeded to the earldom, 1493; lord high chancellor of Scotland, 1494; joint-administrator of the lordship of the Isles, 1499; suppressed revolt of islanders, 1504; governor of the Argyllshire islands, 1506; slain at Flodden. [viii. 312]

CAMPBELL, ARCHIBALD, fourth EARL OF ARGYLL (d. 1558), eldest son of Colin Campbell, third earl [q. v.]; succeeded to the earldom, 1530; suppressed rebellion in Argyllshire islands, 1530; imprisoned on charge of having provoked the rebellion by oppression; joined Huntly and other peers in taking the infant queen Mary from the custody of the Earl of Arran, then regent, 1543; resisted the Earl of Lennox's descent on the Clyde, 1544, and obtained a grant of his forfeited estates; commanded right wing at Pinkie, 1547; generally opposed the aggressions of Henry VIII; became a reformer; entertained John Knox at Castle Campbell, Clackmannanshire, 1556; signed the first protestant engagement, 1557. [viii. 313]

CAMPBELL, ARCHIBALD, fifth EARL OF ARGYLL (1530-1573), eldest son of Archibald Campbell, fourth earl [q. v.]; styled Lord of Lorne up to 1558; a hearer of John Knox, 1556; joined in inviting Knox to return from Geneva, 1557; signed the first protestant engagement, 1557; succeeded to the earldom, August 1558; supported the queen-regent in repressing the protestant mob at Perth, May 1559, but joined Lord James Stuart and 'the lords of the congregation' in signing the protestant engagement; present at the destruction of St. Andrews Cathedral, June 1559; marched with Lord James Stuart against the queen-regent at Cupar-Fife; captured Perth and Edinburgh; brought his highlanders to fight the French garrison of Leith; asked Elizabeth's intervention, 1560, in return for a promise to help her in subduing Ireland; a commissioner to destroy popish monuments in the west, 1560; received Queen Mary at Leith, 1561, and entertained her in Argyllshire, 1563; opposed her marriage with Darnley, 1565; forced by Queen Elizabeth's non-intervention to make his peace with Mary; privy to the plot to murder Darnley, 1567; assented to Mary's marriage with Bothwell, 1567; intrigued to deliver Mary from Lochleven Castle; sentenced by the general assembly to do penance for his domestic quarrels; Mary's defeat at Langside caused by his half-hearted support, 1568; submitted to the regent Moray, 1569; intrigued for Mary's return, 1570; again submitted to the young king James VI's party, 1571; lord high chancellor, 1572. [viii. 314]

CAMPBELL, ARCHIBALD, seventh EARL OF ARGYLL (1576?-1638), eldest son of Colin Campbell, sixth earl [q. v.]; succeeded to the earldom, 1584; defeated by Huntly at Glenlivat, 1594; imprisoned at Edinburgh, 1595; reconciled to Huntly, 1603; joined Huntly in exterminating the Macgregors, 1608; embraced catholicism; subdued the Clandonalds of Kintyre, 1615; fled from his creditors into Flanders, ceding his estates to his son, 1619; attainted on account of his being in the Spanish service, 1619; restored, 1621; returned to London. [viii. 318]

CAMPBELL, ARCHIBALD, MARQUIS OF ARGYLL and eighth EARL (1598-1661), nicknamed, from his squint, 'Gillespie Grumach' and 'the glaed-eyed marquis'; eldest son of Archibald Campbell, seventh earl [q.v.]; styled **Lord** of Lorne till November 1638; fought in Kintyre, 1615; took over the estates from his father, 1619; privy councillor, 1626; extraordinary lord of session, 1634; summoned to London to advise Charles I, after the renewal of the covenant, 1638; discovered that Charles I had empowered the Earl of Antrim to invade Kintyre; succeeded to the earldom, November 1638; accepted the abolition of episcopacy by the general assembly, 1638; raised an army, took Brodick Castle, and encamped at Stirling; negotiated the peace of Berwick between the Scots and Charles I, June 1639; alienated by his continual opposition to the king from Montrose; persuaded the Scottish parliament to sit in defiance of the king's order, and to appoint an executive committee, 1640; ravaged the lands of royalist nobles in Perth, Aberdeen, and Forfar shires; imprisoned Montrose on a charge of slandering him to the king, June 1641; negotiated with the king at Edinburgh, September 1641; fled from Edinburgh, alleging that there was a plot to arrest him, October 1641; forced Charles I to accept the terms of the Scottish parliament, November 1641; intrigued to prevent Charles from getting help from Scotland, 1642; accompanied the Scottish army into England, January 1644; sent to repress Huntly's northern rising, April, and the Irish invasion of the west, July, 1644; resigned his commission, having been out-generalled by Montrose; surprised at Inverary by Montrose, and the Campbell country ravaged, December 1644; routed by Montrose at Inverlochy, February 1645, and at Kilsyth in August; recovered his influence after Montrose's defeat at Philliphaugh, September 1645; negotiated with Charles at Newcastle, May 1646, and at London with the parliament, June 1646; became head of the new executive committee and invited Cromwell to Edinburgh, October 1646; enraged at the execution of Charles I, joined in proclaiming Charles II, February 1650; consented to Montrose's execution, May 1650; joined Charles II, but did not obtain his confidence; set the crown on Charles II's head, January 1651; vainly opposed the invasion of England; was besieged at Inverary; submitted to the Commonwealth, August 1652; engaged in intrigues in London, 1656; M.P. for Aberdeenshire in the Commonwealth parliament, 1658; came to London to welcome Charles II, 1660; charged with high treason; condemned at Edinburgh and executed, May 1661. [viii. 319]

CAMPBELL, ARCHIBALD, ninth EARL OF ARGYLL (d. 1685), eldest son of Archibald Campbell, marquis and eighth earl of Argyll [q. v.]; styled Lord of Lorne till 1663; travelled in France and Italy, 1648-9; a far more energetic royalist than his father; captain of Charles II's Scottish lifeguard, 1650; fought at Dunbar; tried to raise his clan for Charles II, September 1650; joined the highland royalists, 1653; quarrelled with them and withdrew his own men, January 1654; was excepted from Cromwell's act of pardon, May 1654, and remained in arms; directed by Charles II to make his peace with Cromwell, March 1655; submitted accordingly, 1655; suspected of plotting a royalist rising, August 1656; imprisoned at Edinburgh, 1657-60; well received at Charles II's court, 1660; strong efforts made by Middleton to involve him in his father's fall, 1661; supported by Lauderdale; imprisoned, July 1661, and sentenced to death, August, but the date left in Charles II's hands; released, June 1663; sentence of death recalled; restored to earldom and heavily burdened estates, 1663; Scottish privy counsellor, 1664; disarmed covenanters in Kintyre, 1665; hated by the extreme episcopalians, who accused him of favouring the insurgents, 1666; commissioner for quieting the highlands, 1667; raised a militia regiment, 1670; was constantly enjoined to repress conventicles after 1671, and constantly urged gentler measures; extraordinary lord of session, 1674-80; at war with the McCleans of Mull, 1674-8; ordered to disarm and secure highland papists, 1679; ordered to send his highlanders to be quartered in the whig districts; opposed the arbitrary measures resorted to by James, duke of York, then high commissioner for Scotland, 1680; strongly opposed the Scottish test act, 1681; imprisoned on a charge of treason, November, sentenced to death and his estates forfeited, December 1681; escaped to London and to Holland, 1682; in treaty with the Rye House conspirators, 1683; appointed commander of the descent on Scotland, April 1685; published declaration in favour of Monmouth at Campbeltown, May, but was not joined by his clan;

H

worsted by the king's ships at Inverary; taken prisoner, June 1685; executed, without trial, at Edinburgh, in virtue of the sentence passed in 1681. [viii. 329]

CAMPBELL, ARCHIBALD, first DUKE OF ARGYLL (*d.* 1703), eldest son of Archibald Campbell, ninth earl [q. v.]; granted maintenance out of the forfeited estates, *c.* 1682; offered to resist his father's invasion, 1685; failed to obtain restoration of his title and estates by embracing catholicism; joined William of Orange at the Hague, and accompanied him to England; took his place in the Scottish convention as Earl of Argyll, March 1689; commissioner to offer the crown of Scotland to William and Mary; Scottish privy councillor, May; restored to the title and estates, June 1689; undertook to extirpate the Macdonalds of Glencoe, 1692; extraordinary lord of session, 1694; created Duke of Argyll, June 1701. [viii. 338]

CAMPBELL, ARCHIBALD (*d.* 1744), bishop of Aberdeen; said to have taken part in Argyll's invasion, 1685; withdrew to Surinam; a rigid nonjuror on his return; frequently imprisoned; consecrated bishop by three ejected Scottish bishops, 1711; resided in London; negotiated for the union of the nonjurors with the Greek church, 1717; elected bishop of Aberdeen, 1721, but resided in London; resigned, 1724, and formed a separate nonjuring community; published theological tracts. [viii. 339]

CAMPBELL, ARCHIBALD (1691–1756), theologian; educated at Edinburgh and Glasgow; minister of Larbert, 1718; a philosophical treatise by himself published fraudulently under a friend's name, 1728; professor of church history at St. Andrews, 1730; published theological treatises. [viii. 340]

CAMPBELL, ARCHIBALD, third DUKE OF ARGYLL (1682–1761), younger son of Archibald Campbell, first duke [q. v.]; styled Lord Archibald Campbell till 1705; educated at Eton and Glasgow; studied law at Utrecht; served under Marlborough; lord high treasurer of Scotland, 1705; promoted the union; created Earl of Islay, October 1705; a Scottish representative peer, 1707; extraordinary lord of session, 1708; justice-general, 1710; lord register of Scotland, 1714; raised Argyllshire for George I, 1715; fought at Sheriffmuir, 1715; overcame Scottish opposition to the malt tax, 1725, and became Walpole's chief adviser in Scotland; keeper of the privy seal, 1725, and of the great seal, 1734–61; chancellor of Aberdeen University; succeeded to the dukedom, 1743; advised the raising of highland regiments, 1746; rebuilt Inverary Castle. [viii. 341]

CAMPBELL, ARCHIBALD (1726?–1780), satirist; son of Archibald Campbell (1691–1756) [q. v.]; purser of a man-of-war; befriended William Falconer, 1745; satirised Samuel Johnson in 'Lexiphanes' and other writers in 'Sale of Authors,' 1767; died at Kingston, Jamaica. [viii. 342]

CAMPBELL, SIR ARCHIBALD (1739–1791), of Inverneil, general; captain, 1757; served in America, 1757–64, and in India till 1773, becoming lieutenant-colonel; M.P. for Stirling burghs, 1774 and 1789; prisoner of war in America, 1775; brigadier-general, 1776; captured Savannah; major-general, 1782; governor of Jamaica, and active in checking the French; K.C.B., 1785; governor of Madras, 1786–9. [viii. 342]

CAMPBELL, SIR ARCHIBALD (1769–1843), general; ensign, 1787; served in India, 1788–99, distinguishing himself at Seringapatam; captain, 1799; major, 1804; served in Portugal and in Sir John Moore's campaign, 1808; lieutenant-colonel, 1809; commanded Portuguese regiment, 1810, and Portuguese brigade, 1811–14; colonel, 1814; K.C.B., 1815; Portuguese commander at Lisbon, 1816–20; commanded regiment in India, 1821; entrusted with conduct of Burmese war; took Rangoon, May 1824; defeated Bundoola, the chief Burmese general, 1825; took Prome; made major-general; marched on Ava, December 1825; dictated terms of peace, February 1826; governor of British Burmah, 1826–9; created baronet, 1831; lieutenant-governor of New Brunswick, 1831–7; lieutenant-general, 1838. [viii. 343]

CAMPBELL, COLIN, second LORD CAMPBELL and first EARL OF ARGYLL (*d.* 1493), succeeded his grandfather in the peerage, 1453; obtained by marriage and treaty the estates and lordship of Lorne; created Earl of

Argyll, 1457; lord justiciary, 1465; lord high chancellor, 1483; joined the conspiracy against James III, 1487; envoy to England, 1488. [viii. 345]

CAMPBELL, COLIN, third EARL OF ARGYLL (*d.* 1530), eldest son of Archibald Campbell, second earl [q. v.]; succeeded to the earldom, 1513; frustrated the plans of Donald, lord of the Isles, 1513–17; became the chief power in the west highlands; one of the council of regency, 1525; took James V's side against the regent Angus, 1528; made hereditary sheriff of Argyllshire and hereditary justiciary; lord justice-general, 1529. [viii. 346]

CAMPBELL, COLIN, sixth EARL OF ARGYLL (*d.* 1584), second son of Archibald Campbell, fourth earl [q. v.]; succeeded his half-brother, Archibald Campbell, fifth earl [q. v.], 1573; compelled by the regent Morton to surrender the crown jewels, 1575; plotted with Atholl to overthrow Morton, 1578; collected an army, but came to terms; lord high chancellor, 1579; a promoter of Morton's execution, 1581; implicated in the 'raid of Ruthven' to seize James VI, 1582, and in the plot to release him, June 1583. [viii. 347]

CAMPBELL, COLIN (1644–1726), theologian; educated at St. Andrews; minister of Ardchattan, Argyllshire, 1667–1726; corresponded with Isaac Newton; wrote theological treatises. [viii. 348]

CAMPBELL, COLIN (*d.* 1729), architect; designed the Rolls House, Chancery Lane, 1717, and Drumlanrig Castle; published 'Vitruvius Britannicus,' 1717–25. [viii. 348]

CAMPBELL, COLIN (*d.* 1782), of Kilberry, Argyllshire; major in the army; cashiered for the manslaughter of Captain John McKaarg at Martinico, 1762. [viii. 349]

CAMPBELL, COLIN (1754–1814), general; ensign, 1771; lieutenant, 1774; served in North America and West Indies, 1775–95; major, 1783; lieutenant-colonel, 1795; served in Ireland, 1796–1811; at Vinegar Hill, 1798; major-general, 1811; lieutenant-general, 1811; acting governor of Gibraltar, 1811–14. [viii. 349]

CAMPBELL, SIR COLIN (1776–1847), general; ran away to sea, 1792; midshipman on an East Indiaman, 1793; militia officer, 1795; served in West Indies, 1799–1801; lieutenant, 1801; served in India, 1802–6; distinguished himself at Ahmednuggur, 1803; brigade-major at Assaye, 1803; served in Denmark, 1807, and in Portugal, 1808; major, 1808; served in the Peninsula, 1809–14; brevet lieutenant-colonel, 1810; assistant quartermaster-general, 1812; K.C.B., 1814; at Waterloo, 1815; major-general, 1825; appointed governor of Nova Scotia, 1833, and of Ceylon, 1839; returned to England, 1847. [viii. 350]

CAMPBELL, SIR COLIN, BARON CLYDE (1792–1863), field marshal; son of Colin Macliver, a Glasgow carpenter; took the name Campbell through an error of the Duke of York, 1807; ensign, 1808; served in Portugal and under Sir John Moore, 1808; at Walcheren, 1809; lieutenant, 1809; served in the Peninsula, 1810–13, displaying conspicuous courage at Barossa, 1811, San Sebastian, and the Bidassoa, 1813; captain, 1813; served in Nova Scotia, 1814, at Gibraltar, 1816, and in the West Indies, 1819–26; major, 1825; lieutenant-colonel, 1832; served in China, 1842–6; brigadier-general, 1844; served in India, 1846–53; K.C.B., 1849; major-general, 1854; commanded highland brigade at the Alma, 1854; commanded first division in Crimea, 1854–5; returned to England, having been badly treated by the authorities, 1855; lieutenant-general, 1856; D.C.L. Oxford, 1857; commander-in-chief in India, 1857–60; suppressed the Indian mutiny, 1857–8; created Baron Clyde, 1858; field-marshal, 1862; buried in Westminster Abbey. [viii. 351]

CAMPBELL, DANIEL (more correctly DONALD) (1665–1722), divine; educated at Aberdeen and Edinburgh; M.A. Aberdeen, 1686; minister of Glassary, Argyllshire, 1691–1722; published 'Sacramental Meditations,' 1698, and other devotional works. [viii. 352]

CAMPBELL, DANIEL or DONALD (1671?–1753), of Shawfield, member of parliament; a successful Glasgow merchant; M.P., Inverary, 1702; bought Shawfield, 1707; M.P., Glasgow burghs, 1716–34; Shawfield House burnt by the malt-tax mob, 1725; bought Islay, 1727. [viii. 355]

CAMPBELL, DONALD (*d.* 1562), ecclesiastic ; youngest son of Archibald Campbell, second earl of Argyll [q. v.] ; abbot of Cupar-Angus, 1526 till death ; keeper of the privy seal; lord of session, 1541 ; privy councillor, 1543 and 1547; lord of the articles, 1546 and 1554; nominated to the see of Brechin, but refused admission by the pope, 1559. [viii. 355]

CAMPBELL, DONALD (1751-1804), of Barbreck, Indian traveller ; published account of his ' Journey over land to India.' [viii. 355]

CAMPBELL, DUNCAN (1680 ?-1730), charlatan ; born in Lapland ; son of a Scottish seaman and a native; deaf and dumb ; a fortune-teller in London, 1694 ; withdrew, in debt, to Rotterdam ; returned to London ; told fortunes and sold miraculous cures; married a rich widow. Pamphlets on his life and adventures were written by Daniel Defoe, 1720-6. [viii. 356]

CAMPBELL, LORD FREDERICK (1729-1816), lord clerk register of Scotland, 1768-1816 ; M.P., Glasgow burghs, 1761-80 ; M.P., Argyllshire, 1780-99. [viii. 357]

CAMPBELL, FREDERICK WILLIAM (1782-1846), genealogist; eldest son of Donald Campbell (1751-1804) [q. v.] ; captain in the army ; compiled genealogy of the Campbells of Barbreck. [viii. 357]

CAMPBELL, GEORGE (1719-1796), theologian ; educated at Aberdeen and Edinburgh ; minister of Banchory Ternan, Aberdeenshire, 1748 ; minister of Aberdeen, 1757 ; principal of Marischal College, Aberdeen, 1759-92, and professor of divinity there, 1771-92 ; D.D., 1764 ; minister of Grey Friars, Aberdeen, 1771-92. His works include a ' Dissertation on Miracles,' 1762. [viii. 357]

CAMPBELL, GEORGE (1761-1817), poet; shoemaker at Kilmarnock ; studied at Glasgow ; minister of the secession church, Stockbridge, Berwickshire, 1794-1817 ; published ' Poems,' 1787, and ' Sermons,' 1816. [viii. 358]

CAMPBELL, SIR GEORGE (1824-1892). Indian administrator ; educated at Edinburgh New Academy, Madras College, St. Andrews, St. Andrews University, and Haileybury; went to India, 1842 ; collector at Badaon, Rohilcund, 1843 ; in England, 1851-4 ; called to bar at Inner Temple, 1854 ; magistrate and collector of Azimghur, 1854 ; assistant to John Russell Colvin [q. v.] in general government of northern provinces, 1855 ; commissioner of Cis-Sutlej states, 1855 ; served in Indian mutiny; employed by Lord Canning, governor-general, to write official account of mutiny for the home authorities, 1857 ; second civil commissioner of Oude ; judge of high court of Bengal, 1862 ; head of commission to inquire into causes of famine in Bengal, 1866 ; chief commissioner of central provinces, 1867 ; D.C.L. Oxford, 1870 ; lieutenant-governor of Bengal, 1871-4 ; K.C.S.I., 1873 ; liberal M.P. for Kirkcaldy, 1875-92. His works include 'Ethnology of India,' 1865. [Suppl. i. 383]

CAMPBELL, GEORGE DOUGLAS, eighth DUKE OF ARGYLL (1823-1900) ; succeeded his brother, John Henry (*b.* 1821), as Marquis of Lorne, 1837 ; published writings relating to the struggle in church of Scotland, 1842-8 ; succeeded to dukedom, 1847 ; F.R.S., 1851 ; chancellor of St. Andrews University, 1851 ; lord rector of Glasgow University, 1854 ; president of Royal Society of Edinburgh, 1861 ; prominent in politics as a whig ; privy seal, 1853-5, 1859-60, and 1860-6 ; postmaster-general, 1855-8 and 1860 ; secretary of state for India, 1868-74, and adopted foreign policy of friendship to neighbouring states, and financial policy of ' decentralisation '; opposed tory government's policy in Eastern question, and in Afghanistan, 1877-80 ; privy seal, 1880-1 ; opposed home rule, 1886 and 1893 ; K.T., 1856 ; D.C.L. Oxford, 1870 ; K.G., 1883. A follower of the cataclysmal school in geology, and never in agreement with the younger evolutional school, he yet exerted a useful influence on scientific progress. He published works on science, religion, and politics. [Suppl. i. 385]

CAMPBELL, SIR GUY (1786-1849), major-general ; eldest son of Colin Campbell (1754-1814) [q. v.] ; ensign, 1795 ; lieutenant, 1796 ; served in Ireland, 1798, and Canada, 1803 ; captain, 1804 ; served in Portugal and with Sir John Moore, 1808 ; major, 1813 ; served in the Peninsula, 1813 ; baronet, 1815 ; at Waterloo, 1815 ; in Ireland, 1828 ; major-general, 1841. [viii. 358]

CAMPBELL, HARRIETTE (1817-1841), novelist ; published ' The Only Daughter,' 1837, and two other novels. [viii. 359]

CAMPBELL, HUGH, third EARL OF LOUDOUN (*d.* 1731) ; succeeded to the earldom, 1684 ; Scottish privy councillor, 1697; extraordinary lord of session, 1699-1731 : joint secretary of state for Scotland, 1704 ; strongly advocated the union ; keeper of the great seal of Scotland, 1708-13 ; Scottish representative peer ; English privy councillor, 1708 ; lord-lieutenant of Ayrshire, 1715 ; fought at Sheriffmuir, 1715 ; frequently lord high commissioner to the general assembly of the kirk of Scotland. [viii. 359]

CAMPBELL, SIR ILAY (1734-1823), of Succoth, Scottish judge ; advocate, 1757 ; engaged on the Douglas peerage case, *c.* 1764-9 ; solicitor-general for Scotland, 1783 ; lord advocate, 1784 ; M.P. for Glasgow burghs, 1784 ; lord president of the court of session, 1799-1808, styled Lord Succoth; created baronet, 1808 ; published Scots law reports. [viii. 360]

CAMPBELL, SIR JAMES (1570-1642). [See CAMBELL.]

CAMPBELL, SIR JAMES (1667-1745), of Lawers, general ; lieutenant-colonel of the Scots Greys, 1708 ; at Malplaquet, 1709 ; colonel, 1717 ; M.P., Ayrshire, 1727 ; major-general, *c.* 1727 ; governor of Edinburgh Castle, 1738 ; lieutenant-general, 1742 ; knighted at Dettingen, 1743 ; killed at Fontenoy, 1745. [viii. 361]

CAMPBELL, SIR JAMES (1763-1819), of Inverneil, lieutenant-general ; ensign, 1780 ; lieutenant, 1781 ; served in America; captain, 1787 ; in India, 1787-94; major, 1794 ; served in Ireland; lieutenant-colonel, 1804; served in Sicily, 1805-13 ; major-general, 1808 ; lieutenant-general, 1813 ; governor of the Ionian islands, 1814-1816 ; G.C.H., 1817 ; created baronet, 1818. [viii. 362]

CAMPBELL, SIR JAMES (1745-1832), of Ardkinglass ; eldest son of John Callander (*d.* 1789) [q. v.] ; took the name Campbell on succeeding to the estate ; ensign, 1759 ; served with troops in Mediterranean till 1802 ; involved in a celebrated matrimonial suit ; wrote his own ' Memoirs.' [viii. 362]

CAMPBELL, SIR JAMES (1773 ?-1835), general ; captain, 1794 ; served at Minorca, 1798 ; major, 1803 ; lieutenant-colonel 1804 ; served with distinction in India, 1803-7, and the Peninsula, 1810-13 ; colonel, 1813 ; major-general, 1819 ; K.C.B., 1822. [viii. 363]

CAMPBELL, JAMES DYKES (1838-1895), biographer of Coleridge; entered house of Messrs. Cochrane & Co., manufacturers of 'Verreville pottery,' Glasgow, 1854 ; partner in Ireland, Fraser & Co.'s firm in Mauritius, 1873-1881. He spent many years in collecting materials for a biography of Coleridge, which was prefixed to an edition of Coleridge's poetical works, 1893, and appeared in a separate volume, 1894. [Suppl. i. 391]

CAMPBELL, SIR JOHN (1470-1563), of Lundy, Scottish judge ; lord of session, 1532-63 ; captain-general of foot, 1528 ; privy councillor, 1540 ; often employed as envoy by James V of Scotland. [viii. 364]

CAMPBELL, JOHN, first EARL OF LOUDOUN (1598-1663), travelled abroad ; married, 1620, the heiress of the barony of Loudoun ; in his wife's right, took his seat in the Scottish parliament, 1622 ; his patent for an earldom stopped by Charles I because of his strenuous opposition to episcopacy, 1633 ; took leading part in organising the covenant, 1637-8 ; a leader of the armed insurrection in Scotland, 1639 ; envoy from Scotland to Charles I, 1640 ; imprisoned in the Tower ; joined the Scottish army of invasion, August 1640 ; again envoy to London ; lord chancellor of Scotland, 1641-60 ; created Earl of Loudoun, 1641 ; frequently envoy to Charles I from the parliament, 1642-7 ; present at the coronation of Charles II, 1651, and fought at Dunbar ; joined the highland rising, 1653 ; submitted to Monck ; excepted from Cromwell's act of pardon, 1654 ; heavily fined by Charles II, 1662. [viii. 364]

CAMPBELL, JOHN, first EARL OF BREADALBANE (1635-1716), joined the royalist insurgents in the highlands, 1653 ; M.P. for Argyllshire, 1661 ; obtained from the bankrupt Earl of Caithness a cession of his title and estates, 1672 ; took possession of the estates, 1673 ; obtained a patent for the title, 1677; led his highlanders to be quartered on the west-country whigs, 1678 ; made war on the heir-male, who claimed the Caithness peerage, 1680 ; obtained the earldom of Breadalbane, when the privy council decided against his claim to the Caithness peerage and estates, 1681 ; privy councillor, 1685 ; submitted to William III, September 1689 ; employed to bribe the highland chiefs to submit to William III, 1690–1691 ; contrived the massacre of the Macdonalds of Glencoe, 1692 ; encouraged a French invasion, 1707 ; half-heartedly joined Mar's rising, 1715, but withdrew after Sheriffmuir. [viii. 366]

CAMPBELL, JOHN, second DUKE OF ARGYLL and DUKE OF GREENWICH (1678–1743), eldest son of Archibald Campbell, first duke [q. v.] ; entered the army, 1694 ; served in Flanders, 1702 ; succeeded to dukedom of Argyll, 1703 ; a prime agent in bringing about the union, 1705 ; created Earl of Greenwich in the English peerage, 1705 ; served with much distinction in Flanders, 1706–1709 ; lieutenant-general, 1709 ; developed bitter hostility to Marlborough, 1709 ; ambassador and commander-in-chief in Spain, 1711 ; commander-in-chief in Scotland, 1712 ; violently opposed the proposed malt tax, 1713 ; took a leading part in proclaiming George I, 1714 ; sent to suppress Mar's insurrection, 1715 ; collected troops at Stirling, secured Edinburgh, and repulsed Mar at Sheriffmuir, 1715 ; crushed the revolt, January 1716 ; deprived of his offices, 1716 ; restored, 1719 ; created Duke of Greenwich, 1719 ; helped to remove Scottish opposition to the malt tax, 1725 ; field-marshal, 1736 ; defended Edinburgh city from the indignation of the court after the Porteous riot, 1737 ; began violently to oppose Walpole, 1738 ; deprived of his offices, 1740 ; restored, 1742, but speedily resigned. [viii. 369]

CAMPBELL, JOHN (1708–1775), miscellaneous writer ; lawyer's clerk at Windsor ; highly successful as a professional man of letters in London ; LL.D. Glasgow, 1754 ; agent for Georgia, 1765–75 ; contributed much to historical and biographical series, and edited books of travel. His chief works are ' Military History of Prince Eugene,' 1736, ' Travels of ' a fictitious ' Edward Bevan,' 1739, ' Lives of the Admirals,' 1742–4, and ' Political Survey of Britain,' 1774. [viii. 373]

CAMPBELL, JOHN, third EARL OF BREADALBANE (1696–1782) ; educated at Christ Church, Oxford ; styled Viscount Glenorchy, 1716–52 ; envoy to Denmark, 1718 ; K.B., 1725 ; M.P., Saltash, 1727 and 1734 ; ambassador to Russia, 1731 ; M.P., Oxford City, 1741 ; master of the jewel office, 1746 ; succeeded to the earldom, 1752 ; Scottish representative peer, 1752 ; D.C.L. Oxford, 1756 ; a chief-justice in eyre, 1761–5 ; vice-admiral of Scotland, 1776. [viii. 375]

CAMPBELL, JOHN, fourth EARL OF LOUDOUN (1705–1782), only son of Hugh Campbell, third earl [q. v.] ; entered the army, 1727 ; succeeded to the earldom, 1731 ; Scottish representative peer, 1734–82 ; governor of Stirling Castle, 1741 ; supported George II in the highlands, 1745–6 ; commander-in-chief in America, 1756 ; superseded, 1758 ; second in command in Portugal, 1762 ; general, 1770 ; fond of forestry. [viii. 376]

CAMPBELL, JOHN (1753–1784), lieutenant-colonel ; ensign, 1771 ; lieutenant, 1774 ; served in America, 1774–1780 ; major, 1777 ; lieutenant-colonel, 1781 ; in India, 1782 ; defended Mangalore against Tippoo Sultan, May 1783–January 1784. [viii. 376]

CAMPBELL, JOHN (1720 ?–1790), vice-admiral ; apprenticed to the master of a coaster ; midshipman, 1740 ; sailed round the world with Anson : lieutenant, 1745 ; captain, 1747 ; in constant service, 1747–79 ; rear-admiral, 1778 ; vice-admiral, 1779 ; governor of Newfoundland, 1782–6. [viii. 377]

CAMPBELL, JOHN (1766–1840), philanthropist ; a founder of the Scottish Religious Tract Society ; advocated Sunday schools, lay-preaching, Magdalene societies, and abolition of slavery ; minister of an independent congregation, Kingsland, London, 1802 ; inspected the London Missionary Society's stations in South Africa, 1812–14, and 1819–21 ; published accounts of his travels. [viii. 378]

CAMPBELL, SIR JOHN (1807–1855), general ; only son of Sir Archibald Campbell (1769–1843) [q. v.] ; ensign, 1821 ; lieutenant, 1824 ; aide-de-camp in Burmah,

1824–6 ; captain, 1826 ; civil servant in Burmah, 1826–9 ; aide-de-camp in New Brunswick, 1831–7 ; lieutenant-colonel, 1840 ; baronet, 1843 ; commanded brigade in the Crimea, 1854 ; major-general, 1854 ; killed before the Redan, 1855. [viii. 378]

CAMPBELL, JOHN, first BARON CAMPBELL (1779–1861), lord chancellor ; son of the minister of Cupar-Fife ; attended arts classes at St. Andrews, 1790, and divinity classes, 1794 ; private tutor in London, 1798 ; wrote for the press ; entered Lincoln's Inn, 1800 ; parliamentary and law reporter ; read law in chambers, 1804 ; barrister, 1806 ; quickly acquired a profitable practice ; K.C., 1827 ; employed on commission on law of real property, 1828–1833 ; M.P. for Stafford, 1830 took a leading part in the Commons in matters of law reform ; solicitor-general, 1832 ; attorney-general, 1834–41 ; liberal M.P., Edinburgh, 1834–41 ; his wife made Baroness Stratheden, 1836 ; lord chancellor of Ireland, June–September 1841 ; created Baron Campbell, June 1841 ; took a foremost place in the Lords in questions of law ; chancellor of the duchy of Lancaster, 1846 ; chief-justice of the queen's bench, 1850 ; lord chancellor, 1859 ; published ' Nisi Prius Reports,' 1809–16, ' Speeches,' 1842, ' Lives of the Lord Chancellors,' 1845–7, ' Lives of the Chief-Justices,' 1849, 1857, law pamphlets, and ' Lives of Lyndhurst and Brougham,' 1869. [viii. 379]

CAMPBELL, JOHN, second MARQUIS OF BREADALBANE (1796–1862) ; styled Viscount Glenorchy till 1831 ; M.P. for Okehampton, 1820–6 ; styled Earl of Ormelie, 1831–4 ; M.P., Perthshire, 1832 ; succeeded as marquis, 1834 ; entertained Queen Victoria at Taymouth, 1842 ; a strenuous free churchman in the disruption controversy. [viii. 386]

CAMPBELL, SIR JOHN (1780–1863), soldier ; educated at Harrow ; cornet, 1800 ; captain, 1806 ; served in South America, 1807, and Spain, 1808 ; commanded a Portuguese cavalry regiment, 1809–14 ; knighted, 1815 ; military adviser of the Portuguese government, 1815–19 ; Portuguese major-general, 1820 ; English lieutenant-colonel, 1820–4 ; fought for Dom Miguel in Portugal, 1828–34 ; resided in London. [viii. 386]

CAMPBELL, JOHN (1794–1867), miscellaneous writer ; a blacksmith ; studied at St. Andrews and Glasgow ; a congregational minister in Ayrshire, and at Moorfields, London ; started the ' Christian Witness,' 1844, and other newspapers ; published much on missions, ritualism, &c. [viii. 387]

CAMPBELL, SIR JOHN (1802–1878), of Lochend, Indian official : ensign, 1819 ; an officer in the East India Company's forces, 1820–37 ; captain, 1830 ; magistrate over the Khonds of Orissa, 1837–42 ; served in China, 1842 ; lieutenant-colonel, 1842 ; held command in Madras, 1842–7 ; reappointed magistrate over the Khonds, 1847–9 ; colonel, 1853 ; major-general, 1859 ; published narrative of affairs in Orissa, 1864 ; K.C.S.I., 1866 ; general, 1872. [viii. 387]

CAMPBELL, JOHN FRANCIS (1822–1885), of Islay ; Gaelic scholar ; educated at Eton and Edinburgh ; a government official ; published ' Popular Tales of the West Highlands,' 1860–2 ; published Gaelic texts, 1872 ; wrote also on natural science. [viii. 388]

CAMPBELL, JOHN McLEOD (1800–1872), theologian ; educated at Glasgow, 1811–20, and Edinburgh, 1821 ; licentiate of the church of Scotland, 1821 ; minister of Row, Dumbartonshire, 1825 ; ejected for heresy, 1830 ; preached in the highlands, 1830–2 ; minister of a congregation in Glasgow, 1833–59 ; D.D. Glasgow, 1868 ; retired to Roseneath, 1870 ; published ' Sermons,' 1832, and theological tracts. [viii. 388]

CAMPBELL, NEIL (d. 1627), Scottish bishop ; parson of Kilmartin, Argyllshire, 1574 ; bishop of Argyll, 1606–8. [viii. 389]

CAMPBELL, SIR NEIL (1776–1827), general ; ensign, 1797 ; lieutenant, 1799 ; major, 1805 ; stationed in the West Indies, 1798–1800 ; in home garrisons, 1800–6 ; in the West Indies, 1806–10 ; lieutenant-colonel, 1808 ; colonel of Portuguese infantry, 1811–13 ; military attaché with the Russian army invading France, 1813–14 ; colonel, 1814 ; escorted Napoleon to Elba ; served at Waterloo ; major-general, 1825 ; governor of Sierra Leone, 1826. [viii. 389]

CAMPBELL, Sir PATRICK (1773–1841), of Melfort, naval officer; lieutenant, 1794; captain, 1800; on active service, 1799–1815 and 1827–30; rear-admiral, 1830; naval commander at Cape Town, 1834–7; K.C.B., 1836; vice-admiral, 1838. [viii. 390]

CAMPBELL, ROBERT (*d.* 1722), presbyterian; native of Scotland; presbyterian minister at Ray, Donegal, 1671; imprisoned, 1681–2; minister at Roseneath, Dumbartonshire, 1689–91; and then again at Ray, 1691–1722; published sermons. [viii. 391]

CAMPBELL, ROBERT CALDER (1798–1857), miscellaneous writer; cadet in the East India Company's service, 1817; captain, 1826; served in Burmah, 1826–7; invalided home, 1831; settled in London; major, 1836; published verse and prose, 1831–57. [viii. 391]

CAMPBELL, THOMAS (1733–1795), miscellaneous writer; M.A. Trinity College, Dublin, 1761; curate of Clogher, 1761–72; chancellor of St. Macartin's, Clogher, 1773; published works on Irish topography and history; wrote a diary of his visits to England, 1775–92. [viii. 392]

CAMPBELL, THOMAS (1777–1844), poet; son of a ruined Glasgow merchant; at Glasgow University. 1791–1796; tutor in Mull, 1795, and Argyllshire, 1796; settled in Edinburgh as law-clerk and tutor; published 'Pleasures of Hope,' 1799; travelled in Germany and Denmark, June 1800–March 1801; well received in London, 1801; returned to Edinburgh; resided in or near London, as a man of letters, 1804–44; pensioned by the crown, 1805; issued ' Poems,' 1805; visited Paris, 1814; published 'Specimens of the British Poets,' 1819; edited the ' New Monthly Magazine,' 1820–30; advocated a university for London, 1825; lord rector of Glasgow University, 1826–9; visited Algiers 1835; died at Boulogne; buried in Westminster Abbey. [viii. 392]

CAMPBELL, THOMAS (1790–1858), sculptor in bronze and marble; apprenticed to an Edinburgh marble-cutter; studied in London and (1818) at Rome; exhibited at the Royal Academy, 1827–57. [viii. 396]

CAMPBELL, WILLIAM (*d.* 1805), presbyterian; a native of Newry, co. Down; entered Glasgow University, 1744; licensed by Armagh presbytery, 1750; tutor in France; returned to Ireland, 1758; minister at Antrim, 1759; minister of First Armagh, 1764–89; D.D. Glasgow, 1784; minister at Clonmel, 1789–1805; published pamphlets. [viii. 397]

CAMPBELL, WILLIELMA, Viscountess Glenorchy (1741–1786), a daughter of William Maxwell of Preston, Kirkcudbrightshire; married, 1761, John Campbell, viscount Glenorchy (*d.* 1771); adopted peculiar religious views, *c.* 1764; founded chapels for her followers in Edinburgh, Carlisle, Matlock, Strathfillan. [viii. 397]

CAMPDEN, Viscounts. [See Hicks, Baptist, first Viscount, 1551–1629; Noel, Edward, second Viscount, 1582–1643; Noel, Baptist, third Viscount, 1611–1682.]

CAMPEGGIO, LORENZO (1472–1539), papal legate; born at Bologna; studied law at Pavia and Bologna; ordained after his wife's death; bishop of Feltri, 1512; cardinal, 1517; legate to Henry VIII to urge a crusade against the Turks, 1518; bishop of Salisbury, 1524–34; archbishop of Bologna; legate to England to hear Henry VIII's suit to divorce Queen Catherine, October 1528–July 1529. [viii. 398]

CAMPION, EDMUND (1540–1581), jesuit martyr; son of a London bookseller; educated at Christ's Hospital; delivered a speech at Queen Mary's state entry to London, 1553; fellow of St. John's College, Oxford, 1557; M.A., 1564; a speaker at Queen Elizabeth's state visit to Oxford, 1566; patronised by the Earl of Leicester; Anglican deacon, *c.* 1568; junior proctor, April 1568–April 1569; asked B.D. 1569, but did not obtain it; withdrew to Dublin, 1569, expecting promotion in the projected Romanist college; withdrew, as a suspected papist, to London, June 1571; went to Douay, and graduated B.D. there; went to Rome, 1573; joined the jesuits, 1573; passed his novitiate in Prague and Brünn; ordained priest, 1578; chosen, with Robert Parsons, to coerce temporising catholics in England; reached Dover, June 1580; preached privately in London; his ' Decem Rationes' distributed at Oxford, 1581; arrested at Lyford,

Berkshire, 1581; sent to the Tower; examined, under torture, 1581; sentenced to death; executed, 1 Dec. 1581; published controversial works. [viii. 398]

CAMPION, GEORGE B. (1796–1870), water-colour painter; exhibited in London, 1834 onwards; drawing-master at Woolwich; retired to Munich. [viii. 403]

CAMPION, MARIA (1777–1803). [See Pope.]

CAMPION, THOMAS (*d.* 1620), poet and musician; probably educated abroad; mentioned as 'doctor in phisicke,' 1607, and 'physician,' 1616; published Latin verses, 1595, and 'Observations on . . . English Poesie,' 1602; prepared masques presented at court, 1607–17; published ' Books of Ayres,' 1610, 1612, 'Songs' on the death of Prince Henry, and a musical treatise, 1613. [viii. 403]

CAMPION, *alias* Wigmore, WILLIAM (1599–1665), jesuit; joined the jesuits, 1624; missioner in England, and in Wales, 1655; rector of a seminary in Ghent; wrote on transubstantiation. [viii. 404]

CAMVILLE, GERARD DE (*d.* 1215 ?), judge; adhered to Prince John; became, by marriage, sheriff of Lincolnshire, and keeper of Lincoln Castle, *c.* 1190; his removal vainly attempted by Richard I's vicegerents, 1191; removed and fined, on Richard's return, 1194; restored by King John, 1199; justice itinerant for Cambridgeshire, 1209. [viii. 404]

CAMVILLE, THOMAS DE (*d.* 1235), judge; deprived by John of estates in Kent and Essex, 1215; restored, 1217; acted as a justice, 1229. [viii. 404]

CANADA, Viscount (1567 ?–1640). [See Alexander, Sir William.]

CANCELLAR, JAMES (*fl.* 1564), theologian; of the queen's chapel; published devotional treatises, 1553–64. [viii. 405]

CANDIDUS, HUGH (*fl.* 1107 ?–1155 ?). [See Hugh.]

CANDISH. [See Cavendish.]

CANDLER, ANN (1740–1814), versifier, ' the Suffolk cottager '; daughter of a Suffolk glover named More; married a militia-man, 1762; lived in the workhouse, 1780 and 1783; wrote verses, 1785–9; her collected verses published, 1803. [viii. 405]

CANDLISH, ROBERT SMITH (1806–1873), Free church leader; educated at Glasgow; assistant minister in Glasgow, at Bonhill, Dumbartonshire, and (1833) at St. George's, Edinburgh; minister of St. George's; from 1839 took a leading part against the authority of the civil courts in patronage cases; suggested as professor of biblical criticism in Edinburgh, but objected to by Lord Aberdeen; D.D. Princeton, 1841; went out at the disruption, 1843; minister of Free St. George's till death; leader of the Free church; principal of the Free church college, Edinburgh, 1862; D.D. Edinburgh, 1865; wrote theological treatises. [viii. 405]

CANE, ROBERT (1807–1858), writer on Irish history; a chemist's assistant; M.D. Trinity College, Dublin, 1836; practised medicine at Kilkenny. [viii. 408]

CANES, VINCENT (*d.* 1672), Franciscan friar, named in religion John-Baptist; studied at Cambridge; travelled on the continent; joined the Franciscans at Douay; served on the English mission, 1648, in Lancashire and London; published controversial tracts under the initials J. V. C., 1655–72. [viii. 408]

CANFIELD, BENEDICT (1563–1611), Capuchin friar; really William Fitch, of Little Canfield, Essex; of the Middle Temple; withdrew to Douay; joined the Capuchins at Paris; came to England, 1589; imprisoned for three years; master of the novices at Rouen; wrote devotional works. [viii. 409]

CANICUS or **KENNY**, Saint (*d.* 598 ?). [See Cainnech.]

CANN, ABRAHAM (1794–1864), champion wrestler of Devonshire; fought a drawn match with the Cornish champion, 1826; afterwards an innkeeper. [viii. 410]

CANNE, JOHN (*d.* 1667?), theologian; pastor of an independent congregation in London; pastor of the English independents in Amsterdam, 1630–47; visited England, 1640; published a reference bible, 1647; returned to

England, 1648; garrison chaplain at Hull, 1650, and in fierce controversy with his colleague, John Shawe; expelled, 1657; came to London; returned to Amsterdam; published 'Bible with Marginal Notes,' 1664; published other theological and controversial works. [viii. 411]

CANNERA or **CAINNER**, SAINT (d. 530 ?), an Irishwoman; anchorite; wished to join the monastery of St. Senan, on Inis-cathey, but was refused. [viii. 413]

CANNING, CHARLES JOHN, EARL CANNING (1812–1862), governor-general of India; third son of George Canning [q. v.]; educated at Eton, and, 1829–33, at Christ Church, Oxford; M.P., Warwick, 1836; succeeded as Viscount Canning in the Irish peerage, 1837; under-secretary for foreign affairs, 1841–6; attached himself to Sir Robert Peel; postmaster-general, 1853–5; assumed the governor-generalship of India, February 1856; confronted by three difficulties: (i.) war with Persia, to restore Herat to Afghanistan, with the question of subsidising the ameer, (ii.) the assimilation of the terms of service of the Bengal native army with those of the Bombay and Madras armies, especially as regards service oversea, (iii) the settlement of Oudh (annexed, 7 Feb. 1856); his second year marked by the outbreak of the mutiny, February 1857, the wide extent of which he, like other officials, was slow to apprehend; by a happy instinct, gave full freedom of action to Sir Henry Lawrence in Oudh, and John Lawrence in the Punjab, and showed unshaken confidence throughout; involved in a controversy with Lord Ellenborough about the terms of settlement in Oudh, 1858; created earl, 1859; engaged in reorganising the financial, legal, and administrative systems in India, 1859–62. [viii. 414]

CANNING, ELIZABETH (1734–1773), impostor; a sawyer's daughter; maid-servant in Aldermanbury; falsely asserted that she had been kidnapped and kept prisoner by a procuress, 1–29 Jan. 1753; examined before Henry Fielding; secured the conviction of the people she accused; tried for perjury and transported, 1754. Her case led to a war of pamphlets and London public opinion. [viii. 418]

CANNING, GEORGE (1770–1827), statesman; son of a barrister; brought up by an uncle, a whig banker in London; educated at Eton, and, 1788–91, at Christ Church, Oxford; entered Lincoln's Inn, 1791; in horror of the French revolution attached himself to William Pitt, 1793; M.P., Newport, 1794; M.P., Wendover, 1797; under-secretary for foreign affairs in Pitt's administration, 1796–9; member of the India board, 1799–1800; paymaster-general, 1800–1; opposed Henry Addington's administration, 1801–4; treasurer of the navy in Pitt's administration, May 1804–February 1806; refused office in Grenville's administration; foreign secretary in Portland's administration, March 1807; planned seizure of Danish fleet, September 1807; dissatisfied with Castlereagh's policy at the war office, 1808; fought duel with Castlereagh, and resigned office, September 1809; refused office under Spencer Perceval, November 1809; refused the foreign office under Lord Liverpool, May 1812; M.P., Liverpool, 1812–22; visited Portugal and the south of France, 1814–16; designated ambassador extraordinary to Portugal, 1814; joined Lord Liverpool's administration as president of the India board, June 1816; resigned, January 1821, as favouring Queen Caroline; wintered abroad, 1821–2; nominated governor-general of India, 27 March, but resigned, September 1822; M.P., Harwich, 1822; foreign secretary in Lord Liverpool's administration, September 1822; acknowledged independence of Spain's American colonies, 1823; shielded Greece from conquest by Turkey, 1825–7; supported the popular party in Portugal against absolutism, 1826–7; on Lord Liverpool's death, made premier by George IV, and chancellor of the exchequer, April 1827; endeavoured to reform the corn-laws; friend and correspondent of Sir Walter Scott. His 'Poems' were published, 1823, and his 'Speeches,' 1828. [viii. 420]

CANNING, RICHARD (1708–1775), Suffolk antiquary; at Westminster School, 1723; M.A. St. Catharine's College, Cambridge, 1735; rector of Harkstead, Suffolk, 1738–69; rector of Freston, Suffolk, 1755–75; published sermons, pamphlets, a history of Suffolk, and Ipswich collections. [viii. 431]

CANNING, STRATFORD, first VISCOUNT STRATFORD DE REDCLIFFE (1786–1880), diplomatist, styled 'the Great Elchi,' i.e. ambassador *par excellence*; educated at Eton, 1794, and King's College, Cambridge, 1805; clerk in the foreign office, 1807; second secretary to the envoy to Denmark, 1807; secretary to the envoy to Constantinople, 1808; left in charge of the embassy at Constantinople, 1810, to counteract Napoleon's influence, to protect British interests in the Levant, and to prevent war between Russia and Turkey, so as to leave Russia free to fight Napoleon; negotiated the treaty of Bucharest between Russia and Turkey, May 1812; returned to London; pensioned; visited Paris, 1814; plenipotentiary to Switzerland, 1814–20, to settle federal government there; his arrangements sanctioned by the congress of Vienna, 1815; envoy to Washington, 1820–4, but failed to obtain settlement of disputed points; envoy to St. Petersburg to settle the Alaska boundary and discuss the Greek question, 1824; envoy to Constantinople to obtain recognition of Greek independence, 1825; his mediation on behalf of Greece followed by the joint intervention of Great Britain, France, and Russia 1827, but negotiations broken off by the battle of Navarino, October 1827; withdrew to Corfu, and to London, February 1828; negotiated the settlement of Greek affairs at Poros, with the French and Russian envoys, December 1828; M.P., Old Sarum, 1828; resigned his ambassadorship, 1829; G.C.B., December 1829; M.P., Stockbridge, by purchase, 1830; drew up the British case in the American boundary dispute, 1830; sent to Constantinople to obtain enlargement of the Greek frontier, November 1831; fruitlessly advised Palmerston to support the sultan against the viceroy of Egypt, 1832; failed to reconcile the rival parties in Portugal, 1832; named envoy to St. Petersburg, 1833, but the czar refused to receive him; declined governorship of Canada, 1835 and 1841; M.P., King's Lynn, 1835–41; ambassador at Constantinople, 1842; obtained abolition of execution for apostasy, 1844; obtained permission for Sir Henry Layard to explore Nineveh; home on leave, 1846–7; envoy to Switzerland, November 1847; returned to Constantinople, 1848; encouraged Turkey to protect the refugees from Hungary; visited England 1852; created Viscount Stratford de Redcliffe, May 1852; advised the sultan to refuse the czar's demands for a protectorate over the Greek church, 1853; visited the Crimea, 1855; resigned his ambassadorship, 1858; hon. D.C.L. Oxford, 1858; K.G., 1869; published verses and pamphlets. A statue of him was placed in Westminster Abbey. [viii. 431]

CANNON, RICHARD (1779–1865), historian; clerk at the Horse Guards, 1802–54; chief compiler of the incomplete official statement of the services of the several regiments, 'Historical Records of the British Army,' 1836–53. [viii. 444]

CANNON, ROBERT (1663–1722), ecclesiastic; educated at Eton; fellow of King's College, Cambridge; B.A., 1685; D.D., 1707; married the bishop of Ely's daughter; a pluralist in rectories and prebends; dean of Lincoln, 1721; wrote controversial tracts. [viii. 445]

CANON or **CANONICUS**, JOHN (fl. 1329), schoolman; studied at Oxford; joined the Franciscans; studied at Paris; returned to Oxford and graduated D.D.; wrote commentaries on the 'Sentences' of Peter Lombard. His commentary on the 'Physics' of Aristotle, printed 1475, and often afterwards, was a favourite mediæval text-work. [viii. 445]

CANOT, PETER CHARLES (1710–1777), line-engraver; came from France to London, 1740; a member of the Society of Artists, 1766, and an associate of the Royal Academy, 1770. [viii. 446]

CANSFIELD, BENEDICT (1563–1611). [See CANFIELD.]

CANT, ANDREW (1590 ?–1663), covenanting leader; invited by the people to be minister of Edinburgh, but rejected by James I, c. 1623; minister of Pitsligo, Aberdeenshire, 1633; fruitlessly endeavoured to persuade the university and clergy of Aberdeen to adopt the covenant, July 1638; member of the Glasgow general assembly which abolished episcopacy, 1638; minister of Newbattle, Midlothian; chaplain to the Scottish army, 1640; minister of Aberdeen, 1640; courageously advocated monarchy in the time of Cromwell. [viii. 446]

CANTEBRIG or **CAMBRIDGE**, JOHN DE (d. 1335), judge; a large landowner near Cambridge; M.P.,

Cambridgeshire from 1321; king's serjeant, 1330; knighted, October 1330; justice of common pleas, 1331. [viii. 447]

CANTELUPE, CANTILUPE, CANTELO, or **CAN-TELEO,** FULK DE (*fl.* 1209), adherent of King John; sent to expel the monks of Canterbury and to administer the archiepiscopal estates, 1207. [viii. 447]

CANTELUPE, GEORGE DE (*d.* 1273), styled BARON OF BERGAVENNY; son of William, the third baron Cantelupe by tenure (*d.* 1254) [q. v.] and Eva, co-heiress of William de Braose; knighted, 1272; put in possession of his estates, April 1273. [viii. 447]

CANTELUPE, NICHOLAS DE, third BARON CANTE-LUPE by writ (*d.* 1355), lord of Gresley, Nottinghamshire; with Edward II in Scotland, 1320; knighted, 1326; governor of Berwick-on-Tweed, 1336; summoned to parliament, 1337–54; served in Scotland and Flanders, 1339; envoy to France, 1343; attended Edward III at Crecy, 1346; commissioner to defend Lincolnshire, 1352; founded a chantry in Lincoln Cathedral and a Carthusian house in Nottinghamshire. [viii. 447]

CANTELUPE, ROGER DE (*fl.* 1248), legist; adherent of Henry III; envoy to Rome, 1231; perhaps prebendary of St. Paul's, 1248. [viii. 447]

CANTELUPE, SIMON, called LE NORMAN (*d.* 1249), chancellor; envoy to Rome, 1238; archdeacon of Norwich, 1238–40; chancellor, August 1238, but removed for opposing wool tax, 1239. [viii. 447]

CANTELUPE, THOMAS DE (1218?–1282), saint; bishop of Hereford; son of William de Cantelupe, second baron [q. v.]; nephew of Walter de Cantelupe [q. v.], bishop of Worcester; studied possibly at Oxford, 1237, afterwards at Paris; attended council of Lyons, 1245, and obtained papal dispensation to hold benefices in plurality; studied civil law at Orleans and canon law at Paris; taught canon law at Oxford; chancellor of Oxford University, 1262–3; stated the case of the revolted barons before St. Louis at Amiens, 1263–4; lord chancellor of England, February–August 1265; pensioned by Henry III, March 1265, but took refuge at Paris in August; lectured in theology at Paris, and, 1272, at Oxford; possibly again chancellor of Oxford University; prebendary of Hereford, 1273, in a place claimed by Peter de Langona; held several canonries and rich rectories, especially in Herefordshire, in plurality; attended council at Lyons, 1274; elected bishop of Hereford, June, and consecrated, September 1275; chief supporter of Edward I and opponent of Llewelyn of Wales; a bitter enemy of the Jews; active in reforming diocese of Hereford, and in maintaining claims of see against Earl Gilbert of Gloucester, 1278, Lord Corbet, and the bishops of St. Asaph and St. David's; led the opposition to Archbishop Peckham in the council at Reading, July 1279; involved in a bitter dispute with Peckham regarding jurisdiction; withdrew for safety to Normandy, and appealed against Peckham to Rome, *c.* 1281; vigorously sued at Rome for the prebend of Hereford by Peter de Langona, 1281; tried to bribe the curia; excommunicated by Peckham through a dispute as to jurisdiction; appealed to Rome; went in person to Italy to press his appeal, March 1282; died at Orvieto, August; buried in Hereford Cathedral; translated to a new tomb there, 1287; miracles worked at his tomb; popularly accepted as a saint; the pope urged to canonise him, 1290, 1299, 1305; canonised by Pope John XXII as St. Thomas of Hereford, 1320. [viii. 448]

CANTELUPE, WALTER DE (*d.* 1266), bishop of Worcester; defender of English liberties against the encroachments of the crown and the papacy; second son of William, first baron Cantelupe [q. v.]; pluralist, while still in minor orders; at Rome, 1229; justice itinerant, 1231; elected bishop of Worcester, 1236; ordained deacon and priest, and consecrated bishop at Viterbo, May 1237; enthroned, October 1237; defended pluralities against the papal legate, Otho, at the council of St. Paul's, 1237; laboured earnestly to reform his diocese; mediated between Bishop Grosseteste and the chapter of Lincoln, 1239; escorted Otho as far as Burgundy, 1241; urged Henry III to accept William de Raleigh as bishop of Winchester; accompanied Archbishop Boniface to the papal court at Lyons, 1245; promised to join the crusaders, 1247; again at Lyons, 1250; a second time vowed to go on crusade, 1250; resisted Archbishop Boni-

face's claim of the right of visitation, 1251, and the pope's demand of a tenth for Henry III, 1252; joined in excommunicating the infringers of Magna Charta, 1253; went with Henry III to Gascony, 1253, and was sent as envoy to Castile; resisted demand for an aid for the pope and Henry III, 1255; envoy to France, 1257; a representative of the barons on the committee of regency ('provisions of Oxford'), 1258; aided Prince Edward's escape from Bristol, 1264; encouraged the barons at Lewes, 1264, and Evesham, 1265; suspended by Ottoboni and summoned to Rome; died before starting, and was buried in Worcester Cathedral. [viii. 452]

CANTELUPE, WILLIAM DE, first BARON CANTE-LUPE (*d.* 1239), a constant adherent of King John; steward of the household; sheriff of Warwick, Leicester, Worcester, and Hereford for John; justiciar, 1203; attached himself to Henry III, 1216; sheriff of Warwick and Leicester; justice itinerant in Bedfordshire, 1218; a witness to the confirmation of Magna Charta, 1236; founder of Studley Hospital. [viii. 454]

CANTELUPE, WILLIAM DE, second BARON CANTE-LUPE (*d.* 1251), son of William de Cantelupe, first baron [q. v.]; an adherent of King John and of Henry III; steward of the household to Henry III; envoy to the papal court at Lyons, 1245. [viii. 454]

CANTELUPE, WILLIAM DE, third BARON CANTE-LUPE (*d.* 1254), son of William de Cantelupe, second baron [q. v.]; obtained by marriage the honour of Bergavenny; accompanied Henry III to Gascony, 1253. [viii. 455]

CANTERBURY, VISCOUNTS. [See MANNERS-SUT-TON, CHARLES, first VISCOUNT, 1780–1845; MANNERS-SUTTON, JOHN HENRY THOMAS, third VISCOUNT, 1814–1877.]

CANTILLON, RICHARD (*d.* 1734), economist; of Irish extraction; merchant in London and Paris; said to have helped John Law to float his paper-money scheme in Paris, 1716; returned to London; murdered by his cook. His 'Essai sur la Nature du Commerce' (published, 1755), contains striking anticipations of later theories. [viii. 455]

CANTON, JOHN (1718–1772), electrician; a weaver's apprentice; went to London, 1737, and taught school there; conducted valuable experiments in electricity and magnetism; F.R.S., 1749. [viii. 456]

CANTRELL, HENRY (1685?–1773), controversialist; educated at Derby grammar school; M.A. Emmanuel College, Cambridge, 1710; incumbent of St. Alkmund's, Derby, 1712–73; wrote against lay-baptism. [viii. 457]

CANTWELL, ANDREW (*d.* 1764), physician; of Irish birth; graduated in medicine at Montpellier, 1729; migrated to Paris, 1733; M.D. Paris, 1742, and professor of surgery, 1750, and of pharmacy, 1762; a bitter opponent of inoculation against small-pox; visited England; wrote on medical subjects. [viii. 457]

CANUTE or **CNUT** (994?–1035), called 'the Great,' king of the English, Danes, and Norwegians; son of Sweyn, king of the Danes; a pagan in childhood; baptised, *c.* 1000; accompanied Sweyn in his invasion of England, 1013; acknowledged as king of England by the invaders on Sweyn's death, near Gainsborough, February 1014; outlawed, the witan having recalled Æthelred from Normandy; withdrew before the forces of Æthelred, 1014, to Sandwich in Kent, where he mutilated his English hostages, and thence to Denmark; soon supplanted his brother Harold, who had been (1014) acknowledged king of Denmark; made war on the Slavs on the south coast of the Baltic; openly resisted by Olaf Haroldsson, who was made king of Norway, 1014–15; ravaged Wessex, 1015, and Warwickshire, 1016; marched to York, and received the submission of Northumbria; fruitlessly besieged London, May 1016; suffered defeat in Kent, but routed Eadmund, Æthelred's successor, at Assandun (? Ashington, Essex); followed Eadmund into Gloucestershire, and, by the treaty of Olney Isle, arranged that Eadmund should have Wessex, and probably East Anglia, whi e he himself ruled the north; wintered at London; chosen by the witan at London, 1017, king of all England, after the murder of Eadmund (1016); married Emma or Ælfgifu, Æthelred's widow, arranging that if a son were born to her he should succeed to the crown, excluding Cnut's sons, Harold and

Sweyn, by Ælfgifu [q. v.]; levied a large subsidy, 1018; paid and dismissed his Danish forces; held a gemot at Oxford, where he vowed to rule justly; visited Denmark, 1019, and fought against the Wends; returned to England, 1020, and courted English favour, by benefactions to many monasteries and honours to English saints; fought in Wihtland, Esthonia, 1022; demanded the submission of Olaf of Norway; was defeated by the Norse and Swedes in the Helga river; crushed a rising in Denmark, 1026; visited Rome, 1027, and was present at the coronation of the Emperor Conrad, with whom he agreed to make the river Eider the boundary between Denmark and Germany; invaded Scotland, c. 1027; reconquered Norway, 1028; sent his son Sweyn to govern Norway, 1030, and his son Harthacnut to govern Denmark; benefactor to the church; died at Shaftesbury, and was buried at Winchester; bequeathed England and Denmark to Harthacnut, and Norway to Sweyn. [ix. 1]

CANUTE, ROBERT (*fl.* 1170). [See ROBERT OF CRICKLADE.]

CANVANE, PETER (1720–1786), introducer of castor oil into British pharmacy; born in America; studied medicine at Leyden and Rheims; L.C.P. London, 1744; practised at St. Kitts, West Indies, and afterwards at Bath; withdrew to Brussels. [ix. 8]

CANYNGES, WILLIAM (1399?–1474), merchant and five times mayor of Bristol (1441, 1449, 1457, 1461, 1466); brought up by his stepfather, a Bristol merchant, 1405; traded with Iceland and Finmark, 1450; M.P., Bristol, 1451 and 1455; supported the Yorkists and Edward IV; rebuilt St. Mary Redcliffe, Bristol, and the college at Westbury; became a monk at Westbury, 1467, and dean of the college, 1469. [ix. 8]

CAPE, WILLIAM TIMOTHY (1806–1863), Australian colonist; educated at Merchant Taylors' School; taken to Tasmania by his father, 1821, and to Sydney, 1822; assistant to his father in Sydney public school; head-master, 1829; kept private school, 1830; headmaster of Sydney College, 1835–42; kept private school, 1842–55; member of New South Wales legislature, 1859; magistrate; died in London while on a visit. [ix. 10]

CAPEL, ARTHUR, first BARON CAPEL OF HADHAM (1610?–1649), royalist leader; a Hertfordshire squire; M.P. for Hertfordshire in the Short parliament, 1640, and the Long parliament, 1640; attached himself to the court party; created Baron Capel of Hadham, 1641; attended Charles I to York, January 1642; his estates confiscated by parliament, 1643; the king's lieutenant-general in Shropshire, Cheshire, and North Wales, 1643; appointed to attend the Prince of Wales; commissioner for Charles I at Uxbridge, 1645; escorted the queen to Paris, 1646; withdrew to Jersey; obtained leave to reside in Hertfordshire; aided Charles I's escape from Hampton Court, November 1647; joined the insurgents of 1648; surrendered at Colchester, August 1648; escaped from the Tower; re-arrested; condemned by the parliament, 1649, and beheaded. [ix. 10]

CAPEL, ARTHUR, EARL OF ESSEX (1631–1683), eldest son of Arthur Capel, first baron Capel of Hadham [q. v.]; fought in the king's army, 1643; succeeded to barony, 1649; lord-lieutenant of Hertfordshire, 1660; created Earl of Essex, April 1661; opposed Charles II's endeavours to obtain arbitrary power and leanings towards catholicism; travelled in France, 1667; lord-lieutenant of Wiltshire, 1668; envoy to Denmark, 1670; lord-lieutenant of Ireland, 1672; hated by the king's favourites for opposing grants to them; recalled, April 1677; joined the opponents of Danby, 1678; accepted the 'Popish plot' story; first lord of the treasury, March to November 1679; joined Shaftesbury in advocating the Exclusion Bill, 1680; petitioned Charles II against holding the parliament at Oxford, 1681; spoke bitterly against the popish peers; associated himself with Monmouth's schemes, 1682; his share in them betrayed by Lord Howard of Escrick; sent to the Tower; found with his throat cut, July 1683, having probably committed suicide, though many thought him assassinated by order of the court. His extensive correspondence is preserved in the British Museum Library. [ix. 12]

CAPEL, SIR HENRY, BARON CAPEL OF TEWKESBURY (*d.* 1696), second son of Arthur Capel, first baron Capel of Hadham [q. v.]; K.B., 1661; a commissioner of the admiralty, 1679–80; supported the Exclusion Bill in the Commons, 1680; a commissioner of the treasury, 1689 and 1692; created Baron Capel of Tewkesbury, 1692; lord justice in Ireland, 1693; lord deputy, May 1695; induced the Irish parliament to annul James II's acts. [ix. 17]

CAPEL, RICHARD (1586–1656), puritan; demy of Magdalen College, Oxford, 1604; M.A., 1607; fellow, 1608–14; chaplain to Carr, earl of Somerset, 1613; rector of Eastington, Gloucestershire, 1613; resigned, declining to read in his church the 'Book of Sports,' 1633; licensed to practise physic; puritan preacher, 1641; published sermons and tracts. [ix. 17]

CAPEL, SIR THOMAS BLADEN (1776–1853), admiral; put on the navy books, 1782; in active service, 1792–1837; lieutenant, 1797; fought at the battle of the Nile, 1797; captain, 1798; at Trafalgar, 1805; rear-admiral, 1825; K.C.B., 1832; commander-in-chief in East Indies, 1834–7; admiral, 1847. [ix. 18]

CAPEL, WILLIAM, third EARL OF ESSEX (1697–1743), succeeded to earldom, 1709; gentleman of the bedchamber to George, prince of Wales, 1718, and to George II, 1727; lord-lieutenant of Hertfordshire, 1727; envoy to Turin, 1731–6; K.G., 1738. [ix. 19]

CAPELL, EDWARD (1713–1781), Shakespearean commentator; educated at Cambridge; deputy-inspector of plays, 1737; published a text of Shakespeare, 10 vols. 1768; began to publish his commentary, 1774; bequeathed part of his library to Trinity College, Cambridge. His commentary appeared (3 vols.) in 1783. [ix. 19]

CAPELL-CONINGSBY, CATHERINE, COUNTESS OF ESSEX (1794–1882). [See STEPHENS, CATHERINE.]

CAPELLANUS, JOHN (*fl.* 1410?), real name JOHN WALTON; translated into English verse Boethius's 'De Consolatione Philosophiæ.' [ix. 20]

CAPERN, EDWARD (1819–1894), 'the rural postman of Bideford'; employed in lace factory at Tiverton; rural letter carrier at Bideford, 1847; published by subscription, 1856, his 'Poems,' which attracted much favourable attention; subsequently published verses. [Suppl. i. 393]

CAPGRAVE, JOHN (1393–1464), theologian and historian; studied perhaps at Cambridge; an Augustinian friar; resided most of his life in the friary at Lynn; ordained priest, c. 1418; D.D., possibly of Oxford; visited Rome; a client of Humphrey, duke of Gloucester; provincial of the Augustinian friars, 1456; wrote in Latin sermons, theological tracts, and commentaries on many books of scripture. His chief Latin historical works are 'Nova Legenda Angliæ,' 'De illustribus Henricis,' and 'Vita Humfredi Ducis Glocestriæ.' In English he wrote lives of St. Gilbert of Sempringham and of St. Katharine, also a chronicle of English history extending to A.D. 1417. [ix. 20]

CAPON, JOHN, *alias* SALCOT (*d.* 1557), bishop of Salisbury; Benedictine monk; B.A. Cambridge, 1488; prior of St. John's Abbey, Colchester; D.D. Cambridge, 1515; preached at court, 1516–17; abbot of St. Benet's Hulme, Norfolk; client of Cardinal Wolsey; solicited Cambridge University for a decree in favour of Henry VIII's divorce, 1530; abbot of Hyde, near Winchester, 1530–9; nominated bishop of Bangor, 1533; consecrated, 1534, in defiance of the pope's veto; translated to Salisbury, 1539; surrendered Hyde Abbey to the king; reconciled to Rome, 1553. [ix. 22]

CAPON, WILLIAM (*d.* 1550), ecclesiastic; B.A. Cambridge, 1499; D.D., 1517; fellow of Catharine Hall, Cambridge; a pluralist in benefices and prebends; chaplain to Cardinal Wolsey; master of Jesus College, Cambridge, 1516–46; dean of Wolsey's short-lived college at Ipswich, 1528. [ix. 23]

CAPON, WILLIAM (1757–1827), architect and scene-painter; a portrait painter; scene-painter at Drury Lane, 1794–1809, and at Covent Garden, 1802; architectural draughtsman to Duke of York, 1804; exhibited views of buildings at the Royal Academy; made plans of the old palace of Westminster and the substructure of the abbey. [ix. 23]

CAPPE, NEWCOME (1733–1800), unitarian; educated by dissenting ministers; pastor of St. Saviourgate chapel, York, 1756–1800; published sermons and theological tracts. [ix. 24]

CAPPER, FRANCIS (1735–1818), divine; educated at Westminster School and Christ Church, Oxford; rector of Monk Soham and Earl Soham, Suffolk, 1759–1818. [ix. 25]

CAPPER, JAMES (1743–1825), meteorologist; educated at Harrow; colonel in the East India Company's service; afterwards resided in South Wales and Norfolk; wrote Asiatic itineraries and books on meteorological subjects and farming. [ix. 25]

CAPPER, JOSEPH (1727–1804), eccentric; grocer in London; lodged in the Horns inn, Kennington, 1779–1804. [ix. 25]

CAPPER, LOUISA (1776–1840), daughter of James Capper [q. v.]; published an abridgment of 'Locke on the Human Understanding,' 1811. [ix. 25]

CAPPOCH, THOMAS (1719–1746). [See COPPOCK.]

CARACCIOLI, CHARLES (*fl.* 1766), topographer; master of Arundel grammar school; published, 1776, 'The Antiquities of Arundel.' Other works of doubtful authenticity are attributed to him. [ix. 26]

CARACTACUS (*fl.* 50), king of the Britons; his name in English, Caradoc, in Welsh, Caradawg; a son of Cunobelin of Colchester; as chief of the Catuvellauni, took the lead in resisting the Roman invasion, A.D. 43; defeated on the Thames and in Essex; withdrew to South Wales, and continued to harass the Romans; defeated (perhaps near Shrewsbury), A.D. 50; sent captive to Rome; died in captivity. [ix. 26]

CARADOC, SIR JOHN FRANCIS, first BARON HOWDEN (1762–1839), general; only son of John Cradock [q. v.], archbishop of Dublin; changed his name to Caradoc in 1820; cornet, 1777; captain, 1781; major, 1785; M.P. in the Irish parliament, 1785–1800; lieutenant-colonel, 1789; served in West Indies, 1790 and 1793–5; stationed in Ireland, 1795; took active part in suppressing Irish rebellion, 1798; major-general, 1798; served in Egypt, 1801; K.B., 1803; commander-in-chief at Madras, 1804–7; lieutenant-general, 1805; partly responsible for mutiny at Vellore, 1806; took command in Portugal, 1808; removed to the governorship of Gibraltar, 1809; governor of the Cape, 1811–14; general, 1812; created Baron Howden in the Irish peerage, 1819, and in the English peerage, 1831. [ix. 27]

CARADOC, SIR JOHN HOBART, second BARON HOWDEN (1799–1873), diplomatist; only child of Sir John Francis Caradoc, first baron Howden [q. v.]; ensign, 1815; aide-de-camp in France, 1815–18; captain, 1818; aide-de-camp at Lisbon and in Malta; on the embassy staff at Berlin, 1824, and Paris, 1825; major, 1825; envoy to Egypt, 1827; M.P., Dundalk, 1830; military attaché with the French army, 1832, and the Spanish army, 1834; succeeded to barony, 1839; colonel, 1841; minister to Brazil, 1847–50; broke up the British blockade of Buenos Ayres, 1847; minister at Madrid, 1850–8; lieutenant-general, 1859; G.C.B.; died at Bayonne. [ix. 29]

CARADOG (*d.* 1035), a South Welsh prince; a son of Rhydderch; fought against the sons of Edwin, 1032–5; slain by the English. [ix. 30]

CARADOG OF LLANCARVAN (*d.* 1147 ?), Welsh chronicler; of the suite of Earl Robert of Gloucester; a friend of Geoffrey of Monmouth; wrote continuation of Geoffrey's chronicle, and other works, not now extant. [ix. 30]

CARADORI-ALLAN, MARIA CATERINA ROSALBINA (1800–1865), vocalist; born at Milan; daughter of Baron de Munck; took her mother's maiden name, Caradori, for her professional name; married E. T. Allan, secretary of the King's Theatre, London, 1824; sang in the Italian opera in London, 1822–7, in Venice, 1830, and again in London in 1834; quitted the stage, and sang in oratorios and concerts; retired, 1845. [ix. 30]

CARANTACUS, in Welsh CARANNOG, SAINT (*fl.* 450), said to have declined the princedom of Cardigan in order to become a hermit; joined St. Patrick, and laboured with him in the conversion of Ireland; changed his name to Cernach; perhaps to be identified with the St. Cairnech whose festival is 16 May; returned to Wales; died in Ireland. [ix. 31]

CARAUSIUS (245 ?–293), Roman emperor in Britain; originally pilot on the Scheldt; served under the Emperor Maximian against the revolted Gauls, 286; given command of the Boulogne fleet against the Saxon pirates; enriched himself by plunder; suspecting Maximian's hostility, crossed to Britain, proclaimed himself emperor, raised troops, and struck coins, 287; defeated Maximian's fleet; admitted to partnership in the empire, 290; his garrison at Boulogne subdued by Constantius, 292; assassinated by Allectus [q. v.] His coins, chiefly minted at London and Colchester, are exceptionally numerous. [ix. 32]

CARBERY, EARLS OF. [See VAUGHAN, RICHARD, second EARL of, 1600 ?–1686; VAUGHAN, JOHN, third EARL of, 1640–1713.]

CARD, HENRY (1779–1844), miscellaneous writer; educated at Westmᵗⁿsᵗᵉʳ School; B.A. Pembroke College, Oxford, 1800; D.D., 1823; vicar of Great Malvern, 1815, and of Dormington, Herefordshire, 1832; published verses and historical and theological tracts. [ix. 36]

CARDALE, JOHN BATE (1802–1877), founder of the Catholic Apostolic (popularly called the Irvingite) church; son of a wealthy London solicitor; educated at Rugby, 1815–18; practised as solicitor in London, 1824–34; went to Scotland, 1830, to investigate the reported 'speaking with tongues'; opened a prayer-meeting in London, to wait for the gift, October 1830; the gift of speaking 'in a tongue' obtained by his wife, 1831; became, 1831, 'apostle' of the new church; member, with his wife, of Edward Irving's [q. v.] congregation, in which (October 1831) speaking with tongues began; ordained Irving to be minister of the new church, 1833; settled at Albury, Surrey, 1835, where a cathedral was built; issued liturgy, 1842; published sermons and theological tracts. [ix. 36]

CARDALE, PAUL (1705–1775), Socinian; educated at a nonconformist seminary in Derbyshire, 1720; presbyterian preacher at Kidderminster, 1726; minister at Evesham, 1733–75; published, anonymously, many Socinian sermons and tracts, 1740–74. [ix. 38]

CARDER, PETER (*fl.* 1577–1586), a Cornish seaman; appeared in England, November 1586, with a tale that he had sailed with Sir Francis Drake, November 1577, been wrecked in the Straits of Magellan, October 1578, lived with savages, and made his way to Pernambuco. [ix. 39]

CARDIGAN, seventh EARL OF (1797–1868). [See BRUDENELL, JAMES THOMAS.]

CARDMAKER, *alias* TAYLOR, JOHN (*d.* 1555), protestant martyr; an Observant friar; married after the suppression of his order by Henry VIII; vicar of St. Bridget's, Fleet Street, and lecturer at St. Paul's; prebendary of Wells; tried to escape over sea; arrested in London, November 1554; sentenced to death for heresy, May 1555; burnt in Smithfield. [ix. 39]

CARDON, ANTHONY (1772–1813), engraver; a native of Brussels; came to London, 1792; illustrated books; engraved in stipple, chiefly portraits and battle-pieces. [ix. 40]

CARDON, PHILIP (*d.* 1817 ?), engraver. [ix. 40]

CARDONNEL, ADAM [DE] (*d.* 1719), secretary to the Duke of Marlborough from 1692 throughout his campaigns; son of a Huguenot refugee; clerk in the war office; M.P. for Southampton, 1701; his name put forward by Marlborough for the secretaryship of war, January 1710, but rejected by the tories; expelled the house on a charge of receiving gratuities from army contractors, 1712. [ix. 40]

CARDONNEL, afterwards **CARDONNEL-LAWSON**, ADAM [MANSFELDT] DE (*d.* 1820), antiquary; by profession a surgeon; studied antiquities and numismatics; F.S.A. Scotland, 1780; resided in Edinburgh; gave much assistance to Francis Grose; took the name Lawson and removed to Northumberland, on succession to an estate, *c.* 1790; often visited Bath; published treatises on Scottish coins and antiquities. [ix. 41]

CARDONNEL, PHILIP DE (*d.* 1667), author of verses on Charles II's marriage. [ix. 41]

CARDROSS, BARONS. [See ERSKINE, DANIEL, second BARON, 1616–1671; ERSKINE, HENRY, third BARON, 1650–1693.]

CARDWELL, EDWARD (1787-1861), church historian; B.A. Brasenose College, Oxford, 1809; D.D., 1831; fellow and tutor; Camden professor of ancient history, 1826-61; rector of Stoke Bruerne, Northamptonshire, 1828; principal of St. Alban Hall, Oxford, 1831-61; published sermons, editions of Aristotle's 'Ethics,' the Greek Testament, and Josephus, and collections for the history (1546-1717) of the church of England and of the prayer book. [ix. 42]

CARDWELL, EDWARD, VISCOUNT CARDWELL (1813-1886), statesman; son of Liverpool merchant; educated at Winchester and Balliol College, Oxford; B.A., 1835; barrister of the Inner Temple, 1838; M.P. for Clitheroe, 1842; attached himself to Sir Robert Peel; secretary to the treasury, 1845-6; M.P. for Liverpool, 1847-52; M.P. for Oxford city, 1852; president of the board of trade in Lord Aberdeen's coalition cabinet, 1852-5; carried through the Merchant Shipping Act, 1854; served on the commission regarding the manning of the navy, 1858; secretary for Ireland under Lord Palmerston, 1859-61; secretary for the colonies under Lord Palmerston and Russell, 1864-6; withdrew British troops from colonial stations and abolished transportation; secretary for war under Mr. Gladstone, 1868-74; introduced short service and the army reserve; abolished commissions by purchase; created Viscount Cardwell, 1874. [ix. 43]

CARE, HENRY (1646-1688), journalist; edited a partisan anti-Romanist journal, called the 'Weekly Pacquet of Advice from Rome,' 1678-9, suppressed in 1680, but afterwards continued till 1683; published several controversial pamphlets and some translations. [ix. 45]

CARELESS, WILLIAM (d. 1689). [See CARLOS.]

CARENCROSS, ALEXANDER (d. 1701). [See CAIRNCROSS.]

CAREW. [See also CAREY and CARY.]

CAREW, SIR ALEXANDER (1609-1644), second baronet, of Antony, Cornwall; M.P. for Cornwall, 1640; governor for the parliament of St. Nicholas Island in Plymouth harbour; arrested on suspicion of betraying his charge; found guilty, 1644; executed on Tower Hill. [ix. 46]

CAREW, BAMPFYLDE MOORE (1693-1770?), king of the gipsies; son of a Devonshire rector; ran away from Tiverton school, and joined the gipsies; became a clever sharper; went to Newfoundland; returned to Newcastle-on-Tyne; elected king of the English gipsies; transported to Maryland; escaped, and returned to England; followed Prince Charles Edward's army to Derby, 1745. [ix. 47]

CAREW, SIR BENJAMIN HALLOWELL (1760-1834), admiral; named Hallowell up to 1828, when he took the name Carew on succeeding to certain property; born in Canada; served in the navy, chiefly in Mediterranean, 1781-1814; commander, 1790; commanded a ship in the battle of the Nile, 1798; presented Nelson with a coffin made of the timbers of the L'Orient; rear-admiral, 1811; K.C.B., 1815; commanded on home stations, 1816-1824; admiral, 1830. [ix. 47]

CAREW, SIR EDMUND (1464-1513), soldier; adherent of Henry VII; knighted on Bosworth field, 1485; drove Perkin Warbeck from Exeter, 1497; killed at the siege of Thérouanne. [ix. 49]

CAREW, ELIZABETH, LADY (fl. 1590). [See CAREY, ELIZABETH, LADY.]

CAREW, GEORGE (d. 1583), ecclesiastic; third son of Sir Edmund Carew [q. v.]; B.A. Oxford, 1522; a pluralist in rectories and prebends; dean of Bristol, 1552-3 and 1559-71; dean of Christ Church, Oxford, 1559-61; dean of Windsor, 1560-77; dean of Exeter, 1571-1583. [ix. 51]

CAREW, SIR GEORGE (d. 1612), lawyer and diplomatist; probably at Oxford; travelled; barrister; secretary to lord chancellors Hatton and Egerton; M.P. for various Cornish boroughs, 1584-1601; envoy to Sweden and Poland, 1598; a master in chancery, 1599-1612; knighted, 1603; envoy to France, 1605-9; master of court of wards, 1612; drew up reports of causes in chancery. [ix. 50]

CAREW, GEORGE, BARON CAREW OF CLOPTON and EARL OF TOTNES (1555-1629), statesman; son of George

Carew (d. 1583) [q. v.]; educated at Broadgates Hall, Oxford, 1564-73; attended Sir Peter Carew [q. v.] to Ireland, 1574; volunteer in Ireland, 1575; given charge of Leighlin Castle, 1576; repulsed Rory Oge O'More, 1577; captain in navy, 1578; commanded troops in Ireland, 1579-80; knighted, 1586; sent to report on Irish affairs to Queen Elizabeth, 1586; master of ordnance in Ireland, 1588-92; lieutenant-general of ordnance in England, 1592; went with the expeditions to Cadiz, 1596, and the Azores, 1597; envoy to France, 1598; treasurer at war in Ireland, 1599; lord justice, 1599; president of Munster, 1600-3; ruthlessly suppressed Irish rebellion; M.P. for Hastings, 1604; created Baron Carew of Clopton House, 1605; master-general of the ordnance, 1608-17; governor of Guernsey, 1610-21; visited Ireland, 1610; created Earl of Totnes, 1626. Portions of his large collections for Irish history are in the Lambeth and Bodleian libraries. [ix. 51]

CAREW, SIR JOHN (d. 1362), justiciar in Ireland; owned Mulesford Manor, Berkshire, 1327; went to Ireland, 1332; negotiated with the Irish rebels, 1346; justiciar, 1349; king's escheator in Ireland, 1349, 1352, 1355, and 1356; attended the council at Waterford, 1359; at Westminster, 1361; followed Prince Lionel to Ireland. [ix. 53]

CAREW, JOHN (d. 1660), regicide; of Antony, Cornwall; of republican opinions; co-opted by the Long parliament into the seat for Tregony; commissioner at Holdenby, 1646; sat as judge on Charles I and signed the death-warrant; served in the Commonwealth parliaments of 1651 and 1654; imprisoned by Cromwell, 1655; retired to his estates; again imprisoned, 1658; fined for not attending in parliament, 1659; tried at London as a regicide, 1660; executed at Charing Cross. [ix. 54]

CAREW, JOHN EDWARD (1785?-1868), sculptor; assistant in London to Sir Richard Westmacott, 1809-1823; employed at Petworth by the third Earl of Egremont, 1823-37; lived latterly in London; exhibited at the Royal Academy, 1830-48. [ix. 54]

CAREW, SIR MATTHEW (d. 1618), lawyer; educated at Westminster School; fellow of Trinity College, Cambridge; studied law abroad; travelled in Italy; practised in the court of arches; a master in chancery, 1583-1618; knighted, 1603. [ix. 55]

CAREW, SIR NICHOLAS (d. 1539), of Beddington, Surrey; courtier of Henry VIII; attended Henry VIII in France, 1513; knighted before 1517; keeper of Greenwich Park, 1517; sheriff of Surrey and Sussex, 1519 and 1529; removed by the privy council from attendance on the king, 1519; sent to Calais, as lieutenant of the castle; attended Henry VIII in France, 1520; returned to court, 1521; master of the horse, 1522; envoy to France, 1527; M.P., Surrey, 1529; envoy to the Emperor Charles V, 1529-30; entertained Henry VIII at Beddington, 1531; envoy to France, 1532; K.G., 1536; condemned for his share in the Marquis of Exeter's treason; beheaded. [ix. 56]

CAREW, SIR PETER (1514-1575), soldier; went to France as a page; became a muleteer; servant to a French officer in Italy, 1525; in the service of Philibert, prince of Orange, 1525-30; recommended to Henry VIII, who made him a gentleman of the privy chamber; travelled in Italy and Turkey, 1540; served in the war with France, 1544; knighted, 1545; sheriff of Devonshire, 1546; active in repressing the Devonshire rising, 1549; opposed Queen Mary's marriage with Philip of Spain; fled oversea; arrested in Antwerp; imprisoned in the Tower, 1556; went to Ireland to claim estates in Munster, 1568; engaged in civil war with the Butlers; recalled; constable of the Tower, 1572; returned to Ireland, 1574. [ix. 59]

CAREW, RICHARD (1555-1620), antiquary; educated at Christ Church, Oxford; succeeded to the estates at Antony, Cornwall; justice of the peace, 1581; M.P. for Saltash, 1584; high sheriff of Cornwall, 1586; M.P. for Michell, 1597; published a translation of the first five cantos of Tasso's 'Godfrey of Bvlloigne' ('Jerusalem Delivered'), 1594, and a 'Svrvey of Cornwall,' 1602. [ix. 60]

CAREW, SIR RICHARD (d. 1643?), writer on education; eldest son of Richard Carew (1555-1620) [q. v.]; educated at Oxford and the Middle Temple; travelled in France; M.P. for Cornwall, 1614; M.P. for Michell, 1620; created baronet, 1642; wrote tract on teaching Latin. [ix. 62]

CAREW or **CARY**, ROBERT, also called CERVINUS (*fl.* 1325), schoolman; D.D. Oxford; wrote commentaries on Aristotle, Peter Lombard, and the scriptures. [ix. 63]

CAREW, SIR THOMAS (*d.* 1431), soldier in the service of Henry IV and Henry V. [ix. 63]

CAREW, THOMAS (1595 ?-1639 ?), poet; son of Sir Matthew Carew [q. v.]; entered Merton College, Oxford, 1608; B.A., 1611; entered at Middle Temple, 1612; secretary to Sir Dudley Carleton in Italy, 1613-1615; quarrelled with Carleton, 1616; accompanied Lord Herbert of Cherbury to France, 1619; employed in the court of Charles I, who gave him Sunninghill; a man of dissipated habits; wrote masques and songs. [ix. 63]

CAREW, THOMAS (1590-1672 ?), traveller and historian. [See CARVE.]

CAREY. [See also CAREW and CARY.]

CAREY, DAVID (1782-1824), journalist; whig journalist in London, *c.* 1804, in Inverness, 1807, in Boston, 1812, and again in London, 1813; published verses, novels, and notes of travel. [ix. 64]

CAREY or **CAREW**, ELIZABETH, LADY, the elder (*fl.* 1590), daughter of Sir John Spencer of Althorpe; kinswoman of Edmund Spenser, who dedicated his 'Muiopotmos' to her; married Sir George Carey, afterwards second baron Hunsdon [q. v.] [ix. 64]

CAREY or **CAREW**, ELIZABETH, the younger (*d.* 1635), daughter of Lady Elizabeth Carey the elder [q. v.]; patroness of Thomas Nash the satirist; married Sir Thomas Berkeley; possibly authoress of 'The Tragedie of Marian,' 1613. [ix. 64]

CAREY, EUSTACE (1791-1855), missionary; educated in baptist seminaries; baptist missionary at Calcutta, 1814-25; visited baptist churches in Great Britain, advocating missions, from 1826; published tracts on missions. [ix. 65]

CAREY, FELIX (1786-1822), author of a Burmese grammar and dictionary, and translations into Burmese; son of William Carey (1761-1834) [q. v.]; missionary; died at Serampúr, Bengal. [ix. 65]

CAREY, GEORGE, second BARON HUNSDON (1547-1603), eldest son of Henry Carey, first baron Hunsdon [q. v.]; married Lady Elizabeth Carey (*fl.* 1590) [q. v.]; entered Trinity College, Cambridge, 1560; envoy to Scotland, 1569; served against the northern rebels, and the Scots, 1570; knighted, 1570; constable of Bamborough Castle, 1574; envoy to Scotland, 1582; captain-general of the Isle of Wight, 1582; fortified the Isle of Wight in expectation of the Armada, 1587; envoy to Scotland, 1589; succeeded to barony, 1596; lord chamberlain of the household, 1597. [ix. 65]

CAREY or **CARY**, SIR GEORGE (*d.* 1617), of Cockington; treasurer at war in Ireland, 1588; lord justice, 1603. [ix. 52]

CAREY, GEORGE JACKSON (1822-1872), major-general; educated at Elizabeth College, Guernsey; ensign, 1845; served in South Africa, 1846-57; captain, 1848; brevet-colonel, 1854; served in New Zealand, 1863-5; on home stations, 1867-72; major-general, 1868. [ix. 66]

CAREY, GEORGE SAVILLE (1743-1807), miscellaneous writer; posthumous son of Henry Carey (*d.* 1743) [q. v.]; brought up as a printer; took to the stage, 1763; failed as an actor; a successful vocalist and mimic in London and the provinces, 1770-1807; published songs, plays, burlettas, and operas, 1766-1801. [ix. 67]

CAREY, HENRY, first BARON HUNSDON (1524 ?-1596), son of Anne Boleyn's sister and first cousin to Queen Elizabeth; M.P., Buckingham, 1547-55; received lands in Buckinghamshire from Edward VI, 1549; knighted, 1558; created Baron Hunsdon, January 1559, and given lands in Hertfordshire and Kent by Queen Elizabeth; K.G., 1561; in attendance at court; envoy to France, 1564; governor of Berwick, 1568-87; active in repressing the northern rebellion, 1569-70; received Elizabeth at Hunsdon and received lands in Yorkshire, 1571; favoured Queen Elizabeth's projected marriage with the Duc d'Anjou, 1579; lord chamberlain of the

household, 1583; commissioner on various treason trials, 1585-95; commissioner to try Mary Stuart, 1586; envoy to Scotland, 1587; in command of the forces at Tilbury, 1588; envoy to France, 1591. [ix. 68]

CAREY, HENRY, second EARL OF MONMOUTH (1596-1661), translator; eldest son of Robert Carey, first earl of Monmouth [q. v.]; spent his boyhood with his father on the borders and at the court of James I; B.A. Exeter College, Oxford, 1613; travelled, 1613-16; K.B., 1616; succeeded to the earldom, 1639; lived in retirement; published translations from the Italian and French, 1637-58. [ix. 70]

CAREY, HENRY (*d.* 1743), author of 'Sally in our Alley'; published his first poems, 1713; wrote farces, burlesques, and songs for the London theatres, 1715-39. His 'Dramatic Works' appeared 1743. [ix. 71]

CAREY, JAMES (1845-1883), Fenian and informer; a bricklayer of Dublin; a successful Dublin builder; joined the Fenians, 1861; became a leader of the 'Invincibles,' 1881; directed the assassination of Lord Frederick Cavendish [q. v.], May 1882; arrested, January 1883; turned queen's evidence, February; murdered at sea. [ix. 72]

CAREY, JOHN, third BARON HUNSDON (*d.* 1617), second son of Henry Carey, first baron Hunsdon [q. v.]; deputy warden of the eastern marches and marshal of Berwick; proclaimed James I, king of England, at Berwick, 25 March 1603; succeeded to barony, September 1603. [ix. 73]

CAREY, JOHN (1756-1826), classical scholar; born in Ireland; educated in France; visited the United States, 1789; settled in London as a teacher of classics and French; edited Dryden's 'Virgil,' 1803 and 1819; edited many classical texts and school-books. [ix. 73]

CAREY, MATTHEW (1760-1839), bookseller; son of a Dublin baker; apprenticed to a bookseller; went to Paris, 1779, fearing prosecution for a pamphlet reflecting on the penal laws; conducted the Dublin 'Freeman's Journal' and (1783) 'The Volunteer's Journal'; emigrated to Philadelphia, 1784; journalist at Philadelphia, 1785-92; bookseller and publisher, 1792-1824; published 'Vindiciæ Hibernicæ,' 1819, to extenuate the rebellion of 1641; wrote a multitude of papers on political and social subjects. [ix. 74]

CAREY, PATRICK (*fl.* 1651). [See CARY.]

CAREY, ROBERT, first EARL OF MONMOUTH (1560 ?-1639), youngest son of Henry Carey, first baron Hunsdon [q. v.]; employed in the public service in the Netherlands, 1577-81, and in Scotland, 1583; M.P., Morpeth, 1586-93; fought in the Netherlands, 1587, against the Armada, 1588, and in Normandy, 1591; envoy to Scotland, 1588 and 1593; knighted, 1591; employed on the Scottish border, 1593-1603; M.P., Northumberland, 1598 and 1601; conveyed, by three days' riding, news of Elizabeth's death to James VI of Scotland, 1603; master of the robes to Prince Charles, 1611, and chamberlain, 1617-25; created Baron Leppington, 1622; followed Prince Charles to Spain, 1623; created Earl of Monmouth, 1626; wrote an autobiography (printed 1759). [ix. 75]

CAREY, VALENTINE (*d.* 1626). [See CARY.]

CAREY, WILLIAM (1761-1834), orientalist and missionary; son of a Northamptonshire schoolmaster; a shoemaker; joined the baptists, 1783; pastor at Moulton, Northamptonshire, 1786, and Leicester, 1789; devoted himself to study; founded Baptist Missionary Society; went to Calcutta, 1794; made a living as foreman at an indigo factory at Máldah; preached there in Bengali, 1795-9; removed to Serampúr, 1799; professor of Sanskrit at Fort William College, 1801; opened mission chapel at Calcutta, 1805; issued translations of the scriptures; compiled grammars and dictionaries of several native languages and edited the 'Ramayana,' 1806-10. [ix. 77]

CAREY, WILLIAM (1769-1846), bishop of Exeter and St. Asaph; educated at Westminster School; entered Christ Church, Oxford, 1789; M.A., 1796; censor, 1798-1802; vicar of Cowley, Oxford; head-master of Westminster, 1803-14; D.D., 1807; prebendary of Westminster, 1809; vicar of Sutton-in-the-Forest, Yorkshire; bishop of Exeter, 1820; bishop of St. Asaph, 1830-46; benefactor of Christ Church, Oxford. [ix. 77]

CAREY, WILLIAM PAULET (1759–1839), art critic; engraver at Dublin; a dealer in pictures and prints in London; one of the first to recognise the genius of Chantrey, the sculptor; removed to Birmingham, 1834; published many works on artistic and literary questions, 1801–35. [ix. 78]

CARGILL, ANN (1748?–1784), actress and vocalist; acted under the name of Miss Brown at Covent Garden, 1770–80, and under that of Mrs. Cargill at the Haymarket, 1780; went on a professional tour to India, 1782; drowned off Scilly. [ix. 79]

CARGILL, DONALD, or, according to some, DANIEL (1619?–1681), covenanter; educated at Aberdeen and St. Andrews; minister of Barony parish, Glasgow, 1655; ejected by the privy council for rebuking Charles II's conduct, 1662; field preacher in the lowlands; present at battle of Bothwell Bridge, 1679; pronounced Charles II deposed and excommunicated, 1680; captured, 1680; executed at Edinburgh. [ix. 79]

CARGILL, JAMES (*fl.* 1605), botanist; medical practitioner in Aberdeen after studying botany at Basle. [ix. 80]

CARHAMPTON, EARLS OF. [See LUTTRELL, HENRY LAWES, second EARL, 1743–1821; LUTTRELL-OLMIUS, JOHN, third EARL, *d.* 1829.]

CARIER, BENJAMIN (1566–1614), convert to Roman catholicism; B.A. Corpus Christi College, Cambridge, 1586, and fellow, 1589–1602; D.D., 1602; rector of Paddlesworth, Kent, 1598–9; vicar of Thurnham, Kent, 1600–13; rector of West Tarring, Sussex, 1602; rector of Old Romney, Kent, and chaplain to James I, 1603; prebendary of Canterbury, 1608; fellow of Sutcliffe's college at Chelsea; withdrew to Spa; converted to Romanism at Cologne; died in Paris; published treatise in justification of his conversion, 1613. [ix. 80]

CARILEF, WILLIAM DE, SAINT (*d.* 1096), bishop of Durham; secular priest at Bayeux; monk at St. Carilef (or Calais), Maine; abbot of St. Vincent; bishop of Durham, 1081; expelled the secular canons at Durham and put monks in their place, 1083; an adviser of William I; chief minister to William II, 1088; rebelled; took refuge in Normandy; pardoned, 1091; commenced the rebuilding of Durham Cathedral, 1093; helped William II in his proceedings against Anselm, 1095, though he had previously maintained that bishops were exempt from the royal jurisdiction. [ix. 81]

CARKEET, SAMUEL (*d.* 1746), presbyterian; minister at Totnes, 1710; removed to Bodmin, *c.* 1729; published sermons. [ix. 84]

CARKESSE, JAMES (*fl.* 1679), verse writer; educated at Westminster; student of Christ Church, Oxford, 1652; master of Magdalen College School, Oxford; joined the Roman catholic church before 1679; published 'Lucida Intervalla,' a volume of doggerel rhymes, 1679. [ix. 84]

CARKETT, ROBERT (*d.* 1780), naval officer; seaman in the navy, 1734; midshipman, *c.* 1738; lieutenant, 1745; distinguished himself in action, 1758; captain, 1758; failed to understand Rodney's instructions, 17 April 1780, thereby spoiling that commander's plans; his ship wrecked in a hurricane, all hands being lost, 1780. [ix. 84]

CARLEILL, CHRISTOPHER (1551?–1593), military and naval commander; educated at Cambridge; Sir Francis Walsingham's son-in-law; served at sea and on land with the Dutch, 1572–7; served under Condé at La Rochelle; escorted English merchant fleet to Russia, 1582; projected voyage of exploration to America, 1583; commander at Coleraine, 1584; commanded the land forces against the Spanish West Indies, 1585; governor of Ulster, 1588. [ix. 85]

CARLELL, LODOWICK (*fl.* 1629–1664), dramatist; a court official under Charles I and Charles II; published nine plays (eight extant). [ix. 86]

CARLETON, BARON (*d.* 1725). [See BOYLE, HENRY.]

CARLETON, SIR DUDLEY, VISCOUNT DORCHESTER (1573–1632), diplomatist; educated at Westminster School; B.A. Christ Church, Oxford, 1595; travelled, 1595–1600; ambassador's secretary at Paris, 1602–3; M.P., St. Mawes, 1604–11; secretary to Henry, earl of Northumberland; travelled with Francis, lord Norreys,

1605; suspected of complicity in the Gunpowder plot, 1606; knighted, 1610; ambassador to Venice, 1610–15; ambassador at the Hague, 1616–25; envoy to Paris, 1626; M.P., Hastings, 1626; created Baron Carleton of Imbercourt, May 1626; envoy to the Hague, 1626–8; created Viscount Dorchester, July 1628; secretary of state, 1628; left a mass of official correspondence. [ix. 87]

CARLETON, GEORGE (1559–1628), bishop of Chichester; entered St. Edmund Hall, Oxford, 1576; fellow of Merton College, 1580; M.A., 1585; vicar of Mayfield, Sussex, 1589–1605; D.D., 1613; bishop of Llandaff, 1618; represented the church of England at the synod at Dort, 1618–19; bishop of Chichester, 1619; published complimentary verses, theological tracts, and a life of Bernard Gilpin. [ix. 90]

CARLETON, GEORGE (*fl.* 1728), captain; published at London, 1728, an autobiography entitled 'Military Memoirs from 1672 to 1713' (long thought to be one of Defoe's fictions); volunteer in the English fleet, 1672; in the Prince of Orange's service in the Netherlands; stationed in Scotland, 1690?–1705; served in Spain under Peterborough, 1705. [ix. 91]

CARLETON, GUY (1598?–1685), bishop of Chichester; educated at Carlisle school; entered Queen's College, Oxford, 1625; fellow; M.A., 1629; followed Charles I's army, although a divine; imprisoned at Lambeth; escaped oversea; D.D., 1660; dean of Carlisle, 1660; bishop of Bristol, 1671; bishop of Chichester, 1678. [ix. 92]

CARLETON, GUY, first BARON DORCHESTER (1724–1808), governor of Quebec; ensign, 1742; lieutenant-colonel, 1757; served in America, 1758–62; colonel, 1762; acting governor of Quebec, 1766–70; returned to England, 1770; major-general, 1772; advocated the Quebec Act, 1774; governor of Quebec, 1775–7; defeated by an American force, 1775; successfully defended Quebec, December 1775 to May 1776; defeated the Americans on Lake Champlain, October 1776; K.B., 1776; returned to England, 1778; commander-in-chief in America, 1782–3; created Baron Dorchester, August 1786; resided in Quebec as governor, 1786–91 and 1793–6; general, 1793. [ix. 93]

CARLETON, HUGH, VISCOUNT CARLETON (1739–1826), Irish judge; educated at Trinity College, Dublin; solicitor-general, 1779; lord chief justice of the common pleas, 1787–1800; created Baron Carleton, 1789; created Viscount Carleton, 1797; lord chief justice, 1800. [ix. 95]

CARLETON, MARY (1642?–1673), 'the German princess'; criminal; born in Canterbury and named Mary Moders; came from Holland to England, 1661, pretending to be a noble German heiress; married bigamously John Carleton, 1663; went on the stage, 1664; transported for theft to Jamaica, 1671; returned to London; hanged for theft; subject of two broadsides and an 'Historicall Narrative.' [ix. 95]

CARLETON, RICHARD (1560?–1638?), composer; B.A. Clare College, Cambridge, 1577; Mus. Bac.; employed at Norwich Cathedral; rector of Bawsey, Norfolk, 1612; published madrigals. [ix. 96]

CARLETON, THOMAS (1593?–1666). [See COMPTON.]

CARLETON, WILLIAM (*d.* 1309?), judge; justice over the Jews, 1286–90; baron of the exchequer, 1291; senior baron, 1300. [ix. 97]

CARLETON, WILLIAM (1794–1869), Irish novelist; born in Tyrone; son of a poor cottar; taught by a hedge-priest; intended for the church; tutor in Dublin; published numerous realistic tales delineating Irish life, 1830–62; pensioned. [ix. 97]

CARLIELL, ROBERT (*d.* 1622?), poet; published, 1620, 'Britaines Glorie,' an allegorical poem praising the church. [ix. 98]

CARLILE. [See also CARLIELL, CARLISLE, and CARLYLE.]

CARLILE or **CARLISLE,** ANNE (*d.* 1680?), miniaturist; mentioned, 1658, as painting in oil. [ix. 99]

CARLILE, CHRISTOPHER (*d.* 1588?), divine; fellow of Clare Hall, Cambridge; M.A., 1541; B.D., 1552; D.D.; was residing at Monks' Horton, Kent, 1563; published two controversial treatises. [ix. 99]

CARLILE, CHRISTOPHER (1551 ?-1593). [See CAR-LEILL, CHRISTOPHER.]

CARLILE, JAMES (d. 1691), dramatist; an actor at Drury Lane, 1682-4; captain in the army; brought out 'Fortune Hunters,' a comedy, 1689; killed at Aghrim. [ix. 99]

CARLILE, JAMES (1784-1854), divine; born at Paisley; educated at Glasgow; D.D.; joint minister of a Scots church in Dublin, 1813-54; commissioner of education, 1830-9; inaugurated mission to Roman catholics at Parsonstown, 1839; published theological and controversial tracts. [ix. 100]

CARLILE, RICHARD (1790-1843), freethinker; a Devonshire shoemaker's son; chemist's shopboy in Exeter; journeyman tinsmith; mechanic in London, 1813; a disciple of Thomas Paine, 1816; vendor of prohibited papers, 1817; printer and author of freethought papers; issued Paine's works, 1818; imprisoned at Dorchester, 1819-25; issued 'The Republican,' a journal, 1819-26; his wife, sister, and shopmen imprisoned, in spite of which the journal still appeared; opened hall for free discussion, 1830; imprisoned for refusing to pay church rates, 1830-3 and 1834-5; wrote numerous controversial tracts and serials. [ix. 100]

CARLINGFORD, EARLS OF. [See TAAFE, THEOBALD, first EARL, d. 1677; TAAFE, FRANCIS, third EARL, 1639-1704.]

CARLINGFORD, VISCOUNTS OF. [See TAAFE, THEOBALD, second VISCOUNT, d. 1677; TAAFE, FRANCIS, fourth VISCOUNT, 1639-1704; TAAFE, NICHOLAS, sixth VISCOUNT, 1677-1769.]

CARLINGFORD, BARON, 1823-1898. [See FORTESCUE, CHICHESTER SAMUEL PARKINSON.]

CARLINI, AGOSTINO (d. 1790), sculptor and painter; born at Genoa; exhibited at Royal Academy, 1760-86; celebrated for his treatment of drapery. [ix. 103]

CARLISLE. [See also CARLEILL, CARLIELL, CARLILE, and CARLYLE.]

CARLISLE, EARLS OF. [See HARCLAY, ANDREW, d. 1323; HAY, JAMES, d. 1636; HOWARD, CHARLES, first EARL of the second creation, 1629-1685; HOWARD, CHARLES, third EARL, 1674-1738; HOWARD, HENRY, fourth EARL, 1694-1758; HOWARD, FREDERICK, fifth EARL, 1748-1825; HOWARD, GEORGE, sixth EARL, 1773-1848; HOWARD, GEORGE WILLIAM FREDERICK, seventh EARL, 1802-1864.]

CARLISLE, COUNTESS OF (1599-1660). [See HAY, LUCY.]

CARLISLE, SIR ANTHONY (1768-1840), surgeon; apprenticed to practitioners in York and Durham; studied in London; surgeon to the Westminster Hospital, 1793-1840; professor of anatomy at the Royal Academy, 1808-1824; knighted, 1820; introduced the thin-bladed, straight-edged amputating knife; wrote on medical, artistic, and scientific subjects. [ix. 103]

CARLISLE, NICHOLAS (1771-1847), antiquary; born at York; purser in the East India Company's service; secretary to Society of Antiquaries, 1807; assistant librarian, Royal Library, 1812; compiler of topographical dictionaries, family histories, and similar works. [ix. 104]

CARLOS, EDWARD JOHN (1798-1851), antiquary; an official of the lord mayor's court office; wrote descriptions of London churches and old buildings. [ix. 105]

CARLOS, CARLES, or **CARELESS,** WILLIAM (d. 1689), royalist; major or colonel in the civil wars; after Worcester fight, 3 Sept. 1651, hid himself in an oak tree near Boscobel House; shared his retreat with Charles II, 6 and 7 Sept.; escaped to France; was taken into Charles's service; granted one-third of the tax on hay and straw in London and Westminster, 1661; received a bounty from James II, 1687. [ix. 105]

CARLSE, JAMES (1798-1855), engraver; of London; engraved chiefly for annuals and books. [ix. 106]

CARLYLE, ALEXANDER (1722-1805), Scottish divine; nicknamed 'Jupiter Carlyle,' from his fine presence; eye-witness of the Porteous riots, 1736, and the battle of Prestonpans, 1745; entered Edinburgh University, 1735; M.A., 1743; studied also at Glasgow, 1743-4, and Leyden, 1745; D.D.; minister of Inveresk, Midlothian, 1748-1805; leader of the Scottish 'Broad church' party; censured for attending the performance of John Home's 'Douglas,' 1757; published political pamphlets, 1758-64; sent to London to ask exemption of Scottish clergy from window-tax, 1769; moderator of the general assembly, 1770; dean of the Chapel Royal, 1789; his autobiography printed, 1860. [ix. 106]

CARLYLE, JANE BAILLIE WELSH (1801-1866), only child of John Welsh (d. 1819), physician, of Haddington; a self-willed girl; wrote verses, 1815; of feeble health and querulous disposition, but with much shrewd wit; wished to marry Edward Irving [q. v.], 1818-23; made the acquaintance of Thomas Carlyle (1795-1881) [q. v.], 1821; rejected him, 1823; accepted him, 1825; married him, 1826; resided first at Edinburgh and Craigenputtock, and then in Cheyne Row, Chelsea, 1834-66; formed a coterie of lady friends, 1841; impaired her own and her husband's happiness by groundless jealousy, 1845-57; became a great invalid, 1858; died suddenly of the shock of a trivial accident; her letters were published, 1883. [ix. 114]

CARLYLE, JOHN AITKEN (1801-1879), physician; younger brother of Thomas Carlyle (1795-1881) [q. v.]; born at Ecclefechan; master in Annan academy; M.D. Edinburgh, 1825; studied also in Germany; failed to gain practice in London; physician to the Countess of Clare in Italy, 1831-7, and to the Duke of Buccleuch abroad, 1838-43; lodged in Chelsea; published a prose translation of Dante's 'Inferno,' 1849; removed to Edinburgh, c. 1855; latterly resided at Dumfries; studied Icelandic; benefactor to Edinburgh University. [ix. 108]

CARLYLE, JOSEPH DACRE (1759-1804), Arabic scholar; B.A. Queens' College, Cambridge, 1779; fellow; B.D., 1793; published translations from the Arabic, 1792-6; professor of Arabic, 1795; travelled in the Levant, 1799-1801; vicar of Newcastle-on-Tyne, 1801. His poems and Arabic bible appeared posthumously. [ix. 109]

CARLYLE, THOMAS (1803-1855), an apostle of the Catholic Apostolic church; schoolfellow of Edward Irving [q. v.] at Annan; studied at Edinburgh; advocate at the Scottish bar, 1824; published theological tracts, 1827-9; settled at Albury, Surrey, as ninth apostle, 1835; received North Germany as his province, 1838, and travelled widely there; died at Albury; published 'The Moral Phenomena of Germany,' 1845. [ix. 110]

CARLYLE, THOMAS (1795-1881), essayist and historian; son of a mason at Ecclefechan, Dumfriesshire; educated at the parish school, and (1805) at Annan academy; entered Edinburgh University, 1809; studied mathematics; intended for the church; mathematical teacher at Annan, 1814; schoolmaster at Kirkcaldy, 1816, where he became intimate with Edward Irving [q. v.]; read law in Edinburgh, 1819, where he developed extreme sensitiveness to physical discomforts; took pupils; read German; met his future wife [see JANE BAILLIE WELSH CARLYLE], 1821; tutor to Charles Buller [q. v.] at Edinburgh and Dunkeld, 1822-4; contributed a 'Life of Schiller' to the 'London Magazine,' 1824; translated Legendre's 'Geometry' and Goethe's 'Wilhelm Meister,' 1824; visited Paris, 1824; lodged in Islington, 1825; retired to Dumfriesshire, 1825; married and settled in Edinburgh, 1826; contributed to the 'Edinburgh Review,' 1827-9; unsuccessful candidate for the moral philosophy chair at St. Andrews; removed to Craigenputtock, Dumfriesshire, 1828, where he wrote on German literature for the magazines; in great monetary difficulties, 1831; in London, 1831, where he failed to get 'Sartor Resartus' published; returned to Craigenputtock, 1832; removed to Cheyne Row, Chelsea, 1834; the manuscript of the first volume of his 'French Revolution' accidentally burnt by John Stuart Mill, March 1835; met John Sterling [q. v.], 1835; published his 'French Revolution,' 1837, and made his reputation; gave four lecture-courses in London, 1837-40, the last on 'Hero-worship' (published 1841); urged formation of London Library, 1839; published 'Chartism,' 1839, 'Past and Present,' 1843, and 'Oliver Cromwell,' 1845; visited Ireland, 1846 and 1849; published 'Life of Sterling,' 1851; wrote 'Frederick the Great,' 1851-1865 (published 1858-65); travelled in Germany, 1852 and 1858; lord rector of Edinburgh University, 1865-6; lost his wife, 1866; wrote his 'Reminiscences' (published 1881); published pamphlet in favour of Germany in regard to Franco-German war, 1870; his right hand paralysed, 1872; received the Prussian order of merit, 1874; buried at Ecclefechan; benefactor of Edinburgh University. His 'Collected Works' first appeared 1857-8. His 'life' was written with great frankness by his friend and disciple, James Anthony Froude [q. v.]   [ix. 111]

CARLYON, CLEMENT (1777-1864), physician; member of Pembroke College, Cambridge; travelled in Germany; studied medicine in Edinburgh and London; settled in Truro; friend of Coleridge; published an autobiography and miscellaneous tracts.   [ix. 127]

CARMARTHEN, MARQUIS OF (1631-1712). [See OSBORNE, THOMAS.]

CARMELIANUS, PETER (d. 1527), court poet; born at Brescia; came to England, c. 1480?; wrote first in laudation, subsequently in vituperation, of Richard III; pensioned by Henry VII, 1486; Latin secretary and chaplain to Henry VII; lute-player to Henry VIII; prebendary of York, 1498-1527; prebendary of St. Paul's, 1517-26; beneficed in Yorkshire; prebendary of St. Stephen's, Westminster, 1524.   [ix. 127]

CARMICHAEL, FREDERICK (1708-1751), divine; M.A. Glasgow, 1725; minister of Monimail, 1737, and of Inveresk, 1747-51; published sermons.   [ix. 128]

CARMICHAEL, JAMES (fl. 1587), a Scot, published a small Latin grammar at Cambridge.   [ix. 129]

CARMICHAEL, SIR JAMES, first BARON CARMICHAEL (1578?-1672), Scottish judge; successively styled of Hyndford, of Westeraw, and, 1600, of Carmichael; courtier of James VI of Scotland; created baronet of Nova Scotia, 1627; sheriff of Lanark, 1632; lord justice clerk, 1634-6; treasurer-depute, 1636-49; a lord of session, 1636-49, with style of Lord Carmichael; created Baron Carmichael, 1651; fined by Cromwell, 1654.   [ix. 128]

CARMICHAEL, JAMES WILSON (1800-1868), marine painter; went to sea; a shipbuilder's draughtsman; painted at Newcastle in water-colours and (1825) in oils; exhibited at the Royal Academy, 1838-62; wrote on painting.   [ix. 129]

CARMICHAEL, SIR JOHN (d. 1600), of Carmichael; tried to deliver Morton, 1581; involved in the raid of Ruthven, 1584; warden of the west marches, 1588-92; envoy to Denmark, 1589; envoy to England, 1590; again warden, 1598; murdered by the Armstrongs.   [ix. 130]

CARMICHAEL, JOHN, second BARON CARMICHAEL and first EARL OF HYNDFORD (1638-1710), succeeded to the barony, 1672; lord privy seal of Scotland, 1689; commissioner to the general assembly, 1690 and 1694-9; colonel of dragoons, 1693-7; secretary of state, 1696-1702; created Earl of Hyndford, 1701; supported the Act of Union.   [ix. 130]

CARMICHAEL, JOHN, third EARL OF HYNDFORD (1701-1767), diplomatist; army captain, 1733; succeeded to earldom, 1737; Scottish representative peer; sheriff of Lanark, 1739; commissioner to the general assembly, 1739-40; envoy to Prussia, 1741-2, to Russia, 1744-9, and to Vienna, 1752-64.   [ix. 130]

CARMICHAEL, RICHARD (1779-1849), surgeon; assistant-surgeon to the Wexford militia, 1795-1802; practised in Dublin, 1803; surgeon to St. George's Hospital, 1803, to the Lock Hospital, 1810, and to the Richmond Hospital, 1816-36; advocated the improvement of medical education in Ireland; founded and endowed the Carmichael School of Medicine, 1826; wrote on medical subjects; drowned.   [ix. 131]

CARMYLYON, ALICE or ELLYS (fl. 1527-1531), decorative painter to Henry VIII.   [ix. 132]

CARNABY, WILLIAM (1772-1839), composer; chorister of the Chapel Royal; organist at Eye and at Huntingdon; Mus. Bac. Cambridge, 1805; Mus. Doc., 1808; organist to Hanover Chapel, Regent Street, London, 1823-39; composed songs, duets, and pianoforte pieces.   [ix. 132]

CARNAC, SIR JAMES RIVETT (1785-1846), Indian official; entered the East India Company's service, 1801; political officer; resident at Baroda, 1817-19; major; returned to England, 1822; created baronet, 1836; chair-

man of the East India Company, 1836-7; M.P., Sandwich, 1837; governor of Bombay, 1838; returned to England, 1841.   [ix. 133]

CARNAC, JOHN (1716-1800), colonel; captain in the East India Company's service, 1758; major, 1760; brigadier-general, 1764; returned to England, 1767; M.P., Leominster, 1767; served in Bengal, 1771; member of council at Bombay, 1776-9; died at Mangalore.   [ix. 133]

CARNARVON, EARLS OF. [See DORMER, ROBERT, first EARL, d. 1643; HERBERT, HENRY JOHN GEORGE, third EARL of the third creation, 1800-1849; HERBERT, HENRY HOWARD MOLYNEUX, fourth EARL, 1831-1890.]

CARNE, SIR EDWARD (d. 1561), diplomatist; D.C.L. Oxford, 1524; a commissioner for suppressing the monasteries, 1539; bought Ewenny Abbey, Glamorganshire; envoy to the pope, 1531; envoy to the Low Countries, 1538 and 1541; knighted by Charles V; M.P., Glamorganshire, 1554-5; ambassador to the pope, 1555-9; remained at Rome till death.   [ix. 134]

CARNE, ELIZABETH CATHERINE THOMAS (1817-1873), author; fifth daughter of Joseph Carne [q. v.]; head of the Penzance bank, 1858-73; founded several schools in Cornwall; a geologist; published notes of travel.   [ix. 135]

CARNE, JOHN (1789-1844), traveller and author; educated at Queens' College, Cambridge; published poems, 1820; travelled in the East, 1821; ordained deacon, 1826; resided in Penzance; published travels, biographies of eminent missionaries, and tales.   [ix. 135]

CARNE, JOSEPH (1782-1858), geologist; manager of Hayle copper works, 1810; manager of Penzance bank, 1820; wrote papers on Cornish geology, 1816-51, and on mining.   [ix. 136]

CARNE, ROBERT HARKNESS (1784-1844), theologian; son of a Cornish mercer; B.A. Exeter College, Oxford, 1806; curate at Crediton; his licence to preach revoked for doctrinal reasons; withdrew from the Anglican church, 1820; pastor of a chapel at Exeter; withdrew to Jersey; published theological tracts, 1810-30.   [ix. 137]

CARNEGIE, SIR DAVID of Kinnaird, BARON CARNEGIE and EARL OF SOUTHESK (1575-1658), succeeded to the Kinnaird estate, 1598; travelled, 1601; knighted, 1603; supported James I's church policy in Scotland; created Baron Carnegie, 1616; a lord of session, 1616-1625; supported Charles I's church policy in Scotland; created Earl of Southesk, 1633; imprisoned in Edinburgh by the covenanters, 1640; fined by Cromwell, 1654.   [ix. 137]

CARNEGIE, SIR ROBERT (d. 1566), of Kinnaird, Scottish judge; a lord of session, 1547, styled Lord Kinnaird; envoy to England, 1548, and to France, 1551; clerk to the treasurer, 1553; an adherent of Mary of Guise, queen regent, who gave him lands in Forfarshire.   [ix. 138]

CARNEGIE, WILLIAM, seventh EARL OF NORTHESK (1758-1831), admiral; served in the navy, 1771-1806; captain, 1782; styled, by courtesy, Lord Rosehill, from 1788; succeeded as seventh earl, 1792; imprisoned by the Nore mutineers, 1797; rear-admiral, 1804; fought at Trafalgar, 1805; admiral, 1814; commander-in-chief at Plymouth, 1827-30.   [ix. 139]

CARNWATH, EARLS OF. [See DALYELL, ROBERT, second EARL, d. 1654; DALYELL, SIR ROBERT, sixth EARL, d. 1737.]

CAROLINE (1683-1737), queen of George II; daughter of John Frederick (d. 1687), margrave of Brandenburg-Ansbach; resided with her mother chiefly at Dresden, 1692-6; wished to marry Frederick II of Saxe-Gotha, c. 1695; resided at Berlin under the tutelage of Frederick, king of Prussia (in 1701) and his consort Sophia Charlotte (d. 1704), daughter of Electress Sophia of Hanover; became acquainted with Leibniz, and with the Electress Sophia; a proposal to marry her to Archduke Charles, afterwards Charles VI, discussed, 1698-1705, but abandoned in consequence of her protestantism; returned to Ansbach, 1704; married, September 1705, to George Augustus, prince of Hanover; resided at Hanover, intriguing for the English succession, 1706-14; her children born, 1707-24; learnt a little English, 1713; accompanied her husband to England as Princess of Wales, 1714; was included in George I's displeasure against her husband, 1717; lived at Richmond Lodge, 1718, which afterwards became her favourite residence; connived at her husband's amour with her bedchamber-woman (Mrs. Howard, afterwards Countess of Suffolk); found a capable and honest adviser as to English politics in John, lord Hervey; became queen, 1727, and thenceforward gave unwavering support to Sir Robert Walpole; maintained her influence over George II by flattering his vanity and conniving at his amours; had an intense hatred of her eldest son, Frederick, prince of Wales; favoured the low church party; regent in George II's absence, 1729, 1732, 1735, 1736–7; was more German than English to the last in her conceptions; died after an unsuccessful operation for rupture. [ix. 139]

CAROLINE MATILDA (1751–1775), queen of Denmark, posthumous child of Frederick, prince of Wales, eldest son of George II; married Christian VII, king of Denmark, at Frederiksberg Palace, near Copenhagen, 8 Nov. 1766; badly treated from the first by her husband, a profligate sinking into imbecility; birth of her son (afterwards king), January 1768; resided at Frederiksberg during her husband's foreign tour, 1768–9; her husband much influenced by his ambitious German physician, John Frederick Struensee; treated by Christian VII with more respect in consequence of the representations of Struensee (1769), who became all powerful in the palace, 1770, and chief minister, 1771; believed to be Struensee's paramour by the Danes, who detested him; a daughter born to her, July 1771; imprisoned at Kronborg, January 1772; Struensee being arrested (subsequently executed), the queen was said to have acknowledged her guilt, March 1772; divorced, April 1772; left Denmark, May 1772. Her brother, George III of England, accepted the case against her. She retired to Celle in Hanover, where she died suddenly, in the midst of Danish overtures for her recall. [ix. 145]

CAROLINE AMELIA ELIZABETH, of Brunswick-Wolfenbüttel (1768–1821), queen of George IV; second daughter of Duke Charles William Ferdinand of Brunswick-Wolfenbüttel, and of Princess Augusta of England, George III's sister; a kind-hearted but eccentric girl; forced by George III as a bride on the Prince of Wales; embarked at Cuxhaven, March 1795; married at St. James's, 8 April 1795; lived at Carlton House, persecuted by the prince's mistresses; birth of her child, Princess Charlotte Augusta [q. v.], 7 Jan. 1796; deserted by her husband, April 1796; lived at Shooter's Hill; removed to Blackheath, 1801; painful accusations brought against her in consequence of her unguarded speeches, 1806; gained no increased dignity from her husband's becoming regent, 1811; denied access to her child, 1812–13; allowed to travel abroad, August 1813; took into her service, in Italy, 1814, Bartolomeo Bergami and his relatives, and travelled in the Levant; her conduct much talked of; wintered at Marseilles, 1819; started for England on hearing of George III's death; her name omitted from the state prayers; on the way rejected an offer of settlement, on condition of her living abroad and not claiming the title of queen; entered London, June 1820, amid popular rejoicings; a bill promoted in the lords for divorcing her, July, but abandoned, November 1820, from fear of a revolution; denied a palace; voted an allowance by parliament; forcibly excluded from the coronation at Westminster Abbey, 29 July 1821; died in London broken-hearted; buried at Brunswick beside her father. [ix. 150]

CARON, REDMOND (1605?–1666), controversialist; Franciscan friar at Athlone and Drogheda; studied at Salzburg and Louvain; professor at Louvain; commissary-general of the recollects in Ireland; published controversial treatises, 1635–62. [ix. 153]

CARPENTER, ALEXANDER, latinised as FABRICIUS (fl. 1429), called also 'Alexander Anglus'; author of 'Destructorium Vitiorum,' an invective against church abuses, printed frequently before 1516. [ix. 153]

CARPENTER, ALFRED JOHN (1825–1892), physician; apprenticed to his father, a surgeon, at Rothwell, 1839; entered St. Thomas's Hospital, 1847; M.R.C.S. and L.S.A. 1851; practised at Croydon; M.B. London, 1855; M.D., 1859; M.R.C.P. 1883; liberal M.P. for Reigate, 1885, and North Bristol, 1886; president of council of British Medical Association, 1878–81; published 'Principles and Practice of School of Hygiene,' 1887, and other works. [Suppl. i. 393]

CARPENTER, GEORGE, BARON CARPENTER (1657–1732), lieutenant-general; page at Paris embassy, 1671; cavalry officer, 1672–89; lieutenant-colonel, 1690; served in Ireland and Flanders; quartermaster-general to Peterborough in Spain, 1705; attached himself to the Hanoverian party; M.P., Whitchurch, 1714; suppressed the northern rebellion at Preston, 1715; commander-in-chief in Scotland; created Baron Carpenter in the Irish peerage, 1719; M.P., Westminster, 1722–9. [ix. 154]

CARPENTER, JAMES (1760–1845), admiral; served in navy, 1776–1812, chiefly in West Indies; lieutenant, 1782; rear-admiral, 1812; admiral, 1837. [ix. 154]

CARPENTER, JOHN (1370?–1441?), benefactor of London; clerk in the town clerk's office; town clerk of London, 1417–38; M.P., London, 1436, 1439; compiled 'Liber Albus,' an account of city privileges, &c. (printed 1859); left lands for education, out of which the City of London School was erected (1837). [ix. 155]

CARPENTER, JOHN (d. 1476), bishop of Worcester; D.D. Oriel College, Oxford; master of St. Antony's Hospital, London, 1420; provost of Oriel, 1427–35; rector of St. Mary Magdalen, Old Fish Street, London, 1436; chancellor of Oxford University, 1437; bishop of Worcester, 1444–76; benefactor of the college at Westbury and of Oriel College. [ix. 156]

CARPENTER, JOHN (d. 1621), divine; educated at Exeter College, Oxford, 1570–3; rector of Northleigh, Devonshire, 1587–1621; published devotional tracts, 1580–1606. [ix. 156]

CARPENTER, LANT (1780–1840), unitarian; educated in dissenting seminaries; at Glasgow University, 1798–1801; taught school; librarian of Liverpool Athenæum, 1802–5; unitarian minister and master of a boarding-school in Exeter, 1805–17; LL.D. Glasgow, 1806; unitarian minister, 1817–39, and master of a boarding-school, 1817–29, at Bristol; drowned off Leghorn; published sermons and controversial tracts. [ix. 157]

CARPENTER, MARGARET SARAH (1793–1872), portrait-painter; née Geddes; settled in London, 1814; married, 1817, William Hookham Carpenter [q. v.]; exhibited at the Royal Academy, 1818–66; pensioned, 1866. [ix. 159]

CARPENTER, MARY (1807–1877), philanthropist; eldest child of Lant Carpenter [q. v.]; opened a girls' school at Bristol, 1829; superintended a Sunday school, 1831–56; agitated for institutions to rescue juvenile criminals; founded at Bristol a ragged school, 1846, a reformatory, 1852, a girls' reformatory, 1854, and an industrial school, 1859; visited India to improve female education and prison management, 1866, 1868, 1869, 1875; visited Germany, 1872, and America, 1873; published verses, memoirs, and treatises on education and criminal reform, 1845–68. [ix. 159]

CARPENTER, NATHANAEL (1589–1628?), author; son of John Carpenter (d. 1621) [q. v.]; educated at St. Edmund Hall, Oxford; fellow of Exeter College, by mandate from James I, 1607; B.A., 1610; D.D., 1626; schoolmaster of the king's wards in Dublin; wrote sermons and treatises on geography and philosophy, the latter directed against Aristotelianism. [ix. 161]

CARPENTER, PHILIP HERBERT (1852–1891), palæontologist and zoologist; son of William Benjamin Carpenter [q. v.]; educated at University College School, London, and Trinity College, Cambridge; M.A., 1878; Sc.D., 1884; biological master at Eton, 1877; F.L.S., 1886; F.R.S., 1885. He published extensive writings on various groups of fossils. [Suppl. i. 394]

CARPENTER, PHILIP PEARSALL (1819–1877), conchologist; youngest child of Lant Carpenter [q. v.]; B.A. London, 1841; presbyterian minister at Stand, 1841, and Warrington, 1846–61; settled at Montreal, 1865; bought, 1855, a mass of Californian shells; subsequently paid much attention to conchology. [ix. 162]

CARPENTER, RICHARD (fl. c. 1580), alchemist. [ix. 164]

CARPENTER, RICHARD (1575–1627), divine; B.A. Exeter College, Oxford, 1596; fellow, 1596–1606; D.D., 1617; rector of Sherwell and Loxhore, Devonshire, 1606–1627; published sermons. [ix. 163]

CARPENTER, RICHARD (*d.* 1670 ?), ecclesiastic; educated at Eton and King's College, Cambridge, 1622; convert to Roman catholicism; travelled on the continent; Benedictine monk at Douay; sent on the English mission; returned to Anglicanism; vicar of Poling, Sussex, 1635–42; itinerant preacher; went back to Paris and Romanism; came to England and joined the independents; preacher at Aylesbury; returned to Romanism; wrote a play, an autobiography, and various pamphlets. [ix. 164]

CARPENTER, RICHARD CROMWELL (1812–1855), architect; educated at Charterhouse; exhibited at the Royal Academy, 1830–49; designed churches in Birmingham, Brighton, and London. [ix. 164]

CARPENTER, WILLIAM (1797–1874), miscellaneous writer; apprentice to a London bookseller; journalist, 1831–54; an advocate of political and legal reform; wrote on biblical subjects, 1825–68, and published political pamphlets. [ix. 165]

CARPENTER, WILLIAM BENJAMIN (1813–1885), naturalist; eldest son of Lant Carpenter [q. v.]; apprenticed to a physician; visited West Indies; studied medicine in London and (1835) in Edinburgh; lecturer at Bristol Medical School; published papers on physiology, 1837, and 'Principles of . . . Physiology,' 1839; professor of physiology in London, 1844; professor of forensic medicine, University College, London; registrar of the University of London, 1856–79; an unwearied investigator in the sciences of zoology, botany, and mental physiology, 1843–71; contributed much to scientific journals and cyclopædias. [ix. 166]

CARPENTER, WILLIAM HOOKHAM (1792–1866), connoisseur in prints; a London bookseller and publisher; studied prints and drawings; married, 1817 [see CARPENTER, MARGARET SARAH]; keeper of prints in the British Museum, 1845–66; wrote memoir of Antony Vandyck and a catalogue of prints in the British Museum show-cases. [ix. 168]

CARPENTIÈRE or **CHARPENTIÈRE**, —— (*d.* 1737), statuary; employed by the Duke of Chandos at Canons; afterwards settled in London. [ix. 169]

CARPENTIERS, **CARPENTIER**, or **CHARPENTIERE**, ADRIEN (*fl.* 1760–1774), portrait-painter; native of France or Switzerland; came to England, *c.* 1760; exhibited in London, 1760–74. [ix. 169]

CARPUE, JOSEPH CONSTANTINE (1764–1846), surgeon and anatomist; of a catholic family of Spanish origin; educated at Douay; travelled on continent; studied surgery in London; surgeon to the Duke of York's Hospital, Chelsea; private lecturer on anatomy, 1800–32; advocate of vaccination; surgeon of the National Vaccine Institution. [ix. 169]

CARR, JOHN (1723–1807), architect; called Carr of York; workman in York; designed many buildings in the northern counties. [ix. 170]

CARR, JOHN (1732–1807), translator of Lucian; educated at St. Paul's School; head-master of Hertford grammar school; LL.D. Aberdeen; published his translation of Lucian, 1773–98; wrote verses and parodies. [ix. 170]

CARR, SIR JOHN (1772–1832), traveller; barrister of the Middle Temple; travelled, for health, over greater part of Europe; knighted, *c.* 1806; published accounts of his tours, 1803–11, and verses. [ix. 170]

CARR, JOHNSON (1744–1765), landscape-painter. [ix. 171]

CARR, NICHOLAS (1524–1568), Greek scholar; B.A. Pembroke Hall, Cambridge, 1541; fellow; M.A., 1544; fellow of Trinity College, Cambridge, 1546; regius professor of Greek, 1547; consistently adhered to Roman catholicism; M.D. Cambridge, 1558; practised medicine in Cambridge; published Latin versions of Eusebius and Demosthenes. [ix. 171]

CARR, R. (*fl.* 1668), engraver. [ix. 172]

CARR, RICHARD (1651–1706), physician; M.A. Magdalene College, Cambridge, 1674; master of Saffron

Walden grammar school, 1676–83; studied medicine at Leyden, 1683–6; M.D. Cambridge, 1686; practised medicine in London; published medical essays. [ix. 172]

CARR or **KER**, ROBERT, EARL OF SOMERSET (*d.* 1645); a cadet of Ker of Ferniehurst, Roxburghshire; brought up in Scotland; accompanied James I to England as page, 1603; in France for a time; returned to James I's court; knighted, 1607; given Sir Walter Ralegh's manor of Sherborne, 1609; created Viscount Rochester, 1611; private secretary to the king, 1612; obtained the imprisonment in the Tower of his friend Sir Thomas Overbury, who opposed his projected marriage with the Countess of Essex, April 1613; K.G., 23 April; a decree of nullity of her marriage with the Earl of Essex obtained by the countess, 25 Sept. 1613, soon after Overbury had been poisoned, 15 Sept. 1613; created Earl of Somerset, 3 Nov. 1613; lord treasurer of Scotland, 23 Dec.; married the divorced Countess of Essex, 26 Dec. 1613; attached himself to his wife's great-uncle, Henry Howard, earl of Northampton, and the Spanish party; acting lord privy seal, on Northampton's death, June 1614; lord chamberlain, July; dislodged from the place of first favourite of James I by George Villiers (afterwards Duke of Buckingham), November 1614; quarrelled with the king, on Buckingham's account, 1615; accused of poisoning Overbury, September 1615, his countess pleading guilty, May 1616, and receiving a pardon, July 1616; prosecuted by the attorney-general, Francis Bacon, and found guilty, May 1616; kept prisoner in the Tower till January 1622; afterwards pardoned; prosecuted in the Star-chamber, 1630. [ix. 172]

CARR, ROBERT JAMES (1774–1841), bishop of Worcester; M.A. Worcester College, Oxford, 1806; D.D., 1820; vicar of Brighton, 1798; *protégé* of the prince regent; dean of Hereford, 1820; bishop of Chichester, 1824; bishop of Worcester, 1831–41. [ix. 176]

CARR, ROGER (*d.* 1612), divine; B.A. Pembroke Hall, Cambridge, 1570; rector of Rayne, Essex, 1573–1612; published devotional tracts. [ix. 177]

CARR, THOMAS, *alias* MILES PINKNEY (1599–1674). [See CARRE, THOMAS.]

CARR, WILLIAM HOLWELL (1758–1830), art connoisseur; called Holwell till 1798, when he took the name Carr on account of his wife's estate; fellow of Exeter College, Oxford, 1778–93; B.D., 1790; travelled and collected pictures, 1781; vicar of Menheniot, Cornwall, 1792; amateur exhibitor at the Royal Academy, 1797–1820; bequeathed pictures to the nation. [ix. 177]

CARRE, THOMAS (1599–1674), really MILES PINKNEY, Roman catholic divine; born in Durham; educated at Douay; priest, 1625; procurator of Douay College till 1634; founder and confessor of an Augustinian nunnery at Paris; *protégé* of Cardinal Richelieu; died at Paris; published English translations of devotional and controversial tracts. [ix. 177]

CARRE, WALTER RIDDELL (1807–1874), topographer; took the name Carre, *c.* 1853, on succeeding to an estate in Roxburghshire; merchant in London; resided latterly in Roxburghshire; wrote papers on topics connected with the borders. [ix. 178]

CARRICK, EARL OF (1253–1304). [See BRUCE, ROBERT DE VII.]

CARRICK, JOHN DONALD (1787–1837), author; shopman in London, 1807; china-warehouseman in Glasgow, 1811–25; journalist in Glasgow, 1828, in Perth, 1833, and in Kilmarnock, 1834–5; wrote Scottish songs and biographies. [ix. 178]

CARRICK, THOMAS (1802–1875), miniature painter; chemist in Carlisle; a self-taught artist; became famous locally as a miniaturist; removed to Newcastle, 1836, and London, 1839; exhibited at the Royal Academy, 1841–66. [ix. 179]

CARRIER, BENJAMIN (1566–1614). [See CARIER, BENJAMIN.]

CARRINGTON, LORD (1617–1679). [See PRIMROSE, SIR ARCHIBALD.]

CARRINGTON, first BARON (1752–1838). [See SMITH, ROBERT.]

CARRINGTON, SIR CODRINGTON EDMUND (1769–1849), judge; educated at Winchester; barrister of the Middle Temple, 1792; practised at Calcutta, 1793–9; drew up a code for Ceylon, 1800; knighted; chief-justice of Ceylon, 1800–6; resided afterwards in Buckinghamshire and then in Jersey; M.P., St. Mawes, 1826–31; published legal pamphlets. [ix. 180]

CARRINGTON, FREDERICK GEORGE (1816–1864), journalist; son of Noel Thomas Carrington [q. v.]; on the staff of various West of England newspapers; wrote for many magazines and encyclopædias. [ix. 180]

CARRINGTON, NOEL THOMAS (1777–1830), Devonshire poet; son of a Plymouth grocer; served in the fleet; taught school at Maidstone, 1804–9, and at Plymouth Rock, 1809–30; wrote verses describing Devonshire scenery and traditions. [ix. 180]

CARRINGTON, RICHARD CHRISTOPHER (1826–1875), astronomer; son of a wealthy brewer; educated at Trinity College, Cambridge, 1844–8; devoted himself to astronomy; observer to Durham University, 1849–52; witnessed the total solar eclipse in Sweden, 1851; built private observatory at Reigate, Surrey, 1853; engaged in mapping stars and sun-spots; visited German observatories, 1856; managed the Brentford brewery, 1858–65; died suddenly. [ix. 181]

CARRODUS, JOHN TIPLADY (1836–1895), violinist; studied under Molique in London and in Stuttgart; joined orchestra of Royal Italian Opera, 1855, and became leader, 1869; professor of violin at National Training School for Music, 1876; professor at Guildhall School of Music and Trinity College, London; published musical compositions and other writings. [Suppl. i. 395]

CARROLL, ANTHONY (1722–1794), jesuit; born in Ireland; joined the jesuits at St. Omer's, 1744; served on the English mission, 1754–73 and 1775–94; murdered in London. [ix. 183]

CARROLL, LEWIS (1832–1898), pseudonym. [See DODGSON, CHARLES LUTWIDGE.]

CARRUTHERS, ANDREW (1770–1852), Roman catholic prelate; native of Kirkcudbrightshire; educated at Douay; returned to Scotland, c. 1790; priest, 1795; titular bishop of Ceramis, 1832, with jurisdiction over the east of Scotland. [ix. 183]

CARRUTHERS, JAMES (1759–1832), Roman catholic historian; native of Kirkcudbrightshire; educated at Douay; catholic priest at Scottish stations; published a Romanist 'History of Scotland,' 1826–31. [ix. 184]

CARRUTHERS, ROBERT (1799–1878), miscellaneous writer; bookseller's apprentice in Dumfries; national schoolmaster at Huntingdon; published a 'History of Huntingdon,' 1824; editor of the 'Inverness Courier,' 1828–78; wrote verses, and papers on the history of the highlands; edited Pope's works (4 vols.), 1853; LL.D. Edinburgh, 1871. [ix. 184]

CARSE, ALEXANDER (fl. 1812–1820), painter, called 'Old Carse'; came to London, 1812; returned to Edinburgh, 1820. [ix. 185]

CARSE, WILLIAM (fl. 1818–1845), painter; probably son of Alexander Carse [q. v.]; art-student in London, 1818; exhibited at the Royal Academy, London, 1820–9, and at Edinburgh, 1830–45. [ix. 185]

CARSEWELL, JOHN (fl. 1560–1572), bishop of the Isles; rector of Kilmartin, Argyllshire; superintendent of Argyll, 1560; censured by the assembly for accepting the see, 1569. [ix. 185]

CARSON, AGLIONBY ROSS (1780–1850), classical scholar; studied at Edinburgh University, 1797; headmaster of Dumfries grammar school, 1801; classical master, 1806, and rector (1820–45) of Edinburgh High School; LL.D. St. Andrews, 1826; edited Tacitus and Phædrus. [ix. 185]

CARSON, ALEXANDER (1776–1844), baptist; educated at Glasgow; minister at Tobermore, Derry, to a presbyterian congregation, 1798–1804, and to an independent chapel, 1814–44; joined the baptists, 1831; wrote works of controversial divinity. [ix. 186]

CARSON, JAMES (1772–1843), physician; M.D. Edinburgh, 1799; practitioner in Liverpool; wrote medical pamphlets. [ix. 186]

CARSTARES, WILLIAM (1649–1715), Scottish statesman and divine; nick-named 'the cardinal' from his political influence under William III; son of the covenanting minister of Cathcart, Lanarkshire; at Edinburgh University, 1663–7; withdrew to Holland after his father's outlawry; studied at Utrecht, 1669–72; came to London, probably as an agent of William of Orange, 1672; political prisoner in Edinburgh Castle, 1674–9; resided in England; conducted intrigues in Scotland, Holland, and London, preparing for the Earl of Argyll's invasion, 1683; arrested, 1683; political prisoner at Edinburgh; his evidence, taken under torture, used to bring Baillie of Jerviswood to the block, 1684; released; minister of a Scottish congregation at Leyden, 1686; accompanied William of Orange to England as chaplain, 1688; chaplain to William III at court, and in his campaigns in Ireland and Flanders; William's chief adviser in Scottish affairs; principal of Edinburgh University, 1703–15; minister of Grey Friars', Edinburgh; leader of the church of Scotland; a chief promoter of the union; moderator of the general assembly, 1705, 1708, 1711, and 1715. [ix. 187]

CARSWELL, SIR ROBERT (1793–1857), physician; studied medicine at Glasgow, Paris, and Lyons; M.D. Aberdeen, 1826; made drawings illustrative of pathology at Paris, 1826–31; professor of pathological anatomy, University College, London, 1831–40; published his 'Forms of Disease,' 1837; went to Brussels as physician to the king of Belgium, 1840; knighted; wrote on medical subjects. [ix. 191]

CARTE, SAMUEL (1653–1740), antiquary; educated at Magdalen College School, Oxford; beneficed successively in Warwick, Leicester, Lincoln shires. [ix. 191]

CARTE, THOMAS (1686–1754), historian; son of Samuel Carte [q. v.]; admitted at University College, Oxford, 1698; B.A. Brasenose College, 1702; M.A. King's College, Cambridge, 1706; ordained; reader at Bath Abbey, 1707–14; refused the oaths to George I, 1715; lived in retirement at Coleshill, Warwickshire; secretary to Bishop Atterbury; fled to France on Atterbury's imprisonment, 1722; went by the name of Phillips; collected materials to illustrate de Thou's 'Historia sui temporis'; returned to England, 1728; published his 'Life of Ormonde,' 1736, and a 'Collection of . . . Papers,' 1744; energetic in enrolling subscribers to a projected 'History of England'; published his history, vols. i.–iii. 1747–52 (vol. iv. posthumous, 1755). His manuscript collections are now in the Bodleian. [ix. 191]

CARTER, EDMUND (fl. 1753), topographer; schoolmaster; published, 1753, histories of Cambridgeshire and Cambridge University. [ix. 194]

CARTER, ELIZABETH (1717–1806), miscellaneous writer; daughter of a Kent clergyman; learned classical and modern languages; wrote for the 'Gentleman's Magazine' from 1734; published poems, 1738 and 1762; translated from the French and Italian; published a translation of Epictetus, 1758; friend of Dr. Samuel Johnson; lived at Deal, Kent; travelled on the continent. Her correspondence was published posthumously. [ix. 194]

CARTER, ELLEN (1762–1815), artist; née Vavasour; native of Yorkshire; educated in a convent at Rouen; married, 1787, the Rev. John Carter, vicar of St. Swithin's, Lincoln; book-illustrator. [ix. 196]

CARTER, FRANCIS (d. 1783), traveller; published, 1777, a narrative of his tour (1772) in Moorish Spain; collected Spanish books; left in manuscript a history of early Spanish literature. [ix. 197]

CARTER, GEORGE (1737–1794), painter; mercer in London; travelled; exhibited privately, 1785. [ix. 197]

CARTER, HARRY WILLIAM (1787–1863), physician; M.A. Oriel College, Oxford, 1810; M.B., 1811; travelled; M.D., 1819; practised at Canterbury, 1819–35; wrote on medical topics. [ix. 198]

CARTER, HENRY, otherwise FRANK LESLIE (1821–1880), engraver, son of an Ipswich glovemaker; apprenticed to a London draper; early showed talent for drawing and engraving; artist to the 'Illustrated London News'; emigrated to New York, 1848, and took the name of Frank Leslie; worked for illustrated papers; separated from his wife, 1860; commenced 'Frank Leslie's Illustrated Newspaper,' 1855, the 'Chimney Corner,' 1865, and other journals; issued an illustrated history of the American civil war, 1862. [ix. 198]

CARTER, JAMES (1798–1855), of London; engraver of architectural and landscape plates for books.
[ix. 199]

CARTER, JOHN, the elder (1554–1635), puritan divine; educated at Clare Hall, Cambridge; vicar of Bramford, Suffolk, 1583; rector of Belstead, Suffolk, 1617–35; published expository tracts. [ix. 199]

CARTER, JOHN, the younger (d. 1655), divine; son of John Carter the elder [q. v.]; M.A. Corpus Christi College, Cambridge, 1603; curate of St. Peter Mancroft, Norwich, 1631, and vicar, 1638–52; rector of St. Lawrence, Norwich, c. 1654; published a memoir of his father.
[ix. 200]

CARTER, JOHN (1784–1817), draughtsman and architect; a surveyor's clerk, 1764; draughtsman to the 'Builder's Magazine,' 1774–86, and to the Society of Antiquaries, 1780; published many books of views of buildings in England, 1780–1814. [ix. 200]

CARTER, JOHN (1815–1850), silkweaver; paralysed by an accident, 1836; copied pictures by means of a pencil or brush held in the mouth. [ix. 202]

CARTER, LAWRENCE (1672–1745), judge; of Lincoln's Inn; recorder of Leicester, 1697–1729; M.P. for Leicester, 1698, 1701, and 1722, for Beeralston, 1710, 1714, and 1715; crown counsel against the rebels, 1715; knighted, 1724; puisne baron of the exchequer, 1726–45.
[ix. 202]

CARTER, MATTHEW (fl. 1660), loyalist; Kentish squire; joined the Kentish insurgents, 1648; prisoner at Colchester; published, 1650, a narrative of the rising; published 'Honor Redivivus,' a treatise on heraldry, 1655. [ix. 203]

CARTER, OLIVER (1540?–1605), divine; scholar of St. John's College, Cambridge, 1555; fellow, 1563; B.D., 1569; a preacher of Manchester Collegiate Church, after 1571, and fellow before 1576; fellow on the new foundation, 1578–1605; a bitter opponent of Dr. John Dee, warden in 1595; published, 1579, a controversial treatise against Richard Bristow. [ix. 203]

CARTER, OWEN BROWNE (1806–1859), architect; practised as an architect at Winchester; published papers on Winchester Cathedral and Hampshire churches; published, 1840, views taken at Cairo, 1830; exhibited architectural drawings at the Royal Academy, 1847–9.
[ix. 205]

CARTER, PETER (1530?–1590), author of a logical treatise, 1563; fellow of St. John's College, Cambridge, 1555; M.A., 1557; master of Preston School, Lancashire.
[ix. 205]

CARTER, RICHARD (d. 1692), rear-admiral; served in the fleet, 1672–81; commander of a ship at Beachy Head, 1690; rear-admiral, 1691; killed in action at Barfleur. [ix. 205]

CARTER, THOMAS (d. 1795), sculptor of tombstones and memorial tablets. [ix. 206]

CARTER, THOMAS (1735?–1804), musical composer; chorister of Christ Church, Dublin; organist of St. Werburgh's, Dublin, 1751–69; studied music in Italy; musical director of Calcutta Theatre; settled in London, c. 1775, and composed for the theatres; published glees and songs, including 'O Nanny, wilt thou gang wi' me?' [ix. 206]

CARTER, THOMAS (d. 1867), clerk at the Horse Guards, 1839; wrote regimental histories. [ix. 207]

CARTER, WILLIAM (d. 1584), printer; apprentice to John Cawood [q. v.], 1563; secretary to Nicholas Harpsfield; secretly printed Roman catholic books against Queen Elizabeth, 1579–83; executed for treason.
[ix. 207]

CARTERET, SIR GEORGE (d. 1680), governor of Jersey; of an old Jersey family; lieutenant in the navy, 1632; captain, 1633; second in command against the Sallee pirates, 1637; controller of the navy, 1639; offered a command by parliament, 1642; from St. Malo, Brittany, sent supplies and arms to the royalists in the west and in the Channel islands; sent by Charles I to Jersey, 1643; reduced the island; sent out privateers against English ships; gave a refuge to royalists, 1646; created baronet, 1646; granted estates in Jersey and America, 1649; surrendered to the Commonwealth forces, December 1651;

vice-admiral in the French navy; imprisoned, August 1657; banished from France, December 1657; withdrew to Venice; treasurer of the navy, 1660–7; vice-chamberlain of the household, 1660–70; M.P., Portsmouth, 1661–9; a proprietor of Carolina, 1663; deputy-treasurer of Ireland, 1667–73; board of trade commissioner, 1668–72; naval commissioner, 1673–9. [ix. 208]

CARTERET, JOHN, EARL GRANVILLE (1690–1763), politician; succeeded his father as second Baron Carteret of Hawnes, 1695; educated at Westminster School; entered Christ Church, Oxford, 1706; became a good classical scholar; took his seat in the House of Lords, 1711; a champion of the protestant succession; lord-lieutenant of Devonshire, 1716–21; a parliamentary adherent of the Earl of Sunderland, 1717; envoy to Sweden, 1719; secured the opening of the Baltic to British commerce; negotiated peace between the Baltic powers, 1719–20; advocated punishment of South Sea Company's officials, 1721; secretary of state in Walpole's administration, 1721–4; became favourite of George I through speaking German and advocating interests of Hanover; accompanied George I to Hanover, 1723; intrigued to oust Walpole from office: factiously fostered sedition in Ireland; lord-lieutenant of Ireland, 1724–30; friendly to Jonathan Swift; virulently opposed Walpole's administration, 1730–1742; secretary of state, 1742–4; accompanied George II in the campaign of 1743; intensely unpopular through his partiality for Hanover to the prejudice of British interests; succeeded as Earl Granville, on his mother's death, 1744; advised George II to exclude William Pitt from office, 1746; failed to form a ministry, February 1746; K.G., 1750; lord president of the council, 1751–63; hon. D.C.L. Oxford, 1756. His correspondence is in the British Museum. [ix. 210]

CARTERET, SIR PHILIP DE (1584–1643), knight; lieutenant-governor of Jersey, 1626–43; seigneur of St. Ouen, Jersey; at Oxford University, 1594–1601; obtained from the privy council canons assimilating the Jersey churches to the Anglican church; showed kindness to William Prynne during his imprisonment, 1639–41; allowed by parliament to return to Jersey, 1642; declared for the king; besieged by the parliamentary forces.
[ix. 215]

CARTERET, PHILIP (d. 1796), rear-admiral; lieutenant of the Dolphin in John Byron's voyage, 1764–6; sailed round the world in the Swallow, 1767–9, making numerous discoveries in the Pacific; captain, 1771; served in the West Indies, 1777–81; retired as rear-admiral, 1794. [ix. 216]

CARTHACH, SAINT, the elder (d. 580?), of a royal house; visited Rome; disciple of St. Ciaran of Saighir, King's County; succeeded him at Saighir, c. 550; tutor of St. Carthach the younger [q. v.]; commemorated on March 5. [ix. 216]

CARTHACH, SAINT, the younger (d. 636), called also MOCHUDA; son of the king of 'Kerry's swineherd; forsook the court to join St. Carthach the elder [q. v.]; bishop in Kerry; founded the monastery of Rahen, King's County, c. 590; expelled from Rahen, c. 631; founded monastery at Lismore; commemorated on May 14.
[ix. 217]

CARTHEW, GEORGE ALFRED (1807–1882), Norfolk antiquary; mainly self-taught; practised as a solicitor at Framlingham, Suffolk, 1830–9, and East Dereham, Norfolk; wrote much on Norfolk antiquities; chief work, 'History of Launditch Hundred,' 1877–9. [ix. 218]

CARTHEW, THOMAS (1657–1704), serjeant-at-law; barrister of the Middle Temple, 1686; serjeant-at-law, 1700; wrote law reports. [ix. 219]

CARTIER, SIR GEORGE ETIENNE (1814–1873), Canadian statesman; educated at Montreal; barrister of Lower Canada, 1835; member of the legislature, 1848; attorney-general, 1856; a leading member of the cabinet, 1857–8; premier, 1858–62; attorney-general, 1864; minister of militia, 1867–73; created baronet, 1868; died in London; wrote French-Canadian songs. [ix. 219]

CARTWRIGHT, CHRISTOPHER (1602–1658), divine; entered Peterhouse, Cambridge, 1617; M.A., 1624; fellow, 1625; a minister in York; student of rabbinical literature; published sermons and works of controversial divinity. [ix. 220]

CARTWRIGHT, EDMUND (1743-1823), reputed inventor of the power-loom; entered University College, Oxford, 1760; fellow of Magdalen College, Oxford, 1764; M.A., 1766; married an heiress; incumbent of Brampton, Yorkshire; rector of Goadby Marwood, Leicestershire, 1779; visited cotton-spinning mills near Matlock, 1784, and conceived the idea of a weaving-mill; patented a power-loom, 1785-7; removed to Doncaster, where he built a weaving-mill, 1787; prebendary of Lincoln, 1786; patented a wool-combing machine, 1789-92; bankrupt; sold his Doncaster factory, 1793; removed to London; patented an alcohol engine, 1797; agricultural experimenter to the Dukes of Bedford at Woburn, Bedfordshire, 1800-7; D.D., 1806; rewarded by parliament, 1809; farmed in Kent. [ix. 221]

CARTWRIGHT, FRANCES DOROTHY (1780-1863), authoress; youngest child of Edmund Cartwright [q. v.]; published a biography of her uncle, John Cartwright (1740-1824) [q. v.], and devotional poems, and translations from the Spanish. [ix. 223]

CARTWRIGHT, GEORGE (*fl.* 1661), author of 'The Heroick Lover,' a tragedy, printed 1661. [ix. 224]

CARTWRIGHT, JOHN (*fl.* 1763-1808), painter; studied in Rome; returned to England, 1779; exhibited, 1784-1808; a friend of Henry Fuseli. [ix. 224]

CARTWRIGHT, JOHN (1740-1824), political reformer; served in the navy, c. 1758-70, chiefly in Newfoundland; lieutenant, 1766; wrote against taxing the American colonies, 1775; major of militia, 1775-90; resided in Lincolnshire; removed to London, 1805; wrote in favour of strengthening the navy, reforming parliament, abolishing slavery, emancipating Greece, and crushing absolutism in Spain. [ix. 224]

CARTWRIGHT, JOSEPH (1789?-1829), marine painter; appointed paymaster of the forces at Corfu, c. 1811; published 'Views in the Ionian Islands'; exhibited in London. [ix. 225]

CARTWRIGHT, SAMUEL (1789-1864), dentist; an ivory turner; attended medical classes in London; practised as dentist, 1811-57. [ix. 226]

CARTWRIGHT, THOMAS (1535-1603), puritan; entered Clare Hall, Cambridge, 1547; scholar of St. John's, Cambridge, 1550; left Cambridge at Mary's accession, 1553; lawyer's clerk; returned to Cambridge, 1559; fellow of St. John's College, 1560; M.A., 1560; fellow of Trinity College, 1562; one of the disputants at Elizabeth's state visit, 1564; attacked the use of the surplice, 1565; accompanied Bishop Adam Loftus to Ireland as chaplain, 1565; returned to Cambridge, 1567; Lady Margaret professor of divinity, 1569; lectured and preached against the constitution of the church of England; deprived of his professorship, 1570, and of his fellowship at Trinity, 1571; retired to Geneva; returned to England, 1572; withdrew to the continent, 1573; tried to organise the Huguenots of the Channel Islands, 1576; employed by English puritan leaders to criticise the Rhemish version of the New Testament, 1582; pastor of the English congregation at Antwerp; declined divinity chair at St. Andrews, 1584; returned to England, 1585; master of the Earl of Leicester's hospital at Warwick, 1586; imprisoned as a puritan, 1590-2; accompanied Edward, baron Zouche, to Guernsey, 1595-8; published exegetical and controversial treatises. [ix. 226]

CARTWRIGHT, THOMAS (1634-1689), bishop of Chester; tabarder of Queen's College, Oxford, c. 1650; M.A., 1655; chaplain; secretly ordained by Bishop Robert Skinner, c. 1655; vicar of Walthamstow, Essex, 1657; preacher at St. Mary Magdalen, Milk Street, London, 1659; prebendary of Wells, 1660; vicar of Barking, 1660-89; D.D., 1661; prebendary of St. Paul's and vicar of St. Thomas, London, 1665; chaplain in ordinary; dean of Ripon, 1675; a favourite of James, duke of York; rector of Wigan; bishop of Chester, 1686; a chief instrument in carrying out James II's unconstitutional acts; one of James II's ecclesiastical commissioners, 1687; chief visitor of Magdalen College, Oxford, to enforce submission to James II, 1687; withdrew to France, 1688; nominated bishop of Salisbury by King James, 1689, whom he followed to Ireland. [ix. 230]

CARTWRIGHT, SIR THOMAS (1795-1850), diplomatist; entered Christ Church, Oxford, 1812; envoy to Sweden; knighted, 1834; died at Stockholm. [ix. 232]

CARTWRIGHT, WILLIAM (1611-1643), dramatist; educated at Westminster School; student of Christ Church, Oxford, 1628; M.A., 1635; a florid preacher; his 'Royal Slave' acted before Charles I at Oxford, 1636; junior proctor, April 1643; died of pestilence, November. His plays and poems were published, 1651. [ix. 232]

CARTWRIGHT, WILLIAM (*d.* 1687), actor; acted at Whitefriars Theatre before the civil war; turned bookseller when the theatres were closed; joined the king's company of players, c. 1661, and the Duke of York's company, 1682; bequeathed books and portraits to Dulwich College. [ix. 233]

CARUS, THOMAS (*d.* 1572?), judge; barrister of the Middle Temple; serjeant-at-law, 1559; justice of the queen's bench, 1565 till death. [ix. 234]

CARVE, THOMAS (1590-1672?), traveller and historian; really CARUE, i.e. Carew; catholic priest in Leighlin diocese; army chaplain in the imperialist service in Germany, from before 1626 to 1643; visited Ireland, 1630 and 1633; vicar-choral of St. Stephen's Cathedral, Vienna, 1643; published abroad 'Itinerarium,' being an account of his services, 1639-46, a treatise on Irish history, 1651, and other works. [ix. 234]

CARVELL, NICHOLAS (*d.* 1566), poet; educated at Eton; entered King's College, Cambridge, 1545; M.A., 1553; withdrew to Zurich, 1553-9; probably author of two poems in the 'Mirror for Magistrates.' [ix. 235]

CARVER, JOHN (1575?-1621), leader of the 'pilgrim fathers'; an English puritan; withdrew to Holland, 1608; deacon in the English congregationalist church in Leyden; sailed in the Mayflower, September 1620; chosen governor by the colonists at Massachusetts, December; made a treaty with the Indians, March 1621; died of sunstroke. [ix. 236]

CARVER, JONATHAN (1732-1780), American explorer; born in Connecticut; son of the English governor; served in the colonial forces, 1757-63; travelled along Lake Superior and in unexplored Minnesota, 1766-8; claimed to have received large grants of land from the Indians; came to England, 1769; further journeys and colonisation schemes prevented by the American rebellion; published account of his travels, 1778, and a tract on tobacco, 1779. [ix. 237]

CARVER, ROBERT (*d.* 1791), landscape and scene painter; son and pupil of an Irish artist; exhibited in Dublin; scene painter to Drury Lane Theatre and afterwards to Covent Garden Theatre; exhibited landscapes in London, 1765-90. [ix. 238]

CARVOSSO, BENJAMIN (1789-1854), Wesleyan minister; a Cornishman; Wesleyan minister, 1814; went to Tasmania, 1820; thence to New South Wales; started the 'Australian Magazine,' 1820; returned to Tasmania, 1825; returned to England, 1830, and served at different centres; published tracts. [ix. 239]

CARWARDINE, PENELOPE, afterwards MRS. BUTLER (1730?-1800?), miniaturist; exhibited, 1761-72; friend of Sir Joshua Reynolds. [ix. 239]

CARWELL, THOMAS (1600-1664), jesuit; real name THOROLD; of Lincolnshire; embraced Romanism, 1622; studied at St. Omer's; joined the jesuits at Rome, 1633; professor at Liège; sent on the English mission, 1647; served chiefly in London; wrote against Archbishop Laud, 1658. [ix. 239]

CARY. [See also CAREW and CAREY.]

CARY, EDWARD (*d.* 1711), Roman catholic divine; went abroad, 1646; priest, 1651; sent on the English mission; army chaplain to James II; Jacobite agent; published a tract. [ix. 240]

CARY, ELIZABETH, VISCOUNTESS FALKLAND (1585-1639), daughter of Sir Lawrence Tanfield, the judge; married, c. 1600, Sir Henry Cary, afterwards first viscount Falkland [q. v.]; a linguist; secretly embraced Roman catholicism, c. 1604; accompanied her husband to Ireland, 1622; separated from him on account of religion, 1625. [ix. 241]

CARY, FRANCIS STEPHEN (1808-1880), artist; a younger son of Henry Francis Cary [q. v.]; studied art in London, Paris (1829), Italy, and Munich; travelled, 1833-5; exhibited in London from 1836; art teacher in Bloomsbury, 1842-74. [ix. 240]

CARY, SIR HENRY, first VISCOUNT FALKLAND (*d.* 1633), lord-deputy of Ireland; son of a Hertfordshire knight; said to have studied at Oxford; served abroad; gentleman of the bedchamber to James I; K.B., 1608; controller of the household, 1617–21; created Viscount Falkland in the Scottish peerage, 1620; lord-deputy of Ireland, 1622; failed in that office; recalled, 1629. [ix. 240]

CARY, HENRY FRANCIS (1772–1844), translator; of Irish extraction; born at Gibraltar; educated at Birmingham; wrote verses, from 1787, chiefly for the 'Gentleman's Magazine'; entered Christ Church, Oxford, 1790; M.A., 1796; vicar of Abbot's Bromley, Staffordshire, 1796, and of Kingsbury, Warwickshire, 1800; published his translation of Dante's 'Inferno,' 1805, and of the 'Purgatorio' and 'Paradiso,' 1812; became a non-resident parson, 1807; resided in London, taking clerical work and writing for the magazines; translated the 'Birds' of Aristophanes, 1824; an official of the British Museum Library, 1826–37; translated Pindar, 1832; travelled, 1833–5; pensioned, 1841. [ix. 242]

CARY, JOHN (*d.* 1395?), judge; warden of the Devonshire ports, 1373; refused to be serjeant-at-law, 1383; chief baron of the exchequer, 1386; impeached and banished to Waterford for favouring Richard II, 1388. [ix. 244]

CARY, JOHN (*d.* 1720?), merchant and writer on trade; son of a vicar of Bristol; West India sugar merchant; compliant to James II, 1687; published, 1695, 'An Essay on . . . England in relation to its Trade'; advocated workhouses for paupers; consulted by the government on Irish manufactures, 1704; published pamphlets on trade and the currency. [ix. 244]

CARY, LUCIUS, second VISCOUNT FALKLAND (1610?–1643), son of Sir Henry Cary, afterwards first viscount Falkland [q. v.], and Elizabeth Cary [q. v.]; accompanied his parents to Dublin, 1622; studied at Trinity College, Dublin; deprived of command of a company by his father's opponents, 1629; imprisoned in the Fleet to prevent his fighting a duel, January 1630; succeeded to the Burford estate, *c.* 1630; vainly sought service in Holland; lived in retirement at Great Tew, Oxfordshire; succeeded to the viscounty and his father's encumbered estates, 1633; supposed to have sold his life interest in the Burford estate, 1634; resided with his mother, a Roman catholic, 1633–4; retired to Great Tew, 1634; served as volunteer against the Scots, 1639; M.P. for Newport in the Isle of Wight in the Short parliament, April 1640, and in the Long parliament, November 1640; spoke against Laud's ecclesiastical tyranny, February 1641; spoke in favour of Strafford's attainder, April 1641; opposed abolition of episcopacy, May 1641; accepted secretaryship of state, January 1642; accompanied Charles I to York; sent to negotiate with the parliament, September 1642; present at the siege of Gloucester, August 1643; despairing of peace threw away his life at Newbury fight, September 1643. Some of his verses and philosophical tractates were published posthumously. [ix. 246]

CARY, PATRICK (*fl.* 1651), poet; a younger son of Sir Henry Cary, first viscount Falkland [q. v.]; brought up as a Roman catholic in France and Italy; a protégé of Pope Urban VIII; an abbé in Italy, before 1644; Benedictine monk at Douay, *c.* 1650; came to England; wrote verses at Warnford, Hampshire, 1651 (first printed, 1771). [ix. 251]

CARY, ROBERT (1615?–1688), chronologer; of the Carys of Cockington, Devonshire; entered Exeter College, Oxford, 1631; scholar of Corpus Christi College, Oxford, 1634; M.A., 1639; D.C.L., 1644; rector of Portlemouth, Devonshire, 1656–88; archdeacon of Exeter, 1662–4; published 'Palæologia Chronica,' 1677. [ix. 252]

CARY, VALENTINE (*d.* 1626), bishop of Exeter; entered St. John's College, Cambridge; migrated to Christ's College, 1585; B.A., 1589; fellow of St. John's, 1591; fellow of Christ's, 1595; again fellow of St. John's, 1599; prebendary of St. Paul's, 1601; vicar of East Tilbury, 1603; rector of Great Parndon, 1606; vicar of Epping, 1607; prebendary of Lincoln, 1607–21; master of Christ's College, Cambridge, 1609–20; ejected the puritan fellows; rector of Orsett, Essex, and of Toft, Cambridgeshire, 1610; dean of St. Paul's, 1614–21; attended James I to Scotland, 1617; bishop of Exeter, 1621–6; chancellor of Exeter, 1622–4; vicar of Exminster, 1624. [ix. 252]

CARY, WILLIAM (1759–1825), philosophical instrument maker in London, 1790–1825. [ix. 253]

CARYL, JOSEPH (1602–1673), independent divine; M.A. Exeter College, Oxford, 1627; preacher at Lincoln's Inn, 1632–47; a frequent preacher before the Long parliament; member of the Westminster Assembly, 1643; minister of St. Magnus, London, 1645–62; chaplain to Oliver Cromwell in Scotland; pastor of a London nonconformist congregation, 1662–73; published sermons and a commentary on Job, 1651–66. [ix. 253]

CARYLL, JOHN, titular BARON CARYLL (1625–1711), diplomatist; of a Roman catholic family in Sussex; wrote a tragedy, 1666, and a comedy, 1671; translated parts of Ovid and Virgil, 1680–3; envoy to Rome, 1685; secretary to Queen Mary of Modena, 1686; withdrew to France, 1689; secretary of state to the exiled dynasty; his estate forfeited, 1696; published a version of the Psalms, 1700; created by James Edward, the Old Pretender, Baron Caryll, 1701; died at Paris. [ix. 254]

CARYLL, JOHN (1666?–1736), friend of Pope, with whom he corresponded, 1710–35; Roman catholic squire in Sussex. [ix. 255]

CARYSFORT, EARLS OF. [See PROBY, JOHN JOSHUA, first EARL, 1751–1828; PROBY, GRANVILLE LEVESON, third EARL, 1781–1868.]

CARYSFORT, first BARON (1720–1772). [See PROBY, JOHN.]

CASALI, ANDREA (1720?–1783?), painter; born at Città Vecchia, Tuscany; studied painting at Rome; came to England, 1748; styled 'cavaliere' after 1761; returned to Rome, 1769; exhibited at London till 1783. [ix. 256]

CASANOVA, FRANCIS (1727–1805), battle painter; born in London, 1727, his parents being there on an acting tour; studied art at Venice, Paris (1751), and Dresden (1752–6); returned to Paris, 1757; exhibited in London, 1767; died at Vienna. [ix. 256]

CASAUBON, ISAAC (1559–1614), classical scholar; born at Geneva; son of Huguenot refugees; brought up at Crest in Dauphiné; learned Greek at Geneva from Francis Portus, a Cretan; succeeded Portus as professor of Greek, 1581; published notes on Diogenes Laertius, 1583; his second wife a daughter of the great printer, Henri Estienne; published commentaries on several Greek authors, 1587–95; met Sir Henry Wotton, 1596; corresponded with Joseph Scaliger; professor at Montpellier, 1596; began his diary ('Ephemerides,' published 1850), 1597; published his Athenæus at Lyons, 1600; removed to Paris, 1600; pensioned by Henry IV; keeper of the royal library, 1604; importuned to embrace Romanism; published Persius, 1605, and Polybius, 1609 (completed 1617); invited to England, July 1610; came to England, October 1610; prebendary of Canterbury, 1611; attached to the court and pensioned by James I; employed to confute Baronius ('Exercitationes xvi ad Baronii Annales,' published 1614); buried in Westminster Abbey. [ix. 257]

CASAUBON, MERIC (1599–1671), classical scholar; a younger son of Isaac Casaubon [q. v.]; born at Geneva; brought up at Sedan; brought to England, 1611; at Eton; student of Christ Church, Oxford, 1614–27; published vindications of his father against Roman catholic detractors, 1621 and 1624; M.A., 1622; rector of Bleadon, Somerset, 1626; B.D., 1628; prebendary of Canterbury, 1628; vicar of Minster and Monckton, Thanet, 1634; D.D., 1636; ejected by parliament from his benefices, 1644; invited by Oliver Cromwell to write a history of the civil war; invited to Sweden by Queen Christina; married a rich wife, 1651; recovered his benefices, 1660; rector of Ickham, Kent, 1662; published classical commentaries, including Marcus Aurelius, 1643, and Epictetus, 1659, translations and theological treatises, 1631–70. [ix. 261]

CASE, JOHN (*d.* 1600), Aristotelian commentator; chorister at Oxford; scholar of St. John's College, Oxford, 1564; fellow; M.A., 1572; M.D., 1589; canon of Salisbury, 1589; practised medicine in Oxford; published philosophical text-books, 1584–99; wrote also 'Apologia Musices,' 1588. [ix. 262]

CASE, JOHN (*fl.* 1680–1700), astrologer; resided in Lambeth, 1682; friend of John Partridge the astrologer;

published two anatomical treatises, 1695, two astrological treatises, 1696-7, and a medical tract, 1698; styled M.D.; practised medicine and astrology in London. [ix. 263]

CASE, THOMAS (1598-1682), presbyterian divine; educated at Canterbury and Merchant Taylors' School; student of Christ Church, Oxford, 1616; M.A., 1623; curate at North Repps, Norfolk; incumbent of Erpingham, Norfolk; preacher at Manchester and Salford, 1635; prosecuted for contempt of church ceremonies in both dioceses (Norwich and Chester); married into an influential family, 1637; lecturer in several London churches, 1641-2; member of the Westminster assembly, 1643; intruded rector of Stockport, Cheshire, 1645-6; ejected by parliament from the rectory of St. Mary Magdalen, Milk Street, 1649; imprisoned as privy to the presbyterian plot to recall Charles II, 1651; rector of St. Giles-in-the-Fields, London, 1652?; deputed by presbyterians to congratulate Charles II at the Hague, 1660; chaplain to Charles II; member of the Savoy conference, 1661; ejected for nonconformity, 1662; published sermons. [ix. 264]

CASEY, JOHN (1820-1891), mathematician; engaged as national school teacher; scholar, Trinity College, Dublin, 1861; B.A., 1862; honorary LL.D., 1869; mathematical master in Kingston school, 1862-73; member of Royal Irish Academy, 1866, and councillor, 1880; professor of higher mathematics and mathematical physics, Catholic university, 1873-81; F.R.S., 1875; fellow of Royal University, 1881; honorary LL.D., 1885; lecturer in mathematics, University College, Stephen's Green, 1881-1891; published mathematical treatises. [Suppl. i. 395]

CASLON, WILLIAM, the elder (1692-1766), typefounder; born in Worcestershire; engraver on metal; set up shop in London, 1716; began type-founding, 1716, his type becoming famous. [ix. 267]

CASLON, WILLIAM, the younger (1720-1778), typefounder; eldest son of William Caslon the elder [q. v.]; partner in his father's business, 1742; carried it on successfully after his father's death. [ix. 267]

CASS, SIR JOHN (1666-1718), merchant and benefactor of city of London; alderman of Portsoken ward, London, 1710; M.P. for city, 1710 and 1713; sheriff, 1711; knighted, 1712; founded by legacy a school at Hackney. [Suppl. i. 396]

CASSAN, STEPHEN HYDE (1789-1841), ecclesiastical biographer; born at Calcutta; B.A. Magdalen Hall, Oxford, 1815; curate in Somerset and Wiltshire; vicar of Bruton, Somerset, 1831; published sermons and trite lives of the bishops of Salisbury, 1824, of Winchester, and (1830) of Bath and Wells. [ix. 268]

CASSEL or **CASSELS,** RICHARD (d. 1751). [See CASTLE, RICHARD.]

CASSELL, JOHN (1817-1865), publisher; son of a Manchester publican; bred a carpenter; self-taught; a teetotal lecturer; removed to London, 1836; opened a grocer's shop before 1847; commenced publishing magazines and books for popular instruction, 1850. [ix. 268]

CASSIE, JAMES (1819-1879), painter; exhibited in Edinburgh and London. [ix. 269]

CASSILLIS, EARLS OF. [See KENNEDY, GILBERT, second EARL, d. 1527; KENNEDY, GILBERT, third EARL, 1517?-1558; KENNEDY, GILBERT, fourth EARL, 1541?-1576; KENNEDY, JOHN, fifth EARL, 1567?-1615; KENNEDY, JOHN, sixth EARL, 1595?-1668; KENNEDY, JOHN, seventh EARL, 1646?-1701.]

CASSIVELLAUNUS (fl. 54 B.C.), in Welsh, CASWALLAWN, British prince; chief of the Catuvellauni (Hertford, Buckingham, and Berk shires); opposed Julius Cæsar in his second campaign in Britain; defeated at a ford over the Thames; his store-town shown to Cæsar by revolted subject tribes; submitted to Cæsar, and gave hostages. [ix. 270]

CASTEELS, PETER (1684-1749), painter and engraver of still-life; born at Antwerp; came to England, 1703; designer of calico patterns at Tooting, 1735, and Richmond. [ix. 271]

CASTELL, EDMUND (1606-1685), Semitic scholar; entered Emmanuel College, Cambridge, 1621; M.A., 1628; B.D., 1635; began his 'Lexicon Heptaglotton,' 1651 (published 1669); helped Brian Walton in the 'Biblia Polyglotta' (published 1657); published verses congratulating Charles II on the Restoration, 1660; D.D., 1661; chaplain to Charles II, 1666; prebendary of Canterbury, 1667; professor of Arabic at Cambridge; successively incumbent of Hatfield Peverel and Woodham Walter, Essex, and Higham-Gobion, Bedfordshire; bequeathed oriental manuscripts to Cambridge University. [ix. 271]

CASTELL, WILLIAM (d. 1645), author of two pamphlets on America, 1641-4; rector of Courteenhall, Northamptonshire, 1627. [ix. 272]

CASTELLO, ADRIAN DE (1460?-1521?). [See ADRIAN DE CASTELLO.]

CASTILLO, JOHN (1792-1845), or CASTELLO, author of poems in the Cleveland dialect; born of Roman catholic parents near Dublin; brought up near Whitby, Yorkshire; stonemason in Cleveland; joined the Wesleyans, 1818; a local preacher. [ix. 273]

CASTINE, THOMAS (d. 1793?), soldier; a Manxman; serjeant in the 4th foot; deserted; served in the French forces in America; said to have been colonel of foot in France, c. 1789; wrongly identified with General Adam Philip de Custine (guillotined 1793). [ix. 273]

CASTLE, EDMUND (1698-1750), ecclesiastic; educated at Canterbury; scholar of Corpus Christi College, Cambridge, 1716; B.A., 1719; fellow, 1722; public orator at Cambridge, 1726-9; vicar of Elm and Emneth, Isle of Ely, 1729; rector of Barley, Hertfordshire; head-master of St. Paul's School, 1744; master of Corpus Christi College, Cambridge, 1744; vice-chancellor of Cambridge University, 1746; prebendary of Lincoln, 1747; dean of Hereford, 1748. [ix. 274]

CASTLE, GEORGE (1635?-1673), physician; educated at Thame school; B.A. Balliol College, Oxford, 1654; fellow of All Souls', 1655; M.D., 1665; practised in Westminster; physician to the Charterhouse; published a medical tract. [ix. 274]

CASTLE, CASSEL, or **CASSELS,** RICHARD (d. 1751), architect; born in Germany of German parents; went to Ireland before 1720; designed many buildings in Dublin and the provinces; published one pamphlet, 1736. [ix. 274]

CASTLE, THOMAS (1804?-1840?), physician; apprenticed to a surgeon at Hythe; studied at Guy's Hospital, 1826; resident in Brighton; styled himself M.D. in 1838; published medical and botanical text-books, 1826-1837. [ix. 275]

CASTLEHAVEN, third EARL OF (1617?-1684). [See TOUCHET, JAMES.]

CASTLEMAINE, COUNTESS OF (1641-1709). [See VILLIERS, BARBARA, DUCHESS OF CLEVELAND.]

CASTLEMAINE, EARL OF (d. 1705). [See PALMER, ROGER.]

CASTLEREAGH, VISCOUNT (1769-1822). [See STEWART, ROBERT.]

CASTRO, ALFONSO Y (1495-1558), theologian; a Spaniard; Franciscan friar; chaplain to the Spanish merchants at Bruges, 1532; published his famous 'Adversus Hæreses,' 1534; preacher at Salamanca; chaplain to Charles V; published sermons, 1537-40, 'De justa hæreticorum punitione,' 1547, and 'De potestate legis pœnalis,' 1550; sent with Philip of Spain to England as his adviser, 1554; declared the burnings of English heretics to be carried out too hastily, February 1555; had a discussion in prison with John Bradford (1510?-1555) [q. v.]; at Antwerp, 1556; named archbishop of Compostella, 1557; died at Brussels. [ix. 275]

CASWALL, EDWARD (1814-1878), hymn-writer; M.A. Brasenose College, Oxford, 1838; incumbent of Stratford-sub-Castle, Wiltshire; embraced Roman catholicism, 1847; a father of the Birmingham Oratory, 1850; published Oxford jeux d'esprit, 1836-7, sermons, 1846, hymns and verses, 1849-65. [ix. 276]

CAT, CHRISTOPHER (fl. 1703-1733), keeper of the 'Cat and Fiddle' in London and afterwards of the 'Fountain' tavern, in which the Kit-Cat Club met, 1703-20. [ix. 277]

CATCHER or BURTON, EDWARD (1584?-1624?), jesuit; of Oriel College, Oxford, 1597; B.A. Balliol College, 1603; embraced Roman catholicism at Rome, 1606; joined the jesuits at Louvain, c. 1609; procurator of the jesuits at Liège, 1621-3; sent on the English mission; translated theological tracts. [ix. 278]

CATCHPOLE, MARGARET (1773-1841), adventuress; daughter of a Suffolk labourer; domestic servant in Ipswich; stole her master's horse to join a seaman in London, 1797; escaped from Ipswich gaol, 1800; transported to Australia, 1801; married a settler; resided in Sydney, 1828-41. [ix. 278]

CATCOTT, ALEXANDER (1725-1779), divine; eldest son of Alexander Stopford Catcott [q. v.]; entered Winchester School, 1739; B.A. Wadham College, Oxford, 1748; curate in Bristol; vicar of Temple Church, Bristol; wrote in defence of the traditional interpretation of the Mosaic deluge, 1756-68. [ix. 278]

CATCOTT, ALEXANDER STOPFORD (1692-1749), divine and poet; entered Merchant Taylors' School, 1699; scholar of St. John's College, Oxford, 1709; fellow, 1712-1722; B.C.L., 1718; head-master of Bristol grammar school, 1722-44; preacher in Bristol; rector of St. Stephen's, Bristol, 1744; published poems, 1715-17, expositions of the views of John Hutchinson [q. v.], 1738, and sermons. [ix. 279]

CATES, WILLIAM LEIST READWIN (1821-1895), compiler; passed in law at London University; articled as solicitor at Thatcham, 1844; engaged in private tuition; assisted Bernard Bolingbroke Woodward [q. v.] in 'Encyclopædia of Chronology,' 1860-72; edited 'Dictionary of General Biography,' 1867, and published other compilations. [Suppl. i. 396]

CATESBY, SIR JOHN (d. 1486), judge; of Whiston, Northamptonshire; of the Inner Temple, 1458; serjeant-at-law, 1463; justice of common pleas, 1481; knighted, 1482. [ix. 280]

CATESBY, MARK (1679?-1749), naturalist; studied natural science in London; collected plants in North America, 1710-19, and again, 1722-6; resided in London; published a 'Natural History of Carolina,' 1731-43, and descriptions of some American fauna and flora. [ix. 281]

CATESBY, ROBERT (1573-1605), conspirator; son and heir of Sir William Catesby of Lapworth, Warwickshire, a rich Roman catholic squire, often harassed for recusancy; possibly educated at Douay; of Gloucester Hall, Oxford, 1586; inherited Chastleton, Oxfordshire, 1593; took a leading part in the Earl of Essex's rising, 1601; heavily fined; sold Chastleton and retired to his mother's house at Ashby St. Legers, Northamptonshire; imprisoned as a malcontent, 1603; released; joined Thomas Winter and Guy Fawkes in the Gunpowder plot, summer of 1604; fled from Westminster to Ashby St. Legers on Guy Fawkes's arrest, 5 Nov. 1605; killed at Holbeach, Staffordshire, 8 Nov., resisting arrest. [ix. 281]

CATESBY, WILLIAM (d. 1485), squire of the body to Richard III, named in the popular satire ('The cat, the rat, and Lovel,' &c.); a lawyer; favourite of Richard, while Duke of Gloucester; contrived the fall of his patron, William, lord Hastings, 1483; chancellor of the exchequer, 1483; knight of the shire for Northamptonshire and speaker of the House of Commons, 1484; taken prisoner at Bosworth; beheaded. [ix. 284]

CATHARINE. [See CATHERINE.]

CATHCART, CHARLES, ninth BARON CATHCART (1721-1776), soldier; entered the army when very young; succeeded to barony, 1740; lieutenant-colonel, 1742; protégé of the Duke of Cumberland, under whom he served in Flanders, Scotland, and Holland; wounded at Fontenoy, 1745; hostage in Paris, 1748; lieutenant-general, 1760; envoy to Russia, 1768-71; commander of the forces in Scotland. [ix. 285]

CATHCART, CHARLES MURRAY, second EARL CATHCART (1783-1859), general; son of William Schaw Cathcart, first earl [q. v.]; cornet, 1800; served in Italy and Sicily, 1805-6; major, 1807; styled Lord Greenock, from November 1807; served at Walcheren, 1809; lieutenant-colonel, 1810; served in the Peninsula, 1810-12; quartermaster-general, 1814-23; served at Waterloo; took an interest in geology; governor of Edinburgh Castle,

1837-42; discovered the mineral 'Greenockite,' 1841; succeeded to earldom, 1843; commander-in-chief in British North America, 1846-9; general, 1854. [ix. 285]

CATHCART, DAVID, LORD ALLOWAY (d. 1829), Scottish judge; advocate, 1785; lord of session, styled Lord Alloway, 1813 till death. [ix. 286]

CATHCART, SIR GEORGE (1794-1854), general; younger son of William Schaw Cathcart, first earl Cathcart [q. v.]; cornet, 1810; lieutenant, 1811; aide-de-camp to his father with the Russian army, 1813-14; aide-de-camp to Wellington at Waterloo and in France, 1815-18; lieutenant-colonel, 1826; deputy-lieutenant of the Tower, 1846-51; published a book on the 1812-13 campaign, 1815; major-general, 1851; commander-in-chief in South Africa, 1852-4; crushed the Kaffirs and Basutos; K.C.B., 1853; commanded the fourth division in the Crimea; vainly urged an immediate attack on Sebastopol, September 1854; killed at Inkermann, 5 Nov. [ix. 286]

CATHCART, SIR WILLIAM SCHAW, tenth BARON CATHCART in the Scottish peerage, and first VISCOUNT and EARL CATHCART (1755-1843), general; eldest son of Charles Cathcart, ninth baron [q. v.]; at Eton, 1766-71; at St. Petersburg, with his father, 1771; studied law at Dresden and Glasgow; advocate, 1776; succeeded to barony, 1776; captain of dragoons, 1777; served in America, 1777-80, commanding the 'British legion' of colonials, 1778-80, and the 38th foot, 1780; returned to England, 1780; lieutenant-colonel, 1781; representative peer of Scotland, 1788; brigadier-general in the Quiberon expedition, 1793; major-general, 1794; served in Hanover, 1794-5; lieutenant-general, 1801; commander-in-chief in Ireland, 1803-5; served ingloriously in Hanover, 1805; bombarded Copenhagen, 1807; created Viscount Cathcart, 1807; commander-in-chief in Scotland; general, 1812; ambassador and military commissioner with the Russian army, 1813-14; created Earl Cathcart, 1814; ambassador at St. Petersburg, 1814-21; retired from politics, 1831. [ix. 287]

CATHERINE OF VALOIS (1401-1437), queen of Henry V; youngest daughter of Charles VI, the insane king of France; born at Paris; neglected by her mother, Isabel of Bavaria; brought up at a convent at Poissy; asked in marriage for Henry, prince of Wales, 1413; demanded in marriage by Henry, now Henry V, who also asked an immense dowry in money and territory, 1414, war with France ensuing on the rejection of his terms; met Henry V, 1419; married him at Troyes, 2 June 1420; came to England, February 1421; crowned at Westminster, 1421; made a progress in the north; birth of her son (Henry VI), 2 Dec. 1421; accompanied Henry V to France, May 1422; returned with his corpse to England, October 1422; granted Baynard's Castle, Surrey, for a residence, 1424; reported to be intriguing with, or secretly married to Owen Tudor, c. 1425; marriage with her forbidden by parliament except with consent of the privy council, 1428; by Owen Tudor had Edmund (created, 1452, Earl of Richmond, father of Henry VII), and other issue; withdrew to Bermondsey Abbey, 1436; buried in Westminster Abbey, with inscription by Henry VI describing her as widow of Henry V; new inscription afterwards put there by Henry VII, acknowledging her marriage to Tudor. [ix. 289]

CATHERINE OF ARRAGON (1485-1536), first queen of Henry VIII; youngest child of Ferdinand and Isabella of Spain; sought in marriage when two years old by Henry VII for Arthur, prince of Wales (he being one year old), 1487; became an excellent Latin scholar; treaty of marriage concluded, 1500; sailed from Coruña, 1501; reached Plymouth 2 Oct. 1501; married to Prince Arthur at St. Paul's, London, 14 Nov., she being almost sixteen, he just fifteen years of age; deprived of Prince Arthur by death, 1502; proposal made for her marriage with Prince Henry; suggestion made for her marriage with Henry VII (a widower, February 1503); treaty of marriage to Prince Henry signed, 23 June 1503; papal dispensation and brief of Pope Julius II for the marriage granted, 1504; left in poverty and distress through the heartless intrigues of Henry VII, who desired a better match for the prince, 1505-9; married to the prince, now Henry VIII, 11 June 1509 (she well over 23, he just 18); crowned, 24 June; gave birth to and lost four children, 1510-14; regent during Henry VIII's French campaign,

1513; birth of Princess Mary, 1516 ; Henry VIII vexed by her father's duplicity, she vexed by Henry's infidelities (Henry Fitzroy, bastard by Elizabeth Blount, widow of Sir Gilbert Tailbois, born 1519, created Duke of Richmond, 1525, died 1536), 1518 ; visited by her nephew Charles V, May 1520 ; accompanied Henry VIII to France, 1520 ; second visit of Charles V, 1522 ; harassed by intrigues of King Henry to annul his marriage, 1526 ; informed by him that cohabitation must cease till the validity of their marriage be determined, 22 June 1526 ; legatine powers to try the cause given to Cardinal Lorenzo Campeggio [q. v.], who arrived in October 1528 ; persecuted with the intention of making her retire to a nunnery ; appeared before the legatine court, 1529 ; appeared in open court to Henry VIII's justice, and to the pope, 1529 ; her case revoked to Rome ; attended the king's progress to Woodstock as queen, September 1529 ; left at Richmond while the king and Anne Boleyn were in London, February 1530 ; English and foreign universities consulted by Henry VIII for warrant to dissolve his marriage ; ill with fever, 1530 ; urged by the peers to allow her case to be tried by English judges, May and October 1531 ; finally abandoned by Henry VIII (who took Anne Boleyn with him), July 1531 ; separated from her daughter, Princess Mary ; removed to Moor, Hertfordshire, 1531, and to Bishop's Hatfield, 1532 ; much sympathy felt for her by the people, Henry VIII and Anne Boleyn being secretly married, 25 Jan., and the marriage acknowledged, 13 April 1533 ; ordered to be styled 'the princess dowager'; her marriage declared null by Archbishop Cranmer, 1533 ; removed to Buckden, Huntingdonshire, 1533 ; forcibly resisted an attempt to remove her to Somersham, Isle of Ely, 1533 ; in fear of poison, 1534 ; her marriage pronounced valid by the pope, 23 March 1534 ; her jointure transferred by parliament to Anne Boleyn ; steadily refused to accept the Act of Succession, 1534 ; many of her supporters executed, 1535 ; serious illness, December 1535 ; died possibly of cancer of the heart, 7 Jan. 1536 ; buried in Peterborough Abbey.
[ix. 290]

CATHERINE HOWARD (*d.* 1542), fifth queen of Henry VIII ; daughter, by his first wife, of Lord Edmund Howard, a younger son of Thomas, second duke of Norfolk ; her education neglected through her father's poverty ; on her father's second marriage became a dependant in her grandmother's (Agnes, dowager duchess of Norfolk's) house at Horsham, Norfolk, and afterwards at Lambeth ; improperly familiar with Henry Mannock (or Manox) her music-master ; passed privately as wife of Francis Dereham, a retainer of the duchess ; during Dereham's absence in Ireland, was thought likely to marry her cousin, Thomas Culpepper of Kent ; met Henry VIII at Bishop Stephen Gardiner's palace ; claims for promotion pressed on her by her old associates, on the report that Henry would divorce Anne of Cleves and marry her; married secretly to King Henry, July, and acknowledged, August 1540 ; accompanied Henry on his midland progress, September–October 1540, and again, to Yorkshire, July–October 1541 ; clandestinely met Culpepper at Lincoln and Pontefract, 1541, by help of her cousin Jane, viscountess Rochford, and 27 Aug., made Dereham her secretary ; a statement of her former intimacy with Mannock and Dereham, supplied by maid-servants, given to Henry VIII, 2 Nov. ; driven to confess pre-nuptial unchastity with Dereham and familiarities with Mannock, a strict inquiry being held ; given by the king a promise to spare her life and sent to Sion House, November 1541 ; evidence of adultery vainly sought ; all persons supposed privy to her misconduct imprisoned, Culpepper and Dereham being sentenced to death, and several of her relatives and servants to imprisonment and forfeiture, 1541 ; a bill attainting her and Lady Rochford (now insane) brought in, 21 Jan., and passed 7 Feb. 1542 ; a new confession, but only of pre-nuptial unchastity, wrung from her ; taken to the Tower, 10 Feb., and, with Lady Rochford, beheaded 13 Feb. 1542.
[ix. 291]

CATHERINE PARR (1512–1548), sixth queen of Henry VIII ; daughter of Sir Thomas Parr (*d.* 1517) of Kendal ; well educated ; married to Edward Borough (possibly Edward, the insane Baron Borough of Gainsborough, *d.* 1529) ; third wife of John Neville, baron Latimer (*d.* 1542) ; ready to marry Sir Thomas Seymour, brother of Jane, the late queen ; forced to marry Henry VIII, 12 July 1543 ; showed great kindness to Prince Edward and the Princesses Elizabeth and Mary ; tried to diminish religious persecution ; regent during Henry VIII's French expedition, 1544 ; her life endangered by her protestant leanings ; secretly married, *c.* April, Sir Thomas Seymour, now Baron Seymour of Sudeley, Henry VIII having died in January 1547 ; obtained Edward VI's consent to the match ; disgusted by her husband's brutalities to Princess Elizabeth ; gave birth to a daughter at Sudeley Castle, 30 Aug. 1548.
[ix. 308]

CATHERINE OF BRAGANZA (1638–1705), queen of Charles II ; born at Villa Viçosa ; her father king of Portugal in 1640 ; her education utterly neglected ; marriage with Charles, prince of Wales, proposed for her by her father, 1645 ; renewed proposals made by the Portuguese for her marriage with Charles II, May 1660 ; proposals opposed by the Spanish party, on the ground of her probable barrenness ; the match determined upon by Charles II, acting under French influence, November 1660–March 1661 ; formal intimation of the match well received in England and enthusiastically in Portugal ; marriage treaty signed, 23 June 1661 ; Catherine sailing for England, 23 April 1662, and reaching Portsmouth, 13 May ; privately married, 21 May ; arrived at Hampton Court, 29 May ; compelled by Charles to receive at court his mistress, Lady Castlemaine, July ; arrived at Whitehall, 23 Aug. ; submissively accepted Charles II's infidelities ; showed kindness to his illegitimate children, and lived mostly at Somerset House, and not at court, being often in great poverty through non-payment of her allowances ; tried to obtain from the pope recognition of Portuguese independence, 1662 ; seriously ill, October 1663 ; kept court in Oxford during the plague of London, 1665–6 ; proposals rumoured for dissolution of her marriage on account of her childlessness, 1667–70 ; complaints made of the concourse of English people to her chapel services, 1667 ; went a progress in the eastern counties, 1671 ; assailed by the whigs as privy to the 'popish plot,' 1678–1680, but protected by Charles ; attended the Oxford parliament, 1681 ; again abandoned by Charles for the Duchess of Portsmouth ; instrumental in securing Charles II's deathbed profession of Romanism, February 1685 ; afterwards lived in retirement at Somerset House and Hammersmith ; vainly begged James II to spare Monmouth ; present at the birth of the Prince of Wales, 10 June 1688 ; gave evidence as to his legitimacy before the council ; tried to recover damages from Henry, earl of Clarendon, her late chamberlain, for negligence in money matters ; visited by William of Orange, but soon quarrelled with both William and Mary ; travelled through France and Spain, reaching Lisbon, January 1693 ; resided near Lisbon ; regent for her brother Pedro, 1704–5 ; favoured Italian music ; unpopular in consequence of her ignorance of affairs, her haughtiness to her household, and her parsimony.
[ix. 312]

CATHROE or **KADROE**, SAINT (*d.* 976 ?). [See CADROE.]

CATLEY, ANN (1745–1789), vocalist ; sang at Vauxhall, 1762 ; legal proceedings undertaken by her father to regain custody of her, 1763 ; pupil of Charles Macklin ; an extremely popular performer at Dublin, 1763–70, and in London, 1770–84 ; married Major-general Francis Lascelles.
[ix. 319]

CATLIN, SIR ROBERT (*d.* 1574), judge ; reader of the Middle Temple, 1547 ; obtained the manor of Beby, Leicestershire, 1553 ; serjeant-at-law, 1555 ; justice of common pleas, 1558 ; chief-justice of the queen's bench, 1559–74 ; knighted, 1559.
[ix. 320]

CATNACH, JAMES (of the Seven Dials) (1792–1841), publisher ; son of John Catnach ; printer in Newcastle-on-Tyne ; came to London, 1813 ; issued penny and farthing chap-books, ballads, and broadsides ; retired, 1838.
[ix. 321]

CATON, WILLIAM (1636–1665), quaker ; met George Fox at Swarthmore, Ulverston, Lancashire, 1652, and embraced quakerism ; travelled as a quaker preacher, 1654 ; imprisoned at Maidstone ; roughly handled by English residents in Holland, 1655 ; preached in Scotland ; settled in Amsterdam, 1656 ; frequently visited England ; married a Dutch woman, 1662 ; imprisoned at Yarmouth ; published many pamphlets in English, Dutch, and German ; his autobiography printed, 1689.
[ix. 321]

CATRIK, JOHN (*d.* 1419). [See KETTERICH.]

CATTERMOLE, GEORGE (1800–1868), painter; son of a Norfolk squire; employed as draughtsman by John Britton [q. v.]; exhibited at the Royal Academy, 1819–27, and historical and other pictures at the Water Colour Society, 1822–50; a prolific book-illustrator, 1830–48; painted in oils, chiefly biblical subjects, from 1850. [ix. 322]

CATTERMOLE, RICHARD (1795?–1858), miscellaneous writer; educated at Christ's College, Cambridge; B.D., 1831; curate at Brixton, Surrey, 1825–31; secretary of the Royal Society of Literature, 1833–52; vicar of Little Marlow, Buckinghamshire; published verses, sermons, and elegant extracts, 1825–46. [ix. 324]

CATTI, TWM SHON (1530–1620?). [See JONES, THOMAS.]

CATTON, CHARLES, the elder (1728–1798), painter; successful coach-painter in London; exhibited from 1760, chiefly landscapes. [ix. 325]

CATTON, CHARLES, the younger (1756–1819), painter; son of Charles Catton the elder [q. v.]; studied art in London; went on sketching tours in England and Scotland; exhibited, 1775–1800; emigrated to the United States, 1804. [ix. 325]

CATTON, THOMAS (1760–1838), astronomer; of St. John's College, Cambridge; B.A., 1781; fellow and tutor; B.D., 1791; curator of the college observatory, 1791–1832; his observations published, 1853. [ix. 325]

CATTON or **CHATTODUNUS,** WALTER (d. 1343), Franciscan friar of Norwich; died at Avignon. None of his works are extant. [ix. 325]

CATTWG, DDOETH (d. 570?). [See CADOC.]

CAULFEILD, JAMES, fourth VISCOUNT and first EARL OF CHARLEMONT (1728–1799), Irish statesman; born in Dublin; succeeded to the viscounty, 1734; travelled in Italy and the Levant, 1746–54; served against the French at Carrickfergus, 1760; created Earl of Charlemont, 1763; resided in London, frequenting literary coteries, 1764–73; removed to Dublin, 1773; associate of Henry Grattan and Henry Flood; intrigued for Irish independence, 1780–2; opposed catholic emancipation and the union; wrote verses. [ix. 326]

CAULFEILD, SIR TOBY or TOBIAS, first BARON CHARLEMONT (1565–1627), of an Oxfordshire family; served under Martin Frobisher, and (1596) at Cadiz; commanded troop of horse at Newry, 1598; served at Kinsale, 1601; officer at Fort Charlemont on the Blackwater; knighted, c. 1604; receiver of Tyrone's rents, 1607–10; received grants of forfeited lands; M.P., Armagh, 1613; master of ordnance, 1615; created Baron Charlemont, 1620. [ix 328]

CAULFEILD, TOBY or TOBIAS, third BARON CHARLEMONT (d. 1642), M.P., Tyrone, 1639; governor of Fort Charlemont, 1641; surprised by Sir Phelim O'Neill [q. v.]; murdered. [ix. 328]

CAULFEILD, WILLIAM, fifth BARON and first VISCOUNT CHARLEMONT (d. 1671), succeeded to barony and estates, 1642; secured the execution of Sir Phelim O'Neill [q. v.]; created viscount, 1665. [ix. 328]

CAULFEILD, WILLIAM, second VISCOUNT CHARLEMONT (d. 1726), son of William Caulfeild, first viscount [q. v.]; attainted by James II; restored by William III; served in West Indies, 1702, and under Peterborough in Spain, 1705; major-general, 1708. [ix. 328]

CAULFIELD, JAMES (1764–1826), publisher; son of a London music-engraver; printseller and compiler of book-catalogues; published numerous biographies, with engraved portraits of historical personages and criminals, 1790–1824; prevented by Edmund Malone from issuing a volume of extracts from John Aubrey's manuscripts, 1797. [ix. 329]

CAULFIELD, RICHARD (1823–1887), Irish antiquary; B.A. Trinity College, Dublin, 1845; LL.B., 1864; LL.D., 1866; F.S.A., 1862; librarian of Royal Cork Institution, 1864, and to Queen's College, Cork, 1876; published council books of corporation of Cork, 1876, Youghal, 1878, and Kinsale, 1878, with other works. [Suppl. i. 397]

CAUNT, BENJAMIN (1815–1861), pugilist; son of a servant of Lord Byron at Newstead; fought with William Thompson ('Bendigo'), 1835, and was beaten; beat Bendigo, 1838, and was styled 'champion'; beat John Leechman ('Brassey'), 1840, and was styled 'champion of England'; visited the United States, 1841–2; subsequently publican in London. [ix. 331]

CAUNTER, JOHN HOBART (1794–1851), miscellaneous writer; cadet in India, 1809; B.D. Cambridge, 1828; clergyman in London, Sussex, and Essex; published 'Romance of History' (India), 1836, verses, sermons, and novels. [ix. 332]

CAUS, SALOMON DE (1576–1630). [See DE CAUS.]

CAUSTON, MICHAEL DE (d. 1395). [See CAWSTON.]

CAUSTON, THOMAS (d. 1569), composer; gentleman of the Chapel Royal; contributed church music to John Day's issues. [ix. 332]

CAUTLEY, SIR PROBY THOMAS (1802–1871), colonel; joined Bengal artillery, 1819; served at Bhurtpore, 1825; assisted in reconstructing Doâb canal, 1824?–30; in charge of it, 1831–43; planned Ganges canal (his plans being censured by Sir Arthur Cotton [q. v.]); superintended its construction, 1843–5 and 1848–54; visited England, 1845–8; K.C.B., 1854; member of council of India, 1858–68; presented Indian fossils to the British Museum; wrote on canals and on fossils. [ix. 333]

CAUX, JOHN DE (d. 1263). [See CALETO, JOHN DE.]

CAVAGNARI, SIR PIERRE LOUIS NAPOLEON (1841–1879), diplomatist; son of Adolphe Cavagnari, one of Napoleon's officers, by his Irish wife; born in France; entered Christ's Hospital, London, 1851; naturalised, 1857; cadet in the East India Company's service, 1858; lieutenant, 1860; political officer, 1861; employed on Afghan frontier, 1868–78; K.C.B., 1879; appointed British resident in Cabul, 1879; murdered by mutinous Afghans. [ix. 335]

CAVALIER or **CAVALLIER,** JEAN (1681–1740), major-general; son of a Languedoc peasant; baker at Geneva; a leader of the protestant insurgents in the Cevennes, 1702; defeated and obliged to surrender, 1704; taken before Louis XIV at Versailles; escaped into Switzerland; served under the Duke of Savoy; raised regiment in Holland for English service in Spain, 1706; severely wounded at Almanza, 1707; paid addresses to Mademoiselle Dunoyer at the Hague, 1708; pensioned by the British government; resided at Portarlington, Ireland; published his 'Memoirs,' 1726; lieutenant-governor of Jersey, 1738; major-general, 1739. [ix. 335]

CAVALLO, TIBERIUS (1749–1809), natural philosopher; born in Naples; settled in England, before 1775; F.R.S., 1779; investigated electrical and chemical phenomena; invented electrical instruments; wrote on electricity and magnetism. [ix. 337]

CAVAN, EARLS OF. [See LAMBART, CHARLES, first EARL, 1600–1660; LAMBART, RICHARD FORD WILLIAM, seventh EARL, 1763–1836.]

CAVE, ALFRED (1847–1900), congregational divine; studied at New College, London; B.A. London, 1870; minister at Berkhampsted, 1872, and Watford, 1876–80; professor of Hebrew and church history, Hackney College, 1880; principal and professor of theology, 1882–1900; honorary D.D. St. Andrews, 1889; published theological works. [Suppl. i. 397]

CAVE, SIR AMBROSE (d. 1568), of Northamptonshire; knight hospitaller of St. John of Jerusalem; visited Rhodes, 1525; pensioned at the suppression of the Knights' Hospital at Shingay, Cambridgeshire, 1540; sheriff of Warwickshire and Leicestershire, 1548; M.P. for Warwickshire, 1557; chancellor of the duchy of Lancaster, 1558; frequently employed on government commissions, 1558–64. [ix. 338]

CAVE, EDWARD (1691–1754), printer; son of a Rugby cobbler; apprenticed to a London printer; printer and journalist at Norwich; married and settled in London; for a short time clerk in the post office; furnished London news to country papers, and country news to a London paper, 1725; conducted the 'Gentleman's Magazine,' 1731–54; denounced in parliament for publishing George II's answer to an address before it had even been reported from the chair, 1738; invented a spinning-machine, 1740; published many journals and books. [ix. 338]

CAVE, JOHN (*d.* 1657), divine; M.A. Lincoln College, Oxford, 1619; rector of Pickwell, Leicestershire, 1629–42; persecuted by the puritans. [ix. 340]

CAVE, SIR LEWIS WILLIAM (1832–1897), judge; educated at Rugby and Lincoln College, Oxford; B.A., 1855; M.A., 1877; called to bar at Inner Temple, 1859; bencher, 1877; revising barrister, 1865; recorder of Lincoln, 1873; Q.C., 1875; justice of high court, queen's bench division, 1881; knighted, 1881; bankruptcy judge, 1883–91; edited legal works. [Suppl. i. 398]

CAVE, SIR STEPHEN (1820–1880), politician; educated at Harrow and Balliol College, Oxford; M.A., 1846; barrister of the Inner Temple, 1846; M.P., Shoreham, 1859–80; paymaster-general, 1866–8, 1874–80; published pamphlets. [ix. 341]

CAVE, WILLIAM (1637–1713), ecclesiastical historian; son of John Cave [q. v.]; M.A. St. John's College, Cambridge, 1660; D.D., 1672; vicar of Islington, 1662–89; vicar of Allhallows the Great, London, 1679–89; canon of Windsor, 1684, and vicar of Isleworth, Middlesex, 1690 till death; published 'Primitive Christianity,' 1672, and other important works on early ecclesiastical history. [ix. 341]

CAVELLUS, HUGO (1571–1626). [See MacCAGHWELL, HUGH.]

CAVENDISH (1830–1899) (pseudonym). [See JONES, HENRY.]

CAVENDISH, ADA (1839–1895), actress; first appeared at New Royalty, 1863, and subsequently played at many London theatres and in America; her parts include Juliet, Beatrice, Rosalind, and Lady Teazle. [Suppl. i. 398]

CAVENDISH, CHARLES (1620–1643), royalist general; second son of William Cavendish, second earl of Devonshire [q. v.]; travelled in the East, 1638–40; served under the Prince of Orange, 1641; volunteer in the guards; given troop after Edgehill; raised regiment of horse; stationed at Newark; given command in Nottinghamshire and Lincoln; victorious at Grantham, March 1643, Ancaster, April, and Burton-on-Trent, July 1643; defeated and slain at Gainsborough. [ix. 343]

CAVENDISH, SIR CHARLES (1591–1654), mathematician; brother of William Cavendish, first duke of Newcastle [q. v.]; accompanied Sir Henry Wotton [q. v.] to France, 1612; knighted, 1619; M.P. for Nottingham, 1624, 1628, and 1640; served for king under his brother as lieutenant-general of horse, 1642; travelled on continent, 1644–51; suffered sequestration of estates, but made submission and was admitted to compound. He was noted for his mathematical knowledge, and was acquainted with many eminent mathematicians of his day. [Suppl. i. 399]

CAVENDISH, CHRISTIANA, COUNTESS OF DEVONSHIRE (*d.* 1675), daughter of Edward Bruce, baron Kinloss [q. v.]; wife of William Cavendish, second earl of Devonshire [q. v.], who died 1628; zealous supporter of the royalist cause. [ix. 343]

CAVENDISH, ELIZABETH, DUCHESS OF DEVONSHIRE (1758–1824), daughter of the fourth Earl of Bristol; married John Thomas Foster; refused offer of marriage from Edmund Gibbon, 1787; married the fifth Duke of Devonshire, 1809; lived latterly at Rome; subsidised editions of Horace and Virgil, 1816–19. [ix. 344]

CAVENDISH, LORD FREDERICK (1729–1803), field-marshal; third son of the third Duke of Devonshire; ensign, 1750; colonel, 1758; M.P. for Derbyshire, 1751, and for Derby, 1754–80; served in Germany, 1757; prisoner in France, 1758–60; commanded brigade in Hanover, 1760–3; major-general, 1761; field-marshal, 1796. [ix. 344]

CAVENDISH, LORD FREDERICK CHARLES (1836–1882), chief secretary for Ireland; second son of William Cavendish, seventh Duke of Devonshire [q. v.]; B.A. Trinity College, Cambridge, 1858; M.P., Yorkshire West Riding, 1865–82; chief secretary for Ireland, 1882; murdered by members of a secret political society in Phœnix Park, Dublin, 6 May. [ix. 345]

CAVENDISH, GEORGE (1500–1561 ?), biographer of Wolsey; in constant attendance on Wolsey, as his usher, from 1526; retired to Glemsford, Suffolk, 1530; zealous Roman catholic; wrote life of Wolsey, *c.* 1557 (published 1815). [ix. 346]

CAVENDISH, GEORGIANA, DUCHESS OF DEVONSHIRE (1757–1806), eldest daughter of the first Earl Spencer; married, 1774, the fifth Duke of Devonshire; canvassed for Fox in the Westminster election, 1784. [ix. 347]

CAVENDISH, HENRY (*d.* 1616), soldier and politician, eldest son of Sir William Cavendish (1505 ?–1557) [q. v.]; M.P. for Derbyshire, 1572; fought in the Low Countries, 1578; travelled in the East; custodian of Mary Queen of Scots. [ix. 363]

CAVENDISH, SIR HENRY (1732–1804), parliamentary reporter; M.P. for Lostwithiel, 1768–1774; took shorthand notes of the debates (now in the British Museum; partly printed, 1839–43); succeeded to baronetcy, 1776; official in Ireland, 1779. [ix. 348]

CAVENDISH, HENRY (1731–1810), natural philosopher; grandson of the second Duke of Devonshire; born at Nice; educated at Peterhouse, Cambridge, 1749–1753; a millionaire; studied mathematics; experimented in physics and chemistry, 1764; began to communicate papers to the Royal Society, 1766; discovered the constitution of water and atmospheric air before 1783; experimented on electricity, 1772 and 1776, and on the density of the earth, 1798. [ix. 348]

CAVENDISH, SIR JOHN (*d.* 1381), judge; pleader in 1348; serjeant-at-law, 1366; justice of common pleas, 1371; chief-justice of king's bench, 1372–81; murdered in Jack Straw's rising. [ix. 353]

CAVENDISH, LORD JOHN (1732–1796), politician; fourth son of the third Duke of Devonshire; M.A. Peterhouse, Cambridge, 1753; M.P., Weymouth, 1753; M.P., Knaresborough, 1761; M.P., York, 1768–90; chancellor of the exchequer, March to July 1782, and April to December, 1783; M.P., Derbyshire, 1794–6; friend of Edmund Burke. [ix. 353]

CAVENDISH, MARGARET, DUCHESS OF NEWCASTLE (1624 ?–1674), writer; youngest child of Sir Thomas Lucas, of St. John's, Colchester; maid of honour to Queen Henrietta Maria, 1643; accompanied her to Paris, 1645; married (second wife) William Cavendish, marquis (afterwards duke) of Newcastle, April 1645; lived at Paris, Rotterdam, and Antwerp in pecuniary distress; came to London, to solicit an allowance out of her husband's confiscated estates; derided by Charles II's court after the Restoration; lived in retirement; buried in Westminster Abbey; wrote and published a multitude of verses, essays, and plays, 1653–68, together with an autobiographical sketch in 'Nature's Pictures,' 1656, and a life of her husband, 1667. [ix. 355]

CAVENDISH, RICHARD (*d.* 1601 ?), politician; educated at Corpus Christi College, Cambridge; employed by the Duke of Norfolk to carry letters to Mary Queen of Scots, 1568–9; witness against the duke, 1572; M.P. for Denbigh, 1572 and 1585; M.A. Cambridge, 1573; appointed by Elizabeth to a law office, but excluded by the judges, 1587; translated Euclid into English, and published a theological tract. [ix. 357]

CAVENDISH, THOMAS (1560–1592), circumnavigator; supplied and commanded a ship in Sir Richard Greenvile's Virginia voyage, 9 April–18 Sept. 1585; fitted out three ships in imitation of Sir Francis Drake's 1577–9 voyage, 1586; sailed from Plymouth, 21 July 1586; touched at Sierra Leone, 21 Aug.; at Cape Frio, Brazil, 31 Oct.; discovered Port Desire, Patagonia, 17 Dec.; entered Magellan Straits, 6 Jan. 1587; reached the Pacific, 24 Feb.; captured the great treasure-ship off Cape St. Lucas, California, 14 Nov.; reached the Ladrones, 3 Jan. 1588; threaded the Eastern archipelago; sighted Cape of Good Hope, 19 March; touched at St. Helena, 8 June; reached Plymouth, 10 Sept.; planned another voyage, in conjunction with Captain John Davis [q. v.], 1591; sailed from Plymouth, 26 Aug. 1591; reached Brazil, 29 Nov.; at Port Desire, 18 March 1592; got only half-way through Magellan Straits, 21 April; started to return, 15 May; parted from Davis in the night off Port Desire, 20 May 1592; sailed eastwards towards St. Helena, and died at sea, June 1592; search for him undertaken by Davis along the Patagonian coast. His ship in the voyage of 1586 was the Desire; in the voyage of 1591 he commanded the Leicester, Davis sailing in the Desire. [ix. 358]

CAVENDISH, SIR WILLIAM (1505 ?–1557), statesman; agent for Henry VIII in securing the property of the monasteries at the dissolution, 1530–41; received grants of church lands from Henry VIII and Edward VI; knighted, 1546; returned to Roman catholicism under Queen Mary; treasurer of the royal chamber to Henry VIII, 1546, and to Mary, 1553; began to build Chatsworth, 1553. [ix. 363]

CAVENDISH, WILLIAM, first EARL OF DEVONSHIRE (d. 1626), second son of Sir William Cavendish (1505 ?–1557) [q. v.]; M.P., Newport, 1588; courtier of James I; created Baron Cavendish of Hardwicke, 1605; created Earl of Devonshire, 1618. [ix. 364]

CAVENDISH, WILLIAM, second EARL OF DEVONSHIRE (1591 ?–1628), second son of William Cavendish, first earl [q. v.]; pupil of Thomas Hobbes; travelled; knighted, 1609; courtier of James I; M.P. for Derby, 1621–6; succeeded to earldom, 1626; in debt, 1628. [ix. 364]

CAVENDISH, WILLIAM, DUKE OF NEWCASTLE (1592–1676), son of Sir Charles Cavendish of Welbeck, Nottinghamshire, and the heiress of the barony of Ogle, Northumberland; educated at St. John's College, Cambridge; K.B., 1610; travelled; entertained James I at Welbeck, 1619; created Viscount Mansfield, November 1620; created Earl of Newcastle, March 1628; succeeded to the Ogle estates, 1629; spent 20,000l. in entertaining Charles I at Welbeck, 1633, Ben Jonson writing the masques; governor of Charles, prince of Wales, 1638–41; lent Charles I 10,000l. and raised a troop at his own cost against the Scots, 1639; withdrew from court, 1641, to avoid prosecution by parliament for again raising troops for the king; named governor of Hull by Charles I, January 1642, but not accepted by the garrison; joined Charles I at York; sent to secure Newcastle-on-Tyne, June, and to command in the north; raised troops at his own charges; invaded Yorkshire, November 1642; raised the siege of York, and advanced southwards; forced to fall back on York, January 1643; advanced into the West Riding, but was forced back; detached troops to escort the queen to Oxford; secured all Yorkshire by the victory of Adwalton Moor, 1643; advanced as far as Lincoln; recalled to besiege Hull; raised the siege, 11 Oct. 1643; created Marquis of Newcastle, 27 Oct. 1643; sent to oppose the Scots, 1644; forced to fall back on York; fought as volunteer at Marston Moor, having vainly urged Prince Rupert to wait for reinforcements, 1644; at Hamburg, July 1644 to February 1645; in Paris, April 1645–8; married [see CAVENDISH, MARGARET, DUCHESS OF NEWCASTLE]; at Rotterdam, 1648, and Antwerp, 1848–60; for some time lived in great pecuniary difficulties, pawned his wife's jewels, and incurred heavy loans; obtained an allowance out of his confiscated estates; accompanied Charles II to London, 1660; had only part of his lands restored, having spent nearly 1,000,000l. in the royal service; created Duke of Newcastle, March 1665; withdrew to Welbeck; patron of Ben Jonson and Dryden. His works include plays, 1649–77, poems, and 'Methode et Invention . . . de dresser les Chevaux,' Antwerp, 1657, and 'New Method . . . to Dress Horses,' 1667. [ix. 364]

CAVENDISH, WILLIAM, third EARL OF DEVONSHIRE (1617–1684), eldest son of William Cavendish, second earl [q. v.]; pupil of Thomas Hobbes K.B., 1625; succeeded to the earldom, 1628; travelled, 1634–7; lord-lieutenant of Derbyshire, 1638–42; belonged to the court party; joined Charles I at York, 1642; attainted by parliament, 1642, and his estates sequestrated; went abroad; returned, 1645; fined by parliament, 1646; lived at his mother's house, Latimers, Buckinghamshire; lord-lieutenant of Derbyshire, 1660. [ix. 369]

CAVENDISH, WILLIAM, first DUKE OF DEVONSHIRE (1640–1707), eldest son of William Cavendish, third earl [q. v.]; styled Lord Cavendish (of Hardwicke) till 1684; educated abroad; M.P. for Derby, 1661; in Ireland, 1662; hon. M.A. Oxford, 1663; served in the fleet, 1665; envoy to France, 1669; provoked a fracas at the opera in Paris; imprisoned in the Tower for instigating a duel, 1675; a leader of the anti-court and anti-Romanist party in the Commons, 1666–78; active in the 'popish plot' proceedings, 1678–9; advocated exclusion of the Duke of York from the succession, 1680–1; made his peace with Charles II, October, 1681; succeeded to earldom, 1684; fined 30,000l. for brawling at court, 1685; built Chatsworth,

1687–1706; joined in inviting William of Orange to England, 1687 and 1688; arranged with the Earl of Danby to raise the north in favour of William of Orange; seized Derby and Nottingham, 1688; raised regiment of horse; escorted Princess Anne to Oxford; moved an address of welcome to the Prince of Orange, December, 1688; argued for James II's deposition, 1689; lord-lieutenant of Derbyshire, 1689; lord high steward at coronation, 1689; with William III in Flanders, 1690–2; created Duke of Devonshire, 1694 lord high steward at Anne's coronation, 1702; advocated toleration of nonconformists and the union with Scotland; of profligate private life; a patron of horse-racing. [ix. 370]

CAVENDISH, WILLIAM, fourth DUKE OF DEVONSHIRE (1720–1764), styled Marquis of Hartington till 1755; M.P. for Derbyshire, 1741–51; married, 1748, the heiress of the Cork and Burlington estates in Ireland; called to the peers as Baron Cavendish, 1751; succeeded to the dukedom, 1755; lord-lieutenant of Ireland, 1755–6; prime minister, 1756–7; lord chamberlain, 1757–62. [ix. 375]

CAVENDISH, SIR WILLIAM, seventh DUKE OF DEVONSHIRE (1808–1891), great grandson of William Cavendish, fourth duke [q. v.]; educated at Eton and Trinity College, Cambridge; M.A., 1829; honorary LL.D., 1835; M.P. for Cambridge University, 1829–31, Malton, Yorkshire, 1831 Derbyshire, 1831, North Derbyshire, 1832–1834; succeeded his grandfather as second Earl of Burlington, 1834, and his cousin William George Spencer Cavendish, sixth duke of Devonshire [q. v.], 1858; chancellor of London University, 1836–56, of Cambridge University, 1861–91, and of Victoria University, 1880; K.G., 1858; privy councillor, 1876; liberal benefactor of scientific and industrial enterprises. [Suppl. i. 400]

CAVENDISH, WILLIAM GEORGE SPENCER, sixth DUKE OF DEVONSHIRE (1790–1858), B.A. Trinity College, Cambridge, 1811; succeeded to the dukedom, July, 1811; British envoy at the coronation of Nicholas, czar of Russia, 1825; lord chamberlain, 1827–8, and 1830–4; bibliophile and collector of coins. [ix. 376]

CAVENDISH-BENTINCK. [See BENTINCK.]

CAVERHILL, JOHN (d. 1781), physician; licentiate of the London College of Physicians, 1767; wrote on medical topics. [ix. 376]

CAW, JOHN YOUNG (1810 ?–1858), banker; educated at St. Andrews and Cambridge; banker in Manchester, c. 1828–58; published pamphlets. [ix. 376]

CAWDELL, JAMES (d. 1800), comedian in the north of England; retired, 1798; published poems and plays, 1778–98. [ix. 377]

CAWDRY, DANIEL (1588–1664), presbyterian; educated at Peterhouse, Cambridge; rector of Great Billing, Northamptonshire, 1625; member of the Westminster Assembly, 1643; ejected from his living for nonconformity, 1662; wrote against churchmen and independents, 1645–61. [ix. 377]

CAWDRY, ZACHARY (1616–1684), divine; entered St. John's College, Cambridge, 1633; M.A., 1642; rector of Barthomley, Cheshire, 1649–84; published 'A Discourse on Patronage,' 1675. [ix. 377]

CAWLEY, WILLIAM (1602–1667), regicide; son of a rich brewer of Chichester; founded St. Bartholomew's Hospital, Chichester, 1626; M.P., Chichester, 1627; fined for refusing knighthood, 1629; M.P., Midhurst, 1640; an active member of the Long parliament; one of the king's judges; member of the council of state, 1651; M.P., 1659; excepted from pardon, 1660; withdrew to Belgium and Switzerland; his estates bestowed by crown on the Duke of York. [ix. 378]

CAWOOD, JOHN (1514–1572), printer; apprenticed in London; printed in his own name, 1549–72; appointed queen's printer to Mary, 1553, and joint queen's printer to Elizabeth, 1560; active member of the Stationers' Company. [ix. 379]

CAWSTON or **CAUSTON**, MICHAEL DE (d. 1395), master of Michaelhouse, Cambridge; fellow of Peterhouse, Cambridge; D.D.; master of Michaelhouse after 1359; chancellor of Cambridge, 1361; benefactor of the university; dean of Chichester at some date between 1383 and 1400. [ix. 380]

CAWTHORN, JAMES (1719-1761), poet; son of a Sheffield upholsterer; usher in several country schools; of Clare Hall, Cambridge; usher in London; head-master of Tonbridge school, c. 1743; styled M.A., 1748; published 'Abelard and Heloise' in 'Poetical Calendar,' 1746; his collected poems published, 1771. [ix. 380]

CAWTON, THOMAS, the elder (1605-1659), divine; educated at Queens' College, Cambridge; puritan; vicar of Wivenhoe, Essex, 1637-44; minister of St. Bartholomew's, London, 1644; opposed the execution of Charles I; imprisoned, February to August, 1649, for praying for 'King Charles II'; involved in the projected rising of 1651; fled to Holland; minister of an English congregation at Rotterdam. [ix. 381]

CAWTON, THOMAS, the younger (1636?-1677), orientalist; studied at Rotterdam and Utrecht; B.A. Merton College, Oxford, 1660; left Oxford in consequence of his nonconformity, 1662; independent minister at Westminster; published a life of his father, Thomas Cawton the elder [q. v.], 1662, also philological and theological tracts. [ix. 381]

CAXTON, WILLIAM (1422?-1491), the first English printer; born in Kent; apprenticed, 1438, to a London mercer; went, after his master's death, to Bruges, 1441; was at Bruges, in business for himself, 1446-70, visiting London, 1453, and Utrecht, 1464; at Bruges, acted as governor of the English merchants in the Low Countries, 1465-9, and was employed in negotiating commercial treaties with the Dukes of Burgundy, 1464 and 1468; began translating the French romance 'Le Recueil des Histoires de Troye,' March 1469, at Bruges, and finished it, 1471, at Cologne; in the household of Margaret (sister of Edward IV), duchess of Burgundy, 1471-6; learned printing after 1471 and before 1474, perhaps at Cologne and in company of Colard Mansion; printed his 'Recuyell of the Histories of Troy,' folio, probably in 1474, and 'The Game and Playe of the Chesse,' another translation from French, probably in 1475, both perhaps at a press set up in 1473 by Colard Mansion at Bruges and belonging to Caxton; came to England, 1476, and continued in favour with Edward IV, Richard III, and Henry VII; established press at Westminster, from which he issued, 1477-91, nearly eighty separate books, many of them translations by himself from French romances (the first of them was the Earl of Rivers's translation of 'The Dictes and Sayings of the Philosophers,' 1477). Six distinct founts of type were used by Caxton. [ix. 381]

CAY, HENRY BOULT (d. 1795), legal writer; B.A. Clare College, Cambridge, 1752; fellow, 1752-70; barrister of the Middle Temple; published supplements to the 'Abridgment' of his father, John Cay [q. v.]. [ix. 390]

CAY, JOHN (1700-1757), editor of the 'Statutes'; born in Northumberland; barrister of Gray's Inn, 1724; a judge of the Marshalsea, 1750; published an 'Abridgment of the Publick Statutes' (1215-1737), 1739; and 'The Statutes at Large' (1215-1756), issued 1758. [ix. 389]

CAYLEY, ARTHUR (d. 1848), author of trite lives of Sir Walter Ralegh, 1805, and of Sir Thomas More, 1808; B.A. Trinity College, Cambridge, 1796; rector of Normanby, Yorkshire, 1814. [ix. 390]

CAYLEY, ARTHUR (1821-1895), mathematician; senior wrangler and Smith's prizeman, Trinity College, Cambridge, 1842; fellow, 1842-52, and 1875-95, and honorary fellow, 1872; called to the bar at Lincoln's Inn, 1849; practised as conveyancer; Sadlerian professor of pure mathematics, Cambridge, 1863-95; president of British Association, 1883; F.R.S., 1852; Copley medallist, 1882; member of the leading British and foreign scientific societies; contributed many valuable papers to mathematical journals. [Suppl. i. 401]

CAYLEY, CHARLES BAGOT (1823-1883), translator; son of a Russian merchant; born near St. Petersburg; educated at King's College, London, and Cambridge (B.A., 1845). His verse translations include Dante, 1851, Æschylus, 1867, Homer, 1877, and Petrarch, 1879. [ix. 390]

CAYLEY, CORNELIUS (1729-1780?), religious writer; for some years clerk in the treasury of the Prince of Wales; methodist preacher; travelled in Holland and France, 1772; published an autobiography, 1758, travels, 1777, and verses and devotional tracts. [ix. 391]

CEADDA, SAINT (d. 672), better known as CHAD; an Angle of Northumbria; disciple of St. Aidan at Lindisfarne; trained in Rathmelsige monastery, co. Louth, Ireland; called to succeed his brother Cedd [q. v.] as abbot of Lastingham, North Yorkshire, 664; consecrated at Winchester as bishop of Lindisfarne or York (in place of Wilfrith, elected but absent in Gaul), c. 665; acted as bishop, c. 666-9 (Wilfrith not claiming the see); resigned, at the instance of Archbishop Theodore, and retired to Lastingham; sent to be bishop of the Mercians, c. 670; fixed the see at Lichfield, where he built a church and cell; probably built a cell at Barrow, Lincolnshire; died of pestilence; revered as an English saint; commemorated on 2 March. [ix. 391]

CEADWALLA. [See CÆDWALLA.]

CEALLACHAN (d. 954), king of Cashel, 935-54; ravaged the neighbouring districts, 935-9; prisoner in Donegal, 941; victorious at Maghduin, 942; ancestor of the O'Callaghans. [ix. 393]

CEARBHALL (d. 888), lord of Ossory; ravaged the neighbouring districts, sometimes in alliance with the Danes, sometimes with the Irish, 845-872; chosen king of Dublin by the Danes, 875; defeated the Munstermen at Clonmel, 876. [ix. 393]

CEAWLIN (d. 593), king of the West-Saxons; fought at Beranbyrig, near Marlborough, 556; succeeded his father, Cynric, 560; took Silchester; defeated the Jutes of Kent at Wimbledon, 568; by a victory at 'Deorham,' 577, conquered Gloucestershire; ravaged the upper Severn valley, 583; repulsed by the Welsh at Vale Royal, Cheshire; deprived of conquests by his nephew, Ceolric, who headed a revolt, 591; defeated at Wanborough, Wiltshire, 592; fell in battle. [ix. 394]

CECIL, ARTHUR, whose real name was ARTHUR CECIL BLUNT (1843-1896), actor; appeared with the German Reeds in 'No Cards' and 'Box and Cox,' 1869, and subsequently played at many London theatres; was with John Clayton [q. v.] joint-manager of the Court Theatre. His parts include Touchstone, Sir Peter Teazle, and Tony Lumpkin. [Suppl. i. 402]

CECIL, SIR EDWARD, VISCOUNT WIMBLEDON (1572-1638), third son of Thomas Cecil, first earl of Exeter [q. v.]; served in the Low Countries, 1596-1610; captain of foot, 1599; in command of the English contingent, 1610; knighted, 1601; a favourite of the Duke of Buckingham; given, by Buckingham, command of the Spanish expedition, 1625; miserably mismanaged the operations at Cadiz, 20-29 Oct., and missed the treasure-ships; created Baron Cecil of Putney, 1625; created Viscount Wimbledon, 1626; lord-lieutenant of Surrey, 1626; held command in Holland, 1627-9; governor of Portsmouth, 1630-8. [ix. 395]

CECIL, JAMES, third EARL OF SALISBURY (d. 1683), educated at St. John's College, Cambridge; succeeded to earldom, 1669; advocated exclusion of James, duke of York, from the succession; prisoner in the Tower, 1677; made his peace with Charles II, 1679. [ix. 397]

CECIL, JAMES, fourth EARL OF SALISBURY (d. 1693), eldest son of James Cecil, third earl [q. v.]; imprisoned as a Roman catholic, 1689; imprisoned as a Jacobite, 1692. [ix. 397]

CECIL, alias SNOWDEN, JOHN (1558-1626), priest and political adventurer; educated at Trinity College, Oxford; joined Roman catholic seminary at Rheims, 1583; studied at English college, Rome, and took holy orders; at Valladolid with Father Parsons, who (1591) sent him to England; captured, subsequently becoming spy in service of Burghley and Sir Robert Cecil; acted for ten years as political agent of Scottish catholic earls in rebellion against their king; subsequently (1601) joined John Mush [q. v.], Anthony Champney [q. v.], and other priests who laid before the pope grievances against Blackwell and the jesuits; in 1606 with Champney presented to the pope petition of English priests for episcopal government; chaplain and almoner to Margaret of Valois; died at Paris. [Suppl. i. 403]

CECIL, RICHARD (1748-1810), evangelical divine; youngest child of a wealthy London dyer; a dilettante; ordained priest, 1777; B.A. Queen's College, Oxford, 1777; curate in Lincolnshire and Leicestershire; rector of All Saints', 1777-98, and St. Thomas, Lewes, 1777-97; a popular preacher in and near London, 1780–1808 ; vicar of Chobham, Surrey, 1800 ; wrote devotional and biographical tracts, published posthumously. [ix. 398]

CECIL, ROBERT, first EARL OF SALISBURY and first VISCOUNT CRANBORNE (1563 ?–1612), statesman ; son of William Cecil, baron Burghley [q. v.] ; educated privately, being of weak health ; resident in France, c. 1584–7 ; attached to the Earl of Derby's mission to the Spanish Netherlands, 1588 ; M.P. for Hertfordshire, 1589 and 1601 ; acted as secretary of state ; knighted, 1591 ; secretary of state, 1596–1608 ; envoy to France, 1598 ; commissioner to try the Earl of Essex for leaving Ireland, 1600 ; accused by Essex of doubting Elizabeth's title, 1601 ; made overtures to James VI of Scotland ; secured the accession of James VI to the English throne, 1603 ; created Baron Cecil, 1603, Viscount Cranborne, 1604, and Earl of Salisbury, 1605 ; forced by James I to exchange Theobalds for Hatfield, 1607 ; built Hatfield House ; known as the 'crook-backed' earl ; died deeply in debt. [ix. 400]

CECIL, THOMAS, first EARL OF EXETER and second BARON BURGHLEY (1542–1623), eldest son of William Cecil, baron Burghley [q. v.] ; educated privately ; lived dissolutely at Paris and in Germany, 1561–3 ; M.P., Stamford, 1563 ; served against the northern rebels, 1569 ; served in Scotland, 1573 ; knighted, 1575 ; served in the Low Countries, 1585, and against the Armada, 1588 ; succeeded to barony, 1598 ; president of the council of the north, 1599 ; helped to crush the Earl of Essex's rising, 1601 ; created Earl of Exeter, 1605 ; founded a hospital at Liddington, Rutlandshire ; benefactor of Clare College, Cambridge. [ix. 404]

CECIL, THOMAS (*fl.* 1630), one of the few English engravers of the early seventeenth century ; engraved, chiefly portraits, in London, 1627–35. [ix. 405]

CECIL, WILLIAM, BARON BURGHLEY (1520–1598), statesman ; only son of a wealthy Northamptonshire squire (*d.* 1552), in the service of Henry VIII ; educated at Grantham school ; at St. John's College, Cambridge, 1535–41 ; studied Greek ; entered Gray's Inn, 1541 ; allied by marriage with Sir John Cheke, of Cambridge, the Greek scholar ; held the lucrative office of custos brevium in the court of common pleas, 1547–61 ; M.P., Stamford, 1547 ; secretary to Lord Protector Somerset ; imprisoned in the Tower on Somerset's fall, 1549 ; secretary of state, 1550–3 ; recorder of Boston, 1551 ; knighted, 1551 ; began building Burleigh House and Wimbledon House, 1553 ; employed by Queen Mary to recall Cardinal Pole, 1554, and (unsuccessfully) to mediate between the French king and emperor, 1555 ; M.P., Lincolnshire, 1555 ; secretary of state, 1558–72 ; chancellor of Cambridge University, 1559 ; envoy to Scotland, 1560 ; his influence threatened by Elizabeth's partiality to Lord Robert Dudley (earl of Leicester in 1564) ; master of the court of wards, 1561 ; attended Queen Elizabeth on her state visits to Cambridge, 1564, and to Oxford, 1566 ; organised secret police to detect plots against Elizabeth, 1570 ; created Baron of Burghley, February 1571 ; lord high treasurer, 1572–98, and chief minister of Queen Elizabeth ; responsible for execution of Mary Queen of Scots, 1587 ; founded a hospital at Stamford Baron ; his correspondence preserved at Hatfield. [ix. 406]

CECILIA or CECILY (1469–1507), third daughter of Edward IV ; betrothed to James, eldest son of James III of Scotland, 1474 ; betrothed to Alexander, duke of Albany, 1482 ; took sanctuary at Westminster from Richard III, 1483 ; surrendered to Richard III, 1484 ; taken into favour by Henry VII, 1486 ; married John, viscount Wells (*d.* 1498), c. 1487 ; married Thomas Kymbe or Kyne, of the Isle of Wight, c. 1504. [ix. 412]

CEDD or CEDDA, SAINT (*d.* 664), brother of Ceadda [q. v.], with whom he is sometimes confused ; an Angle of Northumbria ; pupil of St. Aidan at Lindisfarne ; sent to Christianise the Middle Angles, 653 ; sent to Essex to Christianise the East Saxons, 653 ; consecrated bishop of the East-Saxons, 654 ; founded a monastery near Maldon, and another at West Tilbury, Essex ; founded and ruled the monastery at Lastingham, Yorkshire ; attended the council at Whitby, 664 ; accepted the Roman computation of Easter ; died of plague ; revered as an English saint ; commemorated on 7 Jan. [ix. 413]

CEDMON, SAINT (*fl.* 670). [See CÆDMON.]

CELECLERECH, SAINT (*d.* 697). [See CILIAN.]

CELESIA, DOROTHEA (1738–1790), authoress of 'Almida,' a tragedy, 1771, and 'Indolence,' a poem, 1772 ; daughter of David Mallet [q. v.] ; married Pietro Paolo Celesia, Genoese ambassador (1755–9) ; resided at Genoa, 1759–90. [ix. 414]

CELESTE, MADAME, properly CELESTE-ELLIOTT (1814 ?–1882), actress ; trained in Paris ; visited America, 1827 ; married a Mr. Elliott there ; appeared in Liverpool, 1830, London, 1831 and 1833, America, 1834–7, London, 1837–41, Liverpool, 1843, and London, 1844–74 ; withdrew to Paris. [ix. 415]

CELLACH, SAINT (6th cent.), bishop of Killala ; otherwise CELLAN ; commemorated on 1 May ; eldest son of a king in Mayo ; monk at Clonmacnois ; cursed by St. Ciaran for leaving the monastery to become king ; returned to monkish life ; chosen bishop in Mayo with his see at Killala (Cell Alaidh) ; murdered by order of Guaire, king in Galway. [ix. 415]

CELLACH, SAINT (1079–1129). [See CELSUS.]

CELLIER, ALFRED (1844–1891), composer and contributor ; one of children of Chapel Royal, 1855 ; held successively several appointments as organist ; first musical director at Court Theatre, 1871 ; director of orchestra at Opera Comique, Manchester, 1871–5, and Opera Comique, London, 1877–9 ; joint-conductor with Sir Arthur Sullivan [q. v.] at Covent Garden, 1878–9 ; composed many comic operas, including 'Dorothy,' 1886, and 'Mountebanks' (produced posthumously, 1892) ; his opera 'Pandora' produced in Boston, U.S.A., 1881. [Suppl. i. 405]

CELLIER, ELIZABETH (*fl.* 1680), *née* Dormer ; married Peter Cellier, a Frenchman ; embraced Romanism ; midwife in London ; agent for distributing alms to the 'popish plot' prisoners, 1679 ; acquitted, 1680, on a charge of plotting the king's murder ('the meal-tub plot') ; fined and pilloried for libel in her pamphlet about her trial ('Malice defeated') ; published two pamphlets on the training of midwives, 1687–8. [ix. 417]

CELLING, WILLIAM, perhaps more properly WILLIAM TILLY OF SELLING (*d.* 1494), born in Kent ; monk at Christ Church, Canterbury ; B.D. Oxford, 1458 ; possibly fellow of All Souls' College ; prior of Christ Church, Canterbury, 1472–94 ; collected Latin and Greek manuscripts on the continent, c. 1473 ; improved the buildings of his convent ; taught Thomas Linacre ; envoy to Rome, 1486 ; commissioner in negotiations between England, France, and Brittany, 1490–1. [ix. 417]

CELSUS or CELLACH, SAINT (1079–1129), archbishop of Armagh ; son of Ædh, of a family which held the see hereditarily ; succeeded as archbishop, September 1105 ; created suffragan bishops ; visited in his province, collecting dues, 1106–20 ; mediator between Irish princes, 1107–28 ; presided at a synod to establish rules of conduct, 1111 ; attended a council to fix the boundaries of Irish dioceses, 1117 ; chosen bishop of Dublin, 1121, but perhaps never made good his title against his rival Gregory ; taught St. Malachy, whom he recommended for his successor ; robbed by the O'Ruarcs and O'Brians, 1128 ; commemorated on 6 April. [ix. 418]

CENNICK, JOHN (1718–1755), divine ; joined methodists under Wesley, 1739 ; made tour among Moravian brethren in Germany, 1745 ; ordained deacon in Moravian church, London, 1749 ; published sermons and hymns. [Suppl. i. 406]

CENTLIVRE, SUSANNAH (1667 ?–1723), actress and dramatist ; acted in the provinces, often in her own comedies ; called herself S. Carroll ; married, at Windsor, 1706, Joseph Centlivre, cook to Queen Anne ; lived with her husband in St. Martin's-in-the-Fields, London, 1712–1723 ; wrote eighteen plays, chiefly comedies, 1700–22. [ix. 420]

CENTWINE or KENTEN (*d.* 685), king of the West-Saxons ; came to the throne, 676 ; took the Quantock hills from the Welsh ; sheltered Wilfrith for a time ; benefactor of Glastonbury Abbey. [ix. 422]

CENWALH, KENWEALH, or COINWALCH (*d.* 672), king of the West-Saxons ; succeeded his father Cynegils [q. v.], 643 ; a pagan ; put away his Mercian wife ; driven from his kingdom by Penda of Mercia, *c.* 645 ; sought asylum in East Anglia ; cónverted to Christianity ; regained his kingdom, 648 ; built St. Peter's, Winchester ; made Agilberht bishop of Winchester, 650 ; defeated the Welsh at Bradford-on-Avon, 652, and annexed North Wiltshire ; defeated the Welsh, 658, and annexed country from the Axe to the Parret ; made Wini bishop of Winchester, 660 ; defeated by Wulfhere of Mercia, 661 ; accepted Hlodhere (Leutherius) as bishop of Winchester, 670. [ix. 423]

CENWULF or KENULF (*d.* 1006), abbot of Peterborough, 992 ; bishop of Winchester, 1005. [ix. 424]

CEOLFRID or CEOLFRITH, SAINT (642–716), abbot of Wearmouth ; monk at Gilling, Yorkshire, and at Ripon ; priest, 669 ; visited Kent and Lincolnshire ; prior, under Benedict Biscop [q. v.], at Wearmouth, 674 ; visited Rome, 678, and *c.* 684 ; abbot of Jarrow, 682 ; abbot of Wearmouth and Jarrow combined, 688–716 ; encouraged transcription of manuscripts ; induced the northern Irish, 704, and the Picts, 710, to observe the Roman Easter ; set out for Rome; died at Langres ; commemorated on 25 Sept. [ix. 424]

CEOLNOTH (*d.* 870), archbishop of Canterbury, *c.* 833 ; made an alliance between Ecgberht and Æthelwulf, kings of the West-Saxons, 838 ; plundered by the Danes, 851 ; bought off the Danes, 864. [ix. 426]

CEOLRED (*d.* 716), king of the Mercians, 709 ; invaded Wessex, 715 ; repulsed at Wanborough, Wiltshire ; oppressed the church ; died insane. [ix. 426]

CEOLRIC or CEOL (*d.* 597), king of the West-Saxons, 592, after defeating Ceawlin [q. v.] [ix. 427]

CEOLWULF, SAINT (*d.* 764), king of Northumbria, 729 ; to him Bæda dedicated his 'Historia Ecclesiastica'; dethroned and restored, 731; made Ecgberht bishop of York, 734 ; resigned, 737, and became a monk at Lindisfarne ; his body translated from Lindisfarne to Norham ; commemorated on 15 Jan. [ix. 427]

CERDIC (*d.* 534), king of the West-Saxons ; a Saxon ealdorman ; landed near Southampton, and fought against the Britons, 495 ; defeated the Britons, 508, and acquired South Hampshire up to the Avon ; reinforced, 514 ; defeated the Britons at Charford, Hampshire, 519 ; took the title of king ; defeated by the Britons at Badbury, Dorset, 520 ; conquered the Isle of Wight, 530. [ix. 427]

CERNACH, SAINT (*fl.* 450). [See CARANTACUS.]

CERVETTO, GIACOBBE (1682 ? – 1783), violoncellist ; really named BASEVI ; an Italian Jew ; resided in London, 1739–83 ; played in the orchestra at Drury Lane. [ix. 428]

CERVETTO, JAMES (1749 ?–1837), violoncellist ; taught by his father, Giacobbe Cervetto [q. v.] ; first performed, 1760 ; travelled on the continent, 1764; performed in London, 1765–83 ; retired on his father's fortune. [ix. 429]

CESTRETON, ADAM DE (*d.* 1269), judge ; chaplain to Henry III ; master of the London *domus conversorum,* 1265 ; justice itinerant in 1268. [ix. 429]

CHABHAM or CHOBHAM, THOMAS DE (*fl.* 1230), theologian ; sub-dean of Salisbury, 1214 ; author of 'Summa de Pœnitentia'; other works lost ; confused with Bishop Thomas de Cobham [q. v.] [ix. 429]

CHABOT, CHARLES (1815–1882), expert in handwriting ; born in Battersea ; originally a lithographer ; examined professionally the letters of Junius, identifying the handwriting with that of Sir Philip Francis, 1871. [ix. 429]

CHACEPORC or CHACEPORT, PETER (*d.* 1254), favourite of Henry III ; a Poitevin ; royal clerk, 1243 ; keeper of the wardrobe, 1245 ; rector of Ivinghoe, Buckinghamshire ; archdeacon of Wells, 1250 ; treasurer, 1253 ; treasurer of Lincoln Cathedral, 1254 ; accompanied Henry III to France ; died at Boulogne. [ix. 430]

CHAD, SAINT (*d.* 672). [See CEADDA.]

CHADERTON, LAURENCE (1536?–1640), theologian ; son of a wealthy Roman catholic gentleman in Lancashire ; disowned on becoming a protestant at Cambridge, *c.* 1566 ; entered Christ's College, Cambridge, 1565 ; B.A., 1567 ; fellow, 1568 ?–1576 ; preacher for fifty

years at St. Clement's, Cambridge ; B.D., 1578 ; chosen by Sir Walter Mildmay, the founder, to be master of Emmanuel College, 1584 ; a member of the Hampton Court conference, 1604 ; one of the translators of the authorised version, 1607–11 ; D.D., 1613 ; resigned mastership, 1622. [ix. 430]

CHADERTON, CHADDERTON, or CHATTERTON, WILLIAM (1540 ?–1608), bishop of Chester and of Lincoln ; born in Manchester ; B.A. Pembroke College, Cambridge, 1558 ; fellow of Christ's College, 1558 ; B.D., 1566 ; D.D., 1568 ; a disputant at Elizabeth's visit ; agent in Cambridge for Sir William Cecil and Leicester ; Lady Margaret professor of divinity, 1567–9 ; president of Queens' College (by court pressure), 1568–79 ; regius professor of divinity, 1569–80 ; opposed the Cambridge puritans ; prebendary of York, 1574, and of Westminster, 1576 ; warden of Manchester College, 1580 ; rector of Bangor ; bishop of Chester, 1579–95, carrying out court orders to suppress popery and puritanism ; translated to Lincoln, 1595, where he repressed popish recusancy. [ix. 432]

CHADS, SIR HENRY DUCIE (1788 ?–1868), admiral ; served in the Mediterranean, 1803–6 ; lieutenant, 1806 ; took part in operations leading to the capture of Mauritius, 1810 ; taken prisoner by the American frigate Constitution, 1812 ; released, 1813 ; served in West Indies, 1813–15 ; served in Burmah, 1823–7 ; commanded ship in East Indies, 1834–45 ; head of the naval gunnery school at Portsmouth, 1845–53 ; rear-admiral in the Baltic, 1854–5 ; K.C.B., 1855 ; admiral, 1863. [ix. 434]

CHADWICK, SIR EDWIN (1800–1890), sanitary reformer ; called to bar at Inner Temple, 1830 ; published, 1829, article on 'Preventive Police' in 'London Review,' which gained him the admiration and friendship of Jeremy Bentham ; assistant commissioner for poor-law, 1832 ; chief commissioner, 1833 ; on royal commission to investigate condition of factory children, 1833 ; secretary to new poor-law commissioners, 1834–46 ; member of sanitary commission, 1839 and 1844 ; C.B., 1848 ; member of board of health, 1848–54 ; presented 'separate system,' which was adopted for drainage of Cawnpore, 1871; knighted, 1889 ; published numerous pamphlets, reports, and papers. [Suppl. i. 406]

CHADWICK, JAMES (1813–1882), Roman catholic prelate ; born at Drogheda ; educated at Ushaw ; missionary priest in the north of England ; professor at Ushaw ; bishop of Hexham, 1866 ; published devotional tracts. [ix. 435]

CHAFFERS, RICHARD (1731–1762), set up pottery fabric for blue and white earthenware at Liverpool, 1752, and became rival of Wedgwood. [Suppl. i. 409]

CHAFFERS, WILLIAM (1811–1892), authority on old plate and pottery ; educated at Merchant Taylors' School ; F.S.A., 1843 ; published 'Hall Marks on Gold and Silver Plate,' 1863, and 'Marks and Monograms on Pottery and Porcelain,' 1863. [Suppl. i. 409]

CHAFY, WILLIAM (1779–1843), benefactor of Sidney Sussex College, Cambridge ; entered King's School, Canterbury, 1788 ; B.A. Sidney Sussex College, 1800 ; fellow, 1801 ; B.D., 1810 ; master of Sidney Sussex College, 1813–1843 ; D.D., 1813 ; king's chaplain. [ix. 436]

CHAIGNEAU, WILLIAM (1709–1781), author of 'Jack Connor,' an Irish novel, 1752, and of a farce ; served in Flanders ; army agent in Dublin. [ix. 436]

CHALK, SIR JAMES JELL (1803–1878), secretary to the ecclesiastical commission ; entered the ecclesiastical commission office, 1836 ; secretary, 1849–71 ; barrister of the Middle Temple, 1839 ; knighted, 1871. [ix. 436]

CHALKHILL, JOHN (*fl.* 1600), poet ; author of a pastoral, 'Thealma and Clearchus,' published, 1683, by Izaak Walton, who knew him in youth. [ix. 437]

CHALKLEY, THOMAS (1675–1741), quaker ; son of a Southwark tradesman ; preached in the south of England, in Scotland, 1697, and in Virginia, 1698 ; emigrated to Philadelphia, 1700 ; visited Barbados, 1701 ; visited Great Britain, Holland, and Germany, 1707–10 ; travelled in America as a preacher, 1712–18 ; visited Barbados, 1735 ; died at the Virgin islands ; published pamphlets, and an autobiography. [ix. 437]

CHALLICE, ANNIE EMMA (1821–1875), author of tales and historical sketches, 1847–73: *née* Armstrong; married John Challice [q. v.] [ix. 438]

CHALLICE, JOHN (1815–1863), physician; M.D. Edinburgh; medical officer of health at Battersea; published tracts on sanitary questions, 1848–56. [ix. 438]

CHALLINOR, MRS. HANNAH (*fl.* 1670). [See WOOLLEY.]

CHALLIS, JAMES (1803–1882), astronomer; entered Trinity College, Cambridge, 1821; senior wrangler, 1825; fellow, 1826–31; rector of Papworth Everard, Cambridgeshire, 1830–52; Plumian professor of astronomy, 1836–82; director of Cambridge observatory, 1836–61; observed Neptune, without knowing it, 4 Aug. 1846; published 'Astronomical Observations made at . . . Cambridge,' 1832–64; published his theory of physical forces, 1869; published his astronomical lectures, 1879; wrote on scriptural and educational topics. [ix. 438]

CHALLONER, RICHARD (1691–1781), Roman catholic prelate: son of a Sussex dissenter; befriended by Roman catholic squires; studied at Douay, 1704; priest, 1716; B.D., 1719; D.D., 1727; professor of philosophy, 1713–20; vice-president and professor of divinity, 1720–1730; missioner in London, 1730; entered into controversy with Bishop Conyers Middleton, 1737; titular bishop of Debra and coadjutor in London, 1741; bishop in charge of the London district, 1758–81; published 'Memoirs of . . . Priests . . . that have suffered Death in England, 1577–1684,' 1741–2, 'Britannia Sancta; Lives of . . . Saints,' 1745, the bible in English for Roman catholics, 1749–50, and numerous devotional and controversial tracts, 1706–67. [ix. 440]

CHALMERS, ALEXANDER (1759–1834), miscellaneous writer; son of a printer; educated at Aberdeen; M.A.; journalist in London, 1777–1834; F.S.A., 1805; a voluminous editor of English prose-writers and poets; author of biographies; published 'History of the Colleges of Oxford,' 1810, and 'The General Biographical Dictionary,' 1812–17. [ix. 443]

CHALMERS or **CHAMBERS**, DAVID (1530 ?–1592). [See CHAMBERS.]

CHALMERS, SIR GEORGE (*d.* 1791), portrait-painter; born in Edinburgh of a family which had lost estates by forfeiture; travelled; exhibited at the Royal Academy, 1775–90. [ix. 445]

CHALMERS, GEORGE (1742–1825), Scottish antiquary; educated at Aberdeen and Edinburgh; emigrated; lawyer at Baltimore; settled in London, 1775; published pamphlets on the American colonies, 1777–82; government clerk, 1786; published biographies of De Foe and Tom Paine; edited Scottish poets and wrote numerous Scottish biographies; his chief work, 'Caledonia: an account of . . . North Britain,' 1807–24. [ix. 445]

CHALMERS, GEORGE PAUL (1836–1878), painter; a shopman; studied art at Edinburgh; exhibited in London, 1863–76; murdered by thieves in Edinburgh. [ix. 446]

CHALMERS, JAMES (1782–1853), post-office reformer; bookseller and newspaper publisher in Dundee; advocated accelerated mail service, 1825; suggested an adhesive stamp, 1834; promulgated this plan, 1837. [ix. 447]

CHALMERS, SIR JOHN (1756–1818), major-general; ensign in Madras, 1775; lieutenant, 1780; defended Coimbatoor, June–November 1791; captain, 1792; major-general, 1812; K.C.B., 1814; held command in India, 1803–18; died at sea. [ix. 447]

CHALMERS, PATRICK (1802–1854), Scottish antiquary; of Queen's College, Oxford, 1818; captain of dragoons; retired to Auldbar, 1826; M.P. for Montrose burghs, 1835–42; published antiquarian papers; author of 'Ancient Sculptured Monuments . . . of Angus,' 1848; died at Rome. [ix. 448]

CHALMERS, THOMAS (1780–1847), theologian; educated at St. Andrews; minister of Kilmeny, Fife, 1803–15; lectured on chemistry at St. Andrews; minister of Tron parish, Glasgow, 1815–20, and of St. John's, Glasgow, 1820–3; D.D. Glasgow, 1816; visited London, 1817; professor of moral philosophy, St. Andrews, 1823–8; professor of divinity, Edinburgh, 1828–43; lectured in London,

1838; an active pioneer of the movement which led to the disruption of the Scottish Established church and to the formation of the Free church, 1843; devised the sustentation fund of the newly founded Free church; principal and divinity professor of the Free Church College, Edinburgh, 1843–7; advocated home missions; author of theological, philosophical, expository, and devotional treatises, from 1813. [ix. 449]

CHALMERS, W. A. (*fl.* 1798), water-colour painter; exhibited at the Royal Academy, 1790–8. [ix. 454]

CHALMERS, SIR WILLIAM (1787–1860), lieutenant-general; lieutenant, 1803; served in Sicily, 1806–7; captain, 1807; served in Portugal, 1808, at Walcheren, 1809, in the Peninsula, 1810–13, in Belgium, 1815, at Waterloo, 1815, and in France, 1815–17; major-general, 1846; knighted, 1848; lieutenant-general, 1854. [ix. 454]

CHALON, ALFRED EDWARD (1780–1860), portrait and subject painter; born in Geneva; studied art in London, 1797; exhibited, 1810–57. [ix. 455]

CHALON, JOHN JAMES (1778–1854), landscape and genre painter; born in Geneva; studied art in London, 1796; exhibited, 1806–44. [ix. 456]

CHALONER, JAMES (1603–1660), regicide; fourth son of Sir Thomas Chaloner the younger [q. v.]; of Brasenose College, Oxford, 1617; of the Middle Temple, 1619; M.P., Aldborough, Yorkshire, 1645–53; parliamentary commissioner in the Isle of Man, 1652; governor of Man, 1658; imprisoned by the army in Peel Castle, 1659. [ix. 456]

CHALONER, RICHARD (*d.* 1643), linendraper, of London; hanged for share in Edmund Waller's royalist plot, 1643. [ix. 456]

CHALONER, SIR THOMAS, the elder (1521–1565), diplomatist; son of a London mercer; attached to the embassy to Spain, 1540–1; clerk to the privy council; served in Scotland and was knighted, 1547; granted Guisborough priory lands, Yorkshire, 1550, Steeple Claydon, Buckinghamshire, 1557, and other lands, 1553–61; envoy to Scotland, 1551–2, to France, 1553, to Scotland, 1556, to the emperor, 1559, the Spanish Netherlands, 1559–60, and Spain, 1561–4; wrote Latin verses (published, 1579); published translations from the Latin. [ix. 457]

CHALONER, SIR THOMAS, the younger (1561–1615), naturalist; only son of Sir Thomas Chaloner the elder [q. v.]; entered Magdalen College, Oxford, 1579; B.A. Magdalen Hall, 1582; travelled, 1580; served in France and was knighted, 1591; in Italy, 1596–7; opened alum mines on his Yorkshire estate, 1600; envoy to Scotland; accompanied James VI of Scotland to England; governor of Prince Henry, 1603, and his chamberlain, 1610; benefactor of St. Bees' School. [ix. 458]

CHALONER, THOMAS (1595–1661), regicide; third son of Sir Thomas Chaloner the younger [q. v.]; of Exeter College, Oxford, 1611; travelled; incensed with Charles I for confiscating his Yorkshire alum mines; M.P. for Richmond, Yorkshire, 1645–53; commissioner in Munster, 1647; one of Charles I's judges; councillor of state, 1651; M.P., Scarborough, 1659; excluded from pardon, 1660; died in Holland. [ix. 460]

CHAMBER or **CHAMBERLAYNE**, JOHN A (*d.* 1489), rebel; knight of influence in the north of England; hanged at York for spreading agitation in the north against payment of a subsidy to Henry VII. [x. 1]

CHAMBER, JOHN (1470–1549). [See CHAMBRE.]

CHAMBER, JOHN (1546–1604), astronomer; B.A. Merton College, Oxford, 1568; fellow, 1569; M.A., 1573; studied medicine; fellow of Eton, 1582; canon of Windsor, 1601; wrote against astrology, 1601. [x. 1]

CHAMBERLAIN. [See also CHAMBERLAINE, CHAMBERLAYNE, CHAMBERLEN, and CHAMBERLIN.]

CHAMBERLAIN or **CHAMBERLAYNE**, GEORGE (1576–1634), bishop of Ypres; of the Shirburn family; born at Ghent; educated at Rome; dean of St. Bavon, Ghent; bishop of Ypres, 1626–34. [x. 1]

CHAMBERLAIN, JOHN (1553–1627), letter-writer; born in London; entered Trinity College, Cambridge, 1570; resided in or near London. His letters date from 1598 to 1625. [x. 2]

CHAMBERLAIN, JOHN HENRY (1831–1883), architect; studied architecture in offices in Leicester and London; visited Italy; much employed in Birmingham and district from 1856; patron of the Birmingham school of art and other educational institutions. [x. 2]

CHAMBERLAIN or **CHAMBERLAYNE**, SIR LEONARD (d. 1561), governor of Guernsey; son of Sir Edward Chamberlayne (1484?–1543?) [q. v.]; keeper of Woodstock Park, 1543; obtained grants of church-lands, 1543; sheriff of Oxfordshire and Berkshire, 1547 and 1552; knighted, 1553; an officer of the Tower, 1549–53; M.P. for Scarborough, 1553, and for Oxfordshire, 1554; governor of Guernsey, 1553–61. [x. 3]

CHAMBERLAIN, ROBERT (fl. 1640–1660), poet; a barrister's clerk; entered Exeter College, Oxford, 1637; published apophthegms and verses, 1638, a comedy entitled 'The Swaggering Damsell' and jests, 1640. [x. 4]

CHAMBERLAIN, ROBERT (fl. 1678), arithmetician; accountant, of London; published 'The Accomptant's Guide,' and 'A Plaine . . . Explanation of . . . Arithmetick,' 1679. [x. 5]

CHAMBERLAIN, ROBERT (d. 1798?), ceramist; employed at the Worcester porcelain works, 1751–83; started business as Chamberlain & Son, Worcester, 1786. [x. 5]

CHAMBERLAIN or **CHAMBERLAYNE**, THOMAS (d. 1625), judge; barrister of Gray's Inn, 1585; serjeant-at-law, 1614; knighted; a judge in North Wales, 1615; chief-justice of Chester, 1616–20; justice of the king's bench, 1620–4: temporary justice of the common pleas, 1625; chief-justice of Chester, 1624–5. [x. 6]

CHAMBERLAIN, WILLIAM (d. 1807), portrait and animal painter; a Londoner; pupil of John Opie; exhibited, 1794–1802. [x. 6]

CHAMBERLAINE, JOHN (1745–1812), antiquary; keeper of the king's drawings, 1791; edited reproductions of drawings in the royal collection, 1792–1812. [x. 7]

CHAMBERLANE, ROBERT (d. 1638), theologian; an Irishman; educated at Salamanca; Franciscan lecturer at Louvain; wrote theological tracts. [x. 7]

CHAMBERLAYNE, SIR EDWARD (1470–1541), of Gedding, Suffolk; succeeded to his maternal estates, 1522. [x. 7]

CHAMBERLAYNE, SIR EDWARD (1484?–1543?), of Shirburn Castle, Oxfordshire; succeeded to his estates, 1497; keeper of Woodstock Park, 1508; served against France, 1512–14 and 1522; sheriff of Oxfordshire and Berkshire, 1518; accompanied Henry VIII to France, 1520; M.P., Wallingford, 1529; attendant on Catherine of Arragon at Kimbolton, 1533–6. [x. 7]

CHAMBERLAYNE, EDWARD (1616–1703), author; of Odington, Gloucestershire; M.A. St. Edmund Hall, Oxford, 1641; travelled, 1642–60; LL.D. Cambridge, 1671; D.C.L. Oxford, 1672; tutor to the Duke of Grafton, 1679, and to Prince George of Denmark; published 'Angliæ Notitiæ, or the Present State of England,' 1669 (20th edition, 1702); published other pamphlets and translations. [x. 8]

CHAMBERLAYNE, SIR JAMES (d. 1699), third baronet, of Wickham, Oxfordshire; published sacred poems, 1680–1. [x. 9]

CHAMBERLAYNE, JOHN (1666–1723), miscellaneous writer; younger son of Edward Chamberlayne (1616–1703) [q. v.]; educated at Oxford, 1685, and Leyden, 1688; usher to Queen Anne and George I; F.R.S., 1702; published a tract on 'Coffee, Tea, and Chocolate,' 1685; translated from French, Italian, and Dutch; continued his father's 'Present State of England'; published 'Oratio Dominica,' the Lord's prayer in various languages, 1715. [x. 9]

CHAMBERLAYNE, WILLIAM (1619–1689), poet; physician at Shaftesbury, Dorset; published a play, entitled 'Love's Victory,' 1658, an epic poem entitled 'Pharonnida,' 1659, and congratulatory verses to Charles II, 1660. [x. 10]

CHAMBERLEN, HUGH, the elder (fl. 1720), manmidwife and projector; eldest son of Peter Chamberlen (1601–1683) [q. v.]; accoucheur in London; translated François Mauriceau's text-book of midwifery, 1672; court physician, 1673; F.R.S., 1681; published 'Manuale Medicum,' 1685; prosecuted for practising medicine without qualification, 1688; too late to witness the birth of the Prince of Wales, 1688; published bank scheme, 1690, and plan for paying doctors out of the taxes, 1694; withdrew to Scotland, 1699; renewed his bank scheme there, 1700; published in favour of the union, 1702; withdrew to Amsterdam; communicated the use of the midwifery forceps to Hendrik van Roonhuisen. [x. 10]

CHAMBERLEN, HUGH, the younger (1664–1728), physician; eldest son of Hugh Chamberlen the elder [q. v.]; educated at Cambridge and Leyden; M.D. Cambridge, 1689; a fashionable London physician and accoucheur. [x. 12]

CHAMBERLEN, PAUL (1635–1717), empiric; second son of Peter Chamberlen (1601–1683) [q. v.]; accoucheur in London; invented 'Anodyne Necklace,' an amulet for children teething and women in labour, recommending it in pamphlets. [x. 12]

CHAMBERLEN, PETER, the younger (1572–1626), surgeon; younger brother of Peter Chamberlen the elder [q. v.]; born at Southampton; surgeon and accoucheur in London, 1600; prosecuted for practising medicine without qualification; advocated incorporation of London midwives, 1616. [x. 14]

CHAMBERLEN, PETER, the elder (d. 1631), surgeon; son of a Paris surgeon and protestant refugee; accoucheur at Southampton; learnt the use of the forceps in midwifery and made it a family secret; came to London, 1596; court accoucheur; prosecuted for practising medicine without qualification, 1612. [x. 13]

CHAMBERLEN, PETER (1601–1683), physician and projector; son of Peter Chamberlen the younger [q. v.]; educated at Merchant Taylors' School and Cambridge; M.D. Padua, 1619; used the midwifery forceps, the family secret; F.R.C.P., 1628–49; advocated incorporation of London midwives, 1634; advocated public baths, 1648; for some time an anabaptist; physician to Charles II, 1660; published theological and other pamphlets. [x. 14]

CHAMBERLIN, MASON (d. 1787), portrait painter; originally a merchant's clerk; exhibited in London, 1760–1787. [x. 15]

CHAMBERS, DAVID, LORD ORMOND (1530?–1592), Scottish judge; educated at Aberdeen; studied theology and law in France and Italy; parson of Suddy; chancellor of Ross; lord of session, with style of Lord Ormond, 1565; partisan of Mary Queen of Scots; privy to Darnley's murder, 1567; attended Mary Queen of Scots at Langside, 1568; attainted, 1568; withdrew to Spain and France; published, 1579, 'Abbregé des Histoires . . .,' a chronological summary of European history, with an appendix on Scotland; returned to Scotland, c. 1582; his attainder reversed, 1584; lord of session, 1586–92. [x. 16]

CHAMBERS, EPHRAIM (d. 1740), encyclopædist; apprenticed to a London map-maker; published his 'Cyclopædia, or . . . Dictionary of Arts and Sciences,' 1728 (two volumes folio); visited France; translated French scientific treatises. [x. 16]

CHAMBERS, GEORGE (1803–1840), marine painter, went to sea, 1813; visited the Baltic and Mediterranean; house-painter at Whitby; scene-painter in London; exhibited pictures of naval battles. [x. 17]

CHAMBERS, JOHN (d. 1556), first bishop of Peterborough; Benedictine monk at Peterborough; studied at Oxford and Cambridge; M.A. Cambridge, 1505; abbot of Peterborough, 1528; entertained Wolsey, 1530; surrendered Peterborough Abbey to the king, 1539; B.D. Cambridge, 1539; king's chaplain; bishop of Peterborough, 1541–56. [x. 18]

CHAMBERS, JOHN (1780–1839), topographer; trained as an architect; of ample private means; resided at Worcester, afterwards at Norwich; published histories of Worcestershire, 1819–20, and Norfolk, 1829. [x. 19]

CHAMBERS, JOHN CHARLES (1817–1874), warden of the 'House of Charity'; eldest son of John Chambers (1780–1839) [q. v.]; educated at Norwich school and Emmanuel College, Cambridge; M.A., 1843; curate of Sedbergh, Yorkshire, 1842; Anglican clergyman at Perth, 1846–55; vicar of St. Mary's, Soho, and warden of the 'House of Charity,' Soho, 1856–74; published sermons. [x. 191]

CHAMBERS, JOHN GRAHAM (1843-1883), athlete and journalist; at Eton, 1856; B.A. Trinity College, Cambridge, 1865; a university athlete and oarsman; patron of athletics; contributor to the 'Standard'; editor of 'Land and Water,' 1871-83. [x. 20]

CHAMBERS, RICHARD (1588?-1658), London merchant; opposed levy of tonnage and poundage without sanction of parliament, 1628; illegally imprisoned by the king, 1629-35; again imprisoned for resisting ship-money, 1636; voted compensation by parliament, but was never paid; alderman of London, 1642-9; surveyor of customs, London, 1648-9; imprisoned for refusing to recognise the Commonwealth, 1649-51; died poor. [x. 21]

CHAMBERS, ROBERT (1571-1624?), Roman catholic priest; born in Yorkshire; at Rheims, 1582; at Rome, 1593; confessor at Brussels, 1599-1623; died in England; published devotional tracts. [x. 21]

CHAMBERS, SIR ROBERT (1737-1803), Indian judge; exhibitioner of Lincoln College, 1754, and fellow of University College, Oxford, 1761; B.C.L., 1765; Vinerian professor of law, 1762-77; friend of Dr. Samuel Johnson, 1766; principal of New Inn Hall, Oxford, 1766-1803; a judge of the supreme court of Bengal, 1774; showed great weakness in the trial of Nuncomar, 1776; knighted, 1778; chief-justice in Bengal, 1789-99; died in Paris. His collection of Sanskrit MSS. is now at Oxford. [x. 22]

CHAMBERS, ROBERT (1802-1871), publisher and author; educated at Peebles and in Edinburgh till 1816; clerk; opened bookstall, c. 1818; founded with his brother the publishing firm of W. & R. Chambers, Edinburgh; attracted notice by his 'Traditions of Edinburgh,' 1823; wrote and issued a multitude of books on Scottish history, biography, and literature, 1824-67; established 'Chambers's Journal,' 1832; wrote and published, anonymously, 'Vestiges of Creation,' 1844; hon. LL.D. St. Andrews, 1861; compiled 'Book of Days,' an antiquarian miscellany, 1862-4. [x. 23]

CHAMBERS, ROBERT (1832-1888), publisher; son of Robert Chambers (1802-1871) [q. v.]; editor of 'Chambers's Journal,' 1874; took active part in production of 'Chambers's Encyclopædia,' 1859-68. [Suppl. i. 409]

CHAMBERS, SABINE (1560?-1633), jesuit; born in Leicestershire; M.A. Broadgates Hall, Oxford, 1583; joined jesuits at Paris, 1587; theological lecturer at Dôle; missioner in London, 1609-33; published devotional tracts. [x. 25]

CHAMBERS, SIR THOMAS (1814-1891), recorder of London; LL.B. Clare Hall, Cambridge, 1846; called to bar at Middle Temple, 1840; bencher, 1861; treasurer, 1872; Q.C., 1861; common serjeant, 1857; recorder of city of London, 1878; knighted, 1872; liberal M.P. for Hertford, 1852-7, and for Marylebone, 1865-85; published legal writings. [Suppl. i. 410]

CHAMBERS, SIR WILLIAM (1726-1796), architect; son of a Scottish merchant at Stockholm; supercargo on a Swedish ship sailing to China, 1742-4; studied architecture in Italy and Paris; settled as architect in London, 1755; employed at Kew Gardens, 1757-62; published 'Treatise of Civil Architecture,' 1759; a Swedish knight, 1771; satirised for his ideas on Chinese gardening, 1772; designed Somerset House, 1775. [x. 26]

CHAMBERS, WILLIAM (1800-1883), publisher and author; apprenticed to an Edinburgh bookseller, 1814; opened bookstall, 1819; joined with his brother Robert Chambers (1802-1871) [q. v.] in founding the publishing house of W. & R. Chambers, Edinburgh; issued a multitude of cheap educational works; issued 'Chambers's Encyclopædia,' 1859; published notes of travel, tales, &c.; lord provost of Edinburgh, 1865-9; hon. LL.D. Edinburgh, 1872; presented a public library to Peebles; restored St. Giles's, Edinburgh. [x. 27]

CHAMBERS, WILLIAM FREDERICK (1786-1855), physician; born in India; came to England, 1793; educated at Westminster School; M.A. Cambridge, 1811; M.D. Cambridge, 1818; studied medicine in London and Edinburgh; physician to St. George's Hospital, London, 1816-39; an eminent consulting physician; retired, 1848. [x. 29]

CHAMBRÉ, SIR ALAN (1739-1823), judge; barrister, of Gray's Inn. 1767; recorder of Lancaster, 1796; serjeant-at-law, 1799; baron of the exchequer, 1799; justice of the common pleas, 1800-15. [x. 30]

CHAMBRE, JOHN (1470-1549), physician; fellow of Merton College, Oxford, 1492; M.D. Padua, 1506; physician to Henry VII and Henry VIII; an original member of the College of Physicians, 1518; rector of Tichmarsh, Northamptonshire, 1490, of Great Bowden, Leicestershire, 1508, and of Aller, Somerset, 1522-49; prebendary of Lincoln, 1494-1549; warden of Merton College, 1525-44; dean of St. Stephen's, Westminster; M.D. Oxford, 1531. [x. 30]

CHAMBRE, WILLIAM DE (fl. 1365?), probable author of a Latin biography of Bishop Richard de Bury. [x. 31]

CHAMIER, ANTHONY (1725-1780), friend of Dr. Samuel Johnson; born in London; of French extraction; government official; deputy secretary at war, 1772; under-secretary of state, 1775; M.P., Tamworth, 1778. [x. 32]

CHAMIER, FREDERICK (1796-1870), novelist; entered navy, 1809; lieutenant, 1815; served, chiefly in Mediterranean, 1810-27; captain, 1856; published nautical novels, 1832-41, a continuation of James's 'Naval History,' 1837, and notes of travel, 1849-55. [x. 32]

CHAMPAIN, SIR JOHN UNDERWOOD BATEMAN (1835-1887). [See BATEMAN-CHAMPAIN.]

CHAMPION, ANTHONY (1725-1801), poet; educated at Eton, 1739, and Oxford, 1743; barrister of the Middle Temple; M.P. for St. Germans, 1754, and for Liskeard, 1761-8; wrote verses. [x. 33]

CHAMPION, JOHN GEORGE (1815?-1854), botanist; ensign, 1831; served in the Ionian islands, Ceylon, and (1847-50) Hongkong; brought plants to England, 1850, and gave them to Kew herbarium; wounded at Inkermann, 1854; lieutenant-colonel; died at Scutari. [x. 33]

CHAMPION, JOSEPH (fl. 1762), calligrapher; pupil of Charles Snell, penman; schoolmaster in London; published text-books of arithmetic and penmanship, 1733-62. [x. 33]

CHAMPION, RICHARD (1743-1791), ceramist; merchant's clerk in Bristol, 1762; commenced making china, 1768; manager of William Cookworthy's Bristol china works, 1770; carried on the works in his own name, 1773-81; a friend of Edmund Burke; government official, 1782-4; emigrated to Carolina. [x. 34]

CHAMPION, THOMAS (d. 1619). [See CAMPION.]

CHAMPNEY, ANTHONY (1569?-1643?), controversialist; born in Yorkshire; studied at Rheims, 1590, and Rome, 1593; D.D. and fellow of the Sorbonne, Paris; vice-president and divinity lecturer at Douay, 1619-26; confessor at Brussels, 1626; returned to Douay, 1628; missioner in England; published controversial tracts, 1601-23; wrote against the validity of Anglican orders, 1616. [x. 35]

CHAMPNEYS, JOHN (fl. 1548), a London layman; prosecuted by Archbishop Cranmer for Calvinistic opinions expressed in his published works. [x. 36]

CHAMPNEYS, JOHN (d. 1556), lord mayor of London; skinner, of London; lord mayor, 1534; knighted; became blind. [x. 36]

CHAMPNEYS, WILLIAM WELDON (1807-1875), dean of Lichfield; entered Brasenose College, Oxford, 1824; M.A. and fellow, 1831; curate of St. Ebbe's, Oxford, 1831; rector of St. Mary's, Whitechapel, London, 1837-60; canon of St. Paul's, 1851; rector of St. Pancras, London, 1860; dean of Lichfield, 1868-75; published sermons and religious biographies. [x. 36]

CHANCELLOR, RICHARD (d. 1556), navigator; sailed to the Levant, 1550; given command of a ship in Sir Hugh Willoughby's [q. v.] expedition to discover a north-east passage to India, 1553; reached Archangel; visited the Russian court at Moscow; sailed back from Archangel, 1554; revisited Archangel and Moscow, 1555; wrecked on the Aberdeenshire coast on his return. [x. 37]

CHANCY or **CHAWNEY**, MAURICE (d. 1581). [See CHAUNCY.]

CHANDLER, ANNE (1740–1814). [See CANDLER.]

CHANDLER, BENJAMIN (1737–1786), surgeon; practised medicine at Canterbury; wrote on 'Inoculation,' 1767, and 'Apoplexies,' 1785. [x. 38]

CHANDLER, EDWARD (1668 ?–1750), bishop of Durham; M.A. Emmanuel College, Cambridge, 1693; D.D., 1701; prebendary of Lichfield, 1697, Salisbury, 1703, and Worcester, 1706; bishop of Lichfield, 1717; bishop of Durham, 1730–50; published sermons and controversial treatises. [x. 38]

CHANDLER, HENRY WILLIAM (1828–1889), scholar; B.A. Pembroke College, Oxford, 1852; fellow, 1853; M.A., 1855; Waynflete professor of moral and metaphysical philosophy, 1867–89; curator of Bodleian Library, 1884. His works include Practical Introduction to Greek Accentuation,' 1864, and catalogue of (1868) and chronological index to (1878) editions of Aristotle's 'Nicomachean Ethics.' [Suppl. i. 410]

CHANDLER, JOHANNA (1820–1875), philanthropist; sold work and collected subscriptions, 1856–9, to found a hospital for paralytics in London. [x. 38]

CHANDLER, JOHN (1700–1780), apothecary; published medical tracts, 1729–61. [x. 39]

CHANDLER, J. W. (d. 1805 ?), portrait painter; exhibited in London, 1787–91; removed to Aberdeenshire, 1800, and Edinburgh; died insane, c. 1805. [x. 39]

CHANDLER, MARY (1687–1745), writer of a metrical 'Description o Bath' (sixth edition, 1744); shopkeeper in Bath, 1705–44. [x. 39]

CHANDLER, RICHARD (d. 1744), printer and bookseller; in partnership with Cæsar Ward in London, York, and Scarborough, published 'The History . . . of the House of Commons . . .' to 1743 (fourteen volumes), 1742–4; failed; committed suicide. [x. 39]

CHANDLER, RICHARD (1738–1810), classical antiquary and traveller; educated at Winchester; demy of Magdalen College, Oxford, 1757, and fellow, 1770; M.A., 1761; D.D., 1773; published fragments of the Greek lyrists, 1759, and 'Marmora Oxoniensia,' 1763; travelled, for the Dilettanti Society in Asia Minor and Greece, 1764–6; published his results in 'Ionian Antiquities,' 1769, 'Inscriptiones Antiquæ,' 1774, and 'Travels,' 1775–6; vicar of East Worldham, Hampshire, 1779, and of Tilehurst, Berkshire, 1800–10; travelled in Switzerland and Italy, 1785–7; published 'History of Ilium,' 1802; wrote 'The Life of (bishop) Waynflete' (published 1811). [x. 40]

CHANDLER, SAMUEL (1693–1766), theologian; educated at Gloucester and Leyden; minister of a presbyterian congregation at Peckham, 1716; bookseller; nonconformist minister at the Old Jewry, 1726–66; hon. D.D. Edinburgh; published pamphlets against deism, 1725–62, and against Roman catholicism, 1732–45, as well as other controversial tracts and sermons. [x. 42]

CHANDLER or **CHAUNDLER**, THOMAS (1418 ?–1490). [See CHAUNDLER.]

CHANDOS, DUKE OF (1673–1744). [See BRYDGES, JAMES.]

CHANDOS, BARONS. [See BRYDGES, SIR JOHN, first BARON, 1490 ?–1556; BRYDGES, GREY, fifth BARON, 1579 ?–1621; BRYDGES, GEORGE, sixth BARON, d. 1655.]

CHANDOS, SIR JOHN (d. 1370), soldier; present at the siege of Cambrai, 1337, and the battle of Crecy, 1346; K.G., c. 1349; saved the Black Prince's life at Poitiers, 1356; granted lands in Lincolnshire and the Coutantin; Edward III's lieutenant in France, 1360; constable of Guienne, 1362; won the battle of Auray, Brittany, 1364; fought at Navarete, Spain, 1367; withdrew from Guienne, 1368; recalled, 1368; seneschal of Poitiers, 1369; died of his wounds at Mortemer. [x. 43]

CHANDOS, SIR JOHN (d. 1428), of Herefordshire. [x. 44]

CHANNELL, SIR WILLIAM FRY (1804–1873), judge; barrister of the Inner Temple, 1827; serjeant-at-law, 1840; baron of the exchequer, 1857; knighted, June 1857. [x. 44]

CHANTREY, SIR FRANCIS LEGATT (1781–1841), sculptor; son of a carpenter; grocer's boy in Sheffield;

apprentice to a Sheffield wood-carver, 1797–1802; learned drawing, stone-carving, and painting in oil; portrait painter in Sheffield, 1802, and continued his visits there till 1808; resided chiefly in London from 1802, studying art, painting portraits, and practising wood-carving; exhibited pictures at the Royal Academy. 1804–7; worked chiefly at statuary from 1804; exhibited statues, 1809; paid by George IV three hundred guineas for his bust, 1822; knighted, 1835; bequeathed his property to the Royal Academy. [x. 44]

CHAPLEAU, SIR JOSEPH ADOLPHE (1840–1898), Canadian statesman; born at Sainte Thérèse de Blainville, in province of Quebec; called to bar of Lower Canada, 1861; Q.C., 1873; conservative member for county of Terrebonne in provincial parliament, 1867–82, and in Canadian House of Commons, 1882–92; solicitor-general, 1873–4; premier and minister of agriculture and public works, 1879; secretary of state for Canada, registrar-general and privy councillor, 1882; lieutenant-governor of Quebec, 1892; K.C.M.G., 1896. [Suppl. i. 411]

CHAPMAN, EDMUND (fl. 1733), surgeon; a country accoucheur, 1708; practitioner in London, 1733; published a treatise on midwifery. [x. 47]

CHAPMAN, FREDERIC (1823–1895), publisher; entered, 1834, house of Chapman & Hall; partner, 1847, and head of firm, 1864; purchased (1870) copyright of Dickens's works, many of which the firm had published; projected and published 'Fortnightly Review,' 1865; published works for the Brownings, Lord Lytton, Trollope, and Mr. George Meredith. [Suppl. i. 412]

CHAPMAN, SIR FREDERICK EDWARD (1815–1893), general; educated at Royal Military Academy, Woolwich; second lieutenant, royal engineers, 1835; lieutenant-colonel, 1859; lieutenant-general and colonel-commandant, 1872; general, 1877; made survey for defences of Dardanelles, 1854; directed operations during latter part of siege of Sebastopol; C.B., 1855; K.C.B., 1867; governor and commander-in-chief of Bermudas, 1867–70; inspector-general of fortifications and director of works at war office, 1870–5; G.C.B., 1877. [Suppl. i. 413]

CHAPMAN, GEORGE (1559 ?–1634), poet; nothing known of his education; published 'The Shadow of Night' (hymns), 1594, and 'Ovid's Banquet of Sence' and other poems, 1595; completed Marlowe's 'Hero and Leander,' 1598; said to have been imprisoned for satirising James I's Scottish followers, 1605; mentioned by the poet John Davies of Hereford as having lived in his later days in straitened circumstances; contributed to plays by Ben Jonson and Shirley. Chapman's first known play, 'The Blind Beggar of Alexandria,' appeared 1596, and was printed in 1598; the comedies 'All Fools' (printed 1605) and 'An Humerous dayes Myrth' belong to 1599, as also other plays now lost. The bulk of his dramas appeared between 1606 and 1612. Chapman published a specimen of his rhyming fourteen-syllable version of the 'Iliad' in 1598, and the whole 'Iliad' in 1611, adding the 'Odyssey' (rhyming ten-syllable) in 1614, and the hymns &c. in 1624. Translations by him from Petrarch appeared in 1612, from Musæus in 1616, Hesiod's 'Georgicks' in 1618, and a satire of Juvenal in 1629. He wrote also copies of verses for his friends' books, court poems, and a masque (1614). His collected works appeared in 1873–5. [x. 47]

CHAPMAN, GEORGE (1723–1806), author of tracts on education; M.A. Aberdeen, 1741, and LL.D.; taught school in Dalkeith, 1747, Dumfries, 1751–74, and Banff; was afterwards a printer in Edinburgh. [x. 53]

CHAPMAN, HENRY SAMUEL (1803–1881), colonial judge; emigrated to Canada, 1823; newspaper editor in Montreal, 1833–4; barrister of the Middle Temple, 1840; judge in New Zealand, 1842–52; barrister and member of the legislature at Melbourne, 1854–65; judge in New Zealand, 1865–77; died at Dunedin; wrote on legal and economical topics. [x. 54]

CHAPMAN, JOHN (1704–1784), divine; educated at Eton; fellow of King's College, Cambridge; M.A., 1731; D.D. Oxford, 1741; rector of Smeeth, Kent, 1739, and of Saltwood, 1739–41, and of Mersham, 1744; archdeacon of Sudbury; presented himself to the precentorship of Lincoln, but was ejected, 1760; wrote on classical antiquities and controversial divinity. [x. 54]

I

CHAPMAN, JOHN (1801–1854), political writer; bred as a clockmaker at Loughborough, Leicestershire; joined baptists, 1822; opened factory for spinning machinery, 1822; failed in business, 1834; withdrew to London; edited the 'Mechanic's Magazine'; patented improvements on the hansom cab, 1836; wrote much for the newspapers; projected railway and irrigation schemes in India; published several treatises on Indian finance and administration. [x. 55]

CHAPMAN, JOHN (1822–1894), physician, author and publisher; apprenticed as watchmaker at Worksop, and was in business in Adelaide; studied medicine in Paris and at St. George's Hospital, London; publisher and bookseller in London; editor and proprietor of 'Westminster Review,' 1851; graduated in medicine at St. Andrews, 1857, and practised as physician; wrote medical and other works. [Suppl. i. 414]

CHAPMAN, MARY FRANCIS (1838–1884), novelist; published 'Mary Bertrand,' 1856, and other novels, under the pseudonym J. C. Ayrton. Her last novel, 'The Gift of the Gods' (1879), appeared under her own name. [x. 56]

CHAPMAN, SIR STEPHEN REMNANT (1776–1851), military engineer; educated at Woolwich; entered royal engineers, 1793; captain, 1805; served in Holland, 1799, Denmark, 1807, and Portugal, 1809; secretary to the master-general of the ordnance, 1810–25; lieutenant-colonel, 1812; secretary at Gibraltar, 1825–31; knighted, 1831; governor of the Bermudas, 1831–9; lieutenant-general, 1846. [x. 57]

CHAPMAN, THOMAS (1717–1760), ecclesiastic; fellow of Christ's College, Cambridge; master of Magdalene College, Cambridge, 1746; D.D., 1749; rector of Kirkby-over-Blow, Yorkshire, 1749; prebendary of Durham, 1750; published a classical tract. [x. 57]

CHAPMAN, WALTER (1473?–1538?). [See CHEPMAN.]

CHAPMAN, WILLIAM (1749–1832), engineer; constructed canals in Ireland, and docks in England and Scotland; wrote on canal navigation and the corn laws. [x. 57]

CHAPONE, HESTER (1727–1801), essayist; née Mulso; married (1760) one Chapone (d. 1761), an attorney; friend of Samuel Richardson; published verses and tales, 1750–3, and essays, 1773–7. Her 'Works' and 'Posthumous Works' appeared in 1807. [x. 58]

CHAPPELL, WILLIAM (1582–1649), bishop of Cork; of Christ's College, Cambridge, 1599; fellow, 1607; for some time college tutor of John Milton; patronised by William Laud; dean of Cashel, 1633; provost of Trinity College, Dublin, 1637–40; treasurer of St. Patrick's, Dublin, 1636–8; bishop of Cork and Ross, 1638; imprisoned at Dublin, 1641, and at Tenby, Pembrokeshire, 1642; withdrew to Nottinghamshire. [x. 59]

CHAPPELL, WILLIAM (1809–1888), musical antiquary; managed, 1834–43, music publishing business, of which his father, Samuel Chappell (d. 1834), had become sole partner, 1826; published 'Collection of National English Airs,' 1838; F.S.A., 1840; one of founders of Percy Society and Musical Antiquarian Society; joined publishing business of Cramer & Co., 1845; retired, 1861; vice-president of Musical Association, 1874. His works include the first volume of a 'History of Music,' 1874. [Suppl. i. 415]

CHAPPELOW, LEONARD (1683–1768), orientalist; M.A. St. John's College, Cambridge, 1716; fellow, 1717–31; rector of Hormead, Hertfordshire; professor of Arabic, 1720; published an Arabic grammar, 1730, translations, and 'Commentary on the Book of Job,' 1752. [x. 61]

CHAPPINGTON or **CHAPINGTON**, JOHN (d. 1606), organ-builder; built an organ for St. Margaret's, Westminster, 1596, and for Magdalen College, Oxford, 1597. [x. 61]

CHAPPLE, SAMUEL (1775–1833), organist; lost his sight before 1785; learned music at Exeter; organist of Ashburton Church, 1795–1833; published music. [x. 61]

CHAPPLE, SIR WILLIAM (1677–1745), judge; M.P., Dorchester, 1722–37; serjeant-at-law, 1724; judge in North Wales, 1728; knighted, 1729; justice of the king's bench, 1737–45. [x. 62]

CHAPPLE, WILLIAM (1718–1781), topographer; self-taught; surveyor's clerk in Exeter, 1738; landsteward to the Courtenay family; compiled vocabulary of Exmoor dialect, 1746; projected recension of Risdon's 'Survey of Devon' (partly printed, 1785). [x. 62]

CHARD, GEORGE WILLIAM (1765?–1849), organist; chorister of St. Paul's, London; lay-clerk of Winchester Cathedral, 1787; organist of Winchester Cathedral, 1802–49, and of Winchester College, 1832–49; Mus. Doc. Cambridge, 1812. [x. 63]

CHARD, JOHN ROUSE MERRIOTT (1847–1897), hero of Rorke's Drift; educated at Royal Military Academy, Woolwich; lieutenant, royal engineers, 1868; lieutenant-colonel, 1893; colonel, 1897; served in Zulu war, 1878; attached to Brigadier-general Glyn's column; defended Rorke's Drift, 22–23 Jan. 1879, with a force numbering 139, against about 3,000 Zulus; received Victoria cross; commanding royal engineers at Singapore, 1892–6. [Suppl. i. 416]

CHARDIN, SIR JOHN (1643–1713), traveller; born in Paris; a wealthy jeweller; travelled as a jewel merchant through Turkey to Persia and India, 1664–70 and 1671–7; published notes of his travels, 1671, 1686, and 1711; protestant refugee, 1681; jeweller to the English court; knighted, 1681; F.R.S., 1682; envoy to Holland, 1684; his biblical illustrations incorporated in Thomas Harmer's 'Observations on . . Scripture,' 1776. [x. 63]

CHARDON, **CHARLDON**, or **CHARLTON**, JOHN (d. 1601), bishop of Down and Connor; fellow of Exeter College, Oxford, 1565–8; M.A., 1572; schoolmaster at Worksop, Nottinghamshire, 1571; vicar of Heavitree, Exeter, 1571; D.D., 1586; bishop of Down and Connor, 1596; warden of Youghal College, 1598; published sermons and translations. [x. 64]

CHARITE, WILLIAM (1422–1502?), prior of St. Mary's Abbey, Leicester; compiled rent-roll and cartulary of the abbey. [x. 65]

CHARKE, CHARLOTTE (d. 1760?), actress and writer; youngest daughter of Colley Cibber [q. v.]; amused herself with masculine pursuits; married Richard Charke, a theatrical musician, c. 1729; separated from him, c. 1730; first appeared on the stage, 1730; performed in various London companies, chiefly in male parts, till 1737; afterwards employed at puppet-shows and low theatres; attempted management of Haymarket Theatre, 1745; published an autobiography, 1755; wrote plays and novels. [x. 65]

CHARKE, WILLIAM (fl. 1580), puritan; fellow of Peterhouse, Cambridge; expelled for nonconformity, 1572; wrote against Edmund Campion [q. v.], 1580; held disputation with Campion in the Tower; preacher to Lincoln's Inn, 1581–93. [x. 67]

CHARLEMONT, first EARL OF (1728–1799). [See CAULFEILD, JAMES.]

CHARLEMONT, VISCOUNTS OF. [See CAULFEILD, WILLIAM, first VISCOUNT, d. 1671; CAULFEILD, WILLIAM, second VISCOUNT, d. 1726; CAULFEILD, JAMES, fourth VISCOUNT, 1728–1799.]

CHARLEMONT, BARONS. [See CAULFEILD, SIR TOBY, first BARON, 1565–1627; CAULFEILD, TOBY, third BARON, d. 1642; CAULFEILD, WILLIAM, fifth BARON, d. 1671.]

CHARLES I (1600–1649), king of Great Britain and Ireland; second son of James VI of Scotland and Anne of Denmark; born at Dunfermline; created Duke of Albany, December 1600; brought to England, 1604; created Duke of York, 1605; a sickly child; became heir-apparent, 1612; created Prince of Wales, November 1616; negotiation for his marriage with Princess Christina of France broken off, 1616; match between him and Princess Maria of Spain formally proposed, 1617, dropped, 1618; went to Madrid to urge his suit, February, 1623, but returned, October, finding the religious difficulty insurmountable; betrothed to Princess Henrietta Maria of France, December 1624, he and his father pledging themselves to toleration for all English catholics; succeeded to the throne, 27 March 1625; married by proxy, May; received his bride at Canterbury, June 1625; refused by his first parliaments, who distrusted the Duke of Buckingham, supplies equal to the undertakings into which he and the favourite rashly plunged; to help the Elector Palatine, equipped by his personal credit an English force to be placed in command of the German adventurer, Ernst von Mansfeld, 1625; promised a subsidy to Christian IV of Denmark to make war on the German catholic states, but was unable to pay, Christian being subsequently routed (August 1626); enabled by the help of loans and pawning the crown jewels to fit out an expedition against Cadiz, which miserably failed, October 1626; lost in a storm a second fleet, obtained by levying ships from the coast-counties; sent an expedition to relieve the protestants of Rochelle, which (1627) failed shamefully, peace being concluded with France, 1629, and with Spain, 1630; out of touch with English sentiment, which as reflected in the houses of parliament was in respect of doctrine overwhelmingly Calvinistic, and in respect of policy anti-Romanist; repudiated the pro-Romanist clauses of his marriage treaty, 1626, but was reasonably suspected of favouring catholics; promoted Arminian clergy, and prevented parliament from prosecuting them, 1625; forbade preaching in favour of Calvinist dogmas, 1629; had recourse to extraordinary expedients for obtaining supplies, exacting forced loans, and removing the judges who dissented from his measures; involved by his foreign, domestic, and ecclesiastical policy in quarrels with his parliaments; his first parliament, which met, June 1625, dissolved in August, in consequence of its attacks on Buckingham and the king's Roman catholic leanings; dissolved in June 1626, after a four months' session, his second parliament, which, in spite of the devices of making the king's chief opponents sheriffs and imprisoning others, pressed charges against Buckingham; signed the statement of grievances which his third parliament, led by Sir Thomas Wentworth, submitted (the 'petition of right'), June 1628; opposed by Commons for his levy of taxes without parliamentary grant, and his ecclesiastical policy; dissolved parliament, 10 March 1629; governed without parliament for eleven years; levied tonnage and poundage, 1629; exacted fines for not taking up knighthood, 1630, and for encroaching on forest lands; raised money by granting monopolies, and by demanding ship-money from the seaports, 1634, and from the inland counties, 1635; showed marked favour to the papal envoys at the queen's court, 1634–7; supported Laud in his severe measures to enforce Arminian doctrine and church ceremonies on the puritan party in the church, 1633–7; obtained verdict in the ship-money case against John Hampden, 1638; was crowned in Scotland, 18 June 1633, giving offence by the episcopal ceremonial he required; caused great irritation by a fruitless order to Scottish ministers to use the surplice; riots in Edinburgh caused by his attempt (1637) to enforce the use of a liturgy, drawn up under Laud's influence; affronted by the signing of the 'national covenant,' 1638, and the abolition of episcopacy by the general assembly at Glasgow, November 1638; collected troops, and invaded Scotland, May 1639; compelled by want of funds to sign the treaty of Berwick, 1639; summoned parliament (April 1640), hoping to obtain supplies for renewing war with Scotland; dissolved it, 5 May 1640, on its demanding, under leadership of John Pym, redress of grievances; elated by Strafford's success in raising an army in Ireland; lost Newcastle and Durham, which were occupied by the Scots, who on the invitation of parliament had crossed the Tweed, 1640; advised, by a council of peers convoked at York, to negotiate with the Scots and summon parliament, 24 Sept. 1640; defied by the Long parliament which met, 3 Nov. 1640, and at once attacked Strafford and Laud; plotted to save Strafford, but finally assented to his execution, May 1641, and pledged himself not to dissolve this parliament except by its own vote; indirectly caused the formation of two parties in the Commons, a party in favour of moderate episcopacy, and an extreme party which desired to abolish bishops and the prayer-book; went to Scotland, seeking support against the extremists, August 1641; discredited by a plot formed among his courtiers to murder the Scottish leaders ('the Incident'); appealed for help to the Irish catholic peers, and was in consequence generally supposed privy to the Ulster massacres, October 1641; well received by London on his return, November 1641; resolved to resist the parliament's demands for a responsible ministry and church reform; tried to seize 'the five members' in the House of Commons, 4 Jan. 1642; left Whitehall to collect troops in the north, 10 Jan. 1642; declared war at Nottingham, 22 Aug. 1642; pushed

aside the parliamentary army at Edgehill, 23 Oct., advanced as far as Brentford, November, but withdrew to winter in Oxford; formed plan, 1643, for Hopton to advance on London from the west, Newcastle through the eastern counties, and Charles himself from Reading; baulked; carried on fruitless negotiations during the winter; entertained design, 1644, of operating from Oxford and attacking the parliamentary army in detail, a design which came to nothing through Rupert's defeat at Marston Moor (2 July); conducted fruitless negotiations at Uxbridge, January–February, 1645; vainly tried to obtain large forces from Ireland and from Lorraine; cheered by Montrose's success in the highlands, September 1644–February 1645; his main army crushed at Naseby, 14 June 1645; again sought help from Ireland and France; left Oxford; surrendered to the Scots at Newark, 5 May 1646, and was conducted to Newcastle, 13 May; tried to negotiate separately with the Scots and with parliament, parliament meanwhile coming to terms with the Scots; taken by parliamentary commissioners to Holmby House, January 1647; tried to get terms from parliament, unfavourable to the army; taken in charge by Joyce's troopers, 4 June, and conducted to Hampton Court, 24 Aug., while the army occupied London; escaped to the Isle of Wight, 16 Nov. 1647, having offended parliament by dallying with the army proposals, but was there kept in custody by Colonel Hammond; refused his assent to fresh proposals of parliament, December 1647; made a secret treaty with the Scots by which he accepted presbyterianism and obtained promise of a Scots army; cavalier risings in his favour crushed before September 1648; negotiated with parliamentary commissioners at Newport, September–October 1648; his death demanded by the army in November; taken to Hurst Castle, 1 Dec., to Windsor, 23 Dec. 1648, and to St. James's, London, 19 Jan. 1649, all who favoured him in parliament having been excluded by the army leaders ('Pride's purge'), 6 Dec. 1648; refused to plead before the court which the Commons constituted for his trial, 20 Jan.; condemned, 27 Jan., and executed, 30 Jan. 1649. [x. 67]

CHARLES II (1630–1685), king of Great Britain and Ireland; second son of Charles I and Henrietta Maria; born at St. James's, London; given an establishment as Prince of Wales, 1638; took his seat in the House of Lords, 1640; joined Charles I at York, March 1642; present at Edgehill; resided in Oxford, October 1642 to March 1645, and at Bristol, March to April 1645; at Barnstaple, June; withdrew to Cornwall, July; tried to hold Devon and Cornwall against Fairfax; at Falmouth, February 1646; withdrew to Scilly, March, and to Jersey, April; at Paris, July 1646; went to Helvoetsluys, July 1648; made a descent on the shipping at Thames mouth; tried to avert Charles I's execution, January 1649; proclaimed king in Edinburgh, 5 Feb., and in Ireland; returned to Paris; went to Jersey, 1649; withdrew to Breda, 1650; accepted the covenant and the terms of the Scottish commissioners, March; reached Cromarty Frith, and took up his residence at Falkland Palace, Fife, June 1650; practically a prisoner in the hands of Argyll and the presbyterian party; secretly negotiated with the English catholics; defeated at Dunbar, 3 Sept. 1650; tried to escape from Argyll to join Huntly ('The Start'); crowned at Scone, 1 Jan. 1651, accepting the covenant; at Stirling, April; marched southwards, 1651; routed at Worcester, 3 Sept. 1651; dismissed all his followers, except Wilmot; reached Fécamp, Normandy, 1651; resided in poverty at Paris, October 1651–June 1654; withdrew to Cologne; went to Middelburg, March 1655, to wait the issue of a cavalier rising; removed his court to Bruges, 1656; dissoluteness of his court much spoken of; formally excluded from the succession by act of parliament, November 1656; offered to raise English troops for the Spanish service in Flanders; removed his court to Brussels, February 1658; withdrew to Breda, August; returned to Brussels, September 1658; went to Brittany, to wait the issue of a cavalier rising, August 1659; followed Mazarin to Spain to ask French and Spanish help; returned to Brussels, December 1659; negotiated with the English presbyterians and with Monck; went to Breda, and issued his declaration there, 4 April 1660; proclaimed king in London; landed at Dover, 26 May; entered London, 29 May; urged the House of Lords to pass Act of Indemnity; issued a declaration for the settlement of Ireland, 30 Nov. 1660; dissolved the Convention parliament, 29 Dec. 1660, which had settled on him 1,200,000l. a year; accepted by the

Scottish parliament, 1661; threatened by Venner's plot; formally crowned, 23 April 1661; married, 20 May 1662, Catherine of Braganza [q. v.], and so became pledged to support Portugal against Spain; coldly supported the administration of Clarendon, 1660–7; aimed at securing toleration for English catholics, but thereby only excited the jealousy of parliament and the severities of the Act of Uniformity, May 1662; was thus forced to violate his promises to the presbyterian party made in his solemn declarations, April and October 1660; the severe Conventicle Act, 1664, and the Five-mile Act, 1665, brought on by his Declaration of Indulgence, 1662; neglected to take efficient measures to recover estates forfeited during the Commonwealth, thereby bringing great odium on Clarendon; secretly allied himself with Louis XIV, receiving a large subsidy to attack Spain, 1661, selling Dunkirk and Mardyke to France, December 1662, and declaring war on the Dutch, February 1665; created a bastard son, James, Duke of Monmouth, 1663; withdrew to Salisbury, to avoid the plague, July 1665, and to Oxford, September, returning to London, January 1666; showed unwonted energy on occasion of the fire in London, September 1666; hoped by means of the Dutch war to obtain the stadtholdership for his nephew, William of Orange, but the Dutch fleet destroyed the shipping in the Medway (June 1667), and Charles was forced to conclude peace, July 1667; the king protected himself by ordering Clarendon to leave England, November 1667; himself conducted secretly the most important negotiations, though the period (1667–74) is nominally that of the ascendency of Buckingham, Arlington, and Lauderdale; received large subsidies from Louis XIV, promising in return to favour French designs on the Netherlands and to reduce England to Romanism; assented to the triple alliance with Sweden and Holland, January 1668, in order to force Louis's hand; concluded with Louis the shameful secret treaty of Dover, May 1670; his Declaration of Indulgence in favour of English catholics, March 1671, cancelled, owing to parliamentary agitation, March 1673, and followed by the Test Act; forced by popular discontent to close the Dutch war (begun March 1672), February 1674; stopped payments by the exchequer, January 1672, and abandoned himself with his court to excess; directed foreign policy, though Danby was nominally at the head of affairs, 1674–8; entered into a secret treaty not to oppose Louis XIV, 1676; forced by popular feeling against France to assent to the marriage of Princess Mary with William of Orange, November 1677, but renewed his secret treaty with Louis, 1678; gave way to the persecution engendered by the pretended 'popish plot,' August 1678, contenting himself with protecting the queen; dissolved parliament, January 1679, to shield Danby; repeatedly declared the Duke of Monmouth illegitimate, in order to foil the anti-court party, led by Shaftesbury, which now set itself to secure the exclusion of James, duke of York, from the succession; ordered the Duke of York to withdraw from England, and offered to accept a protestant regency; dissolved parliament, July 1679 and January 1681, and the Oxford parliament, March 1681, which violently opposed his efforts; warmly received in London, October 1681; laid the foundation-stone of Chelsea Hospital, February 1682; the whigs in Scotland grievously persecuted by his brother, the Duke of York; rigorously enforced penal laws against English nonconformists; his opponents discredited by the discovery of the Rye House plot, June 1683; Charles resolved to govern without a parliament, in compliance with the wishes of Louis XIV; popularly reported as being about to declare himself a Roman catholic, 1684, the Duke of York, in defiance of the Test Act, being reappointed acting lord high admiral, May 1684; had an apoplectic stroke, 2 Feb. 1685, and died 6 Feb., acknowledging himself a Roman catholic; buried at Westminster, 17 Feb. Thirteen of his mistresses are known by name, the chief being the Duchesses of Cleveland, Portsmouth, and Mazarin, and Nell Gwynn. Of his numerous illegitimate children six were created dukes. He was fond of conversation, coarse wit, walking and hunting, patronised the stage, and was interested in chemistry and naval architecture. [x. 84]

CHARLES Edward Louis Philip Casimir (1720–1788), the Young Pretender; eldest son of the titular James III; born and bred at Rome; served at Gaeta, 1734; sent from Rome to head a French invasion of England, 1743; foiled by the English fleet at Dunkirk, 1744; sailed from Belleisle, 1745; reached the Hebrides, August 1745; unfurled his standard at Glenfinnan, entered Edinburgh, and defeated Cope at Prestonpans, 1745; reached Carlisle and Derby; retreated, 6 Dec. 1745; defeated Hawley at Falkirk, 1746; crushed by Cumberland at Culloden, 1746; fugitive in the highlands; escaped to France, 1746; expelled from France, 1748; alienated the Jacobites by drunkenness and by refusing to separate from his mistress, Clementina Walkenshaw [q. v.], a reputed spy; said to have visited London, 1750, 1752, 1754; resided at Basle, 1756; titular king, 1766; resided in Rome; pensioned by France; married Louisa von Stolberg, 1772; separated from her, 1780; removed to Florence; died at Rome. [x. 108]

CHARLES, DAVID (1762–1834), author of sermons; a well-to-do Carmarthen tradesman; lay-preacher, 1808; Calvinistic methodist minister in South Wales, 1811; paralysed, 1828. [x. 111]

CHARLES, DAVID (d. 1878), methodist; co-founder of Bala College, 1837; principal of Trevecca College, 1842–62. [x. 114]

CHARLES, Mrs. ELIZABETH (1828–1896), author; née Rundle; began early to write, and attracted attention of James Anthony Froude and Tennyson; married, 1851, Andrew Paton Charles, with whom she made several journeys in the East. Her works include 'Tales and Sketches of Christian Life in different Lands and Ages,' 1850, and 'Chronicles of the Schönberg-Cotta Family,' 1862. [Suppl. i. 417]

CHARLES, JOSEPH (1716–1786), author of 'The Dispersion of the Men of Babel,' a tract on Genesis, 1755; vicar of Wighton, Norfolk, 1740–86. [x. 111]

CHARLES or CARLES, NICHOLAS (d. 1613), herald; Blanch-Lion pursuivant; Lancaster herald, 1609; visited Derbyshire, 1611, and Huntingdonshire, 1613; his manuscript collections are in the British Museum. [x. 111]

CHARLES, THOMAS (1755–1814), of Bala; Welsh preacher; son of a Carmarthenshire farmer; brought up a methodist; studied at Jesus College, Oxford, 1775–8; curate of Queen's Camel, Somerset, 1778; B.A., 1779; married a wealthy tradeswoman, and settled at Bala, 1783; took occasional clerical duty; Calvinistic methodist minister at Bala, 1784; went on preaching tours through North Wales; established methodist schools, 1785, and Sunday schools, 1789; published Welsh theological tracts and magazines, 1789–1813; set up a press at Bala, 1803; visited London yearly from 1793; visited Ireland, 1807; organised the Welsh Calvinistic methodists, 1810–11. [x. 112]

CHARLESWORTH, EDWARD PARKER (1783–1853), physician; apprenticed to a Horncastle physician; M.D. Edinburgh, 1807; practised at Lincoln; visiting physician to the asylum, 1820; advocated humane treatment of the insane. [x. 114]

CHARLESWORTH, JOHN (1782–1864), divine; B.D. Queens' College, Cambridge, 1826; rector of Flowton, Suffolk, 1814–44; rector of St. Mildred's, London, 1844–62. [x. 115]

CHARLESWORTH, MARIA LOUISA (1819–1880), author; daughter of John Charlesworth [q. v.]; visitor in her father's parishes; retired to Nutfield, Surrey, 1864; published religious tales and devotional tracts, 1846–80. [x. 115]

CHARLETON. [See also CHARLTON.]

CHARLETON, RICE (1710–1789), physician; entered Queen's College, Oxford, 1740; M.A., 1747; M.D., 1757; practised medicine at Bath; physician to Bath General Hospital, 1757–81; published tracts on the Bath waters, 1750–74. [x. 115]

CHARLETON, ROBERT (1809–1872), quaker; pin manufacturer at Bristol, 1833–52; became a quaker; advocated total abstinence; one of the peace deputation to the Czar Nicholas, 1854; a quaker preacher in England and Ireland, 1860–72; published theological tracts. [x. 116]

CHARLETON, WALTER (1619–1707), physician; entered Magdalen Hall, Oxford, 1635; M.D., by king's mandate, 1643; nominally physician to Charles I and Charles II; practised physic in London, 1650–92; withdrew to Nantwich; returned to London before 1698; published medical, philosophical, and antiquarian tracts, 1650–1705, including 'Chorea Gigantum' (1663), to prove that Stonehenge was made by the Danes. [x. 116]

CHARLETT, ARTHUR (1655–1722), master of University College, Oxford; entered Trinity College, Oxford, 1669; M.A., 1676; fellow, 1680; travelled in Scotland, 1683; B.D., 1684; published a theological tract, 1686; tutor to Lord Guilford, 1688; master of University College and D.D., 1692; rector of Hambledon, Buckinghamshire, 1707–22; king's chaplain, 1697–1717; his large correspondence is preserved in the Bodleian. [x. 119]

CHARLEWOOD, CHARLWOOD, or **CHERLWOD,** JOHN (d. 1592), London printer; printed before 1559; issued ballads, tracts, and popular pieces, 1562–92; held the monopoly of printing playbills, 1587–92; often fined for literary piracy. [x. 120]

CHARLOTTE AUGUSTA, PRINCESS (1796–1817), only child of George, prince of Wales (afterwards George IV), and Caroline of Brunswick; brought up by Lady Elgin at Carlton House till 1804; at Lower Lodge, Windsor, 1805–1814; ignored by her father; engaged to William, prince of Orange, 1813; angered her father by breaking off her engagement, 1814; in seclusion at Cranbourn Lodge, Windsor, 1814–16; married Prince Leopold of Saxe-Coburg, May 1816; died in childbirth, 19 Nov. 1817. [x. 120]

CHARLOTTE AUGUSTA MATILDA, PRINCESS ROYAL, afterwards QUEEN OF WÜRTEMBERG (1766–1828), eldest daughter of George III; betrothed, 1796; married (second wife) Frederick William Charles, prince of Württemberg, May 1797; Duchess of Württemberg, December 1797; queen of Württemberg, 1806; queen-dowager, 1816. [x. 122]

CHARLOTTE SOPHIA (1744–1818), queen of George III; of Mecklenburg-Strelitz; married in London, 8 Sept. 1761; crowned, 22 Sept.; managed the royal household during the king's insanity, 1788 and 1810–18. [x. 123]

CHARLTON. [See also CHARLETON.]

CHARLTON or **CHERLETON,** EDWARD, fifth and last BARON CHARLTON OF POWYS (1370–1421), married, 1398, the widowed Countess of March, thus obtaining Usk and Caerleon; took Henry IV's side, 1399; succeeded to the barony, October 1401; attacked by Owen of Glyndwfrdwy, 1402; allowed to make a private truce with the Welsh, 1404; again attacked by Owen, 1409; captured Sir John Oldcastle in Powys, 1417. [x. 123]

CHARLTON, SIR JOB (1614–1697), judge; son of a London goldsmith; B.A. Oxford, 1632; barrister of Lincoln's Inn; M.P., Ludlow, 1659–78; serjeant-at-law, 1660; chief-justice of Chester, 1662–80 and October 1686–1689; speaker of the House of Commons, 4–18 Feb. 1673; justice of common pleas, 1680; removed, April 1686, for opposing James II's dispensing power; created baronet, 1686. [x. 124]

CHARLTON or **CHERLETON,** JOHN DE, first BARON CHARLTON OF POWYS (d. 1353), succeeded to estates at Charlton and Pontesbury, Shropshire, c. 1300; chamberlain to Edward II, 1307; knighted before 1308; obtained by marriage Powys Castle and its domains, 1309; raised Welsh troops for the king's service from 1310; at feud with his Welsh neighbours, 1311–13 and 1315–30; summoned to the peers, 1313–46; joined Lancaster's revolt, 1321; pardoned, 1322; joined Mortimer's rebellion, 1326; viceroy of Ireland, 1337; recalled, 1338; latterly interested himself in religion. [x. 125]

CHARLTON, JOHN (fl. 1571). [See CHARDON, JOHN.]

CHARLTON or **CHERLETON,** LEWIS (d. 1369), bishop of Hereford; an Oxford graduate in law and theology; resided in Oxford; prebendary of Hereford (1336) and Pontesbury; recognised as a benefactor of Oxford University, 1356; bishop of Hereford, 1361. [x. 127]

CHARLTON, LIONEL (1720–1788), author of 'The History of Whitby,' 1779; schoolmaster at Whitby. [x. 128]

CHARLTON or **CHERLETON,** THOMAS (d. 1344), bishop of Hereford; younger brother of John Charlton, first baron Charlton [q. v.]; doctor of civil law; privy seal to Edward II; prebendary of St. Paul's, of St. Mary's, Stafford, and (1316) of Pontesbury; failed to obtain the

see of Durham, 1316, and of Hereford, 1317; bishop of Hereford, 1327; lord-treasurer, 1328–30; chancellor of Ireland, 1337, and viceroy, 1338; returned to England, 1340. [x. 128]

CHARNOCK, JOB (d. 1693), founder of Calcutta; went to India, 1655; entered the East India Company's service; stationed at Kásimbázár, 1658–64, at Patna, 1664, at Kásimbázár, and at Hugli, April 1686; withdrew, in face of native hostility, to the island Hijili, at the mouth of the Ganges, December 1686; superseded and sent to Madras, 1688; re-appointed to the Bengal agency; obtained from Arangzib a grant of land at Sutánati (now Calcutta), 1690. [x. 129]

CHARNOCK, JOHN (1756–1807), author; educated at Winchester and Trinity College, Oxford; journalist; naval volunteer; published 'Biographia Navalis,' 1794–8, 'History of Marine Architecture,' 1801–2, 'Life of Nelson,' 1806, and some political tracts. [x. 132]

CHARNOCK or **CHERNOCK,** ROBERT (1663 ?–1696), Jacobite conspirator; demy of Magdalen College, Oxford, 1680; M.A., 1686; fellow, by mandate from James II, 1686; embraced Roman catholicism; James II's agent in his oppression of the college, 1687; vice-president, January 1688; expelled, October 1688; styled 'captain'; in London, planning the assassination of William III, 1692–6; arrested February 1696; executed, 1696. [x. 132]

CHARNOCK, STEPHEN (1628–1680), puritan; son of a London solicitor; M.A. Emmanuel College, Cambridge; puritan preacher in Southwark; intruded into a fellowship at New College, Oxford, 1650; proctor, 1654; chaplain to Henry Cromwell in Ireland, 1657; withdrew to London, 1658; co-pastor of the Bishopsgate Street presbyterian church, 1675; his theological works published posthumously. [x. 134]

CHARNOCK, THOMAS (1526–1581), alchemist; learned alchemy from a Salisbury clergyman; served at Calais, 1557; lived in retirement in Somerset. [x. 135]

CHARPENTIÈRE. [See CARPENTIÈRE and CARPENTIERS.]

CHARRETIE, ANNA MARIA (1819–1875), miniature and oil painter; née Kenwell; married, 1841, John Charretie (d. 1868); exhibited, 1843–75. [x. 135]

CHARTERIS, FRANCIS (1675–1732), styled 'colonel'; of a Dumfriesshire family; dismissed the army for cheating; dismissed the Dutch service for theft; captain in the 1st foot guards; censured for fraud, 1711; accumulated a fortune by gambling and usury; the typical profligate of Arbuthnot, Pope, and Hogarth; landowner in Haddington and Midlothian; convicted of rape, but pardoned, 1730. [x. 135]

CHARTERIS, HENRY, the elder (d. 1599), bookseller and printer, of Edinburgh; brought out a blackletter edition of Sir David Lyndsay's works, 1568; printed from 1581 theological tracts, bibles, and religious publications. [x. 136]

CHARTERIS, HENRY, the younger (1565–1628), Scottish divine; eldest son of Henry Charteris the elder [q. v.]; M.A. Edinburgh, 1587; a regent of Edinburgh University, 1589; principal and professor of divinity, 1599–1620; minister of North Leith, 1620; professor of divinity, 1627–8. [x. 137]

CHARTERIS, LAWRENCE (1625–1700), Scottish divine; younger son of Henry Charteris the younger [q. v.]; M.A. Edinburgh, 1646; minister of Bathans (or Yester), Haddingtonshire, 1654–75; professor of divinity in Edinburgh, 1675–81; minister of Dirleton, Haddingtonshire, 1688–97; published theological tracts. [x. 137]

CHARY, CHINTAMANNY RAGOONATHA (d. 1880), astronomer; assistant at Madras observatory; a good observer; wrote on astronomical topics. [x. 139]

CHASE, JOHN (1810–1879), water-colour painter; exhibited, chiefly architectural views, 1826–78. [x. 139]

CHASTILLON or **CASTILLUN,** HENRY DE (fl. 1195), archdeacon of Canterbury; a justiciary, 1195; agent in negotiations between Archbishop Hubert and monastery of Christ Church, Canterbury, 1198–9; supported King John against St. Augustine's, Canterbury, 1202. [x. 139]

CHATELAIN, CLARA DE (1807-1876), composer and author; of French extraction; *née* de Pontigny; born in London; resided in France, 1826; returned to London, 1827; married J. B. F. E. de Chatelain [q. v.], 1843; wrote many tales for magazines, under various pseudonyms; composed ballads and songs; died insane. [x. 140]

CHATELAIN, JEAN-BAPTISTE FRANÇOIS ERNEST DE (1801-1881), journalist; born and educated in Paris; French journalist in London, 1826; visited Rome, 1827; journalist in Bordeaux, 1830, and Paris, 1833-8; returned to England, 1842; naturalised, 1848; published literary and political papers. [x. 140]

CHATELAINE, JOHN BAPTIST CLAUDE (1710-1771), draughtsman and engraver; real name, PHILIPPE; of French extraction; resided at Chelsea; of improvident habits; engraved chiefly landscapes. [x. 141]

CHÂTELHERAULT, DUKE OF (d. 1575). [See HAMILTON, JAMES.]

CHATFIELD, EDWARD (1800-1839), painter; son of a Croy lon distiller; pupil of B. R. Haydon; painted portraits and historical scenes, 1821-38; wrote in the magazines under pseudonym of 'Echion.' [x. 141]

CHATHAM, EARLS OF. [See PITT, WILLIAM, first EARL, 1708-1778; PITT, JOHN, second EARL, 1756-1835.]

CHATTERLEY, WILLIAM SIMMONDS (1787-1822), actor; member of the Drury Lane company, 1789-1804; acted also at Birmingham, Cheltenham, 1804, and Bath, 1810; returned to London, 1816. [x. 142]

CHATTERTON, HENRIETTA GEORGIANA MARCIA LASCELLES, LADY (1806-1876), miscellaneous writer; *née* Iremonger; married, 1824, Sir William Abraham Chatterton (d. 1855), of co. Cork; retired to England, 1852; married, 1859, Edward Heneage Dering; embraced Romanism, 1875; published numerous tales, notes of travel, and poems, 1837-76. [x. 143]

CHATTERTON, JOHN BALSIR (1802?-1871), harpist; son of a Portsmouth music-master; harpist in London, 1824-71; composed music for the harp. [x. 143]

CHATTERTON, THOMAS (1752-1770), poet; posthumous child of a poor Bristol schoolmaster; began to show signs of interest in reading, 1759; obtained access to the charters of St. Mary Redcliffe Church, Bristol; wrote his first verses, 1762; published verses in 'Felix Farley's Bristol Journal,' 1763; began to represent his 'antique' verses as genuine old pieces, 1764; began to fabricate 'Thomas Rowley's' verses, 1765; invented a pedigree for a Bristol pewterer, 1767; apprenticed to a Bristol attorney, 1767-70; published in the 'Bristol Journal' a piece dated 1248, 1768; encouraged in his fabrications by the credulity of George Catcott of Bristol, 1768; wrote to James Dodsley, offering old plays, December 1768-February 1769; wrote to Horace Walpole, forwarding ancient histories of painting in England, 1769; neglected by Walpole, who omitted to return his pieces, 1769; satirised leading people in Bristol, 1769; med tated suicide, 1770; came to London, 1770; lodged in Shoreditch, and subsequently in Brooke Street, Holborn; wrote for the journals; poisoned himself with arsenic in desperation at his poverty, 1770; editions of 'Thomas Rowley,' as genuine fifteenth-century poems, published 1777 and 1782. His collected works appeared in 1803. [x. 143]

CHATTO, WILLIAM ANDREW (1799-1864), miscellaneous writer; born at Newcastle-on-Tyne; tea-dealer in London, 1830-4; published, under the pseudonym of 'Stephen Oliver,' notes of rambles in the northern counties, 1834-5; wrote also on wood-engraving, 1839-48; edited 'New Sporting Magazine,' 1839-41, and 'Puck,' a comic paper, 1844. [x. 154]

CHATTODUNUS, WALTER (d. 1343). [See CATTON.]

CHAUCER, GEOFFREY (1340?-1400), poet; son of John Chaucer (d. 1366), vintner, of London; page to Elizabeth de Burgh, wife of Lionel, duke of Clarence, third son of Edward III, 1357; accompanied the expedition to France, 1359; taken prisoner in Brittany; ransomed by Edward III, 1360; married Philippa (? Roet, d. 1387?), a servant of the Duchess of Lancaster (wife of John of Gaunt), probably in 1366, certainly before 1374; received from Edward III pension of

13l. 6s. 8d., in 1367, being then yeoman of the chamber; in service in France, 1369; abroad, on the king's service, 1370; styled 'esquire' (armiger), from 1372; on a mission to Genoa and Florence, 1372-3, when he met Boccaccio and perhaps Petrarch; received additional pension of 13l. 6s. 8d. from Edward III, 1374; appointed comptroller of the customs and subsidy of wools, &c., London, June 1374; received pension of 10l. from John of Gaunt, June 1374; resided over Aldgate, London, 1374-86, except when abroad on the king's service; sent on secret service to Flanders, 1376 and 1377; attached to embassies to France and Lombardy, 1378; a party to the abduction of Cecilia Chaumpaigne, 1380; appointed comptroller of petty customs, London, and allowed to have a deputy, 1382; allowed to have a deputy in his comptrollership of the customs, 1385; knight of the shire for Kent, 1386; removed from both comptrollerships, 1386; went the Canterbury pilgrimage, April 1388; to raise money for his immediate needs, sold his two pensions from the king, 1388; clerk of the king's works at various places, acting by deputy, July 1389-September 1391; robbed by highwaymen, 9 Sept. 1390; joint forester of North Petherton Park, Somerset, 1391; sole forester, 1397; received pension of 20l. from Richard II, 1394; received additional pension of 26l. 13s. 4d. from Henry IV, 1399; leased a house at Westminster, 1399; buried in Westminster Abbey; a monument erected to him, 1555. Chaucer's writings fall into three periods: (1) The period of French influence (1359-72), in which he uses the octosyllabic couplet. To this period belong 'The Boke of the Duchesse,' 1369, and a lost translation of the 'Roman de la Rose.' (2) The period of Italian influence, especially of Dante and Boccaccio, 1372-86, in which he leaves off the octosyllabic couplet, uses mainly the 'heroic' stanza of seven lines, and begins to use the heroic couplet. To this period belong 'The House of Fame'; 'The Assembly of Foules'; 'Troylus and Cryseyde'; 'The Legende of Good Women'; and the first drafts of some of his tales. (3) The period of his maturity, 1386-1400, in which he uses the heroic couplet. To this period belong the 'Canterbury Tales,' designed about 1387. The 'Canterbury Tales' were first printed by Caxton in 1475; the collected works were first issued by W. Thynne in 1532. [x. 154]

CHAUCER, THOMAS (1367?-1434), speaker of the House of Commons; supposed to be son of Geoffrey Chaucer [q. v.] and Philippa Roet; obtained Ewelme, Oxfordshire, by marriage; received two annuities of 10l. from John of Gaunt; chief butler to Richard II, Henry IV, Henry V, and Henry VI; received from Richard II a pension of 13l. 6s. 8d., March 1399; constable of Wallingford Castle; granted Woodstock Manor, 1411; M.P. for Oxfordshire in most parliaments, 1400-31; speaker of the House of Commons, 1407, 1410, 1411, 1414; fought at Agincourt, 1415; envoy to France, 1417; member of the council, 1424; an executor of the Duchess of York's will, 1431; reputed to be of great wealth. [x. 167]

CHAUCOMBE, HUGH DE (fl. 1200), justiciar; of Chalcombe, Northamptonshire, 1168; sheriff of Staffordshire, Warwickshire, and Leicestershire, 1196-8; accompanied King John to Normandy, 1199; in attendance on John, 1203-4, in England; justiciar, 1204; sheriff of Warwickshire and Leicestershire, and keeper of Kenilworth Castle, 1204-7; a monk at Chalcombe Priory, 1209. [x. 168]

CHAUNCEY, CHARLES (1706-1777), physician; M.D. Cambridge, 1739; collected pictures, coins, and books. [x. 168]

CHAUNCEY, ICHABOD (d. 1691), physician; army chaplain at Dunkirk before 1660; beneficed in Bristol; ejected for nonconformity, 1662; practised medicine at Bristol, 1662-84; banished for nonconformity, 1684; returned to Bristol, 1686. [x. 169]

CHAUNCY, CHARLES (1592-1672), puritan; educated at Westminster; entered Trinity College, Cambridge, 1609; fellow; M.A., 1617; B.D., 1624; vicar of Ware, Hertfordshire, 1627-33; vicar of Marston St. Lawrence, Northamptonshire, 1633-7; prosecuted for neglect of church ceremonies, 1630 and 1634; submitted to Laud, 1636; assistant minister at Plymouth, New England, 1637; minister at Scituate, 1641; invited back to England, 1654; president of Harvard College, 1654-72; published sermons, theological tracts, and Latin verses and speeches. [x. 169]

CHAUNCY, Sir HENRY (1632–1719), topographer; entered Caius College, Cambridge, 1647; barrister of the Middle Temple, 1656; recorder of Hertford, 1680; knighted, 1681; succeeded to the family estates, 1681; serjeant-at-law, 1688; justice in South Wales, 1688; published 'The Historical Antiquities of Hertfordshire,' 1700; caused a 'witch' to be arrested in Hertfordshire, 1712. [x. 170]

CHAUNCY, ISAAC (1632–1712), congregationalist; eldest son of Charles Chauncy [q. v.]; taken to New England, 1637; at Harvard College, 1651; studied also at Oxford; intruded rector of Woodborough, Wiltshire; ejected, 1662; congregationalist minister at Andover, Hampshire; L.C.P. London, 1669; practised medicine in London, 1669 till death; was also a congregationalist minister in St. Mary Axe, 1687–1701, and divinity tutor of the London Dissenting Academy; published controversial treatises, 1681–1700. [x. 171]

CHAUNCY, MAURICE (d. 1581), Carthusian monk; studied at Oxford and Gray's Inn, London; entered the Charterhouse; took the oath to Henry VIII, 1535; joined in the surrender of the Charterhouse, 1537; withdrew to Bruges; returned to England, June 1555; prior of the Carthusians at Shene, 1556; withdrew to Bruges, 1559, and to Louvain, 1578; died at Bruges; published 'Historia aliquot nostri sæculi Martyrum,' 1550. [x. 172]

CHAUNDLER or **CHANDLER**, THOMAS (1418?–1490), dean of Hereford; educated at Winchester and New College, Oxford; fellow, 1437; M.A.; proctor, 1444; B.D., 1450; warden of Winchester College, 1450, and of New College, 1451; B.Can.L., 1451; chancellor of Wells Cathedral, 1452; D.D. and warden of New College, 1455–75; chancellor of Oxford University, 1457–61 and 1472–9, and vice-chancellor, 1463–7; prebendary of York, St. Paul's, Southwell, and Hereford; dean of Hereford, 1482; left a sacred drama and other writings in manuscripts which he illustrated with tinted drawings. [Suppl. i. 419]

CHAVASSE, WILLIAM (1785–1814), of the East India Company's service; died near Bagdad on a journey to explore Xenophon's route in the Retreat of the Ten Thousand. [x. 173]

CHEADSEY, WILLIAM (1510?–1574?). [See CHEDSEY.]

CHEAPE, DOUGLAS (1797–1861), Scottish advocate; professor of civil law, Edinburgh, 1827–42; author of legal squibs. [x. 173]

CHEAPE, Sir JOHN (1792–1875), general; second lieutenant, Bengal engineers, 1809; captain, 1821; colonel, 1844; brigadier-general, 1852; K.C.B., 1849; on active service in India, 1809–23; in the first Burmese war, 1824–6; in the Sikh war, 1848–50; conquered Pegu, 1853; returned to England, 1855; promoted general, 1866. [x. 173]

CHEBHAM, THOMAS DE (fl. 1230). [See CHABHAM.]

CHEDSEY or **CHEADSEY**, WILLIAM (1510?–1574?), divine; born in Somerset; scholar of Corpus Christi College, Oxford, 1528; fellow, 1531; M.A., 1534; D.D., 1546; chaplain to Bishop Bonner; prebendary of St. Paul's, 1548; disputed against the reformed doctrines, 1549; imprisoned for preaching against the reformed doctrines, 1551; canon of Windsor, with other promotion, 1554; archdeacon of Middlesex, 1556; canon of Christ Church, Oxford, 1557; president of Corpus Christi College, Oxford, 1558–9; deprived of his benefices and imprisoned in the Fleet as a recusant, 1559; published theological tracts. [x. 174]

CHEDWORTH, fourth BARON (1754–1804). [See HOWE, JOHN.]

CHEDWORTH, JOHN (d. 1471), bishop of Lincoln; of Merton College, Oxford; fellow of King's College, Cambridge, and provost, 1446; prebendary of Salisbury, 1444; prebendary of Lincoln; bishop of Lincoln, 1452; very active against the lollards in his diocese. [x. 175]

CHEEKE, WILLIAM (fl. 1613), author of 'Anagrammata et Chron-Anagrammata'; B.A. Magdalen Hall, Oxford, 1596. [x. 176]

CHEERE, Sir HENRY (1703–1781), statuary; pupil of Peter Scheemakers; worked in marble, bronze, and lead; carved statues for gardens and funeral monuments; knighted, 1760; created baronet, 1766; patron of Louis François Roubillac. [x. 176]

CHEESMAN, THOMAS (1760–1835?), engraver and draughtsman; pupil of Francesco Bartolozzi; resided in London. [x. 177]

CHEFER or **CHEFFER**, RICHARD (fl. 1400?), theological writer; probably an Augustinian friar of Norwich. [x. 177]

CHEKE, HENRY (1548?–1586?), translator; eldest son of Sir John Cheke [q. v.]; M.A. King's College, Cambridge, 1568; M.P. for Bedford, 1572–83; travelled in Italy, 1575–6; secretary to the council of the north at York, 1581 till death; M.P., Boroughbridge, Yorkshire, 1584; translated an Italian morality play by Francesco Negri de Bassano. [x. 178]

CHEKE, Sir JOHN (1514–1557), Greek scholar; born in Cambridge; son of an esquire-bedel; fellow of St. John's College, Cambridge, 1529; M.A., 1533; embraced protestantism; an efficient college tutor; professor of Greek, Cambridge, 1540–51; introduced a new pronunciation of Greek; public orator, Cambridge, 1544; tutor to Edward, prince of Wales, 1544; canon of King Henry VIII's College, Oxford; pensioned by Henry VIII, 1545; granted church lands by Edward VI, 1547; M.P. for Bletchingley, 1547 and 1553; provost of King's College, Cambridge, 1548, by king's mandate; took orders before 1549; knighted, 1552; granted additional lands by Edward VI; clerk of the council; secretary of state, 1553; supported Lady Jane Grey; imprisoned in the Tower by Queen Mary, July 1553–September 1554; withdrew to Basle; travelled in Italy; taught Greek at Strasburg; treacherously invited to Brussels, 1556, by Lord Paget and Sir John Mason, and sent prisoner to England, 1556; imprisoned in the Tower; compelled to abjure protestantism, 1556; published Greek texts, translations into Latin, and theological treatises. [x. 178]

CHELLE or **CHELL**, WILLIAM (fl. 1550), musician; Mus. Bac. Oxford, 1524; prebendary of Hereford, 1532–59, and precentor, 1554–9; perhaps taught music in London. [x. 183]

CHELMESTON or **CHELVESTON**, JOHN (fl. 1297), theological writer; a Carmelite friar; taught at Oxford, Bruges, and Brussels. [x. 183]

CHELMSFORD, first BARON (1794–1878). [See THESIGER, FREDERICK.]

CHELSUM, JAMES (1740?–1801), opponent of Gibbon; educated at Westminster and Christ Church, Oxford; B.A., 1759; D.D., 1773; rector of Droxford, Hampshire, with other preferment; died insane; published sermons, a history of mezzotint engraving, 1786, and two pamphlets on Gibbon's treatment of Christianity, 1776 and 1785. [x. 183]

CHENERY, THOMAS (1826–1884), editor of 'The Times'; born at Barbados; educated at Eton and Cambridge; M.A., 1858; barrister; 'Times' correspondent at Constantinople, 1854–6; leader writer to 'The Times'; editor, 1877–84; a great linguist; professor of Arabic, Oxford, 1868–77; one of the Old Testament revisers; wrote on Arabic and Hebrew. [x. 184]

CHENEVIX, RICHARD (1698–1779), bishop of Waterford and Lismore, of Huguenot extraction; B.A. Peterhouse, Cambridge, 1716; chaplain to the Earl of Scarborough, 171 and to the Earl of Chesterfield, 1728; D.D., 1744; chaplain to Chesterfield when lord-lieutenant of Ireland, 1745; bishop of Killaloe, 1745; translated to Waterford, 1746. [x. 184]

CHENEVIX, RICHARD (1774–1830), chemist and mineralogist; born in Ireland; of Huguenot extraction; began to contribute to French chemical journals, 1798, and to English journals, 1800; F.R.S., 1801; resided in Paris, 1808; published also dramas and poems. [x. 185]

CHEPMAN, WALTER (1473?–1538?), printer, of Edinburgh; clerk in the king's secretary's office, 1494, and was still in the king's service in 1528; general merchant; bought lands in and near Edinburgh, 1505–9; supplied capital to Andrew Myllar, who had learned printing at Rouen, to set up a press in Edinburgh, the first in Scotland; obtained by patent the right to exclude books printed abroad, 1507; issued some poetical pieces, 1508, and the Aberdeen breviary, 1509–10 ; perhaps abandoned printing, 1510 ; dean of guild, 1515 ; founded chantry in St. Giles's, Edinburgh. [x. 186]

CHERBURY or CHIRBURY, DAVID (*fl.* 1430), bishop of Dromore, 1427–30 : afterwards suffragan to the bishop of St. David's ; a Carmelite friar. [x. 188]

CHERMSIDE, Sir ROBERT ALEXANDER (1787–1860), physician ; army surgeon in the Peninsula and at Waterloo ; M.D. Edinburgh, 1817 ; settled as practitioner in Paris, 1821. [x. 188]

CHÉRON, LOUIS (1655–1725), painter and engraver ; born in Paris ; travelled in Italy ; settled as a painter in Paris before 1687 ; Huguenot refugee in London, 1695 ; his reputation mainly based on his book illustrations. [x. 188]

CHERRY, ANDREW (1762–1812), actor and dramatist ; bookseller's apprentice in Dublin ; joined an Irish strolling company, 1779 ; attached to the Dublin theatre, 1787 ; acted in Yorkshire, 1792 ; returned to Dublin, 1794 ; acted at Manchester, and (1798) at Bath ; at Drury Lane, London, 1802–7 ; brought out some ten dramatic pieces, 1793–1807, the most successful being ' The Soldier's Daughter,' a comedy, 1804. [x. 189]

CHERRY, FRANCIS (1665 ?–1713), nonjuror ; of Shottesbrooke, Berkshire ; entered St. Edmund Hall, Oxford, 1682 ; collected books and coins ; benefactor of Thomas Hearne ; friend of Bishop Ken and other nonjurors. [x. 190]

CHERRY, THOMAS (1683–1706), friend of Thomas Hearne ; of St. Edmund Hall, Oxford, 1700 ; M.A., 1706 ; curate of Witney, Oxfordshire. [x. 191]

CHERTSEY, ANDREW (*fl.* 1508–1532), translator into English of French devotional books for Wynkyn de Worde's press. [x. 191]

CHESELDEN, WILLIAM (1688–1752), surgeon and anatomist ; studied surgery in London ; pupil of William Cowper the anatomist, 1703 ; lectured on anatomy in London, 1711 ; F.R.S., 1712 ; surgeon of St. Thomas's Hospital, 1719–38, of St. George's Hospital, 1734–7, and of Chelsea Hospital, 1737–52 ; invented the lateral operation for the stone, 1727 ; published works, including ' The Anatomy of the Human Body,' 1713, and ' Osteographia,' 1733. [x. 192]

CHESHAM, FRANCIS (1749–1806), engraver : first exhibited, 1777. [x. 194]

CHESHIRE, JOHN (1695–1762), physician ; entered Balliol College, Oxford, 1713 ; medical practitioner at Leicester ; published trite treatises on rheumatism, 1723, and gout, 1747. [x. 194]

CHESNEY, CHARLES CORNWALLIS (1826–1876), military critic ; entered Woolwich, 1843 ; sub-lieutenant, royal engineers, 1845 ; stationed in Ireland and the colonies, 1845–56 ; captain, 1854 ; professor of military history at Sandhurst ; lieutenant-colonel, 1868. His principal works are : ' Campaigns in Virginia and Maryland,' 1863, ' Waterloo Lectures,' 1868, and ' Essays in Military Biography,' 1874. [x. 195]

CHESNEY, FRANCIS RAWDON (1789–1872), general ; served as volunteer against the Irish rebels, 1798 ; received commission in the royal artillery, 1805 ; fruitlessly petitioned to be sent on active service ; visited Turkey, 1829 ; surveyed the isthmus of Suez, 1830, and showed that a canal was practicable ; explored valley of the Euphrates, 1831, with a view to a trade-route from the Syrian coast to Kurrachee ; navigated the lower Euphrates and explored the Tigris, 1835–7 ; stationed at Hongkong, 1843–7 ; major-general, 1855 ; surveyed course of projected railway from Antioch to the Euphrates, 1856 ; general, 1868 ; published narratives of his surveys. [x. 195]

CHESNEY, Sir GEORGE TOMKYNS (1830–1895), general ; brother of Colonel Charles Cornwallis Chesney [q. v.] ; studied at East India Company's College, Addiscombe ; second lieutenant, Bengal engineers, 1848 ; captain, 1858 ; lieutenant-colonel, 1874 ; colonel, 1884 ; colonel-commandant, royal engineers, 1890 ; general, 1892 ; served in Indian mutiny ; president of engineering college, Calcutta ; head of department of accounts, 1860 ; prepared scheme for Royal Indian Civil Engineering College, Cooper's Hill, 1868 ; first president, 1871–80 ;

secretary to military department of Indian government, 1880–6 ; member of governor's council, 1886–91 ; K.C.B., 1890 ; M.P. for Oxford, 1892 ; published novels and political writings. [Suppl. i. 420]

CHESNEY, ROBERT DE (*d.* 1166), or DE QUERCETO, bishop of Lincoln ; archdeacon of Leicester ; of a mild disposition ; bishop of Lincoln, 1148 ; injured the see by alienating its estates, pledging the cathedral jewels to Aaron the Jew, and (1163) allowing St. Albans Abbey exemption from episcopal control ; commenced building the bishop's palace at Lincoln, 1155, and bought a London house for the see, 1162 ; urged Archbishop Becket to submit to the king, 1164. [x. 198]

CHESSAR, JANE AGNES (1835–1880), teacher ; educated in Edinburgh ; teacher in a London seminary, 1852–66 ; member of the London School Board, 1873–5 ; died at Brussels. [x. 200]

CHESSHER, ROBERT (1750–1831), surgeon ; studied surgery in London, 1768 ; practised at Hinckley. [x. 200]

CHESSHYRE, Sir JOHN (1662–1738), lawyer ; of Halwood, Cheshire ; entered the Inner Temple, 1696 ; serjeant-at-law, 1705 ; endowed a church and library at Halton, Cheshire ; knighted before 1733. [x. 200]

CHESTER, EARLS OF. [See HUGH, *d.* 1101 ; RANDULF, *d.* 1129 ? ; RANDULF, *d.* 1153 ; HUGH, *d.* 1181 ; BLUNDEVILL, RANDULF DE, *d.* 1232 ; EDMUND, 1245–1296 ; MONTFORT, SIMON OF, 1208 ?–1265 ; EDWARD III, 1312–1377 ; EDWARD, PRINCE OF WALES, 1330–1376.]

CHESTER, JOSEPH LEMUEL (1821–1882), genealogist ; born in Connecticut ; went to New York, 1838 ; merchant's clerk ; published verses under the pseudonym of ' Julian Cramer,' 1843 ; removed to Philadelphia, 1845 ; journalist, and newspaper editor ; aide-de-camp to the governor of Philadelphia and titular colonel,' 1855 ; settled in London, 1858–82 ; collected materials for the history of American families from the wills in Doctors' Commons, parish registers, the registers of Oxford University and the see of London ; chief publications : ' John Rogers, the compiler of the first Authorised English Bible,' 1861, and ' Registers of the Abbey of St. Peter, Westminster,' 1876. [x. 201]

CHESTER, ROBERT (*fl.* 1182), author of astronomical tracts preserved in manuscript in the Bodleian ; his Latin version of an Arabic treatise on alchemy, printed, 1564. [x. 203]

CHESTER, ROBERT (1566 ?–1640 ?), poet ; published ' Love's Martyr,' 1601, republished, 1611, under the title, ' The Anuals of Great Brittaine,' an appendix to the poem containing Shakespeare's ' Phœnix and Turtle.' [x. 203]

CHESTER, ROGER OF (*fl.* 1339), writer of ' Polycratica Temporum ' ; probably a misdescription of Ranulf Higden [q. v.], monk of St. Werburgh's, Chester, and an alternative title of Higden's ' Polychronicon ' or ' Polycraticon.' [x. 203]

CHESTER, WILLIAM OF (*fl.* 1109). [See WILLIAM.]

CHESTER, Sir WILLIAM (1509 ?–1595 ?), lord mayor of London ; son of a London draper ; educated at Peterhouse, Cambridge ; draper in London before 1532 ; partner in the first sugar refinery in England, 1544 ; alderman of London, 1553–72 ; showed kindness to the Protestant martyrs when sheriff, 1554 ; knighted, 1557 ; lord mayor, 1560 ; M.P. London, 1563 ; honorary M.A. Cambridge, 1567 ; traded with Russia, the Levant, and the African coast ; lived in retirement at Cambridge, 1572 till death ; benefactor of Christ's Hospital and of St. Bartholomew's Hospital. [x. 204]

CHESTERFIELD, EARLS OF. [See STANHOPE, PHILIP first EARL, 1584–1656 ; STANHOPE, PHILIP, second EARL 1633–1713 ; STANHOPE, PHILIP DORMER, fourth EARL 1694–1773 ; STANHOPE, PHILIP, fifth EARL, 1755–1815.]

CHESTERFIELD, COUNTESS OF (*d.* 1667). [See KIRKHOVEN, CATHERINE.]

CHESTERFIELD or WORSHOP, THOMAS (*d.* 1451 ?), canon of Lichfield ; prebendary of Lichfield, 1425 and of Hereford, 1450 ; archdeacon of Salop, 1428–30 wrote a chronicle of the bishops of Lichfield down to 1347 (printed 1691). [x. 205]

CHESTERS, LORD (*d.* 1638). [See HENRYSON, SIR THOMAS.]

CHESTRE, THOMAS (*fl.* 1430), author of an Arthurian romance in English, 'The Noble Knighte Syr Launfal' (printed 1802). [x. 206]

CHETHAM, HUMPHREY (1580–1653), founder of the Chetham Hospital and Library, Manchester; son of a Manchester merchant; educated at Manchester grammar school; apprenticed to a linendraper; merchant, woollen-cloth manufacturer, and usurer in Manchester; partner with his brother George in a London grocery business; bought land in and near Manchester, 1620–8; bequeathed 8,000*l.* for educating poor boys (Chetham Hospital, opened 1656) and founding a public library. [x. 206]

CHETHAM, JAMES (1640–1692), writer on angling; published 'The Angler's Vade Mecum,' 1681. [x. 207]

CHETTLE, HENRY (*d.* 1607 ?), dramatist; son of a London dyer; stationer's apprentice, 1577; partner in a printing business, 1591; edited Robert Greene's 'Groatsworth of Wit,' 1592; wrote two satirical pamphlets, 'Kind-Hart's Dreame,' 1593, and 'Pierce Plainnes' . . . Prentiship,' 1595; reputed author of thirteen and joint author of thirty-five plays, produced 1598–1603; imprisoned for debt, 1599; published 'Englande's Mourning Garment,' an elegy on Queen Elizabeth, 1603. [x. 207]

CHETTLE, WILLIAM (*fl.* 1150). [See KETEL.]

CHETWOOD, KNIGHTLY (1650–1720), dean of Gloucester; educated at Eton and Cambridge; M.A., 1679; chaplain to James II; rector of Great Rissington, Gloucestershire, 1686; prebendary of Wells, 1687; intended by James II for the bishopric of Bristol, 1688; chaplain to the forces in Holland, 1689–1704; D.D., 1691; rector of Little Rissington, 1702; dean of Gloucester, 1707; claimant of the barony of Wahull; published translations from the classics, sermons, and verses. [x. 210]

CHETWOOD, WILLIAM RUFUS (*d.* 1766), dramatist; a London bookseller; published pamphlet on the stage, 1720; prompter at Drury Lane Theatre, 1722–40; imprisoned for debt, 1741; prompter at the Dublin theatre, 1742; imprisoned for debt, 1750; published four dramatic pieces, 1720–3, also a 'General History of the Stage,' 1749, 'The British Theatre: Lives of the . . . Dramatic Poets,' 1750, narratives of travels, and tales from the Spanish. [x. 211]

CHETWYND, EDWARD (1577–1639), divine; of the Ingestre, Staffordshire, family; B.A. Exeter College, Oxford, 1595; D.D., 1616; preacher at Abingdon, 1606, and Bristol, 1607; beneficed; dean of Bristol, 1617. [x. 212]

CHETWYND or **CHETWIND**, JOHN (1623–1692), divine; eldest son of Edward Chetwynd [q. v.]; M.A. Exeter College, Oxford, 1648; presbyterian minister at Wells, 1648; took Anglican orders, 1660; vicar of Temple Church, Bristol; prebendary of Bristol, 1668; published sermons. [x. 212]

CHETWYND, WALTER (*d.* 1693), antiquary; of Ingestre, Staffordshire; M.P. for Stafford, 1673–85, and for Staffordshire, 1689; encouraged Robert Plot's 'Natural History of Staffordshire.' [x. 213]

CHETWYND, WILLIAM RICHARD CHETWYND, third VISCOUNT CHETWYND (1685 ?–1770), educated at Westminster and Oxford; envoy to Genoa, 1708–12; M.P. for Stafford, 1714–22, for Plymouth, 1722–7, and for Stafford, 1734 till death; master of the mint, 1744–69; succeeded to the Irish viscounty of Chetwynd, 1767. [x. 213]

CHEVALIER, JOHN (1589–1675), chronicler of Jersey; *vingtenier* of St. Helier's; wrote an account of affairs in Jersey, 1640–51. [x. 214]

CHEVALIER, THOMAS (1767–1824), surgeon; son of a Huguenot refugee; B.A. Pembroke College, Cambridge, 1792; studied anatomy in London; lectured on anatomy and surgery in London; published surgical treatises, 1797–1823. [x. 214]

CHEVALLIER, ANTHONY RODOLPH (1523–1572), hebraist; born in Normandy; learned Hebrew from Francis Vatablus in Paris; embraced protestantism; came to England, *c.* 1548; patronised by the bishops; settled at Cambridge, 1550; withdrew to Strasburg, 1553, to Geneva, 1559, and thence to Caen: returned to London, 1568; Hebrew professor at Cambridge, 1569; prebendary of Canterbury, 1570; at Paris, August 1572; died in Guernsey; his chief writings first published in Bryan Walton's 'Polyglot Bible,' 1657. [x. 214]

CHEVALLIER, JOHN (*d.* 1846), agriculturist; vicar of Aspall, Suffolk, 1817; kept a lunatic asylum there; introduced into practical agriculture the Chevallier barley. [x. 215]

CHEVALLIER, TEMPLE (1794–1873), astronomer; entered Pembroke College, Cambridge, 1813; second wrangler, 1817; B.D. Cambridge, 1825; fellow of Pembroke and of St. Catharine's, Cambridge; vicar of Great St. Andrew's, Cambridge, 1821–4; professor at Durham, 1835–71; canon of Durham, 1865; published sermons, astronomical papers, and translations from the fathers. [x. 215]

CHEWT, ANTHONY (*d.* 1595 ?). [See CHUTE.]

CHEYNE or **CHIENE**, CHARLES VISCOUNT NEWHAVEN (1624 ?–1698), inherited Cogenho, Northamptonshire, 1644; purchased Chelsea estate with the dowry of his wife, Lady Jane Cheyne [q. v.], 1657; created a Scottish viscount, 1681; M.P. for Newport, Cornwall, 1695. [x. 216]

CHEYNE, GEORGE (1671–1743), physician; studied medicine at Edinburgh; published medical and mathematical tracts, 1702–3; settled in London, *c.* 1702; removed to Bath; advocated vegetarianism; published treatises on diet and natural theology. [x. 217]

CHEYNE or **LE CHEN**, HENRY (*d.* 1328), bishop of Aberdeen, *c.* 1282; submitted to Edward I, 1291; declared for Robert Bruce, 1309; said to have built Baldownie Bridge. [x. 219]

CHEYNE, JAMES (*d.* 1602), philosopher and mathematician; studied at Aberdeen and in France; professor at St. Barbe College, Paris, and at Douay; canon of Tournai; published, 1575–87, Latin treatises on various subjects, including astronomy, geography, and the Aristotelian philosophy. [x. 219]

CHEYNE, LADY JANE (1621–1669), elder daughter of William Cavendish, first duke of Newcastle [q. v.]; brought up at Welbeck, Nottinghamshire; married, 1654, Charles Cheyne [q. v.]; wrote verses (not published). [x. 220]

CHEYNE, JOHN (1777–1836), medical writer; educated at Edinburgh; graduated in medicine, 1795; army surgeon; stationed at Leith Fort, 1799; removed to Dublin, 1809; acquired a lucrative practice; appointed physician-general to the forces in Ireland, 1820; retired to Buckinghamshire, 1831; published medical tracts, 1802–21; wrote an autobiography. [x. 220]

CHEYNE, CHEYNEY, or **CHENEY**, SIR THOMAS (1485 ?–1558), treasurer of household, and warden of Cinque ports; knighted, *c.* 1511; sent on mission to Pope Leo X, 1513–14; sheriff of Kent, 1516; squire of body to Henry VIII, *c.* 1519; resident ambassador at French court, 1522 and 1526; served in Brittany, 1523; warden of Cinque ports, 1536; treasurer of household, 1539; K.G., 1539; Henry VIII's deputy in Paris at christening of Henry III of France, 1546; M.P. for Kent, 1542, 1544, 1547, 1553, 1554, and 1558; joined opposition to Somerset, 1549; took field against Wyatt, 1554; retained his offices under Mary and Elizabeth. [Suppl. i. 421]

CHEYNE, SIR WILLIAM (*d.* 1438 ?), judge; serjeant-at-law, 1410; justice of the king's bench, 1415; chief-justice, 1424 till death; knighted, 1426. Probably not identical with the William Cheyne who was recorder of London in 1379. [x. 222]

CHEYNE, WILLIAM, second VISCOUNT NEWHAVEN (1657–1738), lord-lieutenant of Buckinghamshire, 1712–1714; M.P., Buckinghamshire, under Queen Anne; sold Chelsea Manor, 1712. [x. 217]

CHEYNELL, FRANCIS (1608–1665), puritan; son of an Oxford physician; fellow of Merton College, 1629; M.A., 1633; was refused the degree of B.D. because of his Calvinist opinions; vicar of Marston St. Lawrence, Northamptonshire, 1637; plundered by the king's troops, *c.* 1642; chaplain in the parliamentary army; member of the Westminster Assembly, 1643; intruded rector of

Petworth, Sussex, 1643-60; violent adversary of William Chillingworth [q. v.], 1643-4; one of the parliamentary visitors of Oxford University, 1647; intruded president of St. John's College, Oxford, 1648-50; Lady Margaret professor of divinity, 1648-52; D.D., 1649; retired to his estate at Preston, Sussex, c. 1660; published works of controversial divinity, 1643-7. [x. 222]

CHEYNEY, JOHN (*fl.* 1677), congregationalist preacher in Cheshire, 1674; published four bitter pamphlets against quakerism, 1676-7. [x. 224]

CHEYNEY, RICHARD (1513-1579), bishop of Gloucester; fellow of Pembroke Hall, Cambridge; M.A., 1532; B.D., 1540; courtier of Edward VI; beneficed in Buckingham, Hereford, Gloucester, and Warwick shires; disputed against transubstantiation, 1553; canon of Gloucester, 1558, and of Westminster, 1560; bishop of Gloucester, 1562, with Bristol *in commendam*; of decided Lutheran opinions; strongly opposed the Thirty-nine Articles, 1563; gave great offence by preaching Lutheran doctrines, 1568; D.D. Cambridge, 1569; reluctantly signed the articles, 1571. [x. 224]

CHIBALD, JAMES (*b.* 1612), royalist divine; son of William Chibald [q. v.]; chorister of Magdalen College, Oxford, 1624; M.A., 1633; rector of St. Nicholas Cole Abbey, London, 1641; sequestrated by parliament, 1642. [x. 226]

CHIBALD, WILLIAM (1575-1641), divine; chorister of Magdalen College, Oxford, 1588; M.A., 1599; rector of St. Nicholas Cole Abbey, London, 1604-1640-1; published sermons and devotional tracts. [x. 226]

CHICHELE or **CHICHELEY, HENRY** (1362?-1443), archbishop of Canterbury; son of a yeoman of Higham Ferrers, Northamptonshire; patronised by William of Wykeham; educated at Winchester, 1373, and New College, Oxford, 1387,; fellow, 1389; B.C.L., 1390; beneficed in Wales, 1391; D.C.L.; rector of St. Stephen's, Walbrook, 1396-7; advocate in court of arches; prebendary of Salisbury, 1397-1409; archdeacon of Dorset, 1397; canon of Abergwilly, and of Lichfield, 1400; vicar of Odiham, Hampshire, 1402; archdeacon of Salisbury, 1402-4; chancellor of Salisbury, 1404-10; rector of Melcombe, Dorset, and of Sherston, Wiltshire; envoy to Pope Innocent VII, 1405, and to Gregory XII, 1407; bishop of St. David's, 1408 (enthroned, 1411); envoy to the council of Pisa, 1409; envoy to France, 1410 and 1413; archbishop of Canterbury, 1414; assented to the French war; appointed a special thanksgiving for Agincourt, 1415; active in proceedings against lollardism, 1416-22; with Henry V in France, 1418; negotiated surrender of Rouen, 1419; provided for independence of Gallican church, 1420; infringed the independence of the primacy by recalling an indulgence at the order of Pope Martin V, 1422; undertook visitation of his province, 1423; founded college and hospital at Higham Ferrers, 1424; upheld in council the Duke of Gloucester against Bishop Beaufort, 1424-31; endeavoured, under orders from Pope Martin V, to get the anti-papal statutes repealed, 1427-8; slighted by Pope Eugenius IV, 1438-9; benefactor of Canterbury Cathedral; founded the Chichele chest in Oxford University for relief of poor students; built a house for Cistercians in Oxford; founded All Souls' College, Oxford, 1437; consecrated its chapel, 1443. [x. 226]

CHICHELEY, SIR JOHN (*d.* 1691), rear-admiral; captain in the navy, 1663; knighted, 1665; served in Dutch war, 1665-6, in Mediterranean, 1668-71, and in Dutch war, 1672-3; rear-admiral, 1673; commissioner of the navy, 1675-80; commissioner of the admiralty, 1681-4 and 1689-90. [x. 231]

CHICHELEY, SIR THOMAS (1618-1699), mastergeneral of the ordnance; of Wimple, Cambridgeshire; high sheriff, 1637; M.P. for Cambridgeshire, 1640; ejected by the roundheads, 1642; M.P. for Cambridgeshire, 1661; knighted, 1670; master-general of the ordnance, 1670-4; M.P. for Cambridge town, 1678-9, 1685, 1689; lived extravagantly, and was obliged to sell Wimple, 1686. [x. 231]

CHICHESTER, EARLS OF. [See LEIGH, FRANCIS, first EARL, *d.* 1653; WRIOTHESLEY, THOMAS, second EARL, 1607-1677; PELHAM, THOMAS, first EARL of the third creation, 1728-1805; PELHAM, THOMAS, second EARL, 1756-1826; PELHAM, HENRY THOMAS, third EARL, 1804-1886.]

CHICHESTER, ARTHUR, BARON CHICHESTER of Belfast (1563-1625), lord deputy of Ireland; entered Exeter College, Oxford, 1583; assaulted a royal purveyor, and prudently withdrew to Ireland, where he remained till pardon was granted; served against the Armada, 1588, in Drake's expedition, 1595, in Essex's Cadiz expedition, 1596, in France, 1597, and in the Low Countries; knighted, 1597; colonel of a regiment at Drogheda, 1598; governor of Carrickfergus, and active against the Irish insurgents, 1599-1603; lord-deputy, 1604-14; aimed at disarming the natives and breaking down the clan system; forced by James I into repressive measures against Roman catholics, 1605-7; advocated translation of the common prayer book into Irish, 1607-8; endeavoured to pacify Ulster, 1607-8; engaged in planting Ulster with Scottish colonists; created Baron Chichester, 1613; recalled in consequence of his reluctance to resume repression of the Roman catholics, November 1614; lord treasurer of Ireland, 1616-25; envoy to the Elector Palatine, 1622; opposed war with Spain, 1624. [x. 232]

CHICHESTER, ARTHUR, first EARL OF DONEGAL (1606-1675), captain in the Irish army, 1627; M.P., Antrim, 1639; raised troops against Irish rebels, 1641; governor of Carrickfergus, 1643-4; refused the covenant, 1644; created Earl of Donegal, 1647; one of the hostages for Ormonde, 1647; governor of Carrickfergus, 1661-75; benefactor of Trinity College, Dublin. [x. 235]

CHICHESTER, SIR CHARLES (1795-1847), lieutenant-colonel; educated at Stonyhurst; ensign of foot, 1811; lieutenant, 1812; served in Mediterranean stations, 1811-17, in India, 1817-21, and America, 1821; major, 1826; lieutenant-colonel, 1831; brigadier-general of the British legion against the Carlists, 1835-8; knighted, 1840; commanded his regiment in American stations; died at Toronto. [x. 236]

CHICHESTER, FREDERICK RICHARD, styled by courtesy EARL OF BELFAST (1827-1853), author; educated at Eton; gave lectures in Belfast, 1851; died at Naples; wrote essays and tales. [x. 236]

CHICHESTER, HENRY MANNERS (1832-1894), writer on military history; lieutenant in 85th regiment; served at Mauritius and Cape of Good Hope; assisted in compiling and editing works on military history; contributed extensively to 'Dictionary of National Biography'; assisted in preparation of 'Records and Badges of Regiments in British Army,' 1895. [Suppl. i. 423]

CHICHESTER, ROBERT (*d.* 1155), bishop of Exeter, 1138-55; dean of Salisbury. [x. 237]

CHIFFINCH, THOMAS (1600-1666), closet-keeper to Charles II; page to Charles I, 1641; page to Charles, prince of Wales, 1645, attending him during his exile; keeper of the king's jewels, 1660; receiver-general of the revenues of the plantations, 1663. [x. 237]

CHIFFINCH, WILLIAM (1602?-1688), page to Charles II before 1666; closet-keeper after the death of his brother Thomas [q. v.]; employed in secret and confidential transactions; received Charles's French pension for him; closet-keeper to James II. [x. 238]

CHIFFNEY, SAMUEL, the elder (1753?-1807), jockey; jockey and trainer at Newmarket, 1770-1806; won the Oaks, 1782, and the Derby, 1789; suspected, along with his employer, George, prince of Wales, of dishonest riding, 1790-1; published an autobiography, 1795 and 1800; invented a bit for horses. [x. 239]

CHIFFNEY, SAMUEL, the younger (1786-1854), jockey and trainer at Newmarket, 1802-51; won the Oaks five times and the Derby twice; son of Samuel Chiffney the elder [q. v.] [x. 239]

CHIFFNEY, WILLIAM (1784-1862), trainer at Newmarket; son of Samuel Chiffney the elder [q. v.] [x. 239]

CHILCOT, THOMAS (*d.* 1766), organist of Bath Abbey, 1733; composed songs and concertos. [x. 240]

CHILD, SIR FRANCIS, the elder (1642-1713), banker; goldsmith's apprentice in London, 1656-64; married 1671, Elizabeth Wheeler, heiress of the wealthy goldsmith of that name; in partnership with Robert Blanchard (*d.* 1681), his wife's stepfather, 1677, at the 'Marygold'; in partnership as Francis Child and John Rogers, 1681; gave up goldsmith's and pawnbroker's business and confined himself to banking, 1690 ; alderman of London, 1689 ; knighted, 1689 ; sheriff, 1690 ; lord mayor, 1698–9 ; M.P. for city of London, 1705 and 1708, and for Devizes, 1710 ; benefactor of Christ's Hospital. [x. 240]

CHILD, SIR FRANCIS, the younger (1684 ?–1740), banker ; younger son of Sir Francis Child the elder [q. v.] ; head of the firm of Francis Child & Co., 1721 ; alderman of London, 1721 ; sheriff, 1722 ; M.P. for city of London, 1722, and for Middlesex, 1727 and 1734 ; lord mayor, 1731–2 ; knighted, 1732. [x. 242]

CHILD, JOHN (1638 ?–1684), baptist preacher ; born at Bedford ; artisan and baptist preacher at Newport Pagnel ; removed to London ; published pamphlets arguing against dissent from the church, 1682 ; hanged himself ; his death regarded as a ' judgment' against apostasy.
[x. 242]

CHILD, SIR JOHN (d. 1690), governor of Bombay ; brother of Sir Josiah Child [q. v.] ; went to India as a boy ; in the East India Company's service at Rajahpur ; transferred to Surat, 1680 ; tried to suppress the Bombay mutiny, 1683 ; captain-general of the company's forces, 1684 ; created baronet, 1685 ; removed to Bombay, 1685 ; given authority over all the company's possessions, 1686 ; involved the company in war with Arangzib, 1689 ; charged with tyrannical conduct and want of faith with natives ; died at Bombay. [x. 243]

CHILD, SIR JOSIAH (1630–1699), author of ' A new Discourse of Trade,' 1668 (4th edition, 1693) ; son of a London merchant ; naval store-dealer at Portsmouth, 1655 ; mayor of Portsmouth ; bought Wanstead Abbey, 1673 ; created baronet, 1678 ; despotic chairman of East India Company ; retained power by bribing the court.
[x. 244]

CHILD, WILLIAM (1606 ?–1697), musician ; chorister at Bristol ; clerk and assistant organist of St. George's Chapel, Windsor, 1630 ; Mus. Bac. Oxford, 1631 ; sole organist of St. George's Chapel, 1634 ; said to have been also organist of the Chapel Royal, Whitehall ; ejected by the puritans, 1643 ; restored, 1660 ; chanter of the Chapel Royal, Whitehall ; composer to the king ; Mus. Doc. Oxford, 1663 ; published twenty anthems, 1639 ; much of his music still in manuscript. [x. 245]

CHILDE, ELIAS (fl. 1798–1848), landscape painter.
[x. 247]

CHILDE, HENRY LANGDON (1781–1874), inventor of dissolving views ; perfected the magic lantern ; adapted the limelight to it ; gave popular lantern lectures in London and the provinces ; devised double lanterns and dissolving views, 1807. [x. 247]

CHILDE, JAMES WARREN (1780–1862), miniature painter ; exhibited landscapes, 1798 ; exhibited miniatures, 1815–53. [x. 248]

CHILDERLEY, JOHN (1565–1645), divine ; entered Merchant Taylors' School, 1575 ; fellow of St. John's College, Oxford, 1579 ; D.D., 1603 ; beneficed in London and Essex ; sequestrated as a royalist, 1643. [x. 248]

CHILDERS, HUGH CULLING EARDLEY (1827–1896), statesman ; B.A. Trinity College, Cambridge, 1850 ; inspector of schools, Melbourne, 1851, and, later, secretary to education department and emigration agent at port of Melbourne ; auditor-general and member of legislative council, 1852 ; first vice-chancellor of Melbourne University ; collector of customs and member of executive council, 1853 ; member for Portland in parliament of Victoria, 1856 ; agent-general for Victoria in London, 1857 ; M.P. for Pontefract, 1860–85 ; member of royal commission on penal servitude, 1863 ; financial secretary to treasury, 1865–6 ; appointed first lord of admiralty and privy councillor, 1868 ; resigned office, 1871 ; chancellor of duchy of Lancaster, 1872–3 ; secretary of state for war, 1880–2 ; produced successful scheme of army reform, 1881 ; chancellor of exchequer, 1882–5 ; M.P. for South Edinburgh, 1886 ; home secretary, 1886 ; supported Gladstone's home rule bill. [Suppl. i. 423]

CHILDERS, ROBERT CÆSAR (1838–1876), orientalist ; civil servant in Ceylon, 1860 ; studied Sinhalese, Pali, and Buddhist sacred books ; returned to England, 1864 ; sub-librarian at the India Office, 1872 ; professor of Pali, University College, London, 1873 ; edited Pali texts, 1869–74 ; compiled the first Pali dictionary, 1872–5 ; established the Aryan character of Sinhalese, 1873–5.
[x. 248]

CHILDREN, GEORGE (1742–1818), electrician ; B.A. Oriel College, Oxford, 1762 ; barrister of the Middle Temple ; banker at Tunbridge ; studied galvanic electricity, 1802.
[x. 249]

CHILDREN, JOHN GEORGE (1777–1852), scientist ; only son of George Children [q. v.] ; educated at Eton and Cambridge ; F.R.S., 1807 ; published notes on electricity, 1808–15 ; employed in the British Museum, 1816–40 ; translated chemical tracts, 1819–22 ; studied entomology.
[x. 249]

CHILDREY, JOSHUA (1623–1670), antiquary ; clerk of Magdalen College, Oxford, 1640 ; B.A., 1646 ; schoolmaster at Faversham, 1648 ; M.A., 1661 ; prebendary of Salisbury, rector of Upwey, Dorsetshire, and archdeacon of Sarum, 1664 ; published two astrological tracts, 1652–3, and 'Britannia Baconica,' 1660. [x. 250]

CHILDS, CHARLES (1807–1876), head of John Childs & Son, printers, Bungay, Suffolk ; son of John Childs [q. v.] [x. 251]

CHILDS, JOHN, (1783–1853), printer, of Bungay, Suffolk ; issued cheap editions of standard authors and annotated bibles ; refused to pay church rates, 1836. [x. 251]

CHILDS, ROBERT (d. 1837), brother and partner of John Childs [q. v.] [x. 251]

CHILLENDEN, EDMUND (fl. 1656), author of 'Preaching without Ordination,' 1647 ; lieutenant, afterwards captain, in the parliamentary army. [x. 252]

CHILLESTER, JAMES (fl. 1571), translator from the French of 'A most excellent Hystorie of . . . Christian Princes.' [x. 252]

CHILLINGWORTH, JOHN (fl. 1360), mathematician ; fellow of Merton College, Oxford ; wrote on astrology and mathematics. [x. 252]

CHILLINGWORTH, JOHN (d. 1445), astronomer ; fellow of Merton College, Oxford ; junior proctor, 1441.
[x. 252]

CHILLINGWORTH, WILLIAM (1602–1644), theologian ; son of an Oxford mercer ; godson of William Laud ; scholar of Trinity College, Oxford, 1618 ; M.A., 1624 ; fellow, 1628 ; one of Laud's Oxford informers, 1628 ; disputed against Roman catholicism with 'John Fisher,' jesuit ; embraced Romanism and went to Douay, 1630 ; returned to Oxford, 1631 ; abjured Romanism, 1634 ; violently attacked by Romanist writers, especially (1636) by Edward Knott ; published ' The Religion of Protestants a safe Way of Salvation,' 1638 ; prebendary and chancellor of Salisbury, 1638 ; wrote against the Scots ; with the king's army at Gloucester, 1643 ; taken prisoner at Arundel Castle, 1643 ; harassed by Francis Cheynell [q. v.]
[x. 252]

CHILMARK or **CHYLMARK,** JOHN (fl. 1386), schoolman ; M.A. and fellow of Merton College, Oxford.
[x. 257]

CHILMEAD, EDMUND (1610–1654), sometimes erroneously styled Edward,' miscellaneous writer ; clerk of Magdalen College, Oxford, 1625–32 ; M.A., 1632 ; chaplain of Christ Church, Oxford, 1632 ; ejected, 1648 ; hackwriter in London ; compiled a catalogue of Greek manuscripts in Bodleian, 1636 ; published translations and pamphlets, 1640–50 ; composed songs ; his translation of Malalas was published 1691. [x. 257]

CHINNERY, GEORGE (d. 1852), portrait and landscape painter ; exhibited in London, 1766 ; in Dublin, 1798 ; at Canton, 1830 ; visited India ; published etchings of ' Oriental heads,' 1839–40 ; died at Macao. [x. 258]

CHIPP, EDMUND THOMAS (1823–1886), composer ; eldest son of Thomas Paul Chipp [q. v.] ; chorister of the Chapel Royal, Whitehall ; organist of various London churches, 1843–62 ; professional violinist ; Mus.Bac. Cambridge, 1859 ; Mus.Doc., 1860 ; organist in Belfast, 1862–6 ; organist of Ely Cathedral, 1866–86 ; published music. [x. 258]

CHIPP, THOMAS PAUL (1793–1870), musician ; chorister of Westminster Abbey ; harpist ; drummer ; member of London orchestras, 1818–70. [x. 259]

CHIPPENDALE, MARY JANE (1837 ?–1888), actress ; née Seaman ; married William Henry Chippendale [q. v.], 1866 ; at Lyceum and in America with (Sir) Henry Irving. [Suppl. ii. 1]

CHIPPENDALE, THOMAS (*d.* 1779), furniture maker, of London ; published 'The Gentleman and Cabinet Maker's Director,' 1752.   [x. 259]

CHIPPENDALE, WILLIAM HENRY (1801–1888), actor ; apprenticed as printer and auctioneer ; appeared as David in 'Rivals' at Montrose, 1819 at Park Theatre, New York, 1836–53 ; appeared as Sir Anthony Absolute at Haymarket, 1853 ; and later as Malvolio, Adam, and Hardcastle ; at Lyceum, as Polonius, 1874. [Suppl. ii. 1]

CHIRBURY, DAVID (*fl.* 1430). [See CHERBURY.]

CHIRK, LORD OF (1256 ?–1326). [See MORTIMER, ROGER.]

CHISENHALE or **CHISENHALL**, EDWARD (*d.* 1654), historian ; colonel in Charles I's army ; published 'Catholike History,' 1653, in favour of the church of England.   [x. 259]

CHISHOLM, ÆNEAS (1759–1818), Scottish catholic prelate ; educated at Valladolid ; tutor at Douay, 1786 ; priest in Strathglass, 1789 ; titular bishop of Diocæsarea, 1805 ; coadjutor, 1805, and vicar-apostolic, 1814, of the highland district.   [x. 260]

CHISHOLM, ALEXANDER (1792 ?–1847), portrait and historical painter ; weaver's apprentice at Peterhead ; removed to Edinburgh ; came to London, 1818 ; exhibited, 1820–47.   [x. 259]

CHISHOLM, ARCHIBALD (*d.* 1877), officer in the East India Company's service, 1817–45 ; captain, 1833 ; major.   [x. 261]

CHISHOLM, CAROLINE (1808–1877), the emigrant's friend ; *née* Jones ; married Archibald Chisholm [q. v.], 1830 ; opened schools for soldiers' daughters, Madras, 1832 ; opened home for female immigrants, Sydney, 1841 ; came to London, 1846 ; wrote on emigration, 1850 ; returned to Australia, 1854 ; returned to England, 1866 ; pensioned, 1867.   [x. 260]

CHISHOLM, COLIN (*d.* 1825), medical writer ; surgeon in the West Indies, 1796 ; practitioner in Bristol, *c.* 1800.   [x. 261]

CHISHOLM, JOHN (1752–1814), Scottish catholic prelate ; educated at Douay ; titular bishop of Oria, 1792 ; vicar-apostolic of highland district, 1792–1814. [x. 261]

CHISHOLM, WALTER (1856–1877), poet ; a Berwickshire shepherd ; wrote verses in the local papers, 1875. Poems by him appeared in 1879.   [x. 261]

CHISHOLM, WILLIAM I (*d.* 1564), bishop of Dunblane, 1527–64 ; a man of infamous character ; alienated the episcopal estates to his illegitimate children.[x. 262]

CHISHOLM, WILLIAM II (*d.* 1593), bishop of Dunblane ; coadjutor to his uncle, William Chisholm I [q.v.], 1561 ; bishop of Dunblane, 1564 ; envoy for Mary Queen of Scots, 1565–7 ; withdrew to France before 1570 ; deposed, 1573 ; bishop of Vaison, France, 1570–84 ; monk of the Chartreuse ; prior of the Chartreuse at Lyons and Rome.   [x. 262]

CHISHOLM, WILLIAM III (*d.* 1629), bishop of Vaison, 1584, in succession to his uncle, William Chisholm II [q. v.] ; intrigued in Scottish affairs, 1602, wishing to obtain the cardinalate, in the interest of the Scottish catholics ; rector of the Venaissin, 1603–29.   [x. 262]

CHISHULL, EDMUND (1671–1733), antiquary ; scholar of Corpus Christi College, Oxford, 1687 ; M.A., 1693 ; fellow, 1696 ; B.D., 1705 ; chaplain at Smyrna, 1698–1702 ; vicar of Walthamstow, Essex, 1708–33, with other preferment ; published Latin verses, numismatical notes, notes of travel, and 'Antiquitates Asiaticæ,' 1728.   [x. 263]

CHISHULL, JOHN DE (*d.* 1280), bishop of London ; rector of Isleham, Cambridgeshire, 1252, and of Upwell, Norfolk, 1256 ; archdeacon of London, 1262–8 ; clerk of Henry III ; envoy to Paris, 1263 ; baron and chancellor of the exchequer, 1264 ; provost of Beverley, 1264 ; dean of St. Paul's, 1268 ; lord treasurer, 1269 ; bishop of London, 1274–80 ; his duties performed by deputies, 1280.
          [x. 264]

CHISWELL, RICHARD, the elder (1639–1711), publisher at the 'Rose and Crown,' Paul's Churchyard.
          [x. 265]

CHISWELL, RICHARD, the younger (1673–1751), traveller ` son of Richard Chiswell the elder [q. v.] ; a Turkey merchant ; travelled in the East ; M.P., Calne, 1714 ; bought Debden Hall, Essex, 1715.   [x. 265]

CHISWELL, TRENCH, originally RICHARD MUILMAN (1735 ?–1797), antiquary ; son of a Dutch merchant ; changed his name on succeeding to the Debden Hall estate, 1772 ; M.P., Aldborough, Yorkshire ; collected notes relating to history of Essex ; committed suicide.
          [x. 266]

CHITTING, HENRY (*d.* 1638), Chester herald, 1618 ; visited Berkshire, Gloucestershire, and Lincolnshire.
          [x. 266]

CHITTY, EDWARD (1804–1863), legal reporter ; third son of Joseph Chitty the elder [q.v.] ; barrister, 1829 ; equity draughtsman ; published 'Equity Index,' 1831, and bankruptcy cases ('Deacon and Chitty'), 1833–1839 ; subsequently lived in Jamaica.   [x. 266]

CHITTY, JOSEPH, the younger (*d.* 1838), special pleader ; son of Joseph Chitty the elder [q. v.] ; author of 'Chitty on Contracts,' 1841, and other legal works.
          [x. 267]

CHITTY, JOSEPH, the elder (1776–1841), legal writer ; special pleader ; barrister, 1816 ; retired from practice, 1833 ; published law manuals, 1799–1837.
          [x. 266]

CHITTY, SIR JOSEPH WILLIAM (1828–1899), judge ; son of Thomas Chitty [q. v.] ; educated at Eton and Balliol College, Oxford ; M.A., 1855 ; called to bar at Lincoln's Inn, 1856 ; bencher, 1875 ; treasurer, 1895 ; Q.C., 1874 ; M.P. for Oxford, 1880 ; appointed justice of high court, chancery division, and knighted, 1881 ; lord justice of appeal, 1897 ; nominated judge under the Benefices Act, 1898.   [Suppl. ii. 2]

CHITTY, THOMAS (1802–1878), legal writer ; special pleader, 1820–77 ; edited standard law books, 1835–45 ; published 'Chitty's Forms' (of practical proceedings), 1834.   [x. 267]

CHOKE, SIR RICHARD (*d.* 1483 ?), judge ; pleader by 1441 ; serjeant-at-law, 1453 ; bought Long Ashton, Somerset, 1454 ; justice of common pleas, 1461 till death ; knighted, 1464.   [x. 267]

CHOLMLEY, HUGH (1574 ?–1641), controversialist ; schoolfellow of Bishop Joseph Hall ; entered Emmanuel College, Cambridge, 1589 ; M.A., 1596 ; beneficed at Tiverton, 1604 ; canon of Exeter, 1632 ; published 'The State of the Now-Romane Church,' 1629.   [x. 268]

CHOLMLEY, SIR HUGH (1600–1657), royalist ; educated at Cambridge and Gray's Inn ; M.P., Scarborough, 1624–6 and 1640 ; refused to pay ship-money, 1636 ; actively opposed Strafford, 1640 ; raised troops in Yorkshire for parliament, 1642 ; fought half-heartedly for parliament in Yorkshire, 1642–3 ; joined the queen at York, 1643 ; held Yorkshire coast for Charles I ; taken prisoner, 1645 ; withdrew to Rouen ; returned, 1649 ; imprisoned, 1651 ; wrote an autobiography, 1656 (printed, 1787).   [x. 268]

CHOLMLEY, SIR ROGER (*d.* 1565), judge ; of Lincoln's Inn ; serjeant-at-law, 1531 ; recorder of London, 1535–45 ; knighted, 1537 ; M.P. for London, 1542 ; chief baron of the exchequer, 1546 ; commissioner to suppress the chantries, 1547 ; chief-justice of king's bench, 1552 ; deprived by Queen Mary, 1553 ; founded Highgate grammar school, 1562.   [x. 269]

CHOLMLEY, WILLIAM (*d.* 1554), grocer, of London ; wrote, 1553, a political tract (first printed, 1853), entitled 'The Request and Suite of a True-hearted Englishman.'   [x. 270]

CHOLMONDELEY, GEORGE, second EARL OF CHOLMONDELEY (*d.* 1733), general ; brother of Hugh Cholmondeley, first earl [q. v.] ; educated at Westminster and Christ Church, Oxford ; cornet of horse, 1685 ; in arms for Prince of Orange, 1688 ; cavalry officer at the Boyne, 1690, and Steinkirk, 1692 ; hon. D.C.L. Oxford, 1695 ; major-general, 1702 ; created Baron Newborough, 1716 ; succeeded as second Earl of Cholmondeley, 1724 ; general of horse, 1727 ; governor of Guernsey, 1732.
          [x. 271]

CHOLMONDELEY or **CHOLMLEY**, SIR HUGH (1513–1596), soldier ; of Cholmondeley, Cheshire ; knighted for service in Scotland, 1542 ; served against the Scots, **1557** ; high sheriff of Cheshire.   **[x. 271]**

CHOLMONDELEY, HUGH, first EARL of CHOLMONDELEY (*d.* 1724), succeeded as Viscount Cholmondeley of Kells, 1681; created Baron Cholmondeley, in the peerage of England, 1689, and Earl of Cholmondeley, 1706; treasurer of the household, 1708-13 and 1714-24.　[x. 271]

CHOLMONDELEY, MARY, LADY (1563-1626), litigant; daughter of Charles Holford (*d.* 1581), of Holford, Cheshire; married, *c.* 1580, Sir Hugh Cholmondeley [q. v.]; litigation concerning her patrimony, begun 1581, ended, by compromise, *c.* 1620.　[x. 272]

CHOLMONDELEY, ROBERT, EARL OF LEINSTER (1584?-1659), eldest son of Sir Hugh Cholmondeley [q. v.]; created baronet, 1611; created Viscount Cholmondeley of Kells, 1628; raised troops in Cheshire for Charles I, 1642; created Baron Cholmondeley, in the peerage of England, 1645; created Earl of Leinster, 1646; fined by parliament.　[x. 272]

CHORLEY, CHARLES (1810?-1874), journalist at Truro; printed privately translations from various languages.　[x. 272]

CHORLEY, HENRY FOTHERGILL (1808-1872), critic; clerk in Liverpool; wrote for magazines, 1827; contributed musical criticisms to the 'Athenæum,' 1830-1868; resided in London, on the staff of the 'Athenæum,' 1833-66; wrote unsuccessful novels and dramas, 1835-1859, memoirs on music, 1841-62, a life of Mrs. Hemans, 1836, and an autobiography.　[x. 273]

CHORLEY, JOHN RUTTER (1807?-1867), poet; clerk in Liverpool; secretary to Grand Junction railway between Liverpool and Birmingham; removed to London; contributed to the 'Athenæum,' 1846-54; published 'The Wife's Litany,' a rhyming drama, 1865; gave to the British Museum his fine collection of Spanish plays.　[x. 274]

CHORLEY, JOSIAH (*d.* 1719?), presbyterian minister; M.A.; presbyterian minister at Norwich, 1691 till death; published an 'Index to the Bible,' appending 'A Poetical Meditation,' 1711.　[x. 275]

CHORLEY, RICHARD (*fl.* 1757), presbyterian minister in Norfolk; son of Josiah Chorley [q. v.]　[x. 275]

CHORLTON, JOHN (1666-1705), presbyterian divine; educated in Richard Frankland's [q.v.] academy, 1682; presbyterian pastor in Manchester, 1687-1705; conducted a presbyterian divinity college in Manchester, 1699-1705.　[x. 275]

CHRISMAS. [See CHRISTMAS.]

CHRISTIAN, EDWARD (*d.* 1823), lawyer; B.A. St. John's College, Cambridge, 1779; fellow, 1780-9; barrister of Gray's Inn, 1786; failed on circuit; professor of law at Cambridge, 1788; chief-justice of Isle of Ely; published legal treatises, 1790-1821.　[x. 276]

CHRISTIAN, FLETCHER (*fl.* 1789), mutineer; master's mate of the exploring ship Bounty, 1787; headed the mutiny in the Pacific, 28 April 1789, against William Bligh [q. v.], commander of the ship; sailed to Tahiti; reported to have been in England, 1809.　[x. 277]

CHRISTIAN, SIR HUGH CLOBERRY (1747-1798), rear-admiral; served, chiefly in Mediterranean, 1761-71; captain, 1778; served in West Indies, 1779-82; rear-admiral, 1795; knighted, 1796; commander-in-chief in West Indies, 1796, and at the Cape, 1798.　[x. 278]

CHRISTIAN, THOMAS (*d.* 1799), translator into Manx of part of 'Paradise Lost,' 1796; vicar of Kirk Marown, Man, 1779-99.　[x. 279]

CHRISTIAN, WILLIAM (1608-1663), ILLIAM DHÔNE ('Brown-haired William') of Manx story; third son of one of the deemsters of Man; his family, with others, irritated by the land policy of James, seventh earl of Derby and tenth lord of Man; received from his father Ronaldsway estate, 1643; receiver-general of Man, 1648-1658; appointed commander of Manx troops, August 1651, by the Earl of Derby (beheaded 15 Oct.); headed an insurrection against the Countess of Derby; surrendered Man to the parliamentary forces, 1651; compelled the countess to surrender Rushen and Peel castles, November 1651; governor of Man, 1656; superseded and accused of peculation, 1658; escaped to England; imprisoned in London, 1660; returned to Man, confiding in the Act of Indemnity, *c.* 1661; arrested by Charles, eighth earl of

Derby, September 1662; appealed to Charles II; found guilty of treason by the Manx authorities, under great pressure from the earl, 29 Dec. 1662; executed, 2 Jan. 1663. Charles II expressed great indignation at the proceedings, punished the deemsters and governor, and restored Ronaldsway to Christian's son.　[x. 279]

CHRISTIE, ALEXANDER (1807-1860), historical painter; educated in Edinburgh; served apprenticeship to a writer to the signet; studied art in Edinburgh (1833), London, and Paris; art teacher in the Edinburgh School of Art, 1843; exhibited in Edinburgh.　[x. 282]

CHRISTIE, HUGH (1710-1774), schoolmaster; M.A. Aberdeen, 1730; rector of Brechin, afterwards of Montrose, academy; published a Latin grammar and primer, 1758-60.　[x. 283]

CHRISTIE, JAMES, the elder (1730-1803), auctioneer in London, 1766-1803.　[x. 283]

CHRISTIE, JAMES, the younger (1773-1831), antiquary and auctioneer; eldest son of James Christie the elder [q. v.]; educated at Eton; took over his father's business, 1803; wrote on the antiquity of chess, 1801, Etruscan vases, 1806, Greek vases, 1822-5, and sculpture, 1833 (posthumously published).　[x. 283]

CHRISTIE, RICHARD COPLEY (1830-1901), scholar and bibliophile; B.A. Lincoln College, Oxford, 1853; M.A. 1855; professor of ancient and modern history, 1854-66, political economy and commercial science, 1855-66, and jurisprudence and law, 1855-69, Owens College, Manchester, holding chairs in plurality; called to bar at Lincoln's Inn, 1857; governor and member of council of Owens College, Manchester, 1870; member of council and university court, Victoria University, 1880; hon. LL.D., 1895; chancellor of see of Manchester, 1872-94; became joint-legatee of Sir Joseph Whitworth [q. v.], 1887, and was subsequently a munificent benefactor of Owens College; chairman of Chetham Society, 1883-1901; bequeathed his library to Owens College; contributed to the 'Dictionary of National Biography' and 'Encyclopædia Britannica.' His publications include 'Etienne Dolet, the Martyr of the Renaissance,' 1880.　[Suppl. ii. 3]

CHRISTIE, SAMUEL HUNTER (1784-1865), mathematician; son of James Christie the elder [q. v.]; entered Trinity College, Cambridge, 1800; second wrangler, 1805; mathematical teacher and professor at Woolwich Military Academy, 1806-54; F.R.S., 1826; studied magnetism, and served constantly upon the compass committee; contributed to scientific journals.　[x. 284]

CHRISTIE, THOMAS (1761-1796), political writer; banker's clerk; studied science privately; studied medicine in London (1784) and Edinburgh; contributed scientific papers to the 'Gentleman's Magazine,' 1784; wrote for the 'Analytical Review'; published his 'Miscellanies,' 1789; visited Paris, 1789; wrote in defence of the French revolution 1790-1; returned to Paris, 1792; wrote, for the 'National Assembly,' an English version of the new French constitution; partner in a London carpet factory, 1792; died at Surinam.　[x. 285]

CHRISTIE, THOMAS (1773-1829), physician; educated at Aberdeen; surgeon in the East India Company's service, Ceylon, 1797-1810; introduced vaccination there, 1802; M.D. Aberdeen, 1810; practitioner in Cheltenham, 1810-29; physician extraordinary to the prince regent, 1813; wrote on 'Vaccination in Ceylon,' 1811.　[x. 287]

CHRISTIE, WILLIAM (1748-1823), unitarian; merchant in Montrose; opened, and became minister of, a unitarian church in Montrose, 1782, the first of the denomination in Scotland; unitarian minister in Glasgow, 1794; emigrated to America, 1795; published unitarian treatises, 1784-1811.　[x. 287]

CHRISTIE, WILLIAM DOUGAL (1816-1874), diplomatist; son of an army physician; born at Bombay; B.A. Cambridge, 1838; barrister, 1840; M.P., Weymouth, 1842-7; entered the diplomatic service, 1848; envoy to Brazil, 1859-63; pensioned, 1863; edited Dryden's works, 1870; vindicated John Stuart Mill's memory against Abraham Hayward's adverse criticism; published a life of Shaftesbury, 1871.　[x. 288]

CHRISTINA (*fl.* 1086), nun of Romsey; daughter of the ætheling Eadward; born in Hungary; brought to England, 1057; fled to Scotland with her brother Eadgar,

1067 ; submitted to William the Conqueror ; obtained lands in Oxfordshire and Warwickshire ; nun at Romsey, Hampshire, 1086 ; brought up Eadgyth (or Matilda), and opposed her marriage with Henry I, 1100.   [x. 289]

CHRISTISON, Sir ROBERT (1797–1882), toxicologist ; educated in Edinburgh ; M.D., 1819 ; house physician to Edinburgh Infirmary, 1817–20 ; studied in London, under John Abernethy, and in Paris, under Robiquet, the chemist, and Orfila, the toxicologist ; medical professor in Edinburgh, 1822–77 ; physician to Edinburgh Infirmary, 1827 ; medical adviser to the crown, 1829–66 ; created baronet, 1871 ; published ' Treatise on Poisons,' 1829, and contributed largely to medical and scientific periodicals.   [x. 290]

CHRISTMAS, GERARD, or GARRETT CHRISMAS (d. 1634), carver and statuary ; carved funeral monuments ; carver to the navy, 1614–34 ; designer of figures for several lord mayors' shows between 1619 and 1632.   [x. 291]

CHRISTMAS, HENRY, afterwards NOEL-FEARN (1811–1868), miscellaneous writer ; M.A. St. John's College, Cambridge, 1840 ; in holy orders, 1837 ; librarian of Sion College, 1841–8 ; editor of church periodicals, 1840–1860 ; published verses, theological and philosophical pamphlets, and notes of travel ; wrote on numismatics, 1844–64 ; his collection of coins sold, 1864.   [x. 292]

CHRISTOPHERSON, JOHN (d. 1558), bishop of Chichester ; educated at Pembroke Hall and St. John's College, Cambridge ; M.A., 1543 ; fellow of Pembroke Hall, 1541, of St. John's College, and, 1546, of Trinity College, Cambridge ; withdrew to Louvain, c. 1547 ; master of Trinity College, Cambridge, 1553 ; confessor to Queen Mary ; dean of Norwich, 1554 ; rector of Swanton Morley, Norfolk, 1556 ; a visitor of Cambridge University, 1557 ; bishop of Chichester, 1557 ; persecuted protestants in his diocese ; imprisoned for violent preaching, 1558 ; benefactor to Trinity College, Cambridge ; translated into Latin the ecclesiastical historians, four books of Philo, and other Greek authors.   [x. 293]

CHRISTOPHERSON, MICHAEL (fl. 1613), Roman catholic divine ; educated at Douay ; wrote ' A Treatise of Antichrist,' in defence of Bellarmine, 1613.   [x. 295]

CHRISTY, HENRY (1810–1865), ethnologist ; banker in London ; travelled, for ethnological purposes, in the East, 1850, in Scandinavia, 1852–3, in North America, Cuba, and Mexico, 1856–7 ; explored the Vezere valley caves, 1864 ; died in Belgium ; bequeathed his collections to the nation.   [x. 295]

CHRYSTAL, THOMAS (d. 1535). [See CRYSTALL.]

CHUBB, CHARLES (d. 1845), locksmith ; ironmonger in Winchester ; locksmith at Portsea ; founded firm of Chubb & Co., London ; patented locks and safes, 1824–33.   [x. 296]

CHUBB, JOHN (1816–1872), manufacturer of locks and safes ; son of Charles Chubb [q. v.]   [x. 296]

CHUBB, THOMAS (1679–1747), deist ; glover's apprentice at Salisbury, 1694 ; tallow-chandler's assistant, 1705 ; published ' The Supremacy of the Father asserted,' 1715 ; servant to Sir Joseph Jekyll ; helped in a tallow-chandler's shop in Salisbury, c. 1716 till death ; published Arian tracts, 1725–32, and deistical tracts, 1734–46.   [x. 297]

CHUBBES or **JUBBS** or **SHUBYS**, WILLIAM (d. 1505), writer on logic ; B.A. Pembroke Hall, Cambridge, 1465 ; fellow ; D.D., 1491 ; first master of Jesus College, Cambridge, 1497–1505.   [x. 298]

CHUDLEIGH, ELIZABETH, COUNTESS OF BRISTOL (1720–1788), calling herself DUCHESS OF KINGSTON ; daughter of Colonel Thomas Chudleigh (d. 1726) ; beautiful, but weak-minded, and illiterate ; befriended by William Pulteney, afterwards earl of Bath ; maid of honour to Augusta, princess of Wales, at Leicester House, 1743 ; courted by James, duke of Hamilton, a minor, 1744 ; married, secretly, Augustus John Hervey, lieutenant in the navy, brother of the second Earl of Bristol, 1744 ; concealed birth and death of a son, November 1747 ; obtained separation from her husband ; carried on flirtations with George II ; privately took means to establish the fact of her marriage, 1759 ; appeared openly as concubine of Evelyn Pierrepoint, second duke of Kingston, 1760 ;

visited Berlin and Dresden, as ' Madame Chudleigh,' 1765 ; denied the marriage with Hervey, on oath, February 1769, after her husband threatened (1768) a trial for divorce ; being legally declared a spinster, she married the Duke of Kingston, 8 March ; left heiress of the duke's property, September 1773 ; went to Rome ; accused of bigamy by the Duke of Kingston's nephew, 1774 ; quarrelled with Samuel Foote, August 1775 ; found guilty of bigamy by the peers, 1776 ; withdrew to Calais ; her marriage with Hervey, who in 1775 became third Earl of Bristol (d. 1779), declared valid, 1777 ; visited the czarina Catherine, 1777 ; visited Rome and other capitals ; died at Paris.   [x. 298]

CHUDLEIGH, Sir GEORGE (d. 1657), parliamentarian commander ; M.P. for St. Michael, Cornwall, 1601, for Lostwithiel, 1614, 1621, and 1625, and for Tiverton, 1624 ; created baronet, 1622 ; parliamentarian officer in Cornwall, 1643 ; resigned his commission, 1643, after his son James Chudleigh [q. v.] had been accused of treason ; subsequently espoused the royalist cause.   [x. 301]

CHUDLEIGH, JAMES (d. 1643), parliamentarian major-general ; third son of Sir George Chudleigh [q. v.] ; captain in the parliament's army in Yorkshire, 1641 ; sergeant-major-general in Cornwall ; victorious over the royalists, 1643 ; taken prisoner by the royalists, 1643 ; suspected of treachery in the action ; accepted a colonelship in the king's army, May 1643 ; mortally wounded, September 1643.   [x. 302]

CHUDLEIGH, MARY, LADY (1656–1710), authoress ; née Lee ; married Sir George Chudleigh, bart., of Ashton, Devonshire, 1685 ; published verses and essays, 1701–10.   [x. 303]

CHUDLEIGH, THOMAS (fl. 1689), diplomatist ; secretary to the embassy to Sweden, 1673, and to Nimeguen, 1677 ; envoy to Holland, 1678–87 ; converted to Roman catholicism, 1687.   [x. 303]

CHURCH, FREDERICK JOHN (1854–1888), translator of Dante's ' De Monarchia,' 1878 ; eldest son of Richard William Church [q. v.]   [Suppl. ii. 8]

CHURCH, JOHN (1675 ?–1741), musician ; chorister of New College, Oxford ; member of the Chapel Royal, 1697 ; lay vicar of Westminster Abbey, c. 1700 ; published ' Introduction to Psalmody,' 1723.   [x. 303]

CHURCH, RALPH (d. 1787), editor of Spenser's ' Faery Queen,' 1738 ; son of John Church [q. v.] ; M.A. Christ Church, Oxford, 1732 ; vicar of Pyrton and Shirburn, Oxfordshire.   [x. 304]

CHURCH, Sir RICHARD (1784–1873), liberator of Greece ; ensign 13th light infantry, 1800 ; served in Egypt, 1801 ; lieutenant, at Malta, 1803 ; captain of the Corsican rangers, 1806 ; distinguished himself at Capri, 1808, and in the Ionian islands, 1809 ; major, 1809, and colonel, 1812–15, of Greek troops in Ionian islands ; British attaché with the Austrian army, 1815 ; Neapolitan major-general ; suppressed brigandage in Apulia ; defeated by the Sicilian insurgents, 1820 ; K.C.H., 1822 ; generalissimo of the Greek insurgents, 1827 ; defeated, through disobedience of the Greek chief Tzavellas, at Athens ; drove the Turks out of Akarnania, 1827 ; protested against restoring North Greece to Turkey, 1830–2 ; led the Greek revolution, 1843 ; general in the Greek army, 1854 ; lived in retirement at Athens.   [x. 304]

CHURCH, RICHARD WILLIAM (1815–1890), dean of St. Paul's ; born at Lisbon ; lived at Florence, 1818–28 ; B.A. Wadham College, Oxford, 1836 ; fellow of Oriel, 1838–1852 ; formed lasting friendship with Newman ; ordained deacon, 1839 ; junior proctor, 1844 ; one of originators of ' Guardian,' 1845 ; priest, 1852 ; accepted living of Whatley, 1852 ; select preacher at Oxford, 1868, 1876–8, and 1881–2 ; dean of St. Paul's, 1871–90 ; leading member of the high church party. A contributor to the ' English Men of Letters ' series, and author of a ' History of the Oxford Movement ' (posthumously published, 1891).   [Suppl. ii. 6]

CHURCH, THOMAS (1707–1756), controversialist ; M.A. Brasenose College, Oxford, 1731 ; D.D., 1749 ; vicar of Battersea, 1740–56 ; prebendary of St. Paul's, 1744 ; wrote against deism and methodism.   [x. 305]

CHURCHER, RICHARD (1659–1723), founder of ' Churcher's College ' at Petersfield, Hampshire, for naval cadets of the East India Company; apprenticed to a London barber-surgeon, 1675–82 ; in the East India Company's service ; settled at Petersfield.   [x. 306]

CHURCHEY, WALTER (1741-1805), methodist ; attorney of Brecon ; corresponded with John Wesley, 1771 ; wrote religious verse, 1789–1804.   [x. 306]

CHURCHILL, ALFRED B. (1825–1870), journalist; born at Constantinople ; proprietor of the Turkish semi-official journal, the ' Jeride Hawades ' ; published Turkish books ; visited England, 1867.   [x. 306]

CHURCHILL, ARABELLA (1648–1730), mistress of James II ; eldest daughter of Sir Winston Churchill [q. v.] ; maid of honour to Anne, duchess of York, c. 1665 ; intrigued with James, from 1668, by whom she had two sons and two daughters ; pensioned ; married Colonel Charles Godfrey.   [x. 307]

CHURCHILL, AWNSHAM (d. 1728), bookseller and publisher in partnership with his brother John at the ' Black Swan,' London, from 1665 ; bought estates in Dorset ; M.P., Dorchester, 1705–10.   [x. 307]

CHURCHILL, CHARLES (1656–1714), general; younger son of Sir Winston Churchill [q. v.] ; of the household of Christian V of Denmark, and of Prince George of Denmark ; served in Ireland, 1690 ; fought at Landen, 1693, and Blenheim, 1704 ; major-general, 1694 ; lieutenant-general, 1702 ; M.P., Weymouth, 1701–10; governor of Guernsey, 1706–10 ; general, 1707. [x. 308]

CHURCHILL, CHARLES (1731–1764), satirist ; son of a Westminster curate ; at Westminster School, 1739–1748 ; curate in Somerset, 1754 ; curate at Rainham, Essex, 1756 ; curate of St. John's, Westminster, 1758–63, in succession to his father ; separated from his wife, 1761 ; became famous by his ' Rosciad ' and ' Apology,' 1761 ; attached himself to John Wilkes ; satirised authors and politicians, 1762–4 ; died at Boulogne ; his collected works published, 1763–4.   [x. 309]

CHURCHILL, FLEETWOOD (1808–1878), obstetrician ; apprenticed to a Nottingham physician, 1822 ; studied in London, Dublin, Paris, and Edinburgh : M.D. Edinburgh, 1831 ; practitioner in Dublin ; lectured on obstetrics, 1856–64; wrote on midwifery ; a strong supporter of the episcopal church in Ireland. [x. 313]

CHURCHILL, GEORGE (1654 - 1710), admiral ; younger son of Sir Winston Churchill [q. v.] ; naval volunteer, 1666 ; lieutenant, 1672–4 ; in command of a ship, 1678–88; made haste to join the Prince of Orange ; fought at Beachy Head, 1690, and Barfleur, 1692 ; left the service, 1693 ; commissioner of the admiralty, 1699–1702 ; rear-admiral, 1701 ; admiral of the blue, 1702 ; actual manager of naval affairs, though the naval administration was conducted in the name of Prince George of Denmark, 1702–8; rendered odious by his rapacity and incompetence ; M.P. for St. Albans, 1700–8, and later for Portsmouth.   [x. 313]

CHURCHILL, SIR JOHN (d. 1685), master of the rolls ; barrister of Lincoln's Inn, 1647 ; practised in chancery ; possibly M.P., 1661–79 ; knighted, 1670 ; censured by the Commons for appearing as senior counsel against a member, 1675 ; recorder of Bristol, 1683 ; master of the rolls, 1685 ; M.P., Bristol, 1685.   [x. 314]

CHURCHILL, JOHN, first DUKE OF MARLBOROUGH (1650–1722), eldest surviving son of Sir Winston Churchill [q. v.] ; educated at St. Paul's School ; favourite of the Duchess of Cleveland ; page to James, duke of York ; and afterwards his confidential servant; ensign in the foot guards, September 1667 ; served at Tangiers ; captain of foot, 1672 ; served in Flanders, 1672–7; colonel in French service, 1674 ; colonel of foot, February, 1678 ; married, 1678, Sarah Jennings [see CHURCHILL, SARAH] ; envoy to the Prince of Orange and offered to serve under him, 1678 ; accompanied the Duke of York to Holland, 1679, and to Scotland, 1679–82, acting as agent between the duke and Charles II ; created Baron Churchill of Aymouth in the Scottish peerage, 1682 ; colonel of the 1st dragoons, 1683 ; envoy to Louis XIV, 1685 ; created Baron Churchill of Sandridge in the English peerage, 1685 ; chief instrument in crushing Monmouth's rebellion, July 1685 ; major-general and colonel of the 3rd horse guards, 1685 ; lieutenant-general, 1688 ; entered into negotiations with the Prince of Orange, 1687, and expressed readiness to support him, August 1688 ; vowed fidelity to James II, November 1688; in command at Salisbury ; went over to the Prince of Orange, 24 Nov. 1688; employed in quieting

the troops ; openly voted for a regency, but privately induced the Princess Anne to consent that William of Orange should reign over England for life ; created Earl of Marlborough, 1689 ; commanded the English troops in Flanders, 1689 ; commander-in-chief in England, 1690 ; captured Cork and Kinsale, 1690 ; accompanied William III to Flanders, 1691 ; opened negotiations with James II, 1691 ; persuaded Princess Anne to write to her father, 1691 ; intrigued with the army ; dismissed from his offices, 1692 ; imprisoned in the Tower for two months, 1692 ; revenged himself by causing the failure of the Brest expedition, 1694 ; his overtures to William III rejected, 1694 ; voted with the extreme tories in the Lords ; voted for Sir John Fenwick's [q. v.] attainder, 1696 ; received back into favour, 1698 ; governor of the Duke of Gloucester (d. 1700), 1698 ; restored to his commands ; continued to vote with the tories, 1701 ; accompanied William III to Holland, July 1701 ; came into power on Anne's accession, 1702 ; K.G., 1702 ; captain-general of the forces, 1702–11 ; master-general of the ordnance, 1702–11 ; procured declaration of war with France, 1702 ; commander of the forces in Holland : delayed by the supineness of his allies ; crossed the Meuse, July 1702 ; took Venloo, September, and Rüremonde and Liège, October 1702 ; created Duke of Marlborough, December 1702 ; continued to vote with the tories ; lost his only son, February 1703 ; opened his next campaign by taking Bonn, 1703 ; his plans thwarted by the incompetency or treachery of the Dutch generals ; took Limburg, September 1703 ; opposed by the extreme tories ; obtained their dismissal from office, but failed to conciliate the whigs ; persuaded the Dutch to assent to a campaign on the Moselle, 1704 ; transferred his army to Bavaria ; joined Prince Eugene, June 1704 ; forced the Schellenberg, 2 July ; crushed the French and Bavarians at Blenheim, 13 Aug. 1704 ; arranged for a campaign on the Moselle in 1705 ; visited Berlin ; created Prince of Mindelheim by the emperor (November 1705) ; voted Woodstock Manor and Blenheim Palace by parliament ; failed to persuade the Dutch and Germans to support his favourite plan of invading France by the Moselle, April-June, 1705 ; invaded Brabant, July 1705 ; again thwarted by the Dutch general, Slangenberg ; visited Vienna, Berlin, and Hanover in order to pacify the allies ; opposed at home by the extreme tories ; failed to persuade the Dutch to undertake a campaign in Italy, April 1706 ; crushed the French at Ramillies, May 1706 ; occupied Brussels, Antwerp, Ostend, and other fortresses, May–October 1706 ; confronted by great jealousy between the Dutch and the emperor, which was fomented by Louis XIV's overtures; weakened by the growing influence of the whigs at home; began to lose Anne's good will ; pensioned by parliament ; visited the Elector of Hanover, Charles XII of Sweden, and the king of Prussia, 1707 ; deserted by the emperor, who sought to secure Naples by a separate treaty with France : unable to take the field effectually ; became involved in the bitter party strife between the whig and tory leaders, and forced Anne to dismiss Harley, 1708 ; provided for defence against the Pretender's attempted invasion, 1708 ; delayed by the tardiness of the allies, May 1708 ; crushed the French at Oudenarde, July 1708 ; took Lille and Ghent, December 1708 ; took part in abortive peace negotiations at the Hague, May 1709, missing an opportunity of closing the war on reasonable terms ; took Tournay ; his attack on the French at Malplaquet delayed by the allies, and the victory dearly bought in consequence, 11 Sept. 1709 ; took Mons, October 1709 ; completely lost Anne's personal favour through his duchess's bad temper and his application to be captain-general for life; attended the peace conferences at Gertruydenberg, February 1710 ; perceived that the state of English politics encouraged France to continue the war ; began the campaign in April; took Douay and some minor fortresses, 1710 ; lost favour of Queen Anne, January 1711, soon after the fall of the whig ministry ; went abroad to conduct the campaign, March 1711 ; out-manœuvred Villars, August 1711 ; took Bouchain, 14 Sept. 1711 ; accused of peculation soon after peace had been concluded with France by the tory ministry ; returned to England, November ; dismissed from all his offices, 31 Dec. 1711 ; charges against him dropped by the hostile ministry ; withdrew to the continent, November 1712 ; lost his territory at Mindelheim, 1713 ; active in arranging for the Hanoverian succession, 1714 ; returned to England, August 1714 ; captain-general and master of the ordnance ; had a paralytic stroke and fell into senile decay, 1716.   [x. 315]

CHURCHILL, JOHN SPRIGGS MORSS (1801–1875), medical publisher; apprenticed to a London firm of medical booksellers, 1816–23; bought a business, 1832; gave up the retail trade, 1854; issued medical text-books and journals after 1837. [x. 341]

CHURCHILL, JOHN WINSTON SPENCER, sixth DUKE OF MARLBOROUGH (1822–1883), politician; educated at Eton, 1835–8, and Oxford, 1840; as Marquis of Blandford was M.P., Woodstock, 1844, 1847–57; succeeded to the dukedom, 1857; lord-steward of the household, 1866; lord-lieutenant of Ireland, 1866–80. [x. 341]

CHURCHILL, RANDOLPH HENRY SPENCER, commonly known as LORD RANDOLPH CHURCHILL (1849–1894), statesman; third son of John Winston Spencer Churchill, sixth duke of Marlborough [q. v.]; educated at Eton and Merton College, Oxford; B.A., 1870; conservative M.P. for Woodstock, 1874 and 1880; attracted attention by attack on subordinate members of Disraeli government, 1878; became exponent of a resolute and aggressive toryism, assisted by Sir Henry Drummond Wolff, Mr. (afterwards Sir John) Gorst, and, occasionally, Mr. Arthur Balfour; his followers received nickname of the 'Fourth Party'; supported Charles Bradlaugh [q. v.]; attacked Irish Compensation for Disturbance Bill, and while advocating the policy of conciliation in Irish affairs, strongly opposed any compromise with home rule; fostered conservatism among working classes by promoting, with Mr. Gorst's assistance, the establishment of conservative clubs, and by establishing and popularising the Primrose League; took prominent part in discussion of franchise bill, and by advocating extension of franchise to Ireland, came into antagonism with a section of his own party, but was subsequently officially accepted as one of the party leaders; visited India, 1884. secretary of state for India, 1885–6, during which period the annexation of Burmah was effected; unsuccessfully opposed Bright in central division of Birmingham at election of 1885. and was returned for South Paddington; opposed home rule bill; re-elected for South Paddington, 1886; chancellor of exchequer and leader of House of Commons, 1886; resigned offices, December 1886, being unable to agree with the demands on the public purse made by the ministers for the army and navy; honorary LL.D. Cambridge, 1888; travelled for health and recreation in South Africa, 1891, and contributed series of letters to 'Daily Graphic' (published, 1892, as 'Men, Mines, and Animals in South Africa'); re-elected for South Paddington, 1892; attacked home rule bill and Mr. Asquith's Welsh church bill; died of general paralysis. [Suppl. ii. 9]

CHURCHILL, SARAH, DUCHESS OF MARLBOROUGH (1660–1744), née Jennings; maid of honour to Princess Anne before 1676; married John Churchill (1650–1722) [q. v.], 1678; became Lady Churchill, 1682; lady of the bedchamber to Anne, now princess of Denmark, 1683; acquired an absolute ascendency over Anne's weak mind; helped Anne to escape to Nottingham on the news of James II's resolve to fly, 1688; induced Anne to accept William III as king, 1689; became Countess of Marlborough, 1689; helped Anne to secure a large parliamentary allowance, 1689; pensioned by Anne, 1690; persuaded Anne to open negotiations with her father, December 1691; retained by Anne in defiance of William and Mary, 1692; mistress of the robes and keeper of the privy purse on Queen Anne's accession, 1702 ranger of Windsor Park, 1702; began to lose hold on Anne by her want of tact and violence of temper; introduced, before 1707, her relative, Abigail Hill (Mrs. Masham), to the queen's service, by whom she was ousted; behaved imperiously to Queen Anne, 1707–10; sent in her accounts as keeper of the privy purse, deducting 2,000l. a year as her pension since 1702, 1711; went abroad, 1713; after the duke's death in 1722 plunged into family quarrels and lawsuits; at bitter feud with Sir Robert Walpole; wrote memoirs of her life, published 1742. [x. 316]

CHURCHILL, SIR WINSTON (1620?–1688), politician; educated at Oxford, 1636; impoverished by the civil war; M.P., Plymouth, 1661–8; knighted, 1663; comptroller of the board of green cloth; M.P., Lynn Regis, 1685–7; published 'Divi Britannici,' 1675. [x. 342]

CHURCHYARD, THOMAS (1520?–1604), miscellaneous writer; page to Henry, earl of Surrey; lived a wandering life, partly as a soldier in Scotland, Ireland, France, and the Low Countries, partly as a hanger-on of the court and the nobility; at the siege of Leith, 1560; pensioned by Queen Elizabeth, 1592; published, before 1553, 'A myrrour for man'; between 1560 and 1603 issued a multitude of broadsheets and small volumes in verse and prose, several containing autobiographical pieces and notices of current events; sometimes wrote in the hope of getting a little money for the dedication; his best-known pieces are 'Shore's Wife,' 1563, and 'The Worthines of Wales,' 1587. [x. 343]

CHURTON, EDWARD (1800–1874), theologian; second son of Ralph Churton [q. v.]; educated at Charterhouse and Christ Church, Oxford; M.A., 1824; rector of Crayke, Yorkshire, 1835, and archdeacon of Cleveland, 1846–74; published 'Notes on the Basque Churches' and 'Gongora . . . with translations' (from the Spanish), 1862; wrote poems and works on Anglican theology and church history. [x. 346]

CHURTON, RALPH (1754–1831), biographer; entered Brasenose College, Oxford, 1772; M.A. and fellow, 1778; rector of Middleton Cheney, Northamptonshire, 1792, and archdeacon of St. David's, 1805–31; published sermons and lives of the founders of Brasenose College, of Alexander Nowell, dean of St. Paul's, and others. [x. 347]

CHURTON, WILLIAM RALPH (d. 1828), author; third son of Ralph Churton [q. v.]; fellow of Oriel College, Oxford, 1824; M.A., 1825; his 'Remains' privately printed, 1830. [x. 347]

CHUTE or **CHEWT**, ANTHONY (d. 1595?), poet; attorney's clerk; possibly purser with the Portugal expedition, 1589; attached himself to Gabriel Harvey; published 'Beawtie dishonoured, written under the title of Shore's Wife,' and verses against Thomas Nashe, 1593; satirised by Nashe, 1596. [x. 347]

CHUTE, CHALONER (d. 1659), speaker of the House of Commons; barrister of the Middle Temple; practised in chancery; much employed as royalist counsel, 1641; bought the Vyne, Hampshire, 1653; elected M.P. for Middlesex, 1656, but was excluded; M.P. for Middlesex, 1659; speaker, 27 Jan.–9 March 1659. [x. 348]

CIARAN, SAINT (516–549), of Clonmacnoi; commemorated on 9 Sept.; spelt also Keyran, Kieran, and Quiaranus; son of an Ulster refugee; educated by St. Finnian in Meath; obtained Clonmacnois, 548, and founded the monastery there. [x. 349]

CIARAN, SAINT (fl. 500–560), of Saigir, bishop of Ossory; commemorated on 5 March; born on Clear Island; a hermit in King's County; founded the monastery of Saigir or Seirkieran, near Birr. [x. 350]

CIBBER or **CIBERT**, CAIUS GABRIEL (1630–1700), sculptor; born in Holstein; trained at Rome; brought to England by John Stone; his works include figures for Bethlehem Hospital, 1680, and the phœnix above the south door of St. Paul's. [x. 352]

CIBBER, CHARLOTTE (d. 1760?). [See CHARKE.]

CIBBER, COLLEY (1671–1757), actor and dramatist; son of Caius Gabriel Cibber [q. v.]; educated at Grantham school, 1682–7; served in the Earl of Devonshire's levy for the Prince of Orange, 1688; joined united companies at Theatre Royal, 1690; known as 'Mr. Colley'; played minor parts, 1691; failed in tragedy, but made a good impression in comedy, 1692–4; brought out his first play, 'Love's Last Shift,' 1696; recognised as the leading actor of eccentric characters, 1697–1732; brought out some thirty dramatic pieces, 1697–1748, including several smart comedies · obtained a profitable share in the management of Drury Lane, c. 1711, and held it in spite of the machinations of the tories; brought out 'The Nonjuror,' 1717, a play directed against the Jacobites; fiercely attacked by other writers on his appointment as poet laureate, December 1730; 'retired' from the stage, 1733, but reappeared at intervals till 1745; published an autobiography entitled 'Apology for the Life of Colley Cibber, Comedian,' 1740, two letters to Pope, 1742–4, a poor 'Character . . . of Cicero,' 1747, and some worthless official odes; made by Pope the hero of the 'Dunciad' (1742). The title of the chap-book, 'Colley Cibber's Jests,' 1761, shows his notoriety. [x. 352]

CIBBER, SUSANNAH MARIA (1714–1766), actress; née Arne; well educated; married, 1734, Theophilus Cibber [q. v.]; separated from her husband, 1738; first sang in

opera at the Haymarket, 1732; first appeared in tragedy,
1736; highly esteemed as a vocalist, both in oratorio and
opera; an especial favourite with Handel; failed in
comedy; failed in tragedy till she shook off the old-
fashioned style of declamation; acknowledged as a powerful tragedian, 1744; joined Garrick's company at Drury
Lane, 1753; wrote a comedy, 'The Oracle,' 1752.
[x. 359]

CIBBER, THEOPHILUS (1703-1758), actor and
playwright; son of Colley Cibber [q. v.]; educated at
Winchester; first appeared on the stage, 1721; continued
to act at various London theatres with success, till
death; appeared at Dublin, 1743; published a life of Barton
Booth, 'Dissertations on Theatrical Subjects,' 1756, a few
dramatic pieces, 1730-57, and pamphlets. 'Lives of the
Poets,' 1753, which has Cibber's name on the title-page,
was mainly compiled by Robert Shiels [q. v.]	[x. 362]

CILIAN, SAINT (d. 697), apostle of Franconia; com-
memorated on 8 July; spelt also Kilian, Chillianus,
Cœlianus, and Quillianus; born in Cavan; a bishop in
Ireland; went to Franconia, c. 689; martyred at Würz-
burg.	[x. 363]

CIMELLIAUC (d. 927), bishop of Llandaff; given
estates for the church of Llandaff by Brochmael [q. v.],
king of Gwent; excommunicated Brochmael; taken
prisoner by the vikings, 918, but ransomed by Eadward
the elder; his name spelt in modern Welsh, Cyfeiliawg;
supposed by some to be Saint Cyfelach.	[x. 364]

CIPRIANI, GIOVANNI BATTISTA (1727-1785), historical painter and engraver; born in Florence; went to
Rome, 1750; came to London, 1755; taught drawing,
1758; R.A., 1768; exhibited, 1769-83; a prolific book-
illustrator.	[x. 364]

CIRENCESTER, RICHARD OF (d. 1401?), chronicler; monk of St. Peter's, Westminster, 1355; visited
Jerusalem, 1391; returned to the abbey; compiled 'Speculum Historiale,' 447-1066 A.D.; wrote other works now
lost. Charles Bertram [q. v.] fathered on him a famous
forgery, 'De situ Britanniæ.'	[x. 365]

CLAGETT, NICHOLAS, the elder (1610?-1663),
puritan; entered Merton College, Oxford, 1628; M.A.
Magdalen Hall, 1634; vicar of Melbourne, Derbyshire, c.
1636; preacher at Bury St. Edmunds, 1644-62; published
'The Abuse of God's Grace,' 1659.	[x. 366]

CLAGETT, NICHOLAS, the younger (1654-1727),
controversialist; son of Nicholas Clagett the elder [q. v.];
educated at Norwich and Cambridge; D.D., 1704;
preacher at Bury St. Edmunds, 1680-1727; rector of
Thurlow Parva, Norfolk, 1683; archdeacon of Sudbury,
1693; rector of Hitcham, Suffolk, 1707; published pam-
phlets, 1683-1710.	[x. 366]

CLAGETT, NICHOLAS (d. 1746), bishop of Exeter;
son of Nicholas Clagett the younger [q. v.]; D.D. Cambridge; dean of Rochester, 1724; bishop of St. David's,
1732; translated to Exeter, 1742.	[x. 366]

CLAGETT, WILLIAM (1646-1688), controversialist;
eldest son of Nicholas Clagett the elder [q. v.]; entered
Emmanuel College, Cambridge, 1659; M.A., 1667; D.D.,
1683; preacher at Bury St. Edmund's, 1672-80; preacher
at Gray's Inn, 1680, and at St. Michael Bassishaw, 1686;
rector of Farnham Royal, Buckinghamshire, 1683; published treatises against nonconformity and Romanism,
1680-9. His sermons appeared posthumously, 1689-1720.
[x. 367]

CLAGGET, CHARLES (1740?-1820?), musician; in
the orchestra at the Dublin theatre, c. 1766; came to
London, 1776; patented musical inventions, 1776 and
1788; visited by Haydn, 1792; published pamphlets.
[x. 368]

CLAIRMONT, CLARA MARY JANE (1798-1879),
called herself 'Claire'; daughter, by a former marriage, of
Mary Jane, second wife of William Godwin; accompanied
Mary Godwin, her step-sister (1814). in her elopement with
Shelley; became intimate with Lord Byron, 1816; with the
Shelleys, followed Byron to Switzerland; gave birth to a
daughter, Allegra, at Bath, January 1817; accompanied
the Shelleys to Italy, 1818; ner daughter taken from her
by Byron, 1818, and placed in a convent near Ravenna,
1821; governess in Russia and Italy; resided in Paris and
Florence; embraced Romanism.	[x. 369]

CLANBRASSIL, first BARON (1788-1870). [See
JOCELYN, ROBERT.]

CLANCARTY, fourth EARL OF (1668-1734). [See
MACCARTHY, DONOGH.]

CLANCARTY, second EARL of the second creation,
and first VISCOUNT OF (1767-1837). [See TRENCH, RI-
CHARD LE POER.]

CLANEBOYE, first VISCOUNT (1559-1643). [See
HAMILTON, JAMES.]

CLANNY, WILLIAM REID (1776-1850), inventor
(1812) of a mining safety-lamp; educated in Edinburgh;
M.D., 1803; practitioner at Bishopswearmouth; published
medical tracts.	[x. 370]

CLANRICARDE, fifth EARL OF (1604-1657). [See
BURGH, ULICK DE.]

CLANWILLIAM, third EARL OF (1795-1879). [See
MEADE, RICHARD GEORGE FRANCIS.]

CLAPHAM, DAVID (d. 1551), translator (1542-5) of
Cornelius Agrippa; LL.B. Cambridge, 1533; practised at
Doctors' Commons.	[x. 371]

CLAPHAM, HENOCH (fl. 1600), theological writer;
pastor of an English congregation at Amsterdam, 1595-8;
pastor in London, 1603; imprisoned, 1603-5; possibly
vicar of Northbourne, Kent, 1607; published devotional
and doctrinal treatises, 1595-7, tracts against schismatics,
1600-9, and tracts on the plague of 1603, 1603-4.
[x. 371]

CLAPHAM, SAMUEL (1755-1830), divine; M.A. Cambridge, 1784; vicar of Great Ouseburn, Yorkshire, 1797;
vicar of Christ Church, Hampshire, 1802; rector of Gus-
sage St. Michael, Dorset, 1806; published sermons and mis-
cellaneous works.	[x. 372]

CLAPOLE, RICHARD (fl. 1286). [See CLAPWELL.]

CLAPPERTON, HUGH (1788-1827), African explorer;
cabin-boy, 1801; pressed for the navy; midshipman;
served in the East Indies, 1808-13, and in Canada, 1814-
1817; placed on half-pay; travelled in Nigeria, 1822-5;
commander R.N., 1825; travelled again in Nigeria, 1825-
1827; died near Sokota. Accounts of his travels were
published by his companions Dixon Denham, 1826, and
Richard Lander, 1830.	[x. 372]

CLAPWELL or **KNAPWELL**, RICHARD (fl. 1286),
Dominican; spelt also 'Clapole'; D.D. Oxford; wrote
on scholastic theology; condemned for heresy by Franciscan primate (Peckham), 1286, and Franciscan pope
(Nicholas IV), 1288; withdrew to Bologna.	[x. 374]

CLARE, EARLS OF. [See CLARE, RICHARD DE, first
EARL, d. 1090?; CLARE, GILBERT DE, second EARL, d.
1115?; CLARE, RICHARD DE, third EARL, d. 1136?;
CLARE, ROGER DE, fifth EARL, d. 1173; CLARE, GILBERT
DE, seventh EARL, d. 1230; CLARE, RICHARD DE, eighth
EARL, 1222-1262; CLARE, GILBERT DE, ninth EARL, 1243-
1295; CLARE, GILBERT DE, tenth EARL, 1291-1314;
HOLLES, JOHN, first EARL of the second creation, 1564?-
1637; HOLLES, JOHN, second EARL, 1595-1666; HOLLES,
GILBERT, third EARL, 1633-1689; HOLLES, JOHN, fourth
EARL, 1662-1711; PELHAM-HOLLES, THOMAS, first EARL
of the third creation, 1693-1768; FITZGIBBON, JOHN, first
EARL of the fourth creation, 1749-1802.]

CLARE, VISCOUNTS. [See O'BRIEN, DANIEL, first
VISCOUNT, 1577?-1663; O'BRIEN, DANIEL, third VIS-
COUNT, d. 1690; O'BRIEN, CHARLES, fifth VISCOUNT, d.
1706; O'BRIEN, CHARLES, sixth VISCOUNT, 1699-1761.]

CLARE, DE, FAMILY OF; took its name from the
manor of Clare, Suffolk; founded by Richard de Clare
(d. 1090?) [q. v.], who followed the Conqueror to Eng-
land, and was son of Gilbert (d. 1039), count of Eu or
Brionne, and grandson of Godfrey, a bastard of Richard
(d. 996) 'the Fearless,' duke of Normandy. Richard's son,
Gilbert de Clare (d. 1115?), [q. v.], conquered lands in
Wales. From him, by his elder son, descended the Earls
of Hertford or Clare, and by his younger son the Earls of
Pembroke or Strigul. The house attained its zenith in
Gilbert de Clare (d. 1230) [q. v.] The male line ended in
Gilbert de Clare, tenth earl [q. v.] The dukedom of
'Clarence' created 1362, when the tenth Earl's grand-
niece married Edward III's third son Lionel [q. v.]
[x. 375]

CLARE, ELIZABETH DE (1291 ?-1360), third daughter of Gilbert de Clare, ninth earl (1243-1295) [q. v.]; born at Acre; married (1) John de Burgh (d. 1313), son of Richard, second earl of Ulster; (2) Theobald, baron Verdon (d. 1316); (3) Robert (or Roger), baron Damory (d. 1321); became (1314), on the death of her brother Gilbert de Clare, tenth earl [q. v.], Lady of Clare; endowed, 1336, University Hall, Cambridge (afterwards called Clare Hall or College), and gave it a body of statutes, 1359.   [x. 376]

CLARE, GILBERT DE (d. 1115 ?), baronial leader; son of Richard de Clare (d. 1090 ?) [q. v.]; tried to hold Tunbridge Castle against Rufus, 1088; in attendance on Rufus, 1100, and on Henry I, 1101; conquered Cardigan, 1107 or 1111.   [x. 377]

CLARE, GILBERT DE, seventh EARL OF CLARE, fifth EARL OF HERTFORD, and sixth EARL OF GLOUCESTER (d. 1230), among the twenty-five barons appointed to carry out Magna Charta, 1215; excommunicated by Innocent III, 1216; succeeded his father in the earldom of Hertford, c. 1217; inherited, through his mother, the earldom of Gloucester, 1217; fought against the Welsh, 1228; attended Henry III to Brittany, 1230.   [x. 378]

CLARE, GILBERT DE, called the 'Red,' ninth EARL OF CLARE, seventh EARL OF HERTFORD, and eighth EARL OF GLOUCESTER (1243-1295), son of Richard de Clare, eighth earl [q. v.]; married Alice, niece of Henry III, 1253; succeeded to the earldoms, July 1262; refused the oath of allegiance to Prince Edward, 1263; acted with Simon de Montfort, 1263; was reconciled to Henry III, October 1263; in arms against Henry; massacred the Jews of Canterbury, 1264; commanded the centre at Lewes, 1264; quarrelled with De Montfort, November 1264; protected the banished marcher lords; fled to the Welsh marches, 1265; joined Prince Edward, and prevented De Montfort from crossing the Severn; commanded division at Evesham, August 1265; joined Prince Edward in reducing the Cinque ports, 1266; pleaded for the disinherited barons, 266; refused to attend parliament, January 1267; took London, 1267, but was reconciled to Henry III two months afterwards; took the cross, 1268; obtained the restoration of their lands to the disinherited barons, 1271; proclaimed Edward I, November 1272; divorced his first wife, 1271 (or 1285); fought against the Welsh, 1276-1283; married Joan, daughter of Edward I, 1290; took the cross, 1290; imprisoned for making private war, 1291; driven out of Wales by a native rising, 1294.   [x. 378]

CLARE, GILBERT DE, tenth EARL OF CLARE, eighth EARL OF HERTFORD, and ninth EARL OF GLOUCESTER (1291-1314), son of Gilbert de Clare, ninth earl [q. v.]; ward of Ralph de Monthermer, 1296; companion of Edward II; served in Scotland, 1306; summoned to parliament, 1308; commanded the English forces in Scotland, 1309; adhered to Edward II in his dispute with Lancaster, 1310; mediated between Edward II and Lancaster, 1313; killed at Bannockburn, 1314.   [x. 382]

CLARE, JOHN (1577-1628), reputed author of a Romanist tract ('The Converted Jew'), published 1630; born in Wiltshire; jesuit, 1605; tutor at Louvain and Rome; became rector of the jesuits in Wales before 1628.   [x. 383]

CLARE, JOHN (1793-1864), poet; son of a Northamptonshire labourer; a herd-boy; attended night-schools; under-gardener; read Thomson's 'Seasons,' 1808; wrote songs; kept dissolute company; militiaman at Oundle, 1812; a vagrant; issued proposal to print his poems, 1817; published his first volume, 1820; visited London, 1820, 1822, 1824, 1828; failed as a farmer, 1827 and 1831; in constant poverty, although holding annuities of 45l. a year; became imbecile, 1837; published 'Poems . . . of Rural Life,' 1820, 'The Village Minstrel,' 1821, 'Shepherd's Calendar,' 1827, and 'The Rural Muse,' 1835.   [x. 384]

CLARE, OSBERT DE (fl. 1136), hagiologist; monk of Westminster; banished from the monastery, c. 1129-1133; elected prior, 1136; sent to Rome to advocate canonisation of Edward the Confessor, 1141; again expelled from the monastery; wrote lives of Saints Eadmund, Æthelberht, Eadburh, and Edward the Confessor; a volume of his letters published, 1846. [x. 386]

CLARE, PETER (1738-1786), London surgeon; published medical tracts, 1778-80.   [x. 388]

CLARE, SIR RALPH (1587-1670), royalist; fought at Worcester, 1642 and 1651; impoverished by the civil war; opponent of Richard Baxter.   [x. 388]

CLARE, RICHARD DE (d. 1090 ?), founder of the family of de Clare [q. v.]; known as Richard FitzGilbert or Richard of Tonbridge; received estates in Suffolk and Kent; chief justiciar, 1075; in attendance on William I, 1080-1.   [x. 389]

CLARE, RICHARD DE (d. 1136 ?), son of Gilbert de Clare (d. 1115 ?) [q. v.]; perhaps the first to use the surname of Clare; possibly created Earl of Hertford; killed by the Welsh; founded Tonbridge Priory. [x. 389]

CLARE, RICHARD DE, or RICHARD STRONGBOW, second EARL OF PEMBROKE AND STRIGUL (d. 1176), succeeded to the estates, 1148; signed the treaty of Westminster, 1153; allowed to retain the title (one of Stephen's creations); said to have lost his estates, c. 1167; escorted Princess Matilda to Germany, 1168; induced by the dethroned Dermot [see MACMURCHADA, DIARMID] to intervene in Leinster, 1168; stormed Waterford, 1170; married Eva, eldest daughter of Dermot; reached Dublin, September; invaded Meath and wintered at Waterford; tried to soothe Henry II's jealousy by offering him his Irish conquests, 1171; confronted by an Irish rising on Dermot's death, 1171; defeated Roderic O'Connor at Dublin, July 1171; put to death Murrough O'Brien; forced to surrender his castles and seaports to Henry II; kept court at Kildare, while King Henry was marching through Ireland, 1171-2; summoned to Normandy to aid King Henry, 1173; granted Wexford, Waterford, and Dublin; defeated in Munster, 1174; held hostages from all the great Irish princes, 1175; according to legend slew his son for cowardice.   [x. 390]

CLARE, RICHARD DE, eighth EARL OF CLARE, sixth EARL OF HERTFORD, and seventh EARL OF GLOUCESTER (1222-1262), son of Gilbert de Clare, seventh earl [q. v.]; succeeded, while still a minor, 1230; obtained possession of his Glamorgan estates, 1240; defeated by the Welsh, 1244; went on pilgrimage, 1249; visited the pope at Lyons, 1250; refused to join Henry III's expedition to Gascony, 1253; envoy to Scotland, 1255, and to Germany, 1256; defeated by the Welsh, 1257; joined Simon de Montfort against the king, 1258; quarrelled with De Montfort, 1259; in friendly attendance on the king, 1259-61; quarrelled with Prince Edward, 1261.   [x. 393]

CLARE, ROGER DE, fifth EARL OF CLARE and third EARL OF HERTFORD (d. 1173), younger son of Richard de Clare (d. 1136 ?), [q. v.]; succeeded his brother Gilbert in the title and estates, 1152; signed treaty of Westminster, 1153; conquered part of Cardigan, 1157; defeated by Rhys ap Gruffudd, c. 1159; in France, 1160-1; refused Archbishop Becket's claim for homage for Tonbridge Castle, 1163; again defeated by Rhys, 1163; in France, 1171.   [x. 396]

CLARE, WALTER DE (d. 1138 ?), founder of Tintern Abbey, a monastery for Cistercians, 1131.   [x. 397]

CLAREMBALD (fl. 1161), secular priest; made abbot of St. Augustine's, Canterbury, by Henry II, 1161; removed by the pope, 1176; a justiciar, 1170.   [x. 397]

CLARENCE, DUKES OF. [See LIONEL, 1338-1368; THOMAS, 1388 ?-1421; GEORGE, 1449-1478; WILLIAM IV, 1765-1837.]

CLARENCE AND AVONDALE, DUKE OF (1864-1892). [See ALBERT VICTOR.]

CLARENDON, EARLS OF. [See HYDE, EDWARD, first EARL, 1609-1674; HYDE, HENRY, second EARL, 1638-1700; VILLIERS, THOMAS, first EARL of the second creation, 1709-1786; VILLIERS, JOHN CHARLES, third EARL, 1757-1838; VILLIERS, GEORGE WILLIAM FREDERICK, fourth EARL, 1800-1870.]

CLARENDON, SIR ROGER (d. 1402), reputed bastard son of the Black Prince; hanged by Henry IV as being a possible pretender.   [x. 398]

CLARGES, SIR THOMAS (d. 1695), politician; styled M.D.; brother-in-law of George Monck, 1654; sat as a Scottish member in the Commonwealth parliaments, 1656 and 1658; intermediary between Monck and the Commonwealth leaders; muster-master general, 1660; conveyed to Charles II the invitation of parliament to return, May 1660; knighted; M.P. for Westminster, 1660, for Southwark, 1666, for Christchurch, 1679–85, and for Oxford University, 1689, 1690. [x. 398]

CLARIBEL (pseudonym). [See BARNARD, CHARLOTTE ALINGTON, 1830–1869.]

CLARIDGE, RICHARD (1649–1723), quaker minister; B.A. Oxford, 1670; M.A., 1677; rector of Peopleton, Worcestershire, 1673–91; preacher in Oxford, 1692; baptist preacher and schoolmaster in London, 1692; joined the quakers, 1696; quaker minister, 1697; schoolmaster at Barking, 1702, and at Tottenham, 1707–23; published political and controversial tracts, 1689–1714; author of other works, which appeared posthumously. [x. 399]

CLARINA, BARON (1719–1804). [See MASSEY, EYRE.]

CLARIS, JOHN CHALK (1797?–1866), journalist; educated at Canterbury; edited the 'Kent Herald,' 1826–65; published poems, 1816–22, under the name ARTHUR BROOKE. [x. 400]

CLARK. [See also CLARKE, CLERK, and CLERKE.]

CLARK, SIR ANDREW (1826–1893), physician; apprenticed in Dundee; studied at Edinburgh; M.R.C.S. England, 1844; joined naval medical service, 1846; M.R.C.P. London, and M.D. Aberdeen, 1854; F.R.C.P., 1858; Croonian lecturer, 1868; Lumleian lecturer, 1885, and president, 1888 till death; physician to London Hospital, 1866–86; created baronet, 1833; F.R.S., 1885. [Suppl. ii. 23]

CLARK, CHARLES (1806–1880), proprietor of the Great Totham press; farmer at Great Totham; printed a 'History of Great Totham,' 1831, and many satirical broadsides; issued reprints of scarce tracts; withdrew to Heybridge, Essex, before 1859. [x. 400]

CLARK, EDWIN (1814–1894), engineer; brother of Josiah Latimer Clark [q. v.]; superintending engineer of Menai Straits bridge; engineer to Electric and International Telegraph Company, 1850; M.I.C.E., 1850; patented various electric and hydraulic appliances. [Suppl. ii. 26]

CLARK, FREDERICK SCOTSON (1840–1883), organist; organist and music master in London, 1854–1865; organist of Exeter College, Oxford, 1865; Mus. Bac., 1867; Anglican chaplain abroad; organ-master in London, 1875, 1880; composed slight pieces. [x. 400]

CLARK, GEORGE AITKEN (1823–1873), manufacturer and philanthropist; threadmaker in Paisley and America; benefactor of Glasgow University and of Paisley. [x. 401]

CLARK, GEORGE THOMAS (1809–1898), engineer and archæologist; educated at Charterhouse; employed under Brunel on Great Western Railway; engaged on sewerage, salt, and railway works in India, 1843; on board of health; trustee of Dowlais estate and ironworks under will of Sir Josiah John Guest [q. v.], 1852, and administrator of the Dowlais undertakings till 1897; assisted (Sir) Henry Bessemer [q. v.] to perfect his process of steel manufacture; first president of British Iron Trade Association, 1876; sheriff of Glamorganshire, 1868; assisted in founding Archæological Association (now Royal Archæological Institute), 1843. His works include: 'Mediæval Military Architecture in England,' 1884; and contributions to the history of Glamorganshire. [Suppl. ii. 24]

CLARK, JAMES (d. 1819), physician in Dominica; afterwards in London; published a memoir on 'Yellow Fever,' 1797; contributed to scientific journals. [x. 401]

CLARK, SIR JAMES (1788–1870), physician; M.A. Aberdeen; lawyer's clerk; naval surgeon, 1809–15; M.D. Edinburgh, 1817; practitioner in Rome, 1819–26, and in London, 1826–60; court physician; created baronet, 1837; unpopular in consequence of his connection with the case of Lady Flora Hastings [q. v.]; published medical papers, 1817–42. [x. 401]

CLARK, JEREMIAH (d. 1809), organist; chorister of Worcester Cathedral; music teacher in Birmingham, c. 1770; Mus. Bac.; organist of Worcester Cathedral, 1806; published music. [x. 402]

CLARK, JOHN (1688–1736), writing-master of London; published books on penmanship and book-keeping, 1708–32. [x. 403]

CLARK, JOHN (1744–1805), medical philanthropist; studied medicine at Edinburgh; surgeon in the East India Company's service, 1768–75; M.D. St. Andrews; practitioner at Newcastle; founded the Newcastle Dispensary; wrote on medical subjects. [x. 403]

CLARK, JOHN (d. 1807), Gaelic scholar; land agent in Wales; wrote on the Ossianic controversy, 1781; published (1778) what purported to be translations of highland poems. [x. 403]

CLARK, JOHN (d. 1879). [See CLARKE, JOHN.]

CLARK, JOSEPH (d. 1696?), posture-master, of London; nicknamed 'Proteus Clark.' [x. 403]

CLARK, JOSIAH LATIMER (1822–1898), engineer; assistant engineer of Menai Straits bridge, 1848; chief engineer, Electric and International Telegraph Company, 1860–70; M.I.C.E., 1861; in partnership with Sir Charles Tilston Bright [q. v.], 1861–8; formed, 1868, with Henry Charles Forde (1827–1897), firm of Clark, Forde & Taylor, which engaged in cable laying in various parts of the world; joined partnership with John Standfield as hydraulic and canal engineer, 1874; F.R.S., 1889; F.R.G.S.; F.R.A.S.; patented electrical and other inventions; published works relating to engineering. [Suppl. ii. 26]

CLARK, RICHARD (1739–1831), attorney, of London; alderman, 1776–98; sheriff, 1777; lord mayor, 1784; city chamberlain, 1798–1831. [x. 404]

CLARK, RICHARD (1780–1856), musician; chorister of St. George's Chapel, Windsor; choirman of St. George's and Eton College, 1802–11, of the Chapel Royal, 1820, of St. Paul's, 1827, and Westminster, 1828; wrote on musical topics. [x. 404]

CLARK, SAMUEL (1810–1875), promoter of education; son of a quaker basket-maker of Southampton; self-taught; partner in Darton & Clark's publishing firm, London, 1836–43; edited 'Peter Parley's Annuals'; M.A. Magdalen Hall, Oxford, 1846; vice-principal of Chelsea Training College, 1846–50; principal of Battersea Training College, 1851–63; vicar of Bredwardine, Herefordshire, 1863–71; rector of Eaton Bishop, 1871–5; published maps. [x. 405]

CLARK, THOMAS (d. 1792), presbyterian divine; educated at Glasgow University; licentiate of the secession church, 1748; preacher and medical practitioner in Ulster, 1749; emigrated to America, 1764; published controversial tracts, 1751–5. [x. 406]

CLARK, THOMAS (1801–1867), chemist; employed in the St. Rollox chemical works; M.D. Glasgow, 1831; professor of chemistry, Aberdeen, 1833–60; inventor of the soap-test for discovering hardness of water and of a process for softening chalk waters. [x. 407]

CLARK, THOMAS (1820–1876), Scottish landscape painter; studied art at Edinburgh; exhibited, 1840. [x. 408]

CLARK, WILLIAM (d. 1603), Roman catholic priest; educated at Douay, 1587, and Rome, 1589; sent on the English mission, 1592; imprisoned in Southwark, 1602; executed, 1603. [x. 408]

CLARK, WILLIAM (1698–1780?), physician; M.D. Leyden; practitioner in London, and, 1747–72, at Bradford, Wiltshire; wrote on midwifery. [x. 409]

CLARK, WILLIAM (1788–1869), anatomist; son of John Clark (1744–1805) [q. v.]; B.A. Trinity College, Cambridge, 1808; fellow, 1809–27; studied medicine in London; friend of Lord Byron; professor of anatomy, Cambridge, 1817–66; travelled, 1818–20; M.D., 1827; rector of Guiseley, Yorkshire, 1826–59; wrote on science. [x. 409]

CLARK, WILLIAM (1821–1880), civil engineer; in partnership in London, 1851; engineer in Calcutta, 1855–1874; planned the drainage of Madras, 1874, and of several Australian towns, 1876–8. [x. 410]

CLARK, WILLIAM GEORGE (1821–1878), Shakespearean scholar; educated at Shrewsbury; fellow of Trinity College, Cambridge, 1844, till death; public orator, 1857–70; joint-editor of the 'Cambridge Shakespeare,' 1863–6; published notes of travel, sermons and essays; endowed Clark lectureship in English literature at Trinity College, Cambridge. [x. 410]

CLARK, WILLIAM TIERNEY (1783–1852), civil engineer ; millwright at Bristol ; mechanic in foundry at Coalbrookdale ; engineer to the West Middlesex Waterworks ; designed suspension bridges ; F.R.S., 1837. [x. 411]

CLARK-KENNEDY, JOHN (1817–1867), colonel ; cornet, 1833 ; captain, 1841 ; served in China, 1842, 1847, in the Sikh war, 1848–9, and in the Crimea, 1854–5 ; commandant of the military train, 1862 ; died at Cairo. [x. 412]

CLARKE. [See also CLARK, CLERK, CLERKE.]

CLARKE, ADAM (1762 ?–1832), theologian ; educated at Kingswood school, near Bristol ; a methodist, 1778 ; preacher on the Wiltshire circuit, 1782 ; lived near London from 1805 ; LL.D. Aberdeen, 1808 ; published bibliographical works, 1803–6, and a scriptural commentary, 1810–26 ; began to edit Rymer's 'Fœdera,' 1818 ; his miscellaneous works printed, 1836. [x. 413]

CLARKE, ALURED (1696–1742), dean of Exeter ; educated at St. Paul's School, 1712–19 ; entered Corpus Christi College, Cambridge, 1713 ; fellow, 1718 ; M.A., 1720 ; D.D., 1728 ; rector of Chilbolton, Hampshire, 1723 ; prebendary of Winchester, 1723, and Westminster, 1731 ; dean of Exeter, 1741 ; published sermons. [x. 414]

CLARKE, SIR ALURED (1745 ?–1832), field-marshal ; lieutenant, 1760 ; served in Germany ; captain, 1767 ; lieutenant-colonel, 1775 ; served in America and West Indies, 1776–94 ; major-general ; served at the Cape, 1795 ; K.B., 1797 ; commander-in-chief in Bengal, 1797, and in India, 1798–1801 ; field-marshal, 1830. [x. 415]

CLARKE, CHARLES (d. 1750), judge ; barrister of Lincoln's Inn, 1723 ; recorder of Huntingdon, 1731 ; M.P., Huntingdonshire, 1739 ; M.P., Whitchurch, 1741 ; baron of the exchequer, 1743. [x. 416]

CLARKE, CHARLES (d. 1767), antiquary ; of Balliol College, Oxford, 1736 ; F.S.A., 1752. [x. 417]

CLARKE, CHARLES (d. 1840), antiquary ; clerk in the ordnance office, 1783–1807 ; F.S.A., 1796 ; wrote on architectural subjects. [x. 417]

CLARKE, CHARLES COWDEN- (1787–1877), author ; friend of John Keats ; resided at Ramsgate, 1810 ; publisher in London, 1820 ; lectured on Shakespeare and parts of European literature, 1834–56 ; withdrew to Nice, 1856, and to Genoa, 1861. His wife, Mrs. Mary Victoria Cowden-Clarke [q. v.], was also an author. [x. 418]

CLARKE, SIR CHARLES MANSFIELD (1782–1857), accoucheur ; educated at St. Paul's School, St. George's Hospital, and the Hunterian School of Medicine ; lecturer on midwifery, 1804–21 ; M.D. Lambeth, 1827 ; created baronet, 1831 ; published medical treatises. [x. 419]

CLARKE, CUTHBERT (fl. 1777), writer on agriculture and mechanics. [x. 420]

CLARKE, EDWARD (d. 1630), diplomatist ; sent by Charles I to Madrid, 1623, Germany, 1627, and Rochelle, 1628. [x. 420]

CLARKE, EDWARD (1730–1786), traveller ; son of William Clarke (1696–1771) [q. v.] ; M.A. St. John's College, Cambridge, 1755 ; rector of Peperharow, Surrey, 1758 ; embassy chaplain at Madrid, 1760 ; chaplain at Minorca, 1763–8 ; vicar of Willingdon and rector of Buxted, Sussex, 1769 ; published 'Letters on Spain,' 1763, and other works. [x. 420]

CLARKE, EDWARD DANIEL (1769–1822), traveller ; second son of Edward Clarke (1730–1786) [q. v.] ; educated at Tonbridge ; entered Jesus College, Cambridge, 1786 ; fellow ; M.A., 1794 ; LL.D., 1803 ; travelled as tutor in Great Britain, 1790, Italy, 1792, Germany, 1794, Wales, 1794, Scotland, 1797, Northern Europe, 1799, Southern Russia, 1800, and Asia Minor, Palestine, Greece, 1801 ; collected minerals, coins, manuscripts, and marbles ; presented his Greek statues to Cambridge University, 1803 ; rector of Harlton, Cambridgeshire, 1805, and of Yeldham, Essex, 1809–22 ; sold his manuscripts to the Bodleian, 1808 ; professor of mineralogy, Cambridge, 1808 ; university librarian, 1817 ; 'Travels,' published 1810–23 ; wrote on minerals and Greek antiquities. [x. 421]

CLARKE, EDWARD GOODMAN (fl. 1812), physician ; army officer in West Indies ; M.D. Aberdeen, 1791 ; army physician ; wrote medical treatises. [x. 424]

CLARKE, GEORGE (1661–1736), politician and virtuoso ; son of Sir William Clarke (1623 ?–1666) [q. v.] ; B.A. Oxford, 1679 ; fellow of All Souls', 1680–1736 ; D.C.L., 1708 ; M.P. for Oxford University, 1685, for East Looe, 1705, and for Oxford University, 1717–36 ; judge-advocate-general, 1684–1705 ; secretary at war, 1692–1704 ; joint secretary to the admiralty, 1702–5 ; a lord of the admiralty, 1712–14 ; architect ; benefactor of All Souls' and Worcester colleges, Oxford. [x. 424]

CLARKE, GEORGE (1796–1842), sculptor ; exhibited in London, 1821–39 ; called 'the Birmingham Chantrey.' [x. 425]

CLARKE, HARRIET LUDLOW (d. 1866), artist ; wood-engraver, 1837 ; artist in stained glass, 1851. [x. 426]

CLARKE, HENRY (1743–1818), mathematician ; educated at Manchester grammar school ; schoolmaster in Yorkshire ; land surveyor in Manchester ; schoolmaster in Salford, Manchester, and (1799) Bristol ; LL.D. Edinburgh, 1802 ; professor in the military academy, 1802–17 ; published mathematical treatises. [x. 426]

CLARKE, HEWSON (1787–1832 ?), miscellaneous writer ; chemist's assistant at Gateshead ; wrote for the local paper ; for a time at Emmanuel College, Cambridge ; hack-writer in London ; satirised, and was satirised by, Byron ; wrote on contemporary European and English history. [x. 427]

CLARKE, JACOB AUGUSTUS LOCKHART (1817–1880), anatomist ; studied medicine in London ; consulting physician on nervous disorders ; M.D. St. Andrews, 1869 ; wrote on histology and nervous diseases. [x. 428]

CLARKE, JAMES (1798–1861), antiquary ; collected local antiquities ; published 'The Suffolk Antiquary,' 1849. [x. 428]

CLARKE, JAMES FERNANDEZ (1812–1875), medical writer ; apprenticed to a London physician ; studied medicine in Dublin ; wrote for the 'Lancet,' 1834–74 ; practitioner in London ; published an autobiography, 1874. [x. 429]

CLARKE, JAMES STANIER (1765 ?–1834), author ; eldest son of Edward Clarke (1730–1786) [q. v.] ; rector of Preston, Sussex, 1790 ; naval chaplain, 1795–9 ; domestic chaplain to the Prince of Wales, 1799 ; LL.D. Cambridge, 1816 ; canon of Windsor, 1821 ; published sermons, naval history, and lives of Nelson and James II. [x. 429]

CLARKE, JEREMIAH (1669 ?–1707), composer ; chorister of the Chapel Royal ; organist at Winchester ; vicar-choral of St. Paul's, 1699 ; organist at the Chapel Royal, 1704 ; committed suicide ; composed songs, anthems, and music for the theatres. [x. 430]

CLARKE or **CLERK,** JOHN (1582–1653), physician ; M.D. Cambridge, 1615 ; practised in London ; revised the 'Pharmacopœia.' [x. 431]

CLARKE, JOHN (1609–1676), colonist ; physician in London ; one of the first settlers at Rhode Island, 1638 ; physician and baptist preacher there ; in England as agent for the colony, 1651–63 ; obtained a charter for it, 1663 ; returned to Rhode Island, 1663 ; published pamphlets. [x. 432]

CLARKE, JOHN (1662–1723), jesuit ; called the apostle of Belgium ; born at Kilkenny ; educated at St. Omer's ; joined the jesuits, 1681 ; missioner in Belgium, 1690–1718. [x. 432]

CLARKE, JOHN (1687–1734), schoolmaster ; M.A. St. John's College, Cambridge, 1710 ; schoolmaster at Hull (1720) and Gloucester ; published Latin grammars, translations, and philosophical tracts. [x. 432]

CLARKE, JOHN (1682–1757), dean of Salisbury ; M.A. Caius College, Cambridge, 1707 ; D.D., 1717 ; prebendary of Norwich ; canon of Canterbury, 1721 ; dean of Salisbury, 1728 ; published translations and philosophical tracts. [x. 433]

CLARKE, JOHN (1706–1761), schoolmaster ; B.A. Trinity College, Cambridge, 1726 ; fellow, 1729 ; M.A., 1730 ; incumbent of Nun Monkton, Yorkshire ; schoolmaster at Skipton, Beverley, 1735, and Wakefield, 1751. [x. 433]

CLARKE, JOHN (1761–1815), physician ; studied medicine in London ; accoucheur in London ; lectured on midwifery ; wrote medical treatises. [x. 434]

CLARKE, JOHN (1770–1836), Mus. Doc. [See WHIT-FELD.]

CLARKE, JOHN (*d.* 1879), comedian ; a photographer ; acted in the provinces ; acted in London, 1852 ; became celebrated as a burlesque actor, 1856. [x. 434]

CLARKE, JOHN RANDALL (1828 ?–1863), architect ; published architectural histories of Gloucester and Llanthony Abbey, as well as ‘Gloucester Cathedral’ and ‘Manxley Hall,’ two romances. [x. 435]

CLARKE, JOHN SLEEPER (1833–1899), actor ; born in Baltimore ; educated for American law ; first appeared on stage at Boston, 1851 ; joint lessee successively of Arch Street Theatre, Philadelphia, Winter Garden Theatre, New York, and other houses ; managed Haymarket, 1878, and Strand, 1885. [Suppl. ii. 27]

CLARKE, JOSEPH (*d.* 1749), controversialist ; educated at Westminster ; fellow of Magdalene College, Cambridge ; M.A. [x. 435]

CLARKE, JOSEPH (1758–1834), physician ; educated at Glasgow University, 1775–6 ; and Edinburgh University, 1776–9 ; M.D. Edinburgh, 1779 ; studied midwifery in London, 1781 ; accoucheur in Dublin, 1781–1829 ; physician to the lying-in hospital, 1786 ; wrote medical treatises. [x. 435]

CLARKE, JOSEPH (1811 ?–1860), divine ; M.A. St. John’s College, Cambridge, 1841 ; rector of Stretford, Lancashire ; published tracts. [x. 436]

CLARKE, MARCUS ANDREW HISLOP (1846–1881), author ; generally called MARCUS CLARKE ; emigrated to Victoria, 1863 ; journalist in Melbourne, 1867 ; wrote novels, plays, and pantomimes. [x. 436]

CLARKE, MARY ANNE (1776–1852), mistress of Frederick, duke of York ; *née* Thompson ; married Clarke, a stonemason, 1794 ; actress ; lived extravagantly, 1803 ; bribed to use her influence to obtain army promotions from the Duke of York, commander-in-chief ; examined by the Commons, 1809 ; tried for libel, 1809 ; imprisoned for libel, 1813 ; withdrew to Paris, *c.* 1816. [x. 436]

CLARKE, MARY VICTORIA COWDEN- (1809–1898), compiler of a concordance to Shakespeare ; daughter of Vincent Novello [q. v.] ; married Charles Cowden-Clarke [q. v.], 1828 ; produced, 1829–41, ‘Complete Concordance to Shakespeare,’ published in monthly parts, 1844–5 ; she resided in Italy from 1856. Her works include ‘The Shakespeare Key,’ 1879, and of ‘Recollections of Writers,’ 1878, written in collaboration with her husband. [Suppl. ii. 28]

CLARKE, MATTHEW, the elder (1630 ?–1708 ?), congregational minister ; son of a Shropshire parson ; educated at Westminster School ; fellow of Trinity College, Cambridge, 1653 ; army chaplain in Scotland ; intruded rector of Narborough, Leicestershire, 1657–62 ; nonconformist preacher in Leicestershire ; congregational minister at Market Harborough, 1672. [x. 437]

CLARKE, MATTHEW, the younger (1664–1726), congregational minister ; son of Matthew Clarke the elder [q. v.] ; assistant minister at Market Harborough, 1684 ; minister at Sandwich, 1687 ; pastor of the congregational church, Miles Lane, London, 1689 ; preacher at Pinners’ Hall, 1697 ; published sermons. [x. 438]

CLARKE, MATTHEW (1701–1778), physician ; studied medicine at Leyden, 1721 ; M.D. Cambridge, 1728 ; physician to Guy’s Hospital, 1732–54. [x. 439]

CLARKE, SIR ROBERT (*d.* 1607), judge ; barrister of Lincoln’s Inn, 1568 ; baron of the exchequer, 1587 ; knighted, 1603. [x. 439]

CLARKE, ROBERT (*d.* 1675), Latin poet ; real name GRAINE ; educated at Douay ; professor of poetry at Douay ; sent on the English mission, 1629 ; Carthusian at Nieuport, 1632–75 ; wrote, in Latin, plays and a religious epic. [x. 440]

CLARKE, SAMUEL (1625–1669), orientalist ; educated at Merton College, Oxford, 1640–4 ; M.A., 1648 ; schoolmaster at Islington ; contributed to Walton’s ‘Biblia Polyglotta’ ; esquire bedell of law and ‘architypographus,’ Oxford, 1658–69 ; studied Hebrew, Arabic, Persian, and Turkish. [x. 440]

CLARKE, SAMUEL (1599–1683), divine ; entered Emmanuel College, Cambridge, 1616 ; curate in Cheshire ;

puritan preacher at Warwick ; rector of Alcester, Warwickshire, 1633–45 ; curate of St. Bennet Fink, London, 1642–62 ; member of the Savoy conference, 1661 ; withdrew to Isleworth ; published poems, devotional tracts, and numerous biographies. [x. 441]

CLARKE or **CLARK**, SAMUEL (1626–1701), annotator of the bible ; eldest son of Samuel Clarke (1599–1683) [q. v.] ; of Pembroke College, Cambridge ; intruded fellow, 1644–51 ; intruded rector of Grendon Underwood, Buckinghamshire ; ejected, 1662 ; congregational minister at High Wycombe ; published an annotated bible, 1690 ; a concordance, 1696, and other bib cal works. [x. 442]

CLARKE, SAMUEL (1675–1729), metaphysician ; B.A. Caius College, Cambridge, 1695 ; D.D. ; disciple of Isaac Newton ; published Latin translation of the Cartesian Jacques Rohault’s ‘Physics,’ with Newtonian notes, 1697 ; chaplain to Moore, bishop of Norwich, 1698 ; delivered Boyle lectures, ‘On the Being and Attributes of God,’ 1704–5 ; rector of Drayton, near Norwich ; rector of St. Benet’s, Paul’s Wharf, London, 1706, and of St. James’s, Westminster, 1709 ; wrote against Henry Dodwell, 1706 ; published Latin translation of Newton’s ‘Optics,’ 1706 ; published ‘Scripture Doctrine of the Trinity,’ 1712 ; edited Cæsar, 1712 ; accused of Arianism, 1714 ; held a philosophical correspondence with Leibnitz, 1715–16 ; master of Wigston’s Hospital, Leicester, 1718 ; declined the mastership of the mint, 1727 ; edited Homer’s ‘Iliad,’ 1729 ; founder of the ‘intellectual’ school, which deduced the moral law from a logical necessity ; his collected works published, 1738. [x. 443]

CLARKE, SAMUEL (1684–1750), theological writer ; congregational minister at St. Albans ; published ‘The Saints’ Inheritance ; being a Collection of the Promises of Scripture.’ [x. 446]

CLARKE, THEOPHILUS (1776 ?–1831 ?), painter ; pupil of John Opie ; exhibited in London, 1795–1810. [x. 447]

CLARKE, SIR THOMAS (1703–1764), judge ; educated at Westminster, 1717–21 ; M.A., Trinity College, Cambridge, 1728 ; fellow, 1727 ; barrister of Gray’s Inn, 1729 ; M.P. for St. Michael’s, Cornwall, 1747, and for Lostwithiel, 1754–61 ; master of the rolls, 1754 ; knighted, 1754. [x. 447]

CLARKE, THOMAS (*fl.* 1768–1775), painter ; trained in Dublin ; came to London, 1768 ; exhibited, 1769–75. [x. 448]

CLARKE, TIMOTHY (*d.* 1672), physician ; of Balliol College, Oxford ; M.D., 1652 ; F.R.C.P., 1664 ; physician to Charles II ; F.R.S. ; friend of Samuel Pepys. [x. 448]

CLARKE, SIR WILLIAM (1623 ?–1666), secretary at war ; barrister of the Inner Temple, 1653 ; secretary to Monck ; secretary at war, 1661 ; knighted ; mortally wounded in the action off Harwich. [x. 448]

CLARKE, WILLIAM (1640 ?–1684), physician ; B.A. Merton College, Oxford, 1661 ; fellow, 1663–6 ; practitioner at Bath, and afterwards at Stepney ; wrote on ‘Nitre,’ 1670. [x. 449]

CLARKE, WILLIAM (1696–1771), antiquary ; fellow of St. John’s College, Cambridge, 1717 ; M.A., 1719 ; rector of Buxted, Sussex, 1724–68 ; canon of Chichester, 1738, and chancellor, 1770 ; wrote on miscellaneous subjects, including the relation between Roman, Saxon, and English coins. [x. 449]

CLARKE, WILLIAM (1800–1838), writer of juvenile literature. [x. 450]

CLARKE, WILLIAM BRANWHITE (1798–1878), geologist ; M.A. Cambridge, 1824 ; curate of Ramsholt, Suffolk ; made fifteen geological excursions to the continent ; published poems, 1822, and scientific papers, 1833–1838 ; Anglican clergyman in New South Wales, 1840–70 ; discovered gold there in 1841, tin in 1849, and diamonds in 1859 ; studied the Australian coal-measures ; visited Tasmania, 1856 and 1860 ; F.R.S. London, 1876 ; published numerous scientific papers. [x. 450]

CLARKE, WILLIAM FAIRLIE (1833–1884), medical writer ; born in Calcutta ; educated at Rugby, Oxford, and Edinburgh ; studied medicine in London ; M.B. Oxford, 1862 ; surgeon in London ; M.D. Oxford, 1876 ; published a ‘Manual of … Surgery,’ 1866, and a monograph on ‘Diseases of the Tongue,’ 1873. [x. 452]

CLARKSON, DAVID (1622–1686), controversialist; B.A. Clare Hall, Cambridge; intruded fellow, 1645–51; intruded incumbent of Mortlake, Surrey, 1651–62; congregational minister in London, 1682; published sermons and treatises against episcopacy and Romanism. [x. 452]

CLARKSON, JOHN (1697–1763), Dominican friar, 1716; missioner in Leicestershire, 1733–46; confessor in Brussels, 1747; prior of Bornhem, 1753; died at Brussels; published devotional and philosophical tracts. [x. 453]

CLARKSON, LAURENCE (1615–1667). [See CLAXTON.]

CLARKSON, NATHANIEL (1724–1795), painter; coach-painter, of Islington; exhibited portraits, 1762–7; tried historical painting. [x. 453]

CLARKSON, THOMAS (1760–1846), philanthropist; son of the schoolmaster of Wisbeach; educated at St. Paul's School, 1775–80; B.A. St. John's College, Cambridge, 1783; in deacon's orders; published a prize essay against slavery, 1786; agitated for the abolition of slavery, 1787–94, and 1805–33; urged it on the French government, 1789–90, and on the czar, 1818; granted the freedom of London, 1839. His works include pamphlets on slavery, theological tracts, and a memoir of William Penn. [x. 454]

CLATER, FRANCIS (1756–1823), author of 'Every Man his own Farrier,' 1783, and 'His own Cattle Doctor,' 1810; farrier and subsequently druggist. [xi. 1]

CLATER, THOMAS (1789–1867), painter; third son of Francis Clater [q. v.]; exhibited, chiefly genre works, in London, 1819–63. [xi. 1]

CLAUDET, ANTOINE FRANÇOIS JEAN (1797–1867), photographer; born at Lyons; director of glassworks at Choisy-le-Roi; glass warehouseman in London, 1829; invented a glass-cutting machine, 1833; set up as daguerreotype photographer, 1840; soon adopted the collodion process; introduced improvements in photography; wrote on photographic subjects; F.R.S., 1853. [xi. 2]

CLAUGHTON, PIERS CALVERLEY (1814–1884), bishop of Colombo; B.A. Brasenose College, Oxford, 1835; fellow and tutor of University College, Oxford, 1837–42; bishop of St. Helena, 1859–62; bishop of Colombo, 1862–70; archdeacon of London, 1870; chaplain-general of the forces, 1875; published sermons and theological tracts. [xi. 2]

CLAUGHTON, THOMAS LEGH (1808–1892), bishop of St. Albans; brother of Piers Calverley Claughton [q. v.]; educated at Rugby and Trinity College, Oxford; B.A., 1831; fellow, 1832–42; M.A., 1833; public examiner, 1835; select preacher, 1841, 1850, 1860, and 1868; professor of poetry, 1852–7; ordained, 1834; vicar of Kidderminster, 1841–67; bishop of Rochester, 1867–77; first bishop of new diocese of St. Albans, 1877–90; published sermons and religious writings. [Suppl. ii. 29]

CLAVEL, JOHN (1603–1642), highwayman; sentenced to death but pardoned, 1627; published metrical autobiography, 1628. [xi. 3]

CLAVELL, ROBERT (d. 1711), bookseller, of London; published pamphlet against the Dutch, 1665; issued catalogues of current literature, 1668–1700. [xi. 3]

CLAVERHOUSE, JOHN GRAHAM OF (1649?–1689). [See GRAHAM, JOHN, VISCOUNT DUNDEE.]

CLAVERING, SIR JOHN (1722–1777), opponent of Warren Hastings; entered the Coldstream guards; brigadier-general in attack on Guadeloupe, 1759; titular colonel, 1759; military attaché in Hesse-Cassel, 1760–3; lieutenant-general, 1770; given command of the Bengal army, 1774; opposed Warren Hastings in the council of Bengal; K.B., 1776; tried to hold Hastings to his resignation, 1777. [xi. 4]

CLAVERING, ROBERT (1671–1747), bishop of Peterborough; educated at Edinburgh, and Lincoln College, Oxford; M.A., 1696; fellow and tutor of University College, Oxford, 1701; dean and rector of Bocking, Essex, 1714–19; D.D., canon of Christ Church, and professor of Hebrew, Oxford, 1715; bishop of Llandaff, 1725; translated to Peterborough, 1729; published translations from the Hebrew, sermons, and charges. [xi. 5]

CLAXTON or **CLARKSON,** LAURENCE (1615–1667), sectary; presbyterian, subsequently an antinomian; intruded rector of Pulham, Norfolk; joined baptists, 1644; imprisoned at Bury St. Edmunds, 1645; joined the 'seekers'; intruded vicar of Sandridge, Hertfordshire, c. 1646, and of a Lincolnshire church, 1647; his 'Single Eye all Light' burnt, by order of the Commons, 1650; intruded incumbent of churches in Norfolk, c. 1656; joined the Muggletonians, 1658; prisoner for debt, 1666; published sectarian tracts, 1646–60. [xi. 5]

CLAXTON, MARSHALL (1813–1881), historical painter; art student in London, 1831; exhibited, 1832; visited Rome, 1837; returned to England before 1843; exhibited pictures in Australia, 1850, and India; visited Egypt; returned to London, 1858. [xi. 7]

CLAY, ALFRED BORRON (1831–1868), historical painter; second son of John Clay [q. v.]; art student in London, 1852; exhibited, 1854–68. [xi. 7]

CLAY, CHARLES (1801–1893), ovariotomist; apprenticed as surgeon in Manchester; studied at Edinburgh University; L.R.C.S. Edinburgh, 1823; extra-L.R.C.P. London, 1842; practised in Manchester, where he was at one time senior medical officer and lecturer on midwifery at St. Mary's Hospital; placed the operation of ovariotomy on a sure foundation; published 'Complete Handbook of Obstetric Surgery,' 1856, and other surgical works, besides treatises relating to geology and numismatics. [Suppl. ii. 30]

CLAY, FREDERICK (1839–1889), musician; born in Paris; son of James Clay [q. v.]; private secretary to Henry Bouverie William Brand (afterwards Viscount Hampden) [q. v.]; produced two operettas which met with success; collaborated with Tom Taylor in 'Court and Cottage,' 1862; formed friendship with Sir Arthur Seymour Sullivan [q. v.]; subsequently produced, with Mr. W. S. Gilbert, Mr. G. R. Sims, and other librettists, several operettas; set, 1877, libretto constructed by W. G. Wills, from 'Lalla Rookh,' which contains his most successful piece, 'I'll sing thee songs of Araby,' and the quartette, 'Morn wanes, we must away.' [Suppl. ii. 32]

CLAY, JAMES (1805–1873), author of 'A Treatise on . . . Whist,' 1864; son of a London merchant; educated at Winchester; travelled in the East, 1830; M.P. for Hull, 1847–73. [xi. 8]

CLAY, JOHN (1796–1858), chaplain of Preston gaol (1823–58); merchant's clerk in Liverpool; ordained, 1821; B.D. Emmanuel College, Cambridge, 1835; published reports on prison management, sermons, and other works. [xi. 8]

CLAY, JOHN GRANBY (1766–1846), general; ensign, 1782; lieutenant, 1788; served in the West Indies, 1786–1794; major, 1795; at home stations, 1795–1800; in the Egyptian campaign, 1801; lieutenant-colonel, 1804; stationed at Manchester, where he suppressed the riots of 1808 and 1812; major-general, 1813; general, 1841. [xi. 9]

CLAY, SIR WILLIAM (1791–1869), politician; merchant in London; M.P. for Tower Hamlets, 1832–57; created baronet, 1841; published political pamphlets, 1834–56. [xi. 10]

CLAY, WILLIAM KEATINGE (1797–1867), antiquary; ordained, 1823; B.D. Cambridge, 1835; minor canon of Ely, 1837; vicar of Waterbeach, Cambridgeshire, 1854–67; wrote on the prayer book; edited liturgical works; published histories of four Cambridgeshire parishes. [xi. 10]

CLAYMOND, JOHN (1457?–1537), divine; demy of Magdalen College, Oxford, 1483; fellow, 1488; president, 1504–17; D.D., 1510; vicar of Norton, Durham, 1498–1518, with much other preferment; master of St. Cross, Winchester, 1505–24; president of Corpus Christi College, Oxford, 1517–37; wrote notes on classical authors; benefactor of Brasenose, Magdalen, and Corpus Christi colleges. [xi. 11]

CLAYPOOLE or **CLAYPOLE,** ELIZABETH (1629–1658), second daughter of Oliver Cromwell; married, 1646, John Claypoole [q. v.]; said to have interceded for royalist prisoners; buried in Westminster Abbey. [xi. 11]

CLAYPOOLE or **CLAYPOLE,** JOHN (d. 1688), parliamentarian; in arms for the parliament, 1645; married,

1646, Cromwell's second daughter [see CLAYPOOLE, ELIZABETH]; raised a troop of horse, 1651; master of the horse to the Protector; M.P., 1654, 1656; one of Cromwell's peers, 1657; imprisoned as a suspect, 1678.
[xi. 12]

CLAYTON, CHARLOTTE, LADY SUNDON (d. 1742), woman of the bedchamber to Queen Caroline; daughter of John Dyve; married William Clayton, afterwards Baron Sundon in the Irish peerage; became bedchamber woman to Queen Caroline when Princess of Wales in 1714; obtained great influence over her, and controlled court patronage. [lv. 170]

CLAYTON, JOHN (1693–1773), botanist; went to Virginia, 1705; secretary of Gloucester County, Virginia; sent scientific papers to the Royal Society, 1739; collected American plants for European botanists. [xi. 13]

CLAYTON, JOHN (1709–1773), divine; educated at Manchester school and Brasenose College, Oxford; M.A., 1732; joined 'the Oxford Methodists,' c. 1728; curate at Salford, 1733; taught school there; one of the chaplains of Manchester Collegiate Church, 1740, and fellow, 1760; publicly acknowledged the Young Pretender, 1745; published tract on poor relief, and sermons; edited 'Anacreontica,' 1754. [xi. 13]

CLAYTON, JOHN (1728–1800), painter of still-life; surgeon's apprentice; exhibited, 1761–78; his studio accidentally burnt, 1769. [xi. 14]

CLAYTON, JOHN (1754–1843), congregationalist; apothecary's apprentice in Manchester; educated at Trevecca College; preacher in the Countess of Huntingdon's chapel, Tunbridge Wells; failed to obtain ordination, 1777; presbyterian minister at West Looe, Cornwall; pastor of Weighhouse Chapel, London, 1778–1826; published devotional treatises. [xi. 14]

CLAYTON, JOHN (d. 1861), architect; much employed at Hereford; settled in London, 1839; exhibited architectural drawings, 1839–56; published works on architecture, 1846–56. [xi. 15]

CLAYTON, JOHN (1780–1865), congregationalist; son of John Clayton (1754–1843) [q. v.]; pastor of the Poultry Chapel, London; published sermons. [xi. 15]

CLAYTON, JOHN (1843–1888), actor; real name JOHN ALFRED CALTHROP; educated at Merchant Taylors' School; joined Miss Herbert's company at St. James's, 1866, playing Hastings in 'She stoops to Conquer'; subsequently appeared at many London theatres; joint-manager of Court Theatre, 1881–7, during which period he appeared in comic plays by Mr. Pinero and other writers. [Suppl. ii. 32]

CLAYTON, NICHOLAS (1733?–1797), presbyterian divine; educated at Glasgow; pastor at Boston, Lincolnshire, 1759–63, and in Liverpool, 1763–81; divinity tutor at Warrington academy, 1781–3; D.D. Edinburgh, 1782; pastor in Nottingham, 1785–95. [xi. 16]

CLAYTON, RICHARD (d. 1612), dean of Peterborough; entered St. John's College, Cambridge, 1572; B.A. Oxford, 1576; fellow of St. John's College, Cambridge, 1577; M.A., 1579; D.D., 1592; master of Magdalene College, Cambridge, 1593; archdeacon of Lincoln, 1595; master of St. John's College, Cambridge, 1595; built the second court there; canon, 1596, and dean, 1607, of Peterborough. [xi. 16]

CLAYTON, SIR RICHARD (d. 1828), translator; inherited Adlington, Lancashire, 1770; barrister of the Inner Temple, 1771; created baronet, 1774; recorder of Wigan, 1815; consul at Nantes; published essays and translations, 1790–1817. [xi. 17]

CLAYTON or CLETON, SIR ROBERT (1629–1707), politician; a London scrivener; bought Bletchingley, Surrey, 1677; alderman of London, 1670–88; sheriff and knighted, 1671; lord mayor, 1679–80; M.P., London, 1679–1681; advocated the Exclusion Bill; one of the committee to defend the city charter, 1682; M.P., 1689–1707; benefactor of St. Thomas's Hospital and Christ's Hospital. [xi. 17]

CLAYTON, ROBERT (1695–1758), Irish bishop; born in Dublin; educated at Westminster School; B.A. and fellow of Trinity College, Dublin, 1714; LL.D., 1722; D.D., 1730; travelled; inherited estates in Lancashire,

1728; bishop of Killala and Achonry, 1730; bishop of Cork and Ross, 1755; bishop of Clogher, 1745; denied the archbishopric of Tuam, being accused of Arianism, 1752; threatened with prosecution for heresy, 1757; published sermons and theological works, 1738–57. [xi. 19]

CLAYTON, THOMAS (fl. 1706), composer; a member of William III's band, 1692–1702; travelled in Italy, 1702–4; introduced Italian opera at Drury Lane, 1705–11, succeeding with 'Arsinoe,' 1705, but failing with 'Rosamond,' 1707. [xi. 20]

CLEASBY, SIR ANTHONY (1804–1879), judge; at Eton, 1820–3; fellow of Trinity College, Cambridge, 1828; M.A., 1830; barrister of the Inner Temple, 1831; gained lucrative commercial practice; unsuccessful as candidate for parliament, 1852–67; baron of the exchequer, 1868–78; knighted, 1868; unsuccessful on the bench. [xi. 21]

CLEASBY, RICHARD (1797–1847), philologist; broker's clerk in London; studied in Italy and Germany from 1824, becoming a master of German dialects; visited Denmark and Sweden, 1834 and 1839–40; began an 'Icelandic-English Dictionary' (published by Gudbrand Vigfusson, 1873). [xi. 21]

CLEAVER, EUSEBY (1746–1819), archbishop of Dublin; educated at Westminster; M.A. Christ Church, Oxford, 1770; D.D., 1783; rector of Spofforth, Yorkshire, 1774–83; rector of Tillington and Petworth, Sussex, 1783; prebendary of Chichester, 1787; chaplain to the lord-lieutenant of Ireland, 1787; bishop of Cork, 1789, and of Ferns, 1789; archbishop of Dublin, 1809; became imbecile. [xi. 22]

CLEAVER, WILLIAM (1742–1815), bishop of St. Asaph; B.A. Magdalen College, Oxford, 1761; fellow of Brasenose College; M.A., 1764; principal of Brasenose, 1785–1809; prebendary of Westminster, 1784; bishop of Chester, 1787, of Bangor, 1800, and of St. Asaph, 1806; mostly non-resident; published some classical texts; chiefly remembered by De Quincey's encomiums.
[xi. 23]

CLEEVE, BOURCHIER (1715–1760), writer on finance; a London pewterer; bought Foots Cray Place, Kent, c. 1755; published scheme for reducing the national debt, 1756. [xi. 23]

CLEGG, JAMES (1679–1755), presbyterian minister; M.D.; minister and physician at Malcalf, 1702, and, 1711–55, at Chinley; published sermons, 1721–36.
[xi. 24]

CLEGG, JOHN (1714?–1746?), violinist; born in Ireland; trained in Italy; a professional of repute in London, 1723–44; confined in Bedlam, 1744–6. [xi. 24]

CLEGG, SAMUEL, the younger (1814–1856), engineer; son of Samuel Clegg (1781–1861) [q. v.]; surveyor in Portugal, 1836; railway engineer; professor of engineering at Putney, and at Chatham, 1849–56; published treatise on coal-gas, 1850. [xi. 25]

CLEGG, SAMUEL, the elder (1781–1861), gas engineer; educated at Manchester; apprentice to Boulton & Watt, engineers, Soho; a pioneer of gas-lighting in Yorkshire, and (1813) London; invented the water gas-meter; gas engineer at Lisbon. [xi. 24]

CLEGHORN, GEORGE (1716–1789), physician; educated at Edinburgh; army surgeon at Minorca, 1736–49; M.D.; published observations on diseases epidemic in Minorca, 1751; lecturer and professor of anatomy in Dublin, 1751–89. [xi. 25]

CLEGHORN, JAMES (1778–1838), actuary; farmer, and, in 1811, journalist in Edinburgh; became an accountant of repute. [xi. 26]

CLEIN or CLEYN, FRANCIS (1590?–1658), draughtsman; born at Rostock, Germany; patronised by Christian IV of Denmark; studied in Italy; engaged by James I as designer for the Mortlake tapestry works, 1623; pensioned by Charles I, 1625; book-illustrator, 1637–50. [xi. 26]

CLELAND, JAMES (1770–1840), statistician; a Glasgow cabinet-maker; superintendent of public works, London, 1814; took the census of Glasgow, 1819, 1821, 1831; published histories of Glasgow, 1816–36. [xi. 27]

CLELAND, JOHN (1709–1789), novelist; entered Westminster School, 1722; consul at Smyrna; East India

Company's servant at Bombay, 1736; wandered over Europe; published his first novel, 'Fanny Hill,' 1750; pensioned; journalist in London, 1757; published novels and dramatic pieces. [xi. 28]

CLELAND, WILLIAM (1661 ?-1689), covenanter; educated at St. Andrews, 1676; fought at Drumclog and Bothwell Bridge, 1679; took part in Argyll's invasion, 1685; escaped to Holland; returned to Scotland to agitate for the Prince of Orange, 1688; killed in action at Dunkeld; his poems posthumously published, 1697. [xi. 28]

CLELAND, WILLIAM (1674 ?-1741), friend of Pope; student at Utrecht; served in Spain, 1705; commissioner of customs in Scotland; commissioner of taxes in England, 1723. [xi. 30]

CLEMENT SCOTUS I (*fl.* 745), bishop among the Franks; probably a native of Ireland; resisted the Romanising policy of Archbishop Boniface of Mentz; deposed and imprisoned by Boniface as married and a heretic, 744; sentence confirmed, 745. [xi. 30]

CLEMENT SCOTUS II (*fl.* 820), grammarian; left Ireland for France, c. 772; taught at Charles the Great's court; died probably at Würzburg; reputed author of two Latin grammatical tracts; often confused with Clemens Scotus I, and with Claudius (*d.* 839 ?), wrongly called Clemens Claudius, bishop of Turin, a Spaniard. [xi. 31]

CLEMENT OF LLANTHONY (*d.* 1190 ?), known also as CLEMENT OF GLOUCESTER, theological writer; canon, sub-prior, and prior of Llanthony, where he was educated. His works include 'Concordia Quatuor Evangelistarum,' extant in several manuscripts, and other commentaries. [Suppl. ii. 33]

CLEMENT, CÆSAR (*d.* 1626), Roman catholic divine; educated at Douay, Rheims, and Rome; priest, 1585; D.D.; dean of St. Gudule's, Brussels. [xi. 32]

CLEMENT, GREGORY (*d.* 1660), regicide; Spanish merchant in London; M.P., Camelford, 1647-52; sat in the high court of justice and signed Charles I's death-warrant; executed. [xi. 32]

CLEMENT or **CLEMENTS,** JOHN (*d.* 1572), physician; educated at St. Paul's School; tutor in Sir Thomas More's family; M.D.; Cardinal Wolsey's lecturer in rhetoric, Oxford, c. 1519; subsequently reader in Greek; president of the College of Physicians, London, 1544; a strong Romanist; withdrew to Louvain, 1549; practised medicine in Essex, 1554-9; withdrew to Mechlin, 1559. [xi. 33]

CLEMENT or **CLEMENTS,** MARGARET (1508-1570), *née* Giggs; kinswoman of Sir Thomas More; married John Clement [q. v.], c. 1530; died at Mechlin. [xi. 33]

CLEMENT, WILLIAM INNELL (*d.* 1852), part proprietor of the 'Observer,' c. 1814; proprietor of the 'Morning Chronicle,' 1821-34, and of 'Bell's Life.' [xi. 33]

CLEMENTS, MICHAEL (*d.* 1796 ?), naval officer; as lieutenant, distinguished himself in action, 1757; commanded frigate, 1757; took part in capture of Thurot's squadron at Belfast, 1760; served in the Mediterranean, 1760-3 and 1770; defended Admiral Keppel, 1778, and was shamefully neglected by the admiralty in consequence; retired, 1787; titular rear-admiral. [xi. 34]

CLENCH, ANDREW (*d.* 1692), physician; M.D. Cambridge, 1671; fellow of the College of Physicians, London, 1680; murdered, 1692. [xi. 34]

CLENCH, JOHN (*d.* 1607), judge; barrister of Lincoln's Inn, 1568; baron of the exchequer, 1581; justice of the queen's bench, 1584-1603. [xi. 35]

CLENNELL, LUKE (1781-1840), wood engraver and painter; trained by Thomas Bewick [q. v.], 1797-1804; wood engraver in London, 1804-10; exhibited watercolour paintings, 1812-18; was insane from 1817 till death. [xi. 35]

CLENOCKE or **CLYNOG,** MAURICE (*d.* 1580 ?), divine; a Welshman; B.C.L. Oxford, 1548; chaplain to Cardinal Pole; a pluralist; nominated by Queen Mary to the see of Bangor, 1558; withdrew to Rome, 1560; officer of the hospital for English pilgrims, 1567; rector of the English college, 1578-9; drowned at sea. [xi. 37]

CLEPHANE, JOHN (*d.* 1758), physician; M.D. St. Andrews, 1729; army physician; physician to St. George's Hospital, London, 1751. [xi. 37]

CLÉRISSEAU, CHARLES LOUIS (1721-1820), architectural draughtsman; born in Paris; long resident in Rome, sketching ancient buildings; exhibited in London, 1772-90, and in Paris, 1773-1808; invited to St. Petersburg, 1783; died near Paris. [xi. 38]

CLERK. [See also CLARK, CLARKE, and CLERKE.]

CLERK, SIR GEORGE (1787-1867), statesman; of Penicuik; succeeded as sixth baronet, 1798; educated at Edinburgh and, 1806, Trinity College, Oxford; advocate at Scottish bar, 1809; D.C.L. Oxford, 1810; M.P., 1811-32; lord of the admiralty, 1819-27; under-secretary for home affairs, 1830; master of the mint, 1845-6. [xi. 38]

CLERK, SIR GEORGE RUSSELL (1800-1889), Indian civilian; educated at Haileybury College; writer in East India Company's service, 1817, and subsequently held successively several subordinate positions; political agent at Ambála, 1831; British envoy at Lahore; governor of Bombay, 1846-8 and 1860-2; K.C.B., 1848; permanent under-secretary to India board, 1856, and secretary, 1857; permanent under-secretary of state for India, 1858; member of Indian council, 1863; G.C.S.I., 1866. [Suppl. ii. 34]

CLERK, JOHN (*d.* 1541), bishop of Bath and Wells; M.A. Cambridge, 1502; LL.D. Bologna; rector of Hothfield, Kent, 1508, with other benefices; dean of Windsor, 1519; chaplain and agent of Wolsey; envoy to Rome, 1521; master of the rolls, 1522-3; bishop of Bath and Wells, 1523; tried to obtain the papacy for Wolsey, 1523; envoy to France, 1526, and to Rome, 1527; assented to Henry VIII's divorce, 1529; envoy to Cleves, 1540. [xi. 39]

CLERK, JOHN (*d.* 1552), Roman catholic writer; educated at Oxford; visited France and Italy; secretary to Thomas, duke of Norfolk; committed suicide in the Tower; published translations and theological pieces. [xi. 40]

CLERK, SIR JOHN (1684-1755), of Penicuik; antiquary; advocate; M.P. in Scottish parliament, 1702-7; a commissioner for the union, 1707; judge of the exchequer court in Scotland, 1708-55; succeeded as second baronet, 1722; patron of Allan Ramsay; collected antiquities; wrote antiquarian tracts. [xi. 40]

CLERK, JOHN (1728-1812), naval writer; of Eldin; younger son of Sir John Clerk [q. v.]; successful merchant in Edinburgh; practised drawing and etching, 1770; bought Eldin, near Edinburgh, c. 1773; wrote an 'Essay on Naval Tactics,' privately printed, 1782, published, 1790, and enlarged, 1797. [xi. 41]

CLERK, JOHN, LORD ELDIN (1757-1832), Scottish judge; eldest son of John Clerk (1728-1812) [q. v.]; apprentice to a writer to the signet; accountant; advocate, 1785; lord of session, 1823-8; failed as a judge. [xi. 42]

CLERK, JOSIAH (1639-1714), physician; entered Peterhouse, Cambridge, 1656; M.D. 1666; fellow of the London College of Physicians, 1675; president, 1708. [xi. 43]

CLERK, MATTHEW (1659-1735), Irish presbyterian; served in siege of Derry, 1689; minister of Kilrea, co. Derry, 1697-1729; wrote against non-subscription to the Westminster Confession, 1721; minister and schoolmaster at Londonderry, New Hampshire, 1729. [xi. 43]

CLERK, WILLIAM (1655), civilian; LL.D. Cambridge, 1629; practised at Doctors' Commons, 1629; a judge of the admiralty, 1651; published a law pamphlet, 1631. [xi. 44]

CLERK-MAXWELL, SIR GEORGE (1715-1784), of Penicuik; second son of Sir John Clerk [q. v.]; educated at Edinburgh and Leyden; assumed the name Clerk-Maxwell on marrying the heiress of Middlebie, Dumfriesshire; succeeded to baronetcy and Penicuik estate, 1782; wrote on farming. [xi. 44]

CLERK-MAXWELL, JAMES (1831-1879), first professor of experimental physics at Cambridge; contributed papers to the Royal Society of Edinburgh, on curves, 1846 and 1849, and on the equilibrium of elastic solids, 1850; left Edinburgh for Cambridge; fellow of Trinity College, 1855; professor of natural philosophy at Aberdeen, 1856-60, and at King's College, London, 1860-5; elected without opposition to the new chair of experimental physics at Cambridge, 1871; his essay on

'Saturn's Rings' gained the Adams prize, 1857 ; and his studies on the kinetic theory of gases are described in many papers, but his theories are not altogether accepted now ; investigated the theory of colours in relation to colour-blindness, on which he read a paper before the Royal Society, 1860, and gained the Rumford medal. His best-known researches, dealing with electricity and magnetism, commenced 1856 ; and the theories he formulated in his treatise, 1873, daily gain more and more acceptance ; foremost physicists are engaged in developing his ideas ; he also turned his attention to electrical measurements and the velocity of propagation of electro-magnetic waves. He founded a scholarship in experimental physics at Cambridge.　　　　[xxxvii. 118]

CLERKE. [See also CLARK, CLARKE, and CLERK.]

CLERKE, BARTHOLOMEW (1537 ?–1590), civilian ; educated at Eton ; fellow of King's College, Cambridge, 1557 ; M.A., 1562 ; studied at Paris ; proctor at Cambridge, 1564 and 1569 ; LL.D. ; M.P. for Bramber, 1571 ; secretary to Thomas Sackville, lord Buckhurst, 1571 ; dean of arches, 1573 ; archdeacon of Wells, 1582 ; employed in the Low Countries, 1585–7 ; published a reply to Nicholas Sanders, 1573, and other works.　　　　[xi. 45]

CLERKE, CHARLES (1741–1779), circumnavigator ; entered the navy, c. 1755 ; sailed round the world with John Byron [q. v.], 1764–6 : alleged that the Patagonians were eight feet high : master's mate in James Cook's [q. v.] voyage, 1768–71 ; lieutenant in Cook's second voyage, 1772–5 ; commanded ship in Cook's third voyage, 1776.　　　　[xi. 46]

CLERKE or **CLARKE,** FRANCIS (*fl.* 1594), civilian ; practised at Doctors' Commons, 1559 ; B.C.L. Oxford, 1594 ; wrote Latin manuals of the admiralty and ecclesiastical courts.　　　　[xi. 46]

CLERKE, GILBERT (1626–1697 ?), mathematician ; entered Sidney Sussex College, Cambridge, 1641 ; fellow, 1648–55 ; presbyterian minister, 1651 ; lived in retirement ; published Latin mathematical and theological treatises, 1660–95.　　　　[xi. 47]

CLERKE, HENRY (*d.* 1687), physician ; demy of Magdalen College, Oxford ; fellow, 1642–67 ; M.A., 1644 ; M.D., 1652 ; president, 1672–87.　　　　[xi. 47]

CLERKE, RICHARD (*d.* 1634), divine ; D.D. Christ's College, Cambridge ; vicar of Minster, Thanet, 1597 ; one of the six preachers at Canterbury, 1602 ; one of the translators of the Old Testament ; his sermons published, 1637.　　　　[xi. 48]

CLERKE, THOMAS HENRY SHADWELL (1792–1849), military journalist ; ensign, 1808 ; disabled by wounds for field service, 1811 ; major, 1830 ; editor of 'Coulburn's United Service Magazine,' 1829–42.
　　　　[xi. 48]

CLERKE, WILLIAM (*fl.* 1595), reputed author of 'The Triall of Bastardie,' 1594, and ' Polimanteia,' 1595 ; entered Trinity College, Cambridge, 1575 ; fellow, 1579 ; M.A., 1582.　　　　[xi. 48]

CLERKE, SIR WILLIAM HENRY (1751–1818), baronet ; of Christ Church, Oxford, 1769 ; B.C.L. All Souls' College, 1778 ; succeeded as eighth baronet, 1778 ; rector of Bury, Lancashire, 1778 ; imprisoned for debt ; published sermons and pamphlets.　　　　[xi. 49]

CLERY, MICHAEL (1575–1643). [See O'CLEARY.]

CLEVELAND, first DUKE OF, second creation. [See VANE, WILLIAM HARRY, 1766–1842.]

CLEVELAND, DUCHESS OF (1641–1709). [See VILLIERS, BARBARA.]

CLEVELAND, EARL OF (1591–1667). [See WENTWORTH, SIR THOMAS.]

CLEVELAND, AUGUSTUS (1755–1784), magistrate of Boglipoor, Bengal.　　　　[xi. 49]

CLEVELAND, JOHN (1613–1658), cavalier poet ; entered Christ's College, Cambridge, 1627 ; fellow of St. John's College, Cambridge, 1634–45 ; M.A., 1635 ; tutor ; opposed Cromwell's election as M.P. for Cambridge borough, 1640 ; ejected as a royalist, 1645 ; his verses famous in royalist circles ; judge-advocate at Newark,

1645–6 ; imprisoned at Yarmouth, 1655 ; released by Cromwell ; published 'Poems,' 1656 ; his works re-edited, 1677, as ' Clievelandi Vindiciæ.'　　　　[xi. 50]

CLEVELEY, JOHN (1747–1786), marine painter in oil- and water-colours ; twin-brother of Robert Cleveley [q.v.] ; exhibited, as John Cleveley, junior, chiefly views on the Thames, 1767–82 ; draughtsman in Sir Joseph Banks's voyage to the Hebrides, 1772, and Captain Phipps's to the north seas, 1774.　　　　[xi. 53]

CLEVELEY, ROBERT (1747–1809), marine painter in oil- and water-colours ; twin-brother of John Cleveley [q. v.] ; exhibited, 1780–95.　　　　[xi. 53]

CLEVERLEY, SAMUEL (*d.* 1824), physician ; M.D. Edinburgh, 1797 ; went to study on the continent ; prisoner in France, 1803–14 ; practitioner in London, 1815–24.　　　　[xi. 54]

CLEVES, ANNE OF (1515–1557). [See ANNE.]

CLEYN, FRANCIS (1590 ?–1658). [See CLEIN.]

CLEYPOLE. [See CLAYPOOLE or CLAYPOLE.]

CLIDERHOU, ROBERT DE (*d.* 1339 ?), justiciar ; of Bayley, near Clitheroe, Lancashire ; a clerk of chancery under Edward I and Edward II ; justice itinerant for Kent, Surrey, and Sussex, 1311 ; king's escheator, north of Trent, 1316 ?–18 ; parson of Wigan from before 1321 till death ; fined for supporting Lancaster, 1323 ; built chapel at Bayley, 1331.　　　　[xi. 54]

CLIFF, HENRY DE (*d.* 1334), judge ; a master in chancery before 1317 ; auditor of petitions, 1320 ; canon of York, 1324 ; master of the rolls, 1325–34.　　　　[xi. 55]

CLIFFORD, ANNE, COUNTESS OF DORSET, PEMBROKE, and MONTGOMERY (1590–1676), heiress of George Clifford, third earl of Cumberland [q. v.] ; involved in lawsuits over the estates ; educated by Samuel Daniel [q. v.], the poet ; married, firstly, February 1609, Richard Sackville, lord Buckhurst (earl of Dorset, 1609) ; claimed the barony of Clifford, 1628 ; married, secondly, 1630, Philip Herbert, earl of Pembroke and Montgomery (*d.* 1650) ; lived unhappily with both husbands ; inherited the Clifford estates, 1643 ; passionately fond of building ; wrote an autobiography.　　　　[xi. 56]

CLIFFORD, ARTHUR (1778–1830), antiquary ; at Stonyhurst College, 1795 ; published letters of Sir Ralph Sadler [q. v.], 1809, 'Tixall Poetry,' 1813, and 'Tixall Letters,' 1815 ; published also a history of the Cliffords, a history of Tixall parish, and educational pamphlets.
　　　　[xi. 57]

CLIFFORD, SIR AUGUSTUS WILLIAM JAMES (1788–1877), usher of the black rod (1832–77) ; educated at Harrow ; entered the navy, 1800 ; served in West Indies, 1803, and Mediterranean, 1807–12 ; captain, 1812 ; rear-admiral, 1848 ; admiral of the red, 1864 ; M.P. for Irish constituencies, 1818–32 ; knighted, 1830 ; created baronet, 1838.　　　　[xi. 58]

CLIFFORD, SIR CONYERS (*d.* 1599), military commander ; of Bobbing Court, Kent ; knighted, 1591 ; M.P. for Pembroke, 1593 ; hon. M.A. Cambridge, 1595 ; sergeant-major in the Cadiz expedition, 1596 ; president of Connaught, 1597 ; killed in battle with the Irish.
　　　　[xi. 59]

CLIFFORD, GEORGE, third EARL OF CUMBERLAND (1558–1605), naval commander ; eldest son of Henry de Clifford, second earl of Cumberland [q. v.] ; succeeded as third earl, 1570 ; ward of Francis Russell, second earl of Bedford ; at Trinity College, Cambridge, 1571–4 ; M.A., 1576 ; a gambler ; wasted his estates ; commanded a queen's ship against the Armada, 1588 ; a favourite at Elizabeth's court ; fitted out ten privateering expeditions, mostly failures, against Spain and Spanish America, 1586–98, sailing personally with those of 1589, 1591, 1593, and 1598.　　　　[xi. 59]

CLIFFORD, HENRY DE, fourteenth BARON CLIFFORD, tenth BARON OF WESTMORELAND, first BARON VESCI (1455 ?–1523), celebrated in Wordsworth's ' Brougham Castle ' and ' White Doe of Rylstone ' ; eldest son of John de Clifford, thirteenth baron [q. v.], who was attainted and his estates forfeited, 1461 ; brought up as a shepherd ; restored to titles and estates, 1485 ; summoned to parliament, 1485–97 ; received the submission of the Yorkshire rebels, 1486 ; fought at Flodden, 1513 ; studied astrology.　　　　[xi. 61]

CLIFFORD, HENRY DE, first EARL OF CUMBER-LAND, fifteenth BARON CLIFFORD, eleventh BARON OF WESTMORELAND, and second BARON VESCI (1493–1542), eldest son of Henry de Clifford, fourteenth baron [q. v.]; page to Henry VIII; styled Sir Harry Clifford; sheriff of Yorkshire, 1522; led his father's forces against the Scots, 1522; succeeded to the barony, 1523; in constant service against the Scots and often warden of the marches, 1523–34; created Earl of Cumberland, 1525; accepted Henry VIII's divorce, 1529; besieged in Skipton Castle by the northern insurgents, 1536; rewarded with church lands. [xi. 62]

CLIFFORD, HENRY DE, second EARL OF CUMBER-LAND, sixteenth BARON CLIFFORD, twelfth BARON OF WESTMORELAND, and third BARON VESCI (d. 1570), eldest son of Henry de Clifford, first earl [q. v.]; styled Lord Clifford; succeeded to title and estates, 1542; withdrew from court, 1547; favoured Mary Queen of Scots, 1569; alchemist. [xi. 63]

CLIFFORD, HENRY, fifth EARL OF CUMBERLAND (1591–1643), entered Christ Church, Oxford, 1607; B.A., 1609; K.B., 1610; summoned to the peers as Baron Clifford, 1628–9; lord lieutenant of Northumberland, Cumberland, and Westmoreland, 1636–9; raised troops for Charles I's Scottish wars, 1639–40; succeeded to earldom, 1641; commanded royalist forces in Yorkshire, 1642; besieged in York, 1642; wrote verses. [xi. 64]

CLIFFORD, HENRY (1768–1813), legal writer; of a Roman catholic family of Tixall, Staffordshire; educated at Liège; barrister of Lincoln's Inn, 1792; published pamphlets, 1790–1810. [xi. 65]

CLIFFORD, SIR HENRY HUGH (1826–1883), major-general; third son of Hugh Charles Clifford, seventh baron Clifford [q. v.]; entered the army, 1846; served in South Africa, 1847 and 1852–3; served in the Crimea, 1854–6; V.C.; brevet major; served in China, 1857–8; brevet colonel; staff officer at home stations, 1860–75; major-general, 1869; controlled lines of communication in Zulu war, 1879; K.C.M.G., 1879. [xi. 66]

CLIFFORD, HUGH CHARLES, seventh BARON CLIFFORD OF CHUDLEIGH (1790–1858), educated at Stonyhurst; served in the Peninsula; succeeded to barony, 1831; lived chiefly in Italy; died at Rome; published political pamphlets. [xi. 66]

CLIFFORD, JAMES (1622–1698), musician; son of an Oxford cook; chorister of Magdalen College, Oxford, 1632–42; minor canon of St. Paul's, London, 1661; sacrist, 1682; published 'Divine Services and Anthems,' 1663, and sermons. [xi. 66]

CLIFFORD, JOHN DE, thirteenth BARON CLIFFORD, ninth BARON OF WESTMORELAND (1435?–1461), son of Thomas de Clifford, twelfth baron [q. v.]; led troops to London to demand compensation for his father's death, 1458; reconciled to the Yorkist lords and attainted with them, 1459; summoned to parliament, 1460; fought against Yorkists at Wakefield, 1460; nicknamed 'the Butcher,' for his cruelty; fell at Ferrybridge; attainted by the Yorkists, 1461. [xi. 67]

CLIFFORD, MARGARET, COUNTESS OF CUMBERLAND (1560?–1616), youngest daughter of Francis Russell, earl of Bedford; married, 1577, George Clifford, third earl of Cumberland [q. v.]; separated from her husband; engaged in lawsuits to secure her daughter's estates, 1605 [see CLIFFORD, ANNE, COUNTESS OF DORSET]. [xi. 68]

CLIFFORD, MARTIN (d. 1677), author of 'A Treatise of Humane Reason,' 1674; educated at Westminster; B.A. Cambridge, 1643; buffoon about court, 1660; wrote anonymously against Dryden; master of the Charterhouse, 1671. [xi. 68]

CLIFFORD, RICHARD (d. 1421), bishop of London; canon of St. Stephen's, Westminster, 1385; imprisoned as a favourite of Richard II, 1388; guardian of the privy seal, 1388–1400; pluralist; dean of York, 1398; nominated by the pope to the see of Bath and Wells, 1401; bishop of Worcester, August, 1401; translated to London, 1407; presided at the trials for heresy of Sir John Oldcastle, 1413, and of John Clayton, 1415; attended the council of Constance, 1416–17; obtained the papacy for Martin V, 1417. [xi. 69]

CLIFFORD, ROBERT DE, fifth BARON CLIFFORD, first BARON OF WESTMORELAND (1273–1314), succeeded to the Clifford estates, 1285, and to Brougham Castle and half the Vipont estates in Westmoreland, c. 1291?; justice of forests north of Trent, 1297–1305; warden of the marches and governor of Carlisle, 1297; constantly fighting against the Scots from 1297; summoned to parliament, 1299–1313; took Caerlaverock Castle, 1300; granted part of Robert Bruce's English estates, 1306; granted Skipton Castle, 1310; a favourite of Edward II; joined baronial party, 1311; made his peace with Edward II, 1313; failed to relieve Stirling Castle, 23 June 1314; slain next day at Bannockburn. [xi. 70]

CLIFFORD, ROGER DE (d. 1285?), soldier and judge; succeeded to his patrimony, as a minor, c. 1231; attended Henry III to France, 1259; sided with De Montfort, 1262–4; aided Henry III at the siege of Nottingham, 1264; justice of the forests south of Trent; fought for Henry III at Lewes and in the Welsh marches, 1264, and at Evesham, 1265; granted estates in Warwickshire and Leicestershire; attended Prince Edward on the crusade, 1270–4; commissioner in Wales, 1274; envoy to France, 1275; justice in Wales, 1279; taken prisoner by the Welsh insurgents, 1282. [xi. 72]

CLIFFORD, ROGER DE, ninth BARON CLIFFORD, fifth BARON OF WESTMORELAND (1333–1389), served in Flanders, 1345, and against the Spanish fleet, 1350; succeeded his brother in the estates, c. 1352; summoned to parliament, 1356–88; served in Gascony, 1355, 1359–60, in Ireland, 1361, 1368, in France, 1373, and in Brittany, 1388; frequently warden of the west marches, fighting against Scots, 1370–88; governor of Carlisle, 1377. [xi. 74]

CLIFFORD, ROSAMOND (FAIR ROSAMOND) (d. 1176?), daughter of Walter de Clifford [q. v.]; probably acknowledged as mistress of Henry II, 1174; buried in the choir of Godstow Abbey; her remains removed to the chapter-house, c. 1191; her story already famous, 1274. [xi. 75]

CLIFFORD, THOMAS DE, tenth BARON CLIFFORD, sixth BARON OF WESTMORELAND (d. 1391?), eldest son of Roger de Clifford, ninth baron [q. v.]; in attendance on Richard II, 1385; governor of Carlisle and warden of the marches, 1386; banished from court by the baronial party, 1388; succeeded to barony, 1390; summoned to parliament, 1390–1; slain in Germany. [xi. 77]

CLIFFORD, THOMAS DE, twelfth BARON CLIFFORD, eighth BARON OF WESTMORELAND (1414–1455), succeeded to barony, 1422; attended Bedford in France, 1435; raised troops against the Scots, 1435; summoned to parliament, 1436; called on for aid in the relief of Calais, 1452 and 1454; slain at St. Albans. [xi. 77]

CLIFFORD, THOMAS, first BARON CLIFFORD OF CHUDLEIGH (1630–1673), of Ugbrooke, Devonshire; a concealed Romanist entered Exeter College, Oxford, 1647, and the Middle Temple, 1648; travelled; M.P., Totnes, 1660–72; joined court party, 1663; a commissioner for the care of the sick and wounded, 1664; a trustee for the Duke of Monmouth, 1665; knighted; a confidant of Arlington; envoy to Denmark, 1665; served at sea, 1665–6; comptroller (1666), and treasurer (1668) of the household; cognisant of Charles II's wishes to establish Roman catholicism in England, 1669; intrigued in France against the triple alliance, 1669; privy to secret clauses of treaty of Dover, December 1670; granted estates by Charles II, 1671; acting secretary of state, 1672; advised the suspension of exchequer payments, and the Declaration of Indulgence, 1672; created Baron Clifford, 1672; lord high treasurer, 1672; resigned under the Test Act, 1673. [xi. 78]

CLIFFORD, WALTER DE (d. 1190?), inherited estates in Herefordshire and other counties; obtained barony of Clifford before 1138, through his mother or by marriage; owned estates in Shropshire; fought with the Welsh, 1157–64. [xi. 81]

CLIFFORD, WILLIAM (d. 1670), divine; pretender to the barony of Clifford; educated at Douay; missioner in England; rector of the English college, Lisbon; superior of Tournay College, Paris; published devotional tracts. [xi. 82]

CLIFFORD, WILLIAM KINGDON (1845–1879), mathematician and metaphysician; educated at King's

College, London, and Trinity College, Cambridge ; second wrangler ; fellow, 1868 ; professor of applied mathematics, University College, London, 1871 ; wrote philosophical treatises, conceiving of consciousness as being built up out of simple elements of 'mind-stuff'; F.R.S., 1874 : attacked by consumption, 1876 ; died at Madeira; his mathematical works published, 1879-85. [xi. 82]

CLIFT, WILLIAM (1775-1849), naturalist; early showed talent for drawing ; secretary to John Hunter the physician [q. v.], 1792-3 ; caretaker of Hunter's collections, 1793-1844 ; F.R.S., 1823 ; osteologist and medical draughtsman ; contributed to scientific journals.
[xi. 85]
CLIFTON, FRANCIS (d. 1736), physician; M.D. Leyden, 1724 ; practitioner in London ; withdrew to Jamaica, 1734 ; published medical tracts, 1724-34.
[xi. 86]
CLIFTON, JOHN C. (1781-1841), composer of songs and glees ; clerk in the stationery office ; professional musician at Bath, and 1802, at Dublin ; music master in London, 1818 ; died insane. [xi. 87]

CLIFTON, RICHARD (d. 1616), puritan ; possibly vicar of Marnham, 1585, and rector of Babworth, Nottinghamshire, 1586 ; Brownist minister at Scrooby ; minister at Amsterdam, 1610 ; wrote controversial tracts, 1610-12.
[xi. 87]
CLIFTON, ROBERT COX (1810-1861), divine ; B.A. Worcester College, Oxford, 1831 ; fellow, 1833 ; chaplain to Manchester Collegiate Church, 1837, and fellow, 1843 ; rector of Somerton, Oxfordshire, 1843-61 ; canon of Manchester, 1840. [xi. 88]

CLINE, HENRY (1750-1827), surgeon ; trained in London ; practised from 1774 ; lecturer on anatomy to St. Thomas's Hospital, 1781-1811, and surgeon, 1784-1811 ; a strong whig. [xi. 88]

CLINT, ALFRED (1807-1883), etcher and marine painter ; son of George Clint [q. v.]; exhibited, 1828-79, at first portraits, afterwards coast views. [xi. 89]

CLINT, GEORGE (1770-1854), portrait painter and engraver ; a house-painter ; miniature painter, c. 1808 ; much employed on theatrical portraits ; mezzotint engraver. [xi. 90]

CLINT, SCIPIO (1805-1839), medallist and sealengraver ; son of George Clint [q. v.] ; first exhibited, 1825. [xi. 90]

CLINTON, CHARLES (1690-1773), American colonist, of co. Longford ; emigrated, 1729 ; settled as a farmer in New York State, 1731 ; colonel of militia ; commanded regiment against Canada, 1758. [xi. 91]

CLINTON, CHARLES JOHN FYNES (1799-1872), divine ; educated at Westminster and Oriel College, Oxford ; B.A., 1821 ; rector of Cromwell, Nottinghamshire, 1828 ; published sermons. [xi. 91]

CLINTON, EDWARD FIENNES DE, ninth BARON CLINTON and SAYE, and first EARL OF LINCOLN (1512-1585), lord high admiral ; a royal ward, 1517 ; in attendance on Henry VIII, 1532 ; married, 1534, Elizabeth Blount, Henry VIII's mistress ; summoned to parliament, 1536 ; served in the fleet against the Scots and French, 1544-7 ; governor of Boulogne, 1547 ; lord high admiral, 1550-4 and 1558-85 ; governor of the Tower, 1553-4 ; abandoned Lady Jane Grey and made his peace with Mary, 1554 ; held command in expedition to support Spaniards at St. Quentin, 1557 ; commanded the fleet against France, 1558 ; in attendance on Elizabeth, 1564 ; joint-commander against the northern rebels, 1569 ; commanded in North Sea, 1570 ; created Earl of Lincoln, 1572 ; envoy to France, 1572. [xi. 91]

CLINTON, GEOFFREY DE (fl. 1130), chamberlain and treasurer to Henry I ; in attendance on Henry I before 1123 ; founded Kenilworth Priory, 1126 ; accused of treason, 1130. [xi. 93]

CLINTON, SIR HENRY, the elder (1738 ?-1795), general ; born in Newfoundland, of which his father was governor ; captain of the New York militia ; lieutenant, Coldstream guards, 1751 ; lieutenant-colonel ; served in Germany, 1760-3 ; major-general, 1772 ; M.P., 1773-84 ; fought at Bunker's Hill, 1775 ; second in command in America, 1776 ; K.B., 1777 ; commander-in-chief, 1778 ;

took Charleston, 1780 ; quarrelled with his second in command, Lord Cornwallis ; resigned, 1781 ; M.P., 1790 ; general, 1793 ; governor of Gibraltar, 1794 ; died at Gibraltar. [xi. 94]

CLINTON, SIR HENRY, the younger (1771-1829), general ; younger son of Sir Henry Clinton the elder [q. v.]; ensign, 1787 ; served in Holland, 1788-9 ; captain, 1791 ; aide-de-camp to the Duke of York, 1793 ; lieutenant-colonel, 1795 ; prisoner in France, 1796-7 ; military attaché with the Russian army in Italy, 1799 ; adjutant-general in India, 1802-5 ; military attaché with the Russian army at Austerlitz, 1805 ; commandant at Syracuse, 1806-7 ; M.P., 1808-18 ; adjutant-general in Sir John Moore's campaign, 1808-9 ; major-general, 1810 ; commanded sixth division in Peninsula, 1811-14 ; K.B., 1813 ; lieutenant-general, 1814 ; at Waterloo, 1815.
[xi. 95]
CLINTON, HENRY FIENNES, ninth EARL OF LINCOLN and second DUKE OF NEWCASTLE-UNDER-LYME (1720-1794), succeeded his brother in earldom, 1730 ; cofferer of the household, 1764 ; succeeded his uncle in dukedom, 1768 ; gave himself up to sport. [xi. 96]

CLINTON, HENRY FYNES (1781-1852), chronologist ; son of Charles Fynes, a Nottinghamshire clergyman, who assumed the name Clinton in 1821 ; educated at Westminster and Christ Church, Oxford ; M.A., 1805 ; well read in Greek ; M.P., Aldborough, 1806-26 ; inherited a fortune, 1811 ; bought Welwyn, Hertfordshire, 1810 ; issued his standard works, 'Fasti Hellenici, 1824-30, and 'Fasti Romani,' 1845-50 ; epitomes of them published, 1851-3.
[xi. 96]
CLINTON, HENRY PELHAM FIENNES PELHAM, fourth DUKE OF NEWCASTLE (1785-1851), grandson of Henry Fiennes Clinton, second duke [q. v.]; succeeded to dukedom, 1795 ; at Eton, 1796-1803 ; prisoner in France, 1803-7 ; married a wealthy heiress, 1807 ; lord-lieutenant of Nottinghamshire, 1809-39 ; an object of mob violence, 1830-1 ; withdrew from politics, 1832 ; bought Worksop ; published pamphlets. [xi. 98]

CLINTON, HENRY PELHAM FIENNES PELHAM, fifth DUKE OF NEWCASTLE (1811-1864), eldest son of Henry Pelham Fiennes Pelham Clinton, fourth duke [q. v.]; styled Earl of Lincoln ; at Eton, 1826 ; B.A. Christ Church, Oxford, 1832 ; M.P., 1832-51 ; chief secretary for Ireland, February-July 1846 ; divorced his wife, 1850 ; succeeded to dukedom, 1851 ; secretary for war and the colonies, 1852-4 ; secretary for war, 1854-5 ; visited the Crimea, 1855 ; colonial secretary 1859-64 ; visited Canada, 1860. [xi. 98]

CLINTON, SIR WILLIAM HENRY (1769-1846), general ; elder son of Sir Henry Clinton the elder [q. v.]; cornet, 1784 ; captain, 1790 ; served in Flanders, 1793 ; lieutenant-colonel, 1794 ; aide-de-amp to the Duke of York, 1796 ; governor of Madeira, 1801-2 ; M.P., 1806-30 ; major-general, 1808 ; served in Sicily and Spain, 1812-13 ; G.C.B., 1815 ; lieutenant-genera⟩ of ordnance, 1825-9 ; commanded British forces in Portugal, 1826-8 ; general, 1830. [xi. 99]

CLIPSTONE, JOHN (fl. 1378), theological writer ; D.D. Cambridge ; Carmelite friar of Nottingham.
[xi. 100]
CLISSOLD, AUGUSTUS (1797 ?-1882), Swedenborgian ; M.A. Exeter College, Oxford, 1821 ; curate of Stoke Newington ; joined the Swedenborgians, 1838 ; published Swedenborgian tracts, 1838-79 ; benefactor of the 'New Church.' [xi. 100]

CLISSOLD, STEPHEN (1790 ?-1863), writer of pamphlets on trade, 1815-38 ; M.A. Clare College, Cambridge, 1822 ; rector of Wrentham, Suffolk, 1830-53.
[xi. 101]
CLITHEROW, SIR CHRISTOPHER (d. 1641), merchant ; member of the East India Company, 1601 ; subscribed for the discovery of a north-west passage, 1612 ; master of the Ironmongers' Company, 1618 and 1624 ; alderman of London, 1625-41 ; sheriff, 1625 ; M.P. London, 1628 ; lord mayor, 1635 ; knighted, 1636 ; an Eastland merchant, 1638 ; benefactor of Christ's Hospital. [xi. 101]

CLITHEROW, MARGARET (d. 1586), the 'martyr of York'; daughter of Thomas Middleton, wax-chandler, York ; married, 1571, John Clitherow, butcher ; embraced Roman catholicism, 1574 ; imprisoned as a recusant ; barbarously executed for harbouring priests. [xi. 103]

CLIVE, CAROLINE (1801–1873), authoress; *née* Meysey-Wigley; married, 1840, the Rev. Archer Clive (*d.* 1878); accidentally burnt to death; published, chiefly under the initial 'V.,' verses and novels, 1840–72, including 'Paul Ferroll,' 1855. [xi. 103]

CLIVE, CATHERINE, commonly known as KITTY CLIVE (1711–1785), actress; of Irish extraction; *née* Raftor; employed by Colley Cibber at Drury Lane, 1728–1741; made her mark in comedy, 1731; married George Clive, a barrister, before 1734; travestied the part of 'Portia,' 1741; visited Dublin, 1741; a favourite with Handel; sang in Handel's 'Samson,' 1742; employed by Garrick at Drury Lane, 1746–69; pensioned by Horace Walpole; wrote dramatic sketches, 1753–65. [xi. 104]

CLIVE, SIR EDWARD (1704–1771), judge; barrister of Lincoln's Inn, 1725; M.P. St. Michael's, Cornwall, 1741; baron of the exchequer, 1745; justice of common pleas, 1753–70; knighted, 1753. [xi. 107]

CLIVE, EDWARD, first EARL OF POWIS (1754–1839), governor of Madras; eldest son of Robert Clive, baron Clive [q. v.]; succeeded to the Irish barony, 1774; M.P., Ludlow, 1774–94; created Baron Clive of Walcot, in the British peerage, 1794; governor of Madras, 1798–1803; created Earl of Powis, 1804. [xi. 108]

CLIVE, ROBERT, BARON CLIVE (1725–1774), governor of Bengal; eldest son of an impoverished Shropshire squire; exhibited a turbulent and masterful temper at school; offered writership in the East India Company's service, 1743; reached Madras penniless and in debt owing to an exceptionally protracted voyage, 1744; friendless and miserable; tried to shoot himself; taken prisoner by Labourdonnais at Madras, September 1746; escaped to Fort St. David; ensign, 1747; showed great bravery at the unsuccessful siege of Pondicherry, 1748; lieutenant under Major Stringer Lawrence at Devikota; commissariat officer; twice sent in charge of reinforcements to Trichinopoly; captain; allowed to try his plan of attacking Arcot, capital of the Carnatic; marched from Madras, and occupied Arcot, 1751; besieged by ten thousand troops 23 Sept.–14 Nov.; beat off all attacks, having only eighty Europeans and 150 Sepoys efficient; reinforced, 15 Nov.; defeated the enemy at Arni; twice took Conjeveram; defeated the French and natives at Cáveripák; helped Major Lawrence to take Trichinopoly; reduced Covelong and Chingleput; invalided to England, 1753; paid his father's debts; tried to enter parliament; appointed lieutenant-colonel; reached Bombay, 1755; helped to reduce Gheriah, the stronghold of the pirate Angriá, 1756; took charge of Fort St. David, 20 June 1756 (the day before the 'Black Hole' of Calcutta); came to terms with Suráj ud Dowlah, the guilty nawáb of Bengal; captured Chandernagore; discovered the nawáb's intended treachery; negotiated privately with his general Mir Jaffier, through the Hindu Omichand; cheated Omichand by having two treaties drawn up, one of them fictitious; marched against the nawáb, and won the great victory of Plassey, 1757; installed Mir Jaffier as nawáb; accepted from him a large present and the quit-rent of the company's territory; governor of the company's Bengal possessions, 1757–60; repulsed the Dutch attempt to found a rival colony at Chinsura, 1759; sailed for England, 1760; M.P., Shrewsbury, 1760–1774; created Baron Clive in the Irish peerage, 1762; sent out to put down abuses in Bengal; assumed the governorship of Bengal, 1765; reformed the civil administration; restored military discipline and pensioned the nawáb of Bengal; obtained for the company the lordship of the province; created, out of a legacy from Mir Jaffier, a pension fund for disabled officers; returned to England in shattered health, 1766; rancorously attacked by politicians and others; went through a parliamentary inquiry, 1772–3; became a victim to opium; committed suicide. [xi. 108]

CLOBERY, ROBERT (1719–1800). [See GLYN, ROBERT.]

CLOËTÉ, SIR ABRAHAM JOSIAS (1794–1886), general; born at the Cape; cornet, 1809; captain, 1812; lieutenant-colonel, 1837; general, 1871; stationed in England, 1809–13; aide-de-camp to the governor, Cape Colony, 1813–17; in India, 1817–19; superintended the 'settlers of 1820 ' at Cape Colony; town major of Cape Town, 1822–

1840; K.H., 1836; on service in South Africa, 1840–54; knighted, 1854; stationed in West Indies, 1855–61; retired, 1877. [xi. 120]

CLOGIE or **CLOGY**, ALEXANDER (1614–1698), biographer; born in Scotland; educated in Dublin; chaplain to William Bedell [q. v.], bishop of Kilmore, 1629; beneficed, 1637; persecuted by the Irish rebels, 1641; army chaplain in England, 1645, rector of Wigmore, Herefordshire, 1647–98; wrote memoir of Bishop Bedell, 1675. [xi. 120]

CLONCURRY, second BARON (1773–1853). [See LAWLESS, VALENTINE BROWNE.]

CLONMELL, EARL OF (1739–1798). [See SCOTT, JOHN.]

CLONTARFF, VISCOUNT (*d.* 1560). [See RAWSON, JOHN.]

CLOPTON, SIR HUGH (*d.* 1496), lord mayor of London; mercer in London; sheriff of London, 1486; lord mayor, 1492; knighted; built at Stratford-on-Avon, 'New Place' (afterwards bought by Shakespeare), 1483, Trinity Chapel, and the stone bridge over the river. [xi. 121]

CLOPTON, WALTER DE (*d.* 1412 ?), judge; king's serjeant, 1378; chief-justice of king's bench, 1389–1400; K.B., 1389; became a Franciscan friar at Norwich. [xi. 122]

CLOSE, SIR BARRY (*d.* 1813), major-general; cadet at Madras, 1771; distinguished himself at the sieges of Seringapatam, 1792 and 1799; resident of Mysore, 1799; resident of Poona, 1801; returned to England, 1811; created baronet. [xi. 122]

CLOSE, FRANCIS (1797–1882), evangelical divine; B.A. St. John's College, Cambridge, 1820; M.A., 1825; rector of Cheltenham, 1826; D.D Lambeth, 1856; dean of Carlisle, 1856–81; published sermons and pamphlets, 1825–77. [xi. 123]

CLOSE, JOHN (1816–1891), 'Poet Close'; son of a butcher at Gunnerside, Swaledale; published tracts of verse; established himself as printer at Kirkby Stephen; attracted patrons by his rhyming, and obtained, 1860, civil service pension, which was withdrawn, 1861, after much public discussion; continued to issue pamphlets of metrical balderdash until his death. [Suppl. ii. 34]

CLOSE, NICHOLAS (*d.* 1452), bishop; fellow of King's College, Cambridge, 1443; a commissioner to Scotland, 1449; archdeacon of Colchester; D.D.; bishop of Carlisle, 1450; translated to Lichfield, 1452. [xi. 124]

CLOSE, THOMAS (1796–1881), antiquary and genealogist. [xi. 125]

CLOSSE, GEORGE (*fl.* 1585), divine; M.A. Trinity College, Cambridge, 1579; ejected from the vicarage of Cuckfield, Sussex, 1581; libelled the lord mayor of London in a sermon at Paul's Cross, 1585. [xi. 125]

CLOSTERMAN, JOHN (1656–1713), portrait-painter; born at Osnabruck, Hanover; visited Paris, 1679; came to England, 1681; visited Madrid, 1696, and Italy; painted the Blenheim group of the Duke of Marlborough and his family, *c.* 1698. [xi. 125]

CLOTWORTHY, SIR JOHN, first VISCOUNT MASSEREENE (*d.* 1665), an Antrim landowner; opponent of Strafford's Irish administration; M.P., Maldon, 1640; a manager of the proceedings against Strafford; joined in the prosecution of Laud; annoyed Laud on the scaffold, 1645; envoy to Ormonde, 1646; accused by the army leaders of embezzlement, 1647; expelled from the Commons, January 1648; replaced, June 1648; imprisoned, 1648–51; employed in Irish affairs, 1653–4; agent in England for the Irish adventurers and landholding soldiers, 1660; created Viscount Massereene, 1660. [xi. 126]

CLOUGH, ANNE JEMIMA (1820–1892), first principal of Newnham College, Cambridge; sister of Arthur Hugh Clough [q. v.]; resided at Liverpool, where, 1841, she started a school, which she removed to Ambleside, 1852; became acquainted with Miss Emily Davies, Madame Barbara Leigh Smith Bodichon [q. v.], and Miss Buss and others interested in cause of education of women; secretary, 1837–70, and president, 1873–4, of North of England council for promoting higher education of women; head,

1871, of house of residence for women students at Cambridge, which ultimately developed into Newnham College. [Suppl. ii. 35]

CLOUGH, ARTHUR HUGH (1819–1861), poet; son of a Liverpool cotton merchant; educated at Rugby, 1829–36; scholar of Balliol College, Oxford, 1837; B.A., 1841; fellow of Oriel College, 1841–8, and tutor, 1843–8; visited Paris, Rome, and Venice, 1848–50; principal of University Hall, London, 1849–52; visited Boston, America, 1852–3; examiner in the education office, London, 1853; visited, in ill-health, Greece, the Pyrenees, Italy, 1861; died at Florence; published his first poem, 1848; revised a translation of Plutarch's 'Lives,' 1859–60; his poems and letters published, 1869. [xi. 127]

CLOUGH, RICHARD (d. 1570), merchant; chorister at Chester; merchant in London; went on pilgrimage to Jerusalem; knight of the Holy Sepulchre; factor at Antwerp for Sir Thomas Gresham, 1552–69; suggested an exchange, London, 1561; granted a lease of crown lands, 1565; visited Spain, 1567; built Plâs Clough, Denbighshire; died at Hamburg; his wealth proverbial in Wales. [xi. 128]

CLOUTT, THOMAS (1781?–1846). [See RUSSELL.]

CLOVER, JOSEPH (1725–1811), farrier; blacksmith in Norwich; studied farriery, 1750; practised as veterinary surgeon, 1765–81. [xi. 131]

CLOWES, BUTLER (d. 1782), mezzotint-engraver and printseller; exhibited, 1768–73, portraits and sketches in mezzotint. [xi. 131]

CLOWES, JOHN (1743–1831), Swedenborgian; M.A. Trinity College, Cambridge, 1769; fellow; vicar of St. John's, Manchester, 1769; began to read Swedenborg, 1773; founded a Swedenborgian printing society, 1780; issued translations of works by Swedenborg, 1781–1816, and theological pamphlets and sermons, 1799–1826; wrote an autobiography. [xi. 131]

CLOWES, WILLIAM, the elder (1540?–1604), surgeon; surgeon's apprentice in London; army surgeon in France, 1563; naval surgeon, 1563–9; practised surgery in London, 1569; surgeon of St. Bartholomew's Hospital, 1581–5, and of Christ's Hospital; army surgeon in the Low Countries, 1585–7; naval surgeon, 1588; again practised in London; published surgical treatises of some merit, 1579–1602. [xi. 132]

CLOWES, WILLIAM, the younger (1582–1648), surgeon; son of William Clowes the elder (1540?–1604) [q. v.]; practised in London, 1605 till death; surgeon to Charles I; prosecuted Leverett for assuming the royal prerogative of touching for the king's evil, 1637. [xi. 134]

CLOWES, WILLIAM, the elder (1779–1847), printer; apprenticed at Chichester; came to London, 1802; commenced business by himself, 1803; the first to use steam machinery for book-printing, 1823. [xi. 134]

CLOWES, WILLIAM (1780–1851), primitive methodist; a Staffordshire potter; champion dancer; joined Wesleyan methodists, 1805; local preacher, 1808–10; cofounder of the primitive methodists, 1810; preached in north of England. [xi. 135]

CLOWES, WILLIAM, the younger (1807–1883), printer; eldest son of William Clowes the elder (1779–1847) [q. v.]; entered his father's business, 1823. [xi. 135]

CLUBBE, JOHN (1703?–1773), satirical writer; B.A. King's College, Cambridge, 1725; vicar of Debenham, Suffolk, 1730; rector of Whatfield, Suffolk, 1735–73; published a sermon, 1751, and burlesques, 1758–70. [xi. 136]

CLUBBE, WILLIAM (1745–1814), poetical writer; son of John Clubbe [q. v.]; LL.B. Caius College, Cambridge, 1769; rector of Flowton, 1769, and vicar of Brandeston, Suffolk, 1770; published verses, 1793–1806. [xi. 136]

CLULOW, WILLIAM BENTON (1802–1882), dissenting minister; pastor at Shaldon, Devonshire, 1823; tutor at Airedale College, Bradford, 1835–43; published essays, 1843–65. [xi. 136]

CLUNIE, JOHN (1757?–1819), composer of Scottish songs; schoolmaster and precentor of Markinch, Fifeshire, 1785; minister of Borthwick, Midlothian, 1791. [xi. 137]

CLUTTERBUCK, HENRY (1767–1856), medical writer; surgeon's apprentice at Truro; came to London, 1788; qualified as a surgeon, 1790; studied medicine at Edinburgh, 1802, and Glasgow; M.D. Glasgow, 1804; a leading physician in London; lectured on materia medica; published medical treatises, 1794–1846. [xi. 137]

CLUTTERBUCK, ROBERT (1772–1831), topographer; B.A. Exeter College, Oxford, 1794; published a finely illustrated history of Hertfordshire, 1815–27. [xi. 138]

CLYDE, BARON (1792–1863). [See CAMPBELL, SIR COLIN.]

CLYFFE, WILLIAM (d. 1558), divine; LL.B. Cambridge, 1514; LL.D., 1523; admitted to Doctors' Commons, 1522; commissary of London diocese, 1522–9; prebendary of St. Paul's, 1526; archdeacon of London, 1529–33; prebendary of York, 1532, precentor, 1534, treasurer, 1538–1547; archdeacon of Cleveland, 1533; dean of Chester, 1547–58. [xi. 138]

CNUT (994?–1035). [See CANUTE.]

COATES, CHARLES (1746?–1813), antiquary; educated at Reading and Cambridge; M.B., 1767; vicar of Preston, Dorset, 1780; vicar of Osmington, Dorset 1788–1813; F.S.A., 1793; published a history of Reading, 1802, and a supplement, 1809. [xi. 139]

COATES, ROBERT (1772–1848), amateur actor; known as ROMEO COATES; son of a wealthy Antigua planter; acted in school in England; acted in private theatricals in Antigua, 1805; acted in Bath, London, and elsewhere, 1810–16; hissed off the stage; withdrew for a time to Boulogne. [xi. 139]

COATS, THOMAS (1809–1883), thread manufacturer; benefactor of Paisley; collector of Scottish coins. [xi. 140]

COBB, JAMES (1756–1818), dramatist; clerk in the East India Company's office; wrote twenty-four dramatic pieces, 1779–1809. [xi. 140]

COBB, SAMUEL (1675–1713), translator and versifier; educated at Christ's Hospital, London, 1683–94; M.A. Trinity College, Cambridge, 1702; master at Christ's Hospital, 1702–13; published political odes, 1694–1709, and translations from Latin and Greek, published 1709–14. [xi. 141]

COBBE, CHARLES (1687–1765), archbishop of Dublin; educated at Winchester and Trinity College, Oxford; M.A., 1712; chaplain to the lord-lieutenant of Ireland, 1717; dean of Ardagh, 1718; bishop of Killala, 1720, and Dromore, 1727; translated to Kildare, 1731; dean of Christ Church, Dublin; D.D. Dublin, 1735; translated to Dublin, 1743. [xi. 142]

COBBETT, WILLIAM (1762–1835), essayist, politician, and agriculturist; son of a labourer at Farnham, Surrey; self-taught; enlisted as soldier, 1783; served in Nova Scotia, 1784–91; withdrew to France and to Philadelphia, 1792, to avoid prosecution through his agitating for increase of soldiers' pay; bookseller and publisher, on the loyalist side, 1796; prosecuted for libel, 1797; withdrew to New York, 1797, and to London, 1800; an active tory journalist, 1801; but afterwards adopted popular opinions, and from 1804 wrote in the radical interest, with characteristic directness and vigour; farmed in Hampshire, 1804–17; withdrew to America, 1817–19; wrote strongly in favour of Queen Caroline, 1820; farmed land in Surrey, 1821; tried to enter parliament, 1821; M.P. Oldham, 1832; wrote with exceptional perspicuity and force, on grammar, economics, and other subjects. 'Cobbett's Weekly Political Register,' begun in January 1802, was continued till his death. [xi. 142]

COBBIN, INGRAM (1777–1851), congregational minister, 1802–28; published scripture commentaries. [xi. 145]

COBBOLD, ELIZABETH (1767–1824), poetess; née Knipe; published poems, 1787; married William Clarke of Ipswich, 1790; published, as Eliza Clarke, 'The Sword,' a novel, 1791; married John Cobbold of Ipswich, 1792; her collected poems published, 1825. [xi. 145]

COBBOLD, JOHN SPENCER (1768–1837), divine; fellow of Caius College, Cambridge; M.A., 1793; master of Nuneaton school, 1794; rector of Woolpit, Suffolk, 1831; published sermons and essays. [xi. 146]

COBBOLD, RICHARD (1797–1877), novelist; son of Elizabeth Cobbold [q. v.]; M.A. Caius College, Cambridge, 1823; rector of Wortham, Suffolk; published an account of Margaret Catchpole [q. v.], 1845, novels, and sermons. [xi. 146]

COBBOLD, THOMAS SPENCER (1828–1886), helminthologist; third son of Richard Cobbold [q. v.]; surgeon's apprentice in Norwich; studied medicine at Edinburgh, 1847; M.D., 1851; curator of Edinburgh anatomical museum, 1851–6; lectured on botany and zoology in London, 1857–84; studied parasitic worms; wrote treatises on parasites from 1864. [xi. 147]

COBDEN, EDWARD (1684–1764), author of poems and sermons, 1718–58; B.A. Trinity College, Oxford, 1706; M.A. King's College, Cambridge, 1713; D.D. Oxford, 1723; archdeacon of London, 1742; chaplain to George II, 1730–1752. [xi. 147]

COBDEN, RICHARD (1804–1865), statesman; son of a Sussex farmer; clerk (1819) and traveller for a London calico merchant; partner, 1828, in a London calico warehouse, and, 1831, in a Lancashire calico factory; settled in Manchester, 1832; wrote on economics in the 'Manchester Examiner'; published his first free-trade pamphlets, 1835–6; travelled in America, the East, and Germany, 1835–8; tried to enter parliament, 1837; a foremost leader of the Anti-Cornlaw League, 1838–46; M.P., Stockport, 1841–7; voted for the Maynooth grant, 1845; greatly contributed, by his strenuous advocacy, to the repeal of the Corn Laws, 1846; travelled on the continent, 1846–7; M.P., West Riding of Yorkshire, 1847–57; advocated international arbitration and disarmament; defeated the government on the Chinese war question, 1857; failed to secure re-election; visited America, 1859; M.P., Rochdale, 1859; negotiated the commercial treaty with France, 1859–1860; opposed intervention in favour of Denmark, 1864; last spoke in the House of Commons, 22 July 1864; refused office, 1859, and a baronetcy, 1860. A subscription on his behalf in 1845 yielded nearly 80,000*l.*; a second subscription, in 1860, yielded 40,000*l.* [xi. 148]

COBHAM, VISCOUNT (1669?–1749). [See TEMPLE, RICHARD.]

COBHAM, BARONS. [See BROOKE, HENRY, *d.* 1619; OLDCASTLE, SIR JOHN, *d.* 1417.]

COBHAM, ELEANOR, DUCHESS OF GLOUCESTER (*d.* 1446?), originally mistress, and, before 1431, wife of Humphrey, duke of Gloucester [q. v.]; accused by one Roger Bolingbroke, who had induced her to believe that her husband would become king, of being her accuser's accomplice in treason and magic, 1441; imprisoned, 1441; sentenced to penance and imprisonment; imprisoned at Chester and Kenilworth. [xxviii. 243]

COBHAM, SIR HENRY (1538–1605?), diplomatist; accompanied an English embassy to Madrid, 1561; envoy to the emperor Maximilian II at Vienna, 1567; envoy to Antwerp, to the emperor at Speyer, and to Spain, 1570; knighted, 1575; envoy to Madrid, 1575; ambassador at Paris, 1579–83; M.P., Kent, 1586–9. [xi. 154]

COBHAM, JOHN DE, third BARON COBHAM (*d.* 1408), succeeded his father, John de Cobham, 1355; served in France, 1367; several times envoy in Flanders and France, from 1374; often a trier of petitions, 1379–1401; impeached (1397) for serving (1388) as commissioner at the trial of Richard II's favourites; banished to Jersey; recalled, 1399. [xi. 155]

COBHAM, THOMAS DE (*d.* 1327), bishop of Worcester; graduate of Paris, Oxford, and Cambridge; prebendary of Hereford, Wells, London, and York; envoy to the pope, 1306, and to France, 1312; elected archbishop of Canterbury, May 1313, but set aside by the pope, October; visited papal court at Avignon, 1313; made, by the pope, bishop of Worcester, 1317; built a library for Oxford University, *c.* 1320; his books placed in it, 1337. [xi. 157]

COBHAM, THOMAS (1786–1842), actor; a London press reader; played Richard III in London, 1816, and was by some reckoned equal to Edmund Kean; acted in Dublin, 1817. [xi. 158]

COBURG, DUKE OF (1844–1900). [See ALFRED ERNEST ALBERT.]

COCHRAN, WILLIAM (1738–1785), painter; art student in Glasgow, 1754, and Italy, 1761; much employed in Glasgow as portrait-painter and miniaturist. [xi. 159]

COCHRAN-PATRICK, ROBERT WILLIAM (1842–1897), statesman and numismatist; B.A. Edinburgh, 1861; LL.B. Trinity Hall, Cambridge, 1864; F.S.A. Scotland; F.S.A. London, 1871; conservative M.P. for North Ayrshire, 1880–5; assessor to St. Andrews University, 1886; honorary LL.D. Glasgow, 1887; permanent undersecretary for Scotland, 1887–92; vice-chairman of Scottish fishery board, 1896; published works relating to Scottish coins and medals and other writings. [Suppl. ii. 36]

COCHRANE, SIR ALEXANDER FORRESTER INGLIS (1758–1832), admiral; younger son of the eighth Earl of Dundonald; lieutenant in navy, 1778; served in West Indies, 1780–2; captain, 1782; commanded a ship with credit, 1790–1802; M.P., Stirling boroughs, 1802; rear-admiral, 1804; blockaded Ferrol, 1804; held command in West Indies and on the American station, 1805–15; K.B., 1806; admiral, 1819; commander-in-chief at Portsmouth, 1821. [xi. 159]

COCHRANE, ARCHIBALD, ninth EARL OF DUNDONALD, styled LORD COCHRANE (1749–1831), served for a time in the navy and in the army; succeeded to the earldom, 1778; brought to poverty by unprofitable attempts to find industrial applications of chemical discoveries; published pamphlets on agricultural chemistry; died at Paris. [xi. 160]

COCHRANE, SIR JAMES (1798–1883), judge; born in Nova Scotia; barrister of the Inner Temple, 1829; attorney-general of Gibraltar, 1837, and chief-justice at Gibraltar, 1841–77; knighted, 1845; died at Gibraltar. [xi. 161]

COCHRANE, SIR JOHN (*d.* 1650?), royalist; commanded regiment at Edinburgh, 1640; joined Charles I at York, 1642; governor of Towcester, 1643; his estates forfeited, 1644; sent to the continent to raise money for Charles I. [xi. 162]

COCHRANE, SIR JOHN (*d.* 1695?), of Ochiltree, Ayrshire; second son of William Cochrane, first earl of Dundonald [q. v.]; involved in the Rye House plot, 1683; escaped to Holland; attainted, 1685; took part in Argyll's invasion, 1685; taken prisoner; saved himself by turning king's evidence; employed to persuade the presbyterians to accept James II's Declaration of Indulgence, 1687; recovered his estates, 1689; imprisoned on a charge of embezzling public money, 1695. [xi. 162]

COCHRANE, JOHN DUNDAS (1780–1825), traveller; naval officer; travelled through France, Spain, and Portugal, 1815; travelled in Russia and Siberia, 1820–1; published an account of his journey, 1824; died in Venezuela. [xi. 162]

COCHRANE, JOHN GEORGE (1781–1852), bibliographer; bookseller's apprentice in Glasgow; as a London publisher agitated against the Copyright Act, 1813; edited the 'Foreign Quarterly Review,' London, 1827–35; edited the 'Caledonian Mercury,' Edinburgh; catalogued Sir Walter Scott's Abbotsford library, 1838; newspaper editor at Hertford; librarian of the London Library, 1841 till death. [xi. 163]

COCHRANE, ROBERT, EARL OF MAR (*d.* 1482), favourite of James III of Scotland; in favour before 1476; built the great hall in Stirling Castle; procured the murder of Mar, and the exile of Albany, the king's brothers, 1479; offended the nobles by taking the earldom of Mar; depreciated the silver coinage; hanged by the nobles at Lauder. [xi. 163]

COCHRANE, THOMAS, tenth EARL OF DUNDONALD (1775–1860), admiral; son of Archibald Cochrane, ninth earl [q. v.]; styled Lord Cochrane; held commission in the army; first joined his ship, the Hind, 1793; lieutenant, 1796; served on the North American station, 1796–8, and on the French and Spanish coasts, 1798–1800; as commander of the Speedy, captured many vessels, 1800–1; captain, 1801; captured by a French squadron, 1801; exchanged; studied at Edinburgh University, 1802–3; banished to the Orkneys guardship, 1803–4; cruised successfully off the Azores, 1805; cruised successfully in the Bay of Biscay, 1806; M.P., Honiton, 1806, Westminster, 1807; exposed the abuses of the admiralty; ordered to the Mediterranean; tried to check the venality of the administration of Corfu and the Maltese prize court; cruised with conspicuous success on the French and Spanish coasts, 1808; his plan for destroying the French fleet in Aix roads frustrated by the jealousy of his senior officers, 1809; K.B., 1809; placed on half-pay for attacking naval abuses; proposed a 'secret war plan' for destroying an enemy's fleets and coast defences, 1811; appointed flag-captain to his uncle, Sir Alexander Forrester Inglis Cochrane [q. v.], 1813; falsely accused of connivance in a stock exchange fraud, 1814; expelled from the navy, parliament, and the order of the Bath; at once re-elected by his Westminster constituents; harassed by the government with fines and imprisonments, 1814–16; his fines paid by penny subscriptions; accepted command of the Chilian navy, 1817; by a series of brilliant successes against the Spanish forces, 1819–22, secured the independence of Chili and Peru; admiral of the Brazilian fleet, securing the independence of Brazil, 1823–5; admiral if the Greek navy, 1827–8; first employed steam-power in ships of war; obstructed by insubordination and peculation; succeeded to earldom, July 1831; reinstated in the navy and promoted rear-admiral, 1832; urged adoption of screwpropellers, 1843; G.C.B., 1847; commander-in-chief on the North American station, 1848; admiral, 1851; again proposed his 'secret war plan,' to cope with Russia, 1854; published a narrative of his South American services, 1859, and his autobiography, 1860–1. [xi. 165]

COCHRANE, Sir THOMAS JOHN (1789–1872), admiral; eldest son of Sir Alexander Forrester Inglis Cochrane [q. v.]; entered navy, 1796; captain, 1806; rearadmiral, 1841; K.C.B., 1847; admiral of the fleet, 1865. [xi. 175]

COCHRANE, Sir WILLIAM, of Cowdon, first EARL OF DUNDONALD (d. 1686), royalist; a great landowner in Ayrshire and Renfrewshire; M.P., Ayrshire, 1644; created Baron Cochrane of Dundonald, 1647; fined by Cromwell, 1654; created Earl of Dundonald, 1669. [xi. 175]

COCHRANE-BAILLIE, ALEXANDER DUNDAS ROSS WISHART, first BARON LAMINGTON (1816–1890), politician and author; son of Admiral Sir Thomas John Cochrane [q. v.]; educated at Eton and Trinity College, Cambridge; B.A., 1837; conservative M.P. for Bridport, 1841–52, Lanarkshire, 1857, Honiton, 1859–68, and Isle of Wight, 1870–80; created Baron Lamington, 1880; joint editor of, and contributor to, 'The Owl,' 1864–8; published poems, novels, and other writings. [Suppl. ii. 37]

COCK, GEORGE (d. 1679), captain; served in Charles I's army; searcher of the port of Newcastle, 1660; steward for sick and wounded seamen, 1664; F.R.S., 1666; friend of Samuel Pepys. [xi. 176]

COCKAYNE. [See also COKAYNE.]

COCKAYNE, THOMAS OSWALD (1807–1873), philologist; B.A. Cambridge, 1828; in holy orders; assistant master at King's College School, London, till 1869; published philological and historical text-books. [xi. 176]

COCKAYNE, WILLIAM (1717–1798), astronomer; educated at Merchant Taylors' School, 1728–36; M.A. St. John's College, Oxford, 1744; D.D., 1754; professor of astronomy, Gresham College, London, 1752–95; rector of Kilkhampton, Cornwall, 1763–98; published sermons. [xi. 176]

COCKBURN, ADAM, LORD ORMISTON (1656–1735), Scottish judge; inherited Ormiston, Haddingtonshire, 1671; a zealous whig; M.P., Haddingtonshire, 1678, 1681, 1689–92; lord justice clerk, 1692–9, 1705–10, and 1714–35; treasurer depute, 1699–1702; a lord of session, styled Lord Ormiston, 1705–35. [xi. 177]

COCKBURN, Sir ALEXANDER JAMES EDMUND (1802–1880), lord chief-justice of England; educated on the continent; entered Trinity Hall, Cambridge, 1822; fellow and LL.B., 1829; barrister of the Middle Temple, 1829; published election cases reports, 1832; obtained practice in election petitions, 1833–8; served on the commission on municipal corporations, 1834; M.P., Southampton, 1847; made his mark by defending Lord Palmerston's foreign policy, 1850; knighted; solicitor-general; attorney-general, 1851–6; recorder of Bristol, 1854; prosecutor in the Palmer poisoning case, 1856; chief-justice of common pleas, 1856; succeeded to baronetcy, 1858; lord chief-justice of England, 1859; presided over the Tichborne trial, 1873; published legal and political pamphlets. [xi. 177]

COCKBURN, ALICIA or ALISON (1712?–1794). authoress of 'I've seen the smiling of fortune beguiling' to the tune 'Flowers of the Forest'; née Rutherford; married Patrick Cockburn, advocate, 1731; a leader of Edinburgh society; friend of Sir Walter Scott. [xi. 181]

COCKBURN, ARCHIBALD (fl. 1722), M.A.; clergyman in St. Christopher's, West Indies; published pamphlet on the intermediate state. [xi. 183]

COCKBURN, CATHARINE (1679–1749), dramatist and philosophical writer; née Trotter; embraced Romanism; returned to the Anglican communion, 1707; married, 1708, Patrick Cockburn [q. v.]; brought out tragedies and comedies, 1695–1706; wrote in defence of Locke, 1702 and 1726; published ethical treatises, 1743 and 1747; her collected prose works published, 1751. [xi. 183]

COCKBURN, Sir GEORGE (1763–1847), general; ensign, 1781; aide-de-camp to General Eliott at Gibraltar, 1781–3; sent to study army manœuvres on the continent, 1785–8; lieutenant-colonel, 1793; major-general, 1803; travelled in Sicily, 1810–11; K.C.H., 1821; general, 1821; published notes of travel and pamphlets. [xi. 184]

COCKBURN, Sir GEORGE (1772–1853), admiral; put on the ship's books, 1781; joined his ship, 1786; commanded ship in Mediterranean, 1793–1802, in West Indies, 1808, in river Scheldt, 1809, and on French and Spanish coasts, 1810–11; rear-admiral, 1812; sent to harass the American coast, 1812–15; took part in capture of Washington, 1813; K.C.B., 1815; conveyed Napoleon to St. Helena, 1815; governor of St. Helena, 1815–16; M.P. and a lord of the admiralty, at intervals, 1820–46; admiral of the fleet, 1851; succeeded to baronetcy, 1852. [xi. 184]

COCKBURN, HENRY THOMAS, LORD COCKBURN (1779–1854), Scottish judge; educated in Edinburgh; advocate, 1800; a zealous whig; a celebrated pleader in criminal cases; wrote on legal and political subjects in pamphlets and reviews, 1822–30; solicitor-general for Scotland, 1830–4; lord rector of Glasgow University, 1831 and 1833; a lord of session, 1834, and of justiciary, 1837; published a life of Lord Jeffrey, 1852; his autobiography published, 1856, his journal and some of his letters, 1874. [xi. 186]

COCKBURN, JAMES (fl. 1783), colonel; saw thirty-six years' service; present at the capture of Quebec, 1759, and at Bunker's Hill, 1775; governor of St. Eustatius, when it was captured by the French, 1781; cashiered, 1783. [xi. 188]

COCKBURN, JAMES PATTISON (1779?–1847), major-general royal artillery; cadet at Woolwich, 1793; second lieutenant, royal artillery, 1795; lieutenant-colonel, 1825; major-general, 1846; director of the Royal Laboratory, Woolwich, 1838–46; published drawings of Swiss and Italian scenery, 1820–9. [xi. 188]

COCKBURN, JOHN (1652–1729), divine; studied at Edinburgh, 1666, and Aberdeen, 1668 (M.A., 1671); ordained by the bishop of Aberdeen, 1675; minister of Udny, Aberdeenshire, 1676; minister of Old Deer, 1681; minister of Ormiston, Haddingtonshire, 1683–9; imprisoned as a Jacobite, 1689; visited St. Germains; D.D.; Anglican chaplain at Amsterdam, 1698–1709; resided in London, 1709–14; vicar of Northolt, Middlesex, 1714–29; published sermons and theological tracts. [xi. 189]

COCKBURN, PATRICK (1678–1749), divine; son of John Cockburn [q. v.]; M.A. Edinburgh, 1705; in Holland, 1705; curate of Nayland, Suffolk, 1704–12; ejected from the curacy of St. Dunstan's, Fleet Street, 1714, for refusing the oath to George I; taught Latin in Chancery Lane; episcopal minister in Aberdeen, 1726–39; vicar of Long Horsley, Northumberland, from before 1737 till death; published sermons. [xi. 191]

COCKBURN, WILLIAM or PIERS (d. 1529), Scottish freebooter; executed. [xi. 191]

COCKBURN, WILLIAM (1669–1739), physician; M.A. Edinburgh; medical student at Leyden, 1691; licentiate of the London College of Physicians, 1694; physician to the fleet, 1694; probably M.D. of Leyden; discovered a specific for dysentery; a successful practitioner in London before 1710; physician to Greenwich Hospital, 1731; published medical tracts. [xi. 192]

COCKBURN, SIR WILLIAM (1768–1835), lieutenant-general; son of James Cockburn (*fl.* 1783) [q. v.]; ensign, 1778; served in American war, 1779–83; captain, 1783; served in India, 1790–1802; lieutenant-colonel, 1798; major-general, 1811; lieutenant-general, 1821; succeeded as fifth baronet of Cockburn, Berwickshire. [xi. 193]

COCKER, EDWARD (1631–1675), arithmetician; taught writing and arithmetic in London from before 1657 to 1665; a book-collector; published twenty-three manuals of penmanship, 1657–75; published his arithmetic, 1664, which afterwards went through more than a hundred editions; published verses, 1670, 1675. [xi. 193]

COCKERAM, HENRY (*fl.* 1650), author of the earliest published dictionary of English (first published, 1623; eleventh edition issued, 1655). [xi. 195]

COCKERELL, CHARLES ROBERT (1788–1863), architect; son of Samuel Pepys Cockerell [q. v.]; trained by his father; studied architectural remains in Greece, Asia Minor, Sicily, and Italy, 1810–17; discovered, in company with two Germans, the frieze of the temple of Apollo at Phigaleia, 1812; architect in London, 1817; exhibited at the Royal Academy, 1818–58; designed buildings in London; R.A., 1836; professor of architecture to the Royal Academy, 1840–57; designed the Taylorian Building, Oxford, 1842; honorary D.C.L. Oxford, 1845; completed the Fitzwilliam Museum, Cambridge, 1845, and St. George's Hall, Liverpool, 1847; wrote on sculpture and architecture, 1816–62. [xi. 195]

COCKERELL, FREDERICK PEPYS (1833–1878), architect; second son of Charles Robert Cockerell [q. v.]; made a sketching tour in North France, 1850; studied architecture in Paris and Italy, 1853–5; exhibited at the Royal Academy, 1854–77; architect of numerous mansions and some churches; died at Paris. [xi. 198]

COCKERELL, SAMUEL PEPYS (1754–1827), architect; pupil of Sir Robert Taylor; exhibited at the Royal Academy, 1785–1803; designed churches and mansions. [xi. 199]

COCKERILL, JOHN (1790–1840), manufacturer; son of William Cockerill [q. v.]; born in Lancashire; went to Verviers, Belgium, 1802; joint-manager of the factory at Liège, 1807; set up a woollen factory at Berlin, 1815; established the great foundry and machine factory at Seraing, Belgium, 1817; died at Warsaw. [xi. 200]

COCKERILL, WILLIAM (1759–1832), inventor; a Lancashire mechanic; employed in St. Petersburg, 1794; in Sweden, 1796; manufactured spinning and weaving machinery at Verviers, Belgium, 1799, and at Liège, 1807–1812; died near Aix-la-Chapelle. [xi. 200]

COCKIN, WILLIAM (1736–1801), author; writing-master in London, at Lancaster, 1764–84, and at Nottingham, 1784–92; published an arithmetic, essays, and poems. [xi. 200]

COCKINGS, GEORGE (*d.* 1802), author of poems and dramas; an official at Boston, America; registrar of a London society, *c.* 1772 till death. [xi. 201]

COCKIS, JOHN (*fl.* 1572). [See COXE.]

COCKLE, SIR JAMES (1819–1895), chief-justice of Queensland and mathematician; educated at Charterhouse and Trinity College, Cambridge; M.A., 1845; called to the bar at Middle Temple, 1846; practised on Midland circuit; first chief-justice of Queensland, 1863–1879; knighted, 1869; F.R.A.S., 1854; F.R.S., 1865; fellow of London Mathematical Society, 1870, and president, 1886–8. He made noteworthy contributions to the theory of differential equations, and published mathematical writings. [Suppl. ii. 38]

COCKS, ARTHUR HERBERT (1819–1881), Bengal civilian; educated at Haileybury; went to Bengal, 1837; sent to Scinde, 1843; political officer with Lord Gough's army, 1848–9; a district magistrate; returned to England, 1863. [xi. 201]

COCKS, ROGER (*fl.* 1635), divine; possibly of Trinity College, Cambridge, 1612; published, 1630, devotional verses, entitled 'Hebdomada Sacra'; answered, 1642, Sir Edward Peyton's book against kneeling at communion. [xi. 201]

COCKSON or **COXON**, THOMAS (*fl.* 1609–1636), engraver of numerous portraits of contemporary notabilities and authors. [xi. 202]

COOKTON, HENRY (1807–1853), author of 'Valentine Vox,' 1840, and other novels. [xi. 202]

CODDINGTON, HENRY (*d.* 1845), mathematician; senior wrangler, 1820; fellow and tutor of Trinity College, Cambridge; M.A., 1823; vicar of Ware, Hertfordshire; died at Rome; wrote chiefly on optics. [xi. 202]

CODDINGTON, WILLIAM (1601–1678), American colonist; merchant at Boston, New England, 1630; removed to Rhode island, 1638; visited England, 1651; named governor of Rhode island, where he became chief magistrate. [xi. 203]

CODRINGTON, CHRISTOPHER (1668–1710), soldier; son of the governor of the Leeward islands; born in Barbados; entered Christ Church, Oxford, 1685; fellow of All Souls', 1690; M.A., 1695; showed great courage in Flanders, 1694; captain, 1695; governor of the Leeward islands, 1697–1703; died at Barbados; benefactor of All Souls' College, Oxford; left his Barbados estates to found Codrington College, Barbados. [xi. 203]

CODRINGTON, SIR EDWARD (1770–1851), admiral; entered navy, 1783; lieutenant, 1793; commander, 1794; commanded ship at Trafalgar, 1805; served in the Scheldt, 1809, and in the Mediterranean, 1810–13; rear-admiral, 1814; K.C.B., 1815; commander-in-chief in Mediterranean, 1827; in treaty with Ibrahim Pasha, the Turkish admiral, for a suspension of hostilities, 1827, soon after which hostilities were resumed by the Greek insurgents; joined with the French and Russian squadrons in destroying the weak Turkish fleet at Navarino, 20 Oct. 1827; recalled, 1828; visited St. Petersburg, 1830; admiral, 1837; retired from active service, 1842; his memoirs published, 1873. [xi. 204]

CODRINGTON, SIR HENRY JOHN (1808–1877 admiral; third son of Sir Edward Codrington [q. v.] entered navy, 1823; wounded at Navarino, 1827; lieutenant, 1829; commander, 1831; helped to bombard Acre, 1840; served off the Italian coast, 1847–50, and in the Baltic, 1854–5; rear-admiral, 1857; K.C.B., 1867; admiral of the fleet, 1877. [xi. 207]

CODRINGTON, ROBERT (*d.* 1665), author; demy of Magdalen College, Oxford, 1619–27; M.A., 1626; travelled; published verses and translations, chiefly theological and historical, from French and Latin. [xi. 209]

CODRINGTON, THOMAS (*d.* 1691?), Roman catholic divine; educated at Douay; secretary to Cardinal Howard at Rome; returned to England, 1684; chaplain to James II; tried to found in England community of secular priests; followed James II to St. Germains; published sermons. [xi. 210]

CODRINGTON, SIR WILLIAM JOHN (1804–1884), general; second son of Sir Edward Codrington [q. v.]; ensign, 1821; colonel, 1846; major-general, 1854; showed courage and promptitude at Alma and Inkerman; K.C.B., 1855; commander-in-chief at Sebastopol, 1855–6; M.P., Greenwich, 1857; governor of Gibraltar, 1859–65; general, 1863. [xi. 210]

COEMGEN, SAINT (498–618), of Glendalough, co. Wicklow; popularly ST. KEVIN; hermit at Glendalough and in Kildare and Westmeath; built two monasteries at Glendalough, but withdrew to hermitages there; went to Westmeath to meet St. Columba; urged the king of Leinster to fight for his country against Ædh MacAinmire, king of Ireland. [xi. 211]

COENRED or **CENRED** (reigned 704–709), king of Mercia; a minor at the death of his father, Wulfhere, 675; king of the Southumbrians, 702; king of Mercia, when his uncle, Æthelred, resigned, 704; abdicated, 709; became a monk at Rome. [xi. 213]

COETLOGON, CHARLES EDWARD DE (1746?–1820), divine; educated at Christ's Hospital, 1755–66; M.A. Pembroke Hall, Cambridge, 17.3; vicar of Godstone, Surrey, 1794–1820; published sermons and theological tracts. [xi. 214]

COFFEY, CHARLES (*d.* 1745), dramatist; an Irishman; deformed; performed at Dublin; afterwards in London; brought out farces and farcical operas, 1729–45. [xi. 215]

COFFIN, *alias* HATTON, EDWARD (1571–1626), jesuit; educated at Rheims and Rome; mission priest in England, 1594; joined the jesuits, 1598; arrested near Antwerp, 1598; imprisoned in the Tower, 1598–1603; confessor to the English college at Rome; died at St. Omer; published controversial treatises, 1619–23. [xi. 215]

COFFIN, SIR EDWARD PINE (1784–1862), commissary-general; commissariat clerk, 1805; commissary-general, 1840; employed at the Cape, 1805–8; in the Peninsula, 1808–14; in Belgium and France, 1815–16; in Canada, 1819–22 and 1833–5; in China, 1843–5; knighted for services during the Irish famine, 1846. [xi. 216]

COFFIN, SIR ISAAC (1759–1839), admiral; born at Boston, America; entered navy, 1773; commander, 1781; rejected Sir George Rodney's nominees to his ship as unequal to their duty, 1782; convicted of signing false muster-roll, 1788 (conviction quashed, 1789); disabled by accident, while rescuing a drowning seaman, 1790; commissioner of the navy in Corsica, 1795–6, in Minorca, at Halifax, 1798, and at Sheerness; rear-admiral and created baronet, 1804; withdrew from service, 1808; adopted name Greenly, 1811–13; admiral, 1814; M.P., 1818–26. [xi. 216]

COFFIN, SIR ISAAC CAMPBELL (1800–1872), lieutenant-general; cadet in the East India Company's service, 1818; lieutenant in the Madras army, 1821; served in Burmah, 1824; lieutenant-colonel, 1845; major-general, 1857; K.C.S.I., 1866; lieutenant-general, 1869. [xi. 217]

COFFIN, JOHN PINE (1778–1830), major-general; cornet, as John Pine, 1795; took the name Coffin, 1797; lieutenant, 1799; served in Egypt, 1801; attached to quartermaster-general's staff; employed in Italy and Spain, 1808–14; military attaché with Austrian army in south France, 1815; lieutenant-governor of St. Helena, 1819–23; major-general, 1825. [xi. 218]

COFFIN, ROBERT ASTON (1819–1885), Roman catholic prelate; educated at Harrow; student of Christ Church, Oxford, 1838–45; M.A., 1843; vicar of St. Mary Magdalene, Oxford, 1843; embraced catholicism, 1845; Redemptorist father, 1852; rector of St. Mary's, Clapham, 1855; mission preacher, 1852–72; D.D.; bishop of Southwark, 1882; translated theological works. [xi. 219]

COGAN, ELIEZER (1762–1855), nonconformist divine; pupil and tutor in Daventry (nonconformist) academy; presbyterian minister at Cirencester, 1787–9; congregational minister at Walthamstow, 1801–16; kept boarding-school at Walthamstow, 1801–28; published sermons and theological tracts. [xi. 219]

COGAN, THOMAS (1545?–1607), physician; fellow of Oriel College, Oxford, 1563–74; M.B., 1574; practised physic in Manchester; master of Manchester grammar-school, 1574–1600; published Latin school-books, and medical and devotional tracts. [xi. 220]

COGAN, THOMAS (1736–1818), philosopher; educated for congregational ministry; presbyterian minister at Rotterdam, 1759, and at Southampton, 1762; unitarian; pastor at the Hague; married a Dutch heiress; studied medicine at Leyden; M.D. Leyden, 1767; practised medicine in Holland; accoucheur in London, c. 1772–80; founded the Royal Humane Society, 1774; resided in Holland, 1780–95; removed to Bath; afterwards resided in London; published novels, notes of travel, translations from the Dutch, and, 1802–17, treatises 'on the passions' and on ethics. [xi. 221]

COGAN, WILLIAM (d. 1774), philanthropist; mayor of Hull, 1717 and 1736; founded a charity school and an apprentice fund at Hull. [xi. 222]

COGGESHALL, HENRY (1623–1690), mathematician; invented Coggeshall sliding-rule, 1677; wrote on mensuration. [xi. 222]

COGGESHALL, RALPH OF (fl. 1207), chronicler; Cistercian monk; abbot of Coggeshall, Essex, 1207–18. The chronicle known by his name extends from 1066 to 1224, becoming more detailed after 1187. [xi. 223]

COGHLAN, JEREMIAH (1775?–1844), captain in navy; mate of merchant ship at Plymouth, 1796, when he attracted attention of Edward Pellew, viscount Exmouth [q. v.], who placed him on his ship the Indefatigable; commanded Viper frigate, 1800; captured French gun-brig Cerbère after hard fight off Port Louis, and was promoted lieutenant, 1800; commanded sloop on Jamaica station, 1804–7; senior officer of light squadron in Bahamas, 1807–11; captain, 1810; flag-captain to Pellew in Mediterranean, 1812; C.B., 1815; on South American station, 1826–30. [Suppl. ii. 39]

COK, JOHN (1392?–1467?), compiler of the chartulary (1456) of St. Bartholomew's Hospital, London; goldsmith's apprentice; priest, 1417; brother of St. Bartholomew's Hospital, 1419. [xi. 223]

COKAYNE, SIR ASTON (1608–1684), poet; son of Thomas Cokayne [q. v.]; fellow-commoner of Trinity College, Cambridge; at the Inns of Court; travelled in France and Italy, 1632; inherited Pooley, Warwickshire, 1639; received a baronet's patent, 1642; created M.A. Oxford, 1643; obtained Ashbourne, Derbyshire, on his mother's death, 1664; ran through his estate; sold his Derbyshire property, 1671, and his Warwickshire property, 1683; published translations from Italian, 1658, and poems and dramas, 1658 and 1669. [xi. 224]

COKAYNE, GEORGE (1619–1691), independent minister; B.A. Sidney Sussex College, Cambridge, 1640; intruded rector of St. Pancras, Soper Lane, London; ejected, 1660; minister of Redcross Street congregational chapel, London, 1660; published sermons. [xi. 225]

COKAYNE, SIR JOHN (d. 1438), judge; of Ashbourne, Derbyshire; recorder of London, 1394; chief baron of the exchequer, 1400–13; justice of common pleas, 1405–29; accompanied troops to France, 1412; sheriff of Derbyshire and Nottinghamshire, 1422, 1428, and 1435. [xi. 226]

COKAYNE, SIR THOMAS (1519?–1592), author of 'A Treatise of Hunting,' 1591; of Ashbourne, Derbyshire; page to the Earl of Shrewsbury; succeeded to the family estates, 1538; knighted, 1544; served in Scotland, 1548; frequently high sheriff of Derbyshire. [xi. 226]

COKAYNE, THOMAS (1587–1638), lexicographer; of Ashbourne, Derbyshire; educated at Corpus Christi College, Oxford; compiled an English-Greek lexicon, published 1658. [xi. 227]

COKAYNE, SIR WILLIAM (d. 1626), lord mayor of London; succeeded to his father's business of merchant, 1599; sheriff of London, 1609; alderman; governor of Ulster colonists, 1612; knighted, 1616; lord mayor, 1619–1620; bought Rushton, Northamptonshire. [xi. 227]

COKE, DANIEL PARKER (1745–1825), politician; M.A. All Souls' College, Oxford, 1772; barrister, 1768; M.P., Derby, 1775–80; M.P., Nottingham, 1780–1812. [xi. 228]

COKE, SIR EDWARD (1552–1634), judge and law writer, commonly called LORD COKE or COOKE; educated at Norwich and (1567) Trinity College, Cambridge; at Clifford's Inn, London, 1571; barrister of the Inner Temple, 1578; soon obtained good practice; reader of Lyon's Inn, 1579; advanced by Burghley's influence; recorder of Coventry, 1585; recorder of Norwich, 1586; recorder of London, 1592; M.P., Aldborough, 1589; M.P., Norfolk, and speaker of the House of Commons, 1593; solicitor-general, 1592; attorney-general, to Francis Bacon's disappointment, 1594; married, to spite Bacon, Burghley's granddaughter, Lady Elizabeth Cecil, widow of Sir William Hatton, 1598; began publishing his law reports, 1600; entertained Queen Elizabeth at Stoke Pogis, 1601; showed great rancour in the trials of the Earl of Essex, 1600, Ralegh, 1603, and the gunpowder plotters, 1605; chief-justice of common pleas, 1606; opposed James I's claim to tax imports and exports, 1606; decided that the post-nati—persons born in Scotland after the union of the crowns—were English subjects, 1607; resisted Archbishop Bancroft's claim, which James I favoured, to exempt the church from the jurisdiction of the common law courts, 1606–9; decided against the king's authority to make law by proclamation, 1610; resisted Archbishop Abbot's attempt to have ecclesiastical causes decided by the court of high commission, 1611; compelled, through Bacon's influence, and against his own wish, to accept the chief-justiceship of the king's bench, 1613; privy councillor, 1613; opposed the practice of consulting the judges extra-judicially, 1615; favoured the courts of common law in their endeavour to curtail the powers of the chancellor, 1615; refused to obey James I's order to

K

stay proceedings in the commendam case; showed uncourtly desire to ascertain the truth in Sir Thomas Overbury's case, 1615; suspended, partly through Bacon's representations to James I, from the privy council and judicial functions, 1616; ordered to expunge from his 'Reports' opinions unfavourable to the king's prerogative; dismissed from the chief-justiceship, 1616; separated from his wife, in consequence of a violent quarrel as to the marriage of their daughter, 1617; recalled to the privy council, 1617; employed on several commissions of inquiry; M.P., Liskeard, 1620–2; vigorously attacked the monopolies; advocated war with Spain; incensed James I by speaking against the Spanish marriage and denouncing interference with the liberties of parliament; on the committee to impeach Bacon; imprisoned in the Tower, 1622; M.P., Coventry, 1624; M.P., Norfolk, 1625–6; opposed Charles I's demand for subsidies, 1625; precluded from parliamentary action by being pricked sheriff of Buckinghamshire, 1626; M.P., Buckinghamshire, 1628; spoke strongly against the Duke of Buckingham, illegal taxation, and illegal imprisonment; lived afterwards in retirement at Stoke Pogis. His papers were seized by order of Charles I, and detained till 1641. Of Coke's 'Reports,' the first eleven parts were published 1600–15, the unfinished twelfth and thirteenth parts not till 1656–9. His 'Booke of Entries' appeared in 1614. 'The First part of the Institutes of the Laws of England' (Coke upon Littleton) appeared in 1628, the second part in 1642, and the third and the unfinished fourth part in 1644.
[xi. 229]

COKE or **COOKE**, GEORGE (d. 1646), bishop of Hereford; brother of Sir John Coke [q. v.]; fellow of Pembroke Hall, Cambridge; rector of Bygrave, Hertfordshire; D.D.; bishop of Bristol, 1633; translated to Hereford, 1636; one of the twelve protesting bishops, 1641; his palace sacked by the parliamentary troops, 1645.
[xi. 244]

COKE, JEREMIAH (d. 1817). [See BRANDRETH.]

COKE, SIR JOHN (1563–1644), secretary of state; fellow of Trinity College, Cambridge, 1583; employed by Burghley; deputy-treasurer of the navy, 1591; travelled, 1594–6; secretary to Fulke Greville [q. v.], 1597; a commissioner of the navy, 1621–36; M.P., 1621–9; pensioned by James I, 1621; a master of requests, 1622; knighted, 1624; Buckingham's agent in the parliaments of 1625 and 1628; secretary of state, 1625; incensed the Commons by his subservience to Charles I; a commissioner of the treasury, 1635–6; a commissioner on Scottish affairs, 1638; dismissed from office, 1639.
[xi. 244]

COKE, ROGER (fl. 1696), political writer; of Thorington, Suffolk; educated at Cambridge; wrote against Thomas Hobbes, 1660; published pamphlets on trade, 1670–95; published his 'Detection of the Court . . . of England during the four last Reigns' [Stuarts], 1694.
[xi. 246]

COKE, THOMAS (1747–1814), methodist bishop; son of a wealthy Brecon apothecary; entered Jesus College, Oxford, 1764; M.A., 1770; curate of South Petherton, Somerset, 1772–6; D.C.L., 1775; methodist preacher in London, 1778; frequently president of the Methodist conference in Ireland from 1782; suggested that the methodists should undertake foreign missions, 1784; joined with John Wesley in ordaining methodist ministers for America, 1784; went to Baltimore as 'superintendent' of the methodists, 1784; adopted the title of bishop in America, 1787; opposed slavery; methodist secretary of conference; vainly proposed the union of the methodist and Anglican churches in America, 1792, and in England, 1799; tried to establish bishops in the methodist church in England, 1794; president of the methodist conference in England, 1797 and 1805; paid his ninth visit to America, 1803; asked Lord Liverpool, the premier, to make him a bishop in India, 1813; died on the voyage to India; published works, including sermons and biographies. [xi. 247]

COKE, THOMAS WILLIAM, of Holkham, first EARL OF LEICESTER (1752–1842), educated at Eton; travelled; lived some time at Rome; returned to England, 1774; succeeded to his patrimony, 1776; M.P., Norfolk, 1776–1806, and 1807–32; protectionist; favoured parliamentary reform; latterly, 'father' of the House of Commons; began farming on his own account, 1778; bred Southdown sheep and Devon cattle; improved the Suffolk breed of pigs; first grew wheat (instead of rye) in West Norfolk, 1787; raised to the peerage, 1837. [xi. 249]

COKER, JOHN (d. 1635?), antiquary; vicar of Tincleton, Dorset, 1576–9; compiled a 'Survey of Dorsetshire' (published 1732). [xi. 251]

COLBATCH, SIR JOHN (d. 1729), physician; apothecary at Worcester; licentiate of the London College of Physicians, 1696; knighted, 1716; published medical tracts, 1695–1723. [xi. 252]

COLBATCH, JOHN (1664–1748), opponent of Richard Bentley; at Westminster School, 1680–3; fellow of Trinity College, Cambridge; M.A., 1690; D.D., 1706; Anglican chaplain at Lisbon; prebendary of Salisbury; professor of moral philosophy, Cambridge, 1707–44; took part with the fellows of Trinity against Richard Bentley [q. v.], the master, 1714; published pamphlets against Bentley; rector of Orwell, Cambridgeshire, 1720–48; refused Bentley, then archdeacon of Ely, his fees for archidiaconal visitations, 1738. [xi. 252]

COLBORNE, SIR JOHN, first BARON SEATON (1778–1863), general; educated at Christ's Hospital; ensign, 1794; captain, 1800; served in Egypt, 1801, and in Sicily, 1806; secretary to Sir John Moore, 1808–9; lieutenant-colonel, by Moore's dying request, 1809; commanded 52nd foot in Peninsula and at Waterloo; K.C.B., 1815; major-general, 1825; lieutenant-governor of Guernsey, 1825; of Upper Canada, 1830; crushed Canadian revolt, 1838; created Baron Seaton, 1839; governor of the Ionian islands, 1843–9; general, 1854; commander of the forces in Ireland, 1855–60; field-marshal, 1860. [xi. 253]

COLBURN, HENRY (d. 1855), publisher, of London; started a number of London magazines, 1814–29; kept a circulating library, 1816; brought out a library of modern standard novelists, 1835–41. His publications included Evelyn's and Pepys's diaries. [xi. 254]

COLBY, THOMAS FREDERICK (1784–1852), director of the ordnance survey; educated at Woolwich; second lieutenant, royal engineers, 1801; lieutenant-colonel, 1825, major-general, 1846; attached to the ordnance survey of England, 1802; lost his right hand, 1803; chief executive officer of the survey, 1809; conducted survey of Scotland, 1813–21; hon. LL.D. Aberdeen; director of the survey, 1820; F.R.S., 1820; conducted survey of Ireland, 1825–47; joint-designer of a geological map of West England, 1833–1845; placed on the retired list, 1847. [xi. 255]

COLCHESTER, first BARON (1757–1829). [See ABBOT, CHARLES.]

COLCHU, **COELCHU**, or **COLGA**, SAINT (d. 792), chief scribe of Clonmacnoise monastery; corresponded with Alcuin [q. v.]; wrote 'Scuap Crabhaigh' (sweeping brush of devotion). [xi. 259]

COLCLOUGH, JOHN HENRY (1769–1798), Irish rebel; a Wexford landowner; an insurgent leader at New Ross, 1798; executed. [xi. 260]

COLDEN, CADWALLADER (1688–1776), botanist and American loyalist; M.D. Edinburgh, 1705; practitioner in Pennsylvania, 1708–18; surveyor-general of New York colony, 1719; member of council, New York, 1720; lieutenant-governor of New York, 1761; unpopular as a loyalist; withdrew to Long Island, 1775; published medical and scientific papers, including 'History of the five Indian Nations of Canada,' 1727; sent descriptions of American plants to Linnæus and other savants. [xi. 260]

COLDINGHAM, GEOFFREY DE (fl. 1214), writer of a history of the church of Durham from 1152 to 1214; sacrist of Coldingham Priory. [xi. 261]

COLDOCK, FRANCIS (1530–1602), publisher; master of the London Stationers' Company, 1591 and 1595; printed a few books; issued many books in conjunction with Henry Bynneman [q. v.] [xi. 262]

COLDSTREAM, JOHN (1806–1863), physician; M.D. Edinburgh, 1827; practitioner in Leith, 1829–47; advocated medical missions; wrote medical papers. [xi. 262]

COLDWELL, JOHN (d. 1596), bishop of Salisbury; fellow of St. John's College, Cambridge; M.A., 1558; M.D., 1564; chaplain to Archbishop Parker; rector of Aldington, 1558, Tunstall, 1572, and Saltwood, Kent, 1580; dean of Rochester, 1581; made bishop of Salisbury in order that the courtiers might plunder the episcopal estates, 1591; died deeply in debt. [xi. 263]

COLE, ABDIAH (1610 ?–1670 ?), 'doctor of physick'; translated and compiled medical text-books, 1655–62. [xi. 263]

COLE, CHARLES NALSON (1723–1804), lawyer; B.A. St. John's College, Cambridge, 1743; barrister, Inner Temple; registrar of the Bedford Level corporation; published law tracts, an edition of the 'Works of Soame Jenyns,' 1790, and other writings. [xi. 264]

COLE, SIR CHRISTOPHER (1770–1837), post-captain; midshipman, 1780; flag-captain to Lord Hugh Seymour [q. v.] in West Indies, 1799, and, later, to Sir John Thomas Duckworth [q. v.]; post-captain, 1802; served with Sir Edward Pellew (afterwards Viscount Exmouth) [q. v.] in East Indies, 1804; despatched to relieve garrison at Amboyna, 1810; effected capture of Neira, chief of Banda islands; served on Malabar coast, 1811; knighted, 1812; honorary D.C.L. Oxford, 1812; in Channel, 1813–14; K.C.B., 1815; M.P. for Glamorganshire, 1817 and 1820–30; commander of yacht Royal Sovereign, 1828; colonel of marines, 1830. [Suppl. ii. 40]

COLE, SIR GALBRAITH LOWRY (1772–1842), general; younger son of the first Earl of Enniskillen; cornet, 1787; major, 1793; served in the West Indies, 1794; staff officer in Ireland, 1797, and in Egypt, 1801; M.P., Inniskillen, 1798–1800, and for Fermanagh, 1803–23; brigadier-general in Sicily, 1806–8; major-general, 1808; commanded 4th division in Peninsula, 1809–14; K.B., 1813; lieutenant-general, 1813; governor of Mauritius, 1823–8; governor of Cape Colony, 1828–33; general, 1830. [xi. 264]

COLE, GEORGE (1810–1883), painter; self-taught; portrait-painter at Plymouth; painted posters of wild animals for Wombwell's menagerie; studied art in Holland; exhibited in London, 1838–80, chiefly landscapes. [xi. 266]

COLE, GEORGE VICAT (1833–1893), landscape painter; son of George Cole [q. v.]; first exhibited at British Institution and Suffolk Street galleries, 1852, and at Royal Academy, 1853; R.A., 1880. His picture, 'The Pool of London,' is in the National Gallery of British Art, Millbank. [Suppl. ii. 41]

COLE, HENRY (1500 ?–1580), dean of St. Paul's; educated at Winchester; fellow of New College, Oxford, 1521–40, and warden, 1542–51; B.C.L., 1530; D.C.L., 1540; D.D., 1554; studied in Padua and Paris; lectured on civil law in Oxford; submitted to the Reformation; prebendary of Sarum, 1539; advocate of the arches and prebendary of St. Paul's, 1540; rector of Chelmsford, Essex, 1540–8, and of Newton Longueville, Buckinghamshire, 1545–52; joined Roman catholic party at Mary's accession; archdeacon of Ely, 1553–6; canon of Westminster and provost of Eton, 1554–9; held disputation with Cranmer at Oxford, 1554; appointed to preach at Cranmer's execution, 1556; one of Cardinal Pole's commissioners to visit Oxford University, 1556, and Cambridge, 1557; dean of St. Paul's, 1556–9; vicar-general of the archbishop of Canterbury, 1557–8; sent to Ireland to extirpate protestantism, 1558; one of the eight Romanist disputants at Westminster Abbey, 1559; imprisoned, from 1560 to c. 1579. [xi. 266]

COLE, SIR HENRY (1808–1882), official; at Christ's Hospital, 1817–23; sub-commissioner of the new record commission, 1833; assistant-keeper of the Record Office, 1838; elaborated scheme of postal reform for treasury, 1839–42; served on managing committee of London exhibitions of 1851, 1862, 1871–4; British commissioner at the Paris exhibitions of 1855 and 1867; joint-secretary of the Science and Art Department, 1853, and sole secretary, 1858–73; K.C.B., 1875; painted in water-colours, etched, engraved book illustrations, and edited, from time to time, several periodicals. [xi. 268]

COLE, HUMFRAY (*fl.* 1570–1580), engraver of a map of Palestine, 1572, and of brass mathematical instruments; employed at the mint. [xi. 270]

COLE, JOHN (1792–1848), bookseller and antiquary; bookseller's apprentice in Northampton; bookseller in Lincoln, 1817, in Hull, in Scarborough, 1821, at Northampton, 1830; lectured on history and popular science; taught school at Wellingborough, 1835, and other places; failed in business and in teaching; died in poverty; published histories of Northampton, 1815, Lincoln, 1818,

Scarborough, 1822–4, and above a hundred other pieces relating chiefly to Yorkshire and Northamptonshire. [xi. 270]

COLE, SIR RALPH (1625 ?–1704), second baronet, of Brancepeth Castle, Durham; studied painting under Vandyck; learned mezzotint engraving; patronised Italian painters; M.P., Durham, 1676–8; ran through his estate; sold Brancepeth, 1701. [xi. 273]

COLE, THOMAS (*d.* 1571), divine; M.A. King's College, Cambridge, 1550; D.D., 1564; master of Maidstone school, 1552; dean of Salisbury; withdrew to the continent, 1553; rector of High Ongar, 1559, and of Stanford Rivers, Essex, 1564; prebendary of St. Paul's and archdeacon of Essex, 1560; of puritan leanings; published sermons. [xi. 273]

COLE, THOMAS (1627 ?–1697), nonconformist divine; educated at Westminster School; student of Christ Church, Oxford, 1647; M.A., 1651; intruded principal of St. Mary Hall, Oxford, 1656–60; kept a private academy at Nettlebed, Oxford; minister of the congregational church in Silver Street and Pinners' Hall, London, 1674–1697; published sermons. [xi. 274]

COLE, WILLIAM (*d.* 1600), dean of Lincoln; fellow of Corpus Christi College, Oxford, 1545–53; M.A., 1552; D.D., 1574; withdrew to Zurich, 1553, and Geneva, 1557; joined in translating the 'Geneva Bible'; rector of Sudbourne, Suffolk, 1561–71, of Buscott, Berkshire, 1571–3, and of Lower Heyford, Oxfordshire, 1572–1600; made president of Corpus Christi College by the crown in defiance of the wishes of the college, 1568; lived at feud with the fellows; brought the college into debt; prebendary of Salisbury, 1571, Lincoln, 1574, and Winchester, 1579; vice-chancellor of Oxford, 1577; compelled to exchange his presidentship for the deanery of Lincoln, 1598. [xi. 274]

COLE, SIR WILLIAM (*d.* 1653), Irish settler; a Londoner; resident in Fermanagh before 1607; obtained forfeited lands, 1611; provost of Enniskillen; knighted, 1617; leased Enniskillen Castle, 1623; M.P., Fermanagh, 1639; colonel of foot against the Irish rebels, 1641–3; defended his conduct before a parliamentary commission, 1645. [xi. 276]

COLE or **COLES**, WILLIAM (1626–1662), botanist; entered New College, Oxford, 1642; postmaster of Merton College, 1650–1; B.A., 1651; resided at Putney; secretary to the bishop of Winchester, 1660; published 'Herbal,' 1656–7. [xi. 277]

COLE, WILLIAM (*d.* 1701), naturalist; surveyor of customs, Bristol; landowner at Hullavington, Wiltshire. [xi. 277]

COLE, WILLIAM (1635–1716), physician; M.D. Gloucester Hall, Oxford, 1666; practised in London and Worcester; fellow of the London College of Physicians, 1694; published Latin medical tracts, 1674–94. [xi. 277]

COLE, WILLIAM (1714–1782), the Cambridge antiquary; of Baberham, Cambridgeshire; while a schoolboy at Eton began to note antiquities; formed a friendship with Horace Walpole; entered Clare Hall, Cambridge, 1733; migrated to King's College, 1735; M.A., 1740; seriously thought of embracing Roman catholicism; resided in Cambridge; travelled occasionally in Flanders and Portugal; F.S.A., 1747; non-resident rector of Hornsey, Middlesex, 1749–51; resident rector of Bletchley, Buckinghamshire, 1753–67; removed to Waterbeach, near Cambridge, 1767, and to Milton, 1770; his income impaired by the breaking of the dykes; non-resident vicar of Burnham, Buckinghamshire, 1774–82; furnished friends with materials for historical and antiquarian books; bequeathed his manuscript collections, about a hundred folio volumes, chiefly dealing with Cambridgeshire and Cambridge university, Huntingdonshire, and Buckinghamshire, to the British Museum. [xi. 278]

COLE, WILLIAM (1753–1806), classical scholar; foundationer at Eton, 1766; scholar of King's College, Cambridge, 1773; fellow, 1776; M.A., 1781; D.D., Lambeth, 1795; master at Eton, 1777–80; chaplain to the Duke of Marlborough; rector of Mersham, Kent, 1788; prebendary of Westminster, 1792; vicar of Shoreham, Kent; author of a Latin explanation prefixed to 'Marlborough Gems' (vol. ii.) [xi. 281]

COLE, WILLIAM (1754–1812), miscellaneous writer ; educated at Eton ; fellow of King's College, Cambridge ; M.A., 1783 ; vicar of Broad Chalk, Wiltshire ; curate in London ; published a 'Key to the Psalms,' 1788, a poem, 1789, and a novel, 1796. [xi. 282]

COLEBROOKE, HENRY THOMAS (1765–1837), Sanscrit scholar · writer at Calcutta, 1782 ; magistrate at Purneah ; studied Hindu law ; contributed papers on suttee to 'Asiatic Researches,' 1794 ; printed privately 'Remarks on Husbandry in Bengal,' 1795 ; magistrate at Mirzapur, near Benares, 1795 ; published translation of 'A Digest of Hindu Law,' 1798 ; envoy to Nagpūr, 1799–1801 ; judge at Calcutta, 1801, and president of the bench, 1805 ; honorary professor in Fort William College ; published his 'Essay on the Vedas,' 1805, a Sanscrit grammar, 1805, and lexicon, 1808, and translations of Hindu treatises on inheritance and contracts, 1810 ; member of the Bengal council, 1807–12 ; returned to England, 1814 ; presented his Sanscrit manuscripts to the India House ; wrote on Hindu mathematics and philosophy, and on natural science ; became blind ; his occasional papers collected in his 'Miscellaneous Essays,' 1837. [xi. 282]

COLEBROOKE, SIR WILLIAM MACBEAN GEORGE (1787–1870), soldier and colonial governor ; studied at Woolwich ; first lieutenant, royal artillery, 1803 ; major, 1813 ; political agent and commissioner in Palembong, Sumatra, 1813, and in Bengal, 1814 ; one of commissioners of the Eastern inquiry, 1822–32 ; lieutenant-governor of Bahamas, 1834–7 ; governor of Leeward islands, 1837 ; lieutenant-governor of New Brunswick, 1841 ; colonel, 1846 ; governor of Barbados and Windward islands, 1848–56 ; lieutenant-general, 1859 ; colonel commanding royal artillery, 1859–70 ; C.B. (civil), 1848. [Suppl. ii. 42]

COLECHURCH, PETER DE (d. 1205), chaplain of St. Mary Colechurch ; architect of the first stone bridge over the Thames in London, 1176. [xi. 286]

COLEMAN, CHARLES (d. 1664), composer ; member of Charles I's band ; music teacher in London, 1641 ; Mus. Doc. Cambridge, 1651 ; composed part of the music for William D'Avenant's 'First Dayes Entertainment' and 'Siege of Rhodes,' 1656 ; member of Charles II's band, 1660 ; composer to Charles II, 1662 ; left music in manuscript. [xi. 286]

COLEMAN, EDWARD (d. 1669), musician ; son of Charles Coleman [q. v.] ; a celebrated music-master in London ; composed the music for James Shirley's 'The glories of our blood and state,' 1653 ; sang in William D'Avenant's 'Siege of Rhodes,' 1656 ; gentleman of the Chapel Royal, 1660 ; member of Charles II's band, 1662 ; friend of Samuel Pepys. [xi. 287]

COLEMAN, EDWARD (d. 1678), conspirator ; embraced Roman catholicism, c. 1670 ; secretary to Mary of Modena, duchess of York, c. 1674 ; corresponded with France, inviting aid for English catholics, 1674–5 ; sent to Brussels to negotiate with the pope's nuncio ; accused by Titus Oates of participation in the 'popish plot, 28 Sept. 1678 ; his papers seized, 29 Sept. ; surrendered himself, 30 Sept. ; convicted on the evidence of Oates and Bedloe, 27 Nov ; executed, 3 Dec. ; his fate discussed in several broadsheets and pamphlets. [xi. 288]

COLEMAN, THOMAS (1598–1647), divine ; entered Magdalen Hall, Oxford, 1615 ; M.A., 1621 ; a learned hebraist, and nicknamed 'Rabbi Coleman' ; rector of Blyton, Lincolnshire, 1623–42, and of St. Peter's, Cornhill, 1642 ; member of Westminster Assembly, 1643. [xi. 289]

COLEMAN, WALTER (d. 1645). [See COLMAN.]

COLEMAN, WILLIAM HIGGINS (d. 1863), botanist ; M.A. St. John's College, Cambridge, 1838 ; ordained, 1840 ; joint-author (with John William Colenso [q. v.]) of 'Examples in Arithmetic and Algebra,' 1834, and (with R. H. Webb) of 'Flora Hertfordiensis,' 1849, and its supplements, 1851 and 1859 ; first introduced the river-basin delimitation into a county flora ; schoolmaster at Hertford, and, 1847, at Ashby-de-la-Zouch ; his 'Biblical Papers' published 1864. [xi. 290]

COLENSO, FRANCES ELLEN (1849–1887), daughter of John William Colenso [q.v.] ; taken to Natal, 1855 ; joint-author of a 'History of the Zulu War,' 1880. [xi. 293]

COLENSO, JOHN WILLIAM (1814–1883), bishop of Natal ; called by the Zulus 'SOBANTU' ('father of the people ') ; a poor Cornish boy ; sizar of St. John's College, Cambridge ; second wrangler, 1836 ; fellow, 1837 ; a master at Harrow, 1839–42 ; tutor of St. John's College, 1842–6 ; vicar of Forncett St. Mary, Norfolk, 1846–53 ; joint-author (with William Higgins Coleman [q. v.]) of 'Examples in Arithmetic and Algebra,' 1834 ; author of text-books on algebra, 1841, and arithmetic, 1843 ; published sermons, 1853 ; named bishop of Natal, 1853 ; published 'Ten Weeks in Natal,' 1854 ; decided against requiring polygamous Kaffir converts to divorce their wives ; took his family to Natal, 1855 ; held his first diocesan council, 1858 ; taught some Zulus printing and issued between 1859 and 1876 a Zulu grammar, dictionary, instructive reading books, and translations of Genesis, Exodus, 1 and 2 Samuel, and the New Testament ; evoked great opposition by his 'Commentary on the Epistle to the Romans,' 1861, attacking the sacramental system ; issued 'Critical examination of the Pentateuch,' 1862–79, concluding that these books were post-exile forgeries, Deuteronomy, in particular, being a pious fraud of Jeremiah the prophet ; formally deposed and excommunicated by Robert Gray, bishop of Cape Town, 1863 ; confirmed in possession of the see by the law courts, 1866 ; published an examination of the first part of 'The Speaker's Commentary,' 1871–4 ; exposed the corruption and tyranny of some colonial officials towards natives, 1875 ; denounced the Zulu war, 1879. [xi. 290]

COLEPEPER. [See also CULPEPER.]

COLEPEPER, JOHN, first BARON COLEPEPER (d. 1660), of Wigsell, Sussex ; served in foreign armies ; studied rural affairs ; M.P., Kent, 1640 ; denounced monopolies and Strafford, 1641 ; defended episcopacy and the liturgy ; opposed the Grand Remonstrance and the militia bill, 1641 ; taken into court favour, made privy councillor, 1642 ; chancellor of the exchequer, 1642–3 ; advised Charles I's withdrawal to Yorkshire ; joined him at York, 1642 ; presented Charles's ultimatum to parliament, 1642 ; contributed to the victory of Edgehill, 1642 ; master of the rolls, 1643 ; attended Charles's Oxford parliament, 1644 ; his advice in military affairs sought by Charles I ; his plans thwarted by the jealousy of Rupert ; created Baron Colepeper of. Thoresway, 1644 ; urged Charles I to make terms at all costs with the Scots, 1645–6 , attended the Prince of Wales in his flight to the west, 1645 ; ordered to convey him to the continent, August 1645 ; accompanied him in the descent on the Thames, 1648 ; at feud with Rupert, 1648 ; urged Charles II to accept the Scottish overtures, 1649 ; went to Moscow to borrow money from the czar, 1650, and to Holland to ask armed support, 1652 ; expelled from France, 1654 ; urged Charles II's advisers to approach Monck, September 1658 ; attended Charles II on his Spanish journey, September 1659 ; returned to England, 1660. [xi. 293]

COLEPEPER, THOMAS (1637–1708), colonel ; inherited Hackington, Kent, 1643 ; steward to Viscount Strangford ; imprisoned as a royalist conspirator, 1659 ; married secretly a daughter of John, baron Frecheville, 1662 ; failed in a lawsuit to prevent Lord Frecheville selling his estate of Staveley, Derbyshire, to William Cavendish, first duke of Devonshire [q. v.] ; imprisoned and sentenced to lose his hand for striking Devonshire at Whitehall, 1685 ; pardoned ; struck by Devonshire at Whitehall, 1687 ; caned by Devonshire, 1697 ; died in great poverty. His genealogical collections are preserved in the British Museum. [xi. 296]

COLEPEPER, WILLIAM (d. 1726), poet and politician ; of Hollingbourn, Kent ; imprisoned for his share in the Kentish petition, 1701 ; published verses. [xi. 297]

COLERAINE, BARONS. [See HARE, HUGH, first BARON, 1606 ?–1667 ; HARE, HENRY, second BARON, 1636–1708 ; HARE, HENRY, third BARON, 1693–1749 ; HANGER, GEORGE, fourth BARON of the second creation, 1751 ?–1824.]

COLERIDGE, DERWENT (1800–1883), author ; second son of Samuel Taylor Coleridge [q. v.] ; educated at Ambleside school and St. John's College, Cambridge ; M.A., 1829 ; ordained, 1825 ; master of Helston school, Cornwall, 1825–41 ; principal of St. Mark's College, Chelsea, 1841–64 ; rector of Hanwell, 1864–80 ; published pamphlets, theological tracts, and biographies of his brother Hartley and the poet Praed. [xi. 298]

COLERIDGE, HARTLEY (1796–1849), author; eldest son of Samuel Taylor Coleridge [q. v.]; brought up by Robert Southey; educated at Ambleside school; B.A. Merton College, Oxford, 1819; probationer fellow of Oriel College, 1819, but dismissed, 1820, for intemperance; failed in literary work in London, and, 1830, in teaching at Ambleside; published poems, 1833, and biographies of Yorkshire and Lancashire worthies, 1833–6; a master at Sedbergh school, 1837–8; edited Massinger and Ford, 1840; his 'Remains,' verse and prose, published, 1851.
[xi. 298]

COLERIDGE, HENRY JAMES (1822–1893), divine; brother of Sir John Duke, Lord Coleridge [q. v.]; educated at Eton and Trinity College, Oxford; B.A., 1845; fellow of Oriel College, 1845; M.A., 1847; held cure in Devonshire; entered Roman catholic church, 1852; studied at Rome; priest, and D.D., 1855; joined jesuit novitiate; editor of the 'Month,' the periodical of the jesuit fathers, 1865–81; published theological works, including 'The Life of Our Lord,' 1872.
[Suppl. ii. 43]

COLERIDGE, HENRY NELSON (1798–1843), literary executor of Samuel Taylor Coleridge [q. v.]; nephew of Samuel Taylor Coleridge [q. v.], and brother of James Duke Coleridge [q. v.], and of Sir John Taylor Coleridge [q. v.]; educated at Eton; fellow of King's College, Cambridge; visited Barbados, 1825; barrister, 1826; married Sara Coleridge [q. v.], 1829; brought out Coleridge's 'Table Talk,' 1835, and edited some of his works; published pamphlets.
[xi. 300]

COLERIDGE, HERBERT (1830–1861), philologist; son of Henry Nelson Coleridge [q. v.]; educated at Eton and Balliol College, Oxford; double first, 1852; barrister, 1854; collected materials for the 'Oxford English Dictionary.'
[xi. 300]

COLERIDGE, JAMES DUKE (1788–1857), divine; nephew of Samuel Taylor Coleridge [q. v.], and brother of Henry Nelson Coleridge [q. v.] and Sir John Taylor Coleridge [q. v.]; entered Balliol College, Oxford, 1808; D.C.L., 1835; vicar of Kenwyn, 1823–8; rector of Lawhitton, 1826–1839; vicar of Lewannick, Cornwall, 1831–41; vicar of Thorverton, Devonshire, 1839–57; prebendary of Exeter, 1825; published sermons and devotional tracts.
[xi. 301]

COLERIDGE, JOHN (1719–1781), schoolmaster; vicar of Ottery St. Mary, Devonshire, and master of the grammar school; an eccentric; published a biblical tract, 1768, and a Latin grammar, 1772.
[xi. 302]

COLERIDGE, SIR JOHN DUKE, first BARON COLERIDGE (1820–1894), lord chief-justice of England; son of Sir John Taylor Coleridge [q. v.]; educated at Eton and Balliol College, Oxford; M.A. 1846; fellow of Exeter, 1843–6, and honorary fellow, 1882; called to bar at Middle Temple, 1846; bencher, 1861; joined western circuit; recorder of Portsmouth, 1855; Q.C., 1861; liberal M.P. for Exeter, 1865–73; appointed solicitor-general and knighted, 1868; attorney-general, 1871; chief counsel for defendants in 'Tichborne case,' 1871–2; chief-justice of common pleas, 1873–80; created Baron Coleridge, 1874; F.R.S., 1875; D.C.L. Oxford, 1877; chief-justice of queen's bench, 1880–94.
[Suppl. ii. 44]

COLERIDGE, SIR JOHN TAYLOR (1790–1876), judge; nephew of Samuel Taylor Coleridge [q. v.], and brother of James Duke Coleridge [q. v.], and Henry Nelson Coleridge [q. v.]; colleger at Eton; scholar of Corpus Christi College, Oxford, 1809; fellow of Exeter College, 1812–18; M.A., 1817; barrister, Middle Temple, 1819; contributed to the 'Quarterly Review,' and (1834) acted as editor; edited Blackstone's 'Commentaries,' 1825; recorder of Exeter, 1832; justice of the king's bench, 1835–1858; sat on several parliamentary commissions; published pamphlets and a life of Keble.
[xi. 302]

COLERIDGE, SAMUEL TAYLOR (1772–1834), poet and philosopher; youngest child of John Coleridge (1719–1781) [q. v.]; educated at Christ's Hospital, 1782–90; read Plotinus and argued on points of metaphysics; schoolfellow and friend of Charles Lamb; courted Mary Evans, a schoolfellow's sister; read Greek, medicine, and metaphysics; sizar, 1791, and scholar, 1793, of Jesus College, Cambridge; read desultorily; spent much time in conversation; adopted extreme views in politics and religion; went back to London, 1793; enlisted in the 15th dragoons,

as Silas Tomkyn Comberback, 1793; bought out by his brothers, 1794; said to have contributed to the 'Morning Chronicle,' 1793–5; returned to Cambridge, 1794; met Robert Southey in Oxford, and visited Wales; engaged himself to Sara Fricker at Bristol; joined Southey, Robert Lovell, and other 'pantisocrats' in their scheme to found a communistic colony on the Susquehanna, Pennsylvania; wrote the first act of the 'Fall of Robespierre' (published, 1794); left Cambridge, 1794; borrowed money of Joseph Cottle [q. v.], bookseller, of Bristol; lectured against Pitt, 1795; married Sara Fricker, 1795; published his first volume of 'Poems,' 1796; canvassed in Birmingham, Sheffield, Manchester, and other towns, for subscribers to the 'Watchman' newspaper, which failed (May 1796) at its tenth number; preached occasionally in unitarian chapels; began to take laudanum, 1796; maintained by Thomas Poole at Nether Stowey, preaching in unitarian chapels at Taunton and Bath, 1796–7; visited Wordsworth, 1797; joined Wordsworth in writing Lyrical Ballads' (published 1798), contributing 'The Ancient Mariner'; wrote the first part of 'Christabel' and 'Kubla Khan,' 1797; contributed occasional poems and articles to the 'Morning Post,' 1798–1802; went to Shrewsbury as unitarian minister, 1798, and met William Hazlitt; accepted two annuities of 75l. each from Josiah and Thomas Wedgwood, on condition of devoting himself to literature; furnished with funds by the Wedgwoods to visit Germany, 1798–9; published his translation of Schiller's 'Wallenstein,' 1800; settled at Keswick, 1800; wrote the second part of 'Christabel,' 1800; a slave to opium, 1803; visited Malta, 1804–5, and Rome, 1805–6; confirmed in 75l. annuity by the will of Thomas Wedgwood (d. July 1805); first met Thomas De Quincey. at Bridgewater, 1807; lectured, very indifferently, at the Royal Institution, 1808; left his family at Keswick and became dependent on Wordsworth at Grasmere, 1809; canvassed for subscribers to the 'Friend' newspaper; published the 'Friend,' August 1809 to March 1810; contributed to the London 'Courier,' 1809, 1811, and 1814; his 75l. annuity from Josiah Wedgwood stopped, 1811; lectured in London on Shakespeare and other poets, 1810–11, 1812, and 1813; his 'Remorse' acted with success at Drury Lane, 1813; left his family dependent on Southey, allowing his wife his 75l. annuity and quartering himself on his friends; lectured on Shakespeare and Milton, at Bristol, 1813; his slavery to opium now undisguisable; domiciled with John Morgan at Calne, Wiltshire, 1814–16; domiciled with James Gillman, at Highgate, 1816–34; published his autobiography, 'Biographia Literaria,' 1817; last lectured in London, 1818; pensioner of Society of Literature, 1824–1830; published 'Aids to Reflection,' 1825; a 'lion' of London literary circles; visited Germany, 1828; took a leading part in the introduction of English thinkers to the results of German thought; published his collected 'Poetical and Dramatic Works,' 1828.
[xi. 302]

COLERIDGE, SARA (1802–1852), author of 'Phantasmion,' 1837; daughter of Samuel Taylor Coleridge [q. v.]; married, 1829, Henry Nelson Coleridge [q. v.]; annotated and edited her father's writings.
[xi. 317]

COLERIDGE, WILLIAM HART (1789–1849), bishop of Barbados; nephew of Samuel Taylor Coleridge [q. v.]; student of Christ Church, Oxford, 1808–24; M.A., 1814; D.D., 1824; curate of St. Andrew's, Holborn; bishop of Barbados, 1824–41; warden of St. Augustine's Missionary College, Canterbury; published sermons and charges.
[xi. 317]

COLES, COWPER PHIPPS (1819–1870), naval officer; entered navy, 1838; captain, 1856; served in Black Sea, 1853–6; constructed a good gun-raft, 1855; suggested building a turret-ship, with low freeboard, and heavy guns, 1861; the Captain constructed after his plans, and (1870) commissioned; went down with the Captain off Cape Finisterre.
[xi. 318]

COLES, ELISHA (1640?–1680), lexicographer and stenographer; chorister of Magdalen College, Oxford, 1658–61; teacher of Latin and English in London, 1663; usher of Merchant Taylors' School, 1677; master of Galway school, 1678; published devotional verses, 1671, a treatise on shorthand, 1674, primers of English and Latin, 1674–5, an English dictionary, 1676, and a Latin dictionary, 1677.
[xi. 320]

COLES, ELISHA (1608?–1688), Calvinist; intruded maniple of Magdalen Hall, Oxford; deputy-registrar to the parliamentary visitors, 1651; intruded steward of Magdalen College, Oxford, 1657–60; clerk to the East India Company; published 'A Practical Discourse of God's Sovereignty,' 1673. [xi. 319]

COLES, ELISHA (*d.* 1715?), son of Elisha Coles (1608?–1688) [q. v.] [xi. 319]

COLES, GILBERT (1617–1676), divine; educated at Winchester; fellow of New College, Oxford, 1637; M.A., 1643; D.D., 1667; fellow of Winchester College, 1648 and 1660–75; rector of East Meon, 1648, of Easton, Hampshire, 1660–76, and of Ash, Surrey, 1669; published tract against Romanism, 1674. [xi. 320]

COLES or COLE, JOHN (*fl.* 1650), translator of part of 'Cléopatre' (1663); probationer fellow and schoolmaster of New College, Oxford, 1643; ejected by the parliamentary visitors, 1648; schoolmaster at Wolverhampton. [xi. 321]

COLET, SIR HENRY (*d.* 1505), lord mayor of London; mercer's apprentice and mercer in London; alderman, 1476; sheriff, 1477; lord mayor, 1486 and 1495; knighted, 1487. [xi. 321]

COLET, JOHN (1467?–1519), dean of St. Paul's and founder of St. Paul's School; eldest and only surviving child of Sir Henry Colet [q. v.]; studied at Oxford, *c.* 1483; M.A., *c.* 1490; read mathematics and, in Latin versions, Platonic and Neo-platonic philosophy; nonresident rector of Dennington, Suffolk, 1485–1519; vicar of St. Dunstan's, Stepney, 1485–1505; rector of Thurning, Huntingdonshire, 1490–3; prebendary of York, 1494, and of St. Martin-le-Grand, 1494–1504; chaplain of Hilberworth, Norfolk; travelled in Italy, studying the fathers, canon and civil law, and the rudiments of Greek, 1493–6; resided in Oxford, and lectured on the New Testament, 1496–1504; priest, 1498; met Erasmus, 1498; prebendary of Salisbury, 1502; D.D., 1504; dean of St. Paul's, 1504–19; inherited his father's vast fortune, 1505; founded St. Paul's School, writing for it in English a Latin accidence, 1509; endowed the school, 1511–14; preached before convocation against ecclesiastical corruptions, 1512; preached against war with France, 1512–13; accused of heresy by FitzJames, bishop of London, 1513–14; made the Canterbury pilgrimage, 1514; paid an annuity to Erasmus; preached at Wolsey's installation as cardinal, 15˙5; drew up statutes for St. Paul's School, 1518; some of his devotional works published, 1534; his complete works first issued, 1867–76. [xi. 321]

COLEY, HENRY (1633–1695?), mathematician and astrologer; teacher of mathematics in London; published 'Clavis Astrologiæ,' 1669; amanuensis and adopted son of William Lilly, 1677; continued (Lilly's) 'Merlini Anglici Ephemeris' from 1681 to 1695. [xi. 328]

COLFE or CALF, ABRAHAM (1580–1657), divine; B.A. Christ Church, Oxford, 1599; curate, 1604–10, and vicar, 1610–57, of Lewisham, Kent; rector of St. Leonard's, Eastcheap, London, 1609–47; founded grammar school at Lewisham, 1652, and bequeathed money to found a library and an almshouse. [xi. 329]

COLFE, ISAAC (1560?–1597), divine; born at Canterbury; of French refugee parentage; M.A. Broadgates Hall, Oxford, 1582; vicar of Stone, 1585–7, and of Brookland, Kent, 1587; master of Kingsbridge Hospital, Canterbury, 1596; published sermons. [xi. 330]

COLGAN, JOHN (*d.* 1657?), hagiographer; born in Ulster; Franciscan friar and divinity professor at Louvain; published 'Acta Sanctorum . . . Hiberniæ' (in the calendar, January–March), 1645, 'Trias Thaumaturga' (lives of SS. Patrick, Columba, and Bridget), 1647, and a life of Duns Scotus, 1655. [xi. 330]

COLINTON, LORD (*d.* 1688). [See FOULIS, SIR JAMES.]

COLLARD, FREDERICK WILLIAM (1772–1860), pianoforte manufacturer; partner in firm of Clementi & Co., 1800–31, of Collard & Collard, 1832–60. [xi. 330]

COLLARD, WILLIAM FREDERICK (1776–1866), partner in Clementi & Co.; partner with his brother Frederick William Collard [q. v.], 1832–42. [xi. 331]

COLLEDGE, THOMAS RICHARDSON (1796–1879), physician; officially employed in Canton, Macao, and other Chinese ports till 1841; founded medical mission in China, 1837; pensioned; M.D. Aberdeen, 1839; practised at Cheltenham, 1841–79. [xi. 331]

COLLEGE, STEPHEN (1635?–1681), 'the protestant joiner'; a clever London carpenter; of presbyterian and democratic opinions; conformed to the church, 1660; issued ballads and pamphlets against Romanism; during the excitement of the 'popish plot' sold 'protestant flails,' pocket bludgeons to repel anticipated Romanist assassins; came in arms to Oxford, at the sitting of parliament, 1681; arrested in London, 1681; bill against him thrown out by the grand jury, July 1681; taken to Oxford, condemned and executed. His fate was the subject of several ballads and pamphlets. [xi. 331]

COLLES, ABRAHAM (1773–1843), surgeon; studied surgery in Dublin, Edinburgh, and London; M.D. Edinburgh, 1796; practised medicine in Dublin, 1797–9; specialised in surgery; resident surgeon 1799–1813, and visiting surgeon, 1813–41, of Steevens's Hospital, Dublin; professor of anatomy and surgery, 1804–36; an able operator; discoverer of Colles's fracture of the radius; published surgical treatises. [xi. 333]

COLLET, JOHN (1725?–1780), painter; exhibited, chiefly humorous pieces, 1721–80; his pictures pleasing to the popular taste and often engraved. [xi. 334]

COLLETON, JOHN (1548–1635), Roman catholic divine; educated at Lincoln College, Oxford, 1565, Louvain, and, 1576, Douay; priest on the English mission, 1576; prisoner in the Tower, 1581–4; exiled, 1584; returned to England, 1587; laboured in London and Kent; imprisoned, 1610; dean and vicar-general, 1623–6; urged the pope to sanction Prince Charles's marriage with Henrietta Maria, 1624; published polemical tracts. [xi. 335]

COLLEY, SIR GEORGE POMEROY (1835–1881), major-general; an Irishman; educated at Sandhurst; ensign, 1852; border magistrate and surveyor in Cape Colony, 1857; captain, 1860; served in China; brevetmajor, 1863; professor at the Staff College, Sandhurst; lieutenant-colonel in Ashanti campaign, 1873; visited Natal and the Transvaal, 1875; secretary to the viceroy of India, 1876; chief of staff in Zulu war, 1879; K.C.S.I., 1879; major-general and governor of Natal, 1880; defeated by the Boers at Laing's Nek, January 1881; defeated and killed at Majuba Hill, 26 February 1881. [xi. 336]

COLLEY, JOHN (*fl.* 1440), theological writer; Carmelite friar of Doncaster. [xi. 337]

COLLIBER, SAMUEL (*fl.* 1718–1737), author of 'Columna Rostrata,' a history of recent Dutch naval wars, 1727, and of theological tracts. [xi. 338]

COLLIER, ARTHUR (1680–1732), metaphysician; of Balliol College, Oxford, 1698; rector of Langford Magna, Wiltshire, 1704–32; published 'Clavis Universalis,' 1713, a metaphysical treatise, anticipating Berkeley's views, 'A Specimen of True Philosophy,' 1730, and 'Logology,' 1732; wrote in 'Mist's Journal' against Bishop Hoadly's opinions, 1719. [xi. 338]

COLLIER, SIR FRANCIS AUGUSTUS (1783?–1849), rear-admiral; second son of Sir George Collier [q. v.]; entered navy, 1794; lieutenant, 1803; sent against Arab pirates in the Persian Gulf, 1819–20; rear-admiral, 1846. [xi. 339]

COLLIER, SIR GEORGE (1738–1795), vice-admiral; entered navy, 1751; commander, 1761; visited Paris and Brussels, 1773; knighted, 1775; senior officer at Halifax, Nova Scotia, 1776–9; inflicted great damage on American shipping, 1779; commanded ship at the relief of Gibraltar and captured Spanish frigate, 1781; M.P., Honiton, 1784; rear-admiral, 1793; vice-admiral, 1794. [xi. 339]

COLLIER, GILES (1622–1678), author of sabbatical tracts; entered New Inn Hall, Oxford, 1638; M.A., 1648; took the covenant, 1648; vicar of Blockley, Worcestershire, *c.* 1648 till death. [xi. 341]

COLLIER, JEREMY (1650–1726), nonjuror; educated at Ipswich and from 1669 at Caius College, Cambridge; M.A., 1676; rector of Ampton, Suffolk, 1679–85; lecturer of Gray's Inn, London, 1685; published sermons, 1686–7; numerous pamphlets against William III, 1688–93, and essays, 1694–7; publicly absolved on the scaffold two of those executed for the assassination plot, 1696; outlawed,

1696, but unmolested ; published 'Short View of the Immorality and Profaneness of the English Stage,' 1698, and rejoinders to those who replied, 1699-1708 ; minister of a London nonjuring congregation ; published an 'Historical Dictionary,' adapted from Louis Moreri, 1705-21, and his learned 'Ecclesiastical History of Great Britain,' 1708-14 ; was ordained a nonjuring bishop, 1713 ; ordained nonjuring bishops, 1716 and 1722 ; introduced a new (Romanising) communion office, and produced a schism among the nonjurors, 1718.   [xi. 341]

COLLIER, JOEL (18th cent.), musician ; pseudonym of GEORGE VEAL ; tenor-player at the Italian opera ; published 'Musical Travels in England,' 1774, satirising Charles Burney (1726-1814) [q. v.], and 'Joel Collier Redivivus,' 1818, satirising Jean-Baptiste Logier.
                [xi. 347]

COLLIER, JOHN, 'TIM BOBBIN' (1708-1786), author and painter ; usher (1729) and master (1739-86) of Milnrow school, near Rochdale ; painted grotesque figures for tap-room walls ; published twenty-six grotesque engravings, 1772-3 ; under the name 'Tim Bobbin,' published satirical pieces in the Lancashire dialect, 1739-71, and two squibs directed against John Whitaker's 'History of Manchester,' 1771-3.   [xi. 347]

COLLIER, JOHN PAYNE (1789-1883), Shakespearean critic ; brought up at Leeds ; reporter to 'Times,' London, 1809-21 ; barrister, Middle Temple, 1829 ; F.S.A., 1830 ; published anonymously satirical 'Criticisms on the Bar,' 1819 ; on 'Morning Chronicle' staff, 1821-47 ; published 'Poetical Decameron,' 1820, showing much knowledge of less-known Elizabethan poets ; edited 'Old Plays,' supplementing those in Dodsley's collection, 1825-7, 1833, and 1851 ; forged ballads ; falsified documents belonging to Dulwich College, the public records, and the Egerton (Bridgewater House) collection ; published a 'History of English Dramatic Poetry,' 1831, and 'Facts' and 'Particulars' concerning Shakespeare, 1835-6 and 1839, largely utilising his forgeries ; librarian to, and pensioner of, the Duke of Devonshire ; edited papers for the Camden Society, 1838-63, the Percy Society, 1840-4, and the Shakespeare Society, 1841-51 ; secretary to the British Museum commission, 1847-50 ; edited 'Roxburghe Ballads,' 1847, 'Registers of the Stationers' Company,' 1848-9, and Thomas Heywood's works, 1850-1 ; received a civil list pension, 1850 ; forged marginal corrections in a first folio of Shakespeare ('the Egerton folio') before 1841, and in a second folio ('the Perkins folio') before 1852 ; brought out annotated editions of Shakespeare, 1842-4, 1858, and 1875-8, and a text of Shakespeare, 1853, based on these forgeries ; published what he alleged to be Coleridge's (1811) lectures on Shakespeare, 1856 ; his Shakespeare forgeries exposed, 1859-61 ; edited Edmund Spenser's works, 1862 ; reprinted privately old pieces in prose and verse, 1863-71 ; published notes on rare English books, 1865 ; wrote also original verse and an autobiographical fragment.   [xi. 348]

COLLIER, ROBERT PORRETT, first BARON MONKSWELL (1817-1886), judge ; B.A. Trinity College, Cambridge, 1843 ; a liberal in politics ; barrister, Inner Temple, 1843 ; went on the western circuit ; secured pardon of Brazilian pirates, 1845 ; recorder of Penzance ; M.P., Plymouth, 1852-71 ; counsel to the admiralty, 1859 ; solicitor-general, 1863-6 ; attorney-general, 1868-71 ; made justice of common pleas, 1871, to qualify for the judicial committee of the privy council ; created Baron Monkswell, 1885 ; landscape painter ; published law treatises.
                [xi. 353]

COLLIER, THOMAS (*fl.* 1691), baptist ; owned land in Godalming, 1634 ; baptist preacher in Guernsey, in Yorkshire, 1646, and in the south and west of England ; published polemical tracts, 1645-91.   [xi. 354]

COLLIGNON, CATHERINE (1753-1832), translator of Jean-Baptiste Ladvocat's 'Historical Dictionary,' 1792; daughter of Charles Collignon [q. v.]; benefactor of Addenbrooke's Hospital, Cambridge.   [xi. 355]

COLLIGNON, CHARLES (1725-1785), physician ; M.B. Trinity College, Cambridge, 1749 ; M.D., 1754 ; professor of anatomy, Cambridge, 1753-85 ; his 'Miscellaneous Writings' published, 1786.   [xi. 355]

COLLING, CHARLES (1751-1836), stockbreeder ; occupied farm at Ketton, near Darlington, from 1782 ; greatly improved the breed of shorthorn cattle on the

Tees and Skerne, and produced many celebrated animals, including the bull 'Hubback.'   [Suppl. ii. 45]

COLLING, ROBERT (1749-1820), stockbreeder ; brother of Charles Colling [q. v.]; occupied farm at Barmpton, where he became a noted breeder of shorthorns.   [Suppl. ii. 46]

COLLINGES, JOHN (1623-1690), presbyterian ; educated at Cambridge ; presbyterian chaplain at Bures, Essex, 1645 ; intruded vicar of St. Saviour's, 1646-53, and of St. Stephen's, Norwich, 1653-60 ; D.D. ; published controversial tracts, 1651-8, sermons and devotional tracts, 1650-2 and 1675-81 ; contributor to Matthew Poole's bible.   [xi. 356]

COLLINGRIDGE, PETER BERNARDINE (1757-1829), Roman catholic prelate ; born in Oxfordshire ; Franciscan friar at Douay, 1770 ; president of Baddesley College, Birmingham, 1791 ; stationed in London ; provincial, 1806 ; D.D. ; titular bishop of Thespiæ and co-adjutor of the western district, 1807.   [xi. 357]

COLLINGS, SAMUEL (*fl.* 1780-1790 ?), painter and caricaturist ; exhibited at the Royal Academy, 1784-9 ; designed caricatures engraved by Thomas Rowlandson ; wrote verses.   [xi. 357]

COLLINGTON, JOHN (1548-1635). [See COLLETON.]

COLLINGWOOD, CUTHBERT, first BARON COLLINGWOOD (1750-1810), vice-admiral ; served on home stations, 1761-74 ; served at Bunker's Hill, 1775 ; lieutenant, 1775 ; served in West Indies, 1776-81, 1783-6, 1790-1 ; censured for petulance, 1777 ; lieutenant in Nelson's ship, 1778 ; wrecked 1781 ; commanded ship in battle of 1 June, 1794, and in the Mediterranean, 1795-7 ; did good service at Cape St. Vincent, 1797 ; blockaded Cadiz, 1797-8 ; rear-admiral, 1799 ; blockaded Brest, 1799-1805 ; vice-admiral, 1804 ; cruised off Cadiz, 1805 ; took command on Nelson's death at Trafalgar, October 1805 ; lost many of the prizes through neglecting Nelson's last order ; raised to the peerage and pensioned ; cruised off Spain, 1805-7 ; sent to the Dardanelles, 1807 ; cruised off Sicily, 1807-8 ; culpably missed a chance of destroying the Toulon fleet, 1808 ; blockaded Toulon, 1808-10 ; died at sea ; buried in St. Paul's.   [xi. 357]

COLLINGWOOD, GEORGE (*d.* 1716), Jacobite ; taken prisoner at Preston, executed at Liverpool.   [xi. 362]

COLLINGWOOD, ROGER (*fl.* 1513), mathematician ; fellow of Queens' College, Cambridge, 1497-1510 ; M.A., 1499 ; travelled, 1507-10 ; proctor, 1513.   [xi. 362]

COLLINS, ANTHONY (1676-1729), deist ; educated at Eton and King's College, Cambridge ; friend of John Locke, 1703-4 ; published political tracts, 1707-10 ; attacked the first clause ('authority in controversies of faith') of the twentieth Article of Religion, 1709 and 1724 ; visited Holland, 1711 and 1713 ; published his 'Discourse of Freethinking,' 1713 ; ridiculed by Bentley and Swift ; published 'Enquiry Concerning Human Liberty,' 1715, 'The Grounds of the Christian Religion,' 1724, and 'Literal Scheme of Prophecy,' 1726.   [xi. 363]

COLLINS, ARTHUR (1690 ?-1760), author of the 'Peerage'; bookseller in London ; published his 'Peerage of England,' one volume, 1709 (fourth edition, 1717), and 'Baronetage of England,' two volumes, 1720 ; revised issue of the 'Peerage,' three volumes, 1735 (second edition, 1741 ; supplement, 1750) ; pensioned ; enlarged edition of the 'Peerage,' six volumes, 1756 ; published histories of noble families, 1732-56 ; the definitive edition of Collins's 'Peerage,' by Sir Egerton Brydges (nine volumes), appeared in 1812, and that of the 'Baronetage' (five volumes), by Wotton, in 1741.   [xi. 364]

COLLINS, CHARLES ALLSTON (1828-1873), painter and author ; son of William Collins (1788-1847) [q. v.]; a pre-Raphaelite ; exhibited at the Royal Academy ; published essays and novels.   [xi. 366]

COLLINS, CHARLES JAMES (1820-1864), sporting journalist in London ; published burlesques and novels.
                [xi. 366]

COLLINS, DAVID (1756-1810), colonial governor ; lieutenant of marines, 1770 ; served at Bunker's Hill, 1775, and at the relief of Gibraltar, 1782 ; secretary with Arthur Phillip at Botany Bay, 1787-96 ; published 'Account of ... New South Wales,' 1798-1802 ; governor of Tasmania, 1804-10.   [xi. 366]

COLLINS, GREENVILE (*fl.* 1679-1693), hydrographer; director of the coast survey of Great Britain, 1681-8; published 'Great Britain's Coasting Pilot,' 1693. [xi. 367]

COLLINS, HERCULES (*d.* 1702), baptist minister at Wapping; published sermons and controversial tracts, 1680-96. [xi. 367]

COLLINS, JOHN (*d.* 1634), physician; fellow of St. John's College, Cambridge, 1598; M.D., 1608; fellow of the London College of Physicians, 1613; regius professor of medicine, Cambridge, 1626-34. [xi. 368]

COLLINS, JOHN (1625-1683), mathematician; bookseller's apprentice in Oxford; clerk in Prince Charles's kitchen; served at sea off Crete, 1642-9; mathematical teacher in London; published mathematical treatises, 1652-9; government clerk, 1660-72; F.R.S., 1667; published pamphlets on trade, 1680-2; his large scientific correspondence partly printed, 1712. [xi. 368]

COLLINS, JOHN (1632?-1687), congregational minister; taken as a boy to America; fellow of Harvard, *c.* 1649; chaplain in Monck's army, 1659-60; congregational minister in London; published sermons. [xi. 369]

COLLINS, JOHN (1725?-1759?), painter of Italian landscapes; scene-painter to various London theatres. [xi. 370]

COLLINS, JOHN (1741-1797), Shakespearean scholar; educated at Eton and from 1759 at Queen's College, Oxford; B.C.L., 1766; curate of Ledbury, Herefordshire; defended Edward Capell [q. v.] against George Steevens [q. v.], 1777; edited Capell's 'Notes' on Shakespeare, 1781; became imbecile; died in penury. [xi. 370]

COLLINS, JOHN (*d.* 1807), colonel; nicknamed 'King Collins'; cadet in the Bengal army, 1769; major, 1794; lieutenant-colonel, 1796; resident at the court of Daulat Ráo Sindhia, 1795-1803; envoy to Jeypore, 1799; resident at the Nawáb of Oudh's court, Lucknow, 1804-7. [xi. 371]

COLLINS, JOHN (*d.* 1808), actor and poet; son of a tailor at Bath; a staymaker; went on the stage at Bath; acted at Dublin, 1764; gave a popular vocal and anecdotal entertainment in London and the provinces, 1775-1793; published 'Scripscrapologia' (verses), 1804, and contributed verses to the 'Birmingham Chronicle.' [xi. 371]

COLLINS, MORTIMER (1827-1876), man of letters; son of a Plymouth solicitor; mathematical master in Guernsey, 1850-6; published verses, 1855 and 1860; wrote for periodicals; settled in Berkshire, 1862; published humorous novels, political squibs, essays. [xi. 373]

COLLINS, RICHARD (*d.* 1732), draughtsman of the Spalding Society; pupil of Michael Dahl [q. v.]. [xi. 374]

COLLINS, RICHARD (1755-1831), miniature painter in London; pupil of Jeremiah Meyer [q. v.]; exhibited, 1777-1818; retired to Pershore, Worcestershire, 1811; returned to London, 1828. [ix. 374]

COLLINS, SAMUEL (1576-1651), divine: born and educated at Eton; scholar of King's College, Cambridge, 1591; M.A., 1599; D.D., 1613; chaplain to archbishops Bancroft and Abbot; rector of Fen Ditton, Cambridgeshire (ejected 1643); sinecure rector of Milton, Cambridgeshire; provost of King's College, Cambridge, 1615; regius professor of divinity, Cambridge, 1617; prebendary of Ely, 1618; ejected by puritans from provostship, 1645; published pamphlets against Bellarmine. [xi. 374]

COLLINS, SAMUEL (1619-1670), author of the 'Present State of Russia' (published 1671); entered Corpus Christi College, Cambridge, 1635; M.D. Padua, 1651; incorporated M.D. at Oxford, 1659; physician to the Czar of Russia at Moscow, 1660-9; died at Paris. [xi. 375]

COLLINS, SAMUEL (1617-1685), physician; educated at Eton; fellow of King's College, Cambridge, 1637; B.A., 1638; studied medicine at Leyden; M.D. Cambridge, 1648; intruded fellow of New College, Oxford, and incorporated as M.D., 1650; fellow of the London College of Physicians, 1651; practised in London. [xi. 376]

COLLINS, SAMUEL (1618-1710), comparative anatomist; fellow of Trinity College, Cambridge; M.A.,

1642; travelled; M.D. Padua, 1654; incorporated M.D. at Oxford, 1659, and at Cambridge, 1673; fellow of the London College of Physicians, 1668, and president, 1695; practised in London; published 'A Systeme of Anatomy,' 1685. [xi. 376]

COLLINS, SAMUEL (*fl.* 1750-1780), miniature-painter. [xi. 377]

COLLINS, SAMUEL (1802-1878), 'the bard of Hale Moss'; a Lancashire weaver and radical politician; published 'Miscellaneous Poems,' partly in the Lancashire dialect. [xi. 377]

COLLINS, THOMAS (*fl.* 1615), author of 'The Penitent Publican,' a devotional poem, 1610, and 'The Teares of Loue,' a pastoral, 1615. [xi. 377]

COLLINS, WILLIAM (1721-1759), poet; son of a Chichester hatter; educated at Winchester; demy of Magdalen College, Oxford, 1741; B.A., 1743; published verses in the 'Gentleman's Magazine,' 1739; published his 'Persian Eclogues,' 1742, and his 'Odes,' which take a very high rank among English lyrics, 1747; contributed some odes to Dodsley's 'Museum,' 1749; became imbecile; affectionately cared for by his sister; his collected works first published, 1765. [xi. 377]

COLLINS, WILLIAM (*d.* 1793), modeller of bas-reliefs for chimney-pieces and reredoses; exhibited at the Incorporated Society of Artists, 1760-8. [xi. 380]

COLLINS, WILLIAM (1788-1847), landscape, portrait, and figure painter; exhibited, 1807-46; also etched; his paintings very popular, and many of them engraved; R.A., 1820. [xi. 380]

COLLINS, WILLIAM LUCAS (1817-1887), miscellaneous writer; M.A. Jesus College, Oxford, 1841; vicar of Kilsby, 1867-73, and rector of Lowick, Northamptonshire, 1873-87; wrote popular monographs on great writers. [xi. 381]

COLLINS, WILLIAM WILKIE (1824-1889), novelist; son of William Collins (1788-1847) [q. v.]; articled to a firm of tea merchants in London; entered Lincoln's Inn, 1846, and was called to the bar, 1851; published 'Antonina,' 1850, and 'Rambles beyond Railways,' 1851; soon adopted the profession of literature; made acquaintance of Dickens; contributed to 'Household Words' and the 'Holly Tree' from 1855; collaborated with Dickens in 'Lazy Tour of Two Idle Apprentices' and 'Perils of certain English Prisoners,' 1857; contributed 'The Woman in White' to 'All the Year Round,' 1860, and subsequently issued serial stories in this and other magazines, including 'Cornhill' and 'Temple Bar'; joined Dickens in writing 'No Thoroughfare,' 1867; gave public readings in United States, 1873-4. His works include 'The Dead Secret,' 1857, 'Armadale,' 1866, 'Moonstone,' 1868, 'The Two Destinies,' 1876, and several plays. [Suppl. ii. 46]

COLLINSON, JAMES (1825?-1881), painter; one of the pre-Raphaelites; embraced Roman catholicism; exhibited at various institutions, 1847-80; wrote verse. [xi. 381]

COLLINSON, JOHN (1757?-1793), county historian; vicar of Clanfield, Oxfordshire; vicar of Long Ashton, Somerset, 1787-93; published 'Beauties of British Antiquities,' 1779, and 'History . . . of Somerset,' 1791. [xi. 382]

COLLINSON, PETER (1694-1768), naturalist and antiquary; born near Windermere; a North American merchant; F.S.A.; F.R.S., 1728; correspondent of Benjamin Franklin; studied plants and insects; contributed to scientific journals. [xi. 382]

COLLINSON, SIR RICHARD (1811-1883), admiral; entered the navy, 1823; employed on survey work on the South American coast, 1828, and in the China seas, 1840-6; captain, 1842; went through Behring Straits in search of Sir John Franklin, 1850-4; rear-admiral, 1862; admiral and K.C.B., 1875; wrote geographical papers. [xi. 383]

COLLINSON, SEPTIMUS (1739-1827), provost of Queen's College, Oxford; M.A. Queen's College, Oxford, 1767; D.D., 1793; rector of Dowlish, Somerset, 1778, and of Holwell, Dorset, 1794; provost of Queen's College, 1796, and Lady Margaret professor of divinity, Oxford, 1798-1827. [xi. 384]

COLLIS, JOHN DAY (1816–1879), author of classical school-books; educated at Rugby, 1832–4; fellow of Worcester College, Oxford, 1839–47; M.A., 1841; D.D., 1860; head-master of Bromsgrove school, 1842–67; vicar of Stratford-on-Avon, 1867–79. [xi. 384]

COLLOP, JOHN (*fl.* 1660), royalist writer; M.D.; published 'Poesis Rediviva,' 1656, being verses against the sectaries, a plea for religious toleration entitled 'Medici Catholicon,' 1656, and 'Itur (*sic*) Satyricum,' 1660, verses welcoming the Restoration. [xi. 385]

COLLYER, JOSEPH, the elder (*d.* 1776), compiler and translator; published 'History of England,' 1774–5. [xi. 385]

COLLYER, JOSEPH, the younger (1748–1827), engraver; son of Joseph Collyer the elder [q. v.]; engraved chiefly portraits; a book illustrator; exhibited at the Royal Academy, 1770–1822. [xi. 385]

COLLYER, MARY (*d.* 1763), authoress; *née* Mitchell; wife of Joseph Collyer the elder [q. v.]; translated Gesner (1761) and Klopstock. [xi. 386]

COLLYER, WILLIAM BENGO (1782–1854), congregational minister; educated at Homerton College, 1798; minister at Peckham, 1800–54; D.D. Edinburgh, 1808; preacher at Salters' Hall Chapel, 1813; published sermons, hymns, and tracts. [xi. 386]

COLMAN of Cloyne, SAINT (522–600), known as MacLenin; commemorated on 24 Nov.; bard to the king of Cashel; converted to Christianity and named Colman (Columbanus); taught by St. Jarlath of Tuam; missionary in east Cork; settled at Cloyne. [xi. 386]

COLMAN, ELA or ELO, SAINT (553–610), son of Beogna and Mor, sister of St. Columba; commemorated on 26 Sept.; born at Glenelly, Tyrone; ordained presbyter at Hy (Iona); founded Muckamore Abbey, Antrim, and Land-Elo (now Lynally), King's County; visited Iona. [xi. 387]

COLMAN, SAINT (*d.* 676), bishop of Lindisfarne; commemorated on 8 Aug. in Ireland, and on 18 Feb. in Scotland; born in Mayo; monk at Iona; bishop of Lindisfarne, 661; unsuccessfully defended Celtic usages against Wilfrith and the Roman party, 664; withdrew to Iona, and thence (668) to Inishbofin island, Mayo. [xi. 389]

COLMAN, GEORGE, the elder (1732–1794), dramatist; born in Florence, where his father (*d.* 1733) was British envoy; nephew of William Pulteney, afterwards (1742) Earl of Bath; educated at Westminster; entered Christ Church, Oxford, 1751; M.A., 1758; barrister, Lincoln's Inn, 1755; went on the Oxford circuit, 1759; joint-editor of 'The Connoisseur,' 1754–6; friend of David Garrick, 1758; successfully brought out a farce, his first dramatic piece, 1760; made his mark with 'The Jealous Wife,' 1761; between 1762 and 1789 wrote or adapted some thirty dramatic pieces; inherited 945*l.* a year from the Earl of Bath, 1764; translated Terence,1765; manager of Covent Garden Theatre, 1767–74; manager of Haymarket Theatre, 1777–89; edited Beaumont and Fletcher, 1778; translated Horace's 'Art of Poetry,' 1783; published miscellaneous essays, 1787; became insane. [xi. 390]

COLMAN, GEORGE, the younger (1762–1836), dramatist; son of George Colman the elder [q. v.]; entered Westminster School, 1772, Christ Church, Oxford, 1779, and Aberdeen University, 1781; sent to London his first dramatic piece, 1782; returned to London; between 1784 and 1822 wrote or adapted some twenty-five dramatic pieces, the best known being 'The Heir at Law,' a comedy, 1797, and 'John Bull,' a comedy, 1803; manager of Haymarket Theatre, 1789–1813; published coarse comic poems, 1797–1820; showed great scrupulosity as examiner of plays, 1824–36; involved in litigation and debt; used sometimes the pseudonym of Arthur Griffinhoofe; published 'Random Records,' an autobiography, 1830. [xi. 393]

COLMAN, WALTER (*d.* 1645), poet; educated at Douay; an Observant friar; priest on the English mission; imprisoned, 1641–5; published, *c.* 1632, 'La Dance Machabre.' [xi. 396]

COLNAGHI, DOMINIC PAUL (1790–1879), print dealer; son of Paul Colnaghi [q. v.]; chief partner in firm of Colnaghi & Co., London, 1833–65; collected ancient armour. [xi. 397]

COLNAGHI or **COLNAGO**, PAUL (1751–1833), print dealer; born in Milan; Paris agent of Signor Torre, print dealer, of London; partner of Colnaghi & Co.; a naturalised Englishman. [xi. 397]

COLOMB, PHILIP HOWARD (1831–1899), vice-admiral; entered navy, 1846; served in Burmese war, 1852; lieutenant, 1852; flag-lieutenant to Sir Thomas Sabine Pasley [q. v.], 1857, and later to (Sir) Thomas Matthew Charles Symonds [q. v.]; made reports to admiralty on day and night signals, and devised night system known as 'Colomb's Flashing Signals,' 1858; commander, 1863; post-captain, 1870; rear-admiral, 1887; vice-admiral, 1892; published numerous writings on naval and other subjects. [Suppl. ii. 49]

COLOMIÈS or **COLOMESIUS**, PAUL (1638–1692), librarian; son of a physician at La Rochelle; educated at Saumur and Paris; visited Isaac Vossius in Holland, 1665; resided at La Rochelle, 1665–81; reader in Peter Allix's [q. v.] church; rector of Eynesford, Kent, 1687; naturalised, 1688; gave up librarianship of Lambeth Library, 1690; compiled 'Gallia Orientalis,' a bibliography of French orientalists, 1665; published epigrams, collections of 'ana,' historical tracts, and theological pieces, 1668–90; his 'Italia et Hispania Orientalis' published 1730. [xi. 397]

COLONIA, ADAM DE (1634–1685), painter; son of Adam Louisz de Colonia, a Rotterdam painter; painted cattle-pieces, village wakes, and conflagrations by night; etched; made copies of Bassano's pictures; settled in England; died in London. [xi. 399]

COLONSAY, LORD (1793–1874). [See MacNEILL, DUNCAN.]

COLORIBUS, JOHN DE (*fl.* 1525), Dominican friar; a foreigner; D.D. Oxford, 1517; a protégé of Wolsey; lectured at Oxford on theology; member of Wolsey's Oxford college, 1525. [xi. 399]

COLPOYS, SIR JOHN (1742?–1821), admiral; entered navy, 1756; served in West Indies, 1758–62, and in East Indies, 1770–4; captain, 1773; commanded ship in West Indies, and in the Mediterranean, 1776–93; rear-admiral, 1794; on board the London at the mutiny at Spithead, 15 April 1797, and at St. Helens, 7 May; ordered by the admiralty to submit to the mutineers, 14 May; K.B., 1798; admiral, 1801; commander-in-chief at Plymouth, 1803; a lord of the admiralty, 1804; treasurer, 1805, and governor, 1816–21, of Greenwich Hospital. [xi. 399]

COLQUHOUN, ARCHIBALD CAMPBELL- (*d.* 1820), lord clerk register; son of John Campbell of Clathick; took the name Colquhoun, 1804, on inheriting Killermont, Dumbartonshire; advocate, 1768; M.P., 1810–20; lord advocate, 1807–16; lord clerk register, 1816–20. [xi. 400]

COLQUHOUN, JANET, LADY (1781–1846), author of anonymous religious tracts (1822–39); *née* Sinclair; married, 1799, James Colquhoun, afterwards (1805) third baronet, of Luss, Dumbartonshire. [xi. 401]

COLQUHOUN, JOHN (1748 – 1827), theological writer; a Dumbartonshire shepherd; D.D.; studied at Glasgow; minister in South Leith, 1781–1827; published devotional tracts, 1813–18. [xi. 402]

COLQUHOUN, JOHN (1805–1885), writer on sport; son of Janet, lady Colquhoun [q. v.]; educated at Edinburgh; army officer in Connaught, 1828; published 'The Moor and the Loch,' 1840, and similar works, 1849–74. [xi. 402]

COLQUHOUN, JOHN CAMPBELL (1785–1854), writer on psychical research; younger son of the second baronet of Luss; educated at Göttingen; advocate at Scottish bar; sheriff-depute of Dumbartonshire, 1815–54; wrote on 'animal magnetism,' 1833; translated part of Kant, 1806, and Wienholt's 'Somnambulism,' 1845. [xi. 402]

COLQUHOUN, JOHN CAMPBELL- (1803–1870), miscellaneous writer; eldest son of Archibald Campbell-Colquhoun [q. v.]; educated at Edinburgh; B.A. Oriel College, Oxford, 1823; M.P., 1832–47; published biographies and political and religious pamphlets. [xi. 402]

COLQUHOUN, PATRICK (1745–1820), metropolitan police magistrate (1792–1818); merchant in Virginia, and, 1766–89, in Glasgow; removed to London, 1789; hon. LL.D. Glasgow, 1797; published pamphlets on trade, liquor traffic, poor relief, and police questions. [xi. 403]

COLQUHOUN, Sir PATRICK MACCHOMBAICH (1815–1891), diplomatist, author, and oarsman; educated at Westminster and St. John's College, Cambridge; M.A., 1844; LL.D., 1851; honorary fellow, 1886; called to bar at Inner Temple, 1838; bencher, 1869, treasurer, 1888; Q.C., 1868; plenipotentiary to Hanse towns, 1840; aulic councillor to king of Saxony, 1857; member of supreme court of justice in Ionian islands, 1858; knighted and appointed chief-justice of the court, 1861; secretary of the Leander boat club; published legal and other writings. [Suppl. ii. 50]

COLSON, JOHN (1680–1760), mathematician; entered Christ Church, Oxford, 1699; mathematical master at Rochester; F.R.S., 1713; vicar of Chalk, Kent, 1724–1740; M.A. Emmanuel College, Cambridge, 1728; Lucasian professor of mathematics, 1739; rector of Lockington, Yorkshire; published mathematical treatises and translations, 1726–52. [xi. 405]

COLSON, LANCELOT (*fl.* 1668), or COELSON, astrologer, of London; published almanacks, 1660–80; and a treatise on alchemy, 'Philosophia Maturata,' 1668. [xi. 406]

COLSTON, EDWARD (1636–1721), philanthropist; educated at Christ's Hospital, London; resided in Bristol, trading with the West Indies, 1683; resided at Mortlake, Surrey, 1689–1721; M.P., Bristol, 1710–13; founded and endowed almshouses and schools at Bristol, 1690–1712; founded school at Mortlake and an almshouse at Sheen; benefactor of poor benefices in England and of London hospitals; commemorated by the Colston banquets in Bristol. [xi. 406]

COLT, JOHN (*fl.* 1618), sculptor; probably son of Maximilian Colt [q. v.] [xi. 407]

COLT or **COULT**, alias POULTRAIN or POWTRAN, MAXIMILIAN (*fl.* 1600–1618), sculptor; native of Arras; carved monuments in Westminster Abbey, 1605–8; master carver to James I, 1608; carved the decorations of court barges, 1611–24; prisoner in the Fleet, 1641. [xi. 407]

COLTON, CHARLES CALEB (1780?–1832), author of 'Lacon' (1820–2), two volumes of aphorisms; educated at Eton; M.A. King's College, Cambridge, 1804; non-resident rector of Prior's Portion, Tiverton, 1801, and vicar of Kew and Petersham, Surrey, 1818–28; wine merchant in London; bankrupt; withdrew to America; committed suicide; published satires, verses, essays, and sermons, 1809–22. [xi. 408]

COLTON, JOHN (*d.* 1404), archbishop of Armagh; master of Gonville College, Cambridge, and doctor of canon law, 1348; rector of Terrington, Norfolk, 1350; prebendary of York; official in Ireland, raising troops against the natives, 1372; treasurer of Ireland, 1374 and 1381; dean of St. Patrick's, Dublin, 1374–82; chancellor of Ireland, 1379–1381; lord justice, 1381; archbishop of Armagh, 1382. [xi. 408]

COLUMBA, otherwise COLUMCILLE or COLUMBANUS, SAINT (521–597), commemorated on 9 June; son of Feidilmid, an Ulster chief; born at Gartan, Donegal; a pupil of St. Finnian; recluse at Glasnevin, near Dublin; built churches at Derry and other places; went to Scotland, 563; founded the monastery of Hy (Iona) and preached to the Picts; received Aidan [q. v.] into his community, 574; visited Ireland, 575 and 585; his reliques translated to Ireland, 878, and destroyed by the Danes, 1127; several books believed to have been written by him long venerated in Ireland; his life was written by Adamnan [q. v.] [xi. 409]

COLUMBAN, SAINT (543–615), abbot of Luxeuil; commemorated on 21 Nov.; born in Leinster; recluse at Lough Erne; wrote religious verses; monk under St. Comgall [q. v.] at Bangor, co. Down; resided in Burgundy, 585–610; built monasteries at Anegray and (590) Luxeuil, Haute-Saône, for which he drew up a monastic 'rule,' afterwards common in France, till replaced by that of St. Benedict; quarrelled with the Frank bishops about Easter and the tonsure; expelled from Burgundy by Theodorik II, 610; befriended by Hlothair II of Soissons, and by Theodebert II of Metz, 611; preached to the heathen Alemanni and Suevi; settled at Bregenz in the Tyrol; founded the monastery of Bobbio, Piedmont, 613, and died there; his reputed writings edited by Patrick Fleming in 1621. [xi. 413]

COLVILE or **COLDEWEL**, GEORGE (*fl.* 1556), translator of 'Boethius de Consolatione,' 1556. [xi. 416]

COLVILE, Sir JAMES WILLIAM (1810–1880), judge; of Craigflower, Fifeshire; educated at Eton; M.A. Trinity College, Cambridge, 1834; barrister of the Inner Temple, 1835; advocate-general at Calcutta, 1845; justice, 1848, and chief-justice, 1855–9, of Bengal; knighted, 1848; member of the judicial committee of the privy council, 1859–80. [xi. 417]

COLVILL or **COLVILLE**, ALEXANDER (1700–1777), Irish presbyterian minister; M.A. Edinburgh, 1715; studied medicine; licensed by presbytery of Cupar-Fife, 1722; refused ordination by presbytery of Armagh to the presbyterian pastorate of Dromore, 1724–5, for refusing subscription to Westminster Confession; ordained by presbytery of Dublin; joined himself and his followers to the expelled presbytery of Antrim, 1730; M.D.; raised troops for the government, 1745; published pamphlets and sermons. [xi. 417]

COLVILLE, ALEXANDER (1530?–1597), Scottish judge; granted Culross Abbey, 1567; opponent of Mary Queen of Scots; a lord of session, 1575–87 and 1587–97; served on various public commissions, 1578–92. [xi. 418]

COLVILLE, ALEXANDER (1620–1676), Scottish episcopalian; educated at Edinburgh; incumbent of Dysart, Fifeshire; professor at Sedan, France; died in Edinburgh; published pamphlets and verses against the presbyterians. [xi. 418]

COLVILLE, Sir CHARLES (1770–1843), general; ensign, 1781; lieutenant-colonel, 1796; served in West Indies, 1791–7, against the Irish rebels, 1798, in Egypt, 1801, and against Martinique, 1809; commanded brigade, and afterwards division, in the Peninsula, 1810–14, and division in Belgium, 1815; K.C.B., 1815; lieutenant-general, 1819; commander-in-chief at Bombay, 1819–25; governor of Mauritius, 1828–34; general, 1837. [xi. 418]

COLVILLE, ELIZABETH, LADY COLVILLE OF CULROS (*fl.* 1603), poetess; née Melville; wife of John Colville of Wester Cumbrae, who in 1640 became entitled to the barony of Colville of Culros. but never claimed it; reputed authoress of a religious poem, 'Ane Godlie Dreame . . . be M.M.,' 1603, founded on a traditional 'Lady of Culross's Dream.' [xi. 419]

COLVILLE, Sir JAMES (*d.* 1540?), diplomatist; of Easter Wemyss; sat in the Scottish parliament, 1525–36; comptroller of Scotland, 1525–38; exchanged ancestral estate of Ochiltree for Easter Wemyss, 1529; knighted and made a lord of session, 1532; commissioner to England, 1533–4; charged with treason, 1539; withdrew to England; his estates forfeited, 1541, but restored, 1543. [xi. 420]

COLVILLE, JOHN (1542?–1605), Scottish politician; of Cleish, Kinross-shire; M.A. St. Andrews, 1561; non-resident minister of Kilbride, Lanarkshire, 1567, of Carmunnock, Lanarkshire, and of Eaglesham, Renfrewshire; chantor of Glasgow, 1569; master of requests, 1578; spy for Queen Elizabeth in Scotland; attached himself to the Gowrie faction 1581; published justification of the 'raid of Ruthven,' 1582; envoy to England, imprisoned, 1583, and expelled from his offices by parliament; restored, 1586; a lord of session, 1587, at once resigning; sat in the Scottish parliament. 1587; joined the Earl of Bothwell's faction, 1591; outlawed, 1593; pardoned on betraying his associates; renounced protestantism; visited Rome; died in Paris; published his 'Palinod,' 1600, an acknowledgment of James VI's title, and his 'Parænesis,' 1601, a justification of his conversion, and Latin verses and orations; some of his letters printed, 1858. [xi. 420]

COLVILLE or **COLVILL**, WILLIAM (*d.* 1675), Scottish divine; of Cleish, Kinross-shire; M.A. St. Andrews, 1617; minister in Edinburgh, 1635–48; envoy to France, but taken prisoner by Charles I, 1640; deposed, 1649, for favouring the 'engagement'; minister at Utrecht; elected principal of Edinburgh University, 1652, but removed by Cromwell, 1653; minister of Perth, 1654; principal of Edinburgh University, 1662–75; published sermons. [xi. 422]

COLVIN, JOHN RUSSELL (1807–1857), Indian official; in the East India Company's service in Bengal, 1826–35; private secretary to the governor-general, 1836–

1842; resident of Nepaul, 1845; commissioner in Tenasserim, 1846; member of the Sudder revenue court, 1849; lieutenant-governor of the north-west provinces, 1853; died at Agra. [xi. 422]

COLWALL, DANIEL (*d.* 1690), citizen of London; F.R.S., 1663, and treasurer, 1665-79; inaugurated the society's museum, 1666; benefactor of Christ's Hospital. [xi. 424]

COLYEAR, SIR DAVID, first EARL OF PORTMORE (*d.* 1730), a scion of the Robertsons of Strowan, Perthshire; entered Dutch service, 1674; served under William III in Ireland (1689-90) and Flanders; married the Countess of Dorchester, mistress of James II; created Baron Portmore, 1699; major-general, 1702; created Earl of Portmore, 1703; served in Ormonde's futile expeditions to Spain, 1702, and Flanders, 1712; general, 1711; non-resident governor of Gibraltar, 1713-30. [xi. 424]

COLYNGHAM, THOMAS (*fl.* 1387), Cistercian monk; graduate of Paris; theological writer. [xi. 425]

COMBE, ANDREW (1797-1847), physiologist and phrenologist; of a sickly constitution; qualified as a surgeon, 1817; studied anatomy in Paris, 1817; disciple of Johann Gaspar Spurzheim, 1818; practised medicine in Edinburgh, 1823-32, 1836-40; M.D. Edinburgh, 1825; contributed to medical journals; published popular health treatises, 1831-40; joined the Phrenological Society, 1820, and contributed to the 'Phrenological Journal,' 1823-46. [xi. 425]

COMBE, CHARLES (1743-1817), numismatist; son of a London apothecary; educated at Harrow; apothecary in London, 1768; F.S.A., 1771; helped William Hunter to collect coins from 1773; F.R.S., 1776; one of Hunter's trustees, 1783; M.D. Glasgow, 1783; accoucheur in London, 1784-1817; published 'Index nummorum omnium Imperatorum, Augustorum et Cæsarum,' 1773, a catalogue of some coins in Hunter's collection, 1782, and other numismatical tracts; edited Horace, 1792-3. [xi. 426]

COMBE, GEORGE (1788-1858), phrenologist; son of an Edinburgh brewer; educated in Edinburgh; a lawyer's apprentice, 1804; writer to the signet, 1812; became a disciple of Spurzheim; retired from business, 1836; wrote in defence of phrenology, 1818-19; founded the Phrenological Society, 1820, and the 'Phrenological Journal,' 1823; lectured on phrenology in Edinburgh from 1822; published 'Elements of Phrenology,' 1824, and 'Essay on the Constitution of Man,' 1828; lectured in America, 1838-40, and Germany, 1842; published pamphlets on education and social ethics. [xi. 427]

COMBE, TAYLOR (1774-1826), numismatist; son of Charles Combe [q.v.]; educated at Harrow and, 1791, Oriel College, Oxford; M.A., 1798; F.S.A., 1796; keeper of coins, 1803, and of antiquities, 1807-26, in the British Museum; F.R.S., 1806; published catalogues of Museum coins and antique marbles, 1814-26; contributed to 'Archæologia.' [xi. 429]

COMBE, THOMAS (1797-1872), printer; son of a Leicestershire bookseller; connected with the Clarendon press, Oxford, from 1837; a leading benefactor of the church in Oxford. [xi. 430]

COMBE, WILLIAM (1741-1823), author of 'Doctor Syntax'; educated at Eton; said to have been at Oxford, *c.* 1760; travelled in France and Italy; lived extravagantly in London and (1768) in Bristol; nicknamed 'Count Combe'; withdrew to France, hopelessly in debt; returned to London; roamed about in the liberties of the Fleet, *c.* 1772 till death; compiled and translated travels and histories for the booksellers, 1774-1821; made a hit by 'The Diaboliad,' a satire on Simon, lord Irnham, 1776; issued similar metrical satires, 1777-84; published supposititious 'Letters,' 1777-85; published novels, 1784-1790; published political pamphlets, 1789-92, and was pensioned by Pitt, 1789-1806, as a government writer; wrote letterpress for Boydell's 'River Thames,' 1794-6, for Ackermann's 'Thames,' 1811, 'Westminster Abbey,' 1812, 'Oxford,' 1814, 'Cambridge,' 1815, and other illustrated works; contributed to the 'Times,' 1803-9; wrote letterpress for Thomas Rowlandson's third volume of 'The Microcosm of London,' 1810, for his three 'Tours of Dr. Syntax,' 1812, 1820, and 1821, for his 'Dance of Death,' 1815-16, and 'Dance of Life,' 1816, and for his 'Johnny Quæ Genus,' 1822. [xi. 430]

COMBER, THOMAS (1575-1654), dean of Carlisle; scholar of Trinity College, Cambridge, 1593; fellow, 1597; M.A., 1598; visited France; chaplain to James I; rector of Worplesdon, Surrey, 1615; D.D.; dean of Carlisle, 1629; master of Trinity, Cambridge, 1631; ejected by the parliament. [xi. 435]

COMBER, THOMAS (1645-1699), dean of Durham; B.A. Sidney Sussex College, Cambridge, 1663; M.A., 1666; rector of Stonegrave, Yorkshire, 1669; prebendary, 1677, and precentor, 1683, of York; D.D.; dean of Durham, 1691; published 'Companion to the Temple,' 1672-1676, and other treatises expository of the liturgy, 1675-1696, anti-Romanist treatises, 1673-95, and pamphlets in favour of William III, 1689-92. [xi. 435]

COMBERFORD, **COMERFORD**, or **QUEMERFORD**, NICHOLAS (1544?-1599), jesuit; born at Waterford; B.A. Oxford, 1563; went to Louvain; D.D., 1575; joined the jesuits, 1578; published controversial tracts. [xi. 438]

COMBERMERE, VISCOUNT. [See COTTON, SIR STAPLETON, 1773-1865.]

COMERFORD, JOHN (1762?-1832?), miniature-painter in Dublin; exhibited in London, 1804-9. [xi. 438]

COMGALL, SAINT (6th cent.), Latinised as FAUSTUS; commemorated on 10 May; native of Antrim; a soldier; pupil of SS. Finnian and Ciaran; missionary priest; recluse on Lough Erne; founded Bangor Abbey, co. Down, *c.* 558, and other monasteries; friend of St. Columba; author of a monastic 'rule' copied by his pupil St. Columban [q. v.] [xi. 438]

COMIN, COMINES, or **CUMIN**, ROBERT DE, EARL OF NORTHUMBERLAND (*d.* 1069), accompanied William the Conqueror to England; created Earl of Northumberland, and deputed to reduce the north of England, 1068; killed in a tumult at Durham; reputed ancestor of the Comyn family. [xi. 440]

COMMAN or **COMMOC** of Ross-Commain, SAINT, (*fl.* 550); commemorated on 26 Dec., of a noble Ulster family; pupil of St. Finnian; missionary in Connaught; founded Roscommon and other monasteries. [xi. 441]

COMMIUS (*fl.* B.C. 57-51), ambassador from Julius Cæsar to the Britons; a Belgic Gaul set over the Atrebates by Julius Cæsar, B.C. 57; sent, as envoy, to Britain, B.C. 55; served against the Menapii, B.C. 53; joined the revolted Gauls, B.C. 52-51; possibly withdrew to Britain, where three 'sons of Commius' are found inscribed on coins. [xi. 441]

COMPOTISTA or **COMPUTISTA**, ROGER (*fl.* 1360?), monk and prior of Bury St. Edmunds; compiled 'Expositiones vocabulorum Bibliæ.' [xi. 442]

COMPTON, HENRY (1632-1713), bishop of London; younger son of Spencer Compton, second earl of Northampton [q. v.]; possibly served in the civil war; nobleman of Queen's College, Oxford, 1640-52; travelled in Italy; possibly served in Flanders; cornet in the horse guards, 1660; M.A. Cambridge, 1661; incorporated at Christ Church, Oxford, 1666; rector of Cottenham, Cambridgeshire; advanced in the church by his family influence and the favour of Danby; master of St. Cross, Winchester, 1667; canon of Christ Church, Oxford, and D.D., 1669; bishop of Oxford, 1674; translated to London, 1675; dean of the Chapel Royal, 1675; privy councillor, 1676; procured the banishment of Joannes Lyserus; religious instructor of Princesses Mary and Anne; his hopes of the see of Canterbury frustrated by the opposition of the Duke of York, 1677; assisted the persecuted French protestants, 1681; strongly opposed repeal of Test Act, 1685; dismissed from the privy council and the deanery of the Chapel Royal, 1685; suspended from episcopal functions for refusing to inhibit John Sharp [q. v.] at the king's order, 1686; agreed to support William of Orange, 1687; joined the revolutionary committee, 1688; signed the invitation to William, 30 June 1688; reinstated in his see, 1688; joined the bishops' protest against James II's illegal acts, October and November 1688; conveyed Princess Anne to Nottingham; marched, as colonel of a regiment, to Oxford; welcomed William in London, December 1688; ordered omission of prayers for James II and the Prince of Wales, 1689; voted for declaring the throne vacant; reinstated as privy councillor and dean of the Chapel Royal; crowned

William and Mary, April 1689 ; acted as primate during Sancroft's suspension, 1689–90 ; supported the toleration bill, 1691 ; lord almoner, 1702 ; voted for Sacheverell, 1710 ; collected foreign plants ; spent his revenues in charity ; published translations from French and Italian, 1666–77, and 'Letters' and 'Charges' to his clergy, 1679–1701. [xi. 443]

COMPTON, HENRY (1805–1877), comedian ; real name CHARLES MACKENZIE ; merchant's clerk in London ; went on the provincial stage ; first acted in London, 1837 ; at Dublin, 1840–1 ; acknowledged to be the best Shakespearean clown of his epoch ; last acted, at Liverpool, 1877. [xi. 447]

COMPTON, SIR HERBERT ABINGDON DRAPER (1770–1846), judge ; army officer in India ; journalist in London ; barrister, Lincoln's Inn, 1808 ; advocate-general at Madras and Calcutta ; knighted, 1831 ; chief-justice of Bombay, 1831–9. [xi. 448]

COMPTON, SPENCER, second EARL OF NORTHAMPTON (1601–1643), educated at St. John's College, Cambridge ; K.B., 1616 ; styled Lord Compton, 1618 ; M.P., Ludlow, 1621–2 ; master of the robes to Charles, as prince of Wales, 1622, and as king, 1625–8 ; accompanied Prince Charles to Spain, 1623 ; called to the peers as Baron Compton, 1626 ; succeeded to the earldom, 1630 ; supported Charles I against the Scots and the parliament, 1639–42 ; commissioned to raise Warwickshire for the king, 1642 ; fought in several actions, and was killed at Hopton Heath, 1643. [xi. 449]

COMPTON, SPENCER, EARL OF WILMINGTON (1673 ?– 1743), third son of the third Earl of Northampton ; M.P., 1698–1710 and 1713–27, and speaker of the house, 1715–1727 ; acted with the whigs ; flattered the court ; paymaster-general, 1722–30 ; K.B., 1725 ; created Baron Wilmington, 1728, and Earl, 1730 ; lord privy seal, 1730 ; lord president of the council, 1730 ; turned against Walpole, 1739 ; first lord of the treasury, 1742 till death. [xi. 450]

COMPTON, SPENCER JOSHUA ALWYNE, second MARQUIS OF NORTHAMPTON (1790–1851), styled Lord Compton ; M.A. Trinity College, Cambridge, 1810 ; styled Earl Compton ; M.P., 1812–20 ; voted with the whigs ; in Italy, 1820–30 ; succeeded as marquis, 1828 ; president of the Royal Society, 1838–49 ; published verses. [xi. 451]

COMPTON, alias CARLETON, THOMAS (1593 ?– 1666), jesuit ; born in Cambridgeshire ; joined the jesuits, 1617 ; ordained priest at Douay, 1622 ; sent to England, 1625 ; professor at St. Omer and Liège ; published Latin scholastic and theological treatises. [xi. 452]

COMPTON, SIR WILLIAM (1482 ?–1528), soldier ; inherited Compton, Warwickshire, 1493 ; in personal attendance on Henry VIII, 1509–23 ; knighted at Tournay, 1513 ; absentee chancellor of Ireland, 1513–16 ; served in the Scottish war, 1523. [xi. 452]

COMPTON, SIR WILLIAM (1625–1663), royalist ; third son of Spencer Compton, second earl of Northampton [q. v.] ; fought bravely at taking of Banbury, 1642 ; knighted, 1643 ; royalist governor of Banbury, 1642 ; besieged, 1644 ; surrendered, 1646 ; took part in the Kentish rising, 1648 ; imprisoned, 1648, 1655, and 1658 ; master of the ordnance, 1660 ; M.P., 1661. [xi. 453]

COMRIE, ALEXANDER (1708–1774), writer against rationalism ; a Scot ; merchant's clerk in Holland ; Ph.D. Leyden, 1734 ; pastor of Woubrugge, 1734–73 ; wrote in Dutch. [xi. 454]

COMYN, ALEXANDER, second EARL OF BUCHAN (d. 1289), constable of Scotland ; succeeded to earldom, 1233 ; member of the king's council, 1244 ; justiciary of Scotland, 1253 ; banished from court, 1255 ; again in power, 1257 ; head of Comyn family, 1258 ; plundered the revolted Western Isles, 1264 ; inherited great estates in Galloway, 1264 ; sheriff of Wigton, 1266 ; constable of Scotland, 1270 ; pledged himself to support the Maid of Norway, 1283 ; one of the regents, 1286. [xi. 455]

COMYN, JOHN (d. 1212), archbishop of Dublin ; Henry II's emissary against Becket to the emperor, 1163, and the pope, 1166 ; excommunicated by Becket ; justice itinerant, 1179 ; envoy to Spain, 1177 ; a justiciar, 1179 ; elected, by King Henry's command, archbishop of Dublin, 1181 ; first visited Ireland, 1184–5 ; sided with Prince Richard, 1188 ; founded St. Patrick's, Dublin, 1190 ; set on foot controversy with see of Armagh as to precedence ; excommunicated the viceroy, 1197 ; imprisoned in Normandy ; restored, 1198 ; taken into favour by King John, 1199 ; returned to Ireland, 1203. [xi. 455]

COMYN, JOHN (d. 1274), justiciar of Galloway ; held large estates in Nithsdale and Tynedale ; in power at the Scottish court, 1249–55 ; recovered power, 1257 ; conspired against Henry III, 1258 ; took Henry III's part against the barons, 1263 ; captured at Lewes, 1264 ; rewarded by Henry III, 1265. [xi. 458]

COMYN, JOHN, the elder (d. 1300 ?), claimant to Scottish throne ; surnamed THE BLACK ; son and heir of John Comyn (d. 1274) [q. v.] ; inherited Badenoch, 1258 ; assented to marriage of Princess Margaret with Eric II of Norway, 1281 ; acknowledged her daughter Margaret's title to throne, 1284 ; one of the regents, 1286–92 ; claimed the throne, 1291 ; supported his brother-in-law, John de Baliol (1249–1315) [q. v.] ; banished south of Trent by Edward I, 1296 ; restored, 1297. [xi. 459]

COMYN, JOHN, the younger (d. 1306), surnamed THE RED ; son of John Comyn the elder [q. v.] ; fought for his uncle, John Baliol, against Edward I, 1296 ; taken prisoner at Dunbar ; released, 1297 ; visited France ; fought at Falkirk, 1298 ; elected joint-guardian of Scotland by the nobles, 1299 ; expelled Edward I's officials, 1302, and defeated his officer, 1303 ; driven northward by Edward I ; submitted, 1304 ; pardoned, on payment of a fine, 1305 ; murdered at Dumfries by Robert Bruce's followers. [xi. 460]

COMYN, JOHN, third EARL OF BUCHAN (d. 1313 ?), constable of Scotland ; son of Alexander Comyn, second earl [q. v.] ; succeeded, 1289 ; friendly to Edward I, 1290–1293 ; summoned to serve in Gascony, 1294 ; joined John Baliol, 1296 ; banished south of Trent ; sent to Scotland to suppress Wallace's rising, 1297 ; elected joint-guardian of Scotland, 1299 ; envoy to request French intervention, 1303 ; his English estates forfeited, 1304, but soon restored ; acknowledged Edward I as king of Scotland, 1305 ; at blood-feud with Bruce for the murder of his cousin, John Comyn the younger [q. v.] ; opposed by his wife Isabella, who crowned Bruce at Scone, 1306 ; defeated by Bruce, 1307 and 1308 ; his estates seized by Robert Bruce, c. 1313. [xi. 462]

COMYN, SIR ROBERT BUCKLEY (1792–1853), judge ; educated at Merchant Taylors' School ; M.A. St. John's College, Oxford, 1815 ; barrister, Lincoln's Inn, 1814 ; knighted, 1825 ; justice of Bengal, 1825 ; chief-justice of Madras, 1835–42 ; published legal and historical works. [xi. 463]

COMYN, WALTER, EARL OF MENTEITH (d. 1258), half-brother of Alexander Comyn, second earl of Buchan [q. v.] ; in attendance on Alexander II, 1221–7 ; acquired Badenoch, 1229 ; acquired the earldom of Menteith by marriage, 1230 ; built castles in Galloway, 1235 ; acquired the chief power in Scotland, 1249 ; put down by Henry III, 1255 ; regained power, 1257. [xi. 463]

COMYNS, SIR JOHN (d. 1740), judge ; barrister, Lincoln's Inn, 1690 ; M.P., Maldon, 1701–26 ; serjeant-at-law, 1705 ; baron of the exchequer, 1726 ; justice of common pleas, 1736 ; chief baron of exchequer, 1738 ; wrote in law-French 'Reports' and a 'Digest of English Law,' since translated. [xi. 464]

CONÆUS (d. 1640). [See CONN, GEORGE.]

CONANT, JOHN (1608–1694), theologian ; entered Exeter College, Oxford, 1627 ; fellow, 1633–47 ; M.A., 1634 ; D.D., 1654 ; withdrew from Oxford, 1642 ; preached in Somerset and London ; chaplain to George, baron Chandos, at Uxbridge ; rector of Exeter College, 1649–62 ; regius professor of divinity, 1654–60 ; vice-chancellor, 1657–60 ; ejected from his headship for nonconformity, 1662 ; ordained priest, 1670 ; vicar of All Saints, Northampton, 1671 ; archdeacon of Norwich, 1676 ; prebendary of Worcester, 1681 ; became blind ; published sermons. [xi. 465]

CONANT, JOHN (1654 ?–1723), biographer ; son of John Conant [q. v.] ; fellow of Merton College, Oxford, 1676–87 ; D.C.L., 1683 ; practised at Doctors' Commons ; wrote a life of his father (published, 1823). [xi. 467]

CONCANEN, MATTHEW (1701–1749), author ; born in Ireland ; brought out a comedy and poems, 1721–2 ;

hack-writer and government journalist in London; befriended by William Warburton, 1726; wrote against Pope, 1728, and was accordingly placed in the 'Dunciad,' 1729; attorney-general of Jamaica, 1732-48. [xi. 467]

CONCHES, WILLIAM DE (d. 1154). [See WILLIAM.]

CONDÉ, JOHN (fl. 1785-1800), engraver; of French nationality; engraved portraits of celebrities. [xi. 468]

CONDELL, HENRY, or CUNDELL (d. 1627), actor; partner in the Globe and Blackfriars theatres; acted leading parts in plays by Shakespeare, Jonson, Beaumont and Fletcher, Webster, and Marston, 1598-1623; member of the lord chamberlain's company, and, 1603-25, of the king's company of players; received a mourning ring by will from Shakespeare, 1616; with John Heming [q. v.], edited the first folio of Shakespeare's plays, 1623.
[xi. 468]

CONDELL, HENRY (1757-1824), composer; violinist in London orchestras; composed stage-music, 1803-8, also catches, songs, and duets. [xi. 469]

CONDER, JAMES (1763-1823), numismatist; youngest son of John Conder [q. v.]; published a catalogue of modern 'Provincial Coins, Tokens,' &c., 1798. [xii. 1]

CONDER, JOHN (1714-1781), congregational minister; educated in London; pastor at Cambridge, 1739-54; D.D.; theological tutor in a London dissenting academy, 1754-81; preacher in London. [xii. 1]

CONDER, JOSIAH (1789-1855), bookseller and author; son of a London bookseller; assistant in his father's shop, 1802; wrote verses for periodicals, 1806; bookseller in London, 1811-19; edited the 'Eclectic Review,' 1814-37, the 'Patriot,' 1832-55, nonconformist periodicals; brought out the 'Modern Traveller,' thirty volumes of travels, 1825-9; published also verses, essays, and religious tracts. [xii. 2]

CONDLAED OF KILDARE, latinised CONLIANUS (d. 520), bishop and saint; commemorated on 3 May; a relative of St. Brigit [q. v.]; spiritual director of Brigit's convent at Kildare; devoured by wolves in co. Wicklow.
[xii. 3]

CONDUITT, JOHN (1688-1737), master of the mint; at Westminster School, 1701, and Trinity College, Cambridge, 1705; travelled; judge-advocate in Portugal, 1711; captain of dragoons; M.P., 1715-37; married Sir Isaac Newton's niece, 1717; master of the mint, 1727; wrote on the coinage, 1730; collected materials for a life of Newton. [xii. 4]

CONDY or **CUNDY**, NICHOLAS (1793?-1857), landscape painter in water-colours; ensign, 1811; served in the Peninsula; lieutenant, 1818; resided at Plymouth; exhibited in London, 1830-45; joint-author of a book describing Cotehele, on the Tamar. [xii. 5]

CONDY, NICHOLAS MATTHEWS (1818-1851), art-teacher at Plymouth; son of Nicholas Condy or Cundy [q. v.]; exhibited sea-pieces in London, 1842-5. [xii. 5]

CONEY, JOHN (1786-1833), draughtsman and engraver; exhibited architectural drawings, 1805-21; published engravings of Warwick Castle, 1815, London churches, 1820, English ecclesiastical antiquities, 1842, and continental buildings, 1832; other volumes appeared posthumously, 1842-3. [xii. 5]

CONGALLUS I, in Gaelic CONALL, third reputed king of the Scots of Dalriada (511-535?), son of Domangart, son of Fergus Mor Mac Earc. [xii. 6]

CONGALLUS II, in Gaelic CONALL, sixth reputed king of the Scots of Dalriada (557-574), son of Congallus I; gave Iona to St. Columba; fought against the Picts, 574. [xii. 6]

CONGALLUS III, in Gaelic CONALL CRANDONNA (d. 660), king or joint-king of the Scots of Dalriada (642-660), son of Eocha Buidhe; perhaps subdued by the Britons. [xii. 6]

CONGLETON, BARONS. [See PARNELL, HENRY BROOKE, first BARON, 1776-1842; PARNELL, JOHN VESEY, second BARON, 1805-1883.]

CONGREVE, RICHARD (1818-1899), positivist; educated at Rugby and Wadham College, Oxford; M.A., 1843; fellow and tutor; met Barthélemy St.-Hilaire and

Auguste Comte in Paris and adopted positivism; founded positivist community in London, 1855; studied medicine; M.R.C.P., 1866; took part in founding propaganda in Chapel Street, Lamb's Conduit Street, London; published political, historical, religious, and other writings.
[Suppl. ii. 51]

CONGREVE, WILLIAM (1670-1729), dramatist; taken as a boy to Ireland; educated at Kilkenny and (1685) Trinity College, Dublin, being schoolfellow and fellow-student of Swift; entered the Middle Temple; published, as Cleophil, 'Incognita,' a feeble novel; contributed to Dryden's metrical versions of 'Juvenal,' 1692, and 'Virgil,' 1697; brought out his comedies, the 'Old Bachelor,' 1693, the 'Double Dealer,' 1693, 'Love for Love,' 1695, and the 'Way of the World,' 1700, and his tragedy, the 'Mourning Bride,' 1697; replied to Jeremy Collier's [q. v.] 'Short View,' 1697; published his collected works, 1710; well provided for by a commissionership of hackney coaches, 1695-1707, of wine licences, 1705-14, the secretaryship of Jamaica, 1714, and other offices; affected to be a man of fashion; flattered by Alexander Pope; visited by Voltaire; favoured by the second Duchess of Marlborough; buried in Westminster Abbey. [xii. 6]

CONGREVE, SIR WILLIAM (1772-1828), inventor (1808) of the Congreve rocket; eldest son of the comptroller of the Royal Laboratory, Woolwich; officer of the royal artillery, 1791; attached to the Royal Laboratory, 1791, and was comptroller, 1814-28; directed to form two rocket companies, 1809; M.P., 1812-28; served with a rocket company at Leipzig, 1813, and in South France, 1814; succeeded as second baronet, 1814; wrote on currency and his own inventions. [xii. 9]

CONINGHAM, JAMES (1670-1716), presbyterian; M.A. Edinburgh, 1694; presbyterian minister at Penrith, 1694, Manchester, 1700, and London, 1712; tutor of the Manchester dissenting academy, 1705-12. [xii. 9]

CONINGSBURGH, EDMUND (fl. 1479), archbishop of Armagh; LL.D. Cambridge; resided in Cambridge, 1455-72; non-resident rector of St. Leonard, Foster Lane, London, 1448, vicar of South Weald, 1450, rector of Copford, Essex, 1451, and rector of St. James's, Colchester, 1470; envoy to the pope, 1471; made archbishop of Armagh, 1477; resigned in deference to the pope, 1479.
[xii. 10]

CONINGSBY, SIR HARRY (fl. 1664), translator; knighted, 1660; printed a metrical paraphrase of 'Boethius de Consolatione' and a memoir of his father, Thomas Coningsby. [xii. 10]

CONINGSBY, SIR HUMPHREY (d. 1535), serjeant-at-law, 1495; justice of the king's bench and knighted, 1509; will proved 26 Nov. 1535. [xii. 13]

CONINGSBY, SIR THOMAS (d. 1625), soldier; of Herefordshire; visited Italy, 1573; served in Normandy, 1591; knighted, 1591; M.P., Hereford, 1593 and 1601; founded hospital at Hereford, 1614; wrote an account of his French campaign (printed 1847). [xii. 11]

CONINGSBY, THOMAS, EARL CONINGSBY (1656?-1729), M.P., Leominster, 1679-1710, and 1715; a strong whig; wounded at the Boyne, 1690; one of the lords-justices in Ireland, 1690-2; vice-treasurer of Ireland, 1693-4 and 1698-1702; suspected of peculation; created Baron Coningsby of Clanbrassil in Ireland, 1692; granted crown lands in England, 1697; a commissioner to investigate the intrigues ending in the peace of Utrecht, and to impeach Harley, 1715; baron in the English peerage, 1715; created earl, 1719; involved in lawsuits as to his title to the manors of Leominster and Marden, Herefordshire. [xii. 11]

CONINGSBY, SIR WILLIAM (d. 1540?), judge; second son of Sir Humphrey Coningsby [q. v.]; educated at Eton; fellow of Trinity College, Cambridge; of the Inner Temple; justice of the king's bench, and knighted, 1540. [xii. 13]

CONINGTON, FRANCIS THIRKILL (1826-1863), chemist; fellow of Corpus Christi College, Oxford, 1849-1863; M.A., 1853; published a 'Handbook of Chemical Analysis,' 1858. [xii. 13]

CONINGTON, JOHN (1825-1869), classical scholar; educated at Rugby; demy of Magdalen College, Oxford, 1843; scholar, 1846, and fellow, 1848-55, of University

College, Oxford ; contributed to the ' Morning Chronicle,' 1849–50 ; professor of Latin, Oxford, 1854–69 ; edited Æschylus's ' Agamemnon,' 1848, and ' Choëphoroe,' 1857 ; edited Virgil and Persius ; published verse translations of Horace, 1863–9, the ' Æneid,' 1866, and half the ' Iliad,' 1868 ; his ' Miscellaneous Writings ' published posthumously. [xii. 13]

CONN OF THE HUNDRED BATTLES (d. 157), in Irish CONN CEAD CATHACH, king of Ireland ; son of King Fedlimid ' the Lawgiver ' ; succeeded to the throne, 123 ; defeated Leinster and Munster at Castleknock, killing Cumhal ; forced to surrender South Ireland to Mogh Nuadat, of the Ebereans ; after fourteen years' war, killed Mogh Nuadat at Kilbride, King's County ; acknowledged king of all Ireland ; slain at Tara. [xii. 17]

CONN-NA-MBOCHT (d. 1059), ' Conn of the Paupers ' ; head of the Culdees of Ireland and bishop of Clonmacnois ; endowed Culdee hospital at Iseal Chiarain. [xii. 19]

CONN (CONÆUS), GEORGE (d. 1640), Scottish catholic ; educated at Douay, Paris, Rome, and Bologna ; secretary to Cardinals Montalto, 1623, and Barberini, and to the congregation of rites ; papal agent at Queen Henrietta Maria's court, 1636–9 ; died at Rome ; published, in Latin, tracts on Scottish affairs and, 1624, a life of Mary Queen of Scots. [xii. 20]

CONNELL, SIR JOHN (1765 ?–1831), lawyer ; advocate, 1788 ; sheriff-depute of Renfrewshire, 1806 ; law adviser of the church of Scotland, 1806 ; judge of the Scots admiralty court, 1816–30 ; knighted, 1822 ; wrote on Scottish ecclesiastical law. [xii. 21]

CONNELLAN, OWEN (1800–1869), Irish scholar ; transcribed manuscripts for the Royal Irish Academy ; Irish historiographer royal, 1822–37 ; professor of Irish at Cork, 1846–69 ; published Irish linguistic tracts, 1830–44, and translated ' The Four Masters,' 1846, and a bardic tale, 1860. [xii. 21]

CONNELLAN, THADDEUS (d. 1854), author of Irish linguistic works, 1814–25. [xii. 21]

CONNOR or **O'CONNOR**, BERNARD (1666 ?–1698), author ; born in Kerry ; studied medicine in France ; M.D. Rheims, 1691 ; physician to King John Sobieski ; came to London, 1695 ; F.R.S., 1695 ; licentiate of the London College of Physicians, 1696 ; lectured in Oxford and London, 1695, and at Cambridge, 1697 ; published scientific papers, 1691–5, an attack on miracles, entitled ' Evangelium Medici,' 1697, and, 1698, a ' History of Poland.' [xii. 21]

CONNOR, CHARLES (d. 1826), comedian ; born in Ireland ; of Trinity College, Dublin ; represented Irish characters in London, 1816–26. [xii. 23]

CONNOR, GEORGE HENRY (1822–1883), divine ; M.A. Trinity College, Dublin, 1851 ; vicar of Newport, Isle of Wight, 1852–83 ; dean of Windsor, 1883 ; published sermons. [xii. 23]

CONNY, ROBERT (1645 ?–1713), physician ; B.A. Magdalen College, Oxford, 1676 ; M.D., 1685 ; naval physician at Deal, 1692 ; practised at Rochester. [xii. 24]

CONOLLY, ARTHUR (1807–1842 ?), traveller ; educated at Rugby and Addiscombe ; cornet of Bengal cavalry, 1823 ; captain, 1838 ; published, 1834, a description of his overland journey (1829–31) to India ; official in Rajpootana, 1834–8 ; travelled through Turkey in Europe and Asia to India, 1839 ; sent to Cabul, 1840, to Merv, Khiva, and Bokhara ; imprisoned at Bokhara, 1841 ; murdered in prison ; contributed to the Asiatic Society's ' Journal.' [xii. 24]

CONOLLY, EDWARD BARRY (1808–1840), captain of Bengal cavalry ; brother of Arthur Conolly [q. v.] ; killed near Cabul ; contributed to the Asiatic Society's ' Journal.' [xii. 26]

CONOLLY, ERSKINE (1796–1843), writer of Scottish songs ; bookseller's apprentice at Anstruther ; solicitor in Edinburgh. [xii. 26]

CONOLLY, HENRY VALENTINE (1806–1855), Indian civilian ; brother of Arthur Conolly [q. v.] ; educated at Rugby ; civil servant at Madras, 1824–55 ; murdered by fanatics. [xii. 26]

CONOLLY, JOHN (1794–1866), physician ; of Irish extraction ; ensign in the militia, 1812–16 ; lived at Tours ;

medical student at Edinburgh, 1817 ; M.D. Edinburgh, 1821 ; practised medicine at Chichester ; removed to Stratford-on-Avon, 1822–7 ; visiting physician of Warwickshire asylums ; medical professor at University College, London, 1828 ; resident at Warwick, 1830–8, visiting asylums ; resident, 1839–44, and visiting, 1844–52, physician to Hanwell Asylum, introducing the humane treatment of lunatics ; hon. D.C.L. Oxford, 1852 ; published treatises on insanity and asylum methods, 1847–56 ; contributed to medical journals. [xii. 26]

CONOLLY, JOHN BALFOUR (d. 1842), lieutenant of Bengal infantry ; brother of Arthur Conolly [q. v.] ; died at Cabul. [xii. 26]

CONOLLY, THOMAS (1738–1803), Irish politician ; M.P. for Malmesbury, 1759, and for Chichester, 1768–84 ; M.P. for Londonderry in the Irish parliament, 1761–1800 ; held various offices in Ireland ; advocated the union. [xii. 29]

CONOLLY, WILLIAM (d. 1729), Irish politician ; an Irish barrister ; speaker of the Irish House of Commons, 1715–29 ; frequently a lord justice of Ireland, 1717–29 ; chief commissioner of Irish revenues. [xii. 30]

CONQUEST, JOHN TRICKER (1789–1866), accoucheur ; M.D. Edinburgh, 1813 ; L.R.C.P., 1819 ; published insignificant medical treatises. [xii. 30]

CONRY, FLORENCE, in Irish FLATHRI O'MOELCHONAIRE (1561–1629), Irish Roman catholic prelate ; educated in Spain and the Spanish Netherlands ; Observant friar at Salamanca ; provincial of the Observants in Ireland ; sent by Philip II to foment rebellion in Ireland ; archbishop of Tuam, 1609 ; died at Madrid ; wrote theological tracts in Latin, published 1619–44, and two in Irish, published 1616 and 1625. [xii. 31]

CONST, FRANCIS (1751–1839), lawyer ; barrister, Middle Temple, 1783 ; chairman of the Westminster sessions. [xii. 31]

CONSTABLE, ARCHIBALD (1774–1827), publisher ; bookseller's apprentice in Edinburgh, 1788 ; bookseller in Edinburgh, 1795 ; began to publish pamphlets and sermons, 1798 ; commenced the ' Farmer's Magazine,' 1800 ; proprietor of the ' Scots Magazine,' 1801 ; started the ' Edinburgh Review,' 1802 ; part-publisher of Sir Walter Scott's ' Minstrelsy,' 1802, ' Lay of the Last Minstrel,' 1805, and ' Marmion,' 1807 ; requested Scott to edit Swift, 1808 ; partner in a London publishing firm, 1808–11 ; acquired copyright of ' Encyclopædia Britannica,' 1812, and brought out supplementary ' Dissertations' ; advised Scott to publish ' Waverley,' 1814 ; deserted by Scott, through the sinister influence of James Ballantyne [q. v.] ; bankrupt through the failure of his London agents, 1826 ; began ' Constable's Miscellany,' 1827. [xii. 32]

CONSTABLE, CUTHBERT (d. 1746), antiquary ; known as Cuthbert Tunstall, educated at Douay, 1700 ; M.D. Montpellier ; took the name Constable, 1718, on inheriting a Yorkshire estate ; a Roman catholic ; collected manuscripts. [xii. 33]

CONSTABLE, HENRY (1562–1613), poet ; B.A. St. John's College, Cambridge, 1580 ; embraced Roman catholicism ; withdrew to Paris ; in friendly correspondence with the English authorities, 1584–5 ; published ' Diana,' a volume of sonnets, 1592, which he enlarged, 1594 ; failed to obtain his recall to England, 1595 ; papal envoy to Edinburgh, 1599 ; pensioned by the French king ; came to London, 1603 ; imprisoned in the Tower, 1604 ; released, 1604 ; died at Liège ; verses by him embodied in various collections, 1591–1610 ; collected works published, 1859. [xii. 34]

CONSTABLE, HENRY, VISCOUNT DUNBAR (d. 1645), succeeded to Burton Constable estate, Yorkshire, 1608 ; knighted, 1614 ; a Roman catholic ; created Viscount Dunbar, in the Scottish peerage, 1620. [xii. 35]

CONSTABLE, JOHN (fl. 1520), epigrammatist ; educated at St. Paul's School ; M.A. Oxford, 1515 ; published Latin ' Epigrammata,' 1520. [xii. 36]

CONSTABLE, JOHN (1676 ?–1744), jesuit ; educated at St. Omer, as ' John Lacey ' ; joined the jesuits, 1695 ; chaplain to the Fitzherberts of Swinnerton, Staffordshire ; wrote, frequently as ' Clerophilus Alethes,' against Anglican orders, Charles Dodd's [q. v.] ' Church History,' and in reply to other controversialists. [xii. 36]

CONSTABLE, JOHN (1776–1837), landscape-painter ; educated at Dedham school, Essex ; encouraged by Sir George Beaumont [q. v.] ; art-student in London, 1795–1797 ; learnt etching ; resided in London, except for summer tours, from 1799 ; sketched in water-colours ; painted in oils ; exhibited his first landscape at the Royal Academy, 1802 ; painted two altar-pieces for Suffolk churches, 1804 and 1809 ; painted in his own style quiet English landscapes, 1803–37, without recognition in England ; employed in painting portraits and making copies of pictures ; made a great impression at the French Salon, 1824 ; inherited a competency, 1828 ; R.A., 1829 ; twenty of his landscapes engraved by David Lucas, 1833 ; lectured on ' Landscape Art,' 1833 and 1836. [xii. 37]

CONSTABLE, SIR MARMADUKE (1455 ?–1518), landowner and soldier, of Flamborough, Yorkshire ; served in France, 1475 and 1492 ; knighted ; served at the siege of Berwick, 1482 ; steward of Tutbury, Staffordshire, 1483 ; sheriff of Staffordshire, 1486–7, and of Yorkshire, 1487–8 and 1509–10 ; inherited Flamborough, 1488 ; attached to the personal service of Henry VII ; commissioner to Scotland, 1509–10 ; commanded left wing at Flodden, 1513. Scholarships were founded in his name at St. John's College, Cambridge, 1522. [xii. 37]

CONSTABLE, SIR MARMADUKE (1480 ?–1545), second son of Sir Marmaduke Constable (1455 ?–1518) [q. v.] ; knighted for service at Flodden, 1513 ; sheriff of Lincolnshire, 1513–14 ; in personal attendance on Henry VIII, 1520 ; served in Scotland, 1522–3 ; M.P., Yorkshire, 1529 ; sheriff of Yorkshire, 1532–3 ; member of the council of the north, 1537–45 ; obtained a grant of Drax Priory, Yorkshire, 1538. [xii. 44]

CONSTABLE, SIR ROBERT (1478 ?–1537), Roman catholic insurgent ; eldest son of Sir Marmaduke Constable (1455 ?–1518) [q. v.] ; knighted at Blackheath for service against the Cornish insurgents, 1497 ; a leader in the Pilgrimage of Grace, 1536, seizing Hull ; pardoned ; refused to come to London ; taken prisoner to the Tower, 1537 ; executed at Hull. [xii. 44]

CONSTABLE, THOMAS (1812–1881), printer and publisher ; youngest son of Archibald Constable [q. v.] ; learnt printing in London ; queen's printer in Edinburgh, 1839, in which office his son was joined with him, 1869 ; publisher in Edinburgh, bringing out mainly school-books, 1847–60 ; wrote memoirs of his father, 1873, and other works. [xii. 45]

CONSTABLE, SIR THOMAS HUGH CLIFFORD (1762–1823), author ; known as Thomas Hugh Clifford ; of a Roman catholic family ; educated at Liège and Paris ; travelled in Switzerland ; inherited Tixall, Staffordshire, 1786 ; created baronet, 1815 ; took the name Constable on inheriting Burton Constable, Yorkshire, 1821 ; died at Ghent ; wrote both of topography and flora of Tixall, 1817 ; wrote devotional works. [xii. 45]

CONSTABLE, SIR WILLIAM (d. 1655), regicide ; served under Essex in Ireland, 1599 ; knighted at Dublin ; pardoned for his share in Essex's revolt, 1601 ; created baronet, 1611 ; M.P., 1626, 1628, and 1642 ; refused to pay the forced loan, 1627 ; sold Flamborough, Yorkshire, 1636 ; raised regiment for the parliament ; fought at Edgehill, 1642 ; routed the Yorkshire royalists, 1644 ; sided with the army against the parliament, 1647 ; joint-gaoler of Charles I at Carisbrook, January 1648 ; governor of Gloucester, 1648–51 ; regular in his attendance as one of the king's judges, 1649 ; member of the Commonwealth councils of state ; his estates confiscated, 1660. [xii. 46]

CONSTANTIIS, WALTER DE (d. 1207). [See COUTANCES, WALTER DE.]

CONSTANTINE I (d. 879), king of Alba (Scotland, north of Forth), 863–79 ; son of Kenneth Macalpine ; raided by the Norse kings of Dublin, 865–79 ; fell in battle. [xii. 46]

CONSTANTINE II (d. 952), king of Alba (Scotland, north of Forth), 900–43 ; son of Æth ; raided by the northmen, 903 ; crushed the invaders, 904 ; held council at Scone to make agreement between the Pictish and Scottish churches, 906 ; made his brother Donald king of Strathclyde, 908 ; raided by Danish pirates under Regnwald, 912 ; defeated by Regnwald, 918, and driven out of Northumberland ; his right to Northumbria challenged by Æthelstan of Wessex, c. 926 ; part of his dominions

ravaged by Æthelstan, 933–4, his counter-invasion repulsed at Brunanburh, Yorkshire, 937 ; resigned his crown, 943 ; became a Culdee monk at St. Andrews. [xii. 47]

CONSTANTINE III (d. 997), king of Scotland, 995–7 ; son of Colin, his predecessor ; murdered. [xii. 48]

CONSTANTINE MAC FERGUS (d. 820), king of the Picts, 807–20 ; founded a monastic church at Dunkeld ; possibly ruled also over the Scots of Dalriada ; harassed by the Norsemen (Iona being ravaged, 806). [xii. 49]

CONSTANTINE, GEORGE (1501 ?–1559), protestant reformer ; bred a surgeon ; bachelor of canon law, Cambridge, 1524 ; adopted protestantism ; wrote in conjunction with William Tyndal at Antwerp ; surgeon in Brabant ; came to England to sell protestant books ; arrested, 1530 ; saved himself by turning king's evidence ; returned to Antwerp, 1531 ; returned to England before 1536 ; vicar of Llawhaden, Pembrokeshire ; registrar of St. David's diocese, c. 1546 ; archdeacon of Carmarthen, 1549 ; substituted a movable table for the altar, 1549 ; an accuser of Bishop Robert Ferrar, 1555 ; archdeacon of Brecon, 1559. [xii. 49]

CONWAY, ANNE, VISCOUNTESS CONWAY (d. 1679), daughter of Sir Henry Finch [q. v.] ; married, 1651, Edward, third viscount Conway ; an hysterical invalid ; corresponded with Henry More of Cambridge ; joined the quakers ; reputed authoress of a philosophical tract, published, 1690. [xii. 50]

CONWAY, EDWARD, first VISCOUNT CONWAY (d. 1631), son of Sir John Conway [q. v.] ; knighted for service in the Cadiz expedition, 1596 ; governor of Brill ; M.P., 1603 and 1624 ; secretary of state, 1623–30 ; lord president of the council ; envoy to Prague, 1623–5 ; governor of the Isle of Wight, 1625 ; created Baron Conway, 1625, Viscount Killultagh, in Ireland, 1626, and Viscount Conway, 1627. [xii. 50]

CONWAY, FRANCIS SEYMOUR, MARQUIS OF HERTFORD (1719–1794), nephew of Sir Robert Walpole ; succeeded as second Baron Conway, 1732 ; created Earl of Hertford, 1750, and Marquis, 1793 ; lord-lieutenant of Ireland, 1765–6 ; lord chamberlain, 1766–82. [xii. 51]

CONWAY, HENRY SEYMOUR (1721–1795), field-marshal ; nephew of Sir Robert Walpole ; given a commission when a boy ; M.P. Antrim, in the Irish parliament, 1741 ; M.P. for various pocket boroughs in the British parliament, 1741–84 ; served in Flanders, 1742 ; present at the battles of Dettingen, 1743, Fontenoy, 1745, Culloden, 1746, and Lauffeld, 1747 ; aide-de-camp to the Duke of Cumberland, 1745 ; secretary to the lord-lieutenant of Ireland, 1755–6 ; major-general, 1756 ; failed in the Rochfort expedition, 1757, his behaviour becoming the subject of several pamphlets, 1758 ; lieutenant-general, 1759 ; served under Prince Ferdinand of Brunswick, 1761–3 ; dismissed from his offices and employments for opposing George III's arbitrary measures, 1764 ; secretary of state, 1765–8 ; lieutenant-general of the ordnance, 1767–72 ; general, 1772 ; governor of Jersey, where he occasionally resided, 1772–95 ; opposed the continuance of the American war, 1775–81 ; commander-in-chief, 1782–3 ; joined Fox in attacking Pitt, 1784 ; withdrew from politics, 1784 ; dabbled in forestry and verse-writing ; field-marshal, 1793. [xii. 51]

CONWAY, SIR JOHN (d. 1603), governor of Ostend ; of Arrow, Warwickshire ; knighted, 1559 ; governor of Ostend, 1586 ; imprisoned, 1588 ; published devotional tracts and verses. [xii. 57]

CONWAY, ROGER OF (d. 1360), Franciscan ; D.D. Oxford ; provincial of the English Franciscans ; wrote in defence of the mendicant orders against Richard FitzRalph, archbishop of Armagh, c. 1357. [xii. 58]

CONWAY, WILLIAM AUGUSTUS (1789–1828), real name RUGG ; appeared on the provincial stage, c. 1808 ; performed in Dublin, 1812, London, 1813–16, Bath, 1817–1820, and London, 1821 ; attacked by Theodore Hook, 1821 ; acted in America, 1824–8 ; committed suicide. [xii. 59]

CONY, WILLIAM (d. 1707), naval captain, 1704 ; taken prisoner by a French squadron, 1705 ; wrecked off Scilly. [xii. 60]

CONYBEARE, JOHN (1692–1755), bishop of Bristol ; fellow of Exeter College, Oxford, 1710 ; M.A., 1716 ; D.D.,

1730 ; rector of Exeter College, 1730–33 ; dean of Christ Church, Oxford, 1733–55 ; bishop of Bristol, 1750 ; published sermons, and 'Defence of Revealed Religion,' 1732, against Matthew Tindal. [xii. 60]

CONYBEARE, JOHN JOSIAS (1779–1824), geologist ; student of Christ Church, Oxford, 1800–13 ; M.A., 1804 ; vicar of Batheaston, Somerset ; professor of Anglo-Saxon at Oxford, 1807–12, and of poetry, 1812–21 ; published tracts, geological, 1817–24, chemical, 1822–3, and theological, 1824 ; translations from Anglo-Saxon by him published, 1826. [xii. 61]

CONYBEARE, WILLIAM DANIEL (1787–1857), geologist ; educated at Westminster and Christ Church, Oxford ; M.A., 1811 ; vicar of Axminster, Devonshire, 1836–44 ; dean of Llandaff, 1845–57 ; published geological papers ; first to describe the ichthyosaurus. [xii. 61]

CONYBEARE, WILLIAM JOHN (1815–1857), divine ; eldest son of William Daniel Conybeare [q. v.] ; educated at Westminster ; fellow of Trinity College, Cambridge ; B.A., 1837 ; principal of Liverpool Collegiate Institution, 1842–8 ; vicar of Axminster, Devonshire, 1848–54 ; published essays and a novel, 1856 ; joint-author (with J. S. Howson) of 'Life of St. Paul,' 1851. [xii. 62]

CONYERS, SIR JOHN (*fl.* 1469). [See ROBIN OF REDESDALE.]

CONYNGHAM, HENRY, first MARQUIS CONYNGHAM (1766–1832), succeeded as third baron, 1787 ; created viscount, 1789, earl, 1797, and marquis, 1816, in the Irish peerage ; representative Irish peer, 1801 ; created Baron Minster, in the British peerage, 1821 ; lord steward of the household, 1821–30 ; his wife possessed great influence over George IV. [xii. 63]

CONYNGTON, RICHARD (*d.* 1330), Franciscan ; D.D. Oxford ; lectured at Oxford and Cambridge ; provincial of the English Franciscans, 1310 ; wrote on scholastic philosophy and theology. [xii. 63]

COODE, SIR JOHN (1816–1892), civil engineer ; articled to James Meadows Rendel [q. v.] of Plymouth ; practised as consulting engineer in Westminster, 1844–7 ; resident engineer in charge of works at Portland harbour, 1847, and engineer-in-chief, 1856–72 ; knighted, 1872 ; K.C.M.G., 1886 ; M.I.C.E., 1849 ; president, 1889–91 ; associated with several important harbour works in various parts of the world, including (1874–85) those at Colombo, Ceylon ; author of professional reports and papers. [Suppl. ii. 52]

COOK. [See also COKE and COOKE.]

COOK, EDWARD DUTTON (1829–1883), dramatic critic ; son of a London solicitor ; educated at King's College School, London ; brought out a melodrama, 1859 ; dramatic critic of London journals, 1867–83 ; published novels, 1861–77, and essays on the stage. [xii. 64]

COOK, ELIZA (1818–1889), poet ; began to write at early age and published 'Lays of a Wild Harp,' 1835 ; contributed to 'Weekly Dispatch,' in which appeared the 'Old Arm Chair,' the most popular of her poems, 1837, and to other periodicals ; conducted Eliza Cook's Journal, 1849–54. Her complete collected poems were published, 1870. [Suppl. ii. 53]

COOK, FREDERIC CHARLES (1810–1889), editor of the 'Speaker's Commentary' ; M.A. St. John's College, Cambridge, 1844 ; chaplain in ordinary to the queen, 1857 ; preacher at Lincoln's Inn, 1860–80 ; canonresidentiary at Exeter, 1864 ; chaplain to bishop of London, 1869 ; precentor of Exeter Cathedral, 1872 ; appointed, 1864, editor of the 'Speaker's Commentary' (published 1871–81, 10 vols.), a critical commentary on the bible occasioned by the appearance of 'Essays and Reviews.' [Suppl. ii. 54]

COOK, GEORGE (1772–1845), Scottish church leader ; son of a St. Andrews professor ; educated at St. Andrews ; M.A., 1790 ; D.D., 1808 ; minister of Laurencekirk, Kincardineshire, 1796–1829 ; professor of moral philosophy, St. Andrews, 1829–45 ; moderator of the church, 1825 ; a leader of the 'moderate' party in the patronage question, 1833–43 ; published histories of the 'Reformation in Scotland,' 1811, and of the 'Church of Scotland,' 1815, and other works, biographical and theological. [xii. 65]

COOK, HENRY (1642–1700), painter ; studied art in Italy ; employed in England as a decorative artist ; fled to Italy to escape justice ; returned ; repaired Raphael's cartoons ; painted altar-pieces and portraits. [xii. 66]

COOK, JAMES (*d.* 1611), divine ; educated at Winchester ; perpetual fellow of New College, Oxford, 1592 ; D.C.L., 1608 ; rector of Houghton, Hampshire, 1609 ; published a controversial tract. [xii. 66]

COOK, JAMES (1728–1779), circumnavigator ; a labourer's son ; seaman in the Baltic trade ; common seaman in the navy, 1755 ; master, 1759 ; surveyed the St. Lawrence, 1759 ; employed on the North American station, 1759–67 ; published his 'Sailing Directions,' 1766–8 ; lieutenant, 1768 ; sailed, 1768, in the Endeavour, for Tahiti, round Cape Horn ; observed the transit of Venus, 3 June ; charted the coasts of New Zealand, the east coast of Australia, and part of New Guinea, 1769–70 ; returned by the Cape of Good Hope, reaching the Downs, 1771 ; commander, 1771 ; sailed in the Resolution to disprove the existence of an Antarctic continent, 1772 ; rounded the Cape of Good Hope, 22 Nov. 1772 ; visited many Pacific islands ; skirted the Antarctic icefields, 1773–5 ; reached Plymouth, 1775, having, by new hygienic rules, escaped scurvy and fever ; captain, 1775 ; attempted to sail round North America from the Pacific, 1776 ; passed the Cape of Good Hope, and (1778) discovered the Sandwich islands ; charted the Pacific coast of North America, 1778 ; touched at Hawaii, 1779 ; driven off by storm, and on putting back to refit was murdered by natives. [xii. 66]

COOK, JOHN (*d.* 1660), regicide ; travelled ; barrister, Gray's Inn ; appointed by parliament to conduct the prosecution of Charles I ; master of St. Cross, Winchester, 1649 ; justice in Munster, 1649 ; granted Irish lands, 1653 ; justice of the upper bench, Ireland, 1655 ; in England, 1657–9 ; arrested in Ireland, 1660 ; executed in London ; published political and legal pamphlets. [xii. 70]

COOK, JOHN (1771–1824), professor of Hebrew ; M.A. St. Andrews, 1788 ; minister of Kilmany, Fifeshire, 1793–1802 ; D.D. ; professor of Hebrew, St. Andrews, 1802–24 ; moderator of the church, 1816. [xii. 71]

COOK, JOHN (1808–1869), professor of ecclesiastical history ; eldest son of John Cook (1771–1824) [q. v.] ; M.A. St. Andrews, 1823 ; D.D., 1848 ; minister of St. Leonards, St. Andrews, 1845–63 ; moderator of the church of Scotland, 1859 ; professor of ecclesiastical history, St. Andrews, 1860–8 ; published sermons and theological and legal pamphlets. [xii. 71]

COOK, JOHN (1807–1874), Scottish divine ; eldest son of George Cook [q. v.] ; M.A. St. Andrews, 1823 ; D.D., 1843 ; minister at Haddington, 1833–74 ; moderator of the church of Scotland, 1866. [xii. 72]

COOK, JOHN DOUGLAS (1808 ?–1868), journalist ; born in Aberdeenshire ; for some time in India ; wrote for 'Times' and 'Quarterly Review' ; edited the 'Morning Chronicle,' 1848–54, and the 'Saturday Review,' 1855–68. [xii. 72]

COOK, JOHN MASON (1834–1899), tourist agent ; son of Thomas Cook (1808–1892) [q. v.] ; engaged in business as printer ; partner with his father from 1864 ; extended the firm's connections with America and the continent, and became agent for developing traffic to many railways in England and abroad ; appointed by Khedive government agent for passenger traffic on Nile, 1870 ; opened branch office at Cairo, 1873 ; granted by Egyptian government exclusive right of carrying mails, specie, and civil and military officials between Assiout and Assouan, 1889 ; made a like contract with the English government, and performed valuable services in the Nile campaigns, 1885–6 ; greatly developed touring arrangements in Norway from 1875 ; acquired railway up Mount Vesuvius ; carried out schemes for travelling in India ; devised plans for the safer travel and better treatment of pilgrims to Jeddah and Yambo, and to Mecca and Medina ; made arrangements for the German Emperor's visit to the Holy Land, 1898. [Suppl. ii. 56]

COOK, RICHARD (1784–1857), historical painter ; art student in London ; exhibited, 1808–22 ; illustrated many books ; R.A., 1822. [xii. 73]

COOK, ROBERT (*d.* 1593 ?), herald and portraitpainter ; of St. John's College, Cambridge, 1553 ; M.A., 1561 ; Chester herald, 1562 ; Clarenceux king-of-arms, 1567 ; commissioned to visit his province, 1568 ; took out a grant of arms, 1577 ; acted as Garter, 1584–6 ; left manuscript collections, heraldic and genealogical. [xii. 73]

COOK, ROBERT (1646?–1726?), vegetarian; an eccentric Waterford landowner; resided in Ipswich and Bristol, 1688–92; nicknamed 'Linen Cook.' [xii. 74]

COOK, SAMUEL (1806–1859), water-colour painter; house-painter at Plymouth; exhibited coast scenes in London, 1830–59. [xii. 74]

COOK, SAMUEL EDWARD (d. 1856). [See WIDDRINGTON.]

COOK, THOMAS (1744?–1818), engraver, of London; much employed in engraving portraits and book illustrations; copied all Hogarth's works for 'Hogarth Restored,' 1806. [xii. 75]

COOK, THOMAS (1808–1892), tourist agent; apprenticed as wood-turner; entered a printing and publishing firm at Loughborough; joined Association of Baptists; travelled as missionary in Rutland, c. 1828–9; wood-turner at Market Harborough, and secretary to the branch there of the South Midland Temperance Association, in connection with which he organised the first publicly advertised excursion by train in England, 1841; induced by the success of this excursion (Leicester to Loughborough and back) to make the organising of excursions at home and abroad a regular occupation; published handbooks for tourists, and subsequently issued coupons for hotel expenses; issued 'Excursionist,' monthly magazine, from c. 1846; removed to London, 1864. [Suppl. ii. 55]

COOK, WILLIAM (d. 1824), miscellaneous writer; squandered his own and his wife's fortune; barrister, Middle Temple, 1777; published poems, memoirs of actors, and a comedy, 1775–1815. [xii. 75]

COOKE. [See also COKE and COOK.]

COOKE, ALEXANDER (1564–1632), divine; entered Brasenose College, Oxford, 1581; fellow of University College, 1587; B.D., 1596; vicar of Louth, Lincolnshire, 1601; vicar of Leeds, 1615–32; published bitter anti-Romanist tracts, 1610–25. [xii. 75]

COOKE, SIR ANTHONY (1504–1576), politician; of Gidea Hall, Romford, Essex; father-in-law of Lord Burghley; tutor to Edward, prince of Wales; K.B., 1547; M.P., 1547; served on several ecclesiastical commissions, 1547–9; obtained church lands, 1552; imprisoned, 1553; withdrew to Strasburg, 1554; returned to England, 1558; M.P., Essex, 1559–67; served on various commissions, 1559–76. [xii. 76]

COOKE, BENJAMIN (1734–1793), musician; son of a London music-seller; pupil of J. C. Pepusch [q. v.]; deputy-organist, 1746, choir-master, 1757, and organist, 1762–93, of Westminster Abbey; Mus.Doc. Cambridge, 1775, and Oxford, 1782; librarian, 1749, and conductor, 1752–89, of Academy of Ancient Music; organist of St. Martin's-in-the-Fields, 1782–93. [xii. 77]

COOKE, EDWARD (fl. 1678), author of a tragedy, 'Love's Triumph,' 1678. [xii. 78]

COOKE, EDWARD (1772–1799), naval officer; lieutenant, 1790; captain, 1794; served at Toulon, 1793, Calvi, 1794, and in East Indies, 1796–9; mortally wounded in action. [xii. 78]

COOKE, EDWARD (1755–1820), under-secretary of state; son of William Cooke (1711–1797) [q. v.]; educated at Eton and King's College, Cambridge; B.A., 1777; official in Ireland, 1778; under-secretary in the Irish military department, 1789–95, and civil department, 1796–1801; M.P., Leighlin, 1790–1800; quarrelled with Earl Fitzwilliam, 1795; a favourite of Castlereagh; wrote, 1798, and intrigued for the union, 1800; under-secretary in London for war, 1807, and for foreign affairs, 1812–17. [xii. 79]

COOKE, EDWARD WILLIAM (1811–1880), marine painter; son of George Cooke (1781–1834) [q. v.]; drew plants for botanical books; etched coast scenes; made drawings of the progress of new London Bridge, 1825–31; travelled on the continent, 1830–46; R.A., 1864; a frequent exhibitor. [xii. 80]

COOKE, GEORGE (1781–1834), line engraver; pupil of James Basire [q. v.]; a prolific workman; illustrated numerous works on landscape and antiquities. [xii. 81]

COOKE, SIR GEORGE (1768–1837), lieutenant-general; ensign, 10th foot guards, 1784; captain, 1792; served in Flanders, 1794, and in Holland, 1799; captain and lieutenant-colonel, 1798; major-general, 1811; at Cadiz, 1811–13; commanded first division of guards at Waterloo, 1815; K.C.B. and colonel, 1815; lieutenant-general, 1821. [Suppl. ii. 58]

COOKE, GEORGE (1807–1863), actor; first appeared on provincial stage, 1828, and in London, 1837; committed suicide. [xii. 82]

COOKE, GEORGE FREDERICK (1756–1811), actor; printer's apprentice at Berwick; first appeared on provincial stage, 1776, and in London, 1778; a favourite in Newcastle, Manchester, and other northern towns; reappeared in London, 1801–10, at first with success; well received in New York, 1810; occasionally a brilliant performer, but uncertain through intemperance. [xii. 82]

COOKE, GEORGE LEIGH (1780?–1853), mathematician; scholar, 1797, and fellow, 1810–15, of Corpus Christi College, Oxford; B.D., 1812; professor of natural philosophy, 1810–53; beneficed in Warwickshire, 1824; edited part of Newton's 'Principia,' 1850. [xii. 85]

COOKE, GEORGE WINGROVE (1814–1865), man of letters; B.A. Jesus College, Oxford, 1834; barrister, Middle Temple, 1835; employed by the tithe and enclosure commissions; copyhold commissioner, 1862; 'Times' correspondent in China, 1857, and Algeria; published memoirs of Bolingbroke, 1835, and Shaftesbury, a history of party politics, 1837, legal treatises, 1844–57, and notes of travel, 1856–60. [xii. 85]

COOKE, HENRY (d. 1672), musician; chorister of the Chapel Royal; entered Charles I's army, 1642, and became captain; teacher of music in London before 1655, several of his pupils becoming afterwards distinguished composers; part-composer of the music for Sir William D'Avenant's operas, 1656; choir-master of the Chapel Royal; composed the music for the coronation service, 1661; composer to Charles II, 1664; marshal of the Corporation of Musicians, 1670. [xii. 86]

COOKE, HENRY (1788–1868), Irish presbyterian leader; entered Glasgow University, 1802; studied science and medicine at Glasgow, 1815–17, and Dublin, 1817–18; D.D. Jefferson College, U.S.A., 1829; LL.D. Dublin, 1837; presbyterian minister at Duneane, 1808, and Donegore, co. Antrim, 1811, at Killyleagh, co. Down, 1818, and Belfast, 1829–68; professor of sacred rhetoric and catechetics, Assembly College, Belfast, 1847; leader of the orthodox party in the controversy, 1821–40, which excluded the Arian ministers from the presbyterian church; strongly opposed disestablishment of Irish episcopal church; published sermons, pamphlets, hymns, and articles in periodicals; reputed one of the most effective of Irish preachers and debaters. [xii. 87]

COOKE, JO. (fl. 1614), author of 'Greene's Tu Quoque,' comedy, printed 1614; possibly also of 'Epigrams,' 1604. [xii. 90]

COOKE, SIR JOHN (1666–1710), civilian; entered Merchant Taylors' School, 1673; entered St. John's College, Oxford, 1684; lieutenant of foot at the Boyne, 1689; D.C.L., 1694; advocate at Doctors' Commons, 1694; knighted, 1701; dean of arches, 1703; vicar-general of see of Canterbury. [xii. 90]

COOKE, JOHN (1763–1805), naval officer; entered navy, 1776; captain, 1794; put on shore by the Spithead mutineers, 1797; killed at Trafalgar. [xii. 91]

COOKE, JOHN (1731–1810), London bookseller; issued annotated bibles, British poets, and other works in weekly sixpenny parts. [xii. 91]

COOKE, JOHN (1738–1823), chaplain of Greenwich Hospital; M.A. Trinity College, Cambridge, 1764; rector of Denton, Buckinghamshire, 1773; published a history of Greenwich Hospital, 1789, memoirs of Lord Sandwich, 1799, and sermons. [xii. 92]

COOKE, JOHN (1756–1838), physician; dissenting preacher in Lancashire; studied medicine in London, Edinburgh, and Leyden; M.D. Leyden; medical practitioner and lecturer in London; physician to the General Dispensary and, 1784–1807, to the London Hospital; published 'A Treatise on Nervous Diseases,' 1821–3. [xii. 92]

COOKE, ROBERT (1550–1615), divine; fellow of Brasenose College, Oxford, 1573–90; proctor, 1582–3; B.D., 1584; vicar of Leeds, 1590–1615; prebendary of Durham, 1614; wrote and preached actively against Romanism. [xii. 92]

COOKE, ROBERT 1768–1814), musician; son of Benjamin Cooke [q. v.]; organist, St. Martin's in-the-Fields, 1793, and Westminster Abbey, 1802; drowned himself; composed songs and glees. [xii. 93]

COOKE, ROBERT (1820?–1882), Irish Roman catholic divine; mission priest in Leicestershire, Yorkshire, 1847, and London; published biographies of Roman catholics, 1875–82. [xii. 93]

COOKE, ROGER (b. 1553), astrologer; assistant of John Dee [q. v.], 1567–81; perhaps published an almanack, 1585. [xii. 93]

COOKE, SIR THOMAS (d. 1478), lord mayor of London; a warden of the Drapers' Company, 1439; intermediary between Jack Cade and the citizens, 1450; sheriff of London, 1453, alderman, 1454, lord mayor, 1462; K.B., 1465; began Gidea Hall, Romford, 1467; imprisoned and heavily fined by Edward IV, 1467 and 1471. [xii. 94]

COOKE, THOMAS (1703–1756), author, commonly called HESIOD COOKE; son of a Braintree innkeeper; educated at Felstead school; whig journalist and pamphleteer in London, 1722; attacked, anonymously, Pope and Swift, 1725 and 1728, and consequently won a place in the 'Dunciad'; wrote against Pope, 1729–31; published poems, 1726–42; author or joint-author of four dramatic pieces, 1728–39; translated Bion and Moschus, 1724, Hesiod, 1728, Terence, 1734, and parts of Cicero and Plautus, 1754; edited Virgil, 1741; edited the 'Craftsman' from 1741. [xii. 95]

COOKE, THOMAS (1722–1783), eccentric divine; educated at Durham school and, 1743, Queen's College, Oxford; dismissed from the curacy of Embleton, Northumberland, for his strange behaviour; street preacher in London; confined in Bedlam; published two comedies, 1762–71, and sermons. [xii. 96]

COOKE, THOMAS (1763–1818), lecturer and writer on physiognomy. [xii. 97]

COOKE, THOMAS (1807–1868), optician; taught school at Allerthorpe, 1823, and York, 1829–36; made his mark as a constructor of astronomical telescopes, 1851; invented appliances for facilitating telescopic observation, and was largely employed as a maker of turret clocks. [xii. 97]

COOKE, THOMAS POTTER (1786–1864), actor; son of a London surgeon; served in the navy, 1796–1802; appeared on the London stage, 1804; stage manager of the Surrey Theatre, 1809; made a great success at the Lyceum, 1820; acted in Paris, 1825, and Edinburgh, 1827; reputed the 'best sailor . . . that ever trod the stage'; last appearance on the stage, 1860. [xii. 98]

COOKE, THOMAS SIMPSON (1782–1848), composer; member of the Dublin orchestra; sang in opera; came to London, 1813; principal tenor, 1815, and musical director, 1821–42, of Drury Lane; an esteemed singing-master; composed stage music and glees; published a manual of singing. [xii. 99]

COOKE, WILLIAM (d. 1553), judge; educated at Cambridge; barrister, Gray's Inn, 1530; recorder of Cambridge, 1545; serjeant-at-law, 1546; justice of common pleas, 1552. [xii. 100]

COOKE, WILLIAM (d. 1780), numismatist; vicar of Enford, Wiltshire, 1733–80; rector of Oldbury, Gloucestershire; translated Sallust, 1746; wrote on Druidical religion, 1754; his 'Medallic History of Imperial Rome,' published posthumously, 1781. [xii. 100]

COOKE, WILLIAM (1711–1797), divine; entered Harrow, 1718, Eton, 1721, and King's College, Cambridge, 1731; fellow, 1734; B.A., 1735; D.D., 1765; head-master of Eton, 1743–5; vicar of Sturminster-Marshall, Dorset, 1745–8; fellow of Eton, 1748; rector of Denham, Buckinghamshire, 1748, and of Stoke Newington, 1768; provost of King's College, Cambridge, 1772; dean of Ely, 1780; published verses, 1732, and sermons. [xii. 100]

COOKE, WILLIAM (d. 1824), Greek professor; son of William Cooke (1711–1797) [q. v.]; fellow of King's College; professor of Greek, Cambridge, 1780–93; rector of Hempstead, Norfolk, 1785–1824; edited Aristotle's 'Poetics,' 1785; wrote on the Apocalypse, 1789; became insane. [xii. 101]

COOKE, WILLIAM (1757–1832), legal writer; educated at Harrow and Caius College, Cambridge; B.A., 1776; called to bar at Lincoln's Inn, 1782; published a manual of 'Bankrupt Laws,' 1785; practised in chancery and bankruptcy cases; sent to Milan to collect evidence against Queen Caroline, 1818; retired, 1825. [xii. 101]

COOKE, WILLIAM BERNARD (1778–1855), line-engraver; a prolific engraver of landscapes for illustrated books; excelled in sea-views. [xii. 102]

COOKE, SIR WILLIAM FOTHERGILL (1806–1879), electrician; educated at Durham and Edinburgh; army officer in India, 1826–31; studied medicine at Paris and Heidelberg; shown the principle of electric telegraphy by Professor Müncke, 1836; patented, jointly with Sir Charles Wheatstone [q. v.], telegraphic apparatus, 1837, and produced a workable instrument, 1845; quarrelled with Wheatstone; knighted, 1869; pensioned, 1871. [xii. 102]

COOKE, WILLIAM JOHN (1797–1865), line-engraver; employed in illustrating books; withdrew to Darmstadt, c. 1840. [xii. 103]

COOKES, SIR THOMAS (d. 1701), baronet, of Bentley Pauncefot, Worcestershire; benefactor of Bromsgrove and Feckenham schools; bequeathed 10,000l. to Oxford University, with which Gloucester Hall was converted into Worcester College. [xii. 103]

COOKESLEY, WILLIAM GIFFORD (1802–1880), classical scholar; educated at Eton and King's College, Cambridge; M.A., 1827; assistant master at Eton; vicar of St. Peter's, Hammersmith, 1860; rector of Tempsford, Bedfordshire, 1868; published classical school-books, 1838–61; sermons, 1843–4, and pamphlets, 1845–67. [xii. 104]

COOKSON, GEORGE (1760–1835), general; entered navy, 1773; transferred to the royal artillery, 1778; served in the West Indies, and, 1793, the Netherlands; brevet-major, 1800; served with distinction in Egypt, 1801; lieutenant-colonel, 1802; served at Copenhagen, 1807, and with Sir John Moore, 1808; major-general, 1814; lieutenant-general, 1830. [xii. 104]

COOKSON, HENRY WILKINSON (1810–1876), master of Peterhouse; godson of Wordsworth; educated at Sedbergh and, from 1828, at Peterhouse, Cambridge; D.D.; master of Peterhouse, 1847 till death; rector of Glaston, Rutland, 1847–67. [xii. 105]

COOKSON, JAMES (1752–1835), divine; rector of Colmer, Hampshire, 1775; entered Queen's College, Oxford, 1777; M.A., 1786; vicar of Harting, Sussex, 1796; master of Churcher's College, Petersfield, c. 1783; F.S.A., 1814; published theological pieces, 1782–4. [xii. 106]

COOKWORTHY, WILLIAM (1705–1780), porcelain-maker; quaker preacher; discovered 'kaolin' (china-clay) and 'petunze' (china-stone) near St. Austell, 1756, specimens of which from Virginia had been shown him in 1745; obtained patent for porcelain factory at Plymouth, 1768; sold the patent, 1777. [xii. 106]

COOLEY, THOMAS (1740–1784), architect; originally a carpenter; designed the Royal Exchange, Dublin, 1769, the Four Courts, 1784, and other buildings in Ireland. [xii. 107]

COOLEY, WILLIAM DESBOROUGH (d. 1883), geographer; published 'History of . . . Discovery,' 1830–1; exposed Douville's fictitious 'Voyage au Congo,' 1832; pensioned, 1859; honorary free member, Royal Geographical Society of London, 1864; published papers on African geography, 1841–74, and a manual of 'Physical Geography,' 1876. [xii. 107]

COOLING or **COLING, RICHARD** (d. 1697), clerk of the privy council, 1689, and gossip of Samuel Pepys; secretary to the lord chamberlain of the household, 1660–1680; hon. M.A. Oxford, 1665. [xii. 108]

COOMBES, ROBERT (1808–1860), champion sculler; a Thames waterman; rowed his first sculling race, 1836; champion of the Thames, 1846–52; coached the Cambridge crew, 1852; died insane. [xii. 108]

COOMBES, WILLIAM HENRY (1767–1850), Roman catholic divine; born in Somerset; educated at Douay; priest, 1791; driven from France by the revolution; professor of divinity at Old Hall Green; D.D., by the pope, 1801; priest at Shepton Mallet, 1810–49; published devotional tracts and translations. [xii. 109]

COOPER, ABRAHAM (1787–1868), battle and animal painter; patronised by (Sir) Henry Meux, 1809; R.A., 1820; over four hundred pieces by him exhibited, 1812–69. [xii. 109]

COOPER, ALEXANDER (*fl.* 1630–1660), miniature painter; withdrew to Amsterdam, and to the court of Queen Christina of Sweden; possibly painted also landscapes. [xii. 110]

COOPER, ANDREW or, probably erroneously, ANTHONY (*fl.* 1660), author of 'Στρατολογία,' a metrical history of the civil war, by 'An. Cooper,' 1660; identified with Andrew Cooper, a newswriter, author of 'A Speedy Post,' 1642. [xii. 110]

COOPER, ANTHONY ASHLEY, first BARON ASHLEY and first EARL OF SHAFTESBURY (1621–1683), succeeded as second baronet, 1631, inheriting large estates, including (through his mother, *d.* 1628) Wimborne St. Giles, Dorset; put into the court of wards; plundered by the law officers; appealed for protection to attorney-general, 1634; entered Exeter College, Oxford, 1637, and Lincoln's Inn, 1638; elected M.P. for Tewkesbury, for the Short Parliament, 1640, but did not sit; elected, on a double return, for Downton, Wiltshire, for the Long parliament, 1640, but consideration of his election shelved by the Commons; with Charles I, but not committed to him, at Nottingham and Derby, 1642; brought to Oxford an offer of the Dorset gentry to rise for Charles I, 1643; raised, at his own expense, foot and horse for King Charles's service; promised the governorship of Weymouth; had great difficulty in obtaining it, 1643; resigned his commissions to Charles I, 1644; attached himself to the parliamentarians; obtained command of the parliamentary forces in Dorset, 1644; captured royalist strongholds and helped to relieve Taunton, 1644; vainly tried to obtain his seat in parliament, 1645; took Corfe Castle, 1646; withdrew from public affairs, but continued to attend to local administration, serving as parliamentary high sheriff for Wiltshire, 1646–1648; sat for Wiltshire in Cromwell's parliaments, 1653–8; served on the council of state, 1653–4; led the parliamentary opposition to Cromwell, 1656–8; sat for Wiltshire in Richard Cromwell's parliament, 1659, opposing the government; claimed his seat for Downton in the Rump parliament, 1659; sat on the council of state; imprisoned as a political suspect, 1659; promised to co-operate with Monck, 1659; seized the Tower and persuaded the fleet to declare for parliament, December 1659; sat on the new council of state; took his seat for Downton, and became colonel of Fleetwood's horse, 1660; urged the admission of the excluded members; negotiated with Charles II, March 1660; M.P. for Wiltshire in the Convention parliament, April; one of the commissioners to recall Prince Charles; admitted privy councillor, May 1660; received a formal pardon for the past, June 1660; opposed the vindictive actions of the royalists; created Baron Ashley, 1661; under-treasurer, 1661–7; chancellor of the exchequer, 1661–72; steadily opposed Clarendon's repressive measures, the Corporation Act, 1661, Act of Uniformity, 1662, and the Five-mile Act, 1665; advised and supported Charles II's first Declaration of Indulgence, 1662–3; received a grant of Carolina, 1663, and an interest in the Bahamas, 1670; treasurer of prizes in Dutch war, 1665–8; made the acquaintance at Oxford, 1666, of John Locke, who became his one intimate friend; lord-lieutenant of Dorset, 1667; attached himself to Buckingham, 1669, and became a strong partisan of the scheme to legitimise Monmouth, 1670; kept in ignorance of the secret provisions of the treaty of Dover, negotiated by Clifford, December 1670; assented to declaration of war with Dutch; opposed the raising of funds for the war by the stoppage of exchequer payments, 1672; approved Charles II's Declaration of Indulgence for protestant dissenters, 1672; created Earl of Shaftesbury, 1672; president of the board of trade, 1672–6; refused the lord high treasurership; lord chancellor, 1672–3; offended the Commons by issuing writs to fill up the vacant seats; alienated the king's mistresses by refusing to pass grants of money to them, and Lauderdale by interfering with his despotic rule

in Scotland; discovered the deceit practised on him by the king and Clifford in 1670, in the treaty of Dover; contrary to his own principles, supported the Test Act, 1673; dismissed from the chancellorship and ordered to withdraw from London, 1673; rejected overtures of accommodation by Charles and by Louis XIV; set himself, in parliament and in the city of London, to fan the apprehension of a Romanist revival, January 1674; dismissed from the privy council and removed from the lord-lieutenancy of Dorset, 1674; withdrew to Wimborne St. Giles; led agitation for dissolution of parliament, 1675–6; led the opposition to Danby, 1675–6; refused to leave London on an order from Charles II, 1676; imprisoned, with Buckingham, Salisbury, and Wharton, by order of the House of Lords, 1677; released on his submission, 1678; rejected overtures of accommodation with the Duke of York; encouraged the 'popish plot' frenzy as a weapon against the government, 1678; led the opposition in parliament, 1679; accepted presidentship of privy council, 1679; passed the Habeas Corpus Act, 1679; supported the Exclusion Bill, May 1679; dismissed from office, October 1679; brought Monmouth back to London, November 1679; agitated for the re-assembling of parliament; tried to make capital out of an alleged Irish 'popish plot,' 1680; tried to prosecute the Duke of York as a popish recusant, June 1680; foiled, by Halifax, in his attempt to carry the Exclusion Bill, 1680; petitioned Charles II against holding parliament at Oxford, 1681; lodged in Balliol College; brought in a bill to repeal the penalties against protestant dissenters, 1681; committed to the Tower on a charge of high treason; asked leave from Charles to withdraw to Carolina, October 1681; released, the charge against him being dismissed by the whig grand jury, 1681; satirised by Dryden in 'Absalom and Achitophel'; planned a revolt in London, the west, and Cheshire, 1682; fled to Harwich and sailed for Holland, 1682; reached Amsterdam and was admitted a burgher of that city, 1682; died there; buried at Poole, Dorset. [xii. 111]

COOPER, ANTHONY ASHLEY, third EARL OF SHAFTESBURY (1671–1713), moral philosopher; styled Lord Ashley, from January 1683; travelled in Italy, France, and Germany; M.P., Poole, 1695–8; advocated allowing counsel to prisoners charged with treason, 1695; visited Holland and came under Pierre Bayle's influence; his 'Inquiry concerning Virtue,' published surreptitiously, 1699; succeeded as third Earl of Shaftesbury, 1699; voted with the whigs, 1700–2; dismissed from the vice-admiralship of Dorset by Anne, 1702; withdrew to Holland, 1703–4; left England for Naples, 1711; died there; possible originator of the phrase 'moral sense' in its philosophic signification; issued his collected writings, as 'Characteristicks of Men,' &c., 1711; his 'Letters,' published, 1716, 1721, and 1830. [xii. 130]

COOPER, ANTONY ASHLEY, seventh EARL OF SHAFTESBURY (1801–1885), philanthropist; styled Lord Ashley from May 1811; educated at Harrow and Christ Church; M.A., 1832; D.C.L., 1841; M.P., 1826–1851; held minor offices, 1828 and 1834; urged reform of lunacy laws, 1829, and the protection of factory operatives, 1833–44, colliery workers, 1842, and chimney-sweeps; joined whig party, 1847; advocated ragged schools and the reclamation of juvenile offenders, 1848; succeeded to the earldom, 1851; advocated the supervision of lodging houses, 1851, and the better housing of the poor; chairman of the sanitary commission in the Crimea; an active member of religious associations. [xii. 133]

COOPER, SIR ASTLEY PASTON (1768–1841), surgeon; fourth son of Samuel Cooper (1739–1800) [q. v.]; pupil of Henry Cline [q. v.]; studied in London, Edinburgh, and Paris; anatomy demonstrator, 1789, and lecturer, 1791–1825, at St. Thomas's Hospital; acquired a lucrative practice; lecturer on anatomy, 1793–6, and on comparative anatomy, 1813–15, to the College of Surgeons; surgeon, 1800, and consulting surgeon, 1825, to Guy's Hospital; F.R.S., 1802; created baronet, 1821; published surgical and anatomical treatises, 1800–40, and contributed much to professional journals. [xii. 137]

COOPER, CHARLES HENRY (1808–1866), Cambridge antiquary; settled in Cambridge, 1826; admitted a solicitor, 1840; coroner, 1836, and town clerk of Cambridge, 1849–66; published 'Guide to Cambridge,' 1831, 'Annals of Cambridge,' 1842–53, 'Athenæ Cantabrigienses,'

1858–61, and 'Memorials of Cambridge,' 1858–66; left much biographical material in manuscript; his memoir of Margaret, countess of Richmond, published, 1874. [xii. 139]

COOPER, CHARLES PURTON (1793–1873), lawyer; entered Wadham College, Oxford, 1810; took double-first honours, 1814; M.A., 1817; barrister, Lincoln's Inn, 1816; an equity draughtsman; queen's serjeant for the duchy of Lancaster; secretary of the second record commission; published law tracts and reports, 1828–68, an account of the public records, 1832, and pamphlets, 1850–7; died at Boulogne. [xii. 140]

COOPER, DANIEL (1817?–1842), naturalist; medical student; zoological assistant, British Museum; curator of the Botanical Society, London; compiled a 'Flora Metropolitana,' and a list of London shells; lectured on botany; army surgeon, 1840. [xii. 141]

COOPER or COWPER, EDWARD (d. 1725?), a leading London printseller from c. 1685. [xii. 141]

COOPER, EDWARD JOSHUA (1798–1863), astronomer; educated at Eton, and, 1816–18, Christ Church, Oxford; travelled extensively on the continent and in the East; published 'Views in Egypt,' 1824; manager of his imbecile uncle's estates at Markree, Sligo, 1830; succeeded to the estates, 1837; M.P., Sligo county, 1830–41, and 1857–9; built observatory at Markree; accumulated astronomical and meteorological observations, 1833–63; published 'Catalogue of Stars,' observed at Markree, 1851–6, and 'Cometic Orbits,' 1852; F.R.S., 1853. [xii. 142]

COOPER, ELIZABETH (fl. 1737), authoress; an auctioneer's widow; published 'The Muses' Library,' vol. i. 1737, a selection of English verse; brought out two dramas, 'The Rival Widows,' 1735, and 'The Nobleman,' 1736. [xii. 143]

COOPER, GEORGE (1820–1876), organist; son of a London organist; organist of various London churches, 1834–76; assistant organist of St. Paul's, 1838–76; organist of the Chapel Royal, 1856–76; organist of Christ's Hospital, 1843; composed hymn-tunes; published manuals for the organ. [xii. 144]

COOPER, SIR GREY (d. 1801), politician; barrister-at-law; published pamphlets in defence of the Rockingham ministry, 1765; pensioned by the ministry; M.P., 1765–90; a secretary of the treasury, 1765–82; a commissioner of the treasury, 1783. [xii. 144]

COOPER, JOHN (d. 1626). [See COPERARIO, GIOVANNI.]

COOPER, JOHN (fl. 1810–1870), actor; went on the Bath stage, 1811; appeared in London, 1811; acted in the provinces, 1812–20; a favourite London actor, 1820–1858. [xii. 145]

COOPER, JOHN GILBERT (1723–1769), miscellaneous writer; educated at Westminster, and, 1743, Trinity College, Cambridge; contributed verses, as 'Philaretes,' to Dodsley's 'Museum,' from 1746; published treatises on questions of æsthetics, 1745 and 1754, a life of Socrates, 1749, collected poems, 1764, and other works. [xii. 145]

COOPER, RICHARD, the elder (d. 1764), engraver; pupil of John Pine; studied art in Italy; settled in Edinburgh; much employed in engraving portraits. [xii. 146]

COOPER, RICHARD, the younger (1740?–1814?), painter and engraver; son of Richard Cooper the elder [q. v.]; studied in Paris under J. P. Le Bas; exhibited drawings and engravings in London, 1761–4; visited Italy; published tinted drawings of scenes near Rome, 1778–9; exhibited drawings at the Royal Academy, 1778–1809; drawing-master at Eton. [xii. 146]

COOPER, ROBERT (fl. 1681), geographer; entered Pembroke College, Oxford, 1667; B.A., 1670; fellow; M.A., 1673; rector of Harlington, Middlesex, 1681; published an optical tract, 1679, and an 'Introduction to Geography,' 1680. [xii. 147]

COOPER, ROBERT (fl. 1800–1836), engraver; much employed in illustrating books and engraving portraits. [xii. 147]

COOPER, SAMUEL (1609–1672), miniature painter; painted portraits of celebrities of the Commonwealth and Restoration; visited France and Holland. [xii. 148]

COOPER, SAMUEL (1739–1800), divine; B.A. Magdalene College, Cambridge, 1760; D.D., 1777; published sermons and pamphlets; provoked merriment by publishing a dull poem, 'The Task,' shortly after William Cowper's 'Task.' [xii. 137]

COOPER, SAMUEL (1780–1848), surgical writer; studied at St. Bartholomew's Hospital, 1800; qualified as surgeon, 1803; army surgeon, 1813–15; practitioner in London; published treatise on cataract, 1805, and 'Surgical Dictionary,' 1809; surgeon of University College Hospital, 1831; F.R.S., 1846. [xii. 148]

COOPER or COUPER, THOMAS (1517?–1594), bishop of Winchester; son of an Oxford tailor; chorister of Magdalen College, Oxford, 1531; B.A., 1539; fellow, 1539–45; M.A., 1543; master of Magdalen College school, 1549–68; qualified for M.B., 1566; satirised for his wife's misconduct; issued an enlargement of Eliot's Latin dictionary, 1548, a continuation of Languet's 'Chronicle' ('Cooper's Chronicle,' A.D. 17–1547), 1549, 'An Answer,' in defence of Jewel, 1562, and 'Thesaurus Linguæ Romanæ,' known as 'Cooper's Dictionary,' 1565; D.D., 1567; dean of Christ Church, 1567; vice-chancellor of Oxford, 1567–70; dean of Gloucester, 1569; bishop of Lincoln, 1570; published a 'Brief Exposition' of the Sunday lessons, 1573, and sermons, 1575–80; bishop of Winchester, 1584–94; lampooned by 'Martin Mar-Prelate,' 1588–9; published an 'Admonition,' in his own defence, 1589. [xii. 149]

COOPER, COUPER, or COWPER, THOMAS (fl. 1626), divine; educated at Westminster; student of Christ Church, Oxford, 1598; B.D., 1600; vicar of Great Budworth, Cheshire, 1601–4; vicar of Holy Trinity, Coventry, 1604–10; preacher to the fleet, 1626; published tracts against the Gunpowder plot, 1606–9, against witchcraft, 1617, and murder, 1620. [xii. 151]

COOPER, THOMAS (1759–1840), natural philosopher and lawyer; entered University College, Oxford, 1779; studied law and medicine; barrister, Inner Temple, 1787; went as democratic envoy to Paris, 1792; attacked by Edmund Burke; defended himself in a pamphlet; failed as a bleacher at Manchester; a lawyer in Pennsylvania from before 1799 to 1811; M.D.; professor of chemistry in various colleges, 1812–34; published political pamphlets and manuals of American law, 1800–40, and a scientific encyclopedia, 1812–14. [xii. 151]

COOPER, THOMAS (1805–1892), chartist; apprenticed as shoemaker at Gainsborough, where after private study he opened a school, 1827; engaged in journalistic and other work at Lincoln and in London; joined staff of 'Leicester Mercury,' 1840; became chartist and edited the chartist 'Midland Counties Illuminator'; imprisoned on charge of sedition and conspiracy, 1843–5; subsequently took no part in chartist movements; published a political epic entitled 'The Purgatory of Suicides,' 1845, and other works in verse and prose. [Suppl. ii. 58]

COOPER, THOMAS HENRY (1759?–1840?), botanist; compiled a list of Sussex plants, 1835. [xii. 152]

COOPER, THOMAS THORNVILLE (1839–1878), traveller; travelled in Australia; merchant's clerk at Madras, 1859–61; travelled in India and Burmah; at Shanghai, 1863; published 'A Pioneer of Commerce,' describing an attempt, January-November 1868, to travel from China through Thibet, and 'Mishmee Hills,' narrating his endeavours, 1869, to reach China from Assam; employé of the India Office; political agent at Bamò, Burmah, 1876; murdered at Bamò. [xii. 153]

COOPER, WILLIAM (fl. 1653), puritan; vicar of Ringmere, Sussex; chaplain to Elizabeth, queen of Bohemia, at the Hague, 1644–8; ejected from St. Olave's, Southwark, 1662; imprisoned, 1681; published sermons. [xii. 154]

COOPER, WILLIAM DURRANT (1812–1875), antiquary; solicitor, 1832; journalist; solicitor to the Reform Club, 1837, and to St. Pancras vestry, 1858; published a 'Parliamentary History' of Sussex, 1834, a glossary of Sussex words, 1836, and memoirs of Sussex poets, 1842; contributed to archæological journals. [xii. 154]

COOPER, WILLIAM RICKETTS (1843–1878), oriental student; secretary to the Society of Biblical Archæology, 1870–6; published papers on Egyptian and Assyrian antiquities, 1873–7. [xii. 155]

COOPER, WILLIAM WHITE (1816–1886), surgeon-oculist; qualified as a surgeon, 1838; ophthalmic surgeon to St. Mary's Hospital, Paddington; wrote on professional and miscellaneous subjects. [xii. 155]

COOTE, Sir CHARLES (d. 1642), soldier; went to Ireland as captain, 1600; fought at Kinsale, 1602; provost-marshal, 1605, and vice-president, 1620, of Connaught; a great Connaught landowner; created baronet, 1621; M.P., Queen's County, 1639; governor of Dublin, 1641; fought vigorously against the Irish rebels, 1641–2; killed in action. [xii. 156]

COOTE, Sir CHARLES, EARL OF MOUNTRATH (d. 1661), eldest son of Sir Charles Coote (d. 1642) [q. v.]; M.P., Leitrim, 1639; fought vigorously against the Irish rebels, 1641–2; succeeded to baronetcy, 1642; provost-marshal, 1642, and president, 1645, of Connaught; continually in arms against the Irish royalists and rebels, 1649–52; a commissioner to govern Ireland, 1659; joined Roger Boyle, baron Broghill, in securing Ireland for Charles II, 1660; reappointed president of Connaught, granted the lands of barony of Westmeath, and named a lord justice of Ireland, 1660; created Earl of Mountrath, 1661. [xii. 156]

COOTE, CHARLES (1761–1835), historian; son of a London bookseller; at St. Paul's School, 1773–8; B.A. Pembroke College, Oxford, 1782; fellow, 1784; D.C.L., 1789; an advocate at Doctors' Commons, 1789; published an English grammar, 1788, a history of England (to 1802), 1791–1803, a history of the union with Ireland, 1802, and lives of English civilians, 1804; published (1818–27) continuation of Russell's 'Modern Europe.' [xii. 157]

COOTE, EDMUND (fl. 1597), grammarian; often wrongly given as EDWARD; entered Peterhouse, Cambridge, 1566; M.A., 1583; master of Bury St. Edmunds school, 1596–7; published 'The English Schoolmaster,' a method of learning English, 1597, which went through some fifty editions before 1704. [xii. 158]

COOTE, Sir EYRE (1726–1783), general; served against the Scottish insurgents, 1745; sailed for India, 1754; captain, 1755; voted for immediate action at Plassey, and led a division in the battle, June 1757; lieutenant-colonel, 1759; assumed command of the troops in Madras, and took Wandewash, 1759; crushed Lally at Wandewash, 1760; took Pondicherry, 1761; returned to England, 1762; bought West Park, Hampshire; colonel, 1765; M.P., Leicester, 1768; went to Madras as commander-in-chief, 1769, but resigned; K.B., 1771; major-general, 1775; lieutenant-general, 1777; named commander-in-chief in India, 1777; assumed command at Calcutta, 1779; sent to Madras to cope with Hyder Ali; raised the siege of Wandewash, 1781; repulsed at Chelambakam, 1781; routed Hyder Ali at Porto Novo, 1 July, and in several later engagements, August–December, 1781; died at Madras. [xii. 158]

COOTE, Sir EYRE (1762–1823), general; nephew and heir of Sir Eyre Coote (1726–1783) [q. v.]; educated at Eton; ensign, 1774; served in America, 1775–81; lieutenant-colonel, 1788; served in the West Indies, 1793 and 1795; major-general, 1798; fought at Ostend, 1798, and Bergen, 1799; served in Egypt, 1801; K.B., 1802; M.P., Queen's County, 1802; governor of Jamaica, 1805–8; besieged Flushing, 1809; general, 1814; M.P., Barnstaple, 1810–18. [xii. 161]

COOTE, HENRY CHARLES (1815–1885), lawyer; son of Charles Coote [q. v.]; proctor in Doctors' Commons, 1840; solicitor, 1857; published legal treatises, 1846–60, and historical essays, pointing out Roman influence on Anglo-Saxon civilisation, 1864 and 1878. [xii. 162]

COOTE, HOLMES (1817–1872), surgeon; studied in London; surgeon to St. Bartholomew's Hospital, 1863; published professional treatises, 1849–67. [xii. 163]

COOTE, RICHARD, first EARL OF BELLAMONT (1636–1701), governor of New York; succeeded as second Baron Coote of Coloony, 1683; M.P., Droitwich, 1688–95; served in Ireland, 1689; created Earl of Bellamont, 1689; appointed governor of New England to repress piracy, 1695; commissioned ship for Captain William Kidd to arrest pirates; reached New York, 1697; arrested Kidd, 1699; died at New York. [xii. 163]

COPCOT, JOHN (d. 1590), divine; entered Trinity College, Cambridge, 1562; B.A., 1566; fellow; D.D., 1582; an instrument of Burghley in Cambridge; vice-chancellor, 1586–7; made master of Christ's College, Cambridge, 1587; rector of St. Dunstan-in-the-East, London; published sermons. [xii. 164]

COPE, ALAN (d. 1578), Roman catholic divine; fellow of Magdalen College, Oxford, 1549; M.A., 1552; student of civil law; withdrew to Flanders, 1560, and to Rome; created D.D. by the pope; canon of St. Peter's, Rome; died in Rome; published 'Syntaxis Historiæ Evangelicæ,' 1572; edited Nicholas Harpsfield's 'Dialogi sex,' against the English reformers, 1566. [xii. 165]

COPE, Sir ANTHONY (d. 1551), author; of Hanwell, Oxfordshire; travelled; chamberlain to Queen Catherine Parr; knighted, 1547; sheriff of Oxfordshire, 1548; published 'The Historie of . . . Anniball,' 1544, and 'A Meditacion upon . . . Psalmes,' 1547. [xii. 165]

COPE, Sir ANTHONY (1548?–1614), high sheriff of Oxfordshire, 1581; of Hanwell, Oxfordshire; M.P., Banbury, 1586–1604; imprisoned as a puritan, 1587; knighted, 1590. [xii. 166]

COPE, CHARLES WEST (1811–1890), historical painter; studied at Sass's academy, 1827, and the Royal Academy, 1828, and subsequently in Paris, Naples, and Florence; exhibited at Royal Academy, 'Paolo and Francesca, 1837, 'Osteria di Campagna,' 1838, and 'Poor Law Guardians,' 1841; obtained prize of 300l. in competition for decoration of houses of parliament, 1843; was one of the six painters commissioned, 1844, to prepare decorations for the House of Lords, and executed several frescoes; studied fresco painting in Italy and at Munich; R.A., 1848; exhibited 'The Firstborn,' 1849, and subsequently produced many paintings and frescoes illustrating incidents in history and romance; professor of painting to Royal Academy, 1867–75; one of committee of artists employed in decoration of Westminster Palace, 1871; exhibited, 1876, 'The Council of the Royal Academy,' now in council-room of the Academy. [Suppl. ii. 59]

COPE, EDWARD MEREDITH (1818–1873), classical scholar; entered Trinity College, Cambridge, 1837; senior classic, 1841; fellow, 1842; M.A., 1844; tutor, 1845; became insane, 1869; translated Plato's 'Phædo,' and edited Aristotle's 'Rhetoric.' [xii. 166]

COPE, Sir JOHN (d. 1760), lieutenant-general; cornet, 1707; K.B. and lieutenant-general, 1743; commander-in-chief in Scotland, 1745; marched from Stirling against the Jacobite insurgents, August 1745; reached Inverness and came by sea to Dunbar; routed by Prince Charles at Prestonpans, 21 Sept. 1745; stationed in Ireland, 1751. [xii. 166]

COPE, MICHAEL (fl. 1557), English protestant refugee at Geneva; preached in French at Geneva; published 'Expositions' of Ecclesiastes and Proverbs, 1557 and 1564. [xii. 167]

COPE, RICHARD (1776–1856), congregationalist minister; educated at Hoxton Theological College, 1798–9; minister and proprietor of a boarding-school at Launceston, 1800–20; hon. M.A. Aberdeen, 1819; minister in Wakefield, 1822–9, Abergavenny, 1829–36, and Penryn, Cornwall, 1836–56; published sermons, tracts, and verses, 1807–38; his autobiography published, 1857. [xii. 167]

COPE, Sir WALTER (d. 1614), politician; built Cope Castle (now Holland House), Kensington, 1607; chamberlain of the exchequer, 1609; master of the wards, 1613. [xii. 168]

COPELAND, THOMAS (1781–1855), writer on surgery; studied at St. Bartholomew's Hospital; qualified as a surgeon, 1804; army surgeon in Spain, 1809; an eminent practitioner in London; F.R.S., 1834; published 'Diseases of the Rectum,' 1810, and other works. [xii. 168]

COPELAND, WILLIAM JOHN (1804–1885), divine; at St. Paul's School, 1815–24; scholar of Trinity College, Oxford, 1824; M.A., 1831; fellow, 1832–49; B.D., 1840; rector of Farnham, Essex, 1849–85. [xii. 168]

COPELAND, WILLIAM TAYLOR (1797–1868), porcelain manufacturer of Stoke-on-Trent; made a specialty of parian groups and statuettes; sheriff of London, 1829; lord mayor, 1835; M.P., 1831–65. [xii. 169]

COPERARIO or **COPRARIO**, GIOVANNI (d. 1626) musician; said to be an Englishman, JOHN COOPER: trained in Italy; published 'Funeral Teares,' 1606, and 'Songs of Mourning' (for Prince Henry), 1613; composed music for court masques, 1607–13; composer to Charles I, 1625; teacher of William and Henry Lawes; left much unpublished music in manuscript. [xii. 170]

COPINGER, WILLIAM (d. 1416), clerk; to him Bale and Pits erroneously assigned two manuscript treatises on theology. [xii. 170]

COPLAND, JAMES (1791–1870), physician; M.D. Edinburgh, 1815; visited the Gold Coast; travelled in France and Germany; L.R.C.P., 1820; F.R.S., 1833; practitioner in London; contributed to professional journals; published 'Dictionary of Practical Medicine,' 1832, and other medical works. [xii. 171]

COPLAND, PATRICK (1749–1822), professor at Aberdeen of natural philosophy, 1775–9 and 1817–22, and of mathematics, 1779–1817; LL.D.; formed a museum of natural philosophy. [xii. 172]

COPLAND, ROBERT (fl. 1508–1547), author and printer; pupil of Wynkyn de Worde; issued books with his imprint, 1515–47; translated from the French, 'The Kalender of Shepeherdes,' 1508, 'The Rutter of the See,' 1528, three romances and devotional and metrical pieces; his best-known poems, 'The Hye Way to the Spyttel Hous,' 'Jyl of Breyntford's Testament,' and 'The Seuen Sorowes that Women have.' [xii. 172]

COPLAND, WILLIAM (fl. 1556–1569), printer; succeeded Robert Copland [q. v.] in business, 1548; member of the Stationers' Company, 1556; issued books with his imprint, 1548–61; compiled 'A boke of . . . Herbes,' 1552. [xii. 174]

COPLESTON, EDWARD (1776–1849), bishop of Llandaff; scholar of Corpus Christi College, Oxford, 1791; B.A., 1795; fellow of Oriel, 1795–1814; tutor, 1797; vicar of St. Mary's, Oxford, 1800; professor of poetry, 1802–12; D.D., 1815; provost of Oriel College, 1814–28; dean of Chester, 1826; bishop of Llandaff and dean of St. Paul's, 1828–49; published pamphlets on education, the currency, and pauperism; worked hard for his diocese; published charges to his clergy. [xii. 174]

COPLEY, ANTHONY (1567–1607?), poet; third son of Sir Thomas Copley [q. v.]; withdrew to Rouen, 1582, and to Rome, 1584; resided in the Low Countries, 1586–90; prisoner in the Tower, 1590; pardoned; published 'Wits, Fittes, and Fancies,' containing verses, and jests from the Spanish, 1595, and a poem, 'A Fig for a Fortune,' 1596; wrote for the secular priests against the jesuits, 1601–2; conspired to place Arabella Stuart on the throne, 1603; turned king's evidence and was pardoned; in Rome in 1606. [xii. 176]

COPLEY, SIR GODFREY (d. 1709), founder of the Royal Society's Copley medal; succeeded as second baronet, 1684; M.P., Aldborough, 1678–81, Thirsk, 1695–1705; F.R.S., 1691; controller of army accounts, 1704. [xii. 177]

COPLEY, JOHN (1577–1662), divine; youngest son of Sir Thomas Copley [q. v.]; born at Louvain; a Roman catholic priest; published 'Reasons' for embracing protestantism, 1612; vicar of Bethersden, 1612–16; rector of Pluckley, Kent, 1616; ejected by parliament, 1643; restored, 1660. [xii. 189]

COPLEY, JOHN SINGLETON, the elder (1737–1815), portrait-painter in oil and crayons; born at Boston, Massachusetts; taught by his step-father, Peter Pelham (d. 1751), portrait-painter and engraver, of Boston; began painting and engraving portraits, 1753; painted George Washington's portrait, 1755; exhibited 'The Boy with the Squirrel,' in London, 1766; left America, 1774, having executed nearly three hundred pictures; visited London; visited continental galleries, 1774–6; settled in London, 1776; employed as a portrait-painter; exhibited his first imaginative picture, 'A Youth rescued from a Shark,' 1779; became famous as an historical painter by painting 'Chatham's last Appearance in the Lords,' 'Repulse of the Spanish Floating Batteries at Gibraltar,' 1790, and 'Charles I demanding the surrender of the Five Members' (began 1785). [xii. 177]

COPLEY, JOHN SINGLETON, the younger, BARON LYNDHURST (1772–1863), lord chancellor; son of John Singleton Copley the elder [q. v.]; born in Boston, Massachusetts; brought to England, 1775; entered Trinity College, Cambridge, 1790; second wrangler, 1794; fellow, 1795–1804; M.A., 1796; went to Boston to try to recover his father's property, 1795; toured in the United States; took chambers as a special pleader; barrister, Lincoln's Inn, 1804; joined the Midland circuit; became popular at Nottingham by defending a Luddite rioter, 1812; serjeant-at-law, 1813; became responsible for his father's debts, 1815; increased his reputation by gaining the bobbin-net lace case, 1816, and defending Arthur Thistlewood, 1817; engaged by the crown as prosecuting counsel, 1817; tory M.P., 1818–26; chief-justice of Chester, 1819; solicitor-general, 1819; conducted the prosecution of Arthur Thistlewood for treason, and that of Queen Caroline before the lords, 1820; knighted; attorney-general, 1824–6; master of the rolls, 1826; recorder of Bristol, 1826; lord-chancellor, 1827–30; created Baron Lyndhurst, 1827; chief baron of the exchequer, 1831–4; again lord chancellor, 1834–5; took a leading part in the debates in the Lords, 1835–41; high steward of Cambridge University, 1840; a third time lord chancellor, 1841–6; benefited by operations for cataract, 1849–52; declined a fourth tenure of the lord chancellorship, 1851; last speech in the Lords, 1861. [xii. 182]

COPLEY, SIR THOMAS (1534–1584), of Gatton, Surrey, and Roughay, in Horsham parish, Sussex; knighted abroad; created baron by Philip II, and so often styled LORD COPLEY; claimed the barony of Hoo and Hastings; M.P. for Gatton, a private borough, 1553–1567; opposed the measures of Philip and Mary, 1558; a favourite with Elizabeth; embraced Roman catholicism; imprisoned as a recusant; went abroad, 1570; entered the Spanish service; died in Flanders. [xii. 189]

COPLEY, THOMAS (1594–1652?), jesuit; of Gatton, Surrey; took part in planting the colony of Maryland. [xii. 189]

COPPE, ABIEZER, alias HIGHAM (1619–1672), fanatic; of disordered mind and disorderly life; servitor of All Souls' College, Oxford, 1636; post-master of Merton College; baptist preacher in Warwickshire and other midland counties; joined the ranters; his 'Fiery Flying Roll' burnt, as blasphemous, by order of parliament, 1650; imprisoned at Warwick, and, 1651, in Newgate; released, on his recantation, 1651; practised physic, after 1660, at Barnes, Surrey, as 'Dr. Higham.' [xii. 190]

COPPIN or **COPPING**, JOHN (d. 1583), Brownist; disciple of Robert Browne [q. v.]; subjected to nominal imprisonment, 1576; taught his fellow-prisoners that Queen Elizabeth was an idolater and perjured; executed for treason. [xii. 191]

COPPIN, RICHARD (fl. 1646–1659), universalist; Anglican, presbyterian (1646), independent, and baptist; claimed to have had a special revelation to preach, 1648; patronised, 1649, by Abiezer Coppe [q. v.]; preached, 1649–54, in several midland counties; often indicted for heresy, but leniently treated; preacher to familists at Rochester, 1655; published pamphlets, 1649–59. [xii. 191]

COPPINGER, EDMUND (d. 1592), fanatic; supported William Hacket [q. v.], who claimed to be the Messiah; died in prison. [xii. 193]

COPPOCK, JAMES (1798–1857), election agent; draper's clerk, then silk-mercer, in London; qualified as a solicitor, 1836; employed in disputed election cases. [xii. 193]

COPPOCK or **CAPPOCH**, THOMAS (1719–1746), Jacobite; B.A. Brasenose College, Oxford, 1742; a clergyman; joined Prince Charles at Manchester; executed at Carlisle; popularly thought to have been named bishop of Carlisle by the Pretender; subject of various pamphlets. [xii. 193]

COPSI, **COPSIGE**, or **COXO**, EARL OF NORTHUMBERLAND (d. 1067), thegn of Northumberland under Tostig, 1065; submitted to William I at Barking, 1066; created earl and sent to reduce Northumberland; slain by Oswulf. [xii. 194]

CORAM, THOMAS (1668?–1751), philanthropist; born at Lyme, Dorset; shipbuilder at Taunton, Massachusetts, 1694; merchant in London, 1720; a trustee for Georgia, 1732; planned colonisation of Nova Scotia, 1735; advocated the establishment of Foundling Hospital; obtained a charter, 1739; opened the building, 1745; received an annuity by subscription, 1749. [xii. 194]

CORBAUX, MARIE FRANÇOISE CATHERINE DOETTER (1812-1883), painter; usually called FANNY CORBAUX; painted in oil- and water-colours; first exhibited, 1827; book illustrator; wrote on Old Testament history; pensioned, 1871. [xii. 195]

CORBEIL, CURBUIL, or CORBEUIL, WILLIAM OF (d. 1136), archbishop of Canterbury; born at one of the Corbeils in Normandy; pupil of Anselm at Laon; clerk of Ranulf Flambard, bishop of Durham; present at the dedication of Durham Cathedral, 1104; became a canon regular of St. Augustine; prior of St. Osyth, Essex; chosen, under pressure from Henry I, archbishop, and consecrated, 1123; went to Rome for the pallium; opposed there by Thurstan, archbishop of York; his contention with Thurstan left undecided at a legatine court held at Westminster by John of Crema, 1125; summoned to Rome by Thurstan; obtained from Honorius II the position of legate in England and Scotland; took the oath to secure the succession to Matilda, 1126; held council at London to proceed against married clergy, 1129; built Rochester Castle and helped to rebuild the cathedral; completed Canterbury Cathedral and dedicated it, 1130; consented to the election of Stephen, whom he crowned in 1135. [xii. 195]

CORBET, CLEMENT (d. 1652), civilian; scholar of Trinity Hall, Cambridge, 1592; fellow, 1598; LL.D., 1605; professor of law, Gresham College, London, 1607-13; master of Trinity Hall, Cambridge, 1611-26; advocate at Doctors' Commons, 1612; chancellor of Chichester; vicar-general of the bishop of Norwich, 1625. [xii. 198]

CORBET, EDWARD (d. 1658), divine; fellow of Merton College, Oxford, 1624; M.A., 1628; member of the Westminster Assembly, 1643; one of the parliamentary visitors of Oxford University, 1647; intruded canon of Christ Church, Oxford, 1648; D.D., 1648; rector of Great Hasely, Oxfordshire, 1649-58. [xii. 199]

CORBET, JOHN (1603-1641), divine; M.A. Glasgow, 1623; minister of Bonhill, Dumbartonshire, 1637; deposed, 1639; withdrew to Ireland; attacked presbyterianism in 'The Ungirding of the Scottish Armour,' and 'The Epistle Congratulatorie of Lysimachus Nicanor,' 1639-40; incumbent of Killaban, Queen's County; murdered in the rebellion. [xii. 199]

CORBET, SIR JOHN (1594-1662), patriot; of Shropshire; created baronet, 1627; probably not the Sir John Corbet who was imprisoned for refusing to pay the forced loan, 1627; high sheriff of Shropshire, 1629; imprisoned in the Fleet for speaking against the muster-master wages, 1629; again imprisoned, 1635; M.P. for Shropshire, 1640, in the Long parliament; took the parliament side. [xii. 200]

CORBET, JOHN (1620-1680), puritan; son of a Gloucester shoemaker; B.A. Magdalen Hall, Oxford, 1639; incumbent and under-schoolmaster of St. Mary-de-Crypt, Gloucester, 1640; chaplain to Colonel Edward Massey, parliamentary governor; published a narrative of events at Gloucester, 1645; preacher at Bridgwater, and afterwards at Chichester; rector of Bramshot, Hampshire; ejected, 1662; resided in Richard Baxter's [q. v.] house; nonconformist minister at Chichester, 1671-80; published controversial and devotional tracts; his 'Remains' published, 1684. [xii. 201]

CORBET, MILES (d. 1662), regicide; of a Norfolk family; barrister, Lincoln's Inn; M.P., Great Yarmouth, 1628, and in the Long parliament; active against Laud; chairman of the committee of examinations; clerk of the court of wards, 1644; registrar of the court of chancery, 1648; attended one meeting of the commission and signed Charles I's death-warrant, 1649; a commissioner for settling Irish affairs, 1655; arrested in Dublin, 1659; M.P., Yarmouth, 1660, but his election annulled; went abroad; arrested in Holland, 1662; brought to London and executed. [xii. 202]

CORBET, REGINALD (d. 1566), judge; of a Shropshire family; reader of the Middle Temple, 1551; justice of the queen's bench, 1559. [xii. 203]

CORBET, RICHARD (1582-1635), bishop of Oxford and of Norwich; son of a Surrey gardener; educated at Westminster; student of Christ Church, Oxford, 1599;

M.A., 1605; proctor, 1612; D.D., 1617; vicar of Cassington, near Oxford; chaplain to James I; prebendary of Salisbury, 1620-31; vicar of Stewkley, Berkshire, 1620-35; dean of Christ Church, 1620-28; bishop of Oxford, 1628; translated to Norwich, 1632; withdrew from the Walloon congregation the use of the bishop's chapel, 1634; his collected poems issued, 1647. [xii. 203]

CORBET, ROBERT (d. 1810), naval officer; of a Shropshire family; lieutenant, 1796; served off Egyptian coast, 1801; commander, 1802; captain, 1806; his men incited to mutiny by his inhuman cruelty to them, 1808; censured by the admiralty, 1809; served with distinction off the Isle of Bourbon, 1809; a mutiny nearly caused by his appointment to the Africaine, 1810; killed in battle with the French, strange stories being current about the bad management of his ship in action. [xii. 204]

CORBET, WILLIAM (1779-1842), Irish rebel; entered Trinity College, Dublin, 1794; joined the United Irishmen; expelled from Trinity College for seditious practices, 1798; went to France; given a captain's commission; attached to Humbert's expedition, but never landed; arrested at Hamburg, 1798; imprisoned at Kilmainham, 1799; escaped to Paris, 1803; served on French side in Peninsula, 1810-13, and in German campaigns, 1813-14; colonel, 1815; slighted by the Bourbons; went with the French expedition to Greece, 1828; general of brigade; commanded French troops in Greece, 1831-2; general of division, 1833. [xii. 206]

CORBETT, THOMAS (d. 1751), secretary to Admiral George Byng in the Sicilian expedition, 1718-20; senior secretary of the admiralty, 1742. [xii. 207]

CORBETT, WILLIAM (d. 1748), violinist and composer; composed music for Lincoln's Inn Fields Theatre, 1700-3; leader of the opera band, 1705-11; visited Italy, c. 1711-13; member of the court band, 1714-47; visited Italy, c. 1716-24; collecting music and musical instruments; supposed government spy on the Jacobites; returned to England, 1724; composed flute and violin music; published concertos, 1728 and 1742. [xii. 207]

CORBIE or CORBINGTON, AMBROSE (1604-1649), jesuit; son of Gerard Corbie [q. v.]; born near Durham; educated at St. Omer, 1616, and Rome, 1622; joined the jesuits, 1627; rhetoric lecturer at St. Omer; minister at Ghent, 1645; died at Rome; wrote lives of jesuits. [xii. 208]

CORBIE or CORBINGTON, GERARD (1558-1637), Roman catholic exile; native of Durham; withdrew to Ireland and to Belgium; joined the jesuits, 1628. [xii. 209]

CORBIE or CORBINGTON, RALPH (1598-1644), Irish jesuit; son of Gerard Corbie [q. v.]; educated in Belgium and Spain; joined the jesuits, 1626; mission priest in Durham, 1631-44; hanged at Tyburn. [xii. 209]

CORBMAC, SAINT (6th cent.), son of Eogan; commemorated on 13 Dec.; born in Munster; founded a monastery in co. Mayo. [xii. 209]

CORBOULD, HENRY (1787-1844), painter; son of Richard Corbould [q. v.]; studied art in London; first exhibited, 1807; much employed as a book-illustrator; employed by the British Museum to make drawings of the Greek marbles. [xii. 211]

CORBOULD, RICHARD (1757-1831), painter; exhibited at the Royal Academy, 1776-1811; a fine book-illustrator. [xii. 211]

CORBRIDGE, THOMAS OF (d. 1304), archbishop of York; D.D.; prebendary of York; chancellor of York, 1279-90; visited Rome on cathedral business, 1281; resigned chancellorship on becoming sacrist of St. Sepulchre's Chapel, York, 1290; went to Rome in hope of recovering his chancellorship, 1290, but failed; sacrist, 1290-9; elected archbishop of York, 1299; involved in ecclesiastical disputes with the prior of Beverley, the bishop of Durham, and the archbishop of Canterbury; lost favour with the king over a question of patronage. [xii. 212]

CORCORAN, MICHAEL (1827-1863), American general; born in co. Sligo; emigrated, 1849; post office clerk in New York; colonel of militia; wounded at Bull's Run, 1861; brigadier-general, 1862. [xii. 213]

CORDELL, CHARLES (1720–1791), Roman catholic divine; of English birth; educated at Douay; chaplain at Arundel Castle, 1748; priest in Yorkshire, Isle of Man, and (1765–91) at Newcastle-on-Tyne; published theological and biographical works. [xii. 213]

CORDELL, SIR WILLIAM (d. 1581), master of the rolls; educated at Cambridge; barrister, Lincoln's Inn, 1544; M.P., Steyning, 1553; solicitor-general, 1553; conducted prosecution of Sir Thomas Wyatt, 1554; knighted; master of the rolls, 1557–81; M.P Suffolk, and speaker of House of Commons, 1558; M.P. for Middlesex, 1563, and for Westminster, 1572. [xii. 213]

CORDEN, WILLIAM (1797–1867), painter; painted china for the Derby works; painted miniature portraits on ivory and china. [xii. 214]

CORDER, WILLIAM (1804–1828), murderer; murdered Maria Marten, near Ipswich, 1827; executed, amid popular execration, 1828. [xii. 214]

CORDEROY, JEREMY (fl. 1600), divine; B.A. St. Alban Hall, Oxford, 1581; M.A., 1584; chaplain of Merton College, 1590; published theological tracts, 1604 and 1608. [xii. 215]

CORDINER, CHARLES (1746?–1794), antiquary; minister of St. Andrew's Episcopal Church, Banff, 1769–1794. His works include 'Antiquities of the North of Scotland,' 1780. [xii. 215]

CORDINER, JAMES (1775–1836), traveller; third son of Charles Cordiner [q. v.]; M.A. Aberdeen, 1793; army chaplain at Madras, 1797, and at Colombo, 1798–1804; minister of St. Paul's Episcopal Church, Aberdeen, 1807–34; published 'A Description of Ceylon,' 1807, and 'A Voyage to India,' 1820. [xii. 215]

COREY, JOHN (fl. 1700–1731), actor; a favourite London actor, 1702–31; brought out a comedy, 1701, and a farce, 1704. [xii. 216]

CORFE, ARTHUR THOMAS (1773–1863), organist; third son of Joseph Corfe [q. v.]; chorister of Westminster Abbey; organist of Salisbury Cathedral, 1804–63; composed anthems, and wrote on 'The Principles of Harmony and Thorough-bass.' [xii. 216]

CORFE, CHARLES WILLIAM (1814–1883), organist of Christ Church, Oxford, 1846–82; younger son of Arthur Thomas Corfe [q. v.]; Mus.Doc. Oxford, 1852; composed glees and anthems. [xii. 217]

CORFE, JOHN DAVIS (1804–1876), organist of Bristol Cathedral; eldest son of Arthur Thomas Corfe [q. v.] [xii. 217]

CORFE, JOSEPH (1740–1820), composer; chorister, lay vicar, and organist, 1792–1804, of Salisbury Cathedral; gentleman of the Chapel Royal, 1783; composed church music, anthems, and glees. [xii. 217]

CORK, EARLS OF. [See BOYLE, RICHARD, first EARL, 1566–1643; BOYLE, RICHARD, second EARL, 1612–1697; BOYLE, RICHARD, fourth EARL, 1695–1753; BOYLE, JOHN, fifth EARL, 1707–1762.]

CORK, COUNTESS OF (1746–1840). [See MONCKTON, MARY.]

CORKER, JAMES or MAURUS (1636–1715), Benedictine monk; a Yorkshireman; embraced Romanism; Roman catholic chaplain in England, 1665–77; arrested, 1678; sentenced to death, 1680; released, 1685; built a monastery at Clerkenwell; received at court as envoy from Cologne, 1688; abbot of Lambspring, Germany, 1690–6; lived in London, 1696–1715; published memoirs of Viscount Stafford and other 'popish plot' victims, 1681–3, and theological tracts, 1680–1710. [xii. 217]

CORMAC MAC ART, also known as CORMAC UA CUINN and CORMAC ULFADA (d. 260), king of Ireland; procured the murder of Lugaid Mac Con, 217, and of Fergus Dubhdeadach, 218, and so became king, 218; frequently at war with the tribal chiefs; once an exile in Scotland; introduced the first water-mill into Ireland; abdicated, 254; composed laws in retirement at Skreen, near Tara; said to have become a Christian; buried at Ros na righ. [xii. 219]

CORMAC, PRESBYTER (6th cent.) [See CORBMAC.]

CORMAC (836–908), king of Cashel; son of Cuilennan; chief bishop in Leth Mogha; became king of Cashel, 900;

defeated Flann, king of Ireland, at Tullamore, 906; routed and slain by Flann; traditional author of 'Sanas Chormaic,' an ancient glossary (printed, 1862). [xii. 221]

CORMACK, SIR JOHN ROSE (1815–1882), physician; M.D. Edinburgh, 1837; M.D. university of France, 1870; physician to Edinburgh Infirmary, c. 1840–5; practitioner in London, 1847–66, and in Paris, 1869–82; knighted, 1872; wrote on medical subjects. [xii. 221]

CORNBURY, VISCOUNT (1710–1753). [See HYDE, HENRY.]

CORNELISZ, LUCAS (1495–1552?), painter; son and pupil of Cornelis Engelbrechtsen, a Leyden artist; called also DE KOK, as being a cook; painted in oil and distemper; came to London, c. 1527; designer for tapestry works at Ferrara, 1535–47. [xii. 221]

CORNELIUS À SANCTO PATRICIO (fl. 1650). [See MAHONY, CONNOR, CORNELIUS, or CONSTANTINE.]

CORNELIUS, JOHN (1557–1594), jesuit; of Irish descent; fellow of Exeter College, Oxford, 1575–8; withdrew to Rheims, and, 1580, to Rome; Roman catholic chaplain in England, 1583; arrested and executed, 1594. [xii. 222]

CORNELYS, THERESA (1723–1797), ball-manager; née Imer; daughter of an actor; born at Venice; married Pompeati, a dancer; directress of theatres in the Austrian Netherlands, as Mme. Trenti; as Mme. Pompeati, sang in London, 1746 and 1761; as Mme. Cornelys, at Carlisle House, Soho Square, gave subscription balls and masquerades, 1760–72, and concerts, 1764–72; bankrupt, 1772; hotel keeper at Southampton, 1774–6; lived obscurely as a huckstress, under name of Smith; died in the Fleet. [xii. 223]

CORNER, GEORGE RICHARD (1801–1863), antiquary; a London solicitor; F.S.A., 1833; vestry clerk of St. Olave's, Southwark, 1835; contributed papers, chiefly on Southwark antiquities, to archæological journals, 1834–60. [xii. 225]

CORNER, JOHN (fl. 1788–1825), engraver; issued 'Portraits of Celebrated Painters,' 1816. [xii. 225]

CORNER, JULIA (1798–1875), writer for the young; published educational works, stories, and plays. [Suppl. ii. 62]

CORNETO, ADRIAN DE (1460?–1521?). [See ADRIAN DE CASTELLO.]

CORNEWALL, CHARLES (1669–1718), vice-admiral; spelt his name CORNWALL, from May 1709; entered navy, 1683; commanded ship in Mediterranean, 1693–6 and 1705–8; M.P., 1708–9; comptroller of the navy, 1714; rear-admiral, 1716; commanded against Sallee corsairs, 1716–17; vice-admiral, 1717; second in command off Cape Passaro, 1718; died at Lisbon. [xii. 226]

CORNEWALL, FOLLIOTT HERBERT WALKER (1754–1831), bishop of Worcester; M.A. St. John's College, Cambridge, 1780; chaplain to House of Commons, 1780; D.D.; canon of Windsor, 1784; dean of Canterbury, 1792; bishop successively of Bristol, 1797, Exeter, 1803, and Worcester, 1808–31; published sermons. [xii. 227]

CORNEWALL, JAMES (1699–1744), navy captain; captain, 1724; served on North American station, 1724–8, off Morocco coast, 1732–4, off Guinea coast, 1737–8, and in Mediterranean, 1741–3; killed in action off Toulon. [xii. 227]

CORNEY, BOLTON (1784–1870), critic; ensign, 1803; clerk at Greenwich Hospital; very deaf, and a literary recluse; wrote on the Bayeux tapestry, 1836; criticised D'Israeli's 'Curiosities of Literature,' 1837, and the 'General Biographical Dictionary' of Hugh James Rose, 1839; contributed to literary journals. [xii. 227]

CORNHILL, WILLIAM OF (d. 1223), bishop of Coventry and Lichfield; one of King John's clerks; an officer of the exchequer, 1204; rector of Maidstone, 1205; justiciar, 1208; bishop of Coventry and Lichfield, 1215; much employed by King John and faithful to him to the last; supported Henry III; benefactor of Lichfield Cathedral. [xii. 228]

CORNISH, HENRY (d. 1685), alderman of London; presbyterian and whig; elected sheriff of London, 1680, against the strongest court pressure; took leading part in petition for a session of parliament, 1681; witness in favour of Edward Fitzharris, 1681 ; one of the committee to protect the city charter, 1682 ; prosecuted, 1682, for inciting riots (condemned, and fined, May 1683) ; unsuccessful candidate, through court intrigue, for the lord mayorship, 1682 ; condemned and executed for alleged implication (1683) in the Rye House plot ; his attainder reversed by parliament, 1689. [xii. 229]

CORNISH, JOSEPH (1750–1823), nonconformist divine ; entered Hoxton Academy, 1767 ; adopted Arian views ; minister, 1772–1823, and private schoolmaster, 1782–1819, at Colyton, Devonshire ; published pamphlets and tracts, 1772–90, and histories 'of the Puritans,' 1772, and 'of Nonconformity,' 1797. [xii. 230]

CORNISH, SIR SAMUEL (d. 1770), vice-admiral ; lieutenant, 1739 ; served at Cartagena, 1741, and in the Mediterranean, 1742–4 ; rear-admiral, 1759 ; took Manila and the Philippines, 1762 ; vice-admiral, October 1762 ; created baronet, 1766. [xii. 231]

CORNWALL, EARLS OF. [See RICHARD, 1209–1272 ; EDMUND, second EARL, 1250–1300 ; GAVESTON, PIERS, d. 1312 ; JOHN, 1316–1336.]

CORNWALL, BARRY (1787–1874). [See PROCTER, BRYAN WALLER.]

CORNWALL, CHARLES WOLFRAN (1735–1789), politician ; educated at Winchester ; barrister, Gray's Inn ; M.P., 1768–89 ; speaker of the House of Commons, 1780–9. [xii. 232]

CORNWALL, HENRY OF (1235–1271). [See HENRY.]

CORNWALL, JOHN OF (fl. 1170). [See JOHN.]

CORNWALL, CAROLINE FRANCES (1786–1858), authoress ; lived much in Italy ; friend of Sismondi ; published 'Philosophical Theories,' 1842, and other 'small books on great subjects' ; contributed to journals ; her 'Letters' published, 1864. [xii. 233]

CORNWALLIS, SIR CHARLES (d. 1629), diplomatist ; second son of Sir Thomas Cornwallis [q. v.] ; knighted, 1603 ; ambassador in Spain, 1605–9 ; treasurer of the household to Prince Henry, 1610–12 ; a commissioner on Irish affairs, 1613 ; imprisoned in the Tower for hostility to the Scots, 1614 ; wrote memoir of Prince Henry, 1626. [xii. 234]

CORNWALLIS, CHARLES, first MARQUIS and second EARL CORNWALLIS (1738–1805), governor-general of India ; educated at Eton ; styled Viscount Brome from June 1753–62 ; ensign, 1756 ; aide-de-camp to the Marquis of Granby in Germany, 1758–9 ; M.P., 1760 ; lieutenant-colonel, 1761 ; served in Germany, 1761–2 ; succeeded as second Earl Cornwallis, 1762 ; acted with the whig peers, 1765–9 ; constable of the Tower, 1770–83, and 1785–1805 ; major-general, 1775 ; sent out with reinforcements to North America, 1776 ; given command of the reserve division ; subdued New Jersey, 1776 ; occupied Philadelphia, 1777 ; given the second command in America, 1778, but kept inactive by Sir Henry Clinton's [q. v.] supineness ; left in command at Charleston, 1780 ; invaded Virginia, 1781 ; ordered to hold Yorktown, but forced to capitulate, 1781 ; petitioned to be governor-general and commander-in-chief in India, to reform abuses, 1782, 1785, and 1786 ; took command at Calcutta, 1786 ; spent three years in reforming the civil and military administration ; took command against Tippoo Sultan, at Madras, 1790 ; took Bangalore, 1791 ; defeated Tippoo near Seringapatam, 1791 ; fell back on Bangalore ; invested Seringapatam, 1792 ; dictated terms of peace to Tippoo ; created Marquis Cornwallis, 1792 ; tried to settle Bengal by making the zemindars owners of the soil, 1793 ; reorganised the law courts ; general, 1793 ; resigned office, October 1793 ; reached England, 1794 ; despatched to the continent to encourage the allied forces, 1794 ; master-general of the ordnance, 1795–1801 ; was named governor-general of India, 1797, but did not take up the appointment ; appointed viceroy and commander-in-chief in Ireland, 1798, to crush an expected rebellion ; ordered the arrest of the ringleaders, and forced the French under Humbert to capitulate, 1798 ; supported Castlereagh in carrying the act of union by bribery, 1799–1800 ; resigned office, 1801, in consequence of the king's refusal to grant catholic emancipation ; negotiated the unfavourable treaty of Amiens, 1801–2 ; sent to India to try to conclude a lasting peace with the native powers, 1805 ; took command at Calcutta, 1805, but died the same year at Ghazipore. [xii. 234]

CORNWALLIS, CHARLES, second MARQUIS CORNWALLIS (1774–1823), only son of Charles Cornwallis, first marquis [q. v.] ; styled Viscount Brome ; styled Earl Cornwallis after August 1792 ; succeeded as second marquis, 1805. [xii. 241]

CORNWALLIS, FREDERICK (1713–1783), archbishop of Canterbury ; younger son of Charles, fourth Baron Cornwallis ; educated at Eton ; B.A. Christ's College, Cambridge, 1736 ; fellow ; D.D., 1748 ; beneficed in Suffolk and Norfolk, 1740 ; canon of Windsor, 1746 ; bishop of Lichfield and Coventry, 1750 , dean of St. Paul's, 1766 ; archbishop of Canterbury, 1768 ; noted for his hospitality at Lambeth ; published four sermons. [xii. 241]

CORNWALLIS, JAMES, fourth EARL CORNWALLIS (1742–1824), bishop ; third son of Charles, first earl Cornwallis ; educated at Eton ; B.A. Christ Church, Oxford, 1763 ; fellow of Merton ; M.A., 1769 ; a pluralist rector in Kent, 1769–81 ; D.C.L., 1775 ; dean of Salisbury, 1775 ; bishop of Lichfield and Coventry, 1781–1824 ; dean of Windsor, 1791 ; dean of Durham, 1794 ; succeeded as fourth Earl Cornwallis, 1823 ; published five sermons. [xii. 242]

CORNWALLIS, JANE, LADY CORNWALLIS (1581–1659), née Meautys ; second wife of Sir William Cornwallis, of Brome, Suffolk, 1608–11 ; afterwards wife of Sir Nathaniel Bacon, of Culford, Suffolk, 1613 ; her 'Correspondence' (1613–44) published, 1842. [xii. 242]

CORNWALLIS, SIR THOMAS (1519–1604), diplomatist ; of Brome Hall, Suffolk ; knighted, 1548 ; sent against the Norfolk insurgents, 1549 ; sheriff of Norfolk and Suffolk, 1553 ; commissioner to treat with Scotland, 1553 ; sent to escort Princess Elizabeth to London, 1554 ; commissioner for trial of Sir Thomas Wyatt, 1554 ; treasurer of Calais, 1554–7 ; popularly supposed to have sold Calais to France ; comptroller of the household, 1557–8 ; M.P., Suffolk, 1558 ; catholic recusant. [xii. 242]

CORNWALLIS, THOMAS (1663–1731), commissioner of lotteries ; a younger son of Charles, second baron Cornwallis ; educated at Cambridge, 1676 ; officer in the guards ; devised parliamentary lotteries, 1709. [xii. 244]

CORNWALLIS, SIR WILLIAM (d. 1631 ?), essayist ; son of Sir Charles Cornwallis [q. v.] ; knighted, 1602 ; published essays, 1600–17. [xii. 244]

CORNWALLIS, SIR WILLIAM (1744–1819), admiral ; a younger son of Charles, first earl Cornwallis ; entered navy, 1755 ; commander, 1762 ; in constant service, 1755–87, taking part in the actions off Grenada, 1779, St. Kitts, 1782, and Dominica, 1782 ; commander-in-chief in East India waters, 1789–93 ; rear-admiral, 1793 ; vice-admiral, 1794 ; brought his squadron off safely on meeting a great French fleet, 1795 ; quarrelled with the admiralty, 1796 ; admiral, 1799 ; commanded Channel fleet, 1801 and 1803–6 ; G.C.B., 1815. [xii. 244]

CORNYSSHE, WILLIAM (d. 1524 ?), musician ; member of the Chapel Royal, 1493, and master of the chapel children, 1509–22 ; composed music for, and acted in court pageants for Henry VII and Henry VIII ; imprisoned in the Fleet for satirising Sir Richard Empson [q. v.], 1504 ; forced Wolsey to give up one of his choristers to the Chapel Royal, 1518 ; attended Henry VIII to France, 1518 ; obtained corrodies in Thetford and Malmesbury monasteries, 1523. Little of his music has survived. [xii. 247]

CORPRE CROMM, i.e. Corpre the bent, SAINT (d. 900) ; confused in the 'Martyrology of Donegal' with Corpre Cromm, an Irish prince (fl. 540) ; commemorated on 6 March ; son of Decill ; became abbot of Clonmacnois, 886 ; harassed by Connaughtmen, 895. [xii. 249]

CORRANUS, ANTONIO DE (1527–1591). [See CORRO.]

CORRI, DOMENICO (1746–1825), musician ; member of orchestras at Rome, 1756 ; pupil of Porpora at Naples, 1763–7 ; conductor of concerts in Edinburgh, singing-master, and (in partnership with Natale Corri, his brother) music publisher, 1771–87 ; published Scottish and English songs, 'Country Dances,' 1797, 'Art of Fingering,' a 'Musical Dictionary,' 1798, and 'Singer's Preceptor,' 1810 ; produced two successful operas, 1774 and 1806 ; insane in later life. [xii. 250]

CORRIE, ARCHIBALD (1777–1857), agriculturist; gardener in Edinburgh, 1797; estate manager in Perthshire; wrote on agriculture in the journals.   [xii. 251]

CORRIE, DANIEL (1777–1837), bishop of Madras; educated at Cambridge; disciple of Charles Simeon [q. v.]; Bengal chaplain, 1806–15; senior chaplain at Calcutta, 1817; LL.D.; archdeacon of Calcutta, 1823; bishop of Madras, 1835.   [xii. 251]

CORRIE, GEORGE ELWES (1793–1885), divine; B.A. St. Catharine's College, Cambridge, 1817; tutor, 1817–49; Norrisian professor of divinity, 1838–54; master of Jesus College, Cambridge, 1849, and rector of Newton, Cambridgeshire, 1851–85; wrote papers on English church history; edited works of Anglican theology.   [xii. 251]

CORRIGAN, SIR DOMINIC JOHN (1802–1880), physician; born in Dublin; M.D. Edinburgh, 1825; acquired the leading practice in Dublin; created baronet, 1866; M.P., Dublin city, 1870–4; published medical tracts.   [xii. 252]

CORRO, ANTONIO DE, otherwise CORRANUS and BELLERIVE (1527–1591), theologian; born at Seville; a Spanish monk; adopted protestantism, 1557; resided in France and Flanders, 1558–68; doctor of a foreign university; came to London, 1568; by Cecil's influence, was pastor of the Spanish congregation, London, 1568–70, and Latin divinity lecturer at the Temple, 1571–4; by Leicester's influence, was lecturer on divinity in Oxford, 1578–86; prebendary of St. Paul's, 1585; accused of heresy; published theological treatises, 1567–79; compiled a Spanish grammar, 1590.   [xii. 253]

CORRY, HENRY THOMAS LOWRY (1803–1873), politician; second son of Somerset Corry, second earl of Belmore; B.A. Christ Church, Oxford, 1823; M.P., Tyrone, 1826–73; junior lord, 1841–5, secretary, 1845–6 and 1858–9, and first lord, 1867–8, of the admiralty.   [xii. 254]

CORRY, ISAAC (1755–1813), Irish politician; educated at Trinity College, Dublin; M.P., Newry, in the Irish parliament, 1776–1800; attached to the government as surveyor of the ordnance in Ireland, 1788, and a commissioner of revenue, 1789–98; chancellor of the Irish exchequer, 1798–1804; surveyor of Irish crown lands, 1799–1813; chief government speaker in favour of the union, 1799–1800; fought a duel with Henry Grattan, 1800; M.P., 1800–4.   [xii. 255]

CORRY, JOHN (*fl.* 1825), topographer; journalist in Dublin, and, 1792, in London; published, 1782–1820, verses, tales, and memoirs, and, 1810–25, histories of Liverpool, Bristol, Macclesfield, and Lancashire.   [xii. 256]

CORSER, THOMAS (1793–1876), bibliographer; educated at Manchester grammar school, 1808–12; M.A. Balliol College, Oxford, 1818; rector of Stand, near Manchester, 1826, and non-resident vicar of Norton, near Daventry, 1828–76; F.S.A., 1850; collected a fine library of early English poetry, described in 'Collectanea Anglo-Poetica,' 1860–80.   [xii. 256]

CORT, HENRY (1740–1800), ironmaster; navy agent in London, 1765–75; bought premises near Fareham, Hampshire, in which to carry on processes (patented 1783–4) for purifying iron by 'puddling'; ruined, 1789, by the prosecution of his partner, Adam Jellicoe, for embezzlement of naval funds; pensioned, 1794.   [xii. 257]

CORVUS, JOANNES (*fl.* 1512–1544), painter; real name Jan Rave, of Bruges; came to England. His portraits include Bishop Richard Fox (after 1522) and the Princess Mary, 1544.   [xii. 258]

CORY, ISAAC PRESTON (1802–1842), miscellaneous writer; fellow of Caius College, Cambridge; M.A., 1827.   [xii. 258]

CORY, WILLIAM JOHNSON (1823–1892), poet and master at Eton; son of Charles Johnson of Torrington; educated at Eton and King's College, Cambridge; won chancellor's medal for English poem, 1843; fellow, 1845–72; B.A., 1845; assistant master at Eton, 1845–72; assumed name of Cory and retired from fellowship and mastership, 1872; published educational works, besides several volumes of poems, some of which give him a permanent place among English lyrists.   [Suppl. ii. 62]

CORYATE, GEORGE (*d.* 1607), divine; educated at Winchester; fellow of New College, Oxford, 1560–70;

M.A., 1569; rector of Odcombe, Somerset, 1570–1607; prebendary of York, 1594; wrote copies of Latin verses to the nobility.   [xii. 258]

CORYATE, THOMAS (1577?–1617), traveller; son of George Coryate [q. v.]; entered Gloucester Hall, Oxford, 1596; a buffoon at court; of Prince Henry's household; travelled, mainly on foot, through France to Venice, and thence by Switzerland, Germany, and Holland to London, 1608; published his narrative, 'Coryats Crudities,' with commendatory verses from the wits, and two appendices, 'Coryats Crambe' and 'The Odcombian Banquet,' 1611; visited Constantinople (1612), Asia Minor, Greece, and Egypt; travelled through Palestine, Mesopotamia, and Persia, to India, reaching Agra, October 1616; died at Surat; some 'letters' from him published, 1616 and 1618.   [xii. 259]

CORYTON, WILLIAM (*d.* 1651), politician; vice-warden of the stannaries, 1603–27 and 1630–40; M.P., 1623–9; imprisoned, 1627–8, for refusing to pay the forced loan, and, 1629–30, for abetting Sir John Eliot (2 March 1629); M.P., 1640, in the Short parliament; elected to the Long parliament, but unseated and dismissed from his employments for malpractices.   [xii. 261]

COSBY, ALEXANDER (*fl.* 1580), soldier; eldest son of Francis Cosby [q. v.]; killed in skirmish with the Irish.   [xii. 262]

COSBY, ARNOLD (*fl.* 1580), soldier; second son of Francis Cosby [q. v.]; served in Flanders, 1587.   [xii. 262]

COSBY, FRANCIS (*d.* 1580), Irish general; served against the Irish, 1548–58; granted Stradbally Abbey, Queen's County, 1562; assisted in slaughter of the O'Mores, 1567; killed in battle.   [xii. 262]

COSBY, SIR HENRY AUGUSTUS MONTAGU (1743–1822), lieutenant-general; volunteer at the taking of Gheria, 1756; in active service at Madras, 1760–75, becoming lieutenant-colonel, 1773; commander of the nawáb of Arcot's cavalry, 1778; served against Haidar Ali, 1780; invalided to England, 1782; knighted; left India, 1786; lieutenant-general, 1822.   [xii. 262]

COSBY, PHILLIPS (1727?–1808), admiral; born in Nova Scotia; entered navy, 1745; commander, 1760; on active service, 1745–70; receiver-general of St. Kitts, 1771–8; on the North American station, 1779–81; held Mediterranean command, 1786–9; rear-admiral, 1790; admiral, 1799.   [xii. 263]

COSIN or COSYN, EDMUND (*fl.* 1558), vice-chancellor of Cambridge; B.A. King's Hall, Cambridge, 1535; fellow; M.A., 1541; vicar of Grendon, Northamptonshire, 1538–41; fellow of Trinity College, Cambridge, 1546; B.D., 1547; a strong catholic; master of St. Catharine's Hall; pluralist in Norfolk and (1558–60) vice-chancellor of Cambridge; resigned his preferments, 1560; went abroad, 1568.   [xii. 264]

COSIN, JOHN (1594–1672), bishop of Durham; fellow of Caius College, Cambridge; chaplain to Overall, bishop of Lichfield; friend of Laud and Richard Montague; prebendary of Durham, 1624, archdeacon of the East Riding, 1625, and rector of Elwick and Brancepeth, Durham, 1626; defended Montague's 'Appello Cæsarem,' 1626; compiled, by request of Charles I, 'Collection of Private Devotions,' 1627; at once accused of Romanist leanings; introduced ornate ornaments and services into Durham Cathedral, 1627–33; D.D., 1628; procured the ejection of Peter Smart, puritan prebendary of Durham, 1628; was appointed master of Peterhouse, Cambridge, 1635, where he introduced ornate chapel ornaments and services; vice-chancellor of Cambridge, 1639, and dean of Peterborough, 1640; accused by Smart to the Long parliament, and deprived of his benefices, 1641; sent Peterhouse plate to Charles I, 1642; ejected from the mastership, 1644; chaplain to the Anglican royalists at Paris, 1642–60; wrote, but did not publish, a treatise against Romanism (published 1675), and, 1652, an explanation of Anglicanism (published 1707); resumed his ecclesiastical preferments, 1660; bishop of Durham, 1660; member of the Savoy conference, 1661; proposed several slight changes in the liturgy, 1661; visited his diocese, 1661–2; used his ex-officio powers as lord-lieutenant of Durham to employ the militia to drive nonconformists to church, sold the offices in his patronage, and was most exacting in levying dues to provide money for his buildings at

Auckland and Durham, for the library at Durham, for scholarships at Cambridge, for provision for his family, and for general charity ; published 'History of the Canon of Scripture,' 1657 ; his collected works published, 1843-55, and his correspondence, 1868-70. [xii. 264]

COSIN, RICHARD (1549 ?-1597), civilian ; fellow of Trinity College, Cambridge ; LL.D., 1580 ; dean of the arches, 1583 ; M.P., 1586-9 ; a master in chancery, 1588 ; published treatises on ecclesiastical law. [xii. 271]

COSPATRIC, EARL OF NORTHUMBERLAND (*fl.* 1067). [See GOSPATRIC.]

COSTA, EMANUEL MENDES DA (1717-1791), naturalist ; son of a London Jew ; studied conchology and collected fossils ; F.R.S., 1747-63 ; imprisoned, 1767-72 ; published treatises on fossils and shells, 1757-78.
[xii. 271]

COSTA, SIR MICHAEL (1810-1884), composer ; born and trained at Naples ; composed for Italian theatres, 1825-9 ; employed at the King's Theatre, London, 1830-46, reforming the orchestra, 1832, and producing four ballets and two operas, 1831-44 ; director of music at Covent Garden Theatre from 1846 ; conductor of the Philharmonic concerts, 1847-54 ; conducted the festivals at Birmingham, 1849-79, and Leeds, 1874-80, and the Handel festivals, 1857-77 ; produced two oratorios, 'Eli,' 1855, and ' Naaman,' 1864 ; knighted, 1869 ; director of the Italian opera from 1871. [xii. 272]

COSTARD, GEORGE (1710-1782), astronomical writer ; fellow of Wadham College, Oxford ; M.A., 1733 ; vicar of Whitchurch, Dorset ; vicar of Twickenham, 1764-82 ; published tracts on biblical criticism, 1733-52, and treatises on the history of astronomy, especially in antiquity, 1746-67. [xii. 274]

COSTE, PIERRE (1668-1747), translator ; a Frenchman ; Huguenot minister at Amsterdam, 1690 ; translated two of Locke's tracts into French ; French tutor in England ; translated Locke's 'Essay,' under Locke's supervision, 1697 ; translated Newton's 'Optics' ; annotated French standard authors. [xii. 275]

COSTELEY, GUILLAUME (1531-1606), composer of French chansons, published 1554-97 ; of Scottish extraction ; organist to Henry II and Charles IX of France ; lived at Evreux, 1571-1606. [xii. 276]

COSTELLO, DUDLEY (1803-1865), journalist ; of Irish extraction ; ensign, 1821 ; stationed at Bermuda, 1824-8 ; copyist of illuminated manuscripts at Paris ; lived in London, 1833-8 ; foreign correspondent of London journals ; wrote for periodicals, pensioned, 1861 ; published novels and notes of travel, 1845-61. [xii. 276]

COSTELLO, LOUISA STUART (1799-1870), artist and author ; sister of Dudley Costello [q. v.] ; miniature-painter in Paris, 1814, and London ; copyist of illuminated manuscripts ; pensioned, 1852 ; lived latterly at Boulogne ; published poems, 1815-56, 'Specimens of the Early Poetry of France,' 1835, notes of travel, 1840-6, novels, and memoirs, 1844-55. [xii. 277]

COSTELLO, WILLIAM BIRMINGHAM (1800-1867), surgeon ; native of Dublin ; M.D. ; practitioner in London, 1832 ; withdrew to Paris ; wrote on medical topics.
[xii. 277]

COSWAY, MARIA CECILIA LOUISA (*fl.* 1820), miniature-painter ; *née* Hadfield ; born in Florence ; of English extraction ; educated in Rome ; miniature-painter in London of portraits and mythological subjects ; first exhibited, 1781 ; married, 1781, Richard Cosway [q. v.] ; lived much abroad ; a prolific etcher and book-illustrator.
[xii. 278]

COSWAY, RICHARD (1740-1821), painter ; art-student in London ; drawing-master ; designer of snuff-box lids ; dealer in old pictures ; R.A., 1771 ; in great request as portrait-painter in oil and miniature ; a favourite of the prince regent ; his art collection sold, 1822 ; a folio volume of his designs published by his widow, Florence, 1826. [xii. 279]

COSWORTH or **COSOWARTH**, MICHAEL (*fl.* 1600), metrical translator of psalms ; of Cornish family ; B.A. St. John's College, Cambridge, 1580. [xii. 280]

COTES, FRANCIS (1725 ?-1770), portrait-painter in crayons and oil ; of Irish extraction ; R.A. ; worked in London and Bath. [xii. 281]

COTES, ROGER (1682-1716), mathematician ; educated at St. Paul's School ; fellow of Trinity College, Cambridge, 1705 ; M.A., 1706 ; Plumian professor of astronomy, 1706 ; helped Newton in the reissue of the 'Principia,' 1709-13 ; F.R.S., 1711 ; published 'Logometria,' a treatise on ratios, 1713 ; partially observed the total solar eclipse, April 1715 ; his mathematical papers published, 1722 and 1738, and his correspondence, 1850. [xii. 282]

COTES, SAMUEL (1734-1818), miniature-painter ; taught by his brother, Francis Cotes [q. v.] ; executed crayon portraits and miniatures on enamel and ivory ; exhibited, 1760-89 ; fellow of the Incorporated Society of Artists. [xii. 284]

COTGRAVE, JOHN (*fl.* 1655), author of 'The English Treasury . . . of . . . Dramatick Poems,' and ' Wit's Interpreter,' 1655. [xii. 284]

COTGRAVE, RANDLE (*d.* 1634 ?), compiler of the French-English dictionary, 1611 (second edition, 1632) ; scholar of St. John's College, Cambridge, 1587 ; secretary to William Cecil, afterwards second Earl of Exeter.
[xii. 285]

COTMAN, JOHN SELL (1782-1842), landscape-painter, chiefly in water-colours ; art-student in London, 1798 ; exhibited in London, 1800-6 ; drawing-master in Norwich, 1807-34 ; painted portraits and landscapes ; etched plates of buildings and antiquities, chiefly in Norfolk, 1811-39 ; published, 1822, etchings of ' Architectural Antiquities of Normandy,' taken 1817-20 ; exhibited again in London, 1825-39 ; drawing-master in King's College, London, 1834-42. [xii. 285]

COTMAN, JOSEPH JOHN (1814-1878), landscape-painter ; son of John Sell Cotman [q. v.] ; drawing-master in Norwich, 1836 ; became mentally deranged. [xii. 287]

COTMAN, MILES EDMUND (1810-1858), landscape-painter and etcher ; eldest son of John Sell Cotman [q. v.] ; drawing-master in Norwich, 1834, and in London, 1836-c. 1845 ; exhibited river and sea views in oil- and water colours, 1835-56. [xii. 288]

COTTA or **COTTEY**, JOHN (1575 ?-1650 ?), physician ; scholar of Trinity College, Cambridge, 1590-6 ; M.A. Corpus Christi College, Cambridge, 1597 ; M.D., 1603 ; practised medicine in Northampton, 1603 till death ; published 'Discoverie of . . . Ignorant Practisers of Physicke,' 1611, 'The Triall of Witchcraft,' 1616, and ' Cotta contra Antonium,' 1623 (against Francis Anthony [q. v.])
[xii. 288]

COTTAM, THOMAS (1549-1582), jesuit ; born in Lancashire ; M.A. Brasenose College, Oxford, 1572 ; schoolmaster in London ; embraced Roman catholicism ; withdrew to Douay ; afterwards lived at Rome and at Rheims ; joined the jesuits ; imprisoned in London, 1580-2 ; executed at Tyburn. [xii. 288]

COTTENHAM, EARL OF (1781-1851). [See PEPYS CHARLES CHRISTOPHER.]

COTTER, GEORGE SACKVILLE (1755-1831), translator ; educated at Westminster School, and, 1771, Peterhouse, Cambridge ; M.A., 1779 ; beneficed in co. Cork, Ireland ; published poems, 1788 ; translated Terence, 1826, and Plautus, 1827. [xii. 289]

COTTER, PATRICK (1761 ?-1806), Irish giant ; born at Kinsale ; a bricklayer ; exhibited himself in Great Britain as O'BRIEN, 1779-1804 ; his height sometimes given as over eight feet. [xii. 289]

COTTERELL, SIR CHARLES (1612 ?-1702), courtier ; knighted, 1644 ; master of the ceremonies, 1641-9 ; at Antwerp, 1649-52 ; steward at the Hague to Elizabeth, queen of Bohemia, 1652-4 ; secretary to Henry, duke of Gloucester, 1655-60 ; master of the ceremonies, 1660-86 ; master of requests, 1670-86 ; M.P., Cardigan, 1663-78 ; translated French romances and histories, and ' The Spiritual Year,' a Spanish devotional tract. [xii. 290]

COTTERELL, SIR CHARLES LODOWICK (1654-1710), courtier ; son of Sir Charles Cotterell [q. v.] ; LL.D. Trinity College, Cambridge ; knighted, 1687 ; master of the ceremonies, 1686-1710 ; published memoir of Prince George of Denmark, 1708. [xii. 291]

COTTERELL, SIR CLEMENT (*d.* 1758), courtier ; son of Sir Charles Lodowick Cotterell [q. v.] ; knighted, 1710 ; master of the ceremonies, 1710-58 ; assumed the name DORMER, 1741, on inheriting Rousham, Oxfordshire.
[xii. 291]

COTTERELL, WILLIAM (*d.* 1744), bishop in Ireland; son of Sir Charles Lodowick Cotterell [q. v.]; dean of Raphoe, 1725; D.D. Oxford, 1733; bishop of Ferns and Leighlin, 1743. [xii. 291]

COTTESFORD, THOMAS (*d.* 1555), protestant divine; M.A. Cambridge; imprisoned as a protestant, 1541; resigned rectories at Walpole, Norfolk, 1544; vicar of Littlebury, Essex, 1545; rector of St. Martin's, Ludgate, 1553, but withdrew to the continent; died at Frankfort; published theological and devotional tracts, 1543–53. [xii. 291]

COTTESLOE, BARON (1798–1890). [See FREMANTLE, THOMAS FRANCIS.]

COTTINGHAM, LEWIS NOCKALLS (1787–1847), architect; builder's apprentice at Ipswich; architect in London, 1814; much employed in restoration of churches; published drawings of Westminster Abbey and Hall, and other architectural treatises. [xii. 292]

COTTINGHAM, NOCKALLS JOHNSON (1823–1854), architect; elder son of Lewis Nockalls Cottingham [q. v.]; drowned at sea. [xii. 293]

COTTINGTON, FRANCIS, BARON COTTINGTON (1578?–1652), diplomatist; attached to Sir Charles Cornwallis's embassy at Madrid, 1605–9; English agent at Madrid, 1609–11; consul at Seville, 1612; clerk of the council, 1613–16; again envoy to Spain, 1616–18; secretary to Charles, prince of Wales, 1622; created baronet, 1623; ordered to accompany Prince Charles to Madrid, 1623; professed Romanism there; a leader of the party favourable to Spain; dismissed from court by Buckingham's influence, 1623; privy councillor, 1628; chancellor of the exchequer, 1629–42; ambassador to Spain to conclude peace, 1629–31; created Baron Cottington, 1631; a commissioner on Irish affairs, 1634; master of the court of wards, 1635–41; a commissioner of the treasury, then in conflict with Laud, 1635–6; a commissioner on Scottish affairs, 1638; built Hanworth House, Middlesex; constable of the Tower, 1640; joined Charles I at Oxford, 1643; lord treasurer, 1643; went to Rouen, 1646; joined Prince Charles at the Hague, 1648; unsuccessful in an embassy to Spain to raise money for Prince Charles, 1649; embraced Roman catholicism and settled at Valladolid, 1651; died at Valladolid. [xii. 293]

COTTISFORD, JOHN (*d.* 1540?), vice-chancellor of Oxford; B.A. Oxford, 1505; fellow of Lincoln College, 1509–18, and rector, 1519–39; D.D., 1525; vice-chancellor, 1527–32; directed to suppress protestant heresy; arrested Thomas Garret [q. v.], 1528; canon of Henry VIII's Oxford college, 1532; prebendary of Lincoln, 1538. [xii. 296]

COTTLE, AMOS SIMON (1768?–1800), translator; B.A. Magdalene College, Cambridge, 1799; wrote verses; translated, in metre, the Edda of Saemund, 1797. [xii. 296]

COTTLE, JOSEPH (1770–1853), author; bookseller in Bristol, 1791–9; met Coleridge and Southey, 1794; brought out Coleridge's 'Poems' and Southey's 'Joan of Arc,' 1796, and Coleridge and Wordsworth's 'Lyrical Ballads,' 1798; published verses and essays, 1798–1829, and 'Early Recollections' of Coleridge and Southey, 1837. [xii. 296]

COTTON, SIR ARTHUR THOMAS (1803–1899), general, and irrigation engineer; studied at East India Company's college, Addiscombe; obtained commission in Madras engineers, 1819; assistant engineer in Madras, 1821; accompanied expeditionary force to Burmah, 1824; placed in charge, 1828, of irrigation works in Tanjore, which he greatly extended and improved by construction of anicuts on the Coleroon, 1835–6; constructed an anicut across Godávery river below Rájahmundry for irrigation of Godávery district, 1847–52; subsequently projected the anicut on the Krishna river, the construction of which was carried out by Major-general Charles Orr; knighted, 1861; second class K.C.S.I., 1866; retired from government service, 1862, but continued to give his attention to irrigation schemes; retired from army with rank of general, 1877. [Suppl. ii. 63]

COTTON, BARTHOLOMEW DE (*d.* 1298?), historian; monk of Norwich; compiled 'Historia Anglicana,' in which the events of 1291–8 seem to be described from personal knowledge. [xii. 298]

COTTON, CHARLES (1630–1687), poet; of Beresford, Staffordshire; travelled; single copies of his verses printed (1649–74), but they circulated chiefly in manuscript; became deeply involved in debt; army captain in Ireland, 1670; published burlesques of Virgil, 1664, and of Lucian, 1675, and translations from the French, 1667–74; reputed author of 'The Complete Gamester,' 1674; published 'The Planter's Manual' of fruit-trees, 1675, a 'second part' of Walton's 'Complete Angler,' 1676, 'The Wonders of the Peak,' 1681, and a standard translation of Montaigne's 'Essays,' 1685; his poems collected, 1689, and his works, 1715. [xii. 298]

COTTON, SIR CHARLES (1753–1812), admiral; entered navy, 1772; commander, 1779; succeeded as fifth baronet of Madingley, Cambridgeshire, 1795; in active service, 1772–83, and 1793–1801; rear-admiral, 1797; vice-admiral, 1802; held command in Tagus, 1807–8, in Mediterranean, 1810; in command of Channel fleet, 1812. [xii. 301]

COTTON, GEORGE EDWARD LYNCH (1813–1866), bishop of Calcutta; educated at Westminster and Trinity College, Cambridge; a house-master at Rugby, 1837–52; head-master of Marlborough, 1852–8; D.D.; bishop of Calcutta, 1858; founded schools for poor European and Eurasian children; opposed presbyterian claim to use government churches; drowned in the Ganges. [xii. 302]

COTTON, HENRY (1789–1879), bibliographer and historian; at Westminster School, 1803–7; student of Christ Church, Oxford, 1807–19; M.A., 1813; D.C.L., 1820; sub-librarian of the Bodleian, 1814–22; treasurer of Christ Church, Dublin, 1832–72; titular dean of Lismore, 1834–72; became blind; published a bibliography (1505–1820) of the English bible, 1821, and a bibliography of English Roman catholic versions, 1855, 'Typographical Gazetteer,' 1824, 'Fasti Ecclesiæ Hibernicæ,' 1845–78, and other works. [xii. 304]

COTTON, SIR HENRY (1821–1892), judge; son of William Cotton (1786–1866) [q. v.]; educated at Eton and Christ Church, Oxford; B.A., 1843; called to bar at Lincoln's Inn, 1846; practised in equity courts; standing counsel to Bank of England; Q.C., 1866; standing counsel to Oxford University, 1872; appointed lord justice of appeal, sworn privy councillor, and knighted, 1877; honorary D.C.L. Oxford, 1877. [Suppl. ii. 67]

COTTON, JOHN (12th cent.?), author of a treatise on music (published 1784). [xii. 305]

COTTON, JOHN (1584–1652), nonconformist divine; M.A. Trinity College, Cambridge, 1606; fellow of Emmanuel College, *c.* 1607; later, was dean; B.D., 1613; vicar of Boston, Lincolnshire, 1612; temporarily suspended for disuse of the 'ceremonies,' 1615, but subsequently indulged in his nonconformity with James I's sanction; took theological pupils; cited for nonconformity by high commission court, 1633, resigned living, and sailed with Thomas Hooker [q. v.] and others for New England; joint-minister at Trimountain, the name of which town was at this time changed to Boston; rendered considerable assistance in consolidating the Massachusetts government. His numerous publications include sermons, works on church government, doctrinal questions, and controversial and expository treatises. [Suppl. ii. 67]

COTTON, SIR JOHN (1621–1701), eldest son of Sir Thomas Cotton [q. v.]; succeeded as third baronet, 1662; offered the Cottonian Library to the nation, 1700. [xii. 314]

COTTON, SIR JOHN (1679–1731), succeeded his grandfather [see COTTON, SIR JOHN, 1621–1701] as fourth baronet, 1701; transferred the Cottonian Library to the nation, 1702; M.P., Huntingdonshire, 1711. [xii. 314]

COTTON, SIR JOHN (*d.* 1752), son of Sir Robert Cotton [q. v.]; sixth and last baronet. [xii. 314]

COTTON, SIR JOHN HYNDE (*d.* 1752), Jacobite; succeeded (1712) as fourth baronet of Madingley, Cambridgeshire; M.A. Cambridge, 1705; M.P., 1708–52; a pronounced tory; forced on George II as treasurer of the chamber, 1744–6. [xii. 305]

COTTON, JOSEPH (1745–1825), mariner; son of Nathaniel Cotton [q. v.]; entered the navy, 1760; entered marine service of East India Company; an elder brother of the Trinity House, 1788–1808; a director of the East India Company, 1795–1823; compiled history of Trinity House, 1818. [xii. 306]

COTTON, NATHANIEL (1705–1788), physician; studied medicine at Leyden, 1729; medical practitioner and keeper of a lunatic asylum at St. Albans, 1740–88; wrote verses, which were collected and published, 1791. [xii. 307]

COTTON, RICHARD LYNCH (1794–1880), provost of Worcester College, Oxford; educated at the Charterhouse; B.A. Worcester College, Oxford, 1815, fellow, 1816–38, and provost, 1839–80; D.D., 1839; vicar of Denchworth, Berkshire, 1823–38; vice-chancellor of Oxford, 1852–7; published sermons. [xii. 307]

COTTON, ROBERT (*fl.* 1300). [See Cowton.]

COTTON, SIR ROBERT (1669–1749), son of Sir John Cotton (1621–1701) [q. v.]; succeeded his nephew as fifth baronet, 1731. [xii. 314]

COTTON, SIR ROBERT BRUCE (1571–1631), antiquary; of Connington, Huntingdonshire; educated at Westminster School and Jesus College, Cambridge; B.A., 1585; settled in 'Cotton House,' Westminster, and collected manuscripts and coins; gave free use of his library to Bacon, Camden, Ralegh, Selden, Speed, Ussher, and other scholars; made an antiquarian tour with Camden to Carlisle, 1600; wrote papers on questions of precedents and other antiquarian topics; sent a gift of manuscripts to the Bodleian Library on its foundation, 1601; rebuilt Connington House, 1602; knighted by James I, 1603; M.P., Huntingdon, 1604; his advice in public affairs sought by the king; created baronet, 1611; contributed to Speed's 'History of England,' 1611; bequeathed valuable manuscripts by Arthur Agard [q. v.], 1614; contributed to Camden's 'Elizabeth,' 1615; imprisoned for trying to screen the Earl of Somerset by altering dates of letters, 1615–16; received valuable papers by bequest from Camden, 1623; M.P., Old Sarum, 1624, and Thetford, 1625, attaching himself to Eliot and the parliamentary party; openly affronted by Charles I in consequence, 1626; wrote against debasing the coinage, 1626; published political tracts, 'History of Henry III,' 1627, and 'Dangers wherein the Kingdom now standeth,' 1628; M.P., Castle Rising, 1628–9, acting throughout with Eliot; excluded in consequence from his library by order of Charles I, 1629–31; papers by him printed posthumously, 1641–1771. The Cottonian Library was transferred to the nation, 1702; placed in Essex House, 1712; removed to Ashburnham House, 1730, where it suffered severely in the fire of October 1731; deposited in Westminster School, 1731, and removed to the British Museum, 1753. Catalogues of it appeared in 1696, 1732, and 1802. [xii. 308]

COTTON, ROGER (*fl.* 1596), poet; draper in London; published a devotional tract entitled 'A Direction to the Waters of Lyfe,' 1590, and two devotional poems, ' An Armor of Proofe,' and 'A Spirituall Song,' 1596. [xii. 315]

COTTON, SIR ST. VINCENT (1801–1863), sixth baronet of Madingley, Cambridgeshire; eldest son of Sir Charles Cotton [q. v.]; educated at Westminster School and Christ Church, Oxford; lieutenant of dragoons, 1827–1830; played cricket, 1830–5; patron of sport; gambled away his estates; made a living by driving the stage coach between London and Brighton. [xii. 316]

COTTON, SIR STAPLETON, VISCOUNT COMBERMERE (1773–1865), field-marshal; at Westminster School, 1785–9; lieutenant of foot, 1790; lieutenant-colonel of horse, 1794; served in Flanders, 1793–4, at Cape Town, 1795, and against Tippoo Sahib, 1799; returned to England, 1800; major-general, 1805; M.P., Newark, 1806–14; commanded cavalry division in Peninsula, 1808–12; succeeded as sixth baronet of Combermere, 1809; lieutenant-general, and invalided by wounds, 1812; served in Pyrenees campaign, 1813–14; created Baron Combermere and pensioned, 1814; commanded the allied cavalry in France, 1815–16; governor of Barbados, 1817–20; commander-in-chief in Ireland, 1822–5; general, 1825; commander-in-chief of India, 1825–30; captured Bhurtpore, 1826; created Viscount Combermere, 1827; separated from his wife, 1830; constable of the Tower, 1852; field-marshal, 1855. [xii. 316]

COTTON, SIR SYDNEY JOHN (1792–1874), lieutenant-general; cornet (1810) and lieutenant (1812) of dragoons; captain of foot, 1822; lieutenant-colonel, 1843; served in India, in Burmah, and Australia, 1810–58; K.C.B. and major-general, 1858; lieutenant-general, 1866;

governor of Chelsea Hospital, 1872; wrote on military subjects, 1857–68. [xii. 319]

COTTON, SIR THOMAS (1594–1662), son of Sir Robert Bruce Cotton [q. v.]; M.P., St. Germans, 1628–9; succeeded as second baronet, 1631; obtained, with difficulty, possession of his father's library; M.P. for Huntingdon, 1640 (the Short parliament); left Cotton House in the hands of the parliament. [xii. 313]

COTTON, WILLIAM (*d.* 1621), bishop of Exeter; M.A. Queens' College, Cambridge, 1575; prebendary of St. Paul's, 1577–98; bishop of Exeter, 1598–1621; precentor of Exeter, 1599–1606; prebendary of Exeter, 1608–1621; rector of Silverton, Devonshire, 1600–21; opposed the puritans. [xii. 321]

COTTON, WILLIAM (1786–1866), philanthropist; third son of Joseph Cotton [q. v.]; managing partner of a Limehouse rope-factory, 1807–38; resided at Leytonstone, 1819–66; a director of the Bank of England, 1821–65; inventor of the sovereign weighing-machine, 1844; unweariedly advocated school and church extension from 1811. [xii. 321]

COTTON, WILLIAM CHARLES (1813–1879), writer on bees; brother of Sir Henry Cotton [q. v.]; educated at Eton and Christ Church, Oxford; B.A., 1836; held living of Frodsham, Cheshire, 1857 till death; first secretary of Apiarian Society. [Suppl. ii. 67]

COTTON, SIR WILLOUGHBY (1783–1860), general; educated at Rugby; ensign, 1798; lieutenant, 1799; served in Hanover, 1805; at Copenhagen, 1807, and in the Peninsula, 1809–11 and 1813–14; lieutenant-colonel, 1821; served in Burmah, 1825–6; K.C.H. and major-general, 1830; governor of Jamaica, 1829–34; commanded a division in the Afghan war, 1838–9; lieutenant-general, 1841; commander-in-chief in Bombay, 1847–50; general, 1854. [xii. 322]

COTTRELL. [See Cotterell.]

COUCH, JONATHAN (1789–1870), naturalist; studied medicine in London; medical practitioner at Polperro, 1809–70; published 'Illustrations of Instinct,' 1847, 'History of British Fishes,' 1860–5, 'History of Polperro,' and 'Cornish Fauna.' [xii. 323]

COUCH, RICHARD QUILLER (1816–1863), naturalist; eldest son of Jonathan Couch [q. v.]; medical practitioner at Penzance, 1845–63; an able zoologist; contributed to scientific journals. [xii. 324]

COUCHE, WILLIAM (1732–1753), jesuit; a Cornishman; educated at St. Omer; joined the jesuits, 1749; died at Liège. [xii. 325]

COULSON, WALTER (1794?–1860), journalist and lawyer; a Cornishman; amanuensis to Jeremy Bentham; parliamentary reporter of the ' Morning Chronicle'; editor of the 'Globe,' 1823; barrister, Gray's Inn, 1828; conveyancer; counsel for the home office; friend of Charles Lamb and Leigh Hunt. [xii. 325]

COULSON, WILLIAM (1802–1877), surgeon; surgeon's apprentice at Penzance; studied surgery in London and, 1824–6, Berlin; on the staff of the 'Lancet,' 1823; qualified as a surgeon, 1826; practised in London; senior surgeon of St. Mary's Hospital, Paddington; published surgical treatises, 1836–54; contributed to professional journals. [xii. 326]

COULTON, DAVID TREVENA (1810–1857), journalist; conducted the 'Britannia' newspaper, 1839–50, and the 'Press,' 1854–7; published a novel, 1853, and an 'Inquiry into the Authorship of the Letters of Junius.' [xii. 327]

COUPER. [See also Cooper and Cowper.]

COUPER, ROBERT (1750–1818), author; student at Glasgow, 1769; tutor in Virginia; medical student in Glasgow, 1776; M.D.; medical practitioner in Wigtonshire and, 1788–1806, at Fochabers, Banffshire; published 'Poetry, chiefly in the Scottish Language,' 1804. [xii. 328]

COUPERIE, ALBERT ÉTIENNE JEAN BAPTISTE TERRIEN DE LA (*d.* 1894). [See Terrien.]

COURAYER, PIERRE FRANÇOIS LE (1681–1776), French divine; born at Rouen; joined the fraternity of St. Geneviève; appellant against the bull 'Unigenitus,' 1714; corresponded with Archbishop Wake, 1721–2;

published a dissertation admitting the validity of Anglican orders, 1723, a 'Defence' of the dissertation, 1726, and 'Historical Relation,' a further defence, 1729; hon. D.D. Oxford, 1727; pensioned by the government; translated into French Father Paul's 'Council of Trent,' 1736, and Sleidan's 'Reformation,' 1769-77; published theological tracts of Socinian tendency. [xii. 328]

COURCI, JOHN DE (d. 1219?), conqueror of Ulster; went to Ireland with William FitzAldelm, Henry II's minister, 1176; seized Downpatrick, 1177; after five years' fighting, subdued Uladh (i.e. Down and Antrim); married, 1180, Affreca, a daughter of the king of Man; 'justiciar' of Ireland from 1185; savagely revenged the murder of his brother Jordan by a native, 1197; outlawed in Ireland by William de Lacy, King John's officer, 1200, and his English estate forfeited; raided by Hugh de Lacy, 1203; taken prisoner by Hugh de Lacy, 1204; obtained his freedom by giving hostages; withdrew to Tyrone; submitted, and recovered his English estate, 1205; rebelled on Hugh de Lacy's being granted his lands in Ulster, 1205; collected a pirate fleet and ravaged Antrim, but was defeated; licensed to visit England, 1207; pensioned, and in personal attendance on King John, 1210-16. [xii. 330]

COURTEN, SIR PETER (d. 1625), baronet; of Aldington, Northamptonshire; son of Sir William Courten or Curteene [q. v.]; created baronet, 1622. [xii. 334]

COURTEN or **CURTEENE**, SIR WILLIAM (1572-1636), merchant; son of a London silk merchant, a protestant refugee from Menin, Flanders; factor at Haerlem for his father's business; returned to London, 1600; partner in Courten and Moncy, silk and linen merchants, 1606; heavily fined by the Star-chamber, 1619; had a fleet of twenty ships trading with Guinea, Spain, and the West Indies; knighted, 1622; lent large sums, never repaid, to James I and Charles I; obtained grants of Barbados (discovered by one of his ships in 1624), and sent colonists there, 1625 and 1628; his colonists forcibly expelled by the Earl of Carlisle, 1629; bought Northamptonshire estates, 1628-33; traded with the East Indies; sent to China two ships, which were lost. [xii. 333]

COURTEN, WILLIAM, the younger (d. 1655), merchant; younger son of Sir William Courten or Curteene [q. v.]; his East India ships seized by the Dutch, 1641; became bankrupt, 1643; withdrew to Italy; died at Florence. [xii. 334]

COURTEN, WILLIAM (1642-1702), naturalist; went sometimes by the name of Charleton; son of William Courten the younger [q. v.]; studied at Montpellier; resided in England, 1663-70; tried to enforce his grandfather's claims on money lent to the crown and on Barbados, 1660 and 1677; lived abroad, 1670-84; opened botanical museum in London, 1684. [xii. 335]

COURTENAY. [See also COURTNEY.]

COURTENAY, EDWARD, EARL OF DEVONSHIRE (d. 1509), created earl, and granted large estates in Devonshire, 1485; defended Exeter against Perkin Warbeck, 1497. [xii. 336]

COURTENAY, EDWARD, EARL OF DEVONSHIRE (1526?-1556), son of Henry Courtenay, marquis of Exeter [q. v.]; prisoner in the Tower, 1538-53; attainted, 1539; released and taken into favour by Queen Mary, August 1553; lived dissolutely; created Earl of Devonshire, September 1553; his attainder reversed, October 1553; disappointed in his hope of marrying Queen Mary; formed designs of marrying Princess Elizabeth and making her queen, December 1553; imprisoned, 1554; exiled, 1555; died at Padua; translated an Italian devotional treatise, 1548 (printed, 1856). [xii. 335]

COURTENAY, GERTRUDE, MARCHIONESS OF EXETER (d. 1558), daughter of William Blount, fourth baron Mountjoy [q. v.]; second wife of Henry Courtenay, marquis of Exeter [q. v.]; a devout Roman catholic; patronised Elizabeth Barton [q. v.]; prisoner in the Tower, 1538; attainted, 1539; her attainder reversed, 1553; lady-in-waiting to Queen Mary. [xii. 337]

COURTENAY, HENRY, MARQUIS OF EXETER and EARL OF DEVONSHIRE (1496?-1538), son of Sir William Courtenay [q. v.]; cousin of Henry VIII; allowed to succeed to earldom of Devonshire, 1511; served against France,

1513; privy councillor and gentleman of the privy chamber, 1520; attended Henry VIII to France, 1521; granted estates and offices, 1521-3; constable of Windsor Castle, 1525; created Marquis of Exeter, 1525; envoy to France, 1525; supported Henry VIII in his divorce proceedings, 1529-33; king's agent to seize the lands of the smaller monasteries, 1535; commissioner to try Anne Boleyn, 1536; sent to suppress the Pilgrimage of Grace, 1536; lord steward to try Thomas, lord Darcy, 1537; sent to the Tower as an aspirant to the crown, 1538; beheaded and attainted. [xii. 336]

COURTENAY, HENRY REGINALD (1741-1803), bishop of Exeter; at Westminster School, 1755-9; tutor of Christ Church, Oxford, 1763-8; M.A., 1766; D.C.L., 1774; rector of Lee, Kent, 1773; rector of St. George's, Hanover Square, 1774-1803; prebendary of Exeter, 1772-94, of Rochester, 1773-4 and 1783-97; bishop of Bristol, 1794; bishop and archdeacon of Exeter, 1797-1803; published sermons and charges. [xii. 337]

COURTENAY, JOHN (1741-1816), politician; private secretary to George, viscount Townshend, 1767-82; M.P., 1780-1807 and 1812; surveyor-general of the ordnance, 1783; spoke against Warren Hastings, 1786; advocated abolition of slavery; defended French revolution; published essays and verses, 1772-1811. [xii. 338]

COURTENAY, PETER (d. 1492), bishop of Winchester; of the Powderham, Devonshire, family; studied at Oxford and Padua; doctor of laws; dean of Windsor, 1477; bishop of Exeter, 1478-87; attainted by Richard III for raising insurrection in the west, 1484; fled to Brittany; keeper of the privy seal to Henry VII, 1485-7; bishop of Winchester, 1487-92. [xii. 339]

COURTENAY, RICHARD (d. 1415), bishop of Norwich; of Powderham, Devonshire; studied in youth at Oxford; doctor of civil and canon law; prebendary of St. Paul's, 1394, Lincoln, 1401, and York, 1403; precentor of Chichester, 1400; dean of St. Asaph, 1403; archdeacon of Northumberland, 1410; dean of Wells, 1410; inherited his father's lands, 1406; resided in Oxford, where he was chancellor, 1407 and 1411-12, unsuccessfully resisting, 1411, Archbishop Arundel's title to hold a metropolitan visitation of Oxford University, and organising Thomas de Cobham's [q. v.] library; friend to Henry V, when prince, and treasurer of his household, 1413; non-resident bishop of Norwich, 1413; envoy to France, 1414 and 1415; accompanied Henry V to France, August 1415, and died at Harfleur. [xii. 340]

COURTENAY, THOMAS PEREGRINE (1782-1841), politician; younger son of Henry Reginald Courtenay [q. v.]; M.P., Totnes, 1810-31; secretary to the India commission, 1812-28; vice-president, board of trade, 1828-30; published pamphlets, 1808-40, 'Commentaries on Shakespeare's Historical Plays,' 1840, and a memoir of Sir William Temple, 1836. [xii. 342]

COURTENAY, WILLIAM (1342?-1396), archbishop of Canterbury; fourth son of Hugh, second earl of Devon; studied at Oxford; doctor of canon and civil law; the first chancellor of Oxford elected independently of the bishop of Lincoln, 1367; prebendary of Exeter, Wells, and York; bishop of Hereford, 1370; opposed papal and royal exactions, 1373; bishop of London, 1375; commissioner to regulate the realm, 1376; censured for excommunicating the London Florentine merchants at the pope's bidding, 1376; proceeded against Wycliffe for heresy, 1377; lord keeper, 1381; archbishop of Canterbury, 1381; held synod to condemn Wycliffe's opinions, 1382; obtained the king's licence to repress the lollards, 1382; crushed the lollards at Oxford, November; commenced the visitation of his province, 1382, and persevered in it, in spite of the resistance of the bishops of Exeter and Salisbury; reproved Richard II for his bad government, 1385; one of the regents, 1386; crushed the lollards at Leicester, 1389; opposed the statute of provisors, 1390; helped to carry the statute of præmunire, 1393. [xii. 342]

COURTENAY, SIR WILLIAM (d. 1512), courtier of Henry VII; son of Edward Courtenay, earl of Devonshire (d. 1509) [q. v.]; K.B., 1487; attainted, 1503, as a possible claimant to the crown; prisoner in the Tower, 1503-9; allowed his succession to the earldom by Henry VIII, 1511, but died before reversal of the attainder. [xii. 336]

COURTENAY, WILLIAM REGINALD, eleventh EARL OF DEVON (1807-1888), politician and philan-

thropist; educated at Westminster and Christ Church, Oxford; B.A., 1828; B.C.L., 1831; fellow of All Souls' College, 1828-31; D.C.L., 1838; called to bar at Lincoln's Inn, 1832; conservative and Peelite M.P. for South Devon, 1841-9; secretary to poor law board, 1850-9, and president, 1867-8; succeeded to peerage, 1859; chancellor of duchy of Lancaster, 1866-7; privy councillor, 1866.
[Suppl. ii. 70]

COURTEVILLE, RAPHAEL or RALPH (d. 1772), organist and political writer; author of 'Memoirs of . . . Burleigh,' 1738; editor of the 'Gazetteer,' a government organ, and so nicknamed 'Court-evil.' He has been doubtfully identified with Ralph Courteville, formerly chorister of the Chapel Royal, composer of instrumental and vocal music, 1690-5, who was appointed organist of St. James's, Westminster, in 1691.   [xii. 347]

COURTHOPE, WILLIAM (1808-1866), genealogist; clerk in the Heralds' College, 1833; barrister, Inner Temple, 1851; Somerset herald, 1854; edited Debrett and Sir Harris Nicolas's peerages.   [xii. 348]

COURTHOPP, NATHANIEL (d. 1620), sea-captain; entered the East India Company's service, 1609; held captive by the Turks at Aden and Mocha; agent in Borneo; held Pulo Roon against the Dutch, 1616-20; killed in action.   [xii. 348]

COURTNEY. [See also COURTENAY.]

COURTNEY, EDWARD (1599?-1677), jesuit; real name LEEDES; born in Sussex; educated at St. Omer and Rome; joined the jesuits, 1621; political prisoner in London, 1634; rector of the colleges at St. Omer, Rome, and Liège; published Latin complimentary speeches, 1621-56, and a memoir of Peter Wright, jesuit.   [xii. 348]

COUSE, KENTON (1721-1790), architect; employed by the board of works; designed Richmond bridge, 1774-1777.   [xii. 349]

COUSEN, JOHN (1804-1880), line-engraver of landscapes; pupil of John Scott; much employed as a book-illustrator; engraved largely after Turner.   [xii. 349]

COUSINS, SAMUEL (1801-1887), mezzotint engraver; apprentice (1814) and assistant to S. W. Reynolds; engraved on his own account, 1826-83; instituted a fund for the relief of indigent artists.   [xii. 350]

COUTANCES (DE CONSTANTIIS), WALTER DE (d. 1207), statesman; one of Henry II's clerks; styled chaplain of Blythe; rector of Woolpit, Suffolk; canon of Rouen, 1173; vice-chancellor of England, 1173; envoy to Flanders and to France, 1177; sealbearer to Henry II, 1180; bishop of Lincoln, 1183; archbishop of Rouen, 1184; ambassador to France, 1186 and 1188; took the cross, 1188; invested Richard I with the dukedom of Normandy, 1189; in attendance on Richard I in England and Sicily, 1189-90; sent back to govern England, 1191; took over Nottingham and other castles from Prince John; became chief justiciar (1191) in place of Longchamp, the chancellor; caused the bishop of Bath to be translated to Canterbury; caused Hubert FitzWalter to be elected to Canterbury; drove Longchamp to Normandy and excommunicated him; made efforts to raise Richard I's ransom, 1193; joined Richard in Germany and became hostage for him, 1194; returned to Normandy, 1194; quarrelled with Richard for taking church land to build Château Gaillard, 1196; accepted compensation; invested John with the dukedom of Normandy, 1199; invested Philip II of France with the dukedom, 1204.   [xii. 351]

COUTTS, JOHN (1699-1751), merchant; commission agent and bill negotiator, Edinburgh; lord provost, 1742-1744.   [xii. 354]

COUTTS, THOMAS (1735-1822), founder and, 1778, sole partner of the London banking firm, Coutts & Co.; fourth son of John Coutts [q. v.]   [xii. 354]

COVE, MORGAN (1753?-1830), divine; LL.B. Cambridge, 1776; D.C.L. Oxford, 1816; rector of Eaton-Bishop, Herefordshire, 1799; prebendary of Hereford, 1800; published pamphlets on tithe, 1795 and 1800. [xii. 355]

COVEL, COVELL, or COLVILL, JOHN (1638-1722), traveller; B.A. Christ's College, Cambridge, 1658; fellow; M.A., 1661; chaplain at Constantinople, 1670-6; collected plants; visited Asia Minor, 1677; travelled in Italy,

1677-9; D.D., 1679; rector of Littlebury, Essex, 1680, and of Kegworth, Leicestershire, 1681; chaplain to the Princess of Orange at the Hague, 1681-5; chancellor of York, 1687; master of Christ's College, Cambridge, 1688; published an account of the Greek church, 1722; his manuscript travels preserved in the British Museum.   [xii. 355]

COVELL, WILLIAM (d. 1614?), sub-dean of Lincoln; fellow of Queens' College, Cambridge, 1589; D.D., 1601; beneficed in Kent; sub-dean and prebendary of Lincoln; wrote in defence of Hooker's 'Ecclesiastical Polity,' 1603, and of church ceremonies, 1604-6.   [xii. 356]

COVENTRY, ANDREW (1764-1832), agriculturist; educated at Edinburgh University; member of Medical Society, 1782; M.D., 1783; first professor of agriculture at Edinburgh, 1790-1831; frequently arbitrated on land questions; published works on agricultural subjects.
[Suppl. ii. 71]

COVENTRY, ANNE, COUNTESS OF (1673-1763), author of 'Meditations and Reflections,' 1707; daughter of the first Duke of Beaufort; married, c. 1700, Thomas, second earl of Coventry (d. 1710).   [xii. 357]

COVENTRY, ANNE, COUNTESS OF (1690-1788), née Masters; married Gilbert, fourth earl of Coventry (d. 1719), and 1725, Edward Pytts; obtained a verdict in her favour, 1724, with reference to a settlement made on her first marriage.   [xii. 357]

COVENTRY, FRANCIS (1598-1680). [See DAVENPORT, CHRISTOPHER.]

COVENTRY, FRANCIS (d. 1759?), verse-writer; M.A. Cambridge, 1752; incumbent of Edgware; published verses and satires, 1750-3.   [xii. 357]

COVENTRY, HENRY (1619-1686), secretary of state; a younger son of Thomas, first baron Coventry [q. v.]; fellow of All Souls' College, Oxford; B.C.L., 1638; attended Charles II in exile; envoy to Sweden, 1664-6 and 1671, and to Holland, 1667; secretary of state, 1672-9.
[xii. 357]

COVENTRY, HENRY (d. 1752), fellow of Magdalene College, Cambridge; M.A., 1733; published a theological work, 'Philemon to Hydaspes,' 1736-44.   [xii. 358]

COVENTRY, SIR JOHN (d. 1682), after whom the 'Coventry Act' against mutilation was named; M.P., Evesham, 1640; unseated as a royalist, 1645; K.B., 1661; M.P., Weymouth, 1667-82; waylaid by ruffians and his nose slit, 21 Dec. 1670, for having alluded to Charles II's relations with actresses.   [xii. 358]

COVENTRY, JOHN (1735-1812), maker of telescopes and hygrometers.   [xii. 359]

COVENTRY, MARIA, COUNTESS OF (1733-1760), daughter of a poor Irish squire; a famous beauty in London, 1751; married, 1752, George William, sixth earl of Coventry.   [xii. 359]

COVENTRY, SIR THOMAS (1547-1606), judge; B.A. Balliol College, Oxford, 1565; fellow, 1566; barrister, Inner Temple; serjeant-at-law, 1603; justice of the common pleas and knighted, 1606.   [xii. 360]

COVENTRY, THOMAS, first BARON COVENTRY (1578-1640), lord-keeper; eldest son of Sir Thomas Coventry [q. v.]; entered Balliol College, Oxford, 1592; barrister, Inner Temple, 1603; recorder of London, 1616; solicitor-general and knighted, 1617; attorney-general, 1621; M.P., Droitwich, 1621; lord-keeper, 1625; opened the parliaments of February 1626 and March 1628; created Baron Coventry of Aylesborough, 1628; tried to mediate between Charles I and the parliamentary leaders, 1629; judge of Star-chamber; assented to the levying of ship-money, 1634.   [xii. 360]

COVENTRY, WALTER OF (fl. 1293?), reputed author of an historical compilation, 'Memoriale,' of value for the period 1199-1225; possibly a monk of York. [xii. 362]

COVENTRY, WILLIAM OF (fl. 1360). [See WILLIAM.]

COVENTRY, SIR WILLIAM (1628?-1686), politician; a younger son of Thomas, first baron Coventry [q. v.]; entered Queen's College, Oxford, 1642; captain of foot in Charles I's service; withdrew to France; secretary to the Duke of York, 1660-7; M.P., Great Yarmouth, 1661-1679; commissioner of the navy, 1662, and so friend of

Samuel Pepys; knighted, 1665; spoke against Clarendon, 1667; quarrelled with Buckingham; imprisoned, 1668; published pamphlets, 1673 and 1685; reputed author of 'Character of a Trimmer,' published 1688.   [xii. 362]

COVERDALE, MILES (1488–1568), translator of the bible; studied at Cambridge (bachelor of canon law 1531); ordained priest, 1514; resident in the Austin friary, Cambridge, 1514–26; friend of Thomas Cromwell [q. v.]; adopted Lutheran views; assisted Robert Barnes [q. v.] in his defence on a charge of heresy, 1526; preached against images; went abroad; published translations of two theological tracts, 1534; translated at Antwerp, apparently in the pay of Jacob van Meteren, the bible and Apocrypha from German (Zurich, 1531), and from Latin versions with aid of Tyndale's New Testament; his translation first printed perhaps by Christopher Froschouer of Zurich, and brought into England by James Nicolson of Southwark, 1535; modified his version, 1537; translated theological tracts, 1537; superintended the printing of the 1539 'Great Bible' at Paris, 1538–9, and in London, 1539; superintended 'Cranmer's Bible,' 1540; published 'Goostly Psalmes,' translations from German hymns, c. 1540; went abroad, 1540; D.D. Tübingen; pastor and schoolmaster at Bergzabern in Deux-Ponts, 1543–7, under the name of 'Michael Anglus'; returned to England, 1548; employed to preach against anabaptists, 1549–50, and the Devonshire insurgents, 1551, and to visit Magdalen College, Oxford, 1551; translated theological tracts, 1550; bishop of Exeter, 1551–3; allowed to leave England, 1554; returned to Bergzabern; in Geneva, 1558; returned to England; joined in the consecration of Archbishop Parker, 1559; D.D. Cambridge, 1563; published 'Letters of Saintes,' his last book, 1564; rector of St. Magnus, London Bridge, 1563; resigned for puritanical reasons, 1566; preached privately in London, 1567–8; his collected works published, 1844–6. [xii. 364]

COWARD, JAMES (1824–1880), organist; chorister of Westminster Abbey; organist at Lambeth and other churches; organist of the Crystal Palace; composed glees, songs, and other music.   [xii. 372]

COWARD, WILLIAM (1657?–1725), physician; scholar of Wadham College, Oxford, 1675; fellow of Merton, 1680; M.D., 1687; practitioner in Northampton, and, 1693–1706, in London; published medical tracts; rendered notorious by his 'Second Thoughts concerning Human Soul,' 1702, arguing its mortality; 'The Grand Essay,' 1704, and 'The Just Scrutiny,' and 'Ophthalmoiatria,' 1706, deistical pamphlets; published didactic poems, 1705 and 1709.   [xii. 373]

COWARD, WILLIAM (d. 1738), London merchant and Jamaica planter; provided funds for courses of nonconformist sermons in London, 1730–5; bequeathed money for the education of nonconformist ministers. [xii. 374]

COWDEN-CLARKE. [See CLARKE, CHARLES COWDEN; CLARKE, MARY COWDEN.]

COWELL, JOHN (1554–1611), civilian; educated at Eton, and, 1570, King's College, Cambridge; LL.D.; advocate of Doctors' Commons, 1584; regius professor of civil law, Cambridge, 1594–1610; master of Trinity Hall, Cambridge, 1598–1611; vicar-general of the archbishop of Canterbury, 1608; published 'Institutiones Juris Anglicani,' 1605, and 'The Interpreter,' a law dictionary, 1607, censured for its absolutist opinions, 1610.   [xii. 375]

COWELL, JOSEPH LEATHLEY (1792–1863), actor; real name, HAWKINS WITCHETT; midshipman, royal navy, 1805–9; first appeared (1812) on the Plymouth stage; acted in London and the provinces till 1821; scene-painter; acted in the United States, 1821–46; published an autobiography, 1844.   [xii. 376]

COWELL, SAMUEL HOUGHTON (1820–1864), actor; son of Joseph Leathley Cowell [q. v.]; taken to America, 1822; appeared on the stage at Boston, 1829; acted in most American theatres; came to Edinburgh and became a favourite comic singer between acts; acted in London, Glasgow, Belfast, and Dublin; confined himself latterly to character singing; wrote songs.   [xii. 377]

COWEN, SIR JOSEPH (1800–1873), radical M.P. for Newcastle, 1865–73.   [Suppl. ii. 73]

COWEN, JOSEPH (1831–1900), politician and journalist; son of Sir Joseph Cowen [q. v.]; educated at Edin-

burgh University; interested himself in revolutionary movements on the continent, 1848, and became active supporter of chartists and member of northern reform league (founded 1858); contributor to, and subsequently was proprietor and editor of, 'Newcastle Chronicle'; established monthly 'Northern Tribune'; liberal M.P. for Newcastle, 1873–85.   [Suppl. ii. 72]

COWEN, WILLIAM (fl. 1811–1860), painter and etcher; sketched in Great Britain, Switzerland, Italy, and (1840) Corsica; exhibited landscapes, 1811–60; published etchings, 1817–48; wrote 'Six Weeks in Corsica,' 1848.   [xii. 378]

COWHERD, WILLIAM (1763–1816), founder of the Bible Christians or 'Cowherdites'; tutor in a dissenting academy; Swedenborgian preacher in Manchester; built a chapel in Salford, in which he preached as a Swedenborgian, 1800–9, but afterwards founded a new church, requiring vegetarianism and teetotalism; opened a boarding school, 1810; a dispensing chemist, known as 'Dr. Cowherd'; published hymns for the use of his sect.   [xii. 378]

COWIE, BENJAMIN MORGAN (1816–1900), dean of Exeter; senior wrangler, St. John's College, Cambridge, 1839; M.A., 1842; B.D., 1855; D.D., 1880; fellow, 1839–43; entered Lincoln's Inn, 1837; ordained priest, 1842; principal and senior mathematical lecturer at college for civil engineers, Putney, 1844–51; select preacher at Cambridge, 1852 and 1856; Hulsean lecturer, 1853 and 1854; professor of geometry, Gresham College, London, 1855; fifth minor canon and succentor of St. Paul's Cathedral, 1856; rector of St. Lawrence Jewry, 1857; chaplain in ordinary to the queen, 1871; dean of Manchester, 1872, and of Exeter, 1883; published religious works.   [Suppl. ii. 73]

COWIE, ROBERT (1842–1874), author of 'Shetland, Descriptive and Historical'; M.A. Aberdeen; M.D. Edinburgh; practitioner in Lerwick.   [xii. 379]

COWLEY, first EARL (1804–1884). [See WELLESLEY, HENRY RICHARD CHARLES.]

COWLEY, BARON (1773–1847). [See WELLESLEY, HENRY.]

COWLEY, ABRAHAM (1618–1667), poet; king's scholar at Westminster; published 'Poetical Blossoms,' 1633, and 'Sylva,' 1636; scholar of Trinity College, Cambridge, 1637; fellow, 1640; M.A., 1642; published 'Love's Riddle,' a pastoral drama, 1638; brought out, at Cambridge, 'Naufragium Joculare,' a Latin comedy, 1638, and 'The Guardian,' a comedy, 1641; ejected by the parliament, 1644; resided in St. John's College, Oxford; went to France, 1646; published 'The Mistress,' poems, 1647, and 'Miscellanies,' with other poems, including four books of the 'Davideis,' a sacred epic, 1656; cipher secretary to Queen Henrietta Maria, c. 1647; royalist spy in England, 1656; M.D. Oxford, 1657; withdrew to France; published odes on the Restoration and against Cromwell, 1660–1; was refused the mastership of the Savoy, 1661; F.R.S.; published 'Verses upon several Occasions,' 1663; a competence provided for him by Earl of St. Albans and Duke of Buckingham; his collected works published 1668.   [xii. 379]

COWLEY, HANNAH (1743–1809), dramatist; née Parkhouse; married, c. 1768; brought out thirteen dramatic pieces, 1776–95, including 'The Belle's Stratagem,' 1782; published poems, 1780–94; contributed weekly sentimental verses to the 'World,' as 'Anna Matilda.'   [xii. 382]

COWPER. [See also COOPER and COUPER.]

COWPER, SIR CHARLES (1807–1875), Australian statesman; son of William Cowper (1780–1858) [q. v.]; born in Lancashire; government clerk in New South Wales, 1825–33; sheep farmer; member of the legislature, c. 1843; advocated colonial railways, 1846; opposed further transportation of convicts, 1850; several times minister, 1856–70; agent-general for New South Wales, 1870; knighted, 1872.   [xii. 383]

COWPER, DOUGLAS (1817–1839), painter; artstudent in London; exhibited, 1837–9.   [xii. 385]

COWPER, EBENEZER (1804–1880), manufacturer of printing machines in partnership with his brother Edward Cowper [q. v.]   [xii. 385]

COWPER, EDWARD (1790–1852), inventor ; patented a wall-paper printing machine, 1816 ; a printer, 1818 ; patented process for simultaneously printing both sides of paper, 1818 ; invented, jointly with Augustus Applegarth, the newspaper 'four-cylinder' press, 1827.

[xii. 385]

COWPER, HENRY (1758–1840), lawyer ; barrister, Middle Temple, 1775 ; published law reports, 1783 ; clerk of the House of Lords. [xii. 386]

COWPER, MARY, first COUNTESS COWPER (1685–1724), *née* Clavering ; married William, first earl Cowper [q. v.], 1706 ; lady of the bedchamber to the Princess of Wales, 1714 ; her diary published, 1864. [xii. 386]

COWPER, SPENCER (1669–1728), judge ; educated at Westminster ; barrister ; controller of the Bridge House estates, 1690 ; acquitted of the murder of Sarah Stout of Hertford, 1699 ; M.P., Beeralston, 1705, 1708, Truro, 1711 ; chief-justice of Chester, 1717 ; justice of common pleas, 1727. [xii. 386]

COWPER, SPENCER (1713–1774), dean of Durham, 1746–74 ; youngest son of William, first earl Cowper [q. v.] ; M.A. Exeter College, Oxford, 1734 ; D.D., 1746 ; rector of Fordwich, Kent ; published sermons.

[xii. 387]

COWPER or **COUPER**, WILLIAM (1568–1619), bishop of Galloway ; M.A. St. Andrews, 1583 ; usher at Hoddesdon, Hertfordshire ; minister of Bothkennar, Stirlingshire, 1587, and at Perth, 1595 ; assented to episcopacy, 1608 ; dean of the Chapel Royal, Edinburgh, and bishop of Galloway, 1612–19 ; published devotional tracts, 1611–18 ; his 'works' published, 1623. [xii. 387]

COWPER or **COOPER**, WILLIAM (1666–1709), surgeon ; surgeon's apprentice in London, 1682 ; qualified as a surgeon, 1691 ; practised in London ; F.R.S., 1696 ; published (1694) 'Myotomia Reformata,' a treatise on the muscles, and (169?) 'The Anatomy of Humane Bodies'; defended himself, 1701, against Godefridus Bidloo, a Leyden professor ; published, 1702, a description of 'Cowper's glands' ; contributed to medical journals. [xii. 388]

COWPER, WILLIAM, first EARL COWPER (d. 1723), barrister, Middle Temple, 1688 ; volunteered for the Prince of Orange, November 1688 ; recorder of Colchester, 1694 ; M.P., Hertford, 1695 and 1698, Beeralston, 1701 ; crown prosecutor, 1694–9 ; lord-keeper, 1705 ; a commissioner for the union with Scotland, April 1706 ; succeeded as second baronet, 1706 ; created Baron Cowper, November 1706 ; first lord chancellor of Great Britain, May 1707–September 1710 ; presided at Sacheverell's trial, 1710 ; spoke in the whig interest in the Lords' debates, 1711–14 ; helped to dismiss Bolingbroke from the secretaryship of state, 1714 ; again lord chancellor, 1714–18 ; wrote out a description of English parties for George I's guidance, 1714 ; presided at the trial of the Earl of Winton for rebellion, 1716 ; supported the Mutiny bill, 1718 ; created Earl Cowper, 1718 ; took a leading part in the Lords' debates, 1718–23.

[xii. 389]

COWPER, WILLIAM (1701–1767), antiquary ; studied medicine at Leyden, 1719 ; medical practitioner at Chester ; published a life of St. Werburgh, 1749, and 'Il Penseroso : an Evening's Contemplation in ... Chester,' 1767 ; left manuscript collections relating to Chester and Cheshire. [xii. 394]

COWPER, WILLIAM (1731–1800), poet ; son of John Cowper, rector of Great Berkhampstead ; barbarously treated at a private school, 1737–8, in Hertfordshire ; at Westminster School, 1741–9 ; articled to a solicitor, 1750–1752 ; took chambers in the Middle Temple, 1752 ; first attacked by melancholia, c. 1753 ; barrister, Middle Temple, 1754 ; proposed to marry his cousin, Theodora Jane Cowper (d. 1824), but his intention frustrated by her father, who had noticed Cowper's morbidity, 1756 ; contributed verses to various papers, 1756–61 ; a commissioner of bankrupts, 1759–64 ; offered a clerkship of the House of Lords by his cousin, William Cowper, clerk of the parliaments, 1763 ; thrown into a nervous fever by fear of opposition to his appointment ; tried to commit suicide ; an inmate of Nathaniel Cotton's private asylum, 1763–5 ; a boarder in Morley Unwin's house at Huntingdon, 1765 ; ceased corresponding with his cousin Harriet (d. 1807), wife of Sir Thomas Hesketh, in consequence of her indifference to his new pietistic zeal ; removed with Mary, Morley Unwin's widow, to Olney, 1767 ; lay-reader and district visitor to John Newton, the evangelical

curate of Olney ; composed hymns (sixty-seven appearing in Newton's 'Olney Hymns,' 1779) ; became engaged to Mrs. Unwin ; again deranged, 1773 ; a guest in Newton's house, 1773–4 ; recovered before 1776 ; acquainted with William Bull [q. v.] ; wrote much verse, 1777–81 ; published 'Anti-Thelyphthora,' 1781, against his cousin Martin Madan's 'Thelyphthora' ; published poems, 1782 ; at the suggestion of Ann (d. 1802), widow of Sir Robert Austen, wrote 'John Gilpin,' November 1782, and 'The Task,' 1783 ; quarrelled, through Mrs. Unwin's jealousy, with Lady Austen, 1784 ; began to translate Homer, 1784 ; resumed his correspondence with Lady Hesketh, October 1785 ; again became insane, 1787, and never entirely recovered ; published his translation of 'Homer,' by subscription, 1791 ; undertook to edit Milton ; received a government pension, 1794 ; removed by his cousin, John Johnson, with Mrs. Unwin (d. 1796), to East Dereham, Norfolk, 1795 ; wrote 'The Castaway,' 1798. His life was written by William Hayley, 1803 ; his Milton papers published, 1808–10, his letters, 1824, and his 'complete works,' 1834–7. [xii. 394]

COWPER, WILLIAM (1780–1858), Australian divine ; born in Lancashire ; incumbent of St. Philip's, Sydney, 1809 ; archdeacon, 1848. [xii. 402]

COWPER (afterwards **COWPER-TEMPLE**), WILLIAM FRANCIS, BARON MOUNT-TEMPLE (1811–1888), educated at Eton ; cornet in royal horse guards, 1827 ; lieutenant, 1832 ; brevet major, 1852 ; M.P. for Hertford, 1835–63, and South Hampshire, 1868–80 ; junior lord of treasury, 1841 ; lord of admiralty, 1846–52, and 1852–5 ; under-secretary for home affairs, 1855 ; president of board of health and privy councillor, 1855 ; vice-president of committee of council on education, 1857–8, and of board of trade, 1859 ; commissioner of works, 1860–6 ; raised to peerage, 1880. [Suppl. ii. 74]

COWTON, ROBERT (fl. 1300), Franciscan ; educated at Oxford and Paris ; D.D. of the Sorbonne ; confessor in Oxfordshire, 1300 ; wrote scholastic treatises ; traditionally known as 'doctor amœnus.' [xii. 402]

COX. [See also COXE.]

COX, CAPTAIN ——, of Coventry (fl. 1575), collector of ballads and romances ; present at Kenilworth on Queen Elizabeth's visit, 1575. [xii. 403]

COX, ANNE (1766–1830). [See WOODROOFFE, ANNE.]

COX, **COXE**, or **COCKES**, BENJAMIN (fl. 1646), baptist minister ; entered Christ Church, Oxford, 1609 ; M.A. Broadgates Hall, 1617 ; beneficed in Devonshire ; retracted puritan opinions, 1639 ; baptist preacher at Bedford ; imprisoned at Coventry, 1643 ; baptist preacher in London, 1645 ; conformed, 1662 ; again became a baptist ; published controversial tracts, 1645–6. [xii. 403]

COX, DANIEL (d. 1750), physician ; M.D. St. Andrews, 1742 ; physician to the Middlesex Hospital, 1746–1749 ; published medical tracts. [xii. 404]

COX, DAVID (1783–1859), landscape-painter in water-colours ; son of a Birmingham blacksmith ; taught drawing by Joseph Barber [q. v.] ; apprenticed to a Birmingham locket-painter ; assistant to De Maria, an Italian scene-painter ; scene-painter in London, 1804 ; sold sketches of Thames scenery near London ; sketched in Wales, 1805–6 ; drawing-master at Dulwich ; drawn for the militia, and forced to leave home ; went to Hastings, 1812, and sketched in oils ; drawing-master at Hereford, 1814–26, making summer sketching-tours ; began to etch on copper, 1812 ; published 'A Treatise on Landscape Painting,' 1814, 'Lessons in Landscape,' 1816, 'Views of Bath,' 1820, and 'Young Artists' Companion,' 1825 ; taught by W. J. Müller [q. v.] to paint in oils, 1839 ; removed to neighbourhood of Birmingham, 1841, visiting Bettws-y-Coed yearly (1844–56) ; his merits unrecognised during his lifetime. [xii. 404]

COX, DAVID, the younger (1809–1885), water-colour painter ; only child of David Cox (1783–1859) [q.v.] ; educated at Hereford ; exhibited in London, 1827.

[xii. 409]

COX, EDWARD WILLIAM (1809–1879), serjeant-at-law ; educated at Taunton ; published verses, 1829–30 ; barrister, Middle Temple, 1843 ; proprietor and conductor of the 'Law Times,' 1843–79, the 'County Courts Chronicle,' 1846, the 'Field,' the 'Queen,' 1861, and other periodicals ; recorder of Falmouth, 1857–68 ; M.P., 1865 ;

serjeant-at-law, 1868 ; recorder of Portsmouth, 1868–79 ; published law reports and legal treatises, 1846–78, political pamphlets, 1852–66, and spiritualistic pamphlets, 1877–8.
[xii. 409]

COX, FRANCIS AUGUSTUS (1783–1853), baptist preacher ; a wealthy man ; M.A. Edinburgh ; baptist minister in Northamptonshire, 1805, and at Hackney, 1811–53 ; honorary LL.D. Glasgow, 1824 ; librarian of London University, 1828 ; published biographical and biblical works.
[xii. 411]

COX, GEORGE VALENTINE (1786–1875), author of 'Recollections of Oxford,' 1868 ; M.A. New College, Oxford, 1808 ; an esquire bedell of Oxford University, 1806–1866 ; published a novel, 1837, and translations of German works on ancient history, 1845–51.
[xii. 411]

COX, LEONARD (fl. 1572), schoolmaster ; B.A. Cambridge; asked M.A. at Oxford, 1530 ; schoolmaster at Reading, 1541–6 ; travelled ; taught school at Caerleon ; schoolmaster at Coventry, 1572 ; published 'Rhetoryke,' 1524, a grammatical tract, 1540, and translations.
[xii. 411]

COX, RICHARD (1500–1581), bishop of Ely ; educated at Eton ; fellow of King's College, Cambridge ; B.A., 1524 ; canon of Wolsey's Oxford college, 1525 ; M.A. Oxford, 1526 ; head-master of Eton ; D.D. Cambridge, 1537 ; favourite of Archbishop Cranmer ; prebendary of Lincoln, 1542–7 ; lord almoner ; tutor to Prince Edward, 1544–50 ; dean of Osney, 1544, and of Christ Church, Oxford, 1547–53 ; vice-chancellor of Oxford, 1547–52, destroying 'popish' statues, pictures, and books ; rector of Harrow, 1547 ; canon of Windsor, 1548 ; on the commission to draw up the English liturgy, 1548–50 ; dean of Westminster, 1549 ; imprisoned, 1553 ; in exile, 1554–8, chiefly living at Frankfort, where he led the opposition to John Knox : one of the commission to visit Oxford University, 1559 ; bishop of Norwich, 1559 ; bishop of Ely, 1559–80 ; alienated much property of the see to court favourites ; resigned, 1580.
[xii. 412]

COX, Sir RICHARD (1650–1733), Irish judge ; a strong protestant ; an Irish attorney ; barrister, Gray's Inn, 1673 ; practised law in Ireland ; withdrew to Bristol, 1685 ; wrote in favour of the Prince of Orange, 1689 ; published a trite history of Ireland, 1689–90 ; present at the Boyne, 1690 ; justice of the common pleas, 1690 ; military governor of Cork, 1691–2 ; Irish privy councillor and knighted, 1692 ; removed from the privy council for urging observance of the treaty of Limerick, 1695 ; published pamphlets on Irish affairs, 1696–8 ; chief-justice of the common pleas, 1701–3 ; lord chancellor, 1703–7 ; created baronet, 1706 ; published theological tracts, 1709–1713 ; chief-justice of the queen's bench, 1711–14.
[xii. 414]

COX, ROBERT (1810–1872), anti-Sabbatarian writer ; writer to the signet, Edinburgh ; edited the 'Phrenological Journal' ; advocated Sunday trains, 1850 ; published treatises on the Sabbath question, 1853–65.
[xii. 416]

COX, SAMUEL (1826–1893), theological writer ; apprenticed at London docks ; studied for baptist ministry at Stepney College ; pastor of baptist chapel, St. Paul's Square, Southsea, 1852, at Ryde, 1854–9, and at Mansfield Road, Nottingham, 1863–88 ; contributed to religious periodicals ; editor of the 'Expositor,' 1875–84 ; D.D. St. Andrews, 1882 ; published numerous theological works, of which the most influential was 'Salvator Mundi,' 1877.
[Suppl. ii. 75]

COX, THOMAS (d. 1734), topographer ; rector of Chignal-Smealy, 1680–1704 ; vicar of Broomfield, 1685–1734, and rector of Stock-Harvard, Essex, 1703–34 ; published translations and sermons, 1694–1726 ; edited a meritorious recension of Camden's 'Britannia,' 1720–31.
[xii. 417]

COX, WALTER (1770–1837), Irish journalist ; a Dublin gunsmith ; edited two violent newspapers, 'The Union Star,' 1797, and 'Irish Magazine,' 1807–15 ; pensioned ; resident in New York, 1816, and France, 1820 ; forfeited his pension by returning to Ireland, 1835.
[xii. 417]

COX, WILLIAM SANDS (1802–1875), surgeon ; studied medicine in Birmingham, London, 1821–3, and Paris, 1824 ; lectured on anatomy in Birmingham, 1825 ; joint-founder of the Birmingham School of Medicine, 1828, the Queen's Hospital, 1841, and Queen's College, Birmingham, 1843 ; published medical treatises.
[xii. 418]

COXE, FRANCIS (fl. 1560), quack doctor ; prosecuted for sorcery, 1561 ; published an 'Unfained Retractation,' another pamphlet against necromancy, and, 1575, 'De oleis . . . conficiendis,' a volume of receipts.
[xii. 418]

COXE, HENRY OCTAVIUS (1811–1881), palæographer ; educated at Westminster ; M.A. Worcester College, Oxford, 1836 ; assistant in the manuscript department, British Museum, 1833 ; sub-librarian, 1838, and librarian, 1860–81, of the Bodleian Library ; made an archæological tour in the Levant, 1857 ; rector of Wytham, Berkshire, 1868 ; edited historical manuscripts, 1840–50 ; catalogued manuscripts in the Bodleian and Oxford college libraries, 1852–4 ; superintended cataloguing of Bodleian printed books, 1859–80.
[xii. 419]

COXE or COCKIS, JOHN (fl. 1572), translator of some treatises by Bullinger.
[xii. 420]

COXE, PETER (d. 1844), poet ; a London auctioneer ; published pamphlets and verses, 1807–23.
[xii. 420]

COXE or COX, RICHARD (d. 1596), divine ; B.A. Cambridge, 1582 ; M.A. Oxford, 1584 ; rector of Diss, Norfolk, 1589 ; published a catechism, 1591, and sermons.
[xii. 420]

COXE, RICHARD CHARLES (1800–1865), divine ; M.A. Oxford, 1824 ; vicar of Newcastle-on-Tyne, 1841 ; vicar of Eglingham and archdeacon of Lindisfarne, 1853 ; canon of Durham, 1857 ; published sermons and verses.
[xii. 420]

COXE, THOMAS (1615–1685), physician in the parliamentary army ; M.A. Cambridge, 1638 ; M.D. Padua, 1641 ; F.C.P., 1649 ; died, a bankrupt, in France.
[xii. 421]

COXE, WILLIAM (1747–1828), historian ; educated at Eton ; fellow, King's College, Cambridge, 1768 ; M.A., 1772 ; occasionally travelled, as tutor, on the continent ; vicar of Kingston-on-Thames, 1786–8 ; rector of Bemerton, 1788–1828, holding also other benefices ; archdeacon of Wiltshire, 1804 ; published notes of travel, 1779–1801 ; compiled memoirs of the House of Austria, 1807, of the Spanish Bourbons, 1813, of Walpole, 1798, Marlborough, 1818–19, Shrewsbury, 1821, and Henry Pelham, posthumously published, 1829.
[xii. 421]

COXETER, THOMAS (1689–1747), literary antiquary ; entered Trinity College, Oxford, 1705 ; collected old English plays ; forged titles of plays ; his name attached to a worthless edition of Massinger, 1759.
[xii. 422]

COXON, THOMAS (fl. 1609–1636). [See COCKSON.]

COXON, THOMAS (1654–1735), jesuit ; born in Durham ; joined the jesuits, 1676 ; mission priest in England, 1695–1724 ; died at St. Omer.
[xii. 423]

COXWELL, HENRY (TRACEY) (1819–1900), aeronaut ; apprenticed as surgeon-dentist, 1836 ; made his first balloon ascent, 1844 ; projected and edited 'The Balloon,' 1845 ; entrusted with management of a balloon at Brussels, 1848, and subsequently made ascents in British Islands and on the continent ; attained, 1862, with Dr. James Glaisher, F.R.S., with whom he had made meteorological observations, greatest height on record (about seven miles) ; managed war balloons for the Germans in Franco-German war, 1870 ; made his last ascent, 1885 ; published 'My Life and Balloon Experiences,' 1887–9.
[Suppl. ii. 76]

COYNE, JOSEPH STIRLING (1803–1868), dramatist journalist in Dublin ; brought out three farces in Dublin 1835–6 ; settled as journalist in London, 1836 ; wrote nearly sixty dramatic pieces.
[xii. 423]

COYTE, WILLIAM BEESTON (1741?–1810), botanist ; M.B. Cambridge, 1763 ; medical practitioner in Ipswich ; published botanical tracts, 1785–1807.
[xii. 424]

COZENS, ALEXANDER (d. 1786), landscape-painter in water-colours ; born in Russia ; reputed son of Peter the Great ; studied art in Italy ; settled in England, 1746 exhibited, 1760–81 ; drawing-master at Eton, 1763–8 ; published tracts on art, 1771–85.
[xii. 424]

COZENS, JOHN ROBERT (1752–1799), landscape painter in water-colours ; son of Alexander Cozens [q. v.] exhibited, 1767 ; made sketching tour in Switzerland, 1776 and Italy ; returned to England, 1782 ; insane, 1794–9.
[xii. 425]

CRAB, ROGER (1621?-1680), ascetic; became a vegetarian and water-drinker, 1641; in the parliamentary army, 1642-9; hatter at Chesham, 1649-51; quack doctor near Uxbridge; imprisoned in London, 1655; vulgarly said to have foretold the Restoration and the accession of William of Orange; published an autobiography, 1655, and tracts against the quakers. [xii. 426]

CRABB, GEORGE (1778-1851), miscellaneous writer; studied German at Bremen, 1801; published German textbooks; entered Magdalen Hall, Oxford, 1814; M.A., 1822; barrister, Inner Temple, 1829; compiled technical and historical dictionaries and published law treatises. [xii. 426]

CRABB, HABAKKUK (1750-1794), congregational minister; educated at Daventry academy, 1766; minister at Stowmarket, 1772-6, subsequently in other towns; held Arian opinions; his sermons published posthumously, 1796. [xii. 427]

CRABB, JAMES (1774-1851), Wesleyan methodist; private schoolmaster at Romsey, and preacher at Southampton; missionary to the New Forest gipsies; promoted Southampton educational charities. [xii. 427]

CRABBE, GEORGE (1754-1832), poet; born at Aldeburgh, Suffolk; mostly self-taught; worked in a warehouse; servant to a country doctor, 1768-75; met Sarah Elmy, his future wife, 1771; published verses, 1772-5; studied botany and surgery; practised surgery at Aldeburgh; went to London and published the 'Candidate,' 1780; befriended by Edmund Burke; published the 'Library,' 1781; curate of Aldeburgh, 1781; chaplain at Belvoir to the Duke of Rutland, 1782-5; published the 'Village,' 1783; beneficed, but non-resident, in Dorset; LL.B. Lambeth; curate at Stathern, Leicestershire, 1785; published the 'Newspaper,' 1785; rector of Muston, Leicestershire, and non-resident vicar of Allington, Lincolnshire, 1789; inherited property; wrote, and burned, novels and a treatise on botany; absented himself for many years from Muston rectory; recalled thither by the bishop, 1805; published the 'Parish Register,' 1807; the 'Borough,' 1810, and 'Tales in Verse,' 1812; resident rector of Trowbridge, Wiltshire, 1814-32, and non-resident vicar of Croxton, Leicestershire; published 'Tales of the Hall,' 1819; visited Edinburgh, 1822; his collected works published, 1834. [xii. 428]

CRABBE, GEORGE (1785-1857), biographer; son of George Crabbe (1754-1832) [q. v.]; B.A. Cambridge, 1807; vicar of Bredfield, Suffolk, 1834; published a life of his father, 1834. [xii. 431]

CRABTREE or **KRABTREE**, HENRY (fl. 1685), astrologer; published an almanack, 'Merlinus Rusticus,' 1685; curate at Todmorden, Lancashire. [xii. 431]

CRABTREE, WILLIAM (1610-1644?), astronomer; educated at Manchester grammar school; a cloth merchant; studied astronomy; jointly with Jeremiah Horrox [q. v.] observed the transit of Venus, 1639. [xii. 431]

CRACE, FREDERICK (1779-1859), architectural decorator in London; from 1818, collected maps (1560-1859) and views of London; his collections catalogued, 1878, and bought by the British Museum, 1880. [xii. 432]

CRACHERODE, CLAYTON MORDAUNT (1730-1799), bibliophile; entered Westminster School, 1742; student of Christ Church, Oxford, 1746-99; M.A., 1753; curate of Binsey; a great buyer of books from 1775; bequeathed his books and prints to British Museum. [xii. 433]

CRADOCK, EDWARD (fl. 1571), alchemist: student of Christ Church, Oxford, 1552; M.A., 1559; D.D., 1565; Lady Margaret professor of divinity, 1565-94; published a devotional tract, 'The Shippe of Assured Safetie,' 1571; left manuscript treatises on the philosopher's stone. [xii. 434]

CRADOCK, JOHN (1708?-1778), archbishop of Dublin; fellow of St. John's College, Cambridge; B.A. 1728; D.D., 1749; rector of Dry Drayton, Cambridgeshire, and of St. Paul's, Covent Garden; chaplain to the lord-lieutenant of Ireland, 1757; bishop of Kilmore, 1757; translated to Dublin, 1772; published sermons and charges. [xii. 434]

CRADOCK, SIR JOHN FRANCIS (1762-1839). [See CARADOC.]

CRADOCK, JOSEPH (1742-1826), author; of Gumley, Leicestershire; entered Emmanuel College, Cambridge, 1759; honorary M.A., 1765; a patron of the London stage; adapted Voltaire's 'Les Scythes,' 1771; published a pamphlet against John Wilkes, 1773, account of a tour in Wales, 1777, a tragedy, a novel, essays, and, 1826, 'Literary Memoirs.' [xii. 435]

CRADOCK, MARMADUKE (1660?-1716), wrongly called 'Luke,' painter; house-painter's apprentice in London; painted, without recognition, animals, birds, and still-life; some of his pictures engraved, 1743. [xii. 436]

CRADOCK, MATTHEW (d. 1641), first governor (1628-9) of the Massachusetts Company; London merchant; traded with East Indies, 1618; resigned governorship, 1629, to allow headquarters to be transferred to New England; sent help to the colony, 1630-6; M.P., London, in Long parliament; opposed to the king. [xii. 436]

CRADOCK, SAMUEL (1621?-1706), congregational divine; fellow of Emmanuel College, Cambridge, 1645-56; B.D., 1651; rector of North Cadbury, Somerset, 1656-62; inherited Geesings, Suffolk, 1662; kept a congregational chapel and academy there, 1672-96; congregational preacher near Bishop's Stortford, 1696-1706; published theological treatises, 1659-90. [xii. 437]

CRADOCK, WALTER (1606?-1659), congregational minister; curate at Cardiff and Wrexham; chaplain to Sir Robert Harley of Herefordshire; congregational minister at Llanvaches, Monmouthshire; preacher in London, 1646; published sermons, 1646-51; his works collected, 1800. [xii. 438]

CRADOCK, ZACHARY (1633-1695), provost of Eton; fellow of Queens' College, Cambridge, 1654; chaplain at Lisbon, 1656; canon of Chichester, 1670; fellow of Eton, 1671, and provost, 1681-95; published sermons. [xii. 438]

CRAFT, WILLIAM H. (d. 1805?), enamel-painter; exhibited decorative and portrait enamels, 1774-95; employed at Battersea enamel works. [xii. 438]

CRAGGS, JAMES, the elder (1657-1721), postmaster-general; army clothier; imprisoned, 1695, for refusing a parliamentary commission access to his books; M.P., Grampound, 1702-13; member of committee, East India Company, 1702; secretary of the ordnance office till 1714; clerk of the deliveries; agent of Sarah, duchess of Marlborough; joint postmaster-general, 1715-20; accumulated great wealth; proceeded against for promoting the South Sea Company, 1721. [xii. 439]

CRAGGS, JAMES, the younger (1686-1721), secretary of state; younger son of James Craggs the elder [q. v.]; travelled; friend of George, elector of Hanover; M.P., 1713; secretary at war, 1717; secretary of state, 1718; implicated in the South Sea Company scandal; friend of Alexander Pope. [xii. 440]

CRAIG, ALEXANDER (1567?-1627), poet; M.A. St. Andrews, 1586; published 'Poetical Essayes,' flattering James I, 1604; pensioned, 1605; published 'Amorose Songes,' 1606, 'Poetical Recreations,' 1609 and 1623, and, posthumously, 'The Pilgrime and Heremite'; wrote commendatory verses in books; his works collected, 1873-4. [xii. 441]

CRAIG, JAMES (d. 1795), architect; of Edinburgh; published designs for laying out Edinburgh New Town, 1767; continued his architectural designs, 1786. [xii. 442]

CRAIG, SIR JAMES GIBSON (1765-1850), politician; born James Gibson; took the name Craig on inheriting Riccarton, Midlothian, 1823; writer to the signet, Edinburgh, 1786-1850; an ardent whig; created baronet, 1831; opposed the disruption of the church, 1843. [xii. 442]

CRAIG, SIR JAMES HENRY (1748-1812), general; ensign, 1763; captain, 1771; served in North America, 1774-81; lieutenant-colonel, 1781; served in the Netherlands, 1794; major-general, 1794; took Cape Colony, 1795; governor at the Cape, 1795-7; K.B., 1797; in India, 1797-1802; lieutenant-general, 1801; commanded troops in Italy and Sicily, 1805-6; governor of Canada, 1807-11; general, 1812. [xii. 443]

CRAIG, JAMES THOMSON GIBSON (1799-1886), antiquary; second son of Sir James Gibson Craig [q. v.]; educated at Edinburgh High School and University; writer to the signet, Edinburgh; book collector. [xii. 445]

CRAIG, JOHN (1512?-1600), Scottish divine; educated at St. Andrews; became a Dominican friar; imprisoned for adopting protestant tenets, 1536; visited Cambridge; employed in Italy on Dominican missions; rector of the Dominican convent, Bologna; read Calvin's 'Institutes'; sentenced to death by the inquisition at Rome; escaped to Vienna, and, 1560, to England; minister at Holyrood, Edinburgh, 1561; John Knox's colleague in the High Church, Edinburgh, 1562-71; approved Rizzio's murder; protested against Mary Stuart's marriage with Bothwell; chaplain to James VI, 1579-94; urged the abolition of episcopacy, 1575-81, and opposed its restoration, 1584; offended the violent presbyterians, 1585; drew up, 1581, a confession of faith (the original of the 'Covenant'), and a form for examination before communion, 1590. [xii. 445]

CRAIG, JOHN (d. 1620), physician; third son of Sir Thomas Craig [q. v.]; M.D. Basle; physician to James VI, whom he accompanied to England; M.D. Oxford, 1605; corresponded with Tycho Brahe. [xii. 447]

CRAIG, JOHN (d. 1655), physician; son of John Craig (d. 1620) [q. v.]; physician to James I; F.C.P.; M.D.; declared that James I had died by poison; physician to Charles I. [xii. 448]

CRAIG, JOHN (d. 1731), mathematician; prebendary of Salisbury, 1708; published mathematical treatises, 1685-1718. [xii. 448]

CRAIG, SIR LEWIS, LORD WRIGHTSLANDS (1569-1622), Scottish judge; eldest son of Sir Thomas Craig [q. v.]; M.A. Edinburgh, 1597; studied law at Poitiers; advocate, 1600; a lord of session and knighted, 1605. [xii. 448]

CRAIG, ROBERT (1730-1823), Scottish advocate, 1754; a judge of the Edinburgh commissary court, 1756-1791; wrote in favour of the French democracy, 1795; inherited Riccarton, Midlothian, 1814. [xii. 448]

CRAIG, SIR THOMAS (1538-1608), Scottish feudalist; educated at St. Andrews; studied law at Paris, 1555-61; advocate, 1563; as justice-depute, presided over criminal trials, 1564-73; sheriff-depute of Edinburgh, 1573; knighted, 1603; published 'Jus Feudale,' 1603; attended James I to England, 1603; a commissioner for the union, 1604; wrote, but left unpublished, treatises in vindication of James VI's title to the English crown, against the English claim for homage from Scotland, and in favour of the union, 1603-5; advocate for the Scottish church, 1606; published complimentary Latin verses, 1566, 1603. [xii. 448]

CRAIG, WILLIAM, LORD CRAIG (1745-1813), Scottish judge; educated at Edinburgh; advocate, 1768; sheriff-depute of Ayrshire, 1787; a lord of session, 1792-1813; contributed to the 'Mirror' and 'Lounger.' [xii. 451]

CRAIG, SIR WILLIAM GIBSON (1797-1878), second baronet, of Riccarton, Midlothian; eldest son of Sir James Gibson Craig [q. v.]; advocate, 1820; travelled; M.P., Midlothian, 1837-42, and Edinburgh, 1842-52; lord clerk register, 1862-78. [xii. 451]

CRAIG, WILLIAM MARSHALL (fl. 1788-1828), painter; exhibited miniature-portraits, landscapes in water-colours, and other paintings, 1788-1827; a popular book-illustrator; published manuals on drawing, 1793-1821. [xii. 451]

CRAIGHALL, LORD (1605?-1654). [See HOPE, SIR JOHN.]

CRAIGIE, DAVID (1793-1866), physician; M.D. Edinburgh, 1816; practitioner in Edinburgh; published 'Pathological Anatomy,' 1828, and other medical works. [xii. 452]

CRAIGIE, ROBERT (1685-1760), Scottish judge; advocate, 1710; lord advocate, 1742; president of the court of session, 1754. [xii. 452]

CRAIK, MRS. DINAH MARIA (1826-1887). [See MULOCK.]

CRAIK, GEORGE LILLIE (1798-1866), author; studied divinity at St. Andrews; tutor, 1816; editor of the 'Star,' a local newspaper; wrote for Society for the Diffusion of Useful Knowledge; professor of English literature and history at Belfast, 1849-66; chief works, 'Spenser and his Poetry,' 1845, and 'The Pictorial History of England,' 1837-1841. [xiii. 1]

CRAKANTHORPE, RICHARD (1567-1624), divine; student at Queen's College, Oxford; fellow, 1598; appointed one of the chaplains to Lord Evers, ambassador extraordinary to the emperor Rudolf II, c. 1603; admitted to the rectory of Black Notley, Essex, 1605, of Paglesham, 1617; defended with vigour and learning church of England against Antonio de Dominis [q. v.]; chief works, a 'Defensio Ecclesiæ Anglicanæ' (against De Dominis), 1625 (posthumously published), and 'Logicæ libri quinque de Prædicabilibus,' 1622. [xiii. 2]

CRAKE, AUGUSTINE DAVID (1836-1890), devotional writer; B.A. London, 1864; second master and chaplain of All Saints' school, Bloxham, 1865-78; vicar of St. Peter's, Havenstreet, Isle of Wight, 1879-85, of Cholsey, near Wallingford, 1885-90; published devotional works, and stories relating to church history, besides 'History of Church under Roman Empire,' 1873. [Suppl. ii. 77]

CRAKELT, WILLIAM (1741-1812), classical scholar; master of Northfleet grammar school; vicar of Chalk, 1774; edited Entick's Latin dictionaries and translated Mauduit's 'New Treatise of Spherical Trigonometry,' 1768. [xiii. 3]

CRAMER, FRANZ or FRANÇOIS (1772-1848), violinist; son of Wilhelm Cramer [q. v.]; born at Schwetzingen; member of the Royal Society of Musicians, 1794; one of the first professors of the Royal Academy of Music. [xiii. 3]

CRAMER, JOHANN BAPTIST (1771-1858), pianist; son of Wilhelm Cramer [q. v.]; born at Mannheim; studied in boyhood under Clementi and G. F. Abel, 1785, becoming the foremost performer of his time; met Haydn, 1788, Berlioz and Beethoven later; resided both in England and on the continent. His 'Eighty-four Studies' is still a classic composition. [xiii. 3]

CRAMER, JOHN ANTONY (1793-1848), dean of Carlisle, 1844; born at Mittoden, Switzerland; educated at Westminster; M.A. Christ Church, Oxford, 1817; D.D., 1831; regius professor of modern history, 1842; principal of New Inn Hall, Oxford, 1831-47; wrote on classical geography. [xiii. 4]

CRAMER, WILHELM (1745?-1799), violinist; born at Mannheim; originally a member of the elector's band; came to London in 1772; member of the Royal Society of Musicians, 1777; appeared in most of the musical performances of his time. [xiii. 5]

CRAMP, JOHN MOCKETT (1791-1881), baptist minister; founded the baptist church at St. Peter's, Isle of Thanet; D.D.; president of the baptist college, Montreal, 1844, and of Accadia College, Nova Scotia, 1851-69; theological essayist and conductor of periodicals. [xiii. 5]

CRAMPTON, SIR JOHN FIENNES TWISLETON (1805-1886), diplomatist; son of Sir Philip Crampton [q. v.]; became secretary of legation at Berne, 1844; transferred to Washington, 1845; recalled, 1856, from fear of complications with the U.S.A. government, which he had offended by recruiting soldiers in America for the Crimean war; K.C.B., 1856; minister plenipotentiary and envoy extraordinary at Hanover, 1857. [xiii. 6]

CRAMPTON, SIR PHILIP (1777-1858), surgeon; studied medicine in Dublin; surgeon to the Meath Hospital, Dublin, 1798; graduated at Glasgow, 1800; surgeon in ordinary to the queen; created baronet, 1839; F.R.S.; interested in zoology. [xiii. 7]

CRAMPTON, THOMAS RUSSELL (1816-1888), railway engineer; assistant, 1839-44, to the elder Brunel, and later to (Sir) Daniel Gooch, and John and George Rennie; began business independently, 1848; patented design for Crampton engine, 1843; received gold medal at Great Exhibition, 1851, for locomotive; laid transmarine cable between Dover and Calais, 1851; constructed lines in Kent, now merged in London, Chatham, and Dover Railway; M.I.C.E., 1854. [Suppl. ii. 78]

CRAMPTON, VICTOIRE, LADY (1837-1871), soprano singer; second daughter of Michael William Balfe [q. v.]; born in Paris; appeared first at the Lyceum, 1857, as Amina in 'Sonnambula'; married Sir John Fiennes Twisleton Crampton [q. v.]; died at Madrid. [xiii. 7]

CRANBORNE, first VISCOUNT (1563?-1612). [See CECIL, ROBERT.]

CRANCH, JOHN (1751-1821), painter; self-taught; contributed pictures to the Society of Artists and, 1808, the British Institution, excelling in the 'poker' style; wrote discussion on way to improve British art. [xiii. 8]

CRANE, EDWARD (1721-1749), presbyterian minister; assistant minister, Norwich, 1745; began to preach to the Dutch congregation there, 1749, though not approving the Heidelberg catechism. [xiii. 8]

CRANE, SIR FRANCIS (d. 1636), director of the tapestry works established at Mortlake by James I; clerk of the parliament, 1606; secretary to Charles I when Prince of Wales; M.P., Penryn, 1614 and 1621, Launceston, 1624; reported in 1619 to have received the valuable privilege of creating three baronets, in 1623 ten or twelve serjeants-at-law at 500l. apiece; envied by courtiers for the numerous manors granted him by the king as security for advances; died at Paris. [xiii. 9]

CRANE, JOHN (1572-1652), apothecary; sheriff of Cambridgeshire, 1641. [xiii. 10]

CRANE, LUCY (1842-1882), art critic; daughter of the miniaturist Thomas Crane [q. v.]; musician and redactor of nursery tales; delivered lectures on 'Art and the Formation of Taste' which her brothers Thomas and Walter issued, 1882. [xiii. 10]

CRANE, NICHOLAS (1522?-1588?), presbyterian; educated at Christ's College, Cambridge; imprisoned for performing service out of the Geneva prayer-book, 1568-9; subsequently inhibited; died in Newgate. [xiii. 11]

CRANE, RALPH (fl. 1625), poet; educated for the law; a transcriber of popular works; published 'The Workes of Mercy, both Corporeall and Spirituall,' 1621. [xiii. 11]

CRANE, THOMAS (1631-1714), divine and theological writer; ejected from the living of Rampisham at the Restoration. [xiii. 12]

CRANE, THOMAS (1808-1859), artist; gold medallist, Royal Academy, 1825; miniature-painter; produced lithographic views of North Wales; treasurer of the Liverpool Academy, 1841. [xiii. 12]

CRANE, WILLIAM (fl. 1530), master of the children of the Chapel Royal; water-bailiff for the town and harbour of Dartmouth, 1509-10; controller of the tonnage and poundage of customs in the port of London, 1514; licensed to export merchandise not belonging to the staple of Calais, 1514; appointed master of the Chapel Royal choristers, 1526, and water-bailiff of the port of Lynn, 1535. [xiii. 13]

CRANFIELD, LIONEL, EARL OF MIDDLESEX (1575-1645), originally apprenticed to Richard Shephard, a merchant adventurer; member of the Company of Mercers; appearing in its behalf before the privy council, attracted the notice of James I, the Earl of Northampton, and subsequently of the Duke of Buckingham; appointed receiver of customs for Dorset and Somerset, 1605; surveyor-general of customs, 1613, master of the great wardrobe, 1618, and master of the court of wards, and chief commissioner of the navy, 1619; checked waste in all these departments; privy councillor, 1620; attacked Bacon, disliking his views on patents and monopolies, 1621; created Baron Cranfield of Cranfield, 1622, and Earl of Middlesex, 1622; charged by Coke with corrupt practices as master of court of wards, and condemned, 1624; released from the Tower, 1624; pardoned, 1625. [xiii. 14]

CRANFORD, JAMES (1592?-1657), presbyterian divine; M.A. Balliol College, Oxford, 1624; rector of St. Christopher, London, 1643; wrote a 'Confutation of the Anabaptists,' 'Hæreseomachia,' 1646, and various prefaces. [xiii. 16]

CRANKE, JAMES (1746?-1826), portrait-painter; of the school of Reynolds; a successful copyist of great pictures. [xiii. 17]

CRANLEY, THOMAS (1337?-1417), archbishop of Dublin; D.D. Oxford, and fellow of Merton, 1366; first warden of Winchester College, 1382; principal of Hart Hall, 1384; warden, New College, Oxford, 1389-96; chancellor of the university, 1390; archbishop of Dublin, 1397-1417; chancellor of Ireland under Henry IV. [xiii. 17]

CRANLEY, THOMAS (fl. 1635), poet and friend of George Wither [q. v.]; published 'Amanda,' 1635. [xiii. 18]

CRANMER, GEORGE (1563-1600), secretary to Davison, secretary of state, subsequently to Sir Henry Killigrew; educated at Merchant Taylors' School and Corpus Christi College, Oxford; wrote a letter to Hooker 'Concerning the new Church Discipline,' 1598; killed in skirmish with Irish rebels at Carlingford. [xiii. 18]

CRANMER, THOMAS (1489-1556), archbishop of Canterbury; studied philosophy, logic, and classics at Cambridge; M.A., 1515; forfeited fellowship at Jesus College by marriage; re-elected; D.D.; public examiner in theology; expressed privately an opinion that the establishment of the invalidity of Henry VIII's marriage with Catherine of Arragon would justify a divorce, 1529; propounded these views in a treatise; attended the Earl of Wiltshire, ambassador to Charles V, 1530; returned to England, 1533, being appointed archbishop of Canterbury; gave formal sentence of the invalidity of the king's marriage with Catherine of Arragon, 1533; pronounced King Henry's marriage with Anne Boleyn to be lawful; granted bulls and dispensations; maintained the king's claim to be the supreme head of the church of England; pronounced his marriage with Anne Boleyn null and void, 1536; promulgated ten articles of doctrine, 1536; in conjunction with Cromwell had the supposed relics of St. Thomas of Canterbury investigated, 1538, but did not take part in the suppression of the monasteries; unsuccessfully opposed the Act of the Six Articles 'for Abolishing Diversity of Opinions,' 1539; became an instrument for the divorce of Anne of Cleves; did not oppose the bill of attainder against Thomas Cromwell, 1540; conveyed to the king information of the infidelity of his fifth wife, Catherine Howard, 1541; defended the 'Great Bible' against the criticisms of Bishop Gardiner, 1542; vindicated by Henry VIII against charges of heresy; appointed one of the council to govern during the minority of Edward VI, 1547; supervised the production of the first prayer-book, 1548; deserted the falling Protector Somerset, 1549; made overtures to Melanchthon with the view of promoting union of reformed churches; wrote against transubstantiation; made a revision of the prayer-book, but could not induce the Princess Mary to recognise the new use, which was authorised (1552) by an Act of Uniformity; promulgated forty-two articles of religion (afterwards reduced to thirty-nine), 1552; joined in signing a will of Edward VI excluding the Princess Mary from the succession, 1553; committed to the Tower for disseminating seditious bills against the mass and for having been a partisan of Lady Jane Grey, 1553; released that he might argue in justification of his alleged heresies, 1554; adjudged to be in the wrong at a discussion held at Oxford; formally cited to appear before the pope, 1555; refused to recognise papal jurisdiction; condemned for heresy by Cardinal Pole, recently appointed archbishop of Canterbury; degraded, 1556; signed six documents admitting the supremacy of the pope and the truth of all Roman catholic doctrine except transubstantiation, in vain; burned at the stake repudiating these admissions, 21 March 1556; compiled a 'Reformatio Legum Ecclesiasticarum,' 1550, and wrote on Anglican discipline and theology. [xiii. 19]

CRANSTOUN, DAVID (fl. 1509-1526), professor of belles-lettres at the College of Montacute, Paris; Theol. Doc.; wrote additions to the 'Moralia' of Almain, 1526, and to the 'Parva Logicalia' of de Villascusa, 1520. [xiii. 31]

CRANSTOUN, GEORGE, LORD COREHOUSE (d. 1850), Scottish judge; advocate at the Scottish bar, 1793; sheriff-depute for Sutherland, 1806; dean of the Faculty of Advocates, 1823; raised to the bench as Lord Corehouse, 1826; friend of Sir Walter Scott; author of a skit entitled 'The Diamond Beetle Case.' [xiii. 32]

CRANSTOUN, HELEN D'ARCY (1765-1838), songwriter; sister of George Cranstoun, lord Corehouse [q. v.]; wife of Dugald Stewart [q. v.] [liv. 283]

CRANSTOUN, JAMES, eighth BARON CRANSTOUN (1755-1796), naval officer; fought against the French in Basseterre roads, 1782; captain, 1782; commanded Rodney's flag-ship, 1782; died just after being made governor of Grenada island, 1796. [xiii. 32]

CRANSTOUN, WILLIAM HENRY (1714-1752), disowned his marriage with Anne Murray of Leith, 1746, in order to marry Mary Blandy [q. v.] The latter murdered her father for remonstrating, but there is no proof that Cranstoun was implicated. [xiii. 32]

CRANWELL, JOHN (d. 1793), poet; fellow of Sidney Sussex College, Cambridge; M.A., 1751; incumbent of Abbott's Ripton; translator of two modern Latin poems. [xiii. 33]

CRANWORTH, BARON (1790-1868). [See ROLFE, ROBERT MONSEY.]

CRASHAW, RICHARD (1613?-1649), poet; son of William Crashaw [q. v.]; educated at Charterhouse and Pembroke Hall, Cambridge; fellow of Peterhouse, 1637-1643; M.A., 1638; expelled from Peterhouse for refusing to accept the Solemn League and Covenant, 1643; entered the Roman catholic church and travelled to Paris; introduced by Queen Henrietta Maria to Cardinal Palotta of Rome; went to Italy, 1648 or 1649; sub-canon of the Basilica-church of Our Lady of Loretto, 1649; died at Loretto the same year, probably from overheating himself in the journey thither. His 'Steps to the Temple,' appeared 1646, another edition, containing designs by himself, 1652. The book includes a section of secular poems, entitled 'Delights of the Muses.' iii. 33]

CRASHAW, WILLIAM (1572-1626), puritan divine and poet; B.A. St. John's College, Cambridge, 1592?; M.A., 1595; nominated by Queen Elizabeth to the bishop of Ely's fellowship, 1594; B.D., 1603; prebendary of Ripon, 1604; ordered by the archbishop of Canterbury to retract his 'Translation of the Life of the Marchese Caraccioli,' 1609; prebendary of York, 1617; incumbent of St. Mary, Whitechapel, London, 1618-26; wrote, among other works, 'Romish Forgeries and Falsifications,' 1606, and a 'Dialogue betwixt the Soule and the Bodie of a damned Man,' 1616. [xiii. 36]

CRATFIELD, WILLIAM (d 1415), Benedictine; camerarius and, 1390-1414, abbot of Bury St. Edmunds; compiled a 'Registrum' of his house. [xiii. 38]

CRATHORNE, WILLIAM (1670-1740), Roman catholic divine; student, subsequently professor at the English college, Douay; missioner at Hammersmith; translated a 'Life of St. Francis of Sales' and an 'Historical Catechism' from the French. [xiii. 38]

CRAUFURD. [See also CRAWFORD and CRAWFURD.]

CRAUFURD, SIR CHARLES GREGAN- (1761-1821), lieutenant-general; lieutenant, 1781; equerry to the Duke of York, 1785; translated Tielke's work on military science and the history of the Prussian, Austrian, and Russian war from 1756 to 1763, 1787; representative of the English commander-in-chief in the Netherlands at the Austrian headquarters; major-general, 1803; M.P., East Retford, 1806-12; lieutenant-general, 1810; G.C.B., 1820. [xiii. 38]

CRAUFURD, JAMES, LORD ARDMILLAN (1805-1876), Scottish judge; educated at the burgh school, Edinburgh, and at Edinburgh and Glasgow universities; advocate, 1829; solicitor-general for Scotland, 1853; lord of the court of session and lord of justiciary, 1855-76. [xiii. 39]

CRAUFURD, JOHN WALKINSHAW (1721-1793), lieutenant-colonel; fought, as cornet, at Dettingen, 1743, and Fontenoy, 1745; king's falconer for Scotland, 1761; lieutenant-colonel, 1772; laird of Craufurdland, Ayrshire. [xiii. 39]

CRAUFURD, QUINTIN (1743-1819), author; servant of the East India Company till 1780; adhered to the French royal family during the revolution, having settled at Paris; published a history of the Bastille, 1798, researches on the Hindoo civilisation, 1817, and essays on French literature, 1803. [xiii. 40]

CRAUFURD, ROBERT (1764-1812), major-general; brother of Sir Charles Gregan-Craufurd [q. v.]; fought, as captain, against Tippoo Sultan, 1790, 1791, and 1792; lieutenant-colonel, 1797; served as deputy quartermaster-general of Ireland against the Irish rebels, 1798; commanded light brigade in attack on Buenos Ayres, 1807; served in Peninsula with distinction as commander of light troops, 1807 and 1809; major-general, 1811; killed at Ciudad Rodrigo. [xiii. 41]

CRAVEN, ELIZABETH, COUNTESS OF (1750-1828). [See ANSPACH, ELIZABETH, MARGRAVINE OF.]

CRAVEN, JOHN, BARON CRAVEN OF RYTON (d. 1649), founder of scholarships; second son of Sir William Craven [q. v.]; Baron Craven, 1643; founded the Craven scholarships at Oxford and Cambridge. [xiii. 49]

CRAVEN, KEPPEL RICHARD (1779-1851), traveller; settled at Naples, 1805; chamberlain to the Princess of Wales, 1814; friend of Sir William Gell [q. v.]; published 'Excursions in the Abruzzi,' 1838, and 'Italian Scenes,' 1825. [xiii. 42]

CRAVEN, LOUISA, COUNTESS OF (1785?-1860), actress; née Brunton; made her debut as Lady Townley in the 'Provoked Husband' and Beatrice in 'Much Ado,' 1803; married William, first Earl of Craven, of the second creation, 1807. [xiii. 43]

CRAVEN, MRS. PAULINE MARIE ARMANDE AGLAÉ (1808-1891), authoress; daughter of Comte Auguste Marie de La Ferronays, a French emigrant in London; married Augustus, son of Keppel Richard Craven [q. v.], 1834, and lived successively at various continental towns where her husband was attached to English legations; published, 1866, 'Récit d'une Sœur,' relating the history of her family, which met with success. Her subsequent writings include novels and historical and autobiographical works. [Suppl. ii. 79]

CRAVEN, SIR WILLIAM (1548?-1618), lord mayor of London; originally apprenticed to Robert Hulson, merchant taylor; entered into partnership with him, having obtained the freedom of the Merchant Taylors' Company, 1569; warden of the company, 1593; gave 50l. towards the building of the library, St. John's College, Oxford; founded a grammar school at Burnsall, Yorkshire, 1602; knighted, 1603; lord mayor of London, 1610; president of Christ's Hospital, 1611-18. [xiii. 43]

CRAVEN, WILLIAM, EARL OF CRAVEN (1606-1697), eldest son of Sir William Craven [q. v.]; entered the service of Maurice, prince of Orange, 1623; knighted on returning to England, 1627; commanded English troops fighting for Gustavus Adolphus, 1631; contributed 30,000l. to the cause of the palatine house, 1637; fought beside Prince Rupert at Limgea; taken prisoner by the imperialists, 1637; purchased his liberty, 1639; aided Charles I with money; drafted a protest for the then exiled Elizabeth of Bohemia against the parliament's stoppage of her pension; deprived of his estates for loyalty to Charles I, 1651; recovered his lands at the Restoration; privy councillor, 1666 and 1681; created Viscount Craven of Uffington and Earl of Craven, 1664; offered his London mansion, Drury House, to Elizabeth of Bohemia, 1661; said, without much probability, to have been privately married to her; lieutenant-general of the forces, 1685; bidden by James II to hand over the duty of guarding Whitehall to the Dutch troops under Solms, 1688. He was early a fellow of the Royal Society. [xiii. 43]

CRAWFORD. [See also CRAUFURD and CRAWFURD.]

CRAWFORD, EARLS OF. [See LINDSAY, SIR DAVID, first EARL, 1365?-1407; LINDSAY, ALEXANDER, fourth EARL, d. 1454; LINDSAY, DAVID, fifth EARL, 1440?-1495; LINDSAY, DAVID, tenth EARL, d. 1574; LINDSAY, DAVID, eleventh EARL, 1547?-1607; LINDSAY, LUDOVIC, sixteenth EARL, 1600-1652?; LINDSAY, JOHN, seventeenth EARL, 1596-1678; LINDSAY, DAVID, twelfth EARL, d. 1621; LINDSAY, WILLIAM, eighteenth EARL, d. 1698; LINDSAY, JOHN, twentieth EARL, 1702-1749; LINDSAY, ALEXANDER WILLIAM, twenty-fifth EARL, 1812-1880.]

CRAWFORD, ADAIR (1748-1795), physician and chemist; professor of chemistry at the military academy, Woolwich, and physician at St. Thomas's Hospital; published work maintaining the 'phlogiston' hypothesis, 1779; wrote 'On Cancer and the Aerial Fluids,' 1790, and an 'Inquiry into the Effects of Tonics on the Animal Fibre,' published 1817. [xiii. 49]

CRAWFORD, ANN (1734-1801). [See BARRY, ANN SPRANGER.]

CRAWFORD, DAVID (1665–1726), historiographer for Scotland; educated at Glasgow University; wrote two comedies. His 'Memoirs' from 1567 to his own times on the Scottish revolution, published 1706, were asserted by Laing to be untrustworthy. [xiii. 51]

CRAWFORD, EDMUND THORNTON (1806–1885), landscape and marine painter, and one of the earliest members of the Royal Scottish Academy. [xiii. 51]

CRAWFORD, JOHN (1816–1873), Scottish poet; wrote 'Doric Lays,' 1850, and 'Memorials of Alloa,' a posthumous publication. [xiii. 52]

CRAWFORD, LAWRENCE (1611–1645), soldier; served under Gustavus Adolphus and Christian of Denmark; commanded foot regiment in Ireland, 1641; refused to fight against the parliament, and was obliged to leave Scotland, 1643; sergeant-major-general, 1644; quarrelled with Cromwell, but fought bravely for the parliament; killed at the siege of Hereford. [xiii. 52]

CRAWFORD, ROBERT (d. 1733), author of 'Tweedside' and other well-known Scottish songs; contributed to Ramsay's 'Tea-table Miscellany.' [xii. 53]

CRAWFORD or **CRAUFURD**, THOMAS (1530?–1603), soldier; taken prisoner at Pinkie, 1547; entered the service of Henry II of France, 1550; became one of the gentlemen of Lord Darnley, 1561; expressed an opinion that Mary treated Darnley too much like a prisoner; joined association for bringing Darnley's murderers to trial; unsuccessfully demanded justice on Maitland and Sir James Balfour as the murderers, 1569; captured castle of Dumbarton, 1571; received the surrender of Edinburgh Castle, 1573; rewarded with a grant of lands at Dalry, 1578. [xiii. 53]

CRAWFORD, THOMAS JACKSON (1812–1875), Scottish divine; educated at St. Andrews University; D.D. St. Andrews, 1844; professor of divinity, 1859; dean of the Chapel Royal; moderator of the general assembly, 1867; died at Genoa; wrote various theological works on presbyterian lines. [xiii. 55]

CRAWFORD, WILLIAM (1739?–1800), Irish presbyterian minister and historian; minister of Strabane, co. Tyrone, 1766–98; M.A. Glasgow; D.D. 1785; promoted volunteer movement, 1778; founded an unsectarian academy at Strabane, 1785; admitted into the Antrim presbytery, 1798; wrote a critique on Chesterfield's 'Letters to his Son,' 1776, and published a 'History of Ireland' in the form of letters, 1783. [xiii. 56]

CRAWFORD, WILLIAM (1788–1847), philanthropist; obtained an appointment in the naval transport office, 1804; secretary to the London Prison Discipline Society; sent to examine United States prison system, 1833; helped to introduce system of separate cells in England; inspector of prisons for the London and midland district, 1835–47. [xiii. 57]

CRAWFORD, WILLIAM (1825–1869), painter; studied at Rome; especially famous for his crayon portraits. [xiii. 58]

CRAWFORD, WILLIAM SHARMAN (1781–1861), politician; sheriff of Down, 1811; advocated Roman catholic emancipation; M.P. for Dundalk, 1835–7; brought forward a bill to compensate evicted tenants for improvements, 1835, which was not carried; supported the chartists, 1837; M.P. for Rochdale, 1841–52; procured the formation of the Tenant Right Association in Ulster, 1846; promulgated the 'federal scheme' for an Irish parliament in opposition to O'Connell, 1843. [xiii. 58]

CRAWFURD. [See also CRAUFURD and CRAWFORD.]

CRAWFURD, ARCHIBALD (1785–1843), Scottish poet; apprenticed to a baker in boyhood; obtained an engagement in the family of General Hay of Rannes; published 'St. James's in an Uproar,' 1819; started two periodicals, 'The Correspondent' and 'The Gaberlunzie,' and (1824) wrote 'Tales of a Grandfather.' [xiii. 59]

CRAWFURD, GEORGE (d. 1748), genealogist and historian; enabled by his researches Simon Fraser to obtain the barony of Lovat, but was not recompensed; wrote on Scottish history and genealogy. [xiii. 60]

CRAWFURD, JOHN (1783–1868), orientalist; army doctor in N.W. Provinces of India; held appointments under Lord Minto in Java from 1811; envoy to the court of Siam; appointed to administer government of Singapore, 1823; envoy to the court of Ava; published 'History of the Indian Archipelago,' 1820, and 'A Grammar and Dictionary of the Malay Language,' 1852. [xiii. 60]

CRAWFURD or **CRAWFORD**, THOMAS (d. 1662), professor; educated at St. Andrews University; M.A., 1621; professor of humanity, Edinburgh, 1626; rector of the high school, Edinburgh, 1630; professor of mathematics at Edinburgh, 1640–62; wrote a 'History of the University of Edinburgh from 1580 to 1646' (published, 1808). [xiii. 61]

CRAWLEY, SIR FRANCIS (1584–1649), judge; scholar of Caius College, Cambridge, 1592; studied law at Staple Inn and Gray's Inn; serjeant-at-law, 1623; counsel for the Earl of Bristol, 1626; puisne judge in the common pleas, 1632; knighted, 1632; maintained legality of ship-money, 1636; impeached and restrained from going on circuit, 1641. [xiii. 62]

CRAWLEY, RICHARD (1840–1893), scholar; educated at Marlborough and University College, Oxford; B.A., 1866; fellow of Worcester College, 1866–80; barrister, Lincoln's Inn, 1869; translated Thucydides, 1866–74, and wrote in verse and prose. [Suppl. ii. 81]

CRAWSHAY, ROBERT THOMPSON (1817–1879), ironmaster; son of William Crawshay [q. v.]; acting manager of Cyfarthfa ironworks; sole manager, 1867; assented to combination of masters to meet workmen's strikes; closed works on the invention of the Bessemer steel process. [xiii. 62]

CRAWSHAY, WILLIAM (1788–1867), ironmaster; proprietor of the Cyfarthfa ironworks; sheriff of Glamorganshire, 1822; subscribed 500l. on behalf of the Hungarian refugees in Turkey, 1849. [xiii. 63]

CREAGH, PETER (d. 1707), Roman catholic bishop of Cork and Cloyne, 1676; archbishop of Dublin, 1693; died an exile at Strasburg. [xiii. 63]

CREAGH, RICHARD (1525?–1585), Roman catholic archbishop of Armagh; studied at Louvain; B.D. of the Pontifical College, 1555; archbishop of Armagh, 1564; committed to the Tower of London, 1565; tried for high treason in Dublin, 1567; acquitted, but died in the Tower, 1585; wrote works of Irish philology, theology, and an 'Ecclesiastical History.' [xiii. 63]

CREALOCK, HENRY HOPE (1831–1891), soldier, artist, and author; educated at Rugby; lieutenant 90th light infantry, 1852; captain, 1854; served in Crimea; in China, 1856–8; lieutenant-colonel, 1858; in India, 1858–9; military secretary to Lord Elgin in China, 1860; major-general, 1870; served in Zulu war, 1879; C.M.G., 1879; retired as lieutenant-general, 1884. His 'Deer Stalking in Highlands of Scotland' was published posthumously, 1892, with illustrations from his own drawings.
[Suppl. ii. 81]

CREASY, SIR EDWARD SHEPHERD (1812–1878), historian; educated at Eton; fellow, King's College, Cambridge, 1834; barrister, Lincoln's Inn, 1837; professor of modern and ancient history, London University, 1840; knighted, 1860; chief-justice of Ceylon, 1860; best known by his 'Fifteen Decisive Battles of the World,' 1852.
[xiii. 64]

CREECH, THOMAS (1659–1700), translator; scholar of Wadham College, Oxford, 1676; M.A., 1683; B.D., 1696; fellow of All Souls, Oxford, 1683; head-master of Sherborne, 1694–6; committed suicide from disappointed love and pecuniary difficulties, 1700. He translated Lucretius, 1682 (verse), the Odes, Satires, and Epistles of Horace, 1684 (verse), Theocritus, 1684, Manilius, 1697 (verse), the XIIIth satire of Juvenal, 1693, and parts of Plutarch and less famous Greek and Latin writers.
[xiii. 64]

CREECH, WILLIAM (1745–1815), Edinburgh publisher and lord provost of Edinburgh; studied at Edinburgh University; partner with the publisher Kincaid, 1771; on the withdrawal of Kincaid, 1773, became the foremost publisher in Scotland, and was first to bring out the works of Blair, Beattie, Mackenzie, and Burns; quarrelled with Burns; helped to found the Speculative Society; contributed under the pseudonym of 'Theophrastus' essays to the newspapers; lord provost of Edinburgh, 1811–13. [xiii. 67]

CREED, CARY (1708-1775), etcher; published plates from the marbles at Wilton House. [xiii. 68]

CREED, ELIZABETH (1644?-1728), philanthropist; *née* Pickering; married John Creed [q. v.], of Oundle, 1668; gave free instruction to girls in drawing and needlework; painted altar-pieces for churches near Oundle. [xiii. 68]

CREED, JOHN (*fl.* 1663), official; deputy-treasurer of the fleet, 1660; secretary to the commissioners for Tangier, 1662; F.R.S., 1663. [xiii. 68]

CREED or **CREEDE**, THOMAS (*d.* 1616?), stationer; printed the 1599 quarto of 'Romeo and Juliet,' 'Richard III' (1598 quarto), and 'Henry V' (1600 quarto). [xiii. 69]

CREED, WILLIAM (1614?-1663), divine; scholar of St. John's College, Oxford, 1631; M.A., 1639; B.D., 1646; regius professor of divinity, Oxford, 1660; archdeacon of Wiltshire, 1660; prebendary of Salisbury; rector of Stockton, Wiltshire. [xiii. 69]

CREIGHTON. [See also CRICHTON.]

CREIGHTON, MANDELL (1843-1901), bishop of London; fellow of Merton College, Oxford, 1866; B.A., 1867; tutor; held living of Embleton, Northumberland, 1875-84; rural dean of Alnwick, 1879; took prominent part in organising new diocese of Newcastle, 1881; was examining chaplain to Bishop Wilberforce, 1882; honorary canon of Newcastle, 1883; published, 1882, the first two volumes of his 'History of the Papacy' (vols. iii. and iv. appearing in 1887, vol. v. 1894); honorary D.D. Cambridge; first Dixie professor of ecclesiastical history, and fellow of Emmanuel College, Cambridge, 1884; first editor of 'English Historical Review,' 1886-91; canon of Worcester, 1885; canon of Windsor, 1890; bishop of Peterborough, 1891; represented English church at coronation of Emperor Nicholas II at Moscow, 1896; first president of Church Historical Society, 1894-1901; Hulsean lecturer, 1893-4, and Rede lecturer, 1895, at Cambridge; Romanes lecturer at Oxford, 1896; bishop of London, 1897; opposed the extravagances of some of the ritualistic clergy; D.D. Oxford and Cambridge; hon. LL.D. Glasgow and Harvard; hon. D.C.L. Oxford and Durham; hon. Litt.D. Durham. His works include 'The Age of Elizabeth,' 1876, 'Cardinal Wolsey,' 1888, 'Queen Elizabeth,' 1896, and numerous sermons, lectures, and historical and other writings. He contributed several memoirs to the 'Dictionary of National Biography.' [Suppl. ii. 82]

CREIGHTON or **CRICHTON**, ROBERT (1593-1672), bishop of Bath and Wells; educated at Westminster and Trinity College, Cambridge; M.A., 1621; professor of Greek, 1625-39; public orator, 1627-39; prebendary of Lincoln, 1631; dean of St. Burians, Cornwall, 1637; chaplain to Charles I; dean of Wells; restored Wells Cathedral; signalised himself by his outspokenness on the sins of Charles II's court; bishop of Bath and Wells, 1670; translated Sguropulus, 1660. [xiii. 69]

CREIGHTON or **CREYGHTON**, ROBERT (1639?-1734), precentor of Wells; son of Robert Creighton [q. v.]; M.A. Cambridge, 1662; fellow of Trinity College, Cambridge, 1662; professor of Greek, Cambridge, 1662-74; canon and precentor of Wells, 1674; D.D. 1678. [xiii. 70]

CRESSENER, DRUE (1638?-1718), protestant writer; fellow of Pembroke Hall, Cambridge, 1662; M.A., 1685; D.D., 1708; prebendary of Ely, 1700; wrote on the Apocalypse. [xiii. 71]

CRESSINGHAM, HUGH (*d.* 1297), treasurer of Scotland; originally steward of Eleanor, queen of Edward I; audited the debts due to Henry III, 1292; prebendary in several English churches; defeated and slain fighting against Wallace at Cambuskenneth, 1297. [xiii. 71]

CRESSWELL, MADAM (*fl.* 1670-1684), courtesan and self-proclaimed religious devotee; satirised by Rochester. [xiii. 72]

CRESSWELL, SIR CRESSWELL (1794-1863), judge; educated at Charterhouse and Emmanuel College, Cambridge; 'wooden spoon'; M.A., 1818; barrister, Inner Temple, 1819; together with Alexander, leader of the northern circuit; king's counsel, 1834; M.P. for Liverpool, 1837 and 1841; puisne judge of the court of common

pleas, 1842-58; first judge in ordinary and organiser of the probate and divorce court, 1858-63. [xiii. 72]

CRESSWELL, DANIEL (1776-1844), divine and mathematician; fellow of Trinity College, Cambridge; D.D., 1823; vicar of Enfield, 1822-44; F.R.S.; J.P. for Middlesex, 1823; published mathematical works. [xiii. 73]

CRESSWELL, JOSEPH (1557-1623?), jesuit; rector of the English college, Rome, 1589-92; worked also in Spain; rector of the college at Ghent, 1621; died at Ghent; published polemical treatises and religious biographies, also a 'Relacion del Estado de Inglaterra en el gobierno de la Reina Isabella' (unpublished). [xiii. 73]

CRESSY, HUGH PAULINUS or SERENUS (1605-1674), Benedictine monk; B.A. Oxford, 1623; fellow of Merton College, 1626; M.A., 1629; chaplain to Thomas, lord Wentworth; prebendary of Christ Church, Dublin, and St. Patrick's, Dublin, 1636; dean of Leighlin, 1637; publicly renounced protestantism at Rome, 1646; studied theology at Paris; D.D.; confessor to the English nuns at Paris, 1651; servant of Catherine of Braganza, queen of Charles II; definitor of the southern province, 1666; cathedral prior of Rochester, 1669. His chief works were 'Exomologesis,' being reasons for his conversion, 1647-1653, and 'The Church History of Brittany, or England,' in two parts (part I. published 1668). He also edited various books of catholic mysticism. [xiii. 74]

CRESSY, ROBERT (*fl.* 1450?), Carmelite; wrote a book of 'Homiliæ.' [xiii. 76]

CRESTADORO, ANDREA (1808-1879), bibliographer; born and educated at Genoa; Ph.D. Turin; professor of natural philosophy, Turin; took out patents in England which proved useless, one being for aerial locomotion, 1852, 1862, 1868, and 1873; chief librarian of the Manchester Free Libraries, 1864; wrote Italian treatises, and a book on the 'Art of making Catalogues.' [xiii. 76]

CRESWICK, THOMAS (1811-1869), landscape-painter; studied under John Vincent Barber [q. v.]; exhibited for more than thirty years at the Royal Academy, also at the Suffolk Street Gallery, and the British Institution; R.A., 1851; member of the Etching Club; favourably criticised by Ruskin. [xiii. 77]

CRESWICK, WILLIAM (1813-1888), actor; played in travelling companies, and appeared at Queen's Theatre, London, 1835; joined Phelps's company at Sadler's Wells, 1846; at Princess's, 1847, and Haymarket, 1847-8; joint-manager of the Surrey, 1849-62; at Drury Lane, 1862-6; toured in America and Australia; last appeared at Drury Lane, 1885. His parts included Hotspur, Hamlet, Othello, Iago, Macbeth, Iachimo, and King John. [Suppl. ii. 88]

CRESY, EDWARD (1792-1858), architect and civil engineer; travelled in England and on the continent, drawing and measuring ancient buildings; F.S.A., 1820; member of the British Archæological Association; wrote on sanitary engineering, and the architecture of mediæval Italy, also an 'Encyclopædia of Civil Engineering,' 1847. [xiii. 78]

CREW, JOHN, first BARON CREW of Stene (1598-1679), son of Sir Thomas Crew [q. v.]; M.P. for Amersham, 1625, for Brackley, 1626, 1640, for Banbury, 1628, for Northamptonshire, 1640; voted against Strafford's attainder, 1641; supported the 'self-denying ordinance'; arrested among the 'secluded members' for not approving Charles I's trial, 1648; M.P. for Northamptonshire, 1654, 1660; one of the council of state, 1660; met Charles II at the Hague; created Baron Crew of Stene, 1661. [xiii. 78]

CREW, NATHANIEL, third BARON CREW of Stene (1633-1721), bishop of Durham; son of John, first baron Crew of Stene [q. v.]; B.A. Lincoln College, Oxford, 1656; fellow; rector, 1668; dean of Chichester, 1669; bishop of Oxford, 1671; married Duke of York to Maria d'Este, 1673; bishop of Durham, 1674; privy councillor, 1676; rewarded for subserviency to James II with deanery of Chapel Royal; helped to administer diocese of London, 1686; specially excepted from general pardon, 1690, but retained as bishop of Durham; benefactor of diocese of Durham and Lincoln College. [xiii. 79]

CREW or **CREWE**, RANDOLPH (1631-1657), artist; grandson of Sir Ranulphe Crew [q. v.]; executed a map of Cheshire; died from violence at Paris. [xiii. 82]

CREW or CREWE, SIR RANULPHE or RAN-
DOLPH (1558–1646), judge; barrister, Lincoln's Inn,
1584; M.P., Brackley, 1597; bencher of Lincoln's Inn,
1600; knighted, 1614; speaker, 1614; serjeant-at-law,
1615; commissioner for the examination of Edmond
Peacham [q. v.], 1615, also of Weston, as the murderer of
Sir Thomas Overbury, 1615; maintained the contention
of the Lords that the Commons had no right to pass
sentence on Floyde for libelling the princess palatine,
1621; lord chief-justice of the king's bench, 1625; removed for denying the legality of forced loans, 1626.
[xiii. 81]

CREW, THOMAS (*fl.* 1580), author of 'A Nosegay of
Moral Philosophy,' 1580. [xiii. 82]

CREW or CREWE, SIR THOMAS (1565–1634),
speaker of the House of Commons; Lent reader, Gray's
Inn, 1612; M.P. for Lichfield, 1603, for Northampton,
1621, for Aylesbury, 1623, for Gatton, 1625; declared the
liberties of parliament to be 'matters of inheritance,'
1621; placed on an Irish commission, 1622; speaker,
1623 and 1625; knighted, 1623; member of the ecclesiastical commission, 1633. [xiii. 82]

CREWDSON, ISAAC (1780–1844), author; minister
of the Society of Friends, 1816–*c.*; seceded, 1836;
author of several works, including 'A Beacon to the
Society of Friends,' 1835, and 'Trade to the East Indies,'
c. 1827. [xiii. 83]

CREWDSON, JANE (1808–1863), poetess; *née* Fox;
published 'Lays of the Reformation,' 1860, and other
poems, chiefly religious. [xiii. 84]

CREWE, FRANCES ANNE, LADY CREWE (*d.* 1818),
daughter of Fulke Greville; married John (afterwards
Lord) Crewe [q. v.], 1766; a fashionable beauty and friend
of Fox, Burke, and Sheridan. [xiii. 84]

CREWE, JOHN, first BARON CREWE of Crewe
(1742–1829), educated at Trinity College, Cambridge;
sheriff of Cheshire, 1764; M.P., Stafford, 1765, Cheshire,
1768; carried bill for disfranchising excise officers, 1782;
created Baron Crewe, 1806. [xiii. 84]

CREYGHTON. [See CREIGHTON.]

CRIBB, TOM (1781–1848), champion pugilist; champion, 1808; sparred before the emperor of Russia and the
king of Prussia, 1814; guarded the entrance to Westminster Hall at the coronation of George IV. [xiii. 84]

CRICHTON. [See also CREIGHTON.]

CRICHTON, SIR ALEXANDER (1763–1856), physician; M.D. Leyden, 1785; studied at Paris, Stuttgard,
Vienna, and Halle; abandoned surgery and became
L.C.P., 1791; physician, Westminster Hospital, 1794;
F.L.S., 1793; F.R.S., 1800; F.G.S., 1819; physician in
ordinary to Alexander I of Russia, 1804; decorated with
various Russian and Prussian orders; wrote on medical
and geological subjects. [xiii. 85]

CRICHTON, ANDREW (1790–1855), biographer and
historian; educated at Dumfries and Edinburgh University; LL.D. St. Andrews 1837; licensed preacher; contributor to periodicals and the 'Edinburgh Cabinet
Library' series; editor of the 'Edinburgh Advertiser,'
1832–51. [xiii. 86]

CRICHTON, GEORGE (1555?–1611), jurist and classical scholar; studied the classics at Paris and jurisprudence at Toulouse; regent, Collège Harcourt, 1583; professor of Greek, Collège Royal; doctor of canon law,
Paris, 1609. His works consist chiefly of public orations
in Latin. [xiii. 86]

CRICHTON, JAMES, 'THE ADMIRABLE' (1560–
1585?), scholar; son of Robert Crichton [q. v.] of Eliock;
M.A. St. Andrews, 1575; travelled to Paris, 1577, where
he is said to have disputed on scientific questions in
twelve languages; served in French army; visited Genoa,
1579, and Venice, 1580; introduced to the learned world
at Venice by the scholar-printer, Aldus Manutius; disputed doctrines of Thomists and Scotists; entertained by
Cornelius Aloisi at Padua, 1581; successfully challenged
the university there; a good swordsman; killed in a brawl
at Mantua. His authentic and extant works consist
mainly of odes and orations addressed to Italian nobles
and scholars. His title of Admirable originated in Sir
Thomas Urquhart's narrative of his career, 1652.
[xiii. 87]

CRICHTON, JAMES, VISCOUNT FRENDRAUGHT (*d.*
1650), descendant of William, Baron Crichton [q. v.];
created Viscount Frendraught, 1642; killed himself at the
battle of Invercharran, from grief at Montrose's defeat,
1650. [xiii. 91]

CRICHTON, ROBERT (*d.* 1586?), of Eliock, lord
advocate of Scotland, 1562–73 and 1573–81; sole advocate
and senator of the College of Justice, 1581. [xiii. 87]

CRICHTON, SIR ROBERT (*fl.* 1604), son of Robert
Crichton [q. v.] of Eliock; forcibly removed his half-
sister Marion from her guardians at Ardoch Castle, 1591;
denounced by the privy council, 1593; forfeited his property by non-appearance when charged with assaulting a
courtier in James VI's presence, 1602. [xiii. 90]

CRICHTON, ROBERT, sixth BARON SANQUHAR (*d.*
1612), assassin; hanged in Great Palace Yard for having
hired two men to assassinate Turner, a fencing-master,
who had accidentally deprived him of one eye.
[xiii. 91]

CRICHTON, SIR WILLIAM, BARON CRICHTON (*d.*
1454), chancellor of Scotland; knighted, 1424; ambassador to Eric of Norway, 1426; privy councillor of Scotland; self-appointed guardian of James I of Scotland's
infant son, 1437; allied himself with Livingston, who
had been sent by the queen's influence to arrest him in
Edinburgh Castle, 1437; supported the young king against
Livingston and Douglas; created Baron Crichton, 1445;
arranged marriage between James II and Mary, daughter
of the Duke of Gueldres, 1448. [xiii. 92]

CRICHTON, CREIGHTON, or CREITTON, WIL-
LIAM (*fl.* 1615), jesuit; enabled de Gouda, the pope's
legate, to escape from Scotland, 1562; intrigued unsuccessfully to convert James VI to catholicism; saved by Queen
Elizabeth from execution in Holland for supposed complicity in the murder of the Prince of Orange, 1584;
planned rising in England, 1586; sent to Rome in the interest of Scottish catholics, 1592; forced to flee from
Scotland, 1595; founded seminary at Douay. [xiii. 93]

CRIDIODUNUS, FRIDERICUS (*d.* 838), bishop of
Utrecht; said by William of Malmesbury to have been
nephew of St. Boniface; more probably a Frisian, and
unconnected with the saint. [xiii. 94]

CRIPPS, JOHN MARTEN (*d.* 1853), traveller and
antiquary; educated at Jesus College, Cambridge; F.S.A.,
1805; travelled over Europe and the near East; naturalised
kohl-rabi, a Russian vegetable. [xiii. 95]

CRISP, SIR NICHOLAS (1599?–1666), royalist; received from Charles I the exclusive right of trading to
Guinea, in company with five others, 1632; one of the
body which contracted for the 'great' and 'petty' customs farms, 1640; knighted, 1641; M.P. for Winchelsea,
but expelled from parliament as a monopolist, 1641;
fined for having collected duties on merchandise without
parliamentary grant; raised regiment for Charles I,
1643; received commission to equip fifteen war-vessels,
1644; his property sequestered by the parliament, 1645;
fled to France; supported Monck at the Restoration,
1660; compounded the king's debt to the East India
Company, 1662; customs farmer; created baronet, 1665.
[xiii. 95]

CRISP, SAMUEL (*d.* 1783), dramatist; soured by
the severe criticism to which his tragedy of 'Virginia'
was subjected, 1754. [xiii. 97]

CRISP, STEPHEN (1628–1692), quaker; separatist,
then baptist, 1648, and quaker, 1655; imprisoned, 1656;
visited Holland, 1663 and 1667, and also Germany and
Denmark as a missionary; fined for infringing the Conventicle Act, 1670; tried to get the penal laws suspended,
1688; wrote tracts in Dutch and English. [xiii. 98]

CRISP, TOBIAS (1600–1643), antinomian; brother
of Sir Nicholas Crisp [q. v.]; educated at Cambridge;
subsequently removed to Balliol College, Oxford; M.A.,
1626; rector of Newington Butts, also of Brinkworth,
Wiltshire, 1627; his discourses published posthumously.
[xiii. 99]

CRISPIN, GILBERT (*d.* 1117?), abbot of Westminster; educated at Bec; made abbot by Lanfranc, 1085;
exhumed the body of Edward the Confessor, 1102; ambassador to Theobald of Blois, 1118; author of 'Vita
Herluini' and 'Disputatio Judæi cum Christiano.'
[xiii. 100]

CRISTALL, JOSHUA (1767–1847), painter in oil and water colours; china dealer at Rotherhithe; china-painter; first president of reconstituted Water-colour Society, 1821; founded the Sketching Society; leader in the English school of water-colours.   [xiii. 101]

CRITCHETT, GEORGE (1817–1882), ophthalmic surgeon; studied at the London Hospital; M.R.C.S., 1839; F.R.C.S., 1844; demonstrator of anatomy and, 1861–3, surgeon to the London Hospital; member of council of College of Surgeons, 1870; ophthalmic surgeon and lecturer, Middlesex Hospital, 1876–82.   [xiii. 102]

CROCKER, CHARLES (1797–1861), poet; shoemaker's apprentice; sexton, Chichester Cathedral, 1845; bishop's verger; his poems published by subscription, the sonnet 'To the British Oak' being specially praised by Southey.
          [xiii. 102]
CROCKER, JOHANN (1670–1741). [See CROKER, JOHN.]

CROCKFORD, WILLIAM (1775–1844), proprietor of Crockford's Club; originally a fishmonger; set up his famous gambling club, 1827, out of which he amassed 1,200,000*l.* in a few years.   [xiii. 103]

CROFT, EDWARD (*d.* 1601), son of Sir James Croft (*d.* 1591) [q. v.]; M.P. for Leominster, 1571 and 1586; accused of having caused the death of Leicester, his father's enemy, by magic, 1588.   [xiii. 112]

CROFT, GEORGE (1747–1809), divine; educated at the grammar school of Bolton Abbey and University College, Oxford; servitor and bible clerk, 1762; chancellor's English essay prizeman, 1768; M.A., 1769; fellow of his college, 1779; vicar of Arncliffe, 1779; head-master of Brewood school, 1780–91; Bampton lecturer, 1786; rector of Thwing, 1802; author of sermons and tractates, theological and political.   [xiii. 103]

CROFT, SIR HERBERT (*d.* 1622), Roman catholic writer; son of Edward Croft [q. v.]; educated at Christ Church, Oxford; M.P. for Carmarthenshire, 1589, for Launceston, 1597, for Herefordshire, 1592, 1601, 1604, and 1614; Benedictine monk at Douay, 1617; wrote controversial works.   [xiii. 104]

CROFT, HERBERT (1603–1691), bishop of Hereford; son of Sir Herbert Croft (*d.* 1622) [q. v.]; student at Oxford, 1616; placed by his father in the English college, St. Omer, and converted to catholicism; convictor in the English college, Rome, 1626; brought back to the church of England by Morton, bishop of Durham; prebendary of Salisbury, 1639; D.D., 1640; chaplain to Charles I; prebendary of Worcester, 1640; canon of Windsor, 1641; dean of Hereford, 1644; ejected in the great rebellion; bishop of Hereford, 1661–91; dean of the Chapel Royal, 1668–70; wrote controversial pamphlets against Roman catholicism.
          [xiii. 105]
CROFT, SIR HERBERT, bart. (1751–1816), author; matriculated at University College, Oxford, 1771; entered at Lincoln's Inn; barrister; B.C.L., 1785; vicar of Prittlewell, Essex, 1786–1816; imprisoned for debt at Exeter, 1795; withdrew to Hamburg; presented with a gold medal by the king of Sweden; returned to England, 1800; died at Paris, in receipt of a pension of 200*l.* per annum from the English government. He contributed a memoir of Young to Johnson's 'Lives of the Poets,' and planned a new edition of Johnson's 'Dictionary,' but could not proceed for want of subscribers, 1793. In his 'Love and Madness,' which he published in 1780, he introduced letters concerning Chatterton that he had obtained from Chatterton's relations, it is said, under false pretences and without remunerating their owners. Among his works are 'The Abbey of Kilkhampton,' being a collection of satirical epitaphs, 1780, 'Horace éclairci par la Ponctuation,' 1810, and 'The Will of King Alfred,' a translation, 1788.   [xiii. 107]

CROFT, SIR JAMES (*d.* 1590), lord deputy of Ireland and controller of Queen Elizabeth's household; knighted, 1547; governor of Haddington, 1549; served in the Calais marches, 1550; pacified Cork, but was unable to conciliate Ulster and Connaught, 1551; implicated in Wyatt's rebellion, and (1555) fined 500*l.*; seneschal of Hereford and governor of Berwick, 1559; corresponded with Knox on Scottish affairs; M.P. for Herefordshire, 1564, 1570, and 1585–7; privy councillor, 1570; commissioner for the trial of Mary Queen of Scots, 1586; had treasonable intercourse with the Duke of Parma, when on an embassy, 1588.   [xiii. 110]

CROFT, SIR JAMES, the younger (*fl.* 1603), son of Sir James Croft (*d.* 1591) [q. v.]; gentleman-pensioner to Queen Elizabeth; knighted, 1603.   [xiii. 112]

CROFT, JOHN (1732–1820), antiquary; learnt wine trade at Oporto; sheriff of York, 1773; author of 'Annotations on the Plays of Shakespear,' 1810, and 'Excerpta Antiqua,' 1797, the outcome of researches at York.
          [xiii. 112]
CROFT, SIR RICHARD, bart. (1762–1818), accoucheur; brother of Sir Herbert Croft (1751–1816) [q. v.]; attended the Duchess of Devonshire; accused of negligence in connection with the Princess Charlotte's accouchement, 1817; shot himself, 1818.   [xiii. 113]

CROFT, WILLIAM (1677 ?–1727), musician; chorister of the Chapel Royal; organist of St. Anne's, Westminster, 1700–11; organist of the Chapel Royal, 1707; organist, Westminster Abbey, 1708; Mus. Doc. Oxford, 1713; wrote various anthems, as composer at the Chapel Royal.
          [xiii. 113]
CROFTON, ZACHARY (*d.* 1672), Irish nonconformist divine; educated at Dublin; expelled from the living of Wrenbury, Cheshire, for refusing to take the engagement, 1651; vicar of St. Botolph, Aldgate; ejected at the Restoration; committed to the Tower for maintaining that the Solemn League and Covenant was still binding on the English nation, *c.* 1660; published controversial tracts.
          [xiii. 114]
CROFTS or **CROFT**, ELIZABETH (*fl.* 1554), impostor; denounced the projected marriage of Mary and Philip of Spain from within a wall in Aldersgate Street.
          [xiii. 115]
CROFTS or **CRAFTE**, GEORGE (*d.* 1539), divine; fellow of Oriel College, Oxford, 1513–19; B.A., 1513; rector of Shepton Mallet and Winford, Somerset, 1524; chancellor of Chichester Cathedral, 1531; executed for affirming the pope's supremacy, 1539.   [xiii. 115]

CROFTS, JAMES, DUKE OF MONMOUTH (1649–1685). [See SCOTT.]

CROFTS, WILLIAM, BARON CROFTS OF SAXHAM (1611 ?–1677), captain of Queen Henrietta Maria's guards before outbreak of civil war, during which he continued in attendance on the king and queen; given manors in Essex and Suffolk, 1645; gentleman of bedchamber to Charles II, 1652; created peer, 1658; employed on several royal missions after the Restoration.   [Suppl. ii. 88]

CROGHAN, GEORGE (*d.* 1782), captain or colonel, Passayunk, Pennsylvania; British crown agent with the Indians; trader, 1746; deputy-agent with the Pennsylvania and Ohio Indians, 1756; formed settlement near Fort Pitt, 1766.   [xiii. 116]

CROKE, SIR ALEXANDER (1758–1842), lawyer and author; educated at Oriel College, Oxford; D.C.L., 1797; member of the College of Advocates, 1797; answered the strictures of Schlegel, a Danish lawyer, upon the English admiralty court, 1801; judge in the vice-admiralty court, Halifax, Nova Scotia, 1801–15; knighted, 1816; wrote on law and on genealogy and rhyming Latin verses; author of the 'Progress of Idolatry,' a poem, 1841.   [xiii. 116]

CROKE, CHARLES (*d.* 1657), professor; third son of Sir John Croke [q. v.]; tutor of Christ Church College, Oxford; D.D.; professor of rhetoric, Gresham College, London, 1613–19; rector of Waterstock, Oxfordshire, 1616; died in Ireland.   [xiii. 119]

CROKE, SIR GEORGE (1560–1642), judge and law reporter; educated at Oxford; barrister, Inner Temple, 1584; treasurer, 1609; M.P., Beeralston, Devonshire, 1597; knighted, 1623; justice of the king's bench, 1628; spoke against ship-money and the prosecution of Hampden, 1638. His reports, written in Norman-French, extend over sixty years (1580–1640).   [xiii. 117]

CROKE, JOHN (*d.* 1554), lawyer; descended from the family of Le Blount to which Sir Thomas Blount (*d.* 1400) [q. v.] belonged; scholar of King's College, Cambridge, 1507; serjeant-at-law, 1546; M.P., Chippenham, 1547; master in Chancery, 1549; author of 'Ordinances upon the Estate of the Chancery Court,' 1554.
          [xiii. 118]
CROKE, SIR JOHN (1553–1620), judge and recorder of London; grandson of John Croke [q. v.]; entered the

Inner Temple, 1570; treasurer of his inn, 1597; M.P. for London, 1597 and 1601; speaker of the House of Commons, 1601; king's serjeant, 1603; knighted, 1603. [xiii. 118]

CROKE or **CROCUS**, RICHARD (1489 ?–1558), Greek scholar and diplomatist; educated at Eton and King's College, Cambridge; B.A., 1510; studied at Paris, 1513; recommended to Colet by Erasmus for pecuniary assistance without effect; Greek lecturer at Leipzig, 1515–17, where he taught Camerarius; M.A. Cambridge, 1517; taught Henry VIII Greek; lecturer at Cambridge, 1518; fellow of St. John's College, 1523; D.D., 1524; sent to Italy to collect the opinions of canonists on the king's divorce, 1529; deputy vice-chancellor, Cambridge, 1531; rector of Long Buckby, Northamptonshire, 1531; D.D. Oxford, 1532; canon and sub-dean of Cardinal's College, afterwards Christ Church, 1532; testified to Cranmer's heresy at Oxford, 1555; his chief work was an edition of Ausonius, 1515. [xiii. 119]

CROKE, UNTON (*fl.* 1658), parliamentarian colonel; son of Unton Croke (1594 ?–1671) [q. v.]; colonel in parliamentary army; B.C.L. Oxford, 1649; barrister, Inner Temple, 1653; high sheriff of Oxfordshire, 1658. [xiii. 119]

CROKE, UNTON (1594 ?–1671), fourth son of Sir John Croke [q. v.]; bencher of the Inner Temple, 1635; M.P. for Wallingford, 1626 and 1640; commissioner for treason trials, 1656. [xiii. 119]

CROKER, JOHN, or **CROCKER**, JOHANN (1670–1741), engraver of English coins and medals; born at Dresden; came to England, 1691; chief engraver at the mint, 1705; public medallist. [xiii. 121]

CROKER, JOHN WILSON (1780–1857), politician and essayist; B.A. Trinity College, Dublin; student at Lincoln's Inn, 1800; attached to the Munster circuit; M.P. for Downpatrick, 1807; temporarily chief secretary for Ireland, 1808; friend of Canning; contributor to the 'Quarterly Review,' 1809, and afterwards famous for his scathing criticism of Keats's 'Endymion,' 1818; secretary to the admiralty, exposing (1810) defalcations; offended the Duke of Clarence, afterwards William IV; privy councillor and friend of Sir Robert Peel; resigned his office at the admiralty, 1830; spoke against the Reform Bill, 1831; edited Boswell's 'Life of Johnson,' 1831, and was severely criticised by Macaulay; retired from parliament on the passing of the Reform Bill, 1832; introduced the term 'conservatives,' 1830; while in retirement supported Sir Robert Peel until Peel gave in his adherence to Cobden's policy, 1845; the supposed original of Rigby in Disraeli's novel 'Coningsby'; attacked Macaulay's 'History of England,' 1849. Besides his edition of Boswell's 'Johnson' in 1831, his works include 'An Intercepted Letter from Canton' (satire on Dublin society), 1804, 'Military Events of the French Revolution of 1830,' 1831, and 'Essays on the Early Period of the French Revolution,' 1857. [xiii. 123]

CROKER, MARIANNE (*d.* 1854), artist; wife of Thomas Crofton Croker [q. v.] [xiii. 133]

CROKER, TEMPLE HENRY (1730 ?–1790 ?), miscellaneous writer; educated at Westminster School; scholar of Trinity College, Cambridge, 1746; removed to Oxford; M.A., 1760; chaplain to the Earl of Hillsborough; rector of Igtham, Kent, 1769–73; rector of St. John's, Capisterre, St. Christopher's, in the West Indies. He translated the 'Orlando Furioso,' 1755, the 'Satires of Ariosto,' 1759, wrote on 'Experimental Magnetism,' 1761, and compiled a 'Dictionary of Arts and Sciences,' 1764–1766. [xiii. 132]

CROKER, THOMAS CROFTON (1798–1854), Irish antiquary; friend of Tom Moore, to whom he forwarded fragments of ancient Irish poetry, 1818; clerk at the admiralty in London, 1818–50; helped to found the Camden Society, 1839, the Percy Society, 1840, and the British Archæological Association, 1843; best-known works, 'The Fairy Legends and Traditions of the South of Ireland,' 1825, and 'Popular Songs of Ireland,' 1839; edited memoirs and books connected with the topography and archæology of Ireland. [xiii. 132]

CROKESLEY, RICHARD DE (*d.* 1258), ecclesiastic and judge; abbot of St. Peter's, Westminster, 1247; archdeacon of Westminster; arranged marriage between Prince Edward and the daughter of the Duke of Brabant, 1247; chaplain to the pope at Lyons, 1251, whither he

had been sent to bring about a meeting between the pope and Henry III; unsuccessful in his negotiations for the restoration of Henry III's French provinces, 1257; arbitrator for Henry III at the Oxford conference, 1258; baron of the exchequer, 1250 and 1257. [xiii. 134]

CROLL, FRANCIS (1826 ?–1854), line engraver; articled to an Edinburgh draughtsman; executed engravings for the 'Art Journal' and for the Royal Association for the Promotion of the Fine Arts in Scotland. [xiii. 135]

CROLL, JAMES (1821–1890), physical geologist; apprenticed as wheelwright at Collace; worked as joiner at Banchory; kept temperance hotel at Blairgowrie, 1852–3; keeper of Andersonian University and Museum, Glasgow, 1859; keeper of maps and correspondence of Geological Survey of Scotland, 1867–80; F.R.S. and LL.D. St. Andrews, 1876; retired owing to ill-health, 1880; published 'Climate and Time,' 1875, 'Philosophic Basis of Evolution,' 1890, and other writings chiefly on questions in physical geology. [Suppl. ii. 89]

CROLLY, WILLIAM (1780–1849), Roman catholic archbishop of Armagh; entered Maynooth, 1801; priest, 1806; professor at Maynooth; parish priest of Belfast, 1812–25; bishop of Down and Connor, 1825; archbishop of Armagh, 1835. [xiii. 135]

CROLY, GEORGE (1780–1860), author and divine; educated at Trinity College, Dublin; licensed to an Irish curacy, 1804; settled in London, 1810; dramatic critic to the 'New Times' and contributor to the 'Literary Gazette' and 'Blackwood's Magazine'; gained reputation for eloquence when rector of St. Stephen's, Walbrook, 1835–47; afternoon lecturer at the Foundling, 1847; wrote 'Salathiel,' a romance, 1829, 'Catiline,' a tragedy, 1822, 'Paris in 1815,' a poem, 1817, 'Divine Providence, or the Three Cycles of Revelation,' 1834, 'Marston,' a novel, 1846, and numerous narrative and romantic poems. [xiii. 135]

CROMARTY, EARLS OF. [See MACKENZIE, GEORGE, first EARL, 1630–1714; MACKENZIE, GEORGE, third EARL, *d.* 1766.]

CROMARTY, COUNT, in the Swedish peerage (1727–1789). [See MACKENZIE, JOHN.]

CROMBIE, ALEXANDER (1762–1840), philologist and schoolmaster; educated at Marischal College, Aberdeen; M.A. Aberdeen, 1777; LL.D., 1798; licentiate of the church of Scotland; kept private school in Highgate; wrote 'A Defence of Philosophic Necessity,' 1793, 'Gymnasium sive Symbola Critica,' 1812, and 'Natural Theology,' 1829, also tractates on questions of political economy. [xiii. 136]

CROMBIE, JAMES (1730–1790), presbyterian minister; M.A. St. Andrews, 1752; presented to the living of Lhanbryd, near Elgin, 1760; tutor in the family of the Earl of Moray; co-pastor in the first non-subscribing presbyterian congregation of Belfast, 1770; sole pastor, 1781–90; D.D. St. Andrews, 1783; founder of the Belfast Academy, 1786, and its principal; wrote 'An Essay on Church Consecration,' 1777, and a tractate on the question of Sabbath observance. [xiii. 137]

CROME, EDWARD (*d.* 1562), protestant divine; M.A. Cambridge, 1507; D.D. 1526; fellow of Gonville Hall; university preacher, 1516; maintained the nullity of Henry VIII's marriage with Catherine of Arragon, 1530; in sympathy with Roman catholic doctrine; parson of St. Antholin's, London, and subsequently of St. Mary Aldermary; preached against the mass, 1546; recanted; managed to escape the stake in Mary's reign. [xiii. 138]

CROME, JOHN (1768–1821), landscape-painter; born in humble circumstances; apprenticed to a sign-painter, 1783; introduced the art of graining at Norwich; picked up an informal education in art from Thomas Harvey of Catton, Norfolk, who allowed him access to his collection of Flemish and Dutch pictures; taught drawing; founded the Norwich school of painting and a 'joint-stock association of accomplishments and worldly goods,' which exhibited from 1805 to 1833; exhibited at the Royal Academy, first in 1806. His painting of trees was exceptionally sympathetic in its treatment of the subject, the 'Oak at Poringland' and the 'Willow' being among the best pictures in their kind. [xiii. 140]

CROME, JOHN BERNAY (1794–1842), painter; son of John Crome [q. v.]; educated at Norwich grammar school; landscapes by him exhibited (1811–43) at the Royal Academy, and other institutions; travelled in France, Holland, Belgium, and Italy. [xiii. 143]

CROMEK, ROBERT HARTLEY (1770–1812), engraver; studied under Bartolozzi; published an edition of Blair's 'Grave,' with etchings after Blake by Schiavonetti; compiled 'Reliques of Burns,' 1808, and 'Select Scottish Songs,' 1810. [xiii. 144]

CROMER, GEORGE (d. 1543), archbishop of Armagh, 1522; lord chancellor of Ireland, 1532; opposed Henry VIII's attempt to make the reformatory measures passed at Westminster binding upon the parliament of Dublin, 1536; refused to recognise the king as supreme head of the church; intrigued with the pope and the Duke of Norfolk to prevent the Reformation setting foot in Ireland. [xiii. 144]

CROMLEHOLME, SAMUEL (1618–1672), head-master of St. Paul's School; M.A. Corpus Christi College, Oxford; master of the Mercers' Chapel School, London; surmaster of St. Paul's School, 1647–51; master of Dorchester grammar school, 1651–7; head-master, St. Paul's School, 1657–72. [xiii. 145]

CROMMELIN, SAMUEL-LOUIS (1652–1727), director of Irish linen enterprise; born at Armandcourt, Picardy; his family compelled to leave France upon the revocation of the edict of Nantes; arrived at Lisburn, Ireland, by invitation of William III, for the purpose of inquiring into the linen manufacture of the French colony there, 1698; overseer of the royal linen manufacture of Ireland; thanked by the Irish parliament, 1707; promoted settlements for the manufacture of hempen sail-cloth in southern Ireland, 1717; wrote on his work, 1705. [xiii. 145]

CROMPTON, SIR CHARLES JOHN (1797–1865), justice of the queen's bench; graduated at Trinity College, Dublin; barrister, Inner Temple, 1821; joined the northern circuit; postman in the exchequer; counsel for the board of stamps and taxes; assessor of the court of passage, Liverpool, 1836; knighted, 1852; raised to the bench, 1852. [xiii. 146]

CROMPTON, HUGH (fl. 1657), poet; published 'Poems by Hugh Crompton, the Son of Bacchus and Godson of Apollo,' 1657, and 'Pierides,' 1658 (?). [xiii. 147]

CROMPTON, JOHN (1611–1669), nonconformist divine; M.A. Emmanuel College, Cambridge; lecturer at All Saints', Derby; rector of Brailsford; forced to retire at the Restoration; vicar of Arnold, near Nottingham; ejected by the Act of Uniformity. [xiii. 147]

CROMPTON, RICHARD (fl. 1573–1599), lawyer; educated at Brasenose College, Oxford; bencher of the Inner Temple; summer reader, 1573; Lent reader, 1578; edited Fitzherbert's 'Office et Aucthoritie de Justices de Peace,' 1583; wrote 'L'Authoritie et Jurisdiction des Courts de la Maiestie de la Roygne,' 1594, and 'The Mansion of Magnanimitie,' 1599. [xiii. 148]

CROMPTON, SAMUEL (1753–1827), inventor of the spinning mule; induced by the imperfections of Hargreaves's spinning-jenny to invent a substitute, 1779; gave it to the public, but received no pecuniary advantage; granted 5,000l. by the House of Commons, 1812. [xiii. 148]

CROMPTON, WILLIAM (1599?–1642), puritan divine; son of Richard Crompton [q. v.]; educated at Brasenose College, Oxford; M.A., 1623; lecturer at Barnstaple, 1628–40; pastor of the church of St. Mary Magdalene, Launceston. His chief work, 'St. Austin's Religion,' 1624, was written to prove that St. Austin 'agreed with the religion of the protestants.' [xiii. 150]

CROMPTON, WILLIAM (1633–1696), nonconformist divine; educated at Merchant Taylors' School and Christ Church, Oxford; ejected from his living of Collumpton, Devonshire, for nonconformity at the Restoration; author of some puritan tractates. [xiii. 151]

CROMWELL, EDWARD, third BARON CROMWELL (1559?–1607), politician; pupil of Richard Bancroft [q. v.] at Jesus College, Cambridge; M.A., 1593; colonel under Essex when sent to aid Henri IV in Normandy, 1591; served against Spain, 1597; accompanied Essex to Ireland,

1599; sent to the Tower for complicity in Essex's rebellion, 1601; fined 6,000l. and released, 1601; privy councillor, 1603; appointed governor of Lecale, 1605. [xiii. 151]

CROMWELL, HENRY (1628–1674), son of Oliver Cromwell; entered the parliamentary army; colonel, 1650; defeated Lord Inchiquin near Limerick, 1650; entered at Gray's Inn, 1654; represented Ireland in the Barebones parliament, 1653; sent to Ireland to counteract the influence of the anabaptists; major-general of the forces in Ireland, and member of the Irish council, 1654; remonstrated against the oath of abjuration imposed upon Irish catholics in 1657, but did not mitigate the rigour of the transplantation; lord-deputy, 1657; attempted to relieve the financial difficulties of the Irish administration, but was thwarted from home; urged his father to refuse the title of king, 1657; advised the remodelling of the army, 1658; governor-general of Ireland, 1658; unsuccessfully solicited by partisans of Prince Charles, 1659; returned to England and went into retirement, 1659; lost his lands at the Restoration, but subsequently had his possessions in Meath and Connaught confirmed to his trustees in compensation. [xiii. 152]

CROMWELL, OLIVER (1599–1658), the Protector; matriculated from Sidney Sussex College, Cambridge, 1616; said to have been a member of Lincoln's Inn; married Elizabeth Bourchier, 1620; M.P. for Huntingdon, 1628; J.P. for Huntingdon, 1630; said to have intended emigrating to America; became a religious enthusiast, 1638; M.P. for Cambridge, 1640; moved the second reading of Strode's bill for reviving the old law of Edward III for annual parliaments, 1640; proposed committee to put the kingdom in a posture of defence, 1642; fought at Edgehill in the army of Essex, 1642; converted his troop of horse into a regiment, 1643; suppressed a royalist rising at Lowestoft, 1643; recaptured Stamford, 1643; governor of the Isle of Ely, and second in command to the Earl of Manchester, 1643; lieutenant-general, 1644; took part in the siege of Lincoln, 1644; commanded the left wing at the victory of Marston Moor, 1644; urged toleration for differences of religious opinion in the parliamentary army, and demanded the dismissal of Major-general Crawford, an intolerant presbyterian, but subsequently forgave him; fought at Newbury, 1644; accused the Earl of Manchester of half-heartedness, who retaliated by charging him with contempt for the Scots and presbyterians, 1644; largely helped the remodelling of the army and the passing of the 'Self-denying Ordinance,' which he was excused from obeying, 1644; relieved Taunton, 1645; fought with success in Oxfordshire and at Naseby, 1645; took part in the sieges of Bridgewater, Sherborne, and Bristol, 1645; captured Devizes, Winchester, and Basing House, 1645; thanked by the House of Commons, 1646; assisted in negotiations for surrender of Oxford, 1646; recognised the grievances of the army in its quarrel with parliament, 1647; restored military subordination when commissioner, 1647; supposed to have planned the seizure of Charles I, 1647; his policy based on the assumption that terms might ultimately be arrived at with the king; entered into an engagement with the soldiers for the redress of their wrongs, 1647; induced parliament to vote that no further address should be made to the king, the case seeming hopeless, 1648; accused by Lilburn of apostacy and double-dealing, 1648; subdued a Welsh insurrection, 1648; routed the Scots at Preston, 1648; denounced the treaty made by parliament with Charles I at Newport, 1648; active in the prosecution of Charles I, 1648; temporary president of the council of state after Charles's execution; opposed the anarchical designs of the 'levellers,' 1649; commander-in-chief and lord-lieutenant of Ireland, 1649; stormed Drogheda and Wexford, massacring their garrisons, 1649; compelled to raise the siege of Waterford, 1649; reduced Cahir, Cashel, Kilkenny, and Clonmel, 1650; treated non-combatants with leniency, but forbade the exercise of catholic worship; returned to England, 1650; commander-in-chief, 1650; defeated the Scots at Dunbar, 3 Sept. 1650; stirred up dissension among the Scots, some of them being convinced by his arguments and humane policy; captured Perth, 1651; defeated the Scots, in whose army was Prince Charles, at Worcester, 3 Sept. 1651; procured the Act of Pardon and Oblivion, 1652; dissolved the Long parliament, which had shown itself unequal to dealing satisfactorily with the complaints of the army, 1652; convoked the Little parliament; dissolved it in consequence of its rejection of a scheme for the appointment and maintenance of the clergy ; installed as protector and head of the executive power, 1653 ; during the abeyance of parliament issued ordinances, having the force of law until parliament otherwise ordered, providing for the administration of justice in Scotland, the representation of Ireland in the British parliament, and the re-organisation of the church in England on comprehensive lines, 1653–4 ; reorganised the court of chancery, recommended the revision of the criminal code, 1657, and appointed new judges ; engaged in negotiations for the acquisition of Dunkirk, 1652 ; signed an advantageous peace with the Dutch States-General, 1654 ; concluded commercial treaties with Sweden and Denmark, 1654, the latter country having been recently in open hostility to England ; ended a war with Portugal by a commercial treaty, 1653 ; failed to get unanimous recognition of the authority which had been conferred on him by the army from parliament, 1654 ; dissolved parliament, the Commons having delayed a vote of supplies, 1655 ; became the object of conspiracies, which were speedily foiled, 1655 ; parcelled out the country into twelve divisions, each under the command of a major-general, 1655 ; imprisoned lawyers for impugning the validity of his ordinances, and dismissed malcontent judges ; prohibited the use of the prayer-book, 1655 ; found himself compelled to prosecute the anabaptists, but protected the quakers and Jews ; sent Blake to bombard Tunis, 1655 ; championed the cause of the persecuted Vaudois, and, by the influence of Cardinal Mazarin, obliged the Duke of Savoy to respect their rights as his subjects, 1655 ; made a treaty with France against Spain, 1655 ; at war with the latter country owing to its aggressive catholicism and exclusive colonial policy ; refused the title of king, 1657 ; installed Protector a second time, that being a style to which the army did not object, as it objected to the royal title, 1657 ; acquired right to appoint his own successor ; concluded offensive and defensive alliance with France, 1657 ; formed league with Sweden against the Austrian Hapsburgs ; dissolved the parliament of 1658 in consequence of its restiveness ; again intervened on behalf of the Vaudois ; humbled the Spaniards at Dunkirk, 1658 ; alleged to have prejudiced the interests of trade by friendship for Holland and hostility to Spain, 1659 ; assailed by plots, Gerard's, 1654, and Sindercombe's, 1657 ; denounced in a pamphlet entitled ' Killing no Murder,' 1657 ; died of a tertian ague, 3 Sept. 1658 ; buried in Westminster Abbey, 23 Nov. ; disinterred and hung on the gallows at Tyburn, 30 Jan. 1661.

[xiii. 155]

CROMWELL, OLIVER (1742 ?–1821), biographer ; solicitor in the Strand and clerk to St. Thomas's Hospital ; wrote ' Memoirs of the Protector Oliver Cromwell, and of his sons, Richard and Henry,' from whom he was descended. [xiii. 186]

CROMWELL, RALPH, fourth BARON CROMWELL (1394 ?–1456), lord treasurer of England ; fought at Agincourt, 1415 ; first summoned to parliament, 1422 ; chamberlain of exchequer, c. 1423–32 ; lord treasurer, 1433–43 ; served at relief of Calais, 1436 ; master of king's mews and falcons, 1436 ; constable of Nottingham Castle, and warden of Sherwood Forest, 1445 ; led attack on Suffolk, 1449 ; founded a college at Tattershall.

[Suppl. ii. 90]

CROMWELL, RICHARD (1626–1712), Lord Protector ; third son of Oliver Cromwell ; member of Lincoln's Inn, 1647 ; M.P for Hampshire, 1654, for Cambridge, 1656 ; member of committee of trade and navigation, 1655 ; chancellor of Oxford University, 1657 ; member of the council of state, 1657 ; sat in Cromwell's House of Lords ; twice nominated as his father's successor, 31 Aug. and 2 Sept. 1658 ; proclaimed protector amid apparent satisfaction ; refused the petition of a number of officers that a commander-in-chief should be appointed, and increased the pay of the soldiers, 1658 ; compelled to assent to the retirement of his chief adviser, Thurloe, 1658 ; inclined to ignore his father's treaty with Sweden ; recognised as his father's successor by parliament, 1659 ; retained the right to make peace or war ; opposed by parliament in the matter of supplies and by Fleetwood, who took advantage of the grievances of the army to stir up mutiny ; driven to throw in his lot with the army and dissolve parliament, 21 April 1659 ; obliged to recall the Long parliament, 7 May 1659 ; said, probably without much foundation, to have intrigued for the restoration of

the Stuarts ; practically deposed by the army, May 1659 ; appealed to Monck for pecuniary assistance, arrangements formulated by parliament for the payment of his debts having, come to nothing, 1660 ; retired to the continent and lived at Paris under the name of John Clarke, 1660 ; returned to England, c. 1680, and lived in retirement. [xiii. 186]

CROMWELL, THOMAS, EARL OF ESSEX (1485 ?–1540), statesman ; compelled to leave England when young owing to a misdemeanour ; said to have been present at the battle of Garigliano, 1503 ; escaped to Florence in a state of destitution ; much of his early history uncertain in point of date, its obscurity being increased by the fact that he was sometimes called ' Thomas Smyth ' ; clerk at Antwerp ; visited Italy a second time, and introduced himself to Pope Julius II, in company with one Geoffrey Chambers ; stated by Cardinal Pole to have been clerk to a Venetian merchant ; engaged in money-lending, legal practice, and cloth dressing in England, c. 1513 ; appointed by Wolsey collector of the revenues of the see of York, 1514 ; entered parliament, 1523 ; humoured the king's designs upon France, while deprecating their immediate execution ; member of Gray's Inn, 1524 ; one of the commissioners appointed by the influence of Wolsey to inquire into the state of the smaller monasteries, 1525 ; showed great harshness when on this commission ; receiver-general of Cardinal's College, Oxford ; managed all Wolsey's legal business, as his secretary, drawing up the deeds for the foundation of Cardinal's College and Ipswich College ; pleaded Wolsey's cause in the House of Commons, 1529 ; suggested to Henry VIII the policy of making himself head of the church of England, and so facilitating his divorce from Catherine of Arragon ; attempted to convert Cardinal Pole to the doctrines of Machiavelli, 1529 ; privy councillor, 1531 ; master of the jewels and master of the king's wards, 1532 ; obtained grant of the lordship of Romney in Newport, South Wales, 1532 ; medium of communication between Henry VIII and Chapuys, the imperial ambassador ; chancellor of the exchequer, 1533 ; king's secretary, 1534 ; master of the rolls, 1534 ; endorsed the frivolous charge of treason against Bishop Fisher, 1534 ; vicar-general, 1535 ; commissioned to hold a general visitation of churches, monasteries, and clergy, 1535 ; chancellor of the university of Cambridge ; took a great part in procuring the dissolution of the smaller monasteries, 1536 ; conveyed Anne Boleyn to the Tower, 1536 ; made lord privy seal and Baron Cromwell of Oakham, 1536 ; knight of the Garter, 1537 ; dean of Wells, 1537 ; appointed to oversee the printing of the bible for five years, 1539 ; rewarded with confiscated lands of the larger monasteries, 1538–40 ; lord great chamberlain of England, 1539 ; negotiated the marriage of Henry VIII with Anne of Cleves, 1539 ; created Earl of Essex, 1540 ; accused of treason by the Duke of Norfolk and executed, the king, who was dissatisfied with Anne of Cleves and the German protestant alliance, not interposing, 1540. [xiii. 192]

CROMWELL, THOMAS, fourth BARON CROMWELL (d. 1653), son of Edward Cromwell [q. v.] ; created Viscount Lecale, 1624, and Earl of Ardglass, 1645.

[xiii. 151]

CROMWELL, THOMAS [KITSON] (1792–1870), dissenting minister ; entered literary department of Messrs. Longmans ; unitarian minister, Stoke Newington Green, 1839–64 ; F.S.A., 1838 ; minister of the old presbyterian congregation at Canterbury ; chief works, ' Oliver Cromwell and his Times,' 1821, ' The Soul and the Future Life,' 1859, ' The Druid : a Tragedy,' 1832, and a ' History of the Ancient Town and Borough of Colchester,' 1825.

[xiii. 202]

CRONAN, SAINT (7th cent.), abbot and founder of Roscrea, Tipperary ; born in Munster ; travelled over the south and west of Ireland founding monasteries ; appeased the anger of Fingen, king of Cassel, against the people of Ely, a district on the borders of Connaught and Munster.

[xiii. 202]

CRONE, ROBERT (d. 1779), landscape-painter ; a native of Dublin ; exhibited paintings of Italian scenery at the Society of Artists, 1768–9, and the Royal Academy, 1770–8. [xiii. 203]

CROOK, JOHN (1617–1699), quaker ; knight of the shire for Bedfordshire, 1653 ; commissioner of the peace ; joined quakers, and lost his commission, 1654 ; tried at the Old Bailey for refusing the oath of allegiance, 1662 ;

remanded to prison, but soon liberated ; imprisoned again, 1669 ; author of ' An Apology for the Quakers,' 1662, and numerous books of quaker exegesis. [xiii. 204]

CROOKE, HELKIAH (1576–1635), physician ; scholar of St. John's College, Cambridge, 1591 ; B.A., 1596 ; M.D. Leyden, 1597 ; M.D. Cambridge, 1604 ; physician to James I ; F.C.P., 1620–35 ; anatomy reader, 1629 ; governor of Bethlehem Hospital, 1632 ; took no notice of Harvey's discovery of the circulation of the blood ; chief work, ' Mikrokosmographia, a Description of the Body of Man,' 1616. [xiii. 205]

CROOKE, SAMUEL (1575–1649), divine ; son of Thomas Crooke [q. v.] ; educated at Merchant Taylors' School ; scholar of Pembroke Hall, Cambridge ; B.D. Cambridge ; fellow of Emmanuel College ; rhetoric and philosophy reader in the public schools ; rector of Wrington, Somerset, 1602 ; parliamentarian in his leanings, but submissive to the royal commissioners, 1643 ; one of the ministers appointed to superintend the district of Bath and Wrington, under a scheme for the presbyterian government of Somerset, 1648. [xiii. 205]

CROOKE, THOMAS (*fl.* 1582), divine ; scholar, Trinity College, Cambridge, 1562 ; fellow ; M.A., 1566 ; D.D., 1578 ; rector of Great Waldingfield, Suffolk, 1574 ; took part in conferences between English churchmen and Roman catholics, 1582 ; urged Cartwright to publish his book on the Rhemish translation of the New Testament. [xiii. 206]

CROOKSHANKS, JOHN (1708–1795), navy captain ; lieutenant, 1734 ; captain of the Lowestoft frigate, 1742 ; appeared unwilling to risk fighting on three occasions, thereby causing general discontent, 1742, 1746, and 1747 ; charged with neglect of duty, and dismissed by courtmartial at Jamaica, 1747 ; brought groundless accusations of unfairness against the court, 1759 and 1772 ; ultimately restored to the half-pay of his rank. [xiii. 206]

CROONE or **CROUNE**, WILLIAM (1633–1684), physician ; educated at Merchant Taylors' School ; fellow of Emmanuel College, Cambridge ; professor of rhetoric, Gresham College, London, 1659–70 ; M.D. Cambridge, 1662 ; F.R.S., 1663 ; anatomy lecturer on the muscles to the Company of Surgeons, 1670–84 ; F.C.P., 1675 ; left money to the Royal Society, also funds to establish algebra lectures at Cambridge and the Croonian lecture ; published ' De ratione motus Musculorum,' 1664. [xiii. 207]

CROPHILL, JOHN (*fl.* 1420), astrologer ; his writings preserved among the Harleian MSS. (British Museum, 1735). [xiii. 208]

CROPPER, JAMES (1773–1840), philanthropist ; founded mercantile house of Cropper, Benson & Co., Liverpool ; worked for abolition of slavery in West Indies and amelioration of social conditions among Irish poor ; director of the Liverpool and Manchester railway, 1830 ; started agricultural industrial school near Warrington, 1833. [xiii. 208]

CROSBIE, ANDREW (*d.* 1785), Scottish advocate ; stated to have been the original of ' Councillor Pleydell ' in ' Guy Mannering ' ; friend of Johnson and Boswell ; died in distressed circumstances. [xiii. 209]

CROSBY, ALLAN JAMES (1835–1881), archivist ; educated at Worcester College, Oxford ; B.A., 1858 ; clerk in the Record Office ; barrister, Inner Temple, 1865 ; edited, 1871–81, ' Calendar of State Papers ' (Foreign Series) from 1558. [xiii. 210]

CROSBY, BRASS (1725–1793), lord mayor of London ; attorney in London ; city remembrancer, 1760 ; sheriff, 1764 ; alderman, 1765 ; M.P. for Honiton, 1768–74 ; lord mayor, 1770 ; refused to back the press warrants, 1770 ; committed to the Tower for releasing from custody one Miller, printer of the ' London Evening Post,' who had been summoned to the bar of the House of Commons, and had refused to attend, 1771 ; returned to the Mansion House at the close of the session, 1771 ; president of Bethlehem Hospital, 1772 ; governor of the Irish Society, 1785. [xiii. 210]

CROSBY, SIR JOHN (*d.* 1475), alderman of London ; M.P. for London, 1466 ; alderman, 1468 ; sheriff, 1470 ; helped to repel Falconbridge's attack on London, 1471 ; knighted, 1471 ; despatched on missions to the Duke of Burgundy, 1472 and 1473 ; mayor of the Staple of Calais ; built a mansion of some fame in Bishopsgate Street. [xiii. 211]

CROSBY, THOMAS (*fl.* 1740), author of ' History of the Baptists ' ; deacon of the baptist church, Horsleydown ; chief works, a ' History of the English Baptists from the Reformation to the beginning of the Reign of George I,' 1738–40, and ' The Book-keeper's Guide,' 1749. [xiii. 212]

CROSDILL, JOHN (1751 ?–1825), violoncellist ; member of the Royal Society of Musicians, 1768 ; principal 'cello at the Concerts of Antient Music, 1776 ; violist of the Chapel Royal, 1778–1825 ; chamber musician to Queen Charlotte, 1782 ; principal violoncellist at the Handel festival in Westminster Abbey, 1784. [xiii. 212]

CROSFIELD, GEORGE (1785–1847), botanist ; elder in the Society of Friends, 1815 ; published ' Calendar of Flora,' 1810, ' Memoirs of S. Fothergill,' 1837, and religious works. [xiii. 213]

CROSKERY, THOMAS (1830–1886), theologian and reviewer ; entered at the old college, Belfast, 1845 ; reporter in connection with the Belfast press ; licensed to preach, 1851 ; ordained, 1860 ; in charge of the presbyterian congregation at Creggan, at Clonakilty, 1863, and at Waterside, Londonderry, 1866 ; professor of logic and belles-lettres, Magee College, Londonderry, 1875–9 ; professor of theology, 1879–86 ; D.D. of the Presbyterian Theological Faculty, Ireland, 1883 ; published ' Plymouth Brethrenism : a Refutation of its Principles and Doctrines,' 1879, and ' Irish Presbyterianism,' 1884. [xiii. 213]

CROSLAND, MRS. CAMILLA DUFOUR (1812–1895). [See TOULMIN.]

CROSLY, DAVID (1670–1744), baptist minister ; originally stonemason at Walsden ; minister at Tottlebank, near Lancaster, 1695–1705 ; pastor of the particular baptist church, Curriers' Hall, London Wall, 1705 ; groundlessly slandered, and expelled, 1718 ; kept school at Goodshaw ; correspondent of George Whitefield ; published sermons and (1720) a poem, entitled ' Adam, where art Thou ? ' [xiii. 214]

CROSS, JOHN (1630–1689), Franciscan ; provincial of his order in England for three years, 1674–7 ; re-elected, 1686 ; D.D. ; established a small community at Lincoln's Inn Fields, 1687 ; compelled to retire from the place by popular violence, 1688 ; died at Douay ; published devotional works and a treatise, ' De Dialectica.' [xiii. 215]

CROSS, SIR JOHN (1766–1842), judge in bankruptcy ; educated at Trinity College, Cambridge ; barrister, Lincoln's Inn, 1795 ; king's serjeant, 1827 ; attorney-general of the duchy of Lancaster, 1827 ; judge in bankruptcy, 1831 ; knighted, 1831 ; subsequently became chief judge. [xiii. 215]

CROSS, JOHN (1819–1861), painter ; studied at St. Quentin ; director of the old French classical school ; unsuccessful candidate for the decoration of the houses of parliament, 1844 ; exhibited a picture, by which he became famous, called ' The Clemency of Richard Cœur-de-Lion towards Bertrand de Gourdon,' at the exhibition of 1847 ; sent historical pictures to the Royal Academy ; broke down under pecuniary failure. [xiii. 215]

CROSS, MARY ANN or MARIAN (1819–1880), novelist under the name of GEORGE ELIOT ; *née* Evans ; was sent to school at Coventry, 1832 ; reproduced much of her early history in her novels ; converted from evangelism to more liberal views by the influence of Charles Bray [q. v.], a ribbon manufacturer of Coventry, 1842 ; finished Miss Brabant's translation of Strauss's ' Life of Jesus,' 1846 ; visited Geneva, 1849 ; on returning to England contributed to the ' Westminster Review,' of which she became (1851) assistant editor ; resigned the post, 1853 ; translated Feuerbach's ' Essence of Christianity,' 1854 ; attracted by positivism ; formed a lifelong union without legal form with George Henry Lewes, 1854 ; visited Berlin, 1854 ; published ' Amos Barton ' serially in ' Blackwood's Magazine,' 1857, under the pseudonym of ' George Eliot ' ; published ' Scenes of Clerical Life,' 1858, ' Adam Bede,' 1859, ' The Mill on the Floss,' 1860, and ' Silas Marner,' 1861 ; visited Florence, 1860 and 1861, in search of material for an Italian story of the time of Savonarola ; published ' Romola ' in serial instalments in the ' Cornhill Magazine,' 1862–3 ; finished ' Felix Holt,'

1866; travelled in Spain, 1867; produced 'The Spanish Gypsy,' 1868; published 'Middlemarch,' in parts, 1871-2, and 'Daniel Deronda,' in the same way, 1874-6; wrote the 'Impressions of Theophrastus Such,' 1878 (published, 1879); founded, after Lewes's death in 1878 the 'George Henry Lewes Studentship,' 1879; married Mr. J. W. Cross, then a banker at New York, 6 May 1880. In addition to her novels she published 'Agatha,' a poem, 1869, 'Jubal and other Poems,' 1874, and many essays. She claimed in all her books to be an æsthetic teacher and to interpret philosophical ideas. Most of her novels, despite the tendency to didacticism, stand in the first rank of literary fiction. [xiii. 216]

CROSS, MICHAEL (*fl.* 1630-1660), painter; copied pictures for Charles I in Spain and Italy; reported to have executed a copy of a Madonna by Raphael so accurately that it was interchangeable with the original. [xiii. 222]

CROSS, NATHANIEL (18th cent.), English violin-maker; worked in partnership with Barak Norman; excelled as a maker of violoncellos on the model of Jacob Stainer. [xiii. 222]

CROSS, NICHOLAS (1616-1698), Franciscan; provincial, 1662, 1671, 1680, and 1689; chaplain to Anne; duchess of York; died at Douay, 1698; published 'The Cynosura,' a paraphrase on the 50th Psalm, 1670. [xiii. 222]

CROSS, THOMAS (*fl.* 1632-1682), engraver; employed in engraving portraits of authors and celebrities as frontispieces to books; engraved music. [xiii. 223]

CROSSE, ANDREW (1784-1855), electrician; educated at Brasenose College, Oxford, 1802; lived, at Fyne Court in Somerset, the life of an amateur scientist; experimented on electro-crystallisation and metallurgy; gained notoriety by announcing the appearance of insects of genus *Acarus* in connection with the arrangements of a voltaic battery, 1837. [xiii. 223]

CROSSE, JOHN (1739-1816), vicar of Bradford; studied at St. Edmund Hall, Oxford; B.A., 1768; ordained; appointed to the Lock Chapel, London; incorporated B.A. at Cambridge, 1776; M.A. King's College, Cambridge; incumbent of Todmorden and Halifax in Yorkshire, also of White Chapel, Cleckheaton; presented to the vicarage of Bradford, 1784; published religious pamphlets. [xiii. 224]

CROSSE, JOHN (1786-1833), writer on music; F.S.A.; published 'History of the York Festivals,' 1825. [xiii. 225]

CROSSE, JOHN GREEN (1790-1850), surgeon; studied at St. George's Hospital and the school of anatomy, Windmill Street, London; demonstrator, Trinity College, Dublin; surgeon, Norfolk and Norwich Hospital, from 1826; famous as a lithotomist; F.R.S., 1836; president of the Provincial Medical and Surgical Association, 1846; wrote on the urinary calculus (Jacksonian prize-essay, 1833), and (1820) on the variolous epidemic which occurred in 1819 at Norwich. [xiii. 225]

CROSSE, LAWRENCE (1650?-1724), miniature-painter; imitated Samuel Cooper (1609-1672) [q. v.]; said to have created an erroneous type of the features of Mary Queen of Scots by renovating a portrait of her. [xiii. 225]

CROSSE, RICHARD (1742-1810), miniature-painter; exhibited at the Royal Academy, 1770-95, and other institutions; painter in enamel to the king, 1790; portrait-painter in water-colours and oil. [xiii. 226]

CROSSE, ROBERT (1605-1683), puritan divine; fellow of Lincoln College, Oxford, 1627; B.D., 1637; nominated to the assembly of divines, 1643; declined regius professorship of divinity at Oxford, 1648; vicar of Chew Magna, Somerset, c. 1648-83; entered into controversy with Joseph Glanvill on the Aristotelian philosophy; published 'Λόγου ἀλογία,' a denial of reason in matters of faith, 1655. [xiii. 226]

CROSSE, WILLIAM (*fl.* 1630), poet and translator; educated at St. Mary Hall, Oxford; M.A., 1613; preacher to Sir Edward Horwood's regiment at Cadiz, 1626, and to the company of the Nonsuch at Rochelle, 1630; wrote a boo of verses on the Spanish wars in Holland, 1625; collaborator in Edward Grimestone's 'Historie of the Netherlands,' 1627; translated Sallust, 1629. [xiii. 227]

CROSSLEY, DAVID (1670-1744). [See CROSLY.]

CROSSLEY, SIR FRANCIS (1817-1872), carpet manufacturer and philanthropist; with his father, John Crossley, and brothers, constituted the firm of J. Crossley & Sons, carpet manufacturers, Halifax; applied machinery to carpet-making, driving out the hand-looms; mayor of Halifax, 1849 and 1850; M.P. for Halifax, 1852-9, for the West Riding of Yorkshire, 1859, for the northern division of the West Riding, 1869-72; erected almshouses at Halifax, 1855; presented a park to the townspeople, 1857; built orphan school on Skircoat Moor, 1860; created baronet, 1863; gave 20,000*l.* to the London Missionary Society, 1870. [xiii. 227]

CROSSLEY, JAMES (1800-1883), author; articled to Thomas Ainsworth, solicitor, 1817; wrote for 'Blackwood's Magazine' and for the 'Retrospective Review,' 1820; assisted Lockhart in the 'Quarterly Review'; edited Sir Thomas Browne's 'Tracts,' 1822; wrote the 'Fragment on Mummies,' generally ascribed to Sir Thomas Browne, for Wilkin's edition of that author; partner with Thomas Ainsworth, 1823; president of the Incorporated Law Association of Manchester, 1840 and 1857; president of the Manchester Athenæum, 1847-50; formed Chetham Society, 1843, becoming president, 1848; edited Dr. John Worthington's 'Diary,' 1848-52. [xiii. 228]

CROSSMAN, SAMUEL (1624?-1684), divine and poet; educated at Pembroke College, Cambridge; B.D., 1660; rector of Little Henny, Essex; ejected, 1662; prebendary of Bristol, 1667; dean of Bristol, 1683-4; published homiletic poems and sermons. [xiii. 230]

CROSSRIG, LORD (1643-1707). [See HUME, SIR DAVID.]

CROSTON, THOMAS (1603?-1663?). [See CROXTON.]

CROTCH, WILLIAM (1775-1847), composer; performed on the organ in London, 1779; studied at Cambridge, 1786, at Oxford, 1788; organist at Christ Church, Oxford, 1790-1807, at St. John's College, 1797, and at St. Mary's, Oxford; professor of music, 1797-1806; Mus. Doc., 1799; published six etchings of Christ Church, 1809; member of the Philharmonic Society, 1814-19; first principal of the Royal Academy of Music, 1822-32; played the organ at a Handel festival, Westminster Abbey, 1834; composed two oratorios of note, 'Palestine,' 1812, and 'The Captivity of Judah,' 1834, besides a juvenile work, 'The Captivity of Judah,' 1789; published anthems, lectures on music, and (1812) 'Elements of Musical Composition.' [xiii. 230]

CROTTY, WILLIAM (*d.* 1742), Irish highwayman and rapparee; hanged at Waterford. [xiii. 232]

CROUCH, ANNA MARIA (1763-1805), vocalist; *née* Phillips; played Mandane in Arne's 'Artaxerxes,' 1780; appeared as Clarissa in 'Lionel and Clarissa,' 1781, and as Venus in Dryden and Purcell's 'King Arthur'; generally performed at Drury Lane; married Crouch, a lieutenant in the navy, 1785; taught Michael Kelly [q. v.] English, 1787; separated from her husband, 1791; retired from the stage and society, 1801. [xiii. 232]

CROUCH or CROWCH, HUMPHREY (*fl.* 1635-1671), ballad-writer and pamphleteer; published a folio broadside in verse entitled 'A Whip for the back of a backsliding Brownist,' 1640?; wrote numerous poems and ballads, including 'Love's Court of Conscience,' 1637, 'The Heroic History of Guy, Earl of Warwick,' 'The Madman's Morris,' and 'The Welch Traveller,' 1671, as well as a few prose tracts. [xiii. 233]

CROUCH, JOHN (*fl.* 1660-1681), royalist verse-writer; probably brother of Humphrey Crouch [q. v.]; at one time servant to Robert Pierrepoint, marquis of Dorchester; author of numerous elegies, panegyrics, and verses on the events of his time. [xiii. 234]

CROUCH, NATHANIEL (1632?-1725?), miscellaneous author under initials 'R. B.'; apprenticed to a London stationer, 1656; made free of the Stationers' Company, 1663; issued several journals. [xiii. 235]

CROUCH, WILLIAM (1628-1710), quaker; apprenticed to an upholsterer of Cornhill, 1646; imprisoned for refusing to pay tithes; declined to be parish constable, 1662; complained of the persecution of his sect to Archbishop Sancroft, 1683; published 'The Enormous Sin of Covetousness detected,' 1708. [xiii. 235]

CROUNE, WILLIAM (1633–1684). [See CROONE.]

CROW, FRANCIS (d. 1692), nonconformist divine; M.A.; vicar of Hundon, Suffolk; ejected, 1662; preached at Ovington, Essex, and Bury St. Edmunds; retired to Jamaica, 1686; returned to Essex 'upon K. James's liberty'; published 'The Vanity and Impiety of Judicial Astrology' in Jamaica, 1690; his 'Mensalia Sacra' published posthumously. [xiii. 235]

CROW, HUGH (1765–1829), voyager; captain of a merchant vessel in the African trade; his 'Memoirs,' posthumously published, valuable for their descriptions of the west coast of Africa. [xiii. 236]

CROW, MITFORD (d. 1719), colonel; as British diplomatic agent in Catalonia espoused the cause of the Archduke Charles; governor of Barbados, 1707–11; M.P., Southampton; friend of Swift. [xiii. 236]

CROWDER or **CROWTHER**, ANSELM (1588–1666), Benedictine monk; sub-prior and professor of philosophy, Douay; definitor, 1621; cathedral prior of Rochester, 1633, of Canterbury, 1657; provincial of Canterbury, 1653–66; died in the Old Bailey; wrote devotional works. [xiii. 236]

CROWDER, SIR RICHARD BUDDEN (1795–1859), judge; educated at Eton and Trinity College, Cambridge; barrister of Lincoln's Inn, 1821; joined western circuit, 1821; Q.C., 1837; M.P., Liskeard, 1849–54; puisne justice in the court of common pleas and knighted, 1854; counsel to the admiralty and judge-advocate of the fleet. [xiii. 237]

CROWE, CATHERINE (1800?–1876), novelist and writer on the supernatural; née Stevens; chief works, the 'Night Side of Nature,' 1848, 'Spiritualism, and the Age we live in,' 1859, and two novels, 'Susan Hopley,' 1841, and 'Lilly Dawson,' 1847; translated Kerner's 'Seeress of Prevorst,' 1845. [xiii. 237]

CROWE, EYRE EVANS (1799–1868), historian; educated at Trinity College, Dublin; visited Italy, 1822; Paris correspondent of the 'Morning Chronicle'; editor of the 'Daily News,' 1849–51; contributed a 'History of France' to Lardner's 'Encyclopædia,' 1830; published 'The Greek and the Turk,' 1853, 'History of Louis XVIII and Charles X,' 1854, and novels, 1825–53. [xiii. 237]

CROWE, SIR JOSEPH ARCHER (1825–1896), journalist, art-critic, and commercial attaché; son of Eyre Evans Crowe [q. v.]; became correspondent for 'Morning Chronicle' and 'Daily News,' 1843; correspondent to 'Illustrated London News' in Crimea, and to 'Times' during Indian Mutiny, 1857, and war between Austria and Italy, 1859; consul-general for Saxony, 1860; consul-general for Westphalia and Rhenish Provinces, 1872; commercial attaché to embassies at Berlin and Vienna, 1880; commercial attaché for whole of Europe, residing at Paris, 1882; C.B., 1885; K.C.M.G., 1890; published in collaboration with Cavalcaselle, an Italian painter, works relating to Italian painting. [Suppl. ii. 92]

CROWE, WILLIAM (1616–1675), bibliographer; educated at Caius College, Cambridge; chaplain and schoolmaster of the hospital of Holy Trinity, Croydon, 1668–75; committed suicide. His bibliographical work was exclusively concerned with the scriptures. [xiii. 238]

CROWE, WILLIAM (d. 1743), divine; educated at Trinity Hall, Cambridge; fellow, 1713; M.A., 1717; D.D., 1728; rector of St. Botolph's, Bishopsgate, 1730, of Finchley, 1731–43; chaplain in ordinary to George II.; said to have lent his notes on Greek literature to Bentley; published sermons. [xiii. 238]

CROWE, WILLIAM (1745–1829), poet and divine; scholar of Winchester College, 1758; fellow of New College, Oxford, 1767; B.C.L., 1773; rector of Alton Barnes, Wiltshire, 1787–1829; public orator, Oxford, 1784–1829; lectured on poetry at the Royal Institution; author of 'Lewesdon Hill,' a poem, 1788, and of several sermons and orations; edited Collins's poems, 1828. [xiii. 239]

CROWFOOT, JOHN RUSTAT (1817–1875), Hebrew and Syriac scholar; foundation scholar at Eton; B.A. Caius College, Cambridge, 1839; fellow, 1840; M.A., 1842; B.D., 1849; curate, Great St. Mary's, Cambridge, 1851–3; vicar of Wangford-cum-Reydon, Suffolk, 1860; issued pamphlets on university matters; travelled in Egypt in search of Syriac manuscripts of the gospels, 1873; published 'Fragmenta Evangelica,' 1870. [xiii. 240]

CROWLEY, NICHOLAS JOSEPH (1819–1857), painter; exhibited 'The Eventful Consultation' at the Royal Academy, 1835; member of the Royal Hibernian Academy, 1838; painted historical pictures and portraits. [xiii. 241]

CROWLEY, PETER O'NEILL (1832–1867), Fenian; shot in a skirmish with the constabulary at Kilclooney Wood, 1867. [xiii. 241]

CROWLEY, CROLE, or **CROLEUS**, ROBERT (1518?–1588), author, printer, and divine; demy, Magdalen College, Oxford; probationer-fellow and B.A., 1542; printed his metrical version of the Psalms, 1549; printed three impressions of the 'Vision of Pierce Plowman,' 1550; exile at Frankfort, 1554; returned to England on the death of Queen Mary; archdeacon of Hereford, 1559; prebendary of St. Paul's, 1563; opposed Archbishop Parker on the question of the surplice, 1564; vicar of St. Lawrence Jewry, 1576–8; published a few satirical writings, sermons, and controversial tractates, several of which have been reprinted by the Early English Text Society. [xiii. 241]

CROWNE, JOHN (d. 1703?), dramatist; returned to England from Nova Scotia, whither his father had been compelled to emigrate; became gentleman-usher to a lady early in Charles II's reign; wrote 'Pandion and Amphigenia' (romance), 1665, 'Juliana, or the Princess of Poland' (tragi-comedy), 1671, and 'History of Charles the Eighth,' a rhyming tragedy, 1672; satirised Settle's 'Empress of Morocco,' 1673; prepared 'Calisto,' a court masque, 1675; produced 'Sir Courtly Nice,' comedy, 1685, 'Darius,' tragedy, 1688, and 'Dæneids,' burlesque poem, 1692; published 'The Married Beau,' a comedy, 1694; wrote songs and a few other dramas, including 'Thyestes,' founded on Seneca's play, 1681. [xiii. 243]

CROWQUILL, ALFRED (pseudonym) (1804–1872). [See FORRESTER, ALFRED HENRY.]

CROWTHER, JAMES (1768–1847), botanist; worked as draw-boy at a loom and as porter; assisted J. B. Wood in compiling the 'Flora Mancuniensis'; first to discover the lady's-slipper orchid at Malham, Yorkshire. [xiii. 245]

CROWTHER, JONATHAN (1760–1824), methodist preacher; sent to Scotland by John Wesley, 1787; president of conference, 1819; president of the Irish conference, 1820; author of two books on methodism and a life of Thomas Coke, D.C.L. [q. v.] [xiii. 245]

CROWTHER, JONATHAN (1794–1856), Wesleyan minister; nephew of Jonathan Crowther (1760–1824) [q. v.]; head-master of Kingswood school, Gloucestershire, 1823; general superintendent of the Wesleyan missions in India, 1837–43; classical tutor in the Wesleyan Theological Institution at Didsbury, Lancashire, 1849; examiner at Wesley College, Sheffield. [xiii. 246]

CROWTHER, SAMUEL ADJAI (1809?–1892), negro bishop of the Niger territory from 1864 till death; born of negro parents in the Yoruba country, West Africa; carried off as slave, but recovered by British, 1821; studied at Fourah Bay College, Sierra Leone; ordained in England, 1843; missionary in Yoruba country. [Suppl. ii. 93]

CROXALL, RODNEY (fl. 1745), brother of Samuel Croxall [q. v.]; prebendary of Hereford, 1732; treasurer, 1745. [xiii. 247]

CROXALL, SAMUEL (d. 1752), miscellaneous writer; educated at Eton and St. John's College, Cambridge; M.A., 1717; D.D., 1728; prebendary of Hereford, 1727 and 1730; vicar of St. Mary Somerset and St. Mary Mounthaw, London, 1731–52; archdeacon of Shropshire, 1732; chancellor of Hereford, 1738; built a house with the materials of an ancient chapel in Hereford Cathedral; published 'An Original Canto of Spencer (sic),' 1713 and 1714 (satire on the Earl of Oxford), 'The Vision,' 1715, a translation of Ovid's 'Metamorphoses,' 1717, 'The Fair Circassian,' an indelicate adaptation of the Song of Solomon, first printed in 1720, a translation of Æsop's 'Fables,' 1722, and 'Scripture Politics,' 1735. [xiii. 246]

CROXTON, THOMAS (1603?–1663?), colonel in the parliamentary army, 1650; militia commissioner for Chester, 1650; defended Chester Castle against Sir George Booth's royalists for three weeks, 1659; arrested for conspiracy, 1663; possibly released. [xiii. 248]

CROYLAND, ROGER OF (d. 1214?). [See ROGER.]

CROZIER, FRANCIS RAWDON MOIRA (1796?–1848), navy-captain; went to the Cape of Good Hope as mate of the Doterel sloop, 1818; accompanied Captain Parry in Arctic voyages, 1821–7; lieutenant, 1826; served off Portugal, 1831–5; commander of the Cove, 1837; went with Ross to explore Antarctic Ocean, 1839; discovered north-west passage in company with Sir John Franklin (record found, 1859); lost in Arctic regions, 1848. [xiii. 248]

CRUDEN, ALEXANDER (1701–1770), author of the 'Biblical Concordance'; educated at Marischal College, Aberdeen; M.A.; amanuensis to the tenth Earl of Derby, 1729; discharged on account of his ignorance of French, 1729; tutor in the Isle of Man; bookseller in the Royal Exchange, London, 1732; published his 'Concordance,' 1737; became insane, 1738; escaped from confinement, 1738; corrected works of learning for the press; believed himself divinely appointed to reform the nation; received with great respect at Oxford and Cambridge, 1755; wrote pamphlets on his experiences and contemporary events; repulsed by the daughter of Sir Thomas Abney, to whom he paid his addresses, 1755; founded bursary at Marischal College, Aberdeen. [xiii. 249]

CRUDEN, WILLIAM (1725–1785), Scottish divine; M.A. Aberdeen, 1743; minister of the Scottish presbyterian church, Covent Garden, 1773; chief work, 'Nature Spiritualised,' a book of religious poems. [xiii. 251]

CRUIKSHANK, GEORGE (1792–1878), artist and caricaturist; son of Isaac Cruikshank [q. v.]; his earliest important caricature 'Sir Francis Burdett taken from his house, No. 80 Piccadilly, by warrant of the Speaker of the House of Commons,' 1810; supplied etchings to 'The Scourge,' a satirical periodical, 1811–16, and to 'The Meteor,' 1813–14; produced caricatures of Bonaparte, Joanna Southcott, the purchase of the Elgin marbles, and contemporary events; did much to put an end to the death-penalty for forgery of bank-notes by a cartoon entitled 'Bank-note *not* to be Imitated,' 1818; produced coloured etchings for the 'Humourist' (series of tales), 1819–21, and two volumes of etchings for Grimm's 'Popular Tales,' 1824–6, by some considered his masterpiece; produced 'Phrenological Illustrations,' 1826; substituted wood-engraving for etching, 1828; issued the firs tnumber of the 'Comic Almanack,' 1835; engraved for Dickens's 'Sketches by Boz,' 1836 and 1837; designed a cover and supplied 126 plates for Bentley's 'Miscellany,' 1837–43; illustrated Ainsworth's 'Tower of London,' 1840, and 'Guy Fawkes,' 1841, also 'Ainsworth's Magazine,' 1842–4; claimed, without much show of reason, to have suggested to Dickens the story of 'Oliver Twist,' and to Ainsworth the general plan of the 'Miser's Daughter'; started 'The Table Book,' a miscellany, 1845; illustrated for it Thackeray's 'Legend of the Rhine'; published 'The Bottle,' a famous picture, 1847, and 'The Drunkard's Children,' 1848, in support of the cause of total abstinence; essayed a new 'Cruikshank's Magazine,' which he soon dropped, 1854; supplied frontispiece to Lowell's 'Biglow Papers,' 1859; issued satirical pamphlet against General W. Napier's aspersions on the British volunteers of 1803, 1860, and another against spiritualistic séances, 1863; exhibited oil paintings at the Royal Academy on humorous subjects, such as 'Moses dressing for the Fair,' 1830, and, his *magnum opus*, a cartoon entitled 'The Worship of Bacchus: or, the Drinking Customs of Society,' 1862. In the treatment and moral tone of his drawings he resembled Hogarth. [xiii. 252]

CRUIKSHANK, ISAAC (1756?–1811?), caricaturist and water-colour painter; exhibited at the Royal Academy, 1790 and 1792; designed frontispiece for the 'Witticisms and Jests of Dr. Samuel Johnson,' 1791; executed caricatures of Gillray and Rowlandson type, some political and some social. [xiii. 258]

CRUIKSHANK, ISAAC ROBERT, or ROBERT (1789–1856), caricaturist and miniature-painter; son of Isaac Cruikshank [q. v.]; midshipman in the East India Company's ship Perseverance; gave up a seaman's life for an artist's; satirised social extravagances; published cartoon urging neutrality on England, 1823; illustrated various books dealing with the humours of English, and especially London, life, including the 'English Spy,' 1825, and 'The Orphan,' a translation of the 'Mathilde' of Eugène Sue. [xiii. 259]

CRUIKSHANK, WILLIAM CUMBERLAND (1745–1800), anatomist; M.A. Glasgow, 1767; French and Italian scholar; assistant to Dr. William Hunter, 1771; partner with Hunter in the Windmill Street school; F.R.S., 1797; proved the effluence of carbolic acid from the skin; chief work, 'The Anatomy of the Absorbing Vessels of the Human Body,' 1786. [xiii. 260]

CRUISE, WILLIAM (d. 1824), legal writer; member of Lincoln's Inn, 1773; licensed conveyancer; barrister, Lincoln's Inn, 1791, a statute of William III, which excluded him as a catholic, having been repealed; published 'An Essay on the Nature and Operation of Fines and Recoveries,' 1783, 'A Digest of the Laws of England respecting Real Property,' 1804, and a few other legal treatises. [xiii. 261]

CRULL, JODOCUS (d. 1713?), miscellaneous writer; native of Hamburg; M.D. Leyden, 1679; M.D. Cambridge, 1681; L.R.C.P., 1692; translated and compiled for the booksellers; among other books translated Pufendorf, 'On the Nature and Qualification of Religion, in reference to Civil Society,' 1698, and published an account of 'The Antient and Present State of Muscovy,' 1698. [xiii. 262]

CRUMLEHOLME or **CRUMLUM**, SAMUEL (1618–1672). [See CROMLEHOLME.]

CRUMP, HENRY (fl. 1382), theologian; Cistercian of the monastery of Baltinglass, co. Wicklow; probably fellow of University College, Oxford; D.D.; preached against Wycliffe's scheme of putting church property under secular control; subscribed to the document condemning Wycliffe's doctrine of the sacrament, 1381; suspended from his academical 'acts' by Robert Rygge [q. v.], the chancellor, 1382; reinstated by the king, 1382; condemned for heresy and opposition to mendicant orders at Meath, 1385; returned to Oxford; compelled to abjure, 1392; wrote polemics against the friars and a book of scholastic logic, all lost. [xiii. 262]

CRUMPE, SAMUEL (1766–1796), Irish physician; M.D. Edinburgh, 1788; author of 'An Inquiry into the Nature and Properties of Opium,' 1793, and 'An Essay on the best Means of providing Employment for the People of Ireland,' 1793. [xiii. 263]

CRUSIUS, LEWIS (1701–1775), biographer; educated at St. John's College, Cambridge; M.A., 1737; head-master of the Charterhouse School, 1748–69; prebendary of Worcester, 1751; F.R.S., 1754; rector of Stoke Prior, Worcester, 1754, St. John's, Bedwardine, 1764; prebendary of Brecknock; published 'The Lives of the Roman Poets,' a critical and historical work, 1733. [xiii. 264]

CRUSO, JOHN (d. 1681), civilian; entered Caius College, Cambridge, 1632; fellow; M.A. Oxford, 1639; lost his Cambridge fellowship on account of his royalist views; LL.D., 1652; member of the College of Advocates, 1652; chancellor of St. David's; wrote books on military science and 'Euribates,' a drama. [xiii. 264]

CRUSO, TIMOTHY (1656?–1697), presbyterian minister; studied in the Newington Green Academy; M.A. of one of the Scottish universities; pastor at Crutched Friars, 1688; appointed to Pinners' Hall merchants' lectureship, 1694; published homilies and sermons. [xiii. 264]

CRUTTWELL, CLEMENT (1743–1808), author and compiler; surgeon at Bath; took orders; published Bishop Wilson's bible and works, with a life, 1785, a 'Concordance of the Parallel Texts of Scripture,' 'Gazetteer of France,' 1793, 'Gazetteer of the Netherlands,' 1794, and the 'Universal Gazetteer,' 1798. [xiii. 265]

CRUTTWELL, RICHARD (1776–1846), writer on the currency; educated at Exeter College, Oxford; B.C.L., 1803; chaplain of H.M.S. Trident, and secretary to Rear-admiral Sir Alexander John Ball [q. v.]; perpetual curate of Holmfirth, Yorkshire; rector of Spexhall, Suffolk, 1822–46; wrote 'Treatise on the State of the Currency' (against Ricardo), 1825, 'The System of Country Banking defended,' 1828, 'Reform without Revolution,' 1839, and other works on monetary and social questions. [xiii. 265]

CRYSTALL, THOMAS (d. 1535), abbot of the Cistercian monastery of Kinloss, Morayshire; recommended in youth by his musical talent to Galbraith, abbot of Kinloss; novice, 1487; monk, 1488; abbot, 1499; recovered by legal processes the property of his foundation; erected mills at Strathisla and repaired abbey buildings of Kinloss ; benefactor of monastery and church at Ellon ; as visitor of his order restored the foundations of Deer and Culross ; patronised learning.   [xiii. 266]

CUBBON, SIR MARK (1784–1861), commissioner of Mysore ; cadet, Madras infantry, 1800 ; captain, 1816 ; deputy commissary-general, Madras Presidency, 1822, and a commissioner to inquire into Mysore rebellion, 1831 ; colonel, 1831 ; commissioner of Mysore, 1834–61 ; lieutenant-general, 1852 ; K.C.B., 1859 ; died at Suez on his way home, 1861.   [xiii. 267]

CUBITT, JOSEPH (1811–1872), civil engineer ; son of Sir William Cubitt [q. v.] ; constructed the Great Northern railway, the London, Chatham, and Dover railway, and part of the London and South-Western ; built the new Blackfriars Bridge.   [xiii. 269]

CUBITT, THOMAS (1788–1855), builder ; in early life made a voyage to India as ship-carpenter ; master carpenter in London, 1809 ; built the London Institution, Finsbury Circus, 1815 ; carried out building operations in London ; built east front of Buckingham Palace ; supported Thames embankment scheme ; guaranteed a sum of money to the Great Exhibition of 1851 ; much interested in sewage questions.   [xiii. 267]

CUBITT, SIR WILLIAM (1785–1861), civil engineer ; invented self-regulating windmill sails, 1807 ; chief engineer of Messrs. Ransome's establishment, Ipswich, 1812–21 ; partner, 1821–6 ; invented the treadmill, 1818 ; constructed Oxford canal and the Liverpool Junction canal ; F.R.S., 1830 ; constructed docks at Cardiff and Middlesborough ; constructed South-Eastern railway ; consulting engineer to the Great Northern railway and to the Boulogne and Amiens railway ; constructed the waterworks of Berlin ; president of the Institution of Civil Engineers, 1850, 1851 ; knighted, 1851.   [xiii. 268]

CUBITT, WILLIAM (1791–1863), lord mayor of London ; partner in the building firm of his brother, Thomas Cubitt [q. v.], at Gray's Inn Road ; subsequently sole proprietor ; M.P., Andover, 1847–61, 1862 ; sheriff of London, 1847 ; lord mayor, 1860–1, 1861–2 ; president of St. Bartholomew's Hospital.   [xiii. 269]

CUDDON, AMBROSE (*fl.* 1827), Roman catholic publisher and journalist ; began the publication of 'The Catholic Miscellany,' 1822 ; published 'A Complete Modern British Martyrology,' 1824–5.   [xiii. 270]

CUDMORE, RICHARD (1787–1840), musician ; pupil of Salomon ; led the band at the Chichester Theatre, 1799–1808 ; solo pianist and violinist in London after 1808 ; led the Gentlemen's Concerts, Manchester ; composed 'The Martyr of Antioch,' an oratorio.   [xiii. 270]

CUDWORTH, RALPH (1617–1688), divine ; M.A. Emmanuel College, Cambridge, 1639 ; fellow and tutor, 1639 ; master of Clare Hall, 1645 ; regius professor of Hebrew, 1645–88 ; presented to the living of North Cadbury, Somerset, 1650 ; D.D., 1651 ; master of Christ's College, Cambridge, 1654 ; consulted with a committee of the House of Commons on a proposed revision of the translation of the bible, 1657 ; originated theory of a 'plastic nature' to combat doctrines of chance and constant divine interference ; chief works, 'The True Intellectual System of the Universe,' 1678, and a 'Treatise concerning Eternal and Immutable Morality,' published posthumously.   [xiii. 271]

CUFF or **CUFFE**, HENRY (1563–1601), author and politician ; scholar of Trinity College, Oxford, 1578 ; fellow 1583 ; tutor at Merton, 1586 ; M.A., 1589 ; lecturer at Queen's College ; professor of Greek, 1590–6 ; accompanied Essex to Cadiz as secretary, 1596 ; faithful to his master when in disgrace, but a reckless adviser ; imprisoned for complicity in Essex's treason, 1601 ; executed, 1601. Cuff wrote 'The Differences of the Ages of Man's Life,' 1600, and assisted Columbanus in his edition of Longus's 'Pastoral of Daphnis and Chloe.'   [xiii. 272]

CUFF, JAMES DODSLEY (1780–1853), numismatist ; employed in the Bank of England ; F.S.A. ; contributed descriptions of coins to Hearne's 'Supplement' to Ainslie's 'Illustrations of the Anglo-French Coinage,' 1830.   [xiii. 275]

CUIT or **CUITT**, GEORGE, the elder (1743–1818), painter ; sent to study in Italy by Sir Lawrence Dundas,

1769 ; exhibited 'The Infant Jupiter fed with goat's milk and honey,' at the Royal Academy, 1776.   [xiii. 275]

CUITT, GEORGE, the younger (1779–1854), etcher ; son of George Cuit, or Cuitt, the elder [q. v.] ; published etchings of ancient buildings in England and Wales, 1810.   [xiii. 275]

CULBERTSON, ROBERT (1765–1823), Scottish divine ; educated at Edinburgh University ; pastor of the associate congregation, Leith, 1791 ; editor of the 'Christian Magazine,' and author of secessionist treatises of divinity.   [xiii. 276]

CULEN or **COLIN** (967–971 ?), king of Scotland ; defeated Dubh, who had taken the crown by the law of tanistry, 967 ; slain by the Britons, 971.   [xiii. 276]

CULIN, PATRICK (*d.* 1534), bishop of Clogher ; prior of St. John without Newgate, in Dublin, till 1531 ; bishop of Clogher, 1516 ; compiled a register of the antiquities of his church, 1525.   [xiii. 276]

CULLEN, LORDS. [See GRANT, SIR FRANCIS, 1658–1726 ; CULLEN, ROBERT, *d.* 1810.]

CULLEN, PAUL (1803–1878), cardinal ; studied at Carlow College and in the Urban College of the Propaganda, Rome ; made a doctor by the pope in person, 1828 ; priest, 1829 ; rector of the Irish College, Rome ; rector of the Propaganda College, 1848–9, which he saved from Mazzini by placing it under American protection, 1848 ; archbishop of Armagh, 1849–52 ; summoned synod of Irish catholic clergy at Thurles, 1850 ; archbishop of Dublin, 1852 ; delegate apostolic for the foundation of a catholic university in Ireland ; opposed the Fenian brotherhood ; cardinal-priest, 1866 ; presided at the synod of Maynooth, 1875.   [xiii. 277]

CULLEN, ROBERT, LORD CULLEN (*d.* 1810), Scottish judge ; son of William Cullen [q. v.] ; educated at Edinburgh University ; advocate, 1764 ; introduced bill for reform of Scottish representation, 1785 ; lord of session, 1796 ; lord justiciary, 1799.   [xiii. 278]

CULLEN, WILLIAM (1710–1790), physician ; studied at Glasgow University ; studied at the Edinburgh Medical School, 1734–6 ; M.D. Glasgow, 1740 ; professor of medicine, Glasgow, 1751–5 ; professor of chemistry, Edinburgh, 1756 ; clinical lecturer, 1757 ; professor of the theory of physic, 1766 ; president of the Edinburgh College of Physicians, 1773–5 ; F.R.S., 1777 ; attacked by John Brown (1735–1788) [q. v.], founder of the Brunonian system ; chief works, 'An Essay on the Cold produced by Evaporating Fluids,' 1755, and 'First Lines of the Practice of Physic,' 1776–84.   [xiii. 279]

CULLEY, GEORGE (1735–1813), cattle-breeder ; pupil of Bakewell ; author of works on agriculture. [xiii. 282]

CULLIMORE, ISAAC (1791–1852), egyptologist ; began to publish the oriental seals and cylinders of the British Museum, 1842.   [xiii. 282]

CULLUM, SIR DUDLEY, third baronet (1657–1720), horticultural writer ; grandson of Sir Thomas Cullum [q. v.] ; educated at St. John's College, Cambridge, 1675 ; corresponded with Evelyn ; recorded his horticultural experiments at Hawsted, Suffolk, in the 'Philosophical Transactions,' 1694 ; high sheriff, 1690 ; M.P., 1702.
                                                [xiii. 282]

CULLUM, SIR JOHN, sixth baronet (1733–1785), antiquary and divine of Hardwick, Suffolk ; educated at Catharine Hall, Cambridge ; fourth junior optime, 1756 ; fellow ; rector of Hawsted, 1762 ; vicar of Great Thurlow, 1774 ; F.S.A., 1774 ; F.R.S., 1775 ; published 'The History and Antiquities of Hawsted and Hardwick in the County of Suffolk' ; an accomplished botanist.   [xiii. 283]

CULLUM, SIR THOMAS (1587 ?–1664), sheriff of London ; apprenticed to John Rayney, draper ; alderman and member of the Drapers' Company ; sheriff, 1646 ; imprisoned in the Tower as a royalist, 1647 ; created baronet, 1660 ; compelled to disburse a large sum, 1663, in connection with the excise, of which he had formerly been commissioner.   [xiii. 283]

CULLUM, SIR THOMAS GERY (1741–1831), Bath king-at-arms ; educated at the Charterhouse ; member of the Corporation of Surgeons, 1800 ; practised at Bury St. Edmunds ; printed privately 'Floræ Anglicæ Specimen imperfectum et ineditum,' 1774.   [xiii. 284]

CULMER, RICHARD (*fl.* 1660), fanatical divine ; educated at the King's School, Canterbury ; B.A. Magdalene College, Cambridge, 1619 ; rector of Goodnestone, Kent, 1630 ; suspended for refusing to read the ' Book of Sabbath Sports,' 1635 ; rector of Chartham, Kent, 1643 ; appointed by the parliament to destroy the monuments and stained glass of Canterbury Cathedral, 1643 ; appointed to the living of Minster, Thanet, 1644 ; excited great dislike by his fanaticism and personal peculiarities ; ejected, 1660 ; arrested for supposed complicity in Venner's conspiracy, but liberated. [xiii. 284]

CULPEPER. [See also COLEPEPER.]

CULPEPER, NICHOLAS (1616–1654), writer on astrology and medicine : astrologer and physician in Spitalfields, 1640 ; fought for parliament in civil war ; published a translation of the College of Physicians' ' Pharmacopœia,' for which he was virulently lampooned, 1649 ; published ' The English Physician Enlarged,' 1653, ' Semeiotica Uranica,' 1651, and other quaint medleys of astrology and medicine ; many of his manuscripts published posthumously. [xiii. 286]

CULPEPER, SIR THOMAS, the elder (1578–1662), writer on usury ; entered Hart Hall, Oxford, 1591 ; student at one of the Inns of Court ; knighted, 1619 ; published ' Tract against the high rate of Usurie,' 1621. [xiii. 287]

CULPEPER, SIR THOMAS, the younger (1626–1697), writer on usury ; son of Sir Thomas Culpeper (1578–1662) [q. v.] ; B.A. University College, Oxford, 1643 ; probationer-fellow All Souls' College ; knighted ; wrote pamphlets against usury. [xiii. 288]

CULVERWEL, NATHANAEL (*d.* 1651 ?), divine ; M.A. Emmanuel College, Cambridge, 1640 ; fellow, 1642 ; author of the ' Light of Nature,' 1652 ; one of the Cambridge platonists. [xiii. 288]

CULY, DAVID (*d.* 1725), sectary ; founded the Culimite sect of anabaptists. [xiii. 289]

CUMBERLAND, DUKES OF. [See RUPERT, 1619–1682 ; GEORGE, PRINCE OF DENMARK, 1653–1708 ; WILLIAM AUGUSTUS, 1721–1765 ; HENRY FREDERICK, 1745–1790 ; ERNEST AUGUSTUS, 1771–1851.]

CUMBERLAND, EARLS OF. [See CLIFFORD, HENRY DE, first EARL, 1493–1542 ; CLIFFORD, HENRY DE, second EARL, *d.* 1570 ; CLIFFORD, GEORGE, third EARL, 1558–1605 ; CLIFFORD, HENRY, fifth EARL, 1591–1643.]

CUMBERLAND, COUNTESS OF (1560 ?–1616). [See CLIFFORD, MARGARET.]

CUMBERLAND, RICHARD (1631–1718), bishop of Peterborough ; educated at St. Paul's School and at Magdalene College, Cambridge ; fellow, 1656 ; M.A., 1656 ; M.A. Oxford, 1657 ; B.D. Cambridge, 1663 ; rector of Brampton, Northamptonshire, 1658–67 ; respondent at the public commencement, Cambridge, 1680 ; bishop of Peterborough, 1691 ; published ' De Legibus Naturæ Disquisitio philosophica,' 1672, in opposition to the doctrines of Hobbes ; author of a translation of Sanchoniatho, published 1720. [xiii. 289]

CUMBERLAND, RICHARD (1732–1811), dramatist ; great-grandson of Richard Cumberland (1631–1718) [q. v.] ; educated at Westminster School and Trinity College, Cambridge ; fellow ; private secretary to Lord Halifax in the board of trade ; Ulster secretary, 1761 ; clerk of reports in the board of trade ; secretary to the board of trade, c. 1776 ; sent to Spain to arrange a separate treaty with England, 1780 ; wrote pieces of the sentimental comedy type, his best play being the ' West Indian,' acted 1771 ; with Sir James Bland Burges [q. v.] wrote an epic called the ' Exodiad,' 1808 ; author of some tragedies, a translation of Greek comic fragments, and the ' Clouds ' of Aristophanes, two novels, ' Arundel,' 1789, and ' Henry,' 1795, and the ' Observer,' a periodical. [xiii. 290]

CUMBERLAND, RICHARD FRANCIS G. (1792–1870), captain ; grandson of Richard Cumberland (1732–1811) [q. v.] ; captain 3rd foot guards, 1814 ; aide-de-camp to the Duke of Wellington in Peninsula. [xiii. 293]

CUMINE AILBHE or **FINN** (657 ?–669 ?), seventh abbot of Hy ; of the race of Conall Gulban ; attempted to introduce into the ancient Irish church the Roman cycle

for calculating Easter ; author of a life of St. Columba, published by Mabillon, 1733 ; his day, 24 Feb. [xiii. 293]

CUMING. [See also COMYN and CUMMING.]

CUMING or **CUMMING**, SIR ALEXANDER (1690 ?–1775), chief of the Cherokees ; called to the Scottish bar, 1714 ; sailed to America, 1729 ; chosen lawgiver of the Cherokee nation, 1730 ; presented seven Cherokee chiefs in audience to George II, 1730 ; drew up an ' agreement ' with them in the name of the British nation, 1730 ; ineffectually proposed to settle Jewish families in the Cherokee mountains ; accused of having defrauded settlers of South Carolina ; imprisoned, 1737 ; poor brother of the Charterhouse, 1765. [xiii. 294]

CUMING, HUGH (1791–1865), naturalist ; sail-maker at Valparaiso, 1819 ; collected shells and living orchids in the Pacific, on the coast of Chili, and in the Philippine islands, 1835 ; finally returned to England, 1839. [xiii. 295]

CUMMING. [See also COMYN and CUMING.]

CUMMING, ALEXANDER (1733–1814), mathematician and mechanic ; F.R.S. ; wrote largely on the mechanical laws and action of wheels. [xiii. 296]

CUMMING, SIR ARTHUR (1817–1893), admiral ; studied at Royal Naval College, Portsmouth ; mate and lieutenant, 1840 ; served with distinction off South America ; commander, 1846 ; captain, 1854 ; served in Baltic, 1854, and Black Sea, 1855–6 ; with Channel fleet, 1859–63 ; C.B., 1867 ; commander-in-chief in East Indies, 1872–5 ; vice-admiral, 1876 ; admiral, 1880 ; K.C.B., 1887. [Suppl. ii. 93]

CUMMING, JAMES (*d.* 1827), official in the India Office ; head of the revenue and judicial department under the board of control, 1807–23 ; collaborator in a House of Commons report on the government of Madras. [xiii. 296]

CUMMING, JAMES (1777–1861), professor of chemistry at Cambridge ; B.A. Trinity College, Cambridge, 1801 ; fellow, 1803 ; professor of chemistry, 1815–60 ; an independent discoverer of thermo-electricity, publishing ' A Manual of Electro-Dynamics,' 1827. [xiii. 296]

CUMMING, JOHN (1807–1881), divine ; M.A. Aberdeen, 1827 ; licensed to preach, 1832 ; appointed to the National Scottish Church at Crown Court, Covent Garden, 1832 ; took part in Maynooth controversy, 1845 ; opponent of ' papal aggression,' 1850 ; published (1848–70) books on the Apocalypse, maintaining that the ' last vial ' was to be poured out between 1848 and 1867. [xiii. 297]

CUMMING, JOSEPH GEORGE (1812–1868), geologist and divine ; senior optime, Emmanuel College, Cambridge, 1834 ; vice-principal of King William's College, Isle of Man, 1841–56 ; warden and professor, Queen's College, Birmingham, 1858 ; rector of Mellis, Suffolk, 1862–7 ; wrote on the history and geology of the Isle of Man, 1848. [xiii. 298]

CUMMING, ROUALEYN GEORGE GORDON- (1820–1866), African lion-hunter ; cornet, Madras cavalry, 1838–1840 ; joined the Cape mounted rifles, 1843 ; resigned, to take up a sportsman's life, 1843 ; published on his return to England ' Five Years of a Hunter's Life in the Far Interior of South Africa,' 1850. [xiii. 298]

CUMMING, THOMAS (*d.* 1774), quaker ; successfully organised expedition against French posts in South Barbary. [xiii. 299]

CUMMING, WILLIAM (*fl.* 1797–1823), portrait-painter ; one of the first fourteen academicians of the Royal Hibernian Academy, 1821. [xiii. 299]

CUMMING, WILLIAM (1822 ?–1855), pioneer of modern ophthalmology ; demonstrated that light falling on the retina might be reflected back to an observer's eye, 1846. [xiii. 299]

CUNARD, SIR SAMUEL (1787–1865), shipowner ; merchant at Halifax, Nova Scotia ; established British and North American Royal Mail Steam Packet Company, 1839 ; F.R.G.S., 1846 ; created baronet, 1859. [xiii. 300]

CUNDY, JAMES (1792–1826), sculptor ; son of Thomas Cundy the elder [q. v.] [xiii. 301]

CUNDY, JOSEPH (1795–1875), architect in Belgravia ; son of Thomas Cundy the elder [q. v.] [xiii. 301]

CUNDY, NICHOLAS WILCOCKS (*b.* 1778), architect; brother of Thomas Cundy the elder [q. v.]; designed the Pantheon, Oxford Street, London. [xiii. 301]

CUNDY, SAMUEL (*d.* 1866), architect; son of James Cundy [q. v.]; employed on restorations at Westminster Abbey and St. Albans. [xiii. 301]

CUNDY, THOMAS, the elder (1765–1825), architect and builder. His name is associated with Hawarden Castle, Sion House, Osterley Park, and other famous buildings. [xiii. 300]

CUNDY, THOMAS, the younger (1790–1867), architect; son of Thomas Cundy (1765–1825) [q. v.]; surveyor to Earl Grosvenor's London estates, 1825–66; built numerous churches in west end of London. [xiii. 301]

CUNGAR or **CYNGAR**, SAINT (*fl.* 500 ?), anchorite; said to have been the son of an emperor of Constantinople; founded oratories at Congresbury in Somerset and Morganwy in Glamorganshire; granted land by King Iva. [xiii. 301]

CUNINGHAM. [See also CUNNINGHAM and CUNYNGHAM.]

CUNINGHAM or **KENINGHAM**, WILLIAM (*fl.* 1586), physician, astrologer, and engraver; M.B. Corpus Christi College, Cambridge, 1557; M.D. Heidelberg, 1559; public lecturer at Surgeons' Hall, 1563; chief works, 'The Cosmographicall Glasse,' 1559, 'Commentaria in Hippocratem,' and 'Organographia.' [xiii. 302]

CUNLIFFE-OWEN, SIR FRANCIS PHILIP (1828–1894). [See OWEN.]

CUNNINGHAM, ALEXANDER, first EARL OF GLENCAIRN (*d.* 1488), lord of parliament with the title Lord Kilmaurs, *c.* 1450; created Earl of Glencairn, 1488; slain at the battle of Sauchieburn, 1488. [xiii. 303]

CUNNINGHAM, ALEXANDER, fifth EARL OF GLENCAIRN (*d.* 1574), principal promoter of the reformation in Scotland; surrendered by his father as pledge for performance of treaty against England, 1544; invited Knox to return from Geneva, 1557; prevented the queen-regent of Scotland from advancing against the Scottish reformers in Perth, 1559; signed letter to Queen Elizabeth for assistance against the queen-regent, 1559; ambassador to England to claim aid from Elizabeth in repelling French invasion, 1560; commissioned to destroy the monasteries and 'monuments of idolatry' in western Scotland, 1561; privy councillor of Scotland, 1561; declared guilty of lese-majesty for not appearing before Mary Queen of Scots to answer a charge of rebellion in having accompanied Moray in an attack on Edinburgh, 1565; commanded the insurgents under the Earl of Morton; commanded a division at Langside, 1568; nominated for the regency, but defeated by the Earl of Morton, 1571. [xiii. 303]

CUNNINGHAM, ALEXANDER (1655 ?–1730), critic; educated in Holland and at Edinburgh; professor of civil law, Edinburgh, 1698; ousted for political reasons, 1710; retired to the Hague, 1710; attacked Bentley's edition of Horace, 1721; published an edition of Horace, 1721; friend of Burmann and Leclerc; famous as a chess-player; edited Virgil, published, 1743, and Phædrus, published, 1757. [xiii. 306]

CUNNINGHAM, ALEXANDER (1654–1737), historian; sometimes confused with Alexander Cunningham (1655 ?–1730) [q. v.]; tutor to John, marquis of Lorne, 1697; employed by William III as a spy upon the French military preparations, 1701; travelling tutor to Lord Lonsdale in Italy, 1711; British envoy to Venice, 1715–20; wrote in Latin a history of Great Britain 'from the Revolution in 1688 to the accession of George I,' which was translated and published in 1787. [xiii. 306]

CUNNINGHAM, SIR ALEXANDER (1703–1785). [See DICK.]

CUNNINGHAM, SIR ALEXANDER (1814–1893), soldier and archæologist; son of Allan Cunningham (1784–1842) [q. v.]; educated at Christ's Hospital and Addiscombe; second-lieutenant, Bengal engineers, 1831; aide-de-camp to Lord Auckland, 1836; executive engineer to King of Oudh, 1840, and at Gwalior, 1844–5; field-engineer in first Sikh war, 1846, and in second, 1848–9; lieutenant-colonel; chief engineer in Burmah, 1856–8, and in north-western provinces, 1858–61; retired as major-general, 1861; archæological surveyor to government of India, 1861–5; director-general of Indian archæological survey, 1870–85; C.S.I., 1871; C.I.E., 1878; K.C.I.E., 1887; published valuable treatises on Indian archæology and numismatics, including 'The Ancient Geography of India' (Buddhist period), 1871, and 'Coins of Mediæval India,' posthumously, 1894. [Suppl. ii. 94]

CUNNINGHAM, ALLAN (1791–1839), botanist; botanical collector to the royal gardens, Kew, 1814; travelled on a botanical expedition in South America, 1815; in Australia, 1817, and subsequently in Tasmania; declined post of colonial botanist to New South Wales in favour of his brother Richard, 1832; colonial botanist on his brother's death, 1835; reached Sydney, 1836; resigned, 1836; buried at Sydney. [xiii. 308]

CUNNINGHAM, ALLAN (1784–1842), miscellaneous writer; friend of Hogg the Ettrick shepherd; provided R. H. Cromek [q. v.] with 'old ballads' of his own composition, 1809; published in London 'Remains of Nithsdale and Galloway Song,' 1810; parliamentary reporter to the 'Day,' 1810–14; secretary to Francis Chantrey, 1814–41; contributed 'Recollections of Mark Macrabin, the Cameronian' to 'Blackwood's Magazine,' 1819–21; published 'Traditional Tales of the English and Scottish Peasantry,' 1822, 'The Songs of Scotland, Ancient and Modern,' including the famous 'A Wet Sheet and a Flowing Sea,' 1825, 'Lives of the most Eminent British Painters, Sculptors, and Architects,' 1829–33, and an edition of Burns, 1834. [xiii. 308]

CUNNINGHAM, SIR CHARLES (1755–1834), rear-admiral; first lieutenant of the Hinchingbroke with Nelson, 1779; attached to Mediterranean fleet on outbreak of war with France, 1793; practically ended the mutiny at the Nore, 1797; rear-admiral, 1829; knight commander of the Royal Hanoverian Guelphic Order, 1832. [xiii. 310]

CUNNINGHAM or **CALZE**, EDMUND FRANCIS (1742 ?–1795), portrait-painter; son of a Jacobite refugee; studied in Italy; exhibited at the Royal Academy under the name Calze, 1770–81; entered the service of Catharine II of Russia; went to Berlin, 1788; painted portraits of Frederick the Great's court. [xiii. 311]

CUNNINGHAM, FRANCIS (1820–1875), commentator on Ben Jonson; son of Allan Cunningham (1784–1842) [q. v.]; field-engineer at Jellalabad; member of the Mysore commission; edited Marlowe, 1870, Massinger, 1871, and Ben Jonson, 1871. [xiii. 312]

CUNNINGHAM, JAMES (*d.* 1709 ?), botanist; surgeon to the East India Company's factory, Emouï, China, 1698; escaped massacre at Pulo Condore, 1705; driven from Banjar-Massin by a native rising, 1707; chief of Banjar, 1707, under the East India Company; botanical collector in China; author of meteorological and geographical papers. [xiii. 312]

CUNNINGHAM, JAMES, fourteenth EARL OF GLENCAIRN (1749–1791), friend of Burns; captain in the West Fencible regiment, 1778; Scottish representative peer, 1780. [xiii. 313]

CUNNINGHAM, SIR JOHN (*d.* 1684), lawyer; defended Argyll, 1661; created baronet of Nova Scotia, 1669; suspended by Charles II for maintaining the right of appeal from the court of session to parliament, 1674; M.P. for Ayrshire, 1681. [xiii. 313]

CUNNINGHAM, JOHN (1729–1773), poet; published 'Love in a Mist,' a farce, 1747; strolling actor; author of 'The Contemplatist,' 1762, 'Fortune, an Apologue,' 1765, and 'Poems, chiefly Pastoral,' 1766. [xiii. 313]

CUNNINGHAM, JOHN (1819–1893), historian; educated at Glasgow and Edinburgh Universities; minister of Crieff, Perthshire, 1845–86; successfully advocated introduction of instrumental music into church, 1867; moderator of general assembly and principal of St. Mary's College, St. Andrews, 1886; D.D. Edinburgh, 1860; LL.D. Glasgow, 1886; honorary LL.D. Dublin, 1887; published 'Church History of Scotland,' 1859, and other works. [Suppl. ii. 96]

CUNNINGHAM, JOHN WILLIAM (1780–1861), evangelical divine; fifth wrangler, St. John's College, Cambridge, 1802; fellow, 1802; vicar of Harrow, 1811–61; editor of the 'Christian Observer,' 1850–8; wrote on missions and religious work. [xiii. 314]

CUNNINGHAM, JOSEPH DAVEY (1812–1851), historian of the Sikhs; son of Allan Cunningham (1784–1842) [q. v.]; nominated to the Bengal engineers, 1831; fortified Firozpur, 1837; entrusted with various important missions in the Sikh country; fought at Sobraon; captain, 1845; political agent at Bhopal, 1846; published 'History of the Sikhs,' 1849; removed for having revealed governmental secrets in his 'History,' 1850. [xiii. 314]

CUNNINGHAM, PETER (d. 1805), poet; curate at Eyam, near the Peak, 1775–90 ?; author of 'Leith Hill,' 1789, and of 'St. Anne's Hill,' 1800. [xiii. 316]

CUNNINGHAM, PETER (1816–1869), author and critic; son of Allan Cunningham (1784–1842) [q. v.]; educated at Christ's Hospital; chief clerk in the audit office; treasurer of the Shakespeare Society; edited Walpole's 'Letters,' 1857, and the works of Drummond of Hawthornden, 1833; compiled a 'Handbook to London,' 1849. [xiii. 316]

CUNNINGHAM, PETER MILLER (1789–1864), navy surgeon; assistant-surgeon to the English fleet off Spain, 1810; surgeon, 1814; surgeon-superintendent of convict ships sailing to New South Wales; failed as settler in Australia; served at Alexandria, 1840; wrote 'Two Years in New South Wales,' 1827, and a book on the influence of galvanic action on the human constitution, 1834. [xiii. 316]

CUNNINGHAM, RICHARD (1793–1835), botanist; colonial botanist at Sydney, 1833–5; murdered by natives. [xiii. 317]

CUNNINGHAM, THOMAS MOUNSEY (1776–1834), Scottish poet; foreman superintendent of Fowler's chain cable manufactory, London; contributed to the 'Scots Magazine,' 1806, and to the 'Edinburgh Magazine,' 1817; author of 'The Hills o' Gallowa,' and other songs and satires. [xiii. 317]

CUNNINGHAM, TIMOTHY (d. 1789), antiquarian; F.S.A., 1761; founded Cunningham prize in Royal Irish Academy; compiled legal and antiquarian works. [xiii. 318]

CUNNINGHAM, WILLIAM, fourth EARL OF GLENCAIRN (d. 1547), lord high treasurer of Scotland, 1526; sent to France to conclude a treaty for James V's marriage with Mary of Guise, 1538; taken prisoner at Solway Moss, 1542; supported the reformers; acknowledged Henry VIII as protector of Scotland, 1544; defeated by the Earl of Arran, 1544; treacherously lost the battle of Coldingham in the interests of England, 1544; went over to the queen-regent, 1544. [xiii. 318]

CUNNINGHAM, WILLIAM, ninth EARL OF GLENCAIRN (1610 ?–1664), privy councillor and commissioner of the treasury, 1641; lord justice-general, 1646; privy to the attempted rescue of Charles I, 1648; commissioned by Charles II to command the king's forces in Scotland, 1653; defeated at Dunkeld, 1654; arrested by Monck, 1655; excepted from Cromwell's 'grace and pardon'; chancellor of Glasgow University, 1660; lord chancellor of Scotland, 1661. [xiii. 320]

CUNNINGHAM, WILLIAM (1805–1861), church leader and theologian; educated at Edinburgh University; minister of Trinity College Church, Edinburgh, 1834; D.D. Princeton, New Jersey, 1842; professor of church history in the Free church, New College, 1845; principal, 1847; Calvinist controversialist and writer of 'Historical Theology.' [xiii. 321]

CUNNINGTON, WILLIAM (1754–1810), antiquary; F.S.A.; excavated numerous barrows in Wiltshire. [xiii. 323]

CUNOBELINUS (d. 43 ?), British king; supposed son of Cassivelaunus; ally of Augustus and paramount ruler of Britain. Shakespeare's Cymbeline is named after him, but is not historical. [xiii. 323]

CUNYNGHAME, SIR ARTHUR AUGUSTUS THURLOW (1812–1884), general; second lieutenant 60th royal rifles, 1830; aide-de-camp to Lord Saltoun, 1841; present at the investment of Nankin; brevet-colonel, 1854; fought at Inkermann and held the fortress of Kertch, 1855; K.C.B., 1869; commanded in South Africa, 1874–8; general, 1877. [xiii. 324]

CURE, WILLIAM (d. 1632), statuary; master-mason to James I; worked under Inigo Jones at the Banqueting House, Whitehall. [xiii. 324]

CURETON, SIR CHARLES (1826–1891), general; son of Charles Robert Cureton [q. v.]; ensign in East India Company's army, 1843; major-general, 1870; general, 1888; served in Sutlej and Punjab and north-west frontier campaigns, 1846–52; in Indian Mutiny, 1857, and in north-west frontier campaign, 1860; commanded Oude division, Bengal army, 1879–84; K.C.B., 1891. [Suppl. ii. 98]

CURETON, CHARLES ROBERT (1789–1848), brigadier-general; ensign in Shropshire militia, 1806; lieutenant; fled from creditors and enlisted, 1808; served in Peninsular war; gazetted ensign in 40th foot, 1814; lieutenant 20th light dragoons, 1816; adjutant, 1816; captain, 16th lancers, 1825; major, 1833; brevet colonel, 1846; served in India, 1822–6, Afghanistan, 1839, and Gwalior campaign, 1843; C.B., 1844; commanded cavalry in Satlaj campaign, 1846; colonel and aide-de-camp to Queen Victoria, 1846; adjutant-general in East Indies, 1846; killed in action at Ramnagar in second Sikh war. [Suppl. ii. 97]

CURETON, EDWARD BURGOYNE (1822–1894), lieutenant-general; son of Charles Robert Cureton [q. v.]; ensign, 13th foot, 1839; major-general, 1878; colonel, 12th lancers, 1892; served in India and in the Kaffir and Crimean wars. [Suppl. ii. 98]

CURETON, WILLIAM (1808–1864), Syriac scholar; M.A. Christ Church, Oxford, 1833; D.C.L., 1858; chaplain of Christ Church; chaplain in ordinary to the queen, 1847; canon of Westminster, 1849–64; discovered (1845), when assistant-keeper of manuscripts at the British Museum, the epistles of St. Ignatius among manuscripts from the Nitrian monasteries, also the 'Curetonian Gospels'; edited Arabic texts. [xiii. 325]

CURLE, HIPPOLITUS (1592–1638), Scottish jesuit; studied in the Scots seminary, Douay; rector, 1633. [xiii. 326]

CURLING, HENRY (1803–1864), novelist; captain in the 52nd foot. [xiii. 326]

CURLL, EDMUND (1675–1747), bookseller; pamphleteer during the Sacheverell controversy, 1710; offended Pope by ascribing to him the authorship of 'Court Poems,' 1716; published a pirated edition of the trial of the Earl of Wintoun, 1716; convicted of printing immoral books, 1725; claimed to have unearthed a plot against the government, but was ignored, 1728; accused by Pope of selling forged letters under the name of 'Mr. Pope's Literary Correspondence for thirty years,' 1735; published among other books Swift's 'Meditation upon a Broomstick,' 1710, John Hale's 'Discourse,' 1720, and Betterton's 'History of the English Stage from the Restoration to the Present Times,' 1741. [xiii. 327]

CURLL, WALTER (1575–1647), bishop of Winchester; entered at Peterhouse, Cambridge, 1592; fellow; D.D., 1612; chaplain to James I; dean of Lichfield, 1621; bishop of Rochester, 1628–9; bishop of Bath and Wells, 1629; bishop of Winchester, 1632; helped to defend Winchester Castle against Cromwell, 1645; compelled to surrender and deprived of his private property and episcopal income, 1645. [xiii. 331]

CURRAN, JOHN PHILPOT (1750–1817), Irish judge; sizar at Trinity College, Dublin, 1769; studied law at the Middle Temple, 1773; studied declamation in private; called to the bar, 1775; gained a verdict for Neale, a Roman catholic priest, who sued Lord Doneraile for assault, 1780; king's counsel, 1782; M.P., Kilbeggan, Westmeath, 1783; joined Grattan's party; M.P., Rathcormac, co. Cork; spoke in favour of Flood's motion for parliamentary reform, 1783; fought a duel with Fitzgibbon, an old friend, in consequence of a quarrel at a debate on the abuse of attachments in the king's bench, 1785; refused at the price of a judgeship to vote for the adoption by the Irish parliament of Pitt's measure limiting the power of the regent, 1785; spoke on the question of the Portugal trade, 1786; lost his chancery practice in consequence of the hostility of Fitzgibbon (then chancellor and Lord Clare), 1789; attacked the extravagance of the administration, and was indirectly led thereby into fighting one of his five duels, 1790; spoke on Roman catholic disabilities, 1792; defended Archibald Hamilton Rowan, secretary of the Dublin Society of United Irishmen, when prosecuted for a seditious publication, 1794; spoke on the disarming of Ulster, 1797; supported Ponsonby's scheme for parliamentary reform and catholic emancipation,

1797 ; defended all the leaders of the United Irishmen conspiracy when brought to trial, 1798 ; refused to be intimidated ; sympathised with Robert Emmet's insurrection of 1803 ; troubled by domestic misfortunes ; appointed master of the rolls, with a seat in the privy council, by the whig ministry of 1806 ; a famous orator.
[xiii. 332]

CURRER, FRANCES MARY RICHARDSON (1785-1861), book-collector ; possessed a library of fifteen thousand volumes (catalogued 1820 and 1833) ; printed 'Extracts from the Literary and Scientific Correspondence of Richard Richardson, M.D.,' 1835.   [xiii. 340]

CURREY, FREDERICK (1819-1881), mycologist ; educated at Eton ; M.A. Trinity College, Cambridge, 1844 ; secretary of the Linnean Society, 1860-80 ; translated Hofmeister's ' Higher Cryptogamia ' ; fungi *Curreya* named after him.   [xiii. 341]

CURRIE, SIR FREDERICK, first baronet (1799-1875), Indian official ; educated at Charterhouse and the East India Company's College, Haileybury ; cadet, Bengal civil service, 1817 ; judge of sudder adawlut, N.W. Provinces, 1840-2 ; foreign secretary to the Indian government, 1842-9 ; drew up the treaty with the Sikhs after Sobraon ; created baronet, 1847 ; member of the supreme council, 1849-53 ; chairman of the East India Company, 1857 ; vice-president of the council of India ; honorary D.C.L. Oxford, 1866.   [xiii. 341]

CURRIE, JAMES (1756-1805), physician ; entered Dumfries grammar school, 1769 ; trader in Virginia, U.S.A., 1771 ; sailed for Greenock, 1776, and after many hardships, his goods being confiscated by the revolted colony, reached London, 1777 ; studied medicine and metaphysics at Edinburgh University ; graduated at Glasgow, 1780 ; physician at Liverpool from 1780 ; advocated abolition of slave trade, 1787 ; F.R.S., 1792 ; published brochure against war with France, 1793 ; published ' Medical Reports on the Effects of Water, cold and warm, as a Remedy in Fever,' 1797.   [xiii. 341]

CURRIEHILL, LORDS. [See SKENE, SIR JOHN, 1543 ?-1617 ; MARSHALL, JOHN, 1794-1868.]

CURRY, JOHN (d. 1780), historian ; studied medicine at Paris and obtained a diploma at Rheims ; published an 'Historical and Critical Review of the Civil Wars in Ireland,' 1775, in defence of the Irish catholics, and an ' Essay on ordinary Fevers,' 1743.   [xiii. 343]

CURSON, DE COURÇON, DE CORCEONE, or DE CURCHUN, ROBERT (d. 1218), cardinal ; born at Kedleston, Derbyshire ; studied at Oxford and Paris ; canon of Paris, 1211 ; cardinal-priest, 1212 ; legate *a latere* in France and preacher of a crusade, 1213 ; held a council in Paris, 1213 ; arranged truce between King John and Philip of France after battle of Bouvines, 1214 ; actively opposed the heretics of Toulouse and handed over their land to Simon of Montfort, 1215 ; died at Damietta.
[xiii. 344]

CURTEYS, RICHARD (1532 ?-1582), bishop of Chichester ; scholar, St. John's College, Cambridge, 1550 ; M.A., 1556 ; senior fellow, 1559 ; university proctor, 1563 ; dean of Chichester, 1566 ; D.D., 1569 ; bishop of Chichester, 1570 ; an active reformer of abuses, though bigoted ; chief work, ' The Truthe of Christes naturall Bodye,' 1577.   [xiii. 345]

CURTIS, JOHN (*fl.* 1790), landscape-painter ; exhibited ' A View of Netley Abbey ' at the Royal Academy, 1790, and a battle-piece, 1797.   [xiii. 346]

CURTIS, JOHN (1791-1862), entomologist ; writing clerk in lawyer's office ; placed with an engraver at Bungay, where he learned to dissect, draw, and describe insects and engrave them on copper ; executed engravings for many eminent naturalists ; F.L.S., 1822 ; produced in parts, 1824-39, his ' British Entomology ' ; president of Entomological Society, 1855. His writings include ' Farm Insects,' 1860, ' Guide to arrangement of British Insects,' 1829, and numerous papers in scientific journals.
[Suppl. ii. 99]

CURTIS, PATRICK (1740-1832), Roman catholic archbishop of Armagh ; regius professor of astronomy and natural history at Salamanca ; rector at the Irish college ; arrested as a spy by the French, 1811 ; returned to Ireland, 1818 ; archbishop of Armagh, 1819 ; advocated

catholic emancipation before a committee of the Lords, 1825 ; corresponded with the Duke of Wellington on the subject.   [xiii. 347]

CURTIS, SIR ROGER (1746-1816), admiral ; served on the coasts of Africa and Newfoundland ; lieutenant, 1771 ; commander of Lord Howe's flagship, 1777 ; blockaded by the French at Minorca, 1781 ; destroyed floating batteries at Gibraltar, 1782 ; knighted, 1782 ; rear-admiral, 1794 ; created baronet, 1794 ; admiral, 1803 ; commander-in-chief at Portsmouth, 1809 ; G.C.B., 1815.
[xiii. 348]

CURTIS, SAMUEL (1779-1860), florist ; succeeded to the proprietorship of the 'Botanical Magazine' by his marriage, 1801.   [xiii. 349]

CURTIS, WILLIAM (1746-1799), botanist and entomologist ; translated Linnæus's ' Fundamenta Entomologiæ,' 1772 ; undertook the 'Botanical Magazine,' 1781 ; published 'British Grasses' and some entomological pamphlets.   [xiii. 349]

CURTIS, SIR WILLIAM (1752-1829), lord mayor of London ; alderman of the Tower ward, 1785 ; established the present bank of Robarts, Lubbock & Co. ; sheriff, 1789 ; M.P. for London, 1790-1818, and 1820 ; lord mayor, 1795 ; created baronet, 1802 ; M.P. Bletchingley, 1819, Hastings, 1826 ; friend of George IV.   [xiii. 349]

CURWEN, HENRY (1845-1892), journalist ; educated at Rossall school ; worked in London for John Camden Hotten [q. v.], the publisher ; went to India, 1876 ; chief editor of 'Times of India,' 1880 ; a joint-proprietor, 1889 ; published novels, compilations, and volumes of short stories, translations, and essays, including, ' Echoes from French Poets,' 1870, and ' Sorrow and Song,' 1874.
[Suppl. ii. 100]

CURWEN or COREN, HUGH (d. 1568), archbishop of Dublin ; B.C.L. Cambridge, 1510 ; vicar of Buckden, Huntingdonshire, 1514 ; chaplain to Henry VIII ; D.C.L. Oxford, 1532 ; defended Henry VIII's marriage with Anne Boleyn, 1533 ; dean of Hereford, 1541 ; archbishop of Dublin, 1555-67 ; consecrated according to the form of the Roman pontifical, 1555 ; lord chancellor of Ireland, 1555 ; lord justice of Ireland, 1557 ; became a protestant at Elizabeth's accession ; compelled to resign his archbishopric by the hostility and suspicions of Loftus, archbishop of Armagh, and others, 1567 ; bishop of Oxford, 1567.   [xiii. 350]

CURWEN, JOHN (1816-1880), writer on music ; in charge of the independent chapel, Plaistow, 1844 ; first to advocate the tonic sol-fa system, 1842 ; compiled 'People's Service of Song,' 1849-50 ; judge at the Welsh National Eisteddfod, 1873 ; founded the Tonic Sol-fa College (incorporated 1875) ; published numerous books on music.
[xiii. 352]

CURWEN, THOMAS (*fl.* 1665), quaker ; imprisoned at Lancaster, probably for refusing to take the oath of allegiance, 1660, 1663 ; imprisoned, together with his wife, at Boston, as a quaker missionary, 1678 ; sent to Newgate, 1683.   [xiii. 353]

CURZON, ROBERT, fourteenth BARON ZOUCHE (or DE LA ZOUCHE), of Harringworth (1810-1873) ; educated at the Charterhouse and Christ Church, Oxford ; M.P. Clitheroe, 1831 ; travelled in Egypt and Palestine in search of manuscripts, 1833-4 ; visited Mount Athos, 1837 ; attaché at the embassy at Constantinople, 1841 ; joint-commissioner for defining the boundary between Turkey and Persia, 1843 ; decorated by the shah and the sultan ; student of the early history of handwriting ; published a ' Visit to the Monasteries in the Levant,' 1849, and an 'Account of the most celebrated Libraries of Italy,' 1854 ; succeeded his mother in barony of Zouche, 1870.   [xiii. 354]

CUSACK or CUSAKE, SIR THOMAS (1490-1571), lord chancellor of Ireland ; recommended the extension of English law to every part of Ireland ; lord chancellor, 1551 ; lord justice, 1552 ; again lord chancellor, 1563.
[xiii. 355]

CUSINS, SIR WILLIAM GEORGE (1833-1893), pianist and conductor ; studied under Fétis at Brussels, and at Royal Academy of Music, London, where he was subsequently professor ; organist of Queen Victoria's private chapel, Windsor, 1849 ; conducted concerts of Philharmonic Society, 1867-83 ; master of the music to

Queen Victoria, 1870 ; professor of pianoforte at Guildhall, 1885 ; knighted, 1892 : published musical compositions and writings on musical subjects.
[Suppl. ii. 101]

CUSSANS, JOHN EDWIN (1837-1899), antiquary ; engaged in commercial pursuits ; adopted authorship as profession, 1863 ; published genealogical and heraldic works. [Suppl. ii. 102]

CUST, SIR EDWARD (1794-1878), general and military historian ; educated at Eton ; lieutenant, 1810 ; fought in most of the battles of the Peninsular war ; M.P., Grantham, 1818-26, Lostwithiel 1826-32 ; knight commander of the Guelphic order of Hanover, 1831 ; master of the ceremonies to Queen Victoria, 1847 ; honorary D.C.L. Oxford, 1853 ; colonel, 16th light dragoons, 1859 ; general, 1866 ; created baronet, 1876 ; author of 'Annals of the Wars of the Eighteenth Century.' [xiii. 355]

CUST, SIR JOHN (1718-1770), baronet, speaker of the House of Commons ; educated at Eton ; barrister, Middle Temple, 1742 ; M.A. Corpus Christi College, Cambridge, 1739 ; M.P., Grantham, 1743-70 ; speaker, 1761 ; privy councillor, 1762 ; again speaker, 1768-70. [xiii. 356]

CUTCLIFFE, ROCHETAILLADE, or DE RUPES-CISSA, JOHN (*fl.* 1345), Franciscan ; native of Dammage, Devonshire ; studied at Toulouse ; became a Franciscan monk ; imprisoned at Figeac for criticising the abuses of the church, 1345 ; imprisoned at Avignon by Alexander VI, 1349 ; doubtfully said to have been burnt at Avignon ; author of books on alchemy and prophetical writings. [xiii. 357]

CUTHBERT, SAINT (*d.* 687), bishop of Lindisfarne ; kept sheep on the hills near the Lauder, a tributary of the Tweed, 651 ; entered the monastery of Melrose, 651 ; guest-receiver at the monastery of Ripon, but expelled for refusing to adopt the Roman usages, 661 ; prior of Melrose ; adopted the Roman usages, 664 ; abbot of Lindisfarne ; anchorite on Farne island, 676 ; accepted see of Lindisfarne, 684 ; retired to Farne island, 686 ; died in his cell, 687 ; reputed a worker of miracles. His body, which was said to have remained in a state of incorruption for many years, was finally transferred to Durham Cathedral, 1104. [xiii. 359]

CUTHBERT (*d.* 758), archbishop of Canterbury ; abbot of Liminge, Kent ; bishop of Hereford, 736 ; archbishop of Canterbury, *c.* 740 ; assessor of Æthelbald, king of Mercia, at a council held at Clovesho, 742 ; summoned council at Clovesho to regulate the monastic life and duties of priests, 747 ; friend of Boniface, archbishop of Mentz ; built a chapel to St. John Baptist at the east end of Canterbury Cathedral. [xiii. 362]

CUTHBURH or CUTHBURGA, SAINT (*fl.* 700), sister of Ine, king of the West-Saxons ; founder and abbess of Wimborne, Dorset. [xiii. 363]

CUTHRED (*d.* 754), over-lord of the West-Saxon kingdom ; defeated Æthelbald of Mercia at Burford, Oxfordshire, 752 ; defeated the Welsh, 753. [xiii. 363]

CUTLER, SIR JOHN (1608?-1693), London merchant ; promoted the subscriptions raised by the city of London for Charles II, 1660 ; created baronet, 1660 ; treasurer of St. Paul's, 1663 ; founded lectureship on mechanics at Gresham College, London, 1664 ; honorary F.R.S., 1664 ; four times master warden of the Grocers' Company ; benefactor of the College of Physicians, 1679 ; benefactor of the parish of St. Margaret, Westminster, 1682 ; personally parsimonious, and the occasion of Wycherley's 'Praise of Avarice.' [xiii. 364]

CUTLER, WILLIAM HENRY (*b.* 1792), musician ; played pianoforte concerto at the Haymarket, 1800 ; Mus. Bac. Oxford, 1812 ; organist, St. Helen's, Bishopsgate, 1818-23 ; organist at Quebec Street Chapel, 1823 ; founded

an academy, which proved unsuccessful, for teaching music on the Logierian system. [xiii. 365]

CUTPURSE, MOLL (1584?-1659). [See FRITH, MARY.]

CUTTANCE, SIR ROGER (*fl.* 1650-1669), navy captain ; commanded the Sussex in the Dutch war, 1652-3 ; assisted in reduction of Porto Farina, 1655 ; flag-captain of the Naseby, 1657 ; knighted, 1665 ; captain of the fleet, 1665. [xiii. 366]

CUTTINGE, FRANCIS (16th cent.), lutenist and composer ; contributed music to Barley's 'New Booke of Tabliture,' 1596 ; possibly identical with Thomas Cuttinge, lutenist to the king of Denmark, 1607. [xiii. 366]

CUTTS, JOHN, BARON CUTTS of Gowran, Ireland (1661-1707), lieutenant-general ; fellow-commoner, Catharine Hall, Cambridge, 1676 ; published 'La Muse de Cavalier,' 1685 ; volunteer against the Turks in Hungary, 1686 ; adjutant-general to the Duke of Lorraine, 1686 ; colonel, 1st foot guards ; fought for William III at the Boyne, 1690 ; created Baron Cutts of Gowran, 1690 ; honorary LL.D. Cambridge ; hero of siege of Namur, 1695 ; took part in negotiating treaty of Ryswick, 1697 ; with Marlborough in Holland, 1701 ; captured Fort St. Michael, 1702 ; lieutenant-general, 1702 ; fought at Blenheim, 1704 ; commander-in-chief in Ireland, 1705 ; M.P. for Cambridgeshire, 1689-1701, and for Newport, 1702-1707. [xiii. 367]

CUTWODE, THOMAS (*fl.* 1599), poet ; published 'Caltha Poetarum : or the Bumble Bee,' a satire on contemporary poets, which the archbishop of Canterbury condemned to the flames, 1599. [xiii. 370]

CWICHELM (*d.* 636), king of the West-Saxons ; son of, and co-ruler with, Cynegils [q. v.] ; defeated Britons at Beandûn, 614 ; beaten by Eadwine of Northumbria, 626 ; baptised, 636. [xiii. 371]

CYBI, CUBI, or KEBI (*fl.* 560?), Welsh saint ; visited Ireland, but was expelled by Crubthir Fintam, a local chief ; founder, abbot, and bishop of monastery on Holyhead island. [xiii. 371]

CYFEIAWG (*d.* 927). [See CIMELLIAUC.]

CYMBELINE (*d.* 43 ?). [See CUNOBELINUS.]

CYNEGILS or KINEGILS (*d.* 643), king of the West-Saxons ; together with his son Cwichelm [q. v.], defeated the Britons at Beandûn, 614 ; defeated by Eadwine of Northumbria, 626 ; conquered the East-Saxons, 626 ; baptised, 635 ; founder of the see of Dorchester, Oxfordshire. [xiii. 371]

CYNEWULF or CYNWULF (*fl.* 750), Anglo-Saxon poet ; probably a Northumbrian minstrel. The poems ascribed to him are contained in the 'Exeter Codex' and the 'Vercelli Codex,' two manuscript collections of Anglo-Saxon verse. Many poems in them may be by Cynewulf ; four certainly are his, viz. 'The Christ,' 'The Passion of St. Juliana,' 'Elene,' and 'The Dream of the Cross' ; Cynewulf's poems first printed, 1842 ; translated into modern English or into German by various hands between 1871 and 1889. [xxxi. 358]

CYNEWULF (*d.* 785), king of the West-Saxons ; fought with the Welsh ; defeated by Offa, 777 ; slain by the followers of Cyneheard the ætheling, a prince whom he had ordered into banishment. [xiii. 372]

CYNRIC (*d.* 560?), king of the Gewissas or West-Saxons ; probably son, and perhaps grandson, of Cerdic [q. v.], whom he is said to have succeeded, 534 ; traditionally defeated the Britons at Searobyrig, 552.
[Suppl. ii. 102]

CYPLES, WILLIAM (1831-1882), philosophical writer ; published an 'Inquiry into the Process of Human Experience,' 1880 ; author of 'Pottery Poems' and 'Satan Restored,' 1859. [xiii. 373]

D

DABORNE, ROBERT (d. 1628), dramatist and divine; dean of Lismore, 1621; collaborated with Field and Massinger; wrote several plays, two of which, 'A Christian turn'd Turke,' 1612, and 'The Poor-man's Comfort,' are still extant. [xiii. 373]

DACRE, BARONS. [See FIENNES, THOMAS, ninth BARON, 1517–1541; FIENNES, GREGORY, tenth BARON, 1539–1594; LENNARD, FRANCIS, fourteenth BARON, 1619–1662.]

DACRE, BARONESS. [See FIENNES, ANNE, d. 1595; BRAND, BARBARINA, 1768–1854.]

DACRE, twenty-third BARON (1814–1892). [See BRAND, SIR HENRY BOUVERIE WILLIAM.]

DACRE, LEONARD (d. 1573), promoter of the Northern rebellion in the reign of Queen Elizabeth; defeated near Carlisle by Lord Hunsdon, who had been ordered to arrest him, 1570; fled to Scotland, and sat in a convention of the nobles at Leith, 1570; died at Brussels. [xiii. 374]

DACRES, ARTHUR (1624–1678), physician; B.A. Magdalene College, Cambridge, 1645; fellow, 1646; M.D., 1654; assistant-physician at St. Bartholomew's Hospital, 1653–78; professor of geometry, Gresham College, 1664; censor of the College of Physicians, 1672. [xiii. 375]

DACRES, SIR RICHARD JAMES (1799–1886), field-marshal; captain in the royal artillery, 1837; brevet-major, 1851; commanded the royal horse artillery at the Alma, 1854; engaged in the bombardments of Sebastopol; general, 1867; G.C.B., 1869; field-marshal, 1886. [xiii. 375]

DACRES, SIR SIDNEY COLPOYS (1805–1884), admiral; brother of Sir Richard James Dacres [q.v.]; lieutenant in navy, 1827; reduced Kastro Morea, and received the crosses of the Legion of Honour and of the Redeemer of Greece, 1828; commanded the Sans Pareil before Sebastopol, 1854; captain of the Mediterranean fleet, 1859; commander-in-chief in Channel, 1683; vice-admiral, 1865; G.C.B., 1871. [xiii. 375]

DADE, WILLIAM (1740?–1790), antiquary; rector of St. Mary's, Castlegate, York, and Barmston; F.S.A., 1783; his 'History of Holderness' published by Poulson, 1840–1. [xiii. 376]

DAFFORNE, JAMES (d. 1880), writer on art; contributed to the 'Art Journal'; published 'The Life and Works of Edward Matthew Ward, R.A.,' 1879, and translated De la Croix's 'Arts of the Middle Ages.' [xiii. 377]

DAFFY, THOMAS (d. 1680), inventor of Daffy's 'elixir salutis'; rector of Harby, Leicestershire, 1647, and of Redmile, Leicestershire, 1666–80. [xiii. 377]

DAFT, RICHARD (1835–1900), cricketer; amateur, 1857; played for Gentlemen, 1858, and as professional for Nottinghamshire, 1858–81; took team to Canada and United States, 1879; published 'Kings of Cricket,' 1893. [Suppl. ii. 103]

D'AGAR, JACQUES (1640–1716), painter; court painter at Copenhagen; visited London, c. 1700; died at Copenhagen. [xiii. 377]

DAGLEY, RICHARD (d. 1841), subject-painter and engraver; educated at Christ's Hospital; exhibited sixty pictures at the Royal Academy, 1785–1833; illustrated the elder D'Israeli's 'Flim-flams'; author of 'Gems selected from the Antique,' 1804, and other works. [xiii. 377]

D'AGUILAR, SIR GEORGE CHARLES (1784–1855), lieutenant-general; lieutenant, 1802; brigade-major, 1806; served against the Maráthás; sent by Lord William Bentinck on a military mission to Yanina and Constantinople; major in the rifle brigade, 1817; commanded in the Chinese war, receiving the submission of Canton, 1847; lieutenant-colonel and K.C.B., 1851; author of manuals of military discipline. [xiii. 378]

DAHL, MICHAEL (1656–1743), portrait-painter; born at Stockholm; portrait-painter in London from 1688; patronised by Queen Anne and most of the nobility; undeservedly styled the rival of Kneller. [xiii. 379]

DAINTREE, RICHARD (1831–1878), geologist; educated at Bedford grammar school and Christ's College, Cambridge; student in the Royal School of Mines, 1856; field geologist on the geological survey of Victoria, 1858–1864; government geologist, North Queensland, 1869–72; examined the auriferous strata of Queensland; agent-general for Queensland, 1872–8; C.M.G., 1878. [xiii. 379]

DAIRCELL or **TAIRCELL**, otherwise MOLLING (d. 696), Irish saint and bishop; founded a monastery and church at Ross Broc, on the river Barrow; settled the boundary between Leinster and the territories of Diarmuid and Blathmac. kings of Ireland; procured a remission of the boruma tax by stratagem from King Finnachta in favour of the Leinstermen; supposititious author of the 'Baile Molling,' a prophetic rhapsody. [xiii. 380]

DAKINS, WILLIAM (d. 1607), divine; educated at Westminster and Trinity College, Cambridge; major fellow, 1594; M.A., 1594; B.D., 1601; vicar of Trumpington, 1603–5; professor of divinity, Gresham College, London, 1604; junior dean, Trinity College, 1606–7; took part in the 'authorised translation' of the bible. [xiii. 382]

DALBIAC, SIR JAMES CHARLES (1776–1847), lieutenant-general; captain, 4th light dragoons, 1798; fought, as lieutenant-colonel, at Talavera, 1809, and at Salamanca, 1812; commanded the Goojerat district of the Bombay army, 1822–4; president of court-martial for trial of Bristol rioters, 1831; K.C.H.; M.P., Ripon, 1835–7; lieutenant-general, 1838. [xiii. 382]

DALBIER, JOHN (d. 1648), soldier; perhaps in service of Count Mansfeld during thirty years' war; entered English service, c. 1627, and accompanied Buckingham to Isle of Ré; in service of Sweden, c. 1628–32; quarter-master-general and captain of troop of horse under Essex in civil war; commanded forces at siege of Basing; took Donnington Castle, 1646; joined royalists, 1648; killed after defeat at St. Neots. [Suppl. ii. 103]

DALBY, ISAAC (1744–1824), mathematician; mathematical master in the naval school, Chelsea, 1781; trigonometrical surveyor for connecting meridians of Greenwich and Paris, 1787; assisted in trigonometrical survey of England and Wales; professor of mathematics, Sandhurst College, 1799–1820; published books on mathematics, especially trigonometry. [xiii. 382]

DALBY, ROBERT (d. 1589), Roman catholic divine; ordained priest at Douay; sent back to England as a missioner, 1588; executed, 1589. [xiii. 383]

DALDERBY, JOHN DE (d. 1320), bishop of Lincoln; archdeacon of Carmarthen, 1283; chancellor of Lincoln Cathedral; bishop of Lincoln, 1300; denied the right of Edward I to tax ecclesiastics without consent of pope, 1301; papal commissioner to try the templars, 1308; present at the appointment of the 'ordainers,' 1310. [xiii. 383]

DALE, DAVID (1739–1806), industrialist and philanthropist; fixed on New Lanark as a site for the erection of cotton-mills in conjunction with Arkwright; partner in cotton-mills at Catrine; established the first Turkey-red dyeing works in Scotland, 1785; imported at his own risk food-stuffs for the poor in times of dearth. [xiii. 384]

DALE, ROBERT WILLIAM (1829–1895), congregational divine; joined congregational church, 1844; usher successively at Brixton Hill and Leamington; studied theology at Spring College, Birmingham; M.A. London, 1853; assistant minister at Carr's Lane Chapel, Birmingham, 1853; sole pastor, 1859; lecturer on literature, philosophy, and homiletics at Spring Hill, 1858; presided over international council of congregational churches, 1891; LL.D. Glasgow, 1883; published numerous theological works, and compiled 'The English Hymn Book,' 1874. [Suppl. ii. 104]

DALE, SAMUEL (1659?–1739), physician; practised at Braintree, Essex, 1686; chief work, 'Pharmacologia,' 1693; wrote an appendix to Taylor's 'History and Antiquities of Harwich and Dovercourt,' 1730. [xiii. 385]

DALE, Sir THOMAS (d. 1619), naval commander; served in the Low Countries; marshal of Virginia, 1609; governor of Virginia, 1611 and 1614–16; defeated the Dutch off Jacatra, Java, 1618.   [xiii. 385]

DALE, THOMAS (1729–1816), physician; educated at St. Paul's School and Edinburgh University; M.D. Edinburgh, 1775; L.R.C.P., 1786; one of the originators of the Royal Literary Fund.   [xiii. 386]

DALE, THOMAS (1797–1870), dean of Rochester; educated at Christ's Hospital and Corpus Christi College, Cambridge; M.A., 1826; vicar of St. Bride's, Fleet Street, 1835; professor of English at London University, 1828–30, and at King's College, 1836–9; prebendary of St. Paul's Cathedral, 1843; vicar of St. Pancras, 1846–61; dean of Rochester, 1870; D.D. Cambridge, 1870; published theological writings and poems, including 'The Widow of Nain,' 1817, and 'The Outlaw of Taurus,' 1818; translated Sophocles, 1824.   [xiii. 386]

DALE, THOMAS PELHAM (1821–1892), ritualistic divine; son of Thomas Dale (1797–1870) [q. v.]; educated at King's College, London, and Sidney Sussex College, Cambridge; M.A., 1848; rector of St. Vedast's, Foster Lane, with St. Michael-le-Querne, London; instituted ritualistic practices and, after protracted legal proceedings, was lodged in Holloway gaol, 1880; afterwards became rector of Sausthorpe-cum-Aswardby, Lincolnshire; published religious writings.   [Suppl. ii. 106]

DALE, VALENTINE (d. 1589), civilian and diplomatist; fellow of All Souls' College, Oxford, 1542; B.C.L. 1545; D.C.L. Orleans; LL.D. Cambridge, 1562; ambassador in Flanders, 1563; in France, 1573–6; M.P., Chichester, 1572, 1584, 1586, and 1589; dean of Wells, 1575; assisted at trial of Mary Queen of Scots, 1586; ambassador to Prince of Parma, 1588–9.   [xiii. 387]

DALGAIRNS, JOHN DOBREE, in religion BERNARD (1818–1876), priest of the Oratory; born in Guernsey; M.A. Exeter College, Oxford, 1842; converted to catholicism, 1845; superior of the Oratory at Brompton, 1863–5; assisted in translating the 'Catena Aurea,' a mediæval compilation from St. Thomas Aquinas, 1841–5, and wrote mystical and metaphysical works.   [xiii. 388]

DALGARNO, GEORGE (1626?–1687), pasigraphist; educated at the university of New Aberdeen; master of Elizabeth School, Guernsey, 1662–72; chief works, 'Didascalocophus,' 1680, and the 'Ars Signorum,' 1661, an attempt to formulate a philosophical language; the latter is alluded to by Leibnitz.   [xiii. 389]

DALGLIESH, WILLIAM (1733–1807), theological writer; D.D. Edinburgh, 1786; minister at Peebles, 1761–1807; published 'The Self-existence and Supreme Deity of Christ defended,' 1777, in justification of his 'True Sonship of Christ investigated,' 1776.   [xiii. 390]

DALHOUSIE, MARQUIS OF (1812–1860). [See RAMSAY, JAMES ANDREW BROUN.]

DALHOUSIE, EARLS OF. [See RAMSAY, WILLIAM, first EARL, d. 1674; RAMSAY, JAMES ANDREW BROUN, tenth EARL, 1812–1860; MAULE, FOX, eleventh EARL, 1801–1874; RAMSAY, GEORGE, twelfth EARL, 1806–1880; RAMSAY, JOHN WILLIAM, thirteenth EARL, 1847–1887.]

DALISON, SIR WILLIAM (d. 1559), judge; barrister, Gray's Inn, 1537; reader, 1548 and 1552; justice of the county palatine of Lancaster, 1554; knighted, 1556; justice of the king's bench, 1556.   [xiii. 391]

DALL, NICHOLAS THOMAS (d. 1777), landscape-painter; a Dane; in London, c. 1760; A.R.A., 1771.   [xiii. 391]

DALLAM, GEORGE (17th cent.), organ-builder; added a choir organ to Harris's instrument at Hereford Cathedral, 1686.   [xiii. 391]

DALLAM, RALPH (d. 1672), organ-builder; built organs at Rugby, Hackney (1665), and Lynn Regis, as well as one for St. George's Chapel, Windsor, which proved unsatisfactory.   [xiii. 391]

DALLAM, ROBERT (1602–1665), organ-builder; son of Thomas Dallam [q. v.]; member of the Blacksmiths' Company; built organs for Durham Cathedral, York Minster, 1634, Jesus College, Cambridge, 1634, and New College, Oxford, 1661.   [xiii. 391]

DALLAM, THOMAS (fl. 1615), organ-builder; member of the Blacksmiths' Company; built organs for King's College, Cambridge, 1606, and for Worcester Cathedral, 1613.   [xiii. 392]

DALLAN, SAINT (fl. 600), Irish saint; otherwise FORGAILL; wrote verse panegyric on Columba, made public after Columba's death, 597, also panegyrics on Bishop Senan and Abbot Conall Coel.   [xiii. 393]

DALLAS, ALEXANDER ROBERT CHARLES (1791–1869), divine; son of Robert Charles Dallas [q. v.]; treasury clerk, 1805; present at Waterloo, 1815; gentleman-commoner, Worcester College, Oxford, 1820; vicar of Yardley, Hertfordshire, 1827; prebendary of Llandaff, 1827; chaplain to Bishop Sumner; M.A. Lambeth; founded the Society for Irish Church Missions, 1843; wrote theological works.   [xiii. 393]

DALLAS, ELMSLIE WILLIAM (1809–1879), artist; gold medallist of the Royal Academy, 1834; assisted in decoration of garden pavilion at Buckingham Palace, 1840; exhibited at the Royal Scottish Academy, 1842–58.   [xiii. 394]

DALLAS, ENEAS SWEETLAND (1828–1879), journalist and author; born in Jamaica; educated at Edinburgh University; published 'Poetics,' 1852, 'The Gay Science,' 1866, and an abridgment of Richardson's 'Clarissa Harlowe,' 1868.   [xiii. 394]

DALLAS, GEORGE (1630–1702?), lawyer; writer to the signet; deputy-keeper of the privy seal of Scotland, 1660 till death; published 'A System of Stiles,' 1697.   [xiii. 395]

DALLAS, SIR GEORGE (1758–1833), political writer; educated at Geneva; writer in the East India Company's service, 1776; superintendent of the collections at Rajeshahi; created baronet, 1798; M.P., Newport, 1800–2; published pamphlet in vindication of Warren Hastings, 1789, a defence of the Marquis Wellesley's policy in India, 1806, 'Letters on the Political and Commercial State of Ireland,' 1797, and tractates against the French revolution.   [xiii. 395]

DALLAS, SIR ROBERT (1756–1824), judge; educated at Geneva; barrister of Lincoln's Inn, 1782; counsel for Warren Hastings, 1787; counsel for Lord George Gordon, 1788; king's counsel, 1795; M.P., St. Michael's, Cornwall, 1802–5, Kirkcaldy, 1805–6; solicitor-general, 1813; knighted, 1813; chief-justice of common pleas, 1818–23; privy councillor, 1818.   [xiii. 396]

DALLAS, ROBERT CHARLES (1754–1824), miscellaneous writer; born in Jamaica; lived on the continent, in Jamaica, and in America; prohibited by Lord Eldon from publishing his friend Lord Byron's letters, 1824; died in Normandy; wrote tales, poems, a 'History of the Maroons,' 1803, and ethical treatises.   [xiii. 397]

DALLAS, SIR THOMAS (d. 1839), lieutenant-general; great-grandson of George Dallas [q. v.]; fought in the Carnatic and at the siege of Seringapatam.   [xiii. 395]

DALLAWAY, JAMES (1763–1834), topographer and miscellaneous writer; scholar of Trinity College, Oxford; M.A., 1784; appointed to a curacy near Stroud; F.S.A., 1789; M.B. Oxford, 1794; secretary to the earl marshal, 1797–1834; prebendary of Chichester, 1811; edited Burrell's manuscript 'History of the Three Western Rapes of Sussex,' 1811; wrote on heraldry, English architecture, and ancient sculpture, and edited 'The Letters and other Works of Lady Mary Wortley Montagu,' 1803, and 'Walpole's Anecdotes of Painting,' 1826–8.   [xiii. 398]

DALLEY, WILLIAM BEDE (1831–1888), Australian politician; born in Sydney; educated at Sydney and St. Mary's colleges; called to bar, 1856; Q.C., 1877; member for Sydney in first constitutional parliament, 1857, and for Cumberland boroughs, 1858; solicitor-general, 1858–9; attorney-general, 1875–7, 1877, and 1883; acting premier and foreign secretary, 1885; carried out plan of sending troops to aid the imperial forces in Egypt; privy councillor, 1887.   [Suppl. ii. 107]

DALLING AND BULWER, BARON (1801–1872). [See BULWER, WILLIAM HENRY LYTTON EARLE.]

DALLINGTON, SIR ROBERT (1561–1637), master of Charterhouse; educated at Cambridge; gentleman of the privy chamber in ordinary to Prince Henry; master of

Charterhouse, 1624–37; knighted, 1624; published 'A Survey of the Great Duke's State of Tuscany,' 1605, and part of Guicciardini's history, 1613. [xiii. 399]

DALLMEYER, JOHN HENRY (1830–1883), optician; born in Westphalia: educated and apprenticed at Osnabrück; came to England, 1851; workman in, and subsequently scientific adviser to, the firm of Andrew Ross; F.R.A.S., 1861; received the cross of the Legion of Honour and the Russian order of St. Stanislaus; supplied photo-heliographs to the Wilna observatory, 1863, and to the Harvard College observatory, 1864; executed five photo-heliographs for government, 1873; famous as a maker of photographic lenses and object-glasses for the microscope. [xiii. 400]

DALRYMPLE, ALEXANDER (1737–1808), hydrographer to the admiralty; writer in the East India Company's service, 1752–4; as deputy-secretary, effected a commercial treaty with the sultan of Sulu; attempted to open up trade with Sulu, but failed, 1762; published chart of northern part of Bay of Bengal, 1772; member of council, Madras, 1775–7; hydrographer to the East India Company, 1779; hydrographer to the admiralty, 1795; died broken-hearted on his dismissal, 1808; published an 'Account of Discoveries in the South Pacific Ocean before 1764,' 1767. [xiii. 402]

DALRYMPLE, SIR DAVID, first (Nova Scotia) baronet of Hailes (d. 1721), Scottish politician; member of the Faculty of Advocates, 1688; created baronet of Nova Scotia, 1700; solicitor-general to Queen Anne; M.P. for Culross in the Scottish parliament, 1703; M.P. for Haddington in the parliament of Great Britain, 1708–21; commissioner for the treaty of union, 1706; auditor to Scottish exchequer, 1720. [xiii. 403]

DALRYMPLE, SIR DAVID, LORD HAILES (1726–1792), Scottish judge; educated at Eton; studied civil law at Utrecht; admitted to the Scottish bar, 1748; judge of the court of session as Lord Hailes, 1766; refused to revise Hume's 'Inquiry,' considering its principles atheistic, 1753; friend and correspondent of Dr. Johnson, who revised Hailes's 'Annals of Scotland,' 1776; judge of the criminal court, 1776; wrote against Gibbon, 1786. Other of his works are 'An Examination of some of the Arguments for the High Antiquity of Regiam Majestatem, and an Inquiry into the Authenticity of the Leges Malcolmi,' 1769, a translation of the 'Octavius' of Minucius Felix, 1781, 'Ancient Scottish Poems, published from the Manuscript of George Bannatyne, 1568,' 1770, and 'The Canons of the Church of Scotland,' 1769. [xiii. 403]

DALRYMPLE, SIR HEW, LORD NORTH BERWICK (1652–1737), lord president of session; third son of Sir James Dalrymple, first viscount Stair [q. v.]; commissary of Edinburgh; M.P. for New Galloway burgh, 1690, and for North Berwick burgh, 1702, in the Scots parliament; dean of the Faculty of Advocates, 1695; created baronet of Nova Scotia, 1698; lord president of session, 1698–1737; commissioner for the articles of union between England and Scotland, 1702 and 1703. [xiii. 406]

DALRYMPLE, HON. SIR HEW (1690–1755), lord justiciary, 1745; son of Sir Hew Dalrymple [q. v.]; lord of session as Lord Drummore, 1726. [xiii. 407]

DALRYMPLE, SIR HEW WHITEFOORD, baronet (1750–1830), general; great-grandson of Sir James Dalrymple, first viscount Stair [q. v.]; lieutenant, 1766; major 77th royals, 1777; knighted, 1779; colonel, 1790; lieutenant-governor of Guernsey. 1796–1801; commander of the Gibraltar garrison, 1806–8; signed convention of Cintra, 1808; general, 1812; created baronet, 1815; governor of Blackness Castle, 1818. [xiii. 408]

DALRYMPLE, SIR JAMES, first VISCOUNT STAIR (1619–1695), Scottish lawyer and statesman; art graduate of Glasgow University, 1637; commanded a troop under William, earl of Glencairn; regent of Glasgow University, 1641–7; admitted to the Scottish bar, 1648; secretary to commissions for treating with Charles II, 1649 and 1650; judge of the reformed court of session, 1657–60; advised Monck to call a full and free parliament, 1660; judge of the court of session under Charles II, 1661; allowed to make a proviso in taking the declaration against the Solemn League and Covenant, 1664; president of session, 1670; issued regulations for the conduct of judicial business and advocates' fees; M.P. for Wigtownshire, 1672 and 1673–4; privy councillor of Scotland, 1674; protested

against Lauderdale's persecution of the covenanters, 1677; attempted to lessen the severity of the Test Act, 1681; fled from its operation to London; published 'Institutions of the Law of Scotland,' 1681; driven by the hostility of the Duke of York and Claverhouse to Leyden, 1682; published 'Physiologia Nova Experimentalis,' 1686; sailed to England with William of Orange, 1688; created Viscount of Stair, Lord Glenluce and Stranraer, 1690; member of the privy council which advised that Glencoe's oath should not be taken after the day originally appointed, 1692; furnished a report on which was grounded the Act for the Regulation of the Judicatures, 1695; published 'A Vindication of the Divine Perfections,' 1695. [xiii. 409]

DALRYMPLE, SIR JAMES, first (Nova Scotia) baronet of Borthwick (fl. 1714), Scottish antiquary; second son of Sir James Dalrymple, first viscount Stair [q. v.]; member of the Faculty of Advocates, 1675; commissary of Edinburgh; principal clerk of the court of session; created baronet of Nova Scotia, 1698; chief work, 'Collections concerning the Scottish History preceding the death of King David the First in 1153,' 1705. [xiii. 415]

DALRYMPLE, SIR JOHN, first EARL OF STAIR (1648–1707), son of Sir James Dalrymple, first viscount Stair [q. v.]; knighted, 1667; Scottish advocate, 1672; imprisoned, through the hostility of Graham of Claverhouse, in Edinburgh Castle, 1682–3; imprisoned in the Tolbooth, 1684; king's advocate, 1686–88; lord justice-clerk, 1688; moved in convention of estates that James Stuart had forfeited the crown of Scotland, 1688; as lord advocate represented William III's government in the Scottish parliament; opposed by Sir James Montgomery, an extreme covenanter; conciliated the presbyterians by establishing presbyterian church government; Master of Stair, 1690; joint-secretary of state, 1691; commissioned the privy council to make an offer of indemnity to the highland clans, in the hope that its conditions would not be accepted, 1691; bitterly hostile to the Macdonalds of Glencoe, and implicated in the massacre of that clan, 1692; accused by parliament of exceeding instructions in the matter, 1695; resigned office, 1695; succeeded as Viscount Stair, 1695; privy councillor, 1702; created Earl of Stair, 1703; supporter of the Act of Union, 1707. [xiii. 415]

DALRYMPLE, JOHN, second EARL OF STAIR (1673–1747), general and diplomatist; son of Sir John Dalrymple, first earl of Stair [q. v.]; studied at Leyden; present at the battle of Steenkerk, 1692; master of Stair, 1695; lieutenant-colonel in Scots guards; aide-de-camp to Marlborough, 1703; colonel of a regiment in the Dutch service, 1705; colonel of the Cameronians, 1706; sent home with the despatches of the battle of Oudenarde, 1708; major-general, 1709; ambassador to Augustus, elector of Saxony, 1709; knight of the Thistle, 1710; covered the siege of Bouchain, 1711; general, 1712; privy councillor, and ambassador at Paris, 1715; secured expulsion of James Edward, the Old Pretender, from Paris; revealed schemes of Alberoni and Cellamare; recalled, 1720; vice-admiral of Scotland, 1720–33; rural economist; opponent of Sir Robert Walpole; deprived of his vice-admiralty for asserting the right of the Scottish peers to elect representative peers without governmental interference, 1733; field-marshal, 1742; governor of Minorca, 1742; fought at Dettingen, 1743; commander-in-chief in south Britain, 1744; general of the marines, 1746. [xiii. 420]

DALRYMPLE, JOHN, fifth EARL OF STAIR (1720–1789), army captain; advocate of the Scottish bar, 1741; captain in the army; representative peer, 1771; presented a petition on behalf of Massachusetts, 1774; published pamphlets on the national finances. [xiii. 423]

DALRYMPLE, SIR JOHN, fourth baronet of Cranstoun (1726–1810), Scottish judge; educated at Edinburgh University and Trinity Hall, Cambridge; advocate at the Scottish bar, 1748; exchequer baron, 1776–1807; discovered the art of making soap from herrings; chief works, 'Essay towards a General History of Feudal Property in Great Britain,' 1757, and 'Memoirs of Great Britain and Ireland (1681–1692),' 1771. [xiii. 424]

DALRYMPLE, JOHN, sixth EARL OF STAIR (1749–1821), son of John, fifth earl of Stair [q. v.]; captain 87th foot; served in the first American war; minister plenipotentiary to Poland, 1782, and to Berlin, 1785. [xiii. 425]

DALRYMPLE, JOHN (1803–1852), ophthalmic surgeon; son of William Dalrymple (1772–1847) [q. v.]; M.R.C.S., 1827; surgeon to the Royal London Ophthalmic Hospital, 1843; F.R.S., 1850; writer on ophthalmic science. [xiii. 425]

DALRYMPLE, Sir JOHN HAMILTON MACGILL, eighth EARL OF STAIR (1771–1853), son of Sir John Dalrymple (1726–1810) [q. v.]; served as captain in Flanders, 1794 and 1795; general, 1838; devised a substitute for corporal punishment in the army; M.P. for Midlothian, 1832; keeper of the great seal of Scotland, 1840–1, and 1846–52; created Baron Oxenford of Cousland, 1841; K.T., 1847. [xiii. 425]

DALRYMPLE, WILLIAM (1723–1814), religious writer; minister of the first charge at Ayr, 1756; D.D. St. Andrews, 1779; moderator of the general assembly, 1781; eulogised in Burns's 'Kirk's Alarm.' [xiii. 426]

DALRYMPLE, WILLIAM (1772–1847), surgeon; surgeon to the Norfolk and Norwich Hospital, 1814–39; successful as an operator in tying the common carotid artery, and in lithotomy. [xiii. 426]

DALTON, JOHN (1709–1763), poet and divine; tabardar, Queen's College, Oxford, 1730; M.A., 1734; adapted Milton's 'Comus' for the stage, 1738; fellow of Queen's College, Oxford, 1741; canon of Worcester, 1748; rector of St. Mary-at-Hill, 1748; D.D., 1750; published sermons and didactic and descriptive poems. [xiii. 427]

DALTON, JOHN (1726–1811), captain under the East India Company; as second lieutenant in the 8th marines was employed on the Coromandel coast, 1745; captain of European grenadiers under the East India Company, 1749; defended Trichinopoly, 1753; returned to England, 1754. [xiii. 428]

DALTON, JOHN (1766–1844), chemist and natural philosopher; kept a quaker's school, 1778; assistant and subsequently partner in a school at Kendal, 1781–93; commenced meteorological journal, 1787; studied mathematics, zoology, and botany, compiling a 'Hortus Siccus'; professor of mathematics and natural philosophy, New College, Manchester, 1793–9; published 'Meteorological Observations and Essays,' maintaining electrical origin of aurora borealis, 1793; revealed his discovery of colour-blindness, 1794; constituted meteorology a science by his papers on the 'Constitution of Mixed Gases,' and on 'The Expansion of Gases by Heat,' 1801; discovered the law of chemical combinations, and tabulated the atomic weights of various elements, 1805; president of the Manchester Philosophical Society, 1817–44; foreign associate of the Paris Academy of Sciences, 1830; prizeman of the Royal Society 'for his development of the chemical theory of Definite Proportions,' 1825; honorary D.C.L. and LL.D. of Oxford and Edinburgh respectively, 1832 and 1834; published 'A New System of Chemical Philosophy,' 1808 and 1827, in which he partly anticipated (1808) Dulong and Petit's law of specific heats, and wrote the article 'Meteorology' in Rees's 'Cyclopædia.' [xiii. 428]

D'ALTON, JOHN (1792–1867), Irish historian, genealogist and biographer; graduate of Trinity College, Dublin; law student of the Middle Temple, London, 1811; called to the Irish bar, 1813; medallist, Royal Irish Academy, 1827, and prizeman, 1831; published a 'Treatise on the Law of Tithes,' a poem entitled 'Dermid,' 'Memoirs of the Archbishops of Dublin,' 1838, a 'History of the County of Dublin,' 1838, and the 'Annals of Boyle.' [xiii. 434]

DALTON, JOHN (1814–1874), Roman catholic divine; missioner at Northampton, Norwich, and Lynn; member of the chapter of the diocese of Northampton; translated Latin and Spanish devotional works, also a 'Life of St. Winifrede' from a British Museum manuscript, 1857. [xiii. 435]

DALTON, LAURENCE (d. 1561), Norroy king-of-arms; Rouge Croix pursuivant, 1546; Richmond herald, 1547; Norroy king-of-arms, 1557. [xiii. 435]

DALTON, MICHAEL (d. 1648?), legal writer; J.P. for Cambridgeshire; commissioner of sequestrations for the county of Cambridge, 1648; author of 'The Countrey Justice,' 1618, and 'Officium Vicecomitum, or the Office and Authoritie of Sheriffs,' 1623. [xiii. 435]

DALTON, RICHARD (1715?–1791), draughtsman, engraver, and librarian; studied art in Rome; travelled,

1749, in Greece, Constantinople, and Egypt, publishing first drawings of monuments of ancient art in those countries; librarian to George III as Prince of Wales and as king; keeper of pictures and antiquarian to George III; one of original committee which drew up project for establishment of Royal Academy, 1755; original member, 1765, and treasurer of Incorporated Society of Artists; antiquarian to Royal Academy; F.S.A., 1767. [Suppl. ii. 108]

DALY or **O'DALY**, DANIEL or DOMINIC (1595–1662), ecclesiastic and author; a native of Kerry; Dominican monk at Lugo, Galicia, with the name of Dominic de Rosario; professor at the Irish Dominican college of Louvain; established an Irish Dominican college at Lisbon, and was appointed rector, 1634; enlisted men in Limerick for the Spanish service; founded nunnery for Irish Dominicans at Lisbon, 1639; Portuguese envoy to Charles I and Charles II; urged Charles II to give the Irish civil and religious liberty, 1649; bishop-elect of Coimbra and president of the Portuguese privy council; author of an account in Latin of the Geraldine Earls of Desmond, 1655, published at Lisbon. [xiii. 436]

DALY, DENIS (1747–1791), Irish politician; educated at Christ Church, Oxford; M.P. for Galway county, 1768–90, for Galway town, 1790; opposed the measure of independence, 1780; muster-master-general, 1781; opposed Flood's bill for parliamentary reform, 1783. [xiii. 438]

DALY, Sir DOMINICK (1798–1868), governor of South Australia; assistant-secretary to the government of Lower Canada, 1825–7; provincial secretary for the united provinces of Canada, 1840–8; member of the council, 1840; lieutenant-governor, Tobago, 1851–4; lieutenant-governor, Prince Edward island, 1854–9; knighted, 1856; governor of South Australia, 1861–8. [xiii. 439]

DALY, Sir HENRY DERMOT (1821–1895), general; ensign 1st Bombay European regiment, 1840; brevet-colonel, 1864; major-general, 1870; lieutenant-general, 1877; general, 1888; served in Sikh war, 1848–9, and against Afridis, 1849; with field force under Captain Coke, 1851, and under Sir Colin Campbell, 1852; served at Delhi and Lucknow and in campaign in Oude, 1858; commander of Central India Horse and political assistant at Angur for Western Malwa, 1861; agent to governor-general for Central India at Indore and opium agent in Malwa, 1871; K.C.B., 1875; C.I.E., 1880; G.C.B., 1889. [Suppl. ii. 109]

DALY, RICHARD (d. 1813), actor and theatrical manager; fellow-commoner, Trinity College, Dublin; first appeared on the Dublin stage as Lord Townley; opened Smock Alley Theatre, Dublin, 1781; became proprietor of Crow Street Theatre; patentee for a theatre royal at Dublin, 1786; obtained decision for libel against Magee, a journalist, 1790; surrendered his claim to the theatre royal, 1797; pensioned, 1798. [xiii. 439]

DALY, ROBERT (1783–1872), bishop of Cashel and Waterford; son of Denis Daly [q. v.]; M.A. Trinity College, Dublin, 1832; D.D., 1843; dean of St. Patrick's, Dublin, 1842; bishop of Cashel and Waterford, 1843; edited Bishop O'Brien's 'Focaloir Gaoidhilge-Sax-Bhéarla, or Irish-English Dictionary,' 1832. [xiii. 440]

DALYELL, Sir JOHN GRAHAM (1775–1851), antiquary and naturalist; studied at Edinburgh University; member of the Faculty of Advocates, 1796; vice-president, Society of Antiquaries of Scotland, 1797; knighted, 1836; president, Society of Arts for Scotland, 1839–40; preses of the board of directors of the Zoological Gardens, Edinburgh, 1841; published works, including 'Scottish Poems of the Sixteenth Century,' 1801, 'The Darker Superstitions of Scotland,' 1834, and 'The Powers of the Creator displayed in the Creation' (vol. i. 1851, vol. ii. 1853). [xiii. 441]

DALYELL or **DALZELL**, ROBERT, second EARL OF CARNWATH (d. 1654), privy councillor for Scotland, 1641; hostile to the covenanters; fined 10,000l. Scots for refusing to appear in answer to a charge of treasonable correspondence with the queen, 1642; said to have caused the royalist defeat at Naseby by his over-caution, 1645; declared guilty of treason, 1645; committed to the Tower, 1651. [xiii. 442]

DALYELL or **DALZELL**, Sir ROBERT, sixth EARL OF CARNWATH (d. 1737), educated at Cambridge;

captured on Stuart side at Preston, 1715; condemned to death by the House of Lords for favouring the Pretender, 1716, but finally protected by the indemnity. [xiii. 443]

DALYELL, SIR ROBERT ANSTRUTHER (1831–1890), Indian civilian; educated at Haileybury; entered Madras civil service, 1851; secretary of Madras government revenue department, 1868; member of board of revenue and chief secretary to Madras government, 1873; vice-president of council of secretary of state for India, 1883–4; C.S.I., 1879; K.C.I.E., 1887. [Suppl. ii. 110]

DALYELL or **DALZELL**, THOMAS (1599 ?–1685), of Binns; general; took part in Rochelle expedition, 1628; colonel in Ireland, 1642; in charge of the customs at Carrickfergus, 1649; proclaimed banished from Scotland, 1650; taken prisoner at Worcester, and committed to the Tower, 1651; escaped to the continent, 1652; assisted in the Scottish rebellion, 1654; as lieutenant-general in the Russian army, fought against the Poles and Turks; commander-in-chief in Scotland, 1666; defeated the covenanters in the Pentlands, 1666; privy councillor, 1667; M.P. in the Scottish parliament for Linlithgow, 1678–85; reappointed commander-in-chief, 1679; commissioner of justiciary to punish the rebels of Bothwell Bridge, 1679; enrolled the Scots Greys, 1681; commander-in-chief with increased powers, 1685. [xiii. 444]

DALZEL, ANDREW (1742–1806), classical scholar; M.A. Edinburgh; collaborator in Dr. Alexander Adam's 'Latin Grammar,' 1772; professor of Greek, Edinburgh University, 1779–1805; corresponded with Heine; helped to found the Royal Society of Edinburgh, 1783; principal clerk to the general assembly, 1789; compiled 'Ἀνάλεκτα Ἑλληνικὰ Ἥσσονα,' 1789, 'Ἀνάλεκτα Ἑλληνικὰ Μείζονα,' 1805,' translated Chevalier's 'Tableau de la Plaine de Troye,' 1791, and wrote a 'History of the University of Edinburgh,' published 1862. [xiii. 447]

DALZELL, NICOL ALEXANDER (1817–1878), botanist; M.A. Edinburgh, 1837; assistant commissioner of customs, Bombay, 1841; conservator of forests, Bombay, 1841; retired, 1870; author of 'The Bombay Flora,' 1861, and other works on Indian botany. [xiii. 448]

DALZELL, ROBERT (1662–1758), general; said to have been in the direct line of succession to the earldom of Carnwath; town-major of Portsmouth, 1702; fought as lieutenant-colonel under Marlborough in the Netherlands, 1705–6; served in Spain as colonel, 1708; lieutenant-general, 1727; commander of the forces in North Britain, 1732; general, 1745; sold his regimental commissions, 1749; chairman of the directors of the Sun Fire Office, 1750. [xiii. 448]

DAMASCENE, ALEXANDER (d. 1719), musician; a Frenchman by birth; naturalised in England 1682; gentleman extraordinary of the Chapel Royal, 1690; gentleman of the Chapel Royal, 1695; composed numerous songs. [xiii. 450]

DAMER, ANNE SEYMOUR (1749–1828), sculptress; daughter of Field-marshal (Henry Seymour) Conway [q. v.]; studied under Ceracchi and Cruikshank; married John Damer, lord Milton, 1767; friend of Nelson, Walpole, Josephine de Beauharnais, and Napoleon; made a statue of George III for the Edinburgh register office; executed heads of Thame and Isis for Henley Bridge, 1785; executrix and residuary legatee of Horace Walpole, 1797; presented Napoleon with a bust of Fox, and the king of Tanjore with a bronze cast of her bust of Nelson, 1826. [xiii. 450]

DAMON or **DAMAN**, WILLIAM (16th cent.), musician to Queen Elizabeth; first composer to set the psalms in the vernacular to part-music, 1579. [xiv. 1]

DAMPIER, THOMAS (1748–1812), bishop of Ely; educated at Eton and King's College, Cambridge; M.A., 1774; D.D., 1780; dean of Rochester, 1782; bishop of Rochester, 1802–8; bishop of Ely, 1808–12; celebrated for his collection of books and prints. [xiv. 1]

DAMPIER, WILLIAM (1652–1715), pirate; captain R.N., and hydrographer; assistant-manager of a Jamaica plantation, 1674; sailor on board ketch bound for Bay of Campeachy, 1675; log-wood cutter, 1675 and 1676; joined buccaneers in West Indies, 1679; separated, with some others, from the main body and took service on a French pirate ship, 1681; boarded Danish ship at Sierra Leone;

ravaged the coast of South America with a fleet of free cruisers under one Captain Davis; set sail for East Indies; reached Guam, 1686; marooned on Nicobar island, 1688; eventually escaped to Acheen; master-gunner of the fort, Bencoolen; escaped from this position of captivity, 1691; published in England his 'Voyage round the World,' 1697, and a 'Discourse of Winds,' 1699; surveyed for government north, east, and south coasts of New Britain, 1699; sailed for England, and was shipwrecked on Ascension, 1701; rescued by an East Indiaman, 1701; fined by a court-martial for excessive severity to his lieutenant, 1702; incompetently commanded privateer in the South Seas, 1703–7; pilot on board the Duke privateer, which rescued Alexander Selkirk [q. v.], 1708; died in London. [xiv. 2]

DANBY, EARLS OF. [See DANVERS, HENRY, 1573–1644; OSBORNE, SIR THOMAS, first earl of the second creation, 1631–1712.]

DANBY, FRANCIS (1793–1861), painter; native of Ireland; came to London, 1813; A.R.A., 1825; left England owing to domestic troubles, and lived near the Lake of Geneva, 1829–41; excelled as a painter of ideal and poetic landscapes, among which may be mentioned 'Sunset at Sea after a Storm,' 1824, and 'The Departure of Ulysses from Ithaca,' 1854. [xiv. 7]

DANBY, JAMES FRANCIS (1816–1875), painter; son of Francis Danby [q. v.]; exhibited at the Royal Academy and British Institution from 1847. [xiv. 8]

DANBY, JOHN (1757–1798), musician; member of the Royal Society of Musicians, 1785; organist to chapel of Spanish embassy; well known for his collections of glees. [xiv. 9]

DANBY, SIR ROBERT (d. 1471 ?), chief-justice of common pleas; serjeant-at-law, 1443; king's serjeant; raised to bench of common pleas, 1452; chief-justice, 1461–71; knighted, c. 1461. [Suppl. ii. 110]

DANBY, THOMAS (1817 ?–1886), painter; son of Francis Danby [q. v.]; copied pictures at the Louvre; exhibited landscapes in the style of Claude; member of the Society of Painters in Water-colours, 1870. [xiv. 9]

DANBY, WILLIAM (1752–1833), miscellaneous writer; high sheriff of Yorkshire, 1784; visited by Southey, 1829; chief works, 'Ideas and Realities,' 1827, and 'Poems,' 1831. [xiv. 9]

DANCE, CHARLES (1794–1863), dramatist; son of George Dance the younger [q. v.]; registrar, taxing-officer, and chief clerk in the insolvent debtors' court; author of comediettas and extravaganzas. [xiv. 10]

DANCE, GEORGE, the elder (1700–1768), architect and surveyor to the corporation of London; designed the Mansion House, 1739. [xiv. 10]

DANCE, GEORGE, the younger (1741–1825), architect; son of George Dance (1700–1768) [q. v.]; city surveyor, 1768–1815; rebuilt Newgate, 1770; built St. Luke's Hospital and the front of Guildhall; F.S.A., 1794; professor of architecture at the Royal Academy, 1798–1805. [xiv. 11]

DANCE, alias LOVE, JAMES (1722–1774), comedian; son of George Dance the elder [q. v.]; educated at Merchant Taylors' School and St. John's College, Oxford; attracted the notice of Sir Robert Walpole by a party poem; manager of an Edinburgh theatre; invited to Drury Lane, 1762; published 'Cricket; an heroic poem,' 1740, 'Pamela' (comedy), 1742, and some pantomimes. [xiv. 11]

DANCE, NATHANIEL (1734–1811). [See HOLLAND, SIR NATHANIEL DANCE-.]

DANCE, SIR NATHANIEL (1748–1827), commander under the East India Company; nephew of George Dance the younger [q. v.]; commodore of the East India Company's homeward-bound fleet, 1804; deceived into flight a French squadron by show of force off Pulo Aor, 1804; knighted, 1804. [xiv. 11]

DANCE, WILLIAM (1755–1840), musician; member of the King's Theatre orchestra, 1775–93; led at the Handel festival in Westminster Abbey, 1790; director and treasurer of the Philharmonic Society, 1813–40. [xiv. 12]

DANCER, MRS. ANN (1734–1801). [See BARRY, MRS. ANN SPRANGER.]

DANCER, DANIEL (1716–1794), miser; left all his wealth to widow of Sir Henry Tempest, who nursed him in his last illness, 1794. [xiv. 12]

DANCER, JOHN (*fl.* 1675), translator and dramatist; probably at one time in the Duke of Ormonde's service; translated, among other works, Corneille's 'Nicomede,' 1671, Quinault's 'Agrippa,' 1675, and Tasso's 'Aminta,' 1660, the first two in rhyming couplets. [xiv. 13]

DANCER, THOMAS (1755?–1811), botanist; physician to the Bath waters, 1784; M.D.; resigned his position as 'island botanist' in Jamaica, the proposals of his 'Observations respecting the Botanic Garden' not being adopted by the House of Assembly, 1804. [xiv. 13]

DANCKERTS, HENRY (1630?–1680?), landscape-painter and line-engraver; born at the Hague; painted landscapes and views of the royal palaces for Charles II; decorated panelling in the house of Pepys, the diarist, 1669; left England in consequence of the 'popish plot,' 1679; engraved portraits of Charles II and of some Dutch dignitaries. [xiv. 14]

DANCKERTS, JOHN (*fl.* 1660), painter; brother of Henry Danckerts [q. v.]; dean of the guild of St. Luke at the Hague, 1650–2; painted historical subjects. [xiv. 14]

DANDRIDGE, BARTHOLOMEW (*fl.* 1750), portrait-painter. [xiv. 15]

DANELL, JAMES (1821–1881), Roman catholic bishop of Southwark; canon of Southwark, 1857; vicar-general of the diocese, 1862; D.D.; bishop, 1871. [xiv. 15]

DANETT, THOMAS (*fl.* 1566–1601), translator of De Commines's 'Historie,' 1601, and part of Guicciardini, 1593. [xiv. 15]

DANFORTH, THOMAS (1622–1699), magistrate in New England; taken to America by his father, 1634; deputy-governor of Massachusetts, 1679–86; president of Maine, 1681–6; judge of the superior court of Massachusetts; a zealous supporter of the old charter of Massachusetts; treasurer and benefactor of Harvard College. [xiv. 15]

DANGERFIELD, THOMAS (1650?–1685), false witness; rambled over Europe; coiner in England; escaped from prison and was outlawed, 1675; befriended by Mrs. Elizabeth Cellier [q. v.], 'the popish midwife,' 1679; revealed an apocryphal plot of the Duke of Monmouth to Charles II, 1679; appeared against Mrs. Elizabeth Cellier, 1680; supported Oates as second witness against the Earl of Castlemaine, but was discredited, 1680; accused the Duke of York and others of being privy to the Sham Plot before the House of Commons, 1680; personated the Duke of Monmouth and claimed miraculous gifts of healing, 1685; convicted of perjury, 1685; died from a blow inflicted by one Robert Frances, 1685. [xiv. 16]

DANICAN, FRANÇOIS ANDRÉ (1726–1795). [See PHILIDOR.]

DANIEL, SAINT, more correctly DEINIOL (*d.* 584?), bishop of Bangor; founded numerous churches in Wales and an abbey at Bangor; bard, and one of the 'seven happy cousins.' [xiv. 18]

DANIEL, or according to Bæda DANIHEL (*d.* 745), bishop of the West-Saxons; made Winchester his episcopal see, 705; literary coadjutor of Bæda and correspondent of St. Boniface. [xiv. 19]

DANIEL À JESU (1572–1649). [See FLOYD, JOHN.]

DANIEL, ALEXANDER (1599–1668), diarist; born at Middleburg, Walcheren; entered Lincoln College, Oxford, 1617; left in manuscript a 'Brief Chronologicalle of Letters and Papers of and for Mine Own Family, 1617–1668,' and 'Meditations.' [xiv. 20]

DANIEL, EDWARD (*d.* 1657), Roman catholic divine; entered the English college at Douay, 1618; student and, in 1640, D.D. of Don Pedro Continho's recently founded college at Lisbon; president of the college, 1642–1648; regent of the Douay college, 1651; dean of the chapter in England, 1653; author of 'Meditations,' 1649. [xiv. 21]

DANIEL, GEORGE, of BESWICK (1616–1657), cavalier poet; wrote a panegyric 'To the Memorie of the best Dramaticke English Poet, Ben Jonson,' 1638; author of 'Trinarchodia,' 1649, 'Idyllia,' 1650, and 'Scattered Fancies,' 1646. [xiv. 21]

DANIEL, GEORGE (1789–1864), miscellaneous writer and book-collector; engaged through life in business; published in early life squibs on royal scandals, some of which were suppressed; satirised contemporary poetasters in 'The Modern Dunciad,' 1814; friend of Charles Lamb and Robert Bloomfield; edited John Cumberland's 'British Theatre,' 1823–31, and Davison's 'Actable Drama'; wrote two farces for Drury Lane Theatre, and humorous and religious poems. At his residence, 18 Canonbury Square, London, he brought together a splendid collection of Elizabethan books, black-letter ballads, and theatrical curiosities, which were dispersed at his death. [xiv. 22]

DANIEL, HENRY (*fl.* 1379), Dominican friar; left manuscripts of medical and natural science. [xiv. 24]

DANIEL, JOHN (*fl.* 1625), musician; brother of Samuel Daniel [q. v.]; Mus. Bac. Christ Church, Oxford, 1604; inspector of the children of the queen's revels, 1618; published 'Songs for the Lute, Viol, and Voice,' 1606. [xiv. 25]

DANIEL, JOHN (1745–1823), last president of the English college, Douay; president, 1792; imprisoned at Arras and Dourlens, 1792; permitted to return to England, 1795; founded Ushaw College, 1795. [xiv. 24]

DANIEL, NEHEMIAS (*d.* 1609?). [See DONELLAN.]

DANIEL, ROBERT MACKENZIE (1814–1847), novelist; educated at Marischal College, Aberdeen, and Edinburgh University; editor of the 'Court Journal,' and of the 'Jersey Herald,' 1845–6; author of society novels. [xiv. 25]

DANIEL, SAMUEL (1562–1619), poet; entered Magdalen Hall, Oxford, 1579; tutor to William Herbert, third earl of Pembroke; published 'Delia,' collection of sonnets, 1592, 'The Complaynt of Rosamond,' narrative poem, 1592, and 'Cleopatra,' a tragedy in the style of Seneca, 1594; advised by Spenser, who admired his love poems, to attempt tragedy, 1595; published 'Musophilus, or A General Defence of Learning,' a poem of great beauty, 1599; maintained, against Campion, the fitness of the English language for rhyme, 1602; produced a tragedy on the story of Philotas, which he had to defend against the charge of covertly apologising for Essex's rebellion, 1605; issued a new edition of his 'Civill Warres' (of York and Lancaster), extended to eight books, 1609; issued a history of England in prose, 1612–17; composed numerous masques for court festivities, including 'Tethys Festival,' 1610, and 'Hymen's Triumph,' 1615; inspector of the children of the queen's revels, 1615–18. His poems were sharply criticised by Ben Jonson, with whom he was 'at jealousies,' but praised for their 'sweetness of ryming' by Drummond of Hawthornden, and for their purity of language by Sir John Harington. [xiv. 25]

DANIEL, THOMAS (1720–1779). [See WEST.]

DANIEL or O'DOMHNUILL, WILLIAM (*d.* 1628), archbishop of Tuam; fellow of Trinity College, Dublin, 1593; M.A., 1595; D.D., 1602; translated the New Testament into Irish, 1602; translated the Book of Common Prayer into Irish, 1608; archbishop of Tuam, 1609; privy councillor of Ireland, 1611; repaired Tuam Cathedral, 1612. [xiv. 31]

DANIEL, WILLIAM BARKER (1753?–1833), sporting writer; M.A. Christ's College, Cambridge, 1790; took orders; published 'Rural Sports,' 1801. [xiv. 32]

DANIEL, EDWARD THOMAS (1804–1843), archæologist; took orders; died at Adalia in Syria while searching for antiquities in Asia Minor with Edward Forbes [q. v.]; sketches by him preserved in British Museum. [xix. 389]

DANIELL, JOHN FREDERIC (1790–1845), physicist; F.R.S., 1813; invented Daniell's hygrometer, 1820; published 'Meteorological Essays,' 1823; constructed water barometer for Royal Society, 1830; professor of chemistry, King's College, London, 1831–45; invented Daniell's constant battery; Copley medallist, 1836; member of admiralty commission on best way of protecting ships from lightning, 1839; honorary D.C.L. Oxford, 1842. [xiv. 33]

DANIELL, SAMUEL (1775–1811), artist and traveller; secretary and draughtsman on a mission for exploring Bechuanaland, 1801; died in Ceylon; exhibited landscapes at the Society of Artists and the Royal Academy; author of books of travel. [xiv. 33]

DANIELL, THOMAS (1749–1840), landscape-painter; went to India with his nephew, William Daniell [q. v.], 1784; R.A., 1799; F.R.S., F.R.A.S., and F.S.A.; published books of views, including 'Oriental Scenery,' 1808, 'Views in Egypt,' and 'A Picturesque Voyage to China.' [xiv. 34]

DANIELL, WILLIAM (1769–1837), landscape-painter; visited India, 1784; returned to England, 1794; R.A., 1822; exhibited Indian and British views, 1795–1837; author, among other works, of 'Zoography' (with William Wood), and a 'Picturesque Voyage to India.' [xiv. 34]

DANIELL, WILLIAM FREEMAN (1818–1865), botanist; M.R.C.S., 1841; M.D.; assistant-surgeon to army on coast of West Africa, where he made a study of the frankincense tree; published 'Medical Topography and Native Diseases of the Gulf of Guinea,' 1849; *Phrynium Danielli* and *Daniellia* named after him. [xiv. 35]

DANNELEY, JOHN FELTHAM (1786–1834?), musician; teacher of music at Ipswich, 1812; organist at St. Mary-of-the-Tower, Ipswich; best known work, 'An Encyclopædia or Dictionary of Music,' 1825. [xiv. 35]

DANSEY, WILLIAM (1792–1856), canon of Salisbury; Stapledon scholar, Exeter College, Oxford, 1811; M.A., 1817; Med. Bac., 1818; prebendary of Salisbury, 1841–56; translated 'Arrian on Coursing,' 1831, and wrote 'Horæ Decanicæ Rurales,' 1835. [xiv. 35]

DANSON, THOMAS (d. 1694), nonconformist divine; chaplain of Corpus Christi College, Oxford, 1648; B.A. and fellow of Magdalen College, Oxford, 1649; M.A.; minister at Sandwich, Kent; ejected, 1660; ejected from the living of Sibton, Suffolk, 1662; wrote largely against the quakers and in defence of predestination. [xiv. 36]

DANVERS, SIR CHARLES (1568?–1601), soldier; knighted by Lord Willoughby in the Netherlands, 1588; M.A. Oxford, 1590; outlawed with his brother, Henry Danvers, earl of Danby [q. v.], who had killed one Henry Long in a duel; fled to France; pardoned, 1598; colonel under Essex in Ireland, 1599; beheaded for complicity in Essex's rebellion, 1601, in which he was probably induced to engage through his intimacy with Henry Wriothesley, earl of Southampton. [xiv. 36]

DANVERS, HENRY, EARL OF DANBY (1573–1644), statesman; accompanied Sir Philip Sidney to the Low Countries as his page; commanded under Maurice, count of Nassau, 1591; killed one Henry Long, who had challenged his brother, Sir Charles Danvers [q. v.], in a duel, or, according to another account, without provocation, 1594; escaped to France with his brother; pardoned, 1598; sergeant-major-general of the army in Ireland, 1602; created Baron Danvers of Dauntsey, Wiltshire, 1603; lord president of Munster, 1607–15; governor of Guernsey, 1621–44; created Earl of Danby, 1626; privy councillor, 1628; K.G., 1633; commissioner of the regency, 1641; established the Botanic Gardens at Oxford in 1622. [xiv. 37]

DANVERS, HENRY (d. 1687), anabaptist and politician; colonel in the parliament army and governor of Stafford; placed under arrest for supposed conspiracy against Cromwell's life, 1657; published a seditious libel about the death of the Earl of Essex, 1684; undertook to raise London in favour of Monmouth, but deserted his leader, 1685; died at Utrecht; author of 'Theopolis,' 1672, and some other treatises of anabaptist theology. [xiv. 39]

DANVERS, SIR JOHN (1588?–1655), regicide; brother of Sir Charles Danvers [q. v.]; laid out Italian garden at Chelsea; knighted by James I; M.P. for Oxford University, 1625, 1626, 1628, and 1639; colonel in the parliament army, 1642; M.P., Malmesbury, 1645; signed death-warrant of Charles I, 1649; member of the council of state, 1649–53. [xiv. 40]

DANVERS, *alias* VILLIERS, *alias* WRIGHT, ROBERT, called VISCOUNT PURBECK (1621?–1674), Fifth-monarchy man; natural son of Frances, daughter of Sir Edward Coke, and wife of Sir John Villiers, viscount Purbeck; married Elizabeth, daughter of Sir John Danvers [q. v.], assuming her surname; M.P. for Westbury, Wiltshire, 1659; expelled from the House of Commons for delinquency, 1659; M.P. for Malmesbury, 1660; imprisoned for the expression of republican principles, 1660; surrendered his title of viscount, 1660; became a Fifth-monarchy man; died an exile in France. [xiv. 41]

D'ARBLAY, FRANCES (1752–1840). [See ARBLAY, FRANCES (BURNEY), MADAME D'.]

DARBY, ABRAHAM (1677–1717), iron manufacturer; founded the Baptist Mills Brass Works at Bristol; patented a method of casting iron-ware in sand, 1708; dissolved connection with the Baptist Mills, 1709, and leased furnace at Coalbrookdale, Shropshire. [xiv. 42]

DARBY, ABRAHAM (1711–1763), manager of iron-works; son of Abraham Darby (1677–1717) [q. v.]; devised, when manager of the Coalbrookdale Ironworks, a method of smelting iron ore by the use of coke. [xiv. 42]

DARBY, ABRAHAM (1750–1791), manager of iron-works; son of Abraham Darby (1711–1763) [q. v.]; manager of the Coalbrookdale Ironworks; built across the Severn at Coalbrookdale the first iron bridge ever constructed (opened, 1779). [xiv. 43]

DARBY, GEORGE (d. 1790), vice-admiral; lieutenant in the navy, 1742; served at reduction of Martinique, 1761; vice-admiral, 1779; commander-in-chief, 1780; admiralty lord, 1780; relieved Gibraltar, 1781; rear-admiral of Great Britain, 1781. [xiv. 43]

DARBY, JOHN NELSON (1800–1882), Plymouth brother and founder of the Darbyites; educated at Westminster; B.A. Trinity College, Dublin, 1819; resigned curacy and joined Plymouth brethren, 1827; founded the Darbyites, or exclusive party among the Plymouth brethren, 1847; visited Canada, Germany, New Zealand, the West Indies, France, and the United States; published devotional and controversial works. [xiv. 43]

DARBYSHIRE, THOMAS (1518–1604), jesuit; B.A. Broadgates Hall (Pembroke College), Oxford, 1544; D.C.L., 1556; prebendary of St. Paul's Cathedral, 1543; chancellor of the diocese of London; deprived of numerous livings at the accession of Elizabeth; obtained decree from council of Trent against temporising with the protestants; became a jesuit at Rome, 1563; sent on a mission to Scotland; professed father of the Society of Jesus, 1572; died at Pont-à-Mousson in Lorraine. [xiv. 44]

DARCY or DARCIE, ABRAHAM (*fl.* 1625), author; native of Geneva; his works include 'The Honour of Ladies,' a prose treatise, 1622. [xiv. 45]

DARCY, JOHN (d. 1347), baron; sheriff of Nottingham, Derby, and Yorkshire; lord justice of Ireland; fought in Scotland, 1333, in France, 1346, and in Flanders; ambassador to Scotland and France, 1337. [xiv. 46]

DARCY, PATRICK (1598–1668), Irish politician; member of the House of Commons in the Dublin parliament, 1640; member of the supreme council of confederated catholics at Kilkenny during the revolt, 1641; maintained exclusive right of Irish parliament to legislate for Ireland, 1641. [xiv. 46]

D'ARCY, PATRICK, COUNT (1725–1779), maréchal-de-camp in the French army; studied mathematics in France; captured by the English while on expedition to assist Prince Charles Edward, 1745; treated as French prisoner of war; captain under Condé, 1749; fought at colonel at Rosbach, 1757; maréchal-de-camp, 1759; wrote against Maupertuis's 'principle of least action,' 1750, and on artillery, 1760. [xiv. 46]

D'ARCY, ROBERT, fourth EARL OF HOLDERNESS (1718–1778), diplomatist; educated at Westminster and Trinity Hall, Cambridge; lord-lieutenant of the North Riding of Yorkshire, 1740; ambassador to Venice, 1744–6; minister plenipotentiary at the Hague, 1749–51; secretary of state, 1751–61; privy councillor, 1751; dismissed for party reasons, 1761. [xiv. 47]

DARCY, THOMAS, BARON DARCY (1467–1537), statesman and rebel leader; served in the army of Henry VII, 1492; pursued James IV on his retreat into Scotland, 1497; captain of Berwick, 1498; constable and marshal of England to punish Perkin Warbeck's following, 1500; warden of the east marches, 1505; named Baron Darcy, 1505; K.G., 1509; volunteered to aid Ferdinand of Spain against the Moors, but returned to England as his services were not wanted, 1511; raided Scottish borders, 1523; at first approved, but subsequently, 1532, opposed Henry VIII's divorce from Catherine of Arragon; began to intrigue with Chapuys, the imperial ambassador, 1534; surrendered Pomfret Castle to the insurgents of the Pilgrimage of Grace, ostensibly of necessity, 1536;

regarded by Henry VIII as a rebel leader, but pardoned in consideration of his efforts for the suppression of Sir Francis Bigod's rebellion, 1537 ; betrayed by a treasonable letter to Robert Aske, 1537, which was intercepted ; beheaded, 1537. [xiv. 49]

DARELL or **DORELL**, WILLIAM (*d.* 1580), antiquary ; M.A. Corpus Christi College, Cambridge ; chaplain to Queen Elizabeth ; sub-dean of Canterbury, 1560 ; chancellor of Bangor, 1565–70 ; prebendary of Lichfield, 1568 ; author of a Latin treatise on the Kentish castles. [xiv. 53]

DARGAN, WILLIAM (1799–1867), Irish railway projector ; constructed the Ulster canal and the chief Irish railways ; declined a baronetcy, 1853. [xiv. 54]

DARLEY, GEORGE (1795–1846), poet and mathematician ; B.A. Trinity College, Dublin, 1820 ; travelled in Italy, and wrote for the 'Athenæum' on Italian art ; edited Beaumont and Fletcher, 1840, and drew up mathematical works for Taylor's series of scientific treatises. His chief works were 'Nepenthe,' a poem, 1839, 'Sylvia,' 1827, 'The Labours of Idleness,' 1826, and two tragedies. [xiv. 55]

DARLEY, JOHN RICHARD (1799–1884), bishop of Kilmore, Elphin, and Ardagh ; M.A. Trinity College, Dublin, 1827 ; D.D. 1875 ; head-master of the grammar School of Dundalk, 1826, and of the royal school of Dungannon, 1831 ; bishop, 1874 ; published 'The Grecian Drama,' 1840, and 'Homer,' 1848. [xiv. 56]

DARLING, Sir CHARLES HENRY (1809–1870), colonial administrator ; military secretary in the West Indies, 1833–6, in Jamaica, 1836–9 ; lieutenant-governor of St. Lucia, 1847, of Cape Colony, 1851 ; governor of Newfoundland ; captain-general of Jamaica, 1857 ; governor of Victoria, 1863 ; K.C.B., 1865 ; recalled from Victoria, 1866. [xiv. 56]

DARLING, GEORGE (1782 ?–1862), physician ; educated at Edinburgh ; L.R.C.P. ; published anonymously 'An Essay on Medical Economy,' 1814. [xiv. 57]

DARLING, GRACE HORSLEY (1815–1842), heroine ; daughter of a lighthouse-keeper on the Farne islands ; rescued four men and a woman from the wreck of the Forfarshire steamboat, 1838. [xiv. 57]

DARLING, JAMES (1797–1862), bookseller and publisher ; founded Metropolitan Library, 1839 ; brought out in two volumes 'Cyclopædia Bibliographica,' 1854, 1859. [xiv. 58]

DARLING, Sir RALPH (1775–1858), general ; assisted in suppressing negro insurrection in Grenada, 1793 ; lieutenant, 1795 ; commanded 51st regiment in Spain, 1808 ; deputy adjutant-general in Walcheren expedition, 1809 ; lieutenant-general and governor of New South Wales, 1825 ; incurred much unpopularity in consequence of excessive severity to two soldiers who had committed larceny with a view to getting their discharge, 1826 ; alleged to have been influenced by favouritism in disposal of crown lands ; recalled, 1831 ; acquitted by a parliamentary committee and knighted, 1835 ; general, 1841. [xiv. 58]

DARLING, WILLIAM (1802–1884), anatomist ; studied at Edinburgh and the University Medical School, New York, being in the latter professor of anatomy, 1862–1884 ; M.R.C.S., 1856 ; published anatomical works. [xiv. 61]

DARLINGTON, third EARL OF (1766–1842). [See VANE, WILLIAM HARRY.]

DARLINGTON, JOHN OF (*d.* 1284), archbishop of Dublin and theologian ; Dominican friar ; assisted in preparing an edition of the 'Concordances' of Hugh of Saint-Cher ; member of Henry III's council, 1256 ; sided with Henry III against the barons ; helped to formulate provisions of Oxford, 1258 ; obtained for Edward I from Pope Nicholas III the tenth of ecclesiastical revenue assigned for crusading purposes by the council of Lyons, 1278, collecting it with difficulty ; consecrated archbishop of Dublin, 1279. [xiv. 61]

DARLUGDACH, SAINT (*d.* 522), second abbess of Kildare, and St. Brigit's favourite pupil. [xiv. 63]

DARLY, MATTHEW (*fl.* 1778), engraver, caricaturist, and artists' colourman. [xiv. 63]

DARNALL, Sir JOHN, the elder (*d.* 1706), lawyer ; clerk to the parliament during Oliver Cromwell's Protectorate ; king's serjeant, 1698 ; knighted, 1699. [xiv. 63]

DARNALL, Sir JOHN, the younger (1672–1735), serjeant-at-law ; son of Sir John Darnall (*d.* 1706) [q. v.] ; serjeant-at-law, 1714 ; knighted, 1724 ; ruled that George I was entitled to the custody of his grandchildren equally with his subjects, 1717. [xiv. 64]

DARNELL, GEORGE (1798–1857), master of a day school at Islington ; started a series of copybooks, c. 1840. [xiv. 64]

DARNELL, Sir THOMAS (*d.* 1640 ?), patriot ; created baronet, 1621 ; imprisoned for having refused to subscribe to the forced loan of 1627 ; released from custody, 1628. [xiv. 65]

DARNELL, WILLIAM NICHOLAS (1776–1865), theological writer and antiquary ; fellow and tutor, Corpus Christi College, Oxford ; M.A. 1800 ; B.D. 1808 ; F.S.A., 1804 ; university examiner, 1801, 1803, 1804 ; select preacher, 1807 ; prebendary of Durham, 1816–31 ; published some sermons and an edition of the 'Book of Wisdom' ; author of 'The King of the Picts and St. Cuthbert,' a well-known ballad. [xiv. 65]

DARNLEY, EARL OF (1545–1567). [See STEWART, HENRY.]

DARRACOTT, RISDON (1717–1759), independent minister ; pastor at Penzance, 1738–9 ; at Wellington, Somerset, 1741–59 ; published 'Scripture Marks of Salvation,' 1755 or 1756. [xiv. 66]

DARREL, JOHN (*fl.* 1562–1602), exorcist ; B.A. Queens' College, Cambridge, 1579 ; preacher at Mansfield ; prohibited from preaching by reason of his exorcist impostures, 1598 ; imprisoned by an episcopal commission, 1599. [xiv. 67]

DARRELL, THOMAS (*fl.* 1572), Roman catholic divine ; educated at New College, Oxford ; D.D. Douay, 1572 ; chaplain to a French bishop. [xiv. 67]

DARRELL, WILLIAM (1651–1721), jesuit, 1671 ; procurator of the province in Paris, 1696 and 1712 ; professor of casuistry at Liège ; rector of the college, 1708–12 ; chief works, 'A Vindication of St. Ignatius (Loyola) from Phanaticism,' 1688, and a treatise 'Of the Real Presence,' 1721. [xiv. 68]

DART, JOHN (*d.* 1730), antiquary ; curate of Yateley, Hampshire, 1728–30 ; author of 'History and Antiquities of the Cathedral Church of Canterbury,' 1726, and 'Westmonasterium' (published 1742). [xiv. 68]

DART, JOSEPH HENRY (1817–1887), conveyancer ; M.A. Exeter College, Oxford, 1841 ; Newdigate prizeman ; barrister, Lincoln's Inn, 1841 ; senior conveyancing counsel to the high court of justice, 1875–86 ; published 'Compendium of the Law relating to Real Estate,' 1851. [xiv. 69]

DARTIQUENAVE, CHARLES (1664–1737), epicure and humorist ; probably of French descent ; paymaster of the royal works, surveyor-general of the king's gardens, and (1731) surveyor of the king's private roads ; referred to by Swift as a punster, and by Pope as an epicure. [xiv. 69]

DARTMOUTH, EARLS OF. [See LEGGE, WILLIAM, first EARL, 1672–1750 ; LEGGE, WILLIAM, second EARL, 1731–1801 ; LEGGE, GEORGE, third EARL, 1755–1810.]

DARTMOUTH, first BARON (1648–1691). [See LEGGE, GEORGE.]

DARTON, NICHOLAS (1603–1649 ?), divine ; B.A. Exeter College, Oxford, 1622 ; incumbent of Kilsby, Northamptonshire, 1628–45 ; author of the 'True and Absolute Bishop,' 1641. [xiv. 70]

DARUSMONT, FRANCES, better known by her maiden name of FRANCES WRIGHT (1795–1852), philanthropist ; friend of Lafayette ; formed a settlement of negro slaves in the state of Tennessee, hoping that they would work out their liberty, but failed, 1824 ; conducted a socialistic journal in Indiana with the assistance of Robert Dale Owen ; one of the original advocates of female suffrage. [xiv. 70]

DARWIN, CHARLES ROBERT (1809–1882), naturalist ; grandson of Erasmus Darwin [q. v.] ; educated at Shrewsbury, Edinburgh University, and Christ's College,

Cambridge; embarked as naturalist, by invitation of Captain Fitz Roy, on board the Beagle, bound for South America on a scientific expedition, 1831; worked at South American geology; returned to England, 1836; published 'Zoology of the Voyage of the Beagle,' 1840; secretary to the Geographical Society, 1838–41; wrote 'The Volcanic Islands,' 1844, and other works in retirement necessitated by ill-health; first gave definite written shape to his theory of evolution by natural selection, 1844; induced by his friend Lyell, the geologist, to write out the results of his experiments, 1856; received a manuscript from the naturalist, A. R. Wallace, containing a theory of the origin of species identical with his own, 1858; published Wallace's essay and a letter of his own, addressed to Dr. Asa Gray, in 1857, containing a sketch of his theory; produced 'Origin of Species,' 1859; developed theory of Pangenesis in his 'Variation of Animals and Plants under Domestication,' 1868; published 'The Descent of Man,' 1871, and 'The Expression of the Emotions in Man and Animals,' 1872; elaborated a paper which he had read before the Geological Society in 1838 into a book on the 'Formation of Vegetable Mould through the action of Worms,' 1881. In the domain of botany he resuscitated Sprengel's theory of the fertilisation of plants in his 'Fertilisation of Orchids,' 1862 (supplemented by his 'Effects of Cross and Self Fertilisation,' 1876), and published 'The Movements and Habits of Climbing Plants,' 1864, 'Different Forms of Flowers' (the latter being an investigation of heterostyled plants), 1877, 'Insectivorous Plants,' 1875, and 'The Power of Movement in Plants,' in which was formulated his theory of circumnutation, 1880. In 1879 he wrote a biography of Erasmus Darwin for Dr. E. Krause's 'Essay.' [xiv. 72]

DARWIN, ERASMUS (1731–1802), physician; Exeter scholar, St. John's College, Cambridge; B.A., 1754; M.B., 1755; corresponded with Rousseau; established a dispensary at Lichfield and founded the Philosophical Society at Derby, 1784; declined invitation of George III to become his physician; formed botanical garden near Lichfield, 1778; published 'The Loves of the Plants,' 1789, and the 'Economy of Vegetation,' 1792, both forming parts of his poetic work, 'Botanic Garden,' and wrote 'The Temple of Nature, or the Origin of Society' (published, 1803). He was also the author of a few prose works, maintaining a form of evolutionism which was subsequently expounded by Lamarck. [xiv. 84]

DASENT, Sir GEORGE WEBBE (1817–1896), Scandinavian scholar; born in St. Vincent; educated at Westminster and Magdalen Hall, Oxford; M.A., 1843; D.C.L., 1852; secretary to Sir Thomas Cartwright [q. v.]; British envoy at Stockholm, 1840–5; studied Scandinavian literature and mythology; assistant editor of the 'Times,' 1845–70; called to bar at Middle Temple, 1852; professor of English literature and modern history at King's College, London, 1853; civil service commissioner, 1870–92; knighted, 1876; commissioner of historical manuscripts, 1870. He published many translations from Norse, including 'Popular Tales from Norse,' 1859, the 'Story of Burnt Njal,' 1861, and 'The Story of Gisli the Outlaw,' 1866, besides various essays and other writings. [Suppl. ii. 111]

DASHWOOD, FRANCIS, Baron Le Despencer (1708–1781), chancellor of the exchequer; son of Sir Francis Dashwood, baronet, whom he succeeded, 1724; lived riotous life on continent; entered household of Frederick Lewis, prince of Wales; leading member of Dilettanti Society, 1736, and was arch-master, 1746; M.P. for New Romney, 1741, 1747, and 1754, and for Weymouth and Melcombe Regis, 1761 and 1762; F.R.S., 1746; D.C.L. Oxford, 1749; founded 'Hell-fire Club,' or society of the monks of Medmenham Abbey, c 1755; first colonel of Buckinghamshire militia, 1757; chancellor of exchequer, 1762–3; keeper of wardrobe, 1763; succeeded, as fifteenth Baron Le Despencer, his uncle, John Fane, seventh earl of Westmorland and fourteenth baron Le Despencer, 1763; joint postmaster-general, 1770–81. [Suppl. ii. 112]

DASHWOOD, GEORGE HENRY (1801–1869), antiquary; M.A. Lincoln College, Oxford, 1825; F.S.A., 1844; vicar of Stow Bardolph, 1852; wrote on the archæology and antiquities of Norfolk. [xiv. 87]

DASSIER, JAMES ANTHONY (1715–1759), medallist; son of John Dassier [q. v.]; appointed assistant-engraver to the English mint, 1741; worked on the coin-

age of Elizabeth of Russia, c. 1756; struck medals of Pope Clement XII and the most distinguished Englishmen of the time. [xiv. 87]

DASSIER, JOHN (1676–1763), medallist; born at Geneva; employed at the Geneva mint; member of the Geneva council of Two Hundred, 1738; issued numerous sets of medals, including a series of celebrated men of the age of Louis XIV, 1720, and a series of English sovereigns (William I to George II), 1731. [xiv. 88]

D'ASSIGNY, MARIUS (1643–1717), author and translator; B.D. Cambridge, 1668; translated Drelincourt's 'Christian's Defence,' 1701, and Pierre Gautruche's 'Histoire Poëtique,' adding two appendices of his own on Roman curiosities and Egyptian hieroglyphics respectively, 1671; published also theological works. [xiv. 89]

DASTIN, **DASTYN**, or **DAUSTIN**, JOHN (*fl.* 1320), alchemist; correspondent of Pope John XXII and Cardinal Adrian of Naples; left in manuscript a 'Rosarium' and a 'Visio super Artem Alchemicam.' [xiv. 89]

DAUBENEY, GILES, first Baron Daubeney (*d.* 1508), soldier and statesman; commanded four men-at-arms and fifty archers under Edward IV in France, 1475; fled to the Earl of Richmond in Brittany on the failure of Buckingham's rebellion, and was attainted, 1483; privy councillor, 1485; master of the mint, 1485; lieutenant of Calais, 1486; created Baron Daubeney, 1486; K.G., 1487; arranged the first treaty for the marriage of Prince Arthur with Catherine of Arragon, 1488; took Ostend, 1489; commander of a force sent to assist the Duchess Anne in Brittany, 1490; negotiated treaty of Etaples, 1492; lord chamberlain, 1495; put down the second rebellion of Perkin Warbeck and the Cornish revolt, 1497; accompanied Henry VII to Calais, 1500. [xiv. 90]

DAUBENY, CHARLES (1745–1827), archdeacon of Salisbury; educated at Winchester and New College, Oxford; fellow of New College, 1774; prebendary of Salisbury, 1784; minister (1798) of Christ Church, Walcot, Bath, the first free and open church in the country, to the erection of which he was the chief subscriber; archdeacon of Salisbury, 1804; D.C.L. Oxford, 1822; author of numerous theological works, partly anticipating the tractarian movement. [xiv. 92]

DAUBENY, CHARLES GILES BRIDLE (1795–1867), chemist and botanist; educated at Winchester and Magdalen College, Oxford; B.A., 1814; lay-fellow of Magdalen; studied medicine at Edinburgh, 1815–18; M.D. Oxford; professor of chemistry at Oxford, 1822–55; professor of botany, 1834; of rural economy, 1840; F.R.S.; chief works, 'A Description of Active and Extinct Volcanoes,' largely based on investigations in Auvergne, 1826, and an 'Introduction to the Atomic Theory,' 1831. [xiv. 94]

DAUBUZ, CHARLES (1673–1717), divine; born in Guienne; came to England, his father having been allowed to leave France on the revocation of the edict of Nantes, 1685; educated at Merchant Taylors' School and Queens' College, Cambridge; master of Sheffield grammar school, 1696–9; M.A., 1697; vicar of Brotherton, Yorkshire, 1699–1717; chief work, 'A Perpetual Commentary on the Revelation of St. John' (published, 1720). [xiv. 95]

DAUGLISH, JOHN (1824–1866), inventor of aërated bread; studied medicine at Edinburgh, 1852; M.D., 1855; took out his first patent for 'an improved method of making bread,' 1856, silver medallist of the Society of Arts, 1860. [xiv. 96]

DAUNCEY or **DAUNCY**, JOHN (*fl.* 1663), translator of Perefixe's 'Histoire de Henri le Grand,' 1663; published histories of Charles II, 1660, of Henrietta Maria, 1660, and of Portugal, 1661. [xiv. 97]

DAUNT, ACHILLES (1832–1878), dean of Cork; gold medallist in classics at Dublin, 1853; vicar of St. Matthias, Dublin, 1867–78; D.D.; representative canon for the united diocese of Dublin and Glendalough; dean of Cork. [xiv. 97]

DAUS, JOHN (*fl.* 1561), translator of 'Sleidanes Commentaries,' 1560. [xiv. 98]

D'AUVERGNE, EDWARD (1660–1737), military historian; born in Jersey; M.A. Pembroke, College, Oxford, 1686; chaplain to the Scots guards in Flanders, 1691; rector of Great Hallingbury, 1701–37; published narratives of William III's campaigns in Flanders. [xiv. 99]

DAVALL, EDMUND (1763–1798), botanist; F.L.S.; gave name to *Davallia* genus of ferns; resided at Orbe, Switzerland; left an unfinished work on the Swiss flora. [xiv. 99]

DAVENANT, CHARLES (1656–1714), political economist; son of Sir William D'Avenant [q. v.]; entered Balliol College, Oxford, 1671; M.P., St. Ives, Cornwall, 1685; LL.D.; M.P., Great Bedwin, 1698 and 1700; attacked the clergy in his 'Essays upon the Ballance of Power,' 1701; secretary to the commissioners appointed to treat for the union with Scotland, 1702; inspector-general of imports and exports, 1705–14; published 'An Essay upon the Ways and Means of Supplying the War,' 1695, and 'An Essay on the East India Trade,' in which, while upholding the mercantile system, he questioned its applicability to this particular subject, 1697. [xiv. 99]

DAVENANT, JOHN (1576–1641), bishop of Salisbury; fellow of Queens' College, Cambridge, 1597; D.D., 1609; Margaret professor of divinity, 1609–21; master of Queens', 1614; represented the church of England at the synod of Dort, 1618; bishop of Salisbury, 1621; accused before Archbishop Laud of Calvinism, 1631; best-known work, a commentary on St. Paul's Epistle to the Colossians, 1631. [xiv. 101]

D'AVENANT, SIR WILLIAM (1606–1668), poet and dramatist; educated at Oxford; earliest drama 'The Tragedy of Alboine, King of the Lombards,' 1629; wrote masques for the court; printed 'Madagascar and other Poems,' 1635; published 'The Platonick Lovers' (tragicomedy), 1636; his comic masterpiece, 'The Wits,' acted, 1633, published, 1636; poet-laureate, 1638; produced the 'Unfortunate Lovers,' 1643, and 'Love and Honour,' 1649, in the opinion of Pepys 'a very good play'; fled to France when threatened by parliament with arrest on account of his active support of Charles I's cause, but returned; was knighted by Charles I (1643) at the siege of Gloucester; carried a letter of advice from Henrietta Maria, then in France, to Charles I, 1646; sent by Henrietta Maria on a mission to Virginia, but was captured on the way by a parliament ship, 1650; imprisoned in the Tower, 1650–2; published (1651) the first edition of 'Gondibert'; practically founded the English opera by his 'Siege of Rhodes,' 1656; opened Drury Lane Theatre, 1658; produced 'The Cruelty of the Spaniards in Peru,' 1658, and 'The History of Sir Francis Drake,' 1659; imprisoned for complicity in the rising of Sir George Booth (1622–1684) [q. v.], 1659; established the 'Duke's Theatrical Company,' 1660, in spite of the opposition of Sir Henry Herbert, master of the revels; in conjunction with Dryden adapted Shakespeare's 'Tempest,' 1667; produced versions of other of Shakespeare's plays. [xiv. 101]

DAVENANT, WILLIAM (*d.* 1681), translator; son of Sir William D'Avenant [q. v.]; M.A. Magdalen Hall, Oxford, 1680; held a living in Surrey; translated into English 'Notitia Historicorum Selectorum,' 1678; drowned in the Seine, 1681. [xiv. 108]

DAVENPORT, CHRISTOPHER (1598–1680), Franciscan; better known as FRANCISCUS À SANCTÂ CLARÂ; left Merton College, Oxford, and went to Douay, 1615; became a Franciscan at Ypres, 1617; graduated at Salamanca; chaplain to Queen Henrietta Maria; gained friendship of Archbishop Laud by his liberal construction of the Romish position; chaplain to Catherine of Braganza; chief work, 'Deus, Natura, Gratia,' 1634. [xiv. 108]

DAVENPORT, SIR HUMPHREY (1566–1645), judge; studied at Balliol College, Oxford; barrister, Gray's Inn, 1590; serjeant-at-law, 1623; knighted, 1624; puisne judge of common pleas, 1630–1; president of court of exchequer, 1631; maintained legality of ship-money, but gave judgment for Hampden on a technical point, 1637; impeached by Long parliament, but passed over, 1641. [xiv. 109]

DAVENPORT, JOHN (1597–1670), puritan divine; educated at Merton and Magdalen colleges, Oxford; M.A. and B.D., 1625; fled from Laud's hostility; co-pastor of the English church at Amsterdam, 1634–5; founded colony of New Haven, Quinnipiac, 1638; argued against the 'Half Way Covenant,' 1662; published theological works. [xiv. 110]

DAVENPORT, MARY ANN (1765 ?–1843), actress; *née* Harvey; first appeared as Lappet in Fielding's 'Miser,' 1784; engaged at Covent Garden, 1794; most successful in the rôle of an old woman. [xiv. 111]

DAVENPORT, RICHARD ALFRED (1777 ?–1852), miscellaneous writer; published 'The History of the Bastile,' 1838, 'A Dictionary of Biography,' 1831, and numerous other works, besides editing various British poets, Robertson's histories, 1824, Mitford's 'History of Greece,' 1835, and Pilkington's 'Dictionary of Painters,' 1852; died from an overdose of opium. [xiv. 112]

DAVENPORT, ROBERT (*fl.* 1623), poet and dramatist; published 'A Crowne for a Conquerour,' and 'Too Late to call backe Yesterday,' 1623; author of 'King John and Matilda' (tragedy), published 1655, 'A New Trick to Cheat the Divell,' 1639, and 'The City Night-Cap,' licensed, 1624. [xiv. 112]

DAVENPORT, SAMUEL (1783–1867), line-engraver; engraved portraits for biographical works and (1828–42) plates for the 'Forget-me-not Annual.' [xiv. 113]

DAVERS. [See DANVERS.]

DAVID. [See DAVYDD.]

DAVID or **DEWI**, SAINT (*d.* 601 ?), patron saint of Wales; bishop of Menevia (St. David's); credited with the foundation of monasteries at Glastonbury, Leominster, Repton, Crowland, Bath, and Raglan; commemorated 1 March; canonised by Pope Calixtus in 1120. [xiv. 113]

DAVID (*d.* 1139 ?), generally called 'David the Scot,' but probably of Welsh descent; teacher at Würzburg; chaplain to the Emperor Henry V, 1110; attended Henry in his expedition against Pope Paschal II, of which he wrote an account, 1110; chosen bishop of Bangor by the influence of Gruffudd, king of Gwynedd, 1120; took part in Archbishop William of Corbeil's council at Westminster, 1127. [xiv. 115]

DAVID I (1084–1153), king of Scotland; son of Malcolm Canmore; became an English baron by his marriage with Matilda, countess of Northampton; introduced the feudal organisation into Cumbria on becoming its prince, 1107; king of Scotland, 1124; declared for the Empress Matilda against Stephen, but was defeated at the Battle of the Standard, 1138; concluded an advantageous peace at Carlisle, but subsequently (1140) joined Matilda in her flight to Winchester; unsuccessfully invaded England, 1149; founded the sees of Brechin, Dunblane, Caithness, Ross, and Aberdeen; introduced into Scotland the new regular orders of the monastic clergy, especially favouring the Cistercians; founded the burghs of Edinburgh, Berwick, Roxburgh, Stirling, and perhaps Perth; made Norman feudal law the law of Scotland, organised a feudal court, and established the office of chancellor for the administration of the laws and the publishing of the royal charters. [xiv. 117]

DAVID II (1324–1371). [See BRUCE, DAVID.]

DAVID (*d.* 1176), called David the Second, bishop of St. David's; consecrated bishop of St. David's by Archbishop Theobald, on condition of waiving the claims of his see to metropolitan rank, 1148; involved in constant disputes with his chapter and with Mahel, lord of Brecon, who disliked David's Norman connections and policy; attended council of Tours, 1163. [xiv. 120]

DAVID AP GWILYM (14th cent.), Welsh bard; said to have studied in Italy; imprisoned for eloping with Morvydd of Anglesey, but released on the payment of his fine by the men of Glamorgan; chief bard of Glamorganshire; wrote love poems and satires on his personal enemies and the monastic orders. [xiv. 122]

DAVID AB LLEWELYN (*d.* 1415). [See GAM, DAVID.]

DAVID or **DAFYDD**, EDWARD (*d.* 1690), Welsh poet; lampooned Cromwell's Welsh expedition; editor of 'Cyfrinach y Beirdd,' a treatise on the rules of Welsh poetry; president of Gorsedd Morganwg, 1660. [xiv. 122]

DAVIDS, THOMAS WILLIAM (1816–1884), ecclesiastical historian; congregational minister at Colchester, 1840–74; secretary of the Essex Congregational Union; author of 'Annals of Evangelical Nonconformity in the County of Essex,' 1863, and (unfinished) 'Annals of Reformers before the Reformation.' [xiv. 123]

DAVIDSON. [See also DAVISON.]

M

DAVIDSON, ALEXANDER DYCE (1807–1872), divine; educated at Aberdeen University; D.D., 1854; minister of the South church, Aberdeen, 1832, of the West church, 1836; led the evangelical movement in Aberdeen, 1843.   [xiv. 124]

DAVIDSON, HARRIET MILLER (1839–1883), authoress; daughter of Hugh Miller [q. v.]; removed to Adelaide with her husband, the Rev. John Davidson, 1869. A tale, entitled 'A Man of Genius,' published in an Adelaide journal, is considered the best of her writings.   [xiv. 124]

DAVIDSON, JAMES (1793–1864), antiquary and bibliographer; published numerous works on the topography and history of Devonshire, also a 'Glossary of the Obsolete and Unused Words and Phrases of the Holy Scriptures in the Authorised English Version,' 1850.   [xiv. 125]

DAVIDSON, JAMES BRIDGE (d. 1885), miscellaneous writer; son of James Davidson [q. v.]; contributed to various journals.   [xiv. 125]

DAVIDSON, JOHN (1549?–1603), Scottish church leader; regent of St. Leonard's College, St. Andrews; quarrelled with the regent Morton, and fled from Scotland; allowed to return, 1577; minister of Liberton, Edinburgh, 1579; opposed James VI's desire to restore prelacy with much plain speaking; excommunicated Montgomery, bishop of Glasgow, at the desire of the general assembly, 1582; minister of Prestonpans, 1596; opposed James VI's proposal that certain of the clergy should vote in parliament, 1599; interdicted from going beyond his own parish, 1601; author of 'Memorials of his Time.'   [xiv. 125]

DAVIDSON, JOHN (d. 1797), Scottish antiquary; writer to the signet and crown agent; printed privately works on the legal history of Scotland, 1771–92.
                                                    [xiv. 127]

DAVIDSON, JOHN (1797–1836), African traveller; originally a pupil at St. George's Hospital and student at Edinburgh University; F.R.S., 1832; travelled as a physician in the sultanate of Morocco, 1835; murdered in the great desert at Swekeza, on his way to Timbuctoo, 1836; an expert in egyptology and the topography of the near East; his notes of travel printed posthumously, 1839.   [xiv. 127]

DAVIDSON, SAMUEL (1806–1898), theologian and biblical scholar; born in co. Antrim; studied for presbyterian ministry at Royal Academical Institution, Belfast; licensed preacher, 1833; professor of biblical criticism at Belfast, 1835–41; LL.D. Aberdeen, 1838; professor of biblical literature and ecclesiastical history at Lancashire Independent College, Manchester, 1843–57; published, 1856, as part of an edition of Horne's 'Introduction,' 'The Text of the Old Testament considered,' which was objected to on doctrinal grounds by the Lancashire College committee; resigned professorship in consequence, 1857; engaged in tuition at Hatherlow, Cheshire; scripture examiner at London University, 1862; published numerous theological writings.   [Suppl. ii. 115]

DAVIDSON, THOMAS (1747–1827), theologian; educated at Glasgow and Leyden; D.D.; minister at Inchture, 1771–3, at the outer high church, Glasgow, 1773, at Lady Yester's church, Edinburgh, and subsequently, 1785, at the Tolbooth church, Edinburgh.   [xiv. 128]

DAVIDSON, THOMAS (1838–1870), Scottish poet; of English extraction; entered Edinburgh University, 1855; licensed preacher of the united presbyterian church, 1864; wrote songs, including 'Myspie's Den' and 'The Auld Ash Tree,' and 'Yang-Tsi-Kiang,' an extravaganza.
                                                    [xiv. 129]

DAVIDSON, THOMAS (1817–1885), palæontologist; educated in France, Italy, Switzerland, and Edinburgh; medallist of the Royal Society, 1870; LL.D. St Andrews, 1882; wrote a monograph on the British fossil brachiopods for the Palæontological Society, 1850–70.   [xiv. 129]

DAVIDSON, WILLIAM (1756?–1795?), privateersman; able seaman on board H.M.S. Niger, 1791; found in possession of a journal, 1791, which showed that he and other pirates on board a Russian privateer had plundered numerous ships with horrible atrocities in the Levant, 1788–9; deserted, 1794.   [xiv. 130]

DAVIE, ADAM (fl. 1308?). [See DAVY.]

DAVIES. [See also DAVIS and DAVYS.]

DAVIES, BENJAMIN (1814–1875), hebraist; Ph.D. Leipzig, 1838; LL.D.; president of Stepney Baptist College, 1844–7; professor at McGill College, Montreal, 1847; professor of oriental and classical languages at Stepney Baptist College, 1857; one of the revisers of the Old Testament; translated Gesenius's Grammar and Lexicon.
                                                    [xiv. 130]

DAVIES, CATHERINE (1773–1841?), authoress of 'Eleven Years' Residence in the Family of Murat, King of Naples,' published by subscription, 1841; governess in Murat's family, 1802–15.   [xiv. 131]

DAVIES, CECILIA (1750?–1836), vocalist; visited Vienna, and sang before Duke Ferdinand of Parma, 1769; taught the archduchesses, Maria Theresa's daughters, singing; engaged at the King's Theatre in Italian opera, 1773; returned to Italy, where she was the first Englishwoman to appear on the stage; subsequently appeared in oratorios at Drury Lane, 1791.   [xiv. 131]

DAVIES, CHRISTIAN, alias MOTHER ROSS (1667–1739), female soldier; born in Dublin; enlisted under the name of Christopher Welsh, c. 1693; fought in Flanders; at the battle of Blenheim, 1704; her sex revealed by an operation necessitated by a wound at Ramillies, 1706; dismissed the service, but still followed the army; pensioned, 1712; thrice married, all her husbands being soldiers.   [xiv. 132]

DAVIES, DAVID (d. 1819?), writer on poor laws; M.A. Jesus College, Oxford, 1785; D.D., 1800; rector of Barkham, Berkshire; published 'The Case of Labourers in Husbandry stated and considered,' 1795.   [xiv. 133]

DAVIES, DAVID CHARLES (1826–1891), Welsh presbyterian divine; educated at University College, London; M.A., 1849; ordained pastor of a bilingual church at Builth, 1852, and 1856–8; at English church in Windsor Street, Liverpool, 1853–6, Newtown, 1858, Welsh church at Jewin Crescent, London, 1859–76, and at English church, Menai Bridge, 1876; principal of Trevecca, 1888–91; published numerous contributions to Welsh theological literature.   [Suppl. ii. 116]

DAVIES, DAVID CHRISTOPHER (1827–1885), geologist and mining engineer; fellow of the Geological Society, 1872; opened quarries in North Wales, in the south of France, 1880–5, and in Germany; published 'Treatise on Slate and Slate Quarrying,' 1878, and 'Treatise on Metalliferous Minerals and Mining.'
                                                    [xiv. 133]

DAVIES, EDWARD (1756–1831), Welsh antiquary; master of the grammar school at Chipping Sodbury, Gloucestershire, 1783–99; chancellor of Brecon, 1816; associate of the Royal Society of Literature, 1824; chief work, 'Celtic Researches on the Origin, Traditions, and Language of the Ancient Britons,' 1804.   [xiv. 134]

DAVIES, ELEANOR, LADY (d. 1652), daughter of George Touchet, baron Audley; married, firstly, c. 1608, Sir John Davies (1569–1626) [q. v.], and, secondly, Sir Archibald Douglas. She published several fanatical books of prophecy.   [xiv. 143]

DAVIES, EVAN (1805–1864), independent minister; sent to Penang by the London Missionary Society, 1835; superintendent of the Boys' Mission School, Walthamstow, 1842–4; pastor of the congregational church, Richmond, 1844–57; published 'China and her Spiritual Claims,' 1845, with other religious works.   [xiv. 135]

DAVIES, FRANCIS (1605–1675), bishop of Llandaff; M.A. Jesus College, Oxford, 1628; fellow and B.D., 1640; ejected from his rectory of Llangan under the Commonwealth; archdeacon of Llandaff, 1660; D.D. 1661; bishop of Llandaff, 1667.   [xiv. 135]

DAVIES, GEORGE (d. 1811). [See HARLEY.]

DAVIES, GRIFFITH (1788–1855), actuary; gained repute by his 'Key to Bonnycastle's Trigonometry,' 1814; permanent actuary of the Guardian Assurance Company, 1823–55; published 'Tables of Life Contingencies,' 1825; engaged to report on various Indian funds 1829–51; F.R.S., 1831; compiled 'Tables for the Use of Friendly Societies,' 1847.   [xiv. 136]

DAVIES, HENRY (1782–1862), physician; M.C.S., 1803; M.D Aberdeen, 1823; L.R.C.P., 1823; physician to the British Lying-in Hospital, and lecturer on midwifery at St. George's Hospital; published 'The Young Wife's Guide,' 1844.   [xiv. 137]

DAVIES, HERBERT (1818–1885), physician; son of Dr. Thomas Davies (1792–1839) [q. v.]; scholar of Gonville and Caius College, Cambridge, 1838; B.A., 1842; fellow of Queens' College, Cambridge, 1844; M.D., 1848; F.R.C.P., 1850; physician to the London Hospital, 1854–1874; his 'Lectures on the Physical Diagnosis of the Diseases of the Lungs and Heart,' 1851, translated into German and Dutch.   [xiv. 137]

DAVIES, HUGH (1739?–1821), botanist; educated at Peterhouse, Cambridge; rector of Aber; published 'Welsh Botanology,' 1813, and edited second edition of Pennant's 'Indian Zoology,' 1790.   [xiv. 138]

DAVIES, JAMES (1820–1883), classical scholar; scholar and graduate of Lincoln College, Oxford; headmaster of Ludlow grammar school; translated Babrius, in verse, 1860, and Hesiod, Theognis, and Callimachus in prose.   [xiv. 138]

DAVIES, SIR JOHN (*fl.* 1595), marshal of Connaught under Queen Elizabeth.   [xiv. 144]

DAVIES, SIR JOHN (*fl.* 1599), master of the ordnance in Ireland.   [xiv. 144]

DAVIES, SIR JOHN (*fl.* 1601), conspirator; sentenced to death for his share in Essex's conspiracy, 1601; pardoned.   [xiv. 144]

DAVIES, JOHN (1565?–1618), poet and writing-master; published 'Microcosmos,' 1603, 'Humours Heau'n on Earth.... As also The Triumph of Death,' 1605, being a description of the plague of 1603, the 'Holy Roode,' 1609, 'Wittes Pilgrimage (by Poeticall Essaies),' 1611, 'The Muse's Sacrifice,' containing the author's famous 'Picture of an Happy Man,' 1612, and 'Wit's Bedlam,' 1617. He also issued an 'Anatomy of Fair Writing,' 1633. Some of his epigrams are valuable for their notices of Ben Jonson, Fletcher, and other contemporary poets.   [xiv. 138]

DAVIES, SIR JOHN (1569–1626), attorney-general for Ireland and poet; educated at Winchester and Queen's College, Oxford; B.A., 1590; barrister, Middle Temple, 1595; M.P., Corfe Castle, 1601; solicitor-general for Ireland, the miserable state of which country he recounted in his letters to Cecil, 1603; attorney-general for Ireland, 1606–19; serjeant-at-law, 1606; used his influence for the banishment of Romanist priests from Ireland; on commission for plantation of Ulster, 1608; serjeant, 1609; M.P., co. Fermanagh, and speaker of the Irish parliament, 1613; M.P., Newcastle-under-Lyme, 1614 and 1621; appointed chief-justice as a reward for maintaining the legality of Charles I's forced loans, 1626, but died before entering on office. In 1622 he collected in one volume, 'Orchestra,' 1594, 'Astræa,' and a set of quatrains on the immortality of the soul, entitled 'Nosce Teipsum,' 1599. He wrote also 'A Contention betwixt a Wife, a Widdow, and a Maide,' which was performed before the queen in 1602, a treatise on taxation (published 1656), and a discussion on recent Irish discontent, 1612. [xiv. 140]

DAVIES, JOHN (1570?–1644), lexicographer; B.A. Jesus College, Oxford, 1593; rector of Mallwyd, Merionethshire, 1604–8; B.D. Lincoln College, 1608; D.D., 1616; prebendary of St. Asaph, 1607; his most important work, 'Antiquæ Linguæ Britannicæ Dictionarium Duplex,' 1632; assisted Dr. Richard Parry in the preparation of his Welsh translation of the bible, 1620.   [xiv. 144]

DAVIES, JOHN (1627?–1693), translator; educated at Jesus College, Oxford, and St. John's College, Cambridge. His translations include 'Treatise against . . . Descartes,' 1654, 'Les Provinciales,' 1656, Scuderi's 'Clelia,' 1656, Appian's 'History,' 1679, and a few Spanish romances.   [xiv. 144]

DAVIES, JOHN (1679–1732), president of Queens' College, Cambridge; educated at Charterhouse and Queens' College, Cambridge; fellow, 1701; M.A., 1702; rector of Fen Ditton, Cambridge, 1711; prebendary of Ely, 1711; LL.D., 1711; president of Queens' College, 1717; D.D., 1717; vice-chancellor, 1725; edited many of Cicero's philosophical treatises and works of other classical authors.   [xiv. 146]

DAVIES or **DAVIS**, JOHN SCARLETT (*fl.* 1841), painter; visited Amsterdam, 1841; devoted himself more especially to painting interiors; lithographed twelve heads from studies by Rubens.   [xiv. 146]

DAVIES, JONATHAN (1736–1809), provost of Eton; educated at Eton and King's College, Cambridge; M.A., 1763; canon of Windsor, 1781–91; provost of Eton, 1791; founded an exhibition at Eton and the Davies scholarship at Cambridge; bequeathed 2,000*l.* to King's College.
                   [xiv. 147]

DAVIES, LADY LUCY CLEMENTINA (1795–1879), authoress; daughter of Lord Leon de Melfort, titular earl of Perth; married, 1823, Francis Henry Davies; published 'Recollections of Society in France and England,' 1872.   [xiv. 147]

DAVIES, MARIANNE (1744–1816?), musician; performed in public on the armonica, an invention of Benjamin Franklin, which became her exclusive property, 1762; travelled in Italy and visited Vienna.   [xiv. 147]

DAVIES, MILES (1662–1715?), bibliographer; admitted into the English college at Rome, 1686; priest, 1688; missioner in Worcestershire and adjacent counties; recanted, 1705; possibly adopted legal profession; wrote and personally hawked his own works, which include 'Athenæ Britannicæ,' a miscellany, 1715–16. [xiv. 148]

DAVIES, OWEN (1752–1830), superintendent of the Welsh Wesleyan Mission; religious writer. [xiv. 149]

DAVIES, RICHARD (d. 1581), bishop of St. David's; educated at New Inn Hall, Oxford; vicar of Burnham, 1550; D.D.; fled to Geneva in Mary's reign; reinstated, and (1560) consecrated bishop of St. Asaph; bishop of St. David's, 1561; member of the council of Wales and adviser of Archbishop Parker and Cecil on Welsh affairs; commissioner for the suppression of Welsh piracy, 1578; founded Carmarthen grammar school in conjunction with Walter Devereux, earl of Essex [q. v.], 1576; informed Cecil that there were no recusants in his diocese, 1577; collaborated with William Salisbury or Salesbury [q. v.] in translating the New Testament into Welsh, 1567; revised part of first edition of 'Bishops' Bible,' 1568.
                   [xiv. 149]

DAVIES, RICHARD (1635–1708), Welsh quaker; originally an independent, but became a professed quaker while working as a hatter in London, 1659; imprisoned, 1660; obtained the release of some of his followers on their promising to appear at Shrewsbury assizes, 1660; friend of the third Lord Herbert of Cherbury; excommunicated, but restored with other quakers to his former privileges by Dr. Lloyd, bishop of St. Asaph, 1680; a religious autobiography appeared, 1710.   [xiv. 152]

DAVIES, RICHARD (d. 1762), physician; fellow of Queens' College, Cambridge; M.A., 1734; M.D., 1748; F.R.S., 1738; practised at Bath and Shrewsbury; author of an essay on the blood, 1760, and a treatise on university training, 1759.   [xiv. 154]

DAVIES, ROBERT (1684–1728), Welsh antiquary and collector of Welsh manuscripts.   [xiv. 154]

DAVIES, ROBERT (1769?–1835), Welsh poet; better known as BARDD NANTGLYN and ROBIN DDU O'R GLYN; occupied the bardic chair for Powis at the Wrexham Eisteddfod, 1820; published a Welsh grammar, 1808.
                   [xiv. 154]

DAVIES, ROBERT (1793–1875), antiquary of York; solicitor, 1814; town clerk of York, 1827–48; F.S.A., 1842; wrote on the antiquities of York; edited York municipal records.   [xiv. 154]

DAVIES, ROWLAND (1649–1721), dean of Cork; M.A. Trinity College, Dublin, 1681; LL.D., 1706; prebendary of Cork, 1671, 1674, and 1679; prebendary of Cloyne, 1673 and 1676; dean of Ross, 1679; left Ireland, 1689; chaplain to one of William III's regiments at the Boyne, 1690; dean of Cork, 1710; wrote 'Journal' (printed 1857) and theological pamphlets.   [xiv. 155]

DAVIES, ROWLAND (1740–1797), composer of sacred music; pupil of Handel; ordained Roman catholic priest at the college of Douay, 1765.   [xiv. 156]

DAVIES, SNEYD (1709–1769), poet; educated at Eton and King's College, Cambridge; archdeacon of Derby, 1755; prebendary of Lichfield; author of Latin poems, imitations of Milton, and verses in the manner of Swift.   [xiv. 156]

DAVIES, THOMAS (1511 ?–1573), bishop of St. Asaph; rector of Llanbedr and vicar of Caerhun, 1535; studied at St. John's and Queens' Colleges, Cambridge; LL.D., 1548; chancellor of Bangor, 1546; received custody of spiritualities of Bangor from Cardinal Pole, 1558; bishop of St. Asaph, 1561–73; issued charge to his clergy, 1561; founded scholarship at Queens' College, Cambridge, and left money for Bangor school. [xiv. 157]

DAVIES or **DAVIS**, SIR THOMAS (1631–1680), lord mayor of London and bookseller; educated at St. Paul's School; sheriff, 1667; knighted, 1667; twice master of the Stationers' Company, 1668 and 1669; lord mayor, 1676–7. [xiv. 158]

DAVIES, THOMAS (1712 ?–1785), bookseller; educated at Edinburgh University, 1728; played Pierre in 'Venice Preserved,' 1746; engaged at Drury Lane Theatre, 1753; said to have been driven from the stage (1762) by a sneer in Churchill's 'Rosciad'; introduced Boswell to Johnson, 1763; published a pirated edition of Johnson's writings, but was forgiven by the author, 1773; wrote a 'Life of Garrick,' 1780, and 'Dramatic Miscellanies,' 1785; republished Elizabethan and Jacobean works. [xiv. 158]

DAVIES, THOMAS (1792–1839), physician; M.D. Paris, 1821; assistant-physician to the London Hospital, 1827; F.R.C.P., 1838; published 'Lectures on the Diseases of the Lungs and Heart,' 1835. [xiv. 159]

DAVIES, THOMAS (1837–1891), mineralogist; son of William Davies (1814–1891) [q. v.]; assistant in mineral department at British Museum, 1858; editor of 'Mineralogical Magazine'; F.G.S., 1870. [Suppl. ii. 118]

DAVIES, THOMAS STEPHENS (1795–1851), mathematician and writer on science; F.R.S. of Edinburgh, 1831; mathematical master, Royal Military Academy, Woolwich, 1834; F.S.A., 1840; developed in his works a new system of spherical geometry. [xiv. 159]

DAVIES, WALTER (1761–1849), Welsh bard and essayist; B.A. All Souls' College, Oxford, 1795; M.A. Trinity College, Cambridge, 1803; rector of Llanwyddelan, Montgomeryshire, of Manafon, 1807–37, and vicar of Llanrhaiadyr-yn-Mochnant, Denbighshire, 1837–49; author of a book on Welsh industries, 1810, 1813, and 1816, and of poems in the ancient bardic style; edited works of Lewis Glyn Cothi, 1807, and Hugh Morris, 1823. [xiv. 160]

DAVIES, WILLIAM (d. 1593), Roman catholic divine; studied in the English college at Rheims; missioner in Wales, 1585; imprisoned at Ludlow, Bewdley, and Beaumaris; formed a small religious community in Beaumaris prison, 1592; executed as a priest, 1593. [xiv. 161]

DAVIES, WILLIAM (fl. 1614), traveller; taken captive when serving in a trading-ship off Tunis by some Florentine galleys and condemned to slavery at Leghorn; released by the influence of Robert Thornton, an English captain, and taken as ship's doctor on a voyage to the Amazon; imprisoned by the Inquisition in Italy; escaped and published 'A True Relation' of his travels, 1614. [xiv. 161]

DAVIES, WILLIAM (d. 1820), bookseller; partner with Thomas Cadell the younger [q. v.]; published fourth to eighth editions of Boswell's 'Life of Johnson.' [xiv. 161]

DAVIES, WILLIAM (1814–1891), palæontologist; obtained post in British Museum, 1843, and worked successively on mineralogy and vertebrate palæontology; retired, 1887; F.G.S., 1877. [Suppl. ii. 118]

DAVIES, WILLIAM EDMUND (1819–1879), bettingman; known as the LEVIATHAN; originated the bettinglist system, 1846; left to the corporation of Brighton 60,000l., of which his widow obtained the enjoyment till her death, 1879; noted for professional honesty and the magnitude of his transactions. [xiv. 162]

DAVIS, CHARLES (d. 1755), bookseller and publisher; one of the first to issue priced catalogues of second-hand books. [xiv. 162]

DAVIS, DAVID (1745–1827), Welsh poet; ordained co-pastor at Llwyn-rhyd-owen, Cardiganshire, 1773; conducted school at Castle Howel, 1783; initiated resolutions of condolence with Dr. Priestley from Cardiganshire nonconformists, 1791; translated Scougall's 'Life of God in

the Soul of Man' into Welsh, 1779, and published 'Telyn Dewi [Harp of David],' 1824. [xiv. 163]

DAVIS, DAVID DANIEL (1777–1841), physician; M.D. Glasgow, 1801; physician to the Sheffield infirmary, 1803–13; L.R.C.P., 1813; attended the Duchess of Kent at the birth of Queen Victoria, 1819; obstetric physician to University College Hospital, 1834–41; chief work, 'The Principles and Practice of Obstetric Medicine,' 1836. [xiv. 164]

DAVIS, EDWARD (fl. 1683–1702), buccaneer and pirate; joined Cook's band [see DAMPIER, WILLIAM], 1683; commissioned 'to fish and hunt in Hispaniola,' in reality to plunder, by the governor of Petit Goave, 1684; defeated by Spaniards in Panama Bay, 1685; burnt Leon, 1685; accepted king's pardon; settled in Virginia, 1688; commissioned as privateer by the governor of Jamaica, 1702; formed alliance with the Indians of the islands of San Blas, under whose guidance he sailed up a river, possibly the Atrato, and sacked a Spanish settlement. [xiv. 164]

DAVIS, EDWARD (1833–1867), subject painter; first exhibited at the Royal Academy in 1854; died in Rome. [xiv. 166]

DAVIS, HENRY EDWARDS (1756–1784), opponent of Gibbon; B.A. Balliol College, Oxford, 1778; published an 'Examination' of Gibbon's account of the origin of Christianity, but was overmatched, 1778; priest, 1780; fellow and tutor of Balliol, 1780. [xiv. 166]

DAVIS, HENRY GEORGE (1830–1857), topographer; left in manuscript 'Memorials of the Hamlet of Knightsbridge' (published, 1859), 'Recollections of Piccadilly,' and an account of Pimlico. [xiv. 166]

DAVIS, JAMES (d. 1755), Welsh satirist; M.A. Jesus College, Oxford, 1729; M.B. 1732; published 'Origines Divisianæ; or the Antiquities of the Devizes,' a satire on the contemporary school of etymologists, 1754. [xiv. 167]

DAVIS, JOHN (1550 ?–1605). [See DAVYS.]

DAVIS, JOHN (d. 1622), navigator; made voyage to the East Indies as pilot and captain; captured by the Dutch at Pularoon, 1617; released, 1618; died at Batavia, 1622; wrote 'A Ruter . . . for Readie Sailings into the East India,' 1618, published in 'Purchas his Pilgrimes.' [xiv. 167]

DAVIS, JOHN BUNNELL (1780–1824), physician; M.D. Montpellier, 1803; imprisoned at Montpellier and Verdun by Bonaparte; released in 1806 by the influence of Corvisart, Bonaparte's physician, to whom he showed his 'Observations on Precipitate Burial'; M.D. Edinburgh, 1808; L.R.C.P., 1810; physician to the troops invalided home from Walcheren. [xiv. 168]

DAVIS, JOHN FORD (1773–1864), physician; M.D. Edinburgh, 1797; L.R.C.P., 1808; physician to the General Hospital, Bath, 1817–34; chief work,' An Inquiry into the Symptoms and Treatment of Carditis,' 1808. [xiv. 168]

DAVIS, SIR JOHN FRANCIS (1795–1890), diplomatist; writer in East India Company's factory at Canton, 1813; accompanied Lord Amherst on embassy to Pekin, 1816; president of factory at Canton, 1832; joint commissioner in China with Lord Napier, 1834; British plenipotentiary and chief superintendent of British trade in China, and governor and commander-in-chief at Hongkong, 1844–8; created baronet, 1845; K.C.B., 1854; D.C.L. Oxford, 1876; published works on China. [Suppl. ii. 118]

DAVIS, JOHN PHILIP (called 'POPE' DAVIS)(1784–1862), painter; called 'Pope' from his picture of the 'Talbot family receiving the Benediction of the Pope,' painted at Rome, 1824; exhibited at the Royal Academy, 1811–43; published a criticism on the Royal Academy and National Gallery, 1858, and 'Thoughts on Great Painters,' 1866. [xiv. 167]

DAVIS, JOSEPH BARNARD (1801–1881), craniologist; surgeon on an Arctic whaler, 1820; M.C.S., 1843; M.D. St. Andrews, 1862; chief work, 'Crania Britannica,' 1865. [xiv. 168]

DAVIS, LOCKYER (1719–1791), bookseller; nephew of Charles Davis [q. v.]; member of the booksellers' club which produced Johnson's 'Lives of the Poets,' 1778; translated La Rochefoucault's 'Maxims and Moral Reflections,' 1749. [xiv. 169]

DAVIS or **DAVIES**, MARY (*fl.* 1663–1669), actress in the company of Sir William D'Avenant [q. v.], 1660 ; performed in various plays by Etherege, Dryden, and Shirley ; mistress of Charles II, 1668 ; frequently mentioned by Pepys as a dancer and court beauty. [xiv. 169]

DAVIS, NATHAN (1812–1882), traveller and excavator ; resided in an old Moorish palace near Tunis ; engaged on behalf of the British Museum in excavations at Carthage and Utica, 1856–8. His works include 'A Voice from North Africa,' 1844, and 'Israel's true Emancipator,' 1852. [xiv. 170]

DAVIS, RICHARD BARRETT (1782–1854), animal painter ; exhibited at the Royal Academy (1802–53), the British Institute, and the Suffolk Street Exhibition ; animal painter to William IV, 1831. [xiv. 171]

DAVIS, THOMAS OSBORNE (1814–1845), poet and politician ; graduated at Trinity College, Dublin, 1836 ; called to the bar, 1838 ; in conjunction with Duffy and Dillon founded the ' Nation ' newspaper, to which he contributed some stirring ballads, 1842 ; developed Young Ireland party out of the extremists who were dissatisfied with O'Connell's constitutional methods, 1845. [xiv. 171]

DAVIS, WILLIAM (1627–1690), highwayman on Wiltshire, Gloucestershire, and Worcestershire roads ; known as the 'Golden Farmer' from his habitually paying with gold coin to avoid identification of his plunder ; lived unsuspected as a farmer till 1690, when he was identified and hanged. [xiv. 172]

DAVIS, WILLIAM (1771–1807), mathematician and editor of the 'Companion to the Gentleman's Diary' ; bookseller and publisher (1803) of Motte's translation of Sir Isaac Newton's 'Principles' ; largely wrote or edited works on fluxions. [xiv. 173]

DAVIS, WILLIAM (1812–1873), landscape and portrait painter ; professor of painting, 'Liverpool Academy ; exhibited landscapes at the Royal Academy, 1851–72. [xiv. 173]

DAVISON. [See also DAVIDSON.]

DAVISON, ALEXANDER (1750–1829), government contractor ; member of legislative council of Quebec, 1784 ; friend of Nelson ; prize-agent of Lord Nelson after battle of the Nile, 1798 ; clothing contractor to the army and agent for the purchase of barrack supplies, 1795 ; fined and imprisoned for fraudulently accepting government commission on the sale of private stock, 1808. [xiv. 174]

DAVISON, EDWARD (1576 ?–1624 ?). [See DAWSON.]

DAVISON, EDWARD (1789–1863), divine ; M.A. University College, Oxford, 1819 ; rector of Harlington, 1822, and of St. Nicholas, Durham, 1825–56 ; published 'Tentamen Theologicum' (manual on preaching), 1850. [xiv. 175]

DAVISON, FRANCIS (*fl.* 1602), poet ; son of William Davison (1541?–1608) [q. v.] ; member of Gray's Inn, 1593 ; travelled in Italy, 1595 ; contributed some of its best poems to 'A Poetical Rapsody,' 1602 ; left in manuscript metrical translations from the Psalms, 'Tabula Analytica Poetica,' and some historical pamphlets. [xiv. 175]

DAVISON, JAMES WILLIAM (1813–1885), journalist ; studied at the Royal Academy of Music ; composed songs ; wrote monograph on Chopin, 1849 ; musical critic to the 'Times,' 1846–85 ; trained popular taste to appreciate Berlioz and Mendelssohn. [xiv. 176]

DAVISON, JEREMIAH (1695 ?–1750 ?), portrait-painter. Among his sitters were Frederick, prince of Wales, 1730, and Admiral Byng. [xiv. 177]

DAVISON, JOHN (1777–1834), theological writer ; educated at Durham Cathedral school and Christ Church, Oxford ; Craven scholar, 1796 ; fellow of Oriel, 1800 ; rector of Washington, Durham, 1818, of Upton-upon-Severn, 1826 ; prebendary of St. Paul's and (1826) of Worcester. His most important works are the 'Discourses on Prophecy,' emphasising the moral aspect of prophetic revelations, and 'An Inquiry into the Origin and Intent of Primitive Sacrifice,' 1825. [xiv. 177]

DAVISON, MARIA REBECCA (1780 ?–1858), actress ; played children's parts in Dublin, Liverpool, and Newcastle ; played Lady Teazle and Rosalind at Drury Lane, 1804 ; 'created' Juliana in the 'Honeymoon,' 1805 ; last appeared at Drury Lane in 1829 ; styled by Leigh Hunt the best *lady* of the comic stage. [xiv. 178]

DAVISON, WALTER (1581–1608 ?), poet ; son of William Davison (1541 ?–1608) [q. v.] ; educated at King's College, Cambridge ; served in Low Countries, *c.* 1602 ; author of poems in 'Poetical Rapsody,' 1602. [xiv. 179]

DAVISON, WILLIAM (1541 ?–1608), secretary of Queen Elizabeth ; resident agent at Antwerp, 1577 ; obtained for the States-General a loan of 50,000*l.* from the English government, 1579 ; sent to Scotland to prevent a proposed French alliance, 1583 ; commander of Flushing, 1585 ; returned to England to explain the Earl of Leicester's acceptance of the governorship of the Low Countries without instructions from home, 1586 ; privy councillor and secretary to Queen Elizabeth, 1586 ; member of the commission for the trial of Mary Queen of Scots, 1586 ; fined and imprisoned in the Tower, 1587–9, for ' misprision and contempt,' being unfairly charged by the queen with undue precipitation in securing her signature to the death-warrant of Mary Queen of Scots, ; subsequently custos brevium in the king's bench and clerk of the treasury, by a reversion dating from 1579. [xiv. 179]

DAVISON or **DAVIDSON**, WILLIAM (*fl.* 1635–1660), chemist and physician ; physician to the king of France ; keeper of the Royal Botanic Garden of Paris, 1648–50 ; senior surgeon to the king of Poland, 1650 ; follower of Paracelsus in ' Philosophia Pyrotechnica ' complete edition, 1641 ; published prolegomena on the philosophy of Severinus, 1660. [xiv. 182]

DAVY, ADAM (*fl.* 1308 ?), fanatical rhymer ; formerly supposed to be the author of 'Alisaunder' and the entire Bodleian MS. Laud, 622 ; claimed to predict the destiny of King Edward (III ?) in his 'Dreams.' [xiv. 183]

DAVY, CHARLES (1722–1797), miscellaneous writer ; M.A. Caius College, Cambridge, 1748 ; held incumbencies in Norfolk and Suffolk, 1764–97 ; published 'Conjectural Observations on the Origin and Progress of Alphabetical Writing,' 1772, and 'Letters,' in which was embodied a translation of 'Euclid's Section of the Canon, and Treatise on Harmonic,' 1787. [xiv. 184]

DAVY, DAVID ELISHA (1769–1851), Suffolk antiquary and collector ; B.A. Pembroke Hall, Cambridge, 1790 ; receiver-general for Suffolk ; left manuscripts on the genealogical history and heraldry of Suffolk families, now in British Museum. [xiv. 184]

DAVY, EDMUND (1785–1857), professor of chemistry ; operator and assistant in the laboratory of the Royal Institution, 1804–13 ; professor and secretary of the Royal Cork Institution, 1813 ; professor of chemistry of the Royal Dublin Society, 1826 ; F.R.S. and F.C.S. ; author of papers on agricultural chemistry, electro-chemistry, and metallurgy. [xiv. 185]

DAVY, EDWARD (1806–1885), scientific investigator ; M.R.C.S., 1829 ; invented 'Davy's diamond cement,' 1835 ; invented needle telegraph, 1837 ; sailed, as medical superintendent of an emigrant ship, to Australia, 1839 ; editor of the 'Adelaide Examiner,' 1843–5 ; in charge of the government assay office at Adelaide, 1852, and at Melbourne, 1853–4 ; surgeon at Malmesbury, Victoria, where he died ; published 'An Experimental Guide to Chemistry,' 1836. [xiv. 185]

DAVY, HENRY (*fl.* 1829), architect and landscape-painter ; executed etchings of the country seats and antiquities of Suffolk, 1818 and 1827. [xiv. 187]

DAVY, SIR HUMPHRY (1778–1829), natural philosopher ; instructed in the rudiments of science by a saddler of Penzance ; educated at Penzance grammar school and at Truro ; wrote 'The Sons of Genius,' a poem, 1795 ; introduced to Dr. Edwards, the chemist, who directed his attention to some phenomena of what was afterwards known as galvanic action ; superintendent of the laboratory of the 'Pneumatic Institution' at Bristol, 1798–9 ; visited London, 1799 ; published the first volume of the 'West-Country Collections' and 'Researches, Chemical and Philosophical, chiefly concerning Nitrous Oxide and its Respiration,' 1799 ; nearly died in attempt to breathe carburetted hydrogen gas, 1800 ; lectured on galvanism and 'pneumatic chemistry' at the Royal Institution, where he was appointed director of chemical laboratory, 1801 ; chemistry professor, Royal Institution, 1802 ; F.R.S., 1803 ; Copley medallist of the Royal

Society, 1805 ; demonstrated the elementary existence of potassium, sodium, and chlorine by the agency of the galvanic battery, 1807 ; discovered the actual constitution of oxymuriatic acid, 1807 ; gained the Napoleon prize from the Institute of France for his discoveries ; honorary LL.D. Dublin, 1811 ; knighted, 1812 ; appointed Faraday his assistant in the laboratory of the Royal Institution, 1812 ; experimented in Italy on ancient pigments and combustion of diamond, 1812–13 ; invented safety-lamp, 1815 ; created baronet, 1818 ; P.R.S., 1820 ; invented an ultimately abandoned system of protectors for preserving the copper sheathing of the bottoms of ships, 1823 ; died, worn out, at Geneva, 1829.   [xiv. 187]

DAVY, JANE, LADY (1780–1855), wife of Sir Humphry Davy [q. v.] after the death of her first husband, Sir Shuckburgh Ashby Apreece, in 1807 ; née Kerr ; a prominent figure in the society of both Rome and London ; commended by Madame de Staël.   [xiv. 193]

DAVY, JOHN (1763–1824), musical composer ; articled to William Jackson (1730–1803) [q. v.], organist of Exeter Cathedral ; organist at Exeter ; violinist in the orchestra of Covent Garden Theatre, 1800 ; set to music various dramatic pieces ; composed overture for Shakespeare's 'Tempest' ; popular song-writer in his day. [xiv. 194]

DAVY, JOHN (1790–1868), physiologist and anatomist ; brother of Sir Humphry Davy [q. v.] ; M.D. Edinburgh, 1814 ; championed his brother's discovery of the constitution of muriatic acid ; army surgeon and inspector-general of army hospitals ; F.R.S., 1834 ; published 'An Account of the Interior of Ceylon,' 1821, 'Discourses on Agriculture,' 1849, 'Physiological Researches,' 1863, and other works of science and travel.   [xiv. 195]

DAVY, MARTIN (1763–1839), physician and master of Caius College, Cambridge ; M.D. Caius College, Cambridge, 1797 ; master of Caius, 1803–39 ; D.D., 1811 ; prebendary of Chichester ; vice-chancellor, 1803 and 1827 ; adherent of the Brunonian system of medicine.
     [xiv. 196]

DAVY, ROBERT (d. 1793), portrait-painter ; studied at Rome ; under drawing-master at the Royal Military Academy, Woolwich ; exhibited at the Free Society of Artists, 1762–8, and at the Royal Academy, 1771–82.
     [xiv. 196]

DAVY, WILLIAM (d. 1780), lawyer ; entered the Middle Temple, 1741 ; serjeant-at-law, 1754 ; king's serjeant, 1762 ; defended the runaway slave Sommersett against the claims of the slave-owner, 1772 ; famous as a cross-examiner and humorist.   [xiv. 197]

DAVY, WILLIAM (1743–1826), divine ; B.A. Balliol College, Oxford, 1766 ; vicar of Winkleigh, Devonshire, 1825–6 ; author of a 'System of Divinity on the Being, Nature, and Attributes of God,' which he printed himself, 1795–1807 ; his work highly praised after his death.
     [xiv. 198]

DAVYDD. [See also DAVID.]

DAVYDD I (d. 1203), king of North Wales ; son of Owain Gwynedd [q. v.] ; fought vigorously against Henry II's troops in Wales, 1157 ; slew his rival, Howel, and became lord of Gwynedd, 1170 ; allied himself with Henry II, in the hope of getting his help against rival chieftains, 1176 ; entertained Archbishop Baldwin at Rhuddlan Castle, 1188 ; overpowered and dethroned by Llewelyn, son of Iorwerth, 1194.   [xiv. 199]

DAVYDD II (1208 ?–1246), prince of North Wales ; son of Llewelyn ab Iorwerth ; did homage to Henry III, 1229 ; married to Isabella, the daughter of William de Braose [q. v.], 1230 ; defeated Gruffudd, his half-brother and rival for the succession, 1238 ; recognised as prince and knighted by Henry III, 1240 ; became alienated from him by refusing, in 1241, to liberate Gruffudd, whom he had treacherously imprisoned ; capitulated to an invading force led by King Henry in person, 1241 ; sent Welsh troops for the French war, 1242 ; invaded Herefordshire, 1244 ; attempted, but ultimately failed, to enlist the sympathies of the pope against Henry III, 1245 ; carried on a border warfare till his death.   [xiv. 200]

DAVYDD III (d. 1283), last native prince of North Wales ; son of Gruffudd ; joined his brother Llewelyn in his opposition to the designs of the king of England, 1258 ; defeated the marcher lords of south-west Wales, 1258 ; accompanied Edward I in his expedition against

Llewelyn, 1277 ; arranged a treaty between Edward and Llewelyn, for which he was rewarded, though his lands were handed over to his brother ; driven to revolt by Edward's excessive demands and the contempt he showed for the Welsh laws, 1282 ; excommunicated by Archbishop Peckham for refusing to go on a crusade, 1282 ; betrayed by his own countrymen, 1283 ; executed and gibbeted, 1283.   [xiv. 202]

DAVYS, GEORGE (1780–1864), bishop of Peterborough ; educated at Christ's College, Cambridge ; fellow, 1806 ; M.A., 1806 ; tutor to the Princess Victoria, 1827 ; rector of Allhallows-on-the-Wall, London, 1829–39 ; dean of Chester and D.D., 1831–9 ; bishop of Peterborough, 1839–1864 ; compiled educational works and wrote on the English liturgy.   [xiv. 205]

DAVYS, JOHN (1550 ?–1605), navigator ; in company with his friend, Adrian Gilbert, and Dr. John Dee [q. v.], explained the possibility of the north-west passage to Walsingham, 1583 ; discovered Davys Strait, and explored Baffin's Bay, 1587 ; commanded the squadron which captured the Uggera Salvagnia, 1590 ; accompanied Thomas Cavendish [q. v.] in the south seas on his second voyage, for the failure of which he was unjustly blamed, 1591–3 ; published 'Seaman's Secrets,' 1594, and the 'World's Hydrographical Description,' maintaining existence of north-west passage, 1595 ; embarked, at the suggestion of the Earl of Essex, as pilot of the Leeuw, a Dutch East Indiaman, 1598 ; pilot of the Tiger, 1604 ; killed in an affray with Japanese pirates off Singapore, 1605.   [xiv. 206]

DAVYS, MARY (fl. 1756), dramatist and novelist ; corresponded with Dean Swift ; author of society comedies and tales.   [xiv. 209]

DAWE, GEORGE (1781–1829), portrait-painter and mezzotint engraver ; gold medallist of the Royal Academy for his picture of 'Achilles rejecting the Consolations of Thetis,' 1803 ; R.A., 1814 ; commissioned by Alexander of Russia to paint a series of portraits of the higher Russian officers who had fought against Napoleon, 1819 ; painted portraits of the king of Prussia and the Duke of Cumberland at Berlin, 1828.   [xiv. 209]

DAWE, HENRY EDWARD (1790–1848), painter and mezzotint engraver ; son of Philip Dawe [q. v.] ; member of the Society of British Artists, 1830 ; exhibited at Suffolk Street, 1824–45, the Royal Academy, and the British Institution ; employed by Turner upon the 'Liber Studiorum.'   [xiv. 210]

DAWE, PHILIP (fl. 1780), mezzotint engraver ; friend of George Morland [q. v.] ; contributed to the first exhibition of the Royal Academy, 1763.   [xiv. 211]

DAWES, LANCELOT (1580–1654), divine ; M.A. and fellow of Queen's College, Oxford, 1605 ; incumbent of Ashby, Westmoreland, a charge of simony having been invalidated, 1618–54 ; prebendary of Carlisle ; D.D. St. Andrews, c. 1618.   [xiv. 211]

DAWES, MANASSEH (d. 1829), miscellaneous writer ; author of numerous publications, including an 'Essay on Intellectual Liberty,' 1780, and an 'Epitome of the Law of Landed Property,' 1818.   [xiv. 212]

DAWES, RICHARD (1708–1766), Greek scholar and schoolmaster ; fellow of Emmanuel College, Cambridge, 1731 ; M.A., 1733 ; master of Newcastle grammar school and St. Mary's Hospital, Newcastle, 1738 ; resigned school in consequence of differences with the governors, 1749 ; published 'Miscellanea Critica,' containing his canons of Greek moods and tenses, 1745 ; severely criticised Bentley.   [xiv. 212]

DAWES, RICHARD (1793–1867), dean of Hereford ; fourth wrangler, Trinity College, Cambridge, 1817 ; M.A., 1820 ; mathematical tutor and bursar of Downing College, 1818 ; rector of King's Somborne, Hampshire, 1836–1850 ; founded a model lower-class school in his parish, 1842 ; D.D. ; dean of Hereford, 1850 ; author of some pamphlets on the education of the poorer classes.
     [xiv. 213]

DAWES or **DAW,** SOPHIA, BARONNE DE FEUCHÈRES (1790–1840), adventuress ; daughter of a fisherman at St. Helen's, Isle of Wight ; became, in London in 1811, mistress of the Duke of Bourbon, son of the Prince de Condé ; married at Paris by the Duke of Bourbon to Baron Adrien Victor de Feuchères, 1818 ; forbidden the French court by Louis XVIII on being separated from her husband for adultery, 1822; readmitted to the French court by Charles X, 1830; reputed to be concerned in the apparent suicide of the Duke of Bourbon, 1830, and in the sudden death of her nephew, James Dawes. [xiv. 214]

DAWES, Sir WILLIAM, third baronet (1671–1724), archbishop of York; entered Merchant Taylors' School, 1680; wrote a devotional work entitled 'The Duties of the Closet,' c. 1691; fellow of St. John's College, Oxford; master of St. Catharine's Hall, Cambridge, 1696; D.D., 1696; chaplain in ordinary to William III, 1696; prebendary of Worcester, 1698; bishop of Chester, 1708; archbishop of York, 1713; edited the works of Blackall, bishop of Exeter, 1723, and wrote religious poems and treatises. [xiv. 215]

DAWES, WILLIAM RUTTER (1799–1868), astronomer; educated at Charterhouse; studied medicine at St. Bartholomew's Hospital and practised at Haddenham, Buckinghamshire; contributed to the Royal Astronomical Society's 'Memoirs,' 'Micrometrical Measurements of 121 Double Stars, taken at Ormskirk during the years 1830, 1831, 1832, and 1833'; M.R.A.S., 1830; in charge of the observatory at South Villa, Regent's Park, 1839–44; gold medallist of the Astronomical Society, 1855; controverted Nasmyth's supposed discovery of solar 'willow-leaves'; invented the 'wedge photometer,' exhibited 1865; established the non-atmospheric character of the redness of Mars, 1865; F.R.S., 1865. [xiv. 217]

DAWKINS, JAMES (1722–1757), archæologist and Jacobite; born in Jamaica; educated at St. John's College, Oxford; D.C.L., 1749; travelled on continent; assisted James Stuart (1713–1788) [q. v.] and Nicholas Revett [q. v.] in taking measurements of Greek architecture at Athens; visited with Robert Wood [q. v.] ruins of Palmyra and Baalbec, 1751; engaged in Jacobite intrigues in Paris, 1751–4; sent by George Keith, tenth earl Marischal [q. v.], as envoy to Frederick the Great; returned to England, 1754; M.P. for Hindon Borough, Wiltshire, 1754–7. [Suppl. ii. 119]

DAWKS, ICHABOD (1661–1730), printer; son of Thomas Dawks the younger [q. v.]; started 'in script' 'Dawks's News-Letter,' 1696; mentioned in the 'Tatler,' 1709, 1710, and in the 'Spectator,' 1712. [xiv. 219]

DAWKS, THOMAS, the elder (d. 1670), printer. [xiv. 219]

DAWKS, THOMAS, the younger (b. 1636), printer; son of Thomas Dawks the elder [q. v.]; entered Merchant Taylors' School, 1649; employed as compositor on Walton's Polyglott bible, 1653–7; master-printer at Blackfriars, 1674. [xiv. 219]

DAWSON, ABRAHAM (1713 ?–1789), biblical scholar; M.A.; rector of Ringsfield, Suffolk, 1754–89; published various translations, with notes, of the earlier chapters of Genesis. [xiv. 219]

DAWSON, AMBROSE (1707–1794), physician; M.D. Christ's College, Cambridge, 1735; F.R.C.P., 1737; Harveian orator, 1744; physician to St. George's Hospital, 1745–60; best known by his 'Thoughts on the Hydrocephalus Internus,' 1778. [xiv. 220]

DAWSON, BENJAMIN (1729–1814), divine and philologist; brother of Abraham Dawson [q. v.]; M.A. Glasgow, 1753; presbyterian minister, 1754–60; rector of Burgh, Suffolk, 1760–1814; LL.D., 1763; Lady Moyer's lecturer, 1764; wrote 'The Necessitarian,' a defence of necessitarianism, 1783; published first part of a 'Philological and Synonymical Dictionary of the English Language,' 1806. [xiv. 220]

DAWSON or DAVISON, EDWARD (1576 ?–1624 ?), jesuit; studied in Spain and was sent on the English mission; imprisoned, and in 1606 exiled; became a jesuit at Louvain, 1606 or 1609; twice missioner in England; died of the plague at Brussels; translated 'Lives of many Saints,' from the Spanish, 1615. [xiv. 221]

DAWSON, GEORGE (1637–1700), jurist; M.A. St. John's College, Cambridge, 1662; vicar of Sunninghill; wrote 'Origo Legum,' in seven books, 1694. [xiv. 221]

DAWSON, GEORGE (1821–1876), preacher, lecturer and politician; entered Marischal College, Aberdeen, 1837, and Glasgow University, 1838; M.A. Glasgow; baptist pastor, Mount Zion, Birmingham, 1844–5; pastor of the 'Church of the Saviour,' Birmingham, a new insti-

tution on broad and undenominational lines, 1847–76; friend of Carlyle and Emerson, whose teachings he popularised in his lectures and writings; helped to found the Shakespeare Memorial Library at Birmingham; sympathised with the patriots and exiles of Poland. [xiv. 221]

DAWSON, HENRY (1811–1878), landscape-painter; originally employed in the lace-making industry, for which he invented a machine; competed for the decoration of the Houses of Parliament with a picture of Charles I raising his standard at Nottingham, 1847; praised as a colourist by Ruskin; exhibited at the British Institution and the Royal Academy; best known by his later pictures in the style of Turner, such as 'Greenwich' (1874), 'Wooden Walls,' 'Houses of Parliament,' and 'Durham.' [xiv. 223]

DAWSON, JAMES (1717 ?–1746), Jacobite; pensioner, St. John's College, Cambridge, 1737; left the university and joined the Young Pretender, 1745; captain, 1745; executed, his betrothed dying of grief the same day, 1746. [xiv. 225]

DAWSON, JOHN (1734–1820), surgeon and mathematician; studied medicine at Edinburgh; surgeon and teacher of mathematics at Sedbergh, eight senior wranglers being among his pupils, 1781–94; attacked Priestley's doctrine of philosophical necessity, 1781; controverted William Emerson's Newtonian analysis; published, 1768, 'Four Propositions' against Stewart's 'Sun's Distance.' [xiv. 225]

DAWSON, Sir JOHN WILLIAM (1820–1899), geologist; born at Pictou, Nova Scotia; educated at Edinburgh University; made geological survey of Nova Scotia; superintendent of education for common schools in Nova Scotia, 1850; professor of geology and principal at McGill College and University, Montreal, 1855–93; F.G.S., 1854; F.R.S., 1862; first president of Royal Society of Canada; hon. LL.D. McGill University, 1857, and Edinburgh, 1884; D.C.L. Bishop's College, Quebec, 1881; C.M.G., 1882; knighted, 1884; Emeritus principal, professor, and honorary curator of Redpath Museum, 1893; published numerous works and papers on subjects connected with geology and natural history. [Suppl. ii. 120]

DAWSON, MATTHEW (1820–1898), trainer of race-horses; presided over James Merry's stable at Russley, 1860–6; started as public trainer at Newmarket, 1866; had charge of Lord Falmouth's stud, 1869–84. He trained winners for six Derbies, seven St. Legers, and four Gold Cups at Ascot. [Suppl. ii. 122]

DAWSON, NANCY (1730 ?–1767), dancer; figure-dancer at Sadler's Wells; joined Covent Garden Theatre and made her reputation by dancing the hornpipe in the 'Beggar's Opera,' 1759, the tune becoming popular. [xiv. 227]

DAWSON, ROBERT (1776–1860), topographical artist; assistant-draughtsman on the ordnance survey of Great Britain, 1794; first-class draughtsman of the royal military surveyors, 1802; taught at the Royal Military College and, 1810, at the East India Company's military seminary, Addiscombe; excelled in the artistic employment of oblique light. [xiv. 228]

DAWSON, ROBERT KEARSLEY (1798–1861), lieutenant-colonel royal engineers; son of Robert Dawson [q. v.]; employed on the Scotch and Irish surveys; head surveyor of the commons enclosure and copyhold commission; C.B., civil division. [xiv. 228]

DAWSON, THOMAS (1725 ?–1782), physician; brother of Abraham Dawson [q. v.]; M.D. Glasgow, 1753; physician to the Middlesex Hospital, 1759–61; L.R.C.P., 1762; physician to the London Hospital, 1764–1770. [xiv. 228]

DAWSON, WILLIAM (1773–1841), Wesleyan; lay and (from 1837) itinerant preacher. [xiv. 229]

DAY, ALEXANDER (1773–1841), painter and art dealer; lived at Rome, 1794, and was detained by the French during their war with Naples; painted medallions; imported into England many valuable pictures. [xiv. 229]

DAY, ALFRED (1810–1849), musical theorist; took a medical degree at Heidelberg, and practised homœopathy in London; published 'A Treatise on Harmony,' 1845. [xiv. 230]

DAY, ANGELL (*fl.* 1586), miscellaneous writer; chief works, 'The English Secretorie' (letter-writing manual), 1586, and 'Daphnis and Chloe' (translated from Longus), 1587. [xiv. 230]

DAY, DANIEL (1683–1767), founder of Fairlop fair, a popular festival which arose out of his custom of yearly feasting his tenants on his estate near Fairlop Oak in Hainault forest. [xiv. 230]

DAY, FRANCIS (*d.* 1642), founder of Madras; founded a factory at Armaguam, 1625; built Fort St. George on a site less exposed to Dutch attacks, 1639; died at Madras. [xiv. 231]

DAY, FRANCIS (1829–1889), ichthyologist; educated at Shrewsbury; studied medicine at St. George's Hospital, London; M.R.C.S., 1851; entered Madras medical service, 1852; served in second Burmese war; inspector-general of fisheries in India; retired as deputy surgeon-general, 1876; C.I.E., 1885; honorary LL.D. Edinburgh, 1889; F.Z.S., 1864; F.L.S., 1857; published numerous writings relating to ichthyology. Collections formed by him are in the British Museum (natural history) and at Cambridge. [Suppl. ii. 122]

DAY, GEORGE (1501?–1556), bishop of Chichester; master of St. John's College, Cambridge, 1537; provost of King's College, 1538–*c.* 1547; public orator; member of commission which drew up the 'Necessary Doctrine and Erudition of a Christian Man,' 1540; bishop of Chichester, 1543; assisted in drawing up first English prayer-book, 1548, but voted against its use, 1549; deprived of his bishopric for contempt by the council, 1551, and imprisoned in the Tower; released at Mary's accession, 1553, and restored to bishopric of Chichester. [xiv. 231]

DAY, GEORGE EDWARD (1815–1872), physician; M.A. Pembroke College, Cambridge, 1840; F.R.C.P., 1847; Chandos professor of anatomy and medicine at St. Andrews, 1849–63; M.D. Giessen, 1849; translated Russian and German works on pathological anatomy, and published 'Chemistry in its Relations to Physiology and Medicine,' 1860. [xiv. 232]

DAY, JAMES (*fl.* 1637), verse-writer; published 'A New Spring of Divine Poetrie,' 1637. [xiv. 233]

DAY, **DAYE**, or **DAIE**, JOHN (1522–1584), printer; imprisoned for his protestant ardour by Queen Mary; printed first church-music book in English, 1560; produced first English edition of Foxe's 'Martyrs,' 1563; printed earliest collection of psalm-tunes published in England, 1563; first to cast Anglo-Saxon type in England, using it for an edition of Ælfric's 'Homily,' 1567; Asser's 'Life of Alfred,' 1574, and other works; printer of A B C and catechisms by a monopoly which led to litigation in 1582; master of the Stationers' Company, 1580; introduced a new italic, a Roman, and a Greek type. [xiv. 233]

DAY, JOHN (*fl.* 1606), dramatist; at Caius College, Cambridge, 1592–3; referred to with dislike by Ben Jonson, 1619. Among his extant plays are 'The Ile of Gvls,' 1606, 'Law-Trickes' (a play in many points resembling 'Pericles'), 1608, and 'Humour out of Breath' (rhyming comedy), 1608. His best piece is 'The Parliament of Bees,' a moral allegory, 1607 (?). Works first collected by Mr. A. H. Bullen in 1881. [xiv. 235]

DAY, JOHN (1566–1628), divine; son of John Day (1522–1584) [q. v.]; commoner of St. Alban Hall, Oxford, 1582; fellow of Oriel College, 1588; M.A. and B.D.; vicar of St. Mary's, Oxford, 1609–22; chief works, 'Commentarii in octo libros Aristotelis de Auscultatione Physica,' 1589, and 'Day's Dyall,' 1614. [xiv. 237]

DAY, MATTHEW (*d.* 1663), classical scholar; M.A. King's College, Cambridge, 1637; rector of Everdon, Northamptonshire; ejected, 1644; master of the free school, Lewisham; prebendary of St. Paul's, 1660; D.D. Cambridge, 1661; published 'Excerpta in sex priores Homeri Iliados libros,' 1652. [xiv. 238]

DAY, **DAYE**, or **D'AJE**, RICHARD (1552–1607?), printer, translator, and divine; son of John Day (1522–1584) [q. v.]; educated at Eton; fellow of King's College, Cambridge, 1574; B.A., 1575; vicar of Reigate, 1583–4; printed 'The First Part of the Key of Philosophie, by Paracelsus,' 1580; edited Gilby's translation of 'The Testamentes of the Twelve Patriarches,' 1581. [xiv. 238]

DAY, STEPHEN (1610?–1668). [See DAYE.]

DAY, THOMAS (1748–1789), author of 'Sandford and Merton'; educated at Charterhouse and Corpus Christi College, Oxford; barrister of the Middle Temple, 1775; formed friendship with Richard Lovell Edgeworth [q. v.]; educated two orphan girls, intending to marry one and apprentice the other, but subsequently (1778) married a Miss Esther Milnes; took a farm at Anningsley, Surrey, and did something to work out his schemes of moral and social reform among the poor, 1781; published social and philanthropic pamphlets and the 'History of Sandford and Merton,' vol. i. 1783, vol. ii. 1787, and vol. iii. 1789, in which he attempted to reconcile Rousseau's naturalism with a sounder morality. [xiv. 239]

DAY, WILLIAM (1529–1596), bishop of Winchester; brother of George Day [q. v.], bishop of Chichester; educated at Eton and King's College, Cambridge; fellow, 1548; M.A., 1553; prebendary of York, 1560; elected provost of Eton, 1561; B.D., 1562; destroyed all traces of catholicism in Eton College chapel; offended De Foix, the French ambassador, when staying at Eton, by requiring his submission to discipline and causing his subsequent removal, 1563; dean of Chapel Royal, 1572; dean of Windsor, 1572; registrar of the order of the Garter, 1584; chancellor of St. Paul's Cathedral, 1587; bishop of Winchester, 1595; published sermons. [xiv. 241]

DAY, WILLIAM (*fl.* 1666), divine; brother of Matthew Day [q. v.]; educated at Eton and King's College, Cambridge; fellow of King's; M.A., 1632; M.A. Oxford, 1635; vicar of Mapledurham, Oxfordshire, 1637; divinity reader in St. George's Chapel, *c.* 1660; published scripture commentaries. [xiv. 244]

DAYE, STEPHEN (1610?–1668), first printer in New England; employed by President Dunster of Harvard, 1639–49; printed in America the 'Freeman's Oath' and a complete metrical translation of the Psalms, known as the Bay Psalm Book, 1640. [xiv. 244]

DAYES, EDWARD (1763–1804), water-colour painter and engraver in mezzotint; exhibited miniatures, landscapes, and classic and scriptural subjects, at the Royal Academy, 1786–1804, and the Society of Artists; draughtsman to the Duke of York; committed suicide, 1804. [xiv. 245]

DAYROLLES, SOLOMON (*d.* 1786), diplomatist; master of the revels to George II, 1744; secretary to Lord Chesterfield, his godfather, when ambassador to The Hague for the second time, 1745; gentleman usher of the black rod to Chesterfield, when lord-lieutenant of Ireland, 1745; resident at the Hague, 1747–51, at Brussels, 1751–7; assisted Maty in writing his 'Life of Chesterfield.' [xiv. 245]

DEACON, JAMES (*d.* 1750), miniature-painter. [xiv. 246]

DEACON, THOMAS (1697–1753), physician and nonjuring bishop; agent in the Jacobite rising of 1715; physician at Manchester, 1720 (?); was consecrated a nonjuring bishop, 1733; supported Prince Charles Edward, 1745; founded 'The True British Catholic Church' at Manchester; translator of Tillemont and author of some liturgical and theological works. [xiv. 246]

DEACON, WILLIAM FREDERICK (1799–1845), journalist and author; educated at St. Catharine Hall, Cambridge; editor of 'The Déjeuné,' 1820; critic to the 'Sun'; published 'The Innkeeper's Album,' 1823, 'Warreniana' (burlesque), 1824, and the 'Exile of Erin,' a tale, 1835. [xiv. 248]

DEALTRY, THOMAS (1796–1861), third bishop of Madras; LL.B. St. Catharine Hall, Cambridge, 1829; D.D.; appointed to a chaplaincy in Bengal by the influence of Charles Simeon, 1829; archdeacon of Calcutta, 1835–48; bishop of Madras, 1849–61. [xiv. 249]

DEALTRY, WILLIAM (1775–1847), archdeacon of Surrey; educated at St. Catharine Hall and Trinity College, Cambridge; fellow of Trinity, 1798–1814; M.A., 1799; D.D., 1829; professor of mathematics at the East India College, Haileybury; chancellor of the diocese of Winchester, 1830; archdeacon of Surrey, 1845; published 'The Principles of Fluxions,' 1810. [xiv. 250]

DEAN, RICHARD (1727?–1778), divine and author; wrote 'An Essay on the Future Life of Brutes,' 1767. [xiv. 250]

DEAN, THOMAS (18th cent.), musician ; organist at Warwick and Coventry ; Mus. Doc. Oxford, 1731 ; wrote music for Oldmixon's 'Governor of Cyprus,' 1703. [xiv. 250]

DEAN, WILLIAM (*d.* 1588), Roman catholic divine ; educated in the English college, Rheims ; sent on the English mission, 1582 ; executed, 1588. [xiv. 250]

DEANE, SIR ANTHONY (1638 ?–1721), shipbuilder ; friend of Pepys ; master shipwright at Harwich, 1664 ; mayor of Harwich, 1676 and 1682 ; commissioner of the navy, 1675 ; knighted ; built yachts for Louis XIV, 1675 ; M.P., New Shoreham, 1678, Harwich, 1679 and 1685 ; inventor of ' Punchinello' cannon ; F.R.S., 1681. [xiv. 251]

DEANE, HENRY (*d.* 1503), archbishop of Canterbury ; councillor of Henry VII ; chancellor of Ireland, 1494 ; elected bishop of Bangor, 1494 ; deputy-governor of Ireland, 1496 ; deputy and justiciary, 1496 ; built a wall to protect the English pale, 1496 ; retired, 1496 ; rebuilt Bangor Cathedral, 1498, and vindicated its right to the Skerries fisheries ; keeper of the great seal, 1500–2 ; archbishop of Canterbury, 1501 ; chief commissioner for negotiating the marriage of Margaret, daughter of Henry VII, with James IV of Scotland, 1502. [xiv. 252]

DEANE, RICHARD (1610–1653), admiral and general at sea ; commanded parliament artillery in Cornwall, 1644, and at Naseby, 1645 ; commanded right wing at Preston, 1648 ; assisted in framing the 'Remonstrance of the Army,' 1648 ; showed great energy as commissioner for the trial of Charles I, 1649 ; general at sea, in charge of the coast from Portsmouth to Milford Haven, 1649 ; fought as major-general at Worcester, 1651 ; commander-in-chief of the army in Scotland, his chief achievement being the pacification of the highlands, by an agreement with the Marquis of Argyll, 1652 ; imprisoned Ogilvie, governor of Dunnottar Castle, and Grainger, a minister, on the charge of having made away with the Scotch regalia, 1652 ; associated with Blake in the battle off Portland, 1653 ; paid great attention to the details of the administration of the fleet ; killed in action off Solebay, 1653. [xiv. 254]

DEANE, THOMAS (1651–1735), Roman catholic controversialist ; M.A. University College, Oxford, 1676 ; tutor and fellow, 1684–9 ; declared himself a Romanist, 1685 ; pilloried at Charing Cross, 1691 ; published a work to prove that Luther was neither a catholic nor a protestant, 1688. [xiv. 258]

DEANE, SIR THOMAS (1792–1871), builder and architect in Cork ; mayor of Cork, 1830 ; knighted, 1830 ; designed many of the public buildings in Cork, the Venetian addition to Trinity College, Dublin, and the museum at Oxford ; president of the Institute of Irish Architects. [xiv. 259]

DEANE, SIR THOMAS NEWENHAM (1828–1899), architect ; son of Sir Thomas Deane (1792–1871) [q. v.] ; educated at Rugby and Trinity College, Dublin ; B.A., 1849 ; entered his father's firm, 1850 ; his most important works, the Science and Art Museum and the National Library of Ireland, Dublin, 1885–90 ; knighted, 1890 ; inspector of national and ancient monuments. His other works include the Clarendon Laboratory and Examination Schools and the Physiological Laboratory and Anthropological Museum, Oxford. [Suppl. ii. 123]

DEANE, WILLIAM JOHN (1823–1895), theological writer ; B.A. Oriel College, Oxford, 1847 ; M.A., 1872 ; ordained deacon, 1847 ; priest, 1849 ; rector of South Thoresby, Lincolnshire, 1852–3, and of Ashen, Essex, 1853–95 ; published a number of exegetical works. [Suppl. ii. 124]

DEANE, WILLIAM WOOD (1825–1873), architect and painter ; cashier at the Bank of England ; silver medallist of the Royal Academy, 1844 ; associate of the Royal Institute of British Architects, 1848 ; relinquished practical architecture in disappointment, 1856 ; made impressionist sketches of architecture and local incident at Rome, 1850, at Venice, 1865, and in other parts of Europe ; associate of the Society of Painters in Water-colours, 1870. [xiv. 260]

DEARE, JOHN (1759–1798), sculptor ; sent by the king and the Royal Academy to Rome, where he settled, 1785 ; imprisoned by the commander of the French troops, who had fallen in love with Deare's wife, 1798 ; his death sometimes ascribed to this cause. [xiv. 261]

DEARE, JOSEPH (1804 ?–1835), sculptor ; nephew of John Deare [q. v.] ; exhibited marble groups and portrait busts at the Royal Academy, 1826–32. [xiv. 261]

DEAS, SIR DAVID (1807–1876), naval medical officer ; educated at Edinburgh University and high school ; licentiate of the College of Surgeons, Edinburgh, 1827 ; surgeon R.N., 1836 ; served off Syria, subsequently at Sebastopol, 1854 ; inspector-general of hospitals and fleets, 1855–72 ; K.C.B., 1867. [xiv. 261]

DEAS, SIR GEORGE (1804–1887), Scottish judge ; studied law at Edinburgh ; called to the Scottish bar, 1828 ; sheriff of Ross and Cromarty, 1850–1 ; solicitor-general, 1851–2 ; permanent lord ordinary of session, with title of Lord Deas, 1853 ; exchequer judge, 1853 ; lord commissioner of justiciary, 1854 ; knighted, 1858. [xiv. 262]

DEASE, WILLIAM (1752 ?–1798), surgeon ; studied medicine at Paris and Dublin ; professor of surgery, Surgeons' College, Dublin, 1785 ; president, 1789 ; died of an internal wound under mysterious circumstances ; published medical works. [xiv. 262]

DEASY, RICKARD (1812–1883), Irish judge ; M.A. Trinity College, Dublin, 1847 ; called to the Irish bar, 1835 ; queen's counsel, 1849 ; M.P., co. Cork, 1855–61 ; attorney-general for Ireland, 1860 ; LL.D. Dublin, 1860 ; exchequer baron in Ireland, 1861–78 ; lord justice of appeal, 1878. [xiv. 262]

DE BAAN, JACOBUS (1673–1700), portrait-painter ; son of Johannes de Baan [q. v.] ; born at the Hague ; painted in England portraits of William III and his nobility, and in Italy pictures for the Grand Duke of Tuscany ; died at Vienna. [xiv. 264]

DE BAAN or **DE BAEN**, JOHANNES (1633–1702), painter ; born at Haarlem ; director of the Painters' Guild of St. Luke at the Hague ; invited to England by Charles II ; executed portraits of Charles II, Catherine of Braganza, and the Duke of York, and, on his return to Holland, of eminent Dutchmen ; formed Louis XIV's collection of Dutch masters ; three times escaped being assassinated by his rivals. [xiv. 263]

DEBBIEG, HUGH (1731–1810), general ; cadet-gunner, royal artillery, 1745 ; studied at Royal Military Academy, Woolwich ; engineer extraordinary in Flanders, 1747 ; practitioner engineer in Brabant, 1748 ; engaged in survey operations in Scotland and north of England, 1748–51 ; sub-engineer at Chatham, 1751 ; lieutenant in 37th foot, 1756, and in royal engineers, 1757 ; captain-lieutenant, 1758 ; served in North America and Canada ; captain, 1759 ; chief engineer in Newfoundland, 1765 ; went on secret mission to examine seaports of France and Spain, 1767–8 ; brevet-major, 1772 ; brevet lieutenant-colonel, 1777 ; chief engineer on staff of Jeffrey, lord Amherst, 1777 ; chief engineer at Chatham, 1778 ; had charge of defences of public buildings during ' no popery' riots, 1780 ; sub-director and major in royal engineers, 1781 ; colonel, 1782 ; censured and temporarily deprived of rank, owing to disputes with third Duke of Richmond, who was master-general of ordnance, 1789 ; major-general, 1793 ; lieutenant-general, 1798 ; general, 1803. [Suppl. ii. 124]

DEBRETT, JOHN (*d.* 1822), publisher and compiler ; compiled a 'Peerage of England, Scotland, and Ireland,' 1802, and a 'Baronetage of England,' 1808. [xiv. 264]

DE BRIE, DIRK or THEODORE (1528–1598), engraver ; born at Liège ; engraved plates for Boissard's 'Roman Antiquities,' and executed 'The Grand Funeral Procession of Sir Philip Sidney,' a series, 1587. [xiv. 264]

DE BRUYN, THEODORE (*d.* 1804), landscape-painter ; born in Switzerland ; exhibited landscapes at the Royal Academy ; decorated chapel at Greenwich Hospital in monochrome imitation of bas-relief. [xiv. 264]

DE CAUS, ISAAC (*fl.* 1644), mathematician ; son or nephew of Salomon de Caus [q. v.] ; laid out the gardens at Wilton House ; restated the hydraulic theorems of Salomon de Caus, 1644. [xiv. 265]

DE CAUS, CAULS, or **CAUX**, SALOMON (1576–1626 ?), engineer and architect ; native of Normandy ; mathematical tutor to Henry, prince of Wales ; laid out gardens at Heidelberg Castle, 1613 ; left the service of the elector palatine to return to France, 1623. His works include 'Institution Harmonique,' 1615, and a book on the motive power of water, in which he anticipated the steam-engine, 1615. [xiv. 265]

DECKER, Sir MATTHEW (1679–1749), writer on trade; born in Amsterdam; settled in London, 1702; director of the East India Company; M.P. for Bishops Castle; sheriff of Surrey, 1729; created baronet, 1716; much interested in landscape gardening. In 'Serious Considerations on the High Duties,' he advocated a single excise tax on all the houses of Great Britain, 1743. His 'Essay on the Causes of the Decline of the Foreign Trade' (1744) adversely criticised by Adam Smith. [xiv. 266]

DECKER, THOMAS (1570?–1641?). [See DEKKER.]

DECLAN, SAINT (fl. 600–650), bishop of Ardmore, co. Waterford; became in Gaul possessed of the 'duibhin,' a supernatural gift, which was possibly a black altar-cross; crossed to Ireland in a ship which was miraculously supplied to him; founded church and monastery at Meath and Ardmore. [xiv. 267]

DE COETLOGON, CHARLES EDWARD (1746?–1820). [See COETLOGON.]

DE CORT, HENRY FRANCIS (HENDRIK FRANS) (1742–1810), landscape-painter; born at Antwerp; secretary to the new Antwerp Academy, 1788; exhibited at the Royal Academy from 1790. [xiv. 268]

DE CRITZ, EMMANUEL (fl. 1650), sergeant-painter; son of John de Critz (d. 1642) [q. v.]; painted scenery for court masques. [xiv. 269]

DE CRITZ, JOHN, the younger (fl. 1610), sergeant-painter; son of John de Critz (d. 1642) [q. v.]; sergeant-painter by reversion, 1610; killed on the royalist side at Oxford. [xiv. 269]

DE CRITZ, JOHN (d. 1642), sergeant-painter from 1605; native of Flanders; extolled in Meres's 'Palladis Tamia,' 1548; painted portraits of Queen Elizabeth, Walsingham, and Sir Philip Sidney; repaired the royal barges, 1631. [xiv. 268]

DECUMAN or DEGEMAN, SAINT (d. 706?), Welsh hermit; miraculously crossed the Bristol Channel; hermit near Dunster Castle, Somerset. [xiv. 269]

DEE, ARTHUR (1579–1651), alchemist; son of John Dee [q. v.]; travelled in Germany, Poland, and Bohemia; educated at Westminster School, 1592; cited before the College of Physicians as an unlicensed practitioner; appointed physician to the czar on James I's recommendation; author of a Rosicrucian 'Fasciculus Chemicus,' 1631. [xiv. 269]

DEE, DUNCAN (1657–1720), pleader; educated at Merchant Taylors' School and St. John's College, Oxford; common serjeant of the city of London, 1700; defended Sacheverell before the House of Lords, 1710. [xiv. 270]

DEE, FRANCIS (d. 1638), bishop of Peterborough; scholar of Merchant Taylors' School, 1591; M.A. St. John's College, Cambridge, 1603; D.D., 1617; chancellor of Salisbury Cathedral, 1619; 'assistant' in the foundation of Sion College, 1630; dean of Chichester, 1630; bishop of Peterborough, 1634–8; benefactor of St. John's College, Cambridge. [xiv. 270]

DEE, JOHN (1527–1608), mathematician and astrologer; B.A. St. John's College, Cambridge, 1545; foundation-fellow, c. 1546; fellow of Trinity College, Cambridge, where the clever stage effects he introduced into a performance of the 'Peace' of Aristophanes procured him his life-long reputation of being a magician, 1546; M.A. Cambridge, 1548; studied at Louvain, 1548; lectured at Paris on Euclid, 1550; rector of Upton-upon-Severn, 1553; acquitted by the Star-chamber when accused of practising sorcery against Queen Mary's life, but put under the surveillance of Bishop Bonner as a possible heretic; suggested to Queen Mary the formation of a royal library of ancient manuscripts, 1556; acquired at Antwerp (c. 1562) a manuscript of Trithemius's 'Steganographia'; visited Venice, 1563; made a voyage to St. Helena; travelled to Hungary to present his 'Monas Hieroglyphica' to Maximilian II, 1563; explained the appearance of a new star, 1572; described his magic glass to Queen Elizabeth, 1575; sent to Germany to consult physicians on the queen's health, 1578; drew up hydrographical and geographical description of newly discovered countries for

Queen Elizabeth, at her request, 1580; made calculations to facilitate adoption in England of Gregory XIII's calendar, 1583; practised crystallomancy in conjunction with Albert Laski, palatine of Siradz, 1584; went to Prague and had interviews with the Emperor Rodolph II, 1584, and Stephen of Poland, 1585; compelled to leave Prague by representations of Bishop of Piacenza, 1586; head of a small confraternity, which dissolved in 1589, for seeking the philosopher's stone and invoking the angels; warden of Manchester College, 1595–1604; fruitlessly petitioned James I to be formally cleared of the imputation of being a magician, 1604. Among his numerous works were 'De Trigono,' 1565, 'Navigationis ad Cathayam . . delineatio Hydrographica,' 1580, and a 'Treatise of the Rosie Crucian Secrets.' [xiv. 271]

DEERING, GEORGE CHARLES (1695?–1749), botanist; native of Saxony; secretary to Baron Schach; Russian envoy extraordinary to Queen Anne, 1713; graduated at Rheims and Leyden, 1718; member of Dillenius and Martyn's English Botanical Society, 1721; gave up medicine and enlisted as an ensign in the Nottingham foot regiment, 1745. [xiv. 279]

DEERING, formerly GANDY, JOHN PETER (1787–1850), architect; travelled in Greece, 1811–13; M.P., Aylesbury; R.A., 1838; high sheriff of Buckinghamshire, 1840; designed numerous public buildings in London, and published the 'Rural Architect,' 1805, also assisting Sir William Gell [q. v.] in 'Pompeiana,' 1817–19. [xiv. 280]

DEFOE, DANIEL (1661?–1731), journalist and novelist; changed his name from Foe to Defoe, c. 1703; hose factor, 1685; joined Monmouth's rebellion, 1685; joined William III's army, 1688; accountant to the commissioners of the glass duty, 1695–9; published an 'Essay upon Projects,' 1698; advocated war with France in 'The Two Great Questions considered,' 1700; published 'The True-born Englishman, a Satyr,' 1701; wrote 'The Original Power of the Collective Body of the People of England examined and asserted' in approval of the liberation of the lately imprisoned 'Kentish petitioners,' 1701; wrote the 'Mock Mourners,' a lament for William III, 1702; published (1702) 'The Shortest Way with the Dissenters,' a satiric pamphlet which was designed to teach high-churchmen the logical result of suppressing the privilege of 'occasional conformity,' and for which he was fined, imprisoned, and pilloried while the people drank his health, 1703; composed a 'Hymn to the Pillory'; started the 'Review' (suppressed 1713) during his imprisonment, 1704; sent into Scotland on a secret mission by the government, 1705; published 'Jure Divino,' a long political satire, 1706; published a 'History of the Union with Scotland,' 1709; supported Marlborough and Godolphin against the growing discontent with the French war; defended Sacheverell's impeachment in the 'Review'; wrote in Harley's interest, 1710; wrote in favour of peace with France; contributed to the 'Mercator,' a journal of economics, 1713; anti-Jacobite pamphleteer, 1712–13; prosecuted by the whigs for treasonable publications, 1713; condemned, but pardoned under the great seal, 1713; published his 'Appeal to Honour and Justice,' an apologetic, 1715; convicted (1715) of libelling Lord Annesley, Bolingbroke's emissary to Ireland; escaped punishment by favour of Lord Townshend, secretary of state; published 'History of the Wars of Charles XII,' 1715; started 'Mercurius Politicus,' a monthly paper in the service of the government, 1716; redactor of 'Mist's Journal,' a Jacobite organ, 1717–24; published the first volume of his best-known work, 'Robinson Crusoe,' 1719, and 'Serious Reflections during the life . . . of Robinson Crusoe,' a sequel, 1720, both widely pirated; published 'The Anatomy of Exchange Alley,' an attack on stockjobbers, and the 'Chimera,' 1720; published 'Captain Singleton, 1720, 'Moll Flanders' and 'Colonel Jacque,' 1722, and 'Roxana,' 1724; author of 'Journal of the Plague Year,' 1722, and a 'New Voyage Round the World,' 1725, two works of fiction; produced didactic works, as well as books of vulgar supernaturalism and economic and social pamphlets; adopted pseudonym of Andrew Morton, 1725; became acquainted with Henry Baker (1698–1774) [q. v.], who married his daughter, Sophia Defoe, 1729, but apparently quarrelled with him later; published over 250 works. [xiv. 280]

DE GEX, Sir JOHN PETER (1809–1887), law reporter; M.A. Jesus College, Cambridge, 1834; barrister of Lincoln's Inn, 1835; published a volume of 'Cases in

Bankruptcy,' reported by himself, 1852; represented the appellant against the decision of the bankruptcy court that the Duke of Newcastle was exempt from the law of bankruptcy, 1869; treasurer of Lincoln's Inn, 1882; knighted, 1882. [xiv. 293]

DEGGE, Sir SIMON (1612-1704), author of the 'Parson's Counsellor'; barrister, Inner Temple, 1653; justice of the Welsh marches, 1662; knighted, 1669; bencher of the Inner Temple, 1669; high sheriff of Derbyshire, 1673; published the 'Parson's Counsellor and Law of Tithes,' 1676. [xiv. 293]

DE GREY. [See GREY.]

DE HEERE or D'HEERE, LUCAS (1534-1584), painter and poet; born at Ghent; adopted the reformed religion; set up a school of painting at Ghent, and became a member of the Chamber of Rhetoric; published 'De Hof en Boomgaerd der Poesien,' 1565; banished, 1568; lived in England, 1568-77; painted in England some portraits, including (1554) one of Queen Mary, and an allegorical picture of Queen Elizabeth, 1569; employed in mural decoration; designed the pageants at the entry of the Prince of Orange into Ghent, 1577. [xiv. 294]

DEICOLA or DEICOLUS, SAINT (d. 625); attended St. Columbanus for a time in East Anglia and France, 590, as one of the twelve companions; founded, and placed under papal protection, a monastery at Luthra (Lure). [xiv. 295]

DEINIOL, SAINT (d. 584 ?). [See DANIEL.]

DEIOS, LAURENCE (fl. 1607), divine; fellow of St. John's College, Cambridge, 1573; M.A., 1576; B.D., 1583; Hebrew lecturer and junior dean of St. John's College; rector of East Horsley, Surrey, 1590-1. [xiv. 296]

DEIRA, KINGS OF. [See ÆLLA, d. 588; EDWIN, 585 ?-633; OSRIC, d. 634; OSWIN, d. 651.]

DE KEYSER, WILLIAM (1647-1692 ?), painter; native of Antwerp, where he painted altar-pieces; tried his fortune in England; his prospects ruined by the overthrow of his patron, James II. [xiv. 296]

DEKKER, THOMAS (1570 ?-1641 ?), dramatist and pamphleteer; engaged by Philip Henslowe to write plays (most of which are now lost), in collaboration with Drayton, Ben Jonson, Day, and many others; published in 1600 'The Pleasant Comedie of Fortunatus'; ridiculed in Ben Jonson's 'Poetaster,' 1601, on which he retorted in the 'Satiromastix,' 1602; wrote 'The Batchelors Banquet,' a tract founded on 'Les Quinze Joyes de Mariage,' 1603; published 'The Seuen deadly Sinnes of London,' and 'Newes from Hell,' an imitation of Nash, 1606; wrote 'The Belman of London,' a social satire, 1608; published 'The Guls Hornebooke,' 1609, and 'Fowre Birds of Noahs Arke,' a prose devotional work, 1609; collaborated with Middleton in 'Roaring Girl,' 1611, and Massinger in 'The Virgin Martyr,' 1622; published 'Match Mee in London,' a tragi-comedy, 1631; composed the lyrical passages of Ford's 'Sun's Darling' (published 1656) and, with Ford and Rowley, produced 'Witch of Edmonton' (published 1658). His dramatic works were collected by Mr. R. H. Shepherd in 1873, and his miscellaneous works by Dr. Grosart in 'The Huth Library.' [xiv. 297]

DE LACY. [See LACY.]

DELAMAINE, ALEXANDER (fl. 1654-1683), Muggletonian; quaker, 1654; composed song dealing with Muggleton's trial, 1677. [xiv. 301]

DELAMAINE, RICHARD, the elder (fl. 1631), mathematician; tutor to Charles I in mathematics; chief work, 'Grammelogia or the Mathematicall Ring,' 1631. [xiv. 301]

DELAMAINE, RICHARD, the younger (fl. 1654), mathematician; son of Richard Delamaine (fl. 1631) [q. v.]; published computation of rates due on lands in Ireland, 1641; preacher, 1648; helped to defend Hereford against the royalists. [xiv. 301]

DE LA MARE, Sir PETER (fl. 1370), speaker of the House of Commons; knight of the shire for Hereford and speaker of the Commons in the Good parliament, 1376; imprisoned at Nottingham by the influence of the Duke of Lancaster, 1376-7; M.P., Herefordshire, 1377; again speaker, 1377. [xiv. 301]

DELAMER or DE LA MER, BARONS. [See BOOTH, GEORGE, first BARON, 1622-1684; BOOTH, HENRY, second BARON, 1652-1694; BOOTH, GEORGE, third BARON, 1675-1758.]

DE LA MOTTE, FREEMAN GAGE (d. 1862), author of works on alphabets and illumination; son of William de la Motte [q. v.]; friend of Turner. [xiv. 303]

DE LA MOTTE, PHILIP (d. 1805), lieutenant-colonel and (1803) author of a work on British heraldry; cousin of William de la Motte [q. v.] [xiv. 303]

DE LA MOTTE, WILLIAM (1775-1863), painter; by descent a Huguenot refugee; contributed landscapes, sea-scenes, and architectural pictures to the Royal Academy exhibitions, 1796-1848; 'fellow exhibitor' of the Water-Colour Society, exhibiting in 1806, 1807, and 1808; published 'Thirty Etchings of Rural Subjects,' 1816. [xiv. 302]

DE LANCEY, OLIVER, the elder (1749-1822), general; descended from a Huguenot family, which had emigrated to America; lieutenant, 14th dragoons, 1770; captain, 17th dragoons, 1773; brigadier-general of American loyalists, 1774; fought at Brooklyn and White Plains, 1776; present at the surrender of Charleston, 1781; lieutenant-colonel, 17th dragoons, 1781; major-general, 1794; M.P., Maidstone, 1796-1802; removed, in consequence of culpable carelessness in the keeping of his accounts as barrack-master, 1804; general, 1812. [xiv. 303]

DE LANCEY, OLIVER, the younger (1803-1837), Christinist officer; son of Oliver de Lancey the elder [q. v.]; second lieutenant, 60th rifles, 1818; aide-de-camp to Lieutenant-general Sir Charles Colville, G.C.B., at Bombay, 1821; captain, 1829; relieved Santander, 1835; deputy adjutant-general to the legion; killed while repelling Carlist attack on San Sebastian, 1837. [xiv. 304]

DE LANCEY, Sir WILLIAM HOWE (d. 1815), colonel, quartermaster-general's staff; born of a Huguenot family at New York; lieutenant, 16th light dragoons, 1793; served in East Indies, 1795; fought in Spain as assistant quartermaster-general and deputy quartermaster-general, 1809-14; present at capture of Ciudad Rodrigo, 1811, and battle of Vittoria, 1813; K.C.B.; killed at Waterloo, 1815. [xiv. 304]

DELANE, DENNIS (d. 1750), Irish actor; educated at Trinity College, Dublin; appeared first at the Smock Alley Theatre, Dublin, 1728; appeared at Goodman's Fields as Chamont in the 'Orphan,' 1730; played Alexander, Antony, Falstaff, Volpone, and other characters of Elizabethan drama at Covent Garden, 1735; engaged at Drury Lane, 1741; created Mahomet in Miller's adaptation from Voltaire, 1744; resented the hostility of Garrick, and returned to Covent Garden, 1748. [xiv. 305]

DELANE, JOHN THADEUS (1817-1879), editor of the 'Times'; educated at King's College, London, and Magdalen Hall, Oxford; B.A., 1839; barrister of Middle Temple, 1847; editor of the 'Times,' 1841-77; organised a special 'Times' express from Alexandria to London, 1845; published information which compelled Lord Palmerston to apologise to the Neapolitan government for assisting insurgents, 1849; attacked the government for neglecting Crimean commissariat; prevented the government from assisting Denmark, 1864. [xiv. 306]

DELANE, SOLOMON (1727-1784 ?), landscape-painter; settled at Rome, where he painted two landscapes for the Royal Academy exhibition, 1771; returned to England, 1782. [xiv. 308]

DELANY, MARY (1700-1788), friend of Swift; née Granville; married, firstly, against her will to one Alexander Pendarves, of Roscrow, Cornwall, 1718; married, secondly, Patrick Delany, 1743; invented 'flower mosaic,' 1774; corresponded with Swift and introduced Miss Burney, the novelist, at court. [xiv. 308]

DELANY, PATRICK (1685 ?-1768), divine; senior fellow and tutor, Trinity College, Dublin; an intimate friend of Sheridan and Swift, the latter styling him 'the most eminent preacher we have'; made chancellor of Christ Church Cathedral by Lord Carteret, 1727; chancellor of St. Patrick's, 1730; started the 'Tribune,' a periodical, 1738; appointed to the deanery of Down by the influence of his wife, Mary Delany [q. v.], 1744;

published 'Revelations examined with Candour,' 1732, 1734, and 1736, 'Reflections upon Polygamy,' 1738, and a defence of Swift against Lord Orrery, 1754. [xiv. 310]

DELAP, JOHN (1725–1812), poet and dramatist; educated at Trinity and Magdalene Colleges, Cambridge; fellow of Magdalene, 1748; M.A., 1750; D.D., 1762; incumbent of Iford and Kingston, Sussex, 1765–1812, of Woollavington, Sussex, 1774–1812; wrote mediocre tragedies for Drury Lane and elegies. [xiv. 311]

DE LA POLE. [See POLE.]

DELARAM, FRANCIS (d. 1627), engraver; engraved portraits of Tudor notabilities. [xiv. 312]

DE LA RUE, THOMAS (1793–1866), printer; native of Guernsey; founded firm in card and ornamental paper trade in London; chevalier of the Legion of Honour, 1855. [xiv. 313]

DE LA RUE, WARREN (1815–1889), inventor; son of Thomas De la Rue [q. v.]; born at Guernsey; educated in Paris; entered his father's printing firm; studied science; F.R.S., 1850; invented first envelope-making machine, 1851; formed friendship with Wilhelm Hofmann (1818–1892); erected, c. 1850, observatory at Canonbury, which was removed to Cranford, Middlesex, 1857; eminent in celestial photography; devised 'Kew heliograph' for taking daily photographs of sun, 1858; directed expedition to observe solar eclipse at Rivabellosa, Spain, 1860; observed sun spots with Balfour Stewart [q. v.] and Mr. Benjamin Loewy, 1862; engaged in chemical researches, with Dr. Hugo Müller, on Rangoon tar and glyceric acid (1859), terephthalic acid (1861), and on electric discharge through gases, 1868–83; received gold medals from Astronomical (1862) and Royal societies (1864); D.C.L. Oxford; original member of Chemical Society and president, 1867–9, and 1879–80; president, Royal Astronomical Society, 1864–6; published scientific papers. [xlix. 387]

DELATRE or **DELATTRE**, JEAN MARIE (1745–1840), engraver; born at Abbeville; assistant to Bartolozzi. [xiv. 313]

DELAUNE or **DELAWNE**, GIDEON (1565?–1659), apothecary; son of William Delaune (d. 1610) [q. v.]; born at Rheims; apothecary to Anne of Denmark, queen of James I; worked for incorporation of Apothecaries' Company; inventor of Delaune's pills. [xiv. 313]

DELAUNE, PAUL (1584?–1654?), physician; M.A. Emmanuel College, Cambridge, 1610; M.D. Padua, 1614, Cambridge, 1615; senior censor of the College of Physicians, 1643; professor of physic in Gresham College, 1643–52; went to Hispaniola and Jamaica as physician-general to Cromwell's fleet. [xiv. 314]

DELAUNE, THOMAS (d. 1685), nonconformist writer; converted to protestantism when clerk to the proprietor of a pilchard fishery near Kinsale; imprisoned for libel on account of his 'Plea for the Nonconformists,' 1683; died in Newgate, 1685. [xiv. 315]

DELAUNE, WILLIAM (d. 1610), divine and physician; native of France, where he became a protestant minister; studied medicine at Paris and Montpellier; Huguenot refugee in England; L.R.C.P., 1582; epitomised Calvin's 'Institutions,' 1583. [xiv. 315]

DELAUNE, WILLIAM (1659–1728), president of St. John's College, Oxford; educated at Merchant Taylors' and St. John's College, Oxford; M.A., 1683; D.D., 1697; president of St. John's, 1698–1728; canon of Winchester, 1701; vice-chancellor of Oxford, 1702–6; accused of embezzling university funds; Margaret lecturer in divinity, 1715; one of Queen Anne's chaplains. [xiv. 316]

DELAVAL, EDWARD HUSSEY (1729–1814), chemist; M.A. and fellow of Pembroke Hall, Cambridge; F.R.S., 1759; gold medallist of the Royal Society; manufactured the completest set of musical glasses then known in England; chief work, 'The Cause of Changes in Opaque and Coloured Bodies,' 1777. [xiv. 316]

DELAVALL, SIR RALPH (d. 1707), admiral; commander of the York, 1688; vice-admiral of the blue, 1690; knighted, 1690; commanded the rear squadron in the battle of Beachy Head, 1690; as president of the court-martial acquitted Lord Torrington of remissness in that action; vice-admiral of the red squadron at Barfleur, 1692; as Jacobite removed from command, 1693; M.P., Great Bedwin, 1695–8. [xiv. 317]

DE LA WARR, EARLS OF. [See WEST, JOHN, first EARL, 1693–1766; WEST, SIR CHARLES RICHARD SACKVILLE-, sixth EARL, 1815–1873.]

DE LA WARR, BARONS OF. [See WEST, SIR THOMAS, ninth BARON, 1472?–1554; WEST, THOMAS, third or twelfth BARON, 1577–1618; WEST, JOHN, sixth BARON, 1693–1766; WEST, SIR CHARLES RICHARD SACKVILLE-, twelfth BARON, 1815–1873.]

DELEPIERRE, JOSEPH OCTAVE (1802–1879), author and antiquary; born at Bruges; doctor of laws of Ghent; avocat, and 'archiviste de la Flandre Occidentale,' in Bruges; visited England, 1843; Belgian consul, 1849; Belgian secretary of legation; F.S.A.; published, 'Chroniques, traditions, &c., de l'ancienne histoire des Flamands,' 1834, 'Macaronéana,' 1852, 'A Sketch of the History of Flemish Literature,' 1860, and other works. [xiv. 318]

DE LISLE, AMBROSE LISLE MARCH PHILLIPPS (1809–1878), Roman catholic writer; converted to Roman catholicism, 1824; entered Trinity College, Cambridge, 1826; gave 230 acres of land in Charnwood Forest to found a Cistercian monastery, 1835; received habit of Third Order of St. Dominic, at Rome, 1837; principal founder of the 'Association for the Promotion of the Unity of Christendom,' 1857; high sheriff of Leicestershire, 1868; published theological works. [xiv. 321]

DE LISLE, RUDOLPH EDWARD LISLE MARCH PHILLIPPS (1853–1885), sub-lieutenant in the navy; son of Ambrose de Lisle [q. v.]; killed at Abu Klea, 1885. [xiv. 322]

DELL, HENRY (fl. 1766), bookseller; author or adapter of four plays and (1766) of a poem called 'The Bookseller.' [xiv. 322]

DELL, JONAS (d. 1665), quaker; served in the parliamentary army; styled 'the quaking soldier'; published theological polemics. [xiv. 323]

DELL, THOMAS (1740?–1780). [See HALES.]

DELL, WILLIAM (d. 1664), master of Gonville and Caius College, Cambridge; fellow of Emmanuel College, Cambridge; M.A., 1631; secretary to Laud; master of Caius, 1649–60; declaimed against 'the gospel of Christ understood according to Aristotle,' 1653; ejected from his living of Yelden, Bedfordshire, 1662; anticipated the university extension movement in his 'Right Reformation of Learning, Schools, and Universities.' [xiv. 323]

DELMARIIS, CÆSAR À (d. 1569). [See CÆSAR ADELMARE.]

DE LOLME, JOHN LOUIS (1740?–1807), writer on the English constitution; born at Geneva; came to England, 1769; published 'The Constitution of England' (first English edition, 1775), the theory of which led D'Israeli to call its author 'the English Montesquieu'; subsequently member of the Geneva Council of Two Hundred, and sous-prefet under Napoleon; published also 'The History of the Flagellants,' adapted from the Abbé Boileau, 1777, 'The British Empire in Europe,' 1787, and other works. [xiv. 325]

DELONEY, THOMAS (1543?–1607?), ballad writer and pamphleteer; by trade a silk-weaver; author of ballads and broadsides (three on the Spanish Armada, 1588); collected ballads in 'Garland of Good Will,' 1604, and 'Strange Histories,' before 1607. [xiv. 327]

DELORAINE, first EARL OF (1676–1730). [See SCOTT, HENRY.]

DELPINI, CARLO ANTONIO (d. 1828), pantomimist and scene-mechanician at Drury Lane (1774), Covent Garden, and the Haymarket; acted afterwards in 'Robinson Crusoe,' 'Don Juan,' and the 'Deserter of Naples'; stage manager at the opera. [xiv. 328]

DELUC, JEAN ANDRÉ (1727–1817), geologist and meteorologist; native of Geneva; member of the Council of Two Hundred, 1770; settled in England, 1773; reader to Queen Charlotte; F.R.S.; honorary professor of geology at Göttingen, 1798; endeavoured to reconcile science with Mosaic cosmogony; published 'Bacon tel qu'il est,' 1800, 'Geological Travels,' 1803, and an 'Introduction à la Physique Terrestre,' 1803. [xiv. 328]

DELVAUX, LAURENT (1695–1778), sculptor; born at Ghent; studied at Rome, 1728; chief sculptor to the Archduchess Marie Elizabeth and the Emperor Charles VI, 1734–50; chief sculptor to Charles, duke of Lorraine, 1750–78; executed works in England in bronze and marble; died at Nivelles. [xiv. 329]

DELVIN, BARONS. [See NUGENT, SIR RICHARD, tenth BARON, d. 1460?; NUGENT, RICHARD, twelfth BARON, d. 1538?; NUGENT, SIR CHRISTOPHER, fourteenth BARON, 1544–1602; NUGENT, SIR RICHARD, fifteenth BARON, 1583–1642.]

DEMAINBRAY, STEPHEN CHARLES TRIBOUDET (1710–1782), electrician and astronomer; of Huguenot extraction; educated at Westminster School and Leyden; LL.D. Edinburgh; discovered influence of electricity in stimulating growth of plants; fought at Prestonpans, 1745; tutor to George III, when Prince of Wales, 1754; astronomer at the Royal observatory, Kew, 1768–82. [xiv. 330]

DEMAINBRAY, STEPHEN GEORGE FRANCIS TRIBOUDET (1760–1854), astronomer; son of Stephen Charles Triboudet Demainbray [q. v.]; fellow of Exeter College, Oxford, 1778–99; B.D., 1793; astronomer at the Royal observatory, Kew, 1782–1840; rector of Somerford Magna, Wiltshire, 1799–1854. [xiv. 331]

DEMAUS, ROBERT (1829? – 1874), biographical writer; M.A. Edinburgh, 1850; schoolmaster at Aberfeldy, Perthshire, Alnwick, 1856, and Aberdeen, 1858; deacon, 1860, and priest, 1862; chaplain to Thomas George Suther, bishop of Aberdeen, 1860–5; senior curate of St. Luke's, Chelsea, 1865–74; principal of Whitelands Training College, 1869; published biographies of Latimer (1869) and Tyndale (1871) and other works. [Suppl. ii. 127]

DE MOIVRE, ABRAHAM (1667–1754). [See MOIVRE.]

DE MORGAN, AUGUSTUS (1806–1871), mathematician; entered Trinity College, Cambridge, 1823; fourth wrangler, 1827; professor of mathematics, University College, London, 1828; resigned, 1831, but was reappointed, 1836; resigned his professorship, regarding the refusal of the council of University College to elect James Martineau to the chair of mental philosophy and logic as a piece of religious intolerance, 1866; first president of the Mathematical Society, 1865; follower of Berkeley; chief works, 'Formal Logic,' 1847; 'Essay on Probabilities,' 1838, 'Trigonometry and Double Algebra,' 1849, and a 'Budget of Paradoxes,' collected 1872. [xiv. 331]

DE MORGAN, CAMPBELL GREIG (1811–1876), surgeon; brother of Augustus de Morgan [q. v.]; educated at University College, London, and at the Middlesex Hospital; surgeon to the Middlesex Hospital; F.R.S.; professor of anatomy, 1845; published work on the 'Origin of Cancer,' 1872. [xiv. 334]

DEMPSTER, GEORGE (1732–1818), agriculturist; educated at Edinburgh and St. Andrews; member of the Faculty of Advocates, 1755; M.P., Forfar and Fife burghs, 1762–90; provost of St. Andrews, 1780; director of the East India Company, but subsequently withdrew and supported Fox's India Bill; promoted society for extension and protection of Scottish fisheries. His works include 'Magnetic Mountains of Cannay,' and a disquisition on the agriculture of Forfarshire, 1794. [xiv. 334]

DEMPSTER, THOMAS (1579?–1625), biographical and miscellaneous writer; entered Pembroke Hall, Cambridge, in his tenth year; travelled in France, then in a disturbed state, and was sent from the university of Louvain to be educated at Rome; graduated at Douay; graduated in canon law at Paris; appointed professor of humanities at Toulouse; elected professor of oratory at Nîmes; refuted William Cowper (1568–1619) [q. v.] in a theological controversy at Perth; professor in the Collèges des Grassins, de Lisieux, and de Plessy, Paris; published an enlarged edition of Rosinus's 'Antiquitatum Romanarum Corpus absolutissimum' (1620); appointed professor of civil law at Pisa by Cosmo II, grand duke of Tuscany; left Pisa, when an Englishman, whom he had insulted, attempted to assassinate him; became professor of humanities at Bologna; accused of heresy by

his English enemy, to whom he was subsequently reconciled by a court of arbitration at Rome; knighted by Urban VIII; died at Bologna; edited Claudian, was famous as a Latin poet, and wrote 'Historia Ecclesiastica Gentis Scotorum' (published 1627), 'De Etruria Regali' (printed 1723-4), and an autobiography. [xiv. 335]

DENBIGH, EARLS OF. [See FEILDING, WILLIAM, first EARL, d. 1643; FEILDING, BASIL, second EARL, d. 1675.]

DENDY, WALTER COOPER (1794–1871), surgeon; studied at Guy's and St. Thomas's hospitals; M.C.S., 1814; president of the Medical Society of London; published numerous medical and some speculative works, such as 'Zone,' 1841, 'Psyche,' 1853, and a 'Gleam of the Spirit Mystery,' 1861. [xiv. 340]

DENE, WILLIAM (fl. 1350), chronicler; notary public to Haymo, bishop of Rochester; probably author of 'Annales Roffenses' (British Museum, Faustina, B 5). [xiv. 341]

DENHAM, DIXON (1786–1828), lieutenant-colonel and African traveller; entered Merchant Taylors' School, 1793; served in the Peninsular war as second lieutenant, 23rd royal Welsh fusiliers, 1812; first lieutenant, 1813; received the Waterloo medal, 1815; volunteered to explore the country between Timbuctoo and the north coast of Africa, 1821; crossed the Tebu Desert and reached Kuka, 1823; took part in inter-tribal warfare, 1823; partially explored Lake Tchad, 1824; superintendent of liberated Africans on the west coast, the post being specially created for him, 1825; lieutenant-governor of Sierra Leone, where he died, 1828. [xiv. 341]

DENHAM, HENRY (fl. 1591), printer; underwarden of the Stationers' Company, 1586 and 1588; printed the first edition of the New Testament in Welsh, 1567, and the first English translation of Ovid's 'Heroycall Epistles,' by Turbervile. [xiv. 342]

DENHAM, SIR JAMES STEUART, the elder (1712–1780), political economist; assumed surname of Denham, 1733; son of Sir James Steuart [q. v.]; studied law at Edinburgh; member of the Faculty of Advocates, 1735; attended Prince Charles Edward at Edinburgh, 1745; excepted by name from the Act of Oblivion, 1747; wandered about the continent, finally returning to Edinburgh in 1763. His chief work, 'Inquiry into the Principles of Political Economy,' 1767, written from the standpoint of the mercantile system, was the first systematic exposition of the science in English. [xiv. 343]

DENHAM, SIR JAMES STEUART, the younger (1744–1839), general; son of Sir James Steuart Denham the elder [q. v.]; captain 105th royal highlanders, 1763; lieutenant-colonel 13th dragoons, 1776; succeeded as baronet of Coltness and West Shields, 1780; M.P., Lanarkshire, 1781–1801; colonel, 1782; organised regiments of fencible cavalry in Scotland, 1795; local lieutenant-general in Munster, where he behaved with great intrepidity and conciliatoriness during troubled times, 1797-9; lieutenant-general, 1798; general, 1803. [xiv. 344]

DENHAM, SIR JOHN (1559–1639), judge; barrister of Lincoln's Inn, 1587; lord chief-baron of Irish exchequer, 1609; knighted, 1609; privy councillor, 1611; lord chief-justice of king's bench in Ireland, 1612; baron of the English exchequer, 1617; sheriff of Bedfordshire and Buckinghamshire, 1622; on the high commission, 1633; wrote a brief opinion in Hampden's favour, 1638. [xiv. 345]

DENHAM, SIR JOHN (1615–1669), poet; son of Sir John Denham (1559–1639) [q. v.]; matriculated at Trinity College, Oxford, 1631; studied law at Lincoln's Inn; published 'The Sophy,' an historical tragedy, 1642; compelled to surrender Farnham Castle, of which he was governor, to Sir William Waller, 1642; published 'Cooper's Hill,' his best-known poem, 1642; petitioned Charles I to pardon Wither, of whose poems Denham thought meanly; councillor of Charles I, and attendant of Henrietta Maria at Paris; sent to Holland with a letter of instructions for Charles II, 1649; published a translation of Virgil's 'Æneid II,' 1656; licensed by Cromwell to live at Bury in Suffolk, 1658; surveyor-general of works, 1660; K.B., 1661; became mad for a short period, 1666, in consequence of the faithlessness of his second wife, Lady Margaret Denham; lampooned by Samuel Butler, author of 'Hudibras,' 1667; published occasional verses and satires. His 'Cooper's Hill' is the earliest example of strictly descriptive poetry in English. [xiv. 346]

DENHAM, MICHAEL AISLABIE (*d.* 1859), collector of folklore ; merchant at Piersebridge, Durham ; published numerous compilations of proverbs and North British folklore. [xiv. 349]

DENHOLM, JAMES (1772–1818), teacher of drawing in Glasgow ; president of the Glasgow Philosophical Society, 1811–14 ; published 'An Historical and Topographical Description of the City of Glasgow,' 1797. [xiv. 350]

DENIS, SIR PETER (*d.* 1778), vice-admiral ; son of a Huguenot refugee ; lieutenant, 1739 ; took part in Anson's fight with De la Jonquière and carried home the despatches, 1747 ; M.P., Hedon, Yorkshire, 1754 ; fought at Quiberon Bay, 1759 ; created baronet, 1767 ; vice-admiral of the blue, 1775 ; died vice-admiral of the red, 1778. [xiv. 350]

DENISON, ALBERT, first BARON LONDESBOROUGH (1805–1860), son of Henry Conyngham, first marquis Conyngham [q. v.] ; educated at Eton ; secretary of legation at Florence, 1826, and at Berlin, 1829–31 ; K.C.H., 1829 ; deputy-lieutenant of the West Riding of Yorkshire ; M.P., Canterbury, 1835–41 and 1847–50 ; F.S.A., 1840 ; created Baron Londesborough, 1850 ; assumed surname of Denison, 1849 ; F.R.S., 1850 ; president of the British Archæological Association, 1843, and of the London and Middlesex Archæological Society, 1855 ; student of Anglo-Saxon antiquities. [xiv. 351]

DENISON, EDWARD, the elder (1801–1854), bishop of Salisbury ; educated at Eton and Oriel College, Oxford ; fellow of Merton College, 1826 ; M.A. ; select preacher, 1834 ; opposed the admission of dissenters to the colleges at Oxford, 1835 ; D.D. and bishop of Salisbury, 1837 ; author of sermons and charges. [xiv. 352]

DENISON, EDWARD, the younger (1840–1870), philanthropist ; son of Edward Denison the elder [q. v.] ; educated at Eton and Christ Church, Oxford ; built and endowed a school in the Mile End Road, 1867 ; M.P., Newark, 1868 ; committeeman of the Society for Organising Charitable Relief, 1869 ; died at Melbourne, whither he had gone for the sake of his health and to study the workings of colonisation. [xiv. 352]

DENISON, GEORGE ANTHONY (1805–1896), archdeacon of Taunton ; educated at Eton and Christ Church, Oxford ; M.A., 1830 ; fellow of Oriel College, 1828 ; took holy orders, 1832 ; college tutor, 1830–6, and treasurer, 1836 ; vicar of Broadwinsor, Dorset, 1838–51, and of East Brent, Somerset, 1851 ; prebendary of Sarum, 1841, and of Wells, 1849 ; archdeacon of Taunton, 1851 ; examining chaplain to bishop of Bath and Wells, but resigned, 1853, owing to disagreement on the part of the bishop with his eucharistic doctrine ; having defined his doctrinal position, was prosecuted in the ecclesiastical courts, and deprived, 1856, but the decision was reversed, 1857 ; edited 'Church and State Review,' 1862–5 ; took a prominent part in religious controversy as a high churchman of the old school ; published religious and other writings, including a violent political diatribe against Gladstone (1885). [Suppl. ii. 127]

DENISON, JOHN (*d.* 1629), divine ; student and graduate of Balliol College, Oxford ; D.D. ; chaplain to James I ; head-master of the free school, Reading, and successively vicar of the three churches in that town, 1604–29 ; author of some theological works, including (1621) a polemic against Cardinal Bellarmine. [xiv. 353]

DENISON, JOHN EVELYN, first VISCOUNT OSSINGTON (1800–1873), speaker of the House of Commons ; educated at Eton and Christ Church, Oxford ; M.A., 1828 ; M.P. for Newcastle-under-Lyme, 1823, and Hastings, 1826 ; appointed one of the council of the Duke of Clarence (afterwards William IV), 1827 ; M.P. for Nottinghamshire, 1831, and for South Nottinghamshire, 1833 and 1835, for Malton, 1841, 1847, and 1852, and for North Nottinghamshire, 1857 ; privy councillor, 1857 ; speaker, 1857–72 ; honorary D.C.L. Oxford, 1870 ; created Viscount Ossington, 1872. [xiv. 353]

DENISON, WILLIAM JOSEPH (1770–1849), millionaire ; senior partner of Denison, Heywood & Kennard, bankers, Lombard Street ; M.P. for Camelford, 1796–1802, for Kingston-upon-Hull, 1806, and for Surrey, 1818–49. [xiv. 354]

DENISON, SIR WILLIAM THOMAS (1804–1871), lieutenant-general, colonial and Indian governor ; brother of John Evelyn Denison [q. v.] ; entered the Royal Military Academy, Woolwich, 1819 ; constructed the Rideau Canal, Canada, 1827–31 ; in charge of the works at Woolwich dockyard, 1837 ; knighted, 1846 ; lieutenant-governor of Van Diemen's Land, 1846–54 ; opened the first session of the new representative assembly, 1852 ; consolidated system of public works and education ; governor of New South Wales, 1854–61 ; established parliament in New South Wales, 1855 ; civil K.C.B., 1856 ; governor of Madras, 1861–6 ; opposed establishment of legislative councils in minor presidencies and provinces and native representation ; carried out Sitána expedition as acting governor-general, 1863 ; published essays on social and educational topics at Sydney. [xiv. 355]

DENMAN, GEORGE (1819–1896), judge ; son of Thomas, first baron Denman [q. v.] ; educated at Repton and Trinity College, Cambridge ; senior classic and B.A., 1842 ; fellow of Trinity, 1843 ; M.A., 1845 ; called to bar at Lincoln's Inn, 1846 ; joined home circuit ; counsel to Cambridge University, 1857 ; Q.C., 1861 ; M.P. for Tiverton, 1859–65, and 1866–72 ; responsible for Evidence further Amendment Act, known as Denman's Act, 1869 ; succeeded Sir James Shaw Willes [q. v.] in court of common pleas, 1872 ; justice of common pleas division of high court, 1875 ; judge of high court of justice, queen's bench division, 1881–92 ; retired, 1892 ; privy councillor, 1893 ; published translations in Greek, Latin, and English verse. [Suppl. ii. 129]

DENMAN, THOMAS, the elder (1733–1815), physician ; studied medicine at St. George's Hospital, 1753 ; surgeon in the navy, 1757–63 ; M.D. Aberdeen, 1764 ; physician accoucheur to the Middlesex Hospital, 1769–83 ; licentiate in midwifery of the College of Physicians, 1783 ; published works on obstetrics. [xiv. 358]

DENMAN, THOMAS, first BARON DENMAN (1779–1854), lord chief-justice ; son of Thomas Denman the elder [q. v.] ; sent to Eton, 1788 ; entered St. John's College, Cambridge, 1796 ; barrister of Lincoln's Inn, 1806 ; deputy-recorder of Nottingham, and M.P. for Wareham, 1818 ; M.P. for Nottingham, 1820 ; solicitor-general to Queen Caroline, 1820 ; procured the withdrawal of Lord Liverpool's bill of pains and penalties against Queen Caroline, whose innocence he maintained before the bar of the Lords, 1820 ; common serjeant, 1822–30 ; pointed out defects in the law of evidence in a review of Dumont's 'Traité de Législation,' 1824 ; took silk, 1828, the Duke of Wellington having with difficulty pacified George IV, who looked on Denman as a slanderer ; again M.P. for Nottingham, 1830 ; attorney-general, 1830 ; knighted, 1830 ; drafted Reform Bill, 1831 ; undertook prosecution of Reform rioters, 1832 ; privy councillor and lord chief-justice, 1832 ; gazetted Baron Denman of Dovedale, 1834 ; speaker of the House of Lords, 1835 ; opposed privilege of the House of Commons in the libel case Stockdale *v.* Hansard, 1837 ; carried two bills abolishing death-penalty for forgery and some other offences, 1837 ; supported proposal to hold sittings in banc at other times than during the legal terms ; condemned Moxon, publisher of Shelley's complete works, for blasphemy, 1841 ; published pamphlets and spoke in favour of the extinction of the slave trade, 1843–54 ; secured retention of squadron to intercept slavers on the west coast of Africa, 1848 ; resigned lord chief-justiceship, 1850. [xiv. 358]

DENMAN, THOMAS, second BARON DENMAN (1805–1894), son of Thomas Denman, first baron [q. v.] ; educated at Eton and Brasenose College, Oxford ; called to bar at Lincoln's Inn, 1833 ; succeeded to peerage, 1854. [Suppl. ii. 130]

DENMARK, PRINCE OF (1653–1708). [See GEORGE.]

DENNE, HENRY (*d.* 1660 ?), puritan divine ; educated at Cambridge University ; one of the ministers selected for preferment by the House of Commons, 1641 ; imprisoned for holding baptist opinions, 1644 ; obtained the living of Elsly (Eltisley), Cambridgeshire, 1645 ; published controversial works. [xiv. 365]

DENNE, JOHN (1693–1767), antiquary ; M.A. Corpus Christi College, Cambridge, 1716 ; tutor and fellow of his college ; archdeacon and prebendary of Rochester, 1728 ; D.D. Cambridge, 1728 ; wrote on ecclesiastical subjects and arranged archives of Rochester Cathedral. [xiv. 366]

DENNE, SAMUEL (1730–1799), antiquary ; son of John Denne [q. v.] ; M.A. Corpus Christi College, Cambridge, 1756; held various incumbencies in Kent; F.S.A., 1785; published 'The Histories and Antiquities of Rochester and its Environs,' 1772, and other works on English antiquities. [xiv. 367]

DENNETT, JOHN (1790–1852), inventor and antiquary; invented 'Dennett's Life-Saving Rocket Apparatus,' 1832; custodian of Carisbrooke Castle; contributed to journal of British Archæological Association. [xiv. 367]

DENNIE, WILLIAM HENRY (1785 ?–1842), colonel, 13th light infantry; major, 22nd foot, 1821; served in India, 1804–5, at the capture of Mauritius, 1810, in the Channel islands and Ireland, and in Burmah; brevet lieutenant-colonel and C.B.; captured Ghuznee, 1839; defeated Dost Mahomed at Bameean, 1840; aide-de-camp to Queen Victoria; defended Jellalabad during Afghan war, and was slain in a sortie from that city, 1842. [xiv. 368]

DENNIS. [See also DENIS and DENNYS.]

DENNIS, JAMES BLATCH PIGGOTT (1816–1861), histologist; B.A. Queen's College, Oxford; ordained, 1839; elected member of the Geological Society for his scientific discoveries; read a paper before the British Association 'On the Mode of Flight of the Sterodactyles of the Coprolite bed near Cambridge,' 1860. [xiv. 369]

DENNIS, JOHN (1657–1734), critic; B.A. Caius College, Cambridge, 1679; M.A. Trinity Hall, 1683; appointed royal waiter in the port of London by the influence of the Duke of Marlborough, 1705; author of 'Rinaldo and Armida,' 1699, and other tragedies, one of which, 'Appius and Virginia,' acted at Drury Lane, 1709, was satirised for its bombast by Pope, to whom Dennis replied in his 'Reflections, Critical and Satirical,' 1711; defended the stage against Law and Collier; wrote 'Gibraltar,' 1705, and some other comedies; died in distressed circumstances. He is best known as a critic, producing 'The Advancement and Reformation of Modern Poetry,' 1701, 'Three Letters on . . . Shakespeare,' 1711, and 'Remarks on "The Fable of the Bees,"' 1724. [xiv. 369]

DENNIS or **DENYS**, SIR THOMAS (1480 ?–1561), privy councillor; chancellor of Anne of Cleves and custos rotulorum of Devon; frequently sheriff of Devon between 1508 and 1556; recorder of Exeter, 1514–44; put Exeter in a posture of defence against the projected rising of Sir Peter Carew [q. v.], 1554. [xiv. 372]

DENNISTOUN, JAMES (1803–1855), Scottish antiquary; educated at Edinburgh and Glasgow; member of the Faculty of Advocates, 1824; travelled in Italy and Germany collecting antiques, 1825–6 and 1836–47; deputy-lieutenant for Renfrewshire; edited papers and documents illustrative of the history of Scotland, and published among other works 'Memoirs of the Dukes of Urbino,' 1851. [xiv. 373]

DENNY, SIR ANTHONY (1501–1549), favourite of Henry VIII; educated at St. Paul's School and St. John's College, Cambridge; privy councillor; obtained grants of various manors and the lands of dissolved monasteries; knighted at Boulogne-sur-Mer, 1544; appointed by Henry VIII counsellor to his son and successor, Edward VI, 1547; M.P., Hertfordshire, 1547; assisted in suppression of Kett's rebellion, 1549. [xiv. 373]

DENNY, EDWARD, EARL OF NORWICH (1565 ?–1630), grandson of Sir Anthony Denny [q. v.]; M.P. for Liskeard, 1585–6, for Tregony, 1597–8, and for Essex, 1604; knighted, 1587; created Baron Denny of Waltham, 1604, and Earl of Norwich, 1626. [xiv. 374]

DENNY, HENRY (1803–1871), entomologist; curator of the museum of the Literary and Philosophical Society, Leeds; wrote on British parasitic insects. [xiv. 374]

DENNY, SIR WILLIAM (d. 1676), author of 'Pelecanicidium,' 1653, and of 'The Shepheards Holiday,' 1653, a pastoral poem; created baronet, 1642. [xiv. 375]

DENNYS, JOHN (d. 1609), author of 'The Secrets of Angling,' 1613, a poem quoted in Isaak Walton's 'Compleat Angler.' [xiv. 375]

DENT, ARTHUR (d. 1607), puritan divine; M.A. Christ's College, Cambridge, 1579; rector of South Shoebury, Essex, 1580–1607; one of the signatories of a petition declining to recognise the scriptural validity of the prayer-book; author of sermons and treatises of puritan theology. [xiv. 376]

DENT, EDWARD JOHN (1790–1853), chronometer maker; employed by the admiralty and the East India Company; supplied a Graham's escapement for the transit clock of Greenwich observatory; associate of the Institution of Civil Engineers, 1833; established clock-making manufactory, 1843; presented with a gold medal by the emperor of Russia, 1843; published 'A Treatise on the Aneroid,' 1849, and works on the construction and working of chronometers. [xiv. 377]

DENT, PETER (d. 1689), naturalist; M.B. Lambeth, 1678; incorporated at Cambridge, 1680; physician at Cambridge; assisted Ray in his 'Historia Plantarum.' [xiv. 378]

DENTON, HENRY (1633 ?–1681), writer; M.A. Oxford, 1659; fellow of Queen's College, Oxford, 1660; chaplain to the English ambassador at Constantinople, 1664–1672; translated Georginos's 'Description of the Present State of Samos, Nicaria, Patmos, and Mount Athos,' 1678. [xiv. 378]

DENTON, JAMES (d. 1533), dean of Lichfield; educated at Eton and King's College, Cambridge; M.A., 1492; fellow of King's College; student and doctor of canon law at Valencia; prebendary of Lichfield, 1409, of Lincoln, 1514; dean of Lichfield, 1522–33; chancellor to Mary, sister of Henry VIII and wife of Louis XII, whom he had attended in France; chancellor to the council of the Princess Mary, with jurisdiction over the Welsh marches, 1526; benefactor of King's College and St. George's Chapel, Windsor. [xiv. 378]

DENTON, JOHN (1625–1709), nonconformist divine; entered at Clare Hall, Cambridge, 1646; ejected from Oswaldkirk, Yorkshire, 1662, but subsequently given living of Stonegrave and prebend at York; friend of Tillotson. [xiv. 379]

DENTON, NATHAN (1634–1720), last survivor of the ejected ministers; entered at University College, Oxford, 1652; taught grammar school at Cawthorne, Yorkshire; ejected from the perpetual curacy of Bolton, 1662. [xiv. 379]

DENTON, RICHARD (1603–1663), divine; B.A. Catharine Hall, Cambridge, 1623; gave up Coley Chapel, and emigrated to New England, 1640; died at Hempstead, Long Island. [xiv. 380]

DENTON, THOMAS (1724–1777), miscellaneous writer; M.A. Queen's College, Oxford, 1752; rector of Ashtead, Surrey, 1754–77; published, in the style of Spenser, two poems, 'Immortality,' 1754, and 'The House of Superstition,' 1762. [xiv. 380]

DENTON, THOMAS (d. 1789), bookseller and artificer; made speaking and writing automata; translated a French book of parlour-magic, 1784; hanged for coining. [xiv. 380]

DENTON, WILLIAM (1605–1691), physician and political writer; educated at Magdalen Hall, Oxford; M.D. Oxford, 1634; physician to Charles I, 1636; physician in ordinary to the household of Charles II, 1660; F.R.C.P.; author of theological works largely directed against the Roman catholics. [xiv. 381]

DENTON, WILLIAM (1815–1888), divine; B.A. Worcester College, Oxford, 1844; M.A., 1848; ordained priest, 1845; vicar of St. Bartholomew, Cripplegate, 1850–88; published pamphlets relating to social and political questions, and several religious and historical works, including 'England in the Fifteenth Century,' 1888. [Suppl. ii. 130]

D'ÉON DE BEAUMONT, CHARLES GENEVIÈVE LOUIS AUGUSTE ANDRÉ TIMOTHÉE (1728–1810), chevalier; born at Tonnerre in Burgundy; educated as a boy, though his sex was long held to be doubtful; secret agent of the king of France at St. Petersburg, 1755; instrumental in bringing about an alliance between Russia, France, and Austria; received lieutenancy of dragoons as reward for his celerity in carrying news of battle of Prague to Versailles, 1757; secretary to the French embassy at St. Petersburg, 1757–60; captain of dragoons, 1758; minister plenipotentiary in London, secretly corresponding with the king of France on a projected invasion of England; obtained a true bill against Count de Guerchy, the French ambassador, for plotting his assassination; was generally suspected of being a woman; pensioned by the French government on condition of wearing woman's clothes, 1774; adopted female attire,

1777 ; returned to England, 1785 ; made a living by exhibiting his skill as a swordsman ; discovered to be a man at his death, 1810 ; left in manuscript materials for a life of the Count de Vauban ; published historical and autobiographical pamphlets. [xiv. 381]

DE QUINCEY, THOMAS (1785–1859), author of 'Confessions of an Opium Eater' ; educated at Bath grammar school and at Winkfield, Wiltshire ; sent to Manchester grammar school, 1801 ; became acquainted with Roscoe, Currie, and Lady Carbery, who consulted him in her Greek and Latin studies ; left school and rambled about in Wales, 1802, finally going to London, where he led a Bohemian life and met the Ann of his 'Confessions' ; studied Hebrew and German at Worcester College, Oxford, where he matriculated, 17 Dec. 1803, and first began opium-eating ; made the acquaintance of Coleridge, Wordsworth, and Southey, 1807, of Lamb and Sir H. Davy, 1808 ; read German metaphysics and drew up a 'Prolegomena of all future systems of Political Economy' on the lines of Ricardo, 1819 ; editor of the 'Westmoreland Gazette,' 1819–20 ; wrote his 'Confessions of an English Opium-Eater' in London, 1821, for the 'London Magazine' ; translated the 'Laocoon,' 1826, and wrote the first part of 'Murder as one of the Fine Arts,' 1827, for 'Blackwood's Magazine' ; published 'Klosterheim' at Edinburgh, 1832 ; contributed reminiscences of the Lake poets to 'Tait's Magazine,' 1834 ; published 'The Logic of Political Economy,' 1844. He aimed at popularising German philosophy and reviving the English prose style of the seventeenth century. [xiv. 385]

DERBY, EARLS OF. [See FERRERS, ROBERT DE, 1240 ?–1279 ? ; STANLEY, THOMAS, first EARL, 1435 ?–1504 ; STANLEY, EDWARD, third EARL, 1508–1572 ; STANLEY, HENRY, fourth EARL, 1531–1593 ; STANLEY, FERDINANDO, fifth EARL, 1559–1594 ; STANLEY, JAMES, seventh EARL, 1607–1651 ; STANLEY, EDWARD SMITH, thirteenth EARL, 1775–1851 ; STANLEY, EDWARD GEORGE GEOFFREY SMITH, fourteenth EARL, 1799–1869 ; STANLEY, EDWARD HENRY, fifteenth EARL, 1826–1893.]

DERBY, COUNTESSES OF. [See STANLEY, CHARLOTTE, 1599–1664 ; FARREN, ELIZABETH, 1759 ?–1829.]

DERBY, ALFRED THOMAS (1821–1873), painter ; son of William Derby [q. v.] ; painted figure-subjects, portraits, and scenes from Sir Walter Scott's novels. [xiv. 391]

DERBY, WILLIAM (1786–1847), water-colour and miniature-painter ; drew for Lodge's 'Portraits of Illustrious Personages of Great Britain,' 1825 ; exhibited at the Royal Academy and other institutions, 1811–42. [xiv. 391]

DERHAM, SAMUEL (1655–1689), physician ; M.A. Magdalen Hall, Oxford, 1679 ; M.D., 1687 ; published an 'Account of Ilmington Waters in Warwickshire,' 1685, which established the reputation of the place. [xiv. 392]

DERHAM, WILLIAM (1657–1735), divine ; B.A. Trinity College, Oxford, 1679 ; vicar of Wargrave, 1682, of Upminster, Essex, 1689 ; F.R.S., 1702 ; Boyle lecturer, 1711 and 1712 ; chief works, 'Physico-Theology' (his Boyle lectures), published, 1713, and 'Astro-Theology,' 1715, two statements of the argument from final causes. [xiv. 392]

DERHAM, WILLIAM (1702–1757), president of St. John's College, Oxford ; son of William Derham (1657–1735) [q. v.] ; entered Merchant Taylors' School, 1714 ; fellow of St. John's College, Oxford, 1724 ; M.A., 1729 ; Whyte's professor of moral philosophy, 1737 ; D.D., 1742 ; president of St. John's, 1748–57. [xiv. 393]

DERING. [See also DEERING.]

DERING, EDWARD (1540 ?–1576), puritan divine ; B.A., and fellow, Christ's College, Cambridge, 1560 ; M.A., 1563 ; university proctor, 1566 ; chaplain of the Tower of London ; prohibited from preaching in consequence of his denunciations of the clergy, 1570 ; prebendary of Salisbury, 1571 ; lectured on the first part of the Epistle to the Hebrews, 1572 ; summoned before the Star-chamber for unorthodox teaching, but acquitted, 1573 ; his collected works published, 1614. [xiv. 393]

DERING, SIR EDWARD (1598–1644), antiquary and politician ; educated at Magdalene College, Cambridge ; knighted, 1619 ; created baronet, 1627 ; lieutenant of Dover Castle ; M.P. for Kent in the Long parliament, 1640 ;

moved the first reading of the Root and Branch Bill, 1641 ; became an episcopal royalist by his vote on the Grand Remonstrance, 1641 ; imprisoned, 1642 ; escaped and took up arms for the king, but resigned his commission, 1643 ; accepted the parliament's pardon, 1644. [xiv. 395]

DERING, HENEAGE (1665–1750), antiquary and divine ; entered of the Inner Temple, 1678 ; pensioner of Clare College, Cambridge, 1680 ; barrister, Inner Temple, 1690 ; LL.D., *per literas regias,* 1701 ; prebendary of York, 1705–50 ; dean of Ripon, 1711 ; author of 'Reliquiæ Eboracenses,' 1743, and 'De Senectute,' 1746, two Latin poems. [xiv. 396]

DERING or **DEERING,** RICHARD (d. 1630), musician ; studied music in Italy ; organist to the English convent at Brussels, 1617 ; organist to Queen Henrietta Maria, 1625 ; published 'Cantiones Sacræ sex vocum cum basso continuo ad organum' at Antwerp, 1597. [xiv. 398]

DERLINGTON, JOHN DE (d. 1284). [See DARLINGTON.]

DERMOD, MACMURRAGH (1110 ?–1171). [See MAC MURCHADA, DIARMID.]

DERMODY, THOMAS (1775–1802), Irish poet ; served abroad as second lieutenant in the wagon corps ; published 'Poems Moral and Descriptive,' 1800, 'Poems on various Subjects,' 1802, and a pamphlet entitled 'The Rights of Justice,' 1793. [xiv. 399]

DERMOTT, LAURENCE (1720–1791), freemason ; deputy grand-master of the 'Antient' masons of Atholl, 1771–87 ; wrote 'Ahiman Rezon,' a masonic work, 1756. [xiv. 399]

DE ROS, BARONS. [See ROS.]

DERRICK, SAMUEL (1724–1769), author ; friend of Dr. Johnson ; published translations from the French, letters, books of minor criticism, and a few poems ; edited Dryden's 'Works,' 1760. [xiv. 399]

DERRICKE, JOHN (fl. 1578), author of the 'Image of Ireland,' a poem, published, 1581. [xiv. 400]

DERWENTWATER, third EARL OF (1689–1716). [See RADCLIFFE, JAMES.]

DE RYCK, WILLIAM (1635–1697), history painter ; born at Antwerp and bred as a goldsmith ; visited England in the reign of William III and became a painter. [xiv. 400]

DESAGULIERS, JOHN THEOPHILUS (1683–1744), natural philosopher ; born at La Rochelle ; brought to England by his father, a Huguenot refugee, 1685 ; B.A. Christ Church, Oxford, 1710 ; lecturer on experimental philosophy at Hart Hall, Oxford, 1710 ; M.A., 1712 ; F.R.S., 1714 ; presented to the living of Whitchurch, Middlesex, 1714 ; LL.D. Oxford, 1718 ; invented the planetarium ; published works on physics, astronomy, and mechanics, also 'The Contributions of the Free-Masons,' 1732. [xiv. 400]

DESAGULIERS, THOMAS (1725 ?–1780), lieutenant-general and colonel-commandant of royal artillery ; son of John Theophilus Desaguliers [q. v.] ; cadet in the royal artillery, 1740 ; captain, 1745 ; engaged at Fontenoy, 1745 ; lieutenant-colonel, 1757 ; in charge of siege operations at Belleisle, 1761 ; invented a method of firing small shot from mortars and an instrument for verifying the bores of cannon ; colonel commandant of the royal artillery, 1762 ; F.R.S., 1763 ; lieutenant general, 1777. [xiv. 401]

DE SAUMAREZ. [See SAUMAREZ.]

DESBARRES, JOSEPH FREDERICK WALSH or WALLET (1722–1824), military engineer ; of Huguenot origin ; lieutenant 60th regiment, 1756 ; made successful expedition against North American Indians, 1757 ; retook Newfoundland, 1762 ; surveyed coast of Nova Scotia, 1763–73 ; lieutenant-governor of Cape Breton, 1784–1805, of Prince Edward's island, 1805–13 ; colonel, 1798 ; published charts of the Atlantic and North American coasts. [xiv. 402]

DESBOROUGH, DESBOROW, or **DISBROWE,** JOHN (1608–1680), major-general ; commanded Cromwellian horse at storming of Bristol, 1645 ; colonel, 1648 ; fought as major-general at Worcester, 1651 ; commissioner of the treasury, 1653 ; general of the fleet, 1653 ; M.P.,

Cambridgeshire, 1654, Somerset, 1656; privy councillor, 1657; led the army's opposition to Richard Cromwell, 1659; given a colonel's commission by the Rump parliament, but soon cashiered, 1659; imprisoned on suspicion of being concerned in a plot to kill Charles II and Queen Henrietta Maria, 1660; imprisoned for intriguing in Holland, 1666; released, 1667; nicknamed the 'grim Gyant Desborough' in a pasquinade of 1661. [xiv. 403]

DESBOROUGH, SAMUEL (1619–1690), statesman; brother of John Desborough [q. v.]; one of the original settlers of Guilford, Connecticut, 1641; keeper of the great seal of Scotland, 1657; represented Midlothian in parliament, 1656, and Edinburgh, 1658–9. [xiv. 405]

DESENFANS, NOEL JOSEPH (1745–1807), picture-dealer; born at Douay; commissioned by Stanislaus, last king of Poland, to collect pictures in England for a Polish national collection; sold this collection, 1802, Poland being dismembered and Russia repudiating the debt. [xiv. 405]

DES GRANGES, DAVID (*fl.* 1625–1675), miniature-painter; engraver; limner to Charles II in Scotland, 1651. [xiv. 406]

DESMAIZEAUX, PIERRE (1673?–1745), miscellaneous writer; born in Auvergne; came to England with the third Lord Shaftesbury, 1699; F.R.S., 1720; gentleman of his majesty's privy chamber, 1722; friend of Joseph Addison [q. v.] and Anthony Collins [q. v.]; consulted by Hume on his 'Treatise of Human Nature,' 1739; edited Saint-Evremond, 1705, and Bayle's works, 1725–31, translated 'Télémaque,' 1742, and was the author of some biographies and compilations. [xiv. 406]

DESMOND, EARLS OF. [See FITZTHOMAS, MAURICE, first EARL, *d.* 1356; FITZGERALD, GERALD, fourth EARL, *d.* 1398; FITZGERALD, THOMAS, eighth EARL, 1426?–1468; FITZGERALD, JAMES (FITZMAURICE), thirteenth EARL, *d.* 1540; FITZGERALD, JAMES (FITZJOHN), fourteenth EARL, *d.* 1558; FITZGERALD, GERALD, fifteenth EARL, *d.* 1583; FITZGERALD, JAMES, the town EARL, 1570?–1601; FITZGERALD, JAMES, the Sugan EARL, *d.* 1608.]

D'ESPAGNE, JEAN (1591–1659), French protestant pastor and theologian; pastor at Orange, 1620; published 'Antiduello,' a discussion on the morality of the duel, 1632; pastor to a French congregation in London, which came to regard him as a schismatic. [xiv. 408]

DESPARD, EDWARD MARCUS (1751–1803), officer in colonial service; served in Jamaica as lieutenant, 50th regiment, 1772; commandant of the island of Rattan on the Spanish main, 1781; captured the Spanish possessions on the Black River, 1782; superintendent of his majesty's affairs in Yucatan, 1784–90; suspended on frivolous charges by Lord Grenville; imprisoned on account of his claim for compensation, 1798; devised in London plot against the government, 1802; executed for high treason at Newington. [xiv. 408]

DESPARD, JOHN (1745–1829), general; brother of Edward Marcus Despard [q. v.]; fought in the seven years' war; lieutenant in the 12th regiment, 1762; lieutenant, 7th regiment, 1767; fought in the American war of independence; taken prisoner at York Town; released, 1782; colonel, 1795; commandant of troops at Cape Breton, 1799–1807; general, 1814. [xiv. 409]

DESPENSER, EDWARD LE (*d.* 1375), warrior; grandson of Hugh le Despenser the younger [q. v.]; fought in Edward III's French campaigns and under Pope Urban V in 1369; K.G. [xiv. 416]

DESPENSER or **SPENCER,** HENRY LE (*d.* 1406), bishop of Norwich; canon of Salisbury; nominated by Urban V to the bishopric of Norwich, 1370; defeated the Norfolk peasants in their entrenchments at North Walsham, 1381; commanded for Pope Urban VI against the antipope's adherents, in Flanders, whom he defeated at Dunkirk, 1383; raised siege of Ypres; came to terms with the French, September 1383; deprived of his temporalities; denounced as a fighting bishop by Wycliffe; helped to repel the French invasion of Scotland, and was restored to his temporalities, 1385; persecuted the lollards, 1389; imprisoned for his loyal adherence to Richard II; reconciled to Henry IV, 1401. [xiv. 410]

DESPENSER, HUGH LE (*d.* 1265), last justiciary of England; accompanied Richard, king of the Romans, to Germany, 1257; named commissioner for the barons by the 'Provisions of Oxford,' 1258; justiciary of the barons, 1260; reappointed justiciary, 1263; fought for the barons at Lewes, 1264; arbitrator for arranging terms of peace, 1264; summoned to Simon de Montfort's parliament, 1264; killed at Evesham, 1265. [xiv. 412]

DESPENSER, HUGH LE, the elder, EARL OF WINCHESTER (1262–1326), son of Hugh le Despenser (*d.* 1265) [q. v.]; fought at Dunbar; took part in Edward I's expedition to Flanders, 1297; obtained a bull from Clement V absolving Edward I from the oaths he had taken to his people, 1305; upheld Gaveston, Edward II's favourite, 1308; forced to withdraw from the court and the council, 1314; supported Edward II at the parliament of Northampton, 1318; banished, together with his son, Hugh le Despenser the younger [q. v.], the king giving way to a coalition of the nobles, 1321; returned, and was made Earl of Winchester, 1322; captured by Queen Isabella, whom he had induced the king to outlaw and executed, 1326. [xiv. 413]

DESPENSER, HUGH LE, the younger (*d.* 1326), baron; son of Hugh le Despenser the elder [q. v.]; knighted, 1306; king's chamberlain, 1313; attacked by a confederacy of the barons under the Earl of Hereford, partly on account of his desertion to the side of the king, 1321; banished, 1321; recalled, 1322; employed to negotiate a truce with Scotland, 1323; attempted to weaken the barons by enlisting the common people on the side of the king; caught at Llantrissant by the followers of Queen Isabella, and executed at Hereford, 1326. [xiv. 415]

DESPENSER, THOMAS LE, EARL OF GLOUCESTER (1373–1400), son of Edward le Despenser [q. v.]; upheld Richard II against Gloucester, Arundel, and Warwick, 1397; created Earl of Gloucester, 1397; accompanied Richard II to Ireland, 1399; commissioner for pronouncing the sentence of deposition on Richard II, 1399; accused of poisoning the Duke of Gloucester, and degraded from his earldom, 1399; joined in a conspiracy which was betrayed by the Earl of Rutland; beheaded, 1400. [xiv. 417]

D'ESTE, SIR AUGUSTUS FREDERICK (1794–1848), son of the Duke of Sussex, who displeased his father, George III, by an illegal marriage; present as aide-de-camp to Sir John Lambert at the attack on New Orleans, 1814; lieutenant-colonel, 1824; colonel, 1838; knight-commander of the Hanoverian Guelphic order, 1830; unsuccessfully claimed his father's title, 1843. [xiv. 417]

DE TABLEY, BARONS. [See LEICESTER, SIR JOHN FLEMING, first BARON, 1762–1827; WARREN, JOHN BYRNE LEICESTER, third BARON, 1835–1895.]

DETHICK, SIR GILBERT (1519?–1584), Garter king-of-arms; probably of Dutch extraction and naturalised; Rouge Croix pursuivant, 1540; Richmond herald, 1540; Garter king-of-arms, 1550; knighted, 1551; accompanied Somerset in his Scottish expedition, 1547; member of the old Society of Antiquaries. [xiv. 418]

DETHICK, SIR WILLIAM (1543–1612), Garter king-of-arms; son of Sir Gilbert Dethick [q. v.]; Rouge Croix pursuivant, 1567; York herald, 1570; Garter king-of-arms, 1586; suspended for unduly extending his prerogative, but restored by the queen's clemency; member of the old Society of Antiquaries, 1593; proclaimed Essex a traitor, 1601; knighted, 1603; deprived of Garter for irregularities at the investiture of the Duke of Würtemberg, 1605; author of some heraldic works and papers on antiquities, printed in Hearne's 'Curious Discourses.' [xiv. 419]

DETROSIER, ROWLAND (1800?–1834), popular lecturer and political reformer; self-educated; supervised Swedenborgian school at Hulme; framed a liturgy for his chapel at Stockport; corresponded with Bentham and founded mechanics' institutions in Hulme and Salford; founder and president of the Banksian Society, Manchester, 1829; secretary of the National Political Union, 1831; lectured on science at Manchester and Stratford, advocating moral and political instruction for the working classes. [xiv. 421]

DEUSDEDIT (*d.* 663?), sixth archbishop of Canterbury and the first of English origin. [xiv. 422]

DEUTSCH, EMANUEL OSCAR MENAHEM (1829–1873), Semitic scholar; born in Silesia; proceeded to the theological faculty of Berlin, 1845; assistant in the library of the British Museum, 1855–70; best known by his essay on the 'Talmud,' in the 'Quarterly Review,' 1867; deciphered Phœnician inscriptions; died of cancer at Alexandria. [xiv. 422]

DE VERE. [See also VERE.]

DE VERE, SIR AUBREY, second baronet (1788–1846), poet; educated at Harrow; succeeded to baronetcy, 1818; published historical dramas and (1842) 'The Song of Faith, Devout Exercises and Sonnets.' [xiv. 423]

DEVERELL, formerly **PEDLEY**, ROBERT (1760–1841), author; seventh wrangler, St. John's College, Cambridge, 1781; fellow, 1784; M.A. 1784; M.P., Saltash, 1802; published some eccentric works on the knowledge of the ancients, and propounded in 'Hieroglyphics and other Antiquities' (1813) a strange theory that Shakespeare's characters and incidents were suggested by lunar appearances. [xiv. 424]

DEVEREUX, SIR JOHN, second BARON DEVEREUX (d. 1393), warrior; fought with Du Guesclin against Don Pedro in Spain, 1366; governor of Limousin, 1370; defeated by Du Guesclin, 1373; served with the English fleet at sea, 1377; governor of Calais, 1380; commissioner to negotiate a peace with France, 1382; warden of the Cinque Ports, 1387; K.G., 1388. [xiv. 424]

DEVEREUX, ROBERT, second EARL OF ESSEX (1566–1601), eldest son of Walter Devereux, first earl [q. v.]; matriculated at Trinity College, Cambridge, 1579; M.A. 1581; created knight banneret for his bravery at Zutphen, 1586; became a favourite of Queen Elizabeth and master of the horse, 1587; quarrelled with Charles Blount, earl of Devonshire (1563–1606) [q. v.], and offended Ralegh; K.G., 1588; joined the faction of Don Antonio, a claimant to the throne of Portugal, 1589; married Frances, the widow of Sir Philip Sidney, thereby displeasing Elizabeth, 1590; supposed to favour puritanism, 1591; commanded a force sent to the help of Henry of Navarre, 1591; took Gournay, 1591; recalled, 1592; privy councillor, 1593; unsuccessfully appealed to Elizabeth on two occasions to give some preferment to Francis Bacon, then a struggling barrister; received political advice and literary assistance from Bacon; assisted by Don Antonio, tracked out the plot of Roderigo Lopez [q. v.] against the queen's life, 1594; established a sort of foreign intelligence department, 1595; defeated the Spaniards in a naval battle off Cadiz, and took the town, 1596; mistakenly dissuaded by his colleagues from putting out to intercept the Spanish treasure fleet; master of the ordnance, 1597; advised by Bacon to study Irish affairs; set out on an expedition to the Azores, which proved a failure, and was nearly intercepted by Spanish ships at Falmouth on his return, 1597; earl-marshal, 1597; opposed Burghley's policy of peace with Spain, 1598; affronted the queen when discussing the appointment of a lord deputy in Ireland, 1598; chancellor of Cambridge University, 1598; appointed, amid popular rejoicing, lieutenant and governor-general of Ireland, 1599; punished his soldiers by decimation after a defeat at Arklow, 1599; forbidden to return to England, and ordered to proceed against Ulster, 1599; made a truce, renewable every six weeks, with Tyrone, and set out for London, arriving there 28 Sept. 1599; accused before a specially constituted court of leaving his government and entering into a 'dishonourable and dangerous treaty' with Tyrone, 5 June 1600; set at liberty, August 1600; induced by Mountjoy, Southampton, and others (1601) to contrive a plot for securing the dismissal of Elizabeth's counsellors; attempted to raise citizens of London, and was proclaimed traitor, February 1601; tried at Westminster Hall, where his former friend and protégé Bacon spoke for the prosecution, and sentenced to death, 19 Feb.; executed 25 Feb. 1601. Elizabeth is said to have been ready to pardon him had he asked forgiveness, but the story of the ring and of its suppression by the Countess of Nottingham is doubtful. Essex wrote numerous sonnets, and was credited by Wotton with special skill in masques; as a patron of literature he was panegyrised by Daniel, Chapman, Spenser, and Ben Jonson. [xiv. 425]

DEVEREUX, ROBERT, third EARL OF ESSEX (1591–1646), parliamentary general; son of Robert, second earl of Essex [q. v.]; restored in blood and honour by act of

parliament, 1604; vice-admiral in the Cadiz expedition, 1625; supported the Petition of Right, 1628; voted for disallowing Charles I's appeal for assistance to the House of Lords, 1640; privy councillor, 1641, voting for the death of Strafford contrary to Charles I's expectations; general of the parliamentary army, 1642; fought at Edgehill, 1642; took Reading, 1643; declared in favour of Pym's policy of continuing the war, 1643; relieved Gloucester, August 1643; fought without substantial success at Newbury, 1643; resigned from irritation at Cromwell's hostility to the Scots, 1645. [xiv. 440]

DEVEREUX, WALTER, first VISCOUNT HEREFORD (d. 1558), joint-constable of Warwick Castle, 1511; went to act with the Spaniards in an intended invasion of Guienne, 1512; fought under Admiral Howard off Conquêt, 1513; K.G., 1523; chief-justice of South Wales, 1525; privy councillor, 1550; created Viscount Hereford, 1550. [xiv. 443]

DEVEREUX, WALTER, first EARL OF ESSEX and second VISCOUNT HEREFORD (1541?–1576), Irish adventurer; succeeded to his grandfather's titles, Lord of Chartley and Viscount Hereford, 1558; raised a troop to aid in suppressing the northern rebellion of 1569; K.G., 1572; created Earl of Essex, 1572; undertook to conquer Ulster, 1573; attempted to rid Ulster of the Scots under Sorley Boy, but subsequently decided to ally himself with the Scots against the Irishry of O'Neill; treacherously seized and executed Sir Brian Mac Phelim, 1574; earl-marshal of Ireland, 1575; made a useless and cruel raid in Rathlin, and was recalled, 1575; reappointed earl-marshal, 1576; groundlessly reported to have been poisoned at the instigation of the Earl of Leicester, who married his widow. [xiv. 443]

DEVEY, GEORGE (1820–1886), architect; fellow of the Royal Institute of Architects; exhibited at the Royal Academy, 1841–8; added to, and altered many of the English mansions. [xiv. 447]

DEVIS, ARTHUR (1711?–1787), portrait-painter; exhibited at the Free Society of Artists, 1762–80; restored Sir James Thornton's paintings in the hall at Greenwich. [xiv. 447]

DEVIS, ARTHUR WILLIAM (1763–1822), portrait and history painter; son of Arthur Devis [q. v.]; appointed draughtsman in a voyage projected by the East India Company, c. 1783; wrecked on the Pelew islands; proceeded to Canton and thence to Bengal; painted portraits and historical subjects, sixty-five of which he exhibited (1779–1821) at the Royal Academy. [xiv. 448]

DEVISME, LOUIS (1720–1776), diplomatist; of Huguenot origin; educated at Westminster School and Christ Church, Oxford; M.A., 1746; represented England at diet of Ratisbon; envoy extraordinary and minister plenipotentiary at Stockholm; died at Stockholm. [xiv. 448]

DEVON, eleventh EARL OF. [See COURTENAY, WILLIAM REGINALD, 1807–1888.]

DEVONSHIRE, DUKES OF. [See CAVENDISH, WILLIAM, first DUKE, 1640–1707; CAVENDISH, WILLIAM, fourth DUKE, 1720–1764; CAVENDISH, WILLIAM GEORGE SPENCER, sixth DUKE, 1790–1858; CAVENDISH, SIR WILLIAM, seventh DUKE, 1808–1891.]

DEVONSHIRE, DUCHESS OF (1757–1806). [See CAVENDISH, GEORGIANA.]

DEVONSHIRE or **DEVON**, EARLS OF. [See STAFFORD, HUMPHREY, 1439–1469; COURTENAY, HENRY, 1496?–1538; COURTENAY, EDWARD, 1526?–1556; BLOUNT, CHARLES, 1563–1606; CAVENDISH, WILLIAM, first EARL, d. 1626; CAVENDISH, WILLIAM, second EARL, 1591?–1628; CAVENDISH, WILLIAM, third EARL, 1617–1684; CAVENDISH, WILLIAM, fourth EARL, 1640–1707.]

DEVONSHIRE, COUNTESS OF (d. 1675). [See CAVENDISH, CHRISTIANA.]

DEWAR, JAMES (1793–1846), musician; organist at St. George's Episcopal Church, Edinburgh, 1815–35; conducted the Edinburgh Musical Association. [xiv. 449]

D'EWES or **DEWES**, GERRARD, GEERARD, or GARRET (d. 1591), printer; descended from the ancient lords of Kessel in Guelderland; under-warden of the Stationers' Company, 1581. [xiv. 449]

DEWES or DUWES, GILES (d. 1535), writer on the French language; librarian to Henry VII and (from 1509) Henry VIII; teacher of French to Prince Arthur; French teacher to the Princess Mary, 1527, for whom he wrote a French grammar, supplemented by dialogues, 1528. [xiv. 449]

D'EWES or DEWES, PAUL (1567–1631), one of the six clerks in chancery; son of Gerrard D'Ewes [q. v.]. [xiv. 449]

D'EWES, SIR SIMONDS (1602–1650), antiquarian writer; grandson of Gerrard D'Ewes [q. v.]; entered St. John's College, Cambridge, 1618; barrister, Middle Temple, 1623; joined Sir Robert Cotton, who had introduced him to Selden, in establishing the claim of Robert Vere to the earldom of Oxford, 1626; knighted, 1626; high sheriff for Suffolk, 1639; M.P., Sudbury, 1640; created baronet, 1641; expelled from parliament by Colonel Pride, 1648; compiled an Anglo-Saxon dictionary (never printed); author of 'Journals of all the Parliaments during the Reign of Queen Elizabeth' (published, 1682), of an 'Autobiography' (first published, 1845), and of unpublished transcripts of monastic cartularies and registers. [xiv. 450]

DE WILDE, GEORGE JAMES (1804–1871), editor of the 'Northampton Mercury,' and friend of Leigh Hunt, the Cowden Clarkes and Sir James Stephen; son of Samuel de Wilde [q. v.]. [xiv. 454]

DE WILDE, SAMUEL (1748–1832), portrait-painter; born in Holland of Dutch parents; exhibited at the Society of Artists (1776) and the Royal Academy; painted portraits of actors in character. [xiv. 453]

DE WINT, PETER (1784–1849), landscape-painter; member of the Society of Painters in Water-colours; exhibited at the Royal Academy, 1807–28; painted also in oils; his chief subject being the scenery of northern and eastern England. [xiv. 454]

DEWSBURY, WILLIAM (1621–1688), quaker preacher and author; joined the parliament army for a time; converted to quakerism by hearing George Fox preach; frequently imprisoned for his religious opinions; wrote religious tracts. [xiv. 455]

D'EYNCOURT, CHARLES TENNYSON (1784–1861), politician; M.A. Trinity College, Cambridge, 1818; barrister, Inner Temple, 1806; whig M.P. for Great Grimsby, 1818–26, for Bletchingley, 1826–31, and for Stamford, 1831; F.S.A., F.R.S., 1829; M.P. for Lambeth, 1832–1852; privy councillor, 1832; deputy-lieutenant for Lincolnshire; advocated the repeal of the corn and navigation laws. [xiv. 455]

D'HÈLE or D'HELL, THOMAS (1740 ?–1780). [See HALES, THOMAS.]

DIAMOND, HUGH WELCH (1809–1886), photographer; of Huguenot origin; M.R.C.S., 1834; resident superintendent of female patients at the Surrey County Asylum, 1848–58; secretary to the London Photographic Society, 1853; said to have invented the paper or cardboard photographic portrait. [xv. 1]

DIBBEN, THOMAS (d. 1741), Latin poet; educated at Westminster School and Trinity College, Cambridge; fellow, 1698; M.A., 1703; D.D., 1721; chaplain to lord privy seal at congress of Utrecht, 1713; precentor of St. Paul's, 1714; translated Prior's 'Carmen Seculare' for 1700 into Latin verse. [xv. 1]

DIBDIN, CHARLES (1745–1814), dramatist and songwriter; composed 'The Shepherd's Artifice,' a pastoral operetta, 1762; acted at Richmond Theatre, 1762, and later at Covent Garden; composed music for Garrick's Shakespeare jubilee at Stratford, 1769; quarrelled with Garrick, but was reconciled, 1769; discharged by Garrick on account of his ill-usage of a Miss Pitt, his mistress; his 'Cobler' and 'Waterman' produced at the Haymarket; satirised Garrick in 'The Comic Mirror,' a puppet-play; wrote the 'Seraglio,' containing 'Blow high, blow low,' the earliest of his sea-songs, 1776; produced 'Professional Volunteers,' 'The Rent Day,' 'A Thanksgiving,' and 'Commodore Pennant,' his last pieces, at the Lyceum, 1808; composed entertainments and sketches in which were introduced the nautical songs by which he is best remembered, as well as a 'History of the

Stage,' 1795, an autobiography and two novels, 'Hannah Hewit,' 1792, the 'Younger Brother,' 1793. [xv. 2]

DIBDIN, CHARLES, the younger (1768–1833), proprietor and acting-manager of Sadler's Wells Theatre, for which he wrote plays, songs, and spectacles; natural son of Charles Dibdin [q. v.]. [xv. 5]

DIBDIN, HENRY EDWARD (1813–1866), musician; son of Charles Dibdin the younger [q. v.]; played the harp at Paganini's last concert, Covent Garden Theatre, 1832; organist of Trinity Chapel, Edinburgh, 1833–66; published the 'Standard Psalm Book,' 1857, and 'The Praise Book,' 1865. [xv. 6]

DIBDIN, THOMAS FROGNALL (1776–1847), bibliographer; nephew of Charles Dibdin (1745–1814) [q. v.]; born in India; educated at St. John's College, Oxford; M.A., 1825; D.D., 1825; brought under the notice of Lord Spencer by his 'Introduction to the Knowledge of Rare and Valuable Editions of the Greek and Latin Classics,' 1802; published 'Bibliomania,' 1809; was an original member of the Roxburghe Club, 1812; catalogued Lord Spencer's library at Althorp, though hampered by his ignorance of Greek; published a 'Bibliographical, Antiquarian, and Picturesque Tour' (1821), the outcome of travels on the continent; rector of St. Mary's, Bryanston Square, from 1824. His reprints and bibliographical writings, although valued by book-collectors, are often inaccurate. [xv. 6]

DIBDIN, THOMAS JOHN (1771–1841), actor and dramatist; illegitimate son of Charles Dibdin (1745–1814) [q. v.]; shown on the stage as Cupid to Mrs. Siddons's Venus, 1775; apprenticed to London upholsterer; ran away, and obtained theatrical engagement at Eastbourne under name of Merchant; wrote operas and dramatic trifles for Sadler's Wells, 1796; prompter and joint stage manager at Sadler's Wells; wrote 'The British Raft,' a piece containing 'The Snug Little Island,' a song which became very popular, 1797; composed, in honour of Nelson's victory, 'The Mouth of the Nile,' while performing on a seven years' engagement at Covent Garden, 1798; produced (1801–2) 'The Cabinet,' his first and best opera; prompter and pantomime writer at Drury Lane Theatre, when reopened after the fire of 1809; financially ruined by his ill-success as proprietor of the Surrey Theatre, 1822; wrote nearly two thousand songs and about two hundred operas and plays. [xv. 9]

DICCONSON, EDWARD (1670–1752), Roman catholic prelate; educated at the English college, Douay; professor of poetry, 1708–9, of syntax, 1709–10, and of philosophy, 1711–12; D.D.; vice-president and professor of theology, 1714–20; vicar-apostolic of the northern district of England, 1740; bishop of Malla in partibus infidelium, 1741. [xv. 11]

DICETO, RALPH DE (d. 1202 ?), dean of St. Paul's; archdeacon of Middlesex, 1152; dean of St. Paul's, 1180; made survey of capitulary property of deanery, 1181; built deanery-house and chapel within cathedral precincts; author of 'Abbreviationes Chronicorum' and 'Ymagines Historiarum,' two works on contemporary history; frequently mediated between Henry II and the ecclesiastics. [xv. 12]

DICK, SIR ALEXANDER (1703–1785), physician; studied medicine at Edinburgh and Leyden; M.D., 1725; M.D. St. Andrews, 1727; succeeded to the baronetcy of Dick, 1746; president of the College of Physicians of Edinburgh, 1756–63; assisted in obtaining charter for Royal Society of Edinburgh; gold medallist of Society of Arts 'for best specimen of rhubarb,' 1774; correspondent of Dr. Johnson. [xv. 14]

DICK, ANNE, LADY (d. 1741), verse-writer; née Mackenzie; married Sir William Dick of Prestonfield; notorious for the eccentricity of her habits and her virulent epigrams. [xv. 14]

DICK, DIRTY (pseudonym) (1735 ?–1809). [See BENTLEY, NATHANIEL.]

DICK, JOHN (1764–1833), theological writer; studied at King's College, Aberdeen; published 'The Conduct and Doom of False Teachers,' to combat unitarian thought, 1788; maintained plenary inspiration in an 'Essay on the Inspiration of the Scriptures,' 1800; minister of Greyfriars, Glasgow, 1801–33; D.D. Princeton College, New Jersey, 1815; theological professor to the associate synod, 1820–33. [xv. 14]

DICK, ROBERT (1811–1866), geologist and botanist; self-taught; apprenticed to a baker; re-discovered northern holy-grass, 1834; furnished information to Hugh Miller, for whom he also procured fossils. [xv. 16]

DICK, SIR ROBERT HENRY (1785?–1846), major-general; lieutenant 62nd regiment, 1802; captain Ross-shire buffs, 1804; served in Egypt, 1807; major, 1808; commander of battalions in Peninsula, 1809; lieutenant-colonel, 1812; senior major in Flanders, 1815; colonel, 1825; major-general, 1837; K.C.B., 1838; acting commander-in-chief at Madras, 1841–2; commanded third infantry division in Sikh war; killed at Sobraon. [xv. 16]

DICK, THOMAS (1774–1857), scientific writer; entered Edinburgh University, 1794; teacher in secession school at Methven, where he did much to popularise science, and at Perth; LL.D. New York; M.R.A.S., 1853; chief works, 'The Christian Philosopher,' 1823, and 'The Sidereal Heavens,' 1840. [xv. 18]

DICK, SIR WILLIAM (1580?–1655), provost of Edinburgh; advanced 6,000l. to James VI, 1618; customs and excise farmer; lord provost of Edinburgh, 1638 and 1639; extended the trade of the Firth of Forth; advanced money for the cause of Montrose, 1639; knighted by Charles I, 1642; created baronet of Nova Scotia, c. 1642; reduced to destitution by fine imposed by parliament for lending 20,000l. to Charles II in 1650. [xv. 18]

DICKENS, CHARLES JOHN HUFFAM (1812–1870), novelist; son of a government clerk; employed in making up parcels in an office at Hungerford Stairs, c. 1823; shorthand reporter of debates in Commons to 'True Sun,' and, in 1835, to 'Morning Chronicle'; contributed to 'Monthly Magazine,' 1833–5, and to 'Evening Chronicle,' 1835; these articles were collected and published as 'Sketches by Boz,' 1836; commenced 'Pickwick Papers,' 1836; produced 'Oliver Twist' in Bentley's 'Miscellany,' 1837–9, and 'Nicholas Nickleby,' 1838–9, in monthly numbers; wrote 'Master Humphrey's Clock,' a serial, 1840–1, in which first appeared 'Old Curiosity Shop' and 'Barnaby Rudge'; edited 'Pic-Nic Papers' for the benefit of the widow of his old publisher, Macrone, 1841; sailed for America (1842), where he advocated international copyright and abolition of slavery; commenced 'Martin Chuzzlewit' in serial form, 1843; assisted Miss Coutts, afterwards the Baroness Burdett Coutts, in philanthropic work; wrote the 'Christmas Carol,' 1843; settled at Genoa, where he wrote the 'Chimes' and learned Italian, 1844; first editor of 'Daily News,' January 1846, resigning in February; wrote in Switzerland, 1846, 'Dombey and Son' (published, 1848) and 'The Battle of Life'; manager of a theatrical company which performed Elizabethan dramas and modern comedies in the great provincial towns, 1847; started two journals, 'Household Words,' 1849, and subsequently 'All the Year Round'; published 'The Haunted Man,' 1848, and 'David Copperfield' in monthly numbers, 1849–50; produced 'Bleak House' in serial form, 1852–3, 'Hard Times,' 1854, and 'Little Dorrit,' 1855–7; began to give public readings, 1858; published his 'Tale of Two Cities' in 'All the Year Round,' 1859; produced 'Great Expectations,' 1860–1, and 'Our Mutual Friend,' 1864–5, both in monthly instalments; gave public readings in America, 1867 and 1868, and in England on his return, 1868; commenced 'The Mystery of Edwin Drood' in 1870, but died suddenly before completing it. He was buried in Westminster Abbey, 14 June 1870. His novels have probably had the largest number of readers of any English works of fiction. [xv. 20]

DICKENS, CHARLES (1837–1896), compiler; eldest son of Charles Dickens, the novelist [q. v.]; educated at King's College, London, and Eton; entered Baring's bank, 1855; set up in business in city, 1861; sub-editor of 'All the Year Round,' 1869, and sole proprietor on his father's death; chief partner in printing firm of Dickens & Evans; published series of dictionary-guides, 1879–84; gave readings from his father's works in America, 1887; reader in firm of Macmillan & Co., c. 1887. [Suppl. ii. 131]

DICKENSON, JOHN (fl. 1594), romance-writer; author of 'Arisbas,' 1594, 'Greene in Conceipt . . . The Tragique Historie of Faire Valeria of London,' 1598, and a pastoral poem in English hexameters. [xv. 32]

DICKIE, GEORGE (1812–1882), botanist; M.A. Marischal College, Aberdeen, 1830; professor of natural history, Belfast, 1849–60; M.D., professor of botany, Aberdeen, 1860–77; specialised on algæ, and published works on flora of east Scotland and Ulster. [xv. 32]

DICKINSON, CHARLES (1792–1842), bishop of Meath; M.A. Trinity College, Dublin, 1820; chaplain of the Female Orphan House, Dublin, 1822; vicar of St. Anne's, Dublin, 1833; D.D., 1834; bishop of Meath, 1840–2; published sermons and tracts. [xv. 32]

DICKINSON or **DICKENSON**, EDMUND (1624–1707), physician and alchemist; educated at Eton and Merton College, Oxford; probationer-fellow, 1647; M.A., 1649; M.D., 1656; induced by Mundanus, a French adept, to study chemistry; F.C.P., 1677; physician in ordinary to Charles II and James II; published 'Delphi Phœnicizantes,' 1666, and 'Physica vetus et vera,' claiming to base a philosophy on the Pentateuch, 1702. [xv. 33]

DICKINSON, JAMES (1659–1741), quaker; quaker minister, 1678; made three missionary voyages to America, visiting Barbados in 1692; 'commanded' to proclaim the Divine wrath at the death of Queen Mary, 1694. [xv. 34]

DICKINSON, JOHN (1815–1876), writer on India; educated at Eton; published 'Letters on the Cotton and Roads of Western India,' 1851; founded India Reform Society (1853), which insisted on leniency after the mutiny of 1857; corresponded with Holkar, maharajah of Indore; published 'India, its Government under Bureaucracy,' 1852, 'Dhar not Restored,' 1864–5, and other pamphlets. [xv. 35]

DICKINSON, JOSEPH (d. 1865), botanist; M.A. and M.D. Dublin and Cambridge, 1843; physician to the Royal Infirmary (1839) and other Liverpool institutions; F.R.S. and F.R.C.P.; published 'Flora of Liverpool,' 1851. [xv. 36]

DICKINSON, WILLIAM (1756–1822), topographer and legal writer; fellow of Jesus College, Cambridge; M.A., 1780; justice of the peace for Nottingham, Lincoln, Middlesex, Surrey, and Sussex; wrote on Nottinghamshire antiquities and justice law. [xv. 36]

DICKINSON, WILLIAM (1746–1823), mezzotint engraver; awarded premium by Society of Arts, 1767; printseller, 1773; died in Paris; engraved chiefly after Sir Joshua Reynolds. [xv. 37]

DICKONS, MARIA (1770?–1833), vocalist; née Poole; made her début at Covent Garden as Ophelia, 1793; appeared at the Lyceum as Clara in Sheridan's 'Duenna,' 1811, and at the King's Theatre as the Countess in Mozart's 'Nozze di Figaro,' 1812; honorary member of the Instituto Filarmonico of Venice. [xv. 37]

DICKSON, ADAM (1721–1776), writer on agriculture; M.A. Edinburgh; incumbent of Whittinghame in East Lothian, 1769–76; chief works, 'The Husbandry of the Ancients,' published 1788, and a 'Treatise on Agriculture,' vol. i. 1762, vol. ii. 1770. [xv. 38]

DICKSON, SIR ALEXANDER (1777–1840), major-general, royal artillery; second lieutenant, royal artillery, 1794; acting engineer at siege of Valetta, 1800; commander of artillery in South America, 1807; brigade-major in the operations before Oporto, 1809; major and lieutenant-colonel in the Portuguese service; superintended artillery operations in Peninsula, 1811 and 1812; commanded allied artillery at Vittoria, 1813; fought at Waterloo, 1815; inspector of artillery, 1822; director-general of the field-train department, 1833; major-general, 1837; G.C.B., 1838; F.R.G.S. [xv. 39]

DICKSON, ALEXANDER (1836–1887), botanist; graduated in medicine at Edinburgh, 1860; professor of botany at Dublin, at Glasgow, 1868, and at Edinburgh, 1879; regius keeper of the Royal Botanic Garden, Edinburgh, 1879; LL.D. Glasgow; F.R.S. Edinburgh; published scientific papers. [xv. 41]

DICKSON or **DICK**, DAVID (1583?–1663), Scottish divine; M.A. and professor of philosophy, Glasgow; minister at Irvine, 1618; deprived for declining the jurisdiction of the high court of commission, before which he was cited as an assailant of the five articles of Perth, 1622; permitted to return, 1623; professor of divinity at Glasgow, 1640–50; chaplain in the covenanters' army, 1639; professor of divinity at Edinburgh, 1650–60; ejected for refusing the oath of supremacy, 1660; commentator on scripture.   [xv. 41]

DICKSON, DAVID, the elder (1754–1820), theologian; studied at Glasgow and Edinburgh; minister first of the College Church and then of the New North Church, Edinburgh; opponent of Dr. M'Gill.   [xv. 42]

DICKSON, DAVID, the younger (1780–1842), presbyterian divine; educated at Edinburgh University; D.D. Edinburgh, 1824; senior minister of St. Cuthbert's Church, Edinburgh, 1827–42; published 'The Influence of Learning on Religion,' 1814, and other works.   [xv. 43]

DICKSON, ELIZABETH (1793?–1862), philanthropist; née Dalzel; married John Dickson; visited Algiers; made revelations about piracy (1809), which led to Lord Exmouth's expedition; died at Tripoli.
          [xv. 43]

DICKSON, JAMES (1737?–1822), botanist; of humble origin; author of 'Catalogus Plantarum Cryptogamicarum Britanniæ,' 1795, and some other botanical publications.   [xv. 44]

DICKSON, SIR JAMES ROBERT (1832–1901), Australian statesman; served in City of Glasgow Bank; emigrated to Victoria, 1854, and entered Bank of Australasia; auctioneer in Queensland, 1862; member for Enoggera of Queensland House of Assembly, 1872–87, and, 1876–87, held office in ministry; member for Bulimba, 1892, 1893, and 1896; premier, 1898–9; advocated formation of Australian commonwealth; delegate for Queensland; discussed project for commonwealth in London, 1900; minister for defence in first government of United Australia, 1900; K.C.M.G., 1901; honorary D.C.L. Oxford, 1900.
          [Suppl. ii. 131]

DICKSON, ROBERT (1804–1875), physician; M.D. Edinburgh, 1826; F.R.C.P., 1855; lectured on botany at St. George's Hospital.   [xv. 44]

DICKSON, SAMUEL (1802–1869), author of the 'Chrono-thermal System of Medicine'; pupil of Liston at Edinburgh; assistant-surgeon in the 30th regiment of foot at Madras; M.D. Glasgow, 1833; published 'Revelations on Cholera,' 1848; attacked received systems in 'The Fallacy of Physic as taught in the Schools,' 1836, and similar writings; originated hypothesis of the periodicity and intermittency of all vital actions.
          [xv. 44]

DICKSON, WILLIAM (1745–1804), Irish bishop; educated at Eton and Hertford College, Oxford; M.A., 1770; friend of Charles James Fox; bishop of Down and Connor, 1783.   [xv. 45]

DICKSON, WILLIAM GILLESPIE (1823–1876), legal writer; educated at the Edinburgh Academy and University; member of the Faculty of Advocates, 1847; procureur and advocate-general of Mauritius, 1856–67; sheriff-depute of Lanark, 1874; honorary LL.D. Edinburgh, 1874; published 'Treatise on the Law of Evidence in Scotland,' 1855.   [xv. 45]

DICKSON, WILLIAM STEEL (1744–1824), United Irishman; entered Glasgow College, 1761; denounced England's treatment of the American colonies, 1776; advocated enrolment of catholics as volunteers, 1779; minister at Portaferry, 1780; D.D. Glasgow; member of Wolf Tone's society of United Irishmen, 1791; instrumental in bringing about Catholic Relief Act, 1793; adjutant-general of the United Irish forces for co. Down, 1798; imprisoned for sedition at Belfast and, in 1799, at Fort George, Inverness-shire; released, 1802; minister of second Keady, co. Armagh, 1803; resigned in broken health, 1815; died in poverty.   [xv. 46]

DICUIL (fl. 825), Irish geographer; author of a 'Liber de Mensurâ Orbis Terræ,' professing to be based on survey of the world carried out by Theodosius (I?), and embodying the reports of recent travellers.   [xv. 48]

DIEST, ADRIAEN VAN (1656–1704).   [See VAN DIEST.]

DIGBY, EVERARD (fl. 1590), divine and author; bursar of St. John's College, Cambridge, 1567; scholar, 1570; Lady Margaret fellow, 1573; M.A., 1574; B.D., 1581; senior fellow, 1585; deprived for alleged insubordination and Romanist tendencies, 1587; author of the earliest treatise on swimming published in England,

1587; suggested classification of sciences in his 'De Duplici Methodo libri duo,' 1580, and 'Theoria Analytica,' 1579; propounded a theory of perception based on the active correspondence of mind and matter.   [xv. 50]

DIGBY, SIR EVERARD (1578–1606), conspirator; converted to catholicism at court by John Gerard, 1599; knighted, 1603; told off to excite a rising in the Midlands at the time of the Gunpowder plot, 1605; deserted his companions when besieged in Holbeach House, Staffordshire, 8 Nov. 1605; executed, 1606.   [xv. 51]

DIGBY, GEORGE, second EARL OF BRISTOL (1612–1677), son of John Digby, first earl of Bristol [q. v.]; born at Madrid; entered Magdalen College, Oxford, 1626; M.A., 1636; attacked Roman catholicism in correspondence with Sir Kenelm Digby [q. v.], 1638–9; M.P., Dorset, 1640; opposed third reading of bill for Strafford's attainder, though on committee for his impeachment, 1641; succeeded as Baron Digby, 1641; fled to Holland (1642) and was impeached by default for levying royalist troops; fought for Charles I at Edgehill, 1642, but gave up his command after a quarrel with Prince Rupert; secretary of state and privy councillor, 1643; high steward of Oxford University, 1643; lieutenant-general of the king's forces north of the Trent, 1645; defeated at Carlisle Sands; retired to France and took part in the Fronde, 1648; lieutenant-general in French army, 1651; detected in an intrigue against Mazarin, and forced to leave France; reappointed secretary of state to Charles II, 1657; subsequently deprived of the seals as a catholic; K.G., 1661; ineffectually impeached Clarendon (1663), who had foiled his scheme of an Italian marriage for the king; wrote comedies and, according to Walpole, translated from French first three books of 'Cassandra.'   [xv. 52]

DIGBY, JOHN, first EARL OF BRISTOL (1580–1653), diplomatist and statesman; fellow-commoner of Magdalene College, Cambridge, 1595; knighted, 1607; sent on a fruitless embassy to negotiate a marriage between Prince Henry and Anne, the Spanish infanta, 1611, and between Prince Charles and the Infanta Maria, 1614; vice-chamberlain and privy councillor, 1616; again sent to Spain (1617) to arrange the Spanish match, which was temporarily broken off by James I's refusal to grant liberty of conscience to English catholics; created Baron Digby, 1618; commissioned to negotiate peace between elector palatine and Ferdinand II, emperor of Germany, 1621; returned to Spain in 1622 to reopen marriage treaty of 1618; created Earl of Bristol, 1622; offended Prince Charles and Buckingham at Madrid, 1623; vainly demanded a trial in parliament to appease the hostility of Charles I, 1626; impartial in debates over Petition of Right, 1628; refused to vote on the attainder bill against Strafford, 1641; advised Charles I to conciliate the independents, 1644; his expulsion from the court demanded by the parliament in propositions for peace at Oxford, 1643; went into exile after capitulation of Exeter, 1646; died at Paris.   [xv. 56]

DIGBY, SIR KENELM (1603–1665), author, naval commander, and diplomatist; son of Sir Everard Digby (1578–1606) [q. v.]; entered Gloucester Hall (Worcester College), Oxford, 1618; visited Paris and Angers, 1620; removed to Florence to escape the importunities of Marie de Medicis; joined Prince Charles and Buckingham at Madrid, 1623; knighted, 1623; defeated French and Venetian fleet in Scanderoon harbour, 1628; returned to England, 1629; professed protestantism after 1630, but soon returned to Roman catholicism; published 'A Conference with a Lady about Choice of a Religion,' 1638; his removal from the royal councils requested by the House of Commons (1641) for having appealed to the English Roman catholics to support Charles I in Scotland; fought a duel at Paris in defence of Charles I, 1641; published a criticism on Sir Thomas Browne's 'Religio Medici,' 1643; wrote 'Of Bodies' and 'Of the Immortality of Man's Soul,' 1644; chancellor to Queen Henrietta Maria, 1644; pleaded Charles I's cause with Pope Innocent X, but quarrelled with him and left Rome, 1645; returned to England and was banished, 1649; visited by Evelyn at Paris, 1651; became acquainted with Descartes; returned to England on permission, 1654; worked in Cromwell's interest on the continent, 1656; returned to England, 1660, retaining the office of Queen Henrietta's chancellor; forbidden the court, 1664; member of the council of the Royal Society when first incorporated, 1663. He discovered the necessity of oxygen to the life of plants, and claimed to have discovered a 'sympathetic powder' for the cure of wounds (it was of no medicinal value). In philosophy he followed the schoolmen, writing by the aid of Thomas White [q. v.] 'Institutionum Peripateticarum libri quinque,' 1651. His 'Private Memoirs' were first printed in 1827. [xv. 60]

DIGBY, KENELM HENRY (1800-1880), miscellaneous writer ; B.A. Trinity College, Cambridge, 1819 ; converted to Roman catholicism ; author of 'The Broad-Stone of Honour,' 1822, 'Mores Catholici,' 1831-40, some books on the emotional aspects of catholicism, and a few poems. [xv. 66]

DIGBY, LETTICE, LADY (1588?-1658) ; created Baroness Offaley ; heiress-general to the Earls of Kildare on the death of her father, Gerald Fitzgerald ; married Sir Robert Digby of Coleshill, 1608 ; held Geashill Castle against Irish rebels, 1642. [xv. 67]

DIGBY, ROBERT (1732-1815), admiral ; great-grandson of William, fifth baron Digby [q. v.] ; commanded the Dunkirk at the battle of Quiberon Bay, 1759 ; commanded in Palliser's division off Ushant, 1778 ; rear-admiral, 1779 ; second in command in Rodney's expedition for relief of Gibraltar, 1779 ; commander-in-chief in North America, 1781 ; admiral, 1794. [xv. 67]

DIGBY, VENETIA, LADY (1600-1633) ; née Stanley ; married Sir Kenelm Digby [q. v.], 1625 ; commemorated in elegies by Ben Jonson and others. [xv. 60]

DIGBY, WILLIAM, fifth BARON DIGBY (1661-1752) ; B.A. Magdalen College, Oxford, 1681 ; D.C.L., 1708 ; M.P., Warwickshire, 1689 ; included in the Act of Attainder passed by James II's parliament at Dublin, 1689 ; member of the common council for Georgia, 1733. [xv. 68]

DIGGES, SIR DUDLEY (1583-1639), diplomatist and judge ; son of Thomas Digges [q. v.] ; B.A. University College, Oxford, 1601 ; knighted, 1607 ; founded a company to trade with the East by the supposed north-west passage, 1612 ; authorised to lend 10,000l. from the funds of the East India Company to the emperor of Russia, 1618 ; M.P., Tewkesbury, 1621, 1624, 1625, and 1626 ; opened case against Duke of Buckingham, 1626 ; M.P., Kent, 1628 ; influential in preparing the Petition of Right, 1628 ; sharply maintained right of House of Commons to criticise ministers of state, 1628 ; placed on the high commission, 1633 ; master of the rolls, 1636 ; joint-author with his father of 'Foure Paradoxes or Politique Discourses,' 1604. [xv. 68]

DIGGES, DUDLEY (1613-1643), political writer ; son of Sir Dudley Digges [q. v.] ; M.A. University College, Oxford, 1635 ; fellow of All Souls', Oxford, 1633 ; wrote in support of doctrine of passive obedience. [xv. 70]

DIGGES, LEONARD (d. 1571?), mathematician ; studied at University College, Oxford ; author of 'Tectonicon,' 1556, 'A Geometricall Practise, named Pantometria' (published, 1571), and 'An Arithmeticall Militare Treatise, named Stratioticos' (published, 1579) ; said to have anticipated invention of telescope. [xv. 70]

DIGGES, LEONARD (1588-1635), poet and translator ; son of Thomas Digges [q. v.] ; M.A. University College, Oxford, 1626 ; translated Claudian's 'Rape of Proserpine,' 1617, and 'Gerardo,' a Spanish novel, 1622 ; wrote two poems in praise of Shakespeare. [xv. 71]

DIGGES, THOMAS (d. 1595), mathematician ; son of Leonard Digges (d. 1571?) [q. v.] ; M.A. Queens' College, Cambridge, 1557 ; M.P., Wallingford, 1572, Southampton, 1585 ; muster-master-general of the English forces in the Netherlands, 1586 ; commissioned, with others, to equip expedition for exploration of Cathay and Antarctic seas, 1590 ; published some of his father's works, and wrote works on applied mathematics, highly esteemed by Tycho Brahe. [xv. 71]

DIGGES, WEST (1720-1786), actor ; appeared first at the Smock Alley Theatre, Dublin, as Jaffier in 'Venice Preserved,' 1749 ; played Cato at the Haymarket, 1777 ; an admirable exponent of Shakespeare's Wolsey. [xv. 73]

DIGHTON, DENIS (1792-1827), battle painter ; military draughtsman to the Prince of Wales, 1815 ; exhibited at the Royal Academy, 1811-25 ; died at St. Servan, Brittany. [xv. 74]

DIGHTON, ROBERT (1752?-1814), portrait-painter, caricaturist, and etcher ; etched a 'Book of Heads,' caricaturing leading counsel, military officers, actors, and actresses, 1795 ; discovered to have abstracted etchings and prints from the British Museum, 1806. [xv. 74]

DIGNUM, CHARLES (1765?-1827), vocalist ; first appeared at Drury Lane in 'Love in a Village,' 1784 ; particularly successful as Tom Tug in the 'Waterman' and as Crop in 'No Song, No Supper' ; sang at Drury Lane oratorios. [xv. 75]

DILKE, ASHTON WENTWORTH (1850-1883), traveller and politician ; younger son of Sir Charles Wentworth Dilke [q. v.] ; scholar of Trinity Hall, Cambridge ; travelled in Russia and Central Asia ; editor of the 'Weekly Dispatch' ; M.P. for Newcastle, 1880 ; died at Algiers ; translated Tourguenieff's 'Virgin Soil,' 1878. [xv. 75]

DILKE, CHARLES WENTWORTH (1789-1864), antiquary and critic ; brought out continuation of Dodsley's 'Old Plays' between 1814 and 1816 ; acquainted with Charles Armitage Brown [q. v.], Keats, Shelley, and Hood ; edited the 'Athenæum,' 1830-46, procuring contributions from continental writers—an innovation in English journalism ; manager of the 'Daily News,' 1846 ; discussed in the 'Athenæum' after 1847 the authorship of the 'Letters of Junius,' his criticism being mainly destructive of the claim of Sir Philip Francis ; wrote in defence of Wilkes and Peter Pindar ; threw much light on Pope's career and writings in papers published in the 'Athenæum' and 'Notes and Queries.' [xv. 76]

DILKE, SIR CHARLES WENTWORTH, first baronet (1810-1869) ; son of Charles Wentworth Dilke [q. v.] ; educated at Westminster and Trinity Hall, Cambridge ; B.A., 1834 ; among the first to propose the International Exhibition of 1851, and one of the executive committee ; created baronet, 1862 ; M.P., Wallingford, 1865-8 ; died at St. Petersburg. [xv. 77]

DILKES, SIR THOMAS (1667?-1707), rear-admiral ; lieutenant under James II ; fought at La Hogue, 1692 ; brought home West Indies squadron, 1697 ; rear-admiral of the white, 1703 ; captured French merchantmen at Avranches, 1703 ; knighted, 1704 ; defeated French blockading squadron at Gibraltar, 1705 ; died at Leghorn. [xv. 78]

DILLENIUS, JOHN JAMES (1687-1747), botanical professor at Oxford ; born at Darmstadt ; M.D. Giessen ; first professor of botany at Oxford, 1728-47 ; M.D. Oxford 1735 ; highly esteemed as a scientist by Linnæus ; chief work, 'Historia Muscorum,' 1741. [xv. 79]

DILLINGHAM, FRANCIS (fl. 1611), divine ; fellow of Christ's College, Cambridge ; M.A., 1590 ; B.D., 1599 ; renowned as a disputant ; presented to the living of Wilden, Bedfordshire ; one of the translators of the authorised version (1611), and a protestant controversialist. [xv. 79]

DILLINGHAM, THEOPHILUS (1613-1678), master of Clare Hall, Cambridge ; M.A. Emmanuel College, Cambridge, 1637 ; fellow of Sidney Sussex College, Cambridge 1638 ; D.D. ; master of Clare Hall, 1654 ; vice-chancellor of the university, 1655, 1656, and 1661 ; ejected from his mastership at the Restoration ; prebendary of York, 1662. [xv. 80]

DILLINGHAM, WILLIAM (1617?-1689), Latin poet and controversialist ; fellow of Emmanuel College, Cambridge, 1642 ; M.A., 1643 ; master of Emmanuel College 1653-62 ; D.D., 1655 ; vice-chancellor of the university 1659 ; deprived of mastership by the Act of Uniformity 1662 ; rector of Woodhill, Bedfordshire, 1672-89 ; published Latin poems, 1678, 'Ægyptus triumphata,' 1680, and other poems and English tractates. [xv. 80]

DILLON, ARTHUR (1670-1733), general in the French service ; colonel of a Jacobite regiment serving in France, 1690 ; maréchal-de-camp, 1704 ; lieutenant general under Tessé in Provence, 1707 ; superintended entrenchments at siege of Barcelona, 1714 ; 'Pretender' agent at Paris ; died at St. Germain. [xv. 81]

DILLON, ARTHUR RICHARD (1750-1794), general in the French service ; nephew of Archbishop Arthur Richard Dillon [q. v.] ; colonel, under Louis XV, 1767 ; governor of St. Kitt's ; brigadier-general, 1784 ; governor of Tobago and deputy for Martinique in the National Assembly ; Jacobin general ; served in the Argonne, 1792 ; supplanted by Dumouriez, 1792 ; guillotined, 1794. [xv. 82]

DILLON, ARTHUR RICHARD (1721-1806), French prelate; son of Arthur Dillon (1670-1733) [q. v.]; bishop of Evreux, 1753; archbishop of Toulouse, 1758, and of Narbonne, 1763; his diocese abolished by a concordat; died in London.   [xv. 82]

DILLON, EDOUARD (1751-1839), French general and diplomatist; colonel of the Provence regiment; formed a new Dillon regiment at Coblenz, 1791; lieutenant-general, 1814; ambassador to Saxony, 1816-18, and to Tuscany, 1819.   [xv. 82]

DILLON, SIR JAMES (fl. 1667), the first Dillon who served in foreign armies; lieutenant-general and governor of Athlone and Connaught; took part in Leinster revolt, 1652; excepted from pardon under Act of Settlement, 1652; brigadier-general in service of Spain and the Fronde; pensioned by Charles II for his loyalty, 1662.   [xv. 83]

DILLON, JOHN BLAKE (1816-1866), Irish politician; graduate and moderator, Trinity College, Dublin; called to the Irish bar, 1841; joint-founder of the 'Nation' newspaper, 1842; led rebels, 1848, at Mullinahone and Killenance, eventually escaping to the United States; secretary to the Irish National Association, 1865; M.P., Tipperary, 1865; repealer; opponent of fenianism.   [xv. 83]

DILLON, SIR JOHN TALBOT (1740 ?-1805), traveller, critic, and historical writer; M.P. for Blessington, in the Irish parliament, 1776-83; made a free baron of the Holy Roman Empire at Vienna, previous to 1780; created baronet, 1801; published 'Travels through Spain,' 1780, a history of Spanish poetry in the form of letters, 1781, memoirs of the French Revolution, 1790, and 'Sketches on the Art of Painting,' translated from the Spanish, 1782.   [xv. 84]

DILLON, SIR LUCAS (d. 1593), chief-baron of Irish exchequer; son of Sir Robert Dillon (1500 ?-1580) [q. v.]; solicitor-general for Ireland, 1565; attorney-general, 1566; M.P., 1569; chief baron of court of Irish exchequer, 1570; knighted, 1576; seneschal of Kilkenny West, 1583; one of lords justices appointed to administer government pending arrival of Sir John Perrot [q. v.], 1584; commissioner for plantation of Munster, 1587. [Suppl. ii. 132]

DILLON, PETER (1785 ?-1847), navigator in South Seas; engaged in sandal-wood trade between West Pacific islands and China, and, 1822-5, was employed in timber-trade for the East India market; went in search of lost ships of La Pérouse, whose expedition was wrecked on the Santa Cruz group, 1827-8, and published account of voyage, 1829.   [Suppl. ii. 133]

DILLON, SIR ROBERT (1500 ?-1580), Irish judge; attorney-general for Ireland, 1534; second justice of queen's bench, 1554; chief-justice of court of common pleas, 1559-80.   [Suppl. ii. 135]

DILLON, SIR ROBERT (d. 1597), Irish judge; second justice of presidency of Connaught, 1569; chancellor of Irish exchequer, 1572; second justice of court of common pleas, 1577; chief-justice, 1581; accused of corruption and cruelty, imprisoned, and compelled to resign chief-justiceship, 1593; declared innocent; restored to chief-justiceship of Ireland, 1595.   [Suppl. ii. 135]

DILLON, ROBERT CRAWFORD (1795-1847), divine; M.A. St. Edmund Hall, Oxford, 1820; D.D., 1836; chaplain to Alderman Venables when lord mayor, 1826, whom he accompanied on an official visit to Oxford; published a turgid and puerile account of this visit, which the lord mayor vainly requested him to suppress, 1826; suspended for immorality from his proprietary chapel in Charlotte Street, Pimlico, 1840; founded a new church in Friar Street, Blackfriars; 'first presbyter.'   [xv. 85]

DILLON, THEOBALD (1745-1792), general in the French service; lieutenant-colonel in Dillon's regiment, 1780; took part in attack on Grenada, 1779; knight of St. Louis, 1781; brigadier-general, 1792; murdered by his own republican troops in a panic at Tournay, 1792.   [xv. 86]

DILLON, THOMAS, fourth VISCOUNT DILLON (1615 ?-1672 ?), lord of the privy council in Ireland, 1640; joint governor of co. Mayo, 1641; served under Charles I, 1642, being deputed by the Irish parliament to present a statement of its grievances to the king; lord president of Connaught; joined the Marquis of Ormonde's rising, 1649; appointed custos rotulorum by Charles II, 1662.   [xv. 86]

DILLON or **DE LEON**, THOMAS (1613-1676 ?), jesuit; novice of the Society of Jesus at Seville, 1627; professed father; professor of humanities at Cadiz, 1640-1676 ?; a skilled orientalist and theologian.   [xv. 87]

DILLON, WENTWORTH, fourth EARL OF ROSCOMMON (1633 ?-1685); educated at the protestant university of Caen; studied Italian and numismatics at Rome; member of the Irish parliament, 1661; captain of the band of gentlemen pensioners, 1661; honorary LL.D. Cambridge, 1680; D.C.L. Oxford, 1683; chief works, a blank verse translation of Horace's 'Ars Poetica,' 1680, and an 'Essay on Translated Verse,' 1684. He was the first critic who publicly praised Milton's 'Paradise Lost.'   [xv. 87]

DILLON, SIR WILLIAM HENRY (1779-1857), admiral; son of Sir John Talbot Dillon [q. v.]; co-operated with the army as naval lieutenant off Wexford and arrested Skallian, 1798; seized by the Dutch commodore, Valterbach (1803), and handed over to the French for detention; commander, 1805; with one sloop defeated a Danish man-of-war brig, 1808; served at Walcheren, off Spain and in East Indies; K.C.H., and knighted, 1835; vice-admiral of the red, 1853.   [xv. 89]

DILLON-LEE, HENRY AUGUSTUS, thirteenth VISCOUNT DILLON (1777-1832), writer; colonel in the Irish brigade, 1794; M.P., Harwich, 1799; knight for co. Mayo, 1802, 1806, 1807, and 1812; published works of political jurisprudence, an edition of Ælian's 'Tactics,' 1814, and 'The Life and Opinions of Sir Richard Maltravers' (novel), 1822.   [xv. 90]

DILLWYN, LEWIS WESTON (1778-1855), naturalist; published his Natural History of British Confervæ,' 1802-9; in charge of the Cambrian pottery at Swansea, 1802; trained public taste for natural-history designs; high sheriff of Glamorganshire, 1818; M.P., Glamorganshire, 1832-41; wrote 'Flora and Fauna of Swansea' for the British Association, 1848.   [xv. 90]

DILLY, CHARLES (1739-1807), bookseller; at one time in partnership with his brother Edward [q. v.]; noted for the hospitality that he extended towards the writers of the day; published Boswell's 'Tour in the Hebrides,' 1780, and the 'Life of Johnson,' 1791; master of the Stationers' Company, 1803.   [xv. 91]

DILLY, EDWARD (1732-1779), bookseller; brother of Charles Dilly [q. v.]; exported works of dissenting theology to America.   [xv. 92]

DILLY, JOHN (1731-1806), brother of Charles Dilly [q. v.]; Boswell's 'Squire Dilly'; high sheriff of Bedfordshire, 1783.   [xv. 91]

DIMOCK, JAMES (d. 1718 ?). [See DYMOCKE.]

DIMOCK, JAMES FRANCIS (1810-1876), divine; B.A. St. John's College, Cambridge, 1833; M.A., 1837; minor canon of Southwell, 1846-63; rector of Barnborough, 1863 till death; prebendary of Lincoln, 1869-76; published works relating to ecclesiastical and mediæval history.   [Suppl. ii. 136]

DIMSDALE, THOMAS (1712-1800), physician; volunteer under the Duke of Cumberland, 1745; M.D., 1761; inoculated for small pox the Empress Catherine, various Russian princes, and the Hawaiian Omai; councillor of state in Russia with hereditary title of baron, 1768; M.P., Hertford, 1780 and 1784; wrote on inoculation. [xv. 92]

DINELEY-GOODERE, SIR JOHN (d. 1809), poor knight of Windsor; succeeded to baronetcy of Burhope in Wellington, Herefordshire, 1761; subsequently poor knight of Windsor; cherished delusive claims to certain (mythical) estates.   [xv. 93]

DINGLEY, ROBERT (1619-1660), puritan divine; M.A. Magdalen College, Oxford; parliamentarian preacher and rector of Brightstone, Isle of Wight; published religious works.   [xv. 94]

DINGLEY or **DINELEY**, THOMAS (d. 1695), antiquary; student of Gray's Inn, 1670; attended Sir George Downing (1623 ?-1684) [q. v.] when ambassador to the United Provinces, 1671; died at Louvain; left in manuscript 'Travails through the Low Countreys, Anno Domini 1674,' an account of travels in Ireland, a description of Wales, and a 'History from Marble,' dealing with English epigraphy and church architecture (published 1867-8).   [xv. 94]

DIODATI, CHARLES (1608 ?-1638), friend of Milton ; son of Theodore Diodati [q. v.] ; scholar of St. Paul's School, where he first became acquainted with Milton ; M.A. Trinity College, Oxford, 1628 ; M.A. Cambridge, 1629 ; practised physic near Chester. Milton addressed to him two Latin elegies and an Italian sonnet, and bewailed his death in 'Epitaphium Damonis,' 1645.   [xv. 95]

DIODATI, THEODORE (1574 ?-1651), physician ; born at Geneva of a Lucca family ; brought up in England as a physician ; attended Prince Henry and Princess Elizabeth ; M.D. Leyden, 1615 ; L.C.P. London, 1617 ; assisted Florio in his translation of Montaigne. [xv. 95]

DIRCKS, HENRY (1806-1873), civil engineer and author ; life member of the British Association, 1837 ; consulting engineer ; invented 'Pepper's Ghost,' an optical illusion, 1858 ; chief works, 'Jordantype, otherwise called Electrotype,' 1852, 'Perpetuum Mobile,' 1861, and 'A Biographical Memoir of Samuel Hartlib,' 1865.   [xv. 95]

DIRLETON, LORD (1609 ?-1687). [See NISBET, SIR JOHN.]

DIROM, ALEXANDER (d. 1830), lieutenant-general ; deputy adjutant-general in the second Mysore war, 1790-2 ; F.R.S., 1794 ; published account of the campaign against Tippoo Sultan in 1792, 'An Inquiry into the Corn Laws,' 1796, and 'Plans for the Defence of Great Britain and Ireland,' 1797.   [xv. 96]

DISIBOD, SAINT (594 ?-674), bishop ; son of an Irish chieftain : elected bishop against his will ; wandered into Alemannia (Baden), where he founded a Benedictine community.   [xv. 96]

DISNEY, JOHN (1677-1730), divine ; magistrate for Lincolnshire ; rector of St. Mary's, Nottingham, 1722-30 ; wrote on the reformation of manners.   [xv. 98]

DISNEY, JOHN (1746-1816), unitarian clergyman ; grandson of John Disney (1677-1730) [q. v.] ; at Peterhouse, Cambridge, 1764 ; vicar of Swinderby and rector of Panton, Lincolnshire, 1769-82 ; LL.B., 1770 ; D.D. Edinburgh, 1775 ; F.S.A., 1778 ; threw up preferments (1782) and assisted Theophilus Lindsey [q. v.] at Essex Street unitarian church ; sole minister, 1793 ; published memoirs and theological works ; helped to secure the act of 1813 'to relieve persons who impugn the doctrine of the Holy Trinity from certain penalties.'   [xv. 98]

DISNEY, JOHN (1779-1857), collector of classical antiquities ; son of the Rev. John Disney (1746-1816) [q. v.] ; hon. LL.D. Cambridge, and F.R.S. ; barrister, Inner Temple ; founded Disney professorship of archæology at Cambridge, 1851, to which university he bequeathed his Roman marbles ; published two legal works. [xv. 100]

DISNEY, SIR MOORE (1766 ?-1846), general ; lieutenant and captain, first grenadier guards, 1791 ; colonel, 1802 ; commandant of Messina, 1808 ; detailed to cover Sir John Moore's retreat, 1808 ; fought at Betanzos and Coruña, 1809 ; major-general, 1809 ; commanded first brigade of guards at Walcheren, 1809 ; colonel, 15th regiment, 1814 ; K.C.B., 1815 ; general, 1837.   [xv. 100]

DISNEY, WILLIAM (1731-1807), professor of Hebrew ; educated at Merchant Taylors' School and Trinity College, Cambridge ; B.A. and senior wrangler, 1753 ; M.A., 1756 ; major fellow, 1756 ; regius professor of Hebrew, 1757-71 ; vicar of Pluckley, Kent, 1777-1807 ; D.D., 1789.   [xv. 101]

DISRAELI, BENJAMIN, first EARL OF BEACONSFIELD (1804-1881), statesman and man of letters ; eldest son of Isaac D'Israeli [q. v.] ; entered Lincoln's Inn, 1824 ; published 'Vivian Grey,' his first novel, which attracted attention by its brilliance, 1826 ; produced 'Vindication of the British Constitution,' 1835, and some political pamphlets ; published 'The Young Duke,' 1831, 'Contarini Fleming,' 1832, 'Alroy,' 1833, 'The Rise of Iskander,' 'The Revolutionary Epic,' 1834, 'Venetia,' 1837, and 'Henrietta Temple,' 1837 ; M.P., Maidstone, 1837 ; his first speech a failure, 1837 ; spoke in favour of the chartist petition, 1839 ; conservative M.P. for Shrewsbury, 1841 ; a member of the Young England party ; declared himself a supporter of the corn laws on political and social grounds, 1843 ; violently attacked Sir Robert Peel for repealing the corn laws, 1846 ; published 'Coningsby,' 1844, and 'Sybil,' 1845, two novels advocating a combination of monarchy, a sort

of social democracy, and Anglicanism as a political creed, and attacking the whig principles of the upper and middle classes ; published 'Tancred,' 1847 ; a champion of the protectionists, 1845-50 ; M.P. for Buckinghamshire, 1847-76 ; chancellor of the exchequer in Lord Derby's first government, February 1852, but resigned in December, his party being defeated on his budget ; attacked the Aberdeen administration in the 'Press,' a paper conducted under his influence, 1853 ; chancellor of the exchequer and leader of the House of Commons under Lord Derby's second government, February 1858-June 1859 ; introduced a reform bill, which was defeated by Lord John Russell's amendment, 1859 ; criticised Mr. Gladstone's financial system, 1860 and 1862, and Lord John Russell's foreign policy yearly till 1865 ; on defeat of Lord John Russell's reform bill, June 1866, became chancellor of the exchequer in Lord Derby's third government ; carried a bill for giving franchise to all ratepayers, 1867 ; prime minister on Lord Derby's retirement, February 1868 ; resigned after general election, December 1868 ; published 'Lothair,' 1870 ; criticised Mr. Gladstone's Irish and foreign policy, 1868-73 ; prime minister for the second time, 1874 ; caused Queen Victoria to assume the title of Empress of India, 1876 ; created Earl of Beaconsfield, 1876 ; became intimate friend of Queen Victoria ; sought to check the predominance of Russia in Eastern Europe, 1877-8 ; English plenipotentiary at the congress of Berlin, which he forced upon Russia at the close of the Russo-Turkish war, 1878 ; K.G., 22 July 1878 ; procured the occupation of Cyprus, and the retention of Candahar ; resigned on the tory defeat at the general election, April 1880 ; published 'Endymion,' his last novel, 1880 ; died in London, 19 April 1881 ; buried at Hughenden. A public monument in his memory was erected in Westminster Abbey.   [xv. 101]

D'ISRAELI, ISAAC (1766-1848), author ; descended from a Jewish family which had fled from Spain to Venice in time of persecution ; son of Benjamin D'Israeli, who came from Italy to settle in England in 1748 ; studied at Amsterdam ; issued anonymously 'Curiosities of Literature,' 1791 ; published 'Calamities of Authors,' 1812-13, 'Quarrels of Authors,' 1814, and some novels ; withdrew from the Jewish congregation, of which he and his family had hitherto been members, in 1817 ; published between 1828 and 1830 'Commentaries on the Life and Reign of Charles I' ; D.C.L. Oxford, 1832 ; published anonymously the 'Genius of Judaism,' 1833 ; completed his 'Amenities of Literature,' though blind, 1840.
    [xv. 117]

DISS or **DYSSE**, WALTER (d. 1404 ?), Carmelite ; D.D. Cambridge ; subscribed the Blackfriars council's condemnation of Wycliffe's twenty-four conclusions, 1382 ; named papal legate by Pope Urban VI, to give the character of a crusade to John of Gaunt's expedition into Castile, 1386, where the rival pope, Clement VII, had much influence ; never went to Spain ; left theological works in manuscript.   [xv. 120]

DITTON, HUMPHREY (1675-1715), mathematician ; master of a new mathematical school at Christ's Hospital, 1706 ; devised an impracticable scheme with William Whiston [q. v.], for ascertaining longitudes by the firing of a shell timed to explode at a certain height, 1713 ; published mathematical works.   [xv. 121]

DIVE or **DIVES**, SIR LEWIS (1599-1669). [See DYVE.]

DIX, JOHN, alias JOHN ROSS (1800 ?-1865 ?), biographer of Chatterton ; surgeon at Bristol ; published a 'Life of Chatterton,' containing a disputed portrait of the poet, 1837 ; published miscellaneous works.   [xv. 122]

DIXEY, JOHN (d. 1820), sculptor and modeller ; sent by the Royal Academy to complete his art studies in Italy ; vice-president of Pennsylvania Academy of Fine Arts, 1812 ; employed in the embellishment of private and public buildings in the United States.   [xv. 122]

DIXIE, SIR WOLSTAN (1525-1594), lord mayor of London ; sheriff of London, 1575 ; lord mayor, 1585, when George Peele [q. v.] wrote the pageant ; president of Christ's Hospital, 1590 ; benefactor of Christ's Hospital, Emmanuel College, Cambridge, and Market Bosworth school.   [xv. 122]

DIXON, GEORGE (d. 1800 ?), navigator ; served on the Resolution under Cook [see COOK, JAMES] ; commanded the Queen Charlotte for the King George's Sound Company, 1785 ; fur trader in the region of King George's Sound and discoverer (1787) of the Queen Charlotte islands. [xv. 123]

DIXON, GEORGE (1820–1898), educational reformer ; entered a foreign mercantile house in Birmingham, 1838, became partner, 1844, and was ultimately head of the firm ; entered town council, 1863 ; mayor, 1866 ; took active interest in question of popular education ; assisted in forming Birmingham Education Aid Society, and, in 1868, with Mr. Joseph Chamberlain, John Sandford (1801–1873) [q. v.], George Dawson (1821–1876) [q. v.], and Robert William Dale [q. v.], the National Education League, of which he was first president, 1869 ; liberal M.P. for Birmingham, 1867–76 ; member of first Birmingham School Board, 1870, and was re-elected, 1873 and 1876 ; chairman, 1876–97 ; M.P. for Edgbaston division of Birmingham, 1885 till death ; joined liberal unionists, 1886. [Suppl. ii. 136]

DIXON, HENRY HALL (1822–1870), sporting writer ; known as 'The Druid' ; educated at Rugby and Trinity College, Cambridge ; B.A., 1846 ; clerk to an attorney at Doncaster ; contributed to 'Bell's Life' ; called to bar, 1853, and practised on midland circuit ; wrote regularly for 'Sporting Magazine' from c. 1853, and subsequently for 'Illustrated London News,' 'Mark Lane Express,' and 'Daily News.' His works include 'The Law of the Farm,' 1858, 'Breeding of Shorthorns,' 1865, 'Post and Paddock,' 1856, 'Silk and Scarlet,' 1859, and 'Scott and Sebright,' 1862. [Suppl. ii. 138]

DIXON, JAMES (1788–1871), Wesleyan minister ; president of the Wesleyan conference, 1841 ; president of the Canada conference ; English representative at United States conference, 1847 ; D.D. ; a celebrated preacher ; published works on the history and development of methodism. [xv. 124]

DIXON, JOHN (d. 1715), miniature and crayon painter ; pupil of Sir Peter Lely ; 'keeper of the king's picture closet' to William III. [xv. 125]

DIXON, JOHN (1740?–1780?), mezzotint engraver ; engraver of silver plate in Ireland ; engraved, while in England, after the works of Sir Joshua Reynolds ; member of the Incorporated Society of Artists, 1766. [xv. 125]

DIXON, JOSEPH (1806–1866), Irish catholic prelate ; dean of St. Patrick's College, Maynooth ; professor of sacred scripture and Hebrew at Maynooth ; D.D. ; archbishop of Armagh, 1852–66 ; published 'A General Introduction to the Sacred Scriptures,' 1852, and 'The Blessed Cornelius,' 1854. [xv. 125]

DIXON, JOSHUA (d. 1825), biographer ; M.D. Edinburgh, 1768 ; practised at Whitehaven ; author of 'The Literary Life of William Brownrigg, M.D., F.R.S.,' 1801. [xv. 126]

DIXON, RICHARD WATSON (1833–1900), historian, poet, and divine ; son of Dr. James Dixon [q. v.] ; educated at King Edward's School, Birmingham, and Pembroke College, Oxford ; formed close friendship with (Sir) Edward Burne-Jones [q. v.] and William Morris [q. v.] ; projected with Morris 'Oxford and Cambridge Magazine' ; B.A., 1857 ; ordained curate of St. Mary-the-Less, Lambeth, 1858 ; curate of St. Mary, Newington Butts, 1861 ; second master at Carlisle high school, 1863–1868 ; minor canon and honorary librarian of Carlisle Cathedral, 1868–75 ; vicar of Hayton, Cumberland, 1875–1883, and of Warkworth, Northumberland, 1883 till death ; honorary canon of Carlisle, 1874 ; rural dean of Brampton, 1879, and of Alnwick, 1884 ; proctor in convocation, 1890–4 ; honorary D.D. Oxford, 1899 ; published poetical and religious works, besides an elaborate 'History of Church of England from Abolition of Roman Jurisdiction,' 1877–1900. [Suppl. ii. 139]

DIXON, ROBERT (d. 1688), royalist divine ; M.A. St. John's College, Cambridge, 1638 ; imprisoned in Leeds Castle, Kent, for refusing the solemn league and covenant, 1644 ; rector of Tunstall, Kent, 1647 ; sequestered ; restored, 1660 ; prebendary of Rochester, 1660 ; D.D., per literas regias, Cambridge, 1668 ; author of 'The Doctrine of Faith, Justification, and Assurance . . . farther cleared,' 1668, and other theological works, possibly also of 'Canidia,' a satire on society, 1683. [xv. 126]

DIXON, THOMAS (1680?–1729), nonconformist tutor ; studied at Manchester, 1700–5 ; minister of a dissenting congregation at Whitehaven (1708–23), when he founded an academy for the education of nonconformist ministers ; hon. M.A. Edinburgh, 1709 ; M.D. Edinburgh ; practised as a physician. [xv. 126]

DIXON, THOMAS (1721–1754), nonconformist minister ; son of Thomas Dixon (1680?–1729) [q. v.] ; assistant to Dr. John Taylor at Norwich, 1750–2, where he began a Greek concordance ; ordained, 1753. [xv. 127]

DIXON, WILLIAM HENRY (1783–1854), clergyman and antiquary ; M.A. Pembroke College, Cambridge, 1809 ; canon of Ripon, canon-residentiary of York, rector of Etton, and vicar of Bishopthorpe ; F.S.A., 1821 ; left in manuscript a recension of James Torre's manuscript annals of the members of the cathedral of York (part published, with additions, 1863). [xv. 127]

DIXON, WILLIAM HEPWORTH (1821–1879), historian and traveller ; barrister, Inner Temple, 1854 ; controverted Macaulay in a 'Life of William Penn,' 1851 ; published a life of Admiral Blake, 1852 ; editor of the 'Athenæum,' 1853–69 ; published 'The Story of Lord Bacon's Life,' 1862, and other works embodying researches into Bacon's history ; helped to found the Palestine Exploration Fund ; published 'The Holy Land,' 1865 ; discovered (1866) a collection of English state papers in the public library at Philadelphia, which were subsequently restored to the British government ; J.P. for Middlesex and Westminster, 1869 ; member of the London School Board, 1870 ; published 'The Switzers,' 1872, and, while in Spain on a foreign bondholders' mission, wrote his 'History of Two Queens,' 1873 ; embodied the results of a tour through North America in 'The White Conquest,' 1875 ; travelled in Cyprus, 1878 ; published part of 'Royal Windsor,' 1878, and 'British Cyprus,' 1879 ; F.S.A. and F.R.G.S. [xv. 128]

DIXWELL, JOHN (d. 1689), regicide ; M.P., Dover, 1646 ; commissioner for the trial of Charles I, 1649 ; member of council of state, 1651 and 1659 ; excluded from Act of Indemnity, 1660 ; became burgess of Hanau ; settled at Newhaven, Connecticut, 1665. [xv. 130]

DOBBS, ARTHUR (1689–1765), governor of North Carolina ; represented Carrickfergus in the Irish parliament of 1727–30 ; surveyor-general in Ireland, 1730 ; wrote an 'Essay on the Trade and Imports of Ireland,' 1729 and 1731 ; induced admiralty to send expedition to search for north-west passage, 1741 ; published 'An Account of the Countries adjoining Hudson's Bay,' 1744, which led to an expedition for diverting the fur trade from the Hudson's Bay Company, 1746. As governor of North Carolina (1754–65) he persistently upheld the royal prerogative and consulted the interests of the Indians. [xv. 130]

DOBBS, FRANCIS (1750–1811), Irish politician ; graduate of Trinity College, Dublin ; called to the Irish bar, 1773 ; published pamphlets against legislative union with England ; issued a volume of poems, 1788 ; member for Charlemont in the Irish House of Commons, 1799, where in a famous speech he opposed the Union Bill on scriptural grounds, 1800 ; published a 'Universal History,' 1800. [xv. 132]

DOBELL, SYDNEY THOMPSON (1824–1874), poet and critic ; privately educated at his parents' house at Cheltenham ; resided for most of his adult life in Gloucestershire ; owing to delicate health often wintered abroad ; published 'The Roman,' a dramatic poem inspired by sympathy with oppressed nationalities, 1850 ; published 'Balder,' 1853 ; issued sonnets on the Crimean war, 1855 ; lived in Scotland, 1854–7 ; published a volume of verse entitled 'England in Time of War,' 1856 ; one of the first to apply the principle of co-operation in trade ; injured by a fall among the ruins of Pozzuoli, 1866, and was thenceforth an invalid. [xv. 133]

DOBREE, PETER PAUL (1782–1825), Greek scholar ; fourth senior optime, Trinity College, Cambridge, 1804 ; fellow, 1806 ; M.A., 1807 ; professor of Greek at Cambridge, 1823–5 ; edited Porson's manuscript 'Aristophanica,' 1820 ; wrote in the 'Monthly Review' and Valpy's 'Classical Journal,' which latter he helped to found in 1810 ; edited Porson's transcript of Photius, with a lexicon, 1822 ; left notes on the Greek historians and orators, which were published by Scholefield in 'Adversaria,' 1831-3; Greek epigraphist. [xv. 134]

DOBSON, GEORGE EDWARD (1848-1895), zoologist; B.A. Trinity College, Dublin, 1866; M.B. and M.Ch., 1867; M.A., 1875; entered army medical department, 1868; served in India; retired as surgeon-major, 1888; F.L.S., 1874; F.R.S., 1883; F.Z.S.; curator of Royal Victoria Museum, Netley, c. 1878; published 'Catalogue of Chiroptera in Collection of British Museum,' 1878, and other writings on chiroptera and insectivora. [Suppl. ii. 140]

DOBSON, JOHN (1633-1681), puritan divine; M.A. Magdalen College, Oxford, 1659; perpetual fellow, 1662; expelled for writing a libel in vindication of Dr. Thomas Pierce, 1663, but soon restored; B.D., 1667; held various clerical preferments. [xv. 136]

DOBSON, JOHN (1787-1865), architect; designed for Newcastle-on-Tyne public buildings, new streets, and central station; reputed pioneer in the modern Gothic revival. [xv. 136]

DOBSON, SUSANNAH (d. 1795), translator; née Dawson; married Matthew Dobson; translated Sainte-Palaye's 'Literary History of the Troubadours,' 1779, and 'Memoirs of Ancient Chivalry,' 1784, besides Petrarch's 'View of Human Life,' 1791. [xv. 137]

DOBSON, WILLIAM (1610-1646), portrait-painter; introduced to Charles I by Vandyck; sergeant-painter, 1641; one of the earliest English subject and portrait painters of eminence. [xv. 137]

DOBSON, WILLIAM (1820-1884), journalist and antiquary; editor of the 'Preston Chronicle'; wrote on the history and antiquities of Preston. [xv. 138]

DOBSON, WILLIAM CHARLES THOMAS (1817-1898), painter; studied in Royal Academy schools; headmaster of government school of design, Birmingham, 1843-5; exhibited at Royal Academy from 1842; studied in Italy and Germany, and subsequently gained considerable reputation as painter of scriptural subjects in oil- and water-colour; R.A., 1872; retired, 1895. [Suppl. ii. 141]

DOCHARTY, JAMES (1829-1878), landscape-painter; at one time engaged in pattern designing at Glasgow; exhibited highland scenes at the Royal Scottish Academy, associate Royal Scottish Academy, 1877; exhibited at Royal Academy, 1865-77. [xv. 138]

DOCKING, THOMAS OF (fl. 1250), Franciscan; D.D., and seventh Franciscan reader in divinity in Oxford University; left in manuscript scriptural commentaries. [xv. 139]

DOCKWRAY or **DOCKWRA,** WILLIAM (d. 1716), London merchant; established a penny postal system in the metropolis, 1683; cast in a suit instituted by the Duke of York to protect his monopoly; comptroller of the penny post, 1697-1700; dismissed on charges of maladministration, 1700. [xv. 139]

DOCWRA, SIR HENRY, first BARON DOCWRA in Irish peerage (1560?-1631), general; captain under Sir Richard Bingham [q. v.] in Ireland; constable of Dungarvan Castle, 1584; commanded under Essex in the Netherlands and in Spain; knighted; received submission of Art O'Neill and founded modern city of Derry, 1600; governor of Derry, 1603-8; treasurer of war in Ireland, 1616; created Baron Docwra of Culmore, 1621; joint-keeper of the great seal of Ireland, 1627. [xv. 140]

DOCWRA, SIR THOMAS (d. 1527), prior of the knights of St. John at Clerkenwell, 1502; negotiated treaty for Henry VII's marriage with Margaret of Savoy, 1506; received from Louis XII formal acknowledgment of the arrears of tribute due to England, 1510; attended Henry VIII in France, 1513; sent to Terouenne to settle mercantile disputes with the French, 1517; took part in search for suspicious characters in London, 1519-25; attended Wolsey when arbitrating between the French and the imperialists at Calais, 1521; commissioned by Henry VIII to draw up treaty with the imperial ambassador for joint invasion of France, 1524. [xv. 142]

DOD, CHARLES ROGER PHIPPS (1793-1855), author of the 'Parliamentary Companion'; connected with the 'Times' for twenty-three years, contributing obituary notices and redacting the parliamentary reports; compiled 'Parliamentary Pocket Companion,' 1832, and 'Peerage, Baronetage, and Knightage,' 1841. [xv. 144]

DOD, HENRY (1550?-1630?), poet; published 'Certaine Psalmes of David in meter,' 1603, and 'Al the Psalmes of David, with certaine Songes and Canticles,' 1620. [xv. 144]

DOD, JOHN (1549?-1645), puritan divine; scholar and fellow of Jesus College, Cambridge; incumbent of Hanwell, Oxfordshire; suspended for nonconformity, 1604; rector of Fawsley, Northamptonshire, 1624-45; reputed author of a famous sermon on 'malt'; called 'Decalogue Dod' from his exposition of the Ten Commandments (published 1604). [xv. 145]

DOD, PEIRCE (1683-1754), medical writer; B.A. Brasenose College, Oxford, 1701; fellow of All Souls; M.A., 1705; M.D., 1714; Harveian orator, 1729; censor, College of Physicians, 1724, 1732, 1736, and 1739; physician to St. Bartholomew's Hospital, 1725-54; F.R.S., 1730; attacked for his book against inoculation (1746) in 'A Letter to the real and genuine Pierce (sic) Dod, M.D.,' 1746. [xv. 146]

DOD, ROBERT PHIPPS (d. 1865), compiler; son of Charles Roger Phipps Dod [q. v.]; captain, 54th Shropshire regiment of militia, 1855; assisted in his father's compilations. [xv. 144]

DOD, TIMOTHY (d. 1665), nonconformist divine; son of John Dod [q. v.]; preacher at Daventry, 1640; ejected, 1662. [xv. 147]

DODD, CHARLES (1672-1743), Roman catholic divine; real name, HUGH TOOTEL; studied philosophy at Douay, 1688; received the minor orders at Cambray, 1690; B.D. at the English seminary of St. Gregory, Paris; in charge of a congregation at Harvington, Worcestershire, 1726-43; published 'The Church History of England,' 1737-39-42, 'The Secret Policy of the English Society of Jesus,' 1715, severely criticising the order, and 'A Philosophical and Theological Dictionary.' [xv. 147]

DODD, DANIEL (fl. 1760-1790), painter; member of the Free Society of Artists. His works consist principally of oil and crayon portraits and scenes of fashionable life. [xv. 149]

DODD, GEORGE (1783-1827), engineer; son of Ralph Dodd [q. v.]; resident engineer under John Rennie, the designer of Waterloo Bridge; resigned his post, and died, refusing all medicine, in the compter, 1827. [xv. 149]

DODD, GEORGE (1808-1881), miscellaneous writer; edited the 'Cyclopædia of the Industry of all Nations,' 1851; wrote for Charles Knight's 'Weekly Volumes' and other serials; compiled guide-books for Messrs. Chambers's publishing firm; best-known work, 'The Food of London,' 1856. [xv. 149]

DODD, JAMES SOLAS (1721-1805), surgeon, lecturer, and actor; member of the corporation of surgeons, London, 1751; published 'An Essay towards a Natural History of the Herring,' 1752; produced 'A Physical Account of the Case of Elizabeth Canning,' 1753; master-surgeon on board the Hawke, 1762-3; delivered a series of comic lectures on 'Hearts' and 'Noses' at Exeter Exchange, 1766; acted in London in a play written by himself after De Lafont's 'Le Naufrage,' 1779; tricked into accompanying Major John Savage, a soi-disant ambassador to the Russian court, 1781; actor and lecturer at Edinburgh, 1782; translated the 'Ancient and Modern History of Gibraltar' from the Spanish, 1781. [xv. 151]

DODD, JAMES WILLIAM (1740?-1796), actor; first appeared at Drury Lane, 1765; at Drury Lane, 1765-96; favourably criticised by Charles Lamb for his sympathetic impersonation of Sir Andrew Aguecheek; retired after his failure in Colman's 'Iron Chest,' 1796. [xv. 150]

DODD, PHILIP STANHOPE (1775-1852), divine; fellow of Magdalene College, Cambridge; M.A., 1799; chaplain to the lord mayor, 1806; rector of St. Mary-at-Hill, 1807-12; published a work basing arguments for Christianity on the ministry of St. Paul, 1837. [xv. 152]

DODD, RALPH (1756–1822), civil engineer; published 'Account of the principal Canals in the known World,' 1795; largely occupied in forming projects for the construction of canals and a dry tunnel from Gravesend to Tilbury; promoter of steam navigation. [xv. 153]

DODD, ROBERT (1748–1816 ?), marine painter and engraver; exhibited at the Royal Academy, 1782–1809; distinguished for his rendering of storm effects.
[xv. 153]

DODD, SIR SAMUEL (1652–1716), judge; barrister, Inner Temple, 1679; bencher, 1700; employed by various bankers upon a question of the liability of the crown for interest on loans to Charles II. 1693 and 1700; negotiated fusion of old with New East India Company, 1701; counsel for Sacheverell, 1710; knighted, 1714; serjeant, 1714; lord chief-baron, 1714. [xv. 154]

DODD, THOMAS (1771–1850), auctioneer and print-seller; opened day-school near Battle Bridge, St. Pancras, 1794; print-seller, 1796; his dictionary of monograms anticipated by Brulliot, 1817; auctioneer in Manchester, 1819; projected a scheme which was ultimately realised in the Royal Manchester Institution, 1823; commenced publication of his 'Connoisseur's Repertorium,' 1825; catalogued Douce collection of prints in the Bodleian Library, 1839–41. [xv. 154]

DODD, WILLIAM (1729–1777), forger; entered at Clare Hall, Cambridge, 1746; B.A., 1750; acted as chaplain of the 'Magdalen House,' 1758; editor of the 'Christian Magazine,' 1760–7; chaplain to the king and prebendary at Brecon, 1763; LL.D., 1766; founded Charlotte Chapel in Pimlico; nick-named the 'macaroni parson'; rector of Hockliffe and vicar of Chalgrove, 1772; struck off the list of royal chaplains for improper solicitation of preferment from the lord chancellor, 1774; forged a bond for 4,200l. in the name of his former pupil, the fifth Lord Chesterfield, 1777; executed (1777), though numerous petitions were presented on his behalf, one being written for him by Dr. Johnson. His numerous publications include Beauties of Shakespeare,' 1752, a translation of the Hymns of Callimachus,' 1754, 'Reflections on Death,' 1763, and 'Thoughts in Prison,' 1777. [xv. 155]

DODDRIDGE or **DODERIDGE**, SIR JOHN (1555–1628), judge; B.A. Exeter College, Oxford, 1577; serjeant-at-law and Prince Henry's serjeant, 1604; solicitor-general, 1604; M.P., Horsham, Sussex, between 1603 and 1611; knighted, 1607; justice of the king's bench, 1612; M.A., honoris causâ, Oxford, 1614; signed the letter refusing to stay proceedings at the instance of the king in the commendam case of 1616, but subsequently gave way; directed to soften the rigour of the statutes against popish recusants, 1623. His published work includes 'The English Lawyer,' 1631, and 'A Compleat Parson' the substance of some lectures on advowsons), 1630.
[xv. 157]

DODDRIDGE, PHILIP (1702–1751), nonconformist divine; minister at Kibworth, 1723; declined overtures from Pershore, Worcestershire, and Haberdashers' Hall from unwillingness to subscribe the Toleration Act, a probable condition of ordination, 1723; co-minister with his friend, David Some, at Market Harborough, 1725–9; opened an academy at Market Harborough, 1729, subsequently removing it to Northampton; presbyter, 1730; published 'Free Thoughts on the most probable means of reviving the Dissenting Interest,' 1730; tolerant of Arianism, though rejecting its claims; D.D. of the two universities of Aberdeen, 1736; lectured on philosophy and divinity in the mathematical or Spinozistic style; founded charity school at Northampton, 1737; took part in the foundation of a county infirmary, 1743; died at Lisbon; a celebrated hymn-writer; published 'The Rise and Progress of Religion in the Soul,' 1745. 'A Course of Lectures on Pneumatology, Ethics, and Divinity' appeared posthumously in 1763. [xv. 158]

DODDS, JAMES (1813–1874), lecturer and poet; studied at Edinburgh University; solicitor in London; friend of Leigh Hunt and Thomas Carlyle; author of 'Lays of the Covenanters,' posthumously published by the Rev. James Dodds of Dunbar, and 'The Fifty Years' Struggle of the Covenanters, 1638–1688.' [xv. 164]

DODDS, JAMES (1812–1885), religious and general writer; studied at Edinburgh University; minister at Humbie in East Lothian, and, after joining the Free Church, at Dunbar, 1843–85; friend of Thomas Carlyle;

published 'Famous Men of Dumfriesshire,' 'A Century of Scottish Church History,' and theological works and memoirs. [xv. 165]

DODGSON, CHARLES LUTWIDGE (1832–1898), writer of books for children under the pseudonym of LEWIS CARROLL, and mathematician; educated at Rugby and Christ Church, Oxford; nominated student of Christ Church, 1852; B.A., 1854; mathematical lecturer, 1855–81; M.A., 1857; ordained deacon, 1861; resided at Oxford, where he published occasionally humorous pamphlets on matters of local interest. His most popular works are 'Alice's Adventures in Wonderland,' 1865, and 'Through the Looking Glass,' 1871, both illustrated by Sir John Tenniel. His other publications include, 'The Hunting of the Snark,' 1876, and 'Sylvie and Bruno,' 1889, besides various mathematical writings, of which the most valuable is 'Euclid and his Modern Rivals,' 1879.
[Suppl. ii. 142]

DODGSON, GEORGE HAYDOCK (1811–1880), water-colour painter; prepared plans for Whitby and Pickering railway, while apprentice to George Stephenson; exhibited at the Royal Academy a 'Tribute to the Memory of Sir Christopher Wren' (study in architectural drawing), 1838; member of the Society of Painters in Water-colours, 1852; exhibited at the Royal Academy, 1838–50.
[xv. 165]

DODINGTON, BARTHOLOMEW (1536–1595), Greek scholar; Lady Margaret's scholar, St. John's College, Cambridge, 1547; Lady Margaret's fellow, 1552; M.A., 1555; senior fellow, 1558; fellow of Trinity College, Cambridge, c. 1560; regius professor of Greek, 1562–85; wrote Greek poems and Greek and Latin orations.
[xv. 166]

DODINGTON, GEORGE BUBB, BARON MELCOMBE (1691–1762); M.P., Winchelsea, 1715; envoy extraordinary to Spain, 1715; took the surname Dodington on succeeding to his uncle's estate, 1720; M.P., Bridgewater, 1722–54; lord of the treasury, 1724; adherent of Walpole; favourite of Frederick, prince of Wales; attached himself to the Duke of Argyll and attacked Walpole, 1742; treasurer of the navy in Pelham's administration, 1744; paid court to the Pelhams, and in 1754 to the Duke of Newcastle; M.P., Weymouth; treasurer of the navy under Newcastle and Fox, 1755; spoke against the execution of Byng, 1757; created Baron Melcombe of Melcombe Regis, 1761; wit, patron of literature, writer of occasional verses, and political pamphleteer.
[xv. 166]

DODS, MARCUS (1786–1838), theological writer; educated at Edinburgh; presbyterian minister, Belford, 1810–38; D.D.; published a work 'On the Incarnation of the Eternal Word'; criticised Edward Irving's doctrine of the incarnation. [xv. 169]

DODSLEY, JAMES (1724–1797), bookseller; brother of Robert Dodsley [q. v.]; produced an improved edition of Isaac Reed's 'Collection of Old Plays,' 1780, and re-edited Reed's 'Collection of Poems,' 1782; member of the Congeries, a well-known booksellers' club; suggested plan of receipt tax to Rockingham's administration, 1782.
[xv. 169]

DODSLEY, ROBERT (1703–1764), poet, dramatist, and bookseller; while a footman in service of the Hon. Mrs. Lowther published 'Servitude, a Poem,' in the 'Country Journal,' 1729 (afterwards reissued as 'The Footman's Friendly Advice to his Brethren of the Livery'); bookseller, 1735; wrote the plays 'The King and the Miller of Mansfield,' 1737, and 'Sir John Cockle at Court,' a sequel, 1738; published for Pope, Young, and Akenside; published a 'Select Collection of Old Plays,' his best-known work, 1744; started 'The Publick Register,' 1741, 'The Museum,' 1746, and 'The Preceptor'; suggested to Johnson the scheme of an English dictionary; published Johnson's 'Vanity of Human Wishes' and 'Irene' (both in 1749); published an ode entitled 'Melpomene,' 1758; his tragedy, 'Cleone,' acted at Covent Garden,' 1758; founded 'The Annual Register,' 1758; published with his brother James Dodsley [q. v.], Goldsmith's 'Polite Learning,' 1759, and, with Johnson and Strahan, Johnson's 'Rasselas,' 1759; friend of Shenstone, some of whose narrative poems appeared in Dodsley's 'Select Fables,' 1761. [xv. 170]

DODSON, JAMES (d. 1757), teacher of mathematics and master of the Royal Mathematical School, Christ's Hospital; F.R.S., 1755; master at Christ's Hospital,

1755-7; prepared the way for ultimate incorporation of Equitable Society; published 'The Anti-Logarithmic Canon,' 1742; and an 'Accountant, or a Method of Book-keeping,' 1750. [xv. 174]

DODSON, Sir JOHN (1780-1858), judge of the prerogative court; educated at Merchant Taylors' School and Oriel College, Oxford; M.A., 1804; D.C.L., 1808; advocate of the College of Doctors of Laws, 1808; M.P., Rye, 1819-23; advocate-general and knighted, 1834; barrister, Inner Temple, 1834; judge of the prerogative court of Canterbury, and dean of the arches court, 1852-1857; privy councillor, 1852. [xv. 175]

DODSON, JOHN GEORGE, first Baron Monk-Bretton (1825-1897), politician; son of Sir John Dodson [q. v.]; educated at Eton, and Christ Church, Oxford; B.A., 1847; M.A., 1851; called to bar at Lincoln's Inn, 1853; travelled; liberal M.P. for East Sussex, 1857-74, Chester, 1874-80, and Scarborough, 1880-4; chairman of committees and deputy speaker of House of Commons, 1865-72; privy councillor, 1872; president of local government board with seat in cabinet, 1880; chancellor of duchy of Lancaster, 1882-4; raised to peerage, 1884; liberal unionist from 1886. [Suppl. ii. 144]

DODSON, MICHAEL (1732-1799), lawyer; educated at Marlborough grammar school; barrister, Middle Temple, 1783; commissioner of bankruptcy, 1770-99; unitarian; edited Sir Michael Foster's 'Report on the Commission for the Trial of Rebels in the Year 1746,' and published 'A New Translation of Isaiah,' 1790. [xv. 176]

DODSWORTH, ROGER (1585-1654), antiquary; studied in London in the library of Sir Robert Cotton; designed an English baronage, a history of Yorkshire, and a Monasticon Anglicanum, published as 'Monasticon Boreale,' 1655, with name of Dugdale as joint-compiler. [xv. 176]

DODSWORTH, WILLIAM (1798-1861), Roman catholic writer; M.A. Trinity College, Cambridge, 1823; adopted Tractarian opinions and became minister of Margaret Street Chapel, Cavendish Square, London; perpetual curate of Christ Church, St. Pancras, London, 1837; joined the Roman catholic church after the Gorham judgment, 1851; published 'Advent Lectures,' 1837, 'Anglicanism considered in its results,' 1851, and catholic apologetics. [xv. 177]

DODWELL, EDWARD (1767-1832), traveller and archæologist; B.A. Trinity College, Cambridge, 1800; collected vases, including the well-known 'Dodwell Vase' from Corinth, and marbles and coins in Greece and the Archipelago; settled (1806) in Italy, where he enjoyed the friendship of the pope; published 'A Classical and Topographical Tour through Greece, 1819, and views and descriptions of ancient remains; died at Rome. [xv. 178]

DODWELL, HENRY, the elder (1641-1711), scholar and theologian; scholar and fellow of Trinity College, Dublin; resigned his fellowship from unwillingness to take holy orders, 1666; Camden professor of history at Oxford, 1688-91; deprived for refusing oath of allegiance, 1691; returned (1710) to the established church, from which he had been excluded as a nonjuror; published a 'Book of Schism,' which was controverted by Richard Baxter; 'Annales Thucydideani,' for Hudson's 'Thucydides'; 'A Discourse concerning the Time of Phalaris,' 1704, and other learned works. [xv. 179]

DODWELL, HENRY, the younger (d. 1784), deist; son of Henry Dodwell the elder [q. v.]; B.A. Magdalen Hall, Oxford, 1726; published 'Christianity not founded on Argument,' a deistical pamphlet, which some mistook for a defence of Christianity, 1742. [xv. 181]

DODWELL, WILLIAM (1709-1785), archdeacon of Berks and theological writer; son of Henry Dodwell (1641-1711) [q. v.]; M.A. Trinity College, Oxford, 1732; prebendary of Salisbury; D.D. Oxford, 1750; archdeacon of Berks; published controversial works, including, 1743, 'Two Sermons on the Eternity of Future Punishment,' in answer to Whiston, and, 1745, 'Two Sermons on the Nature, Procedure, and Effects of a Rational Faith,' in answer to his brother, Henry Dodwell the younger. [xv. 182]

DOGGET, JOHN (d. 1501), provost of King's College, Cambridge; educated at Eton; M.A. and fellow,

King's College, Cambridge; prebendary of Lincoln, 1474; ambassador to Sixtus IV and the princes of Sicily and Hungary, 1479; chaplain to Richard III, 1483; vicar-general, Sarum, 1483, and chancellor of Lichfield, 1489; doctor of canon law at Bologna; provost of King's College, 1499-1501; benefactor of King's College. [xv. 183]

DOGGETT, THOMAS (d. 1721), actor; 'created' Ben in Congreve's 'Love for Love,' 1695; author of the 'Country Wake,' a comedy, in which he acted himself, 1696; friend of Congreve and Colley Cibber; his dignified style praised by Cibber; joint-manager of the Haymarket, 1709-10, subsequently of Drury Lane; founded in 1716, in honour of the anniversary of George I's accession, a prize for a rowing competition for Thames watermen, which is still continued. [xv. 184]

DOGHERTY. [See also Docharty and Dougharty.]

DOGHERTY, THOMAS (d. 1805), legal writer; of Irish origin; member of Gray's Inn; special pleader, c. 1785; clerk of indictments on the Chester circuit; wrote the 'Crown Circuit Assistant,' 1787. [xv. 185]

DOGMAEL, also called DOGVAEL, SAINT (6th cent.), reputed founder of a monastery at Cemmes, opposite Cardigan, and of some churches in modern Pembrokeshire. [xv. 185]

DOHARTY, JOHN (1677-1755). [See Dougharty.]

DOHERTY, JOHN (1783-1850), chief-justice of Ireland; B.A. Trinity College, Dublin, 1806; LL.D., 1814 called to the Irish bar, 1808; M.P., New Ross, 1824-6 Kilkenny, 1826; solicitor-general, 1827; lord chief-justice of common pleas and privy councillor, 1830; spoke against O'Connell in the debate on the 'Doneraile conspiracy,' 1830. [xv. 186]

DOIG, DAVID (1719-1800), philologist; M.A. St Andrews; rector of the grammar school at Stirling honorary LL.D. Glasgow; fellow of the Royal Society of Edinburgh; wrote 'Two Letters on the Savag< State, 1792, against Lord Kames's views [see Home, Henry Lord Kames], a friendship resulting between author and critic; published 'Extracts from a Poem on the Prospect from Stirling Castle,' 1796. [xv. 186]

DOKET or **DUCKET**, ANDREW (d. 1484), first president of Queens' College, Cambridge; rector of St Botolph, Cambridge, 1444-70; prebendary of Lichfield 1467, and chancellor, 1470-6; authorised by royal charte in 1447 to found 'the College of St. Bernard of Cambridge, which was ultimately called 'Queens' College' in honou of its patronesses, Margaret of Anjou and Elizabeth Wood ville. [xv. 187]

DOLBEN, DAVID (1581-1633), bishop of Bangor M.A. St. John's College, Cambridge, 1609; vicar o Hackney, Middlesex, 1618-33; prebendary of St. Asaph 1625; D.D., 1627; bishop of Bangor, 1631-3. [xv. 188]

DOLBEN, Sir GILBERT (1658-1722), judge; so of John Dolben (1625-1686) [q. v.]; educated at West minster School and at Oxford; barrister of the Inne Temple, 1681; M.P., Ripon, 1685, Peterborough, 1689-1707; puisne judge in the Irish court of common pleas 1701; maintained exclusive jurisdiction of the House o Commons in election questions, 1704; created baronet 1704; M.P., Yarmouth, Isle of Wight, 1710 and 1714. [xv. 189]

DOLBEN, JOHN (1625-1686), archbishop of York son of William Dolben (d. 1631) [q.v.]; educated at West minster under Dr. Busby [q. v.]; student of Chris Church, Oxford, 1640-8; fought for Charles I at Marsto Moor, 1644; captain and major; M.A. by accumulation 1647; deprived of his studentship, 1648; privately main tained the proscribed church of England service; cano of Christ Church, 1660; prebendary of St. Paul's, 1661 dean of Westminster, 1662-83; maintained the immunity of Westminster Abbey from diocesan control; bishop o Rochester, 1666; suspended at the time of Clarendon' fall, 1667; lord high almoner, 1675; archbishop of York 1683-6; reformed cathedral discipline. [xv. 189]

DOLBEN, JOHN (1662-1710), politician; son o John Dolben (1625-1686) [q.v.]; studied at Christ Churcl Oxford; barrister of the Temple; spent his fortune withdrew to the West Indies; M.P., Liskeard, 1707-10 manager of Sacheverell's impeachment, 1709. [xv. 192]

DOLBEN, SIR JOHN (1684–1756), divine ; son of Sir Gilbert Dolben [q. v.] ; canon's student of Christ Church, Oxford, 1702 ; M.A., 1707 ; prebendary of Durham, 1718 and 1719 ; rector of Burton Latimer and vicar of Finedon, 1719 ; succeeded as baronet, 1722 ; visitor of Balliol College, Oxford, 1728 ; sub-dean of Queen Caroline's chapel ; friend of Bishop Atterbury, paying him an annuity when exiled. [xv. 193]

DOLBEN, WILLIAM (d. 1631), prebendary of Lincoln, bishop designate ; educated at Westminster and Christ Church, Oxford ; rector of Stanwick and Benefield, 1623 ; D.D. ; prebendary of Lincoln, 1629 ; said by his great-grandson, Sir John Dolben (1684–1756) [q. v.], to have been nominated bishop of Gloucester. [xv. 194]

DOLBEN, SIR WILLIAM (d. 1694), judge ; son of William Dolben (d. 1631) [q. v.] ; barrister of the Inner Temple, 1655 ; recorder of London and knighted, 1676 ; serjeant-at-law, 1677 ; king's serjeant and steward of the see of Canterbury ; puisne judge of the king's bench, 1678–83, and 1689. [xv. 194]

DOLBEN, WILLIAM (1726–1814), abolitionist ; son of Sir John Dolben [q. v.] ; M.P. for Oxford University, 1768–1806. [xv. 194]

DOLBY, CHARLOTTE HELEN SAINTON- (1821–1885). [See SAINTON-DOLBY, CHARLOTTE HELEN.]

DOLLE, WILLIAM (fl. 1670–1680), engraver ; employed by the booksellers in engraving portraits and frontispieces, including portraits of Sir Henry Wotton and Richard Hooker in Izaak Walton's 'Lives' (1670). [xv. 195]

DOLLOND, GEORGE (1774–1852), optician ; partner with his uncle, Peter Dollond [q. v.], 1805 ; invented an improved altazimuth, 1821, 'a double altitude instrument,' 1823, and an atmospheric recorder ; F.R.S., 1819 ; F.R.G.S. [xv. 195]

DOLLOND, JOHN (1706–1761), optician ; of Huguenot origin ; read his 'Account of some Experiments concerning the different Refrangibility of Light' before the Royal Society (1758) ; Copley medallist, 1758 ; inventor of triple objectives, 1757–8 ; his invention of the achromatic telescope independently made by Chester Moor Hall [q. v.] ; invented modern heliometer, 1754 ; F.R.S. and optician to the king, 1761. [xv. 196]

DOLLOND, PETER (1730–1820), optician ; eldest son of John Dollond [q. v.] ; optician in the Strand, 1750 ; invented improved triple achromatic object-glasses ; improved Hadley's quadrant by a device for bringing the back-observation into use ; member of the American Philosophical Society. [xv. 198]

DOLMAN, CHARLES (1807–1863), Roman catholic publisher ; entered into partnership with his cousin, Thomas Booker, a Roman catholic publisher in London, 1840 ; set on foot new series of the 'Catholic Magazine,' 1838, and 'Dolman's Magazine,' 1845 ; noted for the elaborateness of his typography. [xv. 199]

DOMERHAM, ADAM OF (d. after 1291). [See ADAM.]

DOMETT, ALFRED (1811–1887), colonial statesman and poet ; entered at St. John's College, Cambridge, 1829 ; barrister of the Middle Temple, 1841 ; emigrated to New Zealand, 1842 ; friend of Robert Browning, who lamented his departure in 'Waring,' 1842 ; M.P. for Nelson, 1855 ; prime minister of New Zealand, 1862–3, and registrar-general of land, 1865 ; returned to England, 1871 ; C.M.G., 1880 ; author of 'Ranolf and Amohia, a South Sea Day Dream,' 1872, 'Flotsam and Jetsam,' 1877, and some official publications. [xv. 199]

DOMETT, SIR WILLIAM (1754–1828), admiral ; navy lieutenant, 1777 ; present in the action off Ushant, 1778, and in the engagement of the Chesapeake, 1781 ; signal officer at St. Kitts and off Dominica, 1782 ; sent to England with Sir George Rodney's despatches, 1782 ; flag captain during the French war of 1793 ; captain of Baltic fleet, 1801 ; admiral, 1819 ; G.C.B., 1820. [xv. 200]

DOMINICUS DE ROSARIO (1595–1662). [See DALY, DANIEL or DOMINIC.]

DOMINIS, MARCO ANTONIO DE (1566–1624), divine ; born in the island of Arbe off Dalmatia ; professor of mathematics at Padua, of logic and rhetoric at Brescia ; bishop of Segni ; archbishop of Spalatro ; migrated to England (1616) from annoyance at the pope's imposition of a tax upon the see of Spalatro to be paid to the bishop of Segni ; defended his action in 'Consilium Profectionis,' 1616 ; dean of Windsor and master of the Savoy, 1617 ; published first part of 'De Republicâ Ecclesiasticâ' (1617), maintaining rights of national churches ; left England, to the annoyance of James I, 1622 ; wrote a recantation entitled 'Consilium Reditûs' ; promised pardon by Pope Gregory XV ; imprisoned by the inquisition. [xv. 201]

DOMVILLE, alias TAYLOR, SILAS (1624–1678), antiquary ; educated at Westminster and New Inn Hall, Oxford ; captain in the parliamentary army, and subsequently sequestrator in Herefordshire ; commissary for ammunition under Sir Edward Harley at Dunkirk, 1660 ; surreptitiously obtained from the library of Worcester Cathedral an original grant of King Edgar, dated 964 ; published 'The History of Gavelkind,' 1663 ; left in manuscript collections for a history of Herefordshire. [xv. 203]

DON, DAVID (1800–1841), botanist ; made the acquaintance of Humboldt and Cuvier at Paris, 1821 ; fellow of the Linnæan Society ; professor of botany, King's College, London, 1836–41 ; published 'Prodromus Floræ Nepalensis,' 1825. [xv. 204]

DON, SIR GEORGE (1754–1832), general ; lieutenant, 51st regiment, 1774 ; lieutenant-colonel at Gibraltar, 1789 ; adjutant-general in the Netherlands, 1794 ; major-general, 1798 ; commanded the third division at the Helder, 1799 ; prisoner in France till 1800 ; second in command of the forces of Scotland, 1804 ; lieutenant-general, 1803 ; lieutenant-governor of Jersey, 1806–14 ; general, 1814 ; lieutenant-governor of Gibraltar (1814), where he died ; G.C.B., 1820 ; G.C.M.G., 1825. [xv. 205]

DON, GEORGE (1798–1856), botanist ; collector on behalf of the Royal Horticultural Society in Brazil, the West Indies, and at Sierra Leone, 1821 ; fellow of the Linnæan Society, 1831 ; published 'A General System of Gardening and Botany, founded upon Miller's "Gardener's Dictionary,"' 1832–8. [xv. 206]

DON, SIR WILLIAM HENRY (1825–1862), actor ; seventh baronet of Newtondon, 1826 ; educated at Eton ; lieutenant, 5th dragoon guards, 1845 ; appeared on the stage at New York, 1850, and at the Haymarket, 1857 ; played, in Australia, female characters in burlesques ; died at Hobart Town, Tasmania. [xv. 206]

DONALD IV, BREAC (the Speckled or Freckled) (d. 643), Celtic king of Scottish Dalriada ; fought on the side of Congall Claen, king of the Cruthnigh (Picts), against Donald, king of Ireland, at the battle of Rath, Ireland, 637 ; slain in battle at Strathcarron by Owen, king of the Strathclyde Britons. [xv. 207]

DONALD V, MACALPIN (d. 864), king of Alban, the united kingdom of the Scots and Picts ; established the rights and laws of Aedh, a Dalriad king of the eighth century, at Forteviot ; according to one account was killed at Scone, 864. [xv. 207]

DONALD VI (d. 900), king of Celtic Scotland ; son of Constantine I [q. v.] ; made peace with the Danish chiefs, Ronald and Sitric ; died, worn out by his exertions in reducing the highland robber tribes. [xv. 208]

DONALD, ADAM (1703–1780), called 'the prophet of Bethelnie' ; necromancer and quack physician. [xv. 208]

DONALDSON, JAMES (fl. 1713), Scottish miscellaneous writer ; left farm to serve in regiment of Earl of Angus ; disbanded, 1690 ; published 'Husbandry Anatomized,' 1697–8, 'Money encreas'd and Credit rais'd,' 1705, and other efforts in political economy and verse-writing. [xv. 209]

DONALDSON, JAMES (fl. 1794), writer on agriculture ; land surveyor at Dundee ; drew up county surveys for the board of agriculture ; published 'Modern Agriculture,' 1795–6. [xv. 210]

DONALDSON, JAMES (1751–1830), founder of Donaldson's Hospital, Edinburgh ; proprietor and editor of the 'Edinburgh Advertiser' after 1764 ; left 220,000l. for the maintenance and education of three hundred poor children. [xv. 210]

DONALDSON, JOHN (d. 1865), professor of music ; called to the Scottish bar, 1826 ; Reid professor of music, Edinburgh, 1845–65 ; investigated acoustic problems. [xv. 211]

DONALDSON, JOHN (1799–1876), author of 'Agricultural Biography,' 1854, and other works on agricultural subjects. [Suppl. ii. 145]

DONALDSON, JOHN WILLIAM (1811–1861), philologist; brother of Sir Stuart Alexander Donaldson [q. v.]; sent to Trinity College, Cambridge, 1831; second in classical tripos, 1834; fellow and tutor of Trinity; published 'New Cratylus,' practically starting the science of comparative philology in England, 1839; D.D.; head-master of King Edward's School, Bury St. Edmunds, 1841–55; published 'Varronianus,' advancing theory of the Gothic affinities of the Etruscans, 1844; resigned head-mastership, 1855; classical examiner to the university of London; completed K. O. Müller's 'History of Greek Literature,' 1858; the main author of the 'Theatre of the Greeks'; edited Pindar's 'Epinician Odes' and the 'Antigone' of Sophocles; published 'Jashar' (1854), to prove that a book of Jashar constituted 'the religious marrow of the scriptures.' [xv. 211]

DONALDSON, JOSEPH (1794–1830), author of 'Recollections of the Eventful Life of a Soldier'; fought in Peninsular war, 1811–14; discharged as sergeant, 1815; enlisted in the East India Company's service; head-clerk in the Glasgow district staff-office; surgeon at Oban, 1827. [xv. 213]

DONALDSON, Sir STUART ALEXANDER (1812–1867), Australian statesman; brother of John William Donaldson [q. v.]; magistrate of New South Wales, 1838; realised a fortune in wool and sperm oil; was member of the council of New South Wales, 1848–59; first minister and colonial secretary in accordance with the New Constitution Act, 1856; finance minister, 1856–57; returned to England, 1859; knighted, 1860. [xv. 213]

DONALDSON, THOMAS LEVERTON (1795–1885), architect and author; in merchant's office at Cape of Good Hope, 1809; silver medallist of the Royal Academy, 1817; visited Greece, Italy, and Asia Minor, studying ancient buildings; president of the Institute of Architects, 1864; member of the Institut de France; emeritus professor of architecture at University College, London, 1841–64; designed various London churches and mansions. His works include, 'Handbook of Specifications' 1859, and 'Architectura Numismatica,' 1859. [xv. 214]

DONALDSON, WALTER (*fl.* 1620), philosophical writer; attached to embassy sent by James VI of Scotland to Denmark, 1594; LL.D. Heidelberg; principal of the protestant college of Sedan; published a survey of Greek philosophy in the form of extracts from Diogenes Laertius, 1612, and 'Synopsis Œconomica,' 1620.
[xv. 215]

DONAT (1038–1074). [See DUNAN.]

DONATUS, SAINT (*fl.* 829–876), bishop of Fiesole; of Irish birth; wandered about Europe visiting sacred places; appointed bishop of Fiesole as one divinely sent, *c.* 829; obtained new charter for church of Fiesole from the Emperor Louis, son of Lothair, 866; his day, 22 Oct. [xv. 216]

DONCASTER, first VISCOUNT (*d.* 1636). [See HAY, JAMES.]

DONEGAL, first EARL OF (1606–1675). [See CHICHESTER, ARTHUR.]

DONELLAN, NEHEMIAS (*d.* 1609?), archbishop of Tuam; sizar of King's College, Cambridge, 1580; B.A. Catharine Hall, Cambridge, 1582; archbishop of Tuam, 1595–1609; continued Walsh and Kearney's translation of New Testament into Irish. [xv. 216]

DONKIN, BRYAN (1768–1855), civil engineer and inventor; erected paper-making machine at Frogmore, Kent, 1804; invented polygonal printing-machine, 1813, and composition printing-roller; devised process of 'tinning' meat and vegetables, 1812; F.R.S., 1838; M.R.A.S.; gold medallist of Society of Arts for invention of counting-engine and a machine for registering velocities of rotation. [xv. 217]

DONKIN, Sir RUFANE SHAW (1773–1841), general; educated at Westminster School; lieut. 44th foot 1779; capt. 1793; major, 1795; served at St. Lucia, 1796; commanded brigade at Talavera, 1809; major-general, 1811; served in Mahratta war, 1817–18; K.C.B., 1818; acting-governor, Cape of Good Hope, 1820; founded Port Elizabeth; lieutenant-general, 1821; F.R.S. and F.R.G.S.; M.P., Berwick, 1832 and 1835, and subsequently for Sandwich; surveyor-general of the ordnance, 1835; colonel, 11th foot, 1837; general, 1838; author of 'A Dissertation on the Course and Probable Termination of the Niger,' 1829, and some unpublished tractates. [xv. 218]

DONKIN, WILLIAM FISHBURN (1814–1869), astronomer; entered St. Edmund Hall, Oxford, 1832; double first-class, 1836; Johnson mathematical scholar, 1837; M.A., 1839; fellow of University College; Savilian professor of astronomy at Oxford, 1842–69; F.R.S. and F.R.A.S.; contributed to learned periodicals; a fragment of his projected work on acoustics published, 1870.
[xv. 220]

DONLEVY, ANDREW (1694?–1761?), Irish ecclesiastic; prefect in the Irish college at Paris; licentiate of laws, Paris University; D.D.; published 'The Catechism, or Christian Doctrine,' 1742, extant in Irish and English, with an appendix on 'The Elements of the Irish Language.' [xv. 221]

DONN or **DONNE**, BENJAMIN (1729–1798), mathematician; started mathematical academy at Bristol; master of mechanics to the king; published maps of South-western England, charts of the western ocean, and works on mathematics and book-keeping. [xv. 221]

DONN, JAMES (1758–1813), botanist; curator of the Cambridge Botanic Garden, 1790–1813; fellow of the Linnean Society; best known as having named *Claytonia perfoliata.* [xv. 222]

DONNE or **DUNN**, Sir DANIEL (*d.* 1617), civilian; educated at All Souls' College, Oxford; D.C.L., 1580; principal of New Inn, 1580; dean of arches and master of requests, 1598; member of commission for suppression of English piracy, 1601; appointed Whitgift's vicar-general; master in chancery; commissioner for proposed fisheries treaty with Denmark, 1602; knighted; M.P. for Oxford, 1604 and 1614; a recognised authority on marriage-law.
[xv. 222]

DONNE or **DUNNE**, GABRIEL (*d.* 1558), Cistercian monk; member of St. Bernard's College, Oxford, and M.A.; planned the arrest of William Tyndale at Antwerp, 1535; abbot of Buckfastleigh, Devonshire, which he surrendered to Henry VIII in 1539; keeper of the spiritualities of St. Paul's, 1549; benefactor of Trinity Hall, Cambridge. [xv. 223]

DONNE, JOHN (1573–1631), poet and divine; brought up by his mother in the Roman catholic religion; entered Hart Hall, Oxford, at an early age to avoid the necessity of taking the oath of supremacy, 1584; friend of Sir Henry Wotton and Henry Fitzsimon [q. v.]; admitted at Lincoln's Inn, 1592; sailed in Essex's expedition to Cadiz, 1596; secretary to Sir Thomas Egerton, keeper of the great seal, 1596; dismissed in consequence of an imprudent marriage, 1601; strongly urged by Thomas Morton (1564–1659) [q. v.], one of the king's chaplains, whom he had assisted in writing an 'Apologia Christiana,' to take orders and accept the living of Long Marston in Yorkshire; refused, for religious reasons, 1607; produced the 'Pseudo-Martyr' in answer to Bellarmine's justification of the popish recusants, 1610; M.A. Oxford, by decree of convocation, 1610; wrote 'An Anatomy of the World,' an elegy on the death of Elizabeth, daughter of Sir Robert Drury, 1611; wrote a funeral elegy on Prince Henry, 1612; published an 'Epithalamium' on the marriage of the count palatine and the Princess Elizabeth, 1613; wrote 'Essays in Divinity' (published 1651) about this time; admitted a conditional right of suicide in 'Biathanatos' (printed 1644); ordained, 1615; chaplain to James I, 1615; D.D. Cambridge; rector of Keyston, Huntingdonshire, and Sevenoaks, Kent, 1616; divinity reader at Lincoln's Inn, preaching sermons which rank among the best of the seventeenth century, 1616; preached at Heidelberg before the Princess Elizabeth, 1619; dean of St. Paul's, 1621–31; prolocutor of convocation, 1623 and 1624; frequently preached before Charles I. Collections of his 'Poems by J. D.' appeared in 1633 and 1649, and 'Letters' by him in 1651. He was one of the 'metaphysical' poets of the seventeenth century. [xv. 223]

DONNE, JOHN, the younger (1604–1662), miscellaneous writer; son of John Donne (1573–1631) [q. v.]; educated at Westminster School and Christ Church, Oxford; tried for the manslaughter of a child eight years old, but acquitted, 1633; doctor of laws, Padua; incorporated at Oxford, 1638; held various livings; author of 'Donnes Satyr,' a ribald production, 1661-2.   [xv. 234]

DONNE, WILLIAM BODHAM (1807-1882), examiner of plays; studied at Caius College, Cambridge; librarian of the London Library, 1852-7; examiner of plays in the lord chamberlain's office, 1857-74; published 'Old Roads and New Roads,' 1852, and 'Essays upon the Drama,' 1858.   [xv. 234]

DONNEGAN, JAMES (*fl.* 1841), lexicographer; graduate in medicine of a foreign university; medical practitioner in London, 1820-35; published 'A New Greek and English Lexicon,' 1826.   [xv. 235]

DONNELLY, SIR ROSS (1761?-1840), admiral; lieutenant, 1781; commander, 1794; captain, 1795; served successively in Mediterranean, 1801-5, at Cape of Good Hope, 1805, Buenos Ayres, at capture of Monte Video, and Cadiz, 1808; rear-admiral, 1814; admiral, 1838; K.C.B., 1837.   [Suppl. ii. 146]

DONOUGHMORE, EARLS OF. [See HELY-HUTCHINSON, RICHARD, first EARL, 1756-1825; HELY-HUTCHINSON, JOHN, second EARL, 1757-1832; HELY-HUTCHINSON, JOHN, third EARL, 1787-1851.]

DONOVAN, EDWARD (1768-1837), naturalist and author; founded London Museum and Institute of Natural History, 1807; published works of natural history, illustrated with drawings by himself, including 'The Nests and Eggs of British Birds,' and 'General Illustrations of Entomology,' 1805.   [xv. 235]

DOODY, SAMUEL (1656-1706), botanist; apothecary, 1696; assisted Ray in the 'Historia Plantarum'; F.R.S.; curator of the Apothecaries' Garden, Chelsea, 1693-1706; specialist on cryptogams.   [xv. 236]

DOOLITTLE, THOMAS (1632?-1707), nonconformist tutor; M.A. Pembroke Hall, Cambridge; pastor of St. Alphage, London Wall, 1653; ejected, 1662; opened boarding-school at Moorfields; licensed by the indulgence of 1672 to a meeting-house in Mugwell Street; his academy ruined by its enforced removal from place to place, 1687; published theological treatises, including his catechetical lectures as 'A Complete Body of Practical Divinity,' 1723.   [xv. 236]

DOPPING, ANTHONY (1643-1697), bishop successively of Kildare and Meath; fellow of Trinity College, Dublin, 1662; M.A., 1662; D.D., 1672; chaplain to the Duke of Ormonde; bishop of Kildare, 1679; privy councillor and bishop of Meath by letters patent, 1682; suggested to William III the proclamation of a fast during the struggle with James II; published orations, theological treatises, and political pamphlets.   [xv. 238]

DORAN, JOHN (1807-1878), miscellaneous writer; of Irish parentage; author of 'Justice, or the Venetian Jew,' a melodrama, 1824; doctor of philosophy, Marburg; literary editor of the 'Church and State Gazette,' 1841-1852; editor of the 'Athenæum,' 1869-70; published 'The Queens of the House of Hanover,' 1855, 'Knights and their Days,' 1856, and an historical account of the English stage, entitled 'Their Majesties' Servants,' 1860.   [xv. 239]

DORCHESTER, MARQUISES OF. [See PIERREPONT, HENRY, 1606-1680; PIERREPONT, EVELYN, first marquis of the second creation, 1665?-1726.]

DORCHESTER, COUNTESS OF (1657-1717). [See SEDLEY, CATHARINE.]

DORCHESTER, VISCOUNT (1573-1632). [See CARLETON, SIR DUDLEY.]

DORCHESTER, first BARON (1724-1808). [See CARLETON, GUY.]

DORIGNY, SIR NICHOLAS (1658-1746), painter and engraver; born at Paris; studied painting and etching at Rome; engraver of pictures of the various Italian schools; invited to engrave Raphael's tapestries in the Vatican; came to England to study some of the original cartoons, 1711; presented two complete sets of engravings after Raphael to George I, 1719; knighted, 1720; member of the French Academy, 1725; exhibited paintings at the Salon exhibitions, 1739-1743; died at Paris.   [xv. 240]

DORIN, JOSEPH ALEXANDER (1802-1872), Indian official; nominated to Bengal branch of East India Company's service; assistant to the accountant-general, 1821; deputy accountant-general; entrusted by Lord Ellenborough with re-organisation of Indian finance, 1842; financial secretary, 1843; member of Lord Dalhousie's council, 1853; advocated annexation of Oude, when president of council; assailed in the 'Red Pamphlet' as a member of Lord Canning's government at the time of the Indian mutiny, 1857.   [xv. 241]

DORION, SIR ANTOINE AIMÉ (1818-1891), Canadian judge; born in Canada; advocate, 1842; Q.C., 1863; joined party founded by Louis Joseph Papineau [q. v.]; member for Montreal, 1854-61, and Hochelaga, 1862; provincial secretary, 1862; attorney-general east and leader of French-Canadian liberals, 1863-64; member for Napierville, 1872; minister of justice and privy councillor, 1873; chief-justice of court of queen's bench, Quebec, 1874; knighted, 1877.   [Suppl. ii. 146]

DORISLAUS, ISAAC (1595-1649), diplomatist, born at Alkmaar, Holland; LL.D. Leyden; Grenville lecturer on history, Cambridge, 1627; practically compelled to resign for defending the Dutch resistance to Spain, 1627; member of the College of Advocates, 1645; friend of Wotton and Selden; judge of the admiralty court, 1648; prepared the charge of high treason against Charles I, 1648; assassinated, when envoy to the States-General, by royalists at the Hague.   [xv. 242]

DORISLAUS, ISAAC, the younger (*d.* 1688), manager of the post office, 1660; son of Isaac Dorislaus (1595-1649) [q. v.]; entered Merchant Taylors' School, 1639; translator and interpreter to Thurloe; accompanied embassy to Holland, 1651; solicitor to the court of admiralty, 1653; F.R.S., 1681.   [xv. 244]

DORMAN, THOMAS (*d.* 1577?), Roman catholic divine; educated at Winchester and New College, Oxford; gave up a prospective fellowship for religious reasons; fellow of All Souls' College, 1554; B.C.L., 1558; B.D. Douay, 1565; D.D.; died in possession of a benefice at Tournay; published controversial works.   [xv. 244]

DORMER, JAMES (1679-1741), lieutenant-general; lieutenant and captain, 1st foot guards, 1700; wounded at Blenheim, 1704; levied the present 14th hussars, 1715; colonel of the 6th foot, 1720; envoy extraordinary at Lisbon, *c.* 1728; lieutenant-general and colonel, 1st troop of horse-grenadier guards, 1737; governor of Hull, 1740.   [xv. 245]

DORMER, JANE, DUCHESS OF FERIA (1538-1612), companion of Queen Mary; second daughter of Sir William Dormer; married in 1558 Don Gomez Suarez de Figueroa, count of Feria, who came to England with Philip II; joined her husband in Flanders, 1559; promoted papal interests; took the habit of the third order of St. Francis and founded a monastery near Villalva.   [xv. 245]

DORMER, JOHN (1636-1700), jesuit; his real name HUDDLESTON; professed jesuit father, 1673; preacher to James II; rector of the college of Liège, 1688-91; died at Liège; defended the taking of interest in 'Usury Explain'd,' 1696.   [xv. 247]

DORMER, JOHN (1734?-1796), officer in the Austrian army; first rittmeister in the Kleinhold cuirassier regiment, 1763; transferred to Serbelloni's cuirassier regiment, 1768; major, 1782; died at Grau.   [xv. 248]

DORMER, ROBERT, EARL OF CARNARVON (*d.* 1643), royalist; created Viscount Ascot and Earl of Carnarvon, 1628; commanded a regiment in the second Scottish war, 1641; fought for Charles I at Edgehill, 1642; took part in capture of Cirencester, 1643; advised Lord Wilmot to concentrate his forces against Haselrig's cuirassiers at Roundway Down, 1643; effected submission of Dorset, 1643; fell at the first battle of Newbury, 1643.   [xv. 248]

DORMER, SIR ROBERT (1649-1726), judge; barrister, Lincoln's Inn, 1675; chancellor of Durham; M.P., Aylesbury, 1699; M.P. for Buckinghamshire, 1701, for Northallerton, 1702, and for Buckinghamshire again; justice of common pleas, 1706.   [xv. 249]

DORNFORD, JOSEPH (1794-1868), divine; half-brother of Josiah Dornford [q. v.]; served as a volunteer in the Peninsular war, 1811; B.A. Wadham College,

Oxford, 1816 ; Michel fellow of Queen's College, Oxford, 1817 ; fellow of Oriel, 1819 ; M.A., 1820 ; dean and proctor of Oriel ; rector of Plymtree, Devonshire, 1832 ; prebendary of Exeter, 1844 ; published sermons. [xv. 250]

DORNFORD, JOSIAH (1764–1797), miscellaneous writer ; M.A. Trinity College, Oxford, 1792 ; LL.D. Göttingen ; barrister, Lincoln's Inn ; inspector-general of the army accounts in the Leeward islands, 1795 ; died at Martinique ; translated Pütter's ' Historical Developement of the Present Political Constitution of the Germanic Empire,' 1790, and published ' The Motives and Consequences of the Present War impartially considered,' 1793. [xv. 250]

DORRELL, WILLIAM (1651–1721). [See DARRELL, WILLIAM.]

DORRINGTON, THEOPHILUS (d. 1715), controversialist ; studied medicine at Leyden, 1680 ; published an account of his travels (1698) in Holland and Germany ; rector of Wittersham, Kent, 1698–1715 ; M.A. Magdalen College, Oxford, 1710 ; translated Puffendorf's ' Divine Feudal Law,' 1703, and wrote against the tenets of the dissenters. [xv. 250]

D'ORSAY, ALFRED GUILLAUME GABRIEL, COUNT (1801–1852), artist ; served in the Bourbons' bodyguard, though of imperialist sympathies ; visited England at the coronation of George IV, 1821 ; mentioned by Byron as an ideal Frenchman of the *ancien régime* ; joined the Countess of Blessington in establishing a fashionable coterie in London, 1831 ; painted the last portrait of the Duke of Wellington ; left London in consequence of pecuniary embarrassments, 1849 ; appointed director of the fine arts by Prince Louis Napoleon, 1852, shortly before his death. [xv. 251]

DORSET, DUKES OF. [See SACKVILLE, LIONEL CRANFIELD, first DUKE, 1688–1765 ; SACKVILLE, CHARLES, second DUKE, 1711–1769 ; SACKVILLE, JOHN FREDERICK, third DUKE, 1745–1799.]

DORSET, MARQUISES OF. [See GREY, THOMAS, first MARQUIS, 1451–1501 ; GREY, THOMAS, second MARQUIS, 1477–1530 ; GREY, HENRY, third MARQUIS, d. 1554.]

DORSET, EARLS OF. [See BEAUFORT, SIR THOMAS, first EARL of the second creation, d. 1427 ; BEAUFORT, EDMUND, first EARL of the third creation, d. 1455 ; SACKVILLE, THOMAS, first EARL of the fourth creation, 1536–1608 ; SACKVILLE, ROBERT, second EARL, 1561–1609 ; SACKVILLE, EDWARD, fourth EARL, 1591–1652 ; SACKVILLE, CHARLES, sixth EARL, 1638–1706 ; SACKVILLE, RICHARD, fifth EARL, 1622–1677.]

DORSET, COUNTESS OF (1590–1676). [See CLIFFORD, ANNE.]

DORSET, ST. JOHN (pseudonym) (1802–1827). [See BELFOUR, HUGO JOHN.]

DORSET, CATHERINE ANN (1750 ?–1817 ?) poetess ; *née* Turner ; married, c. 1770, Captain Michael Dorset ; author of ' The Peacock "at Home," ' a poem for children, 1807, and probably of ' The Lion's Masquerade,' a poem, 1807.

DOUBLEDAY, EDWARD (1811–1849), quaker entomologist ; brother of Henry Doubleday [q. v.] ; published papers occasioned by an entomological expedition (1835) to the United States ; assistant in the British Museum, 1839–1849 ; secretary of the Entomological Society ; commenced ' Genera of Diurnal Lepidoptera,' 1846. [xv. 254]

DOUBLEDAY, HENRY (1808–1875), quaker naturalist ; introduced practice of capturing moths at sallowblossoms and ' sugaring ' ; published ' A Nomenclature of British Birds,' 1838 ; member of the Entomological Society of London, 1833 ; attempted to establish a uniform system of entomological nomenclature by his ' Synonymic List of British Lepidoptera,' 1847–50. [xv. 254]

DOUBLEDAY, THOMAS (1790–1870), poet, dramatist, radical politician, and political economist ; agitated for reform, 1832 ; secretary to the northern political union ; joined in presenting address to Earl Grey pointing out deficiencies in the newly passed reform bill, 1832 ; published ' Essay on Mundane Moral Government,' 1832, ' The True Law of Population shown to be connected with the Food of the People,' 1842, ' The Eve of St. Mark ' (poem), and dramas and other works. [xv. 255]

DOUCE, FRANCIS (1757–1834), antiquary ; at one time keeper of the manuscripts in the British Museum ; published ' Illustrations of Shakespeare,' 1807 ; assisted Scott in the preparation of ' Sir Tristram' ; edited ' Arnold's Chronicle,' 1811 ; edited ' The Recreative Review,' 1821–3 ; published with a dissertation ' The Dance of Death,' 1833 ; bequeathed his manuscripts, prints, and coins to the Bodleian Library, and his unpublished essays to the British Museum. [xv. 256]

DOUDNEY, DAVID ALFRED (1811–1894), educational pioneer ; entered printing firm in London, 1832, and started business independently, 1835 ; editor and proprietor of ' Gospel Magazine,' 1840 ; ordained priest, 1847 ; vicar of Kilrush and curate of Monksland, co. Waterford, 1847–59 ; established industrial schools at Bunmahon and, later, at Bedminster, where he was perpetual curate of St. Luke's, 1859 till death ; published religious works. [Suppl. ii. 147]

DOUGALL, JOHN (1760–1822), miscellaneous writer ; studied at Edinburgh University ; private secretary to General Melville ; chief works, ' The Modern Preceptor,' 1810, and ' The Cabinet of Arts,' 1821. [xv. 257]

DOUGALL, NEIL (1776–1862), Scottish poet and musical composer ; served on board a government privateer, and was accidentally wounded by a shot during the rejoicings at Lord Howe's victory, 1794 ; composed psalm and hymn tunes ; published ' Poems and Songs,' 1854. [xv. 257]

DOUGHARTY, JOHN (1677–1755), mathematician ; of Irish extraction ; published ' Mathematical Digests ' and a ' General Gauger,' 1750. [xv. 257]

DOUGHTIE or **DOUGHTY**, JOHN (1598–1672), divine ; B.A., and fellow of Merton College, Oxford, 1619 ; M.A., 1622 ; joined the cavalier forces ; D.D., and prebendary of Westminster Abbey, 1660 ; rector of Cheam, 1662. [xv. 258]

DOUGHTY, WILLIAM (d. 1782), portrait-painter and mezzotint engraver ; pupil of Sir Joshua Reynolds ; painted a portrait of the poet Gray from description and profile outline ; excelled in mezzotint engraving ; exhibited at the Royal Academy, 1779 ; captured by a French squadron while on the way with his wife to India ; died at Lisbon. [xv. 258]

DOUGLAS, SIR ALEXANDER (1738–1812), physician ; son of Sir Robert Douglas of Glenbervie [q. v.] ; M.D. St. Andrews, 1760 ; L.R.C.P., 1796 ; physician to the king's forces in Scotland. [xv. 258]

DOUGLAS, ALEXANDER HAMILTON, tenth DUKE OF HAMILTON (1767–1852), premier peer in the peerage of Scotland ; colonel of Lanarkshire militia and lord-lieutenant of the county, 1801 ; M.P. for Lancaster, 1803 ; privy councillor and ambassador to St. Petersburg, 1806 ; succeeded as Duke of Hamilton, 1819 ; K.G., 1836 ; F.R.S. and F.S.A. ; claimed to be the true heir to the throne of Scotland. [xv. 258]

DOUGLAS, ANDREW (d. 1725), navy captain ; helped to burst the boom at the siege of Londonderry, 1689 ; commander of the Norwich, 1701 ; cashiered, on the charge of having used his commission for private ends at Port Royal, 1704 ; reinstated, 1709. [xv. 259]

DOUGLAS, ANDREW (1736–1806), physician ; educated at Edinburgh University ; surgeon in the navy, 1756–75 ; M.D. Edinburgh, 1775 ; L.R.C.P., 1776 ; published works on uterine surgery. [xv. 260]

DOUGLAS, SIR ARCHIBALD (1296 ?–1333), regent of Scotland ; youngest son of Sir William of Douglas ' the Hardy ' [q. v.] ; Scottish leader during the minority of David II ; defeated Edward de Baliol, the newly crowned king, at Annan, 1332 ; regent, 1333 ; defeated and slain at Halidon, 1333. [xv. 261]

DOUGLAS, ARCHIBALD, third EARL OF DOUGLAS, called ' THE GRIM ' (1328 ?–1400 ?), natural son of ' the Good ' Sir James Douglas (1286 ?–1330) [q. v.] ; knighted during a period of detention in England ; constable of Edinburgh, 1361 ; warden of the western marches, 1364 and 1368 ; ambassador from David II to the French court, 1369 ; renewed the French alliance by the treaty of Vincennes, 1371 ; lord of Galloway by the purchase of land, 1372 ; established and rigorously administered the feudal régime in Galloway; succeeded as Earl of Douglas, 1385; nick-named the 'Black Douglas'; invaded England, 1389; worked towards including Scotland in the peace between England and France, 1389 and 1391; codified the laws of the marches. [xv. 261]

DOUGLAS, ARCHIBALD, fourth EARL OF DOUGLAS, first DUKE OF TOURAINE (1369 ?–1424), called 'TYNEMAN,' son of Archibald 'the Grim' (1328 ?–1400 ?) [q. v.]; married Margaret, daughter of Robert III, 1390; keeper of Edinburgh Castle, 1400; warden of the marches; allied himself with the Duke of Albany, then forming designs upon the throne of Scotland, 1402; probably implicated in murder of Rothesay; defeated and taken prisoner at Mil-field, Northumberland, by the Earl of March and Hotspur, 1402; fought on the side of Hotspur at Shrewsbury, 1403, when he was again made prisoner; ransomed, 1408; con-cluded a treaty with Jean Sans Peur, duke of Burgundy, at Paris, 1412; unsuccessfully besieged Roxburgh, 1417; conciliated by Henry V in 1421; led Scottish contingent to the help of Charles VIII, regent of France, 1423; re-warded by a lieutenant-generalship and the duchy of Touraine; canon of the cathedral of Tours; defeated by the Duke of Bedford at Verneuil and slain; buried at Tours. [xv. 263]

DOUGLAS, ARCHIBALD, fifth EARL OF DOUGLAS and second DUKE OF TOURAINE (1391 ?–1439), son of Archibald, fourth earl [q. v.]; fought for Charles VI against the English at Beaugé, 1421; conducted James I home from his English captivity; arrested by James I for disaffection; released, but (1431) again kept in custody for a short time; member of the council of regency, 1437; lieutenant-general of the kingdom, 1438–9.
[xv. 266]

DOUGLAS, ARCHIBALD, fifth EARL OF ANGUS, 'THE GREAT EARL' (Bell-the-Cat) (1449 ?–1514), son of George Douglas, fourth earl [q. v.]; warden of the east marches, 1481; took part in the alliance which the Scot-tish nobles formed with Edward IV· declared to his con-federates that he would 'bell the cat,' i.e. kill Robert Cochrane, Earl of Mar [q. v.], the hated favourite of James III; followed up his words by leading an attack on Cochrane, after whose execution the king was made prisoner; shared in Albany's intrigues with Edward IV, which he renounced in 1483; intrigued with Henry VII, 1491; received into favour by James IV, 1493; chan-cellor, 1493–8; tried to dissuade James IV from fighting at a disadvantage at Flodden, 1513; died at Whithorn Priory, Wigtownshire, while engaged in his duties of justiciar. [xv. 268]

DOUGLAS, SIR ARCHIBALD (1480 ?–1540 ?), of Kilspindie; high treasurer of Scotland; son of Archibald Douglas, fifth earl of Angus [q. v.]; provost of Edin-burgh, 1519 and 1526–8; member of the privy council of Scotland; searcher-principal for preventing the export of bullion; lord high treasurer, 1526; outlawed in conse-quence of a change in the government of Scotland; fled to the court of Henry VIII; returned to Scotland, 1534, to ask forgiveness from James V, who sent him to France, where he died in exile. [xv. 270]

DOUGLAS, ARCHIBALD, sixth EARL OF ANGUS (1489 ?–1557), grandson of Archibald Douglas, fifth earl [q. v.]; privately married in 1514 to the queen-dowager, Margaret Tudor, Henry VIII's sister, whom the privy coun-cil declared to have forfeited the regency in consequence; deprived Beaton, archbishop of Glasgow, of the great seal for his influence over the privy council; joined Argyll in declaring the Duke of Albany protector, 1515; required Albany to give up the possession of the young king James V, Margaret's son, a demand which the queen resented, though her husband temporised; withdrew to Forfarshire, while Margaret was besieged in Stirling, 1515; appointed member of council of regency by Albany, then just leaving for France; contested the supreme power with the Earl of Arran, whom Margaret favoured; defeated Arran in the streets of Edinburgh, 1520; sent into exile in France on the return of the Duke of Albany, 1520; escaped to the court of Henry VIII, 1524; returned to Scotland, where Margaret had obtained the recognition of her son, a boy of twelve, as King James V, 1524; ordered by Margaret to leave Edinburgh, 1524; trusting to sup-port of Henry VIII and Scottish nobles, demanded that Margaret should give up the custody of her son; lieu-tenant of the east and middle marches, 1525; guardian of

Margaret's son, James V, in turn with the Earl of Arran and some other nobles, but refused to hand over the custody of him at the end of his allotted time; declared the king's majority, 1526; chancellor, 1526; maintained his hold over the young king against the will of the latter, who was an accomplice in most of the attempts to rescue him from Angus's custody; defeated and slew his rival, Lennox; a divorce from him obtained by Margaret, 1528; was ordered to live north of the Spey, but disobeyed, 1528; forfeited for high treason, 1528; his pardon demanded by Henry VIII, but not granted; lived in England till 1542; returned to Scotland on the death of James V, a ruthless enemy of the Douglas family; privy councillor, 1543; lieutenant-general, 1543; entered into hostilities with the regent Arran, but subsequently made compact with him to resist the English; lieutenant of Scotland south of the Forth, 1544; commanded the van at Pinkie, 1547; repelled Lord Wharton's invasion, 1548; recognised, though with some show of ill-humour, the regency of the queen-dowager, Mary of Guise, 1554. [xv. 271]

DOUGLAS, ARCHIBALD (fl. 1565–1586), parson of Glasgow; extraordinary lord of session, 1565; fled to France after murder of Rizzio, favourite of Mary Queen of Scots, in which he was implicated, 1566; lord of session, 1568; made parson of Glasgow after some objections from the kirk, 1572; imprisoned in Stirling Castle for send-ing money to the party of Mary Queen of Scots, 1572; accused before the council of being concerned in Darnley's murder, 1580; fled to England; degraded from the bench and forfeited, 1581; pardoned for all acts of treason, and acquitted of the murder of Darnley by a packed jury, 1586; ambassador to Queen Elizabeth and witness against Queen Mary. [xv. 280]

DOUGLAS, ARCHIBALD, eighth EARL OF ANGUS (1555–1588), nephew of James Douglas, fourth earl of Morton [q. v.]; supported the marriage of Mary Queen of Scots to Darnley, in return for her confirmation of the charter granted by James V to the sixth earl; studied at St. Andrews; member of the privy council, 1573; lieu-tenant-general south of the Forth, 1574; warden of west marches, 1577; adhered to the Earl of Morton, his uncle and guardian, when removed from the regency, 1578; lieutenant-general of the king. on Morton's return to power; planned an invasion of Scotland with Randolph, the English envoy, but was detected and fled to England; friend of Sir Philip Sidney; pardoned by the influence of the Earls of Mar and Gowrie, 1582; attainted for his share in his unsuccessful insurrection, 1584; his re-moval to Cambridge suggested by the Earl of Arran, with the consent of Elizabeth, 1585; took Stirling town and castle in pursuance of a plot formed in exile against Arran, 1585; lieutenant-general, 1586; his death, the result of consumption, attributed to sorcery, 1588.
[xv. 281]

DOUGLAS, ARCHIBALD, EARL OF ORMOND and LORD ANGUS (1609–1655), eldest son of William, eleventh earl of Angus [q. v.]; member of the privy council of Scotland, 1636; vacillated in his opinions on the new service-book, originally (1636) approving its use; extra-ordinary lord of session, 1631; signed the covenant, but was unwilling to take up arms in its defence; commis-sioner for the covenanters in England, 1643; colonel of Douglas regiment in France, 1646; member of committee of estates, 1650; created Earl of Ormond, 1651; fined 1,000l. by Cromwell's act of grace, 1654. [xv. 285]

DOUGLAS, ARCHIBALD (d. 1667), captain; refused to retire before De Ruyter's fleet in the Medway, and perished in the burning of his ship, the Royal Oak.
[xv. 285]

DOUGLAS, ARCHIBALD, first EARL OF FORFAR (1653–1712), son of Archibald, earl of Ormond [q. v.]; created Earl of Forfar, 1661; sat in parliament, 1670; took important part in invitation to Prince of Orange, 1688; lord of the Scots treasury; built the modern Both-well Castle. [xv. 286]

DOUGLAS, ARCHIBALD, second EARL OF FORFAR (1693–1715), son of Archibald Douglas, first earl [q. v.]; colonel of the 10th regiment of infantry, 1713; envoy extraordinary to Prussia, 1714; killed on the king's side at Sheriffmuir, 1715. [xv. 286]

DOUGLAS, ARCHIBALD, third MARQUIS and first DUKE OF DOUGLAS (1694–1761), son of James, second

N

marquis of Douglas [q. v.]; Duke of Douglas by patent, 1703; raised regiment for the king and fought at Sheriff-muir, 1715; actively resented the secret marriage of his sister, Lady Jane Douglas, but, on investigating the circumstances of the case after her death, settled his estates on her son, Archibald James Edward [q. v.]

[xv. 286]

DOUGLAS (formerly STEWART), ARCHIBALD JAMES EDWARD, first BARON DOUGLAS OF DOUGLAS (1748–1827); claimant in the great Douglas lawsuit; son of Lady Jane Douglas [q. v.]; educated at Rugby and Westminster; his right to the Douglas estates assailed by the Duke of Hamilton, heir male of the family, on the ground that he was not a real son of Colonel Stewart and Lady Jane Douglas; the estates confirmed to him by the House of Lords on appeal from the court of session, 1769; lord-lieutenant and M.P. for Forfarshire; created Baron Douglas of Douglas, 1790.

[xv. 287]

DOUGLAS, MISS ARCHIBALD RAMSAY (1807–1886), miniature-painter; daughter of William Douglas (1780–1832) [q. v.]; exhibited at the Royal Academy, 1834, 1836, and 1841.

[xv. 375]

DOUGLAS, BRICE DE (d. 1222). [See BRICIE.]

DOUGLAS, CATHERINE, DUCHESS OF QUEENS-BERRY (d. 1777), an eccentric woman of fashion; second daughter of Henry Hyde, earl of Clarendon and Rochester; wife of Charles Douglas, third duke of Queensberry [q. v.]; correspondent of Swift and friend of Congreve, Thomson, Pope, Prior, and Whitehead.

[xv. 289]

DOUGLAS, CHARLES, third DUKE OF QUEENSBERRY and second DUKE OF DOVER (1698–1778), son of James Douglas, second duke of Queensberry and first duke of Dover [q. v.]; privy councillor and vice-admiral of Scotland; took up the cause of Gay, when a license for his opera 'Polly' was refused, 1728; quarrelled with George II and resigned his appointments, 1728; keeper of the great seal of Scotland, 1760; lord justice-general, 1763–78.

[xv. 288]

DOUGLAS, SIR CHARLES, first baronet (d. 1789), rear-admiral; prevented by ice in the St. Lawrence from carrying stores and reinforcements to Quebec, 1775; relieved Quebec, 1776; created baronet, 1777; captain of the fleet at the battle of Dominica, 1782; sometimes credited wrongly with personally planning the manœuvre of breaking the French line which led to the victory; commander-in-chief on the Halifax station, 1783–6; rear-admiral, 1787; invented improvements in naval gunnery.

[xv. 289]

DOUGLAS, DAVID (1798–1834), botanist and traveller; collected in United States for Royal Horticultural Society, 1823; discovered 'Douglas's spruce,' and introduced into Europe various plants, including the common 'ribes'; fellow of the Linnean, Geological, and Zoological societies; gored to death by a wild bull in the Sandwich islands, 1834.

[xv. 291]

DOUGLAS, FRANCIS (1710?–1790?), miscellaneous writer; started the 'Aberdeen Intelligencer,' a Jacobite organ, 1750; rewarded with the life-rent of Abbots-Inch farm, near Paisley, for a pamphlet maintaining claim of Archibald Douglas (1748–1827) [q. v.] to Douglas estates. His works include 'History of the Rebellion in 1745 and 1746,' 1755, and 'Life of James Crichton of Clunie' (1760?).

[xv. 291]

DOUGLAS, FREDERICK SYLVESTER NORTH (1791–1819), author; son of Sylvester Douglas [q. v.]; educated at Westminster School and Christ Church, Oxford; M.A., 1813; M.P., Banbury, 1812 and 1818; published 'An Essay on certain Points of Resemblance between the Ancient and Modern Greeks,' 1813.

[xv. 349]

DOUGLAS, GAWIN or GAVIN (1474?–1522), Scottish poet and bishop; third son of Archibald, fifth earl of Angus [q. v.]; studied at St. Andrews, 1489–94, and perhaps at Paris; provost of St. Giles, Edinburgh, 1501; named abbot of Aberbrothock and archbishop of St. Andrews, 1514; ousted from the abbacy by James Beaton, archbishop of Glasgow [q. v.], 1514, also from the archbishopric by Hepburn, the prior, 1514; nominated bishop of Dunkeld by Queen Margaret (1515), but imprisoned by the Duke of Albany for receiving bulls from the pope; released on the remonstrance of Leo X; bishop of Dunkeld, 1516–20; accompanied Albany to France, 1517; deprived of his bishopric for going to the English court in the interest of the sixth Earl of Angus, 1520; friend of Polydore

Vergil [q. v.]; died of the plague, 1522. Douglas wrote two allegorical poems, entitled, 'The Palice of Honour' (first published, 1553?), and 'King Hart' (first printed, 1786), also a translation of the Æneid with prologues (first edition, 1553), which constitutes him the earliest classical translator in the language.

[xv. 292]

DOUGLAS, GEORGE, first EARL OF ANGUS (1380?–1403); created Earl of Angus by a charter of Robert II, 1389; fought under Archibald Douglas at Homildon, and was taken prisoner, 1402; died of the plague in England, 1403.

[xv. 295]

DOUGLAS, GEORGE, fourth EARL OF ANGUS and LORD OF DOUGLAS (1412?–1462); commanded James II's forces against the Douglases at Arkinholm, 1455; defeated Douglas and Percy, 1458; supported Henry VI against Yorkists, 1461; resisted queen-dowager's schemes for regency on death of James II; transferred power of Angus Douglases from Forfarshire to the border.

[xv. 295]

DOUGLAS, SIR GEORGE, of Pittendriech, MASTER OF ANGUS (1490?–1552), younger brother of Archibald, sixth earl of Angus [q. v.]; diplomatic leader of the English party in Scotland; master of the household, when James V was in the hands of his brother; negotiated reconciliation between his brother and Governor Arran, 1542; imprisoned in Edinburgh Castle, 1544; favoured, but would never actively support, English aggression.

[xv. 296]

DOUGLAS, LORD GEORGE, EARL OF DUMBARTON (1636?–1692), colonel of the Douglas regiment in the service of Louis XIV; created Earl of Dumbarton, 1675; suppressed Argyll's rising, 1685; accompanied James II to France; died at St. Germain-en-Laye.

[xv. 297]

DOUGLAS, GEORGE, fourth BARON MORDINGTON (d. 1741), author; defended constitutional monarchy in 'The Great Blessing of a Monarchical Government, when . . . bounded by the Laws,' 1724.

[xv. 297]

DOUGLAS, SIR HOWARD, third baronet (1776–1861); general; son of Rear-admiral Sir Charles Douglas [q. v.]; first lieutenant, royal artillery, 1794; commanded regiment at Quebec; employed on mission to the Cherokees, 1797; served with Congreve's mortar-brigade, 1803–4; captain, royal artillery, 1804; major-general and inspector-general of instructions in the Royal Military College, High Wycombe; fought as assistant quartermaster-general at Coruña, 1809; took part in the attack on Flushing, 1809; succeeded to baronetcy, 1809; patented 'Douglas's reflecting circle,' 1811; sent by Lord Liverpool to report on Spanish armies in Galicia and Asturias, 1811; F.R.S., 1812; major-general, 1821; published work on military bridges, 1816; treatise on Carnot's system of fortification 1819, and another treatise on naval gunnery, 1820; governor of New Brunswick, 1823–8, and founder of the university of Fredericton; published 'Naval Evolutions,' 1832, maintaining that his father had originated the manœuvre of breaking the line; G.C.M.G., 1835; lord high commissioner of the Ionian islands, for which he drew up the Douglas code, 1835–40; colonel, 99th foot, 1841; G.C.B. civil division, 1841; M.P., Liverpool, 1842–6; general 1851; F.R.G.S.

[xv. 298]

DOUGLAS, SIR JAMES, of Douglas, 'the Good,' LORD OF DOUGLAS (1286?–1330), son of William de Douglas, 'the Hardy' [q. v.]; deprived of his inheritance by Edward I; three times destroyed an English garrison in his castle of Douglas, which he burnt twice; joined Bruce in raiding the Lord of Lorne; frequently raided England; knighted at Bannockburn, 1314; warden of the marches; defeated the archbishop of York and the bishop of Ely at Mitton in Yorkshire, the engagement being known as the 'Chapter of Mitton,' from the large number of ecclesiastics slain, 1319; surprised troops led by Edward III, after which the English army was dismissed and peace followed; set out on a pilgrimage to the Holy Land carrying the heart of Bruce, in accordance with that king's dying wish, but was killed on the way, or some say on his return journey, while fighting against the Moors in Andalusia.

[xv. 301]

DOUGLAS, JAMES, second EARL OF DOUGLAS (1358?–1388); married by papal dispensation to Isabel, daughter of Robert II, 1373; assisted against England by Sir John de Vienne, admiral of France, 1385; acquiesced on payment of a subsidy, in the departure of his French allies, who were weary of their subordinate position, 1385;

defeated the two sons of the Earl of Northumberland at the battle of Otterburn, but was slain before the victory was assured. [xv. 304]

DOUGLAS, JAMES, seventh EARL OF DOUGLAS, 'the Gross' or 'Fat' (1371 ?-1443), son of Archibald 'the Grim,' third earl (1328 ?-1400 ?) [q. v.]; supported the regent Albany, who allowed him to make profit out of the customs; sat on the assizes which tried the Duke of Albany, 1425; granted lands and baronies at some distance from the border by James I; created Earl of Avondale, 1437; possibly connived at the murder of his grandnephew, William, whom he succeeded in the earldom. [xv. 306]

DOUGLAS, JAMES, ninth EARL OF DOUGLAS (1426-1488), second son of James 'the Gross,' seventh earl [q. v.]; made a journey to Rome, 1450; denounced James II as a traitor after the assassination of his brother William, eighth earl of Douglas [q. v.], 1452; overawed into submission after the forfeiture of his allies, Crawford and Lindsay, promising to do his duty as warden of the marches and relinquish the earldom of Wigton and lordship of Stewarton, 1452; married his brother's widow, the Maid of Galloway, 1453; commissioner for arranging a truce with England, 1453; forced to fly to England, 1455, his brothers and adherents having been routed; forfeited, 1455; knight of the Garter in return for his services to Edward IV. While raiding Scotland he gave himself up, that an old retainer might earn the promised reward for his capture, and died a monk in the abbey of Lindores. [xv. 307]

DOUGLAS, JAMES, fourth EARL OF MORTON (d. 1581), regent of Scotland; son of Sir George Douglas of Pittendriech [q. v.]; Earl of Morton in right of his wife, Elizabeth Douglas, 1553; subscribed the first bond of the Scottish reformers, 1557, but withdrew his support in 1559; privy councillor on arrival of Mary Queen of Scots in Scotland; assisted in suppressing Huntly's conspiracy, 1562; lord chancellor, 1563; supported marriage of Mary Queen of Scots and Darnley, but without much enthusiasm, 1565; procured the murder of Rizzio, Mary's favourite, and joined Ruthven and Maitland in signing a bond which promised the crown matrimonial to Darnley, 1566; fled to England, 1566, being denounced by Darnley; ordered into retirement, 1566; pardoned by the influence of Bothwell, Mary's new favourite, December 1566; disapproved of the murder (1567) of Darnley, but refused to serve as a juryman on the trial of Bothwell; signed bond for Bothwell's marriage with the queen, 1567; seized Edinburgh and called upon the citizens to join the confederacy against Bothwell, whom, however, he allowed to escape on the surrender of Mary at Carberry Hill, 1567; suggested Mary's imprisonment in the fortalice of Lochleven, 1567; lord chancellor and member of the council of regency, 1567; led the van at Langside, 1568; adviser of the regent Moray, whom he prepared to support at Maitland's trial for the murder of Darnley; induced Elizabeth to declare for the young king James VI, in anger at the assassination of Moray, 1569; practically controlled the government during the regency of Lennox, 1569; quarrelled with Lennox; lord-general of the kingdom at the commencement of the Earl of Mar's regency; approved the proposal of Queen Elizabeth that Mary should be handed over to the reformers, 1572; regent, 1572; pronounced a funeral eulogy over John Knox, 1572; obtained promises of support from Elizabeth, and induced Huntly and the Hamiltons to desert the cause of Mary, 1573; reduced Edinburgh Castle, 1573; passed an act against 'ryding and incursions in England,' 1575; established justice eyres to levy fines for criminal acts and nonconformity to protestantism; endeavoured to perpetuate the episcopal system and bring about a practical union with England; accused of avarice for taking into his own hands the management of the third part of the revenues of the benefices, which had been set apart for the support of the reformed clergy; refused to be bribed by France into recommending Mary's liberation; ousted from the regency by Argyll and Atholl, who prevailed on James VI to assume the government, 1578; re-established himself at the head of affairs by consent of a parliament held at Stirling Castle, 1578; had the Hamilton estates sequestrated in retaliation for the murder of Moray and Lennox; accused by Esme Stuart, earl of Lennox, with the connivance of James VI, of having contrived Darnley's murder; brought to trial and convicted of 'being council, concealing, and

being art and part of the king's murder'; executed, 1581. [xv. 309]

DOUGLAS, LORD JAMES or WILLIAM (1617-1645), military commander; second son of William, first marquis of Douglas [q. v.]; commanded Louis XIII's Scots regiment, 1637; killed in a skirmish near Arras. [xv. 322]

DOUGLAS, JAMES, second EARL OF QUEENSBERRY (d. 1671); taken prisoner when on his way to join Montrose after the battle of Kilsyth; fined for his allegiance to Charles I, 1645 and 1654. [xv. 322]

DOUGLAS, JAMES, second MARQUIS OF DOUGLAS (1646 ?-1700), grandson of William Douglas, first marquis of Douglas [q. v.]; became Earl of Angus by the death of his father, 1655; financially ruined by his factor, William Lawrie. [xv. 323]

DOUGLAS, JAMES, second DUKE OF QUEENSBERRY and first DUKE OF DOVER (1662-1711), eldest son of William, first duke of Queensberry [q. v.]; educated at Glasgow University; privy councillor, 1684; lieutenant-colonel of Dundee's regiment of horse; joined William III, 1688, and was appointed colonel of the 6th horse guards; privy councillor, 1689; lord high treasurer, 1693; keeper of the privy seal; king's commissioner at a meeting of the Scottish estates called to further the prosecution of the Darien enterprise, of which he procured the abandonment, 1701; K.G., 1701; one of the secretaries of state for Scotland, 1702; encouraged the Jacobites by his undecided attitude on the question of the settlement, 1703; deluded into unconsciously furthering Jacobite designs of Simon Fraser [q. v.] (1703); withdrew from the government; reinstated as lord privy seal, 1705; commissioner of the estates, 1706; procured signing of treaty of union in face of Scottish opposition, 1706; created Duke of Dover, Marquis of Beverley, and Earl of Ripon, 1708; third secretary of state, 1709. [xv. 323]

DOUGLAS, JAMES, fourth DUKE OF HAMILTON (1658-1712), eldest son of William Douglas, third duke of Hamilton [q. v.]; educated at Glasgow University; ambassador extraordinary to Louis XIV, 1683-5; commanded regiment of horse against Monmouth, 1685; knight-companion of the Thistle, 1687; accompanied James II to Salisbury as colonel of the Oxford regiment, 1688; acquitted of conspiracy on surrendering to a warrant, 1696; Duke of Hamilton by resignation of his mother, 1698; promoted the African Company in the Scottish parliament, 1700; leader of the Scottish national party, 1702; his project for a commercial treaty with England frustrated; spoke against the treaty of union in the last session of the last parliament of Scotland, but prevented armed opposition, 1707; foiled in his scheme of petitioning Anne for a new parliament; taken prisoner to London for complicity in the attempted French invasion of Scotland, 1708; chosen one of the sixteen Scottish representative peers by whig influence, 1708; rewarded for his support of Sacheverell by the lord-lieutenancy of Lancashire, 1710; privy councillor, 1710; master-general of the ordnance, 1712; K.G.; named ambassador-extraordinary to France on the eve of the conclusion of the peace of Utrecht; killed in a duel before starting by Lord Mohun, who had given the lie to, and subsequently challenged, him. The duel was alleged at the time to be a whig plot. [xv. 326]

DOUGLAS, JAMES (1675-1742), physician; M.D. Rheims; F.R.S., 1706; published 'Myographiæ Comparatæ Specimen,' 1707; compiled a general bibliography of anatomy, 1715; wrote a 'Description of the Peritoneum and of the Membrana Cellularis which is on its outside,' in connection with the question of tapping in dropsy and the high operation for stone in the bladder; nearly anticipated the discovery of auscultation; physician to Queen Caroline; referred to by Pope as a bibliophile as well as an obstetric practitioner; published 'The History of the Lateral Operation for the Stone,' 1726. [xv. 329]

DOUGLAS, JAMES, fourteenth EARL OF MORTON (1702-1768); M.A. King's College, Cambridge, 1722; helped to transform the Medical Society of Edinburgh into the Society for Improving Arts and Sciences; first president, 1739; K.T., 1738; lord of the bedchamber and a representative peer of Scotland, 1739; owner of Orkney and Shetland by act of parliament, 1742; imprisoned in the Bastile, 1746; lord clerk register of Scotland, 1760; president of the Royal Society, 1764. [xv. 331]

DOUGLAS, SIR JAMES, first baronet (1703-1787), admiral; member of the court-martial which condemned Admiral Byng, 1757; served at reduction of Quebec, 1759; commander-in-chief on Leeward islands station, 1760-2; captured Dominica, 1761; second in command at reduction of Martinique, 1762; admiral, 1778; created baronet, 1786; M.P. for Orkney. [xv. 332]

DOUGLAS, JAMES (1753-1819), divine, antiquary, and artist; entered the Austrian army as a cadet, and, being sent by Prince John of Lichtenstein to purchase horses in England, procured a lieutenancy in the Leicester militia; entered Peterhouse, Cambridge; took orders; chaplain to the Prince of Wales; F.S.A., 1780; vicar of Kenton, Suffolk, 1803; painted oil and miniature portraits of his friends. His works include 'A Sepulchral History of Great Britain,' 1793. [xv. 332]

DOUGLAS, JAMES, fourth and last BARON DOUGLAS (1787-1857), fifth son of Archibald, first baron [q. v.], rector of Marsh Gibbon, Buckinghamshire, 1819-25; rector of Broughton, Northamptonshire, 1825-57. [xv. 333]

DOUGLAS, SIR JAMES DAWES (1785-1862), general; aide-de-camp to Major-general Sir James Duff; friend of Napier, the military historian; captain, 42nd regiment, 1804; deputy-assistant quartermaster-general in South America, 1806; present at the battles of Roliça, Vimeiro (1808), and Coruña, 1809; lieutenant-colonel, 8th Portuguese regiment, and major, 1809; fought at Busaco, 1810; lieutenant-colonel, 1811; commanded the 7th Portuguese brigade at the battles of the Pyrenees, 1813, and in southern France, 1814; major-general, 1825; lieutenant-governor of Guernsey, 1830-8; G.C.B., 1846; general, 1854. [xv. 333]

DOUGLAS, LADY JANE (1698-1753), daughter of James, second marquis of Douglas [q. v.]; her engagement to Francis, earl of Dalkeith, broken off, 1720; hindered from entering a foreign convent by her mother and brother; married Colonel John Stewart, 1746, a step which she concealed for fear that her brother, Archibald, first duke of Douglas [q. v.], might withdraw her allowance; became the mother (1748) at Paris of twin sons, Archibald and Sholto; deprived of her allowance on informing her brother of their birth; disowned by her brother. Her only surviving son, Archibald James Edward Douglas [q. v.], claimed successfully the Douglas estates in great Douglas lawsuit. [xv. 334]

DOUGLAS, JANET, LADY GLAMIS (d. 1537), granddaughter of Archibald, fifth earl of Angus [q. v.]; married John, sixth lord Glamis, c. 1520; forfeited (1531) for disloyalty; indicted on a charge of poisoning her husband, which was abandoned; charged with conspiring the death of James V, and burnt at the stake in Edinburgh, 'without any substanciall ground,' according to Henry VIII's representative in Scotland. [xv. 335]

DOUGLAS, JOHN (d. 1743), surgeon; brother of James Douglas (1675-1742) [q. v.]; F.R.S.; surgeon-lithotomist to the Westminster Hospital; lectured on anatomy and surgery; keen controversialist in medicine; published 'An Account of Mortifications, 1729, and advocated the high operation for stone, which he claimed as essentially his own discovery, in 'Lithotomia Douglasiana,' 1720. [xv. 336]

DOUGLAS, JOHN (1721-1807), bishop of Salisbury; M.A. Balliol College, Oxford, 1743; present, as chaplain to the 3rd regiment of foot guards, at the battle of Fontenoy, 1745; Snell exhibitioner at Balliol, 1745; vicar of High Ercall, Shropshire, 1750-61; exposed forgeries of William Lauder [q. v.], 1750; attacked Hume's argument against miracles, publishing the 'Criterion,' 1752; attacked the Hutchinsonians in an 'Apology for the Clergy,' 1755; D.D., 1758; canon of Windsor, 1762; F.R.S. and F.S.A., 1778; bishop of Carlisle, 1787-91; dean of Windsor, 1788; bishop of Salisbury, 1791-1807; edited Clarendon's 'Diary and Letters,' 1763. [xv. 337]

DOUGLAS, SIR JOHN SHOLTO, eighth MARQUIS OF QUEENSBERRY (1844-1900); succeeded his father, seventh marquis, 1858; sat as representative peer for Scotland, 1872-80. He is chiefly known as a patron of boxing, the 'Queensberry rules' being drawn up under his supervision, 1867. [Suppl. ii. 148]

DOUGLAS, formerly MACKENZIE, SIR KENNETH, first baronet (1754-1833), lieutenant-general; lieutenant, 33rd regiment, 1775; served in West Indies and throughout Netherlands campaign of 1793 under paternal name of Mackenzie; captain and major in the newly raised Perthshire Light Infantry, 1794; lieutenant-colonel for services at capture of Minorca, 1798; appointed lieutenant-colonel of the 44th before Alexandria, 1801; governor of Antwerp, 1814 and 1815; lieutenant-general, 1821; made baronet 'of Glenbervie' (a second creation), 1831; took the name of Douglas by royal licence, 1831. [xv. 338]

DOUGLAS, LADY MARGARET, COUNTESS OF LENNOX (1515-1578), mother of Lord Darnley; daughter of Archibald Douglas, sixth earl of Angus [q. v.], by Margaret Tudor; placed by Henry VIII in the Princess Mary's establishment at Beaulieu, 1531; friend of Princess Mary; displeased the king by her private betrothal to Lord Thomas Howard, Anne Boleyn's uncle, and was imprisoned in Syon Abbey; married Matthew Stewart, earl of Lennox [q. v.], 1544; excluded from the English succession for her Roman catholic leanings, 1546; planned marriage between her son, Lord Darnley, and Mary Queen of Scots; arrested before its accomplishment for her treasonable intentions towards Elizabeth, 1562; released, but on successfully carrying out her scheme was sent to the Tower; denounced Mary Queen of Scots at the court of Elizabeth for Darnley's murder; reconciled to Mary, c. 1572. Her aspirations were substantially fulfilled by the accession of her grandson, James VI, to the throne of England. [xv. 339]

DOUGLAS, NEIL (1750-1823), poet and preacher; educated at Glasgow University; appeared as a social reformer in 'A Monitory Address to Great Britain,' 1792; minister of Relief Charge at Dundee, 1793-8; published 'The Lady's Scull,' a poem, 1794; wrote (1799) his 'Journal of a Mission to part of the Highlands of Scotland'; 'universalist preacher,' 1809; a vigorous abolitionist; arraigned before the high court of justiciary at Edinburgh for comparing George III to Nebuchadnezzar, 1817; acquitted. [xv. 343]

DOUGLAS, SIR NEIL (1779-1853), lieutenant-general; captain, Cameron Highlanders, 1804; fought at Coruña, 1809, and at the siege of Copenhagen, 1807, and Flushing, 1809; wounded at Busaco, 1810; major, 1811; lieutenant-colonel, 1812; commanded battalion in south of France, 1814, and at Waterloo, 1815; knighted, 1831; major-general and K.C.B., 1837; lieutenant-general, 1846. [xv. 344]

DOUGLAS, PHILIP (1758-1822), master of Corpus Christi College, Cambridge; educated at Harrow and Corpus Christi, Cambridge; M.A., 1784; tutor, 1787; D.D. and master of Corpus Christi, 1795-1822; vicar of Gedney, Lincolnshire, 1796; vice-chancellor, 1795-6 and 1810-11. [xv. 345]

DOUGLAS, ROBERT, VISCOUNT BELHAVEN (1574?-1639); knighted, 1609; master of the household and privy councillor under Charles I; created Viscount Belhaven, 1633; blind. [xv. 345]

DOUGLAS, ROBERT (1594-1674), presbyterian divine; reputed grandson of Mary Queen of Scots; M.A. St. Andrews, 1614; chaplain to a Scots brigade sent to the assistance of Gustavus Adolphus, c. 1630; minister of the Tolbooth Church, Edinburgh, 1641-2; presented the solemn league and covenant to the parliament, 1649; officiated at the coronation of Charles II at Scone, 1651; largely helped to bring about the Restoration; declined bishopric of Edinburgh, refusing to recognise episcopacy. [xv. 346]

DOUGLAS, SIR ROBERT (1694-1770), baronet of Glenbervie, genealogist; compiler of 'The Peerage of Scotland,' 1764, and of a 'Baronage of Scotland,' vol. i. 1798. [xv. 347]

DOUGLAS, SYLVESTER, BARON GLENBERVIE (1743-1823), educated at Aberdeen University; graduated at Leyden, 1766; barrister of Lincoln's Inn, 1776; king's counsel, 1793; member of the Irish parliament for Irishtown, Kilkenny; privy councillor of Ireland and, in 1794, of England; M.P. for Fowey, Cornwall, 1795; lord of the treasury, 1797-1800; nominated governor of the Cape of Good Hope, 1800, but did not take the office; created Baron Glenbervie of Kincardine (in Irish peerage), 1800; M.P., Plympton

Earls, 1801, Hastings, 1802–6; first chief commissioner of the united land and forest department, 1810–14; chairman of the secret committee appointed to inquire into the advance of 100,000*l.* for secret naval services, 1805; published histories of controverted elections, 15 and 16 George III, 1775 and 1777. [xv. 348]

DOUGLAS, THOMAS (*fl.* 1661), divine; ejected from the living of St. Olave's, Silver Street, London, at the Restoration; M.D. Padua; published 'Θεάνθρωπος, or the Great Mysterie of Godlinesse,' 1661. [xv. 350]

DOUGLAS, THOMAS, fifth EARL OF SELKIRK, BARON DAER and SHORTCLEUCH (1771–1820); educated at Edinburgh University; settled emigrants from the highlands of Scotland in Prince Edward's island, 1803, intending to direct towards British colonies the unavoidable emigration of the highlanders; Scottish representative peer, 1806 and 1807; F.R.S., 1808; sent out pioneers to colonise the Red River valley; his colonists twice driven from their settlements, Forts Douglas and Daer, by soldiers of the North-west Company, 1815 and 1816; personally led an attack on Fort William, the chief post of the North-west Company, and re-established his colony under the name Kildonan, 1817; fined 2,000*l.* by Canadian courts on the charge of having plotted the ruin of the North-west Company, 1818; died at Pau; published 'Observations on the Present State of the Highlands of Scotland,' 1805, in defence of his colonisation scheme. [xv. 350]

DOUGLAS, SIR THOMAS MONTEATH (1787–1868), general; lieutenant, 35th regiment of Bengal infantry, 1808; fought in the Bundelkhand campaigns, 1809 and 1810, against the Pindaris, 1818, and against the Mers, 1820; lieutenant-colonel, 1834; took part in capture of Cabul, 1838; second in command at defence of Jellalabad, 1841–2; colonel of his old regiment, 1845; took additional surname of Douglas, 1851; K.C.B., 1865; general, 1865. [xv. 353]

DOUGLAS, WILLIAM DE, 'the Hardy' (*d.* 1298); a crusader and knighted; lord of Douglas, 1288; recognised Baliol as king, after some hesitation; captured at the taking of Berwick, after Baliol's abdication, and imprisoned; released; again took up arms, and, his confederates submitting to Edward I at Irvine water (1297), was imprisoned in the Tower till his death. [xv. 354]

DOUGLAS, SIR WILLIAM, KNIGHT OF LIDDESDALE (1300?–1353), keeper of Lochmaben Castle and warden of the west marches, 1332; slew the Earl of Atholl, Edward Baliol's lieutenant, 1337; given the lordship of Liddesdale by David II, 1342; ambassador to the French court; treacherously wounded and starved in prison Sir Alexander Ramsay, to whom David II had given Roxburgh Castle, not knowing that it was in the possession of Douglas; pardoned, and appointed constable of Roxburgh Castle; taken prisoner by the English at Durham, 1346; released on condition of becoming Edward III's liegeman; murdered by his kinsman, the Lord of Douglas. [xv. 355]

DOUGLAS, WILLIAM, first EARL OF DOUGLAS (1327?–1384), younger son of Sir Archibald Douglas (*d.* 1333) [q. v.]; trained in arms in France; returned to Scotland, *c.* 1348, and restored Ettrick Forest to the Scottish allegiance; took part in treaty of Newcastle, by which David II's ransom from captivity in England was arranged, 1354; slew his kinsman, the Knight of Liddesdale, 1353; present at the battle of Poitiers, 1356; warden of the east marches, and, in 1358, created Earl of Douglas; took up arms against David II, who was supposed to have appropriated the money raised for his ransom and to be intriguing with England; submitted, 1363; swore homage to Robert II, 1371; justiciary south of the Forth from 1371; Earl of Mar, probably by marriage, 1374; defeated Sir Thomas Musgrave at Melrose in border raid, 1378; negotiated truce with John of Gaunt at Berwick, 1380. [xv. 357]

DOUGLAS, SIR WILLIAM, LORD OF NITHSDALE (*d.* 1392?), illegitimate son of Archibald, third earl of Douglas [q. v.]; married Egidia, daughter of Robert II, at the same time receiving the lordship of Nithsdale, 1387; made retaliatory raid on Ireland, burning Carlingford and plundering the Isle of Man, 1388; commanded maritime expedition sent from Danzig against the Lithuanians, 1391. [xv. 360]

DOUGLAS, WILLIAM, second EARL OF ANGUS (1398?–1437), elder son of George, first earl [q. v.]; knighted by James I; sat on the assize at Albany's trial, 1425; warden of the middle marches, 1433; defeated English force at Piperden, 1435. [xv. 361]

DOUGLAS, WILLIAM, sixth EARL OF DOUGLAS and third DUKE OF TOURAINE (1423?–1440), eldest son of Archibald Douglas, fifth earl [q. v.]; said to have behaved as a claimant to the Scottish crown; treacherously seized and beheaded after a banquet at Edinburgh, to which he and his brother David had been invited by James II, 1440. [xv. 361]

DOUGLAS, WILLIAM, eighth EARL OF DOUGLAS (1425?–1452), son of James Douglas, 'the Gross,' seventh earl [q. v.]; used his influence with James II to dispossess the chancellor, Sir William Crichton, of office, 1443; burnt Alnwick, 1448; negotiated the marriage of James II to Mary of Gueldres, 1449; assisted the king and Sir William Crichton to overthrow the Livingstones, 1449; made journey to Rome, 1450; warden of the marches; murdered McLellan, a partisan of the king; inveigled into Stirling Castle, and attacked and killed by James II and his followers. [xv. 362]

DOUGLAS, WILLIAM, ninth EARL OF ANGUS in right of entails (1533–1591); sided with Mary Queen of Scots against the Earl of Huntly at Corrichie, 1562; chancellor of the assize which convicted Francis, earl of Bothwell; privy councillor of Scotland. [xv. 364]

DOUGLAS, SIR WILLIAM, of Lochleven, sixth or seventh EARL OF MORTON (*d.* 1606); denounced as one of the murderers of Rizzio, favourite of Mary Queen of Scots, 1566; joined confederacy for avenging murder of Darnley, husband of Mary Queen of Scots; entrusted with the custody of Mary Queen of Scots after her surrender at Carberry Hill, 1567; commanded in the rear guard at Langside, 1568; surrendered to Queen Elizabeth, for 2,000*l.*, the Earl of Northumberland, who had been delivered into his charge by the regent Moray, 1572; friend of the regent Morton; signed bond of confederate nobles to stand by James VI, 1582; banished by the counter-revolution at St. Andrews, 1583; organised a plot, while in France, which led to the overthrow of Arran in 1585; succeeded as Earl of Morton, 1588, the same title being held by Lord Maxwell in 1592. [xv. 365]

DOUGLAS, WILLIAM, tenth EARL OF ANGUS (1554–1611), son of William, ninth earl [q. v.]; studied at St. Andrews; converted to catholicism at the French court; reconciled the Earls of Atholl and Huntly, 1592; imprisoned for his share in the 'Spanish Blanks' conspiracy; escaped, 1593; forfeited along with the Earls of Huntly and Atholl; made a successful descent on Aberdeen, 1594; returned with his two confederates to presbyterianism, 1597; released from his forfeiture, 1597; royal lieutenant of the borders, 1597; excommunicated by the Scottish church, 1608; died near the abbey of St. Germain-des-Prés, Paris. [xv. 366]

DOUGLAS, SIR WILLIAM, first EARL OF QUEENSBERRY (*d.* 1640); created Viscount of Drumlanrig, 1617; created Earl of Queensberry (1633), on the occasion of Charles I's visit to Scotland. [xv. 367]

DOUGLAS, LORD WILLIAM (1617–1645). [See DOUGLAS, LORD JAMES.]

DOUGLAS, WILLIAM, seventh or eighth EARL OF MORTON (1582–1650), lord high treasurer of Scotland; grandson of Sir William Douglas of Lochleven (*d.* 1606) [q. v.]; privy councillor and gentleman of the chamber to James VI; commanded Scots regiment in Rochelle expedition, 1627; lord high treasurer of Scotland, 1630–5; K.G. and privy councillor of England, 1635; sat in the Scottish parliament, 1641; nominated by Charles I for the chancellorship, but prevented from obtaining it by the rancour of the Earl of Argyll, 1641; rewarded for advances of money to Charles I by a charter of the Orkney and Shetland islands, 1643. [xv. 367]

DOUGLAS, WILLIAM, eleventh EARL OF ANGUS and first MARQUIS OF DOUGLAS (1589–1660), son of William, tenth earl [q. v.]; brought up in the reformed religion; created Marquis of Douglas, 1633; went to England to assist Charles I, 1639; signed the covenant, 1644, but fought at Philiphaugh on the side of Montrose, 1645; imprisoned, 1646; member of committee of estates, 1651; fined by Cromwell, 1654. [xv. 368]

DOUGLAS, WILLIAM, third DUKE OF HAMILTON (1635–1694), eldest son of William, first marquis of Douglas [q. v.] ; fined 1,000*l.* by Cromwell, 1654 ; created Duke of Hamilton on the petition of his wife, Anne, duchess of Hamilton ; privy councillor in Scotland, 1660–1676 ; at first opposed, and then ignored, in the interests of the Scottish nobility, the governor Lauderdale's land tax of a year's assessment, 1672 ; opposed Lauderdale's demand for supplies to carry on the Dutch war, 1673 ; ejected from the council, 1676 ; went to London to lodge complaints against Lauderdale, who intended to have a writ of law-burrows issued against him ; refused to commit himself by detailing his grievances in writing, 1678 and 1679 ; K.G. ; commissioner of the treasury, and, in 1687, privy councillor of England ; royal commissioner under William III, 1689 and 1693. [xv. 370]

DOUGLAS, WILLIAM, third EARL and first DUKE OF QUEENSBERRY (1637–1695), son of James, second earl of Queensberry [q. v.] ; privy councillor, 1667 ; lord justice-general of Scotland, 1680–6 ; lord high treasurer of Scotland, 1682–6 ; created Duke of Queensberry, 1684 ; refused to support James II's measures against the established church, 1685 ; president of the council, 1686 ; accused of maladministration by the Earl of Perth, and stripped of his appointments, 1686 ; one of the lords of privy council of both kingdoms, 1687. [xv. 372]

DOUGLAS, WILLIAM, third EARL OF MARCH and fourth DUKE OF QUEENSBERRY (1724–1810), latterly known as 'Old Q.' ; notorious for his escapades and dissolute life ; endeavoured to develop horse-racing into a science ; K.T., 1761 ; representative peer for Scotland, 1761 ; vice-admiral of Scotland, 1767–76 ; succeeded his cousin Charles [q. v.] in dukedom of Queensberry, 1778 ; created Baron Douglas of Amesbury in British peerage, 1786 ; friend of Prince of Wales ; removed from the office of lord of the bedchamber (1789) for having recommended a regency in 1788 ; satirised by Burns. [xv. 373]

DOUGLAS, WILLIAM (1780–1832), miniature-painter to Princess Charlotte and Prince Leopold of Saxe-Coburg, 1817 ; exhibited at the Royal Academy, 1818, 1819, and 1826. [xv. 374]

DOUGLAS, WILLIAM ALEXANDER ANTHONY ARCHIBALD, eleventh DUKE OF HAMILTON (1811–1863), son of Alexander Hamilton Douglas, tenth duke [q. v.] ; educated at Eton and Christ Church, Oxford ; B.A., 1832 ; knight-marischal of Scotland and lord-lieutenant of Lanarkshire ; married the Princess Marie Amélie, Napoleon III's cousin, 1843 ; died in Paris. [xv. 375]

DOUGLAS, SIR WILLIAM FETTES (1822–1891), artist and connoisseur ; assistant in Commercial Bank, Edinburgh ; studied drawing and adopted profession of artist, 1847 ; exhibited in Royal Scottish Academy from 1845 ; associate, 1851, full member, 1854, and president, 1882 ; curator of National Gallery of Scotland, 1877–82 ; knighted, 1882 ; LL.D. Edinburgh, 1884 ; collector of objects of art. Among his best pictures are 'The Alchemist,' 1855, and 'The Rosicrucians,' 1856. [Suppl. ii. 149]

DOUGLAS, WILLIAM SCOTT (1815–1883), editor of a library edition of Burns, 1877–9 ; wrote 'Picture of the County of Ayr,' 1874. [xv. 375]

DOUGLASS, SIR JAMES NICHOLAS (1826–1898), engineer ; apprenticed to Messrs. Hunter & English at Bow ; manager to Messrs. Laycock on the Tyne ; engineer successively on Gun Fleet Pile, Smalls Rock, and Wolf Rock lighthouses, 1854–70 ; chief engineer to corporation of Trinity House, 1862 ; designed and executed new Eddystone lighthouse, 1878–82 ; knighted, 1882 ; M.I.C.E., 1861 ; F.R.S., 1887 ; published pamphlets relating to lighthouses. [Suppl. ii. 150]

DOUGLASS, JOHN (1743–1812), Roman catholic prelate ; professor of humanities, 1768, and subsequently of philosophy at the English college, Valladolid ; D.D. ; vicar-apostolic of the London district, 1790 ; bishop of Centuria *in partibus*, 1790 ; suggested the employment of the Irish oath of allegiance of 1778 to meet the requirements of the Catholic Relief Act, 1791. [xv. 375]

DOULTON, SIR HENRY (1820–1897), potter ; educated at University College School, London ; entered his father's pottery at Lambeth, 1835, and greatly extended it ; began, *c.* 1870, to develop 'sgraffito' ware, which rapidly gained wide reputation ; received, 1885, gold

Albert medal of Society of Arts, of which he was vice-president, 1890-4 ; knighted, 1887. [Suppl. ii. 150]

D'OUVILLY, GEORGE GERBIER (*fl.* 1661), dramatist and translator ; of Dutch origin ; captain in Lord Craven's regiment in the Netherlands ; published 'The False Favourite Disgrac'd,' a tragi-comedy, 1657 ; translated biographies by André Thevet. [xv. 376]

DOVASTON, JOHN FREEMAN MILWARD (1782–1854), miscellaneous writer ; M.A. Christ Church, Oxford, 1807 ; barrister of the Middle Temple, 1807 ; published 'Lectures on Natural History and National Melody,' 1839, and poetical works. [xv. 376]

DOVE, HENRY (1640–1695), archdeacon of Richmond ; educated at Westminster and Trinity College, Cambridge ; M.A., 1665 ; vicar of St. Bride's, Fleet Street, 1673 ; D.D., 1677 ; archdeacon of Richmond, 1678 ; chaplain to Charles II, James II, and William III ; recommended by Pearson for the mastership of Trinity College, Cambridge, 1683 ; published sermons. [xv. 377]

DOVE, JOHN (1561–1618), divine ; scholar of Westminster ; M.A. Christ Church, Oxford, 1586 ; D.D., 1596 ; rector of St. Mary Aldermary, London, 1596–1618 ; author of 'A Confutation of Atheism,' 1605, and other works. [xv. 377]

DOVE, JOHN (*d.* 1665 ?), regicide ; M.P. for Salisbury, 1645 ; commissioner for Charles I's trial, 1649 ; high sheriff of Wiltshire, 1655 ; taken prisoner by royalist conspirators at Salisbury, 1655 ; submitted at the Restoration. [xv. 378]

DOVE, NATHANIEL (1710–1754), calligrapher ; master of an academy at Hoxton ; contributed to the 'Universal Penman,' published, 1743 ; clerk in the victualling office, Tower Hill. [xv. 378]

DOVE, PATRICK EDWARD (1815–1873), philosophic writer ; farmer near Ballantrae, Aryshire, from 1841 ; published 'The Theory of Human Progression, and Natural Probability of a Reign of Justice,' 1850, a book which earned the praise of Carlyle ; author of 'Elements of Political Science,' 1854 ; inventor of rifled cannon. Though a strong individualist, his attitude on the question of rent anticipated that of Henry George. [xv. 379]

DOVE, THOMAS (1555–1630), bishop of Peterborough ; educated at Merchant Taylors' School ; Wattes' scholar, Pembroke Hall, Cambridge, 1571 ; original scholar of Jesus College, Oxford ; chaplain to Queen Elizabeth, who admired his eloquence ; dean of Norwich, 1589 ; bishop of Peterborough, 1601 ; charged with remissness for allowing silenced ministers to preach, 1611 and 1614. [xv. 380]

DOVER, DUKES OF. [See DOUGLAS, JAMES, first DUKE, 1662–1711 ; DOUGLAS, CHARLES, second DUKE, 1698–1778.]

DOVER, BARONS. [See JERMYN, HENRY, 1636–1708 ; YORKE, JOSEPH, first baron of the second creation, 1724–1792 ; ELLIS, GEORGE JAMES WELBORE AGAR-, first BARON of the third creation, 1797–1833.]

DOVER, JOHN (*d.* 1725), dramatist ; demy of Magdalen College, Oxford, 1661 ; barrister, Gray's Inn, 1672 ; rector of Drayton, Oxfordshire, 1688 ; author of 'The Roman Generalls,' 1667, a rhyming tragedy. [xv. 380]

DOVER, CAPTAIN ROBERT (1575 ?–1641), founder of the Cotswold games on Cotswold Hills, near Evesham c. 1604, which were celebrated by the poets in 'Annalia Dubrensia,' 1636 ; attorney at Barton-on-the-Heath, Warwickshire. [xv. 381]

DOVER, THOMAS (1660–1742), physician ; sailed with the ships Duke and Duchess on a privateering voyage, as captain of the Duke, 1708 ; sacked Guayaquil in Peru, and cured a hundred and seventy-two of his sailors of the plague, 1709 ; rescued Alexander Selkirk from the island of Juan Fernandez, 1709 ; M.D. ; L.C.P. 1721 ; called the 'quicksilver doctor' from his exaggerated encomiums of metallic mercury ; inventor of 'Dover' powder. [xv. 382]

DOVETON, SIR JOHN (1768–1847), general ; captain 1st Madras light cavalry, 1800 ; colonel, 1813 ; brigadier general of the Hyderabad contingent, 1814 ; defeated Apa Sahib, raja of Nagpur, who was in league with the Pindaris, and brought about the evacuation of Nagpur, 1817 ; lieutenant-general and G.C.B., 1837 ; died at Madras. [xv. 382]

DOW, ALEXANDER (*d.* 1779), historian and dramatist; worked his way to Bencoolen, and became secretary to the governor; captain in the East India Company's Bengal infantry, 1764; lieutenant-colonel, 1769; died at Bhágalpur; his tragedies, 'Zingis,' 1769, and 'Sethona,' 1774, acted at Drury Lane; translated Ferishta's history of Hindostan, 1768. [xv. 383]

DOWDALL, GEORGE (1487–1558), archbishop of Armagh; prior of the hospital of St. John of Ardee, Armagh; archbishop of Armagh, 1543; reluctantly submitted to Edward VI's order for the public use of the English liturgy in Ireland, 1550; deprived of the primacy of all Ireland, 1550; reinstated, 1553; member of the Irish privy council, 1556. [xv. 384]

DOWDESWELL, WILLIAM (1721–1775), politician; educated at Westminster and Christ Church, Oxford; studied at Leyden, 1745; M.P., Tewkesbury, 1747–54, Worcester, 1761–75; chancellor of the exchequer, 1765–6; received thanks of the mercantile interest, 1766; privy councillor, 1765; refused to be president of the board of trade or joint-paymaster in Lord Chatham's government, 1766; carried a motion for the reduction of the land tax, 1767; died at Nice. [xv. 385]

DOWDESWELL, WILLIAM (1761–1828), general and print-collector; third son of William Dowdeswell [q. v.]; lieutenant and captain, grenadier guards, 1785; M.P., Tewkesbury, 1792; fought at Valenciennes and in the battles before Dunkirk, 1793; governor of the Bahamas, 1797–1802; colonel, 1797; commanded under Lake at Bhurtpore, 1805; commander-in-chief in India, 1807; lieutenant-general, 1810; collected prints by old English engravers, and made a specialty of 'grangerising.' [xv. 386]

DOWELL, STEPHEN (1833–1898), legal and historical writer; B.A. Corpus Christi College, Oxford, 1855; M.A., 1872; assistant solicitor to board of inland revenue, 1863–96. [Suppl. ii. 151]

DOWLAND, JOHN (1563?–1626?), lutenist and composer; made several journeys to Italy and Germany, becoming acquainted with Gregory Howet of Antwerp, Luca Marenzio, and other famous musicians; Mus. Bac. Oxford, 1588; published three books of 'Songes or Ayres of Foure Partes with Tableture for the Lute,' 1597, 1600, and 1603; dedicated his 'Lachrymæ' to Anne of Denmark, apparently his 'court lutenist, 1605; lutenist to Charles I, 1625. [xv. 387]

DOWLAND, ROBERT (17th cent.), musician; son of John Dowland [q. v.]; published a 'Varietie of Lute-Lessons' and a collection of English and continental airs, entitled 'A Mvsicall Banqvet,' 1610; 'musician in ordinary for the consort,' 1626. [xv. 388]

DOWLEY, RICHARD (1622–1702), nonconformist divine; matriculated at All Souls' College, Oxford, 1639; demy of Magdalen, 1640; B.A., 1643; minister of Stoke Prior, Worcestershire, 1656; ejected at the Restoration; licensed to hold meetings in his own house by the Declaration of Indulgence, 1672; preached at Godalming after the Toleration Act of 1689. [xv. 389]

DOWLING, ALFRED SEPTIMUS (1805–1868), law reporter; brother of Sir James Dowling [q. v.]; barrister of Gray's Inn, 1828; judge of county courts, circuit No. 15, Yorkshire, 1849; commissioner on the management of the county courts, 1853; published collections of statutes passed 11 George IV–3 William IV; compiled case reports. [xv. 389]

DOWLING, FRANK LEWIS (1823–1867), journalist; son of Vincent George Dowling [q. v.]; barrister, Middle Temple, 1848; editor of 'Bell's Life,' 1851, and 'Fistiana,' 1852–64. [xv. 389]

DOWLING, SIR JAMES (1787–1844), colonial judge; admitted to St. Paul's School, London, 1802; barrister, Middle Temple, 1815; author of 'The Practice of the Superior Courts of Common Law,' 1834; puisne judge of the court of New South Wales, 1827; chief-justice, 1837; knighted, 1838; died at Darlinghurst, Sydney. [xv. 390]

DOWLING, JOHN GOULTER (1805–1841), divine; B.A. Wadham College, Oxford; head-master of the Crypt Grammar School, Gloucester, 1827–41; rector of St. Mary-de-Crypt with St. Owen, Gloucester, 1834–41; student of patristics; wrote 'An Introduction to the Critical Study of Ecclesiastical History.' [xv. 390]

DOWLING, THADY (1544–1628), author of 'Annales Hiberniæ'; ecclesiastical treasurer (*c.* 1590) and chancellor (1591) of the see of Leighlin, co. Carlow. [xv. 391]

DOWLING, VINCENT GEORGE (1785–1852), journalist; elder brother of Sir James Dowling [q. v.]; engaged with the 'Star' newspaper and, in 1809, with the 'Day'; crossed the Channel in an open boat to give the 'Observer' the first news of Queen Caroline's return, 1820; editor of 'Bell's Life,' 1824–52; issued annually, from 1840, 'Fistiana'; claimed to have originated scheme of new police system. [xv. 391]

DOWNE, JOHN (1570?–1631), divine; B.D. and fellow, Emmanuel College, Cambridge; vicar of Winsford, Somerset; Latin poet; his 'Treatise of the True Nature and Definition of Justifying Faith' published, 1635. [xv. 391]

DOWNES, BARONS. [See DOWNES, WILLIAM, first BARON, 1752–1826; BURGH, SIR ULYSSES BAGENAL, second BARON, 1788–1863.]

DOWNES, ANDREW (1549?–1628), Greek professor at Cambridge; Lady Margaret scholar, St. John's College, Cambridge, 1567; M.A., 1574; senior fellow, 1581; B.D., 1582; regius professor of Greek, the study of which he had helped to revive, 1585–1624; one of the translators of the Apocrypha for the 'authorised version'; edited the 'Eratosthenes' of Lysias, 1593; published 'Prælectiones in Philippicam de Pace Demosthenis,' 1621. [xv. 392]

DOWNES, JOHN (*fl.* 1666), regicide; sat for Arundel in the Long parliament, 1642; prevailed upon, partly against his will, to sign Charles I's death-warrant; member of the council of state, 1651 and 1659; commissioner for the revenue, 1659; arrested (1660) for his share in the execution of Charles I, and kept a close prisoner in Newgate. [xv. 393]

DOWNES, JOHN (*fl.* 1662–1710), writer on the stage; prompter to Sir William D'Avenant's company at the theatre in Lincoln's Inn Fields, 1662; published 'Roscius Anglicanus, or an Historical Review of the Stage,' 1708. [xv. 394]

DOWNES, THEOPHILUS (*d.* 1726), nonjuror; M.A. Balliol College, Oxford, 1679; fellow; ejected for refusing oath of allegiance, 1690; published anonymously 'A Discourse concerning the Signification of Allegiance' (1689?). [xv. 394]

DOWNES, WILLIAM, first BARON DOWNES (1752–1826), chief-justice of the king's bench in Ireland; B.A. Trinity College, Dublin, 1773; called to the Irish bar, 1776; M.P. for Donegal; lord chief-justice of the king's bench, 1803–22; vice-chancellor of Dublin University, 1806–16; created Baron Downes of Aghanville, 1822. [xv. 395]

DOWNAM or **DOWNAME**, GEORGE (*d.* 1634), bishop of Derry; elder son of William Downham, bishop of Chester [q. v.]; fellow of Christ's College, Cambridge, 1585; university professor of logic; chaplain to James I; bishop of Derry, 1616; published a sermon against Arminianism, 1631, for the suppression of which Laud procured royal letters; treated the presbyterians with moderation; published 'A Treatise concerning Antichrist . . . against . . . Bellarmine,' 1603, and a 'Commentarius in Rami Dialecticam,' 1610. [xv. 395]

DOWNHAM or **DOWNAME**, JOHN (*d.* 1652), puritan divine; son of William Downham, bishop of Chester [q. v.]; B.D. Christ's College, Cambridge; rector of All-hallows the Great, 1630–52; signed petition against Laud's book of canons, 1640; licenser of the press, 1643; wrote largely on religious subjects. [xv. 396]

DOWNHAM, WILLIAM, whose name is sometimes spelt DOWNAME and DOWNMAN (1505–1577), bishop of Chester; M.A. and fellow of Magdalen College, Oxford, 1543; canon of Westminster, 1560; bishop of Chester, 1561–77; reported to the council for remissness in enforcing the Act of Uniformity, 1561 and 1570; D.D. Oxford, 1566. [xv. 397]

DOWNING, CALYBUTE (1606–1644), divine; B.A. Oriel College, Oxford, 1626; M.A. Peterhouse, Cambridge; LL.D. Peterhouse, Cambridge, 1637; vicar of Hackney, London, 1637–43; chaplain to Lord Robartes's regiment in the Earl of Essex's army; licenser of books of divinity, 1643; probably became an independent. [xv. 398]

DOWNING, SIR GEORGE, first baronet (1623 ?–1684), soldier and politician; second graduate of Harvard College; scout-master-general of Cromwell's army in Scotland, 1650; M.P. for Edinburgh, 1654, for Carlisle and Haddington boroughs, 1656; headed movement for offering crown to Cromwell; sent to remonstrate with Louis XIV on Vaudois massacre, 1655; resident at the Hague, 1657, 1659, and 1660; teller of the exchequer, 1660; procured the arrest of three regicides, Barkstead, Okey, and Corbet, at Delft, 1662; created baronet, 1663; began the custom of the appropriation of supplies during the Dutch war, which he promoted, 1665; M.P., Morpeth, 1669–70; resident at the Hague, 1671; compelled by his unpopularity to leave the Hague, 1672. Colbert called him 'le plus grand querelleur des diplomates de son temps.' [xv. 399]

DOWNING, SIR GEORGE, third baronet (1684?–1749), founder of Downing College; grandson of Sir George Downing (1623 ?–1684) [q. v.]; M.P., Dunwich, Suffolk, 1710, 1713, and 1722–49; K.B., 1732; left estates in Cambridgeshire, Bedfordshire, and Suffolk, with which, in default of heirs, to buy land for building a college at Cambridge. After much litigation, Downing College was founded by charter in 1800. [xv. 401]

DOWNMAN, HUGH (1740–1809), physician and poet; B.A. Balliol College, Oxford, 1763; M.A. Jesus College, Cambridge; medical practitioner at Exeter, 1770; author of three tragedies and of a poem, 'Infancy, or the Management of Children,' 3 parts, 1774, 1775, and 1776. [xv. 402]

DOWNMAN, JOHN (1750–1824), portrait and subject painter; A.R.A., 1795; exhibited at the Royal Academy, 1769–1819. [xv. 403]

DOWNMAN, SIR THOMAS (1776–1852), lieutenant-general; served with the guards in the Netherlands, 1793 and 1794; taken prisoner at Mouveaux, 1794; served in San Domingo from 1798 to 1800; commanded cavalry engaged in covering Sir John Moore's retreat from Coruña, 1809; present in the chief battles and sieges of the Peninsular war; lieutenant-colonel, royal horse artillery, 1814; knighted, 1821; lieutenant-general, 1851; K.C.B., 1852. [xv. 403]

DOWNMAN, WILLIAM (1505–1577). [See DOWNHAM.]

DOWNSHIRE, first MARQUIS OF (1718–1793). [See HILL, WILLS.]

DOWTON, NICHOLAS (d. 1615), commander under the East India Company; sailed about among the Red Sea ports establishing a trade, in company with Sir Henry Middleton, 1611; brought home Middleton's disabled ship, the Peppercorn, 1613; general of the company's ships in the East Indies; compelled the Portuguese, under the viceroy of Goa, to retire, after three weeks' fighting off Surat, 1615; undermined by Edwardes, his second in command; set out, in face of a threatened Portuguese attack, for Bantam, where he died. [xv. 404]

DOWRICHE, ANNE (fl. 1589), poetess; née Edgcumbe; wrote 'The French Historie,' a poem in alexandrines describing three events in the religious history of contemporary France, 1589. [xv. 405]

DOWRICHE, HUGH (fl. 1596), husband of Anne Dowriche [q. v.]; published 'Δεσμόφυλαξ, the Iaylors Conversion,' 1596. [xv. 406]

DOWSE, RICHARD (1824–1890), Irish judge; graduated at Trinity College, Dublin, 1849; called to Irish bar, 1852; Q.C., 1863; queen's serjeant-at-law, 1869; liberal M.P., Londonderry, 1868 and 1870; solicitor-general for Ireland, 1870; attorney-general, Irish privy councillor, and baron of Irish court of exchequer, 1872. [Suppl. ii. 152]

DOWSING, WILLIAM (1596?–1679?), iconoclast; parliamentary visitor of the Suffolk churches, 1644; employed also in Cambridgeshire, where an eye-witness described him as having 'battered and beaten downe all our painted glasse,' 1643. [xv. 406]

DOWSON, JOHN (1820–1881), orientalist; tutor at Haileybury; professor of Hindustani at University College, London, and the Staff College, Sandhurst, 1855–77; published an Urdu grammar, 1862, 'History of India as told by its own Historians,' 1867–77, and a dictionary of Hindu mythology and culture, 1879; Indian epigraphist. [xv. 407]

DOWTON, HENRY (b. 1798), actor; son of William Dowton (1764–1851) [q. v.] [xv. 408]

DOWTON, WILLIAM (1764–1851), actor; appeared at Drury Lane as Sheva in Cumberland's comedy of the 'Jew,' 1796; considered the best representative of Malvolio on the English stage; frequently acted in sentimental comedy. [xv. 408]

DOWTON, WILLIAM (d. 1883), actor; son of William Dowton (1764–1851) [q. v.]; manager of the Kent circuit, 1815–35; brother of the Charterhouse, 1846–83. [xv. 408]

DOXAT, LEWIS (1773–1871), journalist; born in the British West Indies; manager of the 'Observer'; manager of the 'Morning Chronicle' after 1821. [xv. 409]

DOYLE, SIR CHARLES HASTINGS (1805–1883), general; son of Lieutenant-general Sir Charles William Doyle [q. v.]; ensign, 87th regiment, 1819; captain, 1825; lieutenant-colonel, 1846; colonel, 1854; invalided home from Varna, 1854; commanded in Nova Scotia, 1861; lieutenant-governor of Nova Scotia, 1867–73; K.C.M.G., 1869; general, 1877. [xv. 409]

DOYLE, SIR CHARLES WILLIAM (1770–1842), lieutenant-general; lieutenant, 14th regiment, 1793; brigade-major in the Netherlands, 1793; aide-de-camp to Abercromby at the battle of Lannoy, and (1797) in the West Indies; served as brigade-major at Cadiz, at Malta, 1800, and in Egypt, 1801; sent by government to help the insurgents in Spain, 1808; distinguished in the campaigns of 1810 and 1811, and made a Spanish lieutenant-general; director and inspector-general of military instruction, 1811; colonel in the English army, 1813; C.B. and knighted; lieutenant-general, 1837; G.C.H., 1839; died in Paris. [xv. 409]

DOYLE, SIR FRANCIS HASTINGS CHARLES, second baronet (1810–1888), poet; grand-nephew of Sir John Doyle (1750 ?–1834) [q. v.]; educated at Eton and Christ Church, Oxford; B.A., 1832; B.C.L., 1843; M.A., 1867; fellow of All Souls', 1835–44; barrister, Inner Temple, 1837; succeeded to baronetcy, 1839; receiver-general of customs, 1846–69; professor of poetry at Oxford, 1867–77; honorary D.C.L. Oxford, 1877; commissioner of customs, 1869–83; published several volumes of verse, including ballads on contemporary events. [Suppl. ii. 152]

DOYLE, HENRY EDWARD (1827–1892), director of National Gallery of Ireland, 1869 till death; son of John Doyle [q. v.]; honorary secretary to National Portrait Gallery, London, 1865–9; C.B., 1880. [Suppl. ii. 154]

DOYLE, JAMES WARREN (1786–1834), Roman catholic bishop of Kildare and Leighlin; Augustinian monk, 1806; entered the university of Coimbra, 1806; volunteer under Sir Arthur Wellesley; accompanied Colonel Murray with the articles of convention to Lisbon, 1808; successively professor of rhetoric, humanity, and theology at Carlow College, 1813–19; bishop of Kildare and Leighlin, 1819; reformed discipline of his diocese and attacked established church; examined by parliamentary committees on the condition of Ireland, 1825, 1830, and 1832; built a cathedral at Carlow; published 'Letters on the State of Ireland,' 1824, 1825; wrote much under initials 'J. K. L.' [xv. 411]

DOYLE, JAMES WILLIAM EDMUND (1822–1892), son of John Doyle [q. v.]; published 'Official Baronage of England,' 1886. [Suppl. ii. 154]

DOYLE, SIR JOHN (1750 ?–1834), general; served at the siege of Charleston, 1780; brigade-major to Lord Cornwallis, 1780; M.P. for Mullingar in the Irish House of Commons, 1783; secretary at war, 1796–9; raised the 87th regiment, 1793, and served with it in the Netherlands, 1794; fought at Alexandria and Marabout, 1801; constructed roads in Guernsey and organised the defences of the island when lieutenant-governor, 1804–15; created baronet, 1805; K.B., 1812; general, 1819. [xv. 412]

DOYLE, JOHN (1797–1868), portrait-painter and caricaturist; produced in lithograph, under the signature of 'H.B.,' satiric portraits of the political celebrities of contemporary England, 1829–51. [xv. 413]

DOYLE, SIR JOHN MILLEY (1781–1856), colonel; nephew of Sir John Doyle (1750 ?–1834) [q. v.]; lieutenant in the 108th regiment, 1794; assisted in the suppression of the Irish insurrection, 1798; aide-de-camp to Brigadier-general John Doyle before Alexandria, 1801 ; lieutenant-colonel in Portuguese service, 1809 ; fought at Fuentes de Onoro and the capture of Ciudad Rodrigo, 1812 ; lieutenant-colonel in the English army, 1811 ; K.C.B. ; took part in Portuguese affairs, 1823 ; imprisoned by Dom Miguel for actively aiding his rival Don Pedro, 1823 ; M.P., co. Carlow, 1831–2 ; his financial claims on the English government repudiated, 1834.   [xv. 414]

DOYLE, RICHARD (1824–1883), artist and caricaturist ; son of John Doyle [q. v.] ; contributor to 'Punch,' 1843–50 ; designed the cover of 'Punch' ; contributed to 'Punch' cartoons and the 'Manners and Customs of ye Englyshe,' 1849 ; resigned his connection with the paper in consequence of its hostility to papal aggression, 1850 ; illustrated Ruskin's 'King of the Golden River,' 1851, Thackeray's 'Newcomes,' 1853–5, and other books ; poetically treated moorland scenes in water-colour. [xv. 415]

DOYLE, THOMAS (1793–1879), Roman catholic divine ; D.D. ; provost of the cathedral chapter of Southwark, 1850 ; the building of St. George's Cathedral, St. George's Fields, mainly due to his exertions.   [xv. 417]

DOYLE, WELBORE ELLIS (d. 1797), general ; brother of Sir John Doyle (1750?–1834) [q. v.] ; commanded the 14th regiment in the attack on Famars, 1793 ; commander-in-chief in Ceylon.   [xv. 413]

DOYLEY or **DOYLY**, EDWARD (1617–1675), governor of Jamaica ; fought for parliament during civil war ; lieutenant-colonel in expedition to West Indies, 1654 ; commander-in-chief of forces in Jamaica, 1655–6 and 1657–61 ; defended island against several Spanish attempts at reconquest.   [Suppl. ii. 155]

D'OYLIE or **D'OYLY**, THOMAS (1548?–1603), Spanish scholar ; M.A. Magdalen College, Oxford, 1569 ; friend of Francis Bacon ; M.D. Basle, c. 1581 ; held medical appointment in the army at Antwerp ; censor, London College of Physicians, 1593, 1596, and 1598 ; assisted in the compilation of Percival's 'Bibliotheca Hispanica,' 1591 ; drew up a Spanish grammar and dictionary in Spanish, Latin, and English, licensed, 1590, which he withdrew in favour of Percival's book.   [xv. 417]

D'OYLY, SIR CHARLES, seventh baronet (1781–1845), Indian civilian and artist ; assistant to the registrar of the Calcutta court of appeal, 1798 ; collector of Dacca, 1808 ; opium agent at Behar, 1821 ; commercial resident at Patna, 1831 ; senior member of the marine board, 1833 ; an amateur artist of Indian and Anglo-Indian life.   [xv. 418]

D'OYLY, SIR FRANCIS (d. 1815), colonel ; brother of George and Sir John D'Oyly [q. v.] ; assistant adjutant-general in the Peninsular campaigns ; K.C.B. ; killed at Waterloo.   [xv. 420]

D'OYLY, GEORGE (1778–1846), theologian and biographer ; brother of Sir Francis and Sir John D'Oyly [q. v.] ; second wrangler, Corpus Christi College, Cambridge, 1800 ; fellow, 1801 ; moderator in the university, 1806–9, and select preacher, 1809–11 ; Hulsean Christian advocate, 1811 ; D.D. ; rector of Lambeth, Surrey, and of Sundridge, Kent, 1820–46 ; published 'Life of Archbishop Sancroft,' 1821, and theological works.   [xv. 419]

D'OYLY, SIR JOHN, first baronet (1774–1824), resident of Kandy ; brother of George and Sir Francis D'Oyly [q. v.] ; educated at Westminster ; collector of Colombo, 1802 ; secretary to the government of Ceylon, 1810 ; largely instrumental, as head of General Brownrigg's intelligence department, in the overthrow of the king of Kandy, 1814 and 1815 ; created baronet, 1821 ; resident and first commissioner of government in the Kandyan provinces ; died at Kandy.   [xv. 419]

D'OYLY, SAMUEL (d. 1748), translator ; scholar of Westminster, 1697 ; fellow of Trinity College, Cambridge ; M.A., 1707 ; vicar of St. Nicholas, Rochester, 1710–48 ; published 'Christian Eloquence in Theory and Practice,' a translation from Blaise Gisbert, 1718.   [xv. 420]

D'OYLY, THOMAS (fl. 1585), antiquary ; admitted at Gray's Inn, 1555 ; D.C.L. ; read archæological papers before the Society of Antiquaries, founded c. 1572.   [xv. 421]

DRAGE, WILLIAM (1637?–1669), medical writer ; apothecary at Hitchin ; author of 'A Physical Nosonomy,' 1665, and 'Pretologie, a Treatise concerning Intermitting Fevers,' 1665 ; a believer in the occult sciences. [xv. 421]

DRAGHI, GIOVANNI BATTISTA (17th cent.), Italian musician ; wrote instrumental interludes for Shadwell's 'Psyche,' 1674 ; organist to Queen Catherine of Braganza, 1677 ; a skilful player on the harpsichord ; left manuscripts and printed songs ; adopted the English style of music.   [xv. 421]

DRAGONETTI, DOMENICO (1755?–1846), performer on the double-bass ; native of Venice ; succeeded his master, Berini, in the orchestra at St. Mark's ; visited England, 1794 ; left Venice for good, 1797 ; friend of Beethoven, Haydn, and Sechter ; engaged in England at concerts and the opera ; played on one occasion in Paris before Napoleon, who desired him to ask a favour on his instrument, his speech being unintelligible ; composed sonatas and three canzonets.   [xv. 422]

DRAKARD, JOHN (1775?–1854), newspaper proprietor and publisher ; started the 'Stamford News,' 1809 ; fined and imprisoned for an article denouncing corporal punishment in the army, 1810 ; proprietor of the 'Stamford Champion,' 1830–4.   [xv. 424]

DRAKE, SIR BERNARD (d. 1586), naval commander ; sent to seize all Spanish ships off Newfoundland, in retaliation for the detention of English ships in Spain, 1585 ; knighted, 1586 ; died of gaol fever or plague caught at the trial at Exeter of the crew of a Portuguese ship, the Lion of Viana, which he had captured off Brittany.   [xv. 424]

DRAKE, CHARLES FRANCIS TYRWHITT (1846–1874), naturalist and explorer in the Holy Land ; educated at Rugby, Wellington, and Trinity College, Cambridge ; explored, in company with Professor Edward Henry Palmer [q. v.], mountains west of the Arabah and parts of Edom and Moab, 1869 ; investigated, for Palestine Exploration Fund, inscribed stones at Hamáh, 1870 ; died of fever at Jerusalem. Chief works : 'Notes on the Birds of Tangier and Eastern Morocco' ('Ibis,' 1867, 1869), and part of 'Unexplored Syria,' 1872.   [xv. 425]

DRAKE, SIR FRANCIS (1540?–1596), circumnavigator and admiral ; commanded the Judith in John Hawkyns's ill-fated expedition, 1567 [see HAWKINS, SIR JOHN] ; made three voyages from Plymouth to the West Indies, 1570, 1571, and 1572 ; landed at Nombre de Dios, and would have plundered the town, had not his men become disheartened at a wound which their commander received, 1572 ; burnt Portobello, 1572 ; sacked Venta Cruz, 1573 ; returned to Plymouth, 1573 ; served under Essex in Ireland ; reduced Rathlin, 1575 ; set sail from Plymouth for the River Plate, 1577 ; executed Thomas Doughty, a deposed officer of his following, on a charge of conspiracy, 1578 ; sailed through the Straits of Magellan, 1578 ; plundered Valparaiso, 1579 ; captured a ship from Acapulco, commanded by one Don Francisco de Çarate, who sent the viceroy of New Spain a letter, still extant, giving an account of Drake, 1579 ; reached Pelew islands and Mindanao, 1579 ; sailed through the Indian Archipelago, and, rounding the Cape of Good Hope, touched at Sierra Leone, 1580 ; knighted at Deptford in 1581 by Queen Elizabeth, who justified him to the Spanish ambassador ; mayor of Plymouth, 1582 ; his assassination plotted by one John Doughty, an agent of the king of Spain, 1583 ; M.P., Bossiney, 1584–5 ; commissioned by Elizabeth with the command of a fleet and letters of marque, 1585 ; burnt St. Iago and plundered Vigo, 1585 ; took San Domingo and Cartagena, by the aid of the land forces under Carleill ; brought back to England the first colonists of Virginia, 1586 ; commissioned to commit acts of war against Spain, in accordance with which he destroyed an armament in the harbour of Cadiz, not being aware that the order, in so far as it related to Spanish territory, had been countermanded, 1587 ; superseded his vice-admiral, William Borough [q. v.], from his command, 1587 ; urged Elizabeth to forestall a Spanish invasion by attacking the king of Spain at home, 1588 ; stationed off Ushant with one of the three divisions of the English fleet to intercept the Spanish Armada ; driven back to Plymouth by a southerly wind, July 1588 ; defeated the Armada off Gravelines and pursued it to the north of Scotland ; quarrelled with Sir Martin Frobisher about spoil of Rosario, a ship captured by Drake in the Channel, 1588 ; associated with Sir John Norris [q. v.] in expedition against coasts of Spain and Portugal, which plundered Coruña, burnt Vigo, and destroyed much Spanish shipping, 1589 ; regulated the water supply of Plymouth by bringing the

Meavy into the town, 1590 ; M.P., Plymouth, 1593 ; commanded an unsuccessful expedition to the West Indies (1595) with Sir John Hawkyns ; died off Portobello, 1596 ; hero of many popular legends.   [xv. 426]

DRAKE, FRANCIS (1696–1771), author of 'Eboracum' ; city surgeon, York, 1727 ; published with numerous copper-plate engravings 'Eboracum : or, the History and Antiquities of the City of York,' 1736 ; dedicated 'Eboracum' to the Earl of Burlington, whose influence procured his release when imprisoned in the Fleet for a debt contracted by incautiously signing a bond for Sir Harry Slingsby ; F.S.A., 1736 ; investigated local antiquarian problems, such as the Micklegate Stone and the site of Delgovitia.   [xv. 442]

DRAKE, FRANCIS (1721–1795), clergyman ; son of Francis Drake (1696–1771) [q. v.] ; Trapp's scholar, Lincoln College, Oxford, 1739 ; M.A., 1746 ; fellow of Magdalen, 1746 ; D.D., 1773 ; rector of Winestead, Holderness, 1775–95.   [xv. 444]

DRAKE, SIR FRANCIS SAMUEL, first baronet (d. 1789), rear-admiral ; served in West Indies, 1757–8 ; present at the defeat of the French in Quiberon Bay, 1759 ; rear-admiral, 1780 ; detached under Sir Samuel Hood [q. v.] to blockade Martinique, 1781 ; commanded under Rodney in the battle of Dominica, 1782 ; created baronet, 1782 ; M.P., Plymouth, 1789 ; junior lord of the admiralty, 1789.   [xv. 445]

DRAKE, JAMES (1667–1707), political writer ; educated at Eton and Caius College, Cambridge ; M.A. ; M.D., 1694 ; F.R.S., 1701 ; F.R.C.P., 1706 ; prosecuted for his tory pamphlet, 'The History of the Last Parliament,' but acquitted, 1702 ; part author of 'The Memorial of the Church of England' (1705), the authors of which would have been prosecuted had their identity been established ; published 'The Antient and Modern Stages Reviewed,' 1700, and 'Anthropologia Nova,' 1707.   [xv. 446]

DRAKE, JOHN POAD (1794–1883), inventor and artist ; painted a picture of Napoleon on board the Bellerophon ; visited Montreal ; patented a diagonal arrangement of ribs and planking for ships and a screw trenail fastening, 1837 ; said to have discovered the principle of the Snider Enfield gun, 1835.   [xv. 447]

DRAKE, NATHAN (1766–1836), literary essayist and physician ; M.D. Edinburgh, 1789 ; practised at Sudbury, 1790–2, and at Hadleigh, Suffolk, 1792–1836 ; published 'Shakespeare and his Times,' 1817, 'Memorials of Shakespeare,' 1828, and miscellaneous essays ; advocated use of digitalis in consumption.   [xv. 448]

DRAKE, ROGER (1608–1669), physician and divine ; M.A. Pembroke College, Cambridge, 1631 ; M.D. Leyden, 1639 ; defended Harveian doctrine of the circulation of the blood against Dr. James Primrose [q. v.], 1641 ; arrested for share in Love's plot, but pardoned, 1651 ; minister of St. Peter's Cheap, 1653 ; published 'Sacred Chronologie,' 1648, and religious tractates and medical dissertations.   [xv. 448]

DRAKE, SAMUEL (d. 1673), royalist divine ; fellow of St. John's College, Cambridge, 1643 ; M.A., 1644 ; ejected from fellowship for refusing to take the covenant ; fought at Newark ; incumbent of Pontefract, 1660 ; D.D., 1661 ; prebendary of Southwell, 1670–1.   [xv. 449]

DRAKE, SAMUEL (1686?–1753), antiquary ; brother of Francis Drake (1696–1771) [q. v.] ; M.A. St. John's College, Cambridge, 1711 ; D.D., 1724 ; rector of Treeton, Yorkshire, 1728–53, and vicar of Holme-on-Spalding Moor, 1733–53 ; wrote on Christian ritual ; edited Bartholomew Clerke's Latin translation of Castiglione's 'Courtier,' 1713.   [xv. 450]

DRAKE, WILLIAM (1723–1801), antiquary and philologist ; son of Francis Drake (1696–1771) [q. v.] ; B.A. Christ Church, Oxford, 1744 ; master of Felstead grammar school, 1750–77 ; vicar of Isleworth, Middlesex, 1777–1801 ; F.S.A., 1770 ; contributed papers on the origin of the English language to 'Archæologia.'   [xv. 450]

DRANE, AUGUSTA THEODOSIA (1823–1894), historian and poet ; brought up in established church, but joined Roman catholics, 1850 ; postulant, 1852, in Dominican convent, Clifton (removed to Stone, 1853) ; pronounced vows, 1856 ; prioress, 1872–81 ; mother provincial of order, 1881–94 ; published numerous historical, biographical, and poetical works, chiefly of a religious tendency.   [Suppl. ii. 155]

DRANT, THOMAS (d. 1578 ?), divine and poet ; B.A. and fellow St. John's College, Cambridge, 1561 ; M.A., 1564 ; domestic chaplain to Archbishop Grindal ; B.D., 1569 ; prebendary of St. Paul's, 1569 ; prebendary of Chichester, 1570 ; archdeacon of Lewes, 1570–8 ; translated Horace's epistles, satires, and 'Ars Poetica' into English verse, 1567 ; published 'Sylva,' a collection of Latin poems, c. 1576 ; advocated the use of classical metres in English verse.   [xvi. 1]

DRAPENTIER, JAN (fl. 1674–1713), engraver ; native of Dordrecht ; engraved portraits for London booksellers and views for Chauncy's 'Hertfordshire' ; engraver to the mint.   [xvi. 2]

DRAPER, EDWARD ALURED (1776–1841), colonel ; cousin of Sir William Draper [q. v.] ; educated at Eton ; page of honour to George III ; lieutenant and captain, 3rd foot guards, 1796 ; brevet-major and military secretary to Lieutenant-general Grinfield, 1802, bringing home despatches after capture of St. Lucia, 1803 ; executive official in Mauritius, taking the popular side in opposing the home government's nomination of a Mr. Jeremie as procureur-general, 1832 ; recalled ; subsequently colonial treasurer of Mauritius.   [xvi. 2]

DRAPER, MRS. ELIZA (1744–1778), friend of Laurence Sterne [q. v.] ; born at Anjengo in India ; daughter of May Sclater ; married at Bombay Daniel Draper, H.E.I.C.S. (1725 ?–1805) ; met on a visit to London, 1766–7, Sterne, who addressed to her amorous letters and a 'Journal to Eliza' ; returned, 1767, to India, where she lived unhappily with her husband, and ran away from him, finally settling in England ; eulogised by Abbé Raynal and James Forbes in 'Oriental Memoirs' ; died at Bristol and buried in cathedral cloisters there.   [liv. 211]

DRAPER, JOHN WILLIAM (1811–1882), chemist ; studied at the London and Pennsylvania universities ; M.D. Pennsylvania, 1836 ; professor of chemistry and physiology, Hampden Sidney College, Virginia, 1836, and at New York, 1839 ; LL.D. ; first to produce daguerreotype portraits, 1839 ; president of the New York University, 1850–73 ; brought out 'Scientific Memoirs, being Experimental Contributions to a Knowledge of Radiant Energy,' 1878 ; devoted special study to ultra-violet rays of spectrum ; published historical works.   [xvi. 3]

DRAPER, SIR WILLIAM (1721–1787), lieutenant-general ; educated at Eton and King's College, Cambridge ; fellow of King's College ; M.A., 1749 ; ensign in Lord Henry Beauclerk's regiment, 1744 ; adjutant, 1st foot guards, 1746 ; lieutenant and captain, 1749 ; commanded the 79th regiment, raised by himself, at the siege of Fort St. George, 1758–9 ; colonel, 1762 ; captured Manilla, 1762, ransoming it for 1,000,000l. in bills on Madrid, which was never paid ; colonel, 16th foot, 1765 ; K.B., 1766 ; defended the Marquis of Granby against 'Junius,' 1769 ; lieutenant-general, 1777 ; lieutenant-governor of Minorca, 1779–82 ; preferred unfounded charges of misconduct against Lieutenant-general Hon. James Murray, who had suspended him, 1782 ; reprimanded by a general court-martial, 1783.   [xvi. 4]

DRAXE, THOMAS (d. 1618), divine ; B.D. Christ's College, Cambridge ; vicar of Dovercourt-cum-Harwich, 1601 ; author of 'Treasurie of Ancient Adagies and Sententious Proverbs,' 1633, and other works.   [xvi. 7]

DRAYCOT, ANTHONY (d. 1571), divine ; principal of White Hall and Pirye Hall, Oxford ; doctor of canon law, 1522 ; rector of Draycot ; prebendary of Lincoln, 1539, of Lichfield, 1556 ; chancellor of Lincoln, Coventry, and Lichfield ; stripped of all his preferments except Draycot, 1559.   [xvi. 8]

DRAYTON, MICHAEL (1563–1631), poet : at one time probably page to Sir Henry Goodere of Powlesworth ; published 'Idea. The Shepheards Garland. Fashioned in nine Eglogs,' 1593 ; published three historical poems, 'Piers Gaveston,' 1593, 'Matilda' (Fitzwater), 1594, and 'The Tragicall Legend of Robert, Duke of Normandie,' 1596 ; composed in rhymed heroics 'Endymion and Phœbe,' c. 1594 ; published 'Ideas Mirrovr,' a series of sonnets in honour of a lady otherwise unknown, 1594 ; republished his 'Mortimeriados' as 'The Barrons Wars,' 1603 ; collaborated in dramatic work with Henry Chettle [q. v.], Thomas Dekker [q. v.], and John Webster (1580 ?–1625 ?) [q. v.] ; possibly employed by Queen Elizabeth on a diplomatic mission to Scotland ; published 'The Owle,' a satire, 1604; produced, *c.* 1605, 'Poemes Lyrick and Pastorall,' containing the famous 'Ballad of Agincourt'; published (1607) 'The Legend of Great Cromwell,' included in the 1610 edition of 'Mirour for Magistrates'; finished 'Poly-Olbion,' a long poetic topography of England, 1622; published 'Nimphidia' and other poems, 1627; friend of Shakespeare; highly esteemed by Drummond of Hawthornden. [xvi. 8]

DRAYTON, NICHOLAS DE (*fl.* 1376), ecclesiastic and judge; warden of King's Hall, Cambridge, 1363; imprisoned for heresy, 1369; exchequer baron, 1376. [xvi. 13]

DREBBEL, CORNELIS (1572-1634), philosopher and scientific inventor; born at Alkmaar; invented machine for producing perpetual motion, which he presented to his patron, James I; visited the court of Rudolph II; imprisoned on the capture of Prague by the elector palatine, 1620; released at James I's intercession; sent in charge of fireships on the Rochelle expedition, 1627; credited with invention of telescope, microscope, and thermometer; author of a Dutch work on the 'Nature of the Elements,' 1608. [xvi. 13]

DREGHORN, LORD (1734-1796). [See MACLAURIN, JOHN.]

DRELINCOURT, PETER (1644-1722), dean of Armagh; son of a Huguenot minister; M.A. Trinity College, Dublin, 1681; LL.D., 1691; archdeacon of Leighlin, 1683; dean of Armagh, 1691-1722. [xvi. 14]

DRENNAN, WILLIAM (1754-1820), Irish poet; M.A. Glasgow, 1771; M.D. Edinburgh, 1778; formulated original prospectus of the Society of United Irishmen, 1791; chairman, 1792 and 1793; tried for sedition, and acquitted, 1794; writer of patriotic lyrics; first Irish poet to call Ireland the 'Emerald Isle.' [xvi. 14]

DREW, EDWARD (1542?-1598), recorder of London; scholar, Exeter College, Oxford; admitted Inner Temple, 1560; serjeant-at-law, 1589; M.P. for Lyme Regis, 1584, for Exeter, 1586 and 1588; recorder (1592-4) and M.P. for London, 1592; queen's serjeant, 1596. [xvi. 15]

DREW, FREDERICK (1836-1891), geologist; studied at Royal School of Mines; joined geological survey, 1855; entered service of maharajah of Kashmir, 1862, and became governor of province of Ladakh; F.G.S., 1858; science master at Eton, 1875-91; published geographical and geological writings. [Suppl. ii. 156]

DREW, GEORGE SMITH (1819-1880), Hulsean lecturer; B.A. St. John's College, Cambridge, 1843; M.A., 1847; vicar of Holy Trinity, Lambeth, 1873-80; Hulsean lecturer (1877) on 'The Human Life of Christ revealing the order of the Universe,' 1878. [xvi. 16]

DREW, JOHN (1809-1857), astronomer; schoolmaster at Southampton, *c.* 1847; part founder of the Meteorological Society, 1850; doctor in philosophy, Bâle. His works include 'Chronological Charts illustrative of Ancient History and Geography,' 1835, and a 'Manual of Astronomy,' 1845. [xvi. 16]

DREW, SAMUEL (1765-1833), metaphysician; of humble origin; Wesleyan preacher, 1788; published 'Remarks upon Paine's "Age of Reason,"' 1799; styled the 'Cornish metaphysician' on the publication of an 'Essay on the Immateriality and Immortality of the Soul,' 1802; superintendent from 1819 of the Caxton press, first at Liverpool and then in London. [xvi. 17]

DRING, RAWLINS (*fl.* 1688), physician; fellow and M.A. Wadham College, Oxford, 1682; medical practitioner at Sherborne; endeavoured to disprove invariability of configurations assumed by crystallising salts. [xvi. 18]

DRINKWATER, JOHN (1762-1844). [See BETHUNE, JOHN DRINKWATER.]

DROESHOUT, JOHN (1596-1652), engraver; brother of Martin Droeshout [q. v.]; engraved a set of plates for De Souza's 'Lusitania Liberata.' [xvi. 19]

DROESHOUT, MARTIN (*fl.* 1620-1651), engraver; born in London, of Flemish parentage; engraved portrait of Shakespeare prefixed to First Folio, 1623. [xvi. 18]

DROGHEDA, first MARQUIS and sixth EARL OF (1730-1822). [See MOORE, CHARLES.]

DROGHEDA, VISCOUNTS. [See MOORE, SIR GARRET, first VISCOUNT, 1560?-1627; MOORE, SIR CHARLES, second VISCOUNT, 1603-1643.]

DROKENSFORD, JOHN DE (*d.* 1329), bishop of Bath and Wells; accompanied Edward I against the Scots, 1291, 1296, and probably also in 1304; rector of Droxford, Hampshire, and prebendary of Southwell, Lichfield, Lincoln, and Wells; chancellor of the exchequer, 1307; bishop of Bath and Wells, 1309-29; petitioned for appointment of ordainers, 1310; regent, 1313; took oath to support Queen Isabella and her son Edward III, 1327. [xvi. 19]

DROMGOOLE, THOMAS (1750?-1826?), Roman catholic agitator; native of Ireland; M.D. Edinburgh; settled as a physician in Dublin; denounced in 1813 all compromise in struggle for Catholic Emancipation, thereby delaying its grant by parliament; died at Rome. [xvi. 20]

DROPE, FRANCIS (1629?-1671), arboriculturist; demy of Magdalen College, Oxford, 1645; ejected, 1648; M.A., 1660; fellow, 1662; B.D., 1667; prebendary of Lincoln, 1670; his 'Short and Sure Guide in the Practice of Raising and Ordering of Fruit-trees,' published, 1672. [xvi. 21]

DROPE, JOHN (1626-1670), physician and poet; brother of Francis Drope [q. v.]; demy of Magdalen College, Oxford, 1642; fought for Charles I in the garrison of Oxford; fellow, 1647; master at John Fetiplace's school, Dorchester, *c.* 1654; M.A., 1660; physician at Borough, Lincolnshire; published poems. [xvi. 21]

DROUT, JOHN (*fl.* 1570), poet; attorney, of Thavies Inn; issued, 1570, a poetic tale 'from the Italian.' [xvi. 21]

DRUE, THOMAS (*fl.* 1631), author of 'The Life of the Dvtches of Svffolke,' an historical play, 1631. [xvi. 21]

DRUID, THE (pseudonym) (1822-1870). [See DIXON, HENRY HALL.]

DRUITT, ROBERT (1814-1883), medical writer; F.R.C.S., 1845; F.R.C.P., 1874; M.D. Lambeth; editor of the 'Medical Times and Gazette,' 1862-72; president of the Metropolitan Association of Medical Officers of Health, 1864-72; published 'The Surgeon's Vade-Mecum,' 1839, and other writings. [xvi. 22]

DRUMCAIRN, LORD, EARL OF MELROSE (1563-1637). [See HAMILTON, SIR THOMAS.]

DRUMMOND, ALEXANDER (*d.* 1769), published 'Travels through .... Germany, Italy, Greece, and parts of Asia,' 1754; consul at Aleppo, 1754-6. [xvi. 22]

DRUMMOND, ANNABELLA (1350?-1402), queen of Robert III of Scotland; daughter of Sir John Drummond of Stobhall; married John Stewart of Kyle (afterwards Robert III), 1367; crowned queen, 1390; proposed a marriage between a relation of Richard II and one of the royal children of Scotland, 1394. David Stewart, duke of Rothesay [q. v.], her son, was murdered, while regent, shortly after her death. [xvi. 22]

DRUMMOND, EDWARD (1792-1843), civil servant; private secretary to the Earl of Ripon, Canning, Wellington, and Sir Robert Peel; shot, in mistake for Peel, by one Macnaghten. [xvi. 25]

DRUMMOND, GEORGE (1687-1766), six times lord provost of Edinburgh; said to have calculated financial details for the union, 1705; accountant-general of excise, 1707-15; raised a company of volunteers for service against the Earl of Mar, 1715; member of council, Edinburgh, 1715; lord provost, 1725, 1746, 1750-1, 1754-5, 1758-9, and 1762-3; established a medical faculty and five professorships in Edinburgh University; joined Sir John Cope [q. v.], 1745; organised schemes for improvement of Edinburgh. [xvi. 25]

DRUMMOND, SIR GORDON (1772-1854), general; lieutenant, 41st regiment, 1791; lieutenant-colonel, 8th regiment, 1794; distinguished himself at Nimeguen; colonel, 1798; fought at the capture of Alexandria and Cairo, 1801; major-general, 1805; commanded division in Jamaica, 1805; lieutenant-general, 1811; defeated Americans at Niagara, 1814; general, 1825; G.C.B., 1837. [xvi. 27]

DRUMMOND, HENRY (1786–1860), politician ; studied at Harrow and Christ Church, Oxford ; M.P., Plympton Earls, 1810 ; carried an act against embezzlement by bankers of securities entrusted to their safe keeping, 1812 ; settled near Geneva, and continued Haldane's movement against Socinianism in the venerable company and the consistory ; founded professorship of political economy at Oxford, 1825 ; joint-founder of the Irvingite church ; M.P., West Surrey, 1847–60. [xvi. 28]

DRUMMOND, HENRY (1851–1897), theological writer ; educated at Edinburgh University ; studied divinity at New College, Edinburgh ; joined, 1873, evangelical movement initiated by Dwight L. Moody and Ira D. Sankey ; lecturer in natural science at the Free Church College, Glasgow, 1877 ; published 'Natural Law in the Spiritual World,' 1883 ; made scientific exploration of Lake Nyasa and Tanganyika district for African Lakes Corporation, 1883–4, and published 'Tropical Africa,' 1888 ; professor of theology in New Church, 1884 ; ordained in College Free Church, 1884 ; supported students' mission in Edinburgh and Glasgow, and made tour of American and Australian colleges ; published 'Ascent of Man,' 1894. [Suppl. ii. 157]

DRUMMOND, JAMES, first BARON MADERTY (1540 ?–1623), 'commendator' of Inchaffray ; lord of the bedchamber to James VI, 1585 ; made depositions concerning the so-called Gowrie plot, 1600. [xvi. 29]

DRUMMOND, JAMES, fourth EARL and first titular DUKE OF PERTH (1648–1716) ; educated at St. Andrews ; supported Lauderdale's policy of giving up the disaffected western shires of Scotland to highland raids, 1677 ; member of Lauderdale's Scottish privy council, 1678 ; subsequently joined Hamilton's faction ; partner with William Penn in the settlement of East New Jersey, 1681 ; justice-general, 1682 ; extraordinary lord of session, 1682 ; lord chancellor, 1684 ; introduced use of thumb-screw ; converted to Roman catholicism ; K.T., 1687 ; imprisoned in Stirling Castle, 1689 ; released on a bond to leave the kingdom, 1693 ; created K.G. by the exiled James II ; created Duke of Perth by James II's will ; died at St. Germain. [xvi. 29]

DRUMMOND, JAMES, fifth EARL, and second titular DUKE OF PERTH (1675–1720), eldest son of James Drummond, fourth earl [q. v.] ; studied at Paris ; imprisoned as a Jacobite, 1708 ; commanded rebel cavalry at Sheriffmuir, 1715 ; attainted ; attended James Edward [q. v.], the Old Pretender, on the continent ; died at Paris. [xvi. 31]

DRUMMOND, JAMES, sixth EARL and third titular DUKE OF PERTH (1713–1747), eldest son of James Drummond, fifth earl [q. v.] ; educated at Douay ; styled himself Duke of Perth in spite of his father's attainder ; eluded government attempt to arrest him, 1745 ; surprised camp of Lord Loudon, a royalist leader, 1746 ; commanded the Young Pretender's left wing at Culloden, 1746. [xvi. 31]

DRUMMOND, JAMES (1784 ?–1863), botanical collector ; elder brother of Thomas Drummond (d. 1835) [q. v.] ; associate of Linnean Society, 1810 ; made up sets of the indigenous vegetation of Western Australia for sale ; died in Western Australia. [xvi. 33]

DRUMMOND, JAMES (1816–1877), subject and history painter ; academician, Royal Scottish Academy, 1852 ; curator of the National Gallery, 1868 ; painted scenes from later Scottish history. [xvi. 33]

DRUMMOND, JAMES LAWSON (1783–1853), professor of anatomy ; brother of William Hamilton Drummond [q. v.] ; navy surgeon in Mediterranean, 1807–13 ; M.D. Edinburgh, 1814 ; first professor of anatomy at the Academical Institution, Belfast, 1818–49 ; published botanical and anatomical works. [xvi. 33]

DRUMMOND, JOHN, first BARON DRUMMOND (d. 1519), statesman ; commissioned to negotiate a marriage between James, prince of Scotland, and Anne de la Pole, 1484 ; created Baron Drummond, 1488 ; privy councillor, 1488 ; justiciary of Scotland, 1488 ; routed the rebel forces under the so-called Earl of Lennox, 1489 ; imprisoned by Albany (1515), really for opposing his election as regent, nominally for striking Lyon king-at-arms ; forfeited, but soon reconciled to Albany (1516), whom he supported against Henry VIII and the queen-dowager Margaret. [xvi. 34]

DRUMMOND, JOHN, first EARL and titular DUKE OF MELFORT (1649–1714), lieutenant-general and master of ordnance, 1680 ; secretary of state for Scotland, 1684 ; created Earl of Melfort, 1686 ; converted to Roman catholicism ; together with his brother James, fourth Earl of Perth [q. v.], practically ruled Scotland ; advocated a wholesale seizure of influential whigs, 1688 ; attended James II for a time in Ireland ; Jacobite envoy to Rome ; made K.G. at St. Germain, 1691 ; attainted, 1695 ; wrote to his brother, then at St. Germain, a letter from Paris, which was intercepted in London, ascribing to Louis XIV the intention of restoring James II, 1701 ; suspected of treachery to Jacobite interests, and sent to Angers ; died at Paris. [xvi. 35]

DRUMMOND, JOHN, fourth DUKE OF PERTH (d. 1747), brother of James, sixth earl of Perth [q. v.] ; educated at Douay ; raised the Royal Scots regiment, and was sent from France to join Prince Charles Edward, 1745 ; called on six thousand Dutch soldiers to withdraw, as having previously capitulated in Flanders ; mainly contributed to the Jacobite victory at Falkirk, 1746 ; fought at Culloden, 1746 ; died before Bergen-op-Zoom. [xvi. 32]

DRUMMOND, MARGARET (1472 ?–1501), mistress of James IV of Scotland ; daughter of John, first baron Drummond [q. v.] ; poisoned, together with her two sisters, one of them being wife of Lord Fleming, 1501. The triple murder has been sometimes attributed to Lord Fleming. [xvi. 37]

DRUMMOND, PETER ROBERT (1802–1879), biographer ; bookseller at Dundee ; farmer, and collector of pictures and engravings ; chief works, 'Perthshire in Bygone Days,' 1879, and 'The Life of Robert Nicoll, poet' (published 1884). [xvi. 38]

DRUMMOND, ROBERT HAY (1711–1776), archbishop of York ; educated at Westminster, where Queen Caroline remarked him, and at Christ Church, Oxford ; M.A., 1735 ; royal chaplain, 1736 ; took the additional surname of Drummond, 1739 ; attended George II on his German campaign, 1743 ; D.D., 1745 ; bishop of St. Asaph, 1748–61 ; successfully defended Bishop Johnson of Gloucester and two other friends on a charge of Jacobitism, 1753 ; bishop of Salisbury, 1761 ; archbishop of York, 1761–76 ; made additions to the archiepiscopal palace. [xvi. 38]

DRUMMOND, SAMUEL (1765–1844), portrait and historical painter ; exhibited at the Royal Academy after 1791 ; A.R.A., 1808 ; curator of the Royal Academy painting school. [xvi. 40]

DRUMMOND, THOMAS (d. 1835), botanical collector ; brother of James Drummond (1784 ?–1863) [q. v.] ; assistant-naturalist in Sir John Franklin's second (1825) land expedition ; made a botanical tour in Texas, sending collections of plants to England ; died at Havana. [xvi. 41]

DRUMMOND, THOMAS (1797–1840), engineer and administrator ; studied at Edinburgh University ; entered the royal engineers, 1815 ; introduced 'Drummond' limelight ; improved heliostat ; head of the boundary commission in connection with the great Reform Bill ; undersecretary at Dublin Castle, 1835–40 ; organised the Dublin police and appointed stipendiaries to control the local magistrates ; told the landlords that 'property' had 'its duties as well as its rights' ; supported by O'Connell ; his administration vindicated by a commission of inquiry, 1839. [xvi. 41]

DRUMMOND, WILLIAM, of Hawthornden (1585–1649), poet ; related to the royal family of Scotland through Annabella Drummond [q. v.] ; M.A. Edinburgh, 1605 ; attended law lectures at Bourges and Paris, 1607 and 1608 ; laird of Hawthornden, 1610 ; lamented Prince Henry in 'Tears on the Death of Meliades,' 1613 ; friend and correspondent of (Sir) William Alexander of Menstrie [q. v.] and of Michael Drayton, and an acquaintance of Ben Jonson ; issued 'Flowers of Zion' (religious verse), and 'The Cypresse Grove,' a prose meditation on death, 1623 ; patented sixteen mechanical inventions, comprising weapons and scientific instruments, 1627 ; drew up a genealogy of the Drummond family, and sent Charles I a manuscript tractate, in which he rebutted the claim of William Graham, seventh earl of Menteith, to the earldom of Strathearn, 1632 ; wrote 'History of Scotland

[1423–1524]' (first printed 1655); wrote 'Irene' in the interest of concord during the Scottish political turmoil of 1638 ; protested against the solemn league and covenant in 'Remoras for the National League between Scotland and England,' 1643 ; wrote in favour of negotiation with Charles I, 1646 ; his death ascribed to grief for Charles I's execution. The first collected edition of his poems issued in 1656. As a sonnetteer Drummond was much influenced by Guarini. He invented the metre employed in Milton's 'Hymn of the Nativity.' [xvi. 45]

DRUMMOND, WILLIAM, first VISCOUNT OF STRATHALLAN (1617 ?–1688), royalist general; studied at St. Andrews ; commanded royalist brigade at battle of Worcester, and was taken prisoner, 1651 ; escaped and entered the Russian service, becoming lieutenant-general of the 'strangers' and governor of Smolensko ; major-general of the forces in Scotland, with seat on the council, 1666 ; popularly supposed to have introduced the thumbscrew ; urged the necessity of a standing army upon Charles II, 1667 ; knighted, c. 1680 ; represented Perthshire in Scottish parliament, 1669–74, 1678, 1681–2, and 1685–6 ; lieutenant-general of the forces in Scotland, and treasury lord, 1685 ; created Viscount Strathallan and Baron Drummond of Cromlix, 1686 ; disapproved James II's proposal of exclusive toleration for Romanists, 1686. [xvi. 49]

DRUMMOND, WILLIAM, fourth VISCOUNT OF STRATHALLAN (1690–1746), Jacobite ; taken prisoner at Sheriffmuir, 1715 ; released by the act of grace, 1717 ; killed while commanding under the Young Pretender at Culloden, 1746. [xvi. 50]

DRUMMOND, SIR WILLIAM (1770 ?–1828), scholar and diplomatist ; M.P., St. Mawes, 1795, Lostwithiel, 1796 and 1801 ; F.R.S., 1799 ; D.C.L. Oxford, 1810 ; privy councillor, 1801 ; minister plenipotentiary to Naples, 1801 and 1806 ; ambassador to the Porte, 1803–6 ; his chief works, 'Origines,' 1824–9, and 'Œdipus Judaicus,' which explained Old Testament stories as astronomical allegories, 1811. [xvi. 51]

DRUMMOND, WILLIAM ABERNETHY (1719 ?–1809), bishop of Edinburgh ; of the Abernethy family at Salton ; M.D. ; episcopalian minister at Edinburgh ; assumed his father-in-law's surname of Drummond, 1760 ; bishop of Brechin, 1787 ; bishop of Edinburgh, 1787–1805 ; urged episcopalians to submit to Hanoverian dynasty after Prince Charles Edward's death, 1788. [xvi. 51]

DRUMMOND, WILLIAM HAMILTON (1778–1865), poet and controversialist ; educated at the Belfast Academy and Glasgow College ; ordained by the Antrim presbytery to Second Belfast, 1800 ; D.D. Marischal College, Aberdeen, 1810 ; colleague to James Armstrong [q. v.] at Strand Street, Dublin, 1815 ; defended unitarianism in his 'Doctrine of the Trinity,' 1827, and wrote an enthusiastic life of Servetus, 1848 ; published poems and (1852) 'Ancient Irish Minstrelsy.' [xvi. 52]

DRUMMOND-HAY, SIR JOHN HAY (1816–1893), diplomatist ; educated at Charterhouse ; attaché at Constantinople, 1840 ; consul-general at Morocco, 1845, chargé d'affaires, 1847–60, minister resident, 1860–72, and minister plenipotentiary, 1872–86 ; K.C.B., 1862 ; G.C.M.G., 1884 ; privy councillor, 1886 ; published 'Western Barbary' and other writings. [Suppl. ii. 158]

DRUMMORE, HEW DALRYMPLE, LORD (1690–1755). [See DALRYMPLE, HEW.]

DRURY, SIR DRU or DRUE (1531 ?–1617), courtier; brother of Sir William Drury [q. v.] ; gentleman-usher of the privy chamber to Elizabeth and James I ; knighted, 1579 ; joint-warder of Mary Queen of Scots at Fotheringay, 1586. [xvi. 54]

DRURY, DRU (1725–1803), naturalist ; silversmith in the Strand ; entomological collector ; F.L.S. ; correspondent of Linnæus, Kirby, and Fabricius ; wrote on natural history and entomology and published 'Thoughts on the Precious Metals,' 1801. [xvi. 54]

DRURY, HENRY (1812–1863), archdeacon of Wilts ; educated at Harrow and Caius College, Cambridge ; Browne medallist, 1833 and 1835 ; M.A., 1840 ; classical lecturer at Caius, 1839–3 ; prebendary of Salisbury, 1855 ; chaplain to the House of Commons, 1857 ; archdeacon of Wilts, 1862–3 ; projected and published 'Arundines Cami,' 1841. [xvi. 55]

DRURY, HENRY JOSEPH THOMAS (1778–1841), scholar ; son of Joseph Drury [q. v.]; educated at Eton and King's College, Cambridge; fellow of King's; M.A., 1804 ; master of Harrow lower school ; edited for Harrow selections from the classics. [xvi. 56]

DRURY, JOSEPH (1750–1834), head-master of Harrow ; scholar of Westminster, 1765 ; elected to Trinity College, Cambridge, 1768 ; assistant-master at Harrow, 1769 ; head-master, 1785–1805 ; D.D., 1789 ; helped to establish Edmund Kean, at Drury Lane Theatre ; prebendary of Wells, 1812 ; repeatedly mentioned as a great schoolmaster by his pupil Byron. [xvi. 56]

DRURY, SIR ROBERT (d. 1536), speaker of the House of Commons ; educated at Cambridge ; barrister-at-law of Lincoln's Inn ; governor, 1488–9, 1492–3, and 1497 ; knight of the shire for Suffolk ; speaker, 1495 ; took part in attempts to conciliate the Scottish borderers, 1510–13 ; knight for the body, 1516 ; commissioner for collection of loan for French war, 1524 ; member of legal committee of privy council. [xvi. 57]

DRURY, ROBERT (1567–1607), Roman catholic divine ; educated at Douay ; ordained priest at Philip II's College, Valladolid ; missioner in London, 1593 ; subscribed protestation of allegiance, 1603 ; executed for remaining in England contrary to 27 Eliz. [xvi. 58]

DRURY, ROBERT (1587–1623), jesuit ; son of William Drury (d. 1589) [q. v.] ; studied in London, and at Douay, St. Omer, and Posna ; rector of the college at St. Omer, 1620 ; missioner in England ; jesuit professed of the four vows, 1622 ; lost his life at the 'Fatal Vespers,' when the floor of a room in the French ambassador's residence at Blackfriars collapsed, 1623. [xvi. 58]

DRURY, ROBERT (fl. 1729), traveller ; forced to land in Androy, Madagascar, on his return from Bengal, the ship being disabled ; escaped from the massacre of his comrades, and subsequently from slavery ; captured by the Sakalavas ; ransomed by his father ; made a subsequent voyage to Madagascar as a slave trader ; published a narrative of his travels, 1729. [xvi. 59]

DRURY, SIR WILLIAM (1527–1579), marshal of Berwick, and lord-justice to the council in Ireland ; educated at Gonville Hall, Cambridge ; took part in sieges of Boulogne and Montreuil, 1544 ; assisted in suppressing Devonshire rising, 1549 ; declared for Queen Mary, 1553, but, being a protestant, retired into private life ; marshal and deputy-governor of Berwick, 1564–76 ; with Earl of Sussex raided Scotland, 1570 ; knighted, 1570 ; commissioned to negotiate a peace in the interest of James VI's party in Scotland, 1571 and 1572 ; narrowly escaped assassination on several occasions ; reduced Edinburgh Castle, 1573 ; president of Munster, 1576–8 ; suppressed the practice of coyne and livery ; lord-justice, 1578. [xvi. 60]

DRURY, WILLIAM (d. 1589), civilian ; LL.B. Trinity Hall, Cambridge, 1553 ; regius professor of civil law, 1559 ; LL.D., 1560 ; advocate at Doctors' Commons, 1561 ; consulted by Elizabeth on points of international law raised by the intrigues of the Bishop of Ross on behalf of Mary Stuart, 1571 ; master of the prerogative court of Canterbury, 1577 ; master in chancery, 1585. [xvi. 62]

DRURY, WILLIAM (fl. 1641), Latin dramatist ; imprisoned as a Roman catholic, but released through intercession of the Spanish ambassador, c. 1616 ; taught poetry and rhetoric at the English College, Douay, 1618 ; author of two Latin tragi-comedies and 'Mors,' a Latin farce. [xvi. 63]

DRY, SIR RICHARD (1815–1869), Tasmanian statesman ; born at Elphin, Tasmania ; nominated to the old council (1844) by Lieutenant-Governor Sir John Eardley Wilmot ; opponent of Wilmot's financial schemes, and one of the 'patriotic six' ; member for Launceston in new legislative council, 1851 ; speaker of new legislative council, 1851–5 ; procured abolition of transportation, 1853 ; knighted, 1858 ; colonial secretary and premier, 1866–9. [xvi. 63]

DRYANDER, JONAS (1748–1810), botanist ; native of Sweden, and graduate of Lund ; original fellow and librarian of the Royal Society ; vice-president of the Linnean Society ; compiled a valuable 'Catalogus Bibliothecæ Historico-Naturalis Josephi Banks, Baronetti,' 1796–1800. [xvi. 64]

DRYDEN, CHARLES (1666–1704), chamberlain to Pope Innocent XII; eldest son of John Dryden (1631–1700) [q. v.]; educated at Westminster and Trinity College, Oxford; translated Juvenal's seventh satire for his father's version, 1692; his horoscope calculated by his father; drowned in the Thames. [xvi. 72]

DRYDEN, SIR ERASMUS HENRY (1669–1710), third son of John Dryden (1631–1700) [q. v.]; scholar at the Charterhouse; studied at Douay; sub-prior of the convent of Holy Cross, Bornheim, 1697–1700; missioner in Northamptonshire; baronet by succession, 1710. [xvi. 73]

DRYDEN, JOHN (1631–1700), poet; scholar of Westminster and Trinity College, Cambridge; B.A., 1654; clerk to his cousin, Sir Gilbert Pickering [q. v.], Cromwell's chamberlain; bewailed Cromwell's death in 'Heroic Stanzas,' 1658; published 'Astræa Redux,' 1660, and a 'Panegyric' in honour of the Restoration, 1661; M.R.S., 1662; failed in his first play, 'The Wild Gallant,' 1663; brought out the 'Rival Ladies,' 1663, and the 'Indian Emperor,' 1665; wrote 'Annus Mirabilis' in 1666 or 1667, and published an 'Essay on Dramatic Poesy,' defending the use of rhyme in tragedy, 1668; M.A. Lambeth, 1668; poet laureate and historiographer, 1670; wrote about fourteen plays between 1668 and 1681; produced 'Amboyna,' a tragedy designed to exasperate England against the Dutch, 1673, and 'The Spanish Friar,' an attack on the papists, 1681; wrote 'Tyrannic Love' and 'Almanzor and Almahide,' 1669 and 1670; produced 'Aurengzebe,' his last rhymed tragedy, 1675; planned an epic poem; produced 'All for Love,' his finest play, 1678; adapted Shakespeare's 'Tempest,' and (1679) 'Troilus and Cressida'; his rhyming tragedies ridiculed in the 'Rehearsal,' 1671; involved in a literary controversy with Elkanah Settle [q. v.], 1673; assaulted, probably at the instigation of John Wilmot, second earl of Rochester, 1679; satirised Shaftesbury in 'Absalom and Achitophel,' 1681; published 'The Medal,' a satire on the ignoramus of the grand jury at Shaftesbury's trial, 1682; lampooned his detractor, Shadwell, in 'Mac Flecknoe,' 1682; revised the whole of the second part of 'Absalom and Achitophel,' 1682; defended Anglicanism in his poem 'Religio Laici,' 1682; collector of customs in the port of London, 1683; panegyrised Charles II in 'Albion and Albanius' and 'King Arthur,' two operas, 1685; converted to Roman catholicism, 1686; employed by James II to answer Stillingfleet; published 'The Hind and the Panther,' 1687; deprived of the laureateship, 1689; finished his career as a playwright with 'Love Triumphant,' a tragi-comedy, 1694; translated Juvenal and Persius, 1693; published a translation of Virgil which pleased the public, but was sharply criticised by Swift and Bentley, 1697; wrote 'Alexander's Feast' for a London musical society, 1697; published 'Fables, Ancient and Modern,' 1700. [xvi. 64]

DRYDEN, JOHN (1668–1701), writer; second son of John Dryden (1631–1700) [q. v.]; educated at Westminster and University College, Oxford; died at Rome; translated Juvenal's fourteenth satire for his father's version, and wrote one mediocre comedy. [xvi. 73]

DRYSDALE, JOHN (1718–1788), Scottish divine; entered Edinburgh University, 1732; presented to Lady Yester's Church, Edinburgh, 1762; D.D. Marischal College, Aberdeen, 1765; minister of the Tron Church, Edinburgh, 1767; royal chaplain; principal clerk of the general assembly, 1785; friend of Adam Smith [q. v.] [xvi. 75]

DUANE, MATTHEW (1707–1785), coin collector, antiquary, and conveyancer; F.R.S. and F.S.A.; published 'Explication de quelques Medailles Pheniciennes du Cabinet de M. Duane,' 1774. [xvi. 76]

DUBHDALETHE (d. 1064), primate (comharb) of Armagh, 1049; made war on the abbot of Clonard, 1055; wrote 'Annals of Ireland,' adopting chronology of the Christian era. [xvi. 76]

DUBOIS, CHARLES (d. 1740), treasurer to the East India Company; cultivated exotics at Mitcham, Surrey; contributed observations to the third edition of Ray's 'Synopsis,' 1724. [xvi. 77]

DU BOIS, LADY DOROTHEA (1728–1774), authoress; daughter of Richard Annesley, sixth earl of Anglesey [q. v.], who repudiated his marriage and disinherited his children, 1740; married Du Bois, a French musician,

1752; exposed her father's heartlessness in 'Poems by a Lady of Quality,' 1764; published 'Theodora' (novel), 1770, and 'The Lady's Polite Secretary,' 1772. [xvi. 77]

DU BOIS, EDWARD (1622–1699?), painter; brother of Simon Du Bois [q. v.]; studied antiques in Italy, and executed some works for Charles Emmanuel, duke of Savoy; painted landscapes and historical subjects. [xvi. 80]

DU BOIS, EDWARD (1774–1850), wit and man of letters; barrister, Inner Temple, 1809; conducted the 'European Magazine,' and edited the 'Lady's Magazine' and the 'Monthly Mirror'; friend of Sir Philip Francis [q. v.]; assistant judge in the court of requests; treasurer and secretary of the Metropolitan Lunacy Commission, 1833–46. His works include tales, verses, and a satire on Sir John Carr's travels, entitled 'My Pocket-book,' 1807, which led Carr to bring against him a lawsuit which failed, 1808. [xvi. 78]

DU BOIS, SIMON (d. 1708), painter; of Dutch or Flemish origin; took to painting cattle pictures after a course of instruction from Wouvermans; sold many of his pictures as the works of the great masters; came to England as a portrait-painter, 1685; befriended by Lord-chancellor Somers. Among his sitters were Archbishop Tenison and William Bentinck, first earl of Portland. [xvi. 79]

DU BOSC, CLAUDE (1682–1745?), engraver; born in France; temporarily assisted (Sir) Nicholas Dorigny [q. v.] in engraving the cartoons of Raphael at Hampton Court, 1712; engraved plates illustrative of the battles of Marlborough and Prince Eugene, 1714–17. [xvi. 80]

DUBOURDIEU, ISAAC (1597?–1692?), French protestant minister at Montpellier; minister of the Savoy Chapel, London; published 'A Discourse of Obedience unto Kings and Magistrates,' 1684. [xvi. 80]

DUBOURDIEU, JEAN (1642?–1720), French protestant minister; son of Isaac Dubourdieu [q. v.]; pastor at Montpellier; argued with Bossuet on mariolatry, 1682; Duke of Schomberg's chaplain at the battle of the Boyne, 1690; chaplain to his son, Duke Charles, at Marsiglia, 1693; pastor of the French church in the Savoy; published 'An Historical Dissertation upon the Theban Legion,' 1696. [xvi. 81]

DUBOURDIEU, JEAN ARMAND (d. 1726), controversialist; son or nephew of Jean Dubourdieu [q. v.]; pastor of the Savoy French church; rector of Sawtrey-Moynes, 1701; cited before the bishop of London for lampooning Louis XIV, 1713; published pamphlets and sermons. [xvi. 81]

DUBOURG, GEORGE (1799–1882), author of 'The Violin, being an account of that leading Instrument and its most eminent Professors,' 1836; grandson of Matthew Dubourg [q. v.] [xvi. 81]

DUBOURG, MATTHEW (1703–1767), violinist; played a solo at the Lincoln's Inn Fields Theatre, 1715; master of the viceroy of Ireland's band, 1728–67; played at Handel's Oratorio concerts at Covent Garden, 1741 and 1742; on one occasion loudly applauded by Handel; master of George II's band, 1752. [xvi. 81]

DUBRICIUS (in Welsh DYFRIG), SAINT (d. 612), reputed founder of the bishopric of Llandaff. The twelfth century 'Lectiones de vita Sancti Dubricii' describe him as founder of a university at Henllan on the Wye, and grandson of Pebiau, a British king. Geoffrey of Monmouth fabulously states that he crowned Arthur king of Britain and was archbishop of Caerleon. [xvi. 82]

DUBTHACH MACCU LUGIR (5th cent.), chief poet and brehon of Laogaire, king of Ireland; baptised by St. Patrick; author of three poems on Leinster history preserved in the 'Book of Leinster' and a poem in the 'Book of Rights'; one of the nine who drew up the 'Senchus Mor' code (completed A.D. 441). [xvi. 83]

DUCAREL, ANDREW COLTEE (1713–1785), civilian and antiquary; born in Normandy; scholar at Eton and gentleman commoner, St. John's College, Oxford; D.C.L., 1742; member of the College of Advocates, 1743; commissary and official of the city and diocese of Canterbury, 1758; F.S.A., 1737; F.R.S., 1762; keeper of the Lambeth library from 1757 until his death; arranged the archives of the state paper office (1763) and augmentation office;

made frequent antiquarian tours. Among his printed works is 'A Tour through Normandy,' 1754. He left in MS. 'Testamenta Lambethana (1312-1636).' [xvi. 84]

DUCHAL, JAMES (1697-1761), Irish presbyterian divine; M.A. Glasgow College; leader of the non-subscribing presbyterians in Antrim, 1730; D.D. Glasgow, 1753; renowned as a liberal thinker and sermon-writer. [xvi. 86]

DUCIE, second EARL OF (1802-1853). [See MORETON, HENRY JOHN REYNOLDS-.]

DUCK, SIR ARTHUR (1580-1648), civilian; B.A. Exeter College, Oxford, 1599; M.A. Hart Hall, 1602; fellow of All Souls', 1604; LL.D., 1612; advocate at Doctors' Commons, 1614; M.P., Minehead, 1624 and 1640; chancellor of the diocese of London, c. 1628; chancellor of Bath and Wells, 1635; pleaded an ecclesiastical case on behalf of Laud, 1633; master in chancery, 1645; published a Latin 'Life of Chichely,' 1617. A book by him on Roman civil law appeared 1653. [xvi. 87]

DUCK, SIR JOHN, first baronet (d. 1691), mayor of Durham; mayor, 1680; created baronet, 1686; his prosperity said to have been prognosticated by a raven dropping a gold Jacobus at his feet. [xvi. 88]

DUCK, NICHOLAS (1570-1628), lawyer; entered Exeter College, Oxford, 1584; barrister of Lincoln's Inn; governor of the Inn, 1615-28; recorder of Exeter, 1618. [xvi. 88]

DUCK, STEPHEN (1705-1756), poet; agricultural labourer in Wiltshire; made yeoman of the guard by Queen Caroline, 1733; published 'Poems on Several Occasions,' 1736; rector of Byfleet, 1752; wrote, in imitation of Denham, 'Cæsar's Camp on St. George's Hill,' 1755; drowned himself in a fit of dejection. [xvi. 89]

DUCKENFIELD, ROBERT (1619-1689), colonel in the parliamentarian army; defeated at Stockport bridge, 1644; governor of Chester, 1650; reduced the Isle of Man, when governor designate, 1651; M.P., Cheshire, 1653; assisted in suppressing Sir George Booth's 'Cheshire Rising,' 1659; imprisoned, 1665-c. 1667. [xvi. 89]

DUCKET, ANDREW (d. 1484). [See DOKET.]

DUCKETT, GEORGE (d. 1732), author; M.P., Calne, 1705, 1708, and 1722; commissioner of excise, 1722-32; issued, perhaps in conjunction with Sir Thomas Burnet (1694-1753) [q. v.], 'Homerides,' an unfavourable criticism of Pope's 'Iliad,' 1715; published 'A Summary of all the Religious Houses in England and Wales' (anonymous), 1717. [xvi. 90]

DUCKETT, JAMES (d. 1601), bookseller; hanged for having Roman catholic books in his possession. [xvi. 91]

DUCKETT, JOHN (1613-1644), Roman catholic priest; educated at the English college, Douay; missioner in Durham; executed by the parliamentarians. [xvi. 91]

DUCKETT, WILLIAM (1768-1841), United Irishman; contributor to the revolutionary 'Northern Star'; outlawed by the Irish parliament; settled in Paris (1796), where he was regarded with unfounded suspicion by Wolfe Tone; professor at the resuscitated college Sainte-Barbe, Paris, c. 1803; issued a 'Nouvelle Grammaire Anglaise,' 1828. [xvi. 92]

DUCKWORTH, SIR JOHN THOMAS, first baronet (1748-1817), admiral; left Eton, and served as a volunteer at the battles of Lagos Bay and Quiberon Bay, 1759; lieutenant, 1771; flag-captain to Rear-admiral Sir Joshua Rowley in Jamaica, 1780; officially mentioned by Howe after action off Ushant, 1794; rear-admiral of the white, 1799; took possession of St. Bartholomew, St. Thomas, and other Swedish and Danish possessions in West Indies, 1801; K.B., 1801; commander-in-chief at Jamaica, 1803-1805; acquitted by court-martial of the charge of using the frigate Acasta as a private merchantman, 1805; completely defeated French squadron off San Domingo, 1806; sent to dictate conditions at Constantinople, but prevented by local circumstances from approaching within eight miles of the city, 1807; governor and commander-in-chief of Newfoundland, 1810-13; admiral, 1810; created baronet, 1813. [xvi. 92]

DUCKWORTH, RICHARD (fl. 1695), author of works on campanology; M.A. New Inn Hall, Oxford, 1653; B.D.

and fellow of Brasenose; rector of Steeple Aston, Oxfordshire, 1679; principal of St. Alban Hall, 1692. [xvi. 96]

DUCROW, ANDREW (1793-1842), equestrian performer; son of a Flemish 'strong man'; chief equestrian at Astley's, 1808; pantomimist at the Royal Circus, St. George's Fields, 1813; travelled professionally through France and Flanders; produced spectacles at Drury Lane, 1833; patronised by William IV. [xvi. 96]

DUDGEON, WILLIAM (fl. 1765), philosophical writer. [xvi. 97]

DUDGEON, WILLIAM (1753?-1813), poet and farmer; author of 'The Maid that tends the Goats' and other songs; commended by Robert Burns. [xvi. 97]

DUDHOPE, VISCOUNTS. [See SCRYMGEOUR, JOHN, d. 1643; SCRYMGEOUR, JAMES, second VISCOUNT, d. 1644; SCRYMGEOUR, JOHN, third VISCOUNT, d. 1668.]

DUDLEY, first EARL OF (1781-1833). [See WARD, JOHN WILLIAM.]

DUDLEY, ALICE, DUCHESS DUDLEY (d. 1669), wife of Sir Robert Dudley (1573-1649) [q. v.]; deserted by her husband, 1605; created Duchess Dudley in her own right, 1645. [xvi. 112]

DUDLEY, AMBROSE, EARL OF WARWICK (1528?-1590), third son of John Dudley, duke of Northumberland [q. v.]; knighted, 1549; convicted of treason for supporting his sister-in-law, Lady Jane Grey, but pardoned, 1554; assisted Spaniards at siege of St. Quentin, 1557; master of the ordnance, 1560; succeeded his father as Earl of Warwick, 1561; sent to help the protestants of Havre, 1562; expelled the inhabitants of Havre, his life being threatened; besieged in Havre, Prince Condé having come to terms with the catholics, 1563; capitulated, 1563; M.A. Cambridge, 1564; D.C.L. Oxford, 1566; privy councillor, 1573; lieutenant of the order of the Garter, 1575; took part in the trial of Mary Queen of Scots, who appealed to his sense of justice, 1586. [xvi. 97]

DUDLEY, LADY AMYE, (1532?-1560), née Robsart; married Robert Dudley, afterwards earl of Leicester, 1550; found dead at the foot of a staircase in Cumnor Hall, Oxfordshire, where she was residing; her death probably due to suicide, though laid by common report to Leicester's charge. [xvi. 112]

DUDLEY, SIR ANDREW (d. 1559), adherent of Lady Jane Grey; son of Edmund Dudley [q. v.]; admiral of the northern seas, 1547; knighted, 1547; keeper of the palace of Westminster and captain of Guisnes; K.G., 1553; condemned for supporting Lady Jane Grey, but set at liberty, 1555. [xvi. 101]

DUDLEY, DUD (1599-1684), ironmaster; summoned from Balliol College, Oxford, to superintend his father's ironworks at Pensnet, Worcestershire, 1619; first to use pit-coal successfully in smelting iron ore; patentee, 1619 and 1639; colonel under Charles I; general of the ordnance to Prince Maurice; condemned, but not executed, 1648; published 'Metallum Martis,' 1665. [xvi. 99]

DUDLEY, EDMUND (1462?-1510), statesman and lawyer; student at Oxford, 1478; studied law at Gray's Inn; privy councillor, 1485?; under-sheriff of London, 1497; associated Sir Richard Empson [q. v.] with himself in work of rearranging taxes and feudal dues under Henry VII; speaker in the House of Commons, 1504; suspected of corruption; argued for absolute monarchy in his 'Tree of Commonwealth' (privately printed, 1859); executed on a charge of constructive treason, 1510, in consequence of his having bidden his friends arm themselves in the event of Henry VII's death. [xvi. 100]

DUDLEY, EDWARD, fourth BARON DUDLEY (d. 1586); served in Ireland (1536) and Scotland (1546); knighted, 1553; lieutenant of Hampnes, Picardy, 1556-8; entertained Queen Elizabeth at Dudley Castle, 1575. [xvi. 108]

DUDLEY, LORD GUILDFORD (d. 1554), husband of Lady Jane Grey; fourth son of John Dudley, duke of Northumberland [q. v.]; married to Lady Jane Grey in accordance with the self-aggrandising policy of Northumberland, 1553; beheaded, 1554. [xvi. 102]

DUDLEY, LORD HENRY (1531?-1557), sixth son of John Dudley, duke of Northumberland; arrested for complicity in his father's conspiracy, 1553; but pardoned, 1554; killed at battle of St. Quentin. [Suppl. ii. 160]

DUDLEY, SIR HENRY (d. 1565 ?), conspirator; son of John (Sutton) de Dudley, sixth baron Dudley; captain of guards at Boulogne, 1547; captain of the guard, 1550; captain of Guisnes, 1551; knighted, 1551; vice-admiral of the Narrow Seas, 1552; devised plot to rob exchequer, marry Princess Elizabeth to Courtenay, and depose Philip and Mary, 1556; proclaimed traitor in England, but received by French king, Henry II, and continued intrigues in France; probably returned to England before 1564, and died c. 1565. [Suppl. ii. 159]

DUDLEY, SIR HENRY BATE, first baronet (1745–1824), journalist; curate of Hendon, c. 1773; editor of the 'Morning Post'; started the 'Morning Herald,' 1780; nicknamed the 'Fighting Parson'; imprisoned, 1781, for libel on Duke of Richmond; bought the advowson of Bradwell-juxta-Mare, Essex, 1781, but, in consequence of charges of simony, was never instituted; chancellor of Ferns, 1805; created baronet, 1813; prebendary of Ely, 1817; author of a satire, comic operas, and dramatic adaptations. [xvi. 102]

DUDLEY, HOWARD (1820–1864), wood engraver; wrote, printed, and engraved description of part of Sussex and Hants, 1835, and a similar work, 1836. [xvi. 104]

DUDLEY, LADY JANE, (1537–1554), commonly called LADY JANE GREY, daughter of Henry Grey, duke of Suffolk; Greek scholar and humanist; married to Lord Guildford Dudley [q. v.], in pursuance of plot for altering succession from Tudor to Dudley family, 1553; proclaimed queen, 1553; her short and unsought sovereignty ruined on the dispersion of the troops under her father-in-law, Northumberland, 1553; executed, after Wyatt's rebellion, 1554. [xvi. 105]

DUDLEY, JOHN (SUTTON) DE, sixth BARON DUDLEY (1401 ?–1487), statesman; regularly summoned to parliament from 1440 to 1487; viceroy of Ireland, 1428–30; employed on various diplomatic missions; K.G., 1451; taken prisoner by the Yorkists at the battle of St. Albans, 1455; received into favour by Edward IV. [xvi. 107]

DUDLEY, JOHN, DUKE OF NORTHUMBERLAND (1502?–1553), son of Edmund Dudley [q. v.]; knighted by the Duke of Suffolk in France, 1523; deputy-governor of Calais, 1538; warden of the Scottish marches, 1542; created Viscount Lisle; great admiral, 1542–7; privy councillor and K.G., 1543; led the assault on Boulogne, 1544; governor of Boulogne, 1544–6; joint-regent, acquiescing in Somerset's sole protectorate, 1547; created Earl of Warwick, and high chamberlain of England, 1547; defeated the Scots at Pinkie, 1547, and Ket's followers at Dussindale, 1549; created earl marshal and Duke of Northumberland, 1551; procured the execution of Somerset, 1552; chancellor of Cambridge University, 1552; obtained from Edward VI letters patent 'for the limitation of the crown,' and, with the same object of altering the succession, married his son, Lord Guildford Dudley [q. v.], to Lady Jane Grey, 1553; executed for resisting actively the succession of Mary to the throne, 1553; avowed himself a Roman catholic upon the scaffold. [xvi. 109]

DUDLEY, JOHN, LORD LISLE and EARL OF WARWICK (d. 1554), son of John Dudley, duke of Northumberland [q. v.]; master of the horse to Edward VI, 1552; condemned to death as a supporter of Lady Jane Grey, but pardoned, 1554. [xvi. 111]

DUDLEY, JOHN (1762–1856), miscellaneous writer; second wrangler, Clare College, Cambridge, 1785; fellow, 1787; tutor and M.A., 1788; vicar of Sileby, 1795–1856; chief works, 'Naology,' 1846, and 'The Anti-Materialist,' 1849. [xvi. 111]

DUDLEY, LETTICE, COUNTESS OF LEICESTER (1541 ?–1634), eldest daughter of Sir Francis Knollys [q. v.]; married as her first husband Walter Devereux, first earl of Essex [q. v.]; married as her second husband Robert Dudley, earl of Leicester, 1578. [xvi. 117]

DUDLEY, ROBERT, EARL OF LEICESTER (1532 ?–1588), Queen Elizabeth's favourite; fifth son of John Dudley, duke of Northumberland [q. v.]; knighted in Edward VI's reign; married Amye Robsart, 1550 [see DUDLEY, AMYE, LADY]; M.P., Norfolk, 1553; proclaimed his sister-in-law, Lady Jane, at King's Lynn, 1553; par-

doned by Queen Mary for supporting Lady Jane, 1554; master of the ordnance before St. Quentin, 1557; K.G. and privy councillor, 1559; favourite of Queen Elizabeth, who, to encourage him, affected to disdain the suit of the Archduke Charles, 1560; supposed by some, including the author of 'Leicester's Commonwealth' (printed 1584), to have brought about the murder of his wife Amye, 1560; attempted, with the queen's consent, to obtain Spanish support for his projected marriage with Elizabeth at the price of acknowledging the papal supremacy, 1561; displeased Elizabeth by his presumptuous behaviour, 1563; high steward of Cambridge University, 1562; created Baron Denbigh and Earl of Leicester, 1564; his efforts for the hand of Elizabeth opposed by Cecil and the nobility; chancellor of Oxford University, 1564; induced by his dislike of Cecil to abet the rebellion of the northern earls, 1569; secretly married Lady Sheffield, 1573, whose husband he was said to have poisoned; entertained the queen with masques at Kenilworth, 1575; took part in Drake's expedition, 1577; married Lettice Knollys, countess of Essex [see DUDLEY, LETTICE], 1578; charged by Elizabeth with being in league with the Prince of Orange, an imputation which he admitted, 1581; suggested association for the protection of the queen's person, 1584; commanded expedition to assist United Provinces against Spain, 1585, and was chosen absolute governor, 1586; allowed by Elizabeth, after some insincere manifestations of displeasure, to remain in the post; carried on an indecisive campaign against the Spaniards; finally recalled, 1587; died 'of a continual fever,' or, according to some authorities, of poison, 1588. Roger Ascham credits him with literary taste. He showed interest in the drama. [xvi. 112]

DUDLEY, SIR ROBERT, styled DUKE OF NORTHUMBERLAND and EARL OF WARWICK (1574–1649), naval commander and inventor; son of Robert Dudley, earl of Leicester [q. v.]; entered Christ Church, Oxford, 1587; explored Guiana, 1594; knighted by Essex at Cadiz, 1596; repudiated his marriage with Alice Leigh, 1605, and settled at Florence with one Elizabeth Southwell; refused to return and answer a charge of having assumed the title of Earl of Warwick, 1607; suggested the building of a new class of warships, called Gallizabras, for the English navy, 1612; created Earl of Warwick, and Duke of Northumberland in the Holy Roman Empire, 1620; drained the morass between Pisa and the sea; died at Villa Castello, the gift of Cosmo II, duke of Tuscany. Chief work, 'Dell' Arcano del Mare,' dealing with naval architecture, navigation, and kindred subjects, published 1646 and 1647. [xvi. 122]

DUDLEY, THOMAS (fl. 1670–1680), engraver; executed etchings representing the life of Æsop, 1678, and portraits of John IV and Peter II of Portugal. [xvi. 124]

DUDLEY, WILLIAM (d. 1483), bishop of Durham; son of John (Sutton) de Dudley, sixth baron [q. v.]; M.A. University College, Oxford, 1457; prebendary of St. Paul's, 1468–73; dean of Windsor, 1473; prebendary of Wells, 1476; bishop of Durham, 1476; chancellor of Oxford University, 1483. [xvi. 124]

DUESBURY, WILLIAM (1725–1786), china manufacturer; learnt the art of making china figures from Andrew Planché, a French refugee; founded the Derby ceramic industry. [xvi. 125]

DUESBURY, WILLIAM (1763–1796), china manufacturer; son of William Duesbury (1725–1786) [q. v.]; proprietor of the Duesbury China Works, Derby. [xvi. 125]

DUFF (Dubh, the Black) (d. 967), king of Celtic Alban (Scotland); killed at Forres, fighting against the usurper Colin. There is a legend that the sun did not shine till his body was found and buried. [xvi. 125]

DUFF, ALEXANDER (1806–1878), missionary; studied at St. Andrews; opened mission school at Calcutta, 1830; encouraged by Lord William Cavendish Bentinck [q. v.], governor-general; wrote against Lord Auckland's policy of making a compromise between 'Orientalist' and European education for India, 1839; chairman of the general assembly of the Free church, 1851; D.D. Aberdeen; LL.D. New York, 1854; condemned Canning's policy in 'The Indian Mutiny: its Causes and Results,' 1858; assisted in framing the constitution of Calcutta University; founded missionary chair in New College,

Edinburgh; first missionary professor; published pamphlets on the church of Scotland and higher education in India. [xvi. 125]

DUFF, ANDREW HALLIDAY (1830-1877). [See HALLIDAY.]

DUFF, JAMES, second EARL OF FIFE (1729-1809); M.P. for Banff, 1754, 1761, 1768, 1774, and 1780, for Elgin county, 1784; created Baron Fife, 1790; lord-lieutenant of county Banff; did much for the improvement of agriculture and cattle-breeding. [xvi. 128]

DUFF, SIR JAMES (1752-1839), general; lieutenant and captain, grenadier guards, 1775; knighted, 1779; major-general, 1794; received command of Limerick district, 1797; kept Limerick quiet during insurrection of 1798; general, 1809. [xvi. 129]

DUFF, JAMES, fourth EARL OF FIFE (1776-1857), Spanish general; volunteered to help the Spaniards against Napoleon; fought at Talavera as major-general in the Spanish service, 1809; fourth Earl of Fife in Scottish peerage, 1811; M.P., Banffshire, 1818; created Baron Fife in British peerage and K.T., 1827. [xvi. 129]

DUFF, JAMES GRANT (1789-1858), historian; educated at Marischal College, Aberdeen; East India cadet, 1805; adjutant and Persian interpreter, Bombay grenadiers; assistant to Mountstuart Elphinstone [q. v.], resident of Poona; served against the Peishwa Bajee Rao; resident of Sattara, 1818-22; published in Scotland a 'History of the Mahrattas,' 1826. [xvi. 130]

DUFF, ROBERT (d. 1787), vice-admiral; when senior officer of a squadron on the south coast of Bretagne, drew the French into the main body of the English fleet, the battle of Quiberon Bay ensuing, 1759; commander-in-chief at Newfoundland, 1775-7; vice-admiral, 1778; co-operated at siege of Gibraltar, 1779. [xvi. 131]

DUFF, SIR ROBERT WILLIAM, for some time styled ROBERT WILLIAM DUFF ABERCROMBY (1835-1895), governor of New South Wales; entered navy, 1848, and was commander, 1865; liberal M.P. for Banffshire, 1861-93; junior lord of treasury and liberal whip, 1882-5; junior lord of admiralty, 1886; privy councillor, 1892; G.C.M.G. and governor of New South Wales, 1893-5.

[Suppl. ii. 160]

DUFF, WILLIAM (1732-1815), miscellaneous writer; M.A.; appointed to the ministry of various parishes by the Scottish presbytery; father of the 'ynod; published 'An Essay on Original Genius,' 1767, and 'Rhedi,' an oriental tale, 1773, and ethical writings. [xvi. 131]

DUFF-GORDON, LUCIE or LUCY, LADY (1821-1869), author and translator; only child of John Austin (1790-1859) [q. v.]; married Sir A. C. Duff-Gordon, bart., 1840; their house in London a rendezvous for English and foreign celebrities; lived in Egypt from 1862 and died at Cairo; translated Niebuhr's 'Ancient Greek Mythology' (1839), Meinhold's 'Mary Schweidlet' (1844), Ranke's 'Memoirs of the House of Brandenburg' (1847), and 'Ferdinand I and Maximilian II' (1853), and Moltke's 'Russians in Bulgaria' (1854); edited Van Sybel's 'History of the Crusades' (1861); published 'Letters from Egypt.'

[xxii. 220]

DUFFERIN, LADY (1807-1867). [See SHERIDAN, HELEN SELINA.]

DUFFET, THOMAS (fl. 1678), dramatist; travestied contemporary plays, including Dryden and D'Avenant's alteration of Shakespeare's 'Tempest,' 1675. [xvi. 132]

DUFFIELD, ALEXANDER JAMES (1821-1890), Spanish scholar; engaged as mining chemist in Bolivia and Peru; travelled widely in Spain and in various parts of the world; published a valuable translation of 'Don Quixote,' 1881, and other writings, including novels and works relating to his travels. [Suppl. ii. 161]

DUFFIELD, WILLIAM (1816-1863), still-life painter; studied at the Royal Academy, and worked under Baron Wappers at Antwerp. [xvi. 132]

DUFFY, EDWARD (1840-1868), Fenian leader in Connaught; sentenced to fifteen years' penal servitude, 1867. [xvi. 132]

DUFIEF, NICOLAS GOUÏN (1776?-1834), French teacher; native of Nantes; served under Count d'Hector,

1792; emigrated to America, 1793; taught French in America and England; chief work, 'Nature displayed in her Mode of teaching Language to Man,' 1818.

[xvi. 132]

DUGARD, SAMUEL (1645?-1697), divine; scholar of Trinity College, Oxford, 1662; fellow and M.A., 1667; rector of Forton; prebendary of Lichfield, 1697; published ethical writings. [xvi. 133]

DUGARD, WILLIAM (1606-1662), schoolmaster; M.A. Sidney Sussex College, Cambridge, 1630; master of Stamford (1630), and Colchester grammar schools, 1637-1643; head-master of Merchant Taylors', 1644-50; dismissed and imprisoned by council of state for printing Salmasius's 'Defensio regia pro Carolo primo,' 1650; reinstated by Bradshaw, 1650; dismissed by the governors, 1661; published works on Latin and Greek. [xvi. 133]

DUGDALE, JOHN (1628-1700), herald; son of Sir William Dugdale [q. v.]; Norroy herald, and knighted, 1686; wrote continuation of his father's autobiography, first published in 1827. [xvi. 142]

DUGDALE, RICHARD (fl. 1697), Surey demoniac; enabled by his liability to hysterical fits to pose as a prophet. [xvi. 134]

DUGDALE, STEPHEN (1640?-1683), informer; steward to Lord Aston at Tixall, Staffordshire, 1677; intimate with Romanist priests; speciously pretended knowledge of the 'Popish plot,' 1678; appeared against his old associate, Stephen College [q. v.], 1681. [xvi. 135]

DUGDALE, SIR WILLIAM (1605-1686), Garter king-of-arms; employed by Sir Symon Archer [q. v.], to collect material for a history of Warwickshire; Rouge Croix pursuivant, 1639; commissioned to prepare drawings of monuments and armorial bearings in Westminster Abbey, St. Paul's, and other churches, 1641; accompanied Charles I to Oxford; M.A., 1642; Chester herald, 1644; brought out the first volume of 'Monasticon Anglicanum' conjointly with Roger Dodsworth [q. v.], 1655 (second volume, 1661); issued 'Antiquities of Warwickshire,' 1656; proclaimed Charles II at Coleshill, 1660; Norroy, 1660; produced a 'History of Imbanking and Drayning of divers Fenns and Marshes,' 1662, and 'Origines Juridiciales, 1666; brought out the third volume of 'Monasticon,' 1673; the 'Monasticon' admitted as circumstantial evidence in the courts at Westminster; Garter king-of-arms and knighted, 1677; published the 'Baronage of England,' 1675-6; correspondent of Sir Thomas Browne [q. v.] [xvi. 136]

DUGRÈS, GABRIEL (fl. 1643), grammarian; born at Saumur; Huguenot refugee, 1631; taught French at Cambridge, and subsequently at Oxford; best known by his 'Regulæ Pronunciandi,' 1652, and other works on French grammar. [xvi. 143]

DU GUERNIER, LOUIS (1677-1716), engraver; born in Paris; member of the Great Queen Street academy; assisted Claude du Bosc [q. v.] in engraving Marlborough's battles, 1714. [xvi. 143]

DUHIGG, BARTHOLOMEW THOMAS (1750?-1813), Irish legal antiquary; librarian to King's Inns, Dublin; assistant-barrister for co. Wexford; wrote on the insolvent laws and (1805-6) the history of King's Inns.

[xvi. 143]

DUIGENAN, PATRICK (1735-1816), Irish politician; scholar of Trinity College, Dublin, 1756; M.A. and fellow, 1761-71; LL.D., 1765; called to Irish bar, 1767; king's counsel; king's advocate-general of the high court of admiralty of Dublin, 1785; vicar-general of Armagh, Meath, and Elphin; judge of the consistorial court of Dublin; M.P. for Old Leighlin in Irish House of Commons, 1790; privy councillor of Ireland; professor of civil law, Trinity College, Dublin; M.P. for the city of Armagh in the first united parliament, 1801; violently opposed catholic emancipation in Ireland. [xvi. 143]

DUKE, EDWARD (1779-1852), antiquary; M.A. Magdalen Hall, Oxford, 1807; Wiltshire magistrate; subsequently engaged in clerical work; fellow of the Linnean Society; F.S.A.; maintained the existence of 'a vast planetarium' on the Wiltshire downs in 'Druidical Temples of the County of Wilts,' 1846. [xvi. 144]

DUKE, RICHARD (1658-1711), poet and divine; educated at Westminster and Trinity College, Cambridge; M.A., 1682; fellow, 1683; prebendary of Gloucester, 1688;

chaplain to Dr. Jonathan Trelawney, 1707, who (1710) gave him the living of Witney ; queen's chaplain ; friend of Atterbury and Prior ; published occasional poems, including a satirical 'Panegyrick upon Oates ' and (1683) an 'Ode on the Marriage of Prince George of Denmark and the Lady Anne.' [xvi. 144]

DUMARESQ, PHILIP (1650 ?–1690), seigneur of Samarés, Jersey ; navy captain ; jurat of the royal court, 1681 ; presented James II with a manuscript account of the Channel islands, 1685 ; friend and correspondent of John Evelyn. [xvi. 145]

DU MAURIER, GEORGE LOUIS PALMELLA BUSSON (1834–1896), artist in black and white and novelist ; born in Paris, where he was educated ; studied chemistry at University College, London, 1851 ; studied art under Gleyre in Paris, 1856–7, and under De Keyser and Van Lerius at Antwerp, 1857–60 ; worked at book illustrations in London, 1860 ; contributed occasional drawings to 'Punch,' 1860 ; joined regular staff of 'Punch,' 1864, as successor to John Leech, and began literary contributions, in verse and prose, 1865 ; illustrated stories for 'Cornhill Magazine,' 1863–83. He published, in the first instance serially, in 'Harper's Magazine,' three novels, 'Peter Ibbetson' (1891), 'Trilby' (1894), and 'The Martian' (posthumously, 1896), the first two of which recorded numerous incidents in his own life ; 'Trilby' was dramatised and produced at the Haymarket, London, 1895. His artistic work for 'Punch' chiefly satirised middle-class society in the spirit of Thackeray. [Suppl. ii. 161]

DUMBARTON, EARL OF (1636 ?–1692). [See DOUGLAS, LORD GEORGE.]

DUMBLETON, JOHN OF (*fl.* 1340), schoolman ; of Dumbleton, Gloucestershire ; incumbent of Rotherfield Peppard, 1332–4 ; fellow of Queen's College, Oxford, 1341, also of Merton College ; left manuscripts including 'Summa Logicæ et Naturalis Philosophiæ.' [xvi. 146]

DUMBRECK, SIR DAVID (1805–1876), army medical officer ; licentiate of the Royal College of Surgeons, Edinburgh, 1825 ; M.D. Edinburgh, 1830 ; surgeon-major in the army, 1847–54 ; senior deputy inspector-general during the Russian war of 1854–5 ; inspector-general of the medical department, 1859–60 ; K.C.B., 1871. [xvi. 147]

DU MOULIN. [See MOULIN.]

DUN, LORD (1670–1758). [See ERSKINE, DAVID.]

DUN, SIR DANIEL (*d.* 1617). [See DONNE.]

DUN, FINLAY (1795–1853), musician ; educated at Edinburgh University ; first viola player at the San Carlo Theatre, Naples ; published solfeggi, 1829 ; edited collections of Scottish songs. [xvi. 147]

DUN, JOHN (1570 ?–1631). [See DOWNE.]

DUN, SIR PATRICK (1642–1713), Irish physician ; probably studied at Aberdeen and on the continent ; five times president, Dublin College of Physicians ; M.D. Dublin ; M.P. in Irish House of Commons for Killileagh, 1692, for Mullingar, 1695 and 1703 ; obtained new charter for Dublin College of Physicians, 1692 ; knighted, 1696 ; physician-general to the army, 1705 ; left money to found professorship of physic in Dublin College of Physicians ; his portrait painted by Kneller. [xvi. 148]

DUNAN or **DONAT** (1038–1074), first diocesan bishop of Dublin ; an Easterling ; founded Christ Church, Dublin, *c.* 1040. [xvi. 149]

DUNBAR, EARL OF (*d.* 1611). [See HOME, SIR GEORGE.]

DUNBAR, first VISCOUNT (*d.* 1645). [See CONSTABLE, HENRY.]

DUNBAR, AGNES, COUNTESS OF DUNBAR, called 'BLACK AGNES' (1312 ?–1369), daughter of Sir Thomas Randolph, first earl of Moray [q. v.] ; married Patrick, tenth earl of Dunbar [q. v.] ; spiritedly defended Dunbar Castle against the English, 1338, when her husband rebelled against Edward III. [xvi. 150]

DUNBAR, COLUMBA (1370 ?–1435), bishop of Moray ; grandson of Patrick and Agnes, earl and countess of Dunbar [q. v.] ; dean of St. Mary Magdalene, Bridgnorth, *c.* 1403 ; bishop of Moray, 1422 ; restored Elgin Cathedral. [xvi. 150]

DUNBAR, GAVIN (1455 ?–1532), bishop of Aberdeen ; dean of Moray, 1487 ; clerk register and privy councillor in Scotland, 1503 ; confirmed a league between Scotland and France, 1512 ; bishop of Aberdeen, 1518 ; imprisoned for his adherence to the regent Albany by the queen-mother, 1524 ; released, on the remonstrance of Pope Clement VII, 1524 ; completed Bishop Elphinstone's bridge across the Dee, and improved St. Machar's Cathedral. [xvi. 151]

DUNBAR, GAVIN (*d.* 1547), tutor of James V ; nephew of Gavin Dunbar (1455 ?–1532) [q. v.] ; educated at Glasgow University ; dean of Moray and tutor to James V ; archbishop of Glasgow, 1525–47 ; solicited Pope Clement VII for exemption from the jurisdiction of the archbishop of St. Andrews ; privy councillor, 1526 ; lord high chancellor, 1528–39 ; a lord of the regency, 1536 ; resigned the chancellorship to David Beaton, cardinal archbishop of St. Andrews [q. v.], 1539. [xvi. 151]

DUNBAR, GEORGE (1774–1851), classical scholar ; of humble origin ; M.A. and professor of Greek, Edinburgh, 1807–51 ; edited Herodotus, 1806–7 ; endeavoured to derive Sanscrit from Greek, 1827 ; compiled Greek lexicon, with E. H. Barker [q. v.], 1831. [xvi. 153]

DUNBAR, JAMES (*d.* 1798), philosophical writer ; 'regent' at King's College, Aberdeen, 1766 ; LL.D. ; wrote on primitive man, 1780. [xvi. 153]

DUNBAR, PATRICK, tenth EARL OF DUNBAR and second EARL OF MARCH (1285–1369), sheltered Edward II after the battle of Bannockburn, 1314 ; put himself under Edward III's protection, 1333 ; renounced his allegiance to Edward III, 1334 ; fought against English at Durham, 1338 ; rebelled against David II, king of Scotland, 1363 ; surrendered his earldoms to his son George, 1368. [xvi. 150]

DUNBAR, ROBERT NUGENT (*d.* 1866), poet ; wrote in verse of the West Indies, where he had resided. [xvi. 154]

DUNBAR, WILLIAM (1465 ?–1530 ?), Scottish poet ; possibly M.A. of St. Andrews ; wrecked off Zealand while carrying out a diplomatic mission for James IV ; for a time a Franciscan friar ; pensioned, 1500 ; accompanied embassy to negotiate marriage between James IV and Margaret Tudor ; wrote 'The Thrissill and the Rois,' his first great poem, in 1503 ; produced a satire, entitled 'The Dance of the Sevin Deidly Synnis,' between 1503 and 1508, 'The Goldyn Targe' (allegorical poem), and the 'Lament for the Makaris,' a magnificent elegy ; described Queen Margaret's visit (1511) to the North of Scotland in 'The Quenis Progress at Aberdeen' ; by some supposed to have fallen at Flodden (1513), by others to have written the 'Orisone' after 1517. [xvi. 154]

DUNBOYNE, BARON (*d.* 1800). [See BUTLER, JOHN.]

DUNCAN I (*d.* 1040), king of Scotland ; probably appointed king over the Strathclyde Welsh, *c.* 1018 ; his Cumbrian subjects harried by Eadulf, earl of the Northumbrians, 1038 ; made yearly progresses through Scotland to restrain oppression ; defeated and slain, some say assassinated, by Maelbaethe or Macbeth, mormaer of Moray. [xvi. 157]

DUNCAN II (*d.* 1094), king of Scotland ; eldest son of Malcolm Canmore ; released from captivity in Normandy and knighted by Robert, William I's son, 1087 ; supported by the Normans against the usurpation of his uncle, Donald Bane, but compelled, when conqueror, to dismiss his allies ; treacherously slain at Donald Bane's instigation. [xvi. 158]

DUNCAN, ADAM, VISCOUNT DUNCAN (1731–1804), admiral ; naval lieutenant, 1755 ; present at the blockade of Brest, 1759 ; commanded the Royal Exchange, a hired vessel, employed in petty convoy service, till it was put out of commission, 1759–60 ; helped to reduce Belle Isle, 1761, and Havana, 1762 ; sat on the court-martial on Keppel, with whom he showed much sympathy, and on that on Sir Hugh Palliser [q. v.], 1779 ; admiral, 1795 ; commander-in-chief in the North Sea, 1795–1801 ; prevented the mutiny of 1797 from extending to his flagship, the Venerable ; defeated the Dutch admiral, De Winter, off Camperdown, 1797 ; created Baron Duncan of Lundie and Viscount Duncan of Camperdown, 1797. [xvi. 159]

DUNCAN, ANDREW, the elder (1744–1828), physician and professor, Edinburgh University; M.A. St. Andrews, 1762; six times president of the Royal Medical Society; surgeon on board the East Indiaman, Asia, bound for China, 1768; M.D. St. Andrews, 1769; founder of the Royal Public Dispensary, Edinburgh (incorporated, 1818); instituted 'Medical and Philosophical Commentaries,' a quarterly journal, 1773; president of the Edinburgh College of Physicians, 1790 and 1824; professor of physiology, Edinburgh, 1790–1821; obtained charter for erecting public lunatic asylum in Edinburgh, 1807; published 'Elements of Therapeutics,' 1770, and other works. [xvi. 161]

DUNCAN, ANDREW, the younger (1773–1832), physician and professor, Edinburgh University; son of Andrew Duncan the elder [q. v.]; M.A. Edinburgh, 1793; M.D., 1794; studied on the continent; F.C.P. of Edinburgh; first professor of medical jurisprudence and medical police at Edinburgh, 1807–19; joint-professor with his father of the institute of medicine (physiology), 1819; professor of materia medica, 1821–32; discovered the isolability of cinchonin; published medical works. [xvi. 163]

DUNCAN, DANIEL (1649–1735), physician; born at Montauban; M.D. Montpellier, 1673; physician-general to the army before St. Omer; assisted the French refugees; professor of physic at Berlin and physician to Frederick I of Prussia, 1702–3; settled in England (1714), where he refused all fees; published iatro-chemical works. [xvi. 163]

DUNCAN, EDWARD (1804–1882), landscape-painter, etcher, and lithographer; exhibited at the Old Water-Colour Society, 1859 and 1860. [xvi. 165]

DUNCAN, ELEAZAR (d. 1660). [See DUNCON.]

DUNCAN, FRANCIS (1836–1888), colonel; M.A. Marischal College, Aberdeen, 1855; obtained commission in royal artillery, 1855; served in Nova Scotia and Canada, 1857–62; captain, 1864; major, 1874; instructor in gunnery at the repository, Woolwich, 1877; chairman of committee of management of Oxford military college, 1877; lieutenant-colonel, 1881; commanded Egyptian artillery, 1883–5; colonel and C.B., 1885; conservative M.P. for Holborn division of Finsbury, 1885 and 1886; LL.D. Aberdeen; D.C.L. Durham. [Suppl. ii. 166]

DUNCAN, HENRY (1774–1846), founder of savings banks; studied for two sessions at St. Andrews; minister of Ruthwell, Dumfriesshire, 1798–1846; brought Indian corn from Liverpool in a time of scarcity; instituted at Ruthwell the first savings bank, 1810; D.D. St. Andrews, 1823; discovered the Ruthwell runic cross; pointed out the footmarks of quadrupeds on the new red sandstone of Corncockle Muir; moderator of the general assembly, 1839; published 'The Sacred Philosophy of the Seasons,' 1835–6, and other works. [xvi. 165]

DUNCAN, JAMES MATTHEWS (1826–1890), physician; M.A. Marischal College, Aberdeen, 1843; M.D., 1846; assistant in Edinburgh to James Young Simpson [q. v.], 1847; F.R.C.P. Edinburgh, 1851; lectured on midwifery; physician for diseases of women in Edinburgh Royal Infirmary, 1861; obstetric physician at St. Bartholomew's Hospital, London, 1877; F.R.C.P. London, and F.R.S., 1883; published works relating principally to obstetrics. [Suppl. ii. 167]

DUNCAN, JOHN (1721–1808), miscellaneous writer; grandson of Daniel Duncan [q. v.]; educated at Merchant Taylors' School and St. John's College, Oxford; M.A., 1746; chaplain of the forces during the siege of St. Philip's, Minorca; D.D., 1757; incumbent of South Warnborough, 1763–1808; wrote 'Essays on Happiness' (verse) and on religious philosophy. [xvi. 166]

DUNCAN, JOHN (1805–1849), African traveller; sailed on the Niger expedition of 1842 as master-at-arms in the Albert; wounded by a poisoned arrow in the Cape de Verde isles; reached Adofidiah in Dahomey, 1845; published 'Travels in Western Africa in 1845 and 1846,' 1847; made vice-consul at Whydah, 1849, but died at sea on voyage out. [xvi. 166]

DUNCAN, JOHN (1796–1870), theologian; studied at Marischal College, Aberdeen; ordained to Milton Church, Glasgow, 1836; LL.D., 1840; appointed missionary to the Jews at Pesth, 1840; professor of oriental languages at New College, Edinburgh, 1843–70; edited Robinson's 'Lexicon of the Greek New Testament,' 1838. [xvi. 167]

DUNCAN, JOHN (1794–1881), weaver and botanist; apprenticed to a Drumlithie weaver; formed herbarium, which he presented to Aberdeen University, 1880; founded by will prizes for the encouragement of natural science in schools of the Vale of Alford. [xvi. 168]

DUNCAN, JOHN SHUTE (fl. 1831), writer; brother of Philip Bury Duncan [q. v.]; keeper of the Ashmolean Museum, Oxford, until 1826; chief work, 'Analogies of Organised Beings,' 1831. [xvi. 172]

DUNCAN, JONATHAN, the elder (1756–1811), governor of Bombay; resident and superintendent at Benares, 1788; first resident to combat infanticide at Benares; governor of Bombay, 1795–1811; instituted in the Bombay presidency the policy of recognising petty chieftains as sovereign princes. [xvi. 170]

DUNCAN, JONATHAN, the younger (1799–1865), currency reformer; son of Jonathan Duncan (1756–1811) [q. v.]; B.A. Trinity College, Cambridge, 1821; denounced S. J. Loyd's monetary system and the 'silly sophisms' of Peel in 'Jerrold's Weekly News.' His works include, 'The Religions of Profane Antiquity: . . . founded on Astronomical Principles,' 1830?, and 'The National Anti-Gold Law League,' 1847. [xvi. 170]

DUNCAN, MARK (1570?–1640), professor of philosophy in the university of Saumur; a native of Maxpoffle, Roxburghshire; M.D.; published 'Institutiones Logicæ,' 1612; irritated the clergy in his 'Discours de la Possession des Religieuses Ursulines de Loudun,' 1634, by ascribing to melancholia some reputed cases of demoniacal possession. [xvi. 171]

DUNCAN, MARK, who adopted the additional surname of DE CÉRISANTIS (d. 1648), diplomatist and Latin poet; son of Mark Duncan (1570?–1640) [q. v.]; agent of Richelieu at Constantinople, 1641; left the French for the Swedish service; Swedish ambassador resident in France, 1645; secretary to the Duke of Guise, 1647; mortally wounded in an engagement with the Spaniards, 1648. [xvi. 171]

DUNCAN, PETER MARTIN (1821–1891), geologist; M.B. London, 1846; practised at Colchester, 1848–60, and at Blackheath, 1860; professor of geology, King's College, London, 1870, and at Cooper's Hill College, c. 1871; F.G.S., 1849, secretary, 1864–70, and president, 1876–8; Wollaston medallist, 1881; F.Z.S., F.L.S.; F.R.S., 1868; made a special study of corals and echinids. [Suppl. ii. 168]

DUNCAN, PHILIP BURY (1772–1863), keeper of the Ashmolean Museum, Oxford; educated at Winchester and New College, Oxford; fellow of New College, 1792; M.A., 1798; called to the bar, 1796; keeper of the Ashmolean, 1826–55, in succession to his brother John Shute Duncan [q. v.]; honorary D.C.L., 1855; established at Bath and Oxford a savings bank and a society for the suppression of mendicity; published 'Reliquiæ Romanæ,' 1836. [xvi. 172]

DUNCAN, THOMAS (1807–1845), painter; studied at the Trustees' Academy, Edinburgh, eventually becoming head-master; professor of colour, and subsequently professor of drawing, to the Scottish Academy; A.R.A., 1843; exhibited portraits, genre pictures, and scenes from Scottish history at various institutions. [xvi. 172]

DUNCAN, WILLIAM (1717–1760), professor of philosophy at Aberdeen; M.A. Marischal College, Aberdeen, 1737; professor of natural and experimental philosophy, Marischal College, 1753–60; translated Cæsar's 'Commentaries,' 1753, and edited, with a translation, 'Cicero's Select Orations.' [xvi. 173]

DUNCAN, WILLIAM AUGUSTINE (1811–1885), journalist; studied at the Scots Benedictine College, Ratisbon, and the new Blairs College, Kincardine; emigrated to Sydney, New South Wales, 1838; editor of 'Australasian Chronicle,' a newly established Roman catholic journal, 1839–43; issued 'Duncan's Weekly Register of Politics, Facts, and General Literature,' 1843; collector of customs for New South Wales, 1859–81; C.M.G., 1881; translated a treatise of 1610 on Australia by Pedro Fernandes de Queiros, 1874. [xvi. 174]

DUNCANNON, BARONS. [See PONSONBY, JOHN WILLIAM, first BARON, 1781–1847; PONSONBY, FREDERICK GEORGE BRABAZON, third BARON, 1815–1895.]

DUNCANSON, ROBERT (*d.* 1705), colonel; second in command to Lieutenant-colonel James Hamilton; delegated conduct of Glencoe massacre, with which he was entrusted, to Captain Robert Campbell, 1692; colonel, 33rd regiment, 1705; fell before Valencia, 1705. [xvi. 174]

DUNCH, EDMUND (1657–1719), politician and bon-vivant; M.P., Cricklade, 1701–2, and 1705–13, Borough-bridge, 1713–15, and Wallingford, 1715–19; master of the royal household, 1708, 1714; member of the Kit-Cat Club. [xvi. 175]

DUNCKLEY, HENRY (1823–1896), journalist; studied for baptist ministry at Accrington, Lancashire; M.A. Glasgow, 1848; LL.D., 1883; baptist minister at Salford, 1848–55; editor of 'Manchester Examiner and Times' (liberal), 1855–89; contributed a number of letters, signed 'Verax,' on constitutional and political questions to 'Manchester Weekly Times' and 'Manchester Guardian,' successively, from 1877. [Suppl. ii. 169]

DUNCOMB, JOHN (1765–1839). [See DUNCUMB.]

DUNCOMBE, SIR CHARLES (*d.* 1711), banker and politician; apprenticed to Edward Backwell [q. v.], a London goldsmith; receiver of the customs under Charles II and James II, 1672; M.P. for Hedon, 1685–7; knighted, 1699; M.P., Downton, 1695–8, and 1702–11; opposed, for party reasons, the inception of the Bank of England; expelled from parliament, 1698, for having falsely endorsed certain exchequer bills; tried, and acquitted through a mistake in the information, 1699; knighted, 1699; nominated lord mayor, 1700 and 1701; elected, 1708; died the richest commoner in England. [xvi. 175]

DUNCOMBE, JOHN (1729–1786), miscellaneous writer; son of William Duncombe [q. v.]; M.A. Corpus Christi College, Cambridge, 1752; fellow of Corpus; held livings of St. Andrew and St. Mary Bredman, Canterbury; one of the six preachers of Canterbury Cathedral; wrote on Kentish archæology and other subjects. [xvi. 177]

DUNCOMBE, SUSANNA (1730?–1812), poetess and artist; *née* Highmore; wife of John Duncombe [q. v.]; wrote 'Fidelio and Honoria' for the 'Adventurer'; furnished a frontispiece to John Duncombe's 'Letters of John Hughes,' 1773, and contributed to the 'Poetical Calendar.' [xvi. 178]

DUNCOMBE, THOMAS SLINGSBY (1796–1861), radical politician; educated at Harrow; lieutenant, 1815; retired from the army, 1819; M.P. for Hertford, 1826, 1830, and 1831; radical M.P. for Finsbury, 1834; exerted himself in defence of Lord Durham, 1838; presented chartist petition, 1842; concerned in Prince Louis Napoleon's escape from Ham, 1846; member of council of 'Friends of Italy,' 1851; worked on behalf of Kossuth in the matter of the Hungarian notes, 1861. [xvi. 178]

DUNCOMBE, WILLIAM (1690–1769), miscellaneous writer; clerk in the navy office, 1706–25; part proprietor of 'Whitehall Evening Post'; wrote against the 'Beggar's Opera' as immoral, 1728, thereby gaining the friendship of Dr. (afterwards Archbishop) Herring; brought out 'Lucius Junius Brutus' at Drury Lane, 1734; reprinted a sermon (of Arbuthnot's) on the evil of rebellion, 1745; unsuspectingly compiled (1749) from the fraudulent lips of Archibald Bower [q. v.] a narrative of Bower's pretended 'escape' from the inquisition. [xvi. 180]

DUNCON, EDMUND (*d.* 1673), clergyman; brother of Eleazar Duncon [q. v.]; sent by Nicholas Ferrar [q. v.] to visit George Herbert in his last illness; promoted the publication of Herbert's 'A Priest to the Temple'; LL.B.; rector of Friern Barnet, Middlesex, 1663–73. [xvi. 181]

DUNCON, ELEAZAR (*d.* 1660), royalist divine; B.A. Caius College, Cambridge; fellow of Pembroke Hall, Cambridge, 1618; prebendary of Durham, 1628, of Winchester, 1629; D.D., 1633; prebendary of York, 1640; chaplain to Charles I; stripped of all his preferments by parliament; died at Leghorn. [xvi. 181]

DUNCON, JOHN (*fl.* 1648), biographer; brother of Eleazar Duncon [q. v.]; held a cure in Essex, *c.* 1645; wrote a religious biography of Lettice, viscountess Falkland, 1648. [xvi. 181]

DUNCON, SAMUEL (*fl.* 1600–1659), political writer; thrice distrained on for refusing to pay ship-money, 1640; 'damnified about 300*l.*' by the commissaries' court and the court of arches; high collector of assessments for the parliament; suggested in two tracts, 1651 and 1659, appointment of 'peacemakers' or public arbitrators as a means of lessening litigation. [xvi. 182]

DUNCUMB, JOHN (1765–1839), topographer; M.A. Trinity College, Cambridge, 1796; editor and printer of Pugh's 'Hereford Journal,' 1788–90; incumbent of various parishes; engaged (1790) by Charles, duke of Norfolk, to compile a history of Herefordshire (second volume completed, 1866, third volume issued [1882] by Judge W. H. Cooke); published a 'General View of the Agriculture of . . . . Hereford,' 1805. [xvi. 182]

DUNDAS, CHARLES, BARON AMESBURY (1751–1832), twice M.P. for Richmond; barrister; M.P. for Orkney and Shetland, 1781–4, and for Berkshire, 1794–1832; was nominated speaker in opposition to Abbot, but withdrew from the contest, 1802; created Baron Amesbury, 1832. [xvi. 183]

DUNDAS, SIR DAVID (1735–1820), general; lieutenant fireworker in the royal artillery, 1754; lieutenant, 56th regiment, 1756; present at the attack on St. Malo, the capture of Cherbourg, and the fight at St. Cas; served in Cuba, 1762; colonel, 1781; major-general, 1790; wrote drill-books which were issued as the official orders for the army; defeated the French at Tuyl, 1794; lieutenant-general, 1797; accompanied Duke of York to the Helder, 1799; general, 1802; K.B., 1804; commander-in-chief, 1809–11; privy councillor, 1809; tactician of Frederick the Great's school in his 'Principles of Military Movements, chiefly applicable to Infantry,' 1788. [xvi. 183]

DUNDAS, SIR DAVID (1799–1877), statesman; educated at Westminster and Christ Church, Oxford; student, 1820; M.A., 1822; barrister, Inner Temple, 1823; went the northern circuit; M.P., Sutherlandshire, 1840–52, and 1861–7; Q.C., 1840; knighted, 1847; judge-advocate-general and privy councillor, 1849. [xvi. 185]

DUNDAS, FRANCIS (*d.* 1824), general; son of Robert Dundas, Lord Arniston the younger [q. v.]; lieutenant and captain, 1st foot guards, 1778; surrendered with Cornwallis at York Town, 1781; took part as adjutant-general in capture of Martinique and Guadaloupe, 1794; acting governor of the Cape, 1798–9, and 1801–3; general, 1812. [xvi. 185]

DUNDAS, HENRY, first VISCOUNT MELVILLE (1742–1811), son of Robert Dundas, Lord Arniston the elder [q. v.]; educated at Edinburgh High School and University; member of the Faculty of Advocates, 1763; solicitor-general for Scotland, 1766; M.P. for Midlothian, 1774–90, except for few months in 1782 when he sat for Newtown, Isle of Wight; lord advocate, 1775–83; supported Powys's amendment for the repeal of the Massachusetts charter, 1778; lord rector of Glasgow University, 1781–3; carried resolution that Warren Hastings be recalled from India, 1782; privy councillor and treasurer of the navy, 1782–3 and 1784–1800; keeper of the Scottish signet, 1782; defended Hastings's Rohilla war, 1786; chancellor of St. Andrews, 1788; LL.D. Edinburgh, 1789; M.P., Edinburgh, 1790–1802; home secretary, 1791–4; president of the board of control, 1793–1801; spoke in support of the East India Company, 1793; secretary of war, 1794–1801; keeper of the privy seal of Scotland, 1800; planned and carried out the Egyptian campaign of 1801 against the opinion of Pitt and the king; created Viscount Melville of Melville, and Baron Dunira, 1802; first lord of the admiralty, 1804–5; erased from the roll of the privy council, 1805, and impeached, 1806, for malversation; guilty of negligence, but acquitted, 1806; restored to the privy council, 1807. [xvi. 186]

DUNDAS, HENRY, third VISCOUNT MELVILLE (1801–1876), general; son of Robert Saunders Dundas, second viscount Melville [q. v.]; captain, 83rd regiment, 1824; active in suppressing the Canadian rebellion, 1837; colonel and aide-de-camp to Queen Victoria, 1841; second in command at the capture of Multán, 1847; general, 1868; G.C.B., 1870. [xvi. 191]

DUNDAS, SIR JAMES, LORD ARNISTON (*d.* 1679), educated at St. Andrews; knighted, 1641; M.P., Edinburgh, 1648; member of committee of estates, 1648; lord of session as Lord Arniston, 1662–3; refused to renounce the covenant, and resigned, 1663. [xvi. 191]

DUNDAS, JAMES (1842–1879), captain, royal engineers; V.C. for distinguished bravery in storming a blockhouse in Bhootan, 1865; killed in attempt to blow up a fort near Cabul, 1879. [xvi. 192]

DUNDAS, SIR JAMES WHITLEY DEANS (1785–1862), admiral; commander in the Baltic, 1807; took the surname of Dundas, 1808; frequently sat for Greenwich after the passing of the Reform Bill; C.B., 1839; vice-admiral, 1852; remiss, when in command of the chief naval operations in the Russian war, 1854; G.C.B.; admiral, 1857. [xvi. 192]

DUNDAS, SIR RICHARD SAUNDERS (1802–1861), vice-admiral; son of Robert Saunders Dundas, second viscount Melville [q. v.]; educated at Harrow; navy captain, 1824; C.B. for his services in the first Chinese war, 1841; junior lord of the admiralty, 1853–61; commander-in-chief of the Baltic fleet, 1855–61; K.C.B., 1856; grand officer of the Legion of Honour; vice-admiral, 1858. [xvi. 193]

DUNDAS, ROBERT, LORD ARNISTON (d. 1726), ordinary lord of session; eldest son of Sir James Dundas (d. 1679) [q. v.]; M.P., Midlothian, 1700–2, and 1702–7; lord of session, 1689. [xvi. 193]

DUNDAS, ROBERT, LORD ARNISTON, the elder (1685–1753), judge; second son of Robert Dundas (d. 1726) [q. v.]; solicitor-general for Scotland, 1717–20; lord advocate, 1720; dean of the Faculty of Advocates, 1721; M.P., Midlothian, 1722–7, 1727–34, and 1734–7; chief adviser of Lord Ilay's opponents; lord president of session, 1748–53; re-introduced into Scottish juries the possible findings 'guilty' or 'not guilty' as against 'proven' or 'not proven,' 1728. [xvi. 194]

DUNDAS, ROBERT, LORD ARNISTON, the younger (1713–1787), judge; eldest son of Robert Dundas, Lord Arniston the elder [q. v.]; educated at Edinburgh University; studied Roman law at Utrecht; solicitor-general for Scotland, 1742–6; lord-advocate, 1754; M.P., Midlothian, 1754; lord-president of session, 1760; lost popularity by giving his casting vote against Archibald (Stewart) Douglas [q. v.] in the Douglas peerage case, 1767. [xvi. 195]

DUNDAS, ROBERT, OF ARNISTON (1758–1819), judge; son of Robert Dundas, Lord Arniston, the younger [q. v.]; solicitor-general for Scotland, 1784; lord advocate, 1789; M.P., Edinburghshire, 1790–6; chief baron of the exchequer in Scotland, 1801. [xvi. 195]

DUNDAS, ROBERT SAUNDERS, second VISCOUNT MELVILLE (1771–1851), statesman; son of Henry Dundas, first viscount [q. v.]; M.P., Hastings, 1794, Rye, 1796; keeper of the signet for Scotland, 1800; M.P., Midlothian, 1801; privy councillor, 1807; president of the board of control, 1807 and 1809; Irish secretary, 1809; first lord of the admiralty, 1812–27; chancellor of St. Andrews University, 1814; K.T., 1821. Melville Sound was so named in recognition of his interest in Arctic exploration. [xvi. 195]

DUNDAS, THOMAS (1750–1794), major-general; served as major 65th foot in America and the West Indies; M.P. for the stewartry of Orkney and Shetland, 1771, 1774, and 1784; joint-commissioner for arranging the capitulation at York Town, 1781; major-general, 1793; died at Guadaloupe after distinguished services in the West Indies, 1794. [xvi. 196]

DUNDAS, WILLIAM (1762–1845), politician; son of Robert Dundas, Lord Arniston, the younger [q. v.]; barrister, Lincoln's Inn, 1788; M.P. for Kirkwall, Wick, Dornoch, Dingwall, and Tain, 1796 and 1797; privy councillor, 1800; M.P., Sutherland, 1802 and 1806, Cullen, 1810, and Edinburgh, 1812–31; secretary-at-war, 1804–6; keeper of the signet, 1814; lord clerk register, 1821. [xvi. 197]

DUNDEE, first VISCOUNT (1649?–1689). [See GRAHAM, JOHN.]

DUNDONALD, EARLS OF. [See COCHRANE, SIR WILLIAM, first EARL, d. 1686; COCHRANE, ARCHIBALD, ninth EARL, 1749–1831; COCHRANE, THOMAS, tenth EARL, 1775–1860.]

DUNDRENNAN, LORD (1792–1851). [See MAITLAND, THOMAS.]

DUNFERMLINE, EARLS OF. [See SETON, SIR ALEXANDER, first EARL, 1555?–1622; SETON, CHARLES, second EARL, d. 1673.]

DUNFERMLINE, BARON (1776–1858). [See ABERCROMBY, JAMES.]

DUNGAL (fl. 811–827), Irish monk in deacon's orders; driven from Ireland by the Danish invasions; invited by Charlemagne (811) to explain two rumoured solar eclipses of 810; recognised as an authoritative teacher at Pavia in a capitular of Lothair, 823. [xvi. 197]

DUNGANNON, VISCOUNTS. [See TREVOR, MARCUS, first VISCOUNT of the first creation, 1618–1670; TREVOR, ARTHUR HILL-, third VISCOUNT of the second creation, 1798–1862.]

DUNGLISSON, ROBLEY (1798–1869), medical writer; M.D. Erlangen, 1824; professor in the university of Virginia, 1825–33; professor of the institutes of medicine in Jefferson Medical College, Philadelphia, 1836–68; published a 'Human Physiology,' a 'History of Medicine,' and other medical works. [xvi. 198]

DUNHAM, SAMUEL ASTLEY (d. 1858), historian; LL.D.; author of works published in Lardner's 'Cabinet Cyclopædia,' including (1832–3) a famous 'History of Spain and Portugal.' [xvi. 199]

DUNK, GEORGE MONTAGU, second EARL OF HALIFAX (1716–1771); educated at Eton and Trinity College, Cambridge; colonel, 1745; president of the board of trade, 1748–61; privy councillor, 1749; aided foundation of colony of Nova Scotia, the town of Halifax being thereupon named after him, 1749; styled the 'Father of the Colonies' for his success in extending American commerce; lieutenant-general, 1759; lord-lieutenant of Ireland, 1761–3; first lord of the admiralty, 1762; secretary of state, 1762; 'triumvir' with Lords Egremont and Grenville, 1763; K.G., 1764; lord privy seal, 1770; secretary of state, 1771. [xvi. 199]

DUNKARTON, ROBERT (fl. 1770–1811), engraver of portraits in mezzotint. [xvi. 201]

DUNKIN, ALFRED JOHN (1812–1879), antiquary and historian; son of John Dunkin [q. v.]; educated at the Military College, Vendôme; original member of the British Archæological Association; wrote on old English customs and the antiquities of Kent; printed and translated the works of Radulphus, abbot of Coggeshall, supposing himself the original editor, 1856. [xvi. 201]

DUNKIN, JOHN (1782–1846), topographer; original member of the British Archæological Association; published 'Outlines of the History and Antiquities of Bromley in Kent,' 1815, and other antiquarian works. [xvi. 202]

DUNKIN, WILLIAM (1709?–1765), poet; B.A. Trinity College, Dublin, 1729; D.D., 1744; received an annuity from Trinity College, Dublin, as stipulated in the will of his aunt, a benefactor of the college; ordained, 1735; master of Portora Royal School, Enniskillen, 1746–1765; friend of Swift; author of some clever poems in English and Latin, including 'Bœotia,' 1747, and 'Vindication of the Libel,' a poem attributed to Swift. [xvi. 203]

DUNLOP, ALEXANDER (1684–1747), Greek scholar; son of William Dunlop, the elder [q. v.]; professor of Greek in Glasgow University, 1706–42; published a Greek grammar, 1736. [xvi. 203]

DUNLOP, ALEXANDER COLQUHOUN-STIRLING-MURRAY- (1798–1870), church lawyer and politician; earnestly supported the 'non-intrusion' party in the church, which he professionally defended on all occasions; M.P., Greenock, 1852–68; carried bill abolishing Gretna Green marriages; attacked government of Lord Palmerston, 1861, for tampering with the despatches of Sir Alexander Burnes, envoy at the Afghan court in 1839; published a treatise on the law of Scotland relating to the poor, 1825, another on the law of patronage, 1833, and a third on parochial law. [xvi. 204]

DUNLOP, FRANCES ANNE WALLACE (1730–1815), friend of Robert Burns; née Wallace; married John Dunlop of Dunlop, Ayrshire, 1747; became a correspondent and friend of Burns on the publication of his 'Cottar's Saturday Night,' but afterwards deserted him. [xvi. 205]

DUNLOP, JAMES (d. 1832), of Dunlop, Ayrshire, lieutenant-general; accompanied the old 82nd foot to

Nova Scotia ; lieutenant, 1779 ; despatched to Charlestown with the news of seizure of Chesapeake estuary, 1781 ; subsequently stationed at Halifax ; served against Tippoo Sultan, 1791 ; lieutenant-colonel, 1795 ; commanded brigade at Sedaseer and at capture of Seringapatam, 1799 ; brigadier-general, 1805 ; M.P. for the stewartry of Kirkcudbright, 1813–26 ; commanded 5th division at Fuentes de Onoro, 1811 ; lieutenant-general, 1817. [xvi. 205]

DUNLOP, JAMES (1795–1848), astronomer ; keeper (1823–7) of the Brisbane observatory at Paramatta ; made most of the observations for the ' Brisbane Catalogue' of 7,385 southern stars (completed 1826) ; gold medallist of the Astronomical Society, 1828 ; F.R.A.S., 1828 ; the number of nebulæ claimed as his discoveries subsequently found to be greater than that actually existing ; director of the Paramatta observatory, 1829–42 ; author of ' An Account of Observations made in Scotland on the Distribution of the Magnetic Intensity,' 1830. [xvi. 206]

DUNLOP, JOHN (1755–1820), song-writer ; lord provost of Glasgow, 1796 ; collector of customs at Borrowstounness and subsequently at Port Glasgow ; author of the well-known lyrics ' Oh dinna ask me gin I lo'e ye' and ' Here's to the year that's awa.' [xvi. 207]

DUNLOP, JOHN COLIN (d. 1842), author ; son of John Dunlop [q. v.] ; advocate, 1807 ; sheriff depute of Renfrewshire, 1816–42 ; published a learned ' History of Fiction,' which was criticised with unwarranted severity by Hazlitt, 1814, a ' History of Roman Literature, from the earliest period to the Augustan Age,' 1823–8, and ' Memoirs of Spain during the Reigns of Philip IV and Charles II,' 1834. [xvi. 208]

DUNLOP, WILLIAM, the elder (1649 ?–1700), principal of Glasgow University ; emigrated to California, remaining there till 1688 ; minister of Ochiltree and afterwards of Paisley ; principal of Glasgow University, 1690 ; director of the Darien Company ; historiographer for Scotland, 1693. [xvi. 209]

DUNLOP, WILLIAM, the younger (1692–1720), professor of church history in Edinburgh University ; son of William Dunlop the elder [q. v.] ; licensed by the presbytery of Edinburgh, 1714 ; appointed by George I professor of divinity and church history, Edinburgh. [xvi. 209]

DUNLUCE, VISCOUNTS. [See MACDONNELL, Sir RANDAL, first VISCOUNT, d. 1636 ; MACDONNELL, RANDAL, second VISCOUNT, 1609–1683.]

DUNMORE, EARLS OF. [See MURRAY, LORD CHARLES, first EARL, 1660–1710 ; MURRAY, JOHN, fourth EARL, 1732–1809.]

DUNN, SIR DANIEL (d. 1617). [See DONNE.]

DUNN, ROBERT (1799–1877), surgeon ; licentiate of the Society of Apothecaries, 1825 ; F.R.C.S., 1852 ; contributed to medical and psychological reviews. [xvi. 210]

DUNN, SAMUEL (d. 1794), mathematician ; inventor of the ' universal planispheres, or terrestrial and celestial globes in plano,' 1757 ; master of an academy at Ormond House, Chelsea, 1758–63 ; mathematical examiner to the East India Company. His works include ' The Navigator's Guide to the Oriental or Indian Seas,' 1775, and ' The Astronomy of Fixed Stars,' part i. 1792. [xvi. 210]

DUNN, SAMUEL (1798–1882), expelled Wesleyan minister ; first Wesleyan minister in the Shetland islands, 1822 ; supposed to have taken part in the publication of the ' Fly Sheets,' pamphlets advocating reforms in the Wesleyan governing body, 1847 ; called upon to discontinue his monthly ' Wesley Banner and Revival Record,' and expelled for contumacy, 1849 ; D.D. of one of the United States universities. [xvi. 212]

DUNN, WILLIAM (1770–1849), mechanic and agriculturist ; proprietor of the Dalnotter Ironworks, 1813 ; built mills at Duntocher for cotton-spinning and weaving. [xvi. 213]

DUNNE, GABRIEL (d. 1558). [See DONNE.]

DUNNING, JOHN, first BARON ASHBURTON (1731–1783), barrister, Middle Temple, 1756 ; drew up a defence of the English East India Company against the Dutch, 1762 ; solicitor-general, 1768–70 ; M.P. for Calne in whig

interest, 1768 ; re-elected for Calne, 1774 ; carried a resolution that ' the influence of the crown has increased, is increasing, and ought to be diminished,' 1780 ; again returned for Calne, 1780 ; privy councillor, 1782 ; created Baron Ashburton of Ashburton, 1782 ; author of an ' Inquiry into the Doctrines lately promulgated concerning Juries, Libels, &c.,' 1764, which Horace Walpole considered ' the finest piece . . . written for liberty since Lord Somers.' [xvi. 213]

DUNRAVEN, third EARL OF (1812–1871). [See QUIN, EDWIN RICHARD WINDHAM WYNDHAM-]

DUNS, JOANNES SCOTUS, known as the DOCTOR SUBTILIS (1265 ?–1308 ?), schoolman ; said, without evidence, to have been fellow of Merton College, Oxford, and in 1301 professor of divinity at Oxford ; stated to have been 'regent' of Paris University ; nicknamed Doctor Subtilis ; possibly died at Cologne, there being a tradition that he was buried alive. Duns was the author of a philosophic grammar, entitled, ' De Modis Significandi sive Grammatica Speculativa ' (printed, 1499), of logical ' Quæstiones ' (edited, 1474), of a work on metaphysics called ' De Rerum Principio' (edited, 1497), and of the ' Opus Oxoniense,' (printed, 1481), a commentary on the ' Sententiæ ' of Peter Lombard. A conceptualist in logic, he borrowed from Ibn Gebirol (fl. 1045) the theory of a universal matter, the common basis of all existences, while in theology he denied the possibility of rationalism. [xvi. 216]

DUNSANY, ninth BARON (d. 1668). [See PLUNKET, PATRICK.]

DUNSINANE, LORD (1731 ?–1811). [See NAIRNE, SIR WILLIAM.]

DUNSTABLE, JOHN (d. 1453), musician and mathematician ; mentioned in the 'Proportionale' of Johannes Tinctoris (1445–1511) as the chief musician in England ; mentioned in a Seville manuscript of 1480 ; compiler of a manuscript collection of latitudes and longitudes, 1438. [xvi. 220]

DUNSTALL, JOHN (fl. 1644–1675), engraver ; published two drawing-books. [xvi. 221]

DUNSTAN, SAINT (924–988), archbishop of Canterbury ; educated by Irish scholars at Glastonbury Abbey ; favourite of King Æthelstan ; falsely accused of being a wizard, and expelled the court ; made his profession of monastic vows to Ælfheah, bishop of Winchester ; practised the arts of metal-working, painting, and transcription ; councillor of King Eadmund [see EDMUND], narrowly escaping a second dismissal on false charges ; abbot of Glastonbury c. 945 ; laid the foundation of a new church, and modified the constitution of the abbey, making it also a famous school ; treasurer and chief adviser of King Eadred [see EDRED] ; procured arrest of Wulfstan, archbishop of York and leader of the Danish insurgents, 952 ; rebuked King Edwy for leaving the coronation feast to visit a mistress ; retired to Flanders in disgrace, 956, Count Arnulf I assigning him a residence at Ghent ; appointed by Eadgar [see EDGAR] bishop of Worcester, 957 ; bishop of London, retaining Worcester, 959–61 ; archbishop of Canterbury, 961 ; concentrated his energies on making the Danes an integral part of the nation ; in company with Oswald, archbishop of York, crowned Eadgar at Bath, 973 ; imposed penance on Eadgar for incontinence ; sympathised with the Benedictine movement and the abolition of secular monasteries ; formulated ecclesiastical discipline in the ' Penitentiale ' ; averted civil war by crowning Eadward, 975 ; foretold to King Æthelred the calamities by which the nation would expiate the murder of Eadward. [xvi. 221]

DUNSTAN, alias KITCHIN, ANTHONY (1477–1563). [See KITCHIN.]

DUNSTAN, JEFFREY (1759 ?–1797), 'mayor' of Garrett ; brought up as a foundling ; dealer in old wigs ; elected, in 1785, mock mayor, according to custom, of the Garrett association for protecting Garrett common from encroachment ; successful at three successive elections. [xvi. 230]

DUNSTANVILLE, BARON (1757–1835). [See BASSET, FRANCIS.]

DUNSTER, CHARLES (1750–1816), miscellaneous writer ; B.A. Oriel College, Oxford, 1770 ; rural dean of

West Sussex; published works on the gospels and an attempt (1800) to demonstrate Milton's obligations to Josuah Sylvester [q. v.]   [xvi. 231]

DUNSTER, HENRY (*d.* 1659), president of Harvard College in Massachusetts; M.A. Magdalene College, Cambridge, 1634; emigrated to America, 1640; president of Harvard College, 1640, resigning (1654) as an anti-pædo-baptist; procured the Harvard charters of 1642 and 1650; revised Eliot's 'Bay Psalm-Book.'   [xvi. 231]

DUNSTER, SAMUEL (1675-1754), translator of Horace; educated at Merchant Taylors' School and Trinity College, Cambridge; M.A., 1700; D.D., 1713; prebendary of Salisbury, 1717-48, of Lincoln, 1720; vicar of Rochdale, 1722-54; author of 'Anglia Rediviva,' 1699; translated into mechanical verse 'The Satyrs and Epistles of Horace,' 1710, publishing a second edition, including the 'Art of Poetry,' 1717.   [xvi. 232]

DUNSTERVILLE, EDWARD (1796-1873), commander R.N. and hydrographer; second master of H.M.S. Valorous, 1824; completed survey of Mosquito coast, 1833-5; lieutenant in operations off Syria, 1840; hydrographer's assistant at the admiralty, 1842-70; produced 'Admiralty Catalogue of Charts, Plans, Views, and Sailing Directions,' 1860.   [xvi. 233]

DUNTHORN, WILLIAM (*d.* 1490), town clerk of London; fellow of Peterhouse, Cambridge, 1455; common clerk of London, 1461; compiled the extant 'Liber Dunthorn'; a devoted Yorkist.   [xvi. 233]

DUNTHORNE, JOHN (*fl.* 1783-1792), artist; of Colchester; exhibited small genre pictures at the Royal Academy, 1783-92; his son John was also an artist.
                                                     [xvi. 235]

DUNTHORNE, JOHN, the younger (1798-1832), painter; son of John Dunthorne the elder [q. v.]; assisted the painter John Constable [q. v.]; exhibited landscapes at the Royal Academy, 1827-32. [xvi. 234]

DUNTHORNE, JOHN, the elder (1770-1844), landscape-painter; friend of the painter John Constable [q. v.]   [xvi. 234]

DUNTHORNE, RICHARD (1711-1775), astronomer; butler of Pembroke Hall, Cambridge, and scientific assistant to Dr. Roger Long [q. v.]; worked on Long's 'Astronomy,' 1770; conducted a survey of the fens, when superintendent of the works of the Bedford Level Corporation; published 'The Practical Astronomy of the Moon,' 1739, and assigned to the acceleration of the moon's mean motion the secular rate of 10″; expert in computing on the basis of mediæval observations.
                                                     [xvi. 235]

DUNTON, JOHN (1659-1733), bookseller; educated for the church, but, being of a restless temperament, was apprenticed to a bookseller; emigrated, and wandered over New England, learning something of Indian customs; bookseller in London; issued the 'Athenian Gazette,' 1690-6; published 'The Dublin Scuffle,' narrating rambles in Ireland, to which domestic discomforts impelled him, 1699; published 'Life and Errors of John Dunton,' 1705; attacked Oxford and Bolingbroke in 'Neck or Nothing,' one of a large number of political satires; issued 'Athenianism, or the New Projects of John Dunton,' 1710; made a fruitless appeal for recognition (1723) to George I.   [xvi. 236]

DUPONT, GAINSBOROUGH (1754?-1797), portrait-painter and mezzotint engraver; nephew of Thomas Gainsborough [q. v.]; first exhibited at the Royal Academy, 1790; engraved in mezzotint from portraits by Gainsborough; painted landscapes in the style of Poussin.
                                                     [xvi. 238]

DUPORT, JAMES (1606-1679), master of Magdalene College, Cambridge; son of John Duport [q. v.]; educated at Westminster School and Trinity College, Cambridge; fellow of Trinity, 1627; M.A., 1630; regius professor of Greek, 1639-54; prebendary of Lincoln, and archdeacon of Stow, 1641; Lady Margaret's preacher, 1646; ejected from his professorship by the parliamentarians, 1654; vice-master of Trinity College, Cambridge, from 1655; king's chaplain, and again regius professor, 1660; D.D., 1660; dean of Peterborough, 1664; master of Magdalene College, Cambridge, 1668; vice-chancellor, 1669; benefactor of Magdalene College and Peterborough grammar school. His works consist of translations into Greek

verse of parts of the Old Testament, Latin lectures on Theophrastus, a 'Homeri Gnomologia,' 1660, and Latin poems.   [xvi. 239]

DUPORT, JOHN (*d.* 1617), biblical scholar; of Norman extraction; M.A. and fellow of Jesus College, Cambridge, before 1580; rector of Fulham, 1583; precentor of St. Paul's, 1585; D.D.; master of Jesus College, 1590; four times vice-chancellor of Cambridge, and (1609) prebendary of Ely; one of the translators of the bible (1611).
                                                     [xvi. 241]

DUPPA, BRIAN (1588-1662), bishop of Winchester; educated at Westminster; student of Christ Church, 1605, and fellow of All Souls' College, Oxford, 1612; M.A., 1614; D.D., 1625; dean of Christ Church, 1629-38; vice-chancellor, 1632 and 1633; chancellor of Salisbury, 1634; tutor to the Prince of Wales and the Duke of Gloucester; bishop of Chichester, 1638-41; bishop of Salisbury, 1641; corresponded with Sheldon and Sir Edward Hyde on the re-establishment of episcopacy, 1659; bishop of Winchester, 1660; lord almoner; benefactor of his colleges and bishoprics.   [xvi. 242]

DUPPA, RICHARD (1770-1831), artist and author; student of the Middle Temple, 1810; LL.B. Trinity Hall, Cambridge, 1814; F.S.A.; published the 'Life and Literary Works of Michael Angelo Buonarotti,' 1806, 'Classes and Orders of Botany,' 1816, and other works.
                                                     [xvi. 243]

DUPUIS, THOMAS SANDERS (1733-1796), musician; M.R.S.M., 1758; organist and composer to the Chapel Royal, 1779-96; Mus. Doc. Oxford, 1790; composed cathedral music.   [xvi. 243]

DURAND, DAVID (1680-1763), French protestant minister and author; born at Sommières; taken prisoner at Almanza, fighting among French refugees, 1707; pastor at Rotterdam; successively pastor of Martin's Lane and the Savoy French churches after 1711; F.R.S., 1728; chief works, a history of the sixteenth century (1725-9), and a history of painting in antiquity, 1725, both in French.   [xvi. 244]

DURAND, SIR HENRY MARION (1812-1871), major-general royal engineers; second lieutenant, Bengal engineers, 1828; blew up Cabul gate of Ghazni, 1839; private secretary to Lord Ellenborough, 1841; captain, 1843; commissioner of Tenasserim provinces, 1844-6; served in the Sikh war; political agent at Gwalior and Bhopal; appointed to Central India agency, 1857; held Indore and reconquered Western Malwa, 1857; C.B.; member of council of India, 1859; foreign secretary in India, 1861; major-general and K.C.S.I., 1867; lieutenant-governor of the Punjab, 1870-1.   [xvi. 244]

DURANT or **DURANCE**, JOHN (*fl.* 1660), puritan divine; denounced in Edwards's 'Gangræna'; ordered to discontinue his preaching in Canterbury Cathedral, *c.* 1660; published theological works.   [xvi. 246]

DURAS or **DURFORT**, LOUIS, EARL OF FEVERSHAM (1640?-1709), general; Marquis de Blanquefort in the French peerage; naturalised in England, 1665; colonel of the Duke of York's guards, 1667; created Baron Duras of Holdenby, 1673; English ambassador at Nimeguen, 1675; succeeded as Earl of Feversham, 1677; submitted proposals at French court for treaty of peace with Flanders, 1677; lord chamberlain to the queen, 1680; privy councillor, 1685; commanded James II's troops at the battle of Sedgemoor, 1685; K.G., 1685; commander-in-chief of James II's forces, 1686; voted for a regency, 1689.   [xvi. 247]

D'URBAN, SIR BENJAMIN (1777-1849), lieutenant-general; captain queen's bays, 1794; served in the Netherlands, Westphalia, and (1796) San Domingo; major, 25th light dragoons; superintendent of the junior department of the Royal Military College, 1803-5; major-general in the Portuguese, and colonel in the English, army, 1813; K.C.B.; K.C.H., 1818; lieutenant-governor and commander-in-chief of British Guiana, 1821-5, of Barbados, 1825-9; lieutenant-general, 1837; G.C.B., 1840; governor and commander-in-chief of the Cape, 1842-7; occupied Natal, 1843; died at Montreal in command of the forces in Canada.   [xvi. 249]

DUREL, JOHN (1625-1683), dean of Windsor; entered Merton College, Oxford, 1640; M.A. of the Sylvanian

College, Caen, 1644; assisted in the royalist defence of Jersey, 1647; founded the Savoy French episcopal chapel, 1660; became first minister, 1660; selected by Charles II to translate English prayer-book into French for use in Channel islands; king's chaplain, 1662; prebendary of Salisbury, 1663, of Windsor, 1664; completed translation of revised prayer-book, 1670; prebendary of Durham, 1668; D.D., 1670; dean of Windsor and Wolverhampton, 1677; published 'Sanctæ Ecclesiæ Anglicanæ . . . Vindiciæ,' 1669. [xvi. 250]

DURELL, DAVID (1728–1775), divine; M.A. Pembroke College, Oxford, 1753; fellow, and from 1757 principal of Hertford College; D.D., 1764; vicar of Ticehurst; prebendary of Canterbury, 1767; vice-chancellor of Oxford, 1766 and 1767; published works including 'The Hebrew Text of the Parallel Prophecies of Jacob and Moses relating to the Twelve Tribes,' with the Samaritan-Arabic and Arabic versions, 1763. [xvi. 251]

D'URFEY, THOMAS (1653–1723), poet and dramatist; generally known as 'Tom Durfey'; by descent a French Huguenot; wrote a bombastic tragedy, entitled 'The Siege of Memphis,' 1676; produced 'Madam Fickle,' 1677, and 'The Virtuous Wife,' 1680; lampooned by Tom Brown (1663–1704) [q. v.]; incidentally replied to the strictures of Jeremy Collier in his 'Campaigners,' a comedy, 1698; author of 'Wonders in the Sun,' a comic opera, in which an imaginary picture of bird-life was presented; issued various recensions of his songs and poems, first using the title, 'An Antidote against Melancholy, made up in Pills,' in 1661; published an 'Elegy upon Charles II and a Panegyric on James II,' 1685; issued 'Tales, Tragical and Comical,' 1704, and 'Tales, Moral and Comical,' 1706; wrote 'The Modern Prophets,' and 'The Old Mode and the New,' two social comedies, 1709; satirised Bellarmine, Porto-Carrero, and the Harley-Bolingbroke ministry; buried in St. James's church, Piccadilly, at the expense of the Earl of Dorset. He had been an intimate of Charles II and James II. Many of his burlesque poems and songs are still heard in Scotland. [xvi. 251]

DURHAM, first EARL OF (1792–1840). [See LAMBTON, JOHN GEORGE.]

DURHAM, JAMES (1622–1658), covenanting divine; studied at St. Andrews; captain of a troop in the civil war; divinity student at Glasgow; chaplain to the king; professor of divinity, Glasgow, 1650; inducted into the 'Inner Kirk,' Glasgow; traditionally reported to have impressed Cromwell by his preaching; published religious works. [xvi. 255]

DURHAM, JOSEPH (1814–1877), sculptor; A.R.A., 1866; his finest work, 'Leander and the Syren,' exhibited at the Royal Academy, 1875; excelled in figures of boy-athletes. [xvi. 256]

DURHAM, SIR PHILIP CHARLES HENDERSON CALDERWOOD (1763–1845), admiral; acting-lieutenant of the Victory, 1781; saved from the sinking of the Royal George, 1782; present at the relief of Gibraltar, and battle off Cape Spartel; brought home convoy from Mediterranean, 1794; took part in French defeat off Tory island, 1798; fought in the action off Cape Finisterre, 1805; wounded at Trafalgar, 1805; rear-admiral, 1810; commander-in-chief of the Leeward islands station, 1813–16; co-operated in reduction of Martinique and Guadaloupe, 1815; G.C.B. and admiral, 1830. [xvi. 256]

DURHAM, SIMEON OF (fl. 1130). [See SIMEON.]

DURHAM, WILLIAM OF (d. 1249). [See WILLIAM.]

DURHAM, WILLIAM (1611–1684), divine; M.A. New Inn Hall, Oxford, 1633; preacher at the Rolls Chapel; B.D., 1649; ejected from his living of Tredington at the Restoration; rector of St. Mildred's, Bread Street, 1663–84; published a life of Robert Harris, D.D., 1660. [xvi. 258]

DURHAM, WILLIAM (d. 1686), clergyman; son of William Durham (1611–1684) [q. v.]; scholar of the Charterhouse and Corpus Christi College, Oxford; M.A., 1660; university proctor, 1668; rector of Letcomb-Bassett, Berkshire, and chaplain to James, duke of Monmouth; D.D. Cambridge, 1676; published sermons. [xvi. 258]

DURIE, LORDS. [See GIBSON, SIR ALEXANDER, d. 1644; GIBSON, SIR ALEXANDER, d. 1656.]

DURIE, ANDREW (d. 1558), bishop of Galloway and abbot of Melrose; brother of George Durie [q. v.]; appointed by Archbishop James Beaton (d. 1539) [q. v.] to the abbacy of Melrose, 1526, against the will of James V, and by means of forged letters of recommendation to the pope; bishop of Galloway, 1541; persecuted the protestants. [xvi. 258]

DURIE, GEORGE (1496–1561), abbot of Dunfermline and archdeacon of St. Andrews; brother of Andrew Durie [q. v.]; abbot of Dunfermline under the direction of his uncle, Archbishop James Beaton (d. 1539) [q. v.]; independent abbot on the archbishop's death, 1539; endeavoured to avenge Cardinal Beaton's murder, 1546; sat in parliament, 1540, 1542, 1543, and 1554; keeper of the privy seal, 1554; member of the regent Arran's privy council, 1545; Scottish privy councillor, 1547; forced on the battle of Pinkie, 1547; deputed to the French court to represent the situation of the Scottish catholics, 1560; attempted to stir up Mary Stuart's religious zeal, 1560; beatified, 1563. [xvi. 259]

DURIE, JOHN (d. 1587), Scottish jesuit; son of George Durie [q. v.]; educated at Paris and Louvain; joined the Society of Jesus; assailed the theological position of William Whitaker, 1582. [xvi. 260]

DURIE, JOHN (1537–1600), presbyterian minister; suspected of heresy when a monk at Dunfermline, and condemned to imprisonment for life; escaped at the time of the Reformation; minister at Leith, ardently supporting John Knox; minister at Edinburgh, c. 1573; imprisoned for inveighing against the court; ordered to leave Edinburgh for reflecting on Lennox, 1582; was soon afterwards accorded an ovation by the people of Edinburgh; pensioned by James VI, 1590. [xvi. 261]

DURIE, JOHN (1596–1680), protestant divine; son of Robert Durie [q. v.]; minister to the English Company of Merchants at Elbing, West Prussia, 1628–30; formed scheme for uniting all the evangelical churches, which Gustavus Adolphus, whom he visited, approved, but Oxenstiern disallowed; ordained priest, 1634; king's chaplain; worked at his idea without success in Sweden and Denmark, but was welcomed by the Dukes of Brunswick, Hildesheim, and Zelle; chaplain and tutor to Mary, princess of Orange, at the Hague; favourably received in Switzerland, the Netherlands, and North Germany, having the approbation of Cromwell and the English universities, 1654–7; his plans finally rejected by the Great Elector, 1668; published theological treatises and writings on Christian unity, including 'Manière d'expliquer l'Apocalyse,' 1674. [xvi. 261]

DURIE, ROBERT (1555–1616), presbyterian minister; son of John Durie (1537–1600) [q. v.]; studied at St. Mary's College, St. Andrews; minister of Abercrombie, Fifeshire, 1588, of Anstruther, 1590; visited the island of Lewis on a civilising and Christianising mission, 1598; banished (1606) for attending the prohibited general assembly at Aberdeen, 1605; first minister of the Scots church at Leyden. [xvi. 263]

DURNFORD, ANTHONY WILLIAM (1830–1879), colonel, royal engineers; second lieutenant, royal engineers, 1848; served in Ceylon, 1851–6; adjutant at Malta; major, 1871; accompanied mission appointed to attend Cetshwayo's coronation; sent to seize Bushman's River pass on revolt of Ama Hlubi tribe, 1873; nearly killed by his horse falling over a precipice, 1873; demolished Drakensberg passes, 1874; lieutenant-colonel, 1873; colonel, 1878; raised a Basuto column, 1879; killed while covering the retreat at Isandhlwana, 1879. [xvi. 264]

DURNFORD, RICHARD (1802–1895), bishop of Chichester; educated at Eton and Magdalen College, Oxford; one of the founders of the Oxford Union, and was first president, 1823; M.A., 1827; fellow of Magdalen College, 1828, and honorary fellow, 1888; ordained priest, 1831; held living of Middleton, Lancashire, 1833–1870; rural dean and honorary canon of Manchester, c. 1848; archdeacon of Manchester, 1867; canon residentiary of Manchester Cathedral, 1868; bishop of Chichester, 1870–95. [Suppl. ii. 170]

DURNO, JAMES (1750?–1795), historical painter; assisted his master, Benjamin West, in preparing repetitions of his pictures; member of the Society of Incorporated Artists; died at Rome. [xvi. 266]

DURWARD, ALAN, EARL OF ATHOLL, otherwise known as ALANUS OSTIARIUS, HOSTIARIUS, DYRWART 'LE USHER' (d. 1268); justiciar of Scotland before 1246; leader of the English party after the death (1249) of Alexander II; accused of treason for attempting to get his children by a natural daughter of Alexander II legitimatised, 1251; fled to England, 1252; attended Henry III on his Gascon expedition, 1253; member of the new council appointed under English auspices to govern Scotland for seven years, 1255; again high justiciar, 1255; shielded by Henry III from the consequences of Alexander III's new anti-English policy, 1258; one of the four temporary regents of Scotland, 1260; Earl of Atholl by marriage. [xvi. 266]

DUSGATE, THOMAS (d. 1532), protestant martyr; scholar of Christ's College and fellow of Corpus Christi, Cambridge; M.A., 1524; dissuaded by Luther from becoming a priest; put up bills on the doors of Exeter Cathedral denouncing the Roman catholic doctrines preached there; burned near Exeter, 1532. [xvi. 268]

DUSSEK, afterwards BUCKLEY, OLIVIA (1799–1847). [See BUCKLEY, OLIVIA.]

DUSSEK, SOPHIA (1775–1830?), musician and composer; daughter of Domenico Corri [q. v.]; deserted by her husband, 1800; performed as a harpist and pianist in Ireland and Scotland, appearing for one season in opera. [xvi. 268]

DUTENS, LOUIS (1730–1812), diplomatist and man of letters; Huguenot refugee; chaplain to the embassy at Turin, 1758; chargé d'affaires at Turin, 1760–2 and 1763–6; presented by the Duke of Northumberland to the living of Elsdon, 1766; historiographer to the king, and F.R.S.; nominated secretary to Lord Walsingham's embassy to Spain, 1786, but did not actually go, Walsingham's appointment being cancelled; edited Leibnitz, 1769, and published (1805) 'Mémoires d'un Voyageur qui se repose'; wrote also works on literary and philosophical topics, which appeared first in French. [xvi. 268]

DUVAL, CHARLES ALLEN (1808–1872), painter; exhibited portraits and subject-pictures at the Royal Academy, 1836–72; best-known works, a characteristic portrait of Daniel O'Connell and 'The Ruined Gamester,' a subject-picture from which 'Punch' designed a cartoon caricaturing Sir Robert Peel. [xvi. 270]

DUVAL, CLAUDE (1643–1670), highwayman; born at Domfront, Normandy; came to England at the Restoration in attendance on the Duke of Richmond; took to the road, and became notorious for his gallantry and daring; captured in London and executed. Samuel Butler satirically commemorated his death in a Pindaric ode. [xvi. 271]

DUVAL, LEWIS (1774–1844), conveyancer; LL.B. Trinity Hall, Cambridge, 1796; fellow of Trinity Hall; barrister, Lincoln's Inn, 1804; famous as a chamber practitioner; acknowledged to be *facile princeps* of contemporary conveyancers; placed on the real property commission, writing the greater part of its second report, 1830. [xvi. 272]

DUVAL, PHILIP (d. 1709?), painter; of French nationality; settled in England, c. 1670; painted a picture of 'Venus receiving from Vulcan the armour for Æneas,' 1672; received an annuity from the Hon. Robert Boyle [q. v.] [xvi. 272]

DUVAL, ROBERT (1644–1732), painter; born at the Hague; director of William III's collections; sent over to England to assist in cleaning and repairing Raphael's cartoons; director of the Hague Academy. [xvi. 272]

DWARRIS, SIR FORTUNATUS WILLIAM LILLEY (1786–1860), lawyer; born in Jamaica; educated at Rugby and University College, Oxford; B.A., 1808; barrister, Middle Temple, 1811; commissioner to inquire into law of West Indies, 1822; knighted, 1838; master of the queen's bench; treasurer of the Middle Temple, 1859; F.R.S.; F.S.A.; vice-president of the Archæological Association; author of 'A General Treatise on Statutes,' 1830–1, some books on the law of the West Indies, 'Alberic, Consul of Rome' (drama, 1832), and 'Some New Facts and a Suggested New Theory as to the Authorship of Junius,' 1850, with other works. [xvi. 272]

DWIGHT, JOHN (fl. 1671–1698), potter; B.C.L. Christ Church, Oxford, 1661; patentee for the manufacture of 'porcelain,' 1671 and 1684; established works at Fulham; achieved production of ware resembling oriental porcelain; executed stoneware statuettes of contemporaries and mythological figures (Mars and Meleager), for which he is doubtfully said to have employed Italian modellers. [xvi. 273]

DWIGHT, SAMUEL (1669?–1737), physician; son of John Dwight [q. v.]; educated at Westminster School and Christ Church, Oxford; M.A., 1693; L.R.C.P., 1731; practised at Fulham; published 'De Hydropibus,' 1725, and other medical works. [xvi. 275]

DWNN, LEWYS, or more properly LEWYS AP RHYS AP OWAIN (d. 1616?), deputy-herald for Wales (1586) and bard. His collections of pedigrees, interspersed with poems by himself, were edited by Sir Samuel Rush Meyrick [q. v.] in 1846. Transcripts by him of bardic verses are among the Peniarth MSS. [xvi. 276]

DWYER, MICHAEL (1771–1826), Irish insurgent; took part in insurrections of 1798 and 1803, but disapproved Emmet's attempt upon Dublin, 1803; sentenced to transportation, dying, according to Grattan, before leaving Britain, though, according to Ross, he was subsequently for eleven years high constable of Sydney. [xvi. 277]

DYCE, ALEXANDER (1798–1869), scholar; educated at the Edinburgh High School and Exeter College, Oxford; B.A., 1819; held two country curacies; published 'Specimens of British Poetesses,' 1825; edited Collins's poems, 1827; edited George Peele, 1828 and 1839; published 'Demetrius and Enanthe' (Fletcher's 'Humorous Lieutenant'), 1830; published edition of Shakespeare in nine volumes, 1857. He edited also the works of Thomas Middleton, 1840, Beaumont and Fletcher, 1843–6, Marlowe, 1850, Gifford's Ford, 1869, Robert Greene, 1831, John Webster, and others. His library was bequeathed to Victoria and Albert Museum, South Kensington. [xvi. 277]

DYCE, WILLIAM (1806–1864), painter; cousin of Alexander Dyce [q. v.]; M.A. Marischal College, Aberdeen, 1822; studied at the Royal Academy and at Rome; first exhibited at the Royal Academy, 1827; originated 'pre-Raphaelite' school of painting in England with 'Madonna and Child,' 1828; Blackwell prizeman at Marischal College for essay on 'Electro-magnetism'; F.R.S. of Edinburgh, 1832; director and secretary to council of school of design, 1840–3; professor of fine arts, King's College, London, 1844; R.A., 1848; was entrusted with the decoration in fresco of the House of Lords, 1846, and of the queen's robing-room, 1848, but did not fully carry out the former contract; an accomplished musician and glass painter; leader in the high church movement. His paintings comprise both portraits and historical subjects; his frescoes consist largely of allegorical and sacred figures. [xvi. 278]

DYCE-SOMBRE, DAVID OCHTERLONY (1808–1851), an eccentric character; born at Sirdhana, Bengal; great-grandson of one Walter Reinhard, a native of Strasburg, who became satrap of Sirdhana under the Mogul emperor, 1777; inherited a large fortune from his foster-mother, the Begum Sombre, 1836; chevalier of the order of Christ; M.P., Sudbury, 1841; unseated for bribery, 1842; held to be of unsound mind by a commission *de lunatico inquirendo*, 1843; published a refutation of the charges of lunacy previously advanced against him, 1849; lived mainly in France; died in England, on a visit undertaken in the hope of obtaining a *supersedeas*, 1851. [xvi. 281]

DYCHE, THOMAS (fl. 1719), schoolmaster; master of Stratford Bow school after 1710; convicted of libel for attempting to expose the peculations of the notorious John Ward of Hackney, 1719; compiled English and Latin grammars and vocabularies. [xvi. 282]

DYER, SIR EDWARD (d. 1607), poet and courtier; educated either at Balliol College or Broadgates Hall, Oxford; introduced at court by the Earl of Leicester, at one time falling under the displeasure of Queen Elizabeth; commissioner for the attachment of forfeited lands in Somerset, 1586; sent on a diplomatic mission to Denmark, 1589; chancellor of the order of the Garter, and knighted, 1596; intimate friend of Sir Philip Sidney; reputed Rosicrucian. His most famous poem is the description of contentment beginning 'My mind to me a kingdom is.'

Meres mentions him as ' famous for elegy,' and, according to Collier, he translated part of Theocritus.
[xvi. 283]

DYER, GEORGE (1755–1841), author; educated at Christ's Hospital and Emmanuel College, Cambridge; B.A., 1778; usher at Dedham grammar school, 1779, subsequently in a school at Northampton; converted to unitarianism by Robert Robinson (1735–1790) [q. v.]; mentioned by Charles Lamb as a gentle and kindly eccentric; nearly drowned in the New River while in a fit of abstraction, 1823. His works include ' The Complaints of the Poor People of England,' 1793, 'Poems,' 1801, and ' Poems and Critical Essays,' 1802. [xvi. 284]

DYER, GILBERT (1743–1820), antiquary and bookseller; formed collection of theological works when bookseller at Exeter; published ' A Restoration of the Ancient Modes of bestowing Names on the Rivers, Hills, &c. of Britain,' tracing back their names to the Gaelic, 1805, ' Vulgar Errors, Ancient and Modern,' and a pamphlet against ' atheism,' 1796. [xvi. 286]

DYER, Sir JAMES (1512–1582), judge; barrister, Middle Temple, c. 1537; M.P., Cambridgeshire, 1547; king's serjeant and knighted, 1552; M.P., Cambridgeshire and speaker of the House of Commons, 1553; judge of the queen's bench; president of the court of common pleas, 1559; compiled what Coke thought ' fruitful and summary collections' of cases covering the period 1573–82, reports which constitute the transition from the year-book to the modern system. [xvi. 286]

DYER, JOHN (1700 ?–1758), poet; educated at Westminster School; itinerant artist in South Wales, publishing his poem of ' Grongar Hill' in 1727; studied painting in Italy; returned to England and held various livings; LL.B. Cambridge, 1752; published ' The Fleece,' 1757.
[xvi. 287]

DYER, JOSEPH CHESSBOROUGH (1780–1871), inventor; born at Stonnington Point, Connecticut; devoted himself to naturalising American inventions in England; patented improvement of Danforth's roving frame for cotton-spinning, 1825; joint-founder of ' North American Review,' 1815, and of ' Manchester Guardian,' 1821; aided in establishing Royal Institution and Mechanics' Institution at Manchester; abolitionist and free trader.
[xvi. 287]

DYER, SAMUEL (1725–1772), translator; matriculated at Leyden, 1743; translated the lives of Pericles and Demetrius for Tonson's Plutarch's ' Lives,' 1758; F.R.S., 1761; obtained war office appointment; lived on intimate terms with Burke, who wrote an obituary notice of him; believed by Sir Joshua Reynolds and Malone to have written ' Junius's Letters.' [xvi. 288]

DYER, THOMAS HENRY (1804–1888), historian; contributed to Dr. William Smith's classical and biographical dictionaries; published ' Tentamina Æschylea,' 1841; published ' A History of the City of Rome,' 1865, and ' The History of the Kings of Rome,' 1868, the latter to confute Niebuhr; LL.D. St. Andrews; explored and published accounts of sites in Pompeii and Athens; investigated origin and nature of European concert in his ' History of Modern Europe,' 1861–4. [xvi. 289]

DYER, WILLIAM (d. 1696), nonconformist divine; minister of Chesham, and subsequently of Cholesbury, Buckinghamshire; ejected, 1662; published theological treatises resembling in literary style those of John Bunyan. [xvi. 290]

DYFRIG (d. 612). [See DUBRICIUS.]

DYGON, JOHN (fl. 1512), Benedictine monk and musician; Mus. Bac. Oxford, 1512; possibly prior of St. Augustine's Monastery, Canterbury; composer of a piece printed in John Hawkins's ' History of Music,' ii. 518.
[xvi. 290]

DYKE, DANIEL (d. 1614), puritan divine; B.A. St. John's College, Cambridge, 1596; M.A. Sidney Sussex College, 1599; fellow of Sidney Sussex, and B.D. 1606; minister of Coggeshall, Essex; suspended, 1583; his restoration refused, though Lord Burghley interceded for him; published theological tracts. [xvi. 291]

DYKE, DANIEL (1617–1688), baptist divine; son of Jeremiah Dyke [q. v.]; M.A. Sidney Sussex College, Cambridge; rector of Great Hadham, Hertfordshire, 1645–60;

chaplain in ordinary to Oliver Cromwell, 1651; trier for the approval of ministers, 1653. [xvi. 291]

DYKE, JEREMIAH (d. 1620 ?), puritan divine; brother of Daniel Dyke (d. 1614) [q. v.]; graduate of Sidney Sussex College, Cambridge; incumbent of Epping, 1609 till death; published tracts. [xvi. 292]

DYKES, JOHN BACCHUS (1823–1876), musician and theologian; grandson of Thomas Dykes [q. v.]; senior optime, St. Catherine's College, Cambridge, 1847; minor canon, 1849, and precentor of Durham, 1849–62; Mus. Doc. Durham; vicar of St. Oswald's, Durham, 1862; composed numerous hymn-tunes. [xvi. 292]

DYKES, THOMAS (1761–1847), divine; B.A. Magdalene College, Cambridge; built St. John's Church, Hull, 1791; first incumbent, 1792; founder of female penitentiary, Hull, 1812; master of the Charterhouse at Hull, 1833; a moderate Calvinist; published sermons.
[xvi. 293]

DYMOCK, ROGER (fl. 1395), theologian; D.D. Oxford; possibly a Dominican friar; author of an unpublished treatise, ' Adversus duodecim errores et hæreses Lollardorum.' [xvi. 293]

DYMOCKE, JAMES (d. 1718 ?), Roman catholic divine; missioner in England; prior of St. Arnoul, near Chartres; chief work, ' Le Vice ridiculé et la Vertu louée,' 1671. [xvi. 294]

DYMOKE, Sir HENRY, first baronet (1801–1865), king's champion at George IV's coronation, 1821; created baronet, 1841. [xvi. 296]

DYMOKE, Sir JOHN (d. 1381), king's champion; owed his advancement to a marriage with Margaret de Ludlow; knighted, 1373; M.P., Lincolnshire, 1372, 1373, and 1377; claimed, as lord of the manor of Scrivelsby, to act as king's champion at the coronation of Richard II; his right challenged by Sir Baldwin de Freville, but upheld by a decision of the lord steward. [xvi. 294]

DYMOKE, Sir ROBERT (d. 1546), king's champion; son of Sir Thomas Dymoke [q. v.]; knight-banneret; sheriff of Lincolnshire, 1484, 1502, and 1509; champion at the coronations of Richard III, Henry VII, and Henry VIII; distinguished himself at the siege of Tournay. [xvi. 295]

DYMOKE, ROBERT (d. 1580), son of Sir Robert Dymoke [q. v.]; imprisoned for recusancy at Lincoln.
[xvi. 295]

DYMOKE, Sir THOMAS (1428 ?–1471); aided his brother-in-law, Sir Robert Wells, in collecting a Lancastrian force in Lincolnshire, 1471; beheaded, 1471. [xvi. 295]

DYMOND, JONATHAN (1796–1828), quaker moralist; founded an auxiliary peace society at Exeter, 1825; chief work, ' Essays on the Principles of Morality and on the Private and Political Rights and Obligations of Mankind' (published 1829), written against Paley's utilitarianism.
[xvi. 296]

DYMPNA, SAINT (6th or 9th cent.), Christian daughter of a pagan king in Ireland; fled to Antwerp from the incestuous designs of her father; overtaken and slain by her father with his own hand. [xvi. 296]

DYOTT, WILLIAM (1761–1847), general; lieutenant, 4th regiment, 1782; major, 103rd regiment, 1794; commanded 25th regiment at capture of Grenada, 1796; colonel, 1800; aide-de-camp to George III, 1801; commanded brigade in battle of Alexandria, 1801, and in Walcheren expedition, 1809; lieutenant-general, 1813.
[xvi. 298]

DYSART, first EARL OF (1600 ?–1651). [See MURRAY, WILLIAM.]

DYSART, COUNTESS OF (d. 1697). See MURRAY, ELIZABETH.]

DYSON, CHARLES (1788–1860), professor of Anglo-Saxon at Oxford; grandson of Jeremiah Dyson [q. v.]; scholar of Corpus Christi College, Oxford; friend of Keble and Arnold; M.A., 1816; Rawlinsonian professor of Anglo-Saxon, 1812–16; incumbent successively of Nunburnholme, Nasing, and Dogmersfield. [xvi. 298]

DYSON, JEREMIAH (1722–1776), civil servant and politician; studied at Edinburgh University; matriculated at Leyden, 1742; settled a pension on his friend Mark Akenside [q. v.]; friend of Richardson; purchased clerkship of House of Commons, 1748; became a tory after George III's accession ; discontinued the practice of selling the clerkships subordinate to his office ; M.P., Yarmouth, Isle of Wight, 1762-8, Weymouth and Melcombe Regis, 1768-74, and Horsham, 1774 ; commissioner for the board of trade, 1764-8 ; a lord of the treasury, 1768-74 ; privy councillor, 1774 ; supported Lord North's treatment of the American colonies ; nicknamed 'Mungo' (the ubiquitous negro slave in Isaac Bickerstaffe's 'Padlock') from his omnipresence in parliamentary business ; defended Akenside's 'Pleasures of Imagination' against Warburton. [xvi. 299]

DYVE, Sir Lewis (1599-1669), royalist; knighted, 1620 ; attended Prince Charles at Madrid ; M.P., Bridport, 1625, 1626, Weymouth, 1628 ; arrested by Hotham, governor of Hull, for conspiracy with ultimate object of admitting Charles I into that town, 1642 ; fled to Holland ; returned, and was wounded at skirmish at Worcester, 1642 ; fought under Rupert at relief of Newark, 1644 ; sergeant-major-general of Dorset, 1644, storming Weymouth, 1645 ; imprisoned in the Tower, 1645-7 ; served in Ireland, publishing (1650) an account of events there from 1648 to 1650 ; finally took refuge in France. [xvi. 301]

E

EACHARD, John (1636 ?-1697), master of Catharine Hall, Cambridge ; fellow of Catharine Hall, 1658 ; M.A., 1660 ; master, 1675-97 ; D.D., 1676 ; vice-chancellor of Cambridge, 1679 and 1695 ; appointed to justify the vice-chancellor's action in disobeying the mandamus of James II to confer the degree of M.A. without oaths on the Benedictine monk, Alban Francis [q. v.], 1687 ; published two 'Dialogues' on the philosophy of Hobbes, 1672 and 1673, and a satirical work entitled 'The Grounds and Occasions of the Contempt of the Clergy and Religion enquired into,' 1670. [xvi. 302]

EACHARD, Laurence (1670 ?-1730). [See Echard.]

EADBALD, ÆODBALD, ÆTHELBALD, or AUDUWALD (d. 640), king of Kent ; son of Æthelberht ; broke off his incestuous connection with his father's wife on being converted to Christianity ; said to have built a church at Canterbury and another church for Folkestone nunnery ; married his sister Æthelburh to the Northumbrian king Eadwine on condition of her being allowed to remain a Christian. [xvi. 303]

EADBERT or EADBERHT, Saint (d. 698), bishop of Lindisfarne, 688 ; buried in the grave which had held St. Cuthbert, whose remains he had translated. [xvi. 304]

EADBERT or EADBERHT (d. 768), king of the Northumbrians ; divided the government between himself and his brother Ecgberht [see Egberht], archbishop of York ; made alliances with the Franks and Picts ; reduced Dumbarton, 756 ; joined the monastery of St. Peter's, York, in grief for the destruction of his army in 756. [xvi. 304]

EADBERT or EADBRYHT PRÆN (fl. 796), king of Kent ; forsook the cloister and headed a revolt against Mercia, founding the independent kingdom of Kent, 796 ; defeated and mutilated by Cenwulf of Mercia, 798. [xvi. 305]

EADBURGA, EADBURH, BUGGA, or BUGGE, Saint (d. 751), abbess of Minster ; daughter of Centwine [q. v.], king of the West-Saxons ; abbess of the nunnery founded in Thanet by the mother of St. Mildred, near which she built a new convent ; friend and correspondent of St. Boniface ; taught Lioba the art of poetry. [xvi. 305]

EADBURGA, EADBURGH, or EADBURH (fl. 802), queen of the West-Saxons ; daughter of Offa ; prepared poison for a favourite of her husband Beorhtric [q. v.], king of the West-Saxons, which the king accidentally drank himself, 802 ; fled to the court of Charlemagne, who made her abbess of a nunnery ; expelled for unchastity and reduced to beg in the streets of Pavia. [xvi. 306]

EADFRID or EADFRITH (d. 721), bishop of Lindisfarne, 698 ; ruled as a monastic bishop of the Celtic type, though following Rome on points of ritual ; promoted the committal of his master St. Cuthbert's acts to writing ; began the compilation of the Lindisfarne gospels manuscripts. [xvi. 306]

EADIE, John (1810-1876), theological author ; studied at Glasgow University ; minister of the Cambridge Street united secession congregation, Glasgow, 1835 ; professor of biblical literature in the United Secession Divinity Hall, Glasgow, 1843-76 ; LL.D. Glasgow, 1844 ; D.D. St. Andrew's, 1850 ; moderator of synod, 1857 ; author of a popular 'Biblical Cyclopædia,' 1848, and an 'Analytical Concordance,' 1856 ; published commentaries on the Greek

text of the Epistles to the Ephesians (1854), the Colossians (1856), the Philippians (1857), the Galatians (1869), and the Thessalonians (the last appearing posthumously). [xvi. 307]

EADMER or EDMER (d. 1124 ?), historian ; monk of Canterbury ; biographer of St. Anselm ; chronicler of contemporary events in 'Historia Novorum' ; elected archbishop of St. Andrews, but, in consequence of the rivalry between the northern and southern primates, never consecrated. [xvi. 309]

EADNOTH (d. 1067), staller, or master of the horse, under Eadward the Confessor and William I ; slain in battle with the sons of Harold, 1067. [xvi. 310]

EADRIC. [See Edric.]

EADSIGE, EADSINE, EDSIE, or ELSI (d. 1050), archbishop of Canterbury ; one of the chaplains of Cnut ; archbishop, 1038 ; crowned Harthacnut ; said to have helped Earl Godwine to seize Folkestone. [xvi. 311]

EAGER, John (1782-1853 ?), organist ; organist to the corporation of Yarmouth, 1803-33 ; defended and introduced J. B. Logier's chiroplast to the public ; wrote pianoforte sonatas, songs, and glees. [xvi. 311]

EAGLES. [See also Eccles.]

EAGLES, John (1783-1855), artist and author ; son of Thomas Eagles [q. v.] ; admitted to Winchester College, 1797 ; studied art in Italy, trying to work his style on Gaspard Poussin and Salvator Rosa ; M.A. Wadham College, Oxford, 1838 ; took orders ; contributed to 'Blackwood's Magazine,' 1831-55 ; wrote sonnets and a Latin macaronic poem ; translated 'Odyssey,' books i. and ii. and five cantos of 'Orlando Furioso.' [xvi. 312]

EAGLES, Thomas (1746-1812), classical scholar ; entered at Winchester College, 1757 ; merchant and collector of customs at Bristol ; F.S.A., 1811 ; translated part of Athenæus ; contributed to 'The Crier,' a periodical essay (in 'Felix Farley's Bristol Journal'), and left dissertations on the Rowley controversy. [xvi. 313]

EALDULF (d. 1002). [See Aldulf.]

EAMES, John (d. 1744), dissenting tutor ; educated at Merchant Taylors' School ; theological tutor in the Fund Academy, Moorfields ; F.R.S., and friend of Sir Isaac Newton ; edited Isaac Watts's 'Knowledge of the Heavens and Earth made easy,' 1726. [xvi. 313]

EANBALD I (d. 796), archbishop of York ; with Alcuin superintended rebuilding of York Minster ; archbishop, 780 ; crowned Eardwulf [q. v.], 796. [xvi. 314]

EANBALD II (d. 810 ?), archbishop of York ; sent by the church of York to consult his master, Alcuin, on the succession, 796 ; archbishop, 796 ; helped Cenwulf of Mercia to depose Eardwulf of Northumbria, 807 ; received letters of advice from Alcuin. [xvi. 314]

EANFLÆD (b. 626), queen of Northumbria ; first Northumbrian to be baptised, 626 ; brought up at the court of her uncle Eadbald [q. v.], king of Kent ; married to Oswiu of Northumbria, 643 ; hastened the synod of Whitby by her adherence to the Roman ritual, while her husband practised the Celtic ; joint-abbess of Whitby with her daughter Ælflæd, c. 685. [xvi. 315]

EARDLEY, Sir Culling Eardley (1805-1863), religious philanthropist ; educated at Eton and Oriel College, Oxford ; M.P., Pontefract, 1830 ; founded the Evangelical Alliance, 1846. Under his direction the Alliance secured the independence of the Bulgarian church, 1861, and the abolition of the penal laws against Roman catholics in Sweden, 1858 ; he obtained firmans of religious liberty from the sultan of Turkey (1856) and from the khedive of Egypt. [xvi. 316]

EARDWULF or **EARDULF** (*d.* 810), king of Northumbria ; said to have been executed by order of Ethelred, but to have been miraculously restored to life ; king of Northumbria, 796 ; expelled by Alfwold, 808, but restored (809) by Charlemagne. [xvi. 317]

EARLE, ERASMUS (1590–1667), serjeant-at-law ; barrister of Lincoln's Inn ; bencher, 1635–41 ; reader, 1639 ; M.P., Norwich, 1647 ; serjeant-at-law, 1648 and 1660 ; counsel to the state, 1653. [xvi. 317]

EARLE, GILES (1678 ?–1758), politician and wit ; colonel in the army and follower of John, second duke of Argyll ; M.P., Chippenham, 1715–22, Malmesbury, 1722–1747 ; clerk-comptroller of the king's household, 1720 ; treasury lord, 1737–42 ; chairman of committees of election, 1727–41 ; boon companion of Walpole. [xvi. 318]

EARLE, HENRY (1789–1838), surgeon ; third son of Sir James Earle [q. v.] ; M.R.C.S., 1808 ; surgeon to St. Bartholomew's Hospital, 1827 ; professor of anatomy and surgery at the Royal College of Surgeons, 1833 ; president of the Royal Medical and Chirurgical Society, 1835–7 ; surgeon-extraordinary to Queen Victoria, 1837 ; published 'Practical Observations in Surgery,' 1823 ; maintained, against Sir Astley Paston Cooper, the possible uniting of fracture of the neck of the thigh-bone. [xvi. 319]

EARLE, JABEZ (1676 ?–1768), presbyterian minister ; pastor in Drury Street, Westminster, 1706 ; established a Thursday-morning lecture at Hanover Street ; D.D. Edinburgh, 1728 ; D.D. King's College, Aberdeen ; chaplain to Archibald, duke of Douglas (1694–1761) [q. v.] ; published sermons and religious poems. [xvi. 319]

EARLE, SIR JAMES (1755–1817), surgeon ; surgeon to St. Bartholomew's Hospital, 1784–1815 ; surgeon-extraordinary to George III ; president of the College of Surgeons and knighted, 1802 ; lithotomist ; improved treatment of hydrocele ; chief work, 'A Treatise on the Hydrocele,' 1791. [xvi. 320]

EARLE, JOHN (1601 ?–1665), bishop of Salisbury ; B.A. Merton College, Oxford, and fellow, 1619 ; M.A., 1624 ; rector of Bishopston, Wiltshire, 1639 ; tutor to Charles, prince of Wales, 1641 ; D.D. Oxford, 1640 ; unexpectedly appointed one of the Westminster Assembly of Divines, 1643 ; chancellor of Salisbury, 1643 ; deprived, as a 'malignant' ; chaplain and clerk of the closet to Charles II in France ; dean of Westminster, 1660 ; bishop of Worcester, 1662–3 ; bishop of Salisbury, 1663–5 ; opposed both the Conventicle and the Five-mile acts ; author of 'Microcosmographie,' 1628, and 'Hortus Mertonensis,' a Latin poem. [xvi. 321]

EARLE, JOHN (1749–1818), Roman catholic divine ; educated at the English college, Douay ; priest at Spanish ambassador's chapel, Dorset Street, Manchester Square, London ; published poem on 'Gratitude,' 1791, and critique (1799) on Geddes's translation of the bible. [xvi. 322]

EARLE, WILLIAM (1833–1885), major-general ; educated at Winchester ; lieutenant, 49th regiment, 1854 ; promoted captain in the Crimea, 1855 ; captain and lieutenant-colonel, grenadier guards, 1863 ; served in Nova Scotia, 1862 and 1863 ; colonel, 1868 ; military secretary to Lord Northbrook in India, 1872–6 ; C.S.I., 1876 ; major-general, 1880 ; commanded garrison of Alexandria, 1882–1884 ; C.B. ; killed at Kirbekan during the war in the Soudan. [xvi. 323]

EARLE, WILLIAM BENSON (1740–1796), philanthropist ; educated at Salisbury Cathedral school, Winchester College, and Merton College, Oxford ; M.A., 1764 ; published descriptions of continental tour extending from 1765 to 1767 ; bequeathed large sums to learned and charitable institutions. [xvi. 323]

EARLOM, RICHARD (1743–1822), mezzotint engraver ; studied under G. B. Cipriani [q. v.], admiration for whose allegorical paintings on the lord mayor's state coach induced him to become an artist ; achieved a fine style in the chalk manner, and in mezzotint representation of the texture of flowers ; executed prints after Claude Lorraine to further the detection of spurious works. [xvi. 324]

EARNSHAW, LAURENCE (*d.* 1767), mechanician ; constructed an astronomical clock ; invented a machine to spin and reel cotton simultaneously, 1753, which he destroyed, under the impression that it would lessen the demand for labour. [xvi. 324]

EARNSHAW, THOMAS (1749–1829), watchmaker ; first to bring chronometers within the means of private individuals ; invented cylindrical balance spring and detached detent escapement. [xvi. 325]

EARWAKER, JOHN PARSONS (1847–1895), antiquary ; M.A. Merton College, Oxford, 1876 ; studied at Middle Temple ; honorary secretary of Oxford Archæological Society ; F.S.A., 1873 ; published 'East Cheshire,' 1877–81, and other writings, relating chiefly to Cheshire and Lancashire ; edited 'Court Leet Records of Manor of Manchester,' 1884–90. [Suppl. ii. 172]

EAST, SIR EDWARD HYDE (1764–1847), chief-justice of Calcutta ; born in Jamaica ; barrister, Inner Temple, 1786 ; M.P., Great Bedwin, 1792 ; knighted ; chief-justice of the supreme court at Fort William, Bengal, 1813–22 ; chief promoter of the Hindoo College ; created baronet, 1823 ; M.P., Winchester, 1823–30 ; member of judicial committee of privy council ; F.R.S., and bencher of the Inner Temple ; published 'Pleas of the Crown,' 1803 ; compiled case reports. [xvi. 325]

EAST, SIR JAMES BULLER (1789–1878), barrister ; eldest son of Sir Edward Hyde East [q. v.] ; educated at Harrow and Christ Church, Oxford ; M.A., 1824 ; D.C.L., 1834 ; barrister, Inner Temple, 1863 ; reader, 1869 ; M.P., Winchester, 1830–2 and 1835–64 ; deputy-lieutenant for Gloucestershire. [xvi. 326]

EAST (also spelt EST, ESTE, and EASTE) MICHAEL (1580 ?–1680 ?), musical composer ; probably son of Thomas East [q. v.] ; wrote 'Hence, stars too dim of light,' a madrigal, for the 'Triumphs of Oriana' (printed, 1601) ; choirmaster of Lichfield Cathedral, *c.* 1618 ; author of 'Madrigales,' pastorals, 'Neopolitanes,' and 'anthemes.' His last book, comprising 'Duos for two Base Viols' and 'Ayerie Fancies of 4 parts' appeared in 1638. [xvi. 326]

EAST (also spelt EST, ESTE, and EASTE), THOMAS (1540 ?–1608 ?), printer and music-publisher ; published Burd's 'Bassus,' 1587 ; printed a new edition of Damon's psalter, showing the ancient and modern methods of harmonising tunes for congregational use, 1591 ; edited 'The Whole Booke of Psalmes,' an early example of 'score,' 1592 ; published (1603) 'The Triumphs of Oriana,' a collection of madrigals in honour of Queen Elizabeth ; connected with most of the musical publications of the time. [xvi. 327]

EAST-ANGLES, KINGS OF. [See REDWALD, *d.* 627 ? ; SIGEBERT, *d.* 637 ? ; ETHELBERT, *d.* 794 ; EDMUND, 841–870.]

EASTCOTT, RICHARD (1740 ?–1828), writer on music ; deprecated the custom of writing fugal music for voices in 'Sketches of the Origin, Progress, and Effects of Music,' 1793 ; chaplain of Livery Dale, Devonshire. [xvi. 329]

EASTCOURT, RICHARD (1668–1712). [See ESTCOURT.]

EASTER KENNET, LORD (*d.* 1594). [See HAY, ALEXANDER.]

EASTHOPE, SIR JOHN (1784–1865), politician and journalist ; M.P., St. Albans, 1826–30, Banbury, 1831, and Leicester, 1837–47 ; magistrate for Middlesex and Surrey, and chairman of various companies ; purchased the 'Morning Chronicle,' 1834 ; created baronet, 1841. [xvi. 329]

EASTLAKE, SIR CHARLES LOCK (1793–1865), president of the Royal Academy ; entered Charterhouse School, 1808 ; studied art under Benjamin Robert Haydon [q. v.] and in the Royal Academy schools ; returning from studying the Louvre masterpieces (1815) to Plymouth, was enabled to visit Italy by the proceeds of a portrait of Napoleon I, devoting himself to landscape-painting at Rome ; visited Athens, Malta, and Sicily, on a sketching tour ; exhibited 'banditti' pictures at the British Institution, 1823 ; exhibited at Royal Academy after 1827 ; praised by Haydon for the 'Titianesque' simplicity of his 'Champion' ; twice refused the chair of fine arts at the London University, 1833 and 1836 ;

secretary of the Fine Arts Commission ; commissioner for the exhibition of 1851 ; president of the Royal Academy, 1850–65 ; director of the National Gallery, 1855 ; died at Pisa ; F.R.S. and honorary D.C.L. Oxford ; published 'Materials for the History of Oil-painting,' some books of art criticism, and a translation of Goethe's 'Theory of Colours,' 1840.   [xvi. 330]

EASTLAKE, ELIZABETH, LADY (1809–1893), authoress ; daughter of Edward Rigby (1747–1821) [q. v.] ; travelled in Germany and Russia, and published, 1841, 'A Residence on the Shores of the Baltic' ; contributed, from 1842, numerous articles to 'Quarterly,' in one of which (1848) she attacked 'Jane Eyre' ; married Sir Charles Lock Eastlake [q. v.], 1849. Her works include translation of Waagen's 'Treasures of Art in Great Britain,' 1854–7, 'Five Great Painters,' 1883, and a revised edition of her husband's issue of Kügler's 'Handbook of Painting : Italian Schools,' 1874. Her 'Journals and Correspondence' appeared, 1895.   [Suppl. ii. 173]

EASTMEAD, WILLIAM (d. 1847 ?), dissenting minister ; pastor at Kirkby Moorside, Yorkshire ; published two theologico-moral essays, also (1824) 'Historia Rievallensis.'   [xvi. 333]

EASTON, ADAM (d. 1397), cardinal ; of humble parentage ; doctor in theology, Oxford ; erroneously described as bishop of Hereford or of London ; cardinal-priest after 1381 ; nominated by papal provision to the deanery of York, 1382 ; thrown into a dungeon at Nocera by Urban II for being concerned in the cardinals' plot against the pope's despotic rule, 1385 ; liberated by the intervention of Richard II, but degraded from the cardinalate ; reinstated by Boniface IX, 1389 ; prebendary of Salisbury before 1392 ; incumbent of Hecham ; died at Rome. Of his numerous writings, among which may be mentioned 'Perfectio Vitæ Spiritualis' and 'Hebraica Saraceni,' none are extant.   [xvi. 333]

EAST-SAXONS, KINGS OF. [See SEBERT, d. 616 ? ; SEXRED, d. 626 ; SIGEBERT, fl. 626 ; SIGEBERT, fl. 653 ; SIGHERI, fl. 665 ; SEBBI, d. 695 ? ; SIGHARD, fl. 695 ; OFFA, fl. 709 ; SELRED, d. 746 ; SIGERED, fl. 799.]

EASTWICK, EDWARD BACKHOUSE (1814–1883), orientalist and diplomatist ; educated at Charterhouse and Merton College, Oxford ; given political employment in Kattiawar and Sindh ; professor of Hindustani at the East India College, Haileybury, 1845 ; assistant political secretary at the India Office, 1859 ; barrister, Middle Temple, 1860 ; secretary of legation to the Persian court, 1860–3 ; commissioner for arranging a Venezuelan loan, 1864 and 1867 ; C.B. ; M.P., Penryn and Falmouth, 1868–74 ; translated Sa'di's 'Gulistan,' 1852, and some Hindustani classics, besides writing works dealing with his diplomatic experiences.   [xvi. 334]

EASTWOOD, JONATHAN (1824–1864), topographer ; M.A. St. John's College, Cambridge, 1849 ; incumbent of Hope, Staffordshire ; wrote a 'History of the Parish of Ecclesfield in the County of York,' 1862, and a 'Bible Word-book,' published 1866.   [xvi. 335]

EATA (d. 686), bishop of Hexham and Lindisfarne ; disciple of St. Aidan and, in 651, abbot of Melrose ; consecrated bishop of the Bernicians, 678 ; bishop of Lindisfarne alone, and subsequently of Hexham alone, his see having been divided in 681.   [xvi. 336]

EATON, MRS. CHARLOTTE ANN (1788–1859). [See WALDIE.]

EATON, DANIEL ISAAC (d. 1814), bookseller ; indicted for selling the second part of Paine's 'Rights of Man,' 1793, and for a supposed libel on George III in 'Politics for the People,' 1794, but acquitted ; fled to America, and was outlawed, 1796 ; translated Helvetius's 'True Sense and Meaning of the System of Nature,' 1810 ; pilloried, 1812 ; tried, for publishing 'Ecce Homo,' 1813, but, being an old man, was not brought up for judgment.   [xvi. 336]

EATON, JOHN (fl. 1619), divine ; M.A. Trinity College, Oxford, 1603 ; vicar of Wickham Market, Suffolk, 1604–19 ; deprived, as a suspected antinomian, 1619 ; imprisoned ; published works including 'The Honey-Combe of Free Justification by Christ alone,' 1642.   [xvi. 336]

EATON, NATHANIEL (1609 ?–1674), president-designate of Harvard College, Massachusetts ; brother of Theophilus Eaton [q. v.] ; educated at Westminster and Trinity College, Cambridge ; emigrated to America, 1637 ; president-designate of Harvard College, 1638–9 ; dismissed by order of the court at Boston for cruelty to his pupils and ushers, 1639 ; doctor of philosophy and medicine, Padua, 1647 ; vicar of Bishops Castle, Shropshire, 1661 ; rector of Bideford, 1668 ; died a prisoner for debt in the king's bench.   [xvi. 337]

EATON, SAMUEL (1596 ?–1665), independent divine ; M.A. Magdalene College, Cambridge, 1628 ; brother of Theophilus Eaton [q. v.] ; colleague of John Davenport [q. v.] at New Haven ; returned to England (1640) for the purpose of gathering a company to settle Toboket, but did not go back to America ; assistant to the parliamentary commissioners of Cheshire ; an influential preacher ; teacher of a congregational church at Dukinfield, Cheshire ; wrote against the Socinians and quakers.   [xvi. 338]

EATON, THEOPHILUS (1590 ?–1658), first governor of New Haven ; friend of John Davenport [q. v.], at New Haven ; deputy-governor of the East Land Company ; agent of Charles I to the court of Denmark ; original patentee and magistrate of Massachusetts, 1629 ; founded settlement of New Haven, 1638 ; annually re-elected governor of New Haven, 1639–58 ; drew up the 'blue' code of laws, so named from its whimsicality and severity (printed 1656) ; treated Dutch and Indians fairly and prudently.   [xvi. 340]

EBBA or **ÆBBE**, SAINT (d. 679 ?), abbess of Coldingham ; daughter of Æthelfrith, king of Northumbria ; founded monastery at Ebchester on the Derwent ; abbess of Coldingham, Berwickshire, a mixed monastery of monks and nuns, which was burnt down in 679 as a divine punishment on the disorderliness of its inmates, according to the dream of a monk named Adamnan ; said to have healed Queen Eormenburh of a malady caused by demoniacal possession.   [xvi. 341]

EBBA (fl. 870), abbess of Coldingham when the house was destroyed by the Danes.   [xvi. 342]

EBDON, THOMAS (1738–1811), organist of Durham Cathedral, 1763–1811. His 'Morning, Communion, and Evening Service in O' is still occasionally heard.   [xvi. 342]

EBERS, JOHN (1785 ?–1830 ?), operatic manager ; lessee of the King's Theatre, opening it in 1821 with 'La Gazza Ladra' ; produced, with alternate success and failure, representative Italian operas ; sublet the theatre to Benelli, his assistant stage manager, who absconded in 1824 ; ruined by the enormous rent of the theatre, 1826 ; became a bookseller, publishing 'Seven Years of the King's Theatre,' 1828.   [xvi. 342]

EBORARD or **EVERARD** (1083 ?–1150), second bishop of Norwich ; archdeacon of Salisbury in 1121 ; consecrated bishop of Norwich, 1121 ; one of the bishops who attested the great charter issued by Stephen, 1135 ; deposed, according to Henry of Huntingdon, for his cruelty, c. 1145 ; built the church of Fontenay Abbey ; died, a Cistercian monk, at Fontenay, 1150.   [xvi. 344]

EBORIUS or **EBURIUS** (fl. 314), bishop of Eboracum or York ; one of the three bishops from the Roman province of Britain who attended the council of Arles, 314.   [xvi. 345]

EBSWORTH, JOSEPH (1788–1868), dramatist and musician ; baritone singer at Covent Garden Theatre ; actor and prompter at the Theatre Royal, Edinburgh ; abandoned the stage to become choir-leader at St. Stephen's Church ; friend of Charles Dibdin the younger [q. v.] ; author of numerous short dramas and a collection of songs in manuscript.   [xvi. 345]

EBSWORTH, MARY EMMA (1794–1881), dramatist ; née Fairbrother ; married to Joseph Ebsworth [q. v.], 1817 ; author of works published in Cumberland's 'Acting Drama.'   [xvi. 347]

EBURY, BARON (1801–1893). [See GROSVENOR, ROBERT.]

ECCARDT or **ECKHARDT**, JOHN GILES (JOHANNES ÆGIDIUS) (d. 1779), portrait-painter ; native of Germany ; succeeded to the practice of his master, Vanloo ; painted portraits of Bentley, Gray, and Mrs. Woffington.   [xvi. 347]

ECCLES, AMBROSE (*d.* 1809), Shakespearean scholar; educated at Trinity College, Dublin; edited 'Cymbeline,' 1793, 'King Lear,' 1793, and 'Merchant of Venice,' 1805, transposing scenes which he thought wrongly placed. [xvi. 348]

ECCLES, HENRY (*fl.* 1720), violinist; son of Solomon Eccles [q. v.]; member of the king's band, 1694–1710; member of the French king's band; published in Paris 'Twelve Excellent Solos for the Violin,' 1720. [xvi. 348]

ECCLES, JOHN (*d.* 1735), musical composer; son of Solomon Eccles [q. v.]; contributed songs to about forty-six plays; master of Queen Anne's band, 1704; composed new-year and birthday songs for the court. [xvi. 348]

ECCLES, SOLOMON (1618–1683), musician and quaker; abandoned music on becoming a quaker, 1660; wandered naked through London streets, prophesying divine wrath, during the plague of 1665; accompanied George Fox to the West Indies, 1671; banished from New England, 1672, and from Barbados, 1680; published 'A Musick-Lector,' 1667, and 'The Quakers Challenge,' 1668, the latter making physical endurance in spiritual exercises a proof of the true religion. [xvi. 349]

ECCLESTON, THOMAS OF (*fl.* 1250), Franciscan; studied at Oxford; wrote 'De Adventu Fratrum Minorum in Angliam' (printed 1858). [xvi. 350]

ECCLESTON, THOMAS (1659–1743), jesuit; educated at St. Omer and the English college, Rome; captain in James II's army after 1688; professed of the four vows, 1712; missioner in Yorkshire; chaplain to Lord Petre. [xvi. 350]

ECCLESTONE or **EGGLESTONE**, WILLIAM (*fl.* 1605–1623), actor; joined the king's company of actors associated with the Blackfriars and Globe theatres after 1605, performing in Jonson's 'Alchemist,' 1610; joined Henslowe's company at the Fortune Theatre, 1611. [xvi. 350]

ECHARD, LAURENCE (1670?–1730), historian; M.A. Christ's College, Cambridge, 1695; prebendary of Lincoln, 1697; archdeacon of Stow, 1712–30; F.S.A.; chief work, 'A History of England,' 1707 and 1718; translated Terence and part of Plautus, 1694, writing also various compendiums; translated D'Orleans' 'History of the Revolutions in England (1603–1690)' (second edition, 1722). [xvi. 351]

ECHLIN, ROBERT (*d.* 1635), bishop of Down and Connor; M.A. St. Andrews, 1596; in charge of second congregation of Inverkeithing, 1601; bishop of Down and Connor, 1613; procured commission to inquire into causes of impoverishment of his diocese, 1615; abandoned policy of toleration and deposed (1634) the presbyterian ministers, Livingstone and Robert Blair. [xvi. 352]

ECTON, JOHN (*d.* 1730), compiler; receiver of the tenths of the clergy in Queen Anne's Bounty office; F.S.A., 1723; bequeathed his manuscripts and books to Oxford University; author of two works of reference in connection with Queen Anne's Bounty Fund. [xvi. 353]

EDBURGE, SAINT (*d.* 751). [See EADBURGA.]

EDDI, **ÆDDE**, or **EDDIUS** (*fl.* 669), biographer; assumed the name of Stephanus, probably on taking orders; brought to Northumbria by Bishop Wilfrid to teach the Roman method of chanting, 669; monk at Ripon; wrote a 'Vita Wilfridi Episcopi,' which William of Malmesbury consulted. [xvi. 354]

EDDISBURY, first BARON (1802–1869). [See STANLEY, EDWARD JOHN.]

EDELBURGE, SAINT (*d.* 676?). [See ETHELBURGA.]

EDEMA, GERARD (1652–1700?), landscape-painter; native of Friesland; travelled in Guiana, Norway, and Newfoundland; came to England, c. 1670. His paintings of novel and unknown scenery earned for him the title of 'the Salvator Rosa of the North.' [xvi. 354]

EDEN, SIR ASHLEY (1831–1887), Indian official; third son of Robert John Eden [q. v.]; educated at Rugby and Winchester; magistrate at Moorshedábád, 1856, doing much to prevent disaffection there, 1857; secretary to the governor of Bengal, 1860–71; envoy to Bhután, where he was constrained to sign a disadvantageous treaty, 1863;

chief commissioner of British Burmah, 1871; lieutenant-governor of Bengal, 1877–82; K.C.S.I., 1878; member of the secretary of state's council, 1882. [xvi. 354]

EDEN, CHARLES PAGE (1807–1885), clerical author and editor; bible clerk, Oriel College, Oxford, 1825; B.A., 1829; Ellerton and chancellor's prizeman; fellow of Oriel, 1832; vicar of St. Mary's, Oxford, 1843–50; prebendary of York, 1870; edited Gunning's 'Paschal or Lent Fast,' 1845, Andrewes's 'Pattern of Catechistical Doctrine,' 1846, and Jeremy Taylor's works. [xvi. 355]

EDEN, EMILY (1797–1869), novelist and traveller; daughter of William Eden, first baron Auckland [q. v.]; accompanied her brother, George Eden [q. v.], to India; published 'Portraits of the People and Princes of India,' 1844, 'Up the Country,' 1866, and two novels, 'The Semi-detached House,' 1859, and 'The Semi-attached Couple,' 1860. [xvi. 356]

EDEN, SIR FREDERICK MORTON (1766–1809), writer on the state of the poor; nephew of William Eden, first baron Auckland [q. v.]; M.A. Christ Church, Oxford, 1789; chairman of the Globe Insurance Company; applied the principles of Adam Smith to investigations into the condition of the poor; chief work, 'The State of the Poor; or an History of the Labouring Classes in England from the Conquest to the present period,' 1797. [xvi. 356]

EDEN, GEORGE, first EARL OF AUCKLAND (1784–1849), statesman and governor-general of India; second son of William Eden, first baron Auckland [q. v.]; M.A. Christ Church, Oxford, 1808; barrister, Lincoln's Inn, 1809; M.P., Woodstock, 1810–12, re-elected, 1813; president of the board of trade, 1830–4 and 1835, and master of the mint, 1830–4; first lord of the admiralty, 1834; G.C.B.; governor-general of India, 1835; instituted famine relief works in the north-west provinces, 1838; adopted the policy of reinstating Sháh Shujá as ameer of Afghanistan, 1837; created Earl of Auckland on successful termination of first Afghan campaign, 1839; recalled by Peel after catastrophe of November 1841; first lord of the admiralty, 1846; president of the Royal Asiatic Society and of the senate of University College, London. [xvi. 357]

EDEN, HENRY (1797–1888), admiral; cousin of George Eden [q. v.]; navy lieutenant, 1817; commanded the Martin off the coast of Greece during the Greek revolution, 1822–4; flag-captain to Sir Graham Moore, commander-in-chief at Plymouth, 1839–42; admiralty lord, 1855–8; rear-admiral, 1854; admiral, 1864. [xvi. 358]

EDEN, MORTON, first BARON HENLEY (1752–1830), diplomatist; matriculated at Christ Church, Oxford, 1770; minister plenipotentiary to the elector of Bavaria; envoy extraordinary at Copenhagen, 1779, at Dresden, 1782; K.B., 1791; ambassador to the Austrian court, 1793; privy councillor, 1794; envoy extraordinary to Vienna, 1794–9; created peer of Ireland as Baron Henley of Chardstock, Dorset, 1799; F.R.S. [xvi. 359]

EDEN, RICHARD (1521?–1576), translator; studied at Queens' College, Cambridge, 1535–44; cited before Bishop Gardiner for heresy, and deprived of his place in the English treasury of the Prince of Spain; entered service of Jean de Ferrières, vidame of Chartres, 1562; translated Münster's 'Cosmography,' 1553, and John Taisner's 'De Natura Magnetis,' 1574, and published 'The Decades of the Newe Worlde, or West India,' 1555. [xvi. 359]

EDEN, ROBERT (1804–1886), bishop of Moray, Ross, and Caithness; son of Sir Frederick Morton Eden [q. v.]; educated at Westminster and Christ Church, Oxford; B.A., 1827; bishop of Moray and Ross, 1851; D.D., 1851; primus of the Scottish church, 1862; founded St Andrew's Cathedral, Inverness; worked for recognition of Scottish orders by the English church; founder of the Representative Church Council; published tracts. [xvi. 360]

EDEN, ROBERT HENLEY, second BARON HENLEY (1789–1841), son of Morton Eden, first baron [q. v.]; M.A. Christ Church, Oxford, 1814; barrister of Lincoln's Inn, 1814; mastery in chancery, 1826–40; M.P., Fowey, 1826–30; wrote on bankruptcy laws and ecclesiastical questions. [xvi. 361]

EDEN, ROBERT JOHN, third BARON AUCKLAND (1799–1870), bishop of Bath and Wells; son of William

Eden, first baron Auckland [q. v.]; M.A. Magdalene College, Cambridge, 1819; D.D., 1847; royal chaplain, 1831–7, and 1837–47; bishop of Sodor and Man, 1847–54; bishop of Bath and Wells, 1854–69; published pamphlets and edited 'Journal' of William, lord Auckland, 1860.

[xvi. 361]

EDEN, THOMAS (d. 1645), master of Trinity Hall, Cambridge; scholar of Trinity Hall, Cambridge, 1596; fellow, 1599; LL.B., 1613; professor of law, Gresham College, London, 1613–40; member of College of Advocates at Doctors' Commons, 1615; LL.D., 1616; M.P. for Cambridge University, 1626, 1628, and 1640; master of Trinity Hall, 1626; chancellor of Ely, 1630; took the solemn national league and covenant, 1644; member of the admiralty committee, 1645; benefactor of Trinity Hall.

[xvi. 361]

EDEN, WILLIAM, first BARON AUCKLAND (1744–1814), statesman and diplomatist; educated at Eton and Christ Church, Oxford; M.A., 1768; barrister, Middle Temple, 1769; under-secretary of state, 1772; M.P., Woodstock, 1774 and 1778–84; a first lord of the board of trade and plantations, 1776; privy councillor of Ireland; sat for Dungannon in the Irish parliament; established National Bank of Ireland; vice-treasurer of Ireland, 1783; privy councillor; M.P., Heytesbury, 1784; negotiated commercial treaty with France, 1786; created Baron Auckland in Irish peerage, 1789; concluded a treaty on the settlement of Holland with the Emperor Leopold and the king of Prussia, 1790; ambassador extraordinary at the Hague during the French revolution; created Baron Auckland of West Auckland, Durham, 1793; joint postmaster-general, 1798–1804, under both Pitt and Addington; excluded from Pitt's second administration, 1804; president of board of trade in Grenville's of 'All the Talents,' 1806–7; published 'Principles of Penal Law,' 1772, and a 'History of New Holland,' 1788.

[xvi. 362]

EDERSHEIM, ALFRED (1825–1889), biblical scholar; born of Jewish parents at Vienna; studied at Vienna University; embraced Christianity; studied theology in Edinburgh and Berlin; entered presbyterian ministry, 1846; preached as missionary at Jassy, Roumania; minister of free church, Old Aberdeen, 1848, and of presbyterian church at Torquay, 1861–72; held living of Loders, near Bridport, Dorset, 1876–82; Warburtonian lecturer at Lincoln's Inn, 1880–4; M.A. Oxford, 1881; select preacher to university, 1884–5; Grinfield lecturer on the Septuagint, 1886–8 and 1888–90; published 'Life and Times of Jesus the Messiah,' 1883, 'Bible History' (of Old Testament), 1876–87, and other religious writings.

[Suppl. ii. 175]

EDES or **EEDES**, RICHARD (1555–1604), dean of Worcester; educated at Westminster and Christ Church, Oxford; student, 1571; M.A., 1578; D.D., 1590; prebendary of Sarum, 1584, of Christ Church Cathedral, 1586, and of Hereford, 1590; treasurer of Hereford, 1596; queen's chaplain; dean of Worcester, 1597; chaplain to James I; prevented by death from taking part in the translation of the bible.

[xvi. 364]

EDEYRN, DAVOD AUR, i.e. THE GOLDEN-TONGUED (fl. 1270), Welsh bard and grammarian; said to have compiled a Welsh grammar and prosody.

[xvi. 365]

EDGAR or **EADGAR** (944–975), king of the English; younger son of Eadmund the Magnificent [see EDMUND, 922?–946]; chosen king of the land north of the Thames by the northern rebels, 957; appointed Dunstan [q. v.] his chief minister; chosen king by the whole people, 959; imposed on the rebellious prince of North Wales a tribute of three hundred wolves' heads for four years, c. 968; pacified Northumbria, 966; entrusted the province to Earl Oslac, 966; said to have purchased the goodwill of Kenneth, king of Scotland, by the grant of Lothian; allowed limited self-government to the Danes of the north; appointed Oswald, a Northumbrian Dane, archbishop of York, 972; solemnly crowned at Bath, possibly as an 'enunciation of the consummation of English unity,' 973; received homage of eight British princes at Chester, 973; made an alliance with the emperor Otto the Great; dispossessed clerks in favour of Benedictine monks at Chertsey, Milton, Exeter, Ely, Peterborough, Thorney, and throughout Mercia; organised a system of naval defence against the northern pirates, and used the territorial division of the hundred as the basis of an efficient police system; according to legend, was ordered by Dunstan to

do penance for incontinence; reports of the looseness of his private life probably exaggerated by the national party, which disliked his Danish sympathies.

[xvi. 365]

EDGAR (1072–1107), king of Scotland; son of Malcolm Canmore; fled to England on Donald Bane's usurpation, 1093; placed on the Scottish throne by William Rufus, 1097; compelled by the Norwegian king, Magnus Barefoot, to surrender all the western islands round which he could steer a helm-carrying vessel, 1098; friend to the church.

[xvi. 370]

EDGAR ATHELING or **EADGAR** the ÆTHELING (fl. 1066–1106), king-elect of England; son of Eadward the Exile; born in Hungary; chosen king by the two archbishops and the northern earls, Eadwine and Morkere, after Harold's defeat, 1066; compelled by defection of his supporters to submit to William I (1066), who received him graciously; took part in insurrections of 1068 and 1069; allied himself with the Danes, 1069; wandered about among the courts of Scotland, Flanders, and France; lived at William I's court, c. 1074–86; joined the Normans in Apulia, 1086; resided at the court of Duke Robert of Normandy; led expedition to Scotland to set his nephew Edgar (1072–1107) [q. v.] on the throne, 1097; crusader, 1099; fought for Robert of Normandy against Henry I at Tenchebrai, where he was taken prisoner, 1106; released, 1106.

[xvi. 371]

EDGAR, JOHN (1798–1866), theologian and philanthropist; educated at Glasgow University and at Belfast; minister of a Belfast congregation, 1820–48; professor of theology in the secession branch of the presbyterian church, 1826; D.D. Hamilton College, U.S.A., 1836; moderator of the general assembly, 1842; LL.D. New York, 1860; warmly championed temperance, although he disapproved of teetotal movement; visited America to enlist sympathy for the starving Irish peasants, 1859.

[xvi. 373]

EDGAR, JOHN GEORGE (1834–1864), miscellaneous writer; travelled on mercantile business in the West Indies; first editor of 'Every Boy's Magazine'; published 'The Boyhood of Great Men,' 1853, and 'Footprints of Famous Men,' 1853.

[xvi. 374]

EDGCUMBE, GEORGE, first EARL OF MOUNT-EDGCUMBE (1721–1795), son of Richard, first baron Edgcumbe [q. v.]; navy lieutenant, 1739; took part in blockade of Brest and battle of Quiberon Bay, 1759; lord-lieutenant of Cornwall, 1761; admiral, 1778; created Viscount Mount-Edgcumbe, 1781, and Earl of Mount-Edgcumbe, 1789; one of the vice-treasurers of Ireland, 1771–3, and 1784–95.

[xvi. 375]

EDGCUMBE, SIR PIERS (d. 1539), son of Sir Richard Edgcumbe (d. 1489) [q. v.]; K.B., 1489; sheriff of Devonshire, 1493, 1494, and 1497; made knight-banneret for his services at the battle of Spurs, 1513.

[xvi. 376]

EDGCUMBE or **EDGECOMBE**, SIR RICHARD (d. 1489), statesman; M.P., Tavistock, 1467; escheator of Cornwall, 1467; took part in the Duke of Buckingham's rebellion, escaping to Brittany after its failure, 1484; knighted by Henry VII for valour at Bosworth Field, 1485; erected a chapel in honour of the victory; privy councillor and chamberlain of the exchequer; sheriff of Devonshire, 1487; ambassador to Scotland; administered the oaths of allegiance in Ireland, 1488; despatched to negotiate truce with Anne, duchess of Brittany, 1488; died at Morlaix.

[xvi. 375]

EDGCUMBE or **EDGECOMBE**, SIR RICHARD (1499–1562), country gentleman, called 'the good old knight of the castle'; son of Sir Piers Edgcumbe [q. v.]; knighted, 1537; sheriff of Devon, 1543 and 1544; commissioner of muster in Cornwall, 1557.

[xvi. 376]

EDGCUMBE, RICHARD, first BARON EDGCUMBE (1680–1758); M.A. Trinity College, Cambridge, 1698; M.P., Cornwall, 1701, Plympton and St. Germans, 1702; treasury lord, 1716 and 1720; vice-treasurer, receiver-general, treasurer of war, and paymaster-general of George I's revenues in Ireland, 1724; adherent of Walpole; raised to the peerage, 1742, to prevent his being examined as to the management of the Cornish boroughs; chancellor of the duchy of Lancaster, 1743–58; privy councillor, 1744.

[xvi. 377]

EDGCUMBE, RICHARD, second BARON EDGCUMBE (1716–1761), son of Richard, first baron [q. v.]; major-general in the army; M.P., Lostwithiel, 1747–54, Penryn,

1754; admiralty lord, 1755-6; comptroller of his majesty's household, 1756; privy councillor, 1756; friend of Horace Walpole; one of the first to recognise the genius of Reynolds.   [xvi. 377]

EDGCUMBE, RICHARD, second EARL OF MOUNT-EDGCUMBE (1764–1839), son of George, first earl [q. v.]; D.C.L. Christ Church, Oxford, 1793; M.P., Fowey, 1786–1795; captain of the band of gentlemen-pensioners, 1808–1812; privy councillor, 1808; wrote, for private circulation, 'Musical Reminiscences of an Old Amateur.'
                                                    [xvi. 378]

EDGEWORTH DE FIRMONT, HENRY ESSEX (1745–1807), confessor to Louis XVI; son of an Irish clergyman; educated by the jesuits of Toulouse and at Paris; took name De Firmont when ordained; declined an Irish see, preferring to work among the poor of Paris; confessor to the French Princess Elizabeth, 1791; attended Louis XVI on the scaffold as friend and confessor, 1793; eventually accepted Pitt's offer of a pension, from fear of becoming a burden to the exiled Louis XVIII, who had appointed him chaplain; died of a fever contracted while attending French prisoners at Mittau.   [xvi. 378]

EDGEWORTH, MARIA (1767–1849), novelist; daughter of Richard Lovell Edgeworth [q. v.]; undertook her brother Henry's education; defended female education in 'Letters to Literary Ladies,' 1795; published, in conjunction with her father, two volumes on 'Practical Education,' 1798, adopting, with modifications, the ideas of Rousseau's 'Émile'; published 'Castle Rackrent,' 1800, and 'Belinda,' 1801; issued 'Essay on Irish Bulls,' 1802; published 'Moral Tales,' 1801; brought out 'Popular Tales' and 'The Modern Griselda,' 1804, 'Leonora,' 1806, and two series of 'Tales of Fashionable Life,' 1809 and 1812; brought out her father's 'Memoirs,' amid the distractions of domestic troubles and society calls, 1820; complimented by Scott on her descriptions of Irish character, 1823; published 'Helen,' her last novel, 1834; did much to relieve the sufferers in the Irish famine, 1846; gave much literary advice to Basil Hall.   [xvi. 380]

EDGEWORTH, MICHAEL PAKENHAM (1812–1881), botanist; son of Richard Lovell Edgeworth [q. v.]; studied at the Charterhouse and at Edinburgh; member of Indian civil service, 1831–81; contributed 'Two Hours' Herborization at Aden' to the 'Journal of the Asiatic Society of Bengal,' describing forty species, eleven quite new, which, 1831, he had collected there; commissioner for the settlement of the Punjab, 1850; author of papers on the botany of India, a volume on 'Pollen,' 1878, and a 'Grammar of Kashmiri.'   [xvi. 382]

EDGEWORTH, RICHARD LOVELL (1744–1817), author; fellow commoner, Trinity College, Dublin, 1761; left Dublin in disgust at his idleness, and entered Corpus Christi College, Oxford, 1761; led to invent a plan for telegraphing by a desire to know the result of a race at Newmarket; silver medallist of the Society of Arts for a new land-measuring machine, 1768; friend of Thomas Day [q. v.], Miss Seward, and Erasmus Darwin; visited Rousseau and settled at Lyons, 1771; settled on his estates in Ireland, 1782; aide-de-camp to Lord Charlemont, 1783; succeeded in getting a government telegraph line erected between Dublin and Galway, 1804; raised a corps against the rebels at Edgeworthstown, 1798, and sat in the last Irish parliament; served on a board for inquiring into Irish education, 1806–11; four times married; published works on educational and mechanical subjects.
                                                    [xvi. 383]

EDGEWORTH, ROGER (d. 1560), Roman catholic divine; B.A. Oxford, 1507; fellow of Oriel, 1508; D.D., 1526; prebendary of Bristol, 1542; canon of Wells and Salisbury; chancellor of Wells, 1554; prebendary of Salisbury; benefactor of Oriel College; published works on church discipline.   [xvi. 385]

EDGUARD, DAVID (fl. 1532), anatomist; educated at Oxford and Cambridge; published 'De Indiciis et Præcognitionibus,' 1532, and 'Introductio ad Anatomicen,' 1532.   [xvi. 386]

EDINBURGH, DUKE OF (1844–1900). [See ALFRED ERNEST ALBERT.]

EDINGTON, WILLIAM OF (d. 1366), bishop of Winchester and chancellor; prebendary of Lincoln, 1342-6, of Salisbury, 1344-6; bishop of Winchester, 1346; prebendary of Hereford, 1345; king's treasurer, 1345–56; carried out

an issue of base coinage, 1351; chancellor, 1356–63; refused the archbishopric of Canterbury on account of ill-health, 1366; founded a college of reformed Austin friars at Westbury, Wiltshire, c. 1347; commenced recasing of Walkelin's nave in Winchester Cathedral.   [xvi. 386]

EDITH or EADGYTH, SAINT (962?–984), daughter of king Eadgar and Wulfthryth by a 'hand-fast' marriage; built church at Wilton; greatly venerated as a saint.
                                                    [xvi. 387]

EDITH or EADGYTH (d. 1075), queen of Eadward the Confessor; daughter of Earl Godwine; divorced from King Eadward and immured either in Wherwell or Wilton nunnery, 1051; brought back to the court on the reconciliation of the king and Earl Godwine, 1052; obtained the abolition of the custom which empowered bishops and abbots to receive kisses from ladies; commended by the dying Eadward to the care of her brother Harold, whose cause she deserted, 1066.   [xvi. 387]

EDLIN or EDLYN, RICHARD (1631–1677), astrologer; contributed to his 'noble science,' 'Observationes Astrologicæ,' 1659, and 'Præ-Nuncius Sydereus,' 1664.
                                                    [xvi. 389]

EDMONDES, SIR CLEMENT (1564?–1622), clerk to the council; matriculated as chorister at All Souls' College, Oxford, 1586; fellow, 1590; M.A., 1593; remembrancer of the city of London, 1605–9; clerk of the council for life, 1609; mustermaster-general, 1613; commissioner to treat with Holland concerning disputes as to throwing open the East India trade and the Greenland fisheries, 1614; knighted, 1617; M.P., Oxford, 1620–1; nominated secretary of state, 1622; wrote mainly on military tactics.
                                                    [xvi. 389]

EDMONDES, SIR THOMAS (1563?–1639), diplomatist; English agent to Henry IV at Paris, 1592, 1597, and 1598; owed his advancement to Sir Robert Cecil; French secretary to Elizabeth, 1596; given a clerkship of the privy council for his careful negotiations with the Archduke Albert at Boulogne, 1598; M.P., Liskeard, 1601; knighted, 1603; M.P., Wilton, 1604; aimed at preserving peace between Spain and the States-General, when ambassador to the archduke at Brussels, 1605; suppressed a despatch instructing him to open negotiations for the marriage of Prince Charles with Princess Christina, sister of Louis XIII, immediately after the death of Prince Henry, 1612; privy councillor, 1616; treasurer of the royal household, 1618; succeeded by reversion to clerkship of crown in king's bench court, 1620; royalist M.P., Bewdley, 1620, Chichester, 1624, Oxford University, 1625, and Penryn, 1628.   [xvi. 391]

EDMONDS, RICHARD (1801–1886), scientific writer; published 'The Land's End District: its Antiquities, Natural History, Natural Phenomena, and Scenery,' 1862; attributed marine disturbances off the Cornish coast to submarine earthquakes; wrote also on antiquarian subjects.   [xvi. 393]

EDMONDS, SIR WILLIAM (d. 1606), Scottish colonel in the Dutch service; in command of a regiment of Scots foot cut to pieces at Leffingen, 1600; killed during defence of Rhineberg, 1606.   [xvi. 394]

EDMONDS, WILLIAM (1550?–1616). [See WESTON.]

EDMONDSON, GEORGE (1798–1863), promoter of education, originally a bookbinder's apprentice; master of a boarding-school at Broomhall; visited Russia as tutor to Daniel Wheeler's children, 1817; reclaimed the bog land round St. Petersburg, 1825; principal of Queenwood Hall, Hampshire, an Owenite school; added agriculture to the curriculum; an early promoter of the College of Preceptors.   [xvi. 394]

EDMONDSON, HENRY (1607?–1659), schoolmaster; tabarder of Queen's College, Oxford; fellow of Queen's; M.A., 1630; master of Northleach free school, Gloucestershire, 1655–9; chief work 'Lingua Linguarum,' a method of learning languages, 1655.   [xvi. 394]

EDMONDSON, JOSEPH (d. 1786), herald and genealogist; led to study heraldry by his employment of emblazoning coat-armour on carriages; Mowbray herald extraordinary, 1764; F.S.A.; compiled 'Complete Body of Heraldry,' 1780, and genealogical works. [xvi. 395]

EDMONDSON, THOMAS (1792–1851), inventor; brother of George Edmondson [q. v.]; quaker; railway clerk at Milton, near Carlisle; inventor of printed railway tickets, 1837.   [xvi. 396]

EDMONDSTON, ARTHUR (1776 ?–1841), writer on the Shetland isles ; army surgeon in Egypt under Sir Ralph Abercromby ; M.D. ; subsequently surgeon at Lerwick ; wrote two treatises on ophthalmia, and a ' View of the Ancient and Present State of the Zetland Islands,' 1809. [xvi. 396]

EDMONDSTON, LAURENCE (1795–1879), naturalist ; brother of Arthur Edmondston [q. v.] ; studied medicine at Edinburgh, and practised in Unst ; M.D. ; familiarised the public with the Shetland chromate of iron ; experimented in agriculture and acclimatised trees in the Shetlands ; Scandinavian scholar, and author of scientific pamphlets. [xvi. 397]

EDMONDSTON, THOMAS (1825–1846), naturalist ; son of Laurence Edmonston [q. v.], of Shetland ; kept a herbarium, in which was found *Arenaria norvegica*, then first discovered as a native plant ; assistant-secretary to the Edinburgh Botanical Society ; left Edinburgh University after a supposed affront ; elected professor of botany and natural history in Anderson's ' University,' Glasgow, 1845 ; issued ' Flora of Shetland,' 1845 ; naturalist on board the Herald ; accidentally shot in Peru, 1846. [xvi. 397]

EDMONSTONE, SIR ARCHIBALD, third baronet (1795–1871), traveller and author ; B.A. Christ Church, Oxford, 1816 ; published account of his travels in Egypt, 1822, 'Tragedies,' 1837, 'Leonora,' 1832, and religious works. [xvi. 398]

EDMONSTONE, SIR GEORGE FREDERICK (1813–1864), Indian civilian ; son of Neil Benjamin Edmonstone [q. v.] ; commissioner and superintendent of the Cis-Sutlej states ; secretary in foreign, political, and secret department, 1856 ; drew up proclamation confiscating the land of Oudh ; lieutenant-governor of the north-western provinces, 1859–63 ; created new government of central provinces ; K.C.B., 1863. [xvi. 399]

EDMONSTONE, NEIL BENJAMIN (1765–1841), Indian civilian ; writer to the East India Company, 1783 ; Persian translator to government, 1794 ; accompanied Lord Mornington's expedition against Tippoo Sultan, 1799, translating and publishing Tippoo's secret documents ; secretary to the foreign, political, and secret department, 1801 ; probably suggested Lord Wellesley's policy of subsidiary treaties ; chief secretary to government, 1809 ; member of the supreme council at Calcutta, 1812–17. [xvi. 399]

EDMONSTONE, ROBERT (1794–1834), artist ; exhibited portraits at the Royal Academy, 1818 ; twice visited Italy ; successful with child subjects. [xvi. 400]

EDMUND or **EADMUND** (841–870), king of the East Angles, martyr and saint ; born at Nüremberg ; son of King Alkmund ; adopted by Offa, king of the East Angles, *c.* 854 ; succeeded to Offa's throne, 855 ; defeated by the Danes at Hoxne (870), though according to another account he surrendered to avoid further slaughter ; bound to a tree, scourged, and beheaded on refusing to renounce Christianity ; interred at Hoxne ; subsequently enshrined at Bury ; canonised. [xvi. 400]

EDMUND or **EADMUND** (922 ?–946), king of the English ; son of Edward the elder ; besieged the independent kings of the north, Olaf and Wulfstan, at Leicester, 943 ; after a truce expelled both of them from Mercia and the Five Boroughs, 944 ; handed over Cumbria to Malcolm of Scotland, on condition that he should be his ' fellow-worker,' 945 ; demanded the release of his nephew, King Lewis, from Hugh, duke of the French ; named the ' deed-doer' or the ' magnificent ' ; stabbed by Liofa, a bandit. His laws were framed with a view to the reformation of manners of clergy and laity. [xvi. 401]

EDMUND or **EADMUND**, called IRONSIDE (981 ?–1016), king ; son of Æthelred the Unready ; married Ealdgyth, widow of the Danish earl Sigeferth, and received the submission of the Five Boroughs of the Danish confederacy, 1015 ; crowned in London, 1016 ; defeated Cnut at Pen in Somerset and at Sherston, Wiltshire ; utterly routed at Assandûn (Ashington in Essex) ; gave the north of England to Cnut by a treaty made in Olney, an island of the Severn, 1016 ; his death due to a sudden sickness, or possibly to the murderous resentment of Eadric (*d.* 1017) [q. v.] ; famous for his bodily strength. [xvi. 403]

EDMUND (RICH), SAINT (1170 ?–1240), archbishop of Canterbury ; brought up in ascetic habits ; sent to study at Paris (? 1185–1190) ; taught at Oxford, where he showed great tenderness towards his pupils (? 1195–1200) ; studied theology at Paris ; returned to Oxford as a teacher of divinity ; treasurer of Salisbury Cathedral, *c.* 1220 ; preached the crusade at Gregory IX's bidding, *c.* 1227 ; prebendary of Calne, *c.* 1233 ; archbishop of Canterbury, 1234 ; procured the dismissal of Henry III's favourites by the threat of excommunicating the king, 1234 ; bade Henry III interrogate his conscience when he disclaimed the murder of Richard, earl marshal, the recognised head of the national party, 1234 ; defended himself at Rome on charges arising out of the exercise of his archiepiscopal authority, 1238 ; acknowledged himself baffled by pope and king ; died at Soisy while on his way to Pontigny to become a monk ; canonised, 1248 ; author of 'Speculum Ecclesiæ ' and other works. [xvi. 405]

EDMUND, EARL OF LANCASTER (1245–1296). [See LANCASTER.]

EDMUND, second EARL OF CORNWALL (1250–1300), a younger son of Richard, earl of Cornwall [q. v.], and nephew of Henry III ; knighted, 1272 ; joint-guardian of the realm, 1272 and 1279 ; guardian and lieutenant of England, 1286–9. [xlviii. 174]

EDMUND OF WOODSTOCK, EARL OF KENT (1301–1330), youngest son of Edward I ; summoned to parliament, 1320 ; created Earl of Kent, 1321 ; joined Edward II in his war against the barons, 1322 ; besieged Lancaster's stronghold of Pontefract and witnessed his execution, 1322 ; lieutenant of the king in the northern marches, 1323 ; after showing himself a weak diplomatist at the French court, was made lieutenant of Aquitaine (1324), where he was soon invaded by Charles of Valois ; joined conspiracy against Edward II, 1326 ; one of the standing council appointed to govern for the young king, Edward III, 1327 ; resisted the ascendency of Queen Isabella and Mortimer, who consequently lured him into treasonable designs against Edward III, and procured his execution. [xvi. 410]

EDMUND, surnamed DE LANGLEY, first DUKE OF YORK (1341–1402). [See LANGLEY.]

EDMUND TUDOR, EARL OF RICHMOND (1420 ?–1456). [See TUDOR.]

EDMUNDS, JOHN (*d.* 1544), master of Peterhouse ; M.A., 1507 ; fellow of Jesus College, Cambridge, 1517, of St. John's, 1519 ; D.D., 1520 ; master of Peterhouse, 1522 ; vice-chancellor, 1523, 1528, 1529, and 1541–3 ; chancellor and prebendary of Salisbury ; assisted in compiling 'The Institution of a Christian Man.' [xvi. 412]

EDMUNDSON, WILLIAM (1627–1712), quaker ; fought in Cromwell's army at Worcester and in the Isle of Man, 1651 ; tradesman at Antrim ; quaker, 1653 ; frequently imprisoned for religious reasons ; worked with George Fox in Virginia and West Indies, 1671 ; imprisoned for not paying tithes (1682), but released by the intervention of the bishop of Kildare ; remonstrated with James II on the persecution of the Irish protestants, 1689 ; thrown into a dungeon at Athlone, 1690 ; worked against an act enabling the Irish clergy to recover tithes in the temporal courts ; published quaker pamphlets ; his ' Journal ' appeared, 1715. [xvi. 412]

EDNYVED, surnamed VYCHAN (Vaughan), i.e. the Little (*fl.* 1230–1240), statesman and warrior ; signed a truce between Henry III and Llewelyn ab Iorwerth [q. v.], 1231 ; took part in the treaty 'apud Alnetum,' near St. Asaph, 1241 ; ancestor of the Tudors. [xvi. 414]

EDRED or **EADRED** (*d.* 955), king of the English ; son of Edward the elder [q. v.] ; crowned 946 ; burnt Ripon to punish the rebellion of Wulfstan, archbishop of York ; caught and imprisoned Wulfstan when heading a second insurrection, 952 ; fought with Eric Bloodaxe, the Danish king of Northumbria, till Eric's death in 954 ; conferred, by the advice of Dunstan, a limited autonomy on the Danes. [xvi. 414]

EDRIC or **EADRIC**, STREONA (*d.* 1017), ealdorman of the Mercians, 1007 ; married Eadgyth, a daughter of King Æthelred, 1009 ; frequently dissuaded Æthelred from attacking the Danes ; treacherously slew Sigeferth and Morkere, chief thegns of the Danish confederacy of the

o

'Seven (or Five) Boroughs,' 1015 ; said to have endeavoured to betray Edmund Ironside to Cnut, and possibly to murder him, 1015 ; marched with Cnut into Mercia, 1016 ; reputed to have spread a rumour of Edmund's death during the battle of Sherston, in order to secure a victory for the Danes, as also at Assandûn, 1016 ; proposed peace of Olney, 1016 ; probably planned murder of Edmund Ironside ; slain by Cnut from fear of his treacherous character. [xvi. 415]

EDRIC or **EADRIC** (*fl.* 1067–1072), called the WILD ; held lands in Herefordshire and Shropshire under Edward the Confessor ; submitted to William I, 1066, but joined the Welsh in ravaging Herefordshire, 1067, and burning Shrewsbury, 1069 ; accompanied William I on his Scottish expedition, 1072. [xvi. 418]

EDRIDGE, HENRY (1769–1821), miniature-painter ; F.S.A., 1814 ; travelled in Normandy, 1817 and 1819 ; A.R.A., 1820 ; executed portraits, landscapes, and architectural studies. [xvi. 418]

EDWARD, EADWARD, or **EADWEARD,** called THE ELDER (*d.* 924), king of the Angles and Saxons ; son of Ælfred ; chosen king by the 'witan,' 901 ; defeated and slew his rival, Æthelwald, 905 ; obtained co-operation of Guthrum Eohricsson [see GUTHRUM or GUTHORN], Danish under-king of East Anglia, in promoting a code which recognised Danish customs ; defeated Danish forces at Tettenhall, 910, and at Wodensfield, 911 ; received the submission of the Danes of East Anglia, Essex, and Cambridge, 918 ; annexed Mercia after the death of his sister, Æthelflæd, 'Lady of the Mercians,' 919 ; subdued the Welsh, who were abetting Danish inroads, 921 ; extended his dominion to the Humber ; introduced the West-Saxon shire-division into Mercia ; increased the number of sees in southern England. [xvii. 1]

EDWARD or **EADWARD** THE MARTYR (963 ?–978), king of the English ; son of Eadgar ; chosen king after some opposition, 975 ; his ecclesiastical policy directed by Dunstan ; assassinated by the thegns of his step-mother, Ælfthryth [q. v.] ; officially styled martyr as early as 1001. [xvii. 5]

EDWARD or **EADWARD,** called THE CONFESSOR (*d.* 1066), king of the English ; son of Æthelred the Unready ; brought up at the monastery of Ely ; kept out of the sovereignty by Cnut ; resided at the court of Harthacnut, 1041–2 ; crowned, 1043 ; allied himself with Henry, king of the French ; received homage of Magnus of Norway ; married Eadgyth [see EDITH, *d.* 1075], daughter of Earl Godwine of Wessex, 1045 ; favoured monasticism ; entrusted the administration of government to personal favourites ; appointed a coadjutor-archbishop of Canterbury with Godwine's co-operation, 1044 ; fitted out a fleet to meet a threatened Scandinavian invasion ; sent representatives to Council of Rheims, 1049 ; built Westminster Abbey as the price of papal absolution for breaking his vow to make a pilgrimage to Rome ; rejected Ælfric, a kinsman of Godwine, who had been canonically elected to the archbishopric of Canterbury, for Robert of Jumièges, bishop of London, 1051 ; discontinued the heregeld, a tax for the maintenance of the fleet, 1051 ; quarrelled with Godwine, and entertained William, duke of the Normans (afterwards William I), at his court ; reconciled to Godwine, who, with his son Harold, had undertaken an invasion of England, 1052 ; intended to make his nephew, Eadward the Ætheling, heir ; banished Ælfgar, earl of the East-Angles, who in revenge assisted Gruffydd, prince of north Wales, to make war on England ; compelled to part with his favourite Tostig, against whose government of Northumbria the Danish population had risen in revolt, 1065 ; buried in the newly consecrated Westminster Abbey ; canonised, 1161. His so-called laws are said to have been drawn up from declarations made on oath by twelve men of each shire in 1070. [xvii. 7]

EDWARD I (1239–1307), king of England ; eldest son of Henry III and Eleanor of Provence ; married to Eleanor of Castile [q. v.], sister of Alfonso X, 1254, his father giving him Gascony, Ireland, Wales, Bristol, Stamford, and Grantham ; countenanced his lieutenant in Wales, Geoffrey Langley, in forcing on the Welsh the English system of counties and hundreds, thereby provoking a war with Llywelyn, prince of Wales, 1256 ; acted with Simon, earl of Leicester, in obtaining the formulation of the provisions of Westminster, 1259 ; made war upon the Welsh, who sympathised with the baronial malcontents, 1263 ; attacked North-

ampton, capturing Simon de Montfort the younger, 1264 ; caused his father Henry III's defeat at Lewes by an ill-advised pursuit of the retreating Londoners, 1264 ; defeated the barons at Evesham, 1265 ; received the submission of the Cinque ports, 1266 ; compelled the surrender of Kenilworth Castle on conditions, 1266 ; overawed into submission the rebel lords who had been disinherited after Evesham, and were then occupying the Isle of Ely, 1267 ; steward of England, 1268 ; warden of the city and Tower of London, 1268 ; gained popularity by abolishing the levy of customs from the city of London, and by urging a statute forbidding the Jews to acquire the property of Christians by means of pledges, 1269 ; sailed for Syria as a crusader, 1271 ; relieved Acre, and won a victory at Haifa ; wounded with a poisoned dagger by an envoy of the emir of Jaffa, 1272 ; made a truce with the emir, 1272 ; succeeded to the English crown, 1272 ; made a triumphal progress through Europe, and defeated the Count of Chalons at the 'little battle of Chalons,' an ostensible tourney, 1273 ; crowned king of England, 1274 ; legislated with a view to the overthrow of feudalism and the growth of the parliamentary system ; promulgated 'Statute of Westminster the First,' 1275 ; made war upon Llywelyn of Wales, who had repeatedly refused to attend any of the king's parliaments, and (1276) obtained his submission ; promulgated ' Statute of Gloucester ' to amend working of territorial jurisdictions, 1278 ; caused all the Jews and goldsmiths in England to be arrested on the charge of clipping the coin, 1278 ; did homage to Philip of France for Ponthieu, and surrendered all claim to Normandy, 1279 ; defeated and slew Llywelyn in Radnorshire, 1282 ; determined that David, Llywelyn's brother, 'should be tried before a full representative of the laity,' which sentenced him to be drawn, hanged, beheaded, disembowelled, and quartered, 1283 ; assimilated the administration of Wales to the English pattern by the 'Statute of Wales,' 1284 ; published 'Statute of Westminster the Second,' 1285 ; spent much time in France and Gascony, 1286–9 ; returned to England, 1289 ; appointed commissioners to inquire into the misdemeanours of his judges during his long absence, 1289 ; forbade sub-infeudation in the statute 'Quia emptores,' 1290 ; banished the Jews, 1290 ; lost his queen, Eleanor of Castile, 1290 ; appointed (1290) Antony Bek governor of Scotland, the throne of which was soon afterwards claimed by thirteen competitors ; put John Baliol in seisin of the Scottish kingdom, 1292 ; deprived of Gascony by Philip IV, 1294 ; received grants for the settlement of Welsh, French, and Scottish difficulties from a parliament in which the three estates of the realm were perfectly represented, 1295 ; stormed Berwick to punish Baliol for contemplating revolt, 1296 ; accepted Baliol's surrender of Scotland, 1296 ; compelled the clergy to make a grant for the defence of the kingdom, 1297 ; met with protracted opposition from his barons in regard to proposed campaign in Gascony, 1297 ; set sail for Bruges in pursuance of a promise to help the Count of Flanders against the French, 1297 ; induced by Boniface VIII to make a truce with France, by which he recovered Gascony, but deserted his ally, the Count of Flanders, 1298 ; defeated William Wallace on Linlithgow Heath, 1298 ; confirmed the Great Charter, but added proviso in favour of the rights of the crown to the confirmation of the ' Forest Charter,' 1299 ; made second expedition to Scotland, refusing demand of Scottish lords that Baliol be allowed to reign, 1300 ; denounced as a marauder by Archbishop Robert de Winchelsea, 1300 ; his troubles with the baronage ended by the death of Humphrey Bohun, earl of Hereford ; captured Stirling Castle, 1304 ; ordered execution of Wallace, who had been betrayed, 1305 ; suspended his old enemy, Archbishop Winchelsea, by the connivance of the new pope, Clement V, 1306 ; died at Burgh-on-Sands while on his way northward to crush the rebellion of Robert Bruce, who threatened to undo the judicial system recently drawn up for Scotland ; was buried in Westminster Abbey on 27 Oct 1307. [xvii. 14]

EDWARD II OF CARNARVON (1284–1327), king of England ; son of Edward I and Eleanor of Castile ; regent during his father's absence in Flanders, 1297–8 ; created Prince of Wales and Earl of Chester, 1301 ; served on the Scottish campaigns of 1301, 1303, and 1304, carrying his habits of extravagance into camp-life ; knighted, 1306 ; devastated the Scottish borders, 1306 ; succeeded to the crown, 1307 ; made Aymer de Valence guardian of Scotland, 1307 ; created Piers Gaveston, his favourite, Earl o

Cornwall, 1307 ; married Isabella, daughter of Philip the Fair, king of France, 1308 ; appointed Gaveston regent of Ireland, 1308, being compelled by the council to banish him ; undermined baronial opposition, and achieved Gaveston's restoration to his earldom, 1309 ; compelled by threats of withdrawal of allegiance to consent to the appointment of twenty-one lords ordainers, 1310 ; marched northwards under the pretence of attacking Bruce, really to avoid Lancaster, his chief opponent, and the ordainers, 1310 ; allowed Gaveston to be exiled, 1311 ; committed to a civil war by the return of Gaveston, 1312, who was soon afterwards seized by the Earl of Warwick and murdered, June, 1312 ; supported by Hugh le Despenser [q. v.] and the Earls of Pembroke and Warenne ; granted an amnesty to the malcontents, 1313 ; took the field against Bruce, and, neglecting the Earl of Gloucester's warning not to join battle under unfavourable circumstances, was defeated at Bannockburn, 1314 ; forced to submit to Lancaster, 1314 ; regained his authority on Lancaster's failure to suppress Irish, Welsh, and Scottish disaffection, 1316 ; negotiated with Lancaster, 1318 ; failed to take Berwick, 1319 ; made a favourite of Hugh le Despenser the younger [q. v.] ; reluctantly agreed to the banishment of both Despensers, 1321 ; besieged Leeds Castle, which had closed its gates against the queen, 1321 ; conducted a campaign in the west against the Mortimers, 1321 ; recalled the Despensers, 1322 ; slew the Earl of Hereford and captured Lancaster, who was beheaded without a hearing at Boroughbridge, 1322 ; vainly attempted to subdue Scotland, 1322 ; concluded truce with Scotland for three years, 1323 ; alienated Queen Isabella by his fondness for the younger Despenser, 1324 ; allowed Isabella to go to France in his stead to pay homage for Aquitaine and Ponthieu, whence she returned (1326) to dethrone him ; fled westward, and after many wanderings was taken at Neath ; forced to resign the throne, 1327 ; brutally treated by his gaolers in Berkeley Castle, and murdered ; currently reported in the next generation to have died a hermit in Lombardy.

[xvii. 38]

EDWARD III (1312–1377), king of England ; eldest son of Edward II ; Earl of Chester, 1320 ; received county of Ponthieu and duchy of Aquitaine, 1325 ; proclaimed guardian of the kingdom in the name of his father, 1326 ; chosen king, 1327 ; was for four years the figure-head of his mother Isabella and of Mortimer's rule ; out-manceuvred in Scotland by Moray and Douglas, 1327 ; gave up all claim to Scotland by the treaty of Northampton, 1328 ; married Philippa of Hainault, 1328 ; claimed the French throne through his mother Isabella, but was set aside for Philip of Valois, 1328 ; paid homage to Philip VI for his French fiefs, 1329, refusing liege homage ; executed Mortimer, and placed the queen-mother in honourable confinement, 1330 ; performed liege homage for Guyenne and Ponthieu, 1331 ; invited Flemish weavers to come to England and teach the manufacture of fine cloth, 1332 ; secured recognition of Edward de Baliol [q. v.] as king of Scotland, 1332 ; defeated Scots at Halidon Hill, 1333, and restored Baliol twice ; his seneschals expelled from Agenois by Philip VI, 1336 ; laid a heavy customs duty on sacks of wool and woolfells to raise money for a war with France, 1337 ; gained the goodwill of James van Artevelde, a citizen of Ghent, who procured him an alliance with Ghent, Ypres, Bruges, and Cassel ; made treaty for hire of troops with the Emperor Lewis of Bavaria, thereby displeasing Pope Benedict XII, 1337 ; appointed imperial vicar by Lewis of Bavaria, 1338 ; laid siege to Cambray, 1339, when cannon is said to have been first used ; assumed title of king of France in order to retain Flemish support, 1340 ; returned to England to get supplies voted by parliament ; defeated French fleet in the Sluys, 1340 ; reproached John de Stratford, archbishop of Canterbury, for retarding supplies, though he had urged him to undertake the war, 1341 ; landed at Brest in consequence of an offer from John of Montfort to hold Brittany of him conditionally, 1342 ; made truce with the king of France for three years at Ste. Madeleine, 1343 ; built round tower of Windsor Castle, 1344 ; wrote to the pope that Philip had broken truce and that he declared war upon him, 1345 ; sacked Barfleur, Valonges, Carentan, St. Lô, and Caen, 1346 ; executed strategic movements culminating in total destruction of French army at Crécy, near Abbeville, 1346 ; the Scots routed at Nevill's Cross by his generals, 1346 ; blockaded Calais, which surrendered at discretion (1347), after the withdrawal of a French relief force ; spared the lives of the citizens of Calais at the request of his queen, 1347 ; returned to England, 1347 ;

founded the order of the Garter, 1349 ; lost his daughter, Joan, by the black death pestilence ; passed 'Statute of Labourers,' 1351 ; defeated a Spanish fleet in the service of France off Winchelsea, 1350 ; enacted the 'Statute of Provisors,' 1351, 'of Treasons,' 1352, and 'of Præmunire,' 1353 ; released King David of Scotland from the Tower, 1357 ; gained Aquitaine, Calais, Guisnes, and Ponthieu by the treaty of Bretigny, in which he renounced all claim to the French crown, 1360 ; entertained knights from Spain, Cyprus, and Armenia, who had come to solicit aid against the Mahometans, 1362 ; erected Gascony and Aquitaine into a principality, 1362 ; passed statute ordering discontinuance of French in the law courts, 1362 ; concerted project with David II for union of England and Scotland, 1363 ; forbade payment of Peter's pence, 1366, from annoyance at the pope's attempt to recover arrears of the tribute promised him by King John ; endeavoured by the 'Statute of Kilkenny' (1367) to check the adoption of Irish customs by the English colonists ; disapproved of the depredations of the English free companies in France ; sent the Black Prince to help Pedro of Castile against his half-brother, Henry of Trastamare, 1367 ; involved in a second French war by Charles V's complaints of the free companies, 1369 ; carried on a desultory warfare in Poitou and Touraine, in revenge for which the French burnt Portsmouth, 1369 ; gave himself up to the influence of Alice Perrers [q. v.], a concubine, on the death of his queen, 1369 ; dissented from the Prince of Wales's conduct of the French war ; laid hands on church property in order to raise supplies, 1371 ; renewed league with Brittany, 1371, and made treaty with Genoa, 1372 ; the Earl of Pembroke, his lieutenant in Aquitaine, defeated by a French and Spanish fleet at Rochelle, 1372 ; despatched armament against Du Guesclin in Brittany, 1373 ; lost Aquitaine, 1374 ; his latter years embittered by national discontent and the rivalry between his chief minister, Lancaster, and the Commons. During the first part of his reign he inaugurated an enlightened commercial policy, and devoted so much attention to naval administration as to be entitled by parliament the 'king of the sea.'

[xvii. 48]

EDWARD IV (1442–1483), king of England ; son of Richard, duke of York ; born at Rouen ; Earl of March ; attainted as a Yorkist, 1459 ; returned from Calais with the Yorkist earls, Warwick and Salisbury, and defeated Henry VI's force at Northampton, 1460 ; swore fealty to Henry VI, 1460 ; defeated Henry's restless queen, Margaret, at Mortimer's Cross, 1461 ; proclaimed himself king, 1461 ; utterly defeated the Lancastrians at Towton, 1461 ; crowned, 1461 ; captured Margaret's strongholds in the north of England, 1463 ; believed himself, on insufficient grounds, to have conciliated Somerset, a prominent Lancastrian, 1463 ; privately married Elizabeth Woodville, widow of Sir John Grey, 1464, ultimately disclosing the fact to his council when a match with Bona of Savoy was under consideration ; married his sister Margaret to Charles the Bold, duke of Burgundy, 1468 ; his position threatened by the intrigues of the Earl of Warwick, who was offended by his rejection of the French marriage alliance which he had proposed, and was, with the Duke of Clarence, plotting his overthrow ; taken prisoner by the archbishop of York, one of the leaders in insurrection of Robin of Redesdale [q. v.], 1469 ; released by Warwick, who, with Clarence, offered his assistance in putting down a rebellion (1470) which he had himself organised ; defeated the rebels at Losecoat Field, 1470 ; proclaimed Warwick and Clarence traitors, 1470 ; compelled to seek refuge in Holland by the joint-attack of Warwick and Clarence, as concerted with Margaret of Anjou, 1470 ; enabled by the money of the Duke of Burgundy to return to England, 1471 ; reconciled to Clarence ; took Henry VI, who had just been reappointed king, in the field, and defeated and slew Warwick at Barnet, 1471 ; captured Queen Margaret at the battle of Tewkesbury, 1471, and slew her son immediately afterwards ; quelled the Kent rising under the Bastard Falconbridge [see FAUCONBERG, THOMAS], whom he compelled to surrender Sandwich and the navy he had brought from Calais, 1471 ; raised money by means of benevolences and in other unprecedented ways for a projected invasion of France, 1474 ; actually invaded France, but was beguiled by the astuteness of Louis XI, who succeeded in making him desert his ally, the Duke of Burgundy, by a seven years' treaty at Picquigny, 1475 ; imprisoned and murdered his brother Clarence, who had aspired to the hand of Mary, daughter of the Duke of Burgundy, 1478 ; ignored the appeal of

Mary of Burgundy for protection against Louis XI from fear of losing his French pension and the stipulated marriage of his daughter to the dauphin, both secured by the treaty of Picquigny ; undertook a partially successful expedition against Scotland to dethrone James III on the plea of illegitimacy, and to procure the abandonment of the old French alliance, 1482 ; died, as French writers believed, of mortification at the treaty of Arras (1482), by which it was arranged between Maximilian of Burgundy and Louis XI that Margaret, daughter of the former prince, should be married to the dauphin.   [xvii. 70]

EDWARD V (1470–1483), king of England ; eldest son of Edward IV, by his queen, Elizabeth Woodville [see ELIZABETH (1437 ?–1492)] ; created Prince of Wales, 1471 ; entrusted by his father to the care of a council of control, of which his uncles, Clarence and Gloucester, and his maternal uncle, Earl Rivers, were members, 1471 ; justiciar of Wales, 1476 ; succeeded to the crown, 1483 ; conducted to London by the Duke of Gloucester, who had previously imprisoned Earl Rivers and Lord Richard Grey at Pomfret, 1483 ; sent to the Tower with his brother, the Duke of York, 1483 ; deposed by an assembly of Lords and Commons, at which was brought in a roll, setting forth Gloucester's right to the crown, by the alleged invalidity of Edward IV's marriage with Elizabeth Woodville ; murdered, with the Duke of York, by order of Gloucester, then Richard III, according to an irrefragable account first given in detail by Sir Thomas More.   [xvii. 82]

EDWARD VI (1537–1553), king of England ; son of Henry VIII, by Jane Seymour ; his education entrusted to Richard Cox [q. v.], Sir John Cheke [q. v.], Sir Anthony Cooke [q. v.], and Roger Ascham [q. v.] ; a finished Greek, Latin, and French scholar ; lutenist and amateur astronomer ; knighted by the Earl of Hertford, his uncle and protector of the realm, 1547 ; appointed Hertford Duke of Somerset, 1547 ; crowned, 1547 ; made John Knox and Bishop Ridley, Latimer, and Hooper court preachers ; commended by Martin Bucer in a letter to Calvin ; agreed to the execution of Lord Seymour (1549), who had attempted to displace his brother, Somerset, taking advantage of Somerset's departure to Scotland to enforce a treaty, by which Edward was to marry Mary Queen of Scots ; his marriage with Princess Elizabeth, daughter of Henry II of France, settled in 1551, but deferred ; nonchalantly agreed to the execution of Protector Somerset on charges brought by Warwick, then Duke of Northumberland, 1552 ; instructed by William Thomas, clerk of the council, in statecraft ; preserved neutral attitude in war between the emperor and the French king, 1552 ; showed deep concern at the illness of Sir John Cheke, his friend and tutor, 1553 ; attacked by consumption, 1553 ; gave palace of Bridewell to corporation of London as a 'workhouse,' 1553 ; converted the old Grey Friars' monastery into Christ's Hospital, 1553 ; induced by Northumberland to 'devise' the succession to Lady Jane Grey, 1553. Numerous portraits of Edward are extant, most of them by Holbein.   [xvii. 84]

EDWARD, PRINCE OF WALES (1330–1376), called the BLACK PRINCE, and sometimes EDWARD IV and EDWARD OF WOODSTOCK ; eldest son of Edward III [q. v.] ; created Duke of Cornwall, 1337 ; guardian of the kingdom in his father's absence, 1338, 1340, and 1342 ; created Prince of Wales, 1343 ; knighted by his father at La Hogue, 1345 ; commanded the van at Crécy, his father intentionally leaving him to win the battle, 1346 ; named the Black Prince after the battle of Crécy, at which he was possibly accoutred in black armour ; took part in Edward III's Calais expedition, 1349 ; appointed king's lieutenant in Gascony, and ordered to lead an army into Aquitaine, 1355 ; pillaged Avignonet and Castelnaudary, sacked Carcassonne, and plundered Narbonne, 1355 ; ravaged Auvergne, Limousin, and Berry, 1356 ; failed to take Bourges, 1356 ; offered terms of peace to King John, who had outflanked him near Poitiers, but refused to surrender himself as the price of their acceptance, 1356 ; routed the French at Poitiers, and took King John prisoner, 1356 ; returned to England, 1357 ; negotiated the treaty of Bretigny, 1360 ; created Prince of Aquitaine and Gascony, 1362 ; his suzerainty disowned by the lord of Albret and other Gascon nobles ; directed by his father to forbid the marauding raids of the English and Gascon free companies, 1364 ; entered into an agreement with Don Pedro of Castile and Charles of Navarre, by which

Pedro covenanted to mortgage Castro de Urdiales and the province of Biscay to him as security for a loan ; a passage was thus secured through Navarre, 1366 ; received letter of defiance from Henry of Trastamare, Don Pedro's half-brother and rival, 1367 ; defeated Henry at Nájara after an obstinate conflict, 1367 ; failed to obtain either the province of Biscay or liquidation of the debt from Don Pedro, 1367 ; prevailed on the estates of Aquitaine to allow him a hearth-tax of ten sous for five years, 1368, thereby alienating the lord of Albret and other nobles ; drawn into open war with Charles V of France, 1369 ; took Limoges, where he gave orders for an indiscriminate massacre (1370) in revenge for the voluntary surrender of that town to the French by its bishop, who had been his private friend ; returned to England, 1371 ; resigned the principality of Aquitaine and Gascony, 1372 ; led the commons in their attack upon the Lancastrian administration, 1376 ; buried in Canterbury Cathedral, where his surcoat, helmet, shield, and gauntlets are still preserved.   [xvii. 90]

EDWARD, PRINCE OF WALES (1453–1471), only son of Henry VI ; created Prince of Wales, 1454 ; taken by his mother, Queen Margaret, for safety to Harlech Castle after the Lancastrian defeat at Northampton, 1460 ; disinherited in parliament, 1460 ; present at the second battle of St. Albans, 1461 ; knighted by his father, 1461 ; carried by Margaret into Scotland, 1461, and into Brittany and France, 1462 ; ultimately given, together with his mother, a refuge in Lorraine ; his cause favoured by Louis XI and René of Lorraine, who arranged with the Earl of Warwick a temporarily successful invasion of England, 1470 ; set sail for England too late to follow up this advantage ; defeated at Tewkesbury, 1471, and slain, after being brutally insulted, by order of Edward IV.   [xvii. 101]

EDWARD, EARL OF WARWICK (1475–1499), eldest son of George, duke of Clarence ; brought up, after his father's murder, by his aunt, Anne, duchess of Gloucester ; knighted by Richard III, 1483 ; imprisoned in the Tower by Henry VII, 1485 ; personated by Simnel in Ireland, 1487, in consequence of which Henry VII showed him for one day in the streets of London ; personated by Wilford, 1498 ; beheaded on the ridiculous pretence that he had conspired against Henry VII, though he had merely helped Warbeck to plan the escape of both from prison.   [xvii. 104]

EDWARD, DAFYDD (d. 1690). [See DAVID, EDWARD.]

EDWARD, THOMAS (1814–1886), the Banff naturalist ; settled in Banff to work at his trade of shoemaker, 1834 ; exhibited at the Banff fair a taxodermic collection, formed by himself, 1845 ; discovered twenty new species of British sessile-eyed crustacea ; curator of the museum of the Banff Institution ; associate of the Linnean Society, 1866 ; placed on the civil list, 1876.   [xvii. 106]

EDWARDES, SIR HERBERT BENJAMIN (1819–1868), Indian official ; attended classes at King's College, London, 1837 ; cadet, Bengal infantry, 1841 ; second lieutenant, Bengal fusiliers, 1842 ; Urdu, Hindi, and Persian 'interpreter' to his regiment ; contributed to the 'Delhi Gazette' 'Letters of Brahminee Bull in India to his cousin John in England' ; aide-de-camp to Sir Hugh Gough at the battles of Moodkee (1845) and Sobraon (1846), and assistant (1847) to Sir Henry Montgomery Lawrence, resident of Lahore ; reformed civil administration of Banu, 1847 ; twice routed, on his own responsibility, the rebel Diwán Mulráj, prince of Multan, 1848 ; brevet-major and C.B. ; D.C.L. Oxford, 1850 ; founded Abbottábád, 1853 ; commissioner of Peshawur, 1853–9 ; prevailed upon Sir John Lawrence to make a treaty of non-interference with the amir of Afghanistan ; induced Sir John Lawrence to sanction the levy of a mixed force, which was employed against the mutineers, 1857 ; knighted ; LL.D. Cambridge ; K.B. ; commissioner of Umballa, 1862 ; returned to England finally, 1865 ; major-general and C.S.I., vice-president of the Church Missionary Society.   [xvii. 107]

EDWARDS, AMELIA ANN BLANFORD (1831–1892), novelist and egyptologist ; contributed to 'Chambers's Journal,' 'Household Words,' and 'All the Year Round,' and served on staff of 'Saturday Review' and 'Morning Post' ; published eight novels between 1855 and 1880 ; first visited Egypt, 1873–4, and began study of egyptology ; did much to bring about foundation of Egypt Exploration Fund, 1882, and was first joint honorary secretary; lectured in United States, 1889–90, and published lectures as 'Pharaohs, Fellahs, and Explorers,' 1891. She bequeathed her egyptological library and collections to University College, London, together with money to found a chair of egyptology. [Suppl. ii. 176]

EDWARDS, ARTHUR (d. 1743), major; F.S.A., 1725; first major of the second troop of horse guards in Grosvenor Street, London; gave 7,000l. and bequeathed two thousand volumes of printed books to the Cotton Library. [xvii. 111]

EDWARDS, BRYAN (1743–1800), West India merchant; partner in, and ultimately possessor of, an uncle's business in Jamaica; member of the colonial assembly, attacking tariff against United States; West India merchant in England, establishing a bank at Southampton, 1792; M.P., Grampound, 1796; anti-abolitionist; satirised 'Peter Pindar'; chief works, 'The History of the British Colonies in the West Indies,' 1793, and an 'Historical Survey of the French Colony in the Island of St. Domingo,' 1797. [xvii. 111]

EDWARDS, CHARLES (d. 1691?), Welsh author; entered at All Souls College, Oxford; expelled by the parliamentary visitors, 1648; elected scholar of Jesus College, Oxford, 1648; honorary fellow, 1649; B.A., 1649; presented to the 'sine cura' of Llanrhaiadr, 1653; deprived, 1660. His works include 'Hanes y Ffydd Ddiffuant,' a kind of history of Christianity, 1671, and 'Hebraicorum Cambro-Britannicorum Specimen,' maintaining the Hebrew origin of the Welsh language, 1675. [xvii. 113]

EDWARDS, EDWARD (1738–1806), painter; of humble origin; gained premium of the Society of Arts for his 'Death of Tatius,' 1764; A.R.A., 1773; travelled in Italy, 1775–6; professor of perspective at the Royal Academy, 1788; published fifty-two etchings, 1792. [xvii. 114]

EDWARDS, EDWARD (1803–1879), marine zoologist; improved construction of aquaria by his invention of a 'dark-water chamber slope-back tank.' [xvii. 115]

EDWARDS, EDWARD (1812–1886), librarian; supernumerary assistant in the printed book department of the British Museum, 1839, where he catalogued the Great Rebellion tracts; published returns, occasionally untrustworthy, of library statistics in the 'Athenæum,' c. 1846; materially assisted William Ewart [q. v.], the originator of free library legislation, 1850; first librarian of the Manchester Free Library, 1850–8. His works include 'Memoirs of Libraries,' 1859, 'Lives of the Founders of the British Museum,' 1870, and a biography of Sir Walter Ralegh, 1865. [xvii. 115]

EDWARDS, EDWIN (1823–1879), painter and etcher; at one time examining proctor in the admiralty and prerogative courts; exhibited Cornish coast scenes at the Royal Academy; published a work upon 'Old Inns of England,' profusely illustrated with etchings, two legal treatises, and 'Ecclesiastical Jurisdiction,' 1833. [xvii. 117]

EDWARDS, GEORGE (1694–1773), naturalist; arrested as a presumable spy by Danish soldiers at Friedrichstadt, 1718; librarian of the Royal College of Physicians, 1733; F.R.S.; F.S.A., 1752; chief work, a 'History of Birds,' 1743–64. [xvii. 117]

EDWARDS, GEORGE (1752–1823), author; M.D. Edinburgh, 1772; author of 'The Practical System of Human Economy,' 1816, and other books of applied sociology. [xvii. 118]

EDWARDS, GEORGE NELSON (1830–1868), physician; medical student at Gonville and Caius College, Cambridge; studied at St. Bartholomew's Hospital; M.D. Cambridge, 1859; lecturer on forensic medicine at St. Bartholomew's Hospital, 1866; physician to the hospital, 1867–8; became gradually blind; published 'The Examination of the Chest in a Series of Tables,' 1862. [xvii. 118]

EDWARDS, HENRY THOMAS (1837–1884), dean of Bangor; Williams exhibitioner at Westminster; B.A. Jesus College, Oxford, 1860; vicar of Aberdare, 1866–9, of Carnarvon, 1869; dean of Bangor, 1876; addressed a letter to W. E. Gladstone entitled 'The Church of the Cymry,' explaining the prevalence of dissent in Wales, 1870; published sermons and religious pamphlets; committed suicide. [xvii. 119]

EDWARDS, HUMPHREY (d. 1658), regicide; joined parliamentarians, finding loyalty to Charles I pecuniarily unprofitable; M.P. for Shropshire; signed Charles I's death-warrant, 1649; thrust himself into the chief ushership of the exchequer, 1650; commissioner of South Wales, 1651. [xvii. 119]

EDWARDS, JAMES (1757–1816), bookseller and bibliographer; purchased the Pinelli library at Venice, 1788, and sold it by auction, 1789; purchased (1786) the Bedford Missal (temp. Henry VI); the 'Rinaldo' of Dibdin. [xvii. 120]

EDWARDS or EDWARDES, JOHN (fl. 1638), Sedleian reader at Oxford; educated at Merchant Taylors' and St. John's College, Oxford; probationer-fellow, 1617; head-master of Merchant Taylors', 1632–4; Sedleian reader of natural philosophy, 1638–48; deprived, 1648; M.D. [xvii. 121]

EDWARDS, JOHN (SION TREREDYN) (fl. 1651), translator; translated the 'Marrow of Modern Divinity' into Welsh, 1651; ejected from living of Tredynock. [xvii. 121]

EDWARDS, JOHN (1637–1716), Calvinistic divine; son of Thomas Edwards (1599–1647) [q. v.]; educated at Merchant Taylors' and St. John's College, Cambridge; B.A., 1657; fellow, 1659; M.A., 1661; lecturer of Bury St. Edmunds; resigned his fellowship and became minister of St. Sepulchre's, Cambridge; D.D., 1699; wrote largely against Socinianism and the Arminians, also against Locke's 'Reasonableness of Christians.' [xvii. 121]

EDWARDS, JOHN (SION Y POTIAU) (1700?–1776), poet and translator (1767–8) of the 'Pilgrim's Progress' into Welsh. [xvii. 123]

EDWARDS, JOHN (1714–1785), dissenting minister of Leeds; published theological works. [xvii. 123]

EDWARDS, JOHN (SION CEIRIOG) (1747–1792), Welsh poet; joint-founder of the Venedotian Society, 1770, and president, 1783; poet, orator, and astronomer. [xvii. 123]

EDWARDS, JOHN (1751–1832), poetical writer; lieutenant-colonel of light dragoons in the volunteer army of Ireland; published 'Interests of Ireland,' 1815, 'Kathleen' (a ballad of Irish history), 1808, and 'Abradates and Panthea : a Tragedy,' 1808. [xvii. 123]

EDWARDS, JONATHAN (1629–1712), controversialist; B.A. Christ Church, Oxford, 1659; fellow of Jesus College, Oxford, 1662; principal, 1686; rector of Kiddington, and, in 1681, of Hinton-Ampner; D.D., 1686; vice-chancellor, 1689–91; treasurer of Llandaff, 1687; treated Socinus as the founder of a new religion in 'A Preservative against Socinianism,' 1693–1703. [xvii. 123]

EDWARDS, LEWIS (1809–1887), Welsh Calvinistic methodist; studied at London and Edinburgh universities; first Calvinist M.A. of Edinburgh; ordained, 1837; editor of 'Y Traethodydd' ('The Essayist'), 1845–55; principal of Bala College for fifty years, lecturing on classics, ethics, metaphysics, and theology; D.D. Edinburgh, 1865; best-known work 'Athrawiaeth yr Iawn' ('Atonement'), 1860. [xvii. 124]

EDWARDS, RICHARD (1523?–1566), poet and playwright; B.A. Corpus Christi College, Oxford, 1544; fellow, 1544; student of Christ Church, and M.A., 1547; master of the children of the Chapel Royal, 1561; composed 'Palamon and Arcite' for Queen Elizabeth's entertainment at Oxford, 1566; eulogised by Meres. The 'Excellent Comedie of . . . Damon and Pithias,' 1571, is his only extant play. [xvii. 125]

EDWARDS, ROGER (1811–1886), Welsh Calvinistic methodist; editor of 'Cronicl yr Oes,' an early Welsh political paper, 1835–9; secretary of the Calvinistic Methodist Association, 1839–74; D.D.; editor of the 'Drysorfa,' 1846–86. [xvii. 125]

EDWARDS, SYDENHAM TEAK (1769?–1819), natural historical draughtsman; founder of the 'Botanical Magazine'; executed drawings from 1798 for the 'Botanical Magazine,' and 'Flora Londiniensis'; started the 'Botanical Register'; supplied plates for the 'New Botanic Garden,' 1805–7. [xvii. 126]

EDWARDS, THOMAS (fl. 1595), poet; author of two long narrative poems (recently discovered), 'Cephalus and Procris' and 'Narcissus'; contributed to Adrianus Romanus's 'Parvum Theatrum Urbium,' fifty-five Latin hexameters on the cities of Italy, 1595 ; possibly identical with a Thomas Edwards (fellow of All Souls College, Oxford ; D.C.L., 1590), who became chancellor to the bishop of London.   [xvii. 126]

EDWARDS, THOMAS (1599-1647), author of 'Gangræna'; M.A. Queens' College, Cambridge ; university preacher at Cambridge, where he became known as 'Young Luther'; ordered to recant, 1628 ; licensed to preach in St. Botolph's, Aldgate, 1629 ; suspended by Laud ; a zealous presbyterian, attacking the independents in 'Antapologia,' 1644 ; published 'Gangræna ; or a . . . Discovery of many Errours, Heresies, Blasphemies, and pernicious Practices,' 1646, an intemperate polemic ; died in Holland.   [xvii. 127]

EDWARDS, THOMAS (1652-1721), divine and orientalist ; M.A. St. John's College, Cambridge, 1677 ; engaged to assist in the Coptic impression of the New Testament, 1685 ; chaplain of Christ Church, Oxford ; rector of Aldwinckle All Saints, 1707-21 ; left a Coptic lexicon ready for the press.   [xvii. 128]

EDWARDS, THOMAS (1699-1757), critic ; entered at Lincoln's Inn, 1721 ; F.S.A. ; 1745 ; published, on the appearance of Warburton's edition of Shakespeare (1747), an ironical supplement, subsequently named 'The Canons of Criticism'; friend of Samuel Richardson [q. v.] ; wrote Miltonic sonnets.   [xvii. 129]

EDWARDS, THOMAS (1729-1785), divine ; M.A. Clare Hall, Cambridge, 1754 ; fellow ; master of the free grammar school and rector of St. John the Baptist, Coventry, 1758-79 ; D.D., 1766 ; published 'Prolegomena in Libros Veteris Testamenti Poeticos,' 1762, and wrote against doctrine of irresistible grace, 1759.   [xvii. 129]

EDWARDS, THOMAS (*fl.* 1810), divine ; son of Thomas Edwards (1729-1785) [q. v.] ; LL.B. Clare College, Cambridge, 1782 ; fellow of Jesus College, 1787 ; LL.D. ; published treatise on free inquiry in religion, 1792.
                    [xvii. 130]

EDWARDS, THOMAS (1775 ?-1845), law reporter ; LL.D. Trinity Hall, Cambridge, 1805 ; fellow of Trinity Hall and advocate at Doctors' Commons ; Surrey magistrate ; compiled a collection of admiralty cases, 1812.
                    [xvii. 130]

EDWARDS, THOMAS (CAERFALLWCH) (1779-1858), Welsh author ; published 'An Analysis of Welsh Orthography,' 1845, and an 'English and Welsh Dictionary,' 1850.   [xvii. 130]

EDWARDS, THOMAS CHARLES (1837-1900), divine ; son of Lewis Edwards [q. v.] ; M.A. London, 1862 ; B.A. Lincoln College, Oxford, 1866 ; M.A., 1872 ; first principal of University College of Wales, Aberystwyth, 1872-91, of Welsh Calvinistic methodist theological college, Bala, 1891 ; D.D. Edinburgh, 1887, University of Wales, 1898 ; published religious works.   [Suppl. ii. 178]

EDWARDS, WILLIAM (1719-1789), bridge-builder in South Wales ; originated (1751) the invention of perforated haunches to remove the pressure to which the single arch of his bridge over the Taff had succumbed ; independent minister.   [xvii. 130]

EDWARDS, WILLIAM CAMDEN (1777-1855), engraver, mainly of portrait-plates.   [xvii. 131]

EDWARDSTON, THOMAS (*d.* 1396), Augustinian friar ; D.D. Oxford ; prior of Clare, Suffolk ; accompanied Lionel, duke of Clarence, to Italy as confessor ; acted as archbishop of some English diocese.   [xvii. 131]

EDWIN or **EADWINE,** Lat. ÆDUINUS (585 ?-633), king of Northumbria ; son of Ælla, king of Deira, on whose death in 588 he fled before Æthelric of Bernicia, conqueror of Deira, to Cearl of Mercia ; subsequently sought asylum with Rædwald, king of the East-Angles, 617 ; his surrender promised by Rædwald to Æthelfrith, Æthelric's son and successor ; accosted by Paulinus, who gave him a sign for future recognition, soon after which Rædwald defeated and slew Æthelfrith, 617. Edwin thereupon became king of Deira, and, annexing Bernicia and neighbouring territory, formed the united Northumbrian kingdom ; extended his power in all directions ; in 625 married Æthelburh, sister of Eadbald, king of Kent ; converted to Christianity by the action of Paulinus in re-

minding him of the sign given him at Rædwald's court ; baptised, 627 ; appointed Paulinus archbishop of York ; defeated and slain in battle with Penda [q. v.] of Mercia.
                    [xvii. 132]

EDWIN, ELIZABETH REBECCA (1771 ?-1854), actress ; *née* Richards ; appeared, when eight years old, at the Crow Street Theatre, Dublin ; acted at Covent Garden in Murphy's 'Citizen,' 1789 ; the original Lady Traffic in 'Riches, or the Wife and Brother,' at the Lyceum, 1810 ; played, 1821, the Duenna in Sheridan's comic opera at Drury Lane, where she had been engaged at the recommendation of T. Sheridan.   [xvii. 134]

EDWIN, SIR HUMPHREY (1642-1707), lord mayor of London ; wool merchant in Great St. Helens ; master of the Barber-Surgeons' Company, 1688 ; member of the Skinners' Company ; sheriff of Glamorganshire, and knighted, 1687 ; present as sheriff of London and Middlesex (1688-9) at the proclamation of William and Mary ; commissioner of excise, 1689-91 ; captain of a trainband regiment and of the horse volunteers ; cashiered from his military appointments for nonconformity, 1690 ; lord mayor, 1697 ; acquiesced in an order to discontinue his much ridiculed practice of attending nonconformist meetings in full civic state, 1697.   [xvii. 135]

EDWIN, JOHN, the elder (1749-1790), comedian ; secretary for one year to the South Sea Trust ; took comic parts at the Smock Alley Theatre, Dublin, and at Bath ; for a long time the mainstay of the Haymarket ; appeared at Covent Garden after 1779 ; associated with John O'Keeffe, who wrote comic songs for him ; created Figaro in the 'Spanish Barber' and Punch in 'Pleasures of the Town' (adaptation from Fielding) ; played Dogberry, Cloten, Sir Anthony Absolute, and similar characters ; praised by Colman as a burletta singer.
                    [xvii. 137]

EDWIN, JOHN, the younger (1768-1805), actor ; son of John Edwin the elder [q. v.] ; appeared at the Haymarket as Hengo in 'Bonduca,' 1778, and as Blister in 'The Virgin Unmasked,' 1792 ; committed suicide from mortification at a lampoon.   [xvii. 139]

EDWY or **EADWIG** (*d.* 959), king of the English ; eldest son of Eadmund and St. Ælfgifu ; became king, 955 ; exiled Dunstan for refusing to authorise his proposed marriage with Ælfgifu [q. v.] ; forced by the 'witan' to resign the country north of the Thames to his brother Eadgar, 957 ; appointed two opponents of Dunstan's monastic reforms to the see of Canterbury.   [xvii. 140]

EDZELL, LORD (1551 ?-1610). [See LINDSAY, SIR DAVID.]

EEDES, JOHN (1609 ?-1667 ?), divine ; B.A. Oriel College, Oxford, 1630 ; ejected from his ministry in the isle of Sheppey during the civil war ; published 'The Orthodox Doctrine concerning Justification by Faith asserted and vindicated,' 1654.   [xvii. 141]

EEDES, RICHARD (1555-1604). [See EDES.]

EEDES, RICHARD (*d.* 1686), presbyterian divine ; M.A. Corpus Christi College, Oxford, 1634 ; subscribed the covenant ; vicar of Beckford, 1647-58 ; attempted, without success, to conciliate the court party after the Restoration ; published homilies.   [xvii. 141]

EFFINGHAM, first EARL of the second creation (1767-1845). [See HOWARD, KENNETH ALEXANDER.]

EFFINGHAM, BARONS. [See HOWARD, LORD WILLIAM, first BARON, 1510 ?-1573 ; HOWARD, CHARLES, second BARON, 1536-1624.]

EGAN, JAMES (1799-1842), mezzotint engraver ; of humble origin ; learnt his art while employed in laying mezzotint grounds for S. W. Reynolds (1773-1835) [q. v.] ; died before attaining success.   [xvii. 141]

EGAN, JOHN (1750 ?-1810), chairman of Kilmainham, co. Dublin ; B.A. Trinity College, Dublin, 1773 ; called to the Irish bar, 1778 ; bencher of King's Inns, Dublin, 1787 ; LL.D., *honoris causâ,* Dublin, 1790 ; chairman of Kilmainham ; sat for Tallagh in the Irish House of Commons.   [xvii. 142]

EGAN, PIERCE, the elder (1772-1849), author of 'Life in London'; attacked the Prince Regent and Mrs. Robinson in 'The Mistress of Royalty ; or the Loves of Florizel and Perdita,' 1814 ; issued 'Boxiana ; or Sketches of Modern Pugilism,' a monthly serial, 1818–24; brought out 'Life in London ; or, The Day and Night Scenes of Jerry Hawthorn . . . and . . . Corinthian Tom, accompanied by Bob Logic,' in monthly numbers from 1821, a book which was frequently dramatised and pirated; published a didactic sequel, 1828; furnished the 'slang phrases' to Francis Grose's 'Dictionary of the Vulgar Tongue,' 1823 ; commenced 'Pierce Egan's Life in London and Sporting Guide,' a weekly newspaper, 1824 ; completed his serial, 'Pierce Egan's Book of Sports and Mirror of Life,' 1832 ; dedicated to Queen Victoria 'The Pilgrims of the Thames in Search of the National,' 1838.

[xvii. 142]

EGAN, PIERCE, the younger (1814–1880), novelist: son of Pierce Egan the elder [q. v.]; executed etchings for 'The Pilgrims of the Thames in Search of the National,' 1837 ; published novels of the feudal period; edited the 'Home Circle,' 1849–51; contributed to 'London Journal' and other periodicals ; best-known works, 'Eve; or the Angel of Innocence,' 1867, and 'The Poor Girl,' 1862–3; pioneer of cheap literature. [xvii. 144]

EGBERT or ECGBERHT, SAINT (639–729), a noble Angle, who 'visited the cells of the masters' to study in Ireland after 652 ; priest and monk in accordance with a vow; remonstrated with the Northumbrian king, Ecgfrith, on his unprovoked war with the Irish, c. 684; visited St. Columba's monasteries in Iona, 716 ; successfully advocated the Roman Easter in Iona, 716, introducing also the Roman tonsure, 718. [xvii. 146]

EGBERT or ECGBERHT (d. 766), archbishop of York; cousin of Ceolwulf [q. v.], king of Northumbria; archbishop of York, 732–66; obtained his pall from Rome, 735 ; supreme in ecclesiastical matters, issuing also coins bearing his own name along with that of his brother Eadbert [q. v.], king of Northumbria; founded the cathedral school of York, in which he himself taught ; wrote Latin ecclesiastical works. [xvii. 147]

EGBERT, ECGBERHT, or ECGBRYHT (d. 839), king of the West-Saxons ; son of Ealhmund, an underking of Kent; banished from England by Offa of Mercia and Beorhtric of Wessex [q. v.], the latter conceiving his throne to be endangered by Egbert's ancestral claims; lived at the court of Charlemagne till 802 ; accepted as king by the West-Saxons, 802 ; routed a force of Cornishmen, c. 825 ; regained the kingdom of Kent; received final submission of Mercia, 828 ; overlord of Northumbria, and eighth Bretwalda, 829 ; defeated by Scandinavian pirates at Charmouth, 835 ; probably brought the shire military organisation to its completion in Wessex ; agreed to a perpetual alliance with the archbishop of Canterbury at Kingston, 838 ; defeated northmen and Cornishmen at Hengestdune, 837. [xvii. 148]

EGERTON, CHARLES CHANDLER (1798–1885), surgeon ; learnt medicine at the then united hospitals of St. Thomas's and Guy's; assistant-surgeon on the Bengal establishment to deal with eye-disease among the Indo-European lads of the lower orphan school, 1823 ; oculist at the Indian Eye Hospital ; first surgeon at the Calcutta Medical College Hospital. [xvii. 151]

EGERTON, DANIEL (1772–1835), actor; bred to the law ; member of the Covent Garden Company, Henry VIII, Tullus Aufidius, Syphax, and Clytus being esteemed his best parts in tragedy ; manager of the Olympic, 1821, and of Sadler's Wells, 1821–4; ruined by the failure (1834) of the Victoria Theatre, of which he was proprietor.

[xvii. 151]

EGERTON, FRANCIS, third and last DUKE OF BRIDGEWATER (1736–1803); devoted himself, after making the grand tour, to the development of his coal mines at Worsley, Lancashire, 1759 ; called the founder of British inland navigation on account of the canal which he employed James Brindley [q. v.] to construct from Worsley to Manchester, 1760 ; constructed, under great pecuniary difficulties, a canal connecting Manchester and Liverpool, 1762–72 ; subscribed 100,000l. to the loyalty loan ; 'the first great Manchester man.' [xvii. 151]

EGERTON, FRANCIS, first EARL OF ELLESMERE (1800–1857), statesman and poet ; educated at Eton and Christ Church, Oxford ; captain in the Staffordshire regiment of yeomanry, 1819 ; M.P., Bletchingley, 1822–6; an early promoter of free-trade and the London University ; M.P. for Sutherland, 1826 and 1830, for South Lancashire, 1835, 1837, and 1841–6; privy councillor, 1828 ;

privy councillor for Ireland, 1828 ; secretary at war, 1830 ; D.C.L. Oxford, 1834 ; rector of King's College, Aberdeen, 1838 ; first president of Camden Society, 1838 ; president of the British Association, 1842, and of other learned bodies : created Viscount Brackley of Brackley and Earl of Ellesmere of Ellesmere, 1846 ; K.G., 1855. His translations include 'Faust . . . and Schiller's Song of the Bell,' 1823, and Amari's 'History of the War of the Sicilian Vespers,' 1850, his original works 'Donna Charitea, poems,' and a 'Guide to Northern Archæology,' 1848. [xvii. 153]

EGERTON, FRANCIS HENRY, eighth EARL OF BRIDGEWATER (1756–1829), founder of the 'Bridgewater Treatises'; son of John Egerton, bishop of Durham [q. v.]; educated at Eton, Christ Church and All Souls College, Oxford ; M.A., 1780 ; fellow of All Souls, 1780 ; prebendary of Durham, 1780 ; held livings in Shropshire ; F.R.S., 1781 ; F.S.A., 1791 ; prince of the Holy Roman Empire; succeeded as Earl of Bridgewater, Viscount Brackley, and Baron Ellesmere, 1823 ; left 8,000l. for the best work on 'The Goodness of God as manifested in the Creation,' which was divided among the eight authors of the 'Bridgewater Treatises'; published translations, family biographies, and other works. [xvii. 154]

EGERTON, JOHN, first EARL OF BRIDGEWATER (1579–1649), son of Sir Thomas Egerton, baron Ellesmere [q. v.]; served in Essex's Irish expedition, 1599 ; M.P., Shropshire, 1601 ; knighted, 1603 ; honorary M.A. of Oxford, whither he accompanied James I, 1605 ; created Earl of Bridgewater, 1617 ; privy councillor, 1626 ; lordlieutenant of Wales, 1631, Milton's 'Comus' being written for the festivities held at Ludlow Castle (1634) on the occasion of his taking up the appointment. [xvii. 156]

EGERTON, JOHN, second EARL OF BRIDGEWATER (1622–1686), eldest surviving son of John, first earl [q. v.]; represented the Elder Brother in Milton's 'Comus' at its first performance, 1634 ; high steward of Oxford University, 1663 ; M.A., 1663 ; privy councillor, 1666 and 1679 ; a commissioner to inquire into the expenditure of the Dutch war vote, 1667. [xvii. 156]

EGERTON, JOHN, third EARL OF BRIDGEWATER (1646–1701), eldest surviving son of John, second earl [q. v.]; K.B., 1660 ; knight of the shire for Buckinghamshire, 1685 ; succeeded as earl, 1686 ; removed from lordlieutenancy of Buckinghamshire, as disaffected, 1687 ; re-instated by William III ; privy councillor; first lord of the admiralty, 1699 ; lord-justice of the kingdom, 1699.

[xvii. 157]

EGERTON, JOHN (1721–1787), bishop of Durham ; educated at Eton and Oriel College, Oxford ; prebendary of Hereford, 1746 ; king's chaplain, 1749 ; dean of Hereford, 1750 ; D.C.L. ; bishop of Bangor, 1756–68; bishop of Lichfield, 1768–71 ; prebendary of St. Paul's, 1768 ; bishop of Durham, 1771 ; granted a new charter to the city of Durham, 1780. [xvii. 158]

EGERTON, SIR PHILIP DE MALPAS GREY- (1806–1881), palæontologist ; educated at Eton and Christ Church, Oxford ; B.A., 1828 ; travelled with a friend over Germany, Italy, and Switzerland, in quest of fossil fishes ; M.P. for Chester, 1830 and 1835–68, for West Cheshire, 1868–81 ; contributed to the 'Decades of the Geological Survey of Great Britain'; F.G.S., 1829 ; F.R.S., 1831 ; Wollaston medallist of the Geological Society, 1873 ; published antiquarian works and catalogues of his collections.

[xvii. 159]

EGERTON, SARAH (1782–1847), actress ; née Fisher ; appeared at Bath, 1803 ; overshadowed as a tragedian at Covent Garden (1811–13) by Mrs. Siddons ; the original Ravina in Pocock's 'Miller and his Men,' 1813 ; excelled in melodrama. [xvii. 159]

EGERTON, STEPHEN (1555 ?–1621 ?), puritan divine ; M.A. Peterhouse, Cambridge, 1579 ; leader in formation of presbytery at Wandsworth ; suspended for refusing to subscribe Whitgift's articles, 1584 ; imprisoned, 1590 ; minister of St. Anne's, Blackfriars, 1598–c. 1621 ; introduced petition to the lower house of convocation for a reformed prayer-book, 1604 ; published sermons.

[xvii. 160]

EGERTON, SIR THOMAS, BARON ELLESMERE and VISCOUNT BRACKLEY (1540 ?–1617), lord chancellor ; barrister of Lincoln's Inn, 1572 ; governor of the inn, 1580 ; treasurer, 1587 ; solicitor-general, 1581 ; attorney-general, 1592 ; knighted, 1593 ; master of the rolls, 1594–1603 ;

lord-keeper, 1596 and 1603; privy councillor; employed by Elizabeth on diplomatic commissions; befriended Francis Bacon, and (1599) counselled Essex to show greater prudence; made Baron Ellesmere and lord chancellor, 1603; obtained a Star-chamber declaration that the deprivation in 1605 of puritan ministers was legal; enforced the catholic penal laws; helped to determine the Act of Union between England and Scotland (1606 and 1607), maintaining the right of a Scotsman born after James I's accession to hold land in England, 1608; chancellor of Oxford, 1610–17; obtained from Bacon an opinion in favour of the equity court against Coke, 1616; created Viscount Brackley, 1616; resigned the lord chancellorship, 1617; complimented by Sir John Davies, Camden, Ben Jonson, and Samuel Daniel; left in manuscript judicial and legal treatises.   [xvii. 161]

EGG, AUGUSTUS LEOPOLD (1816–1863), subject-painter; student in the Royal Academy, 1836, exhibiting his 'Spanish Girl,' 1838; R.A., 1860. His first work of importance, 'The Victim,' was engraved in the 'Gems of European Art.'   [xvii. 162]

EGGLESFIELD, ROBERT (d. 1349). [See EGLES-FIELD.]

EGGLESTONE, WILLIAM (fl. 1605–1623). [See ECCLESTONE.]

EGINTON, FRANCIS (1737–1805), painter on glass; partner with Boulton in the production of 'mechanical paintings' or 'polygraphs,' the process having been perfected by himself; established a factory at Birmingham, in which he revived glass-painting, in the form of transparencies on glass; given commissions for various ecclesiastical buildings.   [xvii. 164]

EGINTON, FRANCIS (1775–1823), engraver; nephew of Francis Eginton (1737–1805) [q. v.]; illustrated topographical and historical works.   [xvii. 165]

EGLESFIELD, ROBERT OF (d. 1349), founder of the Queen's College, Oxford; said to have been B.D. of Oxford; chaplain to Queen Philippa, and rector of Burgh, Westmoreland; established the 'Hall of the Queen's Scholars of Oxford' by royal charter, 1341; drew up statutes for his foundation, 1341; possibly identical with Robert de Eglesfield, knight of the shire for Cumberland in 1328.   [xvii. 165]

EGLEY, WILLIAM (1798–1870), miniature-painter; exhibited portraits at the Royal Academy from 1824 and at other institutions.   [xvii. 166]

EGLINTON, EARLS OF. [See MONTGOMERIE, HUGH, first EARL, 1460?–1545; MONTGOMERIE, HUGH, third EARL, 1531?–1585; MONTGOMERIE, ALEXANDER, sixth EARL, 1588–1661; MONTGOMERIE, HUGH, seventh EARL, 1613–1669; MONTGOMERIE, ALEXANDER, ninth EARL, 1660?–1729; MONTGOMERIE, ALEXANDER, tenth EARL, 1723–1769; MONTGOMERIE, ARCHIBALD, eleventh EARL, 1726–1796; MONTGOMERIE, HUGH, twelfth EARL, 1739–1819; MONTGOMERIE, ARCHIBALD, thirteenth EARL, 1812–1861.]

EGLISHAM, GEORGE (fl. 1612–1642), Scottish physician and poet; M.D., probably of Leyden; physician to James VI, 1616; undertook in his 'Duellum Poeticum' to prove that George Buchanan had been guilty of 'impiety towards God, perfidy to his prince, and tyranny to the muses,' 1618; published (1626) 'Prodromus Vindictæ,' a pamphlet charging the Duke of Buckingham with being a poisoner; retired to Brussels from the anger of the duke, 1626.   [xvii. 166]

EGMONT, EARLS OF. [See PERCEVAL, JOHN, first EARL, 1683–1748; PERCEVAL, JOHN, second EARL, 1711–1770.]

EGREMONT, EARLS OF. [See WYNDHAM, SIR CHARLES, second EARL, 1710–1763; WYNDHAM, SIR GEORGE O'BRIEN, third EARL, 1751–1837.]

EHRET, GEORG DIONYSIUS (1710–1770), botanic draughtsman; born at Erfurt; contributed the drawings to Linnæus's 'Hortus Cliffortianus,' 1737; befriended in England by the Duchess of Portland, Dr. Mead, and Sir Hans Sloane; chief published works, 'Plantæ Selectæ,' 1750, and 'Plantæ et Papiliones selectæ,' 1748–50.
                                                         [xvii. 167]

EINEON (fl. 1093), Welsh prince and warrior; in accordance with promise to Iestin [q. v.], prince of Morganwg, secured Norman aid for him against Rhys, chief king of South Wales, on the condition that he should marry Iestin's daughter; organised a revolt which gave South Wales to the Normans, Iestin having ignored his agreement when victorious.   [xvii. 167]

EIRENÆUS, PHILALETHES (b. 1622?), alchemist; real name unknown; claimed to have discovered philosopher's stone, 1645; friend of Robert Boyle and George Starkey [q. v.]; published works on alchemy, 1654–84.
                                                         [liv. 108]

EKINS, SIR CHARLES (1768–1855), admiral; son of Jeffery Ekins [q. v.]; served at the relief of Gibraltar, 1782; lieutenant, 1790; invalided home from the West Indies with despatches, 1801; took part in expedition against Copenhagen, 1807, operations off Portugal, 1808, and Baltic cruise, 1809; wounded at Algiers, 1816; C.B. and C.W.N.; admiral, 1841; G.C.B., 1852; published work on recent British naval engagements, 1824.
                                                         [xvii. 168]

EKINS, JEFFERY (d. 1791), dean of Carlisle; educated at Eton; fellow of King's College, Cambridge; M.A., 1758; assistant-master at Eton; chaplain to the Earl of Carlisle; rector of Quainton, 1761–75, of Morpeth, 1775, and of Sedgefield, 1777; D.D. Cambridge, 1781; dean of Carlisle, 1782; friend of Richard Cumberland; poet, and translator of 'The Loves of Medea and Jason' from Apollonius Rhodius, 1771.   [xvii. 169]

ELCHIES, LORD (1690–1754). [See GRANT, PATRICK.]

ELCHO, LORD (1721–1787). [See WEMYSS, DAVID.]

ELD, GEORGE (1791–1862), antiquary; editor of the 'Coventry Standard'; last mayor of Coventry before the Municipal Reform Act, 1834–5; restored the fourteenth-century interior of the mayoress's parlour, Coventry, 1834–5.   [xvii. 169]

ELDER, CHARLES (1821–1851), historical and portrait painter; sent to St. Paul's School, 1834; commenced exhibiting at the Academy with a 'Sappho,' 1845.
                                                         [xvii. 170]

ELDER, EDWARD (1812–1858), head-master of Charterhouse; educated at Charterhouse; scholar of Balliol College, Oxford, 1830; Ellerton prizeman; M.A., 1836; tutor of Balliol; head-master of Durham Cathedral grammar school, 1839; head-master of Charterhouse, 1853; D.D., 1853; contributed articles to Smith's 'Dictionary of Classical Biography and Mythology.'   [xvii. 170]

ELDER, JOHN (fl. 1555), Scottish writer; studied at St. Andrews, Aberdeen, and Glasgow universities; presented Henry VIII with a 'plot' or topographical description of Scotland, 1542; denounced Cardinal David Beaton [q. v.] in a letter to Henry VIII; converted to Romanism, 1553.   [xvii. 170]

ELDER, JOHN (1824–1869), marine engineer and shipbuilder; continued Randolph, Elder & Co.'s shipbuilding business, 1868; successfully constructed compound engines; read before the United Service Institute a paper on 'Circular Ships of War, with increased motive power,' 1868; president of the Glasgow Institution of Engineers and Shipbuilders, 1869; regarded as an authority on the capital and labour problem.   [xvii. 171]

ELDER, THOMAS (1737–1799), lord provost of Edinburgh, 1788–90, 1792–4, and 1796–8; broke up the Edinburgh meeting of the British Convention unaided, 1793; first colonel of the Royal Edinburgh Volunteers, 1794; postmaster-general for Scotland, 1795; procured rebuilding of Edinburgh College.   [xvii. 172]

ELDER, WILLIAM (fl. 1680–1700), engraver; an expert engraver of writing; engraved portrait of Ben Jonson for the folio edition of Jonson's works of 1692.
                                                         [xvii. 172]

ELDERFIELD, CHRISTOPHER (1607–1652), divine; M.A. St. Mary Hall, Oxford; chaplain to Sir William Goring, Burton, Sussex; author of 'The Civill Right of Tythes,' 1650, and a theological work.   [xvii. 172]

ELDERTON, WILLIAM (d. 1592?), ballad-writer; master of a company of comedians; attorney in the Sheriff's Court; published 'scurile balates' on Campion's execution, 1581. The opening of one of his ballads is quoted in 'Much Ado about Nothing,' v. 2. [xvii. 173]

ELDIN, LORD (1757–1832). [See CLERK, JOHN.]

ELDON, first EARL OF (1751–1838). [See SCOTT, JOHN.]

ELDRED, JOHN (1552–1632), traveller; visited, in company with some brother merchants (1583), Tripoli, Aleppo, and Bassorah; wrote account of voyage; took cargo of spices from Bassorah to Bagdad; journeyed through Palestine and Arabia; member of the first court of directors of the East India Company, 1600; patentee for the pre-emption of tin, customs farmer, and commissioner for the sale of lands under James I. [xvii. 174]

ELDRED, THOMAS (*fl.* 1586–1622), mariner of Ipswich; sailed in one or both of the voyages of Thomas Cavendish [q. v.]; commander or factor under the East India Company, 1600–9. [xvii. 175]

ELDRED, WILLIAM (*fl.* 1646), master gunner of Dover Castle; mentions his service as gunner in Germany and the Low Countries in 'The Gunner's Glasse,' 1646, an account of the great gun exercise as then practised. [xvii. 175]

ELEANOR, ALIENOR, or **ÆNOR,** DUCHESS OF AQUITAINE, QUEEN successively of FRANCE and ENGLAND (1122?–1204), queen of Henry II; daughter of William X, duke of Aquitaine; married by her father's arrangement to Louis VII of France, 1137; intrigued with her uncle, Raymond I, prince of Antioch, while attending her husband on a crusade, 1146; helped Louis to pacify Aquitaine, 1152; divorced from Louis by a church council on the ostensible plea of consanguinity, 1152; married Henry, count of Anjou and duke of Normandy, afterwards Henry II of England, 1152; enabled by her ancestral claims to induce Henry II to attack Toulouse, 1159; abetted her children's conspiracy against their father, Henry II, 1173; arrested and put under strict guard at Salisbury or Winchester, 1173; present at the reconciliation of Henry II and his sons, 1184; released, 1185; secured the undisturbed recognition of Richard I as king, 1189; prevented John, who was meditating treachery against his brother, from crossing to France, and exacted an oath of fealty to Richard I from the lords of the realm, 1192; organised force to resist contemplated invasion of John and French king, 1193; laid waste Anjou, which had declared for her grandson Arthur against King John, 1199; relieved by John when Arthur and Geoffrey de Lusignan besieged her in Mirabeau Castle, 1202; buried in Fontevraud Abbey, where she had once lived in retirement. [xvii. 175]

ELEANOR OF CASTILE (*d.* 1290), queen of Edward I; daughter of Ferdinand III of Castile; married to Prince Edward, afterwards Edward I, at Las Huelgas, 1254, thereby giving the English crown claims on Gascony and her mother's possessions of Ponthieu and Montreuil; entered London, 1255; refugee in France, 1264–5; accompanied her husband (1270) on his crusade; sometimes said to have saved Edward I's life by sucking a poisoned wound; crowned, 1274; acquired estates by help of Jewish usurers. Edward I marked the route taken by her funeral procession from Nottinghamshire to London by erecting crosses at its halting-places. [xvii. 178]

ELEANOR OF PROVENCE (*d.* 1291), queen of Henry III; daughter of Raymond Berenger IV, count of Provence; married to Henry III, 1236; lost popularity by her alleged partiality to Poitevin adventurers in England; reconciled Henry III and the earl marshal, 1241; accompanied her husband on his abortive expedition to Gascony, 1242; joint-governor of England with the king's brother, 1253; summoned council of Westminster, 1254; impoverished herself, the king, and the archbishop of Canterbury, to support the ambition of Thomas of Savoy, 1255; collected mercenaries at Sluys to fight for Henry in the barons' war, 1264; died a nun at Amesbury. [xvii. 179]

ELERS, JOHN PHILIP (*fl.* 1690–1730), potter; of Saxon descent; came to London with the Prince of Orange, 1688; established pottery works near Burslem, *c.* 1690; with his brother produced a red unglazed ware having slight raised ornamentations of an oriental character; introduced salt-glazing into Staffordshire. [xvii. 180]

ELFLEDA or **ÆLFLÆD** (654–714?), abbess of Whitby; dedicated to the church by her father, Oswiu, as a thank-offering for his victory over Penda, 655; abbess of

Whitby, jointly with her mother, Eanflæd [q. v.], 680; on the side of Wilfrith at the Northumbrian synod, 705. [xvi. 316]

ELFLEDA (*d.* 918?). [See ETHELFLEDA.]

ELFORD, RICHARD (*d.* 1714), vocalist; gentleman of the Chapel Royal, 1702; lay vicar at St. Paul's Cathedral and Westminster Abbey; took part in the performance before Queen Anne of Eccles's 'Birthday Songs,' 1703; famous as a singer of sacred music. [xvii. 181]

ELFORD, SIR WILLIAM (1749–1837), banker, politician, and amateur artist; mayor of Plymouth, 1797; M.P., Plymouth, 1796–1806, and Westbury; M.P., Rye, 1807–8; lieutenant-colonel of the South Devon militia in Ireland, 1798–9; F.R.S., 1790; created baronet, 1800; exhibited at the Royal Academy, 1774–1837; friend of William Pitt (1759–1806). [xvii. 182]

ELFRIDA (945–1000). [See ÆLFTHRYTH.]

ELGIN, EARLS OF. [See BRUCE, ROBERT, second EARL, *d.* 1685; BRUCE, THOMAS, third EARL, 1655?–1741; BRUCE, THOMAS, seventh EARL, 1766–1841; BRUCE, JAMES, eighth EARL, 1811–1863.]

ELGIVA (*fl.* 956). [See ÆLFGIFU.]

ELIAS, JOHN (1774–1841), Welsh Calvinistic methodist; taught in the 'first Sunday school in Carnarvonshire'; itinerant preacher in Carnarvonshire; learnt English and studied the Greek and Hebrew scriptures; ameliorated moral and religious condition of Anglesey; ordained, 1811; helped to draw up the methodists' articles of faith, 1823; opposed Arminian methodism and catholic emancipation; a famous preacher; published religious tractates in Welsh. [xvii. 182]

ELIAS, NEY (1844–1897), explorer and diplomatist; F.R.G.S., 1865; went to Shanghai in employment of a mercantile house, 1866; led expedition to examine courses of Hoang-ho, 1868; travelled across Gobi desert from great wall to Nijni Novgorod, 1872; received founder's medal of Royal Geographical Society, 1873; his services secured by Indian government; held diplomatic posts in India; made numerous journeys in various parts of Asia, solving on one occasion the problem as to which was the upper course of the Oxus; retired from service, 1896; published works relating to his journeys. [Suppl. ii. 178]

ELIBANK, LORD (*d.* 1621). [See MURRAY, SIR GIDEON.]

ELIBANK, fifth BARON (1703–1778). [See MURRAY, PATRICK.]

ELIOCK, LORD (1712–1793). [See VEITCH, JAMES.]

ELIOT. [See also ELIOTT, ELLIOT, ELLIOTT, and ELYOT.]

ELIOT, EDWARD, BARON ELIOT (1727–1804), politician; visited Montesquieu in company with Lord Charlemont; knight of the shire for Cornwall; M.P., St. Germans, 1748–68, Liskeard, 1768–75, Cornwall, 1775–1784; created Baron Eliot of St. Germans, 1784; commissioner of board of trade and plantations, 1760–76; severed his connection with Lord North by voting against employment of Hessian troops in America, 1776; acquaintance of Dr. Johnson and patron of Sir Joshua Reynolds. [xvii. 184]

ELIOT, EDWARD GRANVILLE, third EARL OF ST. GERMANS (1798–1877), diplomatist; educated at Westminster and Christ Church, Oxford; M.P., Liskeard, 1824–32; secretary of legation at Madrid, 1823, at Lisbon, 1824; envoy extraordinary to Spain, where he induced the Carlists and royalists to make the 'Eliot Convention' for the humaner treatment of prisoners, 1834; M.P., East Cornwall, 1837–45; deputy-lieutenant of Cornwall, 1841; chief secretary for Ireland, 1841–5; carried bill for registration of firearms, 1843; honorary LL.D. Dublin, 1843; succeeded as Earl St. Germans, 1845; appointed postmaster-general and (1852) lord-lieutenant of Ireland; Irish viceroy during Palmerston's premiership, 1855. [xvii. 185]

ELIOT, FRANCIS PERCEVAL (1756?–1818), writer on finance; commissioner of audit at Somerset House; chief work, 'Observations on the Fallacy of the supposed Depreciation of the Paper Currency of the Kingdom,' 1811. [xvii. 186]

ELIOT, GEORGE (pseudonym). [See CROSS, MARY ANN, 1819–1880.]

ELIOT, SIR JOHN (1592–1632), patriot; studied at Exeter College, Oxford, 1607–10, and at one of the Inns of Court; sat in the Addled parliament for St. Germans, 1614; knighted, 1618; vice-admiral of Devon, 1619; M.P., Newport, Cornwall, 1624, sympathising with Buckingham's policy of war with Spain; urged the enforcement of the catholic penal laws when M.P. for Newport, 1625; declared his distrust in a war policy which extended to Denmark, Savoy, Germany, and France, 1625; M.P., St. Germans, 1626; attacked Buckingham, 1626, for the Cadiz disaster; summed up the charges against Buckingham, whom he compared to Sejanus, 1626; imprisoned for refusing to pay his share of the forced loan, 1627; M.P., Cornwall, 1628; insisted on the full acceptance of the Petition of Right, 1628; read three resolutions in parliament against the king's religious proceedings and claim to levy provisionally tonnage and poundage without consent of parliament, 2 March, 1629; imprisoned for conspiracy to resist the king's lawful order for the adjournment of parliament on 2 March, 1629, to calumniate the ministers of the crown, and to assault the speaker; sentenced to a fine of 2,000l., 1630; died in prison. He left in manuscript 'The Monarchie of Man' and a vindication of himself in 'An Apology for Socrates,' also 'Negotium Posterorum' and 'De Jure Majestatis' (all first printed, 1879–82). [xvii. 186]

ELIOT, JOHN (1604 – 1690), styled the 'Indian Apostle'; B.A. Jesus College, Cambridge, 1622; emigrated, 1631; 'teacher' of the church at Roxbury, near Boston, Massachusetts, 1632–90; bore witness against the religious enthusiast, Mrs. Anne Hutchinson [q. v.], 1637; preached his first sermon to the aborigines in their own tongue at Nonantum, Massachusetts, 1646; obtained an ordinance in parliament (1649) for the advancement of civilisation and Christianity among the Indians; encouraged by the formation of a society (1649), which afterwards found funds for building an Indian college; founded at Natick the first township of 'praying Indians,' 1651; his 'Christian Commonwealth' suppressed by the governor and council of New England, 1660; translated Baxter's 'Call' into the dialect of the Massachusetts Indians, 1664; his translation of the bible into the same dialect issued by the press, 1663; published 'The Indian Grammar begun,' 1666, an 'Indian Primer,' 1669, and a 'Logick Primer,' 1672; showed great solicitude for the natives during King Philip's war, 1675–6; published 'The Harmony of the Gospels,' 1678; died at Roxbury; narrated the progress of his work in 'Indian tracts.' [xvii. 189]

ELIOT, SIR THOMAS (1490?–1546). [See ELYOT.]

ELIOTT, SIR DANIEL (1798–1872), Indian civilian; educated at the Edinburgh Academy; nominated to the East India Company's civil service; deputy Tamil translator, 1822; Marátha translator to the Madras government, 1823; member of the board of revenue, 1836; Madras member of the Indian law commission, 1838; president of the revenue, marine, and college boards, Madras, 1850–3; Madras member of the legislative council, 1854–1859; K.C.S.I., 1867. [xvii. 194]

ELIOTT, GEORGE AUGUSTUS, first BARON HEATHFIELD (1717–1790), general and defender of Gibraltar; educated at Leyden University and the military college of La Fère; volunteer in the Prussian army, 1735–6; cornet 2nd life guards and field engineer, 1739; present as adjutant at Dettingen, 1743, and Fontenoy, 1745; aide-de-camp to George II, 1755; major-general, 1762; second in command in the Cuban expedition; lieutenant-general, 1763; commander-in-chief of the forces in Ireland, 1774–5; governor of Gibraltar, 1775; defended Gibraltar against D'Arzon and the Spaniards, 1779–83; K.B.; created Baron Heathfield of Gibraltar, 1787. [xvii. 195]

ELIZABETH, queen of Edward IV (1437?–1492), daughter of Sir Richard Woodville, afterwards Earl Rivers; married Sir John Grey, who (1461) was killed at St. Albans; privately married to Edward IV, whom she personally petitioned for her husband's forfeited lands, 1464; crowned, 1465; withdrew into sanctuary at Westminster on Edward IV's flight, 1470; principal executrix of the will made by her husband in 1475; accused by Clarence of having caused the death of his wife by sorcery, 1476; favoured a match, which the council of Flanders rejected, between her brother Anthony and Mary,

daughter of Charles the Bold, late Duke of Burgundy, 1477; took sanctuary at Westminster from the anger of Gloucester and Buckingham after Edward IV's death, 1483; persuaded by Cardinal Bourchier to deliver up the young Duke of York, 1483; her marriage with Edward IV pronounced invalid in a parliament controlled by Richard III, 1484; persuaded by Richard III to quit her sanctuary on a promise of providing for herself and her daughters, by which he long postponed, although he intended to prevent, the marriage arranged for her daughter with the exiled Earl of Richmond, 1484; placed by Henry VII in full possession of her rights as queen-dowager, 1486; her lands forfeited (1487) for the perfidy she was alleged to have shown in 1484; retired to the abbey of Bermondsey. She refounded and endowed Queens' College, Cambridge. [xvii. 196]

ELIZABETH, queen of Henry VII (1465–1503), of York; daughter of Edward IV and Elizabeth Woodville; her marriage with the dauphin made a condition of peace between Edward IV and Louis XI, 1475, but never performed; promised in marriage to the Earl of Richmond, then an exile plotting the dethronement of Richard III, an arrangement which was temporarily frustrated, 1484, by the king's specious promises of protection to her mother; reported to have received a proposal of marriage from Richard III; mentioned in the 'Song of the Lady Bessy,' a contemporary composition, as having induced Lord Stanley to join Richmond; married to Henry VII, 1486, in pursuance of a petition presented to the king by parliament, 1485; crowned, 1487, after the suppression of the Earl of Lincoln's rebellion; received grant of her mother's forfeited lordships and manors of the duchy of Lancaster, 1487; her death attributed to grief occasioned by the decease of her eldest son, Prince Arthur. An elegy upon her was written by Sir Thomas More. [xvii. 200]

ELIZABETH (1533–1603), queen of England and Ireland; only child of Henry VIII and his second wife, Anne Boleyn [q. v.]; declared illegitimate by parliament in the interest of her father's third wife, Jane Seymour, mother of Edward VI, 1536; refused (1547) the hand of Sir Thomas Seymour, lord high admiral, who, however, did not abandon his suit till his execution, 1549; read Latin and Greek with Roger Ascham; refused to use her influence to save the Duke of Somerset, 1552; rode by the side of her elder half-sister, Queen Mary, at the latter's triumphal entry into London, 1553; refused to compromise herself by taking part in the insurrection of Sir Thomas Wyatt, who wished her to marry Edward Courtenay [q. v.], a kinsman of the blood royal, 1554; thrown into the Tower at the instance of Gardiner, 1554; released from custody at Woodstock, 1554; refused to engage in plots against Queen Mary; proclaimed queen, in succession to Mary, November 1558, most of her friends and foes alike being already dead; crowned by Owen Oglethorpe [q. v.], bishop of Carlisle, nearly all the bishops refusing to recognise her as head of the church, 1559; made a proclamation that the English litany should be read in the London churches, 1559; refused the hand of Philip II of Spain; declared to the House of Commons that she had no intention of marrying, 1559; played off three suitors, Eric of Sweden, Adolphus, duke of Holstein, and the Archduke Charles, against one another, 1559; appointed Grindal bishop of London and Parker archbishop of Canterbury, 1559; disturbed by the cordiality existing between Scotland and France, although a treaty had been signed (1559) between those countries and England; signed treaty with Scotland through her agent, Cecil, in which it was laid down that Mary Stuart should give up using the title of queen of England and that the French should quit Scotland, 1560; called in the debased coinage, 1560; pretended a passion for Robert Dudley [q. v.], afterwards created Earl of Leicester; sent help to Condé, leader of the French protestants in their war with the Duke of Guise; compelled, 1563, by the reduction of the garrison after the peace of Amboise to surrender Havre, which, with Dieppe, had been the price of her support; promulgated the Thirty-nine Articles and extended the range of the oath of supremacy, 1563; made writing in defence of the papal authority liable to the penalties of the statute of Præmunire, 1563; suggested that her favourite, Dudley, should marry Mary Queen of Scots; encouraged the advances of the Archduke Charles, while maintaining in parliament her aversion to marriage in itself, 1564; grudgingly thanked Sir Henry Sidney for his services against Shaen O'Neill in Ireland, 1567; imprisoned Mary

Queen of Scots, 1568 and 1569; excommunicated by Pope Pius V, 1570; encouraged the vindictive measures adopted in the north on the suppression of the catholic rebellion, 1571; executed the Duke of Norfolk, 1572, soon after the discovery of the Ridolfi plot; forbade parliament to proceed with the bill of attainder against Mary Stuart; received from Charles IX of France a proposal of marriage with his brother, the Duke of Anjou, 1571; gave orders for the execution of Northumberland, whom the Scots had sold to Lord Hunsdon, 1572; accepted Francis, duke d'Alençon, as a suitor, 1572–84; vainly attempted to get the regent Morton to pay for his English auxiliaries in Scotland, 1573; sent a force to help the United Provinces against Spain, though not fully understanding the significance of her action or Lord Burghley's policy, 1572; recalled Sir Humphrey Gilbert, her general in the Netherlands, 1572; undertook to act as peacemaker between Philip II and the Low Countries, the sovereignty of which she declined, 1573; put in force the penal laws against Romanists and especially against the seminarist priests of Douay, who, after receiving their education at Douay, returned to England to work quietly as 'missioners,' 1574; suspended Grindal, archbishop of Canterbury, for refusing to suppress the prophesyings of the puritans, 1577; the protection of her person guaranteed by a sort of plébiscite, which was signed among others by Mary Queen of Scots, 1584; betrayed into greater severity by the discovery of the Guise conspiracy; transferred Mary Queen of Scots to the custody of Sir Amyas Paulet at Tutbury, at a time when the treasonable acts of Mary's adherents were compromising her safety, 1585; sent troops under Leicester (1585) to fight with the insurgents of the Netherlands against Parma, but soon necessitated his return by withholding supplies, 1586; ordered the torture and execution of the Babington conspirators, 1586; shrank, in fear of the moral condemnation of the world, from signing the death-warrant of Mary Stuart, but ultimately consented, after having ineffectually suggested to Mary's warders the desirability of a secret assassination, 1587; recognised James VI as king of Scotland, 1587; drawn into a war with Spain by Drake's action in destroying a Spanish squadron off Cadiz, 1587; disregarded the advice of Walsingham and her council to precipitate an attack upon the Spanish Armada, 1588; caused the death of many of the sailors by reducing the commissariat of the fleet below the level of bare necessity, 1588; reviewed her troops at Tilbury, 1588; supported Henry of Navarre's claim to inherit the French crown, 1590 and 1591; lost her bravest commanders, Drake and Hawkins, in an expedition to the Spanish main, despatched 1595; deprived by death of the services of her treasurer, Lord Burghley, 1598; her marshal in Ireland, Sir Henry Bagnal, defeated by Tyrone, the leader of an insurrection prompted by maladministration and the abolition of the ancient Brehon law, 1598; appointed Essex 'lieutenant and governor-general of Ireland,' in which post he failed signally, 1599; humoured the Commons by the revocation of monopolies, 1601; threw upon the church courts the burden of dealing with puritans and sectaries; kept many of the sees vacant in order to use their revenues for governmental purposes; sent Essex to the scaffold, his attempted insurrection leaving her no option, 1601; sanctioned a plundering expedition to the coast of Spain, which failed to secure any treasure, 1602; died at Richmond of the effects of a cold supervening on health already broken, 24 March 1602–3; buried in Westminster Abbey, 28 April 1603. [xvii. 203]

ELIZABETH (1635–1650), princess; second daughter of Charles I; appealed to the lords to be allowed to retain in her service the principal members of her household, 1642; devoted herself, when separated from her parents, to the study of languages and theology, in which she made great proficiency; dedicatee of Alexander Rowley's biblical lexicon of Greek and Hebrew, 1648; named 'Temperance' from her gentle bearing; facilitated the escape of the Duke of York, 1648; panegyrised by Christopher Wase in his translation of Sophocles' 'Electra,' 1649; died a prisoner at Carisbrooke Castle. [xvii. 232]

ELIZABETH (1596–1662), queen of Bohemia; daughter of James VI of Scotland; represented the nymph of the Thames in Daniel's 'Tethys's Festival' at Whitehall, 1610; married, after the falling through of many other political plans, to the Count Palatine, Frederick V, 1613; her husband chosen king of Bohemia, till then an appanage of the empire, 1619; crowned, 1619; found a temporary refuge with George William, elector of Bran-

denburg, after her husband's defeat by the Emperor Frederick II at Prague, 1620; the seizure of her husband's dominions by Maximilian, duke of Bavaria, confirmed at the conference of Ratisbon, 1623; named the Queen of Hearts for her winning demeanour; her cause ineffectually championed by her chivalrous cousin, Duke Christian of Brunswick, 1623; her charm immortalised in a poem by Sir Henry Wotton; lost her eldest son, 1629, and her husband, 1632, soon after the death of Gustavus Adolphus at Lutzen; levied a small army on behalf of her eldest surviving son, Charles Lewis, 1633, to whom part of the Palatinate was restored by the peace of Westphalia, 1648; subsidised by William, first earl of Craven [q. v.]; deserted by her children, Charles Lewis allowing his mother to remain dependent on the generosity of Holland; granted 10,000l. by the parliament of the Restoration, 1660; pensioned by her nephew, Charles II, who had at first looked coldly on her coming to England; bequeathed to her favourite son, Prince Rupert, most of her jewellery, 1662; died at Leicester House, Leicester Fields, London, 13 Feb. 1661-2, and buried in Westminster Abbey; long regarded as a martyr to protestantism. [xvii. 233]

ELIZABETH, Princess of England and Landgravine of Hesse-Homburg (1770–1840), artist; daughter of George III; designed a series of pictures, entitled, 'The Birth and Triumph of Cupid,' 1795; established society at Windsor for giving dowries to poor girls, 1808; married, 1818, Frederick Joseph Louis, hereditary prince of Hesse-Homburg, who died 1829; set apart 6,000l. a year to reduce the deficits of Hesse-Homburg; reissued her sketches 'Power and Progress of Genius,' to benefit the poor of Hanover, 1834. [xvii. 240]

ELKINGTON, GEORGE RICHARDS (1801–1865), introducer of electro-plating; Birmingham magistrate, 1856; introduced, in conjunction with his cousin, Henry Elkington [q. v.], the industry of electro-plating and electro-gilding, at first using the voltaic pile and subsequently Wright's solution; patentee for 'mercurial gilding,' 1836 and 1837. [xvii. 240]

ELKINGTON, HENRY (1810–1852), inventor; cousin of G. R. Elkington [q. v.]; invented and patented the pantascopic spectacles. [xvii. 241]

ELLA. [See ÆLLA.]

ELLA, JOHN (1802–1888), violinist and director of concerts; first appeared in the orchestra of Drury Lane Theatre, 1821; founded the Saltoun Club of Instrumentalists and the Società Lirica, c. 1826; musical editor of the 'Athenæum,' c. 1826; wrote a 'Victoria March,' 1837; inaugurated the 'Musical Union,' a set of chamber concerts; musical lecturer to the London Institution, 1855; published 'A Personal Memoir of Meyerbeer' and 'Musical Sketches Abroad and at Home,' 1869. [xvii. 241]

ELLACOMBE or **ELLICOMBE**, HENRY THOMAS (1790–1885), divine and antiquary; B.A. Oriel College, Oxford, 1812; M.A., 1816; vicar of Bitton, 1835-50, and rector of Clyst St. George, 1850-85; restored or built various churches; invented apparatus enabling one man to chime all the bells in a steeple; wrote on campanology and the antiquities of Bitton and Clyst St. George. [xvii. 242]

ELLENBOROUGH, EARL OF (1790–1871). [See LAW EDWARD.]

ELLENBOROUGH, BARONS. [See LAW, EDWARD, first BARON, 1750-1818; LAW, EDWARD, second BARON, 1790-1871.]

ELLERKER, SIR RALPH (d. 1546), warrior; knighted on Flodden Field, 1513; possibly M.P. for Scarborough, 1529; J.P. for the East Riding; M.P., Yorkshire, 1541; marshal of the English army in France; took the crest from the dauphin at the capture of Boulogne, 1544; buried at Boulogne. [xvii. 243]

ELLERKER, THOMAS (1738–1795), jesuit; emigrated from Liège to Stonyhurst, 1794; published 'Tractatus Theologicus de Jure et Justitia,' 1767, and 'De Incarnatione.' [xvii. 243]

ELLERTON, EDWARD (1770–1851), founder of scholarships; M.A. University College, Oxford, 1795; master of Magdalen College School, 1799; fellow of Magdalen; D.D., 1815; held various country curacies; founded the Ellerton theological essay prize, 1825, and exhibitions at Magdalen and Richmond School ; joint-founder of the Pusey and Ellerton scholarships, 1832 ; wrote against Tractarianism, 1845.   [xvii. 244]

ELLERTON, JOHN LODGE, formerly JOHN LODGE (1801–1873), amateur musical composer ; M.A. Brasenose College, Oxford, 1828 ; studied counterpoint at Rome ; produced ' Paradise Lost,' a successful oratorio, 1857, but failed in his English opera ' Domenica,' 1838 ; member of the Musical Union, 1847–71 ; published poems.
                                                          [xvii. 244]

ELLESMERE, BARON (1540 ?–1617). [See EGERTON, SIR THOMAS.]

ELLESMERE, first EARL OF (1800–1857). [See EGERTON, FRANCIS.]

ELLEY, SIR JOHN (d. 1839), lieutenant-general ; distinguished himself at Cateau, 1794 ; lieutenant-colonel by purchase, 1808 ; served in Peninsula ; fought at Waterloo, 1815 ; K.C.B. ; governor of Galway, 1820 ; colonel, 17th lancers, 1829 ; M.P., Windsor, 1835 ; lieutenant-general, 1837.   [xvii. 245]

ELLICE, SIR CHARLES HAY (1823–1888), general ; nephew of Edward Ellice the elder [q. v.] ; studied at Sandhurst ; ensign and lieutenant, 1839 ; captain, 1845 ; served in India, 1846 ; major, 1849 ; lieutenant-colonel, 1851 ; colonel, 1854 ; served in Indian mutiny ; C.B., 1858 ; commanded second battalion of 24th in Mauritius, 1860–2 ; major-general, 1865 ; lieutenant-general, 1873 ; general, 1877 ; K.C.B., 1873 ; G.C.B., 1882.   [Suppl. ii. 179]

ELLICE, EDWARD, the elder (1781–1863), politician ; educated at Winchester and Marischal College, Aberdeen ; M.A., 1800 ; engaged in the Canada fur trade, 1803 ; amalgamated North-west, X.Y., and Hudson's Bay companies, 1821 ; M.P., Coventry, 1818, 1820, 1830, and 1831–63 ; secretary to the treasury, and whip in Lord Grey's government, 1830–2 ; proposed, when secretary at war (1832–4), that appointments in the army should be made directly from his office ; helped to found Reform Club, 1836 ; supported Palmerston as premier ; D.C.L. St. Andrews ; privately urged French government to send troops into Spain, 1836 ; deputy-governor of the Hudson's Bay Company.   [xvii. 246]

ELLICE, EDWARD, the younger (1810–1880), politician ; son of Edward Ellice the elder [q. v.] ; educated at Eton and Trinity College, Cambridge ; M.A., 1831 ; private secretary to Lord Durham in Russia, 1832, in Canada, 1838 ; M.P. for Huddersfield, 1853, and subsequently for St. Andrews burghs ; free-trader and advocate of Irish disestablishment ; proposed that there should be some mediated members in the House of Commons, 1859 ; condemned the Highland administration of the poor law in ' The State of the Highlands in 1854,' 1855.
                                                          [xvii. 247]

ELLICOMBE. [See also ELLACOMBE.]

ELLICOMBE, SIR CHARLES GRENE (1783–1871), general, royal engineers ; educated at the Royal Military Academy, Woolwich ; first lieutenant, royal engineers, 1801 ; associated in the direction of attack on Ciudad Rodrigo, 1812 ; brigade-major to the corps of royal engineers at the siege of San Sebastian, 1813 ; major-general, 1841 ; general and colonel commandant of royal engineers ; K.C.B., 1862.   [xvii. 248]

ELLICOTT, EDWARD (d. 1791), son of John Ellicott [q. v.] ; clockmaker to the king.   [xvii. 250]

ELLICOTT, JOHN (1706 ?–1772), clockmaker and man of science ; clockmaker to George III ; improved the pyrometer, 1736 ; invented a compensated pendulum, 1752 ; F.R.S., 1738 ; made observations of the transit of Venus, 1761 ; published ' Essays towards discovering the Laws of Electricity,' 1748.   [xvii. 249]

ELLIOT. [See also ELIOT, ELIOTT, and ELLIOTT.]

ELLIOT, ADAM (d. 1700), traveller ; B.A. Caius College, Cambridge, 1668 ; taken captive by the Moors, and sold into slavery, 1670 ; ordained priest, 1672 ; accused by Titus Oates of being a jesuit priest and a Mahommedan ; author of a 'Narrative of my Travails, Captivity, and Escape from Salle, in the Kingdom of Fez,' bound up with an attack on Oates, 1682.   [xvii. 250]

ELLIOT, SIR CHARLES (1801–1875), admiral ; son of Hugh Elliot [q. v.] ; present at the bombardment of Algiers, 1816 ; lieutenant on the Jamaica station, 1822 ; advanced to post rank, 1828 ; protector of slaves in Guiana, 1830–3 ; chief superintendent and plenipotentiary on the China Trade Commission, 1837 ; forced to surrender 4,000,000l. worth of opium, 1839 ; virtually directed hostilities in China ; ransomed Canton ; governor of Bermuda, 1846–54, of Trinidad, 1854–6, and of St. Helena, 1863–9 ; K.C.B., 1856 ; admiral, 1865.   [xvii. 251]

ELLIOT, SIR GEORGE (1784–1863), admiral ; second son of Sir Gilbert Elliot, first earl of Minto [q. v.] ; present in the battles of Cape St. Vincent and the Nile ; commander, 1802 ; highly esteemed by Nelson ; served at the reduction of Java, 1811 ; secretary of the admiralty, 1834–1835 ; commander-in-chief at the Cape of Good Hope, 1837–40 ; commander-in-chief and joint-plenipotentiary with Sir Charles Elliot [q. v.] in China, 1840 ; admiral, 1853 ; K.C.B., 1862.   [xvii. 251]

ELLIOT, SIR GILBERT, LORD MINTO (1651–1718), judge ; writer in Edinburgh ; helped to organise the Earl of Argyll's rising, and was forfeited, 1685 ; condemned to death, but pardoned ; advocate, 1688 ; knighted ; clerk of the privy council, 1692 ; created baronet, 1700 ; M.P. for Roxburghshire from 1703 ; judge of session, with the title of Lord Minto, 1705 ; opposed the union.
                                                          [xvii. 252]

ELLIOT, SIR GILBERT, LORD MINTO (1693–1766), Scottish judge ; son of Sir Gilbert Elliot (1651–1718) [q. v.] ; advocate, 1715 ; M.P. for Roxburghshire, 1722–6 ; lord of justiciary, 1733–66 ; justice clerk, 1763–6 ; narrowly escaped seizure by Prince Charles Edward's highlanders, 1745 ; said, rather doubtfully, to have introduced the German flute into Scotland.   [xvii. 253]

ELLIOT, SIR GILBERT, third baronet of Minto (1722–1777), statesman, philosopher, and poet ; son of Sir Gilbert Elliot (1693–1766) [q. v.] ; studied at Edinburgh and Leyden universities ; called to the Scottish bar, 1742 ; M.P. for Selkirkshire, 1754 and 1762–5, for Roxburghshire, 1765–77 ; admiralty lord, 1756 ; keeper of the signet in Scotland, 1767 ; treasurer of the navy, 1770 ; at first a supporter of Pitt and the Grenvilles, afterwards of Lord Bute ; overruled Lord North by haranguing on the threatened liberties of the house, at the time of the London riots, 1771 ; encouraged George III's policy towards America ; declined, from dislike of the sceptical philosophy, to co-operate in his friend Hume's ' Dialogues of Natural Religion ' ; died at Marseilles. His fame as a song-writer rests upon his pastoral ditty, ' Amynta,' and in a less degree upon ' 'Twas at the hour of dark midnight,' 1745.
                                                          [xvii. 253]

ELLIOT, SIR GILBERT, first EARL OF MINTO (1751–1814), governor-general of India ; son of Sir Gilbert Elliot (1722–1777) [q. v.] ; schoolfellow of Mirabeau at the Pension Militaire, Fontainebleau ; gentleman commoner, Christ Church, Oxford, 1768 ; barrister of Lincoln's Inn, 1774 ; M.P. for Morpeth, 1776–84 ; M.P. for Berwick, 1786–90 ; carried motion condemning Sir Elijah Impey's conduct at Fort William, 1787 ; M.P. for Helston, Cornwall, 1790 ; opposed Fox, 1793 ; D.C.L. Oxford, 1793 ; constitutional viceroy of Corsica, 1794–6 ; expelled General Paoli ; created Baron Minto of Minto, 1798 ; minister plenipotentiary at Vienna, 1799 ; F.R.S., 1803 ; president of board of control, 1806 ; governor-general of India, 1807–13 ; subsidised Shah Shuja, ameer of Afghanistan, to secure his loyalty, 1809 ; annexed Amboyna, the Molucca islands, and, in 1811, Java, whither he went in person ; projected the establishment of colleges for Indian Mahommedans ; created Viscount Melgund and Earl of Minto, 1813.   [xvii. 255]

ELLIOT, GILBERT, second EARL OF MINTO (1782–1859), eldest son of Sir Gilbert Elliot, first earl [q. v.] ; educated at Edinburgh University ; whig M.P. for Ashburton, 1806–14 ; privy councillor ; British ambassador to Berlin, 1832–4 ; G.C.B. ; first lord of the admiralty, 1835–1841 ; lord privy seal, 1846 ; prevailed on king of Naples to grant Sicily a separate parliament ; F.R.S.   [xvii. 257]

ELLIOT, SIR HENRY MIERS (1808–1853), Indian civil servant and historian ; educated at Winchester ; first ' competition wallah ' for an immediate post in India 1826 ; secretary to the Sudder board of revenue for the north-west provinces ; foreign secretary to the governor-general in council, 1847 ; negotiated the Sikh treaty of 1849 ; K.C.B. ; died at Simon's Town ; published first volume of ' Bibliographical Index to the Historians of Mohammadan India,' 1849. [xvii. 258]

ELLIOT, HUGH (1752–1830), diplomatist ; school-fellow of Mirabeau at Paris ; studied at Christ Church, Oxford, 1768–70 ; minister plenipotentiary at Munich, 1773 ; minister plenipotentiary to Prussia, 1777, to Denmark, 1782 ; instigated by the queen of Naples, when envoy plenipotentiary, to forbid Sir James Henry Craig [q. v.] to withdraw his English troops from Italy, 1803 ; recalled ; governor of the Leeward islands, 1809–13 ; privy councillor and governor of Madras, 1814. [xvii. 259]

ELLIOT, JANE or JEAN (1727–1805), poet ; daughter of Sir Gilbert Elliot (1693–1766) [q. v.] ; outwitted her father's highland pursuers, 1745 ; authoress of ' Flowers of the Forest,' a celebrated ballad, 1756. [xvii. 259]

ELLIOT, JOHN (1725–1782), antiquary ; articled to a solicitor ; F.S.A., 1780 ; furnished information on the feudal barony to the Rev. John Watson (1725–1783) [q. v.] [xvii. 260]

ELLIOT, JOHN (d. 1808), admiral ; third son of Sir Gilbert Elliot (1693–1766) [q. v.] : navy lieutenant, 1756 ; captured the French frigate Mignonne, 1759 ; defeated Thurot's squadron off the ' Isle of Mann,' 1760 ; fought at Cape St. Vincent, 1780, and under Kempenfelt, 1781 ; governor and commander-in-chief at Newfoundland, 1786–9 ; admiral, 1795. [xvii. 261]

ELLIOT or SHELDON, NATHANIEL (1705–1780), jesuit ; professed of the four vows, 1741 ; rector of St. Omer College, 1748–56, of the English College at Rome, 1756–62, of the Greater College, Bruges, 1766–80 ; provincial in England, 1766 ; translated Pinamonti's ' Cross in its True Light,' 1775. [xvii. 262]

ELLIOT, ROBERT (*fl.* 1822–1833), captain R.N. and topographical draughtsman, 1822–4 ; his sketches published as ' Views in the East,' 1830–3. [xvii. 262]

ELLIOT, SIR WALTER (1803–1887), Indian civil servant and archæologist ; sent to Haileybury College, 1818 ; assistant to the magistrate at Salem, 1823 ; private secretary to Lord Elphinstone, 1836 ; deputed to investigate the revenue difficulties of Guntúr, 1845 ; commissioner for the administration of the Northern Sirkárs till 1854 ; member of the council of the governor of Madras, 1854 ; K.C.S.I., 1866 ; F.R.S., 1877 ; LL.D. Edinburgh, 1878 ; deputy-lieutenant and magistrate for Roxburghshire ; published in the ' Journal of the Royal Asiatic Society ' a paper on ' Hindu Inscriptions,' 1837, and wrote a treatise on the coins of Southern India, 1885. [xvii. 262]

ELLIOTSON, JOHN (1791–1868), physician ; educated at Edinburgh and Jesus College, Cambridge ; M.D., 1821 ; professor of the practice of medicine to London University, 1831–8 ; procured the foundation of University College Hospital ; founder and first president of the Phrenological Society ; professor of clinical medicine, London, 1831 ; compelled to resign the professorship of the practice of medicine for his unauthorised interest in mesmerism, 1838 ; Harveian orator, 1846 ; established a mesmeric hospital, 1849 ; started the 'Zoist,' a journal of mesmeric healing ; first to use the stethoscope ; published his Lumley lectures (1829) on diseases of the heart, 1830. [xvii. 264]

ELLIOTT. [See also ELIOT, ELIOTT, and ELLIOT.]

ELLIOTT, CHARLOTTE (1789–1871), hymn-writer ; friend of Cæsar Malan ; wrote many religious poems, including (1834) ' Just as I am.' [xvii. 266]

ELLIOTT, EBENEZER (1781–1849), ' the corn-law rhymer ' ; commended by Southey for his ' Tales of the Night ' ; started in business in the Sheffield iron trade, 1821 ; withdrew from the chartists on their dissenting from the corn-law agitation ; bitterly condemned the ' bread-tax,' to which he attributed all the national misfortunes, in ' Corn-Law Rhymes,' 1831, ' The Ranter,' ' The Village Patriarch,' 1829, and ' The Splendid Village.' [xvii. 266]

ELLIOTT, EDWARD BISHOP (1793–1875), divine ; brother of Henry Venn Elliott [q. v.] ; third senior optime, Trinity College, Cambridge, 1816 ; fellow, 1817 ; Seatonian prizeman, 1821 and 1822 ; prebendary of Heytesbury, Wiltshire, 1853 ; incumbent of St. Mark's, Brighton ; chief work ' Horæ Apocalypticæ,' 1844. [xvii. 268]

ELLIOTT, GRACE DALRYMPLE (1758 ?–1823), *née* Dalrymple ; married Sir John Elliott [q. v.] ; eloped with Lord Valentia, 1774 ; gave birth to a child whom the Prince of Wales considered his son, 1782 ; described her life in France during the Revolution in a ' Journal,' in which she claimed to have received an offer of marriage from Bonaparte. [xvii. 268]

ELLIOTT, HENRY VENN (1792–1865), divine ; scholar of Trinity College, Cambridge, 1811 ; B.A., 1814 ; fellow of Trinity, 1816 ; travelled to Greece, Constantinople, and Jerusalem, 1817 ; held the priory of St. John's, Wilton ; first preacher of St. Mary's proprietary chapel, Brighton, 1827 ; originated (1832) and helped to manage school for daughters of poor clergymen. [xvii. 269]

ELLIOTT, JOHN (d. 1691), adherent of James II ; M.D. Cambridge, 1681 ; F.R.C.P. and censor, 1687 ; imprisoned, and released on bail, 1690, for publishing a soidisant manifesto of James II, 1689. [xvii. 270]

ELLIOTT, SIR JOHN (1736–1786), physician ; surgeon to a privateer ; M.D. St. Andrews, 1759 ; L.R.C.P., 1762 ; knighted, 1776 ; created baronet, 1778 ; physician to the Prince of Wales ; published ' The Medical Pocket-Book,' 1781, and superficial compilations on physiology and hygiene. [xvii. 270]

ELLIOTT, JOHN (1747–1787), physician ; M.D. ; discharged a pistol at a Miss Boydell, his sweetheart, 1787 ; tried for murder and acquitted as insane ; rearrested for assault ; died in Newgate.

ELLIOTT or ELLIOT, WILLIAM (1727–1766), engraver of landscapes ; exhibited, 1761–6. [xvii. 271]

ELLIOTT, WILLIAM (d. 1792), lieutenant R.N. and marine painter ; president of the Incorporated Society of Artists, 1791 ; exhibited paintings of the naval actions between 1780 and 1790 at the Royal Academy and other works at various institutions. [xvii. 271]

ELLIOTT, SIR WILLIAM HENRY (1792–1874), general ; ensign, 1809 ; lieutenant, 1812 ; served in Peninsula ; fought at Waterloo, 1815 ; lieutenant-colonel, 1838 ; commanded the 51st in Australia, Van Diemen's Land, New Zealand, and at Bangalore till 1852 ; discovered, when commandant at Rangoon, a plot to massacre the English inhabitants, 1853 ; G.C.B., 1870 ; general, 1871. [xvii. 272]

ELLIS, ALEXANDER JOHN (1814–1890), philologist and mathematician ; educated at Shrewsbury, Eton, and Trinity College, Cambridge ; B.A., 1837 ; entered Middle Temple ; wrote extensively on mathematical subjects and published ' Algebra identified with Geometry,' 1874 ; arranged with (Sir) Isaac Pitman [q. v.] a system of printing called phonotypy, which aimed at the accurate representation of sounds in print ; published ' Fonetic Frend,' 1849, and ' Spelling Reformer,' 1849–50, periodicals advocating reform of spelling ; published, in five parts, ' Early English Pronunciation,' 1869–89 ; honorary LL.D. Cambridge, 1890 ; F.R.S., 1864 ; F.S.A., 1870 ; president of Philological Society, 1872–4 and 1880–2 ; fellow of London Mathematical Society, 1865. His works include numerous treatises on philological, mathematical, musical, and other subjects. [Suppl. ii. 180]

ELLIS, ALFRED BURDON (1852–1894), soldier and writer ; lieutenant in 1st West India regiment, 1873 ; served in Ashanti war, 1873 ; seconded for service with Gold Coast constabulary, 1877 ; captain, 1879 ; attached to intelligence department in Zulu campaign ; major, 1884 ; commanded troop on Gold Coast, 1881 and 1886, and in Bahamas, 1889 ; lieutenant-colonel, 1891 ; local colonel in West Africa, 1892 ; C.B., 1892 ; died of fever contracted after expedition against the Sofas, 1893 ; published works relating to native peoples among whom he had been stationed. [Suppl. ii. 182]

ELLIS, ANTHONY (1690–1761). [See ELLYS.]

ELLIS, ARTHUR AYRES (1830–1887), Greek Testament critic ; B.A. Trinity College, Cambridge, 1852 ; fellow, 1854 ; M.A., 1855 ; divinity lecturer at Christ's College ; vicar of Stotfold, 1860–87 ; published Bentley's ' Critica Sacra,' 1862. [xvii. 272]

ELLIS, SIR BARROW HELBERT (1823–1887), Anglo-Indian ; educated at University College School, London University, and Haileybury ; chief commissioner in Sindh,

1857; chief secretary of the Bombay government; member (1865) of the Bombay council; member of the viceroy's council, 1870; K.C.S.I.; M.R.A.S., 1876; left 2,500*l.* for the poor of Ratnajiri, his first charge; edited Stack's 'Dictionary of Sindhi and English,' 1855.
[xvii. 272]

ELLIS, CHARLES AUGUSTUS, sixth BARON HOWARD DE WALDEN and second BARON SEAFORD (1799–1868), diplomatist; elder son of Charles Rose Ellis, M.P. [q. v.]; educated at Eton; captain, 8th regiment, 1822; appointed by Canning under-secretary of state for foreign affairs, 1824; minister plenipotentiary and envoy extraordinary at Stockholm, 1832, at Lisbon, 1833; moulded Portuguese policy during the Miguelite and Pedroite war; G.C.B., 1838, and grand cross of the Tower and the Sword, 1841; minister plenipotentiary at Brussels, 1846; died at Lesve near Namur.
[xvii. 273]

ELLIS, CHARLES ROSE, first BARON SEAFORD (1771–1845); M.P. for Heytesbury, 1793, for Seaford, 1796–1806 and 1812–26, for East Grinstead, 1807; head of the West Indian interest and friend of Canning; created Baron Seaford, 1826.
[xvii. 274]

ELLIS, CLEMENT (1630–1700), divine and poet; taberdar of Queen's College, Oxford; fellow, 1657; M.A., 1656; received, while at Oxford, remittances from anonymous benefactors; celebrated the Restoration in a dull panegyric, 1660; domestic chaplain to William, marquis of Newcastle, 1661; prebendary of Southwell, 1693; published theological works.
[xvii. 274]

ELLIS, EDMUND (*fl.* 1707). [See ELYS.]

ELLIS, EDWIN (1844–1878), musician; solo violinist at Cremorne Gardens, 1851; general musical director at the Adelphi, *c.* 1867; published selections for small orchestra.
[xvii. 275]

ELLIS, FRANCIS WHYTE (*d.* 1819), orientalist; writer in the East India Company's service at Madras, 1796; collector of Madras, 1810; Tamil and Sanskrit scholar; student of Mirâsi right; died at Ramnad; published commentary on 'The Sacred Kurral,' 1816, and dissertations on the Tamil, Telugu, and Malayalim languages; proved the Sanskrit MSS. at Pondicherry to be jesuit forgeries.
[xvii. 276]

ELLIS, GEORGE (1753–1815), author; produced 'Poetical Tales by Sir Gregory Gander,' 1778; a 'favorite' at Versailles, 1783; accompanied Sir James Harris's embassy to the Hague, 1784, where he obtained material for his history of the Dutch revolution (published, 1789); M.P., Seaford, 1796; founded the 'Anti-Jacobin' in concert with Canning; F.R.S. and F.S.A.; published 'Specimens of Early English Romances in Metre,' 1805; friend of Sir Walter Scott.
[xvii. 276]

ELLIS, GEORGE JAMES WELBORE AGAR-, first BARON DOVER (1797–1833); educated at Westminster and Christ Church, Oxford; M.A., 1819; M.P., Heytesbury, 1818, Seaford, 1820; suggested to government purchase of Angerstein collection and formation of national gallery, 1823; M.P., Ludgershall, 1826, Okehampton, 1830; privy councillor, 1830; chief commissioner of woods and forests, 1830; created Baron Dover, 1831; wrote, among other works, a 'Life of Frederick the Second, King of Prussia,' 1832; edited Horace Walpole's 'Letters,' 1833.
[xvii. 277]

ELLIS, HENRY (1721–1806), traveller, hydrographer, and colonial governor; hydrographer, surveyor, and mineralogist to the north-west expedition, 1746; published an itinerary which overthrew the idea that the north-west passage must lie through Hudson's Bay, 1748; F.R.S., 1749; governor of Georgia and Nova Scotia; died at Naples.
[xvii. 278]

ELLIS, SIR HENRY (1777–1855), diplomatist; negotiated treaty of peace with Persia, 1815; third commissioner in Earl Amherst's embassy to China, 1816; wrecked on return journey and forced to make for Java in an open boat; published an authorised account of the mission, 1817; commissioner of the board of control, 1830–5; advised the East India Company to abandon exclusive privileges; privy councillor, 1832; special envoy to the Brazils, 1842; K.C.B., 1848.
[xvii. 279]

ELLIS, SIR HENRY (1777–1869), principal librarian of the British Museum; educated at Merchant Taylors' and St. John's College, Oxford; fellow; assistant in the

Bodleian, 1798; B.C.L., 1802; keeper of printed books in the British Museum, 1806–27; re-catalogued the printed books, 1807–19; secretary to Society of Antiquaries, 1814; edited 'Additamenta' to 'Domesday Book,' 1816; published 'Original Letters illustrative of English History,' 1824, 1827, and 1846; principal librarian of the museum, 1827; knight of Hanover, 1833; virtually superseded in consequence of his unprogressive methods, 1836.
[xvii. 280]

ELLIS, SIR HENRY WALTON (1783–1815), colonel; named ensign in the 89th foot, 1783; captain, 23rd fusiliers, 1796; served in the descent on Ostend, 1798, in Egypt, 1801, at Copenhagen, 1807; shared in the expedition against Martinique, 1809; distinguished himself at Albuhera, 1811; wounded at Badajos, 1812; colonel and K.C.B.; mortally wounded at Waterloo.
[xvii. 282]

ELLIS, HUMPHREY (*d.* 1676), Roman catholic divine, really named WARING; student at Douay and an original member of the English College, Lisbon; D.D. and president of the English College; dean of the chapter in England, 1657–76.
[xvii. 282]

ELLIS, JAMES (1763?–1830), antiquary and solicitor; communicated border traditions to Sir Walter Scott.
[xvii. 283]

ELLIS, JOHN (1599?–1665), divine; M.A. Hart Hall, Oxford, 1625; fellow of Jesus College, Oxford, 1628; B.D., 1632; D.D. St. Andrews, 1634; rector of Wheatfield and subsequently of Dolgelly; published theological works.
[xvii. 283]

ELLIS, JOHN (1606?–1681), author of 'Vindiciæ Catholicæ'; fellow and B.D. St. Catharine Hall, Cambridge; incumbent of the third portion of the rectory of Waddesdon, Buckinghamshire; published 'Vindiciæ Catholicæ, or the Rights of Particular Churches rescued,' 1647, which he retracted at the Restoration; rector of Waddesdon, 1661–81.
[xvii. 283]

ELLIS, JOHN (1643?–1738), under-secretary of state; educated at Westminster School; student of Christ Church, Oxford, 1664; friend of Humphrey Prideaux [q. v.]; secretary to Sir Leoline Jenkins at the Nimeguen conference, 1675; obtained from the States-General recognition of Lord Ossory's claims to the rank of general, 1680; under-secretary of state, 1695–1705; M.P., Harwich, 1705–8; contributed to the Peckwater buildings, Christ Church, Oxford; paramour of the Duchess of Cleveland.
[xvii. 284]

ELLIS, JOHN (1701–1757). [See ELLYS.]

ELLIS, JOHN (1710?–1776), naturalist; agent for West Florida, 1764, for Dominica, 1770; F.R.S., 1754; published 'An Essay towards the Natural History of the Corallines,' 1755; described *Dionœa Muscipula* in 'Directions for bringing over Seeds and Plants from the East Indies,' 1770.
[xvii. 285]

ELLIS, JOHN (1698–1790), scrivener and political writer; partner with one Tanner, a London scrivener; four times master of the Scriveners' Company; member of Dr. Johnson's circle; travestied Maphæus, 1758; published 'The South Sea Dream,' a poem in Hudibrastic verse, 1720; translated, but never published, Ovid's 'Epistles.'
[xvii. 286]

ELLIS, JOHN (1789–1862), member of parliament and railway chairman; promoted Leicester and Swannington railway; M.P., Leicester, 1848–52; J.P. for Leicestershire; chairman of Midland Railway, 1849–58.
[xvii. 287]

ELLIS, PHILIP, in religion MICHAEL (1652–1726), Roman catholic prelate; son of John Ellis (1606?–1681) [q. v.]; foundationer of Westminster School, 1667; professed at St. Gregory's convent, Douay, 1670; missioner in England, and chaplain to James II; vicarapostolic of the western district of England, and bishop *in partibus* of Aureliopolis, 1688–1705; arrested and imprisoned at the revolution; unofficial agent of the exiled James II at Rome; bishop of Segni, 1708; died at Segni.
[xvii. 287]

ELLIS, SIR RICHARD (1688?–1742). [See ELLYS.]

ELLIS, ROBERT (CYNDDELW) (1810–1875), baptist minister and Welsh poet; minister of Llanelian, 1837, and in Denbighshire, Monmouthshire, and Carnarvon; a learned and popular lecturer on ancient Welsh thought and society; author of works, mainly theological, in Welsh and English.
[xvii. 289]

ELLIS, ROBERT (1820?–1885), classical scholar; scholar of St. John's College, Cambridge, 1839; fifth wrangler, 1840; fellow, 1841; M.A., 1843; ordained, 1845; B.D., 1850; chiefly known by his controversy with William John Law [q. v.] on the topography of Hannibal's passage of the Alps, 1854–6; ascribed an Armenian origin to the Etruscans; published ethnological works. [xvii. 289]

ELLIS, ROBERT LESLIE (1817–1859), man of science and letters; senior wrangler, and fellow of Trinity College, Cambridge, 1840; M.A., 1843; undertook, in conjunction with Heath and Spedding, to edit Francis Bacon's works, with annotations; edited 'Cambridge Mathematical Journal.' [xvii. 290]

ELLIS, SIR SAMUEL BURDON (1787–1865), general; second lieutenant, royal marine light infantry, 1804; fought at Trafalgar, 1805; lieutenant, 1806; served in the Walcheren expedition, 1809, and at Guadeloupe, 1810; distinguished himself in naval operations preliminary to siege of Bayonne; brought off the political resident of Bushire during a revolt, being then commander of marines; commanded advance on Canton, 1841; lieutenant-colonel by brevet, and C.B.; colonel, 1851; K.C.B., 1860; general, 1862. [xvii. 290]

ELLIS, SARAH STICKNEY (d. 1872), authoress; married William Ellis (1794–1872) [q. v.]; much interested in temperance and the education of women; chief works, 'The Poetry of Life' and 'Northern Roses.' [xvii. 296]

ELLIS, THOMAS (1625–1673), Welsh antiquary; B.A. Jesus College, Oxford, 1644; fellow, 1646; fought for Charles I in garrison of Oxford, 1644; M.A., 1646; B.D., 1661; rector of St. Mary's, Dolgelly, 1665; undertook to assist Robert Vaughan in editing Powell's 'History of Cambria,' but desisted on finding that he had been forestalled; left history of Owen Glendowr, published 1775. [xvii. 291]

ELLIS, THOMAS FLOWER (1796–1861), law reporter; B.A. Trinity College, Cambridge, 1818; fellow; barrister, Lincoln's Inn, 1824; prepared for publication his friend Macaulay's posthumous essays; a commissioner to determine the boundaries of parliamentary boroughs in Wales, 1831; recorder of Leeds, 1839; part author of three series of law reports. [xvii. 291]

ELLIS, WELBORE (1651?–1734), bishop of Meath; educated at Westminster School; M.A. Christ Church, Oxford, 1687; prebendary of Winchester, 1696; D.D. by diploma, 1697; bishop of Kildare, 1705–31; bishop of Meath, and privy councillor of Ireland, 1731. [xvii. 292]

ELLIS, WELBORE, first BARON MENDIP (1713–1802); son of Welbore Ellis (1651?–1734) [q. v.]; educated at Westminster; student, Christ Church, Oxford, 1732; B.A., 1736; M.P., Cricklade, 1741; admiralty lord, 1747–55; M.P., Weymouth, 1747, 1754, 1774, 1780, and 1784, Melcombe Regis, 1747; vice-treasurer of Ireland, 1755–62, 1765–6, and 1770; privy councillor, 1760; M.P., Aylesbury, 1761; secretary at war, 1762–5; M.P., Petersfield, 1768 and 1791; D.C.L. Oxford, 1773; treasurer of the navy, 1777; secretary of state for America, 1782; frightened by the progress of the French revolution into supporting Pitt, 1793; created Baron Mendip of Mendip, 1794; F.R.S.; called by Horace Walpole Fox's 'Jackal.' [xvii. 292]

ELLIS, SIR WILLIAM (1609–1680), judge; M.A. Caius College, Cambridge, 1636; barrister, Gray's Inn, 1634; M.P. for Boston in the Short and Long parliaments, 1640; solicitor-general, 1654; sat for Boston, 1654, for Grantham, 1656 and 1659; created baronet by Cromwell; returned for Grantham, 1660, but unseated as a republican; reader at Gray's Inn, 1664; king's serjeant, and knighted, 1671; judge of common pleas, 1673–6 and 1679–1680; M.P., Boston, 1679. [xvii. 294]

ELLIS, SIR WILLIAM (d. 1732), secretary of state; second son of John Ellis (1606?–1681) [q. v.]; foundationer of Westminster; student of Christ Church, Oxford, 1665; B.A., 1669; M.A., per literas regias, Cambridge, 1671; customer, comptroller, and searcher for Leinster and Munster, 1678; knighted, 1686; privy councillor to James II in Ireland, 1690; attainted, 1691; secretary to James II at St. Germain; died at Rome. [xvii. 295]

ELLIS, WILLIAM (d. 1758), writer on agriculture; farmer at Little Gaddesden, Hertfordshire; travelling agent for seeds and the sale of farming implements;

engaged as a writer by Osborne the bookseller. His works, which contain fabulous anecdotes and unscientific nostrums, include 'The Modern Husbandman,' 1750. [xvii. 295]

ELLIS, WILLIAM (1747–1810), engraver; exhibited at the Society of Artists, 1780; worked also in aquatint. [xvii. 295]

ELLIS, WILLIAM (1794–1872), missionary; ordained, 1815, and appointed missionary, first to South Africa and afterwards to the South Sea islands; commenced a new mission at Huahine, 1818; returned to England, 1825; chief foreign secretary to the London Missionary Society; sent to Madagascar to ascertain and improve the condition of native converts under Queen Ranavolona, but three times denied access to the capital; helped the government of Madagascar to checkmate French interference, 1861–5; published three books on Madagascar and 'Polynesian Researches.' [xvii. 296]

ELLIS, WILLIAM (1800–1881), economist; assistant underwriter to the Indemnity Marine Insurance Company, 1824; chief manager, 1827; director; advocated teaching of political economy in elementary education, for which object he personally founded (1848–52) the Birkbeck schools [see BIRKBECK, GEORGE]; governor of the school of the Middle-class Corporation, which he helped to establish; utilitarian philosopher; published 'Lessons on the Phenomena of Industrial Life' and similar works. [xvii. 298]

ELLIS, WYNNE (1790–1875), picture collector; London mercer, 1812–71; M.P., Leicester, 1831–4 and 1839–47; free-trader; J.P. for Hertfordshire and Kent; left 402 pictures to the nation, forty-four of which were selected by the National Gallery. [xvii. 298]

ELLISTON, HENRY TWISELTON (1801?–1864), composer of church music and inventor; son of Robert William Elliston [q. v.]; organist at Leamington parish church; librarian of the Leamington public library, 1863; invented a transposing piano; composed church services. [xvii. 299]

ELLISTON, ROBERT WILLIAM (1774–1831), actor; educated at St. Paul's school; played Tressel in 'Richard III' at the Bath Theatre, 1791, and Romeo, 1793; appeared at the Haymarket and at Covent Garden, 1796; engaged by Colman at the Haymarket, 1803; played Rolla at Drury Lane, 1804; manager of the Royal Circus, renamed the Surrey Theatre, 1809; opened the Olympic, and temporarily managed the Leicester theatre; acted Hamlet at re-opening of Drury Lane, 1812; lessee and manager of Drury Lane, 1819–26; inaugurated Drury Lane's reputation for scenery; bankrupt, 1826; again lessee of the Surrey, 1827–31; lived an eccentric life; lauded by Charles Lamb in the lines beginning 'Joyousest of once embodied spirits'; joint-author of 'No Prelude,' 1803, and author of 'The Venetian Outlaw,' 1805. [xvii. 299]

ELLMAN, JOHN (1753–1832), agriculturist; breeder of Southdown sheep; suggested to Lord Egremont formation of Sussex Agricultural Association; took part in institution of Smithfield cattle show; gold medallist for best cultivated farm in Sussex, 1819; commissioner of taxes; maintained school for labourers' children at Glynde; assisted Arthur Young in compiling his 'Annals of Agriculture.' [xvii. 302]

ELLWOOD, THOMAS (1639–1713), quaker and friend of Milton; educated at Thame free school; converted to quakerism by the preaching of Edward Burrough [q. v.], 1659; published 'An Alarm to the Priests,' 1660; formed a friendship (1662) with John Milton, who taught him the foreign mode of pronouncing Latin; committed to Newgate for refusing to take the oath of allegiance, 1662; suggested to Milton by a chance remark the writing of 'Paradise Regained,' 1665; travelled with George Fox through the west of England to organise the quakers; endeavoured to protect the quakers against the Conventicle Act; controversialist and author of 'Davideis,' a sacred poem, 1712, and of an autobiography (1st ed. 1714). [xvii. 303]

ELLYS, ANTHONY (1690–1761), bishop of St. David's; M.A. Clare Hall, Cambridge, 1716; D.D., 1728; fellow; prebendary of Gloucester, 1724; favoured the Test Act; bishop of St. David's, 1752; published anonymously 'Remarks on Mr. Hume's Essay concerning Miracles,' 1752. Parts of his projected 'Defence of the Reformation' appeared posthumously. [xvii. 306]

ELLYS or **ELLIS**, JOHN (1701-1757), portrait-painter; of the Kneller school; tapestry maker to the crown; master keeper of the lions in the Tower; principal painter to the Prince of Wales, 1736. [xvii. 306]

ELLYS, SIR RICHARD (1688 ?-1742), theological writer; became a Greek and Hebrew scholar in Holland; M.P., Boston, 1719, 1722, and 1727; published 'Fortuita Sacra; quibus subiicitur Commentarius de Cymbalis,' 1727. Gronovius dedicated to him his edition of Ælian's 'Varia Historia. [xvii. 307]

ELMER (d. 1137). [See ETHELMÆR.]

ELMER (d. 1260). [See AYMER DE VALENCE.]

ELMER, JOHN (1521-1594). [See AYLMER, JOHN.]

ELMER, STEPHEN (d. 1796), painter of still-life; member of the Free Society of Artists, 1763; A.R.A., 1772. [xvii. 308]

ELMER, WILLIAM (fl. 1799), painter of still-life; nephew of Stephen Elmer [q. v.]; exhibited at the Royal Academy between 1783 and 1799. [xvii. 308]

ELMES, HARVEY LONSDALE (1813-1847), architect; son and pupil of James Elmes [q. v.]; designed St. George's Hall, Liverpool, 1836, also the county lunatic asylum at West Derby; died in Jamaica. [xvii. 308]

ELMES, JAMES (1782-1862), architect and antiquary; admitted at Merchant Taylors', 1796; silver medallist of the Royal Academy; vice-president of the Royal Architectural Society, 1809-48; editor of 'The Annals of the Fine Arts,' 1816-20, printing poems by Keats and Wordsworth; chief works, 'Lectures on Architecture,' 1823, and 'Memoirs of the Life and Works of Sir Christopher Wren,' 1823. [xvii. 308]

ELMHAM, THOMAS (d. 1440 ?), historian; treasurer of St. Augustine's, Canterbury, 1407; prior of Lenton; vicar-general for England and Scotland, 1416; commissary-general for vacant benefices of Cluniac order in England, Scotland, and Ireland, 1426; author of 'Historia Monasterii Sancti Augustini Cantuariensis,' 'Vita et Gesta Henrici V,' and 'Liber Metricus de Henrico Vᵗᵒ.' [xvii. 309]

ELMORE, ALFRED (1815-1881), painter; studied in Italy; his reputation established by his 'Origin of the Guelph and Ghibelline Quarrel,' 1845; R.A., 1877. [xvii. 309]

ELMSLEY or **ELMSLY**, PETER (1736-1802), bookseller; helped to form the club of booksellers which produced Johnson's 'Lives of the Poets'; intimate with Wilkes. [xvii. 310]

ELMSLEY, PETER (1773-1825), classical scholar; educated at Westminster and Christ Church, Oxford; M.A., 1797; incumbent of Little Horkesley, 1798-1825; superintended development of Herculaneum papyri in company with Sir Humphry Davy, 1819; D.D., 1823; principal of St. Alban Hall, Oxford, 1823-5; Camden professor of ancient history, Oxford, 1823-5; best known for his critical labours on Sophocles and Euripides. [xvii. 310]

ELPHEGE (954-1012). [See ÆLFHEAH.]

ELPHINSTON, JAMES (1721-1809), educationalist; educated at Edinburgh University; started academy at Brompton, 1753, keeping it at Kensington, 1763-76; published 'An Analysis of the French and English Languages,' 1753; published 'Education, a Poem,' 1763; his translation of Martial (1782) ridiculed by Burns, 1788; displayed an arbitrary system of phonetic spelling in 'Inglish Speech and Spelling under Mutual Guides,' 1787, and similar works; published his correspondence with 'Geniusses ov boath Sexes,' 1791 and 1794. [xvii. 311]

ELPHINSTON, JOHN (1722-1785), captain R.N.; rear-admiral in the Russian service; lieutenant, 1746; served at the capture of Quebec, 1759; superintended transport service during siege of Havana, 1762; rear-admiral in the Russian service, 1769; ordered as a foreign admiral to discontinue his practice of setting the watch in Portsmouth harbour, 1770; defeated and blockaded Turkish squadron in Gulf of Nauplia, 1770; defeated Turkish fleet in Chesme Bay, though his proposed manœuvre to establish a local superiority was rejected by the jealousy of the Russian officers, 1770; abandoned

Russian service; commanded the Magnificent in the battle off Grenada, 1779, and in Rodney's encounters with De Guichen, 1780. [xvii. 312]

ELPHINSTONE, ALEXANDER, fourth BARON ELPHINSTONE (1552-1648 ?), member of the new privy council of Scotland, 1599; lord high treasurer of Scotland, 1599; lord of the articles, 1604 and 1607; commissioner for the union, 1604. [xvii. 314]

ELPHINSTONE, ARTHUR, sixth BARON BALMERINO (1688-1746), Jacobite; threw up his command in Shannon's regiment and joined the Jacobites after Sheriffmuir, 1715; escaped to the continent; pardoned by government without his knowledge, 1733; joined Prince Charles Edward, 1745; colonel and captain of the prince's guards; present at the battle of Falkirk; delivered up by the Grants after Culloden, 1746; executed. [xvii. 314]

ELPHINSTONE, GEORGE KEITH, VISCOUNT KEITH (1746-1823), admiral; made a voyage to China, 1767; navy lieutenant, 1770; served on shore at the reduction of Charleston, 1780; M.P., Dumbartonshire, 1780, Stirlingshire, 1790; took possession of Fort La Malgue, near Toulon, 1793; rear-admiral, 1794; commander-in-chief of the Indian squadron, 1795; compelled the Dutch to retire from their camp at Muizenberg, 1795; anticipated by Rear-admiral Rainier in taking possession of Ceylon, 1796; received the surrender of a Dutch squadron in Saldanha Bay, 1796; created Baron Keith of Stonehaven Marischal, 1797; the suppression of the Sheerness mutiny largely due to his efforts, 1797; allayed disaffection among the Plymouth sailors; commander in Spanish waters, 1799; pursued a French fleet, which eluded him, from the Mediterranean to Brest, 1799; entered the harbour of Genoa, which he had blockaded in co-operation with an Austrian force, 1800; declined to sanction El Arish Convention, 1800; demanded, but did not enforce, the surrender of the ships of war in Cadiz, and withdrew with Abercromby, 1800; admiral, 1801; commander-in-chief in the North Sea, 1803; created viscount, 1814; intermediary of the government in its correspondence with Bonaparte relative to his being sent to St. Helena. [xvii. 316]

ELPHINSTONE, HESTER MARIA, VISCOUNTESS KEITH (1762-1857), daughter of Henry and Hester Thrale; her education directed by Dr. Johnson; gave herself up to the study of Hebrew and mathematics when her mother married Piozzi; married George Keith Elphinstone, Viscount Keith [q. v.], 1808. [xvii. 321]

ELPHINSTONE, SIR HOWARD (1773-1846), major-general; second lieutenant, royal engineers, 1793; served at the capture of the Cape of Good Hope, 1795; captain-lieutenant in India, 1800; attached to embassy to Portugal, 1806; commanding royal engineer in Peninsula, 1808; wounded at Roliça; major by brevet, 1812; commanding royal engineer at the battles of Nivelle and the Nive, 1814; created baronet and C.B. [xvii. 321]

ELPHINSTONE, SIR HOWARD CRAWFURD (1829-1890), major-general; educated at Royal Military Academy, Woolwich; second lieutenant, royal engineers, 1847; lieutenant, 1851; first captain, 1862; major, 1872; lieutenant-colonel, 1873; colonel, 1884; major-general, 1887; served in Crimea, and received Victoria cross, 1855; governor to Prince Arthur (duke of Connaught), 1859-71, and treasurer and comptroller of his household, 1871-90; C.B. civil, 1865, and military, 1871; C.M.G., 1870; K.C.B., 1871; aide-de-camp to Queen Victoria, 1877; accidentally drowned off Ushant while journeying to Teneriffe. [Suppl. ii. 183]

ELPHINSTONE, JAMES, first BARON BALMERINO (1553 ?-1612), one of the 'Octavians,' 1595; secretary of state in Scotland, 1598; created Baron Balmerino, 1604; commissioner to discuss the union with England, 1604; president of session, 1605; appointed secretary of state; disgraced and attainted for having, when secretary of state for Scotland, written a letter (1599), which James I (then James VI of Scotland) signed without knowing its contents, to Pope Clement VIII in commendation of the Roman catholic faith; condemned to death; imprisoned, but subsequently released. [xvii. 322]

ELPHINSTONE, JOHN, second BARON BALMERINO (d. 1649), son of James, first baron [q. v.]; restored to blood and peerage, 1613; sentenced to death for misprision of treason, 1635, as having read, interlined, and secretly handled a petition against Charles I's ecclesiastical measures, which the king had declined to look at; pardoned to appease popular feeling, 1635; advised the covenanters to complain to Louis XIII against Charles I; president of the Scots parliament, 1641; privy councillor and extraordinary lord of session, 1641; a commissioner to England, 1644. [xvii. 323]

ELPHINSTONE, JOHN, third BARON BALMERINO (1623–1704); fined 6,000l. Scots for having conformed under the Commonwealth, 1662. [xvii. 324]

ELPHINSTONE, JOHN, fourth BARON BALMERINO (1652–1736), privy councillor, 1687–1714; opposed the union; representative of the peers, 1710 and 1713–14. [xvii. 324]

ELPHINSTONE, JOHN, thirteenth BARON ELPHINSTONE (1807–1860), captain in the royal horse guards, 1832; lord-in-waiting to William IV, 1835–7; G.C.H. and privy councillor, 1836; governor of Madras, 1837–42; explored Cashmere; governor of Bombay, 1853–9; prevented a rising in Bombay, 1857; G.C.B., 1858; created Baron Elphinstone in peerage of United Kingdom, 1859. [xvii. 325]

ELPHINSTONE, MARGARET MERCER, COMTESSE DE FLAHAULT, VISCOUNTESS KEITH, and BARONESS NAIRN (1788–1867), daughter of George Keith Elphinstone, Viscount Keith [q. v.]; confidante of Princess Charlotte; married the Comte de Flahault, 1817. [xvii. 325]

ELPHINSTONE, MOUNTSTUART (1779–1859), governor of Bombay; appointed to the Bengal civil service, 1796; escaped from Vazir Ali's massacre of Europeans, 1798; assistant to the governor-general's agent at the peshwa of Poona's court, 1801; military attaché at the battle of Assaye, 1803; charged with the cavalry at Argaum, 1803; resident of Nagpur; ambassador to Shah Shuja at Cabul, 1808; resident of Poona, 1810–16; demanded justice from the peshwa of Poona on one of his favourites, who had murdered a Mahratta envoy, 1815; superseded, 1816; took part in a repulse of Mahratta troops, 1817; instructed to annex Poona, 1817; governor of Bombay, 1819–27; prepared code for Bombay presidency; declined the governor-generalship on retiring; author of a 'History of India' and 'The Rise of British Power in the East,' published 1887. [xvii. 326]

ELPHINSTONE, WILLIAM (1431–1514), bishop of Aberdeen and founder of Aberdeen University; M.A., Glasgow, 1452; regent of Glasgow University, 1465; rector of St. Michael's Church, Trongate, 1465; doctor of decrees at Paris; rector of Glasgow University, c. 1474; official of Glasgow, and (1478) of Lothian; made archdeacon of Argyll for his services as ambassador to Louis XI, 1479; bishop of Ross, 1481; privy councillor, 1483; bishop of Aberdeen, c. 1488–1514; sent to arrange a marriage between James III and Edward IV's niece Anne, 1484; lord auditor of complaints, Edinburgh; consistently supported James III; lord high chancellor, 1488; keeper of the privy seal, 1492–1514; concluded a treaty between Scotland and Holland, 1493; obtained charter from James IV to found King's College, Aberdeen, 1498; rebuilt choir of Aberdeen Cathedral; introduced printing into Scotland; his end said to have been hastened by distress at the English victory at Flodden. [xvii. 328]

ELPHINSTONE, WILLIAM GEORGE KEITH (1782–1842), major-general; lieutenant, 41st regiment, 1804; major, 8th West India regiment, 1811; fought at Waterloo, 1815; C.B.; aide-de-camp to the king, 1825; major-general, 1837; unfortunate in his command of the troops at Cabul, 1841, where he died just before the final catastrophe. [xvii. 330]

ELPHINSTONE-HOLLOWAY, WILLIAM CUTHBERT (1787–1850), colonel, R.E.; son of Sir Charles Holloway (1749–1827) [q. v.]; second lieutenant, royal engineers, 1804; lieutenant, 1805; captain, 1813; lieutenant-colonel, 1828; colonel, 1841; served in Peninsula, 1810–12; commanding royal engineer in Cape of Good Hope, 1818–31, in Canada, 1843–9, and in western military district, 1849 till death; C.B., 1831; took surname of Elphinstone, 1825. [Suppl. ii. 438]

ELRINGTON, CHARLES RICHARD (1787–1850), regius professor of divinity in Dublin University; B.A., Trinity College, Dublin, 1805; mathematical and Hebrew prizeman; fellow, 1810–29; M.A., 1811; Donnellan lecturer, 1819; D.D., 1820; chancellor of Ferns, 1832–40; regius professor of divinity, 1829–50; rector of the union of Armagh, 1841; commenced publication of Archbishop Ussher's complete works, 1847; specialised on the recent ecclesiastical history of Ireland. [xvii. 331]

ELRINGTON, THOMAS (1688–1732), actor; first appeared at Drury Lane, 1709, as Oroonoko; deputy-master of the revels and steward of the king's inns of court; played Hamlet at Lincoln's Inn Fields, 1716; frequently appeared at Drury Lane. [xvii. 331]

ELRINGTON, THOMAS (1760–1835), bishop of Leighlin and Ferns; scholar of Trinity College, Dublin, 1778; fellow, 1781–1806; M.A., 1785; Donnellan divinity lecturer, 1794; D.D., 1795; Archbishop King's lecturer, 1795; Smith's professor of mathematics and (1799) of natural philosophy; provost of Trinity College, Dublin, 1811–20; bishop of Limerick, 1820–2, of Leighlin and Ferns, 1822–35; published ecclesiastical and other works; edited Locke's 'Two Treatises on Government,' as well as Juvenal and Persius. [xvii. 333]

ELSDALE, ROBINSON (1744–1783), autobiographer, narrating his adventures as a privateer (1762–79) off Hispaniola and the west coast of Africa. [xvii. 334]

ELSDALE, SAMUEL (d. 1827), master of Moulton grammar school; son of Robinson Elsdale [q. v.]; M.A. Lincoln College, Oxford, 1809; fellow. [xvii. 334]

ELSI (d. 1050). [See EADSIGE.]

ELSTOB, ELIZABETH (1683–1756), Anglo-Saxon scholar; sister of William Elstob [q. v.]; published 'English-Saxon Homily on the Nativity of St. Gregory,' with translation, 1709; given 100l. by Queen Caroline; commenced edition of Ælfric's 'Homilies,' and published Anglo-Saxon grammar, 1715. [xvii. 334]

ELSTOB, WILLIAM (1673–1715), divine; claimed to descend from Welsh princes; educated at Eton and Catharine Hall, Cambridge; fellow of University College, Oxford, 1696; M.A., 1697; incumbent of St. Swithin and St. Mary Bothaw, London, 1702–15; edited Roger Ascham's 'Letters,' 1703; made proposals for re-editing the Saxon laws. [xvii. 335]

ELSTRACKE, RENOLD (RENIER) (fl. 1590–1630), engraver; of Belgian origin; executed engravings of the kings of England for Henry Holland (1583–1650?) [q. v.], 1618; engraved, among other portraits, a double whole-length of Mary Stuart and Darnley. [xvii. 336]

ELSUM, JOHN (fl. 1700–1705), author; collected 'Epigrams upon the Paintings of the most eminent Masters, Antient and Modern,' 1700, and wrote on painting, 1703–4. [xvii. 336]

ELSYNGE, HENRY (1598–1654), clerk of the House of Commons; educated at Westminster and Christ Church, Oxford; B.A., 1625; resigned his clerkship of the House of Commons to avoid implication in proceedings against Charles I, 1648. [xvii. 336]

ELTHAM, JOHN OF, EARL OF CORNWALL (1316–1336). [See JOHN.]

ELTON, SIR CHARLES ABRAHAM (1778–1853), author; educated at Eton; captain, 48th regiment; served in Holland; translated Hesiod and selections from other Greek and Roman poets; defended unitarianism, 1818, but abjured it in Δεύτεραι Φροντίδες, 1827. [xvii. 337]

ELTON, CHARLES ISAAC (1839–1900), lawyer and antiquary; B.A. Balliol College, Oxford, 1862; fellow of Queen's, and Vinerian law scholar, 1862; called to bar at Lincoln's Inn, 1865; Q.C., 1885; conservative M.P. for West Somerset, 1884–5, and for Wellington division, 1886–1892; F.S.A., 1883; published numerous writings on historical, archæological, legal, and literary topics. [Suppl. ii. 184]

ELTON, EDWARD WILLIAM (1794–1843), actor; trained for the law; appeared at the opening of the Garrick Theatre in Whitechapel, 1831; the original Beauseant in the 'Lady of Lyons' at Covent Garden; played Romeo and Rolla at Drury Lane, 1839–40; perished by shipwreck, 1843; famous in the rôle of Edgar in 'Lear.' [xvii. 337]

ELTON, JAMES FREDERIC (1840–1877), African explorer; took part in relief of Delhi and Lucknow, 1857; present at capture of Pekin, 1860; joined staff of French army in Mexico, 1866; sent to report on South African gold and diamond fields, 1871; member of Natal executive and legislative council; political agent and vice-consul at Zanzibar to assist in the suppression of the slave-trade, 1873; British consul at Mozambique, 1875; explored the Makua country, 1877; endeavoured to ascertain the possibility of a route from the north end of Lake Nyassa to Quiloa, 1877; died of malarial fever in Ugogo.

[xvii. 338]

ELTON, JOHN (d. 1751), adventurer in Persia; sea-captain in Russian service, c. 1735–8; formed scheme for British trade through Russia into Persia and central Asia by way of Caspian Sea, which was temporarily adopted by the Russian company, c. 1741; entered service of shah and was appointed admiral of Caspian; espoused cause of Muhammad Hassan Khán, 1751, and was shot by members of the rival faction. [Suppl. ii. 185]

ELTON, RICHARD (fl. 1650), military writer; lieutenant-colonel, and governor-general of Hull, 1656; author of 'The compleat Body of the Art Military,' 1650.

[xvii. 339]

ELVEY, SIR GEORGE JOB (1816–1893), organist and composer; chorister of Canterbury Cathedral; studied music, and was organist of St. George's Chapel, Windsor, 1835–82; Mus. Bac. New College, Oxford, 1838; Mus. Doc. by special dispensation of chancellor of university, 1840; knighted, 1871. He was a prolific writer of church music, and composed several anthems for royal marriages and other occasions. [Suppl. ii. 186]

ELVEY, STEPHEN (1805–1860), organist and composer; organist of New College, Oxford, 1830; Mus. Doc. Oxon., 1838; organist of St. Mary's Church, and (1846) of St. John's College; university choragus, 1848–60; composed Evening Service (1825), and settings of the Psalter.

[xvii. '339]

ELVIDEN, EDMUND (fl. 1570), poet; published 'A Neweyere's gift to the Rebellious Persons in the North partes of England,' 1570, 'The Closit of Counsells,' 1569, and a 'Metaphoricall History of Pesistratus and Catanea.'

[xvii. 340]

ELWALL, EDWARD (1676–1744), sabbatarian; defended the presbyterian meeting-house at Wolverhampton from a high church mob, 1715; successively a unitarian, a churchman, and an Ebionite; wore at one time 'Turkish habit,' from respect to the unitarianism of Islam; 'transient member' of the sabbatarian baptists, 1720; prosecuted for blasphemy at Stafford, but discharged by Alexander Denton, 1726; published unitarian, sabbatarian, and other religious pamphlets. [xvii. 340]

ELWES, SIR GERVASE (1561–1615). [See HELWYS.]

ELWES OF MEGGOTT, JOHN (1714–1789), miser; educated at Westminster; became an expert in riding at Geneva; heir to his uncle's estate, 1763; M.P. for Berkshire, 1774–87; 'trimmed' between the party of Pitt and Fox; lived a parsimonious rather than a selfish life.

[xvii. 342]

ELWIN, WHITWELL (1816–1900), prose-writer; B.A. Caius College, Cambridge, 1839; ordained priest, 1840; curate of Hardington, Somerset, 1840–9; rector of Booton, 1849–1900; contributed to 'Quarterly Review,' 1843–85; editor, 1853–60. His works include five volumes (1871–2) of the edition of Pope which Mr. W. J. Courthope completed. [Suppl. ii. 187]

ELY, HUMPHREY (d. 1604), Roman catholic divine; studied at Brasenose College, Oxford; scholar of St. John's College, Oxford; licentiate in the canon and civil laws, Douay; LL.D.; made by a mistake gaoler of one of his travelling companions, when visiting England disguised as a merchant, 1580; priest, 1582; professor of the canon and civil laws at Pont-à-Mousson, 1586–1604; wrote 'Certaine Briefe Notes' on the archpriest controversy, 1603. [xvii. 344]

ELY, NICHOLAS OF (d. 1280), chancellor; archdeacon of Ely, 1249; prebendary of St. Paul's; elevated to the keepership of the great seal soon after the provisions of Oxford, becoming chancellor, 1260; dismissed, 1261; treasurer, 1262; reappointed chancellor, but restricted to signing ordinary writs, of which the justiciar was witness, 1263; reappointed treasurer, 1264; bishop of Worcester, 1266–8; one of the board appointed to arrange terms for the submission of the disinherited barons, 1266;

bishop of Winchester, 1268–80; involved in an obstinate quarrel with the chapter of Winchester relative to his nomination of a prior; reconstituted the monastery and appointed Adam of Fareham prior, 1278. [xvii. 344]

ELY, THOMAS OF (fl. 1175). [See THOMAS.]

ELY, WILLIAM (d. 1609), Roman catholic divine; brother of Humphrey Ely [q. v.]; M.A. Brasenose College, Oxford, 1549; refused to shake hands with Cranmer at the stake, 1556; B.D., 1557; second president of St. John's College, Oxford, 1559–63, having temporarily conformed; removed on refusing to acknowledge the queen's supremacy over the English church, 1563; missioner in Herefordshire; died in Hereford gaol.

[xvii. 346]

ELYOT, SIR RICHARD (1450?–1522), judge; commissioner for the collection of an aid in Wiltshire, 1503; serjeant-at-law, 1503; attorney-general to the queen, c. 1504; judge of assize on the western circuit; J.P. for Cornwall, 1509; judge of the common pleas, 1513; knighted before 1517; summoned to the first three parliaments of Henry VIII's reign. [xvii. 347]

ELYOT, SIR THOMAS (1490?–1546), diplomatist and author; son of Sir Richard Elyot [q. v.]; studied Galen and other medical writers; clerk of assize on the western circuit, 1511–28; J.P. for Oxfordshire, 1522; clerk of the privy council, 1523–30; knighted, 1530; owed his appointment (1531) as ambassador to Charles V to his 'Boke called the Governour' (published, 1531); directed, against his inclination, to obtain the emperor's assent to Henry VIII's divorce from Catherine of Arragon; again ambassador to the emperor, 1535; insisted in a letter to Cromwell that, though intimate with Sir Thomas More, he was no catholic, 1536; M.P., Cambridge, 1542. His works, written under the influence of Erasmus and the Italian humanists, include 'The Doctrine of Princes . . . translated out of Greke into Englishe' (from Isocrates), 1534, a Latin-English dictionary, 1538, 'The Image of Governance,' translated from a Greek manuscript of Eucolpius (first published, 1540), and Platonic dialogues and compilations from the fathers. [xvii. 347]

ELYS, EDMUND (fl. 1707), divine and poet; probationer fellow of Balliol College, Oxford, 1655–9; M.A., 1658; rector of East Allington, 1659–89; imprisoned on suspicion of being a royalist, 1659; deprived, 1689; published quaker and anti-Socinian pamphlets and religious poems. [xvii. 350]

EMERSON, WILLIAM (1701–1782), mathematician; unsuccessful as a private teacher; keenly interested in practical mechanics, incidentally constructing a spinning-wheel for his wife; declined, on grounds of economy, to become a member of the Royal Society; published treatise on 'Fluxions,' 1749, and mathematical manuals for young students, including 'Cyclomathesis,' 1763, 'The Arithmetic of Infinites,' 1767, and 'Dialling,' 1770.

[xvii. 351]

EMERY, EDWARD (d. 1850?), numismatist; produced the imitations of coins known as 'Emery's forgeries'; exposed, 1842. [xvii. 352]

EMERY, JOHN (1777–1822), actor; performed at the Brighton Theatre; appeared at the Haymarket in Colman's 'Heir-at-Law,' 1800; member of the Covent Garden Company, 1801–22; exhibited, mainly sea-pieces, at the Royal Academy, 1801–17; declared by Leigh Hunt to be 'almost perfect' in his representation of rustics.

[xvii. 352]

EMERY, SAMUEL ANDERSON (1817–1881), actor; son of John Emery [q. v.]; engaged at the Queen's Theatre, c. 1834; played in Scotland and the Midlands; played Giles in the 'Miller's Maid' and Lovegold in the 'Miser' at the Lyceum, 1843; stage-manager at the Surrey, but not permanently identified with any theatre; excelled in the parts of old man and countryman.

[xvii. 353]

EMES, JOHN (fl. 1785–1805), engraver and water-colour painter; exhibited landscapes at the Royal Academy, 1790 and 1791; best known by his engraving of Jefferys's 'Destruction of the Spanish Batteries before Gibraltar,' 1786. [xvii. 354]

EMES, THOMAS (d. 1707), known as 'the prophet'; quack doctor; his resurrection expected by the Camisard fraternity, to which he belonged, 1707; derided Colbatch's theory of alkali being morbific and 'acid' being curative in 'A Dialogue between Alkali and Acid,' 1698 ; published 'The Reasonableness and Union of Natural and the True Christian Religion,' 1698.   [xvii. 354]

EMILY, EDWARD (1617–1657), Harveian orator ; M.D. Leyden, 1640 ; M.D. Oxford ; L.C.P., 1641 ; censor, 1652 and 1653 ; Gulstonian lecturer, 1649 ; attacked the Commonwealth in his Harveian oration, 1656.
[xvii. 355]

EMLY, BARON (1812–1894). [See MONSELL, WILLIAM.]

EMLYN, HENRY (1729–1815), architect ; published 'A Proposition for a New Order in Architecture ' (founded on a division of the upper portion of the shaft into two columns), 1781 ; introduced the order into the tetra-style portico at Beaumont Lodge, near Windsor, c. 1785.
[xvii. 355]

EMLYN, SOLLOM (1697–1754), legal writer ; son of Thomas Emlyn [q. v.] ; studied at Leyden ; member of Lincoln's Inn ; disparaged the civil law, the criminal law, and the ecclesiastical courts in the preface to his (second) edition of the 'State Trials,' 1730.   [xvii. 355]

EMLYN, THOMAS (1663–1741), first unitarian minister in England ; domestic chaplain to Letitia, countess of Donegal, a presbyterian lady, 1683–8 ; chaplain to Sir Robert Rich, 1689–91 ; colleague to Joseph Boyse [q. v.] at Dublin, 1691–1702 ; made confession of his heresy to a suspicious elder of his congregation, 1702 ; virtually dismissed, 1702 ; put to press 'An Humble Inquiry into the Scripture Account of Jesus Christ,' 1702, for which he was sentenced in the court of queen's bench to a year's imprisonment, to be extended until he had paid a fine of 1,000*l*. and found security for good behaviour during life, 1703 ; the reduction of his fine mooted by Boyse and subsequently allowed by Ormonde, the lord-lieutenant ; released on payment of 90*l*., 1705 ; occasionally preached at the general baptist church in the Barbican (Paul's Alley) ; probably the first preacher who described himself as a unitarian, the term originated by Thomas Firmin [q. v.] ; friend of Samuel Clarke (1675–1729) [q. v.] ; published unitarian pamphlets.   [xvii. 356]

EMMA (*d.* 1052), called ÆLFGIFU, queen ; daughter of Richard the Fearless, duke of the Normans ; called 'the gem of the Normans' in Henry of Huntingdon's chronicle ; married to King Ethelred II, the Unready [q. v.], 1002 ; adopted the English name Ælfgifu ; said to have defended London against Cnut, 1016 ; married to Cnut, 1017 ; endeavoured to make her son Harthacnut king, but was opposed by her step-son Harold, who seized England to the north of the Thames, 1035 ; secured for Harthacnut recognition as king in Wessex, 1035 ; banished by Harold I, the men of Wessex being tired of Harthacnut's prolonged absence, 1037 ; fled to the court of Baldwin V, count of Flanders ; wielded considerable influence during the reign of Harthacnut, 1040–1 ; despoiled of her wealth by King Edward the Confessor, her son by Æthelred, 1043.
[xvii. 360]

EMMET, CHRISTOPHER TEMPLE (1761–1788), barrister ; brother of Robert Emmet [q. v.] ; scholar, Trinity College, Dublin, 1778 ; called to the bar in Ireland, 1781 ; king's counsel, 1787 ; predicted downfall of England, unless Irish wrongs were redressed, in his 'Decree,' an allegorical poem.   [xvii. 361]

EMMET, ROBERT (1778–1803), United Irishman ; entered Trinity College, Dublin, 1793 ; took his name off the books when brought up at the visitation held to discover the political sympathies of the students, 1798 ; visited Paris ; interviewed Talleyrand and Napoleon, the latter of whom promised to secure Irish independence, 1802 ; fell in love with Sarah Curran, daughter of John Philpot Curran [q. v.] ; projected a rising, 1803, the plan of which included the seizure of the person of the viceroy ; lost heart at the violence of his followers and retired to Rathfarnham ; arrested and executed, 1803.   [xvii. 362]

EMMET, THOMAS ADDIS (1764–1827), United Irishman ; brother of Robert Emmet [q. v.] ; scholar of Trinity College, Dublin 1781 ; B.A., 1783 ; M.D. Edinburgh ; LL.B. Dublin ; called to the Irish bar, 1790 ; took the oath of the United Irishmen in open court, 1795 ; one of the directors of the Society of the United Irishmen, 1797 ; arrested with his colleagues, 1798 ; agreed to Castlereagh's proposal that he should be transported to

America, but, in consequence of the American minister's objection, was transferred to Fort St. George in Scotland, 1799 ; sent to Holland, 1802 ; assisted MacSheehy in his scheme for raising a battalion of Irish in the pay of France ; joined the New York bar, 1804 ; died at New York.   [xvii. 363]

EMMETT, ANTHONY (1790–1872), major-general, royal engineers ; second lieutenant, royal engineers, 1808 ; wounded while leading a column to the assault of Badajoz, 1812 ; captain, 1813 ; fought at Orthes and Toulouse, 1814 ; commanding royal engineer at St. Helena ; retired as major-general.   [xvii. 364]

EMPSON or **EMSON**, SIR RICHARD (*d.* 1510), statesman and lawyer ; M.P. for Northamptonshire, 1491 ; speaker, 1491–2 ; knighted, 1504 ; high steward of Cambridge University, 1504 ; chancellor of the duchy of Lancaster, 1504 ; associated with Edmund Dudley [q. v.] in the exaction of taxes and crown fines during Henry VII's reign ; executed on a charge of constructive treason, suggested by his having armed his friends during Henry VII's last illness.   [xvii. 364]

EMPSON, WILLIAM (1791–1852), editor of the 'Edinburgh Review' ; educated at Winchester and Trinity College, Cambridge ; M.A., 1815 ; his article on Bentham in the 'Edinburgh Review' (1843) answered by John Stuart Mill ; professor of 'general polity and the laws of England' at the East India College, Haileybury, 1824–52 ; editor of the 'Edinburgh Review,' 1847–52.   [xvii. 365]

ENDA, or, in the older spelling, **ENNA**, SAINT, of Arran (*fl.* 6th cent.), son of a chief of Oriel (in county Louth) ; persuaded by his sister, St. Fanche, to become a monk ; crossed over to Britain ; ordained presbyter after living with St. Ninian ; founded monastery of 'Latinum' ; missionary in Ireland, founding ten monasteries in Arran of the Saints.   [xvii. 365]

ENDECOTT, JOHN (1588 ?–1665), governor of New England ; probably born at Dorchester ; joined in purchasing a patent of Massachusetts Bay territory, 1628 ; in charge of Naumkeag (afterwards Salem), 1628 ; conducted expedition to Mount Wollaston (now Quincy), and rebuked the inhabitants for their lawlessness ; friend of John Winthrop, the first regularly elected governor of New England ; member of his council of assistants, 1630 and 1636 ; disqualified from holding office for one year by judicial sentence, for having insulted the red cross of St. George, 1634 ; sent on an expedition against the Block Island and Pequot Indians, 1636 ; governor, 1644, 1649, 1651–3, and 1655–65 ; sergeant major-general of Massachusetts, 1645 ; persecuted the quakers ; coined money, 1652–65 ; informed that Charles II was ready to take the colony under his protection, provided that it submitted to be a dependency of the English crown, 1662 ; the royal commissioners refused a hearing by his court, 1664 ; his dismissal recommended by Secretary Sir William Morrice, 1665.   [xvii. 366]

ENFIELD, EDWARD (1811–1880), philanthropist ; grandson of William Enfield [q. v.] ; literary student at Manchester College, York ; moneyer at the mint ; president of the senate of University College, London, 1878–80 ; treasurer of the University College Hospital, 1867–80 ; president of Manchester New College, London ; worked with the domestic mission society for the poor of East London.   [xvii. 368]

ENFIELD, WILLIAM (1741–1797), divine and author ; tutor in belles-lettres and rector of the Warrington academy, 1770–83 ; LL.D. Edinburgh, 1774 ; pastor of two presbyterian congregations ; published 'The Speaker,' 1774, a popular schoolbook, 'Institutes of Natural Philosophy,' 1785, and translations and religious works.
[xvii. 369]

ENGLAND, GEORGE (*fl.* 1735), divine and author ; incumbent of two country parishes ; published 'An Enquiry into the Morals of the Ancients,' 1737. [xvii. 370]

ENGLAND, GEORGE (*fl.* 1740–1788), organ-builder ; built an organ for St. Stephen's, Walbrook (1760), and for various other churches.   [xvii. 370]

ENGLAND, GEORGE PIKE (1765 ?–1814), organ-builder ; son of George England (*fl.* 1740–1788) [q. v.] ; built organs for numerous churches, including one, conjointly with Nicholls, for Durham Cathedral, 1815.
[xvii. 370]

ENGLAND, JOHN (1786-1842), bishop of Charleston ; founded female penitentiary and poor schools for both sexes while a student at Carlow College ; lecturer at Cork Cathedral and chaplain to the Presentation Convent, 1808 ; D.D. ; president of the diocesan college of St. Mary, 1812-17 ; Roman catholic bishop of Charleston, U.S.A., 1820 ; established the pioneer ' United States Catholic Miscellany ' ; befriended the negroes of his diocese ; papal legate to the government of Hayti, 1833 ; his collected works (dealing with topics of controversial theology) published, 1849. [xvii. 370]

ENGLAND, SIR RICHARD (1793-1883), general ; born at Detroit, Upper Canada ; lieutenant, 1809 ; lieutenant-colonel, 1825 ; brigadier-general during the Kaffir war, 1836 and 1837 ; colonel, 1838 ; assisted Nott in defeating Akbar Khán on the Khojak Heights, but suffered some reverses, 1841 ; K.C.B., 1843 ; distinguished himself at Inkerman, 1854 ; directed attack on Redan, 1855 ; G.C.B. ; colonel, 41st regiment, 1861 ; general, 1863. [xvii. 371]

ENGLAND, THOMAS RICHARD (1790-1847), biographer ; brother of John England [q. v.] ; catholic parish priest in Ireland ; published biographies of some Roman catholic ecclesiastics. [xvii. 372]

ENGLEFIELD, SIR FRANCIS (d. 1596 ?), Roman catholic exile ; knighted at Edward VI's coronation, 1547 ; imprisoned for celebrating mass before the Princess Mary, 1551 ; privy councillor, 1553 ; knight of the shire for Berks ; placed on the witchcraft commission, 1555 ; fled to Valladolid, 1559 ; outlawed for high treason, committed at Namur, 1564 ; attainted and forfeited, 1585, Elizabeth seizing even the estates he had alienated ; pensioned by the king of Spain ; corresponded with the pope and the king of Spain on behalf of Mary Stuart, 1586 ; buried at Valladolid. [xvii. 372]

ENGLEFIELD, SIR HENRY CHARLES (1752-1822), antiquary and scientific writer ; F.S.A., 1779 ; P.S.A. ; directed the society's issue of engravings of English cathedrals and churches, 1797-1813 ; F.R.S., 1778 ; gold medallist of the Society of Arts for his ' Discovery of a Lake from Madder ' ; published miscellaneous works. [xvii. 374]

ENGLEHEART, FRANCIS (1775-1849), engraver ; nephew of George Engleheart [q. v.] ; engraved for books from drawings by Richard Cook [q. v.] ; engraved Sir David Wilkie's ' Duncan Gray ' and ' The Only Daughter ' ; exhibited at the Society of British Artists. [xvii. 375]

ENGLEHEART, GEORGE (1752-1839), miniature-painter ; of Silesian extraction ; pupil of Sir Joshua Reynolds ; miniature-painter to the king, 1790 ; exhibited at the Royal Academy, 1773-1812. [xvii. 375]

ENGLEHEART, JOHN COX DILLMAN (1783-1862), miniature-painter ; nephew of George Engleheart [q. v.] ; exhibited at the Royal Academy, 1801-28. [xvii. 375]

ENGLEHEART, THOMAS (d. 1787 ?), sculptor and modeller in wax ; brother of George Engleheart [q. v.] ; gold medallist of the Royal Academy for a bas-relief of ' Ulysses and Nausicaa,' 1772 ; exhibited wax busts and models at the Royal Academy, 1773-86. [xvii. 375]

ENGLEHEART, TIMOTHY STANSFELD (1803-1879), engraver ; engraved Guido Reni's ' Ecce Homo,' 1840, and plates in ' The British Museum Marbles.' [xvii. 375]

ENGLISH, HESTER (1571-1624). [See KELLO.]

ENGLISH, SIR JOHN HAWKER (1788-1840), surgeon-in-chief to the Swedish army ; decorated with the order of Gustavus Vasa, 1813 ; knighted, 1815 ; M.D. Göttingen, 1814 ; M.D. Aberdeen, 1823 ; L.R.C.P., 1823. [xvii. 376]

ENGLISH, JOSIAS (d. 1718 ?), amateur etcher ; etched in the style of Hollar from Clein's designs ; his most important etching, ' Christ and the Disciples at Emmaus ' after Titian. [xvii. 376]

ENGLISH, WILLIAM (fl. 1350). [See GRISAUNT.]

ENGLISH, WILLIAM (d. 1778), Irish poet ; Augustinian monk and writer of ballads, including the well-known ' Cashel of Munster.' [xvii. 376]

ENNISKILLEN, second BARON OF (1616-1645). [See MAGUIRE, CONNOR or CORNELIUS.]

ENSOM, WILLIAM (1796-1832), engraver ; silver medallist of the Society of Arts for a pen-and-ink portrait of William Blake (1757-1827) [q. v.], 1815 ; engraved for annuals ; executed engravings from portraits by Sir Thomas Lawrence. [xvii. 376]

ENSOR, GEORGE (1769-1843), political writer ; B.A. Trinity College, Dublin, 1790 ; author of a philosophical essay, entitled ' The Independent Man,' 1806, and assailant of the English government of Ireland in such books as ' Anti-Union,' 1831, and ' A Defence of the Irish,' 1825 ; wrote against Malthusianism, 1818. [xvii. 376]

ENT, SIR GEORGE (1604-1689), physician ; of Dutch parentage ; M.A. Sidney Sussex College, Cambridge, 1631 ; M.D. Padua, 1636 ; F.C.P., 1639 ; Gulstonian lecturer, 1642 ; knighted, 1665 ; P.C.P., 1670-5, 1682, and 1684 ; F.R.S. ; vindicated Harvey's discovery with an ' Apologia pro circuitione sanguinis,' 1641. [xvii. 377]

ENTICK, JOHN (1703 ?-1773), schoolmaster and author ; published a ' Speculum Latinum,' 1728 ; brought out ' Phædri Fabulæ,' with accents and notes, 1754 ; attacked the government in Shebbeare and Scott's anti-ministerial ' Monitor ' ; obtained damages in 1765 for seizure of his papers by the government three years before ; published histories and compiled English and Latin dictionaries. [xvii. 378]

ENTWISLE, JOSEPH (1767-1841), methodist minister ; preached before his sixteenth year ; sent on the Oxfordshire circuit by Wesley, 1787 ; first missionary secretary, 1805 ; president of conference, 1812 and 1825 ; house governor of the Hoxton Theological Institution, 1834-8 ; published an ' Essay on Secret Prayer,' 1820. [xvii. 378]

ENTY, JOHN (1675 ?-1743), presbyterian minister ; of humble origin ; pastor of a presbyterian congregation at Plymouth, 1698 ; leader of the conservative party in the assembly of united ministers ; published theological pamphlets. [xvii. 379]

EOGHAN, SAINT and BISHOP (d. 618), kinsman of the chieftains of Ulster and Leinster ; carried off to Britain by pirates in boyhood ; educated by St. Ninian ; taken to Armorica by Gaulish raiders ; returned to Ireland and founded a monastery at Hy Cualann, co. Wicklow ; humanised the chieftains of Ardstraw, and helped his friend, Tigernach, to found monasteries in North Ireland. [xvii. 379]

ÉON, CHEVALIER D' (1728-1810). [See D'ÉON DE BEAUMONT.]

EPINE, FRANCESCA MARGHERITA DE L' (d. 1746), Tuscan vocalist ; became associated with the establishment of Italian opera in England by singing in ' Thamyris,' 1707, ' Almahide,' 1710, Handel's ' Pastor Fido,' 1712, and similar pieces ; divided London society into factions by her jealousy of Mrs. Tofts, the Drury Lane favourite, 1704. [xvii. 380]

EPPS, GEORGE NAPOLEON (1815-1874), homœopathic practitioner ; half-brother of John Epps [q. v.] ; M.R.C.S., 1845 ; surgeon to the Homœopathic Hospital, Hanover Square, 1845 ; chief work, ' Spinal Curvature, its Theory and Cure,' 1849. [xvii. 381]

EPPS, JOHN (1805-1869), homœopathic physician ; M.D. Edinburgh, 1826 ; published ' Evidences of Christianity deduced from Phrenology ' ; medical director of the Royal Jennerian and London Vaccine Institution, c. 1830 ; issued ' Homœopathy and its Principles Explained,' 1841, and other works in defence of Hahnemann's system ; lecturer on materia medica at the Homœopathic Hospital, Hanover Square, 1851 ; issued the ' Christian Physician and Anthropological Magazine,' 1835-9 ; friend of Mazzini and Kossuth. [xvii. 382]

ERARD, SAINT and BISHOP (fl. 730-754) ; left Ireland to look for his brother Hildulph, who had gone out as a missionary to Germany, and, finding him a hermit in the Vosges, induced him to teach publicly ; baptised Ottilia, daughter of the Duke of the Allemanni ; possibly a monastic bishop at Ratisbon, where he was buried ; canonised, 1052. [xvii. 383]

ERBURY, WILLIAM (1604 - 1654), independent divine ; B.A. Brasenose College, Oxford, 1623 ; incumbent of St. Mary's, Cardiff, 1623-38 ; pronounced a schismatic by the bishop of Llandaff, 1634 ; forced to resign his living, 1638 ; chaplain of Skippon's regiment ; according to Edwards, taught universal redemption; denied the divinity of Christ, 1645; maintained in various theological treatises that the Holy Spirit departed about the end of the apostolic period. [xvii. 383]

ERCELDOUNE, THOMAS OF, called also the RHYMER and LEARMONT (*fl.* 1220 ?-1297 ?), seer and poet; mentioned in the chartulary (1294) of the Trinity House of Soltra as having inherited lands in Erceldoune, a Berwickshire village; said to have predicted the death of Alexander III, king of Scotland, under the figure of a destructive gale, 1285, also the battle of Bannockburn; traditional fountain of many (fabricated) oracles, one of which 'foretold' the accession of James VI to the English throne; reputed author of a poem on the Tristrem story, which Sir Walter Scott considered genuine; it probably emanated from a French source. The romance of Thomas and the 'ladye gaye,' popularly attributed to him, may be placed after 1401 (edited by Dr. J. A. H. Murray, 1875). [xvii. 385]

ERDESWICKE, SAMPSON (*d.* 1603), historian of Staffordshire; studied at Brasenose College, Oxford, 1553-1554; worked at his 'View' or 'Survey' of Staffordshire from 1593 to 1603; said to have written his pupil William Wyrley's 'True Use of Armorie,' 1592; commended by the antiquary Camden. [xvii. 388]

ERICHSEN, SIR JOHN ERIC (1818-1896), surgeon; born at Copenhagen; studied medicine at University College, London; M.R.C.S., 1839; F.R.C.S., 1845; joint lecturer on anatomy and physiology at Westminster Hospital, 1844, and joint lecturer on anatomy, 1846-8; assistant-surgeon, 1848, and full surgeon, 1850-75, to University College Hospital; professor of surgery in University College, 1850-66; Holme professor of clinical surgery, 1866; F.R.S., 1876; honorary LL.D. Edinburgh, 1884; surgeon-extraordinary to Queen Victoria, 1877; created baronet, 1895; president of council of University College, 1887-96; published 'Science and Art of Surgery,' 1853, and other surgical works. [Suppl. ii. 188]

ERIGENA, JOHN (*fl.* 850). [See SCOTUS.]

ERKENWALD or **EARCONWALD,** SAINT (*d.* 693), bishop of London; founded a monastery with the help of Frithewald, under-king of Surrey, at Chertsey, and another at Barking; consecrated bishop of the East-Saxons, 676, practically founding his see. [xvii. 390]

ERLE, THOMAS (1650 ?-1720), general; M.P. for Wareham, 1678-97, and 1699-1718, for Portsmouth, 1698; deputy lieutenant for Dorset, 1685; colonel of foot, 1689; fought for William III in Ireland, 1690-1, and at Steinkirk, 1692; wounded at Landen, 1693; commander-in-chief in Ireland, 1702; lord justice in Ireland, *c.* 1702; lieutenant of the ordnance on Marlborough's recommendation, 1703; commanded the centre as lieutenant-general at Almanza, 1707; commander-in-chief at siege of Lille, 1708; commander-in-chief in South Britain and governor of Portsmouth, 1709-12; nominated general of foot in Flanders, 1711. [xvii. 391]

ERLE, SIR WILLIAM (1793-1880), judge; educated at Winchester and New College, Oxford; fellow; B.C.L., 1818; barrister, Middle Temple, 1819; bencher, Inner Temple, 1834; M.P. for city of Oxford, 1837; counsel to the Bank of England, 1844; serjeant-at-law, 1844; knighted, 1845; lord chief-justice of common pleas, 1859-66; privy councillor, 1859; member of the Trades' Union Commission, 1867; published 'The Law relating to Trades' Unions,' 1869-80. [xvii. 392]

ERNEST AUGUSTUS, DUKE OF YORK AND ALBANY (1674-1728), fifth son of Ernest Augustus, elector of Hanover and brother of George I; saw military service under the emperor; created Duke of York and Albany and Earl of Ulster, 1716; K.G.; prince bishop of Osnaburg, 1716-28. [xvii. 393]

ERNEST AUGUSTUS, DUKE OF CUMBERLAND and KING OF HANOVER (1771-1851), fifth son of George III; K.G., 1786; student at Göttingen University, 1786; lieutenant-colonel, 9th Hanoverian hussars, 1793; major-general in the English and Hanoverian armies, 1794; wounded at the first battle of Tournay, 1794; created Duke of Cumberland and Earl of Armagh, 1799; general, 1803; chancellor of Trinity College, Dublin, 1805; opposed all relaxation of the catholic penal laws, 1808; voted against the regency bill, 1810; narrowly escaped assassination in his bed, 1810; deputy-elector of Hanover, 1813; field marshal in the British army, 1813; G.C.B., 1815; resigned his colonelcy of the blues, 1830; opposed the Reform Bill of 1832; insulted by Brougham in parliament; grand master of Irish Orangemen; succeeded on William IV's death, in accordance with provisions of Salic law, as King Ernest I of Hanover, 1837; cancelled William IV's constitution, and made himself absolute monarch; gained popularity by the contrast he showed to the absenteeism of his predecessors; granted Hanover a constitution on democratic lines, 1840; died at Herrenhausen. [xvii. 393]

ERNULF or **ARNULF** (1040 - 1124), bishop of Rochester; of French origin; Benedictine monk at Beauvais; made prior of Christ Church, Canterbury, by Archbishop Anselm; abbot of Peterborough, 1107-14; appointed bishop of Rochester against his will and to the sorrow of his monks, 1114; author of the 'Textus Roffensis,' a collection of laws, papal decrees, and documents relating to the church of Rochester (published by Thomas Hearne, 1720). [xvii. 396]

ERPINGHAM, SIR THOMAS (1357-1428), soldier; in service of John of Gaunt, 1380; accompanied him to Spain, 1386; went with John of Gaunt's son, Henry, earl of Derby (afterwards Henry IV), on expeditions to Lithuania, 1390 and 1392, and accompanied him during his banishment, 1398-9; constable of Dover Castle and warden of Cinque ports, 1399-1409; K.G. and chamberlain of king's household, 1400; accompanied Thomas, duke of Clarence (1388 ?-1421) [q. v.], in Ireland, 1401-3; privy councillor and steward of royal household, 1404; took part in Agincourt campaign, 1415; sent with John Wakering [q. v.], bishop of Berwick, to Calais and Beauvais, to treat with king of France, 1416. [Suppl. ii. 189]

ERRINGTON, ANTHONY (1719 ?), Roman catholic divine; D.D.; dedicated 'Catechistical Discourses' to the Princess Henrietta Maria, 1654. [xvii. 398]

ERRINGTON, GEORGE (1804-1886), Roman catholic archbishop; educated at St. Cuthbert's College, Ushaw, 1814-21; D.D. of the English college, Rome, 1827; vice-rector, 1832; presided over St. Mary's College, Oscott, 1843-7; first bishop of Plymouth, 1850-5; archbishop of Trebizond *in partibus*, 1855; coadjutor to Cardinal Wiseman, 1855-62; assistant at the pontifical throne, 1856; in charge of St. Paul's College, Prior Park, 1870-86. [xvii. 398]

ERRINGTON, JOHN EDWARD (1806-1862), civil engineer; resident engineer of the Grand Junction railway; constructed harbour works of Greenock, 1841; brought forward the entire system of railways from Lancaster to Inverness; vice-president of the Institution of Civil Engineers, 1861-2; engineer to London and South-Western Railway; his plan for the line from Yeovil to Exeter accepted, 1856. [xvii. 399]

ERRINGTON, WILLIAM (1716-1768), Roman catholic divine; student and professor at the English college, Douay; established school at Sedgley Park, Staffordshire, 1763; archdeacon and treasurer of the chapter in London. [xvii. 399]

ERROL, ninth EARL OF (*d.* 1631). [See HAY, FRANCIS.]

ERSKINE, CHARLES (1680-1763), lord justice clerk; regent of Edinburgh University, 1700-7; first professor of public law, Edinburgh, 1707; member of the Faculty of Advocates, 1711; M.P., Dumfriesshire, 1722, 1727, and 1734; M.P., Dumfries burghs, 1734; solicitor-general for Scotland, 1725; lord advocate, 1737-42; M.P. for the Wick burghs, 1741; raised to the bench as Lord Tinwald, 1744; lord justice clerk, 1748. [xvii. 400]

ERSKINE, DAVID, second BARON CARDROSS (1616-1671), royalist; fined and excluded from parliament (1649) for having promoted the 'engagement,' 1648. [xvii. 400]

ERSKINE, DAVID, LORD DUN (1670-1758), Scottish judge; studied at Paris and St. Andrews; member of the Scottish bar, 1698; M.P., Forfarshire, 1690-1, 1693, 1695, and 1696; opposed the union; ordinary lord, with title of Lord Dun, 1710-53; lord of justiciary, 1714-44; published 'Friendly and Familiar Advices,' 1754. [xvii. 401]

ERSKINE, SIR DAVID (1772-1837), dramatist and antiquary; natural son of David Steuart Erskine [q. v.]; professor at the Royal Military Academy, Sandhurst; knighted, 1830; F.S.A. Scot.; a founder of the Scots

Military and Naval Academy, Edinburgh; author of 'King James the First of Scotland,' 1827, 'King James the Second of Scotland,' 1828, and other plays, also of 'Annals and Antiquities of Dryburgh,' 1836. [xvii. 401]

ERSKINE, DAVID MONTAGU, second BARON ERSKINE (1776–1855), diplomatist; eldest son of Thomas, first baron Erskine [q. v.]; educated at Westminster and Christ Church, Oxford; barrister, Lincoln's Inn, 1802; M.P., Portsmouth, 1806; minister plenipotentiary to the United States, 1806–9, at Stuttgard, 1825–8, at Munich, 1828–43. [xvii. 401]

ERSKINE, DAVID STEUART, eleventh EARL OF BUCHAN (1742–1829), brother of Henry Erskine (1746–1817) [q. v.]; studied at Glasgow University and Robert Foulis's academy; nominated secretary to the embassy to Spain, but did not go, possibly because the ambassador was his inferior by birth, 1766; freed the election of Scottish representative peers from governmental interference; originated Society of Antiquaries of Scotland, 1780; founded annual festival in commemoration of James Thomson, 1791; presented Washington with a snuff-box made from the tree which sheltered Wallace, 1792; contributed to numerous publications and wrote literary biographies and essays. [xvii. 402]

ERSKINE, EBENEZER (1680–1754), founder of Scottish secession church; M.A. Edinburgh, 1697; ordained by the presbytery of Kirkcaldy to Portmoak, 1703; consistently refused the oath of abjuration; one of the 'twelve apostles' who signed the 'representation,' 1721; admitted to the third charge of Stirling, 1731; moderator of the synod of Stirling and Perth; preached against an act of the assembly to regulate the election to vacant churches, failing presentation by the patron, 1732; censured by the synod, 1732; deposed for protesting against the censure of the assembly, 1733; seceded, and formed an 'associate' presbytery, 1733; issued, in company with three others, his 'judicial testimony' against the church of Scotland, 1736; formally deposed with his followers, 1740; headed two companies of 'seceders' against the Pretender, 1746; professor of divinity to the 'associate synod,' 1747–9, his followers having become divided into two parties by varying interpretations of the civic oath taken by the burgesses of Edinburgh, Glasgow, and Perth; deposed from the ministry (1748) by the antiburgher synod. [xvii. 404]

ERSKINE, EDWARD MORRIS (1817–1883), diplomatist; son of David Montagu, second baron Erskine [q. v.]; secretary of legation at Florence, 1852, at Washington, and at Stockholm, 1858–60; secretary of embassy to St. Petersburg and Constantinople, 1860; minister plenipotentiary to Greece, 1864–72; on the Stockholm legation, 1872–81; C.B., 1873. [xvii. 407]

ERSKINE, HENRY, third BARON CARDROSS (1650–1693), covenanter; son of David, second baron Cardross [q. v.]; fined and imprisoned on account of his own and his wife's presbyterian leanings; released, 1679; denied all redress by Charles II; emigrated; expelled by the Spaniards from his plantation at Charlestown Neck, South Carolina; accompanied the Prince of Orange to England, 1688; fought at Killiecrankie, 1689; privy councillor, and general of the mint, 1689; lieutenant-colonel, 1689. [xvii. 408]

ERSKINE, HENRY (1624–1696), presbyterian minister; minister of Cornhill, Northumberland, 1649; ejected, 1662; his sentence of fine and imprisonment by a committee of privy council commuted to banishment from Scotland; released from imprisonment at Newcastle, 1685; allowed to preach by royal indulgence, 1687. [xvii. 409]

ERSKINE, SIR HENRY or HARRY (d. 1765), fifth baronet of Alva and Cambuskenneth; lieutenant-general; deputy quartermaster-general and lieutenant-colonel in expedition to L'Orient, 1746; M.P., Ayr, 1749, Anstruther, 1754–61; removed from the army for political reasons, 1756; subsequently became lieutenant-general; secretary of the order of the Thistle; endeavoured to prevent publication of Lady Mary Wortley Montagu's letters; erroneously credited with the authorship of the Scottish march, 'Garb of Old Gaul.' [xvii. 409]

ERSKINE, HENRY (1746–1817), lord advocate; studied at St. Salvator and St. Leonard's, Edinburgh, and Glasgow; lord advocate, 1783 and 1806; advocate and

state councillor to the Prince of Wales in Scotland, 1783; dean of the Faculty of Advocates, 1785–95; condemned the 'sedition' and 'treason' bills as unconstitutional, 1795, and so was not re-elected dean, 1796; M.P., Haddington burghs, 1806, Dumfries burghs, 1806–7; a commissioner to inquire into administration of justice in Scotland, 1808; friend of the poor; published 'The Emigrant, an Eclogue,' 1773, and other poems. [xvii. 410]

ERSKINE, HENRY NAPIER BRUCE (1832–1893), commissioner of Scinde, 1879–87; son of William Erskine (1773–1852) [q. v.] [Suppl. ii. 193]

ERSKINE, JAMES, sixth EARL OF BUCHAN (d. 1640), son of John, second or seventh earl of Mar [q. v.]; Earl of Buchan by marriage; lord of the bedchamber to Charles I, 1625. [xvii. 412]

ERSKINE, JAMES, LORD GRANGE (1679–1754), judge; member of the Faculty of Advocates, 1705; lord of justiciary, 1707; lord justice clerk, with the title of Lord Grange, 1710; secretly intrigued with Jacobites, though professing loyalty to Hanoverian dynasty; denied the qualification of heritors, as heritors, to elect a minister, 1731; publicly celebrated his wife's funeral, 1732, though she was still alive in the Hebrides, a prisoner to prevent the disclosure of Jacobite secrets; resigned his judgeship in order to sit in parliament; M.P., Stirlingshire, 1734; opposed Walpole and (1736) the abolition of the statutes against witchcraft; secretary to Frederick, prince of Wales. [xvii. 413]

ERSKINE, JAMES (1722–1796), Scottish judge; son of Charles Erskine [q. v.]; advocate, 1743; sheriff depute of Perthshire, 1748; exchequer baron in Scotland, 1754; knight-marshal of Scotland, 1758; sessions judge as Lord Barjarg, 1761, afterwards as Lord Alva. [xvii. 400]

ERSKINE, JAMES CLAUDIUS (1821–1893), member of Indian civil service; son of William Erskine (1773–1852) [q. v.]; judge of Bombay high court, 1862–3. [Suppl. ii. 192]

ERSKINE, SIR JAMES ST. CLAIR, second EARL OF ROSSLYN (1762–1837), general; son of Sir Henry Erskine (d. 1765) [q. v.]; lieutenant, 38th regiment; lieutenant, 2nd dragoons, 1778; assistant adjutant-general in Ireland, 1782; M.P., Castle Rising, 1781–4, Morpeth, 1784; one of the managers of Warren Hastings's impeachment; M.P., Kirkcaldy burghs, 1790–1805; served as adjutant-general before Toulon, 1793, and in Corsica; aide-de-camp to the king, and colonel, 1795; major-general, 1798; commander-in-chief in the Mediterranean; lieutenant-general, 1805; succeeded his uncle as Earl of Rosslyn, 1805; sent with Simcoe (1806) on a special mission to Lisbon, which resulted in the despatch of Sir Arthur Wellesley to the Peninsula; general, 1814; G.C.B.; lord privy seal and privy councillor; lord president of the council, 1834 [xvii. 414]

ERSKINE, JOHN, sixth BARON ERSKINE, and first or sixth EARL OF MAR of the ERSKINE line (d. 1572), regent of Scotland; put in charge of Edinburgh Castle, 1554; disregarded the warning of the lords of the congregation not to allow the queen regent to fortify Leith, 1559; refused to subscribe the 'Book of Discipline,' though a hearer of Knox, 1560; privy councillor, 1561; favoured the marriage of Mary Queen of Scots and Darnley; created, or possibly recognised as, Earl of Mar, 1565; assisted in suppressing Moray's rebellion, 1566; signed the order for Mary's commitment to Lochleven Castle, 1567; member of the council of government, 1567; fought at Langside, 1568; implored the assistance of Queen Elizabeth, when the safety of the young king, James VI, his ward, was endangered by Moray's murder, 1569; regent on the death of Lennox, 1571; proclaimed Morton the real governor, lieutenant-general of the forces, 1571; consented to the extradition of the Duke of Northumberland in order to obtain Elizabeth's assistance, 1572; joined Morton in agreeing to the proposal of Killigrew, the English ambassador, that Mary should be delivered up to the extreme reformers, 1572. [xvii. 416]

ERSKINE, JOHN (1509–1591), of Dun, Scottish reformer; educated at King's College, Aberdeen; brought from the continent a French gentleman, Petrus de Marsiliers, whom he established at Montrose to teach Greek, 'nocht heard of before' in Scotland; friend of the reformer Wishart; supported the queen dowager, 1547; signed the first bond of the Scottish reformers inviting

Knox to return from Geneva, 1557 ; signed the act suspending the queen regent, who had broken faith, 1559 ; appointed superintendent for Angus and Mearns, 1560 ; allayed the anger of Mary Queen of Scots at the denunciations of Knox ; remonstrated with the regent for proclaiming certain letters dismissing the collectors of the thirds of the benefices, 1571 ; agreed to the modified episcopacy introduced at the Leith convention, 1572 ; assisted in the compilation of the 'Second Book of Discipline,' 1578 ; member of the king's council, 1579 ; superintendent of the general assembly, 1589. [xvii. 419]

ERSKINE, JOHN, second or seventh EARL OF MAR of the ERSKINE line (1558–1634), lord high treasurer of Scotland ; son of John, first or sixth earl [q. v.] ; educated with James VI, who called him 'Jocky o' Sclaittis' (slates) ; obtained the government of Stirling Castle and the guardianship of the young king, James VI, by stratagem, 1578 ; authorised, by the influence of Morton, to apprehend all such persons as entered Stirling Castle in arms while the king was there, 1579 ; accompanied the king from Stirling to Holyrood, 1579 ; foiled a plot of Lennox to carry off the king, 1580 ; excluded from the counsels of the king after Morton's arrest ; regained possession of the king's person by the 'raid of Ruthven,' 1582 ; favourably received at court, the king having escaped from his keeping, 1583 ; banished from England, Scotland, and Ireland, 1584 ; returned, and captured Stirling Castle in the protestant interest, 1584 ; found refuge in England from the resentment of King James ; 'forfaulted,' 1584 ; returned to Scotland in arms ; privy councillor of Scotland, 1585 ; great master of the household ; guardian of the young Prince Henry, 1595 ; instrumental in preventing the success of the Gowrie conspiracy, 1600 ; ambassador to Elizabeth, at first as a cloak for assisting Essex's rebellion, but subsequently to negotiate James VI's accession to the English throne, 1601 ; member of the English privy council ; K.G., 1603 ; created Baron Cardross, 1604 ; lord high treasurer of Scotland, 1616–30. [xvii. 422]

ERSKINE, JOHN, sixth or eleventh EARL OF MAR of the ERSKINE line (1675–1732), Jacobite leader ; joined court party, 1696 ; privy councillor, 1697 ; K.T. ; left court party, 1704 ; rejoined it, 1705 ; commissioner for the union, 1705 ; secretary of state for Scotland ; keeper of the signet ; Scottish representative peer, 1707, 1708, 1710, and 1713 ; privy councillor, 1708 ; advocated the repeal of the union, 1713 ; secretary of state, 1713 ; dismissed, though professing loyalty, 1714 ; set up James Edward, the Old Pretender's, standard at Braemar, 1715 ; his projected attack on Edinburgh foiled by the rapidity of Argyll's movements ; defeated at Sheriffmuir, 1715 ; created duke by the Old Pretender, 1715 ; escaped with the Pretender to Gravelines ; treated with George I for a partial restoration of the Stuarts, possibly to commend himself at the Hanoverian court, 1717 ; memorialised the regent of France with a proposal for dismembering the British empire, 1723 ; lost the confidence of the Pretender. [xvii. 426]

ERSKINE, JOHN (1695–1768), Scottish lawyer ; member of the Faculty of Advocates, 1719 ; professor of Scots law, Edinburgh, 1737–65 ; gave a connected view of the entire Scots law in 'Principles of the Law of Scotland,' 1754, and 'Institutes of the Law of Scotland,' published, 1773. [xvii. 431]

ERSKINE, JOHN (1721 ?–1803), theologian ; son of John Erskine (1695–1768) [q. v.] ; educated at Edinburgh University ; partially adopted Warburton's views ; minister of Kirkintilloch, 1744–53, of Culross, 1753–8, of the New Greyfriars, 1758–67, and from 1767 of the Old Greyfriars, Edinburgh ; D.D. Glasgow, 1766 ; friend of Whitefield and Jonathan Edwards ; published pamphlets deprecating war with America, c. 1774 ; corresponded with Edmund Burke and lords Kames and Hailes ; published controversial and theological works. [xvii. 432]

ERSKINE, RALPH (1685–1752), Scottish seceding divine and poet ; son of Henry Erskine (1624–1696) [q. v.] ; possibly M.A. Edinburgh ; minister of the second charge, Dunfermline, 1711, of the first charge, 1716 ; one of the 'twelve apostles' of 1721 ; seceded, 1737 ; deposed, with his colleagues, 1740 ; published 'Faith no Fancy,' to discountenance Whitefield's revival, 1742, also 'Gospel Sonnets' (25th edit. 1797) and 'Scripture Songs,' collected, 1754. [xvii. 433]

ERSKINE, THOMAS, first EARL OF KELLIE, first VISCOUNT FENTON and first BARON DIRLETON (1566–1639) ; educated with James VI ; gentleman of the bedchamber, 1585 ; privy councillor in Scotland, 1601 ; captain of the yeomen of the guard, 1603–32 ; created Baron Dirleton, 1604, Viscount Fenton, 1606 ; K.G., 1615 ; rewarded for his scheme of respite of homage with the earldom of Kellie, 1619. [xvii. 434]

ERSKINE, THOMAS, first BARON ERSKINE (1750–1823), lord chancellor ; midshipman in the West Indies, 1764–8 ; bought commission in 1st royal regiment of foot, 1768 ; published a pamphlet on 'Abuses in the Army' ; advised by Lord Mansfield to go to the bar ; studied at Lincoln's Inn, 1775 ; gentleman commoner, Trinity College, Cambridge, 1776 ; honorary M.A., 1778 ; called to the bar, 1778 ; gained the day for his client, Thomas Baillie [q. v.], by a fierce onslaught on the opposing party, Lord Sandwich, first lord of the admiralty, 1778 ; obtained a verdict of 'not guilty' for Lord George Gordon, 1781 ; did much to mould English commercial law, an almost new department of jurisprudence ; first barrister to refuse to go on circuit except for a special fee ; intimate friend of Sheridan and Fox ; M.P. for Portsmouth on formation of coalition government, 1783 ; attorney-general to the Prince of Wales, 1783 ; spoke ineffectively on Fox's East India bill ; denounced Pitt's India bill, 1784 ; lost his seat at the dissolution, 1784 ; hissed for unsparing abuse of Pitt in his speech as counsel for the East India Company, 1788 ; contributed by his speech on a libel case to the passing (1792) of Fox's Libel Act ; successfully defended Stockdale on a charge of libelling the managers of Hastings's impeachment, 1789 ; M.P., Portsmouth, 1790–1806 ; lost his office of attorney-general to the Prince of Wales by appearing on behalf of Thomas Paine [q. v.], 1792 ; procured acquittal of most of those prosecuted by the government for conspiracy or constructive treason, 1793–4 ; issued 'Causes and Consequences of the War with France,' 1797 ; supported Peace of Amiens in parliament and spoke (1795) against Seditious Meetings Bill ; lord chancellor, though ignorant of equity, 1806 ; created Baron Erskine of Restormel, 1806 ; his decisions unfairly termed the 'Apocrypha' ; presided at Lord Melville's trial, 1806 ; resigned the seals, 1807 ; moved that the king's personal inclinations ought not to be binding on ministers ; became an advocate of negro emancipation ; retired into private life, studied farming, and wrote 'Armata,' a political romance ; K.T. ; opposed the second reading of the bill of pains and penalties against Queen Caroline, 1820, and the Six Acts, 1819 and 1820 ; protested against the Corn Law Bill, 1822 ; worked for the cause of Greek independence, 1822–3. [xvii. 435]

ERSKINE, THOMAS (1788–1864), judge ; son of Thomas, first baron Erskine [q. v.] ; M.A. Trinity College, Cambridge, 1811 ; barrister, Lincoln's Inn, 1813 ; king's counsel, 1827 ; chief judge in bankruptcy, 1831–42 ; privy councillor ; judge of common pleas, 1839–4 ; friend of Charles Kingsley. [xvii. 443]

ERSKINE, THOMAS (1788–1870), advocate and theologian ; grandson of John Erskine (1695–1768) [q. v] ; educated at Edinburgh High School and University ; member of the Faculty of Advocates, 1810 ; espoused and developed John M'Leod Campbell's doctrine of 'universal atonement,' 1831 ; friend of Carlyle, Dean Stanley, and F. D. Maurice ; seemed to Prévost-Paradol, a 'kind of old prophet' ; upheld Calvinism as making 'God all in all' ; published Christian apologetics and expository works, including 'Remarks on the Internal Evidence for the Truth of Revealed Religion,' 1820. [xvii. 444]

ERSKINE, THOMAS ALEXANDER, sixth EARL OF KELLIE (1732–1781), musical dilettante ; studied music in Germany ; director of the St. Cecilia concerts at Edinburgh ; notorious for his coarse joviality. A collection of his minuets was published in 1836. [xvii. 445]

ERSKINE, WILLIAM (d. 1685) ; son of John, second or seventh earl of Mar [q. v.] ; master of Charterhouse, 1677–85 ; cupbearer to Charles II ; M.R.S. [xvii. 445]

ERSKINE, SIR WILLIAM (1769–1813), major-general ; lieutenant, 15th light dragoons, 1788 ; captain, 1791 ; created baronet, 1791 ; one of the officers who saved the Emperor Leopold at Villiers-en-Couche, 1793 ; M.P., Fifeshire, 1796 and 1802–5 ; major-general, 1808 ; commanded the light division at Torres Vedras, though too recklessly to be successful; commanded Hills's cavalry in the advance on Madrid, 1812; cashiered as insane; killed himself at Lisbon. [xvii. 445]

ERSKINE, WILLIAM, LORD KINNEDER (1769–1822), friend of Sir Walter Scott; educated at Glasgow University; advocate at the Scottish bar, 1790; guided Scott in his studies of German drama and romance; negotiated for Scott's translation of 'Lenore,' 1796; sheriff depute of Orkney, 1809; promoted to the bench as Lord Kinneder, 1822; ruined in health by a groundless accusation of immorality; wrote Scottish songs. [xvii. 446]

ERSKINE, WILLIAM (1773–1852), historian and orientalist; educated at Edinburgh; apprenticed as lawyer; accompanied Sir James Mackintosh [q. v.] to India, 1804; stipendiary magistrate; master in equity in recorder's court of Bombay, 1820; member of committee of three which drew up Bombay code of regulations; accused of defalcations and deprived of offices, 1823; settled in Edinburgh, 1826; provost of St. Andrews, 1836–9. He had made a careful study of Persian, and published in 1826 a translation of 'Bābar's Memoirs,' with valuable preface, introduction, and notes. His writings include 'History of India under Bābar and Humāyūn,' 1854. [Suppl. ii. 190]

ESCOMBE, HARRY (1838–1899), premier of Natal; educated at St. Paul's School; went to Natal, 1860; attorney-at-law; solicitor and standing counsel for Durban; member for Durban in legislative council, 1872; served in Durban rifles through Zulu campaign, 1879–80, and Transvaal war, 1881; again member for Durban, 1879–85; on executive council, 1880–3; member of council for Newcastle, 1886, Klip River, 1888, and Durban, 1890–7; attorney-general, 1893; premier, 1897; privy councillor and LL.D. Cambridge, 1897. [Suppl. ii. 193]

ESDAILE, JAMES (1808–1859), surgeon and mesmerist; M.D. Edinburgh, 1830; put in charge of East India Company's Hooghly hospital, 1838; adopted and successfully employed mesmerism for production of anæsthesia, 1845; entrusted with hospital in Calcutta for purposes of experiment, 1846; presidency surgeon, 1848; marine surgeon, 1850; published records of his cases and works on mesmerism. [xviii. 1]

ESDAILE, WILLIAM (1758–1837), banker and printcollector; employed in the firm of Esdaile, Hammet & Co., Lombard Street; retired, broken down, 1832; visited Italy, 1825 and 1835; possessed a very complete set of Rembrandt etchings and Claude drawings. [xviii. 3]

ESHER, VISCOUNT (1815–1899). [See BRETT, WILLIAM BALIOL.]

ESKGROVE, LORD (1724?–1804). [See RAE, SIR DAVID.]

ESMONDE, SIR LAURENCE, BARON ESMONDE (1570?–1646), governor of Duncannon; served in the Netherlands and (1599) in Ireland; knighted, 1599; governor of Duncannon, 1606–46; joint-commissioner to survey confiscated territory in Wexford, 1611; charged with packing juries and torturing witnesses in order to deprive the O'Byrnes of their land, 1619; created Baron Esmonde, 1622. [xviii. 3]

ESPEC, WALTER (d. 1153), founder of Rievaulx Abbey, 1131, of Warden Abbey, 1135; itinerant justice in the north during Henry I's reign; a leader in the Battle of the Standard, 1138; died a recluse. [xviii. 4]

ESSEX, KINGS OF. [See EAST-SAXONS.]

ESSEX, EARLS OF. [See MANDEVILLE, GEOFFREY DE, first EARL, d. 1144; MANDEVILLE, WILLIAM DE, third EARL, d. 1189; FITZPETER, GEOFFREY, fourth EARL, d. 1213; BOHUN, HUMPHREY DE, first EARL of the second creation, d. 1274; BOHUN, HUMPHREY DE, second EARL, d. 1298; BOHUN, HUMPHREY DE, third EARL, 1276–1322; BOURCHIER, HENRY, first EARL of the third creation, d. 1483; BOURCHIER, HENRY, second EARL, d. 1539; CROMWELL, THOMAS, first EARL of the fourth creation, 1485?–1540; PARR, WILLIAM, first EARL of the fifth creation, 1513–1571; DEVEREUX, WALTER, first EARL of the sixth creation, 1541?–1576; DEVEREUX, ROBERT, second EARL, 1567–1601; DEVEREUX, ROBERT, third EARL, 1591–1646; CAPEL, ARTHUR, first EARL of the seventh creation, 1631–1683; CAPEL, WILLIAM, third EARL, 1697–1743.]

ESSEX, COUNTESS OF (1794–1882). [See STEPHENS, CATHERINE.]

ESSEX, ALFRED (fl. 1837), artist; son of William Essex [q. v.]; executed plates for Muss; published paper on painting in enamel, 1837. [xviii. 8]

ESSEX, JAMES (1722–1784), builder and architect; designed and built west front of Emmanuel College, Cambridge, 1775, with other collegiate buildings; executed restorations and alterations in Ely Cathedral, 1757–62; put up the four spires and battlement of the central tower at Lincoln, 1775; F.S.A., 1772; published architectural pamphlets. [xviii. 8]

ESSEX, TIMOTHY (1765?–1847), composer; Mus.Doc. Magdalen Hall, Oxford, 1812; organist to St. George's Chapel, Albemarle Street; composed canzonets, duets, and sonatinas. [xviii. 7]

ESSEX, WILLIAM B. (1822–1852), artist; son of William Essex [q. v.]; exhibited at the Royal Academy, 1845–51. [xviii. 8]

ESSEX, WILLIAM (1784?–1869), enamel-painter to Princess Augusta, Queen Victoria (1839), and the prince consort; exhibited at the Royal Academy and other institutions. [xviii. 8]

EST, ESTE, or EASTE, MICHAEL (1580?–1680?). [See EAST.]

ESTCOURT, EDGAR EDMUND (1816–1884), canon of St. Chad's Cathedral, Birmingham; M.A. Exeter College, Oxford, 1840; converted to Roman catholicism, 1845; diocesan œconomus in the western district, 1850–1884; best-known work, 'The Question of Anglican Ordinations discussed,' 1873. [xviii. 8]

ESTCOURT, JAMES BUCKNALL BUCKNALL (1802–1855), major-general; ensign, 1820; superintended magnetic experiments in Euphrates Valley expedition, 1834–6; M.P., Devizes, 1848; fought at Inkerman and the Alma, 1854; major-general, 1854; unfairly blamed for sufferings of Crimean troops; died in Crimea. [xviii. 9]

ESTCOURT, RICHARD (1668–1712), actor and dramatist; travelling actor, 1683; first appeared at Drury Lane, 1704; specially selected by Farquhar for the part of Sergeant Kite; commended by his friend Steele; published a drama and an interlude. [xviii. 9]

ESTCOURT, THOMAS HENRY SUTTON SOTHERON (1801–1876), statesman; educated at Harrow and Oriel College, Oxford; M.A., 1826; D.C.L., 1857; conservative M.P., Marlborough, 1829, Devizes, 1835–44, and North Wiltshire, 1844–65; privy councillor, 1858; home secretary, 3 March–18 June 1859. [xviii. 11]

ESTE, CHARLES (1696–1745), bishop of Waterford; queen's scholar, Westminster; M.A. Christ Church, Oxford, 1722; bishop of Ossory, 1736–40; D.D. Dublin, 1736; bishop of Waterford, 1740. [xviii. 12]

ESTE or EST, THOMAS (1540?–1608?). [See EAST.]

ESTLIN, JOHN BISHOP (1785–1855), surgeon; son of John Prior Estlin [q. v.]; studied at Guy's Hospital; established (1812) and conducted (1812–48) ophthalmic dispensary at Bristol; F.R.C.S., 1843; published 'Remarks on Mesmerism,' 1845. [xviii. 12]

ESTLIN, JOHN PRIOR (1747–1817), unitarian minister; co-pastor at Lewin's Mead, Bristol, 1771; LL.D. Glasgow, 1807; friend of Coleridge, Southey, and Robert Hall; his 'Familiar Lectures' published, 1818. [xviii. 12]

ESTON, ADAM (d. 1397). [See EASTON.]

ESTWICK or EASTWICK, SAMPSON (d. 1739), musician; M.A. Christ Church, Oxford, 1680; B.D., 1692; minor prebendary of St. Paul's, 1692; superintendent of the choir, 1698–1739; sacrist, 1699; the 'Sam' of Henry Aldrich's famous smoking catch; published sermon on 'The Usefulness of Church Musick,' 1696. [xviii. 13]

ESTYE, GEORGE (1566–1601), divine; B.A. Caius College, Cambridge, 1581; fellow; M.A., 1584; B.D., 1591; preacher of St. Mary's, Bury St. Edmunds, 1598–1601; author of Calvinistic expositions of scripture. [xviii. 14]

ETHELBALD or **ÆTHELBALD** (*d.* 757), king of Mercia, 716 ; overlord as far north as the Humber ; invaded Wessex, 733 ; defeated at Burford by the revolted Cuthred of Wessex, 752 ; liberal to the church ; slain at Seccandune (Seckington). [xviii. 14]

ETHELBALD or **ÆTHELBALD** (*d.* 860), king of the West-Saxons ; supplanted his father, Æthelwulf, 856 ; married Judith, his father's widow, 858 ; said, without foundation, to have separated from her at St. Swithun's instance. [xviii. 16]

ETHELBERT, ÆTHELBERHT, or **ÆDILBERCT** (552 ?-616), king of Kent, 560 ; defeated by the West-Saxons, 568 ; married Bertha, daughter of the Frankish king, Charibert, giving her St. Martin's Church, Canterbury ; baptised by St. Augustine, 597 ; promulgated a code of laws, 'according to the Roman fashion' ; built a cathedral at Rochester. [xviii. 16]

ETHELBERT, ÆTHELBERHT, ÆGELBRIHT, or **ALBERT,** SAINT (*d.* 794), king of the East-Angles ; beheaded, by command of Offa, king of the Mercians, 794, according to one legend, through the machinations of Cynethryth, Offa's queen, who suspected him of designs on Mercia ; venerated at Hereford as patron of the cathedral. [xviii. 17]

ETHELBERT or **ÆTHELBERHT** (*d.* 866), king of the West-Saxons and Kentishmen ; king of Wessex, 860, of Kent, according to Asser, 855 ; harassed by Danish marauders. [xviii. 18]

ETHELBURGA or **ÆTHELBURH,** SAINT (*d.* 676 ?), abbess of Barking ; appointed abbess of Barking by her brother, Erkenwald [q. v.], bishop of London.
[xviii. 19]

ETHELDREDA, SAINT (630 ?-679), queen of Northumbria and abbess of Ely ; married Tonbert, prince of the fen-men, 652, and, subsequently, Egfrid, son of Oswy of Northumbria ; disowned marriage duties ; induced by Wilfrid to enter a monastery ; founded an abbey at Ely ; consecrated abbess of Ely, 673 ; eulogised by Bæda. The present cathedral of Ely was subsequently erected over her tomb. [xviii. 19]

ETHELFLEDA, ÆTHELFLÆD, or **ÆLFLED** (*d.* 918 ?), the 'lady of the Mercians' ; daughter of King Ælfred ; married to Æthelred, ealdorman of the Mercians, *c.* 880 ; made alliance with Welsh and Scots of Ireland ; inspired defence of Chester against Ingwar, a Norwegian chief who had been given land in the neighbourhood ; 'Lady of the Mercians' after Æthelred's death in 912 ; built fortresses in Mercia ; stormed Brecknock, 916.
[xviii. 21]

ETHELFRID, ÆTHELFRITH, or **AEDILFRID** (*d.* 617), king of the Northumbrians, 593 ; called Flesaurs ; defeated Scots, British, and Irish at Dægstastane, 603 ; defeated Welsh near Chester, 613 ; defeated and slain by Rædwald of East Anglia. [xviii. 22]

ETHELGAR, ÆTHELGAR, or **ALGAR** (*d.* 990), archbishop of Canterbury ; abbot of Newminster (Hyde Abbey), near Winchester, when Æthelwold expelled the secular clergy, 964 ; bishop of Selsey, 980 ; archbishop of Canterbury, 988. [xviii. 23]

ETHELGIVA (*fl.* 956). [See ÆLFGIFU.]

ETHELHARD, ÆTHELHEARD, ADELARD, or **EDELRED** (*d.* 805), archbishop of Canterbury ; elected archbishop of Canterbury, 791 ; consecrated, 793, the delay being due to the Kentish men's dislike of a prelate interested in maintaining the primacy of Lichfield ; refugee at the Mercian court, 797-8 ; recognised as metropolitan, 803. [xviii. 23]

ETHELMÆR, ELMER, or **ÆLMER** (*d.* 1137), also called HERLEWIN, ascetic writer ; prior of Christ Church, Canterbury, 1128 ; supported Archbishop William of Corbeuil against the convent, 1136 ; wrote 'De exercitiis spiritualis vitæ,' also a volume of letters destroyed in the Cottonian Library fire, 1731. [xviii. 25]

ETHELMÆR (*d.* 1260). [See AYMER (or ÆTHELMÆR) DE VALENCE (or DE LUSIGNAN).]

ETHELNOTH, ÆTHELNOTH, Lat. EGELNODUS or EDNODUS (*d.* 1038), archbishop of Canterbury ; related to kings of Wessex ; one of Cnut's chaplains ; archbishop of Canterbury, 1020 ; supported Harthacnut ; called 'the Good.' [xviii. 25]

ETHELRED or **ÆTHELRED I** (*d.* 871), king of the West-Saxons and Kentishmen ; king, 866 ; saved Mercia from Danish invaders, 868 ; defeated by the Danes near Reading, 871 ; routed the Danes at Ashdown in a battle supposed to be commemorated by the 'White Horse' at Uffington ; mortally wounded at Merton. [xviii. 25]

ETHELRED or **ÆTHELRED** (*d.* 889), archbishop of Canterbury ; monk of Christ Church, Canterbury ; archbishop, 870-89. [xviii. 27]

ETHELRED or **ÆTHELRED II,** the UNREADY (i.e. the resourceless) (968 ?-1016), king of England ; son of Eadgar ; came to the crown (978) through the murder of his brother Edward the Martyr [q. v.]; induced by covetousness and the representations of his favourite, Æthelsine, to ravage the see of Rochester, 986 ; bought the alliance of the Norwegian invader, Olaf Tryggvason, 991 ; defeated Olaf's fleet, 992 ; bought off an attack by Olaf and Swend, 994 ; published laws regulating bail and surety and (997) a police code ; unsuccessfully invaded Cotentin, 1000 ; married Emma [q. v.], daughter of Richard the Fearless, duke of Normandy ; massacred the Danes settled in England, 1002 ; attacked by Malcolm, king of Scots, 1006 ; promulgated code of military regulations, 1008 ; ordered 'the whole nation' to be called out against the Danes ; crippled by Danish sympathies of his favourite, Edric or Eadric Streona [q. v.] ; bought off the Danes for 48,000*l.*, 1012 ; fled to Rouen (1013) after Swend of Denmark had been formally chosen king of England, 1013 ; brought back to England by Olaf and the witan after Swend's death, 1014 ; expelled King Cnut, 1014 ; implicated in the assassination of the Danish thegns Sigeferth and Morkere, 1015. [xviii. 27]

ETHELRED, ÆTHELRED, AILRED, or **AELRED** (1109 ?-1166), historical writer ; in the service of Prince Henry of Scotland ; abbot of Revesby ; abbot of Rievaulx, 1146-66 ; brought about meeting of Henry II of England and Louis VII of France with Pope Alexander III at Touci, 1162 ; composed rhythmical prose eulogy of St. Cuthbert ; missionary to Galloway Picts, whose chief he persuaded to become a monk ; canonised, 1191. His works include 'Vita et Miracula S. Edwardi Regis et Confessoris,' 'De Bello Standardii,' and 'Chronicon ab Adam ad Henricum I.' [xviii. 33]

ETHELSTAN, ÆTHELSTAN, or **ÆLFSTAN** (*fl.* 946), ealdorman of East Anglia, *c.* 929 ; member of the royal house of Wessex ; nicknamed 'the Half-king,' by reason of his great power ; became a monk at Glastonbury, 956. [xviii. 35]

ETHELWERD or **ÆTHELWEARD** (*d.* 998 ?), chronicler ; styled himself 'Patricius Consul Fabius Quæstor' (ealdorman) in his Latin chronicle ; possibly the ealdorman who persuaded Olaf of Norway to conclude the treaty of Andover with Æthelred II, 994 ; compiled a history extending from the creation to 973 A.D., first edited by Savile, 1596. [xviii. 35]

ETHELWINE, ÆTHELWINE, or **AILWIN** (*d.* 992), ealdorman of East Anglia ; son of the ealdorman Ethelstan [q. v.]; ealdorman, 962 ; built and endowed Benedictine monastery in the isle of Ramsey in Huntingdonshire at the suggestion of Oswald, bishop of Worcester, 968 ; abbot, though a layman, with Oswald ; defended the monasteries of East Anglia against the Mercian faction, 975 ; chief ealdorman, 983. [xviii. 36]

ETHELWOLD, ÆTHELWOLD, or **ADELWOLD,** SAINT (908 ?-984), bishop of Winchester ; dean of Glastonbury Abbey ; refounded a monastic house at Abingdon, *c.* 954 ; introduced the strict Benedictine rule from Fleury ; bishop of Winchester, 963 ; forcibly expelled the secular clerks from Winchester, Chertsey, Milton, and Ely, with King Eadgar's support ; narrowly escaped being poisoned ; rebuilt church of Peterborough ; built a new cathedral at Winchester ; restored the nunnery at Winchester ; author of a treatise on the circle and translator of the 'Regularis concordia.' [xviii. 37]

ETHELWULF, ÆTHELWULF, ADELWLF, or **ATHULF** (*d.* 858), king of the West-Saxons and Kentishmen ; bishop of Winchester ; made king of Kent, Sussex, and Surrey by his father, Ecgberht, 828 ; king of Wessex, 839 ; defeated by the Danes in a naval engagement, 842 ; routed the Danes at Ockley, 852 ; freed a tenth part of the folclands from all burdens except the *trinoda necessitas,* *c.* 854 ; made a pilgrimage to Rome, possibly originating the payment of Peter's pence ; married Judith, daughter of Charles the Bald, at Verberie, 856; declined to make war upon his rebellious son Æthelbald, and allowed him Wessex; by his will charged every ten hides of his property with the support of a poor man (857 ?). [xviii. 40]

ETHEREGE or ETHRYGG, GEORGE, in Latin EDRYCUS (*fl.* 1588), classical scholar; scholar of Corpus Christi College, Oxford, 1534; probationer-fellow, 1539; M.A., 1543; M.B., 1545; regius professor of Greek, 1547–1550 and 1554–9; deprived as a catholic, 1559. His works include a Latin translation of part of Justin Martyr. [xviii. 43]

ETHEREGE, SIR GEORGE (1635 ?–1691), dramatist; employed by Charles II and James II on diplomatic missions; knighted; produced 'Comical Revenge,' 1664, 'She would if she could,' 1667, and 'The Man of Mode,' 1676, three comedies; helped to popularise rhyme in comedy. [xviii. 44]

ETHERIDGE, JOHN WESLEY (1804–1866), Wesleyan minister; second minister in the Brighton circuit, 1831; Ph.D. Heidelberg, 1847; principal work, 'The Targums of Onkelos and Jonathan Ben Uzziel on the Pentateuch, &c.,' 1862 and 1865. [xviii. 45]

ETKINS, JAMES (1613 ?–1687). [See ATKINE, JAMES.]

ETTY, WILLIAM (1787–1849), painter; studied in the Royal Academy school at Somerset House; first exhibited at the Royal Academy, 1811; travelled on the continent; made a great impression with 'Cleopatra,' 1821; R.A., 1828; sold his 'Joan of Arc' pictures for 2,500*l.* Some minor works are in National Gallery, London, and at South Kensington. [xviii. 45]

EUGENE (*d.* 618). [See EOGHAN.]

EUGENIUS I, unhistorical king of Scotland, (according to Buchanan) thirty-ninth king after Fergus Mac Ferchard. [xviii. 47]

EUGENIUS II, (according to Buchanan) forty-first king of Scotland; supposed son of Fergus Mac Earc. [xviii. 47]

EUGENIUS III, (according to Buchanan) forty-sixth king of Scotland. [xviii. 47]

EUGENIUS IV, (according to Buchanan) fifty-first king of Scotland; identified with Eochoid Buidhe (reigned 606–29). [xviii. 48]

EUGENIUS V, (according to Buchanan) fifty-sixth king of Scotland; identified with Eochoid Rinnenhail (*c.* 670). [xviii. 48]

EUGENIUS VI (*fl.* 650), (according to Buchanan) fifty-seventh king of Scotland; also called Eogan and Ewen; contemporary with Adamnan. [xviii. 48]

EUGENIUS VII, (according to Buchanan) fifty-ninth king of Scotland; reigned 680–97. [xviii. 48]

EUGENIUS VIII, (according to Buchanan) sixty-second king of Scotland; reigned 761–4. [xviii. 48]

EUGENIUS PHILALETHES (pseudonym). [See VAUGHAN, THOMAS, 1622–1666.]

EUSDEN, LAURENCE (1688–1730), poet laureate; scholar of Trinity College, Cambridge, 1706; M.A., 1712; fellow, 1712; given the laureateship (1718) by the Duke of Newcastle, whose marriage he had celebrated, 1717; rector of Coningsby; the 'L.E.' of Pope and Swift's treatise on bathos; published metrical panegyrics and translations from Claudian and Statius. [xviii. 48]

EUSTACE (*d.* 1215), bishop of Ely; vice-chancellor, keeper of the royal seal, and (1197) chancellor; dean of Salisbury; bishop of Ely, 1197; sent by Richard I to remonstrate with Philip Augustus of France on alleged infringements of the five years' peace; one of three prelates selected by Pope Innocent III to urge King John to recognise Stephen Langton as primate, 1208; pronounced the interdict and escaped, 1208; associated with Archbishop Langton in procuring from Rome sentence of deposition on King John. [xviii. 49]

EUSTACE, JAMES, third VISCOUNT BALTINGLAS (*d.* 1585); headed an Irish catholic insurrection in 1580; escaped to Spain; outlawed and attainted; died in Spain. [xviii. 51]

EUSTACE, JOHN CHETWODE (1762 ?–1815), classical antiquary; took the habit at St. Gregory's Convent,

Douay; priest; friend of Edmund Burke; recorded his continental travels in 'A Tour through Italy,' 1813, written in a 'latitudinarian spirit.' [xviii. 52]

EUSTACE, ROLAND FITZ, BARON PORTLESTER (*d.* 1496), lord-treasurer in Ireland, 1454 (confirmed 1461); created Baron Portlester, 1461; twice accused of treason falsely; chancellor in Ireland, 1472–82 and 1488–96; took part in the Lambert Simnel rebellion, 1487. [xviii. 53]

EVANS, ABEL (1679–1737), divine and poet; educated at Merchant Taylors' School; probationer-fellow, St. John's College, Oxford, 1692; M.A., 1699; D.D., 1711; expelled from chaplaincy of his college, but reinstated by Duchess of Marlborough's influence; famous for his satire on 'The Apparition: a dialogue betwixt the Devil and a Doctor concerning the rights of the Christian Church,' 1710; epigrammatist. [xviii. 54]

EVANS, ANNE (1820–1870), poet and musical composer; daughter of Arthur Benoni Evans [q. v.] [xviii. 55]

EVANS, ARISE (*b.* 1607). [See EVANS, RHYS or RICE.]

EVANS, ARTHUR BENONI (1781–1854), miscellaneous writer; son of Lewis Evans (1755–1827) [q. v.]; M.A. St. John's College, Oxford, 1820; D.D., 1828; professor of classics and history in the Royal Military College, 1805–22; held country curacies; head-master of Market Bosworth grammar school, 1829–54. His works include 'Leicestershire Words, Phrases, and Proverbs,' 1848, and poems and sermons. [xviii. 54]

EVANS, BENJAMIN (1740–1821), Welsh congregational minister; published abolitionist and sectarian works in Welsh. [xviii. 55]

EVANS, BROOKE (1797–1862), nickel refiner; partner with a gunmaker in New York; indigo planter and merchant in Central America; amateur navigator; associated with one Askin in a venture for refining nickel from nickel-speiss; built works at Birmingham, 1835; obtained nickel from nickel-ore containing cobalt. [xviii. 56]

EVANS, CALEB (1831–1886), geologist; educated at University College School; clerk in the chancery pay office, 1852–82; F.G.S., 1867; first English geologist to divide Croydon and Oxted limestone into zones. [xviii. 56]

EVANS, CHARLES SMART (1778–1849), vocalist and composer; gentleman of Chapel Royal; alto singer in the chorus of the 'Ancient Concerts' of 1798; composed part-songs, motetts, and a 'Magnificat.' [xviii. 57]

EVANS, CHRISTMAS (1766–1838), one of the great Welsh preachers; originally a farm labourer; baptist minister in Anglesey, 1792–1826, ruling autocratically; called the 'Bunyan of Wales'; his sermons published in Welsh. [xviii. 57]

EVANS, CORNELIUS (*fl.* 1648), impostor; a native of Marseilles; impersonated Charles, prince of Wales, at Sandwich, 1648; escaped from Newgate, 1648. [xviii. 58]

EVANS, DANIEL (1774–1835), independent minister in North Wales, 1796–1835; published Welsh memoirs and sectarian works. [xviii. 58]

EVANS, DANIEL (1792–1846), Welsh poet; commonly called DANIEL DU O GEREDIGION; fellow of Jesus College, Oxford; M.A., 1817; B.D., 1824; took orders; committed suicide, 1846; published Welsh poems. [xviii. 59]

EVANS, DAVID MORIER (1819–1874), financial journalist; assistant city correspondent on the 'Times'; started the 'Hour,' 1873; bankrupt on its failure; published financial works. [xviii. 59]

EVANS, EDWARD (*fl.* 1615), divine; educated at Winchester and New College, Oxford; M.A., 1602; fellow, 1595–1604; published sermons, 1615. [xviii. 59]

EVANS, EDWARD (1716–1798), Welsh poet and bard of Druidic descent; pastor at Aberdare, 1772–98. [xviii. 60]

EVANS, EDWARD (1789–1835), printseller; published 'Catalogue of a Collection of Engraved Portraits.' [xviii. 60]

EVANS, EDWARD DAVID (1818–1860), printseller; son of Edward Evans (1789–1835) [q. v.] [xviii. 60]

EVANS, EVAN (1731–1789), Welsh poet and antiquary; studied at Merton College, Oxford; took orders; embodied his researches in 'Some Specimens of the . . . Antient Welsh Bards, translated into English,' 1764; published one English and several Welsh poems; granted an annuity by Paul Panton of Anglesey on condition of bequeathing him his manuscripts. [xviii. 60]

EVANS, EVAN (1804–1886), founder and pastor (1881–6) of the first Welsh church in Arkansas, U.S.A.; known as EVANS BACH NANTYGLO; published nonconformist treatises in Welsh. [xviii. 61]

EVANS, EVAN HERBER (1836–1896), Welsh divine; studied at Normal College, Swansea, and Memorial College, Brecon; ordained pastor of Libanus Church, Morriston, 1862; pastor of Salem Church, Carnarvon, 1865–94; lecturer on homiletics at 'Bala-Bangor' Congregational College, 1891; became principal, 1894; editor of 'Y Dysgedydd' ('The Instructor'), 1880–96; popular preacher. [Suppl. ii. 194]

EVANS, SIR FREDERICK JOHN OWEN (1815–1885), hydrographer; second-class volunteer in the navy, 1828; surveyed the Coral Sea, the great barrier reef, and Torres Straits, 1841–6; published, when superintendent of the compass department, a 'Report on Compass Deviations in the Royal Navy,' 1860; captain, 1872; hydrographer to the admiralty, 1874–84; K.C.B., 1881. [xviii. 61]

EVANS, GEORGE (1630?–1702), antiquary; fellow of Jesus College, Cambridge; canon of Windsor, 1660; D.D. Cambridge, 1665; his collections on the history of St. George's Chapel printed in Ashmole's 'Berkshire,' 1719. [xviii. 62]

EVANS, SIR GEORGE DE LACY (1787–1870), general; ensign, 1807; served against Amír Khán, 1807; lieutenant, 1809; served in Peninsula; twice wounded before New Orleans, 1814 and 1815; engaged at Waterloo, 1815; lieutenant-colonel by brevet, 1815; M.P., Rye, 1831, Westminster, 1833; commanded British legion aiding Christina of Spain against Don Carlos, 1835–7; rendered great services to the Spanish government at Bilbao, Hernani, and elsewhere; K.C.B., 1837; grand cross of St. Ferdinand and Charles III; M.P., Westminster, 1846, 1852, 1857, and 1859–65; repulsed sortie from Sebastopol, 1854; G.C.B., 1855; honorary D.C.L. Oxford; general, 1861. [xviii. 62]

EVANS, JOHN (d. 1724), bishop of Meath; B.A. Jesus College, Oxford, 1671; minister at Fort St. George, Madras, 1692; engaged in merchandise; bishop of Bangor, 1702; opposed the peace, 1712; bishop of Meath, 1716–24. [xviii. 64]

EVANS, JOHN (1680?–1730), divine; congregational minister at Wrexham, 1702–4; sole pastor of the Hand Alley meeting-house, Westminster, 1716; honorary D.D. Edinburgh and Aberdeen; completed part of a history of nonconformity from the Reformation to the civil war. [xviii. 65]

EVANS, JOHN (1693?–1734?), actor; joint-manager of Smock Alley Theatre, Dublin. [xviii. 66]

EVANS, JOHN (d. 1779), curate of Portsmouth; published a 'Harmony of the Four Gospels,' in Welsh, 1765. [xviii. 66]

EVANS, JOHN (fl. 1812), author; B.A. Jesus College, Oxford, 1792; author of 'North Wales,' 1812, and kindred works. [xviii. 68]

EVANS, JOHN (1767–1827), baptist minister; matriculated at King's College, Aberdeen, 1787; M.A. Edinburgh; general baptist pastor, Worship Street, London, 1792–1827; F.S.A., 1803–25; LL.D. Brown University, 1819; published miscellaneous writings. [xviii. 66]

EVANS, JOHN (1774–1828), printer; printed and edited the 'Bristol Observer,' 1819–23; published work on psalmody, 1823, and a history of Bristol, 1824; killed by the sudden falling of the Brunswick Theatre, Well Street. [xviii. 67]

EVANS, JOHN (d. 1832), miscellaneous writer; kept private schools in Bristol and London; published essays and topographical notices of Bristol. [xviii. 68]

EVANS, JOHN, OF LLWYNFFORTUN (1779–1847), Welsh methodist; methodist deacon, 1808; curate in the episcopal church; returned to methodism; a famous preacher. [xviii. 68]

EVANS, JOHN (1814–1876), better known as I. D. FFRAID, Welsh poet and Calvinistic methodist minister;

published poems, 1835, and a 'History of the Jews,' 1830, in Welsh; translated the 'Night Thoughts' and 'Paradise Lost' into Welsh. [xviii. 69]

EVANS, JOHN, 'EGLWYSBACH' (1840–1897), Welsh Wesleyan divine; shepherd; ordained, 1865; pastor at Liverpool, 1866–9, and 1872–8, Bangor, 1869–72, and 1886–9, Oswestry, 1889–90, and London, 1878–86 and 1890–1893; member of Legal hundred of Wesleyan conference, 1884, and chairman of South Wales district, 1895; organised and conducted 'forward movement' mission in Glamorgan; frequently styled 'the Welsh Spurgeon'; published biographical and religious writings in Welsh. [Suppl. ii. 195]

EVANS, LEWIS (fl. 1574), controversialist; M.A. Christ Church, Oxford, 1557; B.D., 1562; offended Bishop Grindal by his zealous catholicism, and fled the country; published at Antwerp an attack on protestantism, 1565; published attacks on Romanism after 1568. [xviii. 69]

EVANS, LEWIS (1755–1827), mathematician; matriculated at Merton College, Oxford, 1774; vicar of Froxfield, Wiltshire, 1788–1827; first mathematical master, Royal Military Academy, Woolwich, 1799–1820; F.R.S., 1823; F.A.S.; contributed to 'Philosophical Magazine.' [xviii. 70]

EVANS, PHILIP (1645–1679), jesuit; studied at St. Omer; missioner in North Wales, 1675; executed during Popish plot persecution. [xviii. 70]

EVANS, RHYS or RICE (b. 1607), fanatic; adopted name of ARISE EVANS; independent; imprisoned on the charge that he had declared himself to be Christ, 1647; petitioned Cromwell to restore Charles II, 1653; published mystical tracts. [xviii. 70]

EVANS, RICHARD (1784–1871), portrait-painter and copyist; painted in Rome a fresco which he afterwards found hanging at South Kensington as an antique; exhibited portraits at the Royal Academy from 1816. [xviii. 71]

EVANS, ROBERT HARDING (1778–1857), bookseller and auctioneer; son of Thomas Evans (1742–1784) [q. v.]; educated at Westminster; sold the Duke of Roxburghe's library, 1812; edited Thomas Evans's 'Old Ballads,' 1810, and other works. [xviii. 71]

EVANS, ROBERT WILSON (1789–1866), archdeacon of Westmoreland and author; educated at Shrewsbury and Trinity College, Cambridge; fellow, 1813; M.A., 1814; B.D., 1842; archdeacon of Westmoreland, 1856–65. His works include 'Tales of the Ancient British Church,' 1840. [xviii. 72]

EVANS, SAMUEL (d. 1835?), landscape-painter; taught the daughter of George III drawing; drawing-master at Eton. [xviii. 76]

EVANS, THEOPHILUS (1694–1767), divine; educated at Shrewsbury; clergyman in South Wales, 1728–67; published a 'History of Modern Enthusiasm,' 1752 and 1759, and an uncritical relation of Welsh antiquities. [xviii. 73]

EVANS, THOMAS (d. 1633), poet; M.A. Corpus Christi College, Cambridge, 1616; B.D., 1628; rector of Little Holland, 1618–33; published a poem, 'Œdipus,' 1615, which is now very rare. [xviii. 73]

EVANS, THOMAS (1742–1784), bookseller; edited, among other works, Shakespeare's 'Poems,' 1774, and Prior's 'Works,' 1779; published collection of 'Old Ballads,' 1777. [xviii. 73]

EVANS, THOMAS (1739–1803), bookseller; publisher of the 'Morning Chronicle'; printed in his 'London Packet' a letter reflecting on Oliver Goldsmith and Miss Horneck, 1773. [xviii. 74]

EVANS, THOMAS (TOMOS GLYN COTHI) (1766–1833), Welsh poet; pilloried and imprisoned for singing a Welsh song 'On Liberty,' 1797; minister at Aberdare, 1811–33; published theological works. [xviii. 74]

EVANS, THOMAS (TELYNOG) (1840–1865), Welsh poet; sailor, and subsequently collier; his poetical works collected, 1866. [xviii. 74]

EVANS, THOMAS SIMPSON (1777–1818), mathematician; son of Lewis Evans (1755–1827) [q. v.]; assistant at Greenwich Observatory, 1800–5; mathematical master at Woolwich, 1803–10, at Christ's Hospital, 1813–18; LL.D.; translated Cagnoli's 'Trigonometria piana e sferica.' [xviii. 75]

EVANS, WILLIAM (*d.* 1720?), presbyterian divine; pastor in Carmarthenshire, 1688–1718; founder of the Welsh academy system; published theological work in Welsh, 1707.   [xviii. 75]

EVANS, WILLIAM (*d.* 1776?), Welsh lexicographer; presbyterian minister; compiled English-Welsh dictionary, 1771.   [xviii. 76]

EVANS, WILLIAM (1811?–1858), landscape-painter; styled 'Evans of Bristol'; his best-known work 'Traeth Mawr.'   [xviii. 76]

EVANS, WILLIAM (1798–1877), water-colour painter; son of Samuel Evans [q. v.]; exhibited at the Old Society of Painters in Water-colours from 1828; drawing-master at Eton, 1818–27; house-master at Eton, 1840–77; helped to reform the school.   [xviii. 76]

EVANS, SIR WILLIAM DAVID (1767–1821), lawyer; educated at Harrow; attorney, 1789; barrister, Gray's Inn, 1794; stipendiary magistrate for Manchester, 1813–1818; knighted, 1819; recorder of Bombay, 1819–21; translated Pothier's 'Law of Obligations and Contracts,' 1806, and wrote legal works.   [xviii. 77]

EVANS, WILLIAM EDWARD (1801–1869), divine and naturalist; educated at Shrewsbury; scholar of Clare Hall, Cambridge; M.A., 1826; prebendary and prælector of Hereford, 1845; canon, 1861; published 'The Song of the Birds,' 1845.   [xviii. 77]

EVANSON, EDWARD (1731–1805), divine; M.A. Emmanuel College, Cambridge, 1753; incumbent of Longdon; prosecuted in the consistory court for unitarianism, 1771; chaplain to Wedderburne, the solicitor-general, 1775; assailed trinitarianism in 'A Letter to Dr. Hurd,' 1777; resigned Longdon, 1778; established school at Mitcham, 1778. His works include 'The Dissonance of the four . . . Evangelists,' 1792. [xviii. 78]

EVELEIGH, JOHN (1748–1814), provost of Oriel College, Oxford; B.A. Wadham College, Oxford, 1770; fellow of Oriel, 1770; M.A., 1772; B.D., 1782; D.D., 1783; dean of Oriel, 1775–81; provost, 1781; vicar of St. Mary's, Oxford, 1778–81, and of Aylesford, 1782–92; prebendary of Rochester, 1781.   [Suppl. ii. 196]

EVELYN, SIR GEORGE AUGUSTUS WILLIAM SHUCKBURGH- (1751–1804). [See SHUCKBURGH-EVELYN.]

EVELYN, JOHN, the younger (1655–1699), translator; son of John Evelyn (1620–1706) [q. v.]; entered Trinity College, Oxford, 1667; admitted at the Middle Temple, 1692; a commissioner of revenue in Ireland, 1692–1696; translated Rapinus's Latin poem 'Of Gardens,' 1673.   [xviii. 83]

EVELYN, JOHN (1620–1706), virtuoso; student at the Middle Temple, 1637; fellow commoner at Balliol. 1637; joined Charles I, 1642; travelled; bought 'rare tables of veins and nerves' at Padua, 1645; travelling companion of the poet Waller, 1646; translated La Mothe Le Vayer's 'Of Liberty and Servitude,' 1649; settled at Sayes Court, Deptford, 1653; proposed to Robert Boyle a scheme which was afterwards developed into the Royal Society; member of council of foreign plantations, 1671; a commissioner for privy seal, 1685–7; secretary to Royal Society, 1672; his property at Sayes Court wantonly desecrated by Peter the Great when tenant, 1698; appointed Bentley to first Boyle lectureship; a recognised authority on numismatics, architecture, and landscape gardening. His works include 'Sculptura,' 1662, 'Sylva,' 1664, and 'A Character of England,' 1659. His 'Diary' was first published in 1818 and 1819.   [xviii. 79]

EVERARD (1083?–1150). [See EBORARD.]

EVERARD, JOHN (*fl.* 1611), Roman catholic student, converted to catholicism at Clare Hall, Cambridge; probationer in the English College at Rome, 1610; published 'Britanno-Romanvs' (autobiography), 1611. [xviii. 83]

EVERARD, JOHN (1575?–1650?), divine and mystic; M.A. Clare College, Cambridge, 1607; D.D., 1619; imprisoned for censuring Spanish outrages in the Indies, 1621 and 1622; deprived by the high commission court of his living at Fairstead, 1636; fined 1,000*l.*, 1639; translated the 'Pœmander' of Hermes Trismegistus, 1650. His 'Parable of Two Drops reasoning together' was republished in 1865.   [xviii. 84]

EVERARD, MATHIAS (*d.* 1857), major-general; ensign, 1804; captured by the French, 1805; led the forlorn hope at Monte Video, 1807; fought at Coruña and siege of Flushing, 1809; commanded flank battalion at storming of Bhurtpore, 1825; C.B. and brevet lieutenant-colonel; major-general, 1851; knight of Hanoverian order.   [xviii. 85]

EVERARD, ROBERT (*fl.* 1664), Roman catholic writer; captain during the civil war; published work vindicating his conversion to catholicism, 1664.   [xviii. 85]

EVERARD, *alias* EVERETT, THOMAS (1560–1633), jesuit; studied at Cambridge and (1592–3) at Rheims; socius and master of jesuit novices at Louvain; missioner in England, 1604 and 1617; banished, 1621; subsequently missioner in Suffolk; translated Latin and Italian religious works.   [xviii. 86]

EVERDON, SILVESTER DE (*d.* 1254), bishop of Carlisle; held livings in Northamptonshire from 1219; keeper of great seal, 1244; archdeacon of Chester, 1245; bishop of Carlisle, 1246; justice itinerant, 1251–2; joined other bishops in enforcing Magna Carta, 1253.   [Suppl. ii. 196]

EVEREST, SIR GEORGE (1790–1866), military engineer; East India cadet, 1806; made survey of Java for Sir Stamford Raffles, 1813–15; superintendent of survey, Hyderabad, 1823; surveyor-general of India; lieutenant-colonel, 1838; C.B., 1861; knighted, 1861; F.R.A.S. and F.R.G.S.; published two accounts of measurements on the Meridional Arc of India, 1830 and 1847. Mount Everest is named after him.   [xviii. 86]

EVERETT, JAMES (1784–1872), miscellaneous writer; expelled from Wesleyan conference and ministry, 1849, as author of 'Wesleyan Takings' and the suspected author of the 'Fly Sheets' of 1845 and after; established 'United Methodist Free Church,' 1857; first president of secessionist assembly, 1857; published memoirs, brochures, and histories of methodism.   [xviii. 87]

EVERITT, ALLEN EDWARD (1824–1882), artist; executed water-colour drawings of mediæval remains in the midlands, Belgium, France, and Germany; hon. secretary of Royal Society of Artists of Birmingham, 1858–82, of archæological section of Midland Institute, 1870.   [xviii. 88]

EVERSDEN or **EVERISDEN**, JOHN OF (*fl.* 1300), chronicler; cellarer of the Benedictine abbey of Bury St. Edmunds, 1300; proctor for his abbot, 1307; his 'Series temporum ab initio mundi,' originally supposed a continuation of Florence of Worcester.   [xviii. 89]

EVERSLEY, VISCOUNT (1794–1888). [See SHAW-LEFEVRE, CHARLES.]

EVESHAM, HUGH OF (*d.* 1287), cardinal; called Atratus, Il Nero, and Le Noir; studied at Oxford and Cambridge and in France and Italy; nicknamed 'Phœnix'; archdeacon of Worcester, 1275; prebendary of York, 1279; physician to Pope Martin IV, 1280; cardinal, 1281; author of 'Canones Medicinales,' 'Distinctiones predicables,' and other works.   [xviii. 90]

EVESHAM, WALTER OF (*fl.* 1320). [See WALTER.]

EWALD, ALEXANDER CHARLES (1842–1891), historical writer; clerk in public record office, 1861; senior clerk, 1890; published popular historical works and assisted in compilation of a calendar and précis of 'Norman Rolls—Henry V.'   [Suppl. ii. 197]

EWALD, CHRISTIAN FERDINAND (1802–1874), missionary; took Anglican orders, 1836; laboured in Jerusalem for London Society for Propagating the Gospel among the Jews from 1841.   [Suppl. ii. 197]

EWART, JOSEPH (1759–1792), diplomatist; educated at Dumfries and Edinburgh University; envoy plenipotentiary to Prussia, 1788–91; succeeded in getting the Prince of Orange re-established as stadtholder; arranged marriage treaty between Duke of York and Frederick William's daughter.   [xviii. 90]

EWART, WILLIAM (1798–1869), politician; educated at Eton and Christ Church, Oxford; Newdigate prizeman, 1820; B.A., 1821; barrister, Middle Temple, 1827; M.P., Bletchingley, 1828–30, Liverpool, 1830, 1831, 1832, and 1835, Wigan, 1839, and Dumfries burghs, 1841–

1868 ; free trader ; brought about an act for restricting capital punishment, 1837 ; carried bill establishing free public libraries, 1850 ; published speeches. [xviii. 91]

EWBANK, JOHN W. (1799 ?–1847), painter ; foundation member of Royal Scottish Academy, 1830 ; painted historical pieces and marine subjects. [xviii. 92]

EWBANK, THOMAS (1792–1870), writer on practical mechanics ; manufacturer of lead, tin, and copper tubing in New York, 1819–36 ; related his travels in 'Life in Brazil,' 1856 ; commissioner of patents, 1849–52 ; president of American Ethnological Society ; published 'The World a Workshop,' 1855, and works on physics and hydraulics. [xviii. 92]

EWEN, JOHN (1741–1821), supposed author of 'O weel may the boatie row' ; hardware retailer in Aberdeen ; left 14,000l. by a will (disallowed by the House of Lords) to found an educational charity in Montrose. [xviii. 93]

EWENS, alias NEWPORT, MAURICE (1611–1687). [See NEWPORT.]

EWER, EWERS, or **EWRES**, ISAAC (d. 1650), regicide ; parliamentarian colonel of foot ; custodian of Charles I in Hurst Castle ; signed death-warrant, 1649. [xviii. 93]

EWER, JOHN (d. 1774), bishop of Bangor ; educated at Eton ; B.A. King's College, Cambridge, 1728 ; fellow ; M.A., 1732 ; canon of Windsor, 1738 ; prebendary of Hereford, 1751 ; D.D., 1756 ; bishop of Llandaff, 1761–8, of Bangor, 1768–74 ; preached against the American colonists as profligates, 1767. [xviii. 94]

EWIN, WILLIAM HOWELL (1731 ?–1804), usurer ; M.A. St. John's College, Cambridge, 1756 ; LL.D., 1766 ; J.P. for Cambridgeshire ; suspended from his degrees by the vice-chancellor, 1778, for lending money at usury to a student ; restored in 1779, there being no university statute against his offence ; deprived of his commission, 1781. [xviii. 94]

EWING, GREVILLE (1767–1841), congregational minister ; studied at Edinburgh ; first secretary, Edinburgh Missionary Society, 1796 ; forbidden by the East India Company to go as missionary to India ; abandoned church of Scotland ; superintended congregational charge at Glasgow, 1799–1836 ; tutor of the Glasgow Theological Academy, 1809–36 ; published Greek grammar and lexicon for New Testament students, 1801. [xviii. 95]

EWING, JULIANA HORATIA (1841–1885), writer for the young ; née Gatty ; her first story published in the 'Monthly Packet,' 1861 ; produced 'Melchior's Dream,' 1862 ; started 'Aunt Judy's Magazine,' 1866 ; married Major Alexander Ewing, 1867 ; wrote many soldier-stories. [xviii. 96]

EXETER, DUKES OF. [See HOLLAND, JOHN, 1352 ?–1400 ; BEAUFORT, SIR THOMAS, d. 1427 ; HOLLAND, JOHN, 1395–1447.]

EXETER, MARQUIS OF (1496?–1538). [See COURTENAY, HENRY.]

EXETER, MARCHIONESS OF (d. 1558). [See COURTENAY, GERTRUDE.]

EXETER, first EARL OF (1542–1622). [See CECIL, THOMAS.]

EXETER, JOHN OF (d. 1268). [See JOHN.]

EXETER, JOSEPH OF (fl. 1190). [See JOSEPH.]

EXETER, STEPHEN OF (fl. 1265). [See STEPHEN.]

EXETER, WALTER OF (fl. 1301), Cluniac monk ; wrote a variant of the 'Guy of Warwick' romance. [xviii. 96]

EXETER, WILLIAM OF (fl. 1330 ?), author of 'Determinationes' against Ockham ; D.D. ; canon of Exeter. [xviii. 96]

EXETER, WILLIAM OF (fl. 1360 ?), physician to Queen Philippa ; precentor of Lincoln. [xviii. 97]

EXETER, WILLIAM OF (d. 1365 ?), author of sermons on the Beatitudes. [xviii. 96]

EXLEY, THOMAS (1775–1855), mathematician ; M.A. ; joined William Moore Johnson in bringing out 'The Imperial Encyclopædia,' 1812. His other writings include 'Physical Optics,' 1834. [xviii. 97]

EXMEW, WILLIAM (1507 ?–1535), Carthusian ; educated at Christ's College, Cambridge ; steward of the London Charterhouse, 1535 (?) ; hanged for denying the king's supremacy, 1535. [xviii. 97]

EXMOUTH, first VISCOUNT (1757–1833). [See PELLEW, EDWARD.]

EXSHAW, CHARLES (d. 1771), painter and engraver ; first exhibited, 1764 ; etched mainly after Rembrandt. [xviii. 97]

EXTON, JOHN (1600 ?–1665 ?), admiralty lawyer ; M.A. Trinity Hall, Cambridge, 1623 ; LL.D., 1634 ; admiralty judge, 1649–65 ; published 'The Maritime Dicæologie,' 1664. [xviii. 98]

EXTON, SIR THOMAS (1631–1688), admiralty lawyer ; son of John Exton [q. v.] ; educated at Merchant Taylors' School and Trinity Hall, Cambridge ; LL.D., 1662 ; member of Gray's Inn, 1648 ; knighted ; admiralty judge before 1678 ; advocate-general ; M.P. Cambridge University, 1679, 1681, and 1685 ; master of Trinity Hall, Cambridge, 1676–88. [xviii. 98]

EYRE, CHARLES (1784–1864), miscellaneous writer ; B.A. Trinity College, Cambridge, 1807 ; took orders ; unitarian ; newspaper proprietor at Colchester ; committed suicide. His 'Fall of Adam' (1852) is an 'amended' edition of 'Paradise Lost.' [xviii. 98]

EYRE, EDMUND JOHN (1767–1816), dramatist ; educated at Merchant Taylors' School and Pembroke Hall, Cambridge ; played Jaques at Drury Lane, 1806 ; published 'Maid of Normandy' (tragedy), 1794, and 'Consequences' (comedy), 1793. [xviii. 98]

EYRE, SIR GILES (d. 1695), judge ; barrister, Lincoln's Inn, 1661 ; recorder of Salisbury ; M.P., Salisbury, 1688–9 ; justice of the king's bench and knighted, 1689. [xviii. 99]

EYRE, SIR JAMES (1734–1799), judge ; scholar of Winchester, 1747 ; matriculated at St. John's College, Oxford, 1749 ; treasurer of Gray's Inn, 1766 ; recorder of London, 1763 ; counsel for Wilkes in Wilkes v. Wood, 1763 ; refused to present to the king London's remonstrance on the exclusion of Wilkes from parliament, 1770 ; knighted, 1772 ; president of court of exchequer, 1787 ; chief commissioner of great seal, 1792–3 ; chief-justice of common pleas, 1793. [xviii. 99]

EYRE, JAMES (1748–1813), philologist ; educated at Catharine Hall, Cambridge ; head-master of Solihull grammar school ; country clergyman ; annotated Johnson's 'English Dictionary' (in manuscript). [xviii. 100]

EYRE, SIR JAMES (1792–1857), physician ; M.R.C.S., 1814 ; mayor of Hereford, 1830 ; knighted, 1830 ; M.B. Edinburgh, 1834 ; M.R.C.P., 1836 ; wrote medical works. [xviii. 100]

EYRE, JOHN (1754–1803), evangelical clergyman ; dissenting minister ; matriculated at Emmanuel College, Cambridge, 1778 ; priest, 1779 ; minister of Homerton, 1785 ; helped to found London Missionary Society, 1795 ; originated scheme (1796) which developed into Hackney Theological College (opened, 1803). [xviii. 100]

EYRE, SIR ROBERT (1666–1735), judge ; son of Sir Samuel Eyre [q. v.] ; barrister, Lincoln's Inn, 1689 ; recorder of Salisbury, 1696 ; M.P., Salisbury, 1698–1710 ; solicitor-general, 1708 ; manager of Sacheverell's impeachment ; judge of queen's bench, 1710 ; knighted, 1710 ; lord chief baron, 1723 ; lord chief-justice of common pleas, 1725. [xviii. 101]

EYRE, SIR SAMUEL (1633–1698), judge ; barrister, Lincoln's Inn, 1661 ; justice of king's bench, 1694 ; upheld the murderer Knollys's claim to privilege of peerage, 1698. [xviii. 102]

EYRE, THOMAS (1670–1715), jesuit ; student at St. Omer ; chaplain to James II at St. Germain ; professor of theology, Liège, 1701–4 ; professed jesuit, 1706 ; socius to his provincial, 1712. [xviii. 102]

EYRE, THOMAS (1748–1810), Roman catholic divine ; professor at the English college, Douay ; president of Crook Hall, 1795–1808, subsequently removing it to Ushaw ; edited John Goter's 'Spiritual Works,' 1790. [xviii. 102]

EYRE, SIR VINCENT (1811–1881), general ; gazetted to Bengal establishment, 1828 ; commissary of ordnance

to Cabul field force, 1839 ; surrendered as hostage to
Akbar Khán, 1842 ; rescued by Sir George Pollock, 1843 ;
appointed to command artillery of 'Gwalior contingent,'
1844 ; founded Esapore, colony for destitute families of
Portuguese natives ; defeated a large native force, 1857 ;
took part in the relief of Lucknow, 1857 ; lieutenant-
colonel and C.B., 1857 ; lieutenant-general, 1863 ; K.C.S.I.,
1867.   [xviii. 103]

EYRE, SIR WILLIAM (1805–1859), major-general ;
educated at Rugby ; ensign, 1823 ; received company in
73rd regiment, 1829 ; major, 1839 ; served in first Kaffir
war, 1847 ; lieutenant-colonel, 1847 ; defeated Kaffirs at
Quibigui River and Committee's Hill, 1851 ; C.B., aide-
de-camp to the queen, and colonel, 1852 ; fought in
Crimean war ; major-general, 1854 ; K.C.B., 1855 ; decorated by France and Turkey, 1856.   [xviii. 104]

EYSTON, BERNARD (1628–1709), Franciscan friar ;
called in religion Bernard à Sancto Francisco ; lector of
divinity at St. Bonaventure's Convent, Douay ; D.D. ;
died at Douay ; wrote 'The Christian Duty compared,'
1684.   [xviii. 105]

EYSTON, CHARLES (1667–1721), antiquary ; chief
work, a history of Glastonbury abbey and town, 1716.
                                                    [xviii. 105]

EYTHAN, BARON (1589 ?–1652 ?). [See KING,
JAMES.]

EYTON, ROBERT WILLIAM (1815–1881), antiquary ; educated at Rugby ; M.A. Christ Church, Oxford, 1845 ; rector of Ryton, 1841–63 ; maintained in 'A
Key to Domesday,' 1877, fiscal character of domesday hide
of land ; published 'The Antiquities of Shropshire,' 1861.
                                                    [xviii. 106]

EYTON or **EDON**, STEPHEN (fl. 1320 ?), chronicler ;
canon of Warter ; wrote 'Acta Edwardi II.'
                                                    [xviii. 107]

EYTON, THOMAS CAMPBELL (1809–1880), naturalist ; correspondent of Agassiz and Darwin ; opponent of
Darwinism ; his chief works, 'A History of the Oyster
and Oyster Fisheries,' 1858, and 'Osteologia Avium,'
1871–8.   [xviii. 107]

EZEKIEL, ABRAHAM EZEKIEL (1757–1806),
miniature-painter and scientific optician ; engraved portraits.   [xviii. 107]

EZEKIEL, SOLOMON (1781–1867), Jewish writer ;
son of Abraham Ezekiel Ezekiel [q. v.] ; settled at Penzance ; published letter to Sir Rose Price, which led to
suspension of efforts to convert Jews of Penzance to
Christianity ; published lectures on the lives of Abraham
and Isaac, 1844–5.   [xviii. 107]

F

FABELL, PETER (fl. 15th cent.), magician and
dabbler in alchemy ; hero of the 'Merry Devil of Edmonton,' a play, which has been wrongly attributed to Shakespeare (first edition, 1608).   [xviii. 107]

FABER, FREDERICK WILLIAM (1814–1863), superior of the London Oratory ; educated at Shrewsbury and
Harrow ; matriculated at Balliol College, Oxford, 1832 ;
scholar of University College, 1834 ; Newdigate prizeman,
1836 ; B.A., 1836 ; fellow of University, 1837 ; M.A., 1839 ;
rector of Elton, 1842–5 ; formed catholic community of
Brothers of the Will of God, 1845 ; joined oratory of
St. Philip Neri, 1848 ; established London Oratory, 1849 ;
created D.D. by Pius IX, 1854 ; friend of Wordsworth and
Newman ; published poems and devotional treatises.
                                                    [xviii. 108]

FABER, GEORGE STANLEY (1773–1854), controversialist ; scholar of University College, Oxford, 1790 ;
fellow of Lincoln, 1793 ; M.A., 1796 ; Bampton lecturer,
1801 ; B.D., 1803 ; vicar of Stockton-upon-Tees, 1805–8 ;
master of Sherburn Hospital, 1832–54 ; prebendary of
Salisbury, 1831. Characteristic works are 'The Origin of
Pagan Idolatry,' a pre-scientific dissertation, 1816, and
'Letters on Tractarian Secessions to Popery,' 1846, and
'The Revival of the French Emperorship, anticipated
from the Necessity of Prophecy,' 1852.   [xviii. 111]

FABER, JOHN, the elder (1660 ?–1721), draughtsman
and mezzotint engraver ; native of the Hague ; engraved
portraits of founders of Oxford (1712) and Cambridge
Colleges.   [xviii. 112]

FABER, JOHN, the younger (1695 ?–1756), mezzotint
engraver ; son of John Faber the elder [q. v.] ; engraved portraits of Charles II, Ignatius Loyola, and
others.   [xviii. 112]

FABRICIUS (fl. 1429). [See CARPENTER, ALEX-
ANDER.]

FABYAN, ROBERT (d. 1513), chronicler ; sheriff of
London, 1493 ; held Newgate and Ludgate against Cornish
rebels, 1498 ; expanded his diary into 'The Concordance
of Histories,' a compilation extending from the arrival of
Brutus in England to the death of Henry VII (first
printed, 1516 ; edited by Ellis in 1811).   [xviii. 113]

FACCIO, JEAN CHRISTOPHE (d. 1720), brother of
Nicolas Faccio [q. v.] ; F.R.S., 1706 ; described in the
'Philosophical Transactions' a solar eclipse which he had
observed at Geneva, 1706 ; died at Geneva. [xviii. 116]

FACCIO, NICOLAS (1664–1753), of Duillier, mathematician and fanatic ; citizen of Geneva, 1678 ; developed
Cassini's theory of zodiacal light, 1685 ; showed how to
utilise a ship's motion for grinding corn, sawing, &c. ;
betrayed conspiracy to kidnap the Prince of Orange,

1686 ; F.R.S., 1688 ; befriended by Newton ; disparaged
Leibnitz for personal reasons, 1699 ; chief of the 'French
prophets' ; exposed at Charing Cross as an impostor ;
wandered into Asia to propagate his theories ; chief works
'Epistola .. . de mari æneo Salomonis,' 1688, and 'Navigation Improv'd,' 1728.   [xviii. 114]

FACHTNA, SAINT and BISHOP (fl. 6th cent.), bishop
and abbot of Dairinis Maelanfaidh (Molanna, near Lismore) ; founded school of Ross (Ros Ailithir) ; miraculously cured of blindness.   [xviii. 116]

FAED, THOMAS (1826–1900), painter ; studied at
Edinburgh School of Design ; associate of Scottish Academy, 1849 ; exhibited at Royal Academy, London, from
1851, principally incidents in humble Scottish life ; R.A.,
1864.   [Suppl. ii. 198]

FAGAN, ROBERT (d. 1816), diplomatist and amateur
portrait-painter ; consul-general for Sicily and the Ionian
islands ; purchased from Prince Altieri Claude's 'Landing
of Æneas' and 'Sacrifice of Apollo,' which he refused to
deliver up to the French authorities, and was consequently
imprisoned ; succeeded in conveying (1799) the two paintings by Claude to Palermo ; exhibited three portraits at
the Royal Academy.   [xviii. 117]

FAGG, SIR JOHN (d. 1701), parliamentarian ; colonel ;
M.P., Rye, 1640 ; commissioner for Charles I's trial, 1648–
1649 ; M.P., Sussex, 1654, 1656 (unseated), and 1659 ; imprisoned for attempting to raise forces in Sussex to support Haslerig and Morley, 1659 ; state councillor, 1659 ;
created baronet, 1660 ; M.P., Steyning, Sussex, 1661–1701.
                                                    [xviii. 118]

FAGGE, CHARLES HILTON (1838–1883), physi-
cian ; nephew of John Hilton (1804–1878) [q. v.] ; M.D.
London, 1863 ; F.R.C.P., 1870 ; examiner in medicine to
London University ; demonstrator of morbid anatomy,
lecturer on pathology, and curator of the museum at
Guy's ; wrote medical dissertations.   [xviii. 119]

FAGIUS, PAUL (1504–1549), divine ; born at Rhein-
zabern in the Palatinate ; pastor at Isne, 1537–42 ; established Hebrew printing-press at Isne ; professor of Hebrew
at Strasburg, 1544–6, at Heidelberg, 1546–9 ; deposed for
questioning the Interim, 1549 ; Hebrew reader at Cambridge, 1549.   [xviii. 120]

FAHEY, JAMES (1804–1885), water-colour painter ;
studied anatomy at Paris ; first exhibited at the Royal
Academy, 1825 ; secretary of the New Society of Painters
in Water-Colours, 1838–74 ; drawing-master at Merchant
Taylors' School, 1856–83.   [xviii. 120]

FAHIE, SIR WILLIAM CHARLES (1763–1833),
vice-admiral ; entered navy, 1777 ; assisted at capture of

Danish West India islands, 1807 ; served at reduction of Guadeloupe, 1810 ; commander of the order of St. Ferdinand and Merit ; commander-in-chief on Leeward islands station, 1820, at Halifax, 1821–4 ; K.C.B., 1824 ; vice-admiral, 1830 ; died at Bermuda.   [xviii. 121]

FAIRBAIRN, PATRICK (1805–1874), theologian ; studied at Edinburgh ; presented by the crown to North Ronaldshay, Orkney, 1830 ; professor of divinity in the free church theological college, Aberdeen, 1853–6 ; D.D. Glasgow ; principal of the free church college of Glasgow, 1856–74 ; moderator of the general assembly, 1865 ; chief work, 'Typology of Scripture,' 1845 and 1847 ; edited the 'Imperial Bible Dictionary.'   [xviii. 122]

FAIRBAIRN, SIR PETER (1799–1861), engineer and inventor ; brother of Sir William Fairbairn [q. v.] ; improved flax-spinning machinery by modification of roving-frame and introduction of screw and rotary gills ; established foundry for manufacture of war material ; knighted ; mayor of Leeds. 1857–8, and 1858–9.   [xviii. 123]

FAIRBAIRN, SIR WILLIAM (1789–1874), engineer : of humble origin ; befriended by George Stephenson : constructed two water-mills at Zurich, which worked regularly, whatever the height of the river, 1824 ; M.I.C.E., 1830 ; 'chief fabricator' of machinery for the Turkish government in England, 1839 ; superintended construction of tubular Menai Straits bridge in conjunction with Stephenson, 1848, but found his position untenable, 1849 ; patented his new principle of wrought-iron girders ; honorary LL.D. Edinburgh, 1860, Cambridge, 1862 ; president of the British Association, 1861, of the Institution of Mechanical Engineers, 1854 ; created baronet, 1869.   [xviii. 123]

FAIRBORNE, SIR PALMES (1644–1680), governor of Tangiers ; captain in the Tangiers regiment of foot, 1661 ; knighted ; major, 1664 ; governor of Tangiers, 1676–8 ; constructed a mole across the harbour ; quelled mutiny of troops provoked by the neglect of the home government, 1677 ; superseded, 1680 ; defended Tangiers against Muley Hassan, 1680 ; mortally wounded in skirmish with Moors.   [xviii. 125]

FAIRBORNE, SIR STAFFORD (d. 1742), admiral of the fleet ; son of Sir Palmes Fairborne [q. v.] ; commanded the Warspite at battle of Beachy Head, 1690 ; present at battle of Barfleur, 1692 ; scattered Newfoundland pirates, 1700 ; rear-admiral of the blue, 1701 ; knighted, 1701 ; vice-admiral of the red, 1703 ; present at capture of Barcelona, 1705, and reduction of Ostend, 1706 ; admiral of the fleet, 1708.   [xviii. 126]

FAIRCHILD, THOMAS (1667?–1729), gardener ; established, c. 1690, as nurseryman and florist at Hoxton ; conducted experiments which helped to establish the existence of sex in plants ; first to produce scientifically an artificial 'hybrid' ; published 'The City Gardener,' 1722, and contributed to 'Catalogue of Trees and Shrubs propagated near London,' published 1730. [Suppl. ii. 198]

FAIRCLOUGH. [See also FEATLEY.]

FAIRCLOUGH, RICHARD (1621–1682), nonconformist divine ; son of Samuel Fairclough (1594–1677) [q. v.] ; M.A. and fellow of Emmanuel College, Cambridge ; delivered assize sermon in Somerset ; rector of Mells, 1643 ; ejected by the Act of Uniformity.   [xviii. 127]

FAIRCLOUGH, SAMUEL (1594–1677), nonconformist divine ; B.A. Queens' College, Cambridge ; lecturer at Lynn Regis, 1619 ; cited by the bishop of Norwich for omitting the sign of the cross in baptism ; retired ; rector of Barnardiston, 1623 ; rector of Kedington, 1629–1662 ; signed the petition of 1646 ; ejected, 1662 ; published 'The Pastor's Legacy,' 1663, and other works.   [xviii. 128]

FAIRCLOUGH, SAMUEL (1625?–1691), ejected minister ; fellow of Caius College, Cambridge ; ejected from his rectory of Houghton Conquest, 1662.   [xviii. 129]

FAIRFAX, BLACKERBY (fl. 1728), physician ; son of Nathaniel Fairfax [q. v.] ; M.A. Corpus Christi College, Cambridge, 1693 ; M.D. 1728; M.D. Leyden, 1696 ; physician in the navy ; wrote on the 'Union,' 1702 ; published 'Oratio Apologetica pro Re Herbaria contra Medicos Mathematicos,' 1718.   [xviii. 137]

FAIRFAX, BRIAN, the elder (1633–1711), politician ; son of Henry Fairfax (1588–1665) [q. v.] ; M.A. and LL.D. Trinity College, Cambridge ; sent on a mission to General Monck, 1659 ; equerry to Charles II, 1670–85 ; equerry to William III, 1689–92. His works include poems, a life of Buckingham, and an edition of Fairfax's 'Short Memorials,' 1699.   [xviii. 129]

FAIRFAX, BRIAN, the younger (1676–1749), commissioner of customs, 1723–49 ; son of Brian Fairfax the elder [q. v.] ; queen's scholar, Westminster, 1690 ; fellow of Trinity College, Cambridge, 1698 ; M.A., 1700.   [xviii. 130]

FAIRFAX, SIR CHARLES (fl. 1604), soldier ; brother of Thomas, first baron Fairfax [q. v.] ; routed Velasco at siege of Sluys, 1604.   [xviii. 130]

FAIRFAX, CHARLES (1597–1673), antiquary and genealogist ; son of Thomas, first baron Fairfax [q. v.] ; entered Trinity College, Cambridge, 1611 ; barrister, Lincoln's Inn, 1618 ; parliamentarian colonel of foot ; governor of Kingston-upon-Hull, 1660–1 ; pensioned : assisted Roger Dodsworth [q. v.] in collecting and preserving 'Dodsworth MSS.'; left in manuscript, 'Analecta Fairfaxiana.'   [xviii. 130]

FAIRFAX, CHARLES (d. 1723), dean of Down and Connor, 1722–3 ; son of Brian Fairfax the elder [q. v.] ; educated at Westminster and Christ Church, Oxford.   [xviii. 130]

FAIRFAX, EDWARD (d. 1635), translator of Tasso's 'Gerusalemme Liberata' ; imagined two of his daughters bewitched, 1621 ; author of 'Godfrey of Bulloigne' (1600), a translation of Tasso, which solaced Charles I in prison.   [xviii. 131]

FAIRFAX, FERDINANDO, second BARON FAIRFAX of Cameron in the peerage of Scotland (1584–1648), son of Thomas, first baron [q. v.] ; M.P., Boroughbridge, 1622, 1624, 1625, 1626, and 1627 ; M.P. for Yorkshire in the Long parliament, 1640 ; commanded parliamentarians in Yorkshire, 1642 ; defeated on Adwalton Moor, 1643 ; governor of Hull, 1643–4 ; commanded infantry at Marston Moor, 1644 ; governor of York from 1644 to 1645 ; resigned, 1645.   [xviii. 132]

FAIRFAX, FERDINANDO (fl. 1697), son of Brian Fairfax the elder [q. v.] ; educated at Westminster ; B.A. Trinity College, Cambridge, 1697.   [xviii. 132]

FAIRFAX, SIR GUY (d. 1495), judge ; member of Gray's Inn, 1463 ; king's serjeant, 1468 ; recorder of York, 1476 ; judge of king's bench, 1477 ; chief-justice of Lancaster under Edward V.   [xviii. 133]

FAIRFAX, HENRY (1588–1665), friend of George Herbert ; son of Thomas, first baron Fairfax [q. v.] ; fellow of Trinity College, Cambridge, 1608 ; took part in the unsuccessful movement to obtain a university for the north, c. 1640 ; rector of Bolton Percy, 1646–60.   [xviii. 134]

FAIRFAX, HENRY (1634–1702), dean of Norwich ; son of Charles Fairfax (1597–1673) [q. v.] ; D.D. Magdalen College, Oxford, 1680 ; senior fellow, 1687 ; signed petition to James II against decree naming Anthony Farmer [q. v.] president, 9 April 1687 ; expelled from Magdalen, October 1687 ; restored, 1688 ; dean of Norwich, 1689–1702.   [xviii. 134]

FAIRFAX, JOHN (1623–1700), ejected minister ; B.A. Corpus Christi College, Cambridge ; fellow, 1645–50 ; rector of Barking-cum-Needham, 1650–62 ; ejected, 1662 ; in charge of nonconformist congregation at Ipswich, 1680–6, of presbyterians alone, 1687–1700 ; published sermons.   [xviii. 135]

FAIRFAX, JOHN (1804–1877), journalist and member of legislative council, New South Wales ; emigrated, 1838, being unable to pay costs of suit arising out of his Leamington journal ; bought 'Sydney Morning Herald,' 1841 ; sole proprietor of 'Sydney Herald,' 1853 ; member of legislative council, 1874–7.   [xviii. 136]

FAIRFAX, NATHANIEL (1637–1690), divine and physician ; M.A. Corpus Christi College, Cambridge, 1661 ; ejected from perpetual curacy of Willisham, 1662 ; M.D. Leyden, 1670 ; published 'A Treatise of the Bulk and Selvedge of the World,' 1674.   [xviii. 137]

FAIRFAX or **FAYRFAX**, ROBERT (*d.* 1529), musician; organist at St. Albans; Mus. Doc. Cambridge, 1504, Oxford, 1511; gentleman of the King's Chapel in 1509; poor knight of Windsor, 1514; wrote out music-books, a 'prycke-songe book' and a 'balet boke'; composed masses and part-songs; his 'That was my woo is nowe my most gladnesse,' possibly addressed to Henry VII in 1485. [xviii. 137]

FAIRFAX, ROBERT (1666-1725), rear-admiral; grandson of Sir William Fairfax [q. v.]; present at the battle in Bantry Bay and relief of Londonderry, 1689; court-martialled for failing to overtake a French squadron off Cape Palos, but acquitted, 1704; took part in reduction of Gibraltar, of Barcelona, 1705, and in battle of Malaga, 1704; retired in mortification at the cancelling of his appointment as vice-admiral of the blue, 1708; rear-admiral, 1708; M.P. for York city, 1713-14; lord mayor of York, 1715. [xviii. 138]

FAIRFAX, THOMAS, first BARON FAIRFAX of Cameron in the Scottish peerage (1560-1640); employed by Elizabeth on diplomatic communications with James VI; knighted before Rouen, 1591; served in the Low Countries; created Baron Fairfax of Cameron, 1627; country gentleman at Denton, Yorkshire, writing, but not publishing, 'The Order for the Government of the House at Denton,' 'Conjectures about Horsemanship,' and tractates on similar subjects. [xviii. 140]

FAIRFAX, THOMAS, third BARON FAIRFAX OF CAMERON (1612-1671), general; son of Ferdinando, second baron Fairfax [q. v.]; matriculated at St. John's College, Cambridge, 1626; engaged at siege of Bois-le-Duc, 1629; commanded during first Scottish war; knighted, 1640; became a general for the parliament, 1642; recaptured Leeds for the parliament, 1643; captured Wakefield, 1643; defeated at Adwalton Moor, 1643; commanded detachment at Marston Moor, 1644; commander-in-chief of the parliamentary army, 1645; remodelled the army, in accordance with a parliamentary ordinance, 1645; defeated Charles I at Naseby, 1645, where he captured a standard with his own hand; stormed Bristol, 1645; reduced Oxford, 1646; thanked by parliament, 1646; directed to appease the army's resentment at its contemplated reduction, 1647; Charles I seized against his will, 1647; sided with the peace party, 1647; suppressed the levellers; urged parliament to provide for the soldiers' pay; reduced Colchester, 1648; transmitted to the Commons the army's demand for Charles I's punishment, 1648; one of the king's judges, 1649, endeavouring to prevent his execution; state councillor, 1649; M.P., Cirencester, 1649; commander-in-chief, 1649; D.C.L. Oxford, 1649; resigned from unwillingness to invade Scotland, 1650; M.P. for Yorkshire in Richard Cromwell's parliament; M.P., Yorkshire, 1660; headed commission sent to Charles II at the Hague, 1660; bequeathed twenty-eight manuscripts to the Bodleian; author of poems, translations, and two autobiographical works. Milton wrote a sonnet, calling on him to undertake the settlement of the kingdom, 1648. [xviii. 141]

FAIRFAX, THOMAS (1656-1716), jesuit; studied at St. Omer; priest, 1683; D.D. Trèves; fellow of Magdalen College, Oxford, 1688; removed from his fellowship at the revolution, 1688; professed of the four vows, 1693; procurator of the English province, 1701 and 1704; published works, including 'The Secret Policy of the Jesuits' (2nd edit.), 1702. [xviii. 149]

FAIRFAX, THOMAS, sixth BARON FAIRFAX of Cameron (1692-1782); held commission in the blues; intimate with Bolingbroke, Addison, and Steele; retired to his maternal estates of the Northern Neck in Virginia, 1747; trained and encouraged the young George Washington; died broken-hearted soon after the surrender of Cornwallis, 1781. [xviii. 149]

FAIRFAX, SIR WILLIAM (1609-1644), soldier; knighted, 1630; commanded regiment under Essex, 1642; commanded detachments at Nantwich and Montgomery Moor, 1644; mortally wounded before Montgomery Castle. [xviii. 150]

FAIRFAX, SIR WILLIAM GEORGE (1739-1813), vice-admiral; navy lieutenant, 1757; took part in the St. Lawrence operations, 1759; prisoner, 1778-82; fought at Camperdown, 1797; knight-banneret; vice-admiral, 1806. [xviii. 150]

FAIRFIELD, CHARLES (1761?-1804), painter; copied paintings of Dutch and Flemish masters; his original pictures undeservedly neglected. [xviii. 151]

FAIRHOLM, CHARLES (1566-1617). [See FERM, CHARLES.]

FAIRHOLT, FREDERICK WILLIAM (1814-1866), engraver and antiquarian writer; of German origin; Isis medallist of Society of Arts; illustrated Charles Knight's publications, Halliwell's 'Sir John Maundeville,' 1839, and other works; F.S.A., 1844; author of antiquarian researches, including 'Costume in England,' 1846; bequeathed prints to the British Museum, and Shakespearean collections to Stratford-on-Avon. [xviii. 151]

FAIRLAND, THOMAS (1804-1852), lithographer and portrait-painter; student at Royal Academy; 'Raphael's Virgin and Child' his most famous contribution to the new art of lithography. [xviii. 152]

FAIRLESS, THOMAS KERR (1825-1853), landscape-painter; exhibited at the Royal Academy and other institutions, 1848-51. [xviii. 153]

FAIRLIE, ROBERT FRANCIS (1831-1885), civil engineer; superintendent and general manager of Londonderry and Coleraine railway, 1853; obtained post on Bombay and Baroda railway; patented 'double-bogie engine,' 1864; invited to design and construct railways in Venezuela, 1873; compelled by jungle fever to return to England, 1874. [xviii. 153]

FAITHORNE, WILLIAM, the elder (1616-1691), engraver and portrait-painter; banished for refusing to take the oath to Oliver Cromwell; allowed to return to England, 1650; print-seller in London; executed crayon portraits; engraved frontispieces and prints, also two maps, one of London and Westminster, the other of Virginia and Maryland. [xviii. 154]

FAITHORNE, WILLIAM, the younger (1656-1701?), mezzotint engraver; son of William Faithorne the elder [q. v.]; engraved portraits of Queen Anne, Charles I, Charles II, and John Dryden. [xviii. 155]

FALCONBERG or **FALCONBRIDGE**, the BASTARD (*d.* 1226). [See BREAUTÉ, FALKES DE.]

FALCONBERG or **FALCONBRIDGE**, BASTARD OF (*d.* 1471). [See FAUCONBERG, THOMAS.]

FALCONBRIDGE, ALEXANDER (*d.* 1792), surgeon; surgeon, from poverty, on slave-ships; accepted commission from St. George's Bay Company to found settlement for the homeless colonists formerly sent by government to the river Sierra Leone, 1791; founded Granville Town, 1791; superseded in presidency of Sierra Leone Company's council; dismissed, 1792. [xviii. 156]

FALCONBRIDGE, ANNA MARIA (*fl.* 1794), wife of Alexander Falconbridge [q. v.]; published autobiographical 'Narrative,' defending the slave trade and ridiculing her dead husband, 1794. [xviii. 156]

FALCONER, ALEXANDER, BARON FALCONER OF HALKERTOUN (*d.* 1671), judge; ordinary lord of session, 1639 and 1641; represented Kincardineshire in the convention, 1643-4, and in parliament, 1644-5 and 1645-7; commissioner of exchequer, 1645; created Baron Falconer, 1647; removed from College of Justice, 1649, for having subscribed the 'engagement'; reappointed, 1660; commissioner of excise, 1661. [xviii. 156]

FALCONER, SIR DAVID, of Newton (1640-1686), lord president of session; advocate, 1661; knighted; lord of justiciary, 1678; president of session, 1682; M.P., Forfarshire, 1685; lord of the articles; collected decisions of court of session (November 1681-January 1686). [xviii. 157]

FALCONER, EDMUND (1814-1879), actor and dramatist; really EDMUND O'ROURKE; wrote 'The Cagot, or Heart for Heart,' a drama, acted at Lyceum, 1856; manager of Lyceum, 1858-9 and 1861-2; his Irish drama, 'Peep o' Day,' played in London from November 1861 till December 1862; joint-lessee of Drury Lane, 1862-6; attempted to popularise Shakespearean drama; opened Her Majesty's Theatre, Haymarket, with 'Oonagh,' 1866; appeared at New York, 1867. [xviii. 157]

FALCONER, FORBES (1805-1853), Persian scholar; educated at Marischal College, Aberdeen, and at Paris;

professor of oriental languages in University College, London; edited poems by Jámi; published selections from the 'Bústán,' 1839.   [xviii. 158]

FALCONER, HUGH (1808–1865), palæontologist and botanist; M.A. Aberdeen, 1826; M.D. Edinburgh, 1829; assistant-surgeon on the East India Company's Bengal establishment, 1830; superintendent of the Saháranpur botanic garden, 1832; discovered fossil mammals and reptiles in Siválik hills, 1832; superintended manufacture of first Indian tea, 1834; discovered assafœtida of commerce in valley of Astore; appointed to superintend arrangement of Indian fossils in the British Museum, 1844; commenced 'Fauna Antiqua Sivalensis,' 1846; professor of botany, Calcutta Medical College, 1848–55; proved that the cave fauna of England contained *elephas antiquus* and *rhinoceros hemitœchus*, 1860; vice-president of the Royal Society.   [xviii. 158]

FALCONER, JOHN (*fl.* 1547), merchant. 'Maister Falkonner's Boke' is the earliest English record of an herbarium of dried plants.   [xviii. 161]

FALCONER or FALKNER, JOHN (1577–1656), jesuit; studied at St. Mary's Hall and Gloucester Hall, Oxford; joined expedition of Essex to Spain; professed of the four vows, 1619; confessor at Liège and Ghent; helped to defend Wardour Castle, where he was chaplain, 1643; translated hagiological and devotional works.   [xviii. 161]

FALCONER, RANDLE WILBRAHAM (1816–1881), medical writer; son of Thomas Falconer (1772–1839) [q. v.], graduated in medicine at Edinburgh, 1839; mayor of Bath, 1857; physician to Bath General Water Hospital; wrote on therapeutics.   [xviii. 162]

FALCONER, THOMAS (1738–1792), classical scholar; matriculated at Brasenose College, Oxford, 1754; barrister, Lincoln's Inn, 1760; his 'Observations on Pliny's account of the Temple of Diana at Ephesus' published, 1794, and 'Chronological Tables' published, 1796; left materials for edition of Strabo.   [xviii. 162]

FALCONER, THOMAS (1772–1839), classical scholar; son of William Falconer (1744–1824) [q. v.]; scholar of Corpus Christi College, Oxford, 1788; M.A. and fellow, 1795; Bampton lecturer, 1810; M.D. Oxford, 1822; published, among other works, edition of Strabo, 1807, based on materials left by Thomas Falconer (1738–1792) [q. v.]; edited Hanno's 'Voyage,' with translation, 1797.   [xviii. 162]

FALCONER, THOMAS (1805–1882), county court judge; son of Thomas Falconer (1772–1839) [q. v.]; barrister, Lincoln's Inn, 1830; arbitrator on behalf of Canada for determining boundaries between Canada and New Brunswick, 1850; colonial secretary, Western Australia, 1851; resigned, 1851; judge of Rhayader district and Glamorganshire and Breconshire county courts, 1851–81; published works mainly legal.   [xviii. 163]

FALCONER, WILLIAM (1732–1769), poet; servant of Archibald Campbell (*fl.* 1767) [q. v.], who encouraged his literary tastes; second mate on a ship in the Levant trade, which was wrecked between Alexandria and Venice; drew on his own experience for his chief poem, 'The Shipwreck,' 1762; patronised by the Duke of York; became purser on various ships; published 'The Universal Marine Dictionary,' 1769; lost in the Aurora.   [xviii. 164]

FALCONER, WILLIAM (1744–1824), miscellaneous writer; M.D. Edinburgh, 1766; studied at Leyden, becoming (1767) M.D.; extra-licentiate C.P., 1767; physician to Chester Infirmary, 1767–70; F.R.S., 1773; physician to Bath General Hospital, 1784–1819; intimate with Dr. Parr; published essays on the Bath waters, and miscellaneous tracts.   [xviii. 165]

FALCONER, WILLIAM (1801–1885), translator of Strabo'; son of Thomas Falconer (1772–1839) [q. v.]; B.A. Oriel College, Oxford, 1823; M.A., 1827; Petrean fellow of Exeter College, 1827; university mathematical examiner, 1832–3 and 1836–8; rector of Bushey, 1839–1885; brought out his father's manuscript translation of Strabo's 'Geography' in 'Bohn's Classical Library,' 1854–6–7.   [xviii. 167]

FALCONET, PETER [PIERRE ETIENNE] (1741–1791), portrait-painter; born in Paris; exhibited occasionally at the Royal Academy; executed blacklead portraits of eminent artists.   [xviii. 167]

FALDO, JOHN (1633–1690), nonconformist minister; pastor at Plasterers' Hall, Aldermanbury, 1684–90. His 'Quakerism no Christianity,' 1673, led to an animated controversy with William Penn.   [xviii. 168]

FALE, THOMAS (*fl.* 1604), mathematician; M.A. Corpus Christi College, Cambridge, 1586; B.D., 1597; licensed physician, 1604. His 'Horologiographia' (1593) contains what is probably the earliest trigonometrical table printed in England.   [xviii. 169]

FALKENER, EDWARD (1814–1896), architect; articled to John Newman (1786–1859) [q. v.]; studied at Royal Academy; studied architectural remains in Europe, Asia, and Egypt; practised in London; honorary F.R.I.B.A., 1895; published works relating to classical architecture.   [Suppl. ii. 199]

FALKLAND, VISCOUNTS. [See CARY, SIR HENRY, first VISCOUNT, *d.* 1633; and CARY, LUCIUS, second VISCOUNT, 1610?–1643.]

FALKLAND, ELIZABETH, VISCOUNTESS (1585–1639). [See CARY, ELIZABETH.]

FALKNER, SIR EVERARD (1684–1758). [See FAWKENER.]

FALKNER, JOHN (1577–1656). [See FALCONER, JOHN.]

FALKNER, THOMAS (1707–1784), jesuit missionary; surgeon on board a slave ship; nursed through an illness by Buenos Ayres jesuits, 1731; jesuit missionary in Paraguay and Tucuman; expelled from South America as a jesuit, 1768; joined English province, *c.* 1771; wrote on medicine and natural history of South America.   [xviii. 169]

FALKNER, WILLIAM (*d.* 1682), divine; M.A. Peterhouse, Cambridge, 1656; rector of Glemsford, 1679–82; D.D. Cambridge, 1680; wrote in defence of the church of England.   [xviii. 170]

FALLE, PHILIP (1656–1742), historian of Jersey; native of Jersey; entered at Exeter College, Oxford, 1669; M.A. Alban Hall, 1676; incumbent of Trinity parish, Jersey, 1681–7; incumbent of St. Saviour's, Jersey, 1689–1709; deputed by States of Jersey to request William III's protection, 1693; king's chaplain, 1694; prebendary of Durham, 1700; his chief work, an 'Account of Jersey,' 1694 (expanded 1734).   [xviii. 170]

FALLOWS, FEARON (1789–1831), astronomer; of humble origin; third wrangler, St. John's College, Cambridge, 1813; mathematical lecturer at Corpus Christi College and fellow of St. John's, Cambridge; M.A., 1816; director of astronomical observatory planned for Cape of Good Hope by commissioners of longitude, 1820; F.R.S., 1823; catalogued chief southern stars, 1824; completed observatory, 1829; died at Simon's Bay.   [xviii. 171]

FALMOUTH, first EARL OF (1787–1841). [See BOSCAWEN, EDWARD.]

FALMOUTH, first VISCOUNT (*d.* 1734). [See BOSCAWEN, HUGH.]

FANCOURT, SAMUEL (1678–1768), dissenting minister and projector of circulating libraries; minister and tutor in Salisbury, 1718–30; established subscription library in London, 1730 (dissolved, 1745); established 'The Gentlemen and Ladies' Growing and Circulating Library,' 1746; failed of success; published 'Essay concerning Liberty, Grace, and Prescience,' 1729, and similar works.   [xviii. 172]

FANE, SIR EDMUND DOUGLAS VEITCH (1837–1900), diplomatist; educated at Merton College, Oxford; entered diplomatic service, 1858; minister at Belgrade, 1893–1900; K.C.M.G., 1899.   [Suppl. ii. 200]

FANE, FRANCIS, first BARON BURGHERSH and first EARL OF WESTMORLAND (1583–1628), son of Sir Thomas Fane [q. v.]; K.B., 1603; created earl, 1624.   [xviii. 180]

FANE, SIR FRANCIS (*d.* 1689?), dramatist; grandson of Francis Fane, first earl of Westmorland [q. v.]; K.B., 1660; bequeathed money for Olveston poor; wrote 'Love in the Dark' (comedy), 1675, 'The Sacrifice' (tragedy), 1686, and a masque.   [xviii. 173]

P

FANE, FRANCIS WILLIAM HENRY, twelfth EARL OF WESTMORLAND (1825–1891), educated at Westminster and Sandhurst; ensign, 1843; lieutenant, 1844; captain, 1848; served in India and Crimea; C.B., 1855; succeeded to earldom, 1859; retired as colonel, 1860.
[Suppl. ii. 201]

FANE, SIR HENRY (1778–1840), general; cornet, 1792; captain, 1793; M.P., Lyme Regis, 1796–1818; colonel and aide-de-camp to the king, 1805; turned Laborde's right at Roliça, 1808; major-general, 1810; defeated Villatte, 1813; fought at Vittoria, 1813, and Orthes, 1814; colonel, 1814; lieutenant-general, 1819; G.C.B., 1825; M.P., Sandwich, 1829; commander-in-chief in India, 1835; secured unhindered passage of English troops through Sind into Afghanistan, 1839; died off St. Michael's Island in the Azores. [xviii. 174]

FANE, JOHN, seventh EARL OF WESTMORLAND (1682?–1762), distinguished himself under the Duke of Marlborough; lieutenant-colonel, 1710; created Baron Catherlough, 1733; M.P., Hythe, 1708–10, Buckingham, 1726–7 and 1727; knight of the shire for Kent, 1715; Earl of Westmorland, 1736; lord-lieutenant of Northamptonshire, 1737; lieutenant-general of the forces of the kingdom, 1739; chancellor of Oxford University, 1758.
[xviii. 175]

FANE, JOHN, ninth EARL OF WESTMORLAND (1728–1774), educated at Westminster; M.P., Lyme Regis, 1761 and 1762. [xviii. 176]

FANE, JOHN, tenth EARL OF WESTMORLAND (1759–1841), son of John Fane, ninth earl [q. v.]; educated at Charterhouse and Emmanuel College, Cambridge; M.A., 1778; privy councillor, 1789; lord-lieutenant of Ireland, 1790–5; opposed catholic emancipation; recalled by Pitt, 1795; lord privy seal, 1798–1827; K.G., 1793; lord-lieutenant of Northamptonshire. [xviii. 176]

FANE, JOHN, eleventh EARL OF WESTMORLAND (1784–1859), son of John Fane, tenth earl [q. v.]; educated at Harrow and Trinity College, Cambridge; M.A., 1808; M.P., Lyme Regis, 1806–16; assistant adjutant-general in Sicily, 1806–7; served in Peninsula, 1808–10; minister plenipotentiary to Florence, 1814; LL.D. Cambridge, 1814; signed convention of Caza Lanza, 1815; privy councillor, 1822; D.C.L. Oxford, 1834; resident minister at Berlin, 1841–51; G.C.B., 1846; general, 1854; founded Royal Academy of Music, 1823; musical composer, and author of military memoirs. [xviii. 176]

FANE, JULIAN HENRY CHARLES (1827–1870), diplomatist and poet; son of John Fane, eleventh earl of Westmorland [q. v.]; educated at Harrow and Trinity College, Cambridge; chancellor's medallist, 1850; M.A., 1851; secretary of legation at St. Petersburg, 1856–8; first secretary and acting chargé d'affaires at Paris, 1865–7 and 1868; issued 'Poems,' 1852, and a translation of Heine, 1854. [xviii. 178]

FANE, MILDMAY, second EARL OF WESTMORLAND (d. 1666), eldest son of Francis Fane, first earl [q. v.]; educated at Emmanuel College, Cambridge; M.P. Peterborough, 1621; K.B., 1625; fined and sequestrated by parliament, 1642; his sequestration discharged, 1644; joint lord-lieutenant of Northamptonshire, 1660; privately printed 'Otia Sacra,' 1648, and left manuscript poems.
[xviii. 178]

FANE, PRISCILLA ANNE, COUNTESS OF WESTMORLAND (1793–1879), artist; née Wellesley-Pole; married John Fane, afterwards eleventh Earl of Westmorland [q. v.], 1811; exhibited at various institutions, 1833–41, 1842, and 1857. [xviii. 179]

FANE or VANE, SIR RALPH (d. 1552), alleged conspirator; knighted before Boulogne, 1544; fought at Musselburgh, 1547; knight-banneret, 1547; charged with conspiring to murder Northumberland, 1551; executed.
[xviii. 179]

FANE, ROBERT GEORGE CECIL (1796–1864), bankruptcy commissioner; educated at Charterhouse; matriculated at Balliol College, Oxford, 1813; demy and fellow, Magdalen College, Oxford, 1824–35; M.A., 1819; barrister, Lincoln's Inn, 1821; a commissioner of the 'Thirteenth List,' 1823; a commissioner of bankruptcy, 1831; wrote mainly on bankruptcy reform. [xviii. 179]

FANE, SIR THOMAS (d. 1589), politician; attainted for share in Wyatt's rebellion, but pardoned, 1554; knighted, 1573; deputy-commissioner for breeding of horses in Kent, 1580. [xviii. 180]

FANELLI, FRANCESCO (fl. 1610–1665), statuary; native of Florence; worked in metal in England; styled himself Scultore del Re della Gran Bretagna; published engravings, 1642. [xviii. 181]

FANNING, EDMUND (1737–1818), colonial governor; born in Long Island; graduate of Yale, 1757; colonel of militia, North Carolina, 1763; member of the legislature; compelled to leave North Carolina (1771) for his malpractices when recorder of deeds; surveyor-general, 1774; D.C.L. Oxford, 1774; lieutenant-governor of Nova Scotia, 1783–7, of the island of St. John, 1787–99, of Prince Edward island, 1799–1804; British general, 1808.
[xviii. 181]

FANSHAWE, ANNE, LADY (1625–1680), née Harrison; wife of Sir Richard Fanshawe [q. v.]; lutenist, singer, and French scholar; shared in all her husband's wanderings and diplomatic missions; refused offer of pension from the Spanish government on condition of becoming a catholic, 1666; wrote memoir of Sir Richard Fanshawe, 1676 (first printed in 1829).
[xviii. 184]

FANSHAWE, CATHERINE MARIA (1765–1834), poetess; exchanged verses with Cowper; commended by Scott; best-known poem, a riddle on the letter H; several of her pieces included in Joanna Baillie's 'Collection' (1823). [xviii. 182]

FANSHAWE, SIR HENRY (1569–1616), remembrancer of the exchequer; son of Thomas Fanshawe [q. v.]; student of the Inner Temple, 1586; remembrancer, 1601; M.P., Westbury, 1588 and 1593, Boroughbridge, 1597; knighted, 1603; friend of Prince Henry; horticulturist and Italian scholar. [xviii. 183]

FANSHAWE, SIR RICHARD (1608–1666), diplomatist and author; son of Sir Henry Fanshawe [q. v.]; fellow-commoner, Jesus College, Cambridge, 1623; entered the Inner Temple, 1626; given 'credentials for Spain' by Charles I, 1647; ordered to Spain to procure money for the king's cause, 1650; created baronet, 1650; taken prisoner at battle of Worcester, 1651; master of requests and Latin secretary to Prince Charles at the Hague, 1660; M.P., Cambridge University, 1661; privy councillor of Ireland, 1662; ambassador to Portugal, 1662–3; privy councillor, 1663; ambassador to Spain, 1664–6; recalled (1666) for compromising the home government; died at Madrid; left unpublished poems. His published works include translations of Guarini's 'Pastor Fido,' 1647, and of Camoens's 'Lusiad,' 1655. [xviii. 184]

FANSHAWE, THOMAS (1533–1601), remembrancer of the exchequer; of Jesus College, Cambridge, and the Middle Temple; remembrancer, 1568; M.P., Rye, 1571, and Arundel; M.P., Much Wenlock, 1597; wrote 'Practice of the Exchequer Court' (published, 1658) and 'An Answer . . . concerning the Lord Treasurer's Office.'
[xviii. 189]

FANSHAWE, SIR THOMAS, first VISCOUNT FANSHAWE of Dromore, in the peerage of Ireland (1596–1665), remembrancer of the exchequer, 1616; son of Sir Henry Fanshawe [q. v.]; K.B., 1626; M.P. for Hertford, 1624, 1625, and 1640; M.P., Lancaster, 1626 and 1628; fought for Charles I at Edgehill, 1642; sequestrated, 1642; created Viscount Fanshawe, 1661; M.P., Hertfordshire, 1661.
[xviii. 190]

FANSHAWE, THOMAS, second VISCOUNT FANSHAWE, in the peerage of Ireland (1639–1674), son of Sir Thomas Fanshawe, first viscount [q. v.]; M.A. Trinity College, Cambridge; K.B., 1661; remembrancer, 1665; M.P., Hertford, 1661–74. [xviii. 190]

FARADAY, MICHAEL (1791–1867), natural philosopher; apprenticed to Riebau, a London bookseller, 1804; engaged by Sir Humphry Davy as assistant, on showing interest in science, 1812; travelled as Davy's amanuensis in France, Switzerland, Italy, and the Tyrol 1813–15; treated as a menial by Lady Davy; published in the 'Quarterly Journal of Science' analysis of caustic lime from Tuscany, 1816; professed Sandemanianism 1821; wrote 'History of the Progress of Electro-Magnetism,' 1821; analysed hydrate of chlorine, thereby facilitating Davy's discovery of chlorine, 1823; liquefied chlorine and other gases; announced discovery of benzol 1825; Bakerian lecturer, 1829; the chromatrope suggested by his paper 'On a Peculiar Class of Optical Deceptions,' 1831; discovered magneto-electricity, 1831 regarded position of iron filings round a magnet as deter mined by 'lines of force'; discovered 'extra current' by help of facts furnished by one William Jenkin, 1835; pensioned by Lord Melbourne, 1835; decided in favour of 'identity of electricities'; sought to invent neutral terminology for theory of voltaic pile; constructed a 'voltameter'; declared medium necessary for transmission of electric induction; scientific adviser to Trinity House, 1836; propounded 'rotation of plane of polarisation by magnets and electric currents,' 1845; established diamagnetic repulsion; originated theory of atom as 'centre of force'; died in a house given him by Queen Victoria at Hampton Court.   [xviii. 190]

FAREY, JOHN (1766–1826), geologist; consulting surveyor and geologist in London, 1802, following William Smith's principles; published 'Survey of the County of Derby,' 1811–13, and scientific papers.   [xviii. 202]

FAREY, JOHN (1791–1851), civil engineer; son of John Farey (1766–1826) [q. v.]; gold medallist Society of Arts, 1813; constructed ironworks in Russia, 1819; introduced use of steam-engine indicators; M.I.C.E., 1826; published 'A Treatise on the Steam Engine,' 1827.   [xviii. 202]

FARGUS, FREDERICK JOHN (1847–1885), novelist; under pseudonym of HUGH CONWAY; auctioneer of Bristol from 1868; his first story published in 'Thirteen at Table,' 1881; published 'Called Back,' a highly successful sensational novel, 1883; contributed tales to various periodicals; produced 'Dark Days,' 1884; valued and catalogued Strawberry Hill collection; died at Monte Carlo.   [xviii. 203]

FARICIUS (d. 1117), abbot of Abingdon; native of Arezzo; physician to Henry I; abbot of Abingdon, 1100; obtained grants for the abbey; his election to the archbishopric of Canterbury prevented by opposition of suffragan bishops, 1114; wrote a 'Life of St. Aldhelm.'   [xviii. 204]

FARINDON, ANTHONY (1598–1658), royalist divine; scholar of Trinity College, Oxford, 1612; fellow, 1617; M.A., 1620; B.D., 1629; vicar of Bray, 1634; divinity lecturer in the Chapel Royal at Windsor, 1639; ejected during the civil war; friend of John Hales; minister of St. Mary Magdalene, Milk Street, 1647–56; dispossessed, 1656; famous as a preacher; moderate latitudinarian; a hundred and thirty of his sermons are extant.   [xviii. 205]

FARINGDON, alias COOK, HUGH (d. 1539), abbot of Reading, 1520; sent Henry VIII books on matrimonial law to enable him to find justification for divorcing Catherine of Arragon; trier of petitions from Gascony, 1523; in parliament, '523–39; J.P. for Berkshire; executed for supposed complicity in northern rebellion.   [xviii. 206]

FARINGTON, GEORGE (1752–1788), artist; gold medallist of the Royal Academy, 1780; died at Moorshedabad, when making studies for a grand picture of the nabob's court.   [xviii. 207]

FARINGTON, JOHN (1603–1646). [See WOODCOCK.]

FARINGTON, JOSEPH (1747–1821), landscapepainter; R.A., 1785: best known by two collections of engraved views of the English lakes.   [xviii. 207]

FARISH, WILLIAM (1759–1837), Jacksonian professor at Cambridge; senior wrangler, Magdalene College, Cambridge, 1778; fellow; M.A., 1781; professor of chemistry, 1794; incumbent of St. Giles's, Cambridge, 1800; Jacksonian professor of natural and experimental philosophy, 1813–36; B.D., 1820.   [xviii. 208]

FARLEY, CHARLES (1771–1859), actor and dramatist; instructor of Joseph Grimaldi [q. v.]; excelled in melodrama; superintended Covent Garden pantomimes, 1806–34, writing a few himself.   [xviii. 208]

FARLEY, JAMES LEWIS (1823–1885), writer on eastern affairs; chief accountant of Ottoman bank at Beyrout; accountant-general of state bank of Turkey at Constantinople, 1860; traced extension of British trade throughout Turkish empire to the Greeks in 'Resources of Turkey,' 1862; published 'Turks and Christians,' 1876, some of its suggestions being subsequently forced upon the Porte; consul for the sultan at Bristol, 1870–84; fellow of Statistical Society; privy councillor in Bulgarian public works department.   [xviii. 209]

FARMER. [See also FERMOR.]

FARMER, ANTHONY (fl. 1687), president-designate of Magdalen College, Oxford; matriculated at St. John's College, Cambridge, 1672; scholar of Trinity College, Cambridge, 1676; M.A., 1680; joined Magdalen Hall, Oxford, 1683; asked to migrate to Magdalen College, 1685, being a disorderly and quarrelsome man; vainly nominated by James II to presidency of Magdalen, 1687; charges brought against him by the fellows substantiated, 1687.   [xviii. 209]

FARMER, GEORGE (1732–1779), navy captain; lieutenant in West Indies and on home station; assisted in suppressing riot at Norwich, 1766; appointed commander (1768) on the representations of the Norwich magistrates; shipwrecked off Patagonia, 1770; promoted to post rank, 1771; perished in the burning of his ship during encounter with French, 1779.   [xviii. 210]

FARMER, HUGH (1714–1787), independent minister and theological writer; afternoon preacher at Salters' Hall, 1761–72, and one of the preachers at the 'merchants' lecture,' 1762–80; trustee of Dr. Williams's foundations, 1762; published theological works.   [xviii. 211]

FARMER, JOHN (fl. 1591–1601), composer; dedicated to his friend Edward de Vere, seventeenth earl of Oxford [q. v.], a book containing examples in two-part counterpoint of different orders, 1591, and 'The First Set of English Madrigals,' 1599; contributed a madrigal to 'The Triumphs of Oriana,' 1601.   [xviii. 213]

FARMER, RICHARD (1735–1797), master of Emmanuel College, Cambridge; senior optime, Emmanuel College, Cambridge, 1757; M.A. and tutor, 1760; F.S.A., 1763; published 'Essay on the Learning of Shakspeare,' 1767, maintaining that Shakespeare knew the classics through translations only; master of Emmanuel College, 1775; D.D. Cambridge, 1775; vice-chancellor of Cambridge, 1775–6 and 1787–8; broke open the building in which the university seal was kept in order to prepare the address voted to George III in support of his American policy, 1775; prebendary and chancellor of Lichfield, 1780; prebendary of Canterbury, 1782, of St. Paul's, 1788; introduced statuary into St. Paul's.   [xviii. 214]

FARMER, THOMAS (fl. 1685), composer; Mus. Bac. Cambridge, 1684; contributed to musical collections; published 'consorts,' 1686 and 1690.   [xviii. 216]

FARMERY, JOHN (d. 1590), physician; M.A. King's College, Cambridge, 1568; F.C.P., 1589; M.D. Leyden, 1589; assisted in drawing up formulæ for 'Pharmacopœia,' 1589.   [xviii. 216]

FARNABY, GILES (fl. 1598), composer; Mus. Bac. Oxford, 1592; published canzonets, 1598.   [xviii. 217]

FARNABY, THOMAS (1575?–1647), schoolmaster and classical scholar; postmaster, Merton College, Oxford, 1590; studied at a jesuit college in Spain; sailed in Drake and Hawkins's last voyage; opened school in Goldsmiths' Alley, which his abilities made famous; corresponded with G. J. Vossius, 1630–42; commissioned by Charles I to prepare a new Latin grammar, 1641; detained at Ely House, Holborn, 1644–5; friend of Ben Jonson; edited most of the classical authors, co-operating with Meric Casaubon in an edition of Terence, issued in 1651; published among other works an 'Index Rhetoricus,' 1625.   [xviii. 217]

FARNBOROUGH, LADY (1762–1837). [See LONG, AMELIA.]

FARNBOROUGH, BARON, of Bromley Hill Place (1761–1838). [See LONG, CHARLES.]

FARNBOROUGH, BARON, of Farnborough (1815–1886). [See MAY, SIR THOMAS ERSKINE.]

FARNEWORTH, ELLIS (d. 1763), translator; educated at Eton and Jesus College, Cambridge; M.A., 1738; vicar of Rostherne, 1758–62; rector of Carsington, 1762–3. His translations include Davila's 'Civil Wars of France,' 1758, and a widely circulated version of Machiavelli, 1762.   [xviii. 219]

FARNHAM, RICHARD (d. 1642), fanatic; a weaver by profession; together with John Bull (d. 1642) [q. v.] gave himself out to be a prophet, 1636; imprisoned by high commission court, 1636; vainly petitioned Laud for his release; gained some followers.   [xviii. 219]

FARNWORTH, RICHARD (*d.* 1666), quaker; minister, 1651; imprisoned at Banbury for not uncovering to the mayor, 1655; published theological works.
[xviii. 220]

FARQUHAR, SIR ARTHUR (1772–1843), rear-admiral; entered navy when the French war broke out; commander, 1802; captured in charge of convoy, 1805; advanced to post rank, 1805; senior naval officer in the north German operations, 1813–14; C.B., 1815; helped to suppress West Indian negro revolt; knighted, 1833; rear-admiral, 1837.
[xviii. 220]

FARQUHAR, GEORGE (1678–1707), dramatist; sizar of Trinity College, Dublin, 1694–5; patronised by Bishop Wiseman; gave up the stage in consequence of accidentally wounding a fellow-actor; advised by Wilkes to write a comedy; produced 'Love and a Bottle,' 1699, the 'Constant Couple,' 1700, 'Sir Harry Wildair,' 1701, 'The Inconstant,' 1702, 'The Twin Rivals,' 1702, 'The Stage Coach,' 1704, 'The Recruiting Officer,' 1706, and 'The Beaux' Stratagem,' 1707; served in Holland, 1700; died of mortification at not receiving the captaincy Ormonde had promised him.
[xviii. 221]

FARQUHAR, JOHN (1751–1826), millionaire; dangerously wounded when cadet on Bombay establishment; improved government powder factory at Pultah, and was made superintendent, subsequently sole contractor; partner in Basset, Farquhar & Co.'s agency house, London.
[xviii. 222]

FARQUHAR, SIR ROBERT TOWNSEND (1776–1830), politician; son of Sir Walter Farquhar [q. v.]; lieutenant-governor of Penang; commissioner for transference of Moluccas to Batavian Republic, 1802; governor and commander-in-chief of Mauritius, suppressing slave trade there, 1812–23; created baronet, 1821; M.P., Newton, 1825, Hythe, 1826–30.
[xviii. 223]

FARQUHAR, SIR WALTER (1738–1819), physician; M.A. King's College, Aberdeen; studied medicine at Edinburgh and Glasgow; army surgeon in Howe's expedition, 1761; M.D. Aberdeen, 1796; L.R.C.P., 1796; created baronet, 1796; physician in ordinary to the Prince of Wales, 1796.
[xviii. 224]

FARQUHARSON, JAMES (1781–1843), scientific writer; M.A. King's College, Aberdeen, 1798; minister of Alford, 1813; traced aurora borealis to development of electricity, 1830; F.R.S., 1830; LL.D. King's College, Aberdeen, 1837; published 'A New Illustration of the Latter Part of Daniel's Last Vision and Prophecy,' 1838, and essays and scientific papers.
[xviii. 224]

FARQUHARSON, JOHN (1699–1782), jesuit; studied at Scots College, Douay, 1729; missioner in Scotland; professed jesuit, 1736; formed collection of Gaelic poetry, including work assigned to Ossian, which was deposited (1772) in the Scots College, Douay, and forgotten; it was not known to Macpherson.
[xviii. 225]

FARR, SAMUEL (1741–1795), physician; educated at Edinburgh; M.D. Leyden, 1765; translated Hippocrates's 'History of Epidemics'; and wrote on medical topics.
[xviii. 225]

FARR, WILLIAM (1807–1883), statistician; studied medicine at Paris, 1829–31; L.A.S., 1832; inaugurated a new science by his 'Vital Statistics' in Macculloch's 'Account of the British Empire,' 1837; compiler of abstracts in registrar-general's office, 1838–79; honorary M.D. New York, 1847; F.R.S., 1855; honorary D.C.L. Oxford, 1857; commissioner for census of 1871; president of Statistical Society, 1871 and 1872; C.B., 1880; retired from public service, 1879. A selection of his works was edited by Noel Humphreys, 1885.
[xviii. 226]

FARRANT, RICHARD (*fl.* 1564–1580), composer; gentleman of the Chapel Royal before 1564; organist of St. George's Chapel, Windsor, 1564–9; presented two plays before the queen, 1568; possibly one of the first to set lessons for the viol 'lyra-way'; composed various anthems and a 'High Service.'
[xviii. 227]

FARRAR, JOHN (1802–1884), president of Wesleyan methodist conference; classical tutor at Wesleyan Theological Institution, Richmond, 1843–58; chaplain and governor of Woodhouse Grove school, 1858–68; first governor of Headingley College, Leeds, 1868–76; president

of Wesleyan conference, 1854 and 1870; compiled dictionaries of the bible and ecclesiastical history.
[xviii. 228]

FARRE, ARTHUR (1811–1887), obstetric physician; son of John Richard Farre [q. v.]; educated at Charterhouse and Caius College, Cambridge; studied at St. Bartholomew's Hospital; M.D. Cambridge, 1841; professor of obstetric medicine at King's College and physician-accoucheur to King's College Hospital, 1841–62; councillor, Royal College of Physicians; Harveian orator, 1872; examiner in midwifery, Royal College of Surgeons, 1852–75; physician extraordinary to Queen Victoria. [xviii. 229]

FARRE, FREDERIC JOHN (1804–1886), physician; son of John Richard Farre [q. v.]; educated at the Charterhouse and St. John's College, Cambridge; M.A., 1830; M.D. Cambridge, 1837; physician to St. Bartholomew's, 1854–70, to Royal London Ophthalmic Hospital, 1843–86; vice-president, College of Physicians, 1885; one of the editors of the first 'British Pharmacopœia,' 1864.
[xviii. 229]

FARRE, JOHN RICHARD (1775–1862), physician; born in Barbados; went to France on Lord Moira's expedition, 1793; practised as physician in Barbados; M.D. Aberdeen, 1806; L.R.C.P., 1806; co-founder of Royal London Ophthalmic Hospital, and physician there; published pathological works, 1812–14.
[xviii. 230]

FARREN, ELIZABETH, COUNTESS OF DERBY (1759?–1829), actress; appeared at the Haymarket, 1777; the original Nancy Lovel in Colman's 'Suicide,' 1778; appeared at Drury Lane, 1778; married Edward Stanley, twelfth earl of Derby, and retired, 1797; commended by Hazlitt for her 'fine-lady airs and graces.' [xviii. 230]

FARREN, HENRY (1826?–1860), actor; son of William Farren [q. v.]; played Charles Surface at the Haymarket, *c.* 1847; manager of Brighton Theatre; manager of the theatre at St. Louis, U.S.A., where he died.
[xviii. 231]

FARREN, WILLIAM (1786–1861), actor; played Sir Peter Teazle at Covent Garden, 1818; occasionally took such parts as Meg Merrilies and Miss Harlow in the 'Old Maid'; sued by Covent Garden management for appearing at Drury Lane, 1828; manager of Strand and (1850–3) of Olympic theatres; excelled in *rôle* of old man.
[xviii. 232]

FARRER, SIR THOMAS HENRY, first BARON FARRER (1819–1899), civil servant; educated at Eton and Balliol College, Oxford, B.A., 1840; barrister, Lincoln's Inn, 1844; assistant-secretary of marine department of board of trade, 1850; assistant-secretary to the board, 1854, and permanent-secretary, 1865–86; created baronet, 1883; member of London County Council, 1889–98; for several years vice-chairman; raised to peerage, 1893; published writings on economic subjects. [Suppl. ii. 201]

FARRIER, ROBERT (1796–1879), painter; exhibited miniature portraits, domestic subjects, and scenes from schoolboy life at the Royal Academy after 1818.
[xviii. 233]

FARRINGTON, SIR ANTHONY (1742–1823), baronet and general; lieutenant-fireworker, 1755; served at Gibraltar, 1759–63; captain, 1764; fought in early engagements of American war of independence; colonel, 1791; commanded artillery in North Holland, 1799; general, 1812; inspector-general of artillery, 1812; created baronet, 1818; honorary D.C.L. Oxford, 1820. [xviii. 234]

FARRINGTON, SIR WILLIAM (*fl.* 1412), soldier and diplomatist; knighted by the Duke of Lancaster, 1366; governor of Saintes; imprisoned in the Tower for negligently allowing a prisoner of war to escape, 1376; heavily fined for taking part in crusade led by the bishop of Norwich to support claim of Urban VI to papacy; with the Duke of Lancaster in Galicia; envoy to Portugal, 1390; commander of Bordeaux Castle, 1412. [xviii. 234]

FARROW, JOSEPH (1652?–1692), nonconformist divine; M.A. Magdalene College, Cambridge; friend of John Locke; private tutor; episcopally ordained chaplain in various country families. [xviii. 235]

FASTOLF, SIR JOHN (1378?–1459), warrior and landowner; undertook to serve Henry V in France, 1415; distinguished himself at Agincourt, 1415; governor of Condé-sur-Noireau, 1417; knighted before 1418; governor of the Bastille, 1420; king's lieutenant and regent in Normandy, 1423; governor of Anjou and Maine, 1423–6;

banneret; took prisoner John II, duke of Alençon, at the battle of Verneuil, 1424; K.G., 1426; defeated the French at 'the Battle of the Herrings' near Orleans, 1429; groundlessly accused of cowardice for retreating at Patay, 1429; assisted in negotiating peace of Arras, 1434; privy councillor; retired to the Tower on the outbreak of Cade's insurrection, 1450; built castle at Caister, his birthplace; friend of John Paston (1421-1466) [q. v.], author of the greater number of the 'Paston Letters'; contributed towards building the philosophy schools at Cambridge; left will (widely suspected to be a forgery) by which John Paston became owner of Caister Castle. Funds which Fastolf bequeathed to establish a college at Caister were ultimately transferred to the foundation of Magdalen College, Oxford, 1474. The few coincidences between the careers of Fastolf and Shakespeare's creation of Sir John Falstaff are accidental.   [xviii. 235]

FAUCIT, HELENA SAVILLE, afterwards LADY MARTIN (1817-1898), actress; known as HELEN FAUCIT; appeared first as Juliet at Richmond, 1833; engaged, 1836, at Covent Garden, at the Haymarket, 1839-41, and in Dublin and Birmingham, 1842-3; played in company with Macready, her parts including Constance ('King John'), Queen Katherine ('Henry VIII'), Desdemona, Cordelia, Miranda, Rosalind, Lady Macbeth, and Portia ('Julius Cæsar'); in Paris with Macready, 1842; played, with great success, Antigone, at Dublin, 1845; married Mr. (afterwards Sir) Theodore Martin, 1851; played Imogen to (Sir) Henry Irving's Pisanio, Edinburgh, 1857, and Lady Macbeth to Phelps's Macbeth at Her Majesty's, 1858; terminated last engagement in London, 1866, and appeared for the last time on stage at Manchester, 1879; published a book 'On some of Shakespeare's Female Characters,' 1885.   [Suppl. ii. 202]

FAUCONBERG, EARL (1627-1700). [See BELASYSE, THOMAS.]

FAUCONBERG, BARON (d. 1463). [See NEVILLE, WILLIAM, EARL OF KENT.]

FAUCONBERG, THOMAS, THE BASTARD OF, sometimes called THOMAS THE BASTARD (d. 1471), rebel; ordered to raise the county of Kent on behalf of Warwick and Henry VI, 1471; burnt part of London; his ships destroyed at Sandwich; beheaded.   [xviii. 240]

FAUCONBRIDGE, EUSTACE DE (d. 1228), bishop of London; royal justice, 1199 and after; treasurer, 1217; prebendary of St. Paul's; bishop of London, 1221-8; commissioned to demand Normandy from Louis VIII, 1223; ambassador to France, 1204, 1223, and 1225.
          [xviii. 240]

FAULKNER, SIR ARTHUR BROOKE (1779-1845), physician to the forces; B.A. Trinity College, Dublin; M.D. Edinburgh, 1803; incorporated M.A. of Catharine Hall, Cambridge, 1805, and M.D. of Pembroke College, Oxford, 1806; F.R.C.P., 1808; physician to the forces; distinguished himself by investigating the plague and directing quarantine procedure at Malta, 1813; knighted, 1815; published account of Malta plague, 1820, narratives of continental travel, and piquant pamphlets on supposed abuses in church and state.   [xviii. 241]

FAULKNER, BENJAMIN RAWLINSON (1787-1849), portrait-painter; originally Gibraltar agent for an English firm; exhibited at the Royal Academy from 1821.
          [xviii. 242]

FAULKNER, GEORGE (1699?-1775), bookseller; bookseller and printer in Dublin; started 'Dublin Journal,' 1728; reprimanded by Irish House of Lords for reflecting on 'the honour of their house,' 1733; committed to Newgate for publishing Hort's pamphlet containing a satiric reference to Serjeant Bettesworth, 1736; pirated Richardson's 'Pamela,' 1741; acknowledged by Lord Chesterfield, viceroy of Ireland, as his authoritative adviser; withdrew from publication of Richardson's 'Sir Charles Grandison' on finding out that other Dublin booksellers had obtained advance sheets, 1753; turned Roman catholic, 1758; satirised by Foote, 1762; alderman of Dublin, 1770; published 'Ancient Universal History,' 1774; friend of Swift; published Swift's works with notes, 1772.   [xviii. 242]

FAULKNER, GEORGE (1790?-1862), the supposed originator of the foundation of Owens College, Manchester; friend and partner of John Owens [q. v.] in a Manchester firm; suggested that Owens, who thought of

making him his heir, should leave money for the foundation of an undenominational university college; first chairman of the trustees of Owens College, 1851-8,
          [xviii. 244]

FAULKNER, JOSHUA WILSON (fl. 1809-1820), portrait-painter; brother of Benjamin Rawlinson Faulkner [q. v.]; exhibited miniatures at the Royal Academy.
          [xviii. 242]

FAULKNER, THOMAS (1777-1855), topographer of Chelsea; F.S.A. of Normandy; published history of Chelsea, 1810, Fulham, 1813, Kensington, 1820. Hammersmith, 1839, and Brentford, Chiswick, and Ealing, 1845.
          [xviii. 245]

FAULKNOR, ROBERT (1763-1795), navy captain; fought at battle of Grenada, 1779; specially complimented by Admiral Jervis, and promoted to post rank for capturing Fort Royal alone, 1794; foremost at capture of St. Lucia, Guadeloupe, and Fort Fleur d'Épée, 1794; killed on board the Blanche while endeavouring to lash bowsprit of the French frigate, Pique, to his capstan.
          [xviii. 245]

FAUNT, ARTHUR, in religion LAURENCE ARTHUR (1554-1591), jesuit; entered Merton College, Oxford, 1568; placed in the jesuit college at Louvain, 1570; B.A. Louvain; M.A. Munich; befriended by Pope Gregory XIII; first rector of jesuit college at Posen, 1581; professor of Greek, moral theology, and controversy at Posen; highly esteemed by the Polish estates; died at Wilna; published theological and philosophical works, writing also on Polish secular and ecclesiastical dissensions.   [xviii. 247]

FAUNT, NICHOLAS (fl. 1572-1608), clerk of the signet; educated at Caius and Corpus Christi Colleges, Cambridge; brought news of St. Bartholomew massacre to England, 1572; secretary to Sir Francis Walsingham, c. 1580; M.P., Boroughbridge, 1585; clerk of the signet, 1603; friend of Anthony Bacon [q. v.] and Sir Francis Bacon; wrote 'A Discourse touching the Office of Principal Secretary of State,' 1592 (unprinted).   [xviii. 247]

FAUNTLEROY, HENRY (1785-1824), banker and forger; partner in his father's bank of Marsh, Sibbald & Co., London, 1807-1824; arrested (1824) for fraudulently selling stock (1820) and for forging the trustees' signatures to a power of attorney; claimed to have been impelled by the desire of keeping up the credit of his banking house; executed, though numerous petitions were signed on his behalf, 1824.   [xviii. 248]

FAUQUIER, FRANCIS (1704?-1768), lieutenant-governor of Virginia; F.R.S., 1753; lieutenant-governor of Virginia, 1758; dissolved Virginian House of Burgesses on passing of Patrick Henry's resolutions about taxation, 1765; published 'An Essay on Ways and Means of Raising Money for the present War without Increasing the Public Debts,' 1756; died at Williamsburg. [xviii. 249]

FAUSSETT, BRYAN (1720-1776), antiquary; M.A. University College, Oxford, 1745; endeavoured to organise Jacobite volunteer corps, 1746; fellow of All Souls College, Oxford; rector of Monk's Horton; F.S.A., 1762; excavated Anglo-Saxon barrows in Kent and formed collection largely consisting of Anglo-Saxon ornaments.
          [xviii. 250]

FAUSSETT, THOMAS GODFREY, afterwards T. G. GODFREY-FAUSSETT (1829-1877), antiquary; scholar and fellow of Corpus Christi College, Cambridge; F.S.A., 1859; barrister, 1862; honorary secretary, Kent Archæological Society, 1863-73; auditor to Canterbury dean and chapter, 1866-77; contributed to archæological journals.
          [xviii. 250]

FAVERSHAM, SIMON OF (fl. 1300). [See SIMON.]

FAVOUR, JOHN (d. 1624), divine; educated at Winchester and New College, Oxford; fellow of New College, 1578; LL.D. Oxford, 1592; vicar of Halifax, 1594; warden of St. Mary Magdalen's Hospital at Ripon, Yorkshire, 1608 or 1616; prebendary and chantor of York, 1616; residentiary and chaplain to the archbishop; published a controversial 'Antiqvitie trivmphing over Noveltie,' 1619; lawyer and physician.   [xviii. 251]

FAWCETT, BENJAMIN (1715-1780), dissenting minister; minister of Paul's Meeting, Taunton, 1741-5, of Kidderminster, 1745; published 'Candid Reflections,' laying stress on the number of legitimate interpretations of Trinitarianism, 1777.   [xviii. 252]

FAWCETT, HENRY (1833–1884), statesman; educated at King's College School, London, and Peterhouse, Cambridge; B.A. Trinity Hall, Cambridge, 1856; fellow of Trinity Hall, 1856; student at Lincoln's Inn, 1854; lost his eyesight by a shooting accident, 1858; published 'Manual of Political Economy,' 1863; professor of political economy at Cambridge, 1863–84; issued pamphlets in favour of proportional representation, 1860; liberal M.P. for Brighton, after many defeats, 1865; largely contributed to passing of Reform Bill of 1867; re-elected for Brighton, 1868; M.P., Hackney, 1874; obtained appointment of committees upon Indian finance, 1871–3 and 1874; popularly known as the 'member for India'; advocated decided action in the matter of the Bulgarian atrocities, 1876; co-operated with Lord Lawrence in trying to make the Afghan war unpopular; re-elected for Hackney, 1880; postmaster-general in Gladstone's second administration, 1880; established the parcels post, 1882; introduced 'stamp slip deposits' scheme; doctor of political economy, Würzburg, 1882; F.R.S., 1882; corresponding member of the Institute of France, 1884; honorary LL.D. Glasgow, and lord rector, 1883; a consistent follower of John Stuart Mill. Most of his Cambridge lectures on political economy subsequently appeared in book form. [xviii. 252]

FAWCETT, JAMES (1752–1831), Norrisian professor at Cambridge; M.A. St. John's College, Cambridge, 1777; Constable fellow, 1777; Lady Margaret's preacher, 1782; B.D., 1785; Norrisian professor of divinity, 1795–1815; vicar of St. Sepulchre's, Cambridge, and (1801–31) rector of Thursford and Great Snoring. [xviii. 257]

FAWCETT, JOHN (d. 1793), actor; played at Drury Lane and Covent Garden, and in Dublin. [xviii. 258]

FAWCETT, JOHN (1740–1817), baptist theologian; baptist minister at Halifax; D.D.; best known by his 'Devotional Commentary on the Holy Scriptures,' 1811. [xviii. 257]

FAWCETT, JOHN (1768–1837), actor and dramatist; son of John Fawcett (d. 1793) [q. v.]; entered St. Paul's School, 1776; acted in Tate Wilkinson's company at York, 1787; played Jemmy Jumps in O'Keeffe's 'Farmer,' having been advised to devote his attention to low comedy; engaged for Covent Garden, 1791; held to eclipse all his contemporaries except Cooke as Falstaff in the 'Merry Wives of Windsor,' 1796; played Dr. Pangloss in Colman's 'Heir-at-Law,' 1797; stage-manager of the Haymarket, 1799–1802; superseded in the management of Covent Garden, 1829; treasurer and trustee of the Covent Garden Theatrical Fund, 1808–37; composed some pantomimes and spectacular ballets. [xviii. 258]

FAWCETT, JOHN, the younger (1825?–1857), organist; son of John Fawcett the elder [q. v.]; organist of St. John's Church, Farnworth, 1825–42, of Earl Howe's Curzon Street church, and of Bolton parish church; Mus. Bac. Oxford, 1852. [xviii. 259]

FAWCETT, JOHN, the elder (1789–1867), composer; organist, professor of music, and composer at Bolton; choirmaster of three chapels at Kendal and others in the midlands; upheld Lancashire sol-fa system of notation; composed anthems and psalm and hymn tunes. [xviii. 260]

FAWCETT, JOSEPH (d. 1804), dissenting minister and poet; morning preacher at Walthamstow, 1780–7; Sunday-evening lecturer at the Old Jewry; published sermons and poems, including 'War Elegies,' 1801. [xviii. 260]

FAWCETT, JOSHUA (d. 1864), miscellaneous writer; M.A. Trinity College, Cambridge, 1836; honorary canon of Ripon, and chaplain to the bishop, 1860; published 'A Harmony of the Gospels,' 1836, and miscellaneous works, largely on the archæology of Yorkshire churches. [xviii. 261]

FAWCETT, SIR WILLIAM (1728–1804), general; ensign during the '45; volunteer before Maestricht, 1748; ensign, 1751; adjutant; translated Marshal Saxe's 'Reveries or Memoirs of the Art of War,' 1757; aide-de-camp to General Elliott in Germany, 1757; announced victory of Warburg to George II in German, and was rewarded by a lieutenant-colonelcy, 1760; enlisted Hessians and Brunswickers to serve against America, c. 1775; governor of Gravesend; major-general, 1782; K.B., 1786; superseded as adjutant-general after the disastrous campaign in Flanders, 1794–5; general, 1796; privy councillor, 1799. [xviii. 261]

FAWKENER, SIR EVERARD (1684–1758), merchant and official; London merchant, probably in the silk and cloth trade; intimate with Voltaire, who began to write 'Brutus' at his house; knighted, 1735; ambassador to Constantinople, 1735; censured for precipitancy, 1736; secretary to the Duke of Cumberland; witness against his acquaintance, Lord Lovat, who declined to examine him, 1747; joint postmaster-general, 1745–58. [xviii. 262]

FAWKES, FRANCIS (1720–1777), poet and divine; scholar of Jesus College, Cambridge, 1742; M.A., 1745; given church preferment by Archbishop Herring; bewailed Herring's death in 'Aurelius,' an elegy, 1757; curate of Downe, 1774–7; translated Theocritus, 1767, Anacreon, Sappho, Bion, Moschus, and Musæus, 1760; modernised parts of Gawin Douglas, 1752 and 1754; composed 'The Brown Jug,' a famous comic song; considered by his contemporaries the best translator since Pope. [xviii. 264]

FAWKES, GUY (1570–1606), conspirator; of protestant parentage; adopted Roman catholicism; disposed of his estate; enlisted (1593) in the Spanish army in Flanders; present at capture of Calais, 1595; had no share in originating Gunpowder plot; accompanied Catesby to a secret meeting with Velasco, the constable of Castile, 1604; deputed to fire the powder under the Houses of Parliament, 1605; undertook to watch the cellar by himself, unaware that the plot had become known at court, 3 Nov. 1605; discovered, 4 Nov. 1605; revealed under torture the names of his fellow-conspirators, 9 Nov. 1605; exonerated 'the holy fathers' from all share in the conspiracy; executed. [xviii. 265]

FAWKES, WALTER RAMSDEN (1769–1825), miscellaneous writer; M.P., Yorkshire, 1802–7; abolitionist; high sheriff of Yorkshire, 1823; an early patron of Turner; agriculturist and cattle-breeder; chief work, 'The Chronology of the History of Modern Europe,' 1810. [xviii. 269]

FAWKNER, JOHN PASCOE (1792–1869), Australian settler; son of a convict; practised various trades in Tasmania; undertook the 'Launceston Advertiser,' changing its name to 'Tasmanian Advertiser,' 1829; did much to stimulate and direct his associates, the founders of Victoria; started 'Melbourne Advertiser,' 1838; commenced 'Port Phillip Patriot,' 1839; helped to bring about final separation of Victoria from New South Wales in 1850 by getting Melbourne to choose as its representative in the legislative council at Sydney first Lord Grey and then five of the leading English statesmen; member for Anglesea, Dalhousie, and Talbot in the new council of Victoria; helped to found Australian League, 1851. [xviii. 269]

FAZAKERLEY, NICHOLAS (d. 1767), lawyer and politician; barrister, Middle Temple; an authority on conveyancing; occasionally retained in state trials; M.P., Preston, 1732–67; recorder of Preston, 1742–67; resolutely opposed the marriage clause in Lord Hardwicke's Regency Bill, 1751; Jacobite. [xviii. 270]

FEAD, GEORGE (1729?–1815), lieutenant-general; colonel-commandant, fourth battalion royal artillery; lieutenant-fireworker royal artillery, 1756; present at siege of Louisburg, Cape Breton, 1758; commanded artillery in Minorca, 1774–81, subsequently in Jamaica; lieutenant-governor of Port Royal and lieutenant-general, 1810. [xviii. 271]

FEAKE, CHRISTOPHER (fl. 1645–1660), Fifth-monarchy man; vicar of All Saints, Hertford, 1646; vicar of Christ Church, Newgate, 1649; vilified Cromwell, 1653; liberated from confinement, 1655; published millenarian writings and attacks on the quakers. [xviii. 271]

FEARCHAIR or FERCHARDUS I (622?–636?), fifty-second king of Scottish Dalriada according to Boece and Buchanan, ninth according to the rectified list of Father Innes. [xviii. 273]

FEARCHAIR FADA ('The Long') or FERCHARDUS II (d. 697), fifty-fourth king of Scottish Dalriada according to Boece and Buchanan, twelfth according to Father Innes; possibly led a revolt against the Britons and Angles. [xviii. 273]

FEARGAL (d. 785). [See FERGIL.]

FEARN, HENRY NOEL- (1811–1868). [See CHRISTMAS, HENRY.]

FEARN, JOHN (1768–1837), philosopher; served in the royal navy; professed to base on induction a philosophy which he unfolded in ' A Manual of the Physiology of Mind,' 1829, and other works.   [xviii. 273]

FEARNE, CHARLES (1742–1794), legal writer: educated at Westminster; resided for some time at the Inner Temple; discovered new process of dyeing morocco; compared by Lord Campbell to Pascal or Sir Isaac Newton for his 'Essay on the Learning of Contingent Remainders and Executory Devises,' 1772.   [xviii. 274]

FEARY, JOHN (*fl.* 1770–1788), landscape-painter; obtained premium from the Society of Arts for a drawing from Duke of Richmond's gallery, 1766; exhibited at the Free Society of Artists, 1770–1, at the Royal Academy, 1772–88.   [xviii. 275]

FEATHERSTON, ISAAC EARL (1813–1876), New Zealand statesman; M.D. Edinburgh, 1836; settled at Wellington, New Zealand, 1840; advocated cause of settlers under New Zealand Company, his action ultimately leading to New Zealand Constitution Act of 1853; superintendent of the province of Wellington; supported 'provincialism'; denounced Maori war, 1860; agent-general for New Zealand, 1871–6.   [xviii. 275]

FEATLEY or **FAIRCLOUGH**, DANIEL (1582–1645), controversialist; scholar of Corpus Christi College, Oxford, 1594; B.A., 1601; probationer-fellow, 1602; M.A., 1605; domestic chaplain to Abbot, archbishop of Canterbury, till 1625; D.D., 1617; rector of Lambeth, 1619, of All Hallows, Bread Street, before 1625, of Acton, 1627; published, by direction of Archbishop Abbot, report of conference between Featley and some jesuits, 1624; engaged, with James I, in a 'scholastick duel,' 1625; composed 'Ancilla Pietatis,' a devotional manual, much used by Charles I, 1626; provost of Chelsea College, 1630; refused to turn the communion table in his church at Lambeth 'altar-wise'; one of the sub-committee 'to settle religion,' 1641; narrowly escaped being murdered, 1642–1643, as an adherent of the church of England; reported some proceedings against him before the exchequer court (1643) in 'Spongia,' 1644; member of the Westminster assembly, 1643; best-known work, 'Καταβαπτισταὶ καταπτυστοί. The Dippers dipt,' 1645.   [xviii. 276]

FEATLEY or **FAIRCLOUGH**, JOHN (1605 ?–1666), divine; nephew of Daniel Featley [q. v.]; chorister of All Souls College, Oxford; B.A., 1624; 'first preacher of the Gospel' in St. Christopher's, 1626; chaplain to Charles I, 1639–43; chaplain extraordinary to the king, precentor of Lincoln, and prebendary, 1660; D.D. Oxford, by royal mandamus, 1661.   [xviii. 280]

FEATLEY, RICHARD (1621–1682). [See FAIRCLOUGH.]

FECHIN, SAINT (*d.* 664), born in Connaught; bade Themaria, queen of Diarmait, king of Meath, find the way of her salvation in dressing the sores of a leper; founded the abbeys of Cong and Eas-dara with ten other religious houses.   [xviii. 280]

FECHTER, CHARLES ALBERT (1824–1879), actor and dramatist; of German origin; made, as pensionnaire, his début at the Comédie Française in 1844; performed at Berlin, 1846; first appeared in London with a French company in version of Sophocles's 'Antigone' at St. James's Theatre, 1847; played Armand Duval in 'La Dame aux Camélias' with brilliant success at the Vaudeville, Paris, 1852; abandoned the French for the English stage in 1860, and thenceforth acted in English; gave famous representation of Hamlet at the Princess's Theatre, 1861; failed as Othello, 1861; lessee of the Lyceum, 1863–7, acting in English translations or adaptations, sometimes his own, from the French melodrama; manager of the Globe Theatre, New York, 1870–1; excelled in the rôle of lover; died near Philadelphia.   [xviii. 281]

FECKENHAM, JOHN DE (1518 ?–1585), last abbot of Westminster; of humble origin; admitted into Evesham monastery; B.D. Gloucester Hall, Oxford, 1539; rector of Solihull; chaplain to bishops Bell and (1543–9) Bonner; private chaplain and confessor to Queen Mary, 1553; prebendary, and subsequently dean, of St. Paul's, 1554; saved twenty-eight at one time from the stake in Mary's reign; D.D. Oxford, 1556; mitred abbot of the refounded abbey of St. Peter's, Westminster, 1556; revived privileges of sanctuary, 1557; lost the favour of Elizabeth by stoutly maintaining his religious faith; removed from the abbey, 1559; sent to the Tower 'for railing against the changes that had been made,' 1560; committed to the charge of Richard Cox, bishop of Ely, 1577; known to have written 'Commentaries on the Psalms, and some theological treatises.   [xviii. 282]

FEILD, EDWARD (1801–1876), bishop of Newfoundland; educated at Rugby and Queen's College, Oxford; M.A., 1826; Michel fellow, 1825–33; curate of Kidlington, 1827–34; incumbent of English Bicknor, 1834–44; built schools in both these parishes; inspector of schools, 1840; D.D., 1844; bishop of Newfoundland, 1844; procured building of a cathedral at St. John's; worked energetically in his diocese; refused diocese of Montreal, 1868; died in Bermuda.   [xviii. 286]

FEILD, JOHN (1525 ?–1587). [See FIELD.]

FEILDE or **FIELD**, JOHN (*d.* 1588), puritan divine; educated at Oxford University; imprisoned, as a heretic, in Newgate, with Thomas Wilcox [q. v.] for presenting to parliament 'An Admonition' and a petition for relief, 1572–3; preacher and catechist of St. Mary Aldermary, 1573–7; inhibited by Aylmer, 1577; suspended, 1584; published 'A Caveat for Parsons Hovvlet,' 1581, 'A Godly Exhortation,' 1583, and translations from several foreign divines.   [Suppl. ii. 205]

FEILDING. [See also FIELDING.]

FEILDING, BASIL, second EARL OF DENBIGH (*d.* 1674), eldest son of William Feilding, first earl [q. v.]; educated at Emmanuel College, Cambridge; K.B., 1626; summoned to Lords as Baron Feilding of Newnham Paddox, 1628; volunteer at the siege of Bois-le-Duc, 1629; ambassador extraordinary to Venetian republic, 1634–9; fought for parliament at Edgehill, 1642; commander-in-chief of parliamentarian forces in Warwick, Worcester, Stafford, Shropshire, Coventry, and Lichfield, 1643; defeated royalists near Dudley, 1644; suspected of half-heartedness, and superseded, 1644; a commissioner for the treaty of Uxbridge, 1645; refused to have any share in the trial of Charles I, 1648; state councillor, 1649–51; gradually went over to the royalists; created Baron St. Liz, 1664.   [xviii. 287]

FEILDING, ROBERT, called BEAU FEILDING (1651 ?–1712), related to the Denbigh family; given a regiment by James II, whom he followed to Ireland; sat in Irish parliament for Gowran, 1689; married, on 9 Nov. 1705, Mary Wadsworth, whom a matchmaker had enabled to personate Mrs. Deleau, a rich widow; on 25 Nov. 1705 he also married the Duchess of Cleveland; convicted of bigamy, 1706; ridiculed by Swift.   [xviii. 289]

FEILDING, WILLIAM, first EARL OF DENBIGH (*d.* 1643), educated at Emmanuel College, Cambridge; knighted, 1603; married Buckingham's sister, and became (1622) master of the great wardrobe; created Baron Feilding, 1620, and Earl of Denbigh, 1622; followed Buckingham and Prince Charles to Spain, 1623; commanded fleet despatched to relieve Rochelle, 1628; member of council of Wales, 1633; made voyage to India, 1631; volunteer under Prince Rupert; mortally wounded in Rupert's attack on Nottingham.   [xviii. 290]

FEINAIGLE, GREGOR VON (1765 ?–1819), mnemonist; born at Baden; lectured on local and symbolical memory at Paris, 1806; ridiculed on the stage by Dieulafoy in 'Les filles de mémoire'; lectured in England and Scotland, 1811; published 'The New Art of Memory,' 1812, a system founded on the topical memory of Cicero and Quintilian. A mnemonic school was placed under his personal superintendence at Dublin.   [xviii. 291]

FELIX, SAINT (*d.* 647 ?), bishop of Dunwich; a native of Burgundy; consecrated bishop of East-Anglia by Honorius; founded school, perhaps at Cambridge, and, according to the 'Liber Eliensis,' monastery at Soham, near Ely; his day, 8 March.   [xviii. 291]

FELIX, JOHN (*fl.* 1498), Benedictine monk of Westminster; wrote life of John Estney, abbot of Westminster from 1474 to 1498.   [xviii. 292]

FELIX, N. (pseudonym). [See WANOSTROCHT, NICHOLAS, 1804–1876.]

FELL, CHARLES (1687–1763), Roman catholic divine; of French extraction; his real name UMFREVILLE; studied at Paris and Douay; priest, 1713; D.D., 1716; missioner in England; irregularly elected member of chapter, 1732; deposed by a court of appeal; financially ruined by his 'Lives of Saints,' 1729. [xviii. 292]

FELL, HENRY (*fl.* 1672), quaker; missionary in the West Indies; travelling preacher in England; nearly killed (1660) in the Fifth-monarchy rising; his project of preaching in 'Prester John's country and China 'thwarted by the action of the East India Company, 1661; died probably in Barbados; published quaker pamphlets.
[xviii. 292]

FELL, JOHN (1625–1686), dean of Christ Church and bishop of Oxford; son of Samuel Fell [q. v.]; student of Christ Church, 1636; M.A., 1643; ejected from studentship, 1648; dean of Christ Church, 1660; D.D. Oxford, and chaplain to the king, 1660; built the tower over the principal gateway of Christ Church, to which he transferred the re-cast bell, 'Great Tom'; procured every year the publication of some classical author, giving each member of his college a copy; vice-chancellor of Oxford, 1666–9; friend of Humphrey Prideaux [q. v.]; projected printing of a Malay gospel; bishop of Oxford, 1675; reluctantly expelled John Locke from Christ Church, 1684; summoned the undergraduates to take up arms against Monmouth, 1685; theme of Tom Brown's epigram 'I do not like you, Dr. Fell.' His chief publication was a critical edition of St. Cyprian, 1682. [xviii. 293]

FELL, JOHN (1735–1797), congregational minister and classical tutor; minister of congregational church at Thaxted, Essex, 1770–87; classical tutor at Homerton, 1787–97; compelled to resign by insubordination of students, 1797; controverted views of Hugh Farmer [q. v.] and Joshua Toulmin, D.D. [xviii. 295]

FELL, LEONARD (*d.* 1700), quaker; repeatedly imprisoned for interrupting services between 1654 and 1657; imprisoned for refusing to pay tithes, 1666; worked in North Wales and Cumberland; so impressed a highwayman on one occasion by his Christian charity that his stolen property was returned. [xviii. 296]

FELL, MARGARET (1614–1702), quakeress; *née* Askew; married, *c.* 1632, Thomas Fell [q. v.]; converted by George Fox when her guest, 1652; entreated Oliver Cromwell to protect the quakers, 1655–7; called Charles II's attention to his declaration at Breda; prevailed on Charles II to release more than four thousand Friends from prison, 1661; exempted by Charles II from liability to sentence of præmunire, 1664; sentenced by a Lancashire magistrate to the penalties of præmunire, 1664; released from prison, 1668; married, as second husband, George Fox, 1669; petitioned Charles II for the release of her husband, but refused a pardon, considering him innocent, 1673; published religious works. [xviii. 297]

FELL, SAMUEL (1584–1649), dean of Christ Church; educated at Westminster; M.A. Christ Church, Oxford, 1608; D.D., 1619; chaplain to James I; canon of Christ Church, 1619–37; Lady Margaret professor of divinity, 1626–37; dean of Lichfield, 1638; dean of Christ Church, 1638; wrote to Laud about the excessive number of alehouses in Oxford, 1637; vice-chancellor, 1645–7; deprived, 1647; died of grief at Charles I's execution. [xviii. 298]

FELL, THOMAS (1598–1658), vice-chancellor of the duchy of Lancaster; barrister, Gray's Inn, 1631; J.P. for Lancashire, 1641; M.P., Lancaster, 1645; vice-chancellor of the duchy and attorney for the county palatine, 1649; bencher of Gray's Inn, 1651; judge of assize for Chester and North Wales circuit, 1651; lent his house, Swarthmore Hall, for quaker meetings; withdrew from public life, disapproving of the Protector's assumption of authority. [xviii. 299]

FELL, WILLIAM (1758?–1848), author; schoolmaster at Manchester, Wilmslow, and Lancaster; published, among other works, 'A System of Political Economy,' 1808. [xviii. 300]

FELLOWES, JAMES (*fl.* 1710–1730), portrait-painter; known for portraits of eminent clergymen of his time; represented Dr. White Kennett [q. v.] as Judas Iscariot.
[xviii. 300]

FELLOWES, SIR JAMES (1771–1857), physician; brother of Sir Thomas Fellowes [q. v.]; educated at Eton and Peterhouse, and Gonville and Caius College, Cambridge; Perse fellow; M.D., 1803; F.R.C.P., 1805; physician to the forces; sent to investigate and treat pestilential fever in San Domingo, 1804; knighted, 1809; chief of the medical staff at Cadiz till 1815; described in 1815 the Andalusian pestilence. [xviii. 300]

FELLOWES, ROBERT (1771–1847), philanthropist; M.A. St. Mary Hall, Oxford, 1801; editor of 'Critical Review,' 1804–11; friend of Dr. Parr and Queen Caroline; LL.D.; benefactor of Edinburgh University; a promoter of London University; instituted 'Fellowes medals' in University College, London; advocated Jewish emancipation; liberal thinker in religion; published, among other works, 'Morality united with Policy,' 1800, and 'The Religion of the Universe,' 1836. [xviii. 300]

FELLOWES, SIR THOMAS (1778–1853), rear-admiral; brother of Sir James Fellowes [q. v.]; master's mate in royal navy, 1797; lieutenant, 1807; heroically spiked battery at Guadeloupe, 1809; commanded gunboats at Cadiz, 1810–11; decorated by Greece and Russia for his services at the battle of Navarino, 1827; knighted, 1828; D.C.L. Oxford, 1830; rear-admiral, 1847.
[xviii. 301]

FELLOWS, SIR CHARLES (1799–1860), traveller and archæologist; member of the British Association, 1820; discovered ruins of Xanthus and of Tlos, 1838; published 'Journal,' 1839; discovered thirteen ancient cities in Lycia, after 1839; obtained firman from Constantinople permitting him to explore, 1841; published 'An Account of Discoveries in Lycia,' 1841; published, to refute misstatement, 'The Xanthian Marbles, their Acquisition and Transmission to England,' 1843; knighted, 1845; Lycian numismatologist. [xviii. 302]

FELLTHAM, OWEN (1602?–1668), author of 'Resolves'; published, *c.* 1620, 'Resolves,' a series of moral essays, when eighteen years of age; secretary or chaplain to the Earl of Thomond; contributed to 'Jonsonus Virbius,' 1638; called the dead Charles I 'Christ the Second'; published 'Brief Character of the Low Countries,' 1652.
[xviii. 303]

FELTON, HENRY (1679–1740), divine; educated at Westminster, Charterhouse, and St. Edmund Hall, Oxford; M.A., 1702; in charge of the English church at Amsterdam, 1708–9; domestic chaplain to three dukes of Rutland; presented to rectory of Whitwell, 1711; D.D., 1712; controverted Locke's theory of personality and identity, 1725; his Lady Moyer lectures (1728–9) published as 'The Christian Faith asserted against Deists, &c.,' 1732. [xviii. 305]

FELTON, JOHN (*fl.* 1430), divine; fellow of St. Mary Magdalen College, Oxford; professor of theology and 'vicarius Magdalensis Oxonii extra muros'; presented books to Balliol College, 1420; left sermons and an 'Alphabetum theologicum ex opusculis Rob. Grost. collectum.' [xviii. 305]

FELTON, JOHN (*d.* 1570), Roman catholic layman; affixed Pius V's excommunication of Elizabeth to the gates of the bishop of London's palace, 1570; arrested and hanged, 1570. [xviii. 306]

FELTON, JOHN (1595?–1628), assassin of the Duke of Buckingham; of a good Suffolk family; lieutenant at Cadiz, 1625; his application to Buckingham for a captain's commission scornfully refused, 1627; was incited by reading 'The Golden Epistles' to plan Buckingham's assassination, 1628; stabbed Buckingham at Portsmouth, 1628; described as a national benefactor in popular ballads; hanged. [xviii. 307]

FELTON, NICHOLAS (1556–1626), bishop of Ely; son of a sailor; fellow of Pembroke College, Cambridge, 1583; M.A., 1584; D.D., 1602; prebendary of St. Paul's, 1616; bishop of Bristol, 1617–19; master of Pembroke, 1617–19; bishop of Ely, 1619; favoured puritans; compiled statutes for Merchant Taylors' in reference to annual probation days; helped to translate Epistles for Authorised Version. [xviii. 308]

FELTON, SIR THOMAS (*d.* 1381), seneschal of Aquitaine; took part in battle of Crécy, 1346, and capture of Calais, 1347; fought at Poitiers, 1356; signatory to treaty of Bretigny, 1360; seneschal of Aquitaine; despatched to conduct Don Pedro of Castile to his intending ally, the Black Prince; taken prisoner by Henry of Trastamare's

forces, 1367 ; joint-governor of Aquitaine, 1372 ; seneschal of Bordeaux ; caused Guillaume de Pommiers and his secretary to be beheaded for treason, 1377 ; K.G., 1381.
[xviii. 309]

FELTON, THOMAS (1567 ? – 1588), Franciscan friar ; son of John Felton (d. 1570) [q. v.] ; received the first tonsure at Rheims, 1583 ; returned to England, being unable to endure Minims austerities ; hanged for refusing the oath of supremacy. [xviii. 310]

FELTON, SIR WILLIAM (d. 1367), seneschal of Poitou ; took part in battle of Halidon Hill, 1333 ; fought at Crécy, 1346 ; lord justice of all the king's lands in Scotland, 1348 ; fought at battle of Poitiers, 1356 ; seneschal of Poitou, 1360 ; accompanied Black Prince on Spanish campaign, 1367 ; called by Chandos herald ' Felleton Guilliam qui ot cœur de lyon ' ; killed in skirmish at Inglesmundi in Alava. [xviii. 311]

FELTON, WILLIAM (1713–1769), composer ; M.A. St. John's College, Cambridge, 1745 ; chaplain to the Princess Dowager of Wales ; composed three sets of six concertos, modelled on Handel's ; composed the glee, ' Fill, fill, fill the glass.' [xviii. 311]

FENN, ELEANOR, LADY (1743–1813), author ; wife of Sir John Fenn [q. v.] ; wrote, under the names of Mrs. Lovechild and Mrs. Teachwell, educational works for the young. [xviii. 314]

FENN, HUMPHREY (d. 1634), puritan divine ; B.A. Queens' College, Cambridge, 1573 ; M.A. Peterhouse, 1576 ; vicar of Holy Trinity, Coventry, 1578–84 ; suspended (1584) for refusing to subscribe Whitgift's three articles ; restored, 1585 ; again suspended, 1590 ; cited before the Star-chamber, 1591 ; remanded, 1591 ; released, 1592 ; protested against episcopacy in his will.
[xviii. 312]

FENN, JAMES (d. 1584), Roman catholic priest ; scholar of Corpus Christi College, Oxford, 1554 ; fellow, 1558 ; B.A., 1559, but put aside for refusing the oath of supremacy ; ordained priest at Châlons-sur-Marne, 1580 ; missioner in Somerset ; executed as a priest. [xviii. 313]

FENN, JOHN (d. 1615), Roman catholic divine ; brother of James Fenn [q. v.] ; chorister of Wells ; educated at Winchester and New College, Oxford ; perpetual fellow, 1552 ; schoolmaster at Bury St. Edmunds ; confessor to English Augustinian nuns at Louvain, where he died ; martyrologist, hagiologist, and writer or translator of Italian devotional works. [xviii. 313]

FENN, SIR JOHN (1739–1794), antiquary ; M.A. Caius College, Cambridge, 1764 ; J.P. for Norfolk ; M.S.A. ; edited manuscript of Paston letters, which he acquired from Thomas Worth, a chemist at Diss ; knighted, 1787 ; sheriff of Norfolk, 1791. [xviii. 314]

FENN, JOSEPH FINCH (1820–1884), honorary canon of Gloucester ; M.A. Trinity College, Cambridge, 1845 ; fellow, 1844–7 ; B.D., 1877 ; perpetual curate of Christ Church, Cheltenham, 1860 ; chaplain to the bishop of Gloucester and Bristol, 1877 ; honorary canon, 1879 ; promoted free library movement in Cheltenham.
[xviii. 315]

FENNELL, JAMES (1766–1816), actor and dramatist ; educated at Eton and Trinity College, Cambridge ; entered Lincoln's Inn ; engaged at Theatre Royal, Edinburgh, 1787 ; appeared at Covent Garden as Othello, 1787 ; objected to a proposal that he should play Pierre instead of Jaffier in ' Venice Preserved ' at Edinburgh ; after some legal difficulties occasioned by the subsequent riot consented to a compromise, 1788 ; reappeared at Covent Garden as Othello ; brought out at Richmond his ' Linda and Clara,' a comedy, 1791 ; acted in New York, Boston, and elsewhere, 1797–1806 ; kept an academy at Charlestown, Massachusetts ; established saltworks near New London, Connecticut, 1814. [xviii. 315]

FENNELL, JOHN GREVILLE (1807–1885), artist, naturalist, and angler ; drew pictures of the tournament at Eglinton Castle for the ' Illustrated London News ' ; member of ' Field ' staff from 1853 ; intimate with Dickens, Thackeray, and other literary men ; published ' The Rail and the Rod,' and ' The Book of the Roach,' 1870. [xviii. 316]

FENNER, DUDLEY (1558 ?–1587), puritan divine ; fellow-commoner of Peterhouse, Cambridge, 1575 ; expelled for puritanical tendencies ; followed Thomas Cartwright to Antwerp ; induced by the tolerant spirit of Archbishop Grindal to return to England ; curate at Cranbrook, 1583 ; suspended for refusing to subscribe Whitgift's three articles, 1584 ; published works, including ' Sacra Theologia,' 1585, and, posthumously, ' The Whole Doctrine of the Sacramentes,' 1588, as well as verse-rendering ' The Song of Songs,' 1587 and 1594 ; died in charge of the reformed church at Middleburg.
[xviii. 317]

FENNER, EDWARD (d. 1612), judge ; barrister, Middle Temple ; reader, 1576 ; serjeant, 1577 ; J.P. for Surrey ; justice of king's bench, 1590. [xviii. 319]

FENNER, GEORGE (d. 1600 ?), naval commander ; engaged in trading to Gold Coast, 1566, and Low Countries, 1570 ; as freebooter came frequently into conflict with Spanish and French ships ; accompanied Essex on Islands' Voyage, 1597 ; brought news of supposed approach of Armada to Plymouth, 1597, which occasioned naval mobilisation, 1597. [Suppl. ii. 206]

FENNER, THOMAS (d. 1590 ?), naval commander ; flag-captain under Drake on Indies voyage, 1585 ; probably rear-admiral in Drake's Cadiz expedition, 1587 ; vice-admiral against Armada, 1588, and in expedition to Coruña, 1589. [Suppl. ii. 207]

FENNER, WILLIAM (1600–1640), puritan divine ; M.A. Pembroke College, Cambridge, 1619 ; forced to leave cure of Sedgley on account of his puritanical principles, c. 1627 ; B.D., 1627 ; incumbent of Rochford, 1629–40 ; wrote theological treatises. [xviii. 319]

FENNING, ELIZABETH (1792–1815), criminal ; hanged for mixing arsenic in the food of her employer, Orlibar Turner ; strongly asseverated her innocence ; verdict against her twice reconsidered by home office ; hanged, 26 June 1815. [xviii. 319]

FENTON, first VISCOUNT (1566–1639). [See ERSKINE, THOMAS.]

FENTON, EDWARD (d. 1603), captain and navigator ; commanded under Sir Henry Sidney in Ireland, 1566 ; published ' Certaine Secrete Wonders of Nature,' 1569, recently discovered to be a translation of Boaistuau's compilation of Greek and Roman anecdotes ; sailed in Frobisher's second voyage to discover north-west passage to Cathay and Meta Incognita, 1577 ; built a house for the members of Frobisher's third expedition upon the Countess of Warwick's (Kod-lu-aru) Island, 1578 ; sent on a trading expedition to Moluccas and China by way of Cape of Good Hope, nominally to discover the north-west passage, 1582 ; thought of making himself king of St. Helena ; served against Spanish Armada, 1588. [xviii. 320]

FENTON, EDWARD DYNE (d. 1880), author ; lieutenant, 1849 ; captain, 1858 ; served at Gibraltar, 1860–70 ; published sketches, including ' Sorties from Gib. in quest of Sensation and Sentiment,' 1872.
[xviii. 322]

FENTON, ELIJAH (1683–1730), poet ; B.A. Jesus College, Cambridge, 1704 ; secretary to Earl of Orrery in Flanders ; head-master of Sevenoaks grammar school ; published poems (1707) which attracted attention of Duke of Marlborough ; instructed Craggs, secretary of state, in literature, 1720 ; translated the first, fourth, nineteenth, and twentieth books of the ' Odyssey ' for Pope, completely catching Pope's manner ; edited Milton and (1729) Waller. His poems include a successful tragedy, ' Mariamne,' 1723. [xviii. 322]

FENTON, SIR GEOFFREY (1539 ?–1608), translator and statesman ; dedicated to Lady Mary Sydney, from Paris, a collection of novels by Bandello translated from French versions of Boaistuau and Belleforest, 1567 ; published ' Monophylo, a Philosophical Discourse and Division of Love,' 1572 ; translated from the French Guicciardini's ' Wars of Italy,' 1579 ; served on an Irish campaign, 1580 ; principal secretary of state in Ireland from 1580 ; thrown into the debtors' prison at Dublin by Lord deputy Perrot, against whom he had laid accusations, 1586 ; knighted, 1589 ; joint-secretary for Ireland with Sir Richard Coke ; advocated assassination of Earl of Desmond as means of ending Munster rebellion. [xviii. 323]

FENTON, LAVINIA, afterwards DUCHESS OF BOLTON (1708–1760), actress ; learned new songs when a girl from ' a comedian belonging to the old house ' ; appeared at the Haymarket as Monimia in Otway's ' Orphans,' 1726 ; appeared at Lincoln's Inn Fields as Polly Peachum in

Gay's 'Beggar's Opera,' 1728, after which she became the rage; played Ophelia in 'Hamlet,' 1728; mistress, and (1751) wife, of Charles Paulet, third duke of Bolton [q. v.] [xviii. 324]

FENTON, RICHARD (1746–1821), topographer and poet; educated at St. David's cathedral school; barrister, Middle Temple; left manuscript translation of the 'Deipnosophistæ.' His works include 'Poems,' 1773, 'A Historical Tour through Pembrokeshire,' 1811, and 'Memoirs of an Old Wig,' 1815. [xviii. 326]

FENTON, ROGER (1565–1616), divine; fellow of Pembroke Hall, Cambridge; vicar of Chigwell, 1606; prebendary of St. Paul's, 1609; preacher to the readers at Gray's Inn; D.D.; published 'A Treatise of Usurie,' 1611; took part in translation of bible; his theological writings published posthumously. [xviii. 327]

FENTONBARNS, LORD (d. 1616). [See PRESTON, SIR JOHN.]

FENWICK, FRANCIS (1645–1694), Benedictine monk; doctor of the Sorbonne; D.D.; agent of James II at the papal court; abbot-president of St. Gregory's College at Rome; died in Rome. [xviii. 327]

FENWICK, GEORGE (1603?–1657), parliamentarian; barrister at Gray's Inn, 1631; ancient, 1650; agent for the patentees of Connecticut, and governor of Saybrook fort, 1639–44; sold Saybrook to Connecticut under pledges which he broke, 1644; M.P. for Morpeth, 1645; commanded regiment of northern militia for parliament; governor of Berwick, 1648; commissioner for the trial of Charles I, but did not act, 1648; took part in Cromwell's invasion of Scotland; governor of Leith and Edinburgh Castle, 1650; one of the commissioners for the government of Scotland, 1651; M.P. for Berwick, 1654 and 1656; excluded, 1656. [xviii. 328]

FENWICK or FENWICKE, SIR JOHN (1579–1658?), politician; M.P. for Northumberland, 1623–44; baronet by purchase, 1628; commissioner for suppression of violence in border districts, 1635; deputy-lieutenant of Northumberland; muster-master-general of the king's army, 1640; excluded from the House of Commons, 1644; readmitted, 1646; high sheriff of Northumberland. [xviii. 329]

FENWICK, veré CALDWELL, JOHN (1628–1679), jesuit; of protestant parentage; jesuit, 1656; procurator at St. Omer, 1662, and afterwards; professed father, 1675; procurator in London of St. Omer's College, 1675; executed on the information of Titus Oates, 1679. [xviii. 328]

FENWICK, SIR JOHN (1645?–1697), conspirator; colonel of foot, 1675; general, 1688; M.P., Northumberland, 1677, and at intervals till 1685; brought up the bill of attainder against Monmouth, 1685; insulted Queen Mary, 1691; privy to plot for William III's assassination, 1695, and Barclay and Charnock's plot, 1696; named major-general of the troops to be raised for King James; attempted to bribe two men who were likely to be witnesses against him, and was indicted on the information of one of them, 1696; arrested, 1696; offered for a pardon to reveal all that he knew of the Jacobite conspiracies, but did no more than cast aspersion on the whig leaders, 1696; examined before the king and the House of Commons; attainted, the law requiring the evidence of two witnesses in cases of treason being dispensed with; shrank from adopting Monmouth's advice to save himself by challenging inquiry into the truth of his allegations against the whig leaders; beheaded. [xviii. 329]

FENWICKE, GEORGE (1690–1760), divine; fellow of St. John's College, Cambridge, 1710; rector of Hallaton, 1722–60; B.D.; published devotional works. [xviii. 332]

FENWICKE, JOHN (d. 1658), parliamentarian; master of Sherborne Hospital, 1644; lieutenant-colonel in parliamentarian army; defeated Irish rebels near Trim, 1647; mortally wounded in battle of the Dunes, 1658. [xviii. 332]

FEOLOGELD (d. 832), archbishop of Canterbury; abbot of a Kentish monastery, 803; archbishop of Canterbury, 832. [xviii. 333]

FERCHARD, kings of Scotland. [See FEARCHAIR.]

FERDINAND, PHILIP (1555?–1598), hebraist; born in Poland of Jewish parents; converted to Roman catholicism, and subsequently to protestantism; poor student at Oxford, where he taught Hebrew; matriculated at Cambridge, 1596; professor at Leyden, where he died; translated into Latin from the Hebrew a work on the Mosaic law, 1597. [xviii. 333]

FEREBE or FERIBYE, or FERRABEE, GEORGE (fl. 1613), composer; chorister of Magdalen College, Oxford; M.A., 1595; vicar of Bishop's Cannings; entertained Anne, the queen consort, with a four-part song set to wind-instrument music, 1613; and was made chaplain to the king. [xviii. 333]

FERG, FRANCIS PAUL [FRANZ DE PAULA] (1689–1740), painter; born in Vienna; gained reputation at Dresden for small landscapes, sea-pieces, and peasant scenes; employed in Chelsea china manufactory; died of want in London. [xviii. 333]

FERGIL or VIRGILIUS, SAINT (d. 785), bishop of Salzburg; a descendant of Niall of the Nine Hostages; abbot of Aghaboe till 745; abbot of St. Peter's at Salzburg, c. 747; accused to Pope Zachary by St. Boniface [q. v.] of maintaining the existence of antipodes; his expulsion from the church directed by Zachary; bishop of Salzburg, 756; sent missionaries to Carinthia (part of his diocese); 'Apostle of Carinthia'; travelled through Carinthia and as far as Slavonia; concealed his episcopal orders; called 'the Geometer'; canonised, 1233. [xviii. 334]

FERGUS I (fl. 330 B.C.?), son of Ferchard, the first king of Scotland, according to Boece and Buchanan's fictitious chronology; said to have come to Scotland from Ireland to assist the Scots against the joint-attack of the Picts and Britons, and to have been drowned on his return to Ireland, c. 330 B.C. [xviii. 335]

FERGUS II (d. 501), the first Dalriad king in Scotland; came from Ulster with his brothers, Lorn and Angus, and took possession of Cantyre and adjacent islands. [xviii. 336]

FERGUSHILL, JOHN (1592?–1644), Scottish divine; educated at Edinburgh and Glasgow universities and in France; laureatus of Glasgow, 1612; suspended from cure of Ochiltree for declining jurisdiction of high commission court, 1620; reinstituted; transferred to Ayr 1639. [xviii. 336]

FERGUSON, ADAM (1723–1816), professor of philosophy at Edinburgh; bursar of St. Andrews; M.A. St. Andrews, 1742; studied divinity at Edinburgh; preacher as chaplain of Black Watch at battle of Fontenoy, 1745; abandoned clerical profession, 1754; librarian, Advocates' Library, 1757; professor of natural philosophy, Edinburgh, 1759; professor of 'pneumatics and moral philosophy,' Edinburgh, 1764–85; published an 'Essay on Civil Society,' 1766, which was unfavourably regarded by Hume; LL.D. Edinburgh, 1766; republished his lecture notes in 'Institutes of Moral Philosophy,' 1772; dismissed on account of absence, but reinstated (1776) after legal proceedings; visited Voltaire at Ferney; secretary to British commissioners at Philadelphia, 1778; regarded Macpherson's 'Ossian' as genuine; published 'History of the Progress and Termination of the Roman Republic,' 1782; professor of mathematics, 1785; published 'Principles of Moral and Political Science,' 1792. [xviii. 336]

FERGUSON, SIR ADAM (1771–1855), keeper of the regalia in Scotland; son of Adam Ferguson [q. v.]; companion of Sir Walter Scott at Edinburgh University and afterwards; captain, 101st regiment, 1808; read the 'Lady of the Lake' canto VI, to his company in the lines of Torres Vedras; keeper of the regalia of Scotland, 1818; knighted, 1822. [xviii. 340]

FERGUSON, DAVID (d. 1598), Scottish reformer; glover; sent to Dunfermline as minister; preached before the regent against appropriation of church property to governmental purposes, 1572; moderator of the general assembly, 1573 and 1578; formed one of a deputation which admonished James VI 'to beware of innovations court,' 1583; compiled a collection of 'Scottish Proverbs' (published 1641), and wrote a critical analysis of the 'Song of Solomon.' [xviii. 341]

FERGUSON, JAMES (1621–1667), Scottish divine; graduate of Glasgow, 1638; minister of Kilwinning, 164 appointed to the Glasgow professorship of divinity, 1661, but did not take it up; resolutioner; his 'Refutation of the Errors of Toleration,' &c., published, 1692.   [xviii. 342]

FERGUSON, JAMES (*d.* 1705), major-general, colonel of the Cameronians; brother of Robert Ferguson 'the Plotter' [q. v.]; served in Holland as quartermaster in the Scots brigade, 1677; summoned to join royalist forces against Monmouth, 1685; captain, 1687; landed with William of Orange at Torbay, 1688; reduced the western isles; fought at Steinkirk, 1692; led the 1st Cameronians at Landen, 1693, and at siege of Namur, 1695; colonel, 1693; fought at Blenheim, 1704; major-general; his sudden death at Bois-le-Duc possibly due to poison.   [xviii. 342]

FERGUSON, JAMES (1710–1776), astronomer; displayed original genius in mechanics when nine years old; constructed terrestrial globe from Gordon's 'Geographical Grammar'; patronised by Sir James Dunbar and Lady Dipple, the latter of whom enabled him to become a portrait-painter; contrived 'astronomical rotula'; constructed orrery, 1742; invented a tide-dial, an 'eclipsareon,' 1754, and 'a universal dialling cylinder,' 1767; published 'Astronomy explained on Sir Isaac Newton's Principles,' 1756; observed transit of Venus with six-foot reflector; F.R.S., 1763; presented to the Royal Society (1763) a projection of the partial solar eclipse of 1764; lectured on electricity; published 'The Young Gentleman's and Lady's Astronomy,' 1768; frequently discussed mechanics with George III; unhappy in his domestic relations; published, though ignorant of geometry, 'The Art of Drawing in Perspective,' 1775.   [xviii. 343]

FERGUSON, JAMES FREDERIC (1807–1855), Irish antiquary; of French descent; born at Charleston; indexed Irish 'Exchequer Records'; clerk and secretary to commission for arranging records of Irish courts, 1850–2; purchased at his own cost some Irish records in the possession of a Suabian baron, having travelled to Switzerland for the purpose; contributed to 'Topographer and Genealogist' papers illustrative of law and society in seventeenth-century Ireland; chief work, 'Remarks on the Limitations of Actions Bill intended for Ireland,' 1843.   [xviii. 347]

FERGUSON, JOHN (1787–1856), founder of the Ferguson bequest; settled at Irvine, Ayrshire, after arranging an uncle's business concerns in America, 1810; gave 400,000*l.* for advancement of religious education in South of Scotland; founded six scholarships in connection with Scottish universities.   [xviii. 348]

FERGUSON, PATRICK (1744–1780), inventor of the first breech-loading rifle used in the British army; commanded company in the 70th foot against the revolted negroes of Tobago; patented effectual plans of breech-loading, 1776; wounded at the battle of Brandywine, 1777; employed with artillery at siege of Charleston, 1779; major, 71st Highlanders, 1779; accompanied Lord Cornwallis in his march through the Carolinas; lieutenant-colonel; surprised and killed at King's Mountain, North Carolina.   [xviii. 348]

FERGUSON, RICHARD SAUL (1837–1900), antiquary; educated at Shrewsbury, and St. John's College, Cambridge; M.A., 1863; LL.M., 1874; barrister, Lincoln's Inn, 1862; joined northern circuit; travelled in Egypt, Australia, and America, 1871–2; devoted himself to study of local antiquities at Carlisle; president of Cumberland and Westmorland Archæological and Antiquarian Society, 1886; mayor of Carlisle, 1881 and 1882; chancellor of diocese of Carlisle, 1887; F.S.A., 1877; F.S.A. Scotland, 1880; published and edited antiquarian works relating to Cumberland and Westmorland.   [Suppl. ii. 208]

FERGUSON, ROBERT (*d.* 1714), surnamed the 'Plotter'; possibly educated at Aberdeen; incumbent of Godmersham, *c.* 1660; expelled by the Act of Uniformity, 1662; wrote 'a Sober Enquiry into the Nature, Measure, and Principle of Moral Virtue,' 1673; maintained that the story of the 'Black Box' and documents therein contained proving the marriage of Monmouth's mother to Charles II was invented by those who wished to discredit Monmouth's title to the crown, 1680; one of the chief contrivers of the Rye House plot, though probably disapproving of assassination, 1682; outlawed, 1683; author of Monmouth's manifesto, and chaplain in the rebel army,

1685; accompanied expedition of William of Orange to Torbay, 1688; published pamphlets in support of William III; housekeeper at the excise; became a Jacobite, his hopes of reward being unsatisfied; declared the revolution to have been a design of the Vatican in his 'History of the Revolution,' 1706; superseded at the excise, 1692; asked 'Whether the Parliament be not in Law dissolved by the death of the Princess of Orange?' 1695; privy to Sir George Barclay's plot; gave information which led to frustration of the machinations of Simon Fraser, twelfth lord Lovat [q. v.] against the Duke of Atholl, 1703; committed to Newgate for treason, 1704; admitted to bail and never tried.   [xviii. 350]

FERGUSON, ROBERT (1750–1774). [See FERGUSSON.]

FERGUSON, ROBERT (1799–1865), physician; born in India; studied at Heidelberg and Edinburgh; M.D. Edinburgh, 1823; physician to the Westminster Lying-in Hospital; founded 'London Medical Gazette,' 1827; professor of obstetrics, King's College, London, 1831; censor, C.P.; physician-accoucheur to Queen Victoria, 1840; published works on obstetrics.   [xviii. 353]

FERGUSON, SIR RONALD CRAUFURD (1773–1841), general; captain, 1793; lieutenant-colonel, 1794; co-operated from India in reduction of Cape of Good Hope, 1795; colonel, 1800; quitted Pulteney on his refusing to attack Ferrol, 1800; served in Sir David Baird's expedition to recapture Cape of Good Hope, 1805; M.P., Kirkcaldy burghs, 1806–30, Nottingham, 1830–41; major-general, 1808; twice turned Laborde's right at Roliça, 1808; general, 1830; G.C.B., 1831.   [xviii. 354]

FERGUSON, SIR SAMUEL (1810–1886), poet and antiquary; M.A. Trinity College, Dublin, 1832; called to the Irish bar, 1838; Q.C., 1859; deputy-keeper of the public records of Ireland, 1867; thoroughly organised the public records department; knighted, 1878; LL.D., *honoris causâ*, Trinity College, Dublin, 1864; published, among other works, 'Lays of the Western Gael,' 1865, and 'Congal, an Epic Poem,' 1872. 'Ogham Inscriptions in Ireland, Wales, and Scotland,' edited, 1887, is his most important antiquarian work.   [xviii. 355]

FERGUSON, WILLIAM (1820–1887), botanist and entomologist; member of the Ceylon civil service, 1839–1887; died in Ceylon; wrote 'Ceylon Ferns,' 'The Timber Trees of Ceylon,' and similar works.   [xviii. 356]

FERGUSON, WILLIAM GOUW (1633?–1690?), painter of still-life; native of Scotland; lived at the Hague, 1660–8; his works sometimes attributed to Weenix.   [xviii. 357]

FERGUSSON, SIR CHARLES DALRYMPLE (1800–1849), fifth baronet, of Kilkerran; educated at Harrow; advocate, 1822; originated Ayrshire Educational Association; protectionist.   [xviii. 357]

FERGUSSON, DAVID (*d.* 1598). [See FERGUSON.]

FERGUSSON, GEORGE, LORD HERMAND (*d.* 1827), Scottish judge; member of the Faculty of Advocates, 1765; lord of session as Lord Hermand, 1799–1826; lord justiciary, 1808–26; an enthusiastic admirer of Sir Walter Scott's novel of 'Guy Mannering.'   [xviii. 358]

FERGUSSON, SIR JAMES, LORD KILKERRAN (1688–1759), Scottish judge; studied law at Leyden; advocate, 1711; M.P., Sutherlandshire, 1734–5; lord of session as Lord Kilkerran, 1735; justiciary lord, 1749; collected and arranged decisions of court of session from 1738 to 1752 (published, 1775).   [xviii. 358]

FERGUSSON, JAMES (1769–1842), Scottish legal writer; studied at Edinburgh University; member of the Faculty of Advocates, 1791; consistorial judge, clerk of session, and keeper of the general record of entails for Scotland; published legal works.   [xviii. 359]

FERGUSSON, SIR JAMES (1787–1865), general; ensign, 1801; captain, 1806; wounded at Vimeiro, 1808; wounded in assaults on Badajoz and Ciudad Rodrigo; major, 1812; fought in the battles of Nivelle and Nive, aide-de-camp to William IV; lieutenant-general, 1851; general commanding troops at Malta, 1853–5; governor and commander-in-chief at Gibraltar, 1855–9; general, 1860; G.C.B., 1860.   [xviii. 359]

FERGUSSON, JAMES (1808–1886), writer upon architecture; started an indigo factory in India; employed in a Calcutta firm; published 'Picturesque Illustrations of Ancient Architecture in Hindustan'; F.R.A.S., 1840; maintained in 'An Historical Enquiry into the true Principles of Beauty in Art' (1849) that the Greek temples were lighted by a triple roof and clerestory; published work proposing to substitute earthworks for masonry in fortification, 1849; member of royal commission to inquire into defences of the United Kingdom, 1857; inspector of public buildings and monuments; gold medallist of the Institute of British Architects, 1871; maintained the comparatively recent erection of Stonehenge; recast his earlier writings in 'A History of Architecture in all Countries from the Earliest Times to the Present Day,' 1865–7; published 'Fire and Serpent Worship . . . from the Sculptures of the Buddhist Topes at Sanchi and Amravati,' 1868. [xviii. 360]

FERGUSSON, ROBERT (1750–1774), Scottish poet; matriculated at St. Andrews, 1765; extracting clerk in commissary clerk's office, and for a time in sheriff clerk's office; contributed pastorals to Ruddiman's 'Weekly Magazine,' 1771; published 'Poems,' 1773, and subsequently the 'Farmer's Ingle,' the prototype of Burns's 'Cottar's Saturday Night,' 1773; died insane from the effects of a fall. [xviii. 362]

FERGUSSON, ROBERT CUTLAR (1768–1838), judge advocate-general; barrister, Lincoln's Inn, 1797; defended John Allen on a charge of high treason, 1798; fined and imprisoned (1799) for his alleged share in the attempted rescue of Arthur O'Connor from the dock at Maidstone, 1798; attorney-general at Calcutta; liberal M.P., Kirkcudbright stewartry, 1826; judge advocate-general, and privy councillor, 1834; advocated cause of Poland. [xviii. 364]

FERGUSSON, WILLIAM (1773–1846), inspector-general of military hospitals; M.D. Edinburgh; assistant-surgeon in the army in Holland, the West Indies, the Baltic, the Peninsula, and Guadaloupe; pointed out and discussed the frequent occurrence of malarial fevers on arid soils; his 'Notes and Recollections of a Professional Life' published posthumously. [xviii. 365]

FERGUSSON, SIR WILLIAM (1808–1877), surgeon; educated at Edinburgh High School and University; surgeon to Edinburgh Royal Dispensary, 1831–6; tied subclavian artery, 1831; surgeon to Edinburgh Royal Infirmary, 1836–40; professor of surgery, King's College, London, 1840–70; created baronet, 1866; serjeant-surgeon to Queen Victoria, 1867; P.R.C.S., 1870; honorary LL.D. Edinburgh, 1875; F.R.S.; clinical professor of surgery and senior surgeon at King's College Hospital; a great 'conservative' surgeon and dissector; principal work, 'System of Practical Surgery,' 1842. [xviii. 365]

FERIA, DUCHESS OF (1538–1612). [See DORMER, JANE.]

FERINGS, RICHARD DE (d. 1306), archbishop of Dublin; friend of Archbishop Peckham; archdeacon of Canterbury, 1281–99; archbishop of Dublin, 1299; composed feud between Christ Church and St. Patrick's, Dublin, by giving equality to both and precedence to Christ Church, 1300; endowed St. Patrick's, 1303; summoned to the English parliament, 1303. [xviii. 367]

FERM, **FERME**, **FARHOLME**, or **FAIRHOLM**, CHARLES (1566–1617), principal of Fraserburgh University; of humble origin; M.A. Edinburgh, 1588; regent, 1590; accepted the charge (1598) of Philorth, Aberdeenshire, incorporated in 1613 under the name of Fraserburgh, where Sir Alexander Fraser (1537–1623) [q. v.] had obtained a royal grant for the erection of a college and university; principal, 1600. Fraserburgh University came to an end at his death. [xviii. 368]

FERMANAGH, third VISCOUNT (1712?–1791). See VERNEY, RALPH.]

FERMANAGH, LORD OF (d. 1600). [See MAGUIRE, HUGH.]

FERMOR, HENRIETTA LOUISA, COUNTESS OF POMFRET (d. 1761), letter-writer; née Jeffreys; married Thomas Fermor, second baron Leominster, 1720; lady of the bedchamber to Queen Caroline till 1737; wrote a 'life' of Vandyke at Rome; précieuse ridicule, and writer of dull and affected letters. [xviii. 369]

FERMOR, SIR JOHN (d. 1571), son of Richard Fermor [q. v.]; knighted, 1553; M.P. for Northamptonshire, 1553 and 1555; sheriff, 1557. [xviii. 370]

FERMOR or **FERMOUR**, RICHARD (d. 1552), merchant of the staple of Calais; licensed to export six hundred sacks of wool, 1515; personally assisted Wolsey's agent in Florence, 1524; sheriff for Bedford and Buckingham, 1532 and 1533; stripped of all his lands under the statute of præmunire, 1540; restored to his property, 1550. [xviii. 369]

FERMOR, THOMAS WILLIAM, fourth EARL OF POMFRET (1770–1833), general; ensign, 1791; present at Lincelles and the sieges of Valenciennes and Dunkirk, 1793; lieutenant, 1794; F.R.S. and F.S.A.; took part in Helder expedition, 1799; major-general, 1813; received medal for battle of Salamanca, 1812; knight of the Tower and Sword; lieutenant-general, 1825. [xviii. 370]

FERMOR, **FARMER**, or **FERMOUR**, SIR WILLIAM (1623?–1661), royalist; created baronet, 1641; privy councillor to Prince Charles; compounded with the Commonwealth; privy councillor, 1660; M.P. for Brackley, and deputy-lieutenant for Northamptonshire, 1661; K.B., 1661. [xviii. 371]

FERMOR, WILLIAM, BARON LEOMINSTER (d. 1711), connoisseur; son of Sir William Fermor [q. v.]; created Baron Leominster, 1692; laid out country seat at Easton Neston, adorning it with some of the Arundel marbles. [xviii. 371]

FERMOY, seventh VISCOUNT (1573?–1635). [See ROCHE, DAVID.]

FERNE, HENRY (1602–1662), bishop of Chester; son of Sir John Ferne [q. v.]; educated at Uppingham and St. Mary Hall, Oxford; pensioner (1620) and fellow of Trinity College, Cambridge; archdeacon of Leicester, 1641; D.D. Cambridge, 1642; joined royal forces at Nottingham; chaplain extraordinary to Charles I; chaplain in ordinary; obliged to abandon his living of Medbourne for writing in support of Charles I, 1643; D.D. Oxford, 1643; given patent for next vacancy in mastership of Trinity College, Cambridge; censured Harrington's 'Oceana,' 1656; master of Trinity College, Cambridge, 1660–2; vice-chancellor, 1660 and 1661; dean of Ely, 1661; bishop of Chester, 1662; published theological pamphlets, 1647–60. [xviii. 372]

FERNE, SIR JOHN (d. 1610?), writer on heraldry; studied at Oxford and the Inner Temple; brought out 'The Blazon of Gentrie,' 1586, of which the second part dealt with Albertus à Lasco's provedly untenable claim to be descended from the Lacy family; knighted, 1604; joint-secretary and keeper of the signet in the north, 1604. [xviii. 373]

FERNELEY, JOHN (1782–1860), animal painter; given commissions to paint hunting, and occasionally racing or coaching, scenes. [xviii. 374]

FERRABEE, GEORGE (fl. 1613). [See FEREBE.]

FERRABOSCO or **FERABOSCO**, ALFONSO (fl. 1544–1587), musical composer; of Italian origin; pensioned by Elizabeth, 1567; composed, with William Byrd, 'Medulla Musicke' (settings of 'Miserere' plain-song) published, 1603; composed madrigals; took service at the ducal court of Savoy. [xviii. 375]

FERRABOSCO or **FERABOSCO**, ALFONSO (d. 1628), lutenist and composer; son of Alfonso Ferrabosco (1544–1587) [q. v.]; introduced the new Italian style of music into England; extraordinary groom of the privy chamber and musical instructor to Prince Henry, 1605; author of 'Ayres,' 1609, and a 'Fantasie' and 'Pavin,' 1610; composer in ordinary, 1626. [xviii. 376]

FERRABOSCO, ALFONSO (d. 1661), musician and composer; son of Alfonso Ferrabosco (d. 1628) [q. v.]; 'viol' in the king's band, and musician in ordinary, 1628. [xviii. 377]

FERRABOSCO, JOHN (d. 1682), organist of Ely Cathedral; Mus. Bac., per literas regias, Cambridge, 1671; possibly introduced 'Chanting Service' into Ely Cathedral. [xviii. 377]

FERRAR, NICHOLAS (1592–1637), theologian; B.A. and fellow, Clare Hall, Cambridge, 1610; M.A.; attended Elizabeth, queen of Bohemia, to Holland, 1613; devoted himself to the affairs of the Virginia Company, 1619 ; declined readership of geometry at Gresham College, 1619 ; assisted as member of parliament in the impeachment of the Earl of Middlesex, 1624 ; retired to Little Gidding in Huntingdonshire, 1625 ; deacon, 1626 ; chaplain of an Anglican community at Little Gidding, composed of his brother's and brother-in-law's families ; introduced bookbinding trade into his brotherhood ; visited by Charles I, 1633 ; his 'Arminian nunnery' broken up by the parliament, 1647 ; friend of George Herbert ; left in manuscript harmony of the Gospels, and also of the Books of Kings and Chronicles. [xviii. 377]

FERRAR, ROBERT (d. 1555), bishop of St. David's ; studied at Cambridge ; Augustinian canon and monk of St. Mary's Priory, Oxford ; converted to Lutheranism, but (1528) compelled to recant ; accompanied William Barlow (d. 1568) [q. v.] on his embassy to Scotland, 1535 ; prior of St. Oswald's at Nostell ; D.D. ; bishop of St. David's, 1548–54 ; gospeller ; technical errors in the wording of his commission discovered by his prejudiced chapter ; kept in prison till Queen Mary's accession, after being cited to answer charges of præmunire ; deprived of his bishopric, 1554 ; charged by Gardiner with having violated his monastic vow of chastity ; burnt at the stake, 1555. [xviii. 380]

FERRARD, BARON (1663–1731). [See TICHBORNE, SIR HENRY.]

FERRARS, first BARON DE (1755–1811). [See TOWNSHEND, GEORGE.]

FERRERS OF GROBY, eighth BARON (1432–1461). [See GREY, JOHN.]

FERRERS, third BARON (d. 1558). [See DEVEREUX, WALTER.]

FERRERS, EARLS. [See SHIRLEY, LAURENCE, fourth EARL, 1720–1760; SHIRLEY, WASHINGTON, fifth EARL, 1722–1778.]

FERRERS, BENJAMIN (d. 1732), portrait-painter ; deaf and dumb from birth. [xviii. 382]

FERRERS, EDWARD (d. 1564) ; confounded by Wood, who describes him as a distinguished dramatist (after Puttenham and Meres), with George Ferrers [q. v.] [xviii. 382]

FERRERS, GEORGE (1500 ?–1579), poet and politician ; bachelor of canon law, Cambridge, 1531 ; translated Magna Charta into English, 1534 ; member of Lincoln's Inn ; M.P., Plymouth, 1542, 1545, and 1553 ; said to have murdered some Scots with great barbarity when campaigning with the Duke of Somerset, 1548 ; 'master of the king's pastimes,' 1551 and 1552 ; lord of misrule to Queen Mary, 1553 ; assisted in suppressing Wyatt's rebellion, 1554 ; M.P., Brackley, 1554 and 1555, St. Albans, 1571 ; devised (with Baldwin) the series of historical poems entitled 'Mirror for Magistrates' (complete edition, 1578) ; wrote tragedies and court masques. [xviii. 383]

FERRERS, HENRY DE (fl. 1086), Domesday commissioner ; Norman baron ; fought at Hastings, 1066. [xviii. 385]

FERRERS, HENRY (1549–1633), antiquary ; son of Edward Ferrers [q. v.] ; educated at Oxford, probably at Hart Hall ; collected materials (utilised by Dugdale) for the history of Warwickshire, his native county. [xviii. 385]

FERRERS, JOHN (1271–1324), son of Robert Ferrers, earl of Derby or Ferrers [q. v.] ; joined Bohun and Bigod in the struggle for the charters ; summoned to parliament, 1299. [xviii. 388]

FERRERS, JOSEPH (1725–1797), Carmelite friar ; professed abroad, 1745 ; provincial of the English Carmelites. [xviii. 386]

FERRERS, RICHARD (fl. 1590). [See FERRIS.]

FERRERS, ROBERT DE (d. 1139), warrior ; son of Henry de Ferrers [q. v] ; one of the English leaders at Northallerton, 1138 ; created earl, 1138. [xviii. 386]

FERRERS, ROBERT, EARL OF DERBY or FERRERS (1240 ?–1279 ?) ; married one of Henry III's Poitevin relatives, 1249 ; took Prince Edward prisoner, 1263 ; defeated royalists at Chester, 1264 ; shut up in the Tower by Montfort to save him from the king's anger, 1265 ; headed the 'disinherited,' 1266 ; specially exempted from the general composition of the 'Dictum de Kenilworth,' 1266 ; released from prison, 1269. [xviii. 386]

FERREY, BENJAMIN (1810–1880), architect ; of Huguenot origin ; employed on the detail drawings of the National Gallery ; part-author of 'Antiquities of the Priory Church of Christchurch, Hants ; 1834 ; restored, when hon. diocesan architect, 1841–80, nave, transepts, and Lady Chapel of Wells Cathedral, 1842 ; twice vice-president of Royal Institute of British Architects ; F.S.A., 1863 ; published recollections of the two Pugins, 1861. [xviii. 388]

FERRIAR, JOHN (1761–1815), physician ; M.D. Edinburgh, 1781 ; his essay on Massinger reprinted in Gifford's edition (1805) ; physician of the Manchester Infirmary, 1789–1815 ; introduced many sanitary reforms when on the Manchester board of health ; published works including 'Medical Histories and Reflections,' 1792–5–8, and 'Illustrations of Sterne,' 1798. [xviii. 389]

FERRIER, JAMES FREDERICK (1808–1864), meta-physician ; studied at Edinburgh University and Magdalen College, Oxford ; B.A. Magdalen College, Oxford, 1831 ; advocate, 1832 ; studied German philosophy at Heidelberg, 1834 ; professor of civil history, Edinburgh, 1842–5 ; professor of moral philosophy and political economy at St. Andrews, 1845–64 ; published 'Institutes of Metaphysic,' 1854, re-interpreting Berkeley in the light of German idealism. [xviii. 390]

FERRIER, SUSAN EDMONSTONE (1782–1854), novelist ; visited Sir Walter Scott, 1811, 1829, and 1831 ; published 'Marriage,' 1818, 'The Inheritance,' 1824, and 'Destiny,' 1831, three novels. [xviii. 391]

FERRIS. [See also FERRERS.]

FERRIS, RICHARD (fl. 1590), adventurer ; a messenger in Queen Elizabeth's household ; rowed in an open boat from London to Bristol, 1590. [xviii. 392]

FESTING, SIR FRANCIS WORGAN (1833–1886), major-general ; second lieutenant, royal marines, 1850 ; commanded mortar off Sebastopol, 1855 ; present as adjutant of artillery at bombardment of Canton ; defeated Ashantees, burning Ehina, 1873 ; virtually administered government of Gold Coast, 1874 ; colonel, 1874 ; C.B., 1874 ; K.C.M.G., 1874 ; aide-de-camp to Queen Victoria, 1879 ; colonel commandant, royal marine artillery, 1886. [xviii. 392]

FESTING, MICHAEL CHRISTIAN (d. 1752), violinist and composer ; member of George II's band ; director of the Italian opera, 1737 ; director of the 'Philharmonic Society' ; initiated Royal Society of Musicians from subscription for the indigent family of a German oboe-player, 1738 ; composed concertos, solos, sonatas for stringed instruments, and 'Sylvia,' a cantata. [xviii. 393]

FETHERSTON, RICHARD (d. 1540), Roman catholic martyr ; chaplain to Catherine of Arragon ; schoolmaster to the Princess Mary ; wrote against Henry VIII's divorce from Catherine of Arragon ; hanged for refusing the oath of supremacy. [xviii. 394]

FETHERSTONHAUGH, SIR TIMOTHY (d. 1651), royalist ; member of Gray's Inn, 1620 ; knighted, 1628 ; taken prisoner at battle of Wigan Lane ; beheaded. [xviii. 394]

FETTES, SIR WILLIAM (1750–1836), founder of Fettes College, Edinburgh ; merchant, underwriter, and contractor for military stores ; lord provost of Edinburgh, 1800 and 1805 ; created baronet, 1804 ; devoted part of his estate to form endowment for education of orphan or otherwise needy children, 1830, a scheme which developed into the present Fettes College. [xviii. 395]

FEUCHÈRES, BARONNE DE (1790–1840). [See DAWES, SOPHIA.]

FEVERSHAM, EARLS OF. [See SONDES, SIR GEORGE, first EARL, 1600–1677 ; DURAS, LOUIS, second EARL. 1640 ?–1709.]

FFENNELL, WILLIAM JOSHUA (1799–1867), fishery reformer ; J.P., 1834 ; called attention with Lord Glengall to the neglected state of the Suir salmon fisheries ; brought about the salmon-fishery acts of 1842, 1844, and 1845, and 'Ffennell's Act,' 1848 ; inspector of salmon fisheries for England and Wales, 1861. [xviii. 396]

FFRAID, I. D. (1814–1875). [See EVANS, JOHN.]

FIACRE or **FIACHRACH**, SAINT (*d.* 670 ?), Irish noble; founded monastery at Breuil, on land given him by Faro, bishop of Meaux; chiefly celebrated for his miraculous cure of a tumour, since known as 'le fic de St. Fiacre'; enshrined in Meaux Cathedral, 1568; part of his body given to the grand-duke of Tuscany, 1617, part to Cardinal Richelieu, 1637. The saint's name was given to the French hackney carriage from 1640, because at the Hôtel de St. Fiacre in Paris hackney carriages were then first kept on hire. [xviii. 396]

FICH, FYCH, or **FYCHE,** THOMAS (*d.* 1517), ecclesiastic and compiler; studied at Oxford; sub-prior of convent of Holy Trinity, Dublin; author of a Latin necrology of the convent, entitled 'Mortilogium' (printed by the Irish Archæological Society, 1844), and of the 'White Book of Christ Church, Dublin.' [xviii. 397]

FIDDES, RICHARD (1671–1725), divine and historian; B.A. University College, Oxford, 1691; non-resident rector of Halsham, 1696; chaplain of Hull, by Swift's influence, 1713–14; chaplain to the Earl of Oxford, 1713–14; published 'Theologia Speculativa,' 1718, and 'Theologia Practica,' 1720; D.D. Oxford; attacked Mandeville in 'A General Treatise of Morality,' 1724; unfairly represented as a papist on account of his 'Life of Cardinal Wolsey,' 1724. [xviii. 397]

FIELD, BARRON (1786–1846), lawyer and miscellaneous writer; son of Henry Field [q. v.]; intimate with Lamb, Coleridge, Wordsworth, Hazlitt, and Leigh Hunt; barrister, Inner Temple, 1814; theatrical critic to the 'Times'; advocate-fiscal in Ceylon; judge of supreme court of New South Wales, 1817–24; engaged in party conflicts; chief-justice of Gibraltar; published (1811) an analysis of Blackstone's 'Commentaries' (frequently reprinted), and edited 'Geographical Memoirs on New South Wales,' 1825; edited a few of Heywood's, and one of Legge's, plays for the Shakespeare Society; original poet with 'First Fruits of Australian Poetry' (privately printed, 1819). [xviii. 399]

FIELD, EDWIN WILKINS (1804–1871), law reformer and amateur artist; son of William Field [q. v.]; attorney and solicitor, 1826; established firm of Sharpe & Field in Cheapside; the abolition of the court of exchequer as an equity court and the appointment of two additional vice-chancellors (1841) due to his 'Observations of a Solicitor,' 1840; suggested provisions of trust-deed executed by Robert Hibbert [q. v.], 1847; a commissioner to report on accountant-general's department of chancery court, 1861; amateur artist; his views on the option of contract realised by the act of 1870. [xviii. 401]

FIELD, FREDERICK (1801–1885), divine; son of Henry Field [q. v.]; educated at Christ's Hospital; tenth wrangler, chancellor's classical medallist, and Tyrwhitt's Hebrew scholar, Trinity College, Cambridge, 1823; fellow, 1824; examiner for classical tripos, 1833 and 1837; incumbent of Great Saxham and (1842–63) of Reepham; LL.D. Cambridge, 1874; original member of the Old Testament revision company, 1870; edited homilies by St. Chrysostom, 1839 and 1849–62, and Origen's 'Hexapla' (in parts, finished 1874). [xviii. 402]

FIELD, FREDERICK (1826–1885), chemist; chemist to copper-smelting works at Coquimbo in Chili, 1848–52; manager at Caldera, 1852; first to discover lapis lazuli in South America, 1851; vice-consul of Caldera, 1853; sub-manager to smelting-works at Guayacan, 1856–9; professor of chemistry, London Institution, 1862. [xviii. 404]

FIELD, GEORGE (1777 ?–1854), chemist; succeeded in cultivating madder in his own garden, reducing it to its finest consistence by the 'physeter,' his own invention; Isis medallist, Society of Arts, 1816; chief works, 'Chromatography, or a treatise on Colours and Pigments,' 1835, and 'Rudiments of the Painter's Art, or a Grammar of Colouring,' 1850. [xviii. 405]

FIELD, HENRY (1755–1837), apothecary; apothecary to Christ's Hospital, 1807–37; M. Soc. Apoth.; established gratuitous courses of lectures on materia medica at Apothecaries' Hall; one of the medical officers attached to the city of London board of health to meet threatened epidemic of cholera, 1831. [xviii. 405]

FIELD, HENRY IBBOT (1797–1848), pianist; educated at Bath grammar school; performed Johann Hummel's grand sonata, œuvre 92, with the master, 1830; paralysed, 1848. [xviii. 406]

FIELD or **FEILD,** JOHN (1525 ?–1587), 'proto-Copernican' of England; public instructor in science, London; granted crest and confirmation of arms, 1558; representative work, 'Ephemeris anni 1557 currentis juxta Copernici et Reinholdi canones . . . ad Meridianum Londinensem . . . supputata,' 1556. [xviii. 406]

FIELD, JOHN (*d.* 1588). [See FEILDE.]

FIELD, JOHN (1782–1837), composer; composed and performed concerto, 1799; taken by his master, Clementi, to St. Petersburg as a salesman, 1802; his playing admired by Spohr, 1802; settled in Moscow between 1824 and 1828; died at Moscow; chiefly famous for his 'Nocturnes,' romantic music which inspired Chopin. [xviii. 407]

FIELD, JOSHUA (1787 ?–1863), civil engineer; partner in firm of Maudslay, Sons & Field of Lambeth, which constructed (1838) engines capable of propelling a vessel across the Atlantic; part-founder of Institution of Civil Engineers, 1817; F.R.S. 1836; president I.C.E. 1848. [xviii. 408]

FIELD, NATHANIEL (1587–1633), actor and dramatist; one of the six principal comedians of the Children of the Queen's Revels who performed Ben Jonson's 'Cynthia's Revels' in 1600; acted in plays by Shakespeare, Ben Jonson, and Beaumont and Fletcher; his name made synonymous with 'best actor' in Jonson's 'Bartholomew Fair,' 1614; probably performed himself in his 'A Woman's a Weathercock,' published 1612, and 'Amends for Ladies,' published 1618; collaborated in Massinger's 'Fatal Dowry,' 1632. [xviii. 408]

FIELD or **DE LA FIELD,** RICHARD (1554 ?–1606), jesuit; studied at Douay; superior of Irish jesuit mission, *c.* 1600. [xviii. 410]

FIELD, RICHARD (1561–1616), divine; B.A. Magdalen College, Oxford, 1581; M.A., and 'Catechism lecturer,' Magdalen Hall, 1584; D.D., 1596; divinity lecturer, Lincoln's Inn, 1594; chaplain in ordinary to Queen Elizabeth, 1598; installed prebendary of Windsor, 1604, by a grant dating from 1602; chaplain to James I; dean of Gloucester, 1610; discussed theology with James I; friend of Hooker; sincerely mourned by James I. His great work, 'Of the Church Five Bookes' (first published, 1606), is a masterpiece of polemical divinity. [xviii. 410]

FIELD, RICHARD (*fl.* 1579–1624), London printer and stationer; free of the Stationers' Company, 1587; sole licensee for first edition of Harington's translation of 'Orlando Furioso,' 1592; master of the Stationers' Company, 1620; fellow townsman, and probably a personal friend of Shakespeare, printing 'Venus and Adonis,' 1593, 1594, and 1596, as well as the first (1594) edition of 'Lucrece.' [xviii. 412]

FIELD, THEOPHILUS (1574–1636), bishop of Hereford; brother of Nathaniel Field [q. v.]; fellow of Pembroke Hall, Cambridge, 1598; M.A., 1599; M.A. Oxford, 1600; D.D.; chaplain to James I and Lord-chancellor Bacon; consecrated bishop of Llandaff by the influence of Buckingham, 1619; impeached by the Commons for brocage and bribery before his promotion, and admonished in the convocation house, 1621; bishop of St. David's, 1627; obtained see of Hereford, 1635; edited 'Elegies on the Death of Sir Oratio Pallavicino,' 1600. [xviii. 413]

FIELD, THOMAS (1546 ?–1625), jesuit; studied at Paris and Douay; M.A. Louvain; spiritual coadjutor of the Society of Jesus; lived for some years in Brazil and Paraguay; put by English pirates into an open boat, in which he drifted to Buenos Ayres, 1586; died at the Assumption Settlement. [xviii. 414]

FIELD, WILLIAM (1768–1851), unitarian minister; minister of the presbyterian congregation at Warwick, 1790–1843; friend of Dr. Samuel Parr; started a Sunday school (the first in Warwick), which led to a pamphlet war with some local clergy, 1791; kept boarding-school at Leam; published pamphlets, sermons, and a history of Warwick and Leamington, 1815. [xviii. 414]

FIELDEN, JOHN (1784–1849), M.P. for Oldham; partner with his father, and subsequently with his

brothers, in cotton-spinning manufactory at Todmorden ; M.P. for Oldham, 1833, 1835, 1837, and 1841 ; seconded Cobbett's resolution for removing Peel from the privy council, 1833 ; moved second reading of Ten Hours' Bill, 1846 and 1847 ; published 'The Mischiefs and Iniquities of Paper Money,' 1832, with other works and pamphlets, including 'The Curse of the Factory System,' 1836.
[xviii. 415]

FIELDING, ANTONY VANDYKE COPLEY (1787-1855), landscape-painter in water-colour ; son of Nathan Theodore Fielding [q. v.] ; commenced to exhibit at the Royal Academy, 1811 ; awarded a medal at the Paris Salon, 1824 ; president of the Water-colour Society, 1831-55.
[xviii. 416]

FIELDING, BASIL, second EARL OF DENBIGH (d. 1674). [See FIELDING.]

FIELDING, HENRY (1707-1754), novelist ; contemporary with Pitt and Fox at Eton ; sent, after a youthful escapade, to study law at Leyden ; brought out a few comedies of the Congreve school, 1728-32 ; burlesqued all the popular playwrights of the day in 'Tom Thumb,' a farce, 1730 ; supported the 'distressed actors' at Drury Lane on the occasion of the revolt headed by Theophilus Cibber, 1733 ; opened theatre in the Haymarket with 'Pasquin,' 1736, but gave up the career on the passing of a bill, partly due to 'Pasquin,' making a license from the lord chamberlain necessary for all dramatic performances, 1737 ; barrister, Middle Temple, 1740 ; retaliated on Colley Cibber's 'Apology' in his paper, the 'Champion' ; parodied Richardson's 'Pamela' in 'The History of the Adventures of Joseph Andrews and his friend Mr. Abraham Adams,' 1742, copying Parson Adams from William Young, with whom he co-operated in translating Aristophanes's 'Plutus,' 1742 ; published 'Miscellanies,' the third volume containing 'Jonathan Wild the Great,' a powerful satire, 1743 ; issued two weekly papers in support of the government 1745 and 1747-8 ; J.P. for Westminster, 1748 ; produced the novel of 'Tom Jones,' drawing his first wife, then dead, as Sophia, 1749 ; chairman of quarter sessions at Hicks's Hall, 1749 ; attacked social evils, especially excessive gin-drinking, in an 'Inquiry' into the increase of robbers in London, 1750 ; propounded elaborate scheme for erection of county poor-house, 1753 ; published 'Amelia,' 1751 ; provided informers against robberies by a special fund, and succeeded in breaking up a gang, 1753 ; died an invalid at Lisbon ; his 'Journal of a Voyage to Lisbon' published posthumously.
[xviii. 416]

FIELDING, HENRY BORRON (d. 1851), botanist ; fellow of the Linnean Society, 1838 ; published 'Sertum Plantarum,' containing figures and descriptions of seventy-five new or rare plants, 1844. [xviii. 424]

FIELDING, SIR JOHN (d. 1780), magistrate ; half-brother of Henry Fielding [q. v.] ; blind, apparently from birth ; carried on Henry Fielding's plan for breaking up robber-gangs ; originated (1755) scheme for sending 'distressed boys' into the royal navy ; published pamphlet on the Duke of Newcastle's police force, with plan for rescuing deserted girls, 1758 ; denounced in 'A Letter to Sir John Fielding, occasioned by his extraordinary request to Mr. Garrick for the suppression of the "Beggar's Opera,"' 1773 ; unfairly accused of encouraging and then condemning criminals ; published collection of laws concerning breaches of peace in metropolis, 1768. [xviii. 424]

FIELDING, NATHAN THEODORE (fl. 1775-1814), painter ; occasionally exhibited at the British Institution and the Society of Artists ; famous in Yorkshire for his portraits of aged people. [xviii. 425]

FIELDING, NEWTON SMITH (1799-1856), painter and lithographer ; son of Nathan Theodore Fielding [q. v.] ; exhibited at Society of Painters in Water-colours, 1815 and 1818 ; taught family of Louis-Philippe in Paris ; published works on art ; best known for his paintings and engravings of animals. [xviii. 425]

FIELDING, ROBERT (1651?-1712). [See FEILDING.]

FIELDING, SARAH (1710-1768), novelist ; sister of Henry Fielding [q. v.] ; wrote romances, including 'The Adventures of David Simple in search of a Faithful Friend,' 1744 ; translated Xenophon's 'Memorabilia' and 'Apologia,' 1762. [xviii. 425]

FIELDING, THALES (1793-1837), water-colour painter ; son of Nathan Theodore Fielding [q. v.] ; ex-hibited at the British Institution, 1816, and afterwards at the Royal Academy ; associate exhibitor of the Royal Society of Painters in Water-colours ; drawing-master at the Royal Military Academy, Woolwich. [xviii. 426]

FIELDING, THEODORE HENRY ADOLPHUS (1781-1851), painter, engraver, and author ; son of Nathan Theodore Fielding [q. v.] ; taught drawing and perspective at East India Company's Military College, Addiscombe ; first exhibited at the Royal Academy, 1799 ; worked in stipple and aquatint ; published works on the practice of art. [xviii. 426]

FIELDING, THOMAS (fl. 1780-1790), engraver ; executed engravings in Ryland's stipple manner.
[xviii. 427]

FIELDING, WILLIAM, first EARL OF DENBIGH (d. 1643). [See FEILDING.]

FIENNES or FIENES, ANNE, LADY DACRE (d. 1595), daughter of Sir Richard Sackville ; married Gregory Fiennes [q. v.] ; complained to Queen Elizabeth of her sister-in-law, Margaret Lennard, for alleged calumnies ; left money for erection of almshouse at Chelsea.
[xviii. 427]

FIENNES, EDWARD, EARL OF LINCOLN (1512-1585). [See CLINTON, EDWARD FIENNES DE.]

FIENNES or FIENES, GREGORY, tenth BARON DACRE OF THE SOUTH (1539-1594), son of Thomas Fiennes, ninth baron Dacre [q. v.] ; restored by act of parliament to his father's honours, 1558 ; one of the nobles who attended Lord Lincoln to court of Charles IX to ratify confederacy of Blois, 1572. [xviii. 428]

FIENNES, JAMES, BARON SAY (or SAYE) AND SELE (d. 1450) ; given grants in France for service under Henry V in his French wars, 1418 ; governor of Arques, 1419 ; sheriff of Kent, 1437, of Surrey and Sussex, 1439 ; constable of Dover and warden of the Cinque ports by patent, 1447-9 ; M.P., 1447 ; created baron, 1447 ; lord chamberlain and privy councillor ; lord-treasurer, 1449 ; sequestered for his consent to the surrender of Anjou and Maine, 1450 ; generally suspected of extortion and maladministration ; imprisoned in the Tower and handed over by the governor to Jack Cade, who had him beheaded. That he caused printing to be used (Shakespeare, 'Henry VI,' pt. ii. Act iv., sc. 7), is an anachronism. [xviii. 428]

FIENNES, JOHN (fl. 1657), parliamentarian ; son of William Fiennes, first viscount Saye and Sele [q. v.] ; colonel of a regiment of parliamentary horse, 1643 ; fought at Naseby, 1645 ; summoned by Cromwell to the House of Lords, 1657. [xviii. 430]

FIENNES, NATHANIEL (1608?-1669), parliamentarian ; son of William Fiennes, first viscount Say and Sele [q. v.] ; educated at Winchester and New College, Oxford ; perpetual fellow of New College, 1624 ; travelled to Geneva ; M.P., Banbury, 1640 ; sat in the Long parliament ; made a famous speech against episcopacy, 1641 ; member of committee appointed for consideration of church affairs, 1641 ; member of committee of safety, 1642 ; fought at Edgehill, 1642 ; arrested Colonel Essex, the disaffected governor of Bristol, 1643 ; governor of Bristol, 1643 ; sentenced to death for 'improperly surrendering' Bristol to Prince Rupert, 1643 ; pardoned ; exonerated by Cromwell ; member of committee of safety, 1648 ; excluded from the Commons by Pride's Purge, 1648 ; state councillor, 1654 ; one of the keepers of the great seal, 1655 ; M.P., Oxfordshire, 1654, Oxford University, 1656 ; sat in Cromwell's House of Lords, 1658 ; endeavoured to argue Cromwell into accepting the crown ; author, according to Wood, of 'Monarchy Asserted,' 1660. [xviii. 430]

FIENNES or FIENES, THOMAS, ninth BARON DACRE (1517-1541) ; when intent on a poaching frolic mortally wounded, by accident, a man whom he met ; indicted for murder ; executed. [xviii. 432]

FIENNES, WILLIAM, first VISCOUNT SAYE AND SELE (1582-1662) ; fellow of New College, Oxford, 1600 ; succeeded as Baron Saye and Sele, 1613 ; advised Bacon's degradation from the peerage, 1621 ; created viscount, 1624 ; refused to pay forced loan, 1626 ; probably first to discover right of peers to protest ; opposed reservations and amendments to Petition of Right suggested by court party, 1628 ; helped to establish company for colonisation of Providence Island, 1630 ; patentee for land on Connecticut River, 1632 ; purchased plantation in Cocheco, New Hampshire, 1633 ; his suggestion that an hereditary aristocracy should be established in New England rejected by Massachusetts government; relinquished intention of settling in New England; reluctantly followed the king to Scotland, and was sent away on refusing military oath, 1639; saved from accusation of treason by the impeachment of Strafford, 1640; privy councillor and commissioner of the treasury, 1641; lord-lieutenant of Oxfordshire, Cheshire, and Gloucestershire, and member of the committee of safety, 1642; sat in Westminster Assembly, 1643; turned the scale in favour of the self-denying ordinance on two occasions; signed engagement, 1647; urged the king, from selfish motives, to make peace with the parliament at Newport, 1648; privy councillor and lord privy seal, 1660; nicknamed 'Old Subtlety'; wrote two tracts against the quakers.   [xviii. 433]

FIFE, EARLS OF. [See DUFF, JAMES, second EARL, 1729–1809; DUFF, JAMES, fourth EARL, 1776–1857.]

FIFE, THANE or EARL OF (*fl.* 1056?)   [See MAC-DUFF.]

FIFE, SIR JOHN (1795–1871), surgeon; M.R.C.S.; army assistant-surgeon at Woolwich; helped to found Newcastle School of Medicine, 1834; Reform Bill agitator in the north, 1831; mayor of Newcastle, 1838–9 and 1843; knighted (1840) for suppressing chartist outbreak, 1839; F.R.C.S., 1844.   [xviii. 436]

FIGG, JAMES (*d.* 1734), pugilist; taught boxing and swordsmanship at his academy in Marylebone Fields; praised as a swordsman in the 'Tatler' and 'Guardian'; contended with Sparks in a broadsword duel at the Little Theatre in the Haymarket before the Duke of Lorraine, 1731; occasionally exhibited bear-baiting and tiger-baiting.   [xviii. 437]

FILBIE, WILLIAM (1555?–1582), Roman catholic priest; educated at Lincoln College, Oxford, and the English college, Douay; priest, 1581; missioner in England; refused to save his life by conforming to the established church and pleading guilty to communication with Edmund Campion, a prisoner; executed.
            [xviii. 438]

FILCOCK, ROGER (*d.* 1601), jesuit; grammarian and bateler of the English College, Douay; sent to colonise Philip II's new university at Valladolid, 1590; missioner in England, 1598; jesuit, 1600; executed.   [xviii. 438]

FILLAN, FOILAN, or FELAN (with other varieties of form), SAINT (*d.* 777?), Irish missionary in Scotland; son of Feredach, a prince in Munster; Kilkoan and Killellan, two churches in Argyllshire, named after him; joint-founder of abbey at Glendochart, Perthshire; his crosier and bell still preserved in museum of Society of Antiquaries of Scotland, Edinburgh. One of his arms, set in silver, was carried by Bruce to the battle of Bannockburn.   [xviii. 438]

FILLIAN, JOHN (*fl.* 1658–1680), engraver of portraits; pupil of William Faithorne the elder [q. v.]; mentioned by Evelyn in 'Sculptura,' 1662.   [xviii. 439]

FILLS, ROBERT (*fl.* 1562), translator from the French; published 'The Lawes and Statutes of Geneva,' 1562; translated, among other works,'A Briefe and Piththie Summe of the Christian Faith,' from Theodore Beza, 1563.
            [xviii. 440]

FILMER, EDWARD (*fl.* 1707), dramatist: founder's kin fellow, All Souls' College, Oxford, 1672; B.A., 1672; D.C.L., 1681; his tragedy 'The Unnatural Brother,' coldly received on the stage, 1697; defended the stage against Jeremy Collier with 'A Defence of Plays,' 1707.
            [xviii. 440]

FILMER, SIR ROBERT (*d.* 1653), political writer; matriculated at Trinity College, Cambridge, 1604; knighted by Charles I; imprisoned in Leeds Castle, Kent, 1644; wrote, among other works, 'Patriarcha, or the Natural Power of Kings asserted' (published 1680), a manifesto which was sharply criticised by Locke.
            [xviii. 440]

FINAN, SAINT (*d.* 661), bishop of Lindisfarne; monk of Iona; bishop of Lindisfarne, 652; rebuilt church of Lindisfarne; baptised Peada, a Mercian prince, and Sigebert, king of the East-Saxons; consecrated St. Cedd [q. v.] bishop of the East-Saxons; adhered to the Celtic celebration of Easter.   [xviii. 441]

FINCH, ANNE (*d.* 1679). [See CONWAY, ANNE, VISCOUNTESS.]

FINCH, ANNE, COUNTESS OF WINCHILSEA (*d.* 1720), poetess; wife of Heneage Finch, fourth earl, son of Heneage Finch, second earl [q. v.]; maid of honour to the second wife of James, duke of York, and friend of Pope and Rowe, who complimented her in verse as 'Ardelia' and 'Flavia.' Her poem on 'Spleen' appeared in 1701 in Gildon's 'Miscellany,' and her 'Miscellany Poems, written by a Lady,' in 1713.   [xix. 1]

FINCH, DANIEL, second EARL OF NOTTINGHAM and sixth of WINCHILSEA (1647–1730), statesman; eldest son of Heneage Finch, first earl of Nottingham [q. v.]; privy councillor, 1680; first lord of the admiralty, 1681–4; after the flight of James II proposed a regency and opposed the motion declaring the throne vacant; obtained modification of oaths of allegiance and supremacy, and accepted the revolution; secretary-at-war, 1688–93; carried the Toleration Act; failed to get his Comprehension Bill passed; reluctantly dismissed by William III, 1693; remained out of office till the king's death; again secretary of state, 1702–4; resigned when the whigs became predominant; throughout the reign of Anne was active as the head of the high church tories, and (1711) carried an act forbidding the occasional conformity of dissenters; opposed preliminaries of peace with France, 1711; named president of council by George I in 1714, but dismissed in 1716 for advocating leniency to the Jacobite peers.   [xix. 1]

FINCH, EDWARD (*fl.* 1630–1641), royalist divine; probably younger son of Sir Henry Finch [q. v.]; dispossessed of the vicarage of Christ Church, Newgate, by the parliamentary committee, 1641; published 'An Answer to the Articles exhibited in Parliament against Edw. Finch,' 1641.   [xix. 5]

FINCH, EDWARD (1664–1738), composer; fifth son of Heneage Finch, first earl of Nottingham [q. v.]; M.A., 1679; fellow of Christ's College, Cambridge; prebendary of York, 1704, Canterbury, 1710; a 'Te Deum' and anthem by him found in Tudway's manuscript collection; his manuscript 'Grammar of Thorough Bass' preserved in Euing Library, Glasgow.   [xix. 5]

FINCH, EDWARD (1756–1843), general; served with Coldstream guards in Flanders, 1793–5, in Ireland, 1798, and the Helder, 1799; commanded cavalry under Abercromby in Egypt, 1801, and brigade of guards in Copenhagen expedition, 1809; M.P., Cambridge University, 1789–1819; named groom of the bedchamber, 1804.
            [xix. 5]

FINCH, FRANCIS OLIVER (1802–1862), watercolour painter; worked five years under John Varley and joined Society of Painters in Water-colours, 1822; painted many views of Scottish and English landscapes; and printed 'An Artist's Dream,' a collection of sonnets.
            [xix. 6]

FINCH, SIR HENEAGE (*d.* 1631), speaker of the House of Commons; grandson of Sir Thomas Finch [q. v.]; barrister, Inner Temple, 1606; M.P., Rye, 1607; defended royal prerogative in debate on impositions, 1610; M.P., West Looe, 1621; knighted, 1623; serjeant-at-law, 1623; recorder of London, 1620, and M.P. for the city, 1623–6; speaker, 1626.   [xix. 7]

FINCH, HENEAGE, first EARL OF NOTTINGHAM (1621–1682), lord chancellor; eldest son of Sir Heneage Finch [q. v.]; distinguished at the Inner Temple for his knowledge of municipal law; became at the Restoration M.P. for Canterbury and solicitor-general; created baronet, 1660; M.P. for Oxford University, 1661; appointed attorney-general, 1670; lord keeper of the seals, 1673; Baron Finch and lord chancellor, 1674; and Earl of Nottingham, 1681; a zealous and able supporter of policy of court, but independent as judge; the Amri of 'Absalom and Achitophel.'   [xix. 8]

FINCH, HENEAGE, second EARL OF WINCHILSEA (*d.* 1689), provided troops for the king in the great rebellion, and money for Charles II when abroad; ambassador at Constantinople, 1661–9; published account of his embassy (1661), and of an eruption of Mount Etna, 1669.   [xix. 11]

FINCH, HENEAGE, first EARL OF AYLESFORD (1647?–1719), second son of Heneage Finch, first earl of Nottingham [q. v.]; educated at Westminster and Christ Church, Oxford; king's counsel, 1677, and solicitor-general, 1679–86; dismissed by James II, 1686; leading counsel for the seven bishops, 1688; M.P. for Oxford University in several parliaments; created Baron Guernsey and privy councillor, 1703; created Earl of Aylesford, 1714. [xix. 12]

FINCH, SIR HENRY (1558-1625), serjeant-at-law; second son of Sir Thomas Finch [q. v.]; educated at Oriel College, Oxford; barrister, Gray's Inn, 1585; M.P., Canterbury, 1593; recorder of Sandwich, 1613; serjeant-at-law and knighted, 1616; one of those employed upon the attempted codification of statute laws; consulted by James I on monopolies. His 'World's Great Restauration, or Calling of the Jews,' 1621, was suppressed as derogatory to the royal power; but his valuable treatise on common law, 1613, fol., in legal French, was frequently translated, and finally edited by Danby Pickering, 1789. [xix. 12]

FINCH, HENRY (1633-1704), ejected minister; vicar of Walton, Lancashire, 1656; actively engaged in royalist rising under Sir George Booth; ejected for nonconformity, 1662; presbyterian minister of Birch Hall, Lancashire, 1672-97; aided Calamy, historian of the silenced ministers, with corrections. [xix. 13]

FINCH, SIR JOHN, BARON FINCH OF FORDWICH (1584-1660), speaker and lord keeper; son of Sir Henry Finch [q. v.]; barrister, Gray's Inn, 1611; M.P., Canterbury, 1614, and recorder, 1617; king's counsel, 1626; speaker of the House of Commons, 1628; held down in the chair in the following session to prevent his adjourning the house; employed by the court in Star-chamber and high commission cases against Prynne and others; serjeant-at-law, 1634; appointed chief-justice of the common pleas, 1635; mainly responsible for the ship-money judgment, 1637; named lord keeper by influence of Queen Henrietta Maria, January, and created baron, April 1640; impeached in the Long parliament, October 1640; fled to Holland, December 1640, but returned at the Restoration. [xix. 14]

FINCH, SIR JOHN (1626-1682), physician; younger son of Sir Heneage Finch (d. 1631) [q. v.]; after graduating B.A. at Balliol College, Oxford, 1647, and M.A. Christ's College, Cambridge, 1649, went to Padua, where he became English consul and syndic of the university; afterwards professor at Pisa; knighted by Charles II, 1661; admitted to council of Royal Society, 1663; minister to the Grand Duke of Tuscany, 1665; ambassador at Constantinople, 1672-82; died soon after his return to England; buried at Christ's College, Cambridge, near his lifelong companion, Sir Thomas Baines [q. v.] [xix. 18]

FINCH, PETER (1661-1754), presbyterian minister; son of Henry Finch [q. v.]; M.A. Edinburgh, 1680; minister at Norwich, 1691-1754. [xix. 14]

FINCH, ROBERT (1783-1830), antiquary; educated at St. Paul's School and Balliol College, Oxford; M.A., 1809; ordained in 1807; lived chiefly abroad; died at Rome; his literary and fine art collections preserved in the Ashmolean Museum, Oxford. [xix. 18]

FINCH, ROBERT POOLE (1724-1803), divine; educated at Merchant Taylors' and Peterhouse, Cambridge; M.A., 1747; D.D., 1772; rector of St. Michael's, Cornhill, 1771; prebendary of Westminster, 1781; an eminent preacher; published treatise on oaths and perjury, 1788. [xix. 19]

FINCH, SIR THOMAS (d. 1563), military commander; knighted for assisting in suppression of Wyatt's rising, 1553; drowned off Havre when about to act as knight-marshal to the English force engaged there; his body buried at Eastwell, Kent, where he had acquired the Moyle property by his marriage. [xix. 19]

FINCH, WILLIAM (d. 1613), merchant; agent to an expedition which obtained from the Great Mogul trading privileges for the East India Company at Surat in 1610; died at Babylon from drinking poisoned water. [xix. 20]

FINCH, WILLIAM (1747-1810), divine; educated at Merchant Taylors' and St. John's College, Oxford; incumbent of Tackley, Oxfordshire; D.C.L. Oxford, 1775; published 'The Objections of Infidel Historians and other Writers against Christianity' (his Bampton lecture). [xix. 20]

FINCH-HATTON, EDWARD (d. 1771), diplomatist; fifth son of Daniel Finch, second earl of Nottingham [q. v.]; M.A. Trinity College, Cambridge, 1718; M.P., Cambridge University, 1727-64; instituted prize for Latin essay; ambassador in Sweden, Holland, Poland, and Russia (1739); assumed name of Hatton, 1764, under will of aunt, daughter of Viscount Hatton. [xix. 20]

FINCH-HATTON, GEORGE WILLIAM, ninth EARL OF WINCHILSEA and fifth EARL OF NOTTINGHAM (1791-1858), politician; succeeded his cousin, George Finch, fifth earl of Nottingham and ninth of Winchilsea, in 1826; a violent opponent of catholic relief; fought a duel with Wellington, 1829; a frequent speaker in the House of Lords against liberal measures. [xix. 20]

FINDEN, EDWARD FRANCIS (1791-1857), engraver; youngest brother of William Finden [q. v.]; engraved separately 'The Harvest Waggon,' after Gainsborough, and a few other pictures. [xix. 21]

FINDEN, WILLIAM (1787-1852), engraver; apprenticed to James Mitan; established, with his brother, school of engraving; engraved with him the Elgin Marbles for British Museum, Murray's 'Arctic Voyages,' Lodge's 'Portraits,' 1821-34, illustrations to Moore's 'Byron,' 1833, and 'The Royal Gallery of British Art'; engraved also Lawrence's 'George IV' and pictures by Wilkie and Landseer. [xix. 21]

FINDLATER, EARLS OF. [See OGILVY, JAMES, fourth EARL, 1664-1730; OGILVY, JAMES, sixth EARL, 1714?-1770.]

FINDLATER, ANDREW (1810-1885), compiler; graduated at Aberdeen, 1810; LL.D. Aberdeen, 1864; edited Chambers's 'Encyclopædia' and (1857) 'Information for the People'; wrote educational manuals. [xix. 22]

FINDLATER, CHARLES (1754-1838), agricultural writer; graduated at Edinburgh, 1770; minister of Newlands, 1790-1835; published 'General View of the Agriculture of the County of Peebles,' 1802, and contributed to Sinclair's 'Statistical Account of Scotland.' [xix. 22]

FINDLAY, ALEXANDER GEORGE (1812-1875), geographer and hydrographer; F.R.G.S., 1844; compiled atlases of 'Ancient and Comparative Geography,' 'Coasts and Islands of the Pacific Ocean,' six nautical directories with charts; published 'Lighthouses and Coast Fog Signals of the World'; aided Franklin expedition of 1875, and African exploration. [xix. 23]

FINDLAY, SIR GEORGE (1829-1893), railway manager; assistant engineer on Birkenhead railway, 1849; superintended construction of line between Hereford and Ludlow, and on its completion, 1852, became manager under Thomas Brassey [q. v.]; district manager for North-Western railway in Shropshire and South Wales, 1862; general goods manager at Euston, 1864; general traffic manager, 1874; general manager, 1880; A.I.C.E., 1874; knighted, 1892; published 'Working and Management of an English Railway,' 1889. [Suppl. ii. 209]

FINDLAY, JOHN RITCHIE (1824-1898), newspaper proprietor; educated at Edinburgh University; entered, 1842, office of 'Scotsman,' which he subsequently assisted in editing; partner in firm, 1868, and principal proprietor, 1870; spent large sums on public objects, and presented to the nation the Scottish National Portrait Gallery, Edinburgh (opened 1889); received freedom of Edinburgh, 1896; published 'Personal Recollections of De Quincey,' 1886. [Suppl. ii. 211]

FINDLAY, ROBERT (1721-1814), Scots divine; professor of divinity in Glasgow University, 1782; D.D.; carried on a controversy with Kennicott, 1761, and published a work combating Voltaire's views on the credibility of Christian and Jewish writers, 1770. [xix. 24]

FINET or **FINETT**, SIR JOHN (1571-1641), master of the ceremonies. His works include a book on the etiquette of embassies, published 1656. [xix. 24]

FINEUX, SIR JOHN (1441?-1527). [See FYNEUX.]

FINGALL, second EARL OF (d. 1649). [See PLUNKET, CHRISTOPHER.]

FINGER, GODFREY or GOTTFRIED (fl. 1685-1717), composer; born at Olmütz; came to England, c. 1685; published sonatas, and music for Congreve, Lee, and other dramatists, 1695-1701; became chamber-musician to the queen of Prussia, 1702, and chapel-master at Gotha, 1717. [xix. 25]

FINGLAS, PATRICK (*fl.* 1535), Irish judge; chief-justice of king's bench in Ireland, 1534-5; his 'Breviat of the getting of Ireland, and of the Decaie of the same' included in Harris's 'Hibernica,' 1770.   [xix. 27]

FINGLOW, JOHN (*d.* 1586), Roman catholic divine; ordained priest at Douay, 1581; missioner in England; executed at York for high treason.   [xix. 27]

FININGHAM, ROBERT DE (*d.* 1460), Franciscan, of Norwich; author of several works in defence of his order.   [xix. 27]

FINLAISON, JOHN (1783-1860), statistician and government actuary; introduced important reforms in victualling department of admiralty, and plan (1809) for indexing records, which was adopted also on the continent; compiled first official 'navy list,' 1814; initiated fund for orphans and children of civil employés in admiralty, 1819; in the treasury, 1822-51; published 'Life Annuities,' 1829, showing difference between male and female lives; first president of the Institution of Actuaries, 1847-60.   [xix. 27]

FINLASON, WILLIAM FRANCIS (1818-1895), legal writer; called to bar at Middle Temple, 1851; parliamentary and legal reporter for 'Times'; master of bench of Middle Temple; published legal works.   [Suppl. ii. 212]

FINLAY, FRANCIS DALZELL (1793-1857), Irish journalist; began life as a printer's apprentice; founded in 1824 the 'Northern Whig'; twice imprisoned for libel; supported liberal measures, but opposed repeal and Young Irelandism.   [xix. 29]

FINLAY, GEORGE (1799-1875), historian; studied law at Glasgow and Göttingen; went to Greece, 1823, and saw much of Byron; took part in the war of independence, at the close of which he bought an estate in Attica; died at Athens. His 'History of Greece,' covering a period of two thousand years, appeared in sections between 1844 and 1861, and was published collectively in 1877.   [xix. 30]

FINLAY, JOHN (1782-1810), Scottish poet; educated at Glasgow University, where he became a friend of 'Christopher North'; published 'Wallace... and other Poems,' 1802, a collection of Scottish ballads, 1808, and other works.   [xix. 31]

FINLAY, KIRKMAN (*d.* 1828), philhellene; brother of George Finlay [q. v.]; spent his fortune and his life after twenty years' fighting for the Greeks; killed before Scio.   [xix. 32]

FINLAY, KIRKMAN (1773-1842), lord provost of Glasgow; uncle of Kirkman Finlay (*d.* 1828) [q. v.]; M.P., Glasgow, 1812-18; rector of the university, 1819; an advanced economist and founder of Glasgow commerce.   [xix. 32]

FINLAYSON, GEORGE (1790-1823), traveller; as naturalist accompanied the expedition of 1821 to Siam and Cochin China; his journal edited by Sir Stamford Raffles, 1826.   [xix. 32]

FINLAYSON, JAMES (1758-1808), divine; professor of logic in Edinburgh University, 1787-1808, when he nominated his successor; incumbent of Grey Friars, 1793-9; moderator of general assembly, 1802; wrote life of Hugh Blair (published posthumously), and other works.   [xix. 32]

FINLAYSON or **FINLEYSON**, JOHN (1770-1854), disciple of Richard Brothers [q. v.]; published pseudo-scientific pamphlets.   [xix. 33]

FINLAYSON, THOMAS (1809-1872), U.P. minister; incumbent of Rose Street Church, Edinburgh, 1847-72; moderator of supreme court and D.D. of Edinburgh, 1867; promoter of the manse fund.   [xix. 34]

FINN BARR, SAINT and BISHOP (*d.* 623), in popular usage Barra or Bairre; baptised by Bishop MacCorb; founded a school at Lough Eirce, where many famous saints were educated, and churches at Achaidh Durbchon (source of the Lee), and Cluain (Queen's County); finally settled at Cork (Corcach Mor), of which he became bishop; said to have visited Rome and Britain.   [xix. 35]

FINNCHU, SAINT (*fl.* 7th cent.), baptised by Ailbe of Imlach Ibair (Emly); abbot of Bangor (co. Down) till

608; helped the king of Meath to repel British pirates, and assisted the kings of Leinster and Munster in their wars; his day, 12 Nov.   [xix. 37]

FINNERTY, PETER (1766?-1822), journalist; punished for political libel in his paper, the Dublin 'Press,' 1797, though defended by Curran; imprisoned for libel on Castlereagh in 'Morning Chronicle,' 1811.   [xix. 38]

FINNEY, SAMUEL (1719-1798), miniature-painter to Queen Charlotte; his manuscript history of his family printed in 'Cheshire and Lancashire Historical Collector,' vol. i.   [xix. 39]

FINNIAN, SAINT (*d.* 550), 'tutor of the saints of Ireland,' and chief of the second order of Irish saints; baptised by Saint Abban; stayed thirty years at St. David's (Cell Muine) in Wales, where he negotiated with the Saxon invaders; afterwards lived sixteen years at Aghowle (Achad Aball), Wicklow; founded many churches; established, *c.* 530, his great school at Clonard (Cluainiraird), Meath; his day, 12 Dec.   [xix. 39]

FINTAN, SAINT (*d.* 595), 'chief head of the monks of Ireland'; founded, *c.* 548, a monastery at Clonenagh (Cluain-ednech), Queen's County, with a very rigorous rule; his day, 17 Feb. Comgall [q. v.] said to have been his most famous pupil.   [xix. 41]

FINTAN or **MUNNU**, SAINT (*d.* 634), founder of a monastery at Taghmon (Tech Munnu), co. Wexford; a leper for twenty-three years; opposed change in the rule of Easter at council of Magh Ailbe or Whitefield; said to be buried at Kilmun in Cowall, Scotland; his day, 21 Oct.   [xix. 42]

FIRBANK, JOSEPH (1819-1886), railway contractor; son of a Durham miner; constructed forty-nine lines, 1846-86; built Midland goods depôt, St. Pancras; employed thirty years in South Wales.   [xix. 43]

FIREBRACE, HENRY (1619-1691), royalist; as page of the bedchamber and clerk of the kitchen attended Charles I throughout the rebellion, 1648; devised two plans for his escape from Carisbrooke Castle; reinstated after the Restoration.   [xix. 44]

FIRMIN, GILES (1614-1697), ejected minister; educated at Emmanuel College, Cambridge; went to New England, 1632, and was ordained deacon of the first church at Boston; received grant of land at Ipswich, Massachusetts, 1638; shipwrecked off coast of Spain on return to England, *c.* 1647; vicar of Shalford, Essex, 1648, till ejection, 1662; his house at Ridgewell licensed for presbyterian worship, 1672; practised medicine both in America and England; published theological pamphlets.   [xix. 45]

FIRMIN, THOMAS (1632-1697), philanthropist; girdler and mercer in Lombard Street; friend of Tillotson, John Biddle [q. v.], and other divines; a governor of Christ's Hospital, 1673, and of St. Thomas's Hospital, 1693; established depôt where corn and coal were sold to the poor at cost price; started in 1676 a workhouse in Little Britain for employment of poor in linen manufacture, carrying it on at a loss till his death; also interested himself in debtors' prisons and French refugees; a walk named after him in Marden Park, Surrey.   [xix. 46]

FIRTH, MARK (1819-1880), founder of Firth College, Sheffield; carried on large steel works at Sheffield, Birmingham, and Whittington, by which British government was supplied; erected and endowed Ranmoor almshouses, 1869; gave public park to Sheffield, opened, 1875; founded Firth College, 1879.   [xix. 49]

FISCHER, JOHANN CHRISTIAN (1733-1800), oboist and composer; after having been in the Dresden court band and that of Frederick the Great, settled in London, 1768; became musician to Queen Charlotte, 1780; married younger daughter of Gainsborough, who painted his portrait; published concertos and other works at Berlin and London.   [xix. 50]

FISCHER, JOHN GEORGE PAUL (1786-1875), painter; came to England from Hanover in 1810; painted miniatures for the court and nobility, including two of Queen Victoria (1819 and 1820) as an infant; exhibited at Royal Academy, 1817-52.   [xix. 51]

FISH, SIMON (*d.* 1531), theologian and pamphleteer; entered Gray's Inn, *c.* 1525; having incurred the displeasure of Wolsey fled to Holland; wrote there against the clergy his 'Supplication of the Beggars,' circulated in London, 1529, and answered by Sir Thomas More [q. v.] It was printed in Foxe, 1546, and is one of 'The Four Supplications,' edited by Dr. Furnivall, 1871. [xix. 51]

FISH, WILLIAM (1775–1866), musician; organist of St. Andrew's, Norwich; published a sonata, some ballads, an oboe concerto, and pianoforte and harp music. [xix. 52]

FISHACRE, FISSAKRE, FISHAKLE, or **FIZACRE,** RICHARD DE (d. 1248), Dominican divine; wrote commentaries on Peter Lombard's 'Sentences,' the manuscripts of which are at Oriel and Balliol Colleges, Oxford. [xix. 53]

FISHER, CATHERINE MARIA, known as 'KITTY FISHER' (d. 1767), courtesan; afterwards wife of John Norris of Benenden; described under name of Kitty Willis in Mrs. Cowley's 'Belle's Stratagem'; several times painted by Sir Joshua Reynolds. [xix. 53]

FISHER, DANIEL (1731–1807), dissenting minister; tutor at Homerton College from 1771. [xix. 54]

FISHER, DAVID, the elder (1788 ?–1858), actor and musician; appeared at Drury Lane in 1817 in Shakespearean rôles; built several theatres in the eastern counties, and for some time led the Norwich choral concerts. [xix. 54]

FISHER, DAVID, the younger (1816 ?–1887), actor; son of David Fisher the elder [q. v.]; played at the Princess's under Charles Kean, 1853–4; the original Abbé Latour in the 'Dead Heart' at the Adelphi, 1859; final appearance in London, 1884, at the Lyceum, as Sir Toby Belch. [xix. 54]

FISHER, EDWARD (fl. 1627–1655), theological writer; B.A. Brasenose College, Oxford, 1630; author of anti-puritan tracts; identified by some with E. F., author of the 'Marrow of Modern Divinity,' 1645. [xix. 55]

FISHER, EDWARD (1730–1785 ?), mezzotint engraver; engraved over sixty plates of portraits, including several after Reynolds, and published ten after his own designs, 1776. [xix. 56]

FISHER, GEORGE (1794–1873), astronomer; M.A. St. Catharine's College, Cambridge, 1821, having previously acted as astronomer to the Polar expedition of 1818; chaplain and astronomer to Parry's north-west passage expedition, 1821–3; F.R.S., 1825; several times vice-president of Astronomical Society; carried on magnetical experiments in Mediterranean, 1827–32; head-master of Greenwich Hospital school, 1834–60, and principal, 1860–3; erected observatory for the school; propounded theory of the nature and origin of the aurora borealis, 1834; published scientific papers. [xix. 56]

FISHER, JAMES (1697–1775), a founder of the Scottish secession church; studied at Glasgow University; ordained minister of Kinclaven, Perthshire, 1725; joined his father-in-law, Ebenezer Erskine [q. v.], in forming the associate presbytery and in compiling Fisher's 'Catechism,' 1753–60; made professor of divinity by associate burgher synod, 1749; brought out Fisher's 'Catechism' in parts, 1753 and 1760. [xix. 57]

FISHER, JASPER (fl. 1639), divine and dramatist; M.A. Magdalen Hall, Oxford, 1614; D.D., 1639; divinity reader at Magdalen College, Oxford; appointed rector of Wilsden, Bedfordshire, c. 1631; published a play, 'Fuimus Troes, the True Trojans,' 1633. [xix. 58]

FISHER, JOHN (1459–1535), bishop of Rochester; educated at Michaelhouse, Cambridge, of which he became master in 1497; M.A., 1491; senior proctor, 1494; vice-chancellor, 1501; first Lady Margaret professor of divinity, 1503; chancellor of the university and bishop of Rochester, 1504; president of Queens' College, Cambridge, 1505–8; took chief part in the foundation of Christ's, 1505, and St. John's colleges, 1511, acting for his patroness, Margaret, countess of Richmond; opposed in convocation Wolsey's subsidy, 1523; brought Erasmus to Cambridge; wrote three treatises against Luther, 1523–5; opposed church reform, 1529; fined for denying the validity of the divorce of Queen Catherine, 1534; committed to the Tower for refusing to swear to the Act of Succession; deprived, attainted, and beheaded, 1535, for refusing to acknowledge the king as supreme head of the church. His Latin theological works were issued in 1597; vol. i. of his collected English works appeared in 1876. [xix. 58]

FISHER, JOHN (1569–1641), jesuit (real name PERCY); educated at the English colleges at Rheims and Rome; admitted into society by Aquaviva; imprisoned in Bridewell on arrival in London, but escaped, 1595; sent by Garnet to the north; afterwards with Gerard in Northamptonshire and chaplain to Sir Everard Digby [q. v.]; imprisoned in the Gatehouse, 1610, and then banished; after some time in Belgium returned and again imprisoned; disputed with James I and Laud; pardoned on conclusion of Spanish marriage, but again imprisoned, 1634–5; published theological works. [xix. 63]

FISHER, JOHN (1748–1825), bishop of Salisbury; educated at St. Paul's School and Peterhouse; M.A., 1773; fellow of St. John's College, Cambridge, 1773; D.D. Cambridge, 1789; tutor to the duke of Kent, 1780–5, of the Princess Charlotte, 1805; bishop of Exeter, 1803; translated to Salisbury, 1807; published sermons. [xix. 64]

FISHER, JOHN ABRAHAM (1744–1806), violinist; received musical degrees at Oxford, 1777; played at court and on the continent; expelled from Austria for ill-treatment of his second wife, Anna Storace [q. v.]; retired to Ireland; composed violin pieces, six symphonies, songs, an anthem, and dramatic music. [xix. 66]

FISHER, SIR JOHN WILLIAM (1788–1876), surgeon; M.R.C.S., 1809; F.R.C.S., 1836; M.D. Erlangen, 1841; surgeon-in-chief to metropolitan police, 1829–65; knighted, 1858. [xix. 67]

FISHER, JONATHAN (d. 1812), landscape-painter; studied art while a draper in Dublin; painted Irish scenes; employed in stamp office, Dublin. [xix. 67]

FISHER, JOSEPH (d. 1705), archdeacon of Carlisle; fellow of Queen's College, Oxford; M.A., 1682; archdeacon, 1702. [xix. 67]

FISHER, MARY (fl. 1652–1697), Yorkshire quakeress (afterwards Bayley and Cross); imprisoned at Boston, Massachusetts, 1655; attempted to convert sultan Mahomet IV, at Adrianople, 1660; was living in South Carolina, 1697. [xix. 68]

FISHER, PAYNE (1616–1693), poet; of Hart Hall, Oxford, and Magdalene College, Cambridge; served in royalist army in Ireland, becoming captain; deserted at Marston Moor (1644); afterwards wrote Latin poems celebrating the exploits of Cromwell and his generals, and after the Restoration two English prose works on the tombs in London churches, 1668 and 1684. [xix. 68]

FISHER, SAMUEL (1605–1665), quaker; educated at Trinity College and New Inn Hall, Oxford; M.A., 1630; lecturer at Lydd till he joined the baptists, after which he went about 'disputing' on baptism; became a quaker, 1654; with John Stubbs went to Rome and addressed the cardinals; several times imprisoned after his return; died of the plague; published tracts long in use among quakers. [xix. 70]

FISHER, SAMUEL (d. 1681), puritan; M.A. Magdalen College, Oxford, 1640; ejected at the Restoration from Thornton-in-the-Moors rectory, Cheshire. [xix. 72]

FISHER, otherwise HAWKINS, THOMAS (d. 1577), a protégé of John Dudley, duke of Northumberland [q. v.]; afterwards secretary to the Duke of Somerset; obtained grant of estate of St. Sepulchre's Priory, Warwick; M.P. for Warwick, 1554–8; wrongly identified with John Fisher (compiler of 'Black Book of Warwick '). [xix. 72]

FISHER, THOMAS (1781 ?–1836), antiquary; forty-six years in the India House; F.S.A., 1836; published 'Collections, Historical, Genealogical, and Topographical, for Bedfordshire,' 1812–16, also lithographic plates of eastern and other inscribed monuments. [xix. 73]

FISHER, WILLIAM (1780–1852), rear-admiral; served against Villeneuve, 1805; surveyed the Mozambique in the Racehorse, 1809–10; captured slavers and pirates off Guinea coast, 1816–17; senior officer of the Alexandria detached squadron, 1840. [xix. 75]

FISHER, WILLIAM WEBSTER (1798 ?–1874), Downing professor of medicine at Cambridge, 1841–74; fellow of Downing College, Cambridge, 1834–41; M.D., Montpellier, 1825; Cambridge, 1841. [xix. 75]

FISK, WILLIAM (1796–1872), painter; exhibited at the Academy, the British Institution, and Suffolk Street Gallery; his historical pictures chiefly remarkable for their fidelity. [xix. 76]

FISK, WILLIAM HENRY (1827–1884), painter and drawing-master; son of William Fisk [q. v.]; exhibited landscapes in London and Paris; anatomical draughtsman to College of Surgeons; very successful as art teacher at University College School, London, and lecturer. [xix. 76]

FISKEN, WILLIAM (d. 1883), presbyterian minister of the secession church; with his brother Thomas invented the steam plough, the steam tackle (patented 1855), and other machines. [xix. 76]

FITCH, RALPH (fl. 1583–1606), traveller in India; one of the first Englishmen who made the overland route to India; left London with other Levant merchants, 1583, and travelled down the Euphrates valley by caravan and boat; imprisoned by Portuguese at Ormuz and Goa, 1583; escaped across Deccan and visited court of the Great Mogul (Akbar); thence sailed down the Jumna and the Ganges; first Englishman to visit Burmah and Siam, 1586–7; returned by the Malabar coast and Euphrates valley, reaching London, 1591; his narrative in Hakluyt. [xix. 77]

FITCH, THOMAS (d. 1517). [See FICH.]

FITCH, WILLIAM (1563–1611). [See CANFIELD, BENEDICT.]

FITCH, WILLIAM STEVENSON (1793–1859), antiquary; postmaster of Ipswich; made collections for a history of Suffolk. [xix. 79]

FITCHETT, JOHN (1776–1838), poet; a Warrington attorney; left, besides 'Minor Poems' (printed 1836), an unfinished romantic epic, 'King Alfred,' completed by Robert Roscoe, and published, 1841–2. [xix. 79]

FITTLER, JAMES (1758–1835), engraver; A.R.A., 1800; marine engraver to George III. His works include 'Titian's Schoolmaster' (Moroni), Velasquez's 'Innocent X,' and the plates for Forster's 'British Gallery.' [xix. 79]

FITTON, SIR ALEXANDER (d. 1699), lord chancellor of Ireland; barrister, Inner Temple, 1662; lost Gawsworth estates by litigation with Lord Gerard of Brandon; made chancellor by James II, 1687, after whose abdication he was attainted and fled to France; died at St. Germains. [xix. 80]

FITTON, SIR EDWARD, the elder (1527–1579), lord president of Connaught, 1569–72; vice-treasurer of Ireland, 1573; imprisoned Clanricarde, 1572, and carried on war with the Burkes; escorted Kildare and his sons to England, 1575. [xix. 81]

FITTON, SIR EDWARD, the younger (1548?–1606), son of Sir Edward Fitton [q. v.]; grantee of part of the Desmond estates. [xix. 82]

FITTON, MARY (fl. 1600), maid of honour to Queen Elizabeth; daughter of Sir Edward Fitton the younger [q. v.]; most doubtfully identified with the 'dark lady' of Shakespeare's sonnets; mistress of William Herbert, third earl of Pembroke [q. v.]; married Captain W. Polwhele, 1607, and Captain Lougher. [xix. 82]

FITTON, MICHAEL (1766–1852), naval lieutenant; midshipman at relief of Gibraltar, 1782; as commander of Abergavenny tender performed many daring exploits; promoted after attack on Curaçao, 1804; captured forty French privateers, including the Superbe, 1806; admitted into Greenwich Hospital, 1835. [xix. 83]

FITTON, WILLIAM HENRY (1780–1861), geologist; B.A. Dublin, 1799; studied geology under Jameson at Edinburgh; afterwards practised as physician at Northampton; M.D. Cambridge, 1816; after marriage removed to London and devoted himself to geology; several years secretary of Geological Society; president, 1828; F.R.S., 1815; Wollaston medallist, 1852; published scientific pamphlets and laid down proper succession of strata between oolite and chalk, 1824–36. [xix. 84]

FITZAILWIN, HENRY (d. 1212), first mayor of London; appointed probably between 1191 and 1193, and possibly as early as 1189; presided over a meeting of citizens in 1212 after the great fire, and probably held office till his death. [xix. 85]

FITZALAN, BERTRAM (d. 1424), Carmelite of Lincoln, where he founded a library; left theological manuscripts. [xix. 86]

FITZALAN, BRIAN, LORD OF BEDALE (d. 1306), warden of Castles Forfar, Dundee, Roxburgh, and Jedburgh, 1290; a guardian of Scotland during interregnum, 1292 and 1297; served against Welsh, 1294, and against Scots, 1299 and 1303; summoned to English parliament, 1295. [xix. 86]

FITZALAN, EDMUND, EARL OF ARUNDEL (1285–1326), son of Richard I Fitzalan, earl of Arundel [q. v.]; served against Scots, 1306–7; refused to attend council at York, 1309; one of the lords ordainers, 1310; joined Lancaster against Gaveston, and (1314) refused to accompany Edward II to Stirling; captain-general north of Trent, 1316; member of council of barons, 1318; joined the king, 1321; one of Lancaster's judges, justice of Wales, and warden of the Welsh marches; finally captured and executed by Queen Isabella and Mortimer. [xix. 87]

FITZALAN, HENRY, twelfth EARL OF ARUNDEL (1511?–1580), godson of Henry VIII, whom he accompanied to France, 1532; lord-deputy of Calais, 1540–3; K.G., 1544; stormed Boulogne, 1544; created lord chamberlain on his return to England; retained office under Edward VI; member of council; joined Warwick against Somerset, but was removed by former from council; next allied himself with Somerset, on whose fall he was imprisoned and fined; secret partisan of Mary, for whom he raised the city against Northumberland, and then captured the latter; lord steward of the household and member of the council, 1553; one of the English commissioners to mediate between France and the emperor, 1555; lieutenant-general and captain of the forces, 1557; lord steward and privy councillor at accession of Elizabeth; chancellor of Oxford university, 1559; resigned lord stewardship, 1564, and went out of favour; headed the catholic party, whose object was to depose Elizabeth in favour of Mary Stuart and the Duke of Norfolk; restrained to his own houses, 1569; restored to council by influence of Leicester, 1570; opposed the Alençon match; again imprisoned after Ridolfi plot, 1571–2. His portrait was painted by Holbein. [xix. 88]

FITZALAN, JOHN II, LORD OF OSWESTRY, CLUN, AND ARUNDEL (1223–1267), at first fought with the barons against Henry III (1258–61), but afterwards led royal troops against the baronial partisan, Llewelyn of Wales, 1258 and 1260; finally joined the party of Prince Edward; captured by the barons at Lewes, 1264. [xix. 93]

FITZALAN, JOHN VI, EARL OF ARUNDEL (1408–1435), summoned to parliament as a baron, 1429; recognised as earl, 1435 (the title having been contested by the Mowbrays); distinguished himself as a soldier in France; captain of Rouen Castle, 1432; Duke of Touraine and K.G.; wounded and captured at Gournay; died at Beauvais. [xix. 94]

FITZALAN, RICHARD I, EARL OF ARUNDEL (1267–1302), grandson of John II Fitzalan, lord of Oswestry [q. v.]; served against Welsh and Scots and in Gascony; signed the letter to the pope from Lincoln, 1301. [xix. 95]

FITZALAN, RICHARD II, EARL OF ARUNDEL AND WARENNE (1307?–1376), son of Edmund Fitzalan, earl of Arundel [q. v.]; married a daughter of Hugh le Despenser; restored to his estates after fall of Mortimer, 1330; justice of North Wales for life, 1334; commander of English army in north, 1337; as admiral of the ships at Portsmouth distinguished himself at Sluys, 1340; joint warden of Scottish marches; joint lieutenant of Aquitaine, 1344; admiral of the west, 1345–7; commanded division at Crécy, 1346, and took part in siege of Calais; at naval action with Spanish off Winchelsea, 1350; one of the regents, 1355; much employed in diplomatic missions by Edward III, to whom he also lent large sums. [xix. 96]

FITZALAN, RICHARD III, EARL OF ARUNDEL AND SURREY (1346–1397), son of Richard Fitzalan II, earl of Arundel [q. v.]; one of the council appointed by the Good parliament: member of council of regency, 1380; admiral of the west, 1377; joint governor of Richard II, 1381; joined reforming party under Gloucester, 1386; won a naval victory over the French, Spanish, and Flemings off Margate, 1387; took leading part in the opposition to Richard II after his own attempted arrest, 1387 ; one of the lords appellant, 1388 ; removed from the council and admiralty, but soon restored ; quarrelled with John of Gaunt ; imprisoned ; after his release conspired with Gloucester and Warwick and was executed on Tower Hill ; his tomb in the Augustinian church for many years an object of pilgrimage. [xix. 98]

FITZALAN, *alias* ARUNDEL, THOMAS (1353–1414). [See ARUNDEL.]

FITZALAN, THOMAS, EARL OF ARUNDEL AND SURREY (1381–1415), son of Richard III Fitzalan [q. v.] ; escaped from custody of his half-brother to the continent, where he joined his uncle the archbishop ; with him accompanied Henry of Lancaster to England, 1399 ; created by Henry IV one of the first knights of the Bath, and restored to his titles and estates ; defeated and captured Exeter and insurgent nobles ; procured execution of Scrope and Mowbray, 1405 ; joined party of the Beauforts ; one of the commanders of the English expedition to help Burgundy, 1411 ; made lord treasurer and warden of the Cinque ports by Henry V, 1413 ; took part in siege of Harfleur, 1415 ; died of dysentery. [xix. 100]

FITZALAN, WILLIAM (*d.* 1160), rebel ; defended Shrewsbury Castle against Stephen, 1138, and afterwards joined the army of the Empress Matilda and her son, who restored him his fiefs. His younger brother Walter (*d.* 1177) was ancestor of the house of Stuart. [xix. 103]

FITZALDHELM, WILLIAM (*fl.* 1157–1198), steward of Henry II and governor of Ireland ; one of the royal justices, *c.* 1165 ; acted as Henry II's representative before he came to Ireland ; succeeded Strongbow as justiciar in Ireland, 1176–8 ; sheriff of Cumberland and justice in Yorkshire and Northumberland, 1189 ; wrongly identified with William de Burgh (*d.* 1204) [q. v.] [xix. 103]

FITZALWYN, HENRY (*d.* 1212). [See FITZAILWIN.]

FITZBALL, EDWARD (1792–1873), dramatist ; apprenticed as printer at Norwich, 1809–12 ; attempted dramatic writing with some success, and adopted profession of dramatist, *c.* 1819, and subsequently produced numerous melodramas and other pieces, among the most successful of which were 'Peveril of the Peak,' 1823, 'Waverley,' 1824, 'The Pilot,' 1825, 'Jonathan Bradford,' 1833, and 'Nitocris,' 1855 ; wrote also many romances, librettos, and songs, including 'The Bloom is on the Rye,' 1831 ; published 'Thirty-five Years of a Dramatic Author's Life,' 1859. [Suppl. ii. 212]

FITZCHARLES, CHARLES, EARL OF PLYMOUTH (1657 ?–1680), natural son of Charles II by Catherine Pegge. [xix. 106]

FITZCLARENCE, LORD ADOLPHUS (1802–1856), rear-admiral ; younger son of William IV by Mrs. Jordan ; entered navy, 1814 ; commanded royal yacht, 1830–53, when he attained flag-rank. [xix. 106]

FITZCLARENCE, GEORGE AUGUSTUS FREDERICK, first EARL OF MUNSTER (1794–1842), major-general ; eldest son of William IV by Mrs. Jordan ; served in Spain at age of fifteen ; wounded and captured at Fuentes d'Onoro, 1811 ; escaped ; severely wounded at Toulouse, 1814 ; aide-de-camp to Marquis Hastings in Mahratta war, 1816–17 ; sent home overland with news of peace, 1817 ; created a peer, 1831 ; lieutenant of the Tower ; supposed to have influenced his father against reform ; committed suicide. He did much to promote oriental studies, being some time president of the Asiatic Society, and published fragments of military history. [xix. 106]

FITZCOUNT, BRIAN (*fl.* 1125–1142), warrior and author ; brought up and knighted by Henry,I ; one of the chief supporters of the Empress Matilda, in defence of whose right to the crown he wrote a treatise ; thrice besieged by Stephen in his castle of Wallingford. [xix. 108]

FITZGEFFREY, CHARLES (1575 ?–1638), poet and divine ; M.A. Broadgates Hall, Oxford, 1600 ; incumbent of St. Dominic, Eastwellshire ; published a poem on Drake, 1596, and 'The Blessed Birthday,' 1634 (reprinted by Grosart), and a volume of Latin epitaphs and epigrams ; mentioned in 'Palladis Tamia,' 1598, and quoted in 'England's Parnassus,' 1600. [xix. 109]

FITZGEFFREY, HENRY (*fl.* 1617), author ; perhaps a son of Charles Fitzgeffrey [q. v.] ; published satires and epigrams, 1617 (twelve copies reprinted at Beldornie Press, 1843). [xix. 109]

FITZGERALD, DAVID. [See DAVID, *d.* 1176.]

FITZGERALD, LORD EDWARD (1763–1798), Irish rebel ; son of James Fitzgerald, first duke of Leinster [q. v.] ; served in the American war and was wounded at Eutaw Springs, 1781 ; M.P. in the Irish parliament for Athy and Kildare ; as major of the 54th, got Cobbett his discharge ; travelled in America, and was admitted to the Bear tribe of Indians ; cashiered for attending revolutionary banquet at Paris, 1792, in which year he married Pamela ; returned to Ireland, and began to take an active part in politics ; joined United Irishmen, 1796, and with Arthur O'Connor [q. v.], went to Basle to negotiate with Hoche ; declined to re-enter parliament ; headed military committee to co-operate with French invaders ; while being arrested, was wounded by Major Henry Charles Sirr [q. v.] ; died of his wounds. [xix. 110]

FITZGERALD, EDWARD (1770 ?–1807), Irish insurgent ; released from Wexford gaol by mob ; held commands during rebellion of 1798 ; surrendered to Wilford ; imprisoned in Dublin ; after living in England, rearrested, 1800 ; died at Hamburg. [xix. 111]

FITZGERALD, EDWARD (1809–1883), poet and translator ; educated at Bury St. Edmunds and Trinity College, Cambridge ; graduated, 1830 ; lived a retired life in Suffolk ; friend of Carlyle, Thackeray, Spedding, and the Tennysons. His chief work was an English poetic version (from the Persian) of the 'Rubaiyat of Omar Khayyám' (anon., 1859). He also published anonymously a life of Bernard Barton, prefixed to Barton's collected poems (1849), 'Euphranor' (1851), 'Polonius' (1852), English versions of the 'Agamemnon,' and of two plays of Sophocles, and selections from Crabbe ; and under his own name, 'Six Dramas of Calderon freely translated' (1853). [xix. 111]

FITZGERALD, LADY ELIZABETH, 'the Fair Geraldine' (1528 ?–1589), youngest daughter of Gerald Fitzgerald, ninth earl of Kildare [q. v.] ; in the household of Princess Mary, afterwards of Queen Catherine Howard ; was twice married, first, at fifteen, to Sir Anthony Browne [q. v.], and, secondly, to Edward Fiennes de Clinton, earl of Lincoln [q. v.] ; celebrated in verse by Henry Howard, earl of Surrey [q. v.], Michael Drayton, and Sir Walter Scott. [xix. 113]

FITZGERALD, GEORGE, sixteenth EARL OF KILDARE (1611–1660), rebuilt ancestral castle of Maynooth ; befriended Shirley, the dramatist, when in Dublin ; governor of co. Kildare, 1641 ; governor of Dublin for the parliament, 1647. [xix. 114]

FITZGERALD, GEORGE ROBERT (1748 ?–1786), 'Fighting Fitzgerald' ; notorious for his duels, gallantries, and extravagances ; married, against her parents' wishes, a daughter of Thomas Conolly [q. v.] ; took part in volunteer movement ; quarrelled with his family ; executed for murder of Patrick M'Donnell. [xix. 114]

FITZGERALD, GERALD, LORD OF OFFALY (*d.* 1204), son of Maurice Fitzgerald (*d.* 1176) [q. v.], often known as Fitzmaurice ; distinguished himself as an opponent of Roderic O'Connor, 1171 ; received property in Kildare from Strongbow, and built Maynooth ; ancestor of the Earls of Kildare. [xix. 115]

FITZGERALD, GERALD, fourth (properly third) EARL OF DESMOND (*d.* 1398), justiciar of Ireland, 1367–9 ; son of Maurice Fitzthomas, first earl of Desmond [q. v.] ; generally styled Gerald Fitzmaurice ; granted by Edward III the lands of his deceased elder brother Maurice, on condition of marrying the Earl of Ormonde's daughter ; as justiciar of Ireland, 1367–9, carried on policy of amalgamation with natives ; defeated and captured by Brien O'Brien, 1369 ; upheld the king's authority in Munster. [xix. 116]

FITZGERALD, GERALD, eighth ('the great'), EARL OF KILDARE (*d.* 1513), son of Thomas Fitzgerald, seventh earl [q. v.] ; nominated deputy-governor in Ireland by the council at Dublin, 1477, and held office in opposition to a nominee of Edward IV ; afterwards deputy for Richard, duke of York, and his son, Prince Edward ; pardoned by Henry VII, and continued in office ; attainted, and imprisoned in the Tower as a partisan of Warbeck, 1494; reappointed deputy of Ireland, 1496; died of a wound received in battle with a Leinster sept.

[xix. 117]

FITZGERALD, GERALD, ninth EARL OF KILDARE (1487–1534), son of Gerald Fitzgerald, eighth earl [q. v.]; educated in England; appointed lord high treasurer on his return to Ireland, 1504; lord justice and lord deputy, 1513; gained great successes against the Irish; charged with maladministration at instance of Ormonde, and removed, 1520; reappointed, 1524; again removed, being charged with treason by Ossory (Ormonde) and imprisoned in the Tower, 1526; returned to Ireland with Skeffington, whom he displaced as deputy, 1532; wounded at siege of Birr Castle, 1533; again summoned to England, and died prisoner in the Tower. [xix. 118]

FITZGERALD, GERALD, fifteenth EARL OF DESMOND (d. 1583), son of James (Fitzjohn) Fitzgerald, fourteenth earl [q. v.]; summoned to England on account of a quarrel with Thomas Butler, tenth earl of Ormonde [q. v.], and confined, 1562 ; allowed to return to Ireland, 1564; again summoned to England on account of fresh feud with Ormonde, and bound over next year; again imprisoned, for refusing to accept Sir H. Sidney's award in favour of Ormonde, 1567–73; rearrested after return to Ireland; escaped; carried on war in Munster and was outlawed; submitted, but after temporising, again rebelled, 1579; after four years' fighting was captured and killed at Glanaginty. [xix. 120]

FITZGERALD, GERALD, eleventh EARL OF KILDARE (1525–1585), son of Gerald Fitzgerald, ninth earl [q. v.]; educated in France and at Rome; served with knights of Rhodes against Moors and with Cosimo de' Medici; restored to his estates by Edward VI, and to earldom by Mary; warred against the Irish and Spanish invaders; committed to the Tower on suspicion of treason, 1582; allowed to return to Ireland, 1584; died in London.

[xix. 123]

FITZGERALD, GERALD (FITZMAURICE), BARON OF OFFALY (1265 ?–1287 ?), son of Maurice Fitzgerald (d. 1268) [q. v.]; attacked by the native Irish of his barony, 1285. [xix. 139]

FITZGERALD, HENRY VESEY (d. 1860), dean of Emly (1818–26) and dean of Kilmore (1826–60); son of James Fitzgerald (1742–1835) [q. v.] [xix. 131]

FITZGERALD, JAMES (FITZJOHN), fourteenth EARL OF DESMOND (d. 1558), second son of Sir John Desmond; assumed title on death of his grandfather, John Fitzthomas (1536); four years later submitted to the rebel O'Brien of Thomond; received by Henry VIII, who acknowledged his title, 1542; created lord treasurer of Ireland by Edward VI, and continued in office by Mary, though arrested for treason; did much to pacify Munster. [xix. 123]

FITZGERALD, JAMES (FITZMAURICE), thirteenth EARL OF DESMOND (d. 1540); waylaid and slain near Cork by Sir Maurice of Desmond. [xix. 125]

FITZGERALD, JAMES (FITZMAURICE) (d. 1579), 'arch-traitor'; assumed the position of captain of Desmond and rebelled against the English government; submitted to Sir John Perrot, 1573; on return of Desmond (1575), retired to France and saw Catherine de' Medici; visited Spain and Italy; concerted with Pope Gregory XIII and Stukely plan for invasion of Ireland; sailed from Spain with first body of invaders, 1579; killed in a skirmish, soon after landing, by his cousin, Theobald Burke. [xix. 125]

FITZGERALD, JAMES, 'the Tower Earl' or 'the Queen's Earl of Desmond' (1570 ?–1601), son of Gerald Fitzgerald, fifteenth earl of Desmond [q. v.], by his second wife; delivered by his mother to the Irish government on rebellion of his father, 1579; removed to Tower of London and imprisoned there sixteen years; released in 1600 and taken to Munster to bring back the Geraldines to their allegiance; failed, and returned to London, where he died. [xix. 127]

FITZGERALD, JAMES (FITZTHOMAS), the SUGAN EARL OF DESMOND (d. 1608), assumed the title of earl in 1598, and for three years carried on war in Munster; captured in a cave near Mitchelstown by the White knight,

Edmund Fitzgibbon [q. v.]; removed to England and imprisoned in the Tower, where he died insane.

[xix. 129]

FITZGERALD, JAMES, first DUKE OF LEINSTER (1722–1773), M.P. for Athy in Irish parliament (as Lord Offaly), 1741; succeeded as twentieth Earl of Kildare, 1744; created Viscount Leinster in English peerage, 1747; procured recall of Duke of Dorset from Ireland, 1754; himself appointed lord deputy, 1756; created Earl of Offaly and Marquis of Kildare in Irish peerage, and Duke of Leinster, 1761–6. [xix. 129]

FITZGERALD, JAMES (1742–1835), Irish politician; educated at Trinity College, Dublin; called to Irish bar, 1769; had a large practice, and became prime serjeant, 1787; entered Irish parliament for Ennis, 1772; represented co. Kildare in last Irish parliament; distinguished himself as an orator and was dismissed for his speeches against the union; M.P. for Ennis in imperial parliament, 1802–8 and 1812–13; refused a peerage; his wife created Baroness Fitzgerald, 1826. [xix. 130]

FITZGERALD, JAMES EDWARD (1818–1896), prime minister in New Zealand; B.A. Trinity College, Cambridge, 1842; under-secretary of British Museum, 1849; accompanied to New Zealand, 1850, Edward Gibbon Wakefield [q. v.] and John Robert Godley [q. v.], and pioneers of Canterbury settlement; first superintendent of province of Canterbury and member for Lyttelton in first New Zealand parliament, 1853; prime minister, 1854; founded 'Press' newspaper, 1861; controller-general, 1866; commissioner of audit, 1872; controller and auditor-general, 1878. [Suppl. ii. 214]

FITZGERALD, JOHN, first EARL OF KILDARE. [See FITZTHOMAS, JOHN, d. 1316.]

FITZGERALD, SIR JOHN, of Desmond (d. 1581), Irish rebel; brother of Gerald Fitzgerald, fifteenth earl of Desmond [q. v.]; for some time chief of the Irish rebels; hanged at Cork. [xix. 123]

FITZGERALD, JOHN DAVID, LORD FITZGERALD (1816–1889), Irish judge; studied at King's Inns, Dublin, and Gray's Inn; called to Irish bar, 1838; joined Munster circuit; Q.C., 1847; liberal M.P. for Ennis, 1852; solicitor-general for Ireland and bencher of King's Inns, 1855; attorney-general, 1856–8 and 1859; Irish privy councillor, 1856; introduced and passed bill for establishing court of chancery appeal in Ireland, 1856; justice of queen's bench in Ireland, 1860–82; appointed lord of appeal with life peerage, and English privy councillor, 1882; honorary bencher of Gray's Inn, 1883; honorary LL.D. Dublin, 1870. [Suppl. ii. 215]

FITZGERALD, JOHN (FITZEDMUND) (d. 1589), seneschal of Imokilly; joined the rebellion of James (Fitzmaurice) Fitzgerald [q. v.], 'the arch-traitor,' 1569–1573, after whose death he became the virtual head of the second rising; submitted, 1583; arrested four years later; died in Dublin Castle. [xix. 131]

FITZGERALD, SIR JOHN (FITZEDMUND) (1528–1612), dean of Cloyne; granted an annuity for his support of government; knighted, and made dean of Cloyne, though a layman. [xix. 132]

FITZGERALD, SIR JOHN FORSTER (1784 ?–1877), field-marshal; ensign, 1793; distinguished himself while serving with 60th foot at siege of Badajos, 1812; while commanding brigade in the Pyrenees was captured, but exchanged; created C.B. for services in Peninsula; afterwards held commands in Canada and India; major-general, 1830; K.C.B., 1831; lieutenant-general, 1841; general, 1854, G.C.B., 1862, field-marshal, 1875; M.P. for co. Clare, 1852–7; died at Tours, the oldest officer in the service. [xix. 133]

FITZGERALD, KATHERINE, the 'old' COUNTESS OF DESMOND (1500 ?–1604); second wife of Thomas, twelfth earl; said to have lived to the age of 140 (probably a mistake for 104). [xix. 134]

FITZGERALD, MAURICE (d. 1176), an English conqueror of Ireland; brother of David II [q. v.], bishop of St. David's; went to Ireland, 1169, and commanded the English contingent in the expedition of Dermot against Dublin; led the great sally from the city, 1171; received grant of property in Kildare; died at Wexford, where his ruined monument was seen several hundred years later. [xix. 135]

FITZGERALD, MAURICE (*d.* 1268), nephew of Maurice Fitzmaurice Fitzgerald [q. v.]; inherited barony of Offaly; drowned in the Irish Channel. [xix. 139]

FITZGERALD, MAURICE II, BARON OF OFFALY (1194?-1257), justiciar of Ireland; son of Gerald Fitzgerald, lord of Offaly [q. v.]; appointed justiciar, 1232; defeated and captured Richard, the earl marshal, 1234, whom he was suspected to have poisoned; carried on wars in Connaught and Ulster; resigned office, 1245, but was deputy to his successor, and helped him in his wars. [xix. 136]

FITZGERALD, MAURICE FITZMAURICE (1238?-1277?), justiciar of Ireland; son of Maurice Fitzgerald, baron of Offaly (1194?-1257) [q. v.]; was granted (1259) Athlone Castle and the shrievalty of Connaught; justiciar of Ireland, 1272-3; captured O'Brien, king of Thomond, 1277. [xix. 139]

FITZGERALD, MAURICE, first EARL OF DESMOND (*d.* 1356). [See FITZTHOMAS, MAURICE.]

FITZGERALD, MAURICE, fourth EARL OF KILDARE (1318-1390), justiciar of Ireland; youngest son of Thomas Fitzgerald, second earl [q. v.]; generally known as Maurice Fitzthomas; opposed the Anglicising policy of Ralph D'Ufford; present with Edward III at siege and capture of Calais, 1347; justiciar, 1356-7, 1361, 1371, and 1376, and several times deputy. [xix. 140]

FITZGERALD, MAURICE, knight of Kerry (1774-1849), Irish statesman; represented co. Kerry for thirty-seven years in the Irish and imperial parliaments; commissioner of customs in Ireland, 1799-1802; a lord of the treasury in England, 1827; vice-treasurer of Ireland, 1830; unable to regain his seat for Kerry after Reform Act; friend of Wellington and Castlereagh. [xix. 141]

FITZGERALD, PAMELA (1776?-1831), wife of Lord Edward Fitzgerald [q. v.]; described in her marriage contract as of Newfoundland parentage, but popularly supposed to be a daughter of Madame de Genlis, by Philip, duke of Orleans, in whose family she was brought up, although she was never recognised; came to England in 1791 and met Sheridan; was seen by Fitzgerald next year at Paris, and married to him at Tournay; accompanied him to Ireland; visited him during his imprisonment; after leaving Ireland, married a second time, but retained name of Fitzgerald; died in Paris. [xix. 142]

FITZGERALD, SIR PETER GEORGE (1808-1880), nineteenth knight of Kerry; son of Maurice Fitzgerald (1774-1849) [q. v.]; vice-treasurer of Ireland in Sir Robert Peel's administration, 1841-6; created baronet, 1880. [xix. 144]

FITZGERALD, RAYMOND, 'Le Gros' (*d.* 1182?), nephew of Maurice Fitzgerald (*d.* 1176) [q. v.]; landed in Ireland as Strongbow's representative, 1170; took chief part in capture of Waterford, and led centre in Dublin expedition, 1170; returned with Strongbow to Ireland, but soon retired to Wales; came to his relief when besieged in Waterford, 1174, and married his sister; defeated Donald O'Brien, 1176, and ruled Ireland till the arrival of Fitzaldhelm; reduced Cork. [xix. 144]

FITZGERALD, THOMAS, second EARL OF KILDARE (*d.* 1328), justiciar of Ireland; son of John Fitzthomas, first earl [q. v.]; married Joan, daughter of Richard de Burgh, earl of Ulster; led a great army against Edward Bruce, 1316; justiciar, 1320 and 1327; a partisan of Roger Mortimer. [xix. 146]

FITZGERALD, THOMAS, eighth EARL OF DESMOND (1426?-1468), lord deputy of Ireland, 1463-7; superseded, 1467, and attainted on charge of alliance with Irish; executed at Drogheda. [xix. 147]

FITZGERALD, THOMAS, seventh EARL OF KILDARE (*d.* 1477), lord deputy of Ireland, 1455-9, for Richard, duke of York, and 1461-2 for Clarence; lord chancellor of Ireland, 1463; attainted in 1467, but respited and restored; again deputy for Clarence, 1468-75. [xix. 148]

FITZGERALD, THOMAS, BARON OFFALY and tenth EARL OF KILDARE (1513-1537), son of Gerald Fitzgerald, ninth earl [q. v.]; appointed deputy-governor of Ireland, 1534, but renounced his allegiance and slew Archbishop Allen; submitted to Lord Leonard Grey, 1535; executed at Tyburn with his five uncles. [xix. 148]

FITZGERALD, SIR THOMAS JUDKIN (*d.* 1810). [See JUDKIN-FITZGERALD.]

FITZGERALD, WILLIAM (1814-1883), bishop of Killaloe; graduated at Trinity College, Dublin; B.A. 1835; D.D., 1853; professor of moral philosophy in the university, 1847-52, and of ecclesiastical history, 1852-7; archdeacon of Kildare, 1855; bishop of Cork, Cloyne, and Ross, 1857-62; translated to Killaloe, 1862; edited Butler's 'Analogy of Religion,' and published numerous other works. [xix. 150]

FITZGERALD, WILLIAM ROBERT, second DUKE OF LEINSTER (1749-1804), son of James Fitzgerald, first duke [q. v.]; M.P. for Dublin in Irish parliament, 1769-73; colonel of the Dublin regiment of volunteers; the first K.P., 1783; master of the rolls in Ireland, 1788; made great efforts to save his brother, Lord Edward Fitzgerald [q. v.]; supported the union. [xix. 151]

FITZGERALD, SIR WILLIAM ROBERT SEYMOUR VESEY (1818-1885), governor of Bombay; M.A. Oriel College, Oxford, 1844; Newdigate prizeman, 1835; barrister, Lincoln's Inn, 1839; M.P., Horsham, 1852-65; under-secretary for foreign affairs, 1858-9; hon. D.C.L. Oxford, 1863; governor of Bombay, 1867-72; on his return to England was again M.P. for Horsham; became chief charity commissioner, 1875. [xix. 151]

FITZGERALD, WILLIAM THOMAS (1759?-1829), versifier; clerk in navy pay office; author of patriotic effusions; parodied in 'Rejected Addresses.' [xix. 152]

FITZGERALD, WILLIAM VESEY, BARON FITZGERALD AND VESEY (1783-1843), statesman; son of Right Hon. James Fitzgerald (1742-1835) [q. v.]; M.P., Ennis, 1808; Irish privy councillor and lord of treasury, 1810; English privy councillor, 1812; chancellor of Irish exchequer, 1812-16; M.P., co. Clare, 1818; envoy to Sweden, 1820-3; paymaster-general, 1826; president of board of trade, 1828; defeated by O'Connell for Clare; elected for Cornish boroughs, 1829 and 1830; M.P., Ennis, 1831-2; succeeded to his mother's peerage, 1832; created an English peer by Peel, 1835; president of board of control, 1841-3. [xix. 152]

FITZGIBBON, EDMUND (FITZJOHN) (1552?-1608), the 'White Knight'; probably implicated in O'Neill's rebellion, though sheriff of Cork at the time; captured the Sugan Earl (James Fitzthomas Fitzgerald, *d.* 1608) [q. v.], and (1604) was created by James I Baron of Clangibbon; this creation, and the intended restoration of his estates (of which he had been deprived by his father's attainder) did not take effect, since no parliament assembled before his death. [xix. 153]

FITZGIBBON, EDWARD (1803-1857), writer under the name 'Ephemera'; after living six years in France wrote in England for the 'Morning Chronicle' and 'Bell's Life'; published a good 'Handbook of Angling,' 1847, and 'The Book of the Salmon' (with A. Young), 1850; edited 'The Compleat Angler,' 1853. [xix. 154]

FITZGIBBON, GERALD (1793-1882), lawyer and author; M.A. Trinity College, Dublin, 1832; called to the Irish bar, 1830; Q.C., 1841; defended Dr. Gray in the state trials of 1844, when he refused a challenge sent him by the attorney-general; appointed receiver-master in chancery, 1860; published works, including 'Ireland in 1868, the Battlefield for English Party Strife,' and a pamphlet advocating a conditional fixity of tenure in Irish land, 1869. [xix. 155]

FITZGIBBON, JOHN, EARL OF CLARE (1749-1802), lord chancellor of Ireland; distinguished himself at Trinity College, Dublin; M.A. Christ Church, Oxford, 1770; called to the Irish bar, 1772; obtained a large practice, and (1783) became attorney-general; represented Dublin University as a moderate nationalist, 1778-1783, after which he sat for Kilmallock; fought a duel with Curran, in consequence of a speech in support of the commercial treaty with England, 1785; began his policy of repression with the Whiteboy Act, 1787; made powerful speeches in support of Pitt's regency proposals, 1789; lord chancellor of Ireland, 1789-1802; created Baron Fitzgibbon, 1789, Viscount Fitzgibbon, 1793, and Earl of Clare, 1795; became at the union a peer of the United Kingdom; as chancellor a zealous law reformer and strong opponent of catholic emancipation; the passing of the Act of Union mainly due to him. [xix. 156]

FITZGILBERT, RICHARD (*d.* 1090?). [See CLARE, RICHARD DE.]

FITZGILBERT, RICHARD (*d.* 1136 ?). [See CLARE, RICHARD DE.]

FITZHAMON, ROBERT (*d.* 1107), conqueror of Glamorgan; rewarded for his support of the crown in Odo's revolt (1088) by grants of lands in Gloucestershire, Buckinghamshire, and Cornwall; soon afterwards began his conquest of South Wales, aided by twelve knights; supported Henry I against Duke Robert, by whom he was captured in Normandy (1105) and imprisoned at Bayeux; rescued by the king, 1105; procured the surrender of Caen; died from effects of wound received at siege of Falaise; buried in Tewkesbury Abbey, of which he was second founder. [xix. 159]

FITZHARDING, ROBERT (*d.* 1170), founder of the second house of Berkeley; probably grandson of Eadnoth [q. v.], the staller; as reeve of Bristol supported cause of the Empress Matilda, and bought much property in the west from Robert of Gloucester; granted by Henry II the lordship of Berkeley Hernesse; built priory of St. Augustine's, now Bristol Cathedral. [xix. 162]

FITZHARDINGE, BARON (1788–1867). [See BERKELEY, MAURICE FREDERICK FITZHARDINGE.]

FITZHARRIS, EDWARD (1648?–1681), conspirator; an Irish catholic; resigned lieutenancy in the army after Test Act, 1673; impeached for publishing pamphlet advocating the deposition of Charles II in favour of James, duke of York, 1681; his impeachment interrupted by the dissolution of parliament; tried before the king's bench and convicted of libel; executed after vainly endeavouring to fix the authorship on Lord Howard of Escrick and to implicate others in a charge of conspiracy. [xix. 163]

FITZHENRY, MEILER (*d.* 1220), justiciar of Ireland; grandson of Henry I, through his bastard son Henry; accompanied his uncle, Robert Fitzstephen [q. v.], to Ireland, and distinguished himself in the invasion of Ossory, 1169; returning to Ireland received grant of property in Kildare, 1174, and received further grants in Kerry and Cork from King John, for whom he was justiciar, 1200–8; founded (1202) Connall Abbey, Kildare, where he was buried. [xix. 164]

FITZHENRY, MRS. (*d.* 1790 ?), actress; *née* Flannigan; after the death of her first husband, Capt. Gregory, appeared at Covent Garden, 1754; afterwards made a reputation in Dublin; reappeared at Covent Garden in her original part of Hermione in 'The Distressed Mother,' and Lady Macbeth, 1757; married Fitzhenry, a lawyer; played again in Dublin, 1759–64, Calista in 'The Fair Penitent,' and Shakespearean parts; acted at Drury Lane, 1765; rival of Mrs. Yates on the Irish boards. [xix. 165]

FITZHERBERT, ALLEYNE, BARON ST. HELENS (1753–1839), diplomatist; educated at Eton and St. John's College, Cambridge; M.A., 1777; visited while at Cambridge by Gray; ambassador at Brussels, 1777–82; negotiated preliminaries of peace with France and Spain, 1782–3; envoy extraordinary at court of Russia, 1783–7; chief-secretary for Ireland, 1787–9; envoy extraordinary at the Hague, 1789; as ambassador at Madrid, 1791–4, settled the Nootka Sound difficulty, and concluded a treaty with Spain, for which he was created an Irish peer; returned to the Hague; raised to the British peerage for concluding a treaty with Russia, 1801; created a lord of the bedchamber, 1804. [xix. 166]

FITZHERBERT, SIR ANTHONY (1470–1538), judge; barrister, Gray's Inn; serjeant-at-law, 1510; king's serjeant, 1516; knighted and appointed a judge of the common pleas, 1522; one of the commissioners who negotiated pacification in Ireland between Kildare and Ormonde, 1524; signed articles of impeachment against Wolsey, 1529; a member of the courts which tried the Carthusians and Fisher and More. His 'La Graunde Abridgement' (published 1514) is the first important attempt to systematise the whole law; other works are also attributed to him. [xix. 168]

FITZHERBERT, MARIA ANNE (1756–1837), wife of George IV; daughter of Walter Smythe; married first Edward Weld of Lulworth Castle, 1775, and secondly Thomas Fitzherbert of Swynnerton, 1778; lived at Richmond after the death (1781) of her second husband; married to George, Prince of Wales, at her house, December 1785, before witnesses; lived with the Prince of Wales

till 1803; recognised by the royal family in spite of the Royal Marriage Act and the Act of Settlement, which made the marriage illegal on account of the minority of the prince and the Roman catholic religion of Mrs. Fitzherbert. Fox's denial in parliament that the ceremony had taken place was privately repudiated by the prince. [xix. 170]

FITZHERBERT, NICHOLAS (1550–1612), secretary to Cardinal Allen; grandson of Sir Anthony Fitzherbert [q. v.]; studied at Exeter College, Oxford, Douay, and Bologna; attainted, 1580, for his activity in raising funds for the English (catholic) college at Rheims; became secretary to Cardinal Allen at Rome, 1587; opposed the policy of Parsons; drowned at Florence, where he is buried; his published works include a history of Roman catholicism in England, 1608 and 1638. [xix. 171]

FITZHERBERT, THOMAS (1552–1640), jesuit: grandson of Sir Anthony Fitzherbert [q. v.]; educated at Oxford; imprisoned for recusancy at Oxford, 1572; after his release assisted Parsons and Campion; retired to France, 1582, and afterwards to Spain, where he was pensioned by the king; charged with a plot to poison Queen Elizabeth, 1598; ordained priest at Rome; became a jesuit in 1613; for twelve years agent for the English clergy; became superior of the English mission at Brussels, 1616; rector of the English college at Rome, 1618–39, where he died; published works dealing with political aspects of Roman catholicism. [xix. 172]

FITZHERBERT, WILLIAM (*d.* 1154), archbishop of York; generally known as St. William of York; treasurer and canon of York, *c.* 1130; one of King Stephen's chaplains; elected archbishop of York under pressure from King Stephen, 1142; opposed by a minority of Cistercians, and compelled to go to Rome to secure consecration; denied the pallium by Eugenius III under the influence of St. Bernard of Clairvaux; suspended from his see; took refuge with Roger, king of Sicily; deposed at the council of Rheims, 1147; restored to his see and received his pall from Anastasius IV, 1153; died very suddenly, perhaps from poison. In 1227 he was canonised, and his remains were removed to a shrine behind the high altar in York Minster, in the presence of Edward I, 1283. [xix. 173]

FITZHERBERT, SIR WILLIAM (1748–1791), eldest brother of Alleyne Fitzherbert, baron St. Helens [q. v.]; gentleman-usher to George III; created baronet, 1784; author of 'Maxims' and a 'Dialogue on the Revenue Laws.' [xix. 167]

FITZHUBERT, ROBERT (*fl.* 1140), freebooter; a Flemish mercenary, who came over with Stephen; carried on private war, seizing the castles of Malmesbury and Devizes; hanged before the latter by the Earl of Gloucester. [xix. 176]

FITZHUGH, ROBERT (*d.* 1436), bishop of London; master of King's Hall, Cambridge, and vice-chancellor of the university, 1424; ambassador to Rome and Venice, 1429; bishop of London, 1431, being consecrated at Foligno, Italy; one of the English delegates at the council of Basle, 1434, on the way home from which he died; buried in St. Paul's Cathedral. [xix. 177]

FITZJAMES, JAMES, DUKE OF BERWICK (1670–1734), marshal of France; natural son of James, duke of York (James II), by Arabella Churchill [q. v.]; born and educated in France; came to England after his father's accession and was created Duke of Berwick, 1687; distinguished himself in Hungary against the Turks; served in Ireland against William III, 1689–90, and in Flanders as a French officer, being taken prisoner at Neerwinden, 1693; commanded with success French army in Spain, 1704; partially subdued the Camisards and took Nice, for which he was created Maréchal de France; defeated the English under Galway (Ruvigny) at Almanza, 1707; defended south-eastern France against Prince Eugène, 1709–10; after the peace of Utrecht supported the English alliance; appointed to command the French army of the Rhine, 1733; killed at the siege of Philipsbourg in the second campaign, next year. [xix. 178]

FITZJAMES, SIR JOHN (1470?–1542?), judge; nephew of Richard Fitzjames [q. v.], bishop of London; treasurer of the Middle Temple, 1509; recorder of Bristol, 1510; attorney-general, 1519; serjeant-at-law, 1521; chief baron of the exchequer, 1522; chief-justice of the king's bench,

1526 ; signed articles of impeachment against Wolsey, 1529 ; member of the court which tried the Carthusians and More and Fisher ; retired from office, 1538. [xix. 179]

FITZJAMES, RICHARD (d. 1522), bishop of London ; M.A. Merton College, Oxford ; fellow of Merton, 1465 ; proctor, 1473 ; principal of St. Alban Hall, 1477–81 ; chaplain to Edward IV ; warden of Merton, 1483–1507 ; bishop of Rochester, 1497 ; one of the negotiators of the Great Intercourse, 1499 ; bishop of Chichester, 1504, of London, 1506. He introduced reforms at Oxford and built Fulham Palace. [xix. 180]

FITZJOCELIN, REGINALD (1140 ?–1191), archbishop-elect of Canterbury ; called 'the Lombard,' from his education in Italy ; at first a friend of Becket ; became his opponent when Becket excommunicated his father, the Bishop of Salisbury ; employed by Henry II on several embassies to the pope ; bishop of Bath, 1174 ; founded hospital of St. John at Bath, 1180 ; one of the commissioners to repress heresy at Toulouse, 1178 ; attended Lateran Council, 1179 ; helped to overthrow Longchamp, 1191 ; elected to see of Canterbury, 1191. [xix. 181]

FITZJOHN, EUSTACE (d. 1157), judge ; justice-itinerant in the north and governor of Bamborough Castle under Henry I, who gave him much property in Yorkshire ; supported the Empress Matilda ; fought at the battle of the Standard in David's army, 1138 ; founded Alnwick Abbey, 1147, and Gilbertine houses in Yorkshire ; as constable of Chester fell while taking part in Henry II's first expedition into Wales. The Barons de Vescy were descended from his son William. [xix. 183]

FITZJOHN, PAIN (d. 1137), judge ; brother of Eustace Fitzjohn [q. v.] ; justice-itinerant under Henry I ; sheriff of Shropshire and Herefordshire ; supported Stephen ; slain in battle with Welsh rebels. [xix. 184]

FITZJOHN, THOMAS, second EARL OF KILDARE (d. 1328). [See FITZGERALD, THOMAS.]

FITZMAURICE, HENRY PETTY-, third MARQUIS OF LANSDOWNE (1780–1863). [See PETTY-FITZMAURICE.]

FITZMAURICE, JAMES (d. 1579). [See FITZGERALD, JAMES FITZMAURICE.]

FITZMAURICE, MRS. (fl. 1741–1766). [See HIPPESLEY, E.]

FITZMAURICE, PATRICK, seventeenth LORD KERRY and BARON LIXNAW (1551 ?–1600), son and heir of Thomas Fitzmaurice, sixteenth lord Kerry [q. v.] ; joined Desmond's rebellion, 1580 ; escaped, 1581, from Limerick, where he was confined ; again captured, 1587, and imprisoned at Dublin till 1592 ; joined O'Neill's rising and lost Lixnaw. [xix. 184]

FITZMAURICE, THOMAS, sixteenth LORD KERRY and BARON LIXNAW (1502–1590) ; served in imperial army at Milan ; rebelled against Queen Elizabeth's government, 1582 ; pardoned, 1583. [xix. 185]

FITZMAURICE, THOMAS, eighteenth LORD KERRY and BARON LIXNAW (1574–1630), son of Patrick Fitzmaurice, seventeenth lord Kerry [q. v.] ; took an active part in O'Neill's rebellion, but submitted in 1603 ; imprisoned in London for refusing jointure to his son. [xix. 185]

FITZNEALE or **FITZNIGEL**, RICHARD, otherwise RICHARD OF ELY (d. 1198), bishop of London ; son of Nigel, bishop of Ely, whom he succeeded as treasurer of England, 1169 ; became justice-itinerant, 1179 ; dean of Lincoln, 1184 ; his election to the bishopric of Lincoln annulled by Henry II in favour of Hugh ; appointed bishop of London, 1189 ; continued as treasurer by Richard I ; mediated between Prince John and Longchamp ; protected Geoffrey Plantagenet from Longchamp, and was loyal to Richard I against Prince John ; patron of learning ; wrote 'Dialogus de Scaccario' and 'The Acts of King Henry and King Richard' ('Tricolumnus'), the latter wrongly ascribed to Benedict (d. 1193) [q. v.] of Peterborough. [xix. 186]

FITZOSBERN, WILLIAM, EARL OF HEREFORD (d. 1071), son of Osbern the seneschal, who was guardian of William the Conqueror when Duke of Normandy ; urged on William conquest of England, and led right wing at Hastings, 1066 ; granted lands in the west ; joint viceroy

of England during William's absence, 1067 ; as Earl of Hereford defended the border against the South Welsh ; sent to administer Normandy for the queen, 1070 ; killed at Cassel fighting for Countess of Flanders. [xix. 188]

FITZOSBERT, WILLIAM (d. 1196), demagogue ; known as 'Longbeard' ; led agitation in London against the city magnates, particularly in connection with the aids levied for Richard I's ransom, 1194 ; dragged from sanctuary in Bow Church by order of the primate and hanged in chains at Smithfield. [xix. 189]

FITZPATRICK, SIR BARNABY, BARON OF UPPER OSSORY (1535 ?–1581), educated at court with Prince Edward (Edward VI) ; while in France corresponded with the king (correspondence printed in 'Literary Remains of Edward VI') ; active in suppression of Wyatt's rebellion, 1553 ; went to Ireland, where he had lifelong feud with Ormonde ; his wife and daughter abducted, 1573 ; killed the rebel Rory O'More, 1578. [xix. 190]

FITZPATRICK, RICHARD, first BARON GOWRAN (d. 1727), naval commander ; distinguished himself against the French, 1687–1702 ; granted land in Queen's County and created an Irish peer, 1715. [xix. 191]

FITZPATRICK, RICHARD (1747–1813), general, politician, and wit ; grandson of Richard Fitzpatrick, first baron Gowran [q. v.] ; began at Westminster lifelong friendship with C. J. Fox ; entered the army, 1765 ; served in America, 1777–8 ; M.P. for Tavistock, 1774, 1807, and 1812 ; M.P. for Bedfordshire, 1807–12 ; chief secretary for Ireland, 1782 ; secretary of war in coalition of 1783, and in ministry of all the talents, 1806–7 ; one of the chief writers of the 'Rolliad.' [xix. 191]

FITZPATRICK, WILLIAM JOHN (1830–1895), Irish biographer ; educated at Clongowes Wood Roman catholic college, co. Kildare ; honorary professor of history at Royal Hibernian Academy of Arts, 1876 ; honorary LL.D. Royal University of Ireland. He published a number of works, relating chiefly to the secret history of eminent personages, including 'Life and Times of Bishop Doyle,' 1861, 'Lord Edward Fitzgerald,' 1859, 'The Sham Squire,' 1866, 'Ireland before the Union,' 1867, and 'The Correspondence of Daniel O'Connell,' 1888. He also produced a pamphlet, 1856, claiming for Thomas Scott, brother of Sir Walter Scott, the chief credit for a large part of the Waverley novels. [Suppl. ii. 216]

FITZPETER, GEOFFREY, EARL OF ESSEX (d. 1213), one of the five judges of the king's court while Richard I was on crusade ; joined opposition to Longchamp and was excommunicated ; appointed chief justiciar, 1198 ; ennobled by John, whose succession he did much to secure ; joint-vicegerent when the king set out for Poitou. [xix. 192]

FITZRALPH, RICHARD, 'ARMACHANUS' (d. 1360), archbishop of Armagh ; fellow of Balliol College, Oxford, and perhaps chancellor ; dean of Lichfield, 1337 ; archbishop of Armagh, 1347 ; had great repute as a preacher ; attacked the friars, and was cited in 1357 to defend his opinions before the pope at Avignon, where he probably died ; wrote treatises against the errors of Armenian Christians and against the friars' doctrine of obligatory poverty. [xix. 194]

FITZRICHARD, GILBERT (d. 1115 ?). [See CLARE, GILBERT DE.]

FITZROBERT, SIMON (d. 1207). [See SIMON DE WELLS.]

FITZROY, AUGUSTUS HENRY, third DUKE OF GRAFTON (1735–1811), statesman ; educated at Westminster and Peterhouse, Cambridge ; M.A., 1753 ; as Earl of Euston M.P. for Bury St. Edmunds, 1756 ; succeeded to dukedom, 1757, being also named lord-lieutenant of Suffolk ; opposed Bute ; visited Wilkes in the Tower, 1763 ; secretary for the northern department in Rockingham's first ministry, 1765–6, but resigned when it was not supported by Pitt ; became nominal head of the Chatham administration, 1766, and actual first minister when Pitt retired two years later ; outvoted in his own cabinet on the repeal of the American tea duty, and attacked by Junius and Chatham ; resigned, January 1770 ; held the office of privy seal under Lord North, 1771–5, without a seat in the cabinet ; in opposition again till March 1782, when he joined second Rockingham cabinet as lord

privy seal; wrote, in retirement, a work in defence of unitarianism and an autobiography (first published in complete form, 1899). He appointed the poet Gray professor of modern history at Cambridge University.
            [xix. 198]

FITZROY, CHARLES, first DUKE OF SOUTHAMPTON and CLEVELAND (1662–1730), natural son of Charles II by Barbara Villiers [q. v.]; created Baron of Newbury, Earl of Chichester, and Duke of Southampton, 1675; became Duke of Cleveland on death of his mother, 1709.
            [xix. 201]

FITZROY, CHARLES, first BARON SOUTHAMPTON (1737–1797); as Colonel Fitzroy served under Ferdinand of Brunswick in the seven years' war, and was his aide-de-camp at Minden, 1759; created peer, 1780. [xix. 201]

FITZROY, LORD CHARLES (1764–1829), general; second son of Augustus Henry Fitzroy, third duke of Grafton [q. v.]; M.A. Trinity College, Cambridge, 1784; served in Flanders, 1793–4; aide-de-camp to George III, 1795; M.P., Bury St. Edmunds, 1784–90 and 1802–18.
            [xix. 202]

FITZROY, SIR CHARLES AUGUSTUS (1796–1858), colonial governor; son of Lord Charles Fitzroy [q. v.]; present at Waterloo as a member of Sir Hussey Vivian's staff, 1815; M.P., Bury, 1831; lieutenant-governor of Prince Edward island, 1837; governor of the Leeward islands, 1841; as governor of New South Wales (1846–50), resisted the importation of convicts; governor-general of Australia, 1850–5.
            [xix. 202]

FITZROY, GEORGE, DUKE OF NORTHUMBERLAND (1665–1716), youngest son of Charles II by Barbara Villiers; created Baron of Pontefract, 1674, and Viscount Falmouth and Earl of Northampton, 1674; created duke of Northumberland on his return from Venice, 1683; lieutenant-general, 1710; privy councillor, 1713.
            [xix. 203]

FITZROY, GEORGE HENRY, fourth DUKE OF GRAFTON (1760–1844), eldest son of Augustus Henry Fitzroy, third duke [q. v.]; M.A. Trinity College, Cambridge, 1799; as Lord Euston was returned with Pitt for Cambridge University in 1784, and represented it till 1811; after the revolution became a whig. [xix. 203]

FITZROY, HENRY, DUKE OF RICHMOND (1519–1536), natural son of Henry VIII by Elizabeth Blount (afterwards Talboys); suspected to have been poisoned by Anne Boleyn and her brother. [xix. 204]

FITZROY, HENRY, first DUKE OF GRAFTON (1663–1690), second son of Charles II by Barbara Villiers; married whilst a child to a daughter of Henry Bennet, earl of Arlington; created Earl of Euston, 1672, and duke of Grafton, 1675; distinguished himself as a sailor in command of the Grafton at battle of Beachy Head (1690), and saw service as a soldier with the French in Flanders, 1684, and at Sedgemoor, 1685; professed loyalty to James II, 1688, but soon deserted him for William III; mortally wounded while in command at the siege of Cork.
            [xix. 205]

FITZROY, HENRY (1807–1859), statesman; educated at Magdalen College, Oxford; M.A. Trinity College, Cambridge, 1828; M.P., Grimsby, 1831–2, and Lewes, 1837–59; a lord of the admiralty, 1845; under-secretary for home department, 1852–5; chairman of committees, 1855; chief commissioner of works, 1859. [xix. 206]

FITZROY, JAMES, otherwise CROFTS, afterwards SCOTT, DUKE OF MONMOUTH and BUCCLEUCH, 1649–1685. [See SCOTT.]

FITZROY, MARY, DUCHESS OF RICHMOND (d. 1557), daughter of Thomas Howard, third duke of Norfolk [q. v.]; married to Henry Fitzroy, duke of Richmond, [q. v.], 1533, but never lived with him; gave evidence inculpating her brother, the Earl of Surrey, on charge of treason, 1540. [xix. 206]

FITZROY, ROBERT (1805–1865), vice-admiral, hydrographer, and meteorologist; son of Lord Charles Fitzroy [q. v.]; in command of the Beagle, conducted survey of Patagonia and the Straits of Magellan (1828–36), having Darwin as naturalist for the last five years; wrote with Darwin a narrative of the voyage, 1839; elected M.P. for Durham, 1841; governor of New Zealand, 1843–5; F.R.S., 1851; chief of meteorological department, 1854; suggested plan of Fitzroy barometer and instituted a system of storm-warnings, the first weather forecasts; published meteorological works. [xix. 207]

FITZSIMON, HENRY (1566–1643), jesuit; of Hart Hall, Oxford; at first a zealous protestant, but converted to Roman catholicism by Thomas Darbyshire [q. v.]; admitted to Society of Jesus, 1592; afterwards held chair of philosophy at Douay; carried on a mission at Dublin, for which he was arrested (1599) and imprisoned five years, disputing while in prison with Ussher and others; after some time in Spain, Flanders, and Rome was army chaplain in Bohemia, 1620, writing a history of the campaign; returned to Ireland, 1630, and was involved in the rebellion of 1641; published theological works.
            [xix. 209]

FITZSIMONS or **FITZSYMOND**, WALTER (d. 1511), archbishop of Dublin, 1484; the first consecrated in St. Patrick's; espoused cause of Lambert Simnel, 1487, but was pardoned; appointed lord deputy of Ireland, 1492 and 1503, and lord chancellor, 1496, 1501, and 1509–11.
            [xix. 210]

FITZSTEPHEN, ROBERT (d. 1183?), Norman conqueror of Ireland; as constable of Cardigan (Aberteivi) carried on war with the Welsh, and was three years their prisoner; accompanied his half-brother Maurice Fitzgerald (d. 1176) [q. v.] to Ireland, 1169; took Wexford and invaded Ossory; surrendered at Carrig, 1171, but was given up to Henry II on his arrival; with Miles Cogan received from him kingdom of Cork, 1177, where he was besieged, 1182–3. [xix. 211]

FITZSTEPHEN, WILLIAM (d. 1190?), biographer of Becket; dissuaded Becket at the council of Northampton, 1164, from excommunicating his enemies if they laid hands on him; present at his murder. His 'Vita Sancti Thomae' (first printed, 1723) contains an account of London in the twelfth century. [xix. 212]

FITZTHEDMAR, ARNOLD (1201–1274?), alderman of London; of German parentage; as 'alderman of the Germans' took the royalist side in the barons' war; probably the author of 'Chronica Majorum et Vicecomitum Londoniarum' (edited, 1846). [xix. 213]

FITZTHOMAS, JOHN, first EARL OF KILDARE and sixth BARON OF OFFALY (d. 1316), grandson of Maurice Fitzgerald II [q. v.]; took part in the expedition of 1288 against the Irish of Offaly and Leix; accused of treason by justiciar De Vesci in connection with the Connaught succession, 1294; his Sligo and Connaught estates forfeited after his capture of Richard de Burgh, earl of Ulster (1294–5); afterwards served Edward I and his son in Scotland; his territory in Kildare constantly disturbed by the Irish; allied himself by marriage with the De Burghs, 1312; created Earl of Kildare, 1316, after having had his territories invaded by Edward Bruce. [xix. 214]

FITZTHOMAS or **FITZGERALD**, MAURICE, first EARL OF DESMOND (d. 1356), justiciar of Ireland; kinsman and ward of John Fitzthomas, first earl of Kildare [q. v.]; married Catherine de Burgh (1312); created Earl of Desmond with grant of palatine county of Kerry, 1329; imprisoned by the justiciar and viceroy, who had intervened in his feud with the Earl of Ulster; took lead in resistance of Anglo-Irish to the English policy of viceroys, 1341–6; imprisoned, but eventually liberated and received back his forfeited estates, and governed Ireland as viceroy, 1355–6.
            [xix. 217]

FITZURSE, REGINALD (fl. 1170), one of the murderers of Becket; had been one of his tenants when chancellor. According to Hoveden, he died while doing penance in a religious house near Jerusalem, but by another account he went to Ireland and there founded the family of McMahon. [xix. 218]

FITZWALTER, ninth BARON (1452?–1496). [See RADCLIFFE or RATCLIFFE, JOHN.]

FITZWALTER, JOHN (d. 1412?). [See WALTER.]

FITZWALTER, ROBERT (d. 1235), baronial leader; lord of Dunmow and Baynard's Castle, was grandson through his mother of Richard de Lucy [q. v.]; charged for conspiracy against John, 1212; fled to France; returned after the king's submission to the pope, and received back his estates; led barons' army, 1215, when London was seized and the Great Charter extorted; excommunicated, as one of the twenty-five executors of the Great Charter; offered the crown to the dauphin Louis, for whom he raised the siege of Mountsorrel; defeated and captured at Lincoln by William Marshall, 1217; went on the fifth

crusade, and was present at the siege of Damietta, 1219–1220; after his return submitted to the government of Henry III. A legend relating to his daughter Matilda and her supposed solicitation and murder by King John has been the subject of several poems and plays.
[xix. 219]

FITZWARINE, FULK, the name of eleven successive persons having property in Shropshire between 1150 and 1420. A traditional history of the family contained in an old French manuscript in the British Museum was published in French, 1840, and was first printed in English by Thomas Wright, 1855.
[xix. 223]

FITZWARINE, FULK I (*fl.* 1156), head of his family and a powerful noble.
[xix. 223]

FITZWARINE, FULK II (*d.* 1197), son of Fulk Fitzwarine I [q. v.]
[xix. 223]

FITZWARINE, FULK III (*d.* 1256?), baron; opposed King John and was specially excommunicated; made his peace with Henry III, but in 1245 was deputed by the barons to order the papal nuncio to leave the country.
[xix. 223]

FITZWARINE, FULK IV (*d.* 1264), baron; was drowned at the battle of Lewes, 1264.
[xix. 223]

FITZWILLIAM, CHARLES WILLIAM WENTWORTH, third EARL FITZWILLIAM (1786–1857), son of William Wentworth Fitzwilliam, second earl [q. v.]; M.P. (as Viscount Milton) for Yorkshire, 1807–31, and for Northamptonshire, 1831–3; K.G., 1851; supported parliamentary reform, and was one of the earliest advocates of free trade; edited (1844) Burke's correspondence between 1744 and 1797.
[xix. 224]

FITZWILLIAM, EDWARD (1788–1852), actor; played under Elliston at the Olympic and Royal Circus (Surrey), and under Thomas John Dibdin [q. v.] at the latter house; his best parts, Leporello, Dumbiedykes, Partridge, and Humphry Clinker.
[xix. 225]

FITZWILLIAM, EDWARD FRANCIS (1824–1857), song-writer; son of Edward Fitzwilliam [q. v.]; composed a Stabat Mater at twenty-one; musical director at the Lyceum with Madame Vestris, 1847–9, and afterwards at the Haymarket; composed two operettas for the latter theatre, the music for 'Green Bushes' (Adelphi), and a cantata performed by Hullah, 1851, besides songs.
[xix. 225]

FITZWILLIAM, ELLEN (1822–1880), actress; wife of Edward Francis Fitzwilliam [q. v.]; played for twenty-two years under Buckstone at the Haymarket; died at Auckland, New Zealand, after having acted in Australia.
[xix. 226]

FITZWILLIAM, FANNY ELIZABETH (1801–1854), actress; wife of Edward Fitzwilliam [q. v.]; played as a child at Dover, where her father (Copeland) was manager; appeared at the Haymarket, 1817, and at the Olympic and Surrey under Thomas John Dibdin [q. v.]; at Drury Lane, 1821–2; leased Sadler's Wells, 1832; went with Webster to the Haymarket, 1837; played with great success in America in 'The Country Girl,' and after her return to England attained the height of her reputation in 'Green Bushes' and 'Flowers of the Forest' (Adelphi, 1845–7); subsequently returned to the Haymarket.
[xix. 226]

FITZWILLIAM, JOHN (*d.* 1699), nonjuror; fellow of Magdalen College, Oxford, 1661–70; university lecturer on music, *c.* 1662; chaplain to the Duke of York and tutor to Princess (afterwards queen) Anne; subsequently canon of Windsor; refused to take the oaths to William and Mary; left bequests to the Bodleian and Magdalen College Library, Bishop Ken being his executor.
[xix. 227]

FITZWILLIAM, RALPH (1256?–1316), baron of Grimthorpe; served against the Welsh and Scots; joined baronial opposition to Edward II; warden of the northern marches, where he had large property.
[xix. 228]

FITZWILLIAM, RICHARD, seventh VISCOUNT FITZWILLIAM of Meryon (1745–1816), founder of the Fitzwilliam Museum at Cambridge (begun in 1837); M.A. Trinity Hall, Cambridge, 1764; F.R.S.; author of 'The Letters of Atticus' (originally composed in French.)
[xix. 229]

FITZWILLIAM, ROGER, *alias* ROGER DE BRETEUIL, EARL OF HEREFORD (*fl.* 1071–1075), succeeded to title and estates of his father, William Fitzosbern, earl of Hereford

[q. v.]; with his brother-in-law Ralf, earl of Norfolk, conspired against William I, and was sentenced to forfeiture and perpetual imprisonment (1075).
[xix. 229]

FITZWILLIAM, SIR WILLIAM (1460?–1534), sheriff of London; warden of Merchant Taylors' Company, 1494 and 1498, and master, 1499; obtained a new charter for the company, 1502, and left it a bequest; alderman of Bread Street ward and sheriff of London, 1506; refused to serve, 1510; treasurer and chamberlain to Wolsey, whom he entertained when disgraced; knighted, 1522; sheriff of Northampton, 1524.
[xix. 230]

FITZWILLIAM, WILLIAM, EARL OF SOUTHAMPTON (*d.* 1542), lord high admiral; wounded in action off Brest, 1513; knighted at Tournay, 1513, and created vice-admiral of England when treasurer of Wolsey's household; went as ambassador to France, 1521; vice-admiral under Surrey, 1522; comptroller of royal household and K.G., 1526; chancellor of Duchy of Lancaster, 1529; lord privy seal, 1533; lord high admiral, 1536–40; created Earl of Southampton, 1537; served Henry VIII, both at home and abroad, being his intimate friend from childhood; died while in command of the van of Norfolk's expedition against Scotland.
[xix. 230]

FITZWILLIAM, SIR WILLIAM (1526–1599), lord deputy of Ireland; grandson of Sir William Fitzwilliam [q. v.], the sheriff; though a protestant, supported Mary; vice-treasurer in Ireland, 1559–73; assisted Sussex against Shane O'Neill, 1561; lord justice in Ireland, 1571; lord deputy, 1572–5; reduced Desmond to submission; re-appointed, 1588, when he made an expedition into Connaught; pacified Monaghan and suppressed Maguire in Cavan; left Ireland, 1599. He was governor of Fotheringay Castle when Mary Queen of Scots was executed, and was given by her a portrait of her son James.
[xix. 232]

FITZWILLIAM, WILLIAM WENTWORTH, second EARL FITZWILLIAM (1748–1833), statesman; nephew and heir of Charles Wentworth [q. v.], Marquis of Rockingham; educated at Eton and Cambridge; joined Pitt as one of the 'Old Whigs,' and became president of the council, 1794; went to Ireland as lord-lieutenant, 1795, but was recalled within three months, on account of his premature and unauthorised avowal of sympathy with the demand for catholic emancipation; fought duel with Beresford, whom he had tried to dismiss from the commissionership of the customs; lord-lieutenant of the West Riding of Yorkshire, 1798; president of council under Lord Grenville, 1806–7; remained in opposition for the rest of his life, and was dismissed from his lieutenancy (1819) for his censure of the Peterloo 'massacre.'
[xix. 235]

FLAHAULT, COMTESSE DE (1788–1867). [See ELPHINSTONE, MARGARET MERCER.]

FLAKEFIELD, WILLIAM (*fl.* 1700), first weaver of checked linen in Great Britain; served in the army till 1700, when he began to make check handkerchiefs at Glasgow, of which, at his death, he was town drummer.
[xix. 237]

FLAMBARD, RANNULF (*d.* 1128), bishop of Durham and chief minister of William II; according to Florence of Worcester, rose by buying the custody of vacant sees and other benefices for ready money and an annual rent; adviser and instrument of William Rufus's extortions; rewarded with bishopric of Durham, 1099; sent to the Tower by Henry I; escaped and fled with his mother to Normandy; became minister of Duke Robert, but after Robert's defeat at Tenchebrai (1106) was pardoned and restored to his see by Henry I; for three years acting bishop of Lisieux; completed the nave of Durham Cathedral, and renewed the walls of the city; built Norham Castle. The abuse of feudal customs (especially 'the relief') probably originated with him.
[xix. 237]

FLAMMOCK, THOMAS (*d.* 1497), rebel; led a body of Cornishmen, who were discontented at the taxation levied for the contemplated Scottish expedition, to London; defeated at Deptford Strand and hanged at Tyburn.
[xix. 241]

FLAMSTEED, JOHN (1646–1719), first astronomer royal; educated at the free school, Derby; in a tract written in 1667 explained the cause of and gave rules for the equation of time (in Horrocks's 'Posthumous Works,' 1673); began systematic observations with Townley's mensurator, 1671; entered his name at Jesus College,

Cambridge, where he made the acquaintance of Newton, and was created M.A., 1674; made a barometer and thermometer for Charles II and the Duke of York, 1674; appointed astronomer royal, 1675; took orders, 1675; F.R.S., 1677. Though he was overworked and underpaid, with very defective instruments, his observations gave great help to Newton in writing his 'Principia,' and he laid the basis of modern astronomy by ascertaining absolute right ascensions through simultaneous observations of the sun and a star near both equinoxes. In 1707 the first volume of his catalogue and observations of the stars (containing the work done between 1676 and 1689) was printed at the expense of Prince George of Denmark, but disputes then arose with Newton and Halley, who published in 1712, without Flamsteed's consent, an imperfect edition of his later observations. Three-fourths of the copies of this edition were obtained by him and destroyed; the authorised work was completed in 1725 by his assistant, Joseph Crosthwait. [xix. 241]

FLANAGAN, RODERICK (1828–1861), journalist; with his brother founded at Sydney a weekly paper, 'The Chronicle'; afterwards edited 'The Empire,' writing in it severe criticisms upon colonial treatment of the aborigines; died at London when superintending publication of his 'History of New South Wales' (issued 1862). [xix. 248]

FLANAGAN, THOMAS (1814–1865), compiler; president of Sedgley Park Roman catholic school; afterwards prefect of studies at Oscott; published 'Manual of British and Irish History' and 'History of the (Catholic) Church in England to 1850' (1857), with other works. [xix. 249]

FLANN (d. 1056), Irish historian; commonly called 'Mainistrech,' eleven of his poetical histories are in the 'Book of Leinster.' [xix. 249]

FLANNAN, SAINT and BISHOP of Killaloe [Cill-da-Lua] (fl. 7th cent.); said to have been consecrated at Rome and to have visited the Isle of Man; his day 18th December. [xix. 250]

FLATMAN, ELNATHAN (1810–1860), jockey; entered service of William Cooper, the trainer, at Newmarket, 1825, and from 1839 to 1859 was one of the most popular jockeys in the field; his greatest triumph, the winning of the Doncaster Cup, 1850, when, on Lord Zetland's Voltigeur he beat the Flying Dutchman, ridden by Marlow; died of consumption resulting from an accident on Bath racecourse. [Suppl. ii. 217]

FLATMAN, THOMAS (1637–1688), poet and miniature-painter; of Winchester and New College; M.A. Cambridge, 1666; published 'Poems and Songs' (1674), which had appeared separately. Two miniatures of himself from his own hand are preserved. [xix. 251]

FLATTISBURY, PHILIP (fl. 1500), compiler; drew up the 'Red Book of the Earls of Kildare,' now in the possession of the Duke of Leinster, and transcribed a collection of Anglo-Irish annals, first printed in Camden's 'Britannia.' [xix. 252]

FLAVEL, JOHN (1596–1617), logician; educated at Trinity and Wadham colleges, Oxford; M.A., 1617; professor of grammar, 1617; his manuscript 'Tractatus de Demonstratione Methodicus et Polemicus,' edited by A. Huish, 1619. [xix. 253]

FLAVEL, JOHN (1630?–1691), presbyterian divine; educated at University College, Oxford; ejected from Dartmouth, 1662; continued to minister there secretly; published 'Husbandry Spiritualised,' 1669, and many other works, a selection from which appeared in 1823 (ed. Bradley). [xix. 253]

FLAXMAN, JOHN (1755–1826), sculptor and draughtsman; son of a plasterer; cast maker in Covent Garden; at twelve gained the first prize of the Society of Arts for a medal; studied at the Royal Academy schools; began to be employed by the Wedgwoods to design wax models for prizes and medallions in Wedgwood ware, c. 1775; first exhibited at the Royal Academy, 1770, and ten years later showed his design for the Chatterton monument; became acquainted with Blake and Stothard; introduced by Romney to William Hayley [q. v.], who became a useful patron; spent seven years (1787–94) in Rome and Italy; made a great reputation in Italy by his

drawings (executed for the mother of the Hares) for the 'Iliad' and 'Odyssey,' and for Dante and Æschylus; exhibited the Mansfield and Paoli models for Westminster Abbey, and the designs for Sir William Jones's portrait statue at Oxford; A.R.A., 1797, and R.A., 1800; his diploma work the marble relief, 'Apollo and Marpessa'; first professor of sculpture at the Royal Academy, 1810; executed the Baring monument at Micheldever, 1805–11, model for the Reynolds in St. Paul's, 1807, and the pedimental group at Woburn, 1820. In 1817 appeared his outlines to Hesiod, engraved by Blake, and next year the Achilles shield, drawings, and models. Among his later works are the marble groups at Petworth, the statues of Burns and Kemble in Westminster Abbey, and the completion of the friezes at Buckingham Palace. Collections of his drawings are at South Kensington, the British Museum, University College, London, and at Cambridge. [xix. 254]

FLAXMAN, MARY ANN (1768–1833), artist; half-sister of John Flaxman (1755–1826) [q. v.]; published six designs for Hayley's 'Triumphs of Temper,' 1803 (engraved by Blake); and exhibited drawings at the Royal Academy, 1786–1819. [xix. 259]

FLAXMAN, WILLIAM (1753?–1795?) artist; exhibited at the Academy a wax portrait of his brother, John Flaxman (1755–1826) [q. v.], 1781; a good woodcarver. [xix. 259]

FLECCIUS, GERBARUS (fl. 1546–1554). [See FLICCIUS.]

FLECKNOE, RICHARD (d. 1678?), poet; said to have been an Irish priest; printed privately several poems and prose works, including 'A Relation of Ten Years' Travels in Europe, Asia, Affrique, and America,' 1656; satirised by Dryden in 'Mac Flecknoe,' 1682. [xix. 260]

FLEET, SIR JOHN (d. 1712), governor of the East India Company, 1695; amalgamated Old with New East India Company, 1702; sheriff of London, 1688; lord mayor, 1692; M.P. for the city, 1693–1705. [xix. 261]

FLEETWOOD, CHARLES (d. 1692), parliamentarian soldier; admitted at Gray's Inn, 1638; one of Essex's bodyguard, 1642; wounded at first battle of Newbury when captain, 1643; appointed receiver of the court of wards forfeited by his royalist brother, Sir William, 1644; commanded regiment of horse in the new model at Naseby, 1645; M.P., Marlborough, 1646; took leading part in quarrel between army and parliament, 1647, on side of former; joint-governor of Isle of Wight, 1649; lieutenant-general of horse at Dunbar, 1650; member of the third council of state (1651) and commander of the forces in England before Worcester, where he did good service; married as his second wife Cromwell's eldest daughter (Bridget), the widow of Ireton, 1652; named commander-in-chief in Ireland, where in 1654–7 he was also lord-deputy; after the first year came to England and only nominally filled the office; recalled on account of his partiality to the anabaptists; one of the Protector's council, 1654; major-general of the eastern district, 1655; a member of Cromwell's House of Lords, 1656; nominal supporter of Richard Cromwell; headed the army's opposition to the parliament; commander-in-chief, 1659; failed to make terms with General Monck; and at the Restoration was incapacitated for life from holding office. [xix. 261]

FLEETWOOD, GEORGE (fl. 1650?), regicide; M.P. for Buckinghamshire in the Long parliament, 1640; one of the commissioners for trial of Charles I, 1648–9; member of last Commonwealth council of state and M.P. for Buckinghamshire, 1653; for Buckingham, 1654; member of Cromwell's House of Lords, 1657; joined Monck, 1660, and though condemned to death at the Restoration, was never executed. [xix. 265]

FLEETWOOD, GEORGE (1605–1667), general in the Swedish service and baron; brother of Charles Fleetwood [q. v.]; served under Gustavus Adolphus in the thirty years' war; created baron by Queen Christina, 1654; envoy extraordinary to England, 1655; member of Swedish council of war, 1665; died in Sweden, where he left descendants. [xix. 266]

FLEETWOOD, JAMES (1603–1683), bishop of Worcester; brother of George Fleetwood (fl. 1650?) [q. v.]; educated at Eton and King's College, Cambridge; pre-

bendary of Lichfield, 1636; created D.D. of Oxford for services at Edgehill, 1642; ejected from Sutton Coldfield by parliament; chaplain to Charles II; provost of King's College, Cambridge, 1660; bishop of Worcester, 1675.
[xix. 267]

FLEETWOOD, SIR PETER HESKETH, first baronet (1801–1866); changed to Fleetwood in 1831 his original surname of Hesketh; founded the town of Fleetwood, Lancashire, in 1836; M.A. Trinity College, Oxford, 1826; M.P. for Preston, 1832–47; created baronet, 1838.
[xix. 267]

FLEETWOOD, THOMAS (1661–1717), drainer of Marton Meer, Lancashire. The work began in 1692 was completed by Sir Peter Hesketh, afterwards Fleetwood [q. v.]
[xix. 267]

FLEETWOOD, WILLIAM (1535?–1594), recorder of London; of Brasenose College, Oxford; barrister, Middle Temple; counsel for the Merchant Taylors' against the Clothworkers' Company, 1565; M.P. for Marlborough in last parliament of Queen Mary and for Lancaster in first two of Elizabeth; elected recorder of London by Leicester's influence, 1571, and (1572) M.P. for the city; re-elected M.P. for London, 1586 and 1588; famous for his vigorous enforcement of the laws against vagrants and papists.
[xix. 268]

FLEETWOOD, WILLIAM (1656–1723), bishop of Ely; nephew of James Fleetwood [q. v.]; educated at Eton and King's College, Cambridge, where he gained a high reputation as a preacher; M.A., 1683; D.D., 1705; chaplain to William III; canon of Windsor, 1702; bishop of St. Asaph, 1708–14, of Ely, 1714–23. A preface to some of his sermons attacking tory principles was condemned by parliament to be burnt, but was published as No. 384 of the 'Spectator.' Besides many religious works, he published 'Chronicon Pretiosum, or an Account of English Gold and Silver Money' (c. 1707, anon.)
[xix. 269]

FLEMING, MISS, afterwards MRS. STANLEY (1796?–1861), actress; reputed granddaughter of West Digges [q. v.]; chiefly remembered for her connection with the Haymarket, where she played in the rôle of old women.
[xix. 271]

FLEMING, ABRAHAM (1552?–1607), antiquary and poet; B.A. Peterhouse, Cambridge, 1582; chaplain to Countess of Nottingham and rector of St. Pancras, Soper Lane, London; author of verse translation from the classics and some prose works, including a digest of Holinshed and a history of English earthquakes, 1580.
[xix. 271]

FLEMING, ALEXANDER (1824–1875), medical writer; M.D. Edinburgh, 1844. His 'Physiological and Medicinal Properties of Aconitum Napellus (1845) led to introduction of 'Fleming's tincture.'
[xix. 273]

FLEMING, CALEB (1698–1779), dissenting polemic; joint-pastor of Bartholomew Close presbyterian congregation, 1740, pastor of Pinner Hall, 1753–77; D.D. St. Andrews; published 'A Survey of the Search after Souls,' 1758, and numerous controversial pamphlets. [xix. 273]

FLEMING, CHRISTOPHER (1800–1880), surgeon; B.A. Dublin, 1821, and M.D., 1838; president, College of Surgeons (Ireland), 1856.
[xix. 275]

FLEMING, SIR DANIEL (1633–1701), antiquary; of Queen's College, Oxford, and Gray's Inn; sheriff of Cumberland, 1660; knighted, 1681; M.P., Cockermouth, 1685–1687; left in manuscript a 'Description of the County of Westmoreland,' published 1882 (ed. Sir G. F. Duckett).
[xix. 275]

FLEMING, SIR GEORGE (1667–1747), bishop of Carlisle; fifth son of Sir Daniel Fleming [q. v.]; succeeded as second baronet, 1736; M.A. St. Edmund's Hall, Oxford, 1694; domestic chaplain to Dr. Smith, bishop of Carlisle, of which he was canon, 1700, archdeacon, 1705, dean, 1727, and bishop, 1734.
[xix. 276]

FLEMING, JAMES, fourth BARON FLEMING (1534?–1558), lord high chamberlain of Scotland (an office also held by his father Malcolm); accompanied Mary Queen of Scots to France, 1548; was one of the four Scots Commissioners who died on their way home after attending her marriage with the dauphin (Francis II).
[xix. 276]

FLEMING or **FLEMMING**, JAMES (1682–1751), major-general and colonel, 36th foot; wounded at Blenheim, 1704; as brigadier served against Jacobites, 1745–6.
[xix. 277]

FLEMING, JOHN, fifth BARON FLEMING (d. 1572), younger brother of James, fourth baron Fleming [q. v.], whom he succeeded in the title; chamberlain, 1565; governor of Dumbarton Castle, 1567; accompanied Bothwell, husband of Mary Queen of Scots, in his flight to the north of Scotland, 1567; joined the queen's lords, was present with Mary at Langside (1568), and accompanied her to England; interviewed Elizabeth on her behalf in London; represented her at York; held Dumbarton for two years; escaped to France and conducted an unsuccessful expedition in aid of Mary; accidentally killed by French soldiers at Edinburgh.
[xix. 277]

FLEMING, JOHN, first EARL OF WIGTOWN or WIGTON (d. 1619), lord of Cumbernauld; created earl, 1607.
[xix. 278]

FLEMING, JOHN, second EARL OF WIGTOWN or WIGTON (d. 1650), privy councillor, 1641; entered into association in support of Charles I at Cumbernauld, 1650.
[xix. 279]

FLEMING, JOHN (d. 1815), botanist; M.D. Edinburgh; president of Bengal medical service; contributed 'Catalogue of Indian Medicinal Plants and Drugs' to 'Asiatick Researches.'
[xix. 279]

FLEMING, JOHN (1785–1857), naturalist; entered the presbyterian ministry and held charges at Bressay, Flisk, and Clackmannan; joined the free church, 1843; created D.D. of St. Andrews, 1814; appointed professor of natural philosophy, Aberdeen, 1834, of natural science at Edinburgh, 1845 (Free Church College). He published 'Economical Mineralogy of the Orkney and Zetland Islands,' 'The Philosophy of Zoology' (1822), and 'British Animals' (1828).
[xix. 279]

FLEMING, SIR MALCOLM, EARL OF WIGTOWN (d. 1360?), steward of the household to David II (David Bruce); as keeper of Dumbarton Castle received the king after his defeat at Halidon, 1333; accompanied him in his escape to France; created earl and sheriff of Wigtown on the king's return, 1341; captured at battle of Neville's Cross, 1346; confined in Tower of London; one of the commissioners for treaty of Berwick (1357). [xix. 280]

FLEMING, MARGARET (1803–1811), 'Pet Marjorie'; a youthful prodigy; daughter of James Fleming of Kirkcaldy; played with Sir Walter Scott; composed a poem on Mary Queen of Scots, and other verses. [xix. 281]

FLEMING, PATRICK (1599–1631), Franciscan friar of the Strict Observance; studied at Douay, Louvain, and Rome; first superior of the college of the Immaculate Conception, Prague; killed by peasants near Beneschau. His life of St. Columban was published by Thomas O'Sherrin at Louvain, 1667.
[xix. 281]

FLEMING, RICHARD (d. 1431), bishop of Lincoln and founder of Lincoln College, Oxford; junior proctor, 1407; condemned by Archbishop Arundel for Wycliffite tendencies, 1409; prebendary of York and rector of Boston; bishop of Lincoln, 1420; represented England at councils of Pavia and Siena (1428–1429), where he championed the papacy; given by the pope the see of York, but was not confirmed by the king; caused Wycliffe's bones to be exhumed, 1428. [xix. 282]

FLEMING, ROBERT (d. 1483). [See FLEMMING.]

FLEMING, ROBERT, the elder (1630–1694), Scottish divine; ejected from Cambuslang, Lanarkshire, 1662; went to Rotterdam, 1677; died in London; published, among other works, 'The Fulfilling of the Scripture,' re-issued, 1845 (abridgment still current). [xix. 284]

FLEMING, ROBERT, the younger (1660?–1716), presbyterian minister; son of Robert Fleming the elder [q. v.]; studied in Holland, where he was ordained; pastor at Leyden and afterwards at Rotterdam; at Founder's Hall, Lothbury, 1698; lecturer at Salters' Hall. His works include 'Christology,' 1705–8, and 'Apocalyptical Key,' 1701 (reprinted, 1849). [xix. 285]

FLEMING, SIR THOMAS (1544–1613), judge; called to the bar from Lincoln's Inn, 1574; commissioner to Guernsey, 1579; recorder of Winchester and M.P., Winchester, 1584–92; recorder of London, 1594; solicitor-general, 1595; M.P., Hampshire, 1597–1604; chief-baron of the exchequer, 1604; chief-justice of the king's bench, 1607; tried gunpowder plotters; gave judgment for the crown in Bate's case, 1606; commissioner for lord chancellor, 1610.
[xix. 286]

FLEMING, THOMAS (1593-1666), Roman catholic archbishop of Dublin; professor of theology at Louvain; archbishop, 1623; with archbishop of Tuam agreed to treat with Ormonde, 1643, and six years later signed declaration of oblivion, but excommunicated Ormonde when the declaration of oblivion was repudiated by Charles I on the advice of Ormonde.   [xix. 288]

FLEMMING, JAMES (1682-1751). [See FLEMING.]

FLEMMING, RICHARD (*d.* 1431). [See FLEMING.]

FLEMMING, ROBERT (*d.* 1483), dean of Lincoln (1451) and benefactor of Lincoln College, Oxford, founded by his uncle, Richard Fleming [q. v.]; lived chiefly in Italy, where he wrote Latin poems; prothonotary to Pope Sixtus IV.   [xix. 288]

FLEMYNG, MALCOLM (*d.* 1764), physiologist; pupil of Boerhaave and Monro; practised as a surgeon in Hull and Lincolnshire; M.D.; taught physiology in London, and published 'Introduction to Physiology' (1759) and 'Neuropathia,' 1740, with other works.   [xix. 289]

FLETA, name of a Latin text-book of English law (not of a person) probably written in the Fleet prison *c.* 1290 by a judge whom Edward I. had imprisoned.   [xix. 290]

FLETCHER, ABRAHAM (1714-1793), mathematician; self-taught; published 'The Universal Measurer' (Whitehaven, 1753), and 'The Universal Measurer and Mechanic' (1762).   [xix. 290]

FLETCHER, ALEXANDER (1787-1860), presbyterian divine; M.A. Glasgow; came to London, 1811; minister of Albion Chapel, 1816; suspended after breach of promise case, 1824; separated from secession church, and was for thirty-five years minister at Finsbury Circus Chapel (largest in London); ultimately restored; celebrated for his sermons to children and his 'Family Devotions.'   [xix. 291]

FLETCHER, ANDREW, LORD INNERPEFFER (*d.* 1650), judge; ordinary lord of session, 1623-6; member of commissions to revise acts and laws of Scotland, 1633; reappointed judge, 1641; M.P. for Forfarshire, *c.* 1646, 1647, and 1648; commissioner of the exchequer, 1645-9; member of committee of estates, 1647 and 1648; fined by Cromwell, 1648.   [xix. 292]

FLETCHER, ANDREW (1655-1716), Scottish patriot (Fletcher of Saltoun); son of Sir Robert Fletcher of Salton, East Lothian; as a commissioner in the Scots convention of estates opposed policy of Lauderdale and James, duke of York; became an adviser of Monmouth both in London and in Holland; accompanied Monmouth's expedition to England, but left it on account of a private quarrel, 1685; went to Spain and afterwards served in Hungary against the Turks; joined William of Orange at the Hague, 1688, and returned to Scotland; his estates restored; again joined opposition to English rule, which culminated in the Act of Security, 1704; a violent opponent of the Union; for a short time imprisoned in London (1708) for supposed complicity in the attempted French invasion; introduced from Holland an improved barley-mill and fanners; published important pamphlets recommending establishment of a national militia, and compulsory employment of vagrants, also his speeches in the parliament of 1703, and a political dialogue, 1704. In his 'Account of a Conversation,' 1703, appeared his famous dictum that a nation's ballads were more influential than its laws. His library at Salton is still preserved.   [xix. 292]

FLETCHER, ANDREW, LORD MILTON (1692-1766), lord justice clerk; nephew of Andrew Fletcher of Saltoun [q. v.]; became a lord of session, 1724; lord justiciary, 1726; lord justice clerk, 1735-48; keeper of the signet, 1746; presided at the trial of Captain John Porteous [q. v.], 1736.   [xix. 297]

FLETCHER, ARCHIBALD (1746-1828), reformer; called to the Scottish bar, 1790; was gratuitous counsel for Joseph Gerrald and other 'friends of the people,' 1793; commenced agitation for the reform of Scottish burghs, publishing a work on the subject.   [xix. 298]

FLETCHER, BANISTER (1833-1899), architect; began practice at Newcastle-on-Tyne, *c.* 1853; A.R.I.B.A., 1860; F.R.I.B.A., 1876; came to London, 1870; surveyor to board of trade; liberal M.P. for north-west Wiltshire,

1885-6; professor of architecture and building construction, King's College, London, 1890; fellow, 1891; published works on architecture and surveying.
    [Suppl. ii. 218]

FLETCHER, ELIZA (1770-1858), *née* Dawson; wife of Archibald Fletcher [q. v.], whom she married 1791; left 'Autobiography' (privately printed, 1874), published, 1875.   [xix. 298]

FLETCHER, GEORGE (1764-1855), reputed centenarian; pretended to have been born in 1747.   [xix. 299]

FLETCHER, GILES, the elder (1549 ?-1611), civilian, ambassador, and poet; of Eton and King's College, Cambridge, fellow, 1568; M.A., 1573; LL.D., 1581; chancellor of Chichester; M.P., Winchelsea, 1585; envoy to Russia, 1588; remembrancer of London; treasurer of St. Paul's, 1597; his book on Russia (1591), suppressed and partially printed only in Hakluyt and Purchas, was published entire in 1856 (ed. Bond); 'Licia, or Poemes of Love' (1593), printed by Grosart, 1871.   [xix. 299]

FLETCHER, GILES, the younger (1588 ?-1623), poet; younger son of Giles Fletcher the elder [q. v.]; B.A. Trinity College, Cambridge, 1606; reader in Greek grammar, 1615, and language, 1618; rector of Alderton, Suffolk. His 'Christ's Victorie and Triumph in Heaven and Earth' (1610) has been several times reprinted.   [xix. 302]

FLETCHER, HENRY (*fl.* 1710-1750), engraver; executed vignettes and tail-pieces for Voltaire's 'Henriade,' 1728, and drawings of flowers and birds by Peter Casteels [q. v.] and Charles Collins.   [xix. 302]

FLETCHER, SIR HENRY (1727-1807), politician; eighteen years a director of the East India board; whig M.P. for Cumberland, 1768-1806; created baronet, 1782; a commissioner under Fox's India Bill, 1783. [xix. 303]

FLETCHER, JOHN (1579-1625), dramatist; younger son of Richard Fletcher [q. v.]; became intimate with Francis Beaumont about 1607, and between that date and 1616 collaborated with him in many plays, including 'The Scornful Lady' (published, 1616), 'The Maid's Tragedy,' 1619, 'Philaster,' 1620, and 'A King and no King' (licensed, 1611, printed, 1619). He also wrote with Massinger 'The Honest Man's Fortune' (performed, 1613), 'The Knight of Malta' (produced, 1619), 'Thierry and Theodoret' (published, 1621), and many others. He had help from Shakespeare in 'King Henry VIII' (composed, 1617), and perhaps in 'The Two Noble Kinsmen' (published, 1634). From his own pen alone were 'The Faithful Shepherdess' (1609) and fifteen plays, the best of which are the comedies 'Women Pleased' (probably produced, *c.* 1620), 'The Pilgrim' (played, 1621), 'The Wildgoose Chase' (played, 1621), and 'Monsieur Thomas' (first published, 1639).   [xix. 303]

FLETCHER, JOHN (1792-1836), medical writer; M.D. Edinburgh, 1816, lecturing there on physiology and medical jurisprudence; his 'Rudiments of Physiology' published 1835-7, and wrote 'Elements of Pathology,' published posthumously, 1842.   [xix. 311]

FLETCHER, JOHN (*d.* 1848?), Roman catholic divine; professor at St. Omer during the imprisonment of members of the college at Arras and Dourlens; afterwards came to England; created D.D. by Pius VII, 1821; published, among other works, 'The Catholic's Prayer-Book,' 1830.   [xix. 311]

FLETCHER or **DE LA FLECHERE,** JOHN WILLIAM (1729-1785), vicar of Madeley; born at Nyon in Switzerland; educated at Geneva; came to England after several attempts to become a soldier, *c.* 1752; ordained deacon and priest, 1757; intimate with the Wesleys; accepted the living of Madeley (1760), a rough parish, where he spent the rest of his life; superintendent of Lady Huntingdon's College at Trevecca (1768-71), but resigned on account of his Arminian views, which he defended in 'Checks to Antinomianism,' 1771; published theological works.   [xix. 312]

FLETCHER, JOSEPH (1582 ?-1637), religious poet; educated at Merchant Taylors' School and St. John's College, Oxford; M.A., 1608; rector of Wilby, Suffolk, 1609-1637; author of 'The Historie of the Perfect, Cursed, Blessed Man' (1628-9), and, perhaps, of 'Christes Bloodie Sweat' (1613), both reprinted by Grosart.   [xix. 314]

FLETCHER, JOSEPH, the elder (1784–1843), theological writer; M.A. Glasgow, 1807; congregational minister of Blackburn, 1807–23, and afterwards at Stepney; D.D. Glasgow, 1830; author of lectures on the 'Principles and Institutions of the Roman Catholic Religion,' 1817, and other works.   [xix. 315]

FLETCHER, JOSEPH (1813–1852), statistician; inspector of schools, 1844; editor of the 'Statistical Journal'; published 'Summary of the Moral Statistics of England and Wales,' 1850, and several treatises on education.   [xix. 315]

FLETCHER, JOSEPH, the younger (1816–1876), congregational minister; son of Joseph Fletcher (1784–1843) [q. v.], whose life he wrote; published also a 'History of Independency,' 1847–9.   [xix. 315]

FLETCHER, Mrs. MARIA JANE (1800–1833). [See JEWSBURY.]

FLETCHER, PHINEAS (1582–1650), poet; elder son of Giles Fletcher the elder [q. v.]; of Eton and King's College, Cambridge; M.A., 1608; B.D.; fellow, 1611; rector of Hilgay, Norfolk, 1621–50; published, in imitation of the 'Faery Queene,' his 'Purple Island, or the Isle of Man,' 1633, and other poems, English and Latin.
    [xix. 316]

FLETCHER, RICHARD (d. 1596), bishop of London; B.A. Trinity College, Cambridge, 1566; D.D., 1581; fellow of Corpus Christi College, Cambridge, 1569; prebendary of St. Paul's, 1572; chaplain to Queen Elizabeth, 1581; dean of Peterborough, 1583; chaplain at execution of Mary Queen of Scots, having previously drawn up an account of her examination at Fotheringay; bishop of Bristol, 1589, of Worcester, 1593, and London, 1594. He lost the queen's favour for his share in the Lambeth articles, and was suspended by her on account of his second marriage.   [xix. 317]

FLETCHER, SIR RICHARD (1768–1813), lieutenant-colonel, royal engineers; wounded in St. Lucia; served with the Turks, 1799–1800, helping to construct defences at El Arish and Jaffa; captured by the French after reconnoitring Aboukir Bay; released, 1802; joined Copenhagen expedition, 1807; acted as engineer on Wellington's staff in Portugal, 1808; complimented for his conduct at Talavera, 1809; as chief engineer constructed lines of Torres Vedras, 1809–10; distinguished at Busaco, 1810; directed siege operations at Badajoz and Ciudad Rodrigo, 1811–12; wounded at third siege of Badajoz, 1812; received baronetcy and pension, 1811; served at Vittoria and directed sieges of Pampeluna and San Sebastian; fell at capture of San Sebastian.   [xix. 319]

FLETCHER, ROBERT (fl. 1586), verse-writer; fellow of Merton College, Oxford, 1563–9; M.A., 1567; afterwards a schoolmaster at Taunton; published three very rare volumes of verse.   [xix. 321]

FLETCHER, THOMAS (1666–1713), poet; of Winchester and Balliol and New Colleges, Oxford; M.A., 1693; D.D., 1707; fellow of New College, Oxford; fellow of Winchester, 1711–12; prebendary of Wells, 1696–1718; published 'Poems and Translations' (1692). [xix. 321]

FLETE, JOHN (fl. 1421–1465), prior of Westminster, 1448, and author of a Latin chronicle of the monastery of St. Peter's, Westminster, from the earliest times to 1386.   [xix. 322]

FLEXMAN, ROGER (1708–1795), presbyterian minister; minister at Rotherhithe, 1747–83, and lecturer at Little St. Helens, Bishopsgate, 1754; D.D. Aberdeen, 1770; Dr. Williams's librarian, 1786; compiled four volumes of the index to the 'Commons Journals' and appended a bibliography to an edition of Burnet's 'Own Time,' edited by himself.   [xix. 322]

FLEXMORE, RICHARD (1824–1860), pantomimist; son of Richard Flexmore Geatter; imitated the leading dancers of his day at several London theatres and also on the continent, together with his wife (née Auriol).
    [xix. 323]

FLICCIUS or **FLICCUS**, GERBARUS, GERLACHUS, or GERBICUS (fl. 1546–1554), portrait-painter in style of Lucas Cranach; of German origin. He painted the portrait of Cranmer, still preserved in the National Portrait Gallery.   [xix. 323]

FLIGHT, BENJAMIN (1767 ?–1847), organ-builder; with his son and Joseph Robson constructed the apollonicon.   [xix. 324]

FLIGHT, WALTER (1841–1885), mineralogist; educated at Queenwood College and at Halle, Heidelberg, Berlin, and London, becoming doctor of science, London University; assistant in British Museum, 1867; F.R.S., 1883; author of 'A Chapter in the History of Meteorites' (posthumous).   [xix. 324]

FLINDELL, THOMAS (1767–1824), editor and printer; edited the 'Doncaster Gazette'; founded 'Royal Cornwall Gazette,' 1803, and 'Western Luminary,' for a libel in which on Queen Caroline he was imprisoned, 1821; printed works by Polwhele and Hawker at the 'Stannary Press,' Helston, and at Falmouth part of an edition of the bible.   [xix. 325]

FLINDERS, MATTHEW (1774–1814), naval captain, hydrographer and discoverer; assisted George Bass [q. v.] to survey the coast of New South Wales and Van Diemen's Land, 1795–1800; in command of the Investigator and afterwards of the Porpoise and Cumberland, made the first survey of a large part of the Australian coast, 1801–3; detained as a prisoner in Mauritius by the French for more than six years; wrote paper for the Royal Society during his detention, drawing attention to the error in the compass due to attraction of iron in ship; granted post rank on reaching England, 1810; his 'Voyage to Terra Australis' published posthumously.   [xix. 325]

FLINTER, GEORGE DAWSON (d. 1838), soldier of fortune; served in the 7th West India regiment, 1811–16; interpreter at Caracas, 1815; entered Spanish army and served on side of Isabella in Carlist war; in command at Toledo; defeated Carlists, 1838; committed suicide at Madrid on removal from command; published an account of the revolution of Caracas, 1819, and books on Porto Rico, 1834, and Spain and her colonies, 1834. [xix. 329]

FLINTOFT, LUKE (d. 1727), composer; B.A. Queens' College, Cambridge, 1700; minor canon of Westminster; his double chant in G minor perhaps the first of its kind.
    [xix. 329]

FLITCROFT, HENRY (1697–1769), architect; called 'BURLINGTON HARRY' from name of his patron; employed in board of works, becoming comptroller of works in England, 1758; designed churches of St. Giles-in-the-Fields and St. Olave's, Southwark, and made alterations at Woburn Abbey and Wentworth House. [xix. 329]

FLOOD, SIR FREDERICK (1741–1824), Irish politician; M.A. Trinity College, Dublin, 1764; LL.D., 1772; called to the Irish bar, 1763; M.P. for co. Wexford, 1776; created baronet of Ireland, 1780; prominent volunteer and opponent of the union; M.P. for Wexford in imperial parliament, 1800–18.   [xix. 330]

FLOOD, HENRY (1732–1791), statesman and orator; natural son of chief-justice Warden Flood; educated at Trinity College, Dublin, and Christ Church, Oxford; M.A. Oxford, 1752; entered Irish parliament for Kilkenny, 1759, and was returned for Callan, 1760; organised and headed an opposition; carried rejection of money bill, 1769; contributed to 'Baratariana' (an attack on the viceroy); supported the proposed absentee tax, 1773; vice-treasurer of Ireland, 1775; elected for Enniskillen, 1776, continuing to hold office till 1781, though he had been a colonel of volunteers; resumed opposition and co-operated with Grattan in obtaining the independence of the Irish parliament, 1782; quarrelled with Grattan on the expediency of continuing the volunteer movement and on the enfranchisement of Roman catholics; opposed commercial propositions of 1785, and continued to bring forward Irish reform bills; M.P., Winchester, 1783, being at the time M.P. for Kilbeggan in the Irish parliament; returned for Seaford, 1784; spoke in English House of Commons against commercial treaty with France, 1787, and in 1790 brought forward a reform bill based upon household suffrage in counties; mortally wounded James Agar in a duel, 1769; came near fighting a duel with Grattan, 1783.   [xix. 331]

FLOOD, ROBERT (1574–1637). [See FLUDD.]

FLOOD, VALENTINE (d. 1847), anatomist; M.A. Trinity College, Dublin, 1823; M.D., 1830; lecturer on anatomy in Richmond Hospital school, Dublin, c. 1832; chief work, 'The Surgical Anatomy of the Arteries, and Descriptive Anatomy of the Heart,' 1839.   [xix. 355]

FLORENCE OF WORCESTER (*d.* 1118), chronicler ; a monk of Worcester ; author of a ' Chronicon ex Chronicis,' based upon the work of Marianus (an Irish monk), extending to 1117, which was continued by other hands till 1295 (Cambridge MS.) It was first printed in 1592, and translated for Bohn (1847) and for Stevenson's ' Church Historians' (1853). Nine manuscripts exist. [xix. 335]

FLORIO, JOHN (1553 ?-1625), author ; son of Michael Angelo Florio [q. v.] ; entered Magdalen College, Oxford, 1581 ; patronised by the Earls of Leicester, Southampton, and Pembroke ; reader in Italian to Queen Anne, 1603 ; groom of the privy chamber, 1604. His great Italian-English dictionary (1598) was edited by Torriano (with English-Italian added) in 1659. He published translation of Montaigne's ' Essays,' in three books, 1603 (frequently reprinted). [xix. 336]

FLORIO, MICHAEL ANGELO (*fl.* 1550), protestant refugee ; fled from persecution in the Valteline ; preacher to Italian protestant congregation in London, 1550 ; taught Italian in London ; published in Italian a catechism, and a biography of Lady Jane Grey, with translations into Italian of works attributed to her. [xix. 336]

FLOWER, BENJAMIN (1755-1829), political writer ; after a visit to France, in 1791, edited the ' Cambridge Intelligencer,' a pro-revolution and radical paper ; imprisoned for libel on Bishop Watson, 1799 ; afterwards published ' The Political Register,' 1807-11. [xix. 339]

FLOWER, EDWARD FORDHAM (1805-1883), author ; nephew of Benjamin Flower [q. v.] ; a brewer at Stratford-on-Avon thirty years ; published several works on ' bearing reins ' and management of horses. [xix. 339]

FLOWER, ELIZA (1803-1846), musical composer ; elder daughter of Benjamin Flower [q. v.] ; published political songs and music to 'Hymns and Anthems' (1841-6) for South Place Chapel, including settings to words of her sister, Sarah Flower Adams [q. v.] [xix. 340]

FLOWER, JOHN (*fl.* 1658), puritan divine ; B.A. New Inn Hall, Oxford, 1647 ; created M.A. by parliamentary visitors, 1648. [xix. 340]

FLOWER, ROGER (*d.* 1428 ?), speaker ; M.P. for Rutland, 1396-7, 1399, 1402, 1404, and 1413-14 ; four times speaker, 1416, 1417, 1419, and 1422. The Irish viscounts of Ashbrook descend from him. [xix. 340]

FLOWER, WILLIAM (1498 ?-1588), Norroy king of arms ; Rouge Croix, 1544 ; Chester herald, 1546 ; Norroy, 1562 ; published ' Visitation of Yorkshire, 1563-1564 ' (printed, 1881), of Lancashire, 1567 (printed, 1870), and of Durham, 1575 (printed, 1820). [xix. 341]

FLOWER, SIR WILLIAM HENRY (1831-1899), director of Natural History Museum, London ; son of Edward Fordham Flower [q. v.] ; educated at University College, London ; studied medicine and surgery at Middlesex Hospital ; M.B. London, 1851 ; volunteered for medical service in Russian war, 1854 ; assistant-surgeon, Middlesex Hospital ; curator of Hunterian Museum, Royal College of Surgeons, 1861-84, and Hunterian professor of comparative anatomy and physiology, 1870-84 ; president of Zoological Society, 1879 till death ; F.R.S., 1864, and royal medallist, 1882 ; director of Natural History Museum, 1884-98, during which period he developed very successfully both the popular and scientific sides of the museum ; president of Anthropological Institute, 1883-5 ; president British Association for meeting at Newcastle, 1889 ; C.B., 1887 ; K.C.B., 1892 ; honorary LL.D. Edinburgh and Dublin, and D.C.L. Durham. His original investigations related almost exclusively to the mammalia, including man, and he made considerable contributions to scientific literature. His works include, ' Introduction to Osteology of Mammalia,' 1870, ' Fashion in Deformity,' 1881, and ' The Horse,' 1890. [Suppl. ii. 218]

FLOWERDEW, EDWARD (*d.* 1586), judge ; treasurer of the Inner Temple, 1579 ; counsel to the dean of Norwich and town of Yarmouth ; recorder of Great Yarmouth, 1580 ; third baron of the exchequer, 1584 ; died on circuit, of gaol fever. [xix. 342]

FLOWERS, FREDERICK (1810-1886), police magistrate ; barrister, Lincoln's Inn, 1839 ; recorder of Stamford, 1862 ; magistrate at Bow Street, 1864-86. [xix. 342]

FLOWERS, GEORGE FRENCH (1811-1872), musical composer ; brother of Frederick Flowers [q.v.] ; studied in Germany and took musical degrees at Oxford ; founded Contrapuntists' Society, 1843, and taught vocalisation on the lines of Vogler. He published ' Essay on the Construction of Fugue,' 1846, and composed organ and choral fugues. [xix. 342]

FLOYD, FLOUD, or LLOYD, EDWARD (*d.* 1648 ?), Roman catholic barrister, who, having spoken slighting words of the elector palatine and his wife, was impeached and sentenced by the Commons, 1621. The case was afterwards referred to the Lords, who imposed a severer punishment. It was decided during the proceedings that the Lower House had only power to try persons for offences affecting their corporate privileges. [xix. 343]

FLOYD, SIR GODFREY (*fl.* 1667). [See LLOYD.]

FLOYD, HENRY (1563-1641), jesuit ; employed in connection with establishments of Father Parsons in Spain and Portugal ; professed jesuit, 1618 ; missioner in England, and frequently imprisoned. [xix. 344]

FLOYD, JOHN (*d.* 1523). [See LLOYD.]

FLOYD, JOHN (1572-1649), jesuit ; in religion DANIEL À JESU ; brother of Edward Floyd [q. v.] ; joined jesuits while at Rome, 1592, where he was famed as a preacher and teacher ; after frequent arrests in England retired to Louvain, but died at St. Omer ; published, under initials and the pseudonyms, Daniel à Jesu, Hermannus Loemelius, George White, and Annosus Fidelis Verimentanus, twenty-one controversial treatises. [xix. 344]

FLOYD, SIR JOHN (1748-1818), general ; cornet, 1760 ; served in Eliott's light horse (15th hussars) during the seven years' war, being riding-master at the age of fifteen ; went to Madras, 1781, in command of the newly raised 23rd (19th) light dragoons ; commanded cavalry on Coromandel coast and distinguished himself against Tippoo Sultan, 1790-4 ; major-general, 1794 ; second in command under Harris during second war with Tippoo : distinguishing himself at Malavalli ; led the covering army during the siege of Seringapatam, 1799 ; lieutenant-general, 1801 ; general, 1812 ; governor of Gravesend and Tilbury, 1817 ; created baronet, 1816. [xix. 345]

FLOYD, THOMAS (*fl.* 1603), author ; B.A. New Inn Hall, Oxford, 1593 ; M.A. Jesus College, Oxford, 1596 ; published ' The Picture of a Perfect Commonwealth,' 1600. [xix. 346]

FLOYER, SIR JOHN (1649-1734), physician ; M.A. Queen's College, Oxford, 1671 ; M.D., 1680 ; practised at Lichfield ; knighted, *c.* 1686 ; published important works on bathing and upon asthma ; the first to make regular observations upon the rate of the pulse (in the ' Physician's Pulse Watch,' 1707, 1710). [xix. 346]

FLUD, JOHN (*d.* 1523). [See LLOYD.]

FLUDD or FLUD, ROBERT (1574-1637), rosicrucian ; M.A. St. John's College, Oxford, 1598 ; M.D. Christ Church, Oxford, 1605 ; studied chemistry abroad ; four times censor of the College of Physicians ; practised in London ; entered into controversy with Kepler and Gassendi, and published works in defence of the rosicrucians, some of them under the pseudonyms Rudolf Otreb and Joachim Frizius. [xix. 348]

FLUDYER, SIR SAMUEL (1705-1768), lord mayor of London ; great-uncle of Sir Samuel Romilly [q. v.] ; with his brother Thomas made a fortune as a clothier ; alderman, 1751 ; sheriff, 1754 ; mayor, 1761 ; knighted, 1755, and created baronet, 1759 ; M.P., Chippenham, 1754-68. [xix. 350]

FOGG, LAURENCE (1623-1718), dean of Chester ; studied at Emmanuel and St. John's Colleges, Cambridge ; D.D. Cambridge, 1679 ; held various livings ; prebendary of Chester, 1673 ; dean, 1691 ; published theological works. [xix. 350]

FOGGO, GEORGE (1793-1869), historical painter ; associated with his brother James Foggo [q. v.] in painting and lithography, also in foundation of society for obtaining free access to museums and exhibitions ; published the first National Gallery catalogue, 1844, and ' Adventures of Sir J. Brooke, Rajah of Sarawak,' 1853. [xix. 351]

FOGGO, JAMES (1789-1860), historical painter ; studied under Regnault in Paris ; came to London and

in 1816, exhibited at the Academy; painted and lithographed with his brother, 1819-60, among their pictures being 'The Christian Inhabitants of Parga preparing to emigrate,' on which they worked three years; with his brother managed the Pantheon exhibition, 1852-5.
[xix. 351]

FOILLAN, SAINT and BISHOP (d. 655), brother of Fursa [q. v.], who placed him over the monastery of Cnoberesburgh; afterwards followed Fursa abroad, and was placed by Gertrude, daughter of Pepin, in charge of her monastery at Nivelles; killed by robbers in Soignies forest; buried at Fosse.   [xix. 352]

FOLBURY, GEORGE (d. 1540), master of Pembroke Hall, Cambridge, 1537-40; B.A. Cambridge, 1514; B.D., 1524; canon of York; D.D. Montpellier.   [xix. 352]

FOLCARD or **FOULCARD** (fl. 1066), hagiographer; probably came to England in the time of Edward the Confessor from Flanders: at first a monk of Christ Church, Canterbury; set over Thorney Abbey by William I, c. 1066; subsequently returned to Flanders; wrote 'Vita S. Johannis Episcopi Eboracensis,' and lives of several other saints.   [xix. 352]

FOLDSONE, JOHN (d. 1784?), painter; known for his small portraits executed in a day; exhibited at the Society of Artists and (1771-83) at the Royal Academy.
[xix. 353]

FOLEY, DANIEL (1815-1874), of humble parentage; B.D. Trinity College, Dublin; prebendary of Cashel; professor of Irish at Trinity College, Dublin, 1849-61; published an English-Irish dictionary, 1855. [xix. 353]

FOLEY, JOHN HENRY (1818-1874), sculptor; studied in the Royal Dublin Society schools and those of the Royal Academy; A.R.A., 1849; R.A., 1858. The best of his early works were 'Innocence' (1839), 'Ino and Bacchus' (1840), and 'Egeria' (1856). Among his public works are equestrian statues of Sir James Outram, Lord Canning, and Lord Hardinge at Calcutta; statues of O'Connell, Goldsmith, and Burke in Dublin; one of Lord Clyde at Glasgow and of Clive at Shrewsbury; the group of Asia and the figure of the Prince Consort in the Albert Memorial, Hyde Park; a statue of John Stuart Mill on the Thames Embankment and of Sir Charles Barry in the House of Commons; and the sepulchral monument of John Nicholson in Lisburn Cathedral.   [xix. 353]

FOLEY, PAUL (1645?-1699), speaker of the House of Commons; second son of Thomas Foley (1617-1677) [q. v.]; tory M.P. for Hereford in seven parliaments; speaker, 1695-8; ancestor of the Barons Foley of Kidderminster.   [xix. 354]

FOLEY, SAMUEL (1655-1695), bishop of Down and Connor; fellow of Trinity College, Dublin, 1679; chancellor of St. Patrick's, 1689; dean of Achonry, 1691; bishop of Down, 1694.   [xix. 355]

FOLEY, THOMAS (1617-1677), founder of Old Swinford Hospital, Worcestershire; son of an iron manufacturer near Stourbridge, who introduced the Swedish splitting machine; successfully carried on the business, and increased his property by a wealthy marriage; high sheriff of Worcestershire, 1656; represented Bewdley in the convention of 1660; founded Old Swinford Hospital, 1667.   [xix. 355]

FOLEY, THOMAS, baron (d. 1733), grandson of Thomas Foley [q. v.]; M.P., Stafford and Worcester; one of the twelve tory peers created in 1712.   [xix. 356]

FOLEY, SIR THOMAS (1757-1833), admiral; entered navy, 1770; took part in operations under Keppel, 1778, and Sir Charles Hardy, 1779; present at the action off Finisterre and relief of Gibraltar, 1780; served in West Indies, 1781-5; as flag-captain to Gell and Parker off Toulon, 1793; and at St. Vincent, 1797; while in command of the Goliath led the English line into action at the Nile (1798), engaging the French van on the inside; as flag-captain on the Elephant gave great assistance to Nelson at Copenhagen, 1801; rear-admiral, 1808; commander-in-chief in the Downs, 1811; vice-admiral, 1812; admiral, 1825; K.C.B., 1815; G.C.B., 1820; commander-in-chief at Portsmouth, 1830.   [xix. 356]

FOLIOT, GILBERT (d. 1187), bishop of London; after having been prior of Clugny and Abbeville, became abbot of Gloucester; bishop of Hereford, 1147-63, and of London, 1163-87; opposed election of Becket to primacy,

1162; refused to yield him obedience as metropolitan; Henry II's envoy to the French king and the pope on Becket's escape; administrator of Canterbury during Becket's absence; excommunicated by Becket, 1167 and 1169; obtained absolution at Rouen, 1170; again excommunicated as one of those who consecrated Henry II's eldest son; absolved, 1172; exercised great influence over the king till his death.   [xix. 358]

FOLIOT, ROBERT (d. 1186), bishop of Hereford; related to Gilbert Foliot [q. v.]; called 'Melundinensis,' having studied at Melun or Meaux; archdeacon of Oxford, 1151; canon of Hereford, 1155; bishop, 1174; one of the English representatives at the Lateran council, 1179. Bale attributes to him several learned works.
[xix. 360]

FOLKES, LUCRETIA (fl. 1707-1714), actress; née Bradshaw; married Martin Folkes [q. v.], 1714.
[xix. 362]

FOLKES, MARTIN (1690-1754), antiquary; studied at Saumur University; M.A. Clare Hall, Cambridge, 1717; D.C.L. Oxford, 1746; F.R.S., 1713; vice-president, 1723; president, 1741-53; member of the Académie des Sciences, 1742; president of Society of Antiquaries, 1750-4; published 'Tables of English Gold and Silver Coins,' 1736 and 1745; and helped Theobald in his notes to Shakespeare. In 1792 a monument to him was erected in Westminster Abbey.   [xix. 361]

FOLLETT, SIR WILLIAM WEBB (1798-1845), attorney-general; M.A. Trinity College, Cambridge, 1830; called to the bar from Inner Temple, 1824; had large election petition practice, 1831-3; M.P., Exeter, 1835; K.C., 1834; solicitor-general under Peel, 1834-5, and again in 1841; attorney-general, 1844; defended Lord Cardigan in the duel case and appeared for Norton against Lord Melbourne. There is a statue of him in Westminster Abbey.   [xix. 362]

FOLLOWS, RUTH (1718-1809), quakeress; née Alcock; preached extensively throughout England and Wales, and also in Ireland and Scotland.   [xix. 363]

FONBLANQUE, ALBANY (1793-1872), radical journalist; third son of John de Grenier Fonblanque [q. v.]; studied at Woolwich and read law with Chitty; early contributed to 'Times' and 'Morning Chronicle'; wrote for the 'Westminster Review'; leader-writer for the 'Examiner,' 1826; editor of the 'Examiner,' 1830-47; for many years proprietor of the 'Examiner'; statistical officer in board of trade, 1847. His best articles were republished in 'England under Seven Administrations' (1837).   [xix. 363]

FONBLANQUE, JOHN DE GRENIER (1760-1837), jurist; educated at Harrow and Oxford; barrister, Middle Temple, 1783; counsel against the Quebec Bill, 1791; K.C., 1804; M.P., Camelford, 1802-6; died 'father of the bar'; edited Ballow's 'Treatise on Equity,' on which subject he was a great authority; wrote also two tracts.   [xix. 365]

FONBLANQUE, JOHN SAMUEL MARTIN DE GRENIER (1787-1865), legal writer, eldest son of John de Grenier Fonblanque [q. v.]; educated at Charterhouse and Caius College, Cambridge; served in the army in Spain and Italy, and in the second American war; captured at New Orleans, 1815; called to the bar, 1816; commissioner of bankruptcy, 1817; joint-author of 'Medical Jurisprudence' (1823); and one of the founders of 'The Jurist.'   [xix. 365]

FONNEREAU, THOMAS GEORGE (1789-1850), author and artist; while practising as a lawyer entertained artists and wits at his chambers in the Albany; printed privately 'Mems. of a Tour in Italy, from Sketches by T. G. F.' and 'Diary of a Dutiful Son, by H. E. O.' (1849), published in 1864.   [xix. 366]

FONTIBUS (FOUNTAINS), JOHN DE (d. 1225), bishop of Ely; ninth abbot of Fountains, 1211; bishop of Ely, 1219; his skeleton discovered entire in 1770; witnessed Magna Charta.   [xix. 366]

FOOT, JESSE, the elder (1744-1826), surgeon; practised in West Indies (1766-9), at St. Petersburg, and afterwards in London; published lives of John Hunter (hostile), Arthur Murphy, and A. R. Bowes, besides numerous medical tracts and 'A Defence of the Planters in the West Indies,' 1792.   [xix. 367]

Q

FOOT, JESSE, the younger (1780–1850), surgeon; nephew of Jesse Foot the elder [q. v.]; to whose practice he succeeded; published 'Ophthalmic Memoranda,' 1838, and 'The Medical Pocket-Book for 1835,' 1834. [xix. 368]

FOOTE, SIR EDWARD JAMES (1767–1833), vice-admiral; maternal nephew of Sir Horace Mann [q. v.]; entered navy, 1780; present at battle of Dominica, 1782, and St. Vincent, 1797; while in command of the Seahorse captured off Sicily Baraguay d'Hilliers and staff on their way to Egypt, 1798; as senior officer in the Bay of Naples signed capitulation (1799) of Uovo and Nuovo (annulled by Nelson), afterwards publishing a vindication; conducted Abercromby to Egypt, 1800; appointed to the royal yacht Augusta, 1803; vice-admiral, 1821; K.C.B., 1831. [xix. 368]

FOOTE, LYDIA (1844?–1892), actress, whose real name was LYDIA ALICE LEGGE; appeared first at Lyceum, 1852, and subsequently played at many London theatres, her best parts including Esther Eccles in 'Caste,' 1867, and Anna in 'The Danischeffs,' 1877. [Suppl. ii. 221]

FOOTE, MARIA, fourth COUNTESS OF HARRINGTON (1797?–1867), actress; appeared with great success at Covent Garden as Amanthis in 'The Child of Nature' (Inchbald), 1814; played at same theatre till 1825; subsequently acted at Drury Lane; toured extensively throughout Great Britain and Ireland till 1831; married Charles Stanhope, fourth earl of Harrington [q. v.], 1831. She had previously had an intrigue with Colonel Berkeley, and recovered damages for breach of promise from 'Pea Green' Haynes, winning much popular sympathy. [xix. 369]

FOOTE, SAMUEL (1720–1777), actor and dramatist; matriculated at Worcester College, Oxford, 1737; dissipated a fortune at Oxford; while a law student at the Temple appeared as an amateur at the Haymarket, 1744; played comedy parts in imitation of Cibber at Drury Lane, 1745; his 'Diversions of the Morning' prohibited at the Haymarket, 1747; substituted for this prohibited piece an amusing entertainment in which he mimicked leading actors and actresses; produced 'The Knights,' ridiculing Italian opera, 1749; and 1753 'The Englishman in Paris' (Covent Garden and Drury Lane); brought out 'The Englishman Returned from Paris' (Covent Garden), 1756; his 'Author,' given at Drury Lane, suppressed, 1757; failed in the part of Shylock, 1758; his piece ridiculing the methodists, 'The Minor,' when first produced at Dublin (1760), a failure, but successful when given in London in an enlarged form; acted in his co-lessee Murphy's plays at Drury Lane, and (1762) played Peter Paragraph in his own 'Orators'; among his other plays 'The Mayor of Garratt,' 1763, 'The Commissary,' 1765, 'The Devil upon Two Sticks,' 1768, 'The Nabob,' 1772, and 'The Capuchin,' 1776 (an adaptation of 'The Trip to Calais,' which had been suppressed by the influence of the Duchess of Kingston, who was libelled in it). Foote obtained, through the Duke of York, a patent for a theatre in Westminster, 1766, as compensation for a practical joke at a party which had cost him his leg; built the new Haymarket, 1767, which he held till 1777; much broken by the litigation with William Jackson (1737?–1795) [q. v.], the Dr. Viper of the 'Capuchins'; died at Dover while on his way to France for the purpose of recovering his health. His portrait by Reynolds is at the Garrick Club. [xix. 370]

FORANNAN, SAINT and BISHOP (d. 982), bishop of Domhnach mor (Donoughmore), then the metropolis of Ireland; left Ireland, 969, and went to Rome, where he was made abbot; afterwards placed over Count Eilbert's monastery of Walciodor, now Wassor, Belgium, where he died; his day, 30 April. [xix. 375]

FORBES, ALEXANDER, first BARON FORBES (d. 1448), served in France against the English and was present at Beaugé (1421); created a lord of parliament by James II of Scotland between 1436 and 1442. [xix. 376]

FORBES, ALEXANDER, fourth BARON FORBES (d. 1491): fought for James III against his son, but was pardoned and received into favour by James IV. [xix. 376]

FORBES, ALEXANDER (1564–1617), bishop of Aberdeen; M.A. St. Andrews, 1585; supported James VI's efforts to restore episcopacy; bishop of Caithness, 1604; member of the Scotch high commission court; translated to Aberdeen, 1616. [xix. 376]

FORBES, ALEXANDER, fourth and last BARON FORBES OF PITSLIGO (1678–1762), Jacobite; having taken part in the rising of 1715, lived abroad five years; raised a regiment for the Young Pretender in 1745, when he was attainted and remained in hiding many years; published 'Essays Moral and Philosophical,' 1734; his 'Thoughts concerning Man's Condition,' published posthumously, 1763 (republished by Lord Medwyn, 1835). [xix. 377]

FORBES, ALEXANDER PENROSE (1817–1875), bishop of Brechin; second son of John Hay Forbes, baron Medwyn [q. v.]; educated at Glasgow University and Haileybury; after three years in the service of the East India Company in Madras presidency, returned to England and graduated B.A. Brasenose College, Oxford, 1844; ordained, 1844; vicar of St. Saviour's, Leeds, 1847; bishop of Brechin, 1848; censured for promulgating the doctrine of the real presence, 1860; an intimate friend of Pusey and Döllinger, he published 'Explanation of the Thirty-nine Articles,' 1867–8, 'Kalendars of Scottish Saints,' 1872, and edited 'Lives of St. Ninian, St. Kentigern, and St. Columba,' 1875. [xix. 378]

FORBES, ARCHIBALD (1838–1900), war correspondent; educated at Aberdeen and Edinburgh; served in royal dragoons, c. 1857–67; started and ran 'London Scotsman' weekly journal, 1867–71; war correspondent to 'Morning Advertiser' and subsequently to 'Daily News,' in Franco-Prussian war, 1870–1, Russo-Turkish war, 1877, Afghanistan, 1878–9, and Zulu war, 1880, and was on several occasions first to convey to England news of important events; published several volumes of war correspondence and military biography, besides 'Memories and Studies of War and Peace,' 1895. [Suppl. ii. 222]

FORBES, SIR ARTHUR, first EARL OF GRANARD (1623–1696), born and brought up in Ireland; served under Montrose and was imprisoned two years at Edinburgh; returned to Ireland, 1655, whence he went to Breda to represent to Prince Charles the state of the country; a commissioner of court of claims and M.P. for Mullingar, 1660–1; Irish privy councillor, 1670, and several times a lord justice; procured *regium donum* for presbyterians; created Baron Clanehugh and Viscount Granard, 1675; created earl and colonel of 18th foot, 1684; removed from his command by James II; protested against the acts of his parliament, and was besieged by the Irish at Castle Forbes; reduced Sligo for William III. [xix. 379]

FORBES, SIR CHARLES (1774–1849), politician; educated at Aberdeen University; head of the first mercantile house in Bombay, in the town hall of which stands his statue by Chantrey; tory M.P., Beverley, 1812–18, and Malmesbury, 1818–32; supported Wellington on the reform question; created baronet, 1823; lord rector of Aberdeen University. [xix. 380]

FORBES, SIR CHARLES FERGUSSON (1779–1852), army surgeon; M.D. Edinburgh, 1808; saw service in the Peninsular war, Holland, and Egypt, retiring as inspector-general of hospitals, 1814; physician at Westminster Eye Hospital, 1816–27; fought two duels with George James Guthrie [q. v.], his colleague, 1827; F.R.C.P., 1841; G.C.H., 1842. [xix. 381]

FORBES, DAVID (1777?–1849), major-general; entered 78th Highlanders, 1793, and served with distinction in Holland, 1794, and in the Quiberon and Belleisle expedition, 1795; served in India twenty years; took part in Java expedition, 1811; C.B., 1838; major-general, 1846. [xix. 382]

FORBES, DAVID (1828–1876), geologist and philologist; brother of Edward Forbes [q. v.]; ten years superintendent of the Espedal mining works in Norway; thanked by the king of Sweden for arming miners to support the government against a threatened revolution in 1848; F.R.S., 1856; traversed Bolivia and Peru, 1857–60, in search of the ores of nickel and cobalt; studied volcanic phenomena of South Pacific; many years foreign secretary of Iron and Steel Institute; secretary to Geological Society, 1871–6; one of the first to apply the microscope to study of rocks; author of fifty-eight important scientific papers. [xix. 382]

FORBES, DUNCAN (1644?–1704), genealogist; educated at Bourges; M.P., Nairn county, 1678, 1681–2, Inverness county, 1689, 1689–1702, and Nairnshire again, 1702–4; active in Scotland against James II; his estates at Culloden and Ferintosh ravaged by Jacobites, 1689;

published 'The Familie of Innes' (edited by Spalding Club, 1864), to which his wife belonged, and 'Plan for Preserving the Peace of the Highlands'; left in manuscript an interesting diary. [xix. 383]

FORBES, DUNCAN (1685-1747), lord president of the court of session; second son of Duncan Forbes (1644?-1704) [q. v.]; studied law at Leyden; advocate and sheriff of Midlothian, 1709; made depute-advocate for services against rebels in 1715; M.P., Inverness burghs, 1722; lord advocate, 1725; president of court of session, 1737; active in the enforcement of the revenue laws; took a prominent part in opposing punishment of Edinburgh for the Porteous affair, 1737; endeavoured to detach Lovat from the cause of Charles Edward, the Young Pretender, against whom he raised a force, but was obliged to fly to Skye; published theological works on the lines of John Hutchinson (1674-1737) [q. v.] [xix. 384]

FORBES, DUNCAN (1798-1868), orientalist; graduated M.A. St. Andrews, 1823 (created LL.D. 1847); spent three years in Calcutta; became assistant-teacher of Hindustani in London, 1826, and was professor of oriental languages at King's College, London, 1837-61; made first catalogue of Persian manuscripts for British Museum and published 'History of Chess,' 1860, also Persian, Bengali, and Hindustani grammars, and other oriental manuals. [xix. 386]

FORBES, EDWARD (1815-1854), naturalist; brother of David Forbes (1828-1876) [q. v.]; studied at Edinburgh University, where he founded the 'University Magazine'; in vacations made natural-history expeditions to Isle of Man, and to Norway, France, Switzerland, Germany, and Algeria; collected three thousand plant specimens on a tour through Austria, 1838; lectured in various places; as naturalist to the Beacon, collected marine animals and investigated their relation with plants in the Ægean, 1841; made tour through Lycia, collecting molluscs and plants, 1842, aided by a grant from British Association, to which he read a 'Report,' 1843; professor of botany at King's College, London, and lecturer of the Geological Society, 1842; palæontologist of the Geological Survey, 1844; lectured at Royal Institution on 'Light thrown on Geology by Submarine Researches'; F.R.S., 1845; showed that Purbeck beds belonged to oolitic series, 1849; president of Geological Society, 1853; professor of natural history at Edinburgh, 1854, but died within six months of appointment; published 'History of British Mollusca,' 1848, and 'History of British Star-fishes' (1842), besides important geological, botanical, and palæontological papers. [xix. 388]

FORBES, SIR FRANCIS (1784-1841), first chief-justice of New South Wales; called to the bar from Lincoln's Inn, 1812; attorney-general of Bermuda, 1813; chief-justice of Newfoundland, 1816, of New South Wales, 1823; member of legislative and executive councils, 1825; knighted in England, 1837. [xix. 392]

FORBES, GEORGE, third EARL OF GRANARD (1685-1765), naval commander and diplomatist; grandson of Sir Arthur Forbes, first earl [q. v.]; served as midshipman at capture of Gibraltar and battle of Malaga, 1704; appointed brigadier in the horse guards under Argyll, 1707; held a naval command in Mediterranean, and was wounded at Villa Viciosa, 1710; governor of Minorca, 1716-18; went on a special mission to Vienna, 1719; took part in defence of Gibraltar, 1726-7; created Baron Forbes of Ireland, 1727; governor of the Leeward Islands, 1729-30; returned to the navy, 1731; negotiated treaty with Russia, 1733; admiral, 1733; Earl of Granard, 1733; elected M.P. for Ayr boroughs, 1741; a member of the committee of inquiry into Walpole's conduct; privy councillor of Ireland. [xix. 393]

FORBES, GEORGE, sixth EARL OF GRANARD in the peerage of Ireland and first BARON GRANARD in the United Kingdom (1760-1837), lieutenant-general; opposed Buckingham administration in Ireland; raised an Irish regiment, 1794, and commanded another at Castlebar, 1798; opposed the union; created Baron Granard, 1806; lieutenant-general, 1813; died in Paris. [xix. 395]

FORBES, HENRY (1804-1859), pianist and composer; pupil of Smart, Hummel, and Moscheles; organist of St. Luke's, Chelsea, and conductor of the Società Armonica, 1827-50; published 'National Psalmody,' 1843, and other musical compositions. [xix. 396]

FORBES, JAMES (1629?-1712), nonconformist divine; M.A. Aberdeen and Oxford; ejected from Gloucester Cathedral, 1661; imprisoned frequently; for fifty-eight years minister at Gloucester. [xix. 396]

FORBES, JAMES (1749-1819), author of 'Oriental Memoirs'; in service of the East India Company, 1765-1784; imprisoned in France after rupture of peace of Amiens; allowed to return to England, 1804; published 'Letters from France,' 1806, and 'Oriental Memoirs,' 1813-1815; took charge of his grandson, Montalembert, the future historian, who witnessed his death at Aix-la-Chapelle. [xix. 397]

FORBES, JAMES (1779-1837), inspector-general of army hospitals; M.D. Edinburgh; entered army, 1803; staff-surgeon in Peninsular and Walcheren expedition, 1809; had charge of casualties from Waterloo; afterwards served in West Indies and Canada; principal medical officer in Ceylon, 1829-36. [xix. 398]

FORBES, JAMES DAVID (1809-1868), man of science; elected F.R.S.E. at age of nineteen; joined Brewster in founding British Association, 1831; F.R.S., 1832; professor of natural philosophy at Edinburgh, 1833, and dean of Faculty of Arts, 1837; D.C.L. Oxford, 1853; principal of St. Andrews, 1859; received Rumford medal of Royal Society for discovery of polarisation of heat, and the royal medal for his paper on the influence of the atmosphere on the sun's rays; three times Keith medallist of the Edinburgh Society; secretary, Royal Society of Edinburgh, 1840-51. His chief work was 'Travels through the Alps of Savoy and other parts of the Pennine Chain, with Observations on the Phenomena of Glaciers,' 1843. He was the first to study scientifically the phenomena of glaciers, but his claim to be the first observer of their veined structure and other of their characteristics was contested by Agassiz and Tyndall. [xix. 398]

FORBES, JAMES OCHONCAR, seventeenth BARON FORBES (1765-1843), served with the Coldstream guards in Flanders, and (1799) at the Helder; colonel of the 94th and 54th foot, 1809, and of the 21st, 1816; general, 1819; Scottish representative peer, 1806; baronet of Nova Scotia; high commissioner of church of Scotland, 1826; died at Bregenz, Switzerland. [xix. 400]

FORBES, JOHN (1571-1606), Capuchin friar; 'Father Archangel'; escaped from Scotland to Antwerp disguised as a shepherd's boy; took the habit of a Capuchin at Tournay, 1593; said to have converted three hundred Scots soldiers to catholicism at Dixmude; died at Ghent; a Latin 'life' of him by Faustinus Cranius (1620) was translated into English (1623), French, and Italian. [xix. 401]

FORBES, JOHN (1568?-1634), minister of Alford, Aberdeenshire, 1593; went on a special mission to London, 1605; banished from Scotland for denying the jurisdiction of the privy council over the church, 1606; after living some time in France, became pastor of Middelburg, 1611, and Delft, 1621; published theological treatises. [xix. 401]

FORBES, JOHN (1593-1648), professor of divinity; second son of Patrick Forbes of Corse [q. v.]; studied at Heidelberg and other foreign universities; professor of divinity at King's College, Aberdeen, 1620-39; published defence of episcopacy, 1629, and attacked the national covenant, 1638, for refusing to take which he lost his professorship, 1639; went to the Netherlands to avoid taking the solemn league and covenant, 1644; returned to Scotland, 1646, and lived at Corse; published, among other works, 'Instructiones Historico-Theologicæ de Doctrina Christiana' (Amsterdam, 1645). His collected works, 1702-3, include a Latin diary. [xix. 402]

FORBES, JOHN (1710-1759), brigadier; entered Scots Greys, of which regiment he became lieutenant-colonel, 1750; colonel of 17th foot, 1757; adjutant-general and brigadier in America, 1757; led expedition to Fort Du Quesne, which was abandoned by the French, 1758; died at Philadelphia. [Suppl. ii. 223]

FORBES, JOHN (1714-1796), admiral of the fleet; second son of George Forbes, third earl of Granard [q. v.]; commanded the Norfolk at the action off Toulon, 1744; rear-admiral, 1747; commander-in-chief in the Mediterranean, 1749; as a lord of the admiralty refused to sign the warrant for Byng's execution, 1757, and resigned, but was reappointed and held office till 1763; vice-admiral, 1755; admiral of the blue, 1758; general of marines, 1763, admiral of the white, 1770 ; admiral of the fleet, 1781. His 'Memoir of the Earls of Granard' was published in 1868. [xix. 404]

FORBES, JOHN (1733–1808), usually called FORBES-SKELATER ; joined Portuguese service under Lippe-Buckeburg, and became adjutant-general ; general in the Portuguese service, 1789 ; commanded corps in the early Peninsular war, but left for Brazil with Maria Pia, queen of Portugal, prince-regent, and court, when they fled before Junot ; died governor of Rio Janeiro. [xix. 405]

FORBES, JOHN (1799–1823), botanist ; went to east coast of Africa for Horticultural Society, 1822 ; died at Senna ; the genus *Forbesia*, Eckl., named after him. [xix. 405]

FORBES, SIR JOHN (1787–1861), physician ; studied at Aberdeen and Edinburgh ; assistant-surgeon in navy, 1807 ; M.D. Edinburgh, 1817 ; practised at Penzance, Chichester, and London ; became physician to the queen's household, 1840 ; F.R.C.S., 1845 ; hon. D.C.L. Oxford, 1852 ; knighted, 1853 ; joint-editor of a 'Cyclopædia of Practical Medicine,' 1832–5, and chief founder of the ' British and Foreign Medical Review,' 1836–47 ; published 'Illustrations of Modern Mesmerism,' 1845, and 'Nature and Art in the Cure of Disease,' 1857, also translations of Laennec's ' Mediate Auscultation,' 1821, and Auenbrugger's work on the stethoscope, 1824. [xix. 405]

FORBES, JOHN HAY, LORD MEDWYN (1776–1854), Scottish judge ; second son of Sir William Forbes [q. v.] ; a lord of session, 1825 ; lord of justiciary, 1830–47 ; edited 'Thoughts concerning Man's Condition,' by Alexander, fourth baron Forbes [q. v.], with life of the author. [xix. 407]

FORBES, PATRICK (1564–1635), of Corse, bishop of Aberdeen ; studied at Glasgow and St. Andrews ; with Andrew Melville visited Oxford and Cambridge ; ordained minister of Keith, 1610 ; bishop of Aberdeen, 1618–35 ; opposed the church policy of Charles I ; published commentary on the Apocalypse, 1612. [xix. 407]

FORBES, PATRICK (1611 ?–1680), bishop of Caithness ; third son of John Forbes (1568 ?–1634) [q. v.] ; graduated at Aberdeen, 1631 ; minister of Delft, 1641 ; military chaplain in Holland ; bishop of Caithness, 1662. [xix. 409]

FORBES, ROBERT (1708–1775), bishop of Ross and Caithness ; M.A. Marischal College, Aberdeen, 1726 ; episcopal minister at Leith, 1735 ; arrested as a Jacobite, 1745 ; elected bishop of Ross and Caithness, 1769, though still a Jacobite ; published 'The Lyon in Mourning' (1747–1775), extracts from which were given by R. Chambers in 'Jacobite Memoirs' (1834). His 'Journals' were edited by Rev. J. B. Craven (1886). [xix. 409]

FORBES, WALTER, eighteenth BARON FORBES (1798–1868), son of James Ochoncar Forbes, seventeenth baron [q. v.] ; commanded a company of the Coldstream guards at Waterloo ; benefactor of St. Ninian's Cathedral, Perth. [xix. 410]

FORBES, WILLIAM (1585–1634), first bishop of Edinburgh ; M.A. Marischal College, Aberdeen, 1601 ; professor of logic at Marischal College, 1602–6 ; studied abroad and formed friendships with Grotius and Scaliger ; minister of Aberdeen, 1618, of Edinburgh, 1620 ; soon returned to Aberdeen in consequence of the unpopularity of his high church doctrines ; appointed first bishop of Edinburgh, 1634 ; left in manuscript a Latin work (published, 1758) attempting to harmonise the doctrines dividing the Roman and protestant churches. [xix. 411]

FORBES, SIR WILLIAM (1739–1806), of Pitsligo, banker and author ; entered firm of Coutts at Edinburgh, 1754, and soon became a partner, changing the name to Forbes, Hunter & Co. in 1773 ; took leading part in preparation of Bankruptcy Act of 1783 ; consulted by Pitt, who (1799) offered him an Irish peerage ; acquired Pitsligo estates, 1781 ; a member of Johnson's literary club ; author of ' Memoirs of a Banking House,' 1803, and a 'life' of Beattie, 1806. [xix. 412]

FORBES, WILLIAM ALEXANDER (1855–1883), zoologist ; educated at Winchester, Edinburgh University, and University College, London ; fellow of St. John's College, Cambridge ; prosector to the Zoological Society, London, 1879 ; sailed for Pernambuco, 1880 ; died at Shonga on the Niger ; left valuable papers on the anatomy of birds. [xix. 413]

FORBY, ROBERT (1759–1825), philologist ; fellow of Caius College, Cambridge ; M.A., 1784 ; rector of Fincham, Norfolk, 1789 ; F.L.S., 1798–1801 ; published 'The Vocabulary of East Anglia' (edited by Rev. George Turner, 1830). [xix. 414]

FORCER, FRANCIS, the elder (1650 ?–1705 ?), musical composer ; joint-lessee of Sadler's Wells music gardens, c. 1697 ; several of his songs included in Playford's ' Choyce Ayres and Dialogues.' [xix. 414]

FORCER, FRANCIS, the younger (1675 ?–1743), master of Sadler's Wells, 1724–43. [xix. 415]

FORD. [See also FORDE.]

FORD, ANN (1737–1824). [See THICKNESSE, MRS. ANN.]

FORD, DAVID EVERARD (1797–1875), author and musical composer ; congregational minister at Lymington and Manchester ; published 'Decapolis,' 1840, and other religious works, as well as 'Rudiments of Music,' 1829, and several books of psalm and hymn tunes. [xix. 415]

FORD, EDWARD (*fl.* 1647), ballad and verse writer ; four of his ballads found in the Roxburghe Collection and another in Halliwell's ' Norfolk Anthology.' [xix. 415]

FORD, SIR EDWARD (1605–1670), royalist soldier and inventor ; educated at Trinity College, Oxford ; knighted, 1643 ; surrendered Arundel Castle after seventeen days' siege, 1644 ; imprisoned and incapacitated ; escaped to the continent ; returned to negotiate with the army, 1647 ; again imprisoned ; devised an engine for raising the Thames water into the higher streets of London, 1656 ; with Thomas Toogood constructed other water-engines ; died in Ireland, where he had a patent for coining farthings by a new process. [xix. 416]

FORD, EDWARD (1746–1809), surgeon to the Westminster Dispensary, 1780–1801 ; F.S.A., 1792 ; published 'Observations on the Disease of the Hip Joint,' 1794, reissued by his nephew, Thomas Copeland [q. v.], 1810–18. [xix. 417]

FORD, EMANUEL (*fl.* 1607), romance writer ; author of 'Parismus' or 'Parismenos' (1598–9), frequently reprinted till 1704, and two similar works reissued as chap-books. [xix. 417]

FORD, SIR FRANCIS CLARE (1828–1899), diplomatist ; son of Richard Ford [q. v.] ; entered diplomatic service, 1851, and was secretary of embassy at St. Petersburg, 1871, and Vienna, 1872 ; British agent on commission on United States fishery rights, Halifax, 1877 ; C.B. and C.M.G., 1878 ; British minister in Argentine Republic, 1878, Brazil, 1879, Athens, 1881, Madrid, 1884 ; ambassador at Madrid, 1887, Constantinople, 1892, and Rome, 1893–8 ; G.C.M.G., 1886 ; privy councillor, 1888 ; G.C.B., 1889. [Suppl. ii. 224]

FORD, SIR HENRY (1619 ?–1684), Irish secretary ; M.P. for Tiverton, 1664–81 ; secretary to Lord Robartes, viceroy of Ireland, 1669–70, and to the Earl of Essex, 1672, when he was knighted ; F.R.S., 1663. [xix. 418]

FORD, JAMES (1779–1850), antiquary ; fellow of Trinity College, Oxford, 1807 ; M.A., 1804 ; B.D., 1812 ; vicar of Navestock, 1830–50 ; left bequests to Trinity College and Oxford University ; made collections for a new edition of Morant's 'Essex' (at Trinity), and collection for a history of bishops (in British Museum). [xix. 419]

FORD, JOHN (*fl.* 1639), dramatist ; admitted at the Middle Temple, 1602 ; probably spent his last years in Devonshire ; his chief plays, the ' Lovers Melancholy,' 1629, ' 'Tis Pity Shee's a Whore,' 1633, 'The Broken Heart,' 1633, the 'Chronicle Historie of Perkin Warbeck,' 1634, and 'The Ladies Triall,' 1638 ; collaborated with Dekker and Rowley in the 'Witch of Edmonton ' (1624). Four unpublished pieces were destroyed by Bishop Warburton's cook. The best edition of his collected works is Dyce's reissue of Gifford's edition (1869). [xix. 419]

FORD, MICHAEL (*d.* 1758 ?), mezzotint engraver ; probably drowned in the Dublin Trader between Parkgate and Dublin ; his engraved portraits, including Kneller's William III and Hudson's George II, and some from his own paintings (William III and Schomberg), are rare. [xix. 421]

FORD, RICHARD (1796–1858), critic and author; educated at Winchester and Trinity College, Oxford; M.A., 1822; spent several years making riding tours in Spain; contributed from 1837 to the 'Quarterly,' 'Edinburgh,' and 'Westminster' reviews; published 'Handbook for Travellers in Spain,' 1845, 'Gatherings from Spain,' 1846, and other works; his articles first brought Velasquez into notice in England. [xix. 421]

FORD, ROGER OF (*fl.* 1170 ?). [See ROGER.]

FORD, SIMON (1619 ?–1699), divine; of Magdalen College, Oxford, from which he was expelled for puritanism; restored by parliamentary visitors; made delegate, and created B.D., 1650; afterwards vicar of St. Lawrence, Reading, All Saints, Northampton, and St. Mary Aldermanbury; vicar of Old Swinford, 1676–91; published, with other works, three Latin poems on the fire of London. [xix. 422]

FORD, STEPHEN (*d.* 1694), nonconformist divine; ejected from Chipping Norton vicarage, 1662; minister for thirty years in Miles Lane, Cannon Street; subscribed John Faldo's 'Quakerism no Christianity,' 1675; published theological tracts. [xix. 423]

FORD, THOMAS (*d.* 1648), composer; musician to Henry, prince of Wales; published 'Musicke of Sundrie Kindes' (Book I of songs, Book II of instrumental pieces), 1607, and contributed anthems and canons to Leighton's and Hilton's compilations. [xix. 424]

FORD, THOMAS (1598–1674), nonconformist divine; M.A. Magdalen Hall, Oxford, 1627; expelled the university for a puritan sermon, 1631; sometime minister at Hamburg; minister of Aldwinkle All Saints, Northamptonshire, 1637, of St. Faith's, London, and afterwards at Exeter; member of the Westminster Assembly, 1644; published theological works. [xix. 424]

FORD or **FOORD**, WILLIAM (*fl.* 1616), divine; fellow of Trinity College, Cambridge, 1581; M.A., 1582; B.D., 1591; chaplain to the Levant Company at Constantinople; returned, 1614. [xix. 426]

FORD, WILLIAM (1771–1832), bookseller and bibliographer; successively of Manchester and Liverpool; the original edition of Venus and Adonis contained in his first catalogue, 1805; others issued, 1807, 1810–11; contributed to 'Bibliographiana' (Manchester, 1817) and the 'Retrospective Review.' [xix. 426]

FORDE, FRANCIS (*d.* 1770), conqueror of Masulipatam; second in command to Clive in Bengal, 1758; took Masulipatam with a small force and drove the French from the Deccan, 1759; defeated the Dutch at Chinsurah; one of the supervisors sent out in 1769 by the East India Company, who disappeared. [xix. 426]

FORDE, SAMUEL (1805–1828), painter; master in the Cork Mechanics' Institute; friend of Maclise; painted 'Vision of Tragedy' and a crucifixion for Skibbereen chapel. [xix. 427]

FORDE, THOMAS (*d.* 1582), Roman catholic divine; fellow of Trinity College, Oxford; M.A. Trinity College, Oxford, 1567; B.D. of Douay, 1576; executed on charge of conspiracy; beatified, 1886. [xix. 428]

FORDE, THOMAS (*fl.* 1660), author; his 'Times Anatomized' (1647) wrongly attributed to Fuller; published also 'Lusus Fortunæ,' 1649, and 'Virtus Rediviva,' 1660. [xix. 428]

FORDHAM, GEORGE (1837–1887), jockey; won the Cambridgeshire on Little David, 1853; headed the list of winning jockeys, 1855–62, scoring 165 wins in the last year; won the Oaks five times, the Cambridgeshire (Sabinus), 1871, and the Derby (Sir Bevys), 1879; gained the Grand Prix de Paris four times, the French Derby twice, and the French Oaks once. [xix. 429]

FORDUN, JOHN (*d.* 1384?), part author of the 'Scotichronicon'; probably a chantry priest at Aberdeen; said to have collected materials in England and Ireland, as well as Scotland, 1363–84; compiled also 'Gesta Annalia' in continuation of the 'Scotichronicon.' [xix. 430]

FORDYCE, ALEXANDER (*d.* 1789), banker; son of the provost of Aberdeen; partner in London firm of Neale, James, Fordyce & Down; absconded, 1772, after which the bank stopped payment, causing a great panic. [xix. 431]

FORDYCE, DAVID (1711–1751), professor at Aberdeen; brother of Alexander Fordyce [q. v.]; M.A. Marischal College, Aberdeen, 1728; professor of moral philosophy, 1742–51; perished in a storm off the coast of Holland; published his 'Dialogues concerning Education' (1745–8, anon.) and 'Elements of Moral Philosophy' (1754), besides posthumous works. [xix. 432]

FORDYCE, GEORGE (1736–1802), physician; M.D. Edinburgh, 1758; lectured in London on chemistry, materia medica, and practical physic; physician at St. Thomas's Hospital, 1770–1802; F.R.S., 1776; F.R.C.P., *speciali gratia*, 1787; published 'Elements of Physic' (1768–70), 'Treatise on Digestion,' 1791, and five important dissertations on fever, besides chemical works. [xix. 432]

FORDYCE, JAMES (1720–1796), presbyterian divine; uncle of George Fordyce [q. v.]; M.A. Aberdeen, 1753; D.D. Glasgow; minister of Brechin, 1745, Alloa, 1753, and Monkwell Street, London, 1760–82; friend of Dr. Johnson, whose religious character he described in his 'Addresses to the Deity,' 1785. [xix. 433]

FORDYCE, Sir WILLIAM (1724–1792), physician; brother of David, James, and Alexander Fordyce [q. v.]; an army surgeon in war of 1742–8; began to practise in London, 1750; M.D. Cambridge, 1770; knighted, 1787; lord rector of Aberdeen (Marischal College) at death. Some of his works were translated into German. [xix. 435]

FOREST, JOHN (1474?–1538), martyr; member of Franciscan houses at Greenwich and Watergate, Oxford; as confessor of Catherine of Arragon displeased Henry VIII and was removed, 1533; subsequently imprisoned; burnt at Smithfield for his book against the king's assumption of the headship of the church, Bishop Latimer being present. [xix. 435]

FORESTER, JAMES (*fl.* 1611), theological and medical writer; M.A. Clare Hall, Cambridge, 1583; indicted for writing against the queen's prerogative in church matters, 1593; published 'The Pearle of Practise,' 1594, and 'Marrow and Juice of 260 Scriptures,' 1611. [xix. 436]

FORFAR, EARLS OF. [See DOUGLAS, ARCHIBALD, first EARL, 1653–1712; DOUGLAS, ARCHIBALD, second EARL, 1693–1715.]

FORGAILL, DALLAN (*fl.* 600). [See DALLAN.]

FORGLEN, LORD (*d.* 1727). [See OGILVY, SIR ALEXANDER.]

FORMAN, ANDREW (*d.* 1522), archbishop of St. Andrews; as protonotary attended Perkin Warbeck in Scotland, 1495–6; one of the ambassadors to Henry VII, 1498; negotiated marriage of James IV and Margaret Tudor, 1501; bishop of Moray, 1502; ambassador in England, 1509; negotiated alliance between Louis XII and Pope Julius II; archbishop of Bourges, 1513–15; archbishop of St. Andrews after much opposition, 1516; author of 'Contra Lutherum,' 'De Stoica Philosophia,' and 'Collectanea Decretalium'; documents relating to him printed in Robertson's notes to 'Scotiæ Concilia.' [xix. 436]

FORMAN, SIMON (1552–1611), astrologer and quack doctor; left destitute by his father; entered Magdalen College, Oxford, as a 'poor scholar,' 1573; claimed miraculous powers, c. 1579; began to practise as a quack in London, 1580; finally set up in London as an astrologer, 1583; obtained a large disreputable practice, chiefly among court ladies; frequently imprisoned at the instance of medical and other authorities; began to practise necromancy, 1588; granted a license to practise medicine by Cambridge University, 1603; his philtres referred to in Ben Jonson's 'Epicene'; published 'The Grounds of the Longitude,' 1591. Among his manuscripts which came into possession of Ashmole, 'The Bocke of Plaies' contains the earliest account of the performances of 'Macbeth' (1610), the 'Winter's Tale' (1611), and 'Cymbeline.' [xix. 438]

FORREST, ARTHUR (*d.* 1770), commodore; served on West Indian and South American stations; captured merchant fleet off Petit Guave, 1758; died holding Jamaica command. [xx. 1]

FORREST, EBENEZER (*fl.* 1774), attorney; author of 'An Account of what seemed most remarkable in the five days' peregrination of Messrs. Tothall, Scott, Hogarth, Thornhill, and F.' (1782), illustrated by Hogarth. [xx. 2]

FORREST or **FORRES**, HENRY (d. 1533 ?), Scottish martyr ; friar of the Benedictine order ; burned as a heretic at St. Andrews for words spoken in approval of Patrick Hamilton. [xx. 2]

FORREST, JOHN (1474 ?-1538). [See FOREST.]

FORREST, ROBERT (1789 ?-1852), sculptor ; stonemason in Clydesdale : executed the colossal figure of Lord Melville in St. Andrew's Square, Edinburgh, the statue of Knox in the Glasgow necropolis, and that of Mr. Ferguson of Raith at Haddington. [xx. 2]

FORREST, THEODOSIUS (1728-1784), author and lawyer ; son of Ebenezer Forrest [q. v.] ; exhibited at the Royal Academy, 1762-81 ; solicitor to Covent Garden Theatre and friend of Garrick and Colman ; committed suicide. [xx. 2]

FORREST, THOMAS (d. 1540). [See FORRET.]

FORREST, THOMAS (fl. 1580), translator of three orations of Isocrates, 1580. [xx. 3]

FORREST, THOMAS (1729 ?-1802 ?), navigator ; formed for the East India Company new settlement at Balambangan, 1770 ; surveyed coasts of New Guinea and Sulu Archipelago, being the first to place accurately Waygiou on the chart, 1774-6 ; discovered Forrest Strait, 1790 ; published 'Journal of the Esther Brig . . . from Bengal to Quedah,' 1783, and 'Voyage from Calcutta to the Mergui Archipelago,' 1792 ; also wrote 'Treatise on the Monsoons in East India.' [xx. 3]

FORREST, WILLIAM (fl. 1581), Roman catholic priest and poet ; of Christ Church, Oxford ; afterwards one of Queen Mary's chaplains ; his compilation from the 'De Regimine Principum' and his paraphrase of the Psalms dedicated to the Duke of Somerset. His 'Second Gresyld,' a narrative in verse of the divorce of Queen Catherine of Arragon, was printed, 1875. [xx. 4]

FORRESTER, ALFRED HENRY (1804-1872), artist ; worked with his brother, Charles Robert Forrester [q.v.r.], under name of 'Alfred Crowquill' ; exhibited pen-and-ink sketches at the Royal Academy ; contributed sketches (1845) to 'Punch' and the 'Illustrated London News,' and woodcuts to Chambers's 'Book of Days' ; published more than twenty humorous works written and illustrated by himself ; illustrated his brother's works, also 'The Tour of Dr. Syntax,' 1838, Albert R. Smith's 'Beauty and the Beast,' 1843, the Bon Gaultier 'Ballads,' 1849, Cuthbert Bede's 'Fairy Tales,' 1858, 'The Travels of Baron Munchausen,' 1859, and 'Six Plates of Pickwickian Sketches.' [xx. 5]

FORRESTER, CHARLES ROBERT (1803-1850), miscellaneous writer ; elder brother of Alfred Henry Forrester [q. v.] ; published, under the pseudonym 'Hal Willis,' 'Castle Baynard,' 1824, and 'Sir Roland,' 1827, two novels ; contributed to 'Bentley's Miscellany,' as 'A. Crowquill,' his chief articles being reissued (1843) as 'Phantasmagoria of Fun.' 'Absurdities in Prose and Verse,' by 'Alfred Crowquill' (1827), was the joint work of the brothers Forrester. [xx. 7]

FORRESTER, DAVID (1588-1633), Scottish divine ; M.A. St. Andrews, 1608 ; deposed from pastorate of North Leith for opposition to the five articles of Perth ; restored, 1627. [xx. 7]

FORRESTER, JOSEPH JAMES, BARON DE FORRESTER in Portugal (1809-1861), merchant and wineshipper ; went to Oporto, 1831 ; published chart of the Douro from Vilvestre to its mouth, with geological survey and maps of the port-wine districts, 1848 ; exerted himself to obtain reforms in the making and exportation of the wine ; published prize essay on Portugal, 1851 ; drowned in the Douro ; still known as 'Protector of the Douro.' [xx. 8]

FORRESTER, THOMAS (1588 ?-1642), satirist of covenanters ; M.A. St. Andrews, 1608 ; minister of Ayr, 1623, of Melrose, 1627-38 ; deposed for Arminianism ; his satire included in Maidment's 'Book of Scottish Pasquils,' 1828. [xx. 9]

FORRESTER, THOMAS (1635 ?-1706), Scottish theologian ; renounced episcopacy and became a field preacher ;

deposed and imprisoned, 1674 ; minister of Killearn and St. Andrews after the Revolution ; principal of the new college at St. Andrews, 1698 ; wrote 'The Hierarchical Bishop's Claim to a Divine Right tried at the Scripture Bar,' 1699. [xx. 9]

FORRET, THOMAS (d. 1540), Scottish martyr ; studied at Cologne ; canon regular in the monastery of Inchcolm ; when vicar of Dollar, Clackmannanshire, was accused by the friars of heresy ; eventually burned at Edinburgh with four others. [xx. 9]

FORS, WILLIAM DE, EARL OF ALBEMARLE (d. 1242). [See WILLIAM.]

FORS, WILLIAM DE, EARL OF ALBEMARLE (d. 1260). [See WILLIAM.]

FORSETT, EDWARD (d. 1630 ?), political writer ; active as justice of the peace in examination of the Gunpowder plot conspirators ; published 'A Comparative Discovrse of the Bodies Natvral and Politiqve,' 1606, and 'A Defence of the Right of Kings,' 1624, in answer to Robert Parsons. [xx. 10]

FORSHALL, JOSIAH (1795-1863), librarian ; fellow and tutor of Exeter College, Oxford ; keeper of manuscript department, British Museum, 1827-37 ; F.R.S., 1828 ; secretary to the Museum, 1828-50 ; chaplain of the Foundling Hospital, 1829-63 ; edited catalogue of manuscripts (new series), the 'Description of the Greek Papyri,' and catalogues of some of the oriental and Syriac manuscripts ; published editions of the Gospels. [xx. 11]

FORSTER, BENJAMIN (1736-1805), antiquary ; fellow of Corpus Christi College, Cambridge, 1760 ; M.A., 1760 ; B.D., 1768 ; friend of Gray, Mason, and Gough ; rector of Boconnoc, Broadoak, and Cherichayes, Cornwall, 1770. [xx. 11]

FORSTER, BENJAMIN MEGGOT (1764-1829), man of science ; second son of Edward Forster the elder [q. v.] ; published under initials 'Introduction to the Knowledge of Funguses,' 1820 ; invented sliding portfolio and atmospherical electroscope ; one of the first members of the anti-slave trade committee, 1788 ; framed the Child Stealing Act. [xx. 12]

FORSTER, EDWARD, the elder (1730-1812), banker and antiquary ; while in Holland received from his relative, Benjamin Furly, some original letters of Locke ; for nearly thirty years governor of the Russia Company ; consulted by Pitt on paper currency. [xx. 12]

FORSTER, EDWARD (1769-1828), miscellaneous writer ; son of Nathaniel Forster (1726 ?-1790) [q. v.] ; matriculated at Balliol College, Oxford, 1788 ; M.A. St. Mary Hall, Oxford, 1797 ; morning preacher at Berkeley and Grosvenor chapels, and at Park Street and King Street, 1800-14 ; chaplain to the British embassy at Paris, 1818-1828, where he died ; published the 'British Gallery of Engravings,' 1807-13, editions of Jarvis's 'Don Quixote,' 1801, Galland's 'Arabian Nights,' Anacreon, 'Rasselas,' 1805, and various illustrated dramatic collections. [xx. 13]

FORSTER, EDWARD, the younger (1765-1849), botanist ; third son of Edward Forster the elder [q. v.] ; treasurer of the Linnean Society, 1816, and vice-president, 1828 ; died from cholera, after inspecting the Refuge for the Destitute founded by him in Hackney Road. Besides a catalogue of British birds, he printed a 'Supplement to English Botany,' 1834. His herbarium was presented to the British Museum. [xx. 14]

FORSTER, GEORGE (d. 1792), traveller in service of the East India Company ; author of 'A Journey from Bengal to England through the Northern Part of India . . . and into Russia by the Caspian Sea,' 1798, and 'Sketches of the Mythology and Customs of the Hindoos,' 1785. [xx. 14]

FORSTER, HENRY PITTS (1766 ?-1815), orientalist in service of the East India Company ; helped to make Bengali an official and literary language by his 'English and Bengalee Vocabulary,' 1799, 1802. [xx. 14]

FORSTER, JOHANN GEORG ADAM, known as GEORGE (1754-1794), naturalist ; born near Dantzig ; came to England with his father, Reinhold Forster, 1766 ; assisted him as naturalist in Captain Cook's second voyage, and was made F.R.S. for his share in the description of the flora of the South Seas, 1775 ; published a general account of the voyage, 1777 ; afterwards successively professor of natural history at Wilna and librarian at Mainz. [xx. 15]

FORSTER or **FOSTER**, SIR JOHN (1520 ?-1602), warden of the marches ; commander of Harbottle Castle, 1542 ; fought at Solway Moss, 1542, and Pinkie, 1547 ; knighted by Protector Somerset, 1547 ; sheriff of Northumberland, 1549-50 ; captain of Bamborough Castle, 1555 till death ; warden of middle marches, 1560-95 ; dismissed from office, 1586, on charges of maladministration ; restored, 1588. [Suppl. ii. 225]

FORSTER, JOHN (1812-1876), historian and biographer ; educated at Newcastle grammar school and University College, London ; barrister, Inner Temple, 1843 ; made the acquaintance of Lamb and Leigh Hunt ; dramatic critic to the 'Examiner,' 1833 ; contributed to Lardner's 'Cyclopædia ' his ' Lives of the Statesmen of the Commonwealth,' 1836-9, that of Sir John Eliot being issued separately in an enlarged form, 1864 ; edited ' Foreign Quarterly Review,' 1842-3, 'Daily News,' 1846, and ' Examiner,' 1847-55 ; secretary to the lunacy commission, 1855-61, and a lunacy commissioner, 1861-72 ; took part in dramatic performances in connection with Guild of Literature and Art ; contributed to ' Quarterly ' and ' Edinburgh Review ' ; published works, including 'Historical and Biographical Essays,' 1858, ' The Arrest of the Five Members,' and 'The Debates on the Grand Remonstrance,' 1860, lives of his friends Landor (1869) and Dickens, 1872-4, ' Life and Times of Goldsmith,' 1854, and the first volume of a ' Life of Swift,' 1876 ; bequeathed his valuable library and art treasures to the Victoria and Albert Museum, South Kensington. [xx. 16]

FORSTER, JOHN COOPER (1823-1886), surgeon ; educated at King's College School and Guy's Hospital ; M.B. London, 1847 ; F.R.C.S., 1849 ; surgeon at Guy's, 1870-80 ; president of the College of Surgeons, 1884-5 ; published ' The Surgical Diseases of Children,' 1860. [xx. 19]

FORSTER, NATHANIEL (1718 - 1757), scholar ; educated at Eton and Corpus Christi College, Oxford ; fellow, 1739 ; M.A., 1739 ; D.D., 1750 ; domestic chaplain to Bishop Butler from 1750 till Butler's death, and executor ; chaplain to Archbishop Herring ; vicar of Rochdale, 1754 ; prebendary of Bristol, 1755 ; F.R.S., 1755 ; chaplain to George III, 1756 ; published ' Reflections on the Natural Foundation of the high Antiquity of Government, Arts, and Sciences in Egypt,' 1743, 'Appendix Liviana,' 1746, a defence of the genuineness of Josephus's account of Jesus, 1749, ' Biblia Hebraica sine punctis,' 1750, and other works. [xx. 19]

FORSTER, NATHANIEL (1726 ?-1790), writer on political economy ; cousin of Nathaniel Forster (1718-1757) [q. v.] ; M.A. Magdalen College, Oxford, 1748 ; fellow of Balliol College, Oxford ; D.D., 1778 ; rector of All Saints, Colchester, and of Tolleshunt Knights, Essex ; friend of Samuel Parr the Latin scholar ; chief works, ' An Enquiry into the Causes of the present High Price of Provisions,' 1767, and 'Answer to Sir John Dalrymple's pamphlet on the Exportation of Wool,' 1782. [xx. 20]

FORSTER, RICHARD (1546 ?-1616), physician : M.D. Oxford, 1573; president of the College of Physicians, 1601-1604 and 1615-16 ; Lumleian lecturer, 1602 ; published ' Ephemerides Meteorologicæ,' 1575. [xx. 21]

FORSTER, SIR ROBERT (1589-1663). [See FOSTER.]

FORSTER, SIMON ANDREW (1801-1870), part author of the ' History of the Violin,' 1864 ; son of William Forster (1764-1824) [q. v.] [xx. 24]

FORSTER, THOMAS (fl. 1695-1712), limner, known for his excellent pencil miniatures on vellum engraved by Van der Gucht and others. [xx. 21]

FORSTER, THOMAS (1675 ?-1738), James Edward the Old Pretender's general ; M.P., Northumberland, 1708-16 ; surrendered at Preston when in command of the rebel army ; escaped from Newgate, 1716, to France ; died at Boulogne. [xx. 21]

FORSTER, THOMAS FURLY (1761 - 1825), botanist ; eldest son of Edward Forster the elder [q. v.] ; an original member of the Linnean Society ; published ' Flora Tonbrigensis,' 1816 (reissued 1842). [xx. 22]

FORSTER, THOMAS IGNATIUS MARIA (1789-1860), naturalist and astronomer ; son of Thomas Furly Forster [q. v.] ; M.B. Cambridge, 1819 ; discovered a comet, 1819 ; with Spurzheim studied the brain at Edinburgh, and subsequently wrote a sketch of the phrenological system ; published ' Researches about Atmospheric Phenomena,' 1812, original letters of Locke, Shaftesbury, and Algernon Sydney to his ancestor, Benjamin Furly [q. v.], with preface, 1830, ' Observations sur l'Influence des Comètes,' 1836, and ' Sati,' 1843, a Pythagorean treatise. He was the friend of Gray, Shelley, Herschel, and Whewell ; lived at Bruges after 1833, dying at Brussels. His ' Recueil de ma Vie,' 1835, and 'Epistolarium Forsterianum ' contain much biographical information. [xx. 22]

FORSTER, WILLIAM (fl. 1632), mathematician ; pupil of William Oughtred [q. v.], whose treatise on the horizontal instrument for delineating dials upon any plane he translated and published, 1632. [xx. 24]

FORSTER, WILLIAM (1739-1808), musical instrument maker ('Old Forster ') : set up a violin shop near St. Martin's Lane, London, removing afterwards to the Strand. As a publisher he introduced Haydn to the London public. [xx. 24]

FORSTER, WILLIAM (1764-1824), violin-maker ; music-seller to the Prince of Wales and the Duke of Cumberland ; son of William Forster (1739-1808) [q. v.] [xx. 24]

FORSTER, WILLIAM (1788-1824), violin-maker ; son of William Forster (1764-1824) [q.v.] [xx. 24]

FORSTER, WILLIAM (1784-1854), minister of the Society of Friends ; helped his sister-in-law, Elizabeth Fry [q. v.], in philanthropic work ; visited United States, 1820-5 ; checked the spread of unitarian views among quakers ; averted a secession in Indiana caused by the slavery question, 1845 ; investigated the condition of the Irish distressed by the potato famine, 1846-7 ; travelled on the continent in the interests of abolitionism, 1849-52 ; died in East Tennessee ; published ' Christian Exhortation to Sailors ' (1813). [xx. 24]

FORSTER, WILLIAM EDWARD (1818-1886), statesman ; son of William Forster (1784-1854) [q. v.] ; educated at quaker schools in Bristol and Tottenham ; entered woollen trade at Bradford, 1842 ; accompanied his father to Ireland, 1846 ; did much to moderate the chartists in Bradford, lecturing on 'Pauperism and its Proposed Remedies,' 1848 ; reissued Clarkson's ' Life of Penn ' with a preface defending the quakers from Macaulay's charges, 1849 ; left the society on his marriage in 1850 with a daughter of Dr. Arnold ; liberal M.P. for Bradford, 1861-86 ; under-secretary for the colonies, 1865 ; took prominent part in reform debates, 1866-7 ; as vice-president of the council (1868-74), carried the Endowed Schools Bill, the Elementary Education Bill, and in 1871 had charge of the Ballot Bill ; proposed as leader of the opposition, 1874 ; gave way to Lord Hartington ; returned as an independent liberal, 1880 ; appointed by Mr. Gladstone chief secretary for Ireland, 1880 ; failed to carry the Compensation for Disturbance Bill and to obtain the conviction of the leaders of the land league ; resigned office after two years' struggle with them and his opponents in the cabinet whose ' Kilmainham treaty ' he refused to sanction ; again offered his services after the Phœnix Park murders (1882), but never again held office ; during his last four years generally opposed liberal foreign policy, but supported county franchise bill ; first chairman of the Imperial Federation League and of the committee on the Manchester Ship Canal Bill. [xx. 25]

FORSYTH, ALEXANDER JOHN (1769-1843), inventor of the percussion lock, for which he was awarded a pension, after declining 20,000l. from Napoleon to reveal the secret ; LL.D. Glasgow. [xx. 31]

FORSYTH, JAMES (1838-1871), Indian traveller and civilian ; M.A. ; published ' The Sporting Rifle and its Projectiles,' 1862, and a posthumous work describing his tour of the central provinces. [xx. 31]

FORSYTH, JOSEPH (1763-1815), schoolmaster and author ; M.A. King's College, Aberdeen, 1779 ; a prisoner in France, 1803-14 ; published valuable ' Remarks on Antiquities, Arts, and Letters, during an Excursion in Italy in the years 1802 and 1803,' 1813. [xx. 32]

FORSYTH, ROBERT (1766–1846), miscellaneous writer; published, among other works, 'The Beauties of Scotland,' 1805–8, and 'Remarks on the Church of Scotland,' 1843, the latter being severely handled by Hugh Miller in the 'Witness.' [xx. 33]

FORSYTH, SIR THOMAS DOUGLAS (1827–1886), Indian civilian; educated at Sherborne, Rugby, Haileybury, and Calcutta; rendered valuable services at Umballa, 1857, and as special commissioner after the capture of Delhi; created C.B. for his conduct in the mutiny; commissioner of the Punjab, 1860–72; promoted trade with Turkestan, and obtained definition in favour of the amir of Kabul of territories in dispute between him and the Russian government; visited the amir of Yarkand; removed (1872) for measures taken to suppress Ram Singh's rebellion; as envoy to Kashgar, 1873, concluded commercial treaty with the amir; obtained from the king of Burmah agreement that the Karenee States should be acknowledged independent; K.C.S.I. [xx. 33]

FORSYTH, WILLIAM (1722–1800), merchant; made Cromarty, his native town, a great trading centre by introducing flax from Holland and coal from Leith (1770) and originating the manufacture of kelp; an agent of the British Linen Company; eulogised by Hugh Miller. [xx. 34]

FORSYTH, WILLIAM (1737–1804), gardener; succeeded Philip Miller in the Apothecaries' Garden, Chelsea, 1771; superintendent of the royal gardens at St. James' and Kensington, 1784; published 'Observations on the Diseases, &c., of Forest and Fruit Trees,' 1791, and 'Treatise on the Culture of Fruit Trees,' 1802; thanked by parliament for his tree-plaister. [xx. 35]

FORSYTH, WILLIAM (1818–1879), poet and journalist; sub-editor of the 'Inverness Courier' under Carruthers; for thirty years editor of the 'Aberdeen Journal'; assisted in preparation of 'Chambers's Cyclopædia of English Literature'; published 'The Martyrdom of Kelavane,' 1861; and 'Idylls and Lyrics.' [xx. 35]

FORSYTH, WILLIAM (1812–1899), man of letters; B.A. Trinity College, Cambridge, 1834; major fellow and M.A., 1837; barrister, Inner Temple, 1839; bencher, 1857; treasurer, 1872; went Midland circuit; standing counsel for secretary of state for India, 1859–72; member of council of legal education from 1860; conservative M.P. for Marylebone, 1874–80; editor of 'Annual Register,' 1842–68; Q.C., 1857; commissary of Cambridge University, 1868; LL.D. Edinburgh, 1871. His works include 'Hortensius,' 1849, 'History of Captivity of Napoleon at St. Helena,' 1853, 'Life of Cicero,' 1863, 'Novels and Novelists of Eighteenth Century,' 1871, and 'Essays Critical and Narrative,' 1874. [Suppl. ii. 226]

FORTESCUE OF CREDAN, first BARON (1670–1746). [See ALAND, SIR JOHN FORTESCUE.]

FORTESCUE, SIR ADRIAN (1476?–1539), knight of St. John; served against the French, 1513 and 1522; knighted, 1528; knight of St. John, 1532; attainted and executed on a charge of treason, probably on account of his relationship to Queen Anne Boleyn. [xx. 36]

FORTESCUE, SIR ANTHONY (b. 1535?), conspirator; youngest son of Sir Adrian Fortescue [q. v.]; comptroller of the household to Cardinal Pole; arrested on accession of Elizabeth; imprisoned for life for a plot in conjunction with the Poles to proclaim Mary Queen of Scots and restore Romanism by the aid of the Duc de Guise, 1561; allowed to escape from the Tower. [xx. 37]

FORTESCUE, afterwards PARKINSON-FORTESCUE, CHICHESTER SAMUEL, BARON CARLINGFORD (1823–1898), statesman; M.A. Christ Church, Oxford, 1847; student, 1843–56; honorary student, 1867; assumed name of Parkinson, 1862; liberal M.P. for Louth, 1847–74; junior lord of treasury, 1854–5; under-secretary for colonies, 1857–8, and 1859–65; privy councillor, 1864; chief secretary for Ireland, 1865–6 and 1868–70; shared with Gladstone burden and credit of Irish church disestablishment and Irish Land Act of 1870; president of board of trade, 1871–4; raised to peerage, 1874; privy seal, 1881–5; assisted in framing, and conducted through House of Lords, Gladstone's second Irish Land Act; president of council, 1883–5; liberal unionist, 1886. [Suppl. ii. 227]

FORTESCUE, SIR EDMUND (1610–1647), royalist commander; when high sheriff of Devonshire defeated and captured at Modbury by Colonel Ruthven, 1642, and imprisoned in Windsor Castle and Winchester House; released, 1643; held Salcombe (Fort Charles) for the king, 1644–6; created baronet, 1644; died at Delft. [xx. 38]

FORTESCUE, SIR FAITHFUL (1581?–1666), royalist commander; obtained grant of property in Antrim and seat in Irish parliament; frequently at issue with Strafford when lord deputy; named governor of Drogheda, 1641, but was in England during the siege; deserted at Edgehill, 1642, when commanding a troop of horse under Wharton, which was diverted from Ireland to serve the parliament; commanded royalist infantry regiment; went abroad after Worcester, 1651; gentleman of the privy chamber, 1660. [xx. 39]

FORTESCUE, GEORGE (1578?–1659), essayist and poet; grandson of Sir Anthony Fortescue [q. v.]; expelled the kingdom when secretary to the resident of the Duke of Lorraine in London, 1647; proposed by Bolton as member of projected royal academy; corresponded with Galilei, Strada, and Thomas Farnaby [q. v.] His works include 'Feriæ Academicæ' (Latin essays), 1630, and 'The Sovles Pilgrimage,' 1650. [xx. 41]

FORTESCUE, SIR HENRY (fl. 1426), lord chief-justice of the common pleas in Ireland, 1426–7; brother to Sir John Fortescue (1394?–1476?) [q. v.]; M.P., Devonshire, 1421; twice deputed by the Irish parliament to make representations in England concerning their grievances. [xx. 42]

FORTESCUE, JAMES (1716–1777), poetical writer; fellow of Exeter College, Oxford; M.A., 1739; D.D., 1751; chaplain of Merton; senior proctor, 1748; rector of Wootton, Northamptonshire, 1764–77; chief work, 'Essays, Moral and Miscellaneous' (1752 and 1754). [xx. 42]

FORTESCUE, SIR JOHN (1394?–1476?), lord chief-justice of the king's bench (1442) and author; 'gubernator' of Lincoln's Inn, 1425, 1426, 1429; serjeant-at-law, 1430; member of commissions concerning disturbances at Norwich and in Yorkshire, 1443; trier of parliamentary petitions, 1445–55; though a member of the court party declined to be influenced by the crown or the peers in Kerver's and Thorpe's cases; attainted by Edward IV as Lancastrian, 1461; followed the deposed family to Scotland and Flanders and returned with Margaret, 1471; captured at Tewkesbury, 1471; pardoned, and made a member of the council on recognising Edward IV, 1471; wrote several treatises in defence of the title of the house of Lancaster, and a disavowal of them in 1471, besides the 'De Laudibus Legum Angliæ' (first printed, 1537), written for Edward, prince of Wales, and 'On the Governance of the Kingdom of England' ('De Dominio Regali et Politico'), first published, 1714. [xx. 42]

FORTESCUE, SIR JOHN (1531?–1607), chancellor of the exchequer; eldest son of Sir Adrian Fortescue [q. v.]; superintended the studies of the Princess Elizabeth, on whose accession he became keeper of the great wardrobe; M.P., Wallingford, 1572, and afterwards for the county and borough of Buckingham and Middlesex; chancellor of the exchequer and privy councillor, 1589; chancellor of the duchy of Lancaster, 1601; deprived of the exchequer by James I, but continued in his other offices; intimate with Burghley, Bacon, Ralegh, and Essex. His disputed election for Buckinghamshire (1604) raised the important constitutional question whether the house or the law courts had jurisdiction over election petitions. He presented books and manuscripts to his friend Sir Thomas Bodley's library. [xx. 45]

FORTESCUE, SIR NICHOLAS, the elder (1575?–1633), chamberlain of the exchequer; harboured David Baker [q. v.], the Benedictine, for several years at Cookhill, his residence; suspected of complicity in the Gunpowder plot, but cleared himself; commissioner of James I's household and of the navy, 1610; knighted, 1618; chamberlain of the exchequer, 1618–25. [xx. 47]

FORTESCUE, SIR NICHOLAS, the younger (1605?–1644), knight of St. John, 1638; fourth son of Sir Nicholas Fortescue the elder [q. v.]; attempted to revive the order in England, as Queen Henrietta Maria desired, 1637; killed fighting for the king, probably at Marston Moor. [xx. 48]

FORTESCUE, RICHARD (*d.* 1655), governor of Jamaica; lieutenant-colonel in parliamentarian army, 1644; colonel in new model, 1645–7; commanded regiment in expedition to West Indies, 1654; commander-in-chief in Jamaica, 1655. [Suppl. ii. 229]

FORTESCUE, THOMAS (1784–1872), Indian civilian; secretary to Henry Wellesley (Lord Cowley) when lieutenant-governor of Oude; civil commissioner at Delhi, 1803. [xx. 48]

FORTESCUE, WILLIAM (1687–1749), master of the rolls, 1741; introduced by his friend Gay to Pope; barrister, Inner Temple, 1715; private secretary to Walpole; M.P. for Newport (Isle of Wight), 1727–36; K.C., 1730; attorney-general to Frederick, prince of Wales, 1730; baron of the exchequer, 1736; justice of common pleas, 1738; legal adviser to Pope, who addressed to him his first satire. [xx. 49]

FORTH, EARL OF (1573?–1651). [See RUTHVEN, PATRICK.]

FORTNUM, CHARLES DRURY EDWARD (1820–1899), art collector; conducted cattle ranch in South Australia, 1840–5; collected works of art in Europe; F.S.A., 1858; made liberal benefactions, 1892, to Oxford University for erection of suitable buildings for accommodating Ashmolean collections, to which he added his own collections, 1888; honorary D.C.L. Oxford, 1889; published a treatise on 'Maiolica,' 1896, and other writings. [Suppl. ii. 229]

FORTREY, SAMUEL (1622–1681), author of 'England's Interest and Improvement, consisting in the increase of the Store and Trade of this Kingdom,' 1663. [xx. 50]

FORTUNE, ROBERT (1813–1880), traveller and botanist; visited China for the Horticultural Society, 1842, and the East India Company, 1848; sent home the double yellow rose, the Japanese anemone, and the *Chamœrops Fortunei* (fan-palm), named after him; visited Formosa and Japan, 1853; published 'Report upon the Tea Plantations of the N.W. Provinces of India,' 1851, 'Two Visits to the Tea Countries of China and the British Plantations in the Himalayas,' 1853, and 'Yeddo and Peking,' 1863. [xx. 50]

FOSBROKE, THOMAS DUDLEY (1770–1842), antiquary; educated at St. Paul's School and Pembroke College, Oxford; M.A., 1792; vicar of Walford, Herefordshire, 1830–42; F.S.A., 1799; published 'British Monachism,' 1802, 'Encyclopædia of Antiquities,' 1825, and 'History of the City of Gloucester,' 1819, &c. [xx. 51]

FOSS, EDWARD (1787–1870), biographer; member of the Inner Temple, 1822; one of the founders of the Incorporated Law Society, and president, 1842–3; under-sheriff of London, 1827–8; F.S.A., 1822; published 'The Judges of England,' 1848–64, and an abridgment of Blackstone, 1820. [xx. 51]

FOSTER, SIR AUGUSTUS JOHN (1780–1848), diplomatist; plenipotentiary to the United States, 1811–12; to Denmark, 1814–24; and to Turin, 1824–40; privy councillor, 1822; M.P., Cockermouth, 1812–14; G.C.H., 1825; created baronet, 1831; committed suicide, 1848. [xx. 52]

FOSTER, HENRY (1796–1831), navigator; surveyed mouth of Columbia and north shore of La Plata, 1819; assisted Basil Hall, 1820; elected F.R.S. 1824, on return from Sabine's voyage to Greenland; astronomer to Parry's polar expeditions, 1824–5 and 1827; Copley medallist, 1826; given command of government sloop Chanticleer to determine specific ellipticity of the earth, 1828; made pendulum experiments in the South Seas, 1828–9; measured the difference of longitude across the isthmus of Panama by rockets, 1830–1; drowned in the river Chagres. [xx. 52]

FOSTER, JAMES (1697–1753), nonconformist divine; ministered successively at Exeter, Milborne Port, Colesford, Trowbridge, the Barbican chapel (1724), and Pinners' Hall (1744); a famous preacher; had controversies with Tindal and Henry Stebbing (1687–1763) [q. v.]; visited Lord Kilmarnock in the Tower, 1746; D.D. Aberdeen, 1748; published 'Discourses on all the Principal Branches of Natural Religion and Social Virtue,' 1749, and other works; refused the Salters' Hall subscription. [xx. 54]

FOSTER, JOHN (1731–1774), upper master of Eton 1765–73; fellow of King's College, Cambridge, and Craven scholar, 1750; M.A., 1756; D.D., 1766; canon of Windsor, 1772; died in Germany; published an essay in defence of the prevailing accentuation of Greek against Vossius and Gally, 1762. [xx. 55]

FOSTER, JOHN, BARON ORIEL (1740–1828), last speaker of the Irish House of Commons, 1785–1800; student, Middle Temple; called to the Irish bar, 1766; M.P., Dunleer, 1761; co. Louth, 1769–1821; chairman of committees and Irish privy councillor; chancellor of the Irish exchequer, 1784, when his corn law was passed, and after the union, 1804–6 and 1807–11; English privy councillor, 1786; opposed Roman Catholic Relief Bill, 1793; and made able speeches against the union, 1799–1800; entered the imperial parliament; created peer of the United Kingdom, 1821. [xx. 56]

FOSTER, JOHN (1770–1843), essayist and baptist minister; a republican and severe critic of the system of ecclesiastical institutions; published 'Essays,' 1804, contributions to the 'Eclectic Review,' and other works. [xx. 57]

FOSTER, JOHN (1787?–1846), architect; studied under Wyatt; discovered sculptures of pediment of temple of Athene at Ægina; designed Liverpool custom house. [xx. 59]

FOSTER, JOHN LESLIE (*d.* 1842), Irish judge; LL.D. Trinity College, Dublin, 1810; B.A., 1800; called to Irish bar, 1803; tory M.P. for Dublin university, 1807–12, Yarmouth (Isle of Wight), 1816–18, Armagh, 1818–20, Louth county, 1824–30; F.R.S., 1819; baron of the exchequer, 1830; judge of common pleas, 1842; published 'Essay on the Principles of Commercial Exchanges, particularly between England and Ireland,' 1804. [xx. 59]

FOSTER, SIR MICHAEL (1689–1763), judge; entered Exeter College, Oxford, 1705; barrister, Middle Temple, 1713; recorder of Bristol, 1735; serjeant-at-law, 1736; judge of king's bench, 1745; established right of the city of Bristol to try capital offences committed within its jurisdiction in case of Samuel Goodere [q. v.]; at trial of Broadfoot pronounced impressment to be legal; eulogised in the 'Rosciad'; published legal works. [xx. 60]

FOSTER, MYLES BIRKET (1825–1899), painter; engaged independently as illustrator, 1846–58; executed illustrations for editions of poets and prose-writers; devoted himself to painting from 1858; exhibited at Royal Academy from 1859; R.A., 1862. His pictures, chiefly in water-colour, were principally studies of roadside and woodland scenery. [Suppl. ii. 230]

FOSTER, PETER LE NEVE (1809–1879), secretary to the Society of Arts (1853–79); educated at Norwich grammar school and Trinity Hall, Cambridge; B.A., 1830; fellow, 1830; barrister, 1836; helped to organise exhibitions of 1851 and 1862; secretary to mechanical science section of British Association; a chief founder of the Photographic Society. [xx. 61]

FOSTER, SIR ROBERT (1589–1663), lord chief-justice, 1660–3; barrister, Inner Temple, 1610; serjeant-at-law, 1636; justice of common pleas, 1640–3; D.C.L. Oxford, 1643; removed after trial of Captain Turpin, 1644; during Commonwealth practised as chamber counsel; restored, 1660, and made chief-justice for zeal in trial of regicides; procured execution of Sir Harry Vane. [xx. 61]

FOSTER, SAMUEL (*d.* 1652), mathematician; M.A. Emmanuel College, Cambridge, 1623; Gresham professor of astronomy, 1636, and 1641–52; one of the company which preceded the Royal Society; published 'The Use of the Quadrant,' 1624, and 'The Art of Dialling,' 1638; other works by him published posthumously. [xx. 62]

FOSTER, THOMAS (1798–1826), painter; intimate with Lawrence and Nollekens; executed a portrait of H. R. Bishop [q. v.]; and exhibited at the Academy 'Mazeppa,' 1823, and 'Paul and Virginia before their Separation,' 1825; committed suicide. [xx. 63]

FOSTER, THOMAS CAMPBELL (1813–1882), legal writer; barrister, Middle Temple, 1846; Q.C. and bencher, 1875; recorder of Warwick, 1874; leading counsel for the crown at the trial of Charles Peace; published 'Letters on the Condition of the People of Ireland,' 1846 ; various legal works, and (with N. F. Finlason) law reports. [xx. 63]

FOSTER, VERE HENRY LEWIS (1819–1900), philanthropist ; son of Sir Augustus John Foster [q. v.] ; educated at Eton and Christ Church, Oxford ; attaché at Rio de Janeiro, 1842–3, and at Monte Video, 1845–7 ; did much to promote emigration to United States and British colonies ; greatly benefited cause of education in Ireland ; published series of drawing copy-books. [Suppl. ii. 232]

FOSTER, WALTER (*fl.* 1652), mathematician ; elder brother of Samuel Foster [q. v.] ; fellow of Emmanuel College, Cambridge ; M.A., 1621 ; B.D., 1628 ; rector of Allerton, Somerset ; communicated to Twysden his brother's papers. [xx. 63]

FOSTER, WILLIAM (1591–1643), divine ; of Merchant Taylors' and St. John's College, Oxford ; B.A. ; chaplain to the Earl of Carnarvon and rector of Hedgerley, Buckinghamshire ; published a treatise against the use of 'weapon-salve,' 1629 and 1641. [xx. 64]

FOTHERBY, MARTIN (1549 ?–1619), bishop of Salisbury ; fellow of Trinity College, Cambridge ; archdeacon of Canterbury, 1596 ; dean, 1615 ; his 'Atheomastix' published, 1622. [xx. 64]

FOTHERGILL, ANTHONY (1685 ?–1761), author of 'Wicked Christians Practical Atheists,' 1754, and similar works. [xx. 64]

FOTHERGILL, ANTHONY (1732 ?–1813), physician ; M.D. Edinburgh, 1763 ; studied also at Leyden and Paris ; practised at Northampton, London, and Bath ; F.R.S., 1778 ; lived at Philadelphia, 1803–12 ; received gold medal of Royal Humane Society, 1794, for his essay on the revival of persons apparently dead from drowning. [xx. 65]

FOTHERGILL, GEORGE (1705–1760), principal of St. Edmund Hall, Oxford, 1751–60 ; fellow of Queen's College, Oxford ; M.A., 1730 ; D.D., 1749 ; vicar of Bramley ; author of sermons. [xx. 66]

FOTHERGILL, JESSIE (1851–1891), novelist ; published, from 1875, novels, chiefly depicting Lancashire and Yorkshire factory life. [Suppl. ii. 233]

FOTHERGILL, JOHN (1712–1780), physician ; M.D. Edinburgh, 1736 ; began to practise in London, 1740 ; L.R.C.P., 1744 ; F.R.S., 1763 ; fellow of the Royal Society of Medicine at Paris, 1776 ; kept up at Upton, Essex, one of the finest botanical gardens in Europe, his collection of shells and insects passing to Dr. W. Hunter, and his natural history drawings being bought by the empress of Russia ; assisted Benjamin Franklin in drawing up scheme of reconciliation with American colonies, 1774 ; a chief founder of the quaker school at Ackworth. His works (edited by J. C. Lettsom, 1783–4) included 'Account of the Sore Throat,' 1748 (the first recognition of diphtheria in England) ; and a pamphlet advocating the repeal of the Stamp Act. His portrait by Hogarth is at the College of Physicians. [xx. 66]

FOTHERGILL, JOHN MILNER (1841–1888), medical writer ; M.D. Edinburgh, 1865 ; practised in Leeds and London ; wrote valuable essays upon the 'Action of Digitalis ' ; and ' The Antagonism of Therapeutic Agents,' 1878. [xx. 68]

FOTHERGILL, SAMUEL (1715–1772), quaker ; brother of John Fothergill [q. v.] ; undertook missions to Wales, 1739, Ireland, 1744 and 1762, the United States, 1754–6, and Scotland, 1764. [xx. 68]

FOULIS, ANDREW, the elder (1712–1775), brother and partner of Robert Foulis [q. v.] ; undertook the strictly business side of the printing-house. [xx. 74]

FOULIS, ANDREW, the younger (*d.* 1829), printer ; son of Robert Foulis [q. v.] ; printed editions of Virgil and a ' Cicero de Officiis.' [xx. 74]

FOULIS, SIR DAVID, first baronet (*d.* 1642), politician ; great-grandson of Sir James Foulis (*d.* 1549) [q. v.] ; came to England with James I ; naturalised, 1606 ; created an English baronet, 1620 ; the recipient of the letter of advice to James I from Sir Robert Dudley [q. v.] ; titular Duke of Northumberland, 1614 ; dismissed from the council, fined,

and imprisoned for charges against Wentworth as president of the north, 1633–40 ; testified against Wentworth, 1641 [xx. 69]

FOULIS, HENRY (1638–1669), author ; grandson of Sir David Foulis [q. v.] ; M.A. Queen's College, Oxford, 1659 ; B.A. Cambridge, 1658 ; fellow of Lincoln College, Oxford, 1660 ; friend of Anthony à Wood ; published works against presbyterians and Romanists. [xx. 70]

FOULIS, SIR JAMES (*d.* 1549), Scottish judge ; acquired Colinton estates, 1519 ; lord of session, 1526 ; private secretary to James V, 1529 ; knighted, 1539 ; clerk-register of the College of Senators, 1532–46 ; member of the secret council, 1542. [xx. 70]

FOULIS, SIR JAMES, LORD COLINTON (*d.* 1688), lord justice clerk ; M.P. Edinburgh, 1645–8 and 1651 ; member of committee of estates, 1646–7 ; imprisoned as royalist ; lord of session, 1661 ; lord of the articles ; lord commissioner of justiciary and a peer, 1672 ; privy councillor, 1674 ; lord justice clerk, 1684. [xx. 70]

FOULIS, JAMES, LORD REIDFURD (1645 ?–1711), Scottish judge ; eldest son of Sir James Foulis, lord Colinton [q. v.] ; lord of session, 1674 ; nonjuror ; privy councillor, 1703 ; opposed the union. [xx. 71]

FOULIS, SIR JAMES (1714–1791), fifth baronet of Colinton ; contributed to ' Transactions of the Antiquarian Society of Scotland ' a dissertation on the origin of the Scots, 1781. [xx. 71]

FOULIS, SIR JAMES, seventh baronet of Colinton (1770–1842) ; painter and sculptor ; executed portrait of founder of Gillespie's Hospital, Edinburgh. [xx. 71]

FOULIS, ROBERT (1707–1776), printer (originally named Faulls) ; whilst a barber's apprentice at Glasgow attended the lectures of Francis Hutcheson (1694–1746) [q. v.] ; with his brother Andrew visited Oxford and France, collecting rare books, 1738–40 ; bookseller and printer at Glasgow, 1741 ; printed for the university their first Greek book ('Demetrius Phalereus de Elocutione '), 1743, and the 'immaculate' Horace, 1744 ; issued 'Catalogue of Books lately imported from France,' the fine ' Iliad,' 1747, and the Olivet Cicero, 1749 ; founded art academy, 1753 ; gained silver medal of the Edinburgh Select Society for his small folio Callimachus, 1755, for the Iliad, 1756, and Odyssey, 1758, with Flaxman's designs ; issued quarto edition of Gray, 1768, and ' Paradise Lost,' 1770. The Foulis books were sold in 1777. Most of them are now in the Mitchell Library, Glasgow. [xx. 72]

FOULKES, PETER (1676–1747), scholar and divine ; educated at Westminster and Christ Church, Oxford ; M.A., 1701 ; canon of Exeter, 1704 ; sub-dean, 1725–33 ; published (with John Freind) an edition of Æschines and Demosthenes de Coronâ (with Latin translation), 1696. [xx. 74]

FOULKES, ROBERT (*d.* 1679), murderer ; servitor of Christ Church, Oxford ; vicar of Stanton Lacy, Shropshire ; executed at Tyburn for the murder of his illegitimate child. [xx. 75]

FOUNTAINE, SIR ANDREW (1676–1753), virtuoso ; M.A. Christ Church, Oxford, 1700 ; knighted, 1699 ; vice-chamberlain to Queen Caroline and tutor to Prince William ; warden of the mint, 1727–53 ; formed, while travelling in France and Italy, collections of china, pictures, and antiquities (much of the former sold at Christie's, 1884) ; the Annius of Pope's ' Dunciad.' [xx. 75]

FOUNTAINE, JOHN (1600–1671), commissioner of the great seal, 1659–60 ; barrister, Lincoln's Inn, 1629 ; imprisoned for refusing to pay the parliament's war tax, 1642 ; assisted in forming royalist association of western counties, 1645 ; pardoned, 1652, and placed upon parliamentary commissions ; serjeant-at-law, 1658. [xx. 76]

FOUNTAINHALL, LORD (1646–1722). [See LAUDER, SIR JOHN.]

FOUNTAINS, JOHN (*d.* 1225). [See FONTIBUS, JOHN DE.]

FOUNTAYNE, JOHN (1714–1802), dean of York, 1747–1802 ; great-grandson of John Fountaine [q. v.] ; M.A. St. Catharine's Hall, Cambridge, 1739 ; D.D., 1751 ; canon of Salisbury, 1739, of Windsor, 1741. [xx. 78]

FOURDRINIER, HENRY (1766–1854), inventor ; with his brother, Sealy Fourdrinier [q. v.], patented in 1807 a continuous paper-making machine at a cost of 60,000*l*. ; received a parliamentary grant, 1840.   [xx. 78]

FOURDRINIER, PAUL (*d.* 1758), engraver.
[xx. 79]

FOURDRINIER, PETER (*fl.* 1720–1750), engraver of portraits, book illustrations and architectural works.
[xx. 78]

FOURDRINIER, SEALY (*d.* 1847), inventor ; brother of Henry Fourdrinier [q. v.] ; shared with him in parliamentary compensation for losses sustained.   [xx. 78]

FOURNIER, DANIEL (*d.* 1766 ?), engraver and draughtsman ; published ' Treatise of the Theory and Practice of Perspective,' 1761.   [xx. 79]

FOWKE, FRANCIS (1823–1865), captain of royal engineers and architect ; secretary to the British commission at Paris Exhibition, 1854 ; with Redgrave designed the Sheepshanks Gallery ; as architect of the Science and Art Department designed the Edinburgh Museum of Science and Art, the enlarged Dublin National Gallery, the buildings for the Exhibition of 1862, and began the South Kensington Museum ; invented a military fire-engine and patented a photographic camera.   [xx. 79]

FOWKE, JOHN (*d.* 1662), lord mayor, 1652–3 ; imprisoned for refusing to pay tonnage and poundage, 1627–9 ; sheriff of London and leader of the city parliamentarians, 1643 ; fined and imprisoned for conduct as commissioner of customs, 1645 ; presented a petition for peace to parliament, 1648 ; M.P. for the city, 1661 ; benefactor of Bethlehem and Christ's hospitals.   [xx. 81]

FOWKE, PHINEAS (1638–1710), London physician ; fellow of Queens' College, Cambridge, 1658 ; B.A., 1658 ; M.D., 1668 ; F.R.C.P., 1680.   [xx. 82]

FOWLER, ABRAHAM (*fl.* 1577), verse-writer ; educated at Westminster and Christ Church, Oxford.
[xx. 83]

FOWLER, CHRISTOPHER (1610 ?–1678), ejected minister ; B.A. Magdalen College, Oxford, 1632 ; M.A. St. Edmund Hall, Oxford, 1634 ; took covenant and held sequestrated living of St. Mary's, Reading, 1643–62 ; preached in London ; fellow of Eton ; wrote against the quakers, 1656, and the astrologer John Pordage [q. v.]
[xx. 83]

FOWLER, EDWARD (1632–1714), bishop of Gloucester ; B.A. Corpus Christi College, Oxford, 1653 ; M.A. Trinity College, Cambridge, 1656 ; rector of Norhill, Bedfordshire, 1656, All Hallows, Bread Street, 1673 ; D.D. ; canon of Gloucester, 1676 ; vicar of St. Giles, Cripplegate, 1681–5 ; suspended for whiggism, 1685 ; influenced London clergy against reading Declaration of Indulgence, 1687 ; member of commission for revising prayer-book, 1689 ; bishop of Gloucester, 1691–1714 ; published a defence of the latitudinarians, 1670, ' The Design of Christianity,' 1671, which latter occasioned a controversy with Bunyan, several anti-Romanist works, and ' Twenty-eight Propositions ' in explanation of the doctrine of the Trinity, 1693.   [xx. 84]

FOWLER, HENRY (1779–1838), hymn-writer ; minister of Gower Street Chapel, London, 1820 ; published an autobiography and ' Original Hymns . . . with prose reflections,' 1818–24.   [xx. 86]

FOWLER, JOHN (1537–1579), Roman catholic printer and scholar ; educated at Winchester and New College, Oxford ; fellow, 1553–9 ; M.A., 1560 ; printed at Louvain, Antwerp, and Douay many catholic works ; died at Namur ; edited More's ' Dialogue of Comfort,' 1573, and issued a ' Psalter for Catholics,' 1578.   [xx. 86]

FOWLER, JOHN (1826–1864), inventor of the steam plough ; with Albert Fry conducted experiments at Bristol, from which resulted the drain plough, 1850 ; received in 1858 prize of Royal Agricultural Society for his steam cultivator, improved in 1860 by the invention of the double engine tackle ; took out thirty-two patents for himself and partners, 1850–64.   [xx. 87]

FOWLER, SIR JOHN, first baronet (1817–1898), civil engineer ; engaged, under John Urpeth Rastrick [q. v.], on London and Brighton railway ; engineer and general manager of Stockton and Hartlepool line ; consulting engineer in London, 1844 ; designed Pimlico railway bridge, 1860, and Metropolitan railway from 1853 ; K.C.M.G., 1885 ; took into partnership Mr. (now Sir) Benjamin Baker, 1875, the partners being mainly responsible for construction of Forth bridge, 1882–90 ; created baronet, 1890 : member of council of Institution of Civil Engineers, 1849 ; president, 1866–7 ; published professional ' Reports.'   [Suppl. ii. 233]

FOWLER, RICHARD (1765–1863), physician ; M.D. Edinburgh, 1793 ; member of Speculative Society ; physician to Salisbury Infirmary, 1796–1847 ; L.R.C.P., 1796 ; F.R.S., 1802 ; published book on galvanic experiments, 1793, works upon the psychology of defective senses, and ' On Literary and Scientific Pursuits as conducive to Longevity,' 1855.   [xx. 88]

FOWLER, ROBERT (1726 ?–1801), archbishop of Dublin, 1779 ; educated at Westminster and Trinity College, Cambridge ; M.A., 1751 : D.D., 1764 ; chaplain to George II, 1756 ; canon of Westminster, 1765 ; bishop of Killaloe, 1771–9 ; translated to Dublin, 1779.   [xx. 88]

FOWLER, SIR ROBERT NICHOLAS, first baronet (1828–1891), lord mayor of London ; educated at University College, London ; M.A. London, 1850 ; entered banking firm of Drewett & Fowler, in which his father was partner ; conservative M.P. for Penryn and Falmouth, 1868–74 ; engaged in reorganising conservative party in city of London ; alderman for Cornhill ward, 1878 ; M.P. for city of London, 1880–91 ; lord mayor of London, 1883–4, and April 1885 (on death of Alderman Nottage) ; created baronet, 1885 ; published ' Visit to China, Japan, and India,' 1877.   [Suppl. ii. 235]

FOWLER, WILLIAM (*fl.* 1603), Scottish poet ; driven by the jesuits from France ; with Robert Lekprewick published an anti-catholic tract dedicated to Bothwell, 1581 ; secretary to Queen Anne, whom he accompanied to England ; left in manuscript (now in Edinburgh University library) ' The Tarantula of Love ' (seventy-two sonnets) and translations from Petrarch ; uncle of William Drummond of Hawthornden.   [xx. 89]

FOWLER, WILLIAM (1761–1832), artist ; published coloured engravings of Roman pavements ; painted glass subjects and miscellanea between 1799 and 1829 ; said to have introduced lead-lines in representing coloured glass.
[xx. 89]

FOWNES, GEORGE (1815–1849), chemist ; Ph.D. Giessen : chemistry professor to the Pharmaceutical Society, 1842, and at University College, 1846 ; secretary of the Chemical Society ; published text-book of chemistry, 1844 ; gained the Agricultural Society's prize for his ' Food of Plants,' the Actonian prize for an ' Essay on Chemistry,' and a Royal Society medal for researches in organic chemistry.   [xx. 90]

FOWNS, RICHARD (1560 ?–1625), divine ; M.A. Christ Church, Oxford, 1585 ; D.D., 1605 ; chaplain to Prince Henry and rector of Severn Stoke ; published ' Trisagion, or the Three Holy Offices of Iesvs Christ,' 1619.
[xx. 91]

FOX, CAROLINE (1819–1871), diarist ; from 1835 kept a journal, and recorded her intimacy with John Stuart Mill, John Sterling, and Carlyle (extracts edited by H. N. Pym, 1882) ; translated into Italian English religious works.   [xx. 91]

FOX, CHARLES (1749–1809), Persian scholar ; made tour on foot through Sweden, Norway, and Russia, drawing views on the way ; friend of Southey ; assisted Claudius James Rich and Dr. Adam Clarke in oriental studies ; published at Bristol ' Poems . . . of Achmed Ardebeili, a Persian Exile, with notes historical and explanatory,' 1797.   [xx. 91]

FOX, CHARLES (1794–1849), line-engraver ; studied under William Camden Edwards [q. v.] ; assisted John Burnet in his Wilkie plates ; engraved portrait of Sir G. Murray after Pickersgill, Wilkie's ' Village Politicians,' and ' Queen Victoria's First Council.'   [xx. 92]

FOX, SIR CHARLES (1810–1874), engineer ; constructing engineer of London and Birmingham railway ; designed Watford tunnel and extended line from Camden Town to Euston ; as head of firm of Fox, Henderson & Co. invented system of four-feet plates for tanks, and introduced the switch into railway practice ; knighted after designing exhibition buildings in Hyde Park, 1851 ; made first narrow-gauge line in India ; built the Berlin waterworks ; employed in railway construction in Ireland, Denmark, east France, Queensland, Canada, the Cape. [xx. 93]

FOX, CHARLES (1797–1878), scientific writer : uncle of Caroline Fox [q. v.] ; manager of the Perran Foundry Company, 1824–47 ; a founder of the Royal Cornwall Polytechnic Society, 1833 ; president of the Cornwall Geological Society, 1864–7, and Miners' Association, 1861–3, to which he contributed papers on boring machines ; edited ' Spiritual Diary of John Rutty, M.D.,' 1840. [xx. 94]

FOX, CHARLES JAMES (1749–1806), statesman ; third son of Henry Fox, first baron Holland [q. v.] ; while at Eton was taken by his father to Paris and Spa, and encouraged to indulge in dissipation ; studied (1764–6) at Hertford College, Oxford, and afterwards travelled ; M.P., Midhurst, 1768 ; made his mark by anti-Wilkesite speeches, 1769 ; became a lord of the admiralty under North, 1770 ; made himself unpopular by speeches against the liberty of the press ; resigned, 1772 ; opposed Royal Marriage Bill ; rejoined the ministry as a lord of the treasury within ten months, but acted independently, and was dismissed by the king, 1774 ; resided in Paris, 1774, and gambled heavily in London ; joined Johnson's 'club' ; obtained some financial relief by death of his father and elder brother in the same year (1774) ; took leading part in opposing North's American policy, 1774 ; supported the repeal of the tea duty, 1774 ; moved for a committee on the war, 1776 ; continued to attend during the secession of the Rockingham whigs ; attacked Lord George Germain (1716–1785) [q. v.], 1777 ; rejected ministerial overtures and definitely attached himself to the Rockingham party, 1778 ; attacked the admiralty warmly ; advocated the cause of Keppel, 1779 ; wounded in a duel with William Adam (1751–1839) [q. v.] ; spoke in favour of triennial parliaments, 1780 ; took a leading part in debates on economical reform, and made three hours' speech in support of Roman catholic relief ; in spite of great pecuniary distress refused to be bribed by the emoluments of office ; returned with Rodney for Westminster, 1780 ; attacked the financial policy of North, 1781, and on the news of the surrender of Yorktown moved an amendment to the address ; resumed his attacks on the navy, 1782, and much reduced the ministerial majority ; appointed foreign secretary, Rockingham being premier, 1782 ; brought in the measures which created Grattan's parliament ; thwarted in his foreign policy by Shelburne, the other secretary of state ; resigned when Shelburne became premier, May 1782 ; sought reconciliation with Shelburne whigs ; formed coalition with North (April 1783), becoming joint-secretary of state with him under the Duke of Portland ; obtained parliamentary grant for his friend the Prince of Wales, and introduced measure to reform government of India by the creation of a supreme council of seven and a commercial board of assistant-directors nominated by parliament for four years ; defeated on the matter in the House of Lords by the personal influence of the king ; dismissed with his colleague (December 1783) ; enabled by his possession of a majority in the Commons to defeat Pitt's East India Bill, and for three months to defer a dissolution by delaying grants of supply ; elected for Kirkwall, 1784 ; at same time re-elected for Westminster, 1784, although the return of the writ was delayed for two sessions ; formed connection with Mrs. Armitstead, whom he married in 1795 ; opposed Pitt's commercial treaties with Ireland, and (1787) with France, but supported his reform proposals ; attacked Warren Hastings, 1786–7, and moved an impeachment on the Benares charge ; as one of the managers of the proceedings opened the Benares charge in a speech of nearly five hours, 1788 ; spoke against the abatement of the impeachment by dissolution of parliament, 1789 ; supported motions for the removal of dissenters' disabilities, 1788–9 ; moved repeal of corporation and test acts, 1790 ; claimed for the Prince of Wales an inherent right to the regency, 1788–9, during George III's first illness (in spite of the deception which led him to deny in parliament, 1787, the Prince of Wales's marriage with Mrs. Fitzherbert) ; opposed Pitt's policy on the Eastern question, the French revolution, and the treason and sedition bills of 1795–6 ; carried a measure giving juries full powers in libel actions, 1792 ; seldom attended parliament for the next five years, but spent some time on his ' History of the Revolution of 1688' (published after his death), and in literary correspondence with Gilbert Wakefield [q. v.] ; his name erased from the privy council for

giving the toast ' Our sovereign, the people,' 1798 ; toured in the Netherlands and France, and interviewed Buonaparte, 1802 ; made three hours' speech in favour of peace, 1803 ; on Addington's resignation was proposed as member of a coalition ministry with Pitt and the Grenvilles, but was excluded by the king, 1804 ; spoke in favour of catholic emancipation, 1805 ; opposed motion for public honours to Pitt, 1806 ; as foreign secretary under Lord Grenville revealed plot to assassinate Napoleon, and opened negotiations with France ; moved the abolition of the slave trade a few days before his death. [xx. 95]

FOX, CHARLES RICHARD (1796–1873), numismatist : son of Henry Richard Vassall Fox, third baron Holland [q. v.] ; served in navy, 1809–13 ; equerry to Queen Adelaide, 1830 ; M.P., Calne, Tavistock, and (1835) Stroud ; surveyor-general of the ordnance, and aide-de-camp to William IV, 1832 ; general, 1863 ; died receiver-general of the duchy of Lancaster ; his numismatic collection (described in his 'Engravings of Unedited or Rare Greek Coins' (1856, pt. ii., 1862) purchased by the Berlin Royal Museum, 1873. [xx. 112]

FOX, EBENEZER (d. 1886), journalist ; private secretary to Sir Julius Vogel, 1869 ; secretary to the treasury (New Zealand), 1870–86 ; wrote in 'New Zealand Times' on the denudation of forests. [xx. 113]

FOX, EDWARD (1496 ?–1538), bishop of Hereford, 1535–8 ; educated at Eton and King's College, Cambridge ; secretary to Wolsey, 1527 ; accompanied Gardiner to Rome to obtain from Clement VII the dispensation with regard to Catherine of Arragon, 1528 ; D.D. ; elected provost of King's on his return, 1528 ; brought Cranmer into favour by reporting his views on the legality of the royal marriage ; intervened between Latimer and the Romanists at Cambridge ; commissioned to obtain from the English universities and that of Paris a pronouncement on the divorce question, as well as to negotiate treaties with France, 1532–3 ; archdeacon of Leicester, 1531 ; dean of Salisbury, 1533 ; sent to confer with the German protestant divines on the divorce question, 1535 ; while on a similar mission to France supported Alane (Alesius) the reformer ; author of ' De vera Differentia Regiæ Potestatis et Ecclesiæ,' 1534. [xx. 113]

FOX, ELIZABETH VASSALL, LADY HOLLAND (1770–1845), born in Jamaica ; divorced from Sir Godfrey Webster and married to Henry Richard Vassall Fox [q. v.], third baron Holland, 1797 ; presided over the whig circle at Holland House ; a skilful and vivacious, but somewhat overbearing, hostess ; attacked by Byron in ' English Bards and Scotch Reviewers' for her supposed inspiration of a hostile review ; accused by Brougham of spite against himself ; sent Napoleon message at Elba and books at St. Helena, and received from him the bequest of the gold snuff-box given him by Pius VI. [xx. 115]

FOX, FRANCIS (1675–1738), divine ; M.A. St. Edmund Hall, Oxford, 1704 ; rector successively of Boscombe and Potterne ; prebendary of Salisbury, 1713 ; vicar of St. Mary's, Reading, 1726–38 ; published 'The New Testament, with references and notes,' 1722, and ' Introduction to Spelling and Reading.' [xx. 117]

FOX, GEORGE (d. 1661), quaker ; ' the younger in the truth' ; adherent of George Fox (1624–1691) [q. v.] ; his works collected, 1662. [xx. 121]

FOX, GEORGE (1624–1691), founder of the Society of Friends ; son of a Leicestershire weaver : when agent to a grazier and wool-dealer, left home and went south, 1643 ; returned and wandered about, seeking religious advice from the clergy, 1644–6 ; first preached at Dukinfield, at Manchester, and in Leicestershire, 1647–8, when he had a trance ; imprisoned at Nottingham for brawling in church, 1649 ; his society of the 'Friends of Truth' (nicknamed quakers by Gervase Bennet, 1650) a protest against the presbyterian system, rapidly recruited from the lower middle classes, the yearly meeting being first held, 1669 ; made missionary journeys to Scotland, 1657, Ireland, 1669, North America and West Indies, 1671–2, and Holland, 1677–84 ; imprisoned at Lancaster and Scarborough, 1663–6, and Worcester, 1673–4 ; died in London, being buried in Whitecross Street, Bunhill Row. His ' Journal,' revised by a committee under Penn's superintendence, appeared in 1694. His principal writings are contained in ' A Collection of . . . Epistles,' 1698, and ' Gospel Truth,' 1706. [xx. 117]

FOX, GEORGE (1802 ?–1871), author of a 'History of Pontefract,' 1827. [xx. 122]

FOX, HENRY, first BARON HOLLAND (1705–1774), statesman; son of Sir Stephen Fox [q. v.]; at Eton with Pitt and Fielding; ruined himself by gambling and went abroad; M.P. for Hindon, 1738; attached himself to Walpole; surveyor-general of works, 1737–42; M.P., Windsor, 1741–61; a lord of the treasury, 1743; secretary at war, 1746–54; assailed Lord Hardwicke's marriage bill, but continued to hold his office under Newcastle till admitted to the cabinet as secretary of state, 1755; resigned, 1756, but became paymaster-general, 1757; having held office for eight years, made a large fortune; as Bute's leader in the House of Commons carried the peace of 1763 by profuse bribery; created a peer, 1763; the most unpopular of contemporary statesmen; a great social sensation created by his secret marriage to Lady Georgiana Lennox, 1744; said to have written 'The Spendthrift,' a short-lived periodical, 1766. His portraits, by Hogarth and Reynolds, are at Holland House, which he bought in 1767. [xx. 122]

FOX, HENRY EDWARD (1755–1811), general; youngest son of Henry Fox, first baron Holland [q. v.]; served with the 38th foot in the American war; major-general, 1793; as commander of a brigade under the Duke of York repulsed the whole French army at Pont-à-Chin, 1794; lieutenant-general, 1799; general in the Mediterranean, 1801–3; commander-in-chief in Ireland, 1803; lieutenant-governor of Gibraltar, 1804; commander in Sicily and ambassador to the court of Naples, 1806; governor of Portsmouth, 1808. [xx. 125]

FOX, HENRY RICHARD VASSALL, third BARON HOLLAND (1773–1840), nephew of Charles James Fox [q. v.]; educated at Eton and Christ Church; M.A., 1792; travelled in Denmark, Prussia, Spain, and Italy, 1791–4; from 1798 took prominent part in debates of House of Lords as a whig; met Napoleon at Paris, 1802; lived in Spain, 1802–5 and 1808–9; with Lord Auckland concluded the unratified treaty with American commissioners, 1806; lord privy seal, 1806–7; introduced bill for abolition of death penalty for stealing, 1809; led opposition to regency proposals, 1811; urged rescission of order in council prohibiting trade with France, 1812; attacked treaty with Sweden, 1813; visited Murat at Naples, 1814; opposed detention of Napoleon as prisoner of war, 1816, and Sidmouth's measures and the foreign enlistment bill, 1817–19; proposed intervention in Portugal, 1828–30; chancellor of the duchy of Lancaster in the first reform ministry and under Melbourne; published satires on Irish affairs, 1798–9, and translations from Spanish and Italian, and edited Waldegrave's 'Memoirs' and Horace Walpole's 'George II'; left posthumous 'Memoirs of the Whig Party' (edited 1852). [xx. 126]

FOX, HENRY STEPHEN (1791–1846), diplomatist; son of Henry Edward Fox [q. v.]; educated at Eton and Christ Church, Oxford; envoy extraordinary at Buenos Ayres, 1830, Rio de Janeiro, 1832, and Washington, 1835–43. [xx. 128]

FOX, HENRY WATSON (1817–1848), missionary in Masulipatam; educated at Rugby and Wadham College, Oxford; B.A., 1839; author of 'Chapters on Missions in South India,' 1848. [xx. 129]

FOX, JOHN (1516–1587). [See FOXE.]

FOX, JOHN (fl. 1676), nonconformist divine; B.A. Clare Hall, Cambridge, 1624; ejected from Pucklechurch rectory, 1662; published 'Time, and the End of Time,' 1670, 'The Door of Heaven opened and shut,' 1676. [xx. 129]

FOX, JOHN (1693–1763), biographer; educated under Joseph Hallet the elder [q. v.]; his 'Memoirs' and nine 'Characters' printed by the 'Monthly Repository,' 1821; the transcript of his papers made by James Northcote (with additions) preserved in the public library, Plymouth. [xx. 130]

FOX, LUKE (1586–1635), navigator; sailed from London, 1631, in the Charles pinnace in search of a north-west passage; made observations in the channel called after himself on west shore of Baffin Land; returned with his crew intact after a six months' voyage, described in his 'North-west Fox, or Fox from the North-west Passage,' 1635; died neglected. [xx. 131]

FOX, RICHARD (1448 ?–1528). [See FOXE.]

FOX, ROBERT (1798 ?–1843), Huntingdon antiquary; admitted into Society of Antiquaries; published 'History of Godmanchester,' 1831. [xx. 132]

FOX, ROBERT WERE (1789–1877), scientific writer; father of Caroline and Charles Fox (1797–1878) [q. v.]; F.R.S., 1848; made experiments on elasticity of high-pressure steam, and researches into internal temperature of the earth, proving that heat increased with depth, but in a diminishing ratio; constructed the new dipping-needle used by Sir James Clark Ross and Captain Nares. [xx. 133]

FOX, SAMUEL (1560–1630). [See FOXE.]

FOX, SIMEON (1568–1642). [See FOXE.]

FOX, SIR STEPHEN (1627–1716), statesman; aided Charles II to escape after Worcester, 1651, and managed the prince's household while in Holland; employed on secret missions to England, 1658–60; paymaster-general, 1661; M.P. for Salisbury, 1661; knighted, 1665; opposed his patron Clarendon's impeachment, 1667; M.P., Westminster, and a commissioner of the treasury, 1679; first commissioner of horse, 1680, and sole commissioner, 1684; suggested and himself contributed towards the foundation of Chelsea Hospital, and built churches, schools, and almshouses; refused a peerage from James II and opposed the bill for a standing army; remained at the treasury under William III; led the Commons in procession at the coronation of Queen Anne, 1702, and was for a time commissioner of horse; M.P., Salisbury, 1714. [xx. 133]

FOX, TIMOTHY (1628–1710), nonconformist divine; of Christ's College, Cambridge; ejected from Drayton rectory, 1662; twice imprisoned under the Schism Act. [xx. 136]

FOX, WILLIAM (1736–1826), founder of the Sunday School Society; initiated the Sunday schools, 1785; treasurer of Baptist Home Missionary Society, 1797. [xx. 136]

FOX, SIR WILLIAM (1812–1893), prime minister of New Zealand; M.A. Wadham College, Oxford, 1839; barrister, Inner Temple, 1842; resident agent for New Zealand Company at Nelson, New Zealand, 1843, and principal agent in the colony, 1848; attorney-general for south island of colony, 1848; premier of New Zealand, 1856, 1861–2, 1863–4, 1869–72, and 1873; published works relating to the colony of New Zealand. [Suppl. ii. 236]

FOX, WILLIAM JOHNSON (1786–1864), preacher, politician, and author; entered Dr. Pye Smith's independent college at Homerton, 1806; unitarian minister at Chichester, 1812, and Parliament Court, London, 1817; South Place Chapel built for him, 1824, when he had attained celebrity; contributed to the first number of the 'Westminster Review'; co-editor with Robert Aspland [q. v.] of the 'Monthly Repository,' which he purchased in 1831, and obtained contributions from Mill, Harriet Martineau, Crabb Robinson, and Browning; disowned by the unitarians on account of his separation from his wife and the independence of his views; continued much in vogue as a preacher, and made friends with Bulwer, Macready, and John Forster; contributed to the 'Sunday Times' under D. W. Harvey [q. v.], the 'Morning Chronicle,' and the 'Daily News'; wrote the Anti-Corn Law League's address to the nation, 1840; M.P., Oldham, 1847–63; seconded Joseph Hume's motion to extend franchise, 1849; introduced a compulsory education bill, 1850; published popular lectures. [xx. 137]

FOX, WILLIAM TILBURY (1836–1879), physician; M.D. London, 1858; specialised in obstetrics and dermatology; physician at Charing Cross and University College Hospitals; published 'Skin Diseases,' 1864, 'Atlas of Skin Diseases,' 1875–7, and revised Tanner's 'Clinical Medicine,' 1869 and 1876. [xx. 139]

FOX, WILSON (1831–1887), physician; M.D. London, 1855; studied at Paris, Vienna, and under Virchow at Berlin; professor of pathological anatomy at University College, London, 1861; F.R.C.P., 1866; Holme professor, 1867; F.R.S., 1820; physician extraordinary to Queen Victoria, 1870, afterwards becoming physician in ordinary; published papers on cystic tumours, on the artificial production of tubercle in animals, and on the development of striated muscular fibre; published his papers in Reynolds's 'System of Medicine' as 'Diseases of the Stomach' (3rd edition, 1872). [xx. 140]

FOXE, JOHN (1516–1587), martyrologist; native of Boston; sent to Oxford at the expense of a citizen of Coventry and of John Harding or Hawarden, afterwards principal of Brasenose; fellow of Magdalen College, Oxford, 1539; M.A., 1545; intimate with Alexander Nowell [q. v.], Latimer, and Tindal; resigned fellowship, 1545, being unwilling to conform to the statutes in religious matters; tutor successively to Thomas Lucy of Charlecote and to the children of Henry Howard, earl of Surrey; published protestant pamphlets; ordained deacon by Ridley, 1550; preached at Reigate; retired to the continent, 1554; issued at Strasburg his 'Commentarii' (earliest draft of his 'Actes and Monuments'); joined the Geneva party at Frankfort; on the expulsion of Knox removed to Basle, 1555; employed as a reader of the press by Oporinus (Herbst), who published his 'Christus Triumphans,' 1556, his appeal to the English nobility for religious toleration, 1557, and the first issue of 'Rerum in ecclesia gestarum . . . commentarii,' 1559; on his return to England lived first with his pupil Thomas, duke of Norfolk, and afterwards at Waltham and in Grub Street; ordained priest by Grindal, 1560; joined John Day the printer [q. v.], 1564, who, in 1563, had printed the English version of Foxe's 'Rerum in ecclesia gestarum . . . commentarii' as 'Actes and Monuments,' popularly known as 'The Book of Martyrs'; canon of Salisbury and lessee of the vicarage of Shipton, 1563; objected to the surplice and to contributing to the repair of Salisbury Cathedral; preached at Paul's Cross 'A Sermon on Christ Crucified,' 1570, frequently reprinted; published 'Reformatio Legum,' 1571, and an Anglo-Saxon text of the gospels; attended his former pupil, the Duke of Norfolk, at his execution, 1572; buried in church of St. Giles', Cripplegate. Four editions of the 'Actes and Monuments' (1563, 1570, 1576, and 1583) appeared in the author's lifetime; of the posthumous issues that of 1641 contains a memoir of Foxe, attributed to his son, but of doubtful authenticity. The accuracy of the work was impugned by Nicholas Harpsfield, by Robert Parsons, and by Jeremy Collier in the 'Ecclesiastical History' (1702–14), and by S. R. Maitland [q. v.] Foxe's papers, used by Strype in his works, were bought by Edward Harley, earl of Oxford, and are now in the British Museum. [xx. 141]

FOXE or **FOX**, RICHARD (1448?–1528), bishop, statesman, and founder of Corpus Christi College, Oxford; probably educated at Magdalen College, Oxford; employed at Paris by Henry, earl of Richmond, in negotiations with the French court; after Bosworth became secretary of state, lord privy seal, and (1487) bishop of Exeter; baptised Prince Henry, afterwards Henry VIII, 1491; bishop of Bath and Wells, 1492–4, of Durham, 1494–1501, of Winchester, 1501; chief English envoy in the treaty of Estaples and 'The Great Intercourse' (1496); helped to repel invasion of Scots and to conclude peace, 1497; negotiated marriages of Margaret Tudor with James IV and of Prince Arthur with Catherine of Arragon; chancellor of Cambridge University, 1500, and master of Pembroke College, Cambridge, 1507–19; negotiated alliance with the Archduke Charles (Charles V), 1508; one of the executors of Henry VII. Fox shared in the early years of Henry VIII's reign the chief political influence with the Earl of Surrey; concluded treaty with Louis XII, 1510; accompanied the army during the French war; a commissioner at the treaty of 1514; resigned the privy seal and retired from politics, 1516; opposed the subsidy of 1523 in convocation; founded for the secular clergy Corpus Christi College, Oxford, 1515; built and endowed schools at Taunton and Grantham; benefactor of Magdalen College, Oxford, Pembroke College, Cambridge, and other foundations; edited the Sarum 'Processional' (printed at Rouen, 1508), and translated the 'Rule of St. Benedict for women' (printed by Pynson, 1517). [xx. 150]

FOXE, SAMUEL (1560–1630), diarist; eldest son of John Foxe [q. v.]; educated at Merchant Taylors' School and Magdalen College, Oxford; fellow, 1580–1; deprived, 1581; visited Leipzig, Padua, and Basle, 1581–5; M.P., Oxford University, 1590; his diary appended to Strype's 'Annals.' [xx. 156]

FOXE, SIMEON (1568–1642), president of the College of Physicians; youngest son of John Foxe [q. v.]; educated at Eton and King's College, Cambridge; fellow, 1586; M.A., 1591; M.D. Padua; fought in Ireland and the Netherlands; F.R.C.P., 1608; several times censor;

treasurer, 1629, anatomy reader, 1630, president, 1634–40; buried in St. Paul's. [xx. 156]

FOXE, THOMAS (1591–1652), physician; son of Samuel Foxe [q. v.]; fellow, Magdalen College, Oxford, 1613–30; M.A., 1614; M.D. Oxford. [xx. 156]

FOY, NATHANIEL (d. 1707), bishop of Waterford and Lismore; senior fellow, Trinity College, Dublin; M.A., 1671; D.D., 1684; imprisoned by James II for sermons at St. Bride's, Dublin; bishop, 1691; endowed free school at Grantstown. [xx. 157]

FRADELLE, HENRY JOSEPH (1778–1865), historical painter; born at Lille; exhibited at British Institution and Academy, 1817–54. [xx. 158]

FRAIGNEAU, WILLIAM (1717–1788), professor of Greek at Cambridge, 1743–50; educated at Westminster; M.A. Trinity College, Cambridge, 1743; fellow; took orders. [xx. 158]

FRAIZER, SIR ALEXANDER (1610?–1681), physician to Charles II; M.D. Montpellier, 1635; F.R.C.P., 1641; elect, 1666. [xx. 158]

FRAMPTON, JOHN (fl. 1577–1596), merchant; long resident in Spain; translated Marco Polo's 'Travels,' 1579. [xx. 159]

FRAMPTON, MARY (1773–1846), author of a historically valuable 'Journal from the year 1779 until the year 1846' (ed., Mrs. Mundy, 1885). [xx. 159]

FRAMPTON, ROBERT (1622–1708), bishop of Gloucester; graduate of Corpus Christi College, Oxford; headmaster of Gillingham school; fought as a royalist at Hambledon Hill; chaplain to the English factory, Aleppo, 1655–70; famous as a preacher; dean of Gloucester, 1673; bishop of Gloucester, 1680–91; directed his clergy not to read Declaration of Indulgence, and signed bishops' petition; one of the seven bishops committed to the Tower, 1688; deprived as a nonjuror, 1691, but allowed to retain living of Standish; Queen Anne offered to translate him to Hereford. [xx. 159]

FRAMPTON, TREGONWELL (1641–1727), 'father of the turf'; devoted to hawking, 1670; played high at his house at Newmarket, and won many horse races; Hawkesworth's story of his cruelty to his horse Dragon unfounded; his match with Sir William Strickland said to have originated the act forbidding recovery of betting debts; from 1695 trainer of the royal horses at Newmarket. [xx. 161]

FRAMYNGHAM, WILLIAM (1512–1537), author of Latin tractates; educated at Pembroke and Queens' Colleges, Cambridge; M.A., 1533; friend of John Caius [q. v.]; wrote tracts. [xx. 163]

FRANCATELLI, CHARLES ELMÉ (1805–1876), cook; pupil of Carême; manager of Crockford's; maître d'hôtel to Queen Victoria; chef de cuisine at the Reform Club; manager of Freemasons' Tavern; published the 'Modern Cook,' 1845, and other culinary handbooks. [xx. 163]

FRANCE, ABRAHAM (fl. 1587–1633). [See FRAUNCE.]

FRANCIA, FRANÇOIS LOUIS THOMAS (1772–1839), water-colour painter; son of a refugee; exhibited at the Royal Academy, 1795–1821; one of Girtin's sketching society; secretary of Water-colour Society; instructed R. P. Bonington [q. v.] at Calais, where he died. [xx. 163]

FRANCILLON, JAMES (1802–1866), legal writer; barrister, Gray's Inn, 1833; Gloucestershire district county court judge, 1847; died at Lausanne; published 'Lectures in English Law,' 1860–1. [xx. 164]

FRANCIS, ALBAN (d. 1715), Benedictine of St. Adrian's Abbey, Lansperg, Hanover; missioner in Cambridgeshire, when the vice-chancellor of Cambridge was removed for refusing to admit him to a degree without administering tests. [xx. 164]

FRANCIS, ANNE, MRS. (1738–1800), poetess; née Gittins; published 'Poetical Translation of the Song of Solomon,' with introduction and notes, 1781, and other poems. [xx. 165]

FRANCIS, ENOCH (1688–1740), Welsh baptist; moderator of the association at Hengoed, 1730; published devotional works. [xx. 165]

FRANCIS, FRANCIS (1822–1886), writer on angling; son of Captain Morgan, R.N., but changed name on inheriting property; angling editor of the 'Field'; established Thames Rights Defence Association, and suggested plan of National Fish-Culture Association; naturalist; director of Brighton Aquarium; member of oyster commission, 1868–70; published 'The Practical Management of Fisheries,' 1883, books on angling, and novels; his 'Reminiscences' published, 1887.   [xx. 165]

FRANCIS, GEORGE GRANT (1814–1882), Swansea antiquary; mayor of Swansea, 1853–4; F.S.A., 1845; a founder of Royal Institution of South Wales; discovered original contract (1303) of Edward, prince of Wales, and Isabella of France, at Swansea Castle, 1848; edited Swansea charters, 1849; published works, including 'The Smelting of Copper in the Swansea District from the time of Elizabeth,' 1867 (republished, 1881), and 'Original Charters and Materials for a History of Neath and its Abbey,' 1845.   [xx. 166]

FRANCIS, GEORGE WILLIAM (1800–1865), botanical writer; emigrated to Australia, 1849, and became director of the Adelaide garden; published, among other works, 'Catalogue of British Plants and Ferns,' 1835, 'Analysis of British Ferns,' 1837, and 'Chemical Experiments,' 1842.   [xx. 167]

FRANCIS, JAMES GOODALL (1819–1884), Australian statesman; settled in Tasmania, 1834; afterwards removed to Melbourne; director of Bank of New South Wales, 1855; president of chamber of commerce, 1857; in Victorian Legislative Assembly fifteen years; member of William Nicholson's cabinet, 1859–60, of Sir J. M'Culloch's second and third ministries, 1863–8 and 1870–1; as head of administration, 1872–4, passed free education act and large railway measures; re-entered Victoria Assembly, 1878, and held office under James Service.   [xx. 167]

FRANCIS, JOHN (1780–1861), sculptor; pupil of Chantrey; exhibited at the Royal Academy, 1820–56. His works include busts of Miss Horatia Nelson, Queen Victoria, Prince Albert, and the Duke of Wellington.   [xx. 168]

FRANCIS, JOHN (1811–1882), publisher of the 'Athenæum,' 1831–81; in charge of commercial affairs of 'Notes and Queries' from 1872; took leading part in agitation for repeal of fiscal restrictions on the press.   [xx. 168]

FRANCIS, PHILIP (1708?–1773), miscellaneous writer; B.A. Trinity College, Dublin, 1728; kept school at Esher, which Gibbon attended, 1752; as private chaplain to Lady Caroline Fox taught Charles James Fox to read, and accompanied him to Eton; wrote pamphlets against Pitt, 1761–4; rector of Barrow, Suffolk, 1762–73; chaplain at Chelsea Hospital, 1764–8; received a crown pension of 300l., 1764; his version of Horace often republished.   [xx. 169]

FRANCIS, SIR PHILIP (1740–1818), reputed author of 'Letters of Junius'; son of Philip Francis [q. v.]; educated at St. Paul's School with Woodfall, Junius's publisher; junior clerk in office of secretary of state, 1756; became intimate with John Calcraft the elder [q. v.] and Robert Wood, secretary of the treasury; by Wood's influence appointed secretary to General Edward Bligh [q. v.], 1758, and to Lord Kinnoul in Portugal, 1760, and amanuensis to Pitt, 1761–2; copied part of correspondence between Egremont and Bedford in autumn of 1762, referred to by 'Junius'; while first clerk at the war office, 1762–72, contributed to the press under pseudonyms; retired from the war office owing to some disagreement with Barrington, but on the latter's recommendation became one of the four newly appointed councillors of the governor-general of India, 1774; opposed Warren Hastings, charging him with corruption in the case of Nand Kumar (or Nuncomar); quarrelled with his ally, Clavering; wounded in a duel with Hastings, 1779; left India with large fortune, 1780; M.P. for Isle of Wight, 1784, Bletchingley, 1790, and Appleby, 1802; helped Burke to prepare charges against Hastings, and assisted managers of his impeachment, 1787; a founder of 'Society of Friends of the People,' 1793; made elaborate speech upon India, 1805; quarrelled with Fox for refusing to appoint him viceroy; intimate with Prince Regent; created K.C.B.; identified by John Taylor with 'Junius,' 1816; published many political pamphlets. The evidence for the identification of Francis with 'Junius' (first letter, 1768, last, 1773) rests upon the acquaintance of 'Junius' with war office affairs, his displeasure at the removal of Francis, and private letters to the publisher Woodfall, displaying anxiety to conceal authorship of public letters expressing it; correspondence between silences of 'Junius' and absences from London of Francis; expert evidence of Chabot and Netherclift identifying handwriting; similarity of political attitude; Francis's conduct when challenged with authorship, and moral resemblance. Against the Franciscan theory is the denial of that authorship by Pitt and Woodfall, and the almost incredible malignity of 'Junius' towards some of Francis's friends and benefactors.   [xx. 171]

FRANCIS, THOMAS (d. 1574), president of the College of Physicians, 1568; M.D. Christ Church, Oxford, 1555; regius professor of medicine, 1555–61; provost of Queen's, 1561–3; physician in ordinary to Queen Elizabeth.   [xx. 180]

FRANCISCUS à SANCTÂ CLARA (1598–1680). [See DAVENPORT, CHRISTOPHER.]

FRANCK, RICHARD (1624?–1708), captain in parliamentary army; travelled in Scotland, c. 1656; went to America, 1690; published, 1694, the euphuistic 'Northern Memoirs... by Richard Franck, Philanthropus' (edited by Scott), containing accounts of places he had visited between Carlisle and Cromarty, and much about salmon-fishing; also 'Rabbi Moses' (1687), written in America.   [xx. 181]

FRANCKLIN, THOMAS (1721–1784), miscellaneous writer; fellow of Trinity College, Cambridge, 1746–58; M.A., 1746; D.D., 1770; professor of Greek, 1750–9; vicar of Ware, 1759–77; preacher at St. Paul's, Covent Garden; king's chaplain, 1767; chaplain to the Royal Academy through influence of Johnson and Reynolds, and (1774) professor of ancient history; satirised in the 'Rosciad'; translated Sophocles, 1759, Lucian, 1780, and Cicero's 'De Natura Deorum,' 1741; produced three plays, including the 'Earl of Warwick' (acted at Drury Lane, 1766); edited 'The Centinel,' 1757–8, and contributed to Smollett's 'Critical Review.'   [xx. 182]

FRANCKLIN, WILLIAM (1763–1839), orientalist; eldest son of Thomas Francklin [q. v.]; of Westminster and Trinity College, Cambridge; lieutenant-colonel, Bengal native infantry, 1814; died in India; published (1788) 'Observations made on a Tour from Bengal to Persia in ... 1786–7,' 'History of the Reign of Shah-Aulum,' 1798, and other works.   [xx. 184]

FRANK, MARK (1613–1664), theologian; fellow of Pembroke College, Cambridge, 1634; M.A., 1634; ejected by parliamentary visitors, 1644; D.D., 1661; master of Pembroke College, Cambridge, 1662–4; archdeacon of St. Albans and canon of St. Paul's, to which he left books and money; his 'Course of Sermons' (1642) republished in 'Library of Anglo-Catholic Theology.'   [xx. 185]

FRANKLAND, SIR EDWARD (1825–1899), chemist; apprenticed as chemist in Lancaster, c. 1840; studied at Museum of Practical Geology, London, 1845; F.C.S., 1847; studied under Bunsen at Marburg, 1847; Ph.D. Marburg, 1849; professor of chemistry at Putney College for Civil Engineering, 1850, and at Owens College, Manchester, 1851; F.R.S., 1853; royal medallist, 1857; lecturer on chemistry, St. Bartholomew's Hospital, London, 1857; professor of chemistry at Royal Institution, 1863–8, and at Royal College of Chemistry, 1865; served on royal commission on rivers pollution from 1868; D.C.L. Oxford, 1870; LL.D. Edinburgh, 1884; president of Chemical Society, 1871–2 and 1872–3, and of Institute of Chemistry, 1877–80; K.C.B., 1897; made notable contributions to organic chemistry. His works include 'Experimental Researches in Pure, Applied, and Physical Chemistry,' 1877, and 'Inorganic Chemistry,' with F. R. Japp, 1884.   [Suppl. ii. 237]

FRANKLAND, JOCOSA or JOYCE (1531–1587), née Trappes; founder of Saxey fellowships and scholarships at Caius and Emmanuel Colleges, Cambridge; benefactor also of Lincoln and Brasenose Colleges, Oxford.   [xx. 185]

FRANKLAND, RICHARD (1630–1698), nonconformist tutor; educated at Christ's College, Cambridge; M.A., 1655; received presbyterian ordination, 1653; ejected from vicarage of Bishop Auckland, 1662; exhorted Charles II to reform; set up 'academy' for divinity and medical students at Rathmell, from which northern dissenting ministers were chiefly recruited, 1670; removed to Natland, 1674, and afterwards to other places; excommunicated for instigation of first nonconformist ordination in Yorkshire, 1678; returned to Rathmell 1689; again excommunicated, but absolved by order of William III; presided at Wakefield conference of presbyterians and independents, 1691; had a friendly interview with Archbishop Sharp, 1692.   [xx. 186]

FRANKLAND, THOMAS (1633–1690), impostor and annalist; fellow of Brasenose College, Oxford, 1654; M.A., 1655; renounced holy orders to practise medicine; ejected from the College of Physicians as a pretended M.D., 1682; published anonymously 'Annals of James I and Charles I,' 1681.   [xx. 189]

FRANKLAND, SIR THOMAS (1717 ?–1784), admiral; commanded frigate on Bahama station, capturing many vessels and privateers, 1740–5; as commodore at Antigua, 1755, reported on conduct of Sir Thomas Pye [q. v.]; M.P. for Thirsk, 1749–84.   [xx. 189]

FRANKLIN, MRS. ELEANOR ANNE (1797 ?–1825), poetess; née Porden; married Mr. (afterwards Sir John) Franklin, 1823; chief work 'Cœur de Lion,' an epic, 1822.   [xx. 190]

FRANKLIN, JANE, LADY (1792–1875), née Griffin; married Sir John Franklin, 1828; travelled in Syria and Asia Minor, and with her husband in Van Diemen's Land, Australia, and New Zealand, giving much attention to female convicts; fitted out five ships to search for Franklin, and received the founder's medal of the Geographical Society, 1860; sent out the Pandora to make the northwest passage, 1875.   [xx. 191]

FRANKLIN, SIR JOHN (1786–1847), arctic explorer; midshipman in the Polyphemus at Copenhagen, 1801; assisted Matthew Flinders [q. v.] in his observations in the South Pacific; took part in Commodore Sir Nathaniel Dance's [q. v.] engagement with Linois, 1804; at Trafalgar in the Bellerophon; wounded in the Bedford near New Orleans, 1815; commanded the Trent in Buchan's arctic expedition, 1818; headed expedition of 1819–22, which traversed North America from Fort York, at the mouth of the Nelson river, to the mouth of the Coppermine, where it embarked on the Arctic Sea and sailed eastward, returning through the 'Barren Grounds' to Fort Providence and York after terrible privations; elected F.R.S. and promoted to post rank on his return; conducted a second expedition, 1825–7, which, by way of New York, Lake Huron, the Great Bear Lake, and the Mackenzie river, reached Garry Island in the Arctic Sea, and, after wintering at Fort Franklin (Great Bear Lake), divided, the whole expedition ultimately reaching Montreal; knighted, 1829; hon. D.C.L. Oxford, 1829; commanded Rainbow frigate on coast of Greece, 1830–3; as lieutenant-governor of Van Diemen's Land did much to humanise the convicts, 1837–43; started with the Erebus and Terror on his last expedition, May 1845, to make Behring's Strait from Cape Walker; last sighted at the entrance of Lancaster Sound on 26 July 1845. Supplies were sent out under Sir John Richardson (1787–1865) [q. v.], 1847, and many relief expeditions followed. Ommanney discovered traces of ships and provisions on Beechey Island, 1850, and further intelligence, with relics, was obtained from the Eskimos by Rae, 1854. Subsequently Sir Leopold McClintock, in Lady Franklin's yacht, the Fox, came upon boats, skeletons, and a paper stating that the ships had been deserted, 22 April 1848, after nineteen months in the ice, that Franklin had died 11 June 1847, and that the rest, under Crozier, had reached 69° 37' N., 98° 41' W. Accounts of his first two expeditions were published by Franklin (1823 and 1828), who has since been recognised as the discoverer of the north-west passage.   [xx. 191]

FRANKLIN, ROBERT (1630–1684), nonconformist divine; tutor of Jesus College, Cambridge; vicar of Westhall, 1659–62; ejected, 1662; imprisoned for preaching; left manuscript autobiography.   [xx. 196]

FRANKLYN, WILLIAM (1480 ?–1556), dean of Windsor, 1536; educated at Eton and King's College, Cambridge; B.C.L., 1504; chancellor of Durham, 1514; archdeacon, 1515; active in war with Scots, assisted in treaty, 1534; prebendary of Lincoln, 1518, and rector of Houghton-le-Spring; president of Queens' College, Cambridge, 1526–7; alienated deanery revenues.   [xx. 197]

FRANKS, SIR AUGUSTUS WOLLASTON (1826–1897), antiquary; educated at Eton and Trinity College, Cambridge; M.A., 1852; assistant in department of antiquities in British Museum, 1851, and keeper of department of British and mediæval antiquities and ethnography, 1866; presented to British Museum his collections of eastern ceramics and other objects of art; F.S.A., 1853, director, 1858–67 and 1873–80; edited 'Archæologica,' to which and to 'Proceedings' he made important contributions; P.S.A., 1891–7; K.C.B., 1894; honorary Litt.D. Cambridge, 1889, and D.C.L. Oxford, 1895; F.R.S., 1874; 'antiquary' to Royal Academy, 1894; published works chiefly relating to ceramics.   [Suppl. ii. 240]

FRANKS, SIR JOHN (1770–1852), judge; of Calcutta supreme court, 1825–34; of Trinity College, Dublin; called to Irish bar, 1792; K.C., 1823; intimate with Curran.   [xx. 198]

FRANKS, SIR THOMAS HARTE (1808–1862), general; served with 10th foot at Sobraon, 1846, and, was wounded; distinguished himself at the siege of Múltán, 1849, and at Gujrát, 1849; as brigadier in command of 4th infantry division defeated Muhammad Hussein Nazim, but failed before Dohrighat, 1858; created K.C.B. and thanked by parliament.   [xx. 198]

FRANSHAM, JOHN (d. 1753), linendraper and rent-agent to Horace Walpole; published 'The Criterion . . . of High and Low Church,' 1710, and 'A Dialogue between Jack High and Will Low,' 1710.   [xx. 201]

FRANSHAM, JOHN (1730–1810), freethinker; after writing sermons, acting in a company of strolling players, enlisting, and working with a weaver, took pupils at Norwich, and taught in several Norfolk families, including that of James Stark [q. v.]; published anonymously 'Essay on the Oestrum or Enthusiasm of Orpheus,' 1760, and satirical pieces; left in manuscript 'Memorabilia Classica' (containing 'The Code of Aristopia, or Scheme of a perfect Government'); the Dr. Emanuel Last of Foote's 'Devil upon Two Sticks.'   [xx. 199]

FRASER, SIR ALEXANDER (d. 1332), great chamberlain of Scotland, 1319–26; fought with Bruce at Methven, 1306, and aided him to crush the Comyns; present at Bannockburn; married Lady Mary Bruce; killed at battle of Dupplin.   [xx. 202]

FRASER, SIR ALEXANDER (1537 ?–1623), founder of Fraserburgh; inherited from his grandfather baronial burgh of Philorth, establishing (1597) a university there, which was short-lived; knighted by James I; M.P., Aberdeen county, 1596.   [xx. 202]

FRASER, SIR ALEXANDER (1610 ?–1681). [See FRAIZER.]

FRASER, ALEXANDER (1786–1865), painter; exhibited at the Royal Academy, 1810–48; for twenty years painted details and still-life in Wilkie's pictures; his 'Naaman Cured' proclaimed by the British Institution best picture of 1842; associate of Royal Scottish Academy.   [xx. 203]

FRASER, ALEXANDER (1827–1899), landscape-painter; studied at Trustees' Academy, Edinburgh; member of Royal Scottish Academy, 1862.   [Suppl. ii. 243]

FRASER, ALEXANDER GEORGE, sixteenth BARON SALTOUN (1785–1853), general; ensign, 35th foot, 1802; served with the grenadiers in Sicily, 1806, at Coruña, 1808, in Walcheren, 1809, and in Spain and France, 1812–1814; at Quatre Bras commanded light companies of 2nd brigade of guards; at Waterloo held garden and orchard of Hougoumont, and led the charge against the Old Guard; K.C.B., 1818; K.T., 1852; major-general, 1837; commanded first brigade and afterwards the whole force in Chinese war of 1841–3; Scottish representative peer from 1807; a lord of the bedchamber, 1821; G.C.H., 1821; lieutenant-general, 1849.   [xx. 203]

FRASER, ALEXANDER MACKENZIE (1756–1809), lieutenant-general; son of Colin Mackenzie; entered 73rd (71st) highlanders, 1778, and was aide-de-camp to Sir Charles Ross at siege of Gibraltar, 1780; joined Ross-shire buffs, 1793; as lieutenant-colonel distinguished himself at Nimeguen, 1794, and Geldermalsen, 1795; went to the Cape, 1796, with the 2nd battalion 78th, raised by himself; served against Mahrattas, 1798–9; major-general and M.P. for Cromarty, 1802; assumed name of

Fraser, 1803 ; M.P., Ross county, 1806 ; commanded unsuccessful Egyptian expedition, 1807 ; led division at Coruña, 1808, and in Walcheren expedition, 1809. [xx. 204]

FRASER, ANDREW (*d.* 1792). [See FRAZER.]

FRASER, ARCHIBALD CAMPBELL (1736–1815), thirty-eighth Macshimi ; son, by second wife, of Simon Fraser, twelfth baron Lovat [q. v.] ; consul at Tripoli and Algiers, 1766–74 ; succeeded to Fraser estates on death of elder brother, 1782 ; M.P., Inverness-shire, 1782–96 ; set up monument in Kirkhill churchyard detailing his services ; published 'Annals of the Patriots of the Family of Fraser, Frizell, Simson, or FitzSimon,' 1795. [xx. 206]

FRASER, DONALD (1826–1892), presbyterian divine ; educated at University and King's College, Aberdeen ; M.A., 1842 ; honorary D.D., 1872 ; engaged in mercantile business in Canada ; studied theology at 'John Knox' College, Toronto ; licensed preacher, 1851 ; pastor of Free church, Montreal, 1851–9, Free high church, Inverness, 1859–70, Marylebone presbyterian church, London, 1870–1892 ; published religious works. [Suppl. ii. 244]

FRASER, JAMES (1639–1699), covenanting divine ; called FRASER OF BRAE ; imprisoned on the Bass Rock for preaching, 1677–9, in Blackness Castle, 1681, and Newgate, 1683 ; member of the assemblies of 1690 and 1692 ; wrote autobiographical memoirs (published, 1738), and other works. [xx. 207]

FRASER, JAMES (1713–1754), collector of oriental manuscripts ; resided at Surat, 1730–40 ; factor in East India Company's service, 1743–9 ; made collection of Sanscrit manuscripts, which on his death were acquired by Radcliffe Library, Oxford, and were removed to Bodleian Library, 1872 ; published 'History of Nadir Shah,' 1742. [Suppl. ii. 244]

FRASER, JAMES (1700–1769), Scottish divine ; called FRASER OF PITCALZIAN ; son of James Fraser (*d.* 1711) [q. v.] ; presbyterian minister of Alness, 1726 ; published 'The Scripture Doctrine of Sanctification,' 1774. [xx. 208]

FRASER, JAMES (*d.* 1841), publisher in Regent Street, London ; published 'Fraser's Magazine,' 1830–42, 'Gallery of Illustrious Literary Characters,' 1830–8, and Carlyle's 'Heroes.' [xx. 208]

FRASER, JAMES (1818–1885), bishop of Manchester ; educated at Bridgnorth and Shrewsbury Schools and Lincoln College, Oxford ; Ireland scholar, 1839 ; fellow and tutor of Oriel, 1840–60 ; M.A., 1842 ; vicar of Cholderton, 1847 ; chancellor of Salisbury and assistant education commissioner, 1858 ; rector of Ufton Nervet, 1860 ; commissioner to report on education in United States and Canada, 1865, and on employment of children in agriculture, 1867 ; bishop of Manchester, 1870–85 ; arbitrated in Manchester and Salford painting trade dispute, 1874 and 1876 ; interested himself in the co-operative movement ; seconded in convocation the disuse of the Athanasian creed ; supported in the House of Lords the abolition of university tests, 1871 ; benefactor of his diocese. [xx. 209]

FRASER, JAMES BAILLIE (1783–1856), traveller and writer ; with his brother William Fraser (1784 ?–1835) [q. v.] explored Nepal as far as the sources of the Ganges and Jumna, 1815 ; accompanied Dr. Jukes to Persia, and travelled through Kurdistan to Tabriz, 1821 ; rode from Semlin to Constantinople, and from Stamboul to Teheran, 1833–4 ; published 'Military Memoir of Lieutenant-colonel James Skinner, C.B.,' 1851, and works descriptive of his travels, with some romances. [xx. 211]

FRASER, JAMES STUART (1783–1869), general in the Indian army ; aide-de-camp to Sir George Barlow [q. v.] during mutiny of Madras officers ; private secretary to government of Madras, 1810 ; deputy commissary to Mauritius expedition, 1810 ; commandant at Pondicherry, 1816 ; commissioner for restitution of French and Dutch possessions, 1816–17 ; resident of Mysore and commissioner of Coorg, 1834 ; resident of Travancore and Cochin, 1836, of Hyderabad, 1839–52 ; general, 1862. [xx. 212]

FRASER, JOHN (*d.* 1605), Scottish Recollect friar ; abbot of Noyon or Compiègne ; died at Paris ; B.D. ; published controversial treatises and Latin commentaries on Aristotle. [xx. 213]

FRASER, JOHN (*d.* 1711), dissenting minister ; M.A. Aberdeen, 1678 ; imprisoned and deported to New Jersey, 1685 ; preached in Connecticut ; returned to Scotland after the Revolution. [xx. 208]

FRASER, JOHN (1750–1811), botanist ; introduced from America pines, oaks, azaleas, and other plants, 1784–95 ; brought from Russia the Tartarian cherries, 1796 ; went to America as collector for the Tsar Paul, 1799. [xx. 213]

FRASER, SIR JOHN (1760–1843), general ; entered 73rd (71st) highlanders, 1778 ; lost his right leg during siege of Gibraltar, 1780–2 ; judge-advocate at Gibraltar, 1796–8 ; commander of royal African corps, gallantly defending Goree, 1804 ; general, 1838 ; G.C.H., 1832. [xx. 214]

FRASER or **FRAZER**, JOHN (*d.* 1849), poet and cabinet-maker ; of Birr, King's County ; published under name J. de Dean. [xx. 214]

FRASER, LOUIS (*fl.* 1866), naturalist ; curator to the Zoological Society ; naturalist to Niger expedition, 1841–2 ; collected birds in South America and set up shops in London ; afterwards went to San Francisco and Vancouver's island ; published 'Zoologia Typica,' 1849. [xx. 215]

FRASER, PATRICK, LORD FRASER (1819–1889), senator of the College of Justice ; educated at St. Andrews ; called to the bar, 1843 ; sheriff of Renfrewshire, 1864 ; dean of Faculty of Advocates, 1878 ; lord of session and lord ordinary in exchequer cases, 1880. His works include 'Treatise on the Law of Scotland as applicable to the Personal and Domestic Relations,' 1846, with other legal works. [xx. 215]

FRASER, ROBERT (1798–1839), Scottish poet ; editor of 'Fife Herald,' 1838–9. [xx. 216]

FRASER, ROBERT WILLIAM (1810–1876), Scottish divine and author ; minister at Burntisland, 1843, of St. John's, Edinburgh, 1847–76 ; published 'Elements of Physical Science,' 1855, 'The Kirk and the Manse,' 1857, 'The Seaside Naturalist,' 1868, and devotional works. [xx. 216]

FRASER, SIMON, twelfth BARON LOVAT (1667 ?–1747), Jacobite intriguer ; graduated at King's College, Aberdeen, 1683 ; accepted commission in regiment of Lord Murray (afterwards Duke of Atholl) on the assurance that treachery to the government of William III was intended ; secured by violent means the eventual succession to estates of his cousin, Lord Lovat ; being disappointed of a marriage with his cousin, Lord Lovat's daughter (who claimed the title), he imprisoned her uncle and suitor's father, and forcibly married her mother ; outlawed for high treason, 1698 ; assumed title of Baron Lovat, 1699 ; obtained from William III pardon for offences against the state, but had previously visited the exiled James II at St. Germain, 1700 ; outlawed for his outrage on the Dowager Lady Lovat, 1701 ; fled to France, 1702 ; pretended conversion to Romanism, and promised Louis XIV to assist him in invading Scotland ; returned to Scotland with a letter from Mary of Modena, and endeavoured to compromise Atholl and others in a Jacobite plot ; suspected by the highlanders for his relations with Queensberry ; returned to France, where he was imprisoned ; escaped with Major Fraser, 1713 ; arrested in London, but when released rallied his clan to the government, 1715 ; received a full pardon and the life-rent of the Lovat estates, 1716, and after much litigation a recognition of his title, 1733 ; sheriff of Inverness and commander of one of the newly raised highland companies ; for the promise of a dukedom joined association of 1737 to invite the Young Pretender to Scotland ; deprived of regimental command and office of sheriff ; though lukewarm in his support of Prince Charles Edward, 1745, was seized in his castle as hostage for the fidelity of the clan ; escaped to Loch Muilly and afterwards to Loch Morar ; arrested and brought to London ; beheaded for high treason. Treating as invalid his union with the Dowager Lady Lovat, he was twice married during her lifetime, and was succeeded by sons of each wife. [xx. 216]

FRASER, SIMON (*d.* 1777), brigadier and lieutenant-colonel, 24th foot ; served with the Scots brigade in the Dutch army ; with the 78th (Fraser) highlanders at Louisburg, 1758, and Quebec ; with the 24th in Germany, at Gibraltar, and in Ireland ; quartermaster-general in

Ireland, 1770; as brigadier with Burgoyne won victory of Hubbardton, 1777; mortally wounded at Behmise Heights. [xx. 222]

FRASER, SIMON (1726–1782), Master of Lovat, lieutenant-general; eldest son, by first wife, of Simon, twelfth baron Lovat [q. v.]; by his father's instructions headed the Frasers in support of Prince Charles Edward, 1745; attainted and imprisoned at Edinburgh, but pardoned, 1750; practised as an advocate, and was counsel for the widow of Colin Campbell of Glenure against James Stewart of Aucharn, 1752; raised Fraser highlanders (78th), 1757, and commanded them in America, 1757–61, being wounded during the siege of Quebec; brigadier-general in Portugal, 1762; major-general in the Portuguese army; major-general in the British army, 1771; his estates restored on payment of a fine; raised 71st highlanders for the American war; M.P., Inverness county, 1761–82. [xx. 223]

FRASER, SIMON (1765–1803), lieutenant-colonel; son of Archibald Campbell Fraser [q. v.]; entered Wadham College, Oxford, 1786, Lincoln's Inn, 1789, and the Inner Temple, 1793; commanded the Fraser Fencibles in Ireland as lieutenant, 1798; M.P. for Inverness-shire, 1796–1802; died at Lisbon. [xx. 207]

FRASER, SIMON (1738–1813), lieutenant-general; served under Simon Fraser (1726–1782) [q. v.] in Canada; wounded at Sillery, 1760; raised a company and headed it in America, 1778–81, raised 133rd foot, 1793; major-general in Portugal, 1797–1800; lieutenant-general, 1802. [xx. 224]

FRASER, WILLIAM (d. 1297), chancellor of Scotland, 1276; bishop of St. Andrews, 1279–97; as one of the six regents after death of Alexander III went to Gascony to negotiate match between Margaret, Maid of Norway, and Prince Edward of England; invited Edward I to intervene in Scotland, but after accession of Baliol went to France to obtain aid for the latter from Philip IV; died at Arveille. [xx. 225]

FRASER, WILLIAM, eleventh BARON SALTOUN (1654–1715), succeeded his grandfather, 1693; seized and imprisoned in the island of Aigas by Simon Fraser, twelfth baron Lovat [q. v.], on account of his attempt to obtain, by the marriage of his eldest son to Emilia Fraser, heiress of Hugh, baron Lovat, the Lovat barony, 1697; wrote a fragment of family history. [xx. 226]

FRASER, WILLIAM (1784?–1835), Indian civilian; brother of James Baillie Fraser [q. v.]; secretary to Mountstuart Elphinstone at Cabul, 1811; resident of Delhi, 1830–5; murdered by a Muhammadan at instigation of the nawab of Firozpur. [xx. 226]

FRASER, WILLIAM (1817–1879), educationalist; as head-master in the Glasgow Normal Seminary assisted David Stow to carry out his new training system; free church minister at Paisley, 1849–79; made valuable suggestions in his 'State of our Educational Enterprises,' 1857; LL.D. Glasgow, 1872. [xx. 226]

FRASER, SIR WILLIAM (1816–1898), Scottish genealogist and antiquary; solicitor in Edinburgh, 1851; deputy-keeper of sasines, 1852–80; deputy-keeper of records, 1880–92; LL.D. Edinburgh, 1882; K.C.B., 1887; served on royal commission on historical manuscripts from 1869; endowed chair of ancient history and palaeography at Edinburgh; published elaborate compilations on Scottish family history. [Suppl. ii. 245]

FRASER, SIR WILLIAM AUGUSTUS, fourth baronet (1826–1898), politician; succeeded to baronetcy, 1834; educated at Eton and Christ Church, Oxford; M.A., 1852; gazetted cornet, 1st life guards, 1847; captain, 1852; conservative M.P. for Barnstaple, 1857–9, Ludlow, 1863–5, and Kidderminster, 1874–80; F.S.A., 1862; published anecdotic miscellanies on contemporary history. [Suppl. ii. 246]

FRAUNCE, ABRAHAM (fl. 1587–1633), poet; fellow of St. John's College, Cambridge, 1580; M.A., 1583; barrister, Gray's Inn; the Corydon of Spenser's 'Colin Clout's come home again'; intimately associated with Thomas Watson, with whom he translated Tasso's 'Aminta' (fact mentioned in Lodge's 'Phillis' and the 'Faerie Queene'); published in English hexameters 'The Countesse of Pembrokes Yuychurch' (Ivychurch), two parts, 1591, 'Amintas Dale' (pt. iii. of Ivychurch, 1592),

'The Countess of Pembrokes Emanuel' (1591), 'The Arcadian Rhetorike,' 1588, in which the unpublished 'Faerie Queene' is quoted, and 'The Lawiers Logike,' 1588; contributed songs to Sidney's 'Astrophel and Stella,' 1591. [xx. 227]

FRAXINETUS, SIMON (fl. 1200). [See SIMON.]

FRAZER, ANDREW (d. 1792), lieutenant-colonel of engineers; employed to watch demolition of works at Dunkirk, 1767–78, lieutenant-colonel, 1788. [xx. 229]

FRAZER, SIR AUGUSTUS SIMON (1776–1835), colonel; son of Andrew Frazer [q. v.]; entered royal artillery, 1793; commanded artillery at Buenos Ayres, 1807, and horse artillery on Wellington's staff in the Peninsula and at Waterloo, 1813–15; K.C.B., 1814; F.R.S., 1816; colonel, 1825; director of Royal Laboratory, Woolwich, 1828. [xx. 229]

FRAZER, WILLIAM (d. 1297). [See FRASER.]

FREAKE, EDMUND (1516?–1591), bishop of Rochester (1572), Norwich (1575), and Worcester (1584); canon of St. Augustine in Waltham Abbey till the dissolution; D.D. Cambridge; dean of Rochester, 1570, and of Salisbury; had great dispute with John Becon [q. v.]; published translation of treatise by St. Augustine. [xx. 230]

FREAKE, JOHN (1688–1756). [See FREKE.]

FREDERICA CHARLOTTE ULRICA CATHERINA (1767–1820), eldest daughter of Frederick William II, king of Prussia; married Frederick Augustus, duke of York and Albany, 1791; separated from her husband. [xx. 233]

FREDERICK, SAINT (d. 838). [See ORIDIODUNUS, FRIDERICUS.]

FREDERICK, COLONEL, or FREDERICK DE NEUHOFF (1725?–1797), author of 'Description of Corsica': described himself as son of Theodore, baron de Neuhoff, king of Corsica [q. v.]; came to England, c. 1754; taught Italian to Garrick, Macklin, and Alexander Wedderburn, afterwards first baron Loughborough [q. v.]; agent in London of the Grand Duke of Würtemberg; endeavoured to raise loan on continent for English royal princes; when in financial straits shot himself in the porch of Westminster Abbey. [xx. 232]

FREDERICK AUGUSTUS, DUKE OF YORK AND ALBANY (1763–1827), second son of George III; elected to bishopric of Osnaburg, 1764; created Duke of York, 1784; entered the army and studied his profession in Germany; fought a duel with Colonel Lennox, 1789, caused by a speech on the Regency Bill; married eldest daughter of Frederick William II of Prussia, 1791; commanded English army in Flanders, 1793–5; field-marshal, 1795, commander-in-chief, 1798–1809; unsuccessful in Helder expedition, 1799; gave up bishopric of Osnaburg, 1803; removed from head of the army in consequence of the conduct of his mistress, Mary Anne Clarke [q. v.], 1809; reinstated, 1811, and thanked by parliament at conclusion of war; guardian of the king's person, 1818; spoke against catholic emancipation, 1825. [xx. 233]

FREDERICK LOUIS, PRINCE OF WALES (1707–1751), father of George III; born at Hanover; created Duke of Gloucester, 1717, of Edinburgh, 1727; created Prince of Wales, 1729; his projected marriage with the princess royal of Prussia frustrated by George II; wrote or inspired 'Histoire du Prince Titi,' 1735, a caricature of his father and mother; supported Buononcini against Handel; married Princess Augusta of Saxe Gotha, 1736; ordered to quit St. James's on account of his inconsiderate conduct at recent lying-in of his wife, 1737; removed to Kew and Norfolk House, where he gathered together the heads of the opposition; solicited command of the army, 1745. [xx. 235]

FREE, JOHN (d. 1465). [See PHREAS.]

FREEBAIRN, ALFRED ROBERT (1794–1846), engraver; probably son of Robert Freebairn [q. v.]; executed vignettes and illustrations for the 'Book of Gems,' also many engravings by anaglyptograph process published in Art Union, 1846. [xx. 237]

FREEBAIRN, ROBERT (1765–1808), landscape-painter; exhibited at Royal Academy, 1782–6; sent views of Roman scenery to the Academy, 1789 and 1790. [xx. 238]

FREEBURN, JAMES (1808–1876), inventor of metal and wood fuses for exploding live shells; served in royal artillery; in West Indies, 1837–40. [xx. 238]

FREEKE, WILLIAM (1662–1744). [See FREKE.]

FREELING, SIR FRANCIS (1764–1836), postal reformer; helped Palmer in improving his mail coach system, 1785; for many years secretary to the general post office; created baronet, 1828. [xx. 239]

FREELING, SIR GEORGE HENRY (1789–1841), commissioner of customs, 1836–41; son of Sir Francis Freeling [q. v.] [xx. 239]

FREEMAN, EDWARD AUGUSTUS (1823–1892), historian; B.A. and probationary fellow, Trinity College, Oxford, 1845; honorary fellow, 1880; published 'History of Architecture,' 1849; regular contributor to 'Saturday Review,' 1855–78; examiner in school of law and modern history at Oxford, 1857–8, 1863–4, and 1873; honorary D.C.L. Oxford, 1870, and LL.D. Cambridge, 1874; served on royal commission to inquire into constitution and working of ecclesiastical courts, 1881–3; lectured in United States, 1881–2; regius professor of modern history at Oxford, 1884–92; honorary LL.D. Edinburgh, 1884. His works include, 'History and Conquests of the Saracens,' 1856, 'History of Federal Government,' only vol. i. published, 1863, 'History of Norman Conquest,' 1867–79, 'Growth of the English Constitution,' 1872, 'Historical Geography of Europe,' 1881–2, 'Chief Periods of European History,' 1886, and 'History of Sicily,' 1891–2. [Suppl. ii. 247]

FREEMAN, JOHN (fl. 1611), divine; fellow of Trinity College, Cambridge, 1583; M.A., 1584; published 'The Comforter,' 1591. [xx. 239]

FREEMAN, JOHN (fl. 1670–1720), historical painter; rival of Isaac Fuller [q. v.]; was latterly scene-painter to Covent Garden; probably not identical with the artist of the 'Trial of Lord Lovat.' [xx. 239]

FREEMAN, PHILIP (1818–1875), archdeacon of Exeter, 1865; B.A. Trinity College, Cambridge, 1839; Craven University scholar and Browne medallist, 1838; fellow of Peterhouse, 1839; M.A., 1842; principal of Chichester theological college, 1846–8; canon of Cumbrae College, Bute, 1853–8; vicar of Thorverton, 1858; published 'Short Account of the Collegiate Church of Cumbrae,' 1854, 'History ... of Exeter Cathedral,' 1871, and other works. [xx. 240]

FREEMAN, SIR RALPH (fl. 1610–1655), civilian and dramatist; master of requests, 1618; auditor of imprests and master of the mint, 1629; published verse translations from Seneca and 'Imperiale,' a tragedy, 1655. [xx. 240]

FREEMAN, SAMUEL (1773–1857), engraver in stipple. His works include portraits of Johnson after Bartolozzi, Garrick after Reynolds, and L. E. L. after Wright. [xx. 241]

FREEMAN, THOMAS (fl. 1614), epigrammatist; B.A. Magdalen College, Oxford, 1607; published 'Rvbbe and a Great Cast' and 'Rvnne and a Great Cast,' 1614. [xx. 241]

FREEMAN, WILLIAM PEERE WILLIAMS (1742–1832). [See WILLIAMS, afterwards WILLIAMS-FREEMAN.]

FREER, MARTHA WALKER (1822–1888). [See ROBINSON, Mrs.]

FREIND, SIR JOHN (d. 1696). [See FRIEND.]

FREIND, JOHN (1675–1728), physician; educated at Westminster and Christ Church, Oxford; B.A., 1698; M.D., 1707; physician with Peterborough in Spain, 1705–7; published pamphlets in defence of Peterborough; F.R.S., 1712; attended Ormonde in Flanders; F.R.C.P., 1716; Gulstonian lecturer, 1718, Harveian orator, 1720; M.P., Launceston, 1722; implicated in his friend Atterbury's plot; said to have owed his release from the Tower to Richard Mead [q. v.]; physician to Queen Caroline, 1727; published 'History of Physic ... to beginning of the Sixteenth Century' (2 vols. 1725–6). [xx. 241]

FREIND, ROBERT (1667–1751), head-master of Westminster School; brother of John Freind [q. v.]; educated at Westminster and Christ Church, Oxford; B.A., 1690; D.D., 1709; head-master of Westminster, 1711–33; canon

of Windsor, 1729, of Westminster, 1731, of Christ Church, 1737; made Westminster the leading school of the day; helped in the production of Boyle's attack on Bentley. [xx. 243]

FREIND, WILLIAM (1669–1745), divine; brother of Robert and John Freind [q. v.]; educated at Westminster and Christ Church, Oxford; M.A., 1694; rector of Turvey, 1714, of Woodford, Northamptonshire, 1720; won a lottery prize of 20,000l., 1745; author of 'The Christian Minister.' [xx. 245]

FREIND, WILLIAM (1715–1766), dean of Canterbury, 1760–6; son of Robert Freind [q. v.]; of Westminster and Christ Church; M.A., 1738; D.D., 1748; rector of Witney, 1739, of Islip, 1747; canon of Westminster, 1744, of Christ Church, 1756; prolocutor of the lower house, 1761. [xx. 245]

FREKE, JOHN (1688–1756), surgeon; curator of St. Bartholomew's Hospital Museum, and surgeon, 1729–55; F.R.S., 1729; published 'Treatise on the Nature and Property of Fire,' 1752, and 'Essay on the Art of Healing,' 1748; twice mentioned in 'Tom Jones.' [xx. 246]

FREKE, WILLIAM (1662–1744), mystical writer; of Wadham College, Oxford; barrister of the Temple; fined and ordered to make a public recantation for an anti-trinitarian tract distributed to members of parliament, 1694; proclaimed himself 'the great Elijah,' 1709; published 'Lingua Tersancta,' 1703. [xx. 247]

FREMANTLE, SIR THOMAS FRANCIS (1765–1819), vice-admiral; served with Hood and Nelson in the Mediterranean, 1793–7; distinguished himself at Toulon, 1795, and at Leghorn and Elba, 1796; severely wounded in attack on Santa Cruz, 1797; took Nelson home in the Seahorse; at Copenhagen, 1801, in the Ganges; at Trafalgar in the Neptune, 1805; rear-admiral, 1810; commanded in Adriatic, 1812–14, capturing Fiume (1813) and Trieste (1814); K.C.B. and baron of Austria, 1815; G.C.B. and commander-in-chief in Mediterranean, 1818. [xx. 248]

FREMANTLE, THOMAS FRANCIS, first BARON COTTESLOE (1798–1890), son of Sir Thomas Francis Fremantle [q. v.]; B.A. Oriel College, Oxford, 1819; created baronet, 1821; conservative M.P. for Buckingham, 1826–46; one of secretaries of treasury, 1834 and 1841; secretary at war, 1844; chief secretary for Ireland, 1845–6; deputy-chairman, and subsequently chairman of board of customs, 1846–73; raised to peerage, 1874. [Suppl. ii. 251]

FREMANTLE, SIR WILLIAM HENRY (1766–1850), politician; resident secretary for Ireland, 1789–1800; joint-secretary to the treasury under Lord Grenville, 1806; M.P. for Wick, 1808–12, for Buckingham, 1812–27; privy councillor and commissioner of the India board, 1822–6; treasurer of the household, 1826–37. [xx. 249]

FRENCH, GEORGE RUSSELL (1803–1881), antiquary and author of genealogical works. [xx. 250]

FRENCH, GILBERT JAMES (1804–1866), biographer of Samuel Crompton [q. v.]; published, among other works, 'Enquiry into Origin and Authorship of some of the Waverley Novels,' 1856, and 'Life and Times of Samuel Crompton,' 1859. [xx. 251]

FRENCH, JOHN (1616?–1657), physician to the parliamentary army; M.A. New Inn Hall, Oxford, 1640; M.D., 1648; published works, including 'The Art of Distillation, 1651, and 'The Yorkshire Spaw,' 1652, and other works. [xx. 251]

FRENCH, NICHOLAS (1604–1678), bishop of Ferns; president of the Irish College at Louvain; prominent among the confederated catholics during the Irish rebellion; bishop of Ferns before 1646; went on mission to Rome, 1647, to Brussels, 1651, and to Paris, 1652; coadjutor to archbishop of Santiago de Compostella, 1652–1666, afterwards to archbishop of Paris, and to bishop of Ghent, where he died and was buried; published 'Narrative of the Earl of Clarendon's Settlement and Sale of Ireland,' 1668, and other rare tracts. [xx. 252]

FRENCH, PETER (d. 1693), Dominican missionary; laboured for thirty years among Mexican Indians. [xx. 253]

FRENCH, THOMAS VALPY (1825–1891), Indian bishop; M.A. University College, Oxford, 1849; fellow,

1848; ordained priest, 1849; principal of St. John's College, Agra, 1850; first bishop of Lahore, 1877–87; D.D. Oxford, 1877.   [Suppl. ii. 253]

FRENCH, WILLIAM (1786–1849), master of Jesus College, Cambridge; educated at Ipswich and Caius College, Cambridge; second wrangler and Smith's prizeman, 1811; fellow and tutor of Pembroke College, Cambridge; M.A., 1814; master of Jesus College, 1820–49; D.D., 1821; canon of Ely, 1832; published, with George Skinner, translation of the Psalms, with notes, 1830, and of the Proverbs, 1831.   [xx. 254]

FREND, WILLIAM (1757–1841), reformer and scientific writer; educated at Canterbury, St. Omer, and Christ's College, Cambridge; second wrangler and Smith's prizeman, 1780; B.A., 1780; fellow and tutor of Jesus College, 1781; vicar of Madingley, 1783–7, when he became a unitarian; translated for Priestley the historical books of the Old Testament; expelled the university for his 'Peace and Union recommended,' 1793; his expulsion invalidated on technical grounds; actuary of the Rock Life Assurance Company, 1806–26; tutor of Copley (Lyndhurst) and Malthus; published 'Principles of Algebra' (1796 and 1799), and treatises advocating graduated income-tax and a sinking fund.   [xx. 254]

FRENDRAUGHT, first VISCOUNT (d. 1650). [See CRICHTON, JAMES.]

FRERE, BARTHOLOMEW (1778–1851), diplomatist; son of John Frere [q. v.]; M.A. Trinity College, Cambridge, 1806; acting minister in Spain, 1809–10; at Constantinople as secretary and interim minister, 1812, 1815–1817, 1820–1.   [xx. 256]

FRERE, SIR HENRY BARTLE EDWARD, commonly called SIR BARTLE FRERE, first baronet (1815–1884), statesman; nephew of John Hookham Frere [q. v.]; educated at Bath and Haileybury; entered Bombay civil service, 1834; assisted Henry Edward Goldsmid [q. v.] in investigating and reforming land-assessment; resident at Sattara, 1846, and commissioner upon its annexation, 1847, to which he was opposed; as chief commissioner of Sind, 1850–9, conciliated dispossessed amirs and opened up the country by means of public works; during the mutiny sent almost the whole of his armed force to the relief of the Punjab; thanked by parliament; K.C.B.; first non-Bengal civilian appointed to the viceroy's council, 1859; Lord Canning's confidential adviser; as governor of Bombay, 1862–7, instituted the municipality and checked speculation, but was criticised for his conduct with regard to the Bombay Bank; returned to England as member of the council of India, 1867; G.C.S.I.; D.C.L. Oxford; LL.D. Cambridge; president of the Geographical Society, 1873, of the Asiatic Society, 1872; P.C.; sent to Zanzibar to negotiate suppression of slave trade, 1872; privy councillor; accompanied the Prince of Wales to India, 1875; created G.C.B. and a baronet, 1876; governor of the Cape, and first high commissioner of South Africa, 1877; dismissed the cabinet and tried to conciliate the Kaffirs, but was obliged to make war on them, peace being made, 1878; made demands on Cetewayo which resulted in the Zulu war, 1879, when he was held to have exceeded his instructions, censured by the government, and superseded in the high-commissionership; supported Shepstone on the Transvaal question, but after a conference with the Boers promised to urge the redress of some of their grievances, 1879; recalled, 1880, in spite of great popularity in South Africa; defended himself by the publication of correspondence relating to his recall and in 'Afghanistan and South Africa,' 1881; replied to charges of Mr. Gladstone in Midlothian; wrote also memoir of his uncle Hookham Frere prefixed to the 'Works of J. H. Frere.' [xx. 257]

FRERE, JAMES HATLEY (1779–1866), writer on prophecy; sixth son of John Frere [q. v.]; invented phonetic system for teaching blind to read, and cheap method of stereotyping. His works include 'Combined View of the Prophecies of Daniel, Esdras, and St. John,' 1815, and 'On the General Structure of the Apocalypse,' 1826.   [xx. 266]

FRERE, JOHN (1740–1807), antiquary; second wrangler and fellow of Caius College, Cambridge, 1763; M.A., 1766; high sheriff of Norfolk, 1766; F.R.S., 1771; M.P., Norwich, 1799; wrote paper 'On the Flint Weapons of Hoxne in Suffolk' ('Archæologia' for 1800).   [xx. 267]

FRERE, JOHN HOOKHAM (1769–1846), diplomatist and author; eldest son of John Frere [q. v.]; friend of Canning; educated at Eton and Caius College, Cambridge; fellow,1793?–1816; M.A.,1795; a founder of the'Microcosm,' 1786–7; M.P., West Looe, 1799–1802; contributed to the 'Anti-Jacobin' (1797–8) most of the 'Loves of the Triangles,' and parts of 'The Friend of Humanity and the Knifegrinder' and 'The Rovers'; under-secretary for foreign affairs, 1799; envoy extraordinary and plenipotentiary at Lisbon, 1800–2, at Madrid, 1802–4; privy councillor, 1805; as British minister with the Junta, 1808–9; advised Moore to retreat through Galicia; twice refused a peerage; retired to Malta, 1818, where he died; contributed to Ellis's 'Specimens of Early English Poets,' 1801, and to Southey's 'Chronicle of the Cid,' 1808; one of the founders of the 'Quarterly Review'; published metrical versions of Aristophanes's 'Frogs,' 1839, and 'Acharnians, Knights, and Birds,'1840; published 'Theognis Restitutus,' 1842.   [xx. 268]

FRERE, PHILIP HOWARD (1813–1868), agriculturist; eldest son of William Frere [q. v.]: fellow (1837) and bursar (1839) of Downing College, Cambridge; editor of 'Journal of Royal Agricultural Society,' 1862.
          [xx. 270]

FRERE, WILLIAM (1775–1836), master of Downing College, Cambridge, 1812; fourth son of John Frere [q. v.]; educated at Eton and Trinity College, Cambridge; B.A., 1798; Craven scholar and chancellor's medallist; barrister, 1802; serjeant-at-law, 1809; master of Downing College, Cambridge, 1812; LL.D. Cambridge, 1825; D.C.L. Oxford, 1834; edited Baron Glenbervie's 'Reports of Cases,' 1813, and vol. v. of the 'Paston Letters.'   [xx. 270]

FRESNE, SIMON DU (fl. 1200). [See SIMON.]

FRESTON, ANTHONY (1757–1819), divine; B.A. of Christ Church, Oxford, 1780; B.A. and M.A. Clare Hall, Cambridge, 1783; rector of Edgworth, 1801; published theological and poetical works.   [xx. 270]

FREVILLE, GEORGE (d. 1579), baron of the exchequer, 1559–79; recorder of Cambridge, 1553. [xx. 271]

FREWEN, ACCEPTED (1588–1664), archbishop of York; eldest son of John Frewen [q. v.]; fellow of Magdalen College, Oxford, 1612; M.A., 1612; chaplain to Lord Digby (Bristol) in Spain; chaplain to the king and canon of Canterbury, 1625; president of Magdalen, 1626–43; dean of Gloucester, 1631; mainly instrumental in presentation of university plate to Charles I, 1642; bishop of Lichfield and Coventry, 1643; his estate declared forfeited by parliament, 1652; proscribed by Oliver Cromwell; archbishop of York, 1660–4; benefactor of Magdalen College, Oxford.   [xx. 271]

FREWEN, JOHN (1558–1628), puritan divine; rector of Northiam from 1583; indicted by parishioners for nonconformity, 1611; his eight sermons preached in vindication of himself, re-preached from the same pulpit 250 years later by Octavius Lord; published devotional manuals; edited John Bishop's 'Courteous Conference with the English Catholickes Romane,' 1598.   [xx. 273]

FREWEN, THOMAS (1704–1791), physician; M.D. before 1755; one of the first to inoculate for smallpox; published 'Practice and Theory of Inoculation,' 1749.
          [xx. 274]

FREWIN, RICHARD (1681?–1761), physician; of Westminster and Christ Church, Oxford; M.A., 1704; M.D., 1711; Camden professor of ancient history, 1727; left his books to the Radcliffe library and his house (now Frewin Hall) for the regius professor of medicine.
          [xx. 275]

FRIDEGODE (fl. 950). [See FRITHEGODE.]

FRIDESWIDE, FRITHESWITH, or FREDESWITHA, SAINT (d. 735?), said to have founded monastery at Oxford, when miraculously delivered from the persecution of a king, her lover; buried in St. Mary's Church, Oxford; her relics translated, 1180 and 1289; her shrine destroyed, 1538. The monastery (at Oxford) refounded by Roger, bishop of Salisbury, was suppressed, 1524, and handed over to Wolsey.   [xx. 275]

FRIEND, SIR JOHN (d. 1696), conspirator; knighted by James II, 1685; executed for being privy to a conspiracy against William III.   [xx. 276]

FRIPP, GEORGE ARTHUR (1813–1896), water-colour artist; studied under Samuel Jackson (1794–1869) [q. v.]; member of Old Water-colour Society, 1845, and secretary, 1848–54; painted by royal command series of pictures of Balmoral neighbourhood, 1860.   [Suppl. ii. 253]

FRISELL, FRASER (1774–1846), friend of Chateaubriand; studied at Glasgow; prisoner in France, 1793–4 and 1803; intimate with Madame de Guitaut; corresponded with Joubert; wrote 'Étude sur la Constitution de l'Angleterre, avec des remarques sur l'ancienne Constitution de la France' (1820).   [xx. 277]

FRISWELL, JAMES HAIN (1825–1878), miscellaneous writer; published more than thirty works, including essays, 'A Quotation Handbook' (1865), 'The Gentle Life,' 1864, some novels, and 'Modern Men of Letters honestly criticised,' 1870.   [xx. 277]

FRITH, JOHN (1503–1533), protestant martyr; of Eton and King's College, Cambridge; B.A., 1525; junior canon at Wolsey's College, Oxford, 1525; imprisoned for assisting Tyndal to translate the New Testament; on release, 1528, went to Marburg for six years, where he translated Patrick Hamilton's 'Places,' 1529?; in spite of poverty and overtures from Henry VIII wrote 'Disputacion of Purgatorye,' combating More and Fisher, 1531?; imprisoned in the Tower for heresy, 1532, formulated first protestant views on the sacrament; replied to More's answer; burnt at Smithfield for heretical views on purgatory and transubstantiation; his works published by Foxe, 1573.   [xx. 278]

FRITH, MARY (1584?–1659), 'Moll Cutpurse'; notorious as a pickpocket, fortune-teller, and forger; did penance at Paul's Cross, 1612; heroine of Middleton and Dekker's 'Roaring Girle.'   [xx. 280]

FRITHEGODE or **FRIDEGODE** (*fl.* 950), hagiographer; monk of Canterbury; wrote metrical 'Life of Wilfrith.'   [xx. 281]

FROBISHER, SIR MARTIN (1535?–1594), navigator; made his first voyage to Guinea, 1554; examined on suspicion of piracy, 1566; employed on state service off coast of Ireland; made his first voyage in search of northwest passage under auspices of Ambrose Dudley, earl of Warwick [q. v.], 1576, reaching Frobisher Bay; as admiral of the Company of Cathay, sailed to the same region in search of gold, 1577, explored south of Meta Incognita and Jackman's Sound, and brought home two hundred tons of gold from Kodlun-arn (Countess of Warwick's Island); during third voyage with fifteen ships, 1578, landed in southern Greenland and discovered new strait and upper part of Frobisher's Bay; vice-admiral in Drake's West Indian expedition, 1586; commanded the Triumph against Spanish Armada, and led one of the newly formed squadrons; knighted and made commander of squadron in Narrow Seas, 1588–9; vice-admiral in Hawkins's expedition, 1590; captured a Biscayan with valuable cargo, 1592; died from wound received in expedition for relief of Brest and Crozon.   [xx. 281]

FRODSHAM, BRIDGE (1734–1768), actor; twice ran away from Westminster School; the 'York Garrick'; is Hamlet considered by Tate Wilkinson only second to that of Garrick and Barry.   [xx. 284]

FROST, CHARLES (1781?–1862), antiquary; solicitor to Hull Dock Company; F.S.A., 1822; published work on the early history of Hull, 1827.   [xx. 285]

FROST, GEORGE (1754–1821), Ipswich landscape-painter; friend of Constable and imitator of Gainsborough.   [xx. 285]

FROST, JOHN (1626?–1656), nonconformist divine; fellow of St. John's College, Cambridge; B.D., 1656; published 'Select Sermons,' 1667.   [xx. 286]

FROST, JOHN (1803–1840), founder of the Medico-botanical Society, 1821; secretary to Royal Humane Society, 1824; expelled the Medico-Botanical Society for his arrogant behaviour, 1830; having incurred liabilities in respect of Millbank hospital-ship, fled to Paris, 1832; afterwards practised as a physician in Berlin.   [xx. 286]

FROST, JOHN (1750–1842), secretary of the Corresponding Society; prominent member of Thatched House parliamentary reform society, 1782; founded Corresponding Society, 1792; as representative of the Society for Constitutional Information present at trial of Louis XVI,

1792–3; denounced by Burke as 'ambassador to the murderers'; indicted for sedition, and, though defended by Erskine, sentenced to six months' imprisonment and to be struck off the roll of attorneys, 1793; pardoned by the prince regent, 1813, but not replaced on the rolls.   [xx. 287]

FROST, JOHN (*d.* 1877), chartist; imprisoned for libel, 1822; mayor of Newport, Monmouthshire, 1836; after chartist convention of 1839 removed from commission of the peace for seditious language; brought about dissolution of convention and led an armed mob into Newport, 1839; transported to Van Diemen's Land, 1840; conditionally pardoned, 1854; returned to England, 1856, with free pardon; wrote and lectured on convict life and against transportation.   [xx. 288]

FROST, PERCIVAL (1817–1898), mathematician; second wrangler, St. John's College, Cambridge, 1839; M.A., 1842; fellow, 1839; ordained deacon, 1841; mathematical lecturer in Jesus College, 1847–59, and in King's College, 1859–89; F.R.S., 1883; fellow of King's College, 1883–98; D.Sc., 1883; published mathematical works.   [Suppl. ii. 253]

FROST, WILLIAM EDWARD (1810–1877), painter; Royal Academy gold medallist for 'Prometheus Bound,' 1839; exhibited 'Sabrina,' 1845, 'Diana surprised by Actæon,' 1846, 'Una' (purchased by Queen Victoria), 1847, 'Euphrosyne,' 1848, 'Disarming of Cupid,' 1850 (at Osborne), and 'Narcissus,' 1857; R.A., 1870–6.   [xx. 289]

FROUCESTER, WALTER (*d.* 1412), abbot of St. Peter's, Gloucester, 1382, the cloisters of which he completed.   [xx. 290]

FROUDE, JAMES ANTHONY (1818–1894), historian and man of letters; brother of Richard Hurrell Froude [q. v.] and of William Froude [q. v.]; educated at Westminster and Oriel College, Oxford; B.A., 1842; chancellor's English essayist; Devon fellow of Exeter College, 1842; M.A., 1843; wrote life of St. Neot for Newman's 'Lives of the English Saints,' 1844; marked his breach with orthodoxy, 1849, by publication of 'Nemesis of Faith,' a copy of which was publicly burned by William Sewell [q. v.]; resigned his fellowship from annoyance; made acquaintance of Carlyle, 1849, and subsequently became his chief disciple; published 'History of England from Fall of Wolsey to Defeat of Spanish Armada,' 12 vols., 1856–70; editor of 'Fraser's Magazine,' 1860–74; rector of St. Andrews, 1868; published 'The English in Ireland in Eighteenth Century,' 1872–4; lectured in United States, 1872; travelled in South Africa, 1874–5, with object of ascertaining what were the obstacles to confederation of South African States; conducted an unsuccessful political campaign in Cape Colony and Orange Free State in favour of federation, 1875; member of Scottish universities commission, 1876; sole literary executor of Carlyle, 1881; published Carlyle's 'Reminiscences,' 1881, 'Letters and Memorials of Jane Welsh Carlyle,' 1883, 'History of first Forty Years of Carlyle's Life,' 1882, and 'History of Carlyle's Life in London,' 1884; honorary LL.D. Edinburgh, 1884; visited Australia, 1884–5; published 'Oceana, or England and her Colonies,' 1886; visited West Indies, 1886–7, and published 'English in West Indies,' 1888; regius professor of modern history at Oxford, 1892–4. His lectures were published as 'Life and Letters of Erasmus,' 1894, 'English Seamen in Sixteenth Century,' 1895, and 'Council of Trent,' 1896. As a writer of English prose Froude had few rivals in the nineteenth century, though the value of his historical scholarship is matter of controversy.   [Suppl. ii. 254]

FROUDE, RICHARD HURRELL (1803–1836), divine; brother of James Anthony Froude [q. v.] and of William Froude [q. v.]; educated at Ottery, Eton, and Oriel College, Oxford; fellow, 1826; M.A., 1827; intimate with Newman and greatly influenced the Tractarians; with Newman wrote 'Lyra Apostolica' at Rome, 1832–3; contributed three of the 'Tracts for the Times'; his 'Remains' edited by James Bowling Mozley, 1837 and 1839.   [xx. 290]

FROUDE, WILLIAM (1810–1879), engineer and naval architect, brother of Richard Hurrell Froude [q. v.] and James Anthony Froude [q. v.]; of Westminster and Oriel College, Oxford; M.A., 1837; while employed under Brunel on Bristol and Exeter railway propounded 'curve of adjustment'; constructed bilge-keels to prevent rolling of ships; conducted for the admiralty at Torquay experiments on resistance and propulsion of ships; F.R.S., 1870; royal

medallist, 1876 ; constructed dynamometer to determine power of marine engines ; died at Simon's Town.
[xx. 291]

FROWDE, PHILIP (*d.* 1738), poet ; pupil of Addison at Magdalen College, Oxford ; his 'Cursus Glacialis, Anglicè Scating,' published by Curll as Addison's, 1720 ; published two tragedies, 'The Fall of Saguntum,' 1727, and 'Philotas,' 1731, in both of which Quin acted. [xx. 292]

FROWYK, SIR THOMAS (*d.* 1506), judge ; serjeant-at-law, 1494 ; judge of assize in the west, 1501 ; helped to define jurisdiction of university and town of Cambridge, 1502 ; chief-justice of common pleas, 1502. [xx. 293]

FRY, CAROLINE (1787–1846). [See WILSON.]

FRY, EDMUND (1754–1835), type-founder ; son of Joseph Fry [q. v.] ; M.D. Edinburgh ; issued 'specimens of metal-cast ornaments,' 1793 ; published 'Pantographia' (containing more than two hundred alphabets), 1799, and 'Specimen of Printing Types,' 1810 ; sold business to Thorowgood, 1829 ; awarded gold medal for raised type for the blind. [xx. 293]

FRY, ELIZABETH (1780–1845), prison reformer ; sister of Joseph John Gurney [q. v.] ; a quaker minister at twenty-nine ; highly impressive as a preacher ; married Joseph Fry, 1820 ; formed association for improvement of female prisoners in Newgate, 1817 ; interested herself in other prisons, and induced government to make regulation for voyage of convicts to New South Wales ; received by Louis-Philippe and the king of Prussia ; instituted order of nursing sisters ; alleviated condition of vagrants in London and Brighton. [xx. 294]

FRY, FRANCIS (1803–1886), bibliographer ; partner in firm of J. S. Fry & Co. of Bristol ; one of the quaker deputation to monarchs of Europe for abolition of slavery, 1850 ; printed facsimile of Tyndale's New Testament (1525 or 1526), 1862, and in the same year 'Souldier's Pocket Bible' ; published 'Description of the Great Bible of 1539 . . . Cranmer's Bible . . . and editions in large folio of the Authorised Version,' 1865 ; an account of Coverdale's Bible (1535), 1867, and a bibliographical description of Tyndale's version (1534), 1878. [xx. 296]

FRY, JOHN (1609–1657), theological writer ; entered parliament after Pride's Purge ; member of the commission for trial of the king, but took part only in the earlier proceedings ; carried on theological controversy with Francis Cheynell [q. v.] and others concerning the Trinity ; disabled from sitting in parliament on account of his writings. [xx. 297]

FRY, JOHN (1792–1822), Bristol bookseller and author of 'Metrical Trifles,' 1810 ; and 'Bibliographical Memoranda,' 1816 ; printed fragments of mediæval (English) poetry. [xx. 298]

FRY, JOSEPH (1728–1787), type-founder ; practised medicine in Bristol, and afterwards made cocoa and chocolate ; with William Pine began type-founding, 1764 ; removed to London ; brought out bible in 5 vols., 1774–6 ; and 'Specimen of Printing Types made by Joseph Fry & Sons,' 1785 (which he declared to be indistinguishable from the founts of William Caslon).
[xx. 298]

FRY, WILLIAM THOMAS (1789–1843), engraver in stipple. [xx. 299]

FRYE, THOMAS (1710–1762), painter, mezzotint engraver and china manufacturer ; friend of Reynolds ; painted and engraved full lengths of Frederick, Prince of Wales, 1741, and Jeremy Bentham ; engraved and published eighteen life-size heads in mezzotint, including George III, Queen Charlotte, Garrick, and the Gunnings ; patentee, 1744 and 1749, for making porcelain from a new material brought from America. [xx. 300]

FRYER, EDWARD (1761–1826), physician ; M.D. Leyden, 1785 ; L.R.C.P., 1790 ; attended the Duke of Sussex ; published life of Barry, the painter, 1825.
[xx. 301]

FRYER, JOHN (*d.* 1563), physician ; of Eton and King's College, Cambridge ; M.A., 1525 ; expelled from Wolsey's College at Oxford as a Lutheran, and imprisoned in the Savoy and the Fleet ; by assistance of Edward Fox [q. v.] graduated M.D. at Padua, 1535 ; president of College of Physicians, 1549–50 ; attended Fox at Diet of Smalcalde, 1535 ; imprisoned in the Tower for Romanism, 1561–3 ; died of the plague. [xx. 301]

FRYER, JOHN (*fl.* 1571), physician ; M.A. Cambridge, 1548 ; M.D., 1555 ; settled at Padua in Queen Elizabeth's reign ; published the 'Aphorisms of Hippocrates,' versified, 1567 ; and Latin occasional verses.
[xx. 301]

FRYER, JOHN (*d.* 1672), physician ; grandson of John Fryer (*d.* 1563) [q. v.] ; M.D. Padua, 1610 ; excluded from College of Physicians as a Romanist ; honorary fellow, 1664. [xx. 302]

FRYER, JOHN (*d.* 1733), traveller ; M.D. Pembroke College, Cambridge, 1683 ; F.R.S., 1697 ; travelled in the East ; published 'A New Account of East India and Persia, in eight letters,' 1698. [xx. 302]

FRYER, LEONARD (*d.* 1605 ?), serjeant-painter to Queen Elizabeth. [xx. 303]

FRYTH. [See FRITH.]

FRYTON, JOHN DE (*fl.* 1304). [See BARTON, JOHN DE.]

FULBECK, WILLIAM (1560–1603 ?), legal writer ; studied at St. Alban Hall, Christ Church, and Gloucester Hall, Oxford ; M.A., 1584 ; entered Gray's Inn ; chief works : 'A Direction or Preparation to the Study of the Law,' 1600, 'A Parallele, or Conference of the Civil Law, the Canon Law, and the Common Law,' 1601, 1618, 'The Pandectes of the Law of Nations,' 1602, and 'The Misfortunes of Arthur,' a masque (1588). [xx. 303]

FULCHER, GEORGE WILLIAMS (1795–1855), poet, bookseller, and printer of Sudbury ; published, among other works, 'Fulcher's Poetical Miscellany,' 1841 ; selected from the 'Sudbury Pocket Book,' to which James Montgomery, Bernard Barton, and the Howitts contributed, 'The Village Paupers,' 1845, and 'The Farmer's Daybook.' [xx. 304]

FULFORD, FRANCIS (1803–1868), first bishop of Montreal, 1850–60 ; fellow of Exeter College, Oxford, 1824–30 ; M.A., 1838 ; hon. D.D., 1850 ; rector of Trowbridge, 1832–42 ; minister of Curzon Chapel, Mayfair, 1845 ; editor of 'Colonial Church Chronicles,' 1848 ; metropolitan of Canada, 1860 ; attended the Pan-Anglican synod at Lambeth, 1867. [xx. 304]

FULKE, WILLIAM (1538–1589), puritan divine ; M.A. St. John's College, Cambridge, 1563 ; friend of Thomas Cartwright (1535–1603) [q. v.] ; deprived of his fellowship at St. John's by Cecil for preaching against the surplice ; readmitted and elected senior fellow, 1567 ; chaplain to Leicester, through whose influence he became incumbent of Warley and Dennington ; D.D., 1572 ; master of Pembroke Hall, Cambridge, 1578 ; conferred with the deprived bishops, Watson and Feckenham, at Wisbech, 1580, and disputed with Edmund Campion in the Tower, 1581 ; one of the twenty-five theologians in dispute with Romanists, 1582 ; published astronomical and theological works, including treatises against Cardinal Allen, Thomas Stapleton, and other Romanists, and 'Defence of the English Version of the Bible.' [xx. 305]

FULLARTON, JOHN (1780 ?–1849), traveller and writer on currency ; travelled widely in India and the East ; entrusted with important mission to China, 1834 ; published a work 'On the Regulation of Currencies' in support of Tooke's views, 1844. [xx. 308]

FULLARTON, WILLIAM (1754–1808), commissioner of Trinidad ; raised and commanded 98th foot, 1778 ; serving against Haidar Ali in Mysore, 1780–2 ; took part in suppression of the Kollars ; as commander of force south of Coleroon, 1783, took Dharapuram, Pálghát, and Coimbatore ; published 'View of English Interests in India,' 1787 ; raised 23rd dragoons, 1794, and 101st foot, 1800 ; M.P. for Plympton, 1779, Haddington, 1787–90, Horsham, 1793–6, Ayrshire, 1796–1803 ; as commissioner of Trinidad caused Picton to be superseded and tried for torturing a Spanish girl. [xx. 308]

FULLER, ANDREW (1754–1815), baptist theologian ; D.D. Princeton College and Yale ; secretary of Baptist Missionary Society. His works include 'The Gospel worthy of all Acceptation,' 'The Calvinistic and Socinian Systems examined and compared as to their Moral Tendency,' 1794, and 'An Apology for the late Christian Missions to India.' [xx. 309]

FULLER, FRANCIS, the elder (1637 ?–1701), nonconformist divine ; M.A. Queens' College, Cambridge, 1660 ;

xpelled from curacy of Warkworth for nonconformity; preached in the west of England; afterwards assisted Timothy Cruso [q. v.] and his successor in Poor Jewry Lane; published treatises and sermons, 1685-1700.
[xx. 310]

FULLER, FRANCIS, the younger (1670-1706), medical writer; second son of Francis Fuller the elder [q. v.]; M.A. St. John's College, Cambridge,' 1704; published Medicina Gymnastica' (1704). [xx. 311]

FULLER, ISAAC (1606-1672), painter and etcher; studied under Perrier; painted altar-pieces for Magdalen and Wadham Colleges, Oxford; much employed in tavern painting; executed portraits of himself, Samuel Butler the poet, Sir Kenelm Digby, and others.
[xx. 311]

FULLER, JOHN (d. 1558), master of Jesus College, Cambridge; fellow of All Souls', Oxford, 1536; D.C.L., 1546; rector of Hanwell, 1547-51; chancellor to Bishop Thirlby of Norwich, 1550; removed with him to Ely, 1554; master of Jesus, 1557-8. [xx. 312]

FULLER, JOHN (d. 1825), author of 'History of Berwick' (1799); M.D. St. Andrews, 1789. [xx. 312]

FULLER, SIR JOSEPH (d. 1841), general; ensign, Coldstream guards, 1792; captain, 1794; served in Flanders, 1793, Ireland, 1798, and North Holland, 1799; served in Peninsula, 1808-9, commanding 1st battalion at Talavera, 1809; major-general, 1813; K.B., 1826; general, 1838; president of consolidated board of general officers.
[xx. 313]

FULLER, NICHOLAS (1557 ?-1626), hebraist and philologist; secretary to Bishops Horne and Watson of Winchester; graduated at Hart Hall, Oxford, 1586; incumbent of Allington, Wiltshire; canon of Salisbury, 1612; his 'Miscellaneorum Theologicorum . . . libri tres,' incorrectly printed at Heidelberg, 1612, and reissued, with fourth book, at Oxford, 1616. [xx. 313]

FULLER or **FULWAR**, SAMUEL (1635-1700), dean of Lincoln; fellow of St. John's College, Cambridge, 1657; M.A., 1658; D.D., 1679; ordained by his uncle, Thomas Fuller or Fulwar [q. v.], chancellor of Lincoln, 1670; chaplain to the king; dean of Lincoln, 1695-1700; his face painted by Verrio 'for Bacchus astride of a barrel'; his defence of Anglican orders (1690) severely censured by Baxter. [xx. 314]

FULLER, THOMAS (1608-1661), divine; M.A. Queens' College, Cambridge, 1628; perpetual curate of St. Benet's, Cambridge, 1630; prebendary of Salisbury, 1631; rector of Broadwindsor, Dorset, 1634; as curate of the Savoy preached sermons from 1642 in favour of peace between king and parliament; retired to Oxford, 1643; followed the war as chaplain to Sir Ralph Hopton 1643-644; at Exeter as chaplain to the infant Princess Henrietta, 1644-6; returned to London after surrender of Exeter; chaplain to Lord Carlisle; preached in London in sufferance; rector of Cranford and chaplain to Earl Berkeley, 1658; accompanied Berkeley to meet Charles II at the Hague, 1660; after Restoration resumed his canonry and Savoy lectureship and became 'chaplain in extraordinary' to the king; published 'History of the Holy Warre,' viz. the crusades, 1643, 'The Holy State and the Profane State,' 1642, 'A Pisgah-sight of Palestine,' 1650, 'Church History of Britain,' 'History of Cambridge University,' 1655, and ' Worthies of England,' 1662.
[xx. 315]

FULLER or **FULWAR**, THOMAS (1593-1667), archbishop of Cashel, related to Thomas Fuller (1608-1661) [q. v.]; disinherited 'for a prodigal'; went to Ireland; bishop of Ardfert, 1641; D.D. Oxford, 1645; archbishop of Cashel, 1661-7. [xx. 320]

FULLER, THOMAS (1654-1734), physician; M.D. Queens' College, Cambridge, 1681; practised at Sevenoaks, where he effected reform of Senoke charity; published 'Exanthemologia' (on eruptive fevers), 1730, and other medical works, besides three collections of maxims.
[xx. 320]

FULLER, WILLIAM (1580 ?-1659), dean of Durham; fellow of St. Catharine Hall, Cambridge; D.D., 1625; chaplain to James I and Charles I; vicar of St. Giles-without-Cripplegate, 1628; dean of Ely, 1636; attended the king at Oxford, 1645; dean of Durham, 1646; twice summoned as a delinquent. [xx. 321]

FULLER, WILLIAM (1608-1675), bishop of Lincoln; educated at Westminster and Magdalen Hall, Oxford; B.C.L. St. Edmund Hall, Oxford, c. 1632; chaplain to Lord-keeper Lyttelton, 1645; dean of St. Patrick, 1660; D.C.L. Oxford, and D.D. Cambridge, 1660; bishop of Limerick, 1663; repaired St. Patrick's; restored monument of St. Hugh at Lincoln; bishop of Lincoln, 1667-1675; benefactor of Lincoln and Christ Church; intimate with Evelyn and Pepys. [xx. 322]

FULLER, WILLIAM (1670-1717 ?), impostor; described himself as a grandson of Dr. Thomas Fuller; accompanied James II's queen, Mary of Modena, to France; employed by her in Ireland and England; made disclosures to the Earl of Shrewsbury and showed Jacobite letters to William III; lodged with Titus Oates in Westminster, but was prosecuted by him for non-payment of rent; offered to reveal Jacobite plot in which Lord Halifax was implicated; unable to produce witnesses, 1692; imprisoned as an impostor, 1692-5; renewed acquaintance with Oates and published pretended revelations of the warming-pan plot, 1696; issued (1701) autobiography and another version of the warming-pan story, containing letters of Mary of Modena and alleged depositions; convicted of misdemeanor, fined, pilloried, and sent to Bridewell, 1702; while in prison published a second autobiography (1703), representing himself as the tool of Oates and Tutchin, also a confession (1704), and a disavowal of this (1716) stating that he had answered the 'Confession' in 'The Truth at Last' (n.d.) [xx. 323]

FULLERTON, LADY GEORGIANA CHARLOTTE (1812-1885), novelist and philanthropist; youngest daughter of Granville Leveson-Gower, first earl Granville [q. v.]; brought sisters of St. Vincent de Paul to England and founded 'Poor Servants of the Mother of God Incarnate'; published 'Ellen Middleton,' 1844, 'Grantley Manor,' 1847, 'Too Strange not to be True,' 1864, and other novels and biographical works. [xx. 325]

FULLWOOD, WILLIAM (fl. 1562), author; published the 'Enimie of Idlenesse: Teaching the maner and stile how to endite, compose, and write all sorts of Epistles,' 1568. [xx. 329]

FULMAN, WILLIAM (1632-1688), antiquary; educated at Magdalen College School and Corpus Christi College, Oxford; fellow of Corpus, and M.A., 1660; rector of Meysey Hampton, 1669; published 'Academiæ Oxoniensis Notitia,' 1665, vol. i. of 'Rerum Anglicarum Scriptorum Veterum tom. i.,'1684, and 'Works of Henry Hammond,' 1684; real editor of Perrinchief's 'Works' of Charles I, 1662; absurdly supposed to have written 'The Whole Duty of Man.' [xx. 326]

FULWAR. [See FULLER.]

FULWELL, ULPIAN (fl. 1586), poet; rector of Naunton, 1570; published 'Like wil to like,' an interlude, 1568, 'The Flower of Fame,' 1575 (a chronicle of Henry VIII, with appendices in verse), and 'Ars adulandi, the Art of Flattery,' 1576, humorous dialogues; joined St. Mary Hall, Oxford, 1578. [xx. 327]

FULWOOD, CHRISTOPHER (1590 ?-1643), royalist treasurer of Gray's Inn, 1637; tried William Bagshaw [q. v.] at Bakewell sessions; raised forces for Charles I in Derbyshire, 1642; captured by parliamentarians, mortally wounded. [xx. 329]

FURLONG, THOMAS (1794-1827), poet; published 'The Plagues of Ireland,' 1824, and English metrical versions of Irish poets; his 'Doom of Derenzie' published posthumously, 1829. [xx. 330]

FURLY, BENJAMIN (1636-1714), quaker and friend of Locke; assisted John Stubbs [q. v.] in 'The Battle-Door,' 1659-60; entertained George Fox at Rotterdam, and interpreted for him abroad; visited by Algernon Sydney, the third Lord Shaftesbury, and Locke, corresponding with them many years; died at Rotterdam; published translations from the Dutch. [xx. 330]

FURNEAUX, PHILIP (1726-1783), independent minister; friend of Benjamin Kennicott [q. v.]; independent pastor at Clapham, 1753, and Sunday-evening lecturer at Salters' Hall, c. 1752; D.D. Aberdeen, 1767; active in proceedings arising out of fining by the city of nonconformists who refused to qualify for the office of sheriff, 1754-67; entered into controversy with Blackstone for making nonconformity a crime, 1769-70 ; obtained for dissenting clergy partial relief from doctrinal subscription, issuing an 'Essay on Toleration,' 1773. [xx. 330]

FURNEAUX, TOBIAS (1735-1781), circumnavigator ; second lieutenant of the Dolphin in Captain Samuel Wallis's voyage, 1766-8 ; commanded the Adventure in Cook's second voyage ; separately explored the coast of Tasmania, and prepared the first chart of it, giving names now on the map ; returned alone, bringing with him first South Sea islander seen in England, 1774 ; captain of the Syren in Parker's attack on New Orleans, 1777. [xx. 332]

FURNESS, JOCELIN OF (*fl.* 1200). [See JOCELIN.]

FURNESS, RICHARD (1791-1857), Derbyshire poet. [xx. 332]

FURSA, SAINT (*d.* 650), of Peronne : Irishman of noble birth ; built monastery in north-west Clare at Rathmat (Killursa) ; began to wander about Ireland describing his trances, 627 : founded in East Anglia monastery of Cnoberesburg (Burghcastle) ; finally settled in Neustria, where he erected monastery at Lagny, on the Marne, 644 ; died at Macerias (Mazeroeles), and was buried at Peronne. [xx. 333]

FURSDON, JOHN, in religion CUTHBERT (*d.* 1638), Benedictine monk of St. Gregory, Douay, 1620 ; as 'Breton' converted Hugh Paulinus Cressy [q. v.] and Lady Falkland's daughters ; published 'Life and Miracles of St. Benedict,' 1638, and ' The Rule of St. Bennet,' 1638. [xx. 334]

FUSELI, HENRY (JOHANN HEINRICH FUESSLI) (1741-1825), painter and author : native of Zurich : took holy orders with his friend Lavater, with whom he went to Berlin, 1763 ; brought by Sir Andrew Mitchell to England, 1763 ; published translation of Winckelmann's 'The Painting and Sculpture of the Greeks,' 1765 ; encouraged by Reynolds to become an artist, 1767 ; studied Michelangelo and other masters at Rome, 1770-8, and sent several paintings to the Royal Academy : exhibited three pictures at the Academy, 1780, and 'The Nightmare,' 1782 ; painted several works for Boydell's Shakespeare Gallery, including ' Titania and Bottom '; R.A., 1790 ; opened his Milton Gallery, 1799 ; professor of painting at the Academy, 1799-1825 ; keeper, 1804-25 ; buried in St. Paul's Cathedral. Eight hundred sketches (Fuseli's best work) were bought by Lawrence : among his pupils were Haydon, Etty, and Mulready. He edited Pilkington's ' Dictionary of Painters,' translated Lavater's ' Aphorisms,'

wrote prefaces for Blake's illustrations of Blair' 'Grave' and many other works, 'Aphorisms of Art' ap pearing posthumously. [xx. 334]

FUST, SIR HERBERT JENNER- (1778-1852), dea of the arches, 1834 ; son of Robert Jenner ; educated a Reading and Trinity Hall, Cambridge ; LL.D., 1803 ; bar rister, Gray's Inn, 1800 ; king's advocate-general, 1828 vicar-general to the archbishop of Canterbury, 1832 ; pre sided at Gorham case (1847-50) ; master of Trinity Hal (non-resident), 1843-52 ; assumed the name of Fust, 1842. [xx. 339]

FYCH or **FYCHE**, THOMAS (*d.* 1517). [See FICH.]

FYFE, ANDREW, the elder (1754-1824), anatomist dissector under the second and third Monro at Edinburgh published text-books. [xx. 340]

FYFE, ANDREW, the younger (1792-1861), chemist eldest son of Andrew Fyfe the elder [q. v.] ; M.D Edinburgh, 1814 ; president of College of Surgeons (Edin burgh), 1842-3 ; professor of chemistry at Aberdeen 1844-61 ; published 'Elements of Chemistry,' 1827. [xx. 340]

FYFE, WILLIAM BAXTER COLLIER (1836 ?-1882) painter ; first exhibited at Scottish Academy, 1861 ; ex hibited at the English Academy from 1866. [xx. 341]

FYFFE, CHARLES ALAN (1845-1892), historian educated at Christ's Hospital and Balliol College, Oxford M.A., 1870 ; fellow of University College, 1871 ; barrister Inner Temple, 1877 ; published 'History of Moder Europe,' 3 vols. 1880-90. [Suppl. ii. 262]

FYNCH or **FINCH**, MARTIN (1628 ?-1698), ejecte minister ; after leaving vicarage of Tetney, 1662, becam an independent minister at Norwich, where the 'Ol Meeting' was built for him, 1693 ; published theologica works. [xx. 341]

FYNES-CLINTON. [See CLINTON.]

FYNEUX or **FINEUX**, SIR JOHN (1441 ?-1527 chief-justice of king's bench ; barrister, Gray's Inn ; ser jeant-at-law, 1485 ; justice of assize and king's serjean 1489 ; judge of common pleas, 1494 ; an executor c Henry VII's will, 1509 ; chief-justice of king's bench 1495 ; in conference at Baynard Castle upheld jurisdictio of temporal courts over clerks, this being referred to by Lord-chancellor Ellesmere in 1608 as a precedent fo extra-judicial opinions of judges. [xx. 342]

G

GABELL, HENRY DISON (1764-1831), head-master of Winchester ; fellow of New College, Oxford, 1782-90 ; B.A., 1786 ; M.A. Cambridge, 1807 ; head-master of Winchester, 1810-23 ; published pamphlets. [xx. 344]

GABRIEL, afterwards MARCH, MARY ANN VIRGINIA (1825-1877), musical composer : published songs, operettas, and cantatas, including 'Evangeline,' 1873. [xx. 344]

GACE, WILLIAM (*fl.* 1580), translator ; B.A. Clare Hall, Cambridge, 1573 ; Englished N. Hemminge's 'Commentary on the Epistle of St. James,' 1577, selected sermons of Martin Luther, 1578, and Luther's treatise to Duke Frederick of Saxony when sick, 1580. [xx. 344]

GADBURY, JOHN (1627-1704), astrologer : educated at Oxford ; defended Lilly and other astrologers in 'Philastrogus' Knavery Epitomized,' 1652 ; published also 'Genethlialogia, or the Doctrine of Nativities,' 1658, and nativities of Charles I, the king of Sweden, and Sir Matthew Hales ; produced 'De Cometis . . . with an Account of the three late Comets in 1664 and 1665,' 1665, 'Vox Solis ; or a Discourse of the Sun's Eclipse, 22 June 1666,' 'Obsequium Rationabile,' 1675, describing Lilly as an impostor, and 'A Ballad upon the Popish Plot,' 1679 ; he received compensation (1681) for 'wrongous imprisonment' at the time of the 'Popish Plot'; falsely accused of complicity in a plot against William III, 1690. [xx. 345]

GADDERAR, JAMES (1655-1733), restorer of Scottish episcopacy ; M.A. Glasgow, 1675 ; minister of Kilmalcolm,

1682 ; 'rabbled' out, 1688 ; consecrated Scottish bishop 1712, but lived in London ; with Bishop Archibald Camp bell (*d.* 1744) [q. v.] came to Scotland as his 'vicar, 1721 ; obtained sanction of 'the usages' at Holy Commu nion ; confirmed bishop of Aberdeen, 1724 ; elected to se of Moray, 1725. [xx. 346]

GADDESDEN, JOHN OF (1280 ?-1361), physician member of Merton College, Oxford ; practised in London and treated a son of Edward I for smallpox : his treatise 'Rosa Medicinæ' or 'Rosa Anglica,' first printed at Pavia 1492 ; prebendary of St. Paul's, 1342 ; the 'Gatesden' o Chaucer's prologue. [xx. 347]

GADSBY, WILLIAM (1773-1844), particular baptis minister ; pastor of Back Lane chapel, Manchester, fron 1805 ; wrote hymns ; his pamphlets and sermons pub lished by his son, 1851 and 1854. [xx. 348]

GAGE, FRANCIS (1621-1682), president of Doua College, 1676 ; half-brother of Sir Henry Gage [q. v.] studied at Douay and Tournay College, Paris, under Wi liam Clifford [q. v.] ; D.D. of the Sorbonne, 1654 ; ager to the English chapter at Rome, 1659-61 ; left in manu script a journal of his life. [xx. 349]

GAGE, GEORGE (*fl.* 1614-1640), Roman catholi agent : half-brother of Francis Gage [q. v.] ; friend of Si Toby Matthew ; sent by James I to Rome, 1621, to obtai dispensation for marriage of the Spanish Infanta wit Prince Charles ; failed after three years' negotiations. [xx. 349]

GAGE, SIR HENRY (1597-1645), royalist; great-grandson of Sir John Gage [q. v.]; educated in Flanders and in Italy under Piccolomini; in Spanish service at Antwerp; commanded company in Argyll's regiment at Bergen-op-Zoom, 1622, and Breda, 1624; defended St. Omer, 1638; intercepted parliament's supplies from Flanders; during the Rebellion was prominent in defence of Oxford, captured Borstall House, and relieved Basing House, 1644; knighted, 1644; governor of Oxford; mortally wounded at Abingdon.   [xx. 349]

GAGE, SIR JOHN (1479-1556), statesman and military commander; governor of Guisnes and comptroller of Calais, 1522; vice-chamberlain to the king, 1528-40; K.G., 1532; commissioner for surrender of religious houses; constable of the Tower, comptroller of the household, 1540, and chancellor of the duchy of Lancaster on fall of Cromwell; commanded the expedition against Scotland, 1542; with Suffolk conducted siege of Boulogne; expelled from privy council by Somerset; joined Southampton; created lord chamberlain by Queen Mary and restored to the constableship of the Tower, where he received Elizabeth, 1555, having afterwards charge of her at her own house.   [xx. 350]

GAGE, JOHN (1786-1842). [See ROKEWODE, JOHN GAGE.]

GAGE, JOSEPH or JOSEPH EDWARD, COUNT GAGE or DE GAGES (1678?-1753?), grandee of Spain; uncle of Thomas Gage (1721-1787) [q. v.]; went to Spain after losing a great fortune in Mississippi stock; commanded Spanish troops in Italy, 1743-6, and was promoted grandee of the first class, receiving also from the king of Naples the order of St. Januarius and a pension.   [xx. 352]

GAGE, THOMAS (d. 1656), traveller; brother of Sir Henry Gage [q. v.]; when a Spanish Dominican lived for some time among the Indians of Central America; crossed Nicaragua, reached Panama, and, traversing the isthmus, sailed from Portobello; reached Europe, 1637; after a visit to Loreto renounced catholicism and came to England, 1641; preached recantation sermon at St. Paul's (published, 1642); joined parliamentarians and became rector of Acrise, 1642, and Deal, c. 1651; died in Jamaica, as chaplain to Venables. His great work, 'The English-American his Travail by Sea and Land,' 1648, was translated into French by order of Colbert, 1676, also into Dutch and German; portions concerning Laud and rules for learning Central American languages appeared separately.   [xx. 353]

GAGE, THOMAS (1721-1787), general; aide-de-camp to Lord Albemarle in Flanders, 1747-8; as lieutenant-colonel of the 44th served in America under Braddock, 1751-6; raised 80th foot and commanded light infantry at Ticonderoga, 1758; as brigadier-general commanded rear-guard of Amherst; governor of Montreal, 1759-60; major-general, 1761; commander-in-chief in America, 1763-72; lieutenant-general, 1770; governor of Massachusetts, 1774-5; superseded by Howe, October 1775.   [xx. 355]

GAGE, SIR WILLIAM HALL (1777-1864), admiral of the fleet; youngest son of Thomas Gage (1721-1787) [q. v.]; entered navy, 1789; engaged off Toulon, 1795, against the Sabina, 1796, and at St. Vincent, 1797; commanded the Terpsichore at blockade of Malta, and was in the action with the Danish Freja; commanded the Thetis, 1805-8, and the Indus, 1813-14; rear-admiral, 1821; commander in East Indies, 1825-30, at Plymouth, 1848-51; member of board of admiralty, 1842-6; admiral, 1846; K.C.B., 1860; admiral of the fleet, 1862.   [xx. 357]

GAGER, WILLIAM (fl. 1580-1619), Latin dramatist; educated at Westminster and Christ Church, Oxford; M.A., 1580; D.C.L., 1589; chancellor of Ely, 1606, and vicar-general to Bishop Andrewes, 1613, 1616, and 1618; defended performance of plays at Oxford against John Rainolds [q. v.]; wrote five Latin plays acted at Oxford; ranked among comic dramatists in Meres's 'Palladis Tamia,' 1598.   [xx. 357]

GAGNIER, JOHN (1670?-1740), orientalist; born at Paris; studied Hebrew and Arabic at the Collège de Navarre; M.A. Cambridge, 1703; settled at Oxford under patronage of Bishop William Lloyd, taught Hebrew, and became professor of Arabic, 1724; published editions of Ben Gorion's 'History of the Jews,' 1706, and of Abū Alfidā's 'Life of Mahomet,' 1723, also a translation of the Arabic treatise of Rhazes on the smallpox.   [xx. 358]

GAHAGAN, USHER (d. 1749), classical scholar; edited Latin authors for Brindley's classics; rendered in Latin verse Pope's 'Essay on Criticism,' 1747, and 'Messiah' and 'Temple of Fame,' 1749; hanged for coining.   [xx. 359]

GAHAN, WILLIAM (1730-1804), Irish ecclesiastic and author; graduated at Louvain; received back into the Roman church John Butler, twelfth lord Dunboyne [q. v.]; imprisoned, 1802, for refusing to reveal to the court of assize details of his relations with John Butler; published 'Sermons and Moral Discourses' and popular devotional works.   [xx. 360]

GAIMAR, GEOFFREY (fl. 1140?), author of 'Lestorie des Engles,' probably a Norman resident at Scampton, Lincolnshire.   [xx. 360]

GAINSBOROUGH, THOMAS (1727-1788), painter; youngest son of a Sudbury wool manufacturer; studied under Gravelot and Francis Hayman [q. v.] in London; married and lived at Ipswich, 1746-60, where he became acquainted with John Joshua Kirby [q. v.] and Philip Thicknesse; painted 'Gainsborough's Forest' (National Gallery) and portraits of Admiral Vernon and others; resided at Bath, 1760-74; during those years contributed eighteen pictures to the Society of Artists; elected an original member of the Royal Academy, 1768, and exhibited there, 1769-72, as well as, after a misunderstanding with Reynolds, at the Free Society; settled in London, 1774; resumed exhibiting at Academy, 1779-83, but in consequence of a dispute about hanging three portraits, withdrew all his works, 1784, and henceforth showed his pictures in his own house. To the Bath period are assigned his two portraits of Garrick, those of Quin, Foote, Orpin (National Gallery), Lord Camden, Richardson, Sterne, and Chatterton, and 'The Harvest Waggon'; to the London period belong two portraits of the Duchess of Devonshire (including that stolen in 1876), the full-length known as 'The Blue Boy,' Mr. Bate, Mrs. Siddons (both in the National Gallery), and Colonel St. Leger (Hampton Court), 'The View in the Mall of St. James's Park,' 'Girl with Pigs' (bought by Reynolds), and many fine landscapes. Among his intimate friends were Burke and Sheridan, and he was reconciled to Reynolds on his deathbed.   [xx. 361]

GAINSBOROUGH, WILLIAM (d. 1307), ecclesiastic; when divinity lecturer of the Franciscans at Oxford one of the embassy sent by Edward I to Philip IV of France and Pope Boniface VIII; reader in theology to the pope, 1300; appointed to the see of Worcester by 'provision,' 1302, but compelled to renounce the grant; one of the embassy to Clement V, 1305; sent, 1307, to arrange for the marriage of Prince Edward with Isabella of France; died at Beauvais.   [xx. 367]

GAINSFORD, THOMAS (d. 1624?), author; served in Ireland against the Spaniards (1601) and Tyrone; published 'Vision and Discourse of Henry the seventh concerning the unitie of Great Britaine,' 1610, 'The Historie of Trebizond,' 1616, and other works.   [xx. 368]

GAIRDNER, JOHN (1790-1876), medical reformer; M.D. Edinburgh, 1811; studied anatomy under Bell; president of the Edinburgh College of Surgeons, 1830-2; obtained leave for medical students to attend extra-academical lectures, and was active in obtaining by the act of 1859 legal status for every licensed practitioner in Great Britain; published lectures on Edinburgh medical history; his 'Burns and the Ayrshire Moderates' published posthumously.   [xx. 368]

GAIRDNER, WILLIAM (1793-1867), physician; brother of John Gairdner [q. v.]; M.D. Edinburgh, 1813; L.R.C.P., 1823; died at Avignon; published treatise on 'Gout,' 1849.   [xx. 369]

GAISFORD, THOMAS (1779-1855), dean of Christ Church, Oxford; student of Christ Church, 1800; M.A., 1804; appointed regius professor of Greek, 1812; canon of Llandaff and St. Paul's, 1823, Worcester, 1825, Durham, 1831; dean of Christ Church, Oxford, 1831-55; edited the 'Tusculan Disputations,' 1805, and 'De Oratore' of Cicero, 1809; the works of Euripides, Sophocles, and Herodotus, 1824, 'Hephæstion de Metris,' 1810, 'Poetæ Græci Minores,' 1814-20, 'Suidæ Lexicon,' 1834, 'Etymologicon Magnum,' 1848, several works of Eusebius and Theodoret, and an edition of the Septuagint, 1848. The Gaisford prizes at Oxford for Greek prose and verse were founded, 1856.   [xx. 370]

GALBRAITH, ROBERT (*d.* 1543), Scottish judge; advocate to Queen Margaret Tudor; one of the original lords of the College of Senators, 1537; murdered by John Carkettle of Edinburgh.   [xx. 372]

GALDRIC, GUALDRIC, or **WALDRIC** (*d.* 1112), bishop of Laon; chancellor of Henry I; captured Duke Robert of Normandy at Tenchebrai, 1106; bishop of Laon, 1106; expelled from his diocese after the murder by his brother of Gerard, castellan of Laon, but restored by Louis VI, 1109; having attempted to abolish the 'commune' granted in his absence, was murdered in the cellars of his cathedral.   [xx. 372]

GALE, DUNSTAN (*fl.* 1596), poet; author of 'Pyramus and Thisbe,' 1597.   [xx. 373]

GALE, GEORGE (1797 ?–1850), aeronaut; played Mazeppa in New York, 1831; joined a tribe of Indians, with six of whom he was exhibited at the Victoria Theatre, London; made his first ascent from Peckham, 1848; perished at the 114th ascent made in the Royal Cremorne, near Bordeaux.   [xx. 373]

GALE, JOHN (1680–1721), general baptist minister; M.A. and Ph.D. Leyden, 1699; chairman of Whiston's 'society for promoting primitive christianity,' 1715–16; took liberal side at Salters' Hall dispute, 1719; introduced by Shute to whig bishops; published 'Reflections on Mr. Wall's History of Infant Baptism,' 1711.   [xx. 374]

GALE, MILES (1647–1721), antiquary; M.A. Trinity College, Cambridge, 1670; rector of Keighley, 1680–1721; published 'Memoirs of the Family of Gale,' 1703, and 'Description of the Parish of Keighley.'   [xx. 374]

GALE, ROGER (1672–1744), antiquary; eldest son of Thomas Gale (1635 ?–1702) [q. v.]; educated at St. Paul's School and Trinity College, Cambridge; fellow, 1697; M.A., 1698; M.P., Northallerton, 1705–10; commissioner of excise, 1715–35; friend of Stukeley, Willis, and Hearne; first vice-president of Society of Antiquaries, and treasurer of Royal Society; left manuscripts to Trinity College and coins to the university library; his topographical papers collected in 'Bibliotheca Topographica Britannica,' 1781.   [xx. 375]

GALE, SAMUEL (1682–1754), antiquary; brother of Roger Gale [q. v.]; educated at St. Paul's School; first treasurer of revived Society of Antiquaries, 1718; travelled about in England incognito with Dr. Ducarel [q. v.]; published (1715) 'History of Winchester Cathedral,' begun by Henry, earl of Clarendon.   [xx. 376]

GALE, THEOPHILUS (1628–1678), nonconformist tutor; fellow of Magdalen College, Oxford, 1650–60; M.A., 1652; tutor to Thomas (afterwards Marquis) Wharton and his brother, 1662–5; tutor and independent minister at Newington Green; left his library to Harvard College; published 'The Court of the Gentiles,' 1669–77, 'A True Idea of Jansenisme,' 1669, and other theological works.   [xx. 377]

GALE, THOMAS (1507–1587), surgeon; served with the army of Henry VIII in France, 1544, and with that of Philip II at St. Quentin, 1557; master of the Barber-Surgeons' Company, 1561; published a volume on surgery, 1563, containing the prescription for his styptic powder.   [xx. 378]

GALE. THOMAS (1635?–1702), dean of York; educated at Westminster and Trinity College, Cambridge; M.A., 1662; fellow, 1669; Cambridge professor of Greek, 1666–1672; high master of St. Paul's, 1672–97; active member of the Royal Society from 1677; dean of York, 1697–1702; edited 'Opuscula Mythologica, ethica et physica,' 1671, 'Historiæ Poeticæ Scriptores Antiqui,' 1675, 'Rhetores Selecti,' 1676, vol. ii. of 'Historiæ Anglicanæ Scriptores,' 1687, 'Historiæ Britannicæ, Saxonicæ, Anglo-Danicæ Scriptores,' 1691, and 'Antonini Iter Britanniarum,' 1709.   [xx. 378]

GALENSIS, JOHN (*fl.* 1215). [See WALLENSIS.]

GALEON, WILLIAM (*d.* 1507), Augustinian; provincial in England; various theological works ascribed to him.   [xx. 380]

GALEYS, SIR HENRY LE (*d.* 1302 ?). [See WALEYS.]

GALFRIDUS. [See GEOFFREY OF MONMOUTH.]

GALGACUS or **CALGACUS** (*fl. c.* 84), Caledonian chieftain; commander of the tribes defeated at Grampius by Agricola.   [xx. 380]

GALIGNANI, JOHN ANTHONY (1796–1873), publisher in Paris; born in London; issued, with his brother William Galignani [q. v.] till 1852, in Paris, reprints of English books; carried on 'The Messenger' founded by his father, 1815; erected at Neuilly a hospital (now orphanage) for indigent British.   [xx. 380]

GALIGNANI, WILLIAM (1798–1882), publisher in Paris; brother of John Anthony Galignani [q. v.], in all whose undertakings he took part.   [xx. 380]

GALL, SAINT (550 ?–645 ?), originally named CELLACH or CAILLECH, abbot and apostle of the Suevi and Alemanni; reputed son of a noble Irishman and a queen of Hungary; educated by St. Columban at Bangor; followed St. Columban to Gaul, *c.* 585, and at Arbon and Bregenz preached to the people in their own tongue; built cell on the Steinach river, which became the nucleus of the monastery of St. Gall; died at Arbon; commemorated 16 Oct. and 20 Feb.   [xx. 381]

GALL, RICHARD (1776–1801), Scottish poet; friend of Burns and Campbell; his 'Poems and Songs,' published 1819.   [xx. 382]

GALLAGHER, JAMES (*d.* 1751), Roman catholic bishop of Raphoe, 1725, and Kildare, 1737; published 'Irish Sermons, in an easy and familiar style,' 1735.   [xx. 382]

GALLAN, SAINT (*fl.* 500). [See GRELLAN.]

GALLENGA, ANTONIO CARLO NAPOLEONE (1810–1895), author and journalist; born and educated at Parma; took part in political agitation in Italy, 1830, and was compelled to live in exile, assuming name of Luigi Mariotti; successful lecturer, teacher, and writer for magazines in New York, 1836; came to England, 1839, teacher and translator; professor of modern languages at King's College, Windsor, Nova Scotia, *c.* 1841–3; returned to England, 1843; naturalised, 1846; professor of Italian language and literature, University College, London, 1848–59; chargé d'affaires at Frankfort, 1848; resided in Italy, 1854–7; deputy in Piedmontese parliament, and correspondent of 'Daily News'; 'Times' correspondent in Italy, 1859–64; deputy of Italian chamber, 1859–64; 'Times' war correspondent in United States, 1863, and Denmark, 1864; leader-writer for 'Times,' 1866–73, and correspondent in Spain, 1874 and 1879, and at Constantinople, 1875–7. His publications include 'Italy General views of its History and Literature,' 1841 (reprinted as 'Italy, Past and Present,' 1846), and an Italian grammar, 1858.   [Suppl. ii. 262]

GALLEN-RIDGEWAY, first BARON (1565 ?–1631). [See RIDGEWAY, SIR THOMAS, EARL OF LONDONDERRY.]

GALLIARD, JOHN ERNEST (1687 ?–1749), musical composer; son of a hairdresser at Zell; said to have been chamber-musician to Prince George of Denmark; saw Hughes's 'Calypso and Telemachus,' 1712; provided music for pantomimes and farces at Covent Garden and Lincoln's Inn Fields, 1717–36; composed six cantatas to Congreve's, Prior's, and Hughes's words, sonatas for flute, bassoon, and violin, and a setting of the morning hymn from 'Paradise Lost'; translated Tosi's 'Opinioni di Cantori Antichi e Moderni,' 1742.   [xx. 383]

GALLINI, GIOVANNI ANDREA BATTISTA, called SIR JOHN (1728–1805), dancing-master; came to England *c.* 1753; director of dances and stage-manager at Haymarket opera-house; had great vogue as a dancing-master; married Lady Elizabeth Peregrine Bertie, eldest daughter of third Earl of Abingdon; created knight of the Golden Spur by the pope; built Hanover Square concert-rooms; published treatises on calisthenics.   [xx. 384]

GALLOWAY, SIR ARCHIBALD (1780 ?–1850), major-general; entered Bengal native infantry, 1800; colonel of the 58th, 1836; major-general, 1841; K.C.B., 1848; chairman of the East India Company, 1849; published works including 'Notes on Siege of Delhi,' 1804, and 'On Siege of India.'   [xx. 384]

GALLOWAY, JOSEPH (1730–1803), lawyer; born in Maryland; as speaker of Pennsylvania supported the popular against the proprietary interest, and was challenged (1764) by John Dickinson; when member of the rst congress proposed and published (1775) plan for nion between Great Britain and the colonies ; joined British, 1776 ; gave evidence before parliament, 1778 ; ublished pamphlets, including attacks on the Howes for their conduct of the war. [xx. 385]

GALLOWAY, PATRICK (1551 ?–1626 ?), Scottish ivine ; preached against Lennox at Perth, and was uspected of being privy to the raid of Ruthven, 1582 ; ed to England, 1584 ; minister of the royal household of cotland and moderator of the general assembly, 1590 ; ebuked James VI for recalling Arran, 1592, and refused o take the 'band' of 1596 ; again moderator, 1602 ; present at Hampton Court conference, 1604 ; minister of St. Hiles's, Edinburgh, 1607 ; member of the high commission ourt ; signed protestation for liberties of the kirk, 1617, ut supported five articles of Perth ; edited works by James VI. [xx. 386]

GALLOWAY, THOMAS (1796–1851), mathematician ; M.A. Edinburgh ; teacher of mathematics at Sandhurst, 823 ; registrar of Amicable Life Assurance Company, 833 ; F.R.S. and F.R.A.S., 1829 ; contributed to seventh dition of 'Encyclopædia Britannica' and 'Edinburgh Review.' [xx. 387]

GALLY, HENRY (1696–1769), divine and scholar ; M.A. Corpus Christi College, Cambridge, 1721 ; D.D., 728 ; chaplain to Lord King, 1725 ; prebendary of Gloucester, 1728, of Norwich, 1731 ; rector of St. Giles-in-the-Fields, 1732 ; chaplain to George II, 1735 ; edited Theophrastus, with an essay on 'Characteristic Writings,' 725 ; published pamphlets on tenure of corporate estates 1731) and on clandestine marriages (1750) and essays against pronouncing Greek according to accent. [xx. 388]

GALMOY, third VISCOUNT (1652–1740). [See BUTLER, PIERCE.]

GALPINE, JOHN (d. 1806), author of 'Synoptical Compend of the British Flora,' 1806. [xx. 388]

GALT, SIR ALEXANDER TILLOCH (1817–1893), finance minister of Canada ; son of John Galt [q. v.] ; ettled in Sherbrooke, Lower Canada, 1835 ; commissioner a British-American Land Company, 1844 ; active promoter of railways ; liberal M.P. for county of Sherbrooke, 849 and 1853–72 ; inspector-general, 1858–62 and 1864–5 ; delegate to Charlottetown and Quebec conferences, 1864 ; rst minister of finance on inauguration of dominion of Canada, 1867–72 ; nominee of Canada on Halifax commission, 1877 ; high commissioner for the dominion in England, 1880–3 ; G.C.M.G., 1878 ; honorary LL.D. Edinburgh, 1878 ; published pamphlets on political questions. [Suppl. ii. 264]

GALT, JOHN (1779–1839), novelist ; employed in Greenock custom-house and in a mercantile house ; came to London, c. 1803, and published a poem on the 'Battle of Largs' ; entered at Lincoln's Inn ; while on a commercial mission to the continent (1809) travelled with Byron from Gibraltar to Malta, visited Constantinople and Greece ; published (1812) an account of his travels and a life of Wolsey ; edited the 'New British Theatre,' 1814–15, containing his play 'The Witness' ; compiled 'Life . . . nd Studies of Benjamin West' (1816–20) ; published 'The Majolo,' 1816 ; compiled 'Voyages' under pseudonym S. Prior, and 'Tour of Asia' and 'The Wandering Jew' as Rev. T. Clark ; produced novels, 'The Ayrshire Legatees' 1820), 'Annals of the Parish' (1821), 'Sir Andrew Wylie' 1822), and 'The Entail' (1824) ; visited Canada, 1824 nd 1826, as secretary to a company formed for the purchase of crown land ; founded town of Guelph ; imprisoned for debt after his return, 1829 ; published 'Lawrie Todd' and 'Life of Byron,' 1830, and 'Lives of the Players' ; met Carlyle ; issued his 'Autobiography,' 1833, nd 'Literary Life,' 1834, for which William IV sent him 100l. ; paralysed, 1834, but continued literary work. [xx. 388]

GALTON, SIR DOUGLAS STRUTT (1822–1899), man f science and captain, royal engineers ; educated at Rugby nd Royal Military Academy, Woolwich ; lieutenant, royal ngineers, 1843 ; first captain, 1855 ; served in Mediterranean ; joined ordnance survey, 1846 ; secretary to railway commission, 1847, and to royal commission on application of iron to railway structures ; secretary to ailway department of board of trade, 1854 ; chairman of committee to investigate question of electric submarine elegraph cables, 1859–61 ; assistant permanent under-

secretary for war, 1862–9 ; C.B., 1865 ; director of public works and buildings, 1869–75 ; president of British Association, 1895 ; president of senate of University College, London ; K.C.B., 1887 ; honorary M.I.C.E., 1894 ; honorary D.C.L. Oxford, 1875 ; F.R.S., 1859 ; published works on sanitary and educational questions. [Suppl. ii. 266]

GALTON, MARY ANNE (1778–1856). [See SCHIMMEL-PENNINCK.]

GALWAY, EARL OF (1648–1720). [See MASSUE DE RUVIGNY, HENRI DE.]

GAM, DAVID (d. 1415), Welsh warrior ; real name DAVYDD AB LLEWELYN ; rewarded for fidelity to Henry IV during revolt of Glendower by confiscated lands in South Wales, 1401 ; captured by Glendower ; followed Henry V to France and fell at Agincourt. [xx. 392]

GAMBIER, SIR EDWARD JOHN (1794–1879), chief-justice of Madras ; nephew of James, baron Gambier [q. v.] ; fellow of Trinity College, Cambridge ; M.A., 1820 ; barrister, Lincoln's Inn, 1822 ; municipal corporation commissioner, 1833 ; recorder of Prince of Wales island, 1834 ; chief-justice at Madras, 1842–9 ; published 'Treatise on Parochial Settlement,' 1828. [xx. 393]

GAMBIER, JAMES (1723–1789), vice-admiral ; uncle of James, baron Gambier [q. v.] ; present at capture of Louisbourg, 1758, Guadaloupe, 1759, and the battle of Quiberon Bay, 1759 ; commander-in-chief on north American station, 1770–3 ; second in command under Howe at New York ; vice-admiral, 1780 ; commander at Jamaica, 1783–4. [xx. 393]

GAMBIER, JAMES, first BARON GAMBIER (1756–1833), admiral of the fleet ; captured by D'Estaing in the Thunder bomb ; took part in relief of Jersey, 1779, and capture of Charlestown, 1780 ; in the Defence first to break enemy's line in Howe's victory of 1 June 1794 ; a lord of the admiralty, 1795–1801 and 1804–6 ; rear-admiral and vice-admiral, 1799 ; governor of Newfoundland, 1802–4 ; admiral, 1805 ; led the fleet at bombardment of Copenhagen, the Danish fleet being surrendered, 1807 ; created Baron Gambier ; commanded Channel fleet, 1808–11 ; blockaded French fleet in Basque roads and destroyed it by fireships ; a commissioner for treaty with United States, 1814 ; G.C.B., 1815 ; admiral of the fleet, 1830. [xx. 393]

GAMBLE, JOHN (d. 1687), musician in Chapel Royal and composer ; published 'Ayres and Dialogues to be sung to the theorbo, lute, or base violl,' 1656, and 'Ayres and Dialogues, for one, two, and three voyces,' 1659. [xx. 395]

GAMBLE, JOHN (d. 1811), writer on telegraphy ; fellow of Pembroke College, Cambridge ; M.A., 1787 ; chaplain to the Duke of York, and chaplain-general of the forces ; published 'Observations on Telegraphic Experiments,' 1795, and 'Essay on the different Modes of Communication by Signals,' 1797. [xx. 395]

GAMBOLD, JOHN (1711–1771), bishop of the Unitas Fratrum ; while at Christ Church, Oxford, was a member of the Wesleys' 'Holy Club' ; vicar of Stanton-Harcourt, 1735–42 ; formed Anglican branch of Moravians, 1749, and was consecrated a bishop, 1753 ; prominent at synod of Marienborn, 1764 ; founded community at Cootehill, co. Cavan, 1765 ; translated Count Zinzendorf's 'Maxims' into English in 1751 ; published also 'Collection of Hymns,' 1754, and posthumous 'Poems,' 1816 ; edited Bacon, 1765. [xx. 396]

GAMELINE (d. 1271), lord-chancellor of Scotland, 1250–63 ; chaplain of Innocent IV, 1254 ; bishop of St. Andrews, 1255 ; banished from Scotland for prohibiting Alexander III from seizing church property ; died in Scotland. [xx. 397]

GAMGEE, JOSEPH SAMPSON (1828–1886), surgeon ; born and educated in Italy ; Liston prizeman, University College, 1853 ; surgeon to British-Italian legion, 1855, to Queen's Hospital, Birmingham, 1857–81 ; published 'On the Advantages of the Starched Apparatus in the Treatment of Fractures,' 1853, 'On the Treatment of Wounds and Fractures,' 1883, 'On Absorbent and Antiseptic Surgical Dressings,' 1880, and other works. [xx. 398]

GAMMAGE, ROBERT GEORGE (1815–1888), chartist ; deputy from Northampton to national convention of 1838 ; opposed Feargus O'Connor ; published 'History of the Chartist Movement,' 1854. [xx. 399]

GAMMON, JAMES (*fl.* 1660–1670), engraver of portraits valued for their rarity. [xx. 399]

GAMON or **GAMMON**, HANNIBAL (*fl.* 1642), puritan divine; M.A. Broadgates Hall (Pembroke College), Oxford, 1607; rector of Mawgan-in-Pyder, Cornwall, 1619, which county he represented in the Westminster assembly, 1642. [xx. 399]

GANDELL, ROBERT (1818–1887), professor of Arabic at Oxford; B.A. Queen's College, Oxford, 1843; Michel fellow of Queen's College, 1845–50; professor of Arabic, 1861; canon of Wells, 1880; edited Lightfoot's 'Horæ Hebraicæ,' 1859, and contributed to 'Speaker's Commentary.' [xx. 400]

GANDOLPHY, PETER (1779–1821), jesuit; educated at Liège and Stonyhurst; celebrated as a preacher at the Spanish Chapel, Manchester Square; suspended and censured by Bishop Poynter for his 'Liturgy,' 1812, and 'Defence of the Ancient Faith,' 1813–15. [xx. 400]

GANDON, JAMES (1743–1823), architect; articled to Sir William Chambers; with J. Woolfe published continuation of Campbell's 'Vitruvius Britannicus,' 1767–71; won first gold medal for architecture at Royal Academy, 1768, and exhibited drawings, 1774–80; designed at Dublin many public works, including portico and screen wall to Parliament House, 1785, Four Courts, 1786, and King's Inns, 1795–9; original member of Royal Irish Academy. [xx. 401]

GANDY, HENRY (1649–1734), nonjuring bishop; educated at Merchant Taylors' School and Oriel College, Oxford; M.A., 1674; fellow, 1670; proctor, 1683; deprived of fellowship for refusing oath of allegiance, 1690; consecrated bishop, 1716, by Jeremy Collier [q. v.], Nathaniel Spinckes [q. v.], and Samuel Hawes (*d.* 1722); published theological works. [Suppl. ii. 269]

GANDY, JAMES (1619–1689), portrait-painter; pupil of Vandyck, many of whose portraits he copied for the Duke of Ormonde. [xx. 402]

GANDY, JOHN PETER (1787–1850). [See DEERING.]

GANDY, JOSEPH MICHAEL (1771–1843), architect; pupil of Wyatt; received the Pope's medal for architecture, 1795; exhibited at the Academy, 1789–1838; A.R.A., 1803; executed many drawings for Sir John Soane [q. v.]; designed Phœnix and Pelican Insurance offices, Charing Cross; contributed illustrations to Britton's 'Architectural Antiquities.' [xx. 402]

GANDY, MICHAEL (1778–1862), architect; brother of Joseph Michael Gandy [q. v.]; employed in Indian naval service and by Sir Jeffrey Wyatville [q. v.]; exhibited at Academy 'Burning of Onrust and Kupers Island, Batavia,' 1812. [xx. 403]

GANDY, WILLIAM (*d.* 1729), portrait-painter; son of James Gandy [q. v.] His pictures, most of which are to be found in the west of England, were much admired by Reynolds and Northcote. [xx. 403]

GARBET, SAMUEL (*d.* 1751?), author of 'History of Wem' (published 1818), second master at Wem School, 1712–42; M.A. Christ Church, Oxford, 1707; translated Phædrus, Books i. and ii., 1715. [xx. 403]

GARBETT, EDWARD (1817–1887), divine; M.A. Brasenose College, Oxford, 1847; editor of the 'Record,' 1854–67; incumbent of Christ Church, Surbiton, 1863, of Barcombe, 1877; Bampton lecturer, 1867; published Boyle Lectures (1860 and 1863), Bampton Lectures (1867), and other works. [xx. 404]

GARBETT, JAMES (1802–1879), professor of poetry at Oxford; brother of Edward Garbett [q. v.]; fellow of Queen's College, Oxford, 1824–5, of Brasenose, 1825–36; M.A., 1825; incumbent of Clayton-cum-Keymer, 1835–79; Bampton lecturer, 1842; professor of poetry, 1842–52; archdeacon of Chichester, 1851; published anti-tractarian Bampton lectures and 'De Rei Poeticæ Idea,' 1843. [xx. 404]

GARBRAND, HERKS (*fl.* 1556), Dutch protestant refugee; bookseller, and also, after 1546, wine-seller at Oxford. [xx. 405]

GARBRAND, or HERKS, JOHN (1542–1589), divine; son of Herks Garbrand [q. v.]; educated at Winchester

and New College, Oxford; fellow, 1562; M.A., 156?; M.A. Cambridge, 1568; D.D. Oxford, 1582; prebenda[r] of Salisbury, 1565, and of Wells; rector of North Crawle[y] and Farthingstone; edited three works of his patro[n] Bishop Jewel. [xx. 405]

GARBRAND, JOHN (*fl.* 1695), writer of pamphle[t] 'to clear the duke of York from being a papist'; son [of] Tobias Garbrand (*d.* 1689) [q. v.]; B.A. New Inn Ha[ll] Oxford, 1667; barrister, Inner Temple. [xx. 406]

GARBRAND, TOBIAS (1579–1638), probably gran[d] father of John Garbrand (*fl.* 1695) [q. v.]; vice-preside[nt] of Magdalen College, Oxford (1618), and vicar of Finde[n,] Sussex (1618–38). [xx. 406]

GARBRAND, TOBIAS (*d.* 1689), principal of Glo[u]cester Hall, Oxford, 1648–60; M.D. Oxford. [xx. 406]

GARDELLE, THEODORE (1721–1761), miniatur[e] painter and murderer; born at Geneva; executed for th[e] murder of Anne King; his portrait by Hogarth engrave[d] in Ireland's 'Graphic Illustrations.' [xx. 406]

GARDEN, ALEXANDER, the elder (1730 ?–179[1]) botanist; born at Charleston; M.D. Edinburgh; pupil [of] Alston; corresponded with Peter Collinson, Gronovius, [and] Linnæus, in whose 'Systema Naturæ' his name is append[ed] to new species of fish and reptiles; settled in Englan[d,] 1783, and became vice-president of the Royal Society; i[n]troduced many plants; the Cape Jessamine named *Ga[r]denia* after him. [xx. 406]

GARDEN, ALEXANDER, the younger (1757–182[9,] author; son of Alexander Garden the elder [q. v.[;] published 'Anecdotes of the Revolutionary War,' 1822. [xx. 407]

GARDEN, FRANCIS, LORD GARDENSTONE (172[?–] 1793), Scottish judge; educated at Edinburgh University; admitted advocate, 1744; sheriff-depute of Kincardin[e]shire, 1748; joint solicitor-general, 1760; employed in th[e] Douglas cause; lord of session, 1764–93; lord of justiciar[y,] 1776–87; founded Lawrence Kirk, Kincardineshire; pu[b]lished notes of travel. [xx. 407]

GARDEN, FRANCIS (1810–1884), theologian; M.[A.] Trinity College, Cambridge, 1836; intimate with Richa[rd] Chenevix Trench, Frederick Denison Maurice, and Joh[n] Sterling; sub-dean of the Chapel Royal, 1859–84; editor [of] 'The Christian Remembrancer,' 1841; published 'Dic[-] tionary of English Philosophical Terms,' 1878, and oth[er] works. [xx. 408]

GARDEN, GEORGE (1649–1733), Scottish divine; professor at King's College, Aberdeen, 1673; minister [of] Old Machar, Aberdeen, 1679, of St. Nicholas, 1683; 'la[id] aside,' 1692, as a nonjuror; deposed, 1701, in connecti[on] with his 'Apology for Madame Bourignon,' but continue[d] to officiate; imprisoned after rebellion of 1715; edite[d] the works of John Forbes (1593–1648) [q. v.]; and wro[te] pamphlets on behalf of the Scots episcopal clergy. [xx. 409]

GARDEN, JAMES (1647–1726), professor of divinit[y,] Aberdeen; brother of George Garden [q. v.]; deprived [of] professorship, 1696, for refusing to sign Westminst[er] Confession; published 'Comparative Theology.' [xx. 410]

GARDENSTONE, LORD (1721–1793). [See GARDE[N,] FRANCIS.]

GARDINER. [See also GARDNER.]

GARDINER, ALLEN FRANCIS (1794–1851), mi[s]sionary to Patagonia; served in navy; lieutenant, 184[?;] tried to establish Christian churches in Zululand, 1834–[5;] laboured among Chili Indians, 1838–43; attempted [to] establish mission in Patagonia, 1844–5; visited Bolivi[a,] 1845–6; surveyed Tierra del Fuego, 1848; died of starv[a]tion there; published 'Outlines of a Plan for Explorin[g] the Interior of Australia,' 1833, and books describing h[is] missionary travels. [xx. 410]

GARDINER, ARTHUR (1716 ?–1758), captain in th[e] navy; served with Byng in the Mediterranean and (175[6]) gave unwilling testimony against him at his trial; ca[p]tured the Foudroyant off the Spanish coast, but fell in th[e] action. [xx. 411]

GARDINER, BERNARD (1668–1726), warden of A[ll] Souls' College, Oxford; ejected from demyship of Mag[-] dalen by James II; B.A., 1688; D.C.L., 1698; fellow [of]

All Souls', 1689 ; warden, 1702-26 ; vice-chancellor, 1712-1715 ; checked Jacobitism and suppressed the 'terræ filius' (elected undergraduate). [xx. 412]

GARDINER, GEORGE (1535 ?-1589), dean of Norwich ; B.A. Christ's College, Cambridge, 1554 ; fellow of Queens' College, Cambridge, 1558-61 ; M.A., 1558 ; minister of St. Andrew's, Norwich, 1562 ; prebendary of Norwich, 1565 ; one of those who broke down the cathedral organ, 1570 ; rector of St. Martin Outwich, London, 1571 ; dean of Norwich, 1573-89. [xx. 412]

GARDINER, JAMES, the elder (1637-1705), bishop of Lincoln ; M.A. Emmanuel College, Cambridge, 1656 ; D.D., 1669 ; chaplain to Monmouth and incumbent of Epworth, 1660 ; bishop of Lincoln, 1695-1705 ; assisted Simon Patrick [q. v.] to decipher Peterborough charters and muniments. [xx. 413]

GARDINER, JAMES, the younger (d. 1732), sub-dean of Lincoln ; son of James Gardiner the elder [q. v.] ; B.A. Emmanuel College, Cambridge, 1699 ; fellow of Jesus College, 1700 ; master of St. John's Hospital, Peterborough, 1707 ; published sermons. [xx. 414]

GARDINER, JAMES (1688-1745), colonel of dragoons ; wounded at Blenheim, 1704 ; headed storming party at battle of Preston ; lieutenant-colonel, Inniskilling dragoons, 1730 ; colonel in command of light dragoons (now 13th hussars), 1743-5 ; deserted by most of his men at Prestonpans, and mortally wounded ; 'converted,' after a dissolute life ; commemorated in 'Life' by Doddridge, and song by Sir Gilbert Elliot (1722-1777) [q. v.] [xx. 414]

GARDINER, MARGUERITE, COUNTESS OF BLESSINGTON (1789-1849). [See BLESSINGTON.]

GARDINER, RICHARD (1591-1670), divine ; deputy-orator at Oxford before 1620 ; canon of Christ Church, Oxford, 1629 ; M.A., 1614 ; D.D., 1630 ; deprived, 1647, reinstated, 1660 ; chaplain to Charles I, 1630 ; a brilliant, quaint preacher ; published 'Specimen Oratorium,' 1653. [xx. 416]

GARDINER, RICHARD (1723-1781), author ; educated at Eton and St. Catharine's Hall, Cambridge ; published 'History of Pudica ... with an account of her five Lovers' (1754), in which 'Dick Merryfellow' is himself, and 'Account of the Expedition ... against Martinico, Guadeloupe, and other the Leeward Islands,' 1759 ; commanded the marines in the Leeward Islands. [xx. 416]

GARDINER, SIR ROBERT WILLIAM (1781-1864), general ; entered royal artillery, 1797 ; brevet-lieutenant-colonel, 1814 ; major-general, 1841 ; general and colonel-commandant, 1853-4 ; aide-de-camp to Sir John Moore in Sicily, 1806-7, and brigade-major at Coruña, 1809 ; served in the Peninsula and (1809) Walcheren expedition ; prominent at Barossa and Badajoz ; commanded field-battery at Salamanca, 1812 ; commanded E troop royal horse artillery at Vittoria, 1813, and succeeding battles, and at Waterloo ; K.C.B., 1814 ; governor of Gibraltar, 1848-55 ; published life of Admiral Sir Graham Moore and valuable professional papers. [xx. 417]

GARDINER, SAMUEL (fl. 1606), chaplain to Archbishop Abbot and author of 'A Booke of Angling or Fishing. Wherein is shewed ... the agreement betweene the Fishermen ... of both natures, Temporall and Spirituall,' 1606 ; D.D. [xx. 418]

GARDINER, STEPHEN (1483 ?-1555), bishop of Winchester ; educated at Trinity Hall, Cambridge ; fellow ; doctor of civil law, 1520, of canon law, 1521 ; Rede lecturer, 1524 ; tutor to Duke of Norfolk's son ; master of Trinity Hall, 1525-49, re-elected, 1553 ; private secretary to Wolsey ; obtained Clement VII's consent to a second commission in the royal divorce question, 1527 ; attempted to obtain from Cambridge opinions favourable to the divorce, 1530 ; though taking up a 'middle course,' compiled reply to Catherine's counsel at Rome ; after Wolsey's fall acted as secretary to Henry VIII till 1534 ; bishop of Winchester, 1531 ; ambassador in France, 1531-2 ; prepared reply of the ordinaries to the House of Commons' address to the king, stoutly defending his order ; member of the court which invalidated Queen Catherine's marriage, 1533 ; signed renunciation of obedience to Roman jurisdiction, and published oration, 'De verâ Obedientiâ,' repudiating it, and

maintaining supremacy of secular princes over the church, 1535 ; chancellor of Cambridge University, 1540-51 ; opposed Cromwell and Cranmer ; fell temporarily out of favour ; after the fall of Cromwell had supreme political influence, inspiring the six articles, 1539 ; constantly employed in negotiations with the emperor ; imprisoned in the Tower during the greater part of the reign of Edward VI on account of his opposition to doctrinal changes, and (1551) deprived of his see ; reinstated and made lord chancellor on Mary's accession ; procured (1554) re-enactment of 'De Hæretico Comburendo' and took part against Bradford and Rogers, but tried to save Cranmer and Northumberland, and protected Thomas Smith and Peter Martyr ; opposed the Spanish marriage, but advocated great severity towards Elizabeth, whom he caused to be declared illegitimate by act of parliament ; published controversial works against Martin Bucer and Latin letters to John Cheke on the pronunciation of Greek, 1555. [xx. 419]

GARDINER, THOMAS (fl. 1516), monk of Westminster ; compiled 'The Flowers of England,' a chronicle. [xx. 425]

GARDINER, SIR THOMAS (1591-1652), recorder of London, 1636 ; barrister, Inner Temple, 1618 ; bencher, 1635, treasurer, 1639 ; M.P. for Callington in Short parliament, 1640 ; unsuccessful royalist candidate for the city of London ; leading counsel to Sir Edward Herbert, when impeached, 1642 ; himself impeached soon after for his support of ship-money ; solicitor-general to the king at Oxford, 1643 ; commissioner at Uxbridge and royalist attorney-general, 1645 ; pardoned by parliament on payment of fine, 1647. [xx. 425]

GARDINER, WILLIAM or WILLIAM NEVILLE (1748-1806), diplomatist ; lieutenant-general ; served in America, 1775-6 ; wounded at Freehold, New Jersey, 1778 ; lieutenant-colonel, 45th foot (Sherwood Foresters), 1778 ; special envoy at Brussels, 1789-92 ; plenipotentiary at Warsaw, 1792-5 ; major-general, 1793 ; lieutenant-general, 1799 ; M.P., Thomastown, in Irish parliament ; commander of north inland district of Ireland, 1803-5 ; commander-in-chief of Nova Scotia, 1805. [xx. 426]

GARDINER, WILLIAM (1770-1853), musical composer ; member of the Adelphi Philosophical Society, 1790-2 ; composed songs and compiled 'Sacred Melodies from Haydn, Mozart, and Beethoven ... adapted to the best English Poets,' 1812-15, and 'Judah' (1821), an oratorio culled from the same masters ; edited Berry's version of Bombet's 'Life of Haydn' and Brewin's version of Schlichtegroll's 'Life of Mozart,' 1817 ; published popular works on music. [xx. 427]

GARDINER, WILLIAM NELSON (1766-1814), engraver and bookseller ; employed in London by Sylvester, Harding, and Bartolozzi ; B.A. Corpus Christi College, Cambridge, 1797 ; the Mustapha of Dibdin's 'Bibliomania' ; committed suicide. [xx. 428]

GARDNER. [See also GARDINER.]

GARDNER, MRS. (fl. 1763-1782), actress ; as Miss Cheney played Miss Prue in 'Love for Love' at Drury Lane, and Rose in the 'Recruiting Officer,' 1763-4 ; made her reputation in Foote's pieces at the Haymarket, 1768-1774 ; her comedy, 'Advertisement, or a Bold Stroke for a Husband,' played there for her benefit, 1777. [xx. 429]

GARDNER, ALAN, first BARON GARDNER (1742-1809), admiral ; present at Quiberon Bay in the Dorsetshire ; carried to Howe first news of the French approach, and captured on North American coast large French merchantship, 1778 ; commanded the Sultan at Grenada, 1779 ; with Rodney in the Duke in the victory of 1782 ; commander in Jamaica, 1786-9 ; lord of the admiralty, 1790-5 ; created a baronet for his services in Howe's victory, 1794 ; interviewed mutineers at Spithead, 1797 ; admiral of the blue, 1799 ; M.P., Plymouth, 1790-6, and Westminster, 1796-1806 ; created Baron Gardner in Irish peerage, 1800 ; peer of the United Kingdom, 1806. [xx. 430]

GARDNER, DANIEL (1750 ?-1805), portrait-painter ; celebrated for small pictures in oil and crayons. [xx. 430]

GARDNER, GEORGE (1812-1849), botanist ; collected in Brazil many thousand specimens of plants, 1836-40 ; F.L.S., 1842 ; died in Ceylon, superintendent of botanical garden ; published 'Travels in the Interior of Brazil,' 1846. [xx. 431]

GARDNER, JOHN (1804–1880), medical writer; L.R.C.P. Edinburgh, 1860; M.D. Giessen, 1847; translated Liebig's 'Familiar Letters on Chemistry,' 1843; first secretary to Royal College of Chemistry and professor of chemistry to General Apothecaries' Company; published 'The Great Physician,' 1843, 'Household Medicine,' and 'Longevity' [xx. 431]

GARDNER, THOMAS (1690 ?–1769), Southwold antiquary; published 'Historical Account of Dunwich . . . Blithburgh . . . Southwold,' 1754. [xx. 432]

GARDNER, WILLIAM (1844–1887), inventor of the Gardner machine-gun, 1876, and of a quick-firing cannon; a native of Ohio. [xx. 432]

GARDNER, WILLIAM LINNÆUS (1771–1835), Indian officer; nephew of Alan, first baron Gardner [q. v.]; ensign in India, 1789; captain, 30th foot, 1794; employed by the Mahratta Jeswunt Rao Holkar; married a princess of Cambay; escaped to General Lake disguised as a grass-cutter, 1804; commanded irregular horse in Kamaun and Rajpootana; lieutenant-colonel in Indian army, 1819, commanding Gardner's horse. [xx. 432]

GARDNOR, JOHN (1729–1808), painter; vicar of Battersea, 1778–1808; exhibited landscapes at Royal Academy, 1782–96; published views of the Rhine country, engraved in aquatint by himself and others. [xx. 433]

GARDNOR, RICHARD (*fl.* 1766–1793), painter; nephew and assistant of John Gardnor [q. v.]; exhibited with Free Society and at the Academy, 1786–93. [xx. 434]

GARDYNE, ALEXANDER (1585 ?–1634 ?), Scots poet; published 'Garden of Grave and Godlie Flowers,' 1609, and 'Theatre of Scotish Kings.' [xx. 434]

GARENCIÈRES, THEOPHILUS (1610–1680), physician; M.D. Caen, 1636; incorporated M.D. Oxford, 1657; published 'Angliæ Flagellum seu Tabes Anglica,' 1647, and a book of prescriptions for the plague, 1665; translated Nostradamus, 1672. [xx. 434]

GARGRAVE, GEORGE (1710–1785), mathematician; contributed to the 'Gentleman's Magazine' papers on the transit of Venus (1761 and 1769) and (1781) memoirs of Abraham Sharp [q. v.] the mathematician. [xx. 435]

GARGRAVE, SIR THOMAS (1495–1579), speaker and (1560) vice-president of the council of the North; M.P. for York, 1547–55, Yorkshire, 1555; speaker, 1559; active in suppressing rising of 1569. [xx. 435]

GARLAND, AUGUSTINE (*fl.* 1660), regicide; of Emmanuel College, Cambridge, and Lincoln's Inn; M.P. Queenborough, 1648; presided over the committee to consider method of the king's trial, and signed death-warrant; condemned to death, 1660, but suffered only confiscation and imprisonment. [xx. 436]

GARLAND, JOHN (*fl.* 1230), grammarian and alchemist; often confused with Gerlandus, a French writer of twelfth century, and others; studied at Oxford and Paris; professor at Toulouse University, 1229–31; wrote 'Dictionarius Scolasticus' and many other grammatical treatises, 'Compendium Alchymiæ cum Dictionario,' 'Liber de Mineralibus,' and similar works; author of treatises on counterpoint, plain-song, and other musical subjects; some verses by him, including the autobiographical 'De Triumphis Ecclesiæ' and 'De Contemptu Mundi,' wrongly ascribed to St. Bernard. [xx. 436]

GARNEAU, FRANÇOIS XAVIER (1809–1866), historian of Canada; native of Canada; greffier of Quebec, 1844–64; president of Canadian Institute, 1855; member of council of education, 1857; published 'Histoire du Canada,' 1845–6, and 'Voyage en Angleterre et en France,' 1855. [xx. 439]

GARNER, THOMAS (1789–1868), engraver; pupil of Samuel Lines [q. v.]; a founder of Birmingham Society of Artists. [xx. 440]

GARNETT, ARTHUR WILLIAM (1829–1861), engineer; younger son of William Garnett [q. v.]; entered Bengal engineers, 1846; wounded at Mooltan, 1849; held fords of the Chenâb at Goojerât, 1849; designed forts on Afghan frontier; buried in Calcutta Cathedral. [xxi. 1]

GARNETT, HENRY (1555–1606), jesuit; educated at Winchester, 1567; two years corrector of the press to Tottel the law printer; went to Spain and Italy; jesuit novice, 1575; professor of Hebrew in the college at Rome; superior of the English province, 1587–1606; professed of the four vows, 1598; accused of complicity in Gunpowder plot; arrested after three days' search at Hindlip Hall; imprisoned in the Tower; twenty-three times examined before the privy council; condemned on his admission of conversations with Catesby, and executed; published a translation, with supplements, of 'Summa Canisii' (1590), 'A Treatise on Schism,' and other theological works. [xxi. 2]

GARNETT, JEREMIAH (1793–1870), journalist; brother of Richard Garnett [q. v.]; co-founder of the 'Manchester Guardian,' 1821; sole editor, 1844–61; obtained defeat of Milner Gibson and John Bright, 1857. [xxi. 5]

GARNETT, JOHN (1709–1782), bishop of Clogher; fellow of Sidney Sussex College, Cambridge; M.A., 1732; bishop of Ferns, 1752–8, of Clogher, 1758; patron of Philip Skelton [q. v.]; published 'Dissertation on Job,' 1749. [xxi. 5]

GARNETT, JOHN (*d.* 1813), dean of Exeter, 1810; son of John Garnett (1709–1782) [q. v.] [xxi. 6]

GARNETT, RICHARD (1789–1850), philologist; became priest-vicar of Lichfield Cathedral, 1829; incumbent of Chebsey, near Stafford, 1836–8; assistant-keeper of printed books, British Museum, 1838; his philological essays edited by his eldest son, 1859. [xxi. 6]

GARNETT, THOMAS (1575–1608), jesuit; nephew of Henry Garnett [q. v.]; jesuit, 1604; imprisoned in the Tower and banished for life, 1606; executed on his return. [xxi. 7]

GARNETT, THOMAS (1766–1802), physician and natural philosopher; M.D. Edinburgh, 1788; practised at Bradford, Knaresborough, and Harrogate; published first analysis of Harrogate waters; professor of natural philosophy at Anderson's Institution, Glasgow, of natural philosophy and chemistry at Royal Institution, 1799–1801; anticipated modern theory of a quasi-intelligence in plants; published 'Highland Tour,' 1800; his 'Zoonomia' published, 1804. [xxi. 7]

GARNETT, THOMAS (1799–1878), naturalist; brother of Richard and Jeremiah Garnett [q. v.]; wrote on pisciculture and experimented with guano; his papers privately printed, 1883. [xxi. 8]

GARNETT, WILLIAM (1793–1873), civil servant; deputy-registrar and registrar of land tax, 1819–41; inspector-general of stamps and taxes, 1842; published 'Guide to Property and Income Tax.' [xxi. 8]

GARNEYS or **GARNYSSHE**, SIR CHRISTOPHER (*d.* 1534), chief porter of Calais, 1526–34; favourite of Henry VIII, who knighted him at Tournay, 1513. [xxi. 9]

GARNIER or **WARNER** (*fl.* 1106). [See WARNER.]

GARNIER, THOMAS, the younger (1809–1863), dean of Lincoln; of Winchester and Worcester College, Oxford; B.A., 1830; fellow of All Souls, 1830; B.C.L., 1833; chaplain of House of Commons, 1849; incumbent, Holy Trinity, Marylebone, 1850; dean of Ripon, 1859, of Lincoln, 1860; published sermons. [xxi. 9]

GARNIER, THOMAS, the elder (1776–1873), dean of Winchester; educated at Winchester and Worcester College, Oxford; fellow of All Souls', 1796; rector of Bishopstoke, 1807; D.C.L., 1850; dean of Winchester, 1840–72; friend of Palmerston. [xxi. 10]

GARNOCK, ROBERT (*d.* 1681), covenanter; executed for declining the king's authority; his head discovered in 1728; extracts from his autobiography contained in Howie's 'Biographia Scoticana,' and dying testimony in 'Cloud of Witnesses.' [xxi. 10]

GARRARD, GEORGE (1760–1826), animal painter and sculptor; pupil of Sawrey Gilpin [q. v.]; exhibited 'View of a Brewhouse Yard,' 1784, 'Sheep-shearing at Aston Clinton,' 1793; published description of British oxen, 1800; instrumental in obtaining act of 1798 securing copyright in works of plastic art; A.R.A., 1800. [xxi. 11]

GARRARD, MARCUS (1561–1635). [See GHEERAERTS.]

GARRARD, Sir SAMUEL (1650–1724), lord mayor of London; succeeded as baronet, 1700; sheriff of London, 1701; lord mayor, 1709–10; M.P., Agmundesham (Amersham), 1702–14: master of the Grocers' Company, 1710; president of Bridewell and Bethlehem hospitals, 1720. [xxi. 11]

GARRARD, THOMAS (1787–1859), biographer; treasurer of Bristol, 1836–56; published life of Edward Colston, 1852. [xxi. 12]

GARRAWAY, Sir HENRY (1575–1646), lord mayor of London; governor of Greenland, Russia, and Turkey companies, 1639; master of the Drapers' Company, 1627 and 1639; sheriff of London, 1627; lord mayor of London, 1639; knighted, 1640; assisted the king to raise money in the city; expelled from court of aldermen for royalism, 1643; imprisoned; his speech (1642) in answer to Pym's address to the citizens frequently reprinted. [xxi. 12]

GARRETT, JEREMIAH LEARNOULT (*fl.* 1809), dissenting minister; preached in the fields near London; laid foundation-stone of Islington Chapel, 1788; ejected for heresy from Lady Huntingdon's connexion; carried on controversies with Joanna Southcott and William Huntington; published 'Songs of Sion,' and other works. [xxi. 14]

GARRETT, Sir ROBERT (1794–1869), lieutenant-general; educated at Harrow; ensign, 2nd queen's foot, 1811; wounded at Salamanca, 1812; severely wounded in the Pyrenees, 1814; lieutenant-colonel, 1846; led 46th foot in the Crimea, where he commanded first a brigade and subsequently the 4th division; brigadier in China, 1857; lieutenant-general, 1866; K.C.B. [xxi. 15]

GARRICK, DAVID (1717–1779), actor; Dr. Johnson's first pupil at Edial; with him left Lichfield for London, 1737; started a wine business with his brother Peter; introduced by Johnson to Cave; wrote in the 'Gentleman's Magazine'; his 'Lethe' performed at Drury Lane, 1740; became attached to Margaret ('Peg') Woffington [q. v.], to whom he afterwards offered marriage; under name Lyddal made first appearance at Ipswich in 'Oroonoko,' 1741; made his reputation at Goodman's Fields in 'Richard III,' 1741; played Bayes and King Lear, 1742; highly successful at Dublin in 'Hamlet' and 'The Recruiting Officer,' 1742; at Drury Lane played Abel Drugger and other parts, but quarrelled with Macklin, 1742–3; acted Macbeth 'as written by Shakespeare,' 1744, Sir John Brute ('Provoked Wife') and Othello, 1744–5, played Faulconbridge and Iago at Dublin, 1745; first appeared at Covent Garden in Shakespearean parts, 1746; joined Lacy in management of Drury Lane, 1747; played Benedick and Romeo (his own version), 1748, and Demetrius in Johnson's 'Mahomet and Irene,' 1749; his marriage resented by Mrs. Cibber, Quin, Macklin, and Barry; with Miss Bellamy played Romeo and Lear against the same parts by Barry with Mrs. Cibber at Covent Garden, 1750; appeared as Kitely in 'Every Man in his Humour,' 1751; rejoined by Mrs. Cibber and joined by Foote, 1754, when he produced his version of 'Taming of the Shrew' and 'Coriolanus'; threatened to retire from the stage in consequence of riots against French dancers, 1755; appeared in his adaptation of 'Winter's Tale,' 1756; played Don Felix in 'The Wonder,' 1756; produced Foote's 'Author,' 1756; produced his adaptation of 'Cymbeline,' 1761; Sciolto in the 'Fair Penitent,' his last new part, 1763, during which season riots occurred at Drury Lane in consequence of alterations in prices; travelled with his wife in France and Italy, 1763–4; made free of the Comédie Française; met Diderot, Beaumarchais, Marivaux, Marmontel, and Mlle. Clairon; reappearing at Drury Lane as Benedick, 1765, introduced the system of invisible lighting; produced 'The Clandestine Marriage,' written by himself and Colman, 1766; produced his 'Peep Behind the Curtain,' 1767; designed and carried out the Shakespeare jubilee at Stratford, 1769, and produced the 'Jubilee' at Drury Lane; produced Cumberland's 'West Indian' and Dryden's 'King Arthur,' 1770; produced his version of 'Hamlet,' 1772, and his 'Bon Ton, or High Life above Stairs,' 1775; made last appearance as Don Felix, 10 June 1776, selling moiety of his patent to Sheridan and two others for 35,000*l.*; wrote prologue to the 'School for Scandal' and 'All the World's a Stage,' and prologue and epilogue for Fielding's 'Fathers'; made a larger fortune than any actor except Alleyn; last actor buried in Westminster Abbey; his

poetical works published, 1785, his dramatic works (sixteen plays), 1768. His portrait was painted by Reynolds, Hogarth, and Gainsborough. [xxi. 16]

GARROD, ALFRED HENRY (1846–1879), zoologist; studied at University College, London; thrice won medical scholarship at King's College, London; senior in natural science tripos, Cambridge, 1871; prosector of Cambridge Zoological Society, 1871; fellow of St. John's College, Cambridge, 1873; professor of comparative anatomy at King's College, London, 1874–9; Fullerian professor of physiology, Royal Institution, 1875; F.R.S., 1876; made important researches in the anatomy and myology of birds and ruminants; edited Bell's version of Müller on the vocal organs of passerines, and contributed to Cassell's 'Natural History.' [xxi. 27]

GARROW, Sir WILLIAM (1760–1840), baron of the exchequer; barrister, Lincoln's Inn, 1783; made reputation by prosecution of Aikles for stealing bill of exchange, 1784; acted for Fox in Westminster scrutiny; K.C., 1793; M.P., Gatton, 1805, Callington, 1806, and Eye, 1812; solicitor-general, 1812; knighted, 1812; attorney-general, 1813; chief-justice of Chester, 1814; baron of exchequer, 1817–32; privy councillor, 1832. [xxi. 28]

GARSIDE, CHARLES BRIERLEY (1818–1876), Roman catholic divine; educated at Manchester school; M.A. Brasenose College, Oxford, 1844; Anglican curate, 1842–50; graduated at the Collegio Romano, and was ordained Romanist priest, 1854; chaplain to Earl of Shrewsbury, 1855; afterwards assistant-priest in Chelsea and Oxford; died at Posilippo, Italy; published theological works. [xxi. 29]

GARTER, BERNARD (*fl.* 1570), anti-papist poet; published 'The tragicall and true historie which happened betweene two English lovers, 1563,' 1565, and 'A New Yeares Gifte,' 1579. [xxi. 30]

GARTH, JOHN (*fl.* 1757), musical composer; adapted the 'First Fifty Psalms of Marcello' to the English version, 1757–65. [xxi. 30]

GARTH, Sir SAMUEL (1661–1719), physician and poet; M.A. Peterhouse, Cambridge, 1684; M.D., 1691; F.R.C.P., 1693; Gulstonian lecturer, 1694; Harveian orator, 1697; knighted, 1714; physician in ordinary to George I, and physician-general to the army; made a Latin oration over the body of Dryden as it lay in state at the College of Physicians, 1700; wrote much occasional verse, and was a member of the Kit Cat Club; ridiculed in his poem 'The Dispensary,' 1699, the opposition of the apothecaries and their allies to the scheme of out-patient rooms. [xxi. 31]

GARTHSHORE, MAXWELL (1732–1812), physician; M.D. Edinburgh, 1764; L.R.C.P., 1764; F.R.S. and F.S.A.; physician to British Lying-in Hospital; bore striking likeness to great Lord Chatham; provided for widow of John Hunter (1728–1793) [q. v.]; published works on obstetrics. [xxi. 32]

GARTHSHORE, WILLIAM (1764–1806), lord of the admiralty; son of Maxwell Garthshore [q. v.]; educated at Westminster; M.A. Christ Church, Oxford, 1789; private secretary to Dundas, 1794; M.P., Launceston, 1795, Weymouth, 1797–1806; a lord of the admiralty, 1801–4. [xxi. 32]

GARVEY, EDMUND (*d.* 1813), landscape painter; exhibited at Dublin, the Free Society of Artists, and (1769–1808) at the Royal Academy; R.A., 1783. [xxi. 33]

GARVEY, JOHN (1527–1595), archbishop of Armagh; graduated at Oxford; dean of Ferns, 1558, of Christ Church, Dublin, 1565; privy councillor of Ireland; bishop of Kilmore, 1585; archbishop of Armagh, 1589–95. [xxi. 33]

GARWAY, Sir HENRY (1575–1646). [See GARRAWAY.]

GASCAR, HENRI (1635–1701), portrait-painter; born at Paris; *protégé* of Louise de Kéroualle, duchess of Portsmouth [q. v.]; in England, 1674; returned to France, 1680; died at Rome. His portraits include Charles II, the Duchesses of Portsmouth and Cleveland, and Nell Gwyn. [xxi. 34]

GASCOIGNE, Sir BERNARD (1614–1687), soldier and diplomatist; born at Florence; saw military service in Italy and Germany; originally named BERNARDO or

BERNARDINO GUASCONI; captured parliamentarian officers in Cornwall, 1644; commanded a regiment of horse at Colchester, 1648; granted denization as Sir Bernard Gascoigne, 1661; F.R.S., 1667; envoy to Vienna to negotiate marriage of Duke of York with a daughter of the Archduke of Austria, 1672; his memoirs printed at Florence, 1886; his 'Description of Germany' printed in 'Miscellanea Aulica,' 1702. [xxi. 34]

GASCOIGNE, SIR CRISP (1700-1761). [See GASCOYNE.]

GASCOIGNE, GEORGE (1525 ?-1577), poet; a descendant of Sir William Gascoigne (1350 ?-1419) [q. v.]; educated at Trinity College, Cambridge; ancient of Gray's Inn, c. 1557; M.P., Bedford, 1557-9; his 'Supposes,' an adaptation of Ariosto's comedy, acted at Gray's Inn, 1566; married the mother of Nicholas Breton [q. v.], c. 1566; M.P., Midhurst, 1572; went to Holland to avoid his creditors, 1572; saw military service in Holland, 1572-5; captured by the Spaniards; an unauthorised book of poems by him published in his absence; issued the 'Posies of G. Gascoigne, corrected, perfected, and augmented' (1575), containing 'Jocasta,' the second earliest tragedy in English in blank verse, and 'Certayne Notes of Instruction concerning the making of verse or ryme in English,' the earliest English critical essay; published his 'tragicall comedie,' the 'Glasse of Government,' 1575; visited Kenilworth with Queen Elizabeth and Leicester, 1575; contributed to 'The Princelye Pleasures,' 1576. His other works include 'The Steele Glas' (1576), 'The Droomme of Doomesday,' and the posthumously published 'Tale of Hemetes the heremyte,' in English, French, Latin, and Italian. He was praised by Meres, Nash, and other contemporaries. [xxi. 36]

GASCOIGNE, JOHN (fl. 1381), doctor of canon law at Oxford; signatory of the chancellor's condemnation of Wycliffe's views on the Sacrament, 1381; credited by Pits with authorship of a treatise, 'Contra Wiclevum.' [xxi. 39]

GASCOIGNE, RICHARD (1579-1661?), antiquary; B.A. Jesus College, Cambridge, 1599; left books to Jesus College, Cambridge; compiled pedigrees of Gascoigne, Wentworth, and other families. [xxi. 40]

GASCOIGNE, RICHARD (d. 1716), Jacobite; joined the rebels at Preston, 1715; captured and hanged at Tyburn. [xxi. 41]

GASCOIGNE, THOMAS (1403-1458), theologian; of Oriel College, Oxford; D.D., 1434; chancellor of the university, 1434, 1444, and frequently 'cancellarius natus' and vice-chancellor; an active preacher and denouncer of lollardy, but zealous against pluralities and other ecclesiastical abuses; benefactor of Oriel, Balliol, and other colleges; his 'Dictionarium Theologicum' (from which extracts were printed by J. E. T. Rogers, 1881) preserved at Lincoln College. Other works attributed to him include 'The Myroure of our Ladye' (ed. Blunt, 1873), and a 'life' of St. Bridget of Sweden. [xxi. 41]

GASCOIGNE, SIR THOMAS (1593 ?-1686), alleged conspirator; succeeded as baronet of Nova Scotia, 1637; endowed convent near Fountains Abbey, 1678; sent to the Tower on a charge of plotting with other members of his family to murder Charles II, 1679; acquitted, 1679; retired to his brother's monastery at Lambspring, Germany, where he died. [xxi. 44]

GASCOIGNE, SIR WILLIAM (1350 ?-1419), judge; reader at Gray's Inn; king's serjeant, 1397, and attorney to Hereford (Lancaster) on his banishment; chief-justice of king's bench, 1400; raised forces against Northumberland, 1403, and received the submission of his adherents, 1405; probably a member of the court which tried them; improbably said to have refused to try Archbishop Scrope; ceased to be chief-justice soon after Henry V's accession. The story taken by Hall from Sir T. Elyot's 'Governour' (1531) of his committing Henry V when Prince of Wales is without foundation. [xxi. 45]

GASCOIGNE, WILLIAM (1612 ?-1644), inventor of the micrometer; corresponded with Horrocks and Crabtree; his invention of the micrometer not published till Auzout's announcement (1666) of his own; killed on royalist side at Marston Moor. [xxi. 47]

GASCOYNE, BAMBER (1725-1791), lord of the admiralty; eldest son of Sir Crisp Gascoyne [q. v.];

M.P., Malden, 1761-3, Midhurst, 1765-70, Weobly, 1770-4, Truro, 1774-84, Bossiney, 1784-6; receiver-general of customs. [xxi. 48]

GASCOYNE, SIR CRISP (1700-1761), lord mayor of London; master of the Brewers' Company, 1746-7; sheriff of London, 1747-8; passed in common council act for relief of city orphans, 1748; lord mayor, 1752-3; knighted, 1752; first mayor who occupied Mansion House; convicted alleged kidnappers of Elizabeth Canning [q. v.], but afterwards proved her information to be false. [xxi. 47]

GASCOYNE, ISAAC (1770-1841), general; third son of Bamber Gascoyne [q. v.]; served with Coldstream guards in Flanders, 1793-4, and commanded them in Ireland, 1798; major-general on the staff, 1802-8; general, 1819; M.P., Liverpool, 1802-30. [xxi. 48]

GASELEE, SIR STEPHEN (1762-1839), judge; barrister, Gray's Inn, 1793; pupil of Sir Vicary Gibbs [q. v.]; went the western circuit; K.C., 1819; knighted, 1825; justice of common pleas, 1824-37; supposed original of Dickens's Justice Stareleigh. [xxi. 49]

GASELEE, STEPHEN (1807-1883), serjeant-at-law; son of Sir Stephen Gaselee [q. v.]; educated at Winchester and Balliol College, Oxford; M.A., 1832; barrister, Inner Temple, 1832; serjeant-at-law, 1840; M.P., Portsmouth, 1865-8. [xxi. 49]

GASKELL, ELIZABETH CLEGHORN (1810-1865), novelist; daughter of William Stevenson (1772-1829) [q. v.]; brought up by her aunt at Knutsford, the original of 'Cranford'; married William Gaskell [q. v.], 1832; became intimate with the Howitts, 1841; published 'Mary Barton' anonymously, 1848; praised by Miss Edgeworth, Landor, Carlyle, and Bamford; attacked by W. R. Greg and others as hostile to employers; a guest of Dickens, with Carlyle and Thackeray, 1849; contributed to 'Household Words' from 1850, when she also became acquainted with Charlotte Brontë; published 'Life' of Charlotte Brontë, 1857, the first edition being withdrawn because some of its statements were challenged by persons concerned; became intimate with Madame Mohl, 1855; organised sewing-rooms during cotton famine of 1862; died suddenly. Her other works include 'Lizzie Leigh,' 1855, 'The Grey Woman,' 1865, 'My Lady Ludlow,' 1859 (republished as 'Round the Sofa,' 1871), 'Mr. Harrison's Confessions,' 1865, 'Ruth,' 1853, 'Cranford,' 1853, 'North and South,' 1855, 'Sylvia's Lovers,' 1863, and 'Wives and Daughters,' 1865. The first edition of her collected works appeared in 1873. [xxi. 49]

GASKELL, WILLIAM (1805-1884), unitarian minister; M.A. Glasgow, 1824; junior minister of Cross Street Chapel, Manchester, 1828, senior, 1854; secretary to Manchester New College, 1840-6, professor of English history and literature, 1846-53, and chairman of committee from 1854; taught logic and literature at Owens College; his 'Lectures on the Lancashire Dialect' (1844) appended to fifth edition of his wife's novel, 'Mary Barton' [see GASKELL, ELIZABETH CLEGHORN]; some of his hymns included in Martineau's 'Hymns of Praise and Prayer' (1874). [xxi. 54]

GASKIN, GEORGE (1751-1829), divine; M.A. Trinity College, Oxford, 1778; D.D., 1788; for forty-six years lecturer in Islington; incumbent of St. Bennet, Gracechurch Street, and secretary S.P.C.K., 1791; rector of Stoke Newington, 1797; prebendary of Ely, 1822; edited Bishop Dehon's sermons. [xxi. 55]

GASPARS (JASPERS), JAN BAPTIST (1620 ?-1691), portrait-painter; native of Antwerp; worked for General Lambert; assisted Lely and Kneller, and became known as 'Lely's Baptist'; painted portraits of Charles II and Hobbes, and etched 'Banquet of the Gods.' [xxi. 55]

GASPEY, THOMAS (1788-1871), journalist and author; for sixteen years on the staff of the 'Morning Post,' for which he wrote 'Elegy on Marquis of Anglesey's Leg'; sub-editor of 'Courier'; published novels and historical works. [xxi. 56]

GASSIOT, JOHN PETER (1797-1877), scientific writer; chairman of Kew Observatory, which he helped to endow; founder of Royal Society Scientific Relief Fund; proved by experiments with Grove's cells that the static effect of a battery increases with its chemical action, 1844; proved with delicate micrometers the correctness of Grove's arguments against the contact theory, 1844; discovered stratification of electric discharge, 1852; F.R.S.   [xxi. 56]

GAST, LUCE DE (*fl.* 1190 ?), lord of the castle of Gast, near Salisbury; reputed author of the first part of the French poem, 'Tristan.'   [xxi. 57]

GASTINEAU, HENRY (1791–1876), water-colour painter; member of Society of Painters in Water-colours, 1823; exhibited for fifty-eight years.   [xxi. 57]

GASTRELL, FRANCIS (1662–1725), bishop of Chester; educated at Westminster; M.A. Christ Church, Oxford, 1687; D.D., 1700; carried on a controversy with Sherlock on the Trinity, 1696–8; Boyle lecturer, 1697; chaplain to Harley, when speaker, 1700; canon of Christ Church, 1702; queen's chaplain, 1711; bishop of Chester, 1714; published, among other works, 'Christian Institutes,' 1707, and 'Historical Notices of the Diocese of Chester.'   [xxi. 58]

GATACRE, THOMAS (*d.* 1593), divine; educated at Oxford and Magdalene College, Cambridge; student, Middle Temple, *c.* 1553; domestic chaplain to Leicester; rector of St. Edmund's, Lombard Street, 1572. [xxi. 59]

GATAKER, CHARLES (1614?–1680), divine; son of Thomas Gataker [q. v.]; educated at St. Paul's School; B.A. Sidney Sussex College, Cambridge; M.A. Pembroke College, Oxford, 1636; chaplain to Falkland and rector of Hoggeston, Buckinghamshire; published works, including 'Animadversions' on Bull's 'Harmonia Apostolica' and 'Examination of the Case of the Quakers concerning Oaths,' 1675.   [xxi. 62]

GATAKER, THOMAS (1574–1654), puritan divine and critic; son of Thomas Gatacre [q. v.]; scholar of St. John's College, Cambridge; fellow of Sidney Sussex College, 1596; B.D., 1603; M.A. St. John's College, Cambridge; lecturer at Lincoln's Inn, 1601; rector of Rotherhithe, 1611; active member of the Westminster Assembly; favoured a mixture of prelacy and presbyterianism; signed address against Charles I's trial; published, besides controversial works and life of William Bradshaw [q. v.], 'Marci Antonini de Rebus Suis,' 1652 (Greek text with Latin version and commentary), and commentaries on Isaiah, Jeremiah, and Lamentations.
                                                        [xxi. 60]

GATES, BERNARD (1685?–1773), musician; master of children of the Chapel Royal; member of Westminster Abbey choir and of Academy of Vocal Music; sang air in Dettingen 'Te Deum,' 1743; Handel's 'Esther' performed at his house, 1732.   [xxi. 62]

GATES, HORATIO (1728–1806), major-general in United States service; served under Prince Ferdinand of Brunswick; captain, 1754; served at Fort Duquesne, 1755, Fort Pitt, 1760, and Martinique, 1762; major, 1762; in Ireland, 1768–9; retired from service and returned to America, 1769; adjutant-general and brigadier in American army on outbreak of war, 1775; major-general and commander of northern army serving in Canada, 1776; defeated Burgoyne at Bemus Heights, and forced him to surrender at Saratoga, 1777; president of board of war and ordnance, 1777; defeated at Camden, South Carolina, 1780; superseded in the command, 1780.   [Suppl. ii. 269]

GATES, SIR JOHN (1504?–1553), statesman; accompanied Henry VIII to Lincolnshire, 1536; received valuable grants in Essex for confidential services; K.B., 1547; privy councillor and vice-chamberlain, 1551; chancellor of the duchy of Lancaster, 1552; executed as a partisan of Northumberland.   [xxi. 63]

GATES, SIR THOMAS (*fl.* 1596–1621), governor of Virginia; knighted for service in Cadiz expedition, 1596; served in Netherlands, 1604–8; sailed for Virginia as lieutenant-general of the Colonisation Company, 1609; wrecked off the Bermudas; governor, 1611–14, organising the colony; supposed to have died in East Indies; Jourdan's and Purchas's accounts of his adventures in the Bermudas probably groundwork of the 'Tempest.'
                                                        [xxi. 64]

GATFORD, LIONEL (*d.* 1665), royalist divine; fellow of Jesus College, Cambridge; M.A., 1625; B.D., 1633; vicar of St. Clement's, Cambridge, 1631; rector of Dennington, 1637; arrested at Cambridge and imprisoned in Ely House, Holborn, for an unpublished work on passive

obedience, 1643; minister in Jersey and chaplain to Sir Edward Hyde, 1647; D.D., 1660; vicar of Plymouth, 1661, but never had possession; died of the plague when curate of Yarmouth.   [xxi. 65]

GATLEY, ALFRED (1816–1863), sculptor; his 'Hebe' purchased by Art Union; exhibited busts of Espartero, 1846, Archbishop Sumner, 1848, and S. Christie-Miller, 1850, and executed that of Hooker in the Temple Church; after 1852 lived at Rome, where he died; his bas-relief, 'Overthrow of Pharaoh,' statues of 'Echo' and 'Night' and marble statuettes of animals exhibited at International Exhibition, 1862.   [xxi. 66]

GATLIFF, JAMES (1766–1831), divine; educated at Manchester grammar school; perpetual curate of Gorton, Manchester; edited, with life, Wogan's 'Essay on the Proper Lessons,' 1818; imprisoned for debt and sequestrated; issued apologetic pamphlet with eccentric title, 1820.   [xxi. 67]

GATTIE, HENRY (1774–1844), actor; appeared at Bath in vocal characters and old men's parts, 1807–12; at Drury Lane, 1813–33; his best parts, Morbleu in 'Monsieur Tonson' and Dr. Caius in 'Merry Wives.'
                                                        [xxi. 67]

GATTY, MARGARET (1807–1873), writer for children; daughter of Alexander John Scott [q. v.], whose life she and her husband published, 1842; married Alfred Gatty, D.D., 1839; established 'Aunt Judy's Magazine,' 1866; published 'Parables from Nature,' 1855–71, 'Aunt Judy's Tales,' 1859, and 'Aunt Judy's Letters.'
                                                        [xxi. 67]

GAU, JOHN (1493?–1553?), translator; M.A. St. Andrews, 1511; published in Sweden 'Richt Vay to the Kingdome of Heuine' (translation from Christiern Pedersen), 1533, the earliest protestant work in Scottish prose; prebendary of church of Our Lady, Copenhagen.
                                                   [Suppl. ii. 272]

GAUDEN, JOHN (1605–1662), bishop of Worcester; M.A. St. John's College, Cambridge, 1626; entered Wadham College, Oxford; D.D., 1641; vicar of Chippenham and chaplain to Robert Rich, earl of Warwick [q. v.], 1640; dean of Bocking, 1641; 'shuffled out' of the Westminster Assembly for episcopalianism; retained benefices during the Commonwealth; wrote against the Army and the Civil Marriage Act and in defence of the church of England; published 'Ecclesiæ Anglicanæ Suspiria,' 1659; bishop of Exeter, 1660–2; wrote treatises against the covenanters, 1660–1; edited Hooker's 'Ecclesiastical Polity,' 1662; bishop of Worcester, 1662; claimed the authorship of 'Εἰκὼν βασιλική; the Pourtraicture of His Sacred Majestie in His Solitudes and Sufferings,' attributed by royalist writers and Bishop Christopher Wordsworth to Charles I. Gauden's claim was apparently admitted at the Restoration.   [xxi. 69]

GAUGAIN, THOMAS (1748–1810?), stipple engraver, native of Abbeville; exhibited paintings at Royal Academy, 1778–82; executed numerous engravings after Reynolds, Northcote, Morland, Maria Cosway, and Nollekens's bust of Fox.   [xxi. 72]

GAULE, JOHN (*fl.* 1660), divine; studied at Oxford and Cambridge; chaplain to Lord Camden, 1629; vicar of Great Staughton, 1646; published numerous theological works, including 'Select Cases of Conscience touching Witches' (1646).   [xxi. 72]

GAUNT, ELIZABETH (*d.* 1685), the last woman executed for a political offence; burnt at Tyburn for treason in sheltering Burton, a Rye-house conspirator and adherent of Monmouth.   [xxi. 72]

GAUNT, JOHN OF, DUKE OF LANCASTER (1340–1399). [See JOHN.]

GAUNT or **GANT** (or **PAYNELL**), MAURICE DE (1184?–1230), baron of Leeds; granted charter to burgesses of Leeds, 1208; joined insurgent barons, 1216; captured at Lincoln, 1217; paid scutage for lands in eight counties, 1223; justice itinerant for Herefordshire, Staffordshire, Shropshire, Devonshire, Hampshire, and Berkshire, 1227; died in Brittany.   [xxi. 73]

GAUNT, SIMON DE (*d.* 1315). [See GHENT.]

GAUNTLETT, HENRY (1762–1833), divine; vicar of Olney, 1815–33, and friend of Rowland Hill; published 'Exposition of the Book of Revelation,' 1821.   [xxi. 74]

R

GAUNTLETT, HENRY JOHN (1805–1876), organist and composer; son of Henry Gauntlett [q. v.]; played the organ at Olney as a child; organist at St. Olave's, Southwark, 1827–46, at Union chapel, Islington, 1853–61, and St. Bartholomew's, Smithfield, 1872–6; introduced enlarged organs on the Haarlem model; patented electrical-action apparatus, 1852; created Mus.Doc. by Archbishop Howley, 1842; played the 'Elijah' at Birmingham, 1846; edited 'Musical World,' contributing 'Characteristics of Beethoven' and other papers; composed 'St. Alphege,' 'St. Albinus,' 'St. George,' and other hymn-tunes and chants, 'The Song of the Soul,' and 'Notes, Queries, and Exercises in Science and Practice of Music,' 1859. 'Encyclopædia of the Chant,' first published, 1885, was largely his work. [xxi. 74]

GAVESTON, PIERS, EARL OF CORNWALL (d. 1312), favourite and foster-brother of Edward II; banished by Edward I, 1307, but recalled and created an earl on accession of Edward II; betrothed to sister of the Earl of Gloucester; having offended the barons by his conduct at the coronation was banished, but made lieutenant of Ireland, 1308; recalled, 1309; gave fresh offence by insolence and extravagance; accompanied Edward to Scotland, 1310–11; his banishment again demanded by lords ordainers, 1311; returned secretly from Bruges and joined the king at York; surrendered conditionally to Pembroke at Scarborough; kidnapped by Warwick and executed on Blacklow Hill in presence of Lancaster and other barons. [xxi. 76]

GAVIN, ANTONIO (fl. 1726), author of 'A Master-Key to Popery'; M.A. Saragossa; having become a protestant, escaped from Spain to London, and was entertained by Lord Stanhope; officiated as a minister in London and afterwards in Ireland, where his 'Master-Key,' containing mendacious revelations, appeared in 1724. [xxi. 78]

GAVIN, ROBERT (1827–1883), painter; exhibited popular landscapes at the Scottish Academy; A.R.S.A., 1854; travelled in America and Morocco, and lived some years at Tangier; R.S.A., 1879. [xxi. 79]

GAWDIE, SIR JOHN (1639–1699). [See GAWDY.]

GAWDY, FRAMLINGHAM (1589–1654), parliamentary reporter; M.P., Thetford, 1620–1, 1623–4, 1625–6, and 1640; his 'Notes of what passed in Parliament, 1641, 1642,' preserved in British Museum. [xxi. 79]

GAWDY, SIR FRANCIS (d. 1606), chief-justice of common pleas; half-brother of Sir Thomas Gawdy [q. v.]; treasurer of the Inner Temple, 1571; M.P., Morpeth, 1571; serjeant-at-law, 1577; as queen's serjeant, 1582, took part in proceedings against Mary Queen of Scots at Fotheringay, and those against William Davison (1541?–1608) [q. v.]; justice of queen's bench, 1589; knighted, 1603; member of the courts which tried Essex and Ralegh; chief-justice of common pleas, 1605. [xxi. 79]

GAWDY, SIR JOHN (1639–1699), painter; grandson of Framlingham Gawdy [q. v.]; succeeded to baronetcy, 1666. [xxi. 81]

GAWDY, SIR THOMAS (d. 1589), judge; bencher, Inner Temple, 1551; master of requests, 1551; M.P., Arundel, 1553; treasurer of Inner Temple, 1561; serjeant-at-law, 1567; justice of the queen's bench, 1574; knighted, 1579; president of commission to determine fishing rights of Yarmouth and the Cinque ports, 1575; member of the courts which tried Dr. Parry, 1585, William Shelley, 1586, Mary Queen of Scots at Fotheringay, and the Earl of Arundel, 1589. [xxi. 81]

GAWEN, THOMAS (1612–1684), Roman catholic writer; educated at Winchester; fellow of New College, Oxford, 1632; M.A.; met Milton at Rome; prebendary of Winchester, 1645; rector of Bishopstoke, 1660; having become a Romanist, withdrew to France, being admitted to Henrietta Maria's household; devotional works, published, 1686. [xxi. 82]

GAWLER, GEORGE (1796–1869), governor of South Australia; served with 52nd foot in the Peninsula (being twice wounded) and at Waterloo; governor of South Australia, 1838–41. [xxi. 83]

GAWLER, WILLIAM (1750–1809), organist and composer; published collections for piano or harpsichord, with instructions, 1780, 'Harmonia Sacra,' 1781, and other compositions. [xxi. 83]

GAY, JOHN (1685–1732), poet and dramatist; apprenticed to a London mercer; afterwards lived as a private gentleman: his first poem, 'Wine,' denying possibility of successful authorship to water-drinkers, possibly published in 1708; published 'Present State of Wit,' 1711; secretary to the Duchess of Monmouth, 1712–14; issued 'Rural Sports,' 1713; contributed (1713) to Steele's 'Guardian' and 'Poetical Miscellanies'; his 'Shepherd's Week' (satirical eclogues directed against Ambrose Philips [q. v.]), dedicated to Bolingbroke, 1714; accompanied Lord Clarendon to Hanover as secretary, 1714; his first play, 'What-d'ye Call it,' acted at Drury Lane and published, 1715; assisted by Swift in the poem 'Trivia,' 1716, and by Pope and Arbuthnot in 'Three Hours after Marriage,' acted 1717; accompanied William Pulteney to Aix, 1717; issued 'Poems,' 1720, with subscriptions from Burlington, Chandos, and other noble patrons; lost a fortune in South Sea funds; patronised by the Duke and Duchess of. Queensberry ('Kitty'); lottery commissioner, 1722–31; offered post of gentleman-usher to the Princess Louisa, 1727; his 'Captives' acted at Drury Lane, 1724; the first series of his 'Fables' issued, 1727; his 'Beggar's Opera' played for two seasons at Lincoln's Inn Fields, 1728, and throughout the British Isles, making much sensation, while its sequel, 'Polly,' though prohibited (1728) by the court from being acted, was also published with great success; wrote the libretto for Handel's 'Acis and Galatea,' 1732, and 'Achilles,' an opera produced at Covent Garden, 1733; the second series of 'Fables' (1738), his principal posthumous work. He was buried in Westminster Abbey. [xxi. 83]

GAY, JOHN (1699–1745), philosophical writer; M.A. Sidney Sussex College, Cambridge, 1725; fellow, 1724–32; vicar of Wilshampstead, Bedfordshire, 1732–45; prefixed to the translation by Edmund Law [q. v.] of the archbishop of Dublin's 'Essay on the Origin of Evil,' 1731, a 'Preliminary Dissertation' on utilitarian lines. [Suppl. ii. 272]

GAY, JOHN (1813–1885), surgeon; M.R.C.S., 1834; surgeon to Royal Free Hospital, 1836, and Great Northern, 1856–85; published medical works, including treatise 'On Femoral Rupture,' 1848. [xxi. 90]

GAY, JOSEPH (pseudonym) (1680?–1738). [See BREVAL, JOHN DURANT.]

GAYER, ARTHUR EDWARD (1801–1877), Irish ecclesiastical commissioner for Ireland, 1859–69; B.A. Trinity College, Dublin, 1823; LL.D., 1830; called to Irish bar, 1827; Q.C., 1844; chancellor of Ossory, 1848, and of Meath and other dioceses, 1851. His works include 'The Catholic Layman,' 1862, and 'Memoirs of Family of Gayer,' 1870. [xxi. 91]

GAYER, SIR JOHN (d. 1649), lord mayor of London; warden of Fishmongers' Company, 1638; prominent director of East India Company; as sheriff of London, 1635, enforced ship-money; knighted, 1641; lord mayor, 1646; impeached for abetting riots against compulsory militia service, 1647–8; president of Christ's Hospital, 1648; benefactor of Christ's Hospital. [xxi. 91]

GAYER, SIR JOHN (d. 1711?), governor of Bombay; nephew of Sir John Gayer (d. 1649) [q. v.]; received freedom of East India Company, 1682; knighted, 1693; governor of Bombay under Sir John Goldsborough [q. v.], 1693; chief governor on death of latter, 1694; arrested, 1700, and confined several years at Surat, at the instance of Sir Nicholas Waite, representative of the New East India Company; died at Bombay soon after his release. [xxi. 93]

GAYNESBURGH, WILLIAM DE (d. 1307). [See GAINSBOROUGH, WILLIAM.]

GAYTON, CLARK (1720?–1787?), admiral; commanded the St. George at the attack on Martinique and the reduction of Guadaloupe, 1759; commander on Jamaica station, 1774–8; rear-admiral, 1770; admiral, 1782. [xxi. 94]

GAYTON, EDMUND (1608–1666), author; educated at Merchant Taylors' School; M.A. St. John's College, Oxford, 1633; fellow; adopted as a son by Ben Jonson; expelled from post of superior beadle in arts at Oxford by parliamentary visitors, 1648; lived in great pecuniary distress in London; published, among other works, 'Festivous Notes on . . . Don Quixote,' 1654, in prose and verse. [xxi. 94]

GAYWOOD, RICHARD (*fl.* 1650-1680), engraver and etcher; pupil of Wenceslaus Hollar [q. v.] and friend of Francis Barlow [q. v.] [xxi. 95]

GEARE, ALLAN (1622-1662), nonconformist; M.A. Leyden, 1651; incorporated at Oxford; successively minister of St. Peter's, Paul's Wharf, chaplain to the Earl of Bedford, and minister of St. Saviour's, Dartmouth; ejected, 1662. [xxi. 96]

GEARY, SIR FRANCIS (1710?-1796), admiral; entered navy, 1727; while commanding the Chester captured several French and Spanish ships, 1743-5; rear-admiral, 1759; commander of Portsmouth, 1770; admiral of the blue, 1775, of the white, 1778; created baronet, 1782. [xxi. 96]

GED, WILLIAM (1690-1749), inventor of stereotyping; patented development of Van der Mey's method, 1725; made successful experiments, but was foiled in London by the dishonesty of his partner and the jealousy of the trade; returned to Edinburgh, and published in 1744 his stereotyped Sallust; died in poverty. [xxi. 97]

GEDDES, ALEXANDER (1737-1802), biblical critic; studied at Scalan and Paris; priest of Auchinhalrig and Preshome, Banffshire, 1769-79; made literary reputation by his verse translation of Horace's 'Satires,' 1779; LL.D. Aberdeen, 1780; suspended for attending a presbyterian service and hunting; while officiating at the imperial ambassador's chapel in London received from Lord Petre the means to prosecute his scheme for a revised catholic version of the bible; encouraged by Kennicott and Bishop Lowth; issued 'General Answer to Queries, Counsels, and Criticisms,' 1790; published the historical books of the Old Testament and 'Ruth,' 1792, 1797, and 'Critical Remarks on the Hebrew Scriptures,' 1800, the rationalistic character of which caused their prohibition and the author's suspension from ecclesiastical functions; his orthodoxy defended by Charles Butler (1750-1832) [q. v.]; maintained that the Divinity of Jesus Christ was a primitive tenet of Christianity, 1787; published miscellaneous works. [xxi. 98]

GEDDES, ANDREW (1783-1844), painter; educated at Edinburgh; exhibited at Royal Academy after 1806; A.R.A., 1832; in Italy, 1828-31; painted chiefly portraits; excelled as an etcher of portraits, landscapes, and copies of old masters. [xxi. 101]

GEDDES, JAMES (*d.* 1748?), advocate; published 'Essay on the Composition and Manner of Writing of the Ancients, particularly Plato,' 1748. [xxi. 102]

GEDDES, JENNY (*fl.* 1637?), supposed name of the woman who threw a stool at the head of Bishop Lindsay when attempting to read Laud's service-book in St. Giles's, Edinburgh. Her real name is a very open question. [xxi. 102]

GEDDES, JOHN (1735-1799), Roman catholic bishop; educated at the Scots College, Rome; superior of Scalan, 1762-7, of Semple's College in Spain, 1770-9; coadjutor of the Lowlands, with title of Bishop of Morocco, 1779-97; published, 'Life of St. Margaret, Queen of Scotland,' and 'Treatise against Duelling.' [xxi. 102]

GEDDES, MICHAEL (1650?-1713), divine; M.A. Edinburgh, 1668; incorporated at Oxford, 1671; one of the first four Scottish students at Balliol College, Oxford, 1672; chaplain to English factory at Lisbon, 1678-1688; chancellor of Salisbury, 1691; created LL.D. by Archbishop Tenison, 1695; translated Portuguese and Spanish works. [xxi. 103]

GEDDES, WILLIAM (1600?-1694), presbyterian divine and author; graduated at Aberdeen, 1650; minister at Wick and Urquhart; published 'The Saint's Recreation.' [xxi. 104]

GEDDES, SIR WILLIAM DUGUID (1828-1900), Greek scholar; M.A. University and King's Colleges, Aberdeen, 1846; rector of Aberdeen grammar school, 1853; professor of Greek at University and King's College, 1855, and in united university, 1860-85; principal and vice-chancellor of Aberdeen, 1885; LL.D. Edinburgh, 1876; knighted, 1892; published, among other works, an edition of Plato's 'Phædo,' 1863. [Suppl. ii. 273]

GEDEN, JOHN DURY (1822-1886), Wesleyan; educated at Kingswood and Richmond College; joint-editor

of 'London Quarterly Review' (established 1853); member of legal hundred, 1868; hon. D.D. St. Andrews, 1885; Fernley lecturer, 1874; one of the Old Testament revisers. [xxi. 104]

GEDGE, SYDNEY (1802-1883), divine; B.A. St. Catharine's College, Cambridge, 1824; fellow, 1825; second master of King Edward's School, Birmingham, 1835-59; vicar of All Saints', Northampton, 1859-75; active supporter of Church Missionary Society. [xxi. 105]

GEDY, JOHN (*fl.* 1370), abbot of Arbroath; agreed to make a harbour for the burgh, 1394. Southey's story that he placed a bell on the Bell Rock to warn sailors of the dangerous nature of the coast is not supported by evidence. [xxi. 105]

GEE, EDWARD (1565-1618), divine; fellow of Brasenose College, Oxford, 1588; M.A., 1590; D.D., 1616; chaplain to James I and fellow of Chelsea College; prebendary of Exeter, 1616. [xxi. 105]

GEE, EDWARD (1613-1660), presbyterian divine; nephew of Edward Gee (1565-1618) [q. v.]; M.A. Brasenose College, Oxford, 1636; rector of Eccleston, 1643, by choice of the people; prominent member of the Lancashire presbytery; author of 'A Treatise of Prayer' (1653) and 'The Divine Right and Originall of Civil Magistrates' (1658). [xxi. 106]

GEE, EDWARD (1657-1730), dean of Lincoln; M.A. St. John's College, Cambridge, 1683; D.D., after 1701; rector of St. Benet's, Paul's Wharf, and chaplain to William III, 1688; prebendary of Westminster and incumbent of St. Margaret's, 1701; dean of Lincoln, 1722-30; published protestant pamphlets, 1687-9. [xxi. 107]

GEE, JOHN (1596-1639), anti-catholic writer; nephew of Edward Gee (1565-1618) [q. v.]; M.A. Exeter College, Oxford, 1621; beneficed at Newton, 1622, and afterwards at Tenterden; for a short time a Romanist; published on reconversion 'The Foot out of the Snare' (1624) and similar works. [xxi. 107]

GEE, SIR ORLANDO (1619-1705), registrar of court of admiralty, 1660; brother of John Gee [q. v.], benefactor of Isleworth Church. [xxi. 108]

GEERAN or **GUERIN**, THOMAS (*d.* 1871), reputed centenarian; his case discredited by W. J. Thoms, F.S.A. [xxi. 108]

GEFFREY, SIR ROBERT (1613-1703), lord mayor of London; master of Ironmongers' Company, 1667, 1685, 1688; sheriff of London, 1673; knighted, 1673; lord mayor, 1685; president of Bethlehem and Bridewell, 1693; founded school at Landrake; almshouses in Kingsland Road, London, erected from his bequests. [xxi. 109]

GEIKIE, WALTER (1795-1837), painter and draughtsman; a deaf mute from infancy; educated under Thomas Braidwood [q. v.]; exhibited at Scottish Academy from 1827; R.S.A., 1834; published 'Etchings Illustrative of Scottish Character and Scenery,' 1833. [xxi. 110]

GELASIUS or **GILLA MAC LIAG** (1087-1173), count of Armagh and primate of Ireland; erenach of Derry, 1121; asserted primacy of Armagh by visitations; received the pall at the synod of Kells, 1149; summoned synod of Clane to promote uniformity. [xxi. 111]

GELDART, EDMUND MARTIN (1844-1885), unitarian minister; B.A. Balliol College, Oxford, 1867; lived for some time at Athens; joined the unitarians, 1872, and officiated at Hope Street, Liverpool, and at the Croydon Free Christian church; published works on Modern Greek, a translation of Keim's 'Jesus of Nazara,' vol. ii., 1876, 'The Gospel according to Paul,' 1884, and 'A Son of Belial' (i.e. Balliol), 1882; disappeared on voyage to Dieppe. [xxi. 111]

GELDART, JAMES WILLIAM (1785-1876), professor of civil law at Cambridge, 1814-47; fellow of St. Catharine's Hall, Cambridge, 1808, of Trinity Hall, 1809-1820; LL.D., 1814; rector of Kirk Deighton, 1840-76; edited Halifax's 'Analysis of Civil Law,' 1836. [xxi. 112]

GELDORP, GEORGE (*fl.* 1611-1660), portrait-painter; came to England from Antwerp before 1623; intimate with Vandyck; painted portraits of William Cecil, second earl of Salisbury [q. v.] (now at Hatfield), and Lord Totnes. [xxi. 113]

GELL, SIR JOHN (1593–1671), parliamentarian; as sheriff of Derbyshire levied ship-money, 1635; created baronet, 1642; raised regiment for the parliament, which was notorious for its plundering, 1642; prominent at capture of Lichfield and battle of Hopton Heath, 1643; suspected of conniving at escape of the royalists after Naseby, 1645; imprisoned and fined for plots against the Commonwealth, 1650; signed Derbyshire petition to Monck, 1660. [xxi. 113]

GELL, JOHN (d. 1806), admiral; commanded the Monarca in actions of Sir Edward Hughes [q. v.] with De Suffren; rear-admiral, 1793, when he captured a French privateer with the valuable Spanish treasure-ship Santiago; took part in occupation of Toulon; admiral, 1799. [xxi. 114]

GELL, ROBERT (1595–1665), divine; educated at Westminster and Christ's College, Cambridge; fellow; rector of St. Mary, Aldermanbury, c. 1641–65; published 'Essay towards the Amendment of the last English Translation of the Bible,' 1659. [xxi. 115]

GELL, SIR WILLIAM (1777–1836), archæologist and traveller; fellow of Emmanuel College, Cambridge; his 'Topography of Troy,' 1804, made in three days, alluded to by Byron's epithet 'rapid Gell' (originally 'classic'); knighted after mission to Ionian islands, 1803; travelled in Greece with Edward Dodwell [q. v.] and published 'Geography and Antiquities of Ithaca,' 1807, and 'Itinerary of Greece,' 1810; published 'Itinerary of the Morea' (1817) and 'Journey in the Morea' (1823); gave evidence (1820) in favour of Queen Caroline, whose chamberlain he had been; after 1820 lived in Italy; published 'Pompeiana,' 1817–19, and 'Topography of Rome,' 1834; his original drawings preserved in the British Museum. [xxi. 115]

GELLIBRAND, HENRY (1597–1636), mathematician; M.A. Trinity College, Oxford, 1623; friend of Henry Briggs [q. v.]; Gresham professor of astronomy, 1627; prosecuted by Laud for bringing out an almanack in which protestant martyrs were substituted for Romish saints; acquitted; completed Briggs's 'Trigonometria Britannica,' 1633; published other mathematical works and 'Epitome of Navigation.' [xxi. 117]

GEMINI, GEMINIE, or GEMINUS, THOMAS (fl. 1540–1560), engraver and printer; published with copper-plate engravings by himself 'Compendiosa totius Anatomie delineatio,' 1545, an abridgment of Vesalius's work of 1543; printed works for Leonard Digges (d. 1571?) [q. v.] and engraved a portrait of Queen Mary (1559). [xxi. 118]

GENDALL, JOHN (1790–1865), painter, employed by R. Ackermann [q. v.]; exhibited paintings of Devonshire scenery at the Academy, 1846–63. [xxi. 119]

GENEST, JOHN (1764–1839), dramatic historian; educated at Westminster; M.A. Trinity College, Cambridge, 1787; published at Bath 'Account of the English Stage, 1660–1830' (1832). [xxi. 119]

GENINGS, EDMUND (1567–1591), Roman catholic divine; executed at Tyburn for returning to the realm; his life published at St. Omer, 1614. [xxi. 119]

GENINGS, JOHN (1570?–1660), provincial of English Franciscans; brother of Edmund Geninges [q. v.]; first vicar of St. Bonaventure, Douay, 1619; co-founder of convent of St. Elizabeth, Brussels; published 'Institutio Missionariorum,' 1651. [xxi. 120]

GENT, SIR THOMAS (d. 1593), judge; barrister, Middle Temple; M.P., Malden, 1571; serjeant-at-law, 1584; baron of the exchequer, 1586; member of high commission court. [xxi. 120]

GENT, THOMAS (1693–1778), printer and topographer; member of Stationers' Company and admitted to freedom of the city, 1717; employed in Fleet Street by Henry Woodfall [q. v.] and Samuel Richardson [q. v.]; settled at York, 1724, being the sole printer in the city and county; printed his own histories of York (1730), Ripon (1734), and Hull (1735); set up the first press at Scarborough; died in great poverty; his autobiography edited by Rev. Joseph Hunter, 1832. [xxi. 121]

GENTILESCHI, ARTEMISIA (1590–1642?), painter; came to England with her father, Orazio Gentileschi [q. v.]; painted for Charles I 'David and Goliath,' 'Fame,' and a portrait of herself; returned to Italy before 1630; famous for her portraits. [xxi. 123]

GENTILESCHI, ORAZIO (1563–1647), painter; native of Pisa; came to England, 1626, from Paris, at invitation of Vandyck; painted for Buckingham and Charles I, who lodged him and gave him an annuity; some of his pictures at Marlborough House and two at Hampton Court. [xxi. 123]

GENTILI, ALBERICO (1552–1608), civilian; born at Sanginesio; D.C.L. Perugia; obliged to leave Italy with his father on account of heretical opinions; arrived in London, 1580; incorporated D.C.L. at Oxford, 1581; consulted by government as to course to be taken with Mendoza, the plotting Spanish ambassador, 1584; accompanied embassy of Pallavicino to Saxony, 1586; regius professor of civil law at Oxford through Walsingham's influence, 1587; began to practise as an advocate, 1590; admitted at Gray's Inn, 1600; permanent advocate for king of Spain, 1605. His chief works were 'De Juris Interpretibus Dialogi sex,' 1582 (in defence of the older jurists against the 'humanist' school), 'De Legationibus' (1585), 'De Jure Belli Commentationes Tres,' 1589; 'De Jure Belli,' 1598, and 'Hispanicæ Advocationis Libri Duo,' 1613; fifteen volumes of his manuscripts (D'Orville) acquired by the Bodleian, 1805. [xxi. 124]

GENTILI, ALOYSIUS (1801–1848), missionary apostolic in England; came to England, 1835, as missioner of Rosmini's Institute of Charity; superior of the college, Prior Park, Bath, till 1839; removed to Loughborough mission, 1842. [xxi. 127]

GENTILI, ROBERT (1590–1654?), infant prodigy and translator; eldest son of Alberico Gentili [q. v.]; spoke French and Latin at seven; matriculated at Christ Church, Oxford, at nine; B.A. Jesus College, Oxford, at thirteen; nominated probationer fellow of All Souls' College by Archbishop Bancroft in eighteenth year; resigned fellowship, 1612, and disappeared till 1637; translated Servita's 'History of the Inquisition,' several works of Malvezzi, Bacon's 'Historie of Winds' 1653, and 'Le Chemin Abrégé,' 1654. [xxi. 128]

GENTLEMAN, FRANCIS (1728–1784), actor and dramatist; appeared at Dublin in 'Oroonoko'; afterwards played in his own pieces in England and Scotland, the best being 'The Modish Wife' (1774), produced at Chester; published anonymously the 'Dramatic Censor,' 1770; often relieved by Garrick, whom he ridiculed in his 'Stratford Jubilee,' 1769; edited Bell's acting Shakespeare; played Sir Epicure Mammon in his 'Tobacconist,' 1771, an adaptation from the 'Alchemist.' [xxi. 129]

GENTLEMAN, ROBERT (1746–1795), dissenting divine; preached and taught school at Shrewsbury, 1765–1769; divinity tutor at Carmarthen academy, 1779–84; minister at Kidderminster, 1784–95; published, among other works, 'Young English Scholar's Companion.' [xxi. 130]

GENTLEMAN, TOBIAS (fl. 1614), author of a work entitled 'Way to Wealth,' 1614, pointing out advantages of developing herring fisheries. [Suppl. ii. 273]

GEOFFREY (d. 1093), bishop of Coutances, 1048; completed his cathedral, 1056; followed Duke William to England, 1066, and interpreted at his coronation; received vast grants of land, chiefly in the west, where he was active in repressing the rising of 1069; presided at trial of suit between Lanfranc and Odo at Pennenden, 1071; attended councils of Winchester and Windsor, 1072, and the ecclesiastical council at St. Paul's, 1075; helped to put down rising of Ralf, earl of Norfolk, and Roger, earl of Hereford, 1075; took part in the baronial rising against William II, and held Bristol Castle, but was pardoned; upheld privileges of the clergy at Salisbury, 1088; died at Coutances. [xxi. 130]

GEOFFREY, RUFUS (d. 1140). [See RUFUS.]

GEOFFREY GAIMAR (d. 1140?) [See GAIMAR.]

GEOFFREY OF GORHAM (d. 1146), abbot of St. Albans, 1119–46; native of Maine; while teaching a Dunstable composed a miracle-play of St. Katharine built guests' hall, queen's chamber, and a shrine; translated St. Alban's body, 1129; founded leper hospital of St. Julian, and enlarged nunnery at Sopwell. [xxi. 132]

GEOFFREY OF MONMOUTH (1100?-1154), bishop of St. Asaph and chronicler; probably a Benedictine monk of Monmouth; studied at Oxford; archdeacon of Llandaff, c. 1140; bishop of St. Asaph, 1152-4; witnessed Treaty of Wallingford, 1153; buried at Llandaff. His 'Historia Britonum,' compiled from 'Nennius' and a lost book of Breton legends, tracing the descent of British princes from the Trojans, was translated into Anglo-Norman by Gaimar and Wace, and into English by Layamon and Robert of Gloucester; first printed in 1508 (Paris), and edited by Dr. Giles in 1844. Geoffrey's 'Prophetia Anglicana Merlini Ambrosii Britanni' was first printed, 1603. [xxi. 133]

GEOFFREY (d. 1154), first abbot of Dunfermline, 1128; prior of Christ Church, Canterbury, 1126.
[xxi. 136]

GEOFFREY (d. 1178), abbot of Dunfermline, nephew and successor of Geoffrey (d. 1154) [q. v.]; witnessed charters of Malcolm IV and William the Lion; wrote in defence of Scottish church. [xxi. 136]

GEOFFREY (1158-1186), fourth son of Henry II and count of Brittany; betrothed by his father to Constance, daughter of Count Conan, the Little, and adopted as heir, 166; with the French king and his own brothers invaded Normandy, 1173, but did homage to his father on a promise of half the revenues of Brittany, 1175; knighted, 1178; upheld Philip II of France against the rebellious lords, and married Constance, 1181; by order of Henry II made war on his brother Richard; invaded Poitou, and refused to desist, occupying Limoges by treachery, 1183; after temporary reconciliation with Richard, joined Prince John against him, 1184; held 'Assize of Count Geoffrey' at Rennes to preserve rights of the lord, 1185; plotted with Philip II for possession of Anjou; died suddenly at Paris, and was buried in Notre Dame. [xxi. 136]

GEOFFREY DE VINSAUF (fl. 1200). [See VINSAUF.]

GEOFFREY DE MUSCHAMP (d. 1208), bishop of Lichfield and Coventry, 1198; archdeacon of Cleveland, 1189; elected bishop by monks of Coventry at instance of Richard I and Archbishop Hubert, 1198; said to have fled from England, 1207. [xxi. 138]

GEOFFREY (d. 1212), archbishop of York; reputed son of Henry II, at whose accession he was acknowledged and received into the household; made bishop of Lincoln, 173; took prominent part in suppressing the northern rebellion of 1173-4; remained unconsecrated and resigned under pressure from Pope Alexander III, 1182, but became chancellor of England and treasurer of York; faithful to his father in his last war with Richard and Philip Augustus, 1188-9; named archbishop of York by Richard I, 189, but opposed by Hubert Walter and part of the chapter; ordained priest and confirmed in his see after much opposition; retired to Normandy, 1190, and ordered by Richard to remain abroad for three years; consecrated at Tours, 1191, and thereupon returned to England; arrested by William of Longchamp on the ground of Richard's prohibition of his return to England, but supported by Prince John; released and enthroned; excommunicated Bishop Hugh of Durham and other opponents; joined Bishop Hugh against John, 1193; his chapter in open rebellion against him after a demand for contributions for the king's ransom; suspended by the pope and deprived of sheriffdom of Yorkshire by the king, 1195; went to Rome and obtained reversal of sentence from the pope, 1196; temporarily favoured by Richard I, 1198; received with favour at accession of John, 1199; reconciled temporarily with chapter, 1200, but was again involved in disputes; upheld throughout by Innocent III; opposed levy of a tax on church property and fled abroad, 1207; buried at Grandmont, near Rouen. [xxi. 139]

GEOFFREY OF COLDINGHAM (fl. 1214). [See COLDINGHAM.]

GEOFFREY (d. 1235?), prior of Coventry, 1216; chosen by his monks to see of Lichfield and Coventry, 1223, but the election quashed by Archbishop Stephen Langton and Honorius III; suspended for resisting visitation of new bishop, 1232; author of chronicle cited in Dugdale's 'Warwick.' [xxi. 145]

GEOFFREY THE GRAMMARIAN, alias STARKEY (fl. 1440), a friar; preacher at King's Lynn, Norfolk; his 'Promptuarium [store-house] Parvulorum Clericorum,' an English-Latin dictionary, valuable as record of fifteenth-century English and East-Anglian dialect, and for elucidation of debased Latin (printed by Pynson, 1499, and by Wynkyn de Worde). Other works assigned to Geoffrey by Bale and Pits include the first Latin-English dictionary printed in England ('Hortus') W. de Worde, in 1500.
[xxi. 145]

GEORGE I (GEORGE LEWIS) (1660-1727), king of Great Britain and Ireland and elector of Hanover; great grandson of James I; first saw military service under the empire, 1675; came to England to propose for the hand of the Princess Anne, 1680; married his cousin, Sophia Dorothea of Celle, 1682; took part in Sobieski's relief of Vienna, 1683; distinguished himself in Hungary, 1685, and at Neerwinden, 1693; divorced his wife and imprisoned her for life, 1694; succeeded to Hanover, 1698; admitted to the college of electors at the diet, 1708, and named arch-treasurer of the empire, 1710; protected Holstein-Gottorp against Denmark, 1699; joined the Grand Alliance, 1701, contributing 10,000 men and five regiments of horse; formed intimate relations with Marlborough after his mission of 1704-5; commanded imperial army on Upper Rhine, 1707-9; concluded alliances with Poland, 1709, and Denmark, 1710; occupied Verden, 1712; refused to intervene in English politics; reconciled with his son on death (1714) of his mother, Electress Sophia, which made him the next heir after Queen Anne to the English throne; on Queen Anne's death had fresh instrument of regency drawn up for England, 1714; while at the Hague, on his way to fill English throne, displaced Bolingbroke for Townshend as secretary of state, having previously named Marlborough captain-general; became king of England, 1714; his first collective cabinet entirely whig, with the exception of Nottingham [see FINCH, DANIEL]; conformed to the national church, though he was allowed a Lutheran chaplain, but was unpopular on account of his character and the rapacity of his foreign favourites, an attempt on his life being made, 1717; after suppression of Jacobite rebellion of 1715, and passing of Septennial Act, 1716, went to Hanover, where he frequently spent the latter half of each, year, his son Prince George being left as regent; formed an alliance with France and the Netherlands, 1717, in which year Townshend was replaced by Stanhope as chief minister; the quadruple alliance formed in 1718, in accordance with his wishes, and Bremen and Verden added to Hanover, the schemes of Charles XII and Alberoni to aid the Jacobites being foiled; granted a slight measure of relief to the Romanists and dissenters; had convocation silenced, 1717. Walpole, who was called in to deal with the South Sea crisis, remained chief minister from 1721 till the end of the reign. Under Walpole the 'Atterbury plot' was discovered, 1722, further interference with Sweden checked, the treaty of Hanover negotiated, 1725, as a countercheck to that of Vienna, and George I induced to assent to it. George I died of apoplexy at Osnabrück and was buried at Hanover. His will was destroyed by George II. A certain brusqueness of manner, in spite of some kingly qualities, prevented him from attaining popularity. Portraits by Kneller are at Windsor and in the National Portrait Gallery.
[xxi. 146]

GEORGE II (1683-1760), king of Great Britain and Ireland; son of George I; after the divorce of his mother, whom he thought innocent, lived with his grandparents at Hanover; married Charlotte Caroline of Brandenburg-Anspach, 1705; created an English peer, 1706; distinguished himself at Oudenarde, 1708; came to England with his father and was created Prince of Wales, 1714; on friendly terms with John Campbell, second duke of Argyll, formed intimacy with Henrietta Howard (later Countess of Suffolk); popular with English, but not with Hanoverians; confined to his room and excluded from St. James's on account of his conduct to the king and Newcastle at the baptism of his eldest son, Frederick, 1717; removed to Leicester House, which became a centre of opposition, 1718; deprived of custody of his children, partially reconciled to the king through Walpole, 1720; succeeded to the throne, 1727; continued Walpole in office after his favourite, Sir Spencer Compton, afterwards lord Wilmington [q. v.], had failed to form a ministry, but replaced Lord Berkeley (who had propounded a scheme for transplanting him to America when Prince of Wales) by Sir George Byng at the admiralty; went to Hanover to secure possession of his mother's property and that of his uncle, the late bishop of Osnabrück; quarrelled with Frederick William of Prussia, and though reconciled to him by arbitration, 1730, was debarred from carrying out contemplated marriage alliances between the houses of England and Prussia; with difficulty prevented from

involving England in the Polish succession war, 1733 ;
tried to negotiate an alliance between the King of Spain,
Philip V, and the emperor Charles VII ; concluded treaty
with Denmark, 1734 ; became attached to Countess von
Walmoden, 1735 ; reluctantly refused alliance with the emperor ; negotiated marriage for Frederick, prince of
Wales, with Augusta of Saxe-Gotha, 1736 ; spent most
of 1736 in Hanover ; was in great danger from a
storm in returning ; had an open rupture with Frederick, prince of Wales, 1737 ; created Countess Walmoden
Lady Yarmouth, 1738 ; overcame the pacific policy of
Walpole, 1739, and declared war against Spain ; concluded
treaty with Maria Theresa, for whom he obtained a
subsidy, 1741 ; secured Hanover by neutrality agreement
with France ; reluctantly parted with Walpole, 1742 ;
made Lord Wilmington (Compton) head of the treasury,
and in Carteret as secretary of state (1742-5) found
a sympathetic foreign minister ; probably by advice of
Carteret arranged treaty of Breslau between Frederick
the Great of Prussia and Maria Theresa, 1742, and
formed defensive alliances with Prussia and Russia,
1742 ; took Hanoverian troops into British pay and sent
them into the Netherlands ; personally led the allied
troops at Dettingen against the French, the victory
recovering him his popularity, 1743 ; concluded treaty
of Worms with Maria Theresa and Sardinia, 1743 ; compelled by his other ministers to dismiss Carteret, 1744 ;
made largely responsible for the defence of Bohemia when
Frederick the Great declared war upon that country
and renewed hostilities with Maria Theresa ; compelled
by the success of the French and Prussians, and landing
of the Young Pretender in Scotland, to extort Maria
Theresa's consent to the cession of Silesia, 1745 ; tried
to get rid of his ministers and to recall Carteret (Lord
Granville) and Pulteney (Lord Bath) ; refused to accept
Pitt as secretary-at-war ; gained over Newcastle to his
warlike views, and after Culloden sent more troops to
the Netherlands, 1746 ; after unsuccessful operations
obliged to make peace on the basis of mutual restitution, 1748 ; his scheme for procuring election of Archduke Joseph as king of the Romans defeated by Prussia,
1750 ; submitted to the Pelhams on the death of Frederick,
prince of Wales, 1751 ; the subsidy treaties arranged
by him for the defence of Hanover rejected by the
regents, 1755, though next year a treaty was arranged
with Prussia guaranteeing the integrity of Germany ;
obliged by the resignation of Henry Fox [q. v.] to accept
Pitt as secretary of state under Devonshire, 1756, and,
though he dismissed him within three months, on Waldegrave's failure to form a ministry was obliged to re-
appoint him with Newcastle at the treasury, 1757. He
showed much displeasure with his son, the Duke of Cumberland, after his failure in Germany, and considered the
sentence of the court-martial on Sackville too lenient.
At the date of his death the French had been driven
from Canada, checked in Europe, and successfully attacked
in India, Africa, and the West Indies, while the Dutch
were ousted from Bengal. He was buried beside Queen
Caroline in Henry VII's chapel, Westminster Abbey. In
state affairs he was largely guided by Queen Caroline, to
whom he was much attached, in spite of his mistresses. He
put Hanover and his continental interests before England.
Though a patron of Handel, he neglected literature and
pictorial art. Several portraits of him are in the National
Portrait Gallery and at Hampton Court, and a royal group
by Hogarth in the National Portrait Gallery of Ireland.

[xxi. 151]

GEORGE III (GEORGE WILLIAM FREDERICK) (1738-
1820), grandson of George II, and king of Great Britain
and Ireland ; son of Frederick Louis, prince of Wales
[q. v.] ; created Prince of Wales, 1751 ; imbibed political
principles from writings of Bolingbroke and Blackstone ;
completely under influence of his mother, and after attainment of his majority (1756) of Bute ; said to have been in
love with Hannah Lightfoot, a quakeress ; on coming to
the throne, 1760, put forth a proclamation against immorality, and declared that he ' gloried in the name of
Briton ' ; after a flirtation with Lady Sarah Lennox,
married Charlotte Sophia [q. v.] of Mecklenburg-Strelitz,
1761 ; recommended the extension of judge's tenures beyond the demise of the crown ; determined to destroy the
party system and to end the French war ; dismissed Pitt
and Newcastle, and made Bute secretary of state, 1761,
and first minister, 1762 ; dismissed Portland, Rockingham, and other leading whigs, and concluded peace with
France and Spain, 1763 ; was obliged to part with Bute,

but for some time acted on his advice ; called in George
Grenville [q. v.], but made constant attempts to get rid of
him, though concurring generally in his policy ; urged on
prosecution of Wilkes, 1763 ; approved Grenville's Stamp
Act, 1765, but allowed its repeal, 1766 ; the Regency Act
from which ministers at first excluded name of princess
dowager, due to his first mental illness, 1765 ; negotiated
with Pitt and Lyttelton through Cumberland ; again promised to deny access to Bute, probably keeping his word
obliged to accept Rockingham as minister ; intrigued
against Rockingham through ' the king's friends ' ; allowed
Pitt to come in with a free hand, creating him Earl of Chatham, Grafton being nominal premier, 1766 ; entreated
Chatham to retain office, 1767 ; urged firmness in dealing
with the rioters of 1769 and with Wilkes ; insulted by a
mob at St. James's ; induced Charles Yorke [q. v.] to
accept the seals, 1770 ; made North premier, 1770 ; remained unmoved by petitions from the city demanding a
dissolution ; and for twelve years personally directed the
government through distribution of patronage, disposal
of civil list revenue, and manifestations of feeling at
court ceremonials ; frequently wrote to North, but sometimes consulted Charles Jenkinson, afterwards first earl
of Liverpool [q. v.] ; directed the opposition to Savile's
Nullum Tempus Bill ; forbade Cumberland and Gloucester
the court, and promoted the Royal Marriage Bill, which
prohibited members of the royal family from marrying
under twenty-five without the king's consent ; prevented
interference of France between Russia and Turkey ;
showed hostility to Clive, 1773 ; favoured Boston Port
Bill, 1774 ; arranged for Hanoverian garrisons in Gibraltar
and Minorca, and negotiated for the hire of Russian
t.oops, 1775 ; supported the policy which led to outbreak
of war with American colonists, and as the war continued
approved ' every means of distressing America ' ; applied
to parliament for a grant to pay his debts, and though
presenting imperfect accounts, received a sum for arrears
and an addition to the civil list, 1777 ; refused to allow
North to resign or to receive Chatham as chief minister
1778 ; allowed North to negotiate with the opposition ; contemplated retirement to Hanover ; saved London by his
conduct during Gordon riots, 1780 ; spent great sums in
elections of 1781, and is said to have personally canvassed
against Keppel at Windsor ; applied to Shelburne and
Gower on North's resignation, 1782, but was forced again
to take Rockingham as minister ; through Thurlow set
the Shelburne section against the Rockingham whigs
and on Rockingham's death (1782) appointed Shelburne
as his successor ; on Shelburne's resignation applied to
the younger Pitt and Gower before submitting to receive
the coalition, 1783, whom he overthrew by using his personal influence with the peers against their India Bill,
1783 ; supported Pitt both before and after the general
election, which secured him a majority, the ' king's friends '
subsequently disappearing as a party ; followed Pitt's
advice when premier, though disliking his scheme of parliamentary reform and the trial of Warren Hastings ; his
life threatened by the mad Margaret Nicholson [q. v.],
1786 ; suffered second attack of madness, 1788-9 ; agreed
to dismissal of Thurlow, 1792, and recall of Duke of York
from Flanders, 1794 ; remonstrated with Pitt against
negotiating with France, 1797 ; shot at by Hadfield,
1800 ; caused the resignation of Pitt by declaration
against revival of catholic emancipation, 1801 ; suffered
third attack of mania, which was abridged by Pitt's
promise not to revive the Roman Catholic question ; reviewed volunteers in Hyde Park, 1803 ; became deranged
again, 1804, in consequence of the conduct of the Prince
of Wales ; through Eldon consented to receive Pitt back
with the Grenvilles, but without Fox, 1804 ; opened parliament for last time, 1805 ; appointed Manners-Sutton
primate instead of Pitt's nominee, 1805 ; sent for Hawkesbury (Jenkinson), 1806, and on his failure accepted Grenville as minister with Fox, to whom he became reconciled,
but brought about his resignation by demanding a pledge
against catholic emancipation ; by his influence kept the
Portland ministry together, 1809-12 ; condemned the duel
of Canning and Castlereagh ; became blind, and, after
1811, permanently deranged, but retained bodily strength
almost till death. He was very popular with the middle
classes, and generally with the majority of his subjects,
who respected the decorum of his life, and a firmness
which at times verged on obstinacy. He was buried at
St. George's Chapel, Windsor. Portraits of him are at
Windsor, Hampton Court, and in the National Portrait
Gallery.

[xxi. 172]

GEORGE IV (1762–1830), king of Great Britain and Ireland; son of George III and Queen Charlotte; brought up in strict seclusion with his brother Frederick Augustus, duke of York [q. v.], at Kew, but well educated; already involved in intrigue with Mary Robinson [q. v.] ('Perdita'), 1780; came of age, 1783, when he established himself at Carlton House; received 30,000*l.* from parliament to pay debts, and an annual allowance of 50,000*l.* from the king; in close alliance with Charles James Fox [q. v.] and other whig leaders; fell in love with Mrs. Maria Anne Fitzherbert [q. v.] and married her, 1785; denied the marriage in order to conciliate parliament and deceived Fox; received an addition to his income and a parliamentary grant of 161,000*l.* for his debts, 1787; plunged into fresh extravagances in company with York, Fox, Sheridan, and Beau Brummell; built Brighton Pavilion, 1784, and lived much there; intrigued with Thurlow and Loughborough against the queen and Pitt, and openly canvassed for support against the minister's regency resolutions, 1788; drew up a letter of remonstrance in concert with the whigs against the restrictions on his powers as regent, 1789; received an offer of free powers from Irish parliament; excluded from the king's presence on his recovery; addressed remonstrances to him on conduct of the queen and an apologetic memorial; raised money abroad on Osnabrück bishopric and post-obits; their liability repudiated by the prince's agents after 1792; married Caroline of Brunswick, 1795, but soon separated from her, and returned to Mrs Fitzherbert, though recently intimate with Lady Jersey; received another grant from parliament; demanded vice-royalty of Ireland, and intervened on behalf of Lord Edward Fitzgerald [q. v.], 1797–8; applied for service abroad; under influence of Moira [see HASTINGS, FRANCIS RAWDON-, 1754–1826] made overtures to Pitt, 1801; received a fresh money grant and a commutation of his claims on the duchy of Cornwall, 1803; his application for military employment again refused; negotiated through Sheridan with Addington, but at the same time suggested to Pitt a junction between him and Fox under the premiership of Moira, 1804; deprived of the care of his daughter, Princess Charlotte, 1805; obtained commission for examination into charges against Princess Caroline, 1806; practically severed himself from all the whigs except Sheridan, Erskine, and Moira; consulted Grey and Grenville upon his answer to Perceval's regency proposals, when the king was permanently disabled by insanity, but acted on the advice given by Sheridan and Adam, 1811; after further negotiations with the whigs was induced by influence of Lady Hertford to accept the restricted regency; broke with Mrs. Fitzherbert at installation as Prince Regent; deprived of Perceval's services by his death, 1812, after which complicated negotiations for the formation of a coalition ministry under the Marquis Wellesley or Lord Moira followed, but were rendered fruitless owing to the regent's aversion from Grey and Grenville, on which the tories returned to office under Liverpool, 1812; became involved in disputes with his wife and daughter; the re-enactment of the act of 1795 for the security of the king's person necessitated by his unpopularity, 1817; succeeded to the throne, 1820; employed Knighton to deal with his debts; tried to prevent the return of Queen Caroline [q. v.], and on her arrival excluded her from the coronation, and forced ministers to bring in a divorce bill, 1820; visited Ireland and Hanover, 1821, and Scotland, 1822; tried to exclude Canning from office, and thwarted his foreign policy; retired with Lady Conyngham to Brighton and Windsor; strongly opposed catholic emancipation and the recognition of the Spanish-American republics; wished to take command of the army on Wellington's retirement; under the Goderich ministry, 1827–8, distributed appointments without consulting the ministers; reluctantly accepted the repeal of Test and Corporation Acts, and put many obstacles in the way of the passing of Catholic Emancipation Bill, but finally gave way; latterly suffered from failing health and delusions; the power of the crown much diminished in his reign. He was buried in St George's Chapel, Windsor. Portraits by Lawrence are at Windsor and in the National Portrait Gallery. [xxi. 192]

GEORGE, DUKE OF CLARENCE (1449–1478), son of Richard, duke of York (1411–1460) [q. v.]; after his father's death in 1460 was sent for safety to Utrecht, whence he was brought back on his brother Edward IV's accession in 1461 and created Duke of Clarence; lord-lieutenant of Ireland, 1462; at Calais married, contrary to Edward's wishes (1469), Isabella, the elder daughter of the Earl of Warwick [see NEVILLE, RICHARD]; invaded England in company with his father-in-law and made King Edward prisoner at Edgecot, 1469; forced by public opinion to release him; after obtaining an amnesty became implicated with Warwick in an unsuccessful Lancastrian rising in Lincolnshire; fled to France, March 1470; returned to England with Warwick, September 1470, and Edward fled the country; disapproved of the restoration of Henry VI, and in 1471 deserted to his brother at Coventry with four thousand men; fought with Edward at Barnet, 1471, and Tewkesbury, 1471, and assisted in the re-establishment of the York dynasty; became involved in a violent quarrel with his brother, Gloucester, who wished to marry Anne Neville [see ANNE, QUEEN OF RICHARD III] and share her mother's inheritance; reconciled with Gloucester by a parliamentary partition of the Neville estates, 1474; offered himself (1476) as a suitor for the hand of Mary of Burgundy, the successor of Charles the Bold; his scheme vetoed by Edward IV; revenged himself on some of the queen's adherents; charged with compassing the death of the king by necromancy and with other treasonable practices and committed to the Tower; attainted by parliament, January 1478, and sentenced to death; secretly executed within the Tower, 17 or 18 Feb. 1488. The mode of death is uncertain, the statement that he was drowned in a butt of malmsey being perhaps only a London rumour. [xlv. 404]

GEORGE, PRINCE OF DENMARK (1653–1708), consort of Queen Anne; married Princess Anne, 1683; deserted James II, 1688, at Andover; rewarded by act of naturalisation and a peerage, being created Duke of Cumberland, 1689; disliked by William III; on his wife's accession was refused title of king, 1702, but named 'generalissimo' (nominally superior of Marlborough as captain-general) and lord high admiral, receiving a large annuity and exemption from disabilities under Act of Settlement; voted for Occasional Conformity Bill, 1702; his management of the admiralty attacked by the whigs, 1704–8; F.R.S. A portrait by Wissing is in the National Portrait Gallery. [xxi. 204]

GEORGE, JOHN (1804–1871), Irish judge; M.A. Trinity College, Dublin, 1826; barrister, King's Inns, 1826, and Gray's Inn, 1827; Q.C., 1844; M.P. for co. Wexford, 1852–7 and 1859–66; solicitor-general under Lord Derby, 1859; privy councillor of Ireland, and judge of queen's bench, 1866. [xxi. 207]

GEORGE, WILLIAM (d. 1756), dean of Lincoln; educated at Eton and King's College, Cambridge; M.A., 1723; D.D., 1728; seventeen years principal of Eton; provost of King's, 1743, and vice-chancellor of Cambridge; dean of Lincoln, 1748–56; his lines on the death of Prince Frederick highly commended by Pope Benedict XIV. [xxi. 207]

GERALD, SAINT and BISHOP (d. 731), according to the Bollandist Life, a monk who left Winchester for Ireland to lead a solitary life; built a church in Mayo called Oill n-ailither ('Church of the Pilgrims'), where he was buried; termed in 'Annals of the Four Masters' the 'Pontifex of Mayo of the Saxons,' and 'Episcopus' in Litany of Oengus. [xxi. 207]

GERALD, JOSEPH (1763–1796). [See GERRALD.]

GERARD or GIRARD (d. 1108), archbishop of York; when clerk of the chapel and chancery sent by William II on a secret mission to Pope Urban, from whom he obtained the despatch of a legate and pallium, 1095; rewarded with see of Hereford, being ordained only a day before consecration, 1096; witnessed Henry I's charter, 1100; archbishop of York, 1100–8; opposed Archbishop Anselm [q. v.], and successfully represented Henry I against him at Rome in the investiture dispute; eventually repudiated by Pope Paschal and compelled to profess obedience to Anselm; attempted to consecrate bishops; 'invested' by the king and was rebuked by Paschal; reconciled to Anselm, 1107; refused burial in the minster, but transferred thither by Archbishop Thomas II. [xxi. 208]

GERARD, ALEXANDER (1728–1795), philosophical writer; professor of philosophy at Marischal College, Aberdeen, 1750, and of divinity, 1760–71; professor of divinity at King's College, 1771; D.D.; moderator of general assembly, 1764; published prize 'Essay on Taste,' 1759, 'Essay on Genius,' 1774, and apologetic works. [xxi. 210]

GERARD, ALEXANDER (1792–1839), Himalayan explorer; son of Gilbert Gerard [q. v.]; served with 13th Bengal native infantry, 1808–36; while engaged in surveying, 1812–17 and 1825–6, ascended peaks hitherto unscaled and penetrated into Thibet; ascended in 1821 the Charang Pass and Mount Tahigung (22,000 feet); his travels described in Indian scientific journals and in Edinburgh 'Journal of Science,' and noticed in Heber's 'Journal.'   [xxi. 211]

GERARD, CHARLES, first BARON GERARD OF BRANDON and EARL OF MACCLESFIELD (d. 1694), great-grandson of Sir Gilbert Gerard [q. v.]; educated abroad; commanded infantry brigade at Edgehill, 1642; wounded there and at Lichfield, 1643; arranged capitulation of Bristol, 1643; distinguished at first battle of Newbury, 1643; again wounded at relief of Newark, 1644; conducted successful operations in South Wales, 1645; removed for rigorous treatment of Welsh, but created a peer, 1645; commander of Charles I's bodyguard, escorting him from Wales to Oxford, thence to Hereford, and afterwards to Chester, 1645; desperately wounded at Rowton Heath, 1645; retired with the king to Newark, but was dismissed his service for a disorderly protest against the supersession of Sir Richard Willis, 1645; rejoined Charles at Oxford, 1646, and raised a troop of horse; went abroad after the capitulation; vice-admiral of the fleet at Helvoetsluys, 1648; gentleman of the bedchamber to Charles II, 1649; served under Turenne at Arras, 1654; intrigued at Paris on behalf of Henrietta Maria, and encouraged designs of his cousin, John Gerard (1632–1654) [q. v.]; returned with Charles II from Breda, 1660, at the head of the life guards; regained his estates and received a pension; envoy extraordinary to Paris, 1662; supervised defences of Isle of Wight and Portsmouth against Dutch, 1666–7; created Earl of Macclesfield, 1679; dismissed from the bed-chamber as an adherent of Monmouth, 1681; presented by Cheshire grand jury as disaffected, 1684; fled to the continent, 1685; commanded William III's bodyguard, 1688; privy councillor and president of council of Welsh marches, 1689; member of commission to inquire into conduct of fleet, 1690.   [xxi. 212]

GERARD, CHARLES, second EARL OF MACCLESFIELD (1659 ?–1701), son of Charles Gerard, first earl of Macclesfield [q. v.]; M.P., Lancashire, 1679, 1680–1, and 1688–94; committed to the Tower on suspicion of treason, 1683, but acquitted; again arrested as adherent of Monmouth, convicted of complicity in Rye House plot, and sentenced to death, 1685; pardoned, 1687; lord-lieutenant of Lancashire, 1690, of North Wales, 1696; bail for Lord Mohun, 1692; as major-general, 1694, succeeded Talmash after his death before Brest; envoy extraordinary to Hanover, 1701; buried in Westminster Abbey.   [xxi. 217]

GERARD, SIR GILBERT (d. 1593), judge; barrister, Gray's Inn, 1539; joint-treasurer of Gray's Inn, 1556; M.P., Wigan, 1553 and 1555, and Steyning, 1554; attorney-general, 1559; drew up reforms for Irish exchequer court, 1560; counsel to Cambridge University, 1561; commissioner for sale of crown lands, 1563; member of ecclesiastical commission, 1567; member of commission for trial of northern rebels, 1570; took part in prosecution of Norfolk, Northumberland, and others, 1571–2; knighted, 1579; master of the rolls, 1581; M.P., Lancaster, 1584; took part in trials of Somervyle, 1583, Parry, 1585, and Shelley, 1586, for conspiracy, and of Arundel, 1589, and Perrot, 1592; chief commissioner of the great seal, 1591–2.   [xxi. 218]

GERARD, GILBERT (1760–1815), theological writer; son of Alexander Gerard (1728–1795) [q. v.]; minister of Scots church, Amsterdam; professor of Greek at King's College, Aberdeen, 1791, of divinity, 1795; moderator of general assembly, 1803; 'Compendious View of the Evidences of Natural and Revealed Religion,' the joint work of himself and his father, published 1828.   [xxi. 220]

GERARD, JAMES GILBERT (1795–1835), Bengal surgeon; son of Gilbert Gerard [q. v.]; surgeon, 1826; accompanied his brother Alexander Gerard (1792–1839) [q. v.] in Himalayan journeys; gave great scientific assistance to expedition of Sir Alexander Burnes [q. v.] to Bokhara, 1831, but died at Subathoo from exhaustion.   [xxi. 221]

GERARD, JOHN (1545–1612), herbalist; member of court of assistants of Barber-Surgeons, 1595; master, 1607; superintendent of Burghley's gardens; the list of plants in his own garden (Holborn), first published catalogue, 1596 (ed. B. D. Jackson, 1876); his 'Herball' (1597 edited by T. Johnson, 1633.   [xxi. 221]

GERARD, JOHN (1564–1637), jesuit; imprisoned for attempt to leave England without licence, 1585; joined jesuits at Rome, 1588; active on the English mission; betrayed by a servant, imprisoned and tortured; escaped from the Tower, 1597; gave information of Watson's plot, 1603; suspected of complicity in Gunpowder plot; escaped to Rome, 1606; rector at Louvain, 1609; first rector at Liége, 1614–22; director of English college, Rome, 1627–37; his narrative of the Gunpowder plot printed in Morris's 'Condition of the Catholics' (1871), and Latin autobiography translated by G. Kingdon, S.J 1881.   [xxi. 222]

GERARD, JOHN (1632–1654), royalist colonel; cousin of Charles Gerard, first earl of Macclesfield [q. v.]; beheaded for plot to kill Cromwell and proclaim Charles II.   [xxi. 223]

GERARD, MARC. [See GHEERAERTS.]

GERARD, PATRICK (1794–1848), geographical writer; son of Gilbert Gerard [q. v.]; served in Bengal army; captain, 1828; invalided, 1832; died at Simla; contributed meteorological observations to 'Asiatic Researches,' and left in manuscript (British Museum meteorological journal, 1817–29.   [xxi. 224]

GERARD, RICHARD (1613–1686), royalist; served in the Netherlands, 1638–42; escorted Queen Henrietta Maria from the Hague to England; lieutenant-colonel in royal army, 1643; at second battle of Newbury, 1644 attended Charles I at Hurst Castle, and carried letters between him and the queen in France.   [xxi. 224]

GERARD, GARRET, or GARRARD, THOMAS (1500 ?–1540), divine; M.A. Corpus Christi College, Oxford, 1524; entered Christ Church, Oxford; D.D. Cambridge; distributed Lutheran books and Tyndale's translation of the New Testament; examined and forced to recant before the bishops of London and Bath, 1528; pardoned and employed by Wolsey; rector of All Hallows, Honey Lane, and chaplain to Cranmer, 1537; having preached at Paul's Cross, 1540, in answer to Gardiner, was burnt at Smithfield for heresy.   [xxi. 224]

GERARD, SIR WILLIAM (d. 1581), lord chancellor of Ireland; cousin of Sir Gilbert Gerard [q. v.]; barrister, Gray's Inn, 1546; M.P., Preston, 1553, and Chester, 1555, 1572; recorder of Chester, 1565–72; vice-president of council of Wales, 1562; lord chancellor of Ireland, 1576; knighted, 1577; returned to England and became master of requests, 1577; active member of Irish ecclesiastical commission; forwarded to Walsingham an historical treatise on Wales, with suggestions for reform.   [xxi. 225]

GERARDS, MARCUS. [See GHEERAERTS.]

GERBIER, SIR BALTHAZAR (1591 ?–1667), painter, architect, and courtier; native of Middelburg; came to England, 1616, becoming keeper of York House and collector for Buckingham; accompanied Buckingham to Spain, 1623, and Paris, 1625; negotiated with Rubens for a peace with Spain, 1625–7; entered service of Charles and was knighted, 1628; trusted agent of the king at Brussels, 1631, but betrayed for money his negotiation with the Flemish nobles, 1633; became master of the ceremonies, 1641; his house at Bethnal Green attacked by mob as supposed asylum for papists, 1642; retired to France, 1643; returned to England after the king's execution; engaged in mining projects at Cayenne, 1659–60; returned to England, but, being unable to regain his position at court, turned his attention to architecture; a miniature by him of Charles I preserved at South Kensington.   [xxi. 227]

GEREDIGION, DANIEL DU O (1792–1846). [See EVANS, DANIEL.]

GEREE, JOHN (1601 ?–1649), puritan divine; M.A. Magdalen Hall, Oxford, 1621; as incumbent of Tewkesbury 'silenced' for nonconformity (after 1624), but restored, 1641; rector of St. Albans, 1646–7; preacher at St. Faith's, London, 1647; advocated right of the king to abolish episcopacy in 'A Case of Conscience Resolved,' 1646.   [xxi. 229]

GEREE, STEPHEN (1594–1656 ?), puritan; elder brother of John Geree [q. v.]; B.A. Magdalen Hall, Oxford, 1615; vicar of Wonersh, and, c.1641, rector of Abinger; published theological pamphlets.   [xxi 230]

GERMAIN, LADY ELIZABETH, 'LADY BETTY' (1680–1769), daughter of Charles, second earl of Berkeley, and second wife of Sir John Germain [q. v.], who left her large fortune, including the Arundel cameos ; friend of Swift. Young dedicated to her his sixth satire on woman. [xxi. 230]

GERMAIN, GEORGE SACKVILLE, first VISCOUNT SACKVILLE (1716–1785), soldier and statesman (known as LORD GEORGE SACKVILLE till 1770); third son of Lionel Sackville, first duke of Dorset [q. v.]; educated at Westminster and Trinity College, Dublin ; M.A., 1734 ; as lieutenant-colonel of the 28th foot (1st Gloucester) distinguished himself at Fontenoy, 1745, where he was wounded and captured ; colonel of 20th foot (1st Lancashire fusileers), 1746, of 12th dragoons (lancers), 1749, and of present 6th carabineers, 1750 ; major-general, 1755 ; member of the court of inquiry into conduct of Sir John Mordaunt at Rochefort, 1757 ; lieutenant-general of the ordnance, and colonel, 2nd dragoon guards, 1757 ; second in command of St. Malo expedition, 1758 ; as commander of British contingent with Prince Ferdinand neglected to lead British cavalry in pursuit of the French at Minden, 1759, for which he was dismissed the service, declared by court martial unfit to serve in any military capacity, and his name erased from the privy council, 1760 ; M.P., Dover, 1741–61, Hythe, 1761–8, East Grinstead, 1768–82 ; chief secretary to the viceroy of Ireland (Dorset), 1751–6 ; his name restored to privy council by George III ; assumed name of Germain, 1770 ; fought duel with Captain Johnstone, late governor of Pensacola ; commissioner of trade and plantations, and secretary of state for colonies, 1775–82 ; created Viscount Sackville, 1782 ; absurdly credited by some with authorship of 'Junius.' [xxi. 231]

GERMAIN, SIR JOHN (1650–1718), soldier of fortune ; reputed son of William II, prince of Orange ; accompanied William III to England, and served under him in Ireland and Flanders ; created baronet, 1698 ; married Lady Mary Mordaunt, 1701 ; inherited from her Drayton and other property ; his second wife was Lady Betty' Berkeley [see GERMAIN, LADY ELIZABETH]. [xxi. 235]

GERMANUS (378?–448), bishop of Auxerre and missionary to Britain ; one of the six dukes of Gaul ; was forcibly made a cleric by Amator of Auxerre ; succeeded Amator as bishop, 418 ; founded monastery on the Yonne ; with St. Lupus went to Britain, 429, and overcame Pelagians in disputation at Verulamium (St. Albans) ; said to have aided the Britons to overcome the Picts by causing them to cry Alleluia, 430 ; built church at Auxerre in honour of St. Alban ; overcame the Pelagians in a second visit to Britain, 447 ; went to Ravenna to intercede with the empress-mother for the Alans against the Armoricans ; died there, but was buried near Auxerre. [xxi. 236]

GERRALD, JOSEPH (1763–1796), political reformer ; native of St. Christopher, West Indies ; pupil of Samuel Parr [q. v.] at Stanmore, and his lifelong friend ; went to Edinburgh convention as a delegate of the London Corresponding Society, 1793 ; was sentenced by Braxfield to fourteen years' transportation for sedition, 1794 ; died five months after his arrival at Botany Bay. [xxi. 238]

GERVASE OF CANTERBURY (GERVASIUS DOROBERNENSIS) (fl. 1188), chronicler ; became a monk of Christ Church, Canterbury, 1163, and sacrist, 1193 ; engaged in disputes between the archbishop of Canterbury and the abbot of St. Augustine's, 1179–83, and with his own monastery, 1185–91. His works, edited by Bishop Stubbs (Rolls Series, 1879, 1880), include an account of the burning and rebuilding of the cathedral (1174), a history of the archbishops of Canterbury from Augustine to Hubert, 'Mappa Mundi,' a Canterbury Chronicle (1100–99), and 'Gesta Regum,' which after his death was continued to 1328, and is of value for the early years of John's reign. [xxi. 239]

GERVASE OF CHICHESTER (fl. 1170), author of an extant commentary on Malachi ; disciple of Thomas Becket. [xxi. 240]

GERVASE OF TILBURY (fl. 1211), author of 'Otia Imperialia' ; brought up at Rome ; taught law at Bologna, among his pupils being Pignatelli ; present at meeting of Emperor Frederick I and Pope Alexander III, 1177 ; attached to Henry, son of Henry II of England ; high in favour of William II in Sicily ; made marshal of Arles by

the Emperor Otto IV, to whom he dedicated his 'Otia Imperialia' ; probably died in England. [xxi. 241]

GERVAYS, JOHN (d. 1268). [See JOHN.]

GETHIN, GRACE, LADY (1676–1697), learned lady ; daughter of Sir George Norton ; married Sir Richard Gethin ; buried in Westminster Abbey. [xxi. 242]

GETHING, RICHARD (1585?–1652?), calligrapher ; pupil of John Davies of Hereford [q. v.] ; native of Herefordshire ; published at the 'Hand and Pen,' Fetter Lane, a copybook (1616) and 'Chirographia' (1645). [xxi. 242]

GETSIUS, JOHN DANIEL (1592–1672), divine and tutor ; native of the Palatinate ; doctor of philosophy, Marburg, 1618 ; B.A. Cambridge ; taught Hebrew at Exeter College, Oxford, and was incorporated B.A., 1628 ; vicar of Stoke Gabriel, 1636, where he took pupils ; imprisoned, 1643, for a royalist sermon ; published a Greek testament lexicon, with other works. [xxi. 242]

GHEERAERTS, **GEERAERTS**, or **GARRARD**, MARCUS, the elder (1510?–1590?), painter and engraver ; native of Bruges, where he designed the tomb of Charles the Bold ; engraved view of the town, now among the archives, and painted the 'Descent from the Cross' ; came to England as a protestant refugee, 1568 ; said to have died in England. [xxi. 243]

GHEERAERTS, **GHEERAEDTS**, **GEERAERTS**, **GERARDS**, or **GARRARD**, MARCUS, the younger (1561–1635), painter ; son of Marcus Gheeraerts the elder [q. v.] ; accompanied his father to England ; among his portraits were several of Elizabeth and Camden ; his 'Conference of English and Spanish Plenipotentiaries' bought for National Portrait Gallery, 1882 ; published 'Handbook to Art of Drawing.' [xxi. 214]

GHENT or **GAUNT**, JOHN OF, DUKE OF LANCASTER (1340–1399). [See JOHN OF GAUNT.]

GHENT, SIMON DE (d. 1315), bishop of Salisbury ; archdeacon of Oxford, 1284 ; chancellor of the university, 1290–3 ; bishop of Salisbury, 1297–1315 ; one of the lords ordainers, 1310 ; ardent ecclesiastical reformer ; resisted admission of papal nominee to deanery of Salisbury ; preserved his right of tallage against the citizens ; wrote 'Regula Anchoritarum' and drew up 'Statuta ecclesiastica.' [xxi. 245]

GIB, ADAM (1714–1788), Scots anti-burgher divine ; educated at Edinburgh ; joined the 'Associate Presbytery' of 1735 ; minister of secession congregation, Bristo Street, Edinburgh, 1741 ; captured a rebel spy, 1745 ; leader of the anti-burgher synod, 1747 ; when dispossessed of Bristo Street Church ministered in one built for him in Nicholson Street ; called 'Pope Gib' ; published 'Proceedings of the Associate Synod,' 1748. [xxi. 246]

GIBB, FREDERICK (d. 1681), miscellaneous writer ; M.D. Valence, 1651 ; wrote occasionally under the name of Philalethes ; contributed verses to a volume of De Thou 1678. [xxi. 247]

GIBB, JOHN (1776–1850), civil engineer and contractor ; assisted Rennie in construction of Greenock harbour ; repaired Crinan canal, 1817 ; completed Telford's Glasgow bridge. [xxi. 247]

GIBB, ROBERT (d. 1837), landscape-painter ; an original A.R.S.A. ; R.S.A., 1829. [xxi. 247]

GIBB, CHARLES (1604–1681), divine ; M.A. Magdalen Hall, Oxford, 1628 ; D.D., 1662 ; fellow of Merton College, Oxford, 1624 ; prebendary of Wells ; prebendary of Westminster, 1662. [xxi. 247]

GIBBES, SIR GEORGE SMITH (1771–1851), physician to Bath Hospital ; fellow of Magdalen College, Oxford ; B.A., 1792 ; M.D., 1799 ; F.R.C.P., 1804 ; Harveian orator, 1817 ; physician to Bath Hospital, 1804 ; knighted, 1820 ; F.R.S. and F.L.S. His works include treatises on the Bath waters. [xxi. 248]

GIBBES or **GHIBBES**, JAMES ALBAN (1611–1677), Latin poet ; studied under Vesling at Padua ; from 1644 practised as a physician at Rome ; enjoyed favour of four successive popes ; dedicated to Clement IX his 'Carminum Pars Lyrica' ad exemplum Q. Horatii Flacci,' 1668 ; sent to Oxford a gold chain and medal attached to his diploma of poet laureate from the Emperor Leopold I, 1667 ; created M.D. Oxford, 1671, as 'the Horace of his age.' [xxi. 248]

GIBBON, BENJAMIN PHELPS (1802-1851), line-engraver; executed engravings after Landseer and Mulready's 'Wolf and Lamb.' [xxi. 249]

GIBBON, CHARLES (*fl.* 1589-1604), author; published six works, including 'The Order of Equalitie' (1604), an appeal for proportional equalisation of the incidence of taxation. [xxi. 250]

GIBBON, CHARLES (1843-1890), novelist; journalist at Glasgow, *c.* 1860; published about thirty novels; edited 'Casquet of Literature,' 1873-4. [Suppl. ii. 274]

GIBBON, EDWARD (1737-1794), historian; educated at Westminster; owed his taste for books to his aunt, Catherine Porten; spent fourteen 'unprofitable' months at Magdalen College, Oxford, 1752-3; became a Romanist after reading Middleton's 'Free Inquiry' and works by Bossuet and Parsons, 1753; at Lausanne (1753-8), where his tutor, Pavillard, drew him back to protestantism, and where he made friends with Deyverdun and read widely; became attached to Susanne Curchod (afterwards Madame Necker), but in deference to his father broke off the engagement, 1757; published 'Essai sur l'Etude de la Littérature,' 1761 (English version, 1764); served in Hampshire militia, 1759-70, and studied military literature; at Lausanne met Holroyd (afterwards Lord Sheffield); during a tour in Italy, 1764-5, formed plan of his 'History' amid the ruins of the Capitol; with Deyverdun published 'Mémoires Littéraires de la Grande-Bretagne,' 1767-8, contributing a review of Lyttelton's 'Henry II'; issued 'Critical Observations on the Sixth Book of the Æneid,' attacking Warburton, 1770; settled in London, 1772; joined Dr. Johnson's Club, 1774; became professor in ancient history at the Royal Academy in succession to Goldsmith; M.P., Liskeard, 1774-80, Lymington, 1781-3; drew up a state paper against France, and was commissioner of trade and plantations, 1779-82; issued in 1776 the first volume of his 'Decline and Fall of the Roman Empire,' which passed into three editions, and obtained the favourable verdict of Hume, Robertson, Warton, and Walpole; defended the chapters on growth of Christianity in his 'Vindication,' 1779; issued the second and third volumes, 1781, after a visit to Paris, where he met Buffon and disputed with De Mably; retired with Deyverdun to Lausanne, 1783, where he finished the work, 1787 (published, 1788); returned to England, 1793; died suddenly in London; a Latin epitaph written for his monument at Fletching, Sussex, by Dr. Samuel Parr [q. v.] His 'Miscellaneous Works' (edited by his friend Lord Sheffield, 1796) contained an autobiographical memoir, and 'Antiquities of the House of Brunswick' (1814). [xxi. 250]

GIBBON, JOHN (1629-1718), writer on heraldry; educated at Merchant Taylors' and Jesus College, Cambridge; travelled in Europe and America, where he saw Indian aborigines, whose war-paint he took as a proof of the universality of heraldry; created Blue Mantle, 1671; chief work, 'Introductio ad Latinam Blasoniam,' 1682; his 'Heraldo-Memoriale' published in Strype's edition of Stow's 'Survey,' 1720. [xxi. 256]

GIBBON or **GIBBONS**, NICHOLAS, the elder (*fl.* 1600), theological writer; M.A. Clare College, Cambridge, 1592; incorporated at Oxford, 1592; published 'Questions and Disputations concerning the Holy Scripture,' 1601. [xxi. 257]

GIBBON, NICHOLAS, the younger (1605-1697), divine; son of Nicholas Gibbon the elder [q. v.]; M.A. St. Edmund Hall, Oxford, 1629; D.D., 1639; rector of Sevenoaks, 1632-50; consulted by Charles I at Carisbrooke, 1647; worked as farm labourer during the Commonwealth; rector of Corfe Castle, 1660-97; published 'A Summe or Body of Divinity Real' (1653), with a key. [xxi. 257]

GIBBONS. [See also GIBBON.]

GIBBONS, CHRISTOPHER (1615-1676), organist; elder son of Orlando Gibbons [q. v.]; educated in Exeter choir; organist of Winchester Cathedral, 1638-61; at Restoration appointed to Chapel Royal, to Westminster Abbey, and court organist; Mus. Doc. Oxford, 1663; contributed to 'Cantica Sacra,' 1674; collaborated with Lock in music to Shirley's 'Cupid and Death,' 1653. [xxi. 258]

GIBBONS, EDWARD (1570?-1653?), organist; brother of Orlando Gibbons [q. v.]; Mus. Bac. Cambridge and Oxford; organist at King's College, Cambridge,

1592-9; afterwards at Bristol Cathedral, and (1611-44) a Exeter Cathedral; his manuscript compositions pre served in Music School, Oxford. [xxi. 259]

GIBBONS, ELLIS (*fl.* 1600), musical composer brother of Edward Gibbons [q. v.]; probably organist a Salisbury; composed madrigals in 'Triumphs of Oriana, 1603. [xxi. 259]

GIBBONS, GRINLING (1648-1720), wood-carver and statuary; born at Rotterdam; discovered by John Evelyn [q. v.] in 1671 working at Deptford at his carving of Tintoretto's 'Crucifixion,' which was shown to Wren and Pepys, and afterwards to the royal family; employed by Wren to carve stalls in St. Paul's and new London churches; employed in library of Trinity College, Cam bridge, and by the king at Windsor, Whitehall, and Ken sington; carved the throne in Canterbury Cathedral executed statues of Charles II at the Royal Exchang and Chelsea, and of James II at Whitehall; buried in St. Paul's, Covent Garden; his portrait painted b Kneller. [xxi. 259]

GIBBONS, JOHN (1544-1589), jesuit; doctor o philosophy and divinity at German College, Rome, 1576 rector of jesuit college, Trèves; died at Himmelrode his 'Concertatio Ecclesiæ Catholicæ in Anglia, adversu Calvino-Papistas et Puritanos' (1583), enlarged by John Bridgewater [q. v.] [xxi. 261]

GIBBONS, ORLANDO (1583-1625), musical composer entered choir of King's College, Cambridge, 1596, fo which he composed music; Mus. Bac. Cambridge, 1606 Mus. Doc. Oxford, 1622; organist of Chapel Royal, 1604 composed music for the reception of Queen Henriett Maria at Canterbury; buried in Canterbury Cathedral contributed the remarkable fantasia 'The Lord of Salis bury his Pavin,' to Byrd and Bull's 'Parthenia' (1611) published 'First Set of Madrigals and Mottets' (1612 containing 'The Silver Swan,' and other masterpieces composed also settings of George Wither's 'Hymns an Songs of the Church,' 1623, and instrumental 'Fantasies o Three Parts.' His sacred compositions, including service in F and D minor, 'preces,' and many anthems for speci occasions, were edited by Sir F. A. Gore Ouseley [q. v. 1873. [xxi. 261]

GIBBONS, RICHARD (1550?-1632), jesuit; younge brother of John Gibbons [q. v.]; taught mathematic philosophy, Hebrew, and canon law in several continent countries; died at Douay; edited Harpsfield's 'Histori Anglicana Ecclesiastica,' 1622, and translated Bellarmine 'Christian Doctrine,' and other works from Italia Spanish, and Portuguese. [xxi. 264]

GIBBONS, THOMAS (1720-1785), dissenting ministe and author; independent minister of Haberdashers' Hal 1743; tutor of Mile End academy, 1754; D.D. Aberdee 1764; M.A. New Jersey, 1760; published 'Memoirs o Rev. J. Watts, D.D.' (1780), also hymns and devotiona verses. [xxi. 265]

GIBBONS, WILLIAM (1649-1728), physician; o Merchant Taylors' School; B.A. St. John's College, Oxfor 1672; M.D., 1683; F.R.C.P., 1692, and censor, 1716 ridiculed by Garth as Mirmillo; benefactor of Wolver hampton; said to have made mahogany fashionable. [xxi. 265]

GIBBS, MRS. (*fl.* 1783-1844), actress; appeared at th Haymarket as Sally in Colman's 'Man and Wife,' 1783 married the younger George Colman [q. v.], in whos plays she acted, 1797-1803. Her other parts include Katherine, Miss Hardcastle, and Mrs. Candour. [xxi. 266]

GIBBS, MRS. (1804-1854). [See GRADDON, MISS.]

GIBBS, JAMES (*d.* 1724), physician and poet; pub lished metrical version of Psalms i.-xv., 1701, and essa on cure of scrofula. [xxi. 266]

GIBBS, JAMES (1682-1754), architect; M.A Marischal College, Aberdeen; studied under Fontana a Rome; designed St. Mary-le-Strand, St. Peter's, Ver Street, and St. Martin-in-the-Fields, part of the Senat House and of King's College, Cambridge; the monument of Ben Jonson, Prior, and Newcastle in Westminste Abbey; the quadrangle of St. Bartholomew's Hospita and the Radcliffe Library, Oxford; published 'A Boo of Architecture,' 1728, and 'Rules for Drawing th several Parts of Architecture,' 1732, and translate Fonseca's 'De Rebus Emanuelis,' 1752. [xxi. 267]

GIBBS, JOSEPH (1700?–1788), organist of St. Mary-at-Tower, Ipswich; composed 'Eight Solos for a Violin, with a Thorough Bass for the Harpsichord' (1740?). [xxi. 268]

GIBBS, PHILIP (*fl.* 1740), dissenting minister and stenographer; joint-pastor at Hackney, 1729; unitarian, 1737; published 'An Historical Account of Compendious and Swift Writing,' 1736, and 'Essay towards a further Improvement of Short-Hand,' 1736. [xxi. 268]

GIBBS, SIR SAMUEL (*d.* 1815), major-general; ensign, 102nd foot, 1783; commanded the 11th in West Indies, 1799, and 59th foot at Cape, 1805–6, and in Travancore, 1808–9; distinguished himself in the Java expedition, 1811; major-general, 1812, in Holland; mortally wounded at New Orleans, 1815; K.C.B., 1815. [xxi. 269]

GIBBS, SIR VICARY (1751–1820), judge; educated at Eton; contributed to 'Musæ Etonenses'; fellow; M.A. King's College, Cambridge, 1778; Craven scholar, 1772; barrister, Lincoln's Inn, 1783; recorder of Bristol, 1794; assisted Erskine in defence of Thomas Hardy [q. v.] and Horne Tooke [q. v.], 1794, and was highly complimented by the attorney-general, Sir John Scott [q. v.], 1794; M.P., Totnes, and chief-justice of Chester, 1804; solicitor-general, 1805–6; knighted, 1805; M.P., Great Bedwin, 1807; M.P. for Cambridge University, 1807; attorney-general, 1807–12; serjeant-at-law and judge of common pleas, 1812; lord chief-baron and privy councillor, 1813; chief-justice of common pleas, 1814–18; called 'Vinegar Gibbs'; his numerous ex-officio informations noticed in parliament, 1811. [xxi. 270]

GIBSON, SIR ALEXANDER, LORD DURIE (*d.* 1644), Scottish judge; M.A. Edinburgh, 1588; third clerk of session, 1594; lord of session as Lord Durie, 1621; created baronet of Nova Scotia, 1628; commissioner for reviewing the laws and customs, 1633; member of committee of estates, 1640; twice president of the Court of Justice; story of his being kidnapped by Traquair subject of Scott's 'Christie's Will'; 'Lord Durie's Practicks' (1690), the earliest collection of Scottish legal decisions. [xxi. 271]

GIBSON, SIR ALEXANDER, LORD DURIE (*d.* 1656), Scottish judge; son of Sir Alexander Gibson (*d.* 1644) [q. v.]; clerk of session, 1621; opposed ecclesiastical policy of Charles I; commissary-general of forces against Charles I, 1640; knighted, 1641; lord clerk register, 1641; commissioner of the exchequer, 1645; lord of session as Lord Durie, 1646–9. [xxi. 272]

GIBSON, SIR ALEXANDER (*d.* 1693), principal clerk of session and clerk to Scottish privy council; grandson of Sir Alexander Gibson (*d.* 1644) [q. v.], whose 'Practicks' he edited; knighted, 1682. [xxi. 272]

GIBSON, ALEXANDER (1800–1867), botanist; M.D. Edinburgh; surgeon to East India Company; superintendent of Dapuri botanical gardens, 1838–47; conservator of Bombay forests, 1847–60; F.L.S., 1853; published works, including 'Forest Reports,' 1849–55, and 'Bombay Flora.' [xxi. 272]

GIBSON, ALEXANDER CRAIG (1813–1874), Cumberland antiquary; M.R.C.S., 1846; published 'The Old Man, or Ramblings round Coniston,' 1849, and 'The Folk-speech of Cumberland,' 1869. [xxi. 273]

GIBSON, DAVID COOKE (1827–1856), painter; studied in Edinburgh, London, Belgium, and Paris; painted portraits and wrote humorous verse; exhibited Spanish pictures at Royal Academy, 1855–6. [xxi. 273]

GIBSON, EDMUND (1669–1748), bishop of London; nephew of Thomas Gibson (1647–1722) [q. v.]; fellow of Queen's College, Oxford, 1694; M.A., 1694; chaplain to Archbishop Tenison and librarian at Lambeth, where he commenced catalogue of library; combated Atterbury's views on convocation; archdeacon of Surrey, 1710; bishop of Lincoln, 1716–20; bishop of London, 1720–48; used his influence with George I against masquerades; was Walpole's ecclesiastical adviser till his opposition to the Quaker's Relief Bill, 1736; declined primacy, 1747; published numerous works, including an edition of the Saxon Chronicle (1692), a translation of Camden's 'Britannia' (1695), 'Reliquiæ Spelmannianæ' (1698), 'Synodus Anglicana' (1702), 'Codex Juris Ecclesiæ Anglicanæ' (1713). [xxi. 274]

GIBSON, EDWARD (1668–1701), portrait-painter; nephew of William Gibson (1644–1702) [q. v.]; excelled in crayon work. [xxi. 275]

GIBSON, FRANCIS (1753–1805), author; collector of customs at Whitby, 1787; published 'Sailing Directions for the Baltic,' 1791, and 'Streanshall Abbey' (play), 1800. [xxi. 276]

GIBSON, GEORGE STACEY (1818–1883), botanist; quaker banker and benefactor of Saffron Walden; F.R.S., 1847; published 'Flora of Essex,' 1862; contributed to 'Phytologist,' 1842–51, adding six new species to British flora. [xxi. 276]

GIBSON, JAMES (1799–1871), Free church polemic; edited 'Church of Scotland Magazine,' 1834–7; incumbent of Kingston, 1839–43; joined Free church, 1843; professor of theology and church history at Glasgow Theological College, 1856; published theological treatises. [xxi. 276]

GIBSON, SIR JAMES BROWN (1805–1868), physician; M.D. Edinburgh; served in Crimea; director general of army medical department, 1860–7; K.C.B., 1865; died at Rome. [xxi. 277]

GIBSON, JAMES YOUNG (1826–1886), translator from the Spanish; studied at Edinburgh and Halle; contributed some poetical renderings to Duffield's version of 'Don Quixote,' 1881; translated also Cervantes's 'Viage al Parnaso,' 1883, and 'Numantia,' 1885. [xxi. 277]

GIBSON, SIR JOHN (1637–1717), colonel; in Dutch service, 1675–88; lieutenant-colonel in English army, 1689; colonel, 1694; lieutenant-governor of Portsmouth, 1689; M.P., Portsmouth, 1701–2; commander of force sent to capture Newfoundland, 1697; knighted, 1705. [xxi. 278]

GIBSON, JOHN (*d.* 1852), portrait-painter; exhibited at West of Scotland Academy, where a fatal accident caused his death. [xxi. 278]

GIBSON, JOHN (1794–1854), glass-stainer; sheriff of Newcastle, 1854. [xxi. 278]

GIBSON, JOHN (1790–1866), sculptor; of humble parentage; while at Liverpool attracted the attention of William Roscoe [q. v.]; lived at Rome, and received instruction from Canova and Thorwaldsen, 1817; his first commission, the Chatsworth 'Mars and Cupid,' followed by 'Psyche and Zephyrs,' 'Sleeping Shepherd Boy,' 'Hylas and the Nymphs,' 1819–26, 'Cupid disguised as a Shepherd,' 1837, and other works; R.A., 1838; during visit to England (1844) publicly entertained at Glasgow, and received commission for bust of Queen Victoria, his first tinted work; modelled statue of Queen Victoria for Houses of Parliament, 1850–5, which, with his 'Tinted Venus' and 'Pandora' and 'Cupid' (all coloured), were seen at the International Exhibition, 1862; executed three statues of Huskisson, and one of Sir Robert Peel in Westminster Abbey; the last of the purist or abstract school of sculptors; bequeathed his property to the Royal Academy. [xxi. 278]

GIBSON, JOHN (1817–1892), architect; articled to Joseph Aloysius Hansom [q. v.], and (Sir) Charles Barry [q. v.]; successful in competition for National Bank of Scotland, Glasgow, 1844, and carried out work; A.R.I.B.A., 1849; F.R.I.B.A., 1853. His works—chiefly country houses and banks—include the head offices and numerous branches of the National Provincial Bank of England. [Suppl. ii. 274]

GIBSON, KENNET (1730–1772), antiquary; educated at Eton; B.A. Christ's College, Cambridge, 1752; rector of Marham, Northamptonshire; his 'Comment on part of the Fifth Journey of Antoninus through Britain,' printed by Nichols, 1800. [xxi. 281]

GIBSON, MATHEW (*d.* 1741?), antiquary; B.A. Queen's College, Oxford, 1700; rector of Abbey Dore, 1722–41; published 'View of Ancient and Present State of the Churches of Door, Home-Lacy, and Hempsted, 1727,' with memoirs of Scudamore family. [xxi. 281]

GIBSON, MATTHEW (1734–1790), Roman catholic prelate; professor at Douay; vicar-general to Bishop Walton, 1776; vicar-apostolic of Northern England, 1780; joined in issuing 'Protestation oath' encyclical, 1789; with Thomas Eyre (1748–1810) [q. v.] published 'The London, or Little Catechism,' 1784. [xxi. 281]

GIBSON, PATRICK (1782 ?–1829), landscape-painter and writer; exhibited at Royal Academy, 1805–7, and at several Edinburgh galleries; foundation member of Scottish Academy, 1826; professor of painting at Dollar Academy, 1824–9; his 'Landscape Composition' preserved in Scottish National Gallery, and portrait of himself (water-colour) in the Portrait Gallery; published 'Etchings of Select Views in Edinburgh,' 1818; contributed to Brewster's 'Edinburgh Encyclopædia.' [xxi. 282]

GIBSON, RICHARD (1615–1690), dwarf and miniature-painter; page to Charles I and Henrietta Maria; executed several portraits of Cromwell and many miniatures; his marriage to Anne Shepherd, also a dwarf, commemorated by Waller; portrait of him and his wife painted by Lely. [xxi. 283]

GIBSON, SOLOMON (d. 1866), sculptor; brother of John Gibson (1790–1866) [q. v.]; best known for his small Mercury modelled at sixteen; wrote papers on Welsh literature; died at Paris. [xxi. 283]

GIBSON, SUSAN PENELOPE (1652–1700), miniaturist; daughter of Richard Gibson [q. v.] [xxi. 283]

GIBSON, THOMAS (d. 1562), printer, medical practitioner, and author; noted for extraordinary cures; recommended by Latimer to Cromwell, 1537; fled to Geneva in reign of Mary; licensed by Cambridge University to practise physic, 1559; printed in London his own books, including a New Testament concordance (1535), and several medical and anti-papal works. [xxi. 284]

GIBSON, THOMAS (1647–1722), physician; M.D. Leyden, 1675; physician-general to the army, 1718–19; published 'Anatomy of Humane Bodies epitomized,' 1682. [xxi. 284]

GIBSON, THOMAS (1680 ?–1751), portrait-painter; friend of Vertue; painted portraits of Vertue, Locke, Flamsteed, and Archbishop Wake. [xxi. 284]

GIBSON, THOMAS MILNER- (1806–1884), statesman; at school with Disraeli at Higham Hill, Essex, afterwards at Charterhouse; B.A. and thirty-sixth wrangler, Trinity College, Cambridge, 1830; conservative M.P. for Ipswich, 1837–9; resigned on change of views; active member and speaker of Anti-Cornlaw League; liberal M.P., Manchester, 1841; vice-president of board of trade, 1846–8; privy councillor, 1846; seconded Cobden's vote of censure on Palmerston's Chinese policy, 1857; M.P. for Ashton-under-Lyne, 1857–68; carried motion to amend law of conspiracy, which caused Palmerston's resignation, 1858; president of the board of trade in Palmerston's last ministry, 1859–65, and under Lord Russell, 1865–6; active promoter of the commercial treaty with France, and the abolition of the newspaper stamp, advertisement, and paper duties; received a pension of 2,000l. on retirement; died on his yacht off Algiers. [xxi. 285]

GIBSON, WILLIAM (fl. 1540), lord of session; graduated at Glasgow, 1507; dean of Restalrig; lord of session, 1532; employed on embassies to the pope, who bestowed on him armorial bearings; suffragan to Cardinal Beaton and 'Custos Ecclesiæ Scoticæ,' 1540. [xxi. 286]

GIBSON, WILLIAM (1629–1684), quaker; served at one time in parliamentary army; frequently imprisoned for preaching and refusing oaths, 1654–61; his goods distrained for non-payment of tithe, 1676–7; published theological treatises. [xxi. 287]

GIBSON, WILLIAM (1644–1702), miniature-painter; nephew of Richard Gibson [q. v.]; pupil and copyist of Lely. [xxi. 288]

GIBSON, WILLIAM (1720–1791), mathematician; while working as a farmer taught himself reading, writing, geometry, algebra, and trigonometry, and acquired a knowledge of higher mathematics; land-surveyor. [xxi. 288]

GIBSON, WILLIAM (1738–1821), Roman catholic prelate; brother of Matthew Gibson (1734–1790) [q. v.]; president of Douay College, 1781–90; vicar-apostolic of northern England, 1790; founded Ushaw College. [xxi. 288]

GIBSON, WILLIAM (1808–1867), presbyterian divine; established 'Banner of Ulster,' 1842; moderator of general assembly, 1859; author of 'The Year of Grace, a History of the Ulster Revival of 1859' [xxi. 289]

GIBSON, WILLIAM SIDNEY (1814–1871), author; barrister, Lincoln's Inn, 1843; registrar of the Newcastle-upon-Tyne district court of bankruptcy, 1843–69; published works, including 'History of Tynemouth Monastery,' 1846–1847, 'Descriptive and Historical Notices of Northumbrian Antiquities,' 1848–54, 'Memoir of Northumberland,' 1860, and 'Memoir of Lord Lyndhurst,' 1866. [xxi. 289]

GIDDY, DAVIES (1767–1839). [See GILBERT.]

GIDEON, SAMPSON (1699–1762), Jewish financier; of Portuguese extraction; consulted by Walpole and Pelham; raised 1,700,000l. for government, 1745; advised and executed consolidation of National Debt, 1749; paid bounties for recruiting, 1756, and raised several government loans during seven years' war; his son created a baronet and Baron Eardley in peerage of Ireland. [See EARDLEY, SIR CULLING EARDLEY.] [xxi. 289]

GIFFARD. [See also GIFFORD.]

GIFFARD, SIR AMBROSE HARDINGE (1771–1827), chief-justice of Ceylon, 1819–27; barrister, Inner Temple. [xxi. 290]

GIFFARD, BONAVENTURE (1642–1734), Roman catholic bishop; D.D. from the Sorbonne, 1677; chaplain to James II; first vicar-apostolic of midland district, 1688; bishop of Madaura, in partibus, 1688; made by James II president of Magdalen College, Oxford; installed by proxy, 31 March 1688; ejected, on the restoration of his predecessor, John Hough, 25 Oct. 1688; imprisoned in Newgate at the Revolution; transferred to London district on liberation; had also western district, 1708–13 in constant danger; bequeathed his heart to Douay College. [xxi. 291]

GIFFARD, SIR GEORGE MARKHAM (1813–1870), lord justice of appeal; educated at Winchester and New College, Oxford; fellow, 1832; B.C.L., 1841; barrister Inner Temple, 1840; leading chancery junior; Q.C., 1859 lord justice of appeal, 1868–70; privy councillor, 1868. [xxi. 292]

GIFFARD, GODFREY (1235 ?–1302), chancellor of England and bishop of Worcester; younger brother of Walter Giffard [q. v.]; archdeacon of Barnstaple, 1265 and York, 1267, though a deacon; chancellor of England 1266–70; bishop of Worcester, 1268–1302; treated with Llewelyn, 1272; went to meet Edward I on his return from the Holy Land, 1273; justice itinerant, 1278; negotiate with the Scots, 1289; involved in constant disputes with chapter of Worcester; a benefactor of the cathedral. [xxi. 293]

GIFFARD, HENRY WELLS (1810–1854), navy captain; present as midshipman at Navarino, 1827; present at capture of Chusan and Canton, 1839, and reduction of Amoy and Chinghae, 1841; mortally wounded and captured in the Tiger at Odessa. [xxi. 294]

GIFFARD, JOHN, BARON GIFFARD OF BROMSFIELD (1232–1299), fought for de Montfort in the west; captured Warwick Castle, 1264; taken at Lewes, but rescued 1264; attached himself to Gilbert de Clare and fought for the royalists at Evesham, 1265; served Edward I in Wales, Gascony, and Scotland; summoned by writ to parliament of 1295; member of council of regency, 1297; founded Gloucester Hall (now Worcester College), Oxford 1283. [xxi. 295]

GIFFARD, ROGER (d. 1597), president of the College of Physicians; fellow of Merton College, Oxford, and of All Souls'; M.A., 1560; M.D., 1566; physician to Queen Elizabeth; president, College of Physicians, 1581–4. [xxi. 295]

GIFFARD, STANLEY LEES (1788–1858), first editor of the 'Standard'; brother of Sir Ambrose Harding Giffard [q. v.]; M.A. Trinity College, Dublin, 1811; barrister, Middle Temple, 1811; LL.D.; editor of the 'Standard' from 1827; editor of 'St. James's Chronicle'; contributed to the 'Quarterly' and 'Blackwood.' [xxi. 296]

GIFFARD, WALTER (d. 1279), archbishop of York consecrated at Paris bishop of Bath and Wells, 1265 excommunicated Leicester and his followers; chancellor after Evesham, 1265–6; one of the arbitrators at the award of Kenilworth, 1266; archbishop of York, 1266 1279; tutor to Prince Edward's sons; one of the three regents, 1272–4, and 1275. [xxi. 297]

GIFFARD, WILLIAM (d. 1129), bishop of Winchester dean of Rouen and chancellor to William II; nominated to see of Winchester by Henry I on his accession, 1100

inducted by Anselm ; refusing to receive consecration from Gerard or Girard [q. v.], the newly appointed archbishop of York, was banished by the king ; maintained intimate relations with Anselm, whom he accompanied to Rome, 1103 ; consecrated, after settlement of the investiture dispute, 1107 ; as deputy for the primate married Henry I and Queen Adela, 1121 ; his disputes with the monks of Winchester ended by royal intervention, 1124 ; founded at Waverley, Surrey, 1128, the first English Cistercian house ; benefactor of St. Mary Overies, Southwark ; built London residence for bishops of Winchester in Southwark.
[xxi. 298]

GIFFORD. [See also GIFFARD.]

GIFFORD, COUNTESS OF (1807–1867). [See SHERIDAN, HELEN SELINA.]

GIFFORD, ADAM, LORD GIFFORD (1820–1887), lord of session ; called to Scottish bar, 1849 ; advocate-depute, 1861 ; sheriff of Orkney and Zetland, 1865 ; lord of session as Lord Gifford, 1870–81 ; founded Gifford lectureships in natural theology.
[xxi. 299]

GIFFORD, ANDREW (1700–1784), baptist minister and numismatist ; D.D. Aberdeen, 1754 ; chaplain to Sir Richard Ellys [q. v.] and Lady Ellys, 1731–45 ; minister at Eagle Street, London, 1730–84 ; assistant-librarian at British Museum, 1757–84 ; his collection of coins purchased by George II ; left valuable books, manuscripts, pictures, and curios to baptist academy, Bristol ; edited ' Folkes's Tables of English Silver and Gold Coins,' 1763.
[xxi. 300]

GIFFORD, GEORGE (d. 1620), divine ; student at Hart Hall, Oxford, before 1568 ; incumbent of All Saints' with St. Peter's, Maldon, 1582 ; deposed for nonconformity, 1584 ; carried on controversy with the Brownists, Henry Barrow [q. v.], and John Greenwood [q. v.] ; published theological works ; his ' Dialogue concerning Witches and Witchcrafts' (1593) reprinted by Percy Society.
[xxi. 300]

GIFFORD, GEORGE (fl. 1635), engraver ; chiefly known for the portrait of Latimer prefixed to the 1635 edition of Latimer's sermons.
[xxi. 301]

GIFFORD or **GIFFARD,** GILBERT (1561 ?–1590), Roman catholic spy ; of the Chillington family ; while at the English College, Rome, entered English secret service, 1583 ; visited Mary Queen of Scots at Chartley, 1584, and was entrusted with her secret correspondence with the French embassy ; treacherously copied letters, sending originals to Walsingham ; intimate with Anthony Babington [q. v.], whose designs he encouraged and communicated to Walsingham ; carried letters from Mary to Babington approving the conspiracy ; accused by Romanists of concocting the whole plot ; died in prison at Paris.
[xxi. 302]

GIFFORD, HUMPHREY (fl. 1580), poet ; author of ' A Posie of Gilloflowers,' 1580.
[xxi. 303]

GIFFORD, JAMES, the elder (1740 ?–1813), unitarian writer ; educated at Rugby ; served in the 14th foot during American war ; published theological works, including ' Elucidation of the Unity of God,' 1783.
[xxi. 303]

GIFFORD, JAMES, the younger (1768–1853), rear-admiral ; son of James Gifford the elder [q. v.] ; born at Halifax, Nova Scotia ; lieutenant in the navy, 1793 ; rear-admiral, 1846 ; published ' Remonstrance of a Unitarian . . . to Bishop of St. David's,' 1818.
[xxi. 304]

GIFFORD, JOHN (fl. 1636–1642), D.D. Christ Church, Oxford ; rector of St. Michael Bassishaw, 1636–1642 ; expelled as a royalist, 1642.
[xxi. 301]

GIFFORD, JOHN (1758–1818), author ; of Westminster and St. John's College, Oxford ; abandoned his paternal name of Green, and assumed that of Gifford to deceive his creditors, c. 1781 ; London police magistrate ; edited, in imitation of the ' Anti-Jacobin ' of William Gifford (1756–1826) [q. v.], the ' Anti-Jacobin Review and Magazine,' published 1798–1821 : also published ' History of France,' 1791–4 and ' Political Life of Pitt,' 1809.
[xxi. 305]

GIFFORD, RICHARD (1725–1807), author ; B.A. Balliol College, Oxford, 1748 ; vicar of Duffield, 1759 ; rector of North Okendon, 1772 ; his ' Contemplation, a Poem,' 1753, quoted in Johnson's Dictionary ; published

an answer to Priestley's dissertation on matter and mind.
[xxi. 305]

GIFFORD, ROBERT, first BARON GIFFORD (1779–1826), judge ; special pleader ; barrister, Middle Temple, 1808 ; recorder of Bristol, 1812 ; solicitor-general, 1817 ; attorney-general, 1819 ; prosecuted Cato Street conspirators, 1820 ; M.P., Eye, 1817–1824 ; addressed House of Lords against Queen Caroline, 1820 ; serjeant-at-law, 1824 ; chief-justice of common pleas, privy councillor, and created peer, 1824 ; master of the rolls and deputy-speaker of House of Lords.
[xxi. 306]

GIFFORD, WILLIAM (1554–1629), archbishop of Rheims ; studied at Lincoln College, Oxford ; studied at Louvain under Bellarmine and at the Sorbonne and English colleges at Rheims and Rome ; M.A. Louvain ; almoner and chaplain to Cardinal Allen at Rome, 1587 ; dean of Lille, 1596 ; rector of Rheims University, 1608, where he became a Benedictine ; famed as a preacher at Paris and throughout France ; first president of English Benedictines, 1617 ; coadjutor of cardinal of Guise, 1618, at Rheims ; archbishop of Rheims, 1622 ; edited Dr. W. Reynolds's ' Calvino-Turcismus,' 1597, and wrote several works in the interests of the Duc de Guise.
[xxi. 306]

GIFFORD, WILLIAM (1756–1826), first editor of the ' Quarterly Review ' ; son of a glazier at Ashburton ; shoemaker's apprentice ; sent by a surgeon named William Cookesley to Exeter College, Oxford ; B.A., 1782 ; afterwards patronised by Lord Grosvenor ; became known by his satires, the ' Baviad ' (1794) and ' Mæviad ' (1795), against the Della Cruscans and small dramatists ; editor of and writer in ' Anti-Jacobin ' (1797–8) ; published ' Epistle to Peter Pindar,' 1800, attacking Wolcot, who assaulted him at a bookshop in mistake for his namesake, John Gifford [q. v.], of the ' Anti-Jacobin Review' ; editor of the ' Quarterly Review,' 1809–24 ; probably wrote the ' Quarterly's ' attack on Keats's ' Endymion,' 1818 ; inspected Byron's works before publication ; founded exhibitions at Exeter College, Oxford ; edited Juvenal, with autobiography, 1802, and translated Persius, 1821 ; edited the dramatic works of Massinger, 1805 and 1813, of Ben Jonson, 1816, and of Ford, 1827.
[xxi. 308]

GIGLI, GIOVANNI (d. 1498), bishop-elect of Worcester ; came to England as collector for Pope Sixtus IV ; commissioner for sale of indulgences, 1489 ; rewarded for his services for Henry VII at Rome by see of Worcester, 1497, but died at Rome before enthronement ; wrote epithalamium on marriage of Henry VII.
[xxi. 311]

GIGLI, SILVESTRO (1463–1521), bishop of Worcester ; nephew of Giovanni Gigli [q. v.] ; bishop of Worcester, 1499 ; resident ambassador of Henry VII at Rome ; envoy of Pope Julius II to England, 1504 ; stayed at court as master of ceremonies ; envoy to the Lateran council, 1512 ; confidential agent for Wolsey at Rome ; correspondent of Erasmus.
[xxi. 311]

GILBART, JAMES WILLIAM (1794–1863), writer on banking ; banker in London, Birmingham, and Ireland ; manager of the London and Westminster Bank, 1833–59 ; F.R.S. and member of Statistical Society ; chief works, ' Practical Treatise on Banking,' 1827, and ' History and Principles of Banking,' 1834.
[xxi. 312]

GILBERT THE UNIVERSAL (d. 1134 ?), bishop of London ; ' magister ' at Auxerre, c. 1120 ; bishop of London, 1127 or 1128 ; took part in council of London, 1129, which condemned marriage of priests ; his ' infinite ' wealth confiscated by Henry I ; accused by the chronicler, Henry of Huntingdon, of avarice, but highly commended by St. Bernard ; benefactor of sees of London and Auxerre ; owed his title ' Universal ' to his encyclopædic learning ; his only extant work, a treatise on ' Lamentations ' ; many of his works confused with those of Gilbert of Auxerre and Gilbert Foliot [q. v.].
[xxi. 313]

GILBERT OF LOUTH (d. 1153 ?), abbot of Basingwerk, Flintshire ; sent from Louth by Gervase, c. 1140, to obtain grant for an Irish monastery ; the ' Purgatorium Sancti Patricii ' wrongly ascribed to him.
[xxi. 314]

GILBERT THE GREAT or THE THEOLOGIAN (d. 1167 ?), eighth abbot of Cîteaux ; an Englishman ; abbot of Cistercians at Ourcamp, 1143, at Cîteaux, 1163 ; supported Geoffrey of Clairvaux against the pope and king of France ; author of ' Commentaries on the Psalms,' and other works.
[xxi. 314]

GILBERT OF HOYLAND (d. 1172), theological writer; an English Cistercian, often confused with Gilbert the Great [q. v.]; disciple of St. Bernard of Clairvaux; abbot of Swineshead, Lincolnshire, 1163; said to have died at Rivour, near Troyes; his sermons and 'Tractatus Ascetici' printed in Migne's 'Patrologia' and Mabillon's works of St. Bernard.   [xxi. 315]

GILBERT OF SEMPRINGHAM (1083 ?-1189), founder of the Gilbertine order, the head of the thirteen houses being at Sempringham, Lincolnshire, c. 1135; met Pope Eugenius III at Citeaux; received abbot's staves from St. Bernard and St. Malachy; supported Becket against Henry II; held in great regard by Henry II and Queen Eleanor, who protected him against the enemies made by the rapacity of his servants; lived to be over a hundred, but retired from his abbacy long before death; canonised by Innocent III, 1202.   [xxi. 315]

GILBERT OF MORAY (d. 1245), bishop of Caithness, 1223; archdeacon of Moray, 1203; built Dornoch Cathedral; last Scotsman enrolled in calendar of saints.
                                             [xxi. 317]

GILBERT THE ENGLISHMAN (fl. 1250), medical writer; studied and practised abroad, and is said to have been chancellor of Montpellier; his 'Compendium Medicinæ,' or 'Laurea Anglicana,' largely a compilation from Greek and Arab writers, first printed at Lyons, 1510.
                                             [xxi. 318]

GILBERT OF ST. LIFARD (d. 1305), bishop of Chichester; a foreigner, probably named from church of St. Lifard (Leofard), near Meung-sur-Loire; practised as ecclesiastical lawyer chiefly in the north of England; treasurer of Chichester, 1282; employed by Archbishop Peckham on commission to define rights of metropolitical jurisdiction, 1282, and in disputes with monks; bishop of Chichester, 1288-1305; his constitutions of reform (1289) re-enacted by Archbishop William of Greenfield [q. v.]; rebuilt east end of his cathedral.   [xxi. 318]

GILBERT, MRS. ANN (1782-1866), writer of children's poetry; better known under her maiden name, ANN TAYLOR; with her sister Jane wrote 'Original Poems for Infant Minds,' 1804-5, 'Rhymes for the Nursery,' 1806, and 'Hymns,' 1810; married Joseph Gilbert [q. v.], 1813; afterwards published 'Seven Blessings for Little Children,' 1844; contributed to Leifchild's 'Original Hymns,' and compiled memoir of her husband, 1853; her 'Autobiography' issued, 1874.   [xxi. 320]

GILBERT, ASHURST TURNER (1786-1870), bishop of Chichester; fellow of Brasenose College, Oxford; M.A., 1811; D.D., 1822; principal of Brasenose College, Oxford, 1822-42; vice-chancellor, 1836-40; bishop of Chichester, 1842-70; interdicted the Rev. John Purchas, 1868; published sermons and charges.   [xxi. 321]

GILBERT, CHARLES SANDOE (1760-1831), historian of Cornwall; itinerant vendor of medicines in Devon and Cornwall; published two volumes (1817 and 1820) of 'Historical Survey of Cornwall.'   [xxi. 321]

GILBERT, CLAUDIUS, the elder (d. 1696 ?), ecclesiastic; minister under Commonwealth of the precinct of Limerick; active against the quakers; settled at Belfast after the Restoration; published 'The Libertine School'd, or a Vindication of the Magistrates' Power in Religious Matters,' 1657, and other works.   [xxi. 322]

GILBERT, CLAUDIUS, the younger (1670-1743), ecclesiastic; son of Claudius Gilbert the elder [q. v.]; fellow of Trinity College, Dublin, 1693; D.D. and LL.D., 1706; vice-provost, 1716; rector of Ardstraw, 1735; bequeathed many books to Trinity College, Dublin.
                                             [xxi. 323]

GILBERT (formerly GIDDY), DAVIES (1767-1839), president of the Royal Society; assumed wife's name of Gilbert, 1817; educated at Penzance and Pembroke College, Oxford; M.A., 1789; D.C.L., 1832; high sheriff of Cornwall, 1792-3; M.P., Helston, 1804, Bodmin, 1806-32; promoted cause of science and art in parliament; acquired large property in Sussex by marriage, 1808; published 'Plain Statement of the Bullion Question,' 1811; F.S.A., 1820; early encouraged Sir Humphry Davy [q. v.]; treasurer of Royal Society, 1820, president, 1827-30; nominated writers of Bridgewater treatises, and (1830) selected Brunel's design for Clifton bridge; published 'Parochial History of Cornwall,' 1838; edited 'Collection of Christmas Carols' and two Cornish mystery plays. [xxi. 323]

GILBERT, ELIZABETH MARGARETTA MARIA (1826-1885), philanthropist; second daughter of Ashurst Turner Gilbert [q. v.]; rendered blind as a child by scarlet fever; with William Hanks Levy founded 'Association for Promoting the General Welfare of the Blind'; assisted Levy in writing 'Blindness and the Blind,' 1872.
                                             [xxi. 324]

GILBERT, SIR GEOFFREY or JEFFRAY (1674-1726), judge; barrister, Inner Temple, 1698; chief baron of Irish exchequer, 1715-22; resisted claim to jurisdiction of the Irish parliament in case of Annesley v. Sherlock, 1718; English judge of exchequer, 1722; knighted, 1725; a commissioner of great seal, 1725; his 'Law of Uses and Trusts' (1734), edited by Sugden, 1811, and 'Treatise of Tenures' (1754), by Watkins and Vidal, 1824; his 'History and Practice of Civil Actions in the Court of Common Pleas' (1737), praised by Blackstone.
                                             [xxi. 325]

GILBERT, GEORGE (1555-1583), founder (with Thomas Pound of Belmont) of the 'Catholic Association,' 1579; became a jesuit; died at Rome.   [xxi. 326]

GILBERT, SIR HUMPHREY (1539 ?-1583), navigator; step-brother of Ralegh; educated at Eton and Oxford; served under Sir Henry Sidney in Ireland; given charge of Munster, 1569; knighted, 1570; M.P., Plymouth, 1571; rebuked in parliament by Peter Wentworth [q. v.]; unsuccessful against the Spaniards in Zeeland, 1572; composed in retirement his 'Discourse of a Discouery for a New Passage to Cataia' (ed. G. Gascoigne, 1576); obtained charter for discovery and plantation, 1578; failed in his first voyage, 1579; served under Perrot against the Spanish ships off Munster, 1579; left Plymouth with five ships to colonise Newfoundland, 1583; landed at harbour of St. John (5 Aug. 1583) and there founded the first British colony in North America; after a voyage of discovery along the south coast sailed for England (1 Sept.), but was lost in a storm off the Southern Azores; his scheme for the erection in London of an 'Achademy' to educate royal wards and others printed by Dr. Furnivall, 1869.   [xxi. 327]

GILBERT, JOHN (fl. 1680), theological writer; M.A. Hart Hall, Oxford, 1680; published 'Answer to the Bishop of Condom (now of Meaux), his Exposition of the Catholic Faith,' 1686.   [xxi. 330]

GILBERT, JOHN (1693-1761), archbishop of York; B.A. Trinity College, Oxford, 1713; M.A. Merton College, 1718; prebendary (1723), sub-dean (1724-6) and dean (1726) of Exeter; LL.D. Lambeth, 1724; bishop of Llandaff, 1740-9, of Salisbury, 1749; clerk of the closet, 1750; archbishop of York, 1757-61; began the practice of laying hands on each candidate at confirmation.   [xxi. 330]

GILBERT, SIR JOHN (1817-1897), historical painter and draughtsman on wood; entered estate agents' office in city of London, 1833; exhibited two drawings of historical subjects at Suffolk Street, 1836, and two oil-paintings at British Institution, 1837; exhibited at Royal Academy, 1838-51, and from 1867; worked at book illustration, illustrating most of the English poets and other works, including Howard Staunton's edition of Shakespeare, 1856-60; joined staff of 'Illustrated London News,' 1842, as draughtsman on wood, and contributed drawings regularly to 'London Journal,' from 1845; president of Old Water-colour Society, 1871-97; knighted, 1872; R.A., 1876; made presents of collections of his pictures to municipal galleries of London, Birmingham, Liverpool, and Manchester, 1893.   [Suppl. ii. 275]

GILBERT, JOHN GRAHAM- (1794-1866). [See GRAHAM-GILBERT.]

GILBERT, SIR JOHN THOMAS (1829-1898), Irish historian and antiquary; joint honorary secretary to Irish Celtic and Archæological Society, 1855; secretary of Public Record Office, Dublin, 1867-75; vice-president of Royal Irish Academy; LL.D. Royal University, 1892; knighted, 1897. His works include 'Historical Essays on Ireland,' 1851, 'History of the City of Dublin,' 1854-9, 'History of the Viceroys of Ireland,' 1865, and 'Contemporary History of Affairs in Ireland, 1641-1652,' 1879-1880.   [Suppl. ii. 277]

GILBERT, JOSEPH (1779-1852), congregational divine; classical tutor at Rotherham College; minister at Sheffield and Nottingham, 1828-51; published life of

Dr. Edward Williams (1750–1813) [q. v.], 1825, a defence of Williams's hypothesis of origin of evil, 1808, and a work on the atonement, 1836. [xxi. 331]

GILBERT, JOSEPH FRANCIS (1792–1855), painter; exhibited at the Royal Academy after 1813. [xxi. 331]

GILBERT, MARIE DOLORES ELIZA ROSANNA (1818–1861), adventuress; known by her stage name LOLA MONTEZ; daughter of military officer; married Captain Thomas James, 1837; divorced, 1842; appeared at Her Majesty's Theatre, London, as a dancer, 1843, pretending to be a native of Spain; highly successful at Dresden, Berlin, Warsaw, St. Petersburg, and Paris; became mistress of Ludwig I of Bavaria, who created her Baronne de Rosenthal and Comtesse de Lansfeld, 1847; exercised full control over government of Bavaria, 1847–8; banished, owing to Austrian and jesuit influence, 1848; married in England George Trafford Heald, 1849; fled with him to Spain to avoid bigamy proceedings; appeared at New York and Philadelphia, 1852, in Ware's 'Lola Montez in Bavaria'; married P. P. Hull of the 'San Francisco Whig' in California, 1853; played at Sydney and Melbourne, 1855; horsewhipped the editor of the 'Ballarat Times,' 1856; played and lectured at New York, 1857–8, and published 'The Art of Beauty'; devoted herself to helping fallen women; died at Asteria, New York. [xxi. 331]

GILBERT, NICOLAS ALAIN (1762–1821), Roman catholic divine; born at St. Malo; established mission at Whitby; published theological works. [xxi. 333]

GILBERT, RICHARD (1794–1852), printer and compiler, of St. John's Square, Clerkenwell. [xxi. 334]

GILBERT, SAMUEL (d. 1692?), floriculturist; son-in-law of John Rea [q. v.]; rector of Quatt, Shropshire; published 'Florist's Vade-mecum and Gardener's Almanack,' 1683. [xxi. 334]

GILBERT, THOMAS (1610–1673), ejected minister; rector of Cheadle; when ejected from vicarage of Ealing emigrated to New England; pastor of Topsfield, Massachusetts; buried at Charlestown. [xxi. 335]

GILBERT, THOMAS (1613–1694), ejected minister; M.A. St. Edmund Hall, Oxford, 1638; vicar of Upper Winchendon, and c. 1644, St. Lawrence, Reading; rector of Edgmond; took the covenant; nicknamed 'bishop of Shropshire'; lost Edgmond at Restoration; ejected from Winchendon, 1662; preached in family of Lord Wharton; wrote Latin and English poems. [xxi. 335]

GILBERT, THOMAS (1720–1798), poor-law reformer; barrister, Inner Temple, 1744; treasurer, 1789; advised Bridgewater to engage James Brindley [q. v.], whose canals he promoted; M.P., Newcastle-under-Lyme, 1763–8, Lichfield, 1768–95; carried two poor-law measures, 1782; his poor-law bill of 1787 criticised by Sir Henry Bate Dudley; chairman of committees, 1784; carried measures for reform of houses of correction and improvement of highways, and an act for facilitating clerical residence by loans from Queen Anne's Bounty ('Gilbert's Act'); his propositions for helping friendly societies by parochial grants embodied in act of 1793; edited 'Collection of Pamphlets concerning the Poor,' 1787. [xxi. 336]

GILBERT, SIR WALTER RALEIGH (1785–1853), lieutenant-general; lieutenant, 15th Bengal native infantry, 1803; served under Macdonald at Ally Ghur, Delhi, Agra, Laswarrie, and siege of Bhurtpore; colonel, 1832; lieutenant-general, 1851; commanded division in Sikh wars; captured remnant of enemy's force after Goojerat, 1849; G.C.B. and member of council of India, 1850; created baronet, 1851. [xxi. 337]

GILBERT, WILLIAM (1540–1603), physician to Queen Elizabeth and James I; fellow of St. John's College, Cambridge, 1561; M.A., 1564; M.D., 1569; president of College of Physicians, 1600; declared the earth to be a magnet in his 'De Magnete, Magneticisque Corporibus' (1600), the first great scientific book published in England. [xxi. 338]

GILBERT, WILLIAM (1760?–1825?), poet; born in Antigua; educated for the bar; in asylum at Bristol, 1787–8; friend of Coleridge and Southey; published 'The Hurricane: a Theosophical and Western Eclogue,' 1796. [Suppl. ii. 278]

GILBERT, WILLIAM (1804–1890), author; midshipman in East India Company's service, 1818–21; studied at Guy's Hospital, 1825; for short period assistant-surgeon in navy; published novels, many of which dealt with the contrast between the lots of rich and poor; some of his works illustrated by his son, Mr. William Schwenck Gilbert. [Suppl. ii. 279]

GILBURNE or **GILBORNE**, SAMUEL (*fl.* 1605), actor; mentioned as one of Shakespeare's fellow-actors in the Shakespeare First Folio, 1623. [xxi. 338]

GILBY, ANTHONY (d. 1585), puritan divine; M.A. Christ's College, Cambridge, 1535; entertained Foxe at Frankfort; a pastor of the English congregation at Geneva, 1555; assisted in Geneva translation of the bible; presented by Huntingdon to living of Ashby-de-la-Zouch before 1564; his prosecution for nonconformity ordered by Parker, 1571; translated commentaries of Calvin and Beza, and published commentaries on Micah and Malachi and controversial works. [xxi. 339]

GILBY, GODDARD (*fl.* 1561), translator; son of Anthony Gilby [q. v.]; translated Cicero's 'Epistle to Quintus,' 1561, and Calvin's 'Admonition against Judicial Astrology.' [xxi. 339]

GILBY, WILLIAM HALL (d. 1821?), geologist; M.D. Edinburgh, 1815; president of Royal Society of Medicine; contributed geological papers to 'Edinburgh Philosophical Journal.' [xxi. 340]

GILCHRIST, ALEXANDER (1828–1861), biographer; his 'Life of Etty' published, 1855, and that of Blake, 1863. [xxi. 340]

GILCHRIST, ANNE (1828–1885), author; wife of Alexander Gilchrist [q. v.]; finished Alexander Gilchrist's 'Life of Blake,' prefixing a memoir of the author; published 'Life of Mary Lamb,' 1883, essays on Walt Whitman's poetry, and a translation of Hugo's 'Légende des Siècles,' 1884. [xxi. 340]

GILCHRIST, EBENEZER (1707–1774), physician; graduated at Rheims; practised at Dumfries; published 'Use of Sea Voyages in Medicine,' 1756, and 'Essays, Physical and Literary,' 1770. [xxi. 341]

GILCHRIST, JAMES (d. 1777), naval captain; was serving on the Namur when lost, 1749; in command of the Experiment captured sixteen French ships, 1755; fought off Minorca, 1756; captured the Emeraude and two privateers, 1757; severely wounded in taking the Danae, 1759. [xxi. 341]

GILCHRIST, JOHN BORTHWICK (1759–1841), orientalist; educated at Heriot's Hospital, Edinburgh; LL.D. Edinburgh, 1804; surgeon under East India Company at Calcutta, 1794; acquired knowledge of Hindustani, Sanscrit, and Persian; as principal of Fort William College, 1800–4, superintended the production by vernacular scholars of Urdu and Hindi text-books for Europeans; retired from service, 1809; professor of Hindustani at Oriental Institution, Leicester Square, 1818–26; published 'Hindustani Dictionary,' 1787–90, 'Hindustani Grammar,' 1796, 'Dialogues, English and Hindustani,' 1804, and 'British Indian Monitor,' 1806–8, also Persian text-books. [xxi. 342]

GILCHRIST, OCTAVIUS GRAHAM (1779–1823), antiquary; F.S.A., 1803; edited poems of Richard Corbet [q. v.], 1807; published (1808) 'Examination of the Charges maintained by Malone, Chalmers, and others of Ben Jonson's Enmity towards Shakespeare'; had controversies with Stephen Jones, editor of 'Biographia Dramatica,' and with William Lisle Bowles [q. v.] [xxi. 344]

GILDAS (516?–570?), British historian; went to Brittany, c. 550, and is said to have founded monastery of Ruys, near Vannes; a popular Breton saint; called by Alcuin 'the wisest of the Bretons'; his 'De Excidio Britanniæ' first printed by Polydore Vergil, 1525, the first English version being that of Habington, 1638. [xxi. 344]

GILDAS minor or NENNIUS (*fl.* 796). [See NENNIUS.]

GILDERDALE, JOHN (d. 1864), divine; M.A. St. Catharine's Hall, Cambridge, 1830; B.D., 1853; incumbent of Walthamstow and principal of Forest School; published 'Essay on Natural Religion and Revelation,' 1837. [xxi. 346]

GILDON, CHARLES (1665–1724), author; advocated deism in an edition of the works of Charles Blount (1654–1693) [q. v.]; defended orthodoxy in 'Deist's Manual,'

1705 ; attacked Pope as 'Sawney Dapper,' and was included by him in 'The Dunciad'; published 'Life and Adventures of Defoe,' five plays, and an edition, with continuation, of Langbaine's 'Dramatic Poets,' 1699. [xxi. 347]

GILES, FRANCIS (1787–1847), civil engineer ; engaged in surveying under Rennie ; constructed works on South-Western railway and Newcastle and Carlisle railway ; constructed the Warwick bridge, Cumberland ; long opposed as expert railway enterprises of George Stephenson. [xxi. 347]

GILES, JAMES (1801–1870), landscape-painter ; at thirteen maintained mother and sister by painting ; R.S.A., 1829 ; his best works angling pictures. [xxi. 348]

GILES, JOHN ALLEN (1808–1884), editor and translator ; educated at Charterhouse ; M.A. Corpus Christi College, Oxford, 1831 ; fellow, 1832 ; double first and Vinerian scholar ; D.C.L., 1838 ; head-master of the City of London School, 1836–40 ; obliged by Bishop Wilberforce to suppress his 'Christian Records,' 1854 ; imprisoned for making a false entry in Bampton marriage register to shield one of his servants, 1855 ; vicar of Sutton, 1867–84 ; published 'Patres Ecclesiæ Anglicanæ' (1837–43), edited works for Caxton Society (1845–54) ; translated for Bohn Matthew Paris, Bæda's 'Ecclesiastical History,' and the 'Saxon Chronicle' ; published also life of Becket, 1845, and of King Alfred, 1848, and histories of Bampton and Witney. [xxi. 348]

GILES, NATHANIEL (d. 1634), musical composer ; organist at St. George's, Windsor, 1595 ; master of the children of the Chapel Royal, 1597 ; Mus. Doc. Oxford, 1622 ; published 'Lesson of Descant of thirtie-eighte Proportions' on the plain-song, 'Miserere' ; his service in C and anthem, 'O give thanks,' printed in Barnard's collection. [xxi. 349]

GILFILLAN, GEORGE (1813–1878), author ; son of Samuel Gilfillan [q. v.] ; friend of Thomas Aird [q. v.], De Quincey, and Carlyle ; educated at Glasgow College ; united presbyterian minister of the School-Wynd Church, Dundee, 1836–78 ; twice accused of heresy ; helped Sydney Dobell [q. v.] and Alexander Smith [q. v.] ; published works, including 'Hades,' a sermon, 1843, 'Gallery of Literary Portraits,' 'Alpha and Omega,' 1850, 'Bards of the Bible,' 'History of a Man,' 1856, editions of poets with lives, 1853–60 ; the Gilfillan Testimonial Trust formed for founding scholarships from a subscription raised in his honour, 1877–8. [xxi. 350]

GILFILLAN, JAMES (1797–1874), Scottish divine ; brother of George Gilfillan [q. v.] ; ordained in Stirling secession congregation, 1822 ; LL.D. Glasgow, 1866 ; published 'The Sabbath, viewed in the Light of Reason, Revelation, and History,' 1861. [xxi. 351]

GILFILLAN, ROBERT (1798–1850), poet ; his 'Peter M'Craw' praised in 'Noctes Ambrosianæ' ; published, 1831, 'Original Songs' (set by Peter M'Leod). [xxi. 352]

GILFILLAN, SAMUEL (1762–1826), secession minister of Comrie, Strathearn, Perthshire ; educated at Glasgow ; his wife, Rachel Barlas, known as 'the star of the north' ; published 'Discourses on the Dignity, Grace, and Operations of the Holy Spirit,' 1826. [xxi. 352]

GILL, ALEXANDER, the elder (1565–1635), high-master of St. Paul's School ; M.A. Corpus Christi College, Oxford, 1589 ; high-master of St. Paul's School, 1608–35, Milton being one of his pupils ; published 'Logonomia Anglica,' 1619. [xxi. 353]

GILL, ALEXANDER, the younger (1597–1642), high-master of St. Paul's, 1635–9 ; son of Alexander Gill the elder [q. v.] ; M.A. Wadham College, Oxford, 1619 ; D.D. Trinity College, Oxford, 1637 ; his Latin verses praised by Milton ; sentenced to imprisonment, fine, and loss of his ears for speaking disrespectfully of Charles I and drinking a health to Buckingham's assassin, 1628 ; pardoned, 1630 ; dismissed for severity from St. Paul's ; attacked Ben Jonson's 'Magnetick Lady.' [xxi. 353]

GILL, JOHN (1697–1771), baptist minister ; Wednesday-evening lecturer in Great Eastcheap, 1729–56 ; D.D. Aberdeen, 1748 ; published works, including 'Exposition of the Holy Scriptures,' 1746–8, 1766, and 'Dissertation on the Antiquity of the Hebrew Language,' 1767. [xxi. 355]

GILL, WILLIAM JOHN (1843–1882), captain of royal engineers ; served in India, 1869–71 ; travelled with Valentine Baker in Persia, 1873, making a valuable survey ; with E. Colborne Baker in Szechuen, China, and with Mr. Mesny in Eastern Thibet, making a large map and valuable observations, for which the Geographical Society's gold medal was awarded ; assistant commissioner for delimiting Asiatic boundary of Russia and Turkey, 1879 ; travelled in country between Tunis and Egypt, 1881 ; with Professor Palmer and Lieutenant Charrington murdered by Bedouins in the desert when on his way as intelligence officer to cut the telegraph wire from Cairo to Constantinople to prevent its use by Arabi Pasha. [xxi. 355]

GILLAN, ROBERT (1800–1879), Scottish divine ; studied at Edinburgh High School and University ; minister of St. John's, Glasgow, 1847–61, and of Inchinnan, Renfrewshire, 1861–79 ; D.D. Glasgow, 1853 ; moderator of the general assembly, 1873 ; lectured on pastoral theology at four Scottish universities. [xxi. 357]

GILLE or **GILLEBERT** (fl. 1105–1145), bishop of Limerick ; termed by Keating GIOLLA EASBOG ; friend and correspondent of Anselm, who induced him to attempt the introduction into Ireland of the Roman liturgy ; presided over the synod of Rathbreasail as papal legate, about 1111. [xxi. 358]

GILLESPIE, GEORGE (1613–1648), Scottish divine ; Milton's 'Galasp' ; M.A. St. Andrews, 1629 ; issued anonymously 'Dispute against the English Popish Ceremonies obtruded upon the Church of Scotland,' 1637 ; presented to Wemyss, Fifeshire, 1638, and ordained non-episcopally ; preached before Charles I at Holyrood, 1641 ; pensioned, 1641 ; translated to Greyfriars, Edinburgh, 1642 ; the youngest member of the Westminster Assembly, 1643, where he opposed Selden's views on church government ; introduced the directory to Edinburgh assembly, 1645 ; presented confession of faith to general assembly, 1647 ; moderator, 1648 ; elected to the high church of Edinburgh, 1648 ; his tombstone at Kirkcaldy broken by the hangman by order of the committee of estates, 1661 ; published theological works. [xxi. 359]

GILLESPIE, JAMES (1726–1797), founder of hospital at Edinburgh ; owned a snuff-mill at Colinton ; with his younger brother carried on business in High Street, Edinburgh ; left bequests for foundation of a hospital for old people and a school. [xxi. 361]

GILLESPIE, PATRICK (1617–1675), principal of Glasgow University ; brother of George Gillespie [q. v.] ; graduated at St. Andrews, 1635 ; minister at Kirkcaldy, 1642, of the High Church, Glasgow, 1648 ; opposed the 'engagement' to rescue Charles I ; after Dunbar, raised the 'Westland Force' and drew up its 'Remonstrance' condemning the treaty with Charles II, and making grave charges against the Scottish authorities, 1650 ; deposed from ministry for protesting against legality of the resolutions making terms with 'malignants,' 1651 ; leader of the 'protesters,' 1651 ; made principal of Glasgow University by Cromwell, 1652 ; granted 'Gillespie's Charter,' 1653, empowering 'protesters' to remodel the church in their own interest ; again visited London ; became intimate with Lambert and Fleetwood ; obtained revenues for his university from church property ; deprived and (1661) imprisoned. [xxi. 361]

GILLESPIE, SIR ROBERT ROLLO (1766–1814), major-general ; as adjutant-general in San Domingo, 1796, was attacked by eight assassins and killed six ; left Jamaica in command of his regiment, 1801 ; rescued the 69th at Vellore, 1806 ; commanded cavalry against Runjeet Singh, 1809 ; as brigadier headed advance of Auchmuty's Java expedition, directing attack on Cornelis, 1811 ; deposed sultan of Palembang, Sumatra, 1812 ; defended Javanese confederacy at Yodhyakarta ; major-general, 1812 ; killed in attack on Kalunga, Nepaul ; buried at Meerut ; named K.C.B., 1815. [xxi. 363]

GILLESPIE, THOMAS (1708–1774), founder of the relief church ; studied at Edinburgh University ; minister of Carnock, near Dunfermline, 1741 ; deposed by general assembly for refusing to ordain Andrew Richardson, 1752 ; for six and a half years stood alone preaching on the highway and at Dunfermline ; joined by Thomas Boston the younger [q. v.], and by the congregation of Colinsburgh ; formed a presbytery, 1761 ; published 'Practical Treatise on Temptation,' 1774. [xxi. 365]

GILLESPIE, THOMAS (1777–1844), professor at St. Andrews; distinguished at Edinburgh University; LL.D. Glasgow, 1824; professor of humanity at St. Andrews, 1836; contributed to 'Blackwood,' 'Constable's Miscellany,' and 'Tales of the Borders.' [xxi. 366]

GILLESPIE, WILLIAM (1776–1825), poet; minister of Kells, 1800; confined to Kirkcudbrightshire for praying for Queen Caroline, 1820; published 'The Progress of Refinement and other Poems,' 1805, and 'Consolation, and other Poems,' 1815. [xxi. 367]

GILLIES, ADAM, LORD GILLIES (1760–1842), Scottish judge; sheriff-depute of Kincardineshire, 1806; judge, 1811; lord of justiciary, 1812–37; lord commissioner of the jury court, 1816; judge of exchequer, 1837.
[xxi. 367]

GILLIES, JOHN (1712–1796), theological writer; minister of the College Church, Glasgow, from 1742; published 'Historical Collections relating to the Success of the Gospel,' 1754 (supplemented, 1761 and 1780), and 'Life of George Whitefield,' 1772. [xxi. 367]

GILLIES, JOHN (1747–1836), historian and classic; brother of Adam, lord Gillies [q. v.]; educated at Brechin and Glasgow University; LL.D., 1784; F.R.S. and F.S.A.; historiographer royal of Scotland, 1793; published 'History of Greece,' 1786, 'History of the World from Alexander to Augustus,' 1807, 'View of the Reign of Frederick II of Prussia,' 1789, and translations from Aristotle, Lysias, and Isocrates. [xxi. 368]

GILLIES, MARGARET (1803–1887), painter; educated by her uncle Adam, lord Gillies [q. v.]; painted miniatures of Wordsworth and Dickens, and exhibited portraits at Royal Academy; studied at Paris under Hendrik and Ary Scheffer; associate of the Old Society of Painters in Water-colours, 1852–87. [xxi. 368]

GILLIES, ROBERT PEARSE (1788–1858), autobiographer; a member of the Ballantyne circle; the Kemperhausen of Christopher North's 'Noctes Ambrosianæ'; friend of Scott and Wordsworth; contributed to 'Blackwood' translations from German; in constant pecuniary distress; edited 'Foreign Quarterly,' to which Scott, Southey, and Maguire contributed; published, besides 'Memoirs of a Literary Veteran' (1851, 3 vols.), several volumes of poems, prose romance, and translations from the German. [xxi. 369]

GILLILAND, THOMAS (*fl.* 1804–1816), author; said to have haunted the green-room of Drury Lane as 'a spy upon the private conduct of public men'; published 'The Dramatic Mirror,' 1808, and satirical pamphlets.
[xxi. 370]

GILLING, ISAAC (1662 ?–1725), presbyterian minister; relative of John Fox (1693–1763) [q. v.], his biographer; received presbyterian ordination, 1687; ministered at Axminster, Silverton, and Newton Abbot; active member of Exeter assembly for union of presbyterians and independents, 1691; excluded for siding against subscription; published 'Qualifications and Duties of Ministers,' 1708, and 'Life of George Trosse,' 1715. [xxi. 371]

GILLINGWATER, EDMUND (1735 ?–1813), topographer; published 'Essay on Parish Workhouses,' 1786, 'Historical Account of Lowestoft,' 1790, and 'Historical Account of St. Edmund's Bury,' 1804. [xxi. 371]

GILLIS, JAMES (1802–1864), Roman catholic prelate; born at Montreal; ordained at Aquhorties, 1827; founded St. Margaret's Convent, Edinburgh, the first Scottish post-Reformation religious house, 1835; bishop of Limyra *in partibus*, 1838; vicar-apostolic of eastern Scotland, 1852; pronounced panegyric on Joan of Arc at Orleans, 1857, and was presented with the heart of Henry II of England; published pamphlets. [xxi. 372]

GILLOTT, JOSEPH (1799–1873), steel-pen maker of Birmingham; for some time made pens at Birmingham with aid only of a woman, selling them at a shilling each to a stationer; finally employed 450 hands; his collection of pictures, rich in Turners and Ettys, sold for 170,000*l*., and his violins for 4,000*l*. [xxi. 372]

GILLOW, JOHN (1753–1828), president of Ushaw College, 1811–28; professor at Douay; for twenty years in charge of the York mission. [xxi. 373]

GILLOW, THOMAS (1769–1857), Roman catholic divine; at the Revolution escaped from Douay to Crook

Hall, Durham; chaplain at Callaly Castle, Northumberland; missioner at North Shields, 1821–57. [xxi. 374]

GILLRAY, JAMES (1757–1815), caricaturist; apprenticed to a letter-engraver; studied at Royal Academy; said to have etched a caricature at twelve; treated at first anonymously social subjects, turning to political themes after 1780; executed fifteen hundred pieces, mostly issued by Miss Humphrey at 29 St. James's Street, Piccadilly, London, where he lived; imbecile after 1811. Among his caricatures were many ridiculing the habits of the royal family, such as 'Wife or no Wife,' 1788, 'Ancient Music,' 1787, 'Anti-Saccharites,' 1792, 'Temperance Enjoying a Frugal Meal,' 1792, 'A Voluptuary under the Horrors of Digestion,' 1792, and 'Sin, Death, and the Devil,' 1792. He depicted Pitt in 'The Vulture of the Constitution,' 1789, 'God save the King,' 1795, and 'Disciples Catching the Mantle,' 1808; Fox in 'Spouting,' 1792, 'Blue and Buff Charity,' 1793, and 'The Worn-out Patriot,' 1800; Sheridan and Burke in 'The Dagger Scene,' 1792, and Fox, Sheridan, and leading radicals in 'Doublures of Characters' for 'Anti-Jacobin,' 1798 (?). Other caricatures dealt with Napoleon, Nelson, and the Revolution. His serious work included a profile of Arne after Bartolozzi, two portraits of Pitt, and the miniature of himself in the National Portrait Gallery. [xxi. 374]

GILLY, WILLIAM STEPHEN (1789–1855), divine; educated at Christ's Hospital, Caius College, and St. Catharine Hall, Cambridge; M.A., 1817; D.D., 1833; vicar of North Fambridge, Essex, 1817; perpetual curate of St. Margaret, Durham, 1827; vicar of Norham, 1831; canon of Durham, 1853; published works describing his visits to the Vaudois, 'The Peasantry of the Border: an appeal,' 1841, 'Our Protestant Forefathers,' 1835, and other writings. [xxi. 377]

GILMOUR, SIR JOHN (*d.* 1671), Scottish judge; counsel for Montrose, 1641; lord president of the court of session, 1661; privy councillor and lord of the articles; defended Argyll and helped to overthrow Middleton, 1663.
[xxi. 377]

GILPIN, BERNARD (1517–1583), the 'Apostle of the North'; fellow of Queen's College, Oxford; M.A., 1542; B.D., 1549; one of the first elected to Wolsey's foundation; disputed on the Romanist side with John Hooper and Peter Martyr; denounced spoliation of church property in a sermon before Edward VI, 1552; rector of Easington and (1556) archdeacon of Durham; denounced for heresy, but defended by Bishop Tunstall, and promoted to benefice of Houghton-le-Spring; on his way to answer a second charge of heresy when Queen Mary died; refused see of Carlisle, 1559, and provostship of Queen's College, Oxford, 1560; made annual progresses through neglected parts of Northumberland and Yorkshire, preaching and relieving the inhabitants; founded grammar school at Houghton, and supported some of the scholars at his own cost; interceded for rebels of 1569. [xxi. 378]

GILPIN, GEORGE 'the Elder' (1514 ?–1602), diplomatist and translator; elder brother of Bernard Gilpin [q. v.]; agent of English government in Zeeland, and secretary to Gresham; published 'The Beehive of the Romish Church' (translation of St. Aldegonde's 'Apiarium Romanum'), 1571. [xxi. 380]

GILPIN, RANDOLPH (*d.* 1661), divine; educated at Eton; M.A. King's College, Cambridge, 1618; chaplain to the Rochelle expedition and rector of Barningham, Suffolk, 1628; D.D., 1660; rector of Worlingham, 1661; published 'Liturgica Sacra,' 1657. [xxi. 380]

GILPIN, RICHARD (1625–1700), nonconformist divine and physician; M.A. Edinburgh, 1646; as rector of Greystoke, 1653–61, organised his parish on the congregational model, and formed voluntary association of Cumberland and Westmoreland churches; refused see of Carlisle, 1660; removed to Newcastle, 1662, where he preached in defiance of the statutes against dissenters, and practised as a physician; M.D. Leyden, 1676; published 'Dæmonologia sacra; a Treatise of Satan's Temptations,' 1677.
[xxi. 381]

GILPIN, SAWREY (1733–1807), animal painter; worked under Samuel Scott (1710 ?–1772) [q. v.]; employed by the Duke of Cumberland to draw from his stud; exhibited at Incorporated Society of Artists, 1762–83, becoming president, 1774; exhibited at Royal Academy from 1786; R.A., 1797; excelled as a painter of horses.
[xxi. 382]

GILPIN, WILLIAM (1724–1804), author : descendant of Bernard Gilpin [q. v.], and brother of Sawrey Gilpin [q. v.]; M.A. Queen's College, Oxford, 1748 ; kept school at Cheam, Surrey, Sidmouth, Redesdale, and the historian Mitford being among his pupils; an advanced educationalist ; vicar of Boldre, 1777 ; built a new poorhouse and endowed school at Boldre ; published lives of Bernard Gilpin, 1753, Latimer, 1755, Wycliffe, 1765, Cranmer, 1784, and other reformers, 'Essay on Prints,' 1768, 'Lectures on the Church Catechism,' 1779, 'Exposition of the New Testament,' 1790, and five works illustrated by aquatint drawings, describing his summer tours. [xxi. 383]

GILPIN, WILLIAM SAWREY (1762–1843), watercolour painter and landscape gardener; son of Sawrey Gilpin [q. v.]; first president of the Old Water-colour Society, 1804–6 ; seceded, 1813 ; laid out gardens at Danesfield, Enniskillen Castle, and other seats ; published 'Practical Hints for Landscape Gardening,' 1832. [xxi. 385]

GINKEL, FREDERICK CHRISTIAN, second EARL OF ATHLONE (1668–1719), general; served under William III and Anne ; lieutenant-general of Dutch cavalry ; taken prisoner, 1710. [xxi. 387]

GINKEL, GODERT DE, first EARL OF ATHLONE (1630–1703), general ; native of Utrecht ; present at Senef, 1674 ; accompanied William of Orange to England, 1688 ; distinguished at the Boyne and first siege of Limerick, 1690 ; left in command in Ireland on departure of William III ; captured Athlone, won the victory of Aughrim, and took Limerick, 1691 ; created Baron of Aughrim and Earl of Athlone and thanked by the speaker, 1692 ; fought at Steinkirk, 1692, and Landen, 1693 ; commanded Dutch horse at recapture of Namur, 1695, and assisted in surprise of Givet, 1696 ; second in command to Marlborough, 1702 ; died at Utrecht. [xxi. 385]

GIPPS, SIR GEORGE (1791–1847), colonial governor; entered royal engineers, 1809 ; wounded in assault on Badajoz, 1812 ; superintended fortifications of Ostend, 1815 ; while in West Indies, 1824–9, sent home elaborate reports ; private secretary to Lord Auckland, 1834 ; joint-commissioner in Canada, 1835–7 ; governor of New South Wales, 1838–46 ; opened up the country and protected the aborigines, but became unpopular, owing to his arbitrary policy and insistence on the right of the crown to territorial revenue. [xxi. 387]

GIPPS, SIR RICHARD (1659–1708), master of the revels at Gray's Inn, 1682 ; student, 1676 ; knighted by Charles II ; made collections for history of Suffolk. [xxi. 389]

GIPPS, THOMAS (d. 1709), rector of Bury, Lancashire, 1674–1709 ; educated at St. Paul's School ; fellow of Trinity College, Cambridge ; M.A., 1662 ; carried on a controversy with James Owen of Oswestry regarding the presbyterian interpretation of Acts vi. 3. [xxi. 389]

GIRALDUS DE BARRI, called CAMBRENSIS (1146 ?–1220 ?), topographer ; native of Pembrokeshire and son of Nesta, a Welsh princess : lectured on the Trivium at Paris ; as archdeacon of Brecknock, 1172, procured excommunication of bishop of St. Asaph for trespassing on rights of St. David's ; nominated to see of St. David's, 1176, but rejected by Henry II as a Welshman of royal blood ; commissary to the bishop of St. David's, 1180 ; accompanied Prince John to Ireland, 1184, where he refused several sees ; assisted Archbishop Baldwin to preach the crusade in Wales, 1188 ; sent to keep the peace there on death of Henry II ; refused sees of Bangor and Llandaff, 1190–1 ; led a student's life at Lincoln, 1192–8 ; elected to see of St. David's, 1198 ; went to Rome, but failed to obtain metropolitan dignity ; received support from the Welsh princes, but was outlawed and disowned by the chapter, 1202 ; fied abroad and again reached Rome ; imprisoned at Châtillon ; gave way to Henlaw, the newly elected bishop of St. David's, and was reconciled to the king and archbishop, receiving a pension and the expenses of his suit : buried at St. David's. His works (edited by J. S. Brewer and J. F. Dimock, 1861–77) include 'Topographia Hibernica,' 'Expugnatio Hibernica,' 'Itinerarium Cambriæ,' 'Gemma Ecclesiastica,' 'De Rebus a se gestis,' and lives of St. Hugh of Lincoln, St. David, and others. [xxi. 389]

GIRARDUS CORNUBIENSIS (fl. 1350 ?), author of 'De gestis Britonum' and 'De gestis Regum West-Saxonum.' [xxi. 393]

GIRAUD, HERBERT JOHN (1817–1888), physician ; chemist and botanist ; M.D. Edinburgh, 1840 ; principal of Grant Medical College, Bombay ; chief medical officer of Sir Jamsetjee Jeejeebhoy's Hospital, deputy-inspector-general and (1863) dean of faculty of medicine, Bombay University ; author of botanical and chemical papers. [xxi. 393]

GIRDLESTONE, CHARLES (1797–1881), biblical commentator ; B.A. Wadham College, Oxford, 1818 ; fellow of Balliol, 1818 ; M.A., 1821 ; vicar of Sedgley, Staffordshire, 1826, working there during the cholera epidemic of 1832 ; incumbent of Alderley, 1837 ; rector of Kingswinford, 1846–77, where he faced a second cholera epidemic ; published commentary on New Testament, 1832-5, and Old Testament, 1842. [xxi. 394]

GIRDLESTONE, EDWARD (1805–1884), canon of Bristol ; brother of Charles Girdlestone [q. v.] ; scholar of Balliol College, Oxford, 1823 ; M.A., 1829 ; vicar of Deane, 1830 ; canon of Bristol, 1854 ; vicar of Wapley, Gloucestershire, 1858, of Halberton, Devonshire, 1862, of Olveston, Gloucestershire, 1872 ; called 'the Agricultural Labourers' Friend' ; published controversial works. [xxi. 395]

GIRDLESTONE, JOHN LANG (1763–1825), classical translator ; fellow of Caius College, Cambridge ; M.A., 1789 ; master of Beccles School ; translator of Pindar, 1810. [xxi. 395]

GIRDLESTONE, THOMAS (1758–1822), translator of Anacreon ; army doctor at Minorca and in India ; practised thirty-seven years at Great Yarmouth ; translated Anacreon, 1803 ; published medical essays and a work to prove that Arthur Lee wrote 'Junius,' 1813. [xxi. 396]

GIRLING, MARY ANNE (1827–1886), founder of 'The People of God' sect ; daughter of one Clouting, a Suffolk farmer ; married George Stanton Girling ; proclaimed herself to be a new incarnation of the Deity, 1864 ; held meetings in Battersea, 1870 ; her community transferred to New Forest Lodge, purchased for them by Miss Wood, 1872 ; ejected with her followers, 1873 ; obtained Tiptoe Farm, Hordle, Hampshire, 1879, whence she issued 'The Close of the Dispensation,' 1883, signed 'Jesus First and Last.' [xxi. 396]

GIRTIN, THOMAS (1775–1802), water-colour painter ; imprisoned for refusing to serve out his indentures under Edward Dayes [q. v.] ; made a sketching tour with Turner, 1793 ; first exhibited at Royal Academy, 1794 ; sent to the Royal Academy ten drawings, including views of York and St. Cuthbert's, Holy Island, 1797 ; contributed fifteen topographical sketches to J. Walker's 'Itinerary' ; member of the first London sketching-society ; exhibited 'Bolton Bridge,' an oil-painting, 1801 ; drew and etched for Lord Essex twenty sketches of Paris, 1802 and panorama of London from south side of Blackfriar's Bridge ; founder of modern water-colour painting as distinct from 'tinting' ; examples of his work preserved in the British Museum and at South Kensington. [xxi. 397]

GISA or **GISO**, sometimes 'Gila' (d. 1088), bishop of Wells ; native of diocese of Liège ; chaplain of Edward the Confessor ; bishop of Wells, 1060 ; on return from Rome with Tostig and Archbishop Ealdred, robbed by brigands ; complained in his 'Historiola' of Harold's treatment ; recovered manor of Winsham from William I : made his canons conform to Metz rule and live together in Lotharingian fashion. [xxi. 399]

GISBORNE, JOHN (1770–1851), poet ; educated at Harrow ; B.A. St. John's College, Cambridge, 1792 ; called the 'Man of Prayer' ; published 'The Vales of Wever,' 1797, and 'Reflections.' [xxi. 400]

GISBORNE, MARIA (1770–1836), friend of Shelley ; née James ; brought up at Constantinople by her father ; refused William Godwin ; married John Gisborne, 1800 ; lived in Italy ; Shelley's 'Letter to Maria Gisborne' written during her visit to England, 1820 ; introduced Shelley to the study of Calderon. [xxi. 401]

GISBORNE, THOMAS (d. 1806), president of College of Physicians ; fellow of St. John's College, Cambridge ; M.A., 1751 ; M.D., 1758 ; F.R.S., 1759 ; physician to St. George's Hospital, 1757–81 ; Gulstonian lecturer, 1760 ; president, College of Physicians, 1791, 1794, 1796–1803 ; physician in ordinary to the king. [xxi. 401]

GISBORNE, THOMAS, the elder (1758–1846), divine; brother of John Gisborne [q. v.]; of Harrow and St. John's College, Cambridge; B.A., 1780; first chancellor's medallist, 1780; perpetual curate of Barton-under-Needwood, 1783; prebendary of Durham, 1823 and 1826; friend of William Wilberforce; published 'Principles of Moral Philosophy,' 1789, 'Walks in a Forest,' 1794, and other works.   [xxi. 401]

GISBORNE, THOMAS, the younger (1794–1852), politician; son of Thomas Gisborne the elder [q. v.]; whig M.P. for Stafford, 1830–1, north Derbyshire, 1832–7; Carlow, 1839–41, and Nottingham, 1843–52; published 'Essays on Agriculture,' 1854.   [xxi. 402]

GISBURNE, WALTER OF (*fl.* 1300). [See HEMINGFORD.]

GLADSTANES, GEORGE (*d.* 1615), archbishop of St. Andrews; M.A. St. Andrews, 1580; minister successively of St. Cyrus, Arbirlot, and (1597) St. Andrews; member of general assembly; one of the three clerical representatives in parliament, 1598; vice-chancellor of St. Andrews, 1599; bishop of Caithness, 1600; privy councillor of Scotland, 1602; consecrated archbishop of St. Andrews, 1611; attended Hampton Court conference; obtained removal of Andrew Melville [q. v.], principal of St. Andrews University, 1606; permanent moderator, 1607.   [xxi. 402]

GLADSTANES, JOHN (*d.* 1574), Scottish judge; 'Advocatus Pauperum,' 1534; lord of session, 1546; LL.D.   [xxi. 405]

GLADSTONE, SIR JOHN, first baronet (1764–1851), Liverpool merchant; partner in Corrie & Co.; despatched first vessel to Calcutta on the opening up of the trade with India; became sole proprietor of his firm and took six brothers into the business; acquired large East Indian trade; became also West Indian merchant, defending (1823) the slave-trade against James Cropper [q. v.]; issued (1830) 'Statement of Facts connected with the present state of Slavery'; chief supporter of Canning at Liverpool, 1812; Canningite M.P., Lancaster, 1818, Woodstock, 1820, and Berwick, 1826–7; wrote against repeal of the corn laws, but was ultimately convinced by Peel; created baronet, 1846; benefactor of religious and charitable institutions at Leith and Liverpool.   [xxi. 405]

GLADSTONE, WILLIAM EWART (1809–1898), statesman and author; son of (Sir) John Gladstone [q. v.]; educated at Eton and Christ Church, Oxford; president of the Oxford Union Society, 1830; double first in classics and mathematics, 1831; conservative M.P. for Newark, 1832, 1835, and 1837, and again 1841–5; entered Lincoln's Inn, 1833; made first important speech, 1833, favouring 'gradual' emancipation of slaves; successfully opposed appropriation clause in Irish church temporalities bill, 1833; junior lord of treasury in Sir Robert Peel's first administration, 1834; under-secretary for war and colonies in the same government, 1835; published 'The State in its Relations with the Church,' 1838, and 'Church Principles considered in their Results,' 1840; took part in founding Trinity College, Glenalmond, 1840; opposed first opium war with China, 1840; vice-president of board of trade and master of mint in Sir Robert Peel's second administration, 1841; privy councillor, 1841; took charge of customs bill, 1842; became president of board of trade and entered Sir Robert Peel's cabinet, 1843; introduced and carried first general railway bill providing 'parliamentary' trains, 1844; resigned office owing to his disapproval of proposed increase of Maynooth College grant, 1845; published 'Remarks on Recent Commercial Legislation,' 1845; accepted Peel's policy of repealing the corn laws; became secretary of state for colonies in succession to Lord Stanley, who seceded from ministry as a protectionist, 1845–6; vacated seat for Newark on taking office, and did not seek re-election; remained out of parliament through 1846; 'Peelite' M.P. for Oxford University, 1847–65; opposed Palmerston's Greek policy, 1850; visited Naples and published letters condemning the atrocities perpetrated by Ferdinand, king of the Two Sicilies, 1851; opposed Ecclesiastical Titles Bill, 1851; chancellor of exchequer in Aberdeen's coalition ministry, 1852–5; introduced and passed his first budget, suggesting progressive reduction of income tax and extension of legacy duty, under name of succession duty, to real property, 1853; brought in second budget, 1854; resigned office on Palmerston becoming prime minister, 1855; supported Cobden in condemning bombardment of Canton, 1856; vigorously opposed bill for establishing divorce court, 1857; published 'Studies on Homer and the Homeric Age,' 1858; entrusted by Sir Edward Bulwer Lytton, secretary for colonies, with special mission to Ionian islands, and failed to quell agitation for their incorporation with Greek kingdom instead of remaining under British protectorate, 1858–59; spoke in favour of Disraeli's first reform bill, 1859; chancellor of exchequer under Lord Palmerston, 1859–66; introduced budget, and was successful in upholding commercial treaty with France (1859), reducing taxes on articles of food, and granting excise licenses to keepers of eating-houses, but failed to induce House of Lords to repeal paper duty, 1860; lord rector of Edinburgh University, 1860; introduced and passed Post Office Savings Bank Bill, 1861; succeeded in repealing paper duty by including all taxation proposals in one money bill which had to be accepted or rejected in its entirety by House of Lords, 1861; published, with Lord Lyttelton, joint volume of 'Translations,' 1863; supported reform bill moved by (Sir) Edward Baines [q. v.], 1864; opposed bill for removing theological tests for university degrees, 1865; M.P., South Lancashire, 1865–8; chancellor of exchequer and leader of House of Commons on Palmerston's death, 1865; introduced government's reform bill, which failed to pass in committee, and occasioned resignation of government, 1866; introduced budget, pointing out importance of paying off national debt, 1866; proposed successful amendments to Disraeli's reform bill, 1866; leader of liberal party in succession to Lord Russell, 1867; supported bill to abolish compulsory church rates, 1868; successfully moved resolutions embodying principle of Irish church disestablishment, 1868; M.P. for Greenwich, 1868–74 and 1874–80; prime minister for the first time, 1868, the ministry including Robert Lowe (afterwards Viscount Sherbrooke) [q. v.] as chancellor of exchequer, John Bright [q. v.] as president of board of trade, Sir William Page Wood (afterwards Baron Hatherley) [q. v.] as chancellor, and Edward (afterwards Baron) Cardwell [q. v.] as secretary for war; introduced and passed Irish Church Disestablishment Bill, 1869; published 'Juventus Mundi,' 1869; passed first Irish land bill, 1870; procured by royal warrant abolition of purchase in the army, 1871; passed university test bill, 1871; appointed commission to discuss claims of American government for damages caused by cruisers fitted out at British ports during civil war, 1871; passed ballot bill, 1872; introduced Irish University Bill proposing foundation of an undenominational university in Ireland, 1873, and resigned on its rejection at second reading; resumed office on Disraeli's refusal to form ministry, 1873, and, while retaining first lordship of treasury, took chancellorship of the exchequer without resigning seat as member for Greenwich; resigned office on defeat of his party at the general election, 1874, and was succeeded by Disraeli (afterwards Lord Beaconsfield); resigned leadership of liberal party, 1875; vehemently denounced Turkish outrages in Bulgaria and advocated alliance of England and Russia to secure independence of the sultan's Christian provinces, 1875; published 'Homeric Synchronism,' 1876; advocated, unsuccessfully, coercion of the Porte by united Europe, 1877–8; lord rector of Glasgow, 1877; spoke vehemently against Afghan policy of the government, 1878; conducted political campaign in Midlothian, condemning the aggressive imperialism of the prime minister, but dissociating himself from the doctrines of the Manchester school and of peace at any price, 1879–80; M.P. for Midlothian, 1880–95; prime minister for the second time after Beaconsfield's defeat at the general election, 1880; also held office of chancellor of the exchequer, 1880–2; supported Irish Compensation for Disturbance Bill, 1880; succeeded in passing Irish coercion bill, 1881; announced, after defeat of British army at Majuba Hill, conditions of peace with Transvaal, which provided for the maintenance of British suzerainty, self-government for burghers, and British control of foreign relations, 1881; introduced and passed second Irish land bill, proposing to institute a land court for fixing judicial rents, 1881; introduced and passed Irish Arrears Bill, proposing to wipe out arrears of rent in Ireland altogether where tenants were unable to pay them, 1882; adopted policy that it was duty of British government to relieve Egyptian people from military tyranny of Arabi Pasha, 1882; supported military campaign in Egypt, 1882; gave up chancellorship of exchequer to Hugh C. E. Childers [q. v.], 1882; successfully combated two votes of censure in House of Commons on

Egyptian policy, 1883; introduced bill for extension of franchise to agricultural labourers and others, which passed Commons, but was only accepted by Lords after much hesitation, on condition that Gladstone passed simultaneously a bill for redistribution of seats, 1884; adversely criticised for his failure to rescue Gordon, and for his policy of abandonment of Soudan to the Mahdi, 1884; resigned office on passing of amendment opposing points in budget bill, 1885; declined offer of earldom, 1885; was succeeded as prime minister by Lord Salisbury, who, however, failed to obtain a majority for his party at general election at the end of 1885; on defeat of conservatives in House of Commons early in 1886, and the resignation of Lord Salisbury, Gladstone formed ministry for the third time, which included Lord Rosebery in foreign office, Lord Granville as colonial secretary, Mr. John Morley as chief secretary for Ireland, and Mr. Chamberlain (who resigned on introduction of Home Rule Bill) as president of local government board; brought in Home Rule Bill, 8 April 1886, proposing to create legislative body to sit at Dublin for dealing with affairs exclusively Irish, but reserving to British government certain powers affecting the crown, army, navy, and foreign or colonial relations; introduced Irish Land Purchase Bill, which passed only first reading, 16 April 1886; appealed to country on rejection of Home Rule Bill on second reading, 7 June 1886; resigned office with rest of cabinet after general election declared against home rule, 20 July 1886; continued to advocate his Irish policy in session, 1887–92; member of select committee appointed by House of Commons to consider Queen Victoria's message asking for additional grants for maintenance of royal family, 1889; advocated Newcastle programme of radical reforms, 1891; on the defeat of Lord Salisbury's government at general election of 1892, became prime minister for the fourth and last time; also held office of lord privy seal, 1892, his ministry including Lord Rosebery, Mr. Asquith as home secretary, and Sir Edward Grey, under-secretary for foreign affairs; introduced, 13 Feb. 1893, second Home Rule Bill, which, after passing the Commons, was rejected by 419 to 41 in House of Lords, 8 Sept. 1893; made, in support of parish councils bill, his last speech in House of Commons, 1 March 1894; resigned office of prime minister, 3 March 1894; founded St. Deiniol's library for theological students at Hawarden, 1895; urged right and necessity of British intervention in Armenia, 1895–6; published editions of Butler's 'Analogy,' 'Sermons,' and 'Studies Subsidiary to Works of Bishop Butler,' 1896; delivered his last speech at opening of Victoria Jubilee Bridge over Dee, 2 June 1897; died at Hawarden 19 May 1898; buried in Westminster Abbey.

Gladstone's contributions to magazines were collected, under title 'Gleanings from Past Years,' 1879–90, 8 vols. His portrait by Millais, 1879, is in the National Portrait Gallery. As an orator Gladstone's only contemporary rival was John Bright. As a financier he can only be compared with Walpole, Pitt, and Peel. [Suppl. ii. 280]

GLADWIN, FRANCIS (d. 1813 ?), orientalist; of the Bengal army; commissary resident at Patna, 1808; under patronage of Warren Hastings, issued translation of 'Institutes of the Emperor Akbar,' 1783–6, and a Persian-Hindustani-English dictionary, 1809. [xxi. 407]

GLAMMIS, BARONS. [See LYON, JOHN, seventh BARON, 1510 ?–1558; LYON, PATRICK, eighth BARON, d. 1578.]

GLAMMIS, LADY (d. 1537). [See DOUGLAS, JANET.]

GLAMMIS, MASTER OF (d. 1608). [See LYON, SIR THOMAS.]

GLAMORGAN, titular EARL OF (1601–1667). [See SOMERSET, EDWARD, second MARQUIS OF WORCESTER.]

GLANVILL, JOHN (1664 ?–1735), poet and translator; grandson of Sir John Glanville the younger [q. v.]; M.A. Trinity College, Oxford, 1685; barrister, Lincoln's Inn; translated, among other works, Fontenelle's 'Plurality of Worlds,' 1688. [xxi. 407]

GLANVILL, JOSEPH (1636–1680), divine; B.A. Exeter College, Oxford, 1655; M.A. Lincoln College, 1658; rector of the Abbey Church, Bath, 1666–80, and other benefices; an admirer of Baxter, whom he excepted from his attacks on nonconformists in 'The Zealous and Impartial Protestant,' 1681; an original F.R.S., 1664; attacked the scholastic philosophy in 'The Vanity of Dogmatizing' (1661), a work containing the story of the 'Scholar Gipsy'; defended the pre-existence of souls in 'Lux Orientalis,' 1662, and the belief in witchcraft in 'Philosophical considerations touching Witches and Witchcraft,' 1666, generally known as 'Sadducismus Triumphatus.' [xxi. 408]

GLANVILLE, BARTHOLOMEW DE (fl. 1230–1250), minorite friar; properly known as BARTHOLOMEW ANGLICUS, the addition de Glanville being most uncertain; professor of theology at Paris; went to Saxony, 1231, in the interests of his order; author of 'De Proprietatibus Rerum,' the encyclopædia of the middle ages, first printed, c. 1470, at Basle; an English version by John of Trèves was issued by Wynkyn de Worde, c. 1495. [xxi. 409]

GLANVILLE, GILBERT DE (d. 1214), bishop of Rochester, 1185; one of Becket's scholars; archdeacon of Lisieux, 1184; bishop of Rochester, 1185; one of the embassy to Philip Augustus of France, 1186; preached the crusade at Geddington, 1188; supported Longchamp against Prince John; summoned by Richard I to Germany, 1193; excommunicated Prince John on returning, 1194; fled from King John, 1207; absolved Scots from homage to him, 1212. [xxi. 411]

GLANVILLE, SIR JOHN, the elder (1542–1600), judge; the first attorney who reached the bench; barrister, Lincoln's Inn, 1574; serjeant-at-law, 1589; M.P., Launceston, 1585, Tavistock, 1586, and St. Germans, 1592; judge of common pleas, 1598. [xxi. 411]

GLANVILLE, SIR JOHN, the younger (1586–1661), serjeant; son of Sir John Glanville the elder; barrister, Lincoln's Inn, c. 1610; M.P., Plymouth, 1614, 1620, 1623, 1625, 1626, and 1628; opposed the crown; prepared protest against dissolution, 1625; secretary to the council of war at Cadiz, 1625; took leading part in Buckingham's impeachment, 1626–8; eminent as counsel; recorder of Plymouth, 1614; of Bristol, 1638; serjeant, 1637; M.P., Bristol; speaker of the Short parliament, 1640; knighted, 1641; D.C.L. Oxford, 1643; tried Northumberland and other peers; disabled and imprisoned by parliament, 1645–8; M.P. for Oxford University under Commonwealth. [xxi. 412]

GLANVILLE, RANULF DE (d. 1190), chief justiciar of England; sheriff of Yorkshire, 1163–70, and 1174–89; as sheriff of Lancashire, defeated Scots at Alnwick, and captured William the Lion, 1174; ambassador to Flanders, 1177; justice-in-eyre and a member of the permanent royal court, 1179; as justiciar of England, 1180–9, was Henry II's 'eye,' fighting and negotiating with the Welsh and French, and helping the king against his sons; went with Richard I on crusade, 1190, and died at Acre. The authorship of 'Treatise on the Laws and Customs of England' has been doubtfully ascribed to him on the evidence of Roger of Hoveden. [xxi. 413]

GLAPTHORNE, HENRY (fl. 1639), dramatist; published 'Argalus and Parthenia,' 1639, and 'Albertus Wallenstein,' 1639 (tragedies), 'The Hollander,' 1640, 'Wit in a Constable,' 1640, and 'The Ladies Priviledge,' 1640 (comedies), and 'Poems,' 1639; dedicated 'Whitehall' to Lovelace, 1642; his works collected, 1874. xxi. 415]

GLAS, GEORGE (1725–1765), mariner; son of John Glas [q. v.]; discovered between Cape Verde and Senegal a river, which he thought suitable for a settlement; obtained promise of a government grant in exchange for a free cession to the British crown; founded the settlement, naming it Port Hillsborough, 1764; imprisoned by Spaniards at Teneriffe for contraband trading; murdered on his way home; translated from the Spanish 'Account of the Discovery and History of the Canaries,' 1764. [xxi. 415]

GLAS, JOHN (1695–1773), founder of the Glassites; M.A. St. Andrews, 1713; minister of Tealing, Forfarshire, 1719–28, when he was deposed by the general assembly for his 'Testimony of the King of Martyrs' (1727); formed, at Dundee, a sect of independent presbyterians; removed to Perth, 1773, where he was joined by Robert Sandeman [q. v.], afterwards his son-in-law; published an edition (with translation) of the 'True Discourse' of Celsus, 1753, and many other works. [xxi. 417]

GLASCOCK, WILLIAM NUGENT (1787 ?–1847), captain in the navy; present at the action off Finisterre, 1805, and reduction of Flushing, 1809; promoted to post-rank and specially thanked for his services in the Douro, 1832–3; chief work 'Naval Service, or Officers' Manual,' 1836. [xxi. 418]

GLASS, JOSEPH (1791?–1867), philanthropist; received silver medal and 200*l.* for his invention of the chimney-sweeping machine now in use.   [xxi. 419]

GLASS, SIR RICHARD ATWOOD (1820–1873), manufacturer of telegraph cables; educated at King's College, London; adapted Elliot's wire-rope covering to submarine cables, 1852; superintended making of Atlantic cables of 1865–6; knighted, 1866; chairman of Anglo-American Telegraph Company; M.P., Bewdley, 1868–9.   [xxi. 419]

GLASS, THOMAS (*d.* 1786), physician; M.D. Leyden, 1731; practised at Exeter; imparted to his brother Samuel (of Oxford) the process for preparing magnesia alba, afterwards perfected and applied by him; authority on inoculation for smallpox; published medical works.   [xxi. 419]

GLASSE, GEORGE HENRY (1761–1809), classic and divine; son of Samuel Glasse [q. v.]; M.A. Christ Church, Oxford, 1782; rector of Hanwell, 1785; chaplain successively of the Earl of Radnor, Duke of Cambridge, and Earl of Sefton; rendered 'Samson Agonistes' into Greek, 1788; translated 'L'Inconnue, Histoire Véritable, as 'Louisa,' dealing with the lady of the Haystack problem, 1801; spent a fortune; committed suicide.   [xxi. 420]

GLASSE, HANNAH (*fl.* 1747), author of 'The Art of Cookery made Plain and Easy,' 1747, 'The Compleat Confectioner' [1770], and 'The Servant's Directory, or Housekeeper's Companion,' 1770; habit-maker to the Prince of Wales, 1757.   [xxi. 420]

GLASSE, SAMUEL (1735–1812), theologian; educated at Westminster; M.A. Christ Church, Oxford, 1759; D.D., 1769; F.R.S., 1764; chaplain in ordinary to the king, 1772; rector of Hanwell; vicar of Epsom, 1782, Wanstead, 1786; prebendary of St. Paul's, 1798; friend of Bishop Horne; author of a work advocating Sunday schools, 1786.   [xxi. 421]

GLASSFORD, JAMES (*d.* 1845), legal writer and translator; son of John Glassford [q. v.]; sheriff-depute of Dumbartonshire; a commissioner to inquire into Irish education, 1824–6; published 'Remarks on the Constitution and Procedure of the Scottish Courts,' 1812, 'Essay on Principles of Evidence,' 1812, translations from Bacon and the Italian poets.   [xxi. 422]

GLASSFORD, JOHN (1715–1783), tobacco merchant and shipowner; bailie of Glasgow, 1751; purchased Dougalston, Dumbartonshire.   [xxi. 422]

GLASTONBURY, JOHN OF (*fl.* 1400). [See JOHN.]

GLAZEBROOK, JAMES (1744–1803), divine; a Madeley collier, who came under the influence of John Fletcher of Madeley [q. v.]; incumbent of St. James's, Latchford; vicar of Bolton, Lancashire, 1796–1803; published 'Defence of Infant Baptism,' 1781.   [xxi. 422]

GLAZEBROOK, THOMAS KIRKLAND (1780–1855), author; son of James Glazebrook [q. v.]; translated Virgil's first eclogue, 1807, and published poetical works.   [xxi. 423]

GLEICHEN, COUNT (1833–1891). [See VICTOR.]

GLEIG, GEORGE (1753–1840), bishop of Brechin; educated at King's College, Aberdeen; thrice elected bishop of Dunkeld, 1786, 1792, and 1808, but his election made ineffectual by hostility of Bishop Skinner; LL.D. Aberdeen; bishop of Brechin, 1808–40; as primus, 1816–1837, endeavoured to secure *regium donum*; contributed important articles to the 'Encyclopædia Britannica' (3rd edition) and edited the last six volumes, and (1801) wrote most of the 'Supplement'; published 'life' of Principal William Robertson, 1812, and edited Stackhouse's 'History of the Bible,' 1817.   [xxi. 423]

GLEIG, GEORGE ROBERT (1796–1888), chaplain-general of the forces; son of George Gleig [q. v.]; at Glasgow and Balliol College, Oxford; served with the 85th in the Peninsula, 1813–14; wounded at Nivelle and the Nive, and in the American war of 1814; B.A. Magdalen Hall, Oxford, 1818; took orders, 1820; M.A., 1821; perpetual curate of Ash, and rector of Ivy Church, 1822; chaplain of Chelsea Hospital, 1834; chaplain-general of the forces, 1844–75; contributed to the 'Quarterly,' 'Edinburgh,' 'Blackwood,' and 'Fraser' magazines; wrote 'The Subaltern' for 'Blackwood,' 1826; published 'The

Story of Waterloo,' 1847, 'Lives of Military Commanders,' 1831, biographies of Warren Hastings (1841), Clive (1848), and Wellington (1862), and 'Chelsea Pensioners,' 1829, with other works.   [xxi. 424]

GLEMHAM, EDWARD (*fl.* 1590–1594), voyager; of Benhall, Suffolk; in his ship the Edward and Constance destroyed two Spanish vessels, repulsed four galleys, and captured a rich Venetian merchant ship, 1590; made second voyage; his adventures described in black-letter pamphlets (reprinted, 1829 and 1866).   [xxi. 425]

GLEMHAM, SIR THOMAS (*d.* 1649?), royalist; knighted, 1617; M.P., Aldeburgh, in the first two parliaments of Charles I; served on the continent and in first Scottish war; commandant of York, 1642 and 1644; capitulated, 1644; tried to hold Carlisle against the Scots, 1645, and to defend Oxford; took part in the second civil war till Musgrave's seizure of Carlisle, 1648.   [xxi. 426]

GLEN, ANDREW (1665–1732), botanist; M.A. Jesus College, Cambridge, 1687; rector of Hathern, Leicestershire; formed an herbarium, 1685, including two hundred foreign plants, to which he made additions at Turin, 1692.   [xxi. 427]

GLEN, WILLIAM (1789–1826), Scottish poet; published 'Poems, chiefly Lyrical,' 1815, including 'Wae's me for Prince Charlie' and other love and war songs.   [xxi. 427]

GLENBERVIE, BARON (1743–1823). [See DOUGLAS, SYLVESTER.]

GLENCAIRN, EARLS OF. [See CUNNINGHAM, ALEXANDER, first EARL, *d.* 1488; CUNNINGHAM, ALEXANDER, fifth EARL, *d.* 1574; CUNNINGHAM, WILLIAM, fourth EARL, *d.* 1547; CUNNINGHAM, WILLIAM, ninth EARL, 1610?–1664.]

GLENCORSE, LORD (1810–1891). [See INGLIS, JOHN.]

GLENDOWER, OWEN (1359?–1416?) (OWAIN AB GRUFFYDD), Welsh rebel; lord of Glyndwr and Sycharth; claimed descent from Bleddyn ab Cynvyn and from Llewelyn; studied law at Westminster; served with Richard II against the Scots, 1385; witness in suit of Scrope *v.* Grosvenor, 1386; as squire to Earl of Arundel served Henry of Lancaster, but headed Welsh rebellion against him on his accession as Henry IV; assumed title of 'Prince of Wales'; his estates granted by Henry IV to John Beaufort, earl of Somerset [q. v.]; invaded South Wales, and harassed the royal army in the north; repulsed before Carnarvon, 1401; negotiated with Northumberland for peace, but at the same time appealed for help to Scotland and the Irish lords; captured Reginald de Grey [q. v.] and Sir Edmund Mortimer at Pilleth, 1402; baffled the English army and released Mortimer after marrying him to his daughter, November 1402; his chief residences burnt by Prince Henry, 1403; took Carmarthen, Usk, Caerleon, and Newport, failed to join the Percies at Shrewsbury, 1403; ravaged English border; aided by French and Bretons captured Harlech and Cardiff, 1404; concluded an alliance with France, 1405; recognised Benedict XIII as pope, 1405; summoned a Welsh parliament, 1405; probably formed his alliance with Mortimer and Northumberland, *c.* 1405; his sons captured by Prince Henry; retook Carmarthen with help of a French force, 1406; again defeated, 1406; deserted by Northumberland; lost Aberystwith, 1407, and South Wales, 1408; his wife and relations captured, 1413; admitted to the king's grace and obedience, 1415; his end unknown.   [xxi. 427]

GLENELG, BARON (1778–1866). [See GRANT, CHARLES.]

GLENHAM, EDWARD (*fl.* 1590–1594). [See GLEMHAM.]

GLENIE, JAMES (1750–1817), mathematician; M.A. St. Andrews; served in the artillery and engineers during the American war; elected F.R.S., 1779, for papers written while on service; lieutenant, 1787; retired, 1787; emigrated to New Brunswick, and became member of House of Assembly; on return to England appointed engineer extraordinary and (1806) instructor to East India Company's artillery officers; dismissed in consequence of evidence in Wardle case, 1809; died in poverty; published, among other works, 'History of Gunnery,' 1776, 'Doctrine of Universal Comparison,' 1789, 'The Antecedental Calculus,' 1793, and 'Observations on Defence of Great Britain,' 1807.   [xxi. 434]

GLENLEE, BARONS. [See MILLER, SIR THOMAS, 1717–1789; MILLER, SIR WILLIAM, 1755–1846.]

GLENNY, GEORGE (1793–1874), horticultural writer; edited the 'Royal Lady's Magazine'; started the 'Horticultural Journal,' 1832, in which his 'Properties of Flowers' first appeared; edited many other horticultural papers, including 'Glenny's Almanac' (still issued); a successful grower of auriculas, dahlias, and tulips; originated Metropolitan Society of Florists, 1832. [xxi. 436]

GLENORCHY, VISCOUNTESS (1741–1786). [See CAMPBELL, WILLIELMA.]

GLISSON, FRANCIS (1597–1677), physician; M.A. Caius College, Cambridge, 1624; incorporated at Oxford, 1627; M.D. Cambridge, 1634; regius professor of physic, Cambridge, 1636–77; Gulstonian lecturer, 1640; sent out of Colchester to ask for better terms during the siege, 1648; an original F.R.S.; president, College of Physicians, 1667–1669; published (1650) 'Tractatus de Rachitide' (the Rickets), almost the first English medical monograph; published also 'Anatomia Hepatis' (1654), from which the name 'Glisson's capsule' was applied to the sheath of the liver. [xxi. 437]

GLOUCESTER, DUKES OF. [See THOMAS OF WOODSTOCK, 1355–1397; HUMPHREY, 1391–1447; RICHARD III, 1452–1485; HENRY, 1639–1660; WILLIAM HENRY, 1743–1805; WILLIAM FREDERICK, 1776–1834.]

GLOUCESTER, DUCHESS OF. [See COBHAM, ELEANOR.]

GLOUCESTER, EARLS OF. [See CLARE, GILBERT DE, sixth EARL, d. 1230; CLARE, GILBERT DE, eighth EARL, 1243–1295; CLARE, GILBERT DE, ninth EARL, 1291–1314; CLARE, RICHARD DE, seventh EARL, 1222–1262; MONTHERMER, RALPH DE, d. 1325 ?; DESPENSER, THOMAS LE, 1373–1400.]

GLOUCESTER, MILES DE, EARL OF HEREFORD (d. 1143), sheriff of Gloucestershire and Staffordshire from 1128; justice itinerant, a justice of the forest, and royal constable from 1128; adhered to Stephen till 1139, when he joined Gloucester in inviting the Empress Maud to England; relieved Brian Fitzcount [q. v.] at Wallingford, 1139; burnt Worcester, 1139; took Hereford Castle, 1139; present at Lincoln, 1141; accompanied the empress to Winchester as one of her three chief supporters, 1141; fled with her from London, and persuaded her to return to Oxford from Gloucester, 1141; received as a reward the earldom and castle of Hereford, 1141; excommunicated by the bishop of Hereford for demands on church lands, 1143; slain by an arrow shot at a deer. [xxi. 438]

GLOUCESTER, ROBERT OF (fl. 1260–1300). [See ROBERT.]

GLOVER, BOYER (fl. 1758–1771), Muggletonian; watchmaker; contributed to 'Songs of Gratefull Praise,' 1794, and 'Divine Songs of the Muggletonians,' 1829. [xxii. 1]

GLOVER, CHARLES WILLIAM (1806–1863), violinist and composer of popular songs; musical director at Queen's Theatre, 1832. [xxii. 1]

GLOVER, EDMUND (1813 ?–1860), actor and manager; son of Julia Glover [q. v.]; took 'leading business' under Murray at Edinburgh, 1841–8; manager for Jenny Lind in Scotland; leased theatres at Glasgow, Paisley, and Greenock; played Othello at Edinburgh, 1850, and Falkland, 1851; alternated Macbeth and Macduff with Thomas Powrie, 1856. [xxii. 1]

GLOVER, GEORGE (fl. 1625–1650), early English engraver; engraved from life portraits of eminent contemporaries; engraved broadside representing Evans the giant porter, Jeffery Hudson the dwarf, and old Thomas Parr. [xxii. 2]

GLOVER, JEAN (1758–1801), Scottish poetess; daughter of a Kilmarnock weaver and wife of a strolling player; her song 'Ower the Muir among the Heather' taken down by Burns from her singing. [xxii. 2]

GLOVER, JOHN (1714–1774), preacher; author of religious pamphlets. [xxii. 2]

GLOVER, JOHN (1767–1849), landscape-painter; president of the Water-colour Society, 1815; exhibited at Paris 'Landscape Composition'; sketched in Switzerland and Italy; held exhibition of water-colours and oils in Old Bond Street, 1821; a founder of Society of British Artists, with whom he exhibited, 1824–30; emigrated to Western Australia, 1831; died in Tasmania. [xxii. 3]

GLOVER, SIR JOHN HAWLEY (1829–1885), colonial governor; served in navy, 1841–77; joined Baikie's Niger expedition, 1857; captain, 1877; administrator of Lagos, 1863–4 and 1866–72; commanded Houssas in Ashanti campaign, 1873–4; G.C.M.G., 1874; governor of Newfoundland, 1875–81 and 1883–4, of the Leeward islands, 1881–3. [xxii. 4]

GLOVER, MRS. JULIA (1779–1850), actress, née Betterton; played on the York circuit, 1789; performed at Covent Garden, 1797–1801; married Samuel Glover, 1800; played the Queen to Kean's Richard III and Emilia to Othello, 1814; acted Andromache at Macready's first appearance at Covent Garden, 1816; with Benjamin Webster at Haymarket, James Anderson at Drury Lane, and William Farren at the Strand; played Mrs. Malaprop at her farewell (Drury Lane), 1850; first comic actress of the period of her middle life. [xxii. 4]

GLOVER, MOSES (fl. 1620–1640), painter and architect; chiefly known by his large survey vellum of Syon House and Isleworth hundred, 1635. [xxii. 6]

GLOVER, RICHARD (1712–1785), poet; several times addressed the House of Commons as the merchants' representative; as opponent of Walpole received legacy from the Duchess of Marlborough; M.P., Weymouth, 1761–8; published 'Leonidas,' 1737; his ballad, 'Hosier's Ghost,' included in Percy's 'Reliques'; his 'Boadicea' (1753) and 'Medea' (1763) acted at Drury Lane; his 'Athenaid' published, 1787, and 'Memoirs' (1742–57), 1813. [xxii. 6]

GLOVER, ROBERT (d. 1555), protestant martyr; of Eton and King's College, Cambridge; M.A., 1541; burnt for heresy at Coventry. [xxii. 7]

GLOVER, ROBERT (1544–1588), Somerset herald; Portcullis pursuivant at the College of Arms, 1567; Somerset herald, 1571; conducted visitations of Durham (1575), Cheshire (1580), and Yorkshire (1584–5); assisted Camden in his 'Britannia'; 'The Catalogue of Honor' (1610) compiled from his collections. [xxii. 7]

GLOVER, STEPHEN (d. 1869), author of 'History and Gazetteer of Derbyshire' (1831–3, unfinished), and compiler of the 'Peak Guide,' 1830. [xxii. 8]

GLOVER, STEPHEN (1812–1870), composer of songs, ballads, and duets; brother of Charles William Glover [q. v.]. [xxii. 8]

GLOVER, WILLIAM HOWARD (1819–1875), musical composer and writer; second son of Julia Glover [q. v.]; gave operatic performances at Manchester and annual concerts at St. James's Hall and Drury Lane; musical critic to 'Morning Post,' 1849–65; died at New York; composed 'Tam o' Shanter' (produced at the New Philharmonic, 1846), 'Ruy Blas' (Covent Garden, 1861), and 'Manfred,' an overture, and many songs. [xxii. 9]

GLYN, GEORGE GRENFELL, second BARON WOLVERTON (1824–1887), grandson of Sir Richard Carr Glyn [q. v.]; educated at Rugby and University College, Oxford; of banking firm, Glyn, Mills, Currie & Co.; M.P., Shaftesbury, 1857–73; secretary to the treasury, 1868–73; paymaster-general, 1880–5; postmaster-general in home rule ministry, 1886; personal friend of William Ewart Gladstone [q. v.]. [xxii. 9]

GLYN, ISABELLA DALLAS (1823–1889), actress; née Gearns; played under her mother's name of Glyn; made début at Manchester as Constance in 'King John,' 1847; appeared in Shakespearean parts on York circuit and at Sadler's Wells, 1848–51 and 1859; first appeared at Drury Lane, 1851; played Cleopatra at the Princess's, 1867; gave Shakespearean readings and lessons in England and America; obtained divorce from Eneas Sweetland Dallas [q. v.], 1874. [xxii. 10]

GLYN, SIR RICHARD CARR, first baronet (1755–1838), lord mayor of London; partner in Hallifax, Mills, Glyn & Mitton, bankers; sheriff of London, 1790; lord mayor, 1798–9; M.P., St. Ives, 1796–1802; created baronet, 1800. [xxii. 10]

GLYN, WILLIAM (1504 ?–1558), bishop of Bangor; fellow of Queens' College, Cambridge, 1530; dean, 1540; M.A., 1530; D.D., 1544; Lady Margaret professor of divinity, 1544-9 ; original fellow of Trinity, 1546 ; rector of St. Martin's, Ludgate, 1551 ; president of Queens' College, 1553 ; one of the six delegates who disputed with Cranmer, Latimer, and Ridley, 1554 ; bishop of Bangor, 1555 ; Welsh scholar.   [xxii. 11]

GLYNN, JOHN (1722–1779), politician and lawyer ; matriculated at Exeter College, Oxford, 1738 ; barrister, Inner Temple, 1748 ; serjeant-at-law, 1763 ; recorder of Exeter, 1764 ; counsel for Wilkes ; Wilkes's colleague as M.P. for Middlesex, 1768–79 ; leading member of Society of Bill of Rights ; recorder of London, 1772. [xxii. 12]

GLYNN, ROBERT, afterwards CLOBERY (1719–1800), physician ; educated at Eton and King's College, Cambridge ; M.A., 1745 ; M.D., 1752 ; Seatonian prizeman, 1757 ; attended Gray and Bishop Watson ; supported authenticity of Chatterton forgeries against George Steevens, and bequeathed the manuscripts to the British Museum ; said to have assisted Mathias in 'Pursuits of Literature' ; left legacy to King's College. [xxii. 13]

GLYNNE, SIR JOHN (1603–1666), judge ; educated at Westminster and Hart Hall, Oxford ; barrister, Lincoln's Inn, 1628 ; M.P., Westminster, 1640 ; sat on important committees in the Long parliament ; managed conference with the Lords in the Goodman case, 1641 ; conducted several articles of Strafford's impeachment, and replied to his defence, 1642 ; chosen to impeach the bishops, 1641 ; one of committee to consider the attempted arrest of the five members, 1642 ; recorder of London, 1643 ; took the covenant ; one of the eleven excluded members, 1647 ; sent to the Tower, but released and readmitted to parliament, 1648 ; one of the commissioners to treat with the king at Carisbrooke, 1648 ; again excluded before 'Pride's Purge' ; M.P., Carnarvonshire, 1654 and 1660, Flint, 1655 ; serjeant to the Protector and justice of assize, c. 1654 ; prosecuted John Gerard (1632–1654) [q.v.] and other conspirators, 1654 ; tried the conspirator, Miles Sindercombe, 1656 ; chief-justice of the upper bench, 1655–9 ; supported the 'petition and advice,' 1656 ; as king's serjeant prosecuted Sir Henry Vane, 1662 ; his speech before Cromwell (1658) in favour of monarchy printed, 1660 ; knighted, 1660. [xxii. 15]

GLYNNE, SIR STEPHEN RICHARD, ninth and last baronet (1807–1874), antiquary ; brother-in-law of William Ewart Gladstone [q.v.] ; succeeded as baronet, 1815 ; educated at Eton ; M.A. Christ Church, Oxford, 1831 ; M.P., Flint burghs, 1832–7, and Flintshire, 1837–47 ; surveyed and made notes on 5,530 English churches ; his notes concerning Kent published by his nephew, W. H. Gladstone, 1877. [xxii. 18]

GOAD, GEORGE (d. 1671), master at Eton ; M.A. King's College, Cambridge, 1627 ; senior proctor, 1637 ; rector of Horstead and Coltishall, 1646 ; fellow of Eton, 1648 ; continued Eton catalogues. [xxii. 18]

GOAD, JOHN (1616–1689), head-master of Merchant Taylors' School ; fellow of St. John's College, Oxford ; M.A., 1640 ; B.D., 1647 ; vicar of St. Giles's, Oxford, 1643, of Yarnton, 1646–60 ; head-master of Tunbridge, 1660, of Merchant Taylors' School, 1661–81 ; dismissed from Merchant Taylors' as a papist, 1681 ; declared himself a Romanist, 1686 ; afterwards kept private school at Piccadilly, London ; wrote 'Astro-Meteorologia sana,' 1686, and a similar work, published 1690. [xxii. 18]

GOAD, ROGER (1538–1610), provost of King's College, Cambridge, 1570 ; educated at Eton and King's College, Cambridge ; fellow, 1558 ; M.A., 1563 ; master of Guildford school ; D.D., 1573 ; thrice vice-chancellor ; chancellor of Wells, 1577 ; with Dr. Fulke had conferences in the Tower with Edmund Campion [q.v.], 1581 ; re-established college library. [xxii. 19]

GOAD, THOMAS (1576–1638), rector of Hadleigh, 1618–38 ; second son of Roger Goad [q.v.] ; educated at Eton and King's College, Cambridge ; fellow, 1595 ; B.A., 1596 ; D.D., 1615 ; domestic chaplain to Archbishop Abbot ; prebendary of Winchester, 1621 ; succeeded Joseph Hall [q.v.] at synod of Dort, 1619, where he became an Arminian ; disputed with the jesuits ; prolocutor of lower house of convocation, 1625 ; dean of Bocking, 1633 ; embellished Hadleigh Church and rectory with paintings ; published theological tracts. [xxii. 20]

GOAD, THOMAS (d. 1666), regius professor of laws at Cambridge ; brother of George Goad [q.v.] ; of Eton,

King's College, Cambridge, and Gray's Inn ; M.A. and LL.D. ; reader of logic at Cambridge, 1620 ; regius professor, 1635. [xxii. 21]

GOADBY, ROBERT (1721–1778), printer and compiler ; left endowment to Sherborne Church ; chief production, 'Illustration of the Holy Scriptures,' 1759. [xxii. 22]

GOBBAN SAER, 'the Artificer' (fl. 7th cent.), builder of churches and fortresses in north and east of Ireland. [xxii. 22]

GODBOLT, JOHN (d. 1648), judge ; barrister, Gray's Inn, 1611 ; serjeant-at-law, 1636 ; judge of common pleas by vote of parliament, 1647 ; reports revised by him published, 1653. [xxii. 23]

GODBY, JAMES (fl. 1790–1815), stipple-engraver. [xxii. 23]

GODDAM or **WOODHAM**, ADAM (d. 1358), Franciscan ; probably of Norwich ; attended Ockham's lectures on Peter Lombard's 'Sentences' at Oxford ; his 'Commentary on Four Books of the "Sentences,"' as edited (1512) by John Major (1469–1550) [q. v.], probably only an abridgment of Goddam's work. [xxii. 23]

GODDARD, GEORGE BOUVERIE (1832–1886), animal painter ; exhibited at the Academy, 1856–85. [xxii. 24]

GODDARD, JOHN (fl. 1645–1671), engraver ; his 'Seven Deadly Sins' in British Museum. [xxii. 24]

GODDARD, JONATHAN (1617–1675), Gresham professor of physic ; M.B. Christ's College, Cambridge, 1638 ; M.D. Catharine Hall, 1643 ; F.R.C.P., 1646 ; Gulstonian lecturer, 1648 ; as physician-in-chief accompanied Cromwell to Ireland, 1649, and Scotland, 1650 ; warden of Merton College, Oxford, 1651–60 ; member of Little parliament and council of state, 1653 ; on council of Royal Society ; said to have sold the secret of his 'drops' (volatile spirit of raw silk) to Charles II ; appointed Gresham professor of physic, 1655 ; wrote two 'Discourses' against the apothecaries ; according to Seth Ward [q. v.], the first Englishman to make telescopes. [xxii. 24]

GODDARD, THOMAS (d. 1783), Indian general ; lieutenant, 1759 ; served at Madras, 1759–61, and in Bengal, 1763 ; raised sepoy battalion for East India Company, 1764 ; lieutenant-colonel, 1768 ; served at capture of Burrareah, 1770, and against Mahrattas, 1772 ; much trusted by Warren Hastings ; commanded Bengal contingent with Bombay army against Mahrattas, 1778–81 ; brigadier-general ; died at sea. [xxii. 26]

GODDARD, WILLIAM (fl. 1615), satirist ; resided in Holland ; his three works first printed under Dr. Furnivall's editorship, 1878. [xxii. 27]

GODDARD, WILLIAM STANLEY (1757–1845), head-master of Winchester ; M.A. Merton College, Oxford, 1783 ; D.D., 1795 ; second master at Winchester, 1784–96 ; as head-master (1806–1809) raised the school from 60 to 144, among his pupils being Dr. Arnold ; prebendary of St. Paul's, 1814 ; canon of Salisbury, 1829 ; presented 25,000l. to Winchester for masters' salaries ; scholarship founded in memory of him, 1846. [xxii. 27]

GODDEN, properly TYLDEN, THOMAS (1624–1688), controversialist ; B.A. St. John's College, Cambridge, 1642 ; converted to Romanism by John Sergeant [q.v.] ; president of the English college, Lisbon, 1655, and D.D., 1660 ; chaplain to Queen Catharine of Braganza, 1661 ; accused of complicity in murder of Sir Edmund Berry Godfrey [q. v.] ; escaped to Paris, but returned under James II ; carried on theological controversy with Stillingfleet. [xxii. 28]

GODEL, WILLIAM (fl. 1173), historian ; probably a Cistercian in diocese of Sens or Bourges, although of English birth ; his chronicle reaching to 1173 (with continuation to 1320), printed in 'Recueil des Historiens de la France.' [xxii. 29]

GODERICH, VISCOUNT (1782–1859). [See ROBINSON, FREDERICK JOHN, EARL OF RIPON.]

GODFREY OF MALMESBURY (fl. 1081), supposed author of a chronicle extending from the coming of the Saxons to 1129 ; wrongly identified by Tanner with Godfrey, abbot of Malmesbury. [xxii. 29]

GODFREY OF WINCHESTER (d. 1107), Latin poet; native of Cambrai; prior of St. Swithin's, Winchester, 1081–1107; his epigrams in imitation of Martial, and 'De Primatum Angliæ Laudibus,' printed in T. Wright's 'Latin Satirical Poets of the Twelfth Century.'   [xxii. 30]

GODFREY or **GODFREY-HANCKWITZ**, AMBROSE, the elder (d. 1741), chemist; employed by Robert Boyle [q. v.]; F.R.S., 1730; patented machine for extinguishing fires ' by explosion and suffocation,' 1724.   [xxii. 30]

GODFREY, AMBROSE, the younger (d. 1756), chemist; son of Ambrose Godfrey the elder [q. v.]; carried on his father's laboratory in Southampton Street, London; published, with his brother John Godfrey [q. v.], 'A Curious Research into the Element of Water,' 1747.   [xxii. 31]

GODFREY, ARABELLA (1648–1730). [See CHURCHILL, ARABELLA.]

GODFREY, BOYLE (d. 1756 ?), alchemist; brother of Ambrose Godfrey the younger [q. v.]; ruined himself by his passion for alchemy.   [xxii. 31]

GODFREY, SIR EDMUND BERRY (1621–1678), justice of the peace for Westminster; educated at Westminster and Christ Church, Oxford; entered Gray's Inn, 1640; knighted for services during plague, 1665, 1666; offended the court by causing arrest of Sir Alexander Fraizer [q. v.], 1669; reputed best justice of the peace in England; a zealous protestant; received first depositions of Titus Oates [q. v.], 1678; found dead on south side of Primrose Hill a month later; believed murdered by Roman catholics; two Romanists and a protestant were hanged at Tyburn in consequence of the confession (made under torture and once repudiated) of Miles Prance, a catholic silversmith, avowing himself to have been an accomplice in the murder. Prance was punished for perjury, 1686. The crime was perhaps perpetrated at the instigation of Oates himself.   [xxii. 31]

GODFREY, JOHN (fl. 1747), chemist; with his brother Ambrose Godfrey the younger [q. v.] carried on the business of his father Ambrose Godfrey the elder [q. v.]; published, also with his brother, 'A Curious Research into the Element of Water,' 1747.   [xxii. 31]

GODFREY, MICHAEL (d. 1695), financier; nephew of Sir Edmund Berry Godfrey [q. v.]; first deputy-governor of the Bank of England; killed in the trenches at Namur while on his way to establish branch at Antwerp; wrote ' short account' of the Bank of England.   [xxii. 35]

GODFREY, RICHARD BERNARD (b. 1728), engraver of views and antiquities for Grose's 'Antiquarian Repertory' (1775).   [xxii. 35]

GODFREY, THOMAS (1736–1763), poet and dramatist; born at Philadelphia; served in expedition against Fort Duquesne, 1758; while a factor in North Carolina composed 'The Prince of Parthia,' the first play written in America, published, 1765.   [xxii. 35]

GODHAM, ADAM (d. 1358). [See GODDAM.]

GODIVA or **GODGIFU** (fl. 1040–1080), benefactress: wife of Leofric, earl of Mercia [q. v.]; built and endowed monasteries at Stow and Coventry; benefactress of houses at other places. The oldest form of the legend of her riding naked through Coventry to obtain the release of the ' villa' from toll is given by Roger of Wendover (' Flores Historiarum') ; the current story originates with Rapin (1732); the procession at Coventry (last held, 1887) was instituted in 1678.   [xxii. 36]

GODKIN, JAMES (1806–1879), writer on Ireland: established 'Christian Patriot' at Belfast, 1849; edited ' Derry Standard' and Dublin 'Daily Express'; active member of the Tenant League, 1850; received civil list pension, 1873; published works, including 'The Land War in Ireland,' 1870, and 'Religious History of Ireland,' 1873.   [xxii. 38]

GODLEY, JOHN ROBERT (1814–1861), politician; educated at Harrow; B.A. Christ Church, Oxford, 1836; propounded plan for relief of Irish distress by emigration to Canada; friend of Edward Gibbon Wakefield [q. v.]; lived at Canterbury, New Zealand, 1850–2, a settlement founded on his own plan; afterwards income-tax commissioner in Ireland; under-secretary-at-war; selection from his writings and speeches published in New Zealand, 1863.   [xxii. 38]

GODMOND, CHRISTOPHER (fl. 1840), author of ' The Campaign of 1346,' 1836, and ' Vincenzo, Prince of Mantua,' 1840, two dramas; F.S.A., 1837.   [xxii. 39]

GODOLPHIN, FRANCIS, second EARL OF GODOLPHIN (1678–1766), son of Sidney Godolphin, first earl [q. v.]; his education superintended by John Evelyn (1620–1706) [q. v.]; of Eton and King's College, Cambridge; M.A., 1705; M.P. for East Looe, Helston, 1702–10, for Oxfordshire, 1708–10, and Tregony, 1710–12; Viscount Rialton, 1706–12; cofferer of the household, 1704–11 and 1714–23; privy councillor, 1723; groom of the stole and first lord of the bed-chamber, 1727–35; acted as lord justice, 1723, 1725, and 1727; lord privy seal, 1735–40.   [xxii. 39]

GODOLPHIN, HENRY (1648–1733), provost of Eton and dean of St. Paul's, younger brother of Sidney, earl of Godolphin [q. v.]; educated at Eton and Wadham College, Oxford; B.A., 1668; fellow of All Souls, 1668; M.A., 1672; D.D., 1685; fellow of Eton, 1677; provost, 1695–1707 and 1726–33; dean of St. Paul's, 1707–26; benefactor of Eton and Salisbury.   [xxii. 40]

GODOLPHIN, JOHN (1617–1678), civilian; D.C.L. Gloucester Hall, Oxford, 1643; judge of the admiralty, 1653; king's advocate, 1660; published, among other works, 'The Holy Limbec,' 1650, and 'Repertorium Canonicum,' 1678.   [xxii. 41]

GODOLPHIN, MRS. MARGARET (1652–1678), friend of John Evelyn; née Blagge; maid of honour to Duchess of York and to Queen Catharine; privately married Sidney (afterwards earl of) Godolphin [q. v.], 1675; Evelyn's account of her published, 1847.   [xxii. 41]

GODOLPHIN, SIDNEY (1610–1643), poet; educated at Exeter College, Oxford; M.P., Helston, 1628–43; joined Sir Ralph Hopton's force and fell in skirmish at Chagford; friend of Falkland, Hobbes, and Clarendon; Suckling's ' Little Sid'; his 'Passion of Dido' (finished by Waller) contained in Dryden's 'Miscellany,' and songs by him in Ellis's 'Specimens' and the 'Tixall Poetry.'   [xxii. 42]

GODOLPHIN, SIDNEY, first EARL OF GODOLPHIN (1645–1712), statesman; page of honour to the king, 1662; master of the robes, 1678; M.P., Helston, 1668–79, St. Mawes, 1679–81; a lord of the treasury, 1679; allied with Sunderland and the Duchess of Portsmouth; corresponded with the Prince of Orange; secretary of state, 1684; created Baron Godolphin, 1684; chamberlain to Queen Mary of Modena, 1685, with whom he attended mass; a commissioner of the treasury, 1687; one of James II's last adherents; advocated regency on James II's flight; constantly corresponded with St. Germain, sending warning of the projected attack on Brest, 1694; head of the treasury, 1690–6; the only tory lord justice, 1695; implicated in confession of Sir John Fenwick [q. v.], 1696; resigned; again first lord, 1700–1; lord high treasurer and Marlborough's confidential ally, 1702–10; induced by the duchess to force the queen to replace tory by whig ministers; took part in promoting union with Scotland and in Portuguese and Spanish affairs; supported whigs in insisting on barrier treaty with Dutch; attacked by Sacheverell as ' Volpone,' vehemently urged his impeachment, 1709; dismissed by Anne with a pension, 1710; his financial administration defended by Walpole.
                                            [xxii. 42]

GODOLPHIN, SIR WILLIAM (1634 ?–1696), ambassador; educated at Westminster and Christ Church, Oxford; student, 1651; M.A., 1661; D.C.L. Oxford, 1663; M.P., Camelford, 1665; knighted, 1668; envoy extraordinary to Spain, 1669; ambassador at Madrid, 1671–8; recalled under suspicion of Roman catholicism (1678), which he soon openly professed; died at Madrid; his notarial act providing for a posthumous will declared invalid by parliament, 1698.   [xxii. 46]

GODRIC (1065 ?–1170), founder of Finchale; for sixteen years merchant and shipowner; probably the 'Gudericus, pirata de regno Angliæ,' with whom Baldwin I of Jerusalem sailed from Arsuf to Jaffa, 1102; made pilgrimages to Rome, St. James of Compostella, and St. Gilles in Provence; for sixty years lived as a hermit under Rannulf Flambard's protection at Finchale on the Wear, where he built a wooden chapel dedicated to the Virgin.
                                            [xxii. 47]

GODSALVE, EDWARD (d. 1568 ?), Roman catholic divine, original fellow of Trinity College, Cambridge, 1546; B.D., 1554; prebendary of Chichester; rector of

Fulbourn, 1554 ; retired to Antwerp, c. 1560, as professor of divinity in St. Michael's monastery ; edited Christopherson's version of Eusebius (part i.) and translated part iii.   [xxii. 49]

GODSALVE, SIR JOHN (d. 1556), clerk of the signet to Henry VIII, and comptroller of the mint under Edward VI ; knight of the carpet, 1547.   [xxii. 49]

GODWIN or **GODWINE** (d. 1053), earl of the West-Saxons ; described as 'dux' in 1018 ; accompanied Cnut to Denmark, 1019 ; appointed by Cnut earl of the West-Saxons, and married to Gytha, sister of Ulf ; acquired great influence, by his wealth and talent for oratory ; supported claims of Harthacnut to the crown, 1035, but afterwards accepted Harold (Harefoot) ; accused by many writers of causing death (1036) of Ælfred the ætheling [q. v.] ; compelled to clear himself by oath on accession of Harthacnut, 1040 ; procured the peaceful accession of Edward the Confessor, 1042 ; headed the national party against the Norman favourites ; married his daughter Eadgyth (Edith) to King Edward ; obtained for his second son Harold earldom of East Anglia and for his eldest son Swegen earldom of some Mercian shires ; weakened by the accession of Robert of Jumièges to the sees of London (1044) and Canterbury (1050), who revived the old charge against him ; outlawed with his sons, 1051 ; took refuge with Baldwin, count of Flanders, his son Tostig's father-in-law ; made descents on the Isle of Wight and Portland, 1052 ; with the support of Kent, Surrey, Sussex, and London sailed up the Thames ; restored with his family to favour ; died at Winchester of apoplexy while supping with Edward.   [xxii. 50]

GODWIN, MRS. CATHERINE GRACE (1798–1845), poet ; daughter of Thomas Garnett (1766–1802) [q. v.] ; married Thomas Godwin, 1824 ; published 'The Night before the Bridal,' and 'The Wanderer's Legacy,' 1829.
                                                   [xxii. 55]

GODWIN, EDWARD WILLIAM (1833–1886), architect ; practised in Bristol and London ; assisted Burges in designs for new law courts, and Edis in those for the Berlin parliament house ; restored Dromore Castle and Castle Ashby ; designed theatrical costumes and scenery ; published 'Temple Bar Illustrated,' 1877, and an adaptation of 'The Faithfull Shepherdesse,' and other works.
                                                   [xxii. 55]

GODWIN, FRANCIS (1562–1633), bishop of Llandaff and Hereford ; son of Thomas Godwin (1517–1590) [q. v.] ; M.A. Christ Church, Oxford, 1584 ; D.D., 1596 ; sub-dean of Exeter, 1587 ; bishop of Llandaff, 1601, of Hereford, 1617 ; his 'Catalogue of the Bishops of England,' with lives (1601), edited and continued by William Richardson, 1643 ; his Latin 'Annals' (Henry VIII–Mary), translated by his son Morgan. From Godwin's 'Man in the Moone' (published posthumously, 1638), John Wilkins, bishop of Chester, and Cyrano de Bergerac are supposed to have borrowed their imaginary sketches of life in the moon.
                                                   [xxii. 56]

GODWIN, GEORGE (1815–1888), architect ; won British architects' prize for essay on 'Concrete,' 1835 ; hon. secretary Art Union of London, 1836–7 ; became editor of the 'Builder,' 1844 ; restored St. Mary Redcliffe, and erected many buildings in Bristol ; treasurer of Royal Literary Fund ; F.R.S. and F.S.A. ; gold medallist of Institute of Architects, 1881 ; founded Godwin bursary ; active member of royal commission on housing of working classes, 1884 ; noted collector of chairs of celebrities. His works include 'The Churches of London,' 1838, and architectural monographs.   [xxii. 58]

GODWIN, SIR HENRY THOMAS (1784–1853), major-general ; ensign, 9th foot, 1799 ; served in Hanover, 1805, and in the Peninsula ; severely wounded at Barossa, 1811 ; C.B. ; lieutenant-colonel, 41st foot, 1815 ; commanded it in first Burmese war, 1824–6 ; major-general, khed ; commander-in-chief in second Burmese war, 1852–3 ; K.C.B. ; died at Simla.   [xxii. 59]

GODWIN, MRS. MARY WOLLSTONECRAFT (1759–1797), author ; née Wollstonecraft ; kept school at Newington Green with her sister Eliza ; governess to Lord Kingsborough's children, 1787–8 ; employed for five years by Johnson, a London publisher ; at Paris formed connection with Gilbert Imlay, 1793–5 ; attempted to drown herself in despair at his unfaithfulness ; married William Godwin the elder [q. v.], 1797 ; died at the birth of her daughter Mary ; Opie's portraits of her engraved in her

life by C. Kegan Paul. She published 'Thoughts on the Education of Daughters,' 1787, 'Original Stories from Real Life,' 1788, 'Vindication of the Rights of Women,' 1792, and other works ; her 'Letters to Imlay' edited by C. K. Paul, 1879.   [xxii. 60]

GODWIN, MORGAN (fl. 1685), minister in Virginia ; grandson of Bishop Francis Godwin [q. v.] ; B.A. Christ Church, Oxford, 1664 ; minister in Virginia ; died in England ; published 'The Negro's and Indian's Advocate suing for their Admission into the Church,' 1680.
                                                   [xxii. 62]

GODWIN, THOMAS (1517–1590), bishop of Bath and Wells ; fellow of Magdalen College, Oxford, 1545 ; M.A., 1548 ; first head-master of Brackley school, 1549 ; licensed medical practitioner, 1555 ; chaplain to Bishop Nicholas Bullingham [q. v.] ; D.D., 1565 ; dean of Christ Church, 1565, of Canterbury, 1567 ; bishop of Bath and Wells, 1584–90 ; offended Elizabeth by making a second marriage.
                                                   [xxii. 62]

GODWIN, THOMAS (d. 1642), master of Abingdon school ; M.A. Magdalen Hall, Oxford, 1609 ; D.D. ; rector of Brightwell, Berkshire ; published 'Romanæ Historiæ Anthologia' (16th ed., 1696), 'Moses and Aaron' (12th ed., 1685), and other works.   [xxii. 63]

GODWIN, WILLIAM, the younger (1803–1832), reporter to the 'Morning Chronicle,' 1823–32 ; son of William Godwin the elder [q. v.] ; his novel, 'Transfusion,' published by his father, 1835.   [xxii. 64]

GODWIN, WILLIAM, the elder (1756–1836), philosopher and novelist ; began philosophical studies at Hoxton Academy under Dr. Rees ; dissenting minister for four years ; became connected with extreme whigs, and an atheist, under influence of Thomas Holcroft [q. v.] ; married Mary Wollstonecraft [see GODWIN, MRS. MARY WOLLSTONECRAFT], 1797 ; after refusals from Harriet Lee [q. v.] and Mrs. Reveley (Maria Gisborne), married (1801) Mrs. Clairmont, mother of Clara Mary Jane Clairmont [q. v.] ; quarrelled with Dr. Parr and Sir J. Mackintosh, who had criticised his ethics ; converted by Coleridge to theism ; his 'Tragedy of Antonio' unsuccessful at Drury Lane, 1800 ; started (1805) a publishing business, which failed in 1822, though at first successful with Lamb's 'Tales from Shakespeare,' and some children's books written by Godwin under the name Baldwin ; derived pecuniary assistance from his acquaintance with Wedgwood and Shelley ; obtained the sinecure office of yeoman usher of the exchequer from Earl Grey, 1833 ; published 'Enquiry concerning Political Justice,' 1793, which made him known as the philosophical representative of English radicalism, a memoir of Mary Wollstonecraft, 1798, the novels 'Adventures of Caleb Williams,' 1794 (dramatised as the 'Iron Chest'), 'St. Leon,' 1799, and others ; produced 'Life of Chaucer,' 1803, 'Of Population' (answer to Malthus), 1820, and 'History of the Commonwealth,' 1824–8 ; posthumous 'essays' by him issued, 1873.   [xxii. 64]

GODWIN-AUSTEN, ROBERT ALFRED CLOYNE (1808–1884), geologist ; fellow of Oriel College, Oxford, 1830 ; B.A., 1830 ; pupil of Buckland ; F.G.S., 1830 ; F.R.S., 1849 ; took additional surname of Godwin, 1853 ; published essay 'on the possible extension of the coal-measures beneath the south-eastern parts of England,' 1854 ; Wollaston medallist, 1862 ; foreign secretary of Geological Society, 1865–7 ; wrote important papers on the geological formation of Devonshire, southern England, and parts of France ; completed works by Edward Forbes [q. v.]   [xxii. 68]

GOETZ, JOHN DANIEL (1592–1672). [See GETSIUS.]

GOFFE. [See also GOUGH.]

GOFFE or **GOUGH**, JOHN (1610 ?–1661), divine ; perpetual fellow of Magdalen College, Oxford, 1630 ; M.A., 1631 ; D.D., 1660 ; ejected from living of Hackington, and imprisoned for refusing the covenant, 1643 ; restored, 1660, having meanwhile held the living of Norton ; published 'Ecclesiæ Anglicanæ Threnodia,' 1661. [xxii. 69]

GOFFE or **GOUGH**, STEPHEN (1605–1681), royalist divine ; brother of John Goffe [q. v.] ; M.A. Merton College, Oxford, 1627 ; D.D., 1636 ; chaplain in the Low Countries and to Charles I ; employed by the king abroad and in negotiating with the Scots ; became a Romanist ; superior of French Oratorians, 1655 ; chaplain to Henrietta

Maria and tutor to Crofts (Monmouth); befriended English exiles; friend and correspondent of Vossius; died at Paris. [xxii. 69]

GOFFE or **GOUGH**, THOMAS (1591–1629), divine and poet; educated at Westminster and Christ Church, Oxford; M.A., 1616; M.A. Cambridge, 1617; B.D., 1623; incumbent of East Clandon, 1620–9; three of his tragedies acted at Christ Church; his 'Careless Shepherdess' performed before the king and queen at Salisbury (published, 1656); said to have died from his wife's persecution; 'Three Excellent Tragedies' by him published posthumously. [xxii. 70]

GOFFE or **GOUGH**, WILLIAM (d. 1679?), regicide; brother of Stephen Goffe [q. v.]; captain in Harley's new model regiment, 1645; member of deputation which presented charge against the eleven members, 1647; one of the king's judges, 1648; commanded Cromwell's regiment at Dunbar, 1650, and led another at Worcester, 1651; helped to eject Barebones parliament, 1653; active against Penruddock; major-general for Berkshire, Sussex, and Hampshire, 1655; one of the Protector's lords; member of committee of nine, 1658; one of four sent by the army to mediate with Monck, 1659; on the Restoration fled with Whalley to Massachusetts; lived concealed for three years; traditionally supposed to have repelled an attack of Indians at Hadley, Massachusetts, 1675; buried at Hadley. [xxii. 71]

GOLDAR, JOHN (1729–1795), engraver. [xxii. 73]

GOLDESBURG, **GOLDESBOROUGH**, or **GOULDS-BOROUGH**, JOHN (1568–1618), law reporter; barrister, Middle Temple; prothonotary of common pleas. [xxii. 73]

GOLDICUTT, JOHN (1793–1842), architect; received gold medallion from the pope for coloured drawing of the transverse section of St. Peter's, 1818; exhibited at the Academy, 1810–42; hon. secretary of Institute of Architects, 1834–6; published 'Antiquities of Sicily,' 1819, 'Specimens of Ancient Decorations from Pompeii,' 1825, and 'Ancient Wells and Reservoirs,' 1836. [xxii. 73]

GOLDIE or **GOUDIE**, JOHN (1717–1809), author of 'Essay on various important subjects, Moral and Divine,' 1779, known as 'Goudie's Bible.' [xxii. 74]

GOLDING, ARTHUR (1536?–1605?), translator from Latin and French; employed by Somerset; half-brother of Margaret, wife of John De Vere, sixteenth earl of Oxford; friend of Sir Philip Sidney, whose translation of De Mornay's 'Truth of Christianity' he completed, 1589; member of Parker's Society of Antiquaries; his version of Ovid's 'Metamorphoses,' 1565–7 (dedicated to Leicester and praised by Meres), known to Shakespeare; dedicated to Burghley his translation of Cæsar's 'Commentaries,' 1565, of Mela, 1585. [xxii. 75]

GOLDING, BENJAMIN (1793–1863), physician; M.D. St. Andrews, 1823; L.R.C.P., 1825; the extension of the West London Infirmary into the Charing Cross Hospital mainly his work; published 'Historical Account of St. Thomas's Hospital,' 1819, and an account of his own hospital (posthumous). [xxii. 77]

GOLDING, JOHN (d. 1719). [See GOLDWIN.]

GOLDING, RICHARD (1785–1865), line-engraver; engraved West's 'Death of Nelson,' Smirke's designs for 'Don Quixote' and 'Gil Blas,' and portraits. [xxii. 77]

GOLDMAN, FRANCIS (d. 1688?). [See GOULDMAN.]

GOLDNEY, PHILIP (1802–1857), Indian officer; interpreter in the Truckee Hills' expedition; commanded brigade sent to subdue Oudh; in charge of Fyzabad at the outbreak of the mutiny; shot at Begumjee. [xxii. 78]

GOLDSBOROUGH, GODFREY (1548–1604), bishop of Gloucester; major fellow, Trinity College, Cambridge, 1569; M.A., 1569; D.D., 1583; archdeacon of Worcester, 1579, of Shropshire, 1589; canon of Worcester, 1581; bishop of Gloucester, 1598–1604. [xxii. 79]

GOLDSBOROUGH, SIR JOHN (d. 1693), captain in East Indian navy; captured by Dutch in 1673; named chief governor of the East India Company, 1692; knighted, 1692; died of fever at Chatánati (Calcutta). [xxii. 79]

GOLDSBOROUGH, RICHARD (1821–1886), colonial wool-trader; emigrated from Bradford to Australia;

settled at Melbourne, 1848; his wool business amalgamated in 1881 with Australian Agency and Banking Corporation, became a limited company, with Goldsborough as chief director. [xxii. 80]

GOLDSCHMIDT, JENNY LIND (1821–1887). [See LIND, JOHANNA MARIA.]

GOLDSMID, ABRAHAM (1756?–1810), Jewish financier, with his brother Benjamin Goldsmid [q. v.] started as bill-broker, c. 1777; after 1792 largely engaged in government business; committed suicide in consequence of the failure of the government loan of 1810. [xxii. 80]

GOLDSMID, ANNA MARIA (1805–1889), philanthropist; daughter of Sir Isaac Lyon Goldsmid [q. v.]; educated under Campbell the poet, some of whose manuscripts she left to the British Museum. [xxii. 84]

GOLDSMID, BENJAMIN (1753?–1808), financier; brother of Abraham Goldsmid [q. v.]; founder of the Royal Naval Asylum. [xxii. 81]

GOLDSMID, SIR FRANCIS HENRY (1808–1878), lawyer and politician; son of Sir Isaac Lyon Goldsmid [q. v.]; first Jewish barrister (Lincoln's Inn); Q.C., 1858; wrote in favour of the abolition of Jewish disabilities; M.P. for Reading from 1860; spokesman of the Jewish community in parliament; established Jews' infant school, 1841, and Anglo-Jewish Association, 1871; died from an accident at Waterloo station. [xxii. 81]

GOLDSMID, HENRY EDWARD (1812–1855), Bombay civilian; educated at Haileybury; assistant to the revenue commissioner, Bombay, 1835; devised the revenue survey and assessment system of Western India; financial secretary to Bombay government, 1848; chief secretary, 1854; died at Cairo. [xxii. 82]

GOLDSMID, SIR ISAAC LYON (1778–1859), financier and philanthropist; nephew of Abraham Goldsmid [q. v.]; made a large fortune in monetary operations with Portugal, Brazil, and Turkey; created Baron da Palmeira of Portugal, 1846; prominent in foundation of University College, London, 1825, and of the North London Hospital, 1834; interested in prison reform and Robert Owen's system; first Jewish baronet, 1841. [xxii. 83]

GOLDSMITH, FRANCIS (1613–1655), translator of Grotius's 'Baptizatorum Puerorum Institutio,' 1647, and 'Sophompaneas,' 1652; of Merchant Taylors' and Pembroke and St. John's Colleges, Oxford; B.A. [xxii. 84]

GOLDSMITH, HUGH COLVILL (1789–1841), lieutenant in the navy; grandson of Henry, brother of Oliver Goldsmith [q. v.]; moved and replaced the Logan Rock, Cornwall, 1824; died at sea in the West Indies. [xxii. 84]

GOLDSMITH, LEWIS (1763?–1846), political writer and journalist; in Poland during war of independence; attacked the powers who repressed the revolution in 'The Crimes of Cabinets,' 1801; established in Paris, by arrangement with Buonaparte, 'The Argus, or London reviewed in Paris,' 1802; imprisoned for refusing to print articles against English royal family, 1803; entrusted by Napoleon with offer of the Polish crown to the future Louis XVIII in exchange for renunciation of claims in France; escaped to England, 1809; conducted (1811–25) an anti-French weekly ('Anti-Gallican,' afterwards 'British Monitor') which advocated tyrannicide; published brochures against Napoleon; returning to Paris, 1825, became interpreter to Tribunal of Commerce, and published 'Statistics of France' (1832); died in Paris. [xxii. 85]

GOLDSMITH, OLIVER (1728–1774), author; second son of an Irish clergyman; entered Trinity College, Dublin, as a sizar, 1744; sold his books and ran away to Cork on account of 'personal chastisement' received from his tutor at a supper, 1747; returned and graduated B.A., 1749; led an unsettled life in Ireland till 1752, when he went to Edinburgh to study medicine; while on his way to the continent imprisoned at Newcastle on suspicion of recruiting for the French; thence went to Leyden; wandered about for a year in France, Switzerland, and Italy, 1755–6; said to have taken medical degree at Louvain or Padua, and to have visited Voltaire at his house near Lausanne; reached London in destitution, 1756; physician in Southwark; usher at Peckham; met Griffiths, for whose 'Monthly Review' he wrote, 1757; failed to qualify for medical appointment in India, 1758; through his 'Enquiry into the Present State of Polite Learning' (1759) became acquainted with Thomas Percy, afterwards bishop of Dromore [q. v.]; contributed to 'Critical Review' and other magazines; employed by John Newbery [q. v.], in whose 'Public Ledger' his 'Citizen of the World' (1762) appeared as 'Chinese Letters'; made acquaintance of Dr. Johnson, 1761, and afterwards became a member of his club; his 'Traveller' (1764) highly praised by Johnson; introduced by the 'Traveller' to his only patron, Lord Clare; set up for the last time as a physician on the strength of his collected essays, 1765; the 'Vicar of Wakefield' sold by Johnson for him, 1766 (96th edition, 1886); saved by the proceeds from arrest for debt; left Islington for the Temple; wrote for the booksellers a 'History of Rome,' 1769, lives of Parnell and Bolingbroke, 1770, and an English history, 1771; his 'Goodnatured Man' rejected by Garrick, but produced by Colman at Covent Garden, 1768; his comedy 'She stoops to Conquer' played at Covent Garden, 1773; went to Paris with the Hornecks, 1770; had altercation (1771) with Evans, the publisher of the 'London Packet,' in which the insulting letter of 'Tom Tickle' appeared; the 'Deserted Village,' 1770, 'The Retaliation,' 1774, 'The History of Greece,' 1774, and 'Animated Nature,' 1774, were his last works. He was buried in the Temple Church, a monument at the expense of 'the Club' being placed in Westminster Abbey. Dublin editions of poems and plays appeared, 1777 and 1780, English, 1831 and 1846; 'Miscellaneous Works,' with memoir from Bishop Percy's materials, 1831. [xxii. 86]

GOLDSTUECKER, THEODOR (1821–1872), orientalist; of Jewish parentage; graduated at his native Königsberg, 1840; studied at Bonn; while at Paris assisted Burnouf in 'L'Introduction à l'Histoire du Bouddhisme indien'; at Berlin helped A. von Humboldt with his 'Kosmos'; came to England, 1850, to assist Professor H. H. Wilson with new edition of his 'Sanskrit Dictionary'; professor of Sanskrit at University College, London, 1852; member of Royal Asiatic Society; founded Sanskrit Text Society, 1866; attacked Böhtlingk, Roth, and Weber in a work on Pāṇini, 1861; his 'Literary Remains' issued, 1879. [xxii. 95]

GOLDWELL, JAMES (d. 1499), bishop of Norwich; D.C.L. All Souls' College, Oxford, 1452; dean of Salisbury, 1463; secretary of state under Edward IV; negotiated peace with France, 1471; proctor at Rome, 1472; bishop of Norwich, 1472–99; completed the tower of his cathedral, and fitted up the choir and chapels; benefactor of All Souls'. [xxii. 96]

GOLDWELL, THOMAS (d. 1585), bishop of St. Asaph; M.A. All Souls' College, Oxford, 1531; vicar of Cheriton, 1531; chaplain to Reginald Pole [q. v.], with whom he lived at Rome; attainted, 1539; returned to England, 1553; bishop of St. Asaph, 1555–8; romanised his diocese; attended Pole on his deathbed, 1558; escaped to the continent, 1559; superior of Theatines at Naples, 1561; the only English bishop at council of Trent, 1562; attainted, 1562; vicar-general to Archbishop Borromeo, 1563; vicegerent for the cardinal-vicar at Rome, 1574; prevented by illness from heading the English mission; died in Rome; last of the English Romanist bishops. [xxii. 97]

GOLDWIN or **GOLDING**, JOHN (d. 1719), musical composer; organist of St. George's Chapel, Windsor, 1697; master of the choristers, 1703; some of his sacred compositions published in Boyce and Arnold's 'Cathedral Music' and Page's 'Harmonia Sacra.' [xxii. 99]

GOLIGHTLY, CHARLES POURTALES (1807–1885), divine; educated at Eton and Oriel College, Oxford; M.A., 1830; a subscriber to 'Tracts for the Times'; disagreed with Newman, and afterwards wrote largely against the ritualists, especially attacking Cuddesdon College. [xxii. 100]

GOMERSALL, ROBERT (1602–1646?), dramatist and divine; M.A. Christ Church, Oxford, 1621; B.D., 1628; vicar of Thorncombe; published 'The Tragedie of Lodovick Sforza' and 'The Levites Revenge,' a poem (together, 1633). [xxii. 101]

GOMM, SIR WILLIAM MAYNARD (1784–1875), field-marshal; ensign, 1794; served with the 9th foot in Holland, 1799; at Ferrol, 1800, and Hanover, 1805; captain, 1803; assistant quartermaster-general in Copenhagen expedition of 1807, and in Portugal, 1808; at Coruña with Moore; on staff of Walcheren expedition, 1809; served in the Peninsula, 1810–14; lieutenant-colonel, 1812, having greatly distinguished himself at Salamanca, 1812; led his division in subsequent retreat on Portugal and advance to the Ebro; created K.C.B. and transferred to Coldstream guards; on staff at Quatre Bras and Waterloo, 1815; major-general, 1837; commander in Jamaica, 1839–42; governor of Mauritius, 1842–9; commander-in-chief in India, 1850–5; general, 1854; field-marshal, 1868; constable of the Tower, 1872–5; D.C.L. Oxford; LL.D. Cambridge; G.C.B.; his letters from the Peninsula published, 1881. [xxii. 101]

GOMME, SIR BERNARD DE (1620–1685), military engineer; served under Frederick Henry, prince of Orange; knighted by Charles I; engineer and quartermaster-general in royalist army, 1642–6; his plans of Marston Moor, Naseby, and second fight at Newbury in British Museum; as engineer-in-chief (1661) erected fortifications at Dunkirk, Portsmouth, and Plymouth, and made plans for works at Harwich and Dublin; surveyor-general of ordnance, 1685. [xxii. 103]

GOMPERTZ, BENJAMIN (1779–1865), mathematician and actuary; of Jewish extraction; president of the old Mathematical Society of Spitalfields; F.R.S., 1819; member of council of Astronomical Society, 1821–31; with Francis Baily [q. v.] began catalogue of stars, 1822; last of the Newtonian school; published tracts on imaginary quantities and porisms, 1817–18; as actuary of Alliance Assurance Company (1824–48) propounded his law of human mortality, 1825. [xxii. 104]

GOMPERTZ, LEWIS (d. 1861), lover of animals and inventor; brother of Benjamin Gompertz [q. v.]; for some years honorary secretary of Society for Prevention of Cruelty to Animals, which he left when charged with Pythagoreanism; founded Animals' Friend Society, 1832, for which he edited 'The Animals' Friend'; published 'Mechanical Inventions and Suggestions on Land and Water Locomotion,' 1850. His thirty-eight inventions included the expanding chuck still in use. [xxii. 105]

GONDIBOUR or **GOUDIBOUR**, THOMAS (fl. 1484), prior of Carlisle, 1484–1507. [xxii. 105]

GONELL, WILLIAM (d. 1546?), friend of Erasmus; M.A. Cambridge, 1488; 'public professor' at Cambridge; tutor to Sir Thomas More's children; rector of Conington, 1517; possibly author of 'Ad Erasmum Roterodamensem Epistolarum Liber.' [xxii. 106]

GONVILE, EDMUND (d. 1351), founder of Gonville Hall (now Gonville and Caius College, Cambridge; steward of William, earl Warren, and of the Earl of Lancaster; rector of Thelnetham, Suffolk; rector of Rushworth, 1326, and Terrington St. John, 1342; his foundation at Rushworth (1342) for a master and four priests suppressed, 1541. Gonville Hall, originally (1348) a purely theological foundation on the present site of Corpus Christi College, was removed by Bishop Bateman and its statutes remodelled. It was enlarged by Dr. John Caius [q. v.], 1558. [xxii. 106]

GOOCH, BENJAMIN (fl. 1775), surgeon to Shottisham infirmary and (1771) consulting surgeon to Norwich hospital; his works issued, 1792. [xxii. 107]

GOOCH, SIR DANIEL, first baronet (1816–1889), railway pioneer and inventor; trained in Stephenson & Pease's works at Newcastle; twenty-seven years locomotive superintendent of Great Western railway; designed the best broad-gauge engines; invented 'the suspended link motion with the shifting radius link,' 1843, and experimented with a dynamometer carriage; created baronet, 1866, for inauguration of telegraphic communication with America; as chairman, 1865–87, reorganised the Great Western Railway; M.P., Cricklade, 1865–85. [xxii. 107]

GOOCH, ROBERT (1784–1830), physician; descendant of Sir Thomas Gooch [q. v.]; M.D. Edinburgh, 1807; L.R.C.P., 1812; practised in Berners Street as a gynæcologist; librarian to the king, 1826; contributed to the 'Quarterly'; his 'Beguines and Nursing' appended to Southey's 'Colloquies'; wrote on the diseases of women, 1829. [xxii. 108]

GOOCH, SIR THOMAS, second baronet (1674–1754), bishop of Ely; M.A. and fellow, Caius College, Cambridge, 1698; chaplain to Queen Anne; archdeacon of Essex,

1714-37; master of Caius College, Cambridge, 1716-54; vice-chancellor of Cambridge, 1717; bishop of Bristol, 1737-8. of Norwich, 1738-48, Ely, 1748-54; succeeded as baronet, 1751. [xxii. 109]

GOOD, JOHN MASON (1764-1827), physician and author; active member of Guy's Hospital Physical Society; practised at Sudbury; came to London, 1793; M.R.C.S.; published a 'History of Medicine,' 1795; edited 'Critical Review,' and studied Spanish, Portuguese, and Russian, besides Sanskrit and oriental languages; F.R.S., 1805; left unitarianism for the Anglican church, 1807. Among his numerous works the chief are annotated translations of 'The Song of Songs,' 1803, 'Lucretius,' 1805-7 (reissued by Bohn), 'Pantologia,' 1802-13 (in conjunction with Olinthus Gilbert Gregory [q. v.]), and 'The Book of Nature,' 1826. [xxii. 110]

GOOD, JOSEPH HENRY (1775-1857), architect; designed vestry hall and national school, Holborn, and the new hall of the Armourers' Company, Coleman Street; architect to the Pavilion, Brighton, and to the commission for building new churches; clerk of works to the Tower, 1830, and Kensington Palace, 1831; an original fellow of the Institute of Architects. [xxii. 111]

GOOD, THOMAS (1609-1678), master of Balliol College, Oxford; fellow of Balliol, 1630-58; M.A., 1631; rector of Coreley, Shropshire; D.D.; prebendary of Hereford, 1660; master of Balliol, 1672-8; published 'Firmianus and Dubitantius,' 1674. [xxii. 112]

GOOD, THOMAS SWORD (1789-1872), painter, of the school of Wilkie; excelled in pictures of boys, fishermen, and smugglers; exhibited at the principal London exhibitions, 1820-34. [xxii. 112]

GOOD, WILLIAM (1527-1586), jesuit; fellow of Corpus Christi College, Oxford, 1548; M.A., 1552; headmaster and prebendary of Wells in Queen Mary's reign; professed jesuit, 1577; missioner to Ireland, Sweden, and Poland; confessor to English college, Rome; published (1584), engraved pictures of English martyrs (formerly in the English college); reproduced, under supervision of Rev. John Morris, 1888; died at Naples. [xxii. 113]

GOODACRE, HUGH (d. 1553), primate of Ireland, 1553; previously vicar of Shalfleet and chaplain to Bishop Poynet of Winchester. [xxii. 114]

GOODAL, WALTER (1706 ?-1766). [See GOODALL.]

GOODALL, CHARLES, the younger (1671-1689), poet; son of Charles Goodall the elder [q. v.]; of Eton and Merton College, Oxford; published 'Poems and Translations,' 1689. [xxii. 115]

GOODALL, CHARLES, the elder (1642-1712), physician; M.D. Cambridge, 1670; F.R.C.P., 1680; Gulstonian lecturer, 1685; twice Harveian orator; four times censor; president, 1708-12; physician to the Charterhouse, 1691; friend of Sydenham and Sloane; published treatises relating to the College of Physicians, 1684. [xxii. 114]

GOODALL, CHARLOTTE (d. 1830), actress; made a successful début at Bath (as Miss Stanton) in Rosalind, 1784; married Thomas Goodall [q. v.], 1787; first appeared at Drury Lane, 1788; acted there till 1798-9; Sir Harry Wildair and Katharine among her chief parts; divorced by her husband, 1813. [xxii. 115]

GOODALL, EDWARD (1795-1870), line-engraver; engraved many of Turner's pictures and the vignettes for his illustrations of Rogers's 'Italy' and 'Poems'; executed several of the 'Engravings from Pictures in the National Gallery'; engraved figure-subjects after paintings by his son Frederick Goodall, R.A., and plates for the 'Art Journal' and other works. [xxii. 115]

GOODALL, FREDERICK TREVELYAN (1848-1871), painter; grandson of Edward Goodall [q. v.]; Academy gold medallist with 'Return of Ulysses,' 1869; died from an accident at Capri. [xxii. 116]

GOODALL, HOWARD (1850-1874), painter; brother of Frederick Trevelyan Goodall [q. v.]; exhibited at the Royal Academy, 1870-3; died at Cairo. [xxii. 116]

GOODALL, JOSEPH (1760-1840), provost of Eton; fellow of King's College, Cambridge, 1783; Craven scholar, 1782; M.A., 1786; head-master of Eton, 1801; provost, 1809; canon of Windsor, 1808; founded scholarship at Eton. [xxii. 116]

GOODALL, SAMUEL GRANSTON (d. 1801), admiral; captured French privateer on the coast of Norway, 1760; present at reduction of Havana, 1762; commanded the Defiance at Ushant, 1778; in the Valiant at relief of Gibraltar, 1781, and in the actions off Dominica, 1782; commander-in-chief in Newfoundland, 1792; admiral, 1799. [xxii. 116]

GOODALL, THOMAS (1767-1832?), 'admiral of Hayti'; ran away to sea and was wrecked on St. Kitts, 1780; midshipman in Dominica action, 1782; married Charlotte Stanton [see GOODALL, CHARLOTTE], 1787; obtained divorce, 1813; took command of merchant-ship bound for West Indies; captured by French, but allowed to escape; made numerous captures with a privateer before 1801; again captured by the French, 1803; escaped through Germany; assisted Christophe in Hayti. [xxii. 117]

GOODALL, WALTER (1706 ?-1766), Scottish historical writer; sub-librarian of the Advocates' Library, Edinburgh, 1735; his examination (1754) of the letters of Mary Stewart to Bothwell, the first apology for the queen; assisted Keith in 'Catalogue of Scots Bishops'; edited, among other works, Fordun's 'Scotichronicon,' 1759. [xxii. 118]

GOODALL, WALTER (1830-1889), water-colour painter; youngest son of Edward Goodall [q. v.]; member of the Old Water-colour Society, 1862; some of his best work exhibited at Manchester, 1861; and his 'Lottery Ticket' at Philadelphia Exhibition, 1876. [xxii. 119]

GOODCOLE, HENRY (1586-1641), divine; attended prisoners in Newgate, and published their confessions. [xxii. 119]

GOODE, FRANCIS (1797 ?-1842), divine; son of William Goode [q. v.], the elder; of St. Paul's School and Trinity College, Cambridge; fellow and seventh wrangler, 1820; M.A., 1823; Bell university scholar, 1817; C.M.S. missionary in India; published 'The Better Covenant.' [xxii. 119]

GOODE, WILLIAM, the elder (1762-1816), divine; M.A. Magdalen Hall, Oxford, 1787; rector of St. Andrew by the Wardrobe and St. Anne, Blackfriars, 1795; president of Sion College, 1813; his 'Essays on all the Scriptural Names and Titles of Christ' published by his son William, 1822. [xxii. 120]

GOODE, WILLIAM, the younger (1801-1868), divine; son of William Goode the elder [q. v.]; of St. Paul's School and Trinity College, Cambridge; B.A., 1825; M.A., 1828; rector of St. Antholin, Watling Street, 1835-49; of All Hallows the Great, Thames Street, 1849-56; St. Margaret's, Lothbury, 1856-60; dean of Ripon, 1860; edited 'Christian Observer'; published, besides life of his father (1828), many evangelical tracts and pamphlets, and 'The Divine Rule of Faith and Practice,' 1842. [xxii. 120]

GOODEN, JAMES (1670-1730), jesuit; rector of St. Omer, 1722-8; superior of the house of probation, Ghent, 1728-30; issued at Liège 'Trigonometria Plana et Sphærica,' 1704. [xxii. 121]

GOODEN, PETER (d. 1695), Roman catholic controversialist; sent from Lisbon on the English mission; chaplain to Duke of Berwick's regiment; disputed with Thomas Birch on the temporal power of the pope, and with Stillingfleet and with William Clagett [q. v.] on transubstantiation. [xxii. 121]

GOODENOUGH, EDMUND (1785-1845), dean of Wells; son of Samuel Goodenough [q. v.]; of Westminster School and Christ Church, Oxford; M.A., 1807; D.D., 1820; vicar of Warkworth, 1818; head-master of Westminster, 1819-28; prebendary of York, Carlisle, and Westminster; prolocutor of lower house; dean of Wells, 1831-45; member of council of Royal Society, 1828; published sermons. [xxii. 122]

GOODENOUGH, JAMES GRAHAM (1830-1875), commodore; son of Edmund Goodenough [q. v.]; in the Royal William at siege of Bomarsund, 1854; gunnery lieutenant of Hastings at bombardment of Sveaborg, 1855; served in Chinese wars, 1857-8, and 1860-1; went to North America to report on naval gunnery, 1862; served on French Peasant Relief Fund, as naval attaché, and on admiralty designs committee, 1870-2; commodore of the Australian station, 1873-5; died at sea of tetanus from wound caused by a poisoned arrow at Santa Cruz. [xxii. 122]

GOODENOUGH, RICHARD (*fl.* 1686), whig conspirator; under-sheriff of London, 1682; fined for riot and assault on the lord mayor, 1683; outlawed in connection with Rye House plot, 1683; Monmouth's 'secretary of state'; when taken after Sedgemoor turned king's evidence, 1685; afterwards lived in Ireland. [xxii. 124]

GOODENOUGH, SAMUEL (1743–1827), bishop of Carlisle; of Westminster and Christ Church, Oxford; M.A., 1767; D.C.L., 1772; under-master at Westminster; conducted high-class school at Ealing; canon of Windsor, 1798; dean of Rochester, 1802; bishop of Carlisle, 1808–1827; vice-president of Royal Linnæan societies; wrote papers on the genus *Carex* and British *Fuci*; genus *Goodenia* named after him. [xxii. 124]

GOODERE, SAMUEL (1687–1741), murderer; dismissed for misconduct in attack on San Sebastian, 1719; quarrelled with his elder brother, Sir John Dineley-Goodere, uncle of Sir J. Dineley-Goodere [q. v.], and having kidnapped him caused him to be strangled on board his vessel, the Ruby, in King's Road, Bristol, 1741; hanged with his accomplices. [xxii. 125]

GOODFORD, CHARLES OLD (1812–1884), provost of Eton; fellow of King's College, Cambridge; M.A., 1839; D.D., 1853; head-master of Eton, 1853–62; provost, 1862–1884; edited Terence, 1854. [xxii. 126]

GOODGROOME, JOHN (1630?–1704?), composer, lutenist, singer, and teacher; gentleman of the Chapel Royal in three reigns; four airs by him published in Playford's 'Select Airs,' 1669, and three in 'Musical Companion,' 1673. [xxii. 127]

GOODHUGH, WILLIAM (1799?–1842), compiler of part of a Bible cyclopædia, and several linguistic handbooks. [xxii. 127]

GOODINGE, THOMAS (1746–1816), divine; B.A. Trinity College, Oxford, 1766; D.C.L., 1778; M.A. Cambridge, 1778; principal of the college school, Worcester, 1765; head-master of Leeds grammar school, 1779; rector of Cound, Shropshire, 1789. [xxii. 127]

GOODMAN, CARDELL or CARDONNELL (1649?–1699), adventurer; B.A. St. John's College, Cambridge, 1670; page of the backstairs to Charles II; afterwards an actor, winning his chief success as Julius Cæsar and Alexander; pardoned by James II for a highway robbery; paramour of the Duchess of Cleveland, but fined for attempt to poison her children; expert at ombre; bribed by friends of Fenwick not to turn evidence against him, 1697; died in France. [xxii. 128]

GOODMAN, CHRISTOPHER (1520?–1603), puritan divine; B.A. Brasenose College, Oxford, 1541; senior student, Christ Church, 1547; M.A., 1544; B.D., 1551; Margaret professor of divinity; friend and colleague of Knox at Geneva, 1555; issued violent tract against female government, 1558; at Edinburgh, 1559, one of the council concerning religion; minister of Ayr and St. Andrews; chaplain to Sir Henry Sidney in Ireland, 1566; deprived of the benefice of Alford for nonconformity, and obliged to recant his published opinions, 1571; afterwards forbidden to preach; refused subscription to the articles and service-book, 1584; visited on his deathbed at Chester by Archbishop Ussher. [xxii. 128]

GOODMAN, GABRIEL (1529?–1601), dean of Westminster; B.A. Christ's College, Cambridge, 1550; fellow of Jesus College, Cambridge, 1555; M.A., 1553; chaplain to Sir William Cecil (Lord Burghley); dean of Westminster, 1561–1601; member of ecclesiastical commission; one of Burghley's executors; founded Christ's Hospital and the grammar school, Ruthin, and left benefactions to various Cambridge colleges; translated 1 Corinthians in 'Bishops' Bible,' and assisted in William Morgan's Welsh version and in Camden's 'Britannia.' [xxii. 130]

GOODMAN, GODFREY (1583–1656), bishop of Gloucester; nephew of Gabriel Goodman [q. v.]; of Westminster and Trinity College, Cambridge; M.A. and B.D.; vicar of Stapleford Abbots, Essex, 1606–20; chaplain to the queen-consort, Anne of Denmark, 1616; dean of Rochester, 1621; bishop of Gloucester, 1625–43; reprimanded by convocation for a sermon on the real presence, 1626; charged with ritualistic practices; his election to the see of Hereford nullified by the advice of Laud, 1633, on account of his negligence; refused to sign

the new canons (1640), until deprived by convocation and imprisoned; imprisoned by the House of Commons, 1642–3, for signing the canons; compelled to retire from Gloucester, 1643; Laud's treatment of him in the matter of the canons the ninth article of his impeachment; shown by his will to have been a Roman catholic; his 'Court of James I' (a defence of the king) printed by J. S. Brewer, 1839; his 'Fall of Man proved by the Light of his Naturall Reason,' 1616, quoted by Southey. [xxii. 131]

GOODMAN, SIR STEPHEN ARTHUR (d. 1844), major-general; served with 48th foot at reduction of Malta and in the Peninsula, 1809–14, being some time acting adjutant-general; deputy judge-advocate in the Netherlands and at Paris, 1814–15; created C.B. and K.H.; colonial secretary of Berbice, 1819–44, and vendue-master, 1821–44. [xxii. 134]

GOODRICH, RICHARD (d. 1562), ecclesiastical commissioner under Edward VI and Elizabeth; nephew of Thomas Goodrich, bishop of Ely [q. v.]; ancient of Gray's Inn, 1542; attorney of the courts of augmentations and of ward and liveries; M.P., Grimsby, 1547. [xxii. 134]

GOODRICH or **GOODRICKE**, THOMAS (d. 1554), bishop of Ely and lord chancellor; fellow of Jesus College, Cambridge, 1510; M.A., 1514; rector of St. Peter Cheap, London, 1529; D.D.; chaplain of Henry VIII; bishop of Ely, 1534–54; ecclesiastical commissioner under Henry VIII and Edward VI; a compiler of the 'Bishops' Book,' 1537, and the first Book of Common Prayer; privy councillor, 1547; joined opposition to Somerset; commissioner for trial of Gardiner, 1550; ambassador to Henry II of France, 1551; lord chancellor, 1552–3. [xxii. 135]

GOODRICKE, SIR HENRY (1642–1705), second baronet; M.P. Boroughbridge, 1673–9 and 1689–1705; envoy extraordinary to Madrid, 1678–82; lieutenant-general of ordnance, 1689–1702; privy councillor, 1680. [xxii. 136]

GOODRICKE, JOHN (1764–1786), astronomer; Copley medallist, 1783, for discovery of the period and law of Algol's changes; discovered variability of β Lyræ and of δ Cephei, 1784; F.R.S., 1786. [xxii. 137]

GOODSIR, JOHN (1814–1867), anatomist; studied at St. Andrews and Edinburgh; practised with his father at Anstruther; lived at Edinburgh, 1840, with Edward Forbes [q. v.]; curator of College of Surgeons, 1841; curator of university museum and demonstrator in anatomy, 1843–6; professor of anatomy, 1846–67; ruined his health by careless living; wrote thirty scientific papers, 1838–46, including those on the growth of teeth (1839) and on 'Centres of Nutrition'; his 'Anatomical Memoirs' issued 1868; Virchow dedicated to him his 'Cellular-Pathologie' (1859). [xxii. 137]

GOODSON, RICHARD, the elder (d. 1718), organist of Christ Church and New College, Oxford; Oxford professor of music, 1682; Mus. Bac. Oxford. [xxii. 139]

GOODSON, RICHARD, the younger (d. 1741), organist of New College and Christ Church, Oxford; professor of music, 1718; Mus. Bac. Oxford, 1716; son of Richard Goodson the elder [q. v.] [xxii. 139]

GOODSONN, WILLIAM (*fl.* 1634–1662), vice-admiral; captain of the Entrance in the fight off Portland, 25 Jan. 1653; rear-admiral of the blue in the battles of June and July 1653; vice-admiral under Penn, 1654, with him at attempt on Hispaniola, and capture of Jamaica, 1655; took part in siege of Dunkirk, 1658. [xxii. 140]

GOODWIN, ARTHUR (1593?–1643), friend of Hampden at Oxford; B.A. Magdalen College, Oxford, 1614; member of the Inner Temple, 1613; M.P. Chipping Wycombe, 1620–4, Aylesbury, 1625–6; colleague of Hampden as M.P. for Buckinghamshire in Long parliament, 1640; parliamentary commander-in-chief in Buckinghamshire, 1643; present at Hampden's death. [xxii. 141]

GOODWIN, CHARLES WYCLIFFE (1817–1878), Egyptologist; brother of Harvey Goodwin, bishop of Carlisle [q. v.]; fellow of St. Catharine Hall, Cambridge; M.A., 1842; barrister, Lincoln's Inn, 1848; last editor of 'Literary Gazette' and 'Parthenon'; assistant-judge in supreme court of China and Japan, 1865; acting judge, 1868–78; died at Shanghai. His 'Mosaic Cosmogony' was the only lay contribution to 'Essays and Reviews,' 1860. He collaborated with Chabas in 'Voyage d'un

Egyptien en Phénicie ... &c., au XIVᵉ Siècle avant notre ère' (1866), and contributed to his 'Mélanges Egyptologiques' (1864), besides editing 'Story of Saneha' (1866), and Anglo-Saxon texts. [xxii. 142]

GOODWIN, CHRISTOPHER (*fl.* 1542), author of 'The Chaunce of the Dolorous Lover,' printed by Wynkyn de Worde, 1520, and 'The Maydens Dreme,' 1542, two poems. [xxii. 143]

GOODWIN, FRANCIS (1784–1835), architect; exhibited drawings at Royal Academy, 1822–34; designed town-hall and assembly-rooms, Manchester (now Free Reference Library), Derby gaol, Bradford exchange, and Leeds and Salford markets; built churches in the Midlands; published 'Plans of the new House of Commons,' pronounced the best sent in, 1833; his 'Domestic Architecture' (1833–4) republished as 'Rural Architecture,' 1835. [xxii. 143]

GOODWIN, GEORGE (*fl.* 1620), Latin verse-writer. [xxii. 144]

GOODWIN, HARVEY (1818–1891), bishop of Carlisle; educated at Gonville and Caius College, Cambridge; second wrangler and second Smith's prizeman, 1839; M.A., 1843; D.D., 1859; mathematical lecturer, 1840; fellow, 1841; honorary fellow, 1880; ordained deacon, 1842; priest, 1844; assisted in founding Ecclesiological Society, 1848; select preacher at Cambridge, 1845; dean of Ely, 1858; bishop of Carlisle, 1869 till death; honorary D.C.L. Oxford, 1885; published mathematical and religious treatises. [Suppl. ii. 329]

GOODWIN, JAMES IGNATIUS (1603?–1667), jesuit missioner; professor of moral theology and controversy at Liège. [xxii. 144]

GOODWIN, JOHN (1594?–1665), republican divine; fellow of Queens' College, Cambridge, 1617; M.A., 1617; vicar of St. Stephen's, Coleman Street, 1633–45; after his ejection set up an independent congregation there; assisted in drafting London petition against the canons of 1640; held controversies with London ministers on justification, 1638–42, maintaining an Arminian position; published 'Anti-Cavalierisme,' 1642; attacked divine right in 'Os Ossorianum,' 1643, written against the bishop of Ossory, and militant presbyterianism in 'Θεομαχία,' 1644, and 'Hagiomastix,' 1646; translated and edited (1648 and 1651) part of the 'Stratagemata Satanæ' of Jacobus Acontius [q. v.], an early advocate of toleration; applauded Pride's Purge in 'Might and Right well met,' 1648; offered spiritual advice to Charles I; in 'Υβριστοδίκαι,' 1649 (publicly burnt, 1660), defended the proceedings against Charles I; ordered into custody at the Restoration, but finally indemnified; published work in favour of general redemption, 1651 (reprinted 1840), and tracts against the baptists, Fifth-monarchy men, and Cromwell's 'Triers.' [xxii. 145]

GOODWIN, PHILIP (d. 1699), divine; M.A. St. John's College, Cambridge; one of Cromwell's 'Triers'; vicar of Watford, 1645–61; rector of Liston, 1673; published 'The Mystery of Dreames,' 1658, and theological works. [xxii. 148]

GOODWIN, THOMAS, the elder (1600–1680), independent divine; B.A. Christ's College, Cambridge, 1616; M.A. Catharine Hall, 1620; fellow; D.D. Oxford, 1653; pastor of English church at Arnheim, 1639–40; member of Westminster Assembly, 1643, but (1644) joined the 'dissenting brethren,' and became their leader; chaplain to council of state, 1649; president of Magdalen College, Oxford, 1650; a commissioner for inventory of Westminster Assembly, 1650, and approbation of preachers, 1653; attended Cromwell on his deathbed; with John Owen drew up amended Westminster confession, 1658; founded independent congregation in London, 1660; his works issued posthumously, (reprinted) 1861, and condensed 1847–50. [xxii. 148]

GOODWIN, THOMAS, the younger (1650?–1716?), son of Thomas Goodwin the elder [q. v.]; independent minister in London and Pinner; edited his father's works, and published 'History of Reign of Henry V,' 1704. [xxii. 150]

GOODWIN or **GODWIN**, TIMOTHY (1670?–1729), archbishop of Cashel; M.A. St. Edmund's Hall, Oxford, 1697; chaplain to Duke of Shrewsbury; archdeacon of Oxford, 1704; bishop of Kilmore, 1714–27; archbishop of Cashel, 1727–9. [xxii. 150]

GOODWIN, WILLIAM (d. 1620), dean of Christ Church, Oxford; scholar of Westminster; D.D., 1602; chancellor of York, 1605–11; dean of Christ Church, 1611–1620; archdeacon of Middlesex, 1616; chaplain to James I; vice-chancellor of Oxford, 1614, 1615, 1617, and 1618. [xxii. 150]

GOODWYN, EDMUND (1756–1829), medical writer; M.D. Edinburgh; published two medical works. [xxii. 151]

GOODYEAR, JOSEPH (1799–1839), engraver; engraved Eastlake's 'Greek Fugitives' for Finden's 'Gallery.' [xxii. 151]

GOODYER or **GOODIER**, SIR HENRY (1534–1595), colonel; imprisoned in Tower, 1571–2, for complicity in Norfolk's intrigue on behalf of Mary Queen of Scots; served in Low Countries, 1585–6; knighted, 1586; colonel; patron of Michael Drayton. [Suppl. ii. 330]

GOODYER or **GOODIER**, SIR HENRY (1571–1627), literary patron; son of Sir Henry Goodyer (1534–1595) [q. v.]; friend of John Donne; probably knighted in Ireland, 1599; gentleman of privy chamber, 1605; famous for his hospitality to literary men. Verses by him appear in several contemporary publications. [Suppl. ii. 330]

GOOGE, BARNABE (1540–1594), poet; kinsman of Sir William Cecil, who employed him in Ireland, 1574–85; published 'Eglogs, Epytaphes, and Sonnetes,' 1563 (reprinted, 1871), and translations, including Heresbachius's 'Foure Bookes of Husbandrie,' 1577. [xxii. 151]

GOOKIN, DANIEL (1612?–1687), writer on the American Indians; nephew of Sir Vincent Gookin [q. v.]; went to Virginia with his father; obtained grants of land, 1637 and 1642; settled at Boston (Massachusetts), 1644; founded Roxbury school, 1646; removed to Cambridge, Massachusetts, and became speaker of the house, 1651; sent by Cromwell to settle Jamaica, 1655; employed financially at Dunkirk, 1659; returned to America, 1660, with the regicides, Edward Whalley and William Goffe [q. v.], whom he protected; superintendent of Massachusetts Indians, 1661–87; major-general of the colony, 1681; buried at Cambridge; his 'Historical Collections of the Indians in New England' printed by Massachusetts Historical Society, 1792. [xxii. 152]

GOOKIN, CAPTAIN ROBERT (d. 1667), parliamentarian; brother of Vincent Gookin [q. v.]; served parliament in Ireland, and received grants of land. [xxii. 155]

GOOKIN, SIR VINCENT (1590?–1638), anti-Irish writer; knighted; created disturbance in Munster by publishing letter to Lord Deputy Wentworth attacking the Irish nation, 1634; fled to England on issue of warrant for his arrest. His case raised the question of the judicial powers of the Irish parliament. [xxii. 154]

GOOKIN, VINCENT (1616?–1659), surveyor-general of Ireland; son of Sir Vincent Gookin [q. v.]; represented Irish constituencies in Cromwell's parliaments; published pamphlets (1655) deprecating enforcement of orders for transplantation of Irish to Connaught. [xxii. 154]

GOOLD, THOMAS (1766?–1846), Irish master in chancery; barrister, 1791; had large nisi prius practice; king's serjeant, 1830; master in chancery, 1832; opposed the union. [xxii. 155]

GORANUS, GABHRAN (538–560?), king of Scotland; being fourth king of Dalriada; succeeded his brother, Congallus I [q. v.], 538. [xxii. 156]

GORDON, SIR ADAM DE (d. 1305). [See GURDON.]

GORDON, SIR ADAM DE (d. 1333), statesman and warrior; accompanied Edward I to England to arrange for pacification of Scotland, 1304; justiciar of Scotland, 1310–14; granted barony of Stitchel by Robert Bruce, 1315; with Mabinson carried to Avignon letter asserting Scottish independence, 1320; obtained lordship of Strathbogie, which he named Huntly; killed at Halidon Hill. [xxii. 156]

GORDON, SIR ADAM DE (d. 1402), warrior; prominent in raid of Roxburgh, 1377, and subsequent raids present at Otterburn, 1388; fell at Homildon Hill. His daughter Elizabeth was ancestress of the Earls of Huntly and the Dukes of Gordon and Sutherland. [xxii. 157]

GORDON, LORD ADAM (1726?–1801), general; son of Alexander, second duke of Gordon [q. v.]; M.P. Aberdeenshire, 1754–68, Kincardineshire, 1774–88; served with guards in Bligh's expedition, 1758; colonel of 66th in Jamaica, 1762–6; commander of forces in Scotland, 1782–98; general, 1796. [xxii. 158]

GORDON, ADAM LINDSAY (1833–1870), Australian poet; joined Australian mounted police, 1853; member for Victoria in House of Assembly, 1865; migrated to Victoria, 1867; noted steeplechaser; committed suicide; his three volumes of verse edited by Marcus Clarke, 1880. [xxii. 158]

GORDON, ALEXANDER, third EARL OF HUNTLY (d. 1524), rendered valuable assistance in reduction of the Western Isles, 1504; sheriff and castellan of Inverness, 1509, with jurisdiction over Ross and Caithness; led Scots vanguard at Flodden, 1513; member of the queen-mother's council; adherent of Albany; lieutenant of Scotland, 1518, and twice member of the council of regency. [xxii. 158]

GORDON, ALEXANDER (1516?–1575), bishop-elect of Galloway and titular archbishop of Athens; brother of George Gordon, fourth earl of Huntly [q. v.]; favourite of his half-brother, King James V; administrator of Caithness, 1544; his election as archbishop of Glasgow overruled in favour of James Beaton, 1551; bishop of the Isles, 1553; abbot of Inchaffray and Icolmkill; elected to see of Galloway, 1558; joined the reformers, 1560, demanding title of superintendent of Galloway; privy councillor and extraordinary lord of session, 1566; resumed title of bishop; temporised between Mary Queen of Scots and the lords; resigned his see in favour of his son John, 1568, but retained 'supervision'; inhibited for signing bond for restoration of Mary, 1569; her commissioner in England, 1570–1; attended Kirkcaldy of Grange's parliament, 1571; ordered to do penance, 1573. [xxii. 159]

GORDON, ALEXANDER, eleventh or twelfth EARL OF SUTHERLAND (1552–1594), succeeded John Gordon, tenth or eleventh earl [q. v.], 1567; engaged in struggle with Earls of Caithness to secure possession of his earldom; married (1573), as his second wife, Jean Gordon, Bothwell's divorced wife. [xxii. 212]

GORDON, ALEXANDER (1587–1654), of Earlston, covenanter; friend of Samuel Rutherford [q. v.]; fined for refusing to present episcopalian curate; M.P. for Galloway, 1641–9; opposed ecclesiastical policy of Charles I, who called him 'Earl of Earlston.' [xxii. 161]

GORDON, SIR ALEXANDER (1650–1726), of Earlston, covenanter, grandson of Alexander Gordon (1587–1654) [q. v.]; after Bothwell Brigg (1680) escaped to Holland; arrested at Newcastle, 1683, and examined at Edinburgh concerning the Rye House plot; imprisoned till 1689; his estates restored at the Revolution. [xxii. 162]

GORDON, ALEXANDER, second DUKE OF GORDON (1678?–1728), Jacobite; when Marquis of Huntly brought 2,300 men to James Edward, the Old Pretender, at Perth; at Sheriffmuir, 1715; submitted and received pardon; succeeded to dukedom, 1716; visited and corresponded with king of Prussia and grand duke of Tuscany; received presents from Pope Clement XII. [xxii. 163]

GORDON, ALEXANDER (1692?–1754?), antiquary; M.A. Aberdeen; studied music in Italy, and became known as 'Singing Sandie'; travelled in Scotland and northern England; published 'Itinerarium Septentrionale' (1726), with supplement (1732); also 'Lives of Alexander VI and Cæsar Borgia,' 1729, and translation of 'De Amphitheatro' of Maffei, 1730; secretary to Society for the Encouragement of Learning, Society of Antiquaries (1736), and the Egyptian Society; went to South Carolina, 1741, as secretary to the governor; died there. [xxii. 164]

GORDON, SIR ALEXANDER (1786–1815), lieutenant-colonel; brother of George Hamilton-Gordon, fourth earl of Aberdeen [q. v.]; aide-de-camp to his uncle, Sir David Baird [q. v.], at the Cape, 1806, at Copenhagen, 1807, and in Spain, 1808–9; employed by Beresford in negotiations at Buenos Ayres; lieutenant-colonel, 1813; aide-de-camp to Wellington in the Peninsula and in Belgium; K.C.B.; mortally wounded at Waterloo. [xxii. 166]

GORDON, ALEXANDER, fourth DUKE OF GORDON (1743–1827), described by Kaimes as the greatest subject in Britain; Scottish representative peer, 1767; created a British peer, 1784; lord keeper of Scotland; raised regi-ments for American and revolutionary wars; wrote, 'There is Cauld Kail in Aberdeen.' [xxii. 167]

GORDON, ANDREW (1712–1751), natural philosopher; professor of philosophy at Erfurt, 1737; gained great reputation as an electrician; the first to use a cylinder; published, among other works, 'Phænomena Electricitatis exposita,' 1744. [xxii. 167]

GORDON, ARCHIBALD (1812–1886), inspector-general of hospitals; M.D. Edinburgh, 1834; surgeon in Sutlej and Punjaub campaigns; principal medical officer of second division at Sebastopol; chief medical officer in China, 1857, and Oudh, 1858–9; C.B.; inspector-general, 1867–70; knight of the Legion of Honour. [xxii. 168]

GORDON, CHARLES, first EARL OF ABOYNE (d. 1681), fourth son of George Gordon, second marquis of Huntly [q. v.]; created Baron Gordon of Strathavon and Glenlivat, and Earl of Aboyne, 1660; built Aboyne Castle. [xxii. 168]

GORDON, CHARLES, second EARL OF ABOYNE (d. 1702), allowed to sit in Scottish parliament on declaring himself a protestant, 1698. [xxii. 168]

GORDON, SIR CHARLES (1756–1835), governor of St. Lucia; served in the American war; assisted Brunswick in capture of Amsterdam, 1787, and as British commissioner, 1791–2; lieutenant-colonel of 41st, 1787; knight of Prussian order of Military Merit, 1790; took part in capture of Martinique and St. Lucia, 1793; governor of St. Lucia; dismissed from governorship for extortion, 1794. [xxii. 168]

GORDON, CHARLES GEORGE (1833–1885), 'Chinese Gordon'; entered royal engineers, 1852; wounded in trenches before Sebastopol, 1855; took part in attack on the Redan, 1855; received Legion of Honour and Turkish medal; assisted in delimitation of Russo-Turkish boundaries in Europe and Asia, 1856–8; promoted for services in Chinese war, 1860–2; explored section of great wall of China; appointed to command Chinese forces against the Taipings in the Kiangsoo district, 1863; captured Soochow, but retired on account of Li Hung Chang's breach of faith in putting to death rebel leaders (Wangs); refused the honours and gifts offered by the emperor, 1864; induced to resume the command; in four months completed reduction of the rebels by storming of Chanchu-fu, 27 April 1864; made mandarin of the first class, but again refused money present; lieutenant-colonel and C.B., 1865; British member of commission for improving navigation of Sulina mouth of the Danube, 1871; governor of equatorial provinces of Africa (Egyptian), 1874–6, organising a letter-post between Cairo and the Albert Nyanza, and establishing by personal observation the course of the Victoria Nile into Lake Albert; thwarted by Ismail Pasha in his efforts to suppress the slave trade, resigning in consequence, 1876; returned, 1877, as governor-general of the Soudan and of the equatorial provinces and the Red Sea littoral; conquered and pacified Darfour; overawed Suleiman, the slave trader, in personal interview, 1877, and completely suppressed the slave-trade, 1878; failed to come to an understanding with Abyssinia, where he was for a time a prisoner; returned to England, 1880; went to India as secretary to the Marquis of Ripon, 1880; resigned, 1880; induced Chinese government to resume friendly relations with Russia, 1880; commanding royal engineer and head of the troops in Mauritius, 1881–2; major-general, 1882; accepted command of colonial forces in South Africa, 1882; resigned when his negotiations with Masupha, the Basuto chief, were interrupted by the treacherous attack instigated by Mr. Sauer, secretary for native affairs, 1882; in Palestine, 1883; had agreed to go to the Congo for the king of Belgium, but was despatched by the British government (1884) to rescue Egyptian garrisons in the Soudan previous to its abandonment; was appointed at Cairo governor-general of the Soudan, with orders to organise an independent government; his requests for the co-operation of Zebehr and the assistance of Turkish troops refused; hemmed in by the Mahdi at Khartoum, was the only Englishman there after the murder of his companions Colonel Stewart and Frank Power; killed, after having sustained a siege of 317 days, succour being sent from England too late. His memory is perpetuated by statues in London, Chatham, and Khartoum, and by the Gordon Boys' Homes. His Chinese diaries, Khartoum journals, and several volumes of letters have been published. [xxii. 169]

GORDON, DUKE (1739-1800), assistant-librarian to Edinburgh University, 1763-1800 ; M.A. Edinburgh, 1800. [xxii. 176]

GORDON, EDWARD STRATHEARN, BARON GORDON (1814-1879), lord of appeal ; LL.B. Glasgow and Edinburgh ; called to Scottish bar, 1835 ; solicitor-general for Scotland, 1866-7 ; Q.C., 1868 ; lord-advocate, 1867-8 and 1874-6 ; dean of faculty, 1868-74 ; M.P., Thetford, 1867-8, Glasgow and Aberdeen universities, 1869-76 ; privy councillor, 1874 ; lord of appeal, 1876-9. [xxii. 177]

GORDON, ELIZABETH, DUCHESS OF GORDON (1794-1864), daughter of Alexander Brodie ; married, 1813, George Gordon, marquis of Huntly, afterwards fifth Duke of Gordon [q. v.] ; joined Free church of Scotland, 1846. [xxii. 177]

GORDON, GEORGE, second EARL OF HUNTLY (d. 1502 ?), lord high chancellor of Scotland ; succeeded to earldom, 1470 ; commissioner for peace with England, 1484 ; supported James III against the nobles, 1487 ; lord justiciary north of Forth, 1488 ; made privy councillor by James IV, and lieutenant, north of Esk, 1491 ; married Princess Annabella, daughter of James I ; divorced, as being, by a prior marriage, within the forbidden degrees of affinity, 1471 ; chancellor of Scotland, 1498-1501. [xxii. 178]

GORDON, GEORGE, fourth EARL OF HUNTLY (1514-1562), grandson of Alexander Gordon, third earl of Huntly [q. v.] ; succeeded as earl, 1524 ; brought up with James V by Angus ; privy councillor, 1535 ; one of the regents, 1536-7 ; defeated English at Hadden Rig, 1542 ; supported Cardinal Beaton against Arran, and concerted with him carrying off the young queen, 1543 ; as lieutenant of the north crushed the Camerons and Macdonalds, 1544 ; lord chancellor, 1546 ; defeated and captured by Somerset at Pinkie, 1547, after offering single combat ; temporarily supported English in Scotland, but afterwards (1548) favoured French alliance ; disgraced and imprisoned, 1554, owing to the queen regent's jealousy of his power over the north ; joined lords of the congregation against her, 1560 ; made privy councillor on the arrival of Mary Queen of Scots, but his earldom of Moray given to her half-brother ; died at Corrichie in arms against the royal authority. His body was set at the bar of parliament while an act of attainder was passed, 1563, and lay unburied for three years. [xxii. 178]

GORDON, GEORGE, fifth EARL OF HUNTLY (d. 1576), second son of George Gordon, fourth earl of Huntly [q. v.] ; sheriff of Inverness, 1556 ; imprisoned at Dunbar till the marriage of Mary Queen of Scots with Darnley, 1565, when his lands and dignities were nominally restored ; allied himself with Bothwell, 1566 ; joined Queen Mary at Dunbar, after Rizzio's murder, 1566 ; became lord chancellor ; joined Bothwell in plot to murder Moray at Jedburgh ; signed the bond at Craigmillar for Darnley's murder ; accompanied Bothwell and Mary on a visit to Darnley the night before his murder ; his estates actually restored after Bothwell's acquittal, 1567 ; Bothwell's divorce from his sister facilitated by his influence over her ; witnessed marriage contract between Mary and Bothwell, 1567 ; connived at capture of the queen, and accompanied her to Edinburgh ; escaped to the north after her flight ; joined her partisans at Dumbarton ; after a temporary agreement with Moray, conspired for her deliverance from Lochleven, 1567 ; after Mary's escape to England (1568) held all 'the north in alliance with Argyll, but received Mary's order to disperse ; after a temporary submission gained possession of Edinburgh Castle, held a parliament, captured the regent Lennox at Stirling, and (1572) came to terms with the regent Morton. [xxii. 182]

GORDON, GEORGE, first MARQUIS and sixth EARL OF HUNTLY (1562-1636), educated in France ; allied himself with the Duke of Lennox against Morton, and was prominent in the counter-revolution of 1583 ; secretly corresponded with Spain for the restoration of catholicism ; frequently compelled by the kirk to subscribe the confession of faith ; captain of the guard at Holyrood, 1588 ; raised, with Erroll, a rebellion in the north, 1589, but submitted to James VI ; protected by the king after his murder of the 'bonnie Earl' of Moray, 1592, as also after his rebellion and excommunication, 1593 ; joined in a rebellion against James VI's government, 1594 ; his castle of Strathbogie blown up by the king, 1594 ; compelled

(1595) to leave Scotland on his refusal to give up his confederate, Bothwell (the second earl) ; pardoned and received into the kirk, 1597, and created marquis and joint-lieutenant of the north, 1599 ; again excommunicated and compelled to subscribe, 1608 ; imprisoned on refusing a fresh demand for subscription ; on his release went to England and obtained absolution from the archbishop of Canterbury, 1616 ; deprived by Charles I of his family jurisdiction in the north, 1630 ; subsequently twice summoned before the privy council and imprisoned. [xxii. 186]

GORDON, GEORGE, second MARQUIS OF HUNTLY (d. 1649), eldest son of George Gordon, sixth earl and first marquis [q. v.] ; educated in England, and created Earl of Enzie ; commanded company of gens d'armes in France ; created Viscount of Aboyne, 1632 ; succeeded his father, 1636 ; refused to subscribe the covenant, 1638 ; driven, when lieutenant of the north, from Strathbogie by Montrose ; refusing the covenanters' demands was taken to Edinburgh under guard, 1639 ; joined Charles I ; outlawed by the Scots, 1643 ; excommunicated, 1644 ; retired before Argyll to Caithness ; subsequently stormed Aberdeen, 1645 ; raised forces for Charles I ; captured by Colonel Menzies at Dalnabo, 1647 ; beheaded at Edinburgh, 1649. [xxii. 190]

GORDON, GEORGE, first DUKE OF GORDON and fourth MARQUIS OF HUNTLY (1643-1716), succeeded as fourth Marquis of Huntly, 1653 ; educated abroad ; saw military service with the French and the Prince of Orange, 1672-5 ; created Duke of Gordon at instigation of Claverhouse, 1684 ; appointed by James II privy councillor and captain of Edinburgh Castle, 1686 ; surrendered the castle to the convention of estates, 1689 ; several times afterwards imprisoned. [xxii. 194]

GORDON, GEORGE, first EARL OF ABERDEEN (1637-1720), statesman ; second son of Sir John Gordon (d. 1644) [q. v.] ; M.A. King's College, Aberdeen, 1658 ; four years professor at Aberdeen ; succeeded to baronetcy, 1667 ; practised at Edinburgh bar ; represented Aberdeenshire in Scots parliament ; raised to the bench as Lord Haddo, 1680 ; a lord of the articles and president of session, 1681 ; chancellor of Scotland under James, duke of York, 1682-4 ; created Earl of Aberdeen, 1682 ; dismissed from chancellorship for leniency to nonconformists, 1684 ; supported treaty of union, 1705-6. [xxii. 196]

GORDON, LORD GEORGE (1751-1793), agitator ; served in the navy ; M.P. for Ludgershall, 1774-81 ; as president of the Protestant Association for repeal of relieving act of 1778, presented petition which led to the No-Popery riots of 1780 ; acquitted of treason, 1781 ; again appeared as protestant champion, 1784, in the quarrel between the Dutch and the Emperor Joseph ; became a Jew ; imprisoned for libels on the British government and Marie Antoinette, 1788 till death ; died in Newgate. [xxii. 197]

GORDON, GEORGE, fifth DUKE OF GORDON (1770-1836), general ; as Marquis of Huntly served with guards in Flanders, 1793-4 ; raised regiment now known as Gordon Highlanders ; commanded it (1795-9) in Spain, Corsica, Ireland, and Holland, where he was badly wounded ; lieutenant-general, 1808 ; general, 1819 ; commanded division in Walcheren expedition, 1809 ; M.P., Eye, 1806 ; created Baron Gordon, 1807 ; G.C.B., 1820 ; succeeded to dukedom, 1827. [xxii. 198]

GORDON, GEORGE, ninth MARQUIS OF HUNTLY (1761-1853), served in the army as Lord Strathaven ; succeeded as fifth Earl of Aboyne, 1794 ; Scottish representative peer, 1796-1815 ; created peer of United Kingdom, 1815 ; K.T., 1827 ; succeeded as Marquis of Huntly, 1836. [xxii. 199]

GORDON, GEORGE (1806-1879), horticultural writer ; with Robert Glendinning published 'Pinetum' (1858), with supplement (1862). [xxii. 200]

GORDON, GEORGE HAMILTON-, fourth EARL OF ABERDEEN (1784-1860), statesman ; at Harrow with Althorp and Palmerston ; M.A. St. John's College, Cambridge, 1804 ; travelled in Greece and founded the Athenian Society ; 'the travell'd thane' of 'English Bards and Scotch Reviewers' ; Scottish representative peer, 1806-14 ; ambassador extraordinary at Vienna, 1813, and representative at the congress of Châtillon, 1814 ; privy councillor and Viscount Gordon of the United

Kingdom, 1814; president of Society of Antiquaries, 1812–1846; chancellor of the duchy of Lancaster in Wellington's cabinet, and afterwards foreign secretary, 1828–30; secretary for war and the colonies under Peel, 1834–5; endeavoured to prevent schism in the Scottish church by his Non-Intrusion Bill and the act of 1843; foreign secretary, 1841–6, preserving peace with France through his friendship with Guizot; improved relations with America by the Oregon treaty, 1846; followed Peel out of office, and on his death led his adherents; spoke ably against Russell's Ecclesiastical Titles Bill, 1851; brought about the defeat of Lord Derby by joining the whigs on the house-tax resolution, 1852; formed a coalition ministry of whigs and Peelites, 1852; forced into the Crimean war by Palmerston and Stratford Canning, 1854; resigned after the carrying of Roebuck's vote of censure of the ministry's conduct of the war, 1855; naturally inclined to policy of non-intervention; K.G., 1855; published a few miscellaneous works. His bust, by Noble, is in Westminster Abbey. His correspondence was privately printed by his son, Sir A. H. Gordon, afterwards Lord Stanmore.   [xxii. 200]

GORDON, GEORGE ROSS (*fl.* 1832), Gaelic poet; brother of William Gordon (1770–1820) [q. v.]; published poems by himself and brothers, 1804–5.   [xxii. 236]

GORDON, HENRIETTA, 'Lady Henrietta' (*fl.* 1658), maid of honour to Princess Henrietta, Duchess of Orleans; daughter of John Gordon, viscount Melgum; educated in Parisian convents; entered the service of Anne of Austria, 1649; a favourite of the Duc d'Orléans, and attendant on both his wives.   [xxii. 203]

GORDON, SIR HENRY WILLIAM (1818–1887), commissary-general; brother of Charles George Gordon [q. v.]; served in the army, 1835–55; C.B. for services in Crimea, 1857; commissary-general, 1875; K.C.B., 1877; published 'Events in the Life of Charles George Gordon,' 1886.   [xxii. 204]

GORDON, JAMES (1541–1620), jesuit; fifth son of George Gordon, fourth earl of Huntly [q. v.]; while on mission with Father William Crichton [q. v.] to Scotland, 1584, disputed with George Hay (*d.* 1588) [q. v.], and converted Francis, earl of Erroll; held conference with protestants at Holyrood in presence of James VI, 1588; sent by James VI to Rome to arrange for restoration of Romanism, 1592; exiled after his return; author of controversial works; died at Paris.   [xxii. 204]

GORDON, JAMES (1553–1641), jesuit; rector of the colleges at Toulouse and Bordeaux; D.D.; confessor to Louis XIII; died at Paris. His works include biblical commentaries, 1632, and 'Opus Chronologicum,' 1613.   [xxii. 205]

GORDON, JAMES, second VISCOUNT ABOYNE (*d.* 1649), second son of George Gordon, second marquis of Huntly [q. v.]; succeeded as viscount, 1636; defeated by Montrose at bridge of Dee, 1639; outlawed by Scottish council, 1643; joined Montrose against covenanters, and was made lieutenant of the north; excommunicated, 1644, and exempted from pardon, 1648; died of grief in Paris on hearing of Charles I's execution.   [xxii. 206]

GORDON, JAMES (1615?–1686), topographer; son of Robert Gordon (1580–1661) [q. v.]; graduated at King's College, Aberdeen, 1636; pastor of Rothiemay, 1641–86; executed survey of Edinburgh, 1646–7, and views and plan of Aberdeen, 1661. His 'History of Scots Affairs' (wrongly attributed to his father, Robert) was printed, 1841, his 'Aberdoniæ utriusque Descriptio,' 1842.   [xxii. 206]

GORDON, JAMES (1664–1746), Scottish Roman catholic prelate; educated at Scots College, Paris; elected coadjutor of Bishop Thomas Joseph Nicholson [q. v.], and consecrated secretly to see of Nicopolis *in partibus,* 1706; vicar apostolic in Scotland, 1718; first vicar-apostolic of lowland district, 1731–46.   [xxii. 207]

GORDON, JAMES (1762–1825), eccentric; solicitor at Cambridge; made a living in London by waiting at coach offices; his portrait and some of his jests preserved in Hone's 'Everyday Book.'   [xxii. 208]

GORDON, SIR JAMES ALEXANDER (1782–1869), admiral of the fleet; entered navy, 1793; saw service at l'Orient, 1795, and in the Goliath at St. Vincent and the Nile; in the Racoon at capture of the Lodi and the Mutine, 1803; distinguished himself at capture of the Spanish convoy off Rota, 1808; while in command of the Active received gold medal for conduct at Lissa, 1811; lost a leg in the capture of the Pomone, 1812; commanded squadron in American war, which reduced Fort Washington and took city of Alexandria and twenty-one ships, 1814; lieutenant-governor of Greenwich, 1840; governor, 1853; admiral, 1854; G.C.B., 1855; admiral of the fleet, 1868.   [xxii. 208]

GORDON, JAMES ALEXANDER (1793–1872), physician; M.D. Edinburgh, 1814; F.R.C.P., 1836; censor, 1838; physician to the London Hospital, 1828–44; with Dr. Mackenzie established 'Quarterly Journal of Foreign Medicine and Surgery,' 1819.   [xxii. 209]

GORDON, JAMES BENTLEY (1750–1819), historian; B.A. Trinity College, Dublin, 1773; incumbent of Cannaway, Cork, and Killegney, Wexford; published works, including 'History of the Rebellion in Ireland in 1798,' 1801, and 'History of Ireland,' 1805, &c.   [xxii. 209]

GORDON, JAMES EDWARD HENRY (1852–1893), electrical engineer; son of James Alexander Gordon (1793–1872) [q. v.]; B.A. Caius College, Cambridge, 1875; manager of electric lighting department of Telegraph Construction and Maintenance Company, 1883; engineer to Metropolitan Electric Supply Company, 1888–9; started practice with Mr. W. J. Rivington, 1889; M.I.C.E., 1890; published works on electricity.   [Suppl. ii. 332]

GORDON, SIR JAMES WILLOUGHBY (1773–1851), general; served with the 66th in Ireland, the West Indies, Gibraltar, and North America, 1783–1800; lieutenant-colonel of the 85th, 1801, of the 92nd, 1804; military secretary to the Duke of York when commander-in-chief; quartermaster-general in Peninsula, 1811–12, and afterwards at Horse Guards; lieutenant-general, 1825; general, 1841; created baronet, 1818; privy councillor, 1830; G.C.B., 1831; published (1809) 'Military Transactions of the British Empire,' 1803–7. [xxii. 210]

GORDON, JANE, DUCHESS OF GORDON (1749?–1812), wife of Alexander Gordon, fourth duke of Gordon [q. v.]; daughter of Sir William Maxwell of Monreith; married, 1767; head of Tory salon at her house in Pall Mall, 1787–1801; married three of her daughters to dukes and another to a marquis; her portrait painted by Reynolds, 1775.   [xxii. 210]

GORDON, JOHN, tenth or eleventh EARL OF SUTHERLAND (1526?–1567), succeeded his grandfather, Adam, earl of Sutherland, 1537; lieutenant of Moray, 1547–8; accompanied queen mother of Scotland to France, 1550; received earldom of Ross, 1555; employed by his relative, Huntly, in diplomatic negotiations, 1560; said to have been concerned in plot for carrying off the young Queen Mary; attainted while in Flanders, 1563; captured (1565) and detained in England; restored to his estates with Huntly; poisoned at Helmsdale, probably at instigation of George, fourth earl of Caithness.   [xxii. 211]

GORDON, JOHN (1544–1619), dean of Salisbury; probably eldest son of Alexander Gordon (1516?–1575) [q. v.], bishop-elect of Galloway; served Louis, prince of Condé; attended Thomas, duke of Norfolk, 1568, and Mary Queen of Scots, 1569–72; gentleman of the privy chamber to Charles IX, Henri III, and Henri IV; saved lives of several countrymen during massacre of St. Bartholomew, 1572; held public disputations with Benetrius, the chief rabbi at Avignon, 1574, and against Du Perron, 1601; invited to England in consequence of his eulogies of James I; dean of Salisbury, 1604–19; took part in the Hampton Court conference, 1604; D.D. Oxford, 1605; received barony of Glenluce, 1611; benefactor of Salisbury Cathedral; published theological works, some of them in answer to Bellarmine.   [xxii. 212]

GORDON, SIR JOHN, first VISCOUNT KENMURE and BARON LOCHINVAR (1599?–1634), of Lochinvar, brother-in-law of the Marquis of Argyll and friend of Samuel Rutherford [q. v.]; created Scottish peer, 1633.   [xxii. 214]

GORDON, SIR JOHN, first baronet (*d.* 1644), royalist; distinguished himself against the covenanters at Turriff, 1639, and joined Charles I in England; created baronet, 1642; excommunicated and taken at Kellie by Argyll; beheaded at Edinburgh.   [xxii. 215]

s

GORDON, JOHN, thirteenth or fourteenth EARL OF SUTHERLAND (1609–1663), sheriff and coroner of Sutherland ; nephew of Sir Robert Gordon (1580–1656) [q. v.] ; obtained many subscriptions to the covenant in the north ; one of the leaders at battle of Auldearn, 1645 ; lord privy seal in Scotland, 1649 ; raised forces against Cromwell, 1650 ; his piety commemorated by Wodrow. [xxii. 215]

GORDON, JOHN (1644–1726), bishop of Galloway, 1688 ; followed James II to Ireland and France ; D.D. ; converted to Romanism by Bossuet ; appointed by Clement XI to abbey of St. Clement ; died at Rome. [xxii. 216]

GORDON, JOHN, fifteenth or sixteenth EARL OF SUTHERLAND (1660 ?–1733), offered to mediate with William III on behalf of his connection, Dundee, 1689 ; served under William III in Flanders ; succeeded to earldom, 1703 ; privy councillor to Queen Anne, 1704 ; a commissioner for the union ; Scottish representative peer, 1706, 1715, 1722, and 1727 ; president of the board of trade, 1715 ; received pension for services as lieutenant of the north in 1715 ; K.T. [xxii. 217]

GORDON, JOHN (1702–1739), Gresham professor of music ; educated at Westminster and Trinity College, Cambridge ; barrister, Gray's Inn, 1725 ; Gresham professor, 1723–39. [xxii. 217]

GORDON, SIR JOHN WATSON- (1788–1864), portrait-painter ; assumed name of Gordon, 1826 ; the leading portrait-painter after Raeburn's death, 1823 ; exhibited at Scottish Academy, 1830–64 ; president, 1850 ; exhibited at Royal Academy from 1827 ; R.A., 1851 ; knighted, 1850 ; the Watson-Gordon professorship at Edinburgh endowed in his memory, 1879. [xxii. 218]

GORDON, SIR JOHN WILLIAM (1814–1870), major-general ; entered engineers, 1833 ; present at Alma and Inkerman, and prominent in siege of Sebastopol ; severely wounded at the great sortie, but commanded engineers in Kertch expedition ; deputy adjutant-general at the Horse Guards, 1856–61 ; K.C.B. and major-general ; commanded in the Trent affair, 1861 ; inspector-general of fortifications ; killed himself in a fit of insanity resulting from wound. [xxii. 219]

GORDON, LORD LEWIS (d. 1754), Jacobite ; third son of Alexander Gordon, second duke of Gordon [q. v.] ; one of Prince Charles Edward's council, 1745 ; defeated Macleod near Inverury, 1745 ; died at Montreuil. [xxii. 219]

GORDON, LUCY, LADY DUFF- (1821–1869). [See DUFF-GORDON, LUCIE or LUCY.]

GORDON, OSBORNE (1813–1883), divine ; of Christ Church, Oxford ; censor, 1846 ; Ireland scholar, 1835 ; M.A., 1839 ; B.D., 1847 ; reader in Greek, Christ Church, Oxford, 1846 ; active against 'papal aggression,' 1850 ; prominent in the university till presented (1860) to living of Easthampstead, Berkshire ; chairman of commission of inquiry into queen's colleges in Ireland, 1876 ; member of the Oxford commission ; his epitaph at Easthampstead written by Ruskin ; edited Eusebius, 1842. [xxii. 221]

GORDON, PATRICK (fl. 1615–1650), poet ; perhaps author of 'A Shorte Abridgment of Britenes Distemper' (printed, 1844) ; published 'Neptunus Britannicus Corydonis,' 1614, as well as a poem on Bruce, and 'First Booke ... of Penardo and Laissa,' 1615. [xxii. 222]

GORDON, PATRICK (1635–1699), general and friend of Peter the Great ; left Scotland, 1651 ; served alternately the Swedes and the Poles ; attempted assassination at Wender, 1658, of Richard Bradshaw [q. v.], mistaking him for the president at the trial of Charles I ; entered the Russian service, 1661 ; suppressed a revolt, 1662 ; on mission to England, 1664 ; drove Turks from the Ukraine ; lieutenant-general and governor of Kiev, 1679 ; not allowed to retire from Russian service ; general for services against the Crimean Tartars, 1687 ; assisted Peter in his coup d'état ; suppressed the Strelitzes, 1697 ; buried at Moscow ; extracts from his autobiography (in the St. Petersburg archives) edited by Joseph Robertson, 1859. [xxii. 222]

GORDON, PRYSE LOCKHART (fl. 1834), author of 'Personal Memoirs,' 1830, and of 'Holland and Belgium,' 1834 ; from 1815 lived at Brussels. [xxii. 224]

GORDON, SIR ROBERT (1580–1656), historian of house of Sutherland ; fourth son of Alexander Gordon

eleventh or twelfth Earl of Sutherland [q. v.] ; gentleman of the privy chamber to James I and Charles I ; married heiress of John Gordon (1544–1619) [q. v.], dean of Salisbury and Lord of Glenluce, 1613 ; created premier baronet of Nova Scotia, 1625 ; confidential messenger between Charles I and his queen ; sheriff of Inverness-shire, 1629 ; vice-chamberlain of Scotland, 1630 ; privy councillor of Scotland, 1634 ; mediator during the civil war ; founder of family of Gordonstoun ; his 'Genealogical History of the Earldom of Sutherland' edited by Henry Weber, 1813. [xxii. 224]

GORDON, ROBERT (1580–1661), of Straloch, geographer ; first graduate of Marischal College, Aberdeen ; mediated between Huntly and Montrose ; corrected and completed Pont's maps for Scottish section of Bleau's 'Atlas' (vol. vi. of 1662 edition) and contributed 'Remarks on the Charts of the Ancient Scots' ; wrote family history, which William Gordon utilised ; supplied materials for the 'Scots Affairs' of his son James Gordon (1615 ?–1686) [q. v.] of Rothiemay. [xxii. 226]

GORDON, SIR ROBERT (1647–1704), 'Sir Robert the warlock,' of Gordonstoun ; grandson of Sir Robert Gordon (1580–1656) [q. v.] ; knighted, 1673 ; succeeded as baronet, 1685 ; gentleman of James II's household ; member of Scots parliament of 1672–4, and of conventions of 1678, 1681–2, 1685–6 ; correspondent of Boyle ; invented a pump ; F.R.S., 1686. [xxii. 227]

GORDON, ROBERT (1665–1732), founder of Gordon's College (formerly Hospital), Aberdeen ; grandson of Robert Gordon (1580–1661) [q. v.] of Straloch ; acquired fortune as a merchant at Dantzig ; his hospital for thirty boys opened 1750, increased by bequest of Alexander Simpson, 1834, converted into a college, 1881. [xxii. 227]

GORDON, ROBERT (1687–1764), biblical scholar ; prefect of studies at Paris, 1712–18 ; chaplain to Duke of Gordon, 1718–28 ; procurator at Edinburgh, 1728–40 ; arrested in London, 1745, and banished ; died at Lens ; his manuscript translation of the New Testament not approved at Rome. [xxii. 228]

GORDON, SIR ROBERT (1791–1847), diplomatist ; brother of Sir Alexander Gordon (1786–1815) [q. v.] ; plenipotentiary at Vienna, 1815, 1817, 1821 ; privy councillor ; envoy extraordinary to Brazil, 1826 ; at Constantinople, 1828–31 ; at Vienna, 1841–6 ; G.C.B., 1829. [xxii. 228]

GORDON, ROBERT (1786–1853), Free church minister ; D.D. Marischal College, Aberdeen, 1823 ; minister of the High Church, Edinburgh, 1830 ; supported non-intrusionists ; as moderator of the general assembly, 1841, had to pronounce deposition of the Strathbogie ministers ; seconded Thomas Chalmers [q. v.], 1842 ; left established church, 1843, followed by his congregation ; contributed to the 'Edinburgh Encyclopædia.' [xxii. 229]

GORDON, THEODORE (1786–1845), inspector of army hospitals ; M.D. Edinburgh, 1802 ; army surgeon in Germany and the Peninsula ; wounded in crossing Pyrenees ; physician to the forces, 1815 ; professional assistant at medical board of war office ; deputy-inspector-general of hospitals, 1836. [xxii. 229]

GORDON, THOMAS (d. 1750), author ; reputed the Silenus of the 'Dunciad' ; with his patron John Trenchard [q. v.] issued a weekly paper called 'Independent Whig,' collected in volume, 1721 (reissued later as 'A Defence of Primitive Christianity') ; employed by Walpole ; published translation of Tacitus, 1728, and Sallust, 1744, and miscellaneous works. [xxii. 230]

GORDON, THOMAS (1788–1841), major-general in the Greek army ; educated at Eton and Brasenose College, Oxford ; cornet, 2nd dragoons, 1808 ; served in Scots Greys ; captain in Russian army, 1813 ; served under Ipsilanti against the Turks, but retired after massacre at Tripolizza, 1821 ; member of Greek committee in London, 1823 ; returned to Greece, 1826 ; commanded expedition for relief of Athens, 1827 ; lived at Argos, 1828–31 ; served in Greek army, 1833–9 ; published 'History of the Greek Revolution,' 1832, and translations from the Turkish. [xxii. 230]

GORDON, WILLIAM (d. 1577), last pre-reformation bishop of Aberdeen ; fourth son of Alexander Gordon, third earl of Huntly [q. v.] ; bishop of Aberdeen, 1546–1577. [xxii. 232]

GORDON, WILLIAM (1614–1679), of Earlston, covenanter; second son of Alexander Gordon of Earlston (1587–1654) [q. v.]; shared in Glencairn's rising against Cromwell, 1653, but submitted; banished from Scotland for refusing to present an episcopal curate, 1663; shot after Bothwell Brigg. [xxii. 233]

GORDON, WILLIAM, sixth VISCOUNT KENMURE (*d.* 1716), Jacobite; induced by his wife, sister of Sir Robert Dalyell [q. v.], to join rising of 1715; appointed by Mar to command in southern Scotland; failed to surprise Dumfries and marched into England; captured at Preston, 1715; pleaded guilty and made strong appeal to the peers, but was beheaded. [xxii. 234]

GORDON, WILLIAM (1728–1807), independent minister, at Ipswich and Gravel Lane, Southwark; in America, 1770–85, at Roxbury, Massachusetts, and Jamaica Plain; private secretary to Washington, and chaplain to provincial congress of Massachusetts; D.D. New Jersey; pastor of St. Neots, 1789–1802; published 'History of the Rise and Independence of the United States,' 1788. [xxii. 235]

GORDON, WILLIAM (1770–1820), Gaelic poet; brother of George Ross Gordon [q. v.]; while serving with Reay fencibles in Ireland wrote Gaelic hymns and songs, published as 'Dantadh Spioradal,' 1802. [xxii. 235]

GORDON, WILLIAM (1800–1849), philanthropist; M.D. Edinburgh, 1841; physician at Hull; subject of Newman Hall's 'Christian Philanthropist triumphing over Death,' 1849. [xxii. 236]

GORDON-CUMMING, ROUALEYN GEORGE (1820–1866). [See CUMMING.]

GORE, MRS. CATHERINE GRACE FRANCES (1799–1861), novelist and dramatist; *née* Moody; married, 1823, to Captain Charles Arthur Gore; published about seventy works between 1824 and 1862, including the novels 'Manners of the Day' (1830), 'Mrs. Armytage' (1836), 'Cecil, or the Adventures of a Coxcomb' (1841), and 'The Banker's Wife' (1843); her 'School for Coquettes' acted at the Haymarket, 1831, 'Lords and Commons' at Drury Lane, and 'Quid pro Quo' at the Haymarket, 1844; parodied by Thackeray in 'Novels by Eminent Hands'; composed music for 'And ye shall walk in silk attire,' and other favourite songs. [xxii. 236]

GORE, SIR CHARLES STEPHEN (1793–1869), general; served with 43rd in the Peninsula; took part in storming of Ciudad Rodrigo, 1812, and Badajoz, 1812; aide-de-camp to Sir A. Barnard at Salamanca, 1812; to Sir J. Kempt at Vittoria, 1813, and in Canada, 1814; at Quatre Bras and Waterloo; deputy quartermaster-general in Canada, 1838–9; lieutenant-general, 1854; general, 1863; G.C.B. and governor of Chelsea Hospital. [xxii. 238]

GORE, JOHN, BARON ANNALY (1718–1784), Irish judge; B.A. Dublin, 1737; M.P. Jamestown, 1745; solicitor-general for Ireland, 1760; chief-justice of king's bench, 1764; privy councillor; created an Irish peer, 1766. [xxii. 238]

GORE, SIR JOHN (1772–1836), vice-admiral; entered navy, 1781; distinguished himself at Corsica and Toulon, 1794–5; captured by the French; while in command of the Triton in the Channel, 1796–1801, took many prizes; received 40,000*l.* prize-money after capture of Santa Brigida and Thetis, 1799; with the Medusa assisted in capture of Spanish ships off Cadiz, 1804; knighted, 1805; K.C.B., 1815; vice-admiral, 1825; commander of the Nore, 1818–21; in the East Indies, 1831–5. [xxii. 238]

GORE, MONTAGU (1800–1864), politician; whig M.P. for Devizes, 1832–4; conservative M.P. for Barnstaple, 1841–7; supported Peel on corn-law question; published political pamphlets. [xxii. 239]

GORE, THOMAS (1632–1684), writer on heraldry; B.A. Magdalen College, Oxford; member of Lincoln's Inn; gentleman of the privy chamber, 1667; high sheriff of Wiltshire, 1681; chief work 'Nomenclator Geographicus Latino-Anglicus et Anglico-Latinus,' 1667; two valuable manuscripts by him in British Museum. [xxii. 240]

GORGES, SIR ARTHUR (*d.* 1625), poet and translator; commanded the Wast Spite, Ralegh's flagship, on the Islands Voyage, 1597; knighted; his account of the voyage published by Samuel Purchas [q. v.] in 'Pilgrimes,' 1625–6; M.P., Yarmouth, 1584, Camelford, 1588, Dorsetshire, 1592, and Rye, 1601; translated Lucan's 'Pharsalia,' 1614, and Bacon's 'De Sapientiâ Veterum,' 1619, and made French version of the Essays; the 'Alcyon' of Spenser's 'Daphnaida' and 'Colin Clout's come home again.' [xxii. 241]

GORGES, SIR FERDINANDO (1566?–1647), military and naval commander and coloniser; cousin of Sir Arthur Gorges [q. v.]; knighted by Essex for gallantry at siege of Rouen, 1591; with him in the Island Voyage, 1597, and in Ireland, 1599; joined his conspiracy, but gave evidence against him, 1601; governor of Plymouth; became interested in colonisation, and formed two companies which received grants of land in North America, and formed settlement of New Plymouth, 1628; lord proprietary of Maine, 1639. [xxii. 241]

GORHAM, GEOFFREY OF (*d.* 1146). [See GEOFFREY.]

GORHAM, GEORGE CORNELIUS (1787–1857), divine and antiquary; fellow of Queens' College, Cambridge, 1810; third wrangler and second Smith's prizeman, 1808; M.A., 1812; B.D., 1820; vicar of St. Just in Penwith, Cornwall, 1846, of Brampford Speke, Devonshire, 1847–57; refused institution (1847) on account of Calvinistic views on baptismal regeneration by Bishop Henry Phillpotts of Exeter, who was supported by court of arches, but obtained institution soon after the decision had been reversed by the judicial committee of privy council, 1850. Besides his own account of the case, Gorham published books on the two St. Neots (1820), and on the chapel, chauntry, and guild of Maidenhead, and the 'Book of Enoch' (1829), besides genealogical works. [xxii. 243]

GORING, GEORGE, BARON GORING (1608–1657), royalist; son of George Goring, earl of Norwich [q. v.]; wounded in Dutch service at siege of Breda, 1637; held commands in Scotch wars; revealed 'first army plot' to parliament, 1641, but when governor of Portsmouth declared for the king, 1642; raised reinforcements for royalists in Holland; as general of the horse routed Fairfax at Seacroft Moor, 1643, but was captured by him at Wakefield and sent to the Tower; exchanged for the Earl of Lothian, 1644; commanded left wing at Marston Moor, 1644; lieutenant-general of the main army in the south; made successful charge at second battle of Newbury, 1644; conducted unsuccessful operations in the south and west, and injured the royal cause by ambitious intrigues; received command in the west, 1645; defeated at Langport; went abroad and obtained command of English regiments in Spanish service; thenceforth lived in Spain. [xxii. 245]

GORING, GEORGE, EARL OF NORWICH (1583?–1663), royalist; educated at Sidney Sussex College, Cambridge; gentleman of the privy chamber to Henry, prince of Wales, 1610; one of James I's three 'chief and master fools'; accompanied Prince Charles to Spain, 1623; negotiated his marriage with Henrietta Maria of France; became her master of the horse and Baron Goring, 1628; received numerous offices and grants; 'the leader of the monopolists'; privy councillor, 1639; spent money freely for Charles I during the civil war; accompanied the queen to and from Holland, 1642–3; as envoy to France obtained from Mazarin promise of arms and money, 1643; impeached for high treason by parliament, 1644; created Earl of Norwich, 1644; subsequently commanded in Kent and Essex; after capitulation at Colchester (1648) sentenced to death, but respited by casting vote of Speaker Lenthall; with Charles II on the continent, 1649; employed in negotiations with Sexby and the Levellers; captain of the guard and pensioned, 1661. [xxii. 248]

GORRIE, SIR JOHN (1829–1892), colonial judge; educated at Edinburgh; advocate, 1856; honorary advocate-deputy for Scotland, 1860; began practice at English bar, 1862; substitute procureur-général of Mauritius, 1869; second puisne judge, 1870; chief-justice and member of legislative council of Fiji islands, 1876; chief-justice of Leeward islands, and knighted, 1882; chief-justice of Trinidad, 1886; suspended on report of commission to investigate his methods of administering justice, 1892. [Suppl. ii. 332]

GORT, second VISCOUNT. [See VEREKER, CHARLES, 1768–1842.]

GORTON, JOHN (*d.* 1835), compiler; published 'A General Biographical Dictionary,' 1828, and, with G. N. Wright, 'A Topographical Dictionary of Great Britain and Ireland,' 1831–3.   [xxii. 251]

GORTON, SAMUEL (*d.* 1677), founder of the Gortonites; of Gorton, Lancashire; went to New England, 1636; lived at Boston and New Plymouth; obliged to remove to Rhode island; made himself obnoxious to the authorities by his aggressive spirit; purchased land from the Narragansett Indians at Shawomet, 1643; ejected by Massachusetts government and imprisoned for heresy at Charlestown, 1643; came to England, 1644; published 'Simplicities Defence against Seven-Headed Policy,' 1646 (reprinted 1835); having obtained protection against Massachusetts government, returned to Shawomet, 1648, renaming it Warwick in honour of his protector; published religious tracts with an eccentric phraseology.   [xxii. 251]

GOSCELIN or **GOTSELIN** (*fl.* 1099), biographer; came to England with Bishop Hermann of Salisbury; lived in monastery of Canterbury and other houses; wrote lives of St. Augustine (dedicated to Anselm), and St. Swithun and other saints, and 'Historia Translationis S. Augustini'; highly commended by William of Malmesbury.   [xxii. 253]

GOSFORD, BARON (1616?–1679). [See WEDDERBURN, SIR PETER.]

GOSLING, JANE (*d.* 1804), author; published 'Moral Essays,' 1789, and 'Ashdale Village.'   [xxii. 254]

GOSLING, RALPH (1693–1758), topographer; writing-master and schoolmaster at Sheffield; published earliest known map of Sheffield, 1732.   [xxii. 254]

GOSNOLD, BARTHOLOMEW (*d.* 1607), navigator; sailed from Falmouth in the Concord, 1602; discovered Cape Cod and adjoining islands, 1602; a leader of the expedition which, under the auspices of Sir Ferdinando Gorges [q. v.], discovered the Capes of Virginia, and founded Jamestown, 1606; died at Jamestown.   [xxii. 254]

GOSNOLD, JOHN (1625?–1678), anabaptist; of Charterhouse and Pembroke Hall, Cambridge; during the civil war founded baptist congregation in Paul's Alley, Barbican, London, and attracted large audiences; published tracts against infant baptism.   [xxii. 255]

GOSPATRIC or **COSPATRIC**, EARL OF NORTHUMBERLAND (*fl.* 1067), probably the 'Gaius patricius' who accompanied Tostig to Rome, 1061; bought from William I earldom of Northumbria, 1067, but joined rising against the king, 1068; took part in Danes' sack of York, 1069; his earldom restored on submission, but again forfeited, 1072; fled to Scotland and Flanders; received Dunbar from Malcolm of Scotland.   [xxii. 255]

GOSS, ALEXANDER (1814–1872), Roman catholic bishop of Liverpool; vice-president of St. Edward's College, Everton, 1843–53; coadjutor bishop of Liverpool, 1853; bishop, 1856–72; contributor to Chetham, Holbein, and Manx societies.   [xxii. 256]

GOSS, SIR JOHN (1800–1880), musical composer; Chapel Royal chorister and pupil of Thomas Attwood [q. v.]; organist of St. Luke's, Chelsea, 1825; of St. Paul's Cathedral, 1838–72; won Gresham prize, 1833; knighted, 1872; Mus. Doc. Cambridge, 1876; published 'Introduction to Harmony,' 1833, and (with Turle) 'Cathedral Services,' 1841, and 'Chants, Ancient and Modern,' 1841; composed many anthems (including one for Wellington's funeral), orchestral works and glees.   [xxii. 257]

GOSSE, EMILY (1806–1857), religious writer; first wife of Philip Henry Gosse [q. v.]; published devotional verse and religious and educational tracts.   [xxii. 258]

GOSSE, PHILIP HENRY (1810–1888), zoologist; while in a whaler's office at Carbonear, Newfoundland, devoted himself to study of insects; after farming in Canada and the United States returned to England, 1839, and published 'The Canadian Naturalist,' 1840, and 'Introduction to Zoology,' 1843; collected birds and insects in Jamaica for British Museum, 1844–6; issued 'Birds of Jamaica,' 1847 (with plates, 1849), and 'A Naturalist's Sojourn in Jamaica,' 1851; suggested a marine aquarium in 'Rambles on the Devonshire Coast,' 1853, a work followed by 'The Aquarium,' 1854, and 'Manual of Marine Zoology,'

1855–6; F.R.S., 1856; published 'Actinologia Britannica,' 1858–60, and 'Romance of Natural History,' 1860, 1862; devoted last years to *rotifera* and orchids.   [xxii. 258]

GOSSELIN, THOMAS LE MARCHANT (1765–1857), admiral; entered navy, 1778; captured in the Ardent off Plymouth, 1779; assisted in reduction of Surinam, 1799; convoyed troops to the Tagus, 1808, and covered embarkation at Coruña, 1809; vice-admiral, 1825; admiral, 1841.   [xxii. 260]

GOSSET, ISAAC, the elder (1713–1799), modeller of portraits in wax; exhibited with the Incorporated Society of Artists, 1760–78.   [xxii. 261]

GOSSET, ISAAC, the younger (1735?–1812), bibliographer; son of Isaac Gosset the elder [q. v.]; M.A. Exeter College, Oxford, 1770; the Lepidus of Dibdin's 'Bibliomania'; assisted in Dibdin's 'Introduction to the Classics,' 1802, and John Nichols's edition of Bowyer's 'Critical Conjectures and Observations on the New Testament,' 1782; F.R.S., 1772.   [xxii. 261]

GOSSET, MATTHEW (1683–1744), wax modeller and member of Spalding Society; uncle of Isaac Gosset the elder [q. v.]   [xxii. 261]

GOSSET, MONTAGUE (1792–1854), surgeon; a favourite pupil of Sir Astley Cooper [q. v.]; practised in the city thirty-four years; hon. F.R.C.S., 1843; introduced improved tonsil iron for enlarged tonsils and nitric acid for the destruction of nævi.   [xxii. 262]

GOSSON, STEPHEN (1554–1624), author; B.A. Corpus Christi College, Oxford, 1576; ranked by Meres among 'the best for pastorall'; his plays not now extant; attacked poets and players in his 'Schoole of Abuse,' 1579 (often reprinted); defended it in 'Ephemerides of Phialo' (1579); replied to Lodge and 'The Play of Playes' in 'Playes confuted in Fiue Actions,' 1582; evoked by his unauthorised dedications of his works to Sir Philip Sidney, Sidney's 'Apologie for Poetrie' (published, 1595); rector of Great Wigborough, 1591, and St. Botolph's, Bishopsgate, 1600.   [xxii. 263]

GOSSON, THOMAS (*fl.* 1598), publisher of 'Playes Confuted,' 1582; probably brother of Stephen Gosson [q. v.]   [xxii. 264]

GOSTLIN, JOHN (1566?–1626), master of Gonville and Caius College, Cambridge; M.A. Gonville and Caius College, Cambridge, 1590; fellow, 1592–1619; M.D., 1602; M.P., Barnstaple, 1614; twice vice-chancellor; Cambridge regius professor of physic, 1623; master of Gonville and Caius College, Cambridge, 1619–26; benefactor of Caius and St. Catharine's Colleges, Cambridge.   [xxii. 265]

GOSTLIN, JOHN (1632–1704), benefactor of Gonville and Caius College, Cambridge; related to John Gostlin (1566?–1626) [q. v.]; fellow of Peterhouse and (1661) Caius College, Cambridge; M.D. Cambridge, 1661; vice-master of Caius College, 1679.   [xxii. 265]

GOSTLING, JOHN (*d.* 1733), chorister; B.A. St. John's College, Cambridge, 1672; famous bass in the Chapel Royal, for whom Purcell wrote the anthem 'They that go down to the sea in ships'; vicar of Littlebourne, sub-dean of St. Paul's, and prebendary of Lincoln.   [xxii. 265]

GOSTLING, WILLIAM (1696–1777), antiquary; son of John Gostling [q.v.]; M.A. St. John's College, Cambridge, 1719; minor canon of Canterbury, 1727–77; vicar of Littlebourne, 1733–53, of Stone in Oxney, 1753–77; published 'Walk in and about the City of Canterbury,' 1774; his rendering into verse of Hogarth's expedition to Canterbury (1732) inserted in Hone's 'Table-book' (reprinted, 1872).   [xxii. 266]

GOSYNHYLL, EDWARD (*fl.* 1560), poet; author of 'Scole House of Women' (1541, anon.), reprinted by E. V. Utterson ('Select Pieces,' 1817).   [xxii. 266]

GOTAFRIDUS (*fl.* 1290). [See JOFROI.]

GOTER or **GOTHER**, JOHN (*d.* 1704), Roman catholic divine; educated as a presbyterian; at Lisbon, 1668–82; his 'Papist Misrepresented and Represented' (1685, parts ii. and iii., 1687), answered by Stillingfleet, Sherlock, and Clagett; commended by Dryden for his English; died at sea; published 'Pope Pius [IV] his Profession of Faith vindicated,' 1687, and other controversial works; his 'Spiritual Works' (ed. Rev. W. Crathorne, 16 vols., 1718) often reprinted.   [xxii. 267]

GOTSELIN (*fl.* 1099). [See GOSCELIN.]

GOTT, JOSEPH (1785–1860), sculptor; patronised by Benjamin Gott, for whom at Armley his chief work was done; exhibited at Royal Academy, 1830–48; died at Rome. [xxii. 268]

GOUDIE, JOHN (1717–1809). [See GOLDIE.]

GOUDY, ALEXANDER PORTER (1809–1858), presbyterian; minister of Strabane, 1833–58; D.D. Jefferson College, U.S.A., 1851; moderator of general assembly, 1857; took part in controversy with Archibald (afterwards Dean) Boyd [q. v.], publishing 'Presbyterianism Defended,' 1839, 'The Plea of Presbytery,' and other works. [xxii. 268]

GOUGE, ROBERT (1630–1705), independent divine; pupil of Henry More [q. v.] at Christ's College, Cambridge; rector of St. Helen's, Ipswich, 1652–62; afterwards had independent congregations there and at Coggeshall. [xxii. 269]

GOUGE, THOMAS (1609–1681), nonconformist divine and philanthropist; son of Robert Gouge [q. v.]; of Eton and King's College, Cambridge; fellow, 1628; M.A.; vicar of St. Sepulchre's, London, 1638–62; provided work for the poor in flax- and hemp-spinning; friend of Thomas Firmin [q. v.]; organised religious instruction in South Wales, and assisted in forming trust for printing and circulating religious works in the vernacular, 1674; works collected, 1706. [xxii. 269]

GOUGE, THOMAS (1665 ?–1700), independent divine; son of Robert Gouge [q. v.]; pastor of English church at Amsterdam and of independent congregation in Fruiterers' Alley, Thames Street, 1689; merchant lecturer at Pinners' Hall, 1694; praised by Isaac Watts in 'Elegiac Essay' (published 1700). [xxii. 271]

GOUGE, WILLIAM (1578–1653), puritan divine; of St. Paul's School and Eton; fellow of King's College, Cambridge, 1598; M.A., 1602; D.D., 1628; rector of St. Anne's, Blackfriars, 1621–53; imprisoned for his edition of Finch's 'World's Great Restauration,' 1621; joined scheme for buying up impropriations for puritans, 1626; refused to read 'Book of Sports,' 1618 and 1633; an assessor of the Westminster Assembly, 1647; took the covenant, but denounced the king's trial; his commentary on Hebrews reprinted, 1866. [xxii. 271]

GOUGH. [See also GOFFE.]

GOUGH, ALEXANDER DICK (1804–1871), architect and engineer; pupil of B. Wyatt; with R. L. Roumieu exhibited at the Academy, 1837–47; built or restored churches in Islington, North London, and elsewhere; occupied in railway surveying. [xxii. 273]

GOUGH, SIR HUGH, first VISCOUNT GOUGH (1779–1869), field-marshal; adjutant of Colonel Rochford's foot (119th) at fifteen; with 78th highlanders at capture of the Cape, 1795; commanded 2nd battalion at Talavera, 1809, being severely wounded, and promoted lieutenant-colonel; distinguished at Barossa and Tarifa, 1811; again wounded at Nivelle, 1813; knighted and given freedom of Dublin, 1815; major-general, 1830; K.C.B., 1831; G.C.B. for capture of Canton forts, 1841, and a baronet for further services in China, 1842; commander-in-chief in India, 1843, when he defeated the Mahrattas; created Baron Gough at conclusion of first Sikh war, 1845, having won the battles of Mudki, 1845, Ferozeshah, 1845, and Sobraon, 1846; created viscount after the second war, 1848–9, which he brought to a close with battle of Goojerat; received freedom of the city of London and a pension; general, 1854; K.P., 1857; privy councillor, 1859; G.C.S.I., 1861; field-marshal, 1862. [xxii. 274]

GOUGH, GOWGHE, GOWGH, or GOUGE, JOHN (*fl.* 1528–1556), printer, stationer, and translator; of the Mermaid, Fleet Street, and Lombard Street; imprisoned for uttering seditious works, 1541; published first English treatise on book-keeping, 1543. [xxii. 276]

GOUGH, JOHN (*fl.* 1570), divine; rector of St. Peter's, Cornhill, 1560–7; deprived for nonconformity; published a religious work. [xxii. 276]

GOUGH, JOHN (1610 ?–1661). [See GOFFE.]

GOUGH, JOHN (1721–1791), master of the Friends' school, Dublin, 1752–74; afterwards at Lisburn; published 'History of the People called Quakers,' 1789–90, and a popular tract giving reasons for non-payment of tithes. [xxii. 277]

GOUGH, JOHN (1757–1825), scientific writer; lost his sight from small-pox when a child, but so trained his sense of touch that he became an accomplished botanist; taught mathematics to John Dalton, the chemist [q. v.], and William Whewell; contributed to Manchester Philosophical Society and Nicholson's 'Philosophical Magazine'; alluded to in Wordsworth's 'Excursion' and Coleridge's 'Soul and its Organ of Sense.' [xxii. 277]

GOUGH, JOHN BALLANTINE (1817–1886), temperance orator; born at Sandgate, Kent; went to the United States at twelve, and was a bookbinder till 1843; the foremost temperance lecturer in America, he thrice visited England and addressed immense audiences; died at Philadelphia; published 'Autobiography' (1846 and 1871), 'Orations' (1877), and other works. [xxii. 278]

GOUGH, RICHARD (1735–1809), antiquary; educated at Christ's College, Cambridge; F.S.A., 1767, and director of the society, 1771–97; F.R.S., 1775; contributor to 'Gentleman's Magazine' as 'D. H.'; made excursions through England for twenty years, often accompanied by John Nichols [q. v.]; published about twenty works, including 'British Topography' (1768 and 1780), 'Sepulchral Monuments of Great Britain' (1786, 1796, 1799), an edition of Camden's 'Britannia,' translated and enlarged (1789), a translation of the 'Arabian Nights' (1798), and several topographical and numismatic monographs. [xxii. 279]

GOUGH, STEPHEN (1605–1681). [See GOFFE.]

GOUGH, STRICKLAND (*d.* 1752), controversial writer; rector of Swayfield and vicar of Swinstead, Lincolnshire; published 'Enquiry into the Causes of the Decay of the Dissenting Interest' (1730, anon.) [xxii. 282]

GOUGH, THOMAS (1591–1629). [See GOFFE.]

GOUGH, WILLIAM (*d.* 1679 ?). [See GOFFE.]

GOUGH, WILLIAM (1654 ?–1682), antiquary; B.A. St. Alban Hall, Oxford, 1675; published 'Londinum Triumphans,' 1682. [xxii. 282]

GOUGHE or GOFFE, ROBERT (*d.* 1624), actor in Shakespeare's plays. [xxii. 282]

GOULBURN, EDWARD (1787–1868), serjeant-at-law; barrister, Middle Temple, 1815; previously served in horse guards; Welsh judge; recorder of Leicester, Lincoln, and Boston; M.P., Leicester, 1835–7; bankruptcy commissioner, 1842; published two satirical poems and a novel. [xxii. 283]

GOULBURN, EDWARD MEYRICK (1818–1897), dean of Norwich; educated at Eton and Balliol College, Oxford; M.A., 1842; D.C.L., 1850; D.D., 1856; fellow, 1841–6; tutor and dean of Merton College, 1843–5; ordained priest, 1843; chaplain to Samuel Wilberforce bishop of Oxford [q. v.], 1847; head-master of Rugby, 1849–57; accepted ministry of Quebec Chapel, St. Marylebone, 1857; dean of Norwich, 1866–89. His works include 'Life of Burgon,' 1892, and theological manuals. [Suppl. ii. 333]

GOULBURN, HENRY (1813–1843), senior classic and second wrangler, Cambridge, 1835; barrister, Middle Temple, 1840; son of Henry Goulburn (1784–1856) [q. v.] [xxii. 285]

GOULBURN, HENRY (1784–1856), statesman; brother of Edward Goulburn [q. v.]; M.A. Trinity College, Cambridge, 1808; M.P., successively, for Horsham, 1808, St. Germans, West Looe, Armagh city, and Cambridge University (1831–56); under-secretary for home department, 1810, for war and the colonies, 1812–21; commissioner for peace with United States, 1814; privy councillor, 1821; as chief secretary for Ireland, 1821–7, carried Tithe Composition Bill and measure for the suppression of unlawful societies; as chancellor of the exchequer under Wellington reduced interest of 4 per cents to 3½; home secretary under Peel, 1834–5, chancellor of the exchequer, 1841–6; by conversion of stock in budget of 1844 effected an ultimate saving of a million and a quarter; friend and executor of Peel; D.C.L. Oxford, 1834. [xxii. 283]

GOULD (afterwards MORGAN), SIR CHARLES (1726–1806), judge advocate-general; educated at Westminster and Christ Church, Oxford; M.A., 1750; hon. D.C.L.,

1773; barrister, Middle Temple, 1750; judge advocate-general, 1771; chancellor of Salisbury, 1772; M.P., Brecon, 1778–87, Brecon county, 1787–1806; knighted, 1779; created baronet, 1792; privy councillor, 1802; assumed name of Morgan, 1792. [xxii. 285]

GOULD, GEORGE (1818–1882), baptist minister in Dublin, Exeter, and (1849–82) St. Mary's Chapel, Norwich; president of Baptist Union, 1879; a founder of the 'anti-state-church association,' 1844; edited (1862) 'Documents relating to the Settlement of the Church of England ... by the Act of Uniformity, 1662.' [xxii. 285]

GOULD, SIR HENRY, the elder (1644–1710), judge; barrister, Middle Temple, 1667; king's serjeant, 1693; counsel against Sir John Fenwick [q. v.], 1696; judge of the king's bench, 1699–1710. [xxii. 286]

GOULD, SIR HENRY, the younger (1710–1794), judge; grandson of Sir Henry Gould the elder [q. v.]; barrister, Middle Temple, 1734; K.C., 1754; baron of the exchequer, 1761; transferred to common pleas, 1763. [xxii. 286]

GOULD, JAMES ALIPIUS (1812–1886), first Roman catholic archbishop of Melbourne; first bishop of Port Phillip (Victoria), 1848; archbishop of Melbourne, 1876–1886. [xxii. 287]

GOULD, JOHN (1804–1881), ornithologist; taxidermist to the Zoological Society, 1827; travelled in Australasia, 1838–40, making valuable observations and collections; F.R.S., 1843; exhibited collection of humming-birds, 1851, now with his Australian mammals at South Kensington; published forty-one folios on birds, with 2,999 illustrations, including 'A Century of Birds, from the Himalayan Mountains,' 1832, 'Birds of Europe,' 1832–1837, 'Birds of Australia,' 1840–8, and supplement, 1851–69, 'Birds of Asia,' 1850–80, 'Birds of Great Britain,' 1862–73, and numerous monographs. [xxii. 287]

GOULD, ROBERT (d. 1709?), poet; servant of Charles, earl of Dorset; published 'Poems chiefly consisting of Satyrs and Satyrical Epistles,' 1689, and 'The Rival Sisters' (tragedy), 1696, acted at Drury Lane; works collected, 1709. [xxii. 288]

GOULD, THOMAS (1657–1734), controversialist; obtained from Louis XIV abbey of St.-Laon de Thouars for missionary work in Poitou; published several anti-protestant treatises, including 'Lettre à un Gentilhomme du Bas-Poitou.' [xxii. 288]

GOULDMAN, FRANCIS (d. 1688?), lexicographer; M.A. Christ's College, Cambridge, 1630; rector of South Ockendon, Essex, 1634–44, and after Restoration; compiled an English-Latin and Latin-English dictionary with proper names, 1664. [xxii. 289]

GOULSTON or **GULSTON**, THEODORE (1572–1632), founder of Gulstonian lecture; fellow of Merton College, Oxford, 1596; M.A., 1600; M.D., 1610; F.R.C.P., 1611; four times censor; practised in St. Martin-extra-Ludgate; published Latin versions of Aristotle's 'Rhetoric' (1619) and 'Poetics' (1623), and a critical edition of Galen (posthumous), 1640. [xxii. 289]

GOUPY, JOSEPH (d. 1763), water-colour painter and etcher; nephew of Lewis Goupy [q. v.]; 'cabinet-painter' to Frederick, prince of Wales, 1736; pensioned by George III on his accession; executed water-colour copies of Raphael's cartoons; nine etchings by him after Salvator Rosa in the British Museum. [xxii. 290]

GOUPY, LEWIS (d. 1747), painter; of French extraction; seceded from Kneller's academy to that of Louis Chéron [q. v.], 1720; accompanied Lord Burlington to Italy; painted portraits and miniatures, and drew in crayons and tempera. [xxii. 290]

GOURDON, WILLIAM (fl. 1611), traveller; master pilot on two expeditions to north of Russia, described in his 'Voyage made to Pechora' and 'Later Observations' (in 'Purchas's Pilgrimes,' iii.) [xxii. 290]

GOURLIE, WILLIAM (1815–1856), botanist; F.L.S., 1855; studied under Hooker and Balfour; collected mosses, shells, and fossil plants. [xxii. 291]

GOURNEY, SIR MATTHEW (1310?–1406), soldier of fortune; present at Sluys, 1340, Algeciras, 1342–4, Crecy, 1346, and Poitiers, 1356; governor of Brest, 1357; a jurat of peace of Bretigni, 1360; imprisoned in the Tower,

1362; present at Auray, 1364; ambassador of Henry, king of Castile, to Portugal; took service with Black Prince, and assisted in Henry's defeat at Nájara, 1367; created a baron of Guienne; served again in France and fell into ambush near Soissons; defended Bayonne against Anjou and Henry of Castile, 1378; seneschal of the Landes, 1379; constable of the forces in Portuguese expedition, 1388; sat in upper house in first parliament of Henry IV. [xxii. 291]

GOUTER or **GAULTIER**, JAMES (fl. 1636), French lutenist; in service of Charles I of England; referred to by Herrick. [xxii. 292]

GOVE, RICHARD (1587–1668), puritan divine; M.A. Magdalen Hall, Oxford, 1611; incumbent of Hinton St. George, 1618; afterwards rector of East Coker, Somerset; published 'The Saints' Honeycomb,' 1652, 'Pious Thoughts vented in Pithy Ejaculations,' 1658, and other works. [xxii. 293]

GOVER, CHARLES E. (d. 1872), folklorist; principal of Madras Military Male Orphan Asylum, 1864–72; member of Royal Asiatic Society, 1868–72; his essays collected in 'Folk-Songs of Southern India,' 1872. [xxii. 293]

GOW, NATHANIEL (1766–1831), Scottish violinist and composer; son of Niel Gow (1727–1807) [q. v.]; as leader of M'Glashan's band, 1791, frequently played before George, prince of Wales; published two hundred original melodies, and assisted in and continued his father's volumes. [xxii. 293]

GOW, NIEL (1727–1807), violinist and composer; patronised by Duke of Atholl; was much in request at fashionable gatherings in Scotland and England; his portrait four times painted by Raeburn; renowned as composer and player of reels and strathspeys, for some of which Burns wrote words. [xxii. 294]

GOW, NIEL (d. 1823), composer of 'Bonnie Prince Charlie' ('Cam' ye by Athol?'); son of Nathaniel Gow [q. v.] [xxii. 294]

GOWAN, THOMAS (1631–1683), writer on logic; minister of Glasslough, Monaghan, 1658; ejected, 1661; with John Howe [q. v.] carried on school of philosophy and divinity at Antrim; published 'Ars Sciendi,' 1681, and 'Logica Elenctica,' 1683. [xxii. 295]

GOWARD, MARY ANN (1805?–1899). [See KEELEY.]

GOWER. [See also LEVESON-GOWER.]

GOWER, first EARL (d. 1754). [See LEVESON-GOWER, JOHN.]

GOWER, first BARON (1675–1709). [See LEVESON-GOWER, JOHN.]

GOWER, SIR ERASMUS (1742–1814), admiral; in the Medea captured the Dutch Vryheid and retook the Chaser with despatches in East Indies, 1783; knighted after convoying Lord Macartney to China, 1794; commanded the Triumph with Sir William Cornwallis (1744–1819) [q.v.], 1795; vice-admiral, 1804; admiral, 1809. [xxii. 295]

GOWER, FOOTE (1726?–1780), antiquary; M.A. Brasenose College, Oxford, 1750; M.D., 1757; rector of Chignall St. James, Essex, 1761–77; published 'Sketch of the Materials for a new History of Cheshire,' 1771. [xxii. 296]

GOWER, GEORGE (fl. 1575–1585), sergeant-painter to Queen Elizabeth, 1584. [xxii. 296]

GOWER, HENRY (d. 1347), bishop of St. David's; fellow of Merton College, Oxford, and D.C.L.; chancellor of Oxford, 1322–3; archdeacon of St. David's, 1320; employed by Edward III; bishop of St. David's, 1328–47; made 'decorated' additions to his cathedral, and built the rood-screen; built the episcopal palace (now in ruins) and the wall round the close; founded and endowed Swansea Hospital. [xxii. 296]

GOWER, HUMPHREY (1638–1711), master of St. John's College, Cambridge; fellow of St. John's College, Cambridge, 1659; M.A., 1662; incumbent successively of Hammoon, Dorsetshire, Packlesham, 1667–75, Newton, Isle of Ely, and Fen Ditton; prebendary of Ely, 1679; when vice-chancellor entertained Charles II at St. John's, 1681; master of St. John's, 1679–1711; Margaret professor of divinity, 1688; benefactor of his college. [xxii. 298]

GOWER, JOHN (1325?-1408), poet; probably travelled in France in early life, afterwards settling down as a country gentleman; well known at court in his last years; became blind, 1400; died at the priory of St. Mary Overies, Southwark, and was buried in the church (now St. Saviour's); his will extant at Lambeth; friend of Chaucer, who called him 'moral Gower,' but probably quarrelled with him later. Of his chief works, the 'Speculum Meditantis' is a poem written in French, which was discovered by Mr. G. C. Macaulay, and published in his edition of Gower. The 'Vox Clamantis' (in Latin elegiacs), dedicated to Archbishop Arundel, contains an account of the peasants' revolt of 1381, and an indictment of government and society under Richard II. Attached to it in Coxe's collation is Gower's 'Chronica Tripartita,' a Latin poem dealing with events as far as the abdication of Richard II, in which the victims of his *coup d'état* are eulogised (the whole first printed by the Roxburghe Club, ed. H. O. Coxe, 1850). The 'Confessio Amantis' (Gower's only English poem), extant in two versions, the first dedicated to Richard II, the second to Henry IV, contains many stories drawn from Ovid and later sources, with learned digressions, and is preceded by a prologue. Caxton's edition (1483) follows the second version, as does Berthelet's (1532), the latter being the basis of Pauli's text (1857), reprinted by Professor H. Morley (1888). Extracts from a manuscript volume of other poems presented by Gower to Henry IV were printed, 1818. [xxii. 299]

GOWER, RICHARD HALL (1767-1833), naval architect; son of Foote Gower [q. v.]; educated at Winchester; midshipman in East India Company's service, 1780; built sailing yachts on an improved plan; chief work, 'A Treatise on the Theory and Practice of Seamanship,' 1793. [xxii. 304]

GOWER, SIR THOMAS (*fl.* 1543-1577), marshal of Berwick and surveyor of royal estates in Northumberland; captured by Scots at Pinkie, 1547; as master of the ordnance in the north directed siege of Leith, 1560. [xxii. 305]

GOWRAN, first BARON (*d.* 1727). [See FITZPATRICK, RICHARD.]

GOWRIE, EARLS OF. [See RUTHVEN, WILLIAM, first EARL, 1541?-1584; RUTHVEN, JOHN, third EARL, 1578?-1600.]

GRABE, JOHN ERNEST (1666-1711), divine; came to England from Königsberg and received a pension from William III; chaplain of Christ Church, Oxford, 1700; D.D. Oxford, 1706; published 'Spicilegium SS. Patrum,' 1698-9, also editions of Justin Martyr, 1700, and Irenæus, 1702, and of Bishop Bull's works, and a transcript of the 'Codex Alexandrinus' (Septuagint) with numerous emendations (vol. i. 1707, vol. ii. 1709). [xxii. 306]

GRACE, MRS. MARY (*d.* 1786?), painter; exhibited with Incorporated Society of Artists. [xxii. 307]

GRACE, RICHARD (1620?-1691), Irish soldier; carried on guerilla warfare against the Commonwealth; captured at Portumna, and allowed to transport himself and followers to Spain, 1652; joined French service with his regiment, but in 1655 returned to Spanish service, in which he fought at battle of the Dunes, 1658; at the Restoration regained his estates, and received others with a pension; when governor of Athlone joined James II, and compelled Douglas to raise the siege, 1690; killed in second siege. [xxii. 307]

GRACE, SHEFFIELD (1788?-1850), historical writer; patron of Banim; F.R.S. and F.S.A.; published 'Memoirs of the Family of Grace,' 1823, and other works relating to the family; also (1827) Lady Nithsdale's account of the escape (1717) of her husband from the Tower. [xxii. 308]

GRADDON, MISS, afterwards MRS. GIBBS (1804-1854?), vocalist; sang at Drury Lane as Susanna in 'Marriage of Figaro,' 1824, and as Linda in 'Der Freischütz.' [xxii. 309]

GRADWELL, ROBERT (1777-1833), Roman catholic prelate; imprisoned with other students of Douay on the suppression of Douay College; rector of English College of St. Thomas at Rome, 1818; created D.D. by the pope, 1821; coadjutor (bishop of Lydda *in partibus*) to Bishop Bramston, vicar-apostolic of London district, 1828; published 'Winter Evening Dialogue between John Hardman and John Cardwell, 1817. [xxii. 309]

GRAEME, JAMES (1749-1772), poet; his verses published by Robert Anderson (1750-1830) [q. v.], 1773. [xxii. 310]

GRAFTON, DUKES OF. [See FITZROY, HENRY, first DUKE, 1663-1690; FITZROY, AUGUSTUS HENRY, third DUKE, 1735-1811; FITZROY, GEORGE HENRY, fourth DUKE, 1760-1844.]

GRAFTON, RICHARD (*d.* 1572?), chronicler and printer; with Edward Whitchurch had Coverdale's bible reprinted at Antwerp (Matthews's bible), 1537, and Paris, 1538; their 'Great Bible' suppressed at Paris, but printed in England, 1539; ordered to be purchased by every parish, and frequently reissued; with Whitchurch received exclusive patents for church service-books and primers; as 'king's printer' issued prayer-book of 1549, acts of parliament (1552-3), and Lady Jane Grey's proclamation; chief master of Christ's Hospital, 1560; M.P., London, 1553-4 and 1556-7, and Coventry, 1562-3; warden of the Grocers' Company, 1555-6; master of Bridewell, 1559-60; charged by Stow with garbling the editions issued by him of Hardyng's 'Chronicle' (1543) and Hall's 'Union' (1548); himself compiled 'Abridgement of the Chronicles of England' (1562) and a 'Chronicle at Large' (1568). An 'augmented' edition of the latter (1611) was reprinted by Sir H. Ellis, 1809. [xxii. 310]

GRAHAM, MRS. CATHERINE (1731-1791). [See MACAULAY, MRS. CATHERINE.]

GRAHAM, CLEMENTINA STIRLING (1782-1877), authoress of 'Mystifications' (ed. Dr. John Brown, 1865); translated Jonas de Gelieu's 'Bee Preserver' (1829), and wrote songs. [xxii. 313]

GRAHAM, DOUGAL (1724-1779), chap-book writer and bellman of Glasgow; took part in the Jacobite rising of 1745 as a camp follower, and published an account of the Rebellion in doggerel, 1746; his chap-books valuable for folklore; collected writings edited by G. MacGregor, 1883. [xxii. 313]

GRAHAM, SIR FORTESCUE (1794-1880), general; entered royal marine artillery, 1808; served at Walcheren, 1809, in the Peninsula, America, and Canada; commanded marine battalion at Nanking in first Chinese war, and (1855) a brigade of marines at Bomarsund; C.B., 1855; lieutenant-general, 1865; K.C.B., 1865; general, 1866. [xxii. 314]

GRAHAM, GEORGE (1673-1751), mechanician; invented the mercurial pendulum, the 'dead-beat escapement,' and astronomical instruments for Halley, Bradley, and the French Academy; F.R.S.; buried in Westminster Abbey with Tompion. [xxii. 314]

GRAHAM, GEORGE (*d.* 1767), dramatist; assistant-master at Eton and fellow of King's College, Cambridge; M.A., 1754; published a masque, 'Telemachus,' 1763. [xxii. 315]

GRAHAM, GEORGE FARQUHAR (1789-1867), musical amateur; secretary to first Edinburgh festival, 1815; composed 'County Guy' and other songs; republished from seventh edition of 'Encyclopædia Britannica' 'Essay on Theory and Practice of Musical Composition,' 1838; contributed to Wood's 'Songs of Scotland,' and other works. [xxii. 315]

GRAHAM, SIR GERALD (1831-1899), lieutenant-general; educated at Royal Military Academy, Woolwich; lieutenant, royal engineers, 1854; major, 1872; major-general, 1881; lieutenant-general, 1884; colonel-commandant, royal engineers, 1899; served in Crimea, 1854-1856, and received Victoria Cross, 1857; brevet major, 1859; served in Anglo-French expedition against China, 1860-1; brevet lieutenant-colonel; commanding royal engineer in Montreal, 1866-9; C.B. and brevet colonel; commanded second infantry brigade of first division in expedition to Egypt, 1882; won victory at Kassassin; led assault on Tel-el-Kebir; commanded brigade of British army of occupation in Egypt; K.C.B., 1882; commanded expedition against Osman Digna, 1884; won battles of El Teb and Tamai; urged unsuccessfully importance of opening up Suakin-Berber route to assist General Charles George Gordon [q. v.]; advanced from Suakin, 1885, against Osman Digna; repulsed enemy at Hashin and Tamai; G.C.M.G., 1885; published writings on professional and other subjects. [Suppl. ii. 334]

GRAHAM, JAMES, first MARQUIS and fifth EARL OF MONTROSE (1612-1650), succeeded as fifth earl, 1626; on

return from three years' travel coldly received by Charles I,
1636; joined covenanters, 1637; occupied Aberdeen,
carried off Huntly, and defeated his son at the Bridge of
Dee, 1639; invaded England with covenanters, 1640;
joined Charles I, 1641; imprisoned by Argyll, but liberated
on the king's arrival; his advice long rejected for that
of Hamilton; created marquis and lieutenant-general in
Scotland, 1644; won six battles with mixed Irish and
highland force, 1644–5; after Kilsyth entered Glasgow and
summoned a parliament; deserted by the highlanders;
defeated at Philiphaugh, 1645; escaped to the continent;
made field-marshal by the Emperor Ferdinand III, with
leave to levy troops for Charles I, 1648; advised Charles II
against accepting throne of Scotland from covenanters,
and became his lieutenant-governor, 1649; raised money
in Denmark and Sweden, but lost many men by shipwreck; defeated at Invercarron, 1650; betrayed by
Macleod of Assynt, and hanged in the Grassmarket, Edinburgh; wrote vigorous verse.   [xxii. 316]

GRAHAM, JAMES, second MARQUIS OF MONTROSE
(1631 ?–1669), 'the good Marquis'; second son of James,
first marquis [q. v.]; imprisoned as a youth in Edinburgh;
received back his estates, but joined Glencairn's rising,
1653; declined to vote at Marquis of Argyll's trial, 1661;
established claim of 100,664l. Scots against Earl of Argyll,
1667; extraordinary lord of session, 1668.   [xxii. 319]

GRAHAM, JAMES (1649–1730), colonel; of Westminster and Christ Church, Oxford; captain of Scottish
infantry in French service, 1671; entered English service,
1675; lieutenant-colonel of Morpeth's foot, 1678; keeper
of privy purse to Duke of York, 1679, and James II, 1685;
M.P., Carlisle, 1685; corresponded with James II at St.
Germain; outlawed; pardoned, 1692; imprisoned in connection with the 'assassination plot,' 1696; took the oaths,
1701; M.P., Appleby, 1705–7, and Westmoreland, 1708–27;
intimate with the third Earl of Sunderland. [xxii. 320]

GRAHAM, JAMES, fourth MARQUIS and first DUKE
OF MONTROSE (d. 1742), succeeded as fourth Marquis, 1684;
acquired property of the Duke of Lennox, 1702; high
admiral of Scotland, 1705; president of the council, 1706;
created duke for promoting the union, 1707; representative peer; keeper of privy seal (Scotland), 1709–13 and
1716–33; named by George I a lord of the regency and one
of the secretaries of state, 1714; privy councillor, 1717.
                                                 [xxii. 322]

GRAHAM, JAMES (1676–1746), dean of the Faculty
of Advocates; judge of the Scottish admiralty court,
1739; founded family of Graham of Airth Castle.
                                                 [xxii. 323]

GRAHAM, JAMES (1745–1794), quack doctor; studied
medicine at Edinburgh under Monro primus; practised
as oculist and aurist in America; settled at Bristol, 1774,
and began to advertise wonderful cures; removed to Bath,
1777; used electricity, milk baths, and friction; treated
the Duchess of Devonshire at Aix, 1779; set up his
'Temple of Health' in the Adelphi, where he lectured, sold
medicines, and opened a show; caricatured by Colman in
'The Genius of Nonsense,' 1780; Emma Lyon (Lady
Hamilton) said to have represented the Goddess of Health
in his show, which was removed to Pall Mall, 1781; his
property seized for debt, 1782; lectured in Edinburgh,
1783; imprisoned for libelling Edinburgh magistrates;
lectured in Paris, 1786, the Isle of Man, 1788, and Bath,
1789; afterwards became a religious enthusiast and was
confined as a lunatic at Edinburgh; author of twenty
publications.   [xxii. 323]

GRAHAM, JAMES (1765–1811). [See GRAHAME.]

GRAHAM, JAMES, third DUKE OF MONTROSE (1755–
1836), statesman; M.P., Richmond, 1780, Great Bedwin,
1784–90; a lord of the treasury, 1783–9; co-paymaster-
general, 1789–91; privy councillor and vice-president of
the board of trade, 1789; master of the horse, 1790–5 and
1807–30; commissioner for India, 1791–1803; lord justice-
general, 1795–1836; president of the board of trade, 1804–
1806; lord chamberlain, 1821–7 and 1828–30; K.G., 1812;
chancellor of Glasgow University, 1780–1836.
                                                 [xxii. 326]

GRAHAM, JAMES (1791–1845), army pensioner; distinguished himself in Coldstream guards at Waterloo, and
was one of the two Norcross pensioners; said to have
saved Fitzclarence's life at seizure of the Cato Street
conspirators, 1820; died in Kilmainham Hospital.
                                                 [xxii. 327]

GRAHAM, JAMES, seventh MARQUIS and fourth
DUKE OF MONTROSE (1799–1874), statesman; M.P., Cambridge University, 1825–32; a commissioner of India
board, 1828–30; succeeded to dukedom, 1836; lord steward,
1852–3; chancellor of the duchy of Lancaster, 1858; postmaster-general, 1866–8; died at Cannes.   [xxii. 327]

GRAHAM, JAMES GILLESPIE (1777 ?–1855), archi-
tect; on his marriage assumed name of Graham or
Græme; his chef-d'œuvre the convent, with Saxon chapel,
White Horse Lane, Edinburgh, 1835; introduced purer
Gothic into Scotland; with A. W. Pugin designed Vic-
toria Hall, Edinburgh, 1842–4.   [xxii. 328]

GRAHAM, SIR JAMES ROBERT GEORGE (1792–
1861), statesman; educated at Westminster and Christ
Church, Oxford; as secretary to Lord Montgomerie had
chief conduct of negotiations with King Joachim (Murat)
of Naples, 1813–14; whig M.P. for Hull, 1818, for St. Ives,
1820; resigned on petition next year, 1821; during five
years' retirement paid attention to agriculture, and published 'Corn and Currency,' 1826; succeeded to baronetcy,
1824; M.P., Carlisle, 1826, Cumberland, 1827; moved reduction of official salaries, 1830; first lord of the admiralty
under Earl Grey, and one of committee of four which
prepared first Reform Bill; resigned with Lord Stanley
on Irish church question, 1834, becoming one of the
'Derby Dilly'; M.P., Pembroke, 1838, Dorchester, 1841;
as home secretary under Peel, 1841–6, dealt with Scottish
church question and trial of O'Connell; became highly
unpopular, especially after his admissions of tampering
with foreign refugees' letters, 1844; fall of the ministry
occasioned by the defeat of his bill for the protection of
life in Ireland, 1846; acted with Peelites; elected for
Ripon; refused Lord John Russell's offer of governor-
generalship of India, 1847, the admiralty, 1848, and the
board of control, but supported him against protectionists;
again returned for Carlisle, 1852; first lord of the admiralty in Aberdeen's coalition ministry, 1852–5; retained
office under Palmerston, but resigned with Gladstone and
Sidney Herbert.   [xxii. 328]

GRAHAM, JANET (1723–1805), poet; author of 'The
Wayward Wife.'   [xxii. 332]

GRAHAM, SIR JOHN (d. 1298), warrior; rescued
Wallace at Queensberry; killed at Falkirk, where a monument was afterwards erected to him.   [xxii. 332]

GRAHAM, JOHN, third EARL OF MONTROSE (1547 ?–
1608), received renunciation of Scottish crown by Queen
Mary, 1567; fought for the regent at Langside, 1568;
succeeded his grandfather in the earldom, 1571; privy
councillor under the regent Mar; a commissioner for
Morton at the pacification of Perth, 1572; one of James VI's
council from 1578; prominent member of opposition to
Morton and chancellor of assize held on him, 1581; joined in
raid of Ruthven, but rallied to the king on his escape, 1583;
lord chancellor, 1584–5; planned death of Angus, 1584;
reconciled to Angus, 1587; extraordinary lord of session,
1591; president of the council, 1598; lord chancellor,
1599; king's commissioner at union conference, and
viceroy of Scotland, 1604.   [xxii. 333]

GRAHAM, JOHN, of Claverhouse, first VISCOUNT
DUNDEE (1649 ?–1689), studied at St. Andrews; served
under William of Orange; said to have saved William's
life at Seneff, 1674; recommended by him to James, duke
of York; captain under Montrose; sent to repress conventicles in Dumfries and Annandale, 1678; named sheriff-
depute of those districts, 1679; defeated at Drumclog,
1679; held Glasgow; present at Bothwell Brigg, 1679;
procured supersession of Monmouth as commander-in-
chief by Thomas Dalyell [q. v.] and adoption of a severer
policy towards covenanters, 1679; failed in his scheme of
marriage with heiress of Menteith; carried out new policy
in Galloway, 1681, being implacable to ringleaders, but not
wantonly cruel to the people; supported by the council
against Sir John Dalrymple [q. v.], and appointed colonel
of newly raised regiment, 1682; visited Charles II at Newmarket, and obtained money grant and estate of Dudhope,
1683; made privy councillor of Scotland; sent into Ayr
and Clydesdale with civil as well as military powers, 1684,
soon after which the covenanter Renwick's manifesto was
followed by the 'killing time'; lost influence through
quarrel with Queensberry, 1685; temporarily superseded by
Colonel Douglas, 1685; not clearly responsible for deaths of the
'Wigtown martyrs,' but directly concerned in execution

of John Brown (1627 ?–1685) [q. v.] of Priestfield ; briga-dier-general of horse, 1685 ; supported James II's Romanis-ing policy ; appointed major-general, 1686 ; examined Ren-wick, the last of the martyrs (1688), before the council ; provost of Dundee, 1688 ; joined James II at Salisbury as second in command of the force from Scotland, 1688 ; created Viscount Dundee, 1688 ; with Balcarres, the only Scots noble in London who remained faithful ; allowed by William III to return to Scotland with fifty troopers ; found Edinburgh in possession of the covenanters, and escaped through Stirling to Dudhope, 1689 ; outlawed on refusal to return to Edinburgh ; having received James's commission to command for him in Scotland, made his way to the clans at Lochaber ; collected three thousand men, and by Lochiel's advice selected Killiecrankie to await Mackay's attack ; defeated Mackay, but fell mor-tally wounded. [xxii. 335]

GRAHAM, JOHN (*fl.* 1720–1775), history-painter ; settled at the Hague. [xxii. 350]

GRAHAM, JOHN (1754–1817), painter ; director of Trustees' Academy for Scottish manufactures, 1800–17, having Wilkie, Allan, and Watson-Gordon as pupils ; exhibited at Royal Academy, 1780–97. [xxii. 350]

GRAHAM, JOHN (1805–1839), superintendent of botanic garden, Bombay ; deputy postmaster-general of Bombay, 1826–39 ; compiled catalogue of Bombay plants ; died at Khandalla. [xxii. 351]

GRAHAM, JOHN (1776–1844), historian ; M.A. Trinity College, Dublin, 1815 ; rector of Magilligan, 1824–1844 ; published 'Annals of Ireland,' 1819, 'Derriana,' 1823, and (1839) 'History of Ireland, 1689–91.' [xxii. 351]

GRAHAM, JOHN (1794–1865), bishop of Chester ; fourth wrangler and chancellor's medallist, Christ's Col-lege, Cambridge ; fellow, 1816 ; M.A., 1819 ; D.D., 1831 ; master of Christ's College, 1830–48 ; twice vice-chancel-lor ; chaplain to Prince Albert, 1841 ; clerk of the closet, 1849 ; active member of universities' commission ; bishop of Chester, 1848–65 ; published sermons. [xxii. 352]

GRAHAM, JOHN MURRAY (1809–1881), historian ; M.A. Edinburgh, 1828 ; adopted name Graham on succes-sion to part of the estates of Thomas, baron Lynedoch [q. v.], 1859, a memoir of whom he compiled, 1869 ; pub-lished also 'Annals and Correspondence of the Viscount and first and second Earls of Stair,' 1875. [xxii. 352]

GRAHAM, Mrs. MARIA (1785–1842). [See CALL-COTT, MARIA, LADY.]

GRAHAM, PATRICK (*d.* 1478), archbishop of St. Andrews ; dean of arts at St. Andrews, 1457 ; bishop of Brechin, 1463–6 ; succeeded his half-brother, Kennedy, as primate, 1466, but went to Rome till fall of the Boyds, 1469 ; obtained from Sixtus IV the bulls of 1472, consti-tuting St. Andrews a metropolitan see ; his deposition from the archbishopric of St. Andrews by the papal nuncio on charges of heresy and simony procured by William Scheves [q. v.], archdeacon of St. Andrews, and John Lochy, rector of the university, with the assistance of the king, James III, 1478 ; died in prison in Lochleven Castle. [xxii. 353]

GRAHAM, RICHARD, VISCOUNT PRESTON (1648–1695), Jacobite ; educated at Westminster and Christ Church, Oxford ; M.A., 1666 ; created baronet, 1662 ; M.P., Cockermouth, 1675–81 and 1685–8 ; created a Scottish peer for parliamentary services to James, duke of York, 1680 ; as envoy extraordinary to France (1682–5), protested against the seizure of Orange ; with Middleton managed the House of Commons for James II ; lord president of the council, 1688, and one of the council of five left by James in London ; created British peer at St. Germain, 1689 ; arrested and sent to the Tower, 1689 ; his claim of the privilege of a peer disallowed and withdrawn, 1689 ; released on apologising, but arrested next year while carrying treasonable papers on board a smack bound for France ; tried and sentenced for treason, but pardoned after making confessions implicating Penn and others, 1691 ; in retirement revised the translation of Boethius (published, 1695–96), with preface containing allusions to his political conduct. [xxii. 355]

GRAHAM, RICHARD (*fl.* 1680–1720), author of 'Short Account of the most Eminent Painters,' originally supplement to Dryden's version of Du Fresnoy's 'Art of Painting,' 1695. [xxii. 357]

GRAHAM, SIR ROBERT (*d.* 1437), conspirator ; banished for language derogatory to the king, 1435 ; chief agent in conspiracy of Walter, earl of Atholl, in which James I was murdered at Perth, 1437 ; captured in h gh-lands and tortured to death at Stirling. [xxii. 357]

GRAHAM or **GRIMES**, ROBERT (*d.* 1701), colonel and Trappist ; served in Flanders under William III, and afterwards lived at St. Germain ; entered monastery of La Trappe ; much resorted to by the Jacobite court. [xxii. 357]

GRAHAM, afterwards **CUNNINGHAME-GRAHAM**, ROBERT (*d.* 1797 ?), composer of 'If doughty deeds my lady please' ; some time receiver-general of Jamaica ; radical M.P. for Stirlingshire, 1794–6 ; rector of Glasgow University, 1785. [xxii. 358]

GRAHAM, SIR ROBERT (1744–1836), judge ; fellow of Trinity College, Cambridge, and third wrangler, 1766 ; M.A., 1769 ; LL.D., 1835 ; barrister, Inner Temple ; attor-ney-general to Prince of Wales, 1793 ; K.C., 1794 ; baron of the exchequer, 1799 ; knighted, 1800. [xxii. 358]

GRAHAM, ROBERT (1786–1845), M.D. and botanist ; professor of botany at Glasgow, 1818–20 ; regius professor at Edinburgh, 1820–45 ; contributed to Edinburgh botani-cal periodicals and Hooker's 'Companion.' [xxii. 358]

GRAHAM, SIMON (1570 ?–1614). [See GRAHAME.]

GRAHAM, THOMAS, BARON LYNEDOCH (1748–1843), general ; entered Christ Church, Oxford, 1766 ; played in match Scottish cricket match, 1785 ; introduced Cleveland horses and Devon cattle into Scotland ; aide-de-camp to Lord Mulgrave at Toulon, 1793 ; raised 'Perth-shire volunteers' (2nd Scottish rifles) and received tempo-rary rank of lieutenant-colonel commandant, 1794 ; whig M.P. for Perthshire, 1794–1807 ; when British commis-sioner with Austrian army in Mantua made his way, dis-guised as a peasant, to Austrian headquarters, 1796–7 ; distinguished at capture of Minorca, 1798 ; reorganised defences of Messina and commanded troops blockading Malta, 1799–1800 ; obtained permanent military rank by influence of Sir John Moore ; Sir John Moore's aide-de-camp in Coruña campaign ; commanded brigade in Walcheren expedition, 1809 ; lieutenant-general, 1810 ; won victory of Barossa, 1811, but resigned his command on the Spanish generals unfairly claiming the whole credit of the victory ; led division under Wellington and assisted at capture of Ciudad Rodrigo, 1812, and Badajos, 1812 ; commanded left wing at Vittoria, 1813 ; wounded at Tolosa, 1813 ; repulsed before San Sebastian, but after-wards reduced the place, 1813 ; invalided after crossing Bidassoa ; commanded British contingent in Holland, 1814 ; created a peer, 1814, refusing pension ; general, 1821 ; chief founder of United Service Club, where is his portrait by Sir Thomas Lawrence ; G.C.B. and G.C.M.G. [xxii. 358]

GRAHAM, THOMAS (1805–1869), chemist ; M.A. Glasgow, 1824 ; subsequently studied at Edinburgh ; pro-fessor of chemistry at Andersonian University, Glasgow, 1830–7, at University College, London, 1837–55 ; master of the mint, 1855–69 ; vice-president of chemical jury of exhibition of 1851 ; awarded Keith prize for discovery of law of diffusion of gases, 1834, and gold medals of Royal Society, 1840 and 1850 ; first president of Chemical (1840) and Cavendish (1846) societies ; edited 'Chemical Reports and Memoirs,' 1848 ; F.R.S., 1836 ; twice vice-president ; Bakerian lecturer, 1850 and 1854 ; D.C.L. Oxford, 1853 ; discovered the polybasic character of phosphoric acid, and made valuable researches on the compounds of alcohol with salts ; introduced the 'Graham tube' ; published 'Elements of Chemistry,' 1842. [xxii. 361]

GRAHAM, WILLIAM, seventh EARL OF MENTEITH and first EARL OF AIRTH (1591–1661), member of the Scottish privy council, 1626 ; president, 1628 ; justice-general of Scotland, 1628 ; in great favour with Charles I, who made him privy councillor of England ; created Earl of Strathearn, 1631, but, the patent being withdrawn in 1633, was made Earl of Airth instead ; disgraced soon afterwards, being charged with boasting of his descent from Robert II ; restored to favour, 1637 ; served against covenanters. [xxii. 363]

GRAHAM, WILLIAM (1737–1801), secession minister at Whitehaven, 1759, at Newcastle, 1770–1801 ; published, among other works, 'Candid Vindication of the Secession Church,' 1790, and 'Review of Ecclesiastical Establishments in Europe,' 1792. [xxii. 364]

GRAHAM, WILLIAM (1810–1883), Irish presbyterian divine; missionary (1842–83) to Jews at Damascus, Hamburg, and Bonn; wrote commentaries on Ephesians, 1 John, and Titus, and 'An Appeal to Israel' (in four languages). [xxii. 365]

GRAHAM-GILBERT, JOHN (1794–1866), painter; assumed additional name of Gilbert on marriage, 1834; exhibited at Royal Academy, 1820–3; R.S.A., 1829; exhibited constantly at the Scottish and occasionally at the Royal Academy; painted mainly portraits. [xxii. 365]

GRAHAME, JAMES (1765–1811), Scottish poet; educated at Glasgow; successively writer to the signet, advocate, and episcopal clergyman; published (at first anonymously), 1804, 'The Sabbath,' 'Birds of Scotland,' 1806, and 'British Georgics,' 1809, and other verse; praised by 'Christopher North,' but satirised by Byron. [xxii. 366]

GRAHAME, SIMION (1570?–1614), Franciscan; made prebendary of Brodderstanis by James VI; led licentious life as traveller, soldier, and courtier; died a Franciscan at Carpentras; his 'Passionate Sparke of a Relenting Minde' and 'Anatomie of Hvmors,' reprinted, 1830. [xxii. 366]

GRAILE, EDMUND (*fl.* 1611), poet; entered Magdalen College, Oxford, 1593; M.A., 1600; physician of St. Bartholomew's Hospital, Gloucester; published 'Little Timothie, his Lesson,' 1611. [xxii. 367]

GRAIN, RICHARD CORNEY (1844–1895), public entertainer; barrister, Inner Temple, 1866; member of German Reed entertainment, 1870–95; wrote songs and musical sketches. [Suppl. ii. 338]

GRAINGER, EDWARD (1797–1824), anatomical teacher; dresser to Sir Astley Cooper; opened an anatomical school in Southwark, 1819. [xxii. 367]

GRAINGER, JAMES (1721?–1766), physician and poet; army surgeon, 1745–8; M.D. Edinburgh, 1753; friend of Dr. Johnson, Shenstone, and Bishop Percy; contributed to 'Monthly Review,' 1756–8; L.R.C.P., 1758; his version of Tibullus attacked by Smollett, 1759; practised in St. Christopher, 1759–63; published 'The Sugar Cane,' 1764, and 'Essay on the more common West India Diseases,' 1764; died in St. Christopher; contributed a West Indian ballad to Percy's 'Reliques'; his 'Poetical Works' edited by Robert Anderson, 1836. [xxii. 368]

GRAINGER, RICHARD (1798–1861), architect; of Newcastle. [xxii. 370]

GRAINGER, RICHARD DUGARD (1801–1865), anatomist and physiologist; brother of Edward Grainger [q. v.], whose anatomical school he carried on; lecturer at St. Thomas's Hospital, 1842–60; declined to receive a money testimonial, 1860, on which the Grainger testimonial prize was founded with the money collected; as board of health inspector wrote valuable report on cholera, 1850; inspector under Burials Act, 1853; F.R.S.; member of council of College of Surgeons; Hunterian orator, 1848; published 'Elements of General Anatomy,' 1829, and 'Observations on . . . the Spinal Cord,' 1837. [xxii. 370]

GRAINGER, THOMAS (1794–1852), civil engineer; laid down many railways in Scotland and northern England; fatally injured in railway accident. [xxii. 371]

GRAMMONT, ELIZABETH, COMTESSE DE (1641–1708). [See HAMILTON, ELIZABETH.]

GRANARD, EARLS OF. [See FORBES, SIR ARTHUR, first EARL, 1623–1696; FORBES, GEORGE, third EARL, 1685–1765; FORBES, GEORGE, sixth EARL, 1760–1837.]

GRANBY, MARQUIS OF (1721–1770). [See MANNERS, JOHN.]

GRANDISON, VISCOUNTS. [See ST. JOHN, OLIVER, first VISCOUNT, 1559–1630; VILLIERS, GEORGE BUSSY, seventh VISCOUNT, 1735–1805; VILLIERS, GEORGE CHILD-, eighth VISCOUNT, 1773–1859.]

GRANDISON, JOHN (1292?–1369), bishop of Exeter; prebendary of York, 1309, of Lincoln, 1322; archdeacon of Nottingham, 1310; chaplain to Pope John XXII, and

papal legate, 1327; appointed bishop of Exeter by provision, and consecrated at Avignon, 1327; successfully resisted visitation of Archbishop Mepeham, 1332; completed nave of his cathedral and erected episcopal throne; his tomb in St. Radegunde's Chapel ransacked in sixteenth century; his 'Lessons from the Bible' and 'Legends of the Saints' still extant. [xxii. 371]

GRANE, VISCOUNT (*d.* 1541). [See GREY, LORD LEONARD.]

GRANGE, LORD (1679–1754). [See ERSKINE, JAMES.]

GRANGE, JOHN (*fl.* 1577), poet; author of 'The Golden Aphroditis,' 1577. [xxii. 372]

GRANGER, JAMES (1723–1776), biographer and print collector; entered Christ Church, Oxford, 1743; vicar of Shiplake, Oxfordshire; collected fourteen thousand engraved portraits; published 'Biographical History of England, from Egbert the Great to the Revolution . . . adapted to a Methodical Catalogue of Engraved British Heads,' 1769 (with supplement, 1774); a continuation of the work from Granger's manuscripts, by Mark Noble, bringing the history down to 1727, was published, 1806. [xxii. 372]

GRANT, ALBERT, known as BARON GRANT (1830–1899), company promoter; son of W. Gottheimer; assumed name of Grant; achieved extraordinary success as company promoter; gained 100,000*l.* as promotion money for the Emma Silver Mine, which paid investors a shilling for each 20*l.* share; M.P., Kidderminster, 1865–8 and 1874–80; purchased Leicester Square, London, which he converted into a public garden and handed over to metropolitan board of works, 1874; died comparatively poor owing to series of actions in bankruptcy court. [Suppl. ii. 338]

GRANT, ALEXANDER (1679–1720), laird of Grant; brigadier-general; son of Ludovick Grant [q. v.]; M.P. for Inverness-shire in Scottish parliament, 1703–7; a commissioner for the union; served in Flanders; constable of Edinburgh Castle and brigadier-general, 1715; M.P. for Inverness-shire and Elgin and Forres in British parliament. [xxii. 374]

GRANT, SIR ALEXANDER, eighth baronet 'of Dalvey' (1826–1884), principal of Edinburgh University; educated at Harrow; scholar of Balliol College, Oxford; fellow of Oriel College, 1849; succeeded as baronet, 1856; professor of history at the Elphinstone Institution, Madras, 1860, and principal, 1862; vice-chancellor of Bombay University, 1863–8, and director of public instruction; member of legislative council, 1868; as principal at Edinburgh University (1868–84) closed the disagreement with civic authorities, obtained new buildings for the medical department, and (1884) organised tercentenary celebration; hon. D.C.L. Oxford and LL.D. Cambridge, Edinburgh, and Glasgow; prepared first Scottish education code; edited Aristotle's 'Ethics,' 1857; published lives of Aristotle and Xenophon, and 'The Story of the University of Edinburgh,' 1884. [xxii. 374]

GRANT, SIR ALEXANDER CRAY, sixth baronet 'of Dalvey' (1782–1854), civil servant; M.A. St. John's College, Cambridge, 1806; M.P., Tregony, 1812, Lostwithiel, 1818–26, Aldborough, 1826–30, Westbury, 1830–2, and Cambridge, 1840–3, representing interests of West Indian planters; chairman of committees, 1826–32; member of board of control, 1834–5; commissioner of accounts, 1843–54. [xxii. 376]

GRANT, ANDREW (*fl.* 1809), physician; author of 'History of Brazil,' 1809. [xxii. 376]

GRANT, MRS. ANNE (1755–1838), authoress; *née* Macvicar; wife of minister of Laggan, Inverness-shire; from 1810 lived at Edinburgh and was admitted to the best literary society, who procured her (1826) a pension; her 'Letters from the Mountains' (1803) highly popular; published also 'Memoirs of an American Lady,' 1808, and 'Essays on the Superstitions of the Highlands,' 1811. [xxii. 376]

GRANT, ANTHONY (1806–1883), divine; of Winchester and New College, Oxford; fellow, 1827; Ellerton prizeman, 1832; D.C.L., 1842; vicar of Romford, 1838–62, of Aylesford, 1862–77; archdeacon of St. Albans, 1846; canon of Rochester, 1860; published (1844) 'Past and Prospective Extension of the Gospel by Missions' (Bampton Lecture, 1843), and other works. [xxii. 378]

GRANT, CHARLES (1746–1823), statesman and philanthropist; made large fortune in service of East India Company; senior merchant, 1784; fourth member of board of trade at Calcutta, 1787; his pamphlet (1792) advocating toleration of missionary and educational work in the East printed (1813) by order of House of Commons; M.P., Inverness-shire, 1804–18; chairman of court of directors of East India Company from 1805; opposed policy of Wellesley, and supported (1808) motion for his impeachment; procured the assignment of a grant towards education under charter of 1813; promoted building of churches in India and elsewhere; introduced Sunday schools into Scotland; originated scheme for foundation of Haileybury College. [xxii. 378]

GRANT, CHARLES, Baron Glenelg (1778–1866), statesman; eldest son of Charles Grant (1746–1823) [q. v.]; fellow of Magdalene College, Cambridge, 1802; fourth wrangler and chancellor's medallist; M.A., 1804; hon. LL.D., 1819; member of Speculative Society, Edinburgh; M.P. for Inverness and Fortrose, 1811–18, for Inverness-shire, 1818–35; a lord of the treasury, 1813; privy councillor and Irish secretary, 1819–23; vice-president of board of trade, 1823–7; president of board of trade and treasurer of navy, 1827–8; as president of board of control (1830–5) carried charter (1833) vesting the East India Company's property in the crown; as colonial secretary under Melbourne, 1835–9, introduced bill abolishing West Indian slavery; created Baron Glenelg, 1831; refused to sanction action of Sir Benjamin D'Urban [q. v.] after Kaffir invasion of Cape Colony, 1835; offended both tories and radicals by his irresolute Canadian policy; resigned, 1839, receiving a pension and commissionership of the land tax; died at Cannes. [xxii. 380]

GRANT, COLQUHOUN (d. 1792), Jacobite; distinguished at Prestonpans, 1745, and one of Charles Edward's life guards at Culloden, 1746; afterwards practised in Edinburgh as writer to the signet. [xxii. 381]

GRANT, COLQUHOUN (1780–1829), lieutenant-colonel; captured at Ostend with 11th foot, 1798; deputy-assistant adjutant-general and secret intelligence officer in the Peninsula; captured near the Coa, 1812; escaped from Bayonne to Paris, whence he sent intelligence to Wellington; disguised as a sailor reached England, and having arranged for his exchange, rejoined Wellington in Spain; as intelligence officer in 1815 sent news from Condé of Napoleon's intentions; lieutenant-colonel of the 54th, 1821; commanded brigade in first Burmese war; C.B.; died at Aix-la-Chapelle. [xxii. 382]

GRANT, Sir COLQUHOUN (1764?–1835), lieutenant-general; with 25th dragoons at Seringapatam, 1799; lieutenant-colonel of 72nd highlanders, 1802; wounded at recapture of the Cape, 1806; commanded 15th hussars in Moore's retreat and (1813) at Vittoria; K.C.B., 1814; led hussar brigade at Waterloo; lieutenant-general, 1830; M.P., Queensborough, 1831–2. [xxii. 383]

GRANT, DAVID (1823–1886), author of 'Metrical Tales,' 1880, and 'Lays and Legends of the North,' 1884; his 'Book of Ten Songs,' published posthumously. [xxii. 384]

GRANT or **GRAUNT**, EDWARD (1540?–1601), head-master of Westminster; B.A. St. John's College, Cambridge, 1567; B.A. Oxford, 1572; M.A. Oxford, 1572; M.A. Cambridge, 1573; D.D. Cambridge, 1589; canon of Westminster, 1577, of Ely, 1589; friend of Ascham; head-master of Westminster, 1572–93; author of 'Græcæ Linguæ Spicilegium,' 1575, and a revised edition of Crispin's Greek-Latin lexicon, and Greek, Latin, and English verses. [xxii. 384]

GRANT, Mrs. ELIZABETH, afterwards Mrs. Eliza- beth Murray (1745?–1814?), author of the song, 'Roy's Wife.' [xxii. 385]

GRANT, Sir FRANCIS, Lord Cullen (1658–1726), Scottish judge; educated at Aberdeen and Leyden; admitted advocate, 1691; defended power of the estates to settle succession to the crown; created baronet of Nova Scotia, 1705; lord of session, 1709; wrote on societies for the reformation of manners and patronage question in Scottish church. [xxii. 385]

GRANT, Sir FRANCIS (1803–1878), portrait-painter; brother of Sir James Hope Grant [q. v.]; made reputation as a painter of sporting-scenes; fashionable as a portrait-painter after exhibition at the Academy of his equestrian group of the queen, Lord Melbourne, and company, 1840; R.A., 1851; president R.A., 1866–78; knighted, 1866; painted portraits of contemporary celebrities, including Macaulay, Lord-chancellor Campbell, Viscount Hardinge, and Landseer. [xxii. 386]

GRANT, JAMES (1485?–1553), laird of Freuchie ('the Bold'); son of John Grant (d. 1528) [q. v.] of Freuchie; fined for protecting members of the clan Chattan, 1528; took part in expedition against the Clanranald and Mackenzies of Kintail, 1544; exempted by James V from jurisdiction of inferior courts. [xxii. 387]

GRANT, JAMES (1706–1778), Scottish catholic prelate; admitted into the Scots College, Rome, 1726; priest, 1733; missioner in Scotland, 1734; surrendered himself (1746) to some men who threatened to desolate the Isle of Barra, in which he was residing, unless the priest were delivered up to them; imprisoned at Inverness; consecrated bishop of Sinita *in partibus*, 1755. [xxii. 388]

GRANT, JAMES (1720–1806), of Ballindalloch, general; served with 1st royal Scots in Flanders, 1746–8, and at Culloden, 1746; surprised and captured at Fort Duquesne, 1758; lieutenant-colonel of the 40th and governor of East Florida, 1760; defeated Cherokees at Etchoe, 1761; M.P., Wick, 1773, and Sutherlandshire, 1774 and 1787–1806; commanded brigades at Long Island, Brandywine, and Germanstown; captured St. Lucia and held it against d'Estaing, 1778; major-general, 1777; general, 1796. [xxii. 388]

GRANT, Sir JAMES (1738–1811), seventh baronet of Grant, 1773; chief of the clan Grant; M.P., Elgin and Forres, 1761–8, Banff, 1790–95; lord-lieutenant of Inverness-shire, 1794–1809; raised two highland regiments; colonel, 1793. [xxii. 389]

GRANT, JAMES (1743? – 1835), advocate; died senior of Scottish bar; friend of Jeffrey, Erskine, and Scottish whigs; published 'Essays on the Origin of Society,' &c., 1785, and 'Thoughts on the Origin and Descent of the Gael,' containing discussion of the Ossian question, 1814. [xxii. 390]

GRANT, JAMES (1802–1879), journalist; edited 'Elgin Courier,' 'Morning Advertiser' (1850–71), and Grant's 'London Journal'; published 'Random Recollections of the House of Commons and ... Lords,' 1836, 'Sketches in London,' 1838, and 'The Newspaper Press,' 1871–2, and other works. [xxii. 390]

GRANT, JAMES (1840–1885), Scottish antiquary; M.A. Aberdeen; assisted in editing Scots privy council records, and published 'History of the Burgh and Parish Schools of Scotland,' vol. i. 1876. [xxii. 391]

GRANT, JAMES (1822–1887), novelist and historical writer; grandson of James Grant (1743?–1835) [q. v.]; served in the 62nd three years; founded National Association for the Vindication of Scottish Rights, 1852; a military expert. Of his fifty-six novels the best are 'The Romance of War' (1845) and 'Adventures of an Aide-de-Camp.' His other works include memoirs of Kirkcaldy of Grange, Sir J. Hepburn, and Montrose, 'British Battles on Land and Sea,' 1873 (with continuation, 1884), and 'Old and New Edinburgh' (1880). [xxii. 391]

GRANT, JAMES AUGUSTUS (1827–1892), lieutenant-colonel; African traveller; educated at Marischal College, Aberdeen; received commission in 8th native Bengal infantry, 1846; adjutant, 1853–7; attached to 78th highlanders at relief of Lucknow; accompanied John Hanning Speke [q. v.] in African exploring expedition from Ukuni to Karagué, 1861, and from Uganda to falls of Karuma, Faloro, and Gondokoro, 1862–3; made elaborate botanical and meteorological notes, and published 'A Walk across Africa,' 1864; received gold medal of Royal Geographical Society, 1864; C.B., 1866; in intelligence department in Abyssinian expedition, 1868; C.S.I., 1868; lieutenant-colonel, 1868. [Suppl. ii. 339]

GRANT, Sir JAMES HOPE (1808–1875), general; served with the 9th lancers, 1826–58; lieutenant-colonel, 1849; brigade-major to Lord Saltoun in first Chinese war, 1840–2; distinguished himself in the Sikh wars, 1845–1846 and 1848–9; during the mutiny did good service with movable columns; commanded the Trans-Ghogra force; K.C.B., 1858; commanded successfully in the second Chinese war (1860–1); G.C.B.; commander-in-chief at Madras, 1862–3; quartermaster-general at the Horse Guards, 1865; at Aldershot initiated in 1871 the annual autumn manœuvres, and introduced the war game and military lectures. [xxii. 392]

GRANT, JAMES MACPHERSON (1822 – 1885), Australian statesman; emigrated to Sydney when fourteen; solicitor at Sydney and Melbourne; successful gold-digger at Bendigo; acted for Ballarat miners after riots of 1854; member for Bendigo, 1855, Sandhurst, 1856, and Avoca, 1859, in Victoria legislative council; vice-president of lands, 1860–1; president, 1864, 1868–9, and 1871–2; carried Land Act of 1865; minister of justice under Berry, 1875 and 1877–80; chief secretary under Sir Bryan O'Loghlen, 1881–3. [xxii. 394]

GRANT, JAMES WILLIAM (1788–1865), astronomer, in East India Company's service, 1805–49; erected at Elchies, Morayshire, a granite observatory, where was the 'Trophy Telescope' seen at exhibition of 1851; F.R.A.S., 1854; discovered companion of Antares, 1844. [xxii. 395]

GRANT, JOHN (d. 1528), second laird of Freuchie ('The Bard'); fought for James III against his son; rewarded by James IV for his support of Huntly in the northern counties with lands of Glencarny and Ballindalloch, 1489, and barony of Urquhart, 1509. [xxii. 396]

GRANT, JOHN (1568 ?–1622), fifth laird of Freuchie; took part with James VI against George Gordon, first marquis of Huntly [q. v.], in 1589 and 1592; commissioned to suppress witchcraft in highlands, 1602; fined for relations with Macgregors; commissioned to deal with gipsies, 1620; a juror at Orkney's trial, 1615; acquired estates in Strathspey. [xxii. 396]

GRANT, JOHN (1782 – 1842), lieutenant-colonel, Portuguese service; served with the Lusitanian legion in 1808–9, and afterwards under Beresford; a famous spy in the Peninsula war; lieutenant, 2nd royal veteran battalion; secretary to London committee following Beresford's dismissal from Portuguese service, 1820. [xxii. 397]

GRANT, SIR JOHN PETER (1774–1848), chief-justice of Calcutta; barrister, Lincoln's Inn, 1802; M.P., Grimsby and Tavistock; knighted; puisne judge of Bombay, 1827, afterwards of Calcutta; chief works, 'Essays towards illustrating some elementary principles relating to Wealth and Currency,' 1812, and 'Summary of the Law relating to granting New Trials in Civil Suits,' 1817. [xxii. 398]

GRANT, SIR JOHN PETER (1807–1893), Indian and colonial governor; son of Sir John Peter Grant (1774–1848) [q. v.]; educated at Eton, Haileybury, and Edinburgh University; joined Bengal civil service, 1828; assistant in board of revenue, Calcutta, 1832; secretary to government of Bengal, 1848, and virtually ruled province, 1848–1852; foreign secretary, 1853; permanent secretary in home department of government of India, 1853; member of council of governor-general of Bengal, 1854–9; governor-general of Central Provinces, 1857–9; lieutenant-governor of Bengal, 1859–62; K.C.B., 1862; governor of Jamaica, 1866–73, and completely reorganised political and legal status of the island. [Suppl. ii. 341]

GRANT, JOHNSON (1773–1844), divine; grandson of Sir Francis Grant, lord Cullen [q. v.]; M.A. St. John's College, Oxford, 1805; incumbent of Kentish Town, 1822–1844; published, among other works, 'Summary of the History of the English Church,' 1811–26. [xxii. 398]

GRANT, JOSEPH (1805–1835), Scottish poet; author of 'Juvenile Lays,' 1828, 'Kincardineshire Traditions,' 1830, and 'Tales of the Glens' (posthumous). [xxii. 399]

GRANT, LILIAS (d. 1643), poetess; née Murray; wife of John Grant, fifth laird of Freuchie [q. v.]. [xxii. 397]

GRANT, LUDOVICK (1650 ?–1716), of Grant; eighth laird of Freuchie, 1663; fined for protecting covenanters, 1685; sat for Elgin and Inverness-shire in Scottish parliament; as sheriff of Inverness-shire assisted General Mackay against Dundee, 1689; obtained (1694) charter converting Freuchie into regality of Grant, Castleton becoming Grantown. [xxii. 399]

GRANT, MALCOLM (1762–1831), lieutenant-general in East India Company's service; served against Mahrattas, 1779, and in Malabar, 1792–8; held chief command in Malabar and Canara, 1804, and reduced Savendroog; lieutenant-general, 1825. [xxii. 400]

GRANT, PATRICK, LORD ELCHIES (1690–1754), Scottish judge; admitted advocate, 1712; raised to the bench, 1732; lord of justiciary, 1737; collected decisions (1733–54) of session (printed, 1813). [xxii. 400]

GRANT, SIR PATRICK (1804–1895), field-marshal; ensign, 11th Bengal native infantry, 1820; lieutenant, 1823; major, 1845; lieutenant-colonel, 1851; major-general, 1854; colonel, 104th foot, 1862; lieutenant-general, 1862; colonel, Seaforth highlanders, 1863; general, 1870; field-marshal, 1883; colonel, royal horse guards, and gold-stick-in-waiting to Queen Victoria, 1885; served in Gwalior campaign, 1843, first Sikh war, 1845–6; C.B., 1846; adjutant-general of Bengal army, 1846; served in second Sikh war, 1849; brevet colonel and aide-de-camp to Queen Victoria, 1849; commander-in-chief of Madras army, 1856–1861; temporarily commander-in-chief in India, 1857; K.C.B., 1857; G.C.B., 1861; governor and commander-in-chief of Malta, 1867–72; G.C.M.G., 1868; governor of Chelsea Hospital, 1874–95. [Suppl. ii. 343]

GRANT, PETER (d. 1784), Scottish abbé and favourite of the pope; as agent at Rome rendered great services to British travellers; died at Rome. [xxii. 400]

GRANT, RICHARD (d. 1231), also called RICHARD OF WETHERSHED; archbishop of Canterbury; chancellor of Lincoln, 1221–7; appointed primate at request of Henry III and the bishops, 1227; opposed king's demand for scutage, 1228; claimed custody of Tunbridge Castle from Hubert de Burgh, and excommunicated those in possession; went to Rome and brought complaints against Hubert de Burgh; won his cause, but died on the way home at St. Gemini. [xxii. 401]

GRANT, SIR ROBERT (1779–1838), governor of Bombay; second son of Charles Grant (1746–1823) [q. v.]; fellow of Magdalene College, Cambridge, 1802; third wrangler, 1801; M.A., 1804; barrister, Lincoln's Inn, 1807; M.P., Elgin 1818–26, Inverness, 1826–30, Norwich, 1830–2, Finsbury, 1832–4; commissioner of board of control, 1830; judge advocate-general, 1832; carried Jewish emancipation resolution, and two bills in the Commons, 1833–4; governor of Bombay, 1834–8; K.C.H., 1834; published 'Sketch of the History of the East India Company to 1773'; died at Dalpoorie; sacred poems by him edited by Lord Glenelg, 1839. [xxii. 402]

GRANT, ROBERT (1814–1892), astronomer; studied at King's College, Aberdeen; published 'History of Physical Astronomy,' 1852, and received Royal Astronomical Society's gold medal, 1856; F.R.A.S., 1850, edited 'Monthly Notices,' 1852–60; M.A., 1855, and LL.D., 1865, Aberdeen; joined Royal Society, 1865; professor of astronomy and director of observatory, Glasgow University, 1859; published scientific writings. [Suppl. ii. 344]

GRANT, ROBERT EDMOND (1793–1874), comparative anatomist; M.D. Edinburgh, 1814; contributed important papers on sponges to 'Edinburgh Philosophical Journal,' 1825–6; professor of comparative anatomy and zoology at London University, 1827–74; F.R.S., 1836; Fullerian professor of physiology, 1837–40; Swiney lecturer on geology at British Museum; friend of Darwin and correspondent of Cuvier and Saint-Hilaire; left property and collections to University College. [xxii. 402]

GRANT, ROGER (d. 1724), oculist to Anne and George I; alluded to in 'Spectator' as a quack. [xxii. 403]

GRANT, THOMAS (1816–1870), Roman catholic bishop of Southwark; D.D.; rector of the English college, Rome, 1844; active promoter of re-establishment of English hierarchy and bishop of Southwark, 1851–70; latinist to Vatican council, 1869; died at Rome. [xxii. 403]

GRANT, SIR THOMAS TASSELL (1795–1859), inventor; comptroller of victualling and transport service, 1850–8; K.C.B. on retirement; F.R.S.; awarded grant of 2,000l. for his steam biscuit machine, 1829; his 'patent fuel' and apparatus for distillation of sea-water adopted c. 1848. [xxii. 404]

GRANT, WILLIAM, LORD PRESTONGRANGE (1701?-1764), Scottish judge; second son of Sir Francis Grant, lord Cullen [q. v.]; admitted advocate, 1722; procurator for Scottish church and clerk to general assembly, 1731; solicitor-general for Scotland, 1737; lord advocate, 1746; M.P., Elgin, 1747-54; carried bills for abolition of heritable jurisdictions and ward holding and for annexation of forfeited estates to the crown; lord of session and of justiciary, 1754; commissioner of annexed estates, 1755; published pamphlet against patronage in the Scottish church, 1736.   [xxii. 404]

GRANT, WILLIAM (d. 1786), physician; M.D. Aberdeen, 1755; L.R.C.P., 1763; physician to Misericordia Hospital, Goodman's Fields; published treatises on London fevers and (1783) 'Observations on the Influenza of 1775 and 1782.'   [xxii. 405]

GRANT, SIR WILLIAM (1752-1832), master of the rolls; barrister, Lincoln's Inn, 1774; treasurer, 1798; commanded volunteers at siege of Quebec, 1775; attorney-general of Canada, 1776; M.P., Shaftesbury, 1790, Windsor, 1794, Banffshire, 1796-1812; joint-commissioner on laws of Jersey, 1791; chief-justice of Chester, 1798; solicitor-general, 1799-1801; knighted, 1799; privy councillor, 1801; master of the rolls, 1801-17; a highly successful speaker in parliament; supported reform of criminal law; lord rector of Aberdeen, 1809; D.C.L. Oxford, 1820.   [xxii. 405]

GRANT, WILLIAM JAMES (1829-1866), painter; exhibited at Royal Academy, 1847-66; also drew in red and black chalk.   [xxii. 407]

GRANT, SIR WILLIAM KEIR, previously KEIR and GRANT-KEIR (1772-1852), general; distinguished himself in Flanders and at Villiers-en-Couche, 1794; helped to save the Emperor Francis II from capture, 1794; received gold medals and the order of Maria Theresa; served with Russian and Austrian armies in Italy, 1799-1801, being present at Rivoli, 1797, and Marengo, 1800, and siege of Genoa, 1800; adjutant-general in Bengal, 1806; commander-in-chief in Java, 1815; commanded Guzerat field force against the Pindaris, 1817; took hill fort of Raree, and defeated the rajah of Cutch, 1819; suppressed piracy in the Persian Gulf, 1819-20; K.C.B., 1822; general, 1841.   [xxii. 407]

GRANT-DUFF. [See DUFF.]

GRANTHAM, BARONS. [See ROBINSON, THOMAS, first BARON, 1695-1770; ROBINSON, THOMAS, second BARON, 1738-1786.]

GRANTHAM or GRANTHAN, HENRY (fl. 1571-1587), translator; published 'Italian Grammar written in Latin by Scipio Lentulo,' 1571.   [xxii. 408]

GRANTHAM, THOMAS (d. 1664), schoolmaster; B.A. Hart Hall, Oxford, 1630; M.A. Peterhouse, Cambridge, 1634; rector of Waddington, Nottinghamshire, till 1656; taught school in London, where he made a point of doing without corporal punishment; published pamphlets against free schools, 1644, and imprisonment for debt, 1642, also a curious 'Marriage Sermon,' 1641.
                                    [xxii. 408]

GRANTHAM, SIR THOMAS (fl. 1684), naval commander; convoyed twenty-five sail from Virginia to England during Dutch war, 1673; assisted in pacifying the colony, 1676; knighted and given command of the East India Company's fleet, 1683; suppressed Keigwin's mutiny at Bombay, 1684; gentleman of the privy chamber to William III and Anne.   [xxii. 409]

GRANTHAM, THOMAS (1634-1692), general baptist divine; pastor of a small congregation of baptists in south Lincolnshire, 1656; drew up and presented to Charles II 'narrative and complaint' of the general baptists, with a petition for toleration, 1660; imprisoned at Lincoln for preaching, 1662-3, and at Louth, 1670; had another interview with the king, 1672; founded congregations at Norwich, Yarmouth, and King's Lynn, 1685-6; published 'Christianismus Primitivus' (1678) and many controversial tracts, of which 'A Dialogue between the Baptist and the Presbyterian' (1691) contains remarkable verses on Servetus.   [xxii. 410]

GRANTLEY, first BARON (1716-1789). [See NORTON, FLETCHER.]

GRANTMESNIL, HUGH OF (d. 1094). [See HUGH.]

GRANTON, LORD (1763-1851). [See HOPE, CHARLES.]

GRANVILLE. [See also GRENVILLE.]

GRANVILLE, EARLS. [See CARTERET, JOHN, EARL, 1690-1763; LEVESON-GOWER, GRANVILLE, first EARL, 1773-1846; LEVESON-GOWER, GRANVILLE GEORGE, second EARL, 1815-1891.]

GRANVILLE, AUGUSTUS BOZZI (1783-1872) physician and Italian patriot; son of postmaster-general at Milan; assumed name of Granville by his mother's wish; M.D. Pavia, 1802; physician to the Turkish fleet and in Spain; in the English fleet, 1806-12; settled in London as tutor to the sons of William Richard Hamilton [q. v.], 1813; M.R.C.S., 1813; L.R.C.P., 1817; brought warning of Napoleon's expected escape, and introduced iodine, 1814; headed Milan deputation offering Duke of Sussex the crown, 1815; assisted Canova in obtaining restoration of Italian art treasures; F.R.S., 1817; physician-accoucheur to Westminster Dispensary, 1818; established West-end infirmary for children; introduced use of prussic acid for chest affections; president of Westminster Medical Society, 1829; secretary of the visitors of the Royal Institution, 1832-52; published 'Catechism of Health,' 1831, and books on the spas of Germany, 1837, and England, 1841; also 'Counter-irritation,' 1838; practised at Kissingen, 1861-8; published pamphlets advocating the reform of the Royal Society (1830, 1836), the formation of a kingdom of Italy (1848), a work on Thames sewage (1835, 1865) and an 'Autobiography' (posthumous).   [xxii. 412]

GRANVILLE or GRENVILLE, SIR BEVIL (d. 1706), governor of Barbados; grandson of Sir Bevil Grenville [q. v.]; M.A. Trinity College, Cambridge, 1679; knighted by James II; favourite of William III; colonel of Lord Bath's regiment in Flanders, 1694-8; governor of Barbados, 1702-6; acquitted of tyranny and extortion, but recalled from Barbados; died on his way home.
                                    [xxii. 414]

GRANVILLE or GRENVILLE, GEORGE, BARON LANSDOWNE (1667-1735), poet and dramatist; brother of Sir Bevil Granville [q. v.]; educated in France and at Trinity College, Cambridge; M.A., 1679; M.P., Fowey, 1702, Cornwall, 1710-11; secretary-at-war, 1710; one of the twelve peers created for the peace, 1711; privy councillor and comptroller of the household, 1712; treasurer of the household, 1713; imprisoned in the Tower on suspicion of Jacobitism, 1715-17; published plays acted at Lincoln's Inn Fields and Drury Lane, including 'Heroick Love,' 1698, and an opera, with epilogue by Addison. His complete works (1732) include 'Vindication' of Monck and Sir Richard Granville. His poems were praised by Pope (of whom he was an early patron), but declared by Johnson mere imitations of Waller.   [xxii. 415]

GRASCOME, SAMUEL (1641-1708), nonjuror; M.A. Magdalene College, Cambridge, 1674; rector of Stourmouth, Kent, 1680-90; his 'Account of Proceedings in House of Commons in relation to Recoining Clipt Money' (1696) ordered to be burned by the hangman; published numerous controversial tracts.   [xxii. 417]

GRATTAN, HENRY (1746-1820), statesman; graduated at Trinity College, Dublin, 1767; with Flood contributed nationalist articles to the 'Freeman's Journal'; called to Irish bar, 1772; elected to Irish parliament for Charlemont, 1775; carried amendment to the address in favour of free trade, and resolution affirming inexpediency of granting new taxes, 1779; moved in brilliant speeches, but without success, resolutions in favour of legislative independence, and amendments to limit duration of Perpetual Mutiny Bill, 1780-1; after the meeting of the volunteers at Dungannon moved address to the crown demanding legislative independence, and a few months later carried it, 1782; declined office; granted 50,000l. by Irish parliament after consent of British government to his claims; opposed Flood's demand for 'simple repeal,' and favoured disbandment of the volunteers, 1783; successfully opposed Orde's commercial propositions, 1785; brought forward question of tithe commutation, 1788-9; on refusal of the lord-lieutenant to transmit his regency resolutions, formed deputation to present them in person to Prince of Wales, 1789; founded Dublin Whig Club; elected for Dublin, 1790; attacked parliamentary corruption, and supported catholic emancipation, 1791-3; interviewed Pitt, 1794; declined office from Fitzwilliam, on whose recall he renewed opposition: after rejection of Ponsonby's reform resolutions seceded from the house, 1797; in England during the Rebellion of '98, but struck off the Irish privy council; during last session of Irish parliament represented Wicklow; spoke for two hours, sitting, against the union, 1800; fought duel with Isaac Corry [q. v.]; in last speech had altercation with Castlereagh; as M.P. for Malton, 1805-6, in the imperial parliament made impressive maiden speech; M.P. for Dublin, 1806-20; declined office; frequently raised catholic emancipation question; carried motion for committee of inquiry, and second reading of relief bill, 1813; supported continuance of the war, 1815; died in London, and was buried in Westminster Abbey. The best collection of his speeches is that edited by his son, 1822. [xxii. 418]

GRATTAN, THOMAS COLLEY (1792-1864), author; described his French tours in 'Highways and Byways' (three series, 1823-9); at Brussels, 1828-39, issued 'Traits of Travel,' 1829, and 'History of the Netherlands,' 1830; and described the riots of 1834 for the 'Times'; as British consul at Boston, 1839-46, assisted at settlement of northeast boundary question by the Ashburton treaty; published also 'Legends of the Rhine,' 1832, several historical novels, two works on America, and 'Beaten Paths,' 1862 (autobiographical). [xxii. 425]

GRATTAN, JOHN (1641-1712), quaker; joined the Friends, c. 1672; imprisoned at Derby; afterwards travelled ministerially throughout the United Kingdom; his 'Journal' (1720) often reprinted. [xxii. 426]

GRAUNT, EDWARD. [See GRANT.]

GRAUNT, JOHN (1620-1674), statistician; was appointed original member of Royal Society, after his publication of 'Natural and Political Observations . . . made upon the Bills of Mortality,' 1661; falsely charged with being privy to the great fire of 1666. [xxii. 427]

GRAVELOT, HUBERT FRANÇOIS, properly BOURGUIGNON (1699-1773), draughtsman and book-illustrator; came to England, 1732, on the invitation of Claude du Bosc [q. v.]; friend of Garrick; executed illustrations for Theobald's and Hanmer's Shakespeares, Gay's 'Fables,' 'The Dunciad,' and 'Tom Jones,' and (in France) of the works of Voltaire and Racine and Marmontel's 'Contes.' [xxii. 428]

GRAVES, CHARLES (1812-1899), bishop of Limerick and mathematician; educated at Trinity College, Dublin; graduated, 1834; fellow, 1836; professor of mathematics, Dublin University, 1843; dean of the Castle Chapel, Dublin, 1860; dean of Clonfert, 1864; bishop of Limerick, Ardfert, and Aghadoe, 1866 till death; member of Royal Irish Academy, 1837, and president, 1861; F.R.S., 1880; honorary D.C.L. Oxford, 1881; published translation, with many original notes, of Chasles's 'General Properties of Cones of Second Degree and of Spherical Conics,' 1841, and wrote on Irish antiquarian subjects. [Suppl. ii. 345]

GRAVES, HENRY (1806-1892), printseller; brother of Robert Graves [q. v.]; sole proprietor of firm of Henry Graves & Co., 1844; published numerous engravings after Landseer and other eminent painters; one of founders of 'Art Journal' and 'Illustrated London News.' [Suppl. ii. 346]

GRAVES, JAMES (1815-1886), archæologist; B.A. Trinity College, Dublin; incumbent of Inisnag, 1863-86; with J. G. Prim established Kilkenny Archæological Society (Royal Historical Association of Ireland); published work on St. Canice Cathedral, Kilkenny, 1857. [xxii. 429]

GRAVES, JOHN THOMAS (1806-1870), jurist and mathematician; great-nephew of Richard Graves (1763-1829), dean of Ardagh [q. v.]; graduate of Dublin and Oxford; barrister, Inner Temple, 1831; professor of jurisprudence at University College, London, 1839; F.R.S., 1839; poor-law inspector, 1847-70; contributed articles on jurists to Smith's 'Dictionary of Greek and Roman Biography'; friend and correspondent of Sir William Rowan Hamilton [q. v.], towards whose discovery of quaternions he did much by researches concerning imaginary logarithms; his mathematical library bequeathed to University College. [xxii. 430]

GRAVES, RICHARD, the elder (1677-1729), antiquary; educated at Pembroke College, Oxford; said to have been original of Mr. Townsend in the 'Spiritual Quixote.' [xxii. 431]

GRAVES, RICHARD, the younger (1715-1804), poet and novelist; with Whitefield graduated B.A. Pembroke College, Oxford, 1736; fellow of All Souls', 1736; intimate with Shenstone; offended his relations by marrying a farmer's daughter; rector of Claverton, 1749-1804; by influence of Ralph Allen [q. v.] obtained also vicarage of Kilmersdon and chaplaincy to Countess of Chatham; among his pupils Malthus and Prince Hoare; published 'The Spiritual Quixote,' 1772, ridiculing the methodists, 'Recollections of Shenstone,' 1788, a translation of Marcus Aurelius, 1792, and 'The Reveries of Solitude' (1793), besides verses and essays. [xxii. 432]

GRAVES, RICHARD (1763-1829), dean of Ardagh; senior fellow of Trinity College, Dublin, 1799; Donnellan lecturer, 1797 and 1801; DD., 1799; professor of oratory, 1799; regius professor of Greek, 1810, of divinity, 1819; prebendary of St. Michael's, Dublin, 1801; rector of Raheny, 1809; dean of Ardagh, 1813-29; his works collected, 1840. [xxii. 434]

GRAVES, RICHARD HASTINGS (1791-1877), theological writer; son of Richard Graves (1763-1829) [q. v.]; M.A. Trinity College, Dublin, 1818; D.D., 1828; rector of Brigown and prebendary of Cloyne. [xxii. 435]

GRAVES, ROBERT (1798-1873), line-engraver; pupil of John Romney the engraver [q. v.], executed pen-and-ink facsimiles of rare prints; engraved plates for Caulfield's 'Portraits,' Dove's 'English Classics,' Neale's 'Westminster Abbey,' and Burnet's 'Reformation'; exhibited with Society of British Artists, 1824-30, and Royal Academy; associate engraver to Royal Academy, 1836, engraving works after Wilkie, Landseer, and Gainsborough. [xxii. 435]

GRAVES, ROBERT JAMES (1796-1853), physician; third son of Richard Graves (1763-1829) [q. v.], dean of Ardagh; M.B. Dublin, 1818; travelled with Turner in the Alps and in Italy; physician to Meath Hospital and a founder of the Park Street School of Medicine; professor of medicine to the Irish College of Physicians; president, Irish College of Physicians, 1843-4; F.R.S., 1849; gained a European reputation by his 'Clinical Lectures on the Practice of Medicine,' 1848 (reprinted, 1884). [xxii. 436]

GRAVES, SAMUEL (1713-1787), admiral; served under his uncle at Cartagena, 1741; commanded the Barfleur in the Basque Roads, 1757, and the Duke at Quiberon Bay, 1759; vice-admiral, 1770; as commander on North American station attempted to carry out Boston Port Act, 1774; admiral, 1778. [xxii. 437]

GRAVES, THOMAS, first BARON GRAVES (1725?-1802), admiral; cousin of Samuel Graves [q. v.]; commanded the Unicorn at bombardment of Havre, 1758; present in Arbuthnot's action off the Chesapeake, 1781, and commanded at an indecisive action with De Grasse a few months later; despatched by Rodney in charge of prizes to England, losing all but two ships, 1782; vice-admiral, 1787; admiral, 1794; received an Irish peerage and a pension for his conduct as second in command in Howe's action of 1 June 1794, when he was badly wounded. [xxii. 438]

GRAVES, SIR THOMAS (1747?-1814), admiral; nephew of Samuel Graves [q. v.], under whom he served in the seven years' war; severely wounded when in command of the Diana, 1775, in the Charles river; commanded the Bedford in his cousin's action off the Chesapeake, 1781, and in the battles off St. Kitts and Dominica, 1782; with the Magicienne fought the Sybille, 1783; created K.C.B. for conduct as Nelson's second in command at Copenhagen; vice-admiral, 1805; admiral, 1812. [xxii. 440]

GRAVESEND, RICHARD DE (d. 1279), bishop of Lincoln; dean of Lincoln, 1254; associated with dean of London in carrying out papal excommunication of violators of Magna Charta, 1254; bishop of Lincoln, 1258-79; assisted in negotiations for peace with France, 1258-9, and for a pacification between Henry III and the barons, 1263; suspended by the legate as an adherent of De Montfort, 1266; lived abroad till 1269; granted a coadjutor, 1275. [xxii. 441]

GRAVESEND, RICHARD DE (d. 1303), bishop of London; archdeacon of Northampton, 1272-80; prebendary of Lincoln; bishop of London, 1280-1303; sent on mission to France, 1293; one of Prince Edward's coun-

cillors, 1297 ; instituted office of sub-dean ; benefactor of St. Paul's, the poor of London, and Cambridge University ; his executors' accounts printed by Camden Society, 1874.
[xxii. 442]

GRAVESEND, STEPHEN DE (d. 1338), bishop of London ; nephew of Richard de Gravesend (d. 1303) [q. v.] ; rector of Stepney, 1303 ; canon of St. Paul's, 1313 ; bishop of London, 1318–30 ; tried to mediate between Edward II and Isabella, 1326 ; his life menaced by the Londoners ; took part with Lancaster and Kent against Edward III, 1328 ; imprisoned for complicity in Kent's plot, 1330 ; excommunicated Lewis of Bavaria and the anti-pope Nicholas, 1329 ; king's deputy at councils of 1335 and 1336.
[xxii. 443]

GRAVET, WILLIAM (d. 1599), divine ; B.A. Peterhouse, Cambridge, 1558 ; fellow of Pembroke Hall, Cambridge, 1558 ; M.A., 1561 ; vicar of St. Sepulchre, 1566 ; rector of Little Laver and of Bradfield, and prebendary of St. Paul's ; accused by 'Martin Mar-Prelate' of drunkenness.
[xxii. 444]

GRAY. [See also GREY.]

GRAY, ANDREW, first BARON GRAY (1380 ?–1469), hostage in England for payment of ransom of James I of Scotland, 1424–7 ; created Baron Gray of Fowlis (Scotland), 1445 ; master of the household to James II of Scotland, 1452 ; a lord auditor, 1464.
[xxiii. 1]

GRAY, ANDREW (1633–1656), Scottish divine ; graduated at St. Andrews, 1651 ; minister of Outer High Church, Glasgow, 1653–6 ; famous preacher ; last edition of 'Works,' 1839.
[xxiii. 2]

GRAY, ANDREW, seventh BARON GRAY (d. 1663), son of Patrick Gray, sixth baron [q. v.] ; succeeded, 1612 ; lieutenant of Scots gens d'armes in France, 1624 ; member of Scottish council of war, 1628 ; commissioner for Fisheries Treaty, 1630 ; supported Charles I against covenanters ; excommunicated by general assembly as papist, 1649 ; fined by Cromwell, 1654.
[xxiii. 3]

GRAY, ANDREW (d. 1728), divine ; vicar of Mottram, Cheshire ; his 'Door opening into Everlasting Life' (1706) reprinted, 1810.
[xxiii. 4]

GRAY, ANDREW (1805–1861), presbyterian divine ; M.A. Aberdeen, 1824 ; minister of the West Church, Perth, 1836–61 ; joined Free church and drew up 'Catechism of Principles of the Free Church,' 1845 ; his 'Gospel Contrasts and Parallels' edited by Candlish, 1862. [xxiii. 4]

GRAY, CHARLES (1782–1851), captain in the marines and song-writer ; published 'Poems and Songs,' 1811, and 'Lays and Lyrics,' 1841 ; also contributions to Wood's 'Book of Scottish Song' and 'Whistle-Binkie,' and 'Notes on Scottish Song,' 1845.
[xxiii. 4]

GRAY, DAVID (1838–1861), Scottish poet ; friend of Sydney T. Dobell [q. v.] ; his 'Luggie and other Poems' published, 1862, with preface by Lord Houghton, who had befriended him.
[xxiii. 5]

GRAY, EDMUND DWYER (1845–1888), journalist and politician ; son of Sir John Gray [q. v.] ; proprietor of 'Freeman's Journal' and 'Belfast Morning News' ; saved lives of five persons in Dublin Bay, 1866 ; lord-mayor of Dublin, 1880 ; M.P., Tipperary, 1877–80, Carlow, 1880–5, and Dublin, 1885–8 ; imprisoned, when high sheriff of Dublin, for comments on Hynes case in 'Freeman's Journal' ; member of housing of the poor commission, 1884.
[xxiii. 5]

GRAY, EDWARD WHITAKER (1748–1806), botanist ; librarian to College of Physicians before 1773 ; L.C.P., 1773 ; M.D. ; keeper of natural history and antiquities at British Museum ; secretary to Royal Society, 1797 ; original associate of Linnean Society. [xxiii. 7]

GRAY, EDWARD WILLIAM (1787 ?–1860), editor of 'History and Antiquities of Newbury,' 1839. [xxiii. 7]

GRAY, SIR GEORGE (d. 1773), baronet ; colonel of 17th foot and major-general in army ; younger brother of Sir James Gray (d. 1773) [q. v.], with whom he founded Society of Dilettanti, 1732 ; secretary and treasurer to society, 1738–1771.
[Suppl. ii. 347]

GRAY, GEORGE (1758–1819), painter ; went to north America on botanical expedition, 1787, and to Poland on geological expedition, 1791.
[xxiii. 7]

GRAY, GEORGE ROBERT (1808–1872), zoologist ; youngest son of Samuel Frederick Gray [q. v.] ; educated at Merchant Taylors' School ; zoological assistant in British Museum, 1831 ; F.R.S., 1866 ; published ornithological works ; assisted Agassiz in 'Nomenclator Zoologicus,' 1842.
[xxiii. 7]

GRAY, GILBERT (d. 1614), second principal of Marischal College, Aberdeen, 1598 ; delivered a Latin oration, 'Oratio de Illustribus Scotiæ Scriptoribus,' 1611.
[xxiii. 8]

GRAY, HUGH (d. 1604), Gresham professor of divinity ; fellow of Trinity College, Cambridge, 1581 ; M.A., 1582 ; D.D., 1595 ; prebendary of Lincoln, 1600.
[xxiii. 8]

GRAY, SIR JAMES (d. 1773), diplomatist and antiquary ; baronet by succession ; brother of Sir George Gray [q. v.] ; British resident at Venice, 1744–53 ; envoy extraordinary to king of Naples and Two Sicilies, 1753–61 ; K.B. and minister plenipotentiary to king of Spain, 1761 ; privy councillor, 1769.
[Suppl. ii. 347]

GRAY, JAMES (d. 1830), poet ; intimate with Burns at Dumfries ; master in high school, Edinburgh, 1801–22 ; rector of Belfast academy, 1822 ; went to Bombay as chaplain, 1826 ; died at Bhuj in Cutch. He published 'Cona and other Poems,' 1814, edited Robert Fergusson's 'Poems,' 1821, and translated St. Matthew into Cutchee (printed, 1834).
[xxiii. 8]

GRAY, JOHN (1807–1875), legal author ; as solicitor to treasury conducted prosecution of Tichborne claimant, 1873 ; published 'Country Attorney's Practice,' 1836, 'Country Solicitor's Practice,' 1837, and 'Law of Costs,' 1853.
[xxiii. 8]

GRAY, SIR JOHN (1816–1875), journalist ; M.D. and master in surgery, Glasgow, 1839 ; political editor of 'Freeman's Journal,' 1841 ; sole proprietor, 1850 ; indicted for conspiracy, 1843 ; knighted, 1863 ; M.P., Kilkenny, 1865–75 ; advocated disestablishment and land reform ; published 'The Church Establishment in Ireland,' 1866.
[xxiii. 9]

GRAY, JOHN EDWARD (1800–1875), naturalist ; second son of Samuel Frederick Gray [q. v.] ; assistant zoological keeper at British Museum, 1824 ; keeper, 1840–1874 ; F.R.S., 1832 ; vice-president, Zoological Society ; president of Botanical and Entomological societies ; formed largest zoological collection in Europe, 1852 ; doctor of philosophy, Munich, 1852 ; published numerous zoological papers and other works, including 'Handbook of British Waterweeds,' 1864.
[xxiii. 9]

GRAY, JOHN MILLER (1850–1894), curator of Scottish National Portrait Gallery, 1884–94 ; entered commercial Bank, Edinburgh ; worked at art criticism and contributed to various periodicals and other publications, including 'Dictionary of National Biography' ; published monograph on George Monson [q. v.], and other works.
[Suppl. ii. 347]

GRAY, MARIA EMMA (1787–1876), conchologist ; née Smith ; wife of John Edward Gray [q. v.] ; published etchings of molluscans for use of students, and arranged the Cuming collection in British Museum ; her collection of algæ bequeathed to Cambridge University.
[xxiii. 11]

GRAY, PATRICK, fourth BARON GRAY (d. 1582), of Buttergask ; captured at Solway Moss, 1542 ; joined Cardinal Beaton's party ; after Beaton's murder went over to English alliance ; again imprisoned in England, 1561–2 ; joined Queen Mary's lords, 1570 ; one of James VI's council, 1577.
[xxiii. 11]

GRAY, PATRICK, sixth BARON GRAY (d. 1612), Master of Gray till 1609 ; while resident in France intimately connected with the Guises and French friends of Mary Queen of Scots ; betrayed Mary's secrets to James VI and Arran ; concluded an agreement between Elizabeth and James to the exclusion of Arran, but at the same time arranged for deposition of Arran by recall of the banished lords, 1584 ; carried out the scheme with the help of English ambassador, 1585 ; formally remonstrated against condemnation of Mary, but secretly advised her assassination, 1586 ; exiled from Scotland on charge of sedition and of impeding the king's marriage with Anne of Denmark, 1587 ; returned, 1589 ; attempted, with Francis Stewart Hepburn, fifth earl of Bothwell [q. v.], to capture the king at Falkland, 1592.
[xxiii. 12]

GRAY, PETER (1807 ?–1887), writer on life contingencies; published works on logarithms and computation of life contingencies. [xxiii. 16]

GRAY, ROBERT (1762–1834), bishop of Bristol; M.A. St. Mary Hall, Oxford; Bampton lecturer, 1796; canon of Durham, 1804; bishop of Bristol, 1827–34; published 'Religious Union,' 1800, and other works. [xxiii. 16]

GRAY, ROBERT (1809–1872), bishop of Cape Town; son of Robert Gray (1762–1834) [q. v.]; B.A. University College, Oxford, 1831; incumbent of Stockton, 1845–7; bishop of Cape Town, 1847–72; appointed metropolitan of Africa by letters patent, 1853, but his power as such held invalid by privy council in cases of Long and John William Colenso [q. v.], 1863; supported by convocation in appointing new bishop in place of Colenso (excommunicated, 1863); suggested formation of universities mission in Central Africa, and added five new sees to South African church. [xxiii. 17]

GRAY, ROBERT (1825–1887), ornithologist; cashier of Bank of Scotland; a chief founder of Glasgow Natural History Society, 1851; secretary of Royal Physical Society, Edinburgh, 1877; vice-president of Royal Society of Edinburgh, 1882; published 'Birds of the West of Scotland,' 1871. [xxiii. 19]

GRAY, SAMUEL FREDERICK (*fl.* 1780–1836), naturalist and pharmacologist; published 'Supplement to the Pharmacopœia,' 1818; published with his son, John Edward Gray [q. v.], 'Natural Arrangement of British Plants' (according to Jussieu's method), 1821; published 'Elements of Pharmacy,' 1823, and 'The Operative Chemist,' 1828. [xxiii. 20]

GRAY, STEPHEN (*d.* 1736), electrician; pensioner of the Charterhouse; F.R.S., 1732; first to divide substances into electrics and non-electrics, discovering means of their mutual transformation. [xxiii. 20]

GRAY, SIR THOMAS (*d.* 1369 ?), author of the 'Scalachronica'; served in France, 1338–44; fought at Neville's Cross, 1346; warden of Norham Castle; captured by Scots at Norham, 1355; warden of east marches, 1367; his 'Scala-chronica' especially valuable for Scottish and French wars; prologue and latter half printed, 1836, with Leland's abstract of the complete work. [xxiii. 21]

GRAY, THOMAS (1716–1771), poet; educated at Eton with Horace Walpole and Richard West, whom he joined in 'Hymeneals' on marriage of Frederick, prince of Wales, 1736; at Peterhouse, Cambridge, 1734–8; travelled on continent with Walpole, 1739–40, but quarrelled with him; made elaborate notes and wrote Latin ode on the Grande Chartreuse; resided at Cambridge; LL.B. Cambridge, 1743; renewed friendship with Walpole; became intimate with William Mason the poet [q. v.]; removed from Peterhouse to Pembroke College, Cambridge, on account of a practical joke, 1756; refused poet-laureateship, 1757; in London, 1759–61; appointed professor of history and modern languages at Cambridge through the influence of Richard Stonehewer, 1768; formed friendship with Norton Nicholls and Charles Victor de Bonstetten; toured in Scotland and various parts of England; gave plan of a history of English poetry to Warton; classical scholar, linguist, and student of science; buried at Stoke Poges. His letters are among the best of his period. His poems include imitations from the Norse and Welsh, an 'Ode on a distant prospect of Eton College' (at Walpole's suggestion issued anonymously, 1747, and included with those to spring and on the death of his cat in vol. ii. of Dodsley's collection, 1748), 'Elegy in a Country Churchyard,' 1751, the 'Progress of Poesy,' and 'The Bard,' 1758. The collections of Dodsley and Foulis (1768) contained his poem 'The Fatal Sisters,' and other new works. His complete works were edited by T. J. Mathias (1814), by Mitford (Aldine ed. 1835–43), and by Edmund Gosse, 1882. Pembroke College was largely rebuilt (1870–9) from the proceeds of a commemoration fund formed by friends of Gray, whose bust by Mr. Hamo Thornycroft was placed there in 1885; Bacon's bust on the Westminster Abbey monument is from Mason's portrait. [xxiii. 22]

GRAY, THOMAS (1787–1848), railway pioneer; published 'Observations on a General Railway, with Plates and Maps,' 1820. [xxiii. 28]

GRAY, WILLIAM (1802 ?–1835), author; M.A. Magdalen College, Oxford, 1831; edited Sir Philip Sidney's works, 1829; barrister, Inner Temple, 1831; published 'Historical Sketch of Origin of English Prose Literature,' 1835. [xxiii. 28]

GRAYDON, JOHN (*d.* 1726), vice-admiral; commanded the Defiance at Beachy Head, 1690, and the Hampton Court off Cape Barfleur, 1692; rear-admiral with Rooke at Cadiz and Vigo, 1702; vice-admiral in command of fleet to attack French settlement of Placentia, 1703; irregularly cashiered on report of House of Lords committee, 1703. [xxiii. 28]

GRAYLE or **GRAILE**, JOHN (1614–1654), puritan minister; M.A. Magdalen Hall, Oxford, 1637; rector of Tidworth; published work defending himself from charge of Arminianism, 1655. [xxiii. 29]

GRAYSTANES, ROBERT DE (*d.* 1336 ?), chronicler of the church of Durham; sub-prior of St. Mary's, Durham; elected bishop and consecrated, 1333, but refused the temporalities and ousted by Richard de Bury [q. v.]; continued Geoffrey de Coldingham's chronicle from 1213; his work first printed, 1691. [xxiii. 30]

GREATHEAD, HENRY (1757–1816), lifeboat inventor; received grant of 1,200*l.* for his boat. [xxiii. 30]

GREATHED, WILLIAM WILBERFORCE HARRIS (1826–1878), major-general; entered Bengal engineers, 1844; first officer in the breach at storming of Mooltan, 1849; consulting engineer at Allahabad, 1855–7; twice carried despatches from Agra to Meerut through mutineers, 1857; as director of left attack on Delhi severely wounded; field-engineer of Doab force, 1857; directing engineer in Napier's attack on Lucknow; C.B. and brevet major; brevet lieutenant-colonel for services in China, 1860; assistant military secretary at Horse Guards, 1861–5; chief of irrigation department in North-West Provinces, 1867–75; constructed Agra and Lower Ganges canals; major-general, 1877. [xxiii. 31]

GREATHEED, BERTIE (1759–1826), dramatist; the Reuben of Gifford's 'Baviad' and 'Mæviad'; his tragedy, 'The Regent,' acted at Drury Lane, 1788. [xxiii. 32]

GREATOREX, RALPH (*d.* 1712 ?), mathematical-instrument maker; friend of Oughtred and acquaintance of Evelyn and Pepys. [xxiii. 32]

GREATOREX, THOMAS (1758–1831), organist and conductor; musical director to Lord Sandwich at Hinchinbrook; sang in Concerts of Ancient Music; organist of Carlisle Cathedral, 1780–4, Westminster Abbey, 1819; became conductor of Ancient Concerts, 1793; revived Vocal Concerts, 1801; first organ and pianoforte professor at Royal Academy of Music, 1822; F.R.S. for discovery of method of measuring altitude of mountains; published 'Parochial Psalmody,' 1825, and 'Twelve Glees from English, Irish, and Scotch Melodies,' 1833. [xxiii. 33]

GREATRAKES, VALENTINE (1629–1683), 'the stroker'; of Affane, co. Waterford; served in the Cromwellian army in Ireland under Robert Phaire; received offices in co. Cork, 1656; began to cure scrofula and other diseases by laying on of hands, 1662; performed gratuitously cures at Ragley, Worcester, and Lincoln's Inn, 1666; answered attack by David Lloyd (1625–1691) [q. v.] with a 'Brief Account' (1666) of himself and of his cures addressed to Robert Boyle [q. v.], as well as testimonials from Andrew Marvell, Cudworth, Bishop Wilkins, and Whichcote. [xxiii. 34]

GREATRAKES, WILLIAM (1723 ?–1781), barrister; of Trinity College, Dublin; called to Irish bar, 1761; authorship of 'Junius' letters attributed to him, 1799. [xxiii. 36]

GREAVES, SIR EDWARD (1608–1680), physician to Charles II; fellow of All Souls', Oxford, 1634; studied at Padua and Leyden; M.D. Oxford, 1641; Linacre reader of physic, 1643; perhaps created baronet by Charles I, 1645; F.R.C.P., 1657; Harveian orator, 1661. [xxiii. 37]

GREAVES, JAMES PIERREPONT (1777–1842), mystic; joined Pestalozzi, 1817, at Yverdun; secretary of London Infant School Society, 1825; follower of Jacob Boehme; founded educational institution at Ham, Surrey. [xxiii. 37]

GREAVES, JOHN (1602–1652), mathematician and traveller; brother of Sir Edward Greaves [q. v.]; B.A. Balliol College, Oxford, 1621; fellow of Merton College, Oxford, 1624; M.A., 1628; Gresham professor of geometry, London, 1630; visited Paris, Leyden, Italy, Constantinople, and Egypt, measuring the Pyramids and collecting coins, gems, and oriental manuscripts, 1637–40; Savilian professor of astronomy on death (1643) of John Bainbridge; ejected from chair and fellowship by parliament, 1648; published scientific works; his miscellaneous works edited by Thomas Birch, 1737. [xxiii. 38]

GREAVES, THOMAS (fl. 1604), composer and lutenist to Sir H. Pierrepont; published 'Songes of sundrie kinds,' 1604; three madrigals by him edited by G. W. Budd (1843 and 1857). [xxiii. 39]

GREAVES, THOMAS (1612–1676), orientalist; brother of John Greaves [q. v.]; of Charterhouse and Corpus Christi College, Oxford; fellow, 1636; D.D., 1661; deputy-reader of Arabic, 1637; held livings in Northamptonshire; published 'De linguæ Arabicæ utilitate' (1637), and treatises on Persian versions of the scriptures. [xxiii. 39]

GREEN, ALEXANDER HENRY (1832–1896), geologist; B.A. and fellow, Gonville and Caius College, Cambridge, 1855; M.A., 1858; honorary fellow, 1892; worked on geological survey, 1861–74; professor of geology, Yorkshire College, Leeds, 1874, and also professor of mathematics, 1885; professor of geology at Oxford, 1888; honorary M.A. Oxford, 1888; F.G.S., 1862; F.R.S., 1886; chief work, 'Manual of Physical Geology,' 1876. [Suppl. ii. 348]

GREEN, AMOS (1735–1807), flower, fruit, and landscape-painter; friend of Shenstone. [xxiii. 39]

GREEN, BARTHOLOMEW or BARTLET (1530–1556), protestant martyr; burnt at Smithfield. [xxiii. 40]

GREEN, BENJAMIN (1736?–1800?), mezzotint engraver; probably brother of Amos Green [q. v.]; drawing-master at Christ's Hospital; exhibited with Incorporated Society of Artists, 1765–74; engraved illustrations for Morant's 'Essex,' 1768; drew and etched plates of antiquities. [xxiii. 40]

GREEN, BENJAMIN RICHARD (1808–1876), water-colour painter; son of James Green, portrait-painter [q. v.]; exhibited at Royal Academy and Suffolk Street from 1832. [xxiii. 41]

GREEN, CHARLES (1785–1870), aeronaut; made the first ascent with carburetted hydrogen gas, 1821; constructed great Nassau balloon and went up from Vauxhall to Weilburg, Nassau, 1836; invented the guide-rope; made 526 ascents, 1821–52. [xxiii. 41]

GREEN, Mrs. ELIZA S. CRAVEN (1803–1866), poet; née Craven; published 'A Legend of Mona,' 1825, and 'Sea Weeds and Heath Flower,' 1858. [xxiii. 42]

GREEN, GEORGE (1793–1841), mathematician; fellow of Caius College, Cambridge, fourth wrangler, 1837; published 'Essay on the Application of Mathematical Analysis to the Theories of Electricity and Magnetism,' 1828; read before Cambridge Philosophical Society papers on 'Reflection and Refraction of Sound' and 'Reflection and Refraction of Light at the common surface of two non-crystallised Media.' [xxiii. 42]

GREEN, GEORGE SMITH (d. 1762), author; Oxford watchmaker, published 'The Life of Mr. J. Van,' 1750, poems and plays. [xxiii. 43]

GREEN, Sir HENRY (d. 1369), judge; king's serjeant, 1345; knighted and judge of common pleas, 1354; excommunicated by the pope for sentencing the bishop of Ely, 1358; chief-justice of king's bench, 1361–5. [xxiii. 43]

GREEN, HENRY (1801–1873), author; M.A. Glasgow, 1825; presbyterian minister of Knutsford, 1827–72; edited six works for the Holbein Society, and published works, including 'Sir Isaac Newton's Views on Points of Trinitarian Doctrine,' 1856, 'The Cat in Chancery' (1858, anon.), and 'Shakespeare and the Emblem Writers,' 1870. [xxiii. 44]

GREEN, HUGH, alias FERDINAND BROOKS (1584?–1642), Roman catholic martyr; B.A. Peterhouse, Cambridge; studied at Douay; executed at Dorchester under proclamation of 1642. [xxiii. 44]

GREEN, JAMES (fl. 1743), organist at Hull; published 'Book of Psalmody,' 1724. [xxiii. 44]

GREEN, JAMES (1771–1834), portrait-painter; copied Reynolds's pictures; exhibited at Royal Academy after 1792, and at British Institution. [xxiii. 45]

GREEN, Mrs. JANE (d. 1791). [See HIPPISLEY, JANE.]

GREEN, JOHN (fl. 1758), line-engraver; brother of Benjamin Green [q. v.] [xxiii. 40]

GREEN, JOHN (1706?–1779), bishop of Lincoln; fellow of St. John's College, Cambridge, 1730; M.A., 1731; D.D., 1749; as master at Lichfield knew Johnson and Garrick; regius professor of divinity at Cambridge, 1748–56; master of Corpus Christi College, Cambridge, 1750–63; dean of Lincoln and vice-chancellor of Cambridge, 1756; bishop of Lincoln, 1761–79; published anonymously pamphlets on university reform and against methodists; contributed to 'Athenian Letters,' published 1781. [xxiii. 45]

GREEN, JOHN or 'PADDY' (1801–1874), singer and actor; was successively manager and conductor of entertainments at the Cider Cellars and Evans's Hall in Covent Garden; of latter he was proprietor, 1845–65. [lvii. 105]

GREEN, JOHN RICHARD (1837–1883), historian; of Magdalen College school and Jesus College, Oxford; B.A., 1859; in sole charge of Holy Trinity, Hoxton, 1863; incumbent of St. Philip's, Stepney, 1866; librarian at Lambeth, 1869; published 'Short History of the English People,' 1874, 'The Making of England,' 1881, and 'Conquest of England,' 1883; suggested Oxford Historical Society and 'English Historical Review.' [xxiii. 46]

GREEN, JOHN RICHARDS (1758–1818). [See GIFFORD, JOHN.]

GREEN, JONATHAN (1788?–1864), medical writer; M.D. Heidelberg, 1834; M.R.C.S., 1810; patented vapour-bath; died in the Charterhouse; published tracts on fumigating baths and skin diseases. [xxiii. 49]

GREEN, JOSEPH HENRY (1791–1863), surgeon; educated in Germany and St. Thomas's Hospital; surgeon at St. Thomas's, 1820; professor of anatomy at College of Surgeons, 1824; F.R.S., 1825; anatomical professor at Royal Academy, 1825–52; professor of surgery at King's College, London, 1832–7; president of College of Surgeons, 1849–50 and 1858–9; Hunterian orator, 1841 and 1847; president of General Medical Council, 1860; friend and literary executor of S. T. Coleridge; published 'The Dissector's Manual,' 1820, and 'Spiritual Philosophy,' 1865. [xxiii. 49]

GREEN, Sir JUSTLY WATSON (d. 1862), second baronet; son of Sir William Green [q. v.]; officer, 1st royals; selected to attend Prince Edward (afterwards Duke of Kent) in his travels. [xxiii. 60]

GREEN, Mrs. MARY ANNE EVERETT (1818–1895), historian; née Wood; of Wesleyan parentage; married, 1846, George Pycock Green (d. 1893); published 'Letters of Royal Ladies down to Mary's reign' (1846); 'Lives of Princesses of England' (1849–55), 6 vols., and 'Life and Letters of Henrietta Maria,' 1857. She edited at the Public Record Office forty-one volumes of Calendars of Domestic State Papers (1857–95). [lxii. 369]

GREEN, MATTHEW (1696–1737), poet; friend of Richard Glover [q. v.]; his poem 'The Spleen' (1737) admired by Pope and Gray. [xxiii. 51]

GREEN, RICHARD (1716–1793). [See GREENE, RICHARD.]

GREEN, RICHARD (1803–1863), shipowner and philanthropist; helped to establish firm of Green, Wigram & Green, shipowners; built East Indiamen and ships for the voyage to Australia; established Sailors' Home at Poplar; benefactor of many institutions in East London. [xxiii. 51]

GREEN, RUPERT (1768–1804), print publisher and artist; son of Valentine Green [q. v.] [xxiii. 58]

GREEN, SAMUEL (1740–1796), organ-builder. [xxiii. 52]

GREEN, THOMAS (d. 1705), captain of the Worcester East Indiaman; hanged at Edinburgh on charge (apparently baseless) of piracy and murder. [xxiii. 52]

GREEN, THOMAS (1658–1738), bishop; fellow of Corpus Christi College, Cambridge, 1680; M.A., 1682; D.D., 1695; master of Corpus, 1698–1716; vice-chancellor, 1699 and 1713; archdeacon of Canterbury, 1708; incumbent of St. Martin's-in-the-Fields, 1716; bishop of Norwich, 1721–3, of Ely, 1723–38; directed proceedings against Richard Bentley, the classical scholar [q. v.] [xxiii. 53]

GREEN, THOMAS, the elder (1722–1794), political pamphleteer. [xxiii. 54]

GREEN, THOMAS, the younger (1769–1825), author; son of Thomas Green the elder [q. v.]; extracts from his 'Diary of a Lover of Literature,' published, 1810, and 1834–43; published poems and political pamphlets. [xxiii. 54]

GREEN, THOMAS HILL (1836–1882), idealist philosopher; educated at Rugby and Balliol College, Oxford; fellow and tutor, 1860; Whyte professor of moral philosophy, 1878–82; assistant-commissioner on middle-class schools, 1865; benefactor of Balliol College and the Oxford High School, and founder of a university prize; the 'Mr. Gray' of 'Robert Elsmere'; his 'Prolegomena to Ethics' published, 1883; his works edited by Richard Lewis Nettleship, 1885–8. [xxiii. 55]

GREEN, VALENTINE (1739–1813), mezzotint engraver and author; keeper of British Institution, 1805–1813; associate engraver, 1775; F.R.S. and F.S.A.; engraved twenty-two plates from Düsseldorf Gallery, 1789–95; engraved four hundred plates; published 'Review of the Polite Arts in France,' 1782, and other works. [xxiii. 57]

GREEN, WILLIAM (1714?–1794), hebraist; scholar and fellow of Clare Hall, Cambridge; M.A., 1741; rector of Hardingham, Norfolk, 1759–94; chief work, 'Poetical Parts of the Old Testament . . . translated . . . with Notes,' 1781. [xxiii. 58]

GREEN, SIR WILLIAM, first baronet (1725–1811), general; served with engineers in Flanders and Brittany, 1745–8; wounded and captured at Val, 1747; chief engineer of Newfoundland, 1755; took part in capture of Louisberg, 1758; wounded at Quebec, 1759; present at Sillery, 1760, and defence of Quebec; during twenty-two years' service at Gibraltar (1761–83) designed chief fortifications (being promoted director, 1778), general hospital and subterranean galleries; during the siege (1779–83) made kilns for heating shot, and rebuilt Orange bastion under fire; thanked by parliament; created baronet and chief engineer of Great Britain, 1786; president of defence committee, 1788–97; general, 1798. [xxiii. 58]

GREEN, WILLIAM (1761–1823), water-colour painter and engraver; published prints and etchings of English Lake scenery, 1808–14, and 'Tourist's New Guide' (of the Lake district), with forty etchings, 1822. [xxiii. 60]

GREEN, SIR WILLIAM KIRBY MACKENZIE (1836–1891), diplomatist; entered consular service, c. 1854; vice-consul at Tetuan and acting consul at Tangier, 1859–1869; acting agent and consul-general at Tunis, 1869–71, Damascus, 1871–3, Bairût, 1873–6; consul at Scutari, 1876–9; consul-general for Montenegro, 1879–86; envoy to Morocco and consul-general at Tangier, 1886–91; K.C.M.G., 1887. [Suppl. ii. 348]

GREEN, WILLIAM PRINGLE (1785–1846), inventor; entered navy, 1797; promoted lieutenant for services at Trafalgar, 1805; appointed to the Victory, 1842; took out patents, 1836–7, for improvements in capstans and levers; received silver medals from Society of Arts for various naval inventions, 1823; published 'Fragments from remarks of twenty-five years . . . on Electricity, Magnetism, Aerolites,' &c., 1833. [xxiii. 60]

GREENACRE, JAMES (1785–1837), murderer; manufactured 'amalgamated candy' for medical purposes in Camberwell; prepared to marry Hannah Brown, a washerwoman, as his fifth wife, but murdered her, 24 Dec. 1836; hanged. [xxiii. 61]

GREENBURY, ROBERT (*fl.* 1616–1650), painter; executed portraits of William Waynflete and Bishop Arthur Lake, and a picture of Dutch cruelties at Amboyna. [xxiii. 62]

GREENE, ANNE (*fl.* 1650), criminal; revived, and was pardoned, after being hanged for murder of her illegitimate child, 1650. [xxiii. 62]

GREENE, EDWARD BURNABY (*d.* 1788), poet and translator; originally Burnaby, assumed additional name of Greene, 1741; published translations from classical poets and from Gray's Latin verse. [xxiii. 62]

GREENE, GEORGE (*fl.* 1813), traveller; with wife and children imprisoned, when land steward to Prince of Monaco, at Torigny, Normandy, by French revolutionists, 1793–5 and 1799–1800; published account of the revolution in that district, 1802, and 'Journal from London to St. Petersburg by way of Sweden,' 1813. [xxiii. 63]

GREENE, MAURICE (1696?–1755), musical composer; organist of St. Dunstan's-in-the-West, 1716, and St. Andrew's, Holborn, 1717; organist of St. Paul's Cathedral, 1718, of Chapel Royal, 1727; Mus. Doc. and professor of music, Cambridge, 1730; master of George II's band, 1735; sided with Buononcini against Handel; assisted in founding Royal Society of Musicians, 1738; the only English organist named by Mattheson; composed music to Pope's 'Ode on St. Cecilia's Day,' Addison's 'Spacious Firmament,' and Spenser's 'Amoretti,' also two oratorios and songs, including 'Go, Rose,' and 'The Bonny Sailor,' with other works. [xxiii. 64]

GREENE, RICHARD (1716–1793), Lichfield antiquary and surgeon; related to Dr. Johnson; established printing press and collection of curiosities, to which Johnson, Pennant, and Erasmus Darwin contributed. [xxiii. 65]

GREENE, ROBERT (1560?–1592), pamphleteer and poet; B.A. St. John's College, Cambridge, 1579; M.A. Clare Hall, 1583; incorporated at Oxford, 1588; led a dissolute life on the continent and in London; assailed by Gabriel Harvey in 'Fovre Letters' as 'The Ape of Euphues'; defended by Nashe in 'Strange Newes.' He probably had some share in the authorship of the original 'Henry VI' plays, which Shakespeare revised or re-wrote. Among his thirty-eight publications were pamphlets, romances, and five (posthumous) plays, including 'The Honorable Historie of frier Bacon and frier Bongay,' acted, 1594. Of the romances, 'Menaphon' (1589), reprinted as 'Greene's Arcadia' (1599, &c.), and 'Perimedes the Blacke-Smith' (1588) contain passages in verse which are his best efforts in poetry. His numerous pamphlets include 'Euphues, his Censure to Philautus' (continuation of Lyly's work, 1587), 'Greene's Mourning Garment,' 1590, 'Never Too Late,' 1590, and 'Farewell to Folly,' 1591, and the autobiographical 'Groatsworth of Wit bought with a Million of Repentance' (ed. Chettle), which attacks Marlowe and Peele and contains the famous reference to Shakespeare as an 'upstart crow.' His plays and poems were edited by Dyce (1831), his 'Complete Works' by Grosart, 1881–6. [xxiii. 66]

GREENE, ROBERT (1678?–1730), philosopher; fellow and tutor of Clare Hall, Cambridge; M.A., 1703; D.D., 1728; published philosophical works, 1712 and 1727. [xxiii. 74]

GREENE, THOMAS (*d.* 1780), chancellor of Lichfield (1751) and dean of Salisbury (1757); son of Thomas Green (1658–1738) [q. v.]. [xxiii. 54]

GREENFIELD, JOHN (1647?–1710?). [See GROENVELDT.]

GREENFIELD, WILLIAM OF (*d.* 1315), archbishop of York; studied at Oxford and Paris; doctor of civil and canon law; prebendary of Southwell, 1269, Ripon, 1272, and York, 1287; dean of Chichester, 1299; rector of Stratford-on-Avon, 1294; member of royal embassy to Rome, 1290; present at treaty of Tarascon, 1291, of Norham, 1292; summoned to parliaments, 1295–1302; a royal proctor for peace with France, 1302; chancellor, 1302–4; joint-regent, 1307; defended the marches against Robert Bruce; lenient to the Templars; promulgated constitutions, 1306. [xxiii. 74]

GREENFIELD, WILLIAM (1799–1831), philologist; published 'The Comprehensive Bible,' 1827, 'The Polymicrian Greek Lexicon to the New Testament,' 1829, and publications for British and Foreign Bible Society. [xxiii. 76]

GREENHALGH, JOHN (*d.* 1651), royalist; governor of the Isle of Man, 1640; distinguished himself at Worcester; died of wounds. [xxiii. 77]

GREENHAM or **GRENHAM**, RICHARD (1535?–1594?), puritan divine; fellow of Pembroke Hall, Cambridge, 1564; M.A., 1576; rector of Dry Drayton,

Cambridgeshire, 1570-91; cited by Bishop Cox for non-conformity; preached against the Mar-Prelate tracts, 1589; preacher at Christ Church, Newgate; his works edited by Henry Holland, 1599. [xxiii. 77]

GREENHILL, HENRY (1646-1708), governor of the Gold Coast; principal commissioner of the navy, 1691; directed completion of Plymouth dockyard. [xxiii. 79]

GREENHILL, JOHN (1644?-1676), portrait-painter; brother of Henry Greenhill [q. v.]; pupil of Lely; executed portraits of Cowley, Locke, Bishop Seth Ward, Anthony Ashley, earl of Shaftesbury, and Charles II.
[xxiii. 78]

GREENHILL, JOSEPH (1704-1788), theological writer; nephew of Thomas Greenhill [q. v.]; M.A. Sidney Sussex College, Cambridge, 1731; rector of East Horsley and East Clandon, Surrey, 1727-88; published 'Essay on the Prophecies of the New Testament' (7th ed., 1776). [xxiii. 79]

GREENHILL, THOMAS (1681-1740?), author of 'Νεκροκηδεία, or the Art of Embalming,' 1705.
[xxiii. 80]

GREENHILL, WILLIAM (1591-1671), noncon-formist divine; demy of Magdalen College, Oxford, 1605-12; M.A., 1612; incumbent of New Shoreham, Sussex, 1615-33; first pastor of Stepney Congregational Church, 1644-71; member of Westminster Assembly, 1643; parliamentarian chaplain to royal children, 1649; a 'trier,' 1654; vicar of St. Dunstan-in-the-East, 1653-60; published 'Exposition of Ezekiel,' 1645-62. [xxiii. 80]

GREENHILL, WILLIAM ALEXANDER (1814-1894), physician; educated at Rugby and Trinity College, Oxford; studied medicine at Radcliffe Infirmary, Oxford, and in Paris; M.D., 1840; physician to Radcliffe Infirmary, Oxford, 1839-51; practised at Hastings from 1851; founder, 1857, and secretary, 1857-91, of Hastings Cottage Improvement Society; published editions of works by Sir Thomas Browne [q. v.], including 'Religio Medici,' 'Christian Morals,' and other writings, including contri-butions to 'Dictionary of National Biography.'
[Suppl. ii. 349]

GREENHOW, EDWARD HEADLAM (1814-1888), physician; M.D. Aberdeen, 1852; studied at Edinburgh and Montpellier; practised at North Shields and Tyne-mouth; lecturer on public health at St. Thomas's Hospital, 1855; consulting physician to Middlesex Hospital, 1870; chief founder of Clinical Society; president, 1879; Croonian lecturer of College of Physicians, 1875; published medical works. [xxiii. 81]

GREENOUGH, GEORGE BELLAS (1778-1855), geo-grapher and geologist; assumed additional name of Greenough at Eton; studied at Peterhouse, Cambridge, and Göttingen and Freiburg; secretary to Royal Institu-tion; M.P., Gatton, 1807-12; first president of Geo-logical Society, 1811; of Geographical Society, 1839-40; published 'Critical Examination of the first Principles of Geology' (1819), and geological maps of the United King-dom (1820), and of Hindostan; died at Naples.
[xxiii. 81]

GREENWAY, OSWALD (1563-1635). [See TESI-MOND.]

GREENWELL, DORA (1821-1882), poet and essayist; published books of poems, including (1869) 'Carmina Crucis,' and prose works, comprising 'The Patience of Hope,' 1860, and lives of Lacordaire and John Woolman.
[xxiii. 82]

GREENWELL, SIR LEONARD (1781-1844), major-general; with 45th foot at Buenos Ayres and in Peninsular war; frequently wounded; succeeded to the command after Toulouse, 1814; major-general, 1837; K.C.B. and K.C.H. [xxiii. 83]

GREENWICH, DUKE OF (1678-1743). [See CAMP-BELL, JOHN, second DUKE OF ARGYLL.]

GREENWOOD, JAMES (d. 1737), grammarian; sur-master of St. Paul's School, 1721-37; published 'Essay towards a Practical English Grammar,' 1711 (abridged as 'Royal English Grammar'), and 'The London Voca-bulary, English and Latin' (3rd edition, 1713).
[xxiii. 83]

GREENWOOD, JOHN (d. 1593), independent divine; B.A. Corpus Christi College, Cambridge, 1581; imprisoned with Henry Barrow [q. v.] for holding a conventicle;

collaborated with him, 1592; assisted in forming private congregation in Nicholas Lane (possibly the beginning of congregationalism); hanged with Barrow at Tyburn for publishing seditious books [xxiii. 84]

GREENWOOD, JOHN (d. 1609), schoolmaster; fel-low of Catharine Hall, Cambridge; M.A., 1565; master of Brentwood grammar school; published 'Syntaxis et Prosodia' (in verse), 1590. [xxiii. 85]

GREENWOOD, JOHN (1727-1792), portrait-painter; born at Boston, Massachusetts; lived five years at Surinam, and (1758-63) at Amsterdam; settled in London, 1763; original fellow of the Incorporated Society of Artists; his 'Amelia Hone' (1771) perhaps his best work. [xxiii. 85]

GREENWOOD, JOSEPH GOUGE (1821-1894), prin-cipal of the Owens College, Manchester; educated at University College School, and University College, Lon-don; B.A. London, 1840; private tutor and assistant-master at his old school; first professor of classics and history, Owens College, Manchester, 1850; principal, 1857-89, and vice-chancellor, 1880-6; honorary LL.D. Cambridge, 1873, and Edinburgh, 1884; did much to pro-mote public interest in the college. [Suppl. ii. 351]

GREENWOOD, THOMAS (1790-1871), historian; M.A. St. John's College, Cambridge, 1831; barrister, Gray's Inn, 1817, bencher, 1837, and treasurer, 1841-2; fellow and reader in history and polite literature, Durham University; published 'History of Germans' down to 772 A.D., 1836, and 'History of Great Latin Patriarchate,' 1856-65. [Suppl. ii. 352]

GREER, SAMUEL MacCURDY (1810-1880), Irish politician; educated at Belfast Academy and Glasgow; an originator of the tenant league, 1850; liberal M.P. for Londonderry, 1857; recorder, 1870-8; county court judge of Cavan and Leitrim, 1878-80. [xxiii. 86]

GREETING, THOMAS (fl. 1675), musician; pub-lished lessons and instructions for the flageolet, 1675; taught Mrs. Pepys, 1667. [xxiii. 86]

GREG, PERCY (1836-1889), author; son of William Rathbone Greg [q. v.]; published political and religious essays, novels, and poems. [xxiii. 86]

GREG, ROBERT HYDE (1795-1875), economist and antiquary; brother of William Rathbone Greg [q. v.] and of Samuel Greg [q. v.]; contributed archæological memoirs, suggested by his travels, to Manchester Literary Society, 1823-38; M.P., Manchester, 1839-41; president of Chamber of Commerce; published pamphlets on factory question, corn laws, and agriculture. [xxiii. 87]

GREG, SAMUEL (1804-1876), philanthropist; brother of Robert Hyde Greg [q. v.] and of William Rathbone Greg [q. v.]; friend of Dean Stanley; established schools, classes, baths, and libraries for his millhands at Bollington, 1832-47; compelled to retire from business by a strike against cloth-stretching machinery; entertained Kossuth, 1857; gave scientific lectures, and published religious works. [xxiii. 87]

GREG, WILLIAM RATHBONE (1809-1881), es-sayist; brother of Robert Hyde Greg [q. v.] and of Samuel Greg [q. v.]; educated at Edinburgh University; eighteen years a millowner; commissioner of customs, 1856; comp-troller of the stationery office, 1864-77; published works, including 'The Creed of Christendom,' 1851, 'Mistaken Aims and Attainable Ideals of the Working Classes,' 1876, and political and social essays, 1853. [xxiii. 88]

GREGAN, JOHN EDGAR (1813-1855), architect; designed buildings at Manchester. [xxiii. 89]

GREGG, JOHN (1798-1878), Irish bishop; graduated at Trinity College, Dublin, 1824; incumbent of Bethesda chapel, Dublin, 1836, of Trinity church, 1839-62; arch-deacon of Kildare, 1857; bishop of Cork, Cloyne, and Ross, 1862; built new cathedral of St. Finn Barre, Cork.
[xxiii. 89]

GREGG, ROBERT SAMUEL (1834-1896), archbishop of Armagh; son of John Gregg [q. v.]; M.A. Trinity College, Dublin, 1860; incumbent of Christ Church, Belfast; rector of Frankland and chaplain to his father, then bishop of Cork, 1862; rector of Carrigrohane and pre-ceptor of St. Finn Barre's Cathedral, Cork, 1865; dean of Cork, 1874; bishop of Ossory, Ferns, and Leighlin, 1875, and of Cork, 1878; archbishop of Armagh, 1893, till death; D.D. Dublin, 1873. [Suppl. ii. 353]

GREGG, WILLIAM (d. 1708), conspirator; of Scottish origin; under-clerk in office of Robert Harley, secretary of state, 1706; hanged at Tyburn for sending to the French minister, Chamillart, copies of important state documents. [Suppl. ii. 353]

GREGOR, Cacique of Poyais (fl. 1817). [See MACGREGOR, SIR GREGOR.]

GREGOR, WILLIAM (1761 – 1817), chemist and mineralogist; fellow of St. John's College, Cambridge, 1784–7; M.A., 1787; rector of Diptford, Devonshire, 1787–93, of Creed, Cornwall, 1794–1817; discovered Menacchanite, sometimes called after him Gregorite; experimented on zeolite, wavellite, and other substances; published pamphlets. [xxiii. 89]

GREGORY the GREAT (d. 889), GRIG, king of Scotland; according to Skene fifth king of the united kingdom of Scone; succeeded Aed, 878, being associated with Eocha; said to have subjected Bernicia and the greater part of Anglia (probably Northumbria only), and to have been 'the first to give liberty to the Scottish churches'; expelled with Eocha. [xxiii. 90]

GREGORY OF CAERGWENT or WINCHESTER (fl. 1270), historian; perhaps dean of the arches, 1279, and prior of Gloucester, 1284; wrote annals (682–1290) of monastery of St. Peter's, Gloucester. [xxiii. 91]

GREGORY OF HUNTINGDON (fl. 1290), prior of Ramsey and author. [xxiii. 91]

GREGORY, LADY (1815–1895). [See STIRLING, MRS. MARY ANNE.]

GREGORY, MRS. (d. 1790?). [See MRS. FITZHENRY.]

GREGORY, BARNARD (1796 – 1852), journalist; owned and edited, 1831–49, 'The Satirist, or Censor of the Times'; condemned for libel on Duke Charles of Brunswick after seven years' litigation (1843–50). [xxiii. 92]

GREGORY, DAVID (1661–1708), astronomer; son of David Gregory (1627–1720) [q. v.]; professor of mathematics at Edinburgh, 1683–91; appointed Savilian professor of astronomy at Oxford, 1691; M.A. and M.D. Oxford, 1692; master commoner of Balliol College; F.R.S. 1692; published 'Astronomiæ Physicæ et Geometricæ Elementa,' 1702, being the first text-book on gravitational principles, and an edition of Euclid, 1703; observed partial solar eclipse, 13 Sept. 1699. [xxiii. 93]

GREGORY, DAVID (1627–1720), inventor of an improved cannon; practised medicine in Aberdeenshire. [xxiii. 94]

GREGORY, DAVID (1696–1767), dean of Christ Church, Oxford; son of David Gregory (1661–1708) [q. v.]; educated at Westminster and Christ Church, Oxford; M.A., 1721; D.D., 1732; first Oxford professor of modern history and languages, 1724–36; dean of Christ Church, 1756–67; master of Sherborne Hospital, 1759; prolocutor of lower house, 1761; benefactor of Christ Church and Sherborne Hospital. [xxiii. 95]

GREGORY, DONALD (d. 1836), antiquary; secretary to Scottish Antiquaries' Society and the Iona Club; published 'History of the Western Highlands and the Isles of Scotland, 1493–1625,' 1836. [xxiii. 95]

GREGORY, DUNCAN FARQUHARSON (1813–1844), mathematician; youngest son of James Gregory (1753–1821) [q. v.]; educated at Edinburgh, Geneva, and Trinity College, Cambridge; fellow, 1840; fifth wrangler, 1837; M.A., 1841; first editor of 'Cambridge Mathematical Journal'; assistant to chemistry professor; his 'Mathematical Writings' edited by W. Walton, 1865. [xxiii. 96]

GREGORY, EDMUND (fl. 1646), author of 'Historical Anatomy of Christian Melancholy,' 1646; B.A. Trinity College, Oxford, 1636. [xxiii. 96]

GREGORY, FRANCIS (1625?–1707), schoolmaster; of Westminster and Trinity College, Cambridge; M.A., 1648; successively head-master of Woodstock and Witney grammar schools; incumbent of Hambleden, Buckinghamshire, 1671–1707; published lexicons and theological treatises. [xxiii. 96]

GREGORY, GEORGE (1754–1808), divine and author; D.D. Edinburgh, 1792; prebendary of St. Paul's,

1806; edited 'Biographia Britannica,' 1795, and 'New Annual Register.' His works include a 'History of the Christian Church,' 1790, and a 'Dictionary of the Arts and Sciences,' 1808. [xxiii. 97]

GREGORY, GEORGE (1790 – 1853), physician; grandson of John Gregory (1724–1773) [q. v.]; M.D. Edinburgh, 1811; M.R.C.S., 1812; assistant-surgeon to forces in Mediterranean, 1813–15; physician to Small-pox Hospital, 1824; F.R.S.; F.R.C.P., 1839; published 'Elements of the Theory and Practice of Physic,' 1820. [xxiii. 97]

GREGORY, JAMES (1638–1675), mathematician; brother of David Gregory (1627–1720); educated at Aberdeen; published 'Optica Promota,' 1663, describing his reflecting telescope; printed at Padua, 'Vera Circuli et Hyperbolæ Quadratura,' 1667, which provoked controversy with Huygens; F.R.S., 1668: mathematical professor at St. Andrews, 1668; first professor of mathematics at Edinburgh, 1674; struck blind with amaurosis; corresponded with Newton on their respective telescopes; original discoverer in mathematics and astronomy. [xxiii. 98]

GREGORY, JAMES (1753–1821), professor of medicine at Edinburgh; son of John Gregory (1724–1773) [q. v.]; educated at Aberdeen, Edinburgh, and Oxford; M.D. Edinburgh, 1774; professor of institutes of medicine at Edinburgh, 1776, of practice of medicine, 1790; had violent controversies with Dr. Alexander and James Hamilton (managers of Edinburgh Royal Infirmary and College of Physicians); suspended from fellowship, Edinburgh College of Physicians, 1808; published 'Conspectus Medicinæ Theoreticæ,' 1780–2, and miscellaneous works. [xxiii. 99]

GREGORY, JOHN (1607–1646), orientalist; M.A. Christ Church, Oxford, 1631; chaplain to Brian Duppa [q. v.]; collective editions of his writings issued as 'Gregorii Posthuma,' 1649, and 'Opuscula,' 1650; translated works on the Brahmans from Greek into Latin. [xxiii. 101]

GREGORY, JOHN (1724–1773), professor of medicine at Edinburgh; grandson of James Gregory (1638–1675) [q. v.]; studied at Edinburgh and Leyden; M.D. Aberdeen; professor of philosophy, Aberdeen, 1746–9; removed to London, 1754; F.R.S.; professor of medicine, Edinburgh, 1766–73; intimate with Akenside, Hume, Beattie, and other literary celebrities. His works (collected, 1788) include a 'Comparative View of the State and Faculties of Man with those of the Animal World,' 1766. [xxiii. 102]

GREGORY, OLINTHUS GILBERT (1774–1841), mathematician; of humble birth; taught mathematics at Cambridge; mathematical master at Woolwich, 1802; M.A. Aberdeen, 1805, and LL.D., 1808; Hutton's successor at Woolwich, 1807–38; one of the projectors of London University; published treatises on astronomy (1802) and mechanics (1806), besides 'Letters' on Christian evidences (1811), and lives of John Mason Good and Robert Hall. [xxiii. 103]

GREGORY, WILLIAM (d. 1467), chronicler; lord mayor of London, 1451–2; benefactor of St. Anne's, Aldersgate, and other churches and hospitals; his chronicle printed in 'Collections of a London Citizen.' [xxiii. 103]

GREGORY, WILLIAM (fl. 1520), Scottish Carmelite; prior successively at Melun, Albi, and Toulouse; doctor of the Sorbonne and confessor to Francis I. [xxiii. 104]

GREGORY, WILLIAM (d. 1663), composer; violinist to Charles I and Charles II; his compositions contained in Playford's 'Court Ayres' and in the 'Treasury of Musick' and 'Ayres and Dialogues.' [xxiii. 104]

GREGORY, SIR WILLIAM (1624–1696), judge; barrister, Gray's Inn, 1650; recorder of Gloucester, 1672; serjeant-at-law, 1677; M.P., Weobly, 1678; speaker, 1679; baron of the exchequer and knighted, 1679; removed for giving judgment against royal dispensing power, 1685; judge of king's bench, 1689; rebuilt church at How Capel, Herefordshire. [xxiii. 104]

GREGORY, WILLIAM (1766–1840), Irish undersecretary; educated at Harrow and Trinity College, Cambridge; M.A., 1787; studied at Inner Temple; member for Portarlington in Irish parliament, 1798–1800; under-secretary to lord-lieutenant of Ireland, 1812–31, and was confidential adviser of successive viceroys and chief secretaries; retired from public life, 1831; ranger of Phœnix Park from 1812. [Suppl. ii. 354]

GREGORY, WILLIAM (1803–1858), chemist; fourth son of James Gregory (1753–1821) [q. v.]; M.D. Edinburgh, 1828; professor of medicine and chemistry at King's College, Aberdeen, 1839, of chemistry at Edinburgh, 1844–58; edited English editions of Liebig's works; published 'Outlines of Chemistry,' 1845. [xxiii. 105]

GREGORY, SIR WILLIAM HENRY (1817–1892), governor of Ceylon; grandson of William Gregory (1766–1840) [q. v.]; educated at Harrow and Christ Church, Oxford; conservative M.P. for Dublin, 1842–7; actively supported Poor Relief Act, 1847; high sheriff of Galway, 1849; devoted himself to the turf; liberal-conservative M.P. for co. Galway, 1857, and retained seat till 1871; formally joined liberal party on death of Palmerston, 1865; took interest in Irish agrarian legislation; chairman of House of Commons inquiry into accommodation at British Museum, 1860; trustee of National Gallery, 1867–92; Irish privy councillor, 1871; governor of Ceylon, 1871–7; K.C.M.G., 1876. His autobiography was published, 1894. [Suppl. ii. 355]

GREGSON, MATTHEW (1749–1824), antiquary; made a fortune at Liverpool as an upholsterer; elected F.S.A. for his 'Portfolio of Fragments relative to the History and Antiquities of the County Palatine and Duchy of Lancaster,' 1817. [xxiii. 105]

GREIG, ALEXIS SAMUILOVICH (1775–1845), admiral in Russian service; son of Sir Samuel Greig [q. v.]; distinguished himself in Russo-Turkish wars of 1807 and 1828–9; reorganised Russian navy and created Black Sea Fleet. [xxiii. 106]

GREIG, JOHN (1759–1819), mathematician. [xxiii. 106]

GREIG, SIR SAMUEL (1735–1788), admiral of the Russian navy; in British service till 1763; present at Quiberon Bay, 1759, and reduction of Havannah, 1762; entered Russian service, 1764; commanded division under Orloff in Chesme Bay, 1770; appointed grand admiral, governor of Cronstadt and knight of several orders by Tsarina Catherine; commanded against Sweden at action off Hogland, 1788; created the modern Russian navy, manning it largely with Scottish officers. [xxiii. 106]

GREISLEY, HENRY (1615?–1678), translator; of Westminster and Christ Church, Oxford; student, 1634; M.A., 1641; ejected from studentship, 1651; prebendary of Worcester, 1672; translated Balzac's 'Prince,' 1648, and Senault's 'Christian Man,' 1650. [xxiii. 107]

GREISLEY, SIR ROGER (1779–1837). [See GRESLEY.]

GRELLAN, SAINT (*fl.* 500), of Craebh-Grellain, Roscommon; renounced succession to throne of Leinster, and accompanied St. Patrick to Dublin; granted Craebh-Grellain by queen of Connaught for restoring her dead child; intervened in war between Cian and Maine the Great; his crozier said to have been in possession of John Cronelly, 1836. [xxiii. 108]

GRENE, CHRISTOPHER (1629–1697), jesuit; professed, 1669; director at English college, Rome, 1692; collected records of Romanist martyrs. [xxiii. 108]

GRENE, MARTIN (1616–1667), jesuit; brother of Christopher Grene [q. v.]; professed, 1654; professor at Liège, 1642; died at St. Omer; published 'Account of the Jesuites Life and Doctrine,' 1661. [xxiii. 109]

GRENFELL, JOHN PASCOE (1800–1869), admiral in Brazilian navy; served under Cochrane in Chilian navy; wounded in cutting out of the Esmeralda; in Brazilian navy; lost arm in action off Buenos Ayres, 1826; compelled surrender of rebel flotillas in Rio Grande do Sul, 1836; commanded against Argentina, 1851–2; consul-general in England, 1846–50 and 1852–69. [xxiii. 109]

GRENFELL, PASCOE (1761–1838), politician; engaged with Thomas Williams of Temple House, Great Marlow, in developing mining industries of Anglesey and Cornwall; purchased Taplow House; M.P., Great Marlow, 1802–20; Penryn, 1820–6; abolitionist; authority on finance. [xxiii. 110]

GRENVILLE. [See also GRANVILLE.]

GRENVILLE, SIR BEVIL (1596–1643), royalist; B.A. Exeter College, Oxford, 1614; M.P., Cornwall, 1621–4 and 1640–2, Launceston, 1625–40; served against Scots, 1639; defeated parliamentarians at Bradock Down, 1643; killed at Lansdowne. [xxiii. 110]

GRENVILLE, DENIS (1637–1703), Jacobite divine; son of Sir Bevil Grenville [q. v.]; M.A. Exeter College, Oxford, 1660; D.D., 1671; incumbent of Kilkhampton, 1661; archdeacon of Durham, 1662; rector of Sedgefield, 1667; dean of Durham, 1684; raised money for James II and fled the kingdom, 1691; named by James II in exile archbishop of York; died at Paris; two collections of his remains issued by Surtees Society. [xxiii. 112]

GRENVILLE, GEORGE (1712–1770), statesman; educated at Eton and Christ Church, Oxford; barrister, Inner Temple, 1735, bencher, 1763; M.P., Buckingham, 1740–70; joined the 'Boy Patriots,' and long acted with Pitt, even when holding subordinate office under Pelham and Newcastle; resigned treasurership of the navy on dismissal of Pitt and Temple, 1756, but held it again in Newcastle-Pitt ministry, 1757–62; admitted to cabinet, 1761; secretary for the northern department and first lord of the admiralty under Bute, 1762–3; as first lord of the treasury and chancellor of the exchequer, 1763–5, successfully resisted Bute's influence with George III; his ministry chiefly remarkable for the enactment of the Stamp Act (1765) and the early proceedings against Wilkes (1763); alienated the king by omission of the princess-dowager's name from the Regency Bill; while in opposition defeated the budget of 1767, spoke against the expulsion of Wilkes, 1769, and carried a measure transferring the trial of election petitions from the whole house to a select committee, 1770. He was nicknamed 'the Gentle Shepherd' in allusion to Pitt's mocking quotation 'Gentle shepherd, tell me where,' in the course of Grenville's speech in defence of the cider-tax, 1763. [xxiii. 113]

GRENVILLE, GEORGE NUGENT-TEMPLE-, first MARQUIS OF BUCKINGHAM (1753–1813), statesman; second son of George Grenville [q. v.]; M.P., Buckinghamshire, 1774–9; succeeded as second Earl Temple, 1779; privy councillor and lord-lieutenant of Ireland, 1782–3 and 1787–9; advised enactment of Irish Judicature Act, 1783; instituted order of St. Patrick, 1783; George III's instrument in procuring defeat of Fox's India Bill in House of Lords, 1783, and secretary of state for three days (December); created Marquis of Buckingham, 1784; refused to transmit address of Irish parliament to Prince of Wales, 1789. [xxiii. 117]

GRENVILLE, GEORGE NUGENT, BARON NUGENT of Carlanstown, Ireland (1788–1850), author; younger son of George Nugent-Temple-Grenville, first marquis of Buckingham [q. v.]; succeeded to his mother's Irish peerage, 1813; M.P., Aylesbury, 1812–32 and 1847–8; a lord of the treasury, 1830–2; high commissioner of the Ionian islands, 1832–5; published works, including 'Memorials of John Hampden,' 1832, and 'Legends of the Library at Lillies,' 1832. [xxiii. 119]

GRENVILLE, JOHN, EARL OF BATH (1628–1701), eldest surviving son of Sir Bevil Grenville [q. v.]; knighted at Bristol, 1643; wounded at Newbury, 1644; held Scilly islands for Charles II, 1649–51; lord warden of the stannaries, 1660; groom of the stole, 1660; created Earl of Bath, 1661; governor of Plymouth, 1661; ultimately joined William III; lord-lieutenant of Cornwall and Devon and privy councillor, 1689. [xxiii. 120]

GRENVILLE or **GREYNVILE**, SIR RICHARD (1541?–1591), naval commander; knighted; M.P., Cornwall, 1571 and 1584, and sheriff, 1577; commanded, for his cousin, Sir Walter Ralegh, fleet for colonisation of Virginia, and on return voyage captured a Spanish ship, 1585; pillaged the Azores, 1586; engaged in organising defences of the west of England, 1586–8; second in command under Lord Thomas Howard [q. v.] of the Azores fleet, 1591; his ship, the Revenge, being isolated off Flores, he was mortally wounded, after fighting during fifteen hours fifteen Spanish ships. [xxiii. 122]

GRENVILLE, SIR RICHARD (1600–1658), first baronet; grandson of Sir Richard Grenville (1541?–1591) [q. v.]; served in expeditions to Cadiz and the Isle of Ré, writing narrative of the latter; knighted, 1627; created baronet 1630; fought as royalist in Ireland, 1641–3;

arrested by parliament at Liverpool, but released and given a command, 1643; joined Charles I at Oxford, 1644; assisted in defeat of Essex in Cornwall, 1644; failed before Plymouth, 1645; quarrelled with Sir John Berkeley, Goring, and Hopton; imprisoned in Cornwall, 1646; passed last years in Brittany and Holland; published an autobiographical pamphlet; buried at Ghent.   [xxiii. 124]

GRENVILLE, afterwards **GRENVILLE-TEMPLE**, RIOHARD TEMPLE, EARL TEMPLE (1711–1779), statesman; brother of George Grenville [q. v.]; M.P., Buckingham, 1734–41 and 1747–52, Buckinghamshire, 1741–7; succeeded to his mother's peerage, 1752; first lord of the admiralty, 1756–7; greatly disliked by George II, who dismissed him, 1757; lord privy seal, 1757–61; dismissed from the lord-lieutenancy of Buckinghamshire for his patronage of Wilkes, 1763; dissuaded Pitt from forming a ministry on the basis of a reconciliation with George Grenville, 1765; twice refused the treasury, 1765; intrigued against Rockingham, 1766; again refused the treasury and quarrelled with Chatham, 1766; strongly opposed to conciliating the Americans; D.C.L. Oxford, 1771; paid Wilkes's law expenses, and assisted Pitt financially; known to contemporaries as 'Squire Gawkey'; died of an accident. The authorship of Junius's 'Letters' has been ascribed to him.   [xxiii. 127]

GRENVILLE, RIOHARD TEMPLE NUGENT BRYDGES CHANDOS, first DUKE OF BUCKINGHAM AND OHANDOS (1776–1839), statesman; son of George Nugent-Temple-Grenville, first marquis of Buckingham [q. v.]; of Brasenose College, Oxford, 1791; M.P. (as Earl Temple) for Buckinghamshire, 1797–1813; Indian commissioner, 1800–1; privy councillor, 1806; joint paymaster-general and deputy-president of the board of trade, 1806–7; D.C.L. Oxford, 1810; LL.D. Cambridge, 1811; lord-lieutenant of Buckinghamshire, 1813; K.G., 1820; created duke, 1822; collected rare prints; his 'Private Diary' published, 1862.   [xxiii. 129]

GRENVILLE, RIOHARD PLANTAGENET TEMPLE NUGENT BRYDGES CHANDOS, second DUKE OF BUCKINGHAM AND CHANDOS (1797–1861), historical writer; son of Richard T. N. B. C. Grenville [q. v.]; Earl Temple, 1813–1822; matriculated from Oriel College, Oxford, 1815; Marquis of Chandos, 1822–39; M.P., Buckinghamshire, 1818–39; introduced into Reform Bill tenant-at-will clause (Chandos clause), 1832; lord privy seal, 1841–2; protectionist; obliged to sell much of his property, 1847; published court memoirs.   [xxiii. 130]

GRENVILLE, RIOHARD PLANTAGENET CAMPBELL TEMPLE NUGENT BRYDGES CHANDOS, third DUKE OF BUCKINGHAM AND OHANDOS (1823–1889), statesman; son of Richard Plantagenet T. N. B. C. Grenville, second duke of Buckingham [q. v.]; Earl Temple till 1839; Marquis of Chandos, 1839–61; at Eton and Christ Church, Oxford; D.C.L., 1852; M.P., Buckingham, 1846–1857; a lord of the treasury, 1852; chairman of London and North-Western Railway, 1853–61; chairman of executive committee of exhibition commission of 1862; privy councillor, 1866; president of the council, 1866–7, and colonial secretary, 1867–8; governor of Madras, 1875–80; chairman of committees in House of Lords, 1886–9.   [xxiii. 131]

GRENVILLE, THOMAS (1719–1747), navy captain; younger brother of George Grenville (1712–1770) [q. v.]; while commanding the Romney captured off Cape St. Vincent a valuable French ship, 1743; mortally wounded under Anson off Finisterre.   [xxiii. 132]

GRENVILLE, THOMAS (1755–1846), book-collector; third son of George Grenville [q. v.]; educated at Christ Church, Oxford; lieutenant in Rutland regiment, 1779; M.P., Buckinghamshire, 1780–4, Aldborough, 1790–6, Buckingham, 1796–1818; adherent of Fox, subsequently joining the old whigs; began negotiations with America, 1782; envoy extraordinary to Vienna, 1794, to Berlin, 1799; privy councillor, 1798; president of board of control and first lord of the admiralty, 1806–7. His bequest of books to British Museum (including first folio Shakespeare) forms the Grenville Library.   [xxiii. 132]

GRENVILLE, WILLIAM WYNDHAM, BARON GRENVILLE (1759–1834), statesman; youngest son of George Grenville [q. v.]; educated at Eton; B.A. Christ Church, Oxford, 1780; student of Lincoln's Inn, 1780; M.P., Buckingham, 1782–4, Buckinghamshire, 1784–90; created a peer, 1790; chief secretary for Ireland, 1782–3;

privy councillor, 1783; joint-paymaster-general, 1784; vice-president of board of trade, 1786–9; speaker, 1789; home secretary, 1789–90; president of board of control, 1790–3; foreign secretary, 1791–1801; headed war party in ministry; led for ministry in the House of Lords; resigned with Pitt on the catholic question, 1801; refused office without Fox in Pitt's second ministry, 1804; head of 'All the Talents,' 1806–7, which abolished the slave trade, 1807, and resigned on the catholic question, 1807; chancellor of Oxford, 1809; refused several offers to enter a mixed ministry, 1809–12; supported continuance of the war, 1815; allowed his adherents to join Liverpool, 1821; supported repressive measures of 1816, and bill of pains and penalties against Queen Caroline, 1820. [xxiii. 133]

GRESHAM, JAMES (fl. 1626), poet; his 'Picture of Incest' (1626) reprinted by Grosart, 1876.   [xxiii. 138]

GRESHAM, SIR JOHN (d. 1556), lord mayor of London, member of the Mercers', and a founder of the Russia Company; partner of his brother Richard; sheriff of London, 1537, lord mayor, 1547; founded Holt grammar school, Norfolk.   [xxiii. 142]

GRESHAM, SIR RICHARD (1485 ?–1549), lord mayor of London; gentleman usher extraordinary in royal household, 1516; had financial dealings with the king, and lent money to the nobility; confidential correspondent of Wolsey (whose benevolence of 1525 he supported in the common council) and Cromwell; warden of Mercers' Company, 1525, and thrice master; sheriff of London and Middlesex, 1531; a commissioner, 1534, to inquire into value of benefices previous to suppression of the abbeys; alderman; lord mayor of London, 1537; knighted, 1537; suggested appropriation for poor and sick of St. Mary's, St. Bartholomew's, and St. Thomas's hospitals; initiated design of a Royal Exchange; member of Six Articles' commission; bought Fountains Abbey, 1540, and had other grants of monastic lands.   [xxiii. 139]

GRESHAM, SIR THOMAS (1519 ?–1579), founder of the Royal Exchange; second son of Sir Richard Gresham [q. v.]; learnt business under his uncle, Sir John Gresham [q. v.]; assisted his father, on whose death he removed to Lombard Street (now 68); appointed royal agent or king's merchant at Antwerp, 1552, by influence of Northumberland; raised rate of exchange from 16 to 22 shillings for the pound; raised loan in Spain, 1554; received grants in Norfolk from Edward VI and Mary; present at Elizabeth's first council, 1558; intimate friend of Cecil; advised restoration of purity of the coinage; as ambassador to regent of the Netherlands (1559–61) sent important political information to Cecil, besides shipping secretly munitions of war; established at Osterley the first English paper-mills, 1565; finally left Antwerp, 1567; arranged for raising of loans from English merchants instead of foreigners, 1569, and for the settlement of dispute about seizure of Spanish treasure; ceased to be crown financial agent, 1574; the Royal Exchange built at his expense on a site provided by the city, 1566–8 (visited and named by the queen, 1570, destroyed in great fire, 1666); founded also Gresham College, for which he bequeathed (1575) his house in Bishopsgate Street to the corporation and the Mercers' Company; the building sold to the government, 1767, and converted into an excise office; present college built, 1841.   [xxiii. 142]

GRESLEY or **GREISLEY**, SIR ROGER (1799–1837), baronet by succession; M.P., Durham, 1830, New Romney, 1831, South Derbyshire, 1835–7; published pamphlets.   [xxiii. 153]

GRESLEY, WILLIAM (1801–1876), divine; educated at Westminster and Christ Church, Oxford; M.A., 1825; perpetual curate of All Saints', Boyne Hill, 1857–76; published 'Portrait of an English Churchman,' 1838, and religious and social tales, besides 'The Ordinance of Confession,' 1851, and works against scepticism and evangelical doctrines.   [xxiii. 153]

GRESSE, JOHN ALEXANDER (1741–1794), painter and royal drawing-master; of Swiss parentage; exhibited miniatures with Free Society and Incorporated Society of Artists.   [xxiii. 155]

GRESSWELL, DAN (1819–1883), veterinary surgeon; mayor of Louth, Lincolnshire, 1871–2.   [xxiii. 155]

GRESWELL, EDWARD (1797–1869), chronologist; son of William Parr Greswell [q. v.]; M.A. Corpus Christi College, Oxford, 1822; fellow, 1823–69; vice-president

from 1840; B.D., 1830; published works, including 'Harmonia Evangelica,' 1830, 'Fasti Temporis Catholici and Origines Kalendariæ,' 1852, 'Origines Kalendariæ Italicæ,' 1854, and 'Origines Kalendariæ Hellenicæ,' 1861.
[xxiii. 156]

GRESWELL, RICHARD (1800-1881), 're-founder of the National Society'; brother of Edward Greswell [q. v.]; thirty years fellow and tutor of Worcester College, Oxford; M.A., 1825; B.D., 1836; opened subscription on behalf of national education with a donation of 1,000*l.*, 1843; one of the founders of the Museum and the Ashmolean Society, Oxford; chairman of Mr. Gladstone's Oxford election committee, 1847-65.
[xxiii. 156]

GRESWELL, WILLIAM PARR (1765-1854), bibliographer; incumbent of Denton, Lancashire, 1791-1853; published 'Annals of Parisian Typography,' 1818, and 'View of the Early Parisian Greek Press,' 1833, 1840; edited vol. iii. of Chetham Catalogue.
[xxiii. 157]

GRETTON, WILLIAM (1736-1813), master of Magdalene College, Cambridge; educated at St. Paul's School and Peterhouse, Cambridge; M.A., 1761; vice-chancellor, 1800-1; master of Magdalene, 1797-1813; archdeacon of Essex, 1795.
[xxiii. 157]

GREVILLE, ALGERNON FREDERICK (1789-1864), private secretary to Duke of Wellington, 1827-42, having been his aide-de-camp and ensign in grenadier guards at Waterloo; Bath king-of-arms.
[xxiii. 157]

GREVILLE, CHARLES CAVENDISH FULKE (1794-1865), clerk to the council; brother of Algernon Frederick Greville [q. v.]; manager of Duke of York's stud, and racing partner of Lord George Bentinck, his cousin; clerk to the council, 1821-59; intimate with statesmen of both parties, especially Wellington and Palmerston; his diary (mainly political) published 1st series (1817-37), 1875, 2nd and 3rd (to 1860), 1885 and 1887 (ed. H. Reeve); edited Raikes's 'Memoirs' and part of Moore's correspondence.
[xxiii. 158]

GREVILLE, SIR FULKE, first BARON BROOKE (1554-1628), poet and statesman; intimate with Philip Sidney at Shrewsbury; fellow-commoner, Jesus College, Cambridge, 1568; came to court with Sidney, and became favourite of Elizabeth; accompanied Sidney to Heidelberg, 1577; joined Gabriel Harvey's 'Areopagus'; entertained Giordano Bruno at his London house, 1583; pall-bearer at Sidney's funeral at St. Paul's, 1587; secretary for principality of Wales, 1583 till death; M.P., Warwickshire, 1592-1620; 'treasurer of the wars' and the navy, 1598; K.B., 1603; chancellor of the exchequer, 1614-21; created peer, 1621; granted Warwick Castle and Knowle Park by James I; befriended Bacon, Camden, Coke, Daniel, and D'Avenant; stabbed by a servant. A collection of works 'written in his youth' (including tragedies and sonnets) was printed, 1633, his 'Life of Sidney,' 1652 (reprinted by Brydges, 1816), and his 'Remains,' 1670. His complete works were reprinted by Grosart, 1870.
[xxiii. 159]

GREVILLE, HENRY WILLIAM (1801-1872), diarist; brother of Charles Cavendish Fulke Greville [q. v.]; attaché to Paris embassy, 1834-44; gentleman usher at court; his 'Leaves from a Diary' published, 1883-4.
[xxiii. 163]

GREVILLE, ROBERT, second BARON BROOKE (1608-1643), parliamentarian general; adopted by his cousin, Sir Fulke Greville, first baron Brooke [q. v.]; M.P., Warwick, 1628-9; member of company for plantation of Providence and Henrietta islands (incorporated, 1630); commissioner for treaty of Ripon, 1640; speaker, House of Lords, 1642; defeated Northampton at Kineton, 1642; served under Essex in Midlands; took Stratford-on-Avon, 1643, but was killed in attack on Lichfield; published 'The Nature of Truth,' 1640.
[xxiii. 163]

GREVILLE, ROBERT KAYE (1794-1866), botanist; settled at Edinburgh, 1816; joined the Wernerian Society, 1819; F.R.S.E., 1821; LL.D. Glasgow, 1824; made botanical tours in the highlands; vice-president, Antislavery Convention, 1840; M.P., Edinburgh, 1856; published 'Scottish Cryptogamic Flora,' 'Flora Edinensis,' 1824, 'Icones Filicum' (with Hooker), 1829-31, and 'Algæ Britannicæ,' 1830; edited (with Dr. R. Huie), 'The Amethyst' (poems), 1832-4, and (with T. K. Drummond) 'The Church of England Hymn-book,' 1838; his collection of *algæ* acquired by British Museum, insects by

Edinburgh University, flowering plants by Glasgow, and other *cryptogamia* by Edinburgh Botanic Garden.
[xxiii. 164]

GREW, JONATHAN (1626-1711), first presbyterian minister of Dagnal Lane, St. Albans, 1698-1711; nephew of Obadiah Grew [q. v.]
[xxiii. 169]

GREW, NEHEMIAH (1641-1712), vegetable physiologist; son of Obadiah Grew [q. v.]; B.A. Pembroke Hall, Cambridge, 1661; M.D. Leyden, 1671; F.R.S., 1671; secretary to Royal Society, 1677-9; probably first to observe sex in plants; published 'The Anatomy of Plants.' 1682 (4 vols.), embodying previous publications, and 'Cosmologia Sacra,' 1701, against Spinoza, besides scientific pamphlets; genus named *Grewia* after him by Linnæus.
[xxiii. 166]

GREW, OBADIAH (1607-1689), ejected minister; M.A. Balliol College, Oxford, 1632; D.D., 1651; master of Atherstone grammar school, 1632; appointed vicar of St. Michael's, Coventry, 1645; pleaded with Cromwell for the king's life, 1648; favoured royalist rising, 1659; obliged to resign living, 1662, and leave Coventry, 1666; returned, 1672, and with John Bryan (*d.* 1676) [q. v.] founded presbyterian congregation; imprisoned under Five Mile Act, 1682; his 'Sinner's Justification' (1670) translated into Welsh, 1785.
[xxiii. 168]

GREY. [See also GRAY.]

GREY, ANCHITELL (*d.* 1702), compiler of debates; second son of Henry Grey, first earl of Stamford [q. v.]; M.P., Derby, 1665-85, in convention of 1689 and parliament of 1690-4; his notes printed (1769) as 'Debates of the House of Commons, 1667-94.'
[xxiii. 169]

GREY, ARTHUR, fourteenth BARON GREY DE WILTON (1536-1593), son of Sir William, thirteenth baron Grey de Wilton [q. v.]; served at St. Quentin, 1557; wounded during siege of Leith, 1560; succeeded to title, 1562; commissioner at trials of Duke of Norfolk, 1574, Mary Queen of Scots, and William Davison (1541 ?-1608) [q. v.], whom he defended; as lord-deputy of Ireland, 1580-2, had Spenser as secretary; overcame rebels of the pale, and pacified Munster; member of committee of defence of the kingdom, 1587-8.
[xxiii. 169]

GREY, LADY CATHERINE (1538 ?-1568). [See SEYMOUR.]

GREY, CHARLES, first EARL GREY (1729-1807), general; with Wolfe's regiment at Rochefort, 1757, and in Germany; aide-de-camp to Prince Ferdinand at Minden, 1759, being wounded there and at Campen, 1760; lieutenant-colonel of 98th at Belle Isle, 1761, and Havana, 1762; while in America defeated Wayne; commanded third brigade at Germanstown, 1777; annihilated Bayler's Virginian dragoons, 1778; major-general, 1778; K.B., 1782; relieved Nieuport, 1793; co-operated with Jervis in capture of French West Indies, 1794; general and privy councillor, 1795; created baron, 1801, and earl, 1806.
[xxiii. 172]

GREY, CHARLES, second EARL GREY, VISCOUNT HOWICK, and BARON GREY (1764-1845), statesman; son of Charles Grey, first earl [q. v.]; educated at Eton and King's College, Cambridge; M.P., Northumberland, 1786-1807, Appleby (Viscount Howick), 1807; acted with Fox, except on the regency question, during Pitt's first ministry; one of the managers of Warren Hastings's impeachment, 1787; took up reform question for Society of Friends of the People, 1793, and in 1797 brought forward his first bill; attacked Pitt's foreign policy and repressive legislation; seceded from House of Commons with whig party, 1797; returned to resist Irish union, 1800; refused to join Addington, favoured renewal of the war, and acted with Grenville during Pitt's second ministry; first lord of the admiralty, 1806; foreign secretary, 1806-7, resigning when George III required a pledge not to reintroduce catholic emancipation; acted with Grenville as joint adviser to the Prince Regent, 1811; with Grenville refused either to form a whig ministry without control of the household, or to join coalition with tories, but maintained, in opposition to Grenville, the principle of supporting independence of nationalities in foreign affairs, and differed from him in opposing all repressive legislation; opposed the king's divorce bill of 1820, and refused to co-operate with Canning; again took up parliamentary reform, 1830; prime minister of whig administration, 1831; introduced a reform bill, 1831; defeated in committee; dissolved, 1831; carried new bill in Commons, but lost it on second reading in Lords; reintroduced it in Lords, but was defeated on motion to postpone disfranchising clauses, 1832; resigned, but returned in a few days (May 1832) with promise of power to create peers, and finally carried the bill; retired, 1834, in consequence of a disagreement in the cabinet on the renewal of the Irish coercion act of 1833, he himself favouring severity; K.G. [xxiii. 173]

GREY, CHARLES (1804–1870), general; second surviving son of Charles Grey, second earl Grey [q. v.]; lieutenant-colonel, 71st highlanders, 1833–42; general, 1865; private secretary to his father, 1830–4, to Prince Albert, 1849–61, and afterwards to Queen Victoria, 1861–70; M.P., High Wycombe, 1831–7; published biography of his father, 1861, and 'Early Years of The Prince Consort,' 1867. [xxiii. 179]

GREY, SIR CHARLES EDWARD (1785–1865), Indian judge and colonial governor; B.A. University College, Oxford, 1806; fellow of Oriel College, Oxford, 1808; barrister, 1811; bankruptcy commissioner, 1817; judge of Madras supreme court, 1820; knighted, 1820; chief-justice of Bengal, 1825; special commissioner to Canada, 1835; M.P., Tynemouth, 1838–41; governor of Barbados and other islands, 1841–6, of Jamaica, 1847–53. [xxiii. 180]

GREY, EDMUND, first EARL OF KENT (1420?–1489), lord high treasurer; grandson of Reginald de Grey, third baron Grey of Ruthin [q. v.], whom he succeeded, 1440; supported Henry VI; deserted to Yorkists at battle of Northampton, 1460; privy councillor, 1463; lord treasurer, 1463; created Earl of Kent, 1465; commissioner of oyer and terminer in London and home counties, 1483. [xxiii. 180]

GREY, ELIZABETH, COUNTESS OF KENT (1581–1651), authoress; *née* Talbot; married Henry, seventh earl of Kent; said to have been afterwards secretly married to Selden; published 'A Choice Manuall, or Rare and Select Secrets in Physick and Chyrurgery' (2nd ed., 1653), and a book of culinary recipes (19th ed., 1687). [xxiii. 181]

GREY, FORDE, EARL OF TANKERVILLE (*d.* 1701), whig politician; succeeded as third Baron Grey of Werk, 1675; a zealous exclusionist, 1681; convicted of conspiracy to carry off his sister-in-law, Lady Henrietta Berkeley, 1682; fled to Holland on discovery of Rye House plot, 1683; commanded Monmouth's horse at Sedgemoor, 1685; gave evidence against his associates, and was restored to title, 1685; joined William of Orange; created Earl of Tankerville, 1695; privy councillor, 1695; commissioner of trade, 1696; first commissioner of the treasury, 1699; lord privy seal, 1700. [xxiii. 182]

GREY, GEORGE, second EARL OF KENT (*d.* 1503), soldier; styled Lord Grey of Ruthin till 1489; saw military service in France under Edward IV and Henry VII; commanded against Cornish rebels at Blackheath, 1497. [xxiii. 181]

GREY, SIR GEORGE, second baronet (1799–1882), statesman; grandson of Charles Grey, first earl Grey [q. v.]; graduated at Oriel College, Oxford, 1821; barrister, 1826; practised as barrister; succeeded as baronet, 1828; M.P., Devonport, 1832–47, North Northumberland, 1847–52, and Morpeth, 1853–74; under-secretary for colonies, 1834 and 1835–9; judge advocate-general, 1839–41; chancellor of duchy of Lancaster, 1841; home secretary under Russell, 1846–52, and under Palmerston, 1855–8 and 1861–6; colonial secretary in Lord Aberdeen's coalition ministry, 1854–5; chancellor of duchy of Lancaster, 1859–61; carried convict discipline bill, which abolished transportation. [xxiii. 183]

GREY, SIR GEORGE (1812–1898), colonial governor; educated at Sandhurst; received commission in 83rd foot, 1829; captain, 1839; left army, 1839; made exploring expeditions for Royal Geographical Society, north-western coast of Western Australia; governor of South Australia, 1841–5, New Zealand, 1845–53 (both of which colonies he raised from state of disorder to that of peace and comparative prosperity), and Cape Colony, 1853; recalled, 1859, for encouraging, without official permission, a policy of South African federation; restored to office, 1859; again governor of New Zealand, 1861–7, during which period he came into frequent conflict with his ministers and the colonial office; chosen (1874) superintendent of province of Auckland; member of House of Representatives for Auckland city (1874–94), led opposition to centralist

party; prime minister, 1877–9; successfully advocated adult franchise, triennial parliaments, taxation of land values, leasing instead of sale of crown lands, and compulsory repurchase of private estates; returned to England, 1894; privy councillor, 1894; buried publicly in St. Paul's Cathedral; published works relating to language, topography, and history of Australia and New Zealand. [Suppl. ii. 357]

GREY, HENRY, DUKE OF SUFFOLK, third MARQUIS OF DORSET (*d.* 1554), father of Lady Jane Grey; succeeded as third Marquis of Dorset, 1530; K.G., 1547; prominent during Edward VI's minority; privy councillor, 1549; attached himself first to Seymour of Sudeley, and from 1548 to Dudley (Northumberland); created duke on death of wife's male relations, 1551; gave up Lady Jane Grey's cause, 1553, and was pardoned by Mary; joined rising against Spanish marriage; executed for treason. [xxiii. 184]

GREY, HENRY, ninth EARL OF KENT (1594–1651), parliamentarian; M.P. (as Lord Ruthin) for Leicestershire, 1640–3; commissioner of great seal, 1643–4, 1645–6, and 1648–9; speaker of House of Lords, 1645 and 1647. [xxiii. 186]

GREY, HENRY, first EARL OF STAMFORD (1599?–1673), parliamentarian general; succeeded as second Baron Grey of Groby, 1614; created Earl of Stamford, 1628; commanded under Essex in the west, 1642–3; defeated at Stratton, 1643; besieged and compelled to surrender to Prince Maurice at Exeter, 1643; impeached for assaulting Sir Arthur Haselrig, 1645; declared for Charles II, 1659; committed to the Tower, 1659. [xxiii. 187]

GREY, HENRY, DUKE OF KENT, eleventh EARL OF KENT (1664?–1740); grandson of Henry Grey, ninth earl of Kent [q. v.]; created duke, 1710; a lord justice, 1714. [xxiii. 187]

GREY, HENRY (1778–1859), Free church minister; at Stenton, St. Cuthbert's Chapel, Edinburgh, 1813–21, the New North Church, 1821–5, and St. Mary's, 1829; seceded, 1843; chairman of general assembly, 1844; the Grey scholarships at New College, Edinburgh, founded in his honour. [xxiii. 188]

GREY, SIR HENRY GEORGE, VISCOUNT HOWICK, and afterwards third EARL GREY (1802–1894), statesman; son of Charles Grey, second earl Grey [q. v.]; M.A. Trinity College, Cambridge, 1823; whig M.P., Winchelsea, 1826–30, Higham Ferrers, 1830; under-secretary for colonies in his father's administration, 1830–3, and for home affairs, 1834–5; M.P., Northumberland, 1831, and for northern division of Northumberland, 1832–41; privy councillor and secretary-at-war, 1835–9; proposed amendment to Irish franchise bill which resulted in defeat of government, 1841, and abandonment of bill; M.P., Sunderland, 1841; succeeded to earldom, 1845, and became active leader of his party in House of Lords; secretary for colonies, 1846–52; instituted ticket-of-leave system, 1848; strongly advocated transportation of convicts; revived committee of privy council for trade and foreign plantations as a deliberative and advisory body, 1849; published 'Colonial Policy of Lord John Russell's Administration,' 1853; maintained a critical and independent attitude after 1852; strongly opposed Gladstone's home rule policy, 1885–6; published political writings. [Suppl. ii. 361]

GREY, LADY JANE (1537–1554). [See DUDLEY.]

GREY or GRAY, JOHN DE (*d.* 1214), bishop of Norwich, 1200–14; elected by King John's influence to the primacy, 1205, but his election quashed in favour of Langton by Innocent III, 1207; justice itinerant; lent money to John; named by Matthew Paris among the king's evil counsellors; excluded from the general absolution of 1213; as justiciar of Ireland (1210–13) remodelled the coinage on the English pattern; bishop-elect of Durham; died at St. Jean d'Audely while returning from Rome. [xxiii. 189]

GREY, SIR JOHN DE (*d.* 1266), judge; fined and deprived of justiceship of Chester for marrying without royal license, 1251; forgiven after taking the cross, 1253; steward of Gascony, 1253; one of the twelve representatives of the commonalty, 1258; justice in eyre in Somerset, Dorset, and Devon, 1260; fought in Wales against the barons; sheriff of Nottinghamshire and Derbyshire, 1265. [xxiii. 191]

GREY, JOHN DE, second BARON GREY OF WILTON (1268–1323), grandson of Sir John de Grey [q. v.]; summoned to parliament, 1309; a lord ordainer, 1310, and member of barons' council, 1318; justice of North Wales, 1315; joined Edward II, 1322. [xxiii. 191]

GREY, JOHN DE, second BARON GREY OF ROTHERFIELD (1300–1359), soldier; constantly employed in wars of Edward III; one of the original K.G.s, 1344; steward of the household, 1350. [xxiii. 192]

GREY, JOHN DE, third BARON (sixth by tenure) GREY OF CODNOR (1305–1392), soldier; served Edward III in Scotland, Flanders, and France; governor of Rochester Castle, 1360. [xxiii. 192]

GREY or GRAY, JOHN, EARL OF TANKERVILLE (d. 1421), soldier; grandson of Thomas Gray (d. 1369?) [q. v.]; took part in siege of Harfleur and battle of Agincourt, 1415; received executed brother's lands at Heton; served in Henry V's second expedition, 1417, and assisted in conquest of the Cotentin, 1418; created Earl of Tankerville, chamberlain of Normandy, and K.G., 1419; one of the commissioners to negotiate for king's marriage; served at siege of Rouen, 1419; killed at battle of Beaugé. [xxiii. 192]

GREY, JOHN, eighth BARON FERRERS OF GROBY (1432–1461), Lancastrian; not summoned to parliament, and usually styled Sir John; first husband of Elizabeth Woodville (queen of Edward IV); killed at second battle of St. Albans. [xxiii. 193]

GREY, LORD JOHN (d. 1569), youngest son of Thomas Grey, second marquis of Dorset [q. v.]; deputy of Newhaven under Edward VI; received grants of land from Edward VI and Mary; joined Wyatt's rising, 1554, and only obtained his life at intercession of his wife; granted Pyrgo, Essex, and other estates by Elizabeth; one of the four nobles who superintended alterations in prayer-book, 1558; lost favour by espousing cause of Catherine Seymour [q. v.], his niece. [xxiii. 194]

GREY, SIR JOHN (1780?–1856), lieutenant-general; served with 75th against Tippoo Sahib; with 5th in Peninsula, being wounded at storming of Ciudad Rodrigo, 1812; lieutenant-colonel, 2nd battalion, 1812–16; commanded left wing at Punniar, Gwalior, 1843; created K.C.B.; commander-in-chief and member of Bombay council, 1850–2; lieutenant-general, 1851. [xxiii. 195]

GREY, JOHN (1785–1868), of Dilston, agriculturist; managed Greenwich Hospital mining estates, 1833–63, and by applying Liebig's discoveries increased their value; assisted Clarkson and Brougham in anti-slavery agitation; intimate with Earl Grey, Althorpe, and Jeffrey. [xxiii. 195]

GREY or GRAY, LORD LEONARD, VISCOUNT GRANE of Ireland (d. 1541), statesman; sixth son of Thomas, first marquis of Dorset [q. v.]; when marshal of the English army in Ireland, 1535, obtained surrender of Thomas Fitzgerald, tenth earl of Kildare [q. v.], his connection; as deputy-governor of Ireland presided over the important parliament of 1536–7, allied himself with Desmond against Ormonde; defeated Desmond, 1539; beheaded on Tower Hill on charge of supporting native Irish and favouring Geraldines. [xxiii. 196]

GREY, LADY MARY (1540?–1578). [See KEYS.]

GREY, NICHOLAS (1590?–1660), head-master of Eton; educated at Westminster and Christ Church, Oxford; M.A., 1613; M.A. Cambridge, 1614; head-master of Charterhouse, 1614, of Merchant Taylors', 1625–32, and of Tonbridge during Commonwealth; head-master of Eton and fellow, 1632; ejected during the civil war; restored, 1660. [xxiii. 197]

GREY, REGINALD DE, third BARON GREY OF RUTHIN (1362?–1440), succeeded to title, 1388; successful in a suit (1401–10) against Edward Hastings for right to bear Hastings arms and title Earl of Pembroke; governor of Ireland, 1398; as member of Henry IV's council advised recourse to parliament on question of war with France, 1401; carried on war with Owen Glendower, by whom he was captured, 1402, and kept prisoner near Snowdon; continued Welsh war, 1409; member of council of regency, 1415. [xxiii. 197]

GREY, RICHARD DE, second BARON GREY OF CODNOR (fl. 1250), baronial leader; governor of Channel islands,

1226; sheriff of Northumberland, 1236, of Essex and Hertford, 1239; took the cross, 1252; one of the twenty-four and the fifteen perpetual councillors, 1258; custos of Dover and warden of Cinque ports and Rochester for barons; captured by Prince Edward at Kenilworth, 1265; surrendered again, 1266. [xxiii. 199]

GREY, RICHARD DE, second BARON GREY OF CODNOR (d. 1335), served in Scotland under Edward II and Edward III; steward of Aquitaine, 1324; constable of Nottingham, 1326–7. [xxiii. 192]

GREY, RICHARD DE, fourth BARON (seventh by tenure) GREY OF CODNOR (d. 1419), succeeded his grandfather, John Grey, third baron (1305–1392) [q. v.], 1392; admiral of the fleet and governor of Roxburgh, 1400; justice of South Wales, 1404; lieutenant, 1405–6, constable of Nottingham, 1407; much employed on diplomatic missions. [xxiii. 199]

GREY, LORD RICHARD (d. 1483), brother of Thomas Grey, first marquis of Dorset [q. v.]; K.B., 1475; accused by Richard, duke of Gloucester, of estranging Edward V from him; beheaded. [xxiii. 194]

GREY, RICHARD (1694–1771), author; M.A. Lincoln College, Oxford, 1719; chaplain and secretary to Bishop Crew of Durham; rector of Hinton, Northamptonshire, 1720, and Kimcote, Leicestershire, 1725; friend of Doddridge and Dr. Johnson; his 'Memoria Technica' (1730) reprinted as late as 1861; for 'System of English Ecclesiastical Law' created D.D. Oxford, 1731. [xxiii. 200]

GREY, ROGER, first BARON GREY OF RUTHIN (d. 1353), younger son of John de Grey, second baron Grey of Wilton [q. v.]; summoned to parliament as Roger de Grey, 1324; served in Scotland, 1318, 1322, and 1341; custos of Abergavenny Castle, 1331. [xxiii. 201]

GREY, THOMAS, first MARQUIS OF DORSET (1451–1501), succeeded his father, John Grey, eighth Baron Ferrers of Groby [q. v.] as ninth baron, 1461; created Earl of Huntingdon, 1471, having fought for Edward IV at Tewkesbury; K.B. and Marquis of Dorset, 1475; K.G., 1476; privy councillor, 1476; took arms against Richard III and joined Richmond in Brittany, but did not accompany him to England; his titles confirmed, 1486; imprisoned on suspicion, 1487; served with the expedition to aid the Emperor Maximilian, 1492, and against the Cornish rebels, 1497; early patron of Wolsey. [xxiii. 201]

GREY, THOMAS, second MARQUIS OF DORSET (1477–1530), third son of Thomas Grey, first marquis of Dorset [q. v.]; educated at Magdalen College school; styled Lord Harington till 1501; K.G., 1501; imprisoned during last years of Henry VII's reign; won favour of Henry VIII by skill in tournaments; commanded unsuccessful expedition for recovery of Guienne, 1512; took part in French war, 1513; present at meetings of Henry VIII with Francis I and Emperor Charles V, 1520; warden of Scottish marches; witness against Queen Catherine and signer of articles against Wolsey, 1529; pensioner of the emperor and the French king. [xxiii. 202]

GREY, THOMAS, fifteenth and last BARON GREY OF WILTON (d. 1614), succeeded his father, Arthur Grey, fourteenth baron [q. v.], 1593; served against the Armada; a volunteer in the Islands' Voyage, 1597; colonel of horse in Ireland, 1599; in Netherlands army at Nieuport, 1600; general of the horse against Essex and Southampton, and a commissioner at their trial, 1601; involved in 'Bye' plot against James I; reprieved on the scaffold, 1603; detained in the Tower till his death. [xxiii. 204]

GREY, THOMAS, BARON GREY OF GROBY (1623?–1657), regicide; son of Henry Grey, first earl of Stamford [q. v.]; M.P. for Leicester in Long parliament and that of 1654; commander of midland counties association, 1643; present at first battle of Newbury, 1643; thanked by parliament for capture of Duke of Hamilton, 1648; active in 'Pride's Purge,' 1648; one of Charles I's judges; member of council of state, 1649–54; received surrender of Massey after Worcester, 1651; imprisoned as a Fifth-monarchy man, 1655. [xxiii. 206]

GREY, THOMAS, second EARL OF STAMFORD (1654–1720), statesman; son of Thomas Grey, baron Grey of Groby [q. v.]; M.A. Christ Church, Oxford, 1668; succeeded his grandfather, Henry Grey, first earl [q. v.], as second earl, 1673; member of Shaftesbury's party;

imprisoned as connected with Rye House plot, 1683 ; pardoned, 1686 ; member of committee for investigating deaths of Russell and Sydney, 1689 ; privy councillor, 1694 ; commissioner of trade, 1695 ; chancellor of the duchy of Lancaster, 1697 ; president of board of trade and foreign plantations, 1699–1702 and 1707–11 ; F.R.S., 1708.

[xxiii. 207]

GREY, THOMAS PHILIP DE, EARL DE GREY (1781–1859), statesman ; descendant of Henry Grey, ninth earl of Kent [q. v.] ; succeeded his father as third Baron Grantham, 1786 ; assumed name of Weddell, 1803, of De Grey on death of the Countess De Grey, his aunt, 1833 ; first lord of the admiralty, 1834–5 ; viceroy of Ireland, 1841–4 ; F.R.S., 1841 ; first president, Society of British Architects, 1834–59 ; published ' Memoir of the Life of Sir Charles Lucas,' 1845, and ' Characteristics of the Duke of Wellington,' 1853. [xxiii. 208]

GREY or **GRAY**, WALTER DE (d. 1255), archbishop of York ; as chancellor of England, 1205–14, one of King John's chief instruments and recipient of numerous benefices from him ; his election to see of Lichfield, 1210, quashed by papal legate ; bishop of Worcester, 1214 ; one of John's supporters at Runnymead, 1215 ; obtained at Rome the quashing of Simon Langton's election to see of York ; archbishop of York, 1215–55 ; acted against French party during minority of Henry II [q. v.] ; married Alexander II of Scotland to Joanna, sister of Henry III of England, 1221 ; received profession of obedience from bishop-elect of Durham ; employed diplomatically by Henry III ; chief justiciar during Henry III's absence, 1242–3 ; entertained Alexander III of Scotland on his marriage at York with Margaret, daughter of Henry III, 1252 ; ranked among the patriotic prelates in later years ; built south transept of York minster ; benefactor of Ripon and Oxford University. [xxiii. 208]

GREY, WILLIAM (d. 1478), bishop of Ely ; D.D. Balliol College, Oxford ; prebendary of St. Paul's, Lincoln, Lichfield, and York ; chancellor of Oxford, 1440–2 ; lived much in Italy, and was patron of scholars ; proctor of Henry VI at Rome, 1449–54 ; bishop of Ely, 1454–78 ; acted as mediator, 1455 and 1460 ; lord high treasurer, 1469–70 ; head of commission to negotiate with Scotland, 1471–2 ; benefactor of Ely Cathedral and Balliol College library. [xxiii. 212]

GREY, SIR WILLIAM, thirteenth BARON GREY DE WILTON (d. 1562) ; succeeded, 1529 ; distinguished in French war, 1545–6, and as commander at Pinkie, 1547 ; captured and fortified Haddington, 1548 ; pacified west of England, 1549 ; imprisoned on fall of Somerset, 1551 ; governor of Guisnes ; attainted for supporting Northumberland, but pardoned, 1553 ; obliged to surrender Guisnes to the French, 1558 ; restored to his honours by Queen Elizabeth ; governor of Berwick, 1559 ; failed in assault on Leith, 1560. [xxiii. 213]

GREY, WILLIAM (fl. 1649), author of ' Chorographia, or a Svrvey of Nevvcastle upon Tine,' 1649.

[xxiii. 215]

GREY, WILLIAM, first BARON GREY OF WERKE (d. 1674), parliamentarian ; created baronet, 1619 ; created Baron Grey, 1624 ; commander of parliamentarian forces in the east, 1642 ; imprisoned for refusing to go as commissioner to Scotland, 1643 ; speaker of House of Lords, 1643 ; a commissioner of great seal, 1648 ; refused the engagement, 1649 ; pardoned at Restoration.

[xxiii. 215]

GREY, WILLIAM DE, first BARON WALSINGHAM (1719–1781), judge ; educated at Christ's College, Cambridge ; barrister, Middle Temple, 1742 ; K.C., 1758 ; M.P., Newport (Cornwall), 1761–70, Cambridge University, 1770–1 ; attorney-general, 1766–71 ; chief-justice of common pleas, 1771–80 ; created Baron Walsingham, 1780.

[xxiii. 216]

GREY, SIR WILLIAM (1818–1878), Indian and colonial governor ; educated at Haileybury ; secretary to Bank of Bengal, 1851–4, to the government, 1854–7 ; director-general of the post-office during the mutiny ; secretary to government of India, 1859 ; member of governor-general's council, 1862–7 ; lieutenant-governor of Bengal, 1867–71 ; governor of Jamaica, 1874–7.

[xxiii. 216]

GREY, ZACHARY (1688–1766), antiquary ; scholar of Trinity Hall, Cambridge, 1707 ; LL.D., 1720 ; rector of Houghton Conquest, 1725, and vicar of St. Giles and St. Peter's, Cambridge ; published ' Hudibras . . . corrected

and amended, with large annotations and a preface,' and cuts by Hogarth, 1744 (supplement, 1752) ; also controversial pamphlets against dissenting writers, and attacks on Warburton's critical and controversial methods.

[xxiii. 218]

GRIBELIN, SIMON (1661–1733), line-engraver ; came to England, c. 1680 ; engraved seven small plates of Raffaelle's cartoons, 1707 ; engraved portraits and, among other pictures, Rubens's ' Apotheosis of James I,' 1730.

[xxiii. 219]

GRIERSON, MRS. CONSTANTIA (1706 ?–1733), classical scholar ; intimate with Swift ; edited Terence (1727) and Tacitus (1730) for her husband, George Grierson, George II's printer in Ireland ; wrote English verse. [xxiii. 220]

GRIERSON or **GRISSON**, JOHN (d. 1564 ?), Dominican ; principal of King's College, Aberdeen, 1500 ; afterwards prior of St. Andrews and provincial in Scotland,

[xxiii. 220]

GRIERSON, SIR ROBERT (1655 ?–1733), laird of Lag ; notorious for severity towards covenanters ; created a Nova Scotia baronet, 1685 ; presided at trial and execution of ' Wigtown martyrs ' ; fined and imprisoned after the Revolution ; the ' Sir Robert Redgauntlet ' of Scott.

[xxiii. 221]

GRIEVE or **GREIVE**, GEORGE (1748–1809), persecutor of Madame Du Barry ; emigrated to America from Alnwick, c. 1780 ; came to Paris, 1783 ; on Madame Du Barry's return from London, March 1793, caused her name to be placed on list of suspects, published a pamphlet against her, and thrice obtained her arrest ; died at Brussels.

[xxiii. 222]

GRIEVE, JAMES (d. 1773), translator of ' Celsus ' ; M.D. Edinburgh, 1752 ; physician to St. Thomas's, 1764, and the Charterhouse, 1765 ; F.R.S., 1769 ; F.R.C.P., 1771 ; translated Celsus ' De Medicina,' 1756. [xxiii. 223]

GRIEVE, JOHN (1781–1836), Scottish poet and friend of Hogg ; contributed to ' Forest Minstrel.' [xxiii. 223]

GRIEVE, THOMAS (1799–1882), scene-painter at Covent Garden and Drury Lane ; designed the diorama, ' Overland Mail ' (1850), and assisted Telbin and Absolon in panoramas ; illustrated ' Goody Two Shoes,' 1862.

[xxiii. 224]

GRIEVE, WILLIAM (1800–1844), scene-painter ; brother of Thomas Grieve [q. v.] ; at Drury Lane and Her Majesty's. [xxiii. 224]

GRIFFIER, JAN, the elder (1656–1718), painter and etcher ; intimate with Rembrandt and Ruysdael at Amsterdam ; followed Looten to England ; made a drawing during the great fire, 1666 ; lived on a yacht on the Thames, and took views of London and the environs ; etched plates of Barlow's birds and animals. [xxiii. 224]

GRIFFIER, JAN, the younger (d. 1750 ?), landscape-painter ; son of Jan Griffier the elder [q. v.]

[xxiii. 225]

GRIFFIER, ROBERT (1688–1760 ?), landscape-painter ; son of Jan Griffier the elder [q. v.]

[xxiii. 225]

GRIFFIN, B. (fl. 1596), poet (probably Bartholomew Griffin of Coventry), author of ' Fidessa, more chaste than kinde,' 1596 (the third sonnet of which was reproduced in ' The Passionate Pilgrime,' 1599) [xxiii. 225]

GRIFFIN, BENJAMIN (1680–1740), actor and dramatist ; at Lincoln's Inn Fields, 1715–21, and at Drury Lane, 1721–40 ; played Lovegold in Fielding's ' Miser,' Sir Hugh Evans, and Sir Paul Pliant ; wrote farces and ' Whig and Tory ' (comedy), 1720. [xxiii. 225]

GRIFFIN, GERALD (1803–1840), dramatist, novelist, and poet ; came to London from Ireland, 1823 ; assisted by Banim ; returned to Limerick, 1838, and joined the Christian Brothers ; published stories illustrative of Munster life and ' The Collegians,' 1829 ; his play, ' Gisippus,' produced by Macready at Drury Lane, 1842. His novels and poems were edited by his brother, 1842–3, his poetical and dramatic works, 1857–9. [xxiii. 226]

GRIFFIN (originally WHITWELL), JOHN, ninth BARON HOWARD DE WALDEN (1719–1797), field-marshal ; served in Netherlands and Germany during Austrian succession and seven years' wars ; major-general, 1759 ; K.B., 1761 ; general, 1778 ; field-marshal, 1796 ; M.P., Andover, 1749–1784 ; succeeded to barony of Howard de Walden, 1784 ; created Baron Braybrooke, 1788. [xxiii. 227]

GRIFFIN, JOHN JOSEPH (1802–1877), chemist; a publisher till 1852; assisted in foundation of Chemical Society, 1840; did much to popularise chemistry by 'Chemical Recreations,' 1834, and other works.
[xxiii. 227]

GRIFFIN, THOMAS (1706?–1771), organ-builder; Gresham professor of music, 1763.   [xxiii. 228]

GRIFFIN, THOMAS (d. 1771), admiral; incurred much obloquy for not engaging two French ships off Ushant, 1745; vice-admiral, 1748; suspended for negligence while commanding in West Indies, 1750; reinstated, 1752; admiral, 1771; not employed again; M.P., Arundel, 1754–61.   [xxiii. 228]

GRIFFITH. [See also GRIFFIN, GRIFFITHS, and GRUFFYDD.]

GRIFFITH, ALEXANDER (d. 1690), divine; M.A. Hart Hall, Oxford, 1631; deprived of Welsh livings for loyalty; vicar of Glasbury, 1661; wrote against parliamentary itinerant preachers, 1654.   [xxiii. 230]

GRIFFITH, EDMUND (1570–1637), bishop of Bangor; M.A. Brasenose College, Oxford, 1592; canon of Bangor, 1600, dean, 1613, and bishop, 1634–7; D.D.   [xxiii. 230]

GRIFFITH, EDWARD (1790–1858), naturalist; educated at St. Paul's School; master in court of common pleas; F.R.S.; original member of Zoological Society; edited translation of Cuvier's 'Animal Kingdom,' 1827–1834; published collection of Huntingdon records, 1827.
[xxiii. 230]

GRIFFITH, Mrs. ELIZABETH (1720?–1793), playwright and novelist; married, c. 1752, Richard Griffith (d. 1788) [q. v.]; published 'Genuine Letters between Henry and Frances,' 1757, and novels, translations, and plays.   [xxiii. 231]

GRIFFITH, GEORGE (1601–1666), bishop of St. Asaph; of Westminster and Christ Church, Oxford; M.A., 1626; D.D., 1635; chaplain to Bishop John Owen; rector of Llanymynech, 1633; disputed with Vavasor Powell [q. v.], 1652–3; bishop of St. Asaph, 1660–6; helped to draw up form of baptisms for adults.
[xxiii. 231]

GRIFFITH or **GRIFFIN**, JOHN (fl. 1553), præmonstratensian, of Halesowen; published 'Conciones Æstivales' and 'Conciones Hyemales.'   [xxiii. 233]

GRIFFITH, JOHN (1622?–1700), general baptist minister of Dunning's Alley, Bishopsgate Street Without; frequently imprisoned.   [xxiii. 233]

GRIFFITH, JOHN (1714–1798), independent minister; published 'A Brand Plucked out of the Fire,' 1759.
[xxiii. 233]

GRIFFITH, MATTHEW (1599?–1665), master of the Temple; B.A. Gloucester Hall, Oxford, 1618; rector of St. Mary Magdalen, Old Fish Street, and (1640) St. Benet Sherehog; sequestered, 1642; D.D. Oxford, 1643; royal chaplain, 1643; helped to defend Basing House, 1645; his royalist sermon (1660) answered by Milton, 1660; master of the Temple and rector of Bladon, Oxfordshire, c. 1661–5.
[xxiii. 234]

GRIFFITH, **GRIFFYTH**, or **GRIFFYN**, MAURICE (d. 1558), bishop of Rochester; B.D. Oxford, 1582; archdeacon of Rochester, 1537; bishop, 1554–8. [xxiii. 234]

GRIFFITH, MOSES (1724–1785), physician; of Shrewsbury and St. John's College, Cambridge; M.D. Leyden, 1744; said to have invented Pharmacopœia iron mixture.   [xxiii. 235]

GRIFFITH, MOSES (fl. 1769–1809), draughtsman and engraver; employed by Thomas Pennant [q. v.] and Francis Grose [q. v.]   [xxiii. 235]

GRIFFITH, PIERS (d. 1628), naval adventurer; according to tradition commanded a ship against the Armada, and was disgraced for attacks on Spanish after the war; possibly identical with 'Welsh pirate' taken at Cork in 1603.   [xxiii. 235]

GRIFFITH, RICHARD (1635?–1691), physician; fellow of University College, Oxford, 1654; M.A., 1660; M.D. Caen, 1664; F.R.C.P., 1687, and twice censor; published 'A-la-Mode Phlebotomy no good fashion,' 1681.
[xxiii. 236]

GRIFFITH, RICHARD (d. 1719), navy captain; for recapturing with the aid of a boy a merchantman taken by the French, 1691, given command of the Mary galley, tender to the admiral at La Hogue, 1692; suspended for not maintaining discipline, but after 1702 reappointed commander.   [xxiii. 236]

GRIFFITH, RICHARD (d. 1788), author; collaborated with his wife, Elizabeth Griffith [q. v.]; published 'The Triumvirate . . . by Biograph Triglyph' (novel), 1764, and 'Variety' (comedy), acted 1782.   [xxiii. 237]

GRIFFITH, RICHARD (1752–1820), son of Richard Griffith (d. 1788) [q. v.]; deputy-governor, co. Kildare; sat for Askeaton in Irish parliament, 1783–90.
[xxiii. 238]

GRIFFITH, SIR RICHARD JOHN, first baronet (1784–1878), geologist and civil engineer; son of Richard Griffith (1752–1820) [q. v.]; surveyed coalfields of Leinster, 1808; reported on Irish bogs; professor of geology and mining engineer to Royal Dublin Society, 1812; inspector of Irish mines; Wollaston medallist for geological map, 1815; superintended road construction in the south, 1822–30; commissioner of valuation, 1828–68; chairman of Irish board of works, 1850–64; hon. LL.D. Dublin, 1851; created baronet, 1858.   [xxiii. 238]

GRIFFITH, WALTER (d. 1779), captain in the navy; gave Hawke important intelligence of French fleet off Brest, November 1759; took part in defence of Sandy Hook, 1778; present at actions off St. Lucia and Grenada, 1778–9; killed in Fort Royal Bay. [xxiii. 239]

GRIFFITH, WILLIAM (1810–1845), botanist; studied at London University under Lindley; entered East India Company's medical service, 1832; accompanied a botanical expedition to Assam and Burmah (1835–6), Bhotan, Khorassan, and Afghanistan; died at Malacca; works published posthumously by Dr. MacClelland.
[xxiii. 240]

GRIFFITH, WILLIAM PETTIT (1815–1884), architect and archæologist; F.R.I.B.A., 1842; superintended reparations at St. John's and St. James's churches, and St. John's Gate, Clerkenwell, 1845–51. His works include 'Ancient Gothic Churches,' 1847–52, 'Suggestions for a more Perfect and Beautiful Period of Gothic Architecture,' 1855, and papers on ornamental architecture.
[xxiii. 241]

GRIFFITHS, ANN (1780–1805), Welsh hymn-writer.
[xxiii. 242]

GRIFFITHS, DAVID (1792–1863), missionary in Madagascar, 1821–35; published New Testament in language of Madagascar; expelled, 1835; allowed to return as merchant, 1838; finally expelled, 1842; published 'History of Madagascar' in Welsh, and Malagasy grammar and text-books.   [xxiii. 242]

GRIFFITHS, EVAN (1795–1870), Welsh independent minister. His works include a Welsh-English dictionary, 1847, and Welsh versions of Matthew Henry's 'Commentary.'   [xxiii. 243]

GRIFFITHS, FREDERICK AUGUSTUS (d. 1869), major, R.A.; published 'Artillerist's Manual,' 1840.
[xxiii. 244]

GRIFFITHS, GEORGE EDWARD (d. 1829), editor of the 'Monthly Review' till 1825, and verse-writer; son of Ralph Griffiths [q. v.]   [xxiii. 246]

GRIFFITHS, JOHN (1731–1811), congregationalist; pastor of Glandwr, Pembrokeshire, and founder of expository classes; translated English hymns into Welsh; published works, including Welsh versions of the 'Shorter Catechism.'   [xxiii. 244]

GRIFFITHS, JOHN (1806–1885), keeper of the archives at Oxford; educated at Winchester and Wadham College, Oxford; B.A., 1827; fellow, 1830; sub-warden of Wadham College, 1837–54; one of the 'four tutors' who protested against 'Tract XC,' 1841; keeper of the archives at Oxford, 1857; warden of Wadham College, 1871–81; edited Inett's 'Origines Anglicanæ,' 1855, the 'Homilies,' 1859, two plays of Æschylus, and the Laudian 'Statutes,' 1888; published also work on Greek accents, 1831.
[xxiii. 244]

GRIFFITHS, alias ALFORD, MICHAEL (1587–1652). [See ALFORD.]

GRIFFITHS, RALPH (1720–1803), founder, proprietor and publisher of the 'Monthly Review'; previously partner with Thomas (Tom) Davies (1712?–1785) [q. v.] in an evening paper; started the 'Monthly Review,' 1749; assisted by Goldsmith, 1757–8, and his first wife; LL.D. Philadelphia.   [xxiii. 245]

GRIFFITHS, ROBERT (1805-1883), inventor; patented mechanical contrivances, including rivet-machine, 1835, and (with John Gold) glass-grinding and polishing machine, 1836; carried on engineering works at Havre with M. Labruère, 1845-8; his first screw propeller patented, 1849, improvements, 1853, 1858, 1878.
[xxiii. 246]

GRIFFITHS, THOMAS (1791-1847), Roman catholic prelate; president of St. Edmund's (new) College, 1818-33; bishop of Olena *in partibus*, 1833; vicar-apostolic of London district, 1836-47. [xxiii. 247]

GRIGNION or **GRIGNON**, CHARLES, the younger (1754-1804), painter; pupil of Cipriani; exhibited at Royal Academy, 1770-81; afterwards at Rome as history and portrait-painter; painted portrait of Nelson, 1798; died at Leghorn. [xxiii. 247]

GRIGNION or **GRIGNON**, CHARLES, the elder (1717-1810), line-engraver; uncle of Charles Grignion or Grignon the younger [q. v.]; studied under Gravelot and Le Bas; employed by Hogarth on his 'Canvassing for Votes' and 'Garrick as Richard III'; executed plates for Walpole's 'Anecdotes of Painting,' and other publications.
[xxiii. 247]

GRIGNION, REYNOLDS (d. 1787), engraver for the booksellers. [xxiii. 248]

GRIGOR, JAMES (1811?-1848), botanist; published 'Eastern Arboretum, or Register of Remarkable Trees, Seats, &c., in Norfolk,' 1840-1. [xxiii. 248]

GRIM, EDWARD (*fl.* 1170-1177), author of biography of Thomas Becket, c. 1175; eye-witness of Becket's murder. [xxiii. 248]

GRIMALD, **GRIMALDE**, or **GRIMOALD**, NICHOLAS (1519-1562), poet; B.A. Christ's College, Cambridge, 1540; M.A. Oxford, 1544; chaplain to Bishop Ridley; imprisoned as a protestant, 1555, but recanted; contributed verses to Tottel's 'Songs and Sonettes' (1557); published translations from Virgil and Cicero, and two Latin dramas, 'Archi-propheta' (printed 1548), and 'Christus Redivivus,' 1543. [xxiii. 249]

GRIMALDI, JOSEPH (1779-1837), actor and pantomimist; appeared as an infant dancer at Sadler's Wells; acted there and at Drury Lane for many years; played also at Dublin and in the provinces; his greatest successes as Squire Bugle and clown in 'Mother Goose' at Covent Garden. [xxiii. 250]

GRIMALDI, JOSEPH S. (d. 1863), pantomimist, son and successor of Joseph Grimaldi [q. v.] [xxiii. 251]

GRIMALDI, STACEY (1790-1836), antiquary; Marquis Grimaldi of Genoa; second son of William Grimaldi [q. v.]; eminent 'record lawyer' in London; F.S.A., 1824; frequent contributor to 'Gentleman's Magazine'; published 'Origines Genealogicæ,' 1828, and 'Genealogy of the Family of Grimaldi,' 1834; his 'Miscellaneous Writings,' edited, 1874-81. [xxiii. 251]

GRIMALDI,WILLIAM(1751-1830),miniature-painter; apprenticed to his uncle Thomas Worlidge [q. v.], whose 'Antique Gems' he published, 1768; copied in miniature pictures by Reynolds; exhibited at the Royal Academy, 1786-1824; enamel painter to George IV and the Duke of York. [xxiii. 252]

GRIMBALD, **GRIMBOLD**, or **GRYMBOLD**, SAINT (820?-903), abbot of new minster at Winchester; previously prior of St. Bertin in Flanders; came to Eng'and at Alfred's invitation, c. 893; one of Alfred's mass priests and educational assistants; the new minster built for him by Edward the Elder, 903; prominent in mythical story of Oxford. [xxiii. 252]

GRIMES, ROBERT (d. 1701). [See GRAHAM, ROBERT.]

GRIMESTONE, ELIZABETH (d. 1603). [See GRIMSTON.]

GRIMM, SAMUEL HIERONYMUS (1734-1794), water-colour painter; born at Burgdorf, Switzerland; came to London; exhibited at first exhibition of Royal Academy. [xxiii. 254]

GRIMSHAW, WILLIAM (1708-1763), incumbent of Haworth, Yorkshire, 1742-63; of Christ's College, Cambridge; acted with the methodists and John Wesley; preached throughout the north of England with great success. [xxiii. 254]

GRIMSHAWE, THOMAS SHUTTLEWORTH (1778-1850), biographer; M.A. Brasenose College, Oxford, 1800; vicar of Biddenham and rector of Burton Latimer; chief work, 'Life and Works of William Cowper,' 1835.
[xxiii. 255]

GRIMSTON, EDWARD (1528?-1599), comptroller of Calais, 1552-8; studied at Gonville Hall, Cambridge; after capture of Calais by Guise escaped from Bastille to London, 1559; muster-master of the north, 1560; M.P., Ipswich, 1563; employed as a spy in France.
[xxiii. 255]

GRIMSTON or **GRYMESTON**, ELIZABETH (d. 1603), author of 'Miscelanea: Meditations: Memoratives,' in verse, published, 1604. [xxiii. 256]

GRIMSTON, SIR HARBOTTLE, second baronet (1603-1685), speaker and judge; educated at Emmanuel College, Cambridge; barrister, Lincoln's Inn; recorder of Harwich, 1634, of Colchester, 1638-49; M.P., Harwich, 1628; sat for Colchester, 1640, and in Long parliament; prominent in debates of 1640-2, particularly on ecclesiastical questions; president of committee which inquired into escape of Charles I from Hampton Court, 1647; took leading part in negotiations with Charles I in the Isle of Wight; succeeded to baronetcy, 1648; excluded by Pride, 1648, and prevented from resuming his seat in 1656; appointed to council of state on abdication of Richard Cromwell, 1659; speaker of the Convention parliament, 1660; member of commission which tried regicides, 1660; master of the rolls, 1660-85; published 'Strena Christiana,' 1644 (Engl. trans., 1872), and law reports.
[xxiii. 257]

GRIMSTON, ROBERT (1816-1884), sportsman; of Harrow and Christ Church, Oxford; B.A., 1838; barrister, Lincoln's Inn, 1843; chairman, International Telegraph Company; chairman, Indo-European Telegraph Company, 1868; boxer, swimmer, rider, and cricketer.
[xxiii. 259]

GRIMSTON, SIR SAMUEL, third baronet (1643-1700), son of Sir Harbottle Grimston [q. v.]; M.P., St. Albans, 1668, 1679, 1680, and 1689-99; much disliked by James II.
[xxiii. 260]

GRIMSTON, WILLIAM LUCKYN, first VISCOUNT GRIMSTON (1683-1756), succeeded to the Grimston estates, and assumed the name, on death of uncle, Sir Samuel Grimston [q. v.], 1790; fourth baronet in succession to his father, Sir William Luckyn, 1716; M.P., St. Albans, 1710; created Baron Dunboyne and Viscount Grimston in peerage of Ireland, 1719; published 'The Lawyer's Fortune, or Love in a Hollow Tree,' 1705, a play ridiculed by Swift and Pope. [xxiii. 260]

GRINDAL, EDMUND (1519?-1583), archbishop of Canterbury; fellow of Pembroke Hall, Cambridge, 1538; M.A., 1541; D.D., 1564; proctor, 1548-9; chosen by Ridley as a protestant disputant at Cambridge; one of Ridley's chaplains; precentor of St. Paul's, 1551; one of the royal chaplains; at Strasburg and in Germany during Mary's reign; commissioner for revision of the liturgy, and bishop of London, 1558; master of Pembroke Hall, 1558-61; member of the high commission court; when bishop of London sympathised with puritans; as archbishop of York (1570-5) enforced uniformity on the Romish party; elected archbishop of Canterbury by Cecil's influence, 1576; undertook to reform the ecclesiastical courts; under sentence of suspension (1577-82) for refusing to carry out Elizabeth's mandate suppressing 'prophesyings'; eulogised in Spenser's 'Shepherd's Calendar.' [xxiii. 261]

GRINDAL, WILLIAM (d. 1548), tutor to Queen Elizabeth; fellow of St. John's College, Cambridge, 1543; a favourite pupil of Ascham; died of the plague.
[xxiii. 264]

GRINFIELD, EDWARD WILLIAM (1785-1864), biblical scholar; schoolfellow of De Quincey; M.A. Lincoln College, Oxford, 1808; minister of Laura Chapel, Bath; founded and endowed Oxford lectureship on Septuagint, 1859; published Hellenistic edition of New Testament, 'Apology for the Septuagint,' and theological pamphlets. [xxiii. 265]

GRINFIELD, THOMAS (1788-1870), divine and hymnwriter; brother of Edward William Grinfield [q. v.]; B.A. Trinity College, Cambridge, 1811; curate in charge of St. Mary-le-Port, Bristol; published religious verse, 'History of Preaching' (edited by Canon Eden, 1880), and other works. [xxiii. 265]

GRISAUNT, WILLIAM, or WILLIAM ENGLISH (*fl.* 1350), physician ; in youth taught philosophy at Oxford ; physician at Marseilles ; long reputed the father of Pope Urban V. [xxiii. 266]

GRISONI, GIUSEPPE (1692–1769), portrait-painter ; born at Florence ; brought to England by John Talman, 1715 ; died at Rome. [xxiii. 266]

GROCYN, WILLIAM (1446 ?–1519), Greek scholar ; educated at Winchester and New College, Oxford ; fellow, 1467 ; incumbent of Newton Longueville, 1481 ; divinity reader at Magdalen College, Oxford, 1481 ; prebendary of Lincoln, 1485 ; in Italy, 1488–90, with Linacre, studying under Politian and Chalcondyles ; became acquainted with Aldus the printer ; lectured in Greek at Oxford ; became rector of St. Lawrence Jewry, 1496, but did not reside in London till three years later ; criticised Dean Colet's lectures on ' The Ecclesiastical Hierarchy of Dionysius ' ; intimate in London with Linacre, More, and Erasmus ; master of All Hallows, Maidstone, 1506, and rector of Shepperton and Peckham ; catalogue of his library printed, 1889. [xxiii. 266]

GROENVELDT, JOHN (1647 ?–1710 ?), physician ; born at Deventer ; M.D. Utrecht, 1670 ; came to London, 1683 ; twice summoned before College of Physicians for internal use of cantharides ; published medical treatises. [xxiii. 269]

GROGAN, CORNELIUS (1738 ?–1798), United Irishman ; high sheriff of Wexford and M.P. for Enniscorthy, 1783–90 ; commissary-general in insurgent army, 1798 ; beheaded on Wexford Bridge. [xxiii. 269]

GROGAN, NATHANIEL (*d.* 1807 ?), painter of Irish life ; served in American war. [xxiii. 269]

GRONOW, REES HOWELL (1794–1865), writer of reminiscences ; intimate with Shelley at Eton ; served in 1st foot guards in the Peninsula, 1813–14 ; at Quatre Bras and Waterloo ; witnessed *coup d'état* of 1851 ; died in Paris. His ' Reminiscences ' appeared, 1861, 1863, 1865, 1866 (collected, 1888). [xxiii. 270]

GROOMBRIDGE, STEPHEN (1755–1832), astronomer and West India merchant ; published (1838) ' Catalogue of Circumpolar Stars . . . reduced to Jan. 1, 1810,' containing 4,243 star-places, among them No. 1,830, first observed by himself ; F.R.S., 1812 ; a founder of the Astronomical Society ; observed eclipses of the sun in 1816 and 1820. [xxiii. 270]

GROOMBRIDGE, WILLIAM (*fl.* 1770–1790), water-colour painter ; published 'Sonnets,' 1789. [xxiii. 271]

GROOME, JOHN (1678 ?–1760), divine ; B.A. Magdalene College, Cambridge, 1699, where he founded exhibitions ; vicar of Childerditch, Essex, 1709 ; published ' The Dignity and Honour of the Clergy,' 1710. [xxiii. 271]

GROOME, ROBERT HINDES (1810–1889), archdeacon of Suffolk ; M.A. Caius College, Cambridge, 1836 ; archdeacon of Suffolk, 1869–87 ; intimate with Edward Fitzgerald ; edited ' Christian Advocate and Review,' 1861–6 ; his Suffolk stories published posthumously. [xxiii. 272]

GROSART, ALEXANDER BALLOCH (1827–1899), author and editor ; studied at Edinburgh University ; licensed by Edinburgh presbytery, 1856 ; minister at Kinross, Loch Leven, 1856–65, Princes Park, Liverpool, 1865–8, and Blackburn, 1868–92 ; edited reprints of rare Elizabethan and Jacobean literature, besides the works of several puritan divines. His publications include ' Fuller Worthies Library,' 39 vols., 1868–76, ' Occasional Issues of Unique and very Rare Books,' 38 vols., 1875–81 ; ' Chertsey Worthies Library,' 14 vols., 1876–81, ' Huth Library,' 33 vols., 1886, Spenser's ' Works,' 10 vols., 1880–1888, Daniel's ' Works,' 5 vols., finished 1896. He also published several original devotional works. [Suppl. ii. 364]

GROSE, FRANCIS (1731 ?–1791), antiquary and draughtsman ; Richmond herald, 1755–63 ; F.S.A., 1757 ; met Burns during tour in Scotland ; in early life exhibited tinted drawings of architecture at the Academy ; died suddenly at Dublin ; published ' Antiquities of England and Wales,' 1773–87, with many drawings by himself, ' Antiquities of Scotland,' 1789–91, ' Classical Dictionary of the Vulgar Tongue ' (1785, reissued as ' Lexicon Balatronicum,' 1811), and other works. [xxiii. 272]

GROSE, JOHN (1758–1821), divine ; son of John Henry Grose [q. v.] ; M.A. St. Mary Hall, Oxford ; minister of the Tower of London ; rector of Netteswell, Essex ; published ' Ethics, Rational and Theological,' 1782. [xxiii. 273]

GROSE, JOHN HENRY (*fl.* 1750–1783), writer to East India Company ; brother of Francis Grose [q. v.] ; his ' Voyage to the East Indies,' 1757, said to have been compiled from his notes by John Cleland. [xxiii. 274]

GROSE, SIR NASH (1740–1814), judge ; fellow of Trinity Hall, Cambridge ; LL.B., 1768 ; barrister, Lincoln's Inn, 1766 ; serjeant-at-law, 1774 ; judge of king's bench, 1787–1813 ; knighted, 1787. [xxiii. 274]

GROSSE, ALEXANDER (1596 ?–1654), presbyterian divine ; M.A. Gonville and Caius College, Cambridge ; M.A. Exeter College, Oxford ; B.D. Oxford, 1632 ; rector of Bridford, and Ashburton, Devonshire ; published devotional works. [xxiii. 274]

GROSSETESTE, ROBERT (*d.* 1253), bishop of Lincoln ; of humble birth ; educated at Oxford and (probably) Paris ; first rector of Franciscans at Oxford, 1224 ; chancellor of Oxford ; archdeacon successively of Wilts, Northampton, and Leicester ; prebendary of Lincoln, 1221 ; bishop, 1235–53 ; maintained his right of visitation against the Lincoln chapter after a six years' dispute (1239–45) and a journey to Rome ; had disputes also with the Canterbury monks and Henry III ; resisted Archbishop Boniface's visitation, 1250 ; failed in an appeal to the pope against the appropriation by monks of parochial revenues ; preached at Lyons against papal abuses ; suspended by the pope for refusing to appoint an Italian to a benefice, 1251 ; chief opponent of Henry III's demand for a tenth of church revenues, 1252 ; wrote letter refusing to induct pope's nephew to a Lincoln canonry, 1253 ; translated Greek books ; wrote works on theology, philosophy, and husbandry, and commentaries on Aristotle and Boethius, besides French poems. Grosseteste's ' Le Chasteau d'Amour,' was edited by R. F. Weymouth, 1864, ' Carmina Anglo-Normannica,' printed, 1844. [xxiii. 275]

GROSVENOR, GRAVENOR, or GRAVENER, BENJAMIN (1676–1758), dissenting divine ; presbyterian pastor at Crosby Square, 1704–49 ; ' merchants' lecturer ' at Salters' Hall, 1716 ; contributed to ' Bagweell Papers,' 1716 ; said to have drawn up ' Authentick Account ' (1719) of the Salters' Hall proceedings ; Williams trustee, 1723 ; his sermons collected, 1809. [xxiii. 278]

GROSVENOR, HUGH LUPUS, first DUKE OF WESTMINSTER (1825–1899), son of Richard Grosvenor, second marquis of Westminster [q. v.] ; educated at Balliol College, Oxford ; liberal M.P. for Chester, 1847–69 ; opposed government on franchise question, 1866 ; succeeded as third Marquis of Westminster, 1870 ; created Duke of Westminster, 1874 ; master of horse, 1880–5 ; opposed home rule, 1886 ; K.G., 1870 ; privy councillor, 1880 ; aide-de-camp to queen, 1881 ; lord-lieutenant of Cheshire, 1883, and of county of London, 1888 ; breeder of race-horses. [Suppl. ii. 366]

GROSVENOR, JOHN (1742–1823), surgeon ; successful in friction treatment ; proprietor and editor of ' Oxford Journal,' 1795. [xxiii. 280]

GROSVENOR, RICHARD, first EARL GROSVENOR (1731–1802), horse-breeder ; grandson of Sir Thomas Grosvenor [q. v.] ; M.A. Oriel College, Oxford, 1751 ; D.C.L., 1754 ; succeeded as seventh baronet, 1755 ; mayor of Chester, 1759 ; M.P., Chester, 1754–61 ; created baron, 1761, earl, 1784 ; patron of William Gifford (1756–1826) [q. v.] [xxiii. 280]

GROSVENOR, RICHARD, second MARQUIS OF WESTMINSTER (1795–1869), M.P. (Viscount Belgrave) for Chester, 1818–20, and 1826–30, Cheshire, 1831–2, South Cheshire, 1832–5 ; succeeded to marquisate, 1845 ; lord-lieutenant, Cheshire, 1845–67 ; lord steward under Russell, 1850–2. [xxiii. 281]

GROSVENOR, SIR ROBERT (*d.* 1396), defendant in Scrope *v.* Grosvenor ; saw military service at Poitiers, 1356, Najara, 1367, La Roche-sur-Yon, 1369, and siege of Limoges, 1370 ; challenged by Sir Richard Scrope for wearing the arms, ' azure, a bend or,' 1385 ; judgment given against him by the constable, 1389, and confirmed by the king, 1390 ; sheriff of Cheshire, 1394. [xxiii. 281]

GROSVENOR, ROBERT, second EARL GROSVENOR and first MARQUIS OF WESTMINSTER (1767–1845), son of Richard, first earl Grosvenor [q. v.]; M.A. Trinity College, Cambridge, 1786; M.P. (Viscount Belgrave) for St. Looe, 1788–90, Chester, 1790–1802; a lord of the admiralty, 1789–91; commissioner of the board of control, 1793–1801; succeeded as Earl Grosvenor, 1802; created marquis, 1831; K.G., 1841; joined whigs after Pitt's death; laid out Belgravia, 1826, and rebuilt Eaton Hall, Cheshire, 1803; great picture collector and racer; acquired by marriage Egerton estates, 1794. [xxiii. 282]

GROSVENOR, LORD ROBERT, first BARON EBURY (1801–1893), son of Robert Grosvenor, first marquis of Westminster [q. v.]; educated at Westminster and Christ Church, Oxford; B.A., 1821; entered Lincoln's Inn, 1821; whig M.P. for Shaftesbury, 1822–6, Chester, 1826–47, and Middlesex, 1847–57; privy councillor, 1830; treasurer of household, 1846; created Baron Ebury, 1857; devoted himself to cause of protestantism in church of England; opposed home rule; published personal journals, and pamphlets advocating liturgical reform.
[Suppl. ii. 368]

GROSVENOR, SIR THOMAS, third baronet (1656–1700); succeeded his grandfather, 1664; many years M.P. for Chester; sheriff of the county, 1688; by his marriage with Mary Davies, daughter of a London scrivener, obtained the bulk of the present Westminster estates.
[xxiii. 283]

GROSVENOR, THOMAS (1764–1851), field-marshal; nephew of Richard Grosvenor, first earl Grosvenor [q. v.]; with 1st foot guards in Flanders, Holland, and (1799), the Helder expedition; commanded brigades in Copenhagen (1807) and Walcheren (1809) expeditions; general, 1819; field-marshal, 1846; M.P., Chester, 1795–1825, Stockbridge, 1825–30. [xxiii. 283]

GROTE, ARTHUR (1814–1886), Bengal civilian; president of Asiatic Society of Bengal, 1859–62 and 1865; brother of George Grote [q. v.] [xxiii. 284]

GROTE, GEORGE (1794–1871), historian; brother of Arthur Grote [q. v.]; educated at Charterhouse; a banker till 1843; became acquainted through Ricardo with James Mill and Bentham; compiled for Bentham 'Analysis of the Influence of Natural Religion on Temporal Happiness . . . by Philip Beauchamp,' 1822; joined J. S. Mill's reading society; reviewed Mitford's 'Greece' in the 'Westminster,' 1826; an original founder of the first London University, 1828–30; visited Paris, 1830, and began relations with French liberals; took active part in Reform agitation; M.P. for city of London, 1832–41; brought forward four resolutions (1833, 1835, 1838, 1839) and two bills (1836, 1837) in favour of the ballot; retired to devote himself to his history, completing the first two volumes, 1845; re-elected to council of University College, London, 1849; treasurer, 1860, and president, 1868; procured the rejection of Dr. Martineau for the chair of logic on the ground of sectarianism, 1866; guarded the endowment which (dated 1869) he left for a similar professorship by a provision against payment to any minister of religion; advocated examinations and the admission of women to them; trustee of the British Museum, 1859; D.C.L. Oxford, 1853; LL.D. Cambridge, 1861; F.R.S., 1857; vice-chancellor, London University, 1862; foreign associate of the Académie des Sciences, 1864; declined a peerage, 1869; buried in Westminster Abbey. 'The History of Greece' (1846–56, 8 vols.) has been four times reissued (lastly, 1888, 10 vols.), and translated into French and German. His 'Minor Works' were edited by Professor Bain, 1873. [xxiii. 284]

GROTE, HARRIET (1792–1878), biographer; née Lewin; married George Grote [q. v.], 1820; intimate with Mendelssohn and Jenny Lind; published 'Memoir of Ary Scheffer,' 1860, and 'Personal Life of George Grote,' 1873, besides the privately printed 'Philosophic Radicals of 1832.' [xxiii. 293]

GROTE, JOHN (1813–1866), philosopher; brother of George Grote [q. v.]; fellow of Trinity College, Cambridge, 1837–45; B.A., 1835; incumbent of Trumpington, 1847–66; Knightsbridge professor of moral philosophy, 1855–66; published 'Exploratio Philosophica,' 1865; his 'Examination of Utilitarian Philosophy' (1870) and 'Treatise on Moral Ideals' (1876) edited by the Rev. J. B. Mayor. [xxiii. 294]

GROVE, SIR GEORGE (1820–1900), writer on music; articled as civil engineer; M.I.C.E., 1839; superintended

erection of lighthouses at Morant Point, Jamaica, 1842, and on Gibbs' Hill, Bermuda, 1846; secretary to Society of Arts, 1849; secretary at Crystal Palace, where he paid special attention to development of music; compiled weekly, from 1856, analytical programmes of music, of which the more important were published in volume, 1884; editor of 'Macmillan's Magazine,' 1873; contributed to Smith's 'Dictionary of the Bible'; founder of Palestine Exploration Fund, 1865; projected and edited 'Dictionary of Music and Musicians,' 4 vols., 1878–89; first director of Royal College of Music at Kensington, 1883–94; knighted, 1883; C.B., 1894; honorary D.C.L. Durham, and LL.D. Glasgow; published writings on a great variety of subjects. [Suppl. ii. 369]

GROVE, HENRY (1684–1738), dissenting tutor; educated at Taunton grammar school and academy; intimate with Isaac Watts; from 1706 taught at Taunton academy; contributed to revived 'Spectator,' 1714; published 'System of Moral Philosophy' (ed. Amory, 1749) and treatises, including demonstration of the soul's immateriality, 1718. [xxiii. 295]

GROVE, JOSEPH (d. 1764), biographer. His works include 'Life and Times of Cardinal Wolsey,' 1742–4, and 'Lives of all the [Cavendish] Earls and Dukes of Devonshire,' 1764. [xxiii. 297]

GROVE, MATHEW (fl. 1587), poet; author of 'The most famous and tragicall historie of Pelops and Hippodamia' (ballad), 1587. [xxiii. 298]

GROVE, ROBERT (1634–1696), bishop of Chichester; of Winchester and St. John's College, Cambridge; fellow, 1658; M.A., 1660; D.D., 1681; chaplain to Bishop Henchman, 1667; rector of St. Andrew Undershaft, 1670; prebendary of St. Paul's, 1679; chaplain in ordinary, 1690; helped to draw up petition against declaration of indulgence, 1688; bishop of Chichester, 1691–6; published pamphlets against William Jenkyn [q. v.] [xxiii. 298]

GROVE, SIR WILLIAM ROBERT (1811–1896), man of science and judge; M.A. Brasenose College, Oxford, 1835; D.C.L., 1875; LL.D. Cambridge, 1879; barrister, Lincoln's Inn, 1835; member of Royal Institution, 1835, and vice-president, 1844; invented Grove gas voltaic battery, 1839; F.R.S., 1840, and royal medallist, 1847; professor of experimental philosophy, London Institution, 1847; published 'Correlation of Physical Forces,' 1846, establishing theory of mutual convertibility of forces; Q.C., 1853; member of royal commission on law of patents, 1864; judge of court of common pleas, 1871; invested with coif and knighted, 1871; judge of queen's bench, 1880; privy councillor, 1887. [Suppl. ii. 371]

GROVER, HENRY MONTAGUE (1791–1866), author; LL.B. Peterhouse, Cambridge, 1830; rector of Hitcham, Buckinghamshire, 1833–66; published works, including two dramatic poems and 'History of the Resurrection authenticated,' 1841. [xxii. 299]

GROVER, JOHN WILLIAM (1836–1892), civil engineer; educated at Marlborough College; pupil of Sir Charles Fox [q. v.]; employed in office of works of science and art department; set up as consulting engineer at Westminster, 1862; M.I.C.E., 1867; F.S.A.; vice-president of British Archæological Association; carried out several important engineering works, mainly in connection with railways and waterworks; assisted Major-general Walter Scott in design of Albert Hall; published engineering treatises and pamphlets. [Suppl. ii. 372]

GROVES, ANTHONY NORRIS (1795–1853), missionary; friend of John Kitto [q. v.]; a founder of the Plymouth Brethren; unsectarian missionary at Bagdad, 1830–3, and afterwards in India till 1852; died at George Müller's house at Bristol; his journals from 1829 to 1831 published posthumously. [xxiii. 299]

GROVES, JOHN THOMAS (d. 1811), architect; clerk of the works at St. James's, Whitehall, and Westminster, 1794; architect to the General Post Office, 1807; lived in Italy, 1780–90; exhibited Italian subjects at Royal Academy, 1791–2. [xxiii. 300]

GROZER, JOSEPH (fl. 1784–1798), mezzotint engraver. [xxiii. 300]

GRUB, GEORGE (1812–1892), Scottish ecclesiastical historian; educated at King's College, Aberdeen; apprenticed as advocate; admitted advocate, 1836, and was librarian to Society of Advocates, Aberdeen, 1841 till death; lecturer on Scots law, Marischal College, Aberdeen, 1843; professor of law, Aberdeen University, 1881–1891; A.M. Aberdeen, 1856; LL.D., 1864; assisted in formation of Spalding Club, for which he edited several works; published 'Ecclesiastical History of Scotland,' 1861.   [Suppl. ii. 373]

GRUBB, THOMAS (1800–1878), optician; constructed reflectors, including the Armagh fifteen-inch, 1835, the Glasgow observatory reflector (twenty inch), and the great Melbourne reflector (four feet), 1867; F.R.S., 1864; F.R.A.S., 1870.   [xxiii. 301]

GRUFFYDD AB **CYNAN** (1055?–1137), king of Gwynedd or North Wales; said to have been born at Dublin; defeated Trahaiarn and made himself master of Gwynedd, 1081; betrayed to Hugh of Chester and imprisoned before 1087; retaliated on the Normans with help of Rhys ab Tewdwr and a Norse fleet; again compelled to retire to Ireland, 1098; ruled Anglesey after 1099; compelled to pay tribute to Henry I, to whom he is said to have given up Gruffydd ab Rhys [q. v.], 1115; supported Henry I in invasion of Powys, 1121; patron of the clergy and of literature; introduced bagpipes and the Irish element into Welsh music.   [xxiii. 301]

GRUFFYDD AB **GWENWYNWYN** (d. 1286?), lord of Cyveiliog or Upper Powys; son of Gwenwynwyn [q. v.]; brought up in England; did homage for his father's estate to Henry III, 1241; faithful to Henry III during the revolt of Davydd II; deprived by Llywelyn ab Gruffydd [q. v.] of his dominions, fled to England, 1256–7; revolted and did homage to Llywelyn, 1263; plotted with his brother Davydd against Llywelyn, 1276, and thenceforth returned permanently to English allegiance.
                                                     [xxiii. 304]

GRUFFYDD AB **LLYWELYN** (d. 1063), king of the Welsh; slew Iago and made himself king over Gwynedd, 1039, and defeated English at Crossford; defeated Howel and his Norse allies, and secured possession of Deheubarth, 1044; in alliance with the outlawed Ælfgar of Mercia, ravaged Herefordshire and burnt Hereford; compelled by Harold to make peace, with the loss of his lands beyond the Dee, 1052; slew Gruffydd ab Rhydderch and became king of the Britons, 1055; renewed his ravages, 1056; again defeated the English, married Aldgyth (afterwards wife of Harold), and restored the outlawed Ælfgar, 1058; was finally crushed and treacherously slain in combined attack of Harold and Tostig.   [xxiii. 305]

GRUFFYDD AB **LLYWELYN** (d. 1244), Welsh prince; rebelled against his father, Llywelyn ab Iorwerth; headed army against William Marshall, earl of Pembroke, 1223–4; seized and imprisoned by his brother Davydd, 1239; handed over to Henry III, 1241; broke his neck in attempted escape from Tower of London.   [xxiii. 307]

GRUFFYDD AB **MADOG** (d. 1269), called GRUFFYDD OF BROMFIELD, lord of Lower Powys; refused to fight against the English, 1244; driven out by Llywelyn ab Gruffydd [q. v.], 1256, but in alliance with his next year; joined Scottish-Welsh confederacy, 1258.   [xxiii. 308]

GRUFFYDD AB **RHYDDERCH** (d. 1055), king of the South Welsh; headed opposition of the south to Gruffydd ab Llywelyn [q. v.], by whom he was at length slain.   [xxiii. 308]

GRUFFYDD AB **RHYS** (d. 1137), king or prince of South Wales (Deheubarth); returned from Ireland, c. 1113; took refuge with Gruffydd ab Cynan [q. v.], but fled from sanctuary to the south, to avoid being given up to the English; ravaged French and Flemish settlements; driven from his territories to Ireland, 1127; allied himself with king of North Wales; won battle of Aberteivi (Cardigan), 1136; recovered great part of his territory; slain by his wife's treachery.   [xxiii. 309]

GRUFFYDD AB **RHYS** (d. 1201), South Welsh prince; grandson of Gruffydd ab Rhys (d. 1137) [q. v.]; at feud with his brother Maelgwyn; obtained recognition from England, 1197, but fell into his brother's hands and was imprisoned by the English in Corfe Castle; died a monk at Strata Florida.   [xxiii. 310]

GRUFFYDD, THOMAS (1815–1887), harper; played at Buckingham Palace and Marlborough House, 1843; won many prizes at the Eisteddfodau; visited the Comte

de la Villemarqué in Brittany, 1867; harper to Edward VII, when Prince of Wales.   [xxiii. 311]

GRUNDY, JOHN (1782–1843), unitarian; minister at Nottingham, 1806–18, Cross Street, Manchester, 1818–24, and Paradise Street, Liverpool, 1824–35; published religious works.   [xxiii. 311]

GRUNDY, JOHN CLOWES (1806–1867), printseller and art patron.   [xxiii. 312]

GRUNDY, THOMAS LEEMING (1808–1841), engraver; brother of John Clowes Grundy [q. v.]; his best work 'The Lancashire Witch,' after W. Bradley.
                                                     [xxiii. 312]

GRUNEISEN, CHARLES LEWIS (1806–1879), journalist and musical critic; sub-editor of the 'Guardian,' 1832, of the 'Morning Post,' 1833; special correspondent with the Carlist army, 1837; captured by Christinists and saved only by intervention of Palmerston; Paris correspondent, 1839–44; organised an express system between Paris and London and sent despatches by pigeons; afterwards musical critic to 'Illustrated News' and 'Morning Chronicle,' and, from 1868, of the 'Athenæum'; initiated revival of Italian opera at Covent Garden, 1846, and superintended production of 'Le Prophète,' 1849. [xxiii. 312]

GRYG, GRUFFYDD (fl. 1330–1370), Welsh poet; chiefly noted for his poetical contention with David ab Gwilym.   [xxiii. 313]

GRYMESTON, ELIZABETH (d. 1603). [See GRIMSTON.]

GUADER or **WADER,** RALPH, EARL OF NORFOLK (fl. 1070), outlawed by Harold; retired to Brittany; at Hastings, the only British traitor, 1066; created Earl by William I; married, against his own wish, to Emma, daughter of William Fitzosbern [q. v.]; at the bridal conspired with Roger, earl of Hereford, against the king, 1075; fled and was outlawed; crusader with Robert of Normandy; at the siege of Nicæa, 1097; died 'in viâ Dei.'   [xxiii. 314]

GUALDRIC (d. 1112). [See GALDRIC.]

GUALENSIS, THOMAS (d. 1255). [See WALLENSIS.]

GUARO, WILLIAM (1300?). [See WILLIAM OF WARE.]

GUBBINS, MARTIN RICHARD (1812–1863), Anglo-Indian official; financial commissioner in Oudh, 1856–7; prominent at Lucknow during the mutiny; accompanied Sir Colin Campbell to Cawnpore; judge of the Agra supreme court, 1858–62; published 'The Mutinies in Oudh,' 1858; committed suicide at Leamington.   [xxiii. 315]

GUDWAL, SAINT (fl. 650), bishop and confessor; founded monastery in Devonshire (according to the Bollandists), at Cormon (according to Surius and Malebrancq).
                                                     [xxiii. 316]

GUDWAL or **GURVAL** (7th cent.), second bishop of St. Malo; disciple of St. Brendan.   [xxiii. 316]

GUERIN, THOMAS. [See GEERAN.]

GUERSYE, BALTHASAR (d. 1557), Italian physician; surgeon to Catherine of Arragon and Henry VIII; M.D. Cambridge, 1546; F.R.C.P., 1556.   [xxiii. 316]

GUEST, LADY CHARLOTTE. [See SCHREIBER.]

GUEST, GHEAST, or **GESTE,** EDMUND (1518–1577), bishop of Salisbury; M.A. King's College, Cambridge, 1544; while vice-provost of King's College, Cambridge, disputed on the protestant side, 1549; domestic chaplain to Parker and archdeacon of Canterbury, 1559; a reviser of the liturgy; bishop of Rochester, 1560–71; chancellor of the Garter, c. 1560, and chief almoner to Queen Elizabeth, 1560–72; D.D., 1571; bishop of Salisbury, 1571–7; friend of Cecil, Hatton, and Bacon; left his library to Salisbury Cathedral; maintained the real presence, 1564; translated psalms in 'Bishops' Bible.' [xxiii. 316]

GUEST, EDWIN (1800–1880), historical writer, philologist and historian; eleventh wrangler, Caius College, Cambridge, 1824; M.A., 1827; LL.D., 1853; D.C.L. Oxford, 1853; fellow, 1824; master, 1852–80; barrister, 1828; chief founder of the Philological Society, 1842; F.R.S., 1839; hon. sec. S.A., 1852; wrote 'History of English Rhythms,' 1838, papers on philology and Roman-British history, and 'Origines Celticæ,' ed. Stubbs and Deedes, 1883. [xxiii. 318]

GUEST, GEORGE (1771-1831), organist at St. Peter's, Wisbech, 1789-1831; son of Ralph Guest [q. v.]; composed cantatas, organ pieces, quartets, and glees. [xxiii. 319]

GUEST, JOSHUA (1660-1747), lieutenant-general: enlisted in the dragoons, 1685; served in Ireland, Flanders, and Spain; brevet-colonel, 1713; lieutenant-general, 1745; defended Edinburgh Castle against Prince Charles Edward, though, according to Chambers, a Jacobite; buried in Westminster Abbey. [xxiii. 319]

GUEST, SIR JOSIAH JOHN, baronet (1785-1852), ironmaster; as sole manager of Dowlais iron-works introduced chemical and engineering improvements; proprietor, 1849; M.P., Honiton, 1822-31, Merthyr Tydvil, 1832-52; mediator in Merthyr riots of 1831; F.R.S., 1830; created baronet, 1838. [xxiii. 320]

GUEST, RALPH (1742-1830), organist at St. Mary's, Bury St. Edmunds, 1805-22. [xxiii. 319]

GUEST, THOMAS DOUGLAS (*fl.* 1803-1839), historical and portrait painter; exhibited at Academy (1803-1838) and British Institution; published 'Inquiry into Causes of the Decline of Historical Painting,' 1829. [xxiii. 321]

GUIDOTT, THOMAS (*fl.* 1698), physician; M.A. Wadham College, Oxford, 1662; M.B., 1666; practised about Oxford, subsequently at Bath and in London; edited Jorden's 'Discourse of Natural Bathes' (3rd ed. 1669), Theophilus περὶ οὔρων, 1703, and Maplet's 'De Thermarum Bathoniensium Effectis,' 1694; published medical works on English spas. [xxiii. 322]

GUILD, WILLIAM (1586-1657), Scottish divine; member of the 'mutinous assembly' which in Edinburgh protested for the liberties of the kirk, 1617; D.D. and chaplain to Charles I; supported episcopacy, but took the covenant with reservations; principal of King's College, Aberdeen, 1640-51; deprived for lukewarmness, 1651; his 'Moses Unvailed,' 1620, dedicated to Bishop Andrewes; purchased the Trinity Friars' convent at Aberdeen and endowed it as a hospital. [xxiii. 323]

GUILDFORD, SIR HENRY (1489-1532), master of the horse and comptroller of the household; son of Sir Richard Guildford [q. v]; served against the Moors and was knighted by Ferdinand, 1511; king's standard-bearer in French campaign of 1513; accompanied Henry VIII to Field of Cloth of Gold (1520) and to Gravelines, and Wolsey to Calais; master of the horse, 1515-22; comptroller of the household; knight of the shire for Kent, 1529; signed articles against Wolsey, 1529, but remained his friend, though retaining Henry VIII's favour. [xxiii. 324]

GUILDFORD, NICHOLAS DE (*fl.* 1250), poet; supposed author of 'The Owl and the Nightingale' (first printed, 1838), and 'La Passyun Jhu Crist, en Engleys,' printed in Morris's 'Old English Miscellany.' [xxiii. 327]

GUILDFORD, SIR RICHARD (1455?-1506), master of the ordnance under Henry VII; attainted by Richard III; reclaimed land in Sussex (Guildford Level); built ships; attended Henry VII at Boulogne, 1492; sheriff of Kent; comptroller of the household; created banneret for services against Cornish rebels, 1497; K.G., 1500; died at Jerusalem on pilgrimage; his account printed by Pynson, 1511. [xxiii. 327]

GUILFORD, EARLS OF. [See NORTH, FRANCIS, first EARL, 1704-1790; NORTH, FREDERICK, second EARL, 1732-1792; NORTH, GEORGE AUGUSTUS, third EARL, 1757-1802; NORTH, FRANCIS, fourth EARL, 1761-1817; NORTH, FREDERICK, fifth EARL, 1766-1827.]

GUILFORD, BARONS. [See NORTH, FRANCIS, first BARON, 1637-1685; NORTH, FRANCIS, third BARON, 1704-1790.]

GUILLAMORE, VISCOUNTS. [See O'GRADY, STANDISH, first VISCOUNT, 1766-1840; O'GRADY, STANDISH, second VISCOUNT, 1792-1848.]

GUILLEMARD, WILLIAM HENRY (1815-1887), divine; of Christ's Hospital and Pembroke College, Cambridge; fellow, 1839; M.A., 1841; D.D., 1870; headmaster of Royal College, Armagh, 1848-69; vicar of St. Mary-the-Less, Cambridge, 1869-87; introduced Oxford movement at Cambridge; published 'Hebraisms of the Greek Testament,' 1879. [xxiii. 330]

GUILLIM, JOHN (1565-1621), herald; entered Brasenose College, Oxford, 1581; Rouge Croix pursuivant, 1619; systematised science of heraldry; published 'A Display of Heraldrie' (1610). [xxiii. 330]

GUINNESS, SIR BENJAMIN LEE, first baronet (1798-1868), brewer; succeeded his father as sole proprietor, 1855, and developed export side of the business; lord mayor of Dublin, 1851; restored St. Patrick's Cathedral at cost of 150,000*l.*, 1860-5; LL.D. Dublin, 1863; created baronet, 1867; M.P., Dublin, 1865-8. [xxiii. 331]

GUISE, JOHN (1680-1761). [See GUYSE.]

GUISE, JOHN (*d.* 1765), general; served with the 1st foot guards under Marlborough in Flanders; commanded the battalion in Vigo expedition, 1719; brigadier and colonel commanding 6th foot at Carthagena, 1739; major-general, 1742; general, 1762. [xxiii. 332]

GUISE, SIR JOHN WRIGHT, third baronet (1777-1865), general; served with 3rd foot guards at Ferrol, Vigo, and Cadiz, 1800, in Egypt, 1801, and Hanover, 1805-6; commanded light companies at Fuentes d'Onoro, and the first battalion in Spain, 1812-14; general, 1851; G.C.B., 1863; succeeded to baronetcy, 1834. [xxiii. 332]

GUISE, WILLIAM (1653?-1683), orientalist; fellow of All Souls', Oxford, 1674-80; M.A., 1677; his 'Misnæ Pars' (Mishnah), edited by Professor Edward Bernard [q. v.], 1690. [xxiii. 333]

GULL, SIR WILLIAM WITHEY, first baronet (1816-1890), physician to Queen Victoria; M.D. London, 1846; medical tutor and lecturer at Guy's Hospital, and (1856) physician; F.R.C.P., 1848 (councillor, 1863-4); Fullerian professor of physiology, 1847-9; F.R.S., 1869; D.C.L. Oxford, 1868; LL.D. Cambridge and Edinburgh, 1880; member of general medical council, 1871-83; attended Edward VII, when Prince of Wales, during his severe illness, 1871; created baronet, 1872; physician in ordinary to Queen Victoria, 1887-90; Gulstonian lecturer, 1849; Hunterian orator, 1861, and Harveian orator, 1870; pre-eminent as clinical physician. [xxiii. 333]

GULLIVER, GEORGE (1804-1882), anatomist and physiologist; prosector to Abernethy and dresser to Lawrence at St. Bartholomew's Hospital; F.R.S., 1838; F.R.C.S., 1843; Hunterian professor of comparative anatomy and physiology, 1861; surgeon to royal horse guards; edited medical works. [xxiii. 334]

GULLY, JAMES MANBY (1808-1883), physician; studied at Paris; M.D. Edinburgh, 1829; practised in London and afterwards at Malvern, where he and his friend James Wilson introduced the hydropathic treatment of disease; the 'Dr. Gullson' of Charles Reade's 'It is never too late to mend'; his reputation damaged by the Bravo case, 1876; published works, including 'The Water Cure in Chronic Disease,' 1846. [xxiii. 335]

GULLY, JOHN (1783-1863), prize-fighter and horseracer; fought Henry Pearce the 'Game Chicken' at Hailsham, 1805; leading boxer till 1808; won the Derby and the St. Leger, 1832, the Derby and Oaks, 1846, the Two Thousand, 1844, and the Derby and Two Thousand, 1854; M.P., Pontefract, 1832-7. [xxiii. 336]

GULSTON, JOSEPH (1745-1786), collector and connoisseur; born at Greenwich in romantic circumstances; spent a large fortune chiefly in collecting books and prints, the sale of the latter (1786) lasting forty days; M.P., Poole, 1780-4. [xxiii. 337]

GULSTON, THEODORE (1572-1632). [See GOULSTON.]

GUMBLE, THOMAS (*d.* 1676), biographer; chaplain to Monck in Scotland, 1655; entrusted by him with letters to the parliament and city, 1660; D.D. Cambridge and prebendary of Winchester, 1661; rector of East Lavant, Sussex, 1663; published 'Life of General Monck, Duke of Albemarle,' 1671. [xxiii. 338]

GUNDLEUS, SAINT (6th cent.). [See GWYNLLYW.]

GUNDRADA DE WARENNE (*d.* 1085), wife of William de Warrenne, first earl of Surrey, and co-founder with him of Lewes priory, 1077; her tombstone placed in St. John's Church, Southover, Lewes, at end of eighteenth century. [xxiii. 338]

GUNDRY, SIR NATHANIEL (1701 ?–1754), judge; barrister, Middle Temple, 1725; M.P., Dorchester, 1741–1750; K.C., 1742; judge of common pleas, 1750–4; died of gaol fever. [xxiii. 339]

GUNDULF (1024 ?–1108), bishop of Rochester; made a pilgrimage with William, archdeacon of Rouen, to Jerusalem; monk of Bec; followed Lanfranc to Caen and to England, and became his proctor; as bishop of Rochester (1077–1108) remodelled chapter on monastic basis and rebuilt cathedral; architect of the Tower of London, St. Leonard's Tower, West Malling, and other buildings; had charge of see of Canterbury during vacancy, 1089; exercised influence over William II; was attended on his deathbed by Anselm. [xxiii. 339]

GUNN, BARNABAS (d. 1753), musical composer; organist at Gloucester Cathedral, 1732–40, at St. Philip's and St. Martin's, Birmingham, 1740–53, and Chelsea Hospital, 1750–3; published 'Six Solos for Violin and Violoncello,' 1745, and songs and cantatas. [xxiii. 341]

GUNN, DANIEL (1774–1848), congregational minister; celebrated for his unemotional preaching and his schools at Christchurch, Hampshire. [xxiii. 342]

GUNN, JOHN (fl. 1790), musical writer; published 'Treatise on the Origin of Stringed Instruments,' 1789, and a supplemental 'Forty favourite Scotch Airs adapted for Violin, Violoncello, or Flute,' also 'Historical Enquiry respecting the performances of the Harp in the Highlands' (1807) and works on the flute. [xxiii. 342]

GUNN, ROBERT CAMPBELL (1808–1881), naturalist; superintendent of convict prisons in Tasmania, whence he sent home plants and animals; F.L.S., 1850; F.R.S., 1854; died at Hobart Town. [xxiii. 342]

GUNN, WILLIAM (1750–1841), antiquarian writer; B.D. Caius College, Cambridge, 1795; rector of Barton Turf and Irstead, Norfolk, 1786–1829, and afterwards of Gorleston; published 'Extracts' from state papers in the Vatican and other libraries, 1803, a tenth-century manuscript of 'Historia Britonum,' 1819, and an account of the Vatican tapestries, 1831. [xxiii. 343]

GUNNING, ELIZABETH, afterwards DUCHESS OF HAMILTON and OF ARGYLL (1734–1790), famous beauty; youngest daughter of James Gunning, of Castlecoote, Roscommon; secretly married James, sixth duke of Hamilton, at midnight in Mayfair chapel, 14 Feb. 1752, and in 1759 John Campbell, afterwards duke of Argyll; lady of the bedchamber to Queen Charlotte; created Baroness Hamilton, 1776. [xxiii. 343]

GUNNING, ELIZABETH, afterwards MRS. PLUNKETT (1769–1823), novelist; daughter of Susannah Gunning [q. v.] [xxiii. 349]

GUNNING, HENRY (1768–1854), senior esquire bedell of Cambridge University; scholar of Christ's College, Cambridge; sixth wrangler, 1788; M.A., 1791; esquire bedell, 1789 (senior, 1827–54); published 'Reminiscences of the University, Town, and County of Cambridge,' 1854, and new edition of Wall's 'Ceremonies observed in the Senate House.' [xxiii. 344]

GUNNING, JOHN (d. 1798), surgeon to St. George's Hospital, 1765–98; as master of the Surgeons' Company (1789–90) effected many reforms; had violent controversies with John Hunter, whom he succeeded as surgeon-general, 1793. [xxiii. 345]

GUNNING, MARIA, afterwards COUNTESS OF COVENTRY (1733–1760). [See COVENTRY.]

GUNNING, PETER (1614–1684), bishop of Ely; ancestor of the famous beauties; fellow and tutor of Clare Hall, Cambridge, 1633; M.A., 1635; famous as royalist preacher when incumbent of Little St. Mary's; retired to Oxford, 1646; during the Commonwealth celebrated episcopalian service at Exeter Chapel, Strand; D.D., 1660; master of Clare College, Cambridge, and Lady Margaret professor of divinity, 1660; master of St. John's and regius professor, 1661; proctor for Canterbury and Peterborough in the lower house of convocation; prominent in Savoy conference; bishop of Chichester, 1669–75, of Ely, 1675–84; his 'Paschal or Lent Fast' (1662) republished, 1845. [xxiii. 345]

GUNNING, SIR ROBERT, baronet (1731–1816), diplomatist; plenipotentiary at Copenhagen, 1768; transferred to Berlin, 1771; ambassador at St. Petersburg, 1772–5; negotiated for employment of Russian troops in America, 1775; K.B., 1778; created baronet, 1778. [xxiii. 348]

GUNNING, MRS. SUSANNAH (1740 ?–1800), novelist; née Minifie; married John Gunning (afterwards lieutenant-general), brother of the famous beauties, 1768; joined her daughter, Elizabeth Gunning [q. v.], when her husband turned the girl out of the house, both being received by the Duchess of Bedford; published several novels; her 'Memoirs of Mary' (1793) supposed to mention family scandals. [xxiii. 349]

GUNTER, EDMUND (1581–1626), mathematician; educated at Westminster and Christ Church, Oxford; M.A., 1606; B.D., 1615; incumbent of St. George's, Southwark, 1615; Gresham professor of astronomy, 1619–1626; discovered by experiments at Deptford variation of the magnetic needle, 1622; introduced 'Gunter's chain' and the decimal separator; 'Gunter's Line' or rule of proportion described in his 'Book of the Sector'; published 'Canon Triangulorum; or, Table of Artificial Sines and Tangents,' 1620; complete works edited by Samuel Foster (1636) and William Leybourn (1673). [xxiii. 350]

GUNTHORPE or **GUNDORP**, JOHN (d. 1498), dean of Wells; chaplain to Edward IV; warden of the king's hall at Cambridge, 1468–77; prebendary of Lincoln, 1471–98; dean of Wells, 1472–98; keeper of the privy seal, 1483; employed to treat with the Emperor Maximilian, 1486, Ferdinand and Isabella, 1488, and other European princes; built deanery at Wells. [xxiii. 351]

GUNTON, SIMON (1609–1676), divine and antiquary; M.A. Magdalene College, Cambridge, 1634; vicar of Pytchley, 1637, of Peterborough, 1660–6, and of Fiskerton, Lincolnshire, 1666–76; history of Peterborough Cathedral compiled from his collection issued 1686. [xxiii. 352]

GURDON or **GORDON**, SIR ADAM DE (d. 1305), warrior; fought against Henry III in barons' war; repulsed Welsh, 1265; defeated in single combat by Prince Edward, 1266, who restored his estates; a justice of the forest and commissioner of array in Hampshire, Dorset, and Wiltshire under Edward I. [xxiii. 352]

GURDON, BRAMPTON (d. 1741), Boyle lecturer; fellow of Caius College, Cambridge; M.A., 1695; chaplain to Lord Macclesfield; archdeacon of Sudbury, 1727; rector of Denham, 1730, of St. Edmund the King, Lombard Street, 1732; his Boyle lectures (1721–2), 'The Pretended Difficulties in Natural or Reveal'd Religion no Excuse for Infidelity,' printed 1723. [xxiii. 353]

GURDON, JOHN (1595 ?–1679), parliamentarian; M.P. for Ipswich in Long parliament; M.P., Suffolk, 1654; member of Eastern Counties Association; member of council of state, 1650; refused to attend when commissioner for Charles I's trial. [xxiii. 353]

GURDON, THORNHAGH (1663–1733), antiquary; brother of Brampton Gurdon [q. v.]; M.A. Caius College, Cambridge, 1682; F.S.A., 1718; receiver-general of Norfolk; published 'Essay on the Antiquity of the Castel of Norwich,' 1728, and a history of parliament, 1731. [xxiii. 353]

GURNALL, WILLIAM (1617–1679), divine; M.A. Emmanuel College, Cambridge, 1639; rector of Lavenham, Suffolk, 1644–79; published 'The Christian in Complete Armour,' 1655, 1658, 1662. [xxiii. 354]

GURNEY, ANNA (1795–1857), Anglo-Saxon scholar; though paralysed throughout life visited Rome, Athens, and Argos; first female member (1845) of British Archæological Association; published privately 'Literal Translation of the Saxon Chronicle. By a Lady in the Country,' 1819. [xxiii. 354]

GURNEY, ARCHER THOMPSON (1820–1887), divine and author; son of Richard Gurney [q. v.]; chaplain to the Court Chapel, Paris, 1858–71; published books of verse, including 'Songs of the Present,' 1854, and 'Iphigenia at Delphi' (tragedy), 1855; also translations from the German and prose treatises. [xxiii. 354]

GURNEY, DANIEL (1791–1880), banker and antiquary; F.S.A.; printed privately essays on banking and 'Record of the House of Gournay,' 1858. [xxiii. 355]

T

GURNEY or **GURNAY**, EDMUND (d. 1648), divine;
B.A. Queens' College, Cambridge, 1600; Norfolk fellow of
Corpus Christi College, Cambridge, 1601; B.D., 1609;
rector of Edgefield, Norfolk, 1614, of Harpley, 1620; published anti-Romanist treatises. [xxiii. 356]

GURNEY, EDMUND (1847-1888), philosophical
writer; third son of John Hampden Gurney [q. v.];
fourth classic, 1871; fellow of Trinity College, Cambridge, 1872; studied successively music, medicine, and
law; afterwards devoted himself to experimental psychology, and was one of the chief founders of the Society
for Psychical Research, 1882, in whose 'Proceedings' and
'Journal' he wrote on hallucination and hypnotism;
published 'The Power of Sound,' 1880, 'Phantasms of the
Living,' 1886 (with Frederic William Henry Myers [q. v.]
and Mr. F. Podmore), and 'Tertium Quid,' 1887.
[xxiii. 356]

GURNEY, SIR GOLDSWORTHY (1793-1875), inventor; in a course of chemistry lectures at the Surrey
Institution anticipated principle of electric telegraph;
invented oxy-hydrogen blow-pipe, and discovered the so-
called 'Drummond Light'; his steam-jet first applied to
steamboats, 1824; with his steam carriage went from
London to Bath and back at rate of fifteen miles an hour,
1829; extinguished mine fires by his steam-jet; principle
of 'Gurney stove' applied in warming and ventilation of
old House of Commons; superintended lighting and ventilation in new houses of parliament, 1854-63; knighted,
1863; published descriptions of his inventions and 'Observations pointing out a means by which a Seaman may
identify Lighthouses' (1864). [xxiii. 358]

GURNEY, HUDSON (1775-1864), antiquary and
verse-writer; half-brother of Anna Gurney [q. v.]; friend
of Lord Aberdeen; M.P., Newtown, Isle of Wight, from
1816; F.R.S., 1818; vice-president, Society of Antiquaries,
1822-46; published 'Cupid and Psyche,' 1799, 'Heads of
Ancient History,' 1814, a verse translation of 'Orlando
Furioso,' 1843, and 'Norfolk Topographer's Manual' and
'History of Norwich Castle.' [xxiii. 360]

GURNEY, JOHN (1688-1741), quaker; friend of Sir
Robert Walpole; ably defended Norwich wool-trade before
parliamentary committee, 1720. [xxiii. 361]

GURNEY, SIR JOHN (1768-1845), judge; son of
Joseph Gurney (1744-1815) [q. v.]; educated at St. Paul's
School; barrister, Inner Temple, 1793; junior counsel for
Hardy, Horne Tooke, and Thelwall, 1794; defended Cross-
field, 1796, and Arthur O'Connor, 1798; K.C. after prose-
cuting Cochrane, 1816; procured conviction of two Cato
Street conspirators, 1820; baron of the exchequer, 1832-
1845, and knighted, 1832. [xxiii. 361]

GURNEY, JOHN HAMPDEN (1802-1862), author;
eldest son of Sir John Gurney [q. v.]; M.A. Trinity College, Cambridge, 1827; rector of St. Mary's, Bryanstone
Square, 1847-62; prebendary of St. Paul's, 1857. His works
include 'Psalms and Hymns for Public Worship,' 1852,
and three series of 'Historical Sketches.' [xxiii. 362]

GURNEY, JOSEPH (1744-1815), shorthand writer;
son of Thomas Gurney [q. v.]; employed on official reports of civil cases from 1790; ordered to read from his
notes of the Warren Hastings trial words of Burke
accusing Impey of murder, 1789; reported election petition committees, 1791; published thirteen reports, 1775-
1796; edited ninth edition of 'Brachygraphy,' 1778.
[xxiii. 368]

GURNEY, JOSEPH (1804-1879), shorthand writer
and biblical scholar; son of William Brodie Gurney [q. v.];
reporter to houses of parliament, 1849-72; published
'The Annotated Paragraph Bible,' 1850-60, and 'The
Revised English Bible,' 1877. [xxiii. 363]

GURNEY, JOSEPH JOHN (1788-1847), quaker
philanthropist and writer; brother of Daniel Gurney
[q. v.] and Mrs. Elizabeth Fry [q. v.]; studied classics at
Oxford; quaker minister, 1818; interested in prison reform,
negro emancipation, and the abolition of capital punishment; visited the chief European countries, and in 1837-
1840 the United States, Canada, and the West Indies; published 'Essays on the Evidences, Doctrines, and Practical
Operation of Christianity,' 1825, and 'Biblical Notes and
Dissertations,' 1830, his 'Letters to Mrs. Opie,' and 'Autobiography,' printed privately; his 'Chalmeriana' published posthumously. [xxiii. 363]

GURNEY or **GURNARD**, SIR RICHARD, baronet
(1577-1647), lord mayor of London, 1641-2; created baronet
by Charles I; refused to call out the trained bands to keep
the peace when the arrest of the five members was contemplated, 1642; imprisoned in the Tower, 1642-7, for
causing to be read the king's proclamation against parliament's militia ordinance, 1642. [xxiii. 364]

GURNEY, RICHARD (1790-1843), vice-warden of
the stannaries of Devon, and author of 'Fables on Men
and Manners,' 1809, 'The Maid of Prague,' 1841, and other
works; died at Bonn. [xxiii. 354]

GURNEY, RUSSELL (1804-1878), recorder of London; son of Sir John Gurney [q. v.]; B.A. Trinity College, Cambridge, 1826; barrister, Inner Temple, 1828;
common pleader in city of London, 1830; Q.C., 1845;
judge of sheriff's court, 1850; common serjeant, 1856;
recorder, 1857-78; M.P., Southampton, 1865; took charge
of Married Women's Property Bill (1870) and other important measures; commissioner in Jamaica, 1865, and
for treaty of Washington, 1871; privy councillor, 1866;
served on many royal commissions. [xxiii. 365]

GURNEY, SAMUEL (1786-1856), bill-discounter and
philanthropist; brother of Joseph John Gurney [q. v.];
entered firm of Richardson & Overend (afterwards Overend, Gurney & Co.), 1807; became known as 'the banker's
banker'; worked for reform of criminal code; interested
in the Niger expedition of 1841, and the colony of Liberia;
treasurer of British and Foreign School Society from
1843. [xxiii. 366]

GURNEY, THOMAS (1705-1770), shorthand writer;
clockmaker near Blackfriars Road; shorthand teacher;
his engagement at the Old Bailey the first official appointment of a shorthand writer; afterwards practised
in other courts and in the House of Commons; his
'Brachygraphy' (1750) originally an improvement on
William Mason's 'Shorthand,' frequently reissued and improved. Gurney's 'System' was employed by Sir Henry
Cavendish [q. v.], and later for most government and
parliamentary work. [xxiii. 367]

GURNEY, WILLIAM BRODIE (1777-1855), shorthand writer and philanthropist; brother of Sir John
Gurney [q. v.]; reported trials, speeches, &c., throughout
the United Kingdom, 1803-44; official reporter to parliament from 1813; mentioned in 'Don Juan'; edited
fifteenth and sixteenth editions of 'Brachygraphy' (1824-
1835), and the 'Youth's Magazine' (commenced 1805);
president of Sunday School Union; treasurer of Stepney
College and the baptist foreign missions. [xxiii. 369]

GURWOOD, JOHN (1790-1845), editor of the 'Wellington Despatches'; served in Peninsula as subaltern of
52nd till storming of Ciudad Rodrigo, 1812, where he was
severely wounded; exchanged into cavalry; aide-de-
camp to Sir Henry Clinton in the Netherlands; severely
wounded at Waterloo; brevet-colonel, 1841; as private
secretary to Wellington edited his despatches, 1837-44;
C.B. and deputy-lieutenant of the Tower; committed
suicide. [xxiii. 370]

GUTCH, JOHN (1746-1831), antiquary and divine;
M.A. All Souls' College, Oxford, 1771; chaplain of All
Souls', 1770, of Corpus Christi College, Oxford, 1778;
registrar of the university, 1797-1824; rector of St.
Clement's, 1795-1831; published 'Collectanea Curiosa,'
1781, and, from Wood's manuscripts, 'History and Antiquities of the Colleges and Halls in the University of
Oxford,' 1786, 'Fasti Oxonienses,' 1790, and 'History of
the University of Oxford,' 1792-6. [xxiii. 370]

GUTCH, JOHN MATHEW (1776-1861), journalist;
eldest son of John Gutch [q. v.]; at Christ's Hospital
with Coleridge and Lamb; lodged with Lamb, 1800;
removed to Bristol, 1803, and conducted 'Felix Farley's
Bristol Journal' till 1844; prosecuted for libels on
George IV and Lord Lyndhurst in London 'Morning
Journal,' 1829; edited George Wither's 'Poems,' 1820,
and Robin Hood 'Ballads,' 1850 and 1867; called the
'Bristol Junius' from his 'Letters of Cosmo.'
[xxiii. 371]

GUTCH, JOHN WHEELEY GOUGH (1809-1862),
queen's messenger; son of John Mathew Gutch [q. v.];
edited 'Literary and Scientific Register,' 1842-56.
[xxiii. 372]

GUTCH, ROBERT (1777–1851), divine; second son of John Gutch [q. v.]; fellow of Queens' College, Cambridge, 1802; M.A., 1804; rector of Seagrave, Leicestershire, 1809–51; published anonymously satirical tract on a Roman catholic miracle, 1836. [xxiii. 371]

GUTHLAC, SAINT (663 ?–714), of the Mercian royal race; after a youth spent in war entered monastic community at Repton; hermit in the Isle of Crowland for fifteen years; visited by Æthelbald, who, on becoming king of Mercia, built over his shrine Crowland Abbey. [xxiii. 373]

GUTHRIE, SIR DAVID (*fl.* 1479), lord treasurer of Scotland; sheriff of Forfarshire, 1457, and armour-bearer to James II; lord treasurer of Scotland, 1461 and 1467; comptroller of the household, 1466; clerk of the register, 1468; master of the rolls, 1469; lord chief-justice, 1473; founded collegiate church at Guthrie. [xxiii. 374]

GUTHRIE, FREDERICK (1833–1886), scientific writer; B.A. London, 1855; Ph.D. Marburg, 1854; studied under Bunsen at Heidelberg; assisted Frankland at Owens College and Playfair at Edinburgh; professor of chemistry and physics in Royal College, Mauritius, 1861–7; afterwards professor in the Normal School of Science, South Kensington; founded Physical Society of London, 1873; discovered 'approach caused by vibration,' 1870, and 'cryohydrates'; published 'Elements of Heat,' 1868, and 'Magnetism and Electricity,' 1873, and under the pseudonym Frederick Cerny, poems, 'The Jew' (1863) and 'Logroño' (1877). [xxiii. 374]

GUTHRIE, GEORGE JAMES (1785–1856), surgeon; with the 29th in Canada as assistant-surgeon; in the Peninsula, 1808–14; at Waterloo performed several novel operations; declined knighthood; founded eye infirmary (afterwards Westminster Ophthalmic Hospital), 1816; surgeon to Westminster Hospital, 1827–43; professor of anatomy and surgery, 1828–31, and president of College of Surgeons, 1833, 1841, and 1854; gave Hunterian oration without note, 1830; published 'Commentaries on the Surgery of the War' (1808–15), 1853, with supplement, including the Crimean war, 1855, and separate treatises on gunshot wounds, on operative surgery of the eye, and arterial affections. [xxiii. 375]

GUTHRIE or **GUTHRY**, HENRY (1600 ?–1676), bishop of Dunkeld; M.A. St. Andrews, 1620; minister of Stirling, 1632–48; member of the high commission, 1634; opposed Laudian policy and took the covenant, but as a member of the general assembly opposed the 'root and branch' abolition of episcopacy, and favoured the 'engagement' of 1647; dismissed as a malignant, but admitted minister of Kilspindie, 1656, and restored at Stirling, 1661; bishop of Dunkeld, 1665–76; his 'Memoirs of Scottish Affairs, 1637 to Death of Charles I' published 1702. [xxiii. 376]

GUTHRIE, JAMES (1612 ?–1661), presbyterian divine; M.A. and regent, St. Andrews; became presbyterian under influence of Rutherford; minister of Lauder, 1642–9; member of general assembly, 1644–51; commissioner to Charles I at Newcastle, 1646; minister of Stirling, 1649–61; excommunicated Middleton, 1650; deposed as an extreme 'protester,' 1651; named a 'trier' by the English privy council, 1654; refused reparation for insults from 'resolutions' by Cromwell, 1656; hanged at Edinburgh for contriving the 'western remonstrance' and rejecting the king's ecclesiastical authority, 1661; his attainder reversed, 1690. [xxiii. 377]

GUTHRIE, JOHN (*d.* 1649), bishop of Moray; M.A. St. Andrews, 1597; minister successively of Kinnel, Arbirlot, Perth (1617), and St. Giles's, Edinburgh (1621); bishop of Moray, 1623–38; preached before Charles I in his rochet, 1633; deposed and brought by Monro to the estates, who imprisoned him in the Tolbooth, 1639; allowed to retire to Guthrie. [xxiii. 379]

GUTHRIE, THOMAS (1803–1873), preacher and philanthropist; studied at Edinburgh, subsequently in Paris; minister of Arbirlot, 1830–7, Old Greyfriars, Edinburgh, 1837–40, St. John's, 1840–64; joined Free church, 1843, followed by most of his congregation; moderator, 1862; D.D. Edinburgh, 1849; the apostle of ragged schools; platform speaker in cause of temperance; first editor of 'Sunday Magazine,' 1864–73; published 'Plea for Ragged Schools,' 1847–9, 'Plea on behalf of Drunkards,' 1851, and devotional works. [xxiii. 380]

GUTHRIE, WILLIAM (1620–1665), presbyterian divine; cousin of James Guthrie [q. v.]; M.A. St. Andrews, 1638; minister of Fenwick, Ayrshire ('the fool of Fenwick'), 1644–64; army chaplain at Mauchline Moor, 1648; joined 'protesters,' 1651; a 'trier,' 1654; struggled against episcopacy after the Restoration; his 'The Christian's Great Interest' frequently reprinted and translated. [xxiii. 382]

GUTHRIE, WILLIAM (1708–1770), author; educated at Aberdeen; wrote reports for the 'Gentleman's Magazine,' *c.* 1730; obtained pension from Pelham ministry, 1745; published works, including 'A General History of the World,' 1764–7, and 'Geographical, Historical, and Commercial Grammar,' 1770; referred to with respect by Dr. Johnson. [xxiii. 383]

GUTHRUM or **GUTHORM** (*d.* 890), king of East-Anglia; one of the Danish invaders who conquered Mercia, 871, and waged war with Alfred; became a Christian after the battle of Ethandun, and by the treaty of Wedmore, 878, was given East-Anglia (including Essex and London) as his share of the Danish kingdom; broke the treaty by aiding the foreign Norsemen to attack Wessex, and lost London and Western Essex, 886. [xxiii. 384]

GUTHRY, HENRY (1600 ?–1676). [See GUTHRIE.]

GUTO Y GLYN (*fl.* 1430–1468), Welsh poet; domestic bard to abbot of Valle Crucis (Glyn Egwestl); made triennial circuits of Wales; a hundred and nineteen of his poems said to be extant. [xxiii. 385]

GUTTERIDGE, WILLIAM (*fl.* 1813), bandmaster of the 62nd; published 'The Art of playing Gutteridge's Clarinet,' 1824. [xxiii. 385]

GUTTERIDGE, WILLIAM (1798–1872), violinist and organist; led band of Brussels theatre, 1815, and afterwards at Birmingham; member of George IV's and William IV's bands; organist of St. Peter's, Brighton, from 1828; conductor and leader of New Harmonic Society; formed one of a quartet with King George and the future kings of the Belgians and Hanover, and accompanied Queen Victoria in 1837. [xxiii. 385]

GUY OF WARWICK, hero of romance; reputed son of Siward of Wallingford; when page of Roalt or Rohand, earl of Warwick, falls in love with his daughter Felice; wins her after fighting against the Saracens and slaying the Northumbrian dragon; journeys as a palmer to the Holy Land, and on his return slays in single combat, before Winchester, the Danish giant Colbrand; leads ascetic life at Warwick until death. The story, current in Winchester in the fourteenth century, was accepted as authentic by the chroniclers and was versified by Lydgate, *c.* 1450. At Warwick the Beauchamp earls assumed descent from Guy, Earl Richard erecting a chantry for the repose of his soul, 1423, one of the priests of which, John Rous, treated the legends as authentic, and was followed by Dugdale in his 'Warwickshire.' Samuel Pegge (1781) first showed their unhistorical character. The thirteenth-century French poem was first printed, 1525, the English version some years later. [xxiii. 386]

GUY, HENRY (1631–1710), politician; admitted at the Inner Temple, 1652; M.A. Christ Church, Oxford, 1663; M.P. Hedon (Yorkshire), 1670–95 and 1702–5, where he erected a town hall, 1693; boon companion of Charles II; secretary to the treasury, 1679–88 and 1691–5; sent to the Tower for receiving a bribe; granted the manor of Great Tring and other property; left money to William Pulteney [q. v.] [xxiii. 388]

GUY, JOHN (*d.* 1628 ?), governor of Newfoundland; sheriff, 1605–6, mayor, 1618–19; M.P., Bristol, 1620–8; published (1609) appeal for colonisation of Newfoundland; led out a body of planters, 1610; wrote (1612) account of voyage to Trinity Bay; returned to Bristol. [xxiii. 389]

GUY, THOMAS (1645 ?–1724), founder of Guy's Hospital; educated at Tamworth; admitted to Stationers' Company, 1668; set up as bookseller in London, 1668; one of the Oxford University printers, 1679–92; imported Dutch type and sold bibles; M.P., Tamworth, 1695–1707; built Tamworth town hall (1701) and founded an almshouse; lived penurious life, but was liberal; from 1704 an active governor of St. Thomas's Hospital; greatly increased his fortune by selling his South Sea stock; erected at a cost of 18,793*l.* a new hospital (leaving

200,000l. for its endowment), which was to receive incurables and lunatics, though discretion was left to the governors. By his will (reprinted 1732) Guy also left benefactions to Christ's Hospital and the debtors of London, Middlesex, and Surrey. [xxiii. 390]

GUY, WILLIAM AUGUSTUS (1810–1885), medical statistician; educated at Christ's Hospital and Guy's Hospital; studied at Heidelberg and Paris; M.B. Cambridge, 1837; professor of forensic medicine at King's College, London, 1838; assistant-physician at King's College Hospital, 1842, dean of the faculty of medicine, 1846–58; edited 'Journal' of Statistical Society, 1852–6; president of Statistical Society, 1873–5; vice-president of Royal Society, 1876–7; Croonian (1861), Lumleian (1868), and Harveian (1875) lecturer at College of Physicians; a founder of the Health of Towns Association; member of commission on penal servitude and criminal lunacy; published 'Principles of Forensic Medicine,' 1844, 'Public Health,' 1870–4, and statistical papers. [xxiii. 392]

GUYLDFORDE, SIR RICHARD (1455 ?–1506). [See GUILDFORD.]

GUYON, RICHARD DEBAUFRE (1803–1856), general in the Hungarian army; some time in the Austrian service; received command of the landsturm and the honveds in 1848 and won for the Hungarians the battles of Sukoro (1848), Schewechat (1848), and the pass of Branitzko; raised the siege of Komorn (1849) and defeated the ban of Croatia at Hegyes, 1849; after the surrender of Görgey (1849), took service with the sultan; as lieutenant-general (1852) with title of Khourschid Pasha, the first Christian to be given a command; did good service against the Russians in Anatolia, 1853–5; removed after Kurekdere, 1855; died of cholera at Scutari. [xxiii. 393]

GUYSE, JOHN (1680–1761), independent minister at Hertford and in New Broad Street; had controversy with Samuel Chandler [q. v.], 1729–31; D.D. Aberdeen, 1733; published 'Exposition of the New Testament in form of paraphrase,' 1739–52. [xxiii. 394]

GUYTON, MRS. EMMA JANE (1825–1887). [See WORBOISE.]

GWAVAS, WILLIAM (1676–1741), writer in Cornish; corresponded with Thomas Tonkin, Edward Lhuyd, and John Keigwin on the old Cornish language; his writings among British Museum manuscripts. [xxiii. 394]

GWENFREWI. [See WINEFRIDE.]

GWENT, RICHARD (d. 1543), archdeacon of London; fellow of All Souls' College, Oxford, 1515; D.C.L., 1525; advocate for Queen Catherine, 1529; rector of two London parishes; dean of arches, 1532; archdeacon of London, 1534–43; prolocutor of convocation, 1536, 1540, 1541; archdeacon of Huntingdon, 1542; prebendary of St. Paul's, 1542; eulogised by Leland. [xxiii. 395]

GWENWYNWYN (d. 1218 ?), prince of Upper Powys; succeeded Owain Cyveiliog, 1197; fought against the English and Llewelyn ab Iorwerth; granted lands in Derbyshire by King John; joined Llewelyn against King John, 1215; having made peace with the English was driven into Cheshire and lost his territory, 1216; Powys Gwenwynwyn named after him. [xxiii. 396]

GWILT, CHARLES PERKINS (d. 1835), antiquarian writer; eldest son of Joseph Gwilt [q. v.] [xxiii. 399]

GWILT, GEORGE, the elder (1746–1807), architect; surveyor of Surrey, c. 1770, district surveyor of St. George's, Southwark, 1774, and surveyor to Surrey sewers commission, c. 1777; patronised by Henry Thrale the brewer; architect to West India Dock Company. [xxiii. 397]

GWILT, GEORGE, the younger (1775–1856), architect; son of George Gwilt the elder [q. v.]; superintended rebuilding of tower of St. Mary-le-Bow, 1820, and (gratuitously) restoration of St. Mary Overy, Southwark, 1822–5; F.S.A., 1815. [xxiii. 397]

GWILT, JOHN SEBASTIAN (1811–1890), architect; second son of Joseph Gwilt [q. v.]; made drawings for the 'Encyclopædia of Architecture.' [xxiii. 399]

GWILT, JOSEPH (1784–1863), architect and archæologist; son of George Gwilt the elder [q. v.]; educated at St. Paul's School; surveyor of Surrey, 1807–46; designed

Markree Castle, Sligo, the approaches to Southwark Bridge, and St. Thomas's Church, Charlton; F.S.A., 1815; M.R.A.S., 1838; published works, including 'Treatise on the Equilibrium of Arches,' 1811, 'Sciography,' 1822, a translation of Vitruvius, 1826, and 'Encyclopædia of Architecture,' 1842. [xxiii. 397]

GWILYM, DAVID AP (14th cent.). [See DAVID.]

GWIN, ROBERT (fl. 1591), Roman catholic divine; B.A. Corpus Christi College, Oxford, 1568; B.D. Douay, 1575; preacher in Wales; translated 'The Resolution' of Robert Parsons into Welsh. [xxiii. 399]

GWINNE, MATTHEW (1558 ?–1627), physician; of Merchant Taylors' School and St. John's College, Oxford; fellow; M.A., 1582; junior proctor, 1588; M.D., 1593; first Gresham professor of physic, 1598–1607; F.R.C.P., 1605; disputed before Queen Elizabeth (1592) and James I (1605) at Oxford; friend of Florio, to whose works he contributed sonnets, as 'Il Candido'; refuted Francis Anthony's view of 'aurum potabile,' 1611; published also two Latin plays, 'Nero' acted at St. John's College, 1603, 'Vertumnus' at Magdalen College, 1605. [xxiii. 399]

GWINNET, RICHARD (d. 1717), dramatist; corresponded as 'Pylades' with Elizabeth Thomas [q. v.] (Dryden's 'Corinna'); with their published correspondence (1732) appeared his play 'The Country Squire.' [xxiii. 400]

GWYN, DAVID (fl. 1588), poet; published a metrical narrative of his imprisonment in Spain, 1588. [xxiii. 401]

GWYN, ELEANOR (1650–1687), actress and mistress of Charles II; sold oranges in Theatre Royal, Drury Lane; first appeared at Drury Lane as Cydaria in Dryden's 'Indian Emperor,' 1665; continued to play there till 1670; appeared at Dorset Garden, 1677–8, and again at Drury Lane, 1682; illiterate, but good in comedy, prologues, and epilogues; rival of the Duchess of Portsmouth with Charles II, retaining his favour till death; one of her sons by the king created Duke of St. Albans, 1684; her portrait painted by Lely. [xxiii. 401]

GWYN, FRANCIS (1648 ?–1734), politician; friend of Rochester; M.P., Chippenham, 1673–9, Cardiff, 1685, Christchurch, 1689–95, Callington, 1695–8, Totnes, 1699–1701 and 1710–15, Wells, 1673–1727; under-secretary of state, 1681–3 and 1688–9; privy councillor, 1701; Irish secretary, 1701; commissioner of trade, 1711–13; secretary-at-war, 1713–14; his diary of James II's expedition to the west (1688) printed, 1886. [xxiii. 403]

GWYNLLYW or **GUNLYU**, called GWYNLLYW FILWR, 'THE WARRIOR' (6th cent.), Welsh saint (GUNDLEUS); reputed eldest of six sons of Glywys, a South-Welsh king and hermit; Gunlyu's tomb, where miracles were worked, supposed site of St. Woolos Church, Newport-on-Usk. [xxiii. 404]

GWYNN, GWYN, or **GWYNNE**, JOHN (d. 1786), architect; with S. Wale published (1749) Wren's 'Plan for rebuilding the City of London after the great fire in 1666,' and a plan of St. Paul's and other works; member of committee for creating Royal Academy, 1755; an original member, 1768; as surveyor at Oxford designed Magdalen Bridge, 1772; built also the 'English' bridge at Shrewsbury (finished, 1774), and Worcester bridge (finished, 1780); friend of Dr. Johnson, who assisted in several of his writings; proposal for establishing an academy of art contained in his 'Essay on Design' (1749). [xxiii. 405]

GWYNNE, JOHN (fl. 1660), captain in Charles I's guards; distinguished himself in first civil war; with Montrose, 1650, Middleton, 1654, and the Duke of York at Dunkirk, 1658; his statement of services published (1822) by Sir Walter Scott as 'Military Memoirs of the Great Civil War.' [xxiii. 407]

GWYNNE, NELL (1650–1687). [See GWYN, ELEANOR.]

GWYNNE, ROBERT (fl. 1591). [See GWIN.]

GWYNNETH, JOHN (fl. 1557), Roman catholic divine and musician; Mus.Doc. Oxford, 1531; rector of Clynog, St. Peter, Westcheap (1543), and vicar of Luton, 1554; published treatises against John Frith's works and 'My love mourneth' (1530), with other musical compositions. [xxiii. 407]

GYBSON. [See GIBSON.]

GYE, FREDERICK, the elder (1781-1869), entertainment manager; with 30,000*l.* won in a lottery established wine and tea companies; bought and conducted Vauxhall Gardens, 1821-40; M.P., Chippenham, 1826-30.
[xxiii. 408]

GYE, FREDERICK, the younger (1810-1878), director of Italian opera; son of Frederick Gye the elder [q. v.]; assisted Jullien in promenade concerts of 1846, and as acting manager at Drury Lane, 1847; leased Covent Garden for opera, 1849, and as manager produced 'Le Prophète,' 'Rigoletto,' 1853, and other pieces; carried on opera at the Lyceum till the opening of new Covent Garden Theatre, 1858, where Patti (1861), Lucca (1863), and Albani (1873) made their débuts, and the first Wagner operas were given, 1875-6; with Mapleson carried on Covent Garden and Her Majesty's in conjunction, 1869-1870; accidentally shot.
[xxiii. 409]

GYLBY, GODDRED (*fl.* 1561). [See GILBY.]

GYLES or **GILES,** HENRY (1640 ?-1709), glass-painter; friend of Ralph Thoresby [q. v.]; revived pictorial glass work in England, *c.* 1682; his best-known work the east window of University College, Oxford. [xxiii. 410]

GYLES, MASCAL (*d.* 1652), divine; vicar of Ditchling, Sussex, 1621-44, and Wartling, 1648-52; published against Thomas Barton [q. v.]; his 'Treatise against Superstitious Jesu-Worship,' 1642, and 'Defense,' 1643.
[xxiii. 411]

GYRTH (*d.* 1066), earl of East Anglia, 1057-66; fourth son of Godwine; accompanied Tostig to Rome, 1061; probably with Harold at Stamford Bridge, 1066; according to the 'Roman de Rou' advised Harold to leave him (Gyrth) to lead the army against William the Norman; said to have slain William's horse at Hastings before being struck down by him. [xxiii. 411]

H

HAAK, THEODORE (1605-1690), translator; born at Neuhausen; came to England, 1625; studied at Oxford; employed by parliament to translate 'Dutch Annotations upon the whole Bible,' 1657; suggested idea of Royal Society, *c.* 1645, and became an original member, 1663; translated into High Dutch blank verse half of 'Paradise Lost.' [xxiii. 412]

HAAST, SIR JOHN FRANCIS JULIUS VON (1824-1887), geologist and explorer; discovered coal- and goldfields south-west of Nelson, New Zealand, 1859; as surveyor-general of Canterbury carried on ten years' exploration, 1861-71, discovering the Southern Alps; professor of geology in New Zealand university and (1866) founder of Canterbury Museum; F.R.S., 1867; knighted in connection with Colonial Exhibition of 1885; published 'Geology of . . . Canterbury and Westland,' 1879; died at Wellington. [xxiii. 412]

HABERSHON, MATTHEW (1789-1852), architect; exhibited at Royal Academy, 1807-27; visited Jerusalem (1852) to arrange for erection of Anglican cathedral; received from king of Prussia gold medal for his 'Ancient half-timbered Houses of England,' 1836; published works on prophecy. [xxiii. 413]

HABERSHON, SAMUEL OSBORNE (1825-1889), physician; studied at Guy's Hospital; M.D. London, 1851; physician to Guy's Hospital, 1866-80; lecturer on materia medica, 1856-73, and medicine, 1873-7; F.R.C.P., 1856; Lumleian lecturer, 1876, Harveian orator, 1883, and vice-president of College of Physicians, 1887; president of London Medical Society, 1873; published works on diseases of the abdomen, stomach, and liver.
[xxiii. 413]

HABINGTON, ABINGTON, or **ABINGDON,** EDWARD (1553 ?-1586), conspirator in Babington's plot; B.A. Exeter College, Oxford, 1574; a leading conspirator in Babington's plot, 1586; hanged and quartered, denying his guilt. [xxiii. 414]

HABINGTON or **ABINGTON,** THOMAS (1560-1647), antiquary; brother of Edward Habington [q. v.]; studied at Lincoln College, Oxford, Paris, and Rheims; imprisoned for complicity in Babington's plot, 1586; constructed in his house secret chambers and hid jesuits; the letter warning Monteagle of Gunpowder plot said to have been written by his wife; published translation of Gildas, 1638 and 1641; his collections for history of Worcestershire issued, 1717 and 1723. [xxiii. 414]

HABINGTON, WILLIAM (1605-1654), poet; son of Thomas Habington [q. v.]; educated in France; married Lucy Herbert, daughter of William, first baron Powis, whom he celebrated as 'Castara,' 1634; published also 'The Queene of Arragon' (tragi-comedy), 1640, and two historical works. 'Castara' was reprinted by Arber, 1870; the 'Queene of Arragon' is in Dodsley's collection. [xxiii. 415]

HACK, MARIA (1777-1844), writer of children's books, including 'Grecian Stories' (1819) and 'English Stories' (1820, 1825). [xxiii. 416]

HACKER, FRANCIS (*d.* 1660), regicide; captured at Melton Mowbray, 1643, and again at fall of Leicester, 1645; commanded parliamentarian left wing at royalist defeat at Willoughby Field, 1648; commanded regiment in Scottish war under Cromwell; charged with custody of Charles I at Westminster Hall; supervised Charles I's execution; supported protectorate; followed Haslerig in opposition to the army, 1659; hanged as regicide.
[xxiii. 416]

HACKET, GEORGE (*d.* 1756). [See HALKET.]

HACKET, JAMES THOMAS (1805 ?-1876), astrologer; author of 'Student's Assistant in Astronomy and Astrology,' 1836; contributed statistical tables to Herapath's 'Railway and Commercial Journal.' [xxiii. 418]

HACKET, JOHN (1592-1670), bishop of Coventry and Lichfield; educated at Westminster and Trinity College, Cambridge; chaplain to Lord-keeper Williams; incumbent of St. Andrew's, Holborn, 1624-45, and Cheam, Surrey, 1624; chaplain to James I, 1623; prebendary of Lincoln, 1623; archdeacon of Bedford, 1631; attempted to moderate Laud's zeal; as member of committee of religion made able speech before Commons in defence of deans and chapters, 1641; after the Restoration resumed preaching at St. Paul's as canon residentiary; bishop of Coventry and Lichfield, 1661-70; restored Lichfield Cathedral, partly at his own expense; bequeathed money to Trinity College, Cambridge, and his books to the university; chief work, 'Scrinia Reserata' (first published, 1693), a life of Archbishop Williams. [xxiii. 418]

HACKET, HACQUET, or **HECQUET,** JOHN-BAPTIST (*d.* 1676), theologian; originally a Dominican of Cashel; teacher at Milan, Naples, and Rome, where he died; published theological works. [xxiii. 420]

HACKET, ROGER (1559-1621), divine; of Winchester and New College, Oxford; fellow, 1577; M.A., 1583; D.D., 1596; rector of North Crawley, Buckinghamshire, 1590-1621. [xxiii. 420]

HACKET, WILLIAM (*d.* 1591), fanatic; announced mission to prepare the way for the Messiah; imprisoned for reviling Queen Elizabeth; with Edmund Coppinger [q. v.] proposed to dethrone the queen and abolish episcopacy; after riot in Cheapside was tried and executed.
[xxiii. 421]

HACKMAN, ALFRED (1811-1874), sub-librarian at the Bodleian, 1862-73; precentor of Christ Church, Oxford, 1841-73, vicar of St. Paul's, 1844-71; published 'Catalogue of Tanner MSS.' in the Bodleian, 1860.
[xxiii. 422]

HACKMAN, JAMES (1752-1779), murderer; lieutenant in army, 1776; incumbent of Wiveton, Norfolk, 1779; fell in love with Martha Ray, mistress of Lord Sandwich, and on her refusal to marry him shot her outside Covent Garden Theatre. [xxiii. 422]

HACKSTON or **HALKERSTONE,** DAVID (*d.* 1680), covenanter; present at Archbishop Sharp's murder, 1679; fled to the west and helped to draw up the 'Declaration and Testimony,' 1679 ; one of the leaders at Drumclog and Bothwell Brigg, 1679 ; captured at Aird's Moss and executed at Edinburgh. [xxiii. 423]

HACOMBLEN, ROBERT (d. 1528), provost of King's College, Cambridge ; educated at Eton and King's College, Cambridge ; D.D. Cambridge, 1507 ; vicar of Prescot, Lancashire, 1492 ; provost of King's College, Cambridge, 1509-28 ; gave the brass lectern still in use, and fitted up chantry on south side, where he is buried. [xxiii. 423]

HADDAN, ARTHUR WEST (1816-1873), ecclesiastical historian : B.A. Trinity College, Oxford, 1837 ; fellow, 1839 ; M.A.; Johnson theological scholar, 1839 ; curate to Newman at St. Mary's, 1841-2 ; one of the secretaries of Gladstone's election committee, 1847 ; vice-president, Trinity College, Oxford ; incumbent of Barton-on-the-Heath, Warwickshire, 1857-73 ; published editions of the works of Archbishop Bramhall and of H. Thorndike in Anglo-Catholic library, ' Rationalism ' (reply to Mark Pattison), 1862, 'Apostolical Succession in the Church of England,' 1869, and with Bishop Stubbs, ' Councils and Ecclesiastical Documents,' 1869-73 ; his ' Remains ' edited, 1876. [xxiii. 424]

HADDAN, THOMAS HENRY (1814-1873), barrister and first editor of the 'Guardian'; brother of Arthur West Haddan [q. v.]; M.A. Brasenose College, Oxford, 1840 ; fellow of Exeter College, Oxford, 1837-43 ; Vinerian fellow, 1847 ; B.C.L., 1844 ; barrister, Inner Temple, 1841 ; equity draughtsman ; projected and first edited ' Guardian,' 1846 ; published works, including 'Outlines of Administrative Jurisdiction of the Court of Chancery,' 1862 ; died at Vichy. [xxiii. 425]

HADDEN, JAMES MURRAY (d. 1817), surveyor-general of the ordnance ; distinguished himself as an artillery officer with Burgoyne in Canada ; captured at Saratoga, 1777 ; adjutant-general in Portugal, 1797 ; secretary to Richmond when master-general of ordnance, 1794-5 ; surveyor-general of ordnance, 1804-10 ; colonel, 1806 ; major-general, 1811 ; his 'Journal' of 1776 printed at Albany, New York, 1884. [xxiii. 426]

HADDENSTON, JAMES (d. 1443). [See HALDEN-STOUN.]

HADDINGTON, EARLS OF. [See HAMILTON, SIR THOMAS, first EARL, 1563-1637 ; HAMILTON, THOMAS, second EARL, 1600-1640 ; HAMILTON, THOMAS, sixth EARL, 1680-1735 ; HAMILTON, THOMAS, ninth EARL, 1780-1858.]

HADDINGTON, VISCOUNT (1580 ?-1626). [See RAMSAY, SIR JOHN.]

HADDOCK. [See also HAYDOCK.]

HADDOCK, NICHOLAS (1686-1746), admiral ; second son of Sir Richard Haddock [q. v.] ; distinguished himself as midshipman at destruction of Franco-Spanish fleet at Vigo, 1702 ; lieutenant at relief of Barcelona, 1706 ; as captain of the Ludlow Castle, 1707, recaptured the Nightingale in North Sea ; led attack at Cape Passaro, 1718 ; commander at the Nore, 1732 ; as commander-in-chief in Mediterranean, 1738-42, blockaded Spanish coast and took valuable prizes ; vice-admiral, 1741 ; admiral of the blue, 1744 ; M.P., Rochester, 1734-46. [xxiii. 426]

HADDOCK, SIR RICHARD (1629-1715), admiral ; took part in attack on Vlie and Schelling, 1666 ; commanded Sandwich's flagship, the Royal James, in battle of Solebay, 1672, afterwards Prince Rupert's flagship, the Royal Charles ; knighted, 1675 ; commander at the Nore, 1682 ; commissioner of victualling, 1683-90 ; admiral and joint commander-in-chief, 1690 ; afterwards comptroller of the navy. [xxiii. 427]

HADDON, JAMES (fl. 1556), divine ; M.A. Cambridge, 1544 ; original fellow of Trinity College, Cambridge, 1546 ; chaplain to Duke of Suffolk and tutor to Lady Jane Grey, c. 1551 ; dean of Exeter, 1553 ; one of the protestant disputants on the real presence, 1553 ; went to Strasburg, 1554. [xxiii. 428]

HADDON, WALTER (1516-1572), civilian ; brother of James Haddon [q. v.]; educated at Eton and King's College, Cambridge ; B.A., 1537 ; D.C.L., 1549 ; vice-chancellor, 1549-50 ; regius professor of civil law, 1551 ; master of Trinity Hall, 1552 ; engaged with Cheke in

reform of ecclesiastical laws ; president, Magdalen College, Oxford, 1552-3 ; M.P., Thetford, 1558 ; on accession of Elizabeth named master of requests, commissioner for visitation of Cambridge and Eton, ecclesiastical commissioner, and judge of prerogative court ; employed in commercial negotiations with Flanders, 1565-6 ; member of parliamentary committee to petition Queen Elizabeth to marry, 1566 ; defended the Reformation against Osorio da Fonseca ; published, with Cheke, 'Reformatio Legum Ecclesiasticarum,' 1571. His ' Lucubrationes ' (ed. T. Hatcher, 1567) contains Latin letters and orations. [xxiii. 429]

HADENHAM, EDMUND OF (fl. 1307), chronicler ; monk of Rochester ; work ascribed to him by Lambard printed in Wharton's ' Anglia Sacra,' 1691. [xxiii. 432]

HADFIELD, CHARLES (1821-1884), journalist ; edited ' Manchester City News,' 1865-7, ' Warrington Examiner,' and ' Salford Weekly News,' 1880-3. [xxiii. 432]

HADFIELD, GEORGE (d. 1826), architect ; brother of Mrs. Maria Cecilia Louisa Cosway [q. v.]; travelling student of Royal Academy ; at Rome, 1790 ; exhibited in 1795 drawing for a restoration of the temple at Palestrina, and drawings of the temples of Mars and Jupiter Tonans, and an interior of St. Peter's ; designed buildings in Washington ; died in America. [xxiii. 432]

HADFIELD, GEORGE (1787-1879), politician ; radical M.P. for Sheffield, 1852-74 ; introduced measures for registration of judgments and for abolition of qualifications for offices, 1866 ; took part in formation of Anti-Cornlaw League and (1840) establishment of the Lancashire Independent College ; edited charity commission reports, 1829, and other works. [xxiii. 433]

HADFIELD, MATTHEW ELLISON (1812-1885), architect ; with his son Charles designed St. Mary's, Sheffield, the Roman catholic cathedral at Salford ; employed by four dukes of Norfolk. [xxiii. 433]

HADFIELD, WILLIAM (1806-1887), writer on Brazil ; secretary to Buenos Ayres Great Southern Railway and South American Steam Navigation Company ; editor (1863-87) of ' South American Journal '; published works on Brazil and the River Plate (1854 and 1869). [xxiii. 434]

HADHAM, EDMUND OF, EARL OF RICHMOND (1430 ?-1456). [See TUDOR.]

HADLEY, GEORGE (1685-1768), scientific writer ; brother of John Hadley (1682-1744) [q. v.]; of Pembroke College, Oxford, and Lincoln's Inn ; barrister, 1709 ; F.R.S., 1735 ; formulated present theory of trade winds ; published also ' Account and Abstract of the Meteorological Diaries communicated for 1729 and 1730 ' to Royal Society. [xxiii. 434]

HADLEY, GEORGE (d. 1798), orientalist ; served in East India Company's army, 1763-71 ; published 'Grammatical Remarks ' on Moors (dialect of Hindustani), with vocabulary (4th edit. 1796), and on Persian, with vocabulary (1776). [xxiii. 435]

HADLEY, JOHN (1682-1744), mathematician and scientific mechanist ; wrote advanced mathematical papers for Royal Society ; F.R.S., 1717 ; vice-president, Royal Society, 1728 ; invented first serviceable reflecting telescope, 1719-20 ; his reflecting quadrant tested by admiralty, and further improved, 1734. [xxiii. 435]

HADLEY, JOHN (1731-1764), professor of chemistry at Cambridge ; nephew of John Hadley (1682-1744) [q. v.]; fifth wrangler and fellow of Queens' College, Cambridge, 1753 ; M.A., 1756 ; professor of chemistry, 1756 ; M.D., 1763 ; F.R.S., 1758 ; F.R.C.P., 1763 ; physician to Charterhouse, 1763 ; intimate with Thomas Gray (1716-1771) [q. v.] [xxiii. 436]

HADOW, JAMES (1670 ?-1747), ' the Detector '; professor of divinity at St. Mary's College, St. Andrews, 1699, principal, 1707 ; published theological treatises, including ' Antinomianism of the Marrow of Modern Divinity detected,' 1721. [xxiii. 437]

HADRIAN IV (d. 1159). [See ADRIAN IV.]

HADRIAN DE CASTELLO (1460 ?-1521 ?). [See ADRIAN DE CASTELLO.]

HAGGARD, JOHN (1794–1856), civilian; of Westminster and Trinity Hall, Cambridge; fellow, 1815–20; LL.D., 1818; chancellor of Lincoln, 1836, of Winchester, 1845, of Manchester, 1847; edited reports of cases in consistory court of London, admiralty court, and Doctors' Commons. [xxiii. 437]

HAGGART, DAVID (1801–1821), criminal; frequented fairs and race-meetings in Scotland and the north of England; six times imprisoned for theft; four times broke gaol; killed a turnkey at Dumfries, 1820; arrested in Ireland; hanged at Edinburgh; compiled an autobiography in Scottish thieves' cant, published, with notes by George Combe [q. v.] [xxiii. 438]

HAGHE, CHARLES (d. 1888), lithographer; brother of Louis Haghe [q. v.]. [xxiii. 439]

HAGHE, LOUIS (1806–1885), lithographer and watercolour painter; born at Tournay; worked only with his left hand; in his youth left Belgium for England; in partnership with William Day lithographed David Roberts's 'Holy Land and Egypt,' and his own 'Sketches in Belgium and Germany'; president of the New Watercolour Society, 1873–84; exhibited regularly from 1854, chiefly Flemish interiors. [xxiii. 438]

HAGTHORPE, JOHN (fl. 1627), poet; probably identical with the Captain John Hagthorpe who took part in Cadiz expedition, 1625; published 'Divine Meditations and Elegies,' 1622 (selection edited by Brydges, 1817), 'Visiones Rervm,' 1623, and 'Englands-Exchequer,' in prose and verse, 1625. [xxiii. 439]

HAGUE, CHARLES (1769–1821), professor of music at Cambridge; gained repute as a violinist; professor of music, Cambridge, 1799–1821; Mus.Doc. Cambridge, 1801; published glees, Haydn's symphonies arranged as quintets, and setting of William Smyth's ode at the installation of the Duke of Gloucester. [xxiii. 440]

HAIGH, DANIEL HENRY (1819–1879), priest and antiquary; converted to Romanism, 1847; became priest, 1840; built St. Augustine's, Erdington, near Birmingham, chiefly at his own expense; the chief English authority on runic literature; assisted Professor Stephens in his 'Runic Monuments,' and published works on early numismatics, the Saxon conquest, and the Anglo-Saxon sagas. [xxiii. 440]

HAIGH, THOMAS (1769–1808), violinist, pianist, and composer; studied under Haydn; composed sonatas (chiefly for pianoforte), and ballads. [xxiii. 441]

HAIGHTON, JOHN (1755–1823), physician and physiologist; M.D.; demonstrator under Henry Cline [q. v.] at St. Thomas's Hospital; lectured for St. Thomas's and Guy's on physiology and midwifery, 1789; called 'the merciless doctor'; joint-editor of 'Medical Records and Researches,' 1798; silver medallist of London Medical Society for paper on 'Deafness,' 1790. [xxiii. 441]

HAILES, third BARON (d. 1508). [See HEPBURN, PATRICK.]

HAILES, LORD (1726–1792). [See DALRYMPLE, SIR DAVID.]

HAILS or **HAILES**, WILLIAM ANTHONY (1766–1845), author; while working as a shipwright acquired knowledge of classics and Hebrew; published 'Nugæ Poeticæ' (1806) and controversial tracts against Socinianism and unitarianism. [xxiv. 1]

HAILSTONE, EDWARD (1818–1890), author of 'Portraits of Yorkshire Worthies' (1869); son of Samuel Hailstone [q. v.]. [xxiv. 2]

HAILSTONE, JOHN (1759–1847), geologist; second wrangler, Trinity College, Cambridge, 1782; fellow, 1784; Woodwardian professor of geology, Cambridge, 1788–1818; vicar of Trumpington, 1818–47; F.R.S., 1801; original member of Geological Society; made additions to Woodwardian Museum. [xxiv. 1]

HAILSTONE, SAMUEL (1768–1851), botanist; brother of John Hailstone [q. v.]; solicitor at Bradford; leading authority on Yorkshire flora. [xxiv. 2]

HAIMO (d. 1054). [See HAYMO.]

HAINES, HERBERT (1826–1872), archæologist; M.A. Exeter College, Oxford, 1851; as undergraduate, published 'Manual for the Study of Monumental Brasses,' 1848; second master, college school, Gloucester, 1850–72; published guide to Gloucester Cathedral, 1867. [xxiv. 2]

HAINES, JOHN THOMAS (1799?–1843), actor and dramatist; author of many popular melodramas, in some of which he acted, including 'My Poll and my Partner Joe' (1835), and several nautical dramas. [xxiv. 2]

HAINES or **HAYNES**, JOSEPH (d. 1701), actor; known as 'Count Haines'; educated at Queen's College, Oxford; Latin secretary to Sir Joseph Williamson [q. v.]; dancer and afterwards actor at Theatre Royal; Benito in Dryden's 'Assignation,' written expressly for him, 1672; the original Sparkish in the 'Country Wife,' 1673, and Lord Plausible in the 'Plain Dealer,' 1674; his best parts, Noll Bluff in Congreve's 'Old Batchelor,' and Roger in 'Æsop'; recited prologues and epilogues. [xxiv. 3]

HAINES, WILLIAM (1778–1848), engraver and painter; worked on Boydell-Shakespeare plates; made drawings at the Cape, and engravings at Philadelphia, 1800–5; painted miniatures in London. [xxiv. 5]

HAITE, JOHN JAMES (d. 1874), musical composer; published 'Favourite Melodies as Quintets,' 1865, 'Principles of Natural Harmony,' 1855, and other musical compositions. [xxiv. 5]

HAKE, EDWARD (fl. 1579), satirist; mayor of Windsor, 1586; M.P., Windsor, 1588–9; satirised clerical and other abuses in pieces, including 'Newes out of Powles Churchyarde,' 1567, 1579 (reprinted in 'Isham Reprints,' 1872), and 'A Touchstone for this Time Present,' 1574; translated the 'Imitatio Christi,' 1567. [xxiv. 5]

HAKE, THOMAS GORDON (1809–1895), physician and poet; educated at Christ's Hospital; studied medicine at St. George's Hospital and at Glasgow and Edinburgh; practised successively at Brighton, Bury St. Edmund's, and Roehampton (filling post of physician to West London Hospital), and finally settled at St. John's Wood, London. He published, between 1839 and 1890, several volumes of poems, the earlier of which were highly appreciated by Dante Rossetti, whom Hake attended during his last days (1872). His 'Memoirs of Eighty Years' appeared, 1892. [Suppl. ii. 374]

HAKEWILL, ARTHUR WILLIAM (1808–1856), architect; elder son of James Hakewill [q. v.]; published 'Apology for the Architectural Monstrosities of London,' 1835, and other architectural works. [xxiv. 9]

HAKEWILL, EDWARD CHARLES (1812–1872), architect, younger son of Henry Hakewill [q. v.]; designed churches in Suffolk and East London; published 'The Temple,' 1851. [xxiv. 9]

HAKEWILL, GEORGE (1578–1649), divine; fellow of Exeter College, Oxford, 1596–1611; M.A., 1602; D.D., 1611; rector of Exeter College, 1642–9; chaplain to Prince Charles, 1612, but dismissed on account of manuscript treatise against the Spanish match; archdeacon of Surrey, 1617; rector of Heanton Purchardon during civil war; built chapel for Exeter College (consecrated 1624); one of the writers on whom Johnson formed his style. His works include 'The Vanitie of the Eie' (last edit. 1633), a Latin treatise against regicides, 1612, and 'Apologie . . . of the Power and Providence of God,' 1627. [xxiv. 6]

HAKEWILL, HENRY (1771–1830), architect; eldest son of John Hakewill [q. v.]; designed Gothic buildings and chapel at Rugby, Rendlesham House, and Cave Castle. [xxiv. 8]

HAKEWILL, HENRY JAMES (1813–1834), sculptor; son of James Hakewill [q. v.]; exhibited at Royal Academy, 1832. [xxiv. 9]

HAKEWILL, JAMES (1778–1843), architect; son of John Hakewill [q. v.]; published 'Views of the Neighbourhood of Windsor,' 1813, 'Picturesque Tour of Italy,' 1817 (with drawings finished by Turner), and 'Picturesque Tour in the Island of Jamaica,' 1821. [xxiv. 9]

HAKEWILL, JOHN (1742–1791), painter and decorator; employed on decorative work at Blenheim and other mansions; exhibited at Society of Artists, mainly portraits. [xxiv. 9]

HAKEWILL, JOHN HENRY (1811–1880), architect; elder son of Henry Hakewill [q. v.] [xxiv. 9]

HAKEWILL, WILLIAM (1574-1655), legal antiquary; brother of George Hakewill [q. v.]; M.P., Bossiney, 1601, Michell, 1604-11, Tregony, 1614-28, and Amersham, 1628-9; kinsman and executor of Sir Thomas Bodley; M.A. Oxford, 1613; member of commission to revise the laws, 1614; solicitor-general to James I's queen, 1617; bencher of Lincoln's Inn; master of chancery, 1647; chief works, 'Libertie of the Subject against the pretended Power of Imposition,' 1641, and 'The Manner how Statutes are enacted in Parliament,' 1641. [xxiv. 10]

HAKLUYT, RICHARD (1552?-1616), geographer; of Westminster and Christ Church, Oxford; M.A., 1577; published 'Divers Voyages touching the Discovery of America,' 1582; chaplain to Sir Edward Stafford, ambassador at Paris, 1583-8; prebendary of Bristol, 1586; rector of Wetheringsett, 1590; archdeacon of Westminster, 1603; a chief adventurer in the South Virginian Company; buried in Westminster Abbey; his 'Principall Navigations, Voiages, and Discoveries of the English Nation,' issued, 1589, and (much enlarged) 3 vols. 1598-1600; published also 'A notable History, containing four Voyages made by certain French Captains into Florida,' 1587, and translations. [xxiv. 11]

HALCOMB, JOHN (1790-1852), serjeant-at-law; barrister, Inner Temple; M.P., Dover, 1831-5; published 'Practical Treatise on passing Private Bills,' 1836. [xxiv. 12]

HALDANE, DANIEL RUTHERFORD (1824-1887), physician; son of James Alexander Haldane [q. v.]; M.D. Edinburgh, 1848; president, Edinburgh College of Physicians; LL.D. at tercentenary of Edinburgh University. [xxiv. 13]

HALDANE, JAMES ALEXANDER (1768-1851), religious writer; made voyages to India and China as midshipman on an East Indiaman; first congregational minister in Scotland, 1799; founded Society for Propagating the Gospel at Home, 1797; baptist, 1808; took part in most contemporary religious controversies; published journal of his first evangelistic tour, and devotional works. [xxiv. 13]

HALDANE, ROBERT (1764-1842), religious writer; brother of James Alexander Haldane [q. v.]; spent largely in founding and endowing tabernacles and seminaries; co-operated with his brother at Edinburgh; carried on evangelistic work in Geneva and southern France, 1816-1819; from 1824 attacked British and Foreign Bible Society for circulating the Apocrypha; published 'Evidences and Authority of Divine Revelation,' 1816, and 'Exposition of the Epistle to the Romans,' 1835-9. [xxiv. 14]

HALDANE, ROBERT (1772-1854), divine; named after Robert Haldane (1764-1842) [q. v.]; professor of mathematics at St. Andrews, 1807-20; principal of St. Mary's, and primarius of divinity, 1820-54; moderator of general assembly, 1827, and at the disruption. [xxiv. 15]

HALDENSTOUN or **HADDENSTON**, JAMES (d. 1443), prior of St. Andrews, 1418; member of James I's embassy to Rome, 1425. [xxiv. 16]

HALDIMAND, SIR FREDERICK (1718-1791), lieutenant-general; of Swiss birth; some years in Dutch service; lieutenant-colonel, 62nd royal Americans (king's royal rifle corps), 1756, afterwards commanding it as 60th foot; distinguished at Ticonderoga, 1758, and Oswego, 1759; with Amherst's expedition against Montreal, 1760; commanded in Florida, 1766-78; governor and commander-in-chief of Canada, 1778-85; died at Yverdun; his correspondence (1758-85) in British Museum. [xxiv. 16]

HALDIMAND, WILLIAM (1784-1862), philanthropist; grand-nephew of Sir Frederick Haldimand [q. v.]; a director of the Bank of England; M.P., Ipswich, 1820-6; gave pecuniary support to cause of Greek independence; founded Hortense Hospital, Aix-les-Bains, and a blind asylum at Lausanne; died at Denantou. [xxiv. 17]

HALE, SIR BERNARD (1677-1729), judge; barrister, Gray's Inn, 1704; lord chief baron Irish exchequer, 1722; puisne baron of English exchequer and knighted, 1725. [xxiv. 17]

HALE, BERNARD (fl. 1773), general; son of Sir Bernard Hale [q. v.]; governor of Chelsea Hospital, 1773; lieutenant-general of the ordnance. [xxiv. 17]

HALE, HORATIO (1817-1896), anthropologist; born at Newport, New Hampshire, United States; M.A. Harvard; ethnologist and philologist to exploring expedition under Captain Wilkes, 1838-42; admitted to Chicago bar, 1855; resided at Clinton, Ontario, 1856-96; supervised anthropological work of British Association in Canadian North-west and British Columbia; published, 1883, with translation and introduction, 'Iroquois Book of Rites' (1714-35), the only literary American-Indian work extant, and anthropological writings. [Suppl. ii. 376]

HALE, JOHN (d. 1806), general; son of Sir Bernard Hale [q. v.] [xxiv. 18]

HALE, SIR MATTHEW (1609-1676), judge; of Magdalen Hall, Oxford, and Lincoln's Inn; counsel for Sir John Bramston (1641) and Archbishop Laud (1643) on impeachment; counsel for Lord Macguire, 1645, and the eleven members accused by Fairfax, 1646; defended James, duke of Hamilton, 1649; said to have tendered his services to Charles I; took the oath to the Commonwealth, but defended Christopher Love [q. v.], 1651; member of committee for law reform, 1652; serjeant-at-law, 1654; justice of common pleas, 1654; M.P., Gloucestershire, 1654, and in Convention parliament (1660), for Oxford University, 1659; prominent in the convention; lord chief baron of the exchequer, 1660; knighted, 1660; member of special court to adjudicate on questions of property arising out of the fire of 1666; presided at conviction of two women for witchcraft, 1662; endeavoured to mitigate severity of conventicle acts, and to forward 'comprehension'; lord chief-justice of king's bench, 1671; friend of Baxter and Selden and of the latitudinarian bishops; published two scientific works answered by Henry More [q.v.] His posthumous works include 'Contemplations, Moral and Divine,' 'Pleas of the Crown,' 1678, 'The Primitive Origination of Mankind Considered,' 'Historia Placitorum Coronæ' (ordered by parliament to be printed), and 'The Judgment of the late Lord Chief Justice of the Nature of True Religion,' edited by Baxter, 1684; 'Works Moral and Religious,' edited by Rev. T. Thirlwall, 1805. [xxiv. 18]

HALE, RICHARD (1670-1728), physician; M.A. Trinity College, Oxford, 1695; F.R.C.P., 1716; gave 500l. to the Royal College of Physicians library; his Harveian oration on English mediæval physicians published, 1735. [xxiv. 24]

HALE, WARREN STORMES (1791-1872), lord mayor of London; master of Tallow Chandlers' Company, 1849 and 1861; alderman of London, 1856; sheriff, 1858-9; lord mayor, 1864-5; chief founder of City of London School on the old foundation of John Carpenter (1370?-1441?) [q. v.] [xxiv. 25]

HALE, WILLIAM HALE (1795-1870), divine and antiquary; educated at Charterhouse and Oriel College, Oxford; M.A., 1820; domestic chaplain to Bishop Blomfield, 1824; prebendary of St. Paul's, 1829-40; archdeacon of St. Albans, 1840-2, and of London, 1842; master of the Charterhouse, 1842-70; edited (1858) 'The Domesday of St. Paul's of 1222,' &c., the 'Epistles of Bishop Hall' (1840), and 'Institutiones piæ,' ascribed to Bishop Andrewes; published also accounts of Charterhouse and Christ's Hospital. [xxiv. 25]

HALES, ALEXANDER OF (d. 1245). [See ALEXANDER.]

HALES, SIR CHRISTOPHER (d. 1541), master of the rolls; ancient of Gray's Inn, 1516; M.P., Canterbury, 1523; solicitor-general, 1525; attorney-general, 1529; preferred indictment against Wolsey, 1529; justice of assize, 1532; conducted proceedings against More, Fisher, and Anne Boleyn, 1535; granted church lands in Kent. [xxiv. 26]

HALES, SIR EDWARD, baronet, titular EARL OF TENTERDEN (d. 1695); at University College, Oxford, under Obadiah Walker [q. v.]; professed himself a papist, 1685; convicted for having acted as colonel of foot without taking the statutory oaths and the sacrament, but his plea of the king's dispensation allowed by king's bench, 1686; lieutenant of the Tower; dismissed, 1688; arrested while with James II at Faversham and imprisoned; went to St. Germain, 1690; received a Jacobite title, 1692. [xxiv. 27]

HALES, SIR JAMES (*d.* 1554), judge; son of John Hales (*d.* 1539) [q. v.]; ancient of Gray's Inn, 1528; serjeant-at-law, 1540; king's serjeant, 1544; K.B., 1547; judge of common pleas, 1549; member of courts which tried Bonner and Gardiner, and of commission for reforming ecclesiastical laws, 1551; refused to affix his seal to act of council settling the crown on Lady Jane Grey, 1553; imprisoned at instance of Gardiner, 1553–4; drowned himself after release. [xxiv. 28]

HALES, JOHN (*d.* 1539), baron of the exchequer, 1522–39. [xxiv. 28]

HALES or **HAYLES**, JOHN (*d.* 1571), author; clerk of the hanaper to Henry VIII, Edward VI, and Elizabeth; converted his grant of St. John's Hospital, Coventry, into free school, 1548; as M.P. for Preston introduced measures for benefiting the poor, 1548; at Frankfort in Mary's reign; his property confiscated, 1557; imprisoned by Elizabeth for pamphlet affirming legality of marriage of Lord Hertford and Lady Katherine Grey, 1564; published 'Highway to Nobility,' 1543, and 'Introductiones ad Grammaticam'; translated Plutarch's 'Precepts for the Preservation of Health,' *c.* 1543. [xxiv. 29]

HALES, JOHN (1584–1656), 'the ever-memorable': educated at Bath grammar school and Corpus Christi, Oxford; fellow of Merton, 1605; M.A., 1609; public lecturer in Greek, 1612; fellow of Eton, 1613–49; as chaplain to Sir Dudley Carleton [q. v.] attended synod of Dort, 1618–19; canon of Windsor and chaplain to Laud, 1639; his tract on 'Schism and Schismaticks' printed anonymously and unsanctioned, 1642; during the Commonwealth lived in retirement; published oration on Sir Thomas Bodley, also several remarkable sermons, 1613; his 'Golden Remains' first issued, 1659; his works printed by Foulis (Glasgow, 1765), edited by Lord Hailes. [xxiv. 30]

HALES, JOHN (*d.* 1679). [See HAYLS.]

HALES, STEPHEN (1677–1761), physiologist and inventor; fellow of Corpus Christi College, Cambridge, 1703; M.A., 1703; B.D., 1711; D.D. Oxford, 1733; perpetual curate of Teddington, 1709 until death; also incumbent of Farringdon, Hampshire, during same period, but resided chiefly at Teddington; F.R.S., 1718; Copley medallist, 1739; a founder and (1755) vice-president of Society of Arts; clerk of the closet to the princess-dowager, and chaplain to her son (afterwards George III), 1751; trustee of colony of Georgia; invented artificial ventilators and numerous other mechanical contrivances; his 'Vegetable Staticks' (1727) the most important contribution of the eighteenth century to plant-physiology; his contributions to animal physiology in 'Statical Essays' (1733) second only to those of Harvey in the inauguration of modern physiology. His monument was placed in Westminster Abbey by the Princess-dowager of Wales. His works include two pamphlets against spirit-drinking as well as 'Philosophical Experiments' (1739), containing *inter alia* suggestions for distilling water and preserving provisions at sea, proposals for cleaning harbours, and 'A Description of Ventilators,' 1743. [xxiv. 32]

HALES, THOMAS (*fl.* 1250), Franciscan; famous for his learning; his poem 'A Luve Ron' printed in Morris's 'Old English Miscellany.' [xxiv. 36]

HALES, THOMAS (1740?–1780), French dramatist; known as D'HÈLE, D'HELL, or DELL; of English birth; served in the English navy; went to Paris, *c.* 1770; contributed to Grimm's 'Correspondance Littéraire' 'Le Roman de Mon Oncle,' 1777; published comedies, with music by Grétry, of which 'Le Jugement de Midas' was acted and printed, 1778, 'Les Fausses Apparences,' acted 1778 (revived 1850), 'Les Évènemens Imprévus' (acted 1779), translated by Holcroft, 1806, and 'Gilles Ravisseur' (acted 1781). [xxiv. 36]

HALES, WILLIAM (1747–1831), chronologist; fellow of Trinity College, Dublin, 1768; B.A. and D.D.; professor of oriental languages, Trinity College, Dublin; rector of Killeshandra, Cavan, 1788–1831. His twenty-two works include 'A New Analysis of Chronology,' 1809–1812, also mathematical papers in Maseres's 'Scriptores Logarithmici,' and theological treatises. [xxiv. 38]

HALFORD, SIR HENRY, first baronet (1766–1844), physician; son of Dr. James Vaughan; B.A. Christ Church, Oxford, 1788; M.D., 1791; physician to Middlesex Hospital,

1793–1800; F.R.C.P., 1794; changed his name on inheriting property, and was created baronet, 1809; attended George IV, William IV, and Queen Victoria; president, College of Physicians, 1820–44; published 'Account of what appeared on opening the Coffin of King Charles I,' 1813, and 'Essays and Orations delivered at the Royal College of Physicians,' 1831. [xxiv. 28]

HALFORD, SIR HENRY ST. JOHN, third baronet (1828–1897), rifleman; educated at Eton and Merton College, Oxford; B.A., 1849; succeeded to baronetcy, 1868; C.B., 1886; shot for England in first match for Elcho shield, 1862, and in many subsequent years till 1893; made highest scores in 1862 and 1872; won Albert prize, 1862 and 1893, Duke of Cambridge prize and Association cup, 1871, and Dudley, 1893; member of government small arms committee, 1880; published 'Art of Shooting with the Rifle,' 1888. [Suppl. ii. 376]

HALFPENNY, JOSEPH (1748–1811), topographical draughtsman and engraver; clerk of the works to John Carr (1723–1807) [q. v.] at restoration of York Cathedral; published 'Gothic Ornaments in the Cathedral Church of York,' 1795–1800, and 'Fragmenta Vetusta,' 1807. [xxiv. 39]

HALFPENNY, WILLIAM, *alias* MICHAEL HOARE (*fl.* 1752), credited with invention of drawing arches by intersection of straight lines; published 'Practical Architecture,' 'Useful Architecture,' 1751, 'Geometry, Theoretical and Practical,' 1752, and handbooks on rural architecture. [xxiv. 40]

HALGHTON, JOHN OF (*d.* 1324). [See HALTON.]

HALHED, NATHANIEL BRASSEY (1751–1830), orientalist; at Harrow with Richard Brinsley Sheridan; knew Sir William Jones while at Christ Church, Oxford; entered East India Company's service; translated the Gentoo Code from the Persian, 1776; issued from first press set up in India Bengali grammar, 1778; first called attention to affinity between Sanskrit words and 'those of Persian, Arabic, and even of Latin and Greek'; returned to England; M.P., Lymington, 1790–5; became a believer in Richard Brothers [q. v.]; moved that Brothers's 'Revealed Knowledge' be laid before the House of Commons, 1795; entered East India House, 1809; published (1771) verse translation (with Sheridan) of 'The Love Epistles of Aristænetus' and 'Imitations of some of the Epigrams of Martial,' 1793. [xxiv. 41]

HALIBURTON, GEORGE (1616–1665), bishop of Dunkeld; graduated at King's College, Aberdeen, 1636; attended Scots army at Newcastle, 1643; deposed from ministry for holding communication with Montrose, 1644; restored, 1645; silenced for preaching in the king's interest, 1651; parliamentary commissioner for visiting Aberdeen University, 1661; bishop of Dunkeld, 1662–5. [xxiv. 42]

HALIBURTON, GEORGE (1628–1715), bishop of Aberdeen; M.A. St. Andrews, 1646; D.D., 1673; minister of Coupar-Angus, 1648; bishop of Brechin, 1678–82, of Aberdeen, 1682–9; conducted episcopal services at Newtyle, 1698–1710. [xxiv. 42]

HALIBURTON, formerly BURTON, JAMES (1788–1862), egyptologist; M.A. Trinity College, Cambridge, 1815; resumed his father's first name of Haliburton, 1838; while engaged on geological survey of Egypt for Mehemet Ali decided position of Myos Hormos or Aphrodite; travelled with Edward W. Lane [q. v.]; published 'Excerpta Hieroglyphica,' 1822–8; again in the eastern desert, 1830–2; worked with Joseph Bonomi the younger [q. v.] and Sir John Gardner Wilkinson [q. v.]; his 'Collectanea Egyptiaca' presented to British Museum, 1864. [xxiv. 43]

HALIBURTON, THOMAS (1674–1712). [See HALYBURTON.]

HALIBURTON, THOMAS CHANDLER (1796–1865), author of 'Sam Slick'; born and educated in Nova Scotia; chief-justice in Nova Scotia of common pleas, 1828–40, and judge of supreme court, 1842–56; afterwards lived in England; M.P., Launceston, 1859–65; D.C.L. Oxford, 1858. In his 'Clockmaker, or Sayings and Doings of Sam Slick' (1837, 1838, and 1840) he founded American school of humour. His other works include 'The Attaché, or Sam Slick in England,' 1843–4, besides two books on Nova Scotia, and 'The Old Judge, or Life in a Colony,' 1843. [xxiv. 43]

HALIDAY, ALEXANDER HENRY (1728?-1802), physician and politician; son of Samuel Haliday [q. v.]; physician at Belfast; saved Belfast from destruction by 'Hearts of Steel' rioters, 1770; corresponded with Charlemont. [xxiv. 45]

HALIDAY, CHARLES (1789-1866), antiquary; brother of William Haliday [q. v.]; secretary of Dublin chamber of commerce, director of Bank of Ireland, and consul for Greece; published pamphlets on social subjects, harbour and lighthouse reform, &c.; his 'Scandinavian Kingdom of Dublin' edited by J. P. Prendergast, 1881. [xxiv. 45]

HALIDAY or **HOLLYDAY**, SAMUEL (1685-1739), Irish non-subscribing divine; graduated at Glasgow; ordained at Geneva, 1708; chaplain to Scots Cameronians in Flanders; when minister at Belfast refused to subscribe Westminster confession, 1720, defending his conduct in 'Reasons against Imposition of Subscription...,' &c., 1724.] [xxiv. 46]

HALIDAY, WILLIAM (1788-1812), Irish grammarian; learnt Irish from three Munstermen in Dublin; a founder of the Gaelic Society of Dublin, 1807; published, as 'Edmond O'Connell,' 'Uraicecht na Gaedhilge' (Irish grammar), 1808, and vol. i. of a translation of Keating's 'History of Ireland,' 1811. [xxiv. 47]

HALIFAX, MARQUISES OF. [See SAVILE, SIR GEORGE, 1633-1695; SAVILE, WILLIAM, second MARQUIS, 1665-1700.]

HALIFAX, EARLS OF. [See MONTAGU, CHARLES, first earl of second creation, 1661-1715; DUNK, GEORGE MONTAGU, first earl of third creation, 1716-1771.]

HALIFAX, first VISCOUNT (1800-1885). [See WOOD, SIR CHARLES.]

HALIFAX, JOHN (fl. 1230). [See HOLYWOOD.]

HALKERSTON, PETER (d. 1833?), Scottish lawyer; hon. LL.D.; bailie of Holyrood Abbey; published 'Treatise on the History, Law, and Privileges of Holyrood House,' 1831, and several legal works. [xxiv. 47]

HALKERSTONE, DAVID (d. 1689). [See HACKSTON.]

HALKET, ELIZABETH, afterwards LADY WARDLAW (1677-1727). [See WARDLAW.]

HALKET, GEORGE (d. 1756), Scottish song-writer; schoolmaster and session-clerk of Rathen, 1714-25, and Cairnbulg, 1725-50; published works, including 'Occasional Poems upon several Subjects,' 1727, two ballads entitled 'Logie o' Buchan,' and 'Whirry Whigs, Awa' Man'; 'Dialogue between the Devil and George II' also ascribed to him. [xxiv. 48]

HALKETT, ANNE or ANNA, LADY (1622-1699), royalist and author: née Murray; skilled in surgery; with her lover, Joseph Bampfield [q. v.], contrived escape of James, duke of York, 1647; attended soldiers wounded at Dunbar, 1650, and was thanked by Charles II; married Sir James Halkett, 1656; left manuscript devotional works; her autobiography printed, 1875. [xxiv. 48]

HALKETT, SIR COLIN (1774-1856), general; son of Frederick Godar Halkett [q. v.]; served in the Dutch foot-guards, 1792-5, and light infantry (in British pay); commanded 2nd light battalion of the German legion in Germany, 1805-6, Ireland, 1806, the Peninsula and the Walcheren expedition, 1809; led the German light brigade at Albuera, 1811, during Burgos retreat, 1812, and Vittoria, 1813, and succeeding battles; commanded British brigade at Quatre Bras and Waterloo; lieutenant-general, 1830; general, 1841; commander at Bombay, 1831-2; governor of Chelsea Hospital, 1849; G.C.B. and G.C.H. [xxiv. 49]

HALKETT, FREDERICK GODAR (1728-1803), major-general; lieutenant-colonel, 2nd battalion of the Dundas regiment, in Holland, 1777; retired, 1782; raised a Scots battalion for English army; major-general, 1802. [xxiv. 51]

HALKETT, HUGH, BARON VON HALKETT (1783-1863), Hanoverian general and British colonel; son of Frederick Godar Halkett [q. v.]; served in India in Scots brigade, 1798-1801; distinguished himself at Copenhagen, 1807; led battalion at Albuera, 1811, Salamanca, 1812, the Burgos retreat and Venta de Pozo, 1812; organised

Hanoverian levies, 1813; commanded brigade at Göhrde, 1813, and Schestedt, 1813; led the 3rd and 4th brigades of Hanoverian militia at Waterloo, 1815, and captured Cambronne (chief of the imperial guard) with his own hand; commanded 10th army corps of German confederation in Schleswig-Holstein, 1848; created baron with full pension, 1858; O.B. and G.C.H.; died at Hanover. [xxiv. 51]

HALKETT, SAMUEL (1814-1871), keeper of Advocates' Library, Edinburgh, 1848-71; began 'Dictionary of Anonymous and Pseudonymous Literature of Great Britain' (published, 1882-8). [xxiv. 53]

HALL, MRS. AGNES C. (1777-1846), author; wife of Robert Hall (1763-1824) [q. v.]; contributed to various cyclopædias; translated Alfieri's 'Autobiography,' 1810, and works by Madame de Genlis; published novels. [xxiv. 53]

HALL, MRS. ANNA MARIA (1800-1881), author; née Fielding; married Samuel Carter Hall [q. v.], 1824; edited 'St. James's Magazine,' 1862-3; received civil list pension, 1868; assisted in foundation of Brompton Consumption Hospital and other benevolent institutions; published nine novels, including 'Marian, or a Young Maid's Fortunes,' 1840, and 'Lights and Shadows of Irish Life,' 1838; published two plays and 'Tales of the Irish Peasantry,' 1840, and 'Midsummer Eve, a Fairy Tale of Love,' 1848; collaborated with her husband. [xxiv. 54]

HALL, ANTHONY (1679-1723), antiquary; fellow of Queen's College, Oxford, 1706; M.A., 1704; D.D., 1721; rector of Hampton Poyle, 1720; edited Leland's 'Commentaries,' 1709, and works of Nicholas Trivet, 1719; superintended publication of Hudson's 'Josephus,' 1720. [xxiv. 55]

HALL, ARCHIBALD (1736-1778), divine; studied at Edinburgh and Glasgow universities; minister of Torphicen, West Lothian, and from 1765 of the Secession church, Well Street, London; published religious works. [xxiv. 56]

HALL, ARTHUR (fl. 1563-1604), translator and politician; ward of Sir William Cecil (Lord Burghley); M.P., Grantham, 1571-81 and 1585; reprimanded by speaker for lewd speaking, 1572; expelled the house, 1581, for offensive pamphlet impugning action of speaker and members in the case of his servant, who, being freed from ordinary arrest as privileged, was sent to the Tower by the House of Commons for assault; confined in the Tower two years, 1581-3; offered political advice to Burghley (1591) and to James I (1604); his 'Ten Books of Homer's Iliades, translated out of French' (1581), the first English version of Homer's 'Iliad.' [xxiv. 56]

HALL, BASIL (1788-1844), captain in the navy and author; son of Sir James Hall [q. v.]; witnessed battle of Coruña, 1809; accompanied Lord Amherst's Chinese embassy; carried out pendulum observations off South America; interviewed Napoleon; F.R.S., 1816; travelled in North America, 1827-8; died insane in Haslar Hospital; his 'Fragments of Voyages and Travels,' 1831-3, often reprinted. [xxiv. 56]

HALL, SIR BENJAMIN, first BARON LLANOVER (1802-1867), politician; of Westminster and Christ Church, Oxford; M.P., Monmouth, 1831-7, Marylebone, 1837-59; created baronet, 1838; active in cause of ecclesiastical reform; privy councillor, 1854; president of board of health, 1854; as chief commissioner of works, 1855-8, established metropolitan board of works; created Baron Llanover, 1859. [xxiv. 59]

HALL, CHAMBERS (1786-1855), virtuoso; presented to British Museum drawings by Girtin and antiquities, and to Oxford University antiquities and pictures. [xxiv. 60]

HALL, CHARLES (1720?-1783), line-engraver. [xxiv. 60]

HALL, CHARLES (1745?-1825?), writer on economics; M.D. Leyden; published 'Effects of Civilisation on the People in European States,' 1805; died in the Fleet. [xxiv. 60]

HALL, SIR CHARLES (1814-1883), vice-chancellor; barrister, Middle Temple, 1838; assisted and subsequently succeeded Lewis Duval [q. v.] in conveyancing practice; conveyancer to court of chancery, 1864; authority on real property law; vice-chancellor, 1873; knighted, 1873; twice refused silk. [xxiv. 61]

HALL, SIR CHARLES (1843–1900), recorder of London ; son of Sir Charles Hall (1814–1883) [q. v.] ; educated at Harrow and Trinity College, Cambridge ; M.A., 1870 ; barrister, Lincoln's Inn, 1866 ; attorney-general to Prince of Wales, 1877–92 ; Q.C., 1881 ; K.C.M.G., 1890 ; recorder of London, 1892 ; privy councillor, 1899 ; M.P. for Western Cambridgeshire, 1885–6 and 1886–92, and for Holborn division of Finsbury, 1892.   [Suppl. ii. 377]

HALL, CHARLES HENRY (1763–1827), dean of Durham ; educated at Westminster and Christ Church, Oxford ; M.A., 1786 ; D.D., 1800 ; won university prizes for Latin and English essays ; dean of Christ Church, 1809–24 ; Bampton lecturer and prebendary of Exeter, 1798 ; regius professor of divinity and vicar of Luton, 1807 ; dean of Durham, 1824–7.   [xxiv. 61]

HALL, CHESTER MOOR (1703–1771), inventor of the achromatic telescope, 1733 ; bencher, Inner Temple, 1763.   [xxiv. 62]

HALL, EDMUND (1620 ?–1687), divine ; left Oxford to fight for parliament ; fellow of Pembroke, 1647 ; M.A., 1650 ; imprisoned for attacking Cromwell, 1651–2 ; rector of Chipping Norton and (1680–7) of Great Risington ; published 'Scriptural Discourse of the Apostacy and the Antichrist,' 1653, and anonymous monarchical pamphlets.   [xxiv. 62]

HALL, EDWARD (d. 1547), historian ; educated at Eton and King's College, Cambridge ; B.A., 1518 ; reader at Gray's Inn, 1533 and 1540 ; common serjeant, 1532 ; M.P., Bridgnorth, 1542 ; commissioner to inquire into transgressions of Six Articles, 1541–4 ; his 'Union of the Noble and Illustre Famelies of Lancastre and York,' 1542 (completed by Grafton, 1550), followed by Shakespeare, prohibited by Queen Mary, and not reprinted till 1809.   [xxiv. 63]

HALL, ELISHA (fl. 1562), fanatic ; examined by Bishop Grindal, 1562.   [xxiv. 64]

HALL, FRANCIS (1595–1675). [See LINE.]

HALL, FRANCIS RUSSELL (1788–1866), theological writer ; educated at Manchester and St. John's College, Cambridge ; fellow ; M.A., 1813 ; D.D., 1839 ; rector of Fulbourn, 1826–66 ; published theological pamphlets, including 'Reasons for not contributing to circulate the Apocrypha,' 1825.   [xxiv. 64]

HALL, GEORGE (1612 ?–1668), bishop of Chester ; son of Joseph Hall [q. v.] ; fellow of Exeter College, Oxford, 1632 ; M.A., 1634 ; D.D., 1660 ; deprived by parliament of vicarage of Menheniot and archdeaconry of Cornwall, but allowed to officiate in London ; canon of Windsor and archdeacon of Canterbury, 1660 ; bishop of Chester, 1662–8 ; held with his see rectory of Wigan. [xxiv. 64]

HALL, GEORGE (1753–1811), bishop of Dromore ; scholar, fellow, senior fellow (1790–1800), professor of Greek, modern history, and mathematics, and provost (1806–11) of Trinity College, Dublin ; M.A., 1778 ; D.D., 1790 ; bishop of Dromore, 1811.   [xxiv. 65]

HALL, HENRY (d. 1680), covenanter ; joined covenanters on Pentland Hills, 1676 ; imprisoned ; after his release wandered about with Cargill and others ; assisted in drawing up covenanting manifesto, 1679 ; one of the leaders at Drumclog and Bothwell Brigg, 1679 ; fled to Holland ; captured on his return by Thomas Dalyell [q. v.] ; died of a wound ; 'Queensferry Paper' found on him.   [xxiv. 65]

HALL, HENRY, the elder (1655 ?–1707), organist ; chorister of the Chapel Royal ; studied with Purcell under Blow ; organist of Exeter (1674) and Hereford (1688) Cathedrals ; services and anthems by him in Tudway's collection.   [xxiv. 66]

HALL, HENRY, the younger (d. 1713), organist ; son of Henry Hall the elder [q. v.] ; organist of Hereford Cathedral, 1707 ; admired by contemporaries as composer of light verse.   [xxiv. 66]

HALL, JACOB (fl. 1668), rope-dancer ; seen by Pepys at Bartholomew Fair, Smithfield, 1668 ; much favoured by Lady Castlemain.   [xxiv. 67]

HALL, JAMES (d. 1612), navigator ; made two voyages (1605, 1606) to Greenland as pilot of Danish expeditions, described by Purchas ; commanded English expedition to Greenland, 1612 ; mortally wounded by an Eskimo.   [xxiv. 67]

HALL, JAMES (1755–1826), presbyterian divine ; educated at Glasgow University ; pastor of associate congregations at Cumnock, 1777, and Edinburgh, 1786 ; chairman of reunion committee, 1820.   [xxiv. 68]

HALL, SIR JAMES, fourth baronet (1761–1832), geologist and chemist ; intimate with Hutton and Playfair ; tested Huttonian system by study of continental and Scottish formations ; refuted Wernerian views by laboratory experiments ; president of Royal Society of Edinburgh ; M.P., Mitchell or Michael, Cornwall, 1807–12 ; published 'Essay on Gothic Architecture,' 1813.   [xxiv. 68]

HALL, JAMES (1800 ?–1854), amateur painter ; son of Sir James Hall [q. v.] ; friend of Wilkie and Watson Gordon ; exhibited Scottish landscapes and portraits, including Wellington (1838) and Scott, at Royal Academy, 1835–54 ; presented manuscript of 'Waverley' to Advocates' Library.   [xxiv. 69]

HALL or HALLE, JOHN (1529 ?–1566 ?), poet and medical writer ; member of Worshipful Company of Chirurgeons ; published metrical versions of Proverbs, Ecclesiastes, and some Psalms, 1549 ; translated Lanfranc's 'Chirurgia Parva,' 1565 ; published other medical tracts, of which one was reprinted, 1844.   [xxiv. 69]

HALL, JOHN (1575–1635), physician, of Stratford-on-Avon ; married Susanna, Shakespeare's eldest daughter, 1607 ; with her acted as Shakespeare's executor, and inherited New Place ; their daughter Elizabeth (d. 1670), Shakespeare's last direct descendant ; his 'Select Observations on English Bodies, and Cures both Empericall and Historicall,' issued by James Cooke, 1657. [xxiv. 70]

HALL, JOHN (1627–1656), poet and pamphleteer ; of Durham and St. John's College, Cambridge ; friend of Hobbes and Samuel Hartlib [q. v.] ; accompanied Cromwell to Scotland, 1650, and wrote 'The Grounds and Reasons of Monarchy,' and other political pamphlets. His works include 'Horæ Vacivæ, or Essays,' 1646, 'Poems,' 1647 (reprinted, 1816), and 'Satire against Presbytery,' 1648.   [xxiv. 71]

HALL, JOHN (d. 1707), author of 'Jacobs Ladder' (1676) ; fellow of Trinity College, Cambridge, 1658 ; M.A. ; B.D., 1666 ; prebendary of St. Paul's, 1664 ; president of Sion College ; rector of Finchley, 1666.   [xxiv. 72]

HALL, JOHN (d. 1707), criminal ; sentenced to death for housebreaking, 1700 ; pardoned on condition of removing to America ; deserted the ship and returned, 1704 ; executed at Tyburn ; credited with 'Memoirs of the Right Villanous John Hall' (published, 1708).   [xxiv. 72]

HALL, JOHN (1633–1710), bishop of Bristol ; nephew of Edmund and Thomas Hall (1610–1665) [q. v.] ; of Merchant Taylors' School and Pembroke College, Oxford ; scholar, fellow (1653), and master (1664–1710) ; M.A., 1653 ; D.D., 1669 ; Margaret professor of divinity, 1676 ; bishop of Bristol, 1691–1710 ; the last puritan bishop ; benefactor of his college and Bromsgrove. [xxiv. 72]

HALL, JOHN (1739–1797), line-engraver ; executed plates in Bell's 'Shakespeare' and 'British Theatre' ; exhibited with Incorporated Society of Artists, 1766–76 ; historical engraver to George III, 1785 ; engraved Benjamin West's works and portraits after Reynolds, Gainsborough, and others.   [xxiv. 73]

HALL, SIR JOHN (1795–1866), army surgeon ; M.D. St. Andrews, 1845 ; principal medical officer in Kaffraria, 1847 and 1851, in Crimea, 1854–6 ; K.C.B. and inspector-general of hospitals ; defended Crimean medical service, 1857 and 1858 ; died at Pisa.   [xxiv. 74]

HALL, JOHN VINE (1774–1860), author of 'The Sinner's Friend' ; bookseller at Maidstone, 1814–50 ; his 'Sinner's Friend' originally composed of extracts from Bogatzky, but completely rewritten in later editions, and translated into thirty languages.   [xxiv. 74]

HALL, JOSEPH (1574–1656), bishop of Exeter and Norwich ; educated at Ashby-de-la-Zouch and Emmanuel College, Cambridge ; fellow, 1595 ; M.A., 1596 ; D.D., 1612 ; published 'Virgidemiarum,' vol. i. 1597, vol. ii. 1598, satires (ed. Grosart, 1879) ; attacked by Marston, 1598 ; incumbent of Halsted, Suffolk, 1601 ; accompanied Sir Edmund

Bacon to Spa, 1605 ; chaplain to Henry, prince of Wales, 1608 ; incumbent of Waltham, Essex, 1608 ; chaplain to Lord Doncaster in France, 1616 ; dean of Worcester, 1616 ; accompanied James I to Scotland, 1617 ; deputy at synod of Dort, 1618 ; bishop of Exeter, 1627–41 ; conciliatory towards puritans ; issued (with Laud's alteration) 'Divine Right of Episcopacy,' 1640 ; defended the liturgy both in the House of Lords and in controversy ; member of the Lords' committee on religion, 1641 ; bishop of Norwich, 1641–7 ; defended canons of 1640, and was impeached and imprisoned, 1642 ; his episcopal revenues were sequestrated, 1643, and his cathedral desecrated ; expelled from his palace, c. 1647. Besides satires and controversial works against Brownists and presbyterians, he published poems (ed. Singer, 1824, Grosart, 1879), meditations, devotional works, and autobiographical tracts, also 'Observations of some Specialities of Divine Providence,' 'Hard Measure,' 1647, and 'The Shaking of the Olive Tree' (posthumous, 1660) ; collective editions issued, 1808, 1837, and 1863.   [xxiv. 75]

HALL, MARSHALL (1790–1857), physiologist, son of Robert Hall (1755–1827) [q. v.] ; M.D. Edinburgh, 1812 ; visited medical schools at Paris, Göttingen, and Berlin, 1814–15 ; practised in Nottingham, 1817–25 ; F.R.G.S., 1818 ; F.R.S., 1832 ; practised in London, 1826–53, making his speciality nervous diseases ; F.R.C.P., 1841 ; Gulstonian lecturer, 1842, Croonian, 1850–2 ; prominent in foundation of British Association. During his investigations into the circulation of the blood he made his important discovery of reflex action, 1832, which he applied to the explanation of convulsive paroxysms. He rationalised the treatment of epilepsy, and introduced the ready method in asphyxia. Besides numerous scientific and medical works, he published 'Twofold Slavery of the United States' (1854). He devised the system now in use for restoring animation to the partially drowned.
                                                                        [xxiv. 80]

HALL, PETER (1802–1849), divine and topographer ; of Winchester and Brasenose College, Oxford ; M.A., 1830 ; successively minister of Tavistock Chapel, Drury Lane, Long Acre Chapel, St. Martin's, and St. Thomas's, Walcot, Bath ; edited Bishop Joseph Hall's works, 1837–9, and 'Satires' (1838), also Bishop Andrewes's 'Preces privatæ' (1848), some 'Remains' of Bishop Lowth of disputed authenticity ; published topographical works on Winchester, Salisbury, Wimborne Minster, and the New Forest.   [xxiv. 83]

HALL, RICHARD (d. 1604), Roman catholic divine ; fellow of Pembroke Hall, Cambridge, 1556 ; M.A., 1559 ; D.D. Rome ; professor of holy scripture at Douay, and canon of St. Omer, where he died ; his 'Life of John Fisher, bishop of Rochester,' printed surreptitiously and incorrectly, 1655 ; published Latin writings on the revolt of the Netherlands and other works.   [xxiv. 84]

HALL, ROBERT (1763–1824), medical writer ; greatgrandson of Henry Hall (d. 1680) [q. v.] the covenanter ; M.D. Edinburgh ; naval surgeon on Jamaica station and medical officer to a Niger expedition ; works include translation of Spallanzani on the 'Circulation,' 1801, and Guyton de Morveau's 'Means of Purifying Infected Air,' 1802.   [xxiv. 85]

HALL, ROBERT (1755–1827), first user of chlorine for bleaching, and inventor of a new crane. [xxiv. 80]

HALL, ROBERT (1764–1831), baptist divine ; said to have preached when eleven ; educated at baptist academy, Bristol, and King's College, Aberdeen ; M.A. Aberdeen, 1784 ; assistant to Caleb Evans at Broadmead Chapel, 1785–90 ; succeeded Robert Robinson at Cambridge, 1791–1806 ; temporarily insane, 1804–5 and 1805–6 ; at Harvey Lane, Leicester, 1807–25 ; preached celebrated sermon on death of Princess Charlotte, 1817 ; D.D. Aberdeen, 1817 ; created much sensation by his 'Modern Infidelity considered with respect to its Influence on Society,' 1800 ; returned to Bristol, 1826 ; 'Fifty Sermons' by him issued, 1843, 'Miscellaneous Works and Remains' (Bohn), 1846.   [xxiv. 85]

HALL, ROBERT (1753–1836), raised Devon and Cornwall Fencibles, 1794.   [xxiv. 87]

HALL, ROBERT (1817–1882), vice-admiral ; entered navy, 1833 ; commanded the Stromboli in Baltic and Black seas, 1854–5 ; took part in Kertch expedition, 1855 ; naval secretary to admiralty, 1872–82.   [xxiv. 87]

HALL, SAMUEL (1769?–1852), 'the Sherwood Forest Patriarch' ; cobbler at Sutton-in-Ashfield ; invented machine for simultaneous sowing, manuring, and pressing of turnip-seed.   [xxiv. 87]

HALL, SAMUEL (1781–1863), engineer and inventor ; son of Robert Hall (1755–1827) [q. v.] ; took out patent for 'gassing' lace and net, 1817 and 1823, and for a 'surface condenser' for use at sea, 1838.   [xxiv. 87]

HALL, SAMUEL CARTER (1800–1889), author and editor ; son of Robert Hall (1753–1836) [q. v.] ; left Cork for London, 1821 ; literary secretary to Ugo Foscolo, 1822, and a reporter in House of Lords, 1823 ; founded and edited 'The Amulet,' 1826–37 ; connected with 'New Monthly Magazine,' 1830–6, edited 'Art Union Monthly' (afterwards 'Art Journal'), 1839–80 ; received civil list pension, 1880 ; published works, including 'Book of British Ballads,' 1842, 'Gallery of Modern Sculpture,' 1849–54, and 'Memoirs of Great Men and Women . . . from personal acquaintance,' 1871.   [xxiv. 87]

HALL, SPENCER (1806–1875), librarian of the Athenæum Club, 1833–75 ; F.S.A., 1858 ; among other works translated and edited 'Documents from Simancas relating to Reign of Elizabeth,' 1865.   [xxiv. 89]

HALL, SPENCER TIMOTHY (1812–1885), 'the Sherwood Forester' ; son of Samuel Hall (1769?–1852) [q. v.] ; gained the co-editorship of the 'Iris' and governorship of Hollis Hospital, Sheffield, by his 'Forester's Offering' (1841), set up in type by himself ; lectured on phrenology and mesmerism ; published 'Mesmeric Experiences,' 1845 ; cured Harriet Martineau, 1844 ; issued 'Homœopathy, a Testimony,' 1852 ; received degrees from Tübingen ; published miscellaneous works.
                                                                        [xxiv. 90]

HALL, THOMAS (1610–1665), ejected minister ; uncle of John Hall (1633–1710) [q. v.] ; B.A. Pembroke College, Oxford, 1629 ; B.D., 1652 ; perpetual curate and master of the grammar school, King's Norton ; signed Baxter's Worcestershire petition ; ejected, 1662 ; wrote against unlicensed preachers, indiscriminate baptism, Fifth-monarchy men, and cavalier customs.
                                                                        [xxiv. 91]

HALL, THOMAS (1660?–1719?), Roman catholic divine ; brother of William Hall (d. 1718?) [q. v.] ; D.D. Paris ; philosophy professor at Douay, 1688–90 ; died at Paris.   [xxiv. 92]

HALL, TIMOTHY (1637?–1690), titular bishop of Oxford ; B.A. Pembroke College, Oxford ; ejected from Norwood and Southam, 1662 ; afterwards conformed ; incumbent of Allhallows Staining, 1677 ; denied installation to bishopric of Oxford by canons of Christ Church, 1688 ; read the declaration of indulgence at Staining, 1687.   [xxiv. 92]

HALL, WESTLEY (1711–1776), eccentric divine ; pupil of John Wesley at Lincoln College, Oxford ; married Wesley's sister Martha after engaging himself to Keziah ; active in management of methodist society, but adopted Moravian views and (1743) formed new society at Salisbury ; afterwards preached deism and polygamy ; disturbed Charles Wesley's meetings at Bristol, 1750–1.
                                                                        [xxiv. 92]

HALL, WILLIAM (d. 1700), violinist ; son of Henry Hall the elder [q. v.]   [xxiv. 66]

HALL, WILLIAM (d. 1718?), Carthusian ; chaplain and preacher in ordinary to James II ; afterwards prior of Nieuwpoort, in Flanders.   [xxiv. 87]

HALL, WILLIAM (1748–1825), poet and antiquary ; gozzard and cow-leech in the fens ; afterwards bookseller at Lynn ; published 'Sketch of Local History' (1812), and 'Reflections upon Times, and Times, and Times !' 1816–18.   [xxiv. 93]

HALL, WILLIAM EDWARD (1835 – 1894), legal writer ; M.A. University College, Oxford, 1859 ; barrister, Lincoln's Inn, 1861 ; travelled widely, making valuable collection illustrative of the archæology of art ; published 'International Law,' 1880, and other writings ; elected member of Institut de Droit International, 1882.
                                                                 [Suppl. ii. 378]

HALL, SIR WILLIAM HUTCHEON (1797?–1878), admiral ; with Basil Hall [q. v.] in China, 1815–17 ; employed in steamboats on the Hudson and Delaware, 183υ–9 ; in command of the Nemesis (paddle-steamer) ; rendered valuable service in Chinese war, 1840-3, and was given naval rank; F.R.S., 1847; commanded the Hecla and the Blenheim in the Baltic, 1854-5; K.C.B., 1867; vice-admiral, 1869; admiral, 1875; published pamphlets on Sailors' Homes and National Defences. [xxiv. 94]

HALL, Sir WILLIAM KING (1816-1886), admiral; mate of the Benbow under Houston Stewart at bombardment of Acre, 1840; flag-captain to Napier and Sir M. Seymour in the Baltic, 1854-5; distinguished himself during second Chinese war, 1856-8; K.C.B., 1871; admiral, 1879; commander at the Nore, 1877-9. [xxiv. 95]

HALL-HOUGHTON, HENRY (1823-1889). [See Houghton.]

HALL-STEVENSON, JOHN (1718 - 1785). [See Stevenson, John Hall-.]

HALLAHAN, MARGARET MARY (1803-1868), foundress of the English congregations of St. Catherine of Siena; founded five convents in England, besides schools, churches, and orphanages. [xxiv. 96]

HALLAM, ARTHUR HENRY (1811-1833), subject of Tennyson's 'In Memoriam'; elder son of Henry Hallam [q. v.]; educated at Eton and Trinity College, Cambridge, where he met Tennyson; studied at the Inner Temple; died suddenly at Vienna (buried at Clevedon). His 'Remains' issued, 1834. [xxiv. 98]

HALLAM, HENRY (1777-1859), historian; educated at Eton and Christ Church, Oxford; B.A., 1799; barrister; commissioner of stamps; treasurer of the Statistical Society; vice-president of the Society of Antiquaries; occasionally contributed to 'Edinburgh Review'; published 'State of Europe during the Middle Ages,' 1818, 'Constitutional History of England from Henry VII's Accession to the death of George II,' 1827, and 'Introduction to Literature of Europe,' 1837-9, besides a privately printed memoir of his son Arthur. [xxiv. 96]

HALLAM, HENRY FITZMAURICE (1824-1850), younger son of Henry Hallam [q. v.]; of Eton and Trinity College, Cambridge; second chancellor's medallist; founder of the 'Historical' debating club, and one of the 'Apostles'; friend of Maine and Franklin Lushington; died suddenly at Rome; buried at Clevedon. [xxiv. 98]

HALLAM, JOHN (d. 1537), conspirator; took part in Pilgrimage of Grace, 1536; rebel governor of Hull; hanged for participation in the second 'pilgrimage.' [xxiv. 99]

HALLAM or **HALLUM**, ROBERT (d. 1417), bishop of Salisbury; prebendary of Salisbury, 1395, of York, 1400; archdeacon of Canterbury, 1400; chancellor of Oxford University, 1403; his nomination by the pope as archbishop of York disallowed by the king, 1405; bishop of Salisbury, 1407-17; one of the English representatives at council of Pisa, 1409; took lead of English 'nation' at council of Constance, 1414, opposing John XXII and urging consideration of ecclesiastical reform before election of a new pope; died at Gottlieben Castle, and was buried in Constance Cathedral. [xxiv. 99]

HALLÉ, Sir CHARLES (CARL HALLÉ) (1819-1895), pianist and conductor; born at Hagen, Westphalia; studied under Rinck and Gottfried Weber at Darmstadt; performed with Alard and Franchomme in Paris; visited England, 1843, and made it his home, 1848, settling at Manchester; fulfilled numerous engagements as conductor, Hallé's orchestra, instituted 1857, at Manchester, becoming celebrated in north of England; began series of pianoforte recitals, 1850; first principal, Royal College of Music, Manchester, 1893; honorary LL.D. Edinburgh, 1880; knighted, 1888. [Suppl. ii. 379]

HALLE, JOHN (d. 1479), merchant of Salisbury; mayor of Salisbury, 1451, 1458, 1464, and 1465; M.P., Salisbury, 1453, 1460, and 1461; the hall of his house in New Canal, Salisbury, still remains with its stained glass. [xxiv. 101]

HALLETT or **HALLET**, JOSEPH, I (1628?-1689), ejected minister; held the sequestered living of West Chinnock, Somerset, 1656-63; fined and imprisoned under Conventicle Act, 1673; first presbyterian minister at Exeter. [xxiv. 102]

HALLETT or **HALLET**, JOSEPH, II (1656-1722), nonconformist minister of Exeter; son of Joseph Hallett or Hallet (1628?-1689) [q. v.]; pastor of James's

meeting, 1713; his academy reputed unitarian; James Foster [q. v.] and Peter King (afterwards lord chancellor) [q. v.] among his pupils. [xxiv. 102]

HALLETT or **HALLET**, JOSEPH, III (1691?-1744), nonconformist; son of Joseph Hallett or Hallet (1656-1722) [q. v.]; corresponded with Whiston and adopted his form of unitarianism; from 1722 pastor at Exeter; published 'Free and Impartial Study of the Holy Scriptures,' 1729-36, and controversial tracts. [xxiv. 103]

HALLEY, EDMUND (1656-1742), astronomer; educated at St. Paul's School and Queen's College, Oxford; laid the foundation of southern astronomy during residence in St. Helena, 1676-8, and made the first complete observation of a transit of Mercury, 1677; published on his return 'Catalogus Stellarum Australium,' 1678; M.A. Oxford, 1678; F.R.S., 1678; arbitrated at Danzig between Hooke and Hevelius, 1679; made observations of the comet of 1680; travelled in Italy, 1681; originated (by his suggestions) Newton's 'Principia,' which he introduced to the Royal Society, and published (1687) at his own expense, correcting all the proofs; assistant-secretary to the Royal Society and editor of its 'Transactions,' 1685-93, contributing first detailed description of trade winds; while deputy-controller of the mint at Chester, 1696-8, ascended Snowdon to test his method of determining heights by the barometer; in command of the Paramour Pink explored Atlantic, and prepared 'General Chart' of variation of compass with the 'Halleyan lines,' 1699-1701; surveyed coasts and tides of British Channel and published map, 1702; inspected harbours of Adriatic for Emperor Leopold; Savilian professor of geometry at Oxford, 1703; D.C.L. Oxford, 1710; a leading member of committee which prepared Flamsteed's observations for the press, and editor of first (1712) version of Flamsteed's 'Historia Coelestis'; predicted accurately total solar eclipse of 1715; observed eclipse and great aurora, 1715; secretary to Royal Society, 1713; astronomer royal, 1721; foreign member of Académie des Sciences, 1729. His lunar and planetary tables appeared posthumously, 1749, 'Astronomiæ Cometicæ Synopsis' (1705) being reprinted with them. He accurately predicted the return in 1758 of the comet of 1531, 1607, and 1682, first recommended employment of transits of Venus for ascertaining the sun's distance, and demonstrated (1686) law connecting atmospheric elevation with density. In addition he originated the science of life statistics by 'Breslau Table of Mortality,' and that of physical geography by his scientific voyages. [xxiv. 104]

HALLEY, ROBERT (1796-1876), nonconformist divine and historian; classical tutor at Highbury College, 1826-39; D.D., 1834; minister of Mosley Street Chapel, Manchester, 1839 (Cavendish Street, 1848); chairman of Congregational Union, 1855; principal of New College, St. John's Wood, 1857-72; published 'Lancashire: its Puritanism and Nonconformity,' 1869. [xxiv. 109]

HALLIDAY. [See also HALIDAY.]

HALLIDAY, Sir ANDREW (1781-1839), physician; M.D. Edinburgh, 1806; served with Portuguese in the Peninsula and with British at Waterloo; L.R.C.P., 1819; knighted, 1821; domestic physician to Duke of Clarence; inspector of West Indian hospitals, 1823; wrote on lunatic asylums (1808 and 1828), the campaign of 1815, and the West Indies (1837). [xxiv. 110]

HALLIDAY, ANDREW (1830-1877), essayist and dramatist; son of William Duff, but dropped his surname; educated at Aberdeen; contributed to the magazines; president of Savage Club, 1857, and editor of 'Savage Club Papers,' 1868-9; collaborated with William Brough in 'The Area Belle,' and other farces; produced also 'The Great City' (1867), domestic dramas, and adaptations from Dickens and Scott. [xxiv. 111]

HALLIDAY, MICHAEL FREDERICK (1822-1869), amateur artist; one of the first English eight in the rifle-shooting competition at Wimbledon for the Elcho shield, 1862; an early pre-Raphaelite; exhibited at the Royal Academy. [xxiv. 112]

HALLIFAX, SAMUEL (1733-1790), bishop of Gloucester and St. Asaph; third wrangler and chancellor's medallist at Cambridge, 1754; fellow of Jesus College, Cambridge, 1756-60, of Trinity Hall, Cambridge, 1760-75; M.A., 1757; LL.D., 1764; D.D., 1775; held both professorships of Arabic, 1768-70, and chair of civil law, 1770-1882 ; letters of 'Erasmus' in favour of continued subscription to Thirty-nine Articles attributed to him, 1772 ; chaplain to the king, 1774 ; rector of Warsop, 1778 ; bishop of Gloucester, 1781-9, of St. Asaph, 1789-90 ; his 'Analysis of the Roman Civil Law' (1774) reissued with additions. [xxiv. 112]

HALLIFAX, SIR THOMAS (1721-1789), lord mayor of London ; prime warden of Goldsmiths' Company, 1768-1769 ; knighted ; as sheriff of London acted as returning officer when Wilkes was elected for Middlesex, 1769 ; one of the court nominees for the mayoralty against him, 1772 ; lord mayor, 1776-7 ; opposed press-gang system ; M.P., Aylesbury, 1784-9. [xxiv. 114]

HALLIFAX, WILLIAM (1655 ?-1722), divine ; fellow of Corpus Christi College, Oxford, 1682 ; M.A., 1678 ; D.D., 1695 ; chaplain at Aleppo, 1688-95 ; rector of Old Swinford, 1699, and vicar of Salwarpe : his account of Palmyra printed in 'Philosophical Transactions,' 1695 ; bequeathed books and collections to Corpus Christi College. [xxiv. 115]

HALLIWELL, HENRY (1765-1835), classical scholar ; M.A. Brasenose College, Oxford, 1789 ; fellow, 1790 ; rector of Clayton-cum-Keymer, 1803 ; assisted the Falconers with their edition of Strabo (1807) [see FALCONER, THOMAS, 1772-1839] ; satirised by Heber in the 'Whippiad,' 1843. [xxiv. 115]

HALLIWELL, afterwards HALLIWELL-PHILLIPPS, JAMES ORCHARD (1820-1889), biographer of Shakespeare ; scholar and librarian of Jesus College, Cambridge ; published 'Life and Inventions of Sir Samuel Morland,' 1838, and an edition of Mandeville's 'Travels,' 1839 ; F.S.A. and F.R.S., 1839 ; in 1840-1 prepared for press twenty-three works, including three tracts on Cambridge manuscripts, 'Rara Mathematica,' and his earliest Shakespearean works ; edited works for Camden Society, 1839-1844, Percy Society, 1842-50 (including 'Nursery Rhymes of England'), and Shakespeare Society ; catalogued Chetham Library manuscripts, 1841-2 ; married Henrietta, daughter of Sir Thomas Phillipps, 1842, whose surname he assumed thirty years later ; LL.D. Edinburgh, 1883. His 'Dictionary of Archaic and Provincial Words' appeared, 1847, 'Life of Shakespeare,' 1848, 'New Boke about Shakespeare and Stratford-on-Avon,' 1850 ; folio edition of Shakespeare, 1853-65, lithograph facsimiles of the Shakespeare quartos, 1862-71, 'Dictionary of Old English Plays,' 1860, 'Illustrations of the Life of Shakespeare,' 1874, and 'Outlines of the Life' (private issue), 1881 ; published, 1882, 1883, 1884, 1887. He arranged and described the Stratford-on-Avon archives, and wrote much on the history of the town, besides initiating the movement (1863) for purchase of the site of New Place, Shakespeare's residence there. [xxiv. 115]

HALLORAN or O'HALLORAN, LAWRENCE HYNES (1766-1831), author ; published poems, 1790-1, and 1801 ; chaplain to Earl of Northesk at Trafalgar, 1805 ; dismissed from chaplaincy to forces at Cape Town for his 'Cap-Abilities, or South African Characteristics,' 1811 ; transported for forging a frank, 1818. [xxiv. 120]

HALLOWELL, BENJAMIN (1760-1834). [See CAREW, SIR BENJAMIN HALLOWELL.]

HALLS, JOHN JAMES (fl. 1791-1834), painter ; his 'Witch' and full-length of Charles Kean in Richard III engraved by Charles Turner ; published lives of Henry Salt, F.R.S. (1834) and Nathaniel Pearce (1831). [xxiv. 121]

HALPEN or HALPIN, JOHN EDMOND (fl. 1780), painter ; son of Patrick Halpen [q. v.] [xxiv. 122]

HALPEN or HALPIN, PATRICK (fl. 1750-1790), line-engraver. [xxiv. 122]

HALPIN or HALPINE, CHARLES GRAHAM (1829-1868), writer under name of 'Miles O'Reilly' ; son of Nicholas John Halpin [q. v.] ; emigrated from Ireland, 1851 ; journalist at Boston, Washington, and New York, where he edited the 'Times,' and from 1851 the 'Leader' ; enlisted in federal army, 1861 ; assistant-adjutant-general to General David Hunter and General Henry W. Halleck ; published 'Life and Adventures, &c., of Private Miles O'Reilly' (1864) and 'Baked Meats of the Funeral . . . by Private M. O'Reilly' (1866) ; registrar of New York county, 1867-8 ; died from an overdose of chloroform. [xxiv. 122]

HALPIN, NICHOLAS JOHN (1790-1850), author ; B.A. Dublin, 1815 ; edited 'Dublin Evening Mail' ; published three works of Shakespearean criticism and 'Observations on certain Passages in the Life of Edmund Spenser,' 1850. [xxiv. 123]

HALS, WILLIAM (1655-1737 ?), Cornish writer ; grandson of Sir Nicholas Halse [q. v.] ; made collections for 'History of Cornwall,' part ii., published about 1750. [xxiv. 123]

HALSE, SIR NICHOLAS (d. 1636), inventor of new mode of drying malt and hops by iron plates ; knighted, 1605 ; governor of Pendennis Castle, 1608 ; left in manuscript 'Great Britain's Treasure.' [xxiv. 124]

HALSWELLE, KEELEY (1832-1891), artist ; engaged as book illustrator ; exhibited at Royal Scottish Academy from 1857 ; A.R.S.A., 1866 ; subsequently exhibited many landscapes at Royal Academy ; member of Institute of Painters in Oils, 1882. [Suppl. ii. 380]

HALSWORTH or HOLDSWORTH, DANIEL (1558 ?-1595 ?), classical scholar ; of the English colleges of Douay and Rome ; theologian to St. Charles Borromeo ; made Greek translation of Virgil's 'Bucolics,' 1591, and Latin version of epigrams of Archias, 1596 ; died at Rome. [xxiv. 125]

HALTON, IMMANUEL (1628-1699), astronomer ; auditor to the household of Thomas, earl of Arundel ; friend of Flamsteed, who communicated to Royal Society Halton's observations of a solar eclipse, 1675. [xxiv. 125]

HALTON or HALGHTON, JOHN OF (d. 1324), bishop : prior of St. Mary's, Carlisle ; bishop of Carlisle, 1292-1324 ; ambassador to King John of Scotland, 1295 ; excommunicated Bruce for murder of Comyn, 1309 ; sat in Lancaster's council, 1318 ; envoy to Scotland, 1320 ; his register still preserved. [xxiv. 126]

HALTON, TIMOTHY (1632 ?-1704), provost of Queen's College, Oxford ; probably brother of Immanuel Halton [q. v.] ; fellow of Queen's College, Oxford, 1657 ; D.D., 1674 ; archdeacon of Brecknock, 1672, of Oxford, 1675 ; provost of Queen's College, Oxford, 1677-1704 ; vice-chancellor of Oxford, 1679-81 and 1685. [xxiv. 127]

HALYBURTON, GEORGE (d. 1682), Scots nonconformist minister ; ejected, 1662. [xxiv. 129]

HALYBURTON or HALIBURTON, JAMES (1518-1589), provost of Dundee ; M.A. St. Andrews, 1538 ; distinguished at capture of Broughty Castle, 1549 ; provost of Dundee, 1553-86 ; captured by the Grahams in Liddesdale, 1556, but soon rescued ; a lord of the congregation, commander of musters of Fife and Forfar against the queen regent, 1559 ; took part in defence of Edinburgh, and signed 'last band at Leith' and (1561) first Book of Discipline ; commissioner to administer Act of Oblivion, 1563 ; joined Moray's movement against Darnley marriage ; present at Langside, 1568, and at Restalrig, 1571 ; afterwards captured by queen's forces and barely escaped execution, 1571 ; Morton's representative at conference of 1578 ; privy councillor, 1582 ; one of the king's commissioners to general assembly, 1582 and 1588. [xxiv. 127]

HALYBURTON, THOMAS (1674-1712), theologian ; son of George Halyburton [q. v.] ; educated at Rotterdam and St. Andrews ; professor of divinity at St. Leonard's College, 1710-12 ; his writings against deists reissued, 1865, as 'Essay on the Ground or formal Reason of a saving Faith' ; his 'Memoirs' (2nd ed., 1715) frequently reprinted ; works collected, 1835. [xxiv. 129]

HAMBOYS, JOHN (fl. 1470). [See HANBOYS.]

HAMBURY, HENRY DE (fl. 1330), justice of common pleas in Ireland, c. 1324 ; chief-justice, 1327 ; judge of the king's bench (England), 1328. [xxiv. 130]

HAMERTON, PHILIP GILBERT (1834-1894), artist and essayist ; studied art in London ; resided on isle of Innistrynich, Loch Awe, 1858 ; published 'A Painter's Camp in the Highlands,' 1862 ; art critic to 'Saturday Review' ; established with Mr Richmond Seeley, the publisher, 'The Portfolio' periodical, 1869 ; directed 'Portfolio' till his death ; LL.D. Aberdeen, 1894. He published two novels, besides numerous valuable contributions to art literature. His autobiography was completed and published by his widow, 1897. [Suppl. ii. 380]

HAMEY, BALDWIN, the elder (1568–1640), physician to the czar of Muscovy, 1592–8; M.D. Leyden; L.R.C.P., 1610. [xxiv. 130]

HAMEY, BALDWIN, the younger (1600–1676), physician; son of Baldwin Hamey the elder [q. v.]; M.D. Leyden, 1626, Oxford, 1629; visited Paris, Montpelier, and Padua; F.R.C.P., 1633; eight times censor; treasurer, 1664–6; Gulstonian lecturer, 1647; benefactor of the Royal College of Physicians; left manuscript account of contemporary physicians; his dissertation on the ὅρκος Ἱπποκράτους edited 1693. [xxiv. 131]

HAMILTON, DUKES OF. [See HAMILTON, JAMES, first DUKE, 1606–1649; HAMILTON, WILLIAM, second DUKE, 1616–1651; DOUGLAS, WILLIAM, third DUKE, 1635–1694; DOUGLAS, JAMES, fourth DUKE, 1658–1712; DOUGLAS, ALEXANDER HAMILTON, tenth DUKE, 1767–1852; DOUGLAS, WILLIAM ALEXANDER ANTHONY ARCHIBALD, eleventh DUKE, 1811–63.]

HAMILTON, MRS. (*fl.* 1745–1772), actress; appeared for some years as Mrs. Bland, playing with Garrick at Covent Garden in Shakespearean parts, 1746; reappeared at Covent Garden, 1752–62; afterwards went to Ireland; her distresses the cause of the establishment of the Theatrical Fund. [xxiv. 132]

HAMILTON, ALEXANDER (*d.* 1732?), merchant and author; published 'New Account of the East Indies,' 1727. [xxiv. 133]

HAMILTON, ALEXANDER (1739–1802), professor of midwifery at Edinburgh University; deacon of the Edinburgh College of Surgeons; professor of midwifery, Edinburgh, 1780–1800; chief founder of Lying-in Hospital, 1791; published treatises on midwifery. [xxiv. 133]

HAMILTON, ALEXANDER (1762–1824), orientalist; while hostage in France drew up for Paris Library analytical catalogue of Sanskrit manuscripts, and taught the language to Schlegel and Fauriel; F.R.S., 1808; professor of Sanskrit and Hindoo literature at Haileybury; published works on Sanskrit. [xxiv. 134]

HAMILTON, ANDREW (*d.* 1691), rector and prebendary of Kilskerry, 1666; raised troops against James II; published 'True Relation of the Actions of the Inniskilling Men,' 1690. [xxiv. 134]

HAMILTON, ANNE, DUCHESS OF HAMILTON (1636–1716), daughter of the first Duke of Hamilton; married William Douglas (1635–1694) [q. v.], who became on her petition Duke of Hamilton. [xv. 370]

HAMILTON, LADY ANNE (1766–1846), lady-in-waiting to Queen Caroline; daughter of Archibald, ninth duke of Hamilton; accompanied Queen Caroline to England, 1820; her 'Secret History of the Court' (1832), published in her name, but without her sanction. [xxiv. 135]

HAMILTON, ANTHONY (1646?–1720), author of 'Mémoires du Comte de Grammont'; third son of Sir George Hamilton [q. v.]; as governor of Limerick, 1685, openly went to mass; privy councillor, 1686; commanded Jacobite dragoons at Enniskillen and Newtown Butler, 1689; present at the Boyne, 1690; spent the rest of his life at St. Germain-en-Laye, being intimate with Berwick; addressed letters and verses to the Duchess of Berwick and Laura Bulkeley, and wrote for Henrietta Bulkeley four satirical 'Contes' in French. His 'Epistle to the Comte de Grammont' (his brother-in-law) announcing intention of writing his memoirs was approved by Boileau, 1705. The 'Mémoires' appeared anonymously, 1713, and were edited by Horace Walpole, 1772, Sir Walter Scott, 1811, and M. de Lescure, 1876; 'Œuvres Complètes' were issued, 1749–76. [xxiv. 135]

HAMILTON, ARCHIBALD (*d.* 1593), Roman catholic controversialist; disputed publicly with Knox; published Latin works against Scottish Calvinists and a treatise on Aristotle; died at Rome. [xxiv. 138]

HAMILTON, ARCHIBALD (1580?–1659); archbishop of Cashel and Emly; D.D. Glasgow; bishop of Killala and Achonry, 1623; archbishop of Cashel and Emly, 1630; after rebellion of 1641 fled to Sweden, where he died. [xxiv. 138]

HAMILTON, LORD ARCHIBALD (1770–1827), politician; brother of Lady Anne Hamilton [q. v.]; M.A. Christ Church, Oxford, 1795; barrister, Lincoln's Inn, 1799; M.P., Lanarkshire, 1802–27; published pamphlet (1804) condemning Pitt's second ministry and that of Addington; moved vote of censure on Castlereagh as president of board of control, 1809; carried resolution for referring petition from Scottish royal burghs to select committee, 1819; moved insertion of Queen Caroline's name in the liturgy, 1820. [xxiv. 139]

HAMILTON, CHARLES (by courtesy LORD BINNING) (1697–1733), poet; son of Thomas Hamilton, sixth earl of Haddington [q. v.]; fought for government at Sheriffmuir, 1715; M.P., St. Germans, 1722; died at Naples; his pastoral 'Ungrateful Nanny' in Ritson's 'Scottish Songs,' 1794. [xxiv. 139]

HAMILTON, CHARLES (1691–1754), historian; natural son of James Douglas, fourth duke of Hamilton [q. v.], and Lady Barbara Fitzroy; styled Count Arran; accompanied his father in duel with Mohun, 1707, and himself fought General Macartney; settled in Switzerland; died at Paris; 'Transactions during the Reign of Anne' (1790) attributed to him, but written by his son. [xxiv. 140]

HAMILTON, CHARLES (1753?–1792), orientalist; in military service of East India Company; published historical work on the Rohilla Afghans (1787), and translation of the Persian 'Hedaya,' 1791. [xxiv. 140]

HAMILTON, SIR CHARLES, second baronet (1767–1849), admiral; commanded the Dido at sieges of Bastia, Calvi, and San Fiorenzo (1793), the Melpomene on Dutch coast, and at capture of Goree and in West Indies, 1799–1802; vice-admiral, 1814; admiral, 1830; M.P., Dungannon, 1801–7, Honiton, 1807–12; governor of Newfoundland, 1818–24. [xxiv. 140]

HAMILTON, CHARLES WILLIAM (1670–1754), painter at Augsburg; son of James Hamilton (*fl.* 1640–1680) [q. v.] of Murdieston. [xxiv. 185]

HAMILTON, CLAUD, BARON PAISLEY (1543?–1622), known as LORD CLAUD HAMILTON; fourth son of James Hamilton, duke of Châtelherault [q. v.]; convoyed Mary Queen of Scots from Lochleven to Niddry and Hamilton, 1568, and (probably) led the van for her at Langside, 1568; concerned in plot by which Moray was assassinated, 1570; led attempt to capture Lennox and king's lords at Stirling, 1571; recovered his estates by pacification of Perth, 1573; privy to plot against Morton, 1578; denounced by council for murder of the regents; fled to England, 1579; took part in Gowrie conspiracy, 1584; recalled from Paris by James VI, 1586; with Huntly shared leadership of Scottish catholics, and was commissioned by the Guises to reconcile Mary and her son James, 1586; entered into communication with Spain, and urged on Armada project; created Baron Paisley, 1587; became insane. [xxiv. 141]

HAMILTON, SIR DAVID (1663–1721), physician to Queen Anne; M.D. Rheims, 1686; F.R.C.P., 1703; F.R.S., 1708; knighted; published religious and medical tracts. [xxiv. 144]

HAMILTON, DAVID (1768–1843), architect; designed many buildings in western Scotland, including Hamilton Palace, Lennox Castle, and the Glasgow Exchange. [xxiv. 144]

HAMILTON, SIR EDWARD, first baronet (1772–1851), admiral; brother of Sir Charles Hamilton [q. v.]; while in command of Surprise said to have taken or destroyed eighty privateers and merchantmen, 1797–9; knighted and awarded the freedom of the city for cutting out the Hermione at Puerto Cabello, 1799; captured by French, but exchanged; engaged in blockading northern French coast, 1801; dismissed the service for inflicting excessive punishment, 1802, but specially reinstated, 1802; commanded royal yacht and Prince Regent, 1806–19; created baronet, 1818; vice-admiral, 1837; admiral, 1846. [xxiv. 145]

HAMILTON, ELIZABETH, COMTESSE DE GRAMMONT (1641–1708), 'la belle Hamilton'; sister of Anthony Hamilton [q. v.], who brought about her marriage with Philibert, comte de Grammont, 1663; lived in France from 1664. [xxiv. 146]

HAMILTON, ELIZABETH, DUCHESS OF HAMILTON, afterwards of ARGYLL (1734–1790). [See GUNNING.]

HAMILTON, ELIZABETH (1758–1816), author; sister of Charles Hamilton (1753?–1792) [q. v.]; published

'The Hindoo Rajah,' 1796, 'Memoirs of Modern Philosophers,' 1800, and several educational works, besides 'The Cottagers of Glenburnie' (1808) and 'My ain Fireside' (song). [xxiv. 147]

HAMILTON, EMMA, LADY (1761?-1815), wife of Sir William Hamilton (1730-1803) [q. v.] the ambassador; *née* Lyon; went to London, 1778, probably as a nursemaid to family of Dr. Richard Budd [q. v.]; said to have been the 'Goddess of Health' in exhibition of James Graham (1745-1794) [q. v.]; lived under protection of Sir Harry Fetherstonhaugh and Hon. Charles Greville as Emily Hart, 1780-4; refined by innocent intimacy with Romney, 1782; became mistress of Sir William Hamilton at Naples, 1786, and was married to him in England, 1791; intimate with Queen Maria Carolina at Naples; first saw Nelson, 1793; intimate with Nelson on his return from the Nile, 1798; together with her husband accompanied Nelson to Palermo, 1800, and afterwards to England, giving birth to Horatia, 30 Jan. 1801; received the cross of Malta from the czar for supposed services to the Maltese, 1799; claimed to have rendered important political services while at Naples, but these claims, although endorsed by Nelson, were ignored by British ministry; involved in debt by her extravagances, in spite of legacies from Nelson and Hamilton; assisted by Alderman Joshua J. Smith to escape from king's bench to Calais, where she died in obscurity. [xxiv. 148]

HAMILTON, FERDINAND PHILIP (1664-1750), painter to Charles V at Vienna; eldest son of James Hamilton (*fl.* 1640-1680) [q. v.] of Murdieston. [xxiv. 185]

HAMILTON, FRANCIS (1762-1829). [See BUCHANAN.]

HAMILTON, GAVIN (1561?-1612), bishop of Galloway; graduated at St. Andrews, 1584; minister of Hamilton; bishop of Galloway, 1605 (consecrated, 1610); dean of Chapel Royal, Holyrood, 1606. [xxiv. 154]

HAMILTON, GAVIN (1730-1797), painter and excavator; lived principally at Rome; during short residence in London member of committee for forming Royal Academy, 1755; occasionally exhibited at the Royal Academy; his 'Apollo' seen at International Exhibition of 1862; published 'Schola Italica Picturæ,' 1773; carried on excavations at Hadrian's villa below Tivoli, Monte Cagnuolo, the district of the Alban hills and the territory of ancient Gabii, selling his 'finds' to the Museo Pio-Clementino, the Townley collection, Lord Lansdowne, and other collectors; his marbles now in the Louvre. [xxiv. 155]

HAMILTON, GAVIN (1753-1805), friend of Burns; prominent in 'New Light' dispute in Mauchline; defended in Burns's theological satires. [xxiv. 156]

HAMILTON, SIR GEORGE, first baronet (*d.* 1679), royalist; fourth son of James Hamilton, first earl of Abercorn [q. v.]; created an Irish baronet, 1660, for services during the rebellion. [xxiv. 177]

HAMILTON, LORD GEORGE, EARL OF ORKNEY (1666-1737), general; fifth son of William Douglas, third duke of Hamilton [q. v.]; distinguished under William III in Ireland and Flanders; severely wounded at Namur, 1695, and promoted brigadier; married (1695) Elizabeth Villiers, William's mistress; created a Scottish peer, 1696; lieutenant-general, 1704; K.T., 1704; captured 12,000 men and 1,300 officers at Blenheim, 1704; saved citadel of Liège, 1705; led pursuit after Ramillies, 1706; prominent at Oudenarde, 1706, favouring immediate advance on Paris; commanded the van at passage of Scheldt, 1708; opened attack at Malplaquet, 1709; elected a Scottish representative peer, 1707; privy councillor, 1710; lord of the bedchamber, 1714; governor of Virginia, 1714; fieldmarshal, 1736. [xxiv. 156]

HAMILTON, GEORGE (1783-1830), biblical scholar; fourth son of Hugh Hamilton (1729-1805) [q. v.]; M.A. Trinity College, Dublin, 1821; rector of Killermogh, 1809-1830; published 'Introduction to Study of the Hebrew Scriptures,' 1813; 'Codex Criticus of the Hebrew Bible,' 1821, and controversial tracts. [xxiv. 158]

HAMILTON, GEORGE ALEXANDER (1802-1871), politician; of Rugby and Trinity College, Oxford; B.A., 1821; D.C.L., 1853; elected on petition for Dublin, 1836; sat for Dublin University, 1843-59; formed Conservative Society for Ireland; presented protestant petition of 1837;

financial secretary to treasury, 1852, and 1858-9; permanent secretary, 1859; privy councillor, 1869. [xxiv. 158]

HAMILTON, GUSTAVUS, VISCOUNT BOYNE (1639-1723), grandson of Claud Hamilton, baron Paisley [q. v.]; defended Enniskillen and Coleraine against Jacobites, 1689; commanded a regiment at the Boyne, 1690, Athlone, 1691, and Vigo, 1707; major-general, 1703; privy councillor under William III, Anne, and George I; created Irish baron, 1715; created Viscount Boyne in Irish peerage, 1717. [xxiv. 159]

HAMILTON, HENRY PARR (1794-1880), dean of Salisbury; son of Alexander Hamilton (1739-1802) [q. v.]; fellow of Trinity College, Cambridge; ninth wrangler, 1816; M.A., 1819; rector of Wath, Yorkshire, and incumbent (1833-44) of St. Mary the Great, Cambridge; F.R.S., 1828; contributed largely to restoration of his cathedral; published educational pamphlets and works on analytical geometry and conic sections. [xxiv. 160]

HAMILTON, HUGH or HUGO, first BARON HAMILTON OF GLENAWLEY (*d.* 1679), soldier; having served in Swedish army was naturalised and ennobled; created an Irish peer, 1660; settled in Ireland. [xxiv. 160]

HAMILTON, HUGH, BARON HAMILTON in Sweden (*d.* 1724), Swedish general; nephew of Hugh Hamilton (*d.* 1679) [q. v.]; distinguished himself against the Danes, 1710, and Russians, 1719; ancestor of Swedish counts. [xxiv. 161]

HAMILTON, HUGH (1729-1805), bishop of Clonfert and Ossory; M.A. Dublin, 1750; D.D., 1762; fellow of Trinity College, Dublin, 1751-64; professor of natural philosophy, 1759; dean of Armagh, 1768-96; F.R.S.; bishop of Clonfert, 1796-9, of Ossory, 1799; collected works issued, 1809. [xxiv. 161]

HAMILTON, HUGH DOUGLAS (1734?-1806); portrait-painter; exhibited with Incorporated Society (1771, and 1773-5) and Free Society of Artists, 1772; went to Rome, 1778; returned to Dublin, 1791. [xxiv. 161]

HAMILTON, SIR JAMES, of Cadzow, first BARON HAMILTON (*d.* 1479), connected with house of Douglas by his marriage with widow of fifth earl and that of her daughter (Fair Maid of Galloway) with William, eighth earl; lord of parliament, 1445; accompanied the eighth Earl of Douglas to Rome, 1450, and attended him to his fatal meeting with James II at Stirling, 1452; joined James, ninth earl of Douglas, in renunciation of allegiance and subsequent submission, 1453; advised another rebellion, but went over to the king owing to Douglas's weakness; commissioner for peace with England and sheriff of Lanarkshire, 1455; married Mary Stewart, sister of James III, 1469. [xxiv. 162]

HAMILTON, JAMES, second BARON HAMILTON and first EARL OF ARRAN (1477?-1529), son of Sir James Hamilton, first baron Hamilton [q. v.]; made privy councillor by James IV, whose marriage with Margaret Tudor he negotiated, 1503; created Earl of Arran for skill in tournament, 1503; when lieutenant-general of Scotland helped to reduce Western Isles (1504) and to re-establish king of Denmark; detained in England by Henry VII after embassy to France, 1507; during minority of James V opposed Angus and the English party; plotted against the regent Albany; president of council of regency during Albany's absence in France, 1517-20; defeated in attempt to overpower Angus in Edinburgh, 1520; again member of council of regency, 1522, and lieutenant of the south; joined queen-dowager in ousting Albany and proclaiming James V, 1524; compelled by Henry VIII to re-admit Angus to council; supported Angus against Lennox, 1526, but on escape of James V from the Douglases received Bothwell from Angus's forfeited estates. [xxiv. 165]

HAMILTON, SIR JAMES, of Finnart (*d.* 1540), royal architect; natural son of James Hamilton, second baron Hamilton [q. v.]; prominent as the 'Bastard of Arran' in his father's feuds with the Douglases, especially at 'Cleanse the Causeway,' 1520; assassinated Lennox when a prisoner after Linlithgow, 1526; legitimated by James V, as designer of Craignethan and restorer of Linlithgow and Falkland; executed for alleged plot to murder the king. [xxiv. 166]

HAMILTON, JAMES, second EARL OF ARRAN and DUKE OF CHÂTELHERAULT (*d.* 1575), governor of Scotland; eldest son of James Hamilton, second baron Hamilton [q. v.]; chosen governor of Scotland (as 'second person in the realm '), 1542 ; for a short time head of the English party, but came to terms with Cardinal David Beaton [q. v.], 1543 ; successfully resisted transference of power to queen-dowager, 1545 ; created Duke of Châtelherault, 1548 ; obliged to abdicate regency, 1554 ; returned to English alliance on capture of Edinburgh by lords of congregation, 1559 ; revived his project for marriage of his son with Queen Mary on her arrival in Scotland ; for his opposition to Darnley marriage banished to France, 1566 ; returned to Scotland, 1569, as supporter of the queen and was imprisoned with Moray. [xxiv. 167]

HAMILTON, JAMES, of Bothwellhaugh (*fl.* 1566-1580), assassin of the regent Moray ; captured at Langside, 1568, but pardoned at Knox's intercession ; shot the regent Moray at Linlithgow, 1570 [see STEWART, LORD JAMES, 1531 ?-1570] ; escaped to France and tried to obtain aid for Mary ; excepted from pacification of Perth : refused to assist in murder of Coligny, but acted as agent for the Spanish king in attempts on life of William the Silent, 1573 and 1575 ; disinherited ; probably died abroad. [xxiv. 170]

HAMILTON, JAMES, third EARL OF ARRAN (1530-1609), eldest son of James, second earl of Arran [q. v.] ; proposed by Henry VIII as husband for Princess Elizabeth, 1543, but destined by his father for Mary Queen of Scots ; served in Scots guards in France, 1550-8 ; distinguished at St. Quentin, 1557 ; styled Earl of Arran after 1553 ; became a protestant while in France, and by Knox's advice was brought to England to confer with the government, 1558 ; despatched secretly to Scotland, 1559 ; strengthened his father in protestant policy ; with Lord James Stuart (Moray) attempted to capture Bothwell, and by defending Dysart saved Fife from the French ; took part in siege of Leith, and signed the 'last band' and the first Book of Discipline ; again made proposals for hand of Elizabeth, 1560-1 ; on Knox's advice renewed also his suit to Mary ; reconciled with Bothwell by Knox, 1562 ; revealed to latter alleged advice of Bothwell to him to carry off Mary, marry her, and murder Moray and Maitland, 1562 ; imprisoned till 1566, now almost insane ; afterwards lived in retirement at Craignethan till brought to Linlithgow by James VI, 1579. [xxiv. 173]

HAMILTON, JAMES, first EARL OF ABERCORN (*d.* 1617), son of Claud Hamilton, baron Paisley [q. v.] ; gentleman of the bedchamber to James VI ; privy councillor (as master of Paisley), 1598 ; sheriff of Linlithgow, 1600 ; created Baron Abercorn (Scotland), 1603 ; created earl for services as commissioner for union with England, 1606. [xxiv. 176]

HAMILTON, JAMES, second MARQUIS OF HAMILTON (1589-1625) ; succeeded his father, Lord John Hamilton [q. v.], as marquis, 1604, and his uncle as Earl of Arran, 1609 ; privy councillor of Scotland, 1613, of England, 1617 ; created an English peer (Earl of Cambridge), 1619 ; advocated leniency to Bacon, 1621 ; as high commissioner to Scottish parliament, 1621, carried Five Articles of Perth ; a commissioner for marriage of Prince Charles to the Spanish Infanta, 1623 ; lord-steward, 1624 ; opposed Buckingham's French policy, 1624 ; said to have been poisoned by Buckingham. [xxiv. 177]

HAMILTON, JAMES, first VISCOUNT CLANEBOYE in Irish peerage (1559-1643), Ulster planter ; educated at St. Andrews University ; despatched by James VI on secret mission to Ireland, 1587 ; carried on Latin school in Dublin, which Ussher attended : original fellow of Trinity College, Dublin, 1592 ; James VI's agent in London, 1600 ; knighted and given large grants in Ulster, 1605 ; M.P., co. Down, 1613 ; commissioner for plantation of Longford, 1619 ; created Irish peer, 1622 ; granted dissolved monastery of Bangor, 1630 ; privy councillor, 1634 ; armed Scots in Ulster, 1641. [xxiv. 178]

HAMILTON, JAMES, third MARQUIS and first DUKE OF HAMILTON in the Scottish peerage, second EARL OF CAMBRIDGE in the English peerage (1606-1649), succeeded as third marquis, 1625 ; master of the horse, 1628 ; privy councillor, 1628 ; commanded British force under Gustavus Adolphus, 1630-4 ; as Charles I's adviser on Scottish affairs, persuaded him to revoke the prayer-book, canons, and high commission, and to call a parliament, 1638 ; commanded against covenanters, but resigned commissionership, 1639 ; carried on intrigues between Charles and covenanters, and opposed Strafford and

Montrose ; allied himself (1641) for a time with Argyll, but (1642) endeavoured to prevent Scots from supporting English parliament ; refused to take the covenant, 1643, and joined the king at Oxford, but was imprisoned, 1644 ; liberated by Fairfax, 1646 ; again attempted to mediate between Charles and the Scots, 1646 ; led Scottish army into England, but was defeated at Preston, 1648 ; condemned and executed, 1649. [xxiv. 179]

HAMILTON, JAMES (*d.* 1666), divine ; educated at Glasgow University ; incumbent of Ballywalter, 1626-36 ; deposed for heresy after public disputation, 1636 ; afterwards minister at Dumfries and Edinburgh. [xxiv. 183]

HAMILTON, JAMES (1610-1674), bishop of Galloway ; graduated at Glasgow, 1628 ; minister of Cambusnethan, 1634 ; deposed, 1638, but restored, 1639 ; supported the 'Engagement,' 1648 ; bishop of Galloway, 1661-74. [xxiv. 184]

HAMILTON, JAMES, of Murdieston (*fl.* 1640-1680), painter of animals and still-life at Brussels. [xxiv. 185]

HAMILTON, JAMES, sixth EARL OF ABERCORN (1656-1734), grandson of Sir George Hamilton [q. v.] ; assisted in defence of Derry, 1689 ; succeeded as Earl of Abercorn, 1701 ; created Viscount Strabane (Irish peerage), 1701 ; privy councillor. [xxiv. 185]

HAMILTON, JAMES, seventh EARL OF ABERCORN (*d.* 1744), second son of James Hamilton, sixth earl of Abercorn [q. v.] ; privy councillor of England (1738) and Ireland (1739) ; F.R.S. ; published 'Calculations and Tables relating to Attractive Power of Loadstones,' 1729. [xxiv. 185]

HAMILTON, JAMES, eighth EARL OF ABERCORN (1712-1789), eldest son of James Hamilton, seventh earl of Abercorn [q. v.] ; summoned to Irish House of Peers as Baron Mountcastle, 1736 ; representative peer of Scotland, 1761-86 ; created British peer as Viscount Hamilton, 1786. [xxiv. 185]

HAMILTON, JAMES (1769-1829), author of Hamiltonian linguistic system ; derived rudiments of his system from D'Angeli, an *emigré* ; detained in Paris at rupture of peace of Amiens ; began to teach his system at Philadelphia, 1816, and to print texts for use of pupils ; very successful at Boston, the American universities, and in Canada ; came to London, 1823, and taught in chief cities of United Kingdom ; was defended in 'Edinburgh Review,' 1826, by Sydney Smith, and in 'Westminster Review.' [xxiv. 186]

HAMILTON, JAMES, the elder (1749-1835), Edinburgh physician ; noted for old-fashioned dress and manners and his works on purgative treatment. [xxiv. 187]

HAMILTON, JAMES, the younger (*d.* 1839), professor of midwifery at Edinburgh, 1800, succeeding his father, Alexander Hamilton (1739-1802) [q. v.] ; recovered damages from Dr. James Gregory, 1753-1821 [q. v.] for assault, 1793 ; succeeded in getting obstetrics made compulsory in medical course of Edinburgh University, 1830 ; published medical works. [xxiv. 187]

HAMILTON, JAMES (1814-1867), presbyterian minister ; graduated at Glasgow, 1835 ; Candlish's assistant at St. George's, Edinburgh, 1838 ; minister of National Scottish Church, Regent Square, London, 1841-1867 ; published devotional and biographical works ; his 'Book of Psalms and Hymns,' adopted by presbyterian churches. [xxiv. 188]

HAMILTON, JAMES, first DUKE OF ABERCORN (1811-1885), succeeded his grandfather as second Marquis of Abercorn, 1818 ; groom of the stole to Prince Albert, 1846-59 ; lord-lieutenant of Ireland, 1866-8 and 1874-6 ; created duke, 1868. [xxiv. 188]

HAMILTON, JAMES ALEXANDER (1785-1845), compiler of musical handbooks, including the 'Pianoforte Tutor' (1728th ed. 1890). [xxiv. 189]

HAMILTON, JAMES ARCHIBALD (1747-1815), astronomer ; educated at Armagh and Trinity College, Dublin ; B.A. ; D.D., 1784 ; made observations on transit of Mercury from private observatory in Cookstown ; archdeacon of Ross, 1790 ; dean of Cloyne, 1804 ; first astronomer at Armagh Observatory, 1790. [xxiv. 190]

HAMILTON, JANET (1795-1873), Scottish poetess ; daughter of a Lancashire shoemaker ; her 'Poems and Prose Works' collected by her son, 1880. [xxiv. 190]

HAMILTON, JOHN (1511?-1571), archbishop of St. Andrews; natural son of James Hamilton, first earl of Arran [q. v.]; keeper of the privy seal, 1543; bishop of Dunkeld, 1545; archbishop of St. Andrews, 1546; reconciled Arran with Beaton; promulgated Hamilton's catechism at synod of 1552; endowed St. Mary's College, St. Andrews; persecuted protestants; accepted new confession, 1560; imprisoned for popish practices, 1563; member of councils of Mary Queen of Scots, 1566; divorced Bothwell from Lady Jane Gordon, 1567; present at Langside, 1568; hanged at Stirling on charge of being accessory to Darnley's murder and of complicity in that of Moray. [xxiv. 190]

HAMILTON, JOHN, first MARQUIS OF HAMILTON (1532-1604), second son of James Hamilton, duke of Châtelherault [q. v.]; assisted Bothwell and negotiated with England for deliverance of Mary; furthered assassination of Moray (1570) in revenge for forfeiture; represented his family at pacification of Perth, 1573; head of his family after death of Châtelherault, 1575; in constant danger of his life from Sir William Douglas (d. 1606) [q. v.]; escaped to France, 1579; joined his brother, Lord Claud Hamilton [q. v.], in England, and thence went to Scotland, 1584; recovered his estates; in favour with James VI; went on embassy to Denmark, 1588; a lord of the articles, 1594; accompanied James VI against Huntly; sat on Huntly's trial; created marquis, 1599. [xxiv. 192]

HAMILTON, JOHN (fl. 1568-1609), anti-protestant writer; described himself as the queen's 'daily orator'; probably Mary Stuart's messenger to Alva, 1568-9; tutor to Cardinal de Bourbon, 1576; rector of Paris University, 1584; prominent member of French Catholic League; adjutant of thirteen hundred armed ecclesiastics, 1590; on the entry of Henri Quatre (1594) escaped to Brussels; executed in effigy for murder of Tardif; returned to Scotland, 1600, with Edmund Hay [q. v.], and secretly celebrated mass; captured, 1608; died in prison. He published at Paris (1581) tract in favour of transubstantiation, with appendix dedicated to James VI, and at Louvain (1600) a treatise, with prayers, also dedicated to the king. [xxiv. 195]

HAMILTON, SIR JOHN, first BARON BARGENY (d. 1658), royalist; grandson of John, first marquis of Hamilton [q. v.]; created a Scottish peer, 1639. [xxiv. 197]

HAMILTON, JOHN, second BARON BARGENY (d. 1693), son of Sir John Hamilton, first baron Bargeny [q. v.]; imprisoned as disaffected, 1679-80; raised regiment for William of Orange, 1689. [xxiv. 197]

HAMILTON, JOHN, second BARON BELHAVEN (1656-1708), imprisoned and compelled to apologise for remarks on Duke of York, 1681; contributed to settlement of Scottish crown on William III, 1689, and became privy councillor; strong supporter of Darien scheme; advocated Act of Security, 1703, and strongly opposed the union, his speech of 1706 becoming famous as 'Belhaven's Vision'; imprisoned (1708) on suspicion of favouring French invasion. [xxiv. 197]

HAMILTON, JOHN (d. 1755), captain in the navy; second son of James Hamilton, seventh earl of Abercorn [q. v.]; distinguished at wreck of the Louisa, 1736; had the Kinsale fitted with nine-pounders and canvas screens, 1742; drowned near Spithead. [xxiv. 199]

HAMILTON, JOHN (fl. 1765-1786), painter; director of Incorporated Society of Artists, 1773. [xxiv. 199]

HAMILTON, JOHN (1761-1814), Scottish songwriter; contributed to Johnson's 'Museum,' and helped Scott with 'Border Minstrelsy'; composed songs, including 'Up in the Mornin' Early' and 'The Ploughman.' [xxiv. 199]

HAMILTON, SIR JOHN, first baronet (1755-1835), lieutenant-general; served in East Indian army in Cutch Behar and against Mahrattas (1778), and in British against Tippoo Sahib, 1790-1; lieutenant-colonel of the 81st in San Domingo and Kaffir war of 1800; inspector-general of Portuguese army, 1809; commanded divisions at Albuera, 1811, and the Nivelle, 1813; lieutenant-general, 1814; created baronet, 1815. [xxiv. 200]

HAMILTON, JOHN GEORGE (1662-1736?), painter at Vienna; son of James Hamilton (fl. 1640-1680) [q. v.] [xxiv. 185]

HAMILTON, MALCOLM (1635-1699), Swedish general; naturalised as Swedish noble, 1664; created Baron Hamilton de Hageby, 1693. [xxiv. 200]

HAMILTON, MARY, DUCHESS OF HAMILTON (1613-1638), lady of the bedchamber to Henrietta Maria; Waller wrote 'Thyrsis Galatea' in her praise. [xxiv. 183]

HAMILTON, LADY MARY (1739-1816), novelist; née Leslie; lived with her second husband in France, and was intimate with Sir Herbert Croft (1751-1816) [q. v.] and Charles Nodier; published four novels. [xxiv. 201]

HAMILTON, PATRICK (1504?-1528), Scottish martyr; grandson of Sir James Hamilton of Cadzow, lord Hamilton [q. v.]; M.A. Paris, 1520; M.A. St. Andrews, 1524; saw Luther and Melanchthon at Wittenberg; at Marburg, 1527, composed his 'Loci Communes' ('Patrick's Pleas'); after return to Scotland charged with seven articles of heresy; sentenced by Archbishop Beaton and burnt at St. Andrews; had previously converted Alexander Alesius [q. v.] [xxiv. 201]

HAMILTON, RICHARD (fl. 1688), Jacobite lieutenant-general; brother of Anthony Hamilton [q. v.]; served with distinction in French army; banished French court for seeking Princess de Conti in marriage; despatched by Tyrconnel with troops to help James II in England, 1688; sent by William III with offers to Irish catholics; deserted to Tyrconnel, 1689; commanded at siege of Derry, 1689; captured at the Boyne; sent to the Tower, 1690; rejoined James in France. [xxiv. 203]

HAMILTON, RICHARD WINTER (1794-1848), independent minister; minister of Albion (afterwards of Belgrave) Chapel, Leeds; LL.D. Glasgow, 1844; chairman of Congregational Union, 1847; published 'Horæ et Vindiciæ Sabbaticæ,' 1847. [xxiv. 204]

HAMILTON, SIR ROBERT, second baronet (1650-1701), covenanting leader; educated under Burnet at Glasgow; one of the composers of Rutherglen declaration, 1679; showed cowardice in command at Drumclog and at Bothwell Brigg, 1679; fled to Holland; visited Germany and Switzerland as commissioner for Scottish presbyterian church; returned and succeeded as baronet, 1688; imprisoned on suspicion of having drawn up Sanquhar declaration, 1692-3. [xxiv. 205]

HAMILTON, ROBERT (1721-1793), physician; published work on scrofula, 1791. [xxiv. 207]

HAMILTON, ROBERT (1743-1829), professor of natural philosophy and mathematics at Aberdeen, 1779-1829; published 'Inquiry concerning the Rise and Progress, Reduction and Present State, and the Management of the National Debt,' 1813. [xxiv. 207]

HAMILTON, ROBERT (1749-1830), physician; M.D. Edinburgh, 1780; served in the army; practised at Ipswich; published 'Duties of a Regimental Surgeon,' 1788, and a book on the cure of hydrophobia. [xxiv. 207]

HAMILTON, ROBERT (1750?-1831), legal writer and genealogist; served in American war; sheriff of Lanarkshire; clerk of session; accompanied Scott on voyage (1814) as commissioner of northern lights; edited (1803) 'Decisions of Court of Session, from November 1769 to January 1772.' [xxiv. 208]

HAMILTON, SIR ROBERT GEORGE CROOKSHANK (1836-1895), governor of Tasmania; educated at University and King's College, Aberdeen; M.A., 1854; honorary LL.D., 1885; clerk in commissariat department in Crimea, 1855; in charge of finance of education department, 1861; accountant, 1869, and assistant-secretary, 1872-8, to board of trade; accountant-general of navy, 1878; permanent secretary to admiralty, 1882; permanent under-secretary for Ireland, 1883-6; K.C.B., 1884; governor of Tasmania, 1886-93. [Suppl. ii. 382]

HAMILTON, SIR ROBERT NORTH COLLIE, sixth baronet (1802-1887), Indian official; educated at Haileybury; acting secretary in political department, Benares, 1830; resident with Holkar of Indore, 1844-57; succeeded to baronetcy, 1853; viceroy's agent for Central India, 1854-9; his plan for pacification of Central India adopted; K.C.B.; member of supreme council of India, 1859-60. [xxiv. 208]

HAMILTON, Sir THOMAS, LORD DRUMCAIRN, EARL OF MELROSE, and afterwards first EARL OF HADDINGTON (1563–1637); educated under his uncle, John Hamilton (*fl.* 1568–1609) [q. v.] at Paris; admitted advocate, 1587; lord of session as Lord Drumcairn, 1592; probably suggester and was a member of the 'Octavians'; favourite of James VI; king's advocate, 1596; knighted soon after James VI's accession as James I of England; a commissioner for union, 1604; procured imprisonment of Andrew Melville and execution of Sprot for connection with Gowrie conspiracy of 1600; one of the new Octavians, 1611; secretary of state, 1612–26; created Baron Binning and Byres, 1613; president of court of session, 1616–26; created Earl of Melrose, 1619, for obtaining adoption of episcopalianism by six articles of Perth, 1618; lord privy seal, 1626; his title changed to Earl of Haddington, 1626. 'Notes of the Charters, &c., by the Earl of Melrose,' was issued in 1830, his 'State Papers' in 1837. [xxiv. 209]

HAMILTON, THOMAS, second EARL OF HADDINGTON (1600–1640), covenanter; son of Sir Thomas Hamilton, first earl of Haddington [q. v.]; signed 'king's covenant,' 1638; drew up Glasgow proclamation, 1638; defended borders, 1640; perished in explosion at Dunglass Castle. [xxiv. 212]

HAMILTON, THOMAS, sixth EARL OF HADDINGTON (1680–1735), member of the *squadrone volante*; wounded at Sheriffmuir, 1715; elected a representative peer, 1716; caricatured as 'Simon the Skipper'; his treatise on forest trees printed, 1761. [xxiv. 212]

HAMILTON, THOMAS (1789–1842), author; second son of William Hamilton (1758–1790) [q. v.]; wounded at Albuera, 1811; settled in Edinburgh, *c.* 1818; one of the 'Blackwood' writers praised in 'Noctes Ambrosianæ,' 1826; intimate with Scott at Chiefswood and Wordsworth at Elleray; published 'Cyril Thornton' (1827), 'Annals of the Peninsular Campaign' (1829), 'Men and Manners in America' (1833); died at Pisa and was buried at Florence. [xxiv. 213]

HAMILTON, THOMAS, ninth EARL OF HADDINGTON (1780–1858); educated at Edinburgh and Christ Church, Oxford; M.A. Oxford, 1815; tory M.P. for St. Germans, 1802–6, Callington, 1807–14, Michael-borough, 1814–18, Rochester, 1818–26, and Yarmouth (Isle of Wight), 1826; Indian commissioner, 1814–22; created Baron Melros of Tynninghame, 1827; succeeded to Scottish peerage, 1828; lord-lieutenant of Ireland, 1834–5; first lord of the admiralty, 1841–6; lord privy seal, 1846. [xxiv. 213]

HAMILTON, THOMAS (1784–1858), architect; designed Burns monuments at Alloway, 1818, and Edinburgh, 1830, Knox column at Glasgow, 1825, Edinburgh High School (opened 1829), and town buildings and spire at Ayr, 1828; a founder and first treasurer of R.S.A.; F.R.I.B.A., 1836–46. [xxiv. 214]

HAMILTON, WALTER KERR (1808–1869), bishop of Salisbury; nephew of William Richard Hamilton [q. v.]; at Eton and as private pupil of Dr. Arnold of Rugby at Laleham; student of Christ Church, Oxford, 1827; B.A., 1830; fellow of Merton College, 1832; vicar of St. Peter's-in-the-East, Oxford, 1837–41; canon of Salisbury, 1841; bishop of Salisbury, 1854–69, establishing theological college, 1861; published pamphlet on 'Cathedral Reform,' 1853. [xxiv. 216]

HAMILTON, WILLIAM DE (*d.* 1307), chancellor of England; vice-chancellor to the king, 1286; dean of York, 1298; chancellor of England, 1305–7. [xxiv. 217]

HAMILTON, WILLIAM, second DUKE OF HAMILTON (1616–1651), brother of James Hamilton, first duke [q. v.]; created Earl of Lanark, 1639 (so styled till 1649); secretary of state for Scotland, 1640–3 and 1646; fled with his brother (1641) after the Incident, but was at peace with the king till arrest at Oxford, 1643; escaped and made his peace with Scottish estates, 1644; one of commissioners at Newcastle, 1646; again reconciled to Charles I, 1646; protested against his surrender to English army; concluded treaty with the king at Carisbrooke on basis of introduction of presbyterianism into England, 1647; commanded force against Westland whigs, but had to submit to Argyll; succeeded to dukedom while in Holland; made K.G. and privy councillor by Charles II, whom he accompanied to Scotland, 1650; mortally wounded at Worcester. [xxiv. 218]

HAMILTON, WILLIAM (*d.* 1724), of Wishaw; antiquary; his 'Account of the Shyres of Renfrew and Lanark' edited by William Motherwell [q. v.], 1832. [xxiv. 220]

HAMILTON, WILLIAM (*d.* 1729), archdeacon of Armagh; M.A. Trinity College, Dublin, 1696; LL.B., 1700; archdeacon of Armagh, 1700–29; published life of James Bonnell, 1703. [xxiv. 221]

HAMILTON, WILLIAM (1665?–1751), of Gilbertfield; poet; corresponded in verse with Allan Ramsay in 'Seven Familiar Epistles which passed between Lieutenant Hamilton and the Author' (1719); wrote elegy on his dog, 'Bonny Heck,' and 'Willie was a Wanton Wag'; abridged and modernised Blind Harry's 'Wallace,' 1722. [xxiv. 221]

HAMILTON, WILLIAM (1704–1754), of Bangour; poet; contributed lyrics to Allan Ramsay's 'Tea-Table Miscellany,' between 1724 and 1727; celebrated victory of Prestonpans in 'Gladsmuir'; and while hiding after Culloden wrote 'Soliloquy . . . in June 1746'; composed ballads and 'Episode of the Thistle'; made the earliest Homeric translation into English blank verse; his poems issued by Foulis, 1749, and posthumously; died at Lyons. [xxiv. 222]

HAMILTON, WILLIAM (1758–1790), surgeon; M.A. Glasgow, 1775; professor of anatomy and botany at Glasgow, 1781. [xxiv. 222]

HAMILTON, WILLIAM (1755–1797), naturalist and antiquary; fellow of Trinity College, Dublin, 1779; M.A., 1779; rector of Clondavaddog or Fannet, Donegal, 1790; published 'Letters concerning the Northern Coast of Antrim,' 1786; murdered by banditti at Sharon, 1797. [xxiv. 223]

HAMILTON, WILLIAM (1751–1801), painter; studied under Zucchi in Italy; R.A., 1789; exhibited from 1774 historical pictures, arabesques, and ornaments, scriptural and Shakespearean pictures, and portraits, including full-lengths of Mrs. Siddons and John Wesley. [xxiv. 223]

HAMILTON, Sir WILLIAM (1730–1803), diplomatist and archæologist; grandson of William Douglas, third duke of Hamilton [q. v.]; M.P., Midhurst, 1761–4; plenipotentiary at Naples, 1764–1800; K.B., 1772; made twenty-two ascents of Vesuvius, witnessing 1776 and 1777 eruptions; visited Etna; F.R.S., 1766; published 'Campi Phlegræi,' 1776 (also a supplement, 1779), and other works describing observations of volcanoes and Calabrian earthquakes; sent account of Pompeian discoveries to Society of Antiquaries; sold collections of Greek vases and antiquities to British Museum, 1772; and to Thomas Hope, 1801; purchased from Gavin Hamilton (1730–1797) [q. v.] 'Warwick Vase,' and from Byres, the architect, 'Portland Vase'; privy councillor, 1791; married Emma Hart [see HAMILTON, EMMA], 1791; entertained Nelson at Naples, 1798; accompanied Neapolitan court to Palermo, 1798; travelled to England with Nelson; D.C.L. Oxford, 1802. [xxiv. 224]

HAMILTON, WILLIAM (1780–1835), theological writer; minister of Strathblane, Stirlingshire, 1809–35; moved resolution against lay patronage in general assembly, 1834; published theological works, 1820–35. [xxiv. 227]

HAMILTON, Sir WILLIAM, baronet (1788–1856), metaphysician; educated at Glasgow and Balliol College, Oxford, where he was intimate with J. C. Lockhart; M.A., 1814; established claim to baronetcy, 1816; introduced by 'Christopher North' to De Quincey at Edinburgh, 1814; visited Germany, 1817 and 1820; elected professor of civil history at Edinburgh, 1821; had controversy with Combe on phrenology; solicitor of teinds, 1832; his philosophical reputation made by articles in 'Edinburgh Review,' 1829–36; elected to chair of logic and metaphysics at Edinburgh, 1836; made great impression by lectures (ed. Mansel and Veitch, 1859); attacked 'non-intrusion' principle in ecclesiastical controversy of 1843; partially paralysed after 1844; edited Reid's works, 1846 (completed by Mansel); Hamilton philosophical examination founded in his honour, 1865. His doctrine of the 'quantification of the predicate' was assailed by De Morgan, and that of the unknowability of the infinite by Calderwood. He contributed to psychology and logic the theories of the association of ideas, of unconscious mental modifications, and the inverse relation of perception and sensation. Posthumous criticism was led by Mill and Hutchison Stirling. [xxiv. 227]

HAMILTON, WILLIAM GERARD (1729-1796), 'Single-speech Hamilton'; grandson of William Hamilton (*d.* 1724) [q. v.]: educated at Winchester and Oriel College, Oxford; student of Lincoln's Inn, 1744; as M.P. for Petersfield made celebrated maiden speech, 1755 (the so-called 'single speech'); a commissioner of trade, 1756; M.P., Pontefract, 1761, Killebegs (Irish parliament), 1761-1768; chief secretary for Ireland, 1761-4, and chancellor of Irish exchequer, 1763-84; spoke ably in Irish parliament, 1761-2; obtained, 1763, but subsequently appropriated, pension for Burke, who was for a time his private secretary; M.P., Old Sarum, 1768, Wareham, 1774, Wilton, 1780, and Haslemere, 1790; his conversational powers highly praised by Dr. Johnson; 'Letters of Junius' attributed to him by some of his contemporaries; his works published after his death by Malone under title of 'Parliamentary Logick.' [xxiv. 232]

HAMILTON, WILLIAM JOHN (1805-1867), geologist; son of William Richard Hamilton [q. v.]; educated at Charterhouse and Göttingen; pupil of Murchison; F.G.S., 1831; secretary of Geological Society, 1832-54, president, 1854 and 1865; M.P., Newport (Isle of Wight), 1841-7; his tour in the Levant, 1835-7, described in 'Researches in Asia Minor, Pontus, and Armenia,' 1842; president of Royal Geographical Society, 1837, 1841, 1842, and 1847; made excursions in France and Belgium, and wrote papers on rocks of Tuscany and geology of the Mayence basin and Hesse-Cassel. [xxiv. 234]

HAMILTON, WILLIAM RICHARD (1777-1859), antiquary and diplomatist; cousin of William Gerard Hamilton [q. v.]; lamed for life at Harrow; as secretary to Lord Elgin prevented France carrying off Rosetta stone; superintended safe transportation to England of Grecian marbles, 1802; under-secretary for foreign affairs, 1809-22; minister at Naples, 1822-5; obtained restoration by France of works of art taken from Italy, 1815; trustee of British Museum, 1838-58; published 'Ægyptiaca' (1809), containing first translations of Rosetta inscriptions. [xxiv. 234]

HAMILTON, SIR WILLIAM ROWAN (1805-1865), mathematician; discoverer of science of quaternions; as a child competed with Zerah Colburn, the 'calculating boy'; at sixteen detected an error of reasoning in Laplace's 'Mécanique Céleste'; at Trinity College, Dublin, obtained the 'double optime' and twice won vice-chancellor's prize for English verse; while an undergraduate predicted 'conical refraction'; appointed Andrews professor of astronomy, 1827; astronomer royal of Ireland; gold medallist of Royal Society for optical discovery and for (1834) theory of a general method of dynamics; knighted, 1835; president of Royal Irish Academy, 1837; published 'Lectures on Quaternions,' 1853. His 'Elements of Quaternions' appeared posthumously, 1866. [xxiv. 235]

HAMILTON-ROWAN, ARCHIBALD (1751-1834). [See ROWAN.]

HAMLEY, EDWARD (1764-1834), poet; fellow of New College, Oxford, 1785; B.C.L., 1791; rector of Cusop, 1805-34, and Stanton St. John, 1806-34; published poems (1795), translations from Petrarch and Metastasio, 1795, and sonnets, 1795. [xxiv. 238]

HAMLEY, SIR EDWARD BRUCE (1824-1893), general; studied at Royal Military Academy, Woolwich; lieutenant, royal artillery, 1843; stationed at Gibraltar; adjutant to Colonel (Sir) Richard James Dacres [q. v.] in Crimea; brevet lieutenant-colonel, 1855; contributed to Fraser's and Blackwood's magazines; edited first series of 'Tales from Blackwood,' 1858; professor of military history, Sandhurst, 1859-64; published 'Operations of War,' 1866; lieutenant-colonel, 1864; member of council of military education, 1866-70; commandant of staff college, 1870-7; major-general, 1877; British commissioner for delimitation of Bulgaria, 1879, Armenian frontier, 1880, and Greek frontier, 1881; K.C.M.G., 1880; lieutenant-general, 1882; commanded division in Egypt, 1882; fought at Tel-el-Kebir; K.C.B., 1882; M.P. for Birkenhead, 1885, and 1886-92; colonel-commandant, royal artillery, 1886; general, 1890; published novels, 'Shakespeare's Funeral,' 1869, and military works. [Suppl. ii. 382]

HAMMERSLEY, JAMES ASTBURY (1815-1869), painter; master of Manchester School of Design, 1849-62; first president, Manchester Academy of Fine Arts, 1857-61. [xxiv. 238]

HAMMICK, SIR STEPHEN LOVE, first baronet (1777-1867), surgeon extraordinary to George IV and William IV; surgeon to Naval Hospital, Plymouth, 1803; created baronet, 1834; an original member of London University senate; published 'Practical Remarks on . . . Strictures of the Urethra,' 1830. [xxiv. 238]

HAMMOND. [See also HAMOND.]

HAMMOND, ANTHONY (1668-1738), poet and pamphleteer; grand-nephew of William Hammond [q. v.]; M.P., Huntingdonshire, 1695-8, Cambridge University, 1698-1701, Huntingdon, 1702-8; M.A. St. John's College, Cambridge, 1698; commissioner of public accounts, 1701; commissioner of the navy, 1702; declared incapable of sitting in parliament as holding the latter office, 1708; treasurer of forces in Spain, 1711; published pamphlets on finance and parliamentary practice; edited 'New Miscellany of Original Poems,' 1720; died debtor in the Fleet. [xxiv. 239]

HAMMOND, ANTHONY (1758-1838), legal writer; prepared draft of act of 1827 consolidating and amending the criminal law. [xxiv. 240]

HAMMOND, EDMUND, BARON HAMMOND (1802-1890), diplomatist; son of George Hammond [q. v.]; of Harrow and University College, Oxford; fellow, 1828-46; M.A., 1826; accompanied Stratford Canning to Constantinople, 1831, Madrid, and Lisbon, 1832; chief of the oriental department of foreign office; permanent under-secretary, 1854-73; privy councillor, 1866; created a peer, 1874; died at Mentone. [xxiv. 240]

HAMMOND, GEORGE (1763-1853), diplomatist; educated at Merton College, Oxford; fellow, 1787; M.A., 1788; secretary to David Hartley the younger [q. v.] at Paris, 1783; chargé d'affaires at Vienna, 1788-90; first British minister at Washington, 1791-5; as under-secretary for foreign affairs (1795-1806 and 1807-9) intimate with Grenville and Canning; joint-editor of 'Anti-Jacobin'; D.C.L. Oxford, 1810. [xxiv. 241]

HAMMOND, HENRY (1605-1660), chaplain to Charles I; son of John Hammond (*d.* 1617) [q. v.]; of Eton and Magdalen College, Oxford; fellow, 1625, M.A., 1625, D.D., 1639; incumbent of Penshurst, 1633; archdeacon of Chichester, 1643; became known to Charles I by 'Practical Catechism,' 1644; canon of Christ Church and public orator at Oxford, 1645; chaplain to royal commissioners at Uxbridge, 1645, and to Charles I, 1647; deprived and imprisoned, but afterwards allowed to live with Sir Philip Warwick [q. v.] and Sir John Pakington; published 'Paraphrase and Annotations on the New Testament,' 1653; his collected works edited by William Fulman [q. v.], 1674-84, 'Miscellaneous Theological Works,' by Nicholas Pocock, 1847-50. [xxiv. 242]

HAMMOND, JAMES (1710-1742), poet; son of Anthony Hammond (1668-1738) [q. v.]; educated at Westminster; equerry to Frederick, prince of Wales, 1733; M.P., Truro, 1741-2; said to have died for love of Kitty Dashwood; his 'Love Elegies' (1743) (with preface by Chesterfield) condemned by Dr. Johnson for 'frigid pedantry.' [xxiv. 246]

HAMMOND, JOHN (1542-1589), civilian; fellow of Trinity Hall, Cambridge; LL.D., 1569; commissary of deanery of St. Paul's, 1573; master of chancery, 1574; chancellor of London, 1575; delegate to diet of Smalkald, 1578; M.P., Rye, 1585, St. Looe, 1586; as member of high commission examined Campion (1581) and other jesuits under torture. [xxiv. 247]

HAMMOND, JOHN (*d.* 1617), physician to James I; son of John Hammond (1542-1589) [q. v.]; fellow of Trinity College, Cambridge, 1573; M.A., 1577; M.D. Oxford, 1603; F.R.C.P., 1608; made post-mortem examination of Henry, prince of Wales. [xxiv. 247]

HAMMOND, ROBERT (1621-1654), parliamentarian; grandson of John Hammond (*d.* 1617) [q. v.]; member of Magdalen Hall, Oxford, 1636; captain in parliamentary army, 1642; distinguished himself at Tewkesbury, 1644; as colonel of foot in the 'new model,' 1645, captured Powderham Castle and St. Michael's Mount; taken by royalists at Basing House, 1645; governor of Isle of Wight, 1647; custodian of Charles I, who had mistakenly taken refuge with him in the Isle of Wight, November 1647 to November 1648; member of the Irish council, 1654. [xxiv. 248]

HAMMOND, SAMUEL (*d.* 1665), nonconformist divine; fellow of Magdalene College, Cambridge; chaplain to Sir Arthur Hesilrige [q. v.]; while minister at Newcastle (1652-60) assisted in exposing the impostor, Thomas Ramsay; assisted in writing a tract against quakers, 1654. [xxiv. 250]

HAMMOND, WILLIAM (*fl.* 1655), poet; his 'Poems' (1655) reprinted, 1816. [xxiv. 251]

HAMMOND. [See also HAMMOND and HAMONT.]

HAMOND, SIR ANDREW SNAPE, first baronet (1738-1828), comptroller of the navy; present at Quiberon Bay, 1759; captain, 1770; knighted for services in Chesapeake expedition and defence of Sandy Hook, 1778; governor of Nova Scotia, 1780-2; created baronet, 1783; commander at the Nore, 1785-8; commissioner of the navy, 1793; M.P., Ipswich, 1796-1806; comptroller of the navy, 1794-1806. [xxiv. 251]

HAMOND, GEORGE (1620-1705), ejected divine; M.A. Exeter College, Oxford; studied at Trinity College, Dublin; ejected from St. Peter's and Trinity, Dorchester, 1662; presbyterian minister and schoolmaster at Taunton, 1672-85; pastor of Armourers' Hall, London, and lecturer at Salters' Hall. [xxiv. 252]

HAMOND, SIR GRAHAM EDEN, second baronet (1779-1862), admiral; son of Sir Andrew Snape Hamond [q. v.]; midshipman on Howe's flagship at victory of 1794; commanded the Blanche at Copenhagen, 1801; captured Spanish treasure ships, 1804; at reduction of Flushing, 1809; commander on South American station, 1834-8; admiral, 1847; admiral of the fleet, 1862; G.C.B., 1855. [xxiv. 252]

HAMOND, WALTER (*fl.* 1643), author of tracts on Madagascar, 1640 and 1643. [xxiv. 253]

HAMONT, MATTHEW (*d.* 1579), heretic; burnt at Norwich. On his case Philip van Limborch corresponded with Locke, 1699. [xxiv. 253]

HAMPDEN, VISCOUNTS. [See TREVOR, ROBERT HAMPDEN-, first VISCOUNT, 1706-1783; TREVOR, JOHN HAMPDEN-, third VISCOUNT, 1749-1824; BRAND, SIR HENRY BOUVERIE WILLIAM, 1814-1892, first VISCOUNT of new creation.]

HAMPDEN, JOHN (1594-1643), statesman; educated at Thame School and Magdalen College, Oxford; also studied at Inner Temple; M.P. for Grampound, 1621-5, and for Wendover in first three parliaments of Charles I; afterwards represented Buckinghamshire; imprisoned (1627) for refusing to pay forced loan of 1626; prominent in Charles I's third parliament; closely associated with Sir John Eliot [q. v.], corresponding with him when Eliot was in prison; one of the twelve grantees of land in Connecticut, 1632; by resisting second ship-money writ, 1635 (declared legal by exchequer court, 1638), caused it to be paid with increasing reluctance; most popular member in the Short parliament, 1640; led the opposition to the king's demand for twelve subsidies in exchange for the abandonment of ship-money, 1640; exercised great influence over Pym in the Long parliament, and proved a powerful debater and strategist; as one of the managers of Strafford's impeachment opposed the resolution for a bill of attainder, and (1641) obtained leave for Strafford's counsel to be heard; supported the root-and-branch bill; attended the king to Scotland, 1641; calmed House of Commons after the carrying of the Grand Remonstrance, 1641; impeached by the attorney-general, 1642 (3 Jan.), but escaped the attempted arrest by the king next day; returned to move (10 Jan. 1642) the resolution giving control of the militia and the Tower to parliament; leading member of the committee of safety; raised regiment of foot and executed the militia ordinance in his own county after Edgehill, joining the main army (1642) under Essex, whose retreat after Edgehill he condemned; resisted acceptance of Charles I's overtures for peace, 1642-3, and urged an immediate attack on Oxford; mortally wounded in a skirmish with Prince Rupert at Chalgrove Field; died at Thame, and was buried in Great Hampden Church. [xxiv. 254]

HAMPDEN, JOHN, the younger (1656 ?-1696), politician; son of Richard Hampden [q. v.]; M.P., Buckinghamshire, 1679, Wendover, 1681-90; imprisoned and fined on charge of plotting an insurrection, 1684;

condemned to death for high treason after Monmouth's rising, 1685, but bribed Jefferies and Petre, and was pardoned; prominent in Convention parliament (1689) as an extreme whig; opposed employment by William III of Halifax and other ex-ministers; committed suicide. [xxiv. 262]

HAMPDEN, RENN DICKSON (1793-1868), bishop of Hereford; fellow of Oriel College, Oxford, 1814; double first, 1814; M.A., 1816; D.D., 1833; intimate with Arnold and Whately; Bampton lecturer, 1832; principal of St. Mary Hall, 1833; professor of moral philosophy, 1834; his appointment by Melbourne to the regius professorship of divinity (1836) opposed on ground of his unorthodoxy, as also his nomination to bishopric (1848); bishop of Hereford, 1848-68; published 'The Scholastic Philosophy considered in its Relation to Christian Theology' (Bampton lectures), 1833. [xxiv. 264]

HAMPDEN, RICHARD (1631-1695), chancellor of the exchequer; son of John Hampden (1594-1643) [q. v.]; M.P., Buckinghamshire, 1656, and 1681-90, Wendover, 1660-79, and 1690-5; member of Protector's House of Lords; entertained Baxter during the plague, 1665; moved Exclusion Bill of 1679; chairman of Commons' committee that declared the throne vacant, 1689; privy councillor, 1689; commissioner of the treasury, 1689; chancellor of the exchequer, 1690-4; refused emoluments from William III. [xxiv. 266]

HAMPDEN-TREVOR. [See TREVOR.]

HAMPER, WILLIAM (1776-1831), antiquary; F.S.A., 1821; contributed to 'Gentleman's Magazine'; assisted John Britton [q. v.] and other topographical writers; published 'Observations on certain Ancient Pillars of Memorial called Hoar-Stones,' 1820, and 'Life, Diary, and Correspondence of Sir W. Dugdale,' 1827. [xxiv. 267]

HAMPOLE, RICHARD (1290 ?-1349). [See ROLLE, RICHARD.]

HAMPSON, JOHN (1760-1817 ?), author; M.A. St. Edmund Hall, Oxford, 1792; rector of Sunderland, 1801; published works including 'Memoirs of Rev. John Wesley,' 1791; translated 'The Poetics of Marcus Hieronymus Vida,' 1793. [xxiv. 268]

HAMPTON, first BARON (1799-1880). [See PAKINGTON, SIR JOHN SOMERSET.]

HAMPTON, CHRISTOPHER (1552-1625), archbishop of Armagh; probably fellow of Trinity College, Cambridge, 1585; nominated to see of Derry, 1611, but not consecrated; archbishop of Armagh, 1613-25; restored Armagh Cathedral; maintained primacy of Armagh. [xxiv. 268]

HAMPTON, JAMES (1721-1778), translator of Polybius; of Winchester and Corpus Christi College, Oxford; M.A., 1747; rector of Monkton Moor, 1762, and Folkton, Yorkshire, 1775; translated Polybius, first five books, 1756-61; issued extracts from sixth book of Polybius, 1764. [xxiv. 269]

HANBOYS or **HAMBOYS**, JOHN (*fl.* 1470), doctor of music; his commentary on works of the two Francos printed by Coussemaker. [xxiv. 269]

HANBURY, BENJAMIN (1778-1864), nonconformist historian; first treasurer of Congregational Union, 1831-64; published 'Historical Memorials relating to the Independents . . . from their Rise to the Restoration' (1839-44), and an edition of Hooker (1830). [xxiv. 270]

HANBURY, DANIEL (1825-1875), pharmacist; treasurer of Linnean Society; F.R.S., 1867; visited Palestine with Sir Joseph Hooker, 1860; published 'Pharmacographia' (with Professor Flückiger), 1874. [xxiv. 270]

HANBURY, SIR JAMES (1782-1863), lieutenant-general; served with the 58th in Egypt, 1801; present at operations of Coruña, 1808-9; with the guards at Walcheren (1809) and in the Peninsular war; major-general, 1830; K.B., 1830; lieutenant-general, 1841. [xxiv. 271]

HANBURY, JOHN (1664-1734), politician; developed his estate and ironworks at Pontypool; M.P., Gloucester, 1701-15, Monmouthshire, 1720-34; director of the New South Sea Company, 1721; one of Marlborough's executors, 1722. [lxi. 379]

HANBURY, WILLIAM (1725–1778), clergyman; B.A. St. Edmund Hall, Oxford, 1748 ; rector of Church Langton, Leicestershire, 1753–78 ; M.A. St. Andrews, 1769 ; issued (1758) ' Essay on Planting, and a Scheme for making it conducive to the Glory of God and the advantage of Society ' ; his scheme carried out by court of chancery, 1864 ; published ' Complete Body of Planting and Gardening ' (1770–1). [xxiv. 271]

HANCE, HENRY FLETCHER (1827–1886), botanist; vice-consul at Whampoa, 1861–78 ; consul at Canton, 1878–81 and 1883 ; acting consul at Amoy at his death ; contributed papers on Chinese plants to Hooker's ' Journal of Botany,' and supplement to Bentham's ' Flora Hong-kongensis.' [xxiv. 272]

HANCKWITZ, AMBROSE GODFREY (d. 1741). [See GODFREY, AMBROSE.]

HANCOCK, ALBANY (1806–1873), zoologist; received the royal medal of Royal Society for paper on ' The Organisation of Brachiopoda,' 1857 ; F.L.S., 1862 ; collaborated with Joshua Alder [q. v.] in ' Monograph of British Nudibranchiate Mollusca,' 1845–55 ; with Dr. D. Embleton investigated structure of genera *æolis* and *doris*. [xxiv. 273]

HANCOCK, JOHN (d. 1869), sculptor ; exhibited at Royal Academy from 1843. [xxiv. 274]

HANCOCK, ROBERT (1730–1817), mezzotint engraver and draughtsman ; engraver to Worcester porcelain works, 1757–74 ; executed small crayon portraits of Lamb, Wordsworth, Coleridge, and Southey. [xxiv. 274]

HANCOCK, THOMAS (1783–1849), quaker physician ; M.D. Edinburgh, 1809 ; practised in London and Liverpool ; published (1825) ' Principles of Peace exemplified in conduct of Society of Friends in Ireland during the Rebellion of 1798,' and treatises on epidemics ; edited ' Discourses ' from Nicole's ' Essays by John Locke,' 1828. [xxiv. 275]

HANCOCK, THOMAS (1786–1865), founder of the indiarubber trade in England ; took out patent for applying indiarubber springs to articles of dress, 1820 ; first made ' vulcanised ' indiarubber, 1843 ; published ' Personal Narrative of the Origin and Progress of the Caoutchouc or Indiarubber Manufacture in England,' 1857. [xxiv. 276]

HANCOCK, WALTER (1799–1852), engineer ; brother of Thomas Hancock (1786–1865) [q. v.] ; invented steam-engines for road traffic, 1824–36 ; described experiments in ' Narrative,' 1838 ; obtained patent for cutting india-rubber into sheets, and for a method of preparing solutions of indiarubber, 1843. [xxiv. 276]

HAND, THOMAS (d. 1804), painter ; friend and imitator of Morland ; exhibited at Royal Academy. [xxiv. 277]

HANDASYDE, CHARLES (fl. 1760–1780), miniature-painter. [xxiv. 277]

HANDEL, GEORGE FREDERICK, properly GEORG FRIEDRICH HAENDEL (1685–1759), musical composer; son of the town surgeon of Giebichenstein, Saxony; studied music under Zachau at Halle ; presented to elector of Brandenburg at Berlin, c. 1696 ; went to Hamburg, 1703, and became conductor of the opera ; fought a duel with Mattheson (first tenor) ; composed his first opera, ' Almira,' 1705 ; went to Italy, 1707 ; produced the operas ' Rodrigo ' at Florence and ' Agrippina ' at Venice, 1708 ; at Rome composed the oratorios ' Il Trionfo del Tempo ' and ' La Resurrezione ' ; visited Naples, 1708–9, composing songs and cantatas ; went to Hanover and became kapellmeister, 1710 ; came to England, 1710 ; his opera ' Rinaldo ' produced with great success at the Queen's Theatre, Haymarket, 1711 ; returned to Hanover, but was again in England in 1712, where, breaking his pledge to the elector of Hanover (afterwards George I) to return to Hanover, he thenceforth remained ; his operas ' Pastor Fido ' and ' Teseo ' and the ' Utrecht Te Deum and Jubilate,' performed before the death of Anne, the composer receiving for the last an annuity of 200l., increased by George I after Handel's reconciliation with him, effected through Burlington and Kielmannsegge by means of the ' Water-music,' 1715 ; as director for the Duke of Chandos at Canons (1718–20) composed twelve anthems, ' Esther ' (his first English oratorio, performed 1720), and ' Acis and Galatea ' (performed 1720 or 1721) ; director of the Royal

Academy of Music, 1720–8, composing thirteen operas, besides collaborating in ' Muzio Scevola ' with Buononcini, thenceforth his rival in popular favour ; naturalised, 1726 ; appointed court composer ; produced coronation anthems on the accession of George II, 1727 ; carried on (1729–35) a second operatic undertaking at the King's Theatre, Covent Garden, producing several new operas, and giving performances of ' Esther ' and ' Acis and Galatea,' 1732, and ' Deborah,' 1733 ; ' Athaliah ' first heard at Oxford, 1733 ; ousted from the King's Theatre by his rivals, 1735 ; gave more operas, and repeated his oratorios in Lent at Rich's new theatre, Covent Garden, 1735–7, when he became bankrupt and partially paralysed ; composed a fine anthem for the funeral of Queen Caroline, 1737, and two new operas, 1738, when his debts were paid by a benefit concert; his statue by Roubilliac set up at Vauxhall, 1738 ; his last operas given at Lincoln's Inn Fields, 1740–1, also setting of Dryden's shorter ' Ode on St. Cecilia's Day,' 1739 ; the first annual performance of ' Alexander's Feast ' for the Society of Musicians, with himself at the organ, given 1739 ; his ' Saul ' and ' Israel in Egypt,' produced at the King's Theatre, 1739 ; his oratorio the ' Messiah ' (composed in twenty-three days) first heard at Dublin, 1741, in London, 1743 (Covent Garden), and in Germany (Hamburg), 1772 ; his ' Samson ' given at a subscription concert at Covent Garden, and the Dettingen ' Te Deum ' at St. James's Palace, 1743 ; ' Joseph and his Brethren ' and ' Semele,' 1744 (Covent Garden) ; ' Hercules ' and ' Belshazzar ' (King's Theatre), 1744–5 ; ' Judas Maccabæus,' 1747 ; ' Alexander Balus ' and ' Joshua,' 1748 (Covent Garden) ; his oratorios ' Susanna ' and ' Solomon,' produced, 1749 ; his ' Music for the Fireworks ' performed at Vauxhall and the Green Park to celebrate the peace of Aix-la-Chapelle, 1749 ; his ' Theodora,' 1750, a failure ; conducted a performance of the ' Messiah ' (with the organ presented by himself) at the Foundling Hospital, 1750 ; his last oratorio, ' Jephthah,' produced at Covent Garden, 1752 ; his last composition, ' The Triumph of Time and Truth,' 1757 ; buried in Westminster Abbey. His manuscript scores passed from John Christopher Smith to George III. He carried choral music to its highest point, but in instrumental did not advance beyond his contemporaries. His almost certain appropriation (notably in ' Israel in Egypt ') of the work of others is in strong contradiction with his known character. A collection of his works, begun in Germany, 1856, with the help of the king of Hanover, was continued under the auspices of the Prussian government. Roubilliac executed his monument in Westminster Abbey and three busts. [xxiv. 277]

HANDLO, ROBERT DE (fl. 1326), writer on music ; author of ' Regulæ ' (printed by Coussemaker). [xxiv. 291]

HANDYSIDE, WILLIAM (1793–1850), engineer ; employed by the Russian government. [xxiv. 292]

HANGER, GEORGE, fourth BARON COLERAINE (1751 ?–1824), eccentric ; educated at Eton and Göttingen ; served during American war in Hessian Jäger corps and in Tarleton's light dragoons ; aide-de-camp to Sir Henry Clinton at Charlestown, 1779 ; his ' Life, Adventures, and Opinions,' issued by William Combe [q. v.], 1801 ; succeeded his brother in peerage, 1814, but did not assume title ; caricatured by Gillray and George Cruikshank ; published ' Lives and Adventures . . . of Eminent Gamesters,' 1804, and military pamphlets. [xxiv. 292]

HANKEFORD, SIR WILLIAM (d. 1422), judge ; king's serjeant, 1390 ; justice of common pleas, 1398 ; K.B., 1399 ; chief-justice of king's bench, 1413–22. [xxiv. 293]

HANKEY, THOMSON (1805–1893), politician ; senior partner in his father's West Indian mercantile firm ; elected a director of Bank of England, 1835 ; governor, 1851–2 ; liberal M.P. for Peterborough, 1853–68, and 1874–1880 ; published works on questions of political economy. [Suppl. ii. 385]

HANKIN, EDWARD (1747–1835), author ; rector of West Chiltington, Sussex ; published pamphlets on clerical grievances and political subjects. [xxiv. 293]

HANKINSON, THOMAS EDWARDS (1805–1843) poet ; M.A. Corpus Christi College, Cambridge, 1831 ; incumbent of St. Matthew's Chapel, Denmark Hill ; won Seatonian prize at Cambridge nine times ; his ' Poems ' collected, 1844. [xxiv. 294]

HANMER, JOHN (1574-1629), bishop of St. Asaph; matriculated at Oriel College, Oxford, 1592; fellow of All Souls' College, Oxford, 1596; M.A., 1600; D.D., 1616; chaplain to James I; prebendary of Worcester, 1614; bishop of St. Asaph, 1624-9. [xxiv. 294]

HANMER, JOHN (1642-1707), nonconformist minister; son of Jonathan Hanmer [q. v.]; graduated at St. John's College, Cambridge, 1662; pastor at Barnstaple, 1692-1705. [xxiv. 296]

HANMER, SIR JOHN, BARON HANMER (1809-1881), poet; succeeded as third baronet, 1828; educated at Eton and Christ Church, Oxford; whig M.P. for Shrewsbury, 1832-7, Hull, 1841-7, and Flint, 1847-72; created a peer, 1872; published 'Fra Cipolla and other poems,' 1839, 'Sonnets,' 1840, and 'Memorials of Family and Parish of Hanmer,' 1877. [xxiv. 295]

HANMER, JONATHAN (1606-1687), divine; M.A. Emmanuel College, Cambridge, 1631; ejected from vicarage of Bishop's Tawton and lectureship of Barnstaple, 1662, where he founded, with Oliver Peard, the first nonconformist congregation; published 'An Exercitation upon Confirmation,' 1657; and 'A View of Antiquity,' 1677. [xxiv. 295]

HANMER, MEREDITH (1543-1604), historian; chaplain of Corpus Christi College, Oxford, 1567; M.A., 1572; D.D., 1582; vicar of St. Leonard's, Shoreditch, 1581-92; vicar of Islington, 1583-90; accused of celebrating an illegal marriage; went to Ireland, becoming archdeacon of Ross (1591), treasurer of Waterford (1593), vicar choral and prebendary of Christ Church, Dublin (1594-5), chancellor of Kilkenny (1603); published a translation of the histories of Eusebius, Socrates, and Evagrius, 1577; his 'Chronicle of Ireland' printed by Sir James Ware, 1633. [xxiv. 297]

HANMER, SIR THOMAS, fourth baronet (1677-1746), speaker; of Westminster and Christ Church, Oxford; succeeded his uncle as baronet, 1701; tory M.P. for Thetford, 1701 and 1705-8, Flintshire, 1702-5, and Suffolk, 1708-27; chairman of the committee which made the 'representation' of 1712; received in great state by Louis XIV at Paris, 1712; refused office from Harley and procured rejection of two articles of the commercial treaty of 1713; speaker, 1714-15; chief of the Hanoverian tories; while in retirement, prepared sumptuous, but not critically very valuable, edition of Shakespeare, 1743-4; alluded to in the 'Dunciad' as Montalto. [xxiv. 298]

HANN, JAMES (1799-1856), mathematician; calculator in Nautical Almanack office; mathematical master at King's College School, London, till death; published works on mechanics and pure mathematics, including 'Principles and Practice of the Machinery of Locomotive Engines,' 1850, and, with Olinthus Gilbert Gregory [q. v.], 'Tables for the Use of Nautical Men,' 1841. [xxiv. 299]

HANNA, SAMUEL (1772?-1852), presbyterian divine; M.A. Glasgow, 1789; D.D., 1818; minister of Rosemary Street, Belfast, 1799; professor of divinity, Belfast Presbyterian College, 1817; first moderator of general assembly, 1840. [xxiv. 300]

HANNA, WILLIAM (1808-1882), theological writer; son of Samuel Hanna [q. v.]; colleague of Thomas Guthrie [q. v.] at Edinburgh, 1850-66; LL.D. Glasgow, 1852; D.D. Edinburgh, 1864; son-in-law of Chalmers, whose life he issued in 1849-52, afterwards editing his posthumous works; edited also 'Essays by Ministers of the Free Church of Scotland,' 1858, and 'Letters of Thomas Erskine of Linlathen,' 1877. [xxiv. 300]

HANNAH, JOHN, the elder (1792-1867), Wesleyan minister; delegate to United States of Wesleyan conference, 1824 and 1856; secretary to conference, 1840-2, and 1854-8, president, 1842 and 1851; tutor of Didsbury, 1843-1867; published works, including a defence of infant baptism, 1866. [xxiv. 301]

HANNAH, JOHN, the younger (1818-1888), archdeacon of Lewes; son of John Hannah the elder [q. v.]; scholar of Corpus Christi College, Oxford, 1837; fellow of Lincoln, 1840; B.A., 1840; D.C.L., 1853; rector of the Edinburgh Academy, 1847-54; principal of Glenalmond, 1854-70; Bampton lecturer, 1862; vicar of Brighton, 1870-87; archdeacon of Lewes, 1876-88; published, besides Bampton lectures, 1863, 'Courtly Poets from Raleigh to Montrose,' 1870. [xxiv. 302]

HANNAM, RICHARD (d. 1656), robber; imprisoned for burglary; escaped from England, robbed the Danish treasury and the queen of Sweden; returned to England with money entrusted to him by Rotterdam broker merchants; broke prison at Paris and in London after being sentenced to death; hanged for murder at Smithfield. [xxiv. 303]

HANNAN, WILLIAM (d. 1775?), draughtsman and decorative painter. [xxiv. 303]

HANNAY, JAMES (1827-1873), author and journalist; dismissed the navy for insubordination, 1845; edited 'Edinburgh Evening Courant,' 1860-4; consul at Barcelona, 1868-73; published 'Singleton Fontenoy,' 1850, and 'Eustace Conyers,' 1855, naval novels; published 'Satire and Satirist,' 1854, and 'Studies on Thackeray,' 1869. [xxiv. 303]

HANNAY, PATRICK (d. 1629?), poet; master of chancery in Ireland, 1627; said to have died at sea; his 'Happy Husband' (1618-19) and Brathwait's 'Good Wife' (1619) reissued with 'The Nightingale' and other poems, 1622; facsimile of 1622 collection printed, 1875. [xxiv. 304]

HANNEMAN, ADRIAEN (1601?-1668?), portrait-painter; resided in England, c. 1625-40; returned to the Hague and became first director of the new guild of St. Luke, 1656; executed portraits of Charles II, the duke of Hamilton, Vandyck, and William III and Mary. [xxiv. 305]

HANNEN, SIR JAMES, BARON HANNEN (1821-1894), judge; educated at St. Paul's School and Heidelberg University; barrister, Middle Temple, 1848; bencher, 1878; joined home circuit; junior counsel to treasury, 1863; judge of court of queen's bench, 1868; knighted, 1868; appointed serjeant-at-law, 1868; privy councillor, 1872; judge of courts of probate and divorce, 1872; president of probate, divorce, and admiralty division of high court, 1875-91; life baron and lord of appeal in ordinary, 1891; D.C.L. Oxford, 1888; president of Parnell commission, 1888; arbitrator in question of Behring Sea seal fisheries, 1892. [Suppl. ii. 386]

HANNES, SIR EDWARD (d. 1710), physician; of Westminster and Christ Church, Oxford; M.A., 1689; M.D. 1695; attended William, duke of Gloucester, 1700; physician to Queen Anne, 1702; knighted, 1705. [xxiv. 305]

HANNEY or **DE HANNEYA**, THOMAS (fl. 1313), author of Bodleian manuscript 'Memoriale Juniorum' (a work on grammar). [xxiv. 306]

HANNIBAL, THOMAS (d. 1531), master of the rolls; D.C.L. Oxford, 1513; LL.D. Cambridge; ambassador at Rome, 1522-4; master of the rolls, 1523-7; frequently employed as diplomatist. [xxiv. 306]

HANNINGTON, JAMES (1847-1885), bishop of Eastern equatorial Africa; M.A. St. Mary Hall, Oxford, 1875; D.D., 1884; curate in charge of St. George's, Hurstpierpoint, 1875-82; went out for the Church Missionary Society to Uganda, 1882; visited Palestine on way to Africa as bishop (1884-5); led expedition which reached Lake Victoria Nyanza, 1885; murdered by order of king of Uganda, 1885. [xxiv. 307]

HANOVER, KING OF. [See ERNEST AUGUSTUS, 1771-1851.]

HANSARD, LUKE (1752-1828), printer; printed for the Dodsleys; printed House of Commons' Journals from 1774. [xxiv. 308]

HANSARD, THOMAS CURSON (1776-1833), printer; eldest son of Luke Hansard [q. v.]; began to print parliamentary debates in 1803; imprisoned for libel as Cobbett's printer, 1810; patented improved hand-press; published 'Typographia,' 1825. [xxiv. 308]

HANSBIE, MORGAN JOSEPH (1673-1750), Dominican; rector at Louvain, 1717; provincial, 1721; prior of Bornhem and vicar-provincial of Belgium; vicar-provincial in England, 1738-42; vicar-general, 1747; an ardent Jacobite; published theological treatises. [xxiv. 309]

HANSELL, EDWARD HALIFAX (1814-1884), biblical scholar; educated at Norwich and Oxford; fellow of Magdalen College Oxford, 1847-53; M.A., 1838; B.D.,

1847; afterwards divinity lecturer; Grinfield lecturer, 1861-2; vicar of East Ilsley, 1865-84; edited 'Nov. Test. Græc. . . . Acc. Collatio Cod. Sinaitici' (1864). [xxiv. 309]

HANSOM, JOSEPH ALOYSIUS (1803 - 1882), architect and inventor: erected the Birmingham town hall, 1833; registered 'Patent Safety Cab,' 1834, differing in many respects from present hansom; established 'The Builder,' 1842. [xxiv. 309]

HANSON, JOHN (fl. 1604), poet; B.A. Peterhouse, Cambridge, 1604; author of 'Time is a Turn-coate, or England's Threefold Metamorphosis' (1604). [xxiv. 310]

HANSON, JOHN (fl. 1658?), author of 'The Sabbatarians confuted by the New Covenant,' 1658; of Pembroke College, Oxford. [xxiv. 310]

HANSON, 'SIR' LEVETT (1754-1814), author; schoolfellow of Nelson and friend of Warren Hastings; of Trinity and Emmanuel Colleges, Cambridge; councillor to the Grand Duke of Holstein and knight of St. Philip, 1780; knight vice-chancellor of St. Joachim, 1800; lived in many European states; imprisoned in Austria, 1794; published account of European orders of knighthood, 1803, and poems, 1811; died at Copenhagen. [xxiv. 311]

HANSON, SIR RICHARD DAVIES (1805-1876), chief-justice of South Australia; edited the 'Globe' in London; supported Edward Gibbon Wakefield's colonisation schemes; one of the founders of South Australia; accompanied Lord Durham to Canada, 1838; crown prosecutor in New Zealand, 1840-6; drafted constitution of South Australia, 1851-6; attorney-general, 1857-60; chief-justice of South Australia, 1861-74; knighted, 1869; sometime acting-governor; published works, including 'The Jesus of History,' 1869. [xxiv. 311]

HANWAY, JONAS (1712 - 1786), traveller and philanthropist; as partner of a St. Petersburg merchant made journey (1743-5) down the Volga and by the Caspian to Persia with a caravan of woollen goods, and returned after perilous adventures by the same route, 1745; left Russia and lived in London after 1750; published an account of his travels, 1753, an essay attacking tea-drinking (severely criticised by Johnson and Goldsmith) and other works mostly connected with his philanthropic undertakings; appointed commissioner of victualling office, 1762, as reward for public services. He is best known as one of the chief founders of the Marine Society (1756) and the Magdalen charity (1758) the reformer of the umbrella; a monument was erected to him in Westminster Abbey, 1788. [xxiv. 312]

HARBERT. [See HERBERT.]

HARBIN, GEORGE (fl. 1713), nonjuror; B.A. Emmanuel College, Cambridge, 1686; chaplain to Bishop Turner of Ely and Viscount Weymouth; friend of Ken. [xxiv. 316]

HARBORD, EDWARD, third BARON SUFFIELD (1781-1835), philanthropist; M.P., Great Yarmouth, 1806-1812, Shaftesbury, 1820-1; succeeded as peer, 1821; carried reforms concerning prison discipline and game-laws; abolitionist. [xxiv. 316]

HARBORD, WILLIAM (1635 ?-1692), politician; secretary to Earl of Essex, 1672; took active part in attack on Danby in connection with popish plot; M.P., Thetford, 1679, Launceston, 1680 and 1681; volunteered in imperial army at Buda, 1686; accompanied William of Orange to England, 1688; privy councillor and paymaster-general, 1688-90; vice-treasurer of Ireland, 1690; sent as ambassador to Turkey to mediate between sultan and the emperor Leopold, 1691; died on his way at Belgrade. [Suppl. ii. 387]

HARBORNE, WILLIAM (d. 1617), first English ambassador in Turkey, 1582-8; concluded treaty for the establishment of Turkey company, 1579; account of his return journey (1588) printed in Hakluyt's 'Voyages'; manuscript account of his proceedings in Turkey in British Museum. [xxiv. 316]

HARCARSE, LORD (1635 ?-1700). [See HOG, SIR ROGER.]

HARCLAY, HARCLA, or HARTCLA, ANDREW, EARL OF CARLISLE (d. 1323), sheriff of Cumberland, warden of the west marches and of Carlisle Castle;

summoned as a baron to parliament, 1321; defeated and captured Earl Thomas of Lancaster at Boroughbridge and executed him at Pontefract, 1322; created earl by Edward II, with patent specifying his services; executed at Carlisle for making compact with Bruce. [xxiv. 317]

HARCOURT, CHARLES (1838-1880), actor; real name CHARLES PARKER HILLIER; first appeared at St. James's Theatre, 1863; lessee of Marylebone Theatre, 1871-2; best exponent of Mercutio after Vining's death. [xxiv. 319]

HARCOURT, EDWARD (1757 - 1847), archbishop of York; took name Harcourt on succession to family estates, 1831, being previously known as Vernon; educated at Westminster and Oxford; fellow of All Souls' College, Oxford, 1777; D.C.L., 1786; canon of Christ Church, 1785, and vicar of Sudbury; prebendary of Gloucester, 1785-91; bishop of Carlisle, 1791-1807; archbishop of York, 1807-47; privy councillor, 1808; member of Queen Charlotte's council; member of ecclesiastical commission, 1835. [xxiv. 319]

HARCOURT, HENRY (1612-1673), jesuit; real name BEAUMONT; spiritual coadjutor, 1643; published 'England's Old Religion faithfully gathered out of the Church of England,' 1650. [xxiv. 320]

HARCOURT, alias PERSALL, JOHN (1632-1702). [See PERSALL.]

HARCOURT, LEVESON VERNON (1788-1860), chancellor of York; author of 'Doctrine of the Deluge,' 1838; son of Edward Harcourt [q. v.] [xxiv. 320]

HARCOURT, OCTAVIUS HENRY CYRIL VERNON (1793-1863), admiral; son of Edward Harcourt [q. v.]; saw active service in Egypt and at Toulon and Tarragona; captured martello tower and convoy at Piombo, 1814; surveyed coast of Central America, 1834-6; vice-admiral, 1861; built several churches and Masham almshouses. [xxiv. 320]

HARCOURT, ROBERT (1574 ?-1631), traveller; gentleman-commoner, St. Alban Hall, Oxford, 1590; went to Guiana and took possession of land for the crown 1609; obtained letters patent for colonisation of Guiana; his company incorporated with Roger North's, 1626; his 'Relation of a Voyage to Guiana' (1613) reprinted in Purchas. [xxiv. 321]

HARCOURT, SIR SIMON (1603 ?-1642), soldier of fortune; son of Robert Harcourt [q. v.]; knighted, 1627; served Prince of Orange against Spaniards; commanded regiment against Scots, 1639-40; governor of Dublin, 1641; mortally wounded by rebels at Kilgobbin Castle. [xxiv. 321]

HARCOURT, SIMON (1684-1720), second son of Simon Harcourt, first viscount Harcourt [q. v.]; M.A. Christ Church, Oxford, 1712; secretary to the society of 'Brothers'; M.P., Wallingford and Abingdon; wrote verses in preface to Pope's 'Works' (1717); his epitaph composed by Pope. [xxiv. 324]

HARCOURT, SIMON, first VISCOUNT HARCOURT (1661 ?-1727), of Stanton Harcourt, Oxfordshire; B.A. Pembroke College, Oxford, 1678; D.C.L., 1702; barrister, Inner Temple, 1683; recorder of Abingdon, 1683; tory M.P. for Abingdon, 1690-1705, Bossiney, 1705-8, Cardigan, 1710; directed impeachment of Somers, 1701; as solicitor-general (1702-7) took part in prosecuting Defoe (1703) and asserting jurisdiction of the Commons in election petitions, 1704; as commissioner for the union drafted Ratification Bill, 1707; attorney-general, 1707-8; ably defended Sacheverell, 1710; privy councillor, 1710; lord-keeper, 1710; created Baron Harcourt, 1711; lord chancellor, 1713-14; obtained acquittal of Oxford and pardon of Bolingbroke; created viscount, 1721, re-admitted privy councillor, 1722; several times a lord justice; best speaker of his day; friend of Bolingbroke, Pope, and Swift. [xxiv. 322]

HARCOURT, SIMON, first EARL HARCOURT (1714-1777), son of Simon Harcourt (1684-1720) [q. v.]; educated at Westminster; attended George II at Dettingen, 1743; created Viscount Harcourt of Nuneham-Courtney and Earl Harcourt of Stanton Harcourt, 1749; privy councillor, 1751; governor to Prince of Wales, 1751-2; envoy to Mecklenburg-Strelitz for the Prince of Wales's marriage with Princess Charlotte, 1761; ambassador at Paris, 1768-

1772; viceroy of Ireland, 1772-7; recommended tax on absentees, and created numerous peers; drowned in attempt to extricate his dog from a well at Nuneham. [xxiv. 325]

HARCOURT, THOMAS (1618-1679), jesuit; real name WHITBREAD; professed, 1652; on English mission thirty-two years; while provincial refused Titus Oates admission to the jesuit order; was convicted of complicity in the 'popish plot' on Oates's evidence, and was executed. [xxiv. 326]

HARCOURT, *alias* WARING, WILLIAM (1610-1679). [See WARING.]

HARCOURT, WILLIAM (1625-1679), jesuit; real name AYLWORTH; missioner in England and Holland; died at Haarlem; manuscript account at Brussels of his escape during 'popish plot.' [xxiv. 326]

HARCOURT, WILLIAM, third EARL HARCOURT (1743-1830), field-marshal; son of Simon Harcourt, first earl [q. v.]; succeeded his brother in peerage, 1809; aide-de-camp to Lord Albemarle at Havannah, 1762; M.P., Oxford, 1768-74; commanded 16th light dragoons in America, and captured General Charles Lee, 1776; lieutenant-general, 1793; commanded cavalry in Flanders under Duke of York, 1793-4, whom he succeeded in chief command; general, 1796; field-marshal and G.C.B. at coronation of George IV. [xxiv. 327]

HARCOURT, WILLIAM VERNON (1789-1871), general secretary to first meeting of British Association (York, 1831); son of Edward Harcourt [q. v.]; M.A. Christ Church, Oxford, 1814; student of Christ Church; canon of York, 1824; rector of Wheldrake and Bolton Percy; F.R.S., 1824; carried on chemical experiments with Davy and Wollaston; president of British Association at Birmingham, 1839. [xxiv. 328]

HARDCASTLE, THOMAS (*d.* 1678?), ejected minister; B.A. St. John's College, Cambridge, 1655; ejected from Bramley, Yorkshire, 1662; frequently imprisoned for nonconformity; baptist minister at Broadmead, Bristol, 1670-8. [xxiv. 328]

HARDEBY, GEOFFREY (*fl.* 1360?), Austin friar; provincial of his order; confessor (and perhaps councillor) to Richard II; wrote treatise in answer to Archbishop Fitzralph's attack upon 'evangelical poverty.' [xxiv. 329]

HARDECANUTE, HARDACNUT, or **HARTHACNUT** (1019?-1042), king; younger son of Canute or Cnut [q. v.] and Emma [q. v.]; succeeded his father on throne of Denmark, 1035; chosen king of Wessex in absence, 1037; concerted measures for invasion of England at Bruges with Emma, 1039; chosen king of England on death of Harold, his reputed half-brother, 1040; disinterred and insulted the body of King Harold; levied heavy danegelds, 1041; invited his half-brother Edward (the Confessor) to court, 1041; died suddenly at a bridal feast. [xxiv. 330]

HARDHAM, JOHN (*d.* 1772), tobacconist; employed by Garrick at Drury Lane; at his shop in Fleet Street sold the celebrated '37' snuff, which Reynolds used to take; left money to pay poor rates at his native place, Chichester. [xxiv. 332]

HARDIMAN, JAMES (1790?-1855), Irish writer; sub-commissioner of the records at Dublin, afterwards librarian of Queen's College, Galway; published works, including 'History of County and Town of Galway,' 1820, and 'Irish Minstrelsy . . . with English Poetical Translations,' 1831. [xxiv. 333]

HARDIME, SIMON (1672-1737), flower-painter, of Antwerp; lived in London, 1720-37. [xxiv. 333]

HARDING or ST. STEPHEN (*d.* 1134), abbot of Cîteaux; born and educated at Sherborne; visited Scotland, Paris, and Rome; received tonsure at Molême in Burgundy; left it in order to observe a stricter rule; founded with Robert, abbot of Molême, house at Cîteaux, from which the Cistercian order derived its name; abbot, 1110-33; founded thirteen other abbeys (including Clairvaux, 1115, of which he made Bernard abbot) under the severe Cistercian rule; by his 'charter of charity' (confirmed by Calixtus II, 1119) exempt from episcopal visitation; his constitutions approved at council of Troyes (1127), and the white habit adopted; canonised; Cistercian houses exempted from episcopal jurisdiction and payment of tithe by Innocent II, 1132. [xxiv. 333]

HARDING, MRS. ANNE RAIKES (1780-1858), novelist and miscellaneous writer. [xxiv. 335]

HARDING, EDWARD (1755-1840), librarian to Queen Charlotte, 1803-18, and to the Duke of Cumberland, 1818-1840; brother of Silvester Harding [q. v.] [xxiv. 338]

HARDING, GEORGE PERFECT (*d.* 1853), portrait-painter and copyist; son of Silvester Harding [q. v.]; made water-colour copies of old portraits; exhibited at Royal Academy; helped to establish Granger Society, 1840; published portraits of deans of Westminster (1822-1823), and supplied plates to J. H. Jesse (1840) and other writers. [xxiv. 335]

HARDING, JAMES DUFFIELD (1798-1863), landscape-painter and lithographer; exhibited with Watercolour Society from 1818 (member, 1821); unsuccessfully tried oil-painting; abandoned exclusive use of transparent colours. He brought lithography to perfection, invented lithotint, and introduced tinted paper for sketches; published 'Principles and Practice of Art' and other manuals; 'Picturesque Selections' (1861) his first achievement in lithography. [xxiv. 336]

HARDING, JOHN (1378-1465?). [See HARDYNG.]

HARDING, JOHN (1805-1874), bishop of Bombay; of Westminster and Worcester College, Oxford; B.A., 1826; D.D., 1851; rector of St. Andrew's and St. Anne's, Blackfriars, 1836-51; bishop of Bombay, 1851-69; secretary of Pastoral Aid Society. [xxiv. 337]

HARDING, SAMUEL (*fl.* 1641), dramatist; B.A. Exeter College, Oxford, 1638; his tragedy, 'Sicily and Naples,' issued 1640. [xxiv. 338]

HARDING, SILVESTER (1745-1809), artist and publisher; established with his brother, Edward Harding [q. v.], a book- and print-shop, 1786, and issued works illustrated by himself, including 'The Biographical Mirrour,' 1795. [xxiv. 338]

HARDING, THOMAS (1516-1572), divine; educated at Winchester and New College, Oxford; fellow of New College, 1536; M.A., 1542; Hebrew professor and chaplain to Henry Grey, marquis of Dorchester (afterwards Duke of Suffolk); named warden of New College by Edward VI; abandoned protestantism and became chaplain to Gardiner and (1555) treasurer of Salisbury; in reign of Elizabeth retired to Louvain; carried on a long controversy with John Jewel [q. v.], 1564-8; died at Louvain. [xxiv. 339]

HARDING, THOMAS (*d.* 1648), historian; B.D. Oxford; second master of Westminster, 1610; rector of Souldern, 1622-48; his history of England to 1626 recommended for publication by parliament, 1641, but never issued. [xxiv. 339]

HARDING, WILLIAM (1792-1886), author of 'History of Tiverton,' 1847; served in the Peninsular campaign from 1812; retired as lieutenant-colonel, 1841. [xxiv. 340]

HARDINGE, SIR ARTHUR EDWARD (1828-1892), general; second son of Sir Henry Hardinge, first viscount Hardinge [q. v.]; educated at Eton; ensign, 1844; served in first Sikh war; lieutenant, 1845; lieutenant and captain, 1849; served in Crimea on quartermaster-general's staff, 1854-6; lieutenant-colonel, 1855; C.B., 1857; brevet colonel, 1858; equerry successively to Prince Albert and Queen Victoria; major-general, 1871; general, 1883; commanded Bombay army, 1881-5; governor of Gibraltar, 1886-90; K.C.B. and C.I.E., 1886. [Suppl. ii. 389]

HARDINGE, CHARLES STEWART, second VISCOUNT HARDINGE (1822-1894), son of Sir Henry Hardinge, first viscount Hardinge [q. v.]; educated at Eton and Christ Church, Oxford; B.A., 1844; private secretary to his father in India from 1844; conservative M.P. for Downpatrick, 1851-6; under-secretary for war, 1858-9; trustee of National Portrait Gallery, 1868-94, and chairman of board from 1876. [Suppl. ii. 389]

HARDINGE, GEORGE (1743-1816), author; the Jefferies Hardsman of Byron's 'Don Juan'; son of Nicholas Hardinge [q. v.]; of Eton and Trinity College, Cambridge; M.A. by royal mandate, 1769; barrister, Middle Temple, 1769; solicitor-general (1782) and attorney-general to Queen Charlotte, 1794; senior justice of Brecon, Glamorgan, and Radnor, 1787-1816; counsel for East India Company against Fox's India Bill, 1783; tory

M.P. for Old Sarum, 1784-1807; friend of Horace Walpole; F.S.A., 1769; F.R.S., 1788; published 'Letters to Rt. Hon. E. Burke,' an impeachment of Hastings, 1791, 'Essence of Malone,' 1800 and 1801, and ' Rowley and Chatterton in the Shades,' 1782. His 'Miscellaneous Works' edited, 1818. [xxiv. 340]

HARDINGE, GEORGE NICHOLAS (1781-1808), captain in the navy; nephew and adopted son of George Hardinge [q. v.]; received post-rank for cutting out the Dutch Atalante in Vlie Roads, Texel, 1804; took part in capture of the Cape; killed at capture of French cruiser Piedmontaise off Ceylon; voted public monument in St. Paul's Cathedral. [xxiv. 341]

HARDINGE, SIR HENRY, first VISCOUNT HARDINGE OF LAHORE (1785-1856), field-marshal; brother of George Nicholas Hardinge [q. v.]; deputy assistant quartermaster-general of force under Brent Spencer, which joined Wellesley and fought at Roliça and Vimeira; with Moore in last moments at Coruña, 1809; deputy quartermaster-general of Portuguese army; urged final advance of Sir Galbraith Lowry Cole [q.v.] at Albuera, 1811; wounded at Vittoria, 1813; commanded Portuguese brigade at storming of Palais, 1814; K.C.B., 1815; watched Napoleon's movements for Wellington on escape from Elba, 1815; British commissioner with Blücher at battle of Quatre Bras; commissioner with Prussians in France till 1818; tory M.P. for Durham, 1820-30, Newport (Cornwall), 1830-4, Launceston, 1834-44; secretary at war, 1828-30 and 1841-1844; Irish secretary, 1830 and 1834-5; lieutenant-general, 1841; G.C.B., 1844; governor-general of India, 1844-7; served as second in command to Sir Hugh Gough [q. v.] in first Sikh war, 1845; created a peer, with pension for three lives, 1846; annulled Bentinck's order abolishing corporal punishment in native regiments; endeavoured to abolish suttee in native states; originated carrying of soldiers' kits at public expense. Though not a general till 1854, he was commander-in-chief, 1852-5; field-marshal, 1855. [xxiv. 342]

HARDINGE, NICHOLAS (1699-1758), clerk to the House of Commons; of Eton and King's College, Cambridge; fellow; M.A., 1726; clerk to House of Commons, 1731-52; M.P., Eye, 1748-58; joint secretary to the treasury, 1752; his 'Poems, Latin, Greek, and English,' published, 1818. [xxiv. 346]

HARDMAN, EDWARD TOWNLEY (1845-1887), geologist; accompanied Hon. J. Forrest's expedition to report on mineral resources of Kimberley, West Australia, and discovered goldfield near the Napier Range, 1883-5; a range of Australian mountains named after him. [xxiv. 346]

HARDMAN, FREDERICK (1814-1874), novelist and journalist; joined British legion in Spain, 1834; foreign correspondent of the 'Times' at Madrid, Constantinople, in the Crimea and Danubian provinces, Italy, France, and Paris; published stories, contributed to 'Blackwood'; died at Paris. [xxiv. 347]

HARDRES, SIR THOMAS (1610-1681), serjeant-at-law; barrister, Gray's Inn, 1669; king's serjeant, 1675; M.P., Canterbury, 1679-81; knighted; his 'Reports of Cases in the Exchequer, 1655-70' issued, 1693. [xxiv. 347]

HARDWICK, CHARLES (1821-1859), archdeacon of Ely; fellow of St. Catharine's Hall, Cambridge, 1845; M.A., 1847; professor of divinity, Queen's College, Birmingham, 1853; divinity lecturer at King's College, Cambridge, 1855; archdeacon of Ely, 1857; edited catalogue of Cambridge University MSS. (vols. i-iii. 1856-8) and works for Percy Society and Rolls Series; published also history of the Articles of Religion (1851) and of the Christian Church (ed. Stubbs, 1872); killed by falling over a precipice in the Pyrenees. [xxiv. 347]

HARDWICK, CHARLES (1817-1889), antiquary; published works, including ' History . . . of Friendly Societies,' 1859 and 1869, 'Traditions, Superstitions, and Folk-Lore,' 1872, and ' On Some Antient Battlefields in Lancashire,' 1882. [xxiv. 348]

HARDWICK, JOHN (1791-1875), magistrate at Lambeth (1821) and Marlborough Street, 1841-56; eldest son of Thomas Hardwick [q. v.]; fellow of Balliol College, Oxford, 1808-22; barrister, Lincoln's Inn, 1816; D.C.L., 1830. [xxiv. 351]

HARDWICK, PHILIP (1792-1870), architect; youngest son of Thomas Hardwick [q. v.]; exhibited drawings at Academy, including his buildings at St. Katharine's Docks and Euston Railway station, and designs for Lincoln's Inn; F.S.A., 1824; F.R.S., 1831; R.A., 1841; vice-president of Institute of British Architects, 1839 and 1841; treasurer of Royal Academy, 1850-61. [xxiv. 348]

HARDWICK, THOMAS (1752-1829), architect; pupil and biographer of Sir W. Chambers; exhibited at Academy, 1772-1805; designed Galway Gaol, Marylebone Church, and other London buildings; F.S.A., 1781; advised J. M. W. Turner to abandon architecture. [xxiv. 350]

HARDWICKE, EARLS OF. [See YORKE, PHILIP, first EARL, 1690-1764; YORKE, PHILIP, second EARL, 1720-1790; YORKE, PHILIP, third EARL, 1757-1834; YORKE, CHARLES PHILIP, fourth EARL, 1799-1873.]

HARDY, SIR CHARLES, the elder (1680?-1744), vice-admiral; entered navy as volunteer, 1695; served under Norris and Wager in the Baltic and at Gibraltar; commanded royal yacht Carolina, 1730-42; knighted, 1742; vice-admiral and a lord of the admiralty, 1743. [xxiv. 351]

HARDY, SIR CHARLES, the younger (1716?-1780), admiral; son of Sir Charles Hardy the elder [q. v.]; entered navy as volunteer, 1731; tried for loss of convoy to Newfoundland, 1744, but acquitted, 1745; governor of New York, 1755-7; knighted, 1755; rear-admiral, 1756; second in command under Hawke at Brest and Quiberon Bay, 1759; admiral, 1770; governor of Greenwich, 1771; M.P., Portsmouth, 1774; commander, Channel fleet, 1779. [xxiv. 352]

HARDY, ELIZABETH (1794-1854), novelist (anonymous); died in Queen's Bench Prison. [xxiv. 353]

HARDY, FRANCIS (1751-1812), biographer; B.A. Trinity College, Dublin, 1771; barrister, 1777; M.P., Mullingar, in Irish parliament, 1782-1800; commissioner of appeals, 1806; friend of Grattan; published 'Memoirs . . . of James Caulfield, Earl of Charlemont,' 1810. [xxiv. 353]

HARDY, JOHN STOCKDALE (1793-1849), antiquary and ecclesiastical lawyer; F.S.A., 1826; his 'Literary Remains' published by John Gough Nichols, 1852. [xxiv. 354]

HARDY, MARY ANNE, LADY (1825?-1891), novelist and traveller; daughter of Charles MacDowell; married Sir Thomas Duffus Hardy [q. v.]; travelled in America and other countries; published novels and books of travel. [Suppl. ii. 390]

HARDY, NATHANIEL (1618-1670), dean of Rochester; B.A. Magdalen Hall, Oxford, 1635; M.A. Hart Hall, Oxford, 1638; D.D., 1660; rector of St. Dionis Backchurch, Fenchurch Street, 1660; dean of Rochester, 1660; vicar of St. Martin's-in-the-Fields, 1661; archdeacon of Lewes, 1667; active in restoring churches; his lectures on 1st Epistle of St. John (1656 and 1659) republished, 1865. [xxiv. 354]

HARDY, SAMUEL (1636-1691), nonconformist minister; B.A. Wadham College, Oxford, 1659; minister of 'peculiars' at Charminster, 1660-7, and Poole, 1667-82; ejected by royal commission for nonconformity, 1682; 'Guide to Heaven' attributed to him by Calamy. [xxiv. 355]

HARDY, SIR THOMAS (1666-1732), vice-admiral; cousin of Sir Charles Hardy the elder [q. v.]; first lieutenant under George Churchill [q. v.] at Barfleur; knighted for services under Rooke at Vigo, 1702; present at Malaga, 1704; commander at the Nore, 1711; M.P. Weymouth, 1711; captured convoy in North Sea, 1712; second in command under Norris in Baltic, 1715; said to have been dismissed for Jacobitism, but reinstated; vice-admiral; buried in Westminster Abbey. [xxiv. 356]

HARDY or **HARDIE**, THOMAS (1748-1798), Scottish divine; published 'Principles of Moderation' (1782), advocating repeal of Queen Anne's acts (1712) and substitution of parochial committee for single patron; colleague of Hugh Blair [q. v.] in high church, Edinburgh, 1783-6; minister of New North Church (now west St. Giles), 1786, and professor of church history at Edinburgh; moderator, 1793; dean of Chapel Royal, 1794. [xxiv. 357]

HARDY, THOMAS (1752–1832), radical politician and bootmaker; founded 'London Corresponding Society' to promote parliamentary reform, 1792; charged with high treason with Horne Tooke and others, but defended by Erskine, and acquitted, 1794; pensioned by Sir Francis Burdett; autobiographical memoir issued posthumously, 1832. [xxiv. 357]

HARDY, SIR THOMAS DUFFUS (1804–1878), archivist; trained under Petrie; edited 'Modus tenendi Parliamentum,' 1846; as deputy-keeper of Record Office from 1861 to 1876 edited documents for Rolls Series; member of Historical MSS. Commission, 1869; knighted, 1873; D.C.L. and LL.D. [xxiv. 358]

HARDY, SIR THOMAS MASTERMAN, first baronet (1769–1839), vice-admiral; lieutenant in the Minerve at her capture of the Sabina, defending which prize he was made prisoner, 1796; exchanged in time to be present at St. Vincent, 1797; at Santa Cruz directed cutting out of the Mutine, which he commanded at the Nile, 1798; flag-captain of Nelson in the Vanguard and Foudroyant, 1799, in the San Josef and the St. George, 1801, in the Amphion and the Victory, 1803–5; created baronet, 1806; commodore and commander on South American station, 1819–24; first sea lord at admiralty, 1830; G.C.B., 1831; governor of Greenwich Hospital, 1834; vice-admiral, 1837. [xxiv. 359]

HARDY, SIR WILLIAM (1807–1887), archivist; brother of Sir Thomas Duffus Hardy [q. v.]; keeper of duchy of Lancaster records, 1830–68; deputy-keeper of public records, 1878–86; on Historical MSS. Commission, 1878; knighted, 1883; calendared Lancaster records; edited 'Charters of Duchy of Lancaster,' 1845, and Jehan de Waurin's 'Recueil des Croniques' (Rolls Series). [xxiv. 361]

HARDYMAN, LUCIUS FERDINAND (1771–1834), rear-admiral; midshipman at Dominica, 1782; first lieutenant of the Sibylle at her capture of the Forte, 1799; commanded the Unicorn at Monte Video, 1807, and at the Basque Roads, 1809; C.B., 1815; rear-admiral, 1830. [xxiv. 362]

HARDYNG, JOHN (1378–1465?), chronicler; in the service first of Hotspur (Sir Henry Percy), afterwards of Sir Robert Umfreville; present at battle of Homildon, 1402, and of Agincourt, 1415; constable of Kyme Castle, Lincolnshire; received grants of land for documents which he pretended to have procured in Scotland containing admissions of the feudal subordination of Scottish kings to English crown. His chronicle in its original form (Lancastrian) ended 1436; the version (Yorkist) presented to Edward IV reached 1461. Grafton printed two versions varying from these original forms and each other, 1543. [xxiv. 362]

HARE, AUGUSTUS WILLIAM (1792–1834), divine; son of Francis Hare-Naylor [q. v.]; adopted by his aunt, widow of Sir William Jones, 1797; of Winchester and New College, Oxford; tutor of New College, 1818; incumbent of Alton-Barnes, 1829–34; joint author of 'Guesses at Truth,' 1827; died at Rome. [xxiv. 364]

HARE, FRANCIS (1671–1740), bishop of Chichester; of Eton and King's College, Cambridge, where he was tutor of (Sir) Robert Walpole; M.A., 1696; D.D., 1708; chaplain-general in Flanders, 1704; a royal chaplain; defended Marlborough and answered Swift's 'Conduct of the Allies,' 1711; fellow of Eton, 1712; rector of Barnes, 1713–23; dean of Worcester, 1715–26; took part against Hoadly in Bangorian controversy, c. 1718; dean of St. Paul's, 1726–40; bishop of St. Asaph, 1727–31; bishop of Chichester, 1731–40; his preaching complimented in the 'Dunciad' (iii. 204); rival of Bentley in Latin scholarship; patron of Warburton and Markland; his Hebrew edition of Psalms attacked by Lowth, 1736; his 'Difficulties and Discouragements . . . in the way of Private Judgement' (1714) censured by convocation, but often reprinted; published edition of Terence, forestalling Bentley, 1724. [xxiv. 365]

HARE, HENRY, second BARON COLERAINE (1636–1708), antiquary; succeeded his father, Hugh Hare, first baron Coleraine [q. v.], 1667; built vestry and family vault at Tottenham, of which he left manuscript account. [xxiv. 366]

HARE, HENRY, third BARON COLERAINE (1693–1749), antiquary; grandson of Henry Hare, second baron

Coleraine [q. v.]; of Corpus Christi College, Oxford; F.S.A., 1725 (frequently vice-president); F.R.S., 1730; member of Spalding Society; patron of Vertue; M.P., Boston, 1730–4; visited Italy with Conyers Middleton, collecting prints and drawings of antiquities. [xxiv. 367]

HARE, HUGH, first BARON COLERAINE in Irish peerage (1606?–1667), eccentric royalist; created Irish peer, 1625; supplied Charles I with money in the civil war, during which he lost 40,000l.; declined an English peerage; his translation of Loredano's paraphrases on 'The Fifteen Psalms of Degrees' issued 1681, and 'The Situation of Paradise found out' (spiritual romance), 1683. [xxiv. 368]

HARE, HUGH (1668–1707), translator; son of Henry Hare, second baron Coleraine [q. v.]; took part in translation of Lucian (published 1710) and rendered from Italian Mascardi's account of the conspiracy of Count de Fieschi against Genoa, 1693. [xxiv. 369]

HARE, JAMES (1749–1804), wit and friend of Charles James Fox; educated at Eton and Balliol College, Oxford; M.A. St. Edmund Hall, Oxford, 1791; M.P., Stockbridge, 1772–4, Knaresborough, 1781–1804; ambassador at Warsaw, 1779–82; ruined by losses at cards. [xxiv. 369]

HARE, JULIUS CHARLES (1795–1855), archdeacon of Lewes; son of Francis Hare-Naylor [q. v.]; educated at Charterhouse and Trinity College, Cambridge; intimate with Whewell and Kenelm Digby; fellow of Trinity College, 1818; classical lecturer, 1822; incumbent of Hurstmonceaux, 1832, where John Sterling [q. v.] was his curate and Bunsen his neighbour; joint author of 'Guesses at Truth,' 1827; published translations (with notes) of Niebuhr's 'History of Rome' (with Thirlwall), 1828–32, and other German works, also 'The Victory of Faith,' 1840, 'The Mission of the Comforter,' 1846, vindications of Niebuhr, Luther, and others, and 'Miscellaneous Pamphlets on Church Questions,' 1855; edited 'Philological Museum,' 1833. [xxiv. 369]

HARE, SIR NICHOLAS (d. 1557), judge; educated at Gonville Hall, Cambridge; autumn reader of Inner Temple, 1532; M.P., Downton, 1529, Norfolk, 1539–40, Lancaster, 1544–5; defended Wolsey, 1530; recorder of Norwich, 1536; knighted, 1537; master of requests, 1537 (again, 1552); when speaker imprisoned for advising Sir John Skelton how to evade Statute of Uses in his will, 1540; chief-justice of Chester and Flint, 1540–5; instrumental in passing Treason Act of 1551–2; master of the rolls, 1553; commissioner during vacancy of great seal, 1555. [xxiv. 372]

HARE, ROBERT (d. 1611), antiquary; son of Sir Nicholas Hare [q. v.]; clerk of the pells, 1560–71; M.P., Dunwich, 1563; presented manuscripts and books to Caius College and Trinity Hall, Cambridge, and to the universities collections relating to their history and privileges. [xxiv. 373]

HARE, THOMAS (1806–1891), political reformer; barrister, Inner Temple, 1833; bencher, 1872; reported in Vice-chancellor Wigram's court from 1841; inspector of charities, 1853, and assistant-commissioner, with seat on board, 1872; published works relating to a scheme to secure proportional representation in electoral assemblies of all classes in the kingdom, and other political questions. [Suppl. ii. 390]

HARE, WILLIAM (fl. 1829), criminal; accomplice of the murderer William Burke (1792–1829) [q. v.]; indicted for the murder of James Wilson, one of the victims; et at liberty, 1829, from the Tolbooth, the law officers having decided that he could not legally be put on his trial. [vii. 371]

HARE-NAYLOR, FRANCIS (1753–1815), author; grandson of Francis Hare [q. v.]; intimate with Fox and the Duchess of Devonshire, who gave him an annuity to enable him to marry her cousin; lived many years at Bologna in friendly intercourse with Clotilda Tambroni (female professor) and Mezzofanti, and afterwards at Weimar; published works, including 'History of Germany from the landing of Gustavus to Treaty of Westphalia,' issued 1816; died at Tours. [xxiv. 374]

HAREWOOD, second EARL OF (1767–1841). [See LASCELLES, HENRY.]

HARFLETE, HENRY (*fl.* 1653), author; member of Gray's Inn, 1630; published 'The Hunting of the Fox, or Flattery Displayed,' 1632, 'Vox Cœlorum' (a defence of William Lilly), and 'A Banquet of Essayes, fetcht out of Famous Owens Confectionary,' 1653. [xxiv. 375]

HARFORD, JOHN SCANDRETT (1785–1866), biographer; educated at Christ's College, Cambridge; one of the founders of Lampeter College; D.C.L. Oxford, 1822; F.R.S., 1823; the 'Cœlebs' of Hannah More, of whom he published reminiscences in 'Recollections of W. Wilberforce during nearly thirty years,' 1864; published also lives of Michael Angelo (1857, 2 vols.) and of Bishop Burgess, 1840. [xxiv. 376]

HARGOOD, SIR WILLIAM (1762–1839), admiral; served under Sir Peter Parker (1721–1811) [q. v.] in attack on Sullivan's island, 1776; captured by Spaniards at Pensacola, 1781; with Rodney at Dominica, 1782; captain, 1790; captured the Concorde, 1792; commanded the Belleisle under Nelson at Toulon and Trafalgar, 1804–5; vice-admiral, 1814; admiral and G.C.B., 1831; corresponded with William IV. [xxiv. 377]

HARGRAVE, FRANCIS (1741?–1821), legal antiquary; treasurer of Lincoln's Inn; prominent in the Sommersett habeas corpus case, 1772; recorder of Liverpool, 1797; edited 'State Trials' (Henry IV to 19 George III), 1776, 'Hale's Jurisdiction of the Lords' House,' 1796, and (with Charles Butler) 'Coke upon Lyttleton,' 1775; published also 'Collection of Tracts relative to the Law of England,' 1787, 'Collectanea Juridica,' 1791–2, and other works. [xxiv. 379]

HARGRAVES, EDWARD HAMMOND (1816–1891), pioneer of gold-mining in Australia; sheep-farmer in Sydney, 1834–49; began gold-mining at Lewis Ponds Creek, near Bathurst, 1851; temporary commissioner of crown lands, 1851; published 'Australia and its Goldfields,' 1855. [Suppl. ii. 391]

HARGREAVE, CHARLES JAMES (1820–1866), lawyer and mathematician; LL.D. London; hon. LL.D. Dublin, 1852; barrister, Inner Temple, 1844; bencher, 1851; reader, 1866; professor of jurisprudence at University College, London, 1843–9; F.R.S., 1844; commissioner of incumbered estates, 1849–58; judge of landed estate court, 1858–66; drew Record of Title Bill; gold medallist, Royal Society, for paper 'On the Solution of Linear Differential Equations'; wrote other important mathematical essays. [xxiv. 379]

HARGREAVES, JAMES (*d.* 1778), inventor of the spinning-jenny; employed by Robert Peel (grandfather of the statesman) to construct improved carding-machine, *c.* 1760; supposed to have invented spinning-jenny, *c.* 1764 (patented, 1770); his house and machinery destroyed by mob, 1768; appropriated Arkwright's improved carding-machine. [xxiv. 380]

HARGREAVES, JAMES (1768–1845), baptist minister; at Bolton, Ogden (1798–1822), Wild Street, London, and Waltham Abbey Cross (1828–45); secretary to Peace Society; published 'Life and Memoir of the Rev. John Hirst of Bacup,' 1816, and 'Essays and Letters on important Theological Subjects,' 1833. [xxiv. 381]

HARGREAVES, THOMAS (1775–1846), miniature-painter; apprenticed to Sir Thomas Lawrence [q. v.]; original member of Society of British Artists; executed miniatures of Mr. Gladstone and his sister as children, of Mrs. Gladstone, and Sir Thomas Lawrence. [xxiv. 381]

HARGROVE, ELY (1741–1818), author of 'History of . . . Knaresborough,' 1769, 'Anecdotes of Archery,' with life of Robin Hood, 1792, and 'Yorkshire Gazetteer,' 1806. [xxiv. 382]

HARGROVE, WILLIAM (1788–1862), topographer and journalist; son of Ely Hargrove [q. v.]; thirty-five years editor of the 'York Herald'; sheriff of York, 1831; published 'History and Description of the ancient city of York,' 1818, and 'New Guide to York,' 1842, and other works. [xxiv. 382]

HARINGTON, SIR EDWARD (1753?–1807), author; son of Henry Harington (1727–1816) [q. v.]; knighted as mayor of Bath, 1795; published 'Excursion from Paris to Fontainebleau,' 1786, 'A Schizzo on the Genius of Man,' 1793, and other works. [xxiv. 383]

HARINGTON, EDWARD CHARLES (1804–1881); chancellor and sub-dean of Exeter; grandson of Sir Edward Harington [q. v.]; M.A. Worcester College, Oxford, 1833; chancellor of Exeter, 1847, and canon residentiary, 1856; gave money for repair of Exeter Cathedral; left bequests to the chapter; published theological works. [xxiv. 383]

HARINGTON, HENRY (1755–1791), compiler of 'Nugæ Antiquæ' (family papers belonging to his father, Henry Harington, 1727–1816 [q. v.]); M.A. Queen's College, Oxford, 1777; D.D., 1788; minor canon of Norwich; second enlarged edition of his 'Nugæ Antiquæ,' 1779. [xxiv. 384]

HARINGTON, HENRY (1727–1816), musician and author; M.A. Queen's College, Oxford, 1752; M.D., 1762; physician at Wells and Bath; mayor of Bath; founded Bath Harmonic Society; published collections of songs, glees, trios, and duets, and separate compositions. His other works include 'Geometrical Analogy of the Doctrine of the Trinity,' 1806. [xxiv. 384]

HARINGTON, JOHN (*fl.* 1550), treasurer to Henry VIII's camps and buildings; married the king's natural daughter, Etheldreda, 1546, and inherited monastic forfeitures in Somerset; imprisoned in the Tower with his second wife, in company with Princess Elizabeth, 1554. [xxiv. 385]

HARINGTON, SIR JOHN (1561–1612), wit and author; son of John Harington (*fl.* 1550) [q. v.]; godson of Queen Elizabeth; educated at Eton and Christ's College, Cambridge; studied at Lincoln's Inn; compelled by Queen Elizabeth to translate 'Orlando Furioso' (issued 1591, with preface, 'An Apologie of Poetrie'); as high sheriff of Somerset, 1592, entertained Elizabeth at Kelston for 'Metamorphosis of Ajax' and other satires, 1596 banished from court; accompanied Essex to Ireland 1598; knighted by Essex, 1598; deputed by Essex to appease the queen's anger against him, but sent out of her presence; wrote and handed to the queen a journal of the proceedings of Essex; wrote an account of Elizabeth's last days, and a 'Tract on the Succession to the Crown in the interest of James VI (printed, 1880); offered to go to Ireland as chancellor and archbishop, 1605; for instruction of Henry, prince of Wales, wrote appendix to Godwin's 'De Præsulibus Angliæ' ('Briefe View of Church of England in Q. Elizabeth's and K. James his Reigne,' 1653); his collected 'Epigrams' issued, 1618 letters and miscellaneous writings in 'Nugæ Antiquæ' (first published, 1769). [xxiv. 385]

HARINGTON, JOHN, first BARON HARINGTON of EXTON (*d.* 1613), cousin of Sir John Harington [q. v.] created a peer at coronation of James I, 1603; guardian of Princess Elizabeth at Combe Abbey; prevented her abduction by gunpowder plotters, 1605; escorted her to Germany on her marriage to the elector palatine, 1613 died at Worms on return journey; given (1613) three years' patent for coining brass-farthings ('Haringtons'). [xxiv. 388]

HARINGTON, JOHN, second BARON HARINGTON of EXTON (1592–1614), son of John Harington, first baron [q. v.]; friend and correspondent of Henry, prince of Wales; benefactor of Sidney Sussex College, Cambridge funeral ode on him written by Donne. [xxiv. 389]

HARINGTON, JOHN HERBERT (*d.* 1828), orientalist; chief judge of the Sudder Dewanny and Nizamut Adawlut, 1811; governor-general's agent at Delhi, 1823 member of supreme council and president of board of trade, 1825; edited 'Persian and Arabic Works of Sâ'dee,' 1791–5. [xxiv. 389]

HARIOT, THOMAS (1560–1621). [See HARRIOT.]

HARKELEY, HENRY (*fl.* 1316), chancellor of Oxford University, 1313–16; author of theological works. [xxiv. 390]

HARKNESS, ROBERT (1816–1878), geologist; educated at Dumfries and Edinburgh University; professor of geology, Queen's College, Cork, 1853–78; F.R.S.E., 1854 F.R.S., 1856; wrote papers on geology of south-western Scotland and English Lake district. [xxiv. 390]

HARLAND, JOHN (1806–1868), reporter and antiquary; introduced improvements in stenography; edited works for Chetham Society; published 'Lancashire Lyrics,' 'Lancashire Ballads,' and 'Lancashire Folk-lore.' [xxiv. 390]

HARLAND, SIR ROBERT, baronet (1715 ?–1784), admiral; prominent in capture of Magnanime, 1748; second in command under Keppel at Ushant, 1778; a lord of the admiralty, 1782–3; admiral, 1782. [xxiv. 391]

HARLEY, BRILLIANA, LADY (1600 ?–1643), letter-writer; daughter of Edward, afterwards viscount, Conway [q. v.]; third wife of Sir Robert Harley [q. v.], 1623; died while besieged at Brampton Bryan Castle, 1643; her letters (1625–43) printed, 1854. [xxiv. 391]

HARLEY, SIR EDWARD (1624–1700), governor of Dunkirk; eldest son of Sir Robert Harley [q. v.]; distinguished as parliamentarian officer at Red Marley, 1644; general of horse for Herefordshire and Radnor, 1645; M.P., Herefordshire, 1646 and 1656; impeached for supporting the disbanding ordinance, 1648; member of council of state, 1659; governor of Dunkirk, 1660–1; opposed sale of Dunkirk, 1661; K.B.; during reign of Charles II opposed in parliament legislation against nonconformists; sat also in first, third, and fourth parliaments of William III; published theological tracts. [xxiv. 392]

HARLEY, EDWARD (1664–1735), auditor of the imprest; son of Sir Edward Harley [q. v.]; educated at Westminster; barrister, Middle Temple; acted in revolution of 1688; recorder of Leominster, 1692; M.P., Leominster, 1698–1722; published 'Harmony of the Four Gospels,' 1733 (anon.) [xxiv. 394]

HARLEY, EDWARD, second EARL OF OXFORD (1689–1741), collector; son of Robert Harley, first earl [q. v.], whom he succeeded, 1724; friend and correspondent of Pope and Swift; patron of Vertue and Oldys; circulated second edition of the 'Dunciad,' 1729; an assignee of the copyright of third edition; added to his father's collection of books and manuscripts; his books, prints, and pamphlets sold to Thomas Osborne, 1742, and manuscripts to the British Museum. [xxiv. 394]

HARLEY, GEORGE (1791–1871), water-colour painter and drawing-master. [xxiv. 396]

HARLEY, GEORGE (1829–1896), physician; M.D. Edinburgh, 1850; house surgeon and physician to Edinburgh Royal Infirmary; studied physiology and chemistry at Paris; president of Parisian Medical Society, 1853; lecturer on practical physiology and histology at University College, London, 1855; fellow of Chemical Society and F.C.P. Edinburgh, 1858; professor of medical jurisprudence at University College, 1859, and physician to the hospital, 1860; F.R.S., 1865; published medical works. [Suppl. ii. 392]

HARLEY, GEORGE DAVIES (d. 1811 ?), actor and author; known as the 'Norwich Roscius'; real name DAVIES; played Richard III and other Shakespearean parts at Covent Garden, 1789–91, and old men in the country; supported Mrs. Siddons at Dublin, 1802; published verse and biographical sketch of William Henry West Betty, 'the celebrated young Roscius,' 1802. [xxiv. 396]

HARLEY, JOHN (d. 1558), bishop of Hereford; M.A. Magdalen College, Oxford, 1540; probationer-fellow, 1537–42; master of Magdalen School, 1542–8; chaplain to John Dudley, earl of Warwick, 1548, to Edward VI, 1551; prebendary of Worcester, 1552; bishop of Hereford, 1553-4. [xxiv. 397]

HARLEY, JOHN PRITT (1786–1858), actor and singer; succeeded to John Bannister's parts; appeared at Drury Lane and the Lyceum, 1815–35, and under Bunn's management, 1841–8; at Covent Garden with Macready and Madame Vestris, 1838 and 1840; excelled in rôle of Shakespearean clowns; played Bobadil to Edmund Kean's Kitely, 1816; seized with paralysis while playing Lancelot Gobbo at the Princess's. [xxiv. 397]

HARLEY, SIR ROBERT (1579–1656), master of the mint; B.A. Oriel College, Oxford; K.B., 1603; M.P., Radnor and Herefordshire; master of the mint, 1626–35 and 1643–9; active in Long parliament against 'idolatrous monuments,' against Strafford, and in Scottish and Irish affairs; lent plate and money to parliament; organised the militia; his castle at Brampton Bryan captured by royalists, 1644; imprisoned, 1648–9, for voting to treat with the king. [xxiv. 398]

HARLEY, ROBERT, first EARL OF OXFORD (1661–1724), statesman; eldest son of Sir Edward Harley [q. v.]; member of the Inner Temple, 1682; high

sheriff of Herefordshire, 1689; M.P., Tregony, 1689–90; New Radnor, 1690–1711; a moderate tory, but always on terms with the whigs; brought in Triennial Bill, 1694; established National Land Bank, 1696; carried reductions in the army, 1697, 1698; speaker, 1701–5; secretary of state for northern department, 1704; commissioner for union, 1706; intrigued against colleagues through Abigail Hill's influence with the queen; resigned, 1708; chancellor of the exchequer and head of solid tory ministry, 1710; his life attempted by Guiscard, 1711; initiated scheme for funding national debt through South Sea Company, 1711; created Baron Harley, Earl of Oxford and Mortimer, and named lord treasurer, 1711; obtained dismissal of Marlborough and creation of twelve peers to carry peace of Utrecht; K.G., 1712; ousted by Bolingbroke from favour of queen and tory party; dismissed for neglect of business and disrespect to queen, 1714; his impeachment (1717) on charges of making the peace, secretly favouring James Edward, the Old Pretender, and advising dangerous exercise of prerogative dismissed mainly on account of differences on the question of procedure between the two houses, 1717; excepted from the Act of Grace; forbidden the court; continued to appear in the House of Lords, and to correspond with the Old Pretender, though refusing to lead the Jacobite tories. High characters of him are given by Pope and Swift; but he corresponded simultaneously with Hanoverians and Jacobites, and though a skilful party leader was an incapable statesman. He formed a great library, purchasing the manuscript collections of Foxe, Stow, and D'Ewes. [xxiv. 399]

HARLEY, THOMAS (1730–1804), lord mayor of London; grandson of Edward Harley, second earl of Oxford [q. v.]; prime warden of Goldsmiths' Company, 1762–3; M.P., city of London, 1761; re-elected against Wilkes, 1768; M.P., Herefordshire, 1776–1802; as sheriff of London and Middlesex caused No. 45 of the 'North Briton' to be burnt, 1763; lord mayor of London, 1767–8; privy councillor for services during Wilkite riots, 1768; mobbed, 1770; senior alderman, 1785; lord-lieutenant of Radnorshire. [xxiv. 406]

HARLISTON, SIR RICHARD (fl. 1480), governor of Jersey; captured Mont-Orgueil from the French, 1460 or 1467; captain-in-chief of Jersey, 1473; attainted for participating in Simnel's rising, 1486, and in that of Perkin Warbeck, 1495; in service of Duchess of Burgundy. [xxiv. 407]

HARLOW, GEORGE HENRY (1787–1819), painter; eighteen months in Lawrence's studio; a declared opponent of the Academy; exhibited portraits and historical pieces at the Academy from 1804; attracted notice by group of portraits of Charles Mathews (1814) and 'Trial Scene' from 'Henry VIII,' containing portraits of Mrs. Siddons and the Kembles, 1817; while in Italy, 1818, made acquaintance with Canova; member of Academy of St. Luke, Rome; painted portraits of various artists; painted, by invitation, his own portrait for Uffizi Gallery, Florence. [xxiv. 408]

HARLOWE, SARAH (1765–1852), actress; wife of Francis Waldron; after making a name at Sadler's Wells, appeared at Covent Garden, 1790, Haymarket, Drury Lane, English Opera House, and Royalty; retired, 1826; her best parts, Lucy ('Rivals'), Widow Warren ('Road to Ruin'), Miss MacTab ('Poor Gentleman'), and old Lady Lambert ('Hypocrite'). [xxiv. 409]

HARLOWE, THOMAS (d. 1741), captain in the navy; commanded the Burford at Barfleur, 1692; engaged unsuccessfully French squadron carrying spoils from Carthagena, 1697; acquitted by court-martial under Rooke; engaged at Vigo in the Grafton, 1702; died senior captain. [xxiv. 410]

HARMAN, SIR GEORGE BYNG (1830–1892), lieutenant-general; educated at Marlborough; ensign, 1849; captain, 1855; served in Crimea, 1854; brevet major, 1855; served in Indian mutiny, 1857; on staff in West Indies, 1866–72; brevet colonel, 1871; on staff in expeditionary force in Egypt, 1882; deputy adjutant-general at headquarters, 1883; military secretary, 1885; K.C.B., 1887; lieutenant-general, 1890. [Suppl. ii. 393]

HARMAN, alias VEYSEY or VOYSEY, JOHN (1465 ?–1554). [See VEYSEY.]

HARMAN, SIR JOHN (d. 1673), admiral; commanded the Welcome at battle of Portland, 1653, and in action off the Thames, 1653 ; in Worcester under Blake at Santa Cruz ; flag-captain to Duke of York in Royal Charles in action with Dutch, 1665 ; knighted, 1665 ; rear-admiral, 1665 ; prominent in four days' fight off North Foreland, 1666 ; as commander-in-chief in West Indies destroyed French fleet at Martinique and seized Cayenne and Surinam, 1667 ; rear-admiral of the blue at Solebay, 1672 ; vice-admiral in second action with De Ruyter, 1673 ; admiral, 1673. [xxiv. 410]

HARMAN, THOMAS (*fl.* 1567), writer on beggars ; his ' A Caueat, or Warening for commen cvrsetors Vvlgarely called Vagabones ' (first edition, 1566 ; reprinted, 1869) ; plagiarised by Dekker. [xxiv. 411]

HARMAR or **HARMER,** JOHN (1555 ?–1613), professor of Greek at Oxford ; educated at Winchester and New College, Oxford ; fellow of New College ; M.A., 1582 ; B.D., 1605 ; disputed at Paris with Romanists ; patronised by Leicester ; regius professor of Greek, Oxford, 1585 ; head-master of Winchester, 1588–95 ; warden of St. Mary's College, 1596 ; a translator of the New Testament, 1604 ; edited Chrysostom's ' Homilies,' 1586 and 1590. [xxiv. 412]

HARMAR or **HARMER,** JOHN (1594 ?–1670), professor of Greek at Oxford ; nephew of John Harmar or Harmer (1555 ?–1613) [q. v.] ; educated at Winchester and Magdalen College, Oxford ; M.A., 1617 ; M.B., 1632 ; master of free school, St. Albans, 1626 ; professor of Greek, Oxford, 1650 – *c.* 1660 ; translated Heinsius's ' Mirrour of Humility,' 1618, and published ' Life of Cicero,' 1662, with other works. [xxiv. 413]

HARMER, ANTHONY (pseudonym). [See WHARTON, HENRY, 1664–1695.]

HARMER, JAMES (1777–1853), alderman of London, 1833–40 ; sheriff, 1834–5 ; gave important evidence before the committee for reform of criminal law ; a founder of Royal Free Hospital. [xxiv. 413]

HARMER, THOMAS (1714–1788), independent minister of Wattisfield, Suffolk, 1734–88 ; left manuscript accounts of Norfolk and Suffolk dissenting churches ; published ' Observations on Divers Passages of Scripture . . . from . . . Books of Voyages and Travels,' 1764, and ' Outlines of New Commentary on Solomon's Song,' 1768 ; ' Miscellaneous Works ' issued, 1823. [xxiv. 414]

HARNESS, SIR HENRY DRURY (1804–1883), general ; brother of William Harness [q. v.] ; studied mining engineering in Mexico ; instructor in fortification at Woolwich, 1834–40, professor, 1844–6 ; secretary to railway commission, 1846–50 ; deputy-master of the mint, 1850–2 ; commissioner of Irish works, 1852–4 ; lieutenant-colonel, 1855 ; chief-engineer under Lord Clyde in the mutiny ; director at Chatham, 1860 ; K.C.B., 1873 ; general, 1878. [xxiv. 414]

HARNESS, WILLIAM (1790–1869), divine and author ; brother of Sir Henry Drury Harness [q. v.] ; of Harrow and Christ's College, Cambridge ; M.A., 1816 ; friend and correspondent of Byron ; Boyle lecturer at Cambridge, 1822 ; incumbent of Regent Square Chapel, 1826–44 ; perpetual curate of All Saints', Knightsbridge, 1849–69 ; published an edition of Shakespeare with ' life,' 1825, plays of Massinger and Ford, ' Life of Mary Russell Mitford,' 1870 ; the Harness prize for a Shakespearean essay founded at Cambridge in his memory. [xxiv. 416]

HAROLD, called HAREFOOT (*d.* 1040), king of the English ; reputed son of Canute and Ælfgifu of Northampton [q. v.] ; elected by the witan through Danish support king north of the Thames, and (apparently) over-king of all England, 1035 ; said to have lured to England by forged letter his half-brothers, and to have slain Ælfred, 1037 ; chosen king of all England, 1037 ; banished his step-mother Emma from Wessex ; buried in St. Clement Danes after disinterment by Hardicanute. [xxiv. 417]

HAROLD (1022 ?–1066), king of the English ; second son of Godwin or Godwine [q. v.] and Gytha ; earl of East Anglia, 1045 ; received half of Swegen's earldom (1046), and opposed his restoration ; raised forces in Ireland, ravaged Somerset coast, and sailed with Godwin from Portland to London, 1052 ; succeeded his father in Wessex, 1053, and as head of the national party probably caused unjust banishment of Ælfgar, earl of the East Angles, 1055 ; arranged peace between Gruffydd ab Llywelyn [q. v.] and the English king, 1056 ; probably prevented

meeting between Edward the confessor and his intended heir, the ætheling Edward, 1057 ; received earldom of Hereford, 1058 ; went on pilgrimage to Rome, and visited France, *c.* 1058 : his church at Waltham dedicated by Cynesige of York, 1060 ; sailed round the Welsh coast, 1062–3, and, aided by Tostig, subdued and dethroned Gruffydd, ravaged the land, and exacted tribute ; wrecked on the coast of Ponthieu, and delivered by Count Guy to William of Normandy ; after serving William against the Bretons, swore on the relics to be his man in England and to marry his daughter, *c.* 1064 ; on his return married Aldgyth and advised the outlawing of Tostig and his supersession in Northumbria by Morkere to gain Mercian support for his own succession to the English throne ; chosen king, January 1066, by the nobles, as Edward the Confessor enjoined on his deathbed, and crowned ; obtained recognition from the Northumbrians ; sailed to the Isle of Wight, and for four months kept together an army for defence against Normandy ; defeated Harold Hardrada of Norway and Tostig at Stamford Bridge (25 Sept. 1066) ; left York for London, and thence marched to Senlac on Battle near Hastings with men of the east and south ; fortified a position on the hill, where he was attacked (14 Oct. 1066) by the Normans, and, after repelling one attack, was defeated and slain owing to the enemy's stratagem of pretended flight. His body is supposed first to have been buried at William's order on the sea-coast, and afterwards transferred to Waltham. [xxiv. 418]

HAROLD, FRANCIS (*d.* 1685), chronographer of the order of St. Francis ; nephew of Luke Wadding [q. v.] ; chief works : epitome (1662) of Wadding's ' Franciscan Annals,' with ' life,' and (1683) ' life ' of Mogrobeio, archbishop of Lima ; died at Rome. [xxiv. 426]

HARPER, JAMES (1795–1879), theologian ; educated at Edinburgh ; sixty years secession minister of North Leith ; chairman of the synod, 1840 ; secession church professor of pastoral theology, 1843, of systematic theology, 1848 ; hon. D.D. Jefferson College, America, 1843 ; effected union of secession and relief bodies ; moderator of united presbyterian synod, 1860 ; honorary D.D. Glasgow, 1877. [xxiv. 426]

HARPER, JOHN (*d.* 1742), actor ; played at Lincoln's Inn Fields, 1719–21, Dr. Caius and Ajax, and several original parts ; at Drury Lane, Falstaff, Sir Epicure Mammon, Jobson the Cobbler (' The Devil to Pay'), Sir Wilful Witwould (' Way of the World '), Cacafogo (' Rule a Wife and have a Wife') ; prosecuted in a test action for vagrancy and discharged, 1733. [xxiv. 427]

HARPER, JOHN (1809–1842), architect ; friend of Etty and Stanfield ; with the Wyatts prepared designs for Apsley House and York House ; died at Naples. [xxiv. 427]

HARPER, THOMAS (1787–1853), inspector of musical instruments to the East India Company ; trumpet-player engaged at Drury Lane and Lyceum English opera, 1806, at Ancient Concerts and Italian Opera, 1821, and at Philharmonic Concerts. [xxiv. 428]

HARPER, SIR WILLIAM (1496 ?–1573), lord mayor of London ; master of Merchant Taylors' Company, 1553, sheriff of London, 1557–8 ; lord mayor, 1561–2 ; knighted, 1562 ; helped to found Merchant Taylors' School ; founded school at Bedford, 1566. [xxiv. 428]

HARPER, WILLIAM (1806–1857), author and journalist ; published two volumes of religious verse and ' Memoir of Benjamin Braidley,' 1845. [xxiv. 429]

HARPSFIELD or **HARPESFELD,** JOHN (1516 1578), chaplain to Bishop Bonner ; of Winchester and New College, Oxford ; fellow of New College, 1534–*c.* 1551 ; M.A., 1538 ; D.D., 1554 ; archdeacon of London, 1554 ; dean of Norwich, 1558 ; zealous persecutor of protestants ; disputed with Cranmer, Ridley, and Latimer, at Oxford ; active in convocation against Reformation, 1559 ; deprived and imprisoned in the Fleet ; published homilies. [xxiv. 429]

HARPSFIELD or **HARPESFELD,** NICHOLAS (1519 ?–1575), theologian ; brother of John Harpsfield or Harpesfield [q. v.] ; educated at Winchester and New College, Oxford ; fellow, 1535 ; principal of Whitehall hostel, 1544 ; first regius professor of Greek, *c.* 1546 ; lived at Louvain during reign of Edward VI ; D.C.L. Oxford, 1554 ; proctor in court of arches, 1554 ; vicar of Laindon, Essex, 1554 ; archdeacon of Canterbury and official of court of arches; as prolocutor of lower house of convocation presented remonstrance against reformation, 1559; one of the eight Romanist disputants, 1559; imprisoned in the Tower. 1559-75; his 'Historia Anglicana Ecclesiastica' edited by Richard Gibbons, 1622, 'Treatise on the pretended Divorce between Henry VIII and Catherine of Arragon' by Nicholas Pocock, 1878, and six Latin dialogues attacking 'pseudo-martyrs' by Alan Cope, 1566 (Antwerp); left manuscript lives of Cranmer and More. [xxiv. 431]

HARPUR, JOSEPH (1773-1821), critic; matriculated at Trinity College, Oxford, 1790; deputy professor of civil law at Oxford, 1806 (D.C.L., 1813); published 'Essay on the Principles of Philosophical Criticism applied to Poetry,' 1810. [xxiv. 432]

HARRADEN, RICHARD (1756-1838), artist and engraver; published views of Cambridge, 1797-8, and 1800, 'Costume of the various orders in the University,' 1803, and 'Cantabrigia Depicta,' 1811. [xxiv. 432]

HARRADEN, RICHARD BANKES (1778-1862), artist; son of Richard Harraden [q. v.]; made drawings for 'Cantabrigia Depicta,' 1811, and published further 'Illustrations,' 1830. [xxiv. 433]

HARRIES, MARGARET (1797-1846). [See WILSON, MRS. CORNWELL BARON.]

HARRILD, ROBERT (1780-1853), inventor of 'composition rollers' for inking types, 1810; preserved Benjamin Franklin's press, and left money for a 'Franklin pension' for printers. [xxiv. 433]

HARRIMAN, JOHN (1760-1831), botanist; clergyman in Northumberland and Durham; F.L.S.; furnished plants for Smith's 'English Botany,' and observed many species of lichens; the microscopic dot lichen named after him. [xxiv. 433]

HARRINGTON, EARLS OF. [See STANHOPE, WILLIAM, first EARL, 1690?-1756; STANHOPE, WILLIAM, second EARL, 1719-1779; STANHOPE, CHARLES, third EARL, 1753-1829; STANHOPE, CHARLES, fourth EARL, 1780-1851; STANHOPE, LEICESTER FITZGERALD CHARLES, fifth EARL, 1784-1862.]

HARRINGTON or **HARINGTON**, JAMES (1611-1677), political theorist; great-nephew of John Harington, first baron Harington of Exton [q. v.]; studied at Trinity College, Oxford; some time in service of elector palatine; visited Rome and Venice; groom of the bedchamber to Charles I at Holmby and in the Isle of Wight; published 'The Commonwealth of Oceana,' 1656, the 'Art of Lawgiving' (abridgment of 'Oceana'), 1659, and several tracts in defence of it; formed the 'Rota' club for political discussion, 1659-60; imprisoned in the Tower, 1661, and afterwards at Plymouth; works edited by Toland, 1700. [xxiv. 434]

HARRINGTON, JAMES (1664-1693), lawyer and poet; educated at Westminster and Christ Church, Oxford; M.A., 1690; barrister, Inner Temple; published Latin hexameter poem on the death of Charles II, 'Defence of the Rights and Privileges of the University of Oxford' (1690), and other pamphlets; contributed preface and introduction to first edition of 'Athenæ Oxonienses.' [xxiv. 436]

HARRINGTON, SIR JOHN (1561-1612). [See HARINGTON.]

HARRINGTON, MARIA, fourth COUNTESS OF. [See FOOTE, MARIA, 1797?-1867.]

HARRINGTON, ROBERT (fl. 1815), writer on natural philosophy; published, as 'Richard Bewley, M.D.,' a 'Treatise on Air' (1791), and other works against Lavoisier's theory of combustion and in favour of phlogiston, 'Chemical Essay,' (against Priestley), 1794, and other works. [xxiv. 436]

HARRINGTON, WILLIAM (d. 1523), divine; prebendary of St. Paul's, 1497; rector of St. Anne's, Aldersgate, 1505-10; published a work in commendation of matrimony. [xxiv. 437]

HARRIOT, THOMAS (1560-1621), mathematician and astronomer; B.A. St. Mary Hall, Oxford, 1580; mathematical tutor to Sir W. Ralegh, who sent him, 1585, to survey Virginia; his 'Brief and True Report' (1588) reproduced in De Bry's 'Americæ Descriptio' and in Hakluyt; pensioned by Henry, earl of Northumberland,

one of whose 'three magi' he became. His 'Artis Analyticæ Praxis ad Æquationes Algebraicas resolvendas,' edited, 1631, by Walter Warner, embodies inventions which gave algebra its modern form. He used telescopes simultaneously with Galileo: he observed sun-spots and the comets of 1607 and 1618. Collections of his papers are at the British Museum and Sion House. [xxiv. 437]

HARRIOTT, JOHN (1745-1817), projector of the London Thames police; served in the navy and in the merchant service; also in military employ of East India Company; received gold medal from Society of Arts for reclaiming from the sea (1781-2) Rushley isle, Essex; lived in America, 1790-5; patented improved ship's pump (1797) and other inventions; resident magistrate at Thames police court, 1798-1816; addressed (1797) letter to the Duke of Portland, secretary of state, broaching his scheme of Thames police (marine police established, 1798); published 'Struggles through Life,' 1815. [xxiv. 439]

HARRIS, AUGUSTUS GLOSSOP (1825-1873), actor and manager; appeared on American stage when eight years old; managed Princess's Theatre, London, 1859-62; manager of Covent Garden; introduced Fechter to London. [xxv. 1]

HARRIS, SIR AUGUSTUS HENRY GLOSSOP (1852-1896), actor, impresario, and dramatist; son of Augustus Glossop Harris [q. v.]; manager at Covent Garden, c. 1875; became lessee of Drury Lane, 1879, and produced, in collaboration with various authors, a succession of highly popular melodramas and pantomimes, besides operas; sheriff of London and knighted, 1891. [Suppl. ii. 394]

HARRIS, CHARLES AMYAND (1813-1874), bishop of Gibraltar; M.A. Oriel College, Oxford, 1837; fellow of All Souls' College, Oxford, 1835-7; rector of Wilton, 1840-1848; prebendary of Salisbury, 1841; archdeacon of Wilts, 1863; vicar of Bremhill-with-Highway, 1863-8; bishop of Gibraltar, 1868-73. [xxv. 1]

HARRIS, SIR EDWARD ALFRED JOHN (1808-1888), admiral; brother of James Howard Harris, third earl of Malmesbury [q. v.]; M.P., Chippenham, 1844-52; consul-general in Denmark, 1852, Peru, 1852, Chili, 1853, and Austrian coasts of the Adriatic, 1858; minister at Berne and (1867) the Hague; K.C.B., 1872; admiral, 1877. [xxv. 12]

HARRIS, FRANCIS (1829-1885), physician; B.A. Caius College, Cambridge, 1852; M.D., 1859; studied at St. Bartholomew's Hospital, and in Paris and Berlin; assistant-physician at St. Bartholomew's Hospital, 1861; published thesis on amyloid degeneration, 1859. [xxv. 2]

HARRIS, GEORGE (1722-1796), civilian; D.C.L. Oriel College, Oxford, 1750; chancellor of Durham, Hereford, and Llandaff; bequeathed 40,000l. to St. George's and 15,000l. to Westminster Lying-in hospitals; edited Justinian's 'Institutes,' with translation, 1756. [xxv. 2]

HARRIS, GEORGE, first BARON HARRIS (1746-1829), general; served with 5th fusiliers in America; wounded at Bunkers Hill, 1775; commanded grenadier battalion at capture of St. Lucia, 1778; second in command at defence of La Vigie; served against Tippoo Sahib, 1790-2; commanded troops in Madras, 1796-1800; captured Seringapatam and subdued Mysore, 1799; lieutenant-general, 1801; general, 1812; created a peer, 1815; G.C.B., 1820. [xxv. 3]

HARRIS, GEORGE (1794-1859), unitarian minister; studied at Glasgow University; secretary of Scottish Unitarian Association; minister at Liverpool, 1817-22, Bolton, 1822-5, Glasgow, 1825-41, Edinburgh, 1841-5, and Newcastle, 1845-59; eager controversialist and successful preacher. [xxv. 4]

HARRIS, GEORGE (1809-1890), author; educated at Rugby; barrister, Middle Temple, 1843; deputy county court judge of Bristol district, 1853; acting judge of county court, Birmingham, 1861; registrar of court of bankruptcy, Manchester, 1862-8; headed deputation to Palmerston suggesting formation of Historical Manuscripts Commission, 1859; vice-president of Anthropological Society of London, 1871; joint founder and vice-president of Psychological Society, 1875. His works include 'Life of Lord-chancellor Hardwicke,' 1847, 'Civilization considered as a Science,' 1861; and an 'Autobiography,' 1888. [Suppl. ii. 394]

HARRIS, GEORGE FRANCIS ROBERT, third BARON HARRIS (1810–1872), governor of Madras; grandson of George Harris, first baron [q. v.]; educated at Eton and Merton and Christ Church Colleges, Oxford; B.A., 1832; D.C.L., 1863; governor of Trinidad, 1846; governor of Madras, 1854–9; reinforced Earl Canning during the mutiny; G.C.S.I., 1859; chamberlain to Princess of Wales. [xxv. 5]

HARRIS, HENRY (d. 1704?), chief engraver to the mint, 1690–1704; engraver of public seals. [xxv. 6]

HARRIS, HOWEL (1714–1773), Welsh methodist pioneer; worked with Daniel Rowlands [q. v.] till methodist disruption, 1751; founded 'family' or community at Trevecca, 1752; served in Brecknockshire militia, 1759; visited and corresponded with Countess of Huntingdon [see HASTINGS, SELINA]; preached at Whitefield's tabernacle. [xxv. 6]

HARRIS, JAMES (1709–1780), author of 'Hermes, or a Philosophical Inquiry concerning Universal Grammar,' 1751, and other works (collected, 1801); M.P., Christchurch, 1761–80; a lord of the treasury, 1763–5; secretary to George III's queen, 1774. [xxv. 7]

HARRIS, JAMES, first EARL OF MALMESBURY (1746–1820), diplomatist; son of James Harris [q. v.]; educated at Winchester, Merton College, Oxford, and Leyden; when chargé d'affaires at Madrid prevented Spanish expedition against Falkland isles, 1770; minister at Berlin, 1772–6; ambassador at St. Petersburg, 1777–82; named minister at the Hague by Pitt, 1784; promoted counter-revolution in favour of house of Orange; negotiated alliance with Prussia and Holland, 1788; created Baron Malmesbury, 1788; supported Fox on regency question, but (1793) left him with 'old whigs'; negotiated fresh alliance with Prussia, 1794, and match between the Prince of Wales and Princess Caroline of Brunswick; engaged in fruitless negotiations at Paris and Lille, 1796–1797; incapacitated by deafness, but much consulted by Pitt and Canning on foreign affairs; created Earl of Malmesbury and Viscount Fitzharris, 1800; 'Diaries' edited by grandson, 1844, family letters issued, 1870. [xxv. 8]

HARRIS, JAMES HOWARD, third EARL OF MALMESBURY (1807–1889), statesman; grandson of James Harris, first earl of Malmesbury [q. v.]; educated at Eton and Oriel College, Oxford; B.A., 1827; during continental trips became acquainted with Louis Napoleon; M.P., Wilton, 1841; succeeded to peerage, 1841; protectionist whip in the Upper House; joined Disraeli in urging reform on Lord Derby; as foreign secretary (February–December 1852) recognised Napoleon III, whom he interviewed in Paris, 1853; during second tenure of office (1858–9) re-established good relations with him, helped to compose dispute between France and Portugal, exacted reparation from Naples for 'Cagliari' affair, 1858, delayed war between Austria and Sardinia, and strove to localise it when declared (1859), adopting policy of strict neutrality; created G.C.B. on retirement; offered support to Palmerston against Russell, 1860; attempted to remove Napoleon's prejudices against the conservatives, 1861; carried vote of censure on Palmerston for policy on Danish question, 1864; lord privy seal in Lord Derby's last ministry, 1866–8, and under Disraeli, 1874–6; published 'Memoirs of an Ex-minister,' 1884. [xxv. 9]

HARRIS, JOHN (1588?–1658), warden of Winchester College; M.A. New College, Oxford, 1611; D.D.; fellow, 1606–22; regius professor of Greek, 1619–22; prebendary of Wells, 1622; member of Westminster Assembly; warden of Winchester College, 1630–58; published life of Bishop Arthur Lake. [xxv. 13]

HARRIS, JOHN (1667?–1719), divine and author; M.A. St. John's College, Cambridge, 1691; D.D. Lambeth, 1706; prebendary of Rochester, 1708; incumbent of St. Mildred, Bread Street, London, with St. Margaret Moses; rector of East Barming, 1715; ridiculed in 'Picture of a High-flying Clergyman,' 1716; F.R.S., 1696 (secretary, 1709); lectured on mathematics in Birchin Lane, London; died a pauper. His works include defence of the Woodwardian system, 1697, Boyle lectures, 1698, 'Lexicon Technicum,' 1704, and 'Navigantium atque Itinerantium Bibliotheca,' 1705. [xxv. 13]

HARRIS, JOHN (fl. 1737), organ-builder: son of Renatus Harris [q. v.] [xxv. 22]

HARRIS, JOHN (fl. 1680–1740), architectural and topographical engraver. [xxv. 14]

HARRIS, JOHN (d. 1834), water-colour painter exhibited at Royal Academy, 1802–15. [xxv. 14]

HARRIS, JOHN (1756–1846), publisher: assisted John Murray and F. Newbery, and succeeded to latter's business. [xxv. 15]

HARRIS, JOHN (1802–1856), principal of New College, London; 'boy preacher' near Bristol; theological professor at Cheshunt College, 1837; D.D. Brown University, Rhode Island, U.S.A., 1838; principal of New College, London, and its professor of theology, 1851; chairman of Congregational Union, 1852; published 'The Great Teacher,' 1835, and theological prize essays. [xxv. 15]

HARRIS, JOHN (1820–1884), Cornish poet; worked in Dolcoath mine; won first prize for Shakespeare tercentenary poem, 1864; received grants from Royal Literary Fund and Royal Bounty Fund; published 'Lays from the Mine, the Moor, and the Mountain' (1853) and other verse. [xxv. 16]

HARRIS, JOHN RYLAND (IEUAN DDU O LAN TAWY) (1802–1823), writer in Welsh; son of Joseph Harris (Gomer) [q. v.]; contributed to 'Seren Gomer' newspaper, 1818–23; made Welsh version of 'Paradise Regained'; published Welsh guide to reading of music. [xxv. 16]

HARRIS, JOSEPH (?) (fl. 1661–1681), actor; played in Sir William D'Avenant's company at Lincoln's Inn Fields and Dorset Garden; Romeo to Betterton's Mercutio, 1662; took original rôles in plays by D'Avenant, Dryden, Etherege, and Otway; intimate with Pepys. [xxv. 17]

HARRIS, JOSEPH (fl. 1661–1702), actor and dramatist; member of king's company at Theatre Royal; engraver to the mint on accession of Anne; four plays ascribed to him. [xxv. 18]

HARRIS, JOSEPH (1702–1764), assay master of the mint, 1748; author of monometallist 'Essay on Money and Coins' (two parts, 1756 and 1758), cited by Lord Liverpool, 1805, and praised by McCulloch, and posthumous (1775) treatise on optics. [xxv. 18]

HARRIS, JOSEPH (d. 1814), organist of St. Martin's, Birmingham (1787); composed songs and harpsichord quartetts. [xxv. 19]

HARRIS, JOSEPH (GOMER) (1773–1825), Welsh author; baptist pastor at Swansea; edited 'Seren Gomer' (first newspaper in Welsh), 1814–15, and afterwards as monthly magazine; published selection of Welsh hymns (Ychydig o hymnau), 1796, the bible in Welsh and English, 1825, 'Cofiant Ieuan Ddu' (memoir of his son), 1823, and other works. [xxv. 19]

HARRIS, JOSEPH JOHN (1799–1869), organist at Manchester, 1848–69; published 'The Cathedral Daily Service,' 1844, 'The Musical Expression,' 1845. [xxv. 19]

HARRIS, JOSEPH MACDONALD (1789–1860), musician; arranged Burgoyne's 'Collection of Psalms,' 1827; published musical compositions. [xxv. 20]

HARRIS, JOSEPH THORNE (1828–1869), pianist and composer; son of Joseph John Harris [q. v.] [xxv. 20]

HARRIS, MOSES (fl. 1766–1785), entomologist and artist; published with plates by himself 'The Aurelian or Natural History of English Insects,' 1766, 'English Lepidoptera,' 1775, 'Exposition of English Insects,' 1776, and other works; his 'Natural System of Colours' edited by Thomas Martyn, 1811. [xxv. 20]

HARRIS, PAUL (1573–1635?), Roman catholic divine, banished from Dublin for attacking Franciscans; published tracts against Archbishop Thomas Fleming [q. v.] and against Francis Matthews. [xxv. 21]

HARRIS, RENATUS, or RÉNÉ (1640?–1715?), organ-builder; defeated by 'Father Smith' (Bernard Smith, q. v.) in contest for building organ in Temple Church, 1684; afterwards built thirty-nine organs, including those in King's College Chapel, Cambridge (1686) and in cathedrals of Chichester (1678), Winchester (1681), Ely, Bristol (1685), Gloucester, Worcester, Hereford (1686), St. Patrick (1697), and Salisbury (1710), [xxv. 21]

HARRIS, RICHARD (*fl.* 1613), theologian; fellow of St. John's College, Cambridge, 1580; senior fellow, 1593; M.A., 1583; D.D., 1595; rector of Gestingthorp, 1597, and Bradwell-juxta-Mare, 1613; published 'Concordia Anglicana' (1612) in reply to Becane 'de dissidio Anglicano.' [xxv. 22]

HARRIS, ROBERT (1581–1658), president of Trinity College, Oxford; B.A. Worcester College, Oxford, 1600; D.D., 1648; incumbent of Hanwell, Oxfordshire, 1614–42; member of assembly of divines; visitor to the university, 1647–52 and 1654–8; president of Trinity College, Oxford, 1648–58; an eminent preacher; sometime incumbent of St. Botolph's, Bishopsgate. [xxv. 23]

HARRIS, ROBERT (1809–1865), captain in the navy; brother of Sir William Cornwallis Harris [q. v.]; midshipman at Algiers, 1824, and at Navarino, 1827; promoted commander for services at capture of Bogue forts, 1841; captain, 1849; commanded Illustrious training-ship, 1854–9, and Britannia till 1862. [xxv. 23]

HARRIS, SAMUEL (1682–1733), first regius professor of modern history at Cambridge; M.A. Peterhouse, Cambridge, 1707; Craven scholar, 1701; fellow of Peterhouse; professor of modern history, 1724–33. [xxv. 24]

HARRIS, THOMAS (1705–1782), clothing contractor to the army; brother of Howel Harris [q. v.] [xxv. 19]

HARRIS, THOMAS (*d.* 1820), proprietor and manager of Covent Garden; had violent dispute with Colman the elder as to management, 1769–70; stage-manager, 1774. [xxv. 24]

HARRIS, WALTER (1647–1732), physician; M.D. Bourges and Cambridge; scholar of Winchester and (1666) fellow of New College, Oxford; B.A., 1670; F.R.C.P., 1682, five times censor and treasurer, 1714–17; physician to Charles II, 1683; physician to William III; Lumleian lecturer, 1710–32; Harveian orator; attended Queen Mary on her deathbed, 1694; published medical works; admirer of Sydenham. [xxv. 25]

HARRIS, WALTER (1686–1761), Irish historiographer; scholar of Trinity College, Dublin, 1707; hon. LL.D. Dublin, 1753; vicar-general of the protestant bishop of Meath, 1753; published translation with continuation of Sir James Ware's 'Works concerning Ireland,' 1739–46; also history of Irish writers, 1736, 'Hibernica,' 1747–50, and 'History of William III' (1749). [xxv. 26]

HARRIS, WILLIAM (1546?–1602), Roman catholic divine; fellow of Lincoln College, Oxford; M.A., 1570; left England and was ordained priest at Louvain; missioner in England, 1575; wrote 'Theatrum, seu Speculum verissimæ et antiquissimæ Ecclesiæ Magnæ Britanniæ.' [xxv. 27]

HARRIS, WILLIAM (1675?–1740), presbyterian divine; hon. D.D. Edinburgh, 1728, and Aberdeen; minister of Crutched Friars from 1698; Friday evening lecturer at Weighhouse, Eastcheap, 1708; merchants' lecturer at Salters' Hall, 1727; a non-subscriber; original Williams trustee; published 'Exposition of Philippians and Colossians,' 1710, and other works. [xxv. 27]

HARRIS, WILLIAM (1720–1770), biographical writer; hon. D.D. Glasgow, 1765. His collected works (1814) contain lives of Hugh Peters, James I, Charles I, Cromwell, and Charles II. [xxv. 28]

HARRIS, WILLIAM (1776?–1830), independent minister at Cambridge and Stoke Newington, tutor at Hoxton and Highbury; author of 'Grounds of Hope for salvation of all dying in Infancy,' 1821. [xxv. 28]

HARRIS, SIR WILLIAM CORNWALLIS (1807–1848), engineer and traveller; superintending engineer of northern provinces of India, 1848; with Richard Williamson made a big game expedition to country between Orange River and the Matabele chief Moselikatze's kraal, 1835–7 (narratives published, 1838 and 1841); knighted, 1844, for negotiating treaty with Shoa; published 'Portraits of the Game Animals of South Africa,' 1840, and account of his Abyssinian expedition; died at Surwur. [xxv. 28]

HARRIS, WILLIAM GEORGE, second BARON HARRIS (1782–1845), lieutenant-general; son of George, first baron Harris [q. v.]; served against Tippoo Sahib 1799, in the Copenhagen expedition (1801), and in Canada,

1802; volunteer at recapture of the Cape, 1805; commanded 2nd battalion of 73rd in North Germany and the Netherlands, 1813–14; wounded at Waterloo, 1815; lieutenant-general, 1837; commanded northern district, 1825–8; succeeded to peerage, 1829. [xxv. 29]

HARRIS, SIR WILLIAM SNOW (1791–1867), electrician; knighted in 1847 for his improved lightning-conductor; F.R.S., 1831; Copley medallist, 1835; gave Bakerian lecture, 1839, on elementary laws of electricity; received government grant of 5,000*l.*; appointed scientific referee, 1860. [xxv. 30]

HARRISON, BENJAMIN, the elder (1771–1856), treasurer of Guy's Hospital, 1797–1856; F.R.S. and F.S.A.; deputy-governor of Hudson's Bay and South Sea companies; chairman, Exchequer Loan Board. [xxv. 31]

HARRISON, BENJAMIN, the younger (1808–1887), archdeacon of Maidstone; son of Benjamin Harrison the elder; student of Christ Church, Oxford, 1828; M.A., 1833; Ellerton, Kennicott, and chancellor's prizeman; Ellerton Hebrew scholar; chaplain to Archbishop Howley, 1843–8; archdeacon of Maidstone, 1845–87; a reviser of the Old Testament, 1885; presented his library to Canterbury Cathedral; edited Bishop Broughton's sermons, 1857, and 'Christianity in Egypt,' 1883. [xxv. 31]

HARRISON, SIR GEORGE (*d.* 1841), legal writer; auditor for life of the duchy of Cornwall, 1823; of Lancaster, 1826; G.C.H., 1831; published 'Memoir respecting the hereditary revenues of the crown,' 1838, and other works. [xxv. 32]

HARRISON, GEORGE HENRY (1816–1846), water-colour painter; son of Mary Harrison [q. v.]; exhibited at Royal Academy and elsewhere, 1840–6; associate of Old Water-colour Society, 1845. [xxv. 32]

HARRISON, JOHN (*fl.* 1630), envoy to Barbary and author; groom of the privy chamber to Prince Henry; afterwards in service of electress palatine; sheriff of Bermuda, 1622; after several visits to Barbary obtained release of 260 British subjects, 1625–30; published work against Jews (3rd ed., 1656), and books relating to the elector palatine and Bohemia, and to 'Mvley Abdala Melek, the late king of Barbarie,' 1633. [xxv. 33]

HARRISON, JOHN (1579–1656), philanthropist; first chief magistrate of Leeds, 1626, and again, 1634; built New Street or Kirkgate with St. John's Church and almshouses and the market-cross, Leeds; removed Leeds grammar school to present site. [xxv. 33]

HARRISON, JOHN (1613?–1670), presbyterian divine; rector of Ashton-under-Lyne, 1642–62; active member of Manchester classis, 1646–60; imprisoned as royalist, 1651 and 1659–60. [xxv. 34]

HARRISON, JOHN (1693–1776), horologist; son of a carpenter; devised gridiron pendulum (1726), recoil escapement, 'going ratchet' (secondary spring), and 'new musical scale'; competed for board of longitude's prizes for determining longitude at sea within sixty, forty, and thirty geographical miles respectively with his first chronometer, 1736; Copley medallist for third chronometer, 1749; awarded 5,000*l.* (part of the board of longitude's prize) by parliament for fourth chronometer, 1763; after the construction of fifth and interposition of George III received the whole reward, 1773; published narrative relating to his discovery of longitude at sea and other inventions; his tomb in Hampstead churchyard reconstructed by Clockmakers' Company, 1879. [xxv. 35]

HARRISON, JOSEPH (*d.* 1858?), horticulturist; edited 'Floricultural Cabinet' (now 'Gardener's Magazine'), 1833–55, and similar publications. [xxv. 36]

HARRISON, MARY (1788–1875), flower-painter; *née* Rossiter; married William Harrison, 1814; an original member and exhibitor of New Water-colour Society, 1831. [xxv. 37]

HARRISON, RALPH (1748–1810), nonconformist divine and tutor; minister at Cross Street, Manchester, 1771; professor of classics and belles lettres at Manchester Academy, 1786–9; published educational manuals. [xxv. 37]

HARRISON, ROBERT (*d.* 1585?), Brownist; M.A. Corpus Christi College, Cambridge, 1572; removed from mastership of Aylsham school for objections to the prayer-book, 1574 ; when master of a hospital at Norwich, helped Robert Browne [q. v.] to form a nonconformist congregation ; migrated to Middelburg, 1581 ; published theological tracts; corresponded with Cartwright. [xxv. 38]

HARRISON, ROBERT (1715-1802), mathematician and linguist ; master of Trinity House School, Newcastle, 1757 ; published (with Isaac Thomson) 'Short Account of a Course of Natural and Experimental Philosophy,' 1757. [xxv. 39]

HARRISON, SAMUEL (1760 - 1812), vocalist ; soprano at Ancient Concerts and Society of Sacred Music, 1776 ; principal tenor at Gloucester festival, 1781 ; engaged for Handel Commemoration, 1784, at instance of George III ; sang at Hereford, 1786-1808, and at Gloucester and Worcester, 1801-8, at the Ancient Concerts, 1785-91, and afterwards at the Vocal Concerts. [xxv. 39]

HARRISON, STEPHEN (fl. 1603), joiner and architect ; designed arches for entry of James I into London, 1604, described in rare work issued that year. [xxv. 39]

HARRISON, SUSANNAH (1752-1784), religious poet ; sometime a domestic servant ; published 'Songs in the Night,' 1780. [xxv. 40]

HARRISON, THOMAS (1555-1631), biblical scholar ; B.A. St. John's College, Cambridge, 1576 ; fellow and vice-prefect of Trinity College ; a reviser of James I's bible. [xxv. 40]

HARRISON, THOMAS (1606 - 1660), regicide ; when a member of Inns of Court enlisted in Essex's bodyguard, 1642 ; major in Fleetwood's horse at Marston Moor, 1644 ; entered the 'new model' ; present at Naseby, 1645, Langport, and captures of Winchester and Basing ; M.P., Wendover, 1646 ; colonel of horse, 1647 ; opposed further negotiation with Charles I, 1647 ; distinguished himself under Lambert at Appleby, and was wounded, 1648 ; negotiated with levellers, 1648 ; zealous for trial of Charles I, whom he escorted from Hurst to London ; regularly attended meetings of high court of justice ; held chief command in England during Cromwell's absence, 1650-1 ; directed pursuit after Worcester, 1651 ; elected to council of state, 1651 ; a promoter of army petition of 12 Aug. 1652 ; assisted in expelling Long parliament, 1653 ; member of council of thirteen, and a leading spirit in 'Barebones parliament,' 1653 ; deprived of his commission under the instrument of government, 1653 ; reprimanded by Cromwell for relations with anabaptists, 1654 ; imprisoned, 1655-6 and 1658-9 ; refused flight or compromise at the Restoration ; exempted from Act of Indemnity, 1660 ; justified his action against Charles I by the authority of parliament ; showed great courage at his execution. [xxv. 41]

HARRISON, THOMAS (1619 - 1682), nonconformist divine ; chaplain to governor of Virginia ; succeeded Dr. Godwin at St. Dunstan's-in-the-East, c. 1650 ; accompanied Henry Cromwell to Ireland, 1657 ; D.D. Cambridge ; founded dissenting church at Dublin ; published 'Topica Sacra : Spiritual Logick,' 1658 (second part added by John Hunter of Ayr. 1712). [xxv. 41]

HARRISON, THOMAS (1693-1745), divine and poet ; pastor of particular baptists in Little Wild Street, 1715-29 ; conformed and was vicar of Radcliffe-on-the-Wreke, 1729-45 ; published 'Poems on Divine Subjects,' 1719. [xxv. 44]

HARRISON, THOMAS (1744 - 1829), architect ; studied at Rome ; admitted to academy of St. Luke, and awarded medals by Clement XIV ; rebuilt Chester Castle, and (1829) erected the Grosvenor Bridge ; built Broomhall, Fifeshire, 1796 ; suggested to Lord Elgin collection of Greek works of art. [xxv. 45]

HARRISON, THOMAS ELLIOTT (1808 - 1888), civil engineer ; worked with Robert Stephenson, and succeeded as chief engineer of York, Newcastle, and Berwick line ; designed Jarrow (1858) and Hartlepool docks ; president of Institute of Civil Engineers, 1874. [xxv. 45]

HARRISON, WILLIAM (1534-1593), topographer and chronologist ; educated at St. Paul's School and Westminster, Cambridge, and Christ Church, Oxford ;

M.A., 1560 ; rector of Radwinter, 1559-93 ; canon of Windsor, 1586 ; his 'Description of England,' 1577, printed with Holinshed, as also his version of Bellenden's translation of Boece's ' Description of Scotland ' ; extracts from his 'Great Chronologie' (unprinted) in Furnivall's edition of 'Description of England ' (1877). [xxv. 46]

HARRISON, WILLIAM (1553-1621), last archpriest of England ; D.D. Douay ; professor of theology at Douay, 1597-1603 ; arch-priest of England, Scotland, and Ireland, 1615 ; obtained freedom of clergy from jesuit control and restoration of episcopal government. [xxv. 47]

HARRISON, WILLIAM (1685-1713), poet ; educated at Winchester and New College, Oxford ; fellow of New College, 1706 ; protégé of Addison and Swift ; secretary to Lord Raby at the Hague, 1711, afterwards to Utrecht embassy ; continued the 'Tatler' (January to May 1711), with assistance of Swift and St. John ; his 'Woodstock Park' in Dodsley's collection. [xxv. 47]

HARRISON, WILLIAM (1812-1860), commander of the Great Eastern steamship ; selected in 1856 to command the Great Leviathan, afterwards called the Great Eastern ; brought her into Portland after trial trip, 1859 ; capsized in ship's boat near Southampton dock. [xxv. 48]

HARRISON, WILLIAM (1813-1868), opera singer and manager ; appeared at Covent Garden, 1839 ; sang at Drury Lane in English operas ; accompanied Louisa Pyne to America, 1854 ; with her directed English opera at Lyceum, 1857, and Covent Garden, 1858-64 ; sole manager of Her Majesty's, 1864-5, when he played Charles Surface. [xxv. 49]

HARRISON, WILLIAM (1802-1884), antiquary ; established Manx Society, 1858 ; published ' Bibliotheca Monensis,' 1861, and other works. [xxv. 49]

HARRISON, WILLIAM FREDERICK (1815-1880), water-colour painter ; eldest son of Mary Harrison [q. v.] [xxv. 50]

HARRISON, WILLIAM GEORGE (1827-1883), lawyer ; B.A. St. John's College, Cambridge, 1850 ; barrister, Middle Temple, 1853 ; Q.C., 1877 ; part author of ' Joint-Stock Companies Act,' 1856. [xxv. 50]

HARROD, HENRY (1817-1871), professional antiquary ; secretary to Norfolk Archæological Society ; F.S.A., 1854 ; published 'Gleanings among Castles and Convents of Norfolk' (1857) ; arranged records of Norwich, Lynn, and other boroughs. [xxv. 50]

HARROD, WILLIAM (d. 1819), compiler of histories of Stamford, 1785, Mansfield (pt. i. 1786, pt. ii. 1801), and Market Harborough, 1808. [xxv. 50]

HARROWBY, EARLS OF. [See RYDER, DUDLEY, first EARL, 1762-1847 ; RYDER, DUDLEY, second EARL, 1798-1874 ; RYDER, DUDLEY FRANCIS STUART, 1831-1900.]

HARRY, BLIND (fl. 1470-1492). [See HENRY THE MINSTREL.]

HARRY, GEORGE OWEN (fl. 1604), Welsh antiquary ; rector of Whitchurch, Pembrokeshire ; assisted Camden in his 'Britannia' and published a genealogy of King James (1604) and ' The Well-sprynge of True Nobility.' [xxv. 51]

HARRY, NUN MORGAN (1800 - 1842), congregational minister at Banbury, and (1832-42) New Broad Street ; hon. secretary of Peace Society, 1837 ; editor of 'Herald of Peace.' [xxv. 51]

HARSNETT, ADAM (d. 1639), divine ; B.A. Pembroke Hall, Cambridge, 1601 ; M.A. St. John's College, 1604 ; B.D., 1612 ; vicar of Hutton, 1609-39 ; rector of Cranham, 1612-39 ; published religious works. [xxv. 51]

HARSNETT, SAMUEL (1561-1631), archbishop of York ; scholar and fellow (1583) of Pembroke Hall, Cambridge ; M.A., 1584 ; D.D., 1606 ; master of Pembroke Hall, 1605-16 ; censured by Whitgift for sermon against predestination, 1584 ; vicar of Chigwell, 1597-1605 ; chaplain to Bancroft when bishop of London ; archdeacon of Essex, 1603-9 ; rector of Stisted, 1609-19 ; vice-chancellor of Cambridge, 1606 and 1614 ; bishop of Chichester, 1609-19, of Norwich, 1619-28 ; archbishop of York, 1629-31 ; unpopular with puritans ; published an exposure (1599) of the exorcist, John Darrel, and 'A Declaration of egregious

Popish impostures,' 1603, from which Shakespeare took the names of the spirits in 'Lear'; his 'Considerations for the better settling of Church government' ordered by Charles I to be circulated among bishops, 1629; founded schools at Chigwell; bequeathed his library to corporation of Colchester. [xxv. 52]

HART, AARON (1670–1756), chief rabbi; rabbi of first synagogue of German and Polish Jews, Mitre Square, 1692, at Duke's Place, Aldgate, 1721–56; published 'Urim ve-Thumim,' the first Hebrew book printed in London, 1707. [xxv. 55]

HART, AARON (1722–1800), first British merchant in Lower Canada. [xxv. 56]

HART, ADOLPHUS M. (1813–1879), Canadian writer ('Hampden'); son of Ezekiel Hart [q. v.]; published 'History of Discovery of Valley of the Mississippi,' 1852. [xxv. 56]

HART, ANDREW or ANDRO (d. 1621), Edinburgh printer and publisher; issued works of Sir William Alexander and Drummond of Hawthornden; published editions of the Bible (1610) and Barbour's 'Bruce'; imported many works; imprisoned as a leader of tumult of 17 Dec. 1596. [xxv. 56]

HART, Sir ANDREW SEARLE (1811–1890), vice-provost of Trinity College, Dublin; fellow of Trinity College, Dublin, 1835; M.A., 1839; LL.D., 1840; senior fellow, 1858; vice-provost, 1876–90; knighted, 1886; contributed to mathematical journals, and published elementary treatises on mechanics (1844), hydrostatics, and hydrodynamics (1846). [xxv. 56]

HART, Sir ANTHONY (1754?–1831), lord chancellor of Ireland; barrister, Middle Temple, 1781; K.C., 1807; solicitor-general to Queen Charlotte, 1816; vice-chancellor of England, 1827; privy councillor and knighted, 1827; lord chancellor of Ireland, 1827–30. [xxv. 57]

HART, CHARLES (d. 1683), actor; grand-nephew of Shakespeare: played the Duchess in Shirley's 'Cardinal,' 1641; lieutenant in Prince Rupert's regiment during rebellion; arrested while playing Beaumont and Fletcher's 'Bloody Brother,' 1646; after Restoration played at Vere Street house, and with Killigrew at Theatre Royal; his best tragic parts, Arbaces ('King and No King'), Amintor ('Maid's Tragedy'), Alexander, Othello, and Brutus; his best comic parts, Mosca ('Volpone'), Don John ('The Chances'), Wildblood ('Mock Astrologer'); said to have introduced Nell Gwyn to the stage. [xxv. 57]

HART, CHARLES (1797–1859), organist and composer; gained Gresham prize with 'Te Deum,' 1831; published hymns, anthems, an oratorio, and other musical compositions. [xxv. 58]

HART, ERNEST ABRAHAM (1835–1898), medical journalist and reformer; educated at City of London School; Lambert Jones scholar, 1848; studied medicine at St. George's Hospital, and was surgical registrar and demonstrator of anatomy; M.R.C.S., 1856; surgeon, West London Hospital, 1860–3; ophthalmic surgeon at St. Mary's Hospital, 1863–8; dean of medical school, 1863–8; edited 'British Medical Journal,' 1886–98; adviser on medical publications to George Smith [q. v.], head of firm of Smith, Elder & Co., to whom he suggested possibilities of developing the Apollinaris spring; president of Harveian Society, 1868; honorary D.C.L. Durham, 1893; organised numerous medical and sanitary reforms; published addresses, pamphlets, and other works. [Suppl. ii. 396]

HART, EZEKIEL (1770–1843), Canadian Jew; son of Aaron Hart (1722–1800) [q. v.]; established political rights of Jews in Lower Canada, 1831. [xxv. 56]

HART, GEORGE VAUGHAN (1752–1832), general; served with the 46th in American war; present at Long Island, Brandywine, 1777, and Monmouth; afterwards served in India (Bangalore, Seringapatam, Mullavelly); lieutenant-general, 1811; M.P., co. Donegal, 1812–31. [xxv. 59]

HART, HENRY (fl. 1549), author of devotional treatises. [xxv. 59]

HART, HENRY GEORGE (1808–1878), lieutenant-general; editor and proprietor of 'Hart's Army List'; of the 49th foot; colonel, 1860; lieutenant-general, 1877;

published first quarterly army list, 1839, first annual, 1840. [xxv. 59]

HART, JAMES (fl. 1633), physician; studied at Paris and in Germany; graduated abroad; practised at Northampton; published 'Anatomie of Urines,' 1625, and 'Κλινική, or Diet of the Diseased,' 1633. [xxv. 60]

HART, JAMES (1663–1729), minister of Greyfriars, Edinburgh; M.A. Edinburgh, 1687; minister of Ratho, 1692–1702, of Greyfriars, Edinburgh, 1702–29; opposed the union; called by Steele 'the hangman of the Gospel'; his 'Journal in 1714' edited, 1832. [xxv. 61]

HART, JOHN (d. 1574), orthographer; Chester herald, 1566; his 'Orthographie' (on the phonetic system), 1569, reprinted by Pitman, 1850. [xxv. 61]

HART, JOHN (d. 1586), jesuit; B.D. Douay, 1577; priest, 1578; condemned to death as a priest; recanted on the hurdle; withdrew recantation and disputed with John Rainoldes [q. v.] at Oxford; sent back to the Tower, where (1582) he became a jesuit; banished, 1585; landed in Normandy, 1585; died in Poland. [xxv. 61]

HART, JOHN (1809–1873), pioneer colonist and premier of South Australia; engaged in mercantile service to Tasmania; director of Adelaide Auction Company, 1840; member for Victoria district in old legislative council, 1851; member for Port Adelaide in first House of Assembly, 1857; treasurer, 1857; colonial secretary, 1863 and 1864–5; premier, 1865–6, 1868, and 1870–1; C.M.G., 1870. [Suppl. ii. 397]

HART, JOSEPH (1712?–1768), independent preacher at Jewin Street Chapel, London, 1760–8; author of hymns, 1759. [xxv. 62]

HART, JOSEPH BINNS (1794–1844), organist and composer; wrote songs when chorus-master and pianist at the English opera, 1818–21; composed dance music. [xxv. 62]

HART, MOSES (1676?–1756), builder of the great synagogue, Aldgate, 1721; brother of Aaron Hart (1670–1756) [q. v.] [xxv. 55]

HART, PHILIP (d. 1749), organist and composer; played at Britton's with Handel and Pepusch; set Hughes's 'Ode in Praise of Music,' 1703, and Milton's 'Morning Hymn,' 1729; composed fugues, songs, and anthems. [xxv. 63]

HART, SOLOMON ALEXANDER (1806–1881), painter; exhibited in Suffolk Street his 'Elevation of the Law,' 1830; R.A., 1840; professor of painting, Royal Academy, 1854–63; librarian from 1865; exhibited, 1826–1880; his 'Reminiscences' edited, 1882. [xxv. 63]

HARTCLIFFE, JOHN (1651–1712), schoolmaster; of Eton, Edmund Hall, Oxford, and King's College, Cambridge; M.A. King's College, Cambridge, 1676; fellow; D.D., 1689; head-master of Merchant Taylors' School, 1681–6; canon of Windsor, 1691–1712; chief work, 'Treatise of Moral and Intellectual Virtues,' 1691. [xxv. 64]

HARTE, HENRY HICKMAN (1790–1848), mathematician; fellow of Trinity College, Dublin, 1819; incumbent of Cappagh, 1831–48; translated and added to La Place's 'Système du Monde' and Poisson's 'Mécanique Céleste.' [xxv. 65]

HARTE, WALTER (1709–1774), author; M.A. St. Mary Hall, Oxford, 1731; friend of Pope and Arthur Young; travelling tutor to Chesterfield's natural son; vice-principal of St. Mary Hall, Oxford, 1740; canon of Windsor, 1750; published 'History of the Life of Gustavus Adolphus,' 1759, 'Essays on Husbandry,' 1764, and religious poems. [xxv. 65]

HARTGILL or HARTGYLL, GEORGE (fl. 1594), author of 'Generall Calenders, or Most Easie Astronomicall Tables,' 1594. [xxv. 66]

HARTLEY, DAVID, the elder (1705–1757), philosopher; educated at Bradford grammar school and Jesus College, Cambridge; fellow, 1727–30; M.A., 1729; physician in Newark, Bury St. Edmunds, and London; supporter of Byrom's shorthand and Mrs. Stephens's medicine for the stone; friend of Bishops Butler and Warburton; F.R.S.; acquaintance of Hales. His 'Observations on Man,' 1749 (abridged by Priestley, 1775), containing the doctrine of association, influenced Coleridge. [xxv. 66]

HARTLEY, DAVID, the younger (1732–1813), statesman and inventor; son of David Hartley the elder [q. v.]; B.A. Corpus Christi College, Oxford, 1750; fellow of Merton College, Oxford; M.P., Hull, 1774–80 and 1782–4; opposed American war and slave trade; with Franklin drew up and signed treaty between Great Britain and the United States, 1783; published 'Letters on the American War,' 1778–9, editions of his father's 'Observations on Man,' 1791, 1801, and 'Account of a Method of Securing Buildings and Ships against Fire,' 1785.   [xxv. 68]

HARTLEY, MRS. ELIZABETH (1751–1824), actress; *née* White; appeared at Haymarket in 'Oroonoko,' 1769; played at Covent Garden, 1772–80, in Mason's 'Elfrida' and 'Caractacus'; played Lady Frances Touchwood ('Belle's Stratagem'), Cleopatra ('All for Love'), and Shakespearean parts; painted by Reynolds as Jane Shore, Calista, and a Bacchante.   [xxv. 69]

HARTLEY, JAMES (1745–1799), Indian officer; aide-de-camp to governor of Bombay, 1770; saved expeditionary force against the Konkan, 1779; repulsed Mahrattas at Doogaur, 1780; his promotion overruled by directors; appointed lieutenant-colonel, 75th regiment; quartermaster-general of Bombay army, 1788; defeated Hussein Ali at Calicut, 1790; captured French settlement of Mahé, 1793; major-general, 1796; supervisor and magistrate for province of Malabar; second in command of Bombay army against Tippoo Sahib, 1799; died at Cannanore.   [xxv. 70]

HARTLEY, JESSE (1780–1860), engineer for Bolton and Manchester railway and canal.   [xxv. 71]

HARTLEY, THOMAS (1709?–1784), translator of Swedenborg; M.A. St. John's College, Cambridge, 1745; rector of Winwick, 1744–70; paid frequent visits to Swedenborg; translated Swedenborg's 'De Commercio Animæ et Corporis,' 1769; author of 'Nine Queries' concerning Swedenborg's doctrine of the Trinity (published 1785), and 'Paradise Restored,' against Warburton, 1764.   [xxv. 71]

HARTLIB, SAMUEL (*d.* 1670?), friend of Milton; came to England from Poland, *c.* 1628; introduced writings of Comenius; praised by Milton in treatise on education, 1644; received pension from parliament for works on husbandry, 1646; published pamphlets on education and husbandry, including 'Description of the famous Kingdom of Macaria,' 1641, and 'Discours of Husbandrie used in Brabant and Flanders,' 1652.   [xxv. 72]

HARTOG, NUMA EDWARD (1846–1871), senior wrangler and second Smith's prizeman, 1869; B.A. and B.Sc. London, 1864; scholar of Trinity College, Cambridge, 1866; admitted B.A. by special grace as a Jew, 1869; gave evidence before select committee of House of Lords on university tests, 1871.   [xxv. 73]

HARTOPP, SIR JOHN, third baronet (1637?–1722), nonconformist; succeeded to baronetcy, 1658; M.P., Leicestershire, 1678–81; heavily fined for nonconformity, 1682; alderman of London; member of Dr. John Owen's congregation and friend of Isaac Watts; left endowment for education of dissenting ministers.   [xxv. 74]

HARTRY, MALACHY, *alias* JOHN (*fl.* 1640), compiler of Latin works on Irish Cistercian houses (unpublished); died in Flanders.   [xxv. 74]

HARTSHORNE, CHARLES HENRY (1802–1865), antiquary; M.A. St. John's College, Cambridge, 1828; incumbent of Cogenhoe, 1838–50; rector of Holdenby, 1850–1865; published 'Book Rarities of the University of Cambridge,' 1829, 'Ancient Metrical Tales,' 1829, and archæological works.   [xxv. 75]

HARTSTONGE, JOHN (1654–1717), bishop of Derry; M.A. Trinity College, Dublin, 1680; fellow of Caius College, Cambridge, 1681; chaplain to first and second dukes of Ormonde; bishop of Ossory, 1693; D.D. Oxford, 1693; bishop of Derry, 1714.   [xxv. 75]

HARTWELL, ABRAHAM, the elder (*fl.* 1565), Latin poet; educated at Eton and King's College, Cambridge; fellow, 1562–7; M.A., 1567.   [xxv. 75]

HARTWELL, ABRAHAM, the younger (*fl.* 1600), translator and antiquary; M.A. Trinity College, Cambridge, 1575; incorporated at Oxford, 1588; secretary to Archbishop Whitgift; rector of Toddington; member of old Society of Antiquaries; published translations of Italian works by Minadoi and Pigafetta, and the 'Ottoman of Lazaro Soranzo,' 1603.   [xxv. 76]

HARTY, WILLIAM (1781–1854), physician; M.A. Trinity College, Dublin, 1804; M.D., 1830; F.R.C.P., 1824–7; physician to Dublin prisons; published 'Dysentery and its Combinations,' 1805, and 'Historic Sketch of Contagious Fever Epidemic in Ireland in 1817–19.'   [xxv. 77]

HARVARD, JOHN (1607–1638), principal founder of Harvard College, Massachusetts; of humble origin; M.A. Emmanuel College, Cambridge, 1635; settled in Charlestown, Massachusetts, 1637; bequeathed half his estate and library for new college at Cambridge, Massachusetts.   [xxv. 77]

HARVEY, BEAUCHAMP BAGENAL (1762–1798), politician; of Trinity College, Dublin; Irish barrister, 1782; presided at meetings of United Irishmen, 1793; appointed to command Wexford rebels, May 1798; deposed after repulse at Ross; arrested on island near Wexford; court-martialled and hanged.   [xxv. 78]

HARVEY, CHRISTOPHER (1597–1663), poet and friend of Isaak Walton; M.A. Brasenose College, Oxford, 1620; rector of Whitney, 1630; vicar of Clifton, Warwickshire, 1639–63; chief work 'The Synagogue' (devotional poems appended anonymously to 1640 edition of George Herbert's 'Temple').   [xxv. 78]

HARVEY, DANIEL WHITTLE (1786–1863), radical politician; fellow of the Inner Temple, 1818; attorney at Colchester; twice refused admission to bar; M.P., Colchester, 1818–20, and 1826–34, Southwark, 1835–40; founded 'Sunday Times,' 1822; commissioner of London police, 1840–63.   [xxv. 79]

HARVEY, EDMOND (*fl.* 1661), regicide; colonel of horse under Essex, 1642; commissioner for trial of Charles I; refused to sign warrant, 1649; imprisoned for fraud as first commissioner of customs, 1655; sentenced to death, 1660; imprisoned in Pendennis Castle, 1661.   [xxv. 80]

HARVEY, EDMUND GEORGE (1828–1884), musical composer and author; son of William Woodis Harvey [q. v.]; B.A. Queens' College, Cambridge, 1850; rector of St. Mary's, Truro, 1860; vicar of Mullyon, 1865; composed Gregorian chants, hymn-tunes, and waltzes; edited 'The Truro Use,' 1877; published 'History of Mullyon,' 1875.   [xxv. 81]

HARVEY, SIR EDWARD (1783–1865), admiral; third son of Captain John Harvey (1740–1794) [q. v.], with whom he served in action of 1 June 1794; present at Camperdown, 1797, and bombardment of Acre, 1840; rear-admiral, 1847; commander at the Nore, 1857–60; admiral, 1860; G.C.B., 1865.   [xxv. 81]

HARVEY, SIR ELIAB (1758–1830), admiral; M.P., Maldon, 1780, Essex, 1803–12; and 1820–6; a reckless gambler; commanded the Téméraire at blockade of Brest and at Trafalgar, after which he was promoted rear-admiral, 1805; with Gambier in Basque Roads, 1809; dismissed for abuse of Lord Cochrane, 1809; reinstated, 1810; K.C.B., 1815; admiral, 1819.   [xxv. 82]

HARVEY, GABRIEL (1545?–1630), poet; B.A. Christ's College, Cambridge, 1570; M.A., 1573; as fellow of Pembroke Hall became acquainted with Spenser; the Hobbinol of 'The Shepheards Calender'; claimed to be father of English hexameter; lectured on rhetoric; fellow of Trinity Hall, 1578; junior proctor, 1583; D.C.L. Oxford, 1585; published satirical verses which gave offence at court, 1579; attacked Robert Greene in 'Foure Letters,' 1592; wrote 'Pierce's Supererogation,' 1593, and 'Trimming of Thomas Nashe,' 1597, against Nashe, both Nashe and Harvey being silenced by authority, 1599; published Latin works on rhetoric, 1577; English works, including correspondence with Spenser (1579–80), edited by Dr. Grosart.   [xxv. 83]

HARVEY, SIR GEORGE (1806–1876), painter; an original associate, Royal Scottish Academy, and contributor (1827) to first exhibition; full member, 1829; president, 1864–76; knighted, 1864; became known by figure-pictures; excelled later as landscape-painter; published 'Notes on Early History of the Royal Scottish Academy,' 1870.   [xxv. 85]

HARVEY, GIDEON, the elder (1640 ?–1700 ?), physician ; studied at Oxford, Leyden and Paris ; F.C.P., Hague ; M.D. ; doctor-general to king's army in Flanders after the Restoration ; physician to Charles II, *c.* 1675 ; attacked College of Physicians in his ' Conclave of Physicians,' 1683 ; physician to the Tower, 1689 ; his ' Art of Curing Disease by Expectation,' 1689, translated into Latin by George Ernest Stahl, 1730 ; published also ' Discourse of the Plague,' 1665, and ' Vanities of Philosophy and Physick,' 1699. [xxv. 86]

HARVEY, GIDEON, the younger (1669 ?–1754), physician ; son of Gideon Harvey the elder [q. v.] ; M.D. Leyden, 1690, Cambridge, 1698 ; F.R.C.P., 1703 ; king's physician to the Tower, *c.* 1702. [xxv. 87]

HARVEY or **HERVEY**, HENRY (*d.* 1585), master of Trinity Hall, Cambridge ; LL.D. Trinity Hall, Cambridge, 1542 ; vicar-general of London and Canterbury ; commissioner for detection of heretical books at Cambridge, 1556 ; prebendary of Southwell, 1558, Salisbury, 1558 ; master of Trinity Hall on Elizabeth's accession ; vicechancellor, 1560 ; canon of Ely, 1567 ; master in chancery, 1568 ; founded scholarships at Trinity Hall. [xxv. 87]

HARVEY, SIR HENRY (1737–1810), admiral ; wrecked off Cape François in the Hussar, 1762 ; in Martin sloop at relief of Quebec ; commanded the Convert at Dominica, 1782 ; in the Ramillies under Howe at action of 1 June, 1794 ; rear-admiral, 1794 ; took part in action off Lorient, 1795 ; captured Trinidad, 1796 ; K.B., 1800 ; admiral, 1804. [xxv. 88]

HARVEY, JOHN (1563 ?–1592), astrologer ; brother of Gabriel Harvey [q. v.] ; M.A. Queens' College, Cambridge, 1584 ; M.D. ; physician at King's Lynn ; published astrological works. [xxv. 89]

HARVEY, JOHN (1740–1794), captain in the navy ; brother of Sir Henry Harvey [q. v.] ; took part in defence of Gibraltar, 1779–82 ; mortally wounded as captain of the Brunswick in Howe's victory, 1 June, 1794 ; his monument in Westminster Abbey. [xxv. 90]

HARVEY, SIR JOHN (1772–1837), admiral ; second son of John Harvey (1740–1794) [q. v.] ; flag-captain to his uncle, Sir Henry, at Lorient, 1795 ; commanded the Agamemnon under Calder at Finisterre ; rear-admiral, 1813 ; commander in West Indies, 1816–19 ; K.C.B., 1833 ; admiral, 1837. [xxv. 90]

HARVEY, MARGARET (1768–1858), poet ; published ' Lay of the Minstrel's Daughter,' 1814, and ' Raymond de Percy,' 1822. [xxv. 91]

HARVEY, RICHARD (*d.* 1623 ?), astrologer ; brother of Gabriel Harvey [q. v.] ; fellow of Pembroke Hall, Cambridge ; M.A., 1581 ; incurred much ridicule for his predictions, 1583 ; with his ' Plaine Percevall, the Peacemaker of England ' (*c.* 1590) (in Martin Marprelate controversy), provoked Greene's ' Quippe for an Upstart Courtier,' 1592 ; his ' Astrological Discourse ' (1583) parodied (1592) by Nashe, who also ridiculed his ' Theologicall Discovrse of the Lamb of God and his Enemies,' 1590. [xxv. 91]

HARVEY, SIR THOMAS (1775–1841), vice-admiral ; fourth son of Sir Henry Harvey [q. v.], under whom he served, 1794–5 ; captain, 1797 ; took part in destruction of Turkish squadron in Dardanelles, 1807 ; K.C.B., 1833 ; vice-admiral, 1837 ; died at Bermuda as commanderin-chief in West Indies. [xxv. 92]

HARVEY, THOMAS (1812–1884), quaker ; accompanied Joseph Sturge [q. v.] to West Indies to inquire into condition of negroes, 1836 ; to Finland, 1856 ; visited Jamaica, 1866, and relieved sufferers from ' Gordon ' riots ; removed Mennonites from South Russia to Canada ; published theological works. [xxv. 92]

HARVEY or **HERVEY**, WILLIAM (*d.* 1567), Clarenceux king-of-arms, 1557 ; as Norroy paid seven official visits to Germany and declared war on France, 1557 ; many of his visitations of English counties printed. [xxv. 93]

HARVEY, WILLIAM (1578–1657), discoverer of circulation of the blood ; educated at King's School, Canterbury, and Caius College, Cambridge ; B.A., 1597 ; M.D. Padua and Cambridge, 1602 (Oxford, 1642) ; F.R.C.P., 1607 ; physician to St. Bartholomew's Hospital, 1609 ;

Lumleian lecturer from 1616, when he first publicly stated his theory of circulation ; named physician extraordinary to James I, 1618 ; published at Frankfort ' Exercitatio Anatomica de Motu Cordis et Sanguinis in Animalibus,' 1628, describing his great discovery ; with Charles I in Scotland, 1633 ; superintended physical examination of women accused of witchcraft, 1634 ; attended Lord Arundel in Germany and Italy, 1636 ; with Charles I at Edgehill, 1642, and at Oxford, where he was made warden of Merton College, 1645 ; published at Cambridge ' Exercitatio Anatomica de Circulatione Sanguinis,' 1649 (English version, 1653), in reply to Riolanus ; his last work, ' Exercitationes de Generatione Animalium,' 1651 ; his statue erected at Royal College of Physicians in London, 1652, for whom he built a library ; his collected works (Latin) edited by Dr. Lawrence, 1766 ; English edition (Sydenham Society), 1847. [xxv. 94]

HARVEY, WILLIAM (1796–1866), wood-engraver and designer ; pupil of Bewick and Haydon ; designed for Charles Knight ; illustrations to ' Northcote's Fables ' (1828–33) and Lane's ' Thousand and One Nights ' (1838–1840) his masterpieces. [xxv. 99]

HARVEY, WILLIAM HENRY (1811–1866), botanist ; discovered *Hookeria læte virens* at Killarney, 1831 ; colonial treasurer at Cape Town, 1836–42 ; hon. M.D. Dublin, 1844, and professor of botany, 1856 ; lectured in America, 1849 ; visited India, Australia, and the South Seas, 1853–6 ; published ' Genera of S. African Plants,' 1838, and works on British and Australasian *algæ*. [xxv. 100]

HARVEY, WILLIAM WIGAN (1810–1883), divine ; of Eton and King's College, Cambridge ; fellow of King's, 1831 ; M.A., 1836 ; B.D., 1855 ; the equity of his appointment by Mr. Gladstone to rectory of Ewelme shortly after incorporation as M.A. at Oxford (1871) warmly discussed in parliament, 1872 ; published an edition of Irenæus, 1857, and theological works. [xxv. 100]

HARVEY, WILLIAM WOODIS (1798–1864), author ; M.A. Queens' College, Cambridge, 1835 ; vicar of Truro, 1839–60 ; edited Wesley's minor works, and published ' Sketches of Hayti,' 1827, with other writings.
[xxv. 81]

HARWARD, SIMON (*fl.* 1572–1614), divine and author ; M.A. Christ's College, Cambridge, 1578 ; rector of Warrington, 1579–81 ; vicar of Banstead, 1604 ; published miscellaneous works. [xxv. 101]

HARWOOD, SIR BUSICK (1745 ?–1814), professor of anatomy at Cambridge ; after having practised as a surgeon in India graduated at Christ's College, Cambridge ; M.B., 1785 ; M.D., 1790 ; F.S.A., 1783 ; F.R.S., 1784 ; knighted, 1806 ; professor of anatomy (1785) and Downing professor of medicine (1800) at Cambridge ; celebrated for his experiments on transfusion of blood. [xxv. 101]

HARWOOD, SIR EDWARD (1586 ?–1632), colonel ; killed at Maestricht ; ' Advice of Sir Edward Harwood ' issued with life by Hugh Peters, 1642. [xxv. 102]

HARWOOD, EDWARD (1729–1794), scholar and biblical critic ; educated at Blackburn grammar school ; presbyterian minister at Bristol, 1765 ; D.D. Edinburgh, 1768, for ' Introduction to New Testament Studies.' His works include ' Liberal Translation of New Testament, with select Notes,' 1768, a reconstructed text of the Greek Testament, 1776, editions of Tibullus, Propertius, and Catullus, 1774, ' Biographia Classica ' (2nd ed., 1778), and theological and devotional writings. [xxv. 102]

HARWOOD, EDWARD (*d.* 1814), numismatist ; son of Edward Harwood (1729–1794) [q. v.] ; published ' Populorum et Urbium selecta numismata Græca ex aere descripta,' 1812. [xxv. 104]

HARWOOD, ISABELLA (1840 ?–1888), novelist and dramatist ; daughter of Philip Harwood [q. v.] ; published successful novels, 1864–70, and, as ' Ross Neil,' dramas, including ' Inez ' (1871) and ' Pandora ' (1883).
[xxv. 104]

HARWOOD, PHILIP (1809–1887), journalist ; in early life an unitarian minister ; when assistant to William Johnson Fox [q. v.] introduced to John Forster ; subeditor successively of the ' Examiner,' ' Spectator,' ' Morning Chronicle,' 1849–54, and ' Saturday Review,' 1855–68 ; editor of ' Saturday Review,' 1868–83 ; published ' Materialism in Religion,' 1840, ' German Anti-Supernaturalism,' 1841, and other works. [xxv. 104]

HARWOOD, THOMAS (1767–1842), author ; educated at Eton, University College, Oxford, and Emmanuel College, Cambridge ; D.D. Cambridge, 1822 ; head-master of Lichfield grammar school, 1791–1813 ; incumbent of Hammerwich and Burntwood ; F.S.A. ; published ' Alumni Etonenses,' 1797, ' History of Lichfield,' 1806, and other works. [xxv. 105]

HASELDEN, THOMAS (d. 1740), mathematician ; published ' Description and Use of . . . Mercator's Chart,' 1722. [xxv. 106]

HASELEY, WILLIAM DE (fl. 1266), sub-prior of Westminster ; compiler of ' Consuetudinarium Monachorum Westmonasteriensium' (Cotton. MSS. Otho C. xi.) [xxv. 106]

HASELL, ELIZABETH JULIA (1830–1887), author ; published books on Calderon and Tasso, 1877, and devotional works. [xxv. 106]

HASELRIG, SIR ARTHUR (d. 1661). [See HESILRIGE.]

HASELWOOD, THOMAS (fl. 1380), author of ' Chronicon Compendiarium Cantuariense' ; canon regular of Leeds, Kent. [xxv. 106]

HASLAM, JOHN (1764–1844), medical writer ; apothecary to Bethlehem Hospital ; hon. M.D. Aberdeen, 1816 ; L.R.C.P., 1824 ; published ' Observations on Insanity,' 1798, and similar works. [xxv. 107]

HASLEM, JOHN (1808–1884), china and enamel painter ; exhibited at the Academy, 1836–65 ; published ' The Old Derby China Factory,' 1876. [xxv. 107]

HASLETON, RICHARD (fl. 1595), traveller ; published ' Strange and Wonderful Things ' (narrative of travel), 1595. [xxv. 108]

HASLEWOOD, JOSEPH (1769–1833), antiquary ; a founder of the Roxburghe Club, of which he left a manuscript account ; F.S.A. ; edited ' Tusser's Five Hundred Points,' 1810, the ' Mirror for Magistrates,' 1815, and other works ; published ' Green-Room Gossip,' 1809, and an account of Joseph Ritson, 1824. [xxv. 108]

HASSALL or **HALSALL**, EDWARD (fl. 1663), royalist ; supposed author of diary of defence of Lathom House, 1644 (Draper's ' House of Stanley ') ; one of the assassins of Antony Ascham [q. v.] at Madrid, 1650 ; engaged in plot against Cromwell, 1655 ; equerry to Charles II's queen, 1663. [xxv. 108]

HASSALL, JAMES (fl. 1667), royalist ; brother of Edward Hassall or Halsall [q. v.] ; imprisoned in Tower for plot to murder Cromwell, 1655–60 ; corresponded with Aphra Behn [q. v.] ; captain of foot at Portsmouth, 1667. [xxv. 109]

HASSÉ, CHRISTIAN FREDERICK (1771–1831), musical composer ; native of Russia ; organist at Fulneck (Moravian settlement near Leeds) ; arranged music for ' Polyhymnia ' (words by James Montgomery), 1822 ; compiled ' Sacred Music.' [xxv. 109]

HASSELL, EDWARD (d. 1852), water-colour painter ; son of John Hassell [q. v.] ; secretary to Society of British Artists ; exhibited at Royal Academy and British Institution. [xxv. 110]

HASSELL, JOHN (d. 1825), water-colour painter and engraver ; friend and biographer of George Morland [q. v.] ; published ' Speculum, or Art of Drawing in Water-colours,' 1809, ' Art of multiplying Drawings,' 1811, treatise on etching (posthumous ,1836), and other works. [xxv. 109]

HASSELLS, WARNER (fl. 1680–1710), portrait-painter of the school of Kneller. [xxv. 110]

HASTED, EDWARD (1732–1812), historian of Kent ; of Eton and Lincoln's Inn ; F.R.S., 1766 ; F.S.A. ; occupied for forty years in compilation of ' History and Topographical Survey of Kent' (4 vols. 1778–99 ; 2nd ed. 12 vols. 1797–1801) ; published also genealogical tables, 1797 ; died master of Corsham Hospital. [xxv. 110]

HASTIE, JAMES (1786–1826), civil agent of Great Britain in Madagascar ; served in the ranks during Mahratta war ; as civil agent (1817–26) negotiated treaty with Radama I of Madagascar, whom he helped to conquer the eastern, northern, and western tribes. [xxv. 111]

HASTINGS, SIR CHARLES (1794–1866), founder of British Medical Association ; M.D. Edinburgh, 1818 ; physician to Worcester Infirmary ; formed ' Provincial Medical and Surgical Association,' 1832 (styled British Medical Association from 1856), and established its ' Journal,' 1840 ; knighted, 1850 ; Hastings medal and prize in his memory awarded annually by British Medical Association ; published ' Illustrations of Natural History of Worcestershire,' 1834. [xxv. 111]

HASTINGS, EDMUND, BARON HASTINGS OF INCHMAHOME (d. 1314 ?) ; younger son of Henry Hastings, first baron Hastings [q. v.] ; served in Scotland, 1298–1300 ; summoned to parliament, 1299 ; signed ' letter of remonstrance ' to the pope, 1301 ; warden between Forth and Orkney, 1308, of Berwick, 1312 ; last summoned, 1313. [xxv. 126]

HASTINGS, SIR EDWARD (1381–1437), claimant of the Hastings barony ; descendant of John Hastings, second baron Hastings [q. v.], through his second wife. The right to bear the family arms was contested by Reginald Grey, third baron Grey of Ruthin [q. v.], and decided in favour of Grey, 1410. The barony was in abeyance till 1841. [xxv. 112]

HASTINGS, SIR EDWARD, first BARON HASTINGS OF LOUGHBOROUGH (d. 1573), third son of George Hastings, first earl of Huntingdon [q. v.] ; knighted, 1546 ; M.P., Leicestershire, 1547 and 1552 ; a strong Romanist ; created privy councillor and master of the horse by Queen Mary ; opposed Mary's marriage with Philip of Spain ; M.P., Middlesex, 1554 and 1555 ; K.G., 1555 ; accompanied Clinton against French, and became lord chamberlain, 1557 ; created a peer, 1558 ; imprisoned for hearing mass, 1561, but released on taking oath of supremacy. [xxv. 113]

HASTINGS, LADY ELIZABETH (1682–1739), philanthropist and beauty ; eulogised as Aspasia in the ' Tatler ' by Steele and Congreve ; friend of William Law [q. v.] and Bishop Thomas Wilson ; founded scholarships at Queen's College, Oxford, and endowed charities at Ledsham and in Isle of Man. [xxv. 114]

HASTINGS, LADY FLORA ELIZABETH (1806–1839), lady of the bedchamber to Duchess of Kent ; daughter of Francis Rawdon Hastings, first marquis of Hastings [q. v.] ; subject of a court scandal, 1839 ; her poems published, 1841. [xxv. 114]

HASTINGS, FRANCIS, second EARL OF HUNTINGDON (1514 ?–1561), eldest son of George Hastings, first earl of Huntingdon [q. v.] ; summoned to parliament as Baron Hastings, 1529 ; succeeded as earl, 1545 ; adherent of Dudley ; K.G., 1549 ; chief captain of army and fleet abroad, 1549 ; privy councillor, 1550 ; attempted to save Boulogne, 1550 ; granted Leicestershire estates of John Beaumont (fl. 1550) [q. v.], 1552 ; captured with Northumberland at Cambridge, 1553, but released ; as lord-lieutenant of Leicestershire arrested Henry Grey, duke of Suffolk [q. v.], 1554. [xxv. 115]

HASTINGS, SIR FRANCIS (d. 1610), puritan politician ; fifth son of Francis Hastings, second earl of Huntingdon [q. v.] ; sheriff of Leicestershire, 1572 and 1581 ; M.P., Leicestershire, 1571, 1585, 1597, Somerset, 1592, 1604 ; knighted, c. 1589 ; cited before privy council for promoting petition in favour of nonconformists, 1605 ; issued anti-catholic pamphlets. [xxv. 116]

HASTINGS, FRANCIS RAWDON-, first MARQUIS OF HASTINGS and second EARL OF MOIRA (1754–1826), soldier and statesman ; educated at Harrow and University College, Oxford ; distinguished himself at Bunker's Hill, 1775 ; fought in battles of Brooklyn and White Plains, 1776 ; adjutant-general to forces in America, 1778 ; commanded left wing at Camden, 1780 ; defeated Greene at Hobkirk's Hill, 1781 ; captured by French on voyage home ; created Baron Rawdon, 1783 ; joined the opposition, 1789 ; intimate with Prince of Wales ; championed his cause on regency question, 1789 ; assumed additional name of Hastings, 1790 ; succeeded as Irish Earl of Moira, 1793 ; commanded expedition to Brittany, 1793, and reinforcements for Duke of York in Flanders, 1794 ; spoke against Irish union, 1799 ; general, 1803 ; commander-in-chief in Scotland, 1803 ; master of the ordnance, 1806–7 ; active in support of Prince of Wales, 1810–11 ; attempted, with Wellesley, to form a ministry, 1812 ; governor-general of Bengal, 1813–22 ; carried on a successful war against Nepaul, 1814–16 ; created Marquis of Hastings

1817; extirpated Pindáris, and by defeating Mahrattas established British supremacy in Central India, 1817–18; secured cession of Singapore, 1819; opened relations with Siam, 1822; pursued liberal policy towards natives; granted 60,000*l.* by the East India Company, but resigned on account of the annulling by court of directors of his permission to banking house of Palmer to lend money to Hyderabad; named governor of Malta, 1824; died at sea in Baia Bay; published a summary of his Indian administration (1824); his statue, by Chantrey, is at Dalhousie Institute, Calcutta.   [xxv. 117]

HASTINGS, FRANK ABNEY (1794–1828), naval commander in Greek war of independence; fought at Trafalgar, 1805; dismissed British navy for sending a challenge; joined Greeks, 1822; raised fifty men and purchased the steamer Karteria; attacked Turkish camp near Athens, 1827; captured several ships, destroyed fleet in Bay of Salona (1827) and took Vasiladi, 1827; died of wounds after attack on Anatolikon.   [xxv. 122]

HASTINGS, GEORGE, first EARL OF HUNTINGDON and third BARON HASTINGS OF HASTINGS (1488?–1545), favourite of Henry VIII; grandson of William Hastings, baron Hastings [q. v.]; succeeded as Baron Hastings, 1508; joined Suffolk's expedition against France, 1523; created Earl of Huntingdon, 1529; leader against rebels in the Pilgrimage of Grace.   [xxv. 123]

HASTINGS, GEORGE FOWLER (1814–1876), vice-admiral; second son of HansFrancis Hastings, eleventh earl of Huntingdon [q. v.]; served in the Harlequin in Chinese war and against Sumatra pirates, 1841–5; captain of the Curaçoa during Crimean war; C.B., 1857; vice-admiral, 1869; commanded in Pacific, 1866–9, at the Nore, 1873–6.   [xxv. 124]

HASTINGS, HANS FRANCIS, eleventh EARL OF HUNTINGDON (1779–1828), sailor; wounded in Quiberon Bay expedition, 1795; first lieutenant of Thisbe in Egyptian expedition, 1800; tried for murder while superintending impressing of seamen in Weymouth Roads, 1803; right to peerage established, 1818; governor of Dominica, 1822–4; post-captain, 1824.   [xxv. 124]

HASTINGS, HENRY, first BARON HASTINGS by writ (d. 1268), baronial leader; supported Montfort in parliament of 1262; excommunicated as rebel, 1263; commanded Londoners at Lewes, 1264; summoned to parliament of 1265; captured at Evesham, 1265; joined Derby at Chesterfield and held Kenilworth against the king; leader of 'the disinherited' at Ely; submitted, 1267.   [xxv. 125]

HASTINGS, HENRY, third EARL OF HUNTINGDON (1535–1595), son of Francis Hastings, second earl of Huntingdon [q. v.]; married the Duke of Northumberland's daughter Catherine, 1553; summoned to parliament as Baron Hastings, 1559; succeeded to earldom, 1561; heir-presumptive to crown through mother; supporter of puritans; associated with Shrewsbury in custody of Mary Queen of Scots, 1569–70; lord-lieutenant of Leicester and Rutland, 1572; president of the north, 1572; assisted at trial of Norfolk, 1573; K.G., 1579; raised force in north, 1581; active against threatened Spanish invasion, 1588; benefactor of Emmanuel College, Cambridge; compiled family history.   [xxv. 126]

HASTINGS, HENRY (1551–1650), sportsman; nephew of Henry Hastings, third earl of Huntingdon [q. v.], of Woodlands, Dorset; account of him written by his neighbour, Sir Anthony Ashley Cooper, first earl of Shaftesbury [q. v.]   [xxv. 128]

HASTINGS, HENRY, first BARON LOUGHBOROUGH (d. 1667), royalist; second son of Henry Hastings, fifth earl of Huntingdon; raised and commanded troop of horse at Edgehill, 1642; held Ashby House against parliament till 1646; called 'Rob-carrier' for frequent interception of communications between London and the north; created Baron Loughborough, 1643; distinguished at relief of Newark, 1644; governor of Leicester, 1645; escaped to Holland, 1649; royalist conspirator; received pension and lieutenancy of Leicester, 1661.   [xxv. 128]

HASTINGS, SIR HUGH (1307?–1347), soldier; elder son of John Hastings, second baron Hastings [q. v.]; summoned to parliament, 1342; served in Flanders, 1343, and Gascony, 1345–6.   [xxv. 129]

HASTINGS, JOHN, second BARON HASTINGS (eighth by tenure) and BARON BERGAVENNY (1262–1313), claimant

to Scottish throne; married Isabella de Valence, niece of Henry III, 1275; served against Scots, 1285, and Welsh, 1288; claimed (1290) Scottish succession through his grandmother, Ada, third daughter of David, earl of Huntingdon; served in Ireland, 1294; first summoned to parliament, 1295; commanded Durham contingent at siege of Caerlaverock, 1300; at parliament of Lincoln, 1301, denied pope's right to adjudicate on dispute with Scotland; king's lieutenant in Aquitaine, 1302; seneschal, 1309; received grant of Menteith estates, 1306; signed baronial letter to the pope, 1306.   [xxv. 130]

HASTINGS, JOHN, third BARON HASTINGS (1287–1325), served in Scottish wars, 1311–19; sided first with barons, but afterwards joined Edward II; governor of Kenilworth, 1323.   [xxv. 131]

HASTINGS, JOHN, second EARL OF PEMBROKE (1347–1375), soldier and protector of Froissart; son of Laurence Hastings, first earl of Pembroke [q. v.]; K.G., 1369; served with Earl of Cambridge and Black Prince in France; when lieutenant of Aquitaine was defeated and captured by Spanish fleet at La Rochelle, 1372; imprisoned three years in Spain; died in France, having been handed over to Duguesclin.   [xxv. 131]

HASTINGS, LAURENCE, first EARL OF PEMBROKE (1318?–1348), warrior; son of John Hastings, third baron Hastings [q. v.]; succeeded as fourth Baron Hastings (by writ), 1325; created earl palatine as representative of Aymer de Valence [q. v.], 1339, when first summoned to parliament; present at Sluys, 1340; according to Murimuth, a knight of Round Table, 1344; prominent in Gascon campaigns, 1345–6; with Northampton defeated French fleet near Crotoy, 1347.   [xxv. 132]

HASTINGS, SELINA, COUNTESS OF HUNTINGDON (1707–1791), founder of 'Lady Huntingdon's Connexion'; wife of Theophilus Hastings, ninth earl of Huntingdon; 'converted' by her sister-in-law, Lady Margaret Hastings; intimate with the Wesleys; member of first methodist society in Fetter Lane, 1739; first supporter of itinerant lay preaching; employed among her chaplains, Whitefield, Romaine, and Venn; intimate also with Toplady, Doddridge, and Dr. Watts; established first regular chapel at Brighton, 1761; set up churches in London, Bath, Tunbridge, and other aristocratic centres; her chapels registered as dissenting meeting-houses after 1779; her training college at Trevecca opened, 1768, removed to Cheshunt, 1792. She supported Whitefield against the Wesleys, but attempted a reconciliation, 1749, and took an active part in protest against the anti-Calvinistic minutes of Wesley's conference, 1770, and against relaxation of subscription, 1772.   [xxv. 133]

HASTINGS, THEOPHILUS, seventh EARL OF HUNTINGDON (1650–1701), volunteer in French army, 1672; privy councillor, 1683; ecclesiastical commissioner and lord-lieutenant of Leicester and Derby, 1687–8; imprisoned for attempt to seize Plymouth for James II, 1688; a manager of conference with Commons, 1689; imprisoned on suspicion of treason, 1692.   [xxv. 135]

HASTINGS, THOMAS (1740?–1801), itinerant bookseller; known as 'Dr. Green'; author of political pamphlets.   [xxv. 136]

HASTINGS, THOMAS (fl. 1813–1831), amateur etcher; published 'Etchings from works of Richard Wilson,' 1825, and other works.   [xxv. 136]

HASTINGS, SIR THOMAS (1790–1870), admiral; commanded gunboat in Walcheren expedition, 1809; first lieutenant of the Undaunted at Elba, 1814; captain of the Excellent (training ship), 1832–45, and superintendent of R.N. College, Portsmouth; knighted, 1839; K.C.B., 1859; admiral, 1866.   [xxv. 136]

HASTINGS, WARREN (1732–1818), governor-general of India; first king's scholar at Westminster, 1747; went to India, 1750; when member of council at Kásim-Bazár imprisoned by nawab of Bengal, 1756; as resident of Moorshedabad, 1757–60, corresponded with Clive; member of Calcutta council, 1761; despatched on mission to Patna, 1762; returned to England, 1764; gave evidence on Indian affairs before parliamentary committee, 1766; sent out as second in council at Madras, 1769; governor of Bengal, 1772; reorganised the financial and judicial system of Bengal, Behar, and Orissa; investigated conduct of native deputy-governors; assisted, in accordance with treaty of

alliance of 1764, nawab of Oude against the Rohillas, 1773 ;
took measures against dacoity ; created governor-general
by the Regulating Act, 1773 ; opposed by a majority of
his new council and accused by Nand Kumar (Macaulay's
Nuncomar) of corruption ; sent home a conditional resignation and brought a countercharge of conspiracy
against Nand Kumar, who was condemned and hanged
for forgery (1775) on a private suit before the case
came on ; had the opium trade farmed for a term of years,
the proceeds being credited in the public accounts ; supported by supreme court, which ignored the acceptance
of his resignation by the directors, 1777 ; checked confederacy between Mahrattas and Haidar ; freed himself
from the opposition in council of Sir Philip Francis (1740–
1818) [q. v.] by wounding him in a duel, 1780 ; drove
Haidar Ali from the Carnatic ; attacked the French settlements ; deposed Chait Singh and appropriated (1781) his
treasure ; suspected of conniving at imprisonment of the
Begums of Oude and the seizure of their land and money ;
concluded treaty of Salbai with Tippu Sultan, 1783 ; obtained reversal of vote of censure by directors on his treatment of Chait Singh ; founded Asiatic Society of Bengal
and Calcutta Madrisa, 1784 ; left India, 1785. His impeachment on ground of corruption and cruelty in his
Indian administration, begun, 1788, and concluded, 1795,
resulted, after a trial of 145 days, in an acquittal, but cost
him 70,000*l.* The company gave him pecuniary assistance ;
he was created privy councillor and D.C.L. of Oxford, was
presented by the prince regent to the allied sovereigns in
London, and was enabled to repurchase the family estate
of Daylesford.   [xxv. 136]

HASTINGS, WILLIAM, BARON HASTINGS (1430 ?–
1483), sheriff of Leicestershire and Warwickshire ; a devoted Yorkist ; created by Edward IV a peer, 1461 ;
master of the mint, 1461 ; lieutenant of Calais, 1471 ;
lord chamberlain, 1461–83 ; joint-ambassador with Warwick to Charles the Bold, 1465–6 ; assisted Edward IV's
escape to Holland, 1470 ; acted for him in his absence and
gained over Clarence ; prominent at Barnet, 1471, and
Tewkesbury, 1471 ; commanded English force in France,
1475 ; on accession of Edward V opposed Rivers, and, declining Gloucester's overtures, was beheaded.   [xxv. 148]

HATCH, EDWIN (1835–1889), theologian ; B.A. Pembroke College, Oxford, 1857 ; professor of classics at
Toronto, 1859–62 ; rector of high school, Quebec, 1862–
1867 ; vice-principal of St. Mary Hall, Oxford, 1867–
1885 ; first editor of university 'Gazette,' 1870 ; pub-
lised Bampton lectures (1880) on 'Organisation of Early
Christian Churches,' 1881 ; D.D. Edinburgh, 1883 ; Grinfield lecturer, 1882–4 ; reader in ecclesiastical history,
1884 ; Herbert lecturer on 'Greek Influence on Christianity,' 1888 ; published also 'Growth of Church Institutions,' 1887, 'Essays in Biblical Greek,' 1889, and 'Towards
Fields of Light.'   [xxv. 149]

HATCHARD, JOHN (1769–1849), publisher ; issued
'Christian Observer,' 1802–45, and publications of Society
for Bettering the Condition of the Poor.   [xxv. 150]

HATCHARD, THOMAS GOODWIN (1817–1870),
bishop of Mauritius ; grandson of John Hatchard [q. v.] ;
M.A. Brasenose College, Oxford, 1845 ; D.D., 1869 ; rector
of Havant, 1846–56, of St. Nicholas, Guildford, 1856–69 ;
bishop of Mauritius, 1869–70 ; died of fever in Mauritius.
                                                  [xxv. 150]

HATCHER, HENRY (1777–1846), Salisbury antiquary ; published translation, with commentary, of
Richard of Cirencester's 'Description of Britain,' 1809,
and 'Historical Account of Old and New Sarum,' 1834 ;
contributed to Hoare's 'Modern Wiltshire' and Britton's
'Beauties of Wiltshire,' 1825, and 'Picturesque Antiquities,' 1830.   [xxv. 150]

HATCHER, THOMAS (*d.* 1583), antiquary ; of Eton
and King's College, Cambridge ; M.A., 1563 ; admitted at
Gray's Inn, 1565 ; friend and correspondent of Stow and
Dr. John Caius [q. v.] ; began catalogue of King's
College, Cambridge, and edited Haddon's 'Lucubrationes,'
1567, and Carr's 'De scriptorum Britannicorum pauci-
tate,' 1576.   [xxv. 151]

HATCHER, THOMAS (1589 ?–1677), parliamentary
captain ; grandson of Thomas Hatcher (*d.* 1583) [q. v.] ;
M.P., Lincoln, Grantham, Stamford (in Long parliament),
and Lincolnshire, 1654–9 ; commissioner to Scotland,
1643 ; present at Marston Moor, 1644, and siege of York,
1644.   [xxv. 152]

HATCHETT, CHARLES (1765 ?–1847), chemist ;
F.R.S., 1797 ; treasurer of the Literary Club, 1814 ; chief
works, treatise on 'Spikenard of the Ancients,' 1836, and
'Analysis of the Magnetical Pyrites,' 1804.   [xxv. 153]

HATCLIFFE, VINCENT (1601–1671). [See SPENCER,
JOHN.]

HATFIELD, JOHN (1758 ?–1803), forger ; married
and deserted a natural daughter of Lord Robert Manners ;
twice released from a debtor's prison by Duke of Rutland ;
imprisoned seven years at Scarborough, from 1792 ; released and married by Miss Nation, 1800 ; deserted her
and lived in Cumberland as brother of Lord Hopetoun ;
married Mary Robinson, the 'Buttermere Beauty,' 1802 ;
tried at Carlisle for forgery and hanged.   [xxv. 153]

HATFIELD, MARTHA (*fl.* 1652), cataleptic ; her
case described in 'The Wise Virgin,' 1653.   [xxv. 154]

HATFIELD, THOMAS OF (*d.* 1381), bishop of Durham ; keeper of the privy seal, 1343 ; accompanied
Edward III to France, 1346 and 1355 ; bishop of Durham,
1345–81 ; commissioner to treat for peace with Scotland,
1350–7 and subsequently ; resisted visitations of archbishops of York ; at Durham built part of south side of
cathedral choir and hall of castle ; founded Carmelite
house of Northallerton and college at Oxford for Durham monks ; his survey of Durham edited by W. Greenwell, 1857.   [xxv. 154]

HATHAWAY, RICHARD (*fl.* 1702), impostor ; sentenced to fine, pillory, and hard labour for imposture, riot,
and assault, 1702.   [xxv. 156]

HATHERLEY, BARON (1801–1881). [See WOOD,
WILLIAM PAGE.]

HATHERTON, first BARON (1791–1863). [See
LITTLETON, EDWARD JOHN.]

HATHWAY, RICHARD (*fl.* 1602), dramatist ; mentioned by Meres (1598) among best contemporary writers
of comedy ; part author of 'First Part of the True and
Honorable Historie of the Life of Sir John Old-castle,'
1599, and of unprinted plays.   [xxv. 157]

HATSELL, SIR HENRY (1641–1714), judge ; B.A.
Exeter College, Oxford, 1659 ; barrister, Middle Temple,
1667 ; serjeant-at-law, 1689 ; knighted, 1697 ; baron of
the exchequer, 1697–1702 (removed).   [xxv. 158]

HATSELL, JOHN (1743–1820), clerk of House of
Commons ; of Queens' College, Cambridge, and Middle
Temple ; senior bencher ; clerk of House of Commons,
1768–97 ; published 'A Collection of Cases of Privilege of
Parliament . . . to 1628,' 1776, and 'Precedents of Proceed-
ings in House of Commons,' 1781.   [xxv. 158]

HATTECLYFFE, WILLIAM (*d.* 1480), physician
and secretary to Edward IV ; original scholar of King's
College, Cambridge, 1440 ; physician to Henry VI, 1454 ;
captured by Lancastrians, 1470 ; afterwards master of
requests and royal councillor.   [xxv. 158]

HATTECLYFFE, WILLIAM (*fl.* 1500), under-
treasurer of Ireland, 1495.   [xxv. 159]

HATTON. [See also FINCH-HATTON.]

HATTON, SIR CHRISTOPHER (1540–1591), lord
chancellor ; gentleman-commoner, St. Mary Hall, Oxford,
c. 1555 ; took part in masque at Inner Temple, 1561 ;
became one of Elizabeth's gentlemen-pensioners, 1564 ; received grant of estates, court offices, and an annuity ; M.P.,
Higham Ferrers, 1571, Northamptonshire, 1572, 1584, and
subsequently ; captain of the body-guard, 1572 ; charged
with being Elizabeth's paramour by Mary Queen of Scots,
1584 ; the bishop of Ely ordered to surrender fee-simple
of Ely Place, Holborn, for his benefit ; made vice-chamberlain and knighted, 1578 ; the queen's mouthpiece in
parliament ; opposed the queen's match with the duke of
Anjou, 1581 ; member of committees for trials of Babington, 1586, and Mary Queen of Scots, 1586 ; spoke strongly
in parliament against Mary, and advised Davison to
despatch warrant for her execution, 1587 ; lord chancellor. 1587–91 ; assisted by Sir Richard Swale, and had
four masters in chancery as assessors ; K.G., 1588 ; chancellor of Oxford, 1588 ; friend and patron of Spenser and
Churchyard ; wrote act iv. of 'Tancred and Gismund,'
acted at Inner Temple, 1568 ; buried in St. Paul's cathedral ; his correspondence printed, 1847.   [xxv. 159]

HATTON, CHRISTOPHER, first BARON HATTON (1605?-1670), royalist; relative of Sir Christopher Hatton [q. v.]; K.B., 1626; M.P., Higham Ferrers, 1640; hon. D.C.L. Oxford, 1642; created Baron Hatton and privy councillor, 1643; comptroller of Charles I's household, 1643-6; royal commissioner at Uxbridge, 1645; retired to Paris, 1648; allowed to return, 1656; privy councillor and governor of Guernsey, 1662; published psalter with prayers, 1644. [xxv. 162]

HATTON, CHRISTOPHER, first VISCOUNT HATTON (1632-1706), governor of Guernsey; elder son of Christopher, first baron Hatton [q. v.]; succeeded as second baron, 1670; his mother and first wife killed by explosion of powder magazine in Guernsey, 1672; presented to Bodleian Anglo-Saxon Homilies, 1675; created Viscount Hatton, 1683; custos rotulorum of Northampton, 1681-9; hon. D.C.L. Oxford, 1683; selection from correspondence edited, 1878. [xxv. 163]

HATTON, EDWARD (1701-1783), Dominican; provincial, 1754 and 1770; his 'Memoirs of the Reformation of England' appeared with pseudonym 'Constantius Archæophilus,' 1826 and 1841. [xxv. 164]

HATTON, FRANK (1861-1883), mineral explorer to British North Borneo Company, 1881-3; accidentally killed in jungle; left interesting letters and diaries. [xxv. 164]

HATTON, JOHN LIPTROT (1809-1886), musical composer; organist in three Lancashire churches at sixteen, afterwards at St. Nicholas, Chapel Street, Liverpool; appeared in London as an actor, 1832; directed opera choruses at Drury Lane, 1842-3; produced his 'Queen of the Thames,' 1843; his 'Pascal Bruno' given at Vienna for Staudigl's benefit, 1844; on return published trios and eighteen songs, including 'To Anthea'; sang and played on tour and in America, 1848-50; conductor of Glee and Madrigal Union, c. 1850; conductor for Charles Kean at Princess's Theatre, London, 1853-9; his cantata 'Robin Hood' produced at Bradford, 1856; his opera 'Rose' at Covent Garden, 1864, and his oratorio 'Hezekiah' at Crystal Palace, 1877; edited collections of old English songs; composed 300 songs and excellent part-songs. [xxv. 165]

HAUGHTON, SIR GRAVES CHAMPNEY (1788-1849), orientalist; served in Indian army and studied at Baraset and Fort William; professor of Sanskrit and Bengali, at Haileybury, 1819-27; hon. M.A. Oxford, 1819; F.R.S., 1821; foreign member of Paris Asiatic Society and Institute of France; hon. secretary of Royal Asiatic Society, 1831-2; K.H., 1833; issued Bengali grammar, glossaries, and texts, an edition of 'Institutes of Menu,' 1825, Bengali-Sanskrit dictionary, 1833, 'Prodromus,' 1839, and other metaphysical treatises; died of cholera at St. Cloud. [xxv. 166]

HAUGHTON, JAMES (1795-1873), philanthropist; friend and supporter of Father Mathew and O'Connell; prominent in anti-slavery, temperance, and other social movements; president of Vegetarian Society; published 'Slavery Immoral,' 1847, 'Memoir of T. Clarkson,' 1847, and 'Plea for Teetotalism,' 1855. [xxv. 168]

HAUGHTON, JOHN COLPOYS (1817-1887), lieutenant-general; nephew of Sir Graves Champney Haughton [q. v.]; as adjutant of 4th Ghoorkas distinguished himself in defence of Char-ee-kar, 1841, publishing an account, 1867; escaped wounded to Cabul; commissioner at Cooch Behar, 1865-73; C.S.I., 1866; lieutenant-general, 1882. [xxv. 168]

HAUGHTON, MOSES, the elder (1734-1804), still life and enamel-painter; exhibited at Academy, 1788-1804. [xxv. 169]

HAUGHTON, MOSES, the younger (1772?-1848?), miniaturist and engraver; nephew of Moses Haughton the elder [q. v.]; friend of Fuseli; exhibited at Royal Academy, 1808-48. [xxv. 170]

HAUGHTON, SAMUEL (1821-1897), man of science; son of James Haughton [q. v.]; B.A. and fellow, Trinity College, Dublin, 1844; M.A., 1852; senior fellow, 1881; ordained priest, 1847; professor of geology, Dublin University, 1851-81; M.D. Dublin, 1862; registrar of medical school, subsequently chairman of medical school committee, and university representative on general medical council; member of council of Royal Zoological Society of Ireland, 1860 (president, 1883); F.R.S, 1858; honorary D.C.L. Oxford, 1868; LL.D. Cambridge, 1881; honorary LL.D. Edinburgh, 1884; president of Royal Irish Academy, 1887; published scientific works and papers. [Suppl. ii. 398]

HAUGHTON, WILLIAM (fl. 1598), dramatist; author of English-Men for my Money,' 1616; collaborator with Dekker, Chettle, John Day, and others. [xxv. 170]

HAUKSBEE, FRANCIS, the elder (d. 1713?), electrician; F.R.S., 1705; contrived first electrical machine, 1706; published 'Physico-Mechanical Experiments,' 1709; suggested an improved air-pump; determined relative weight of water and air. [xxv. 171]

HAUKSBEE, FRANCIS, the younger (1687-1763), writer on science; perhaps son of Francis Hauksbee the elder [q. v.]; clerk and housekeeper to Royal Society, 1723; published (with P. Shaw) 'Essay for introducing a Portable Laboratory,' 1731, and syllabus for courses of experimental lectures (which he was the first to give, c. 1714), also 'Course of Mechanical, Optical, and Pneumatical Experiments' (with W. Whiston). [xxv. 171]

HAUSTED, PETER (d. 1645), dramatist; rector of Hadham, vicar of Gretton; D.D. Oxford, 1642; died at Banbury Castle during the siege; published, among other works, 'The Rival Friends' (comedy), 1632, and 'Senile Odium' (Latin play), 1633; his 'Hymnus Tabaci,' by 'Raphael Thorius,' appeared 1650. [xxv. 171]

HAUTEVILLE, JOHN DE (fl. 1184), Latin poet; his satire 'Architrenius' first printed at Paris, 1517. [xxv. 172]

HAVARD, WILLIAM (1710?-1778), actor and dramatist; appeared at Goodman's Fields, 1730-7; at Drury Lane till retirement, 1769, playing generally secondary parts; depreciated in 'Rosciad'; appeared also in his own plays, 'King Charles I,' at Lincoln's Inn Fields, 1737, 'Regulus,' Drury Lane, 1744, and 'The Elopement,' Drury Lane, 1763. [xxv. 172]

HAVELL, ROBERT, the elder (fl. 1800-1840), engraver and art publisher; issued aquatint engravings from drawings by W. Havell and others, 1812-28; published Audubon's 'Birds of America,' Salt's 'Views in Africa,' and other works. [xxv. 173]

HAVELL, ROBERT, the younger (fl. 1820-1850), painter; son of Robert Havell the elder [q. v.]; settled in America as landscape-painter. [xxv. 174]

HAVELL, WILLIAM (1782-1857), landscape-painter; original member of Old Water-Colour Society; visited China and India, 1816-25; after his return painted in oil, exhibiting (Italian subjects) at Royal Academy, British Institution, and Suffolk Street; died a Turner pensioner. [xxv. 174]

HAVELOCK, SIR HENRY, first baronet (1795-1857), major-general; intimate at Charterhouse with Julius Hare [q. v.]; studied at Middle Temple under Joseph Chitty [q. v.]; entered army, 1815; went to India as subaltern in 13th, 1823; deputy assistant adjutant-general in Burmese expedition, 1824-6, publishing narrative, 1828; while stationed at Chinsurah became a baptist; regimental adjutant, 1835-8; aide-de-camp to Sir Willoughby Cotton [q. v.] in first Afghan campaign, 1839, of which he published an account; Persian interpreter to General William G. K. Elphinstone [q. v.] in Afghanistan, 1840; accompanied Sir R. Sale to the passes, and assisted him in holding Jellalabad, 1841; returned with Pollock to Cabul, and accompanied Hindoo Khoosh and Kohistan expedition; C.B. and brevet-major, 1842; interpreter to Sir Hugh Gough in Gwalior campaign, 1843; present at Mudki, 1845, Ferozeshah, 1845, and Sobraon, 1846; deputy adjutant-general, Bombay, 1847; visited England for last time, 1849-51; planned the operations at Mohumra in Persian war of 1857; during the Indian mutiny commanded a column which recaptured Cawnpore, after winning four victories and marching 120 miles in nine days, 17 July 1857; major-general, 1857; defeated the sepoys at Onao and thrice at Busseerutgunge, but owing to sickness and want of ammunition was compelled to fall back on Cawnpore, August 1857; reinforced by Outram; carried the Allumbagh and effected first relief of Lucknow, September, 1857; co-operated with Sir Colin

Campbell in second relief, November 1857; died of diarrhœa on morning of withdrawal. He had been created K.C.B. and a baronet, with a pension of 1,000*l*., November, 1857. [xxv. 174]

HAVELOCK, WILLIAM (1793–1848), lieutenant-colonel; brother of Sir Henry Havelock [q. v.]; aide-de-camp in Peninsula and at Waterloo to Count Alten; distinguished at Vera, 1813; aide-de-camp to Sir Charles Colville [q. v.] at Bombay; military secretary to Lord Elphinstone at Madras; lieutenant-colonel, 14th dragoons, 1841; mortally wounded at Ramnuggur in second Sikh war, 1848. [xxv. 179]

HAVELOCK-ALLAN, SIR HENRY MARSHMAN, first baronet (1830–1897), lieutenant-general; son of Sir Henry Havelock [q. v.]; ensign, 1846; adjutant, 10th foot, 1852; captain, 18th foot (royal Irish regiment), 1857; brevet lieutenant-colonel, 1859; unattached major, 1864; brevet-colonel, 1868; major-general, 1878; lieutenant-general, 1881; colonel of royal Irish regiment of foot, 1878; in Persian war and Indian mutiny, 1857–9; took part in defence of Lucknow; received Victoria cross, 1858; created baronet on death of his father, 1858; in Maori war, 1863–4; C.B., 1866; assistant quartermaster-general in Canada, 1867–9, and in Dublin, 1869; liberal M.P. for Sunderland, 1874–81, and south-east Durham county, 1885; assumed additional name of Allan, 1880; liberal-unionist M.P. for south-east Durham county, 1886–92 and 1895; K.C.B., 1897; killed while visiting British troops on Afghan frontier. [Suppl. ii. 400]

HAVERGAL, FRANCES RIDLEY (1836–1879), writer of religious verse; daughter of William Henry Havergal [q. v.]; published 'Ministry of Song,' 1870, and other hymns and poems; 'Poetical Works,' issued, 1884; autobiography in 'Memorials' (2nd edit. 1880). [xxv. 180]

HAVERGAL, FRANCIS TEBBS (1829–1890), author; son of William Henry Havergal [q. v.]; M.A. New College, Oxford, 1857; vicar-choral (1853–74) and prebendary of Hereford, 1877–90; published 'Fasti Herefordenses,' 1869, 'Herefordshire Words and Phrases,' 1887, and other works. [xxv. 182]

HAVERGAL, HENRY EAST (1820–1875), musician; son of William Henry Havergal [q. v.]; M.A. Magdalen Hall, Oxford, 1846; chaplain at Christ Church and New College, Oxford; while vicar of Cople, Bedfordshire, 1847–1875, constructed organ and chiming apparatus; vocalist and instrumentalist; author of musical publications. [xxv. 180]

HAVERGAL, WILLIAM HENRY (1793–1870), composer of sacred music; educated at Merchant Taylors' School and St. Edmund Hall, Oxford; M.A., 1819; rector of Astley, 1829, of St. Nicholas, Worcester, 1845; vicar of Shareshill, 1860; gained Gresham prize for evening service in A, 1836, and for anthem, 'Give Thanks,' 1841; composed 'A Hundred Psalm and Hymn Tunes,' 1859; published 'Old Church Psalmody,' 1847, and other works. [xxv. 181]

HAVERS, ALICE (1850–1890). [See MORGAN MRS. ALICE MARY.]

HAVERS, CLOPTON (*d.* 1702), physician and anatomist; of Catharine Hall, Cambridge; M.D. Utrecht, 1685; L.R.C.P., 1687; F.R.S., 1686; his chief anatomical work, 'Osteologia Nova,' giving the first minute account of the structure of bone, printed, 1691; the 'Haversian canals' named after him. [xxv. 182]

HAVERSHAM, first BARON (1647–1710). [See THOMPSON, SIR JOHN.]

HAVERTY, JOSEPH PATRICK (1794–1864), painter; executed portraits of O'Connell and Bishop Doyle. [xxv. 183]

HAVERTY, MARTIN (1809–1887), historian; brother of Joseph Patrick Haverty [q. v.]; educated at Irish college, Paris; sub-librarian of King's Inns, Dublin; published 'History of Ireland,' 1860, and 'Wanderings in Spain,' 1844. [xxv. 183]

HAVILAND, JOHN (1785–1851), professor of medicine at Cambridge; of Winchester and St. John's College, Cambridge; twelfth wrangler, 1807; fellow; M.A., 1810; professor of anatomy, Cambridge, 1814; regius professor of medicine, 1817–51; F.R.C.P., 1818; M.D., 1817; Harveian orator, 1837. [xxv. 183]

HAVILAND, WILLIAM (1718–1784), general; aide-de-camp to Blakeney, 1745–6; lieutenant-colonel of 27th, 1752; served in North America, 1757–60, under Abercromby and Amherst, rendering valuable assistance in capture of Montreal, 1760; invented a pontoon for rapids; second in command at reduction of Martinique; commanded brigade at capture of Havanna, 1762; general, 1783; friend and connection of Burke. [xxv. 183]

HAVILLAND, THOMAS FIOTT DE (1775–1866), lieutenant-colonel in Madras army; served at siege of Pondicherry, 1793, reduction of Ceylon, 1795–6, in operations against Tippoo Sahib 1799, and in Egypt, 1801; as architect of Madras, 1814–25, built cathedral and St. Andrew's presbyterian church; lieutenant-colonel, 1824; member of Guernsey legislature. [xxv. 184]

HAWARD, FRANCIS (1759–1797), engraver; exhibited at Academy engravings after Reynolds and other artists; associate engraver, 1783. [xxv. 185]

HAWARD, NICHOLAS (*fl.* 1569), author; of Thavies Inn; published 'The Line of Liberalitie dulie directinge the wel bestowing of Benefites,' &c., 1569. [xxv. 185]

HAWARD, SIMON (*fl.* 1572–1614). [See HARWARD.]

HAWARDEN, EDWARD (1662–1735), Roman catholic controversialist; vice-president of Douay College, 1690–1707; head of Romanist colony at Oxford, 1688–9; disputed with Samuel Clarke on the Trinity before Queen Caroline, 1719; published against Leslie's 'The Case Stated' 'The True Church of Christ,' 1714–15, 'Charity and Truth,' 1728 (against Chillingworth's 'Religion of Protestants'), and 'Answer to Dr. Clarke and Mr. Whiston concerning the Divinity of the Son and of the Holy Spirit,' 1729. [xxv. 185]

HAWEIS, THOMAS (1734–1820), divine; studied at Christ Church and Magdalen Hall, Oxford; assistant to Martin Madan [q. v.] at Lock Chapel; rector of Aldwinkle, Northamptonshire, 1764–1820; LL.B. Cambridge, 1772; manager of Trevecca College; trustee and executor of Selina Hastings, countess of Huntingdon [q. v.], 1791; published, among other works, 'Life of William Romaine,' 1797, and 'History of Rise, Declension, and Revival of the Church,' 1800; edited John Newton's 'Authentic Narrative,' 1764. [xxv. 186]

HAWES, SIR BENJAMIN (1797–1862), under-secretary for war; whig M.P., Lambeth, 1832–47, Kinsale, 1848–52; caused appointment of fine arts commission and opening of British Museum on holidays; advocate of penny postage and electric telegraph; under-secretary for colonies, 1846; K.C.B., 1856; under-secretary for war, 1857–62; published narrative of ascent of Mont Blanc in 1827. [xxv. 187]

HAWES, EDWARD (*fl.* 1606), poet; author, while at Westminster School, of 'Trayterous Percyes and Catesbyes Prosopopeia,' 1606. [xxv. 187]

HAWES, RICHARD (1603?–1668), puritan divine; M.A. Corpus Christi College, Cambridge, 1627; when rector of Kentchurch tried by royalists for supposed conspiracy; ejected from vicarage of Leintwardine, 1662, but occasionally allowed to preach. [xxv. 187]

HAWES, ROBERT (1665–1731), topographer; part of his manuscript history of Framlingham and Loes-Hundred printed by R. Loder, 1798. [xxv. 188]

HAWES, STEPHEN (*d.* 1523?), poet; groom of the chamber to Henry VII; his 'Passetyme of Pleasure, or History of Graunde Amoure and la Bel Pucel,' first printed by Wynkyn de Worde, 1509 (reprinted by Southey, 1831); other works by him reprinted (ed. David Laing), 1865. [xxv. 188]

HAWES, WILLIAM (1736–1808), founder of Royal Humane Society; educated at St. Paul's School; M.P.; physician to London Dispensary; founded Royal Humane Society, 1774; published account of Goldsmith's illness, 1774, examination of 'John Wesley's Primitive Physic,' 1776, and tracts on premature interment and suspended animation. [xxv. 190]

HAWES, WILLIAM (1785–1846), singer and composer; chorister, gentleman, and master of children (1817) at Chapel Royal; original associate of Philharmonic Society; almoner and vicar-choral at St. Paul's, 1814;

lay vicar of Westminster, 1817-20; assisted Arnold in management of English opera at Lyceum; conducted Madrigal Society and directed oratorios; composed songs and glees and edited, among other works, 'Triumphs of Oriana,' 1818.   [xxv. 190]

HAWFORD, EDWARD (d. 1582), master of Christ's College, Cambridge; B.A. Jesus College, Cambridge, 1543; fellow of Christ's College; M.A., 1545; master of Christ's College, 1559-82; D.D., 1564; vice-chancellor, 1563-4; took part in framing of university statutes (1570).
            [xxv. 191]

HAWKE, EDWARD, first BARON HAWKE (1705-1781), admiral of the fleet; brought up by his uncle, Martin Bladen [q. v.]; entered navy as volunteer, 1720; first saw fighting as commander of the Berwick in battle of Toulon, 1744; promoted rear-admiral of the white by special interposition of George II, 1747; defeated and captured great part of French squadron protecting convoy from Rochelle, 1747; K.B., 1747; M.P., Portsmouth, 1747; commanded home fleet, 1748-52; presided over court-martials (1750) on admirals Sir Charles Knowles [q. v.] and Thomas Griffin [q. v.]; commanded western fleet, 1755-6, Mediterranean fleet, 1756; admiral, 1757; co-operated with Sir John Mordaunt [q. v.] in the Rochefort expedition, 1757; succeeded in delaying, but failed to destroy, French convoy for America, 1758; struck his flag owing to his treatment by admiralty, but resuming his command blockaded Brest from May to November, 1759; in heavy weather defeated Conflans in Quiberon Bay, 20 Nov. 1759, capturing five ships and running others ashore; thanked by parliament and given a pension of 1,500l. for two lives; after capturing Spanish treasure-ships finally struck his flag, 1762; first lord of the admiralty, 1766-71; admiral of the fleet, 1768; created Baron Hawke of Great Britain, 1776.   [xxv. 192]

HAWKER, EDWARD (1782-1860), admiral; son of James Hawker [q. v.]; entered navy, 1793; successful in cruising against privateers in Mediterranean; flag-captain to Sir Richard Keats at Newfoundland, 1813-15, to Earl of Northesk at Plymouth, 1827-30; admiral, 1853; correspondent of 'Times' as 'A Flag Officer.' [xxv. 199]

HAWKER, JAMES (d. 1787), captain in the navy; posted, 1768; with the Iris fought drawn battle with La Touche Tréville in the Hermione off New York, 1780; commanded the Hero in Porto Praya under Commodore G. Johnstone [q. v.], 1781.   [xxv. 200]

HAWKER, PETER (1786-1853), soldier and author; served with 14th light dragoons in Peninsula; badly wounded at Talavera, 1809; retired, 1813; patented improvements in pianoforte, 1820; published military journal, 1810, 'Instructions to Young Sportsmen,' 1814.
            [xxv. 200]

HAWKER, ROBERT (1753-1827), divine and author; member of Magdalen Hall, Oxford, 1778; curate of Charles, near Plymouth, 1778, vicar, 1784; D.D. Edinburgh, 1792; highly popular as extempore preacher; published numerous devotional works, also 'Concordance and Dictionary to Sacred Scriptures'; collected works edited, 1831.   [xxv. 201]

HAWKER, ROBERT STEPHEN (1803-1875), poet and antiquary; grandson of Robert Hawker [q. v.]; matriculated at Pembroke College, Oxford, 1823; M.A. Magdalen Hall, 1836; Newdigate prizeman, 1827; vicar of Morwenstow, 1834, with Wellcombe, 1851; became Romanist in last days; published 'Quest of the Sangraal,' 1864, 'Cornish Ballads and other Poems,' 1869, and other verse, including 'And shall Trelawny die,' 'Records of the Western Shore,' 1832, 1836, and 'Footprints of Former Men in Far Cornwall,' 1870.   [xxv. 202]

HAWKER, THOMAS (d. 1723?), portrait-painter.
            [xxv. 203]

HAWKESBURY, first BARON (1727-1808). [See JENKINSON, CHARLES, first EARL OF LIVERPOOL.]

HAWKESWORTH, JOHN (1715?-1773), author; said to have succeeded Johnson as compiler of parliamentary debates for 'Gentleman's Magazine,' 1744; with him and Warton carried on the 'Adventurer,' 1752-4; edited Swift's works, 1755; LL.D. Lambeth, 1756; his 'Edgar and Emmeline' produced at Drury Lane, 1761; published an account of voyages in the South Seas, 1773, when he became a director of the East India Company; early friend and imitator of Johnson.   [xxv. 203]

HAWKESWORTH, WALTER (d. 1606), dramatist; major fellow Trinity College, Cambridge, 1595; M.A., 1595; acted in his own comedies, 'Leander' and 'Pedantius,' 1603; secretary to Sir Charles Cornwallis [q. v.] in Spain, c. 1605; died of the plague in Spain. [xxv. 205]

HAWKEY, JOHN (1703-1759), classical scholar; graduate of Trinity College, Dublin, 1725; edited Virgil, 1745, Horace, 1745, and Terence, 1745, Juvenal and Persius, 1746, Sallust, 1747.   [xxv. 205]

HAWKINS, SIR CÆSAR, baronet (1711-1786), surgeon; surgeon to St. George's Hospital, 1735-74; sergeant-surgeon to George II and George III; created baronet, 1778; invented the cutting gorget. [xxv. 206]

HAWKINS, CÆSAR HENRY (1798-1884), surgeon; grandson of Sir Cæsar Hawkins [q. v.]; educated at Christ's Hospital and St. George's Hospital; surgeon to St. George's Hospital, 1829-61; consulting surgeon, 1861; Hunterian orator, 1849; president of College of Surgeons, 1852 and 1861; sergeant-surgeon to Queen Victoria, 1862; F.R.S.; first successful practiser of ovariotomy; collected works issued, 1874.   [xxv. 206]

HAWKINS, EDWARD (1780-1867), numismatist; keeper of antiquities at British Museum, 1826-60; F.R.S., 1821, F.S.A., 1826 (vice-president of both); president of London Numismatic Society; published 'Silver Coins of England,' 1841, and 'Medallic Illustrations of the History of Great Britain and Ireland,' 1885; his collection of medals and political caricatures purchased by British Museum, 1860.   [xxv. 207]

HAWKINS, EDWARD (1789-1882), provost of Oriel College, Oxford; brother of Cæsar Henry Hawkins [q. v.]; educated at Merchant Taylors' School and St. John's College, Oxford; M.A., 1814; D.D., 1828; fellow of Oriel, 1813; vicar of St. Mary's, 1823-8; provost of Oriel, 1828-1874; canon of Rochester, 1828-82; Bampton lecturer, 1840; first Ireland professor of exegesis, 1847-61; though a high churchman opposed tractarian movement and (1841) drew up condemnation of Tract XC; retired to Rochester, 1874; published an edition of Milton's poetry with Newton's life, 1824, 'A Manual for Christians,' 1826, and sermons and pamphlets on university affairs. [xxv. 208]

HAWKINS, ERNEST (1802-1868), canon of Westminster; M.A. Balliol College, Oxford, 1827; B.D., 1839; fellow of Exeter College, 1831; sub-librarian of Bodleian, 1831; secretary of the S.P.G., 1843-64, canon of Westminster, 1864-8; minister of Curzon Chapel, Mayfair, 1850; vice-president, Bishop's College, Cape Town, 1859; published works relating to history of missions. [xxv. 209]

HAWKINS, FRANCIS (1628-1681), jesuit; son of John Hawkins (fl. 1635) [q. v.]; professor of holy scripture at Liège College, 1675-81; translated, at age of eight, 'Youth's Behaviour,' first printed, 1641.   [xxv. 210]

HAWKINS, FRANCIS (1794-1877), physician; brother of Cæsar Henry Hawkins [q. v.]; educated at Merchant Taylors' School and St. John's College, Oxford; fellow; Newdigate prizeman, 1813; B.C.L., 1819; M.D., 1823; F.R.C.P., 1824; first professor of medicine at King's College, London, 1831-6; physician to Middlesex Hospital, 1824-58, and to royal household; registrar of College of Physicians, 1829-58, of Medical Council, 1858-76.
            [xxv. 211]

HAWKINS, GEORGE (1809-1852), lithographic artist.   [xxv. 211]

HAWKINS, HENRY (1571?-1646), jesuit; studied at St. Omer and Rome; exiled from England, 1618; published translations from Latin, French, and Italian, and 'Partheneia Sacra,' 1632; died at Ghent. [xxv. 211]

HAWKINS, JAMES, the elder (1662-1729), organist; Mus. Bac. St. John's College, Cambridge, 1719; organist of Ely Cathedral, 1682-1729; arranged Ely MS. choir-books, of which vol. vii. contains music by himself. [xxv. 212]

HAWKINS, JAMES, the younger (fl. 1714-1750), organist of Peterborough Cathedral, 1714-50; son of James Hawkins the elder [q. v.]   [xxv. 212]

HAWKINS or **HAWKYNS**, SIR JOHN (1532-1595), naval commander; second son of William Hawkyns [q. v.]; freeman of Plymouth, 1556; made voyages to the Canaries before 1561; in three ships fitted out with assistance of his father-in-law and Sir William Wynter [q. v.] sailed to Sierra Leone, kidnapped negroes, and exchanged them with Spaniards in San Domingo (Hispaniola) for hides and other commodities, 1562-3; in second voyage, 1564-5, having loan of the Jesus (queen's ship) and support of Pembroke and Leicester, forced his negroes on Spaniards at Rio de la Hacha, and relieved French colony in Florida: his third expedition, delayed by Spanish remonstrances with Elizabeth, left Plymouth, October 1567, with six ships (two queen's), took money from the Portuguese and negroes from Sierra Leone; brought some of the slaves to Vera Cruz; most of his ships destroyed and treasure seized in the harbour of San Juan de Lua by a Spanish fleet; forced by famine to land some of his men in Mexico; reached Vigo; arrived in England January 1569; pretended, with Burghley's connivance, to favour a Spanish invasion of England, thereby obtaining from Philip II the release of his captured sailors, 40,000l., and the patent of grandee of Spain; M.P., Plymouth, 1572; treasurer and comptroller of the navy; introduced many improvements in the construction of ships for the navy; member of council of war at Plymouth during fight with Armada, 1588; commanded rear squadron during fighting in Channel, 1588; knighted after action off Isle of Wight; commanded centre of Howard's division at Gravelines, 29 Nov. 1588; joint commander with Frobisher of squadron sent to Portuguese coast, 1590; while serving with Drake's expedition to West Indies died at sea off Porto Rico. He founded the hospital called after him at Chatham, 1592, where is a genuine portrait. [xxv. 212]

HAWKINS, JOHN (*fl.* 1635), translator; brother of Henry Hawkins [q. v.]; M.D. Padua; published 'Briefe Introduction to Syntax' (1631) and translations of Andreas de Soto's 'Ransome of Time' and an Italian 'Paraphrase upon the seaven Penitential Psalms,' 1635. [xxv. 219]

HAWKINS, SIR JOHN (1719-1789), author; claimed descent from Sir John Hawkins (1532-1595) [q. v.]; Middlesex magistrate; knighted, 1772; became known to Dr. Johnson through connection with 'Gentleman's Magazine'; member of the club at King's Head, Ivy Lane, and of famous club of 1763; drew up Johnson's will, 1784; published Johnson's 'Life and Works,' 1787-9; edited Walton's 'Compleat Angler,' 1760; his 'General History of Music' issued, 1776. [xxv. 220]

HAWKINS, JOHN (1758?-1841), author; F.R.S.; travelled in Greece and the east; contributed to Walpole's 'Memoirs of European and Asiatic Turkey,' 1818, and 'Travels in . . . the East.' [xxv. 221]

HAWKINS, JOHN SIDNEY (1758-1842), antiquary; son of Sir John Hawkins (1719-1789) [q. v.]; F.S.A.; edited Ruggle's 'Ignoramus,' 1787, and Rigaud's version of Da Vinci 'On Painting,' 1802; published work on Gothic architecture, 1813, 'Inquiry into . . . Greek and Latin Poetry,' 1817, and 'Inquiry into . . . Thorough Bass on a new plan' [1817]. [xxv. 221]

HAWKINS, MAJOR ROHDE (1820-1884), architect to the committee of council on education; third son of Edward Hawkins (1780-1867) [q. v.]; accompanied Sir Charles Fellows's expedition to Asia Minor, 1841. [xxv. 207]

HAWKINS, NICHOLAS (*d.* 1534), bishop-designate of Ely; of Eton and King's College, Cambridge; LL.D.; in youth imprisoned for Lutheranism; as archdeacon of Ely attended convocation of 1529; resident ambassador at imperial court, 1532; had interview with Clement VII at Bologna about Henry VIII's divorce from Catherine of Arragon, 1533; communicated to Charles V in Spain news of the divorce and Henry's private marriage with Anne Boleyn; bishop-designate of Ely, 1533; died at Balbase, Arragon. [xxv. 222]

HAWKINS or HAWKYNS, SIR RICHARD (1562?-1622), naval commander; son of Sir John Hawkins or Hawkyns (1532-1595) [q. v.]; captain of the Duck galliot in Drake's West Indian expedition, 1585-6; commanded the Swallow against Armada, 1588, and the Crane in his father's Portuguese expedition, 1590; left Plymouth in the Dainty on roving commission against Spaniards, 1593; put in at Santos in Brazil, October 1593; passed Straits of Magellan, plundered Valparaiso, and took prizes; had to surrender, severely wounded, in bay of San Mateo, 1594; taken to Lima and (1597) sent to Spain; imprisoned at

Seville and Madrid till 1602; knighted, 1603; M.P., Plymouth, 1604; vice-admiral of Devon, 1604; vice-admiral under Sir Robert Mansell [q. v.] in expedition against Algerine corsairs, 1620-1; published 'Observations in his Voiage into the South Sea, A.D. 1593,' 1622; died suddenly in the council chamber. [xxv. 223]

HAWKINS, SUSANNA (1787-1868), Scottish poet; daughter of a Dumfriesshire blacksmith; published and herself sold local and occasional verse, 1838-61. [xxv. 225]

HAWKINS, THOMAS (*d.* 1577). [See FISHER.]

HAWKINS, SIR THOMAS (*d.* 1640), translator; brother of John Hawkins (*fl.* 1635) [q. v.]; knighted, 1618; friend of Edmund Bolton [q. v.] and James Howell [q. v.]; published 'Odes and Epodes of Horace in Latin and English Verse,' 1625, and translations of Caussin's 'Holy Court,' 1626, and 'Christian Diurnal,' 1632, and other French works. [xxv. 226]

HAWKINS, THOMAS (1810-1889), geologist; F.G.S., 1831; his collection of Devon, Somerset, and Dorset fossils bought by the nation; published 'Memoirs of Ichthyosauri and Plesiosauri,' 1834, 'My Life and Works,' 1887, and poems. [xxv. 227]

HAWKINS or HAWKYNS, WILLIAM (*d.* 1554?), sea-captain; made voyages to Guinea and Brazil, 1528-30; twice mayor of Plymouth; M.P., Plymouth, 1539, 1547, 1553. [xxv. 227]

HAWKINS or HAWKYNS, WILLIAM (*d.* 1589), sea-captain and merchant; son of William Hawkins or Hawkyns (*d.* 1554?) [q. v.]; mayor of Plymouth, 1567, 1578, and 1587-8; partner with his brother, Sir John Hawkins (1532-1595) [q. v.] in ownership of privateers; with Sir Arthur Champernowne seized Spanish treasure at Plymouth, 1568; commanded West Indian expedition, 1582; fitted out ships against Armada. [xxv. 228]

HAWKINS or HAWKYNS, WILLIAM (*fl.* 1595), sea-captain and merchant; son of William Hawkins or Hawkyns (*d.* 1589) [q. v.]; served in Drake's voyage, 1577; lieutenant to Edward Fenton [q. v.] in his East Indian voyage, 1582; probably commander of the Advice on Irish coast, 1587, and of the Griffin against the Armada, 1588; not identical with the William Hawkyns who went to Surat and resided with Great Mogul. [xxv. 229]

HAWKINS, WILLIAM (*d.* 1637), poet; M.A. Christ's College, Cambridge, 1626; master of Hadleigh School; published 'Apollo Shroving,' 1627, 'Corolla Varia,' 1634, and Latin complimentary verses. [xxv. 230]

HAWKINS, WILLIAM (1673-1746), serjeant-at-law; M.A. St. John's College, Cambridge, 1693; member of the Inner Temple, 1700; serjeant-at-law, 1723; chief work, 'Treatise of Pleas of the Crown,' 1716. [xxv. 230]

HAWKINS, WILLIAM (1722-1801), author; son of William Hawkins (1673-1746) [q. v.]; fellow of Pembroke College, Oxford, 1742; M.A., 1744; professor of poetry, 1751-6; rector of Whitchurch, Dorset, 1764-1801; Bampton lecturer, 1787; published 'The Thimble,' 1743, 'Henry and Rosamond,' 1749, and 'The Siege of Aleppo,' and other plays; 'Poems,' 1781, and theological works; collected works issued, 1758. [xxv. 231]

HAWKSHAW, BENJAMIN (*d.* 1738), divine; B.A. St. John's College, Cambridge, 1691; B.A. Dublin, 1693; M.A., 1695; incumbent of St. Nicholas-within-the-Walls, Dublin; published 'Poems,' 1693, and 'Reasonableness of constant Communion with Church of England,' 1709. [xxv. 232]

HAWKSHAW, SIR JOHN (1811-1891), civil engineer; worked under Alexander Nimmo [q. v.], 1821; engaged in mining work in Venezuela, 1832-4; employed by Jesse Hartley [q. v.], 1834, engineer to Manchester and Leeds Railway, 1845; consulting engineer in London, 1850. His works include the railways at Cannon Street and Charing Cross, with bridges over Thames, East London Railway, Severn tunnel, 1887, and completion, with W. H. Barlow, of Clifton suspension bridge; reported favourably on site of proposed Suez canal, 1863; F.R.S., 1855; knighted, 1873; M.I.C.E., 1836, and president, 1862 and 1863; president of British Association, 1875; published professional papers. [Suppl. ii. 402]

HAWKSLEY, THOMAS (1807–1893), civil engineer ; architect and surveyor at Nottingham ; engineer to water companies supplying Nottingham, 1845–80 ; engineer-in-chief to water supply works at Liverpool, 1874–1885, and Sheffield, 1864–93 ; planned Thornton Park and Bradgate reservoirs, Leicester, and carried out numerous other waterworks ; M.I.C.E., 1840 ; president, 1872–3 ; president of Institution of Mechanical Engineers, 1876–7 ; F.R.S., 1878 ; published professional reports. [Suppl. ii. 404]

HAWKSMOOR, NICHOLAS (1661–1736), architect ; employed by Wren as deputy-surveyor at Chelsea Hospital, 1682–90 ; clerk of the works at Greenwich Hospital, 1698, Kensington Palace, 1691–1715, and at Whitehall, St. James's, and Westminster, 1715–18 ; secretary to board of works and deputy-surveyor ; assisted Wren at St. Paul's, 1678–1710, and Vanbrugh at Castle Howard, 1702–14, and Blenheim, 1710–15 ; erected library, 1700–14, and south quadrangle, 1710–59, of Queen's College, Oxford, and part of north quadrangle (including towers) of All Souls, c. 1730 ; directed repairs at Beverley Minster, 1713 ; joint-surveyor of Queen Anne's new churches, 1716 ; designed numerous London churches ; surveyor-general of Westminster Abbey, 1723 ; published ' Short Historical Account of London Bridge,' 1736, with plates. [xxv. 232]

HAWKWOOD, SIR JOHN DE (d. 1394), general ; Froissart's 'Haccoude' ; said to have served under Edward III ; with troop of free lances stormed Pau, 1359 ; with Bernard de la Salle levied contributions from Innocent VII, 1360 ; shared in English victory of Brignais, 1362 ; took service with Monferrato against Milan, his troops becoming known as the White Company ; held to ransom the Count of Savoy ; defeated Visconti's Hungarian mercenaries, 1363 ; served unsuccessfully Pisa against Florence, 1363–4, and assisted Agnello to make himself doge of Pisa, 1364 ; with company of St. George ravaged country between Genoa and Siena, 1365–6, pillaged the Perugino ; escorted Agnello to meet the Pope at Viterbo, 1367 ; took service with Milan, 1368 ; captured by the pope's mercenaries at Arezzo, but ransomed by Pisa, 1369 ; defeated at Rubiera the army of Monferrato, 1372 ; won a great victory for Pope Gregory XI over Gian Galeazzo Visconti at Gavardo, 1374 ; levied contributions on Florence, Pisa, Siena, Lucca, and Arezzo, 1375 ; received pension from Florence, 1375 ; obtained Cotignola and other places in Romagna in default of papal pay, but joined anti-papal league, 1377, marrying a natural daughter of Bernabò Visconti ; with Count Landau forced Verona to pay tribute to Milan, 1378 ; defeated by Stephen Laczsk, and proscribed by Visconti ; generally served Florence from 1380, but won the victory of Castagnaro against Verona for Padua, 1386 ; joint-ambassador for England at Rome, 1382, and at Florence and Naples, 1385 ; as commander-in-chief at Florence carried on successful war against Milan, 1390–92 ; died at Florence and was buried in the Duomo. At the request of Richard II leave was given his widow to transfer his body to England ; it was probably buried at Hedingham Sibil. [xxv. 236]

HAWLES, SIR JOHN (1645–1716), whig lawyer ; educated at Winchester and Queen's College, Oxford ; barrister, Lincoln's Inn ; M.P., Old Sarum, 1689, Wilton, 1695, and 1702–5, St. Michael, 1698, Truro, 1700, St. Ives, 1702, Stockbridge, 1705–10 ; knighted, 1695 ; solicitor-general, 1695–1702 ; a manager of the Sacheverell impeachment, 1710 ; published ' Remarks ' on contemporary state trials, 1689, and other works. [xxv. 242]

HAWLEY, FREDERICK (1827–1889), Shakespearean scholar ; as Frederick Haywell appeared with Wallack at Théâtre aux Italiens, Paris, with Phelps at Sadler's Wells, and with Charles Calvert at Manchester ; produced two plays at the Gaiety ; as librarian at Stratford-on-Avon, 1886–9, completed (1889) catalogue of editions in all languages of Shakespeare's plays. [xxv. 243]

HAWLEY, HENRY or HENRY C. (1679 ?–1759), lieutenant-general ; served with the (present) 4th hussars, 1706–17 ; present at Almanza, 1707 ; wounded at Dunblane, 1715, when lieutenant-colonel ; colonel of 33rd foot, 1717, of 13th dragoons, 1730 ; lieutenant-general, 1744 ; present at Dettingen, 1743, and Fontenoy, 1745 ; when commander-in-chief in Scotland defeated at Falkirk, 1746 ; commanded cavalry at Culloden, 1746,

and in Flanders ; governor of Portsmouth, 1752 ; a severe disciplinarian, known as the ' chief-justice.' [xxv. 243]

HAWLEY, SIR JOSEPH HENRY, third baronet (1813–1875), patron of the turf ; succeeded as baronet, 1831 ; lieutenant, 9th lancers, 1833 ; left army, 1834 ; raced in partnership with J. M. Stanley in Italy and England ; won the Oaks, 1847 ; cleared about 43,000l. by his win (with Beadsman) of the Derby, 1858 ; again won the Derby, 1859 and 1868, and the St. Leger, 1869 ; advocated turf reform, 1870. [xxv. 245]

HAWLEY, THOMAS (d. 1557), Clarenceux king-of-arms ; last Roseblanche pursuivant ; as Rougecroix negotiated with Scots before Flodden ; when Carlisle herald accompanied Henry VIII to Ardres, 1520 ; Norroy, 1534 ; Clarenceux king-of-arms, 1536–57 ; employed to treat with northern rebels, 1536 ; accompanied Northumberland to Cambridge, 1553 ; induced Sir Thomas Wyatt to submit, 1554 ; made visitations of Kent, Surrey, Hampshire, and Essex (printed, 1878). [xxv. 245]

HAWORTH, ADRIAN HARDY (1767–1833), entomologist and botanist ; F.L.S., 1798 ; founded Aurelian Society and Entomological Society of London, 1806 ; made large collection of *lepidoptera* ; sub-division of aloe named after him ; published works, including ' Lepidoptera Britannica ' (pt. i. 1803, pt. ii. c. 1810, pt. iii. 1812), and ' Synopsis Plantarum Succulentarum,' 1812. [xxv. 246]

HAWORTH, SAMUEL (fl. 1683), empiric ; M.D. Paris ; author of ' True Method of curing Consumptions,' 1682. [xxv. 247]

HAWTREY, EDWARD CRAVEN (1789–1862), provost of Eton ; educated at Eton ; scholar (1807) and fellow (1810) of King's College, Cambridge ; B.A. ; as assistant-master at Eton under Keate, 1814–34, encouraged early efforts of Praed, Cornewall Lewis, and Arthur Hallam ; as head-master of Eton, 1834–52, nearly doubled the numbers in twelve years, opened new buildings for foundationers (1846) and the sanatorium, suppressed ' montem ' (1847), introduced principle of competition for king's scholars, founded English essay prize ; provost, 1852–62 ; last person buried in college chapel. He printed translations into Italian, German, and Greek verse, 1839, and translations from Homer into English hexameters, 1843 ; edited Goethe's lyrics, 1833 and 1834. [xxv. 247]

HAXEY, THOMAS (d. 1425), treasurer of York minster ; prebendary of Lichfield, 1391, Lincoln, 1395, and Salisbury ; attended parliament of 1397 (according to Hallam as a member) and brought forward an article in bill of complaints directed against non-residence of bishops and a tax on clergy ; tried and condemned to death, but claimed as a clergyman and pardoned, 1397 ; prebendary of York, 1405, of Southwell, 1405 ; treasurer of York minster, 1418–25. [xxv. 249]

HAY, ALEXANDER, LORD EASTER KENNET (d. 1594), Scottish judge ; clerk to Scots privy council, 1564 ; clerk-register and senator of College of Justice, 1579. [xxv. 250]

HAY, ALEXANDER, LORD NEWTON (d. 1616), clerk-register, 1612 ; son of Alexander Hay (d. 1594) [q. v.] ; author of ' Manuscript Notes of Transactions of King James VI written for use of King Charles.' [xxv. 250]

HAY, ALEXANDER (d. 1807 ?), topographer ; M.A. of a Scottish university ; chaplain of St. Mary's Chapel, Chichester ; vicar of Wisborough Green ; published ' History of Chichester,' 1804. [xxv. 250]

HAY, ALEXANDER LEITH (1758–1838), general ; assumed name of Hay, 1789 ; raised regiment called by his name, 1789 ; general, 1813. [xxv. 251]

HAY, ANDREW (1762–1814), major-general ; raised Banffshire fencible infantry, 1798 ; lieutenant-colonel, 3rd battalion 1st royals at Coruña ; commanded a brigade at Walcheren, 1809, and in Peninsula ; major-general, 1811 ; mortally wounded before Bayonne. [xxv. 251]

HAY, SIR ANDREW LEITH (1785–1862), soldier and author ; son of Alexander Leith Hay [q. v.] ; served in Peninsula, 1808–14, as aide-de-camp to Sir James Leith (his uncle) ; M.P., Elgin, 1832–8 and 1841–7 ; clerk of the ordnance, 1834 ; K.H., 1834 ; published ' Narrative of the Peninsular War,' 1831, and ' Castellated Architecture of Aberdeenshire,' 1849. [xxv. 251]

HAY, ARCHIBALD (*fl.* 1543), Scottish monk of Paris and Latin writer.   [xxv. 252]

HAY, ARTHUR, ninth MARQUIS OF TWEEDDALE (1824–1878), soldier and naturalist; son of George Hay, eighth marquis of Tweeddale [q. v.]; entered grenadier guards, 1841; aide-de-camp to Hardinge in Sutlej campaign, 1845; travelled in Europe and the Himalayas; served in Crimea; colonel, 1866; Viscount Walden, 1862–1876; marquis, 1876; president of Zoological Society; F.R.S.; F.L.S.; his papers on natural history collected, 1881.   [xxv. 252]

HAY, LORD CHARLES (*d.* 1760), major-general; brother of John Hay, fourth marquis of Tweeddale [q. v.]; present at siege of Gibraltar, 1727; volunteer with Prince Eugene on the Rhine, 1734; M.P., Haddingtonshire, 1741; distinguished himself with first foot guards at Fontenoy, 1745, and was severely wounded; major-general, 1757; court-martialled for reflections on conduct of Lord Loudoun in Nova Scotia.   [xxv. 253]

HAY, DAVID RAMSAY (1798–1866), decorative artist and author; employed by Scott at Abbotsford; decorated hall of Society of Arts, *c.* 1846; 'Ninety Club' founded by his pupils; published, among other works, 'Laws of Harmonious Colouring adapted to House Painting,' 1828, and 'Natural Principles of Beauty as developed in the Human Figure,' 1852, &c.   [xxv. 253]

HAY, EDMUND (*d.* 1591), Scottish jesuit; accompanied secret embassy from Pius IV to Mary Queen of Scots, 1562; first rector of Pont-à-Mousson, and provincial of French jesuits; assistant for Germany and France to Aquaviva, general of the jesuits. [xxv. 255]

HAY, EDWARD (1761 ?–1826), Irish writer; active in the cause of catholic emancipation; tried for treason but acquitted, 1798; published 'History of the Insurrection of County of Wexford, 1798,' 1803.   [xxv. 255]

HAY, FRANCIS, ninth EARL OF ERROL (*d.* 1631), succeeded to earldom, 1585; joined Huntly [see GORDON, GEORGE, 1562–1636] in schemes for re-establishing Romanism in Scotland; his letter to Duke of Parma intercepted in England and forwarded to James VI, 1589; joined in rebellion of Huntly and Crawford, and did not submit till king's second visit (1589) to the north; imprisoned on suspicion of complicity with Bothwell, 1591; again in rebellion after 'Spanish Blanks' affair, 1592; excommunicated, outlawed, and exiled, 1593; defeated king's troops, but was severely wounded, 1594; his castle at Slains destroyed by the king, 1594; persuaded by Lennox to leave Scotland, 1594; detained at Middelburg; returned secretly, 1596; restored and absolved on abjuring popery, 1597; commissioner for union with England, 1602; excommunicated and imprisoned at Dumbarton, 1608; absolved, 1617.   [xxv. 255]

HAY, GEORGE (*d.* 1588), controversialist; minister of Eddlestone and Rathven; preached with Knox in Ayrshire, 1562; disputed with abbot of Crossraguel, 1562; moderator of the assembly, 1571; published work against the jesuit Tyrie, 1576; deputy to council at Magdeburg, 1577.   [xxv. 258]

HAY, SIR GEORGE, first EARL OF KINNOULL (1572–1634), lord chancellor of Scotland; gentleman of the bedchamber, 1596; knighted, *c.* 1609; clerk-register and a lord of session, 1616; supported five articles of Perth; lord high chancellor of Scotland, 1622–34; created Viscount Dupplin, 1627, Earl of Kinnoull, 1633; resisted king's regulations for lords of session (1626), and upheld precedency over archbishop of St. Andrews. [xxv. 259]

HAY, GEORGE, seventh EARL OF KINNOULL (*d.* 1758), as Viscount Dupplin M.P., Fowey, 1710; created peer of United Kingdom, 1711; succeeded as earl, 1719; suspected of Jacobitism, 1715 and 1722; British ambassador at Constantinople, 1729–37; maintained right of presentation to parish of Madderty in ecclesiastical courts, 1739–40.   [xxv. 260]

HAY, SIR GEORGE (1715–1778), lawyer and politician; of Merchant Taylors' School and St. John's College, Oxford; D.C.L., 1742; chancellor of Worcester, 1751–64; dean of arches, judge of prerogative court of Canterbury, and chancellor of diocese of London, 1764–78; vicar-general of Canterbury and king's advocate, 1755–64; M.P., Stockbridge, 1754, Calne, 1757, Sandwich, 1761,

Newcastle-under-Lyme, 1768; a lord of the admiralty, 1756–65; judge of admiralty court, 1773–8; knighted, 1773; intimate with Hogarth and Garrick. [xxv. 260]

HAY, GEORGE (1729–1811), Roman catholic bishop of Daulis and vicar-apostolic of the lowland district of Scotland; imprisoned for Jacobitism, 1746–7; became a Romanist, 1748; entered Scots College at Rome, 1751; despatched with John Geddes [q. v.] on Scottish mission, 1759; bishop of Daulis *in partibus* and coadjutor to Bishop James Grant [q. v.], 1769; vicar-apostolic of lowland district, 1778; his furniture and library burnt in protestant riots at Edinburgh, 1779; went to Rome to get plan for reorganising Scots College sanctioned, 1781; had charge of Scalan seminary, 1788–93, and founded that of Aquhorties, whither he retired, 1802; published theological works, edited by Bishop Strain, 1871–3.   [xxv. 261]

HAY, GEORGE, eighth MARQUIS OF TWEEDDALE (1787–1876), field-marshal; succeeded to title, 1804; served in Sicily, 1806, the Peninsula, 1807–13, and America, 1813; wounded at Busaco, 1810, and Vittoria, 1813, also at Niagara, 1813, where he was captured; governor of Madras and commander of troops, 1842–8; general, 1854; field-marshal, 1875; K.T., 1820; G.C.B., 1867; representative peer of Scotland and lord-lieutenant of Haddingtonshire; agricultural reformer and president of Highland Society.   [xxv. 263]

HAY, SIR GILBERT (*fl.* 1456), poet and translator; knighted; sometime chamberlain to Charles VII of France; afterwards resided with Earl of Caithness, and translated from French Bonnet's 'Buke of Battailes,' also 'The Buke of the Order of Knyghthood'; translated the spurious Aristotelian 'Secretum Secretorum' as 'Buke of the Governaunce of Princes'; rendered into Scottish verse 'Buke of the Conqueror Alexaunder the Great.'   [xxv. 264]

HAY, JAMES, first EARL OF CARLISLE, first VISCOUNT DONCASTER, and first BARON HAY (*d.* 1636), courtier; came from Scotland to England with James I; knighted, and became gentleman of the bedchamber; received numerous grants of land, and (1607) the hand of an heiress; K.B., 1610; master of the wardrobe, 1613; created baron for life, though without a seat in the Lords, 1606, Baron Hay, 1615, Viscount Doncaster, 1618, and Earl of Carlisle, 1622; married Lucy Percy [see HAY, LUCY, COUNTESS OF CARLISLE], 1617; sent on missions to Heidelberg and the imperial court, 1619–20; recommended war on behalf of king of Bohemia; envoy to Paris, 1623, to Lorraine and Piedmont, 1628; advised rejection of Richelieu's terms for marriage of Henrietta Maria; advocated war with Spain, 1624, and support of Huguenots, 1628; celebrated for splendid hospitality.   [xxv. 265]

HAY, JOHN (1546–1607), Scottish jesuit; disputed with protestants at Strasburg, 1579; ordered to leave Scotland, 1579; professor of theology and dean of arts at Tournon, 1581; rector of college at Pont-à-Mousson; published 'Certaine Demandes concerning the Christian Religion and Discipline, proposed to the Ministers of the new pretended Kirk of Scotlande,' 1580, also 'De Rebus Japonicis, Indicis et Peruvianis Epistolæ recentiores,' 1605; edited Sisto da Siena's 'Bibliotheca Sancta,' 1591.   [xxv. 267]

HAY, SIR JOHN, LORD BARRA (*d.* 1654), Scottish judge; town-clerk of Edinburgh; lord clerk register, 1633; ordinary lord of session, 1634; as provost of Edinburgh, 1637, tried to present petitions against new prayerbook; obliged to take refuge in England; imprisoned on his return, 1641; tried by a parliamentary committee, 1642; captured at Philiphaugh; his life saved by intervention of Lanark, 1645.   [xxv. 268]

HAY, JOHN, second EARL and first MARQUIS OF TWEEDDALE (1626–1697), lord chancellor of Scotland; joined Charles I at Nottingham, 1642, but fought for parliament at Marston Moor, 1644, on account of his attitude towards covenanters; held command in army of 'the engagement' party, 1648; succeeded as second Earl of Tweeddale, 1654; imprisoned for support of James Guthrie [q. v.], 1660; president of the council, 1663; extraordinary lord of session, 1664; used influence as church commissioner to moderate proceedings against covenanters; dismissed from office and privy council by advice of Lauderdale, 1674; readmitted to treasury, 1680, and the council 1682; chancellor of Scotland 1692–6;

supported revolution in Scotland; created Marquis of Tweeddale, 1694; as high commissioner ordered inquiry into Glencoe massacre, 1695; dismissed from chancellorship for supporting Darien scheme, 1696. [xxv. 268]

HAY, LORD JOHN (d. 1706), brigadier-general; second son of John Hay, second marquis of Tweeddale [q. v.]; commanded Scots dragoons (Scots Greys) under Marlborough; died of fever at Courtrai. [xxv. 270]

HAY, JOHN, second MARQUIS OF TWEEDDALE (1645–1713), eldest son of John Hay, first marquis of Tweeddale [q. v.]; created privy councillor, 1689; succeeded to title, 1697; high commissioner to Scottish parliament, 1704; lord chancellor, 1704–5; led *squadrone volante*, but ultimately supported the union; representative peer, 1707. [xxv. 270]

HAY, JOHN, titular EARL OF INVERNESS (1691–1740), Jacobite; brother of George Hay, seventh earl of Kinnoull [q. v.]; employed by his brother-in-law Mar in preparing Jacobite outbreak of 1715; made governor of Perth; went to France to urge the Chevalier James Edward's immediate sailing, 1715; master of the horse to the Chevalier James Edward; joined St. Germains court; revealed Mar's perfidy, and succeeded him as secretary, 1724 (removed, 1727); created Earl of Inverness, 1725. [xxv. 270]

HAY, JOHN, fourth MARQUIS OF TWEEDDALE (d. 1762), succeeded to title, 1715; extraordinary lord of session, 1721; representative peer, 1722; secretary of state for Scotland, 1742–6; lord justice-general, 1761. [xxv. 271]

HAY, LORD JOHN (1793–1851), rear-admiral; lost his left arm in Hyères Roads, 1807; commanded squadron on north coast of Spain during civil war; C.B., 1837; rear-admiral, 1851; M.P., Haddington, 1826–30, Windsor, 1847; a lord of the admiralty, 1847–50. [xxv. 272]

HAY, SIR JOHN (1816–1892), Australian statesman; M.A. University and King's College, Aberdeen, 1834; emigrated to New South Wales, 1838; member of legislative assembly for Murrumbidgee, 1856; secretary of lands and public works, 1856–7; member for Murray division, 1858–64, and Central Cumberland, 1864–7; speaker of legislative assembly, 1862–5; member of legislative council, 1867, and president, 1873–92; K.C.M.G., 1878. [Suppl. ii. 406]

HAY, SIR JOHN HAY DRUMMOND- (1816–1893). [See DRUMMOND-HAY.]

HAY, LUCY, COUNTESS OF CARLISLE (1599–1660), beauty and wit; daughter of Henry Percy, ninth Earl of Northumberland [q. v.]; married James Hay, first earl of Carlisle [q. v.], 1617; praised and addressed by Carew, Herrick, Suckling, Waller, and D'Avenant; exercised great influence over Queen Henrietta Maria, and was intimate with Strafford and Pym; revealed intended arrest of the five members; during civil wars acted with presbyterians; active in support of Holland's preparations for second civil war; intermediary between Scottish and English leaders; imprisoned in the Tower, 1649–50. [xxv. 272]

HAY, MARY CECIL (1840?–1886), novelist; her works (published, 1873–86) highly popular, especially in America and Australia; the best known being 'Old Myddelton's Money,' 1874. [xxv. 274]

HAY, RICHARD AUGUSTINE (1661–1736?), Scottish antiquary; grandson of Sir John Hay [q. v.] of Barra; canon regular of Sainte-Geneviève's, Paris, 1678; attempted to establish the order in Great Britain; compelled to leave the kingdom, 1689; prior of Bernicourt, 1694, of St.-Pierremont-en-Argonne, 1695; published 'Origine of Royal Family of the Stewarts,' 1722, 'Genealogie of the Hayes of Tweeddale, including Memoirs of his own Times,' privately printed, 1835, and other works; died in Scotland. [xxv. 274]

HAY, ROBERT (1799–1863), of Linplum, egyptologist; leading member of Egyptian expedition, 1826–38; published 'Illustrations of Cairo,' 1840; presented drawings and antiquities to British Museum. [xxv. 275]

HAY, THOMAS, eighth EARL OF KINNOULL (1710–1787), statesman; eldest son of George Hay, seventh earl of Kinnoull [q. v.]; as Viscount Dupplin M.P., Cambridge, 1741–58; commissioner of Irish revenue, 1741; a lord of trade, 1746, of the treasury, 1754; joint-paymaster, 1755; chancellor of the duchy of Lancaster, 1758; privy councillor, 1758; succeeded to earldom, 1758; ambassador extraordinary to Portugal, 1759; chancellor of St. Andrews, 1765. [xxv. 275]

HAY, WILLIAM, fifth BARON YESTER (d. 1576), succeeded as baron, 1559; subscribed 'Book of Discipline,' 1561, but commanded the van in raid against Moray, 1565; joined Mary and Bothwell on their flight to Dunbar; signed the band for Mary's deliverance from Lochleven; fought for Mary at Langside, 1568; after 1572 joined 'king's party.' [xxv. 276]

HAY, WILLIAM (1695–1755), author; of Glyndebourne, Sussex; matriculated at Christ Church, Oxford, 1712; barrister, Middle Temple, 1723; M.P., Seaford, 1734–55; commissioner for victualling the navy, 1738; introduced measures for poor relief; keeper of Tower records, 1753. His collected works (1794) include 'Essay on Civil Government,' 'Religio Philosophi' (reprinted 1831), and a translation of Martial. [xxv. 277]

HAYA, SIR GILBERT DE (d. 1330), lord high constable of Scotland, and ancestor of the earls of Errol; at first faithful to Edward I; joined Bruce in 1306, and was granted Slains, c. 1309, and the hereditary constableship, 1309; his funeral inscription and effigy recently discovered at Cupar. [xxv. 278]

HAYDAY, JAMES (1796–1872), bookbinder; introduced Turkey morocco. [xxv. 278]

HAYDEN, GEORGE (*fl.* 1723), musical composer. [xxv. 279]

HAYDN, JOSEPH (d. 1856), compiler of 'Dictionary of Dates' (1841) and 'Book of Dignities' (1851); received government pension, 1856. [xxv. 279]

HAYDOCK, GEORGE LEO (1774–1849), biblical scholar; of Douay and Crook Hall, Durham; interdicted from saying mass at Westby Hall, 1831; restored, 1839; editor of the Douay Bible and Rheims Testament, 1812–1814. [xxv. 279]

HAYDOCK or **HADDOCK**, RICHARD (1552?–1605), Roman catholic divine; assisted in foundation of English college at Rome, whither he returned as *maestro di camera* to Cardinal Allen, 1590; friend of Parsons; dean of Dublin; died at Rome; his 'Account of Revolution in English College at Rome' printed in Dodd's 'Church History.' [xxv. 280]

HAYDOCK, RICHARD (*fl.* 1605), physician; of Winchester and New College, Oxford; fellow, 1590; M.A., 1595; M.B., 1601; practised at Salisbury; translated from Jo. Paul Lomatius 'Tracte containing the Artes of Curious Paintinge, Carvinge, and Buildinge,' 1598. [xxv. 281]

HAYDOCK, ROGER (1644–1696), quaker; imprisoned and fined for preaching in Lancashire, 1667; disputed at Arley Hall with John Cheyney [q. v.], 1677; visited Scotland, Ireland, 1680, and Holland, 1681, and subsequently obtained protection for quakers in Isle of Man; collected writings edited by J. Field, 1700 (posthumous). [xxv. 281]

HAYDOCK, THOMAS (1772–1859), printer and publisher; brother of George Leo Haydock [q. v.] [xxv. 282]

HAYDOCK, WILLIAM (d. 1537), Cistercian, of Whalley; executed for participation in Pilgrimage of Grace; his body found at Cottam Hall early in nineteenth century. [xxv. 282]

HAYDON. [See also HEYDON.]

HAYDON, BENJAMIN ROBERT (1786–1846), historical painter; came to London, 1804; attended Academy schools and Charles Bell's lectures on anatomy; his first picture, 'Joseph and Mary,' well hung at the Academy, 1806; visited, with Wilkie, the Elgin marbles in Park Lane, and drew studies from them for his 'Dentatus'; offended by position of 'Dentatus' in Academy exhibition of 1809; awarded premium for it by British Gallery, 1810; attacked Payne Knight and the Academy in 'Examiner,' 1812; created sensation with 'Judgment of Solomon' (Water-colour Society), 1814; did much by his letters on the Elgin marbles (1815) towards determining the national purchase; his 'Christ's Entry into Jerusalem' exhibited at Egyptian Hall, 1820, and in Edinburgh and Glasgow; 'Lazarus' (National Gallery) finished 1822; imprisoned for debt in King's Bench, 1822–3, and again three times before 1837; his scheme for government school of design accepted, 1835 ; compelled introduction of models by starting rival school at Savile House ; began lectures on art in northern towns, 1839 ; committed suicide after failure of exhibition of 'Aristides' and 'Nero.' His later pictures include 'Punch,' 'Meeting of Anti-Slavery Society,' and 'Wellington musing at Waterloo.' Wordsworth and Keats addressed sonnets to him. Among his pupils were Eastlake, the Landseers, Lance, and Bewick. He published works on historical painting in England, 1829, the pernicious effect of academies on art, 1839, the relative value of oil and fresco (in connection with decoration of houses of parliament), 1842, and 'Lectures on Painting and Design,' 1844–6, and left part of an autobiography. [xxv. 283]

HAYDON, FRANK SCOTT (1822–1887), editor of 'Eulogium Historiarum' (1868) ; eldest son of Benjamin Robert Haydon [q. v.] ; committed suicide. [xxv. 287]

HAYDON, FREDERICK WORDSWORTH (1827–1886), inspector of factories (dismissed, 1867) ; son of Benjamin Robert Haydon [q. v.] ; published 'Correspondence and Table-Talk' of his father, 1876 ; died at Bethlehem Hospital. [xxv. 287]

HAYES, MRS. CATHERINE (1690–1726), murderess : executed for murder of her husband in Tyburn (Oxford Street) ; convicted of petty treason and sentenced to be burned alive. [xxv. 288]

HAYES, CATHERINE, afterwards MRS. BUSHNELL (1825–1861), vocalist : first sang at Sapio's concert, Dublin, 1839 ; studied under Garcia at Paris and Ronconi at Milan ; sang at La Scala, Milan, at Vienna, and Venice ; made her *début* at Covent Garden in 'Linda di Chamouni,' 1849 ; sang in New York, California, South America, Australia, India, and the Sandwich islands, 1851–6 ; at Jullien's concerts, 1857. [xxv. 288]

HAYES, CHARLES (1678–1760), mathematician and chronologist : sub-governor of Royal African Company till 1752 ; published 'Treatise on Fluxions,' 1704, 'Dissertation on Chronology of the Septuagint,' 1751, and similar works. [xxv. 289]

HAYES, EDMUND (1804–1867), Irish judge ; B.A. Trinity College, Dublin, 1825 ; LL.D., 1832 ; Irish barrister, 1827 ; Q.C., 1852 ; law adviser to Lord Derby's first and second administrations ; judge of queen's bench in Ireland, 1859–66 ; published treatise on Irish criminal law (2nd edit. 1843) and reports of exchequer cases. [xxv. 290]

HAYES, SIR GEORGE (1805–1869), justice of the queen's bench ; barrister, Middle Temple, 1830 ; serjeant-at-law, 1856 ; recorder of Leicester, 1861 ; leader of Midland circuit ; justice of the queen's bench, 1868 ; knighted, 1868 ; author of humorous elegy and song on the 'Dog and the Cock.' [xxv. 290]

HAYES, JOHN (1775–1838), rear-admiral ; commanded the Alfred at Coruña, 1809, Achille in Walcheren expedition, 1809, and Freya frigate at reduction of Guadeloupe, 1810 ; called 'Magnificent Hayes' from his handling of the Magnificent in Basque Roads, 1812 ; C.B., 1815 ; rear-admiral, 1837. [xxv. 290]

HAYES, JOHN (1786 ?–1866), portrait-painter ; exhibited at Royal Academy, 1814–51. [xxv. 291]

HAYES, SIR JOHN MACNAMARA, first baronet (1750 ?–1809), physician ; M.D. Rheims, 1784 ; army surgeon in North America and West Indies ; L.R.C.P., 1786 ; physician extraordinary to Prince of Wales, 1791 ; physician to Westminster Hospital, 1792–4 ; created baronet, 1797 ; inspector-general at Woolwich. [xxv. 291]

HAYES, MICHAEL ANGELO (1820–1877), painter : secretary to Royal Hibernian Academy, 1856 ; marshal of Dublin ; exhibited with new Water-colour Society, London ; painted military and equestrian pictures ; accidentally drowned in a tank. [xxv. 292]

HAYES, PHILIP (1738–1797), professor of music at Oxford ; son of William Hayes the elder [q. v.] ; Mus. Bac. Magdalen College, Oxford, 1763 ; member of Royal Society of Musicians, 1769 ; professor of music, Oxford, 1777–97 ; Mus. Doc. and organist of Magdalen, 1777, of St. John's, 1790 ; composed six concertos, eight anthems,

songs, glees, an oratorio, and odes ; edited and continued Jenkin Lewis's memoirs of Prince William Henry, Duke of Gloucester, 1789, and 'Harmonia Wiccamica' (1780). [xxv. 292]

HAYES, WILLIAM, the elder (1706–1777), professor of music at Oxford ; organist at Worcester Cathedral, 1731, and Magdalen College, Oxford, 1734 ; professor of music, Oxford, 1742–77 ; created Mus. Doc., 1749 ; conducted Gloucester festival, 1763 ; defended Handel against Avison ; set Collins's 'Ode on the Passions' ; composed popular glees and canons. [xxv. 293]

HAYES, WILLIAM, the younger (1742–1790), musical writer ; third son of William Hayes the elder [q. v.] ; B.A. Magdalen Hall, Oxford, 1761 ; M.A. New College, 1764 ; minor canon of Worcester, 1765, of St. Paul's, 1766 ; musical contributor to 'Gentleman's Magazine,' 1765. [xxv. 293]

HAYES, WILLIAM (*fl.* 1794), ornithologist. [xxv. 293]

HAYGARTH, JOHN (1740–1827), physician ; F.R.S. ; M.B. St. John's College, Cambridge, 1766 ; as physician to Chester Infirmary, 1767–98, first carried out treatment of fever by isolation, 1783 ; afterwards practised at Bath ; published 'Plan to Exterminate Small-pox and introduce General Inoculation,' 1793, and other medical works ; his plan for self-supporting savings banks adopted at Bath, 1813. [xxv. 294]

HAYLEY, ROBERT (*d.* 1770 ?), Irish artist in black and white chalk. [xxv. 295]

HAYLEY, THOMAS ALFONSO (1780–1800), sculptor ; natural son of William Hayley [q. v.] ; modelled busts of Flaxman (his master) and Thurlow, and a medallion of Romney. [xxv. 295]

HAYLEY, WILLIAM (1745–1820), poet ; of Eton and Trinity Hall, Cambridge, and the Middle Temple ; friend of Cowper, Romney, and Southey ; published successful volumes of verse ; his 'Triumphs of Temper,' 1781, and 'Triumphs of Music,' 1804, ridiculed in 'English Bards and Scotch Reviewers' ; his 'Ballads founded on Anecdotes of Animals' (1805) illustrated by Blake ; published also lives of Milton, 1794, Cowper, 1803, and Romney, 1809 ; his 'Memoirs' (1823) edited by Dr. John Johnson (*d.* 1833) [q. v.] [xxv. 295]

HAYLS or HALES, JOHN (*d.* 1679), portrait-painter and miniaturist ; rival of Lely and S. Cooper [q. v.] ; painted portraits of Pepys and Pepys's wife and father. [xxv. 296]

HAYMAN, FRANCIS (1708–1776), painter ; designed illustrations for Hanmer's 'Shakespeare,' 1744–6, and Smollett's 'Don Quixote' ; best known for ornamental paintings at Vauxhall ; chairman of committee of exhibition of works by living British painters, 1760 ; president of Society of British Artists, 1766 ; an original academician, 1768, and librarian, 1771–6 ; friend of Hogarth and Garrick. [xxv. 296]

HAYMAN, ROBERT (*d.* 1631 ?), epigrammatist ; B.A. Exeter College, Oxford ; governor of Newfoundland, *c.* 1625 ; published volume of ancient and modern epigrams, 1628 ; died abroad. [xxv. 297]

HAYMAN, SAMUEL (1818–1886), antiquarian writer ; B.A. Trinity College, Dublin, 1839 ; rector of Carrigaline and Douglas, 1872–86 ; canon of Cork ; assisted Sir Bernard Burke in genealogical works ; edited 'Unpublished Geraldine Documents,' 1870–81 ; published works dealing with Youghal. [xxv. 298]

HAYMO or HAIMO (*d.* 1054), archdeacon of Canterbury ; often confused with Haymo, bishop of Halberstadt. [xxv. 298]

HAYMO OF FAVERSHAM (*d.* 1244), fourth general of the Franciscans ; one of the first Franciscans to come to England ; envoy of Gregory IX for union with Greek church, 1233 ; general of Franciscans, 1240 ; called 'Speculum honestatis' ; edited 'Breviarium Romanum' ; died at Anagnia. [xxv. 299]

HAYNE, THOMAS (1582–1645), schoolmaster : M.A. Lincoln College, Oxford, 1612 ; master at Merchant Taylors' School (1605–8) and Christ's Hospital, 1608 ; benefactor of Lincoln College, Oxford, and Thrussington, Leicestershire ; published theological works. [xxv. 299]

HAYNE or **HAYNES**, WILLIAM (*d.* 1631 ?), schoolmaster ; M.A. Christ's College, Cambridge ; head-master of Merchant Taylors' School, 1599-1624 ; published grammatical treatises. [xxv. 300]

HAYNES. [See also HAINES.]

HAYNES, HOPTON (1672 ?-1749), unitarian writer ; intimate with Newton at the mint ; his posthumous 'Scripture Account of . . . God and . . . Christ' first edited by John Blackburn, 1750. [xxv. 301]

HAYNES, JOHN (*d.* 1654), New England statesman ; sailed in the Griffin for Boston with Cotton ; governor of Massachusetts, 1635-6 ; first governor of Connecticut, 1639, re-elected, 1641 and 1643 ; promoted confederation of the four colonies, 1643. [xxv. 301]

HAYNES, JOHN (*fl.* 1730-1750), draughtsman and engraver. [xxv. 302]

HAYNES, JOSEPH (*d.* 1701). [See HAINES.]

HAYNES, JOSEPH (1760-1829), etcher and engraver. [xxv. 302]

HAYNES, SAMUEL (*d.* 1752), historical writer ; son of Hopton Haynes [q. v.] ; M.A. King's College, Cambridge, 1727, D.D., 1748 ; rector of Hatfield, 1737-52, Clothall, 1747-52 ; canon of Windsor, 1743 ; edited Hatfield State Papers (1542-70). [xxv. 302]

HAYNESWORTH, WILLIAM (*fl.* 1659), early engraver. [xxv. 303]

HAYTER, CHARLES (1761-1835), miniature-painter ; exhibited at Royal Academy, 1786-1832 ; published 'Introduction to Perspective,' 1813, and 'Practical Treatise on the three Primitive Colours,' 1826. [xxv. 303]

HAYTER, SIR GEORGE (1792-1871), portrait and historical painter ; son of Charles Hayter [q. v.] ; studied at Rome ; member of Academy of St. Luke ; painted for Duke of Bedford, 'Trial of Lord William Russell,' 1825, portraits of Princess Victoria for King Leopold and the city of London ; portrait and historical painter to the queen, 1837 ; painter in ordinary, 1841 ; knighted, 1842 ; exhibited, at British Institution, 'Moving of the Address in first Reformed Parliament,' 1848. [xxv. 303]

HAYTER, HENRY HEYLYN (1821-1895), statistician ; educated at Charterhouse ; emigrated to Victoria, 1852 ; entered department of registrar-general, 1857, and became head of statistical branch ; government statist, 1874-93 ; brought annual statistical returns of colony of Victoria to elaborate and perfect shape, which formed model for whole of Australian colonies ; originated 'Victorian Year-Book,' published educational and other works. [Suppl. ii. 406]

HAYTER, JOHN (1756-1818), antiquary ; of Eton and King's College, Cambridge ; fellow ; M.A., 1788 ; incorporated at Oxford, 1812 ; chaplain in ordinary to the Prince of Wales ; superintended deciphering of Herculaneum papyri, 1802-6 ; his facsimiles with engravings of the 'Carmen Latinum' and 'Περὶ Θανάτου' presented to Oxford University, 1810 ; died at Paris. [xxv. 304]

HAYTER, RICHARD (1611 ?-1684) theological writer ; M.A. Magdalen Hall, Oxford, 1634 ; published 'The Meaning of Revelation,' 1675. [xxv. 305]

HAYTER, THOMAS (1702-1762), bishop of Norwich and of London ; B.A. Balliol College, Oxford, 1724 ; M.A. Emmanuel College, Cambridge, 1727 ; D.D. Cambridge, 1744 ; chaplain to Archbishop Blackburne of York, 1724 ; sub-dean, 1730, and archdeacon of York, 1730-51 ; prebendary of Westminster, 1739-49, Southwell, 1728-49 ; bishop of Norwich, 1749-61 ; preceptor to Prince of Wales (George III), 1751 ; supported Jews' Naturalisation Bill, 1753 ; bishop of London, 1761-2 ; privy councillor, 1761 ; published pamphlets. [xxv. 305]

HAYTER, SIR WILLIAM GOODENOUGH, first baronet (1792-1878), liberal whip ; educated at Winchester and Trinity College, Oxford ; B.A., 1814 ; barrister, Lincoln's Inn, 1819, treasurer, 1853 ; Q.C., 1839 ; M.P., Wells, 1837-65 ; judge-advocate-general, 1847-9 ; patronage secretary to the treasury, 1850-8 ; privy councillor, 1843 ; created baronet, 1858 ; found drowned at South Hill Park, Berkshire. [xxv. 307]

HAYTHORNE, SIR EDMUND (1818-1888), general ; served with 98th under Colin Campbell in China, 1841-3 ; his aide-de-camp in second Sikh war and in Momund expedition (1851) ; with Napier at forcing of Kohat pass, 1850 ; lieutenant-colonel, 1854 ; commanded 1st royals in Crimea ; chief of the staff in north China, 1859 ; adjutant-general in Bengal, 1860-5 ; K.C.B., 1873 ; general, 1879. [xxv. 307]

HAYTLEY, EDWARD (*d.* 1762 ?), painter of full-length of Peg Woffington. [xxv. 308]

HAYWARD, ABRAHAM (1801-1884), essayist ; educated by Francis Twiss [q. v.] and at Tiverton school ; studied at Inner Temple, 1824 ; edited 'Law Magazine,' 1828-44 ; visited Germany, 1831 ; published translation of 'Faust,' with critical introduction, 1833 ; gave literary assistance to Prince Louis Bonaparte ; Q.C., 1845 ; not elected bencher ; contributed to 'Quarterly,' 'Edinburgh,' and 'Fraser's' ; supported Aberdeen's government in 'Morning Chronicle' ; his reply to De Bazancourt's 'Expédition de Crimée' circulated on the continent by Palmerston ; contributed regularly to 'Quarterly,' 1869-83, and occasionally to the 'Times' ; published 'The Art of Dining,' 1852, and 'Sketches of Eminent Statesmen and Writers,' 1880 ; edited Mrs. Piozzi's 'Autobiography,' 1861, and 'Diaries of a Lady of Quality from 1797 to 1844,' 1864. His three series of 'Essays' (1858, 1873, 1874) include a vigorous attack on the theory identifying 'Junius' with Sir Philip Francis [q. v.] Selections from his correspondence were issued, 1886. [xxv. 308]

HAYWARD, SIR JOHN (1564 ?-1627), historian ; M.A. Pembroke College, Cambridge, 1584 ; LL.D. ; imprisoned for publishing 'First Part of the Life and Raigne of Henrie the IIII,' dedicated to Essex, 1599-1601 ; practised in court of arches under James I ; historiographer of Chelsea College, 1610 ; knighted, 1619 ; published (1603) reply to Parsons's 'Conference about the Next Succession' of 1594, 'Lives of the III Normans, Kings of England,' 1613, and tract in favour of union between England and Scotland, 1604, with devotional works ; his 'Life and Raigne of King Edward the Sixt' (posthumous), 1630, reprinted with 'Beginning of Reign of Elizabeth,' 1840. [xxv. 311]

HAYWARD, THOMAS (*d.* 1779 ?), editor of the 'British Muse' (1738), reprinted as 'Quintessence of English Poetry' (1740) ; F.S.A., 1756. [xxv. 313]

HAYWARD, THOMAS (1702-1781), barrister of Lincoln's Inn ; M.P., Ludgershall, 1741-7 and 1754-61. [xxv. 313]

HAYWARD, SIR THOMAS (1743-1799), clerk of the cheque to corps of gentlemen-pensioners ; knighted, 1799. [xxv. 313]

HAYWOOD, MRS. ELIZA (1693 ?-1756), novelist ; *née* Fowler ; employed by Rich to re-write 'The Fair Captive,' 1721 ; wrote and acted (at Drury Lane) 'A Wife to be Lett,' 1723 ; published 'Frederick, Duke of Brunswick-Lunenburgh' (tragedy), 1729 ; satirised in the 'Dunciad' (1728) for her libellous 'Memoirs of a certain Island adjacent to Utopia' (1725) and 'Secret History of the Present Intrigues of the Court of Caramania' (1727) ; retaliated in contributions to Curll's 'Female Dunciad,' 1729 ; issued 'Female Spectator,' 1744-6 ; published 'History of Jemmy and Jenny Jessamy,' 1753 ; her 'Secret Histories, Novels, and Poems' (1725) dedicated to Steele ; doubtfully identified with Steele's 'Sappho.' [xxv. 313]

HAYWOOD, FRANCIS (1796-1858), translator ; published translation of Kant's 'Critick of Pure Reason' (1828) and other works. [Suppl. ii. 407]

HAYWOOD, WILLIAM (1600 ?-1663), royalist divine ; fellow of St. John's College, Oxford ; M.A., 1624 ; D.D., 1636 ; chaplain to Charles I and Laud ; prebendary of Westminster, 1638 ; ejected from St. Giles-in-the-Fields, 1641, and imprisoned. [xxv. 315]

HAYWOOD, WILLIAM (1821-1894), architect and civil engineer ; pupil of Mr. George Aitchison, R.A. ; chief engineer to commissioners of sewers for city of London, 1846 till death ; M.I.C.E., 1853 ; constructed Holborn Viaduct, 1863-9 published professional reports. [Suppl. ii. 407]

HAZELDINE, WILLIAM (1763-1840), ironfounder ; erected locks on Caledonian canal (1804-12) and supplied ironwork for Menai (1819-25) and Conway (1822-6) bridges. [xxv. 316]

HAZLEHURST, THOMAS (*fl.* 1760-1818), miniature-painter, of Liverpool. [xxv. 316]

HAZLEWOOD, COLIN HENRY (1823-1875), dramatist and low comedian at City of London Theatre; author of popular dramas, farces, and burlesques. [xxv. 316]

HAZLITT, WILLIAM (1778-1830), essayist; educated for unitarian ministry; heard Coleridge's last sermon and visited him at Stowey, 1798; studied painting; painted Lamb as a Venetian senator, 1805; defended Godwin against Malthus, 1807; married Sarah Stoddart, 1808; lectured on modern philosophy at Russell Institution, and wrote parliamentary reports; dramatic critic to 'Morning Chronicle,' 1814; contributed to Hunt's 'Examiner'; wrote for 'Edinburgh Review' from November 1814; lectured at Surrey Institution, 1818-20; assisted Leigh Hunt in the 'Liberal'; attacked Coleridge, Wordsworth, and Southey in the 'Chronicle,' and Shelley in 'Table Talk'; obtained divorce from first wife, 1822; his 'Liber Amoris' (1823) the outcome of amour with Miss Walker; married Mrs. Bridgewater, 1824, who left him on his return from continental tour of 1824-5; contributed to 'London Magazine' and (1826-7) 'Colburn's New Monthly,' where appeared his 'Conversations with Northcote'; appears as 'an investigator' in Haydon's 'Christ's Entry.' His writings include 'Essay on the Principles of Human Action,' 1805, 'The Round Table' (from 'Examiner,' 1815-17), 'The Characters of Shakespeare's Plays,' 1817, 'Review of English Stage,' 1818, 'Lectures on English Poets,' 1818, 'Lectures on the Dramatic Literature of the Reign of Queen Elizabeth,' 1821, 'Table Talk,' 1821-2, 'Spirit of the Age,' 1825, 'The Plain Speaker,' 1826, and 'Life of Napoleon Buonaparte' (four vols. 1828-30); his 'Literary Remains' issued 1836. [xxv. 317]

HEAD, SIR EDMUND WALKER, baronet (1805-1868), colonial governor; fellow of Merton College, Oxford, 1830-7; M.A., 1830; succeeded as baronet, 1838; poor-law commissioner, 1841; governor of New Brunswick, 1847; governor-general of Canada, 1854-61; P.C., 1857; D.C.L. Oxford, 1862; F.R.S. and K.C.B.; edited Sir G. C. Lewis's 'Essays on the Administrations of Great Britain,' and Kugler's 'Handbook of Painting.' [xxv. 323]

HEAD, SIR FRANCIS BOND, first baronet (1793-1875), colonial governor and author; brother of Sir George Head [q. v.]; served in royal engineers, 1811-25, being present at Waterloo; travelled in South America as manager of Rio Plata Mining Association, 1825-6; as lieutenant-governor of Upper Canada, 1835-7, quelled a rising; K.C.H., 1835; created baronet, 1836; privy councillor, 1867; contributed to 'Quarterly Review'; published, among other works, 'Rough Notes of Journeys in the Pampas and Andes,' and lives of Bruce the traveller, 1830, and Sir J. M. Burgoyne, 1872. [xxv. 324]

HEAD, SIR GEORGE (1782-1855), assistant commissary-general; brother of Sir Francis Bond Head [q. v.]; served in commissariat during Peninsular war; assistant commissary-general, 1814; served in North America; deputy marshal at coronations of William IV and Queen Victoria; knighted, 1831; published, among other works, 'A Home Tour . . . with Memoirs of an Assistant Commissary-general,' 1840, and translations of Apuleius and Cardinal Pacca's memoirs. [xxv. 326]

HEAD, GUY (*d.* 1800), painter; copyist of works of Titian, Correggio, and Rubens. [xxv. 326]

HEAD, RICHARD (1637?-1686?), author of first part of 'The English Rogue' (1665); studied at New Inn Hall, Oxford; ruined by gambling; published also 'Proteus Redivivus, or the Art of Wheedling,' 1675; 'The Canting Academy,' 1673, 'Life and Death of Mother Shipton,' 1677, and other works; drowned at sea. [xxv. 326]

HEADDA, SAINT. [See HEDDI.]

HEADLAM, THOMAS EMERSON (1813-1875), judge advocate-general; M.A. Trinity College, Cambridge, 1839; barrister, Inner Temple, 1839, treasurer, 1867; Q.C., 1851; chancellor of Ripon and Durham, 1854; liberal M.P., Newcastle, 1847-74; judge advocate-general, 1859-66; privy councillor, 1866; carried Trustee Act, 1850. [xxv. 328]

HEADLEY, HENRY (1765-1788), poet and critic; educated under Parr at Colchester and Norwich; friend of Bowles at Trinity College, Oxford; B.A., 1786; published 'Select Beauties of Ancient English Poetry, with Remarks,' 1787; his 'Poems' (1786) included in Davenport's and Parr's collections. [xxv. 328]

HEALD, JAMES (1796-1873), Wesleyan philanthropist; M.P., Stockport, 1847-52; founder of Stockport Infirmary. [xxv. 330]

HEALD, WILLIAM MARGETSON (1767-1837), surgeon and divine; M.A. Catharine Hall, Cambridge, 1798; vicar of Birstal, 1801-36; published 'The Brunoniad,' 1789. [xxv. 330]

HEALDE, THOMAS (1724?-1789), physician; M.D. Trinity College, Cambridge, 1754; F.R.C.P., 1760; Harveian orator, 1765; Gulstonian, 1763, Croonian, 1770 and 1784-6, and Lumleian, 1786-9, lecturer; F.R.S., 1770; physician to London Hospital, 1770; Gresham professor, 1771; translated 'New Pharmacopœia,' 1788. [xxv. 330]

HEALE, WILLIAM (1581?-1627), divine; chaplain-fellow of Exeter College, Oxford, 1608-10; M.A., 1606; vicar of Bishop's Teignton, 1610-27; published 'Apologie for Women,' 1609. [xxv. 331]

HEALEY, JOHN (*d.* 1610), translator; friend of Thomas Thorpe (1570?-1635?) [q. v.]; published 'Philip Mornay, Lord of Plessis, his Teares,' 1609, 'Discovery of a Newe World' (version of Bishop Hall's 'Mundus alter et idem'), *c.* 1609, 'Epictetus his Manuall And Cebes his Table,' 1610, and 'St. Augustine of the Citie of God,' with Vives's commentary, 1610. [xxv. 331]

HEALY, JAMES (1824-1894), Roman catholic divine and humorist; educated at Maynooth; curate in Dublin, 1852, and at Bray, co. Wicklow, 1858; administrator of Little Bray, 1867-93; parish priest of Ballybrack and Killiney, co. Dublin, 1893 till death. [Suppl. ii. 408]

HEAPHY, CHARLES (1821?-1881), New Zealand official; son of Thomas Heaphy the elder [q. v.]; assisted in purchase of Chatham islands, 1840-1; published 'Residence in New Zealand,' 1842; land surveyor of Auckland, 1858; chief surveyor of New Zealand, 1864; received Victoria Cross (1867) for conduct during third Maori war as guide at Mangapiko River, 1864; member of House of Representatives, 1867-70; commissioner of native reserves, 1869; judge of native land court, 1878; died at Brisbane. [xxv. 331]

HEAPHY, THOMAS, the elder (1775-1835), water-colour painter; exhibited at Water-colour Society, 1804-12 (member, 1807); painted, on the spot, Wellington and his officers before an action in the Peninsula; established Society of British Artists, 1824. [xxv. 332]

HEAPHY, THOMAS (FRANK), the younger (1813-1873), painter; son of Thomas Heaphy the elder [q. v.]; exhibited at Royal Academy portraits and subject-pictures from 1831; member of Society of British Artists, 1867; investigated origin of the traditional likeness of Christ; his 'Likeness of Christ,' with illustrations, edited by Mr. Wyke Bayliss, 1880; published 'A Wonderful Ghost Story.' [xxv. 333]

HEARD, SIR ISAAC (1730-1822), Garter king-of-arms; Blue-mantle pursuivant, 1759; Lancaster herald, 1761; Norroy, 1774; Clarenceux, 1780; Garter king-of-arms, 1784; knighted, 1794. [xxv. 334]

HEARD, WILLIAM (*fl.* 1778), poet and dramatist. [xxv. 334]

HEARDER, JONATHAN (1810-1876), electrician to South Devon Hospital; patented sub-oceanic cable and thermometer for lead-soundings at sea; assisted researches of Sir William Snow Harris [q. v.] [xxv. 334]

HEARN, WILLIAM EDWARD (1826-1888), legal and sociological writer; of Trinity College, Dublin; professor of Greek, Queen's College, Galway, 1849-54; first professor of modern history and literature at Melbourne University, 1854-72, afterwards dean of the law faculty; as member of legislative council of Victoria devoted himself to codification; published 'The Government of England, its Structure and its Development,' 1867, 'The Aryan Household,' 1879, and other works. [xxv. 335]

HEARNE, SAMUEL (1745–1792), traveller; explored north-western America for Hudson's Bay Company, 1768–1770; captured by La Perouse, 1782; his 'Account of a Journey from Prince of Wales's Fort . . . to the North-West' issued, 1795. [xxv. 335]

HEARNE, THOMAS (1678–1735), historical antiquary; educated at expense of Francis Cherry [q. v.]; M.A. St. Edmund Hall, Oxford, 1703; second keeper of Bodleian Library, 1712; deprived as a nonjuror, 1716; refused chief librarianship and other academical offices on political grounds; published 'Reliquiæ Bodleianæ,' 1703, and editions of Latin classics, of Leland's 'Itinerary,' 1710–12, and 'Collectanea,' 1715, Camden's 'Annales,' 1717, and many English chronicles; his diaries and correspondence printed by Oxford Historical Society; the Wormius of Pope's 'Dunciad.' [xxv. 335]

HEARNE, THOMAS (1744–1817), water-colour painter; F.S.A.; made drawings during residence in Leeward islands, 1771–5; executed fifty-two illustrations for Byrne's 'Antiquities of Great Britain,' 1777–81; exhibited at Royal Academy, 1781–1802; his drawings copied by Girtin and Turner. [xxv. 338]

HEATH, BENJAMIN (1704–1766), book-collector and critic; town clerk of Exeter, 1752–66; hon. D.C.L. Oxford, 1762; prominent in agitation for repeal of cider duty, 1763–6; published notes on Æschylus, Sophocles, and Euripides (1762), and 'Revisal of Shakespear's Text' (1765, anon.); left manuscript notes on Latin poets and supplement to Seward's edition of Beaumont and Fletcher. [xxv. 339]

HEATH, CHARLES (1761–1831), topographer and painter; twice mayor of Monmouth; published histories of Monmouth, 1804, and neighbouring places of interest. [xxv. 340]

HEATH, CHARLES (1785–1848), engraver and publisher of illustrated 'Annuals'; natural son of James Heath (1757–1834) [q. v.]; executed small plates for popular English classics; engraved works after Benjamin West and other painters. [xxv. 340]

HEATH, CHRISTOPHER (1802–1876), minister of catholic apostolic church, Gordon Square; succeeded Edward Irving at Newman Street Hall, and caused erection of new church, Gordon Square (opened 1853). [xxv. 341]

HEATH, DOUGLAS DENON (1811–1897), classical and mathematical scholar; senior wrangler, first Smith's prizeman, and fellow, Trinity College, Cambridge, 1832; barrister, Inner Temple, 1835; county clerk of Middlesex, 1838–46; county court judge, Bloomsbury district, 1847–1865; edited Bacon's legal works for Spedding's edition of Bacon's works, 1859; published 'Doctrine of Energy,' 1874, and mathematical, legal, and classical writings. [Suppl. ii. 408]

HEATH, DUNBAR ISIDORE (1816–1888), heterodox divine; fellow of Trinity College, Cambridge; fifth wrangler, 1838; M.A., 1841; deprived of living of Brading, Isle of Wight, 1861, for 'Sermons on Important Subjects'; edited 'Journal of Anthropology'; translated Egyptian 'Proverbs of Aphobis,' 1858. [xxv. 341]

HEATH, HENRY (1599–1643), Franciscan, of St. Bonaventure, Douay; B.A. Corpus Christi College, Cambridge, 1621; published 'Soliloquia seu Documenta Christianæ Perfectionis,' 1651; executed at Tyburn as a recusant. [xxv. 342]

HEATH, JAMES (1629–1664), royalist historian; of Westminster and Christ Church, Oxford; deprived of studentship, 1648; published 'Brief Chronicle of the late Intestine War,' 1663, 'Flagellum' (a book on Cromwell), and poems. [xxv. 343]

HEATH, JAMES (1757–1834), engraver; pupil of Joseph Collyer the younger [q. v.]; associate engraver of Royal Academy, 1791; historical engraver to George III, George IV, and William IV, 1794–1834; engraved designs for illustrations by Stothard and Smirke; engraved West's 'Death of Nelson,' Copley's 'Death of Major Pierson,' and pictures by foreign masters; re-engraved Hogarth's plates. [xxv. 343]

HEATH, JOHN (fl. 1615), epigrammatist and translator; M.A. New College, Oxford, 1613; fellow, 1609–16; published 'Two Centuries of Epigrammes,' 1610. [xxv. 344]

HEATH, JOHN (1736–1816), judge; M.A. Christ Church, Oxford, 1762; barrister, Inner Temple, 1762; serjeant-at-law and recorder of Exeter, 1775; judge of common pleas, 1780–1816. [xxv. 344]

HEATH, NICHOLAS (1501?–1578), archbishop of York and lord chancellor; fellow, Christ's College, 1521, and Clare Hall, Cambridge, 1524; M.A., 1522; D.D., 1535; archdeacon of Stafford, 1534; accompanied Edward Fox [q. v.] to Germany to negotiate with Smalcaldic League, 1535; king's almoner, 1537; bishop of Rochester, 1539, Worcester, 1543; imprisoned and deprived, 1551, but restored on accession of Mary, 1553; as archbishop of York (1555–9) procured restitution of Ripon, Southwell, and other manors to York, and built York House, Strand; as chancellor (1556–8) proclaimed Elizabeth in House of Lords; arranged preliminaries of disputation at Westminster; released from Tower on promise to abstain from public affairs. [xxv. 345]

HEATH, RICHARD (d. 1702), judge; barrister, Inner Temple, 1659; serjeant-at-law, 1683; judge of exchequer court, 1686–8; excepted from indemnity at revolution. [xxv. 346]

HEATH, SIR ROBERT (1575–1649), judge; of Tunbridge and St. John's College, Cambridge; barrister, Inner Temple, 1603, treasurer, 1625; clerk of pleas in king's bench, 1607; recorder of London, 1618–21, and M.P. for the city, 1620; solicitor-general, 1621; knighted, 1621; M.P., East Grinstead, 1623 and 1625; as attorney-general (1625–31) was engaged with cases of Sir T. Darnell [q. v.], Felton, Eliot, and Star-chamber prosecutions of 1629–30; prepared answer to Petition of Right, 1628; chief-justice of common pleas, 1631; dismissed for supposed puritan sympathies, 1634; king's serjeant, 1636, puisne judge, 1641, and chief-justice of king's bench, 1642; tried Lilburne at Oxford and other parliamentarians at Salisbury, 1642; impeached by parliament and his place declared vacant, 1645; died at Calais; his 'Maxims and Rules of Pleading' published, 1694, and autobiography in 'Philobiblon Society Miscellany.' [xxv. 346]

HEATH, ROBERT (fl. 1650), poet; author of 'Clarastella' and other poems, 1650. [xxv. 349]

HEATH, ROBERT (d. 1779), mathematician; edited 'Ladies' Diary,' 1744–53; after supersession by Thomas Simpson (1710–1761) [q. v.] carried on rival publications; helped to popularise mathematics in periodicals; his 'History of the Islands of Scilly' (1750) reprinted in Pinkerton. [xxv. 349]

HEATH, THOMAS (fl. 1583), mathematician; friend of John Dee [q. v.]; M.A. All Souls' College, Oxford, 1573. [xxv. 350]

HEATHCOAT, JOHN (1783–1861), inventor of lace-making machines known as the horizontal pillow and the 'old Loughborough' (1808–9); after Luddite riots at Loughborough in 1816 removed to Tiverton, which he represented, 1832–59; patented rotary self-narrowing stocking-frame and other inventions. [xxv. 350]

HEATHCOTE, SIR GILBERT (1651?–1733), lord mayor of London; M.A. Christ's College, Cambridge, 1673; chief founder of new East India Company, 1693; member of first board of directors of Bank of England, 1694; knighted, 1702; sheriff of London, 1703; lord mayor, 1710–11; senior alderman, 1724; president of St. Thomas's Hospital; commissioner for Georgia, 1732; whig M.P. for the city, 1700–10, Helston, 1714, New Lymington, 1722, St. Germans, 1727; his parsimony ridiculed by Pope. [xxv. 351]

HEATHCOTE, RALPH (1721–1795), divine and author; M.A. Jesus College, Cambridge, 1748; D.D., 1759; Boyle lecturer, 1763–5; vicar-general of Southwell, 1788; took part in Middletonian controversy, 1752, and that between Hume and Rousseau; published 'Historia Astronomiæ,' 1746, and 'The Irenarch or Justice of the Peace's Manual,' 1771. [xxv. 353]

HEATHER or **HEYTHER**, WILLIAM (1563?–1627), musician; friend and executor of Camden; gentleman of the Chapel Royal, 1615; Mus. Doc. Oxford, 1622; founder of the music lectureship at Oxford, 1626. [xxv. 354]

HEATHERINGTON, ALEXANDER (d. 1878), mining agent; opened at Halifax, Nova Scotia, International Mining Agency, 1867; compiled 'The Gold

Yield of Nova Scotia,' 1860-9, reissued 1870-4 as 'Mining Industries.' [xxv. 355]

HEATHFIELD, first BARON (1717-1790). [See ELIOTT, GEORGE AUGUSTUS.]

HEATON, CLEMENT (1824-1882), glass-painter and church decorator; founded firm of Heaton & Butler. [xxv. 355]

HEATON, MRS. MARY MARGARET (1836-1883), writer on art; *née* Keymer; married Professor Charles William Heaton, 1863; contributed to Bryan's 'Dictionary of Painters and Engravers'; published 'Life of Dürer,' 1870, 'Masterpieces of Flemish Art,' 1869, and 'Concise History of Painting,' 1873. [xxv. 355]

HEBER, REGINALD (1783-1826), bishop of Calcutta; of Brasenose College, Oxford; won prizes for the English essay, Latin poem, and English verse ('Palestine'); fellow of All Souls' College, Oxford, 1805; incumbent of Hodnet, 1807; prebendary of St. Asaph, 1812; Bampton lecturer, 1815; preacher at Lincoln's Inn, 1822; bishop of Calcutta, 1822-6; completed establishment of Bishop's College, Calcutta; travelled in all parts of India; his hymns appeared first in 'Christian Observer,' 1811; published 'Poetical Works,' 1812, and also life and critical examination of works of Jeremy Taylor and accounts of journeys through India; died at Trichinopoly. [xxv. 355]

HEBER, RICHARD (1773-1833), book-collector; half-brother of Reginald Heber [q. v.]; M.A. Brasenose College, Oxford, 1797; intimate with Scott; candidate for Oxford University, 1806; M.P., 1821-6; D.C.L., 1822; a founder of the Athenæum Club, 1824; travelled widely to collect books, spending on them about 100,000l.; his library rich in choice English works, the English portion being ultimately sold for 56,774l.; edited Persius, 1790, Silius Italicus, 1792, and Claudian, 1793-6, and Cutwode's 'Caltha Poetarum,' 1815. [xxv. 357]

HEBERDEN, WILLIAM, the elder (1710-1801), physician; B.A. St. John's College, Cambridge, 1728; senior fellow, 1749; M.D., 1739; contributed to 'Athenian Letters,' 1741; F.R.C.P., 1746; Gulstonian (1749) and Croonian lecturer (1760); Harveian orator (1750) and censor; F.R.S., 1749; practised in London from 1748; first described *angina pectoris*; attended Johnson, Cowper, and Warburton; published at his own expense plays of Euripides edited by Markland, and Middleton's 'Appendix to his Dissertation on servile condition of Physicians among the Ancients.' His works (edited in Germany by Soemmering) include 'Commentarii de Morborum Historiâ et Curatione' (transl., 1803), and contributions to 'Transactions' of College of Physicians and Royal Society. [xxv. 359]

HEBERDEN, WILLIAM, the younger (1767-1845), physician; son of William Heberden the elder [q. v.]; fellow, St. John's College, Cambridge, 1788-96; M.A., 1791; incorporated M.A. Oxford; M.D. Oxford, 1795; physician at St. George's Hospital, 1793-1803; F.R.C.P., 1796; F.R.S.; physician in ordinary to the queen, 1806, and the king, 1809; published miscellaneous works, including a dialogue on education, 1818, translations of Cicero's 'Letters to Atticus,' 1825, and medical tracts. [xxv. 360]

HECHT, EDUARD (1832-1887), musical composer; born at Dürkheim-on-the-Haardt; settled at Manchester, 1854; conducted musical societies at Manchester, Bradford, and Halifax. [xxv. 361]

HEDDI, **HÆDDI**, **HEADDA**, or **ÆTLA** (d. 705), bishop of Gewissas or West-Saxons, 676; fixed his see at Winchester; friend of Archbishop Theodore. [xxv. 361]

HEDDIUS, STEPHEN (*fl.* 669). [See EDDI.]

HEDGES, SIR CHARLES (d. 1714), politician and lawyer; B.A. Magdalen Hall, Oxford, 1670, M.A. Magdalen College, 1673; D.C.L., 1675; chancellor of Rochester, 1686; judge of admiralty court, 1689; knighted, 1689; M.P., Orford (1698-1700), Dover, 1701, Malmesbury, 1701 (November), Calne, 1702, West Looe, 1705, 1708, and 1710, East Looe, 1713-14; secretary of state, 1700-6; judge of prerogative court of Canterbury, 1711-14; reputed author of 'Reasons for Setling [sic] Admiralty Jurisdiction,' 1690. [xxv. 362]

HEDGES, SIR WILLIAM (1632-1701), governor of Bengal; cousin of Sir Charles Hedges [q. v.]; head of

Levant Company's factory at Constantinople; governor of Bengal, 1682-4; failed in effecting reforms in Bengal; knighted, 1688; sheriff of London, 1693; director of the Bank, 1694; his diary and other documents edited by Sir Henry Yule, 1887-8. [xxv. 363]

HEDLEY, WILLIAM (1779-1843), inventor; patented smooth wheel and rails for locomotives, 1813; discovered principle of blast-pipe; introduced at Callerton colliery improved system of pumping water. [xxv. 364]

HEEMSKERK, EGBERT VAN (1645-1704), painter of subject-pictures; came to London from Haarlem. [xxv. 365]

HEERE, LUCAS VAN (1534-1584). [See DE HEERE.]

HEETE, ROBERT, or ROBERT OF WOODSTOCK (d. 1428), canonist and civilian; fellow of New College, Oxford, 1417, of Winchester College, 1422; M.A. and LL.B.; lectured on first book of decretals, 1413; probably author of manuscript life of William of Wykeham; benefactor of Winchester. [xxv. 365]

HEGAT, WILLIAM (*fl.* 1600), professor of philosophy at Bordeaux; native of Glasgow; friend of Robert Balfour (1550?-1625?) [q. v.]; author of Latin poems and orations. [xxv. 366]

HEGGE, ROBERT (1599-1629), author; M.A. Corpus Christi College, Oxford, 1620, probationer fellow, 1624; his treatises on St. Cuthbert's churches printed, 1777. [xxv. 366]

HEIDEGGER, JOHN JAMES (1659?-1749), operatic manager; the 'Swiss Count' of the 'Tatler' and 'Count Ugly' of Fielding's 'Pleasures of the Town'; managed Italian opera at Haymarket, 1713, for Royal Academy of Music, 1720-8; at the Haymarket in partnership with Handel, 1728-34; and alone, 1737-8; carried on masquerades and 'ridottos'; entertained George II at Barn Elms; caricatured by Hogarth. [xxv. 367]

HEIGHAM, SIR CLEMENT (d. 1570), judge; barrister, Lincoln's Inn, autumn reader, 1538 and 1547, and governor; privy councillor and speaker of House of Commons under Queen Mary; knighted, 1555; lord chief baron of the exchequer, 1558-9. [xxv. 368]

HEIGHAM, JOHN (*fl.* 1639), Roman catholic printer, writer, and translator; his 'Devout Exposition of the Holie Masse' (1614), edited by A. J. Rowley, 1876; version of Luis de la Puente's 'Meditations on the Mysteries of our holie Faith,' reprinted, 1852. [xxv. 368]

HEIGHINGTON, MUSGRAVE (1690-1774?), musical composer; of Queen's College, Oxford; organist at Yarmouth, Leicester, 1739, and the episcopal chapel, Dundee, before 1760; member of Spalding Society; composed 'The Enchantress' and odes of Anacreon and Horace. [xxv. 369]

HEINS, JOHN THEODORE (1732-1771), engraver, draughtsman, and painter; painted miniature of Cowper's mother, which occasioned Cowper's poem 'On receipt of my mother's picture.' [xxv. 369]

HELE, SIR JOHN (1565-1608), serjeant-at-law; Lent reader at Inner Temple; recorder of Exeter, 1592-1606, and M.P., 1592-1601; serjeant-at-law, 1594; queen's serjeant, 1602; knighted, 1603; employed at Ralegh's trial, 1603; founded boys' hospital at Plymouth. [xxv. 370]

HELE or **HELL**, THOMAS D' (1740?-1780). [See HALES.]

HELLIER, HENRY (1662?-1697), divine; M.A. Corpus Christi College, Oxford, 1682, D.D., 1697, vice-president at his death; published 'Treatise concerning Schism and Schismaticks,' 1697; committed suicide. [xxv. 370]

HELLINS, JOHN (d. 1827), mathematician and astronomer; assistant in Greenwich Observatory; vicar of Potterspury, 1790; B.D. Trinity College, Cambridge, 1800; F.R.S., 1796; Copley medallist for solution of problem in physical astronomy, 1798; published 'Mathematical Essays,' 1788; made calculations for war office, 1806. [xxv. 371]

HELLOWES, EDWARD (*fl.* 1574-1600), translator; groom of the chamber, 1597; translated works of Guevara. [xxv. 371]

HELMES, THOMAS (d. 1616). [See TUNSTALL, THOMAS.]

HELMORE, THOMAS (1811–1890), musical writer and composer; M.A. Magdalen Hall, Oxford, 1845; vice-principal (1840) and precentor of St. Mark's College, Chelsea, 1846–77; priest-ordinary of Chapel Royal, St. James's, 1847; composed carols and hymn-tunes; translated Fétis on choral singing, 1855; published 'Catechism of Music' and 'Plain-Song,' 1878, and other works. [xxv. 371]

HELPS, SIR ARTHUR (1813–1875), clerk of the privy council; of Eton and Trinity College, Cambridge; M.A., 1839; clerk of privy council, 1860–75; hon. D.C.L. Oxford, 1864; private secretary to Spring Rice and Lord Morpeth; K.C.B., 1872; revised works by Queen Victoria; published, among other works, 'Friends in Council' (four series, 1847–59), 'Conquerors of the New World' (1848), 'Spanish Conquest in America' (1855–61). [xxv. 372]

HELSHAM, RICHARD (1682?–1738), friend of Swift; B.A. Trinity College, Dublin, 1702, fellow, 1704, lecturer in mathematics, 1723–30, Erasmus Smith professor, 1724–1738; regius professor of physic (1733–8) of Dublin University; his 'Lectures on Natural Philosophy' edited by Bryan Robinson [q. v.], 1739. [xxv. 373]

HELWYS, EDWARD (fl. 1589), author of 'A Marvell Deciphered,' 1589; member of Gray's Inn, 1550; brother of Thomas Helwys [q. v.] [xxv. 375]

HELWYS, SIR GERVASE (1561–1615), lieutenant of the Tower; nephew of Thomas Helwys [q. v.]; of St. John's College, Cambridge, and Lincoln's Inn; lieutenant of the Tower, 1613–15; conducted torture of Edmond Peacham [q. v.], 1615; hanged on Tower Hill for complicity in murder of Sir Thomas Overbury (1581–1613) [q. v.] [xxv. 373]

HELWYS, THOMAS (1550?–1616?), puritan divine; uncle of Sir Gervase Helwys [q. v.]; member of Brownist congregation at Amsterdam; formed at Pinners' Hall, London, first general baptist congregation; published tract against 'Persecution for Religion,' 1615. [xxv. 375]

HELY-HUTCHINSON, CHRISTOPHER (1767–1826), soldier and politician; fifth son of John Hely-Hutchinson (1724–1794) [q. v.]; Irish barrister, 1792; M.P., Taghmon (in Irish parliament), 1795; as a volunteer distinguished himself at Ballinamuck, 1798; on the Helder (1799) and Egyptian (1801) expeditions; lieutenant-colonel, 1801; M.P., Cork, 1801–12 and 1819–26, and Co. Longford, 1812–1819; served (1807) in Russian army at Eylau and Friedland. [xxv. 376]

HELY-HUTCHINSON, JOHN (1724–1794), lawyer and statesman; B.A. Trinity College, Dublin, 1744; Irish barrister, 1748; assumed additional name of Hutchinson, 1751; M.P. (in Irish parliament) for Lanesborough, 1759, Cork, 1761–90, and Taghmon, 1790–4; privy councillor and prime serjeant, 1760; secretary of state, 1778; provost of Trinity College, 1774; attacked for abusing his powers; founded modern languages professorship; advocated free trade in 'Commercial Restraints of Ireland,' 1779 (anon.), also home rule, catholic emancipation, and parliamentary reform; supported commercial propositions of 1785, but joined opposition on regency question; friend of Burke and William Gerard Hamilton; his wife created Baroness Donoughmore, 1785. [xxv. 376]

HELY-HUTCHINSON, JOHN, first BARON HUTCHINSON, afterwards second EARL OF DONOUGHMORE (1757–1832), general; second son of John Hely-Hutchinson (1724–1794) [q. v.]; educated at Eton and Dublin; lieutenant-colonel of Athole highlanders, 1783; served with Duke of York, 1793; major-general on Irish staff when troops at Castlebar fled from Humbert, 1798; represented Lanesborough, 1776–83, and Cork, 1790–1800, in Irish parliament; supported the union; severely wounded at Alkmaar while in charge of Craven's brigade, 1799; commanded first division under Abercromby in Egypt; succeeded to chief command, 1801; captured (1801) Cairo and Alexandria; created Baron Hutchinson, with a pension; general, 1813; G.C.B., 1814; undertook mission to Prussia and Russia, 1806–7; carried George IV's proposals to Queen Caroline at St. Omer, 1820; succeeded as Earl of Donoughmore, 1825. [xxv. 378]

HELY-HUTCHINSON, JOHN, third EARL OF DONOUGHMORE (1787–1851), soldier; grandson of John

Hely-Hutchinson (1724–1794) [q. v.]; served with grenadiers in Peninsula and at Waterloo; captain, 1812; deprived of his commission for assisting escape (1815) of General Lavalette at Paris; subsequently reinstated; succeeded his uncle as third earl, 1832; K.P., 1834. [xxv. 380]

HELY-HUTCHINSON, RICHARD, first EARL OF DONOUGHMORE (1756–1825), advocate of catholic emancipation; eldest son of John Hely-Hutchinson (1724–1794) [q. v.]; M.P., Sligo and Taghmon in Irish parliament; created Viscount Suirdale, 1797; commanded Cork legion, 1798; supported the union; created earl, 1800; Irish representative peer, 1800; postmaster-general in Ireland, 1805–9. [xxv. 381]

HELYAR, JOHN (fl. 1535), classical scholar and friend of Erasmus; fellow of Corpus Christi College, Oxford; M.A., 1525; B.D., 1532; his 'Carmina in obitum Erasmi' (Greek and Latin) in 'Epitaphs on Erasmus.' [xxv. 381]

HEMANS, CHARLES ISIDORE (1817–1876), antiquary; son of Felicia Dorothea Hemans [q. v.]; hon. secretary and librarian of English Archæological Society at Rome; published works on Roman history and archæology; died at Lucca. [xxv. 382]

HEMANS, FELICIA DOROTHEA (1793–1835), poet; née Browne; married Captain Alfred Hemans, 1812, but separated from him, 1818; made acquaintance of Scott and Wordsworth, 1829; intimate at Dublin with Sir William Rowan Hamilton, Whately, and Blanco White; her writings highly popular in America; the 'Egeria' of Maria Jane Jewsbury's 'Three Histories.' Her collected works (issued 1839) include 'Translations from Camoens and other Poets,' 'Lays of Many Lands,' 'The Forest Sanctuary,' and 'Songs of the Affections.' [xxv. 382]

HEMING, EDMUND (fl. 1695), projector. [xxv. 384]

HEMING or **HEMMINGE**, JOHN (d. 1630), actor and co-editor of the first folio of Shakespeare; played in King Henry IV, Part I (said to have been the original Falstaff), and in plays of Ben Jonson; before Elizabeth's death a chief proprietor of Globe Theatre and closely associated with Shakespeare; with Henry Condell (d. 1627) [q. v.] issued first folio, 1623. [xxv. 384]

HEMING or **HEMMINGE**, WILLIAM (fl. 1632), dramatist; son of John Heming or Hemminge [q. v.]; of Westminster and Christ Church, Oxford; M.A., 1628; his extant plays, 'The Fatal Contract' (1653), revived as 'Love and Revenge,' and reprinted as 'The Eunuch' (1687), and 'The Jewes Tragedy' (1662). [xxv. 385]

HEMINGFORD or **HEMINGBURGH**, WALTER DE, also WALTER DE GISBURN (fl. 1300), chronicler and subprior of St. Mary's, Gisburn; his chronicle (1066–1346) printed in part by Gale and Hearne; fully edited by H. C. Hamilton, 1848. [xxv. 385]

HEMMING (fl. 1096), chronicler; sub-prior of Worcester; his Worcester chartulary edited by Hearne, 1723. [xxv. 386]

HEMPEL, CHARLES or CARL FREDERICK (1811–1867), musical composer; son of Charles William Hempel [q. v.]; Mus. Doc. Oxford, 1862; organist of St. Mary's, Truro, and St. John's episcopal church, Perth; published songs and part of 'The Seventh Seal' (oratorio). [xxv. 386]

HEMPEL, CHARLES WILLIAM (1777–1855), composer and poet; organist of St. Mary's, Truro, 1804–44; composed, among other works, 'Sacred Melodies,' 1812, and a satirical poem; died in Lambeth workhouse. [xxv. 387]

HEMPHILL, BARBARA (d. 1858), novelist; née Hare; married John Hemphill; her 'Lionel Deerhurst, or Fashionable Life under the Regency' (1846), edited by Lady Blessington. [xxv. 387]

HEMPHILL, SAMUEL (d. 1741), Irish presbyterian; M.A. Glasgow, 1716, Edinburgh, 1726; minister of Castleblayney, Monaghan; published pamphlets in favour of subscription, 1722–6. [xxv. 387]

HENCHMAN, HUMPHREY (1592–1675), bishop of London; M.A. Christ's College, Cambridge, 1616; D.D., 1628; fellow of Clare Hall, 1616–23; canon and precentor of Salisbury, 1623, and rector of Isle of Portland; deprived during rebellion; assisted Charles II to escape after Worcester, 1651; bishop of Salisbury, 1660–3; took influential part in Savoy conference, 1661; bishop of London, 1663-75; restored cathedral and palace at Salisbury, and contributed to rebuilding of St. Paul's, Aldersgate palace, and Clare Hall. [xxv. 388]

HENCHMAN, HUMPHREY (1669-1739), civilian; grandson of Humphrey Henchman (1592-1675) [q. v.]; M.A. Christ Church, Oxford, 1694; D.C.L., 1702; friend of Atterbury; chancellor of Rochester, 1714, London, 1715; counsel for Sacheverell and against Whiston.
[xxv. 390]

HENDERLAND, LORD (1736-1795). [See MURRAY, ALEXANDER.]

HENDERSON. [See also HENRYSON.]

HENDERSON, ALEXANDER (1583?-1646), presbyterian divine and diplomatist; M.A. St. Andrews, 1603; minister of Leuchars, 1614, of the High Kirk, Edinburgh, 1639; opposed five articles of Perth, 1618; headed agitation against new prayer book, 1637; promoted remonstrance against episcopacy, 1637; one of presbyterian committee of four; prepared and read in Greyfriars, Edinburgh, the 'national covenant,' 1638; created burgess of Dundee for public services, 1638; moderator of Glasgow assembly (1638), which laid down lines of presbyterian organisation; commissioner at pacification of Berwick, 1639; ruling spirit at Edinburgh assembly which passed first 'Barrier Act,' 1639; entered England with covenanting army, 1640; negotiated treaty of 1641; as rector of Edinburgh University (1640-6), introduced teaching of Hebrew and 'circles'; as moderator of St. Andrews assembly (1641) proposed confession of faith, catechism, and directory of worship; chaplain to Charles I; at Oxford, 1643, urged him to call a Scottish parliament; drafted 'solemn league and covenant' taken by Westminster Assembly (September, 1643), and drew up the directory of worship; manager of proposed religious settlement at Uxbridge conference, 1645; corresponded with Charles I on episcopacy and the coronation oath, 1646; his 'Bishop's Doom' (1638) reprinted, 1762; 'Sermons, Prayers, and Addresses,' edited by R. T. Martin, 1867; his deathbed 'Declaration' of doubtful authenticity. [xxv. 390]

HENDERSON, ALEXANDER (1780-1863), physician; M.D. Edinburgh, 1803; published, among other works, 'A Sketch of the Revolutions of Medical Science' (translated from Cabanis), 1806, and 'History of Ancient and Modern Wines,' 1824. [xxv. 395]

HENDERSON, ANDREW (fl. 1734-1775), author and bookseller; M.A. of a Scottish university; published 'History of the Rebellion, 1745-6, by an impartial hand, who was an Eyewitness' (1748), and biographical works; published 'Letters' (1775) attacking Dr. Johnson for 'Tour in the Hebrides.' [xxv. 395]

HENDERSON, ANDREW (1783-1835), Glasgow portrait-painter; exhibited at Scottish Academy, 1828-30; published 'Scottish Proverbs,' with etchings, 1832; contributed to the 'Laird of Logan.' [xxv. 396]

HENDERSON, CHARLES COOPER (1803-1877), equestrian painter and etcher; brother of John Henderson (1797-1878) [q. v.] [xxv. 396]

HENDERSON, EBENEZER, the elder (1784-1858), missionary; founded bible societies in Denmark, Scandinavia, Russia, and Iceland, acquiring many languages; went to Iceland, 1814; Ph.D. Kiel, 1816; printed the bible at St. Petersburg in ten languages; lived several years in Russia; tutor of Highbury College, 1830-50; published translations from Hebrew and accounts of visits to Iceland, Russia, and Piedmont; edited Buck's 'Theological Dictionary,' 1833, and other works. [xxv. 397]

HENDERSON, EBENEZER, the younger (1809-1879), mechanician and author; nephew of Ebenezer Henderson the elder [q. v.]; constructed an orrery and astronomical clock, 1827, and wheels to show sidereal time, 1850; published treatises on horology and astronomy, also 'Annals of Dunfermline,' 1879. [xxv. 398]

HENDERSON, SIR EDMUND YÉAMANS WALCOTT (1821-1896), lieutenant-colonel, royal engineers; educated at Woolwich; first lieutenant, royal engineers, 1841; lieutenant-colonel, 1862; engaged on boundary survey between Canada and New Brunswick, 1846-8; comptroller of convicts in western Australia, 1850-63; chairman of directors of prisons and inspector-general of military

prisons, 1863; C.B., 1868; chief commissioner of metropolitan police, 1869-86; instituted criminal investigation department; K.C.B., 1878; resigned on fault being found with police arrangements at Trafalgar Square riots, 1886.
[Suppl. ii. 409]

HENDERSON, GEORGE (1783-1855), lieutenant-colonel, royal engineers; distinguished in Peninsular war, 1812-14; lieutenant-colonel, R.E., 1824; superintendent and director of London and South-Western Railway.
[xxv. 398]

HENDERSON, JAMES (1783?-1848), geographical writer; consul-general for Colombia; F.R.S., 1831; published 'History of the Brazil' (1822), and works on Spain; died at Madrid. [xxv. 399]

HENDERSON, JOHN (1747-1785), 'the Bath Roscius'; appeared under name of Courtney at Bath as Hamlet, 1772; played Shylock at Haymarket, 1777; appeared at Drury Lane, 1777-9, and subsequently at Covent Garden, and chief provincial towns; considered second only to Garrick; regarded with jealousy by him; among his best parts, Shylock, Sir Giles Overreach, Hamlet, and Falstaff; drew, etched, and wrote poems; with Thomas Sheridan (1719-1788) [q. v.] published 'Practical Method of Reading and Writing English Poetry,' 1796; buried in Westminster Abbey.
[xxv. 399]

HENDERSON, JOHN (1757-1788), eccentric student: at twelve taught Greek and Latin at Trevecca; sent to Pembroke College, Oxford, at expense of Dean Tucker, 1781; a skilled linguist, with knowledge of medicine; accompanied Johnson and Hannah More over Pembroke College, 1782; B.A., 1786; refused to adopt any profession, and abandoned himself to solitary study of Lavater and spiritualism. [xxv. 401]

HENDERSON, JOHN (1804-1862), Scottish architect; designed Trinity College, Glenalmond, 1847. [xxv. 402]

HENDERSON, JOHN (1780-1867), philanthropist; drysalter and East India merchant; for twenty years contributed over 30,000l. annually to religious and charitable schemes; founded Evangelical Alliance; active opponent of Sunday travelling. [xxv. 403]

HENDERSON, JOHN (1797-1878), art collector and archaeologist; M.A. Balliol College, Oxford, 1820; bequeathed antiquities to Oxford University, water-colour collections, porcelain, glass, and manuscripts to British Museum, and pictures to National Gallery. [xxv. 403]

HENDERSON or HENRYSON, ROBERT (1430?-1506?). [See HENRYSON.]

HENDERSON, THOMAS (1798-1844), astronomer; secretary to Earl of Lauderdale and Lord Jeffrey, 1819-31; as astronomer royal at the Cape (1832-3) observed Encke's and Biela's comets, and (1832) transit of Mercury; discovered first authentic case of annual parallax in a fixed star; F.R.A.S., 1832; F.R.S., 1840; first Scottish astronomer royal and professor of practical astronomy at Edinburgh, 1834-44; Edinburgh observations published, 1838-43, and (edited by Piazzi Smyth), 1843-52. [xxv. 404]

HENDERSON, WILLIAM (1810-1872), homoeopathist; M.D. Edinburgh, 1831; studied also at Paris, Berlin, and Vienna; physician to Edinburgh Fever Hospital, 1832; pathologist to Royal Infirmary; professor of general pathology, 1842-69; adopted homoeopathy, 1845, and defended it against Sir John Forbes (1787-1861) [q. v.] and others. [xxv. 406]

HENDLEY, WILLIAM (1691?-1724), divine; B.A. Pembroke College, Cambridge, 1711; lecturer of St. James's, Clerkenwell, 1716, at St. Mary, Islington, 1718; his trial (1719) on charge of procuring unlawful gains under guise of collecting charities the subject of Defoe's 'Charity still a Christian Virtue.' [xxv. 407]

HENEAGE, GEORGE (d. 1549), dean of Lincoln, 1528-44; archdeacon, 1542-9; LL.B. Cambridge, 1510; incorporated at Oxford, 1522. [xxv. 407]

HENEAGE, MICHAEL (1540-1600), antiquary; brother of Sir Thomas Heneage (d. 1595) [q. v.]; fellow of St. John's College, Cambridge, 1563; M.A., 1566; M.P., Arundel, 1571, East Grinstead, 1572, Tavistock, 1589, and Wigan, 1593; joint-keeper of Tower records with his brother, c. 1578; assisted Robert Hare [q. v.] with Cambridge records. [xxv. 409]

HENEAGE, SIR THOMAS, the elder (*d.* 1553), gentleman usher to Wolsey, and of privy chamber; knighted, 1537.   [xxv. 407]

HENEAGE, SIR THOMAS (*d.* 1595), vice-chamberlain to Queen Elizabeth; nephew of George Heneage [q. v.]; M.P., Stamford, 1553, Boston, 1562, Lincolnshire, 1571–2, and Essex, 1585–95; treasurer of queen's chamber, 1570; knighted, 1577; keeper of Tower records, *c.* 1577; member of commissions to try Lopez, 1594, and others; built Copthall Essex; sent to Low Countries, 1586; paymaster of forces, 1588; vice-chamberlain, 1589; privy councillor, 1589; chancellor of Lancaster, 1590; friend of Sidney, Hatton, and John Foxe.   [xxv. 407]

HENFREY, ARTHUR (1819–1859), botanist; F.L.S., 1844; professor of botany at King's College, London, 1853; published 'Elementary Course of Botany,' 1857, and several translations; edited (with Huxley) 'Scientific Memoirs,' 1837, 'Micrographic Dictionary,' 1854 (with J. W. Griffith) and Francis's 'Anatomy of British Ferns,' 1855.   [xxv. 409]

HENFREY, HENRY WILLIAM (1852–1881), numismatist; son of Arthur Henfrey [q. v.]; principal work, 'Numismata Cromwelliana,' 1877.   [xxv. 410]

HENGHAM or **HINGHAM**, RALPH DE (*d.* 1311), judge; chancellor of Exeter, 1275–9; justice of king's bench, 1270, of common pleas, 1272; chief-justice of king's bench, 1274–90; dismissed and heavily fined; the fine traditionally applied to building a tower in Palace Yard; chief-justice of common pleas, 1301; puisne judge, 1307; reputed author of 'Hengham Magna' and 'Hengham Parva,' edited (1616) by Selden.   [xxv. 410]

HENGIST (*d.* 488), joint-founder with his brother Horsa [q. v.] of the kingdom of Kent; said to have arrived at Ebbsfleet from Jutland, 449 (according to Nennius, 428), to have settled in Thanet, and, after defeat by Britons at Aylesford (455), to have founded Leyden; returned and established himself in Kent.
                                        [xxv. 411]

HENGLER, FREDERICK CHARLES (1820–1887), circus proprietor; purchased Palais Royal, Argyll Street, London, 1871 (rebuilt, 1884).   [xxv. 413]

HENLEY, BARONS. [See EDEN, MORTON, first BARON, 1752–1830; EDEN, ROBERT HENLEY, second BARON, 1789–1841.]

HENLEY, ANTHONY (*d.* 1711), wit; of Magdalen College, Oxford; whig M.P., Andover (1698–1700), Weymouth (1702–11); contributed to the 'Tatler' and 'Medley'; member of Kit-Cat Club; patron of musicians and men of letters.   [xxv. 413]

HENLEY, JOHN (1692–1756), 'Orator Henley'; M.A. St. John's College, Cambridge, 1716; contributed to the 'Spectator' as 'Dr. Quir'; began his 'orations' at Newport, 1726; established himself in Lincoln's Inn Fields, 1729; employed by Walpole to write in whig 'Hyp Doctor,' 1730–9; his claims as restorer of church oratory ridiculed in the 'Dunciad'; caricatured by Hogarth; edited works of John Sheffield, duke of Buckingham, 1722; published works on oratory, theology, and grammar, and translations; his autograph lectures in British Museum.   [xxv. 414]

HENLEY, JOSEPH WARNER (1793–1884), conservative politician; M.A. Magdalen College, Oxford, 1834 (hon. D.C.L., 1854); M.P., Oxfordshire, 1841–78; president of board of trade, 1852 and 1858–9; resigned on reform question, 1859; declined home office, 1866.
                                        [xxv. 416]

HENLEY, PHOCION (1728–1764), musical composer; nephew of Robert Henley, first earl of Northington [q. v.]; B.A. Wadham College, Oxford, 1749; rector of St. Andrew's and St. Anne's, Blackfriars, 1759–64; some of his compositions are in T. Sharp's 'Divine Harmony' (psalms and hymns), 1798.   [xxv. 416]

HENLEY, ROBERT, first EARL OF NORTHINGTON (1708?–1772), lord chancellor; second son of Anthony Henley [q. v.]; fellow of All Souls' College, Oxford; M.A., 1733; barrister, Inner Temple, 1732; practised on western circuit; M.P., Bath, 1747–57; K.C., 1751, and recorder of Bath; attorney-general, 1756; lord keeper (the last), 1757; speaker of House of Lords, 1757–60, though not a

peer till 1760; lord chancellor, 1761; created an earl, 1764; procured dismissal of Rockingham; president of council under Grafton, 1766–7; intimate with George III.
                                        [xxv. 417]

HENLEY, ROBERT, second EARL OF NORTHINGTON (1747–1786), lord-lieutenant of Ireland; of Westminster and Christ Church, Oxford; M.A., 1766; M.P., Hampshire, 1768; succeeded as earl, 1772; K.T., 1773; viceroy of Ireland (1783–4) during volunteer convention; advocated annual parliaments and promoted Irish industries.
                                        [xxv. 419]

HENLEY, SAMUEL (1740–1815), commentator; professor of moral philosophy at Williamsburg, Virginia; afterwards assistant-master at Harrow; F.S.A., 1778; principal of East India College, Hertford, 1805–15; published English translation, with notes, of 'Vathek,' 1784, and works of scriptural exegesis and classical scholarship.   [xxv. 420]

HENLEY, WALTER DE (*fl.* 1250), author of 'Hosebondrie' (13th cent.)   [xxv. 420]

HENLEY or **HENLY**, WILLIAM (*fl.* 1775), electrician; F.R.S., 1773.   [xxv. 421]

HENLEY, WILLIAM THOMAS (1813?–1882), telegraphic engineer; self-taught; made apparatus for Wheatstone and first Electric Telegraph Company; invented magnetic needle telegraph and formed company (1852) to take over patent; obtained medal at exhibition of 1851; made electric light apparatus, and manufactured fourteen thousand miles of submarine cable.   [xxv. 421]

HENN, THOMAS RICE (1849–1880), lieutenant of royal engineers; fell at Maiwand.   [xxv. 422]

HENNEDY, ROGER (1809–1877), botanist; professor at Andersonian Institution, Glasgow, 1863–77; published 'Clydesdale Flora,' 1865.   [xxv. 422]

HENNELL, CHARLES CHRISTIAN (1809–1850), author of 'Inquiry concerning the Origin of Christianity' (1838) and 'Christian Theism' (1839); brother-in-law of Charles Bray [q. v.]; with J. T. B. Beaumont [q. v.] established New Philosophical Institution, Mile End.
                                        [xxv. 423]

HENNELL, MARY (1802–1843), author of 'Outline of the various Social Systems and Communities which have been founded on Principle of Co-operation' (published 1844); sister of Charles Christian Hennell [q. v.]
                                        [xxv. 424]

HENNEN, JOHN (1779–1828), army surgeon; served in Peninsula and at Waterloo; staff-surgeon, 1812; principal medical officer for Scotland, 1817; M.D. Edinburgh, 1819; died medical officer at Gibraltar; published, among other works, 'Observations on . . . Military Surgery,' 1818.   [xxv. 424]

HENNESSY, WILLIAM MAUNSELL (1829–1889), Irish scholar; assistant deputy-keeper in Dublin Record Office; Todd professor at Royal Irish Academy, 1882–4; edited 'Chronicon Scotorum' of Dubhaltach MacFirbisigh, 1866, 'Annals of Loch Cé,' 1871, and other works; translated 'Tripartite Life of St. Patrick,' 1871; wrote on Ossian.   [xxv. 424]

HENNIKER, SIR FREDERICK, baronet (1793–1825), traveller; of Eton and St. John's College, Cambridge; B.A., 1815; succeeded as baronet, 1816; published 'Notes during a Visit to Egypt, Nubia, the Oasis, Mount Sinai, and Jerusalem,' 1823.   [xxv. 425]

HENNIKER-MAJOR, JOHN, second BARON HENNIKER (1752–1821), antiquary; M.A. St. John's College, Cambridge, 1772; LL.D., 1811; F.S.A., 1785; F.R.S., 1785; took additional name, 1792; succeeded to Irish peerage, 1803; M.P., Rutland, 1805–12, Stamford, 1812–18; published 'Account of Families of Major and Henniker,' 1803, and antiquarian pamphlets.   [xxv. 425]

HENNING, JOHN (1771–1851), modeller and sculptor; a founder of Society of British Artists; modelled copies of Parthenon and Phigaleian friezes and Raphael's cartoons; executed busts of Mrs. Siddons and Princess Charlotte.   [xxv. 426]

HENRIETTA or **HENRIETTE ANNE**, DUCHESS OF ORLEANS (1644–1670), fifth daughter of Charles I; born at Exeter; secretly carried off from St. James's Palace to France, 1646; brought up as a Roman catholic by her mother; came to England at Restoration and became popular at court; married Philippe, duc d'Orléans (brother of Louis XIV), 1661; patronised Molière, Corneille, and Racine; intermediary between Louis XIV and Charles II; often consulted by former on state affairs; with Louise de Keroualle [q. v.] came to Dover, 1670, and negotiated the secret treaty of Dover, 1670; died suddenly soon after her return to France, being poisoned, according to St. Simon, with connivance of her jealous husband, by agents of his favourite, the Chevalier de Lorraine; her funeral oration delivered by Bossuet.   [xxv. 426]

HENRIETTA MARIA (1609-1669), queen consort of Charles I; youngest daughter of Henri IV and Marie de Médicis; married by proxy and came to England, 1625; on indifferent terms with her husband during lifetime of Buckingham; at first abstained from politics, but attracted courtiers and poets; evoked Prynne's 'Histrio-Mastix' by taking part in rehearsal of 'Shepherd's Pastoral,' 1632; under influence of George Conn [q. v.] thwarted Laud's proclamation against catholic recusants, 1636; obtained money from the catholics for Scottish war, 1639; after meeting of Long parliament carried on intrigues with the papal court, but could obtain no help for the royalists except on condition of Charles becoming a Romanist; after failure of overtures to parliamentary leaders, authorised Henry Jermyn and Sir John Suckling to carry out the army plot, 1641; tried to save Strafford; urged on attempted arrest of the five members, 1642; left England early in 1642, and bought munitions of war and obtained money in Holland; landed at Bridlington, February 1643, under fire; impeached by parliament, 23 May 1643; failed to surprise Hull and Lincoln, 1643; entertained by Shakespeare's daughter at Stratford-on-Avon; joined Charles at Edgehill and accompanied him to Oxford, 1643; advised bringing in of foreign or Irish army; escaped from Falmouth to France, 1644; pawned her jewels; negotiated with Mazarin and obtained promise of ten thousand men from Duke of Lorraine, 1644-5; urged Charles to accept Scottish help on basis of presbyterianism, 1646; active in negotiations with Irish catholics and the anti-parliamentarian English fleet, 1648; in state of destitution at the Louvre, 1648; retired into Carmelite nunnery; alienated Charles II's advisers by attempts to convert to Roman catholicism her younger son, Duke of Gloucester; came to England, 1660, to get portion for her daughter Henrietta Anne [q. v.] and to break off engagement between her second son Duke of York and Anne Hyde [q. v.]; lived at Somerset House; finally left England, 1665; died at Colombes and was buried in St. Denis.   [xxv. 429]

HENRY I (1068-1135), king of England; younger son of William I and Matilda; well educated in England; heir of his mother's possessions in England, 1083; bought the Avranchin and Côtentin from his elder brother Robert, duke of Normandy; imprisoned by him at Bayeux, 1088-9; helped to put down revolt of Rouen, 1090; attacked by both William II and Robert, and obliged to evacuate Mont St. Michel; became lord of Domfront, 1092, whence he carried on war against Robert and his vassals; visited William II in England, 1094, and returned to Normandy with money; received counties of Coutances and Bayeux, 1096; on the news of William II's death (1100) secured the treasure at Winchester; chosen king by the witan and crowned at Westminster, issuing at his coronation (1100) charter which formed the basis of Magna Charta; invited Archbishop Anselm [q. v.] to return, 1100, and filled vacant sees; ruled by craft rather than force; agreed, on Anselm's refusal to do homage for his temporalities, to refer the question to the pope, but maintained his position till a compromise was agreed to (1105); married Eadgyth or Matilda (1080-1118) [q. v.], 1100, thereby introducing intermarriages between Normans and English, and becoming the re-founder of the English nation; chose his councillors and officials from lower ranks, and ennobled them as a counterpoise to the great barons; promised at Alton to give up all his Norman possessions (except Domfront) in return for a renunciation by Duke Robert of the English crown and a pension, 1101; defeated and banished Robert of Bellême [q. v.], 1101, and William of Mortain, 1104; compelled Robert to give up his pension and cede Evreux; with help of Anjou, Maine, and Brittany, conquered the whole of Normandy at Tinchebrai, 1106, capturing Robert and Mortain; returned to England and concluded the investiture agreement; developed the judicial and fiscal administration, sending out itinerant justices and organising the exchequer court; reformed the coinage, 1107, but levied heavy taxes; went to Normandy to seize

William 'Clito' (Robert's son), 1108; began a war wit Louis VI of France about the border fortress of Gisor 1109; banished more barons, 1110; put down privat war and restrained his mercenaries; captured Robert c Bellême, 1111; obtained acknowledgment of his right t Bellême, Maine, and Brittany; led an army into Wales 1114; caused all barons to do homage to William, his heir in Normandy, 1115, and England, 1116; began fresh wa with Louis VI, who was aided by Baldwin of Flanders an Fulk of Anjou; detached Fulk from the confederacy, 112(by marrying to Fulk's daughter his son Prince Willian (lost in the White Ship the same year); defeated Louis in a encounter of knights at Brenneville; subdued rebel baron and made peace at Gisors with Louis and Baldwin b mediation of Pope Calixtus II, 1120; made a secon marriage with Adela of Louvain, 1121; exacted tribut from Welsh by second invasion, 1121; upheld rights of Can terbury against both the pope and Thurstan, archbishop c York; reduced fresh Norman rebellion, 1123-4; exacte from nobles (including Stephen of Boulogne) promise t support succession to crown of his daughter, the ex empress Matilda, 1126; married her to Geoffrey of Anjou 1128; engaged again in war with France; exacted fine from clergy for keeping wives; supported Pope Inno cent II against anti-pope Anaclete; exacted oaths t Matilda, 1131; went to Normandy, 1133; had fres trouble with the Angevins and Normans; died at Angers buried at Reading.   [xxv. 436]

HENRY II (1133-1189), king of England; grandso of Henry I, and son of Geoffrey of Anjou and Matild (1102-1167) [q. v.]; inherited Angevin territories, 1151 obtained Aquitaine by marriage with Eleanor (1122? 1204) [q. v.], 1152; came to terms with Stephen, 1153 succeeded to crown, 1154; issued charter based on that c Henry I; expelled Flemish mercenaries and reduced re bellious barons, 1155; exacted homage and restoration c border counties from Malcolm of Scotland; acquire county of Nantes and recognition of overlordship of Brit tany, 1158; re-established exchequer in England; deve loped curia regis; issued new coinage, 1158; extended i a 'great assize' the system of inquest by sworn recog nitors to settlement of land disputes; broke down by th 'great scutage' military dependence of crown on feuda tenants, 1159; gained possession of the Vexin by Frencl marriage of eldest surviving son Henry, 1160; helped Pop Alexander III against the emperor, 1162; made Thoma Becket [q. v.] archbishop, 1162, but was resisted by hin especially in his attempt to bring the clergy within civ jurisdiction, through the constitutions of Clarendon, 1164 caused Becket's condemnation at Northampton, 1164; o his flight enforced the constitutions; applied the prin ciple of jury inquest to criminal matters by the assiz of Clarendon, 1166, the first attempt in England to issu a new code of laws, and to break down feudalism by sub ordinating independent jurisdictions to a central court allied himself, through his daughters' marriages, wit the emperor Frederick Barbarossa and the kings c Castile, 1168-9, and Sicily, 1169; defeated the Bretons 1166-9; by treaty of Montmirail (1169) obtained sanctio of France to establishment of his sons Henry, Geoffrey and Richard; had Prince Henry crowned by the arcl bishop of York, 1170; suspended, and, after inquiry int their conduct, replaced by exchequer officials most of th sheriffs, 1170; made formal peace with Becket and hi ally, Louis of France; after Becket's murder (1170) purge himself and abjured the 'customs,' which had been th chief cause of quarrel; by an expedition to Ireland (1171 1172) received the submission both of Normans in Irelan and natives, divided the land into fiefs, and left Hugh d Lacy as royal vicegerent; drove Louis from Normandy 1173; crushed Breton revolt, 1173; and (after doing penanc at Canterbury) the baronial rising in England; exacte homage from his prisoner, William, king of Scots; checke by these successes combination headed by the young Kin Henry (crowned heir) and his mother (1173-4); issue assize of Northampton, 1176, including among its clause the 'assize of mort d'ancester' and a provision requirin an oath of fealty from all Englishmen; obtained partia recognition of his constitutions from the pope; ordere a return of all crown tenements, 1177; constituted inne tribunal for higher work of curia regis, 1178; establishe judicial circuits, 1176-80; issued assize of arms, 1181 making defensive service obligatory, and personal pro perty subject to taxation; received homage from king o Connaught, 1175; arbiter between Arragon and Toulous

173, and Castile and Navarre, 1177 ; mediator in France, 180-2 ; was asked to deliver the Holy Land, 1185, but was engaged in war with his sons Henry and Geoffrey on behalf of Richard, 1183, and afterwards with Richard and Philip Augustus of France, to whose claims he was reduced (1189) to submit at Colombières ; died at Chinon ; buried at Fontevraud, where is his tomb and effigy. He was a lover of learning and a great builder ; his works of his kind including many palaces, the embankment of the Loire, and the Grand Pont at Angers.   [xxvi. 1]

HENRY III (1207–1272), king of England ; grandson of Henry II and son of John ; crowned at Gloucester, 216, and did homage to Gualo, the Pope's legate ; accompanied William Marshall [q. v.], the regent, to siege of London and to negotiate peace with Louis of France and his supporters, 1217 ; received homage from Alexander II of Scotland ; crowned again at Westminster, 1220, by direction of the pope ; marched with the legate and the Earl of Chester to force William of Aumale to give up Biham Castle, 1221 ; agreed to confirm the Great Charter, 223 ; compelled the Welsh to make peace ; took Fulk de Breauté's castle at Bedford, 1224 ; declared himself of full age, 1227, having during his minority had a 'continual' council distinct from his court ; lost most of his French possessions, 1224, but recovered Gascony, 1225 ; negotiated with Brittany, the emperor, and Bavaria ; compelled by barons to restore the forest liberties ; defeated by Welsh, 228 ; secretly agreed to pope's demand for a tenth of all property, 1229 ; invaded Poitou and Gascony, 1230 ; obtained scutage in exchange for affirmation of liberties of Church, 1231 ; refused aid for Welsh war ; dismissed Hubert de Burgh [q. v.] and made Segrave justiciar, 1232 ; replaced English officers by Poitevin friends of Bishop Peter des Roches ; compelled after a contest by Richard Marshall and Archbishop Edmund Rich [q. v.] to dismiss Poitevins and to be reconciled with De Burgh and the barons, 1234 ; henceforth (1234) became his own minister ; married his sister Isabella to the Emperor Frederic II, 1235 ; wedded Eleanor of Provence, 1236, in which year was passed the Assize of Merton ; depended on guidance of his wife's uncle, William de Valence, and Provençal favourites ; invited the legate Otho to England ; favoured Simon de Montfort (husband of his sister Eleanor), but quarrelled with him, 1239 ; opposed by Richard, Earl of Cornwall [q. v.] and citizens of London ; made concessions ; entertained Baldwin II, emperor of the East, 1238 ; his life attempted by a crazy clerk, 1238 ; kept see of Winchester vacant, the monks refusing (1238) to elect William of Valence ; founded Netley Abbey, 1239 ; gave the archbishopric of Canterbury to Boniface of Savoy [q. v.], 1241, and see of Hereford to another foreigner ; allowed the pope to take fifth of the clergy's goods and many benefices, c. 1240 ; made Peter of Savoy Earl of Richmond ; joined the Count of La Marche and others in an expedition to Gascony, 242, but was deserted by him and forced by Louis IX to retreat, 1243 ; brought back more foreigners, detaching his brother Richard from the opposition by marrying him to Sanchia of Provence ; compelled by Innocent IV to recall the banished bishop of Winchester ; obliged, in order to get a scutage, to admit four 'guardians of liberties' to his council ; made other concessions to the baronage ; with money furnished by Richard of Cornwall undertook successful Welsh campaign, 1245 ; joined in remonstrance against the pope's exactions, but gave way, and laid a heavy tallage on London, 1246 ; enriched his foreign half-brothers from church revenues ; refused an aid, 1249 ; exacted more money from Londoners and Jews ; received homage for Lothian from Alexander III of Scotland on his marriage, 251 ; appointed Simon de Montfort governor of Gascony ; insulted de Montfort with accusations, 1252 ; was refused money for a crusade, 1252 ; confirmed the charters in return for money, 1253, and made a second expedition into Gascony ; visited Pontigny, Fontevraud, and Paris ; agreed to bear cost of Pope Alexander II's war with Manfred in return for grant of Sicilian crown to his son Edmund ; unable to obtain regular grants ; demanded from parliament at Westminster (1258) a third of all property, the barons attending in armour and led by Roger Bigod, fourth earl of Norfolk [q. v.] ; met barons in ' Mad Parliament ' at Oxford (1258), which drew up ' Provisions,' giving barons control of the executive and the nomination of half the council, a committee of twenty-four being appointed to carry out reforms ; made peace with France by giving up Normandy and his hereditary possessions ; on his return from France to England brought accusation against

Simon de Montfort, 1260 ; dismissed the barons' justiciar, 1261 ; seized Dover Castle, 1261 ; exhibited papal bull absolving him from keeping the provisions, 1261 ; ordered the knights of the shire to attend him at Windsor instead of the barons at St. Albans, 1261 ; decision given in his favour by Louis IX of France in the ' Mise of Amiens,' to whom the provisions had been referred for arbitration, 1264, the award being upheld by Pope Urban IV ; captured the younger de Montfort at Northampton, April 1264, the barons having refused to accept the award, and allied themselves with the Welsh ; took Leicester, Nottingham, and Tonbridge ; compelled to march into Sussex for provisions ; routed at Lewes, 14 May, 1264 ; compelled to summon a parliament (including four knights from each shire) and to forbid his queen to raise money for him, 1264 ; gave his assent to the constitution drawn up in the famous parliament of 1265 ; restored to power by his son Prince Edward's victory at Evesham, 1265, when he was wounded, being at the time detained in Montfort's army ; revoked all his recent acts, declared the rebels' lands forfeited, fined the Londoners, reduced Kenilworth, and came to terms with Gloucester in London and Llywelyn in Wales ; at the Marlborough parliament (1267) granted many reforms, but retained the executive ; assented to statute forbidding the Jews to acquire debtors' land, 1269 ; completed (1269) and opened Westminster Abbey, the body of Edward the Confessor being translated ; buried in Westminster Abbey before the high altar, his heart being sent to Fontevraud. Most of the troubles of his reign were due to his foreign sympathies.

    [xxvi. 12]

HENRY IV (1367–1413), king of England ; son of John of Gaunt [q. v.] ; sometimes called Henry of Bolingbroke from his birthplace ; styled Earl of Derby in early life ; K.G., 1377 ; married Mary de Bohun, coheiress of Hereford, 1380 ; praised by Froissart ; as one of the five lords appellant opposed Robert de Vere [q. v.], who, marching on London, compelled Richard II to grant their demands, 1387 ; took part in proceedings of ' Merciless parliament,' 1388, but gradually regained Richard's favour ; joined ' crusade ' of the Teutonic knights against Lithuania, 1390 ; went on pilgrimage to Jerusalem, 1392–1393, being entertained by the kings of Bohemia and Hungary, the Archduke of Austria, and the Venetians ; one of the council during Richard's absence in Ireland, 1395 ; took a decided part for the king against his former allies, and was created Duke of Hereford, 1397 ; appealed Norfolk of treason, but was not allowed to fight with him, being banished the realm for ten years, 1398 ; exiled for life, his Lancaster estates also being confiscated during his stay at Paris ; with the two Arundels and others, secretly left France and landed near Bridlington, 1399 ; joined by northern nobles ; held council at Doncaster, and with a large army marched to Bristol, where some of the royal officers were executed, July 1399 ; met King Richard, who had been deserted by his army, at Flint ; was promised restoration of his estates ; took the king to London, where Richard resigned the crown, 29 Sept. 1399 ; obtained the throne by popular election ; founded the order of the Bath before his coronation, 1399 ; condemned Richard, who soon died, possibly starved, to perpetual imprisonment, 1399 ; crushed rising of Richard's dispossessed supporters, 1400 ; made expeditions against the Scots (1400) and Welsh (1400 and 1401) and entertained the Greek emperor, Manuel Palaiologos, 1400 ; married as his second wife Joan, regent of Brittany, 1402 ; was attacked by the dukes of Orleans and Burgundy in France and by Franciscan conspirators in England, 1402 ; failed to subdue the Welsh, 1402 ; defeated the discontented Percies at Shrewsbury, 1403 ; received submission of Northumberland, 1403 ; compelled to agree to expulsion of aliens ; was strengthened by defeat of French at Dartmouth, 1404 ; received liberal supplies from ' Unlearned parliament ' at Coventry, 1404 ; escaped assassination at Eltham, 1404 ; suppressed revolt of Northumberland, Archbishop Scrope [q. v.], and the earl marshal, 1405 ; captured the heir to the Scottish throne, 1405 ; compelled by parliament to nominate a constitutional council, to submit to an audit of accounts, and reform his household, 1406 ; debarred the Beauforts from the succession, 1407 ; finally defeated Northumberland and Bardolf at Bramham Moor, 1408 ; declined in health and energy, but interested himself in Archbishop Arundel's attempt to heal the papal schism ; supported the church party in preventing proposed confiscation of their temporalities, but was himself refused a revenue for life, 1410 ; defeated attempt to force him to abdicate in favour of Prince Henry, broke off Burgundian alliance, and undertook a progress, 1411–12 ; increased Chaucer's pension and patronised Gower ; died in Jerusalem Chamber, Westminster ; his tomb at Canterbury opened, 1832.   [xxvi. 31]

HENRY V (1387–1422), king of England ; eldest son of Henry IV, by Mary de Bohun ; born at Monmouth ; said to have been educated by his uncle Henry Beaufort (d. 1447) [q. v.] at Queen's College, Oxford ; attended Richard II, 1398–9 ; accompanied his father to Wales, 1400, where he represented him for the next three years, recovering Conway, reducing Merioneth and Carnarvon, and checking Glendower [q. v.] ; assisted his father at Shrewsbury, 1403 : returned to the Welsh marches and relieved Coyty Castle, 1405; after joining in petition against lollards, 1406, captured Aberystwith and invaded Scotland, 1407 ; warden of the Cinque ports and constable of Dover, 1409 ; probably governed in his father's name during chancellorship of Thomas Beaufort [q. v.], 1410–11 ; sent an expedition to help Burgundy against the Armagnacs ; withdrew from the council, 1412, his French policy being reversed ; succeeded to the throne, 1413 ; the supposed wildness of his youth unsupported by contemporary authority, while his traditional conduct towards Gascoigne (taken by Shakespeare from Hall) is improbable, and is first mentioned in Sir T. Elyot's 'Governour' (1531) ; appointed Henry Beaufort (d. 1447) [q. v.] chancellor, and the Earl of Arundel treasurer; gave the remains of Richard II honourable burial ; had Oldcastle arrested, and lollardy repressed, 1414 ; demanded the restoration of French territories ceded at Brétigny, together with the Norman and Angevin lands, as a condition of his marriage with Catherine of France ; left Portsmouth to make war with France (August 1415), just after a conspiracy to proclaim the Earl of March king had been discovered ; took Harfleur and challenged the dauphin to single combat, 1415 ; sent back Clarence in charge of many sick, and marched with the rest towards Calais ; after futile negotiations attacked the greatly superior French army, himself commanding the centre, at Agincourt (25 Oct. 1415), where the French were routed with great slaughter ; reached Calais a few days later, crossed the Channel within a fortnight, and after a triumphal entry into London was granted by parliament tonnage and poundage for life, the custom on wool, and other taxes, 1415 ; while in England restored the heirs of Mortimer, Percy, and Holland to their estates ; made an alliance with Sigismund, king of the Romans, which led to the termination of the papal schism, 1416 ; came to an understanding with Burgundy, October, 1416 ; laid the foundations of a national navy and of military, international, and maritime law ; took Caen, leading the assault in person, 1417 ; sent lieutenants against Cherbourg, Coutances, Avranches, and Evreux, subduing the greater part of Normandy ; surrounded Rouen, cutting it off from the sea with the aid of a Portuguese fleet, and reduced it by famine after a long siege, 1419, while keeping open the feud between Armagnacs and Burgundians by alternate negotiations with each ; after a short truce surprised Pontoise, 1419, and on the murder of John, duke of Burgundy, concluded an alliance with the new duke Philip ; after more fighting and negotiation, accepted the treaty of Troyes (1420), by which Henry was declared heir of Charles VI, regent of France, and lord of Normandy, the dauphin being excepted from the arrangement ; married Catherine of France, 1420; personally directed capture of Melun, November 1420, meeting the Sire de Barbazan in single combat ; entered Paris in triumph, December 1420 ; arranged for the government of Normandy ; took his wife to England to be crowned ; reformed the Benedictine monasteries ; sent back James I to Scotland ; returned to France to reassert his sway, 1421 ; relieved Chartres, 1421 ; drove the dauphin across the Loire ; took Meaux, 1422 ; while on his way to succour Burgundy at Cosne died at Bois de Vincennes. After a funeral procession through France his body was buried in Westminster Abbey, a chantry being endowed in his honour. The silver head of his effigy was stolen from the Confessor's chapel in 1545. He was a patron of the poets Lydgate and Hoccleve. Inflexible justice, affability, and religious spirit were among his chief characteristics, and he was the first of contemporary generals and an able diplomatist.   [xxvi. 43]

HENRY VI (1421–1471), king of England ; son of Henry V ; born at Windsor ; ruled through a council during his minority, his uncle, Humphrey of Gloucester, being protector, and Richard Beauchamp, earl of Warwick, his 'master' ; appeared in public functions in early childhood ; crowned at Westminster, 1429, and at Paris, 1430 ; opened parliament in person, 1432 ; mediated at a great council between Gloucester and Bedford, 1434 ; his precocious interest in politics restrained by the council ; admitted to share in government, 1437, but warned that he was exercising it unprofitably ; identified himself with Cardinal Beaufort's peace policy ; greatly interested in scheme for his marriage with a daughter of the Comte d'Armagnac, 1441–3 ; attained legal majority, 1442 ; concluded two years' truce with France, 1443 ; married Margaret of Anjou, daughter of the Duke of Lorraine, 1445 ; under influence of Beaufort and Suffolk, ordered Gloucester's arrest, 1447 ; surrendered Maine for prolongation of truce with France, 1448 ; made constant progresses through England ; secretly supported Suffolk, but was obliged to exile him, 1450 ; attempted to suppress Cade's rising, but fled to Kenilworth, leaving the work to Archbishop Kemp and Waynflete, 1450 ; lost Normandy ; obliged to make Richard, duke of York [q. v.], a councillor, and agree to arrest of Edmund Beaufort, duke of Somerset [q. v.] ; made Somerset captain of Calais, and refused to remove him from court, 1451 ; lost Guienne, 1451 ; deeply in debt ; attempted a general pacification and pardon, 1452 ; won back part of Guienne, 1452, but lost it all, 1453 ; temporarily lost his reason, 1453 ; on his recovery released Somerset and excluded York from the council, 1455 ; slightly wounded at first battle of St. Albans, 1455 ; again became ill ; persuaded on recovery to remove York from office, 1456, but allowed him to remain in the council, and with the help of Buckingham maintained peace for two years ; after Salisbury's victory (1459) at Bloreheath marched against Ludlow and drove York and the Nevilles from England, 1459, afterwards attainting them at Coventry ; was defeated and captured by Warwick at Northampton, and compelled to acknowledge York as heir to the crown, 1460 ; in spite of the defeat of the Yorkists by his queen (Margaret) at Wakefield (1460) and St. Albans (1461). Henry fled northward after Edward, duke of York, was proclaimed king, 1461 ; at York while Towton Field was fought unsuccessfully by his friends, 1461 ; attainted by the Yorkists, 1461 ; took refuge with the Scots, 1461 ; granted charter to Edinburgh, 1464 ; narrowly escaped capture at Hexham, 1464 ; lurked disguised for a year on the Lancashire and Yorkshire border ; was captured and imprisoned in the Tower for five years (1465–70) ; restored by Warwick, 1470 ; presided at a parliament, but (1471) fell into the hands of Edward IV, and was taken by him to Barnet ; after battle of Barnet (1471) was recommitted to the Tower ; murdered on the night of Edward's return, Richard of Gloucester being held responsible ; worshipped as a martyr by north countrymen ; his canonisation proposed by Henry VII. Henry VI was too weak to rule men, but was genuinely pious, and a liberal patron of learning. Besides taking great interest in the universities of Oxford and Caen, he founded Eton (1440) and King's College, Cambridge (1441), and suggested to his queen Margaret the foundation of Queens' College, Cambridge, 1448.   [xxvi. 56]

HENRY VII (1457–1509), king of England ; son of Edmund Tudor, earl of Richmond, and Margaret Beaufort [q. v.], heiress of John of Gaunt ; brought up in Wales by his uncle, Jasper Tudor ; captured at Harlech by the Yorkist Herbert, 1468, but reclaimed by his uncle and presented to Henry VI, 1470 ; head of house of Lancaster on Henry VI's death, 1471 ; refugee in Brittany during reign of Edward IV ; prevented by a storm from joining Buckingham's rebellion against Richard III, 1483 ; at council of refugees held at Rennes promised to marry Elizabeth of York on obtaining the English crown ; after warning from Morton of contemplated betrayal to Richard escaped from Brittany to France ; with Oxford and some French troops landed at Milford Haven, 1485 ; joined by Welshmen and others ; with the help of Sir William Stanley (d. 1495) [q. v.] defeated and slew Richard at Bosworth, 1485 ; crowned, 1485 ; created peers and instituted a bodyguard ; married Princess Elizabeth, 1486 ; defeated the conspirator Simnel at Stoke-on-Trent, 1487 ; failed to mediate between France and Brittany, 1488 ; employed Surrey to suppress discontent in the north, 1489 ; in alliance with Maximilian, king of the Romans, and Ferdinand and Isabella, besieged Boulogne (1492), but concluded the treaty of Etaples with Charles VIII, 1492 ; took prompt action against Yorkists, and delayed for three years the invasion of England by Perkin Warbeck [q. v.]; drove Warbeck from Ireland by the action of Sir Edward Poynings [q. v.], 1494, and through Spanish diplomacy procured Warbeck's dismissal from the Scottish court; lenient in suppressing Cornish insurrection, 1497; executed Warwick and Warbeck after their attempted escape from the Tower, 1499; concluded treaties with Scotland, 1499, Burgundy, 1500, and the Emperor Maximilian, 1502; lost his queen, 1503; arranged marriages of his children with Spain and Scotland; entertained Philip and Joanna of Castile, and made commercial treaty with Flanders, 1506; died at Richmond in the palace named and built by himself. Through his agents Empson and Dudley he practised much extortion. He was considered one of the wisest princes of his time, and was a great promoter of commerce and learning. He built the chapel in Westminster Abbey called by his name. [xxvi. 69]

HENRY VIII (1491–1547), king of England; second son of Henry VII; nominal lieutenant of Ireland, 1494; created Prince of Wales, 1503, on the death of his elder brother Arthur (1486–1502) [q. v.], to whose widow, Catherine of Arragon [q. v.], he was contracted, but marriage was delayed till his accession, 1509, owing to disputes about her dowry; had Empson and Dudley, the agents of his father's extortions, executed, 1510; helped his father-in-law against the Moors, 1511, and the regent of the Netherlands against Gueldres, 1511, joined the pope, Ferdinand, and Venice, in a league against France, 1511; some important naval victories won by his admirals, the Howards, one of whom captured Andrew Barton [q. v.], 1511; sent an unsuccessful expedition for the recovery of Guienne, 1512; built the Henry Grace de Dieu (largest ship hitherto floated); with the help of the Emperor Maximilian won 'the battle of Spurs,' 1513 (the Scots being defeated at Flodden in his absence); deserted by his allies; made separate peace with France on the basis of a marriage between his sister Mary and Louis XII, 1514; made Cardinal Wolsey chancellor; followed Wolsey's advice in helping Maximilian with money to check the French in Italy, and in keeping on good terms with him, in securing Charles in Castile, and (1518) in making peace with Francis I of France; became, against Wolsey's advice, a secret candidate for the empire, 1519; met Francis at the Field of the Cloth of Gold, 1520, but had previous and subsequent interviews with the Emperor Charles V also; while pretending to mediate between them allied himself with Charles; next year at home had Buckingham executed on a vague charge of treason; his demand for a forced loan, in consequence of the threatened hostilities with France, successfully resisted by London, 1525; helped by Wolsey's negotiations to a secret understanding with France; began negotiations with the pope for a divorce from Catherine of Arragon, 1527; given a commission to hear the case in England, 1528, which met (1529), but was revoked to Rome unfinished, 1529; dismissed Wolsey, October 1529, and took Cranmer as his adviser on the divorce; consulted English, French, and Italian universities, 1530; eight decisions against the validity of marriage with a brother's wife and against the pope's power to dispense being obtained by bribery; wrung from the clergy a qualified acknowledgment of his title as supreme head of the church in exchange for a pardon for having incurred the penalties of præmunire by recognising Wolsey as papal legate, 1531; separated from Catherine on her refusal of arbitration, 1531; secretly married his second wife, Anne Boleyn, and, Cranmer having decided against the validity of the marriage with Catherine, had Anne crowned publicly, 1533; secretly encouraged the Commons to present 'supplication against the ordinaries,' 1532; took away independent powers of convocation; named Cranmer archbishop; provisionally withdrew first-fruits of benefices (annates) and abolished appeals to Rome; was excommunicated, 1533; confirmed abolition of annates; caused Elizabeth Barton [q. v.] to be attainted, 1533; abolished Roman jurisdiction and revenues in England, 1534; obtained act of succession (1534) compelling all subjects to acknowledge Anne Boleyn's issue as heirs to the crown; imprisoned More and Fisher; executed the Nun of Kent and her adherents, 1534; suppressed the observants, and imprisoned recusant friars; obtained severe treason law, parliamentary confirmation of headship of church, and transference of first-fruits and tenths to crown (1534–5); executed Fisher, More, and

some Charterhouse monks for refusing to accept the king's headship, 1535; opened negotiations with German protestants; instituted visitations of monasteries and universities by royal officers under Thomas Cromwell (1485?–1540) [q. v.], and appropriated the revenues of the smaller houses, 1535; beheaded Anne Boleyn and married his third wife, Jane Seymour, 1536; had succession act passed in interests of Jane Seymour, 1536; at first temporised with and then crushed rising in the north and east caused by religious changes and heavy taxation, 1536–7; lamented death of Jane Seymour, 1538; resumed dissolution of monasteries, but failed in negotiations with German protestants; maintained old doctrines; procured statute of the Six Articles, 1539; executed last descendants of the Yorkist house; married his fourth wife, Anne of Cleves, January 1540; executed Cromwell and divorced Anne of Cleves, July 1540; at once married his fifth wife, Catherine Howard; had Barnes and other protestants burned for heresy (1538–40); beheaded Queen Catherine Howard, 1542; proclaimed Ireland a kingdom, 1542; revived the feudal claim on Scotland, and defeated James V, 1542; concluded alliance with Emperor Charles V, 1543; married his sixth and last wife, Catherine Parr [q. v.], 1543; debased the currency; sent an army into Scotland, which burned Leith and Edinburgh, 1544; captured Boulogne, 1545; was granted the endowments of many colleges, chantries, and hospitals, 1545; deserted by Charles V; made peace with France, 1546; gained possession of St. Andrews by aiding the conspiracy against Beaton, 1546; authorised many persecutions for heresy; caused the Earl of Surrey to be beheaded and the Duke of Norfolk attainted, 1547. Henry was technically constitutional, but practically absolute, and a consummate statesman. He completed Wolsey's college at Oxford, calling it Henry VIII's College (Christ Church), erected six new bishoprics from monastical endowments, and established suffragans. He wrote 'Assertio Septem Sacramentorum' against Luther (1521) and preface to revised edition ('king's book') of 'Institution of a Christian Man' ('bishops' book'). Many portraits of him by Holbein are extant. [xxvi. 76]

HENRY OF SCOTLAND (1114?–1152), son of David I of Scotland; granted by Stephen the earldoms of Carlisle, Doncaster, and Huntingdon; fought at battle of the Standard, 1138; created Earl of Northumberland, 1139. [xxvi. 94]

HENRY, 'the Young King' (1155–1183), second son of Henry II of England; married while a child to Margaret, daughter of Louis VII of France, 1160; educated by Becket; crowned at Westminster, 1170, and again with his queen at Winchester, 1172; on being refused lands by his father fled to the French court and joined his father's enemies; reconciled with his father, 1174; made war on his brother Richard in Aquitaine, 1182, and afterwards also on Henry II; struck down by fever, died penitent at Martel; buried at Rouen. [xxvi. 95]

HENRY OF CORNWALL or OF ALMAINE (1235–1271), son of Richard, earl of Cornwall and king of the Romans [q. v.], and Isabella Marshall; accompanied his father to France, 1247 and 1250, and witnessed his coronation at Aachen, 1257; one of the royal nominees to draw up constitution at Oxford, 1258; as partisan of Simon de Montfort imprisoned at Boulogne, 1263; joined Prince Edward and fought for royalists at Lewes, 1264, when he gave himself up as a hostage; sent to France to treat with Louis IX, 1265; commanded expedition against Robert, earl Ferrers [q. v.], 1266; co-opted referee under Dictum de Kenilworth, 1267; mediated between Henry III and Gloucester, 1267; took the cross, 1268; followed Edward to Tunis and Sicily, 1270, but returned to settle the affairs of Gascony, where he had weight through his marriage with the daughter of Gaston, vicomte de Béarn; accompanied the kings of France and Sicily through Italy to Viterbo; murdered at church by De Montfort's sons and Count Rosso, though he had not even been present at Evesham; his heart deposited in Westminster Abbey. [xxvi. 96]

HENRY OF LANCASTER, EARL OF LANCASTER (1281?–1345), grandson of Henry III and second son of Edmund, earl of Lancaster [see LANCASTER, EDMUND, EARL OF]; lord of Monmouth and Lancaster's Welsh estates, 1296; summoned as baron, 1299; served with Edward I in Flanders (1297–8) and Scotland, 1298; helped to subdue Llywelyn Bren, 1315; created Earl of Lancaster and Leicester and steward of England on death of his brother Thomas (1277–1322) [q. v.], 1324; joined Queen Isabella, 1326, and captured Edward II and the younger Despenser, 1326; guardian and chief councillor of the young Edward III; formed confederacy against Mortimer, but was obliged to submit, 1329; sent on embassy to France, 1330; became blind; devised overthrow of Mortimer; founded hospital near Leicester. [xxvi. 100]

HENRY OF LANCASTER, first DUKE OF LANCASTER (1299?–1361), son of Henry, earl of Lancaster (1281?–1345) [q. v.]; a crusader in his youth; distinguished at capture of Dalkeith, 1333; summoned as Henry de Lancaster, 1334; created Earl of Derby, 1337; sent with Sir Walter Manny [q. v.] against Cadsant, 1337; with Edward III in Flanders, 1338–9, lending him money; distinguished himself at Sluys, 1340; captain-general against Scotland, 1341–2, overcoming Sir William Douglas, knight of Liddesdale [q. v.] in a tournament; went on missions to the pope and Alfonso XI of Castile; served against the Moors at Algeciras, 1343; lieutenant of Aquitaine, 1345–7; succeeded to his father's earldoms, 1347; took Bergerac, 1345, and defeated a much superior French force at Auberoche, and stormed Lusignan and Poitiers, 1346; reinforced Edward at Calais, 1347; an original K.G.; negotiated with French and Flemish, 1348–9; created Earl of Lincoln and captain of Gascony and Poitou, 1349; prominent in sea-fight called Espagnols-sur-mer, 1350; created Duke of Lancaster, with palatine jurisdiction, and admiral of western fleet, 1351; attacked Boulogne, 1351; went to Prussia and Poland, 1351–2, and to Paris to fight Otto of Brunswick for an attempt to waylay him in Germany, 1352; head of embassy to king of Navarre, 1354; conducted campaigns in Normandy and Brittany, 1356–7; created Earl of Moray by David II, 1359; co-operated with Edward in France, 1359–60; chief negotiator at peace of Bretigny, 1360; died of the pestilence at Leicester, where he added to his father's foundation the collegiate church of St. Mary-the-Greater. He was Edward III's most trusted counsellor, and esteemed throughout western Europe as a perfect knight. His daughter Blanche (wife of John of Gaunt) was ancestress of the house of Lancaster. [xxvi. 101]

HENRY FREDERICK, PRINCE OF WALES (1594–1612), eldest son of James VI of Scotland (James I of England); his guardianship by the Earl of Mar objected to by the queen but upheld by the king; came to England with Anne of Denmark; matriculated at Magdalen College, Oxford, 1605; a Spanish marriage proposed for him; friend of Ralegh; created Prince of Wales, 1610; died of typhoid fever; buried in Westminster Abbey. [xxvi. 106]

HENRY, DUKE OF GLOUCESTER (1639–1660), third son of Charles I; styled HENRY OF OATLANDS; placed under care of Earl of Northumberland, and afterwards of Countess of Leicester; while in France pressed by his mother, Henrietta Maria, to become a Romanist, and disowned on his refusal; joined his brother Charles at Cologne; distinguished himself as a volunteer with the Spanish in Flanders, 1657–8; died of small-pox in London; buried in same vault as Mary Queen of Scots at Westminster; highly praised by Clarendon. [xxvi. 108]

HENRY FREDERICK, DUKE OF CUMBERLAND AND STRATHEARN (1745–1790), fourth son of Frederick, Prince of Wales; privy councillor and K.G., 1767; 10,000l. recovered against him for criminal conversation with Countess Grosvenor, 1770; alienated his brother, George III, by clandestine marriage with Mrs. Horton, 1771; satirised by 'Junius.' [xxvi. 109]

HENRY BENEDICT MARIA CLEMENT, CARDINAL YORK (1725–1807), the Jacobite HENRY IX; second son of Chevalier de St. George, or 'James III'; came to England to support his brother Charles Edward [q. v.], 1745; on return to Italy became bishop of Ostia and prefect of St. Peter's, Rome, cardinal (1747), archbishop of Corinth (1759), and bishop of Tusculum (1761); assumed title Henry IX, 1788; his residence at Frascati sacked by French, 1799; fled to Padua and Venice; relieved by gift of money from George III; died at Frascati, leaving crown jewels (carried off by James II) to George IV. [xxvi. 110]

HENRY MAURICE OF BATTENBERG, PRINCE (1858–1896), third son of Prince Alexander of Hesse (1823–1888); married Princess Beatrice, youngest daughter of Queen Victoria, 1885; volunteered with Ashanti expeditionary force, 1895, and died of fever. [Suppl. ii. 411]

HENRY, SAINT (fl. 1150), apostle of Finland; of English birth; as bishop of Upsala assisted (Saint) Eric IX of Sweden in his reforms, and accompanied him to Finland, remaining behind to found churches after its conquest; slain by one Lalli, whom he had reproved for homicide; his bones translated to St. Henry's Cathedral, Abo, 1300. [xxvi. 111]

HENRY OF ABENDON (d. 1437), warden of Merton College, Oxford; fellow of Merton College, 1390; as delegate from Oxford to council of Constance defended priority of England over Spain, 1414; warden of Merton College, 1421; completed Merton chapel and provided bells; attended council of Basle, 1432; prebendary of Wells. [xxvi. 112]

HENRY OF BLOIS (d. 1171), bishop of Winchester; son of Stephen, count of Blois, and younger brother of King Stephen of England; educated at Clugny; abbot of Glastonbury, 1126–71, where he built a palace and abbey buildings; bishop of Winchester, 1129–71; procured the crown for Stephen by guaranteeing liberty of the church, and supported him at siege of Exeter; said to have failed to secure the papal sanction for his translation to Canterbury (1138) through the king's influence; named legate in England, 1139; rebuked Stephen for imprisoning bishops of Salisbury and Ely; persuaded Stephen to allow the Empress Matilda to join Gloucester at Bristol, 1139; negotiated for Stephen with Matilda at Bath, 1140; conferred with Louis VII on English affairs, 1140; his proposals rejected by Stephen; joined Matilda, and advocated her claim on the ground of Stephen's treachery to the church, 1141; offended by her and won over by the queen; besieged by the empress and David of Scotland in Wolvesey Castle, Winchester, but receiving help from Stephen besieged her afterwards in Winchester; destroyed Hyde Abbey, and allowed the city to be sacked; formed scheme for making his see metropolitan; said to have received pall from Rome, 1142; held council to mitigate the evils of civil war, 1142; upheld election of his nephew, William Fitzherbert [q. v.], to see of York, but lost legateship after death (1143) of Innocent II; opposed at Rome by Bernard of Clairvaux; suspended from his bishopric for advising Stephen to forbid Archbishop Theobald to attend papal council at Rheims, 1148; obtained absolution at Rome, 1151; active in forwarding treaty of Wallingford, 1153; left England (where Henry II destroyed three of his castles), 1155; stayed at Clugny, becoming the greatest benefactor; on his return consecrated Becket as primate, 1162; gave Becket some support against Henry II, though pronouncing judgment against Becket at Northampton, 1164; disapproved Becket's conduct after his flight, but sent him assistance; gave away all his goods in charity, c. 1168; on his deathbed rebuked the king for Becket's murder; probably buried before the high altar at Winchester, where he built a treasure-house, besides founding the hospital of St. Cross. [xxvi. 112]

HENRY OF EASTRY (d. 1331), prior of Christ Church, Canterbury, 1286–1331, of which he was a great benefactor; revived claim to exercise spiritual jurisdiction over Canterbury during vacancies; quarrelled with the citizens and abbot of St. Augustine's; supported Archbishop Robert de Winchelsea [q. v.] in resisting taxation, but was starved into submission by Edward I, 1297; his letters to Archbishop Reynolds printed in 'Letter Books of Christ Church' (ed. Dr. Sheppard, 1887); corresponded with Archbishop Meopham; died celebrating mass; earliest existing registers of the convent compiled by his direction; his MS. 'Memoriale Henrici Prioris' in British Museum. [xxvi. 117]

HENRY OF HUNTINGDON (1084?–1155), historian; archdeacon of Huntingdon from 1109; accompanied Archbishop Theobald to Rome, 1139, meeting at Bec the Norman historian Robert de Torigny. His 'Historia Anglorum,' compiled at request of Bishop Alexander (d. 1148) [q. v.] of Lincoln, extends in latest form to 1154. It was first printed in 'Scriptores post Bedam,' 1596 (reprinted by Migne, 1854); a complete edition (including biographical epistle 'De Contemptu Mundi') was published, 1879. [xxvi. 118]

HENRY DE LEXINTON (d. 1258). [See LEXINTON or LESSINGTON, HENRY DE.]

HENRY DE LOUNDRES (*d.* 1228). [See LOUNDRES.]

HENRY OF MARLBOROUGH or MARLEBURGH (*fl.* 1420), annalist; vicar of Balscaddan and Donabate, co. Dublin; his Latin annals (1133–1421) of England and Ireland printed by Ware, 1633 (reprinted, 1809), as 'Chronicle of Ireland.' [xxvi. 119]

HENRY the MINSTREL, or BLIND HARRY or HARY (*fl.* 1470–1492), Scottish poet; author of poem on Wallace; mentioned in Dunbar's 'Lament for the Makaris' (1508); probably a native of Lothian, writing under James III; his work largely a translation from John Blair [q. v.]; its chronology and general accuracy discredited by Hailes and others, but in some instances corroborated; complete manuscript (1488) in Advocates' Library. The best printed editions are those of Jamieson and Moir (1885–6); William Hamilton of Gilbertfield's modern version (1722) became more familiar than the original. [xxvi. 120]

HENRY DE NEWARK or NEWERK (*d.* 1299). [See NEWARK.]

HENRY DE NEWBURGH, EARL OF WARWICK (*d.* 1123). [See NEWBURGH.]

HENRY OF SALTREY (*fl.* 1150), Cistercian of Saltrey or Sawtrey, Huntingdonshire; obtained from his friend, Gilbert of Louth [q. v.], story of his 'Purgatorium Sancti Patricii,' included in Matthew Paris's 'Chronica Majora,' and first printed in Massingham's 'Florilegium insulæ Sanctorum Hiberniæ,' 1624. [xxvi. 122]

HENRY, JAMES (1798–1876), physician and classic; gold medallist, Trinity College, Dublin; M.A., 1822; M.D., 1832; practised in Dublin till 1845, after which he travelled through Europe making Virgilian researches; published verse translation of Æneid i. and ii., 1845, and poems; his 'Æneidea' appeared 1873–9. [xxvi. 122]

HENRY, MATTHEW (1662–1714), commentator; son of Philip Henry [q. v.]; studied law at Gray's Inn; nonconformist minister at Chester, 1687–1712, afterwards at Mare Street, Hackney; his 'Exposition of the Old and New Testament' (1708–10), completed by thirteen nonconformist divines after his death, edited (1811) by G. Burder [q. v.] and John Hughes, and often abridged; 'Miscellaneous Writings' edited, 1809 and 1830. [xxvi. 123]

HENRY, PHILIP (1631–1696), nonconformist divine; played with princes Charles and James as a child; favourite pupil of Richard Busby [q. v.] at Westminster; student of Christ Church, Oxford, 1647; M.A., 1652; witnessed execution of Charles I, 1649; minister of Worthenbury, and tutor in family of Mr. Justice Puleston, 1653–60; refused re-ordination; imprisoned on suspicion of conspiracy, 1663; preached as a nonconformist, 1672–81; fined for keeping conventicles; disputed publicly with quakers and with Bishop William Lloyd [q. v.] and the elder Dodwell, 1682; confined at Chester, 1685; ministered at Broad Oak, Flintshire, after Toleration Act; his 'Life' written by his son; 'Remains' edited by Sir J. B. Williams, 1848; 'Diaries' published, 1882. [xxvi. 124]

HENRY, ROBERT (1718–1790), historian; studied at Edinburgh; D.D. Edinburgh, 1771; presbyterian minister successively at Carlisle, Berwick, New Grey Friars, Edinburgh (1768) and old Grey Friars, 1776–90; moderator of general assembly, 1774; received pension in 1781 for his 'History of England' (5 vols. 1771–85, 6th vol. 1793). [xxvi. 126]

HENRY, THOMAS (1734–1816), chemist; practised as a surgeon-apothecary in Manchester; secretary, Manchester Literary and Philosophical Society, 1781, and president, 1807; patented process for preparing calcined magnesia; issued 'Experiments and Observations,' 1773; F.R.S., 1775; member of American Philosophical Society; translated Lavoisier's chemical essays, 1776 and 1783; first observed use of carbonic acid to plants; published 'Memoirs of Albert de Haller,' 1783; assisted in foundation of College of Arts and Sciences at Manchester. [xxvi. 127]

HENRY, SIR THOMAS (1807–1876), police magistrate at Lambeth Street, Whitechapel, 1840–6, chief magistrate at Bow Street, 1864; knighted, 1864; barrister, Middle Temple, 1829; drew Extradition Act and treaties connected therewith. [xxvi. 128]

HENRY, WILLIAM (*d.* 1768), dean of Killaloe; D.D. Dublin, 1750; chaplain to Bishop Josiah Hort [q. v.]; rector of Killesher, 1731, of Urney, 1734; dean of Killaloe, 1761–8; F.R.S., 1755; his 'Description of Lough Erne' printed, 1873. [xxvi. 128]

HENRY, WILLIAM (1774–1836), chemist; son of Thomas Henry [q. v.]; M.D. Edinburgh, 1807; published 'General View of Nature and Objects of Chemistry,' 1799, 'Epitome of Chemistry,' 1801; expanded into 'Elements of Experimental Chemistry' (11th ed. 1829); F.R.S., 1808, and Copley medallist. [xxvi. 129]

HENRYSON, EDWARD (1510?–1590?), Scottish judge; graduate of Bourges and professor of Roman law there, 1554; defended Equinar Baron's treatise on law of jurisdiction against Govea; published also 'Commentatio in Tit. x. Libri Secundi Institutionum de Testamentis Ordinandis,' 1555; commissary in Scotland, 1563; extraordinary lord of session, 1566; edited revision of Scottish laws (1424–1564). [xxvi. 129]

HENRYSON or **HENDERSON,** ROBERT (1430?–1506?), Scottish poet; original member of Glasgow University, 1462; probably a clerical schoolmaster attached to Dunfermline Abbey; his 'Tale of Orpheus' first printed, 1508; his 'Testament of Cresseid' attributed to Chaucer till 1721, though printed as his own in 1593; his 'Morall Fables of Esope the Phrygian' printed, 1621; 'Poems and Fables' collected and edited by Dr. D. Laing, 1865. [xxvi. 130]

HENRYSON or **HENDERSON,** SIR THOMAS, LORD CHESTERS (*d.* 1638), lord of session, 1622–37; knighted; son of Edward Henryson [q. v.] [xxvi. 131]

HENSEY, FLORENCE (*fl.* 1758), spy; M.D. Leyden; physician in Paris and London; supplied information to French foreign office during seven years' war, contributing to failure of Rochefort expedition, 1757; convicted and condemned to death, 1758; pardoned, 1759. [xxvi. 131]

HENSHALL, SAMUEL (1764?–1807), philologist; educated at Manchester and Brasenose College, Oxford (fellow); M.A., 1789; rector of Bow, 1802–7; published 'The Saxon and English Languages reciprocally illustrative' (1798), 'The Gothic Gospel of St. Matthew,' 1807, and some topographical works. [xxvi. 132]

HENSHAW, JOSEPH (1603–1679), bishop of Peterborough; educated at Charterhouse and Magdalen Hall, Oxford; B.A., 1624; D.D., 1639; chaplain to the Earl of Bristol and Duke of Buckingham; held benefices in Sussex; as 'delinquent' had to compound for his estate, 1646; precentor and dean of Chichester, 1660; dean of Windsor, 1660; bishop of Peterborough, 1663–79; his 'Horæ Successivæ' (1631) edited by W. Turnbull, 1839, and 'Meditations' (1637) reprinted at Oxford, 1841. [xxvi. 133]

HENSHAW, NATHANIEL (*d.* 1673), physician; M.D. Leyden and Dublin; F.R.S., 1663; practised in Dublin; published 'Aero-Chalinos: or a Register for the Air,' 1664 (second edition, 1677, printed by Royal Society). [xxvi. 134]

HENSHAW, THOMAS (1618–1700), author; brother of Nathaniel Henshaw [q. v.]; of University College, Oxford, and Middle Temple; served in French army, remaining abroad some years; barrister; gentleman of the privy council and French under-secretary to Charles II, James II, and William III; an original F.R.S., 1663; envoy extraordinary in Denmark, 1672–5. His works include a translation of Samedo's history of China, 1655, and an edition of Stephen Skinner's 'Etymologicon Linguæ Anglicanæ,' 1671. [xxvi. 134]

HENSLOW, JOHN STEVENS (1796–1861), botanist; educated at Rochester and St. John's College, Cambridge; sixteenth wrangler, 1818; M.A., 1821; F.L.S., 1818; assisted Sedgwick in founding Cambridge Philosophical Society; Cambridge professor of mineralogy, 1822–7, of botany, 1827–61; recommended his pupil Charles Robert Darwin [q. v.] as naturalist to the Beagle; vicar of Hitcham, Suffolk, 1839; published 'Letters to the Farmers of Suffolk' on scientific agriculture, 1843; discovered phosphatic nodules in Suffolk Crag, 1843; member of London University senate and examiner in botany; presided over discussion on 'Origin of Species' at British Association, 1861; assisted Sir W. J. Hooker at Kew; works include 'Catalogue of British Plants,' 1829, 'Dictionary of Botanical Terms,' 1857. [xxvi. 135]

HENSLOWE, PHILIP (*d.* 1616), theatrical manager; settled in Southwark, 1577, where he became a dyer, pawn-broker, and money-lender; groom of royal chamber, 1593, and sewer, 1603; rebuilt and managed the Rose play-house on Bankside till 1603, and afterwards the theatre at Newington Butts and the Swan on Bankside; associated with Edward Alleyn [q. v.] in management of the Fortune in Golden Lane, Cripplegate Without, 1600–16, and in other enterprises; bought plays from Dekker, Drayton, Chapman, and other dramatists, most of which are lost: extracts from his diary (preserved at Dulwich) printed by Malone, and the whole (with forged interpolations) by J. P. Collier, 1845. [xxvi. 136]

HENSMAN, JOHN (1780–1864), divine; fellow of Corpus Christi, Cambridge; ninth wrangler, 1801; assistant to Charles Simeon [q. v.] at Cambridge; brought about building of new parish church at Clifton, 1822; incumbent of Trinity, Hotwells, 1830–44; held living of Clifton, 1847–64; chapel of ease consecrated as a memorial of him, 1862. [xxvi. 138]

HENSON, GRAVENER (1785–1852), author of a work on the frame-work knitting and lace trades (1831) and similar subjects; imprisoned for complicity in Luddite riots; expert in detection of smugglers. [xxvi. 138]

HENSTRIDGE, DANIEL (*d.* 1736), organist at Rochester and (1700–36) Canterbury, and composer. [xxvi. 139]

HENTON or **HEINTON**, SIMON (*fl.* 1360), Dominican provincial in England and commentator. [xxvi. 139]

HENTY, EDWARD (1809–1878), pioneer of Victoria, forming Portland Bay settlement, 1834; member for Normanby in Legislative Assembly, 1856–61. [xxvi. 139]

HENWOOD, WILLIAM JORY (1805–1875), mineralogist; supervisor of tin for Cornwall, 1832–8; F.G.S., 1828; F.R.S., 1840; took charge of Gongo-Soco mines, Brazil, 1843; reported to Indian government on metals of Kumaon and Gurhwal, 1855; president of Royal Institute of Cornwall, 1869; Murchison medallist, 1874; his name given to hydrous phosphate of aluminium and copper. [xxvi. 139]

HEPBURN, FRANCIS, or FRANCIS KER (1779–1835), major-general; served with 3rd foot (now Scots) guards in Ireland, 1798, Holland, 1799, and Sicily; wounded at Barossa, 1811; present (1813) at Vittoria, Nivelle, and the Nive; commanded 2nd battalion in Netherlands, 1814–15; commanded at Hougoumont, 1815; C.B.; major-general, 1821. [xxvi. 140]

HEPBURN, FRANCIS STEWART, fifth EARL OF BOTHWELL (*d.* 1624), known by name of his mother (Lady Jane Hepburn), sister of James Hepburn, fourth earl of Bothwell [q. v.], whose title and offices he received on the report of his death, 1576; his father a natural son of James V; supporter of the regent Morton; abroad at time of Morton's fall; on return posed as protestant champion and successor of his uncle Moray; a favourite with James VI till discovery of his complicity in raid of Ruthven, 1582; joined Patrick Gray's conspiracy against Arran, 1585; with Home fortified Kelso for the banished lords, 1585; killed Sir William Stewart at Edinburgh, 1588; urged James to take advantage of the Spanish Armada to invade England; his influence destroyed by rise of Maitland; joined catholic rebellion, but was pardoned by intercession of the kirk; during James's absence in Denmark assisted Lennox as president of privy council; on his return accused of consulting witches and out-lawed, 1591; attempted to capture the king and Maitland in Holyrood, 1591; denounced by James to parliament as a pretender to the throne, 1592; attempted to capture him in Falkland Palace, 1592; sentenced to forfeiture, but introduced by Maitland's enemies into James's presence disguised, 1593; temporarily pardoned, but soon denounced again; appeared with force at Leith and was unsuccessfully pursued by James, 1594; expelled from England; again joined the catholic lords in the north, 1594; fled from Caithness to Normandy, 1595; died in poverty at Naples. [xxvi. 140]

HEPBURN, SIR GEORGE BUCHAN, first baronet (1739–1819), baron of the Scottish exchequer; solicitor to lords of session, 1767–90; judge of admiralty court, 1790–1; baron of Scottish exchequer, 1791–1814; created baronet, 1815; published work on agriculture of East Lothian, 1796. [xxvi. 145]

HEPBURN, JAMES, fourth EARL OF BOTHWELL (1536?–1578), husband of Mary Queen of Scots; son of Patrick Hepburn, third earl [q. v.]; succeeded to hereditary offices of his father, 1556; though nominally protestant, was strong supporter of the queen-dowager and the French party; intercepted money sent by the English to lords of the congregation, 1559; his castle at Crichton seized by Arran and Lord James Stuart after his escape with the treasure, sent on a foreign mission by the queen-dowager, 1560; visited Denmark; at Paris became gentleman of the royal chamber, 1560; returned to Scotland as a commissioner for Mary Queen of Scots, 1561; banished from Edinburgh for a brawl with the Hamiltons; reconciled to Arran by Knox at Kirk-o'-Field; charged by Arran with design to carry off the queen to Dumbarton; escaped from ward, 1562; detained by the English while escaping to France and sent to the Tower, 1564; allowed to go to France on representations of Mary and Maitland; on return to Scotland offered to meet his accusers, but failed to appear, 1565; by favour of Mary allowed to retire to France; recalled by the queen to help her against Moray, 1565; escaped capture by the English, and obtained great influence with Mary; married Lady Jean Gordon, but remained protestant, 1566; though in Holyrood, had no share in murder of Rizzio, 1566; joined Mary and Darnley on their escape to Dunbar, 1566; acquired increasing influence over the queen, who granted him lands and Dunbar Castle; temporarily reconciled with Moray and Maitland; wounded by an outlaw near the Hermitage, 1566; entertained Mary at Dunbar; at Craigmillar said to have favoured Mary's divorce from Darnley, and afterwards signed the bond for his removal, 1566; failed to obtain Morton's help; superintended arrangements for Darnley's lodging at Kirk-o'-Field; escorted Darnley and Mary into Edinburgh (31 Jan. 1567); consulted subordinate plotters in apartments at Holyrood; had powder brought from Dunbar and placed in the queen's room below that of Darnley at Kirk-o'-Field (9 Feb.); went above before Mary set out for a ball; appeared there, but left at midnight and directed the firing of the train; attributed the explosion to lightning; was generally suspected of Darnley's murder, but still favoured by Mary and (with Huntly) given charge of Prince James 1567; accused by Lennox, but prevented Lennox's appearance, and obtained formal acquittal (12 April 1567); obtained written agreement of protestant lords to support his marriage with the queen (19 April); carried her off (perhaps by consent) to Dunbar (21 April); obtained an irregular divorce from his wife (7 May); married to Mary at Holyrood (15 May 1567); created Duke of Orkney and Shetland, 1567; threatened at Holyrood by the nobles; fled with the queen to Borthwick Castle; left her and fled to Dunbar; marched on Edinburgh, but when met by the lords at Carberry Hill was persuaded by Mary to leave her, 1567; rode to Dunbar and thence went north to join Huntly; escaped to Kirkwall; gathered together a pirate fleet, which was pursued by Kirkcaldy of Grange to the North Sea; landed in Norway, whence he was sent to Denmark, 1567; his surrender refused by the king of Denmark, who kept him in confinement; while at Copenhagen composed 'Les Affaires du Conte de Boduel'; removed to Malmö; offered cession of Orkney and Shetland in exchange for release, 1568; his divorce from Mary passed by the pope, 1570; removed to closer prison at Drangholm, 1573; became gradually insane; buried in Faareveile Church; deathbed confession not authentic. [xxvi. 146]

HEPBURN, JAMES (1573–1620), linguist; in religion BONAVENTURE; travelled in Europe and the east; entered order of Minims at Avignon; six years oriental keeper in Vatican Library; published an Arabic grammar (1591), translation into Latin of 'Kettar Malcuth,' and other works; died at Venice. [xxvi. 157]

HEPBURN, SIR JAMES (*d.* 1637), soldier; succeeded his cousin, Sir John Hepburn [q. v.], as commander of Scots brigade; killed at Damvillers. [xxvi. 157]

HEPBURN, JOHN (*d.* 1522), prior of St. Andrews 1482; brother of Patrick Hepburn, first earl of Bothwell [q. v.]; founder of St. Leonard's College, 1512; sometime keeper of the privy seal of Scotland; unsuccessful candidate for archbishopric of St. Andrews, 1514. [xxvi. 157]

HEPBURN, SIR JOHN (1598?–1636), soldier of fortune; though a Roman catholic, joined Scottish force in service of elector palatine, 1620; fought under Mansfeld

1622-3; colonel of Scottish regiment under Gustavus Adolphus, 1625; Swedish governor of Rügenwalde, 1630; commander of the Scots brigade, 1631; wounded at siege of Frankfort-on-Oder, 1631; took decisive part in capture of Landsberg and battle of Breitenfeld, 1631; publicly thanked by Gustavus after capture of Donauwörth, 1632; left the Swedish service and raised two thousand men in Scotland for that of France, 1633; his recruits incorporated with Scots archery guard nicknamed 'Pontius Pilate's guards'; took part as *maréchal-de-camp* in conquest of Lorraine, 1634-5; captured by imperialists, but released; assisted in relief of Hagenau, 1636; obtained precedence for his brigade, augmented by Scots in Swedish service, 1636; killed at siege of Saverne; his monument in Toul Cathedral destroyed at revolution. [xxvi. 158]

HEPBURN, PATRICK, third BARON HAILES and first EARL OF BOTHWELL (*d.* 1508), succeeded his father as third Baron Hailes; defended Berwick against English, 1482; fought against James III at Sauchieburn, 1488; governor of Edinburgh, lord high admiral and master of the household, and created Earl of Bothwell, 1488; received grants in Orkney and Shetland, 1489, and Liddesdale, 1492; took part in various embassies; a commissioner for marriage of James IV and Margaret Tudor, 1501. [xxvi. 160]

HEPBURN, PATRICK, third EARL OF BOTHWELL (1512?-1556), grandson of Patrick Hepburn, first earl of Bothwell [q. v.]; succeeded on his father's death at Flodden, 1513; received share of Angus's forfeited estates, 1529; imprisoned (1529) for protecting border marauders; offered his services to Northumberland against Scotland, 1531; imprisoned at Edinburgh and banished from Scotland, 1533; returned, 1542, and resumed possession of Liddesdale and Hermitage Castle; acted with Cardinal Beaton against English party, and brought queen-dowager and her daughter to Stirling, 1543; supported regency of Mary of Guise and divorced his wife to become a suitor for her hand; arrested George Wishart (1513?-1546) [q. v.], 1546, and was induced to hand him over to Beaton; imprisoned for intrigue with England, 1547-8; fled across the border; recalled by queen-dowager, 1553; lieutenant of the border, 1553. [xxvi. 160]

HEPBURN, PATRICK (*d.* 1573), bishop of Moray; prior of St. Andrews, 1522; secretary to James V, 1524-7; one of those who condemned Patrick Hamilton [q. v.], 1527; bishop of Moray and abbot of Scone, 1535; member of privy council, 1546; border commissioner, 1553; his palace and church at Scone burnt by townsmen of Dundee in revenge for execution of Walter Mylne [q. v.], 1559; deprived of his rents for protecting Bothwell, and tried as accessory to Darnley's murder, 1567; notorious profligate. [xxvi. 162]

HEPBURN, ROBERT (1690?-1712), author; edited the 'Tatler, by Donald MacStaff of the North,' 1711; three posthumous works by him. [xxvi. 163]

HERAPATH, JOHN (1790-1868), mathematician; contributed to the 'Annals of Philosophy'; rejection of his paper offered to Royal Society, 1820, followed by controversy; his 'Tables of Temperature' controverted by Tredgold; corrected Brougham's mathematical works; proprietor and manager of 'Railway Magazine' from 1836; published 'Mathematical Physics,' 1847. [xxvi. 163]

HERAPATH, WILLIAM (1796-1868), analytical chemist; cousin of John Herapath [q. v.]; a founder of the London Chemical Society; professor of chemistry at Bristol Medical School, 1828; often called as an expert in poisoning cases; president of Bristol political union, 1831. [xxvi. 164]

HERAUD, JOHN ABRAHAM (1799-1887), author and critic; assistant-editor of 'Fraser's Magazine,' 1830-1833; contributed to 'Quarterly'; friend of the Carlyles, Lockhart, and Southey; dramatic critic of 'Illustrated London News' (1849-79) and 'Athenæum'; Charterhouse brother, 1873; published 'The Descent into Hell' (1830), 'Judgment of the Flood' (1834), and other poems, as well as plays and miscellaneous works. [xxvi. 165]

HERAULT, JOHN (1566-1626), bailiff of Jersey; of All Souls' College, Oxford; as bailiff, 1615, vindicated against Sir John Peyton (1544-1630) [q. v.] right of crown to appoint and of bailiff to exercise civil and judicial power. [xxvi. 165]

HERBERT DE LOSINGA (1054?-1119). [See LOSINGA.]

HERBERT OF BOSHAM (*fl.* 1162-1186), biographer of Becket; attended the archbishop as special monitor and master in study of holy writ at councils of Tours (1163), Clarendon (1164), and Northampton (1164), escaping with him from the last; brought him money and plate, and secured his reception abroad; shared his exile, encouraging him to hold his ground at Montmirail, 1169; returned with him to England, 1170, but was sent on a message to the French king and remained abroad till 1184; treated well by Henry II; his 'Life of St. Thomas of Canterbury,' with letters and other works, printed in Dr. Giles's 'Sanctus Thomas Cantuariensis' (1846), and edited by Canon J. C. Robertson in 'Materials for History of Archbishop Becket.' [xxvi. 166]

HERBERT, ALFRED (*d.* 1861), water-colour painter; son of a Thames waterman; exhibited at Royal Academy, 1847-60. [xxvi. 168]

HERBERT, ALGERNON (1792-1855), antiquary; educated at Eton and Oxford; fellow of Merton College, 1814, dean, 1828; M.A., 1825; published 'Nimrod, a Discourse upon Certain Passages of History and Fable,' 1828-1830, edition of 'Nennius,' 1848, and other works. [xxvi. 168]

HERBERT, ANNE, COUNTESS OF PEMBROKE AND MONTGOMERY (1590-1676). [See CLIFFORD, ANNE.]

HERBERT, ARTHUR, EARL OF TORRINGTON (1647-1716), admiral of the fleet; second son of Sir Edward Herbert (1591?-1657) [q. v.]; entered navy, 1663; served against the Dutch, 1666, and against Algerine corsairs, 1669-71; commanded the Dreadnought at Solebay, 1672, and the Cambridge, 1673-5; lost an eye in capture of a corsair in Mediterranean, 1678; as admiral in the straits relieved Tangier, 1680, and continued to command against the Algerines till 1683; rear-admiral and master of the robes, 1684; M.P., Dover, 1685; cashiered for refusing to support repeal of Test Act, 1687; commander of fleet which conveyed William of Orange to England, 1688; first lord of the admiralty and commander of Channel fleet, 1689; created Earl of Torrington, 1689, after indecisive action with French in Bantry Bay; resigned the admiralty, 1690; with insufficient squadron obliged by queen's order to engage whole French fleet off Beachy Head, 1690; his cautious tactics frustrated by Dutch contingent; charged before courtmartial with hanging back, 1690; acquitted, but never again held command; corresponded with William III. [xxvi. 169]

HERBERT, ARTHUR JOHN (1834-1856), historical painter; son of John Rogers Herbert [q. v.]; died in Auvergne. [xxvi. 204]

HERBERT, CYRIL WISEMAN (1847-1882), painter; son of John Rogers Herbert [q. v.]; curator of antique school, Royal Academy, 1882; exhibited, 1870-5. [xxvi. 172]

HERBERT, EDWARD, first BARON HERBERT OF CHERBURY (1583-1648), philosopher, historian, and diplomatist; while at University College, Oxford, taught himself the Romance languages and became a good musician, rider, and fencer; went to court, 1600; sheriff of Montgomeryshire, 1605; during a continental tour became intimate with Casaubon and the Constable Montmorency, and fought several duels, 1608-10; volunteer at recapture of Juliers, 1610; joined Prince of Orange's army, 1614; visited the elector palatine and the chief towns of Italy; offered help to the Savoyards, but was imprisoned by the French at Lyons, 1615; stayed with Prince of Orange, 1616; on his return became intimate with Donne, Carew, and Ben Jonson; named by Buckingham ambassador at Paris, 1619; tried to obtain French support for elector palatine, and suggested marriage between Henrietta Maria and Prince Charles; recalled for quarrelling with the French king's favourite De Luynes, 1621, but reappointed on De Luynes's death, 1622; recalled, 1624, owing to his disagreement with James I about the French marriage negotiations; received in Irish peerage the barony of Cherbury, 1629, and seat in council of war, 1632; attended Charles I on Scottish expedition, 1639-40; committed to the Tower for royalist speech in House of Lords, 1642, but released on apologising; aimed at neutrality during the war; compelled to admit parliamentary force into Montgomery Castle, 1644; submitted to parliament and received a pension, 1645; steward of duchy of Cornwall and warden of the Stannaries, 1646; visited Gassendi, 1647; died in London, Selden being one of his executors. His autobiography (to 1624), printed by Horace Walpole, 1764 (thrice reissued), and edited by Mr. Sidney Lee, 1886, scarcely mentions his serious pursuits. His 'De Veritate' (Paris, 1624, London, 1645), the chief of his philosophical works, is the first purely metaphysical work by an Englishman. It was unfavourably criticised by Baxter, Locke, and others, but commended by Gassendi and Descartes. Though named the father of English deism, Herbert's real affinity was with the Cambridge Platonists. His poems were edited by Mr. Churton Collins, 1881; his 'Life of Henry VIII' (apologetic) first published, 1649. [xxvi. 173]

HERBERT, SIR EDWARD (1591?-1657), judge; cousin of Edward Herbert, first baron Herbert of Cherbury [q. v.]; barrister, Inner Temple, 1618, treasurer, 1638; M.P., Montgomery, 1620, Downton, 1625-9, Old Sarum, 1641; a manager of Buckingham's impeachment, 1626; one of Selden's counsel, 1629; attorney-general to Charles I's queen, 1635; assisted in prosecution of Prynne, Burton, and Bastwick, 1637; solicitor-general, 1640; attorney-general, 1641; knighted, 1641; impeached, imprisoned, and incapacitated, 1642, for his share in abortive impeachment of six members; joined royalists; declined lord-keepership, 1645; sequestrated as 'delinquent,' 1646; went to sea with Prince Rupert, 1648; attorney-general to Charles II while abroad; lord-keeper, 1653; died at Paris. [xxvi. 181]

HERBERT, EDWARD, third BARON HERBERT OF CHERBURY (d. 1678), grandson of Edward Herbert, first baron Herbert of Cherbury [q. v.] [xxvi. 180]

HERBERT, SIR EDWARD, titular EARL OF PORTLAND (1648?-1698), judge; younger son of Sir Edward Herbert (1591?-1657) [q. v.]; educated at Winchester and New College, Oxford; B.A., 1669; barrister, Middle Temple; K.C. in Ireland, 1677; chief-justice of Chester, 1683; knighted, 1684; attorney-general to the queen of James II; M.P. for Ludlow, 1685; privy councillor, 1685: chief-justice of king's bench, 1685; gave judgment for dispensing power in case of Godden v. Hales, 1686; transferred to common pleas, 1687; as member of ecclesiastical commission opposed James II in Magdalen College case, 1687; followed James into exile, and was created lord chancellor, but offended James by his protestantism; died at St. Germains. [xxvi. 183]

HERBERT, EDWARD, second EARL OF POWIS (1785-1848), tory politician; grandson of Robert Clive, first baron Clive of Plassey [q. v.]; assumed his mother's surname, 1807; educated at Eton and St. John's College, Cambridge; M.A., 1806; M.P., Ludlow, 1806-39; as lord-lieutenant, Montgomeryshire, active in suppressing Chartist riots, 1839; succeeded to peerage, 1839; his defeat of scheme for creation of see of Manchester by union of Bangor and St. Asaph celebrated by foundation of Powis exhibitions, 1847; president of Roxburghe Club, 1835; candidate for chancellorship of Cambridge, 1847; accidentally killed. [xxvi. 184]

HERBERT, GEORGE (1593-1633), divine and poet; brother of Edward Herbert, first baron Herbert of Cherbury [q. v.]; of Westminster and Trinity College, Cambridge; major fellow, 1616; M.A., 1616; public orator, 1619-27; induced to adopt religious life by Nicholas Ferrar [q. v.]; prebendary of Lincoln, 1626; while deacon accepted benefice of Bemerton, Wiltshire, by Laud's advice, 1630; ordained priest, 1630; 'The Temple; Sacred Poems and Private Ejaculations' (prepared for press by Ferrar, 1633), read by Charles I in prison, and highly commended by Crashaw, Henry Vaughan, Baxter, and Coleridge; his chief prose work, 'A Priest to the Temple,' first printed in his 'Remains,' 1652; complete works edited by Dr. Grosart, 1874. His literary style was influenced by that of Donne. [xxvi. 185]

HERBERT, GEORGE AUGUSTUS, eleventh EARL OF PEMBROKE and eighth EARL OF MONTGOMERY (1759-1827), general (son of Henry Herbert, tenth earl of Pembroke [q. v.]); entered army, 1775, lieutenant-colonel, 2nd dragoon guards, 1783; vice-chamberlain, 1785; M.P., Wilton, 1784-94; served in Flanders, 1793-4; major-general, 1795; K.G., 1805; governor of Guernsey, 1807; ambassador extraordinary to Vienna, 1807; general, 1812; said to have trebled value of his estates. [xxvi. 189]

HERBERT, GEORGE ROBERT CHARLES, thirteenth EARL OF PEMBROKE and ninth EARL OF MONTGOMERY (1850-1895), son of Sidney Herbert, first baron

Herbert of Lea [q. v.], whom he succeeded, 1861; succeeded his uncle in the earldoms, 1862; educated at Eton; travelled abroad with Dr. George Henry Kingsley [q. v.], with whom he published 'South Sea Bubbles,' 1872; under-secretary for war, 1874-5. His 'Letters and Speeches' were published, 1896. [Suppl. ii. 411]

HERBERT, HENRY, second EARL OF PEMBROKE (1534?-1601), elder son of Sir William Herbert, first earl [q. v.]; educated at Peterhouse, Cambridge; styled Lord Herbert, 1551-70; K.B., 1553; married Catherine, sister of Lady Jane Grey, 1553; gentleman of the chamber to King Philip of Spain, 1554; succeeded as earl, 1570; prominent at trials of Norfolk (1572), Arundel (1589), and Mary Queen of Scots (1586); president of Wales and admiral of South Wales, 1586. [xxvi. 189]

HERBERT, SIR HENRY (1595-1673), master of the revels; brother of George Herbert (1593-1633) [q. v.]; knighted, 1623; introduced Baxter at court: as master of the revels claimed jurisdiction over all public entertainments, even licensing some books; his judgment in licensing Middleton's 'Game of Chesse,' 1624, questioned; gentleman of privy chamber, attending Charles I in Scottish expedition, 1639; obliged to compound for his estates during rebellion; resumed his licensing functions at Restoration; his privileges confirmed, 1661, but his functions disputed by D'Avenant and others; claimed to license plays, poems, and ballads, 1663; leased his office to deputies, 1663; M.P., Bewdley, from 1661; friend of Evelyn. [xxvi. 190]

HERBERT, HENRY, fourth BARON HERBERT OF CHERBURY (d. 1691), cofferer of the household to William III and Mary; succeeded his brother Edward Herbert, third baron Herbert of Cherbury [q. v.], 1678; served under Monmouth in France, and supported him in England, afterwards promoting the revolution. [xxvi. 181]

HERBERT, HENRY, created BARON HERBERT OF CHERBURY (1654-1709), son of Sir Henry Herbert [q. v.]; of Trinity College, Oxford; M.P., Bewdley, 1673-94; promoted revolution in Worcestershire; created Baron Herbert, 1694, and Castleisland (Ireland), 1695; commissioner of trade, 1707; chairman of committees in House of Lords; a zealous whig. [xxvi. 193]

HERBERT, HENRY, second BARON HERBERT OF CHERBURY of the second creation (d. 1738), son of Henry Herbert, baron Herbert of Cherbury (1654-1709) [q. v.]; educated at Westminster; M.P., Bewdley, 1707; committed suicide. [xxvi. 193]

HERBERT, HENRY, ninth EARL OF PEMBROKE and sixth EARL OF MONTGOMERY (1693-1751), 'the architect earl'; groom of the stole, 1735; thrice a lord justice; F.R.S., 1743; lieutenant-general, 1742; promoted erection of first Westminster Bridge (1739-50); designed improvements at Wilton House and elsewhere. [xxvi. 194]

HERBERT, HENRY, tenth EARL OF PEMBROKE and seventh EARL OF MONTGOMERY (1734-1794), general; commanded cavalry brigade in Germany, 1760-1; published 'Method of Breaking Horses,' 1762; lord of the bedchamber, 1769; deprived of lieutenancy of Wiltshire for voting against the court, 1780; restored, 1782; governor of Portsmouth, 1782; general, 1782. [xxvi. 194]

HERBERT, HENRY HOWARD MOLYNEUX, fourth EARL OF CARNARVON (1831-1890), statesman: eldest son of Henry John George Herbert, third earl [q. v.]; of Eton and Christ Church, Oxford; B.A., 1852; succeeded to earldom, 1849; with Lord Sandon visited the Druses, 1853; moved address in House of Lords, 1854; under-secretary for colonies in Lord Derby's second administration, 1858-9; high steward of Oxford University, 1859; as colonial secretary in Lord Derby's and Disraeli's administration (1866-7) brought in British North America Confederation Bill, 1867; resigned on the reform question before the Confederation Bill became law (March 1867); while in opposition, supported Irish disestablishment and the Land Bill of 1870; again colonial secretary in Disraeli's second administration, 1874-8; abolished slavery on the Gold Coast, 1874; sent Sir Garnet Wolseley as governor of Natal to report on the native and defence questions, 1875; attempted the confederation of South Africa; arranged for purchase of Boer claims in Griqualand West by Cape Colony, 1876; sent out Sir Theophilus Shepstone [q. v.] and Sir Bartle Frere [q. v.] to settle colonial and native differences, 1876; introduced a permissive confederation Bill, 1877; sanctioned and upheld annexation of Transvaal,

1877 ; resigned (January 1878), being opposed to breach of neutrality in Russo-Turkish affairs ; chairman of colonial defence commission, 1879–82 ; opposed Franchise Bill of 1884 till concurrent redistribution of seats conceded ; joined Imperial Federation League, 1884 ; as lord-lieutenant of Ireland under Lord Salisbury (1885–6) attempted government by ordinary law, held conference with Mr. Parnell, and personally favoured limited self-government ; afterwards opposed Mr. Gladstone's Home Rule and Land Purchase bills ; suggested (1887) appointment of special commission for investigating charges of 'The Times' against Parnell ; visited South Africa and Australia, 1887–8 ; interested in questions of colonial defence ; president of Society of Antiquaries, 1878–85 ; published verse translations of the 'Agamemnon' (1879) and the 'Odyssey' (1886) ; edited (1869) his father's travels in Greece, Mansel's 'Gnostic Heresies,' 1875, and unpublished letters of Lord Chesterfield, 1889. [xxvi. 195]

HERBERT, HENRY JOHN GEORGE, third EARL OF CARNARVON (1800–1849), traveller ; educated at Eton and Christ Church, Oxford ; styled Viscount Porchester till his succession to earldom, 1833 ; travelled in Barbary, Spain, Portugal, and (later) in Greece ; his tragedy, 'Don Pedro,' acted by Macready and Ellen Tree at Drury Lane, 1828 ; published 'Last Days of the Portuguese Constitution,' 1830, and 'Portugal and Galicia,' 1830 ; tory M.P., Wootton Basset, 1831–2 ; his 'Reminiscences of Athens and the Morea in 1839,' issued, 1869. [xxvi. 201]

HERBERT, HENRY WILLIAM (1807 – 1858), author ; son of William Herbert (1778–1847) [q. v.] ; educated at Eton and Caius College, Cambridge ; B.A., 1830 ; became a classical tutor at New York, and established 'American Monthly Magazine,' 1833 ; shot himself at New York ; published as 'Frank Forester,' 'Field Sports of the United States and British Provinces' (1848), and similar works ; published, under his own name, 'The Roman Traitor,' 1846, and other historical novels, translations from Dumas and Eugène Sue, and popular historical works. [xxvi. 202]

HERBERT, JOHN ROGERS (1810–1890), portrait and historical painter ; won his first success with Italian subject-pictures, 1834–40 ; became a Romanist, and thenceforth chiefly devoted himself to religious studies ; a master of design at Somerset House, 1841 ; R.A., 1846 (retired, 1886), his diploma work being 'St. Gregory the Great teaching Roman Boys to sing' ; painted for houses of parliament 'King Lear disinheriting Cordelia,' in fresco, and 'Human Justice' series. [xxvi. 203]

HERBERT, LADY LUCY (1669–1744), devotional writer ; daughter of William Herbert, first marquis of Powis [q. v.] ; prioress of English convent, Bruges, 1709–44 ; her 'Devotions' edited by Rev. John Morris, S.J., 1873. [xxvi. 204]

HERBERT, MARY, COUNTESS OF PEMBROKE (1561–1621), sister of Sir Philip Sidney [q. v.] ; married Henry Herbert, second earl of Pembroke [q. v.], 1577 ; the Urania of Spenser's 'Colin Clout' ; suggested composition of her brother Philip's 'Arcadia' (first printed, 1590), which she revised and added to ; collaborated with Philip in metrical psalms, first printed complete, 1823 ; her elegy on him appended to Spenser's 'Astrophel' ; translated from Plessis du Mornay 'A Discourse of Life and Death,' 1593 ; patron of Samuel Daniel [q. v.], Nicholas Breton [q. v.], Ben Jonson [q. v.], and other poets ; fine epitaph on her by Ben Jonson or William Browne, first printed, 1660. [xxvi. 204]

HERBERT, SIR PERCY EGERTON (1822–1876), lieutenant-general ; second son of Edward Herbert, second earl Powis [q. v.] ; at Eton and Sandhurst ; promoted brevet lieutenant-colonel for services in the Kaffir war, 1851–3 ; assistant quartermaster-general of Sir de Lacy Evans's division in Crimea ; wounded at the Alma, 1854 ; C.B. and aide-de-camp to the queen, 1855 ; commanded left wing in Rohilcund campaign, 1858 ; deputy quartermaster-general at Horse Guards, 1860–5 ; privy councillor, and treasurer of the household, 1867–8 ; major-general, 1868 ; K.C.B., 1869 ; M.P., Ludlow, 1854–60, South Shropshire, 1865–76 ; lieutenant-general, 1875. [xxvi. 207]

HERBERT, PHILIP, EARL OF MONTGOMERY and fourth EARL OF PEMBROKE (1584–1650), parliamentarian ; younger son of Henry Herbert, second earl of Pembroke [q. v.] ; matriculated at New College, Oxford, 1593 ; favourite of James I, and gentleman of the bedchamber, 1605–25 ; created Earl of Montgomery, 1605 ; K.G., 1608 ; high steward of Oxford, 1615 ; privy councillor, 1624 ; lord-lieutenant of Kent, 1624 ; lord chamberlain, 1626–41 ; received grant of Trinidad, Tobago, and Barbados, 1628 ; succeeded his brother William Herbert (1580–1630) [q. v.] as Earl of Pembroke, and lord warden of the Stannaries, 1630 ; commissioner to negotiate with Scots, 1640 ; voted against Strafford, 1641 ; member of committee of safety and parliamentary governor of the Isle of Wight, 1642 ; parliamentary commissioner at Oxford, 1643, and Uxbridge, 1645 ; received Charles I from the Scots, 1647 ; commissioner of the admiralty, 1645 ; as vice-chancellor of Oxford (1641–50) superintended visitation of the colleges and ejection of royalists ; member of first council of state and M.P., Berkshire, 1649 ; a patron of Massinger and Vandyck ; addicted to sport ; rebuilt front of Wilton House, and laid out gardens. [xxvi. 208]

HERBERT, PHILIP, fifth EARL OF PEMBROKE (1619–1669), eldest surviving son of Philip Herbert, fourth earl of Pembroke [q. v.] ; M.P., Glamorgan, in Long parliament ; succeeded to his father's seat for Berkshire, 1650 ; president of council of state (June, July), 1652 ; councillor for trade and navigation, 1660 ; sold Wilton collections. [xxvi. 211]

HERBERT, PHILIP, seventh EARL OF PEMBROKE (1653–1683), son of Philip Herbert, fifth earl [q. v.] ; convicted of manslaughter, 1678. [xxvi. 212]

HERBERT, RICHARD, second BARON HERBERT OF CHERBURY (1600 ? – 1655), royalist ; son of Edward Herbert, first baron Herbert of Cherbury [q. v.] ; conducted Henrietta Maria from Bridlington to Oxford, 1643. [xxvi. 180]

HERBERT, ST. LEGER ALGERNON (1850–1885), war correspondent ; scholar of Wadham College, Oxford, 1869 ; in Canadian civil service, 1875–8 ; private secretary to Sir Garnet Wolseley in Cyprus and South Africa ; 'The Times' correspondent, 1878–9 ; C.M.G. ; secretary to Transvaal commission, 1881–2 ; correspondent of 'Morning Post' in Egypt, 1883–4 ; wounded at Tamai ; killed at Gubat during Soudan war while on the staff of Sir Herbert Stewart. [xxvi. 212]

HERBERT, SIDNEY, first BARON HERBERT OF LEA (1810–1861), statesman ; second son of George Augustus, eleventh earl of Pembroke [q. v.] ; educated at Harrow and Oriel College, Oxford ; B.A., 1831 ; conservative M.P., South Wiltshire, 1832–60 ; secretary to board of control, 1834–5 ; secretary to admiralty, 1841–5 ; war secretary under Peel, 1845–6, Aberdeen, 1852–5 (during the Crimean war), and Palmerston, 1859–60 ; primarily responsible for Miss Florence Nightingale going to the Crimea ; freed by Roebuck committee from suspicion of favouring Russia ; led movement in favour of medical reform in the army and education of officers ; encouraged volunteer movement ; created peer, 1860 ; injured his health by administrative labour. [xxvi. 212]

HERBERT, THOMAS (1597–1642 ?), seaman and author ; brother of Edward Herbert, first baron Herbert of Cherbury [q. v.] ; distinguished himself at Juliers, 1610 ; commanded East Indiaman against Portuguese, 1616 ; visited the Great Mogul at Mandow, 1617 ; served against Algerines, 1620–1 ; brought Prince Charles from Spain to England, 1623, and Count Mansfeldt to the Netherlands, 1625 ; published elegy on Strafford, 1641, and pasquinades, including 'Newes out of Islington,' 1641 (reprinted by Halliwell, 1849). [xxvi. 214]

HERBERT, SIR THOMAS, first baronet (1606–1682), traveller and author ; studied at Oxford and Trinity College, Cambridge ; went to Persia, 1628, with Sir Dodmore Cotton and Sir Robert Shirley [q. v.] ; travelled in Europe ; commissioner with Fairfax's army, 1644, and for surrender of Oxford, 1646 ; attended Charles I, 1647–9, and received presents from him, including the Shakespeare second folio now at Windsor ; created baronet, 1660 ; published 'Description of the Persian Monarchy' (1634), reprinted as 'Some Yeares Travels into divers parts of Asia and Afrique' (1638, &c.) ; collaborated with Dugdale ; his reminiscences (1678) of Charles I's captivity reprinted as 'Memoirs of the last two years of the Reign,' &c., 1702 and 1813. [xxvi. 215]

X

HERBERT, THOMAS, eighth EARL OF PEMBROKE (1656-1733), lord high admiral ; third son of Philip Herbert, fifth earl [q. v.] ; entered at Christ Church, Oxford, 1672 ; succeeded elder brothers in title, 1683 ; lieutenant of Wiltshire ; dismissed, 1687 ; first lord of the admiralty, 1690 ; one of Queen Mary's council, 1690 ; lord privy seal, 1692 ; opposed Fenwick's execution, 1697, and Resumption Bill of 1700 ; first plenipotentiary at treaty of Ryswick, 1697 ; K.G., 1700 ; president of the council, 1702 ; lord high admiral, 1702 and 1708 ; a commissioner for the union, 1706-7 ; lord-lieutenant of Ireland, 1707 ; a lord justice, 1714-15 ; lord-lieutenant of Wiltshire, Monmouth, and South Wales ; P.R.S., 1689-90.   [xxvi. 217]

HERBERT, SIR THOMAS (1793-1861), rear-admiral ; promoted lieutenant for services at reduction of Danish West Indies, 1809 ; commander, 1814 ; as senior officer on Canton River commanded operations against Chuenpee and Bogue forts, and took part in capture of Amoy and Chusan and reduction of Chinghae, 1840 ; K.C.B., 1841 ; junior lord of the admiralty, 1852 ; rear-admiral, 1852 ; M.P., Dartmouth, 1852-7.   [xxvi. 217]

HERBERT, WILLIAM (d. 1333 ?), Franciscan ; preacher and philosopher at Oxford.   [xxvi. 218]

HERBERT, SIR WILLIAM, EARL OF PEMBROKE of the first creation (d. 1469), Yorkist ; knighted by Henry VI, 1449 ; taken prisoner at Formigny, 1450 ; during wars of the Roses did good service against Jasper Tudor ; made privy councillor and chief-justice of South Wales by Edward IV, 1461 ; created Baron Herbert, 1461 ; K.G., 1462 ; chief-justice of North Wales, 1467 ; after capture of Harlech Castle (1468) and attainder of Jasper Tudor (1468) was created Earl of Pembroke and guardian to Henry (afterwards Henry VII), 1468 ; defeated and captured by Lancastrians at Hedgecote and executed.   [xxvi. 218]

HERBERT, WILLIAM, second EARL OF PEMBROKE, afterwards EARL OF HUNTINGDON (1460-1491), son of Sir William Herbert, earl of Pembroke of the first creation (d. 1469) [q. v.] ; English captain in France, 1475 ; exchanged earldom of Pembroke for that of Huntingdon, 1479 ; chief-justice of South Wales, 1483.   [xxvi. 220]

HERBERT, SIR WILLIAM, first EARL OF PEMBROKE of the second creation (1501 ?-1570), grandson of William Herbert, earl of Pembroke of the first creation (d. 1469) [q. v.] ; esquire of the body to Henry VIII, 1526 ; married a sister of Catherine Parr [q. v.] ; granted the dissolved abbey of Wilton, where he built part of the present mansion ; granted property in Wales, 1546 ; gentleman of the privy chamber, 1546 ; one of Henry VIII's executors ; member of Edward VI's council ; K.G. and master of the horse, 1548 ; helped to quell Cornish rising, 1549 ; supported Warwick against Somerset, and was made president of Wales, 1550 ; took part in Somerset's trial, 1551, and obtained Somerset's Wiltshire estates ; created Earl of Pembroke, 1551 ; joined Northumberland in proclaiming Lady Jane Grey, but (19 July 1553) declared for Mary ; commanded against Sir Thomas Wyatt [q. v.], 1554 ; intimate with King Philip ; an envoy to France, 1555 ; governor of Calais, 1556 ; captain-general of English contingent at St. Quentin, 1557 ; under Queen Elizabeth supported Cecil and the protestant party ; lord steward, 1568 ; cleared himself when arrested for supporting scheme for Duke of Norfolk's marriage with Mary Queen of Scots, 1569 ; buried in St. Paul's.   [xxvi. 220]

HERBERT or **HARBERT**, SIR WILLIAM (d. 1593), Irish 'undertaker' and author ; of St. Julians, Monmouthshire ; sole legitimate heir-male of William, first earl of Pembroke (d. 1469) [q. v.] ; knighted, 1578 ; friend of John Dee [q. v.] ; an 'undertaker' for plantation of Munster, being subsequently allotted Desmond property in Kerry, 1587 ; vice-president of Munster in absence of Sir Thomas Norris [q. v.], c. 1589 ; his 'Croftus ; siue de Hibernia Liber' (named in compliment to Sir James Croft (d. 1591) [q. v.]) edited by W. E. Buckley, 1887 ; his Irish tracts and letters to Walsingham and Burghley in 'Calendars of Irish State Papers.'   [xxvi. 223]

HERBERT or **HARBERT**, WILLIAM (fl. 1604), poet ; of Christ Church, Oxford ; author of 'A Prophesie of Cadwallader,' 1604.   [xxvi. 225]

HERBERT, WILLIAM, third EARL OF PEMBROKE of the second creation (1580-1630), eldest son of Henry Herbert, second earl of the second creation [q. v.] ;

educated by Samuel Daniel [q. v.], of New College, Oxford ; succeeded as earl, 1601 ; disgraced for an intrigue with Mary Fitton [q. v.] ; patron of Ben Jonson, Philip Massinger, Inigo Jones, and William Browne (1591-1643 ?) [q. v.] ; thrice entertained James I at Wilton ; lordwarden of the Stannaries, 1604 ; member of the council of New England, 1620 ; interested in the Virginia, Northwest passage, Bermuda, and East India companies ; lord chamberlain, 1615 ; opposed foreign policy of James I and Buckingham ; commissioner of the great seal, 1621 ; member of the committee for foreign affairs and council of war under Charles I, 1626 ; lord steward, 1626 ; chancellor of Oxford University from 1617, Pembroke College being named after him ; presented Barocci library to Bodleian ; wrote poems which were issued with those of Sir Benjamin Rudyerd, 1660. To him as lord chamberlain and to his brother Philip the first folio of Shakespeare's works was dedicated in 1623, but there is no good ground for identifying him with the subject of Shakespeare's sonnets, or with the 'Mr. W. H.' noticed in the publisher Thorpe's dedication of that volume (1609).   [xxvi. 226]

HERBERT, WILLIAM (fl. 1634-1662), author of pious manuals and French conversation-books.
                [xxvi. 226]

HERBERT, WILLIAM, first MARQUIS and titular DUKE OF POWIS (1617-1696), succeeded as third Baron Powis, 1667 ; created Earl of Powis, 1674 ; as chief of the Roman catholic aristocracy imprisoned in connection with the 'Popish plot,' 1679-84 ; privy councillor, 1686 ; created Marquis of Powis, 1687 ; commissioner to 'regulate' corporations, 1687 ; lord-lieutenant of Cheshire, 1688, and vice-lieutenant of Sussex, 1688 ; created by James I, in exile, a duke and chamberlain of his household ; his estates in England confiscated ; died at St. Germains.   [xxvi. 231]

HERBERT, WILLIAM, second MARQUIS and titular DUKE OF POWIS (d. 1745), son of William Herbert, first marquis of Powis [q. v.] ; styled Viscount Montgomery till 1722, when his title as marquis and his estates were restored ; imprisoned, 1689 and 1696-7, on suspicion of complicity in Sir J. Fenwick's plot ; again arrested, 1715.
                [xxvi. 232]

HERBERT, WILLIAM (1718-1795), bibliographer ; went to India, c. 1748, and drew plans of settlements for the East India Company ; published 'A new Directory for the East Indies,' 1758 ; issued second edition of Atkyns's 'Ancient and Present State of Gloucestershire' (rare), 1768, and an enlarged edition of Ames's 'Typographical Antiquities,' 1785-90.   [xxvi. 232]

HERBERT, WILLIAM (1778-1847), dean of Manchester ; edited 'Musæ Etonenses,' 1795 ; B.A. Exeter College, Oxford, 1798 ; M.A. Merton College, 1802, and D.C.L., 1808 ; M.P., Hampshire, 1806, Cricklade, 1811 ; dean of Manchester, 1840-7 ; published 'Select Icelandic Poetry' (1804-6) and translations, also 'Attila, or the Triumph of Christianity,' an epic (1838), and other poems, English, Greek, and Latin ; assisted in editions of White's 'Selborne' (1833 and 1837) ; published monographs on 'Amaryllidaceæ' (1837) and crocuses (edited by J. Lindley, 1847) ; ferns named after him by Sweet ; collected works issued, 1842.   [xxvi. 234]

HERBERT, WILLIAM (1771-1851), antiquarian writer ; librarian of the Guildhall, 1828-45 ; published 'History of the Twelve great Livery Companies' (1836-1837), 'Antiquities of the Inns of Court' (1804), and similar works.   [xxvi. 235]

HERBISON, DAVID (1800-1880), Irish poet ; known as 'The Bard of Dunclug' ; chief work, 'The Fate of McQuillan, and O'Neill's Daughter and . . . other Poems' (1841).   [xxvi. 235]

HERD, DAVID (1732-1810), collector of 'Ancient and Modern Scottish Songs, Heroic Ballads,' &c., 1776 (reprinted, 1869) ; president of the Cape Club, Edinburgh ; literary adviser of Archibald Constable.   [xxvi. 236]

HERD, JOHN (1512 ?-1588), author of 'Historia Anglicana' in Latin verse ; of Eton and King's College, Cambridge ; fellow, 1532 ; M.A., 1546 ; M.D., 1558 ; prebendary of Lincoln, 1557, and York, 1559.   [xxvi. 237]

HERDMAN, JOHN (1762 ?-1842), medical writer M.D. Aberdeen, 1800 ; M.A. Trinity College, Cambridge

1817; physician to Duke of Sussex and city dispensary; ordained; published 'Essay on the Causes and Phenomena of Animal Life,' 1795, and other works. [xxvi. 237]

HERDMAN, ROBERT (1829–1888), Scottish painter; studied at St. Andrews, Edinburgh, and in Italy; exhibited at Royal Scottish Academy from 1850, and at Royal Academy from 1861; R.S.A., 1863; painted portraits of Carlyle, Sir Noel Paton, principals Shairp and Tulloch, and others, and of many ladies. His other works comprise studies of female figures and figure-subjects from Scottish history. [xxvi. 237]

HERDMAN, WILLIAM GAWIN (1805–1882), artist and author; expelled from Liverpool Academy, 1857, for opposition to pre-Raphaelite artists; exhibited at Royal Academy and Suffolk Street, 1834–61; published 'Pictorial Relics of Ancient Liverpool,' 1843, 1856, technical treatises on art, 'Treatise on Skating,' and other works. [xxvi. 238]

HERDSON, HENRY (*fl.* 1651), author of 'Ars Mnemonica,' 1651, and 'Ars Memoriæ,' 1651; 'professor of the art of memory' at Cambridge. [xxvi. 239]

HEREBERT or **HERBERT,** SAINT (*d.* 687), hermit of Derwentwater and friend of St. Cuthbert. [xxvi. 239]

HEREFERTH (*d.* 915). [See WERFERTH.]

HEREFORD, DUKE OF. [See HENRY IV.]

HEREFORD, EARLS OF. [See FITZOSBERN, WILLIAM, *d.* 1071; FITZWILLIAM, ROGER, *alias* ROGER DE BRETEUIL, *fl.* 1071–1075; GLOUCESTER, MILES DE, *d.* 1143; BOHUN, HENRY DE, first EARL (of the Bohun line), 1176–1220; BOHUN, HUMPHREY V, DE, second EARL, *d.* 1274; BOHUN, HUMPHREY VII, DE, third EARL, *d.* 1298; BOHUN, HUMPHREY VIII, DE, fourth EARL, 1276–1322.]

HEREFORD, VISCOUNTS. [See DEVEREUX, WALTER, first VISCOUNT, *d.* 1558; DEVEREUX, WALTER, second VISCOUNT, 1541?–1576.]

HEREFORD, NICHOLAS OF (*fl.* 1390). [See NICHOLAS.]

HEREFORD, ROGER OF (*fl.* 1178). [See ROGER.]

HEREWALD (*d.* 1104), bishop of Llandaff; elected (1056) by Gruffydd ab Llywelyn, Meurig ab Hywel, and Welsh magnates; confirmed by Archbishop Kinsi of York, 1059; suspended by Anselm. [xxvi. 239]

HEREWARD (*fl.* 1070–1071), outlaw; first called 'the Wake' by John of Peterborough; mentioned in Domesday as owner of lands in Lincolnshire; perhaps identical with owner of Marston Jabbett, Warwickshire, and Evenlode, Worcestershire; legendary account of his wanderings given by Ingulf of Crowland and in 'Gesta Herewardi'; headed rising of English at Ely, 1070; with assistance of Danish fleet plundered Peterborough, 1070; joined by Morcar [q. v.], Bishop Æthelwine of Durham, and other refugees; escaped when his allies surrendered to William the Conqueror; said to have been pardoned by William; slain by Normans in Maine, according to account of Geoffrey Gaimar [q. v.] [xxvi. 240]

HERFAST or **ARFAST** (*d.* 1084?), first chancellor of England; chaplain to William I before the Conquest; chancellor of England, 1068–70; bishop of Elmham, 1070; bishop of Thetford, 1078; tried to defeat monastic claims to exemption from episcopal jurisdiction. [xxvi. 242]

HERICKE. [See also HERRICK and HEYRICK.]

HERICKE or **HERRICK,** SIR WILLIAM (1562–1653), goldsmith and money-lender; uncle of Robert Herrick [q. v.]; went on mission from Elizabeth to the Grand Turk, 1580–1; M.P., Leicester, 1601; principal jeweller to James I; knighted, 1605; exempted from liability to serve as sheriff, 1605; refused to pay ship-money. [xxvi. 243]

HERING, GEORGE EDWARDS (1805–1879), landscape-painter; of German parentage; published 'Sketches on the Danube, in Hungary, and Transylvania,' 1838; exhibited at Royal Academy from 1836; his 'Amalfi' and 'Capri' purchased by Prince Consort. [xxvi. 244]

HERIOT, GEORGE (1563–1624), founder of Heriot's Hospital, Edinburgh (opened, 1659); jeweller to James VI, 1601, to his queen, 1597, and to James VI on his

accession as James I of England, 1603; was granted imposition on sugar for three years, 1620; the 'Jingling Geordie' of Scott's 'Fortunes of Nigel.' [xxvi. 244]

HERIOT, JOHN (1760–1833), author and journalist; present as a marine in Rodney's action of 17 April, 1780; published two novels (1787 and 1789), and 'Historical Sketch of Gibraltar,' 1792; edited the 'Sun' and the 'True Briton,' 1793–1806; deputy paymaster-general in West Indies, 1810–16; comptroller of Chelsea Hospital, 1816–33. [xxvi. 246]

HERKS, GARBRAND (*fl.* 1556). [See GARBRAND, HERKS.]

HERKS, *alias* GARBRAND, JOHN (1542–1589). [See GARBRAND.]

HERLE, CHARLES (1598–1659), puritan divine; M.A. Exeter College, Oxford; presented by Stanley family to rectory of Winwick, Lancashire, 1626; represented Lancashire in Westminster Assembly of Divines, 1643, and was appointed prolocutor, 1646; refused to pray for Commonwealth; his chief work, 'The Independency on Scriptures of the Independency of Churches,' 1643; friend of Fuller. [xxvi. 246]

HERLE, WILLIAM DE (*d.* 1347), judge; as serjeant-at-law summoned to assist parliaments of Edward II; judge of common pleas, 1320; chief-justice of common pleas, 1327–9 and 1331–7. [xxvi. 248]

HERLEWIN (*d.* 1137). [See ETHELMÆR.]

HERMAN, HENRY (1832–1894), dramatist and novelist; fought in confederate ranks in American civil war; produced independently and in collaboration with Mr. Henry Arthur Jones and other authors plays at London theatres from 1875. [Suppl. ii. 412]

HERMAND, LORD (*d.* 1827). [See FERGUSSON, GEORGE.]

HERMANN (*fl.* 1070), hagiographer; archdeacon of Thetford under Herfast [q. v.]; afterwards monk of Bury; wrote 'De Miraculis S. Ædmundi,' printed in 'Memorials of St. Edmund's Abbey' (ed. T. Arnold, 1890). [xxvi. 249]

HERMANN (*d.* 1078), first bishop of Old Sarum (Salisbury); native of Lorraine; bishop of Ramsbury or Wilton, 1045; went to Rome for Edward the Confessor, 1050; monk of St. Bertin's Abbey at St. Omer, 1055–8; bishop of Sherborne with Ramsbury, 1058; removed his see to Old Sarum, 1075; assisted at Lanfranc's consecration and several councils. [xxvi. 249]

HERNE, JOHN (*fl.* 1644), lawyer; barrister, Lincoln's Inn; bencher, 1637; defended, among others, Prynne, 1634, and Archbishop Laud, 1644. [xxvi. 250]

HERNE, JOHN (*fl.* 1660), son of John Herne (*fl.* 1644) [q. v.]; author, among other works, of 'The Pleader' (collection of precedents), 1657; translated 'The Learned Reading of John Herne, Esq.' (his father), 1659. [xxvi. 250]

HERNE, THOMAS (*d.* 1722), controversialist; scholar of Corpus Christi College, Cambridge, 1712; B.A., 1715; incorporated at Oxford, 1716; fellow of Merton College, 1716; tutor to third and fourth Dukes of Bedford; as 'Phileleutherus Cantabrigiensis,' published 'False Notion of a Christian Priesthood,' against William Law, 1717–18, and some tracts; issued account of the Bangorian controversy, 1720. [xxvi. 250]

HERON, HALY (*fl.* 1565–1585), author of 'A new Discourse of Morall Philosophie entituled the Kayes of Counsaile,' 1579; B.A. Queens' College, Cambridge, 1570. [xxvi. 251]

HERON, SIR RICHARD, baronet (1726–1805), chief secretary to lord-lieutenant of Ireland, 1776–80; created baronet, 1778; published genealogical table of Herons of Newark, 1798. [xxvi. 251]

HERON, ROBERT (1764–1807), author; son of a Kirkcudbrightshire weaver; edited Thomson's 'Seasons,' 1789 and 1793; wrote part of a 'History of Scotland' (1794) while imprisoned for debt; ruling elder for New Galloway; edited the 'Globe' and other London papers; published, among other works, translations from the French, a life of Burns (1797), and an edition of Junius, 1802. [xxvi. 251]

HERON, SIR ROBERT, baronet (1765–1854), whig politician; of St. John's College, Cambridge; succeeded his uncle, Sir Richard Heron [q. v.], in the baronetcy, 1805; M.P., Grimsby, 1812–18, Peterborough, 1819–47; published political and social 'Notes,' 1851. [xxvi. 252]

HERRICK. [See also HERICKE and HEYRICK.]

HERRICK, ROBERT (1591–1674), poet; apprenticed to his uncle, Sir William Hericke [q. v.], for ten years; afterwards went to St. John's College, Cambridge, but graduated from Trinity Hall, 1617; M.A., 1620; incumbent of Dean Prior, Devonshire, 1629; ejected, 1647; lived in Westminster, restored, 1662; many of his poems published anonymously in 'Witts Recreations,' 1650; several of his pieces set to music by Henry Lawes [q. v.] and other composers; his 'Hesperides' with 'Noble Numbers' first issued, 1648; complete editions edited by Thomas Maitland (1823), Edward Walford (1859), W. Carew Hazlitt (1869), and Dr. Grosart (1876). [xxvi. 253]

HERRIES, BARONS. [See MAXWELL, SIR JOHN, fourth BARON, 1512?–1583; MAXWELL, WILLIAM, fifth BARON, d. 1603.]

HERRIES, SIR CHARLES JOHN (1815–1883), financier; son of John Charles Herries [q. v.]; of Eton and Trinity College, Cambridge; M.A., 1840; commissioner of excise, 1842; deputy-chairman of inland revenue, 1856; chairman of the board of inland revenue, 1877–81; K.C.B., 1880. [xxvi. 255]

HERRIES, JOHN CHARLES (1778–1855), statesman and financier; educated at Leipzig; drew up for Pitt his counter-resolutions against Tierney's financial proposals, 1800; private secretary to Vansittart, 1801, and Perceval, 1807; translated Gentz's treatise 'On the State of Europe before and after the French Revolution,' 1802; defended financial policy of government, 1803; secretary and registrar of the Order of the Bath, 1809–22; commissary-in-chief, 1811–16; auditor of civil list, 1816; drew up second report of Irish revenue commission, 1822; M.P., Harwich, 1823–41; and financial secretary to treasury, 1823–7; privy councillor, 1827; chancellor of the exchequer in Goderich's ministry from 8 Aug. 1827 to 8 Jan. 1828; wrote a statement of events which led to dissolution of Goderich ministry; master of the mint, 1828–30; drew up fourth report of Sir Henry Parnell's finance committee, 1828, first making public accounts intelligible; president of board of trade, 1830; moved resolution against Russian-Dutch loan, 1832; secretary-at-war under Peel, 1834–5; his motion for return of public accounts carried against whig government, 1840; M.P., Stamford, 1847–53; protectionist; president of board of control in Lord Derby's first government, 1852 (February–December). [xxvi. 255]

HERRING, FRANCIS (d. 1628), physician; M.D. Christ's College, Cambridge; M.A., 1589; F.R.C.P., 1599, and seven times censor; published treatises on the plague and Latin poem on the Gunpowder plot ('Pietas Pontificia'), 1609. [xxvi. 258]

HERRING, JOHN FREDERICK (1795–1865), animal-painter; drove coaches between Wakefield and Lincoln, Doncaster and Halifax, and London and York; painted winners of the St. Leger for thirty-two years, and many other sporting subjects; member of Society of British Artists, 1841; exhibited at Royal Academy and Society of British Artists. [xxvi. 258]

HERRING, JULINES (1582–1644), puritan divine; M.A. Sidney Sussex College, Cambridge; ordained by an Irish bishop; incumbent of Calke, Derbyshire, c. 1610–c. 1618; afterwards preached at Shrewsbury from 1618; suspended for nonconformity; co-pastor of English church at Amsterdam, 1637–44. [xxvi. 259]

HERRING, THOMAS (1693–1757), archbishop of Canterbury; B.A. Jesus College, Cambridge, 1713; fellow of Corpus Christi, 1716; M.A., 1717; D.D., 1728; preacher at Lincoln's Inn, and chaplain to George I, 1726; rector of Bletchingley, 1731; dean of Rochester, 1732; bishop of Bangor, 1737–43; as archbishop of York (1743–7) raised a large sum for government during the rebellion; archbishop of Canterbury, 1747–57; repaired Lambeth and Croydon palaces, and left benefactions to the sons of the clergy and Corpus Christi College; his letters (1728–57) to William Duncombe edited by John Duncombe [q. v.], 1777. [xxvi. 259]

HERRING, WILLIAM (d. 1774), dean of St. Asaph, 1751–74; brother of Thomas Herring [q. v.]. [xxvi. 260]

HERSCHEL, CAROLINE LUCRETIA (1750–1848), astronomer; sister of Sir William Herschel [q. v.]; came to live with her brother at Bath, 1772, and became his assistant; discovered eight comets (five undisputed) between 1786 and 1797; received a salary from George III, 1787; her 'Index to Flamsteed's Observations of the Fixed Stars,' with list of Flamsteed's errata, published by Royal Society, 1798; on Sir William's death went to Hanover, 1822; gold medallist of Astronomical Society for her catalogue in zones of Sir W. Herschel's star-clusters and nebulæ, 1828, and was created honorary member, 1835; awarded Prussian gold medal for science on ninety-sixth birthday; entertained crown prince and princess next year; minor planet Lucretia named after her by Palisa, 1889. [xxvi. 260]

HERSCHEL, SIR JOHN FREDERICK WILLIAM, first baronet (1792–1871), astronomer; son of Sir William Herschel [q. v.]; senior wrangler and first Smith's prize-man, 1813; subsequently fellow of St. John's College, Cambridge; M.A., 1816; helped to found Analytical Society, Cambridge, 1813; with George Peacock (1791–1858) [q. v.] translated Lacroix's 'Elementary Treatise on the Differential Calculus,' with appendix on finite differences, 1816; F.R.S., 1813; Copley medallist, 1821; first foreign secretary of Royal Astronomical Society; Lalande prize-man, Royal Astronomical Society, 1825, and gold medallist for revision of his father's double stars; secretary to Royal Society, 1824–7; received medals for catalogue of northern nebulæ, 1836; president of Astronomical Society, 1827–32; discovered and catalogued many double stars; described new graphical method of investigating stellar orbits, 1832; wrote article on 'Light' in 'Encyclopædia Metropolitana' (1827), which gave European currency to undulatory theory; his 'Preliminary Discourse on Study of Natural Philosophy' (1830) translated into French, German, and Italian, his 'Outlines of Astronomy,' 1849 (12th edit. 1873), into Russian Chinese, and Arabic; during residence (1834–8) at Feldhausen, near Cape Town, discovered 1,202 pairs of close double stars and 1,708 nebulæ and clusters, 'monographed' the Orion nebula, prepared a chart of the Argo, made first satisfactory measure of direct solar radiation, and suggested (1836–7) relation between solar and auroral activity; initiated while at the Cape system of national education, and sent tidal observations to Whewell; created baronet, 1838; assisted in royal commission on standards (1838–43); D.C.L. Oxford, 1839; lord rector of Aberdeen, 1842, and president of British Association, 1845; received many foreign orders; prepared charts of all the lucid stars; invented photographic use of sensitised paper, 1839; introduced use of hyposulphite of soda as a fixing agent; discovered 'epipolic dispersion' of light, 1845; the results of his Cape observations printed, 1847, at expense of Duke of Northumberland; received the Copley medal, 1847, and a special testimonial from the Astronomical Society, 1848; master of the mint, 1850–5; assisted at the Great Exhibition and in the universities commission of 1850; his last great undertaking, a general and descriptive catalogue of double stars; buried in Westminster Abbey near the grave of Newton. His miscellaneous writings were collected in 'Essays' (1857) and 'Familiar Lectures on Scientific Subjects' (1867). [xxvi. 263]

HERSCHEL, SIR WILLIAM (1738–1822), astronomer born at Hanover; as a boy played the hautboy and violin in Hanoverian guards; secretly sent to England by his parents, 1757; patronised by Dr. Edward Miller [q.v.]; organist at Halifax, 1765, at Octagon Chapel, Bath, 1766; began to construct optical instruments, 1773 and to observe stars, 1774; discovered Uranus (Georgium Sidus), 1781; Copley medallist and F.R.S., 1781; exhibited his telescope to George III, and was appointed court astronomer, 1782; removed to Slough, 1786; his polishing machine perfected, 1788; visited by distinguished men of science; his great forty-foot mirror begun (aided by royal grant), 1785, first used, 1789 (a sixth satellite of Saturn being discovered), finished (with further aid), 1811, and used till 1839; discovered 'Enceladus' and 'Mimas,' 1789; received numerous degrees and decorations; first president of the Astronomical Society; had interviews with Bonaparte and Laplace, 1802; sent sixty-nine memoirs to Royal Society; discovered more than two thousand nebulæ, and suggested their true nature; discovered mutually revolving stars, over eight hundred double stars (measuring them with the revolving wire and lamp micrometers), and (1783) the translation of the solar system towards a point in Hercules; invented 'method of sequences'; published six memoirs relative to Saturn, 1790–1808; suggested 'trade wind' explanation of Jupiter's belts, 1781; investigated rotation of Mars; made physical observations on comets of 1807 and 1811; discovered infra-red solar rays, 1800; K.H., 1816.   [xxvi. 268]

HERSCHELL, FARRER, first BARON HERSCHELL (1837–1899), lord chancellor; son of Ridley Haim Herschell [q. v.]; educated at University College, London; B.A. London, 1857; barrister, Lincoln's Inn, 1860, bencher, 1872; took silk, 1872; liberal M.P., Durham, 1874–85; knighted and appointed solicitor-general, 1880; created lord chancellor, with title of Baron Herschell of city of Durham, 1886; again lord chancellor, 1892–5; D.C.L. Durham; LL.D. Cambridge; G.C.B., 1893; died at Washington while at work on Anglo-American commission, 1898.   [Suppl. ii. 413]

HERSCHELL, RIDLEY HAIM (1807–1864), dissenting minister; born in Prussian Poland of Jewish parents; settled in England, 1830; took charge of Lady Olivia Sparrow's missions; opened a chapel in London, 1838; one of the founders of mission to Jews and of evangelical alliance; published works concerning relation of Judaism to Christianity.   [xxvi. 274]

HERSCHELL, SOLOMON (1761–1842). [See HIRSCHEL.]

HERSHON, PAUL ISAAC (1817–1888), hebraist; born in Galicia; director of House of Industry for Jews at Jerusalem and the model farm at Jaffa; published 'Talmudic Miscellany,' 1880.   [xxvi. 275]

HERT, HENRY (fl. 1549. [See HART.]

HERTELPOLL or HARTLEPOOL, HUGH OF (d. 1302?). [See HUGH.]

HERTFORD, MARQUISES OF. [See SEYMOUR, WILLIAM, first MARQUIS, 1588–1660; CONWAY, FRANCIS SEYMOUR, first MARQUIS of the second creation, 1719–1794; SEYMOUR, FRANCIS (INGRAM), 1743–1822; SEYMOUR-CONWAY, FRANCIS CHARLES, third MARQUIS, 1777–1842.]

HERTFORD, EARLS OF. [See CLARE, GILBERT DE, seventh EARL (of the Clare family), 1243–1295; CLARE, GILBERT DE, eighth EARL, 1291–1314; CLARE, RICHARD DE, said to be first EARL, d. 1136?; CLARE, RICHARD DE, sixth EARL, 1222–1262; CLARE, ROGER DE, third EARL, d. 1173; MONTHERMER, RALPH DE, d. 1325?; SEYMOUR, EDWARD, first EARL of the second creation, 1506?–1552; SEYMOUR, SIR EDWARD, EARL of the third creation, 1539?–1621.]

HERTFORD, COUNTESS OF. [See SEYMOUR, CATHERINE, 1538?–1568.]

HERTSLET, LEWIS (1787–1870), librarian to the foreign office, 1810–57; published collections of treaties between Great Britain and Foreign Powers, 1820 (continued by his son Edward), and between Turkey and Foreign Powers (1835–55), 1855.   [xxvi. 275]

HERVEY or HERVÆUS (d. 1131), first bishop of Ely; made bishop of Bangor by William II, 1092, but driven from his diocese by the Welsh; confessor to Henry I; made administrator of the Abbey of Ely, 1107; bishop of Ely, 1109–31; attended council on clerical marriages, 1129.   [xxvi. 276]

HERVEY, LORD ARTHUR CHARLES (1808–1894), bishop of Bath and Wells; fourth son of Frederick William Hervey, first marquis of Bristol; educated at Eton and Trinity College, Cambridge; B.A., 1830; ordained priest, 1832; rector of Horringer and Ickworth, 1856; archdeacon of Sudbury, 1862; bishop of Bath and Wells, 1869–1894; on committee of revisers of authorised version of Old Testament, 1870–84; published 'Genealogies of our Lord,' 1853.   [Suppl. ii. 415]

HERVEY, AUGUSTUS JOHN, third EARL OF BRISTOL (1724–1779), admiral; grandson of John Hervey, first earl of Bristol [q. v.]; married Elizabeth Chudleigh [q. v.], 1744, divorced by collusion, 1769; post-captain, 1747; served under Byng in Mediterranean; gave evidence at Byng's trial, 1757; of great service to Hawke in the Channel, 1759; served under Keppel at Belleisle, 1760; took part in capture of Martinique, St. Lucia, and the

Havannah, 1762; M.P., Bury St. Edmunds, 1757–63 and 1768–75, Saltash, 1763–8; groom of the bedchamber, 1763; chief secretary for Ireland, 1766–7; a lord of the admiralty, 1771–5; succeeded to earldom, 1775; rear-admiral, 1775; vice-admiral, 1778; supported Keppel and opposed Sandwich, 1778–9; his correspondence with Lord Hawke in Record Office, other journals in British Museum.   [xxvi. 277]

HERVEY, CARR, LORD HERVEY (1691–1723), reputed father of Horace Walpole; elder son of John Hervey, first earl of Bristol [q. v.]; M.A. Clare Hall, Cambridge, 1710; M.P., Bury St. Edmunds, 1713–22.   [xxvi. 288]

HERVEY, FREDERICK AUGUSTUS, fourth EARL OF BRISTOL and fifth BARON HOWARD DE WALDEN (1730–1803), bishop of Derry; third son of John Hervey, baron Hervey of Ickworth [q. v.]; educated at Westminster and Corpus Christi College, Cambridge; M.A., 1754; D.D., 1770; principal clerk of privy seal, 1761; travelled in Italy and Dalmatia and studied volcanic phenomena; bishop of Cloyne, 1767–8, where he offered Philip Skelton [q. v.] a chaplaincy, and reclaimed the great bog; as bishop of Derry (1768–1803) spent much money on public works and the see; succeeded his brother Augustus John [q. v.] in earldom, 1779; advocated relaxation of catholic penal laws and abolition of tithe; took prominent part at volunteers' convention, 1783; favoured parliamentary reform and the admission of Roman catholics to House of Commons; travelled on the continent; imprisoned by the French at Milan; succeeded to barony of Howard de Walden through his grandmother, 1799; died at Albano; buried at Ickworth.   [xxvi. 279]

HERVEY, GEORGE WILLIAM, second EARL OF BRISTOL (1721–1775), eldest son of John Hervey, baron Hervey of Ickworth [q. v.]; succeeded his father as third baron, 1743, and his grandfather as second Earl of Bristol, 1751; envoy extraordinary to Turin, 1755–8; ambassador at Madrid, 1758–61; nominated lord-lieutenant of Ireland, but did not go, 1766; privy councillor, 1766; lord privy seal, 1768–70; groom of the stole, 1770.   [xxvi. 282]

HERVEY, JAMES (1714–1758), devotional writer; at Lincoln College, Oxford, while John Wesley was fellow; B.A.; M.A. Clare Hall, Cambridge 1752; incumbent of Weston Favell and Collingtree, 1752; his 'Meditations and Contemplations' brought out in two parts, 1746–7; published also 'Dialogues between Theron and Aspasio,' 1755, attacked by Wesley, his reply being issued posthumously, 1766; collected works published, 1769 (6 vols.)   [xxvi. 282]

HERVEY, JAMES (1751?–1824), physician; M.A. Queen's College, Oxford, 1774; M.D., 1781; physician to Guy's Hospital, 1779; F.R.C.P., 1782; Gulstonian lecturer, 1783; six times censor, 1783–1809; Harveian orator, 1785, Lumleian lecturer, 1789–1811.   [xxvi. 284]

HERVEY, JOHN (1616–1679), treasurer to Catherine of Braganza; M.P., Hythe, 1661–79; patron of Cowley.   [xxvi. 284]

HERVEY, JOHN, BARON HERVEY OF ICKWORTH (1696–1743), pamphleteer and memoir writer; younger son of John Hervey, first earl of Bristol [q. v.]; of Westminster and Clare Hall, Cambridge; M.A., 1715; styled Lord Hervey after death of elder brother Carr Hervey [q. v.], 1723; M.P., Bury St. Edmunds, 1725; granted pension by George II on his desertion of Frederick, prince of Wales; vice-chamberlain and privy councillor, 1730; fought a duel with William Pulteney [q. v.], 1731; summoned to House of Lords in his father's barony, 1733; exercised great influence over Queen Caroline; lord privy seal, 1740–2; afterwards joined opposition; friend of Lady Mary Wortley Montagu; attacked by Pope as 'Lord Fanny,' 1733; replied in 'Verses addressed to the Imitator of Horace,' and 'Epistle to a Doctor of Divinity,' 1733; the 'Sporus' of Pope's 'Epistle to Arbuthnot'; wrote pamphlets in behalf of Sir Robert Walpole; 'Letters between Lord Hervey and Dr. Middleton concerning the Roman Senate,' edited by T. Knowles, 1778; Hervey's 'Memoirs of Reign of George II,' edited by J. W. Croker, 1848 (reprinted, 1884).   [xxvi. 284]

HERVEY, JOHN, first EARL OF BRISTOL (1665–1751), whig politician; LL.D. Clare Hall, Cambridge, 1705; M.P., Bury St. Edmunds, 1694–1703; created Baron Hervey of Ickworth, 1703, by influence of the Marlboroughs; created Earl of Bristol, 1714; his portrait by Kneller at Guildhall, Bury.   [xxvi. 288]

HERVEY, MARY, LADY (1700–1768), daughter of brigadier-general Lepell ; eulogised by Pope, Gay, Chesterfield, and Voltaire ; married to John Hervey, baron Hervey of Ickworth [q. v.], 1720; her letters to Rev. Edmund Morris (1742–68) published, 1821, and others in Lady Suffolk's 'Letters' (1824); epitaph composed by Horace Walpole. [xxvi. 289]

HERVEY, THOMAS (1699–1775), eccentric pamphleteer ; second son of John Hervey, first earl of Bristol [q. v.] ; M.P., Bury, 1733–47 ; equerry to Queen Caroline, 1728–37, and vice-chamberlain to her, 1733 ; eloped with wife of Sir Thomas Hanmer [q. v.] ; published pamphlets, including ' Answer to a Letter he received from Dr. Samuel Johnson to dissuade him from parting with his Supposed [second] Wife,' 1763. [xxvi. 290]

HERVEY, THOMAS KIBBLE (1799–1859), poet and critic ; entered at Trinity College, Cambridge, c. 1818; while at Cambridge published ' Australia,' a poem (3rd edit. 1829), edited ' Friendship's Offering,' 1826–7, and the ' Amaranth,' 1839; contributed to annuals ; edited ' Athenæum,' 1846–53. [xxvi. 291]

HERVEY, WILLIAM (d. 1567). [See HARVEY.]

HERVEY, WILLIAM, BARON HERVEY OF KIDBROOKE (d. 1642), distinguished himself against the Spanish Armada, 1588 ; knighted for services at capture of Cadiz, 1596 ; created Irish peer for services in Ireland, 1620 ; promoted to English barony, 1628. [xxvi. 292]

HESELTINE, JAMES (1690–1763), organist of Durham Cathedral, 1710–63, and composer. [xxvi. 292]

HESILRIGE or **HASELRIG**, SIR ARTHUR, second baronet (d. 1661), parliamentarian ; as M.P. for Leicestershire opposed Laud's religious policy ; introduced bill of attainder against Strafford ; promoted ' Root-and-Branch Bill,' and (1641) proposed Militia Bill ; one of the five members impeached by Charles I, 1642 ; raised a troop of horse and fought at Edgehill, 1642 ; as Waller's second in command distinguished himself at Lansdowne, 1643 ; wounded at Lansdowne and Roundway Down, 1643 ; present at Cheriton, 1644 ; a leader of the independents after the self-denying ordinance ; while governor of Newcastle recaptured Tynemouth, 1648 ; refused nomination as one of the king's judges ; accompanied Cromwell to Scotland, 1648, and supported him with a reserve army, 1650 ; Lilburne's charges against him declared false by the House of Commons, 1652 ; purchased confiscated lands of see of Durham ; member of every council of state during the Commonwealth ; opposed Cromwell's government after dissolution of Long parliament, 1653 ; M.P., Leicester, 1654, 1656, and 1659 ; refused to pay taxes and to enter or recognise the new upper chamber, 1657 ; opposed in Commons recognition of Richard Cromwell, and intrigued with army leaders against him ; became recognised leader of parliament ; obtained cashiering of Lambert and others, 1659 ; gained over Portsmouth and raised troops against Lambert, 1659 ; was outwitted by Monck ; arrested at the Restoration, but Monck interposed to save his life ; died in the Tower. [xxvi. 292]

HESKETH, HARRIET, LADY (1733–1807), cousin and friend of the poet Cowper ; married Thomas Hesketh (created baronet, 1761). [xxvi. 296]

HESKETH, HENRY (1637 ?–1710), divine ; B.A. Brasenose College, Oxford, 1656 ; vicar of St. Helen, Bishopsgate, 1678–94 ; chaplain to Charles II and William III ; published religious works. [xxvi. 296]

HESKETH, SIR PETER (1801–1866). [See FLEETWOOD, SIR PETER HESKETH.]

HESKETH, RICHARD (1562–1593), Roman catholic exile ; incited Ferdinando Stanley, fifth earl of Derby, to claim the crown ; executed at St. Albans on the earl's information. [xxvi. 296]

HESKETH, ROGER (1643–1715), Roman catholic controversialist ; vice-president of English college, Lisbon, 1678–86 ; came to England ; wrote a treatise on transubstantiation. [xxvi. 297]

HESKETH or **HASKET**, THOMAS (1561–1613), botanist ; brother of Richard Hesketh [q. v.] [xxvi. 297]

HESKYNS or **HESKIN**, THOMAS (fl. 1566), Roman catholic divine ; fellow of Clare Hall, Cambridge ;

M.A., 1540 ; D.D., 1557 ; rector of Hildersham, 1551–6 ; chancellor of Sarum, 1558–9, and vicar of Brixworth, 1558–9 ; retired to Flanders and became a Dominican, but returned to England secretly ; published ' The Parliament of Chryste,' 1565 (Brussels). [xxvi. 297]

HESLOP, LUKE (1738–1825), archdeacon of Buckingham ; fellow (1769) of Corpus Christi College, Cambridge ; senior wrangler, 1764 ; M.A., 1767 ; B.D., 1775 ; prebendary of St. Paul's, 1776 ; archdeacon of Buckingham, 1778 ; prebendary of Lincoln, 1778 ; rector of Adstock, Buckinghamshire, for twenty-five years ; rector of Marylebone, London, 1809 ; published economic pamphlets. [xxvi. 298]

HESLOP, THOMAS PRETIOUS (1823–1885), physician ; M.D. Edinburgh, 1848 ; lecturer on physiology at Queen's College, Birmingham, 1853–8 ; physician to Queen's Hospital, 1853–60 and 1870–82 ; chairman of Mason's College. [xxvi. 298]

HESSE, PRINCESS OF (1723–1772). [See MARY.]

HESSE-HOMBURG, LANDGRAVINE OF (1770–1840). [See ELIZABETH, PRINCESS.]

HESSEL, PHŒBE (1713 ?–1821), reputed female soldier and centenarian ; a Brighton ' character.' [xxvi. 298]

HESSEY, JAMES AUGUSTUS (1814–1892), divine ; educated at Merchant Taylors' School and St. John's College, Oxford ; M.A., 1840 ; B.D., 1845 ; D.C.L., 1846 ; vicar of Helidon, Northamptonshire, 1839 ; head-master of Merchant Taylors' School, 1845–70 ; prebendary of St. Paul's Cathedral, 1860–75 ; examining chaplain to John Jackson (1811–1885), bishop of London [q. v.], 1870 ; archdeacon of Middlesex, 1875–92 ; published theological writings. [Suppl. ii. 415]

HESTER, JOHN (d. 1593), distiller, of St. Paul's Wharf ; author and translator of medical works ; mentioned in Gabriel Harvey's ' Pierces Supererogation,' 1593. [xxvi. 298]

HESTON, WALTER (fl. 1350), Carmelite of Stamford ; Cambridge scholar and D.D. [xxvi. 299]

HETHERINGTON, HENRY (1792–1849), printer and publisher of unstamped newspapers ; drew up ' Circular for the Formation of Trades Unions,' 1830 ; began to issue the weekly ' Poor Man's Guardian,' unstamped, July, 1831 ; twice imprisoned for defying the law ; indicted for publication of ' Poor Man's Guardian,' and trade-union ' Poor Man's Conservative,' 1834, when the ' Guardian ' was declared legal ; imprisoned for publishing ' Haslam's Letters to the Clergy of all Denominations,' 1840 ; obtained conviction against Edward Moxon [q. v.] for publishing Shelley's works, 1841; died of cholera. [xxvi. 299]

HETHERINGTON, WILLIAM MAXWELL (1803–1865), divine and poet ; studied at Edinburgh ; joined Free church ; became minister of Free St. Paul's, Edinburgh, 1848 ; professor of apologetics in New College, Glasgow, 1857 ; published, among other works, histories of the church of Scotland, 1843, and the Westminster Assembly, 1863 (ed. R. Williamson, 1878). [xxvi. 300]

HETON, MARTIN (1552–1609), bishop of Ely ; of Westminster and Christ Church, Oxford ; M.A., 1578 ; D.D., 1589 ; canon, 1582 ; vice-chancellor, 1588 ; dean of Winchester, 1589 ; bishop of Ely, 1599–1609 ; agreed to alienate to the crown richest manors of Ely. [xxvi. 301]

HETON, THOMAS (fl. 1573), London cloth-merchant and receiver of protestant refugees. [xxvi. 301]

HEUGH, HUGH (1782–1846), presbyterian divine ; moderator of general associate synod, 1819 ; minister of Regent Place, Glasgow, 1821–46 ; D.D. Pittsburg, 1831 ; his life and works issued by Hamilton Macgill, 1850. [xxvi. 301]

HEURTLEY, CHARLES ABEL (1806–1895), Lady Margaret professor of divinity at Oxford ; worked in timber merchant's office at Liverpool, 1822 ; scholar of Corpus Christi College, Oxford, 1823 ; M.A., 1831 ; fellow, 1832 ; D.D., 1853 ; vicar of Fenny Compton, 1840–72 ; Bampton lecturer, 1845 ; Margaret professor, 1853–95. [Suppl. ii. 416]

HEVENINGHAM, WILLIAM (1604–1678), regicide; sheriff of Norfolk, 1633; M.P., Stockbridge, 1640; served on committee of Eastern Association, 1646; member of high court, but refused to sign death-warrant of Charles I, 1649; member of council of state, 1649; vice-admiral of Suffolk, 1651; at the Restoration his life saved by the exertions of his wife's relations, 1661; imprisoned at Windsor, 1664. [xxvi. 302]

HEWETT, SIR GEORGE, first baronet (1750–1840), general; with 70th foot in West Indies, 1764–74, and at siege of Charleston; exchanged with 43rd, and was deputy quartermaster-general to O'Hara; adjutant-general in Ireland, 1793–9; raised regiment in Ireland; major-general, 1796; chief of recruiting department, 1799; inspector-general of royal reserve, 1803; commander-in-chief in East Indies, 1807–11, in Ireland, 1813–16; created baronet, 1818; colonel of 61st; general. [xxvi. 303]

HEWETT, SIR PRESCOTT GARDNER, first baronet (1812–1891), surgeon; studied in Paris; M.R.C.S., 1836; lecturer on anatomy at St. George's Hospital, 1845; full surgeon, 1861, and consulting surgeon, 1875; F.R.C.S., 1843, and president, 1876; F.R.S., 1874; surgeon extraordinary to Queen Victoria, 1867; sergeant-surgeon, 1884; surgeon to Prince of Wales, 1875; created baronet, 1883; published surgical papers. [Suppl. ii. 417]

HEWETT, SIR WILLIAM (d. 1567), lord-mayor of London; master of Clothworkers' Company, 1543; alderman of Vintry, 1550–4, afterwards of Candlewick; sheriff of London, 1553; lord mayor, 1559–60; knighted, 1560; a governor of Highgate school. [xxvi. 304]

HEWETT, SIR WILLIAM NATHAN WRIGHTE (1834–1888), vice-admiral; midshipman during Burmese war, 1851; promoted for gallantry in the Crimea, 1854; one of the first recipients of Victoria cross, 1857; commanded on royal yacht, 1858; captain, 1862; served on China station, 1865–72; as commander-in-chief in West Africa had charge of naval operations in Ashantee war, 1873–4; K.C.B., 1874; rear-admiral, 1878; commander-in-chief in East Indies, 1882, conducting naval operations in Red Sea; assisted in defence of Suakin, 1884; undertook successful mission to Abyssinia, 1884; vice-admiral, 1884; commanded Channel fleet, 1886–8. [xxvi. 305]

HEWIT or **HEWETT**, JOHN (1614–1658), royalist divine; of Pembroke College, Cambridge; D.D. Oxford, 1643; minister of St. Gregory's by St. Paul's, London; said to have harboured Ormonde, 1658; beheaded for royalist plot, though interceded for by Mrs. Claypoole; published devotional works. [xxvi. 306]

HEWITSON, WILLIAM CHAPMAN (1806–1878), naturalist; left to British Museum fine collection of diurnal *lepidoptera*, some birds and pictures; published 'British Oology' (1833–42), and works on *lepidoptera*. [xxvi. 307]

HEWITT, JAMES, VISCOUNT LIFFORD (1709–1789), lord chancellor of Ireland; barrister, Middle Temple, 1742; M.P., Coventry, 1761; king's serjeant, 1760; judge of the king's bench, 1766; lord chancellor of Ireland, 1768–89; created Baron Lifford in Irish peerage, 1768, and viscount, 1781; his decisions as chancellor printed, 1839. [xxvi. 308]

HEWITT, JOHN (1719–1802), mayor of Coventry, 1755, 1758, and 1760; published 'Journal,' 1779–90, Memoirs of Lady Wilbrihammon,' c. 1778, and 'Guide for Constables,' 1779. [xxvi. 308]

HEWITT, JOHN (1807–1878), antiquary; wrote under name 'Sylvanus Swanquill'; published 'Ancient Armour and Weapons,' 1855–60, 'Old Woolwich,' 1860, handbooks on Lichfield, and other works. [xxvi. 309]

HEWLETT, EBENEZER (fl. 1747), writer against the deists. [xxvi. 309]

HEWLETT, JAMES (1789–1836), flower-painter. [xxvi. 309]

HEWLETT, JOHN (1762–1844), biblical scholar; B.D. Magdalene College, Cambridge, 1796; rector of Hilgay, Norfolk, 1819; published 'Vindication of the authenticity of the Parian Chronicle,' 1789, 'The Holy Bible . . . with Critical, Philosophical, and Explanatory Notes,' 1812, and other works. [xxvi. 310]

HEWLETT, JOSEPH THOMAS JAMES (1800–1847), novelist; educated at Charterhouse and Worcester College, Oxford; M.A., 1826; published 'Peter Priggins,

the College Scout,' 1841 (illustrated by Phiz and edited by Theodore Hook), 'Parsons and Widows,' 1844, and other works. [xxvi. 310]

HEWLEY, SARAH, LADY (1627–1710), founder of the Hewley trust; heiress of Robert Wolrych and wife of Sir John Hewley; left land for support of dissenting ministers. [xxvi. 310]

HEWSON, JOHN (d. 1662), regicide; some time a shoemaker; led forlorn hope at Bridgwater, 1647; one of the commissioners to represent soldiers' grievances, 1647; signed Charles I's death-warrant, 1649; commander of foot under Cromwell in Ireland, and governor of Dublin; M.A. Oxford, 1649; favoured anabaptists, and headed faction against Henry Cromwell; represented Ireland, 1653, Dublin, 1654, and Guildford, 1656; member of Cromwell's House of Lords, 1657, of committee of safety, 1659; much satirised after suppression of London 'prentice riot, 1659; escaped at Restoration, and died abroad. [xxvi. 311]

HEWSON, WILLIAM (1739–1774), surgeon and anatomist; partner of Dr. William Hunter [q. v.], 1762–1771; Copley medallist, 1769; F.R.S., 1770; published 'Experimental Inquiry into the Properties of the Blood,' in three parts, 1771, 1774, and 1777 (ed. Falconar); fatally wounded himself while dissecting; works edited for Sydenham Society, 1846. [xxvi. 312]

HEWSON, WILLIAM (1806–1870), theological writer; educated at St. Paul's and St. John's College, Cambridge; M.A., 1833; head-master of St. Peter's School, York, 1838–47; perpetual curate of Goatland, 1848–70; published works, including 'The Key of David,' 1855. [xxvi. 313]

HEXHAM, HENRY (1585 ?–1650 ?), military writer; page in service of Sir Francis Vere [q. v.] at siege of Ostend, 1601, and till 1606; quartermaster under Sir Horace (afterwards baron) Vere [q. v.] in expedition to relieve Breda, 1625, and subsequently under George (afterwards baron) Goring (1608–1657) [q. v.]; in Dutch service, c. 1642, till death. His works include an edition of Mercator's 'Atlas,' 1637, 'English-Dutch Dictionary,' 1648, and accounts of various military operations in which he took part. [Suppl. ii. 418]

HEXHAM, JOHN OF (fl. 1180). [See JOHN.]

HEXHAM, RICHARD OF (fl. 1141). [See RICHARD.]

HEY, JOHN (1734–1815), divine; brother of William Hey (1736–1819) [q. v.]; M.A. Catharine Hall, Cambridge, 1758; fellow of Sidney Sussex College, 1758–79; Seatonian prizeman, 1763; Norrisian professor of divinity, 1780–95; his lectures (1796) edited by Turton, 1841. [xxvi. 314]

HEY, RICHARD (1745–1835), essayist; brother of John Hey [q. v.]; third wrangler and chancellor's medallist, Cambridge, 1768; fellow of Sidney Sussex College, 1771, of Magdalene, 1782–96; published, among other works, dissertation on gaming, 1783, on duelling, 1784, and on suicide, 1785. [xxvi. 314]

HEY, WILLIAM (1736–1819), surgeon; brother of John Hey [q. v.]; senior surgeon to Leeds Infirmary, 1773–1812; F.R.S., 1775; friend of Priestley; mayor of Leeds, 1787–8 and 1801–2; president of Leeds Literary and Philosophical Society, 1783; devised operation of partial amputation of the foot; published medical works. [xxvi. 315]

HEY, WILLIAM (1772–1844), author of 'Treatise on Puerperal Fever' (1815); son of William Hey (1736–1819) [q. v.] [xxvi. 315]

HEY, WILLIAM (1796–1875), surgeon to Leeds Infirmary, 1830–51; son of William Hey (1772–1844) [q. v.] [xxvi. 316]

HEYDON, SIR CHRISTOPHER (d. 1623), writer on astrology; M.P., Norfolk, 1588; knighted at capture of Cadiz, 1596; suspected of complicity in Essex rising, 1601; chief work 'Defence of Judiciall Astrologie,' 1602. [xxvi. 316]

HEYDON, SIR HENRY (d. 1503), steward of the household of Cecilia, duchess of York; knighted, 1485. [xxvi. 316]

HEYDON, SIR JOHN (d. 1653), lieutenant of the ordnance; son of Sir Christopher Heydon [q. v.]; knighted, 1620; lieutenant-general of the ordnance to Charles I during civil war; D.C.L. Oxford, 1642. [xxvi. 317]

HEYDON, JOHN (*fl.* 1667), astrologer; imprisoned for two years by Cromwell for foretelling his death by hanging, and for treasonable practices, 1663 and 1667; wrote many works on Rosicrucian mysticism, borrowing largely from anterior writers.   [xxvi. 317]

HEYLIN, JOHN (1685?–1759), divine; 'the Mystic Doctor'; educated at Westminster and Trinity College, Cambridge; M.A., 1714; D.D., 1728; first rector of St. Mary-le-Strand, 1724–59; prebendary of St. Paul's and Westminster, and chaplain to George II; published 'Theological Lectures at Westminster Abbey,' 1749.   [xxvi. 318]

HEYLYN, PETER (1600–1662), ecclesiastical writer; first cousin (once removed) of Rowland Heylyn [q. v.]; demy and fellow of Magdalen College, Oxford; M.A., 1620; D.D., 1633; published 'Geography,' 1621, and 'Survey of France,' 1656; royal chaplain, 1630; prebendary of Westminster, 1631; incumbent of Alresford, Hants, 1633; controverted puritan views; assisted Noy (1633) in preparation of case against Prynne; proposed conference between convocation and Commons, 1640; obtained money grant from convocation for Charles I, 1640; asserted right of bishops to share in all proceedings of upper house; joined Charles I at Oxford and chronicled the war in 'Mercurius Aulicus'; obliged to compound for his estate; attacked L'Estrange's 'Life of Charles I,' 1656, and, in 'Examen Historicum' (1658–9), Fuller and William Sanderson; issued 'Certamen Epistolare' (1659) against Baxter, Nicholas Bernard [q. v.], and others; sub-dean of Westminster at coronation of Charles II, 1661; disabled by infirmities from promotion; chief works 'Ecclesia Restaurata, or History of the Reformation,' 1661 (edited by J. C. Robertson, 1849), 'Cyprianus Anglicus' (i.e. Archbishop Laud) (published 1668), in answer to 'Canterburies Doom,' and 'Aerius Redivivus, or History of Presbyterianism,' published 1670.   [xxvi. 319]

HEYLYN or **HEYLIN**, ROWLAND (1562?–1631), sheriff of London; master of Ironmongers' Company, 1614 and 1625; alderman of Cripplegate, 1624; sheriff of London, 1624–5; published Welsh bible, 1630; left bequests to Shrewsbury, the Ironmongers' Company, and London charities.   [xxvi. 323]

HEYMAN, SIR PETER (1580–1641), politician; knighted by James I for services in Ireland; M.P., Hythe, 1620–1, and subsequently; ordered to serve abroad at his own expense on account of opposition to the government, *c.* 1622; imprisoned, 1629; elected to Long parliament for Dover, 1640; money voted to his heirs, 1646, for his service to Commonwealth.   [xxvi. 324]

HEYNES, SIMON (*d.* 1552), dean of Exeter; fellow of Queens' College, Cambridge, 1516; M.A., 1519; president, 1528; D.D., 1531; vice-chancellor of Cambridge, 1533–4; vicar of Stepney, 1534; ambassador to France, 1535; dean of Exeter, 1537; joint-envoy to Spain, 1538; prebendary of Westminster, 1540; assisted in compilation of first liturgy.   [xxvi. 325]

HEYRICK, RICHARD (1600–1667), warden of Manchester Collegiate Church; son of Sir William Hericke [q. v.]; of Merchant Taylors' School and St. John's College, Oxford; M.A., 1622; fellow of All Souls', Oxford, 1625; warden of Manchester Collegiate Church, 1635; attacked Romanists and high churchmen, 1641; member of Westminster Assembly; main establisher of presbyterianism in Lancashire; published 'Harmonious Consent of the Ministers within the County Palatine of Lancaster,' 1648; obtained restoration of church revenues; imprisoned for implication in movement of Christopher Love, 1615; conformed at Restoration.   [xxvi. 325]

HEYRICK, THOMAS (*d.* 1694), poet; grand-nephew of Robert Herrick [q. v.]; M.A. Peterhouse, Cambridge, 1675; curate of Market Harborough; published 'Miscellany Poems,' 1691.   [xxvi. 327]

HEYSHAM, JOHN (1753–1834), physician; M.D. of Edinburgh, 1777; practised at Carlisle; his statistics (published 1797) used for Carlisle Table (1816); said to have assisted Paley on question of structural design in nature.   [xxvi. 327]

HEYTESBURY, BARON (1779–1860). [See A'COURT, WILLIAM.]   [xxvi. 327]

HEYTESBURY, WILLIAM (*fl.* 1340), logician; fellow of Merton College, Oxford, 1330; possibly original

fellow (Heightilbury) of Queen's College, 1340; chancellor of university, 1371; works printed under name of 'Hentisberus' or 'Tisberius' at Pavia and Venice. [xxvi. 327]

HEYTHER, WILLIAM (1563?–1627). [See HEATHER.]

HEYWOOD, SIR BENJAMIN, first baronet (1793–1865), banker; founder and president (1825–40) of Manchester Mechanics' Institution; created baronet, 1838; F.R.S., 1843.   [xxvi. 328]

HEYWOOD, ELIZA (1693?–1756). [See HAYWOOD.]

HEYWOOD, ELLIS or ELIZÆUS (1530–1578), jesuit; brother of Jasper Heywood [q. v.]; fellow of All Souls', Oxford, 1548; B.C.L., 1552; secretary to Cardinal Pole; jesuit father at Antwerp; published (in Italian) fictitious conversations of Sir Thomas More (Florence, 1556); died at Louvain.   [xxvi. 329]

HEYWOOD, JAMES (1687–1776), author; published 'Letters and Poems on several Occasions,' 1722.   [xxvi. 329]

HEYWOOD, JASPER (1535–1598), jesuit; son of John Heywood [q. v.]; page of honour to Princess Elizabeth; probationer-fellow of Merton College, Oxford, 1554; fellow of All Souls', 1558; M.A., 1558; became a jesuit at Rome, 1562; professor at Dillingen seventeen years; superior of English jesuit mission, 1581; deported to France, 1585; died at Naples; his translations from Seneca's tragedies reprinted in Thomas Newton's 'Seneca,' 1581; contributed poems to 'Paradyse of Daynty Deuises' (1576).   [xxvi. 329]

HEYWOOD, JOHN (1497?–1580?), 'the old English epigrammatist'; under Henry VIII a singer and player on the virginals; wrote 'Description of a most noble Ladye' (on Princess Mary); publicly recanted his denial of the royal supremacy, 1544; in great favour with Queen Mary as a kind of superior jester; on accession of Elizabeth (1558) retired to Malines, where he probably died. He published interludes, including 'The Four P's,' first printed, 1569 (in Hazlitt's 'Dodsley,' 1874), 'The Play of the Wether,' 1533, and 'The Play of Love'; published also 'Dialogue on Wit and Folly' (reprinted, 1846) and another dialogue containing proverbs and epigrams, 1562 (reprinted, 1867), besides ballads, and 'The Spider and the Flie,' 1556.   [xxvi. 331]

HEYWOOD, NATHANIEL, the elder (1633–1677), ejected minister; B.A. Trinity College, Cambridge, 1650; minister of Ormskirk, Lancashire, 1656–62; compelled to desist from preaching, 1674.   [xxvi. 334]

HEYWOOD, NATHANIEL, the younger (1659–1704), nonconformist minister at Ormskirk; son of Nathaniel Heywood the elder [q. v.]   [xxvi. 334]

HEYWOOD, OLIVER (1630–1702), nonconformist divine; brother of Nathaniel Heywood the elder [q. v.]; B.A. Trinity College, Cambridge, 1650; minister of Coley Chapel, Halifax, 1650; excommunicated for not using the prayer-book, 1662; licensed presbyterian teacher, 1672–5; imprisoned at York for 'riotous assembly,' 1685; his Northowram meeting-house licensed under Toleration Act; introduced into Yorkshire the 'happy union' between presbyterians and congregationalists, 1691; his works collected by R. Slate, 1825–7; 'Diaries' edited by J. Horsfall Turner, 1881–5 (4 vols.), as well as his 'Nonconformist Register.'   [xxvi. 334]

HEYWOOD, PETER (1773–1831), navy captain; sailed in the Bounty, 1786; confined by mutineers, 1789; remained with the party at Tahiti and joined the Pandora, 1791; treated as a mutineer; though in irons escaped when the Pandora went down in Endeavour Strait, 1791; convicted at Spithead with mutineers, 1792; obtained pardon by interposition of Lord Chatham, 1792; promoted lieutenant by Howe, 1794; attained post-rank, 1803; surveyed part of east coast of Ceylon.   [xxvi. 336]

HEYWOOD, ROBERT (1574?–1645), poet; of Heywood Hall, Lancashire; his 'Observations and Instructions, Divine and Morall,' first edited by James Crossley, 1869.   [xxvi. 337]

HEYWOOD, SAMUEL (1753–1828), chief-justice of Carmarthen circuit; of Trinity Hall, Cambridge; barrister, Inner Temple, 1772; serjeant-at-law, 1794; chief justice, Carmarthen circuit, 1807–28; friend of Charles James Fox; published 'Right of Protestant Dissenters to a Compleat Toleration asserted,' 1787, digests of election law, and other works. [xxvi. 338]

HEYWOOD, THOMAS (*d.* 1650?), dramatist; said to have been a fellow of Peterhouse, Cambridge; member of the lord admiral's company, 1598; afterwards retainer of Henry Wriothesley, earl of Southampton, and Edward Somerset, earl of Worcester; one of the queen's players, 1619; composed lord mayor's pageants for many years; many of his plays lost; an ardent protestant. His chief plays were 'The Four Prentices of London' (produced, *c.* 1600, published, 1615), ridiculed in Fletcher's 'Knight of the Burning Pestle'; 'Edward IV' (two parts, 1600, 1605; ed. Barron Field, 1842); 'The Royal King and the Loyal Subject,' 1637 (ed. J. P. Collier, 1850); 'A Woman Killed with Kindness' (acted, 1603, printed, 1607; ed. Collier, 1850; revived, 1887); 'The Rape of Lucrece,' 1608; 'The Captives' (ed. Bullen, 1885); and 'The Wise Woman of Hogsdon,' 1638. He also published 'An Apology for Actors.' 1612 (reprinted, 1841), and poems (including Hierarchy of the Blessed Angels,' 1635), translations, and compilations. [xxvi. 338]

HEYWOOD, THOMAS (1797–1866), antiquary; brother of Sir Benjamin Heywood [q. v.]; of Hope End, Herefordshire; edited for Chetham Society, 'Norris Papers' (1846), 'Diary of the Rev. Henry Newcome' (1849), and other works; his library sold at Manchester, 1868. [xxvi. 342]

HIBBART or **HIBBERT**, WILLIAM (*fl.* 1760–1800), etcher. [xxvi. 342]

HIBBERD, SHIRLEY (1825–1890), journalist and horticultural writer; edited 'Floral World,' 1858–75, and Gardener's Magazine,' 1861–90; published horticultural works. [xxvi. 342]

HIBBERT, GEORGE (1757–1837), West Indian merchant and collector; alderman of London, 1798–1803; M.P., Seaford, 1806–12; F.R.S., 1811; active in establishment of West India Docks and (1805) London Institution; edited for Roxburghe Club Caxton's version of Ovid's 'Metamorphoses,' 1819; his collections sold, 1829. [xxvi. 343]

HIBBERT, HENRY (1600?–1678), divine; B.A. Brasenose College, Oxford, 1622; D.D. St. John's, Cambridge, 1665; vicar of Holy Trinity, Hull, 1651–60, of All Hallows-the-Less and St. Olave's Jewry, 1662; prebendary of St. Paul's, 1669; published 'Syntagma Theologicum,' 1662. [xxvi. 343]

HIBBERT, ROBERT (1770–1849), founder of the Hibbert trust; B.A. Emmanuel College, Cambridge, 1791; Jamaica merchant and slave owner, 1791–1836; author of radical pamphlets; his trust (designed for elevation of unitarian ministry) widened in scope by efforts of Edwin Wilkins Field [q. v.] [xxvi. 344]

HIBBERT-WARE, SAMUEL (1782–1848), antiquary and geologist; M.D. Edinburgh; secretary, Scottish Society of Antiquaries, 1823–7; awarded gold medal by Society of Arts for discovery of chromate of iron in Shetland, 1820; assumed name of Ware, 1837; published, among other works, 'Description of the Shetland Islands,' and an account of Ashton-under-Lyne in the fifteenth century, 1822, 'Sketches of the Philosophy of Apparitions,' 1824, 'Lancashire Memorials of the Rebellion in 1715' (1845), and geological memoirs. [xxvi. 344]

HIBBS, RICHARD (1812?–1886), author; M.A. St. John's College, Cambridge, 1844; established New Church England Chapel, St. Vincent Street, Edinburgh, 1855; afterwards chaplain at Lisbon, Rotterdam, and Utrecht; published 'Prussia and the Poor; or Observations upon the Systematised Relief of the Poor at Elberfield,' 1876. [xxvi. 345]

HIBERNIA, THOMAS DE (*d.* 1270), Franciscan; to be distinguished from Thomas Hibernicus [q. v.]; wrote the 'Promptuarium Morale.' [lvi. 175]

HIBERNICUS, DE HIBERNIA, or DE ISERNIA, PETER (*fl.* 1224). [See PETER.]

HIBERNICUS, THOMAS (1306–1316). [See THOMAS.]

HICKERINGILL or **HICKHORNGILL**, EDMUND (1631–1708), divine and pamphleteer; junior fellow of

Caius College, Cambridge, 1651–2; chaplain to Lilburne's regiment, 1653; successively baptist, quaker, and deist; afterwards a soldier in Scotland and in Swedish service, and captain in Fleetwood's regiment; after residence in Jamaica published an account of it, 1661; ordained by Bishop Robert Sanderson, 1661; vicar of All Saints', Colchester, 1662–1708, and Boxted, 1662–4; quarrelled with Compton, bishop of London, and was condemned to pay damages for slander, Jeffreys being counsel against him, 1682; publicly recanted, 1684; excluded, 1685–8; convicted of forgery, 1707. [xxvi. 346]

HICKES, FRANCIS (1566–1631), translator of Lucian; B.A. St. Mary Hall, Oxford, 1583; his translation of Lucian published, 1634. [xxvi. 349]

HICKES, GASPAR (1605–1677), puritan divine; M.A. Trinity College, Oxford, 1628; held Cornish livings and was consulted by parliament; member of the Westminster Assembly, 1643; ejected from Landrake, 1662; fined under Conventicle Act, 1670. [xxvi. 349]

HICKES, GEORGE (1642–1715), nonjuror; B.A. Magdalen College, Oxford, 1663; fellow of Lincoln College, 1664; M.A., 1665; chaplain to Duke of Lauderdale, 1676; prebendary of Worcester, 1680; vicar of All Hallows Barking, 1680; chaplain to the king, 1681; dean of Worcester, 1683; rector of Alvechurch, 1686; opposed declaration of indulgence; deprived for refusing to take oath of allegiance to William and Mary, 1690; in hiding till proceedings against him stopped, 1699; went to St. Germain, 1693, and was named suffragan of Sancroft, with title 'Bishop of Thetford'; was consecrated in a private chapel by Bishops Turner, Lloyd, and White, 1694; his house on Bagshot Heath searched, 1696; with two Scottish bishops consecrated, in St. Andrew's, Holborn, Samuel Hawes, Nathaniel Spinckes, and Jeremy Collier, 1713. His chief works were 'Case of Infant Baptism,' 1683, 'Records of the New Consecrations,' editions of the 'Imitatio Christi,' and of Fénelon's 'Instructions for the Education of a Daughter,' and 'Linguarum veterum septentrionalium thesaurus grammatico-criticus et archæologicus,' 1703–5. [xxvi. 350]

HICKES or **HICKS**, JOHN (1633–1685), nonconformist divine; brother of George Hickes [q. v.]; fellow of Trinity College, Dublin; ejected from Saltash, Cornwall, 1662; presented petition to Charles II in favour of nonconformists; joined Monmouth (1685) and was sheltered by Alice Lisle [q. v.]; tried and executed at Taunton. [xxvi. 354]

HICKES, THOMAS (1599–1634), son of Francis Hickes [q. v.]; M.A. Balliol College, Oxford. 1623; chaplain of Christ Church, Oxford. [xxvi. 349]

HICKEY, ANTONY (*d.* 1641), Irish Franciscan; professor of theology and philosophy at Louvain and Cologne; definitor of the order at Rome, 1639; published (under pseudonym 'Dermitius Thadæus') 'Nitela Franciscanæ religionis,' 1627, and an edition, with commentary, of the works of Duns Scotus, 1639; died at Rome. [xxvi. 355]

HICKEY, JOHN (1756–1795), Irish sculptor. [xxvi. 356]

HICKEY, THOMAS (*fl.* 1760–1790), portrait-painter; brother of John Hickey [q. v.]; accompanied Macartney to China, 1792; probably visited India; published 'History of Painting and Sculpture' (Calcutta, 1788). [xxvi. 356]

HICKEY, WILLIAM (1787?–1875), Irish philanthropist and author; B.A. St. John's College, Cambridge, 1809, and Trinity College, Dublin, 1809; M.A. Dublin, 1832; incumbent of Bannow, Ferns, 1820; helped to found agricultural school at Bannow; with Thomas Boyce established South Wexford Agricultural Society; rector of Kilcormick, 1826, Wexford, 1831, Mulrankin, 1834; as 'Martin Doyle' published 'Hints to Small Farmers' (1830) and similar works; edited 'Illustrated Book of Domestic Poultry,' 1854, and 'Irish Farmer's and Gardener's Magazine,' 1834–42; gold medallist of Royal Dublin Society; received pension from Royal Literary Fund. [xxvi. 356]

HICKMAN, CHARLES (1648–1713), bishop of Derry; educated at Westminster and Christ Church, Oxford; M.A., 1674; D.D., 1685; chaplain to William III, Anne, and Lawrence Hyde, earl of Rochester; rector of Burnham, Buckinghamshire, 1698–1702; bishop of Derry, 1703–13. [xxvi. 357]

HICKMAN, FRANCIS (*fl.* 1690), scholar; of Westminster and Christ Church, Oxford; M.A., 1688; nonjuror; Bodleian orator, 1693; contributed to 'Musæ Anglicanæ.' [xxvi. 357]

HICKMAN, HENRY (*d.* 1692), controversialist; B.A. St. Catharine Hall, Cambridge; fellow of Magdalen College, Oxford, 1648; M.A., 1649; ejected at the Restoration; retired to Holland; carried on controversies with Peter Heylyn [q. v.], John Durel [q. v.], and others; died at Leyden. [xxvi. 357]

HICKMAN, subsequently **WINDSOR**, THOMAS, seventh BARON WINDSOR OF STANWELL and first EARL OF PLYMOUTH (1627 ?-1687). [See WINDSOR.]

HICKS or **HICKES**, BAPTIST, first VISCOUNT CAMPDEN (1551-1629), mercer and money-lender; contractor for crown lands, 1609; created baronet, 1620; M.P., Tavistock, 1620, Tewkesbury, 1624, 1625, 1626, and 1628; built Hicks's Hall, Clerkenwell; purchased manor of Campden, from which he took his title when created viscount, 1628. [xxvi. 358]

HICKS, HENRY (1837-1899), geologist; studied at Guy's Hospital; L.S.A. and M.R.C.S., 1862; practised as surgeon at St. David's and, from 1871, at Hendon; studied geology with John William Salter [q. v.]; president of Geologists' Association, 1883-5; secretary of Geological Society, 1890-3, and president, 1896-8; F.R.S., 1885; published geological papers. [Suppl. ii. 419]

HICKS, SIR MICHAEL (1543-1612), secretary to Lord Burghley and Sir Robert Cecil; brother of Baptist Hicks or Hickes, first viscount Campden [q. v.]; of Trinity College, Cambridge, and Lincoln's Inn; lent money to Bacon and Fulke Greville [q. v.]; knighted, 1604; ancestor of Sir Michael Hicks-Beach, baronet, M.P. [xxvi. 359]

HICKS, WILLIAM (1621-1660), puritan; of Wadham College, Oxford; fought in parliamentarian army; published an exposition of Revelation, 1659. [xxvi. 360]

HICKS, WILLIAM, 'Captain Hicks' (*fl.* 1671), editor and part writer of 'Oxford Drollery' (1671), 'Grammatical Drollery' (1682), and similar publications. [xxvi. 360]

HICKS, WILLIAM (1830-1883), general in Egyptian army ('Hicks Pasha'); saw service as British officer in India and Abyssinia, attaining rank of colonel, 1880; while in command of Egyptian army for suppression of Mahdi was led into an ambuscade and slain in the 'battle of Kashgil.' [xxvi. 360]

HICKS, WILLIAM ROBERT (1808-1868), humorist; superintendent of Bodmin Asylum and auditor of metropolitan asylums; known as 'Yorick of the West'; wrote stories in western dialect, the most famous being 'The Jury.' [xxvi. 361]

HICKSON, WILLIAM EDWARD (1803-1870), educational writer; member of royal commission on unemployed hand-loom weavers, 1837, presenting a separate report, 1841; studied German, Dutch, and Belgian school systems, and published results in 'Westminster Review' (edited by him, 1840-52); wrote also music manuals. [xxvi. 362]

HIEOVER, HARRY (1795-1859). [See BINDLEY, CHARLES.]

HIERON, SAMUEL (1576 ?-1617), puritan divine; of Eton and King's College, Cambridge; incumbent of Modbury, Devonshire; published the 'Preacher's Plea,' 1604, and other works, collected, 1614, reprinted, 1624-5, by Robert Hill. [xxvi. 362]

HIFFERNAN, PAUL (1719-1777), author; M.B., Montpellier; published in Dublin 'The Tickler' in opposition to Charles Lucas (1713-1771) [q. v.], 1750; issued in London 'The Tuner,' 1753, and composed farces acted at Drury Lane and Covent Garden; published 'Miscellanies in Prose and Verse,' 1770, and 'Dramatic Genius,' 1770, dedicated to Garrick, who raised a subscription for him. [xxvi. 363]

HIGBERT or **HYGEBRYHT** (*fl.* 787), archbishop of Lichfield in 787, being bishop from 779. Lichfield was a Mercian see created by Pope Hadrian at request of Offa, but was soon subordinated to Canterbury. [xxvi. 364]

HIGDEN, HENRY (*fl.* 1693), author of a comedy, 'The Wary Widdow,' 1693, and essays on satires x. and xiii. of Juvenal, 1686 and 1687; of the Middle Temple. [xxvi. 365]

HIGDEN, RANULF (*d.* 1364), chronicler; Benedictine of St. Werburg's, Chester; his 'Polychronicon' printed in English version (dated 1387) of John of Trevisa [q. v.] by Caxton, 1482, Wynkyn de Worde, 1495, and Peter Treveris, 1527; another translation made in the fifteenth century; the original Latin was issued in Rolls Series, with both English versions and continuation. [xxvi. 365]

HIGDEN, WILLIAM (*d.* 1715), divine; M.A. King's College, Cambridge, 1688; D.D., 1710; prebendary of Canterbury, 1713; defended taking the oaths to the Revolution monarchy, 1709 and 1710; wrote also theological treatises. [xxvi. 366]

HIGFORD, WILLIAM (1581 ?-1657), puritan; B.A. Corpus Christi College, Oxford, 1599; his 'Institutions, or Advice to his Grandson,' first printed, 1658. [xxvi. 366]

HIGGINS, BRYAN (1737 ?-1820), physician and chemist; graduated at Leyden; established school of chemistry in Soho, 1774; invited to Russia by Tsarina Catherine, *c.* 1785; assisted in improvement of Muscovado sugar and rum in Jamaica, 1797-9; published 'Experiments and Observations relating to Acetous Acid, Fixable Air,' &c., 1786, and other works. [xxvi. 366]

HIGGINS, CHARLES LONGUET (1806-1885), benefactor of Turvey, Bedfordshire; of Trinity College, Cambridge (M.A. 1834), Lincoln's Inn, and St. Bartholomew's Hospital. [xxvi. 367]

HIGGINS, FRANCIS (1669-1728), archdeacon of Cashel; M.A. Trinity College, Dublin, 1693; prebendary of Christ Church Cathedral, Dublin, 1705; 'the Irish Sacheverell'; prosecuted for seditious preaching, 1707 and 1712; archdeacon of Cashel, 1725-8. [xxvi. 367]

HIGGINS, FRANCIS (1746-1802), Irish adventurer imprisoned for fraud in connection with his marriage, and became known as the 'Sham Squire'; as owner of 'The Freeman's Journal' supported the government; magistrate, 1788-91; exposed by John Magee [q. v.]; removed from the bench and law list; informed against Lord Edward Fitzgerald [q. v.] and others. [xxvi. 368]

HIGGINS, GODFREY (1773-1833), writer on the history of religion; of Trinity Hall, Cambridge; Yorkshire magistrate and reformer; wrote, besides political and social pamphlets, 'Anacalypsis . . . Inquiry into the Origin of Languages, Nations, and Religions,' published 1836 (reprinted, 1878), and other works. [xxvi. 368]

HIGGINS, JOHN (*fl.* 1570-1602), poet and compiler; revised 'Huloet's Dictionarie,' 1572; published also 'Flowers' (selections from Terence by himself and Nicholas Udall, 1575), and supplements to the 'Mirrour for Magistrates,' containing forty new poems (some of which were printed in 1574, and others in 1587), and other works. [xxvi. 369]

HIGGINS, MATTHEW JAMES (1810-1868), journalist; of Eton and University College, Oxford; known as 'Jacob Omnium,' from title of first published article (1845); twice visited British Guiana, where he owned an estate; active on behalf of sufferers from Irish famine, 1847; contributed to the Peelite 'Morning Chronicle,' also to 'The Times,' 'Pall Mall Gazette,' and 'Cornhill Magazine' (under Thackeray), exposing many abuses; his 'Essays on Social Subjects' edited, 1875. [xxvi. 370]

HIGGINS, WILLIAM (*d.* 1825), chemist; nephew of Bryan Higgins [q. v.]; librarian to Royal Dublin Society, 1795; in 'Comparative View of Phlogistic and Antiphlogistic Theories' (1789) enunciated law of multiple proportions; claimed discovery of atomic theory against Dalton in 'Experiments and Observations,' 1814. [xxvi. 371]

HIGGINSON, EDWARD (1807-1880), unitarian divine; minister successively at Hull (1828-46), Wakefield (1846-58), and Swansea (1858-76); president of Home Institute of South Wales, 1877-9; published theological works. [xxvi. 372]

HIGGINSON, FRANCIS (1587-1630), puritan divine; of Jesus and St. John's Colleges, Cambridge; M.A., 1613; deprived of preachership of St. Nicholas, Leicester, for nonconformity, 1627; when threatened with prosecution by high commission became assistant-minister at Salem, Massachusetts, 1629; published accounts of his voyage and of Massachusetts. [xxvi. 372]

HIGGINSON, FRANCIS (1617–1670), author of 'Relation of Irreligion of Northern Quakers,' 1653; son of Francis Higginson (1587–1630) [q. v.]; studied at Leyden; vicar of Kirkby Stephen. [xxvi. 373]

HIGGINSON, JOHN (1616–1708), minister at Saybrook, Guilford (U.S.A.), and Salem, where he died; brother of Francis Higginson (1617–1670) [q. v.] [xxvi. 373]

HIGGONS, BEVIL (1670–1735), historian and poet; son of Sir Thomas Higgons [q. v.]; of St. John's College, Oxford, and Trinity Hall, Cambridge; student of Lincoln's Inn; followed his family (Jacobites) into exile; arrested on charge of conspiracy against William III, 1696; published verses addressed to Dryden and Congreve, and a tragedy (acted, 1702); his 'Historical Works' (1736), consisted of 'Short View of the English History' (1723), and a criticism of Burnet's 'Own Time,' 1725. [xxvi. 373]

HIGGONS, THEOPHILUS (1578?–1659), divine; M.A. Christ Church, Oxford, 1600; chaplain to bishop Ravis and lecturer of St. Dunstan's, Fleet Street; converted to Romanism; retired to France: reconverted and given rectory of Hunton, Kent; published theological works. [xxvi. 374]

HIGGONS, SIR THOMAS (1624–1691), diplomatist and author; of St. Alban Hall, Oxford; M.P., Malmesbury, 1661, St. Germans, 1685; knighted, 1663; envoy extraordinary to Saxony, 1669, to Vienna, 1673–6; published 'History of Isuf Bassa,' 1684; translated Busenello's 'Prospective of the Naval Triumph of the Venetians over the Turk,' 1658. [xxvi. 375]

HIGGS, GRIFFIN or GRIFFITH (1589–1659), dean of Lichfield; B.A. St. John's College, Oxford, 1610; fellow of Merton, 1611; M.A., 1615; senior proctor, 1622–3; chaplain to Elizabeth, queen of Bohemia, 1627–38; D.D. Leyden, 1630; dean of Lichfield, 1638; left bequests to South Stoke, the Bodleian, and Merton and St. John's Colleges; his 'Account of the Christmas Prince exhibited in the University of Oxford in 1607,' printed by Bliss, 1816. [xxvi. 375]

HIGHAM, JOHN (fl. 1639). [See HEIGHAM.]

HIGHAM, THOMAS (1795–1844), line-engraver. [xxvi. 376]

HIGHMORE, ANTHONY (1719–1799), draughtsman, son of Joseph Highmore [q. v.] [xxvi. 378]

HIGHMORE, ANTHONY (1758–1829), legal writer; son of Anthony Highmore (1719–1799); friend of Granville Sharp [q. v.]; published 'Digest of the Doctrine of Bail,' 1783, 'Succinct View of History of Mortmain,' 1787, 'Treatise on the Law of Idiotcy and Lunacy,' 1807, and other works. [xxvi. 376]

HIGHMORE, JOSEPH (1692–1780), painter; nephew of Thomas Highmore [q. v.]; studied under Kneller; executed portrait-drawings for 'Installation of Knights of the Bath,' 1725; painted portraits of the Prince and Princess of Wales, the Duke of Cumberland, the Gunnings, Samuel Richardson, General Wolfe and others, also conversation-pieces and subject-pictures; published pamphlets on perspective. [xxvi. 377]

HIGHMORE, NATHANIEL (1613–1685), physician; M.D. Trinity College, Oxford, 1642; practised at Sherburne, Dorset; endowed exhibition to Oxford from Sherburne school; friend of Harvey; published 'History of Generation,' 1651, and other works; the cavity in the superior maxillary bone named after him. [xxvi. 378]

HIGHMORE, THOMAS (d. 1720), serjeant-painter to William III; cousin of Nathaniel Highmore [q. v.] [xxvi. 379]

HIGHTON, HENRY (1816–1874), author; under Arnold at Rugby; M.A. Queen's College, Oxford, 1840, Michel fellow, 1841; principal of Cheltenham, 1859–62; published revised translation of the New Testament, 1862, translation of Victor Hugo's poems and theological pamphlets; silver medallist, Society of Arts, for 'Telegraphy without Insulation' (1872); patented artificial stone for building. [xxvi. 379]

HIGINBOTHAM, GEORGE (1826–1892), chief-justice of Victoria; B.A. Trinity College, Dublin, 1848; M.A.,

1853; barrister, Lincoln's Inn, 1853; went to Victoria, and was admitted to the local bar, 1854; editor of the 'Argus,' 1856–9; independent liberal member for Brighton in legislative assembly, 1861 and 1863; attorney-general, 1863–8; chairman of education commission, 1866; vice-president of board of works, 1868–9; member for East Bourke borough, 1874–6; puisne judge of supreme court of Victoria, 1880; chief-justice, 1886. [Suppl. ii. 420]

HIGSON, JOHN (1825–1871), topographer; compiled 'Gorton Historical Recorder,' 1852, and history of Droylsden. [xxvi. 379]

HILARY (fl. 1125), Latin poet; supposed to have been an Englishman; disciple of Abelard and canon of Ronceray; his poems printed by M. Champollion-Figeac, 1838; extracts in Wright's 'Biographia Britannica Literaria.' [xxvi. 380]

HILARY (d. 1169), bishop of Chichester, 1147; elected archbishop of York, 1147, but not confirmed by the pope; reconciled King Stephen and Archbishop Theobald, 1148; failed to enforce jurisdiction over the abbot of Battle, 1157; urged Becket to accept the 'ancient customs'; included in embassy to the pope against Becket; granted absolution to those excommunicated by Becket. [xxvi. 380]

HILDA (or, more properly, **HILD**), SAINT (614–680), abbess of Whitby; baptised by Paulinus at York, 627; abbess of Hartlepool, 649; Ælflæd, daughter of Oswy of Northumbria, entrusted to her care, 655; founded monastery of Whitby (657), and ruled it with great wisdom; adopted Roman rule after council of Whitby, 664. [xxvi. 381]

HILDERSAM or **HILDERSHAM**, ARTHUR (1563–1632), puritan divine; entered at Christ's College, Cambridge, 1576; disinherited for refusing to become a Romanist; M.A., 1586; fellow of Christ's College, 1586; vicar of Ashby-de-la-Zouch, 1593; an active manager of 'millenary petition,' 1604; silenced by his bishop, 1605, but licensed in diocese of Lichfield; restored, 1609, but suspended by high commission, 1613, and imprisoned for refusing the 'ex officio' oath, 1615; sentenced to imprisonment and fine as schismatic, 1616; returned to Ashby, 1625, again suspended, 1630, but restored next year; published 'Treatise on Ministry of the Church of England,' 1595; his 'CLII Lectures on Psalm LI' translated into Hungarian, 1672. [xxvi. 382]

HILDERSAM or **HILDERSHAM**, SAMUEL (1594?–1674), divine; son of Arthur Hildersam [q. v.]; fellow of Emmanuel College, Cambridge: B.A. and B.D.; member of Westminster Assembly; ejected from West Felton, Shropshire, 1662. [xxvi. 384]

HILDESLEY, JOHN (d. 1538). [See HILSEY.]

HILDESLEY, MARK (1698–1772), bishop of Sodor and Man; of Charterhouse and Trinity College, Cambridge; fellow, 1723; M.A., 1724; rector of Holwell, Bedfordshire, 1735–67; prebendary of Lincoln, 1754; chaplain to Henry St. John, lord Bolingbroke, and John, viscount St. John; D.D. Lambeth, 1755; bishop of Sodor and Man, 1755–72; master of Christ's Hospital, Sherburn, Durham, 1767; promoted Manx translations of the bible and the Book of Common Prayer. [xxvi. 384]

HILDEYARD, THOMAS (1690–1746), jesuit; rector of the 'college' of St. Francis Xavier, 1743; made astronomical clocks. [xxvi. 385]

HILDILID, SAINT (fl. 700), abbess of Barking. [xxvi. 386]

HILDITCH, SIR EDWARD (1805–1876), inspector-general of hospitals; on West Indian station, 1830–55; at Plymouth, 1855, Greenwich, 1861; inspector-general, 1854–1865; first honorary physician to Queen Victoria, 1859; knighted, 1865. [xxvi. 386]

HILDROP, JOHN (d. 1756), divine; M.A. St. John's College, Oxford, 1705; D.D., 1743; master of free grammar school, Marlborough, 1703–33; rector of Maulden, Bedfordshire, and, 1734, of Wath-juxta-Ripon; friend of Zachary Grey [q. v.] His 'Miscellaneous Works' (1754) include satires against the deists. [xxvi. 386]

HILDYARD, JAMES (1809–1887), classical scholar; educated at Shrewsbury; Tancred student, afterwards fellow of Christ's College, Cambridge; second classic and chancellor's medallist, 1833; M.A., 1836; D.D. 1846;

senior proctor, 1843 ; preacher at Whitehall, 1843–4 ; incumbent of Ingoldsby, 1846–87 ; edited plays of Plautus ; issued pamphlets advocating revision of liturgy and reform of university education.   [xxvi. 387]

HILL, AARON (1685–1750), dramatist ; educated at Westminster ; travelled in the East ; obtained patent for extracting oil from beechmast, 1713 ; proposed colonisation of Georgia, 1718 ; addressed complimentary poems to Peterborough and Peter the Great ; satirised by Pope ; attacked Pope in ' Progress of Wit' (1730) and other publications, but afterwards corresponded amicably with him ; corresponded with Richardson ; produced plays and operas, including words of Handel's 'Rinaldo' (1711), ' Athelwold' (1732), 'Zara,' ' Merope,' and other translations from Voltaire ; joint-author with William Bond (d. 1735) [q. v.] of the 'Plaindealer,' 1724.   [xxvi. 387]

HILL, ABIGAIL (d. 1734). [See MASHAM, ABIGAIL, LADY.]

HILL, ABRAHAM (1635–1721), treasurer of Royal Society, 1663–5 and 1679–1700 ; commissioner of trade, 1689 ; comptroller to Archbishop Tillotson, 1691 ; published life of Barrow, 1683 ; Pepys and Evelyn among his correspondents.   [xxvi. 389]

HILL, ADAM (d. 1595), divine ; fellow of Balliol College, Oxford, 1568–73 ; M.A., 1572 ; D.D., 1591 ; prebendary of Salisbury, 1586.   [xxvi. 390]

HILL or HYLL, ALBAN (d. 1559), physician ; graduated at Bologna ; F.R.C.P., 1552 ; censor, 1555–8.   [xxvi. 390]

HILL, ALEXANDER (1785–1867), professor of divinity at Glasgow ; son of George Hill (1750–1819) [q. v.] ; graduated at St. Andrews, 1804 ; D.D., 1828 ; minister of Dailly, 1816 ; divinity professor, 1840–62 ; moderator of general assembly, 1845 ; published tracts.   [xxvi. 390]

HILL, ARTHUR (1601 ?–1663), parliamentarian colonel ; formed manor of Hillsborough from grants in county Down ; M.P., counties Down, Antrim, and Armagh, 1654 ; constable and Irish privy councillor, 1660.   [xxvi. 391]

HILL, DAVID OCTAVIUS (1802–1870), landscape and portrait painter ; secretary to Scottish Society of Arts, 1830–8, and after its incorporation in the Royal Scottish Academy ; his ' Land of Burns ' series of pictures issued, 1841 ; painted many other Scottish landscapes, and 'Signing the Deed of Demission,' 1865 ; first artist to apply photography to portraiture ; a commissioner of Scottish board of manufactures, 1850 ; originated Edinburgh Art Union.   [xxvi. 391]

HILL, SIR DUDLEY ST. LEGER (1790–1851), major-general ; served with 95th (rifle brigade) at Monte Video and Buenos Ayres, 1807, being captured wounded ; also in the Peninsula, 1808–10 ; held Portuguese commands at Busaco, 1810, and succeeding battles, being seven times wounded ; continued in Portuguese service after the peace ; lieutenant-governor of Saint Lucia, 1834–8 ; major-general, 1841 ; K.C.B., 1848 ; died at Umballa, holding a Bengal command.   [xxvi. 392]

HILL, EDWIN (1793–1876), inventor and author ; brother of Sir Rowland Hill [q. v.] ; supervisor of stamps at Somerset House, 1840–72 ; with Mr. De la Rue invented machine for folding envelopes, exhibited, 1851 ; published ' Principles of Currency,' 1856.   [xxvi. 393]

HILL, GEORGE (1716–1808), king's serjeant, 1772 (' Serjeant Labyrinth') ; of Lincoln's Inn.   [xxvi. 393]

HILL, GEORGE (1750–1819), principal of St. Mary's College, St. Andrews ; graduated from St. Andrews, 1764 ; joint-professor of Greek, 1772–88, of divinity, 1788 ; D.D., 1787 ; principal of St. Mary's College. 1791–1819 ; dean of Chapel Royal, 1799 ; moderator of general assembly, 1789 ; his ' Lectures on Divinity ' published, 1821.   [xxvi. 393]

HILL, SIR HUGH (1802–1871), judge of the queen's bench ; B.A. Dublin, 1821 ; barrister, Middle Temple, 1841, after being a successful special pleader ; Q.C., 1851 ; judge of queen's bench, 1858–61.   [xxvi. 394]

HILL, JAMES (d. 1728 ?), antiquary ; F.S.A., 1718 ; F.R.S., 1719 ; corresponded with William Stukeley ; made collections for history of Herefordshire.   [xxvi. 394]

HILL, JAMES (d. 1817 ?), actor and vocalist ; appeared at Bath and Covent Garden, 1796–1806 ; said to have died in Jamaica.   [xxvi. 395]

HILL, JAMES JOHN (1811–1882), painter ; exhibited with Society of British Artists ; best known by his rustic figure-pictures.   [xxvi. 395]

HILL, JOHN ? (d. 1697 ?), lieutenant-colonel and governor of Inverlochy (Fort William) at time of Glencoe massacre (1692), carried out by his second in command ; both tried for murder and acquitted.
          [xxvi. 396]

HILL, JOHN (d. 1735), major-general ; brother of Abigail, lady Masham [q. v.] ; made page to Queen Anne and (1703) officer in army through Marlborough influence ; commanded brigade at Almanza, 1707 ; wounded at Mons, 1709 ; brigadier-general in command of Quebec expedition, 1711 ; major-general, 1712 ; afterwards in charge of Dunkirk.   [xxvi. 396]

HILL, JOHN, calling himself SIR JOHN (1716 ?–1775), author ; knight of Swedish order of Vasa ; flourished as an apothecary and quack doctor in James Street, Covent Garden ; patronised by Bute ; conducted the ' British Magazine,' 1746–50 ; contributed to ' London Advertiser ' as ' The Inspector,' 1751–3 ; attacked Royal Society, Fielding, Christopher Smart (who replied with the ' Hilliad '), and Garrick, who composed on him a celebrated epigram ; published ' The Vegetable System ' (1759–75), for which he obtained his Swedish order, and translations and compilations dealing with medicine, botany, and horticulture, ' Naval History of Britain,' 1756, and other works ; authorship of Mrs. Glasse's ' Art of Cookery ' (1747) erroneously ascribed to him.
          [xxvi. 397]

HILL, JOHN HARWOOD (1809–1886), antiquary ; F.S.A., 1871 ; B.A. Peterhouse, Cambridge, 1834 ; librarian to Lord Cardigan at Deene ; rector of Cranoe, 1837, and vicar of Welham, 1841 ; published ' History of Market Harborough,' 1875.   [xxvi. 401]

HILL, JOSEPH (1625–1707), nonconformist divine and lexicographer ; fellow of Magdalene College, Cambridge ; M.A., 1649 ; his name removed for nonconformity, 1662 ; pastor of Scottish church at Middelburg, Holland, 1667–73, where he published pamphlet advocating English alliance ; English presbyterian minister on Haringvliet, Rotterdam, 1678–1707 ; edited and enlarged Schrevelius's Greek-Latin lexicon, 1663.
          [xxvi. 402]

HILL, JOSEPH (1667–1729), presbyterian minister at Rotterdam, 1699–1718, and Haberdashers' Hall, London, 1718–29.   [xxvi. 402]

HILL, JOSEPH SIDNEY (1851–1894), missionary bishop ; studied at Church Missionary Society's College, Islington ; deacon, 1876 ; joined mission at Lagos, 1876 ; appointed to New Zealand mission, 1878 ; priest, 1879 ; bishop in Western Equatorial Africa, 1893 ; died at Lagos.   [Suppl. ii. 421]

HILL, MATTHEW DAVENPORT (1792–1872), reformer of criminal law ; eldest son of Thomas Wright Hill [q. v.] ; barrister, Lincoln's Inn, 1819 ; defended John Cartwright (1740–1824) [q. v.], the Nottingham rioters (1831), the Canadian prisoners (1839), and Rebecca rioters (1843) ; counsel for Daniel O'Connell, 1844, and for Baron de Bode ; took part in founding Society for the Diffusion of Useful Knowledge, 1826 ; as M.P. for Hull, 1832–5, had charge of colonisation of South Australia bill (1834) and caused scene between Lord Althorp and Richard Lalor Sheil [q. v.] ; Q.C., 1834 ; first recorder of Birmingham, 1839 ; advocated, in charges (collected in ' Suggestions for Repression of Crime,' 1857), changes in treatment of criminals adopted in Penal Servitude Acts of 1853 and 1864 ; supported establishment of reformatories and industrial schools ; commissioner of bankrupts (Bristol district), 1851–69.   [xxvi. 402]

HILL, NICHOLAS (1570 ?–1610), philosopher ; of Merchant Taylors' School and St. John's College, Oxford ; fellow, 1592 ; B.A., 1592 ; secretary to Edward de Vere, earl of Oxford ; published ' Philosophia Epicurea, Democritiana, Theophrastica,' 1601 ; died abroad.
          [xxvi. 404]

HILL, PASCOE GRENFELL (1804–1882), author ; B.A. Trinity College, Dublin, 1836 ; chaplain in navy, 1836–45 ; to Westminster Hospital, 1852–7 ; rector of St. Edmund the King and Martyr, 1863 ; published ' Life of Napoleon,' 1869, and other works.   [xxvi. 405]

HILL, RICHARD (1655–1727), diplomatist ; educated at Shrewsbury and St. John's College, Cambridge, fellow and benefactor; B.A., 1675; envoy extraordinary to elector of Bavaria, 1696; ambassador at the Hague and a lord of the treasury, 1699; member of admiralty council, 1702; as envoy to Savoy, 1703–6, gained adhesion of the duke to grand alliance and toleration of Vaudois (correspondence published, 1845); fellow of Eton, 1714; F.R.S. and hon. D.C.L. of Oxford.   [xxvi. 405]

HILL, SIR RICHARD, second baronet (1732–1808), controversialist; grand-nephew of Richard Hill [q. v.]; educated at Westminster; M.A. Magdalen College, Oxford, 1754; attacked university for expelling methodist undergraduates, 1768; carried on controversies with Wesley, Charles Daubeny [q. v.], and others; M.P., Shropshire, 1780–1806; succeeded as baronet, 1783.
               [xxvi. 406]

HILL or **HULL**, ROBERT (d. 1425), judge; king's serjeant, 1399; judge of common pleas, 1408; chief-justice of Isle of Ely, 1422.   [xxvi. 407]

HILL, ROBERT (d. 1623), divine; M.A. Christ's College, Cambridge, 1588; fellow of St. John's College, 1589; perpetual curate of St. Andrew, Norwich, 1591–1602; rector of St. Margaret Moyses, Friday Street, London, 1607; of St. Bartholomew Exchange, London, 1613–1623; published devotional works.   [xxvi. 407]

HILL, ROBERT (1699–1777), learned tailor, compared by Joseph Spence with Magliabechi; acquired Greek and Hebrew, and wrote theological treatises.   [xxvi. 408]

HILL, ROBERT GARDINER (1811–1878), surgeon; brother of John Harwood Hill [q. v.]; M.R.C.S., 1834; as house-surgeon to Lincoln lunatic asylum (1835–40) dispensed with the restraint system; joint-proprietor of Eastgate House asylum, 1840–63; mayor of Lincoln, 1852; proprietor of Earl's Court House, Old Brompton, 1863–78; published works on treatment of lunatics.
               [xxvi. 408]

HILL, ROGER (1605–1667), judge; barrister, Inner Temple, 1632; bencher, 1649; junior counsel against Laud, 1644; M.P., Bridport, 1645; assistant to Commonwealth attorney-general; judge of assize, 1656; baron of exchequer, 1657; transferred to upper bench, 1660.
               [xxvi. 409]

HILL, SIR ROWLAND (1492?–1561), lord mayor of London; warden of Mercers' Company, 1536, and four times master; sheriff, 1541; knighted; alderman, Castle Baynard ward, 1542, and Walbrook, 1545; first protestant lord mayor, 1549–50; a commissioner against heretics, 1557; built Hodnet and Stoke churches, Shropshire; endowed school at Drayton and exhibitions to universities.   [xxvi. 410]

HILL, ROWLAND (1744–1833), preacher; brother of Sir Richard Hill [q. v.]; educated at Shrewsbury, Eton, and St. John's College, Cambridge; B.A., 1769; was refused priest's orders owing to his itinerant preaching; from 1783 preached in Surrey Chapel, London, where he had Sunday schools; published hymns, 'Village Dialogues,' 1810, and a tract in favour of inoculation.
               [xxvi. 411]

HILL, ROWLAND, first VISCOUNT HILL (1772–1842), general; nephew of Rowland Hill (1744–1833) [q. v.]; studied at Strasburg military school while subaltern; aide-de-camp at Toulon, 1793; lieutenant-colonel, 90th foot (Graham's regiment), 1794; brevet-colonel, 1800; commanded regiment in Egypt, 1801 (wounded at Aboukir), and in Ireland, establishing regimental school and sergeants' mess; major-general, 1805; commanded brigades in Hanover, and at Roliça and Coruña; led second division at Talavera, 1809; invalided after campaign of 1810; resumed command, May 1811, and defeated Gerard at Merida (October 1811); lieutenant-general and K.B., 1812; stormed Almaraz (May); commanded right at Vittoria, 1813; blockaded Pampeluna; distinguished at Nivelle and the Nive, 1813; won victories of Bayonne (13 Dec. 1813) and Toulouse (10, 11 April, 1814); created Baron Hill and given pension of 2,000l., and the freedom of the city of London. 1814; sent on mission to Prince of Orange, 1815; given command of army corps in Belgium; headed Adam's brigade at Waterloo before the last charge, 1815; second in command of army of occupation in France, 1815–18; general, 1825; commander-in-chief in England, 1825–39; created viscount, 1842.
               [xxvi. 411]

HILL, SIR ROWLAND (1795–1879), inventor of penny postage; son of Thomas Wright Hill [q. v.];

educated in his father's school at Hill Top, Birmingham, where he afterwards taught; established school on his own plan and self-disciplined at Hazelwood (afterwards removed to Bruce Castle, Tottenham), as described in the 'Public Education' (1822) of his brother, Matthew Davenport Hill [q. v.]; invented rotatory printing-press and other machines; secretary to South Australian commission, 1835; submitted to Lord Melbourne his 'Post Office Reform: its Importance and Practicability,' 1837; described his invention of adhesive stamp before commission, 1837; obtained parliamentary committee which recommended twopenny postage, 1838; secured adoption of penny postage in budget of 1839; was given appointment in the post office; his scheme of penny postage established, 1840; dismissed from post office, 1842; as chairman of Brighton railway, 1843–6, introduced express and excursion trains; received public testimonial, 1846; secretary to postmaster-general, 1846; as secretary to the post office, 1854–64; established promotion by merit; F.R.S., 1857; K.C.B., 1860; D.C.L. of Oxford, 1864; received freedom of the city of London, 1879; as member of railway commission published separate report (1867) recommending state purchase and working by companies holding leases; buried in Westminster Abbey.   [xxvi. 416]

HILL, ROWLEY (1836–1887), bishop of Sodor and Man; of Christ's Hospital and Trinity College, Cambridge; M.A., 1863; D.D., 1877; vicar of St. Michael's, Chester Square, London, 1871, of Sheffield, 1873; bishop of Sodor and Man, 1877–87.   [xxvi. 420]

HILL, SAMUEL (1648?–1716), archdeacon of Wells; B.A. St. Mary Hall, Oxford, 1666; rector of Kilmington, 1687; archdeacon of Wells, 1705–16; published controversial works against Bishop Burnet and the nonjurors.   [xxvi. 421]

HILL, SIR STEPHEN JOHN (1809–1891), colonial governor; entered army, 1823; captain, 1842; served in West Africa; brevet major, 1849; governor and commander-in-chief of Gold Coast, 1851; lieutenant-governor of Sierra Leone, 1854, and governor-in-chief, 1860–2; governor-in-chief of Leeward and Caribbee islands, 1863–1869, and of Newfoundland, 1869–76; colonel of West India regiment, 1854; K.C.M.G., 1874. [Suppl. ii. 422]

HILL, THOMAS (fl. 1590), compiler and translator of horticultural and astrological works.   [xxvi. 422]

HILL, alias BUCKLAND, THOMAS (1564–1644), Benedictine; ordained at Rome, 1594, where he opposed the jesuits; sent on English mission, 1597; condemned to death, 1612; reprieved; banished, 1613; published 'A Quartron of Reasons of Catholike Religion' (1600); died at St. Gregory's monastery, Douay.   [xxvi. 422]

HILL, THOMAS (d. 1653), master of Trinity College, Cambridge; scholar and fellow of Emmanuel College, Cambridge; M.A., 1626; B.D., 1633; original member of Westminster Assembly of Divines, 1643; master of Trinity College, Cambridge, 1645–53; vice-chancellor of Cambridge, 1646; Calvinist.   [xxvi. 423]

HILL, THOMAS (1628?–1677?), nonconformist minister; B.A. Corpus Christi College, Cambridge; presbyterian pastor at Orton, Leicestershire, 1653–60; perpetual curate of Shuttington, 1660–5.   [xxvi. 423]

HILL, THOMAS (d. 1720), nonconformist tutor; son of Thomas Hill (1628?–1677?).   [xxvi. 424]

HILL, THOMAS (1661–1734), portrait-painter.
               [xxvi. 424]

HILL, THOMAS (1760–1840), book-collector; patron of Bloomfield and Kirke White; entertained literary and theatrical celebrities at Sydenham; the 'Hull' of Hook's 'Gilbert Gurney'; his collection, the basis of Longmans' 'Bibliotheca Anglo-Poetica,' 1815.   [xxvi. 424]

HILL, THOMAS (1808–1865), topographer; M.A. Clare Hall, Cambridge, 1832; incumbent of Holy Trinity, Queenhithe, 1850–65; author of 'History of Nunnery of St. Clare and Parish of Holy Trinity,' 1851, and 'The Harmony of the Greek and Latin Languages,' 1841.
               [xxvi. 425]

HILL, THOMAS FORD (d. 1795), antiquary; F.S.A., 1792; travelled on continent; collected 'Ancient Erse Songs,' 1784; died at Ariano.   [xxvi. 425]

HILL, SIR THOMAS NOEL (1784–1832), colonel ; brother of Rowland, viscount Hill [q. v.] ; commanded Portuguese regiment, 1810–14 ; lieutenant-colonel, 1st foot-guards, 1814 ; assistant adjutant-general in Waterloo campaign ; deputy adjutant-general in Canada, 1827–30 ; K.C.B.   [xxvi. 425]

HILL, THOMAS WRIGHT (1763–1851), school-master and stenographer ; a disciple of Priestley ; kept school at Hill Top, Birmingham, 1803–19 ; his 'Remains' issued, 1859, and 'Selection from his Papers,' 1860 ; they included his studies in letter-sounds, systems of shorthand and numerical nomenclature, and scheme of minority representation.   [xxvi. 425]

HILL, WILLIAM (*fl.* 1662), informer ; of Merton College, Oxford ; gave information of plot to seize Charles II, 1662.   [xxvi. 427]

HILL, WILLIAM (1619–1667), classical scholar ; fellow of Merton College, Oxford, 1639 ; M.A., 1641 ; D.D. Dublin ; master of Sutton Coldfield school, 1640 ; after-wards of St. Patrick's, Dublin ; edited 'Dionysius Perie-getes,' 1658.   [xxvi. 426]

HILL, WILLIAM NOEL, third BARON BERWICK (*d.* 1842), ambassador at Naples, 1824–33 ; succeeded his brother in title, 1832 ; F.S.A.   [xxvi. 427]

HILL, WILLS, first MARQUIS OF DOWNSHIRE (1718–1793), statesman ; M.P., Warwick, 1741–56 ; succeeded as second Viscount Hillsborough (Ireland), 1742 ; privy councillor of Ireland, 1746 ; created Irish earl, 1751 ; comptroller and treasurer to George II, 1754–6 ; created Baron Harwich (peerage of Great Britain), 1756 ; presi-dent of board of trade and plantations, 1763–5, and 1766 ; joint postmaster-general, 1766–8 ; as secretary of state for colonies, 1768–72, and for northern department, 1779–82, pursued harsh policy towards America ; attacked by 'Junius' ; created Irish marquis, 1789 ; recommended union with Ireland.   [xxvi. 427]

HILL-TREVOR, ARTHUR, third VISCOUNT DUN-GANNON of the second creation in peerage of Ireland (1798–1862). [See TREVOR.]

HILLARY, WILLIAM (*d.* 1763), physician ; M.D. Leyden, 1722, and pupil of Boerhaave ; practised in Ripon, Bath, Barbados, and London ; published 'Observations on Changes of the Air, and the concomitant Epidemical Diseases in Barbadoes,' 1759.   [xxvi. 429]

HILLARY, SIR WILLIAM, first baronet (1771–1847), founder of Royal National Lifeboat Institution ; equerry to Duke of Sussex ; raised First Essex Legion of infantry and cavalry, 1803 ; created baronet, 1805 ; settled in Isle of Man, 1808 ; first proposed Royal National Lifeboat Institution, 1823, and became president of district associa-tion in Isle of Man ; proposed schemes for public benefit in various pamphlets.   [Suppl. ii. 422]

HILLIARD, NICHOLAS (1537–1619), first English miniature-painter ; as goldsmith, carver, and limner to Elizabeth engraved her second great seal, 1586 ; granted sole right to execute portraits of James I, 1617 ; praised by Donne in 'The Storm' ; painted miniature of himself at thirteen, and drew portrait of Mary Queen of Scots at eighteen ; executed miniatures of chief contemporaries, twenty-three of which were exhibited at the Royal Aca-demy, 1879.   [xxvi. 429]

HILLIER, CHARLES PARKER (1838–1880). [See HARCOURT, CHARLES.]

HILLIER, GEORGE (1815–1866), topographer ; pub-lished works, including 'Topography of the Isle of Wight,' 1850, and a guide to Reading, 1859.   [xxvi. 430]

HILLS, HENRY (*d.* 1713), printer to Cromwell, Charles II, and James II ; provision in statute (8 Anne) directing that fine paper copies of all publications should be sent to public libraries occasioned by his piracies.   [xxvi. 431]

HILLS, ROBERT (1769–1844), water-colour painter and etcher ; exhibited at Society of Painters in Water-colours, being many years secretary.   [xxvi. 431]

HILLSBOROUGH, first EARL and second VISCOUNT (1718–1793). [See HILL, WILLS.]

HILLYAR, SIR JAMES (1769–1843), rear-admiral ; midshipman under Lord Hood, 1793 ; as lieutenant under Captain Robert Stopford [q. v.] present in action of 1 June 1794 ; commanded armed boats at Barcelona and on Egyptian coast, 1800–1 ; commanded Niger cruiser in Mediterranean, 1800–7 ; recommended for post-rank by Nelson, 1804 ; assisted in reduction of Mauritius (1810) and Java (1811) ; captured American ship Essex, 1813 ; K.C.H., 1834 ; rear-admiral, 1837 ; K.C.B., 1840.   [xxvi. 432]

HILSEY or **HILDESLEIGH**, JOHN (*d.* 1538), bishop of Rochester ; B.D. Oxford, 1527, D.D., 1532 ; prior of Dominican house at Bristol, 1533 ; appointed by Thomas Cromwell provincial and commissioner (with George Browne (*d.* 1556) [q. v.]) to visit friaries, 1534 ; bishop of Rochester, 1535–8 ; censor of press, 1536 ; exposed the Boxley Rood and other impostures, 1538 ; compiled 'Manuall of Prayers, or the Prymer in Englyshe,' pub-lished, 1539 ; assisted in compiling 'Institution of a Christian Man.'   [xxvi. 433]

HILTON, JOHN (*d.* 1657), musical composer ; Mus. Bac. Trinity College, Cambridge, 1626 ; parish clerk and organist of St. Margaret's, Westminster, 1628 ; published 'Ayres, or Fa La's for Three Voyces,' 1627 ; wrote elegy on William Lawes, 1645 ; contributed madrigals to 'Triumphs of Oriana,' 1601, and canons and catches to 'Catch that catch can,' 1652.   [xxvi. 434]

HILTON, JOHN (1804–1878), surgeon at Guy's Hos-pital, 1849–70 ; professor of human anatomy and surgery at College of Surgeons, 1860–2 ; president, 1867 ; his treatise 'On Rest and Pain' (1863) a surgical classic.   [xxvi. 435]

HILTON, WALTER (*d.* 1396), religious writer ; Au-gustinian canon at Thurgarton, Nottinghamshire ; his 'Scala Perfectionis' (English) printed by Wynkyn de Worde, 1494, and Pynson, 1506 (translated into Latin by Thomas Fyslawe and edited by Robert Guy, 1869, and John Dobree Dalgairns, 1870).   [xxvi. 435]

HILTON, WILLIAM (1786–1839), historical painter ; exhibited at Royal Academy from 1803 ; R.A., 1818, and keeper, 1827 ; his works exhibited at British Institution, 1840 ; his 'Christ Crowned with Thorns' purchased for Chantrey bequest. His paintings include 'Edith discover-ing dead body of Harold,' 1834, and 'Sir Calepine rescuing Serena,' 1831.   [xxvi. 436]

HINCHINBROKE, first VISCOUNT (1625–1672). [See MONTAGU, SIR EDWARD.]

HINCHLIFF, JOHN ELLEY (1777–1867), sculptor ; assistant to Flaxman, for whom he finished statues of Hastings and John Philip Kemble ; chiefly known for mural tablets and sepulchral monuments.   [xxvi. 437]

HINCHLIFF, JOHN JAMES (1805–1875), engraver ; son of John Elley Hinchliff [q. v.]   [xxvi. 437]

HINCHLIFF, THOMAS WOODBINE (1825–1882), president of Alpine Club ; M.A. Trinity College, Cam-bridge, 1852 ; barrister, Lincoln's Inn ; took part in founding Alpine Club, 1857, and was first honorary secre-tary and president, 1874–7 ; published books relating to his travels.   [Suppl. ii. 423]

HINCHLIFFE, JOHN (1731–1794), bishop of Peter-borough ; educated at Westminster, where he was assistant-master seven years and (1764) head for three months ; scholar of Trinity, Cambridge, 1751 ; fellow, 1755 ; master, 1768–88 ; M.A., 1757 ; D.D., 1764 ; vice-chancellor, 1768 ; bishop of Peterborough, 1769–94 ; offended government by liberal speeches in House of Lords, and was made dean of Durham (1788) on condition of resigning the master-ship of Trinity College.   [xxvi. 437]

HINCKLEY, JOHN (1617?–1695), controversialist ; M.A. St. Alban Hall, Oxford, 1640 ; D.D., 1679 ; rector of Northfield, Worcestershire, 1661–95 ; prebendary of Lich-field, 1673 ; published, among other works, 'Fasciculus Literarum' (1680), containing controversy with Baxter.   [xxvi. 438]

HINCKS, EDWARD (1792–1866), orientalist ; son of Thomas Dix Hincks [q. v.] ; gold medallist and B.A. Trinity College, Dublin, 1811 ; rector of Killyleagh, 1825–1866 ; according to Brugsch first employed true method of deciphering Egyptian hieroglyphics ; simultaneously with Rawlinson discovered Persian cuneiform vowel system ; contributed to 'Transactions' of Royal Irish Academy.   [xxvi. 438]

HINCKS, SIR FRANCIS (1807–1885), Canadian statesman; brother of Edward Hincks [q. v.]; emigrated to Canada, 1831; joined liberals, 1837; entered parliament, 1841; inspector-general of public accounts in first Baldwin-Lafontaine ministry, 1842–4; started 'Montreal Pilot,' 1844; inspector-general in second Baldwin ministry, 1848–51; as premier, 1851–4, developed Canadian railway and commercial system, negotiated reciprocity treaty with United States and passed Parliamentary Representation Act; governor of Barbados and Windward isles, 1855–62, of British Guiana, 1862–9; K.C.M.G., 1869; finance minister, 1869–73; wrote on Canadian politics. [xxvi. 439]

HINCKS, THOMAS (1818–1899), zoologist; B.A. London, 1840; minister at Mill Hill unitarian chapel, Leeds, 1855–69; F.R.S., 1872; published 'History of British Hydroid Zoophytes,' 1868, and 'History of British Marine Polyzoa,' 1880. [Suppl. ii. 424]

HINCKS, THOMAS DIX (1767–1857), Irish presbyterian divine; left Trinity College, Dublin, for Hackney New College, 1788; ordained by southern presbytery, 1792; lecturer at Royal Cork Institution and Fermoy academy; classical master of Belfast Academical Institution and professor of Hebrew, 1821–36; LL.D. Glasgow, 1834; contributed Irish articles to Rees's 'Cyclopædia'; wrote educational manuals. [xxvi. 441]

HINCKS, WILLIAM (1794–1871), professor of natural history at Queen's College, Cork, 849–53, and University College, Toronto, 1853–71; son of Thomas Dix Hincks [q. v.] [xxvi. 441]

HIND, JAMES (d. 1652), royalist and highwayman; escaped in woman's clothes from Colchester after its capture, 1648; served under Ormonde in Ireland, 1649; fought in Charles II's army at Worcester, 1651; arrested in London, 1651; hanged for treason. [xxvi. 442]

HIND, JOHN (1796–1866), mathematician; second wrangler and Smith's prizeman, 1818; M.A. Sidney Sussex College, Cambridge, 1821; fellow, 1823–5; published works on the differential calculus and other mathematical subjects. [xxvi. 442]

HIND, JOHN RUSSELL (1823–1895), astronomer; entered magnetic and meteorological department of Royal Observatory, Greenwich, 1840; director of observatory founded by George Bishop [q v.] in Regent's Park, 1844–1895; superintended 'Nautical Almanack,' 1853–91; member of Royal Astronomical Society, 1844, president, 1880–1881; F.R.S., 1863; honorary LL.D. Glasgow, 1882; published astronomical works. [Suppl. ii. 424]

HINDE, WILLIAM (1569?–1629), puritan divine; of Queen's College, Oxford; fellow; M.A., 1594; perpetual curate of Bunbury, Cheshire, 1603–29; published devotional works; edited works by John Rainolds, and Cleaver's 'Bathshebaes Instructions,' 1614. [xxvi. 443]

HINDERWELL, THOMAS (1744–1825), author of 'History of Scarborough,' 1798; mayor of Scarborough, 1781, 1784, 1790, and 1800; published 'Authentic Narratives of Affecting Shipwrecks,' 1799. [xxvi. 443]

HINDLE, JOHN (1761–1796), vocalist and composer; Mus. Bac. Magdalen College, Oxford; lay vicar of Westminster Abbey; sang at Worcester festival, 1788, and London Vocal Concerts, 1791 and 1792; composed glees for words of English poets, and songs. [xxvi. 443]

HINDLEY, JOHN HADDON (1765–1827), orientalist; M.A. Brasenose College, Oxford, 1790; chaplain of Manchester Collegiate Church; Chetham librarian, 1792–1804; published 'Persian Lyrics from the Diwan-i-Hafiz, with paraphrases,' 1800; edited 'Pendeh-i-Attar,' 1807. [xxvi. 444]

HINDMARSH, SIR JOHN (d. 1860), rear-admiral and colonial governor; saved the Bellerophon at battle of the Nile (1798), where he lost an eye; lieutenant of the Phœbe at Trafalgar, 1805; with the Beagle in Basque road, 1809; K.H., 1836; first governor of South Australia, 1836–7; lieutenant-governor of Heligoland, 1840–56; rear-admiral, 1856. [xxvii. 1]

HINDMARSH, ROBERT (1759–1835), organiser of the 'new church'; formed Swedenborgian Society, 1783, opened chapel in Eastcheap, 1788, built another in Cross Street, Hatton Garden; organised hierarchy, 1793; afterwards preached at Salford; 'Rise and Progress of New Jerusalem Church,' issued, 1861. [xxvii. 2]

HINDS, SAMUEL (1793–1872), bishop of Norwich; M.A. Queen's College, Oxford, 1818; D.D., 1831; principal of Codrington College, Barbados; vice-principal of St. Alban Hall, Oxford, 1827–31; chaplain to Archbishop Whately, and earls of Bessborough and Clarendon; dean of Carlisle, 1858; bishop of Norwich, 1849–57; published 'Inquiry into Proofs, &c., of Inspiration and into the Authority of Scripture,' 1831, and other works. [xxvii. 3]

HINE, HENRY GEORGE (1811–1895), landscape-painter; apprenticed as draughtsman to Henry Meyer [q. v.]; practised as wood engraver at Brighton; on staff of 'Punch,' 1841–4; subsequently contributed to 'Illustrated London News' and other publications; exhibited landscapes at Royal Academy and Suffolk Street Gallery; member of Institute of Painters in Water-colours, 1864. [Suppl. ii. 425]

HINE, WILLIAM (1687–1730), organist of Gloucester Cathedral (1712–30), and composer. [xxvii. 3]

HINGSTON, JOHN (d. 1683), composer and organist; employed by Charles I, Cromwell, and Charles II. [xxvii. 4]

HINGSTON, THOMAS (1799–1837), physician; of Queens' College, Cambridge; M.D. Edinburgh, 1824; practised at Penzance and Truro; edited Harvey's 'De Motu Cordis' (1824), and contributed to D. Gilbert's 'Parochial History of Cornwall.' [xxvii. 4]

HINTON, JAMES (1822–1875), surgeon and philosophical writer; son of John Howard Hinton [q. v.]; made voyages to China, Sierra Leone, and Jamaica as medical officer; practised as aural surgeon in London, and became acquainted with Dr. (Sir William Withey) Gull [q. v.]; contributed to Holmes's 'System of Surgery,' 1862; edited 'Year-Book of Medicine,' 1863, and published aural monographs; published 'Mystery of Pain,' 1866, and joined Metaphysical Society; died in the Azores. Hinton's 'Chapters on the Art of Thinking and other Essays,' were printed, 1879, 'Philosophy and Religion,' 1881, 'The Lawbreaker and the Coming of the Law,' 1884. [xxvii. 4]

HINTON, SIR JOHN (1603?–1682), royalist physician; studied at Leyden; present at Edgehill, 1642; M.D. Oxford, 1642; attended Henrietta Maria at Exeter, 1644; practised in London during Commonwealth; physician to Charles II and his queen; knighted, 1665; his 'Memoires' printed, 1814. [xxvii. 7]

HINTON, JOHN HOWARD (1791–1873), baptist minister; M.A. Edinburgh, 1816; minister of Devonshire Square Chapel, Bishopsgate, 1837–63; secretary of Baptist Union; edited 'History and Topography of United States,' and many theological, biographical, and educational works (collected, 1864). [xxvii. 7]

HIPPISLEY, E., subsequently MRS. FITZMAURICE (fl. 1741–1766), actress; daughter of John Hippisley (d. 1748) [q. v.] [xxvii. 9]

HIPPISLEY, JANE, afterwards MRS. GREEN (d. 1791), actress; sister of E. Hippisley [q. v.]; Garrick's Ophelia at Goodman's Fields; original Mrs. Malaprop, 1747–8. [xxvii. 9]

HIPPISLEY, JOHN (d. 1748), actor and dramatist; owned theatres at Bristol and Bath; at Lincoln's Inn Fields, 1722–33, played Fondlewife ('Old Bachelor'), Polonius, and Sir Hugh Evans, and 'created' Peachum; at Covent Garden played Shallow, Dogberry, Fluellen, and other characters; created Sir Simon Loveit ('Miss in her Teens'); also played in his own 'Journey to Bristol' (1731), and 'Drunken Man' (1732). [xxvii. 8]

HIPPISLEY, JOHN (d. 1767), actor and author; probably governor of Cape Coast Castle; son of John Hippisley (d. 1748) [q. v.] [xxvii. 9]

HIPPISLEY, SIR JOHN COXE, first baronet (1748–1825), politician; D.C.L. Hertford College, Oxford, 1776; barrister, Inner Temple, 1771; treasurer, 1816; agent of British government in Italy, 1779–80 and 1792–6; employed by East India Company, 1786–9; negotiated marriage of Princess Royal with Duke of Würtemberg, and was created baronet, 1796; recorder of Sudbury and M.P., 1790–6 and 1802–19; wrote pamphlets in favour of catholic emancipation. [xxvii. 10]

HIRAETHOG, GRUFFYDD (*d.* 1568 ?), Welsh poet, named from Denbighshire mountains; manuscript poems by him in British Museum and at Peniarth House. [xxvii. 11]

HIRSCHEL, SOLOMON (1761–1842), chief rabbi of German and Polish Jews in London, 1802–42. [xxvii. 11]

HIRST, THOMAS ARCHER (1830–1892), mathematician; articled as land agent and surveyor at Halifax, Yorkshire; studied at Marburg and was Ph.D., 1852; lecturer in mathematics, Queenwood College, Hampshire, 1853–6; mathematical master of University College School, 1860; F.R.S., 1861; F.R.A.S., 1866; professor of physics, University College, London, 1865, and of pure mathematics, 1866–70; director of naval studies, Royal Naval College, Greenwich, 1873–83; fellow of London University, 1882; published mathematical writings. [Suppl. ii. 426]

HIRST, WILLIAM (*d.* 1769 ?), astronomer; M.A. Peterhouse, Cambridge, 1754; F.R.S., 1755; naval chaplain at sieges of Pondicherry and Vellore; observed transit of Venus at Madras, 1761; while at Calcutta described two eclipses and an earthquake; described transit of Venus of 1769; lost at sea on a second voyage to India. [xxvii. 11]

HISLOP, JAMES (1798–1827). [See HYSLOP.]

HISLOP, STEPHEN (1817–1863), missionary and naturalist; studied at Edinburgh and Glasgow; joined Free church of Scotland, 1843; went to India as missionary, 1844; founded school at Nagpore, near which he was drowned; his 'Papers relating to Aboriginal Tribes of Central Provinces' edited by Sir R. Temple, 1866. [xxvii. 12]

HISLOP, SIR THOMAS, first baronet (1764–1843), general; with 39th at siege of Gibraltar (1779–83), commanding it at capture of Demerara, Berbice, and Essequibo, 1796; headed first division at capture of Guadeloupe (1809); lieutenant-governor of Trinidad, 1803–11; captured on way to India by American frigate, 1812; created baronet and commander-in-chief at Madras, 1813; led army of Deccan in Mahratta war, 1817–18; won victory of Mahidpore, 1817; incurred blame for severity at Talner; G.C.B., 1818; left Madras, 1820. [xxvii. 13]

HITCHAM, SIR ROBERT (1572 ?–1636), king's serjeant; of Pembroke Hall, Cambridge; barrister, Gray's Inn; M.P., West Looe, 1597, Lynn Regis, 1614, Orford, 1625; attorney-general to James I's queen, 1603; knighted, 1603; king's serjeant, 1616. [xxvii. 14]

HITCHCOCK, RICHARD (1825–1856), Irish archæologist. [xxvii. 14]

HITCHCOCK, ROBERT (*fl.* 1580–1591), military writer; commissioned to raise volunteers in Buckinghamshire for service in Low Countries, 1586; published 'A Politique Platt,' 1580, expounding scheme for developing Newfoundland herring fisheries, and an edition of William Garrard's 'Arte of Warre,' 1591, and other works; left also military writings in manuscript. [Suppl. ii. 427]

HITCHCOCK, ROBERT (*d.* 1809), dramatic author; published 'The Macaroni,' 1773, 'The Coquette,' 1777, and 'Historical View of the Irish Stage,' 1788–94. [xxvii. 15]

HITCHINS, FORTESCUE (1784–1814), Cornish poet and historian; son of Malachy Hitchins [q. v.] [xxvii. 15]

HITCHINS, MALACHY (1741–1809), astronomer; B.A. Exeter College, Oxford, 1781; M.A. St. John's College, Cambridge, 1785; computer and comparer at Greenwich under Neville Maskelyne [q. v.]; vicar of St. Hilary and Gwinear, Cornwall; verified calculations for 'Nautical Almanack.' [xxvii. 15]

HOADLY, BENJAMIN (1706–1757), physician; son of Benjamin Hoadly (1676–1761) [q. v.]; M.D. Corpus Christi College, Cambridge, 1728; F.R.S., 1728; F.R.C.P., 1736; Gulstonian lecturer, 1737; Harveian orator, 1742; physician to George II, 1742; his comedy, 'The Suspicious Husband' (1747), acted at Covent Garden, Garrick taking part. [xxvii. 16]

HOADLY, BENJAMIN (1676–1761), bishop successively of Bangor, Hereford, Salisbury, and Winchester;

son of Samuel Hoadly [q. v.]; fellow of Catharine Hall, Cambridge, 1697–1701; M.A., 1699; lecturer of St. Mildred's, Poultry, London, 1701–11, rector of St. Peter-le-Poor, Broad Street, London, 1704–21, of Streatham, 1710–23; chaplain to George I, 1715; opposed occasional conformity bill, but published against Calamy 'Persuasive to Lay Conformity,' 1704, 'Defence of Reasonableness of Conformity,' 1707, and similar treatises; upheld whig doctrine of resistance against Atterbury and Bishop Blackall, 1709–10; wrote satirical 'Dedication to Pope Clement XI' for Steele's 'Account of state of Roman Catholic Religion,' 1715; bishop of Bangor, 1715–21; by his 'Preservative against Principles and Practices of the Nonjurors,' 1716, and sermon on 'Nature of the Kingdom or Church of Christ,' 1717, caused Bangorian controversy (1717–20) and the silencing of convocation; his 'Reply to Representation of Convocation' Hoadly's chief contribution; bishop of Hereford, 1721–3; as 'Britannicus' attacked Atterbury in 'London Journal,' 1721; bishop of Salisbury, 1723–34; published pamphlets on foreign affairs, 1725, and 'Essay on Life and Writings of Dr. Samuel Clarke,' 1732; bishop of Winchester, 1734–61; Waterland's treatise on the Eucharist elicited by his 'Plain Account of the Nature and End of the Sacrament,' 1735; advocated repeal of Corporation and Test Acts, 1736; eulogised by Akenside, but derided by Pope and Swift. [xxvii. 16]

HOADLY, JOHN (1678–1746), archbishop successively of Dublin and Armagh; brother of Benjamin Hoadly (1676–1761) [q. v.]; B.A. Catharine Hall, Cambridge, 1697; chaplain to Bishop Burnet; prebendary (1706), archdeacon (1710), and chancellor (1713) of Salisbury; friend of Chubb the deist; rector of Ockham, Surrey, 1717; bishop of Leighlin and Ferns, 1727; archbishop of Dublin, 1730; primate of Ireland; archbishop of Armagh, 1742; shared with Shannon chief direction of Irish politics. [xxvii. 21]

HOADLY, JOHN (1711–1776), poet and dramatist; son of Benjamin Hoadly (1676–1761) [q. v.]; LL.B. Corpus Christi College, Cambridge, 1735; chancellor of Winchester, 1735; chaplain to Frederick, prince of Wales, and princess dowager; LL.D. Lambeth, 1748; master of St. Cross, Winchester, 1760–76; friend of Garrick and Hogarth; had poems in Dodsley's 'Collection'; wrote words to oratorios and musical plays; assisted his brother, Benjamin Hoadly (1706–1757) [q. v.] in 'The Suspicious Husband'; edited his father's works. [xxvii. 22]

HOADLY, SAMUEL (1643–1705), schoolmaster; studied at Edinburgh; head-master of Norwich school, 1700–5; published 'Natural Method of Teaching' (1683), with school editions of Phædrus and Publius Syrus, 1700. [xxvii. 22]

HOADLY, SARAH (*d.* 1743), portrait-painter; *née* Curtis; first wife of Bishop Benjamin Hoadly [q. v.] [xxvii. 23]

HOAR, LEONARD (1630 ?–1675), president of Harvard College; emigrated to America and graduated at Harvard, 1650; returned to England, 1653; ejected from Wanstead, Essex, 1662; returned to Harvard; M.D. Cambridge, 1671; president of Harvard College, 1672–5; published 'Index Biblicus' (1668) and 'First Catalogue of Members of Harvard College' (printed, 1864). [xxvii. 23]

HOARD, SAMUEL (1599–1658), divine; M.A. St. Mary Hall, Oxford, 1621; B.D., 1632; prebendary of St. Paul's, 1637; published theological works. [xxvii. 23]

HOARE, CHARLES JAMES (1781–1865), archdeacon of Surrey; second wrangler and Smith's prizeman, St. John's College, Cambridge, 1803; fellow, 1806; M.A., 1806; Seatonian prizeman, 1807; vicar of Blandford, 1807–21, of Godstone, 1821–65; archdeacon of Winchester, 1829, and canon, 1831; archdeacon of Surrey, 1847–60; published religious works. [xxvii. 24]

HOARE, CLEMENT (1789–1849), vine-grower and writer on viticulture. [xxvii. 25]

HOARE, MICHAEL (*fl.* 1752). [See HALFPENNY, WILLIAM.]

HOARE, PRINCE (1755–1834), artist and author; son of William Hoare [q. v.]; exhibited at Royal Academy, 1781–5; made hon. foreign secretary of Academy, 1799; published 'Academic Correspondence,' 1804, and 'Academic Annals of Painting,' 1805; best known of his plays, 'No Song, No Supper' (Drury Lane, 1790). [xxvii. 25]

HOARE, SIR RICHARD (1648–1718), lord mayor of London; founded bank and raised government loans; knighted, 1702; sheriff of London, 1709; tory M.P. for the city, 1710–15; master of Goldsmiths' Company, 1712; lord mayor, 1712. [xxvii. 25]

HOARE, SIR RICHARD (d. 1754), lord mayor of London; grandson of Sir Richard Hoare (1648–1718) [q. v.]; journal of his shrievalty (1741) printed by Sir Richard Colt Hoare [q. v.], 1815. [xxvii. 26]

HOARE, SIR RICHARD COLT, second baronet (1758–1838), historian of Wiltshire; grandson of Sir Richard Hoare (d. 1754) [q. v.]; published works, including 'History of Modern Wiltshire,' 1822–44, 'Ancient History of North and South Wiltshire,' 1812–21, journals of tours in Ireland (1807), Elba (1814), Italy and Sicily (1819), a topographical catalogue of the British isles (1815), and monographs on Wiltshire genealogy, topography, and archæology; F.R.S. and F.S.A. [xxvii. 26]

HOARE, WILLIAM (1707 ?–1792), portrait-painter; reputed the first English artist who visited Rome to study; lodged with Scheemakers, and made acquaintance of Batoni; travelled in France and the Netherlands, 1749; one of those who attempted to form an academy in England, 1755; an original academician, 1768; exhibited till 1783, chiefly crayons; painted portraits of Chatham, Beau Nash, and others; executed also a whole length of Grafton, and crayons of Chesterfield and Pope. [xxvii. 28]

HOARE, WILLIAM HENRY (1809–1888), divine; fellow of St. John's College, Cambridge, 1833; M.A., 1834; took part in Colenso controversy; published 'Outlines of Ecclesiastical History before the Reformation,' 1852. [xxvii. 29]

HOBART, GEORGE, third EARL OF BUCKINGHAMSHIRE (1732–1804), son of John Hobart, first earl [q. v.]; M.P., St. Ives, 1754–61, Beeralston, 1761–80; secretary of St. Petersburg embassy, 1762; succeeded as third earl, 1793; manager of the opera. [xxvii. 30]

HOBART, SIR HENRY, first baronet (d. 1625), judge; great-grandson of Sir James Hobart [q. v.]; barrister, Lincoln's Inn, 1584, governor, 1591; M.P., St. Ives, 1588, Yarmouth, 1597 and 1601, Norwich, 1604–10; serjeant-at-law, 1603; attorney-general, 1606–13; appeared for plaintiffs in 'post-nati' case; created baronet, 1611; chief-justice of common pleas, 1613–25; chancellor to Prince Charles, 1617; successfully opposed Coke in Suffolk case, 1619; his reports published, 1641. [xxvii. 30]

HOBART, SIR JAMES (d. 1507), attorney-general, 1486–1507; of Lincoln's Inn; knighted, 1503; friend of John Paston. [xxvii. 31]

HOBART, JOHN, first EARL OF BUCKINGHAMSHIRE (1694 ?–1756), politician; of Clare Hall, Cambridge; M.P., St. Ives, 1715 and 1722–7, Norfolk, 1727–8; a commissioner of trade, 1721; treasurer of the chamber, 1727; created Baron Hobart, 1728, Earl of Buckinghamshire, 1746; lord-lieutenant of Norfolk and privy councillor, 1745. [xxvii. 31]

HOBART, JOHN, second EARL OF BUCKINGHAMSHIRE (1723–1793), lord-lieutenant of Ireland; son of John Hobart, first earl of Buckinghamshire [q. v.]; of Westminster School and Christ's College, Cambridge; M.P., Norwich, 1747–56; comptroller of the household, 1755; lord of the bedchamber, 1756–67; ambassador to Russia, 1762–5; as viceroy of Ireland (1777–80) had to concede free trade and measures for relief of Romanists and dissenters. [xxvii. 32]

HOBART, SIR MILES (d. 1632), politician; knighted, 1623; when M.P. for Great Marlow locked the door of the house during debate of 2 March, 1629; imprisoned for two years; died by carriage accident; monument voted to him by parliament, 1647. [xxvii. 33]

HOBART, ROBERT, BARON HOBART, fourth EARL OF BUCKINGHAMSHIRE (1760–1816), statesman; eldest son of George Hobart, third earl of Buckinghamshire [q. v.]; of Winchester College; served in American war; represented Bramber and Lincoln, 1788–94, and in Irish parliament Portarlington and Armagh; aide-de-camp to viceroy of Ireland, 1784–8; as chief secretary, 1789–93, acted with protestant party; English privy councillor, 1793; as governor of Madras, 1794–8, conducted expedition against Malacca; took part in war against Tippoo Sahib; recalled owing to difference with Sir John Shore

(afterwards Lord Teignmouth) [q. v.], 1798; summoned as Baron Hobart, 1798; assisted Auckland (1799) in arranging details of Irish union; secretary for war and the colonies, 1801–4; Hobart Town named after him; chancellor of the duchy of Lancaster, 1805 and 1812; postmaster-general under Grenville, 1807; president of board of control, 1812–16; killed by an accident while riding. [xxvii. 34]

HOBART, VERE HENRY, BARON HOBART (1818–1875), governor of Madras; B.A. Trinity College, Oxford, 1840; clerk in board of trade, 1840–61; reported on Turkish finance, and became director-general of Ottoman Bank; governor of Madras, 1872–5, where he died of typhoid; his 'Essays and Miscellaneous Writings' edited by Lady Hobart, 1885. [xxvii. 35]

HOBART-HAMPDEN, AUGUSTUS CHARLES, known as HOBART PASHA (1822–1886), vice-admiral; brother of Vere Henry Hobart, baron Hobart [q. v.]; entered British navy and distinguished himself on South American station against slavers; during Russian war did good service in Baltic (1854–5), and was promoted; retired as captain, 1863; ran blockade off North Carolina during American civil war; became naval adviser to sultan of Turkey, 1867; created pasha (1869) and mushir (1881) for services in reduction of Crete; commanded Black Sea fleet in Russian war, 1877–8; reinstated in British navy (as vice-admiral), 1885; died at Milan; 'Sketches of My Life' issued, 1887. [xxvii. 36]

HOBBES, ROBERT (d. 1538), last abbot of Woburn, 1529–38; acknowledged royal supremacy, 1534, but proved recalcitrant and was executed. [xxvii. 37]

HOBBES, THOMAS (1588–1679), philosopher; educated at Malmesbury and Magdalen Hall, Oxford; B.A., 1608; twenty years tutor and secretary to William Cavendish [q. v.], afterwards second Earl of Devonshire, and his son; his translation of Thucydides published, 1629; at Paris with Sir Gervase Clifton's son, 1629–31; visiting Italy and Paris, 1634, met Galileo, Gassendi, and Mersenne; said to have been Bacon's amanuensis; intimate with Harvey, Ben Jonson, Cowley, and Sidney Godolphin (1610–1643) [q. v.]; resided at Paris, 1641–52; transmitted anonymous objections to Descartes's positions, published his 'Leviathan' (1651), and acted as mathematical tutor to Charles II; on his return to England submitted to council of state; saw much of Harvey and Selden; engaged in controversies with Bramhall in defence of his religion and philosophy, and with Seth Ward [q. v.], Boyle, and John Wallis (1616–1703) [q. v.], on mathematical questions, the last exposing many of his blunders; received pension from Charles II, and was protected by him against Clarendon and the church party; his 'Behemoth' suppressed; left London, 1675; wrote autobiography in Latin verse at eighty-four and completed translation of Homer at eighty-six; buried in Hault Hucknall church. In metaphysics a thoroughgoing nominalist; his political philosophy (chiefly in 'Leviathan'), arguing that the body politic has been formed as the only alternative to a natural state of war, was attacked by Sir Robert Filmer [q. v.], but mentioned with respect in Harrington's 'Oceana.' It influenced Spinoza, Leibnitz, and Rousseau, and was revived in England by the utilitarians. The chief critics of his metaphysical and ethical writings were Clarendon, Tenison, the Cambridge Platonists, and Samuel Clarke. The standard edition of his works is that of Sir W. Molesworth (1839–45). His works include, besides those mentioned, 'De Cive' (1642; English, 1651), 'Human Nature' (1650), 'De Corpore Politico' (originally 'Elements of Law'), 1680, 'De Homine' (1658), 'Quadratura Circuli,' and other geometrical treatises, and 'Behemoth, or the Long Parliament' (edited by Dr. Ferdinand Tönnies, 1889). [xxvii. 37]

HOBDAY, WILLIAM ARMFIELD (1771–1831), portrait-painter; exhibited many years at Academy; opened galleries in Pall Mall for sale of pictures on commission but failed; best work, picture of Carolus the hermit Tong. [xxvii. 45]

HOBHOUSE, SIR BENJAMIN, first baronet (1757–1831), politician; M.A. Brasenose College, Oxford, 1781; barrister, Middle Temple, 1781; M.P., Bletchingley, 1797, Grampound, 1802, and Hindon, 1806–18; secretary to board of control under Addington, 1803; chairman of committees, 1805; created baronet, 1812; published legal treatises. [xxvii. 46]

HOBHOUSE, HENRY (1776–1854), archivist; of Eton and Brasenose College, Oxford; M.A., 1799; D.C.L., 1827; barrister, Middle Temple, 1801; solicitor to the customs, 1806, to Treasury, 1812; permanent under-secretary for home department, 1817–27; privy councillor, 1828; keeper of state papers, 1826–54; superintended publication of 'State Papers of Henry VIII.' [xxvii. 46]

HOBHOUSE, JOHN CAM, BARON BROUGHTON DE GYFFORD (1786–1869), statesman; son of Sir Benjamin Hobhouse [q. v.]; of Westminster and Trinity College, Cambridge; won Hulsean prize, 1808; M.A., 1811; founded Cambridge Whig Club; travelled with Byron in Spain, Portugal, Greece, and Turkey; wrote, from personal observation, Bonapartist account of the 'Hundred Days,' 1816; visited Byron in Switzerland and Italy and wrote notes for Canto IV of 'Childe Harold'; unsuccessfully contested Westminster as a radical, 1819; sent to Newgate for breach of privilege, 1819; returned for Westminster, 1820; as Byron's executor advised destruction of his 'Memoirs,' 1824; active member of Greek committee in London; succeeded as baronet, 1831; secretary at war, 1832–3; chief secretary for Ireland, March–April, 1833; resigned on house and window-tax, 1833; defeated when candidate for Westminster; elected for Nottingham, 1834; commissioner of woods and forests under Melbourne, 1834; president of board of control, 1835–41 and 1846–52; defeated at Nottingham, 1847; elected for Harwich, 1848; created peer, 1851; said to have invented phrase 'his majesty's opposition'; as Byron's 'best man' drew up reply (unpublished) to Lady Byron's 'Remarks'; left manuscript 'Diaries, Correspondence, and Memoranda, &c., not to be opened till 1900.' His works include 'Italy: Remarks made in several visits' (1859), and 'Recollections of a Long Life,' 1865. [xxvii. 47]

HOBLYN, RICHARD DENNIS (1803–1886), educational writer; M.A. Balliol College, Oxford, 1828; chief work, 'Dictionary of Terms used in Medicine.' [xxvii. 50]

HOBLYN, ROBERT (1710–1756), book collector; of Eton and Corpus Christi College, Oxford; B.C.L., 1734; M.P., Bristol, 1742–54; F.R.S., 1745; twice speaker of Stannary parliament; his 'Bibliotheca Hobliniana' printed, 1768; library sold, 1778. [xxvii. 50]

HOBSON, EDWARD (1782–1830), botanist and entomologist; first president of Banksian Society, 1829; published 'Musci Britannici' (1818–24). [xxvii. 51]

HOBSON, RICHARD (1795–1868), physician; of St. George's Hospital and Queens' College, Cambridge; M.D., 1830; physician to Leeds Infirmary, 1833–43; attended Charles Waterton [q. v.] and wrote a book on him (1866). [xxvii. 51]

HOBSON, THOMAS (1544?–1631), Cambridge carrier; referred to in 'Spectator'; presented to Cambridge site of Spinning House, and provided for a conduit; refused always to let out any horse out of its proper turn ('Hobson's choice,' this or none). [xxvii. 52]

HOBY, SIR EDWARD (1560–1617), favourite of James I; son of Sir Thomas Hoby [q. v.]; of Eton and Trinity College, Oxford; M.A., 1576; knighted, 1582; accompanied his father-in-law, Lord Hunsdon, to Scotland, 1584; M.P. for Queenborough, Berkshire, Kent, and Rochester; accompanied Cadiz expedition, 1596; constable of Queenborough, 1597; gentleman of privy chamber to James I; often entertained James I at Bisham; carried on controversies with Theophilus Higgons [q. v.] and John Floyd [q. v.]; translated from French and Spanish; friend and patron of Camden. [xxvii. 52]

HOBY, ELIZABETH, LADY (1528–1609), linguist; wife of Sir Thomas Hoby [q. v.]; afterwards married John, lord Russell, 1574. [xxvii. 56]

HOBY, PEREGRINE (1602–1678), natural son and heir of Sir Edward Hoby; M.P., Great Marlow, 1640, 1660, and 1661. [xxvii. 53]

HOBY, SIR PHILIP (1505–1558), diplomatist; knighted after capture of Boulogne, 1544; ambassador to the Emperor Charles V, 1548; treated for marriage of Edward VI with a French princess, 1551; employed financially in Flanders; privy councillor, master of the ordnance, and grantee of Bisham, 1552; ambassador in Flanders, 1553; brought message from Philip II to Queen Mary, 1556; friend of Titian and Aretino. [xxvii. 54]

HOBY, SIR THOMAS (1530–1566), diplomatist and translator; half-brother of Sir Philip Hoby [q. v.]; of St. John's College, Cambridge; knighted, 1566; translated Martin Bucer's 'Gratulation' to the church of England, 1549, and 'The Courtyer of Count Baldessar Castilio,' 1561; died in Paris, while ambassador to France. [xxvii. 55]

HOCCLEVE or OCCLEVE, THOMAS (1370?–1450?), poet; clerk in privy seal office; granted annuity by Henry IV; portrait of Chaucer contained in his 'De Regimine Principum,' written c. 1411–12 (English), edited by Thomas Wright, 1860; his 'Mother of God' and 'La Male Regle' (autobiography), printed, 1796; the former once attributed to Chaucer. [xxvii. 56]

HODDER, JAMES (fl. 1661), arithmetician; author of 'Arithmetick,' 1661, 'The Penman's Recreation,' and 'Decimal Arithmetick,' 1668. [xxvii. 57]

HODDESDON, SIR CHRISTOPHER (1534–1611), master of Merchants Adventurers' Company; accompanied Richard Chancellor [q. v.] on voyages to Russia; head of English factory at Moscow, 1557–62; sent to develop English trade in Baltic, 1567; chief of English factory at Narva, 1569; employed as financial agent to Queen Elizabeth in Germany from c. 1574; master of Merchants Adventurers at Hamburg, 1578; M.P., Cambridge, 1593; sheriff of Bedfordshire, 1591–2; master of Merchants Adventurers' Company before 1600; knighted, 1603. [Suppl. ii. 428]

HODDESDON, JOHN (fl. 1650), religious writer; friend of Dryden; published 'Sion and Parnassus,' 1650, and biographical compilation on Sir Thomas More, 1652. [xxvii. 57]

HODGE, ARTHUR (d. 1811), West Indian planter; executed for causing death of negroes on his estate in Tortola. [xxvii. 58]

HODGES, CHARLES HOWARD (1764–1837), mezzotint-engraver and portrait-painter; engraved portraits after Reynolds, Romney, C. G. Stuart, and Hoppner, and subject-pictures after old masters; settled at Amsterdam, 1794, and painted portraits of William I of the Netherlands, Louis, king of Holland, himself, and his daughter. [xxvii. 58]

HODGES, EDWARD (1796–1867), organist at Clifton, Bristol, and New York, 1839–63; Mus. Doc. Sidney Sussex College, Cambridge; composed and wrote works on church music, 1825. [xxvii. 59]

HODGES, EDWARD RICHMOND (1826–1881), orientalist; missionary to Jews in Palestine and Algeria; assisted George Smith (1840–1876) [q. v.] in cuneiform researches, and Gotch with 'Paragraph Bible'; edited Craik's 'Principia Hebraica,' 1863, Cory's 'Ancient Fragments,' 1876, and revised Mickle's 'Lusiadas,' 1877. [xxvii. 59]

HODGES, NATHANIEL (1629–1688), physician; scholar of Westminster and Trinity College, Cambridge; student of Christ Church, Oxford; M.A., 1654; M.D., 1659; attended patients throughout plague of 1665; published an account, 1672; F.R.C.P., 1672; censor, 1682; died while in prison for debt. [xxvii. 59]

HODGES, SIR WILLIAM, first baronet (1645?–1714?) Spanish merchant; created baronet, 1697, for financial assistance to government; published pamphlets advocating relief of British seamen from extortion. [xxvii. 60]

HODGES, WILLIAM (1744–1797), landscape-painter; exhibited at Society of Artists, 1766–72; draughtsman in Captain Cook's second expedition, 1772–5; exhibited at Academy view of Otaheite, 1776; painted views in India under patronage of Warren Hastings, 1778–84; published 'Travels in India,' 1793; R.A., 1789; visited St. Petersburg, 1790. [xxvii. 61]

HODGES, SIR WILLIAM (1808–1868), chief-justice of Cape of Good Hope; barrister, Inner Temple, 1833; published reports of common pleas, queen's bench cases, and treatises on railway law; recorder of Poole, 1846; drafted Public Health Act, 1848; knighted, 1857; chief-justice of Cape of Good Hope, 1857–68. [xxvii. 62]

HODGKIN, JOHN (1766–1845), calligraphist; described in manuscript autobiography events during residence at Vincennes, 1792; tutor in London; works include 'Calligraphia' and 'Pœcilographia Græca,' 1807, and 'Introduction to Writing' (4th edit. 1811). [xxvii. 62]

HODGKIN, JOHN (1800–1875), barrister and quaker; son of John Hodgkin (1766–1845) [q. v.] ; friend of John Stuart Mill ; advocated register of titles ; assisted in preparation of Encumbered Estates Act, 1849 ; visited quakers in Ireland, France, and America. [xxvii. 63]

HODGKIN, THOMAS (1798–1866), physician ; brother of John Hodgkin (1800–1875) [q. v.] ; M.D. Edinburgh, 1823 ; curator and pathologist at Guy's Hospital, 1825 ; member of London University senate ; published 'Essay on Medical Education,' 1828, 'Lectures on Morbid Anatomy of Serous and Mucous Membranes,' 1836, and biographical works ; glandular disease named after him ; a founder of Aborigines Protection Society, 1838 ; died at Jaffa. [xxvii. 63]

HODGKINSON, EATON (1789–1861), writer on the strength of materials ; made experiments resulting in 'Hodgkinson's beam,' and gave theoretical expositions ; F.R.S., with royal medal for paper on 'Strength of Pillars of Cast Iron and other Materials,' 1840 ; royal commissioner on application of iron to railways, 1847–9 ; professor of mechanical engineering of University College, London, 1847 ; president of Manchester Literary and Philosophical Society, 1848–50 ; published 'Experimental Researches on the Strength, etc. of Cast Iron,' 1846. [xxvii. 64]

HODGKINSON, GEORGE CHRISTOPHER (1816–1880), meteorologist and educationalist ; M.A. Trinity College, Cambridge, 1842 ; principal of Royal Agricultural College, Cirencester, of Diocesan Training College, York ; head-master of Louth grammar school, 1864–76 ; secretary of National Society ; made astronomical observations on Mont Blanc. [xxvii. 65]

HODGSON, BERNARD (1745 ?–1805), principal of Hertford College, Oxford ; captain of Westminster, 1764 ; student of Christ Church, Oxford ; M.A., 1771 ; D.C.L., 1776 ; principal of Hertford College, 1775–1805 ; translated Solomon's Song, Proverbs, and Ecclesiastes. [xxvii. 66]

HODGSON, BRIAN HOUGHTON (1800–1894), Indian civilian and orientalist ; nominated to Bengal writership, 1816 ; studied at East India Company's College, Hailey-bury, and at college of Fort William ; assistant-commissioner of Kumaon, c. 1818–20 ; assistant-resident at Kathmandu, 1820–9, acting resident, 1829–31, and resident, 1833–1843 ; came to England, 1843, but returned to India in private capacity to continue researches ; studied ethnology at Darjiling ; finally left India, 1858 ; F.R.S., 1877 ; honorary D.C.L. Oxford, 1889 ; while in India made valuable collections of original Sanskrit and Tibetan manuscripts, which he distributed among public libraries. His works include 'Illustrations of Literature and Religion of the Buddhists,' 1841, and 'Essays on Language, Literature, and Religion of Nepal and Tibet,' 1874. [Suppl. ii. 429]

HODGSON, CHRISTOPHER PEMBERTON (1821–1865), traveller ; vice-consul at Pau, 1851–5, Caen, and in Japan, 1859–61 ; published 'Reminiscences of Australia,' 'El Udaivar,' 1849, and other works ; died at Pau. [xxvii. 66]

HODGSON, EDWARD (1719–1794), flower-painter ; treasurer to Associated Artists of Great Britain. [xxvii. 66]

HODGSON, FRANCIS (1781–1852), provost of Eton ; at Eton under Keate ; fellow of King's College, Cambridge, 1802, tutor, 1807 ; M.A., 1807 ; B.D., 1840 ; archdeacon of Derby, 1836 ; provost of Eton, 1840–52 ; friend of Lord Byron ; translated Juvenal (1807) and published English verse. [xxvii. 66]

HODGSON, JAMES (1672–1755), mathematician ; master of Royal School of Mathematics, Christ's Hospital ; F.R.S., 1703 ; helped to edit Flamsteed's 'Atlas Cœlestis' ; published also 'Doctrine of Fluxions founded on Sir Isaac Newton's Method,' 1736, and other works. [xxvii. 67]

HODGSON, JOHN (d. 1684), author of 'Memoirs' (published, 1806, with Sir Henry Slingsby's 'Original Memoirs ') ; served under Fairfax in Yorkshire ; taken by Newcastle at Bradford, 1643 ; present at sieges of Pontefract, 1645 and 1648, and battle of Preston, 1648 ; described battle of Dunbar, 1650 ; refused to fight against Lambert, 1659. [xxvii. 67]

HODGSON, JOHN (1779–1845), antiquary ; schoolmaster at Sedgefield, Lanchester, and other places ; incumbent of Jarrow, 1808, Kirk Whelpington, 1823, and

Hartburn, 1833 ; published part of a large history of Northumberland, guide-book to Newcastle, 1812, 'Account of the [colliery] Explosion at Felling,' 1813, and other works; assisted Davy in invention of safety lamp; built Heworth Church (consecrated, 1822). [xxvii. 68]

HODGSON, JOHN (1757–1846), general ; son of Studholme Hodgson [q. v.] ; served in North America ; wounded in Holland, 1799; governor of Bermuda and Curaçoa ; general, 1830. [xxvii. 70]

HODGSON, JOHN EVAN (1831–1895), painter ; educated at Rugby ; student at Royal Academy, 1853 ; exhibited at Royal Academy from 1856 ; R.A., 1879 ; librarian and professor of painting at Royal Academy, 1882 till death ; published lectures and other writings. [Suppl. ii. 432]

HODGSON, JOHN STUDHOLME (1805–1870), major-general in Bengal army ; second son of John Hodgson (1757–1846) [q. v.] ; wounded at Sobraon, 1846 ; raised and commanded 1st Sikh regiment, 1848–9 ; promoted for capture of Ukrot ; organised Punjab irregular force, 1850 ; major-general, 1861. [xxvii. 70]

HODGSON, JOSEPH (1756–1821), Roman catholic divine ; when vice-president of Douay College, imprisoned by revolutionists ; published an account ; vicar-general to bishops Douglas and Poynter in England. [xxvii. 71]

HODGSON, JOSEPH (1788–1869), surgeon ; studied at St. Bartholomew's Hospital ; surgeon to Birmingham Dispensary, 1818–48 ; president of Medico-Chirurgical Society, 1851, of College of Surgeons, 1864 ; F.R.S. ; published treatise on diseases of arteries and veins, 1815. [xxvii. 71]

HODGSON, STUDHOLME (1708–1798), field-marshal ; aide-de-camp of Duke of Cumberland at Fontenoy, 1745, and Culloden, 1746 ; raised royal West Kent regiment (then 52nd), 1756 ; commanded brigade in Rochefort expedition, 1757 ; conducted siege of Belleisle, 1761 ; general, 1778 ; field-marshal, 1796. [xxvii. 72]

HODGSON, STUDHOLME JOHN (d. 1890), general ; son of John Hodgson (1757–1846) [q. v.] ; commanded forces in Ceylon and Straits Settlements. [xxvii. 70]

HODGSON, WILLIAM (1745–1851), politician and author ; imprisoned and fined for revolutionary speech, 1793 ; M.D. ; published educational manuals and other works. [xxvii. 72]

HODGSON, WILLIAM BALLANTYNE (1815–1880), educational reformer ; studied at Edinburgh ; principal of Liverpool Mechanics' Institute, 1844 ; LL.D. Glasgow, 1846 ; principal of Chorlton High School, Manchester, 1847–51 ; assisted in inquiry into primary education, 1858 ; leading member of council of University College, London ; first professor of political economy and mercantile law at Edinburgh, 1871–80 ; president of Educational Institute of Scotland, 1875 ; published, among other works, 'Turgot' (1870), and lectures and treatises on girls' education and the study of economic science ; joint-editor of William Johnson Fox's works ; died at Brussels. [xxvii. 73]

HODSON, FRODSHAM (1770–1822), principal of Brasenose College, Oxford ; M.A. Brasenose College, Oxford, 1793 ; D.D., 1809 ; principal of Brasenose, 1809–22 ; vice-chancellor, 1818 ; regius professor of divinity, 1820 ; edited Falconer's 'Chronological Tables,' 1796. [xxvii. 73]

HODSON, Mrs. MARGARET (1778–1852), authoress ; née Holford ; married Septimus Hodson [q. v.], 1826 ; friend and correspondent of Southey ; works include 'Wallace,' 'Margaret of Anjou' (1815), and 'Lives of Vasco Nuñez de Balboa and Francisco Pizarro' from the Spanish, 1832. [xxvii. 74]

HODSON, SEPTIMUS (1768–1833), rector of Thrapston and chaplain to Prince of Wales ; published 'Address on High Price of Provisions,' 1795. [xxvii. 74]

HODSON, WILLIAM (fl. 1640), theological writer ; M.A. Peterhouse, Cambridge, 1624 ; published theological works. [xxvii. 74]

HODSON, WILLIAM STEPHEN RAIKES (1821–1858), cavalry leader ; B.A. Trinity College, Cambridge, 1844 ; entered Indian army, 1845 ; served with 2nd grenadiers in Sikh war ; adjutant of the guides, 1847 ; assistant-commissioner under Sir Henry Lawrence in Punjab, 1849 ; commander of guides, 1852–4 ; removed on charge of dishonesty, 1855, but cleared by a second inquiry, 1856 ; served with 1st fusiliers till given commission during Mutiny to raise 'Hodson's horse'; after capture of Delhi seized the king in Humayoon's tomb and shot the Shahzadas when rescue attempted ; did good service at Cawnpore and Lucknow ; was shot at Lucknow and buried there. [xxvii. 75]

HODY, HUMPHREY (1659-1707), divine : scholar, 1677, fellow, 1685, dean, 1688, and bursar, 1691 and 1692, of Wadham College, Oxford ; M.A., 1682 ; D.D., 1692 ; chaplain to Bishop Stillingfleet, and afterwards to Archbishops Tillotson and Tenison ; regius professor of Greek at Oxford, 1698 ; archdeacon of Oxford, 1704 ; founded Greek and Hebrew exhibitions at Wadham ; attacked the genuineness of Aristeas's account of the Septuagint, 1684 ; assisted in editing Aristeas's 'History,' 1692 ; conducted controversy with Henry Dodwell the elder [q. v.] on nonjuring schism, 1691-9 ; published also 'Resurrection of the Body asserted,' 1694, 'De Bibliorum Textibus Originalibus,' 1705, and other works ; his 'De Græcis Illustribus' edited by Samuel Jebb, 1742. [xxvii. 77]

HODY, Sir JOHN (d. 1441), judge : M.P., Shaftesbury, 1423, 1425, 1428, and 1438, Somerset, 1434 and 1440 ; chiefjustice of the king's bench, 1440 ; assisted Lyttelton. [xxvii. 78]

HODY, Sir WILLIAM (d. 1522 ?), chief baron of the exchequer, 1486 ; second son of Sir John Hody [q. v.] ; attorney-general and serjeant-at-law, 1485. [xxvii. 78]

HOFLAND, BARBARA (1770-1844), authoress and friend of Miss Mitford ; married, first, T. Bradshaw Hoole, 1796, and secondly (1808) Thomas Christopher Hofland [q. v.] ; published novels, including 'The Son of a Genius,' 1816. [xxvii. 78]

HOFLAND, THOMAS CHRISTOPHER (1777-1843), landscape-painter ; exhibited at Academy, 1799-1805 ; gained British Institution prize for 'Storm off Scarborough,' 1814 ; held exhibition in Bond Street, 1821 ; foundation member of Society of British Artists ; published 'British Angler's Manual' (1839). [xxvii. 79]

HOG or **HOGG**, JAMES (1658 ?-1734), leader of 'Marrow men' in church of Scotland ; M.A. Edinburgh, 1677 ; declined oath of allegiance, 1693 ; minister of Carnock, 1699-1734 ; republished 'Marrow of Modern Divinity,' 1718 ; denounced by general assembly, 1720 ; published controversial pamphlets. [xxvii. 80]

HOG, Sir ROGER, LORD HARCARSE (1635 ?-1700), lord of session, 1677 ; knighted, 1677 ; lord of justiciary, 1678 ; removed, 1688 ; compiled 'Dictionary of Decisions,' (1681-92),' published, 1757. [xxvii. 80]

HOG, THOMAS (1628-1692), Scottish divine ; M.A. Marischal College, Aberdeen ; minister of Kiltearn, 1654-1661 and 1691-2 ; deposed as protester, 1661 ; imprisoned for keeping conventicles ; fined and banished, 1684 ; chaplain to William of Orange in Holland and when king. [xxvii. 81]

HOGAN, JOHN (1800-1858), Irish sculptor ; during residence at Rome, 1824-49, executed his 'Eve,' 'Drunken Faun,' and 'Dead Christ'; statues of O'Connell and Thomas Drummond by him at Dublin. [xxvii. 81]

HOGARTH, GEORGE (1783-1870), musical critic ; inserted in 'Evening Chronicle' sketches of London life by Dickens, afterwards his son-in-law ; musical critic of 'Daily News,' 1846-66, also of 'Illustrated London News'; secretary of Philharmonic Society, 1850-64 ; published 'Musical History, Biography, and Criticism,' 1835, and other works on music. [xxvii. 82]

HOGARTH, WILLIAM (1697-1764), painter and engraver ; apprenticed to silver-plate engraver in Cranbourne Street, London ; engraved and designed plates for booksellers and printsellers, including (1726) illustrations to 'Hudibras'; painted conversation-pieces, including scenes from 'Beggar's Opera,' 1728-9 ; engraved 'Large Masquerade Ticket,' 1727, and 'Taste,' 1731 ; married clandestinely, at old Paddington Church, Jane Thornhill, 1729 ('Sigismunda') ; assisted in decoration of Vauxhall and designed pass-tickets ; his paintings of 'The Harlot's Progress' engraved, 1732 ; took house in Leicester Square (then Fields) and executed portrait of Sarah Malcolm, murderess, 1733 ; his engraving of 'Rake's Progress' and 'Southwark Fair' issued complete, 1735, when 'Hogarth's Act,' protecting designers from piracy, became operative ; apostrophised by Swift in the 'Legion Club'; painted

historical pictures at St. Bartholomew's Hospital, 1736 ; issued the prints 'The Distrest Poet,' 'Company of Undertakers,' and 'Sleeping Congregation,' 1736 ; his 'Four Times of the Day,' 'Strolling Actresses dressing in a Barn,' produced, 1738 ; his 'Enraged Musician' praised by Fielding, 1741 ; his portraits of Captain Coram painted 1739, Martin Folkes [q. v.], 1741 ; his 'Marriage-à-la-Mode,' 1745, engraved by French masters ; etched Lord Lovat, 1746 ; painted himself and dog, 1749 ; engraved 'Industry and Idleness' and 'Stage Coach,' 1747 ; visited France and revenged himself for arrest by his 'Gate of Calais,' 1749 ; painted 'The March to Finchley' and 'Four Stages of Cruelty' (partly engraved on wood), 1750-1, 'Moses and Pharaoh's Daughter' and 'Paul before Felix,' 1752 ; published (with assistance) the 'Analysis of Beauty,' with etched ticket, 'Columbus breaking the egg,' 1753 ; issued the four 'Election' prints, 1755-8, 'England' and 'France,' 1756, 'The Bench,' 1758, 'Cockpit,' 1759, and 'Five Orders of Periwigs,' 1761 ; serjeant-painter, 1757 ; exhibited 'Picquet, or the Lady's Last Stake' and 'Sigismunda,' 1761 ; caricatured Wilkes and Churchill in 'The Times,' 1762, and etched Fielding ; his last plate, 'The Bathos,' 1764. His epitaph was written by Garrick. Many of his works are at the National Gallery, National Portrait Gallery, and Soane Museum. The 'Apprentice' and 'Cruelty' series, 'France and England,' 'Beer Street,' and 'Gin Lane,' were probably never painted. A large collection of his engravings was acquired by the British Museum, 1828. Hogarth hated foreigners, and attacked art connoisseurs for neglect of native talent. He excelled as a pictorial satirist in depicting both tragic and humorous scenes, always with a sincerely ethical intention. [xxvii. 83]

HOGARTH, WILLIAM (1786-1866), Roman catholic bishop ; professor and general prefect at Ushaw ; vicar-apostolic of northern district, 1848 ; first Roman catholic bishop of Hexham and Newcastle, 1850-66. [xxvii. 97]

HOGENBERG, FRANZ (d. 1590), engraver ; brother of Remigius Hogenberg [q. v.] [xxvii. 98]

HOGENBERG, REMIGIUS (d. 1580 ?), engraver ; came to England, c. 1573 ; employed by Archbishop Parker in constructing genealogies ; his engraving of Parker's portrait by Lyne said to be the first executed in England ; engraved maps and portraits of Henri IV, Erasmus, and others. [xxvii. 98]

HOGG, HENRY (1831-1874), Nottingham poet. [xxvii. 98]

HOGG, JABEZ (1817-1899), ophthalmic surgeon ; apprenticed to medical practitioner, 1832-7 ; joined staff of 'Illustrated London News'; editor and subeditor in various publishing undertakings ; studied at Hunterian School of Medicine and Charing Cross Hospital, 1845 ; M.R.C.S., 1850 ; surgeon to Royal Westminster Ophthalmic Hospital, 1871-8, and to hospital for women and children ; F.L.S., 1866 ; published scientific works. [Suppl. ii. 432]

HOGG, JAMES (1770-1835), the Ettrick Shepherd ; shepherd at Willanslee, c. 1785 ; while employed by the father of William Laidlaw [q. v.] began to write verse ; printed 'Donald M'Donald,' 1800, and 'Scottish Pastorals,' 1801 ; made acquaintance of Scott and gave material for 'Border Minstrelsy'; his ballads published by Constable as 'The Mountain Bard,' 1807 ; returned to Ettrick bankrupt, having failed as a farmer in Dumfriesshire ; came to Edinburgh, 1810, and published the 'Forest Minstrel'; obtained poetical reputation by 'The Queen's Wake,' 1813, and acquaintance, through Byron, of John Murray ; formed friendships with Professor John Wilson, Wordsworth, and Southey ; issued 'Pilgrims of the Sun,' 1815 ; 'The Poetic Mirror,' 1816 ; settled at Eltrive Lake, 1816 ; assisted in the Chaldee MS. for Blackwood's Magazine,' 1817, and began prose tales ; published 'Jacobite Relics' and 'Winter Evening Tales,' 1820, 'The Three Perils of Man,' 1822, 'Confessions of a Fanatic,' 1824, 'Queen Hynde,' 1826, 'Shepherd's Calendar' and 'Songs,' 1829 ; was entertained publicly in London, 1832, and at Peebles, 1833 ; issued 'Domestic Manners and Private Life of Sir Walter Scott,' 1834. A monument to him was erected on St. Mary's Lake, 1860. [xxvii. 98]

HOGG, JAMES (1806-1888), Edinburgh publisher ; edited 'The Weekly Instructor' or 'Titan,' 1845-59 ; published De Quincey's and Gilfillan's works, and 'London Society.' [xxvii. 101]

HOGG, SIR JAMES MACNAGHTEN McGAREL, first BARON MAGHERAMORNE (1823–1890), son of Sir James Weir Hogg [q. v.]; of Eton and Christ Church, Oxford; served in 1st life guards, 1843–59; conservative M.P., Bath, 1865–8, Truro, 1871–85, Hornsey, 1885–7; chairman of metropolitan board of works, 1870–89; created peer, 1887. [xxvii. 101]

HOGG, SIR JAMES WEIR, first baronet (1790–1876), East India director; scholar and gold medallist of Trinity College, Dublin; B.A., 1810; registrar of Calcutta supreme court, 1822–33; a director of East India Company, 1839, chairman, 1846–7 and 1852–3; M.P., Beverley, 1835–47, Honiton, 1847–57; created baronet, 1846; member of Indian council, 1858–72; privy councillor, 1872. [xxvii. 102]

HOGG, JOHN (1800–1869), scholar and naturalist; brother of Thomas Jefferson Hogg [q. v.]; fellow of Peterhouse, Cambridge, 1827; M.A., 1831; foreign secretary and vice-president of Royal Society of Literature, 1866; F.R.S., 1839; published 'Catalogue of Sicilian Plants,' 1842, and other works of natural history. [xxvii. 103]

HOGG, THOMAS JEFFERSON (1792–1862), friend and biographer of Shelley; at University College, Oxford, with Shelley; sent down on the publication of Shelley's 'Necessity of Atheism'; joined the poet and Harriet Shelley at Edinburgh; quarrel caused by his behaviour to Shelley's wife; published 'Memoirs of Prince Alexy Haimatoff,' 1813; called to bar, 1817; united himself to widow of Shelley's friend, Edward Elliker Williams [q. v.]; quarrelled with John Stuart Mill; contributed reminiscences of Shelley at Oxford to Bulwer's 'New Monthly Magazine,' 1832; municipal corporation commissioner, 1833; afterwards revising barrister; published two volumes of life of Shelley, 1858; contributed to 'Edinburgh Review' and 'Encyclopædia Britannica.' [xxvii. 104]

HOGGARDE, MILES (*fl.* 1557). [See HUGGARDE.]

HOGHTON, DANIEL (1770–1811), major-general; major, 1794; served in Jamaica and India; brevet lieutenant-colonel, 1796; lieutenant-colonel, 1804; brevet-colonel, 1805; brigadier at Cadiz, 1810; major-general, 1810; killed at Albuera. A public monument to him in St. Paul's Cathedral. [Suppl. ii. 433]

HOHENLOHE-LANGENBURG, PRINCE VICTOR OF, COUNT GLEICHEN (1833–1891). [See VICTOR.]

HOLBEACH or RANDS, HENRY (*d.* 1551), bishop of Lincoln; assumed name of birthplace (Holbeach) on entering Crowland monastery; D.D. Cambridge, 1534; prior of Buckingham College, 1535, of Worcester, 1536; bishop suffragan (Bristol) to Latimer, 1538; assisted in drawing up prayer-book (1548); first dean of Worcester, 1540; bishop of Rochester, 1544–7, bishop of Lincoln, 1547–51. [xxvii. 105]

HOLBEIN, HANS (1497–1543), painter; born at Augsburg; went to Lucerne; at Basle designed marginal illustrations in copy of Erasmus's 'Encomium Moriæ,' 1515, and painted portraits of Jacob Meyer and Hans Herbster, 1516, and mural paintings and religious works, 1521–2; executed paintings and designs at Lucerne, 1518; painted, c. 1526, the Darmstadt 'Madonna with Meyer family'; designed illustrations for Luther's German Testament and Pentateuch, 1522–3; painted three portraits of Erasmus, 1523; came to England, 1526, with introduction to Sir Thomas More; painted portraits of More, 1527, Warham, and others; designed large picture of More's household; during residence at Basle (1528–32) completed mural paintings at the town-hall, and probably executed portraits of his wife and children and of Erasmus; many of his religious works destroyed in an iconoclastic outbreak; returned to England and executed portraits of merchant goldsmiths; drew 'Queen of Sheba before Solomon'; painted 'The Ambassadors,' 1533, and the 'Morett' portrait; designed title-pages to Coverdale's (1535) and Cranmer's (1540) bible and other protestant publications; painted Cromwell and Jane Seymour, 1536; his 'Henry VIII with Parents' destroyed, 1698, but a copy preserved at Hampton Court; took part (1538) in negotiations for marriage of Henry VIII to Christina of Denmark and painted her portrait; publicly entertained at Basle, and brought out designs to Old Testament and 'The Dance of Death,' 1538; painted portraits of Anne of Cleves, 1539, Norfolk, Surrey, Sir John Russell, and others; began large picture at Barber-Surgeons' Hall, 1542; died of the plague in London. He was one of the earliest miniaturists, painting in that manner Catherine Howard and Anne of Cleves. Authentic pictures by Holbein are rare in England. [xxvii. 106]

HOLBORNE, ANTHONY (*fl.* 1597), musical composer; published 'Cittharn Schoole,' 1597, and 'Pavans, Galliards, Almains,' &c., for wind instruments, 1599. [xxvii. 110]

HOLBORNE, SIR ROBERT (*d.* 1647), lawyer; of Furnival's and Lincoln's Inn (bencher and reader in English law); counsel for Hampden in ship-money case; M.P. for Southwark in Short parliament and for St. Michael in Long parliament; attorney-general to Prince of Wales; knighted, 1643; published legal tracts. [xxvii. 111]

HOLBROOK, ANN CATHERINE (1780–1837), actress; published 'Memoirs of an Actress,' 1807, 'Memoirs of the Stage,' 1809, and tales. [xxvii. 111]

HOLBROOK, JOHN (*d.* 1437), master of Peterhouse, Cambridge; fellow of Peterhouse, 1412, D.D., 1418, master, 1418–31; chaplain to Henry V and Henry VI; chancellor of Cambridge, 1428 and 1429–31; vicar of Hinton, 1430; reputed mathematician. [xxvii. 112]

HOLBURNE, FRANCIS (1704–1771), admiral; while commander in Leeward islands obtained dismantling of Martinique fortifications; rear-admiral, 1755; served with Biscay fleet, 1756; member of court-martial on Byng, 1757; his fleet almost destroyed before Louisbourg; admiral of the blue, 1767, of the white, 1770; eight years commander at Portsmouth; a lord of the admiralty, 1770–1; died governor of Greenwich. [xxvii. 112]

HOLCOMBE, HENRY (1690?–1750?), musical composer; published collections of songs and instrumental pieces. [xxvii. 113]

HOLCOT, ROBERT OF (*d.* 1349), divine; Dominican and doctor in theology of Oxford; won repute for expositions of the bible; said to have died of the plague; author of subsequently published commentaries; 'Quæstiones' on Peter Lombard's 'Sentences'; 'Conferentiæ,' and 'Moralitates Historiarum'; perhaps author of 'Philobiblon sive de amore librorum.' [xxvii. 113]

HOLCROFT, FRANCIS (1629?–1693), puritan divine; M.A. and fellow, Clare Hall, Cambridge; ejected from Bassingbourne, 1662; imprisoned at Cambridge, 1663–1672, and in the Fleet; promoter of independency in Cambridgeshire. [xxvii. 115]

HOLCROFT, THOMAS (1745–1809), dramatist and author; successively stable-boy, shoemaker, tutor in family of Granville Sharp [q. v.], and actor; his first comedy, 'Duplicity,' produced at Covent Garden, 1781; correspondent of 'Morning Herald' in Paris, 1783; translated 'Mariage de Figaro' from memory, and produced adaptation at Covent Garden, himself playing Figaro, 1784; produced 'The Road to Ruin,' 1792 (nine editions printed within the year); indicted for high treason, 1794, but discharged; his musical adaptation, 'Tale of Mystery,' produced at Covent Garden, 1802, during his absence on continent; set up printing business in London, but failed; intimate with William Godwin the elder [q. v.], and spoken highly of by Lamb; his 'Memoirs,' published 1816, mainly compiled by Hazlitt; published numerous comedies and comic operas, also 'Human Happiness' (poem), 1783, some novels, including 'Alwyn, or the Gentleman Comedian,' 1780; translations, including 'Life of Baron Trenck,' 1788, Lavater's 'Physiognomy,' 1793, and Goethe's 'Hermann und Dorothea,' 1801. [xxvii. 116]

HOLDEN, GEORGE (1783–1865), theological writer; graduated at Glasgow; incumbent of Maghull, Liverpool, 1811–65; his library bequeathed to Ripon clergy; published theological works. [xxvii. 119]

HOLDEN, HENRY (1596–1662), Roman catholic divine; D.D. and professor at the Sorbonne and vicar-general of Paris; petitioned for toleration of English catholics, 1647; engaged in controversy with Arnault, 1656; criticised writings of Thomas White (1593–1676) [q. v.]; published 'Divinæ Fidei Analysis' (1652, Eng. translation, 1658); died at Paris, leaving bequests to English subjects in France. [xxvii. 119]

HOLDEN, HUBERT ASHTON (1822–1896), classical scholar; B.A. Trinity College, Cambridge, 1845; fellow, 1847–54; LL.D., 1863; ordained priest, 1859; vice-principal of Cheltenham College, 1853–8; headmaster of Queen Elizabeth's school, Ipswich, 1858–83; fellow of London University, 1890; Litt. D. Dublin, 1892; edited classical works for students. [Suppl. ii. 434]

HOLDEN, SIR ISAAC, first baronet (1807–1897), inventor; worked in cotton mill; shawl weaver; assistant-teacher at schools successively at Paisley, Leeds, Huddersfield, and Reading; book-keeper in Townend Brothers' firm of worsted manufacturers, 1830–46; associated with Samuel Cunliffe Lister, afterwards first Baron Masham, with whom he obtained patent (1847) for new method of carding and combing and preparing genappe yarns; opened manufactory at St. Denis, near Paris, 1848; concentrated business at Bradford, 1864; M.P., Knaresborough, 1865–8, and Keighley division, 1882–95; created baronet, 1893. [Suppl. ii. 434]

HOLDEN, LAWRENCE, the elder (1710–1778), dissenting divine; published 'Paraphrase on ... Job, Psalms, Proverbs, Ecclesiastes,' 1763, and 'A Paraphrase on ... Isaiah,' 1776. [xxvii. 120]

HOLDEN, LAWRENCE, the younger (1752–1844), dissenting divine at Tenterden, 1774–1844; son of Lawrence Holden the elder [q. v.] [xxvii. 121]

HOLDEN, MOSES (1777–1864), Preston astronomer; constructed large orrery and magic lantern; published small celestial atlas, 1818, and an almanack, 1835. [xxvii. 121]

HOLDER, WILLIAM (1616–1698), divine; M.A. and fellow, Pembroke Hall, Cambridge, 1640; rector of Bletchington and Northwold; taught a deaf-mute to speak; F.R.S., 1663; canon of St. Paul's; sub-dean of Chapel Royal, 1674–89; rector of Therfield, Hertfordshire, 1687; helped to educate Sir Christopher Wren; published 'Elements of Speech,' 1669, and treatises on harmony and the Julian calendar. [xxvii. 121]

HOLDERNESS, EARLS OF. [See RAMSAY, SIR JOHN, 1580?–1626; RUPERT, PRINCE, 1619–1682; D'ARCY, ROBERT, fourth EARL of the third creation, 1718–1778.]

HOLDING, FREDERICK (1817–1874), Manchester water-colour painter. [xxvii. 122]

HOLDING, HENRY JAMES (1833–1872), painter; brother of Frederick Holding [q. v.] [xxvii. 122]

HOLDSWORTH, DANIEL (1558?–1595?). [See HALSWORTH.]

HOLDSWORTH, EDWARD (1684–1746), classical scholar; of Winchester and Magdalen College, Oxford; M.A., 1711; held Jacobite views; travelled in Italy and France; published 'Muscipula sive Cambro-muo-machia,' 1709, often reissued, and translated by Samuel Cobb [q. v.] and others; 'Remarks and Dissertations on Virgil,' with notes by Spence, issued 1768. [xxvii. 122]

HOLDSWORTH, RICHARD (1590–1649), master of Emmanuel College, Cambridge; scholar of St. John's College, Cambridge, 1607; fellow, 1613; B.A., 1610; incorporated M.A. Oxford, 1617; rector of St. Peter-le-Poor, London, 1624; Gresham professor of divinity, 1629; archdeacon of Huntingdon, 1634; master of Emmanuel College, Cambridge, 1637–43; president of Sion College, 1639; when vice-chancellor of Cambridge, 1640, resisted interference of parliament with Emmanuel fellowships; sequestrated from mastership and rectory and imprisoned (1643) for withholding aid from parliament and publishing royal proclamation; visited Charles I at Holmby House, and was made dean of Worcester, 1647; his library bought by Cambridge University. [xxvii. 124]

HOLE, HENRY FULKE PLANTAGENET WOOLICOMBE (d. 1820), wood-engraver. [xxvii. 126]

HOLE, MATTHEW (d. 1730), rector of Exeter College, Oxford; M.A., 1664; D.D., 1716; vicar of Stogursey, 1688–1730; rector of Exeter College, 1716–30; made bequests to his college and to Oxford charities; tracts by him on the liturgy republished, 1837–8. [xxvii. 126]

HOLE, RICHARD (1746–1803), poet; B.C.L. Exeter College, Oxford, 1771: vicar of Buckerell, 1777; rector of Faringdon, 1792, and of Inwardleigh; published 'Poetical Translation of Fingal,' with 'Ode to Imagination,' 1772; his version of 'Homer's Hymn to Ceres' (1781) in many collections; his 'Essay on Character of Ulysses' edited, 1807; many poems by him in Richard Polwhele's collection. [xxvii. 127]

HOLE or **HOLLE**, WILLIAM (fl. 1600–1630), earliest English engraver of music on copper plates; also engraved portraits and title-pages of maps for Camden's 'Britannia,' 1607. [xxvii. 128]

HOLFORD, MARGARET (1778–1852). [See HODSON, MRS. MARGARET.]

HOLGATE or **HOLDEGATE**, ROBERT (1481?–1555), archbishop of York; master of the order of St. Gilbert of Sempringham and prior of Watton; chaplain to Henry VIII; bishop of Llandaff, 1537; assisted in composing 'Institutes of a Christian Man'; president of the north, 1538–50; archbishop of York, 1545–54; impoverished his see; favoured reformed doctrines, and was deprived for being married, 1554; imprisoned, but released on submission; endowed hospital at Hemsworth. [xxvii. 128]

HOLINSHED or **HOLLINGSHEAD**, RAPHAEL (d. 1580?), chronicler; came to London early in reign of Elizabeth; employed as translator by Reginald Wolfe, and to continue a chronicle of universal history, which Wolfe had begun; his 'Chronicles' of England (to 1575), Scotland (to 1571), and Ireland (to 1547) published in 1578 (expunged passages inserted in copy in Grenville Library, British Museum). The 'Chronicle' was reissued, with continuation, edited by John Hooker, *alias* Vowell [q. v.], 1586, and politically offensive passages again taken out; it was utilised by Shakespeare and other dramatists. [xxvii. 130]

HOLKER, JEAN LOUIS (1770–1844), discoverer of the method of continuous combustion in vitriol manufacture; son of John Holker (1745–1822) [q. v.] [xxvii. 133]

HOLKER, JOHN (1719–1786), Jacobite; captured with Manchester volunteers at Carlisle, 1745; escaped from Newgate to France, 1746; in Irish brigade, 1747–51; accompanied Young Pretender on secret visit to England, 1750; engaged workmen from Manchester for Rouen cotton-mill, 1754; as inspector-general of manufactures established spinning schools and first French vitriol factory; knight of St. Louis, 1770; ennobled, 1775; buried at Rouen. [xxvii. 133]

HOLKER, JOHN (1745–1822), French consul-general at Philadelphia from 1777; son of John Holker (1719–1786) [q. v.] [xxvii. 133]

HOLKER, SIR JOHN (1828–1882), lord justice; barrister, Gray's Inn, 1854, and treasurer, 1875; Q.C., 1866; knighted, 1874; had large practice in patent cases; M.P., Preston, 1872–82; solicitor-general, 1874; attorney-general, 1875–80; lord justice, 1882; carried Summary Procedure and Public Prosecution Acts, 1879. [xxvii. 133]

HOLL, FRANCIS (1815–1884), engraver; son of William Holl the elder [q. v.]; engraved pictures for Queen Victoria, portraits by George Richmond, Frith's 'Railway Station,' and many chalk drawings; A.R.A., 1883. [xxvii. 134]

HOLL, FRANCIS MONTAGUE, known as FRANK HOLL (1845–1888), painter; son of Francis Holl (1815–1884) [q. v.]; educated at University College and Royal Academy schools; gold medallist, 1863; gained travelling studentship, 1868; exhibited at Academy from 1864; R.A., 1883; exhibited 'No Tidings from the Sea,' 1871, and 'Leaving Home,' 1873; painted 198 portraits, 1879–88, including the Duke of Cambridge, Sir William Jenner, Sir Henry Rawlinson, John Bright, Lord Roberts, and two of King Edward VII while Prince of Wales. [xxvii. 135]

HOLL, WILLIAM, the elder (1771–1838), stipple-engraver; noted for portraits. [xxvii. 136]

HOLL, WILLIAM, the younger (1807–1871), stipple and line engraver; son of William Holl the elder [q. v.]; executed portraits, subject-pictures after Frith, and book illustrations. [xxvii. 137]

HOLLAND, first EARL OF (1590–1649). [See RICH, HENRY.]

HOLLAND, BARONS. [See Fox, HENRY, 1705–1774, first BARON; FOX, HENRY RICHARD VASSALL, 1773–1840, third BARON.]

HOLLAND, LADY (1770–1845). [See FOX, ELIZABETH VASSALL.]

HOLLAND, ABRAHAM (d. 1626), poet; son of Philemon Holland [q. v.]; B.A. Trinity College, Cambridge, 1617; author of 'Naumachia, or Hollands Sea-Fight' (1622), describing Lepanto; 'Hollandi Posthuma,' edited by his brother, 1626. [xxvii. 137]

HOLLAND, CHARLES (1733–1769), actor; appeared at Drury Lane, 1755–69; played Iago, Iachimo, Jaffier, Hamlet, Macbeth, Romeo, Chamont; praised by Chatterton, but satirised by Churchill for imitation of Garrick; intimate with Powell; inscription written by Garrick for his monument in Chiswick Church. [xxvii. 137]

HOLLAND, CHARLES (1768–1849?), actor; nephew of Charles Holland (1733–1769) [q. v.]; appeared at Drury Lane, 1796–1820, at Haymarket, 1809–10; played Horatio to Elliston's Hamlet at Lyceum, 1812, Mendizabel to Kean's Manuel, 1817, Buckingham to his Richard III, 1819, Gloucester to his Lear, 1820. [xxvii. 138]

HOLLAND, CORNELIUS (fl. 1649), regicide; of Merchant Taylors' School and Pembroke Hall, Cambridge; B.A., 1618; clerk-comptroller to Prince of Wales, 1635; M.P., New Windsor, 1640; a commissioner for Scottish treaty, 1643; as member of council of state, 1649, said to have drawn up charges against the king, but did not sign warrant; liberally rewarded by parliament; escaped to Holland, 1660; said to have died at Lausanne. [xxvii. 139]

HOLLAND, EDMUND, fourth EARL OF KENT (d. 1408); second son of Sir Thomas Holland, second earl [q. v.]; mortally wounded at Briant. [xxvii. 157]

HOLLAND, GEORGE CALVERT (1801–1865), physician; M.D. Edinburgh, 1827; B.-ès-Lettres Paris; practised at Manchester and Sheffield; defended the corn laws; abandoned practice to direct banks and railway companies, and failed; adopted homœopathy, 1851; published 'Experimental Enquiry into Laws of Animal Life,' 1829, 'Physiology of the Fœtus,' 1831, and other scientific works. [xxvii. 139]

HOLLAND, GUY, sometimes known as HOLT (1587?–1660), jesuit; B.A. St. John's College, Cambridge, 1605; entered English College, Valladolid, 1608; joined jesuits in England, 1615; arrested in London, 1628; forty-five years on English mission; attacked Falkland's 'Discourse of the Infallibility of the Church of Rome,' 1645; defended immortality of the soul, 1653. [xxvii. 140]

HOLLAND, HENRY (d. 1604), divine; B.A. Magdalene College, Cambridge, 1580; vicar of Orwell, 1580–94, of St. Bride's, London, 1594–1604; works include 'Treatise against Witchcraft' (1590) and 'Spirituall Preservatives against the Pestilence' (1593). [xxvii. 140]

HOLLAND, HENRY (d. 1625), Roman catholic divine; of Eton and St. John's College, Oxford; B.A., 1569; B.D. Douay, 1578; on English mission, 1582; divinity reader at Marchiennes and Anchine; published 'Urna Aurea,' 1612, and Latin life of Thomas Stapleton, 1620; died at Anchine. [xxvii. 141]

HOLLAND, HENRY (1583–1650?), compiler and publisher; son of Philemon Holland [q. v.]; free of Stationers' Company, 1608; issued his own 'Monumenta Sepulchraria Sancti Pauli,' 1614 (continued and reissued, 1633), and 'Baziliωlogia,' with engravings by Elstracke, Pass, and Francis Delaram, 1618, and 'Herωologia Anglica' (with portraits), 1620; edited Philemon Holland's Bauderon's 'Pharmacopœia,' 1639, and 'Regimen Sanitatis Salerni,' 1649; served in parliamentary army, 1643. [xxvii. 141]

HOLLAND, HENRY (1746?–1806), architect; designed Claremont House, Esher, for Clive, 1763–4, Battersea Bridge, 1771–2, Brooks's Club, 1777–8, and Brighton Pavilion, 1787; altered and enlarged Carlton House, 1788; designed Drury Lane for Sheridan, 1791, and new East India House, demolished in 1862; laid out Sloane Street; member of committee to report on houses of parliament, 1789; F.S.A., 1797; drew up architects' report on fires, 1792. [xxvii. 143]

HOLLAND, SIR HENRY, first baronet (1788–1873), physician; M.D. Edinburgh, 1811; studied at Guy's and St. Thomas's hospitals; visited Iceland and contributed to Sir George S. Mackenzie's account, 1810; medical attendant to Princess of Wales (Caroline) on the continent, 1814; gave evidence in her favour, 1820; F.R.S., 1816; F.R.C.P., 1828; physician in ordinary to Prince Albert, 1840, to Queen Victoria, 1852; created baronet, 1853; travelled much on continent; published 'Travels,' 1815, 'Chapters on Mental Physiology,' 1852, 'Essays,' 1862, and 'Recollections,' 1872. [xxvii. 144]

HOLLAND, HEZEKIAH (fl. 1638–1661), puritan divine; rector of Sutton Valence, Kent; author of 'Exposition or . . . Epitome of . . . Commentaries upon . . . Revelations,' 1650. [xxvii. 146]

HOLLAND, HUGH (d. 1633), poet; queen's scholar at Westminster and fellow of Trinity College, Cambridge; converted to Romanism; travelled as far as Jerusalem; patronised by Buckingham; a member of Mermaid Club; wrote sonnet prefixed to first folio Shakespeare; published 'Pancharis,' 1603, and 'A Cypres Garland,' 1625. [xxvii. 146]

HOLLAND, JAMES (1800–1870), water-colour painter; exhibited at Water-colour Society, Royal Academy, Society of British Artists, and British Institution; drew for illustrated annuals, visiting France, Venice, Geneva, Portugal, and Italy. [xxvii. 146]

HOLLAND, JOHN, DUKE OF EXETER AND EARL OF HUNTINGDON (1352?–1400), third son of Sir Thomas Holland, first earl of Kent [q. v.], and half-brother to Richard II; K.G., 1381; justice of Chester, 1381; murdered Ralph Stafford, 1385; married Elizabeth, daughter of John of Gaunt, under whom he distinguished himself in Spain, 1386; created Earl of Huntingdon, 1387; chamberlain of England, 1389; made pilgrimage to Palestine, 1394; commissary, west marches towards Scotland, 1393; rewarded by dukedom for activity against Gloucester and Arundel, 1397; accompanied Richard II to Ireland, 1399; conspired against Henry IV; executed. [xxvii. 147]

HOLLAND, JOHN, DUKE OF EXETER AND EARL OF HUNTINGDON (1395–1447), second son of John Holland, duke of Exeter (1352?–1400) [q. v.]; K.B., 1413; distinguished at Agincourt, 1415; restored to earldom, 1416, and created K.G.; commanded fleet against Genoese off Harfleur, 1417; took part in sieges of Caen and Rouen; distinguished at surprise of Pontoise, 1419; won victory of Fresney, 1420; took part in capture of Melun, 1420; constable of Tower of London, 1420; captured by dauphinists, 1421; exchanged, 1425; English representative at Arras, 1435; commanded expedition for relief of Guisnes, 1438; governor of Aquitaine, 1440; restored to dukedom, 1443. [xxvii. 148]

HOLLAND, JOHN (d. 1722), founder of Bank of Scotland and first governor, 1695; with his son, Richard Holland (1688–1730) [q. v.], projected Irish bank; published financial pamphlets. [xxvii. 150]

HOLLAND, JOHN (1766–1826), nonconformist minister; nephew of Philip Holland [q. v.] [xxvii. 154]

HOLLAND, JOHN (1794–1872), poet and miscellaneous writer; edited 'Sheffield Iris,' 1825–32; joint-editor of 'Sheffield Mercury,' 1835–48; published 'Sheffield Park,' 1820, and 'Diurnal Sonnets,' 1851; friend of James Montgomery; joint-editor of 'Memoirs of Life and Writings of James Montgomery,' 1854–6; completed Newsam's 'Poets of Yorkshire,' 1845; published also 'History of Worksop,' 1826, 'Cruciana,' 1835, and other works. [xxvii. 150]

HOLLAND, SIR NATHANIEL DANCE-, first baronet (1735–1811), painter; third son of the elder George Dance [q. v.]; original member of Royal Academy, to whose first exhibition he sent full lengths of George III and Queen Charlotte; assumed additional name; M.P., East Grinstead; created baronet, 1800. [xxvii. 151]

HOLLAND, PHILEMON (1552–1637), translator; M.A. Trinity College, Cambridge, 1574, major fellow, 1574; claimed degree of M.D.; master of free school, Coventry, 1628; received pension from city, 1632; epitaph by himself in Holy Trinity Church; his chief translations those of Livy, 1600, Pliny's 'Natural History,' 1601,

Plutarch's 'Morals,' 1603, Suetonius, 1606, Ammianus Marcellinus, 1609, Camden's 'Britannia,' 1610, and Xenophon's 'Cyropædia,' 1632 ; praised by Fuller, Hearne, and Southey. [xxvii. 151]

HOLLAND, PHILIP (1721-1789), nonconformist divine ; minister of Bank Street Chapel, Bolton, 1755-80 ; assisted Seddon in establishment of Warrington academy ; active in agitation against subscription. [xxvii. 153]

HOLLAND, SIR RICHARD (*fl.* 1450), Scottish poet and adherent of the Douglases ; author of the 'Buke of the Howlat,' edited by David Laing, 1823 ; praised by Blind Harry, Dunbar, and Lyndsay. [xxvii. 154]

HOLLAND, RICHARD (1596-1677), mathematician ; educated at Oxford ; author of astronomical manuals. [xxvii. 155]

HOLLAND, RICHARD (1688-1730), medical writer ; son of John Holland (*d.* 1722) [q. v.] ; M.A. Catharine Hall, Cambridge, 1712 ; M.D., 1723 ; F.R.C.P., 1725 ; F.R.S., 1726 ; published 'Observations on Smallpox,' 1728. [xxvii. 150]

HOLLAND, ROBERT (1557-1622 ?), Welsh poet ; M.A. Jesus College, Cambridge, 1581 ; incumbent in Pembrokeshire and rector of Llanddowror, Carmarthen. [xxvii. 155]

HOLLAND, SABA, LADY (*d.* 1866), second wife of Sir Henry Holland [q. v.] ; published memoir of her father, Sydney Smith, 1855. [xxvii. 145]

HOLLAND, SETH (*d.* 1561), dean of Worcester ; M.A. All Souls College, Oxford, 1539 ; fellow ; warden, 1555 ; dean of Worcester, 1557-9 ; chaplain to Cardinal Pole ; died in prison. [xxvii. 156]

HOLLAND, SIR THOMAS, first EARL OF KENT of the Holland family (*d.* 1360), soldier ; present at Sluys, 1340 ; an original K.G., 1344 ; prominent at siege of Caen, and at Crecy, 1346 ; royal lieutenant in Brittany, 1354 ; governor of Channel islands, 1356 ; summoned to parliament as Baron Holland, 1353-6 ; captain-general in France and Normandy, 1359 ; Earl of Kent in right of his wife Joan, daughter of Edmund of Woodstock, earl of Kent [q. v.] [xxvii. 156]

HOLLAND, SIR THOMAS, second EARL OF KENT of the Holland family (1350-1397), favourite and half-brother of Richard II ; son of Thomas Holland, first earl of Kent [q. v.] ; succeeded as Baron Holland, 1360 ; knighted in Castile, 1366 ; K.G., 1375 ; earl-marshal, 1380-5 ; ambassador to the Emperor Wenceslaus, 1380 ; Earl of Kent, 1381 ; constable of the Tower and privy councillor, 1389. [xxvii. 157]

HOLLAND, THOMAS, DUKE OF SURREY and EARL OF KENT (1374-1400), eldest son of Sir Thomas Holland, second earl of Kent [q. v.] ; K.G., 1397 ; active in arrest and execution of Arundel ; created Duke of Surrey, 1397 ; marshal and lieutenant of Ireland, 1398 ; deprived of dukedom, 1399 ; conspired against Henry IV, holding Maidenhead bridge three days ; executed by men of Cirencester. [xxvii. 157]

HOLLAND, THOMAS (*d.* 1612), regius professor of divinity at Oxford ; M.A. Balliol College, Oxford, 1575 ; D.D., 1584 ; chaplain to Leicester in Netherlands, 1585 ; regius professor of divinity at Oxford, 1589-1612 ; rector of Exeter College, 1592 ; one of the six translators of the prophets in authorised version, 1611. [xxvii. 158]

HOLLAND, THOMAS (1600-1642), jesuit ; addressed Prince Charles at Madrid, 1623 ; prefect and confessor at St. Omer ; came to England, 1635 ; executed. [xxvii. 159]

HOLLAND, THOMAS (1659-1743). [See ECCLESTON, THOMAS.]

HOLLAND, THOMAS AGAR (1803-1888), poet ; of Westminster and Worcester College, Oxford ; M.A., 1828 ; rector of Poynings, 1846-88 ; published 'Dryburgh Abbey and other Poems,' 1826. [xxvii. 159]

HOLLAR, WENCESLAUS, in Bohemian VACLAV HOLAR (1607-1677), engraver ; native of Prague ; lived at Frankfort, Cologne, and Antwerp ; came to England with Thomas Howard, second earl of Arundel [q. v.], 1635 ; teacher of drawing to Prince Charles ; engraved 'Ornatus Muliebris Anglicanus,' 1640, Charles I and his queen (after Vandyck), 1641, and 'Theatrum Mulierum,'

1643 ; captured by parliamentarians at Basing ; escaped to Antwerp ; returned, 1652 ; illustrated Dugdale's 'St. Paul,' Ogilby's Virgil, and Stapleton's Juvenal ; as Hill's designer produced 'Coronation of Charles II' ; executed fine map of London after the fire of 1666 ; sent to Tangier, 1669 ; engraved picture of Kempthorne's fight with Algerine pirates ; illustrated Thoroton's 'Antiquities of Nottinghamshire' ; 2,733 of his prints enumerated. [xxvii. 160]

HOLLES, DENZIL, first BARON HOLLES OF IFIELD (1599-1680), statesman ; second son of John Holles, first earl of Clare [q. v.] ; M.P., St. Michael, 1624, Dorchester, 1628, and in Long parliament ; opposed Buckingham's foreign policy ; held the speaker in his chair, 2 March, 1629 ; imprisoned and fined ; escaped abroad ; compensated by Long parliament, 1641 ; tried to save his brother-in-law, Strafford ; carried up impeachment of Laud ; supported Grand Remonstrance and impeachment of Digby and Bristol, 1641 ; impeached among the five members, 3 Jan. 1642 ; advocated Militia Bill and impeachment of royalist peers ; member of committee of safety 4 July, 1642 ; led regiment at Edgehill and Brentford ; advocated peace, 1643 ; parliamentary representative at negotiations of 1644, 1645 (Uxbridge), and 1648 (Newport) ; headed presbyterians against independents and (1644) projected impeachment of Cromwell ; charged with intrigues with Charles I, 1645 and 1647 ; impeached by the army among the eleven members, 1647 ; disabled from sitting, but restored, 1648 ; escaped to France under threat of another impeachment ; readmitted by Monck and appointed to council of state, 1660 ; commissioner to Charles II at the Hague ; privy councillor and created peer, 1661 ; ambassador at Paris, 1663-6 ; a negotiator of treaty of Breda, 1667 ; protested against the Test Act, 1675 ; supported impeachment of Danby, 1678, and disbandment of army, 1678 ; opposed Exclusion Bill ; one of the new privy councillors, 1679 ; his 'Memoirs, 1641-8,' printed, 1699. [xxvii. 162]

HOLLES, SIR FRESCHEVILLE (1641-1672), captain in the navy ; son of Gervase Holles [q. v.] ; volunteer in naval campaign, 1665 ; knighted, 1666 ; commanded the Henrietta, 1666 ; abused by Pepys ; M.P., Grimsby, 1667 ; commanded the Cambridge under Sir Robert Holmes [q. v.], 1672 ; killed in battle of Solebay ; buried in Westminster Abbey. [xxvii. 166]

HOLLES, GERVASE (1606-1675), antiquary ; comptroller of Middle Temple, 1635 ; royalist mayor and M.P. for Grimsby ; suspended and disabled from sitting for denunciation of Scots, 1641-2 ; fought at Edgehill, Banbury, Brentford, Newbury ; captured at Colchester ; allowed to retire to France, 1649 ; in Holland till 1660 ; master of the requests and M.P., Grimsby, 1661-75 ; some of his Lincolnshire collections in British Museum. [xxvii. 167]

HOLLES, GILBERT, third EARL OF CLARE (1633-1689), member of the country party, 1660-88 ; son of John Holles, second earl of Clare [q. v.] [xxvii. 170]

HOLLES, JOHN, first EARL OF CLARE (1564 ?-1637), soldier and politician ; served against Armada, 1588, and in Azores expedition, 1597 ; fought against Turks in Hungary ; comptroller to Henry, prince of Wales, 1610-12 ; friend of Somerset and enemy of Coke and Gervase Markham ; created Baron Holles, 1616, and Earl of Clare, 1624 ; opposed Buckingham ; advocated compromise on Petition of Right ; reprimanded for implication in proceedings of Sir Robert Dudley [q. v.], 1629. [xxvii. 168]

HOLLES, JOHN, second EARL OF CLARE (1595-1666), son of John Holles, first earl [q. v.] ; represented East Retford as Lord Haughton, 1624-9 ; volunteer at Bois-le-Duc, 1629 ; succeeded to peerage, 1637 ; took part in negotiations with Scots, 1640 ; sided with five popular peers, 1641, but defended Strafford, 1641 ; changed sides several times during the rebellion. [xxvii. 169]

HOLLES, JOHN, DUKE OF NEWCASTLE (1662-1711), son of Gilbert Holles, third earl of Clare [q. v.] ; known as Lord Haughton till father's death ; M.P. for Nottinghamshire ; gentleman of bedchamber to William III ; married Margaret Cavendish, coheiress of Duke of Newcastle, 1690 ; created duke, 1694 ; K.G., 1698 ; lord privy seal, 1705-11. [xxvii. 170]

HOLLES, THOMAS PELHAM-, DUKE OF NEWCASTLE-UPON-TYNE and NEWCASTLE-UNDER-LYME (1693-1768). [See PELHAM.]

HOLLES or **HOLLIS**, Sir WILLIAM (1471?-1572), lord mayor of London; master of Mercers' Company, 1538; sheriff of London, 1527; knighted, 1533; lord mayor, 1539-40; left bequests to Coventry, the Mercers' Company, and St. Helen's, Bishopsgate; ancestor of earls of Clare and dukes of Newcastle. [xxvii. 171]

HOLLIDAY, JOHN (1730?-1801), author; barrister, Lincoln's Inn, 1771; practised as conveyancer; F.R.S. and F.S.A.; published 'Life of Lord Mansfield' (1797) and poems. [xxvii. 171]

HOLLINGS, EDMUND (1556?-1612), physician; B.A. Queen's College, Oxford, 1575; studied at Rheims and Rome; intimate with Pits; professor of medicine at Ingolstadt; published medical works; died at Ingolstadt. [xxvii. 172]

HOLLINGS, JOHN (1683?-1739), physician-general and physician in ordinary; M.D. Magdalene College, Cambridge, 1710; F.R.S., 1726; F.R.C.P., 1726; Harveian orator, 1734. [xxvii. 172]

HOLLINGWORTH, RICHARD (1639?-1701), controversialist; M.A. Emmanuel College, Cambridge, 1662; D.D., 1684; vicar of West Ham, 1672-82, of Chigwell, 1690-1701; published pamphlets in defence of Charles I's authorship of 'Εἰκὼν βασιλικὴ,' and reissued Edward Symmons's 'Vindication,' 1693. [xxvii. 172]

HOLLINS, JOHN (1798-1855), painter; A.R.A., 1842; exhibited portraits and historical subjects, and, later, figure-pieces and landscapes. [xxvii. 173]

HOLLINS, PETER (1800-1886), sculptor; son of William Hollins [q. v.]; exhibited at Royal Academy. His works include statues of Peel and Sir Rowland Hill for Birmingham. [xxvii. 174]

HOLLINS, WILLIAM (1754-1843), architect and sculptor; cousin of John Hollins [q. v.]; designed public buildings at Birmingham and plans for St. Petersburg mint. [xxvii. 174]

HOLLINWORTH or **HOLLINGWORTH**, RICHARD (1607-1656), divine; educated at Manchester and Magdalene College, Cambridge; M.A., 1630; minister of Trinity Chapel, Salford, 1636; fellow of Manchester Collegiate Church; assisted Richard Heyrick [q. v.] in establishing Lancashire presbyterianism, which he also defended controversially; imprisoned on charge of implication in Love's plot, 1651; one of Chetham's feoffees; his 'Mancuniensis' printed, 1839. [xxvii. 174]

HOLLIS, AISKEW PAFFARD (1764-1844), vice-admiral; present in battle off Ushant, 1778; lieutenant, 1781; wounded in action of 1 June, 1794; brought Crescent into Table Bay, 1797; commanded Thames frigate at action off Gibraltar, 1801; served in Baltic, 1809; vice-admiral, 1837. [xxvii. 176]

HOLLIS, GEORGE (1793-1842), topographical engraver; pupil of George Cooke [q. v.] [xxvii. 176]

HOLLIS, THOMAS (1720-1774), 'republican'; entered at Lincoln's Inn, 1740; travelled much on continent; gave books to Harvard, Berne, and Zurich, and portraits of Newton and Cromwell to Trinity and Sidney Sussex Colleges, Cambridge; F.R.S., 1757; edited Toland's 'Milton,' 1761, Algernon Sidney's works, 1772, and other publications. [xxvii. 176]

HOLLIS, THOMAS (1818-1843), son and assistant of George Hollis [q. v.] [xxvii. 176]

HOLLOND, ELLEN JULIA (1822-1884), authoress and philanthropist; née Teed; as wife of Robert Hollond, M.P., held liberal salon in Paris; published 'Les Quakers,' 1870; and a work on Channing, 1857; established first crèche in London, 1844, and nurses' home at Paris and Nice. [xxvii. 177]

HOLLOND or **HOLLAND**, JOHN (fl. 1638-1659), naval writer; paymaster of navy before 1635 till c. 1642; one of commissioners for navy, 1642 till c. 1645; member of 'committee of merchants for regulation of navy and customs,' 1649; surveyor of the navy, 1649; member of parliament's commission of navy, 1649-52; wrote 'First Discourse of the Navy,' 1638, and 'Second Discourse,' 1659. [Suppl. ii. 436]

HOLLOWAY, BENJAMIN (1691?-1759), divine; of Westminster and St. John's College, Cambridge; LL.B., 1713; F.R.S., 1723; rector of Middleton-Stoney and Bladon, 1736-9; translated Woodward's 'Naturalis Historia Telluris,' 1726; published works, including 'Primævity and Pre-eminence of Hebrew,' 1754, and 'Originals physical and theological,' 1751. [xxvii. 177]

HOLLOWAY, Sir CHARLES (1749-1827), major-general, royal engineers; second-lieutenant, royal engineers, 1776; lieutenant, 1783; captain-lieutenant, 1793; captain, 1795; lieutenant-colonel, 1804; colonel, 1811; major-general, 1814; at Gibraltar, 1779-83, during siege; brigade-major, 1781; assisted Major-general William Roy [q. v.] in survey triangulations, 1784-87; commanding royal engineer in military mission to assist Turks in re-organisation of army, 1798; commander of Turkish army in Syria and Egypt against French, 1801-2; knighted, 1803; commanding royal engineer at Gibraltar, 1807-17. [Suppl. ii. 437]

HOLLOWAY, JAMES (d. 1684), conspirator; formed scheme for improvement of linen manufacture; engaged in extensive plot against government, himself undertaking (1682) to secure Bristol; escaped by France to West Indies; betrayed by his factor in Nevis; while in Newgate wrote confession; refused trial and was executed at Tyburn. [xxvii. 178]

HOLLOWAY, Sir RICHARD (d. 1695?), judge; barrister, Inner Temple, 1658; recorder of Wallingford, 1666; counsel against Stephen College [q. v.], 1681; knighted; judge of king's bench, 1683; member of courts that tried Sidney and condemned Oates and Devonshire for assaulting Thomas Colepepper [q. v.]; dismissed by James II, 1688, for action in trial of seven bishops, excepted from indemnity after revolution. [xxvii. 180]

HOLLOWAY, THOMAS (1748-1827), engraver; exhibited seals at Academy; engraved gems and miniatures; executed plates for Lavater's 'Physiognomy,' 1789-98; engraved portraits after Pine and West and five of Raphael's cartoons. [xxvii. 180]

HOLLOWAY, THOMAS (1800-1883), patent medicine vendor; son of Penzance innkeeper; obtained idea of his ointment from Felix Albinolo; set up in the Strand as medicine vendor, 1839; advertised extensively in all languages, but failed to introduce medicines into France; made large fortune; bought pictures; endowed ladies' college at Egham and sanatorium at Virginia Water. [xxvii. 181]

HOLLOWAY, WILLIAM CUTHBERT (1787-1850). [See ELPHINSTONE-HOLLOWAY.]

HOLLYDAY, SAMUEL (1685-1739). [See HALIDAY.]

HOLLYWOOD or **SACROBOSCO**, CHRISTOPHER (1562-1616). [See HOLYWOOD.]

HOLMAN, FRANCIS (fl. 1760-1790), marine painter; exhibited with Free Society, 1767-72, and Royal Academy, 1774-84. [xxvii. 182]

HOLMAN, JAMES (1786-1857), blind traveller; travelled unattended in Europe, Siberia, Africa, America, and Australasia; published 'Voyage round the World (1827-32),' 1834-5, and other narratives. [xxvii. 182]

HOLMAN, JOSEPH GEORGE (1764-1817), actor and dramatist; of Queen's College, Oxford; at Covent Garden, 1784-1800, played Romeo, Macbeth, Chamont ('The Orphan'), Hamlet; 'created' Harry Dornton in 'Road to Ruin,' 1792; drew up statement of grievances of chief actors, 1800; acted in his own 'What a Blunder' at Haymarket, 1800 (produced at Covent Garden, 1803); re-appeared at Haymarket, 1812; with his daughter played at New York, Philadelphia, and Charleston in 'The Provoked Husband'; died in Long Island; published comedies and comic operas. [xxvii. 183]

HOLMAN, WILLIAM (d. 1730), Essex antiquary; his collections used by Morant; compiled catalogue of Jekyll MSS. [xxvii. 185]

HOLME, BENJAMIN (1683-1749), quaker; visited 'Friends' and preached in Ireland, Holland (1714), the West Indies (1719), Jersey, and America; published 'Tender Invitation and Call,' 1713, with other religious works; 'A Serious Call in Christian Love' (1725), and an autobiography, published in 1753. [xxvii. 185]

HOLME, EDWARD (1770–1847), physician ; M.D.
Leyden, 1793 ; physician to Manchester infirmary ; president of Literary and Philosophical Society (1844), Natural
History and Chetham societies ; first president of medical
section at British Association, 1831 ; left large bequest
and library to University College, London. [xxvii. 186]

HOLME, RANDLE (1571–1655), deputy to College of
Arms for Cheshire, Shropshire, and North Wales ; mayor
of Chester, 1633–4. [xxvii. 186]

HOLME, RANDLE (1601 ?–1659), genealogist ; son
of Randle Holme (1571–1655) [q. v.] ; sheriff of Chester,
1633–4 ; mayor, 1643–4 ; added to Holme collection of
MSS. [xxvii. 187]

HOLME, RANDLE (1627–1699), principal contributor
to Holme MSS. ; son of Randle Holme (1601 ?–1659)
[q. v.] ; deputy Garter for Cheshire, Shropshire, Lancashire, and North Wales ; published 'The Academy of
Armory,' 1688. [xxvii. 187]

HOLME, RANDLE (d. 1707), completer of family
manuscripts ; son of Randle Holme (1627–1699) [q. v.] ;
manuscripts acquired by British Museum, 1753. [xxvii. 187]

HOLMES, ABRAHAM (d. 1685), rebel ; anabaptist
major in Monck's army ; arrested for conspiracy against
Charles II, 1660 ; imprisoned at Windsor, 1664–7 ; engaged in Argyll's plot, 1681–3 ; accompanied Monmouth
to England and commanded battalion at Sedgemoor,
1685 ; executed. [xxvii. 187]

HOLMES, ALFRED (1837–1876), violinist and composer ; with his brother Henry played Kalliwoda's double
concerto, 1853, and distinguished himself by rendering of
Spohr's music during concert tours in Belgium, Germany
(1856), Austria, Sweden, Denmark, Holland, and Paris,
where he settled, 1864 ; produced at St. Petersburg symphony 'Jeanne d'Arc,' 1868, 'Jeunesse de Shakespeare,'
and other works given in Paris ; died at Paris. [xxvii. 188]

HOLMES, CHARLES (1711–1761), rear-admiral ;
commanded Stromboli in Carthagena expedition, 1741 ;
took part in action with Spanish in Gulf of Florida, 1748 ;
member of court-martial on Byng, 1757 ; cut enemy's communications in the Ems, 1758 ; rear-admiral, 1758 ; third
in command under Sir Charles Saunders [q. v.] in St.
Lawrence, 1759 ; commander-in-chief at Jamaica, 1760–1 ;
monument in Westminster Abbey. [xxvii. 189]

HOLMES, EDWARD (1797–1859), writer on music ;
friend of Keats and Charles Cowden Clarke [q. v.] ; with
Vincent Novello [q. v.] raised subscription for Mozart's
widow ; published 'Ramble among Musicians of Germany' (1828), and lives of Mozart (1845) and Purcell ;
composed songs. [xxvii. 190]

HOLMES, GEORGE (fl. 1673–1715), organist at Lincoln, 1704–15 ; grandson of John Holmes (fl. 1602) [q. v.] ;
contributed to 'Musical Companion,' 1673 ; composed
anthems and songs. [xxvii. 190]

HOLMES, GEORGE (1662–1749), deputy-keeper of
the Tower records ; F.R.S. and F.S.A. ; prepared first
seventeen volumes of Rymer's 'Fœdera,' 1727–35. [xxvii. 191]

HOLMES, JAMES (1777–1860), water-colour painter
and miniaturist ; exhibited with Society of British
Artists, 1829–59 ; his two miniatures of Byron engraved. [xxvii. 191]

HOLMES, JOHN (fl. 1602), composer ; organist of
Winchester and Salisbury (1602–10). [xxvii. 191]

HOLMES, SIR JOHN (1640 ?–1683), admiral ; brother
of Sir Robert Holmes [q. v.] ; commanded the Paul at
Lowestoft, 1665, and in fight of June, 1666 ; commanded
the Bristol in fight of 25 July, 1666 ; served under Sir
Edward Spragge [q. v.] in Algerine war, 1670–1 ; wounded
in fight with Dutch Smyrna fleet, 1672, and knighted ;
commanded the Rupert at Solebay, 1672, and in battles of
1673 ; commander in the Downs, 1677–9 ; M.P., Newtown
(Isle of Wight), 1677–83. [xxvii. 192]

HOLMES, JOHN (1800–1854), antiquary ; adviser of
Bertram, earl of Ashburnham, collector of manuscripts ;
compiled catalogue of manuscripts, maps, and plans in
British Museum, 1844 ; edited Evelyn's 'Life of Mrs.
Godolphin,' 1847, Cavendish's 'Wolsey,' 1852, and Wordsworth's 'Ecclesiastical Biography,' 1853. [xxvii. 192]

HOLMES, JOHN BECK (1767–1843), Moravian bishop
of Fulneck ; published historical works concerning his
church. [xxvii. 193]

HOLMES or **HOMES**, NATHANIEL (1599–1678),
puritan divine ; B.A. Exeter College, Oxford, 1620 ; M.A.
Magdalen Hall, 1623 ; D.D. Exeter College, 1637 ; joined
Henry Burton [q. v.] in founding independent congregation, 1643 ; published millenarian works. [xxvii. 193]

HOLMES, SIR ROBERT (1622–1692), admiral ; served
under Prince Rupert in civil war ; governor of Sandown
Castle, 1660 ; seized Dutch possessions on Guinea coast and
in North America, 1664 ; captain of the Revenge at battle
of Lowestoft, 1665 ; knighted, 1666 ; rear-admiral of the
red, 1666 ; distinguished in fight of 1–4 June, 1666 ;
fought duel with Sir Jeremiah Smith or Smyth [q. v.]
arising out of his conduct in fight of 25 July, 1666 ; destroyed shipping and stores at Vlie and Schelling ; admiral
at Portsmouth, 1667 ; one of Buckingham's seconds in
duel with Shrewsbury ; governor of Isle of Wight, 1669 ;
attacked Dutch Smyrna fleet in Channel, 1672 ; took
part in battle of Solebay, 1672 ; M.P., Winchester,
Yarmouth (Isle of Wight), and Newport. [xxvii. 194]

HOLMES, ROBERT (1748–1805), biblical scholar ;
of Winchester and New College, Oxford ; fellow ; M.A.
1774 ; D.D., 1789 ; first winner of chancellor's prize
for Latin verse, 1769 ; rector of Stanton St. John ;
Bampton lecturer, 1782 ; professor of poetry, 1783 ;
collated Septuagint, 1788–1805 ; prebendary of Salisbury,
Hereford, and Christ Church ; dean of Winchester, 1804 ;
F.R.S., 1797 ; published poems, theological works, and
annual accounts of his collections. [xxvii. 197]

HOLMES, ROBERT (1765–1859), Irish lawyer ;
brother-in-law of Robert Emmet [q. v.] ; B.A. Trinity
College, Dublin, 1787 ; imprisoned on suspicion of rebellion, 1803 ; defended John Mitchel, 1848 ; published antiunion pamphlets. [xxvii. 198]

HOLMES, THOMAS (d. 1638), musical composer ;
gentleman of the Chapel Royal, 1633. [xxvii. 192]

HOLMES, WILLIAM (1689–1748), dean of Exeter ;
educated at Merchant Taylors' School ; fellow of St.
John's College, Oxford, 1700 ; M.A., 1715 ; proctor, 1721 ;
B.D. ; president of St. John's College, Oxford, 1728 ; vicechancellor, 1732–5 ; revived the act and invited Handel to
play at Oxford, 1733 ; regius professor of history, 1736–
1742 ; dean of Exeter, 1742–8 ; left estates to his college. [xxvii. 198]

HOLMES, WILLIAM (d. 1851), thirty years tory
whip ; B.A. Trinity College, Dublin, 1795 ; served in the
army ; M.P., Grampound, 1808–12, Tregony, 1812–18,
Totnes, 1819–20, Bishop's Castle, 1820–30 ; Haslemere,
1830–2, Berwick, 1837–41 ; treasurer of the ordnance,
1820–30. [xxvii. 199]

HOLMES, WILLIAM ANTHONY (1782–1843),
chancellor of Cashel ; scholar of Trinity College, Dublin ;
B.A., 1803 ; D.D., 1834 ; incumbent of Holywood, Down,
1810, of Ballyroan, 1818, and Core Abbey, 1822 ; chancellor of Cashel, 1832 ; helped to found Mendicity Institution, Belfast ; published pamphlets. [xxvii. 200]

HOLROYD, SIR GEORGE SOWLEY (1758–1831),
judge ; educated at Harrow ; special pleader, 1779–87 ;
barrister, Gray's Inn, 1878 ; appeared for Burdett against
Speaker Abbott, 1811 ; commissioner to Guernsey, 1815 ;
judge of king's bench, 1816–28. [xxvii. 200]

HOLROYD, JOHN BAKER, first EARL OF SHEFFIELD (1735–1821), statesman and friend of Gibbon ;
purchased Sheffield Place, Sussex, 1769 ; raised and commanded dragoon regiment ; M.P., Coventry, 1780–3,
Bristol, 1783–1802 ; active in suppressing Gordon riots,
1780 ; created Irish baron, 1781 ; created Earl of Sheffield and Viscount Pevensey in peerage of Ireland, 1816 ;
British peer, 1802 ; president of board of agriculture,
1803 ; privy councillor, 1809 ; lord of board of trade,
1809 ; published pamphlets on social and commercial
questions ; edited Gibbon's 'Miscellaneous Works,' 1796,
and 'Memoirs,' 1826. [xxvii. 200]

HOLST, THEODORE VON (1810–1844). [See VON
HOLST.]

HOLT, FRANCIS LUDLOW (1780 - 1844), legal
writer ; of Westminster and Christ Church, Oxford ;

barrister, Middle Temple, 1809; K.C., 1831; treasurer of Inner Temple, 1840; vice-chancellor of Lancaster, 1826–1844; published 'Law of Libel' (1812-1816), nisi prius reports, 1815-17, shipping laws, 1820, bankrupt laws, 1829, and 'The Land we live in' (comedy), 1804.
[xxvii. 202]

HOLT, GUY (1587?–1660). [See HOLLAND.]

HOLT, JOHN (*d.* 1418), judge; king's serjeant, 1377; judge of common pleas, 1383; knight-banneret, 1384; banished to Ireland, 1388, for decision against legality of permanent council; recalled, 1397.
[xxvii. 202]

HOLT, SIR JOHN (1642–1710), judge; of Winchester and Oriel College, Oxford; barrister, Gray's Inn, 1663; counsel for Danby and Lords Powis and Arundell, 1679; appeared for crown against Slingsby Bethel [q. v.], for Lord Russell, and for East India Company against Sandys, 1683; recorder of London, 1686–7; knighted, 1686; king's serjeant, 1686; M.P. Beeralston; manager of conference with peers on vacancy of throne, 1689; lord chief-justice of king's bench, 1689–1710; pronounced dispensing power legal; decided in favour of bankers, 1700; against House of Commons in case of Ashby *v.* White, 1701; declined great seal, 1700; the Verus of the 'Tatler'; his judgment in Coggs *v.* Bernard, chief authority on law of bailments; edited reports of cases in pleas of the crown under Charles II, 1708. As judge he discouraged prosecutions for witchcraft, and put liberal construction on statute compelling attendance at church, but took high view of treason and seditious libel.
[xxvii. 202]

HOLT, JOHN (1743–1801), author; master of Walton grammar school, near Liverpool; published 'Characters of Kings and Queens of England,' 1786-8, and a survey of Lancashire agriculture, 1794.
[xxvii. 205]

HOLT, JOSEPH (1756–1826), Irish rebel; headed rebellion in co. Wicklow, 1798; joined Edward Roche and won victory at Ballyellis, 1798; separated from him and was defeated at Castle Carberry; held out in Wicklow three months; transported to Botany Bay, 1799; successful farmer in New South Wales; banished to Norfolk island on suspicion of rebellion, 1804; pardoned, 1809; wrecked on Eagle island during voyage to England, 1813.
[xxvii. 206]

HOLT, THOMAS (1578?–1624), architect; designed Wadham College, Oxford, and great quadrangle of the examination schools (now part of the Bodleian).
[xxvii. 207]

HOLT, WILLIAM (1545–1599), jesuit; B.A. Brasenose College, Oxford, 1566; fellow of Oriel, 1568; M.A., 1572; studied at Douay, 1574–6; jesuit novice, 1578; intrigued with Lennox in Scotland, 1581–2; arrested through English influence, 1583, but allowed to escape; rector of English college, Rome, 1586–7; Spanish agent at Brussels, 1588–98; died at Barcelona. [xxvii. 208]

HOLTBY, RICHARD (1553–1640), jesuit; of Cambridge and Hart Hall, Oxford; on English mission in north, 1579–81; joined jesuits, 1583; superior of Scots college at Pont-à-Mousson, 1587–9; vice-prefect of English mission, 1606–9; though fifty years in England never imprisoned; his account of persecution in the north in Morris's 'Troubles of our Catholic Forefathers.'
[xxvii. 209]

HOLTE, JOHN (*fl.* 1495), author of first Latin grammar in England (printed by Wynkyn de Worde, *c.* 1510, and Pynson, 1520); fellow of Magdalen College, Oxford, 1491; M.A., 1494. [xxvii. 210]

HOLTE, JOHN (*d.* 1540), bishop of Lydda, and suffragan to Fitzjames, bishop of London, 1506–22.
[xxvii. 210]

HOLTE, SIR THOMAS, first baronet (1571–1654), royalist; sheriff of Warwickshire, 1599; created baronet, 1612; built Aston Hall; entertained Charles I before Edgehill. [xxvii. 210]

HOLTZAPFFEL, CHARLES (1806–1847), mechanician; published 'Turning and Mechanical Manipulation,' 1843. [xxvii. 211]

HOLWELL, JOHN (1649–1686?), astrologer and mathematician; said to have surveyed New York, and been poisoned there; author of works, including 'A Sure Guide to the Practical Surveyor,' 1678, and 'Trigonometry made easy,' 1685. [xxvii. 211]

HOLWELL, JOHN ZEPHANIAH (1711–1798), governor of Bengal; grandson of John Holwell (1649–1686?) [q. v.]; surgeon in East India Company, 1732–49; drew up scheme for reform of zemindar's court, Calcutta; zemindar of the Twenty-four Parganas, Calcutta, 1751; as member of council defended Calcutta against Suráj ud Dowlah, 1756; succeeded Clive as temporary governor; dismissed from council for remonstrating against Vansittart's appointment, 1761; first European who studied Hindoo antiquities; published narrative of 'Black Hole' (1758), and works on Indian politics and mythology.
[xxvii. 212]

HOLWELL, WILLIAM (1726–1798), classical compiler; M.A. Christ Church, Oxford, 1748; B.D., 1760; vicar of Thornbury and chaplain to George III; compiled 'Beauties of Homer,' 1775. [xxvii. 213]

HOLWORTHY, JAMES (*d.* 1841), water-colour painter and friend of Turner. [xxvii. 214]

HOLYDAY or **HOLIDAY**, BARTEN (1593–1661), divine and translator; M.A. Christ Church, Oxford, 1615; chaplain to Sir Francis Steuart in Spain, 1618, and afterwards to Charles I; archdeacon of Oxford before 1626; D.D., *per literas regias*, 1642; translated Persius, Juvenal (published, 1673), and Horace. [xxvii. 214]

HOLYMAN, JOHN (1495–1558), bishop of Bristol; of Winchester and New College, Oxford; fellow of New College, 1512; B.C.L., 1514; M.A., 1518; D.D., 1531; preached against Lutheranism and opposed divorce of Queen Catherine; bishop of Bristol, 1554–8; helped to try the Oxford martyrs. [xxvii. 214]

HOLYOAKE, FRANCIS (1567–1653), lexicographer; studied at Queen's College, Oxford; rector of Southam, 1604; ejected by parliamentarians, 1642; his 'Dictionarium Etymologicum Latinum' (1633) enlarged by his son, 1677. [xxvii. 215]

HOLYOAKE, HENRY (1657–1731), head-master of Rugby; son of Thomas Holyoake [q. v.]; chaplain of Magdalen College, Oxford, 1681–90; M.A., 1681; head-master of Rugby, 1687–1731; held three Warwickshire livings; left money to poor of Rugby and to Magdalen College. [xxvii. 216]

HOLYOAKE, THOMAS (1616?–1675), divine; son of Francis Holyoake [q. v.]; M.A., 1639, and chaplain, Queen's College, Oxford; captain of undergraduate royalists; practised medicine till Restoration; prebendary of Wolverhampton. [xxvii. 215]

HOLYWOOD, CHRISTOPHER (1562–1616), jesuit; joined jesuits, 1582; professor of divinity at Dôle and Padua; imprisoned by English government, 1599; denounced by James I when superior of jesuits' mission in Ireland, 1604–16; published controversial works.
[xxvii. 216]

HOLYWOOD or **HALIFAX**, JOHN, in Latin JOHANNES DE SACRO BOSCO (*fl.* 1230), mathematician; died at Paris; author of 'Tractatus de Sphæra' (first printed at Ferrara, 1472, and frequently translated; his 'Algorismus' edited by J. O. Halliwell, 1838.
[xxvii. 217]

HOME. [See also HUME.]

HOME or **HUME**, SIR ALEXANDER (*d.* 1456), of Home; warden of the marches, 1449; accompanied William, earl of Douglas, to Rome, 1450, and founded collegiate church of Dunglass. [xxvii. 217]

HOME or **HUME**, SIR ALEXANDER, first BARON HOME (*d.* 1491), eldest son of Sir Alexander Home (*d.* 1456) [q. v.]; created lord of parliament, 1473; joined the Hepburns in driving Albany from Scotland; conspired against James III, 1482 and 1484; in the van at Sauchieburn, 1480; had great influence under James IV.
[xxvii. 218]

HOME or **HUME**, ALEXANDER, second BARON HOME (*d.* 1506), lord chancellor of Scotland; grandson of Sir Alexander Home or Hume, first baron [q. v.]; joined conspiracy against James III; privy councillor, 1488; lord chancellor of Scotland, 1488–1506; succeeded to barony, 1491; made pilgrimage to Canterbury, 1493; made raid in support of the pretender Perkin Warbeck, 1496–7. [xxvii. 219]

HOME, ALEXANDER, third BARON HOME (*d.* 1516), lord high chamberlain of Scotland ; son of Alexander Home or Hume, second baron [q. v.] ; lord high chamberlain, 1506 ; as warden of the borders invaded Northumberland, 1513 ; with Huntly commanded van at Flodden, 1513 ; as chief-justice south of Forth, 1514, proposed to recall Albany ; joined Angus against him and intrigued with England and Arran ; pardoned, but arrested at Edinburgh, and beheaded by the regent Albany.
[xxvii. 219]

HOME, ALEXANDER, fifth BARON HOME (*d.* 1575) ; succeeded his father, George Home, fourth baron [q. v.], 1547, while prisoner after Pinkie ; recaptured his castle, 1548 ; assisted French at Haddington ; warden of east marches, 1550 ; commissioner for treaty of Upsettlington, 1559 ; made privy councillor by Mary Queen of Scots, 1561 ; supported her till the Bothwell marriage ; tried to capture Bothwell at Borthwick, 1567 ; prominent at Carberry Hill, 1567 ; prevented Mary's escape at Edinburgh ; member of regent's council on Mary's abdication ; fought in van at Langside, 1568 ; saved Moray from capture, 1569 ; rejoined queen's party after his death ; Kirkcaldy's lieutenant during siege of Edinburgh Castle ; died in prison.
[xxvii. 221]

HOME or **HUME**, ALEXANDER, sixth BARON and first EARL OF HOME (1566 ?-1619), son of Alexander, fifth baron Home [q. v.] ; warden of the east marches, 1582-99 ; engaged in raid of Ruthven, 1582 ; imprisoned, 1583-4, for brawl with Francis Stewart Hepburn, fifth earl of Bothwell [q. v.] ; co-operated with Bothwell against Arran and befriended him in disgrace ; as captain of James VI's bodyguard aided him against Bothwell ; excommunicated as a papist, but absolved on subscribing confession of faith, 1593 ; lord of the articles, 1594 ; with James in the Tolbooth, 1596 ; accompanied James to England and became lieutenant of the marches, 1603 ; created Earl of Home, 1605.
[xxvii. 223]

HOME, DANIEL DUNGLAS (1833–1886), spiritualist medium ; related to the earls of Home ; while in Connecticut claimed to be warned by telepathy of his mother's death ; turned out of the house by his aunt on account of alleged spiritualistic rappings ; his *séances* attended by well-known Americans, including William Cullen Bryant and Judge Edmonds ; said to have been 'levitated,' 1852, at house of Ward Cheney ; came to England, 1855 ; phenomena attested by Sir David Brewster ; *séances* attended by Sir Edward Bulwer and the Brownings ; while in Italy became a Roman catholic ; held *séances* before sovereigns of France, Prussia, and Holland, 1857-8 ; held *séances* in London at houses of Thomas Milner-Gibson [q. v.] and other well-known persons, 1860–1 ; expelled from Rome as a sorcerer, 1864 ; secretary of Spiritual Athenæum in London, 1866 ; his 'levitations' in England attested by Lord Lindsay (earl of Crawford), Lord Adare (earl of Dunraven), and Mrs. Samuel Carter Hall ; followed German army from Sedan to Versailles, 1870 ; convinced (Sir) William Crookes, F.R.S., by submitting to tests in full light, 1871 ; published 'Incidents of My Life' (1863 and 1872), and, with William Howitt, 'Lights and Shadows of Spiritualism' (1877) ; died at Auteuil. [xxvii. 225]

HOME, SIR EVERARD, first baronet (1756–1832), surgeon ; king's scholar at Westminster, 1770 ; pupil of John Hunter ; F.R.S., 1785 ; lecturer on anatomy, 1792, and surgeon to St. George's Hospital, 1793–1827 ; keeper of Hunterian collection ; master (1813) and first president (1821) of Royal College of Surgeons ; Hunterian orator, 1814 and 1822 ; created baronet, 1813 ; surgeon to Chelsea Hospital, 1821–32 ; destroyed Hunter's manuscripts after utilising them ; edited Hunter's 'Treatise on the Blood,' prefixing short life, 1794 ; published 'Lectures on Comparative Anatomy,' 1814, and other medical works.
[xxvii. 227]

HOME, FRANCIS (1719–1813), professor of materia medica at Edinburgh ; studied medicine at Edinburgh ; surgeon of dragoons in seven years' war ; M.D. Edinburgh, 1750 ; professor of materia medica, 1768-98 ; published 'Principia Medicinæ,' 1758, and other works.
[xxvii. 228]

HOME, GEORGE, fourth BARON HOME (*d.* 1547), brother of Alexander Home, third baron [q. v.] ; was restored to title and lands, 1522 ; frustrated Scott of Buccleugh's attempt on James V, 1526 ; joined Argyll against Angus, 1528 ; helped to defeat English at Haddenrig, 1542 ; routed by Grey, 1547.
[xxvii. 229]

HOME or **HUME**, SIR GEORGE, EARL OF DUNBAR (*d.* 1611), lord high treasurer of Scotland ; of Primroknows, afterwards of Spott ; accompanied James VI to Denmark, 1589 ; master of the wardrobe, 1590 ; ally of Maitland and opponent of Bothwell ; special privy councillor, 1598 ; lord high treasurer, 1602 ; created an English baron, 1604, and Scottish earl, 1605 ; commissioner of the border for both kingdoms, 1606 ; managed for James the Linlithgow trial (1606), Glasgow assembly (1610), and measures for introduction of episcopacy in Scotland ; K.G., 1608 ; obtained confession from George Sprott, 1608, and James Elphinstone, first baron Balmerino [q. v.]
[xxvii. 230]

HOME, HENRY, LORD KAMES (1696–1782), Scottish judge and author ; called to Scots bar, 1724 ; published 'Remarkable Decisions of Court of Session' (1716–28), 1728 ; lord of session as Lord Kames, 1752 ; lord of justiciary, 1763–82 ; charged with heresy on account of his 'Essays on the Principles of Morality and Natural Religion' (1751), written against Hume ; his 'Elements of Criticism' (1762) praised by Dugald Stewart ; published also 'Sketches of History of Man,' 1774, 'The Gentleman Farmer,' 1776, and many legal and historical works.
[xxvii. 232]

HOME, SIR JAMES, OF COLDINGKNOWS, third EARL OF HOME (*d.* 1666), succeeded as earl, 1633 ; at first a covenanter ; signed band at Cumbernauld, 1641, and thenceforth supported the king ; served under Hamilton at Preston, 1648 ; his estates seized by Cromwell ; reinstated, 1661, and named privy councillor of Scotland ; member of high commission, 1664. [xxvii. 234]

HOME, JAMES (1760–1844), professor of materia medica, Edinburgh, 1798, in succession to his father, Francis Home [q. v.] ; professor of medicine at Edinburgh, 1821–44. [xxvii. 235]

HOME, JOHN (1722–1808), author of 'Douglas' ; educated at Leith grammar school and Edinburgh University ; volunteer, 1745 ; captured at Falkirk, 1746 ; minister of Athelstaneford, 1747 ; intimate with Hume, Robertson, and the poet Collins ; his 'Douglas' (rejected by Garrick) performed in Edinburgh, 1756, and produced by Rich at Covent Garden, 1757 ; resigned his ministerial charge, owing to proceedings of presbytery, 1757 ; private secretary to Bute and tutor to Prince of Wales ; his 'Agis' (previously rejected) produced by Garrick at Drury Lane, 1758 ; his 'Siege of Aquileia' (1760) and 'Fatal Discovery' (1769) failures ; received pension from George III and sinecure from Bute ; his 'Alonzo' played successfully by Mrs. Barry, 1773, but 'Alfred' (1778) a failure ; settled at Edinburgh, 1779, and was visited by Scott ; published 'History of Rebellion of 1745,' 1802 ; works edited by Henry Mackenzie, 1822. [xxvii. 235]

HOME, ROBERT (*d.* 1836 ?), painter ; brother of Sir Everard Home [q. v.] ; exhibited at the Academy and at Dublin ; chief painter to king of Oude ; died at Calcutta.
[xxvii. 238]

HOME, ROBERT (1837–1879), colonel of royal engineers ; ably reported on defence of Canadian frontier, 1864 ; deputy-assistant quartermaster-general at Aldershot, 1865 ; secretary to royal engineers' committee, 1870 ; commanded royal engineers in Ashanti war, 1873 ; assistant quartermaster-general at headquarters, 1876 ; reported on defence of Constantinople ; published 'Précis of Modern Tactics,' 1873. [xxvii. 238]

HOME, WILLIAM, eighth EARL OF HOME (*d.* 1761), soldier ; served under Cope (1745) and commanded Glasgow volunteer regiment, 1745 ; lieutenant-general ; governor of Gibraltar, 1757–61 ; Scottish representative peer. [xxvii. 239]

HOMER, ARTHUR (1758–1806), author of 'Bibliographia Americana,' 1789 ; son of Henry Homer the elder [q. v.] ; fellow of Magdalen College, Oxford, 1782–1802 ; M.A., 1781 ; D.D., 1797. [xxvii. 240]

HOMER, HENRY, the elder (1719–1791), author of works on enclosures ; M.A. Magdalen College, Oxford, 1743 ; rector of Birdingbury. [xxvii. 240]

HOMER, HENRY, the younger (1753–1791), classical scholar and friend of Dr. Parr ; eldest son of Henry Homer the elder [q. v.] ; fellow of Emmanuel College, Cambridge, 1778-88 ; M.A., 1776 ; B.D., 1783 ; edited Tacitus (1790), Livy (1794), Ovid's 'Heroides' (1789), Persius (1789), Sallust (1789), and Cæsar (1790). [xxvii. 240]

HOMER, PHILIP BRACEBRIDGE (1765–1838), assistant-master at Rugby; brother of Henry Homer the younger [q. v.]; fellow of Magdalen College, Oxford, 1802–6, of Rugby, 1825; M.A., 1788; B.D., 1804; published original poems, translations from Metastasio, and the Eton Greek grammar, with notes (1825); completed his brother Henry's classics. [xxvii. 241]

HONDIUS (DE HONDT), ABRAHAM (1638 ?–1691), painter of animals and hunting scenes; in England, 1665–91. [xxvii. 241]

HONDIUS, JODOCUS [JOOS or JOSSE DE HONDT] (1563–1611), engraver; came to England from Ghent; made large globes, illustrated voyages of Drake and Cavendish, and engraved portraits; at Amsterdam, 1594–1611. [xxvii. 242]

HONE, HORACE (1756–1825), miniature-painter; son of Nathaniel Hone [q. v.]; exhibited at Academy, 1772–1782, and in Dublin; A.R.A., 1799. [xxvii. 243]

HONE, JOHN CAMILLUS (d. 1837), miniature-painter in London and the East Indies; brother of Horace Hone [q. v.] [xxvii. 243]

HONE, NATHANIEL (1718–1784), portrait-painter; studied in Italy; excelled in enamel-painting; exhibited with Society of Artists; an original R.A.; caricatured Reynolds in 'The Conjuror,' 1775; painted also Whitefield, John Wesley, Sir John Fielding, and his son, John Camillus Hone [q. v.], as 'David' and 'Spartan Boy.' [xxvii. 242]

HONE, WILLIAM (1780–1842), author and bookseller; commenced publishing (1817) political satires on the government (including 'John Wilkes's Catechism' and 'The Sinecurist's Creed'), illustrated by Cruikshank; prosecuted for his 'Political Litany,' but acquitted, 1817; aided by public subscription, set up shop in Ludgate Hill, where Cruikshank illustrated his 'Political House that Jack Built,' 1819, 'Man in the Moon,' 1820, 'Bank-Restriction Barometer,' 1820, 'Political Showman,' 1821, 'Facetiæ and Miscellanies,' 1827; his 'Apocryphal New Testament' (1820) attacked in 'Quarterly Review'; published sixpenny reprints, 'Ancient Mysteries,' 1823, 'Every Day Book,' 1826–7 (dedicated to Lamb and praised by Scott and Southey), and 'Table Book,' 1827–8; edited Strutt's 'Sports and Pastimes,' 1830; 'Early Life and Conversion of William Hone, by Himself,' edited by his son, 1841. [xxvii. 243]

HONEY, GEORGE (1822–1880), actor and vocalist; played in opera till 1863; afterwards took eccentric rôles, such as Eccles in Robertson's 'Caste,' and Cheviot Hill in W. S. Gilbert's 'Engaged.' [xxvii. 247]

HONEY, LAURA (1816 ?–1843), actress; very successful as Psyche in 'Cupid' and as Lurline (Adelphi); at the City of London played in 'The Waterman' and 'Riquet with the Tuft,' and sang 'My beautiful Rhine.' [xxvii. 247]

HONNER, MRS. MARIA (1812–1870), actress; née Macarthy; excelled in pathetic parts; played Rosalie Somers with Edmund Kean; played Julia in 'The Hunchback,' 1835; married Robert William Honner [q. v.], 1836; filled place of Mrs. Yates. [xxvii. 248]

HONNER, ROBERT WILLIAM (1809–1852), actor and manager; played under Andrew Ducrow, Grimaldi, Elliston, Benjamin Webster, and Davidge; lessee of Sadler's Wells, 1835–40; manager of the Surrey, 1835–8, and 1842–6. [xxvii. 248]

HONORIUS, SAINT (d. 653), fifth archbishop of Canterbury; consecrated by Paulinus at Lincoln, 628; exercised jurisdiction over Kent and East Anglia. [xxvii. 249]

HONYMAN, SIR GEORGE ESSEX, fourth baronet (1819–1875), judge; barrister, Middle Temple, 1849; Q.C., 1866; serjeant-at-law, 1873; justice of common pleas, 1873–5. [xxvii. 249]

HONYWOOD, MRS. MARY (1527–1620), daughter of Robert Waters of Lenham; celebrated for longevity, piety, and number of lineal descendants (367). [xxvii. 249]

HONYWOOD, MICHAEL (1597–1681), dean of Lincoln; grandson of Mrs. Mary Honywood [q. v.]; fellow of Christ's College, Cambridge; M.A., 1618; D.D., 1661; with Henry More and Edward King ('Lycidas') as fellows and Milton when student; rector of Kegworth; during Protectorate lived at Utrecht; dean of Lincoln, 1660–81; at Lincoln built cathedral library and gave books. [xxvii. 250]

HONYWOOD, SIR ROBERT (1601–1686), of Charing; translator of Battista Nani's 'History of the Affairs of Europe,' 1673; served in Palatinate; knighted as steward to queen of Bohemia, 1625; member of council of state, 1659; went on embassy to Sweden. [xxvii. 251]

HONYWOOD, SIR THOMAS (1586–1666), parliamentarian; of Marks Hall, Essex; knighted, 1632; joined Fairfax before Colchester, 1648; commanded regiment at Worcester, 1651; knight of the shire for Essex, 1654, 1656; sat in Cromwell's House of Lords, 1657. [xxvii. 251]

HOOD, LADY (1783–1862). [See STEWART-MACKENZIE, MARIA ELIZABETH FREDERICA.]

HOOD, ALEXANDER (1758–1798), navy captain; brother of Sir Samuel Hood (1762–1814) [q. v.]; served on the Resolution in Captain Cook's second voyage, 1772; captain of the Barfleur off Cape Henry, 1781, and St. Kitts, 1782; fought at battle of Dominica, 1782; captured the Cérès; put ashore by Spithead mutineers, 1797; captured the Hercule off the Bec du Raz, but was killed; epitaph by Southey on monument at Butleigh. [xxvii. 252]

HOOD, ALEXANDER, first VISCOUNT BRIDPORT (1727–1814), admiral; brother of Samuel Hood, first viscount Hood [q. v.]; flag-captain to Sir Charles Saunders [q. v.] in Mediterranean, 1756–9; took part in Hawke's victory of 20 Nov. 1759; captured the Warwick in Bay of Biscay, 1761; treasurer of Greenwich, 1766; commanded the Robust at Ushant, 1777, and gave evidence in favour of Palliser against Keppel; assisted in relief of Gibraltar, 1782; entered parliament, 1784; K.B., 1787; admiral of the blue, 1794; second in command to Lord Howe on 1 June 1794, and was created Baron Bridport (Irish peerage); defeated Villaret-Joyeuse and captured three French ships, 1795; vice-admiral of England, 1796; created a British baron, 1796; as commander of Channel fleet blockaded Brest almost continuously, 1797–1800; created viscount, 1801; often confused with his brother; portraits of him by Reynolds at Greenwich. [xxvii. 253]

HOOD, CHARLES (1826–1883), major-general; led attack on Redan, 1855; commanded the buffs on entry into Sebastopol, and 58th in Bengal, 1860; major-general, 1870. [xxvii. 256]

HOOD, EDWIN PAXTON (1820–1885), congregational divine and author; minister in London, Brighton, and Manchester; benefactor of Hospital for Incurables; published 'Self-Education,' 1851, and 'The Peerage of Poverty' (1st ser. 3rd ed., 1861); published also popular works on great writers, statesmen, and preachers; died in Paris. [xxvii. 256]

HOOD, FRANCIS GROSVENOR (1809–1855), lieutenant-colonel of grenadier guards, 1841; grandson of Samuel Hood, first viscount Hood [q. v.]; led (as major 3rd battalion) 3rd battalion of grenadiers at the Alma, 1854; shot in trenches before Sebastopol. [xxvii. 257]

HOOD, JOHN (1720–1783 ?), surveyor; invented Hood's compass theodolite; said to have anticipated Hadley's quadrant. [xxvii. 258]

HOOD, ROBIN, legendary outlaw; the name, which originally represented a mythical forest-elf, 'Hodeken,' is part of the designation of places and plants in every part of England. His historical authenticity is ill-supported. As an historical character Robin Hood appears in Wyntoun's 'Chronicle of Scotland' (c. 1420), and is referred to as a ballad hero by Bower, Major, and Stow. The first detailed history, 'Lytell Geste of Robyn Hoode' (printed, c. 1495), locates him in south-west Yorkshire; later writers placing him in Sherwood and Plumpton Park (Cumberland), and finally making him Earl of Huntingdon. Plays dealing with his exploits were written by Munday, Chettle, and others (1600–1784). The 'True Tale of Robin Hood' (verse) was issued, 1632, 'Robin Hood's Garland,' 1670, and prose narrative, 1678. Major first assigned him to the reign of Richard I. A date (18 Nov. 1247) was given for his death by Martin Parker ('True Tale,' c. 1632) and by Thoresby, and his pedigree was supplied by Stukeley. According to Joseph Hunter [q. v.] he was a contemporary of Edward II and adherent of Thomas of Lancaster. [xxvii. 258]

HOOD, SIR SAMUEL, first baronet (1762-1814), vice-admiral; brother of Alexander Hood (1758-1798) [q. v.]; on the Courageux, 1776; fought off Ushant, 1778; lieutenant at actions off Martinique, 1781, Cape Henry, 1781, and St. Kitts, 1782, Dominica, 1782, and Mona Passage, 1782; commanded Juno in Mediterranean, 1793-5; with the Zealous under Nelson at Santa Cruz, 1797; distinguished at the Nile, 1798; as commander-in-chief on Leeward station captured St. Lucia and Tobago and Dutch South American settlements, 1803-4; took French ships off Rochefort, but lost an arm, 1805; under Gambier at Copenhagen, 1807; reduced Madeira, 1807; second in command under Saumarez in Baltic, 1808; created baronet after Coruña, 1809; vice-admiral, 1811; commanded in East Indies, 1812-14; died at Madras. [xxvii. 261]

HOOD, SAMUEL, first VISCOUNT HOOD (1724-1816), admiral; entered navy, 1741; saw junior service under captains Thomas Smith (d. 1762) [q. v.], Thomas Grenville (1719-1747) [q. v.], and Rodney; while in temporary command of the Antelope captured French privateers, 1757; commanded the Vestal in Basque roads, 1758; captured the Bellona off Finisterre, 1759; commander on North American station, 1767-70; created baronet, 1778; joined Rodney in expedition against St. Eustatius, 1781; while blockading Martinique engaged by superior French force; commanded rear in Graves's action off the Chesapeake, September, 1781; repulsed De Grasse off Basseterre, 1782; second in command under Rodney at Dominica (12 April); created Baron Hood of Catherington (Irish peerage), and given freedom of the city, 1782; M.P., Westminster, 1784; vice-admiral, 1787; a lord of the admiralty, 1788-93; as commander in the Mediterranean occupied Toulon, and when abandoning it took away anti-revolutionary refugees; captured Corsica, 1794; recalled for political reasons; admiral, 1794; created Viscount Hood and governor of Greenwich, 1796; G.C.B., 1815. [xxvii. 263]

HOOD, SAMUEL (1800 ?-1875), author of treatise 'On the Law of Decedents,' 1847; member of Philadelphia bar, 1836-75; grandson of John Hood [q. v.] [xxvii. 258]

HOOD, THOMAS (fl. 1582-1598), mathematician; fellow of Trinity College, Cambridge, 1578; M.A., 1581; first Thomas Smith lecturer in mathematics in London, 1582; translated Ramus's 'Elements of Geometry,' 1590; published works on mathematical appliances. [xxvii. 270]

HOOD, THOMAS (1799-1845), poet; contributed to 'London Magazine,' 1821-3, becoming acquainted with Lamb, Hazlitt, and De Quincey; collaborated with John Hamilton Reynolds [q. v.] in 'Odes and Addresses to Great People,' 1825; issued 'Whims and Oddities,' 1826-7; became editor of the 'Gem,' 1829 (in which 'Eugene Aram's Dream' appeared); began 'Comic Annual,' 1830; lived at Coblentz, 1835-7, and Ostend, 1837-40; published 'Hood's Own,' 1838, and 'Up the Rhine,' 1839; returned, 1840, and edited 'New Monthly Magazine,' 1841-3, writing for it 'Miss Kilmansegg'; his 'Song of the Shirt' published anonymously in 'Punch,' 1843; established 'Hood's Magazine,' 1844; issued 'Whimsicalities,' 1844; received pension; collected works issued, 1882-4. [xxvii. 270]

HOOD, THOMAS, the younger (1835-1874), known as TOM HOOD, humorist; son of Thomas Hood (1799-1845) [q. v.]; of Pembroke College, Oxford; became editor of 'Fun,' 1865; began 'Tom Hood's Comic Annual,' 1867; works include 'Pen and Pencil Pictures,' 1857, and 'Captain Masters's Children,' 1865. [xxvii. 272]

HOOK, JAMES (1746-1827), organist at Vauxhall Gardens, 1774-1820, and composer; composed over two thousand songs, including 'Within a Mile' and 'The Lass of Richmond Hill,' also dramatic and concerted pieces; died at Boulogne. [xxvii. 272]

HOOK, JAMES (1772 ?-1828), dean of Worcester; son of James Hook (1746-1827) [q. v.]; while at Westminster edited 'The Trifler'; graduated from St. Mary Hall, Oxford, 1796; private chaplain to Prince of Wales; archdeacon of Huntingdon, 1814; rector of Whippingham, 1817; dean of Worcester, 1825-8; published novels and other works. [xxvii. 273]

HOOK, JOHN (1634-1710), master of Savoy Hospital, 1699-1702; son of William Hook [q. v.] [xxvii. 280]

HOOK, THEODORE EDWARD (1788-1841), novelist and wit; son of James Hook (1746-1827) [q. v.]; educated at Harrow; as a boy wrote words for his father's comic operas and melodramas; early entered Prince of Wales's set and became known as an improviser and practical joker; went to Mauritius as accountant-general, 1813; dismissed for deficiencies in accounts, 1817; imprisoned, 1823-5, and his property confiscated; published, as 'Richard Jones,' 'Exchange no Robbery' (farce) and 'Tentamen' (satire on Queen Caroline), 1819-20; began to edit the tory 'John Bull,' 1820; published 'Sayings and Doings' (nine novels), 1826-9, 'Maxwell,' 1830, 'Gilbert Gurney,' 1836, 'Gurney Married,' 1838, 'Jack Brag,' 1836, and 'Births, Marriages, and Deaths,' 1839; edited 'New Monthly Magazine,' 1836-41; his effects seized by the crown; the Lucian Gay of 'Coningsby' and Mr. Wagg of 'Vanity Fair.' [xxvii. 274]

HOOK, WALTER FARQUHAR (1798-1875), dean of Chichester; son of James Hook (1772 ?-1828) [q. v.]; educated at Winchester and Christ Church, Oxford; M.A., 1824; D.D., 1837; curate at Whippingham; incumbent of Holy Trinity, Coventry, 1828-37; preached at Chapel Royal his sermon 'Hear the Church,' 1838, affirming apostolical succession of English bishops; as vicar of Leeds, 1837-59, built new parish church (1841) and many others, with schools and parsonage houses; obtained act of parliament for subdivision of parish (1844); propounded in letter to Bishop Thirlwall (1846) scheme of rate-paid schools with separate religious instruction; dean of Chichester, 1859-75. His works include 'Church Dictionary,' 1842, 'Dictionary of Ecclesiastical Biography,' 1845-52, and 'Lives of Archbishops of Canterbury,' 1860-1875 (index, 1876). [xxvii. 276]

HOOK, WILLIAM (1600-1677), puritan divine; M.A. Trinity College, Oxford, 1623; vicar of Axmouth; emigrated to New England, 1640, and became minister at Taunton, Massachusetts, and 'teacher' at Newhaven; sent description of affairs in New England to Cromwell, 1653; Cromwell's chaplain in England, 1656; published 'New England's Teares for Old England's Feares,' 1640, and with John Davenport [q. v.] 'A Catechisme . . . for the . . . Church . . . at New Haven.' [xxvii. 279]

HOOKE, JOHN (1655-1712), serjeant-at-law; of Trinity College, Dublin; barrister, Gray's Inn, 1681; serjeant-at-law, 1700; chief-justice of Carnarvon, Merioneth, and Anglesey, c. 1703 and 1706; removed for receiving a present, 1707, but subsequently cleared. [xxvii. 280]

HOOKE, LUKE JOSEPH (1716-1796), Roman catholic divine; son of Nathaniel Hooke (d. 1763) [q. v.]; D.D. Sorbonne, 1736; professor of theology, 1742; virtually compelled to resign by Archbishop de Beaumont; when librarian at the Mazarin Library visited by Dr. Johnson, 1775; dismissed from librarianship by Paris Directory, 1791; edited 'Memoirs of Duke of Berwick,' 1778; died at St. Cloud. [xxvii. 281]

HOOKE, NATHANIEL, the elder (1664-1738), Jacobite; brother of John Hooke [q. v.]; of Dublin and Glasgow Universities and Sidney Sussex College, Cambridge; sent by Monmouth to raise London, 1685; pardoned by James II; joined Dundee and was captured, 1689; served with Jacobites in Ireland and with French in Flanders; undertook secret missions to Scottish Jacobites, 1705 and 1707; corresponded with Marlborough and Stair; his correspondence (1703-7) edited by the Rev. W. D. Macray, 1870-1. [xxvii. 281]

HOOKE, NATHANIEL or NATHANAEL, the younger (d. 1763), author; nephew of Nathaniel Hooke the elder [q. v.]; friend of Pope and Martha Blount and disciple of Fénelon; admitted at Lincoln's Inn, 1702; wrote 'Account of Conduct of the Dowager Duchess of Marlborough' (1742) at her dictation; published 'Roman History,' 1738-71, translation of Sir Andrew Michael Ramsay's 'Travels of Cyrus,' 1739, and a work denouncing Chesterfield's 'Letters,' published, 1791. [xxvii. 282]

HOOKE, ROBERT (1635-1703), experimental philosopher; educated at Westminster under Busby and at Christ Church, Oxford; M.A., 1663; assisted Thomas Willis [q. v.] in his chemistry and Robert Boyle [q. v.] with his air-pump; elected curator of experiments to Royal Society, 1662; F.R.S., 1663; secretary, 1677-82; Gresham professor of geometry, 1665; as surveyor of London designed Montague House, Bethlehem Hospital, and College of Physicians; in his 'Micrographia' (1665) pointed out real nature of combustion; proposed to measure force of gravity by swinging of pendulum, 1666; showed experimentally that centre of gravity of earth and moon is the point describing an ellipse round the sun; in astronomy discovered fifth star in Orion, 1664, inferred rotation of Jupiter, 1664, first observed a star by daylight, and made earliest attempts (1669) at telescopic determination of parallax of a fixed star; in optics helped Newton by hints; first applied spiral spring to regulate watches; expounded true theory of elasticity and kinetic hypothesis of gases, 1678; his anticipation of law of inverse squares admitted by Newton; first asserted true principle of the arch; constructed first Gregorian telescope, 1674; described a system of telegraphy, 1684; invented marine barometer and other instruments; posthumous works edited by R. Waller, 1705, and Derham, 1726. [xxvii. 283]

HOOKER or **HOKER**, JOHN (*fl.* 1540), of Maidstone: poet and dramatist; fellow of Magdalen College, Oxford, 1530; M.A., 1535; B.D., 1540. [xxvii. 289]

HOOKER, *alias* VOWELL, JOHN (1526?-1601), antiquary; educated at Oxford; visited Cologne and Strasburg; first chamberlain of Exeter, 1555; M.P., Athenry (Irish parliament), 1568; contributed to new edition of Holinshed, 1586; wrote also 'The Lyffe of Sir Peter Carewe,' and works concerning Exeter. [xxvii. 287]

HOOKER, RICHARD (1554?-1600), theologian; nephew of John Hooker *alias* Vowell [q. v.]; admitted at Corpus Christi College, Oxford, by influence of Bishop Jewel; scholar, 1573; M.A. and fellow, 1577; deputy Hebrew professor, 1579; intimate at Oxford with (Sir) Edwin Sandys and George Cranmer [q. v.]; incumbent of Drayton-Beauchamp, 1584-5; master of the Temple, 1585; rector of Boscombe, Wiltshire, and (1595-1600) of Bishopsbourne, Kent, where the inscription on his monument first calls him 'Judicious.' Five books (four books, 1594, fifth book, 1597) of 'The Laws of Ecclesiasticall Politie' appeared in his lifetime, the so-called sixth and the eighth in 1648. The seventh was first included in Gauden's edition, 1662. The sixth book is demonstrably spurious. The whole was reissued, with life by Izaak Walton, 1666, and frequently re-edited. It was attacked by the puritans in 'A Christian Letter to certaine English Protestants' (1599) and defended by William Covell [q. v.], admired by James I and Charles I, and praised for its style by Fuller and Swift. Other works by Hooker were issued at Oxford, 1613. [xxvii. 289]

HOOKER, THOMAS (1586?-1647), New England divine; fellow of Emmanuel College, Cambridge; M.A., 1611; rector of Esher, 1620; as lecturer at Chelmsford cited for nonconformity, 1629; withdrew to Holland (1630) to avoid citation of high commission; sailed for New England, 1633; pastor of the eighth church in Massachusetts, till removal to Hartford, Connecticut, 1636; published theological works, including 'A Survey of the Summe of Church Discipline,' issued 1648. [xxvii. 295]

HOOKER, WILLIAM DAWSON (1816-1840), eldest son of Sir William Jackson Hooker [q. v.]; privately printed 'Notes on Norway,' 1837. [xxvii. 298]

HOOKER, SIR WILLIAM JACKSON (1785-1865), director of Kew Gardens; formed collection of Norfolk birds; visited Iceland and printed 'Recollections,' 1811; became acquainted with foreign botanists during tour of 1814; regius professor of botany at Glasgow, 1820; K.H., 1836; greatly extended and threw open to the public Kew Gardens, where, with John Stevens Henslow [q. v.], he founded a museum of economic botany, 1847; his herbarium purchased by the nation; F.L.S., 1806; F.R.S., 1812; LL.D. Glasgow; D.C.L. Oxford, 1845. His works include 'Muscologia Britannica,' 1818-27, 'Flora Boreali-Americana,' 1833-40, 'Species Filicum,' 1846-64. [xxvii. 296]

HOOKES, NICHOLAS (1628-1712), poet; scholar of Westminster and Trinity College, Cambridge; B.A., 1653; published 'Amanda' (1653) and other verses. [xxvii. 299]

HOOLE, CHARLES (1610-1667), educational writer; M.A. Lincoln College, Oxford, 1636; master of Rotherham school; rector of Great Ponton, 1642; sequestrated; became known as teacher in London; prebendary of Lincoln

and rector of Stock, Essex; published 'Terminationes et Exempla,' 1650, and other school manuals. [xxvii. 299]

HOOLE, ELIJAH (1798-1872), orientalist; while Wesleyan missionary in Southern Indian was member of committee for revising Tamil versions of the bible; published translations into Tamil, 'Personal Narrative' (1820-8), and other works; secretary of Wesleyan Missionary Society, 1836. [xxvii. 300]

HOOLE, JOHN (1727-1803), translator; principal auditor at India House; visited Johnson in his last illness; his translations of Tasso's 'Jerusalem Delivered' (1763) and Ariosto's 'Orlando Furioso' (1783) frequently reprinted; published also versions of Metastasio's 'Dramas,' 'Life of John Scott of Amwell' (1785), and three tragedies, acted at Covent Garden. [xxvii. 300]

HOOPER, EDMUND (1553?-1621), organist of Westminster Abbey, 1606-21, and composer of church music; gentleman of the Chapel Royal, 1603. [xxvii. 301]

HOOPER, GEORGE (1640-1727), bishop of Bath and Wells; scholar of St. Paul's and Westminster and student of Christ Church, Oxford; M.A., 1663; D.D., 1677; classical, Hebrew, and Arabic scholar; chaplain to Bishop Morley and Archbishop Sheldon; rector of Lambeth, 1675; precentor of Exeter; as almoner to Princess Mary confirmed her in Anglican principles and offended William of Orange; dean of Canterbury, 1691; prolocutor of the lower house of convocation, 1701; bishop of St. Asaph, 1702-3; accepted see of Bath and Wells, 1703 at importunity of his friend Ken, who dedicated to him his 'Hymnarium'; collective edition of his works, issued 1757, includes 'Calculation of the Credibility of Human Testimony,' and treatise on Tertullian's 'De Valentinianorum Hæresi.' [xxvii. 301]

HOOPER, JOHN (*d.* 1555), bishop of Gloucester and Worcester; B.A. Oxford, 1519; said to have been a Cistercian; adopted protestant views and disputed with Gardiner; fled from England, 1539, to avoid persecution; while at Zurich, 1547-9, adopted views of John à Lasco [see LASKI]; as chaplain to Somerset, 1549, led advanced reformers and denounced Bonner; when nominated to see of Gloucester (1550) refused to wear vestments, and only gave in after committal to the Fleet, 1551; showed great zeal in his diocese and was liberal to the poor; followed Zurich usage in appointing 'superintendents'; member of commission to report on ecclesiastical laws, 1551; bishop of Worcester, *in commendam*, 1552, Gloucester being subsequently made an archdeaconry; opposed attempt to set aside Mary; deprived by Queen Mary and sentenced for heresy; burned at Gloucester. His works consist mainly of homilies and biblical expositions (collected edition issued, 1855). [xxvii. 304]

HOOPER, ROBERT (1773-1835), medical writer; M.A. and M.B. Pembroke College, Oxford, 1804; M.D. St. Andrews, 1805; practised in Savile Row, making special study of pathology. His works include 'Compendious Medical Dictionary,' 1798, and 'Anatomist's Vade-Mecum,' 1798. [xxvii. 306]

HOOPER, WILLIAM HULME (1827-1854), lieutenant in the navy; shared in expedition of the Plover, 1848-50, in search of Sir John Franklin [q. v.], publishing an account, 1853. [xxvii. 307]

HOOPPELL, ROBERT ELI (1833-1895), antiquary; M.A. St. John's College, Cambridge, 1858; LLD., 1865; ordained priest, 1859; English chaplain at Menai Bridge, 1859-61; first head-master of Dr. Winterbottom's nautical college, South Shields, 1861-75; rector of Byers Green, co. Dublin, 1875; published writings relating to excavated Roman camp at South Shields and other antiquarian subjects. [Suppl. ii. 438]

HOOTEN, ELIZABETH (*d.* 1672), first female quaker minister; imprisoned at Derby, 1651, York, 1652, and Lincoln, 1654; went to Boston, Massachusetts, 1662; barbarously treated at Cambridge, U.S.A.; returned to England; accompanied George Fox to Jamaica, 1670, and died there. [xxvii. 308]

HOOTON, CHARLES (1813?-1847), novelist; lived savage life in Texas; journalist in New Orleans, New York, and Montreal; published 'Colin Clink' (in 'Bentley's Miscellany,' and republished, 1841), 'St. Louis's Isle,' 1847, and other works. [xxvii. 308]

HOPE, SIR ALEXANDER (1769–1837), general; second son of the second Earl of Hopetoun; served in Flanders and Holland, 1794–5, as aide-de-camp to Sir Ralph Abercromby; wounded while commanding the 14th in attack on Gueldermasen, 1795; major-general, 1808; governor of Royal Military College, Sandhurst, 1812; undertook mission to Sweden, 1813; honorary D.C.L. Oxford, 1824; lieutenant-governor of Chelsea Hospital, 1826; M.P., Dumfries, 1796, Linlithgowshire, 1802–34; general and G.C.B. [xxvii. 308]

HOPE (afterwards BERESFORD-HOPE), ALEXANDER JAMES BERESFORD (1820–1887), politician and author; son of Thomas Hope (1770?–1831) [q. v.]; of Harrow and Trinity College, Cambridge; M.A., 1844; D.C.L., 1848; tory M.P., Maidstone, 1841–52 and 1857–9, Stoke, 1865–8, and Cambridge University, 1868–87; inherited Marshal Lord Beresford's English estates, 1854; prominent opponent of Deceased Wife's Sister Bill, 1859, abolition of church rates, Reform Bill of 1867, and Burials Bill, 1873; privy councillor, 1880; founded missionary college at Canterbury, and built All Saints' Church, Margaret Street, London; established 'Saturday Review,' 1855, with John Douglas Cook [q. v.] as editor; president of Institute of Architects, 1865–7; trustee of British Museum and National Portrait Gallery; published 'Hymns of the Church literally translated' (1844), 'The English Cathedral of the Nineteenth Century' (1861), works on the American civil war and on church politics, and two novels. [xxvii. 309]

HOPE, MRS. ANNE (1809–1887), authoress; *née* Fulton; wife and biographer of James Hope (1801–1841) [q. v.]; converted to Romanism, 1850; published 'Acts of the Early Martyrs,' 1855, lives of St. Philip Neri (1859) and St. Thomas Becket (1868), 'Conversion of the Teutonic Race,' 1872, and 'Franciscan Martyrs in England,' 1878. [xxvii. 311]

HOPE, ARCHIBALD, LORD RANKEILLOR (1639–1706), lord of session, 1689, and of justiciary, 1690; second son of Sir John Hope, lord Craighall [q. v.] [xxvii. 321]

HOPE, CHARLES, first EARL OF HOPETOUN (1681–1742); supported union with England; created Scots peer, 1703; representative peer from 1722; lord high commissioner of church of Scotland, 1723. [xxvii. 311]

HOPE, CHARLES, LORD GRANTON (1763–1851), president of court of session; eldest son of John Hope (1739–1785) [q. v.]; studied law at Edinburgh University; admitted advocate, 1784; sheriff of Orkney, 1792; lord advocate, 1801; M.P., Edinburgh, 1803; lord justice clerk, 1804; president of court of session, 1811–41; privy councillor, 1822; lord justice general from 1836; active colonel of Edinburgh volunteers. [xxvii. 312]

HOPE, FREDERICK WILLIAM (1797–1862), entomologist and collector; M.A. Christ Church, Oxford, 1823; presented to the university his collection of insects and prints, and founded professorship of zoology; president of Entomological Society, 1835 and 1846; published the 'Coleopterist's Manual,' 1837–40.
[xxvii. 313]

HOPE, GEORGE (1811–1876), Scottish agriculturist; his holding at Fenton Barns, Haddingtonshire, regarded as model farm; wrote against corn laws and game laws; contributed to Sir A. Grant's 'Recess Studies,' 1870.
[xxvii. 313]

HOPE, SIR HENRY (1787–1863), admiral; served under his cousin (Admiral Sir James Hope (1808–1881) [q. v.]) in the Kent; captured in Swiftsure, 1801; commanded cruisers in Mediterranean, 1808–12; while in command of the Endymion captured the U.S. ship President off Sandy Hook, 1815; rear-admiral, 1846; K.C.B., 1855; admiral, 1858. [xxvii. 314]

HOPE, HENRY PHILIP (*d.* 1839), picture and diamond collector; brother of Thomas Hope (1770?–1831) [q. v.] [xxvii. 329]

HOPE, SIR JAMES (1614–1661), of Hopetoun; lawyer and lead-worker; sixth son of Sir Thomas Hope, first baronet (*d.* 1646) [q. v.]; general of the cunzie-house, 1642; a lord of session, 1649; member of committee of estates; commissioner of justice, 1652; member of English council of state, 1653. [xxvii. 315]

HOPE (afterwards HOPE JOHNSTONE), JAMES, third EARL OF HOPETOUN (1741–1816), with foot-guards

at Minden; succeeded to earldom, 1781; representative peer, 1784 and 1794; succeeded to estates of Marquis of Annandale and assumed name of Johnstone, 1792; created British baron, 1809, for raising Hopetoun fencibles.
[xxvii. 316]

HOPE, JAMES (1801–1841), physician; studied at Edinburgh, St. Bartholomew's Hospital, and on the continent; early practised auscultation; physician to Marylebone Infirmary, 1831; assistant at St. George's Hospital, 1834, full physician, 1839; F.R.C.P., 1840; F.R.S., 1832; published 'Treatise on Diseases of the Heart,' 1832, and a work on morbid anatomy, 1833–4. [xxvii. 316]

HOPE, JAMES (1764–1846?), United Irishman; cotton-weaver; supported union between Romanists and presbyterians in Ulster; joined Roughford volunteer corps and (1795) the reconstructed United Irish Society; founded branch at Dublin; present at Ballinahinch, 1798; assisted Robert Emmet [q. v.] and organised rising in co. Down, 1803, but was amnestied. [xxvii. 317]

HOPE, SIR JAMES (1808–1881), admiral of the fleet; cousin of Sir Henry Hope [q. v.]; distinguished in engagement with Obligado batteries, 1845; C.B., 1846; commanded the Majestic in the Baltic, 1854–6; rear-admiral, 1857; commander-in-chief in China, 1859; repulsed and wounded in attempt to force passage of the Peiho, 1859; took Taku forts, 1860; created K.C.B., 1860; wounded while serving against Taepings, 1862; commander in North America, 1863; G.C.B., 1865; commander at Portsmouth, 1869–72; admiral, 1870; admiral of the fleet, 1879. [xxvii. 318]

HOPE, SIR JAMES ARCHIBALD (1785–1871), general; served with 26th in Hanover, 1805–6, and at Copenhagen, 1807; on staff of Sir John Hope (1765–1836) [q. v.] in Spain, 1808–9, and Walcheren expedition, 1809; aide-de-camp to Graham at Barossa, 1811, Ciudad Rodrigo, 1812, and Badajoz, 1812; assistant adjutant-general at Salamanca, Vittoria, and St. Sebastian, and with Beresford in France; exchanged into Scots Guards, 1814; major-general in Lower Canada, 1841–7; G.C.B.; general, 1859. [xxvii. 320]

HOPE, SIR JOHN, LORD CRAIGHALL (1605?–1654), eldest son of Sir Thomas Hope, first baronet (*d.* 1646) [q. v.]; lord of session, 1632; knighted, 1632; member of committee of estates, 1640, of Cromwell's judicial committee, 1652; represented Scotland in English parliament, 1653. [xxvii. 320]

HOPE, SIR JOHN (1684?–1766). [See BRUCE, SIR JOHN HOPE.]

HOPE, JOHN (1739–1785), author; grandson of Charles Hope, first earl of Hopetoun [q. v.]; M.P., Linlithgowshire, 1768–70; published 'Letters on Credit,' 1784, and other works. [xxvii. 321]

HOPE, JOHN (1725–1786), professor of botany at Edinburgh; grandson of Archibald Hope, lord Rankeillor [q. v.]; M.D. Glasgow, 1750; professor of botany and materia medica, Edinburgh, 1761; regius professor of medicine and botany, 1768; president, Edinburgh College of Physicians; F.R.S.; founded new Edinburgh botanic gardens, 1776; genus *Hopea* named after him by Linnæus, whose 'Genera Animalium' he edited, 1781.
[xxvii. 321]

HOPE, JOHN, fourth EARL OF HOPETOUN (1765–1823), general; M.P., Linlithgowshire, 1790; adjutant-general under Abercromby in West Indies, 1796, and in Holland, 1799; wounded at Alexandria, 1801; lieutenant-general, 1808; second in command under Sir John Moore in Sweden and in the Peninsula; commanded left wing at Coruña and directed embarkation; headed division in Walcheren expedition, 1809; succeeded Graham in the Peninsula; led first division at Nivelle and the Nive, 1813; conducted blockade of Bayonne; wounded and captured in final sortie of Bayonne garrison, 1814; created Baron Niddry; succeeded his half-brother James, third Earl of Hopetoun [q.v.], 1816; general, 1819. [xxvii. 322]

HOPE, SIR JOHN (1765–1836), lieutenant-general; son of John Hope (1739–1785) [q. v.]; in Dutch service, 1778–82; aide-de-camp to Sir William Erskine in Flanders and Germany, 1792–3; commanded 28th, 1796–9, and 37th, 1799–1804; deputy adjutant-general under Cathcart at Hanover, 1805, and Copenhagen, 1807; commanded brigade at Salamanca, 1812; lieutenant-general, 1819; knighted, 1821; G.C.H. [xxvii. 324]

HOPE, JOHN (1794–1858), Scottish judge; eldest son of Charles Hope (1763–1851) [q. v.]; advocate, 1816; summoned to Commons' bar for breach of privilege, 1822; solicitor-general for Scotland, 1822–30; dean of Faculty of Advocates, 1830; lord justice clerk, 1841–58; privy councillor, 1844; edited diary of Sir David Hume of Crossrigg, 1828. [xxvii. 324]

HOPE, JOHN WILLIAMS (1757–1813), banker and merchant; son of William Williams; assumed name of Hope on marriage; banker at Amsterdam; one of the eight statesmen of Holland, 1794–1806. [xxvii. 325]

HOPE, SIR THOMAS (1606–1643), of Kerse; son of Sir Thomas Hope, first baronet [q. v.]; admitted advocate, 1631; knighted, 1633; commissioner for Clackmannan, 1639–41; colonel of Leslie's bodyguard, 1639–40; negotiated compromise between Charles I and the estates; lord justice-general, 1641–3; wrote the 'Law Repertorie.' [xxvii. 325]

HOPE, SIR THOMAS, first baronet (d. 1646), lord-advocate of Scotland; advocate, 1605; made reputation by defence of John Forbes (1568?–1634) [q. v.], and other ministers at Linlithgow, 1606; prepared deed revoking James I's grants of church property, 1625; lord advocate, 1626; created Nova Scotia baronet, 1628; conducted case against Balmerino, 1634; as lord high commissioner to general assembly maintained the king's temporising policy, 1643; his 'Minor Practicks' published by Bayne, 1726. [xxvii. 326]

HOPE, THOMAS (1770?–1831), virtuoso and author; of the Hopes of Amsterdam; settled in England, c. 1796; collected marbles and sculptures, and deposited them in Duchess Street, London, and at Deepdene, Surrey; patron of Canova, Thorwaldsen, and Flaxman; caricatured with his wife by Dubost as 'Beauty and the Beast,' 1810; published 'Anastasius' (anonymously), 1819, 'Household Furniture,' 1807, and other works. [xxvii. 327]

HOPE, THOMAS CHARLES (1766–1844), professor of chemistry at Edinburgh; third son of John Hope (1725–1786) [q. v.]; professor of chemistry at Glasgow, 1787–9; professor of chemistry, Edinburgh, 1799–1843; proved that strontian contained a peculiar earth; estimated maximum density point of water; founded chemical prize at Edinburgh. [xxvii. 329]

HOPE, SIR WILLIAM JOHNSTONE (1766–1831), vice-admiral; son of John Hope (1739–1785) [q. v.]; lieutenant of the Boreas under Nelson, 1787; flag-captain to Rear-admiral Pasley in action of 1 June, 1794, to Duncan in the Venerable and the Kent, 1795–6, and 1798–9; served in Egypt, 1800–1; M.P., Dumfries, 1800–4, Dumfriesshire, 1804–30; a lord of the admiralty, 1807–9; vice-admiral, 1819; member of admiralty board, 1820–8; G.C.B., 1825. [xxvii. 329]

HOPE, WILLIAM WILLIAMS (1802–1855), man of fashion and virtuoso; son of John Williams Hope [q. v.] [xxvii. 325]

HOPE-SCOTT, JAMES ROBERT (1812–1873), parliamentary barrister; third son of Sir Alexander Hope [q. v.]; travelled in Germany and Italy before going to Eton; at Christ Church, Oxford, became the friend of William Ewart Gladstone and Roundell Palmer, afterwards Earl of Selborne; fellow of Merton, 1833; D.C.L., 1843; barrister, Inner Temple, 1840; named chancellor of Salisbury, 1840, after arguing before House of Lords against Ecclesiastical Duties and Revenues Bill, 1840; joined tractarians, becoming Newman's chief adviser; with Manning received into Roman church, 1851; soon obtained immense parliamentary practice; Q.C., 1849; married John Gibson Lockhart's daughter, and assumed additional name of Scott, 1853, on becoming possessor of Abbotsford; wrote against Ecclesiastical Titles Act, 1867. [xxvii. 330]

HOPETOUN, EARLS OF. [See HOPE, CHARLES, first EARL, 1681–1742; HOPE, JAMES, third EARL, 1741–1816; HOPE, JOHN, fourth EARL, 1765–1823.]

HOPKIN, HOPKIN (1737–1754), famous dwarf; son of Lewis Hopkin [q. v.] [xxvii. 331]

HOPKIN, LEWIS (1708–1771), Welsh poet; registered bard, 1760; with Edward Evans (1716–1798) [q. v.] made rhymed version of Ecclesiastes, 1767; translated 'Chevy Chase,' 1770; collected works ('Y Fel Gafod') edited by J. Miles, 1813. [xxvii. 332]

HOPKINS, CHARLES (1664?–1700?), poet; son of Ezekiel Hopkins [q. v.]; friend of Dryden and Congreve; of Trinity College, Dublin, and Queens' College, Cambridge; B.A. Cambridge, 1688; published 'Epistolary Poems,' 1694, 'Whitehall,' 1698, and three tragedies. [xxvii. 333]

HOPKINS, EDWARD (1600–1657), governor of Connecticut; emigrated, 1637; governor of Connecticut, 1640–52 (alternate years); helped to form union of New England colonies, 1643; navy commissioner in England, 1653; M.P., Dartmouth, 1656; Hopkinton bought from his donation to Harvard. [xxvii. 333]

HOPKINS, EZEKIEL (1634–1690), bishop of Derry; of Merchant Taylors' School and Magdalen College, Oxford; M.A., 1656; chaplain to Lord Robartes (viceroy of Ireland); archdeacon of Waterford, 1669; bishop of Raphoe, 1670–81; bishop of Derry, 1681–90; left Ireland at Revolution; works edited by Josiah Pratt, 1809. [xxvii. 334]

HOPKINS, GEORGE (1620–1666), rector of Evesham (ejected, 1662), and author of 'Salvation from Sin' (1655). [xxvii. 338]

HOPKINS, JOHN (d. 1570), contributor to metrical Psalms; B.A. Oxford, 1544; Suffolk schoolmaster; rector of Great Waldingfield, 1561–70; the 'Old Hundredth' psalm often attributed to him.' [xxvii. 334]

HOPKINS, JOHN (fl. 1700), verse-writer; brother of Charles Hopkins [q. v.]; M.A. Jesus College, Cambridge, 1698; chief works, 'Milton's Paradise Lost imitated in Rhyme,' 1699, and 'Amasia,' 1700. [xxvii. 336]

HOPKINS, JOHN LARKIN (1819–1873), organist of Rochester (1841) and Trinity College, Cambridge (1856); Mus. Doc. Cambridge, 1857; composed 'Five Glees and a Madrigal,' 1842, and church music; published 'New Vocal Tutor,' 1855. [xxvii. 336]

HOPKINS, MATTHEW (d. 1647), witch-finder; said to have been a lawyer at Ipswich and Manningtree; made journeys for discovery of witches in eastern counties and Huntingdonshire, 1644–7; procured special judicial commission (1645) under John Godbolt [q. v.] by which sixty were hanged in Essex in one year, nearly forty at Bury, and many at Norwich and in Huntingdonshire; published 'Discovery of Witches,' 1647; exposed by John Gaule; hanged as a sorcerer; referred to in 'Hudibras.' [xxvii. 336]

HOPKINS, RICHARD (d. 1594?), translator; of St. Alban's Hall, Oxford, and Middle Temple; studied at Spanish universities, Louvain, Rheims, and Paris; translated Spanish religious works. [xxvii. 337]

HOPKINS, WILLIAM (fl. 1674), stenographer; published 'The Flying Pen-Man,' 1670. [xxvii. 338]

HOPKINS, WILLIAM (1647–1700), divine; son of George Hopkins [q. v.]; M.A. St. Mary Hall, Oxford, 1668; D.D., 1692; chaplain to Henry Coventry (1619–1686) [q. v.] in second embassy to Sweden, 1671; prebendary of Worcester, 1675, and master of St. Oswald's Hospital, 1697; published 'Book of Bertram or Ratramnus concerning the Body and Blood of the Lord,' 1686; assisted Gibson with edition of 'Saxon Chronicle' and Camden in 'Britannia.' [xxvii. 338]

HOPKINS, WILLIAM (1706–1786), theological writer; B.A. All Souls College, Oxford, 1728; master of Cuckfield School, 1756; as vicar of Bolney, made alterations in the liturgy; published Arian pamphlets attacking liturgy. [xxvii. 339]

HOPKINS, WILLIAM (1793–1866), mathematician and geologist; of Peterhouse, Cambridge; seventh wrangler, 1827; M.A., 1830; as coach, had Stokes, Sir W. Thomson, Fawcett, and Todhunter among his pupils; studied geology; Wollaston medallist, 1850; president of Geological Society, 1851, and of British Association, 1853; prize founded in his honour by Cambridge Philosophical Society; published works, including 'Elements of Trigonometry,' 1833, and 'Theoretical Investigations on Motion of Glaciers,' 1842. [xxvii. 339]

HOPKINSON, JOHN (1610–1680), antiquary; of Lincoln's Inn; secretary to Dugdale during visitation of Yorkshire; made large collections for history of Yorkshire. [xxvii. 340]

HOPKINSON, JOHN (1849-1898), electrical engineer; educated at the Owens College, Manchester, and Trinity College, Cambridge; senior wrangler, 1871; Smith's prizeman; fellow; D.Sc. London, 1871; manager and engineer in lighthouse and optical department of Messrs. Chance Brothers, Birmingham, 1872-8; consulting engineer in London, 1878; F.R.S., 1878, and member of council, 1886-7 and 1891-3; patented three-wire system of distributing electricity, 1882; published, with his brother, Edward Hopkinson, paper describing improvements in dynamos, which was foundation of accurate design of dynamos in accordance with theory, 1886; professor of electrical engineering, King's College, London, 1890; consulting engineer to contractors of City and South London Railway; member of council of Institute of Civil Engineers, 1895; member of Institution of Electrical Engineers; killed in Alpine accident. A collection of his scientific papers was published, 1901. [Suppl. ii. 439]

HOPKINSON, WILLIAM (*fl.* 1583), divine; B.A. St. John's College, Cambridge, 1567; published translation from Beza's vindication of Calvin's predestination. [xxvii. 341]

HOPKIRK, THOMAS (1790 ?-1851 ?) Glasgow botanist; F.L.S., 1812; published 'Flora Anomoia,' 1817. [xxvii. 341]

HOPLEY, EDWARD WILLIAM JOHN (1816-1869), painter; exhibited at British Institution and Royal Academy; invented trigonometrical system of facial measurement. [xxvii. 341]

HOPPER, HUMPHREY (*fl.* 1799-1834), sculptor. [xxvii. 341]

HOPPER, THOMAS (1776-1856), architect and surveyor; built Arthur's Club and various mansions. [xxvii. 341]

HOPPNER, JOHN (1758-1810), portrait-painter; born in London of German parentage; chorister in Chapel Royal; exhibited at Royal Academy (1780-1809) 168 pictures, mostly portraits, including 'A Sleeping Nymph'; R.A., 1795; portrait-painter to Prince of Wales, 1789; Lawrence's chief rival; 'Lady Culling (Eardley) Smith and Children' and 'Mrs. Lascelles' among his finest works. [xxvii. 342]

HOPPUS, JOHN (1789-1875), professor at University College, London; M.A. Glasgow; LL.D., 1839; independent minister at Carter Street Chapel, London; first professor of philosophy and logic, University College, London, 1829-66; F.R.S., 1841; published 'Account of Bacon's "Novum Organon,"' 1827, 'Thoughts on Academical Education,' 1837, and other works. [xxvii. 343]

HOPSON, CHARLES RIVINGTON (1744-1796), physician to Finsbury Dispensary; educated at St. Paul's School and Leyden; M.D., 1767; published 'Essay on Fire,' 1782, and translations from German of J. G. Zimmermann and Wiegleb. [xxvii. 344]

HOPSONN or **HOPSON**, EDWARD (*d.* 1728), vice-admiral. [xxvii. 345]

HOPSONN, SIR THOMAS (1642-1717), vice-admiral; served against Dutch, 1672-3; commanded the York at Beachy Head, 1690, and the St. Michael at Barfleur, 1692; rear-admiral, 1693; commanded squadron off French coast, 1694-5, and Channel squadron, 1699; vice-admiral, 1702; as second in command under Rooke forced boom protecting French and Spanish fleet at Vigo, 1702, and was knighted and pensioned; M.P., Newtown (Isle of Wight), 1698-1705. [xxvii. 344]

HOPTON, ARTHUR (1588 ?-1614), astrologer and mathematician; of Clement's Inn; friend of Selden; published prognostications for years, 1607-14, 'Bacvlum Geodæticum,' 1610, and similar works. [xxvii. 346]

HOPTON, SIR ARTHUR (1588 ?-1650), diplomatist; of Lincoln College, Oxford; secretary to Lord Cottington's embassy in Spain, 1629, ambassador, 1638, and throughout civil wars; knighted, 1638. [xxvii. 345]

HOPTON, JOHN (*d.* 1558), bishop of Norwich; prior of Oxford Dominicans; D.D. Oxford, 1532; rector of St. Anne's, London, 1539, of Fobbing, Essex, 1548; chaplain to Princess Mary at Copt Hall; bishop of Norwich, 1554-1558; persecuted the protestants. [xxvii. 346]

HOPTON, RALPH, first BARON HOPTON (1598-1652), royalist commander; nephew of Sir Arthur Hopton [q. v.]; of Lincoln College, Oxford; served under elector

palatine and Mansfeld; K.B., 1625; M.P., Bath, in first parliament of Charles I, and Somerset in Short parliament; M.P., Wells, 1628-9, and in Long parliament; supported Strafford's attainder and presented Grand Remonstrance to king, 1641, but was sent to Tower by parliament for denouncing militia ordinance, 1642; expelled the house; defeated parliamentarians at Bradock Down and Stratton, Cornwall, 1643; joined Maurice's attack on Waller at Lansdown, 1643, and, though wounded, directed defence of Devizes, 1643; created Baron Hopton on resignation of governorship of Bristol to Rupert, 1643; defeated at Cheriton, 1644; succeeded to command of Goring's undisciplined force in the west; routed at Torrington, 1646; capitulated at Truro, 1646; left England with Prince Charles, 1648; opposed concessions to presbyterians and retired to Wesel, 1650; died at Bruges. [xxvii. 347]

HOPTON, SUSANNA (1627-1709), devotional writer; *née* Harvey; wife of Richard Hopton, Welsh judge. [xxvii. 350]

HOPWOOD, JAMES, the elder (1752 ?-1819), engraver; secretary, Artists' Benevolent Fund. [xxvii. 350]

HOPWOOD, JAMES, the younger (*fl.* 1800-1850), stipple-engraver; son of James Hopwood the elder [q. v.] [xxvii. 351]

HOPWOOD, WILLIAM (1784-1853), engraver; brother of James Hopwood the younger [q. v.] [xxvii. 351]

HORBERY, MATTHEW (1707 ?-1773), divine; M.A. Lincoln College, Oxford, 1733; fellow of Magdalen College, Oxford, 1733; defended Waterland against John Jackson (1686-1763) [q. v.]; published treatise on 'Scripture Doctrine of Eternal Punishment,' 1744; canon of Lichfield, 1736; vicar of Hanbury, 1740, of Standlake, 1756; collected works issued, 1828. [xxvii. 351]

HORDEN, HILDEBRAND (*d.* 1796), actor; member of Drury Lane and Dorset Garden Company, 1695-6; said to have written 'Neglected Virtue'; killed in tavern brawl. [xxvii. 351]

HORMAN, WILLIAM (*d.* 1535), vice-provost of Eton; fellow of New College, Oxford, 1477-85; master of Eton, 1485, and fellow, 1502; his Latin aphorisms ('Vulgaria') printed by Pynson, 1519, and De Worde, 1540; in 'Antibossicon' (1521) attacked grammatical works of Robert Whitynton. [xxvii. 352]

HORN, ANDREW (*d.* 1328), chamberlain of London, 1320-8; compiled 'Liber Horn'; author or editor of 'La Somme appelle Miroir des Justices' (printed, 1624). [xxvii. 352]

HORN, CHARLES EDWARD (1786-1849), vocalist and composer; made reputation as Caspar in 'Der Freischütz,' at Drury Lane, 1824; subsequently music publisher at New York; director at Princess's, London, 1843-1847; conductor of Handel and Haydn Society, Boston, 1848; composed popular airs, including 'Cherry Ripe' and 'I know a bank,' operas and oratorios, and glees and pianoforte music; edited 'Hindustani Melodies,' 1813. [xxvii. 353]

HORNBLOWER, JABEZ CARTER (1744-1814), engineer; son of Jonathan Hornblower [q. v.]; employed by Dutch and Swedish governments; patented machine for glazing calicoes. [xxvii. 354]

HORNBLOWER, JONATHAN (1717-1780), engineer. [xxvii. 354]

HORNBLOWER, JONATHAN CARTER (1753-1815), engineer; son of Jonathan Hornblower [q. v.]; employed by Watt; his steam engine on the expansion principle (1781) declared infringement of Watt's patent, 1799; contributed to Nicholson's 'Journal.' [xxvii. 354]

HORNBLOWER, JOSIAH (1729 ?-1809), speaker of New Jersey assembly; brother of Jonathan Hornblower [q. v.] [xxvii. 354]

HORNBY, SIR GEOFFREY THOMAS PHIPPS (1825-1895), admiral of the fleet; son of Admiral Sir Phipps Hornby [q. v.]; entered navy, 1837; lieutenant, 1844; flag-lieutenant to his father in Pacific, 1846; commander, 1850; captain, 1852; at Vancouver's island, 1858; under Sir William Fanshawe Martin [q. v.] in Mediterranean, 1861-2; flag-captain to Rear-admiral Sidney Colpoys Dacres [q. v.] in Channel, 1862-5; first class commodore on west coast of Africa, 1865-7; rear-admiral, 1869; commanded flying squadron, 1869-71, and

Channel squadron, 1871–4; lord of admiralty, 1875–7; vice-admiral, 1875; commander-in-chief in Mediterranean, 1877–80; conducted fleet through Dardanelles to Constantinople during Russo-Turkish war, 1878; K.C.B., 1878; admiral, 1879; president of Royal Naval College, 1881–2; commander-in-chief at Portsmouth, 1882–5; commanded evolutionary squadron, 1885; G.C.B., 1885; principal naval aide-de-camp to the queen, 1886; admiral of the fleet, 1888.   [Suppl. ii. 441]

HORNBY, Sir PHIPPS (1785–1867), admiral; midshipman in the Victory, 1804; while commanding the Duchess of Bedford engaged two privateers off Gibraltar, 1806; in the Volage took part in action off Lissa, 1811; C.B., 1815; commander in Pacific, 1847–50; a lord of the admiralty, 1851–2; admiral, 1858; G.C.B., 1861.   [xxvii. 355]

HORNBY, WILLIAM (*fl.* 1618), poet; author of 'The Scovrge of Drvnkennes,' 1618, and 'Hornbyes Hornbook,' 1622.   [xxvii. 355]

HORNE, GEORGE (1730–1792), bishop of Norwich; B.A. University College, Oxford, 1749; fellow of Magdalen College, Oxford, 1750, and president, 1768–90; M.A., 1752; royal chaplain, 1771–81; vice-chancellor, 1776; dean of Canterbury, 1781; bishop of Norwich, 1790–2; allowed John Wesley to preach in his diocese; defended Hutchinsonian views against Newton; published 'Commentary on the Psalms,' 1771; and wrote against Law, Swedenborg, and Kennicott.   [xxvii. 356]

HORNE, JOHN (1614–1676), puritan divine; of Trinity College, Cambridge; incumbent of Sutton St. James and All Hallows, Lynn Regis; attacked quakers, independents, and presbyterians; published 'The Open Door,' 1650, and other devotional works.   [xxvii. 357]

HORNE, RICHARD HENRY or HENGIST (1803–1884), author; educated at Sandhurst; in Mexican navy against Spain; travelled in America and Canada; advocated establishment of Society of Literature and Art, 1833; edited 'Monthly Repository,' 1836–7; published 'Cosmo de Medici,' 1837, 'Death of Marlowe,' 1837, and other tragedies; corresponded with Mrs. Browning (Miss Barrett), 1839–46; collaborated with her in 'New Spirit of the Age,' 1844; his epic, 'Orion,' published at a farthing, 1843; issued 'Ballad Romances,' 1846, and 'The Poor Artist,' 1850; in Australia, 1852–69, as commissioner for crown lands, and magistrate; granted civil list pension, 1874; published 'Australian Facts and Prospects,' 1859.   [xxvii. 358]

HORNE, ROBERT (1519?–1580), bishop of Winchester; fellow of St. John's College, Cambridge, 1537; M.A., 1540; D.D., 1549; rector of All Hallows, Bread Street, 1550; dean of Durham, 1551; removed St. Cuthbert's tomb with his own hands; helped in preparation of forty-five articles; refused see of Durham, 1552; deprived of deanery on accession of Mary; fled to Zurich; chief minister at Frankfort, 1556, at Strasburg, 1557–8; restored at Durham, 1559; led disputations against the Romanists at Westminster; bishop of Winchester, 1560–1580; had custody of Feckenham, and John Leslie (1527–1596) [q. v.], bishop of Ross; vigorous enforcer of conformity; purged Corpus Christi, Christ's, and St. John's Colleges, Cambridge, of Romanism; pulled down tabernacle work at New College, Oxford; silenced organs and tried to abolish vestments; assisted in drawing up 'Book of Advertisements,' 1564, canons of 1571; in 'Bishops' Bible' (1568), revised Isaiah, Jeremiah, and Lamentations.   [xxvii. 359]

HORNE, ROBERT (1565–1640), divine; probably chaplain of Magdalen Hall, Oxford, 1585–96; M.A. Magdalen Hall, Oxford, 1587; published theological works.   [xxvii. 362]

HORNE, THOMAS (1610–1654), master of Eton; M.A. Magdalen Hall, Oxford, 1633; master of Tunbridge, 1640–8, of Eton, 1648–54; author of classical manuals.   [xxvii. 362]

HORNE, THOMAS HARTWELL (1780–1862), biblical scholar, bibliographer, and polemic; at Christ's Hospital with Samuel Taylor Coleridge; at Record Office, 1817–19; honorary M.A. Aberdeen, 1818; rector of St. Edmund and St. Nicholas Acons, London, 1833; sublibrarian at Surrey Institution, 1809–23; senior assistant in printed books department, British Museum, 1824–60; F.S.A., 1828; B.D. Cambridge, 1829; his 'Introduction to Critical Study and Knowledge of the Holy Scriptures'

(1818; Suppl. 1821) frequently reissued and enlarged; fifth volume of seventh edition published separately as 'Manual of Biblical Bibliography,' 1839; published also 'Introduction to Study of Bibliography,' 1814, 'Deism Refuted,' 1819, 'Manual of Parochial Psalmody,' 1829, and treatises against Romanism, catalogues, and compilations; contributed to 'Encyclopædia Metropolitana'; edited Bishop Beveridge's 'Works,' 1824, and other publications.   [xxvii. 363]

HORNE, Sir WILLIAM (1774–1860), master in chancery; barrister, Lincoln's Inn, 1798; K.C., 1818; attorney-general to Queen Adelaide, 1830; M.D., Helston, 1812–18, Bletchingley, Newtown (Isle of Wight), 1831–2, and Marylebone, 1833–4; solicitor-general, 1830; knighted, 1830; attorney-general, 1832; having scruples against pronouncing death-sentence, resigned exchequer judgeship rather than go on circuit; master in chancery, 1839–53.   [xxvii. 365]

HORNE TOOKE, JOHN (1736–1812). [See TOOKE.]

HORNEBOLT or **HORNEBAUD**, **HORENBOUT**, **HOORENBAULT**, **HOREBOUT**, GERARD (1480?–1540), painter to Henry VIII; came to England from Ghent about 1528.   [xxvii. 365]

HORNEBOLT, **HORNEBAUD**, or **HOORENBAULT**, LUCAS (*d.* 1544), king's painter, 1534; relative of Gerard Hornebolt [q. v.]; instructed Holbein in miniature-painting.   [xxvii. 366]

HORNEBOLT, SUSANNA (1503–1545), illuminator; daughter of Gerard Hornebolt [q. v.]   [xxvii. 366]

HORNEBY, HENRY (*d.* 1518), master and benefactor of Peterhouse, Cambridge; D.D. Clare Hall, 1491; dean of Wimborne; held various prebends; master of Peterhouse, 1509–18; as secretary and chancellor to Margaret, duchess of Richmond, assisted in opening of St. John's College.   [xxvii. 366]

HORNECK, ANTHONY (1641–1697), divine; came to England from Germany, *c.* 1661; M.A. Heidelberg (incorporated at Queen's College, Oxford, 1664); chaplain of Queen's College, Oxford, and vicar of All Saints', Oxford; preacher at the Savoy, 1671; king's chaplain, 1689; prebendary of Westminster, 1693, and Wells, 1694; popular as preacher and casuist; gave offence by supporting social reform; ancestor of Goldsmith's 'Jessamy Bride'; devotional works frequently reprinted.   [xxvii. 367]

HORNER, FRANCIS (1778–1817), politician; studied at Edinburgh; member of Edinburgh Speculative Society; called to Scottish bar, 1800; joined English bar, 1807; contributed to first number of 'Edinburgh Review,' 1802; M.P., St. Ives, 1806, Wendover, 1807; as chairman of bullion committee (1810) recommended early resumption of cash payments; returned for St. Mawes, 1813; took part in debates on corn laws and negro slavery, 1813–15; thanked by common council of the city, 1815; proposed measure to regulate proceedings of Irish grand juries, 1816; spoke ably against ministerial foreign policy, and again advocated cash payments; translated Euler's 'Elements of Algebra,' 1797; published 'Short Account of a late Short Administration,' 1807; died at Pisa and was buried at Leghorn.   [xxvii. 368]

HORNER, LEONARD (1785–1864), geologist and educationalist; studied at Edinburgh University; brother and biographer of Francis Horner [q. v.]; secretary of Geological Society, 1810; president, 1846; F.R.S., 1813; organised whig meetings at Edinburgh, 1821–6; founded London Institution, 1827; warden of London University, 1827–31; commissioner to inquire into employment of children in factories, 1833, and a chief inspector under Factories Act; anticipated some of Murchison and Sedgwick's work on palæozoic rocks.   [xxvii. 371]

HORNER, WILLIAM GEORGE (1786–1837), mathematician; head-master of Kingswood school (1806–9), and afterwards of Grosvenor Place, Bath (1809–37); discovered method of solving numerical equations by continuous approximation.   [xxvii. 372]

HORNSBY, THOMAS (1733–1810), astronomer; fellow of Corpus Christi College, Oxford; M.A., 1757; Savilian professor of astronomy and F.R.S., 1763; first Radcliffe observer, 1772; Radcliffe librarian, 1783; Sedleian professor, 1782; D.D., 1785; observed transit of Venus in

1761 and 1769, and deduced solar parallax ; edited vol. i. of Bradley's 'Astronomical Observations,' 1798. [xxvii. 372]

HORROCKS, JEREMIAH (1617 ?-1641), astronomer : sizar at Emmanuel College, Cambridge, 1632-5 : commenced acquaintance with William Crabtree [q. v.], 1636 ; observed partial solar eclipse of 1639 with half-crown telescope at Toxteth Park ; when curate of Hoole predicted and observed transit of Venus across the sun, 24 Nov. (O.S.) 1639 ; began first tidal observations, 1640 ; obligations for his ascription to moon of an elliptic orbit acknowledged by Newton ; detected 'long inequality' of Jupiter and Saturn, and probably identified solar attraction with terrestrial gravity ; marble scroll in his memory, with inscription by Dean Stanley, in Westminster Abbey, 1875 ; his 'Venus in Sole visa' first printed by Hevelius at Danzig, 1662 ; 'Opera Posthuma' issued by Royal Society, 1672 and 1678. [xxvii. 373]

HORROCKS, JOHN (1768-1804), manufacturer : erected cotton-spinning mill at Preston, 1786 ; acquired large fortune as muslin-manufacturer ; as M.P. for Preston consulted by Pitt on commercial matters. [xxvii. 375]

HORROCKS, JOHN AINSWORTH (1818-1846), Australian explorer and pioneer ; grandson of John Horrocks [q. v.] [xxvii. 375]

HORSA (d. 455), joint-founder of Kent ; brother of Hengist [q. v.] ; a Jute ; arrived with his brother at Ebbsfleet, Thanet, 449 ; resisted by Vortigern ; killed at Aylesford. [xxv. 411]

HORSBURGH, JAMES (1762-1836), hydrographer ; when first mate on a trading ship wrecked on Diego Garcia from error in chart, 1786 ; made charts of Straits of Macassar, of western Philippines, and track from Dampier's Strait to Batavia ; published 'Directions for Sailing to and from East Indies, China, New Holland, Cape of Good Hope, and interjacent Ports,' 1809-11 ; F.R.S., 1806 ; hydrographer to East India Company, 1810. [xxvii. 376]

HORSBURGH, JOHN (1791-1869), historical engraver ; executed plates after Turner ; illustrated Scott's works ; engraved Scott's portraits by Lawrence and Watson Gordon. [xxvii. 376]

HORSEY, SIR EDWARD (d. 1583), naval and military commander ; served under the emperor ; implicated in Throgmorton and Dudley conspiracy, 1556 ; confidant of Leicester ; served under Warwick at Havre, 1562-3 ; captain of Isle of Wight, 1566-83 ; commanded horse against northern insurgents, 1569 ; negotiated pacification between French king and Huguenots, 1573 ; ambassador in Netherlands ; knighted, 1577 ; privy councillor ; died in Isle of Wight of the plague. [xxvii. 377]

HORSEY, SIR JEROME (fl. 1573-1627), traveller ; probably nephew of Sir Edward Horsey [q. v.] ; went to Moscow as clerk in Russia company, 1573 ; sent by Czar Ivan to purchase munitions of war in England. 1580 ; became esquire of the body to Queen Elizabeth ; after return was sent by Czar Feodor with despatches to Elizabeth, 1585 ; obtained monopoly of trade for English company, 1587 ; obliged to leave Russia, 1587 ; charged with malversation and illegal trading, and refused audience by the czar, 1590 ; knighted, 1603 ; high sheriff of Buckinghamshire, 1610 ; M.P. for Cornish boroughs, 1593-1622 ; account of Russian travels edited by E. A. Bond, 1856. [xxvii. 378]

HORSFIELD, THOMAS (1773-1859), naturalist ; born and educated in Pennsylvania ; served in East Indies under Dutch and English, 1799-1819 ; keeper of East India Company's Museum, Leadenhall Street, 1820-59 ; published 'Plantæ Javanicæ rariores,' 1838-52, and (with Sir W. Jardine) 'Illustrations of Ornithology,' 1830. [xxvii. 379]

HORSFIELD, THOMAS WALKER (d. 1837), topographer ; F.S.A., 1826 ; published 'History and Antiquities of Lewes,' 1824-7, and (with William Durrant Cooper [q. v.]) 'History and Topography of Sussex,' 1835. [xxvii. 380]

HORSFORD, SIR ALFRED HASTINGS (1818-1885), general ; served with 1st battalion rifle brigade in Kaffir war, 1847-8, and commanded it in war of 1852-3 and the Crimea ; led 3rd battalion at Cawnpore and advance on Lucknow ; commanded brigade at siege of Lucknow,

1858, and in subsequent operations ; deputy adjutant-general at Horse Guards, 1860-6 ; military secretary, 1874-80 ; lieutenant-general, 1874 ; represented England at Brussels conference, 1874 ; G.C.B., 1875 ; general, 1877. [xxvii. 380]

HORSFORD, SIR JOHN (1751-1817), major-general in Bengal artillery ; of Merchant Taylors' School and St. John's College, Oxford ; fellow, 1768-71 ; enlisted under false name ; received commission, 1778 ; served in second Mysore war, 1790-1 ; commanded artillery under Lake, 1803-5, and brigade at siege of Komanur, 1807 ; head of Bengal artillery from 1808 ; major-general, Bengal artillery, 1811 ; directed siege of Háthras, 1817 ; K.C.B., 1815 ; died at Cawnpore. [xxvii. 381]

HORSLEY, CHARLES EDWARD (1822-1876), musical composer ; son of William Horsley [q. v.] ; studied under Moscheles, Hauptmann, and Mendelssohn ; composed instrumental works in Germany, in England three oratorios, ode for opening of Melbourne Town Hall (1870), music to 'Comus,' and other music while in America ; died at New York ; his 'Text-book of Harmony' published, 1876. [xxvii. 381]

HORSLEY, JOHN (1685-1732), archæologist ; M.A. Edinburgh, 1701 ; presbyterian minister and schoolmaster at Morpeth ; lectured on natural science at Newcastle ; F.R.S., 1730 ; published 'Britannia Romana,' 1732 ; his 'Materials for History of Northumberland' printed in 'Inedited Contributions,' 1869. [xxvii. 382]

HORSLEY, SAMUEL (1733-1806), bishop of St. Asaph ; LL.B. Trinity Hall, Cambridge, 1758 ; rector of Newington Butts, 1759-93 ; F.R.S., 1767 ; secretary, Royal Society, 1773 ; D.C.L. Oxford, 1774 ; prebendary of St. Paul's, 1777, Gloucester, 1787 ; archdeacon of St. Albans, 1781 ; vicar of South Weald, 1782 ; bishop of St. Davids, 1788, of Rochester, 1793 (with Westminster) ; member of Johnson's club at Essex Head, 1783 ; left Royal Society after dispute of 1783-4 ; carried on controversy with Priestley on the Incarnation, 1783-90 ; edited Sir Isaac Newton's works, 1779-85 ; preached impressive sermon on revolutionary spirit before House of Lords, 1793 ; spoke against peace of Amiens, 1801 ; bishop of St. Asaph, 1802-6 ; published mathematical and theological works. [xxvii. 383]

HORSLEY, WILLIAM (1774-1858), musical composer ; organist of Ely Chapel, Holborn, 1794 ; of Female Orphans Asylum, 1802-54, or Charterhouse, 1838 ; Mus. Bac. Oxford, 1800 ; assisted in founding Philharmonic Society, 1813 ; published five collections of glees (including 'By Celia's Arbour'), 1801-37, and 'The Musical Treasury,' 1853 ; edited Calcott's 'Musical Grammar,' 1817, and 'Glees, with Memoir,' 1824, and Byrd's 'Cantiones Sacræ.' [xxvii. 386]

HORSMAN, EDWARD (1807-1876), whig politician ; educated at Rugby and Trinity College, Cambridge ; M.P. Cockermouth, 1836-52, Stroud, 1853-68, and Liskeard, 1869-76 ; junior lord of treasury, 1841 ; chief secretary for Ireland, 1855-7 ; attacked ecclesiastical commissioners, 1847, and the bishops, 1850 ; with Lowe formed 'Cave of Adullam' against Reform Bill of 1866 ; died at Biarritz. [xxvii. 387]

HORSMAN, NICHOLAS (fl. 1689), divine ; fellow of Corpus Christi College, Cambridge ; M.A., 1659 ; B.D., 1667 ; published 'The Spiritual Bee,' 1662. [xxvii. 388]

HORT, FENTON JOHN ANTHONY (1828-1892), scholar and divine ; educated at Rugby and Trinity College, Cambridge ; M.A., 1853 ; B.D., 1875 ; D.D., 1876 ; fellow of Trinity College, 1852-7 ; assistant-editor of 'Journal of Classical and Sacred Philology' from 1854 ; ordained priest, 1856 ; examiner for natural sciences tripos, 1856 ; held living of St. Ippolyts cum Great Wymondley, Hertfordshire, 1857-72 ; Hulsean lecturer, 1871 ; one of revisers of New Testament, 1870-80 ; fellow of Emmanuel College, Cambridge, 1871, and lecturer in theology, 1872-6 ; contributed to Smith's 'Dict'onary of Christian Biography' (vol. i. published, 1877) ; Hulsean professor of divinity, 1878 ; published, with Dr. Westcott, edition of text of Greek New Testament, 1881 ; Lady Margaret reader, 1887 ; honorary D.C.L. Durham, 1890 ; published religious writings. His 'Life and Letters' appeared, 1896. [Suppl. ii. 443]

HORT, JOSIAH (1674 ?-1751), archbishop of Tuam ; educated by nonconformists ; friend of Isaac Watts ; chaplain to John Hampden, M.P. ; chaplain to Lord

Wharton in Ireland, 1709; dean of Cloyne, 1718, of Ardagh, 1720; bishop of Ferns, 1721, Kilmore and Ardagh, 1727; archbishop of Tuam, 1742-51; mentioned in Swift's 'Great Storm of Christmas, 1722.' [xxvii. 388]

HORTON, CHRISTIANA (1696?-1756?), actress; taken by Barton Booth [q. v.] from Southwark fair to Drury Lane, 1714; moved to Covent Garden, 1734; reappeared at Drury Lane, 1752, in benefit performance; distinguished as Millamant ('Way of the World') and Belinda ('Old Bachelor'); praised by Steele. [xxvii. 389]

HORTON, SIR ROBERT JOHN WILMOT, third baronet (1784-1841), politician; assumed name of Horton on death of father-in-law, 1823; of Eton and Christ Church, Oxford; M.A., 1815; M.P., Newcastle-under-Lyme, 1818-1830; took additional name of Horton, 1823; under-secretary for war and colonies, 1821-8; privy councillor, 1827; supported repeal of Test Act, 1828, and catholic emancipation, 1829; governor of Ceylon, 1831-7; knighted, 1831; succeeded as baronet, 1834; as Lady Leigh's representative destroyed Byron's 'Memoirs'; published letters and pamphlets. [xxvii. 390]

HORTON, THOMAS (d. 1649), regicide; originally falconer to Sir Arthur Hesilrige [q. v.]; colonel in Fairfax's army, 1643; defeated Stradling and Lingen in South Wales, 1648; signed Charles I's death-warrant; died in Ireland. [xxvii. 391]

HORTON, THOMAS (d. 1673), president of Queens' College, Cambridge; fellow of Emmanuel College, Cambridge; M.A., 1630; D.D., 1649; president of Queens' College, 1638-60; Gresham professor of divinity, London, 1641; petitioned for presbyterianism; preacher at Gray's Inn, 1647-57; vice-chancellor of Cambridge, 1650; named a trier, 1653; conformed in 1662, and was vicar of St. Helen's, Bishopsgate Street, London, 1666-73; his works issued posthumously. [xxvii. 392]

HORTOP, JOB (fl. 1591), seaman; with Sir John Hawkins (1532-1595) [q. v.], 1567; escaped in the Minion from San Juan de Lua, and travelled from the river Panuco to Mexico; imprisoned at Seville and sent to the galleys at San Lucar; escaped to England, 1590; his narrative in Hakluyt. [xxvii. 393]

HORWITZ, BERNARD (1807-1885), author of 'Chess Studies and End-games' (1884), and joint-author of 'Chess Studies' (1851); came to England from Mecklenburg, 1845. [xxvii. 393]

HOSACK, JOHN (d. 1887), police magistrate at Clerkenwell (1877) and author; of the Middle Temple; legal treatises and books by him defending Mary Queen of Scots published 1869 and 1888. [xxvii. 393]

HOSIER, FRANCIS (1673-1727), vice-admiral; lieutenant in Rooke's flagship at Barfleur, 1693; captured the Heureux off Cape Clear, 1710; distinguished in action with Spanish off Cartagena, 1711; suspended as suspected Jacobite, 1714-17; vice-admiral, 1723; died of fever in Jamaica while commanding squadron in West Indies; the event misrepresented in Glover's ballad. [xxvii. 394]

HOSKEN, JAMES (1798-1885), pioneer of ocean steam navigation; served in royal navy; took Great Western steamship from Bristol to New York in fifteen days, 1838, and in thirteen days, 1839; commanded the Great Britain, 1844-6; chief magistrate at Labuan, 1848-9; commanded Belleisle hospital ship in Baltic, 1854-5; captain, 1857; vice-admiral, 1879. [xxvii. 395]

HOSKING, WILLIAM (1800-1861), architect and civil engineer; worked as builder in Sydney; came to England, 1819; exhibited drawings made in Italy and Sicily at Academy and Suffolk Street, 1826-8; F.S.A., 1830; F.R.I.B.A., 1835; engineer to West London railway; professor of architecture and engineering construction at King's College, London, 1840-61; published 'Theory, Practice, and Architecture of Bridges,' 1843; claimed to have originated design for British Museum reading-room; contributed to 'Encyclopædia Britannica' (7th and 8th editions). [xxvii. 395]

HOSKINS, ANTHONY (1568-1615), jesuit; joined jesuits, 1593; vice-prefect of English mission in Belgium, 1609, and Spain, 1611; modernised Richard Whytford's version of 'De Imitatione Christi,' 1613; translated French works; died at Valladolid. [xxvii. 397]

HOSKINS, JOHN, the younger (1579-1631), brother of John Hoskins (1566-1638) [q. v.]; fellow of New College, Oxford, 1600-13; D.C.L., 1613; prebendary of Hereford, 1612; chaplain to James I, and master of St. Oswald's Hospital, Worcester, 1614. [xxvii. 398]

HOSKINS, JOHN (1566-1638), lawyer and wit; of Westminster, Winchester, and New College, Oxford; fellow of New College, 1586; M.A., 1592; when M.P. for Hereford committed to Tower, 1614, for reflections on Scottish favourites; serjeant-at-law, 1623; Welsh judge; said to have revised Ralegh's 'History of the World' and Ben Jonson's poems; intimate with Camden, Donne, and Selden; gave information to Aubrey. [xxvii. 397]

HOSKINS, JOHN (d. 1664), miniature-painter; painted many contemporary celebrities, including Falkland, Sir Kenelm Digby, and Selden. [xxvii. 399]

HOSKINS or **HOSKYNS**, SIR JOHN, second baronet (1634-1705), of Westminster; barrister, Middle Temple; president of Royal Society, 1682-3, and secretary, 1685-7; knighted; master in chancery and friend of Lord-keeper Guilford; M.P., Herefordshire, 1685. [xxvii. 399]

HOSKINS, SAMUEL ELLIOTT (1799-1888), physician; of Guy's Hospital; F.R.S., 1843; F.R.C.P., 1859; practised in Channel islands; published 'Stethoscopic Chart,' 1830, 'Tables of Corrections for Temperature to Barometric Observations,' 1842, and works on Channel islands. [xxvii. 399]

HOSKYNS, CHANDOS WREN- (1812-1876), writer on agriculture; of Shrewsbury and Balliol College, Oxford; B.A., 1834; assumed additional name (1837) on marriage with descendant of Wren; barrister, Inner Temple, 1838; M.P., Hereford, 1869-74; published works, including 'Land in England, Ireland, and other Lands,' 1869, and 'Land Laws of England,' 1870. [xxvii. 400]

HOSTE, SIR GEORGE CHARLES (1786-1845), colonel, royal engineers; educated at Royal Military Academy, Woolwich; lieutenant, royal engineers, 1802; captain, 1812; brevet-major, 1814; lieutenant-colonel, 1825; brevet-colonel, 1838; colonel, 1841; served under lieutenant-general Sir James Henry Craig (q. v.], in Italy, 1805-6; in Egypt, 1807, Sicily, 1808-9, and Holland, 1813; at bombardment of Antwerp, and assault of Bergen-op-Zoom, 1814; commanding engineer of 1st army corps under Prince of Orange at Quatre Bras and Waterloo, assault of Peronne and occupation of Paris, 1815; C.B., 1815; gentleman usher of privy chamber to Queen Adelaide, 1830. [Suppl. ii. 447]

HOSTE, SIR WILLIAM, first baronet (1780-1828), captain in the navy; served under Nelson in actions off Toulon (1795), at St. Vincent and Santa Cruz; promoted to Mutine brig after the Nile, 1798; attained post rank, 1802; with the Amphion and other ships (1808-9) took or destroyed two hundred French or Venetian vessels in Adriatic; captured Grao, 1808-9, and destroyed forty-six sail in 1810; defeated greatly superior squadron at Lissa and took many prizes, but was severely wounded, 1811; with the Bacchante captured many gunboats, and assisted Austrians in taking Cattaro and Ragusa, 1813-14; created baronet, 1814; K.C.B., 1815. [xxvii. 401]

HOTHAM, BEAUMONT, second BARON HOTHAM in Irish peerage (1737-1814), educated at Westminster; barrister, Middle Temple, 1758; baron of the exchequer, 1775-1805; M.P., Wigan, 1768-75; commissioner of great seal, 1783; succeeded his brother, William Hotham, first baron [q. v.], in Irish peerage. [xxvii. 403]

HOTHAM, BEAUMONT, third BARON HOTHAM in Irish peerage (1794-1870), general; grandson of Beaumont Hotham, second baron [q. v.]; wounded at Salamanca, 1812; present at Waterloo, 1815; tory M.P., Leominster, 1820-41, East Riding, Yorkshire, 1841-68. [xxvii. 404]

HOTHAM, CHARLES (1615-1672?), divine; son of Sir John Hotham [q. v.]; M.A. Christ's College, Cambridge, 1639; fellow of Peterhouse, Cambridge, 1640-51; deprived by parliament, 1651; rector of Wigan, 1653-62; F.R.S., 1667; minister in the Bermudas; translated Boehme's 'Consolatory Treatise of the Four Complexions,' 1654. [xxvii. 404]

HOTHAM, SIR CHARLES (1806–1855), naval commander; as captain in the navy took part in Para expedition against Rosas, 1845; K.C.B., 1846; governor of Victoria, 1854–5; died at Melbourne. [xxvii. 405]

HOTHAM, DURANT (1617?–1691), author of 'Life of Jacob Boehme' (1654); translated, 1650, 'Ad Philosophiam Teutonicam Manuductio' of his brother Charles Hotham [q. v.] [xxvii. 405]

HOTHAM, SIR HENRY (1777–1833), vice-admiral; youngest son of Beaumont Hotham, second baron Hotham [q. v.]; served in Mediterranean operations, 1793–8; commanded Immortalité in Bay of Biscay, 1799–1801; with Sir Richard Strachan, 1805; with the Defiance drove ashore three French frigates at Les Sables d'Olonne, 1809; destroyed two frigates and a brig off Lorient, 1812; K.C.B., 1815; by knowledge of Biscay coast prevented Napoleon's escape to America: a lord of the admiralty, 1818–22 and 1828–30; vice-admiral, 1825; died at Malta as commander in Mediterranean. [xxvii. 406]

HOTHAM or **HOTHUN**, JOHN (d. 1337), bishop of Ely and chancellor; chancellor of Irish exchequer, 1309; dismissed as one of Gaveston's stewards, 1311; as chancellor of English exchequer accompanied Edward II to France, 1312; sent to Ireland, 1314, and Rome, 1317; bishop of Ely, 1316–37; treasurer of exchequer, 1317–18; lord chancellor, 1318–20 and 1327–8; joined Queen Isabella, 1326; built octagon tower at Ely. [xxvii. 407]

HOTHAM, SIR JOHN, first baronet (d. 1645), parliamentarian; served under elector palatine and Mansfeld, knighted, 1617; created baronet, 1622; M.P., Beverley; as sheriff of Yorkshire levied ship-money; after removal from governorship of Hull (1639) went into opposition; committed to the Fleet, 1640; a chief contriver of Yorkshire petition, 1640; as parliamentary commander of Hull refused to admit Charles I, 1642; recovered Scarborough for parliament, 1643; while negotiating with Newcastle with a view to rejoining royalists was arrested, expelled from parliament, and sent to the Tower, 1643; condemned by military commission and executed. [xxvii. 408]

HOTHAM, JOHN (d. 1645), parliamentarian; son of Sir John Hotham [q.v.]; served in Netherlands; M.P., Scarborough, 1640; secured Hull for parliament, 1642; joined Fairfax, 1642; fought at Tadcaster and Sherburn; defeated at Ancaster Heath, 1643; imprisoned at Nottingham on charges of misconduct and suspicion of treachery, 1643; opened negotiations with Charles I's queen and escaped; arrested with his father; tried by court-martial and beheaded. [xxvii. 410]

HOTHAM, WILLIAM, first BARON HOTHAM in Irish peerage (1736–1813), admiral; educated at Westminster and Naval Academy, Portsmouth; promoted captain for capture of French privateer, 1757; cruised in North Sea, 1758–9; served at Belleisle, 1761; as commodore on North American station shared in action off St. Lucia, 1778, and in action under Rodney in April–May, 1780; under Howe at relief of Gibraltar and battle of Cape Spartel, 1782; vice-admiral, 1790; second in command under Lord Hood, 1793–4; commander in Mediterranean, twice engaging inferior French fleet without result, 1795; created Irish peer, 1797. [xxvii. 411]

HOTHAM, SIR WILLIAM (1772–1848), admiral; nephew of William, first baron Hotham [q.v.]; under Nelson at Bastia, 1794; commanded the Adamant at Camperdown, 1797, and blockade of Mauritius; K.C.B., 1815; admiral, 1837; G.C.B., 1840. [xxvii. 413]

HOTHBY, JOHN (d. 1487), Carmelite and writer on music; lived many years at Ferrara; went to Lucca, 1467; invited to England by Henry VII, 1486; works by him in British Museum and at Lambeth; his treatises on 'Proportion,' 'Cantus Figuratus,' and 'Counterpoint' printed by Coussemaker. [xxvii. 414]

HOTHUM or **HODON** or **ODONE**, WILLIAM OF (d. 1298), archbishop of Dublin; graduated in theology at Paris; Dominican prior and provincial in England, 1282–7; employed by Edward I on mission to Rome, 1289; provincial of England and Scotland, 1290; summoned to parliament at Norham, 1291; advised the king on Scottish succession; archbishop of Dublin, 1296–8; accompanied the king to Flanders, 1297, and negotiated with French; represented him at Rome when Boniface VIII mediated truce between England and France; wrote scholastic works; died at Dijon. [xxvii. 414]

HOTON or **HOGHTON**, RICHARD OF (d. 1307), prior of Durham; probable founder of Durham College, 1289; deposed and imprisoned for resisting visitation of Bishop Antony Bek I [q. v.], 1300; reinstated by the pope, 1301, but again suspended; died at Rome. [xxvii. 416]

HOTSPUR (1364–1403). [See PERCY, SIR HENRY.]

HOTTEN, JOHN CAMDEN, originally JOHN WILLIAM HOTTEN (1832–1873), publisher and author; in America, 1848–56; established himself in Piccadilly on his return; first published in England the 'Biglow Papers,' 1864, and other works of American humour; compiled slang dictionary, 1859; published 'Handbook of Topography and Family History,' 1863, and other compilations. [xxvii. 416]

HOUBLON, SIR JAMES (d. 1700), alderman; knighted, 1692: deputy-governor of the Bank of England, and M.P. for the city (1698–1700); brother of Sir John Houblon [q. v.] [xxvii. 417]

HOUBLON, SIR JOHN (d. 1712), first governor of the Bank of England, 1694; sheriff of London, 1689; knighted, 1689; lord mayor, 1695; lord of the admiralty, 1694–9; master of Grocers' Company, 1696; commissioner of accounts, 1704. [xxvii. 417]

HOUGH, JOHN (1651–1743), bishop of Worcester; M.A. Magdalen College, Oxford, 1676; D.D., 1687; fellow; elected president, 1687, but ejected by James II; reinstated, 1688; resigned, 1699; bishop of Oxford, 1690–9, of Lichfield and Coventry, 1699–1717, of Worcester, 1717–1743; refused primacy, 1715; benefactor to Magdalen College, Lichfield, and Worcester. [xxvii. 417]

HOUGHTON. [See also HOTON and HOUTON.]

HOUGHTON, first BARON (1809–1885). [See MILNES, RICHARD MONCKTON.]

HOUGHTON or **HOUTONE**, ADAM DE (d. 1389), bishop of St. David's and chancellor of England; LL.D. Oxford; bishop of St. David's, 1362–89; trier of parliamentary petitions; lord chancellor, 1377; chief negotiator of peace with France, 1377, and with Sir Simon Burley of marriage of Richard II, 1380; established cathedral school at St. David's and founded college or chantry of St. Mary's, 1365. [xxvii. 419]

HOUGHTON, ARTHUR BOYD (1836–1875), bookillustrator and painter; exhibited at Academy, 1860–70, and afterwards at Water-colour Society; illustrated Dalziel's 'Arabian Nights,' 1865, and 'Don Quixote,' 1866. [xxvii. 419]

HOUGHTON, DANIEL (1740?–1791), African traveller; left England in employ of African Association, 1790; journeyed from Gambia, 1790, to Medina (capital of Wolli); crossed uninhabited country between Wolli and Bondou and reached Bambouk, where he negotiated a commercial treaty; set out for Timbuctoo, but was not again heard of. [xxvii. 420]

HOUGHTON, HENRY HALL- (1823–1889), jointfounder (with Canon Hall) of biblical prizes at Oxford, 1868–71; of Sherborne School and Pembroke College, Oxford; M.A., 1848; benefactor of Church Missionary Society. [xxvii. 421]

HOUGHTON, JOHN (1488?–1535), prior of the London Charterhouse; B.A. and LL.B. Cambridge; prior of Beauvale, 1530; prior of Charterhouse, 1531; imprisoned for refusing oath of allegiance to Princess Elizabeth as heir-apparent, 1534; executed for refusing to accept royal headship of the church; beatified, 1886. [xxvii. 421]

HOUGHTON, JOHN (d. 1705), writer on agriculture and trade; F.R.S., 1680; first noticed potato plant as agricultural vegetable. [xxvii. 422]

HOUGHTON, SIR ROBERT (1548–1624), judge; barrister, Lincoln's Inn, 1577; governor of Lincoln's Inn, 1588–1603; serjeant-at-law, 1603; judge of king's bench, 1613–24; knighted, 1613. [xxvii. 422]

HOUGHTON or **HOGHTON**, WILLIAM HYACINTH (1736–1823), Roman catholic divine; prefect at Bornhem

(Dominican) College, 1758–62, and afterwards procurator; professor of philosophy at Louvain, 1779; returned to England; edited 'Catholic Magazine and Reflector,' 1801. [xxvii. 423]

HOULING, JOHN (1539?–1599), Irish jesuit; established Irish college at Lisbon, 1593, where he died of the plague; his Elizabethan catholic martyrology printed by Cardinal Moran in 'Spicilegium Ossoriense.' [xxvii. 423]

HOULTON, ROBERT (*fl.* 1801), dramatist and journalist; demy of Magdalen College, Oxford, 1757–65; M.A., 1762; practised inoculation in Ireland; M.B. Trinity College, Dublin; wrote librettos for operas; editor of 'Morning Herald'; with James Hook (1746–1827) [q. v.] produced 'Wilmore Castle' (comic opera) at Drury Lane, 1800. [xxvii. 423]

HOUSEMAN, JACOB (1636?–1696). [See Huysmans.]

HOUSMAN, ROBERT (1759–1838), divine; intimate when at Cambridge with Charles Simeon and Henry Venn; B.A., 1784; minister of church built by himself at Lancaster, 1795–1836; known as 'the evangelist'; published sermons. [xxvii. 424]

HOUSTON, JOHN (1802–1845), anatomist; curator of Dublin College of Surgeons' Museum, 1824–41; M.D. Edinburgh, 1826; surgeon to Dublin Hospital, 1832; lecturer at Park Street School of Medicine, 1837; contributed to medical journals. [xxvii. 424]

HOUSTON, RICHARD (1721?–1775), mezzotint engraver; pupil of John Brooks; engraved portraits after Reynolds, Zoffany, and William Hoare, and subject-plates after old masters, especially Rembrandt. [xxvii. 425]

HOUSTON or **HOUSTOUN**, WILLIAM (1695?–1733), botanist; M.D. Leyden, 1729; with Van Swieten investigated animal respiration; F.R.S.; collected plants in West Indies and Venezuela ('Reliquiæ Houstonianæ,' catalogue, 1781); died in Jamaica. [xxvii. 425]

HOUSTON, SIR WILLIAM, first baronet (1766–1842), general; commanded 19th foot in Flanders, 1794, and 58th at Minorca and in Egypt, 1798–1801; brigadier in Egypt, 1801, and Walcheren, 1809; commanded 7th division in Peninsula, 1811–12; governor of Gibraltar, 1831–35; created baronet, 1836. [xxvii. 426]

HOUTON, JOHN DE (*d.* 1246), justice; archdeacon of Bedford, 1218, of Northampton, 1231–46; represented Henry III in negotiations with Falkes de Breauté [q. v.], and at Rome, 1224 and 1228. [xxvii. 426]

HOVEDEN, JOHN (*d.* 1275), Latin poet; chaplain of Queen Eleanor and prebendary of Hoveden or Howden, where he built choir; reverenced as saint; his chief poem, 'Philomela sive meditacio de nativitate, &c., Domini nostri Jesu Christi,' printed at Ghent, 1516, at Luxemburg as 'Christias,' 1603; his prose treatise 'Practica Chilindri,' translated by E. Brock. [xxvii. 427]

HOVEDEN or **HOWDEN**, ROGER OF (*d.* 1201?), chronicler; envoy to Henry II to chiefs of Galloway, 1174; justice for northern forests, 1189; his 'Cronica' (732–1201), first printed, 1596, and edited by Bishop Stubbs, 1868–71. [xxvii. 428]

HOVELL-THURLOW, EDWARD, second BARON THURLOW (1781–1829). [See THURLOW.]

HOVENDEN or **HOVEDEN**, ROBERT (1544–1614), warden of All Souls College; fellow of All Souls College, 1565; M.A., 1570; D.D., 1581; warden, 1571–1614; chaplain to Archbishop Parker; prebendary of Lincoln, Bath, and Canterbury; vice-chancellor, 1582; admitted poor scholars to the college and recovered property from crown; wrote life of Archbishop Chichele. [xxvii. 429]

HOW. [See also Howe.]

HOW, WILLIAM WALSHAM (1823–1897), first bishop of Wakefield; M.A. Wadham College, Oxford, 1847; ordained priest, 1847; rural dean of Oswestry, 1854; honorary canon of St. Asaph, 1860; suffragan to bishop of London, with title of bishop of Bedford, 1879; prebendary of St. Paul's Cathedral; D.D. Canterbury, 1879, and Oxford, 1886; bishop of Wakefield, 1888; published religious writings; widely known for his work in connection with the poor in East End of London. [Suppl. iii. 1]

HOWARD, LADY ANNE (1475–1513), third daughter of Edward IV, and first wife of Thomas, third duke of Norfolk. [xxviii. 64]

HOWARD, BERNARD EDWARD, twelfth DUKE OF NORFOLK (1765–1842), succeeded his third cousin Charles Howard, eleventh duke (1746–1815) [q. v.], in dukedom, 1815; though Roman Catholic, he was made earl-marshal by parliament, 1824; privy councillor, 1830; K.G., 1834; supported Reform Bill. [xxviii. 1]

HOWARD, CATHERINE, QUEEN (*d.* 1542). [See CATHERINE.]

HOWARD, CHARLES, second BARON HOWARD OF EFFINGHAM, first EARL OF NOTTINGHAM (1536–1624), lord high admiral; eldest son of William Howard, first baron Howard of Effingham [q. v.]; ambassador to France, 1559; M.P., Surrey; commander of horse against northern rebels, 1569, of squadron to watch Spanish fleet, 1570; knighted; succeeded to peerage, 1573; lord chamberlain, 1574–85; lord high admiral, 1585–1618; commissioner for trial of Mary Queen of Scots, 1586; held chief command against Spanish Armada, 1588, leading mid-channel squadron and ordering and directing attack on the San Lorenzo; officially organised 'the chest at Chatham,' 1590; colleague of Essex in Cadiz expedition, 1596; created Earl of Nottingham, 1596; commander both by land and sea during alarm of 1599; commissioner at Essex's trial, 1601; commissioner for James I's coronation, 1603; ambassador extraordinary to Spain, 1605; commissioner for union with Scotland, 1604, and trial of gunpowder plotters, 1606; improbably supposed of recent years to have been a Roman catholic. [xxviii. 1]

HOWARD, CHARLES, first EARL OF CARLISLE (1629–1685), great-grandson of Lord William Howard (1563–1640) [q. v.]; rendered distinguished service to parliamentarians at Worcester, 1651; member of council of state, 1653; M.P., Westmoreland, 1653, Cumberland, 1654, 1656, and 1660; commanded against Scots, 1654; councillor of state for Scotland, 1655; captain of Cromwell's bodyguard; major-general of Northumberland, Cumberland, and Westmoreland; member of Cromwell's House of Lords, 1657; imprisoned by army leaders, 1659; privy councillor, 1660; lord-lieutenant of Cumberland and Westmoreland, 1660; created earl of Carlisle, 1661; ambassador extraordinary to Russia, Sweden, and Denmark, 1663–4; governor of Jamaica, 1677–81; lieutenant-general, 1667. [xxviii. 6]

HOWARD, CHARLES, third EARL OF CARLISLE (1674–1738), statesman; as Viscount Morpeth, M.P. for Morpeth, 1690–2; succeeded to peerage, 1692; deputy earl-marshal, 1701–6; lord-lieutenant of Cumberland and Westmoreland, 1694–1712; first lord of the treasury, 1701–2 and 1715 (May–October); commissioner for Scottish union; a lord justice, 1714–15. [xxviii. 7]

HOWARD, SIR CHARLES (*d.* 1765), general; second son of Charles Howard, third earl of Carlisle [q. v.]; colonel of 19th foot ('Green Howards'), 1738; commanded brigade at Dettingen, 1743, and Fontenoy, 1745, and the infantry at Val and Roucoux; K.B., 1749; president of court-martial on Lord George Sackville [see GERMAIN, GEORGE SACKVILLE]; M.P., Carlisle, 1727–61. [xxviii. 8]

HOWARD, CHARLES, tenth DUKE OF NORFOLK (1720–1786), author of 'Historical Anecdotes of some of the Howard Family,' 1769; a Roman catholic; succeeded his second cousin, Edward Howard, ninth duke, 1777; F.S.A. and F.R.S. [xxviii. 8]

HOWARD, CHARLES, eleventh DUKE OF NORFOLK (1746–1815), son of Charles Howard, tenth duke of Norfolk [q. v.]; became protestant and a whig; F.R.S., 1767; F.S.A., 1779; M.P., Carlisle, 1780–6; a lord of the treasury under Portland, 1783; dismissed from lord-lieutenancy of the West Riding for democratic speech at Crown and Anchor banquet, 1798; friend of Prince of Wales (George IV); lord-lieutenant of Sussex, 1807; president of Society of Arts, 1794. [xxviii. 9]

HOWARD, SIR EDWARD (1477?–1513), lord high admiral; second son of Thomas Howard, second duke of Norfolk [q. v.]; knighted while serving in Scotland, 1497; standard-bearer, 1509; said to have assisted in capturing Robert and Andrew Barton [q. v.], 1511; as admiral of the fleet landed and ravaged coast of Brittany,

1512, afterwards defeating and burning many French ships; confirmed as lord high admiral, 1513; lost his life while attempting to cut out French galleys from Whitsand Bay; nominated K.G. just before his death.
[xxviii. 10]

HOWARD, EDWARD (*fl.* 1669), dramatist; brother of Sir Robert Howard (1626?-1698) [q. v.]; published 'The Usurper' (tragedy), 1668, 'Six Days' Adventure,' and 'The Women's Conquest' (comedies), 1671; his 'United Kingdom' ridiculed in 'The Rehearsal' and 'The British Princes,' by Rochester.   [xxviii. 12]

HOWARD, EDWARD, first BARON HOWARD OF ESCRICK (*d.* 1675), parliamentarian; son of Thomas Howard, first earl of Suffolk [q. v.]; K.B., 1616; created peer, 1628; one of the twelve petitioning peers, 1640; represented Carlisle after abolition (1649) of upper house; member of council of state, 1650; convicted of taking bribes from delinquents, 1651.   [xxviii. 12]

HOWARD, EDWARD (*d.* 1841), novelist; served in the navy with Marryat, for whom he sub-edited the 'Metropolitan Magazine'; afterwards wrote for Hood's 'New Monthly'; his 'Rattlin the Reefer' (1836) wrongly attributed to Marryat; published other maritime novels.
[xxviii. 13]

HOWARD, EDWARD GEORGE FITZALAN, first BARON HOWARD OF GLOSSOP (1818-1883), second son of Henry Charles Howard, thirteenth duke of Norfolk [q. v.]; liberal M.P. for Horsham, 1848-53, Arundel, 1853-68; vice-chamberlain, 1846-52; created Baron Howard, 1869; chairman of Catholic Poor Schools Committee, 1869-77.   [xxviii. 13]

HOWARD, EDWARD HENRY (1829-1892), cardinal; ordained priest in English college, Rome, 1854; archbishop of Neocæsaria *in partibus infidelium*, 1872, and coadjutor bishop of Frascati; cardinal-priest, 1877; archpriest of basilica of St. Peter, and prefect of congregation of St. Peter, 1881; cardinal-bishop of Frascati, 1881.
[Suppl. iii. 2]

HOWARD, ELIZABETH, DUCHESS OF NORFOLK (1494-1558), daughter of Edward Stafford, duke of Buckingham [q. v.]; second wife of Thomas Howard, third duke of Norfolk.   [xxviii. 65]

HOWARD, FRANK (1805?-1866), painter; son of Henry Howard (1769-1847) [q. v.]; assistant to Sir Thomas Lawrence; exhibited at British Institution, 1824-43, at the Academy, 1825-33, and later; gained prize for cartoon in Westminster Hall competition, 1843; published 'Spirit of Plays of Shakspeare' (plates), 1827-1833, and art manuals.   [xxviii. 14]

HOWARD, FREDERICK, fifth EARL OF CARLISLE (1748-1825), statesman; succeeded to earldom, 1758; of Eton and King's College, Cambridge; friend of Charles James Fox; treasurer of the household, 1777; head of commission to treat with Americans, 1778; president of board of trade, 1779; viceroy of Ireland, 1780-2; lord steward, 1782-3; resigned and (1783) moved amendment against the peace; lord privy seal in coalition ministry, 1783; opposed Pitt on Regency question (1788-9), but went over to him with the old whigs; K.G., 1793; chancery guardian to Lord Byron; attacked in 'English Bards and Scotch Reviewers'; his tragedy 'The Father's Revenge,' 1783, praised by Johnson and Walpole; 'Tragedies and Poems' issued, 1801.   [xxviii. 14]

HOWARD, SIR GEORGE (1720?-1796), field-marshal; commanded 3rd buffs at Fontenoy, 1745, Falkirk, 1746, Culloden, 1746, Val, and the Rochefort expedition; commanded brigade in Germany during seven years' war; K.B., 1763; M.P., Lostwithiel, 1762-6, Stamford, 1768-96; governor of Minorca, 1766-8, afterwards of Jersey and Chelsea Hospital; field-marshal, 1793.   [xxviii. 17]

HOWARD, GEORGE, sixth EARL OF CARLISLE (1773-1848), statesman; son of Frederick Howard, fifth earl [q. v.]; of Eton and Christ Church, Oxford; M.A., 1792; D.C.L., 1799; M.P., Morpeth (while Viscount Morpeth), 1795-1806. Cumberland, 1806-28; commissioner for affairs of India in ministry of All the Talents, 1806; advocated catholic emancipation, 1812; lord-lieutenant of East Riding, 1824; chief commissioner of woods and forests in Canning's cabinet, 1827; lord privy seal, 1827-8 and 1834; trustee of British Museum; contributed to 'Anti-Jacobin.'   [xxviii. 18]

HOWARD, GEORGE WILLIAM FREDERICK, seventh EARL OF CARLISLE (1802-1864), statesman; eldest son of George Howard, sixth earl of Carlisle [q. v.]; won prizes for English and Latin verse at Oxford, 1821; M.A. Christ Church, Oxford, 1827; as Viscount Morpeth, M.P., Morpeth, 1826-30, Yorkshire, 1830-2, the West Riding, 1832-41 and 1846-8; as Irish secretary under Melbourne, 1835-41, carried Irish Tithe, Irish Municipal Reform, and Irish Poor Law bills; admitted to cabinet, 1839; chief commissioner of woods and forests under Russell, 1846-50; carried Public Health Bill, 1848; chancellor of duchy of Lancaster, 1850-2; viceroy of Ireland, 1855-8 and 1859-64; presided at Shakespeare tercentenary, 1864; published poems, travels, and lectures.
[xxviii. 19]

HOWARD, GORGES EDMOND (1715-1786), author; educated under Thomas Sheridan; given freedom of Dublin for public services, 1766; ridiculed for worthless tragedies and occasional verse; published valuable legal works.   [xxviii. 21]

HOWARD, HENRIETTA, COUNTESS OF SUFFOLK (1681-1767), mistress of George II; daughter of Sir Henry Hobart, baronet; married to Charles Howard (afterwards ninth earl of Suffolk), with whom she lived at Hanover; followed George I to England and became bedchamber woman to Princess of Wales; her house at Marble Hill, Twickenham, the resort of Pope, Arbuthnot, and Swift; admired by Lord Peterborough; much courted as mistress of George II; became countess, 1731; retired from court, 1734; married Hon. George Berkeley, 1735; selection from her letters edited by Croker, 1824.
[xxviii. 22]

HOWARD, HENRY, EARL OF SURREY (by courtesy) (1517?-1547), poet; son of Thomas Howard (afterwards third duke of Norfolk) [q. v.]; educated by John Clerk (*d.* 1552) [q. v.]; proposed as husband for Princess Mary; married Frances Vere, 1532; in France, 1532-3; earl marshal at Anne Boleyn's trial, 1536; accompanied his father against Yorkshire rebels, 1536; K.G. and steward of Cambridge University, 1541; imprisoned for a quarrel, 1542, and for annoying London citizens, 1543; with imperial troops at Landrecy, 1543; wounded when marshal before Montreuil, 1544; when commander of Boulogne (1545-6) defeated at St. Etienne, 1546; superseded by his enemy, Lord Hertford, 1546; condemned and executed on frivolous charge of treasonably quartering royal arms and advising his sister to become the king's mistress; his body discovered at Framlingham Church, Suffolk, 1835. Forty poems by Surrey, including 'Description and Praise of his love Geraldine,' were printed in Tottel's 'Songes and Sonettes,' 1557 (reprinted, 1867 and 1870). His translations of the Æneid (books ii. and iii.), reprinted 1814, introduced blank verse in five iambic feet. The poems (with those of Wyatt) were edited by Dr. George Frederick Nott, 1815-16, and others, and for Aldine poets by James Yeowell, 1866. Surrey first imitated Italian models, especially Petrarch, and (with Wyatt) introduced the sonnet from Italy into England.   [xxviii. 23]

HOWARD, HENRY, first EARL OF NORTHAMPTON (1540-1614), second son of Henry Howard, earl of Surrey [q. v.]; M.A. King's College, Cambridge, 1564; went to court, *c.* 1570; received pension, but failed to gain secure position owing to his relations with Mary Queen of Scots; sent to the Fleet after publishing work against judicial astrology, 1583; suspected of intrigues with Spain; attached himself to Essex; gained goodwill of Sir Robert Cecil; re-admitted to court, 1600; corresponded with James VI of Scotland, advising toleration of Romanists; created Earl of Northampton, 1604; warden of Cinque ports, 1604; K.G., 1605; lord privy seal, 1608; chancellor of Cambridge University; commissioner for trials of Ralegh, 1603, Guy Fawkes, 1605, and Garnett, 1606; accused of having secretly apologised to Bellarmine for speech against catholics; a commissioner of the treasury, 1612; supported divorce of grand-niece from Essex, 1613, and procured imprisonment of Sir Thomas Overbury; opposed summoning of parliament, 1614; drew up James I's edict against duelling, 1613; erected monument of Mary Queen of Scots at Westminster; lived and died a Roman catholic; the most learned noble of his day; built Northumberland House.   [xxviii. 28]

HOWARD, HENRY, sixth DUKE of NORFOLK (1628-1684), friend of Evelyn; second son of Henry Frederick Howard, third earl of Arundel [q. v.]; visited Evelyn at

Padua, 1645; entertained by Leopold I at Vienna, 1664; F.R.S., 1666; presented library to Royal Society and Arundel marbles to Oxford University, 1667; D.C.L. Oxford, 1668; created Baron Howard of Castle Rising, 1669; envoy to Morocco, 1669; succeeded his brother as duke, 1677. [xxviii. 32]

HOWARD, HENRY, seventh DUKE OF NORFOLK (1655–1701), son of Henry Howard, sixth duke [q. v.]; M.A. Magdalen College, Oxford, 1668; summoned as Baron Mowbray, 1679; styled Earl of Arundel, 1678–84; lord-lieutenant of Norfolk, Berkshire, and Surrey; brought over eastern counties to William III; privy councillor, 1689. [xxviii. 33]

HOWARD, HENRY (1684–1720), coadjutor-elect of Bishop Bonaventure Giffard [q. v.] in London districts, 1720; grandson of Henry Howard, sixth duke of Norfolk [q. v.] [xxviii. 34]

HOWARD, HENRY, fourth EARL OF CARLISLE (1694–1758), son of Charles Howard, third earl of Carlisle [q. v.]; M.P., Morpeth, 1722, 1727, and 1734–8; K.G., 1756. [xxviii. 8]

HOWARD, HENRY (1757–1842), of Corby Castle, author of 'Memorials of the Howard Family,' 1834; friend and correspondent of Louis Philippe. [xxviii. 34]

HOWARD, HENRY (1769–1847), painter; went to Italy with introduction from Reynolds, 1791; exhibited 'Dream of Cain' at Royal Academy, 1794; R.A., 1808; secretary, Royal Academy, 1811, and professor of painting, 1833; his finest works, 'Birth of Venus,' 1819, and 'Fairies,' 1818; executed portraits, among others, of Flaxman and James Watt. [xxviii. 35]

HOWARD, HENRY CHARLES, thirteenth DUKE OF NORFOLK (1791–1856), son of Bernard Edward Howard, twelfth duke [q. v.]; as Earl of Arundel and Surrey, M.P., Horsham, 1829–41, and treasurer of the household, 1837–41; master of the horse, 1846–52; K.G., 1848; lord steward, 1853–4; though a Romanist, supported Ecclesiastical Titles Bill. [xxviii. 37]

HOWARD, HENRY EDWARD JOHN (1795–1868), dean of Lichfield; youngest son of Frederick Howard, fifth earl of Carlisle [q. v.]; of Eton and Christ Church, Oxford; M.A., 1822; succentor of York, 1822; dean of Lichfield, 1833–68; published translations from Claudian and the Septuagint. [xxviii. 37]

HOWARD, HENRY FREDERICK, third EARL OF ARUNDEL (1608–1652); K.B., 1616; son of Thomas Howard, second earl of Arundel [q. v.]; as Lord Maltravers, M.P., Arundel, 1628 and 1640; Irish privy councillor, 1634; created Baron Mowbray, 1640; committed for quarrel with Philip Herbert, fourth earl of Pembroke [q. v.], 1641; fought as royalist in civil war; succeeded his father as third earl of Arundel and earl-marshal, 1646. [xxviii. 38]

HOWARD, HENRY GRANVILLE FITZALAN-, fourteenth DUKE OF NORFOLK (1815–1860), son of Henry Charles Howard, thirteenth duke [q. v.]; of Trinity College, Cambridge; as Lord Fitzalan (Earl of Arundel from 1842) represented Arundel, 1837–50, Limerick, 1850–2; opposed Ecclesiastical Titles Bill, 1850; friend of Montalembert and a zealous catholic; edited 'Lives of Philip Howard, Earl of Arundel, and . . . his wife,' 1857. [xxviii. 38]

HOWARD, HUGH (1675–1737), portrait-painter and art collector; son of Ralph Howard (1638–1710) [q. v.]; keeper of state papers and paymaster of works belonging to crown; some of his portraits and drawings acquired by British Museum. [xxviii. 39]

HOWARD, JAMES (fl. 1674), dramatist; brother of Sir Robert Howard (1626–1698) [q. v.], and brother-in-law of Dryden; his comedy 'All Mistaken, or the Mad Couple' (1672), first acted, 1667; his 'English Mounsieur' (1674) played in by Nell Gwyn and Hart, 1666. [xxviii. 40]

HOWARD, JAMES, third EARL OF SUFFOLK and third BARON HOWARD DE WALDEN (1619–1688), eldest son of Theophilus Howard, second earl of Suffolk [q. v.]; K.B., 1626; joint-commissioner of the parliament to Charles I, 1646; lord-lieutenant of Suffolk and Cambridgeshire and gentleman of the bedchamber, 1660–82. [xxviii. 40]

HOWARD, JAMES (1821–1889), agriculturist; took out patents for agricultural machines, including first iron wheel plough (1841); president of Farmers' Alliance; mayor of Bedford, 1863–4; M.P., Bedford, 1868–74, Bedfordshire, 1880–5; wrote on scientific farming. [xxviii. 41]

HOWARD, JOHN, first DUKE OF NORFOLK of the Howard family (1430?–1485), present at battle of Châtillon, 1453; entered service of his relative, John Mowbray, duke of Norfolk; knight of the shire for Norfolk, 1455, Suffolk, 1466; named sheriff of Norfolk and Suffolk by Edward IV; constable of Norwich, 1462; served against Lancastrians and in Brittany; envoy to France and Flanders; created Baron Howard by the restored Henry VI, 1470; commanded fleet against Lancastrians, 1471; deputy-governor of Calais, 1471; accompanied Edward IV to France and received pension from Louis XI, 1475; again employed in France, 1477, 1479, and 1480; privy councillor, 1483; created Duke of Norfolk and earl-marshal by Richard III, 1483; admiral of England, Ireland, and Aquitaine, 1483; commanded vanguard at Bosworth and was slain. [xxviii. 42]

HOWARD, JOHN (1726?–1790), philanthropist; captured on the way to Lisbon and imprisoned in France, 1756; high sheriff of Bedfordshire, though a dissenter, 1773; visited county and city gaols and bridewells and obtained acts for abolition of gaoler's fees and for sanitary improvements, 1774; inspected Scottish, Irish, French, Flemish, Dutch, German, and Swiss, and revisited British prisons, 1775–6; published 'State of the Prisons,' 1777, 'Appendix to State of Prisons,' 1780, translation of 'Historical Remarks on the Bastille,' 1774; visited Denmark, Sweden, and Russia, 1781; LL.D. Dublin, 1782; made third inspection of British prisons, 1783; inspected penal institutions of Spain and Portugal, 1783; issued third enlarged edition of 'State of the Prisons,' 1784; visited lazarettos in France, Italy, and Turkey, purposely underwent quarantine at Venice, 1785–6, and published an 'Account,' 1789; died of camp fever while with Russian army at Kherson. [xxviii. 44]

HOWARD, JOHN (1753–1799), mathematician; self-educated; kept schools at Carlisle and Newcastle; published 'Treatise on Spherical Geometry,' 1798. [xxviii. 48]

HOWARD, JOHN ELIOT (1807–1883), author of 'Illustrations of the "Nueva Quinologia" of Pavon, and Observations on the Barks described' (1862), and 'Quinology of the East Indian Plantations' (1869); son of Luke Howard (1772–1864) [q. v.]; F.R.S., 1874. [xxviii. 48]

HOWARD, KENNETH ALEXANDER, first EARL OF EFFINGHAM of the second creation (1767–1845), general; served with Coldstream guards in Flanders, 1793–5, Ireland, and Holland, 1799; inspector-general of foreign troops in British service; aide-de-camp to the king, 1805; major-general, 1810; commanded brigades in the Peninsular war from 1811, and first division of army of occupation after Waterloo; K.C.B., 1815; succeeded as eleventh Baron Howard of Effingham, 1816; deputy earl-marshal at coronation of George IV, 1821; general, 1837; created earl, 1837. [xxviii. 49]

HOWARD, LEONARD (1699?–1767), compiler of 'A Collection of Letters from original Manuscripts of many Princes, great Personages and Statesmen,' 1753; D.D.; rector of St. George's, Southwark, 1749–67; chaplain to Augusta, princess dowager of Wales. [xxviii. 50]

HOWARD, LUKE (1621–1699), quaker; previously a baptist; imprisoned at Dover, 1660, 1661, and 1684; wrote against baptists; his 'Journal' prefixed to works issued, 1704. [xxviii. 50]

HOWARD, LUKE (1772–1864), pioneer in meteorology; chemist in London in partnership with William Allen (1770–1843) [q. v.]; began to keep meteorological register, 1806; published 'Climate of London,' 1818–20 (enlarged, 1830), containing current classification of clouds; F.R.S., 1821; edited 'The Yorkshireman' (quaker journal), 1833–1837; corresponded with Goethe and John Dalton. [xxviii. 51]

HOWARD, PHILIP, first EARL OF ARUNDEL of the Howard family (1557–1595), eldest son of Thomas Howard III, fourth duke of Norfolk [q. v.]; went to Cambridge with courtesy title Earl of Surrey; M.A., 1576; court profligate; succeeded to earldom of Arundel,

1580, in right of his mother, Mary Fitzalan (daughter of Henry, twelfth earl); under influence of his wife (Anne Dacre) became Roman catholic, 1584; after attempting to escape from England (1585) was fined and rigorously imprisoned for life; condemned to death (1589) on charge of saying mass for success of the Armada, but, although not executed, remained in Tower till death.
[xxviii. 52]

HOWARD, PHILIP THOMAS (1629–1694), known as CARDINAL OF NORFOLK, third son of Henry Frederick Howard, third earl of Arundel [q. v.]; educated at Utrecht and Antwerp; became a Dominican; studied at Naples and Rennes; ordained priest, 1652; first prior of his own English foundation at Bornhem, East Flanders, 1657; went on secret royalist mission to England, 1659; promoted marriage of Charles II, 1662, and was first chaplain to Queen Catherine, and afterwards grand almoner; his appointment as vicar-apostolic in England withdrawn; driven from England by popular feeling, 1674; created cardinal-priest by Clement X, 1675; thenceforth lived at Rome; as cardinal-protector of England and Scotland, 1679, obtained restoration of the episcopate; remonstrated against policy of James II.   [xxviii. 54]

HOWARD, RALPH (1638–1710), regius professor of physic at Dublin, 1670–1710; M.D. Dublin, 1667.
[xxviii. 57]

HOWARD, RALPH, VISCOUNT WICKLOW and first BARON CLONMORE (d. 1786), grandson of Ralph Howard (1638–1710) [q. v.]; M.P., co. Wicklow, 1761–75; Irish privy councillor, 1770; created Baron Clonmore, 1776, Viscount Wicklow, 1785.   [xxviii. 58]

HOWARD, RICHARD BARON (1807–1848), Manchester physician; M.D. Edinburgh; published 'Inquiry into Morbid Effects of Deficiency of Food,' 1839.
[xxviii. 58]

HOWARD, SIR ROBERT (1585–1653), royalist; fifth son of Thomas Howard, first earl of Suffolk [q. v.]; K.B., 1616; imprisoned by high commission and publicly excommunicated, 1625, for intrigue with Frances, viscountess Purbeck (Buckingham's brother's wife); M.P., Bishop's Castle, 1624–40; voted compensation by Long parliament, 1640, but expelled for royalism, 1642; his estates sequestered.   [xxviii. 58]

HOWARD, SIR ROBERT (1626–1698), dramatist: nephew of Sir Robert Howard (1585–1653) [q. v.]; rescued Wilmot from parliamentarians at Cropredy Bridge and was knighted, 1644; whig M.P., Stockbridge, 1660, Castle Rising, 1679–98; auditor of the exchequer; built Ashtead House, Surrey, 1684; privy councillor, 1689; commander of militia horse, 1690; ridiculed as Sir Positive At-All in Shadwell's 'Sullen Lovers'; perhaps the Bilboa of 'The Rehearsal'; author of 'The Committee' (revived at Covent Garden as 'The Honest Thieves,' 1797), published with four other plays, 1692 and 1722, in one of which, the 'Indian Queen,' Dryden assisted; opposed use of rhyme in drama; published also historical works and poems.   [xxviii. 59]

HOWARD, ROBERT (1683–1740), bishop of Elphin; son of Ralph Howard (1638–1710) [q. v.]; fellow of Trinity College, Dublin, 1703; bishop of Killala, 1726, of Elphin, 1729–40.   [xxviii. 58]

HOWARD, SAMUEL (1710–1782), organist and composer; Mus.Doc. Cambridge, 1769; best known by his 'musettes.'   [xxviii. 61]

HOWARD, THEOPHILUS, second EARL OF SUFFOLK and second BARON HOWARD DE WALDEN (1584–1640), succeeded his father, Thomas Howard, first earl of Suffolk [q. v.], 1626; M.A. Oxford, 1605; M.P., Maldon, 1605–10; summoned as Baron Howard de Walden, 1610; governor of Jersey, 1610; quarrelled with Lord Herbert of Cherbury at Juliers, 1610; joint lord-lieutenant of northern counties, 1614; lord-lieutenant of Cambridgeshire, Suffolk, and Dorset, 1626; K.G., 1627; warden of Cinque ports, 1628.   [xxviii. 61]

HOWARD, THOMAS I, EARL OF SURREY and second DUKE OF NORFOLK of the Howard house (1443–1524), warrior; only son of Sir John Howard, afterwards first duke of Norfolk [q. v.]; fought for Edward IV at Barnet, 1471; knighted, 1478; Earl of Surrey from 1483; became K.G., 1483; fought for Richard III at Bosworth,

1485; imprisoned in the Tower by Henry VII, but ultimately recovered his estates; subdued Yorkshire rising, 1489; as lieutenant-general of the north compelled the Scots to retreat, 1497, and negotiated marriage treaty; lord-treasurer, 1501–22; earl marshal, 1510; ousted from power by Wolsey; when again lieutenant-general of the north won battle of Flodden, 1513, and was created Duke of Norfolk, 1514; vainly opposed Wolsey's foreign policy; put down London apprentices on 'evil May-day,' 1517; guardian of the kingdom, 1520; presided as high steward at trial of his friend and connection, Buckingham, 1521.
[xxviii. 62]

HOWARD, THOMAS II, EARL OF SURREY and third DUKE OF NORFOLK of the Howard house (1473–1554), eldest son of Thomas Howard I [q. v.]; as Lord Thomas Howard with his brother, Sir Edward Howard [q. v.], captured Andrew Barton [q. v.], 1511; lord admiral, 1513; led vanguard at Flodden, 1513; as Earl of Surrey (1514–1524) strongly opposed Wolsey; lord-lieutenant of Ireland, 1520–1; raided French coast, 1521–22; lord-treasurer, 1522; as warden-general of the marches devastated Scottish border and forced Albany to retreat, 1523; pacified Suffolk insurgents, 1525; as president of the privy council incensed Henry VIII against Wolsey; earl-marshal, 1533; acquiesced in execution of his niece, Anne Boleyn, 1536; put down Pilgrimage of Grace; headed opposition to Cromwell and brought forward the six articles, 1539; again commanded against the Scots, 1542; lieutenant-general of army in France, 1544; ousted from favour by Hertford, and condemned to death, but saved by Henry VIII's death; remained in the Tower till accession of Mary (1553), when he was released and restored; presided at Northumberland's trial, 1553; showed great rashness when commanding against Wyatt, 1554.
[xxviii. 64]

HOWARD, THOMAS III, fourth DUKE OF NORFOLK of the Howard house (1536–1572), son of Henry Howard, earl of Surrey [q. v.]; pupil of John Foxe [q. v.]; K.B., 1553; succeeded his grandfather as duke and earl-marshal, 1554; employed in Scotland, 1559–60; K.G., 1559; privy councillor, 1562; contributed largely towards completion of Magdalene College, Cambridge; quarrelled with Leicester in Elizabeth's presence, 1565; one of the commissioners to inquire into Scottish affairs at York, 1568; formed project of marriage with Mary Queen of Scots; imprisoned, 1569–70; involved in Ridolfi's plot; executed for treason; denied having been a papist.   [xxviii. 67]

HOWARD, LORD THOMAS, first EARL OF SUFFOLK and first BARON HOWARD DE WALDEN (1561–1626), second son of Thomas Howard III, fourth duke of Norfolk [q. v.]; as Lord Thomas Howard distinguished himself against Armada, 1588; commanded in attack on Azores fleet, 1591; admiral of the third squadron in Cadiz expedition, 1596; K.G. and Baron Howard de Walden, 1597; marshal of forces against Essex and constable of Tower, 1601; created Earl of Suffolk by James I, 1603; lord chamberlain, 1603–14; M.A. Oxford and Cambridge, 1605; lord-lieutenant of Suffolk, Cambridgeshire, and Dorset; chancellor of Cambridge University, 1614; lord high treasurer, 1614–18; fined and imprisoned for embezzlement, 1619.
[xxviii. 71]

HOWARD, THOMAS, second EARL OF ARUNDEL AND SURREY (1586–1646), art collector; only son of Philip Howard, first earl of Arundel [q. v.]; restored in title and blood, 1604; made first continental tour, 1609–10; K.G., 1611; became protestant, 1615; privy councillor, 1616; president of committee of peers on Bacon's case, 1621; joint-commissioner of great seal, 1621; earl-marshal, 1621; imprisoned for hostility to Buckingham, 1626–1628; attempted mediation in debates on petition of right, 1628; sent to Vienna to urge restitution of palatinate to Charles I's nephew, 1636; general of army against Scots, 1639; presided at Strafford's trial, 1641; escorted Queen Henrietta Maria to the continent, 1642; thenceforward lived at Padua, contributing large sums to royal cause. He formed at Arundel House the first considerable art collection in England, including statues, busts, pictures, and the marbles (described in Selden's 'Marmora Arundeliana,' 1628), presented to Oxford university, 1667.   [xxviii. 73]

HOWARD, WALTER (1759–1830?), 'The Heir of Poverty'; claimed kinship with the Dukes of Norfolk and received allowances from several; his claim found fictitious; imprisoned, 1812, for importuning the prince regent and the eleventh Duke of Norfolk.   [xxviii. 76]

HOWARD, SIR WILLIAM (d. 1308), judge; justice of assize for northern counties, 1293; summoned to parliament as a justice, 1295; justice of common pleas, 1297. [xxviii. 77]

HOWARD, LORD WILLIAM, first BARON HOWARD OF EFFINGHAM (1510?-1573), lord high admiral; eldest son of Thomas Howard I, second duke of Norfolk [q. v.]; of Trinity College, Cambridge; employed on embassies to Scotland, 1531, 1535, and 1536, and in France, 1537 and 1541; convicted of misprision of treason in connection with Queen Catherine Howard, but pardoned, 1541; governor of Calais, 1552-3; privy councillor, 1553; lord high admiral, 1554-73; K.G., 1554; created peer for defence of London against Wyatt, 1554; remonstrated against harsh treatment of Princess Elizabeth; lord chamberlain, 1558; a negotiator of treaty of Câteau Cambrésis, 1559; lord privy seal, 1572. [xxviii. 77]

HOWARD, LORD WILLIAM (1563-1640), Scott's 'Belted Will'; third son of Thomas Howard III, fourth duke of Norfolk [q. v.]; married Elizabeth Dacre ('Bessie with the braid apron'), 1577; became a Romanist, 1584; twice imprisoned; restored Naworth Castle; active as commissioner of the borders, being known to contemporaries as 'Bauld Willie'; formed large library, and published edition of Florence of Worcester's chronicle, 1592; assisted Camden in 'Britannia'; intimate with Cotton and other antiquaries. [xxviii. 79]

HOWARD, WILLIAM, first VISCOUNT STAFFORD (1614-1680), fifth son of Thomas Howard, second earl of Arundel and Surrey [q. v.]; K.B., 1626; created Viscount Stafford, 1640; remained abroad during rebellion; allowed to return, 1656; discontented with the king, who refused his petition (1664) for restoration of Stafford earldom to his wife; member of council of Royal Society, 1672; accused by Oates of being paymaster of catholic army, and by others of persuading them to murder Charles II; beheaded for treason, 1680; attainder reversed, 1824. [xxviii. 81]

HOWARD, WILLIAM, third BARON HOWARD OF ESCRICK (1626?-1694), second son of Edward Howard, first baron Howard [q. v.]; served in parliamentary army; imprisoned for republican plots, 1657; M.P., Winchelsea, in Convention parliament; succeeded his brother in peerage, 1678; imprisoned, 1674 and 1681; informed against Russell and Sidney, 1683. [xxviii. 83]

HOWARD DE WALDEN, BARONS. [See HOWARD, LORD THOMAS, first BARON, 1561-1626; HOWARD, THEOPHILUS, second BARON, 1584-1640; HOWARD, JAMES, third BARON, 1619-1688; GRIFFIN (formerly WHITWELL), JOHN GRIFFIN, fourth BARON, 1719-1797; HERVEY, FREDERICK AUGUSTUS, fifth BARON, 1730-1803; ELLIS, CHARLES AUGUSTUS, sixth BARON, 1799-1868.]

HOWARD-VYSE, RICHARD WILLIAM (1784-1853). [See VYSE.]

HOWDEN, BARONS. [See CARADOC, SIR JOHN FRANCIS, first BARON, 1762-1839; CARADOC, SIR JOHN HOBART, second BARON, 1799-1873.]

HOWE, CHARLES (1661-1742), author of 'Devout Meditations,' published, 1751; brother of John Grubham Howe [q. v.] [xxviii. 83]

HOWE, EMANUEL SCROPE (d. 1709), diplomatist; brother of Scrope Howe, first viscount Howe [q. v.]; groom of the bedchamber to William III; M.P., Morpeth, 1701-5, Wigan, 1705-8; envoy-extraordinary to Hanover, 1705-9; lieutenant-general, 1709. [xxviii. 84]

HOWE, GEORGE (1655?-1710), physician; son of John Howe (1630-1705) [q. v.]; M.D. Leyden; censor, Royal College of Physicians, 1707; the Querpo of Garth's 'Dispensary.' [xxviii. 84]

HOWE, GEORGE AUGUSTUS, third VISCOUNT HOWE (1725?-1758), grandson of Scrope Howe, first viscount Howe [q. v.], in Irish peerage; succeeded to title, 1735; M.P., Nottingham, 1747 and 1754-65; served in Flanders, 1747; colonel, 1757; commanded 60th foot in Halifax, 1757; killed in skirmish with French at Trout Brook, Lake George. [Suppl. iii. 3]

HOWE, HENRY (1812-1896), actor; his real name HENRY HOWE HUTCHINSON; appeared at Victoria Theatre, London, 1834; with Macready at Covent Garden,

1837; at Haymarket for forty years, his parts including Sir Peter Teazle, Malvolio, Jaques, and Macduff; in 1896 accompanied Sir Henry Irving to America, where he died. [Suppl. iii. 3]

HOWE, JAMES (1780-1836), Scottish animal-painter; exhibited at Royal Academy (1816) picture of Waterloo. [xxviii. 85]

HOWE, JOHN (1630-1705), ejected minister; nephew of Obadiah Howe [q. v.]; B.A. Christ's College, Cambridge, 1648, where he was intimate with Henry More (1614-1687) [q. v.]; M.A. Magdalen College, Oxford, 1652; fellow and chaplain of Magdalen College; perpetual curate of Great Torrington, 1654-62; as domestic chaplain to Cromwell preached against fanaticism; befriended Fuller and Seth Ward; chaplain to Richard Cromwell; preached at houses in the west after ejection; joint pastor at Haberdashers' Hall, London, 1676; began controversy on predestination, 1677; answered sermon on schism by Stillingfleet, 1680; expostulated with Tillotson, 1680; refused to support dispensing power; advocated mutual forbearance of conformists and dissenters, 1689; prominent in 'happy union' of presbyterians and congregationalists, 1690; had controversy with Defoe on occasional conformity, 1700; conferred privately with William III before his death; visited by Richard Cromwell in last illness; chief work, 'The Living Temple of God,' 1675; included in works collected, 1724 (enlarged, 1810-22, 1862-3). [xxviii. 85]

HOWE, JOHN, fourth BARON CHEDWORTH (1754-1804), of Harrow and Queen's College, Oxford; succeeded his uncle Henry Frederick Howe in title and estates, 1781; left 3,000l. to Charles James Fox; his 'Notes upon some of the Obscure Passages in Shakespeare's Plays' issued, 1805. [xxviii. 88]

HOWE or **HOW**, JOHN GRUBHAM (1657-1722), politician ('Jack How'); forbidden court for slandering Duchess of Richmond, 1679; a strong whig and vice-chamberlain to Queen Mary, 1689-92; after dismissal a violent tory, especially denouncing William III's partition treaty (1698) and Dutch favourites; M.P., Cirencester, 1689-98, Gloucestershire, 1698-1701 and 1702-5; privy councillor and joint-clerk of privy council under Anne. [xxviii. 89]

HOWE, JOSEPH (1804-1873), Nova Scotian statesman; from 1828 edited the 'Nova Scotian'; vindicated liberty of the press in successful defence against crown prosecution, 1835; as member for Halifax agitated for responsible government, 1837; member of executive council and speaker, 1840; frequently delegate to England; secretary of state for Nova Scotia in Dominion government, 1870; governor of Nova Scotia, 1873. [xxviii. 90]

HOWE, JOSIAS (1611?-1701), divine; fellow of Trinity College, Oxford, 1637-48, restored, 1660; M.A., 1638; B.D., 1646. [xxviii. 91]

HOWE, MICHAEL (1787-1818), Tasmanian bushranger; transported for highway robbery, 1811; killed while resisting arrest after six years' outlawry. [xxviii. 91]

HOWE, OBADIAH (1616?-1683), divine; M.A. Magdalen Hall, Oxford, 1638; incumbent of Stickney, Horncastle, and Gedney; vicar of Boston, 1660-83; published controversial works. [xxviii. 92]

HOWE, RICHARD, EARL HOWE (1726-1799), admiral of the fleet; grandson of Scrope Howe, first viscount Howe [q. v.]; educated at Eton; sailed in the Severn as far as Cape Horn with Anson, 1740; present at attack on La Guayra, 1743; wounded in action with French frigates off west of Scotland, 1746; by capture of the Alcide off mouth of St. Lawrence opened seven years' war, 1755; M.P., Dartmouth, 1757-82; took leading part in Rochefort expedition, 1757; succeeded brother as fourth Viscount (Irish) Howe, 1758; commanded covering squadron in attacks on St. Malo and Cherbourg, 1758; distinguished at blockade of Brest and battle of Quiberon Bay, 1759; a lord of the admiralty, 1762-5; treasurer of the navy, 1765-70; rear-admiral, 1770; vice-admiral, 1775; as commander-in-chief on North American station co-operated with his brother, Sir William Howe [q. v.]; forced passage of Delaware, 1777, and watched French fleet under D'Estaing off Sandy Hook, 1777; resigned command owing to discontent with ministry, 1778, remaining four years in retirement; admiral, 1782; commander in the Channel, 1782; created a British peer,

1782; effected relief of Gibraltar against superior forces, 1782; as first lord of the admiralty (1783–8) was much attacked in parliament and the press; created Earl Howe, 1788; commanded Channel fleet, 1790; vice-admiral of England, 1792–6; with Channel fleet won the great victory of 1 June 1794, capturing six French ships; incurred some unpopularity owing to insufficient mention of distinguished officers; admiral of the fleet and general of marines, 1796; K.G., 1797; presided over court-martial on Vice-admiral Cornwallis, 1796; after retirement pacified mutineers at Portsmouth, 1797. The signalling code was perfected and refined by him. [xxviii. 92]

HOWE, SCROPE, first VISCOUNT HOWE (1648–1712), whig politician; brother of Charles Howe [q. v.]; knighted, 1663; M.P., Nottinghamshire, 1673–98 and 1710–12; active at the revolution; groom of the bedchamber, 1689–1702; comptroller of the exchequer; created Irish viscount, 1701. [xxviii. 101]

HOWE or **HOW, WILLIAM** (1620–1656), botanist; of Merchant Taylors' School and St. John's College, Oxford; M.A., 1644; published 'Phytologia Britannica' (anonymous, 1650), the earliest work exclusively on British plants. [xxviii. 102]

HOWE, SIR WILLIAM, fifth VISCOUNT HOWE (1729–1814), general; brother of Richard, earl Howe [q. v.]; educated at Eton; commanded 58th (now 1st Northampton) regiment at capture of Louisbourg and defence of Quebec, 1759–60; led forlorn hope at Heights of Abraham, 1759; commanded brigade in Montreal expedition, 1760, and at siege of Belleisle, 1761; adjutant-general at conquest of Havana, 1762; major-general, 1772; lieutenant-general, 1775; M.P., Nottingham, 1758–80; commanded at battle of Bunker Hill, 1775; K.B., 1775; succeeded Gage as commander in American colonies; evacuated Boston and took up position at Halifax, Nova Scotia, 1776; associated with his brother in American conciliation commission, 1776; defeated Americans on Long Island, 1776; captured New York and won battles of White Plains and Brandywine, 1776; repulsed attack on Germantown, 1776; failed to draw Washington into further action, 1777; resigned command, 1778; spoke in parliament on American affairs, and obtained (1779) committee of inquiry; published 'Narrative,' 1780; lieutenant-general of ordnance, 1782–1803; general, 1793; commanded northern, and afterwards eastern, district; succeeded brother in Irish viscountcy, 1799. [xxviii. 102]

HOWEL VYCHAN, or THE LITTLE (d. 825), Welsh prince; fought with Cynan for Anglesey. [xxviii. 105]

HOWEL DDA, or THE GOOD (d. 950), early Welsh king; doubtfully said to have become king of Gwynedd and all Wales, 915; became directly subject to Edward the elder, c. 918; attested many charters at witenagemots in reign of Athelstan and Eadred; made pilgrimage to Rome, 928. His 'Laws' survive in Latin manuscripts at Peniarth (twelfth century) and the British Museum (thirteenth century), and the Welsh 'Black Book of Chirk' (Peniarth, thirteenth century); they exist only as amended by later rulers, and show traces of English and Norman influence. They were in operation till Edward I's conquest. [xxviii. 105]

HOWEL AB IEUAV, or HOWEL DDRWG, the BAD (d. 984), North Welsh prince; expelled Iago from Gwynedd, and (979) slew his son; slain by Saxon treachery. [xxviii. 107]

HOWEL AB EDWIN (d. 1044), South Welsh prince; descended from Howel Dda [q. v.]; succeeded in Deheubarth, 1033; expelled by Gruffydd ab Llywelyn [q. v.], 1039, and finally defeated and slain by him. [xxviii. 107]

HOWEL AB OWAIN GWYNEDD (d. 1171?), warrior and poet; seized part of Ceredigion, 1143; ravaged Cardigan, 1144; with Gruffydd ab Rhys [q. v.] took Carmarthen Castle, 1145, but afterwards joined the Normans; lost his territory, 1150–2; took part in Henry II's defeat at Basingwerk, 1157; killed by his brother David in Ireland, or in Anglesey; eight of his odes in 'Myvyrian Archæology.' [xxviii. 108]

HOWEL Y FWYALL (fl. 1356), 'Howel of the Battleaxe'; fought gallantly at Poitiers, 1356; knighted by the Black Prince, 1356; a mess of meat served before his axe and given to the poor till Queen Elizabeth's time. [xxviii. 108]

HOWELL, FRANCIS (1625–1679), puritan divine; M.A. Exeter College, Oxford, 1648, fellow, 1648–58; senior proctor, 1652; one of the visitors; professor of moral philosophy, 1654; principal of Jesus College, 1657–1660. [xxviii. 109]

HOWELL, JAMES (1594?–1666), author; B.A. Jesus College, Oxford, 1613; fellow, 1623; travelled through Holland, France, Spain, and Italy; went on diplomatic missions to Spain and Sardinia, and while at Madrid wrote accounts of Prince Charles's courtship of the infanta, 1622–4; M.P., Richmond, 1627; secretary to Leicester's embassy to Denmark, 1632; employed by Strafford in Edinburgh and London; intimate with Ben Jonson; corresponded with Lord Herbert of Cherbury [q. v.] and Sir Kenelm Digby [q. v.]; published 'Dodona's Grove' (political allegory), 1640 (2nd part, 1650), and 'Instructions for Forreine Travel,' 1642 (enlarged, 1650; reprinted, 1868); royalist prisoner in the Fleet, 1643–51; wrote in prison royalist pamphlets, 'England's Tears for the present Wars,' a description of Scotland and the Scots (reprinted by Wilkes, 1762), and 'Survey of the Seignorie of Venice' (1651); defended Cromwell against Long parliament, 1653; advocated Restoration, 1660; historiographer-royal, 1661; his 'Cordial for Cavaliers' (1661) attacked by Roger L'Estrange; 'Poems' edited by Payne Fisher, 1663. His reputation rests on 'Epistolæ Ho-elianæ: Familiar Letters,' mostly written in the Fleet, and generally to imaginary correspondents (collected, 1655, frequently reissued; edited by Mr. Joseph Jacobs, 1890–1). His other works include political and historical pamphlets, a revision of Cotgrave's 'French and English Dictionary,' 1650, an English-French-Italian-Spanish dictionary (1659–60), with appendix of Welsh proverbs, translations, and an edition of Sir Robert Cotton's 'Posthuma,' 1657. [xxviii. 109]

HOWELL, JOHN (1774–1830), Welsh poet (IOAN AB HYWEL), fife-major in Carmarthenshire militia; schoolmaster at Llandovery; published 'Blodau Dyfed,' 1824. [xxviii. 114]

HOWELL, JOHN (1788–1863), polyartist, invented 'plough' for cutting edges of books; introduced manufacture of Pompeian plates; published 'Life of Alexander Selkirk,' 1829; contributed to Wilson's 'Tales of the Borders.' [xxviii. 114]

HOWELL, LAURENCE (1664?–1720), nonjuror; M.A. Jesus College, Cambridge, 1688; ordained by George Hickes [q. v.], 1712; sentenced to fine, imprisonment, and whipping for his 'Case of Schism in the Church of England stated,' 1717; died in Newgate. His works include 'Synopsis Canonum SS. Apostolorum, et Conciliorum Œcumenicorum et Provincialium,' &c., 1708, 'Synopsis Canonum Ecclesiæ Latinæ,' 1710, 'View of the Pontificate,' 1712. [xxviii. 115]

HOWELL, THOMAS (fl. 1568), author of 'The Arbor of Amitie' (1568), 'Newe Sonets and pretie Pamphlets' (1567–8), and 'H. His Deuises' (1581). [xxviii. 116]

HOWELL, THOMAS (1588–1646), bishop of Bristol; brother of James Howell [q. v.]; fellow of Jesus College, Oxford; M.A., 1612; D.D., 1630; chaplain to Charles I; canon of Windsor, 1636; rector of Fulham, 1642; bishop of Bristol, 1644–6; died of effects of maltreatment at siege (1645) of Bristol. [xxviii. 116]

HOWELL, THOMAS BAYLY (1768–1815), editor of 'State Trials' (vols. i.–xxi.), 1809–15; of Christ Church, Oxford; barrister, Lincoln's Inn, 1790. [xxviii. 117]

HOWELL, THOMAS JONES (d. 1858), continuer of 'State Trials' (vols. xxii.–xxxiii.); son of Thomas Bayly Howell [q. v.]; of Lincoln's Inn. [xxviii. 117]

HOWELL, WILLIAM (1638?–1683), historian; fellow of Magdalene College, Cambridge; M.A., 1655; chancellor of Lincoln; published 'An Institution of General History' (1661) and 'Medulla Historiæ Anglicanæ,' 1679. [xxviii. 117]

HOWELL, WILLIAM (1656–1714), devotional writer; M.A. New Inn Hall, Oxford, 1676; curate and schoolmaster of Ewelme. [xxviii. 118]

HOWELLS, WILLIAM (1778–1882), minister at Long Acre Chapel, London, 1817; of Wadham College, Oxford; his 'Remains' edited, 1833. [xxviii. 118]

HOWES, EDMUND (*fl.* 1607-1631), continuator of Stow's ' Abridgement' (1607 and 1611) and Stow's ' Annales or Chronicle' (1615 and 1631).   [xxviii. 118]

HOWES, EDWARD (*fl.* 1650), mathematician ; rector of Goldanger, Essex, 1659 ; sent John Winthrop (1588-1649) [q. v.] tract defining locality of North-West Passage ; published 'A Short Arithmetick,' 1659.
[xxviii. 119]

HOWES, FRANCIS (1776-1844), translator of Persius and Horace ; of Trinity College, Cambridge ; eleventh wrangler, 1798 ; M.A., 1804 ; minor canon of Norwich, 1815 ; rector of Alderford, 1826-9, Framingham Pigot, 1829-44 ; his translations collected, 1845.   [xxviii. 119]

HOWES, JOHN (*fl.* 1772-1793), miniature and enamel painter.   [xxviii. 120]

HOWES, THOMAS (1729-1814), author of ' Critical Observations on Books, Ancient and Modern' (1776) ; B.A. Clare Hall, Cambridge, 1746 ; rector of Morningthorpe, 1756-71, Thorndon, 1771-1814.   [xxviii. 119]

HOWGILL, FRANCIS (1618-1669), quaker ; successively churchman, independent, and anabaptist ; with Anthony Pearson held first quaker meetings in London, 1653 ; preached in Ireland till banished by Henry Cromwell ; sentenced to perpetual imprisonment for refusing oath of allegiance, 1664 ; published quaker works.
[xxviii. 120]

HOWGILL, WILLIAM (*fl.* 1794), musical composer.
[xxviii. 121]

HOWICK, VISCOUNT, afterwards second EARL GREY (1764-1845). [See GREY, CHARLES.]

HOWIE, JOHN (1735-1793), author of 'Scots Worthies' (1774 and 1781-5) ; farmer of Lochgoin, Ayrshire ; publishing works concerning the covenanters.
[xxviii. 121]

HOWISON, WILLIAM (*fl.* 1823), author and friend of Sir Walter Scott.   [xxviii. 122]

HOWISON or **HOWIESON**, WILLIAM (1798-1850), line-engraver ; the only engraver ever elected A.R.S.A. ; best known for engravings of Sir George Harvey's pictures.   [xxviii. 121]

HOWITT, MARY (1799-1888), author ; *née* Botham ; married William Howitt [q. v.], 1821, and collaborated with him in many works ; published translations from Fredrika Bremer and Hans Andersen and successful children's books ; other works include 'Popular History of the United States' (1859) ; received civil list pension, 1879 ; died at Rome.   [xxviii. 122]

HOWITT, RICHARD (1799-1869), poet ; brother of William Howitt [q. v.] ; druggist at Nottingham ; lived in Australia, 1839-44 ; published 'Impressions of Australia Felix,' 1845, 'Wasp's Honey,' 1868.   [xxviii. 123]

HOWITT, SAMUEL (1765?-1822), painter and etcher ; brother-in-law of Rowlandson ; exhibited at Academy, 1785-94, chiefly sporting subjects ; published 'Miscellaneous Etchings of Animals,' 1803, and other works.   [xxviii. 123]

HOWITT, WILLIAM (1792-1879), author ; educated at Friends' School, Ackworth ; published a poem at thirteen ; published, with his wife, 'The Forest Minstrel' and other poems ; chemist at Nottingham ; published 'Book of the Seasons,' 1831, 'Popular History of Priestcraft,' 1833, first series of 'Visits to Remarkable Places,' 1840, second series, 1842, 'Rural and Domestic Life of Germany,' 1842, when at Heidelberg ; after three years in Australia issued 'History of Discovery in Australia, Tasmania, and New Zealand' (1865), and Australian tales ; became spiritualist ; received civil list pension, 1865 ; wrote for Cassell's ' Popular History of England,' 1856-62 ; died at Rome.   [xxviii. 124]

HOWLAND, RICHARD (1540-1600), bishop of Peterborough ; B.A. St. John's College, Cambridge, 1561 ; fellow of Peterhouse, 1562 ; M.A., 1564 ; rector of Stathern, 1569 ; at first an adherent of Thomas Cartwright (1535-1603) [q. v.], but afterwards a strong opponent ; chaplain to Lord Burghley ; master of Magdalene (1576-7), and (1577-86) St. John's Colleges, Cambridge ; vice-chancellor of Cambridge, 1578 and 1583 ; bishop of Peterborough, 1584-1600 ; friend of Whitgift ; attacked by Martin Mar-Prelate.   [xxviii. 125]

HOWLET, JOHN (1548-1589), jesuit ; fellow of Exeter College, Oxford, 1566 ; B.A., 1566 ; resided at Douay ; died at Wilna.   [xxviii. 127]

HOWLETT, BARTHOLOMEW (1767-1827), topographical and antiquarian draughtsman and engraver.
[xxviii. 127]

HOWLETT, JOHN (1731-1804), political economist ; M.A. St. John's College, Oxford, 1795 ; B.D., 1796 ; incumbent of Great Dunmow and Great Badow ; published works on enclosures and population combating the views of Price.   [xxviii. 127]

HOWLETT, SAMUEL BURT (1794-1874), military surveyor and inventor ; invented an anemometer and method of construction for large drawing-boards ; published treatise on perspective, 1828.   [xxviii. 128]

HOWLEY, HENRY (1775?-1803), Irish insurgent ; took part in rebellion of 1798, and Robert Emmet's rising ; executed.   [xxviii. 128]

HOWLEY, WILLIAM (1766-1848), archbishop of Canterbury ; of Winchester and New College, Oxford (fellow and tutor) ; M.A., 1791 ; D.D., 1805 ; vicar of Andover, 1802 ; rector of Bradford Peverell, 1811 ; canon of Christ Church, Oxford, 1804 ; regius professor of divinity, Oxford, 1809-13 ; bishop of London, 1813-28 ; supported bill of pains and penalties against Queen Caroline, 1820 ; archbishop of Canterbury, 1828-48 ; opposed catholic emancipation, 1829, parliamentary reform, 1831, and Jewish relief, 1833 ; carried vote of censure on Lord John Russell's education scheme, 1839.   [xxviii. 128]

HOWMAN, JOHN, or **FECKENHAM**, JOHN DE (1518?-1585). [See FECKENHAM, JOHN DE.]

HOWSON, JOHN (1557?-1632), bishop of Durham ; of St. Paul's School and Christ Church, Oxford ; M.A., 1582 ; D.D., 1601 ; prebendary of Hereford, 1587, Exeter, 1592 ; chaplain to Queen Elizabeth and James I ; canon of Christ Church, 1601 ; vice-chancellor, 1602 ; bishop of Oxford, 1619-28, of Durham, 1628-32 ; buried in St. Paul's.
[xxviii. 129]

HOWSON, JOHN SAUL (1816-1885), dean of Chester ; wrangler, Trinity College, Cambridge ; M.A., 1841 ; D.D., 1861 ; principal of Liverpool College, 1849-66 ; Hulsean lecturer at Cambridge, 1862 ; vicar of Wisbech, 1866 ; dean of Chester, 1867-85 ; did good service in restoration of Chester Cathedral ; active on behalf of Chester educational institutions ; with W. J. Conybeare published 'Life and Epistles of St. Paul,' 1852 ; published 'Character of St. Paul,' 1862, and other Pauline studies ; Bohlen lecturer at Philadelphia, 1880 ; contributed to Smith's 'Dictionary of the Bible' and biblical commentaries ; wrote also controversial and archæological works.
[xxviii. 130]

HOWTH, BARONS. [See ST. LAWRENCE, ROBERT, third BARON, *d.* 1483 ; ST. LAWRENCE, SIR CHRISTOPHER, eighth BARON, *d.* 1589 ; ST. LAWRENCE, SIR CHRISTOPHER, tenth BARON, 1568?-1619 ; ST. LAWRENCE, NICHOLAS, fourth BARON, *d.* 1526.]

HOY, THOMAS (1659-1718?), physician and author ; fellow of St. John's College, Oxford, 1675 ; M.A., 1684 ; M.D., 1689 ; regius professor of physic, 1698 ; published essay on Ovid's 'De Arte Amandi' and Musæus's 'Hero and Leander,' 1682, and 'Agathocles' (poem), 1683 ; possibly died in Jamaica.   [xxviii. 132]

HOYLAND, FRANCIS (*fl.* 1763), poet ; B.A. Magdalene College, Cambridge, 1748 ; introduced by Mason to Horace Walpole, who printed his 'Poems' at Strawberry Hill, 1769 ; published 'Odes,' 1783.   [xxviii. 132]

HOYLAND, GILBERT OF (*d.* 1172). [See GILBERT.]

HOYLAND, JOHN (1783-1827), organist at St. James's, Sheffield, and at Louth, Lincolnshire ; composed sacred music.   [xxviii. 132]

HOYLAND, JOHN (1750-1831), quaker author of 'Historical Survey of Customs, Habits, and Present State of the Gypsies' (1816), and euhemeristic 'Epitome of History of the World,' 1812.   [xxviii. 132]

HOYLE, EDMOND (1672-1769), writer on cardgames ; gave lessons on whist in Queen Square, London, 1741 ; issued first edition of his 'Short Treatise on Whist' (1742) at a guinea, second edition (1743) at two shillings ;

incorporated in eighth edition (1748) treatises on quad-rille, piquet, and backgammon, and in the eleventh edition treatise on chess; Hoyle's 'Laws' of 1760 ruled whist till 1864. His book on chess was reissued, 1808. [xxviii. 133]

HOYLE, JOHN (*d.* 1797 ?), author of dictionary of musical terms (1770 and 1791). [xxviii. 134]

HOYLE, JOSHUA (*d.* 1654), puritan divine; fellow of Trinity College, Dublin, 1609; D.D.; master of University College, Oxford, and regius professor of divinity, 1648–54; vicar of Stepney, 1641; member of Westminster Assembly of Divines. [xxviii. 134]

HOYLE, WILLIAM (1831–1886), Lancashire cotton-spinner and temperance reformer; published 'Our National Resources and how they are wasted,' 1871, and other works, including temperance hymns and songs. [xxviii. 135]

HUBBARD, JOHN GELLIBRAND, first BARON ADDINGTON (1805–1889), director of Bank of England, 1838; chairman of public works loan commission, 1853–1889; conservative M.P., Buckingham, 1859–68, London, 1874–87; privy councillor, 1874; created Baron Addington, 1887; obtained inquiry into assessment of income tax, 1861; built and endowed St. Alban's, Holborn, 1863. [xxviii. 135]

HUBBARD, WILLIAM (1621 ?–1704), New England historian; left England, 1635; graduated at Harvard, 1642 (acting president, 1688); pastor of congregational church, Ipswich, Massachusetts; his 'History of New England' printed, 1815 and 1848. [xxviii. 136]

HUBBERTHORN, RICHARD (1628–1662), quaker writer; officer in parliamentary army; accompanied Fox in his journeys in Lancashire and the eastern counties, and with him had interview with Charles II; collaborated with Fox and James Nayler; died in Newgate. [xxviii. 136]

HUBBOCK, WILLIAM (*fl.* 1605), chaplain of the Tower; B.A. Magdalen College, Oxford, 1581; fellow of Corpus Christi College, Oxford; M.A., 1585; cited for puritanical sermon, 1590; published 'Apologie of Infants,' 1595. [xxviii. 137]

HUBERT, SIR FRANCIS (*d.* 1629), poet; clerk in chancery, 1601; author of 'Historie of Edward the Second,' 1629, and 'Egypt's Favorite,' 1631. [xxviii. 137]

HUBERT WALTER (*d.* 1205), archbishop of Canterbury and statesman; trained under Glanville; a baron of exchequer, 1184–5; dean of York, 1186; justice of the curia regis, 1189; bishop of Salisbury, 1189; accompanied Richard I to Palestine and negotiated for him with Saladin; led back English crusaders to Sicily; visited the king in prison and came back to collect ransom; justiciar, 1193; suppressed Prince John's attempt at revolt; archbishop of Canterbury, 1193–1205; officiated at Richard's second coronation, 1194; developed Henry II's judicial and financial system; maintained good relations with Scotland; as legate held council at York, 1195, and London, 1200; unpopular with the clergy for forcing William Fitzosbert [q. v.] from sanctuary, 1196; negotiated alliance with Flanders, truce with France, and pacification of Richard's quarrel with Archbishop of Rouen, 1197; settled succession dispute in South Wales, 1197; caused land-tax to be assessed by help of locally elected landowners and representatives of townships and hundreds, 1198; compelled by Innocent III to resign justiciarship, 1198; joined Richard in Normandy; returned as member of regency after his death; asserted elective character of the monarchy at John's coronation, 1199; chancellor, 1199–1205; on missions to France, 1201 and 1203; dissuaded John from expedition against France, 1205; recovered for his see right of coining money. His bones were identified in Canterbury Cathedral, 1890. [xxviii. 137]

HUCHOWN (*fl.* 14th cent.), author of romances in alliterative verse. [Suppl. iii. 4]

HUCK, RICHARD (1720–1785). [See SAUNDERS, RICHARD HUCK-.]

HUCKELL, JOHN (1729–1771), poet; B.A. Magdalen Hall, Oxford, 1751; curate of Hounslow; his 'Avon' printed by Baskerville, 1758. [xxviii. 141]

HUDDART, JOSEPH (1741–1816), hydrographer and manufacturer; during ten years' service in the East India Company constructed charts of Sumatra and the Indian coast from Bombay to the Godavery; F.R.S., 1791; made fortune by manufacture of patent cordage. [xxviii. 141]

HUDDESFORD, GEORGE (1749–1809), satirical poet; fellow of New College, Oxford, 1771–2; M.A., 1780; pupil of Sir Joshua Reynolds, who painted his portrait in 'Two Gentlemen' (National Gallery); vicar of Loxley and incumbent of Wheler's Chapel, Spital Square, London; political satirist; contributed to 'Salmagundi' (1791). [xxviii. 141]

HUDDESFORD, WILLIAM (1732–1772), antiquary; brother of George Huddesford [q. v.]; fellow of Trinity College, Oxford, 1757; M.A., 1756; B.D., 1767; keeper of the Ashmolean, 1755–72; vicar of Bishop's Tachbrook, 1761; edited Edward Lhuyd's 'Lithophylacii Britannici Ichnographia,' 1760, Martin Lister's 'Synopsis Methodica Conchyliorum,' 1760, and catalogue of Anthony à Wood's manuscripts, 1761. [xxviii. 142]

HUDDLESTON or **HUDLESTON**, JOHN (1608–1698), Benedictine; of Lancashire; while on the English mission was one of those who watched over Charles II at Moseley after Worcester, 1651; joined Benedictines; after Restoration received quarters in Somerset House; chaplain to Queen Catherine, 1669; received Charles II into Roman church on his deathbed; his account of Charles II's death reprinted in Foley's Jesuit records. [xxviii. 143]

HUDDLESTON *alias* DORMER, JOHN (1636–1700). [See DORMER.]

HUDDLESTON, SIR JOHN WALTER (1815–1890), last baron of the exchequer; educated in Ireland; barrister, Gray's Inn, 1839 (treasurer, 1859 and 1868); defended Cuffy the chartist, 1848; with Cockburn in Rugeley poisoning case; Q.C., 1857; M.P., Canterbury, 1865–8, Norwich, 1874–5; judge-advocate of the Fleet, 1865–75; judge of common pleas, 1875–80; last baron of the exchequer, 1875; judge of queen's bench, 1880–90. [xxviii. 144]

HUDDLESTON or **HUDLESTON**, RICHARD (1583–1655), Benedictine; uncle of John Huddleston [q. v.]; converted many Yorkshire and Lancashire families; his 'Short and Plain Way to the Faith and Church' published by his nephew, 1688 (reprinted, 1844 and 1850). [xxviii. 145]

HUDSON, GEORGE (1800–1871), 'railway king'; son of a Yorkshire farmer; made fortune as a draper at York; founded a banking company, and became mayor of York, 1837 and 1846; manager of York and North Midland Railway Company, opened 1839, of the Newcastle and Darlington, 1842, and of the newly formed Midland Railway; M.P., Sunderland, 1845–59; chairman of Sunderland Dock Company; owing to questionable business and over-speculation resigned chairmanship of Midland, Eastern Counties, Newcastle and Berwick, and York and North Midland companies, and retired to continent, 1854; annuity bought for him, 1868. [xxviii. 145]

HUDSON, HENRY (*d.* 1611), navigator; made voyage in the Hopeful for Muscovy Company to realise Thorne's scheme of passage across North Pole to 'islands of spicery,' 1607; searched for north-east passage by the Waigatz or Kara Strait, 1608; in a voyage for the Dutch East India Company reached Novaya Zemlya, and, by examining the coast from Nova Scotia to Sandy Hook, discredited the notion of a strait across North America in low latitude; afterwards ascended the Hudson River to Albany, 1609; in final expedition to attempt north-west passage (1610), reached Hudson's Strait, and spent some time in the bay beyond; ice-bound in south of James's Bay; after struggle with mutineers was sent adrift in a small boat with his son and others, and lost, 1611. Though he explored further than his predecessors, Hudson actually discovered neither the bay, nor straits, nor river called after him. [xxviii. 147]

HUDSON, HENRY (*fl.* 1784–1800), mezzotint-engraver. [xxviii. 149]

HUDSON, SIR JAMES (1810–1885), diplomatist; as private secretary to William IV sent to summon Peel from Rome, 1834; envoy to Rio Janeiro, 1850, and at Turin, 1851–63; showed great sympathy with the Italian cause; G.C.B., 1863; died at Strasburg. [xxviii. 149]

HUDSON, JEFFERY (1619–1682), dwarf; eighteen inches high till thirty; served up in a pie at dinner to

Charles I; afterwards reached three feet six or nine inches; entered service of Queen Henrietta Maria; his capture by Flemish pirates, 1630, celebrated in D'Avenant's 'Jeffreidos'; captain of horse in civil wars; went to Paris, 1649; captured by pirates while off the coast of France and carried to Barbary as a slave; managed to escape and return to England; imprisoned for supposed complicity in 'Popish plot,' 1679; released.
[xxviii. 149]

HUDSON, JOHN (1662-1719), classical scholar; M.A. Queen's College, Oxford, 1684; fellow and tutor of University College, 1686; Bodley's librarian, 1701; principal of St. Mary Hall, 1712; patron of Thomas Hearne (1678-1735) [q. v.]; edited Thucydides (with Latin version of Æmilius Portus), 1696, Dionysius Halicarnassus, 1704, 'Geographiæ veteris Scriptores Græci minores,' 1698-1712, and other classical works. [xxviii. 150]

HUDSON, SIR JOHN (1833-1893), lieutenant-general; lieutenant, 64th regiment, 1855; served in Persia, 1856-7, and Indian mutiny, 1857-8; captain, 43rd light infantry, 1858; in Abyssinia, 1867-8; in Afghan war, 1878-80; lieutenant-colonel, 1879; C.B., 1881; commanded Indian contingent in Soudan, 1885; K.C.B., 1885; lieutenant-general, 1892; commander-in-chief in Bombay, 1893.
[Suppl. iii. 5]

HUDSON, MARY (d. 1801), organist and composer; daughter of Robert Hudson (1731-1815) [q. v.]
[xxviii. 152]

HUDSON, MICHAEL (1605-1648), royalist divine; M.A. Queen's College, Oxford, 1628; fellow, c. 1630; tutor to Prince Charles, who, when king, gave him various livings; his chaplain at Oxford; scout-master to northern army, 1643-4; attended Charles I to Newark, 1646; escaped from prison, but was again captured, 1647, and sent to the Tower; again escaped, 1648, and promoted royalist rising in eastern counties; wrote treatise in defence of divine right (printed, 1647), and 'Account of King Charles I' (printed, 1731); killed while defending Woodcroft, Northamptonshire. [xxviii. 152]

HUDSON, ROBERT (fl. 1600), poet; Chapel Royal musician of James VI; friend of Alexander Montgomerie; four of his sonnets extant. [xxviii. 153]

HUDSON, ROBERT (1731-1815), vicar-choral (1756) and master of the children (1773) at St. Paul's Cathedral; Mus.Bac. Cambridge, 1784; published 'The Myrtle' (songs), 1762, and church music. [xxviii. 153]

HUDSON, THOMAS (fl. 1610), poet; probably brother of Robert Hudson (fl. 1600) [q. v.]; master of James VI's Chapel Royal, 1586; author of a version of Du Bartas's 'Historie of Judith,' 1584; contributor to 'England's Parnassus,' 1600. [xxviii. 153]

HUDSON, THOMAS (1701-1779), portrait-painter; pupil and son-in-law of Jonathan Richardson the elder [q. v.]; for two years Reynolds's master; painted Handel and George II. [xxviii. 154]

HUDSON, WILLIAM (d. 1635), lawyer; barrister, Gray's Inn, 1605; bencher, 1623, Lent reader, 1624; opened case against Prynne, 1633; his 'Treatise of the Court of Star Chamber' printed, 1792. [xxviii. 154]

HUDSON, WILLIAM (1730?-1793), botanist; sub-librarian, British Museum, 1757-8; F.R.S., 1761; 'præfectus horti,' Chelsea, 1765-71; original member of Linnean Society, 1791; published 'Flora Anglica,' 1762 (enlarged, 1778); genus Hudsonia named after him.
[xxviii. 155]

HUEFFER, FRANCIS (FRANZ HÜFFER) (1845-1889), musical critic; born at Münster; Ph.D. Göttingen, 1869; came to London, 1869; naturalised, 1882; assistant-editor of the 'Academy,' c. 1871; edited 'New Quarterly Magazine' and 'Musical World,' 1886; musical critic of 'The Times,' 1879; published 'Richard Wagner and the Music of the Future,' 1874, 'The Troubadours,' 1878, and other works; translated 'Correspondence of Wagner and Liszt,' 1888. [xxviii. 155]

HUES, ROBERT (1553?-1632), geographer; B.A. Magdalen Hall, Oxford, 1578; sailed round the world with Thomas Cavendish [q. v.]; friend of Chapman; published 'Tractatus de Globis et eorum Usu,' 1594.
[xxviii. 156]

HUET or HUETT, THOMAS (d. 1591), Welsh biblical scholar; B.A. Corpus Christi College, Cambridge, 1562;

master of Holy Trinity College, Pontefract; precentor of St. David's, 1562-88; translated Revelation in Welsh version of New Testament, 1567. [xxviii. 156]

HUGESSEN, EDWARD HUGESSEN KNATCH-BULL- (1829-1893), first BARON BRABOURNE. [See KNATCHBULL-HUGESSEN.]

HUGFORD, FERDINANDO ENRICO (1696-1771), monk of Vallombrosa and promoter of the art of scagliola.
[xxviii. 157]

HUGFORD, IGNAZIO ENRICO (1703-1778), painter and art critic at Florence; born of English parents at Florence; brother of Ferdinando Enrico Hugford [q. v.]; compiler of 'Raccolta di cento Pensieri diversi di Anton Domenico Gabbiani,' 1762. [xxviii. 157]

HUGGARDE or HOGGARDE, MILES (fl. 1557), poet and writer against the Reformation; published 'The Abuse of the Blessed Sacrament' (1548), 'The Displaying of the Protestants' (1556), and other controversial works in prose and verse. [xxviii. 157]

HUGGINS, JOHN (fl. 1729). [See BAMBRIDGE, THOMAS.]

HUGGINS, SAMUEL (1811-1885), architectural writer; president of Liverpool Architectural Society, 1856-8; Society for the Protection of Ancient Buildings largely due to his papers against 'restorations' of cathedrals. [xxviii. 158]

HUGGINS, WILLIAM (1696-1761), annotator of Croker's translation of Ariosto's 'Orlando Furioso,' 1757; M.A. Magdalen College, Oxford, 1719; fellow, 1722; wardrobe-keeper at Hampton Court, 1721. [xxviii. 158]

HUGGINS, WILLIAM (1820-1884), animal-painter; brother of Samuel Huggins [q. v.]; exhibited at Royal Academy from 1846. [xxviii. 159]

HUGGINS, WILLIAM JOHN (1781-1845), marine-painter to George IV and William IV. [xxviii. 159]

HUGH OF GRANTMESNIL or GRENTEMAISNIL (d. 1094), baron and sheriff of Leicestershire; restored abbey of St. Evroul, and became abbot, 1059; expelled by Duke William, 1063; went to Italy; recalled to Normandy; present at Hastings, 1066; left in command of Hampshire, 1067; returned to Normandy, 1068; joined barons against William II, 1088; carried on war against Robert of Bellême [q. v.], 1091; died a monk in England.
[xxviii. 159]

HUGH OF MONTGOMERY, second EARL OF SHREWS-BURY AND ARUNDEL (d. 1098), second son of Roger of Montgomery [q. v.]; helped to hold Rochester Castle against William II, 1088; succeeded to his father's earl-doms, 1094; warred with the Welsh; slain in Anglesey by Norse allies of Welsh. [xxviii. 160]

HUGH OF AVRANCHES, EARL OF CHESTER (d. 1101); perhaps nephew of William I; as Viscount of Avranches contributed sixty ships to invasion of England; received earldom of Chester with palatine powers, 1071, and lands in twenty shires; faithful to William II in England, but supported his brother Henry in Normandy, and became one of his chief advisers when king; endowed monastery of St. Werburgh's, Chester; carried on savage wars with the Welsh, gaining name of Lupus (the Wolf); conquered Anglesey and North Wales. [xxviii. 161]

HUGH ALBUS or CANDIDUS (fl. 1107?-1155?), chronicler; monk and sometime sub-prior of Peterborough; his (Latin) 'History of Peterborough Abbey' to 1155, printed by Joseph Sparke [q. v.], 1723; author-ship of Peterborough English 'Chronicle' probably wrongly ascribed to him. [xxviii. 163]

HUGH (d. 1164), abbot of Reading and archbishop of Rouen; born in Laon; abbot of Reading, 1125; arch-bishop of Rouen, 1130; founded abbey of St. Martin of Aumale; supported Innocent II against the anti-pope Anacletus; attended council of Pisa, 1134, and Henry I on his deathbed; supporter of Stephen; reconciled Earl of Gloucester and Count of Boulogne; his works in Migne's 'Patrologiæ Cursus.' [xxviii. 163]

HUGH OF CYVEILIOG, palatine EARL OF CHESTER (d. 1181); succeeded his father Ranulf II in Chester, Avranches, and Bayeux, 1153; present at council of Clarendon, 1164; raised Bretons against Henry II, but was forced to surrender at Dol, 1173 ; imprisoned in England and Normandy, and not restored till 1177 ; went to Ireland with William Fitzaldhelm [q. v.] ; succeeded by son and four co-heiresses. [xxviii. 164]

HUGH OF AVALON, SAINT (1135 ?–1200), bishop of Lincoln ; entered Grande Chartreuse, *c.* 1160, afterwards becoming bursar ; invited to England by Henry II, *c.* 1175, to become head of the Carthusian house of Witham, Somerset ; adviser of Henry II ; liberal to the poor and the lepers ; bishop of Lincoln, 1186–1200 ; excommunicated chief forester in his diocese, and successfully resisted election of royal nominee to a Lincoln prebend ; regarded alleged miracles with dislike ; went on embassy to France, 1189 ; joined opposition to Longchamp, and refused to suspend Geoffrey of York ; excommunicated John, 1194 ; a leader in first refusal of a money grant, 1198 ; pacified Richard I in interview at Roche d'Andeli ; much courted by John ; canonised, 1220, and twice translated. He rebuilt the greater part of his cathedral, where his shrine was much frequented. [xxviii. 165]

HUGH OF WELLS (*d.* 1235), bishop of Lincoln ; deputy to Chancellor Walter de Grey ; archdeacon of Wells, 1204 ; bishop of Lincoln, 1209–35 ; having joined Langton against King John, lived abroad, 1209–13 ; received favours from King John and supported him against the barons ; after John's death acted with the French party and had to pay large sums to recover his see, 1217 ; justice itinerant, 1219. As bishop he established vicarages in parishes where the tithes had been appropriated by monastic bodies, and with the help of Grosseteste made a great visitation ; built nave of Lincoln Cathedral and completed hall of the palace, besides establishing future palace at Buckden ; co-operated with his brother, Jocelyn (*d.* 1242) [q. v.], in reorganisation of Wells Cathedral and foundation of hospital of St. John Baptist. [xxviii. 168]

HUGH OF LINCOLN, SAINT (1246 ?–1255), a child supposed to have been crucified by a Jew named Copin at Lincoln after having been tortured or starved. His body was buried near that of Grosseteste in the cathedral. The story, a frequent theme for poets, is referred to by Chaucer and Marlowe. [xxviii. 169]

HUGH OF BALSHAM (*d.* 1286). [See BALSHAM, HUGH DE.]

HUGH OF EVESHAM (*d.* 1287). [See EVESHAM.]

HUGH OF HERTELPOLL or HARTLEPOOL (*d.* 1302 ?), Franciscan ; one of the two 'proctors' for Balliol College, Oxford, 1282 ; one of Edward I's proctors to negotiate with France, 1302. [xxvi. 275]

HUGH OF NEWCASTLE (*fl.* 1320). [See NEWCASTLE.]

HUGH, WILLIAM (*d.* 1549), author of 'The Troubled Mans Medicine' (two parts, 1546, another edition, 1567 ; reprinted, 1831) ; M.A. Corpus Christi College, Oxford, 1543. [xxviii. 171]

HUGHES, DAVID (1813–1872), Welsh writer ; graduated at Glasgow ; independent minister at St. Asaph, Bangor, and Tredegar ; published 'Geiriadur Ysgrythyrol a Duwinyddol' ('Scriptural and Theological Dictionary'), 1852 ; edited English-Welsh dictionary of Caerfallwch [see EDWARDS, THOMAS.] [xxviii. 171]

HUGHES, DAVID EDWARD (1830–1900), electrician and inventor ; born in London ; went to Virginia, 1837 ; educated at St. Joseph's College, Bardstown, Kentucky, and became professor of music, 1849 ; patented improved type-printing telegraph, 1855 ; invented microphone almost simultaneously with Lüdtge, 1878 ; F.R.S., 1880 ; received society's gold medal, 1885 ; president of Society of Telegraph Engineers, 1886 ; manager (1889) and vice-president (1891) of Royal Institution ; Albert medallist, Society of Arts, 1898. [Suppl. iii. 5]

HUGHES, SIR EDWARD (1720 ?–1794), admiral ; at reduction of Porto Bello, 1739, and attempt on Cartagena, 1741 ; attained post-rank, 1748 ; commanded the Somerset at Louisbourg, 1758, and Quebec, 1759 ; commander in East Indies, 1773–7 ; rear-admiral and K.B., 1778 ; vice-admiral, 1780 ; during second command in East Indies (1778–83) co-operated in capture of Negapatam, 1781, and Trincomalee, 1782, from Dutch, and fought five indecisive battles with French under M. de Suffren (1782–3) ; admiral of the blue, 1793. [xxviii. 172]

HUGHES, EDWARD HUGHES BALL (*d.* 1863) ; step-son of Sir Edward Hughes [q. v.] ; social celebrity known as the 'Golden Ball.' [xxviii. 174]

HUGHES, GEORGE (1603–1667), puritan divine ; M.A. Pembroke College, Oxford, 1625 ; fellow, 1625 ; lecturer of All Hallows, Bread Street, London, 1631 ; suspended for nonconformity, 1663 ; chaplain to Lord Brooke and rector of Tavistock ; vicar of St. Andrew's, Plymouth, 1643–62 ; imprisoned in St. Nicholas island, 1665 ; published theological works. [xxviii. 175]

HUGHES, GRIFFITH (*fl.* 1750), author of 'Natural History of Barbados,' 1750 ; F.R.S., 1750 ; rector of St. Lucy's, Barbados. [xxviii. 175]

HUGHES, HENRY GEORGE (1810–1872), Irish judge ; of Trinity College, Dublin ; Irish barrister, 1834 ; published 'Chancery Practice,' 1837 ; Q.C., 1844 ; solicitor-general for Ireland under Russell, 1850–2, and Palmerston, 1858–9 ; baron of Irish exchequer, 1859–72. [xxviii. 176]

HUGHES, HUGH (Y BARDD COCH) (1693–1776), Welsh poet, whose works are in 'Diddanwch Teuluaidd neu waith Beirdd Môn' (1763) ; published also translations from English. [xxviii. 176]

HUGHES, HUGH (1790 ?–1863), Welsh artist and author ; expelled by Welsh Calvinistic methodists for support of catholic emancipation ; joined Plymouth Brethren ; drew and engraved 'Beauties of Cambria' (1823), and published 'Hynaphion Cymreig,' 1823, and other works. [xxviii. 176]

HUGHES, HUGH (TEGAI) (1805–1864), Welsh poet ; independent minister in Carnarvonshire, at Jackson Street, Manchester, and at (1859) Aberdare ; competed at Eisteddfodau ; published works on Welsh grammar and composition, poems, and theological works. [xxviii. 177]

HUGHES, JABEZ (1685 ?–1731), translator of Suetonius' 'Lives of the XII. Cæsars,' 1717, parts of Lucan and Claudian, and novels by Cervantes. [xxviii. 178]

HUGHES, JAMES (IAGO TRICHRUG) (1779–1844) Welsh Calvinistic methodist ; author of 'New Testament Expositor,' 1829–35. [xxviii. 178]

HUGHES, JOHN (1677–1720), poet ; brother of Jabez Hughes [q. v.] ; employed in ordnance office ; secretary to commissions of the peace in court of chancery, 1717 ; wrote two volumes of Kennett's 'History of England,' 1706 ; edited Spenser, 1715 (reissued, 1750) ; his 'Siege of Damascus' (1720) successfully produced at Drury Lane, and 'Calypso and Telemachus' at Queen's Theatre, Haymarket, 1712 ; contributed to 'Tatler,' 'Spectator,' and 'Guardian' ; with Sir Richard Blackmore [q. v.] wrote 'The Lay Monk,' 1713–14 ; friend of Thomas Britton [q. v.], at whose concerts he played the violin ; his 'Venus and Adonis' set by Handel ; 'Poems on Several Occasions' edited by his brother-in-law, William Duncombe [q. v.], 1735 ; translated works by Fontenelle and others. [xxviii. 178]

HUGHES, JOHN (1776–1843), Wesleyan preacher in Wales and Manchester ; author of 'Essay on Ancient and Present State of the Welsh Language' (1823) and other works. [xxviii. 180]

HUGHES, JOHN (1790–1857), author and artist ; of Westminster and Oriel College, Oxford ; M.A., 1815 ; published 'Itinerary of Provence and the Rhone,' 1822 ; edited 'The Boscobel Tracts' (1830 and 1857). [xxviii. 181]

HUGHES, JOHN (1787–1860), Welsh divine ; vicar of Aberystwith, 1827 ; archdeacon of Cardigan, 1859 ; translated part of Henry's 'Commentary' and Hall's 'Meditations' into Welsh. [xxviii. 181]

HUGHES, JOHN (1796–1860), Calvinistic methodist pastor at Liverpool, 1838–60 ; published 'History of Welsh Calvinistic Methodism' (1851, 1854, 1856, 3 vols.), and Welsh theological works. [xxviii. 182]

HUGHES, JOHN CEIRIOG (1832–1887), Welsh poet ; farmer, clerk at Manchester, and finally station-master on Cambrian railway ; won prizes at the London Eisteddfod, 1856, at Llangollen, 1858, and Merthyr, 1860 ; his 'Owain Wyn' (1856) the best Welsh pastoral ; published about six hundred songs, including the original song for which

Brinley Richards wrote the air, 'God Bless the Prince of Wales'; contributed to Welsh periodicals.   [xxviii. 182]

HUGHES, JOSHUA (1807-1889), bishop of St. Asaph; of St. David's College, Lampeter; intimate with Thirlwall; vicar of Llandovery, 1846-70; D.D. Lambeth; bishop of St. Asaph, 1870-89; promoted Welsh services and higher education.   [xxviii. 183]

HUGHES, LEWIS (*fl.* 1620), chaplain in the Bermudas; among early settlers, 1612; member of council, 1615; quarrelled with Governor Tucker; again member of council, 1622; settled in England, *c.* 1625; wrote against the church service, 1640-1.   [xxviii. 184]

HUGHES, MARGARET (*d.* 1719), actress and mistress of Prince Rupert; the first recorded Desdemona (1663); original Theodosia of Dryden's 'Evening's Love,' 1668; played in Duke of York's company, Dorset Garden, in plays by D'Urfey, Sedley, and others, 1676-7.   [xxviii. 185]

HUGHES, OBADIAH (1695-1751), presbyterian minister; D.D. King's College, Old Aberdeen, 1728; secretary to presbyterian board, 1738-50; Williams trustee; Salters' Hall lecturer, 1746.   [xxviii. 185]

HUGHES, SIR RICHARD, second baronet (1729?-1812), admiral; took part in reduction of Pondicherry, 1760-1; commander-in-chief at Halifax, Nova Scotia, 1778-80 and 1789-92; rear-admiral, 1780; commanded division in relief of Gibraltar, 1782; commander-in-chief in West Indies, 1784-6; admiral, 1794.   [xxviii. 186]

HUGHES, ROBERT (ROBIN DDU O FÔN) (1744?-1785), Welsh poet; his 'Cywydd Molawd Môn' and two Englynion printed in 'Diddanwch Teuluaidd,' 1817; other poems in 'Brython' and other publications.   [xxviii. 187]

HUGHES, ROBERT BALL (1806-1868), sculptor; exhibited busts of Wellington and the Duke of Sussex and other works at the Academy; lived in the United States from 1829; exhibited statue of Oliver Twist at exhibition of 1851.   [xxviii. 187]

HUGHES, THOMAS (*fl.* 1587), dramatist; fellow of Queens' College, Cambridge, 1576; B.A., 1576; of Gray's Inn; chief author of 'The Misfortunes of Arthur,' played before Elizabeth at Greenwich, 1588, by members of Gray's Inn.   [xxviii. 188]

HUGHES, THOMAS (1822-1896), author of 'Tom Brown's School Days'; educated at Rugby and Oriel College, Oxford; B.A., 1845; entered Lincoln's Inn, 1845; barrister, Inner Temple, 1848; Q.C., 1869; bencher, 1870; follower of Frederick Denison Maurice [q. v.]; assisted in work of Christian socialism; published anonymously, 1857, 'Tom Brown's School Days,' which was immediately successful; active in founding and carrying on Working Men's College, Great Ormond Street, being principal, 1872-83; liberal M.P., Lambeth, 1865, Frome, 1868-74; established (1879) in Tennessee a model community which proved unsuccessful; county court judge, 1882-96. His publications include 'The Scouring of the White Horse,' 1859, and 'Tom Brown at Oxford,' 1861, lives of Bishop Fraser (1887), Daniel Macmillan (1882), Livingstone (1889), and Alfred the Great (1869).   [Suppl. iii. 7]

HUGHES, THOMAS SMART (1786-1847), author; of Shrewsbury and St. John's College, Cambridge; M.A., 1811; Browne medallist, 1806 and 1807, members' prizeman, 1809 and 1810; Seatonian prizeman, 1817; B.D., 1818; described his travels in Sicily, Greece, and Albania, 1820; fellow successively of St. John's, Trinity Hall, and Emmanuel Colleges; prebendary of Peterborough, 1827; published continuation of Hume and Smollett's history from 1760 (3rd ed., 1846), and editions of English divines.   [xxviii. 188]

HUGHES, WILLIAM (*d.* 1600), bishop of St. Asaph; fellow of Christ's College, Cambridge, 1557; M.A., 1560; D.D., 1570; chaplain to Thomas, fourth duke of Norfolk; gave offence by sermon at Leicester on the descent into hell, 1567; bishop of St. Asaph, 1573-1600; guilty of pluralism and maladministration as bishop, but encouraged the use of Welsh and aided William Morgan (1540?-1604) [q. v.] in his Welsh bible.   [xxviii. 189]

HUGHES, WILLIAM (*fl.* 1665-1683), author of 'The Complete Vineyard,' 1665, and other horticultural works.   [xxviii. 190]

HUGHES, WILLIAM (*d.* 1798), vicar of St. Peter's, Worcester, and from 1741 minor canon of Worcester; published 'Remarks upon Church Music,' 1763.   [xxviii. 190]

HUGHES, WILLIAM (1793-1825), wood-engraver in style of Thurston.   [xxviii. 191]

HUGHES, WILLIAM (1803-1861), writer on law and angling; nephew of Sir Richard Hughes [q. v.]; conveyancer, of Gray's Inn; published 'Concise Precedents in Modern Conveyancing,' 'Practice of Sales of Real Property,' and books by 'Piscator.'   [xxviii. 191]

HUGHES, WILLIAM LITTLE (1822-1887), translator from English into French; *employé* in French ministry of the interior.   [xxviii. 191]

HUGO, THOMAS (1820-1876), historian and Bewick collector; B.A. Worcester College, Oxford, 1842; vicar of St. Botolph's, Bishopsgate, London, 1852-8; perpetual curate of All Saints, Bishopsgate, 1858-68; rector of West Hackney, 1868-76; high church preacher and hymnologist; active F.S.A.; published tragedies and other works, including 'The Bewick Collector,' 1866 (supplement, 1868), and 'Mediæval Nunneries of Somerset,' 1867.   [xxviii. 191]

HUICKE, ROBERT (*d.* 1581?), physician to Henry VIII, Edward VI, and Elizabeth; fellow of Merton College, Oxford, 1529; M.A., 1533; principal of St. Alban Hall, 1535; deprived for denunciation of schoolmen, 1535; M.D. Cambridge, 1538; five times censor of College of Physicians, and president, 1551, 1552, and 1564.   [xxviii. 192]

HUISH, ALEXANDER (1594? - 1668), biblical scholar; first graduate of Wadham College, Oxford, 1614; fellow, 1615-29; M.A., 1616; B.D., 1627; prebendary of Wells, 1627; deprived of benefices in Somerset, but restored, 1660; assisted Brian Walton [q. v.] in 'Polyglott Bible,' collating the Alexandrian MS.   [xxviii. 193]

HUISH, ROBERT (1777-1850), miscellaneous writer; his publications include a 'Treatise on Nature, Economy, and Practical Management of Bees,' 1815.   [Suppl. iii. 10]

HULBERT, CHARLES (1778-1857), author, cotton manufacturer, and publisher; drew up report on management of factories, 1808; published 'History of Salop,' 1837, and 'Cheshire Antiquities' (1838).   [xxviii. 193]

HULBERT, CHARLES AUGUSTUS (1804-1888), divine and parochial annalist; son of Charles Hulbert [q. v.]; of Shrewsbury and Sidney Sussex College, Cambridge; M.A., 1837; incumbent of Slaithwaite, Yorkshire, 1839-67; vicar of Almondbury, 1867-88.   [xxviii. 194]

HULET, CHARLES (1701-1736), actor; played at Lincoln's Inn Fields, 1722-32, and afterwards at Goodman's Fields; among his best parts, Macbeath, and Henry VIII ('Virtue Betrayed'); played Falstaff in 'Henry IV' and the 'Merry Wives.'   [xxviii. 194]

HULETT, JAMES (*d.* 1771), engraver.   [xxviii. 195]

HULKE, JOHN WHITAKER (1830-1895), surgeon; studied at Moravian College, Neuwied, and King's College school and hospital, London; attached to medical staff of general hospital in Crimea, 1855; F.R.C.S., 1857; surgeon at Middlesex Hospital, 1870, at Royal London Ophthalmic Hospital, Moorfields, 1868-90; president of Royal College of Surgeons, 1893-5; F.R.S., 1867; president of Geological Society, 1882-4, and Wollaston medallist, 1887.   [Suppl. iii. 10]

HULL, JOHN (1761-1843), botanist; M.D. Leyden, 1792; physician at Manchester; published 'British Flora,' 1799, and 'Elements of Botany,' 1800. [xxviii. 195]

HULL, ROBERT (*d.* 1425). [See HILL, ROBERT.]

HULL, THOMAS (1728-1808), actor, dramatist, and author; managed Bath Theatre for John Palmer; played at Covent Garden forty-eight years; manager for Colman, 1775-82; first appeared in Farquhar's 'Twin Rivals,' 1759, and last as the uncle in 'George Barnwell'; excelled in 'heavy' parts; initiated the Theatrical Fund; his tragedy of 'Henry the Second' (1774) first played, 1773, several times revived and reprinted; author of adaptations from Shakespeare and French dramatists, oratorio librettos, two novels, poems, and translations.   [xxviii. 195]

HULL, WILLIAM (1820–1880), artist ; educated by the Moravians ; travelled on the continent, 1841–4 ; member of Manchester Academy of Fine Arts and of the Letherbrow Club ; friend of Ruskin. Among his best black and white works were views of Oxford and Cambridge, and illustrations to Langton's 'Charles Dickens and Rochester.'   [xxviii. 196]

HULL, WILLIAM WINSTANLEY (1794–1873), distinguished writer and hymnologist ; son of John Hull (1761–1843) [q. v.] ; fellow of Brasenose College, Oxford, 1816–20 ; B.A., 1814 ; barrister, Lincoln's Inn, 1820 ; practised at chancery bar till 1846 ; friend of Whately and Dr. Arnold ; drew up petition for revision of liturgy, 1840 ; supported Dr. Hampden, 1836 ; opposed proceedings against William George Ward [q. v.], 1845 ; published 'Occasional Papers on Church Matters,' 1848, containing 'Inquiry after the original Books of Common Prayer,' hymns, and other works.   [xxviii. 197]

HULLAH, JOHN PYKE (1812–1884), musical composer and teacher ; organist of the Charterhouse, 1858–84 ; his 'Village Coquettes' (words by Dickens) produced at the St. James's, 1836 ; began singing-classes on the Wilhem model (tonic sol-fa) at Battersea, 1840 ; established at St. Martin's Hall, Long Acre, 1850–60 ; the system awarded medal at Paris Exhibition, 1867 ; became connected with Academy of Music, 1869 ; musical inspector of training schools, 1872 ; LL.D. Edinburgh, 1876 ; composed songs (including settings of Kingsley's lyrics), duets, and motets. His works include manuals on the Wilhem method, lectures on musical history, and 'Part Music,' 1842–5.   [xxviii. 198]

HULLMANDEL, CHARLES JOSEPH (1789–1850), lithographer ; issued (1818) 'Views of Italy,' drawn and lithographed by himself ; prepared his 'Art of Drawing on Stone,' 1824 ; defended his improvements against representative of Engelmann ; with Cattermole perfected lithotint ; supported by James Duffield Harding [q. v.] and Faraday.   [xxviii. 199]

HULLOCK, SIR JOHN (1767–1829), judge ; barrister, Gray's Inn, 1794 ; serjeant-at-law, 1816 ; took part in prosecution of Henry Hunt [q. v.] and Andrew Hardie, 1820 ; baron of the exchequer, 1823–9 ; knighted, 1823 ; published 'Law of Costs,' 1792 (enlarged, 1810).
          [xxviii. 200]

HULLS or **HULL**, JONATHAN (fl. 1737), author of ' Description and Draught of a new-invented Machine for carrying Vessels or Ships . . . against Wind and Tide or in a Calm,' 1737 (reprinted, 1855), detailing his invention of the principle of steam navigation (patented, 1736).
          [xxviii. 200]

HULME, FREDERICK WILLIAM (1816–1884), landscape-painter and art-teacher ; exhibited at British Institution, 1845–62, Royal Academy, 1852–84.
          [xxviii. 201]

HULME, NATHANIEL (1732–1807), physician ; M.D. Edinburgh, 1765 ; physician to the Charterhouse, 1774–1807 ; F.R.S., 1794 ; published treatise on scurvy (1768) and puerperal fever (1772) ; gold medallist, Paris Medical Society, 1787.   [xxviii. 201]

HULME, WILLIAM (1631–1691), founder of Hulme's charity. His original bequest of four exhibitions at Brasenose College, Oxford, was largely extended by increased value of property ; as resettled, 1881, it provided for foundation of schools at Manchester, Oldham, and Bury, and grant to Queen's College.   [xxviii. 202]

HULOET, RICHARD (fl. 1552), author of 'Abcedarium Anglico-Latinum,' 1552.   [xxviii. 202]

HULSBERG, HENRY (d. 1729), engraver of architectural works ; warden of Savoy Lutheran Church.
          [xxviii. 203]

HULSE, EDWARD (1631–1711), court physician to Prince of Orange ; M.A. Emmanuel College, Cambridge, 1660 ; ejected for nonconformity ; M.D. Leyden ; F.R.C.P., 1677, and treasurer, 1704–9.   [xxviii. 203]

HULSE, SIR EDWARD, first baronet (1682–1759), physician to George II ; son of Edward Hulse [q. v.] ; M.D. Emmanuel College, Cambridge, 1717 ; leading whig physician ; censor, 1720, and 1750, 1751, and 1753 ; 'consiliarius' of College of Physicians ; created baronet, 1739.
          [xxviii. 203]

HULSE, JOHN (1708–1790), founder of the Hulsean lectures at Cambridge ; B.A. St. John's College, Cam-

bridge, 1728 ; bequeathed to his university estates in Cheshire for advancement of religious learning ; Hulsean professor substituted for Christian advocate, 1860.
          [xxviii. 203]

HULSE, SIR SAMUEL, third baronet (1747–1837), field-marshal ; grandson of Sir Edward Hulse [q. v.] ; commanded first battalion of 1st foot guards in Flanders, 1793, and afterwards as major-general a brigade ; in Helder expedition, 1799 ; general, 1803 ; governor of Chelsea Hospital, 1820 ; treasurer, 1820, and vice-chamberlain, 1827, of the household to George IV ; privy councillor and G.C.H. ; field-marshal, 1830.   [xxviii. 204]

HULTON, WILLIAM ADAM (1802–1887), lawyer and antiquary ; barrister, Middle Temple, 1827 ; treasurer of county of Lancaster, 1831–49 ; county court judge, 1847 ; published 'Treatise on the Law of Convictions,' 1835 ; edited works for Chetham Society.   [xxviii. 204]

HUMBERSTON, FRANCIS MACKENZIE, or FRANCIS HUMBERSTON MACKENZIE, first BARON SEAFORTH AND MACKENZIE (1754–1815), lieutenant-general ; succeeded his brother, Thomas Frederick Mackenzie Humberston [q. v.], in estates and hereditary chieftainship, 1783 ; M.P., Ross-shire, 1784 ; raised 'Ross-shire buffs,' 1793–4 ; created peer, 1797 ; colonel of 2nd North British militia (now 3rd Seaforths), 1798 ; major-general, 1802 ; lieutenant-general, 1808 ; as governor of Barbados (1800–6) protected slaves ; F.R.S., 1794 ; patron of Lawrence and West.   [xxviii. 204]

HUMBERSTON, THOMAS FREDERICK MACKENZIE (1753 ?–1783), soldier ; assumed mother's maiden name (Humberston) on coming of age ; served in dragoon guards ; captain in then 78th (now 1st Seaforth highlanders), 1778 ; present at repulse of French attack on Jersey, 1779 ; commanded newly raised 100th in Cape and India ; captured several of Hyder Ali's forts, 1782 ; repulsed attack of Tippoo Sahib, 1782 ; commandant of 78th in 1782 ; captured, mortally wounded, by Mahratta fleets.
          [xxviii. 206]

HUMBERT, ALBERT JENKINS (1822–1877), architect ; rebuilt Whippingham Church and Sandringham House ; designed mausoleums at Frogmore. [xxviii. 207]

HUMBY, MRS. ANNE (fl. 1817–1849), actress ; née Ayre ; first appeared at Hull as a singer ; at Bath, 1818–1820, Dublin, 1821–4 ; from 1825 at Haymarket and Drury Lane ; engaged by Macready, 1837 ; at Lyceum, 1849 ; excelled in light parts.   [xxviii. 207]

HUME. [See also HOME.]

HUME, ABRAHAM (1616 ?–1707), ejected divine ; M.A. St. Andrews ; attended John Maitland (Lauderdale) on the continent, and (1643) in Westminster Assembly ; vicar of Long Benton ; banished from England for royalism ; vicar of Whittingham, Northumberland, 1653–1662 ; subsequently presbyterian minister. [xxviii. 208]

HUME, SIR ABRAHAM, second and last baronet (1749–1838), virtuoso ; M.P., Petersfield, 1774–80 ; F.R.S., 1775 ; vice-president of Geological Society, 1809–13 ; a director of British Institution ; collected minerals, precious stones, and old masters ; published (anonymously) 'Notices of Life and Works of Titian,' 1829.   [xxviii. 208]

HUME, ABRAHAM (1814–1884), antiquarian and social writer ; B.A. Dublin, 1843 ; hon. LL.D. Glasgow, 1843 ; vicar of Vauxhall, Liverpool, 1847 ; explored Chili and Peru for South American Missionary Society, 1867 ; vice-chairman of Liverpool school board, 1870–6, and secretary of bishopric committee, 1873–80 ; F.R.S. ; F.S.A. ; published 'Learned Societies and Printing Clubs of the United Kingdom,' 1847 (enlarged, 1853), 'Condition of Liverpool,' 1858, and works on Irish dialect and Cheshire antiquities.   [xxviii. 209]

HUME or **HOME**, ALEXANDER (1560 ?–1609), Scottish poet ; studied law in Paris ; graduated at St. Andrews, 1597 ; minister at Logie, 1598–1609 ; his 'Description of the Day Estivall' and poem on defeat of the Armada in Sibbald's 'Chronicle,' former also reprinted by Leyden, 1803, and Campbell, 1819 ; 'Hymns and Sacred Songs' (1599) reprinted from Drummond of Hawthornden's copy, 1832.   [xxviii. 210]

HUME, ALEXANDER (d. 1682), covenanter ; hanged at Edinburgh after capture by Charles Home (eighth earl).   [xxviii. 211]

HUME, ALEXANDER, second EARL OF MARCHMONT (1675-1740). [See CAMPBELL.]

HUME, ALEXANDER (1809-1851), poet; brewer's agent in London; published 'Poems and Songs,' 1845. [xxviii. 211]

HUME, ALEXANDER (1811-1859), poet and composer; cabinet-maker in Edinburgh and Glasgow; chorusmaster in Theatre Royal, Edinburgh; edited 'Lyric Gems of Scotland' (1856), containing fifty of his own pieces; composed also glees, and music to Burns's 'Afton Water.' [xxviii. 211]

HUME, ALEXANDER HAMILTON (1797-1873), Australian explorer; born at Paramatta; when seventeen, with his brother, John Kennedy Hume, discovered Bong Bong and Berrima in south-west of New South Wales; shared exploration of Jervis Bay, 1819; discovered Yass Plains, 1821; undertook (with W. H. Howell) first overland journey from Sydney to Port Philip, 1824, discovering five rivers; granted twelve hundred acres; accompanied Captain Sturt on Macquarie expedition, 1828-9; died at Fort George, Yass. [xxviii. 212]

HUME, ANNA (*fl.* 1644), daughter of David Hume (1560?-1630?) [q. v.]; translated Petrarch's 'Triumphs of Love, Chastitie, Death,' 1644; superintended publication of her father's 'History of House and Race of Douglas and Angus.' [xxviii. 213]

HUME, DAVID (1560?-1630?), historian, controversialist, and Latin poet; studied at St. Andrews University; secretary to Archibald Douglas, eighth earl of Angus [q. v.], *c.* 1583; published part of Latin treatise on the union of Britain, 1605; upheld presbyterianism against Law, bishop of Orkney, 1608-11, and Cowper, bishop of Galloway, 1613; his 'History of House and Race of Douglas and Angus' printed with difficulty by his daughter, owing to opposition of eleventh Earl of Angus; 'History of House of Wedderburn,' first printed, 1839; Latin poems twice issued at Paris, 1632 and 1639. [xxviii. 213]

HUME or **HOME**, SIR DAVID, of Crossrig, LORD CROSSRIG (1643-1707), M.A. Edinburgh, 1662; studied law at Paris; advocate, 1687; judge, 1689; lord of justiciary, 1690; knighted, 1690; lost his papers in Edinburgh fire of 1700; his 'Diary of Parliament and Privy Council of Scotland, 1700-7,' printed, 1828, 'Domestic Details,' 1843. [xxviii. 214]

HUME, DAVID (1711-1776), philosopher and historian; studied law; lived in France, 1734-7; his 'Treatise of Human Nature' appeared anonymously, 1739 (ed. Mr. S. Bigge, 1888); the book neglected; his 'Essays Moral and Political' (1741-2) written at Ninewells, Berwickshire, commended by Bishop Butler and favourably received; unsuccessful candidate for chair of ethics at Edinburgh, 1745; lived with Marquis of Annandale at Weldhall, Hertfordshire, 1745-6; judge-advocate to General St. Clair in expedition against Port L'Orient, 1747; accompanied St. Clair on military embassy to Vienna and Turin, 1748, when his 'Philosophical Essays' (including that on miracles) appeared; issued 'Enquiry concerning Principles of Morals,' 1751; gained reputation by his 'Political Discourses,' 1752; published 'Four Dissertations' (including 'Natural History of Religion'), 1757; unsuccessful candidate for chair of logic at Glasgow, but keeper of the Advocates' Library, Edinburgh, 1752; published first volume of 'History of England during reigns of James I and Charles I,' 1754, succeeding better with the second (1649-88); issued two volumes on the Tudor period, 1759, and the last two (backwards from Henry VII), 1761; secretary to Edinburgh Philosophical Society, 1752; being censured by curators of Edinburgh library for buying La Fontaine's 'Contes' and other French works, resigned, 1757; attacked for sceptical views; accompanied Lord Hertford to Paris, 1763; secretary to the embassy, 1765, and for some months chargé d'affaires; intimate with Comtesse de Boufflers, Madame Geoffrin, D'Alembert, and Turgot, and well received at court; brought home Rousseau and procured him a pension, but afterwards quarrelled with him in consequence of Rousseau's suspicious nature; received a pension and invitation from the king to continue his history; under-secretary to Henry Seymour Conway [q. v.], 1767-8; returned to Edinburgh, 1769; made journey (1776) to London and Bath with John Home [q. v.], who recorded it. His autobiography (with letter of Adam Smith) and essays on 'Suicide and Immortality,' published, 1777; 'Dialogues on Natural Religion,' 1779. The best edition of his philosophical works is that of T. H. Green and T. H. Grose (1874-5); abbreviations of his history were edited by (Sir) William Smith and John Sherren Brewer. His thoroughgoing empiricism formed a landmark in the development of metaphysics. [xxviii. 215]

HUME, DAVID (1757-1838), judge; nephew of David Hume (1711-1776) [q. v.]; sheriff of Berwickshire, 1784, of Linlithgowshire, 1793; professor of Scots law at Edinburgh, 1786; clerk to court of session, 1811; baron of Scottish exchequer, 1822; published commentaries on Scottish criminal law, 1797, and reports from 1781 to 1822 (posthumous, 1839). [xxviii. 226]

HUME, SIR GEORGE, EARL OF DUNBAR (*d.* 1611). [See HOME.]

HUME, LADY GRIZEL (1665-1746) [See BAILLIE, LADY GRIZEL.]

HUME, HUGH, third EARL OF MARCHMONT (1708-1794), politician; studied in Dutch universities; as Lord Polwarth represented Berwick, 1734-40; opponent of Walpole; president of court of police in Scotland, 1747; Scottish representative peer, 1750-84; lord keeper of great seal of Scotland, 1764; intimate with Bolingbroke and Chesterfield; executor of Pope and the Duchess of Marlborough; offered information to Johnson for life of Pope; skilful horticulturist and horseman. [xxviii. 226]

HUME, JAMES (*fl.* 1639), mathematician; son of David Hume (1560?-1630?) [q. v.]; lived in France; published nine mathematical works in Latin, and others in French, including 'Algèbre de Viète d'une Méthode nouuelle,' 1636. [xxviii. 228]

HUME, JAMES DEACON (1774-1842), free trader; educated at Westminster; consolidated customs laws into ten acts of 1825; thirty-eight years in the customs; joint-secretary to board of trade, 1828-40; joint-founder of Political Economy Club, 1821; deputy-chairman of Atlas Assurance Company; attacked protection in evidence before parliament, 1840. [xxviii. 228]

HUME, JOHN ROBERT (1781?-1857), physician to Wellington in Peninsula and afterwards in England; M.D. St. Andrews, 1816; L.R.C.P., 1819; commissioner in lunacy, 1836; inspector-general of hospitals. [xxviii. 229]

HUME, JOSEPH (1777-1855), radical politician; entered medical service of East India Company, 1797; army surgeon, interpreter, and paymaster in Mahratta war; returned to England, 1807; travelled; elected tory member for Weymouth, 1812; radical M.P., Aberdeen, 1818-30, Middlesex, 1830-7, Kilkenny, 1837-41, and Montrose, 1842-55; obtained select committees on revenue collection, 1820, and the combination laws, 1824; moved repeal of corn-laws, 1834; carried repeal of combination laws and those prohibiting emigration and export of machinery; devoted himself to question of public expenditure, adding 'retrenchment' to his party's watchwords; privy councillor; F.R.S.; member of board of agriculture, and twice lord rector of Aberdeen University. [xxviii. 230]

HUME, PATRICK (*fl.* 1695), London schoolmaster, and (1695) first commentator on Milton. [xxviii. 231]

HUME or **HOME**, SIR PATRICK, second baronet (of Polwarth), first EARL OF MARCHMONT and BARON POLWARTH (1641-1724), studied law in Paris; elected to Scottish parliament for Berwick, 1665; opposed Lauderdale's policy; imprisoned for five years and incapacitated from office for petition against council's action against covenanters, 1675-9; in England joined Monmouth's party; escaped by Ireland and France to Holland; joined Argyle's expedition, 1684; being outlawed (1685) in connection with Rye House plot escaped by Ireland, France, and Geneva, to Utrecht; surgeon at Utrecht under name of Wallace; adviser of William of Orange, accompanying him to England, 1688; privy councillor and Scottish peer (Baron Polwarth), 1689; sheriff of Berwickshire, 1692-1710; extraordinary lord of session, 1693; lord chancellor of Scotland, 1696-1702; created Earl Marchmont, 1697; high commissioner to parliament, 1698, to general assembly, 1702; prevented an act for the abjuration of the Pretender, passed act for security of presbyterianism, and

proposed settlement of succession on house of Hanover; supported union with England; reappointed by George I to sheriffdom and made lord of court of police.
[xxviii. 231]

HUME, THOMAS (1769?–1850), physician; under Wellesley in Peninsula; B.A. Trinity College, Dublin, 1792; M.D., 1803; four times censor of College of Physicians. [xxviii. 235]

HUME, TOBIAS (d. 1645), soldier of fortune and musician; poor brother of the Charterhouse from 1629; published 'First Part of Ayres, French, Pollish, and others,' 1605, and 'Captain Hume's Musicall Humors,' 1607. [xxviii. 235]

HUMFREY, JOHN (1621–1719), ejected minister; M.A. Pembroke College, Oxford, 1647; received presbyterian ordination, 1649; vicar of Frome Selwood till 1662; re-ordained episcopally; defended his action, but afterwards renounced it; formed congregational church in Duke's Place, London, afterwards in Petticoat Lane; continued ministry to ninety-ninth year; advocated union of all protestants; published 'Account of the French Prophets,' 1708, treatises on justification, and other works.
[xxviii. 235]

HUMFREY, PELHAM (1647–1674), lutenist and composer; with Blow and Turner composed the 'Club Anthem,' 1664; studied music in France and Italy, 1665–6; introduced Lully's methods into England; gentleman of Chapel Royal, 1667; master of the children, 1672–4; composer in ordinary for violins, 1673; composed anthems, services, and songs, contained in the Tudway collection and Boyce's 'Cathedral Music,' and other works.
[xxviii. 237]

HUMPHREY. [See also HUMFREY and HUMPHRY.]

HUMPHREY, DUKE OF GLOUCESTER (1391–1447), 'the Good Duke Humphrey'; youngest son of Henry IV; perhaps educated at Balliol College, Oxford; K.G., 1400; great chamberlain of England, 1413; created Duke of Gloucester, 1414; commanded one of the English divisions in Agincourt expedition; wounded at Agincourt, 1415; as warden of Cinque ports received Emperor Sigismund, 1416; in Henry V's second expedition took Lisieux, 1417, and Cherbourg, 1418; governor of Rouen, 1419; at siege of Melun, 1420; regent of England, 1420–1; on death of Henry V claimed regency, but was only allowed to act as Bedford's deputy, with title of protector, 1422; married Jacqueline of Hainault, 1422, and reconquered Hainault, 1424, but allowed Philip of Burgundy to recapture her and her territory, 1425; quarrelled with his uncle, Henry Beaufort (d. 1447) [q. v.], but was reconciled to him by Bedford; again protector, 1427–9; attempted to give further help to Jacqueline, 1427; his marriage with her having been annulled (1428), married his mistress, Eleanor Cobham [q. v.]; refused to recognise Beaufort as papal legate, 1428; lieutenant of the kingdom, 1430–2; actively prosecuted quarrel with Beaufort; opposed Beaufort's French policy; went to France as captain of Calais and lieutenant of the new army; appointed count of Flanders, but effected nothing, 1436; returned to denounce Beaufort as the friend of France, 1436; lost influence over the king and was powerless to prevent proceedings (1441) against his wife for witchcraft; vainly advocated Armagnac marriage for Henry VI, and (1445) violation of truce with France; suspected by the king of designs on his life, and arrested; died in custody, popular suspicions of foul play being groundless; owed his name of 'the Good' only to his patronage of men of letters (including Titus Livius of Forli, Leonard Aretino, Lydgate, and Capgrave) and to his patriotic sentiment. A strong churchman, he persecuted the lollards and favoured monasteries, especially St. Albans. He read Latin and Italian literature, collected books from his youth, and gave the first books for a library at Oxford; his collection was dispersed in the reign of Edward VI. [xxviii. 241]

HUMPHREY or HUMFREY, LAURENCE (1527?–1590), president of Magdalen College, Oxford; of Christ's College, Cambridge, and Magdalen College, Oxford; perpetual fellow of Magdalen College; M.A., 1552; in Switzerland during reign of Mary; regius professor of divinity at Oxford, 1560; president of Magdalen College, 1561–90; D.D., 1562; cited for refusing to wear vestments, 1564; was refused institution to a living by his friend Bishop Jewel, 1565; after several protests, conformed; dean of Gloucester, 1571, of Winchester, 1580–90; vice-chancellor

of Oxford, 1571–6; deputy to diet of Smalcald, 1578; collaborated with Robert Crowley (1556) in answering Huggarde's Displaying of the Protestants'; published Latin 'Life of Jewel,' 1573, translations from Origen, Cyril, and Philo, and other works. [xxviii. 245]

HUMPHREY, WILLIAM (1740?–1810?), engraver and printseller. [xxviii. 248]

HUMPHREYS, DAVID (1689–1740), divine; educated at Merchant Taylors' School, Christ's Hospital, and Trinity College, Cambridge; fellow; M.A., 1715; D.D., 1728; supported Bentley at Trinity; secretary to the S.P.G., 1716–40; vicar of Ware, 1730, and Thundridge, 1732; published 'Historical Account' (of the S.P.G.), 1730, and translations. [xxviii. 249]

HUMPHREYS, HENRY NOEL (1810–1879), numismatist, naturalist, and artist; illustrated works on natural history; published miscellaneous works, including treatises on coins and missal painting. [xxviii. 249]

HUMPHREYS, HUMPHREY (1648–1712), bishop successively of Bangor and Hereford; fellow of Jesus College, Oxford; M.A., 1673; D.D., 1682; dean of Bangor, 1680; bishop of Bangor, 1689–1701, of Hereford, 1701–12; amplified Wood's works on Oxford; compiled for Wood catalogue of deans of Bangor and St. Asaph.
[xxviii. 249]

HUMPHREYS, JAMES (d. 1830), author of 'Observations on the Actual State of the English Laws of Real Property, with outlines of a Code,' 1826; barrister, Lincoln's Inn, 1800; friend of Charles Butler (1750–1832) [q. v.] [xxviii. 250]

HUMPHREYS, SAMUEL (1698?–1738), author; published miscellaneous works, including translations from Italian and French, and 'Peruvian Tales,' 1734.
[xxviii. 250]

HUMPHRIES, JOHN (d. 1730?), violinist and composer. [xxviii. 251]

HUMPHRY, SIR GEORGE MURRAY (1820–1896), surgeon; studied at St. Bartholomew's Hospital, London; M.R.C.S., 1841; L.S.A., 1842; surgeon at Addenbrooke's College, Cambridge; deputy-professor of anatomy, 1847–1866; M.B. Downing College, Cambridge, 1852; M.D., 1859; professor of human anatomy, Cambridge, 1866–83; professor of surgery, 1883; professorial fellow, King's College, Cambridge, 1884; F.R.C.S., 1844; F.R.S., 1859; knighted, 1891; published anatomical works; instrumental in procuring for the medical school at Cambridge its high reputation. [Suppl. iii. 11]

HUMPHRY, OZIAS (1742–1810), portrait-painter; friend of Romney and Blake; patronised by Duke of Dorset and others; studied four years in Italy; painted miniatures in India, 1785–8; R.A., 1791; abandoned miniature-painting for crayon-drawing; lost his eyesight, 1797. [xxviii. 251]

HUMPHRY, WILLIAM GILSON (1815–1886), divine and author; captain of Shrewsbury School; fellow of Trinity College, Cambridge, 1839; senior classic and second chancellor's medallist, 1837; vicar of St. Martin-in-the-Fields, London, 1855–86; member of commissions on clerical subscription (1865) and ritual (1869); a New Testament reviser; published, besides Hulsean and Boyle lectures, commentaries on the Acts (1847) and the revised version (1882), 'Treatise on Book of Common Prayer,' 1853 (last ed. 1885), and other works. [xxviii. 252]

HUMPHRYS, WILLIAM (1794–1865), engraver; in America illustrated poets and engraved bank-notes; returned to England, 1822; engraved the queen's head on postage-stamps, and executed plates after old and contemporary masters; died at Genoa. [xxviii. 253]

HUMPSTON or HUMSTON, ROBERT (d. 1606), bishop of Down and Connor, 1602–6. [xxviii. 253]

HUNGERFORD, AGNES, LADY (d. 1524), second wife of Sir Edward Hungerford (d. 1522); executed for murder of first husband, John Cotell. [xxviii. 259]

HUNGERFORD, SIR ANTHONY (1564–1627), controversialist; M.A. St. John's College, Oxford, 1594; knighted, 1608; brought up by his mother, Bridget Shelley, as a Romanist; deputy-lieutenant of Wiltshire; his treatises in defence of Anglicanism published, 1639.
[xxviii. 253]

HUNGERFORD, ANTHONY (d. 1657), royalist; younger son of Sir Anthony Hungerford [q. v.]; represented Malmesbury in Short and Long parliaments; fined and imprisoned, 1644, for attending Charles I's parliament at Oxford. [xxviii. 254]

HUNGERFORD, ANTHONY (d. 1657), parliamentarian colonel in Ireland; perhaps half-brother of Anthony Hungerford (d. 1657) [q. v.] [xxviii. 254]

HUNGERFORD, SIR EDWARD (1596–1648), parliamentarian; eldest son of Sir Anthony Hungerford [q. v.]; K.B., 1625 ; sheriff of Wiltshire, 1632 ; M.P., Chippenham, 1620, and in Short and Long parliaments ; occupied and plundered Salisbury, 1643 ; took Wardour and Farleigh castles. [xxviii. 254]

HUNGERFORD, SIR EDWARD (1632–1711), founder of Hungerford Market; son of Anthony Hungerford (d. 1657) [q. v.] ; K.B., 1661 ; M.P., Chippenham, 1660-81, New Shoreham, 1685-90, Steyning, 1695-1702 ; removed from lieutenancy for opposing the court, 1681 ; Hungerford Market built to recruit his fortune, 1682, on site of house destroyed by fire (1669). Charing Cross station was built on site of market house, 1860. [xxviii. 255]

HUNGERFORD, JOHN (d. 1729), lawyer ; M.A. Cambridge *per literas regias*, 1683 ; of Lincoln's Inn ; M.P., Scarborough, 1692, 1707-29 ; expelled for receiving a bribe, 1695 ; counsel for East India Company ; defended Francia (1717), Matthews (1719), and Sayer (1722), charged with Jacobitism. [xxviii. 256]

HUNGERFORD, MRS. MARGARET WOLFE (1855 ?-1897), novelist; daughter of Canon Fitzjohn Stannus Hamilton; married Mr. Thomas H. Hungerford ; published 'Molly Bawn,' 1878, and more than thirty other novels. [Suppl. iii. 13]

HUNGERFORD, ROBERT, second BARON HUNGERFORD (1409-1459), eldest surviving son of Sir Walter Hungerford, first baron Hungerford (d. 1449) [q. v.]; summoned to parliament as baron, 1450-5 ; acquired large property in Cornwall through mother and wife. [xxviii. 259]

HUNGERFORD, ROBERT, BARON MOLEYNS and third BARON HUNGERFORD (1431-1464), son of Robert Hungerford, second baron Hungerford [q. v.] ; summoned as Baron Moleyns in right of his wife, 1445 ; quarrelled with John Paston regarding ownership of manor of Gresham, Norfolk, 1448 ; while serving with Shrewsbury in Aquitaine was captured (1452) and kept prisoner seven years, till 1459 ; after ransom an active Lancastrian ; fled with Henry VI to the north after Towton (1461), and visited France to obtain help ; captured at Hexham and executed. [xxviii. 256]

HUNGERFORD, SIR THOMAS (d. 1398), speaker in last parliament of Edward III ; M.P., Wiltshire, and Somerset, 1357-90 ; purchased Farleigh, 1369 ; knighted before 1377 ; steward of John of Gaunt ; first person formally entitled speaker, 1377. [xxviii. 257]

HUNGERFORD, SIR THOMAS (d. 1469), eldest son of Robert Hungerford, third baron Hungerford [q. v.] ; executed as supporter of Warwick. [xxviii. 257]

HUNGERFORD, SIR WALTER, first BARON HUNGERFORD (d. 1449), warrior and statesman ; son of Sir Thomas Hungerford (d. 1398) [q. v.] ; M.P., Wiltshire, 1400, 1404, 1407, 1413, and 1414, Somerset, 1409 ; speaker, 1414 ; English envoy at council of Constance, 1414-15 ; at Agincourt, 1415, and siege of Rouen, 1418 ; admiral of fleet, 1418 ; K.G., 1421 ; executor of Henry V's will and member of Gloucester's council ; steward of household to Henry VI, 1424 ; first summoned as baron, 1426 ; treasurer, 1427-32 ; buried in Salisbury Cathedral in iron chapel erected by himself. [xxviii. 258]

HUNGERFORD, SIR WALTER (d. 1516), privy councillor of Henry VII and Henry VIII ; son of Robert Hungerford, third baron Hungerford [q. v.] ; M.P., Wiltshire, 1477 ; knighted ; slew Sir Robert Brackenbury at Bosworth, 1485. [xxviii. 257]

HUNGERFORD, WALTER, first BARON HUNGERFORD OF HEYTESBURY (1503-1540), grandson of Sir Walter Hungerford (d. 1516) [q. v.] ; squire of the body to Henry VIII ; sheriff of Wiltshire, 1533 ; created peer, 1536 ; beheaded with Thomas Cromwell, 1540. [xxviii. 259]

HUNGERFORD, SIR WALTER (1532-1596), 'the Knight of Farley' ; eldest son of Walter Hungerford, first baron Hungerford of Heytesbury [q. v.]; restored to confiscated estate of Farleigh, 1554, his father's attainder being reversed ; sheriff of Wiltshire, 1557. [xxviii. 260]

HUNNE, RICHARD (d. 1514), supposed martyr ; found hanged in the Lollards' Tower after prosecution for heresy ; verdict of wilful murder brought in against Bishop of London's chancellor, Dr. Horsey, in civil court. [xxviii. 261]

HUNNEMAN, CHRISTOPHER WILLIAM (d. 1793), portrait and miniature painter. [xxviii. 261]

HUNNIS, WILLIAM (d. 1597), musician and poet ; gentleman of Chapel Royal under Edward VI ; imprisoned for protestant conspiracy, 1555 ; restored by Elizabeth, granted arms, and made master of the children, 1566 ; published metrical psalms, 'A Hyve full of Hunnye,' 1578, and other works. [xxviii. 261]

HUNSDON, BARONS. [See CAREY, HENRY, first BARON, 1524?-1596 ; CAREY, GEORGE, second BARON, 1547-1603 ; CAREY, JOHN, third BARON, d. 1617.]

HUNT, ALFRED WILLIAM (1830-1896), landscape-painter ; son of Andrew Hunt [q. v.]; B.A. Corpus Christi College, Oxford, 1852 ; fellow, 1853-61; honorary fellow, 1882 ; member of Liverpool Academy, 1850 ; exhibited landscapes at Royal Academy, 1854-62, and from 1870 ; member of Old Water-colour Society, 1864 ; disciple of Turner. [Suppl. iii. 13]

HUNT, ANDREW (1790-1861), landscape-painter ; exhibited at Liverpool. [xxviii. 262]

HUNT, ARABELLA (d. 1705), vocalist and lutenist ; painted by Kneller and celebrated by Congreve. [xxviii. 263]

HUNT, FREDERICK KNIGHT (1814-1854), journalist and author ; established 'Medical Times,' 1839 ; sub-editor of 'Illustrated London News'; editor of 'Pictorial Times,' and (1851) the 'Daily News,' after having been on Dickens's staff ; published 'The Fourth Estate,' 1850. [xxviii. 263]

HUNT, GEORGE WARD (1825-1877), statesman ; of Eton and Christ Church, Oxford ; M.A., 1851 ; D.C.L., 1870 ; barrister, Inner Temple, 1851 ; bencher, 1873 ; M.P., North Northamptonshire, 1857-77 ; financial secretary to treasury, 1866-8 ; chancellor of the exchequer, 1868 (February-December) ; first lord of the admiralty, 1874-1877 ; died at Homburg. [xxviii. 263]

HUNT, HENRY (1773-1835), radical politician ; farmed property at Upavon, Wiltshire ; fined and imprisoned for challenging colonel of yeomanry, 1800, and for assaulting a gamekeeper, 1810 ; active in political life of Wiltshire ; contested Bristol, 1812, Westminster, 1818, Somerset, 1826 ; took part in Spa Fields meeting, 1816 ; published pamphlet against Burdett, 1819 ; presided at Manchester meeting, 1819, and was sentenced to two years' imprisonment in connection with it ; M.P., Preston, 1830-33 ; afterwards a blacking manufacturer ; published 'Memoirs,' 1820. [xxviii. 264]

HUNT, JAMES (1833-1869), ethnologist and writer on stammering ; son of Thomas Hunt (1802-1851) [q. v.]; hon. secretary of Ethnological Society, 1859-62 ; founder and first president of Anthropological Society, 1863-7 ; edited 'Anthropological Review' and (1865) Vogt's 'Lectures on Man' ; obtained recognition of anthropology as separate section at British Association ; defended slavery in paper on 'The Negro's Place in Nature' (Brit. Assoc.), 1863 ; published work on 'Stammering and Stuttering,' 1861. [xxviii. 266]

HUNT, JAMES HENRY LEIGH (1784-1859), essayist and poet ; named after James Henry Leigh, father of first Lord Leigh ; at Christ's Hospital ; his verses entitled 'Juvenilia' printed, 1801 ; his 'Critical Essays on Performers of the London Theatres' and 'Classic Tales' reprinted from his brother John's 'The News,' 1807 ; began to edit the 'Examiner,' 1808, and the 'Reflector,' 1810 ; prosecuted for article against army flogging, but defended by Brougham and acquitted, 1811 ; sentenced with his brother to fine and two years' imprisonment, 1813, for reflections on the Prince Regent ; visited in Surrey gaol by Byron, Moore, Bentham, and Lamb ; continued editing the 'Examiner' while in prison; entertained Shelley at Hampstead, and brought about his meeting with Keats,

1816 ; introduced Keats and Shelley to the public in 'Examiner,' 1816 ; Shelley's 'Cenci' dedicated to him, 1819 ; published 'The Story of Rimini,' 1816 (subsequently revised and corrected) ; published 'Foliage' (poems), 1818 ; savagely attacked by 'Quarterly' and 'Blackwood' ; issued 'Hero and Leander,' 1819 ; began 'The Indicator,' 1819 ; joined Byron at Pisa, 1822 ; carried on the 'Liberal' with Byron, 1822-3 ; at Florence, 1823-5, continuing to write ; published 'Lord Byron and some of his Contemporaries,' 1828, and 'The Companion' (weekly), 1828 ; carried on the 'Tatler' (daily), 1830-2 ; introduced by his 'Christianism' (privately printed) to Carlyle ; began 'Leigh Hunt's Journal,' 1834 ; published 'Captain Sword and Captain Pen,' 1835 ; his play 'A Legend of Florence' successfully produced at Covent Garden, 1840 ; issued critical notices of dramatists, 1840, 'Imagination and Fancy' and second collective edition of poems, 1844, 'Wit and Humour,' and 'Stories from Italian Poets,' 1846, 'Men, Women, and Books,' 1847 ; received pension, 200*l.*, 1847 ; published 'Jar of Honey from Mount Hybla,' 1848, 'Autobiography,' 1850 (enlarged, 1860), 'Table-Talk,' 1851, 'Old Court Suburb,' 1855, and edition of Beaumont and Fletcher, 1855 ; bust by Joseph Durham [q. v.] placed at Kensal Green (where he was buried), 1869. His 'Book of the Sonnet' (with S. Adams Lee) appeared posthumously, also (1862) his correspondence. His portrait was painted by Haydon. [xxviii. 267]

HUNT, JEREMIAH (1678-1744), independent minister ; studied at Edinburgh and Leyden ; preached at Amsterdam ; pastor at Pinners' Hall, Old Broad Street, London, 1707 ; non-subscriber at Salters' Hall, 1719 ; hon. D.D. Edinburgh, 1729 ; Williams trustee, 1730 ; friend of Nathaniel Lardner [q. v.] ; published theological works. [xxviii. 274]

HUNT, SIR JOHN (1550 ?-1615), politician ; M.P., Sudbury, 1571 ; knighted, 1611. [xxviii. 275]

HUNT, JOHN (1806-1842), organist of Hereford Cathedral, 1835-42 ; song-writer. [xxviii. 275]

HUNT, JOHN (1812-1848), Wesleyan missionary and translator of bible into Fiji. [xxviii. 276]

HUNT, JOHN HIGGS (1780-1859), translator ; fellow of Trinity College, Cambridge, and Browne medallist ; M.A., 1804 ; vicar of Weedon Beck, 1823-59 ; translated Tasso's 'Jerusalem Delivered,' 1818. [xxviii. 276]

HUNT, NICHOLAS (1596-1648), arithmetician and divine ; B.A. Exeter College, Oxford, 1616 ; proctor of the arches. [xxviii. 276]

HUNT, ROBERT (*d.* 1608 ?), chaplain to first settlers in Virginia and minister at James Town, 1607 ; LL.B. Trinity Hall, Cambridge, 1606. [xxviii. 277]

HUNT, ROBERT (1807-1887), scientific writer ; president of Royal Cornwall Polytechnic Society, 1859 ; published first English treatise on photography, 1841 ; keeper of mining records, 1845-78 ; professor of experimental physics at School of Mines ; issued 'Mineral Statistics,' 1855-84 ; F.R.S., 1854 ; member of coal commission, 1866 ; published handbooks of 1851 and 1862 exhibitions, and other works, including 'British Mining,' 1884, and three editions of Ure's 'Dictionary of Arts' ; contributed to 'Dictionary of National Biography.' [xxviii. 277]

HUNT, ROGER (*fl.* 1433), speaker of the House of Commons ; M.P., Bedfordshire, 1414 and 1420, and afterwards Huntingdonshire ; speaker, 1420 and 1433 ; baron of exchequer, 1438. [xxviii. 278]

HUNT, THOMAS (1611-1683), schoolmaster ; M.A. Pembroke College, Oxford, 1636 ; published works on orthography. [xxviii. 278]

HUNT, THOMAS (1627 ?-1688), lawyer ; M.A. and fellow Queens' College, Cambridge ; of Gray's Inn ; counsel for Lord Stafford, 1680 ; wrote in support of Exclusion Bill, 1680, bishops' right as peers to judge in capital causes, 1682, and municipal rights of city of London, 1683 ; ridiculed by Dryden ; outlawed ; died in Holland. [xxviii. 278]

HUNT, THOMAS (1696-1774), orientalist ; fellow of Hart Hall, Oxford ; M.A., 1721 ; D.D., 1744 ; Laudian professor of Arabic, 1738 ; regius professor of Hebrew, 1747 ; F.R.S., 1740 ; F.S.A., 1757 ; collaborated with Gregory Sharpe in preparation of Thomas Hyde's

'Dissertations' ; quarrelled with him before (1767) publication ; edited 'Fragment of Hippolytus from Arabic MSS.,' 1728, and works of Bishop George Hooper [q. v.], 1757. [xxviii. 279]

HUNT, THOMAS (1802-1851), inventor of a method of curing stammering ; of Trinity College, Cambridge. [xxviii. 280]

HUNT, THOMAS FREDERICK (1791-1831), architect. [xxviii. 280]

HUNT, THORNTON LEIGH (1810-1873), journalist ; son of James Henry Leigh Hunt [q. v.] ; director of political department of the 'Constitutional,' 1836 ; helped George Henry Lewes [q. v.] to establish the 'Leader,' 1850 ; published 'The Foster Brother,' 1845 ; edited Leigh Hunt's 'Autobiography,' 1850, 'Poetical Works,' 1860, and 'Correspondence,' 1862. [xxviii. 280]

HUNT, WALTER (VENANTIUS) (*d.* 1478), theologian ; perhaps professor at Oxford ; represented England at councils of Ferrara and Florence, 1438-9, being a leading exponent of the Latin view as to re-union of western with eastern church ; wrote thirty lost Latin treatises. [xxviii. 281]

HUNT, WILLIAM (1550 ?-1615). [See WESTON.]

HUNT, WILLIAM HENRY (1790-1864), water-colour painter ; apprenticed to Varley ; employed in early days by Dr. Thomas Monro and the Earl of Essex ; exhibited landscapes and interiors at Royal Academy, 1807-11, and a few oils at Old Water-colour Society ; member Society of Painters in Water-colours, 1826 ; exhibited 153 drawings (including sixty fisher-folk pieces), 1824-31 ; excelled in painting still-life and in humorous drawings ; preferred pure colour to mixed tints ; exhibited at Paris, 1855 ; elected to Amsterdam Academy, 1856. [xxviii. 281]

HUNTER, ALEXANDER (1729-1809), physician and author ; M.D. Edinburgh, 1753 ; studied also at London, Paris, and Rouen ; practised at York from 1763 ; established York Lunatic Asylum ; edited 'Georgical Essays' in connection with the Agricultural Society, 1770-2 ; F.R.S., 1777 ; F.R.S.E., 1790 ; hon. member of Board of Agriculture ; edited Evelyn's 'Sylva,' 1776, and 'Terra,' 1778 ; published 'Culina Famulatrix Medicinæ,' 1804 (reprinted as 'Receipts in Modern Cookery,' 1820), and 'Men and Manners' (third ed. 1808). [xxviii. 283]

HUNTER, ANDREW (1743-1809), professor of divinity at Edinburgh University ; studied at Edinburgh and Utrecht ; professor of divinity, 1779-1809 ; minister of Greyfriars, Edinburgh, 1779, of the Tron Church, 1786 ; D.D. ; moderator of general assembly, 1792. [xxviii. 284]

HUNTER, ANNE (1742-1821), poet ; sister of Sir Everard Home [q. v.] ; married John Hunter (1728-1793) [q. v.], 1771. [xxviii. 284]

HUNTER, CHRISTOPHER (1675-1757), antiquary ; M.B. St. John's College, Cambridge, 1698 ; physician successively at Stockton and Durham ; published enlarged edition of Davies's 'Rites and Monuments of the Church of Durham,' 1733 ; excavated Roman altars ; assisted antiquaries ; left manuscript topographical collections. [xxviii. 285]

HUNTER, SIR CLAUDIUS STEPHEN, first baronet (1775-1851), lord mayor of London ; alderman, 1804 ; sheriff of London, 1808 ; lord mayor, 1811-12 ; created baronet, 1812. [xxviii. 286]

HUNTER, GEORGE ORBY (1773 ?-1843), translator of Byron into French ; lieutenant, 7th royal fusiliers, 1785. [xxviii. 286]

HUNTER, HENRY (1741-1802), divine and author ; minister of South Leith, 1766, of London Wall (Scottish), 1771 ; D.D. Edinburgh, *c.* 1771 ; secretary to S.P.C.K. in highlands and islands of Scotland, 1790 ; works include 'Sacred Biography' (8th ed. 1820), and translations from Lavater, Euler, and St. Pierre. [xxviii. 286]

HUNTER, JOHN (1728-1793), surgeon and anatomist ; helped a brother-in-law at Glasgow in cabinet-making ; in London assisted his brother William in dissecting, 1748 ; pupil of William Cheselden [q. v.] at Chelsea Hospital and of Pott at St. Bartholomew's ; house surgeon at St. George's, 1756 ; surgeon, 1768 ; student at St. Mary Hall, Oxford, 1755-6 ; in Belleisle expedition, 1761 ; with army in Portugal, 1762 ; began to practise in

Golden Square, London, 1763; at house in Earl's Court kept dissecting apparatus and wild animals; F.R.S., 1767; had Jenner as house pupil in Jermyn Street, London; began lectures on surgery, 1773, having Astley Cooper and Abernethy in his class; surgeon extraordinary to George III, 1776; drew up 'Proposals for Recovery of People apparently Drowned,' 1776; Croonian lecturer, 1776-82; bought land in Leicester Square and Castle Street, London, and built large museum, 1784-5; first tied femoral artery for popliteal aneurysm, 1785; Copley medallist, 1787; surgeon-general, 1790; died suddenly. His body was removed by College of Surgeons from St. Martin's vaults to Westminster Abbey. His chief works were 'Treatise on the Blood, Inflammation, and Gunshot Wounds,' 1794 (edited by Sir Everard Home [q. v.], 1812, &c.), 'On the Venereal Disease,' 1786, 'Observations on certain parts of the Animal Œconomy,' 1786, 'Observations and Reflections on Geology,' published, 1859, and 'Memoranda on Vegetation,' published, 1860. His manuscripts were destroyed by Sir Everard Home, but his collections were bought by the nation and acquired by the College of Surgeons, 1800, the annual Hunterian oration being first given, 1813. His portrait was painted by Reynolds. [xxviii. 287]

HUNTER, JOHN (d. 1809), physician; M.D. Edinburgh, 1775; superintendent of military hospitals in Jamaica, 1781-3; practised in London; F.R.C.P., 1793; Gulstonian lecturer (on 'softening of the brain'), 1796; Croonian lecturer, 1799-1801; F.R.S.; published 'Observations on Diseases of the Army in Jamaica,' 1788; his Edinburgh thesis ('De Hominum Varietatibus') republished in English, 1865. [xxviii. 293]

HUNTER, JOHN (1738-1821), vice-admiral; studied at Aberdeen; served in Rochefort expedition (1757) and at capture of Quebec, 1759; served as master in North America under Hood and Howe, 1768-78; at the Doggerbank, 1781, and at relief of Gibraltar, 1782; as captain of the Sirius sailed from Port Jackson to the Cape of Good Hope by Cape Horn, 1788-9; wrecked on Norfolk island, 1789; volunteer; with Howe in action of 1 June, 1794; governor of New South Wales, 1795-1801; directed exploration of Terra Australis; wrecked off Paignton, 1804; vice-admiral, 1810. [xxviii. 294]

HUNTER, JOHN (1745-1837), classical scholar; of Edinburgh University; private secretary to Lord Monboddo; professor of humanity at St. Andrews, 1775-1835; LL.B.; principal of St. Salvator's and St. Leonard's colleges, 1835-7; published editions of Livy (i.-v.), 1822, Horace, 1797, Cæsar, 1809, Virgil, 1797, and Sallust, 1796, and Ruddiman's 'Latin Rudiments,' with additions, 1820. [xxviii. 295]

HUNTER, JOHN KELSO (1802-1873), Scottish artist, author, and cobbler; exhibited at Royal Academy portrait of himself as cobbler, 1847; published 'Retrospect of an Artist's Life' (1868), a work on Burns's friends and characters (1870), and 'Memorials of West-Country Men and Manners.' [xxviii. 296]

HUNTER, JOSEPH (1783-1861), antiquary; presbyterian minister at Bath, 1809-33; member of the 'Stourhead Circle'; sub-commissioner of public records, 1833, assistant-keeper, 1838; vice-president, Society of Antiquaries; published 'Hallamshire,' 1819 (enlarged, 1869), 'South Yorkshire,' 1828-31; collections concerning founders of New Plymouth, 1854; edited Cresacre More's 'Life of More,' 1828, Thoresby's 'Diary,' 1830, and Dr. Thomas Cartwright's 'Diary,' 1843; wrote also on Robin Hood, the 'Tempest,' and other subjects; many of his manuscripts in British Museum. [xxviii. 296]

HUNTER, SIR MARTIN (1757-1846), general; with 52nd foot in America, 1775-8, and India; wounded at Seringapatam, 1792; lieutenant-colonel of the 91st, 1794; commanded 60th royal Americans in West Indies under Abercromby, troops in Nova Scotia, 1803; general, 1825; K.B., G.C.M.G., and G.C.H. [xxviii. 298]

HUNTER, MRS. RACHEL (1754-1813), novelist. [xxviii. 299]

HUNTER, ROBERT (d. 1734), governor of New York; at Blenheim (1704) with Ross's dragoons; captured by French on voyage to Virginia, 1707; correspondent of Swift, 1709; as governor of New York (1710-1719) took out refugees from the Rhine palatinate and settled them on the Hudson; had constant disputes with the assembly; major-general, 1729; governor of Jamaica, 1729-34. [xxviii. 299]

HUNTER, ROBERT (fl. 1750-1780), portrait-painter; exhibited at Dublin; painted portrait of John Wesley. [xxviii. 300]

HUNTER, ROBERT (1823-1897), lexicographer and theologian; graduated at Aberdeen, 1840; colleague of Stephen Hislop [q. v.] at free church mission at Nagpore, Central India, 1846-55; resident tutor of presbyterian church of England in London, 1864-6; edited 'Lloyd's Encyclopædic Dictionary,' published, 1889; LL.D. Aberdeen, 1883. His publications include 'History of Missions of Free Church of Scotland in India and Africa,' 1873. [Suppl. iii. 14]

HUNTER, SAMUEL (1769-1839), editor of the 'Glasgow Herald,' 1803-35. [xxviii. 301]

HUNTER, THOMAS (1666-1725), jesuit; joined jesuits, 1684; professor at Liège; chaplain to Duchess of Norfolk; published 'An English Carmelite' (printed, 1876); defended jesuits against Charles Dodd [q. v.]. [xxviii. 301]

HUNTER, THOMAS (1712-1777), author; of Queen's College, Oxford; master of Blackburn grammar school, 1737-50; vicar of Weaverham, 1755-78; chief work, 'Sketch of the Philosophical Character of Lord Bolingbroke,' 1770. [xxviii. 301]

HUNTER, WILLIAM (1718-1783), anatomist; brother of John Hunter (1728-1793) [q. v.]; educated at Glasgow, Edinburgh, and St. George's Hospital; assistant-dissector to Dr. James Douglas (1675-1742) [q. v.]; assisted by John Hunter, 1748-59; surgeon-accoucheur to Middlesex, 1748, and British Lying-in hospital, 1749; M.D. Glasgow, 1750; physician extraordinary to Queen Charlotte, 1764; F.R.S., 1767; first professor of anatomy, Royal Academy, 1768; F.S.A., 1768; claimed several of John Hunter's discoveries; president of Medical Society, 1781; his museum acquired by Glasgow University; portrait painted by Reynolds. His 'Anatomical Description of Human Gravid Uterus' (1774, Latin), was edited by Baillie, 1794, and Edward Rigby, 1843. He published 'Medical Commentaries' (1762-4), and important papers on 'Medical Observations and Inquiries.' [xxviii. 302]

HUNTER, WILLIAM (1755-1812), orientalist; M.A. Marischal College, Aberdeen, 1777; went to India, 1781; published 'Concise Account of . . . Pegu,' 1785; as surgeon at Agra accompanied Palmer's expedition to Oujein, 1792-3; surgeon to the marines, 1794-1806; secretary to Asiatic Society of Bengal, 1798-1802 and 1804-11, of Fort William College, 1805-11; published Hindustani-English dictionary, 1808; his collection of proverbs in Persian and Hindustani published, 1824; died in Java. [xxviii. 305]

HUNTER, WILLIAM ALEXANDER (1844-1898), lawyer; M.A. King's College, Aberdeen, 1864; barrister, Middle Temple, 1867; professor of Roman law, University College, London, 1869-78; of jurisprudence, 1878-82; LL.D. Aberdeen, 1882; liberal M.P., North Aberdeen, 1885-96; moved successfully for free elementary education in Scotland, 1890; published, legal writings. [Suppl. iii. 15]

HUNTER, SIR WILLIAM WILSON (1840-1900), Indian civilian, historian, and publicist; graduated at Glasgow, 1860; entered Indian civil service, 1861; assistant-magistrate and collector in Birbhum district; published 'Annals of Rural Bengal,' 1868, 'Orissa,' 1872, and 'Comparative Dictionary of Non-Aryan Languages of India and High Asia,' 1868; appointed by Lord Mayo to organise statistical survey of Indian empire, 1869; occupied with it twelve years, the compilation reaching 128 volumes, condensed into 'The Imperial Gazetteer of India,' 9 vols., 1881; his article on 'India' reissued, 1895, as 'The Indian Empire: its Peoples, History, and Products'; an additional member of governor-general's council, 1881-7; settled near Oxford; made extensive collections for a history of India; published first volume of work tracing growth of British dominion in India, 1899, second volume, 1900; C.I.E., 1878; C.S.I., 1884; K.C.S.I., 1887; LL.D. Glasgow, 1869; M.A. Oxford, by decree of convocation, 1889; hon. LL.D. Cambridge, 1887. [Suppl. iii. 16]

HUNTINGDON, EARLS OF. [See WALTHEOF, d. 1076; SENLIS or ST. LIZ, SIMON DE, d. 1109; DAVID I, king of Scotland, 1084-1153; HENRY OF SCOTLAND, 1114?-1152; MALCOLM IV, king of Scotland, 1141-1165; WILLIAM THE LYON, king of Scotland, 1143-1214; HERBERT, WILLIAM, 1460-1491; HOLLAND, JOHN, first EARL (of the

Holland family), 1352 ?-1400 ; HOLLAND, JOHN, second EARL (of the Holland family), 1395-1447 ; HASTINGS, GEORGE, first EARL (of the Hastings family), 1488 ?-1545 ; HASTINGS, FRANCIS, second EARL, 1514 ?-1561 ; HASTINGS, HENRY, third EARL, 1535-1595 ; HASTINGS, THEOPHILUS, seventh EARL, 1650-1701 ; HASTINGS, HANS FRANCIS, eleventh EARL, 1779-1828.]

HUNTINGDON, COUNTESS OF (1707-1791). [See HASTINGS, SELINA.]

HUNTINGDON, GREGORY OF (*fl.* 1290). [See GREGORY.]

HUNTINGDON, HENRY OF (1084 ?-1155). [See HENRY.]

HUNTINGFIELD, WILLIAM DE (*fl.* 1220), justice itinerant; constable of Dover, 1203 ; sheriff of Norfolk and Suffolk, 1210-14 ; one of the twenty-five appointed to enforce Magna Carta ; reduced Essex and Suffolk for Louis of France ; captured at Lincoln, 1217 ; licensed to go on crusade, 1219. [xxviii. 306]

HUNTINGFORD, GEORGE ISAAC (1748-1832), bishop successively of Gloucester and Hereford ; fellow of New College, Oxford, 1770 ; M.A., 1776 ; D.D., 1793 ; warden of Winchester, 1789-1832 ; bishop of Gloucester, 1802-1815, of Hereford, 1815-32 ; compiled account of his friend Henry Addington's administration, 1802 ; published also ' Short Introduction to Writing of Greek ' (frequently reissued), original Latin and Greek verse, and pamphlets. [xxviii. 306]

HUNTINGFORD, HENRY (1787-1867), author of editions of Pindar (1814 and 1821) and of Damm's ' Pindaric Lexicon ' (1814) ; nephew of George Isaac Huntingford [q. v.] ; fellow of Winchester and New College, Oxford ; B.C.L., 1814 ; prebendary of Hereford, 1838. [xxviii. 307]

HUNTINGTON, JOHN (*fl.* 1553), author of ' Genealogy of Heretics ' (doggerel), 1540, reprinted and replied to by Bale ; protestant preacher ; canon of Exeter, 1560. [xxviii. 308]

HUNTINGTON, ROBERT (1637-1701), orientalist ; M.A. Merton College, Oxford, 1663 ; fellow ; chaplain of Levant Company at Aleppo, 1671-81 ; visited Palestine, Cyprus, and Egypt, acquiring valuable manuscripts and corresponding with Narcissus Marsh, Pocock, and Bernard ; provost of Trinity College, Dublin, 1683-92 ; bishop of Raphoe, 1701 ; many of his manuscripts in the Bodleian, and library of Merton College, Oxford, and Trinity College, Dublin. [xxviii. 308]

HUNTINGTON, WILLIAM, S.S. (1745-1813), coalheaver and preacher ; preached in Surrey and Sussex ; built ' Providence Chapel,' Titchfield Street, London, and preached there, 1783-1810 ; opened New Providence Chapel, Gray's Inn Lane, London, 1811 ; had controversies with Rowland Hill and others ; published ' God the Guardian of the Poor,' ' The Naked Bow,' and other works. [xxviii. 309]

HUNTLEY, FRANCIS (1787 ?-1831), actor ; played Othello to Kean's Iago at Birmingham ; appeared under Elliston as Lockit, 1809 ; at Covent Garden, 1811-12 ; the ' Roscius of the Coburg ' (Theatre). [xxviii. 311]

HUNTLEY, SIR HENRY VERE (1795-1864), naval captain and colonial governor ; cruised successfully against slavers on west African coast ; lieutenant-governor of the Gambia, 1839, of Prince Edward island ; knighted, 1841 ; published ' California, its Gold and its Inhabitants,' 1856, and other works ; died consul at Santos, Brazil. [xxviii. 311]

HUNTLY, MARQUISES OF. [See GORDON, GEORGE, first MARQUIS, 1562-1636 ; GORDON, GEORGE, second MARQUIS, *d.* 1649 ; GORDON, GEORGE, fourth MARQUIS, first DUKE OF GORDON, 1643-1716 ; GORDON, ALEXANDER, fifth MARQUIS, second DUKE OF GORDON, 1678 ?-1728 ; GORDON, ALEXANDER, seventh MARQUIS, fourth DUKE OF GORDON, 1745 ?-1827 ; GORDON, GEORGE, eighth MARQUIS, fifth DUKE OF GORDON, 1770-1836 ; GORDON, GEORGE, ninth MARQUIS, 1761-1853.]

HUNTLY, EARLS OF. [See SETON, ALEXANDER DE, first EARL, *d.* 1470 ; GORDON, GEORGE, second EARL, *d.* 1502 ? ; GORDON, ALEXANDER, third EARL, *d.* 1524 ; GORDON, GEORGE, fourth EARL, *d.* 1562 ; GORDON, GEORGE, fifth EARL, *d.* 1576.]

HUNTON, PHILIP (1604 ?-1682), author of ' Treatise of Monarchie,' 1643 ; M.A. Wadham College, Oxford, 1629 ; vicar of Westbury till 1662 ; provost of Cromwell's university of Durham, 1657-60. [xxviii. 312]

HUNTSMAN, BENJAMIN (1704-1776), inventor of cast steel ; originally a Doncaster clockmaker ; experimented and perfected his invention at Handsworth ; removed to Attercliffe, 1770, where his son carried on the business. [xxviii. 313]

HUQUIER, JAMES GABRIEL (1725-1805), portrait-painter and engraver ; came to England from Paris with his father. [xxviii. 313]

HURD, RICHARD (1720-1808), bishop of Worcester ; fellow of Emmanuel College, Cambridge ; M.A., 1742 ; D.D., 1768 ; his editions of Horace's ' Ars Poetica ' (1749) and ' Epistola ad Augustum,' 1751, praised by Warburton and translated into German ; defended Warburton against Jortin (1755) and edited (1757) his ' Remarks ' on Hume's ' Natural History of Religion ' ; issued ' Moral and Political Dialogues,' 1759, and ' Letters on Chivalry and Romance,' 1762 ; his attacks on Leland and Jortin reprinted, with caustic preface by Parr, 1789 ; preacher at Lincoln's Inn, 1765 ; archdeacon of Gloucester, 1767 ; Warburtonian lecturer, 1768 ; bishop of Lichfield and Coventry, 1774-81, of Worcester, 1781-1808 ; preceptor to Prince of Wales, 1776 ; declined the primacy, 1783 ; complete works issued, 1811. [xxviii. 314]

HURD, THOMAS (1757 ?-1823), hydrographer ; lieutenant of the Unicorn at capture of Danaë, 1779 ; present at Dominica, 1782 ; captain, 1802 ; made first exact survey of Bermuda ; hydrographer to the admiralty, 1808-23. [xxviii. 316]

HURDIS, JAMES (1763-1801), author of ' The Village Curate and other Poems ' (1788), and friend of Cowper ; B.A. Magdalen College, Oxford, 1785 ; incumbent of Bishopstone, 1791 ; professor of poetry at Oxford, 1793 ; attempted to vindicate Oxford from Gibbon's aspersions. [xxviii. 316]

HURDIS, JAMES HENRY (1800-1857), amateur artist ; son of James Hurdis [q. v.] ; pupil of Heath and friend of Cruikshank. [xxviii. 317]

HURLESTON, RICHARD (*fl.* 1764-1780), painter ; with Joseph Wright [q. v.] in Italy, 1773-80 ; killed by lightning on Salisbury Plain. [xxviii. 317]

HURLSTONE, FREDERICK YEATES (1800-1869), portrait and historical painter ; grand-nephew of Richard Hurleston [q. v.] ; pupil of Beechey and Lawrence ; began to exhibit at Royal Academy, 1821 ; exhibited from 1831 chiefly at Society of British Artists, being president, 1840-69 ; received gold medal at Paris Exhibition of 1855, sending ' La Mora,' ' Boabdil,' and ' Constance and Arthur.' [xxviii. 317]

HURRION, JOHN (1675 ?-1731), independent minister of Hare Court Chapel, London, and Merchants' lecturer at Pinners' Hall, London ; works edited by Rev. A. Taylor, 1823. [xxviii. 318]

HURRY, SIR JOHN (*d.* 1650). [See URRY.]

HURST, HENRY (1629-1690), nonconformist divine ; made probationary fellow of Merton College, Oxford, by parliamentary visitors, 1649 ; M.A., 1652 ; ejected from St. Matthew's, Friday Street, London, 1662 ; preached at conventicles ; published religious works. [xxviii. 318]

HURWITZ, HYMAN (1770-1844), professor of Hebrew at London University, 1828 ; born at Posen ; acquaintance of Coleridge ; published ' Vindiciæ Hebraicæ,' 1820, ' Elements of the Hebrew Language,' 1829, a Hebrew grammar (2nd edit. 1835), and poems. [xxviii. 319]

HUSBAND, WILLIAM (1823-1887), civil engineer and inventor ; superintended erection of Leigh water engine for drainage of Haarlem Lake ; became managing partner of Harvey & Co., 1863 ; patented (1859) balance valve for waterworks, four-beat pump-valve, the oscillating cylinder stamps called after him, and other inventions ; president of Mining Association and Institute of Cornwall, 1881-2. [xxviii. 319]

HUSE, SIR WILLIAM (*d.* 1495). [See HUSSEY.]

HUSENBETH, FREDERICK CHARLES (1796-1872), Roman catholic divine and author ; educated at Sedgley Park and Oscott ; chaplain at Cossey Hall, Norfolk, from 1820; D.D., 1850; vicar-general of Northampton, 1852. His fifty-four works include a defence of catholicism against Blanco White, 1826, missal and vesper books for the laity, notices of English colleges and convents after the dissolution, 1849, 'Emblems of Saints,' 1850 (ed. Jessopp, 1882), and a translation of the Vulgate based on the Douay and Rhemish versions.   [xxviii. 320]

HUSK, WILLIAM HENRY (1814-1887), writer on music; librarian to Sacred Harmonic Society, 1853-82; published 'Account of Musical Celebrations on St. Cecilia's Day,' 1857; contributed to Grove's 'Dictionary'; edited 'Songs of the Nativity,' 1868.   [xxviii. 321]

HUSKE, ELLIS (1700-1755), deputy postmaster-general in America; brother of John Huske [q. v.]; reputed author of 'Present State of North America,' 1755.   [xxviii. 322]

HUSKE, JOHN (1692?-1761), general; aide-de-camp to Lord Cadogan in Holland; major-general for services at Dettingen, 1743; second in command at Falkirk, 1746; led second line at Culloden; lieutenant-general, 1747; in Flanders and Minorca; general, 1756; governor of Jersey, 1760.   [xxviii. 322]

HUSKISSON, THOMAS (1784-1844), captain in the navy; half-brother of William Huskisson [q. v.]; present in the Defence at Trafalgar, 1805; signal-lieutenant to Gambier at Copenhagen, 1807; served in West Indies, attaining post-rank, 1811; paymaster of the navy, 1827-30.   [xxviii. 323]

HUSKISSON, WILLIAM (1770-1830), statesman; privately educated at Paris; private secretary to Lord Gower, English ambassador at Paris; under-secretary at war, 1795; M.P., Morpeth, 1796-1802, Liskeard, 1804-7, Harwich, 1807-12, Chichester, 1812-23, and Liverpool, 1823-30; secretary to the treasury under Pitt, 1804-5, and Portland, 1807-9; resigned with Canning, 1809; supported Canning on the regency and other questions; published pamphlet on 'Depreciation of the Currency,' 1810; colonial agent for Ceylon, 1811-23; privy councillor, 1814; minister of woods and forests under Liverpool, 1814; took frequent part in debates on corn-laws and (1816) bank restriction; member of finance committee, 1819; drafted report of committee on agricultural distress, 1821; defeated Londonderry's proposed relief loan, 1822, but his offer to resign refused by Liverpool; treasurer of the navy and president of board of trade, 1823-7; passed measures for regulating the silk manufactures and for removal of restrictions on Scotch linen industry; greatly reduced importation duties on sugar, foreign cotton, woollen goods, glass, paper, and other commodities, 1825; spoke effectively on shipping interest and silk trade; much attacked for his free trade tendencies; colonial secretary and leader of House of Commons under Goderich and Wellington, 1827-8; disagreed with Wellington on corn bill, and resigned on question of redistribution of the disfranchised seats at East Retford and Penrhyn, 1828; supported catholic emancipation, 1828, and additional representation for Leeds, Liverpool, and Manchester, 1829; gave much attention to Indian questions; killed by being run over at opening of Manchester and Liverpool railway.   [xxviii. 323]

HUSSEY, BONAVENTURA (d. 1614). [See O'HUSSEY.]

HUSSEY, GILES (1710-1788), painter; studied under the Venetian, Vincenzo Damini, who while travelling with him decamped with his money; friend and pupil of Ercole Lelli at Rome, where he elaborated and illustrated his theory of beauty in nature, and drew chalk portraits of the Young Pretender; in England painted little.   [xxviii. 328]

HUSSEY, SIR JOHN, BARON HUSSEY (1466?-1537), eldest son of Sir William Hussey [q. v.]; comptroller of Henry VII's household; employed diplomatically by Henry VIII; chief butler of England, 1521; summoned to House of Lords, 1529; chamberlain to Princess Mary, 1533; executed on charge of complicity in 'Pilgrimage of Grace.'   [xxviii. 329]

HUSSEY, PHILIP (d. 1782), Irish portrait-painter.   [xxviii. 330]

HUSSEY, RICHARD (1715?-1770), attorney-general to Queen Charlotte; barrister, Middle Temple, 1742; M.P., St. Mawes, 1761-8, East Looe, 1768-70; auditor of duchy of Cornwall, 1768; counsel to East India Company and admiralty; prominent debater.   [xxviii. 330]

HUSSEY, ROBERT (1801-1856), first professor of ecclesiastical history at Oxford; king's scholar of Westminster; double-first from Christ Church, 1824; censor, 1835-42; M.A., 1827; B.D., 1837; professor of ecclesiastical history, 1842-56; edited Socrates, 1844, Evagrius, 1844; Bæda, 1846, and Sozomen (published, 1860); established against William Cureton [q. v.] the accepted view as to Epistles of St. Ignatius, 1849; published also 'Rise of the Papal Power,' 1851.   [xxviii. 330]

HUSSEY, THOMAS (1741-1803), Roman catholic bishop of Waterford and Lismore; after studying at the Irish college, Salamanca, entered La Trappe; chaplain to Spanish embassy and rector of Spanish church, London, 1767; undertook confidential political mission to Madrid; F.R.S., 1792; employed by ministers to check disaffection among Romanists in the public services in Ireland, 1794; president of Maynooth, 1795; bishop of Waterford and Lismore, 1795.   [xxviii. 331]

HUSSEY, WALTER (1742-1783). [See BURGH, WALTER HUSSEY.]

HUSSEY or HUSE, SIR WILLIAM (d. 1495), chief-justice; as attorney-general conducted impeachment of Clarence; serjeant-at-law, 1478; chief-justice of king's bench, 1481-95; successfully protested against practice of consultation of judges by the crown.   [xxviii. 332]

HUSTLER, JOHN (1715-1790), Bradford philanthropist; quaker and wool-stapler; projected Leeds and Liverpool Canal (opened 1777); advocated in pamphlets, 1782 and 1787, prohibition of export of wool.   [xxviii. 332]

HUTCHESON, FRANCIS, the elder (1694-1746), philosopher; educated in Ireland and at Glasgow; while keeping a private school in Dublin became acquainted with Lord Carteret, Archbishop King, and Edward Synge; as professor of moral philosophy at Glasgow, 1729-46, greatly influenced 'common-sense' school of philosophy; upheld ethical principles of Shaftesbury against those of Hobbes and Mandeville; his 'System of Moral Philosophy' published by his son, 1755.   [xxviii. 333]

HUTCHESON, FRANCIS, the younger, also known as FRANCIS IRELAND (fl. 1745-1773), musical composer; only son of Francis Hutcheson the elder [q. v.]; M.A. Trinity College, Dublin, 1748; M.D., 1762; composed part-songs.   [xxviii. 334]

HUTCHESON, GEORGE (1580?-1639), joint-founder of Hutcheson's Hospital, Glasgow.   [xxviii. 335]

HUTCHESON, THOMAS (1589-1641), joint-founder with his brother George Hutcheson [q. v.] of Hutcheson's Hospital, Glasgow; keeper of register of sasines, Glasgow.   [xxviii. 335]

HUTCHINS, EDWARD (1558?-1629), canon of Salisbury, 1589; fellow of Brasenose College, Oxford, 1581; M.A., 1581; B.D., 1590.   [xxviii. 335]

HUTCHINS, SIR GEORGE (d. 1705), king's serjeant; barrister, Gray's Inn, 1667; serjeant-at-law, 1686; king's serjeant, 1689; knighted, 1689; third commissioner of great seal, 1690-3.   [xxviii. 335]

HUTCHINS, JOHN (1698-1773), historian of Dorset: B.A. Balliol College, Oxford, 1722; M.A. Cambridge, 1730; held livings in Dorset; two volumes of his history of Dorset issued, 1774; second edition partially destroyed by fire, 1808; two further volumes, edited by Gough, 1813 and 1815.   [xxviii. 336]

HUTCHINSON, BARON. [See HELY-HUTCHINSON, JOHN, afterwards second EARL OF DONOUGHMORE, 1757-1832.]

HUTCHINSON, MRS. ANNE (1590?-1643), preacher; née Marbury; followed John Cotton to Massachusetts, 1634; formed an antinomian sect; condemned by ecclesiastical synod, 1637, and banished; settled in Aquidneck (Rhode Island), 1638; after death of husband moved to Hell Gate, New York county; murdered there by Indians.   [xxviii. 337]

HUTCHINSON, CHRISTOPHER HELY- (1767-1826). [See HELY-HUTCHINSON.]

HUTCHINSON, EDWARD (1613-1675), settler in Massachusetts, son of Mrs. Anne Hutchinson [q. v.]; murdered while negotiating with Nipmuck Indians.   [xxviii. 337]

HUTCHINSON, FRANCIS (1660–1739), bishop of Down and Connor; M.A. Catharine Hall, Cambridge, 1684; while incumbent of St. James's, Bury St. Edmunds, published 'Historical Essay concerning Witchcraft,' 1718; bishop of Down and Connor, 1720–39; published 'Life of Archbishop Tillotson,' 1718, 'Church Catechism in Irish,' 1722, 'Defence of the Ancient Historians,' 1734, and other works.　　　[xxviii. 338]

HUTCHINSON, JOHN (1615–1664), regicide; of Peterhouse, Cambridge, and Lincoln's Inn; held Nottingham for the parliament as governor; as member for Nottinghamshire from 1646 attached himself to the independents; signed the king's death-warrant; member of first two councils of state, but retired, 1653; took his seat in restored parliament, 1659; worked with Monck and Hesilrige against Lambert; saved from death and confiscation at Restoration by influence of kinsmen, but imprisoned in the Tower and Sandown Castle, 1663–4.
　　　[xxviii. 339]

HUTCHINSON, JOHN (1674–1737), author of 'Moses's Principia,' 1724; while steward to Duke of Somerset employed by Woodward (his physician) to collect fossils; riding purveyor to George I; invented improved timepiece for determination of longitude; published works of religious symbolism, gaining distinguished adherents.
　　　[xxviii. 342]

HUTCHINSON, JOHN HELY- (1724–1794). [See HELY-HUTCHINSON.]

HUTCHINSON, LUCY (b. 1620), author; daughter of Sir Allen Apsley; married John Hutchinson (1615–1664) [q. v.], 1638; in early life made verse translation of Lucretius; adopted baptist views; exerted herself to save her husband in 1660. Her 'Life of Colonel Hutchinson' was first printed, 1806, her treatise 'On Principles of the Christian Religion' in 1817.　　　[xxviii. 340]

HUTCHINSON or **HUCHENSON**, RALPH (1553?–1606), president of St. John's College, Oxford; of Merchant Taylors' School, and St. John's College, Oxford; M.A., 1578; D.D., 1602; president, 1590–1606; a translator of New Testament (A. V.)　　　[xxviii. 343]

HUTCHINSON, RICHARD HELY-, first EARL OF DONOUGHMORE (1756–1825). [See HELY-HUTCHINSON.]

HUTCHINSON, ROGER (d. 1555), divine; fellow of St. John's College, Cambridge, 1543, and of Eton, 1550; M.A., 1544; his works edited by John Bruce.
　　　[xxviii. 343]

HUTCHINSON, THOMAS (1698–1769), scholar; of Lincoln College and Hart Hall, Oxford; M.A., 1721; D.D., 1738; vicar of Horsham and Cocking; edited Xenophon's 'Anabasis,' 1735, and 'Cyropædia,' 1727.
　　　[xxviii. 343]

HUTCHINSON, THOMAS (1711–1780), governor of Massachusetts Bay; descendant of Mrs. Anne Hutchinson [q. v.]; graduated at Harvard, 1727; member of colonial legislature; sent on mission to England, 1740; speaker of House of Representatives, 1746–8; judge, 1752; as commissioner to Albany congress drew up with Franklin plan of union of colonies, 1754; lieutenant-governor of Massachusetts, 1758, and chief-justice, 1760; carried out Grenville's policy, after which his house was sacked, 1765; on withdrawal of Bernard, 1769, acted as governor, being formally appointed, 1771; his removal petitioned for by Massachusetts assembly after disclosure (1773) by Franklin of his correspondence with Whately; left America, 1774; consulted by George III and ministers; deprecated penal measures against Boston and Massachusetts; D.C.L. Oxford, 1776. Of his 'History of Massachuset's [sic] Bay,' vol. i. appeared, 1764, vol. ii. 1767, vol. iii. (written in England) was edited by the Rev. John Hutchinson, 1828. His 'Collection of Original Papers relative to History of Massachusets Bay' (1769) was reissued as 'Hutchinson Papers,' 1823–5; 'Diary and Letters,' edited by P. O. Hutchinson, 1883–6.
　　　[xxviii. 343]

HUTCHINSON, WILLIAM (1715–1801), mariner and writer on seamanship; dock-master at Liverpool, 1760; published treatise on seamanship, 1777, enlarged in fourth edition as 'Treatise on Naval Architecture'; said to have introduced parabolic reflectors for lighthouses.
　　　[xxviii. 346]

HUTCHINSON, WILLIAM (1732–1814), topographer; F.S.A., 1781; published histories of Durham, 1785–1794, and Cumberland, 1794, 'View of Northumberland, 1776–8, and other works.　　　[xxviii. 346]

HUTH, HENRY (1815–1878), merchant-banker and bibliophile; travelled in Germany and France; lived some time in the United States and Mexico; finally joined his father's firm in London, 1849; collected voyages, Shakespearean and early English literature, and early Spanish and German books; printed 'Ancient Ballads and Broadsides,' 1867, 'Inedited Poetical Miscellanies' (1584–1700), 1870, 'Prefaces, Dedications, and Epistles' (1540–1701), 1874, 'Fugitive Tracts' (1493–1700), 1875. [xxviii. 347]

HUTHWAITE, SIR EDWARD (1793?–1873), lieutenant-general; with Bengal artillery in Nepaul, 1815–16, Oude, 1817, the Mahratta war of 1817–18, and Cachar, 1824; commanded battery at Bhurtpore, 1825–6, the artillery of the Megwar field force, 1840–4, and 3rd brigade Bengal horse-artillery in first Sikh war; brigadier of foot-artillery in second Sikh war; major-general, 1857; lieutenant-general, 1868; K.C.B., 1869.
　　　[xxviii. 348]

HUTT, SIR GEORGE (1809–1889), artillery officer; brother of Sir William Hutt [q. v.]; distinguished in Meeanee; commanded artillery in Persian war; K.C.B., 1886.　　　[xxviii. 349]

HUTT, JOHN (1746–1794), captain in the navy; captured by the French, 1781; distinguished as flag-captain to Sir Alan Gardner [q. v.]; mortally wounded in Howe's action of 1 June 1794; his monument in Westminster Abbey.　　　[xxviii. 349]

HUTT, SIR WILLIAM (1801–1882), politician; nephew of John Hutt [q. v.]; M.A. Trinity College, Cambridge, 1831; M.P., Hull, 1832–41, Gateshead, 1841–1874; paymaster-general and vice-president of board of trade, 1865; negotiated commercial treaty with Austria, 1865; K.C.B., 1865; commissioner for foundation of South Australia; leading member of New Zealand Company.　　　[xxviii. 349]

HUTTEN, LEONARD (1557?–1632), divine and antiquary; of Westminster and Christ Church, Oxford; M.A., 1582; D.D., 1600; sub-dean of Christ Church; vicar of Floore, 1601–32; a translator of the bible, 1604; prebendary of St. Paul's, 1609; published 'Answere to … A Short Treatise of the Crosse in Baptisme,' 1605; his 'Antiquities of Oxford' printed, 1720.　[xxviii. 350]

HÜTTNER, JOHANN CHRISTIAN (1765?–1847), author and translator; his account of Macartney's mission to China surreptitiously published in Germany, 1797, and translated into French, anticipating the official narrative; translator to foreign office, 1807.
　　　[xxviii. 350]

HUTTON, ADAM (d. 1389). [See HOUGHTON.]

HUTTON, CATHERINE (1756–1846), author; daughter of William Hutton (1723–1815) [q. v.]; published 'Life of W. Hutton,' 1816 (ed. Llewellyn Jewitt, 1872), 'History of Birmingham' (4th edit. 1819), and novels; left valuable letters (selections published, 1891). [xxviii. 351]

HUTTON, CHARLES (1737–1823), mathematician; son of a colliery labourer; opened mathematical school at Newcastle, 1760; prepared map of Newcastle, 1770; professor of mathematics at Woolwich Academy, 1773–1807; edited 'Ladies' Diary,' 1773–1818; F.R.S., 1774 (foreign secretary, 1779); Copley medallist, 1778; LL.D. Edinburgh, 1779; computed mean density of the earth, 1778; published 'Principles of Bridges,' 1772, 'Mathematical Tables,' 1785, and similar works; abridged 'Philosophical Transactions, 1809.　　　[xxviii. 351]

HUTTON, GEORGE HENRY (d. 1827), archæologist; son of Charles Hutton [q. v.]; lieutenant-general, 1821; LL.D. Aberdeen.　　　[xxviii. 353]

HUTTON, HENRY (fl. 1619), satirical poet; author of 'Follie's Anatomie,' 1619, edited by E. F. Rimbault, 1842.　　　[xxviii. 353]

HUTTON, JAMES (1715–1795), founder of the Moravian church in England; educated at Westminster; became connected with the methodists and published Whitefield's 'Journal,' 1738–9; visited German Moravians, 1739; broke with Wesley, 1740; 'referendary' of Society for Furtherance of the Gospel; published appreciation of Zinzendorf, 1755.　　　[xxviii. 353]

HUTTON, JAMES (1726–1797), geologist; educated at Edinburgh, Paris, and Leyden; M.D. Leyden, 1749; studied agriculture and travelled in Holland, Belgium, and Picardy; partner with James Davie in production of salammoniac from coal-soot; settled in Edinburgh, 1768; published his 'Theory of the Earth,' 1795, verified by visits to Glen Tilt, Galloway, Arran, and the Isle of Man; his 'Theory of Rain' attacked by J. A. Deluc [q. v.] and others; published 'Dissertations,' 1792, and 'Investigations of Principles of Knowledge,' 1794; originator of modern theory of formation of the earth's crust and uniformitarian theory of geology; joint-editor of Adam Smith's 'Essays on Philosophical Subjects,' 1795. [xxviii. 354]

HUTTON, JOHN (d. 1712), physician (originally a herd-boy at Caerlaverock); M.D. Padua; attended Mary (afterwards queen) in Holland and William III as first king's physician in Ireland; M.D. Oxford, 1695; F.R.S., 1697; first physician to Queen Anne; M.P., Dumfries, 1710–12, and local benefactor. [xxviii. 356]

HUTTON, JOHN (1740 ?–1806), author of 'Tour to the Caves . . . of Ingleborough and Settle' with glossary (2nd edit. 1781); fellow of St. John's College, Cambridge; third wrangler, 1763; M.A., 1766; vicar of Burton in Kendal. [xxviii. 356]

HUTTON, LUKE (d. 1598), reputed author of 'Luke Hutton's Repentance' and 'The Black Dogge of Newgate' (reprinted, 1638); executed at York for robbery. [xxviii. 356]

HUTTON, MATTHEW (1529–1606), archbishop of York; fellow of Trinity College, Cambridge; M.A., 1555; D.D., 1565; master of Pembroke Hall, 1562–7; regius professor of divinity, 1562–7; disputed before Elizabeth at Cambridge, 1564; dean of York, 1567; bishop of Durham, 1589; interceded successfully for Lady Margaret Neville, 1594 and 1595; president of the north, 1596–1600; archbishop of York, 1596–1660; founded Warton grammar school and almshouses. [xxviii. 357]

HUTTON, MATTHEW (1639–1711), antiquary; great-grandson of Matthew Hutton (1529–1606) [q. v.]; fellow of Brasenose College, Oxford; M.A. and D.D.; rector of Aynhoe, Northamptonshire, 1677–1711; friend of Anthony à Wood; collections of his manuscripts in British Museum. [xxviii. 358]

HUTTON, MATTHEW (1693–1758), archbishop of York and Canterbury; descended from Matthew Hutton (1529–1606) [q. v.]; M.A. Jesus College, Cambridge, 1717; D.D., 1728; fellow of Christ's College, Cambridge, 1717; rector of Trowbridge, 1726, of Spofforth, 1729; chaplain to George II; bishop of Bangor, 1743–7; archbishop of York, 1747–57, of Canterbury, 1757–8. [xxviii. 358]

HUTTON, SIR RICHARD (1561 ?–1639), judge: of Hutton Hall, Cumberland; studied at Jesus College, Oxford; barrister, Gray's Inn, 1586; ancient, 1598; member of council of the north, 1599–1619; serjeant-at-law, 1603; for the defendant in Calvin's case, 1608; knighted, 1617; puisne judge, 1617–39; knighted, 1617; a grantee of Bacon's fine; gave judgment for Hampden in ship-money case, 1638; some of his reports printed, 1656, and conveyancing precedents ('Young Clerk's Guide'), 1658. [xxviii. 359]

HUTTON, RICHARD HOLT (1826–1897), theologian, journalist, and man of letters; educated at University College school and University College, London; B.A., 1845; M.A., 1849; studied at Heidelberg and Berlin; prepared for unitarian ministry at Manchester New College, 1847; principal of University Hall, London; edited unitarian magazine, 'The Inquirer,' 1851–3; studied at Lincoln's Inn; joint-editor with Walter Bagehot [q. v.] of 'National Review,' 1855–64; professor of mathematics at Bedford College, London, 1856–65; assistant-editor of the 'Economist,' 1858–60; joint-editor and part-proprietor of the 'Spectator,' 1861–97; definitively abandoned unitarianism and accepted principles of English church. His publications include 'Essays on some Modern Guides of English Thought,' 1887, and 'Criticisms on contemporary Thought and Thinkers,' 1894. [Suppl. iii. 19]

HUTTON or **HUTTEN**, ROBERT (d. 1568), divine; of Pembroke Hall, Cambridge; rector of Little Braxted and Wickham Bishops, Essex, and Catterick, Yorkshire; published translation of Spangenberg, called 'The Sum of Diuinitie,' 1548. [xxviii. 360]

HUTTON, ROBERT HOWARD (1840–1887), bonesetter; joined his uncle (Richard) about 1869 in London, afterwards setting up for himself; accidentally poisoned. [xxviii. 360]

HUTTON, THOMAS (1566–1639), divine; of Merchant Taylors' School and St. John's College, Oxford; probationary fellow, 1585; M.A., 1591; B.D., 1597; vicar of St. Kew, rector of North Lew, and prebendary of Exeter, 1616; defended subscription to prayer-book, 1605–6. [xxviii. 360]

HUTTON, WILLIAM (1735 ? – 1811), antiquary; rector of Beetham, Westmoreland, 1762; his dialect 'Bran New Wark' (1785) reprinted, 1879. [xxviii. 363]

HUTTON, WILLIAM (1723–1815), topographer; employed in silk-mills at Derby and Nottingham; bookseller in Birmingham, 1750, opening first circulating library, 1751; opened paper-warehouse, 1756; president of local 'Court of Requests,' 1787; as friend of Priestley suffered heavily in riots of 1791; published 'History of Birmingham,' 1782, 'Description of Blackpool,' 1789, 'History of Derby,' 1791, 'Dissertation on Juries,' &c., 1789, poems, and other works; an autobiography and family history by him issued posthumously. [xxviii. 361]

HUTTON, WILLIAM (1798–1860), geologist; with John Lindley prepared 'Fossil Flora of Great Britain' (1831-7); his collection of fossils at Newcastle. [xxviii. 363]

HUXHAM, JOHN (1692–1768), physician; studied under Boerhaave at Leyden; graduated at Rheims, 1717; practised at Plymouth; F.R.S., 1739; Copley medallist for observations on antimony, 1755; the tincture of cinchona bark in British Pharmacopœia devised by and named after him; his medical works published in Latin at Leipzig, 1764, 1773, and 1829. [xxviii. 363]

HUXLEY, THOMAS HENRY (1825–1895), man of science; studied at Charing Cross Hospital; announced, 1845, discovery of the layer of cells in root sheath of hair which now bears his name; M.B. London, 1845; made as assistant-surgeon on H.M.S. Rattlesnake, 1846–50, investigations relating to hydrozoa; established morphological plan dividing hydrozoa into 'Radiata' and 'Nematophora'; sent, 1848, to Royal Society memoir 'On the Affinities of the Family of the Medusa'; F.R.S., 1850; published two memoirs on the Ascidians; lecturer on natural history at Royal School of Mines, 1854; naturalist to geological survey, 1855; published writings dealing with subject of fossil forms, including memoirs on cephalaspis and pteraspis (1858), the eurypterina, 1856–1859, and the dicynodon, rhamphorhynchus, and other reptiles; read Croonian lecture before Royal Society on 'Theory of the Vertebrate Skull,' 1858; published 'Zoological Evidences as to Man's Place in Nature,' 1863, and 'On the Causes of the Phenomena of Organic Nature,' 1863; served on royal commissions, including those on sea-fisheries of United Kingdom, 1864–5, Royal College of Science for Ireland, 1866, Administration and Operation of Contagious Diseases Acts, 1870–1, Scientific Instruction and Advancement of Science, 1870–5, on vivisection, 1876, and on Scottish Universities, 1876–8; Hunterian professor at Royal College of Surgeons, 1863–1869; Fullerian professor at Royal Institution, 1863–7; published 'Manual of the Comparative Anatomy of Vertebrated Animals,' 1871, 'Elementary Lessons in Physiology,' 1866, 'Elementary Biology' (in conjunction with Mr. H. N. Martin), 1875; an original member of school board for London, 1870–2, greatly influencing scheme of education finally adopted; president of Royal Society, 1883–5; inspector of fisheries, 1881–5; retired from public work owing to ill-health, 1885; delivered Romanes lecture at Oxford on 'Evolution and Ethics,' 1893; rector of Aberdeen University, 1872–4; hon. D.C.L. Oxford, 1885; privy councillor, 1892. His 'Collected Essays' were published in nine volumes, 1893–4. [Suppl. iii. 22]

HUYSMANS (HOUSEMAN), JACOB (1636 ?–1696), portrait-painter; came to England, c. 1660; executed portrait of Queen Catharine of Braganza as a shepherdess, of Izaak Walton, and others. [xxviii. 364]

HUYSSING or **HYSING**, HANS (fl. 1700–1735), portrait-painter; came to England with Michael Dahl [q. v.], 1700; adopted Dahl's manner. [xxviii. 365]

HUYSUM, JACOB VAN (1687 ?–1746). [See VAN HUYSUM.]

HYATT, JOHN (1767–1826), minister of the London Tabernacle; published sermons. [xxviii. 365]

HYDE, BARONS. [See VILLIERS, THOMAS, first BARON, 1709–1786; VILLIERS, JOHN CHARLES, third BARON, 1757–1838; VILLIERS, GEORGE WILLIAM FREDERICK, fourth BARON, 1800–1870.]

HYDE, ALEXANDER (1598–1667), bishop of Salisbury; fellow of New College, Oxford; D.C.L., 1632; sub-dean of Salisbury, 1637; dean of Winchester, 1660; bishop of Salisbury, 1665–7. [xxviii. 366]

HYDE, ANNE, DUCHESS OF YORK (1637–1671), eldest daughter of Edward Hyde, afterwards earl of Clarendon [q. v.]; maid of honour to Princess of Orange, 1654, of whom she wrote a 'portrait'; became engaged to James, duke of York, at Breda, 1659; privately married him in London, 1660; of their children only two daughters—Mary (wife of William III) and (Queen) Anne—survived childhood. She was secretly received into the Roman church, 1670; many portraits of her were painted by her protegé, Lely. [xxviii. 366]

HYDE, CATHERINE, afterwards DUCHESS OF QUEENSBERRY (d. 1777). [See DOUGLAS, CATHERINE.]

HYDE, DAVID DE LA (fl. 1580), classical scholar; M.A. Merton College, Oxford, 1553; probationary fellow, 1549; ejected for denying the queen's supremacy, 1560; wrote learned works. [xxviii. 369]

HYDE, EDWARD (1607–1659), royalist divine; of Westminster and Trinity College, Cambridge; fellow; M.A., 1637; D.D. Oxford, 1643; rector of Brightwell, 1643–5; dean-elect of Windsor, 1659; published theological works. [xxviii. 369]

HYDE, EDWARD, first EARL OF CLARENDON (1609–1674), B.A. Magdalen Hall, Oxford, 1626; friend of Falkland, Ben Jonson, Selden, and Waller; barrister, Middle Temple, 1633; keeper of writs and rolls of the common pleas, 1634; as M.P. for Wootton Bassett in Short parliament (1640) attacked jurisdiction of the marshal's court, and practically obtained its abolition; represented Saltash in Long parliament; chairman of committees of investigation into proceedings of councils of the north and of Wales; took prominent part against the judges; helped to prepare impeachment of Strafford; defended episcopacy, 1641; successfully obstructed Root and Branch Bill, 1641; in second session opposed the Grand Remonstrance, and composed the king's reply; with Falkland and Colepeper arranged to manage king's parliamentary affairs; kept ignorant of design to arrest the five members, 1642; joined Charles I at York, 1642, and for three years drew up all his declarations; advised adherence to law and constitutional methods, with refusal of further concessions; thwarted by influence of the queen and Lord Digby; privy councillor and chancellor of the exchequer, 1643; one of the 'junto' of five; raised loans from Oxford university and the catholics; prominent in negotiations, especially at Uxbridge, 1645, refusing real concessions, but endeavouring to win over opposition leaders by personal offers; obtained calling of Oxford parliament as counterpoise to that of Westminster, 1643; leading spirit of Prince Charles's council in the west, 1645; followed him to Scilly and Jersey, 1646, where he began his history; opposed queen's wish for concessions to Scots and plans for using foreign armies; issued reply to Long parliament's declaration of reasons against further addresses to the king, 1648; captured by corsair on way to Paris; ultimately joined the prince at the Hague; advised him against accepting Scottish proposals; accompanied Cottington to obtain help from Spain and negotiate alliance between Ormonde and O'Neill for recovery of Ireland, 1649–50; after Worcester (1651) Charles II's chief adviser, as secretary of state, and (from 1658) lord chancellor; opposed concessions to presbyterians and Romanists and isolated movements in England, but favoured negotiations with levellers; as chancellor and member of secret committee of six became virtual head of the government, 1660; chancellor of Oxford, 1660–7; created Baron Hyde, 1660, and Viscount Cornbury and Earl of Clarendon, 1661; forwarded Act of Indemnity; in church matters favoured comprehension rather than toleration; opposed to severe treatment of nonconformists, but firm in enforcing Act of Uniformity (1662) and subsequent measures; zealous for restoration of episcopacy in Scotland; one of the eight proprietors of Carolina, 1663; tolerant in colonial affairs, but supported

navigation laws and measures tending to promote mutual division among the colonies; desired peace policy in foreign affairs, but was forced into war; refused bribe from France, but solicited loan; did not initiate, but carried out, sale of Dunkirk, 1662; deprecated attack on Dutch African possessions, but defended seizure (1664) of New Amsterdam; looked upon as French in his sympathies, though really opposed to French alliance; ill-success of Dutch war partly due to his administrative conservatism; overthrown by court intrigues and hostility of parliament, whose authority he had endeavoured to restrict; dismissed, 1667; subsequently impeached; though the Lords declined to commit him, fled to France, 1667; banished; three years at Avignon and Montpellier; removed to Moulins, 1671, and Rouen, 1674, completing his 'History' and writing autobiography; died at Rouen; buried in Westminster Abbey. A consistent upholder of constitutional monarchy, he refused to recognise the altered conditions introduced by the civil war. He took Tacitus and Hooker as models in his 'History of the Rebellion,' which is very unequal in its historical and literary value, being a blend of his later written 'Life' with an unfinished 'History,' the former supplying the more accurate element. 'The True Historical Narrative of the Rebellion and Civil Wars in England' was printed from a transcript under supervision of Clarendon's son, Rochester, 1702–4, the original manuscript being first used in Bandinel's edition (1826); the best text that of W. D. Macray, 1888; profits used to build printing-press at Oxford (Clarendon Buildings). A supplement was issued, 1717. The 'Life of Clarendon,' by himself, was published, 1759, 'History of Rebellion and Civil War in Ireland,' 1720, and selections from his correspondence ('Clarendon State Papers'), edited by Scrope and Monkhouse, 1767–86. [xxviii. 370]

HYDE, HENRY, second EARL OF CLARENDON (1638–1709), eldest son of Edward Hyde, first earl [q. v.]; as Viscount Cornbury represented Wiltshire, 1661–74; private secretary, 1662, and chamberlain, 1665, to Queen Catherine; intimate with Evelyn; defended his father in parliament, and on his fall opposed the court and the cabal; privy councillor by influence of Duke of York, 1680; lord privy seal, 1685; viceroy of Ireland, 1685–6, but was thwarted and ousted by Tyrconnel; high steward of Oxford University, 1686; received pension of 2,000l., 1688; adhered to James II for some time; opposed settlement of the crown on William and Mary; imprisoned in the Tower, 1690; implicated in Lord Preston's plot and again sent to the Tower, 1691; his history of Winchester Cathedral published, 1715, and his 'Diary and Correspondence,' 1828. [xxviii. 389]

HYDE, HENRY, VISCOUNT CORNBURY and BARON HYDE (1710–1753), friend of Bolingbroke; grandson of Laurence Hyde, first earl of Rochester [q. v.]; Jacobite M.P. for Oxford University, 1732–50; called to the Lords as Baron Hyde, 1650; addressed to Pope verses upon his 'Essay on Man,' 1735 (printed with it, 1739); Bolingbroke's 'Letters on the Study of History,' 1735, addressed to him; killed by fall from his horse at Paris. [xxviii. 393]

HYDE, JANE, COUNTESS OF CLARENDON AND ROCHESTER (d. 1725), mother of Henry Hyde, viscount Cornbury [q. v.]; married Henry Hyde, second earl of Rochester, 1693; a celebrated beauty, the Myra of Prior's 'Judgment of Venus.' [xxviii. 394]

HYDE, LAURENCE, first EARL OF ROCHESTER (1641–1711), statesman; second son of Edward Hyde, first earl of Clarendon [q. v.]; M P., Newport (Cornwall), 1660–1, Oxford University, 1661–79; master of the robes, 1662–75; warmly defended his father on his impeachment; ambassador extraordinary to Poland, 1676, and the congress of Nimeguen, 1677–8; M.P., Wootton Bassett, 1679; a commissioner of the treasury, 1679; privy councillor and first lord of the treasury in first tory administration, 1679–85; created Viscount Hyde and Earl of Rochester, 1681; negotiated secret subsidy treaty with France, 1681; opposed summoning of new parliament; lord president of the council, 1684; appointed by James II lord high treasurer, 1685; K.G., 1685; served (1686) on high commission, and supported suspension of Bishop Compton; dismissed for aversion to Roman catholicism, 1687, though receiving large pension; joined Halifax in negotiations with William of Orange, 1688, but opposed his accession to the crown and supported a regency; having taken the oaths was re-admitted privy councillor, 1692; head of the church party; opposed Fenwick's attainder, 1696; named viceroy of Ireland, 1700; retained in office by Queen Anne, but resigned, 1703; adopted non-committal policy as to succession; again president of council, 1710–11; patron of Dryden, and the Hushai of 'Absalom and Achitophel'; wrote prefaces and dedications to Clarendon's 'Rebellion.' [xxviii. 394]

HYDE or **HIDE**, Sir NICHOLAS (d. 1631), chief-justice of England; uncle of Edward Hyde, first earl of Clarendon [q. v.]; barrister, Middle Temple; M.P., Andover, 1601, Christchurch, 1603–4; prominent in opposition, but retained for Buckingham's defence, 1626; knighted, 1627; chief-justice of England, 1627–31; died of gaol fever. [xxviii. 399]

HYDE, Sir ROBERT (1595–1665), chief-justice of the king's bench; nephew of Sir Nicholas Hyde or Hide [q. v.]; barrister, Middle Temple, 1617; serjeant-at-law, 1640; recorder of Salisbury, 1638–46, and M.P. in Long parliament; imprisoned, 1645; deprived of recordership, 1646; sheltered Charles II after Worcester (1651) at Heale; judge of common pleas, 1660; knighted; chief-justice of king's bench, 1663–5; died on the bench. [xxviii. 400]

HYDE, THOMAS (1524–1597), Roman catholic exile and author of 'Consolatorie Epistle to the afflicted Catholikes,' 1579; of Winchester and New College, Oxford; fellow, 1543–50; M.A., 1549; head-master of Winchester, 1551–8; imprisoned by Elizabeth, but escaped abroad; died at Douay. [xxviii. 401]

HYDE, THOMAS (1636–1703), orientalist; while at King's College, Cambridge, assisted Walton in Persian and Syriac versions of the Polyglott; Hebrew reader, Queen's College, Oxford, 1658; M.A. Oxford, 1659; Bodley's librarian, 1665–1701; archdeacon of Gloucester, 1673; D.D., 1682; Laudian professor of Arabic, 1691; regius professor of Hebrew and canon of Christ Church, 1697; government interpreter of oriental languages; chief work, 'Historia religionis veterum Persarum,' 1700. [xxviii. 401]

HYDE, WILLIAM (1597–1651), president of Douay College; graduated at Christ Church, Oxford, under name of Beyard, 1614; M.A., 1617; converted to Romanism and admitted at Douay as Hyde, 1623; professor of divinity, Douay; Roman catholic archdeacon of Worcester and Salop; vice-president of Douay, 1641–5, professor of history, 1649, and president, 1646–51; left money to the college. [xxviii. 402]

HYGDON, BRIAN (d. 1539), dean of York; brother of John Hygdon [q. v.]; principal of Broadgates Hall, Oxford, 1505; D.C.L., 1506; sub-dean of Lincoln, 1511–1523; archdeacon of the West Riding, 1515; dean of York, 1516–39; commissioner for peace with Scotland, 1526. [xxviii. 403]

HYGDON or **HIGDEN**, JOHN (d. 1533), president of Magdalen College, Oxford, and first dean of Christ Church; brother of Brian Hygdon [q. v.]; of Westminster and Magdalen College, Oxford, where he became fellow, c. 1495, dean, 1500–1 and 1503–4, bursar, 1502–3, and president, 1516–25; D.D., 1514; founded demyships and fellowships; placed at head of Cardinal College (Christ Church) by Wolsey, 1525. [xxviii. 404]

HYGEBRYHT (fl. 787). [See HIGBERT.]

HYLL. [See HILL.]

HYLTON, first BARON (1800–1876). [See JOLLIFFE, WILLIAM GEORGE HYLTON.]

HYLTON, WALTER (d. 1396). [See HILTON.]

HYMERS, JOHN (1803–1887), mathematician; second wrangler, St. John's College, Cambridge, 1826; fellow of St. John's College, 1827, tutor, 1832, and president, 1848–1852; D.D., 1841; rector of Brandesburton, 1852–87; caused portrait of Wordsworth to be painted for the college; left money for foundation of school at Hull; published mathematical treatises. [xxviii. 405]

HYND, JOHN (fl. 1606), romancer; probably grandson of Sir John Hynde [q. v.]; M.A. Cambridge, 1599; published 'Eliosto Libidinoso,' 1606. [xxviii. 405]

HYNDE, Sir JOHN (d. 1550), judge of common pleas; educated at Cambridge; barrister, Gray's Inn; reader, 1517, 1527, and 1531; recorder of Cambridge, 1520; serjeant-at-law, 1531; king's serjeant, 1535; prosecuted western rebels, 1536; judge of common pleas, 1545–50; knighted, 1545. [xxviii. 406]

HYNDFORD, EARLS OF. [See CARMICHAEL, JOHN, first EARL, 1638–1710; CARMICHAEL, JOHN, third EARL, 1701–1767.]

HYSLOP, JAMES (1798–1827), Scottish poet; successively shepherd, schoolmaster, tutor on board ship, reporter in London, and again teacher; died of fever off Cape Verde; his poems collected, 1887. [xxviii. 406]

HYWEL. [See HOWEL.]

I

IAGO AB IDWAL VOEL (fl. 943–979), king of Gwynedd; succeeded, 943; at war with sons of Howel Dda; hanged his brother Ieuav, 967; one of the kings who rowed Edgar on the Dee, 972; driven from throne by Ieuav's son and the English; captured by Danes, 980. [xxviii. 407]

IAGO AB IDWAL AB MEIRIG (d. 1039), king of Gwynedd; seized the throne, 1023; killed in battle with Gruffydd ab Llywelyn. [xxviii. 408]

IAGO AB DEWI, or JAMES DAVIES (1648–1722), Welsh bard; translator of English religious works. [xxviii. 407]

I'ANSON, EDWARD (1812–1888), architect; educated at Merchant Taylors' School and the College of Henri IV; designed Royal Exchange Buildings and offices in the city of London; P.R.I.B.A., 1886. [xxviii. 408]

IBBETSON, Mrs. AGNES (1757–1823), vegetable physiologist. [xxviii. 409]

IBBETSON, JULIUS CÆSAR (1759–1817), painter; exhibited at the Academy from 1785; made drawings during a voyage to China, 1788; friend of Morland; excelled as painter (oil) of cattle and pigs; published 'Accidence or Gamut of Painters in Oil and Water-colours,' 1803. [xxviii. 409]

IBBOT, BENJAMIN (1680–1725), divine; B.A. Clare Hall, Cambridge, 1699; M.A. Corpus Christi College, 1703; Norfolk fellow, 1706–7; chaplain to Archbishop Tenison and to George I; treasurer of Wells, 1708; rector of St.

Paul's, Shadwell; prebendary of Westminster, 1724; as Boyle lecturer, 1713–14, replied to Anthony Collins's 'Discourse of Free-thinking.' [xxviii. 410]

IBBOTSON, HENRY (1816?–1886), Yorkshire botanist and schoolmaster; compiler of 'Catalogue of Phænogamous Plants' (1846–8). [xxviii. 410]

IBHAR or **IBERIUS**, SAINT (d. 500?), bishop of Begerin (Wexford); locally known as St. Ivory; his day, 23 April. [xxviii. 411]

ICKHAM, PETER OF (fl. 1290?), reputed author of 'Chronicon de Regibus Angliæ'; monk of Canterbury. [xxviii. 411]

ICKWORTH, BARON HERVEY OF (1696–1743). [See HERVEY, JOHN.]

IDA (d. 559), first Bernician king; began to reign, 547; built Bamborough (Bebbanburch). [xxviii. 411]

IDDESLEIGH, first EARL OF (1818–1887). [See NORTHCOTE, SIR STAFFORD HENRY.]

IDRISYN (1804–1887). [See JONES, JOHN.]

IDWAL VOEL (d. 943), prince of Gwynedd; succeeded, 915; under-king to Æthelstan; helped Welsh to regain freedom, 940; killed by English. [xxviii. 412]

IDWAL AB MEIRIG (d. 997), king of Gwynedd; defeated the usurper Meredydd ab Owain ab Howel Dda, 995; slain in repelling the Danes. [xxviii. 412]

IESTIN AB GWRGANT (*fl.* 1093), prince of Gwent and Morganwg ; succeeded Howel ab Morgan, 1043 ; said to have invoked Norman aid against Rhys ab Tewdwr, but to have been subsequently driven out by Robert Fitzhamon [q. v.]   [xxviii. 412]

IEUAN AB RHYDDERCH AB IEUAN LLWYD (*fl.* 1410–1440), Welsh bard and collector of Welsh manuscripts ; extracts from his works in Iolo MSS. and in 'Cyfrinach y Beirdd '; 'Llyfr Gwyn Rhydderch,' preserved at Peniarth, belonged to him.   [xxviii. 413]

IEUAN AB HYWEL SWRDWAL (*fl.* 1430–1480), Welsh poet and historian of the three principalities ; his English ode (1450) printed in 'Cambrian Register.'   [xxviii. 413]

IEUAN DDU AB DAFYDD AB OWAIN (*fl.* 1440–1480), poet and bardic patron.   [xxviii. 414]

IEUAN DDU O LAN TAWY (1802–1823). [See HARRIS, JOHN RYLAND.]

IEUAN DDU (1795–1871). [See THOMAS, JOHN.]

ILCHESTER, RICHARD OF (*d.* 1188). [See RICHARD.]

ILIVE, JACOB (1705–1763), printer, letter-founder, and author; printed his 'Layman's Vindication of the Christian Religion,' 1730 ; lectured on religious subjects ; imprisoned, 1756–8, for blasphemy in commenting on Sherlock's sermons; published works on reform of the house of correction, and on management of Stationers' Company.   [xxviii. 414]

ILLIDGE, THOMAS HENRY (1799–1851), portrait-painter ; exhibited from 1842 at the Academy.   [xxviii. 415]

ILLINGWORTH, CAYLEY (1758 ?–1823), topographer ; M.A. Pembroke College, Cambridge, 1787 ; D.D., 1811 ; archdeacon of Stow, 1808 ; published 'Topographical Account of ... Scampton,' 1808 ; brother of William Illingworth [q. v.]   [xxviii. 416]

ILLINGWORTH, WILLIAM (1764–1845), deputy-keeper of the records, 1805–19 ; attorney of the king's bench, 1788 ; published 'Inquiry into Laws respecting Forestalling, Regrating and Ingrossing,' 1800 ; transcribed and collated the statutes from Magna Carta to the end of Henry VIII's reign and other important documents; arranged and catalogued Westminster chapter-house records, 1808 ; gave important (unacknowledged) assistance to record commission of 1832, and evidence before Commons' committee, 1836.   [xxviii. 415]

ILLTYD or ILTUTUS (*fl.* 520), Welsh saint ('The Knight'; born in Britanny, where he was a disciple of St. Germanus [q. v.]; came to Glamorganshire and built a monastery at Llantwit Major ; had among his scholars St. David and St. Pol de Leon ; said to have reclaimed land from the sea.   [xxviii. 416]

IMAGE, THOMAS (1772–1856), geologist ; M.A. Corpus Christi College, Cambridge, 1798 ; rector of Whepstead, 1798, and Stanningfield, 1807 ; his fossils acquired by Cambridge University.   [xxviii. 417]

IMISON, JOHN (*d.* 1788), Manchester mechanic and printer ; his best work, 'The School of Arts' (1785).   [xxviii. 417]

IMLAH, JOHN (1799–1846), Scottish poet; published 'May Flowers,' 1827, 'Poems and Songs,' 1841 ; died of fever in Jamaica.   [xxviii. 417]

IMLAY, GILBERT (*fl.* 1793), soldier and author; served against British in American war of independence ; lived with Mary Wollstonecraft, 1793–5, in Havre and London ; published 'Topographical Description of Western Territory of North America,' 1792, and the 'Emigrants,' 1793.   [xxviii. 417]

IMMYNS, JOHN (*d.* 1764), founder of Madrigal Society, 1741 ; active member of Academy of Ancient Music ; lutenist to the Chapel Royal.   [xxviii. 418]

IMPEY, SIR ELIJAH (1732–1809), chief-justice of Bengal ; at Westminster with Warren Hastings; fellow of Trinity College, Cambridge, 1757 ; junior chancellor's medallist, 1756 ; M.A., 1759 ; barrister, Lincoln's Inn, 1756 ; recorder of Basingstoke, 1766 ; counsel for East India Company before House of Commons, 1772 ; went to India, 1774 ; knighted, 1774 ; chief-justice of Bengal,

1774–89 ; confirmed committal of Nand Kumar (Nuncomar) for forgery, and condemned and sentenced him to death, 1775 ; decided for Hastings on question of his resignation of the governor-generalship, 1777 ; his judicial power restricted as a condition of compromise with Sir Philip Francis [q. v.], against whom he awarded damages for criminal conversation, 1779 ; president of new appeal court over local tribunals, 1780 ; recalled to defend himself against Francis's charges of illegality, 1783 ; impeached by the House of Commons ; defended himself successfully at bar of House of Commons against six charges, including the Nuncomar proceedings and exercise of extended judicial powers contrary to his patent, 1788 ; his impeachment dropped, 1788 ; M.P., New Romney, 1790–6.   [xxviii. 418]

IMPEY, JOHN (*d.* 1829), legal writer ; attorney of the sheriff's court ; published treatises on practice of courts of king's bench (1782) and common pleas (1784) and other works.   [xxviii. 422]

INA (*d.* 726). [See INE.]

INCE, JOSEPH MURRAY (1806–1859), landscape-painter ; pupil of David Cox the elder [q. v.]   [xxviii. 423]

INCHBALD, MRS. ELIZABETH (1753–1821), novelist, dramatist, and actress ; *née* Simpson ; married Joseph Inchbald, an actor, 1772 ; appeared as Cordelia to Inchbald's Lear at Bristol, 1772 ; played other parts with him in Scotland ; acted under Tate Wilkinson [q. v.] in Yorkshire, 1778–80, her husband dying at Leeds ; appeared at Covent Garden as Bellario in 'Philaster' and other parts, 1780 ; at the Haymarket and Dublin, 1782 ; retired from the stage, 1789; her 'Mogul Tale' produced at the Haymarket, 1784, 'I'll tell you what,' 1785, 'Appearance is against them' at Covent Garden, 1785 ; produced many other comedies and farces, 1786–1805, chiefly adaptations from French; edited 'The British Theatre,' 1806–9. Her romances, 'A Simple Story' (1791) and 'Nature and Art' (1796), have been often reprinted. [xxviii. 423]

INCHBOLD, JOHN WILLIAM (1830–1888), landscape-painter ; much admired by Ruskin and contemporary poets ; 'The Moorland,' 'The Jungfrau,' and 'Drifting' among his chief works ; published 'Annus Amoris,' 1877.   [xxviii. 426]

INCHIQUIN, EARLS OF. [See MURROUGH, first EARL, 1614–1674; O'BRIEN, WILLIAM, second EARL, 1638 ?–1692 ; O'BRIEN, JAMES, seventh EARL, 1769–1855.]

INCHIQUIN, BARONS. [See O'BRIEN, MURROUGH, first BARON, *d.* 1551 ; O'BRIEN, MURROUGH, sixth BARON, 1614–1674.]

INCLEDON, BENJAMIN (1730–1796), recorder of Barnstaple and Devonshire genealogist.   [xxviii. 426]

INCLEDON, CHARLES (1763–1826), tenor vocalist ; after singing in the Exeter choir spent some time at sea ; sang at Southampton (1784), Bath (1785), and Vauxhall Gardens, 1786–9 ; appeared in operas by Shield and in 'Beggar's Opera' at Covent Garden, 1790–1815 ; sang in sacred concerts under Linley, 1792 ; took part in first performance of Haydn's 'Creation' at Covent Garden, 1800 ; unsuccessful at New York, 1817–18 ; retired, 1822.   [xxviii. 427]

INCLEDON, CHARLES (1791–1865), vocalist; son of Charles Incledon (1763–1826) [q. v.] ; died at Bad Tüffer.   [xxviii. 428]

INDULPHUS (*d.* 962), king of Alba or Scotland 954–62 ; defeated Norse fleet in Buchan.   [xxviii. 428]

INE, INI, or (Latin) **INA** (*d.* 726), West-Saxon king ; chosen king in father's lifetime, 688 ; invaded Kent, 693, and established his supremacy over all England south of Thames; created see of Sherborne, 705 ; defeated Gerent, king of the British Dyvnaint, 710, and extended West-Saxon territory over western Somerset; fought Ceolred [q. v.] of Mercia at Wanborough, 715 ; suppressed rising of the æthelings of the race of Cerdic, 715 ; made war on South-Saxons, 725 ; his laws (promulgated 690–3) earliest extant West-Saxon legislation; benefactor to Glastonbury and Abingdon ; abdicated, 726, and died at Rome.   [xxviii. 428]

INETT, JOHN (1647–1717), author of 'Origines Anglicanæ,' 1710 (ed. Griffiths, 1855) ; M.A. University College, Oxford, 1669 ; successively incumbent of St.

Ebbe's, Oxford, Nuneaton, Tansor, Clayworth, and Wirksworth; precentor of Lincoln, 1682, and chaplain to William III, 1700; published popular devotional manuals. [xxviii. 430]

INGALTON, WILLIAM (1794-1866), painter and builder. [xxviii. 431]

INGE or **YNGE**, HUGH (d. 1528), archbishop of Dublin and lord chancellor of Ireland; scholar at Winchester, 1480; fellow of New College, Oxford, 1488-96; B.A.; D.D.; held preferments in dioceses of Bath and Wells, Lincoln, and Worcester; at Rome in 1504; promoted by Wolsey to see of Meath, 1512; archbishop of Dublin, 1521-8; lord chancellor of Ireland, 1527-8; friend of Gerald Fitzgerald, ninth earl of Kildare [q. v.]. [xxviii. 431]

INGELEND, THOMAS (fl. 1560), author of 'The Disobedient Child,' interlude, published c. 1560 (reprinted by Halliwell, 1848). [xxviii. 432]

INGELO, NATHANIEL (1621?-1683), divine and musician; M.A. Edinburgh (incorporated at Cambridge, 1644); fellow of Queens' College, Cambridge, 1644-6, and of Eton, 1650-83; accompanied Whitelocke to Sweden as chaplain and 'rector chori,' 1653; addressed by Marvell in a Latin poem; D.D. Oxford, 1658; published 'Bentivolio and Urania' (religious romance), 1660; his 'Hymnus Eucharisticus' set by Benjamin Rogers [q. v.]. [xxviii. 432]

INGELOW, JEAN (1820-1897), poetess; lived in London, c. 1863-97. Her works include ' A Rhyming Chronicle of Incidents and Feelings,' 1850, three series of 'Poems,' 1871, 1876, and 1885, and novels and stories for children. [Suppl. iii. 31]

INGELRAM (d. 1174), bishop of Glasgow, 1164-74, and chancellor of Scotland under David and Malcolm IV; upheld Scottish church at Norham, 1159. [xxviii. 433]

INGENHOUSZ, JOHN (1730-1799), physician and physicist; came to England from the Netherlands, c. 1765; went to Vienna to inoculate the Austrian imperial family, 1768, and became body-surgeon and aulic councillor; returned to London. 1779; F.R.S., 1779; published 'Experiments on Vegetables,' 1779, also issued at Vienna, 1786, containing discovery of respiration of plants. [xxviii. 433]

INGHAM, BENJAMIN (1712-1772), Yorkshire evangelist; studied at Queen's College, Oxford, where he was an active 'methodist'; B.A., 1734; accompanied the Wesleys to Georgia, 1735; on his return joined Moravians and preached extensively in the north; married Lady Margaret Hastings, 1741; gave the Moravians settlement at Fulneck, but separated from them, and in 1760 adopted Sandemanian views. [xxviii. 434]

INGHAM, CHARLES CROMWELL (1796-1863), portrait-painter; left Ireland for New York, and became vice-president of National Academy of Design. [xxviii. 434]

INGHAM, SIR JAMES TAYLOR (1805-1890), police magistrate; M.A. Trinity College, Cambridge, 1832; barrister, Inner Temple, 1832; magistrate at Thames police court, Hammersmith, and Wandsworth; knighted, 1876; chief metropolitan magistrate, 1876-90. [xxviii. 435]

INGHAM, OLIVER DE, BARON INGHAM (d. 1344), seneschal of Aquitaine, 1325-6 and 1333-43; supported Edward II, and was made justice of Chester; summoned as baron by Mortimer, 1327; imprisoned by Edward III, 1330. [xxviii. 435]

INGLEBY, SIR CHARLES (fl. 1688), Roman catholic judge; barrister, Gray's Inn, 1671; acquitted of complicity in Gascoigne plot, 1680; made baron of the exchequer by James II, 1688, but dismissed by William III; knighted, 1688; resumed practice. [xxviii. 435]

INGLEBY, CLEMENT MANSFIELD (1823-1886), Shakespearean critic and author; M.A. Trinity College, Cambridge, 1850; LL.D., 1859; published 'Complete View of the Shakespeare Controversy,' 1861, closing the Payne Collier correspondence, 'Introduction to Metaphysic,' 1864 and 1869, 'Revival of Philosophy at Cambridge,' 1870, 'Shakespeare Hermeneutics,' 1875, 'Centurie of Prayse,' 1875, and 'Shakespeare: the Man and the Book,' 1877 and 1881; proposed examination of Shakespeare's skull for identification of portrait, 1882; edited 'Cymbeline,' 1886; vice-president and foreign secretary of Royal Society of Literature. [xxviii. 436]

INGLEFIELD, SIR EDWARD AUGUSTUS (1820-1894), admiral; lieutenant, 1842; flag-lieutenant to his father, Rear-admiral Samuel Hood Inglefield, then commander-in-chief on South American station, 1845; commander, 1845; accompanied Lady Franklin's private steamer in expedition to Arctic, 1852; published 'A Summer Search for Sir John Franklin,' 1853; F.R.S., 1853; again visited Arctic, 1853 and 1854; captain, 1853; in Black Sea, 1855; in Channel and Mediterranean, 1866-1868; rear-admiral, 1869; second in command in Mediterranean, 1872-5; knighted, 1877; commander-in-chief on North American station, 1878-9; admiral, 1879; retired, 1888; K.C.B., 1887. [Suppl. iii. 32]

INGLEFIELD, JOHN NICHOLSON (1748-1828), navy captain; served under Sir Samuel (afterwards Viscount) Hood [q. v.]; at Ushant under Alexander Hood (1727-1814) [q. v.], 1778; flag-captain to Samuel Hood in actions of 1781-2; one of the survivors of wreck of Centaur, 1782; captain of fleet in Mediterranean, 1794; declined flag-rank, but was commissioner of the navy, 1795-1811. [xxviii. 437]

INGLETHORP or **INGOLDSTHORP**, THOMAS (d. 1291), bishop of Rochester; archdeacon of Middlesex and Sudbury; dean of St. Paul's, 1277; bishop of Rochester, 1283-91; had disputes with Rochester monks and abbot of St. Augustine's, Canterbury. [xxviii. 438]

INGLIS, CHARLES (1731?-1791), rear-admiral; present at Hawke's action with L'Étenduère, 1747; commanded a sloop in Rochefort expedition, 1757, and the Carcass bomb at Rodney's bombardment of Havre, 1759; took part in relief of Gibraltar, 1781, and the operations of Sir Samuel (Viscount) Hood [q. v.] in West Indies, 1782; rear-admiral, 1790. [xxix. 1]

INGLIS, CHARLES (1734-1816), first bishop of Nova Scotia; went to America and assisted in evangelical work among the Mohawk Indians; advocated establishment of American episcopate; M.A. by diploma, Oxford, 1770; D.D., 1778; incumbent of Holy Trinity, New York, 1777-83; attainted as a loyalist, 1779; bishop of Nova Scotia, 1787-1816. [xxix. 1]

INGLIS, HENRY DAVID (1795-1835), traveller and author of 'Tales of the Ardennes' (by Derwent Conway), 1825, 'Spain in 1830,' 1831, 'Ireland in 1834' (fifth edition, 1838), and other books of travel. [xxix. 2]

INGLIS, HESTER (1571-1624). [See KELLO.]

INGLIS, JAMES (d. 1531), abbot of Culross; clerk of the closet to James IV; secretary to Queen Margaret, 1515; chancellor of royal chapel at Stirling and abbot of Culross, 1527; wrote poems, which are lost; murdered by John Blacater of Tulliallan and William Lothian. [xxix. 2]

INGLIS, JOHN (1763-1834), Scottish divine; graduated at Edinburgh, 1783; D.D., 1804; successor of Principal Robertson at the Old Greyfriars Church; moderator of general assembly, 1804; a dean of Chapel Royal, 1810; originated scheme for evangelisation of India, 1824. [xxix. 3]

INGLIS, JOHN, LORD GLENCORSE (1810-1891), lord justice-general of Scotland; youngest son of John Inglis (1763-1834) [q. v.]; of Glasgow University and Balliol College, Oxford; M.A. Oxford, 1836; advocate, 1835; solicitor-general and afterwards lord advocate of Scotland, 1852 and 1858; carried Universities of Scotland Act, 1858; lord justice-clerk, 1858-67; lord justice-general of Scotland, 1867-91; privy councillor, 1869; D.C.L. Oxford, 1859; elected chancellor of Edinburgh against Mr. Gladstone, 1869; rector of Aberdeen, 1857, of Glasgow, 1865; president of Scottish Texts Society; published 'Historical Study of Law,' 1863. [xxix. 3]

INGLIS, SIR JOHN EARDLEY WILMOT (1814-1862), major-general; born in Nova Scotia; grandson of bishop Charles Inglis (1734-1816) [q. v.]; with the 32nd in Canada, 1837, and the Punjaub, 1848-9; succeeded Sir Henry Lawrence [q. v.] in command at Lucknow; major-general and K.C.B. for his gallant defence of Lucknow, 1857; commander in Ionian islands, 1860; died at Hamburg. [xxix. 5]

INGLIS, MRS. MARGARET MAXWELL (1774-1843), Scottish poetess; née Murray; published 'Miscellaneous Collection of Poems, chiefly Scriptural Pieces,' 1828. [xxix. 5]

INGLIS, SIR ROBERT HARRY, second baronet (1786–1855), tory politician ; of Winchester, and Christ Church, Oxford ; M.A., 1809 ; D.C.L., 1826 ; of Lincoln's Inn ; private secretary to Lord Sidmouth ; F.S.A., 1816 ; F.R.S. ; M.P., Dundalk, 1824–6, Ripon, 1828–9 ; defeated Peel on the catholic question at Oxford, 1829 ; represented Oxford University till 1854 ; opposed parliamentary reform, Jewish relief, repeal of the corn laws, and (1845) the Maynooth grant ; commissioner on public records, 1831 ; privy councillor, 1854 ; president of the Literary Club ; antiquary of Royal Academy, 1850 ; edited works by Henry Thornton and sermon by Heber. [xxix. 6]

INGLIS, SIR WILLIAM (1764–1835), general ; joined 57th at New York, 1781, and served with it in Flanders, 1793, in St. Lucia, 1796, and Grenada, 1797 ; formed 2nd battalion, 1803 ; commanded 2nd battalion in Peninsula, holding also a brigade command in Hill's division ; led his regiment with great distinction at Albuera, 1811, where he was wounded ; major-general, 1813 ; distinguished himself at head of first brigade of seventh division, especially at second battle of Sauroren, 1813, and the action at Vera, 1813, and at Orthez, 1814 ; lieutenant-general, 1825 ; colonel of 57th, 1830 ; K.C.B. [xxix. 7]

INGLOTT, WILLIAM (1554–1621), organist of Norwich Cathedral. [xxix. 9]

INGMETHORPE, THOMAS (1562–1638), schoolmaster ; B.A. St. Mary Hall, Oxford, 1584 ; M.A. Brasenose College, 1586 ; head-master of Durham school, c. 1610 ; incumbent of Stainton-in-Strata, 1594–1638 ; learned hebraist. [xxix. 9]

INGOLDSBY, SIR HENRY, first baronet (1622–1701), parliamentarian ; brother of Sir Richard Ingoldsby [q. v.] ; created baronet by Cromwell, 1658, and Charles II, 1660. [xxix. 10]

INGOLDSBY, SIR RICHARD (d. 1685), regicide ; as colonel of a 'new model' regiment took part in storming of Bridgwater and Bristol ; signed Charles I's death-warrant under compulsion, as he asserted, 1649 ; M.P., Wendover, 1647, and Buckinghamshire, 1654 and 1656 ; member of council of state, 1652, and of Cromwell's House of Lords, 1657 ; supported his kinsman, Richard Cromwell, 1659 ; seized Windsor for parliament and suppressed Lambert's rising, 1659 ; pardoned and created K.B., 1661 ; M.P., Aylesbury, 1660–85. [xxix. 9]

INGOLDSBY, RICHARD (d. 1712), lieutenant-general ; probably nephew of Sir Richard Ingoldsby [q. v.] ; adjutant-general of the expedition to French coast, 1692 ; commanded royal Welsh fusiliers in Flanders under William III ; brigadier, 1696 ; major-general, 1702 ; lieutenant-general, 1704 ; second in command of first line at Blenheim, 1704 ; M.P. for Limerick in Irish parliament from 1703 ; commander of the forces in Ireland, 1707–12. [xxix. 11]

INGOLDSBY, RICHARD (d. 1759), brigadier-general ; great-grandson of Sir Richard Ingoldsby [q. v.] ; served in 1st foot guards ; while commanding a brigade failed to take French redoubt near Fontenoy, 1745, and was dismissed by court-martial. [xxix. 11]

INGRAM, SIR ARTHUR (d. 1642), courtier ; comptroller of the customs of London for life, 1607 ; M.P., Stafford, 1609, Romney, 1614, Appleby, 1620, and York, 1623–9 ; knighted, 1613 ; secretary of council of the north, 1612 ; high sheriff of Yorkshire, 1620 ; built hospital at Bootham. [xxix. 12]

INGRAM, DALE (1710–1793), surgeon ; practised in Barbados, 1743–50 ; surgeon to Christ's Hospital, 1759–91 ; published 'Practical Cases and Observations in Surgery,' 1751, containing accounts of early abdominal operations. [xxix. 13]

INGRAM, HERBERT (1811–1860), founder of the 'Illustrated London News' (1842) ; removed to London from Nottingham when Nathaniel Cooke to advertise a pill ; purchased 'Pictorial Times' and other illustrated papers ; attempted a threepenny daily, 1848 ; M.P., Boston, 1856–60 ; associated with John Sadleir [q. v.] ; while travelling in America, drowned in Lake Michigan. [xxix. 13]

INGRAM, JAMES (1774–1850), Anglo-Saxon scholar ; educated at Westminster and Winchester ; scholar of Trinity College, Oxford, 1794, fellow, 1803, president,

1824–50 ; M.A., 1800 ; D.D., 1824 ; professor of Anglo-Saxon, 1803–8 ; keeper of the archives, 1815–18 ; published 'Memorials of Oxford,' 1832–7 ; edited the 'Saxon Chronicle' (1823), and Quintilian (1809). [xxix. 14]

INGRAM, JOHN (1721–1771 ?), line-engraver. [xxix. 15]

INGRAM, ROBERT (1727–1804), divine ; M.A. Corpus Christi College, Cambridge, 1753 ; vicar of Wormingford and Boxted, Essex ; published apocalyptic works. [xxix. 15]

INGRAM, ROBERT ACKLOM (1763–1809), political economist ; son of Robert Ingram [q. v.] ; senior wrangler, Queens' College, Cambridge, 1784 ; fellow ; M.A., 1787 ; B.D., 1796 ; rector of Seagrave, 1802–9 ; chief works, 'Syllabus of a System of Political Philosophy,' 1800, and 'Disquisitions on Population,' 1808 (against Malthus). [xxix. 16]

INGRAM, WALTER (1855–1888), yeomanry officer ; son of Herbert Ingram [q. v.] ; volunteer in Soudan expedition, 1884 ; killed by an elephant in east Africa. [xxix. 14]

INGULF (d. 1109), abbot of Crowland or Croyland ; secretary to William the Conqueror ; entered monastery of St. Wandrille under Gerbert ; abbot of Crowland, 1086–1109. The 'Crowland History,' known by his name, though accepted as genuine by Spelman, Dugdale, and Selden, has been shown to be a forgery (probably of the early fifteenth century) by Sir Francis Palgrave, Riley, and others. It was printed by Savile (1596), Fulman (1684, with continuations), and by Mr. Birch (1883). [xxix. 16]

INGWORTH, RICHARD OF (fl. 1224), Franciscan ; came to England with Agnellus, 1224 ; founded first Franciscan houses in London, Oxford, and Northampton ; afterwards custodian of Cambridge and provincial minister of Ireland ; died as missionary in Palestine. [xxix. 17]

INMAN, GEORGE ELLIS (1814–1840), song-writer and poet ; committed suicide in St. James's Park. [xxix. 18]

INMAN, JAMES (1776–1859), writer on nautical science ; educated at Sedbergh and St. John's College, Cambridge ; fellow ; M.A., 1805 ; D.D., 1820 ; senior wrangler and first Smith's prizeman, 1800 ; astronomer with Flinders in the Investigator and Porpoise, 1803–4 ; professor of mathematics at Royal Naval College, Portsmouth, 1808–39 ; principal of school of naval architecture, 1810 ; published 'Navigation and Nautical Astronomy for British Seamen,' 1821, the tables of which are still used, 'Introduction to Naval Gunnery,' 1828, and other works. [xxix. 18]

INMAN, THOMAS (1820–1876), mythologist ; M.D. London, 1842 ; physician to Royal Infirmary, Liverpool ; published, among other works, 'Phenomena of Spinal Irritation,' 1858, and 'Ancient Faiths embodied in Ancient Names' (vol. i. 1868, vol. ii. 1869). [xxix. 19]

INMAN, WILLIAM (1825–1881), founder of the Inman line of steamships ; brother of Thomas Inman [q. v.] ; partner of Richardson brothers of Liverpool, 1849, for whom he purchased the City of Glasgow (screw steamer) for American voyages, 1850 ; founded Inman line, 1857 ; introduced weekly service to New York, 1860 ; after failure of Collins line carried American mails ; launched City of Berlin, 1875. [xxix. 20]

INNERPEFFER, LORD. [See FLETCHER, ANDREW, d. 1650.]

INNES, COSMO (1798–1874), antiquary ; educated at Aberdeen, Glasgow, and Balliol College, Oxford ; M.A. Oxford, 1824 ; engaged in peerage cases ; sheriff of Moray, 1840–52 ; principal clerk of session, 1852 ; professor of constitutional law at Edinburgh, 1846–74 ; edited 'Rescinded Acts' and assisted in folio edition of 'Acts of the Scots Parliament' (1124–1707), besides many works for the Spalding and Bannatyne clubs ; published also works on Scottish history. [xxix. 20]

INNES or **INNES-KER**, JAMES, fifth DUKE OF ROXBURGHE (1738–1823). [See KER.]

INNES, JOHN (d. 1414), bishop of Moray ; canon of Elgin, 1389 ; archdeacon of Caithness, 1396 ; bishop of Moray, 1406–14 ; rebuilt Elgin Cathedral and erected part of the palace. [xxix. 21]

INNES, JOHN (1739–1777), anatomist; dissector under Alexander Monro secundus [q. v.] at Edinburgh. [xxix. 22]

INNES, LEWIS (1651–1738), principal of the Scots College, Paris, 1682–1713; printed charter establishing the legitimacy of Robert III, and vindicated its authenticity, 1695; lord-almoner at St. Germain, 1714; probably compiled 'Life of James II' (printed, 1816). [xxix. 22]

INNES, THOMAS (1662–1744), historian and antiquary; brother of Lewis Innes [q. v.]; studied at Scots College and College of Navarre, Paris; M.A. Paris, 1694; three years on Scottish mission; vice-principal of Scots College, 1727; his 'Critical Essay on the Ancient Inhabitants of the Northern Parts of Britain,' 1729, reprinted in 'Historians of Scotland,' 1879; his 'Civil and Ecclesiastical History of Scotland' edited by George Grub for Spalding Club, 1853. [xxix. 23]

INSKIPP, JAMES (1790–1868), painter; exhibited at British Institution, Society of British Artists, and Royal Academy. [xxix. 24]

INSULA, ROBERT DE, or ROBERT HALIELAND (d. 1283), bishop of Durham, 1274–83; refused to admit visitation of Archbishop Wickwaine of York and was excommunicated, 1280. [xxix. 24]

INVERARITY, ELIZABETH, afterwards MRS. MARTYN (1813–1846), vocalist and actress. [xxix. 25]

INVERKEITHING, RICHARD (d. 1272), bishop of Dunkeld, 1250–72; chancellor of Scotland, 1255–7. [xxix. 25]

INVERNESS, titular EARL OF (1691–1740). [See HAY, JOHN.]

INWOOD, CHARLES FREDERICK (1798–1840), architect; son of William Inwood [q. v.] [xxix. 26]

INWOOD, HENRY WILLIAM (1794–1843), architect; son of William Inwood [q. v.]; travelled in Greece; his collection of antiquities purchased by British Museum; published archæological works. [xxix. 25]

INWOOD, WILLIAM (1771?–1843), architect and surveyor; designed (with assistance of his son) St. Pancras New Church, 1819–22; published (1811) 'Tables for the Purchasing of Estates' (21st ed. 1880). [xxix. 26]

IOLO GOCH, or the RED (fl. 1328–1405), Welsh bard and lord of Llechryd; real name EDWARD LLWYD; said to have been made a 'chaired bard' at the Eisteddfod of 1330; friend of Owen Glendower, for whom he created enthusiasm by his verses; composed also religious poems; eighteen of his poems printed. [xxix. 26]

IONIDES, CONSTANTINE ALEXANDER (1833–1900), public benefactor; entered London Stock Exchange, 1864; bequeathed valuable collections of works of art to South Kensington Museum. [Suppl. iii. 33]

IORWERTH AB BLEDDYN (d. 1112), Welsh prince; being detached from the cause of his lord, Robert of Bellême [q. v.], contributed greatly to his defeat, 1102; imprisoned by Henry I, 1103–11; slain by Madog, his outlawed nephew, and Llywerch at Caereineon. [xxix. 27]

IRBY, CHARLES LEONARD (1789–1845), captain in the navy and traveller; present at reduction of Monte Video and Mauritius; commanded the Thames in attack on New Orleans; travelled with Captain James Mangles [q. v.], Belzoni, and others up the Nile and through Syria to Jerusalem, 1817–18, their 'Travels' being published, 1823 (reissued, 1844); served in the Levant, 1826–7. [xxix. 28]

IRBY, FREDERICK PAUL (1779–1844), rear-admiral; brother of Charles Leonard Irby [q. v.]; present at Howe's victory of 1 June, 1794, and at Camperdown, 1797; attained post rank, 1802; had four hours' indecisive fight with the Aréthuse off Sierra Leone, 1813; C.B., 1831; rear-admiral, 1837. [xxix. 28]

IRELAND, DUKE OF (1362–1392). [See VERE, ROBERT DE.]

IRELAND, ALEXANDER (1810–1894), journalist and man of letters; a native of Edinburgh; made acquaintance there of the brothers Chambers, Dr. John Gairdner [q. v.], and Emerson, for whom (1847–88) he organised lecturing tour in England; one of three persons entrusted by Robert Chambers with secret of authorship of Chambers's 'Vestiges of Creation,' 1843; settled in Manchester, 1843; there engaged in business; publisher and business manager of 'Manchester Examiner,' 1846–86. His publications include 'The Book-Lover's Enchiridion,' 1882, and bibliographies of Leigh Hunt and Hazlitt. [Suppl. iii. 33]

IRELAND, MRS. ANNIE (d. 1893), second wife of Alexander Ireland [q. v.]; sister of Henry Alleyne Nicholson [q. v.]; married, 1866; published biography of Jane Welsh Carlyle, 1891. [Suppl. iii. 34]

IRELAND, FRANCIS (fl. 1745–1773). [See HUTCHESON, FRANCIS, the younger.]

IRELAND, JOHN (d. 1808), biographer of Hogarth; some time a watchmaker in Maiden Lane; published 'Letters and Poems, with Anecdotes,' of his friend, John Henderson (1747–1785) [q. v.], 1786, and 'Hogarth Illustrated,' 1791, with a biography as supplement, 1798. [xxix. 29]

IRELAND, JOHN (1761–1842), dean of Westminster; son of an Ashburton butcher; friend of William Gifford (1756–1826) [q. v.]; bible-clerk at Oriel College, Oxford, 1779; M.A., 1810; D.D., 1810; vicar of Croydon and chaplain to Lord Liverpool, 1793–1816; prebendary of Westminster, 1802, sub-dean, 1806, dean, 1816–42; rector of Islip, 1816–35; published 'Paganism and Christianity compared,' 1809; founded professorship of exegesis and (1825) classical scholarships at Oxford. [xxix. 30]

IRELAND, SAMUEL (d. 1800), author and engraver; etched plates after Mortimer, Hogarth, and Dutch masters; issued 'Graphic Illustrations of Hogarth' (2 vols. 1794, 1799), from pictures and prints in his collection, and 'Picturesque Tour through France, Holland, Brabant,' 1790, and a series of English 'Picturesque Views,' illustrated from his own drawings. Much of his correspondence respecting the Shakespearean forgeries of his son, William Henry Ireland [q. v.], is in British Museum. [xxix. 31]

IRELAND, alias IRONMONGER, WILLIAM (1636–1679), jesuit; educated at St. Omer; procurator of the province in London; tried and executed on testimony of Oates and Bedloe on charges connected with the 'Popish plot.' [xxix. 36]

IRELAND, WILLIAM HENRY (1777–1835), forger of Shakespeare manuscripts; son of Samuel Ireland [q. v.]; of doubtful legitimacy; partially educated in France; early impressed with story of Chatterton; had access to Elizabethan parchments at the lawyer's chambers in New Inn, where he was employed; forged deeds and signatures of or relating to Shakespeare, 1794–1795; made in feigned handwriting a transcript of 'Lear' and extracts from 'Hamlet'; deceived his father and many men of letters and experts, including Dr. Parr, Joseph Warton, and George Chalmers; fabricated in forged handwriting pseudo-Shakespearean plays, 'Vortigern and Rowena' and 'Henry II,' the former being produced unsuccessfully by Sheridan at Drury Lane, with Kemble in the cast, March, 1796; was caricatured by Gillray, 1797; authenticity of his documents attacked by Malone. On the failure of 'Vortigern' young Ireland left his father's house and made an avowal of his fraud ('Authentic Account'), afterwards expanded into 'Confessions' (1805, reissued, 1872); sold imitations of the forgeries; employed by publishers in London; lived some time in Paris; published ballads, narrative poems, romances, and other works of some literary merit. A collection of his forgeries destroyed by fire at Birmingham Library, 1879. Many specimens are in British Museum. [xxix. 32]

IRETON, HENRY (1611–1651), regicide; B.A. Trinity College, Oxford, 1629; of the Middle Temple; fought at Edgehill, 1642; Cromwell's deputy-governor of the Isle of Ely; as quartermaster-general in Manchester's army took part in Yorkshire campaign and second battle of Newbury, 1644; supported Cromwell's accusation of Manchester; surprised royalist quarters before Naseby, 1645; as commander of the cavalry of the left wing was wounded and captured in the battle, but afterwards escaped, 1645; at siege of Bristol, 1645; a negotiator of treaty of Truro, 1646; received overtures from Charles I at Oxford, 1646; married Bridget, Cromwell's daughter, 1646; M.P., Appleby, 1645; justified the army petition and consequently quarrelled with Holles, 1647; one of the four commissioners to pacify the soldiers; sanctioned

z

Joyce's removal of the king from Holdenby; drew up the 'engagement' of the army and 'Heads of the Army Proposals,' 1647, endeavouring to bring about an agreement between king and parliament; opposed the levellers' constitution and was denounced by them; led conservative party in the council of the army till the flight of Charles I to the Isle of Wight, after which he supported his deposition in favour of one of his sons; served under Fairfax in Kent and Essex, and as commissioner for the surrender of Colchester (1648) defended the execution of Lucas and Lisle; with Ludlow concerted 'Pride's Purge,' 1648; attended regularly the high court of justice and signed the warrant for Charles I's execution; chief author of the 'Agreement of the People' drawn up by the council of war, 1649; went to Ireland as Cromwell's second in command, 1649, and remained as his deputy; captured Carlow, Waterford, and Duncannon, 1650, and Limerick, 1651; died of fever before Limerick. He carried out the Cromwellian policy with indefatigable industry and honesty. He was buried in Westminster Abbey, but his body was disinterred and dishonoured after the Restoration. [xxix. 37]

IRETON, JOHN (1615–1689), lord mayor of London, 1658; brother of Henry Ireton [q. v.] [xxix. 42]

IRETON, RALPH (d. 1292), bishop of Carlisle; prior of Gisburne, 1261; elected to see of Carlisle, 1278, but not confirmed by the king and archbishop till after a visit to Rome, where he was consecrated; accused of great extortions in chronicle of Lanercost; with Antony Bek I or II [q. v.] negotiated treaty of Brigham, 1290. [xxix. 43]

IRLAND, BONAVENTURE (1551–1612?), professor of law at Poitiers; son of Robert Irland [q. v.]; wrote 'Remontrances au roi Henri III' and a philosophical treatise 'De Emphasi et Hypostasi,' 1599. [xxix. 44]

IRLAND, JOHN (fl. 1480), Scottish diplomatist; sent by Louis XI to Scotland on an anti-English mission, 1480; Scottish ambassador to France, 1484. [xxix. 44]

IRLAND, ROBERT (d. 1561), professor of law at Poitiers, 1502–61; went to France, c. 1496, and was naturalised, 1521. [xxix. 44]

IRONS, JOSEPH (1785–1852), evangelical preacher; minister of Grove Chapel, Camberwell, 1818–52. [xxix. 45]

IRONS, WILLIAM JOSIAH (1812–1883), theological writer; son of Joseph Irons [q. v.]; M.A. Queen's College, Oxford, 1835; D.D., 1854; vicar of Brompton, 1840–70; contributed (1862) to 'Replies to Essays and Reviews'; rector of Wadingham, Lincolnshire, 1870; of St. Mary Woolnoth, London, 1872–83; Bampton lecturer, 1870; published 'Analysis of Human Responsibility,' 1869; edited 'Literary Churchman'; translated 'Dies Iræ.' [xxix. 45]

IRONSIDE, EDWARD (1736?–1803), author of 'History and Antiquities of Twickenham,' 1797. [xxix. 45]

IRONSIDE, GILBERT, the elder (1588–1671), bishop of Bristol; of Trinity College, Oxford; fellow, 1613; M.A., 1612; D.D., 1660; rector of Winterbourne Steepleton, 1618, of Winterbourne Abbas, 1629; bishop of Bristol, 1661–71. [xxix. 46]

IRONSIDE, GILBERT, the younger (1632–1701), bishop of Bristol and Hereford; son of Gilbert Ironside the elder [q. v.]; M.A. Wadham College, Oxford, 1655; D.D., 1666; fellow, 1656; warden of Wadham College, Oxford, 1667–92; as vice-chancellor, 1687–9, resisted James II; bishop of Bristol, 1689–91, of Hereford, 1691–1701. [xxix. 46]

IRVINE, SIR ALEXANDER, OF DRUM (d. 1658), royalist; sheriff of Aberdeen, 1634; aided Huntly in obtaining subscription to Charles I's covenant, 1638; assisted Montrose to capture Aberdeen, 1639; surrendered to General Monro and was fined and imprisoned, 1640–1; released, 1641; several times refused to subscribe the solemn league and covenant, and had to submit to plunder of Drum in 1645. [xxix. 47]

IRVINE, ALEXANDER, tenth LAIRD OF DRUM (d. 1687), royalist; son of Sir Alexander Irvine [q. v.]; outlawed and imprisoned as royalist, 1644–5; declined earldom of Aberdeen; married as second wife 'the weel-faured May' (Margaret Coutts) of the ballad. [xxix. 48]

IRVINE, ALEXANDER (1793–1873), botanist; opened school in Chelsea, 1851; accompanied by John Stuart Mill on botanical excursions; published 'London [so-called] Flora,' 1838, and 'Illustrated Handbook of British Plants,' 1858; edited 'Phytologist,' 1855–63. [xxix. 48]

IRVINE, CHRISTOPHER (fl. 1638–1685), physician and philologist; ejected from college of Edinburgh for refusing the covenant, 1638; surgeon in Charles II's camp, 1651, to Monck's army, 1653–60, and to horseguards, 1660–81; published 'Bellum Grammaticale,' 1658 (reprinted, 1698), 'Medicina Magnetica,' 1656, translations of medical works, and 'Historiæ Scoticæ nomenclatura Latino-vernacula,' 1682 (reprinted 1817 and 1819). [xxix. 49]

IRVINE, JAMES (1833–1889), Scottish portrait-painter; friend of George Paul Chalmers [q. v.]. [xxix. 50]

IRVINE, ROBERT (d. 1645), royalist; son of Sir Alexander Irvine [q. v.]. [xxix. 48]

IRVINE, WILLIAM (1743–1787), chemist; M.D. Glasgow; assisted Joseph Black [q. v.] in experiments on steam; professor of chemistry at Glasgow, 1770–87; his 'Essays, chiefly on Chemical Subjects,' published, 1805. [xxix. 50]

IRVINE, WILLIAM (1741–1804), American brigadier; born in Ireland; surgeon in British navy during seven years' war; settled in Pennsylvania; captured while commanding a regiment of infantry in Canada by the British, 1776; commanded 2nd Pennsylvanian brigade at Staten island and Bull's Ferry, 1780, and afterwards on western frontier; member of the continental congress, 1786; recommended purchase of 'The Triangle,' to give Pennsylvania an outlet on Lake Erie. [xxix. 50]

IRVINE, WILLIAM (1776–1811), physician to the forces; son of William Irvine (1743–1787) [q. v]; M.D. Edinburgh, 1798; L.R.C.P., 1806; published observations on diseases in Sicily, 1810; died at Malta. [xxix. 51]

IRVING, DAVID (1778–1860), biographer; M.A. Edinburgh, 1801; published 'Elements of English Composition,' 1801, 'Lives of the Scotish Poets,' 1804, 'Life of George Buchanan,' 1805 (enlarged 1817), and 'Introduction to Study of the Civil Law,' 1837; edited Selden's 'Table-Talk,' 1819, and other works; honorary LL.D. Aberdeen, 1808; librarian of the Faculty of Advocates, Edinburgh, 1820–48; his 'History of Scotish Poetry' edited by Dr. John Carlyle, 1861. [xxix. 51]

IRVING, EDWARD (1792–1834), founder of the 'Catholic Apostolic Church'; son of a tanner at Annan; M.A. Edinburgh, 1809; schoolmaster at Haddington, 1810–12, and afterwards at Kirkcaldy, where he became acquainted with Carlyle, 1816; assistant to Dr. Chalmers at St. John's, Glasgow, 1819–22; came to London, 1822, as minister at Hatton Garden Chapel, where his preaching soon made him famous; translated Aben Ezra's (Lacunza) 'Coming of the Messiah,' 1827; intimate with Henry Drummond (1786–1860) [q. v.]; built new church in Regent Square; issued 'Lectures on Baptism,' 1828; undertook preaching tour in Scotland, 1828; established the 'Morning Watch,' 1829; was compelled to retire from Regent Square on account of his approval of the 'tongues,' 1832; title of the 'Holy Catholic Apostolic Church' assumed by his followers, 1832; deprived, by presbytery of Annan, for heretical views in tract on the Incarnation, 1833; personally laid no claim to supernatural gifts; died at Glasgow. The Irvingite church in Gordon Square was built in 1854. [xxix. 52]

IRVING, GEORGE VERE (1815–1869), Scottish lawyer and antiquary. [xxix. 56]

IRVING, JOSEPH (1830–1891), author and journalist; edited Dumbarton 'Herald,' 1854; contributed to 'Morning Chronicle' and 'Glasgow Herald'; published 'History of Dumbartonshire,' 1857, 'Annals of our Time,' 1869, 'The Book of Eminent Scotsmen,' 1882, and other works. [xxix. 56]

IRVING, SIR PAULUS ÆMILIUS, first baronet (1751–1828), general; served with 47th foot in America and Canada; captured at Saratoga, 1777; commanded the regiment, 1783–94; major-general, 1794; captured La Vigie in St. Vincent, 1795; created baronet, 1809; general 1812. [xxix. 57]

IRWIN, EYLES (1751?–1817), traveller and author; superintendent of Madras, 1771; dismissed for protest against deposition of Lord Pigot, 1776; his journey to England narrated in 'Series of Adventures in the course of a Voyage up the Red Sea,' &c., 1780 (3rd edit. with suppl. 1787); returned to India, 1780, on reinstatement; revenue officer in Tinnevelly; commissary to negotiate for cession of Dutch settlements, 1785; in China, 1792–4; published poems, political tracts, and 'The Bedouins' (comic opera), 1802. [xxix. 57]

IRWIN, SIR JOHN (1728–1788), general; protegé of Lionel, duke of Dorset; correspondent of Lord Chesterfield; lieutenant-colonel of 5th foot, 1752; served with distinction under Ferdinand of Brunswick, 1760; major-general, 1762; M.P., East Grinstead, 1762–83; governor of Gibraltar, 1766–8; commander-in-chief in Ireland, 1775–82; K.B., 1779; favourite with George III; general, 1783; obliged by extravagance to retire to the continent; died at Parma. [xxix. 58]

ISAAC, SAMUEL (1815–1886), projector of the Mersey tunnel (opened, 1885); had previously, as army contractor, supplied the confederates during the American civil war (1861–5). [xxix. 60]

ISAACSON, HENRY (1581–1654), theologian and chronologer; of Pembroke Hall, Cambridge; friend of Bishop Andrewes; published 'Satvrni Ephemerides, sive Tabvla Historico-Chronologica,' 1633, a life of Bishop Andrewes, 1650, and other works. [xxix. 60]

ISAACSON, STEPHEN (1798–1849), author; B.A. Christ's College, Cambridge, 1820; translated Bishop Jewel's 'Apologia,' with life and preface, 1825, which involved him in controversy with Charles Butler (1750–1832) [q. v.], 1825–6; edited Henry Isaacson's life of Bishop Andrewes, 1829, with life of the author; rector of St. Paul's, Demerara; defended slave proprietors; published also devotional manuals and 'The Barrow Digger,' a poem. [xxix. 61]

ISABELLA (1214–1241), empress; daughter of John, king of England, and Isabella of Angoulême; married to the emperor Frederic II, 1235; kept in great seclusion; died at Foggia; buried at Andria; called by Matthew Paris 'the glory and hope of England.' [xxix. 62]

ISABELLA OF ANGOULÊME (d. 1246), queen of John, king of England; daughter of Aymer, count of Angoulême, by Alicia, granddaughter of Louis VI of France; betrothed to Hugh of Lusignan, but married to John, king of England, at Angoulême, 1200; crowned in England, 1201; inherited Angoumois, 1213; imprisoned at Gloucester, 1214; left England, 1217; married Hugh of Lusignan, her old lover, 1220; in alliance with her son (Henry III) made war on Alfonso, count of Poitou, and Louis IX of France, 1241; died at Fontevrand. [xxix. 63]

ISABELLA OF FRANCE (1292–1358), queen of England; daughter of Philip the Fair of France; married to Edward II at Boulogne, 1308; neglected by her husband for the sake of Piers Gaveston; helped to mediate between Edward II and the barons, 1313, 1316, and 1321; twice escaped capture by the Scots; deprived of her estates by influence of the Despensers, 1324; went to France, 1325, and formed connection with Roger Mortimer; raised troops in Germany and the Netherlands; landed in England with Mortimer, John of Hainault, and many exiles, 1326; having obtained the adhesion of London, advanced to Gloucester; joined by armies from the north and Welsh marches, executed the Despensers, deposed Edward II and had her eldest son proclaimed king as Edward III, 1327; procured her husband's murder, and with Mortimer virtually ruled England; made peace with France, 1327; renounced overlordship of Scotland for money, 1328; alienated the nobility by her own and Mortimer's rapacity, and execution of Edmund, earl of Kent; arrested with Mortimer at Nottingham by Lancaster, with the concurrence of Edward III, 1330; compelled to give up her riches, but allowed to live at various places in honourable confinement; took the habit of Santa Clara; buried in the Franciscan church, Newgate. [xxix. 64]

ISABELLA (1332–1379), eldest daughter of Edward III and Philippa; proposed as wife for Louis, count of Flanders, who was forced by his subjects to promise assent, but escaped before the day arranged for the ceremony, 1347; after failure of two other matches married

Enguerraud VII, lord of Coucy, then a hostage in England, 1365; lived in England during her six years' absence in Italy, and after his final renunciation of English allegiance. [xxix. 67]

ISABELLA OF FRANCE (1389–1409), second queen of Richard II; daughter of Charles VI of France; her marriage in 1396 the pledge of peace between England and France and the prelude to Richard's *coup d'état*; confined by Henry IV at Sonning and not allowed to see her husband, whose death was concealed from her; allowed to return to France, 1401, but her marriage portion withheld; married to Charles of Angoulême (afterwards Duke of Orleans), 1406; died in childbirth. [xxix. 68]

ISBISTER, ALEXANDER KENNEDY (1822–1883), educational writer; M.A. Edinburgh, 1858; LL.B. London, 1866; master of Stationers' Company's school, 1858–82; edited 'Educational Times' from 1862; barrister, Middle Temple, 1864; dean of College of Preceptors, 1872; published educational manuals. [xxix. 71]

ISCANUS, JOSEPHUS (*fl.* 1190). [See JOSEPH OF EXETER.]

ISHAM or **ISUM**, JOHN (1680?–1726), composer; Mus. Bac. Merton College, Oxford, 1713; organist of St. Anne's, Westminster, 1711, of St. Margaret's and St. Andrew's, Holborn, London, 1718–26; published (with William Morley) songs. [xxix. 71]

ISHAM, SIR JUSTINIAN, second baronet (1610–1674), royalist; of Christ's College, Cambridge; imprisoned as delinquent, 1649; forced to compound on succeeding to baronetcy, 1651; M.P., Northamptonshire, 1661–74; founded Lamport Hall library. [xxix. 72]

ISHAM, SIR THOMAS, third baronet (1657–1681), son of Sir Justinian Isham [q. v.]; his Latin diary translated and printed, 1875. [xxix. 72]

ISHAM, ZACHEUS (1651–1705), divine; M.A. Christ Church, Oxford, 1674; D.D., 1689; tutor to Sir Thomas Isham [q. v.]; chaplain to Bishop Compton, c. 1685; prebendary of St. Paul's, London, 1686; canon of Canterbury, 1691; rector of St. Botolph's, London, 1694, and of Solihull, 1701; published sermons. [xxix. 73]

ISLES, LORDS OF THE. [See SUMERLED, d. 1164; MACDONALD, JOHN, first LORD, d. 1386?; MACDONALD, DONALD, second LORD, d. 1420?; MACDONALD, ALEXANDER, third LORD, d. 1449; MACDONALD, JOHN, fourth LORD, d. 1498?]

ISLIP, JOHN (d. 1532), abbot of Westminster, 1500–1532; obtained removal of Henry VI's body from Windsor; built Henry VII's Chapel; privy councillor, 1513; trier of parliamentary petitions; signed letter to the pope in favour of the divorce, 1530; at Westminster raised western tower to level of the roof, filled niches with statues, and built mortuary chapel known by his name. [xxix. 73]

ISLIP, SIMON (d. 1366), archbishop of Canterbury; fellow of Merton College, Oxford, 1307, and doctor of canon and civil law; vicar-general of Lincoln, 1337; archdeacon of Canterbury, 1343–6; dean of arches; chaplain, secretary, and keeper of the privy seal to Edward III; ambassador to France, 1342; one of the regent's council, 1345; as archbishop (1349–66) issued a canon (1350) ordering chaplains to be content with salaries received before the Black Death; limited rights of friars in favour of secular clergy; arranged compromise with archbishop of York on right of northern primate to carry his cross erect in the southern province, 1353; maintained rights of Canterbury against the Prince of Wales, 1357; caused rejection of the king's demand of a clerical tenth for six years, 1356, and by his remonstrance helped to procure statute of 1362, against purveyance; founded at Oxford a college in connection with Christ Church, Canterbury, of mixed monks and seculars, 1361, of which Wycliffe the reformer may have been the second warden; his foundation monasticised, 1370, and afterwards absorbed in Wolsey's. [xxix. 74]

ISLWYN (1832–1878). [See THOMAS, WILLIAM.]

ISMAY, THOMAS HENRY (1837–1899), shipowner; apprenticed to a firm of shipbrokers in Liverpool, and subsequently started business independently; acquired White

Star line of Australian clippers, 1867; formed, with William Imrie, Oceanic Steamship Company, 1868; began to run steamers between Liverpool and America, 1871.
[Suppl. iii. 34]

ISRAEL, MANASSEH BEN (1604-1657). [See MANASSEH BEN ISRAEL.]

ITE (d. 569), Irish saint; sometimes called Mary of Munster; founded religious house at Cluaincreadhail (Killeedy in present co. Limerick); visited St. Comgan when dying. [xxix. 77]

IVE, PAUL (fl. 1602), writer on fortification; of Corpus Christi College, Cambridge. [xxix. 78]

IVE, SIMON (1600-1662), musician; eighth minor prebendary of St. Paul's, 1661; assisted the brothers Lawes in setting Shirley's 'Triumph of Peace,' 1634; composed vocal and instrumental works. [xxix. 78]

IVE or **IVY**, WILLIAM (d. 1485), theologian; fellow and lecturer at Magdalen College, Oxford; head-master of Winchester, 1444-54; D.D.; canon and (1470) chancellor of Salisbury; some time master of Whittington's College at St. Michael Royal, London; author of theological works. [xxix. 78]

IVERS, MARY ANN (1788-1849). [See ORGER, MARY ANN.]

IVES, EDWARD (d. 1786), naval surgeon and traveller; served on flagship of Vice-admiral Charles Watson [q. v.], 1753-7, and travelled home overland from India; published description of the campaign of 1755-7, and his own travels, 1773. [xxix. 79]

IVES, JEREMIAH (fl. 1653-1674), general baptist; ministered in Old Jewry; imprisoned, 1661; defended adult baptism, and published controversial tracts against quakers and sabbatarians. [xxix. 79]

IVES, JOHN (1751-1776), Suffolk herald extraordinary, 1774; F.S.A., 1771; F.R.S., 1772; published 'Select Papers chiefly relating to English Antiquities,' 1773-5.
[xxix. 80]

IVIE, EDWARD (1678-1745), author of 'Epicteti Enchiridion' in Latin verse, 1715 (reprinted by Simpson);

of Westminster and Christ Church, Oxford; M.A., 1702; vicar of Floore, 1717-45. [xxix. 81]

IVIMEY, JOSEPH (1773-1834), author of history of English baptists, 1811-30; pastor of particular baptist church, Eagle Street, Holborn, London, from 1805; first secretary of Baptist Missionary Society for Ireland; opposed catholic emancipation; published miscellaneous works. [xxix. 81]

IVO OF GRANTMESNIL (fl. 1101), crusader; son of Hugh of Grantmesnil [q. v.] [xxvii. 160]

IVOR HAEL, or the GENEROUS (d. 1361), patron of David ab Gwilym [q. v.] and other Welsh bards; lord of Maesaleg, Y Wenallt, and Gwernycleppa, Monmouthshire. [xxix. 82]

IVORY, SAINT (d. 500?). [See IBHAR or IBERIUS.]

IVORY, SIR JAMES (1765-1842), mathematician; of St. Andrews and Edinburgh universities; professor of mathematics at Royal Military College, Marlow, 1805-19; F.R.S., 1815: Copley medallist, 1814; received the royal medal, 1826 (for paper on refractions), and 1839 ('Theory of Astronomical Refractions'); enounced the 'Ivory Theorem,' 1809; knighted, 1831; received civil list pension.
[xxix. 82]

IVORY, JAMES, LORD IVORY (1792-1866), Scottish judge; nephew of Sir James Ivory [q. v.]; admitted advocate, 1816; advocate-depute, 1830; sheriff of Caithness, 1832, of Buteshire, 1833; solicitor-general for Scotland, 1839; lord of session, 1840; lord of justiciary, 1849-1866. [xxix. 83]

IVORY, THOMAS (1709-1779), architect; designed buildings at Norwich, including (1757) the theatre.
[xxix. 83]

IVORY, THOMAS (d. 1786), master of architectural drawing at Royal Dublin Society's schools, 1759-86; designed Blue Coat Hospital, Dublin. [xxix. 84]

IZACKE, RICHARD (1624?-1698), antiquary; of Exeter College, Oxford; barrister, Inner Temple, 1650; chamberlain (1653) and town-clerk of Exeter (c. 1682); wrote on antiquities of Exeter, 1677. [xxix. 84]

J

JACK, ALEXANDER (1805-1857), brigadier; educated at King's College, Aberdeen; with 30th Bengal native infantry at Aliwal, 1846; brigadier of the force sent against Kangra, 1846; commanded his battalion in second Sikh war; colonel, 1854; brigadier, 1856; treacherously shot at Cawnpore. [xxix. 85]

JACK, GILBERT (1578?-1628), metaphysical and medical writer; as professor of philosophy at Leyden, 1604-28, first taught metaphysics there; M.D. Leyden, 1611; published physical, metaphysical, and medical 'Institutiones.' [xxix. 85]

JACK, THOMAS (d. 1598), master of Glasgow grammar school, quæstor of the university (1577), and thrice member of general assembly; published dictionary of classical names in Latin verse, 1592. [xxix. 86]

JACK, WILLIAM (1795-1822), botanist and Bengal army surgeon; M.A. Aberdeen, 1811; his contributions to 'Malayan Miscellanies,' reprinted by Sir W. J. Hooker; genus *Jackia* named after him. [xxix. 86]

JACKMAN, ISAAC (fl. 1795), joint-editor of 'Morning Post,' 1786-95; author of farces and comic operas.
[xxix. 86]

JACKSON, ABRAHAM (1589-1646?), divine and author; B.A. Exeter College, Oxford, 1611; M.A. Christ Church, Oxford, 1616; prebendary of Peterborough, 1640.
[xxix. 87]

JACKSON, ARTHUR (1593?-1666), ejected divine; of Trinity College, Cambridge; rector of St. Michael's, Wood Street, London, and afterwards of St. Faith's under St. Paul's, London; fined and imprisoned for refusing to give evidence against Christopher Love [q. v.], 1651; presbyterian commissioner at Savoy conference, 1661; ejected, 1662; published exegetical works. [xxix. 87]

JACKSON, ARTHUR HERBERT (1852-1881), composer; professor of harmony and composition at Royal Academy of Music, 1878-81; published orchestral works and vocal and piano pieces. [xxix. 88]

JACKSON, BASIL (1795-1889), lieutenant-colonel; lieutenant, 1813; at St. Helena, 1815-21; captain, 1825; assistant-professor of fortification at East India Company's college, Addiscombe, 1835, and of military surveying, 1836-57; lieutenant-colonel, 1846; published work on military surveying. [Suppl. iii. 35]

JACKSON, CATHERINE HANNAH CHARLOTTE, LADY (d. 1891), authoress; daughter of Thomas Elliott of Wakefield; became second wife, 1856, of Sir George Jackson (1785-1861) [q. v.], whose diaries and letters she edited; published works relating to French society.
[Suppl. iii. 35]

JACKSON, CHARLES (1809-1882), antiquary; treasurer of Doncaster from 1838; published 'Doncaster Charities,' 1881; edited for Surtees Society 'Yorkshire Diaries and Autobiographies of 17th and 18th Centuries,' 1877. [xxix. 88]

JACKSON, CYRIL (1746-1819), dean of Christ Church, Oxford; educated at Westminster under Markham; student of Christ Church, Oxford, 1764; canon, 1779; M.A., 1771; D.D., 1781; sub-preceptor to elder sons of George III, 1771-6; preacher at Lincoln's Inn, 1779-83; as dean of Christ Church (1783-1809) had large share in 'Public Examination Statute'; declined offer of several bishoprics; helped to bring about retirement of Addington from premiership, 1804; his bust by Chantrey in Oxford Cathedral. [xxix. 88]

JACKSON, FRANCIS JAMES (1770-1814), diplomatist; son of Thomas Jackson (1745-1797) [q. v.]; secretary of legation at Berlin and Madrid, 1789-97; ambassador at Constantinople, 1796; plenipotentiary to France, 1801, Prussia, 1802–6, Washington, 1809–11; envoy to Denmark, 1807. [xxix. 90]

JACKSON, afterwards **DUCKETT**, SIR GEORGE, first baronet (1725–1822), secretary to navy board, 1758; second secretary to admiralty, 1766–82; judge-advocate of the fleet, 1766; present at court-martial (1778) on Keppel and Palliser; M.P., Weymouth and Melcombe, 1762–8, Colchester, 1790–6; created baronet, 1791; assumed name of Duckett, 1797; Port Jackson, New South Wales, and Point Jackson, New Zealand, named after him by Captain Cook. [xxix. 90]

JACKSON, SIR GEORGE (1785–1861), diplomatist; brother of Francis James Jackson [q. v.]; chargé d'affaires in Prussia, 1805–6; secretary of legation to John Hookham Frere [q. v.] in Spain, 1808–9; accompanied Sir Charles Stewart to Germany, 1813; minister at Berlin, 1814–15; secretary of embassy at St. Petersburg, 1816; special envoy to Madrid, 1822; commissioner at Washington, 1822–7; K.C.H., 1832; chief commissioner for abolition of slave trade at Rio de Janeiro, 1832–41, Surinam, 1841–5, St. Paul de Loando, 1845–59; his 'Diaries and Letters' issued, 1872–3. [xxix. 91]

JACKSON, HENRY (1586–1662), editor of Hooker's 'Opuscula'; friend and kinsman of Anthony à Wood; M.A. Corpus Christi College, Oxford, 1608; B.D., 1617; rector of Meysey Hampton, Gloucestershire, 1630–62; edited Hooker's minor works, 1612–13; supervised Stansby's reprints of Hooker (1618 and 1622); his own recension of the unpublished eighth book of the 'Ecclesiastical Polity' utilised by Keble; published also editions of 'Wickliffes Wicket,' 1612, and other works. [xxix. 91]

JACKSON, HENRY (1831–1879), author of 'Argus Fairbairn' (1874) and other novels. [xxix. 92]

JACKSON, JOHN (d. 1689?), organist of Wells Cathedral from 1676; composed anthems and chants. [xxix. 93]

JACKSON, JOHN (1686–1763), theological writer; B.A. Jesus College, Cambridge, 1707; denied M.A. degree, 1718, on account of his writings on the Trinity; rector of Rossington, Yorkshire, 1708; expressed Samuel Clarke's views on the Trinity after 1714; advocated Hoadly's position on church government; defended infant baptism; succeeded Clarke as master of Wigston's Hospital, Leicester, 1729; wrote treatises against the deists, and compiled 'Chronological Antiquities,' 1752. [xxix. 93]

JACKSON, JOHN (fl. 1761–1792), actor, manager, and dramatist; played leading parts at Edinburgh, 1761; under Garrick at Drury Lane, 1762–4, Dublin, 1765; appeared with his wife at the Haymarket, 1775, in his own 'Eldred' (1782), also at Covent Garden, 1776; managed theatres in Edinburgh, Glasgow, Dundee, and Aberdeen, 1782–90; again a manager, 1801–9; wrote 'History of the Scottish Stage,' published, 1793; none of his plays except 'Eldred' printed. [xxix. 95]

JACKSON, JOHN (d. 1807), traveller; F.S.A., 1787; published account of a journey from India overland, 1799; made excavations on site of Carthage and at Udena. [xxix. 96]

JACKSON, JOHN (1778–1831), portrait-painter; of humble origin; freed from apprenticeship by Lord Mulgrave and Sir George Beaumont; studied at Royal Academy with Haydon and Wilkie, and introduced them to his patrons; first exhibited, 1804; R.A., 1817; made sketching tour in Netherlands with General Phipps, 1816; travelled with Chantrey in Italy, 1819–20, painting a portrait of Canova and being elected to Academy of St. Luke; liberal to his Wesleyan co-religionists. Of his portraits those of Lady Dover and Flaxman are considered the best. He was also a skilful copyist. [xxix. 96]

JACKSON, JOHN (1769–1845), pugilist ('Gentleman Jackson'); champion of England, 1795–1803; afterwards kept a boxing-school in Bond Street, London, at which Byron was a pupil; referred to by Byron and Moore as a popular character. [xxix. 98]

JACKSON, JOHN (1801–1848), wood-engraver; apprenticed to Bewick; engraved Northcote's 'Fables' and illustrations for the 'Penny Magazine'; with William Andrew Chatto [q. v.] brought out an illustrated history of wood-engraving, 1839. [xxix. 98]

JACKSON, JOHN (1811–1885), bishop successively of Lincoln and London; scholar of Pembroke College, Oxford, 1829; B.A., 1833; Ellerton prizeman, 1834; headmaster of Islington proprietary school, 1836; Boyle lecturer, and vicar of St. James's, Piccadilly, London, 1853; bishop of Lincoln, 1853–68, of London, 1868–85; created diocese of St. Albans and suffragan bishopric of East London; contributed section on the pastoral epistles in the 'Speaker's Commentary,' and published religious works. [xxix. 99]

JACKSON, JOHN BAPTIST (1701–1780?), wood-engraver; worked under Papillon at Paris; during residence in Venice revived colour-engraving, publishing (1745) seventeen engravings of Venetian pictures; established manufactory of chiaroscuro paperhangings at Battersea; published 'Essay on the Invention of Engraving and Printing in Chiaroscuro' and its application to paperhanging, 1754. [xxix. 100]

JACKSON, JOHN EDWARD (1805–1891), antiquary; brother of Charles Jackson [q. v.]; M.A. Brasenose College, Oxford, 1830; vicar of Norton Coleparle, Wiltshire, 1846; librarian to Marquis of Bath; hon. canon of Bristol, 1855; published topographical monographs; edited Aubrey's Wiltshire collections, 1862. [xxix. 100]

JACKSON, JOHN RICHARDSON (1819–1877), engraver in mezzotint of portraits. [xxix. 101]

JACKSON, JOSEPH (1733–1792), letter-founder; while apprentice to the elder William Caslon [q. v.] clandestinely discovered the art of cutting the punches; some years in the navy; in Dorset Street, Salisbury Square, cut Hebrew, Persian, and Bengali letters, 1773; cut fount for Macklin's bible (1800), and another for Hume's history (1806). [xxix. 101]

JACKSON, JULIAN (wrongly called JOHN RICHARD) (1790–1853), colonel on the imperial Russian staff, and geographer; served in Bengal artillery, 1808–13; in Russian service with army of occupation in France; colonel on Russian staff, 1829; retired, 1830; secretary of Royal Geographical Society, 1841–7; F.R.S., 1845; published 'Guide du Voyageur,' 1822, reproduced as 'What to Observe,' 1841, and an edition (with translation) of La Vallée's 'Military Geography,' and other works. [xxix. 102]

JACKSON, LAURENCE (1691–1772), divine; fellow of Sidney Sussex College, Cambridge; M.A., 1716; B.D., 1723; prebendary of Lincoln, 1747; published religious works. [xxix. 103]

JACKSON, RANDLE (1757–1837), parliamentary counsel of the East India Company and the corporation of London; M.A. Exeter College, Oxford, 1793; barrister, Middle Temple, 1793; bencher, 1828. [xxix. 103]

JACKSON, RICHARD (fl. 1570), reputed author of the ballad on Flodden Field (first printed, 1664); B.A. Clare Hall, Cambridge, 1570; master of Ingleton school, Yorkshire. [xxix. 103]

JACKSON or **KUERDEN**, RICHARD (1623–1690?), antiquary; B.A. Emmanuel College, Cambridge, 1642; M.A. and vice-principal of St. Mary Hall, Oxford, 1646; M.D., 1663; friend of Dugdale; left materials for history of Lancashire. [xxix. 104]

JACKSON, RICHARD (1700–1782), founder of Jacksonian professorship at Cambridge; M.A. Trinity College, Cambridge, 1731 (incorporated at Oxford, 1739); fellow. [xxix. 104]

JACKSON, RICHARD (d. 1787), politician ('Omniscient Jackson'); barrister, Lincoln's Inn, 1744, bencher, 1770, reader, 1779, treasurer, 1780; counsel to South Sea Company and Cambridge University; law officer to board of trade; M.P., Weymouth, 1762–8, New Romney, 1768–84; secretary to George Grenville, 1765; F.S.A., 1781; a lord of the admiralty, 1782–3. [xxix. 104]

JACKSON, ROBERT (1750–1827), inspector-general of army hospitals; assistant-surgeon in Jamaica, 1774–80; afterwards served in 71st regiment; studied at Paris; M.D. Leyden, 1786; surgeon to the buffs in Holland and West Indies, 1793–9; overthrew monopoly of College of Physicians in army medical appointments, 1803–9; medical director in West Indies, 1811–15; published 'Systematic View of the Formation, Discipline, and Economy of Armies,' 1804, and treatises on febrile diseases. [xxix. 105]

JACKSON, afterwards **SCORESBY-JACKSON**, ROBERT EDMUND (1835–1867), nephew and biographer of William Scoresby (1789–1857) [q. v.]; M.D. Edinburgh, 1857; F.R.C.S., 1861; F.R.C.P. and F.R.S.E., 1862; physician to Edinburgh Royal Infirmary and lecturer in Surgeons' Hall; published 'Medical Climatology,' 1862, and 'Notebook on Materia Medica, etc.' 1866.   [xxix. 106]

JACKSON, SAMUEL (1786–1861), president of Wesleyan conference, 1847; brother of Thomas Jackson (1783–1873) [q. v.]   [xxix. 109]

JACKSON, SAMUEL (1794–1869), landscape-painter; Associate of the Society of Painters in Water-colours, 1823; founded Bristol sketching society, 1833.   [xxix. 106]

JACKSON, THOMAS (1579–1640), president of Corpus Christi College, Oxford, and dean of Peterborough; fellow of Corpus Christi College, Oxford, 1606; M.A., 1603; D.D., 1622; incumbent of St. Nicholas, Newcastle, 1623, and Winston, Durham, 1625; president of Corpus Christi College, Oxford, 1630–40; attacked by Prynne; dean of Peterborough, 1639–40; highly praised by Pusey; author of 'Commentaries on the Apostles' Creed' (twelve books, three posthumous); collective works issued, 1672–3 and 1844.   [xxix. 107]

JACKSON, THOMAS (d. 1646), prebendary of Canterbury, 1614–46; M.A., 1600, and B.D., 1608, Christ's College, Cambridge; D.D. Emmanuel College, Cambridge, 1615; published sermons.   [xxix. 108]

JACKSON, THOMAS (1745–1797), prebendary of Westminster, 1782–92, and canon of St. Paul's, 1792; M.A. Christ Church, Oxford, 1770; D.D., 1783.
                              [xxix. 90]

JACKSON, THOMAS (1783–1873), Wesleyan minister; itinerant preacher; editor of the connexional magazine, 1824–42; president of conference, 1838–9, and 1849; divinity professor at Richmond College, 1842–61; published life of Charles Wesley, 1841, and other religious biographies, and 'The Centenary of Wesleyan Methodism,' 1839; edited John Wesley's 'Works,' 1829–31, and 'Journals,' 1864; 'Journals, etc.,' of Charles Wesley, 1849; his 'Collection of Christian Biography' published, 1837–40; his 'Recollections' edited by Rev. Benjamin Frankland, 1873.   [xxix. 108]

JACKSON, THOMAS (1812–1886), divine and author; son of Thomas Jackson (1783–1873) [q. v.]; of St. Mary Hall, Oxford, where he wrote 'Uniomachia'; M.A., 1837; principal of Battersea training college, 1844; prebendary of St. Paul's, London, 1850; nominated to see of Lyttelton, New Zealand, 1850, but not consecrated; rector of Stoke Newington, 1852–86; published miscellaneous works.   [xxix. 109]

JACKSON, WILLIAM (1737?–1795), Irish revolutionist; preacher at Tavistock Chapel, Drury Lane, London; when secretary to the Duchess of Kingston satirised by Foote as Dr. Viper; induced Foote's ex-coachman to make an infamous charge against him; whig editor of the 'Public Ledger' and 'Morning Post'; while in France commissioned to ascertain probable success of a French invasion of England and Ireland; betrayed by Duchess of Kingston's attorney, and charged with treason in Dublin, 1794; defended by Curran and Ponsonby; died in the dock, probably from poison supplied by his wife.
                              [xxix. 110]

JACKSON, WILLIAM (1730–1803), musical composer ('JACKSON OF EXETER'); organist and lay vicar of Exeter Cathedral, 1777–1803; friend of the Sheridans, Samuel Rogers, Wolcot, and Gainsborough; composed 'The Lord of the Manor' (Drury Lane, 1780) and the 'Metamorphosis,' 1783 (two operas); set 'Lycidas,' 1767, Warton's 'Ode to Fancy,' and Pope's 'Dying Christian to his Soul'; composed madrigals, songs, services, and other musical works; published miscellaneous works; posthumous compositions issued, 1819.   [xxix. 111]

JACKSON, WILLIAM (1751–1815), bishop of Oxford; brother of Cyril Jackson [q. v.]; of Westminster and Christ Church, Oxford; M.A., 1775; D.D., 1799; chancellor's medallist, 1770; regius professor of Greek at Oxford, 1783; preacher at Lincoln's Inn, 1783; dean of Wells, 1799; canon of Christ Church, 1799; bishop of Oxford, 1812–15.   [xxix. 112]

JACKSON, WILLIAM (1815–1866), musical composer; of Masham, Yorkshire; when a boy worked as a miller; music-seller in Bradford, 1852; organist to St. John's

Church, Bradford; conducted the Church Union and the Festival Choral Society from 1856; composed oratorios 'Deliverance of Israel from Babylon,' 1844–5, and 'Isaiah,' 1851; 'The Year' (cantata), 1859; with glees and other works.   [xxix. 112]

JACOB, ARTHUR (1790–1874), oculist; M.D. Edinburgh, 1814; while demonstrator of anatomy at Trinity College, Dublin, discovered (1816, announced, 1819) a membrane of the eye; Dublin professor of anatomy, 1826–69; thrice president of Irish College of Surgeons; edited 'Dublin Medical Press,' 1839–59; published treatises on inflammation of the eyeball (1849) and on removal of cataract by absorption.   [xxix. 113]

JACOB, BENJAMIN (1778–1829), organist; organist at Salem Chapel, Soho, at age of ten; chorister at Handel commemoration, 1791; organist at Surrey Chapel, 1794–1825; gave public recitals with the elder Wesley, Crotch, and Salomon the violinist; published settings of Dr. Watts's 'Divine and Moral Songs,' c. 1800. [xxix. 113]

JACOB, EDWARD (1710?–1788), antiquary and naturalist.   [xxix. 114]

JACOB, EDWARD (d. 1841), editor (1821–3 and 1828) of chancery reports; son of William Jacob [q. v.]; fellow of Caius College, Cambridge; senior wrangler and first Smith's prizeman, 1816; M.A., 1819; barrister, Lincoln's Inn, 1819; K.C., 1834.   [xxix. 123]

JACOB, SIR GEORGE LE GRAND (1805–1881), major-general in the Indian army; son of John Jacob (1765–1840) [q. v.]; entered 2nd Bombay native infantry, 1820; political agent in Kattywar, 1839–43, Sawunt Warree, 1845–51, Cutch, 1851–9; lieutenant-colonel, 31st Bombay native infantry, 1853; commanded native light battalion in Persia, 1857; put down the mutiny at Kolapore, 1857; special commissioner of South Mahratta country, 1857–1859; retired as major-general, 1861; C.B., 1859; K.C.S.I., 1869; early transcriber of Asoka inscriptions; published 'Western India before and during the Mutiny,' 1871.
                              [xxix. 114]

JACOB, GILES (1686–1744), compiler of the 'Poetical Register' (1719–20), and 'New Law Dictionary' (1729); introduced in the 'Dunciad.'   [xxix. 116]

JACOB, HENRY (1563–1624), early congregationalist; M.A. St. Mary Hall, Oxford, 1586; precentor of Corpus Christi College, Oxford; retired with Brownists to Holland, 1593; again compelled to take refuge in Holland, 1598; collected congregation at Middelburg; afterwards joined John Robinson (1575–1625) [q. v.]; established in Southwark first congregational church, 1616; formed settlement in Virginia, 1622; died in London; published controversial works.   [xxix. 117]

JACOB, HENRY (1608–1652), philologist; son of Henry Jacob (1563–1624) [q. v.]; B.A. and (1629–48) fellow of Merton College, Oxford; authorship of Dickinson's 'Delphi Phœnicizantes' attributed to him by Wood.
                              [xxix. 118]

JACOB, HILDEBRAND (1693–1739), poet; published 'The Curious Maid,' 1721, 'The Fatal Constancy' (tragedy), 1723, and other poems, collected in 1735.
                              [xxix. 118]

JACOB, SIR HILDEBRAND, fourth baronet (d. 1790), Hebrew scholar; son of Hildebrand Jacob [q. v.]
                              [xxix. 118]

JACOB, JOHN (1765–1840), Guernsey topographer; son of Edward Jacob (1710?–1788) [q. v.]   [xxix. 114]

JACOB, JOHN (1812–1858), brigadier-general; cousin of Sir George le Grand Jacob [q. v.]; commanded artillery in Billamore's Cutchee expedition, 1834–40; published memoir of the campaign, 1852; given command of Scinde irregular horse and political charge of Eastern Cutchee by Outram, 1841; led his regiment with great distinction at Meanee, 1843, Shah-dad-poor, and other battles; political superintendent of Upper Scinde, 1847; C.B., 1850; Jacobabad named after him by Dalhousie to commemorate his pacification of the country, 1851; negotiated treaty with khan of Khelat, 1854; acting commissioner in Scinde, 1856; commanded cavalry under Outram in Persia, 1857; raised 'Jacob's Rifles' (infantry), 1858, armed with rifle and bullet of his own invention; died suddenly at Jacobabad. He published letter to Napier's attack in his 'Conquest of Sind' on Outram, 'Rifle Practice with Plates,' 1855, and several works on the re-organisation of the Indian army.   [xxix. 119]

JACOB, JOSEPH (1667 ?–1722), congregational divine; preacher at Parish Street, Southwark (1698–1702), Turners' Hall, Philpot Lane, and Curriers' Hall, London Wall, London. [xxix. 121]

JACOB, JOSHUA (1805 ?–1877), sectary; disowned by Society of Friends, 1838; founded the 'White Quakers' at Dublin, 1843; imprisoned for contempt of court in connection with chancery suit; established community at Newlands, Clondalkin, 1849. [xxix. 121]

JACOB, ROBERT (d. 1588), physician to Queen Elizabeth; fellow of Trinity College, Cambridge; M.A., 1573; M.D. Basle (incorporated at Cambridge, 1579); attended the tsarina, 1581; F.R.C.P., 1586; died abroad.
[xxix. 122]

JACOB, WILLIAM (1762 ?–1851), statistical writer; F.R.S., 1807; M.P., Rye, 1808–12; comptroller of corn returns, 1822–42; wrote on the corn trade, corn laws, and precious metals, and published 'Travels in Spain,' 1811.
[xxix. 122]

JACOB, WILLIAM STEPHEN (1813–1862), astronomer; brother of John Jacob (1812–1858) [q. v.]; some years in Bombay engineers; director of Madras Observatory, 1848–59; discovered triplicity of ν Scorpii, 1847; catalogued 244 double stars observed at Poonah; reobserved and corrected 317 stars from 'British Association Catalogue'; F.R.A.S., 1849; noticed transparency of Saturn's dusky ring, 1852; died at Poonah.
[xxix. 123]

JACOBSEN, THEODORE (d. 1772), architect; designed Foundling Hospital (1742) and the Haslar Hospital, Gosport. [xxix. 124]

JACOBSON, WILLIAM (1803–1884), bishop of Chester; educated at Homerton nonconformist college, Glasgow University, and Lincoln College, Oxford; B.A. Oxford, 1827; fellow of Exeter College, Oxford, 1829; M.A., 1829; vice-principal of Magdalen Hall, 1830; public orator, 1842; regius professor of divinity, 1848; bishop of Chester, 1865–84; published editions of the Patres Apostolici,' 1838, 1840, 1847, 1863, works of Bishop Robert Sanderson, 1854, and Nowell's 'Catechismus,' 1835. [xxix. 124]

JACOMBE, SAMUEL (d. 1659), puritan divine; fellow, Queens' College, Cambridge, 1648; B.D., 1644; incumbent of St. Mary Woolnoth, London, 1655.
[xxix. 126]

JACOMBE, THOMAS (1622–1687), nonconformist divine; brother of Samuel Jacombe [q. v.]; fellow of Trinity College, Cambridge, 1646; M.A., 1647; incumbent of St. Martin's, Ludgate Hill, London, 1647–62; a trier, 1659; commissioner for review of the prayer-book, 1661; imprisoned for holding conventicles in Silver Street, but protected by Countess-dowager of Exeter; published sermons. [xxix. 125]

JAENBERT, JANBRIHT, JAMBERT, GENG-BERHT, LAMBERT, or **LANBRIHT** (d. 791), archbishop of Canterbury; abbot of St. Augustine's, 760; archbishop of Canterbury, 766–91; deprived of much of his jurisdiction after Offa's conquest of Kent, Lichfield being made a metropolitan see. [xxix. 126]

JAFFRAY, ALEXANDER (1614–1673), director of the chancellary of Scotland; bailie of Aberdeen and its representative in Scottish parliament, 1644–50; commissioner for suppressing royalist rising, 1644, and for treating with Charles II, 1649–50; wounded and captured at Dunbar, 1650; as provost of Aberdeen negotiated with Monck, 1651; director of chancellary, 1652–60; member of Little parliament, 1653–4; joined independents, and, in 1661, the quakers; his 'Diary' printed by John Barclay, 1833. [xxix. 127]

JAFFRAY, ANDREW (1650–1726), quaker minister; son of Alexander Jaffray [q. v.] [xxix. 128]

JAGO, JAMES (1815–1893), physician; B.A. St. John's College, Cambridge, 1839; incorporated at Wadham College, Oxford, 1843; M.D. Oxford, 1859; practised in Truro; F.R.S., 1870; published medical works.
[Suppl. iii. 36]

JAGO, RICHARD (1715–1781), poet; friend of Shenstone and Somerville; M.A. University College, Oxford, 1739; vicar of Snitterfield, 1754–81, and Kimcote, 1771–81; his poems in Chalmers's, Anderson's, Park's, and Davenport's collections. [xxix. 128]

JAMES the CISTERCIAN or JAMES the ENGLISHMAN (fl. 1270), first professor of philosophy and theology in Lexington's college at Paris. [xxix. 129]

JAMES I (1394–1437), king of Scotland; third son of Robert III; placed under guardianship of Henry Wardlaw at St. Andrews, 1403; captured while on his way to France by an English ship, probably in 1406; detained in England nineteen years and well educated, but confined first in the Tower, afterwards at Nottingham and Evesham, and, on accession of Henry V, at Windsor, accompanying that king to France in 1420; released, 1423, on condition of his paying a ransom, withdrawing Scottish troops from France, and marrying an English wife; married Jane [q. v.], daughter of the Earl of Somerset, 1424; returned to Scotland and was crowned, 1424; twenty-seven acts passed in his first parliament, 1424, by the lords of the articles, including confirmation of the privileges of the church, prohibition of private war, and measures strengthening the royal authority, granting the customs to the king, and appointing officers to administer justice to the Commons (the statute-book dates from this parliament); registration of titles to land, parliamentary attendance of prelates, barons and freeholders, punishment of heretics by the secular arm, regulation of weights and measures, and a central judicial court provided for by parliament of 1425–6. James I had the late regent Albany and his chief adherents tried and executed for misgovernment, 1425; summoned a parliament at Inverness, reducing the highlands to order, 1427; concluded marriage treaty with France, 1428; renewed truce with England, 1429; made commercial treaty with Flanders, 1429; put down heresy, but reformed clerical abuses and resisted the demands of popes Martin V and Eugenius IV; defeated the Lord of the Isles, 1429; imported cannon from Flanders, 1430; sent representatives to council of Basle, 1433; sent the Princess Margaret to marry the dauphin, 1436; held a parliament at Edinburgh; was murdered at Perth by Sir Robert Graham and conspirators in his own household; buried in the convent of the Carthusians. In spite of his premature attempt to reform the Scottish constitution on the English model he left the monarchy stronger, and improved Scotland's position in Europe. His poem, 'The Kingis Quair,' composed in England, was discovered and printed by Lord Woodhouselee, 1783; other works have also been attributed to him. He was nominal founder and great benefactor of St. Andrews University. [xxix. 129]

JAMES II (1430–1460), king of Scotland; son of James I [q. v.]; crowned at Holyrood, 1437; removed by queen-mother to Stirling, 1439, but kidnapped and brought back to Edinburgh by Sir William Crichton [q. v.]; regained liberty with help of William Douglas, eighth earl of Douglas [q. v.], and Sir Alexander Livingstone [q. v.], 1443; captured Edinburgh Castle, 1445; married Mary of Gueldres, 1449; had Livingstone and his family tried and executed, 1450; re-enacted in parliament of 1450 statutes of James I; proclaimed a general peace, 1450, and afforded protection to tillers of the soil; stabbed Douglas at Stirling, 1452, and wasted his lands, on discovery of the confederacy of Douglas, Crawford, and Ross; forced James, new earl of Douglas, to submit, his brothers being defeated at Arkinholm, 1455; attainted the Douglases, 1455; annexed the Douglas, Crawford, and other estates to the crown, 1455; proposed joint action with France against England; ravaged Northumberland, 1456, but concluded a two years' truce with Henry VI, afterwards prolonged, 1457; pacified the highlands; strengthened the crown by marriages of his sisters with a Gordon and a Douglas, 1458; appointed supreme central court to meet at Edinburgh, Perth, and Aberdeen, and established annual circuits of the justiciary court in his parliament of 1458, the burgh courts also being reformed in the interests of the people, and the coinage re-established; favoured the Lancastrians, and received Queen Margaret and her son after the battle of Northampton, 1460; killed by accident while besieging Roxburgh Castle; buried at Holyrood. [xxix. 136]

JAMES III (1451–1488), king of Scotland; son of James II [q. v.]; crowned at Kelso, 1460; during his minority Henry VI received, Berwick acquired, and truce with England prolonged; his person seized by Sir Alexander Boyd, 1466; his marriage with Margaret of Denmark, and the cession of Orkney and Shetland, arranged,

1468–9 ; threw off the Boyds and assumed power, 1469 ; reduced the highlands by submission of Ross, 1475, and procured archiepiscopal pall for Scotland ; alienated the nobles by partiality to favourites ; attacked by an English army, Albany, his own brother, being in the English camp, 1482, when his forces mutinied, hanged the favourite, Robert Cochrane [q. v.], and imprisoned him in Edinburgh Castle, Berwick being finally retaken by the English, 1482 ; reconciled with Albany, who, however, continued his intrigues with England till driven abroad after the unsuccessful raid of Lochmaben, where Douglas was captured, 1484 ; was attacked anew owing to his extravagance and choice of fresh favourites by the lowland nobles, including Angus, Gray, and Hume, who put the king's eldest son at their head ; was defeated at Sauchieburn and murdered ; buried at Cambuskenneth. His portrait is in the altar-piece at Holyrood.   [xxix. 141]

JAMES IV (1473–1513), king of Scotland ; son of James III [q. v.] ; crowned at Scone, 1488 ; did penance for his father's death, but revoked grants made by him ; crushed the rebellion of Lennox, Lyle, and Forbes, 1489 ; provided for defence of the east coast against English pirates and fostered the navy ; passed acts for musters of the forces in each shire and legal reforms, 1491 ; visited the western isles, 1493–5, and began his pilgrimages to Whithern and St. Duthac's ; received Perkin Warbeck [q. v.] and married him to Lady Katherine Gordon, 1495 ; made border raids in Warbeck's favour, 1496–7, but carried on negotiations with the Spanish and French, who endeavoured to detach him from Warbeck ; having made a truce for seven years with England and strengthened his hold over the west, agreed to treaty of marriage with Margaret, daughter of Henry VII, in 1502 ; married Margaret, 1503 ; crushed rising of Donald Dubh in the west ; introduced royal law into the isles ; instituted a daily council to hear civil cases at Edinburgh, confirmed burgh privileges, secured fixity of tenure by the 'feu' statutes, and revoked acts prejudicial to crown and church, 1504 ; assisted Denmark against the Swedes and Hanse league, 1507 and 1508 ; sent embassy to Venice, 1506 ; favoured English alliance while Henry VII lived, in spite of the national opposition ; was asked to enter the league of Cambrai and consulted as to the marriage of Louis XII of France, 1508 ; sided with Louis XII against the Holy league, 1511 ; signed treaty with France, 1512, and sent fleet to help Louis against Henry VIII ; invaded Northumberland with a large force ; took Norham and smaller castles, but was outgeneralled by Surrey and defeated and slain at Flodden with the flower of his nation, 1513 ; left several natural children. He was a wise legislator and a good diplomatist. He encouraged education, patronised men of letters, and dabbled in astrology and surgery.
[xxix. 145]

JAMES V (1512–1542), king of Scotland ; son of James IV [q. v.] ; taken by his mother to Stirling, but brought to Edinburgh after her surrender to the regent Albany, 1515 ; educated by Gavin Dunbar (d. 1547) [q. v.], John Bellenden [q. v.], David Lindsay [q. v.], and James Inglis [q. v.] ; carried off to Edinburgh by the queenmother and the English party, 1524, and proclaimed competent to rule, 1524 ; under control of Angus, 1525–8 ; prompted by James Beaton (d. 1539) [q. v.], escaped from Falkland, caused parliament to forfeit the Douglas estates, captured Tantallon and compelled Angus to fly to England, 1528 ; pacified western isles ; aided by clergy and Commons crushed power of nobles ; established college of justice, 1532 ; carried on border raids till peace of 1534 ; was offered choice of German and French princesses for his wife ; received cap and sword of most favoured son of the church and title of 'defender of the faith' from Paul III, 1537 ; married Madeleine, daughter of Francis I, in France, 1537 ; on the death of Madeleine married Mary of Guise, 1538, having meanwhile executed conspirators of the Angus family ; persecuted heretics, but forced some reforms on the church, and inspired Buchanan's works against the friars ; refused to follow English advice to support the Reformation ; accompanied the fleet, which extorted submission of western isles, 1540 ; annexed to the crown all the isles, and the lands of the Douglases, Crawfords, and other nobles ; refused Henry VIII's demand for a conference, 1541 ; and, after forbidding the discontented barons to cross the borders, collected a force on the west marches ; placed Oliver Sinclair in command instead of Lord Maxwell, the warden ; on hearing of the rout at Solway Moss, 1542, died at Falkland ; buried at

Holyrood ; was succeeded by Mary Queen of Scots, his only legitimate daughter. Among his natural children were the regent Moray and the father of Francis Stewart Hepburn, fifth earl of Bothwell [q. v.] ; their legitimation by the pope precipitated the Reformation. His popularity with the people earned him the name of 'king of the commons.'
[xxix. 153]

JAMES VI, king of Scotland, afterwards **JAMES I**, king of England (1566–1625) ; son of Mary Queen of Scots, and Henry Stewart, lord Darnley [q. v.] ; crowned on his mother's abdication, 1567 ; entrusted to Mar and afterwards to Sir Alexander Erskine ; well educated under George Buchanan (1506–1582) [q. v.] ; nominally king on first fall of Morton, 1578 ; under influence of Lennox (Esmé Stuart) sanctioned Morton's execution, 1581 ; seized by protestant nobles at the Raid of Ruthven, 1582, and compelled to proscribe Lennox and Arran, to reverse their policy, and to submit to the clergy ; escaped from Falkland to St. Andrews, and took refuge with Argyll and Huntly, 1583 ; recalled Arran, imprisoned Andrew Melville [q. v.], and drove the protestant lords into England ; made overtures to the Guises and the pope, 1584 ; allowed Arran to procure Gowrie's execution and obtain control of the government ; forced by his concern for protestantism and return of the banished raiders to conclude treaty of Berwick (1586) with England, receiving pension from Elizabeth ; made formal protests and intercessions for his mother, but was incensed at being disinherited by her in favour of Philip II ; quickly reconciled himself to his mother's execution in February 1587 ; married Anne of Denmark in Norway, 1589 ; consented to act annulling jurisdiction of the bishops, 1592 ; intrigued with Spain and Parma ; appointed the Octavians to improve the revenue (1596) ; provoked clergy by recalling northern earls from exile, 1596 ; made proclamation for removal of the courts of justice, after tumult in Edinburgh caused by his expulsion of discontented presbyterians, 1596 ; at the general assemblies of Perth and Dundee (1597) obtained limitation of clerical interference, but agreed to confer with clerical commissioners on church affairs ; his proposals for the appointment of parliamentary representatives rejected by further conferences, three bishops only being appointed to seats (1600) ; his relations with the clergy again embittered after failure of the Gowrie conspiracy, 1600 ; before his accession to the English throne (1603) engaged in further intrigues with Rome and secret correspondence with Robert Cecil and others ; after accession made peace with Spain, 1604, and dismissed and imprisoned Ralegh ; called the Hampton Court conference for discussion of puritan objections to the liturgy, 1604 ; issued proclamation (1604) banishing Romanist priests ; after the Gunpowder plot sanctioned a severe recusancy act (1606), but modified it in favour of Romanists who rejected papal power of deposition, 1606 ; thwarted by parliament in his scheme of a union of Great Britain, but obtained from the judges a decision in favour of the post-nati, 1608 ; made defensive league with Dutch republic, 1608 ; joined France in negotiating truce between it and Spain, 1609 ; attempted to secure peace by alliance with catholic powers, 1609 ; carried on controversy with Bellarmine on the papal power ; ordered cessation of common law 'prohibitions' against ecclesiastical courts, 1609 ; obtained decision (1606) in favour of the right to levy 'impositions,' but agreed to abandon the heaviest of them, 1610 ; dissolved his first parliament after failure of negotiations concerning the great contract, 1611 ; treated with Spain and Tuscany for the marriage of his eldest son, but betrothed the Princess Elizabeth to the leader of the German protestants, making defensive treaty with the protestant union, 1611 ; obtained introduction of episcopacy into Scotland, 1610 ; favoured plantation of Ulster with English and Scotsmen ; instituted order of baronets, 1611 ; dissolved second parliament almost immediately, 1614, imprisoning four members ; obtained a benevolence ; consulted the judges separately on Peacham's case, 1615 ; had to submit to condemnation of his favourite Somerset (Robert Carr), 1616 ; renewed negotiations with Spain, 1617 ; reduced independence of Scottish clergy by appointment of bishops as 'constant moderators' and raising of stipends conditionally on their acceptance of Articles of Perth (1618) ; executed Ralegh to please Spain, 1618 ; refused to support ambitious schemes of his son-in-law Frederick, the elector palatine, 1619 ; on advice of Buckingham agreed to redress grievances complained of in his third parliament, and consented to Bacon's condemnation (1621), but held his own in case of Edward Floyd [q. v.] ; dissolved parliament and punished leading members, 1622 ; continued negotiations with Spain, agreeing to relieve the English catholics, 1623, but on the failure of Charles's and Buckingham's mission to Spain was compelled by them to break off the marriage treaty, allow impeachment of Middlesex and Bristol, 1624, and consent to a French marriage, with a provision for religious liberty of the catholics, 1624 ; failed in attempts on behalf of the Palatinate ; buried in Westminster Abbey. Conciliation was the keynote of James I's policy. His chief works were 'Basilikon Doron' (1599), 'True Law of Free Monarchies' (1603), and 'Apology for the Oath of Allegiance' (1607). Collected works published, 1616. Portraits of him are in the National Portrait Gallery.   [xxix. 161]

JAMES II (1633–1701), king of England ; second son of Charles I ; created Duke of York ; handed over to parliament after the surrender of Oxford, 1646 ; escaped to Holland, 1648 ; went to Paris, 1649 ; left Paris for Holland, 1650 ; after battle of Worcester (1651) entered French service as a volunteer, and distinguished himself under Turenne against the Fronde and its allies, 1652-5 ; took service with the Spanish in Flanders, 1657 ; in command of fleet at Cromwell's death, 1658 ; secretly contracted himself to Anne Hyde [q. v.] at Breda, 1659 ; created lord high admiral, 1660 ; received revenues of the post-office, 1663 ; dissuaded disbandment of the troops after Venner's rising, 1661 ; as head of the admiralty reconstituted the board, and issued 'Instructions,' 1662, which remained in force till beginning of nineteenth century, and memoirs of naval affairs, 1660-73 ; governor of the Royal Africa Company, c. 1664 ; received patent of New York (New Amsterdam), 1664 ; commanded fleet in first Dutch war, winning battle of Solebay, 1665, but failed to complete the victory ; defended Clarendon in House of Lords ; estranged from Charles II, but early entered into his French policy ; probably became Roman catholic soon after treaty of Dover (1670) ; won victory of Southwold Bay over De Ruyter, 1672 ; ceased to be high admiral after passing of the Test Act, 1673 ; his second marriage (1673) with Mary Beatrice of Modena (a catholic) censured by House of Commons ; became increasingly unpopular after discovery of the correspondence with Père La Chaise ; at Charles II's request, withdrew to the Hague, and afterwards to Brussels, 1679, the first Exclusion Bill being introduced in his absence ; recalled on the king's illness, and afterwards sent to Scotland as high commissioner, 1679 ; returned, 1680 ; again forced to retire after a few months, another Exclusion Bill being subsequently passed by the Commons, 1680, who, in spite of its rejection by the Lords, adhered to the plan, 1681 ; his religious policy in Scotland at first conciliatory, but afterwards more severe ; his return to London effected by influence of the Duchess of Portsmouth, 1682 ; readmitted to the council ; regained his powers at the admiralty (1684), and witnessed Charles's deathbed conversion ; ascended the throne on his brother's death, 6 Feb. 1685 ; during first year of his reign (1685) openly professed catholicism ; appointed the Anglican Rochester lord treasurer, and banished Duchess of Portsmouth, 1685 ; levied customs duties on his own authority ; lost his pension from Louis XIV by summoning a parliament and maintaining good relations with William of Orange, 1685 ; refused to pardon Monmouth after Sedgemoor (July 1685) ; rewarded Jeffreys for the Bloody Assize (August 1685) with the chief-justiceship ; dismissed Halifax, October 1685 ; with the help of Sunderland, Petre, and Talbot (Tyrconnel) remodelled the army ; made changes on the bench to insure a decision in favour of the dispensing power, 1686 ; revived the high commission, 1686 ; dismissed Rochester and Clarendon, 1687 ; made Roman Catholics officers and justices of the peace ; his first declaration of indulgence (preceded by a similar proclamation in Scotland) issued 4 April 1687 ; publicly received the papal nuncio, 3 July 1687 ; dissolved parliament, 4 July 1687 ; by personal influence forced catholics on Magdalen College, Oxford, 1688 ; ordered the second declaration to be read in churches (May 1688), the seven bishops petitioning against it being tried for seditious libel, but acquitted (30 June 1688) ; ordered recall of the six English regiments in the Dutch service (January 1688) ; accepted money from Louis XIV for equipment of a fleet, April 1688 ; declined French ships and offer of a joint declaration of war against Holland, September 1688 ; brought over soldiers from Ireland, and (September 1688) recalled the parliamentary writs ; circulated general pardon on same day as William of Orange's declaration (29 Sept. 1688) ; re-

stored Bishop Compton, the protestant fellows, and the charter of London ; made formal declaration as to the genuine birth of his son, October 1688 ; dismissed Sunderland, 1688 ; augmented the army and navy ; marched to Salisbury, but after desertion of his adherents returned to London, 1688 ; issued writs for a parliament, 1688 ; named commissioners to meet William, but after the Hungerford conference secretly left London (11 Dec.), embarked at Sheerness, was brought back to Faversham, and finally escaped with Berwick to France (22–25 Dec. 1688) ; established by Louis at St. Germains ; made unsuccessful appeals for help to various powers ; landed in Ireland with French force, 1689 ; held a parliament in Dublin (May 1689), which passed a toleration act, transferred tithes to Roman catholics, and repealed the act of settlement ; joined his army and was present at the Boyne, 1690, after which he left Ireland ; corresponded with Marlborough and others from St. Germains ; witnessed defeat of expedition off Cape La Hogue, 1692, and with Berwick prepared another invasion, 1695 ; rejected proposal of Louis XIV for succession of his son after death of William III, and after peace of Ryswick (1697) devoted himself to religious exercises ; died at St. Germains, having received from Louis a promise to recognise his son's title. His remains were re-interred at St. Germains in 1824. The manuscript of his 'Original Memoirs' was destroyed during the French revolution. By Arabella Churchill he had four natural children and a daughter by Catharine Sedley, besides issue by both his wives. His talent for business was spoilt by religious and political bigotry. Kneller painted his portrait (National Portrait Gallery).   [xxix. 181]

JAMES FRANCIS EDWARD STUART (1688–1766), PRINCE OF WALES ; the CHEVALIER DE ST. GEORGE or 'OLD PRETENDER' ; only son of James II by Mary of Modena ; popularly believed to be a supposititious child ; at the revolution secretly conveyed with his mother to France ; proclaimed king of England on his father's death at St. Germains, 1701 ; accompanied a French expedition to Scotland, but was prevented by English fleet and bad weather from landing, 1706 ; served with the French army and distinguished himself at Oudenarde, 1708, and Malplaquet, 1709 ; retired to Lorraine at peace of Utrecht, 1713 ; on hearing news of Sheriffmuir (1715) sailed in a small privateer from Dunkirk, landed at Peterhead, and being joined by Mar threw off his disguise at Fetteresso, 1715 ; established a court at Scone, but made bad impression on his army, and, flying before Argyll to Montrose, embarked with Mar for France, 1716 ; returned to Bar-le-Duc ; dismissed Bolingbroke, making Mar his chief minister ; finally settled in Rome ; after failure of Alberoni's attempt in his favour, 1719, returned from Madrid to Rome ; married Maria Clementina Sobieski, 1719 ; appointed John Hay (1691–1740) [q. v.] his secretary on discovering Mar's treachery, 1724 ; alienated his followers by neglecting his wife ; received papal pension, 1727 ; gave money for the rising of 1745 ; buried at St. Peter's, where George III employed Canova to erect a monument over his tomb (completed, 1819.)   [xxix. 199]

JAMES, DUKE OF BERWICK (1670–1734). [See FITZ-JAMES, JAMES.]

JAMES, BARTHOLOMEW (1752–1827), rear-admiral ; in the Orpheus at reduction of New York, 1776 ; captured by French while cruising on the Jamaica station, 1778 ; took part in reduction of Omoa, 1779, and defence of Yorktown, 1781 ; in command of the Aurora's boats at wreck of Royal George, 1782, engaged on transport service in connection with capture of Martinique, 1794 ; afterwards held naval commands in Mediterranean and off Teneriffe.   [xxix. 203]

JAMES, CHARLES (d. 1821), major and author ; travelled through France during the revolution, which he defended in 'Audi alteram Partem,' 1793 ; major of the corps of artillery drivers, 1806 ; published poems and military manuals, including 'Regimental Companion,' 1799.   [xxix. 205]

JAMES, DAVID (1839–1893), actor, whose real name was BELASCO ; appeared at Royalty, 1863, and subsequently played at many London theatres ; joint-manager, 1870, of the Vaudeville, where his most successful part was Perkyn Middlewick in 'Our Boys,' which was played more than a thousand times, 1875-9.   [Suppl. iii. 36]

JAMES, EDWARD (1807–1867), barrister; M.A. Brasenose College, Oxford, 1834; barrister, Lincoln's Inn, 1835; assessor of Liverpool court of passage from 1852; Q.C., 1853; attorney-general of duchy of Lancaster, 1863; M.P., Manchester, 1865–7; died in Paris. [xxix. 206]

JAMES, EDWIN JOHN (1812–1882), barrister; admitted, Inner Temple, 1836; defended Dr. Simon Bernard, 1858; engaged in the Palmer (1856) and Anderson (1861) cases; Q.C., 1853; recorder of Brighton, 1855–61; M.P., Marylebone, 1859–61; visited Garibaldi's camp, 1860; became bankrupt and was disbarred for unprofessional conduct, 1861; practised at New York bar and played on the American stage, 1861–72; published 'Political Institutions of America and England,' 1872; died in London. [xxix. 206]

JAMES, ELEANOR (*fl.* 1715), printer and political writer; wife of Thomas James, a London printer; committed to Newgate for 'dispersing scandalous and reflective papers,' 1689; interviewed Charles II and James II, and admonished George I; mentioned by Dryden. [xxix. 207]

JAMES, FRANCIS (1581–1621), Latin poet; of Westminster and Christ Church, Oxford; M.A., 1605; D.D., 1614; rector of St. Matthew's, Friday Street, London, 1616. [xxix. 208]

JAMES, FRANK LINSLY (1851–1890), African explorer; M.A. Downing College, Cambridge, 1881; penetrated the Soudan to Berber, 1877–8; described his subsequent explorations in the Basé country in 'Wild Tribes of the Soudan,' 1883; ascended the Tchad-Amba, 1883; explored the Somali country to the Webbe Shebeyli, 1884–5, relating his experiences in 'The Unknown Horn of Africa' (1888); killed by an elephant near San Benito, West Africa. [xxix. 208]

JAMES, GEORGE (1683–1735), printer to city of London; brother of John James (*d.* 1746) [q. v.] [xxix. 214]

JAMES, GEORGE (*d.* 1795), portrait-painter, A.R.A., 1770; imprisoned during the revolution at Boulogne, where he died. [xxix. 209]

JAMES, GEORGE PAYNE RAINSFORD (1799–1860), novelist and historical writer; grandson of Robert James [q. v.]; historiographer royal to William IV; British consul in Massachusetts, 1850–2; removed to Norfolk, Virginia, 1852; consul-general at Venice (1856–60), where he died; published, besides historical novels ('Richelieu,' 1829, 'Philip Augustus,' 1831, and others), 'Memoirs of great Commanders,' 1832, 'Life of the Black Prince,' 1836, and other popular historical works and poems; the style of his romances parodied by Thackeray. [xxix. 209]

JAMES, SIR HENRY (1803–1877), director-general of the ordnance survey; entered royal engineers, 1826; appointed to ordnance survey, 1827; local superintendent of geological survey of Ireland, 1843; superintendent of construction at Portsmouth, 1846; director-general of ordnance survey, 1854–75; lieutenant-colonel, 1854, colonel, 1857, major-general, 1868, lieutenant-general, 1874, director of topographical department of the war office, 1857; knighted, 1860; applied photo-zincography to ordnance maps, 1859; published comparisons of standards of lengths in various countries, 1866, 'Photozincography,' 1860, and other works. [xxix. 210]

JAMES, HUGH (1771–1817), surgeon; son of John James (1729–1785) [q. v.] [xxix. 215]

JAMES, JOHN (*d.* 1661), Fifth-monarchy man; though not concerned in Venner's rising (1661), was arrested with his baptist congregation and executed for treason. [xxix. 213]

JAMES, JOHN (*d.* 1746), architect; son of Eleanor James [q. v.]; clerk of the works at Greenwich Hospital, 1705–46; surveyor of St. Paul's, Westminster Abbey, and (1716) the fifty new churches; master of Carpenters' Company, 1734; designed St. George's, Hanover Square, London; rebuilt Twickenham Church and Manor-house; wrote on architecture and gardening. [xxix. 213]

JAMES, JOHN (*d.* 1772), 'last of old English letter-founders'; nephew of John James (*d.* 1746) [q. v.] [xxix. 214]

JAMES, JOHN (1729–1785), schoolmaster; M.A. Queen's College, Oxford, 1755; D.D., 1782; head-master of St. Bees School, 1755–7; rector of Arthuret and Kirk Andrews, 1782–5. [xxix. 215]

JAMES, JOHN (1760–1786), rector of Arthuret and Kirk Andrews, 1785–6; son of John James (1729–1785) [q. v.]; B.A. Queen's College, Oxford, 1782. [xxix. 215]

JAMES, JOHN (1811–1867), Yorkshire antiquary; F.S.A., 1856; published 'History and Topography of Bradford,' 1841 (continued, 1866), and other works. [xxix. 215]

JAMES, JOHN ANGELL (1785–1859), independent minister; studied at Gosport academy; minister at Carr's Lane Chapel, Birmingham, from 1803 (rebuilt, 1820), where he took part in municipal work; chairman of Spring Hill College; a projector of Evangelical Alliance, 1842; published religious works, including 'The Anxious Inquirer after Salvation,' 1834 (often reprinted and translated). [xxix. 215]

JAMES, JOHN HADDY (1788–1869), surgeon; studied at St. Bartholomew's, 1808–12; assistant-surgeon to 1st life guards at Waterloo, 1815; surgeon to the Devon and Exeter Hospital, 1816–58, and curator of the museum; mayor of Exeter, 1828; honorary F.R.C.S., 1843; won Jacksonian prize for treatise on inflammation, 1821. [xxix. 217]

JAMES, JOHN THOMAS (1786–1828), bishop of Calcutta; son of Thomas James (1748–1804) [q. v.]; educated at Rugby, Charterhouse, and Christ Church, Oxford; M.A., 1810; published 'Journal of a Tour in Germany, Sweden, Russia, and Poland, during 1813 and 1814,' 1816, works on painting, 1820 and 1822, and 'The Semi-Sceptic,' 1825; vicar of Flitton-cum-Silsoe, 1816–27; bishop of Calcutta, 1827–8. [xxix. 217]

JAMES, RICHARD (1592–1638), scholar; nephew of Thomas James (1573?–1629) [q. v.]; scholar and (1615) fellow of Corpus Christi College, Oxford; M.A., 1615; B.D., 1624; chaplain to Sir Dudley Digges [q. v.] in Russia, 1618; assisted Selden in examining the Arundel marbles, 1624; librarian to Sir Robert Bruce Cotton [q. v.] and his son; friend of Ben Jonson, Sir Kenelm Digby [q. v.], and others; published 'Anti-Possevinus,' 1625, 'The Muses Dirge,' 1625, and other poems, and a translation of Minucius Felix's dialogue 'Octavius,' 1636. His manuscripts acquired by the Bodleian (1676) include 'Decanonizatio T. Becket,' 'Iter Lancastrense' (poem, ed. Thomas Corser, 1845), translations, and an Anglo-Saxon dictionary; his 'Poems' edited by Dr. Grosart, 1880. [xxix. 218]

JAMES, ROBERT (1705–1776), physician; educated at Lichfield and St. John's College, Oxford; B.A., 1726; M.D. Cambridge, 1728; L.R.C.P., 1745; friend of Dr. Johnson, who contributed to his 'Medical Dictionary,' 1743; patented a powder and pill, 1746, recommended in his 'Dissertation on Fevers,' 1748, and other works. [xxix. 220]

JAMES, THOMAS (1573?–1629), Bodley's librarian; of Winchester and New College, Oxford; fellow of New College, 1593–1602; M.A., 1599; D.D., 1614; first librarian of Bodleian, 1602–20; sub-dean of Wells, 1614; rector of Mongeham, 1617; published 'Ecloga Oxonio-Cantabrigiensis' (1600), containing list of manuscripts at Oxford and Cambridge, Aungervile's 'Philobiblon,' 1599, Wycliff's treatises against the Begging Friars and (probably) 'Fiscus Papalis' (1617); published also, besides the first two Bodleian catalogues (1605 and 1620), patristic and anti-catholic works. [xxix. 221]

JAMES, THOMAS (1593?–1635?), navigator, of Bristol; set out to discover a north-west passage in the Henrietta Maria, 3 May, 1631; sailed round Greenland to the south of Hudson's Bay, met Luke Fox [q. v.], and after leaving James's Bay and wintering on an island, arrived in Bristol, with slight loss of crew, 22 Oct., 1633; James's narrative (1633) identified by some as original of Coleridge's 'Rime of the Ancient Mariner.' [xxix. 223]

JAMES, THOMAS (1748–1804), head-master of Rugby; at Eton contributed to 'Musæ Etonenses'; scholar and fellow (1770) of King's College, Cambridge, of which he wrote an account; M.A., 1774; D.D., 1786; head-master at Rugby, 1778–94; raised numbers at Rugby from 52 to 245; rector of Harvington and prebendary of Worcester, 1797–1804. [xxix. 224]

JAMES, THOMAS SMITH (1809–1874), author of 'History of Litigation and Legislation respecting Presbyterian Chapels and Charities' (1867); son of John Angell James [q. v.] [xxix. 216]

JAMES, WILLIAM (1542–1617), bishop of Durham; M.A. Christ Church, Oxford, 1565; D.D., 1574; master of University College, Oxford, 1572; archdeacon of Coventry, 1577–84; dean of Christ Church, 1584; vice-chancellor, 1581 and 1590; chaplain to Leicester; dean of Durham, 1596–1606; bishop of Durham, 1606–17; ordered to receive Arabella Stuart, 1611. [xxix. 225]

JAMES or **JAMESIUS**, WILLIAM (1635?–1663), scholar; king's scholar at Westminster, 1646; student of Christ Church, Oxford, 1650; M.A., 1656; assistant-master under Busby, whom he helped with his 'English Introduction to the Latin tongue,' 1659; published an introduction to Chaldee, 1651. [xxix. 226]

JAMES (*fl.* 1760–1771) landscape-painter; imitator of Canaletto. [xxix. 226]

JAMES, SIR WILLIAM, first baronet (1721–1783), commodore of the Bombay marine; of humble birth; entered service of East India Company, 1747; as commander of Bombay marine (1751–9) captured Severndroog, stronghold of the pirate Angria, 1755, and Gheriah, 1757; carried news of French declaration of war up the Hooghly against north-east monsoon, 1757; returned to England, 1759; created baronet, 1778; M.P., West Looe; chairman of directors of East India Company. [xxix. 226]

JAMES, WILLIAM (*d.* 1827), naval historian; practised in Jamaica supreme court, 1801–13; detained prisoner in United States, 1812; escaped to Nova Scotia, 1813; published pamphlet on comparative merits of English and American navies, 1816; issued in England an account of the war between England and America (naval, 1817, military, 1818); his 'Naval History' of the great war (1793–1820) published, 1822–4. [xxix. 228]

JAMES, WILLIAM (1771–1837), railway projector; solicitor and land-agent in Warwickshire; afterwards chairman of West Bromwich Coalmasters' Association; removed to London, 1815; partner with Stephenson, 1821; projected Manchester and Liverpool Railway, and began survey concluded by George Stephenson; drew up plans for various railways; failed, and was imprisoned for debt, 1823. [xxix. 229]

JAMES, WILLIAM HENRY (1796–1873), engineer; son of William James (1771–1837) [q. v.]; patented loco-motives, boilers, and similar appliances. [xxix. 230]

JAMES, SIR WILLIAM MILBOURNE (1807–1881), lord justice; M.A. and hon. LL.D. Glasgow; barrister, Lincoln's Inn, 1831, treasurer, 1866; Q.C., 1853; vice-chancellor of duchy of Lancaster, 1853; engaged in the Colenso, Lyon *v.* Home, and Martin *v.* Mackonochie cases; vice-chancellor of court of chancery, 1869; knighted, 1869; lord justice, 1870–81; his 'British in India' issued, 1882. [xxix. 230]

JAMESON, ANNA BROWNELL (1794–1860), author; eldest daughter of D. Brownell Murphy [q. v.]; married Robert Jameson (afterwards speaker and attorney-general of Ontario), 1825, but soon separated from him; published, among other works, 'Diary of an Ennuyée,' 1826, 'Characteristics of Women,' 1832, 'Visits and Sketches,' 1834, 'Companion to Public Picture Galleries of London,' 1842, essays, including 'The House of Titian,' 1846, and 'Sacred and Legendary Art,' 1848–52; friend of Ottilie von Goethe and for a time of Lady Byron; devoted much attention to sick nursing. [xxix. 230]

JAMESON, JAMES SLIGO (1856–1888), naturalist and African traveller; discovered the black pern in Borneo, 1877; hunted in Matabeleland and Mashonaland, 1879; shot in Rocky Mountains, 1882; visited Spain and Algeria, 1884; naturalist to Emin Pacha Relief Expedition, 1887; as second in command of the rear expedition witnessed and made sketches of a cannibal banquet; after Major Barttelot's leave (1888) prepared to conduct the rear-guard in search of H. M. Stanley, but died of hæmaturic fever at Bangala; his 'Diary of the Emin Expedition' published, 1890. [xxix. 232]

JAMESON, ROBERT (1774–1854), mineralogist; studied at Edinburgh University; regius professor of natural history and keeper of the museum at Edinburgh, 1804–54; founded Wernerian Society, 1808; with Sir David Brewster established 'Edinburgh Philosophical Journal,' 1819; published 'Mineralogy of the Scottish Isles,' 1800,

and other works; edited Cuvier's 'Theory of the Earth,' 1813, 1817, 1818, and 1827, and Wilson and Bonaparte's 'American Ornithology,' 1826. [xxix. 234]

JAMESON, ROBERT WILLIAM (1805–1868), journalist and author; nephew of Robert Jameson [q. v.]; educated at Edinburgh; writer to the signet. [xxix. 235]

JAMESON, WILLIAM (*fl.* 1689–1720), blind lecturer on history at Glasgow University, 1692–1720; published 'Spicilegia Antiquitatum Ægypti,' 1720, 'Verus Patroclus,' 1689, and anti-episcopalian treatises. [xxix. 235]

JAMESON, WILLIAM (1796–1873), botanist; studied at Edinburgh University; professor of chemistry and botany at Quito, 1827, assayer to Quito mint, 1832, and director, 1861; published 'Synopsis Plantarum Quitensium,' 1865; sent home plants, some of which were named after him; died at Quito. [xxix. 236]

JAMESON, WILLIAM (1815–1882), pioneer of tea-planting in India; nephew of Robert Jameson [q. v.]; studied at Edinburgh University; superintendent of Saharunpore garden, 1842–75. [xxix. 236]

JAMESONE, GEORGE (1588?–1644), Scottish portrait-painter; perhaps studied under Rubens; visited Italy, 1634; painted James I, Charles I, Montrose, and other eminent contemporaries. [xxix. 236]

JAMIESON, JOHN (1759–1838), antiquary and philologist; studied at Glasgow University; anti-burgher minister at Forfar, 1781–97, and Nicolson Street, Edinburgh, 1797–1830; friend of Scott; D.D. Princeton for his reply to Priestley's 'History of Early Opinions,' 1795; edited Barbour's 'Bruce,' 1820, and Blind Harry's 'Wallace,' 1820; compiled 'Etymological Dictionary of the Scottish Language,' 1808 (ed. Longmuir and Donaldson, 1879–87). [xxix. 237]

JAMIESON, JOHN PAUL (*d.* 1700), Roman catholic divine; D.D. during residence at the Scots College, Rome; transcribed original documents relating to history of Scotland, some being deposited at Paris. [xxix. 238]

JAMIESON, ROBERT (1780?–1844), compiler of 'Popular Ballads and Songs,' 1806; collaborated with Scott in 'Illustrations of Northern Antiquities,' 1814. [xxix. 238]

JAMIESON, ROBERT (*d.* 1861), philanthropist; directed exploration of Niger and other West African rivers; rescued African colonisation expedition, 1841; published 'Commerce with Africa,' 1859. [xxix. 239]

JAMIESON, ROBERT (1802–1880), Scottish divine; studied at Edinburgh University; minister of Weststruther, 1830, Currie, 1837, and St. Paul's, Glasgow, 1844–80; moderator of general assembly, 1872; published 'Eastern Manners illustrative of Old and New Testaments,' 1836–8; part author of 'Commentary on the Bible,' 1861–1865. [xxix. 239]

JAMIESON, THOMAS HILL (1843–1876), keeper of the Advocates' Library, Edinburgh, 1871–6; privately printed 'Life of Alexander Barclay,' 1874; edited Barclay's version of Brandt's 'Ship of Fools,' 1874. [xxix. 240]

JAMRACH, JOHANN CHRISTIAN CARL (1815–1891), dealer in wild animals; born in Hamburg. [xxix. 240]

JANE or **JOHANNA** (*d.* 1445), queen of Scotland; daughter of John Beaufort, earl of Somerset; married James I, 1424, whose love for her is told in the 'Kingis Quair'; wounded at James I's assassination; married Sir James Stewart, the Knight of Lorne, before 1439; obliged by Livingstone to surrender custody of James II, her dowry, and Stirling Castle, 1439. [xxix. 240]

JANE SEYMOUR (1509?–1537), third queen of Henry VIII; daughter of Sir John Seymour of Wolf Hall, Savernake; lady-in-waiting to Catherine of Arragon and Anne Boleyn; resisted dishonourable proposals from the king; privately married to Henry VIII in York Place, 30 May 1536; reconciled Princess Mary to Henry; died soon after the birth of her son (Edward VI); was several times painted by Holbein. [xxix. 241]

JANE (1537–1554), queen of England. [See DUDLEY, LADY JANE.]

JANE, JOSEPH (*fl.* 1600–1660), controversialist; mayor and M.P. for Liskeard in Long parliament; royal commissioner in Cornwall during great rebellion; defended 'Eikon Basilike' against Milton, 1651. [xxix. 243]

JANE or **JANYN**, THOMAS (*d.* 1500), bishop of Norwich; fellow of New College, Oxford, 1454–72; doctor of decrees; chancellor's commissary, 1468; archdeacon of Essex, 1480; privy councillor, 1495; canon of Windsor, 1497; dean of Chapel Royal, 1497; bishop of Norwich, 1499–1500. [xxix. 244]

JANE, WILLIAM (1645–1707), divine; son of Joseph Jane [q. v.]; of Westminster and Christ Church, Oxford; M.A., 1667; D.D., 1674; canon of Christ Church, Oxford, 1669; archdeacon of Middlesex, 1679; regius professor of divinity at Oxford, 1680–1707; framed Oxford declaration in favour of passive obedience, 1683; dean of Gloucester, 1685; prolocutor of the lower house, 1689, procuring defeat of the comprehension scheme in convocation, 1689. [xxix. 244]

JANEWAY, JAMES (1636?–1674), nonconformist divine; brother of John Janeway [q. v.]; B.A. Christ Church, Oxford, 1659; preached in Jamaica Row, Rotherhithe; his 'Token for Children' (1671) frequently reprinted. [xxix. 246]

JANEWAY, JOHN (1633–1657), puritan; brother of James Janeway [q. v.]; of St. Paul's School and Eton; first scholar of King's College, Cambridge, 1656; fellow, 1654. [xxix. 246]

JANIEWICZ, afterwards **YANIEWICZ**, FELIX (1762–1848), violinist and composer; native of Wilna; came to London from Paris during the revolution; original member of London Philharmonic Society; published violin and piano music. [xxix. 247]

JANSSEN or **JANSEN**, BERNARD (*fl.* 1610–1630), stonemason and tombmaker; engaged with Nicholas Stone (1586–1647) [q. v.] on tomb of Thomas Sutton in the Charterhouse, and of Sir Nicholas Bacon in Redgrave Church, Suffolk. [xxix. 247]

JANSSEN, GERAERT or GERARD (*fl.* 1616), tombmaker; executed the portrait-bust of Shakespeare at Stratford-on-Avon, 1616. [xxix. 248]

JANSSEN, SIR THEODORE, first baronet (1658?–1748), South Sea director; came to England from Holland, 1680; naturalised, 1685; knighted by William III; created baronet, 1714; M.P., Yarmouth, 1714–21; expelled the house, 1721; author of 'General Maxims in Trade,' 1713. [xxix. 248]

JANSSEN (JONSON) VAN CEULEN, CORNELIUS (1593–1664?), portrait-painter; famous for portrait of Lady Bowyer and groups of the Rushout, Lucy, and Verney families; subsequently practised in Holland. [xxix. 248]

JARDINE, ALEXANDER (*d.* 1799), lieutenant-colonel; captain, royal invalid artillery; went on mission to Morocco, described in 'Letters from Morocco,' 1790; brevet lieutenant-colonel, 1793. [xxix. 249]

JARDINE, DAVID (1794–1860), historical and legal writer; M.A. Glasgow, 1813; police magistrate at Bow Street, 1839; published 'Narrative of the Gunpowder Plot,' 1857; indexed (1828) and (1832–3) abridged Howell's 'State Trials'; wrote legal tracts. [xxix. 249]

JARDINE, GEORGE (1742–1827), professor at Glasgow; in Paris, 1770–3; professor of Greek at Glasgow, 1774; professor of logic at Glasgow, 1787–1824; secretary of Royal Infirmary. [xxix. 250]

JARDINE, JAMES (1776–1858), engineer; constructed Union Canal; first to determine mean level of the sea. [xxix. 250]

JARDINE, JOHN (1716–1766), Scottish divine; minister of Lady Yester's Church, Edinburgh, 1750, of the Tron Church, 1754; D.D. St. Andrews, 1758; dean of order of the Thistle, 1763; contributed to the first 'Edinburgh Review,' 1755. [xxix. 251]

JARDINE, SIR WILLIAM, seventh baronet (1800–1874), naturalist; succeeded as seventh baronet, 1820; published (with Prideaux Selby) 'Illustrations of Ornithology,' 1830; edited 'Naturalists' Library,' 1833–45, contributing sections on birds and fish; conducted also

'Annals and Magazine of Natural History'; joint-editor of 'Edinburgh Philosophical Journal'; commissioner on salmon fisheries, 1860. [xxix. 251]

JARLATH or **IARLAITHE** (424–481), third archbishop of Armagh, 464. [xxix. 252]

JARLATH or **IARLATH** (*fl.* 540), Irish saint; founded a church on site of the modern Tuam; possibly identical with Jarlath (424–481) [q. v.] [xxix. 252]

JARMAN, FRANCES ELEANOR, afterwards Mrs. TERNAN (1803?–1873), actress; appeared as a child at Bath, 1815; appeared in Ireland, 1822; played Juliet to Charles Kemble's Romeo, Imogen, and other parts, at Covent Garden, 1827–8; well received at Edinburgh, 1829, in Desdemona and Juliana ('The Honeymoon'); accompanied her husband in American and Canadian tour, 1834–6; at Drury Lane, 1837–8; played Paulina in 'Winter's Tale' at the Princess's, 1855; acted blind Alice with Fletcher in 'The Bride of Lammermoor,' 1866. [xxix. 252]

JARRETT, THOMAS (1805–1882), linguist; seventh classic at Cambridge, 1827; fellow and lecturer at St. Catharine's College, Cambridge, 1828–32; Cambridge professor of Arabic, 1831–54; regius professor of Hebrew, 1854; rector of Trunch, Norfolk, 1832–82; published 'Hebrew-English and English-Hebrew lexicon,' 1848, 'New Way of marking sounds of English Words without change of Spelling,' 1858, and Sanskrit and Hebrew texts transliterated into Roman characters. [xxix. 253]

JARROLD, THOMAS (1770–1853), physician; M.D. Edinburgh; practised at Manchester; published 'Anthropologia,' 1808, 'Instinct and Reason philosophically investigated,' 1836, and other works. [xxix. 254]

JARRY, FRANCIS (1733–1807), military officer; said to have been in Prussian service during Seven Years' War, and to have presided over military school at Berlin under Frederick the Great; adjutant-general in French army (1791) and maréchal de camp (1792), serving against the Austrians; came to England, 1795; first commandant of the Royal Military College, 1799–1806; his 'Employment of Light Troops' issued, 1803. [xxix. 254]

JARVIS, CHARLES (1675?–1739). [See JERVAS.]

JARVIS, SAMUEL (*fl.* 1770), blind composer; organist of Foundling Hospital and St. Sepulchre's. [xxix. 255]

JARVIS, THOMAS (*d.* 1799). [See JERVAIS.]

JAY, JOHN GEORGE HENRY (1770–1849), violinist and composer; Mus.Doc. Cambridge, 1811. [xxix. 255]

JAY, WILLIAM (1769–1853), dissenting minister; stonemason at erection of Fonthill Abbey; preached for Rowland Hill (1744–1833) [q. v.] at Surrey Chapel, London, 1788; pastor of Argyle Independent Chapel, Bath, from 1791; commended as a preacher by Sheridan and Beckford; published popular devotional works. [xxix. 255]

JEACOCKE, CALEB (1706–1786), baker and orator; author of 'Vindication of the Moral Character of the Apostle Paul,' 1765. [xxix. 256]

JEAKE, SAMUEL, the elder (1623–1690), puritan antiquary; some time town clerk of Rye; detained in London as a nonconformist, 1682–7; his translation (with annotations) of the charters of the Cinque ports printed, 1728. [xxix. 256]

JEAKE, SAMUEL, the younger (1652–1699), astrologer; son of Samuel Jeake the elder [q. v.]; edited his father's 'Logisticelogia,' 1696. [xxix. 257]

JEAN, PHILIP (1755–1802), miniature-painter; native of Jersey. [xxix. 257]

JEANES, HENRY (1611–1662), puritan divine; M.A. New Inn Hall, Oxford, 1633; vicar of Kingston and rector of Chedzoy, Somerset; published theological works and carried on controversies with Dr. Hammond, William Creed, and Jeremy Taylor. [xxix. 257]

JEAVONS, THOMAS (1816–1867), engraver. [xxix. 258]

JEBB, ANN (1735–1812), contributor to 'London Chronicle' ('Priscilla'); wife of John Jebb (1736–1786) [q. v.] [xxix. 259]

JEBB, JOHN (1736–1786), theological and political writer; nephew of Samuel Jebb [q. v.]; second wrangler, Peterhouse, Cambridge, 1757; fellow, 1761; M.A., 1760; as lecturer on the Greek Testament expressed unitarian views, but held church livings in Suffolk till 1775; engaged actively in movement for abolition of clerical and university subscription, 1771; proposed public examinations at Cambridge, 1773–4; M.D. St. Andrews, 1777; practised in London; F.R.S., 1779; his works edited by Dr. John Disney, 1787.   [xxix. 258]

JEBB, JOHN (1775–1833), bishop of Limerick; M.A. Trinity College, Dublin, 1801; rector of Abington, 1809; archdeacon of Emly, 1820; D.D., 1821; bishop of Limerick, 1822–33; defended Irish establishment in House of Lords, 1824; chief works, 'Essay on Sacred Literature,' 1820; pioneer of Oxford movement.   [xxix. 259]

JEBB, JOHN (1805–1886), divine; son of Richard Jebb [q. v.]; of Winchester and Dublin; M.A., 1829; B.D., 1862; rector of Peterstow, Herefordshire, 1843; canon of Hereford, 1870; published 'Literal Translation of the Book of Psalms,' 1846, and works on cathedrals and liturgy; Old Testament reviser, but resigned his position.   [xxix. 261]

JEBB, Sir JOSHUA (1793–1863), surveyor-general of convict prisons; with royal engineers in Canada and America, 1813–20; surveyor-general of convict prisons, 1837; assisted in construction of 'model prison' at Pentonville; designed prisons at Portland and elsewhere; inspector-general of military prisons, 1844; as chairman of convict prisons developed progressive system; honorary major-general on retiring from the army, 1850; K.C.B., 1859; published works on prisons, artesian wells, and fortification.   [xxix. 261]

JEBB, Sir RICHARD, first baronet (1729–1787), physician; son of Samuel Jebb [q. v.]; M.D. Aberdeen, 1751; physician to Westminster Hospital, 1754–62, to St. George's, 1762–8; attended Duke of Gloucester in Italy; F.R.S. and F.S.A.; F.R.C.P., 1771, Harveian orator, 1774, and censor, 1772, 1776, and 1778; created baronet, 1778; physician to Prince of Wales, 1780, and to the king, 1786; friend of Wilkes and Churchill.   [xxix. 262]

JEBB, RICHARD (1766–1834), Irish judge, 1818–34; brother of John Jebb (1775–1833) [q. v.]; published pamphlet in favour of union (1799).   [xxix. 260]

JEBB, SAMUEL (1694?–1772), physician and scholar; B.A. Peterhouse, Cambridge, 1713; librarian to Jeremy Collier; M.D. Rheims, 1728; practised at Stratford-le-Bow; edited Roger Bacon's 'Opus Majus,' 1733, and the works of Aristides, 1722 and 1730; published lives of Mary Queen of Scots and Robert, earl of Leicester.
                    [xxix. 263]

JEEJEEBHOY, Sir JAMSETJEE, first baronet (1783–1859), philanthropist; born at Bombay; made several voyages to China; captured by the French and taken to the Cape; returned, 1807, and made large fortune as a merchant; besides benefactions to his Parsee co-religionists, founded hospital at Bombay (1843), endowed schools at many places, and constructed Mahim-Bandora causeway, Poonah waterworks, and other public institutions; knighted, 1842; created baronet, 1857; fund established in his name for translations into Gujarati.
                    [xxix. 263]

JEENS, CHARLES HENRY (1827–1879), engraver.
                    [xxix. 264]

JEFFCOCK, PARKIN (1829–1866), mining engineer; killed by explosion in Oaks Pit colliery, near Barnsley, while directing rescue operations.   [xxix. 264]

JEFFERIES. [See also JEFFREY and JEFFREYS.]

JEFFERIES, RICHARD (1848–1887), naturalist and novelist; son of a Wiltshire farmer; early contributed to Wiltshire papers; after attempts at literature removed to London and wrote for the 'Pall Mall Gazette,' in which first appeared his 'Gamekeeper at Home' (1877) and 'Wild Life in a Southern County' (1879); returned to the country and published, besides other works, 'Wood Magic,' 1881, 'Bevis,' 1882, 'After London,' 1885, and 'The Story of my Heart,' 1883.   [xxix. 265]

JEFFERSON, SAMUEL (1809–1846), author of 'History and Antiquities of Carlisle,' 1838; editor of 'Carlisle Tracts,' 1839–44.   [xxix. 266]

JEFFERY, DOROTHY (1685–1777), Cornish fish-seller; known by her maiden name, DOLLY PENTREATH; erroneously said to be the last person who spoke Cornish; her monument erected at Paul in 1860 by Prince Louis Lucien Bonaparte.   [xxix. 267]

JEFFERY, JOHN (1647–1720), archdeacon of Norwich; M.A. St. Catharine Hall, Cambridge, 1672; D.D., 1696; incumbent of St. Peter Mancroft, Norwich, 1678; archdeacon, 1694–1720; published devotional works; edited Sir Thomas Browne's 'Christian Morals,' 1716.
                    [xxix. 267]

JEFFERY, THOMAS (1700?–1728), nonconformist divine; minister of Little Baddow; published (1725) reply to the deist Collins's 'Grounds and Reasons'; published 'Christianity the Perfection of all Religion,' 1728.
                    [xxix. 268]

JEFFERYS, JAMES (1757–1784), historical painter; studied in Rome; his 'Scene before Gibraltar on morning of 14 Sept. 1782,' engraved by Woollett and John Emes [q. v.]   [xxix. 268]

JEFFERYS, THOMAS (d. 1771), map-engraver; published miscellaneous works.   [xxix. 269]

JEFFREY. [See also GEOFFREY.]

JEFFREY, ALEXANDER (1806–1874), author of history of Roxburghshire, 1836 (re-written, 1853–64).
                    [xxix. 269]

JEFFREY, FRANCIS, LORD JEFFREY (1773–1850), Scottish judge and critic; educated at the Edinburgh High School and at Glasgow and Edinburgh universities; a few months at Queen's College, Oxford; admitted to the Scots bar, 1794; obtained little practice for many years owing to his whiggism; as member of Speculative Society made acquaintance of Scott and others; joined in foundation of 'Edinburgh Review,' 1802, and edited it from 1803 to 1829; himself wrote the Cevallos article (No. 26), after which Scott ceased his contributions, and the review became decidedly whig; challenged by Moore for an article on his 'Epistles, Odes, and other Poems,' but both duellists arrested at Chalk Farm before fighting, 1806; afterwards became intimate with Moore; from 1807 appeared with success before the general assembly, and gradually extended his practice in the courts; visited New York, 1813; active in British politics, 1821–6; dean of the Faculty of Advocates, 1829; lord advocate, 1830–4; M.P. for Malton, 1831–2, and after the Reform Bill for Edinburgh; acquainted with Wordsworth; judge of the court of session, 1834–50, giving a decision for the free church at the disruption; became intimate with Dickens; read proofs of first two volumes of Macaulay's 'History'; an impartial and acute critic. His contributions to the 'Edinburgh Review' (selected) appeared in 1844 and 1853 (4 vols.)   [xxix. 269]

JEFFREY or **JEFFERAY**, JOHN (d. 1578); judge; barrister, Gray's Inn, 1546; queen's serjeant, 1572; judge of queen's bench, 1576; chief baron of the exchequer, 1577.   [xxix. 276]

JEFFREYS, CHRISTOPHER (d. 1693), musician; son of George Jeffreys (d. 1685) [q. v.]; of Westminster and Christ Church, Oxford; M.A., 1666.   [xxix. 277]

JEFFREYS, GEORGE (d. 1685), organist to Charles I at Oxford, 1643, and composer; steward to the Hattons of Kirby from 1648; many of his compositions in British Museum and Royal College of Music library.
                    [xxix. 276]

JEFFREYS, GEORGE, first BARON JEFFREYS of Wem (1648–1689), judge; educated at Shrewsbury, St. Paul's School, and at Westminster; left Trinity College, Cambridge, without graduating; barrister, Inner Temple, 1668; common serjeant, 1671; introduced at court by Chiffinch; solicitor-general to Duke of York, 1677; knighted, 1677; as recorder of London (1678–80) exercised severity in 'Popish plot' cases; reprimanded by House of Commons for obstructing petitions for the assembling of parliament, and compelled to resign, 1680; his conduct as chief-justice of Chester also censured; after his prosecution of Fitzharris and Colledge created baronet, 1681; active in obtaining quo warranto against the city of London and in prosecution of Lord Russell; named (in spite of Charles II's low estimate of him) lord chief-justice, 1682; privy councillor, 1683; conducted the trials of Algernon Sidney, 1683, and Sir Thomas Armstrong, 1684; after the accession of James II advised levying of the customs and revival of the high commission court; presided at trial of Titus Oates, 1685; created Baron Jeffreys of Wem, 1685 (an exceptional favour); tried Richard Baxter [q. v.], 1685; held 'bloody assize' in the west after suppression of Monmouth's rebellion, 1685; appointed lord chancellor, September, 1685; chief ecclesiastical commissioner, 1686; one of the privy councillors who regulated the municipal corporations, 1687; present at birth of Prince James Edward [q. v.], 1688; carried out James II's tardy reforms; member of council of five in the king's absence with the army, 1688; arrested in disguise at Wapping, 1688; died in the Tower after petitioning for a pardon. He displayed great acuteness in civil cases, but as a criminal judge was notorious for his brutality. [xxix. 277]

JEFFREYS, GEORGE (1678-1755), poet and dramatist; son of Christopher Jeffreys [q. v.]; of Westminster and Trinity College, Cambridge; fellow, 1702-9; M.A., 1702; published 'Edwin' (1724) and 'Merope' (1731), two tragedies, acted at Lincoln's Inn Fields; author of 'Miscellanies in Verse and Prose,' 1754. [xxix. 284]

JEFFREYS, JOHN, second BARON JEFFREYS of Wem (1670?-1702), son of George Jeffreys, first baron [q. v.]; head of Westminster, 1685; took his seat as peer, 1694; instrumental in obtaining public funeral for Dryden, 1700. [xxix. 283]

JEFFREYS, JOHN GWYN (1809-1885), conchologist; treasurer of Linnean and Geological societies; F.R.S., 1840; honorary LL.D. St. Andrews; vice-president of British Association, 1880; conducted dredging operations in the British seas, the Bay of Biscay, the Portuguese coast, Baffin's Bay, and the Norwegian coast, and discovered seventy-one unknown species of shells; published 'British Conchology,' 1862-9; his collection of European molluscs purchased by the American government. [xxix. 284]

JEFFREYS, JULIUS (1801-1877), inventor of the respirator; studied medicine at Edinburgh and London; while in the Bengal medical service recommended Simla as a health resort; invented respirator, 1836; F.R.S., 1840; patented various appliances for ships; wrote on diseases of the respiratory organs. [xxix. 285]

JEGON, JOHN (1550-1618), bishop of Norwich; fellow of Queens' College, Cambridge, 1572; B.A., 1572; vice-president of Queens' College, Cambridge; master of Corpus Christi College, Cambridge, 1590-1601; vice-chancellor, 1596-1601; bishop of Norwich, 1602-18. [xxix. 286]

JEHNER, afterwards **JENNER**, ISAAC (1750-1806?), portrait-painter and mezzotint-engraver; published 'Fortune's Football' (autobiographical), 1806. [xxix. 287]

JEKYLL, SIR JOSEPH (1663-1738), master of the rolls; barrister, Middle Temple, 1687; chief-justice of Chester, 1697-1717; king's serjeant, 1700; knighted, 1700; M.P., Eye, 1697-1713, Lymington, 1713-22, Reigate, 1722-1738; opened the case against Sacheverell, 1710; manager against Lord Wintoun, Francia, and Lord Oxford; master of the rolls, 1717-38; privy councillor, 1717; prominent in exposing South Sea directors, 1720; steady supporter of Walpole; introduced Gin and Mortmain acts, 1736; left money for relief of the national debt. [xxix. 287]

JEKYLL, JOSEPH (d. 1837), wit and politician; great-nephew of Sir Joseph Jekyll [q. v.]; of Westminster and Christ Church, Oxford; M.A., 1777; barrister, Lincoln's Inn, 1778; reader at Inner Temple, 1814, treasurer, 1816; M.P., Calne, 1787-1816; contributed whig pasquinades to 'Morning Chronicle' and 'Evening Statesman'; attacked in 'Jekyll, an Eclogue,' 1788; K.C. and solicitor-general to Prince of Wales, 1805; master in chancery, 1815; compiled 'Facts and Observations relating to the Temple Church,' 1811, which he restored. [xxix. 288]

JEKYLL, THOMAS (1570-1653), antiquary; secondary of the king's bench and clerk of the papers; many of his collections for history of Essex, Norfolk, and Suffolk in British Museum. [xxix. 289]

JEKYLL, THOMAS (1646-1698), divine; of Merchant Taylors' School and Trinity College, Oxford; M.A., 1670; minister of the New Church in St. Margaret, Westminster, 1681-98; instituted free school in Westminster. [xxix. 290]

JELF, RICHARD WILLIAM (1798-1871), principal of King's College, London; educated at Eton and Christ

Church, Oxford; fellow of Oriel College, 1820; M.A., 1823; D.D., 1839; preceptor to Prince George (afterwards king of Hanover), 1826-39; canon of Christ Church, 1830; Bampton lecturer, 1844; principal of King's College, London, 1844-68; one of the doctors who condemned Pusey's sermon, 1847; compelled Maurice to resign professorship, 1853; edited Jewel's works, 1848. [xxix. 290]

JELF, WILLIAM EDWARD (1811-1875), divine and scholar; brother of Richard William Jelf [q. v.]; of Eton and Christ Church, Oxford; tutor, 1836-49, and some time senior censor; M.A., 1836; B.D., 1844; Bampton lecturer, 1857; vicar of Carleton, 1849-54; published Greek grammar (1842-5) and controversial tracts. [xxix. 291]

JELLETT, JOHN HEWITT (1817-1888), provost of Trinity College, Dublin; fellow of Trinity College, Dublin, 1840; M.A., 1843; D.D., 1881; professor of natural philosophy, Dublin, 1848; commissioner of Irish education, 1868; president of Royal Irish Academy, 1869; provost of Trinity College, Dublin, 1881-8; published mathematical and theological works. [xxix. 292]

JEMMAT, WILLIAM (1596?-1678), puritan divine; B.A. Magdalen College, Oxford, 1614; M.A. Margaret Hall, Oxford, 1617; vicar of St. Giles's, Reading, 1648-78; author and editor of theological works. [xxix. 292]

JENISON, FRANCIS, COUNT JENISON WALWORTH (1764-1824), diplomatist; settled with his family in Heidelberg, 1777; revisited England as ambassador for Hesse-Darmstadt, 1793; high chamberlain of Würtemberg, 1797-1816; died at Heidelberg. [xxix. 293]

JENISON or **JENNISON**, ROBERT (1584?-1652), puritan divine; fellow of St. John's College, Cambridge, 1607-19; D.D.; first master of St. Mary Magdalen's Hospital, Newcastle, 1619-52; vicar of St. Nicholas, Newcastle, 1645-52; author of theological works. [xxix. 293]

JENISON, ROBERT (1590-1656), jesuit; grandson of Thomas Jenison [q. v.]; of Gray's Inn; seized as 'Beaumont' at Clerkenwell, 1628; rector of house of probation, Ghent, 1645-9. [xxix. 294]

JENISON, ROBERT, the younger (1649-1688), informer; grand-nephew of Robert Jenison (1590-1656) [q. v.]; studied at Douay and Gray's Inn; pretended conversion to catholicism and made revelations concerning the 'Popish plot.' [xxix. 294]

JENISON, THOMAS (1525?-1587), auditor-general of Ireland and controller of the works at Berwick; bought Walworth, Durham, from Ayscough family. [xxix. 295]

JENKES, HENRY (d. 1697), Gresham professor of rhetoric; M.A. Aberdeen, 1646; fellow of Caius College, Cambridge; incorporated M.A. Cambridge, 1649; Gresham professor of rhetoric, 1670-6; F.R.S., 1674; published theological works. [xxix. 295]

JENKIN, HENRIETTA CAMILLA (1807?-1885), novelist; née Jackson; published 'Who breaks, pays,' 1861, and other novels. [xxix. 295]

JENKIN, HENRY CHARLES FLEEMING (1833-1885), engineer and electrician; son of Henrietta Camilla Jenkin [q. v.]; M.A. Genoa; with Sir William Thomson (Lord Kelvin) made important experiments on the resistance and insulation of electric cables; engaged in fitting out submarine cables, 1858-73; F.R.S. and professor of engineering in University College, London, 1865, at Edinburgh, 1868; published 'Magnetism and Electricity,' 1873, and 'Healthy Houses,' 1878; invented telpherage (transport of goods by electricity), 1882; his 'Miscellaneous Papers' edited by Mr. Sidney Colvin and Professor J. A. Ewing, 1887. [xxix. 296]

JENKIN, ROBERT (1656-1727), master of St. John's College, Cambridge; fellow of St. John's College, Cambridge, 1680-9; M.A., 1681; D.D., 1709; chaplain to Bishop Lake; refused to take the oaths to William and Mary, but complied under Anne; master of St. John's College, Cambridge, 1711-27; Lady Margaret professor of divinity, 1711-27; published 'Historical Examination on the Authority of General Councils,' 1688 (reprinted in Gibson's 'Preservative'), and theological works. [xxix. 297]

JENKINS, DAVID (1582-1663), Welsh judge and royalist; B.A. St. Edmund Hall, Oxford, 1600; barrister, Gray's Inn, 1609, ancient, 1622; judge of great sessions for Carmarthen, Pembroke, and Cardiganshire, 1643 ; indicted Welsh parliamentarians; captured at Hereford, 1645 ; imprisoned till the Restoration ; contested right of the parliament to try him, and published several royalist treatises (collected, 1648), as well as 'Eight Centuries of Reports,' 1661 ; bencher of his inn, 1660 ; patron of Welsh bards in Glamorganshire. [xxix. 298]

JENKINS, HENRY (*d.* 1670), 'the modern Methuselah' ; of Ellerton-upon-Swale, Yorkshire ; claimed to have been born about 1501 ; buried at Bolton-on-Swale. [xxix. 300]

JENKINS, JOHN (1592–1678), earliest English composer of instrumental music ; gave lessons to Roger l'Estrange and Roger North ; skilful on the lute and lyra-viol ; his 'Twelve Sonatas for two Violins and a Base, with Thorough Base for the Organ or Theorbo,' issued, 1660 ; composed also 'Fancies' and 'Rants,' and vocal pieces. [xxix. 301]

JENKINS, JOSEPH (*fl.* 1730), general baptist minister. [xxix. 302]

JENKINS, JOSEPH (1743–1819), particular baptist ; educated at King's College, Aberdeen ; D.D. Edinburgh, 1790 ; minister at Wrexham, Blandford Street, London, and (from 1798) at East Street, Walworth, London ; published theological tracts. [xxix. 301]

JENKINS, JOSEPH JOHN (1811–1885), engraver and water-colour painter ; left New Water-colour Society for the Old, 1847, becoming secretary, 1854–64 ; introduced private views. [xxix. 302]

JENKINS, SIR LEOLINE (1623–1685), civilian and diplomatist ; travelled with pupils, 1655–8 ; fellow of Jesus College, Oxford, 1660, LL.D., 1661, and principal, 1661–73 ; assisted Sheldon in the foundation of his theatre ; Sheldon's commissary at Canterbury ; deputy-professor of civil law, 1662 ; judge of the admiralty court, 1665, and of prerogative court of Canterbury, 1669 ; knighted, 1670, after he had obtained the setting aside in favour of Charles II of Duchess of Orleans's claims to Henrietta Maria's personalty ; M.P., Hythe, 1673–8, and Oxford University, 1679–85 ; English representative at congress of Cologne, 1673, at Nimeguen, 1676–9, being alone after Temple's recall ; privy councillor, 1680 ; secretary of state, 1680–4 ; led opposition to exclusion bills and Hotham's proposal to print parliamentary proceedings, 1681 ; gave money for enlargement of Jesus College, Oxford, and endowed it with bulk of his property. As a judge he was responsible for the Statute of Distributions and partly for the Statute of Frauds. [xxix. 302]

JENKINS, SIR RICHARD (1785–1853), Indian statesman ; intimate with Mountstuart Elphinstone [q. v.] ; acting resident at court of Dowlut Rao Scindia, 1804–5, and at Nagpore, 1807 ; resident of Nagpore, 1810–27 ; suggested annihilation of Pindáris ; distinguished himself at repulse of Appa Sahib's attack on Sitabaldi, 1817 ; arrested and imprisoned Appa Sahib, 1818 ; chairman of East India Company, 1839 ; M.P., Shrewsbury, 1830–1 and 1837–41 ; K.C.B. ; hon. D.C.L. Oxford. [xxix. 305]

JENKINS, ROBERT (*fl.* 1731–1738), master mariner, the cutting off of whose ear by the Spanish captain Fandino at Havana, 1731, precipitated war with Spain in 1739. [xxix. 306]

JENKINS, THOMAS (*d.* 1798), painter ; banker in Rome, and dealer in antiquities. [xxix. 306]

JENKINSON, ANTHONY (*d.* 1611), merchant, sea-captain, and traveller ; wrote account of entry of Solyman the Great into Aleppo, 1553, and obtained permission to trade in Turkish ports ; went to Russia, 1557, as captain-general and agent of the Muscovy Company, sailing round the North Cape and up the Dwina, afterwards sledging to Moscow ; after being well received by the tsar went by water to Astrakhan, 1558 ; visited king of Bokhara, 1558 ; returned to Moscow, 1559, and England, 1560 ; being despatched with letters to the tsar and the shah, 1561, attempted to open up trade with Persia, but failed ; while in command of a queen's ship captured Wilson, a Scottish pirate, 1565 ; obtained grant of White Sea trade for Muscovy Company, 1567, and in final mission secured its confirmation, 1571–2 ; sent on special mission to Embden, 1577 ; granted arms, 1569 ; the first Englishman in Central Asia. [xxix. 307]

JENKINSON, CHARLES, first EARL OF LIVERPOOL and first BARON HAWKESBURY (1727–1808), statesman ; educated at Charterhouse and University College, Oxford ; M.A., 1752 ; under-secretary of state, 1761 ; M.P., Cockermouth, 1761–7, Appleby, 1767–72, Harwich, 1772–4, Hastings, 1774–80, Saltash, 1761–86 ; secretary to the treasury, 1763–5 ; led the 'king's friends' after retirement of Bute ; privy councillor and vice-treasurer of Ireland, 1772 ; master of the mint, 1775 ; secretary-at-war, 1778 ; president of board of trade, 1786 ; chancellor of the duchy of Lancaster, 1786 ; created Baron Hawkesbury, 1786 ; created earl, 1796 ; published 'Collection of Treaties from 1648 to 1783' (1785) ; his 'Coins of the Realm' reprinted by the Bank, 1880. [xxix. 309]

JENKINSON, CHARLES CECIL COPE, third EARL OF LIVERPOOL (1784–1851), second son of Charles Jenkinson, first earl of Liverpool [q. v.] ; volunteer in Austrian army at Austerlitz, 1805 ; M.P., Sandwich, 1807–12, Bridgnorth, 1812–18, and East Grinstead, 1818–28 ; under-secretary for home department, 1807–9, for war, 1809 ; succeeded to earldom, 1828 ; lord steward, 1841–6. [xxix. 310]

JENKINSON, JOHN BANKS (1781–1840), bishop of St. David's ; nephew of Charles Jenkinson, first earl of Liverpool [q. v.] ; of Winchester and Christ Church ; M.A., 1807 ; D.D., 1817 ; dean of Worcester, 1817–25, of Durham, 1827–40 ; bishop of St. David's, 1825–40 ; maintained charity school at Carmarthen. [xxix. 311]

JENKINSON, ROBERT BANKS, second EARL OF LIVERPOOL (1770–1828), statesman ; eldest son of Charles Jenkinson, first earl of Liverpool [q. v.] ; of Charterhouse and Christ Church, Oxford ; in Paris at taking of the Bastille ; elected for Appleby, 1790 ; M.P., Rye, 1796–1803 ; appointed member of the India board by Pitt ; master of the mint, 1799 ; as foreign secretary under Addington, 1801–3, postponed the evacuation of Malta ; created Baron Hawkesbury, 1803 ; reconciled Pitt and Addington, 1804 ; home secretary and leader in the upper house in Pitt's second ministry, 1804–6 ; led opposition to Grenville ministry ; again home secretary, 1807–9 ; succeeded to earldom, 1808 ; secretary for war and the colonies under Perceval, 1809–12 ; introduced regency resolutions, 1810 ; proposed measure for strengthening the army, 1811 ; premier, 1812–27 ; opposed to catholic emancipation, but left it an open question in his cabinet ; vigorously supported Wellington in the Peninsula, carried on war with the United States, sent Napoleon to St. Helena, promoted international prohibition of the slave trade ; had to suspend Habeas Corpus Act, 1817, and pass six repressive acts, 1819–20 ; brought in a bill for the divorce of Queen Caroline ; renewed Insurrection Bill in Ireland, 1822 ; introduced legislation against the Catholic Association in Ireland, 1825 ; while opposed to the principle of catholic emancipation favoured minor concessions ; supported Canning in his foreign policy, and (1826) prepared to reduce the corn duties. [xxix. 311]

JENKS, BENJAMIN (1646–1724), divine ; rector of Harley, Shropshire ; author of devotional works. [xxix. 315]

JENKS, SYLVESTER (1656 ?–1714), Roman catholic divine ; professor of philosophy at Douay, 1680–6 ; preacher in ordinary to James II ; elected vicar-apostolic of northern district, 1713 ; his 'Practical Discourses on the Morality of the Gospel' (1699), reprinted, 1817, and 'Blind Obedience of a Humble Penitent' (1699), 1872. [xxix. 315]

JENKYN, WILLIAM (1613–1685), ejected minister ; M.A. Emmanuel College, Cambridge, 1635 ; vicar of Christ Church, Newgate, London, 1643 ; his living sequestrated, 1650, on account of his remonstrance against the trial of Charles I ; imprisoned for participation in plot of Christopher Love [q. v.] ; restored to his living, 1655 ; ejected, 1662 ; one of the first 'merchants'' lecturers at Pinners' Hall, 1672 ; preached in Jewin Street ; arrested, 1684 ; died in Newgate ; his 'Exposition of the Epistle of Jude' (1652–1654) edited by James Sherman, 1840 ; published controversial works. [xxix. 316]

JENKYNS, RICHARD (1782–1854), master of Balliol College, Oxford ; fellow of Balliol College, Oxford, 1802, tutor, 1813, bursar, 1814, master, 1819–54 ; M.A., 1806 ; D.D., 1819 ; vice-chancellor, 1824–8 ; dean of Wells, 1845–54 ; inaugurated open competition for scholarships ; raised the college to the first rank in Oxford. [xxix. 318]

JENNENS, CHARLES (1700–1773), friend of Handel; a nonjuror; nicknamed 'Solyman the Magnificent'; wrote words for 'Saul' (1735), 'Messiah' (1742), and 'Belshazzar' (1745); printed worthless edition of Shakespeare's tragedies; collected a library at Gopsall.
[xxix. 318]

JENNENS, SIR WILLIAM (*fl.* 1661–1690), captain in the navy and Jacobite; knighted; captain of the Ruby in action of 3 June 1665, against the Dutch, and in that of 1–4 June 1666; commanded in the second post at the Vlie, 1666; captain of the Victory under Prince Rupert, 1673; entered French navy and served under Tourville at Beachy Head, 1690.
[xxix. 319]

JENNER, CHARLES (1736–1774), novelist and poet; great-grandson of Sir Thomas Jenner [q. v.]; of Pembroke Hall (M.A., 1760) and Sidney Sussex College, Cambridge; incumbent of Claybrook and Craneford St. John; published 'The Placid Man, or Memoirs of Sir Charles Beville' (1770), and other works.
[xxix. 320]

JENNER, DAVID (*d.* 1691), divine; fellow of Sidney Sussex College, Cambridge; M.A., 1662, and B.D., 1668, *per literas regias*; prebendary of Salisbury, 1676; chaplain to the king; published 'The Prerogative of Primogeniture,' 1685.
[xxix. 321]

JENNER, EDWARD (1749–1823), discoverer of vaccination; pupil of John Hunter (1728–1793) [q. v.], 1770–1772; began to practise at Berkeley, Gloucestershire, 1773; F.R.S., 1788; M.D. St. Andrews, 1792 (Oxford, 1813); first vaccinated from cow-pox, 1796; published 'Inquiry into Cause and Effects of the Variolæ Vaccinæ' (cow-pox), 1798, 'Further Observations,' 1799, and 'Complete Statement of Facts and Observations,' 1800; made experiments in transmission of lymph; after parliamentary inquiry received grant of 10,000*l*., 1802, a further sum of 20,000*l*. being voted in 1806; had interviews with the tsar and the king of Prussia, 1814. In 1808 the National Vaccine Establishment was founded. Vaccination was made compulsory in England, 1853, having previously been enforced in Bavaria, Denmark, Sweden, Würtemberg, and Prussia. Statues of Jenner are in Kensington Gardens, Gloucester Cathedral, and at Boulogne and Brünn.
[xxix. 321]

JENNER, EDWARD (1803–1872), author of 'Flora of Tunbridge Wells,' 1845.
[xxix. 324]

JENNER, SIR HERBERT (1778–1852). [See FUST.]

JENNER, THOMAS (*fl.* 1631–1656), author, engraver, and publisher; kept a print-shop near the Royal Exchange; published 'Soules Solace,' with engravings, 1631, which George Wither answered; also descriptive tracts, with portraits and other works.
[xxix. 325]

JENNER, THOMAS (*fl.* 1604–1670), author of 'Quakerism Anatomiz'd and Confuted,' 1670; of Christ's College, Cambridge.
[xxix. 325]

JENNER, SIR THOMAS (1637–1707), baron of the exchequer; of Queens' College, Cambridge; barrister, Inner Temple, 1663; recorder of London, 1683; knighted, 1683; king's serjeant, 1684; baron of the exchequer, 1686; gave judgment in favour of the dispensing power, 1686; when on the Magdalen commission opposed expulsion of the fellows; justice of common pleas, 1688; arrested while attempting to escape with James II, and sent to the Tower; resumed practice at the bar.
[xxix. 325]

JENNER, SIR WILLIAM, first baronet (1815–1898), physician; studied medicine at University College, London; L.S.A. and M.R.C.S., 1837; M.A. London, 1844; professor of pathological anatomy at University College, London, 1849; physician to University College Hospital, 1854–76; consulting physician, 1879; Holme professor of clinical medicine at University College, 1860, and professor of principles and practice of medicine, 1863–72; F.R.C.P., 1852, and president, 1881–8; F.R.S., 1864; hon. D.C.L. Oxford, 1870; hon. LL.D. Cambridge, 1880; hon. LL.D. Edinburgh, 1884; physician extraordinary to Queen Victoria, 1861; physician in ordinary to the queen, 1862, and to Prince of Wales, 1863; created baronet, 1868; K.C.B., 1877; G.C.B. (civil), 1889; established the distinct identities of typhus and typhoid fevers; published medical works.
[Suppl. iii. 37]

JENNINGS, DAVID (1691–1762), dissenting tutor; pastor of independent congregation, Wapping New Stairs, London, 1718–62; non-subscriber, 1719; Coward trustee and lecturer, 1743; divinity tutor from 1744; D.D. St. Andrews, 1749; his 'Jewish Antiquities' (1766) edited by Philip Furneaux.
[xxix. 327]

JENNINGS, FRANCES, afterwards **HAMILTON** (*d.* 1730), elder sister of Sarah Jennings, duchess of Marlborough; mentioned by Pepys; courted by Richard Talbot, earl and titular duke of Tyrconnel [q. v.]; married (Sir) George Hamilton.
[Iv. 332]

JENNINGS, HARGRAVE (1817?–1890), author; some time secretary to Mapleson; published, besides romances, 'The Indian Religions,' 1858, 'The Rosicrucians,' 1870, 'Phallicism,' 1884, and other works of occult learning.
[xxix. 328]

JENNINGS, HENRY CONSTANTINE (1731–1819), virtuoso; educated at Westminster; resided eight years in Italy, where he bought at Rome the famous marble dog, sold for one thousand guineas (now at Duncombe Park, Yorkshire); while in Chelsea made collections of shells, precious stones, books, and prints; published 'Free Inquiry into the Enormous Increase of Attornies,' 1785, and other works; died within the rules of the King's Bench.
[xxix. 329]

JENNINGS, JOHN (*d.* 1723), nonconformist minister and tutor; brother of David Jennings [q. v.]; had Philip Doddridge [q. v.] among his pupils at Kibworth.
[xxix. 328]

JENNINGS, SIR JOHN (1664–1743), admiral; commander-in-chief in the Medway, 1698; with Rooke at Cadiz, 1702, Vigo, 1702, the capture of Gibraltar, 1704, and battle of Malaga, 1704; knighted, 1704; rear-admiral, 1705; vice-admiral, 1708; admiral of the white, 1709; commanded off Lisbon, 1708–10; as commander-in-chief in the Mediterranean convoyed allied troops to Italy, 1713; a lord of the admiralty, 1714–27; governor of Greenwich, 1720; commanded fleet of observation on coast of Spain, 1726; rear-admiral of England, 1733.
[xxix. 330]

JENNINGS, LOUIS JOHN (1836–1893), journalist and politician; special correspondent of 'The Times' in India, 1863, and, after civil war in America, editor of 'New York Times'; engaged in literary pursuits in London from 1876; conservative M.P., Stockport, 1885–93; edited 'The Croker Papers,' 1884.
[Suppl. iii. 38]

JENNINGS, SIR PATRICK ALFRED (1831–1897), premier of New South Wales; born at Newry, Ireland; emigrated to goldfields of Victoria, 1852; settled at St. Arnaud, 1855; migrated as squatter to Warbreccan, in Riverina district, New South Wales, 1863; member of legislative council, 1867–9; member of assembly for Murray district, 1869–72; K.C.M.G., 1880; member of assembly for the Bogan, 1880; vice-president of executive council, 1883; colonial treasurer, 1885, and premier, 1886–7; member of legislative council, 1890.
[Suppl. iii. 39]

JENNINGS, SARAH, DUCHESS OF MARLBOROUGH (1660–1744). [See CHURCHILL, SARAH.]

JENOUR, JOSHUA (1755–1853), author; member of Stationers' Company; author of poems, tales, pamphlets, translations of Boileau, 1827, and other works.
[xxix. 331]

JENYE, THOMAS (*fl.* 1565–1583), rebel and poet; accompanied Thomas Randolph (1523–1590) [q. v.] to Scotland, and Sir Henry Norris [q. v.] to Paris; composed proclamation issued by northern rebels of 1569; was attainted; Spanish agent on the continent; implicated in the Throckmorton conspiracy, 1584; his 'Maister Randolphes Phantasey' (describing Moray's revolt), 1565, first printed, 1890; published also (from Ronsard) 'The Present Troobles in Fraunce,' 1568.
[xxix. 331]

JENYNGES, EDWARD (*fl.* 1574), poet; author of 'Notable Hystory of two faithfull Louers named Alfagus and Archelaus,' 1574.
[xxix. 332]

JENYNS, LEONARD (1800–1893). [See BLOMEFIELD.]

JENYNS, SOAME (1704–1787), author; of St. John's College, Cambridge; published 'Poems,' 1752; M.P., Cambridgeshire, 1742–54 and 1760–80, Dunwich, 1754–60; a commissioner of trade, 1753; his 'Free Enquiry into the Nature and Origin of Evil' (1757) reviewed by Johnson in 'Literary Magazine'; 'View of the Internal Evidence of the Christian Religion,' 1776 (10th ed. 1798), translated into various foreign languages; works collected, 1790. [xxix. 332]

JENYNS, SIR STEPHEN (*d.* 1524), lord mayor of London; master of the Merchant Taylors' Company, 1489; sheriff of London, 1498; lord mayor, 1508; knighted, 1509; founded Wolverhampton grammar school. [xxix. 333]

JEPHSON, ROBERT (1736–1803), dramatist and poet; friend of William Gerard Hamilton [q. v.]; master of the horse in Ireland from 1767; his tragedy, 'Braganza' (with epilogue by Horace Walpole), successfully produced at Drury Lane, 1775; his 'Conspiracy' acted by Kemble, 1796; his 'Count of Narbonne' played by Henderson at Covent Garden, 1781 (epilogue by Malone), and afterwards by John Philip Kemble in Dublin, and his 'Julia, or the Italian Lover,' performed by Kemble and Mrs. Siddons (Drury Lane, 1787); published also poems and other works. [xxix. 334]

JEPHSON, WILLIAM (1615 ? – 1659 ?), colonel; M.P., Stockbridge, in Long parliament (one of those expelled by Pride); served against rebels in Ireland; lieutenant-governor of Portsmouth, 1644; governor of Bandon, 1646; deserted with Lord Inchiquin, 1648; as representative of Cork in second protectorate parliament (1656) proposed to offer the crown to Cromwell; envoy extraordinary to Sweden, 1657. [xxix. 335]

JERDAN, WILLIAM (1782–1869), journalist; came to London from Kelso, 1801; began journalistic career on the 'Aurora,' 1806, and the 'Pilot,' 1808; joined 'Morning Post'; first to seize Perceval's assassin in lobby of House of Commons, 1812; conducted 'The Satirist,' 1807–1814; edited 'The Sun,' 1813–17; intimate with Canning; in Paris at entry of Louis XVIII, 1814; edited 'Literary Gazette,' 1817–50, being sole proprietor from 1843; helped to found Royal Society of Literature, 1821, and Royal Geographical Society, 1830; F.S.A., 1826; edited for Camden Society, 'Rutland Papers' (1842) and 'Perth Correspondence'; published 'National Portrait Gallery of the Nineteenth Century,' 1830–4; obtained civil list pension, 1853; published 'Autobiography,' 1852–3, and 'Men I have known,' 1866; figures in Maclise's 'Fraserians.' [xxix. 336]

JERDON, THOMAS CLAVERHILL (1811–1872), zoologist; author of 'Birds of India,' 1862–4. [xxix. 338]

JEREMIE, JAMES AMIRAUX (1802–1872), dean of Lincoln; born in Guernsey; fellow of Trinity College, Cambridge, 1826; M.A., 1827; D.D., 1850; prebendary of Lincoln, 1834, and dean, 1864–72; professor of classics and literature at Haileybury, 1830–50; dean of Haileybury, 1838; Christian advocate at Cambridge, 1833–50. and regius professor of divinity, 1850–70; founded Septuagint prizes; published 'History of the Church in the Second and Third Centuries,' 1852. [xxix. 338]

JEREMIE, SIR JOHN (1795–1841), colonial judge; advocate in Guernsey; chief-justice of St. Lucia, 1824–30; published 'Four Essays on Colonial Slavery,' 1831; his appointment as procureur-général of the Mauritius resisted by supporters of slavery, 1832–3; judge in Ceylon, 1836; governor of Sierra Leone, 1840–1; knighted, 1840. [xxix. 339]

JERMAN, EDWARD (*d.* 1668), architect of the Royal Exchange (burnt, 1838), Fishmongers' Hall, and other buildings erected after the fire. [xxix. 340]

JERMIN or **GERMAN**, MICHAEL (1591–1659), divine; fellow of Corpus Christi College, Oxford, 1615; M.A., 1615; D.D. Leyden, and, 1624, Oxford; chaplain to the electress palatine and afterwards to Charles I; rector of St. Martin's, Ludgate, 1628; ejected as royalist; published commentaries on Proverbs and Ecclesiastes. [xxix. 340]

JERMY, ISAAC (1789–1848), recorder of Norwich, 1831–48; B.A. Christ Church, Oxford, 1812; barrister, Lincoln's Inn, 1815; known as Preston till 1838; his succession to Stanfield Hall forcibly resisted, 1838; murdered there by James Blomfield Rush. [xxix. 340]

JERMY, ISAAC JERMY (1821–1848), son of Isaac Jermy [q. v.]; M.A. Trinity College, Cambridge, 1848; murdered by James Blomfield Rush. [xxix. 341]

JERMY, SETH (*d.* 1724), captain in the navy; lieutenant of the Northumberland at Barfleur, 1692; while on convoy duty at mouth of the Thames, 1707, captured by six French galleys. [xxix. 341]

JERMYN, GEORGE BITTON (1789–1859), antiquary; nephew of Henry Jermyn (1767–1820) [q. v.]; of Caius College and Trinity Hall, Cambridge; LL.D., 1826; died in Sardinia; made genealogical collections for history of Suffolk and compiled a family history. [xxix. 341]

JERMYN, HENRY, first EARL OF ST. ALBANS (*d.* 1684), courtier; vice-chamberlain to Queen Henrietta Maria, 1628, and her master of the horse, 1639; M.P., Liverpool, 1628, Corfe Castle in Short parliament, and Bury St. Edmunds in Long parliament; after being engaged in 'first army plot,' 1641, escaped to France, 1641; returned, 1643; secretary to Queen Henrietta Maria, commander of her body-guard; created Baron Jermyn, 1643; accompanied Henrietta Maria to France, 1644; governor of Jersey, 1644; proposed to cede Jersey to France in exchange for help; persuaded Charles II to accept the terms offered by the Scots; remained at Paris till the Restoration; created Earl of St. Albans, 1660; lord chamberlain, 1674; as ambassador at Paris negotiated Charles II's marriage, a treaty with France (1667), and in 1669 preliminaries of treaty of Dover; planned St. James's Square and gave his name to Jermyn Street; the patron of Cowley, but satirised by Marvell. [xxix. 342]

JERMYN, HENRY, first BARON DOVER (1636–1708), nephew of Henry Jermyn, first earl of St. Albans [q. v.]; master of the horse to Duke of York, 1660; intrigued with Lady Castlemaine and Lady Shrewsbury; wounded in duel with Colonel Thomas Howard, 1662; being a Romanist was created Baron Dover by James II, 1685; a commissioner of the treasury, 1687; entrusted with the Prince of Wales at the revolution; followed James to France; commanded troop at the Boyne, 1690; reconciled to William III; buried at Bruges. [xxix. 344]

JERMYN, HENRY (1767–1820), Suffolk antiquary; of St. John's College, Cambridge; barrister, Lincoln's Inn; his manuscript collections in British Museum. [xxix. 345]

JERMYN, JAMES (*d.* 1852), philologist; cousin of Henry Jermyn (1767–1820) [q. v.]; author of 'Book of English Epithets,' 1849, and other works. [xxix. 345]

JERNINGHAM, EDWARD (1727–1812), poet and dramatist; friend of Chesterfield and Horace Walpole; satirised by Gifford and Mathias; published 'Rise and Progress of Scandinavian Poetry' (poem), 1784, and other verse; his 'Siege of Berwick' acted at Covent Garden, 1793, re-edited by H. E. H. Jerningham, 1882; his 'Margaret of Anjou' (1777) and 'The Welch Heiress' (1795) produced at Drury Lane. [xxix. 346]

JERNINGHAM or **JERNEGAN**, SIR HENRY (*d.* 1571), received manor of Costessy, Norfolk, 1547, and founded that branch of the family; first important adherent of Queen Mary, 1553; master of the horse, 1557–8; K.B., 1553; privy councillor, vice-chamberlain, and captain of the guard; routed Wyatt, 1554. [xxix. 347]

JEROME, STEPHEN (*fl.* 1604–1650), author; M.A. St. John's College, Cambridge, 1607; author of 'Origen's Repentance,' 1619, and other works. [xxix. 348]

JERRAM, CHARLES (1770–1853), evangelical divine; M.A. Magdalene College, Cambridge, 1800; Norrisian prizeman, 1796; successor of Richard Cecil [q. v.] as vicar of Chobham, 1810; rector of Witney, 1834; published theological works. [xxix. 348]

JERRARD, GEORGE BIRCH (*d.* 1863), mathematician; B.A. Trinity College, Dublin, 1827; published writings relating to theory of equations. [Suppl. iii. 40]

JERROLD, DOUGLAS WILLIAM (1803–1857), author; appeared on the stage as a child; midshipman, 1813–15; while a printer's assistant began to contribute to papers and magazines; made reputation as playwright with 'Black-eyed Susan,' at the Surrey, 1829 (Drury Lane, 1835); his 'Bride of Ludgate' acted at Drury Lane, 1831; produced at the Haymarket, 1845, 'Time works Wonders'; contributed to 'Athenæum,' 'Blackwood,' and other publications; published in 'Punch' (1846) 'Mrs. Caudle's Curtain Lectures,' and was a constant contributor, 1841–57; started 'Douglas Jerrold's Shilling

Magazine,' 1845, and 'Douglas Jerrold's Weekly Newspaper,' 1846 ; published 'The Story of a Feather,' 1844, and several novels ; from 1852 till death edited 'Lloyd's Weekly Newspaper' ; enjoyed great reputation as a wit. [xxix. 349]

JERROLD, WILLIAM BLANCHARD (1826–1884), journalist and author ; son of Douglas Jerrold [q. v.] ; contributed to 'Douglas Jerrold's Weekly Newspaper' and 'Daily News' ; Crystal Palace commissioner in Norway and Sweden, 1853 ; produced 'Cool as a Cucumber' at Lyceum, 1851, edited 'Lloyd's Weekly' from 1857 ; collaborated with Gustave Doré in Paris ; published 'Life of Napoleon III,' 1874–82, with help of the empress ; also gastronomic manuals, lives of Douglas Jerrold and George Cruikshank, 'History of Industrial Exhibitions,' 1862, and novels, including 'Cent. per Cent.,' 1871 ; founder and president of English branch of International Association for Assimilation of Copyright Laws. [xxix. 352]

JERSEY, EARLS OF. [See VILLIERS, EDWARD, first EARL, 1656–1711 ; VILLIERS, WILLIAM, second EARL, 1682 ?–1721 ; VILLIERS, GEORGE BUSSY, fourth EARL, 1735–1805 ; VILLIERS, GEORGE CHILD-, fifth EARL, 1773–1859.]

JERVAIS or JARVIS, THOMAS (d. 1799), glass-painter ; executed Reynolds's design for New College Chapel, Oxford (1787), and West's for the east window of St. George's, Windsor. [xxix. 353]

JERVAS or JARVIS, CHARLES (1675 ?–1739), portrait-painter and translator of 'Don Quixote' ; studied under Kneller ; copied antiques at Rome ; painted portraits of George II and Queen Caroline ; taught Pope and painted his portrait thrice, as well as those of Swift, Arbuthnot, Newton, and the Duchess of Queensberry ; his version of 'Don Quixote' (published, 1742) frequently reprinted. [xxix. 354]

JERVIS, JOHN (1752–1820), mineralogist ; unitarian minister at Lympstone, 1773–1820 ; brother of Thomas Jervis [q. v.] [xxix. 365]

JERVIS, JOHN, EARL OF ST. VINCENT (1735–1823), admiral of the fleet ; in West Indies as able seaman and midshipman ; lieutenant, 1755 ; engaged a French privateer off Cape Gata, 1757 ; led advanced squadron in charge of transports past Quebec, and was entrusted by Wolfe with his last message to his fiancée, 1759 ; carried important despatches to Lord Amherst, 1760 ; exacted satisfaction for seizure of Turkish slaves in the Alarm at Genoa, 1769 ; saved the Alarm in violent gale at Marseilles, 1770 ; with Samuel Barrington [q. v.] visited Cronstadt, Stockholm, Carlscrona, and Copenhagen, 1774, and the western ports of France, 1775 ; commanded the Foudroyant at Ushant, 1778 (afterwards giving strong evidence in favour of Keppel) and at the three reliefs of Gibraltar, 1780–2 ; captured the Pégase, 1782 ; K.B., 1782 ; M.P., Launceston, 1783, Yarmouth, 1784 ; on fortification commission, 1785–6 ; rear-admiral, 1787 ; vice-admiral, 1793 ; co-operated with Sir Charles (afterwards earl) Grey [q. v.] in capture of Martinique and Guadeloupe, 1794 ; admiral, 1795, and commander-in-chief in the Mediterranean ; defeated Spanish fleet off Cape St. Vincent, 14 Feb. 1797, capturing four ships and disabling many others ; received pension of 3,000l. and the freedom of the city ; created Earl of St. Vincent, 1797 ; kept Cadiz sealed and sent Nelson to Aboukir and Duckworth to Minorca, 1798 ; successfully repressed mutiny ; censured by the admiralty for sending home Sir John Orde [q. v.], and obliged by failing health to resign his post, 1799 ; after a few months assumed command of the Channel fleet, in which he enforced the severe discipline recently applied in the Mediterranean ; as first lord of the admiralty in Addington ministry organised attack on the armed neutrality, 1801, and defence of the coast against French invasion ; obtained (1802) commission of inquiry which resulted (1806) in impeachment of Melville and thorough reform of naval administration ; being attacked by Pitt for not building sufficient ships, he undertook no further public service till after Pitt's death ; resumed command in Channel, 1806 ; retired, 1807 ; admiral of the fleet, 1821. [xxix. 355]

JERVIS, SIR JOHN (1802–1856), lord chief-justice of common pleas ; second cousin of John Jervis, earl of St. Vincent [q. v.] ; of Westminster, Trinity College, Cambridge, and the Middle Temple ; called, 1824 ; reported in exchequer court, 1826–32 ; liberal M.P. for Chester, 1832–1850 ; voted against Melbourne on Jamaica bill, 1839 ; as attorney-general under Russell (1846–50) introduced the

measures (1848) relating to justices of the peace known by his name ; knighted, 1846 ; president of common law pleading commission, 1850 ; privy councillor, 1850 ; lord chief-justice of common pleas, 1850–6 ; contributed to the 'Jurist' ; published treatise on the office and duties of coroners, 1829, and edited 'Reports.' [xxix. 363]

JERVIS, SIR JOHN JERVIS WHITE, first baronet (1766–1830), author ; B.A. Dublin, and LL.D. ; barrister-at-law ; assumed name of Jervis ; raised volunteer corps, 1796 and 1803 ; created Irish baronet, 1797 ; published works, including 'Refutation of M. M. de Montgaillard's Calumnies against British Policy,' 1812. [xxix. 364]

JERVIS, THOMAS (1748–1833), unitarian minister and Dr. Williams's trustee ; successor of Kippis at Prince's Street, Westminster, 1796 ; afterwards at Mill Hill, Leeds ; contributor to 'Gentleman's Magazine,' and hymn-writer. [xxix. 365]

JERVIS, WILLIAM HENLEY PEARSON- (1813–1883), author of 'History of the Church of France' (1872) and 'The Gallican Church and the French Revolution' (1882) ; son of Hugh Nicolas Pearson [q. v.] ; of Harrow and Christ Church, Oxford ; M.A., 1838 ; assumed name of Jervis, 1865 ; rector of St. Nicholas, Guildford, 1837. [xxix. 365]

JERVISE, ANDREW (1820–1878), Scottish antiquary ; examiner of registers, 1856 ; published 'Epitaphs and Inscriptions from Burial Grounds and Old Buildings in North East Scotland' (vol. i. 1875, vol. ii. (posthumous) 1879), and similar works. [xxix. 366]

JERVISWOODE, LORD. [See BAILLIE, CHARLES, 1804–1879.]

JERVOIS, SIR WILLIAM FRANCIS DRUMMOND (1821–1897), lieutenant-general ; second lieutenant, royal engineers, 1839 ; lieutenant, 1841 ; brevet-major, 1854 ; lieutenant-colonel, 1862 ; colonel, 1872 ; major-general, 1877 ; lieutenant-general, 1882 ; colonel-commandant of royal engineers, 1893 ; went to Cape of Good Hope, 1841, and made valuable surveys of many districts ; served in Kaffir war ; commanded company of sappers and miners at Woolwich and Chatham, 1849–52, and at Alderney, 1852–4 ; commanding royal engineer of London military district, 1855 ; assistant inspector-general of fortifications at war office, 1856 ; secretary to royal commission on defences of United Kingdom, 1859–60 ; director of works for fortifications, 1862 ; C.B. (civil), 1863 ; made frequent visits to British colonies to inspect fortifications ; K.C.M.G., 1874 ; governor of Straits Settlements, 1875 ; appointed adviser to Australian colonies as to defence of chief ports, 1877 ; governor of South Australia, 1877, and of New Zealand, 1882–9 ; G.C.M.G., 1878 ; F.R.S., 1888 ; published writings relating to defences. [Suppl. iii. 40]

JESSE, EDWARD (1780–1868), writer on natural history ; deputy-surveyor of royal parks and palaces ; friend of Croker and John Mitford ; published 'Gleanings in Natural History' (three series, 1832–4–5), 'A Summer's Day at Hampton Court,' 1839, and other works ; edited Walton's 'Angler' and White's 'Selborne.' [xxix. 366]

JESSE, JOHN HENEAGE (1815–1874), historical writer ; son of Edward Jesse [q. v.] ; educated at Eton ; clerk in the admiralty ; author of 'Memoirs of the court of England, of George Selwyn and his contemporaries, 1843, of the Pretenders, 1845, of Richard III, 1862, and George III, 1867, works on London, and 'Celebrated Etonians,' published, 1875. [xxix. 367]

JESSEL, SIR GEORGE (1824–1883), master of the rolls ; educated at London University, of which he was vice-chancellor, 1881–3 ; M.A., 1844 ; barrister, Lincoln's Inn, 1847 (treasurer, 1883) ; practised as conveyancer ; leading junior in rolls court ; Q.C., 1865 ; liberal M.P. for Dover, 1868–73 ; solicitor-general, 1871–3 ; master of the rolls, 1873–83 ; privy councillor, 1873 ; working head of the Patent Office, 1873–83 ; one of the greatest English equity judges ; active member of the commission on working of the medical acts, 1881 ; a baronetcy conferred on his heir after his death, 1883. [xxix. 368]

JESSEY or JACIE, HENRY (1601–1663), baptist divine ; B.A. St. John's College, Cambridge, 1623 ; episcopally ordained, 1627 ; deprived of vicarage of Aughton for nonconformity, 1634 ; independent pastor in Southwark, 1637 ; adopted baptist views, 1645 ; assisted

in founding first Welsh independent church, 1639; baptist 'teacher' in Swan Alley, Coleman Street, 1653; a 'trier' and 'expurgator'; collected money for Jews in Jerusalem, 1657; frequently arrested after the Restoration; published annual 'Scripture Kalendars,' 1645-64, and devotional works, and planned a revision of the bible.
[xxix. 370]

JESSOP, CONSTANTINE (1602?-1658), presbyterian minister; B.A. Trinity College, Dublin, and (1632) M.A. Jesus College, Oxford; obtained sequestered benefices of Fyfield, 1643, and St. Nicholas, Bristol, 1647; rector of Wimborne Minster. 1654-8; published theological works.
[xxix. 372]

JEUNE, FRANCIS (1806-1868), bishop of Peterborough; M.A. Pembroke College, Oxford, 1830; D.C.L., 1834; fellow of Pembroke College, 1830-7; secretary to Sir John Colborne in Canada, 1832; headmaster of King Edward's School, Birmingham, 1834-8; dean of Jersey, 1838-43; master of Pembroke College, Oxford, 1843-64; active member of Oxford commission, 1850; vice-chancellor, 1858-62; dean of Lincoln, 1864; bishop of Peterborough, 1864-8.
[xxix. 372]

JEVON, THOMAS (1652-1688), actor and dramatist; brother-in-law of Thomas Shadwell [q. v.]; played low comedy parts in plays by D'Urfey, Shadwell, Mountford's 'Dr. Faustus,' and his own play, 'The Devil of a Wife,' 1686.
[xxix. 373]

JEVONS, MRS. MARY ANNE (1795-1845), author of 'Sonnets and other Poems, chiefly devotional' (1845); daughter of William Roscoe [q. v.]; married Thomas Jevons, 1825.
[xxix. 374]

JEVONS, WILLIAM STANLEY (1835-1882), economist and logician; son of Mrs. Mary Anne Jevons [q. v.]; educated at University College, London; assayer, Sydney mint, 1854-9; published 'Remarks on the Australian Goldfields,' 1859; returned to England and graduated M.A. London, with the gold medal for philosophy and political economy, 1862; went to Owens College as tutor, 1863; issued his 'Pure Logic' (founded on Boole's mathematical method), 1864; predicted future exhaustion of British coal supply, 1865; professor of logic, political economy, and philosophy at Owens College, 1866-79; exhibited his reasoning machine in Manchester and Liverpool, 1866; published 'Substitution of Similars,' 1869, 'Elementary Lessons in Logic,' 1870, 'Studies in Deductive Logic,' 1880, and 'Principles of Science,' 1874; wrote on currency, 1868-9; defended Lowe's match tax, 1871; issued 'Theory of Political Economy' (treated as a mathematical science), 1871, with 'Primer,' 1878; F.R.S., 1872; hon. LL.D. Edinburgh, 1875; professor of political economy, University College, London, 1876-80; published 'The State in Relation to Labour,' 1882; his 'Methods of Social Reform' published posthumously; drowned at Bulverhythe, Sussex; a fund for the encouragement of economic research was founded in his honour.
[xxix. 374]

JEWEL, JOHN (1522-1571), bishop of Salisbury; fellow of Corpus Christi College, Oxford, 1542-53; M.A., 1545; trained in biblical criticism by John Parkhurst (1512?-1575) [q. v.]; vicar of Sunningwell, 1551; deprived of his fellowship under Mary; notary to Cranmer and Ridley in their disputation, 1554; fled to Frankfort to avoid persecution, 1555, though he had signed Romish articles; joined Richard Cox [q. v.] against Knox; afterwards stayed with Peter Martyr at Strasburg and Zurich; returned to England, 1559; one of the protestant disputants at the Westminster conference, 1559; bishop of Salisbury, 1560-71; challenged Romanist antagonists to prove their doctrines; carried on controversies with Henry Cole [q. v.] and Thomas Harding (1516-1572) [q. v.]; issued in Latin his 'Apologia pro Ecclesia Anglicana,' 1562, and 'Defence of the Apology,' 1570; D.D. Oxford, 1575; ultimately identified himself with Anglicanism and opposed the puritans; his answer to Cartwright and 'View of a Seditious Bull' issued posthumously; entrusted by convocation with revision of the articles, 1571; built cathedral library at Salisbury; encouraged education, Hooker being among his protégés. His complete works have been edited by Fuller (1609), Jelf (1848), and Eyre (1845-50).
[xxix. 378]

JEWETT, RANDOLPH or RANDAL (d. 1675), composer of anthems and organist of St. Patrick and Christ Church, Dublin; Mus. Bac. Trinity College, Dublin;

minor canon of St. Paul's Cathedral, 1661; organist of Winchester.
[xxix. 382]

JEWITT, ARTHUR (1772-1852), topographer; author of 'History of Lincolnshire' (1817), of Buxton (1810), 'The Northern Star, or Yorkshire Magazine' (1817-18), and mathematical handbooks.
[xxix. 382]

JEWITT, LLEWELLYNN FREDERICK WILLIAM (1816-1886), antiquary; son of Arthur Jewitt [q. v.]; executed drawings for Charles Knight's publications and Parker's architectural works; chief librarian of Plymouth, 1849-53; edited 'Derby Telegraph,' 1853-68; established 'Reliquary,' 1860; F.S.A., 1853; published 'Ceramic Art of Great Britain,' 1878, 'The Wedgwoods,' 1865, 'Graves, Mounds, and their Contents,' 1870, and other works; collaborated with Samuel Carter Hall [q. v.] in 'Stately Homes of England,' 1874-7.
[xxix. 383]

JEWITT, THOMAS ORLANDO SHELDON (1799-1869), wood-engraver; brother of Llewellynn Frederick William Jewitt [q. v.]; illustrated Parker's architectural works and other publications.
[xxix. 384]

JEWSBURY, GERALDINE ENDSOR (1812-1880), novelist; friend of the Carlyles, Helen Faucit, and William Edward Forster; published 'Zoe,' 1845, 'The Half-Sisters,' 1848, 'Marian Withers,' 1851, and 'Right or Wrong,' 1859; and juvenile fiction.
[xxix. 384]

JEWSBURY, MARIA JANE, afterwards MRS. FLETCHER (1800-1833), authoress; sister of Geraldine Endsor Jewsbury [q. v.]; contributed to the 'Athenæum'; went to India with her husband; praised by Wordsworth and Christopher North; published 'Phantasmagoria,' 1824, 'The Three Histories,' 1830, and other works; died of cholera at Poonah.
[xxix. 385]

JEZREEL, JAMES JERSHOM (1840-1885), founder of the 'New and Latter House of Israel,' 1876; originally named JAMES WHITE; began life as private in the army; married Clarissa Rogers ('Queen Esther'), 1879, and with her visited America and made converts; published 'Extracts from the Flying Scroll,' 1879-81; erected extensive building for his sect at Gillingham.
[xxix. 385]

JOAN, JOANNA, JONE, or JANE (1165-1199), queen of Sicily; third daughter of Henry II of England; married to William II, king of Sicily, 1177; detained after his death (1189) by Tancred, the new king of Sicily, by whom she was given up to her brother Richard, 1190; accompanied him and Queen Berengaria to Palestine, 1191; proposed as wife for Saphadin, brother of Saladin; married Raymond VI, count of Toulouse, 1196; died at Rouen at birth of her second child; buried at Fontevraud, where she was, when dying, veiled as a nun.
[xxix. 386]

JOAN, JOANNA, ANNA, or JANET (d. 1237), princess of North Wales; according to 'Tewkesbury Annals' a daughter of King John; married to Llywelyn ab Iorwerth [q. v.], 1206; obtained terms for her husband from King John, 1211; mediated between Henry III and the Welsh; Franciscan house founded in Anglesey at her burial place; her stone coffin now in Baron Hill Park, Beaumaris.
[xxix. 388]

JOAN or JOANNA (1210-1238), queen of Scotland; eldest daughter of King John of England; betrothed to the younger Hugh of Lusignan, but (1221) married, at York, Alexander II of Scotland; died in England; buried at Tarent nunnery, Dorset.
[xxix. 388]

JOAN or JOANNA OF ACRE, COUNTESS OF GLOUCESTER AND HERTFORD (1272-1307), third daughter of Edward I and Eleanor of Castile; after five years in Spain was betrothed to Hartmann, son of Rudolf of Habsburg, 1279; married at Westminster Abbey, 1290, Gilbert de Clare (1243-1295) [q. v.]; after his death privately married Ralph de Monthermer [q. v.], 1297.
[xxix. 389]

JOAN (1321-1362), queen of Scotland; youngest child of Edward II; married to David Bruce of Berwick, 1327, both parties being children; crowned at Scone, 1331; accompanied David to France when Baliol seized the crown, 1332; lived at Chateau Gaillard, 1334-41; allowed by Edward III to visit her husband while a prisoner in England; settled in England on account of the infidelity of David, receiving Hertford Castle as a residence; highly popular in Scotland.
[xxix. 390]

JOAN (1328–1385), 'Fair Maid of Kent,' daughter of Edmund of Woodstock, earl of Kent [q. v.] ; her marriage with William de Montacute, second earl of Salisbury [q. v.], set aside on the ground of pre-contract with Sir Thomas Holland (d. 1360) [q. v.], 1349 ; became Countess of Kent and Lady Wake of Liddell in her own right, 1352 ; married, as her second husband, Edward the Black Prince, 1361 ; lived with him in Aquitaine, 1362–71 ; protected John of Gaunt from the Londoners, 1377 ; mediated between Richard II and John of Gaunt, 1385. [xxix. 392]

JOAN or JOANNA OF NAVARRE (1370 ?–1437), queen of Henry IV of England ; second daughter of Charles the Bad of Navarre ; married first to John IV, duke of Brittany, 1386 ; when regent married by proxy to Henry IV, 1401, and in person at Winchester, 1403, leaving her Breton children under Burgundy's guardianship ; accused of witchcraft, deprived of her revenues and imprisoned at Pevensey, 1419–22 ; buried at Canterbury. [xxix. 393]

JOAN, queen of Scotland (d. 1445). [See JANE or JOHANNA.]

JOAN OF KENT (d. 1550). [See BOCHER, JOAN.]

JOBSON, SIR FRANCIS (d. 1573), lieutenant of the Tower, 1564 ; knighted by Edward VI. [xxix. 395]

JOBSON, FREDERICK JAMES (1812–1881), Wesleyan minister ; thrice assistant for a three years' term at the City Road Chapel ; delegate at methodist episcopal conference, Indianapolis, 1856, and the Sydney conference, 1862 ; book steward, 1864 ; president of Wesleyan methodist conference, 1869 ; published religious works. [xxix. 396]

JOBSON, RICHARD (fl. 1620–1623), traveller and author ; ascended the Gambia, 1620 ; published 'The Golden Trade, or a Discovery of the River Gambra,' 1623. [xxix. 396]

JOCELIN. [See also JOSCELYN and JOSSELYN.]

JOCELIN (d. 1199), bishop of Glasgow ; abbot of Melrose, 1170 ; bishop of Glasgow, 1175–99 ; attended council of Northampton, 1176 ; sent by William the Lion to Rome to obtain removal of an interdict, 1181 ; built crypt and began choir, lady-chapel, and central tower, Glasgow Cathedral. [xxix. 396]

JOCELIN DE BRAKELOND (fl. 1200), chronicler ; monk of Bury St. Edmunds. His chronicle of St. Edmund's Abbey (1173–1202), translated by T. E. Tomlins, 1843, and edited by J. G. Rokewood, 1840, and T. Arnold, 1890, inspired Carlyle's 'Past and Present.' [xxix. 397]

JOCELIN or JOSCELIN (fl. 1200), Cistercian ; compiled lives of St. Patrick (first printed, 1624 ; translated by E. L. Swift, 1809) and other saints. [xxix. 397]

JOCELIN or JOSCELINE OF WELLS (d. 1242), bishop of Bath and Wells ; justiciar of fines, 1203–5 ; bishop of Bath and Glastonbury, 1206–18, of Bath (and Wells) alone, 1206–42 ; named in preamble of Great Charter ; justice itinerant in western counties, 1218 ; took part with Langton against Falkes de Breauté, 1224 ; witnessed confirmation of the charter, 1236 ; buried at Wells, where he built the nave, choir, and west front, as well as the oldest part of the palace. [xxix. 398]

JOCELIN, MRS. ELIZABETH (1596–1622), author of 'The Mother's Legacie to her Unborne Childe,' published, 1624 (3rd edition reprinted, 1852) ; née Brooke ; died in childbirth. [xxix. 399]

JOCELYN, PERCY (1764–1843), bishop of Clogher ; son of Robert, first earl of Roden [q. v.] ; B.A. Trinity College, Dublin, 1785 ; bishop of Ferns and Leighlin, 1809, of Clogher, 1820 ; deposed for scandalous crime. [xxix. 399]

JOCELYN, ROBERT, first (Irish) VISCOUNT JOCELYN (1688 ?–1756), lord chancellor of Ireland ; Irish barrister, 1706 ; entered Irish parliament, 1725 ; solicitor-general, 1727 ; attorney-general, 1730 ; lord chancellor of Ireland, 1739–56 ; created Baron Newport, 1743, Viscount Jocelyn, 1755 ; ten times lord justice. [xxix. 399]

JOCELYN, ROBERT, first EARL OF RODEN (1731–1797), auditor-general of Ireland, 1750–97 ; son of Robert, first viscount Jocelyn [q. v.] ; created Irish earl, 1771. [xxix. 400]

JOCELYN, ROBERT, third EARL OF RODEN (1788–1870), grand master of the Orange Society ; M.P., Dundalk, 1810–20 ; created British peer (Baron Clanbrassil), 1821 ; J.P. (removed after Dolly's Brae riots, 1849). [xxix. 400]

JODRELL, SIR PAUL (d. 1803), physician ; fellow of St. John's College, Cambridge ; eleventh wrangler, 1769 ; M.A., 1772 ; M.D., 1786 ; knighted, 1787 ; physician to the nabob of Arcot, 1787 ; died at Madras. [xxix. 401]

JODRELL, RICHARD PAUL (1745–1831), classical scholar and dramatist ; brother of Sir Paul Jodrell [q. v.] ; contributed to 'Musæ Etonenses' ; of Hertford College, Oxford ; barrister, Lincoln's Inn, 1771 ; M.P., Seaford, 1794–6 ; F.R.S. and F.S.A. ; published 'Illustrations of Euripides,' 1778, 'The Philology of the English Language,' 1820, and plays, including 'A Widow and no Widow' and 'Seeing is Believing,' produced at the Haymarket, 1779 and 1783. [xxix. 401]

JODRELL, SIR RICHARD PAUL, second baronet (1781–1861), poet ; son of Richard Paul Jodrell [q. v.] ; of Eton and Magdalen College, Oxford ; M.A., 1806 ; barrister, Lincoln's Inn, 1803 ; succeeded to baronetcy of his maternal great-uncle, Sir John Lombe, 1817. [xxix. 402]

JOFROI or GEOFFROY OF WATERFORD (fl. 1290), translator (Gotafridus). [xxix. 402]

JOHANNES ÆGIDIUS (fl. 1230). [See JOHN OF ST. GILES.]

JOHANNES DE SACRO BOSCO (fl. 1230). [See HOLYWOOD, JOHN.]

JOHN (1167 ?–1216), king of England ; youngest son of Henry II ; called LACKLAND in boyhood by his father, whose favourite son he was : declared king of Ireland, 1177 ; taken to Normandy, 1183 ; with his brother, Geoffrey of Brittany, made war on Richard, 1184, who refused to give him Aquitaine ; sent to Ireland, 1185, where he alienated the natives by his insolence and the mercenaries by spending their pay ; given a command in Normandy, 1187 ; hastened Henry II's death by his treachery, 1189 ; married Avice of Gloucester, 1189, and received from Richard I the counties of Mortain, Derby, Dorset, Somerset, Devon, and Cornwall, the town of Nottingham, and several castles, with full rights of jurisdiction ; returned to England, 1191, and kept royal state at Marlborough and Lancaster ; headed the opposition to William Longchamp (chancellor) ; had himself declared heir to the throne, 1191 ; with the assistance of the Londoners compelled Longchamp to leave England, 1191 ; on the news of Richard's imprisonment did homage to his enemy, Philip of France, for his continental dominions, 1193 ; made raids with foreign mercenaries on Richard's English territory, but was compelled to flee with Philip into France ; attempted to prolong Richard I's captivity ; excommunicated and deprived of his English lands, but forgiven by Richard through the mediation of their mother, Eleanor, 1194 ; made war for him against Philip, and received back some of his lands and a pension, 1195 ; retired to Brittany on being accused by Philip to Richard, but was declared his brother's heir, 1199 ; acknowledged in Normandy, but resisted in the Angevin provinces by the adherents of Arthur of Brittany ; crowned at Westminster, 27 May 1199 ; returned to Normandy and made treaty with Philip of France, being acknowledged king of England and Duke of Normandy, with the homage of Brittany from Arthur ; renounced alliance of the emperor and the count of Flanders, and gave his niece, Blanche, in marriage to Louis of France, 1200 ; divorced his wife, Avice, but retained her inheritance, 1200 ; married Isabella of Angoulême [q. v.], 1200 ; received homage from William of Scotland, 1200 ; proceeded against the Poitevin lords who were allied with Isabella's betrothed, Hugh le Brun ; sentenced by the French peers to forfeit all his fiefs for refusing to submit to his suzerain, Philip, his claims to continental possessions, 1202 ; raised siege of Mirebeau and captured his nephew, Arthur [q. v.], Eleanor, his sister, and many French nobles ; attempted to blind Arthur, removed him to Rouen, and there probably murdered him, 1203 ; being defeated in Normandy returned to England, 1204 ; lost all Normandy and most of Poitou, 1204–5 ; agreed to a truce for two years, surrendering all territory north of Loire, 1206 ; refused to accept Stephen Langton [q. v.] as archbishop, and drove out the monks of Canterbury, in consequence of which the kingdom was laid under interdict, 1208 ;

seized property of bishops who had published it, and confiscated property of the clergy and monks and outlawed them, 1208–9; exacted hostages from William of Scotland and the English nobles; went to Ireland to establish English supremacy, overthrew power of the Lacys, and revenged himself on William de Braose, 1210; extorted money from the Jews; reduced North Wales, 1211; excommunicated by the pope, 1212; oppressed the nobles, but mitigated forest exactions, and allied himself with the counts of Flanders and Boulogne against France; influenced by rumours of conspiracy surrendered his kingdom to the pope, 1213, promising to pay annual tribute and to receive back the exiled prelates, 1213; after the English naval victory at Damme, 1213, renewed his coronation promises to the returned bishops at Winchester; displeased the barons by appointment of Peter des Roches as justiciar, October 1213; issued writ for a council at which representatives of counties were to be present, November 1213; sent an embassy to Morocco; filled up vacant benefices; invaded Poitou, and obtained some successes in Anjou, but fled before the dauphin, and after the defeat of his allies at Bouvines (1214) made a truce for five years, and returned to England; compelled, in spite of papal support, to agree to the barons' demands at Runnymede, 15 June 1215; obtaining excommunication of his opponents and aid of mercenaries, caused division among the barons, and took Rochester, Colchester, and many of the northern castles; deserted on landing of Louis of France, 1216, by Salisbury and other adherents; lost most of England except the west; pursued from Windsor to the east; ravaged the country mercilessly, and after marching north through Lincolnshire, died, possibly poisoned, at Newark; buried in Worcester Cathedral.
[xxix. 402]

JOHN of Eltham, Earl of Cornwall (1316–1336), second son of Edward II; regent for Edward III while in France, 1329 and 1331, and Scotland, 1332; commanded first division at Halidon Hill, 1333; died at Perth while commanding in Scotland. [xxix. 417]

JOHN of Gaunt, Duke of Lancaster (1340–1399), fourth son of Edward III; born at Ghent; created Earl of Richmond, 1342; married Blanche of Lancaster and accompanied expedition to France, 1359; succeeded to Lancaster estates in right of his wife, and was created duke, 1362; led first division of the Black Prince's army into Spain, distinguishing himself at Najera, 1367; captain of Calais and Guisnes, 1369; with Black Prince at recapture of Limoges (1370); lieutenant of Aquitaine, 1371; captured Périgord, but resigned his command, July 1371; married (as his second wife) Constance of Castile, assuming title of king of Castile, 1372; accompanied Rochelle expedition, 1372; as captain-general led force from Calais to Bordeaux, but effected nothing, 1373; took part in Bruges negotiations, 1375–6; attacked through his adherents in the Good parliament, 1376, but on its dissolution, July 1376, reversed its measures; upheld Wycliffe (his ally against the prelates), and when insulted by the Londoners, obtained dismissal of their officers; on accession of Richard II (1377) retired from court; called upon for advice on French war; incurred great odium by failure of his attempt on St. Malo and outrages of his followers, 1378; as commander of the border made truce with Scotland, 1380; acted as justiciar to inquire into rebellion of 1381; presided over commission to reform the royal household, 1381; negotiated truce with France, 1384; unsuccessfully invaded Scotland, 1384; quarrelled with Richard and fortified Pontefract Castle, but accompanied Richard's Scottish expedition, 1385; in alliance with Portugal possessed himself of part of Galicia, but resigned Castilian claims in favour of his daughter Catharine on her marriage with John of Castile, 1387; lieutenant of Guienne, 1388–9; mediated between Richard II and his opponents; named Duke of Aquitaine, 1390; conducted negotiations with France, 1393–4; put down Cheshire revolt, 1393; said to have claimed recognition of his son as heir to the throne; failed to obtain recognition in Aquitaine as duke; married Catharine Swynford, 1396; presided at trial of Arundel, 1397; head of the committee of government, 1398; his tomb in St. Paul's destroyed during the Commonwealth. [xxix. 417]

JOHN of Lancaster, Duke of Bedford (1389–1435), third son of Henry IV; constable of England, governor of Berwick, and warden of the east marches in Henry IV's reign; K.G., 1400; created duke, 1414; lieutenant of England during Henry V's first French expedi-

tion, 1415, and presided over the succeeding parliament, 1415; relieved Harfleur, 1416; while lieutenant of the kingdom repelled the 'Foul raid' of the Scots, 1417; directed proceedings against Sir John Oldcastle [q. v.], 1417; joined Henry V in France, 1419; again lieutenant of England, 1421; assumed command of the army in France during the king's illness, 1422; on Henry's death (1422) became regent of France, and protector of England; negotiated alliance with Burgundy and Brittany against Charles VII of France, himself marrying Philip of Burgundy's sister Anne, 1423; reformed the French coinage, encouraged trade, and promoted good administration; defeated the French and Scots at Verneuil, 1424; forbade his brother, Humphrey, duke of Gloucester [q. v.], to proceed with his challenge to Philip of Burgundy; after a visit to England to settle the quarrel between Gloucester and Henry Beaufort (d. 1447) [q. v.], returned to France, 1427; conducted the war with success till raising of the siege of Orleans, 1429; temporarily resigned the regency to Burgundy; purchased Joan of Arc from her Burgundian captors and caused her to be burnt as a witch at Rouen, 1431; caused Henry VI to be crowned king of France at Notre Dame, 1431; offended Burgundy by his second marriage with Jacqueline of Luxemburg, 1433; on a visit to England defended his French administration against Gloucester's charges, 1433; forced to send delegates to the peace congress at Arras, 1435; died and was buried at Rouen. [xxix. 427]

JOHN of Beverley, Saint (d. 721), bishop of York; educated at Canterbury by Theodore; some time monk at Whitby (Streonshalch); ordained Bede; Bishop of Hexham, 687; at synod of the Nidd (705) opposed restoration of Wilfrid [q. v.], bishop of York, 705–18; retired to monastery built by himself at Beverley, where he died; canonised, 1037, twice translated; his remains discovered, 1664. [xxix. 435]

JOHN SCOTUS, Erigena (d. 875). [See Scotus.]

JOHN de Villula (d. 1122), bishop of Bath; originally a physician of Tours; bishop of Somerset, 1088–1122; bought from William II the city of Bath, and removed his see thither; rebuilt the abbey church; destroyed Gisa's buildings at Wells and forced the canons to live among the laity; present at synod of Westminster, 1102; supposed founder of two baths at Bath.
[xxix. 436]

JOHN (d. 1147), bishop of Glasgow, 1115; suspended by Archbishop Thurstan of York, 1122; some time suffragan to the patriarch at Jerusalem; censured by Pope Honorius at Rome, 1125; withdrew to Tiron (Picardy) till 1128; chancellor to David of Scotland, 1129; rebuilt Glasgow Cathedral. [xxix. 437]

JOHN of Cornwall, or Johannes de Sancto Germano (fl. 1170), probably of St. Germans, Cornwall, but perhaps a Breton: studied at Paris under Peter Lombard, and afterwards lectured there; his only undoubted work, 'Eulogium ad Alexandrum Papam III' (printed in Martène's 'Thesaurus Novus Anecdotum,' and in Migne's 'Patrologia'). [xxix. 438]

JOHN of Salisbury (d. 1180), bishop of Chartres; called Parvus; born at Salisbury; studied at Paris under Peter Abailard and Alberic of Rheims, 1136–8, and at Chartres; returned to Paris (1140) and attended lectures on theology and logic by Gilbert de la Porrée and Robert Pullus; studied and taught with Peter of la Celle at Provins; presented by St. Bernard to Archbishop Theobald at council of Rheims, 1148; attended Pope Eugenius III at Brescia and Rome; came to England probably c. 1150; at Canterbury till 1164, secretary to Theobald and sent on important missions; intimate with Hadrian IV; obtained bull for the conquest of Ireland, 1155; fell into disgrace with Henry II for denouncing exactions demanded from the church in connection with the Toulouse expedition, 1159; applied to Becket (then chancellor) to intercede for him; left England, 1164, owing probably to his enthusiastic support of Becket's cause; during residence with Peter of la Celle at abbey of St. Remigius, Rheims, composed the 'Historia Pontificalis'; counselled moderation to Becket in his exile, but firmly upheld his cause, though seeking the good offices of Gilbert Foliot [q. v.] and others with Henry II; present at meeting of Henry and Louis VII at Angers, 1166; returned to England after pacification of Fréteval, 1170; with Becket at the time of his murder at Canterbury, 1170;

wrote his life and advocated his canonisation; named treasurer of Exeter, 1174; as bishop of Chartres (1176–80) excommunicated Count of Vendôme, and was present at the peace made between England and France near Ivry, 1177; took active part at third Lateran council, 1179; the most learned classical writer of the middle ages. His works (printed by J. A. Giles, 1848) consist of Letters, the 'Policraticus' (first printed, 1476), the 'Metalogicus,' 'Entheticus,' 'Vita Sancti Anselmi,' and other Latin writings. [xxix. 439]

JOHN OF HEXHAM (*fl.* 1180), prior of Hexham; continued Symeon of Durham's 'Chronicle' to 1154. [xxix. 446]

JOHN OF OXFORD (*d.* 1200). [See OXFORD.]

JOHN OF THE FAIR HANDS (*d.* 1203?). [See BELMEIS, JOHN.]

JOHN (*fl.* 1215), called WALLENSIS. [See WALLENSIS.]

JOHN OF ST. GILES (*fl.* 1230), Dominican and physician; sometimes called from his birthplace, St. Albans; lectured on medicine at Montpellier and on philosophy and theology at Paris; first physician to Philip Augustus, *c.* 1209; presented Hôpital de St. Jacques to the Dominicans; perhaps the first Englishman of the order; lectured against the Albigenses at Toulouse, 1233–5; invited to England by Grosseteste; head of the Dominican schools at Oxford; chancellor of Lincoln, 1239; archdeacon of Oxford, *c.* 1239; a royal councillor, 1239; attended Grosseteste and Richard de Clare, earl of Gloucester; his only extant treatise the 'Experimenta Joannis de S. Ægidio.' [xxix. 446]

JOHN BASING or BASINGSTOKE (*d.* 1252). [See BASING.]

JOHN DE LEXINTON (*d.* 1257). [See LEXINTON.]

JOHN OF SCHIPTON (*d.* 1257), Augustinian prior at Newburgh, 1252; counsellor of Henry III. [xxix. 448]

JOHN OF WALLINGFORD (*d.* 1258). [See WALLINGFORD.]

JOHN OF LONDON (*fl.* 1267), mathematician; expounded Roger Bacon's three chief works to Pope Clement IV, 1267. [xxix. 448]

JOHN GERVAYS or OF EXETER (*d.* 1268), bishop of Winchester, 1262; previously chancellor of York; a baronial negotiator at Brackley, 1264, and with Louis IX; suspended, 1266, after Evesham (1265); died at Rome. [xxix. 448]

JOHN DE SANDFORD (*d.* 1294). [See SANDFORD.]

JOHN BEVER or OF LONDON (*d.* 1311), author of 'Commendatio lamentabilis in transitum magni Regis Edwardi Quarti' (Edward I); supposed by some to be writer of 'Flores Historiarum'; monk of Westminster. [xxix. 449]

JOHN DE SANDALE (*d.* 1319). [See SANDALE.]

JOHN OF DALDERBY (*d.* 1320). [See DALDERBY, JOHN DE.]

JOHN DE THORPE or THORP, BARON THORPE (*d.* 1324). [See THORPE.]

JOHN DE TROKELOWE, THROKLOW, or THORLOW (*fl.* 1330). [See TROKELOWE.]

JOHN DE SHOREDITCH or SHORDYCH (*d.* 1345). [See SHOREDITCH, SIR JOHN.]

JOHN DE ST. FAITH'S (*d.* 1359). [See ST. FAITH'S.]

JOHN DE ST. PAUL (1295?–1362). [See ST. PAUL.]

JOHN OF TINMOUTH (*fl.* 1366). [See TINMOUTH.]

JOHN THORESBY (*d.* 1373). [See THORESBY.]

JOHN OF BRIDLINGTON (*d.* 1379), prior of St Mary's, Bridlington, 1360; was formally canonised by Pope Boniface IX on 24 Sept. 1401; the 'prophecies of Bridlington' probably ascribed to him erroneously. [xxix. 451]

JOHN OF PETERBOROUGH (*fl.* 1380), alleged author of 'Chronicon Petroburgense' (654–1368); probably an imaginary person. [xxix. 451]

JOHN DE NEWENHAM (*d.* 1382?). [See NEWENHAM.]

JOHN THOMPSON, THOMSON, or TOMSON (*fl.* 1382). [See THOMPSON.]

JOHN WELLS (*d.* 1388). [See WELLS.]

JOHN OF WALTHAM (*d.* 1395). [See WALTHAM.]

JOHN OF GLASTONBURY (*fl.* 1400), historian of Glastonbury Abbey. [xxix. 452]

JOHN DE TREVISA (1326–1412). [See TREVISA.]

JOHN OF BURY or JOHN BURY (*fl.* 1460), Augustinian; provincial at Erfurt, 1459, 1462, and 1476; wrote 'Gladius Salomonis' in answer to Bishop Reginald Pecock's 'Repressor of Overmuch Learning.' [xxix. 452]

JOHN OF PADUA (*fl.* 1542–1549). [See PADUA, JOHN OF.]

JOHN LLYWELYN (1520?–1616). [See LLYWELYN OF LLANGEWYDD.]

JOHN THE PAINTER (1752–1777). [See AITKEN, JAMES.]

JOHNES, ARTHUR JAMES (1809–1871), Welsh county court judge; studied at London University; barrister, Lincoln's Inn, 1835; advocated legal reforms; published (as 'Maelog') translations from David ab Gwilym [q. v.]; awarded prize by Cymmrodorion Society for essay on causes of Welsh dissent, 1831; issued 'Philological Proofs of original unity and recent origin of the Human Race,' 1843. [xxx. 1]

JOHNES, BASSET (*fl.* 1634–1659). [See JONES.]

JOHNES, THOMAS (1748–1816), translator of the chronicles of Froissart, 1803–5, and Monstrelet, 1809, and 'Memoirs of de Joinville,' 1807; of Shrewsbury, Eton, and Jesus College, Oxford; M.P., Cardigan, 1774–80, Radnorshire, 1780–96, Cardiganshire, 1796–1816; F.R.S., 1809; lord-lieutenant of Cardiganshire. [xxx. 2]

JOHNS, AMBROSE BOWDEN (1776–1858), Devonshire painter; some time friend of J. M. W. Turner. [xxx. 2]

JOHNS, CHARLES ALEXANDER (1811–1874), B.A. Trinity College, Dublin, 1841; second master at Helston school under Derwent Coleridge [q. v.], afterwards (1843–7) head-master; F.L.S., 1836; published popular works of natural history and educational manuals. [xxx. 3]

JOHNS, DAVID (1794–1843), missionary to Madagascar, 1826–36; published Malagasy dictionary, 1835; died at Nossi Bé. [xxx. 3]

JOHNS, WILLIAM (1771–1845), unitarian minister at Nantwich and afterwards at Cross Street, Manchester; joint-secretary of Manchester Literary and Philosophical Society; published theological and educational works. [xxx. 4]

JOHNSON. [See also JOHNSTON, JOHNSTONE, and JONSON.]

JOHNSON, BENJAMIN (1665?–1742), actor; joined Drury Lane company, 1695, and played original parts in plays by Farquhar, Vanbrugh, and others; appeared at the Haymarket as Corbaccio ('Volpone'), First Gravedigger ('Hamlet'), and Morose ('Epicœne'), 1706–7; again at Drury Lane, 1708–9; remained there almost continuously from 1710, adding Justice Shallow, Old Gobbo, and many other parts to his répertoire. [xxx. 4]

JOHNSON, CAPTAIN CHARLES (*fl.* 1724–1736), author of 'General History of the Robberies and Murders of the most Notorious Pyrates,' 1724, and 'General History of the Lives and Adventures of the most famous Highwaymen,' 1734. [xxx. 5]

JOHNSON, CHARLES (1679–1748), dramatist; friend of Robert Wilks [q. v.]; satirised in the 'Dunciad'; author of nineteen plays. [xxx. 6]

JOHNSON, CHARLES (1791–1880), botanist; lecturer at Guy's Hospital; re-edited Smith's (1832) and edited Sowerby's 'English Botany,' 1832–46; published monographs on British ferns, poisonous plants, and grasses. [xxx. 7]

JOHNSON or JONSON, CHRISTOPHER (1536?–1597), Latin poet and physician; fellow of New College, Oxford, 1555; M.A., 1561; head-master of Winchester, 1560–70; M.D. Oxford, 1571; F.R.C.P., 1580, several times censor, and treasurer, 1594–6; his Latin poems in Richard Willes's 'Poemata' (1573). [xxx. 7]

JOHNSON, CORNELIUS (1593–1664 ?). [See JANS-SEN VAN CEULEN, CORNELIUS.]

JOHNSON, CUTHBERT WILLIAM (1799–1878), agricultural writer; barrister, Gray's Inn, 1836; F.R.S., 1842; published 'The Farmers' Encyclopædia,' 1842, 'Farmer's Medical Dictionary,' 1845, 'Life of Sir Edward Coke,' 1837; translated Thaër's 'Principles of Agriculture,' 1844; collaborated with W. Shaw and his brother, George William Johnson [q. v.]. [xxx. 8]

JOHNSON, DANIEL (1767–1835), author of 'Sketches of Indian Field-Sports,' 1822; surgeon in East India Company's service, 1805–9. [xxx. 8]

JOHNSON, EDWARD (*fl.* 1601), musical composer; Mus.Bac. Caius College, Cambridge, 1594. [xxx. 8]

JOHNSON, EDWARD (1599 ?–1672), author of 'History of New England from . . . 1628 untill 1652' ('Wonder-working Providence'); settled in Massachusetts, 1630; represented Woburn in the state assembly from 1643, being speaker, 1655. [xxx. 8]

JOHNSON, SIR EDWIN BEAUMONT (1825–1893), general; studied at East India Company's College, Addiscombe; lieutenant, Bengal artillery, 1845; captain, 1857; lieutenant-colonel, 1865; major-general, 1868; general, 1877; colonel-commandant, royal (late Bengal) artillery, 1890; served in Sikh wars, 1845–6 and 1848–9; assistant adjutant-general of artillery in Oude division, 1855–6?; in Indian mutiny, 1857–8; C.B. (military), 1858; military secretary for Indian affairs at headquarters of army in London, and extra aide-de-camp to the field-marshal commanding-in-chief, the Duke of Cambridge, 1865–72; quartermaster-general in India, 1873; returned to England as member of council of secretary of state for India, 1874; K.C.B., 1875; military member of council of governor-general of India, 1877–80; C.I.E., 1878; director-general of military education at war office in London, 1884–6; G.C.B., 1887. [Suppl. iii. 43]

JOHNSON, ESTHER (1681–1728), friend of Dean Swift; an inmate of Sir William Temple's family, where Swift met her; the 'Stella' of Swift's 'Journal to Stella'; possibly, but improbably, married to Swift. [iv. 208]

JOHNSON, FRANCIS (1562–1618), presbyterian separatist; brother of George Johnson (1564–1605) [q.v.]; fellow of Christ's College, Cambridge, 1584; M.A., 1585; imprisoned and expelled the university, 1589, for maintaining presbyterianism to be of divine right; preacher to English merchants at Middelburg, 1589–92; with John Greenwood (*d.* 1593) [q.v.] formed separatist church in London, 1592; several times imprisoned; from 1597 separatist pastor at Amsterdam; published Brownist treatises and other works. [xxx. 9]

JOHNSON, FRANCIS (1796 ?–1876), orientalist; professor of Sanskrit, Bengali, and Telugu, East India Company's college at Haileybury, 1824–55; published 'Persian Dictionary,' 1829 (enlarged, 1852), an edition of the 'Gulistán,' 1863. and editions of Sanskrit classics. [xxx. 11]

JOHNSON, GEORGE (1564–1605), puritan; M.A. Christ's College, Cambridge, 1588; imprisoned for separatism, 1593; sailed for America in the company of other separatists, 1597, but was obliged to return; escaped to Holland; quarrelled with his brother Francis Johnson (1562–1618) [q.v.] about his wife's fondness for fine clothing and was excommunicated, 1604; returned and prepared an account of the dissensions (Amsterdam, 1603); died in Durham gaol. [xxx. 11]

JOHNSON, SIR GEORGE (1818–1896), physician; studied medicine at King's College, London; M.D. London, 1844; F.R.C.P., 1850; Gulstonian lecturer, 1852; materia medica lecturer, 1853; Lumleian lecturer, 1877; Harveian orator, 1882; vice-president, 1887; assistant-physician to King's College Hospital, 1847, physician, 1856, professor of materia medica and therapeutics, 1857–1863, of medicine, 1863–76, of clinical medicine, 1876–86, and emeritus professor of clinical medicine and consulting physician, 1886; F.R.S., 1872; physician extraordinary to Queen Victoria, 1889; knighted, 1892; published medical works. [Suppl. iii. 44]

JOHNSON, GEORGE HENRY SACHEVERELL (1808–1881), dean of Wells; fellow, tutor, and dean of Queen's College, Oxford; Ireland scholar, 1827; M.A.,

1833; Savilian professor of astronomy, 1839–42; Whyte professor of moral philosophy, 1842–5; F.R.S., 1838; member of the Oxford commissions of 1850 and 1854; dean of Wells, 1854–81; edited 'Psalms' for 'Speaker's Commentary,' 1880. [xxx. 12]

JOHNSON, GEORGE WILLIAM (1802–1886), writer on gardening; barrister of Gray's Inn, 1836; collaborated with his brother Cuthbert William Johnson [q. v.] in 'Essay on Uses of Salt for Agriculture' (13th edit. 1838), 'Outlines of Chemistry,' 1828, and an edition of Paley's works, 1839; professor of political economy at Hindoo college, Calcutta, and editor of the government gazette, 1837–41; published 'History of English Gardening,' 1829, 'Principles of Practical Gardening,' 1845 (reissued as 'Science and Practice,' 1862), and other works; established 'The Cottage Gardener' ('Journal of Horticulture'), 1848. [xxx. 12]

JOHNSON, GERARD (*fl.* 1616). [See JANSSEN, GERAERT.]

JOHNSON, GUY (1740 ?–1788), American loyalist; served against the French, 1757–60; succeeded his uncle, Sir William Johnson [q. v.], as superintendent of Indians, 1774; his estates in Tryon county, New York, confiscated by the Americans, against whom he fought in Canada; died in London. [xxx. 13]

JOHNSON, HARRY JOHN (1826–1884), water-colour painter; friend and fellow-townsman of the elder David Cox [q. v.]; member of Institute of Painters in Water-colours, 1870. [xxx. 14]

JOHNSON, HENRY (1698 ?–1760), South American traveller and translator from the Spanish. [xxx. 14]

JOHNSON, SIR HENRY, first baronet (1748–1835), general; commanded light battalion of 28th, 1775–8, and the 17th regiment, 1778–81, during American war; defeated Irish rebels at New Ross, 1798; general, 1809; created baronet, 1818. [xxx. 14]

JOHNSON, HUMPHRY (*fl.* 1713), calligrapher and mathematician. [xxx. 15]

JOHNSON, ISAAC (*d.* 1630), one of the founders of Massachusetts; accompanied Winthrop to America, 1630. [xxx. 15]

JOHNSON, JAMES (1705–1774), bishop of Worcester; of Westminster and Christ Church, Oxford; M.A., 1731; D.D., 1742; second master at Westminster, 1733–48; rector of Berkhampstead, 1743; canon of St. Paul's and chaplain to George II, 1748; bishop of Gloucester, 1752–9, of Worcester, 1759–74. [xxx. 15]

JOHNSON, JAMES (*d.* 1811), engraver and publisher of 'The Scots Musical Museum,' 1787–1803. [xxx. 16]

JOHNSON, JAMES (1777–1845), physician; naval surgeon during the great war, being at Walcheren in 1809; attended Duke of Clarence and became physician extraordinary (1830) on his accession to the throne as William IV; edited 'Medico-Chirurgical Review,' 1818–44; M.D. St. Andrews, 1821; published 'Influence of Tropical Climates on European Constitutions,' 1812, and popular medical works. [xxx. 16]

JOHNSON, JOHN (*fl.* 1641), author of the 'Academy of Love' (poem), 1641. [xxx. 17]

JOHNSON, JOHN, of Cranbrook (1662–1725), divine; B.A. Magdalene College, Cambridge, 1681; M.A. Corpus Christi College, Cambridge, 1685; vicar of Boughton-under-the-Blean and Hernhill, 1687, of St. John's, Margate, and Appledore, 1697; vicar of Cranbrook, Kent, 1707–25; published works of controversial divinity. [xxx. 18]

JOHNSON, JOHN (1706–1791), baptist minister; pastor in Stanley Street, Liverpool, 1750–91; founded Johnsonian baptists; published 'Advantages and Disadvantages of the Married State' (5th edit. 1760) and other works; his 'Original Letters' issued, 1796–1800. [xxx. 18]

JOHNSON, JOHN (*d.* 1797), wood-engraver. [xxx. 28]

JOHNSON, JOHN (*d.* 1804), dissenting minister of Lady Huntingdon's connexion; pastor of St. George's, Rochdale Road, Manchester; published 'The Levite's Journal.' [xxx. 19]

JOHNSON, JOHN (1754–1814), architect; architect and county surveyor for Essex; erected buildings at Chelmsford. [xxx. 19]

JOHNSON, SIR JOHN, second baronet (d. 1830), superintendent of Indian affairs, 1783–1830, and commander of ' Johnson's Greens '; son of Sir William Johnson [q. v.] [xxx. 51]

JOHNSON, JOHN (d. 1833), kinsman and friend of Cowper; LL.D. Caius College, Cambridge, 1803; rector of Yaxham with Welborne, Norfolk, 1800–33; edited Cowper's correspondence, 1824, and vol. iii. of Cowper's ' Poems,' 1815, and Hayley's ' Memoirs,' 1823. [xxx. 19]

JOHNSON, JOHN (1759–1833), divine; of Charterhouse and Oriel College, Oxford; M.A., 1782; vicar of North Mimms, Hertfordshire, 1790–1833, and translator. [xxx. 20]

JOHNSON, JOHN (1777–1848), printer; compositor to Sir Egerton Brydges's private press at Lee Priory; printed at his own office in Brooke Street, Holborn, ' Typographia, or the Printer's Instructor,' 1824 (four sizes). [xxx. 20]

JOHNSON, JOHN MORDAUNT (1776 ?–1815), diplomatist; of Trinity College, Dublin, and Trinity College, Cambridge; chargé d'affaires at Brussels, 1814; afterwards consul at Geneva; died at Florence. [xxx. 21]

JOHNSON, JOHN NOBLE (1787–1823), author of ' Life of Linacre ' (ed. Robert Graves, 1835); M.A. Magdalen Hall, Oxford, 1810; M.D., 1814; Gulstonian lecturer, 1816; physician to Westminster Hospital, 1818–1822. [xxx. 21]

JOHNSON, JOSEPH (1738–1809), bookseller and publisher for Priestley, Cowper, Horne Tooke, Erasmus Darwin, and other authors; fined and imprisoned for issuing pamphlet by Gilbert Wakefield [q. v.], 1797; published ' Analytical Review,' 1788–99. [xxx. 21]

JOHNSON, LAWRENCE (fl. 1603), early engraver. [xxx. 22]

JOHNSON, MANUEL JOHN (1805–1859), astronomer; while in charge of the St. Helena Observatory observed solar eclipse of 27 July 1832; catalogued 606 fixed stars in the southern hemisphere (1835); M.A. Magdalen Hall, Oxford, 1842; keeper of the Radcliffe observatory, 1839; made observations and measurements with large heliometer, and (1858) utilised electrical transit-recorder; F.R.S., 1856; president of Royal Astronomical Society, 1857–8; astronomical prize founded to commemorate him at Oxford, 1862. [xxx. 22]

JOHNSON, MARTIN (d. 1686 ?), seal-engraver and landscape-painter. [xxx. 23]

JOHNSON, MAURICE (1688–1755), antiquary; founded ' Gentlemen's Society ' at Spalding, 1709–10, and the Stamford Society, c. 1721; barrister, Inner Temple, 1710; hon. librarian of Society of Antiquaries, 1717; left large manuscript collections relating chiefly to Lincolnshire and Peterborough antiquities; writings by him in Nichols's ' Bibliotheca Topographica Britannica.' [xxx. 23]

JOHNSON, RICHARD (1573–1659 ?), romance writer; freeman of London; author of ' Famous Historie of the Seaven Champions of Christendom,' c. 1597, ' The Nine Worthies of London,' 1592, ' The Crowne Garland of Golden Roses,' 1612 (reprinted by Percy Society), and ' Pleasant Conceites of Old Hobson,' 1607 (reprinted, 1843). [xxx. 24]

JOHNSON, RICHARD (1604–1687). [See WHITE.]

JOHNSON, RICHARD (d. 1721), grammarian; B.A. St. John's College, Cambridge, 1679; head-master of Nottingham free school, 1707–18; published ' Grammatical Commentaries,' 1706, ' Aristarchus Anti-Bentleianus,' 1717, and other works. [xxx. 25]

JOHNSON, ROBERT (fl. 1550), musical composer; perhaps chaplain to Anne Boleyn. [xxx. 25]

JOHNSON, ROBERT (d. 1559), canon and chancellor of Worcester, 1544; B.C.L. Cambridge, 1531 (incorporated at Oxford, 1551); his book against Hooper published posthumously. [xxx. 25]

JOHNSON, ROBERT (1540–1625), archdeacon of Leicester; fellow and steward of Trinity College, Cambridge; M.A., 1564 (incorporated at Oxford, 1565);

chaplain to Sir Nicholas Bacon; canon of Peterborough and Norwich, 1570, and of Windsor, 1572–1625; archdeacon of Leicester, 1591; founded schools at Oakham and Uppingham, and divinity scholarships at Clare, St. John's, Emmanuel, and Sidney Sussex Colleges, Cambridge. [xxx. 26]

JOHNSON, ROBERT (fl. 1626), lutenist and composer; musician to Prince Henry and Charles I; member of Shakespeare's company; first set Ariel's songs in the ' Tempest '; composed music for plays by Beaumont and Fletcher, Middleton, and Jonson; contributed to Leighton's ' Teares or Lamentacions,' 1614. [xxx. 27]

JOHNSON, ROBERT (1770–1796), engraver and water-colour painter; executed drawings for Bewick's ' Fables.' [xxx. 28]

JOHNSON, SAMUEL (1649–1703), whig divine; of St. Paul's School and Trinity College, Cambridge; rector of Corringham, Essex, 1670; domestic chaplain to Lord William Russell; imprisoned and fined, 1683, for his ' Julian the Apostate ' (tract against the Duke of York), 1682; wrote also ' Julian's Arts and Methods to undermine and extirpate Christianity,' 1683; degraded, pilloried, fined, and whipped for circulating his ' Humble and Hearty Address to all the English Protestants in the present Army,' 1686; published numerous protestant pamphlets; received pension and bounty from William III, but declined a deanery as inadequate; the Ben-Jochanan of ' Absalom and Achitophel.' [xxx. 28]

JOHNSON, SAMUEL (1691–1773), Manchester dancing-master and dramatist; produced in London, 1729, his extravaganza, ' Hurlothrumbo,' himself appearing as Lord Flame (satirised in Fielding's ' Author's Farce '), and afterwards ' Chester Comics,' the ' Mad Lovers,' and other pieces. [xxx. 30]

JOHNSON, SAMUEL (1709–1784), lexicographer; son of a Lichfield bookseller; educated at Lichfield, Stourbridge, and Pembroke College, Oxford; usher at Market Bosworth grammar school; subsequently assisted publisher of the ' Birmingham Journal '; married Mrs. Porter, 1735; took pupils at Edial, among them being David Garrick; went up to London with Garrick, 1737; found his first patron in Henry Hervey; contributed to ' Gentleman's Magazine,' assisting William Guthrie (1708–1770) [q. v.] with parliamentary debates, and himself compiling them from July 1741 to March 1744; published ' London ' through Dodsley, 1738; employed by Osborne to catalogue library of Edward Harley, second earl of Oxford [q. v.], 1742; issued ' Life of Savage,' 1744; began his ' English Dictionary,' 1747; published ' The Vanity of Human Wishes,' 1749; produced ' Irene ' at Drury Lane, 1749; formed the Ivy Lane Club, 1749; the ' Rambler ' written by him with occasional contributions from Mrs. Carter, Samuel Richardson, and others, 1750–1752; lost his wife, 1752; repelled Chesterfield's tardy offer of patronage, 1755, when his dictionary was published, and he received his M.A. from Oxford; gained the acquaintance of Dr. Charles Burney (1726–1814) [q. v.] and Bennet Langton [q. v.] through the ' Rambler,' and that of Sir Joshua Reynolds through the life of Savage; first met Goldsmith and Burke in 1761; when arrested for debt, 1756, released by a loan from Richardson; contributed to ' Literary Magazine,' 1756–8, reviews of works by Hanway and Soame Jenyns; wrote the ' Idler ' for Newbery's ' Universal Chronicle,' 1758–60, and ' Rasselas ' (his most popular work), 1759, when he went to live in Inner Temple Lane (now Johnson Buildings); helped to expose the Cock Lane Ghost, 1762; received through Wedderburn's application a pension of 300l. from Lord Bute, 1762; wrote pamphlets against Wilkes, 1770, a defence of the government policy in the affair of the Falkland islands, 1771, and towards America, 1775; became acquainted with Boswell in May 1763, and probably in the same winter founded his Literary Club held at the Turk's Head in Gerrard Street till 1783; introduced the ' Rambler,' and that of Sir Joshua Reynolds through the life of Savage to the Thrales, 1764, in whose town houses in Southwark and Grosvenor Square and country house at Streatham he was received hospitably; had an interview with George III, 1767, and with Wilkes, 1776; brought out his long delayed edition of Shakespeare in 1765; wrote Goldsmith's epitaph, 1776; named his own price for ' Lives of the Poets,' vols. i.–iv., 1779, v.–x., 1781; travelled with Boswell in Scotland, 1773 (publishing his

'Journey to the Western Isles of Scotland,' 1775); accompanied the Thrales to Wales, 1774, and Paris, 1775; Thrale's executor, 1781; quarrelled with Mrs. Thrale on her marriage with Piozzi; formed Essex Head Club, 1783; buried in Westminster Abbey, a monument being erected to him in St. Paul's by the club, and statues at Lichfield and Uttoxeter (1878); LL.D. Dublin, 1765, and Oxford, 1775, but rarely styled himself 'Dr.'; called by Carlyle the 'last of the tories.' Of the four portraits by Reynolds, one is in the National Gallery. Johnson holds the highest rank among conversationalists, and his style shows some dialectical power. His 'Prayers and Meditations,' 'Letters to Mrs. Piozzi,' and an autobiographical fragment appeared posthumously. The best edition of his works is that edited by Professor F. P. Walesby, 1825. [xxx. 31]

JOHNSON, THOMAS (d. 1644), botanist and royalist; published an enlarged and corrected edition of Gerard's 'Herball,' 1633, as well as the first local catalogue of plants issued in England (1629), and other works; M.D. Oxford, 1643; died from effects of a wound received at defence of Basing House; genus *Johnsonia* named after him; his minor works edited by T. S. Ralph, 1847. [xxx. 47]

JOHNSON, THOMAS (fl. 1718), classical scholar; of Eton and King's College, Cambridge; M.A., 1692; headmaster of Chigwell school, 1715–18; edited seven plays of Sophocles (collected, 1745), 'Gratii Falisci Cynegeticon,' 1699, and other works; his compilation, 'Novus Græcorum Epigrammatum et Poematiωn Delectus,' still in use at Eton. [xxx. 48]

JOHNSON, SIR THOMAS (1664–1729), founder of the modern Liverpool; bailiff of Liverpool, 1689, mayor, 1695, and M.P., 1701–23; purchased site of the old castle for a market, 1707; knighted, 1708; chief promoter of first floating dock at Liverpool, and erection of St. Peter's and St. George's churches, 1708; retired to Virginia, 1723; died in Jamaica. [xxx. 48]

JOHNSON, THOMAS (d. 1737), classical scholar; fellow of Magdalene College, Cambridge; M.A., 1728; one of the editors of Stephens's 'Latin Thesaurus,' 1734–5; edited Puffendorf's 'De Officio Hominis et Civis,' 1735. [xxx. 48]

JOHNSON, THOMAS? (1772–1839), smuggler; twice escaped from prison; received pardons for piloting expedition to Holland (1799) and the Walcheren expedition, 1809. [xxx. 49]

JOHNSON, THOMAS BURGELAND (d. 1840), author of 'The Sportsman's Cyclopædia,' 1831, and other books on field-sports. [xxx. 49]

JOHNSON, SIR WILLIAM, first baronet (1715–1774), superintendent of Indian affairs in North America: went to America and established himself south of the Mohawk river, 1738; traded with the Mohawk Indians, and was named Sachem; colonel of the six nations, 1744; commissary for Indian affairs, 1746; member of New York council, 1750; reconciled the Indians and colonials, 1753; superintendent of Indian affairs, 1755; commanded Crown Point expedition, 1755; received baronetcy and money grant, 1755; as second in command carried out successfully Fort Niagara expedition, 1759; led the Indians under Amherst in Canada, 1760; received grant of the 'Kingsland' on north of the Mohawk, and built Johnson Hall, 1764; concluded treaty at Fort Stanwix, 1768; contributed memoir on the Indians to the Philosophical Society, 1772. [xxx. 50]

JOHNSON, WILLIAM (1784–1864), promoter of education; B.D. St. John's College, Cambridge, 1827; friend of Wordsworth and Southey; had charge of the National Society's model schools in Holborn and Baldwin's Gardens, London, 1812–40; rector of St. Clement's, Eastcheap, 1820–1864. [xxx. 52]

JOHNSTON. [See also JOHNSON and JOHNSTONE.]

JOHNSTON, SIR ALEXANDER (1775–1849), reorganiser of the government of Ceylon; barrister, Lincoln's Inn; advocate-general of Ceylon, 1799, chief-justice, 1805, and president of the council, 1811–19; knighted, 1811; vice-president of Royal Asiatic Society, 1823; privy councillor, 1832; member of judicial committee, 1833. [xxx. 52]

JOHNSTON, ALEXANDER (1815–1891), painter; exhibited at Royal Academy from 1836; his popularity established by the 'Gentle Shepherd' (1840) and 'Sunday Morning' (1841). [xxx. 53]

JOHNSTON, ALEXANDER JAMES (1820–1888), colonial judge; barrister, Middle Temple, 1843; chief-justice of New Zealand, 1867 and 1886; puisne judge of the supreme court, New Zealand, 1860–86; tried native prisoners in Te Kooti and Tito Kowaru wars; member of several legal commissions and author of legal works. [xxx. 53]

JOHNSTON, ALEXANDER KEITH, the elder (1804–1871), geographer; educated at Edinburgh; hon. LL.D., 1845; published his first maps, 1830; awarded medal at exhibition of 1851 for first globe of physical geography; Victoria medallist, Royal Geographical Society, 1871; travelled in Palestine, 1863; published at Humboldt's suggestion the first English atlas of physical geography, 1848; also 'Dictionary of Geography, 1850, and numerous atlases and maps. [xxx. 54]

JOHNSTON, ALEXANDER KEITH, the younger (1844–1879), geographer; son of Alexander Keith Johnston the elder [q. v.]; studied at Edinburgh and in Germany; geographer to the Paraguay survey 1873–5; published maps of Africa (1866) and East Africa (1870) and school geographies; died at Berobero while leading Royal Geographical Society's expedition to head of Lake Nyassa. [xxx. 55]

JOHNSTON, ALEXANDER ROBERT CAMPBELL-(1812–1888), colonial official; son of Sir Alexander Johnston [q. v.]; administrator of Hong Kong, 1841–2; F.R.S., 1845; died in California. [xxx. 53]

JOHNSTON, ARCHIBALD, LORD WARRISTON (1610?–1663), Scottish statesman; assisted Henderson in framing the Scots national covenant, 1638; procurator of the kirk, 1638; assisted in negotiating pacification of Berwick, 1639, and treaty of Ripon, 1640; lord of session as Lord Warriston, 1641; as commissioner for Midlothian opposed neutrality in English affairs, 1643; took prominent part in the Westminster Assembly, and became (1644) one of the committee representing Scotland in London; named king's advocate by Charles I, 1646; resisted the 'engagement,' 1648, and perhaps drew up the Act of Classes, 1649; lord clerk register, 1649; said to have given Lesley fatal advice at Dunbar, 1650, after which he lost his offices; as a leading 'remonstrant' renamed by Cromwell lord clerk register, 1657; member of Oliver and Richard Cromwell's House of Lords; member of council of state on restoration of the Rump, and on its suppression permanent president of committee of safety; arrested at Rouen at the Restoration; tried before Scottish parliament, and hanged at Edinburgh. [xxx. 56]

JOHNSTON, ARTHUR (1587–1641), writer of Latin verse; M.D. Padua, 1610; intimate with Andrew Melville (1545–1622) [q. v.] at Sedan; physician at Paris; returned to Scotland after an absence of twenty-four years; patronised by Laud as a rival to George Buchanan; rector of King's College, Aberdeen, 1637; published metrical Latin versions of the Psalms, 1637, and Solomon's Song, 1633, and 'Epigrammata,' 1632, 'Elegia,' 1628, and other Latin poems. [xxx. 58]

JOHNSTON, DAVID (1734–1824), founder of the Blind Asylum, Edinburgh, 1793; minister of North Leith, 1765–1824; hon. D.D. Edinburgh, 1781; chaplain in ordinary to George III, 1793. [xxx. 60]

JOHNSTON, FRANCIS (1761–1829), architect; founder of the Royal Hibernian Academy (1813), and frequently president. [xxx. 61]

JOHNSTON, GEORGE (1797–1855), naturalist; surgeon at Berwick; M.D. Edinburgh, 1819; hon. LL.D. Aberdeen; an editor of 'Magazine of Zoology and Botany'; published 'Flora of Berwick' (vol. i. 1829, vol. ii. 1831), 'History of British Zoophytes,' 1838, and other scientific works. [xxx. 61]

JOHNSTON, GEORGE (1814–1889), obstetrician; grand-nephew of Francis Johnston [q. v.]; M.D. Edinburgh, 1845; assistant-physician to Dublin Lying-in Hospital, 1848–55; master of Rotunda Hospital, 1868–75; president of Dublin College of Physicians, 1880; collaborated with (Sir) Edward B. Sinclair in 'Practical Midwifery,' 1878. [xxx. 61]

JOHNSTON, HENRY (*d.* 1723), Benedictine; brother of Nathaniel Johnston [q. v.]; on the English mission till 1696; prior of English Benedictines at Paris (St. Edmund's), 1697–8 and 1705–10; translated (1685) and defended Bossuet's exposition of Roman catholic doctrine. [xxx. 62]

JOHNSTON, HENRY ERSKINE (1777–1830 ?), actor; (the 'Scottish Roscius'); first appeared at Edinburgh as Hamlet, 1794; at Covent Garden, 1797–1803; acted in 'Douglas' and other plays at Drury Lane, 1803–5, 1817–18, and 1821; again at Covent Garden, 1805 and 1816; retired to Edinburgh, 1823. [xxx. 63]

JOHNSTON or **JOHNSTONE**, JAMES (1655–1737), 'Secretary Johnston'; son of Archibald Johnston, Lord Warriston [q. v.]; studied law at Utrecht and was sent to prepare the way for William of Orange's invasion; envoy to Brandenburg, 1689; secretary of state in Scotland, 1692–6; obtained inquiry (1695) into the Glencoe massacre; dismissed for promoting the African Company Bill, 1696, but given money grant; lord clerk register, 1704–5; afterwards a leader of *squadrone volante*, though living in England. [xxx. 64]

JOHNSTON, JAMES FINLAY WEIR (1796–1855), chemist; M.A. Glasgow, 1796; studied in Switzerland under Berzelius; reader in chemistry at Durham University, 1833–55; chemist to Agricultural Society of Scotland, 1843; F.R.S. and F.R.S.E.; his 'Catechism of Agricultural Chemistry' (1844) translated into many European languages. His 'Chemistry of Common Life' (1853–5) was continued by George Henry Lewes (1859) and Prof. A. H. Church (1879). [xxx. 65]

JOHNSTON, JAMES HENRY (1787–1851), controller of East India Company's steamers; in royal navy till 1815, being at Trafalgar (1805) in the Spartiate; proposed plan for establishing steam communication with India by the Mediterranean and Red Sea, 1823; his plan for steam navigation in the Ganges accepted; controller of East India Company's steamers, 1833–50. [xxx. 66]

JOHNSTON, JOHN (1570 ?–1611), Scottish poet; studied at King's College, Aberdeen, and abroad, being intimate with Lipsius at Rostock; co-operated with Andrew Melville (1545–1622) [q. v.] in Scotland; professor of divinity at St. Andrews, *c.* 1593–1611; published 'Inscriptiones Historicæ Regum Scotorum,' 1602, 'Heroes,' 1603, and other works. [xxx. 66]

JOHNSTON, SIR JOHN (*d.* 1690), soldier and criminal; son of a Nova Scotia baronet; hanged at Tyburn for participation in abduction of Mary Wharton.
[xxx. 67]

JOHNSTON, NATHANIEL (1627–1705), physician; M.D. King's College, Cambridge, 1656; F.R.C.P., 1687; friend of Thoresby; after the Revolution lived under protection of Peterborough; chief work, 'The Excellency of Monarchical Government,' 1686; left collections on Yorkshire antiquities. [xxx. 67]

JOHNSTON, PELHAM (*d.* 1765), physician; M.D. Cambridge, 1728; F.R.C.P., 1732; grandson of Nathaniel Johnston [q. v.] [xxx. 68]

JOHNSTON, ROBERT (1567 ?–1639), historian and friend of George Heriot [q. v.]; M.A. Edinburgh, 1587; clerk of deliveries of the ordnance, 1604; left money for eight scholars at Edinburgh; wrote 'Historia Rerum Britannicarum, 1572–1628,' published Amsterdam, 1655; a part of his 'History of Scotland during minority of King James' translated, 1646. [xxx. 69]

JOHNSTON, SAMUEL (1733–1816), American statesman and judge; son of John Johnston of Dundee; member of continental congress, 1781–2; governor of North Carolina, 1788–9; U.S. senator, 1789–93; judge of supreme court, 1800–3. [xxx. 69]

JOHNSTON, SIR WILLIAM, seventh baronet of Johnston (1760–1844), soldier; descendant of Sir John Johnston [q. v.]; M.P., New Windsor, 1801–6; died at the Hague. [xxx. 70]

JOHNSTON, SIR WILLIAM (1773–1844), lieutenant-general; fought in Mediterranean and West Indies; commanded 68th in Walcheren expedition, 1809, and in the Peninsula; seriously wounded at Vittoria, 1813; major-general, 1825; K.C.B., 1837; lieutenant-general, 1838. [xxx. 70]

JOHNSTON, WILLIAM (1800–1874), presbyterian minister; M.A. Glasgow, 1817; minister of Limekilns, 1823–74; moderator of the synod, 1854. [xxx. 70]

JOHNSTON, SIR WILLIAM (1802–1888), lord provost of Edinburgh; joined his brother Alexander Keith Johnston the elder [q. v.] in founding firm of W. & A. K. Johnston at Edinburgh, 1826; high constable of Edinburgh, 1828; engraver to Queen Victoria 1837; bailie, 1840; lord provost, 1848–51. [xxx. 70]

JOHNSTONE. [See also JOHNSON and JOHNSTON.]

JOHNSTONE, ANDREW JAMES COCHRANE (*fl.* 1814), adventurer; assumed name of Johnstone on first marriage, 1793; M.P. for Stirling, 1791–7; lieutenant-colonel of the 79th, 1794; governor of Dominica, 1797–1803; brigadier of Leeward islands, 1799–1803; his commission suspended for tyranny, 1803; elected M.P. for Grampound, 1807, unseated, 1808, re-elected, 1812; committed acts of fraud at Tortola, 1807; being found guilty of conspiracy on the Stock Exchange fled the country, and was expelled the House of Commons, 1814. [xxx. 71]

JOHNSTONE, BRYCE (1747–1805), minister of Holywood, Dumfries, 1772–1805; of St. Andrews University; agriculturist. [xxx. 72]

JOHNSTONE, CHARLES (1719 ?–1800 ?), author of 'Chrysal, or the Adventures of a Guinea,' 1760–5; died at Calcutta. [xxx. 73]

JOHNSTONE, MRS. CHRISTIAN ISOBEL (1781–1857), novelist; assisted her husband, John Johnstone, in editing the 'Inverness Courier' and 'The Edinburgh Weekly Chronicle'; edited 'Tait's Magazine' after its incorporation with Johnstone's 'Edinburgh Magazine,' 1834; published 'The Cook and Housewife's Manual ... by Mistress Margaret Dods,' 1826, 'Clan Albin,' 1815, and other works. [xxx. 73]

JOHNSTONE, EDWARD (1757–1851), physician; son of James Johnstone (1730 ?–1802) [q. v.]; M.D. Edinburgh, 1799; president of Birmingham medical school, 1827; first principal of Queen's College, Birmingham. [xxx. 74]

JOHNSTONE, EDWARD (1804–1881), claimant of Annandale peerage (1876–81); M.A. Trinity College, Cambridge, 1828; barrister, Lincoln's Inn, 1828, and Inner Temple, 1838; son of Edward Johnstone (1757–1851) [q. v.]; joint-founder of Literary Association of Friends of Poland, 1832. [xxx. 74]

JOHNSTONE, GEORGE (1730–1787), commodore; distinguished himself in attack on Port Louis, 1748; his appointment as governor of West Florida (1765) attacked in the 'North Briton'; M.P., Cockermouth, 1768, Appleby, 1774, Lostwithiel, 1781, and Ilchester, 1784; when commissioner to treat with the Americans (1778) tried to win over one of the opposite party by a private arrangement; rewarded for support of government by command of small squadron on the Portuguese coast as commodore, 1779; while leading expedition against the Cape of Good Hope gained some successes, but failed in his objective; elected an East India director, 1783. [xxx. 75]

JOHNSTONE, JAMES, the younger (1754–1783), physician; son of James Johnstone the elder [q. v.]; M.D. Edinburgh, 1773; died of gaol fever when physician to the Worcester Infirmary. [xxx. 79]

JOHNSTONE, JAMES (*d.* 1798), Scandinavian antiquary; chaplain to English envoy in Denmark; translated Danish and Norwegian classics; published 'Antiquitates Celto-Scandicæ,' 1784, and 'Antiquitates Celto-Normannicæ,' 1786, and other works. [xxx. 78]

JOHNSTONE, JAMES, CHEVALIER DE JOHNSTONE (1719–1800 ?), Jacobite; aide-de-camp to the Young Pretender in 1745; lay hid after Culloden, eventually escaping to London and Holland; served with the French at Louisbourg and (1759) Quebec, and received the cross of St. Louis and a pension; extracts from his memoirs published as 'History of the Rebellion of 1745,' in 1820, the whole being translated, 1870. [xxx. 78]

JOHNSTONE, JAMES, the elder (1730 ?–1802), physician; M.D. Edinburgh, 1750; practised at Kidderminster and Worcester; published essays on the 'Malignant Epidemical Fever of 1756' (1758), 'Use of the Ganglions of the Nerves' (1771), and other works.   [xxx. 79]

JOHNSTONE, JAMES (1806–1869), physician; son of Edward Johnstone (1757–1851) [q. v.]; M.D. Trinity College, Cambridge, 1833; F.R.C.P., 1834; professor of materia medica, Queen's College, Birmingham, and extraordinary physician to Birmingham Hospital, 1841; chief work, 'Therapeutic Arrangement and Syllabus of Materia Medica,' 1835.   [xxx. 74]

JOHNSTONE, JAMES (1815–1878), proprietor of the 'Standard' and 'Morning Herald' from 1857; revived 'Evening Standard,' 1860.   [xxx. 80]

JOHNSTONE, JAMES HOPE, third EARL OF HOPETOUN (1741–1816). [See HOPE, JAMES.]

JOHNSTONE or **JONSTON**, JOHN (1603–1675), naturalist; born in Poland; studied at St. Andrews, Cambridge, and Leyden; M.D. Leyden, 1632; practised at Leyden; lived on his estate in Silesia from 1655; published scientific treatises; his works on natural history (1649–53) frequently re-edited and translated.
          [xxx. 80]

JOHNSTONE, JOHN (1768–1836), physician; brother of Edward Johnstone (1757–1851) [q. v.]; of Merton College, Oxford, M.A., 1792; M.D., 1800; F.R.C.P., 1805; Harveian orator, 1819; physician to Birmingham General Hospital, 1801–33; author of 'Memoirs of Dr. Samuel Parr' [q. v.], 1828; published 'Account of Discovery of the Power of Mineral Acid Vapours to Destroy Contagion,' 1803.   [xxx. 81]

JOHNSTONE, JOHN HENRY (1749–1828), actor and tenor singer; after performing on the Irish operatic stage appeared at Covent Garden, 1783–1803, and at Drury Lane, 1803–20; called 'Irish Johnstone,' from his excellence as an exponent of Irish comedy parts.   [xxx. 82]

JOHNSTONE, WILLIAM, third EARL OF ANNANDALE and first MARQUIS OF ANNANDALE (d. 1721); of Glasgow University; succeeded to earldom, 1672; friend of Monmouth; nominally supported revolution, but joined 'The Club' of Jacobite malcontents and was imprisoned in connection with Montgomery plot; restored to favour on making confession; created extraordinary lord of session, 1693, and a lord of the treasury; pensioned for services in connection with Glencoe inquiry; created marquis, 1701; lord high commissioner to general assembly, 1701 and 1711; lord privy seal (Scotland), 1702, and president of privy council, 1702–6; K.T., 1704; joint-secretary of state, 1705; opposed the union; Scots representative peer; keeper of the great seal, 1714.   [xxx. 82]

JOHNSTONE, WILLIAM BORTHWICK (1804–1868), landscape and historical painter; Royal Scottish Academy, 1848, treasurer, 1850; first curator of National Gallery of Scotland, 1858; painted miniatures and collected works of art and antiquities.   [xxx. 84]

JOHNYS, SIR HUGH (fl. 1417–1463), knight-marshal of England and France; fought under the eastern emperor against the Turks, 1436–41; suitor for hand of Elizabeth Woodville, c. 1452.   [xxx. 85]

JOLIFFE, GEORGE (1621–1658). [See JOYLIFFE.]

JOLIFFE, HENRY (d. 1573), dean of Bristol; of Clare Hall and Michaelhouse, Cambridge; M.A., 1527; B.D.; canon of Worcester, 1542; resisted Bishop Hooper and wrote against Ridley; dean of Bristol, 1554–8; attended Cranmer's second trial; lived at Louvain after accession of Elizabeth.   [xxx. 85]

JOLLIE, JOHN, the elder (1640?–1682), ejected minister; brother of Thomas Jollie the elder [q. v.]; of Trinity College, Dublin; received presbyterian ordination at Manchester, 1672.   [xxx. 87]

JOLLIE, JOHN, the younger (d. 1725), nonconformist minister; son of John Jollie the elder [q. v.]   [xxx. 88]

JOLLIE, THOMAS, the elder (1629–1703), ejected minister; became intimate with Oliver Heywood [q. v.] at Trinity College, Cambridge; formed a 'gathered church' at Altham, Lancashire, 1649; frequently imprisoned; licensed to preach at Wymondhouses, Whalley, 1672, where he built meeting-houses after the revolution; one of those

who exorcised Richard Dugdale [q. v.], 1689–90; joined 'the happy union,' 1693; published tracts on the Surrey demoniac (Dugdale).   [xxx. 86]

JOLLIE, THOMAS, the younger (d. 1764), independent minister; son of Timothy Jollie the elder [q. v.]
          [xxx. 88]

JOLLIE, TIMOTHY, the elder (1659?–1714), independent tutor; son of Thomas Jollie (1629–1703) [q. v.]; received presbyterian ordination, 1682; imprisoned at York, 1683; his congregation at Sheffield the largest nonconformist meeting in Yorkshire; started, 1689, and conducted, 1689–1714, an academy at Attercliffe.
          [xxx. 88]

JOLLIE, TIMOTHY, the younger (1692–1757), son of Timothy Jollie the elder [q. v.]; succeeded his father at Sheffield and Matthew Clarke (1664–1726) [q. v.] at Miles Lane, Cannon Street, London.   [xxx. 89]

JOLLIFFE, WILLIAM GEORGE HYLTON, first BARON HYLTON (1800–1876), politician; created baronet, 1821; conservative M.P., Petersfield, 1833–5 and 1837–66; under-secretary for home department, 1852; secretary to treasury and conservative whip, 1858–9; privy councillor, 1859; created Baron Hylton, 1866.   [xxx. 89]

JOLLY, ALEXANDER (1756–1838), bishop of Moray; educated at Marischal College, Aberdeen; episcopal minister at Turriff, 1777, and Fraserburgh, 1788; coadjutor of Moray and Ross, 1796; bishop of Moray, 1798–1838; hon. D.D. Washington College, Connecticut, 1826; published religious works.   [xxx. 89]

JONES, AMBROSE (d. 1678), bishop of Kildare; son of Lewis Jones [q. v.]; educated at Dublin; archdeacon of Meath, 1661; bishop of Kildare, 1667–78.
          [xxx. 147]

JONES, AVONIA, afterwards MRS. BROOKE (1839?–1867), actress; native of New York, where she died; married Gustavus Brooke [q. v.]; played in England, Ireland, America, and Australia.   [xxx. 90]

JONES, BASSET (fl. 1634–1659), physician and grammarian; of Jesus College, Oxford; author of 'Lapis Chymicus Philosophorum Examini subjectus,' 1648, and 'Hermæologium,' 1659.   [xxx. 90]

JONES, CHARLES HANDFIELD (1819–1890), physician; educated at Rugby, Catharine Hall, Cambridge (B.A., 1840, M.B., 1843), and at St. George's; F.R.C.P., 1849, senior censor, 1886, vice-president, 1888; physician to St. Mary's Hospital, 1851–90; F.R.S., 1850; Lumleian lecturer, 1865; published 'Manual of Pathological Anatomy' (with Sir E. H. Sieveking), 1854, 'Clinical Observations on Functional Nervous Disorders,' 1864. [xxx. 91]

JONES, CHARLOTTE (1768–1847), miniature-painter; pupil of Cosway; exhibited at Royal Academy, 1801–23; chiefly known for her twelve miniatures of Princess Charlotte, now at Cranmer Hall, Norfolk.   [xxx. 91]

JONES, DAVID (fl. 1560–1590), Welsh poet and antiquary; vicar of Llanfair Dyffryn Clwyd.   [xxx. 92]

JONES, DAVID (fl. 1676–1720), historical writer and translator; said to have been captain in the horse guards; some time secretary interpreter to Louvois; author of 'Secret History of White Hall from the Restoration ... to the Abdication of the late King James,' 1697, 'Compleat History of Europe,' 1705–20 (annual), 'History of the Turks, 1655–1701' (1701), and other works.   [xxx. 92]

JONES, DAVID (1663–1724?), eccentric preacher; of Westminster and Christ Church, Oxford; B.A., 1685; curate of St. Mary Woolnoth and St. Mary Woolchurch Haw, London; afterwards vicar of Great Budworth, Cheshire, and Marcham, Berkshire.   [xxx. 93]

JONES, DAVID (1711–1777), Welsh hymn-writer and translator of Dr. Watts's hymns.   [xxx. 93]

JONES, DAVID (fl. 1750–1780), Welsh poet and antiquary (DAFYDD SION DAFYDD or DEWI FARDD); edited 'Blodeugerdd Cymru,' 1759, and 'Y Cydymaith Dyddan,' 1776.   [xxx. 94]

JONES, DAVID (1735–1810), Welsh revivalist; active member of Welsh Methodist 'Association' and preacher at Lady Huntingdon's chapel; vicar of Llangan, Glamorganshire, 1768, of Maenornawan, Pembrokeshire, 1794; opposed separation from the church.   [xxx. 94]

JONES, DAVID (1765–1816), 'the Welsh Freeholder'; succeeded Priestley as minister of the new meeting-house, Birmingham, 1792; practised as a barrister, having been called from Lincoln's Inn, 1800; as 'the Welsh Freeholder' defended unitarianism against Bishop Samuel Horsley [q. v.], and published tracts in his own name. [xxx. 95]

JONES, DAVID (1796–1841), missionary to Madagascar; went to Madagascar, 1818; with David Griffiths [q. v.] and David Johns [q. v.] settled Malagasy orthography on the phonetic system, 1822; visited the queen at Ambatomanga to petition against persecution of Christians, 1840; died in Mauritius. [xxx. 95]

JONES, EBENEZER (1820–1860), poet; author of 'Studies of Sensation and Event,' 1843 (reissued, 1878), and some maturer lyrics written at the close of life. [xxx. 96]

JONES, EDWARD (1641–1703), bishop of St. Asaph; of Westminster and Trinity College, Cambridge; fellow, 1667; M.A., 1668; while master of Kilkenny school had Swift as pupil; dean of Lismore, 1678; bishop of Cloyne, 1683–92, of St. Asaph, 1692–1700; deprived of St. Asaph for simony and maladministration, 1701. [xxx. 97]

JONES, EDWARD (1752–1824), 'Bardd y Brenin' (the King's Bard); gained repute as a harpist; published 'Musical and Poetical Relicks of the Welsh Bards,' 1784, and other collections of music. [xxx. 98]

JONES, EDWARD (*fl.* 1771–1831), author ('Ned Mon'); of the Gwyneddigion Society; published 'Cicero's Brutus,' 1776, 'Index to Records called the Originalia and Memoranda' (vol. i. 1793, vol. ii. 1795), and 'Cyfreithiau Plwyf' (parish laws), 1794. [xxx. 98]

JONES, EDWARD (1777–1837), founder of Welsh Wesleyan methodism. [xxx. 99]

JONES, ELIZABETH EMMA (1813–1842). [See SOYER.]

JONES, ERNEST CHARLES (1819–1869), chartist and poet; educated abroad; barrister, Middle Temple, 1844; defended Feargus O'Connor against Thomas Cooper, 1846; advocated physical force, and suffered two years' imprisonment (1848–50) for seditious speeches; twice contested Halifax and Nottingham; edited 'The People's Paper'; published sensational novels, 'The Battle Day and other Poems' (1855), political songs, and other verse. [xxx. 99]

JONES, EVAN, or IEUAN GWYNEDD (1820–1852), Welsh poet and journalist; independent minister at Tredegar, 1845–8; published 'Facts and Figures and Statements' (1849) defending Welsh nonconformists against report of commission of 1847 on Welsh education; conducted 'Y Gymraes' (magazine for women) and 'Yr Adolygydd' (national quarterly), 1850–2; his collected poems edited by the Rev. T. Roberts, 1876. [xxx. 100]

JONES, FREDERICK EDWARD (1759–1834), manager of Crow Street Theatre, Dublin, 1796–1814, and in 1819; of Trinity College, Dublin; met with persistent opposition and misfortune, and was imprisoned for debt; called 'Buck Jones' from his handsome appearance; Jones Road, Dublin, named after him. [xxx. 101]

JONES, GEORGE (1786–1869), painter; son of John Jones (1745?–1797) [q. v.]; volunteer in the Peninsula; painted views of Waterloo and Vittoria; R.A., 1824, librarian, 1834–40, keeper, 1840–50, and acting president, 1845–50; friend of Turner and Chantrey; chief adviser of Robert Vernon [q. v.] [xxx. 102]

JONES, GEORGE MATTHEW (1785?–1831), captain in the navy; brother of Sir John Thomas Jones [q. v.]; lieutenant of the Amphion under Nelson and Hoste, 1803–8, being severely wounded in the Adriatic; posted, 1818; visited and described in 'Travels' (1827) the courts of most of the countries of Europe. [xxx. 103]

JONES, GILES (*fl.* 1765), brother and collaborator of Griffith Jones (1722–1786) [q. v.] in 'Lilliputian Histories.' [xxx. 104]

JONES, GRIFFITH (1683–1761), founder of Welsh charity or circulating schools; incumbent of Llandilo Abercowyn, 1711; rector of Llanddowror, 1716; attacked by John Evans, vicar of Eglwys Cymmun, 1752; published

'Welsh Piety' (annual, 1737–61) and various theological works in Welsh; said to have 'converted' Daniel Rowlands of Llangeitho [q. v.] [xxx. 103]

JONES, GRIFFITH (1722–1786), writer for the young and editor of the 'London Chronicle,' 'Daily Advertiser,' and 'Public Ledger'; printed the 'Literary' and 'British' magazines. [xxx. 104]

JONES, SIR HARFORD (1764–1847). [See BRYDGES, SIR HARFORD JONES.]

JONES, SIR HARRY DAVID (1791–1866), lieutenant-general; brother of Sir John Thomas Jones [q. v.]; entered royal engineers, 1808; served in Walcheren expedition (1809) and Peninsula, being present at capture of Badajoz, 1812, and battle of Vittoria, 1813; captured severely wounded while leading 'forlorn hope' at San Sebastian (25 July, 1813); again wounded at the Nive, 1813; at New Orleans, 1814, and with the army of occupation after Waterloo; secretary to Irish railway commission and first commissioner of boundaries, 1836; chairman of Irish board of works, 1845–50; director of engineers at Chatham, 1851; commanded as brigadier land operations in Baltic, 1854; commanding engineer at Sebastopol, 1855, being severely wounded at the unsuccessful assault of 18 June; created K.C.B., receiving Legion of Honour and other foreign orders; governor of Sandhurst, 1856–66; chairman of defence commission of 1859; lieutenant-general, 1860; G.C.B. and D.C.L. of Oxford, 1861. [xxx. 105]

JONES, HARRY LONGUEVILLE (1806–1870), founder (1846) and first editor of 'Archæologia Cambrensis'; fellow of Magdalene College, Cambridge; seventh wrangler, 1828; M.A., 1832; proposed formation of a Manchester university, 1836; inspector of schools for Wales, 1849–64; published (with Thomas Wright) 'Memorials of Cambridge,' 1841, and other works. [xxx. 107]

JONES, HENRY (1605–1682), bishop of Meath; son of Lewis Jones [q. v.]; M.A. Trinity College, Dublin, 1624 (vice-chancellor, 1646); dean of Ardagh, 1625, of Kilmore, 1637; when prisoner in hands of the rebels presented the Cavan remonstrance, 1641; bishop of Clogher, 1645; engaged on the settlement of Ulster (1653) and other commissions; bishop of Meath, 1661–82; active in procuring evidence of a 'popish plot' in Ireland. [xxx. 107]

JONES, HENRY (*d.* 1727), abridger of 'Philosophical Transactions,' 1700–20; of Eton and King's College, Cambridge; fellow of King's College; M.A., 1720; F.R.S., 1724. [xxx. 109]

JONES, HENRY (1721–1770), poet and dramatist; patronised by Chesterfield, who assisted him to produce 'Poems on Several Occasions' (1749), and by Cibber; his 'Earl of Essex' acted with success at Covent Garden Theatre, 1753; took to drink and was run over in St. Martin's Lane, London. [xxx. 109]

JONES, HENRY (1831–1899), known as CAVENDISH; writer on whist; educated at King's College School; studied at St. Bartholomew's Hospital; M.R.C.S. and L.S.A., 1852; practised in London; retired, 1869; an enthusiastic student of whist; published, 1862, 'Principles of Whist stated and explained by Cavendish'; whist editor of the 'Field' from 1862; issued works on card games and other pastimes. [Suppl. iii. 45]

JONES, HENRY BENCE (1814–1873), physician and chemist; of Harrow and Trinity College, Cambridge; M.A., 1849; M.D., 1849; F.R.S., 1846; physician to St. George's Hospital, 1846–72; F.R.C.P., 1849, afterwards senior censor; secretary to Royal Institution from 1860; studied chemistry under Graham and Liebig; friend and biographer of Faraday; works include 'Lectures on Animal Chemistry,' 1860, and 'Croonian Lectures on Matter and Force,' 1868. [xxx. 110]

JONES, SIR HORACE (1819–1887), city of London architect; designed Smithfield and reconstructed Billingsgate and Leadenhall markets, the Guildhall library and museum (1872), and the new council chamber (1884); with Sir J. Wolfe Barry, made plans for the Tower Bridge; P.R.I.B.A., 1882–3; knighted, 1886. [xxx. 111]

JONES, SIR HUGH (*fl.* 1417–1463). [See JOHNYS.]

JONES, HUGH (1508–1574), bishop of Llandaff, 1567–74; B.C.L. Oxford, 1541. [xxx. 111]

JONES, INIGO (1573–1652), architect; son of a Roman catholic clothworker of London; in his youth travelled on the continent at expense of William Herbert, third earl of Pembroke [q. v.]; summoned from Venice to Denmark by Christian IV; designed shifting scenes, machines, and dresses for many masques by Ben Jonson, Samuel Daniel, Aurelian Townshend, Heywood, D'Avenant, and others; quarrelled with Ben Jonson, and was satirised as In-and-In Medlay in his 'Tale of a Tub,' 1633; surveyor of works to Henry, prince of Wales, 1610–1612; again visited Italy, 1613–15, purchasing works of art for lords Arundel and Pembroke; supposed to have designed buildings at Leghorn; surveyor-general of works, 1615; designed the queen's house at Greenwich (1617–35), Lincoln's Inn Chapel (1617–23), west side of Lincoln's Inn Fields, banqueting house at Whitehall (1619–22) as part of a projected new palace; also the water-gate in Buckingham Street, Adelphi, St. Paul's Church, Covent Garden (rebuilt from his designs, 1795), and the piazza of Covent Garden, Ashburnham House, Westminster, and other buildings; as surveyor directed extensive repairs to the old St. Paul's Cathedral; in Basing House during the siege (1643–5), but on payment of a fine received back his estate; prepared designs for Wilton House, 1648. Large collections of his drawings are at Worcester College, Oxford, and at Chatsworth.
                                             [xxx. 111]

JONES, ISAAC (1804–1850), Welsh translator; educated at Aberystwith, where he was head-master, 1828–34, and Lampeter (Eldon scholar, 1835); curate in Anglesey, 1840–50; translated into Welsh Gurney's 'Dictionary of the Bible,' 1835, Adam Clarke's 'Commentary,' 1847, and other works; joint-editor of 'Y Geirlyfr Cymraeg' (Welsh encyclopædia), 1835.   [xxx. 119]

JONES, JAMES RHYS (1813–1889), Welsh writer and lecturer; known as KILSBY JONES; independent minister at Kilsby, Northamptonshire, 1840–50; preached at Llandrindod Wells from 1868; edited works of W. Williams of Pantycelyn (Welsh), Welsh versions of the 'Pilgrim's Progress,' and other works; contributed to Welsh periodicals; popular lecturer.   [xxx. 120]

JONES, JENKIN (1700?–1742), Welsh Arminian; founded in 1726 Llwynrhydowen, the first Arminian church in Wales; published and translated theological works.   [xxx. 121]

JONES, JEREMIAH (1693–1724), independent tutor at Nailsworth and biblical critic; nephew of Samuel Jones (1680?–1719) [q. v.]; author of 'New and Full Method of settling the Canonical Authority of the New Testament,' published 1726.   [xxx. 121]

JONES, JEZREEL (d. 1731), traveller; as clerk to the Royal Society visited Barbary, 1698 and 1701; British envoy to Morocco, 1704; contributed valuable specimens to the Sloane collection.   [xxx. 122]

JONES, JOHN (fl. 1579), physician; studied at Oxford and Cambridge; practised at Bath and Buxton; translated 'Galens Bookes of Elementes,' 1574; published books on baths and other medical works.   [xxx. 122]

JONES, JOHN, alias BUCKLEY, alias GODFREY MAURICE (d. 1598), Franciscan; went to Pontoise on dissolution of the Greenwich house, 1559, and thence to Rome; arrested in England, 1596; hanged, 1598.
                                             [xxx. 123]

JONES, JOHN (1575–1636), Benedictine ('Leander à Sancto Martino'); educated at Merchant Taylors' School and St. John's College, Oxford (fellow); B.C.L., 1600; entered abbey of St. Martin at Compostella, 1599; D.D. Salamanca; professor of theology at Douay; vicar-general of Anglo-Spanish Benedictines, 1612; prior of St. Gregory's, Douay, 1621–8 and 1629–33; took the oath of allegiance as papal agent in England, 1634; accusation of intercourse with him denied by Laud, 1643; wrote and edited many theological works; his 'Rule of St. Benedict' translated by Canon Francis Cuthbert Doyle, 1875; correspondence concerning English catholics printed in 'Clarendon State Papers.'   [xxx. 123]

JONES, JOHN (d. 1660), regicide; colonel, 1646; negotiated surrender of Anglesey to parliament, 1646; helped to suppress Sir John Owen's rising, 1648; M.P., Merionethshire, 1647; signed Charles I's death-warrant; commissioner to assist lord-deputy of Ireland, 1650; was removed for republicanism, but married Cromwell's sister

Catherine; one of Cromwell's peers and governor of Anglesey, 1657; member of committee of safety and council of state, 1659; arrested as supporter of Lambert, but released on submission, 1659; executed as a regicide.
                                             [xxx. 125]

JONES, JOHN (1645–1709), chancellor of Llandaff; fellow of Jesus College, Oxford; M.A., 1670; D.C.L., 1677; chancellor of Llandaff, 1691–1709; wrote a treatise on intermittent fevers (1683) and invented a clock.
                                             [xxx. 126]

JONES, JOHN (1693–1752), classical scholar; of Merchant Taylors' School and St. John's College, Oxford; B.A., 1716; B.C.L., 1720; head-master of Oundle school, 1718; rector of Uppingham, 1743–52; edited Horace, 1736.   [xxx. 127]

JONES, JOHN (1700–1770), controversialist; B.A., 1721, and chaplain of Worcester College, Oxford; vicar of Alconbury, Huntingdonshire, 1741–50; rector of Bolnhurst, Bedfordshire, 1750–7; curate at Welwyn, 1757–65; vicar of Sheephall, 1767–70; advocated revision of the liturgy in 'Free and Candid Disquisitions relating to the Church of England,' 1749.   [xxx. 127]

JONES, JOHN (d. 1796), organist of St. Paul's, 1755–1796, and composer of chants.   [xxx. 128]

JONES, JOHN (1745?–1797), engraver in mezzotint and stipple.   [xxx. 128]

JONES, JOHN (fl. 1797), sub-director of Handel Commemoration, 1784, and composer.   [xxx. 128]

JONES, JOHN (1767–1821), Welsh satirical songwriter ('Siôn Glanygors'); active member of the Gwyneddigion Society, which met at the King's Head, Ludgate Hill, London, then owned by him; his humorous pieces collected in 'Yr Awen Fywiog,' 1858. [xxx. 128]

JONES, JOHN (1766?–1827), unitarian critic; hon. LL.D. Aberdeen, 1818; educated at Christ's College, Brecon, and at Hackney, under Gilbert Wakefield [q. v.]; 'presbyterian' minister at Plymouth, 1795–8; minister and tutor at Halifax, 1798–1804; a Williams trustee, 1821; published 'Illustrations of the Four Gospels,' 1808, 'Greek-English Lexicon,' 1823 and other works.
                                             [xxx. 129]

JONES, JOHN (fl. 1827), author of 'Attempts in verse by John Jones, an Old Servant,' 1831 (introduction by Southey).   [xxx. 130]

JONES, JOHN (1772–1837), Welsh historian; LL.D Jena; author of 'History of Wales,' 1824, an original translation into Welsh of the gospels, 1812, and other works.   [xxx. 130]

JONES, JOHN (1792–1852), Welsh poet and antiquary and hebraist ('Tegid'); M.A. Jesus College, Oxford, 1821; precentor at Christ Church, Oxford, 1823, and perpetual curate of St. Thomas's, Oxford, 1823; incumbent of Nevern, Pembrokeshire, 1841–52; prebendary of St. David's, 1848–52; transcribed the 'Mabinogion' for Lady Charlotte Guest; joint-editor of 'Poetical Works of Lewis Glyn Cothi' (1837–9); upheld etymological system of Welsh spelling; his poems published, 1859. [xxx. 131]

JONES, JOHN (TALSARN) (1796–1857), Welsh preacher; composer of psalm and hymn tunes.
                                             [xxx. 131]

JONES, JOHN (1788–1858), Welsh verse-writer; served as a sailor in the Napoleonic war; afterwards a cotton-spinner; collected poems issued, 1856.
                                             [xxx. 132]

JONES, JOHN (1810–1869), Welsh poet ('Talhaiarn'); as manager to Sir Joseph Paxton employed in France; wrote Welsh words to old Welsh airs; published three volumes of poetry (1855, 1862, and 1869).   [xxx. 132]

JONES, JOHN (1835–1877), geologist and engineer; secretary to Cleveland Ironmasters' Association from 1866; founded Iron and Steel Institute, 1868; chief work, 'Geology of South Staffordshire.'   [xxx. 133]

JONES, SIR JOHN (1811–1878), lieutenant-general; lieutenant-colonel of 1st battalion 60th rifles at siege of Delhi, commanding the left attack in September 1857; as brigadier of Roorkhee field-force acquired name of 'the Avenger'; afterwards in Oude; K.C.B.; lieutenant-general, 1877; received distinguished service pension.
                                             [xxx. 133]

JONES, JOHN (1821?–1878), Welsh baptist ('Mathetes'); contributed to 'Seren Gomer,' 1846; minister at Rhymney, Monmouthshire, 1862–77; published 'Geiriadur Beiblaidd a Duwinyddol' (biblical dictionary), (vol. i. 1864, vol. ii. 1869, vol. iii. published 1883), and 'Areithfa Mathetes' (sermons), 1873.   [xxx. 133]

JONES, JOHN (1800?–1882), virtuoso; a tailor in Waterloo Place; his pictures, furniture, and objects of vertu bequeathed to South Kensington Museum; benefactor of Ventnor convalescent hospital.   [xxx. 134]

JONES, JOHN (1804–1887), Welsh biblical commentator ('Idrisyn'); vicar of Llandyssilio Gogo, Cardiganshire, 1858–87; published 'Y Deonglydd Beirniadol' (biblical commentary), 1852.   [xxx. 134]

JONES, JOHN (1791–1889), archdeacon of Liverpool; M.A. St. John's College, Cambridge, 1820; incumbent successively of St. Andrew's, Liverpool, and Christ Church, Waterloo, Liverpool; published sermons and expository lectures.   [xxx. 135]

JONES, JOHN ANDREWS (1779–1863), baptist minister, and author of 'Bunhill Memorials' (1849); minister in London from 1831 (at 'Jireh Chapel,' Brick Lane, till 1861, afterwards at East Street, City Road).   [xxx. 135]

JONES, JOHN EDWARD (1806–1862), sculptor of busts; exhibited at the Academy from 1844. [xxx. 136]

JONES, JOHN FELIX (d. 1878), captain in the Indian navy and surveyor; employed in survey of Red Sea, 1829–1834, Ceylon, and Mesopotamia; during survey of Euphrates and Tigris discovered site of Opis, 1850; author of 'Assyrian Vestiges'; political agent in the Persian Gulf, 1855–8.   [xxx. 136]

JONES, JOHN GALE (1769–1838), radical; educated at Merchant Taylors' School, London; caricatured by Gillray as a speaker at London Corresponding Society's meeting in Copenhagen Fields, London, 1795; imprisoned for sedition, 1798, and for libel on Castlereagh, 1810; committed to Newgate by the House of Commons for breach of privilege, 1810.   [xxx. 136]

JONES, JOHN OGWEN (1829–1884), Welsh biblical scholar; B.A. London, 1858; Calvinistic methodist minister at Liverpool, Oswestry, and Rhyl; published lectures and Welsh commentaries.   [xxx. 137]

JONES, JOHN PAUL (1747–1792), naval adventurer; son of a Kircudbrightshire gardener named Paul; after five years in the slave trade engaged in smuggling and trading in West Indies; entered American navy under name of Jones, 1775; while in command of the Ranger took the fort at Whitehaven, plundered Lord Selkirk's house on St. Mary's Isle, and captured the Drake off Carrickfergus, 1778; in the Bonhomme Richard, accompanied by three French ships and an American, threatened Edinburgh and captured the Serapis while convoying the Baltic trade, 1779; afterwards served in French navy; present as rear-admiral in the Russian service in battle of the Liman, 1788; quarrelled with Potemkin; died at Paris.   [xxx. 138]

JONES, JOHN PIKE (1790–1857), antiquary; B.A. Pembroke College, Cambridge, 1813; was refused institution to benefices, 1819; vicar of Alton, Staffordshire, 1829, and Butterleigh, Devonshire, 1832; published 'Historical and Monumental Antiquities of Devonshire,' 1823, and part of 'Ecclesiastical Antiquities,' 1828, and 'Flora Devoniensis,' 1829.   [xxx. 141]

JONES, SIR JOHN THOMAS, first baronet (1783–1843), major-general; adjutant of royal engineers at Gibraltar, 1798–1802; employed on construction of Chelmsford lines of defence, 1804; present at battle of Maida, 1806, and directed attack on Scylla Castle, which he afterwards refortified; aide-de-camp to General Leith with Spanish army, 1808; chief of engineers' staff in Walcheren expedition, 1809; completed the works at Torres Vedras, 1810; brevet lieutenant-colonel, 1812; disabled at Burgos, 1812; while invalided published a 'Journal' of the sieges in Spain, severely criticising their conduct; named C.B. after serving on commission to report upon defences of Netherlands, 1815, being sole inspector, 1816, while holding a command at Woolwich; colonel and aide-de-camp to George IV, 1825; created baronet, 1831, for services in the Netherlands; major-

general, 1837; K.C.B., 1838; drew up plans for defence of United Kingdom and of Gibraltar, 1840; his statue erected by engineers in St. Paul's Cathedral, London; published works of contemporary military history; his reports on Netherland fortresses privately circulated among engineers.   [xxx. 141]

JONES, JOHN WINTER (1805–1881), principal librarian of the British Museum; nephew of Stephen Jones [q. v.]; educated at St. Paul's School, London; travelling secretary to charity commissioners, c. 1835–7; entered British Museum, 1837; had principal hand in framing the rules for cataloguing; assistant-keeper of printed books, 1850, keeper, 1856–66, principal librarian, 1866–78; president of Library Association, 1877; edited works for Hakluyt Society; contributed to 'Biographical Dictionary' of Society for the Diffusion of Useful Knowledge.   [xxx. 145]

JONES, JOSEPH DAVID (1827–1870), Welsh musical composer and schoolmaster; his chief compositions the cantata 'Llys Arthur' or 'Arthur's Court,' 1864, and 'Tonau ac Emynau' (hymns and tunes), 1868.   [xxx. 146]

JONES, JOSHUA (d. 1740), independent minister at Cross Street, Manchester, 1725–40; brother of Jeremiah Jones [q. v.]   [xxx. 122]

JONES, LESLIE GROVE (1779–1839), soldier and radical politician; in the guards during Peninsular war; commandant at Brussels before Waterloo.   [xxx. 146]

JONES, LEWIS (1550?–1646), bishop of Killaloe; fellow of All Souls' College, Oxford, 1568; B.A., 1568; dean of Ardagh, 1606–25, and of Cashel, 1607–33; bishop of Killaloe, 1633–46; restored Cashel Cathedral.   [xxx. 146]

JONES, LEWIS TOBIAS (1797–1895), admiral; lieutenant, 1822; commander, 1838; under Sir Robert Stopford [q. v.] on coast of Syria, 1840; captain, 1840; commanded expedition against slavery at Lagos, 1851; C.B., 1854; in Black Sea, 1854; rear-admiral, 1859; K.C.B., 1861; commander-in-chief at Queenstown, 1862–5; retired as admiral, 1871; G.C.B., 1873.   [Suppl. iii. 46]

JONES, LLOYD (1811–1886), advocate of co-operation; supporter of Robert Owen; joint-author of 'Progress of the Working Classes,' 1867; his life of Robert Owen published, 1889.   [xxx. 147]

JONES, MATTHEW (1654–1717), prebendary of Donoughmore, 1687–1717; brother of Edward Jones (1641–1703) [q. v.]   [xxx. 97]

JONES, MICHAEL (d. 1649), Irish parliamentarian; son of Lewis Jones [q. v.]; of Lincoln's Inn; after fighting for the king against the Irish rebels entered service of parliament and distinguished himself as a cavalry leader in northern England, 1644–5; governor of Chester, 1646; as governor of Dublin, 1647–9, routed the Irish at Dungan Hill, 1647, and Ormonde at Rathmines, 1649; died of fever when Cromwell's second in command.   [xxx. 147]

JONES, OWEN (fl. 1790), president of the Gwyneddigion Society, 1793 ('Côr y Cyrtie'); brother of Edward Jones (fl. 1771–1831) [q. v.]   [xxx. 99]

JONES, OWEN (1741–1814), Welsh antiquary ('Owain Myvyr'); London furrier; founded Gwyneddigion Society, 1770; published 'The Myvyrian Archæology of Wales,' 1801–7; joint-editor of poems of Davydd ab Gwilym, 1789.   [xxx. 149]

JONES, OWEN (1809–1874), architect and ornamental designer; son of Owen Jones (1741–1814) [q. v.]; visited Paris and Italy, 1830, Greece, Egypt, and Constantinople, 1833, and Granada, 1834 and 1837; superintendent of 1851 exhibition; joint-director of decoration of Crystal Palace; designed St. James's Hall, London, and decorated the khedive's palace in Egypt; published works, including 'Plans, Elevations, &c., of the Alhambra' (1842–5), 'The Polychromatic Ornament of Italy,' 1846, and 'The Grammar of Ornament,' 1856.   [xxx. 150]

JONES, OWEN (1806–1889), Welsh writer ('Meudwy Môn'); methodist pastor at Mold, Manchester, and Llandudno, 1866–89; published (in Welsh) works, including an historical, topographical, and biographical dictionary of Wales, 1875, and a Welsh concordance and commentary.   [xxx. 151]

JONES, PAUL (1747-1792). [See JONES, JOHN PAUL.]

JONES, PHILIP (1618 ?-1674), Welsh parliamentarian governor of Swansea, 1645, and colonel, 1646 ; with Colonel Horton defeated the royalists at St. Fagans, 1648 ; governor of Cardiff ; M.P., Brecknockshire, 1650; Glamorganshire, 1656 ; one of Cromwell's peers, 1657 ; member of the council of state from 1653 ; controller of the household to Oliver and Richard Cromwell ; acquired large fortune ; charged with corruption by the military party and extreme republicans ; governor of the Charterhouse, 1658 ; made his peace with the king and was sheriff of Glamorgan, 1671 ; purchased Fonmon Castle, 1664. [xxx. 151]

JONES, RHYS (1713-1801), Welsh poet and compiler of 'Gorchestion Beirdd Cymru,' 1773. [xxx. 153]

JONES, JHONES, or JOHNES, RICHARD (*fl.* 1564-1602), printer of plays, chap-books, romances, and popular literature, including Nicholas Breton's works, 'Tamburlaine' and 'Pierce Penilesse.' [xxx. 153]

JONES, RICHARD (1603-1673), Welsh nonconformist divine and author of metrical mnemonic digests of the bible ; M.A. Jesus College, Oxford, 1628 ; ejected from mastership of Denbigh school for nonconformity ; translated into Welsh works by Baxter. [xxx. 154]

JONES, RICHARD, third VISCOUNT and first EARL OF RANELAGH (1636 ?-1712), succeeded as third viscount, 1669 ; chancellor of the Irish exchequer, 1668 ; farmed Irish revenues, 1674-81 ; as paymaster-general (1691-1702) was convicted of defalcation, but escaped prosecution ; sat in the English parliament, 1685-1703 ; Ranelagh Gardens formed out of his Chelsea estate. [xxx. 154]

JONES, RICHARD (1767-1840), animal-painter. [xxx. 156]

JONES, RICHARD (1779-1851), actor and dramatist ('Gentleman Jones'); appeared at Crow Street, Dublin, under Frederick Edward Jones [q. v.], 1799 ; at Covent Garden, London, 1807-9; afterwards took Lewis's parts at the Haymarket ; claimed authorship of 'The Green Man' (1818) and 'Too Late for Dinner' (1820), in which he acted; collaborated with Theodore Hook [q. v.] in 'Hoaxing'; excelled in eccentric rôles. [xxx. 156]

JONES, RICHARD (1790-1855), political economist ; M.A. Caius College, Cambridge, 1819 ; professor of political economy at King's College, London, 1833-5, at Haileybury, 1835-55; secretary to the capitular commission, and a charity commissioner; published essay on 'Rent' (1831), attacking Ricardo ; his works collected, 1850. [xxx. 157]

JONES, RICHARD ROBERTS (1780-1843), self-educated linguist ('Dick of Aberdaron'); son of a carpenter ; acquired a knowledge of Greek, Latin, Hebrew, French, Italian, and Spanish, as well as some Chaldaic and Syriac ; compiled a Welsh, Greek, and Hebrew dictionary, but was unable to publish it. [xxx. 157]

JONES, ROBERT (*fl.* 1616), musical composer, poet, and lutenist; published four books of ayres, also madrigals, and (1610) 'The Muses' Garden of Delights'; some of his songs reprinted in Mr. A. H. Bullen's 'Lyrics from Elizabethan Song Books.' [xxx. 158]

JONES, ROBERT (1810-1879), writer on Welsh literature ; B.A. Jesus College, Oxford, 1837 ; vicar of All Saints, Rotherhithe, London, 1841-79; first editor of 'Y Cymmrodor,' 1876; author of 'History of the Cymmrodorion'; edited works (with life and correspondence) of Rev. Goronwy Owen, 1876. [xxx. 159]

JONES, ROWLAND (1722-1774), philologist ; of the Inner Temple; published 'The Origin of Language and Nations' (1764), an attempt to prove Welsh the primæval language, also 'Hieroglyfic,' 1768, and other works. [xxx. 159]

JONES, SAMUEL (1628-1697), early Welsh nonconformist ; fellow of Jesus College, Oxford, 1652, and bursar, 1655 ; M.A., 1654 ; received presbyterian ordination; incumbent of Llangynwyd, Glamorganshire, 1657-1662 ; established (1689) first Welsh nonconformist academy (afterwards presbyterian college, Carmarthen). [xxx. 160]

JONES, SAMUEL (1680 ?-1719), nonconformist tutor at Gloucester and Tewkesbury; studied at Leyden ; had among his pupils Secker (afterwards archbishop), Joseph Butler [q. v.], and Daniel Scott [q. v.] [xxx. 161]

JONES, SAMUEL (*d.* 1732), poet ; queen's searcher at Whitby, 1709-31 ; published 'Poetical Miscellanies' (1714) and 'Whitby : a poem,' 1718. [xxx. 161]

JONES, STEPHEN (1763-1827), editor of the 'Biographia Dramatica'; nephew of Griffith Jones (1722-1786) [q. v.]; educated at St. Paul's School ; edited 'European Magazine' (from 1807) and 'Freemasons' Magazine'; compiled 'The Spirit of the Public Journals,' 1797-1814 (illustrated by Cruikshank, 1823-5); published among other works a revised edition of Baker's 'Biographia Dramatica,' 1812, with a continuation as far as 1811. [xxx. 162]

JONES, SIR THEOPHILUS (*d.* 1685), scoutmaster-general in Ireland; son of Lewis Jones [q. v.]; saved Lisburn from the Scots under Robert Monro [q. v.], 1644 ; governor of Dublin, 1649-59; elected to British parliament, 1656 ; after his dismissal (1659) took part against the commonwealth; privy councillor, 1661 ; scoutmaster-general in Ireland, 1661-85. [xxx. 162]

JONES, THEOPHILUS (1758-1812), deputy-registrar of Brecon, and author of 'History of County of Brecknock,' 1805-9. [xxx. 163]

JONES, THOMAS (1550 ?-1619), archbishop of Dublin and lord-chancellor of Ireland ; M.A. Christ's College, Cambridge ; dean of St. Patrick's, 1581-4 ; bishop of Meath, 1584-1605 ; archbishop of Dublin and lord chancellor of Ireland, 1605-19 ; a lord justice, 1613 and 1615. [xxx. 163]

JONES, alias MOETHEU, THOMAS (1530-1620 ?), Welsh bard and genealogist ('Twm Shon Catti'); employed by Welsh gentry to draw up pedigrees ; claimed kinship with Lord Burghley ; the traditional Welsh Robin Hood. [xxx. 164]

JONES, THOMAS (1618-1665), civilian ; fellow of Merton College, Oxford ; M.A., 1644 ; D.C.L., 1659 ; some time deputy to Oxford professor of civil law ; published 'Prolusiones Academicæ,' 1660 ; died of the plague. [xxx. 165]

JONES, THOMAS (1622 ?-1682), Welsh divine ; fellow of University College, Oxford, 1648 ; M.A., 1650 ; rector of Castell Caereinion, 1655-61, of Llandyrnog, 1666-70 ; as chaplain to Duke of York, 1663-6, accused Bishop Morley of negligence, and was prosecuted by him ; wrote against Romanism. [xxx. 166]

JONES, SIR THOMAS (*d.* 1692), chief-justice of common pleas ; educated at Shrewsbury and Emmanuel College, Cambridge ; B.A., 1632 ; barrister, Lincoln's Inn, 1634 ; king's serjeant, 1671 ; knighted, 1671 ; judge of the king's bench, 1676 ; chief-justice of common pleas, 1683-6 ; tried Lord Russell, 1683, and pronounced revocation of the London charter, 1683, but was dismissed (1686) for refusing to declare for the dispensing power ; committed by House of Commons, 1689, for judgment against the serjeant-at-arms in 1682. [xxx. 166]

JONES, THOMAS (1743-1803), painter ; exhibited Welsh and Italian views at the Society of Artists and the Academy ; visited Italy, 1776-84. [xxx. 167]

JONES, THOMAS (1756-1807), fellow and tutor of Trinity College, Cambridge, 1781-1807 : of Shrewsbury and Trinity College, Cambridge ; senior wrangler, 1778 ; M.A., 1782 ; friend of Bishop Herbert Marsh [q. v.] [xxx. 167]

JONES, THOMAS (DENBIGH) (1756-1820), Calvinistic methodist ; printed at Ruthin translation of Gurnall's 'Christian in full Armour,' and (1808) of 'The Larger Catechism'; published at Denbigh his 'History of Martyrs,' 1813, and other works. [xxx. 168]

JONES, THOMAS (1768-1828), Welsh poet ('Y Bardd Cloff'); London coach-builder ; thrice president of the Gwyneddigion Society. [xxx. 168]

JONES, THOMAS (1752-1845), promoter of British and Foreign Bible Society; rector of Great Creaton, Northamptonshire, 1828-33; gained great repute as preacher and translator into Welsh of evangelical works; founded prize at Lampeter for Welsh essay. [xxx. 168]

JONES, THOMAS (1775-1852), optician; assisted in formation of Astronomical Society, 1820 ; F.R.S., 1835. [xxx. 169]

JONES, THOMAS (1810–1875), Cheetham librarian, 1845–75 ; B.A. Jesus College, Oxford, 1832 ; catalogued Neath library, 1842 ; F.S.A., 1866.   [xxx. 170]

JONES, THOMAS (1819–1882), 'the Welsh poet-preacher' ; as 'Jones Treforris' known throughout Wales as an independent preacher and lecturer ; preached English sermons at Bedford Chapel, Oakley Square, London ; chairman of Congregational Union, 1871–2 ; pastor of Congregational church at Melbourne, 1877–80 ; spent his last years at Swansea ; selection of his sermons published, 1884, with preface by Robert Browning, the poet.
                    [xxx. 170]

JONES, THOMAS RYMER (1810–1880), zoologist ; M.R.C.S., 1833 ; first professor of comparative anatomy at King's College, London, 1836–74 ; Fullerian professor of physiology at Royal Institution, 1840–2 ; chief work, 'General Outline of the Animal Kingdom,' 1838–41.
                    [xxx. 171]

JONES, WILLIAM (*fl.* 1612–1631), chaplain to the Countess of Southampton ; devotional writer.
                    [xxx. 171]

JONES, WILLIAM (1561–1636), author of commentaries on Hebrews and Philemon, 1636 ; foundation fellow of Clare Hall, Cambridge ; D.D., 1597 ; incumbent of East Bergholt, 1592–1636.   [xxx. 171]

JONES, SIR WILLIAM (1566–1640), judge ; of St. Edmund's Hall, Oxford ; barrister, Lincoln's Inn, 1595 ; serjeant, 1617 ; knighted, 1617 ; chief-justice of the king's bench in Ireland, 1617–20 ; judge of common pleas in England, 1621, of the king's bench, 1624–40 ; member of Irish commissions and of the council of Wales : gave judgment against Eliot, Holles, and Valentine, 1630, and in favour of ship-money, 1638 ; his 'Reports' issued, 1675.
                    [xxx. 171]

JONES, SIR WILLIAM (1631–1682), lawyer ; of Gray's Inn ; knighted, 1671 ; K.C., 1671 ; solicitor-general, 1673–5 ; attorney-general, 1675–9 ; directed 'Popish plot' prosecutions ; as M.P. for Plymouth, 1680–2, was manager of Stafford's trial, 1680, and a strong supporter of the Exclusion Bill ; the 'Bull-faced Jonas' of 'Absalom and Achitophel.'   [xxx. 172]

JONES, WILLIAM (1675–1749), mathematician ; mathematical tutor to Philip Yorke (Hardwicke) and the first and second Earls of Macclesfield, living many years with them at Shirburn Castle ; friend of Halley and Newton ; edited some of Newton's mathematical tracts, 1711 ; F.R.S., 1712 (afterwards vice-president) ; published also 'Synopsis Palmariorum Matheseos,' 1706, and a treatise on navigation.   [xxx. 173]

JONES, SIR WILLIAM (1746–1794), orientalist and jurist ; son of William Jones (1675–1749) [q. v.] ; educated at Harrow, and at University College, where he became fellow, 1766 ; tutor to Lord Althorp (second Earl Spencer) ; M.A., 1773 ; published French translation of a Persian life of Nadir Shah, 1770, a Persian grammar, 1771, and established his reputation by 'Poeseos Asiaticæ Commentariorum Libri Sex,' 1774 ; F.R.S., 1772 ; member of Johnson's Literary Club, 1773 ; intimate with Burke and Gibbon ; barrister, Middle Temple, 1774 ; became a commissioner of bankrupts, 1776 ; published his 'Essay on Bailments,' 1781 (often reprinted both in England and America) ; judge of the high court at Calcutta, 1783 till death ; knighted, 1783 ; his version of the Arabic 'Moallakat' published, 1783 ; founded Bengal Asiatic Society, 1784 ; mastered Sanskrit and published 'Dissertation on the Orthography of Asiatick Words in Roman Letters,' and translations of the 'Hitopadesa,' and 'Sakúntala,' also extracts from the 'Vedas'; began publication of 'The Institutes of Hindu Law, or Ordinances of Mánu'; his collected works edited by Lord Teignmouth, 1799 (reprinted, 1807); monuments erected to him in St. Paul's Cathedral, London, and at University College, Oxford (the latter by Flaxman).   [xxx. 174]

JONES, WILLIAM, OF NAYLAND (1726–1800), divine ; educated at the Charterhouse and University College, Oxford, where he became the friend of George Horne [q. v.] ; B.A., 1749 ; vicar of Pluckley, Kent ; F.R.S., 1775, delivering the Fairchild 'Discourses on Natural History' ; perpetual curate of Nayland, Suffolk, 1777 ; published, among other works, 'The Catholic Doctrine of the Trinity,' 1756, 'Physiological Disquisitions,' 1781, and some church music.   [xxx. 177]

JONES, WILLIAM (1763–1831), optician ; F.R.A.S.; author of geometrical and graphical essays, and editor (1799 and 1812) of George Adams's works on natural philosophy.   [xxx. 169]

JONES, WILLIAM (1784–1842), independent minister at Bolton ; wrote religious works for the young.
                    [xxx. 178]

JONES, WILLIAM (1762–1846), pastor of Scots baptist church, Finsbury ; author of 'History of the Waldenses' (1811) and other works.   [xxx. 178]

JONES, SIR WILLIAM (1808–1890), general ; created C.B. for services in command of the 61st during Punjaub campaign of 1848–9 ; commanded third infantry brigade at siege of Delhi, 1857 ; K.C.B., 1869 ; general, 1877 ; G.C.B., 1886.   [xxx. 179]

JONES, WILLIAM ARTHUR (1818–1873), antiquary; M.A. Glasgow, 1841 ; unitarian minister at Taunton, 1852–66 ; founded Taunton school of science and art ; hon. secretary of the Somerset Archæological and Natural History Society ; with Wadham P. Williams compiled 'Glossary of Somersetshire Dialect.'   [xxx. 179]

JONES, WILLIAM BASIL (1822–1897), bishop of St. David's ; educated at Shrewsbury and Trinity College, Oxford ; M.A., 1847 ; Michel scholar, 1845, Michel fellow, 1848, at Queen's College, Oxford ; fellow of University College, Oxford, 1851–7 ; examining chaplain, 1861, to William Thomson [q. v.], then bishop of Gloucester ; prebendary of York, 1863 ; archdeacon of York, 1867 ; rural dean of Bishopthorpe, 1869 ; chancellor of York, 1871 ; canon residentiary of York, 1873 ; bishop of St. David's and D.D. by diploma of Archbishop Tait, 1874 ; chaplain of House of Lords, 1878–82 ; visitor of St. David's College, Lampeter ; brought about the almost total disappearance of non-residence, and effected a very complete organisation of diocesan work.   His publications include writings on Welsh antiquities, religious commentaries, and editions of classical authors.   [Suppl. iii. 47]

JONES, WILLIAM BENCE (1812–1882), Irish agriculturist ; brother of Henry Bence Jones [q. v.] ; educated at Harrow and Balliol College, Oxford ; M.A., 1836 ; barrister, Inner Temple ; introduced improvements on his estate at Lisselan, co. Cork ; resisted the Land League ; published works on the Irish church and an autobiography.   [xxx. 179]

JONES, WILLIAM ELLIS (1796–1848), Welsh poet ('Gwilym Cawrdaf') and printer ; won bardic chair at Brecon Eisteddfod, 1822 ; his collected poetry published as 'Gweithoedd Cawrdaf,' 1851.   [xxx. 180]

JONES, WILLIAM HENRY RICH (1817–1885), antiquary ; Boden Sanskrit scholar at Oxford, 1837; M.A. Magdalen Hall, Oxford, 1844 ; vicar of Bradford-on-Avon, 1851–85 ; canon of Salisbury, 1872 ; F.S.A., 1849. His works include editions of the 'Domesday Book for Wiltshire' (1865), the 'Registers of St. Osmund' (Rolls series), and 'Fasti Ecclesiæ Sarusberiensis,' 1879.
                    [xxx. 180]

JONES-LOYD, SAMUEL, BARON OVERSTONE (1796–1883.) [See LOYD.]

JONSON, BENJAMIN (1573 ?–1637), dramatist and poet ('Ben Jonson'); of Border descent, but born probably in Westminster ; at Westminster school under William Camden ; according to Fuller a member of St. John's College, Cambridge ; escaped from trade to the army in Flanders ; returned to England, *c.* 1592 ; began to work for the admiral's company of actors both as player and playwright, 1597 ; included by Meres (1598) among English tragedians ; killed a fellow-actor in a duel or brawl, but escaped death by benefit of clergy, 1598 ; became a Roman catholic during imprisonment, but abjured twelve years later ; his 'Every Man in his Humour' (with Shakespeare in the cast) performed by the lord chamberlain's company at the Globe, 1598, and 'Every Man out of his Humour,' 1599 ; his 'Cynthia's Revels,' 1600, and 'The Poetaster' (attacking Dekker and Marston), 1601, performed by the children of the Queen's chapel ; his first extant tragedy, 'Sejanus,' given at the Globe by Shakespeare's company, 1603 ; his first court masque 'of Blacknesse' (with scenery by Inigo Jones) given on Twelfth Night, 1605 ; temporarily imprisoned (1605) for his share in 'Eastward Ho,' a play reflecting on the Scots ; his 'Volpone' acted both at the Globe and the two universities, 1605; produced, besides 'Twelfth Night' and 'Marriage Masques,' five plays (including 'Epicœne,' 'The Alchemist,' and 'Bartholomew Fayre') between 1605 and 1615; went on foot to Scotland, 1618–19; was made a burgess of Edinburgh, and entertained by Drummond of Hawthornden; guest of Richard Corbet [q. v.] at Oxford, 1619, and created M.A.; his 'Masque of Gypsies' performed, 1621, when he was in high favour with James I; produced 'The Staple of News' (last great play), 1625; elected chronologer of London, 1628; wrote 'Ode to Himself' after failure of 'The New Inn,' 1629; quarrelled with Inigo Jones [q. v.] after production of the masque 'Chloridia,' 1630, and withdrew from court; produced 'The Magnetic Lady,' 1632, and 'Tale of a Tub' (comedies), 1633; his last masques produced, 1633–4; last laureate verses, 1635; buried in Westminster Abbey and celebrated in a collection of elegies entitled 'Jonsonus Virbius.' His friends included Bacon, Selden, Chapman, Fletcher, Donne, and Shakespeare, and of the younger writers (his 'sons') Beaumont, Herrick, Suckling, Sir Kenelm Digby, and Lord Falkland. Among his patrons were the Sidneys, the Earl of Pembroke, and the Duke and Duchess of Newcastle. His poems (1616) include 'Epi- grammes,' 'The Forrest,' and 'Underwoods' (epistles and songs), and translations. His chief prose work is 'Timber,' or Discoveries made upon Men and Matter,' 1641. His works have been edited by William Gifford (1816) and Colonel Cunningham (1875). [xxx. 181]

JOPLIN, THOMAS (1790?–1847), writer on banking; founded the National and Provincial Bank, 1833; chief work, 'Essay on the General Principles and Present Prac- tices of Banking in England and Scotland' (1822), sug- gesting establishment of a joint-stock bank; died at Böhmischdorf, Silesia. [xxx. 191]

JOPLING, JOSEPH MIDDLETON (1831–1884), painter; queen's prizeman at Wimbledon, 1861. [xxx. 192]

JORDAN, DOROTHEA or DOROTHY (1762–1816), actress; née Bland; appeared at Dublin as Phœbe in 'As you like it,' 1777, and afterwards at Waterford and Cork under the management of Richard Daly [q. v.]; ran away to Leeds and, under the name of Mrs. Jordan, played Calista and other parts on the York circuit under Tate Wilkinson, 1782–5; made her début at Drury Lane as Peggy in 'The Country Girl,' 1785, and there or at the Haymarket till 1809 played Viola, Rosalind, Miss Tomboy, Hypolita, Sir Harry Wildair, Miss Prue, and original parts in adaptations by Kemble, and 'The Spoiled Child' (a farce attributed to herself); acted at Covent Garden, 1811–14, Lady Teazle being her last part; highly praised by Hazlitt, Lamb, Leigh Hunt, and the elder Mathews; had children by Richard Daly and Sir Richard Ford, and was for long mistress of the Duke of Clarence (Wil- liam IV); went to France in 1815, and died at St. Cloud, where she was buried. [xxx. 192]

JORDAN, JOHN (1746–1809), 'the Stratford poet'; wheelwright near Stratford-on-Avon; published 'Wel- combe Hills,' 1777; corresponded with Malone; his 'Original Collections on Shakespeare and Stratford-on- Avon' and 'Original Memoirs and Historical Accounts of the Families of Shakespeare and Hart,' printed by Halli- well. [xxx. 196]

JORDAN, SIR JOSEPH (1603–1685), vice-admiral; rear-admiral on the Irish station, 1643; retired to Hol- land, 1648, but was soon re-admitted to the service; as vice-admiral of the blue took part in the battles of June and July, 1653, against the Dutch; rear-admiral with Blake in the Mediterranean, 1654–5; knighted after the battle of 3 June 1665; rear-admiral of the red under Albemarle, 1–4 June, 1666, and vice-admiral on 25 July 1666; commanded squadron at Harwich, 1667; as vice- admiral of the blue led the van at Solebay, 1672; his por- trait by Lely at Greenwich. [xxx. 196]

JORDAN, THOMAS (1612?–1685), poet; recited a poem before Charles I, 1639; an actor till 1642, and after- wards (1668) in his own 'Money is an Ass' (published, 1663); wrote numerous dedications, prologues, epilogues, and pamphlets; as poet to the corporation of London de- vised the lord mayors' shows, 1671–85. Other works include 'Poeticall Varieties,' 1637, 'A Royall Arbour of Loyall Poesie,' 1664, and Pictures of Passions, Fancies, and Affections (1665). [xxx. 198]

JORDAN, THOMAS BROWN (1807–1890), engineer; secretary of Royal Cornwall Polytechnic after 1839; first keeper of mining records, 1840–5; helped Robert Were Fox [q. v.] in constructing dipping-needle; invented a declination magnetograph, a self-recording actinometer, and other instruments. [xxx. 200]

JORDAN, WILLIAM (fl. 1611), Cornish dramatist; supposed author of 'Gwreans an Bys, the Creation of the World.' [xxx. 200]

JORDEN, EDWARD (1569–1632), physician and chemist; of Hart Hall, Oxford; M.D. Padua; F.R.C.P., 1597; attributed to natural causes a supposed case of demoniacal possession which James I employed him to investigate; published 'Discourse of Natural Bathes and Mineral Waters,' 1631. [xxx. 201]

JORTIN, JOHN (1698–1770), ecclesiastical historian; son of Renatus Jortin [q. v.]; educated at the Charter- house and Jesus College, Cambridge (fellow), 1721–8; M.A., 1722; preacher at chapels of ease in New Street, St. Giles, London, and in Oxenden Street, London; Boyle lecturer, 1749; rector of St. Dunstan's-in-the-East, London, 1751; vicar of Kensington, 1762; D.D. Lambeth, 1755; archdeacon of London, 1764; published 'Remarks on Ecclesiastical History' (vol. i. 1751, vol. ii. 1752, vol. iii. 1754; enlarged, 1773), 'Life of Erasmus' (1758), and critical and theological tracts; later editions of his works collected as 'Various Works,' 1805–10. [xxx. 201]

JORTIN or **JORDAIN**, RENATUS (d. 1707) Huguenot refugee; gentleman of the privy chamber; secretary successively to Sir Edward Russell, Sir George Rooke, and Sir Clowdisley Shovell [q. v.], with whom he perished. [xxx. 201]

JORZ or **JOYCE**, THOMAS (d. 1310), 'Thomas the Englishman'; prior of Dominicans at Oxford, and pro- vincial of England, 1296–1308; cardinal-priest, 1305; con- fessor of Edward I; English representative at papal court; one of those appointed to hear the charges brought by Philip IV against the late pope, Boniface VIII; died at Grenoble; author of 'Commentarii super quattuor libros Sententiarum,' and other works; often confused with Thomas Wallensis (d. 1350?) [q. v.] [xxx. 203]

JORZ or **JORSE**, WALTER (fl. 1306), archbishop of Armagh, 1306–7; brother of Thomas Jorz [q. v.]; fined by Edward I for receiving consecration in Italy. [xxx. 204]

JOSCELIN. [See GOSCELIN and JOCELIN.]

JOSCELYN or **JOSSELIN**, JOHN (1529–1603), Anglo-Saxon scholar; fellow of Queens' College, Cam- bridge, 1549–57; M.A., 1552; Latin secretary to Arch- bishop Parker, 1558; prebendary of Hereford, 1560–77; incumbent of Hollingbourn, Kent, 1577; contributed 'Lives of the Archbishops' to Parker's 'De Antiquitate Bri- tannicæ Ecclesiæ,' 1572, and a collection of Anglo-Saxon pieces to his Paschal Homily of Ælfric Grammaticus, c. 1567; his 'Historiola Collegii Corporis' printed, 1880. [xxx. 204]

JOSEPH OF EXETER (fl. 1190), Latin poet (JOSEPHUS ISCANUS); studied at Gueldres; accompanied Archbishop Baldwin (d. 1190) [q. v.] to Palestine, 1188; his principal poem, 'De Bello Trojano,' long current under names of Dares Phrygius and Cornelius Nepos, first published as his own at Frankfort, 1620, and edited by Jusserand, 1877. [xxx. 205]

JOSEPH, GEORGE FRANCIS (1764–1846), portrait and subject painter; A.R.A., 1813; painted portraits of Spencer Perceval, Sir Stamford Raffles, and Charles Lamb. [xxx. 206]

JOSEPH, SAMUEL (d. 1850), sculptor; cousin of George Francis Joseph [q. v.]; best known by his statues of Wilkie in the National Gallery and of William Wilber- force in Westminster Abbey. [xxx. 206]

JOSI, CHRISTIAN (d. 1828), engraver and print- dealer; native of Utrecht; studied in London under John Raphael Smith; practised at Amsterdam; inherited Ploos van Amstel's collections, and catalogued his Rem- brandt etchings; settled in Gerrard Street, London, 1819, and published van Amstel's 'Collection d'imitations de dessins,' completed by himself, 1821. [xxx. 207]

JOSI, HENRY (1802–1845), keeper of prints and drawings, British Museum, 1836–45; born at Amsterdam; son of Christian Josi [q. v.]; some time print-seller in Newman Street, London. [xxx. 207]

A a

JOSSE, AUGUSTIN LOUIS (1763–1841), grammarian and catholic missioner at Gloucester ; born in France ; taught French to the Princess Charlotte, Wellington, and John Kemble ; published Spanish and French grammars and other works. [xxx. 207]

JOSSELYN, HENRY (d. 1683), deputy-governor of Maine, U.S.A., 1645, having gone to New England, 1634 ; brother of John Josselyn [q. v.] [xxx. 208]

JOSSELYN, JOHN (fl. 1675), author of 'New-Englands Rarities discovered,' 1672 (reprinted, 1865), and 'Account of Two Voyages to New-England,' 1674 (reprinted, 1834 and 1869). [xxx. 208]

JOULE, JAMES PRESCOTT (1818–1889), physicist ; studied under Dalton ; in paper on ' Electro-magnetic Forces' (1840) described an attempt to measure an electric current in terms of a unit ; elected to Manchester Literary and Philosophical Society, 1842, becoming president, 1860 ; determined by two distinct methods the physical constant known as Joule's equivalent or ' J,' describing his discovery in two papers ' On the Production of Heat by Voltaic Electricity,' communicated to Royal Society, 1840, and ' On the Heat evolved during the Electrolysis of Water' in Manchester Society's ' Memoirs' ; read paper ' On the Calorific Effects of Magneto Electricity and on the Mechanical Value of Heat,' before British Association at Cork, 1843 ; results of further experiments made by him at Whalley Range communicated in paper 'On the Mechanical Equivalent of Heat' to Royal Society by Faraday, 1849 ; results of his final experiments by direct method of friction communicated, 1878 ; F.R.S., 1850 ; royal medallist, 1852, and Copley medallist, 1860 ; received honorary degrees from Dublin, Oxford, and Edinburgh ; awarded a civil list pension, 1878. Besides the determination of the mechanical equivalent and the discovery of the conservation of energy, he investigated the thermo-dynamic properties of solids, and suggested improvements in the apparatus for measuring electric currents. He collected his 'Scientific Papers' in two volumes, 1885, 1887. [xxx. 208]

JOURDAIN, IGNATIUS (1561–1640), mayor and (1625, 1625–6, and 1627–8) M.P. for Exeter ; promoted bills against adultery and swearing. [xxx. 215]

JOURDAIN, JOHN (d. 1619), captain under East India Company ; cousin of Ignatius Jourdain [q. v.] ; visited Surat and Agra, 1609–11 ; 'president of the English' at Bantam, 1612, and at Jacatra, 1618 ; president of the council of India, 1618 ; surprised and slain by the Dutch of Patani. [xxx. 214]

JOURDAIN or **JOURDAN**, SILVESTER (d. 1650), author of 'A Discovery of the Barmudas, otherwise called the Ile of Divels' (1610), where he had been wrecked ; brother of Ignatius Jourdain [q. v.] ; his 'Discovery' probably known to Shakespeare. [xxx. 214]

JOWETT, BENJAMIN (1817–1893), master of Balliol College, Oxford, and regius professor of Greek at Oxford ; educated at St. Paul's School, London ; scholar of Balliol College, Oxford, 1835 ; obtained Hertford (University) scholarship, 1837 ; fellow of Balliol College, 1838 ; M.A., 1842 ; gained chancellor's prize for Latin essay, 1841 ; tutor at Balliol, 1842–70 ; ordained priest, 1845 ; public examiner, 1849, 1850, 1851, and 1853 ; published edition of St. Paul's Epistles to Thessalonians, Galatians, and Romans, 1855 ; regius professor of Greek at Oxford, 1855 ; owing to his having incurred suspicions of heresy by the liberality of his religious opinions, was deprived for ten years of the emoluments of the office ; contributed essay on ' Interpretation of Scripture' to 'Essays and Reviews' (1860), a liberal work which increased the suspicion of heresy already entertained against Jowett ; master of Balliol College, 1870–93 ; strongly advocated reforms with the object of lessening expense of an Oxford career, and supported claims of secondary education and university extension ; published translations of Plato (4 vols. 1871), Thucydides (2 vols. 1881), and Aristotle's 'Politics,' 1885 ; vice-chancellor of Oxford, 1882–6 ; hon. doctor of theology, Leyden, 1875 ; LL.D. Edinburgh, 1884, and LL.D. Cambridge, 1890. His essays and translations secured him a high place among the writers of his time, but he definitely identified himself with no party in religion or thought. [Suppl. iii. 49]

JOWETT, JOSEPH (1752–1813), professor of civil law ; fellow and tutor of Trinity Hall, Cambridge, 1775 ; LL.D., 1780 ; Cambridge professor of civil law, 1782 ; vicar of Wethersfield, Essex, 1795. [xxx. 215]

JOWETT, WILLIAM (1787–1855), divine and missionary ; nephew of Joseph Jowett [q. v.] ; fellow of St. John's College, Cambridge ; twelfth wrangler, 1810 ; M.A., 1813 ; missionary in Mediterranean countries and Palestine, 1815–24 ; secretary of C.M.S., 1832–40 ; incumbent of St. John, Clapham Rise, London, 1851 ; works include ' Christian Researches in the Mediterranean,' 1822, and in Syria and the Holy Land, 1825. [xxx. 215]

JOY, FRANCIS (1697 ?–1790), printer, paper-maker, and founder (1737) of the ' Belfast Newsletter.' [xxx. 216]

JOY, JOHN CANTILOE (1806–1866), marine-painter ; collaborated with his brother William Joy (1803–1867) [q. v.] [xxx. 216]

JOY, THOMAS MUSGRAVE (1812–1866), subject and portrait painter first exhibited at Royal Academy, 1831. [xxx. 216]

JOY, WILLIAM (d. 1734), 'the English Samson,' began to perform at the Duke's Theatre, Dorset Garden, London, c. 1699 ; afterwards a smuggler. [xxx. 217]

JOY, WILLIAM (1803–1867), marine-painter ; brother of John Cantiloe Joy [q. v.] ; government draughtsman. [xxx. 217]

JOYCE, GEORGE (fl. 1647), parliamentarian officer ; when cornet in Fairfax's regiment seized Holmby House and took Charles I to the army at Newmarket, 1647 ; active in promoting the king's trial ; colonel and governor of the Isle of Portland, 1650 ; imprisoned and cashiered for opposition to Cromwell, 1653 ; employed against royalists, 1659 ; lived at Rotterdam, 1660–70. [xxx. 217]

JOYCE, JEREMIAH (1763–1816), author of 'Scientific Dialogues' (1807) and other educational works ; many years secretary of the Unitarian Society ; while tutor to Earl Stanhope's sons imprisoned on a charge of treason, but liberated without trial after the acquittal of Hardy and Horne Tooke, 1794. [xxx. 218]

JOYCE, THOMAS (d. 1310). [See JORZ.]

JOYE, GEORGE (d. 1553), protestant controversialist ; fellow of Peterhouse, Cambridge, 1517 ; M.A., 1517 ; being charged with heresy fled to Strasburg, 1527, and published an answer, 1527, and a translation of Isaiah, 1531 ; printed at Antwerp translations of Jeremiah and the Psalms ; helped Tyndale in his controversy with Sir Thomas More, but quarrelled with him after surreptitiously reissuing (1534) his New Testament ; returned to England, 1535, but again retired, 1542 ; carried on controversy with Bishop Gardiner, 1543–4 ; issued ' Exposicion of Daniel' at Geneva, 1545, and ' The Conjectures of the ende of the worlde' (translation), 1548 ; died in England. [xxx. 219]

JOYLIFFE, GEORGE (1621–1658), physician ; M.A. Pembroke College, Oxford, 1643 ; M.D. Clare Hall, Cambridge, 1652 ; F.R.C.P., 1658 ; his discovery of the lymph ducts published by Francis Glisson [q. v.], 1654. [xxx. 221]

JOYNER, alias LYDE, WILLIAM (1622–1706), author of ' The Roman Empress' (tragedy, acted 1671) and ' Some Observations on the Life of Reginaldus Polus ' (1686) ; fellow of Magdalen College, Oxford, 1642–5 ; M.A., 1643 ; one of the Romanist fellows introduced at Magdalen by James II, 1687 ; friend of Hearne and Anthony à Wood. [xxx. 222]

JUBB, GEORGE (1718–1787), professor at Oxford ; of Westminster and Christ Church, Oxford ; M.A., 1742 ; D.D., 1780 ; chaplain to Archbishop Herring ; archdeacon of Middlesex, 1779 ; regius professor of Hebrew at Oxford, 1780–7 ; prebendary of St. Paul's, 1781 ; chancellor of York, 1781. [xxx. 222]

JUDKIN-FITZGERALD, SIR THOMAS, first baronet (d. 1810), high sheriff of co. Tipperary ; notorious for his severity in suppressing the rebellion of 1798 ; created baronet, 1801. [xxx. 223]

JUGGE, JOAN (fl. 1579–1587), widow of Richard Jugge [q. v.], whose business she carried on. [xxx. 224]

JUGGE, JOHN (d. 1579 ?), printer ; probably son of Richard Jugge [q. v.] [xxx. 224]

JUGGE, RICHARD (*fl.* 1531–1577 ?), printer; of Eton and King's College, Cambridge; original member of the Stationers' Company (1556), being several times master and warden; queen's printer, 1560; famous for his editions of the bible and New Testament. [xxx. 223]

JUKES, FRANCIS (1745–1812), aquatinta engraver. [xxx. 224]

JUKES, JOSEPH BEETE (1811–1869), geologist; a favourite pupil of Sedgwick while at St. John's College, Cambridge; B.A., 1836; geological surveyor of Newfoundland, 1839–40; naturalist with H.M.S. Fly in the survey of the north-east coast of Australia, 1842–6; after employment in North Wales was director of the Irish survey, 1850–69; member of royal commission on coalfields, 1866. His works include 'Excursions in and about Newfoundland,' 1842, and manuals of geology. [xxx. 224]

JULIANA (1343–1443), Norwich anchoret; author of 'XVI Revelations of Divine Love' (first printed, 1670; ed. H. Collins, 1877). [xxx. 226]

JULIEN or **JULLIEN**, LOUIS ANTOINE (1812–1860), musical conductor; after some success in Paris gave summer concerts at Drury Lane, 1840, and annual winter concerts, 1842–59, at which classical music was given by the best artists; organised opera season of 1847–8, when Sims Reeves made his début; became bankrupt; produced an opera by himself at Covent Garden, 1852; arrested for debt, 1859; composed many popular quadrilles; died insane at Neuilly. [xxx. 226]

JULIUS, CHARLES (1723–1765). [See BERTRAM, CHARLES.]

JUMIÈGES, ROBERT OF (*fl.* 1051). [See ROBERT.]

JUMPER, SIR WILLIAM (*d.* 1715), navy captain; commanded the Lennox at attack on Cadiz, 1703, and reduction of Gibraltar, 1704; wounded in action with Count of Toulouse off Malaga, 1704; knighted. [xxx. 227]

JUNE, JOHN (*fl.* 1740–1770), engraver. [xxx. 227]

JUNIUS (pseudonym). [See FRANCIS, SIR PHILIP, 1740–1818.]

JUNIUS, FRANCIS, or DU JON, FRANÇOIS, the younger (1589–1677), philologist and antiquary; born at Heidelberg; librarian to Thomas Howard, second earl of Arundel [q. v.], and tutor to his son, 1621–51; for a time at Amsterdam; presented Anglo-Saxon manuscripts and philological collections to the Bodleian Library; published 'De Pictura Veterum,' 1637, and editions of Cædmon,' 1655, and of 'Codex Argenteus' of the Mœso-Gothic version of Ulphilas, with glossary, 1664–5; his 'Etymologicum Anglicanum' (first printed, 1743) largely used by Dr. Johnson; buried in St. George's Chapel, Windsor. [xxx. 227]

JUPP, EDWARD BASIL (1812–1877), clerk to the Carpenters' Company, of which he wrote (1848) a historical account; son of Richard Webb Jupp [q. v.]; F.S.A.; published illustrated catalogues of the Academy, Society of Artists, and the Free Society; collected works of Bewick. [xxx. 229]

JUPP, RICHARD (*d.* 1799), chief architect and surveyor to the East India Company; an original member of the Architects' Club (1791). [xxx. 228]

JUPP, RICHARD WEBB (1767–1852), clerk to the Carpenters' Company; son of William Jupp the elder [q. v.] [xxx. 229]

JUPP, WILLIAM, the elder (*d.* 1788), architect; brother of Richard Jupp [q. v.] [xxx. 229]

JUPP, WILLIAM, the younger (*d.* 1839), architect to the Skinners' and other companies. [xxx. 229]

JURIN, JAMES (1684–1750), physician; of Christ's Hospital and Trinity College, Cambridge (fellow), 1706; M.A., 1709; M.D., 1716; master of Newcastle grammar school, 1709–15; president, Royal College of Physicians, 1750; physician to Guy's Hospital, 1725–32; F.R.S., 1718, secretary, 1721–7; an ardent Newtonian; defended mathematicians against Berkeley; attended Sir Robert Walpole in his last illness; attempted to make physiology an exact science; edited Varenius's 'Geographia Generalis,' 1712, and W. Cowper's 'Myotomia Reformata' (2nd edit. 1724). [xxx. 229]

JUST, JOHN (1797–1852), archæologist; assistant-master at Kirkby Lonsdale, and afterwards at Bury grammar school; botanical lecturer at Pine Street (Manchester) School of Medicine, 1834–52; wrote for 'Transactions' of Manchester Literary and Philosophical Society; compiled Westmorland glossary; deciphered Runic inscriptions in Isle of Man. [xxx. 230]

JUSTEL, HENRI (1620–1693), librarian; born in Paris; succeeded his father as secretary to Louis XIV; left France to avoid persecution as a protestant; D.C.L. Oxford, 1675, for gift of valuable manuscripts to the Bodleian; librarian at St. James's Palace, 1681–8; published his father's 'Bibliotheca Juris Canonici veteris,' 1661. [xxx. 231]

JUSTUS, SAINT (*d.* 627), missionary from Rome, first bishop of Rochester, 604–24, and fourth archbishop of Canterbury, 624–7. [xxx. 232]

JUSTYNE, PERCY WILLIAM (1812–1883), artist and book-illustrator; lived in Grenada, 1841–8. [xxx. 232]

JUTSUM, HENRY (1816–1869), landscape-painter. [xxx. 233]

JUXON, WILLIAM (1582–1663), archbishop of Canterbury; educated at Merchant Taylors' School, London, and St. John's College, Oxford; B.C.L., 1603; D.C.L., 1622; vicar of St. Giles, Oxford, 1609–16; rector of Somerton, 1615; president of St. John's College, Oxford, 1621–33; vice-chancellor, 1627–8; dean of Worcester, 1627; clerk of the closet on Laud's recommendation, 1632; as bishop of London, 1633–49, directed the restoration of St. Paul's and enforced conformity without giving offence; a lord of the admiralty, 1636–8; lord high treasurer, 1636–41; summoned as a witness against Strafford, whose attainder he advised Charles I to veto; attended the king at Newport and during his trial; received his last words on the scaffold; archbishop of Canterbury, 1660–3; buried in the chapel of St. John's College, Oxford, to which he left 7,000*l.* [xxx. 233]

K

KALISCH, MARCUS (1825–1885), biblical commentator; educated at Berlin and Halle; came to England after 1848 and was secretary to the chief rabbi in London; afterwards tutor to sons of Baron Lionel Rothschild; published scriptural commentaries, a Hebrew grammar, 1862–1863, and other works. [xxx. 237]

KAMES, LORD (1696–1782). [See HOME, HENRY.]

KANE, JOHN (*d.* 1834), compiler of royal artillery lists; adjutant, late royal invalid artillery, 1799. [xxx. 237]

KANE, RICHARD (1666–1736 ?), brigadier-general; wounded while captain in the 18th (Royal Irish) at Namur, 1695, and at Blenheim (major); commanded regiment at Malplaquet, 1709; lieutenant-governor of Minorca, afterwards of Gibraltar; governor of Minorca, 1730–6; brigadier-general, 1734; wrote narrative of campaigns of William III and Anne and handbook of infantry drill. [xxx. 237]

KANE, SIR ROBERT JOHN (1809–1890), Irish man of science; of Trinity College, Dublin; professor of chemistry, Apothecaries' Hall, Dublin, 1831–45, and of natural philosophy to Royal Dublin Society, 1834–47; president of Royal Irish Academy, 1877; F.R.S., 1849; president of Queen's College, Cork, 1845–73; director of 'Museum of Irish Industry,' Dublin, 1846; knighted, 1846; hon. LL.D. Dublin, 1868; commissioner of Irish education, 1873; vice-chancellor of Royal University of Ireland, 1880; published 'Elements of Chemistry,' 1841–3, 'Industrial Resources of Ireland,' 1844, and other works. [xxx. 238]

KARKEEK, WILLIAM FLOYD (1802–1858), veterinary surgeon and author of essays on agriculture and cattle.   [xxx. 239]

KARSLAKE, SIR JOHN BURGESS (1821–1881), lawyer; barrister, Middle Temple, 1846; Q.C., 1861; solicitor-general, 1866; knighted, 1866; attorney-general, 1867–8 and 1874–5; privy councillor, 1876; member of the judicature commission.   [xxx. 239]

KAT, KIT (*fl.* 1703–1733). [See CAT, CHRISTOPHER.]

KATER, HENRY (1777–1835), man of science; while serving in the 12th foot took part in survey of country between Malabar and Coromandel coasts; afterwards in 62nd; F.R.S., 1815 (some time treasurer); prepared standard measures for Russian government; made important pendulum and telescopical experiments, and produced a seconds pendulum by application of Huyghen's principle of the reciprocity of the centres of suspension and oscillation; Copley medallist, 1817; Bakerian lecturer, 1820; invented the floating collimator.   [xxx. 240]

KATHARINE or KATHERINE.   [See CATHERINE.]

KATTERFELTO, GUSTAVUS (*d.* 1799), conjurer and empiric; appeared in London during the influenza epidemic of 1782, exhibiting in Spring Gardens; referred to by Peter Pindar and Cowper; gave microscopic and magnetic demonstrations.   [xxx. 241]

KAUFFMANN, ANGELICA (1741–1807), historical and portrait painter; of Swiss extraction; gained popularity as a portrait-painter at Milan; painted 'Female Figure allured by Music and Painting,' 1760; studied at Florence and Rome, where she became acquainted with Winckelmann; met English people at Naples and Venice; introduced to London society by Lady Wentworth, 1766; painted Queen Charlotte and Christian VII of Denmark, and decorated the flower room, Frogmore; married the impostor Count de Horn, 1767, but separated from him next year; twice painted by Sir Joshua Reynolds, who was one of her admirers; one of the original Academicians, 1769; exhibited eighty-two pictures, 1769–97; visited Ireland, 1771; after Horn's death married Antonio Zucchi; left England, 1781; spent the rest of her life at Rome, where she was intimate with Goethe, and painted pictures for the Emperor Joseph II, the Czarina Catherine II, Pope Pius VI, and other potentates; her funeral superintended by Canova, the Academicians of St. Luke bearing the pall. Her works were highly esteemed by her contemporaries, and frequently engraved. Her 'Religion Surrounded by the Virtues' is in the National Gallery.   [xxx. 241]

KAVANAGH, ARTHUR MACMORROUGH (1831–1889), Irish politician and sportsman; though born with only the stumps of arms and legs became an expert angler, shot, huntsman, and yachtsman, and could write legibly and draw well; volunteer scout during movement of 1848; travelled through Russia and Persia to India, 1849–51; for a short time in survey department, Poonah; succeeded to family estates in Ireland, 1853, becoming a magistrate, railway director, and chairman of board of guardians; as conservative M.P. for co. Wexford, 1866–8, and Carlow, 1868–80, opposed Irish disestablishment; supported Land Bill of 1870; after losing his seat in 1880 became lord-lieutenant of Carlow; drew up separate report at close of Bessborough commission; initiated Irish Land Committee and (1883) Land Corporation; Irish privy councillor, 1886.   [xxx. 244]

KAVANAGH, CAHIR MAC ART, LORD OF ST. MOLYNS, BARON OF BALLYANN (*d.* 1554), took part in rebellion of the Leinster Geraldines, but submitted, 1538; sat in St. Leger's parliament, 1541; defeated Gerald Kavanagh at Hacketstown, 1545, but was obliged to renounce the title MacMurrough, 1550; received lordship of St. Molyns, 1543; was created baron, 1554.   [xxx. 245]

KAVANAGH, JULIA (1824–1877), novelist and biographical writer; daughter of Morgan Peter Kavanagh [q. v.] Her works include 'Madeleine' (1848), 'Daisy Burns,' and many other stories, and 'Woman in France in the Eighteenth Century,' 1850; died at Nice. [xxx. 246]

KAVANAGH, MORGAN PETER (*d.* 1874), poetical writer and philologist.   [xxx. 246]

KAY.   [See also CAIUS.]

KAY, SIR EDWARD EBENEZER (1822–1897), judge; M.A. Trinity College, Cambridge, 1847; barrister, Lincoln's Inn, 1847; bencher, 1867; treasurer, 1888; took silk, 1866; knighted and appointed justice of high court (chancery division), 1881; lord justice of appeal, 1890; retired, 1897.   [Suppl. iii. 56]

KAY, JOHN (*fl.* 1733–1764), of Bury, inventor of the fly-shuttle (1733); removed to Leeds, 1738, but returned to Bury; his invention largely utilised; ruined in consequence of litigation necessary to protect his patent; his house broken into by the Bury mob, 1753; said to have died a pauper in France.   [xxx. 247]

KAY, JOHN (1742–1826), miniature-painter and caricaturist; barber at Dalkeith and Edinburgh till 1785; etched nearly nine hundred plates, including portraits of Adam Smith and most of chief contemporary Scotsmen; 'Series of Original Portraits and Caricature Etchings,' with biographical matter, issued 1837–8 (3rd ed. 1877).   [xxx. 248]

KAY, JOSEPH (1821–1878), economist; M.A. Trinity College, Cambridge, 1849; as travelling bachelor of the university examined and reported upon social and educational condition of the poor in several continental countries, 1845–9; barrister, Inner Temple, 1848; Q.C., 1869; judge of the Salford Hundred Court of Record, 1862–78; his 'Free Trade in Land' issued, 1879.   [xxx. 248]

KAY, ROBERT (*fl.* 1760), inventor of the 'shuttle drop box'; son of John Kay (1733–1764) [q. v.]   [xxx. 248]

KAY, WILLIAM (1820–1886), biblical scholar; fellow, 1840, and tutor, 1842, of Lincoln College, Oxford; M.A., 1842; Pusey and Ellerton scholar, 1842; principal of Bishop's College, Calcutta, 1849–64; rector of Great Leighs, Essex, 1866–86; Grinfield lecturer, 1869; one of the Old Testament revisers; contributed commentaries on Isaiah (1875) and Hebrews (1881) to the 'Speaker's Bible.'   [xxx. 250]

KAY-SHUTTLEWORTH, SIR JAMES PHILLIPS, first baronet (1804–1877), founder of English popular education; brother of Joseph Kay [q. v.]; assumed his wife's name, 1842; M.D. Edinburgh, 1827; secretary to Manchester board of health; published 'The Physiology, Pathology, and Treatment of Asphyxia,' 1834; assistant poor law commissioner, 1835; first secretary of the committee of council on education, 1839–49; joint-founder of Battersea training college for pupil-teachers, 1839–40; created baronet, 1849; vice-chairman of central relief committee during Lancashire cotton famine (1861–5); high sheriff of Lancashire, 1863; hon. D.C.L. Oxford, 1870; member of scientific commissions, 1870–3; published two novels and works on education and social questions.   [xxx. 250]

KAYE, JOHN (1783–1853), bishop of Lincoln; educated under Dr. Charles Burney (1757–1817) [q. v.]; senior wrangler and senior chancellor's medallist, 1804; M.A. Christ's College, Cambridge, 1807; D.D., 1815; fellow and tutor of Christ's College, Cambridge, and (1814–30) master; as regius professor of divinity at Cambridge, 1816, revived public lectures; published courses on 'The Ecclesiastical History of the Second and Third Centuries' (1825) and some of the fathers; bishop of Bristol, 1820–7, of Lincoln, 1827–53; F.R.S., 1848; supported repeal of Test and Corporation Acts, 1828; opposed revival of convocation and upheld Gorham judgment; his collected works issued, 1888.   [xxx. 252]

KAYE, SIR JOHN WILLIAM (1814–1876), military historian; educated at Eton and Addiscombe; in Bengal artillery, 1832–41; entered East India civil service, 1856; secretary of India Office, political and secret department, from Mill's retirement till 1874; K.C.S.I., 1871. His works include 'History of the Sepoy War' (3 vols. 1864–1876), continued by Colonel Malleson, and history of the 'Administration of the East India Company,' 1853.   [xxx. 253]

KEACH, BENJAMIN (1640–1704), baptist divine; imprisoned for preaching at Winslow, and sentenced to fine and the pillory for his 'Child's Instructor,' 1664; pastor of Calvinistic baptists in Tooley Street, London, 1668; caused schism by advocating congregational singing; practised imposition of hands; preached in Goat Yard Passage, Horsleydown, London, from 1672; published expository, controversial, and allegorical works, and religious poems.   [xxx. 254]

KEAN, CHARLES JOHN (1811 ? – 1868), actor; second son of Edmund Kean [q. v.]; educated at Eton; appeared at Drury Lane as Young Norval, 1827; played at the Haymarket, Romeo, Mortimer (the 'Iron Chest'), and other parts, 1829; successful as Richard III at New York, 1830; acted Iago to his father's Othello at Covent Garden, 25 March 1833; played in Hamburg, 1833, and Edinburgh, 1837; gave Hamlet, Richard III, and Sir Giles Overreach at Drury Lane, 1838; revisited America, 1839 and 1846; first played at Windsor, 1849, and during his management of the Princess's (1850–9) obtained much success in the 'Corsican Brothers,' and 'Louis XI'; produced Byron's 'Sardanapalus' and Charles Reade's 'Courier of Lyons,' besides numerous Shakespearean revivals, which were adversely criticised for their profuse scenic arrangements; visited Australia, America, and Jamaica, 1863–6; acted for the last time at Liverpool, May 1867; excelled only as Hamlet and Louis XI.
[xxx. 255]

KEAN, EDMUND (1787–1833), actor; son of an itinerant actress; deserted by his mother; said to have appeared as a child at Her Majesty's and Drury Lane theatres, London, during an adventurous boyhood; received lessons from his uncle, a ventriloquist, and Miss Tidswell, a Drury Lane actress; played Prince Arthur with Mrs. Siddons and Kemble at Drury Lane, 1801, but ran away to Bartholomew Fair; broke both his legs tumbling in Saunders's circus; recited before George III at Windsor; in retirement, 1803–6; played subordinate parts at the Haymarket, 1806, and acted at Belfast; married Mary Chambers, 1808, and for six years underwent many hardships, but declined a London engagement as premature; attracted attention of Drury Lane stage-manager while acting at Dorchester, and was engaged by him for three years; on 26 Jan. 1814, in spite of hindrances, made a triumphant appearance as Shylock; increased his reputation with Richard III, and played also Hamlet, Othello, and Iago, being praised by Hazlitt, Kemble, and Byron, and invited to her house by Mrs. Garrick; first appeared as Macbeth and Sir Giles Overreach, 1814–15; played Barabas, Young Norval, and King John, 1817; he saw Talma at Paris, 1818, and essayed the part of Orestes in emulation; played Leon (' Rule a Wife and have a Wife') and Rolla (' Pizarro '); failed as Abel Drugger and declined Joseph Surface, 1819; failed as Coriolanus, but triumphed as Lear, 1820; after first visit to America reappeared at Drury Lane as Richard III; gained a success in comedy as Don Felix in the 'Wonder,' 1821; played Othello and Cymbeline with Young; after the action of Cox v. Kean (1825), when he had to pay damages for crim. con., was badly received in London, Scotland, and America; elected a Huron chief in Canada; reappeared with success at Drury Lane as Shylock, 1827, repeating the part at Covent Garden; played at Paris, 1828, and at Covent Garden, 1829; failed in Henry V at Drury Lane, 1830, playing there for the last time (as Richard III) on 12 March 1833; was taken ill at Covent Garden on 25 March while acting Othello, and died at Richmond on 15 May; unrivalled as a tragedian. Though receiving large sums, he ruined himself by drunkenness and ostentation, but was generous to his friends. A portrait of him as Sir Giles Overreach is at the Garrick Club, London.
[xxx. 258]

KEAN, ELLEN (1805–1880), actress; as Ellen Tree played Olivia to the Viola of her sister Maria (Mrs. Bradshaw) at Covent Garden, 1823; appeared at Drury Lane in comedy, 1826–8; at Covent Garden 1829–36, 'created' several parts, and played Romeo to Fanny Kemble's Juliet; in America, 1836–9; married Charles John Kean [q. v.], and played with him in Tobin's 'Honeymoon,' the same evening in Dublin, 1842; played leading parts with him at the Princess's Theatre, London; retired on his death. Among her best impersonations were Viola, Constance, Gertrude (' Hamlet '), and Mrs. Beverley.
[xxx. 265]

KEAN, MICHAEL (d. 1823), miniature-painter and proprietor of the Derby china factory. [xxx. 266]

KEANE, JOHN, first BARON KEANE (1781–1844), lieutenant-general; aide-de-camp to Lord Cavan in Egypt, 1799–1801; at reduction of Martinique, 1809; led a brigade of the third division at Vittoria, 1813, the Pyrenees, Toulouse, 1814, and other engagements; major-general, 1814; K.C.B., 1815; directed landing of first troops at New Orleans and led left column in attack of 8 Jan.

1815; commanded troops in Jamaica, 1823–30; lieutenant-general, 1830; commander-in-chief at Bombay, 1834–9; co-operated with Sir Henry Fane [q. v.] in Scinde 1838–9; took Ghuznee and occupied Cabul, 1839; though adversely criticised, received peerage and pension, 1839; G.C.H. [xxx. 266]

KEANE, JOSEPH B. (d. 1859), Irish architect.
[xxx. 268]

KEARNE, ANDREAS (fl. 1650), sculptor; assisted his brother-in-law, Nicholas Stone the elder [q. v.]
[xxx. 268]

KEARNEY, BARNABAS (BRIAN O CEARNAIDH) (1567–1640), Irish jesuit; said to have converted Thomas Butler, tenth earl of Ormonde [q. v.] [xxx. 268]

KEARNEY or CARNEY, JOHN (SEAN O CEARNAIDH) (d. 1600 ?), Irish protestant divine; B.A. Magdalene College, Cambridge, 1565; some time treasurer of St. Patrick's, Dublin; brought out the first extant work in Irish ('Aibidil air Caiticiosma,' 2nd ed. 1571); his Irish translation of the New Testament not extant. [xxx. 268]

KEARNEY, JOHN (1741–1813), bishop of Ossory; brother of Michael Kearney [q. v.]; provost of Trinity College, Dublin, 1799; bishop of Ossory, 1806–13.
[xxx. 269]

KEARNEY, MICHAEL (1733–1814), archdeacon of Raphoe; brother of John Kearney (1741–1813) [q. v.]; fellow of Trinity College, Dublin, 1757; Erasmus Smith professor of history at Dublin, 1769–78; archdeacon of Raphoe, 1798–1814. [xxx. 269]

KEARNEY, WILLIAM HENRY (1800–1858), water-colour-painter; foundation-member and subsequently vice-president of Institute of Painters in Water-colours.
[xxx. 269]

KEARNS, WILLIAM HENRY (1794–1846), musical composer; played the violin at Ancient Concerts, 1832, and was afterwards first viola; composed 'Bachelors' Wives' (operetta), 1817, 'Cantata, with Accompaniment' (1823), and arranged works by Handel, Haydn, Mozart, and others. [xxx. 270]

KEARY, ANNIE (1825–1879), author of 'Castle Daly' (1875) and other novels; published also children's books, 'Heroes of Asgard,' 1857, and other educational works.
[xxx. 270]

KEATE, GEORGE (1729–1797), author, painter, and friend of Voltaire; exhibited (1766–89) at Royal Academy and Society of Artists; published 'Poetical Works,' 1781, including 'The Alps' (dedicated to Young) and 'Ferney' (to Voltaire); published 'The Distressed Poet' (1787) and an account of Geneva (1761); also dedicated to Voltaire, whom he had met there. [xxx. 271]

KEATE, GEORGIANA JANE, afterwards MRS. HENDERSON (1770–1850), painter; daughter of George Keate [q. v.] [xxx. 271]

KEATE, JOHN (1773–1852), head-master of Eton; son of William Keate [q. v.]; fellow of King's College, Cambridge, Browne medallist, and Craven scholar; M.A., 1799; D.D., 1810; assistant-master at Eton, 1797, head-master, 1809–34; canon of Windsor, 1820; rector of Hartley Westpall, Hampshire, 1824–52; a popular head-master, but remarkable for severity of his discipline.
[xxx. 272]

KEATE, ROBERT (1777–1857), surgeon; brother of John Keate [q. v.]; surgeon at St. George's Hospital, 1813–53; sergeant-surgeon to William IV and Queen Victoria; inspector-general of hospitals, 1810; president of College of Surgeons, 1830, 1831, 1839. [xxx. 273]

KEATE, ROBERT WILLIAM (1814–1873), colonial governor; son of Robert Keate [q. v.]; of Eton and Christ Church, Oxford; governor of Natal, 1867–72, and the Gold Coast, 1872–3. [xxx. 273]

KEATE, THOMAS (1745–1821), surgeon of St. George's Hospital, 1792–1813, surgeon-general, 1793; master of the College of Surgeons, 1802, 1809, and 1818; died surgeon to Chelsea Hospital. [xxx. 273]

KEATE, WILLIAM (d. 1795), master of Stamford school, afterwards rector of Laverton, Somerset; M.A. King's College, Cambridge, 1767. [xxx. 273]

KEATING, GEOFFREY (1570?–1644?), author of 'Foras Feasa ar Eirinn' (' Foundation of Knowledge on

Ireland'), a history of Ireland to the English invasion, never printed (except in translation), but widely circulated in manuscript; his 'Tri Biorghaoithe an Bhais' printed by Dr. R. Atkinson, 1890. [xxx. 274]

KEATING, GEORGE (1762–1842), engraver and Roman catholic bookseller and publisher. [xxx. 275]

KEATING, Sir HENRY SINGER (1804–1888), judge; barrister, Inner Temple, 1832; Q.C, 1849; solicitor-general, 1857–8 and 1859; judge of common pleas, 1859–75; co-editor of 'Leading Cases' (3rd ed. 1849, 4th ed. 1856). [xxx. 275]

KEATING, JOHN (*fl.* 1680), Irish judge; chief-justice of common pleas in Ireland, 1679–89, and Irish privy councillor; supported Clarendon against Tyrconnel and (1686) advocated renewal of the commission of grace; imprisoned by James II; dismissed as a Jacobite. [xxx. 275]

KEATING, MAURICE BAGENAL St. LEGER (*d.* 1835), lieutenant-colonel; M.P., co. Kildare, 1790 and 1801; lieutenant-colonel, 1793; author of 'Travels through France, Spain, and Morocco' (1816–17), and other works. [xxx. 276]

KEATS, JOHN (1795–1821), poet; son of a livery stableman in Moorfields, London; educated at Enfield by John Clarke, with whose son, Charles Cowden Clarke [q. v.], he became intimate; acquired a knowledge of Latin and history, and some French, but no Greek; continued his study of literature after being apprenticed to a surgeon; broke his indentures, but continued medical studies at the hospitals; a dresser at Guy's, 1816; soon abandoned surgery; introduced by Clarke to Leigh Hunt, who printed a sonnet for him in the 'Examiner,' on 5 May 1816, and in whose house at Hampstead he first met his friend, John Hamilton Reynolds [q. v.] and Shelley; published the sonnet on Chapman's Homer in the 'Examiner,' December 1816, and other sonnets, 1817; influenced by Haydon and Hunt; with the help of Shelley published (March 1817) 'Poems by John Keats,' financially a failure; began 'Endymion' during visit to the Isle of Wight; lived with his brothers in Well Walk, Hampstead, London, and became intimate with Charles Wentworth Dilke [q. v.], Charles Armitage Brown [q. v.], and Joseph Severn [q. v.]; finished 'Endymion' at Burford Bridge, Surrey, his health having begun to fail; recited a part of the work to Wordsworth; published 'Endymion,' May 1818; on returning from a walking tour with Brown, nursed his brother Tom until the latter's death; pained by the hostile criticism of 'Blackwood's Magazine' and the 'Quarterly Review,' 1818; commenced 'Hyperion' and wrote some lyrics, 1818; finished 'The Eve of St. Agnes' early in 1819; wrote his best odes and 'La Belle Dame sans Merci,' 1819 (printed in the 'Indicator,' 1820); fell meanwhile deeply in love with Fanny Brawne; financially assisted by Brown, who collaborated with him in 'Otho the Great'; wrote 'Lamia,' broke off 'Hyperion' for a time, but afterwards recast it, and lived for a time in Westminster with a view to journalistic work; nursed by Brown, the first overt symptoms of consumption having appeared; his 'Lamia and other Poems' (July 1820) praised in the 'Edinburgh Review'; nursed first by the Hunts and afterwards by the Brawnes; sailed with Severn from London for Italy, September 1820; landed on the Dorset coast and composed his last poem ('Bright Star'); stayed a fortnight at Naples, and having declined Shelley's invitation to Pisa, reached Rome in November. Here he died, February 1821, and was buried in the protestant cemetery at Rome, where Severn designed a monument for him. A quarrel between George Keats and the poet's friends delayed the publication of his life, and a false impression as to his character prevailed till the issue of Monckton Milnes's 'Life and Letters of John Keats,' 1848. [xxx. 276]

KEATS, Sir RICHARD GOODWIN (1757–1834), admiral; lieutenant of the Ramillies at Ushant, 1778; present at relief of Gibraltar, 1780–1; served on the North American station till end of the war; promoted to post rank, 1789, and saw service on French coast, 1794–6, and again after the mutiny of 1797 till 1800, sending news of the expedition starting for Ireland in 1798; with Nelson off Toulon and in West Indies, 1803–5, and at battle of San Domingo, 1806; rear-admiral, 1807; convoyed Moore's troops to Gottenburg, 1807; K.B. for his seizure of Danish ships containing Spanish soldiers, 1807; second in command of the expedition to the Scheldt, 1809; com-

manded squadron defending Cadiz, 1810–11; vice-admiral, 1811; was governor of Newfoundland, 1813–15, and of Greenwich Hospital, 1821; admiral, 1825; a bust, by Chantrey, erected to his memory at Greenwich Hospital by William IV, his early naval friend. [xxx. 288]

KEBLE, JOHN (1792–1866), divine and poet; educated by his father; scholar of Corpus Christi College, Oxford, 1806; fellow of Oriel, 1811, also tutor, 1818–1823; B.A., 1811; won the university prizes for English and Latin essays, 1812; had Richard Hurrell Froude [q. v.] and Isaac Williams [q. v.] among his pupils when curate at Southrop; declined offers of benefices during his father's lifetime; professor of poetry at Oxford, 1831–41; vicar of Hursley, Hampshire, 1836–66. Keble College, Oxford (opened, 1869), was founded in his memory. Keble's sermon of 1833 on national apostasy initiated the 'Oxford Movement,' which he also supported in seven 'Tracts for the Times,' by his translation of Irenæus in 'The Library of the Fathers,' and his 'Life' and 'Works' of Bishop Thomas Wilson. He also edited Hooker's works (1836), and helped Newman with Richard Hurrell Froude's 'Remains.' 'The Christian Year' appeared anonymously in 1827, and attained extraordinary success. His 'De Poeticæ Vi Medicâ' (Oxford poetry lectures) appeared, 1841; 'Lyra Innocentium,' 1846, 'Sermons Academical and Occasional,' 1847, and the treatise 'On Eucharistical Adoration,' 1857. Chief among the posthumous publications were 'Miscellaneous poems,' 1869, and 'Occasional Papers and Reviews,' 1877. [xxx. 291]

KEBLE, JOSEPH (1632–1710), author of 'Reports in the Court of Queen's Bench' (1685); son of Richard Keble [q. v.]; fellow of All Souls College, Oxford; B.C.L, 1654; barrister, Gray's Inn, 1658. [xxx. 295]

KEBLE, KEEBLE, or KEBBEL, RICHARD (*fl.* 1650), parliamentary judge in Wales; barrister, Gray's Inn, 1614, Lent reader, 1639; serjeant, 1648; commissioner of the great seal, 1649–54; tried Lilburne and Christopher Love [q. v.], 1651; excepted from the Act of Indemnity. [xxx. 295]

KEBLE, THOMAS (1793–1875), divine; brother of John Keble [q. v.]; scholar and fellow of Corpus Christi College, Oxford; B.A., 1811; rector of Bisley, 1827–75; wrote four 'Tracts for the Times' and forty-eight of the 'Plain Sermons,' besides translating Chrysostom's 'Homilies.' [xxx. 296]

KECK, Sir ANTHONY (1630–1695), second commissioner of the great seal, 1689–90; barrister, Inner Temple, 1659, bencher, 1677; knighted, 1689; M.P., Tiverton, 1691. [xxx. 296]

KEDERMYSTER or **KYDERMINSTRE**, RICHARD (*d.* 1531?), abbot of Winchcomb, Gloucestershire, 1487; one of the English representatives at the Lateran council, 1512; defended retention of benefit of clergy as applied to minor orders; some of his Winchcomb register printed in Dugdale's 'Monasticon.' [xxx. 297]

KEDINGTON, ROGER (*d.* 1760), divine; fellow of Caius College, Cambridge; M.A., 1737; D.D., 1749; rector of Kedington, Suffolk; published religious works. [xxx. 297]

KEEBLE. [See also KEBLE.]

KEEBLE, JOHN (1711–1786), composer and organist of St. George's, Hanover Square, 1737, and at Ranelagh from 1742; published 'Theory of Harmonics,' 1784. [xxx. 298]

KEEGAN, JOHN (1809–1849), Irish ballad-writer. [xxx. 298]

KEELEY, Mrs. MARY ANN (1805?–1899), actress, whose maiden name was Goward; appeared at Lyceum Theatre, London, 1825; married Robert Keeley [q. v.], 1829; one of the finest comedians of modern days; last appeared professionally at Lyceum, 1859. Her parts include Jack Sheppard, 1839, Nerissa, Audrey, Maria ('Twelfth Night'), Dame Quickly, and Mrs. Page. [Suppl. iii. 56]

KEELEY, ROBERT (1793–1869), actor; the original Leporello in 'Don Giovanni' (Olympic, 1818) and Jemmy Green in 'Tom and Jerry' (Adelphi); made a great hit as Rumfit, a tailor in Peake's 'Duel, or my two Nephews,' 1823; married Mary Goward and acted with her at Covent Garden, the Lyceum, and other London theatres; with Madame Vestris at the Olympic, 1838–41, Macready at

Drury Lane 1841-2, Strutt at the Lyceum (Dickens's plays), 1844-7, and Charles John Kean [q. v.] at the Princess's; retired, 1857, but reappeared, 1861-2.   [xxx. 298]

KEELING, JOSIAH (*fl.* 1691), conspirator; revealed existence of Rye House plot and gave evidence against Russell, Sidney, and the chief conspirators, 1683; received reward and a place; after Revolution dismissed for Jacobitism; died in prison.   [xxx. 300]

KEELING, WILLIAM (*d.* 1620), naval commander and East India Company's agent; captain of the Susan in voyage of Sir Henry Middleton [q. v.] to the Indies, 1604-1606; commander in the company's voyage of 1607-10; commander-in-chief in India, 1615-17; afterwards captain of Cowes.   [xxx. 300]

KEELING, WILLIAM KNIGHT (1807-1886), painter; in early years assisted William Bradley [q. v.]; exhibited at the New Society; president of the Manchester Academy, 1864-77.   [xxx. 301]

KEENE, Sir BENJAMIN (1697-1757), diplomatist; LL.B. Pembroke Hall, Cambridge, 1718; agent for South Sea Company in Spain and consul at Madrid, 1724; ambassador at Madrid, 1727-39 and 1748-57; negotiated treaty of Seville (1729) and commercial treaty of 1750; member of board of trade, 1742-4; envoy to Portugal, 1746-8; K.B., 1754; died at Madrid.   [xxx. 301]

KEENE, CHARLES SAMUEL (1823-1891), humorous artist; after apprenticeships to an architect and a wood-engraver worked for 'Punch' from 1851, and the 'Illustrated London News'; illustrated stories in 'Once a Week' and Jerrold's 'Caudle Lectures,' and contributed plates to the 1879 edition of Thackeray; gold medallist, Paris Exhibition of 1890.   [xxx. 302]

KEENE, EDMUND (1714-1781), bishop of Ely; brother of Sir Benjamin Keene [q. v.]; of Charterhouse and Caius College, Cambridge (junior fellow, 1736-9); M.A., 1737; fellow of Peterhouse, 1739, and master, 1748-1754; vice-chancellor, 1749-51; rector of Stanhope, Durham, 1740-70; bishop of Chester, 1752-71, and of Ely, 1771-81; sold Ely House, Holborn, London, and built the present residence in Dover Street, London.   [xxx. 303]

KEENE, HENRY (1726-1776), architect and surveyor to Westminster Abbey; designed the Radcliffe Infirmary and Observatory and some collegiate buildings at Oxford.   [xxx. 304]

KEENE, HENRY GEORGE (1781-1864), Persian scholar; grandson of Henry Keene [q. v.]; while in Madras army took part in storming of Seringapatam, 1799; afterwards entered civil service and studied at Fort William College, Calcutta; B.A. Sidney Sussex College, Cambridge, 1815, fellow, 1817; professor of Arabic and Persian at Haileybury, 1824-34; published text and translations of 'Akhlák-i-Mahsini' and 'Anwás-i-Suhaili,' and 'Persian Fables' (edited by his daughter, 1883).   [xxx. 305]

KEEPE, HENRY (1652-1688), author of 'Monumenta Westmonasteriensia' (1682) and other antiquarian works (one under pseudonym of 'Charles Taylour'); of New Inn, Oxford, and Inner Temple; member of Westminster Abbey choir.   [xxx. 306]

KEEPER, JOHN (*fl.* 1580). [See KEPER.]

KEIGHTLEY, THOMAS (1650?-1719), Irish official; married Frances Hyde, sister of the Duchess of York; vice-treasurer of Ireland, 1686; sent by Clarendon to induce James II to stay in England, 1688; commissioner of Irish revenue, 1692; a lord justice, 1702; commissioner for the Irish chancellor, 1710.   [xxx. 306]

KEIGHTLEY, THOMAS (1789-1872), author; of Trinity College, Dublin; published 'Fairy Mythology' (1828, anon.) and histories, including one of the war of Greek independence; also editions of Virgil's 'Bucolics and Georgics,' and other Latin classics, and of Milton and Shakespeare; issued 'Shakespeare Expositor,' 1867; received civil list pension.   [xxx. 307]

KEIGWIN, JOHN (1641-1716), Cornish scholar; his translations of 'Pascon Agan Arluth' (mystery play) and of the 'Gwreans an Bys' of William Jordan [q. v.], printed by Davies Gilbert, 1826-7, and re-edited by Whitley Stokes in 1860 and 1863.   [xxx. 308]

KEIGWIN, RICHARD (*d.* 1690), naval and military commander; present at the four days' fight of June

1666; took part in capture of St. Helena, 1673, and succeeded Munden as governor; as commandant at Bombay defeated the Mahratta fleet, 1679; headed revolt of 1683 against the company holding Bombay for the king till the arrival of Sir Thomas Grantham [q. v.]; fell while leading the attack on Basseterre, St. Christopher's.   [xxx. 308]

KEILL, JAMES (1673-1719), physician; hon. M.D. Cambridge; practised at Northampton; published 'Account of Animal Secretion,' 1708, enlarged as 'Essays on several Parts of the Animal Œconomy,' 1717, the fourth edition containing an account of his controversy with Jurin.   [xxx. 309]

KEILL, JOHN (1671-1721), mathematician and astronomer; brother of James Keill [q. v.]; pupil of David Gregory (1661-1708) [q. v.] at Edinburgh; M.A. Edinburgh; incorporated at Oxford, 1694; at Hart Hall, Oxford, gave the first experimental lectures on natural philosophy; as deputy to the Sedleian professor delivered lectures, published as 'Introductio ad Veram Physicam'; as 'treasurer of the Palatines' conducted German refugees to New England, 1709; patronised by Harley; 'decypherer' to Queen Anne, 1712; professor of astronomy at Oxford, 1712; F.R.S., 1701; defended against Leibnitz Newton's claim to be the inventor of the fluxional calculus; published (1715) Latin editions of Euclid and the elements of trigonometry, and (1718) 'Introductio ad Veram Astronomiam.'   [xxx. 310]

KEILWAY, KELLWAY, or KAYLWAY, ROBERT (1497-1581), law reporter; autumn reader at Inner Temple, 1547, and treasurer, 1557-8; serjeant-at-law, 1552; employed by the crown on various commissions; selections from his law reports issued, 1602.   [xxx. 311]

KEIMER, SAMUEL (*fl.* 1707-1738), quaker printer; while imprisoned in the Fleet wrote 'A Brand Pluck'd from the Burning' (containing a letter from Defoe), 1718; printer in Philadelphia, 1723, with Franklin as foreman; assisted by Franklin in his edition of Sewel's 'History of the Quakers,' 1728; published at Bridgetown, Barbados, first newspaper in Caribbee islands, 1731-8.   [xxx. 312]

KEIR, JAMES (1735-1820), chemist; studied at Edinburgh; friend of Erasmus Darwin; issued 'Treatise on the different kinds of Elastic Fluids or Gases,' 1777; while managing Boulton & Watt's engineering works, patented a metal said to resemble 'Muntz-metal,' 1779; with Alexander Blair opened alkali works at Tipton, the method of extraction being Keir's discovery, 1780; established Tividale colliery; discovered the distinction between carbonic acid gas and atmospheric air; F.R.S., 1785; contributed paper concerning experiments and observations on the dissolution of metals in acids, 1790; wrote memoir of Thomas Day [q. v.]   [xxx. 313]

KEIR, WILLIAM GRANT (1772-1852). [See GRANT, Sir WILLIAM KEIR.]

KEITH, VISCOUNT (1746-1823). [See ELPHINSTONE, GEORGE KEITH.]

KEITH, VISCOUNTESSES. [See ELPHINSTONE, HESTER MARIA, 1762-1857; ELPHINSTONE, MARGARET MERCER, 1788-1867.]

KEITH, ALEXANDER (*d.* 1758), Mayfair parson; excommunicated for celebrating marriages without banns or licence, and afterwards imprisoned for contempt of the church, in the Fleet, where he died.   [xxx. 314]

KEITH, ALEXANDER (*d.* 1819), of Ravelston; founder of the Keith prizes at Edinburgh; friend and connection of Sir Walter Scott.   [xxx. 315]

KEITH, ALEXANDER (1791-1880), writer on prophecy; son of George Skene Keith [q. v.]; D.D. Aberdeen, 1833; pastor of St. Cyrus, Kincardineshire, 1816-40; visited Palestine and eastern Europe for the Scottish church, 1839, and in 1844 took daguerrotype views; joined the free church; published works of Christian evidences founded on the fulfilment of prophecy.   [xxx. 315]

KEITH, GEORGE, fifth EARL MARISCHAL (1553?-1623), founder of Marischal College, Aberdeen; educated at King's College, Aberdeen, and under Beza at Geneva; succeeded his grandfather in the earldom, 1581; privy councillor of Scotland, 1582; a commissioner for executing laws against papists; as ambassador extraordinary to Denmark acted as James VI's proxy in marrying the

Princess Anne, 1589; founded Marischal College, Aberdeen, 1593; king's commissioner for apprehension of Huntly and trial of the catholic lords, 1593; member of parliamentary commission of 1604 for union with England; royal commissioner to Scottish parliament, 1609; member of the ecclesiastical commission.   [xxx. 316]

KEITH, GEORGE (1639?–1716), 'Christian quaker' and S.P.G. missionary; M.A. Marischal College, Aberdeen; became a quaker, 1662; frequently imprisoned for preaching; collaborated with Robert Barclay (1648–1690) [q. v.], and was imprisoned with him at Aberdeen, 1676; accompanied George Fox [q. v.] and William Penn [q. v.] to Holland and Germany on a missionary tour, 1677; after having been twice imprisoned in England, emigrated to Philadelphia, 1689; accused of heresy and interdicted from preaching, 1692; held meetings of 'Christian Quakers'; came to London to defend his views, but was disowned by the 'yearly meeting' of 1694, after which he established a meeting at Turners' Hall, Philpot Lane, London, where, retaining the quaker externals, he administered baptism and the Lord's Supper, 1695–1700; conformed to the Anglican church, 1700; conducted a successful mission in America for the S.P.G., 1702–4; died rector of Edburton, Sussex. Among his chief publications were 'The Deism of William Penn and his Brethren,' 1699, 'The Standard of the Quakers examined,' 1702, and 'A Journal of Travels,' 1706.   [xxx. 318]

KEITH, GEORGE, tenth EARL MARISCHAL (1693?–1778), Jacobite and favourite of Frederick the Great; succeeded to earldom, 1712; commanded cavalry at Sheriffmuir, 1715; entertained James Edward, the Old Pretender, at Newburgh and Fetteresso, 1715; led Spanish Jacobite expedition of 1719, and after Glenshiel escaped to the western isles, and thence to Spain; corresponded from Valencia with the Pretender, but took no part in the Forty-five; named Prussian ambassador at Paris, 1751, governor of Neufchatel, 1752, and ambassador to Madrid, 1758; pardoned by George II, probably for sending intelligence of the Family Compact, 1759; succeeded to the Kintore estates, 1761, but was recalled to Prussia by the king's personal entreaties, 1764; intimate with Voltaire and Rousseau.   [xxx. 321]

KEITH, GEORGE SKENE (1752–1823), author of 'General View of the Agriculture of Aberdeenshire,' 1811; graduated at Aberdeen, 1770; D.D. Marischal College, Aberdeen, 1803; minister of Keith-Hall and Kinkell, 1778–1822, and Tulliallan, 1822–3; published 'Tracts on Weights, Measures, and Coins,' 1791; voted 500l. by parliament for his experiments in distillation; edited Principal George Campbell's 'Lectures on Ecclesiastical History,' with life, 1800.   [xxx. 322]

KEITH, JAMES FRANCIS EDWARD (1696–1758), known as MARSHAL KEITH; brother of George Keith, tenth earl Marischal [q. v.]; carefully educated under Robert Keith (1681–1757) [q. v.] and Meston the Jacobite poet; took part in the Fifteen, and escaped with his brother to Brittany; studied mathematics in Paris under Maupertuis; engaged in Alberoni's unsuccessful Jacobite expedition, 1719; served in the Spanish army; lieutenant-colonel of the Tsarina Anne's bodyguard; second in command in Polish succession war, 1733–5, and Russian general, 1737; wounded in Turkish war, 1737; took prominent part in Russo-Swedish war, 1741–3, but fell into disgrace as a foreigner; made field-marshal by Frederick the Great, 1747; governor of Berlin, 1749; after sharing in the early victories of the Seven Years' war was mortally wounded at Hochkirch; inventor of Kriegsschachspiel. A marble statue of him was erected at Berlin.   [xxx. 324]

KEITH, SIR JOHN, first EARL OF KINTORE (d. 1714), fourth son of William Keith, sixth earl Marischal [q. v.]; held Dunnottar Castle against Cromwell, and preserved the regalia, 1650; created knight marischal of Scotland at the Restoration; created Earl of Kintore and privy councillor, 1677.   [xxx. 325]

KEITH, SIR ROBERT (d. 1346), great marischal of Scotland; received lands of Keith from King John Baliol, 1294; captured by the English, 1300, but released, 1302; one of the four wardens of Scotland till he joined Bruce, 1308; justiciar of Scotland; led Scottish horse at Bannockburn, 1315; fell at battle of Durham.   [xxx. 326]

KEITH, ROBERT (1681–1757), bishop of Fife and historian; at Marischal College, Aberdeen; when coadjutor (1727–33) to Bishop Millar of Edinburgh obtained extinction of project of college of bishops, 1732; bishop of Fife, 1733–43; after his resignation of Fife continued to act as bishop of Orkney and Caithness, and (1743) was chosen 'primus'; published a history of Scotland from the Reformation to 1568, 1734 (reprinted, 1844–5), and 'Catalogue of the Bishops of Scotland to 1688,' 1755 (continued by M. Russell, LL.D., 1824).   [xxx. 326]

KEITH, ROBERT (d. 1774), British ambassador at Vienna, 1748–58, at St. Petersburg, 1758–62; friend of Hume and Robertson.   [xxx. 328]

KEITH, SIR ROBERT MURRAY (1730–1795), lieutenant-general and diplomatist; son of Robert Keith (d. 1774) [q. v.]; served in Scottish brigade in Dutch service, 1747–52; on staff of Lord George Sackville at Minden, 1759; as commander of 87th foot (1759–63) won distinction in the Seven Years' war; British minister in Saxony, 1769–71; while envoy at Copenhagen rescued from the anger of the mob Sophia Matilda of Denmark (sister of George III), and was created K.B., 1772; ambassador at Vienna, 1772–92; lieutenant-general, 1781; privy councillor, 1789.   [xxx. 329]

KEITH, ROBERT WILLIAM (1787–1846), musical composer and organist at the New Jerusalem Church, Friars Street, London; published sacred melodies and 'Musical Vade Mecum,' c. 1820.   [xxx. 330]

KEITH, THOMAS (1759–1824), mathematical writer and teacher, and accountant to the British Museum.   [xxx. 331]

KEITH, SIR WILLIAM (d. 1407?), great marischal of Scotland; nephew of Sir Robert Keith [q. v.]; favourite of David II; built Dunnottar Castle on site of the parish church.   [xxx. 331]

KEITH, WILLIAM, fourth EARL MARISCHAL (d. 1581), 'William of the Tower'; succeeded his grandfather in the peerage, 1530; extraordinary lord of session, 1541; privy councillor, 1543; present at Pinkie, 1547; subscribed the confession of faith, 1560, and 'Book of Discipline,' 1561; opposed proposal to deprive Mary Queen of Scots of the mass; retired from affairs after Darnley's death; the wealthiest Scotsman of his time.   [xxx. 331]

KEITH, WILLIAM (d. 1608?). [See KETHE.]

KEITH, WILLIAM, sixth EARL MARISCHAL (d. 1635), succeeded George, fifth earl, 1623; captain of three ships on Scottish coast, 1626; fitted out a fleet to help the king of Poland, 1634.   [xxx. 332]

KEITH, WILLIAM, seventh EARL MARISCHAL (1617?–1661), covenanter; co-operated with Montrose and twice seized Aberdeen, 1639; chosen a lord of the articles after pacification of Berwick, 1639; again seized Aberdeen and enforced signature of the covenant, 1640; nominated privy councillor, 1641; attended covenanting committees in the north, but remained inactive, 1643–4; refused to give up fugitives to Montrose, and was besieged at Dunnottar, 1645; joined Hamilton's expedition into England, 1648; entertained Charles II at Dunnottar, 1650; arrested and imprisoned in the Tower till the Restoration, when he was appointed keeper of the privy seal of Scotland.   [xxx. 333]

KEITH-FALCONER, ION GRANT NEVILLE (1856–1887), Arabic scholar and bicyclist; educated at Harrow and Trinity College, Cambridge; B.A., 1878; Tyrwhitt Hebrew scholar and first class in the Semitic languages tripos; president of the London Bicycle Club, 1877–86; rode from John o' Groat's to Land's End in thirteen days, less forty-five minutes, 1882; studied Arabic at Assiout, 1881–2; published translation from Syriac version of 'Fables of Bidpai,' 1885; lord almoner's professor of Arabic at Cambridge, 1886; died of fever near Aden, at a station whence he had made excursions to study Somali.   [xxx. 336]

KELBURN, SINCLARE (1754–1802), Irish presbyterian divine; B.A. Trinity College, Dublin, 1774; studied also at Edinburgh; minister at Belfast, 1780–99; imprisoned on suspicion of connection with United Irishmen, 1797; published work on the divinity of Christ, 1792.   [xxx. 337]

KELDELETH or KELDELECH, ROBERT (d. 1273), chancellor of Scotland; abbot of Dunfermline, 1240–51; of Melrose, 1268–73; chancellor of Scotland, 1250–1; deposed as partisan of Alan Durward.   [xxx. 338]

KELHAM, ROBERT (1717–1808), attorney in the king's bench; author of dictionary of Norman-French, 1779, index to abridgments of law and equity, 1758, and other works. [xxx. 338]

KELKE, ROGER (1524–1576), master of Magdalene College, Cambridge; M.A. St. John's College, Cambridge, 1547; senior fellow of St. John's, 1552; lived at Zurich during reign of Mary; Lady Margaret preacher, 1558–65; master of Magdalene College, 1558–76; vice-chancellor, 1567 and 1571–2; opposed Archbishop Parker's 'Advertisements'; archdeacon of Stowe, 1563. [xxx. 338]

KELLAND, PHILIP (1808–1879), mathematician; senior wrangler and first Smith's prizeman, Queens' College, Cambridge, 1834; M.A., 1837, and tutor; professor of mathematics at Edinburgh, 1838–79; secretary of the Senatus Academicus till 1867; F.R.S., 1838; president, Edinburgh Royal Society, 1878–9; wrote on mathematics and Scottish education; contributed the article 'Algebra' to 'Encyclopædia Britannica' (ninth edition). [xxx. 339]

KELLAWE, RICHARD DE (d. 1316), bishop of Durham, 1311–16; refused to receive Gaveston, 1313; his register the earliest extant of the Palatinate. [xxx. 340]

KELLER, GOTTFRIED or GODFREY (d. 1704), harpsichord player and composer; author of a manual of thorough-bass. [xxx. 341]

KELLETT, EDWARD (d. 1641), divine; of Eton and King's College, Cambridge; fellow; incorporated M.A. at Oxford, 1617; D.D., 1621; prebendary of Exeter, 1630; friend of Selden; published 'Miscellanies of Divinitie', 1635, and other works. [xxx. 341]

KELLETT, SIR HENRY (1806–1875), vice-admiral; named C.B. for services as surveyor and pilot in Chinese war of 1840; co-operated with Franklin search expeditions in the Herald, 1848–50; went in search of Franklin in the Resolute, 1852, but abandoned her under orders, May 1854; commodore at Jamaica, 1855–9; rear-admiral, 1862; vice-admiral, 1868; K.C.B., 1869; commander-in-chief in China, 1869–71. [xxx. 342]

KELLEY, EDWARD (1555–1595), alchemist; said to have studied at Oxford under an *alias*; pilloried for fraud or coining at Lancaster, 1580; 'skryer' to John Dee [q. v.], going with him to Prague and staying with him at the Emperor Rudolph II's court; parted from Dee in 1588, but remained in Germany; lost his life in attempting to escape from prison; his Latin treatises on the philosopher's stone issued, 1676; mentioned in 'Hudibras.' [xxx. 342]

KELLIE, EARLS OF. [See ERSKINE, THOMAS, first EARL, 1566–1639; ERSKINE, THOMAS ALEXANDER, sixth EARL, 1732–1781.]

KELLISON, MATTHEW (1560?–1642), president of the English college, Douay; professor of scholastic theology at Rheims, 1589; rector of the university, 1606; member of Arras College, 1611; as president (1613–42) rid Douay of jesuit influence; published 'The Gagge of the Reformed Gospell,' 1623 (frequently reprinted as 'Touchstone of the Reformed Gospel'), and other works. [xxx. 344]

KELLNER, ERNEST AUGUSTUS (1792–1839), musician; played a concerto of Handel before the royal family when five years old; made tours with Incledon as a baritone; sang and played in Switzerland and Germany and at Philharmonic concerts in London, 1820–3; appeared at Venice; gave concerts in Russia and Paris; composed masses and songs. [xxx. 345]

KELLO, MRS. ESTHER or HESTER (1571–1624), calligrapher and miniaturist: *née* English or Inglis (in French Langlois); born in France; perhaps nurse to Prince Henry; manuscripts written or illuminated by her in British Museum, the Bodleian, and continental libraries. [xxx. 346]

KELLO, SAMUEL (d. 1680), rector of Spexall, Suffolk, 1620–80; son of Mrs. Esther Kello [q. v.]; M.A. Edinburgh, 1618; admitted to Christ Church, Oxford. [xxx. 346]

KELLY, EDWARD (1555–1595). [See KELLEY.]

KELLY, EDWARD (1854–1880), bushranger; with his brother and two others held out for two years against the police on the borders of Victoria and New South Wales, occasionally plundering banks; captured and hanged. [xxx. 347]

KELLY, SIR FITZROY (1796–1880), lord chief baron; barrister, Lincoln's Inn, 1824; K.C., 1834; standing counsel to the Bank and the East India Company; defended Tawell the poisoner, 1845; knighted, 1845; prosecuted Dr. Bernard, 1858; appeared in Gorham case, 1847, and Shrewsbury and Crawford peerage cases; conservative M.P. for Ipswich, 1837–41, Cambridge, 1843–1847, and east Suffolk, 1852–66; solicitor-general, 1845–6 and 1852, attorney-general, 1858–9; lord chief baron, 1866–80; privy councillor, 1866. [xxx. 347]

KELLY, FRANCES MARIA (1790–1882), actress and singer; friend of the Lambs; niece of Michael Kelly [q. v.]; made her first appearance at Drury Lane when seven; impressed by her Arthur ('King John') Sheridan, Fox, and Mrs. Siddons; played at Drury Lane and the Italian Opera, 1800–6; associated with the former from its reopening (1812) till 1835, playing Ophelia to Edmund Kean's 'Hamlet' and other Shakespearean parts; excelled in melodrama; her acting celebrated in two sonnets by Lamb, who offered her marriage; after her retirement conducted a dramatic school (for which the Royalty was built) and gave readings and monologues. [xxx. 349]

KELLY, GEORGE (*fl.* 1736), Jacobite; B.A. Trinity College, Dublin, 1706; having acted as Atterbury's amanuensis in his correspondence with the Pretender, was imprisoned in the Tower, 1723–36, but escaped; published translation of Castlenau's 'Memoirs of the English Affairs,' 1724, of Morabin's 'History of Cicero's Banishment,' 1725. [xxx. 350]

KELLY, HUGH (1739–1777), playwright and author; came to London as a staymaker, 1760; edited 'Court Magazine' and 'Ladies' Museum,' and afterwards 'The Public Ledger'; published 'Memoirs of a Magdalen,' 1767, and dramatic criticism; his comedy 'False Delicacy' successfully produced by Garrick at Drury Lane, 1768, in rivalry with Goldsmith's 'Good-Natured Man,' and acted at Paris and Lisbon; produced 'A Word to the Wise,' 1770 (revived with prologue by Johnson at Covent Garden, 1777), and other plays; received pension for political writings; practised as a barrister in his last years. [xxx. 351]

KELLY, JOHN (1680?–1751), journalist and playwright; of the Inner Temple; works include reprint of 'Universal Spectator,' 1747, and four plays. [xxx. 352]

KELLY, JOHN (1750–1809), Manx scholar; transcribed and superintended printing of Manx bible, 1766–1772, revised New Testament, 1775, and with Philip Moore (1705–1783) [q. v.] the whole bible, prayer-book, and other works, 1776; graduated LL.D. St. John's College, Cambridge, 1799; vicar of Ardleigh, 1791–1807; rector of Copford, 1807–9; his Manx grammar (1804) reprinted, 1859, and part of his 'Triglot Dictionary of the Celtic Language,' 1866. [xxx. 353]

KELLY, JOHN (1801–1876), independent minister at Liverpool, 1829–73; chairman of Congregational Union, 1851. [xxx. 354]

KELLY, MATTHEW (1814–1858), Irish antiquary; professor at the Irish college, Paris, 1839–41, and at Maynooth, 1841–58; made D.D. by the pope and canon of Ossory, c. 1854; published 'Calendar of Irish Saints,' 1857, a translation of Gosselin's 'Power of the Popes,' 1853, and editions of Irish antiquarian classics; his 'Dissertations chiefly on Irish Church History' issued, 1864. [xxx. 354]

KELLY, MICHAEL (1764?–1826), vocalist, actor, and composer; successful treble singer on the Dublin stage; studied at Naples and Palermo, and sang at Florence (1780), Venice, and other Italian cities; when principal tenor in Italian opera at Vienna (1783–6) was prepared by Gluck to sing in 'Iphigenia in Tauride' and by Mozart for Basilio in the first performance of 'Nozze di Figaro,' sang in Mozart's Sunday concerts; appeared in opera at Drury Lane Theatre, 1787–1808, singing also in oratorios at the Ancient Concerts, 1789–91, and in Scotland and Ireland; as musical director at Drury Lane Theatre and joint-director at the King's Theatre, London, composed settings of Sheridan's 'Pizarro,' Coleridge's 'Remorse,' and other plays; last seen on the stage at Dublin, 1811. His songs include 'Flora Macdonald' and 'The Woodpecker'; his 'Reminiscences' written by Theodore Hook, 1826. [xxx. 355]

KELLY, PATRICK (1756–1842), mathematician and astronomer; hon. LL.D. Glasgow; master of the 'Mercantile School,' Finsbury Square; published 'The Universal Cambist and Commercial Instructor,' 1811, and other works. [xxx. 357]

KELLY or **O'KELLY**, RALPH (d. 1361), archbishop of Cashel; prolocutor of the Carmelites, 1336; archbishop of Cashel, 1345–61; opposed levy of a subsidy, 1346; assaulted Cradock, bishop of Waterford, 1353. [xxx. 357]

KELSEY, THOMAS (d. 1680?), parliamentarian officer; deputy-governor of Oxford, 1646–50; lieutenant of Dover Castle, 1651; a commissioner for the navy and major-general of the Kent and Surrey militia, 1655; M.P., Sandwich, 1654, Dover, 1656 and 1659; supported Fleetwood and Lambert. [xxx. 358]

KELTON, ARTHUR (fl. 1546), author of rhymed works on matters of Welsh history. [xxx. 359]

KELTRIDGE, JOHN (fl. 1581), divine; M.A. Trinity College, Cambridge, 1575 (incorporated at Oxford, 1579); author of 'Exposition and Readynges . . . upon the wordes of our Saviour Christe, that bee written in the xi. of Luke' (1578). [xxx. 359]

KELTY, MARY ANN (1789–1873), author of a novel, 'The Favourite of Nature' (1821), of 'Memoirs of the Lives and Persecutions of Primitive Quakers,' 1844, and devotional works. [xxx. 360]

KELWAY, JOSEPH (d. 1782), organist and harpsichord player; had Queen Charlotte and Mrs. Delany among his pupils. [xxx. 360]

KELWAY, THOMAS (d. 1749), organist of Chichester Cathedral, 1726–49; brother of Joseph Kelway [q. v.]; composed church music. [xxx. 361]

KELYNG, SIR JOHN (d. 1671), judge; barrister, Inner Temple, 1632; imprisoned for royalism, 1642–60; serjeant-at-law, 1660; knighted, 1661; M.P., Bedford, 1661; employed in drafting Act of Uniformity and in proceedings against the regicides; ridiculed evidence of witchcraft given before Sir Matthew Hale [q. v.], 1662; puisne judge, 1663; chief-justice of the king's bench, 1665–71; censured by parliament (1667) for ill-treatment of jurors; compelled to apologise for a libel on Lord Hollis, 1671; his reports of pleas of the crown edited by R. Loveland Loveland, 1873. [xxx. 361]

KELYNG, SIR JOHN (1630?–1680), serjeant-at-law, 1680; knighted, 1679; son of Sir John Kelyng (d. 1671) [q. v.]; barrister, Inner Temple, 1660. [xxx. 362]

KEM or **KEME**, SAMUEL (1604–1670), puritan divine; demy of Magdalen College, Oxford, 1624–6; B.A., 1625; B.D.; rector of Albury, Oxfordshire, and vicar of Low Leyton, Essex; chaplain to Earl of Essex; captain in parliamentary army; often preached in military dress; spy on royalists at Rotterdam, 1648; became loyal on the Restoration. [xxx. 362]

KEMBLE, ADELAIDE, afterwards MRS. SARTORIS (1814?–1879), vocalist and author; daughter of Charles Kemble [q. v.]; first sang at the Ancient Concerts, 1835; in Germany and at Paris, 1837–8; had lessons from Pasta and appeared with success at Venice as Norma; sang in Italian opera at Covent Garden. 1841–2; married Edward John Sartoris, 1843; published 'A Week in a French Country House,' 1867, and other works. [xxx. 363]

KEMBLE, CHARLES (1775–1854), actor; son of Roger Kemble [q. v.]; appeared at Drury Lane as Malcolm in 'Macbeth,' 1794; Norval in 'Douglas,' 1798, and Alonzo in 'Pizarro,' 1799; first appeared as Charles Surface, Falconbridge, and Young Mirabel, 1800; played Hamlet, 1803; joining his brother at Covent Garden, played Romeo, 1803; appeared in adaptations by himself from Kotzebue; after playing at Brussels and in France returned to Covent Garden as Macbeth, 1815; began his management of Covent Garden, 1822, playing Falstaff (1824) and many leading parts; met with little success financially till the appearance of his eldest daughter, Fanny, with whom, in 1832–4, he made a successful tour in America; his Mercutio first seen at Covent Garden, 1829; gave farewell performance as Benedick (Haymarket), 1836, but acted for a few nights at Covent Garden, 1840. He had a greater range than any actor except Garrick, but was pre-eminent only in comedy. [xxx. 365]

KEMBLE, MRS. ELIZABETH (1763?–1841), actress; née Satchell; appeared at Covent Garden as Polly ('Beggar's Opera'), 1780; played Juliet, Ophelia, and other leading parts next season; Desdemona to Stephen Kemble's Othello, 1783, marrying him the same year; afterwards eclipsed her husband. [xxx. 367]

KEMBLE, FRANCES ANNE, afterwards MRS. BUTLER, generally known as FANNY KEMBLE (1809–1893), actress; daughter of Charles Kemble [q. v.] and Maria Theresa Kemble [q. v.]; appeared with great success as Juliet to her father's Mercutio, Covent Garden, 1829; appeared subsequently as Mrs. Haller (Stranger), Lady Macbeth, Portia, Beatrice, Constance, Julia, Mariana, and Queen Katherine; visited America, 1833, and married, 1834, Pierce Butler (d. 1867), whom she divorced, 1848; began series of Shakespearean readings, 1848; lived in America, 1849–68, and 1873–8; published poetical and dramatic writings and several autobiographical works. [Suppl. iii. 57]

KEMBLE, HENRY STEPHEN (1789–1836), actor; son of Stephen Kemble [q. v.]; of Winchester and Trinity College, Cambridge; after playing in the country appeared at the Haymarket, 1814; acted at Bath and Bristol and played Romeo and other leading parts at Drury Lane, 1818–19; afterwards appeared at minor theatres. [xxx. 368]

KEMBLE, JOHN (1599?–1679), Roman catholic priest; missioner in Herefordshire; executed for saying mass; ancestor of Charles Kemble [q. v.] [xxx. 369]

KEMBLE, JOHN MITCHELL (1807–1857), philologist and historian; elder son of Charles Kemble [q. v.]; educated at first under Richardson, the lexicographer; whilst at Trinity College, Cambridge, intimate with Tennyson, Richard Chenevix Trench [q. v.], and William Bodham Donne [q. v.], and one of 'the apostles'; accompanied Trench to Spain to join a rising against Ferdinand VII, 1830; M.A. Cambridge, 1833; studied philology under Jacob Grimm in Germany; edited the poems of Beowulf, 1833, and lectured at Cambridge on Anglo-Saxon; edited 'British and Foreign Review,' 1835–44; examiner of stage-plays, 1840; studied prehistoric archæology at Hanover, making excavations in Lüneburg, and drawings at Munich, Berlin, and Schwerin, 1854–5; died in Dublin. His chief works were 'Codex Diplomaticus ævi Saxonici,' 1839–48, 'The Saxons in England,' 1849 (ed. Birch, 1876), and 'State Papers' illustrating the period 1688–1714. [xxx. 369]

KEMBLE, JOHN PHILIP (1757–1823), actor; eldest son of Roger Kemble [q. v.]; played as a child in his father's company, but was educated for the Roman catholic priesthood at Sedgley Park and Douay; appeared in Lee's 'Theodosius' at Wolverhampton, 1776; produced a tragedy and a poem at Liverpool; played on York circuit under Tate Wilkinson and lectured at York, 1778–1781; appeared at Edinburgh and gained great success at Dublin as Hamlet and Raymond (Jephson's 'Count of Narbonne'), 1781; during engagement at Drury Lane Theatre (1783–1802) presented over 120 characters, beginning with Hamlet; played with Mrs. Siddons (his sister) in 'King John,' 'Othello,' 'King Lear,' and many other plays, and also with his wife and Miss Farren; as manager, from 1788, began to dress characters unconventionally; played Coriolanus and Henry V in arrangements by himself, and gave also Romeo, Petruchio, Wolsey, and Charles Surface (a failure); reopened Drury Lane with Macbeth, 1794, having played meanwhile at the Haymarket; acted in adaptations by himself of many Shakespearean plays, in Ireland's 'Vortigern' (1796), and pieces by Madame D'Arblay and 'Monk' Lewis; visited Paris, Madrid, and Douay; manager at Covent Garden from 1803 till 1808, when the theatre was burned down, playing Hamlet, Antonio, Iago, Pierre, Prospero, and original parts in plays by Mrs. Inchbald, Coleman, Reynolds, and Morton; reopened Covent Garden Theatre, 1809, with increased prices, thereby occasioning the O. P. riots; played Brutus, 1812, and Coriolanus for his farewell, 1817; went abroad for his health and died at Lausanne; chief founder of the declamatory school of acting; admired by Lamb and intimate with Sir Walter Scott. [xxx. 372]

KEMBLE, MARIA THERESA or MARIE THÉRÈSE (1774-1838), actress; *née* De Camp; came to England from Vienna, and as Miss De Camp appeared at Drury Lane Theatre, 1786; pleased the public as Macheath in the 'Beggar's Opera,' 1792; the original Judith in the 'Iron Chest' and Caroline Dormer in the 'Heir at Law,' 1797; also played Portia, Desdemona, and Katherine, and in her own 'First Faults' (1799); married Charles Kemble [q. v.], 1806; acted at Covent Garden Theatre, 1806-19, in her own plays 'The Day after the Wedding' (1808) and 'Smiles and Tears' (1815), also playing Ophelia, Beatrice, and Mrs. Sullen; created Madge Wildfire in Terry's 'Heart of Midlothian.' [xxx. 378]

KEMBLE, PRISCILLA (1756-1845), actress; *née* Hopkins; acted in Garrick's company at Drury Lane Theatre, 1775; the original Harriet ('The Runaway'), Eliza ('Spleen, or Islington Spa'), and Maria ('School for Scandal'); played secondary parts as Mrs. Brereton, 1778-1787; married John Philip Kemble [q. v.], 1787, and played the Lady Anne ('Richard III'), Hero, Sylvia; retired, 1796. [xxx. 379]

KEMBLE, ROGER (1721-1802), actor and manager; married Sarah Ward (daughter of his manager at Birmingham), 1753, and formed a travelling company, in which his children (Sarah, afterwards Mrs. Siddons, John, Charles, Stephen, and others) acted; played Falstaff and in the 'Miller of Mansfield' at the Haymarket, 1788. [xxx. 380]

KEMBLE, STEPHEN or GEORGE STEPHEN (1758-1822), actor and manager; son of Roger Kemble [q. v.]; first played in Dublin; appeared in Othello and other parts with his wife (Elizabeth Kemble) at Covent Garden Theatre, 1784; played secondary parts at the Haymarket, 1787-91; during his management of the Edinburgh Theatre (1792-1800) engaged John Kemble and Mrs. Siddons, and brought out Henry Erskine Johnston [q. v.], but became involved in litigation and failed financially; after managing theatres in several northern towns, played Falstaff at Covent Garden, 1806, and Drury Lane, 1816, also Sir Christopher Curry ('Inkle and Yarico'), his best part. He published 'Odes, Lyrical Ballads, and Poems,' 1809. [xxx. 381]

KEME, SAMUEL (1604-1670). [See KEM.]

KEMP. [See also KEMPE.]

KEMP, GEORGE MEIKLE (1795-1844), architect of the Scott monument, Edinburgh (begun, 1840); in early life a shepherd, carpenter's apprentice, and millwright. [xxx. 383]

KEMP or KEMPE, JOHN (1380?-1454), lord chancellor and archbishop successively of York and Canterbury; fellow of Merton College, Oxford; practised in ecclesiastical courts; dean of arches and vicar-general of Canterbury, 1415; archdeacon of Durham, c. 1416; keeper of the privy seal, 1418; bishop of Rochester, 1419, of London, 1421-6; chancellor of Normandy, 1419-22, being much employed as a diplomatist by Henry V; member of Henry VI's council and partisan of Cardinal Beaufort; became archbishop of York and chancellor of England, 1426, holding the secular office till Gloucester recovered power in 1432; supported peace with France, but was prevented by his instructions from effecting anything at congress of Arras, 1432, or at the Calais conferences in 1439; appointed cardinal-priest by Pope Eugenius IV, 1439; supported Henry VI's marriage with Margaret of Anjou, but subsequently opposed Suffolk, on whose fall (1450) he again became chancellor; broke up the Kentish rebellion by temporary concessions; made archbishop of Canterbury by provision, and created cardinal-bishop by Pope Nicholas, 1452; resisted the Yorkists till his death; founded college of secular priests at Wye, Kent (his birthplace), with a grammar school and church. [xxx. 384]

KEMP, JOHN (1665-1717), antiquary; F.R.S., 1712; his museum of antiquities described in Ainsworth's 'Monumenta vetustatis Kempiana' (1719-20). [xxx. 388]

KEMP, JOHN (1763-1812), mathematician; M.A. Aberdeen, 1781; LL.D.(America); professor at Columbia College, New York. [xxx. 389]

KEMP, JOSEPH (1778-1824), musical composer and teacher; organist of Bristol Cathedral, 1802; Mus.Doc. Sidney Sussex College, Cambridge, 1809; founded musical

college at Exeter, 1814; composed songs, glees, and anthems, and the 'Jubilee,' 1809; published 'New System of Musical Education,' 1810-19. [xxx. 389]

KEMP, THOMAS READ (1781?-1844), founder of Kemp Town (Brighton); M.A. St. John's College, Cambridge, 1810; M.P., Lewes, 1812-16 and 1826-37; began building Kemp Town, c. 1820; founded a religious sect. [xxx. 389]

KEMP or KEMPE, WILLIAM (*fl.* 1590), author of 'The Education of Children in Learning,' 1588, and 'The Art of Arithmeticke,' 1592; M.A. Trinity Hall, Cambridge, 1584; master of Plymouth grammar school, 1581-1605. [xxx. 390]

KEMP, WILLIAM (*fl.* 1600), comic actor and dancer; member of the company whose successive patrons were Leicester, Lord Strange, and Lord Hunsdon; succeeded to Richard Tarleton's rôles and reputation; chiefly popular for his dancing of jigs accompanied with comic songs; summoned with Richard Burbage [q. v.] and William Shakespeare [q. v.] to act before Queen Elizabeth at Greenwich, 1594; had parts in plays by Shakespeare and Jonson, including Peter ('Romeo and Juliet') and Dogberry; danced a morris-dance from London to Norwich, 1599; performed dancing exploits on the continent; played in the Earl of Worcester's company at the Rose. 'Kemps Nine Daies Wonder' (written by himself, 1600) has been twice reprinted. [xxx. 390]

KEMP, WILLIAM (1555-1628), of Spains Hall, Finchingfield, Essex; remained silent for seven years as a penance. [xxx. 393]

KEMPE. [See also KEMP.]

KEMPE, ALFRED JOHN (1785?-1846), antiquary; friend of Charles Alfred Stothard [q. v.] and Thomas Crofton Croker [q. v.]; F.S.A., 1828; formed Society of Noviomagus; on staff of 'Gentleman's Magazine'; published works on antiquities of Holwood Hill, Kent, and of St. Martin-le-Grand Church, London; edited the Loseley manuscripts, 1836. [xxx. 394]

KEMPE, MARGERIE (*temp. incert.*), religious writer; 'of Lyn.' [xxx. 394]

KEMPENFELT, RICHARD (1718-1782), rear-admiral; with Vernon at Portobello, 1739; as captain of the Elizabeth and commodore served in East Indies, 1758; commanded the Grafton under Steevens in expedition of 1759; present at reduction of Pondicherry, 1761; flag-captain to Cornish at reduction of Manila, 1762; member of court-martial on Palliser, 1778; rear-admiral, 1780; captured part of a French convoy and dispersed the rest off Ushant, 1781; went down with the Royal George; his alteration in signalling system adopted and improved by Lord Howe. [xxx. 395]

KEMPT, SIR JAMES (1764-1854), general; aide-de-camp to Sir Ralph Abercromby [q. v.] in Holland, 1799, the Mediterranean, 1800, and Egypt, 1801, and afterwards to Hely-Hutchinson; commanded light brigade at Maida, 1806; commanded brigade under Picton in the Peninsula; severely wounded at Badajoz, 1812; commanded brigade of light division in 1813-14; succeeded to command of Picton's division on his fall during battle of Waterloo; G.C.B., 1815; governor of Nova Scotia, 1820-1828; governor-general of Canada, 1828-30; privy councillor, 1830; master-general of the ordnance, 1834-8; general, 1841. [xxx. 396]

KEMPTHORNE, SIR JOHN (1620-1679), vice-admiral; after commanding for Levant company entered royal navy, 1664; flag-captain to Prince Rupert; flag-captain to Albemarle in the fight off the North Foreland, 1666; rear-admiral of the blue in the action of 27 July 1666; knighted for gallantry against the Algerines, 1670; took part in battle of Solebay, 1672, and the action of 11 Aug. 1673, after which he was promoted vice-admiral and pensioned. [xxx. 397]

KEMYS, LAWRENCE (d. 1618), sea-captain; accompanied Sir Walter Ralegh up the Orinoco, 1595-6; imprisoned with Ralegh in the Tower, 1603; as his pilot and captain commanded his last expedition to Guiana, on the failure of which he killed himself. [xxx. 398]

KEN or KENN, THOMAS (1637-1711), bishop of Bath and Wells; fellow of Winchester and New College, Oxford; M.A., 1664; D.D., 1679; rector of Little Easton,

Essex, 1663-5, of Brightstone (Isle of Wight), 1667-9, of East Woodhay, Hampshire, 1669-72; chaplain to Bishop Morley of Winchester; took gratuitous charge of St. John in the Soke, Winchester; as chaplain to Princess Mary at the Hague, 1679-80, remonstrated with William of Orange on his unkind behaviour to her; when chaplain to Charles II refused to receive Nell Gwyn at Winchester, 1683; chaplain to Lord Dartmouth at Tangier, 1683-4; bishop of Bath and Wells, 1684-91; attended Charles II's deathbed, 2 Feb. 1685; attended Monmouth in the Tower and at his execution, 1685; interceded with James II on behalf of Kirke's victims; twice preached at Whitehall against Romish practices; one of the 'seven bishops' who petitioned against the Declaration of Indulgence, 1688; voted for a regency, January 1689, and refused to take the oaths to William and Mary; deprived of his see as a nonjuror; opposed the clandestine consecration of nonjuring bishops, and was offered restoration (1702) by Queen Anne, who gave him a pension; lived chiefly with Lord Weymouth at Longleat. His prose works include 'Manual of Prayers for Winchester Scholars' (edition containing the well-known morning, evening, and midnight hymns, 1695, the hymns being published separately, 1862), and 'Practice of Divine Love,' 1685-6 (translated into French and Italian); his poetical works edited by Hawkins, 1721. [xxx. 399]

KENDAL, DUCHESS OF (1667-1743). [See SCHULENBURG, COUNTESS EHRENGARD MELUSINA VON DER.]

KENDALE, RICHARD (d. 1431), grammarian. [xxx. 404]

KENDALL, EDWARD AUGUSTUS (1776?-1842), author of books for children, translations from the French, and other works; conducted the 'Literary Chronicle,' 1819-28, 'The Olio,' 1828-33. [xxx. 404]

KENDALL, GEORGE (1610-1663), controversialist; fellow of Exeter College, Oxford, 1630-47; M.A., 1633; D.D., 1654; rector of Blisland, Cornwall, 1643, and prebendary of Exeter, 1645; rector of Kenton, 1660-2; defended Calvinism in numerous polemics. [xxx. 405]

KENDALL, HENRY CLARENCE (1841-1882), poet of the Australian bush; some time in New South Wales public service; his two chief volumes, 'Leaves from an Australian Forest,' 1869, and 'Songs from the Mountains,' 1880; collected works issued, 1886. [xxx. 406]

KENDALL, JOHN (fl. 1476), vicar-choral of Southwell, 1476-86. [xxx. 408]

KENDALL, JOHN (d. 1485), secretary to Richard III and from 1481 a comptroller of public works; said to have fallen at Bosworth. [xxx. 407]

KENDALL, JOHN (d. 1501?), general of infantry ('Turcopolier') to the knights of St. John, 1477-89; prior of the English Hospitallers, 1491; employed diplomatically by Henry VII. [xxx. 407]

KENDALL, JOHN (1726-1815), quaker; paid several visits to Holland; founded at Colchester almshouses, a school, and a library; published an abstract of the bible, 1800, and other works; 'Memoirs of the Life and Religious Experiences of John Kendall,' issued posthumously. [xxx. 408]

KENDALL, JOHN (1766-1829), architect; author of a work on Gothic architecture, 1818. [xxx. 409]

KENDALL, TIMOTHY (fl. 1577), compiler of 'Flowers of Epigrammes'; of Eton and Magdalen Hall, Oxford; mentioned by Meres among epigrammatists. [xxx. 409]

KENDRICK, EMMA ELEONORA (1788-1871), miniature-painter; author of 'Conversations on the Art of Miniature-Painting,' 1830. [xxx. 409]

KENDRICK, JAMES (1771-1847), botanist; M.D. and F.L.S.; president of the Warrington Natural History Society; friend of Howard the philanthropist. [xxx. 410]

KENDRICK, JAMES (1809-1882), writer on Warrington antiquities; son of James Kendrick (1771-1847) [q. v.]; M.D. Edinburgh, 1833; made excavations at Wilderspool, and collected seals. [xxx. 410]

KENEALY, EDWARD VAUGHAN HYDE (1819-1880), barrister; of Trinity College, Dublin; LL.D., 1850; called to Irish bar, 1840; barrister, Gray's Inn, 1847; Q.C., 1868; junior counsel for Palmer the poisoner; imprisoned for cruelty; prosecuted Overend and Gurney, 1869; leading counsel for the Tichborne claimant, 1873, and was disbarred (1874) for his violent conduct of the case [see ORTON, ARTHUR]; raised agitation for inquiry into it; M.P. for Stoke-on-Trent, 1875-80; published poetical translations and other works. [xxx. 410]

KENINGHALE, JOHN (d. 1451), Carmelite; student at Oxford; provincial, 1430-44; confessor to Richard, duke of York. [xxx. 411]

KENINGHALE, PETER (d. 1494), Carmelite prior at Oxford, 1466. [xxx. 412]

KENINGHAM, WILLIAM (fl. 1586). [See CUNINGHAM.]

KENMURE, VISCOUNTS. [See GORDON, SIR JOHN, first VISCOUNT, 1599?-1634; GORDON, WILLIAM, sixth VISCOUNT, d. 1716.]

KENNAWAY, SIR JOHN, first baronet (1758-1836), diplomatist; served in the Carnatic, 1780-6; created baronet (1791) for his successful mission to Hyderabad, 1788, where he became first resident; concluded treaty with Tippo Sultan, 1792. [xxx. 412]

KENNEDY or FARRELL, MRS. (d. 1793), actress and contralto singer; instructed by Dr. Arne; gained great successes in male parts at Covent Garden. [xxx. 412]

KENNEDY, ALEXANDER (1695?-1785), founder of family of violin-makers. [xxx. 413]

KENNEDY, SIR ARTHUR EDWARD (1810-1883), colonial governor; of Trinity College, Dublin; governor successively of Gambia (1851-2), Sierra Leone (1852-4), West Australia (1854-62), Vancouver's island (1863-7), West Africa (1867-72), Hong Kong (1872-7), and Queensland (1877-83); knighted, 1868. [xxx. 413]

KENNEDY, BENJAMIN HALL (1804-1889), headmaster of Shrewsbury and regius professor of Greek at Cambridge; son of Rann Kennedy [q. v.]; educated at King Edward School, Birmingham, and at Shrewsbury; at St. John's College, Cambridge, won numerous distinctions, being senior classic and first chancellor's medallist, 1827; was president of the union and one of 'the Apostles'; fellow of St. John's College, Cambridge, 1828-1830; assistant-master at Harrow, 1830-6; as head of Shrewsbury (1836-66) became the greatest classical master of the century; canon of Ely, 1867; regius professor of Greek at Cambridge, 1867-89; hon. LL.D. Dublin, 1885; a New Testament reviser; the Latin professorship founded at Cambridge from part of his testimonial was held successively by his pupils, Hugh Andrew Johnstone Munro [q. v.] and Mr. J. E. B. Mayor. The 'Public School Latin Primer' generally adopted by the chief schools (1866) was based upon his work of 1843. Besides his Latin primer (revised 1888) and grammar (1871), he published metrical versions of three Greek plays, 'Between Whiles,' 1877, and other works. [xxx. 414]

KENNEDY, CHARLES RANN (1808-1867), lawyer and scholar; brother of Benjamin Hall Kennedy [q. v.]; educated at Birmingham and Shrewsbury; fellow of Trinity College, Cambridge; senior classic, 1831; Bell and Pitt scholar; Porson prizeman; M.A., 1834; barrister, Lincoln's Inn, 1835; engaged in Stockdale v. Hansard; appeared for the plaintiff in Swinfen v. Swinfen (failing to recover fees); published translations of Demosthenes and Virgil, poems, and legal treatises. [xxx. 416]

KENNEDY, DAVID (1825-1886), Scottish tenor singer; gave concerts in Scotland, London, America, South Africa, India, and Australasia; died at Stratford, Ontario. [xxx. 417]

KENNEDY, EDMUND B. (d. 1848), Australian explorer; as second in command of Sir Thomas Livingstone Mitchell's expedition traced the Barcoo or Victoria river, 1847; killed by natives while exploring Cape York peninsula. [xxx. 417]

KENNEDY, GILBERT, second EARL OF CASSILLIS (d. 1527), partisan of Arran against Angus; afterwards joined Lennox; slain by sheriff of Ayr at instigation of Arran's bastard son. [xxx. 418]

KENNEDY, GILBERT, third EARL OF CASSILLIS (1517?-1558), son of Gilbert Kennedy, second earl of Cassillis [q. v.]; pupil of Buchanan in Paris; lord of James V's secret council, 1538; captured at Solway Moss,

1542; after his release intrigued with the English; lord high treasurer, 1554; one of the seven Scottish commissioners at marriage of Mary Queen of Scots to the dauphin, 1558; died at Dieppe on his way back.

[xxx. 418]

KENNEDY, GILBERT, fourth EARL OF CASSILLIS (1541?-1576), 'King of Carrick'; succeeded his father, Gilbert Kennedy, third earl of Cassillis [q. v.], as gentleman of the bedchamber to Henry II of France; fought for Mary Queen of Scots at Langside, 1568, and subsequently corresponded with her; tortured the abbot of Crosraguel, 1570, in order to obtain a renunciation of his claims, and was imprisoned by the regent Lennox; obtained liberty by an agreement with Morton, 1571; privy councillor, 1571.

[xxx. 419]

KENNEDY, GILBERT (1678-1745), Irish presbyterian minister; moderator of Ulster, 1720; published 'New Light set in a Clear Light,' 1721, and 'Defence of the Principles and Conduct of the General Synod of Ulster,' 1724.

[xxx. 420]

KENNEDY, GRACE (1782-1825), author of religious tales; German translation of her works issued, 1844.

[xxx. 420]

KENNEDY, JAMES (1406?-1465), bishop of St. Andrews; while bishop of Dunkeld (1438-1441) attended council of Florence; bishop of St. Andrews, 1441-65; prominent in political affairs during James II's minority; attempted to mediate in papal schism; founded St. Salvator's College (1450) and the Grey Friars monastery at St. Andrews; one of the regents during minority of James III.

[xxx. 421]

KENNEDY, JAMES (1793?-1827), author of 'Conversations on Religion with Lord Byron,' 1830; garrison physician at Cephalonia, 1823.

[xxx. 422]

KENNEDY, JAMES (1785?-1851), medical writer; M.D. Glasgow, 1813; died while compiling a medical bibliography.

[xxx. 422]

KENNEDY, afterwards **KENNEDY - BAILIE**, JAMES (1793-1864), classical scholar; fellow of Trinity College, Dublin, 1817; M.A., 1819; D.D., 1828; published 'Fasciculus Inscriptionum Græcarum' (1842-9) and editions of Greek classics.

[xxx. 422]

KENNEDY, SIR JAMES SHAW (1788-1865), general; assumed name of Kennedy, 1834; at Copenhagen, 1807, and in the Peninsula, being aide-de-camp to Robert Craufurd [q. v.], 1809-12; attached to the quartermaster-general's staff in Alten's division at Quatre Bras; at Waterloo drew up the division in a novel formation which successfully withstood very severe cavalry attacks; stationed at Calais till 1818; while assistant adjutant-general at Manchester (1826-35) drew up a masterly report concerning methods of keeping order in labour disputes; as inspector-general raised the Irish constabulary, 1836; appointed to Liverpool command during chartist alarms, 1848; lieutenant-general, 1854; general, 1862; K.C.B., 1863; intimate with Sir William Napier; published 'Notes on the Defence of Great Britain and Ireland,' 1859, and 'Notes on Waterloo,' &c., 1865.

[xxx. 423]

KENNEDY, JOHN, fifth EARL OF CASSILLIS (1567?-1615), son of Gilbert Kennedy, fourth earl [q. v.]; lord high treasurer of Scotland, 1598; killed Gilbert Kennedy of Bargany at Maybole, near Ayr, 1601.

[xxx. 425]

KENNEDY or **KENNEDIE**, JOHN (*fl.* 1626), author of 'History of Calanthrop and Lucilla,' 1626 (reprinted as 'The Ladies' Delight,' 1631), and 'Theological Epitome,' 1629.

[xxx. 426]

KENNEDY, JOHN, sixth EARL OF CASSILLIS (1595?-1668), nephew of John Kennedy, fifth earl of Cassillis [q. v.]; lord justice-general, 1649; joined the covenanters; privy councillor, 1641 and 1661; opposed the engagement, 1648; took part in the Whiggamores' raid, 1648; commissioner to treat with Charles II, 1649-50; his first wife (Lady Jean Hamilton) sometimes identified with the heroine of 'The Gypsy Laddie.'

[xxx. 426]

KENNEDY, JOHN, seventh EARL OF CASSILLIS (1646?-1701), opposed Lauderdale's government, and was outlawed; made privy councillor and a lord of the treasury by William III.

[xxx. 427]

KENNEDY, JOHN (*d.* 1760), numismatist; M.D.; lived some time at Smyrna; published 'Numismata

Selectiora,' describing his coins of Carausius and Allectus; his 'Dissertation upon Oriuna,' 1751, making Oriuna Carausius' guardian-goddess, due to Stukeley's misreading of 'Fortuna' on a coin of Carausius.

[xxx. 427]

KENNEDY, JOHN (1698-1782), writer on chronology; rector of All Saints, Bradley, 1732-82.

[xxx. 428]

KENNEDY, JOHN (1730?-1816), violin-maker; nephew of Alexander Kennedy [q. v.]

[xxx. 413]

KENNEDY, JOHN (1789-1833), Scottish poet; author of 'Fancy's Tour with the Genius of Cruelty, and other Poems,' 1826, and the romance of 'Geordie Chalmers,' 1830.

[xxx. 428]

KENNEDY, JOHN (1769-1855), Manchester cotton-spinner and friend of Watt; introduced the 'jack frame' and other improvements.

[xxx. 428]

KENNEDY, JOHN (1819-1884), highland divine; M.A. King's College, Aberdeen, 1840; hon. D.D., 1873; free church minister at Dingwall, Ross-shire, 1844; assisted James Begg [q. v.] in opposing union of the free and united presbyterian churches and wrote against disestablishment and instrumental music in churches; preached in Gaelic; published religious works.

[xxx. 429]

KENNEDY, JOHN CLARK (1817-1867). [See CLARK-KENNEDY.]

KENNEDY, JOHN PITT (1796-1879), lieutenant-colonel; secretary and director of public works in Cephalonia under Sir Charles Napier [q. v.], 1822-8, and sub-inspector of militia in the Ionian islands, 1828-31; interested in agricultural education in Ireland; inspector-general under Irish national education department, 1837-1839; secretary to the Devon commission, 1843; member of famine relief committee, 1845-6; superintended measures for defence of Dublin, 1848; military secretary to Sir Charles Napier in India, 1849-52; consulting engineer for railways to Indian government, 1850; made the road from Simla to Thibet; lieutenant-colonel, 1853; managing director of Bombay and Central Indian railway, from 1853; published works on Irish subjects (especially agriculture) and on finance and public works in India.

[xxx. 430]

KENNEDY, PATRICK (1801-1873), Irish writer and Dublin bookseller; author of 'Legendary Fictions of the Irish Celts,' 1866, and other works.

[xxx. 432]

KENNEDY, QUINTIN (1520-1564), abbot; son of Gilbert Kennedy, second earl of Cassillis [q. v.]; educated at St. Andrews and Paris; abbot of Crosraguel, 1547; disputed with Knox at Maybole, 1562; wrote against the Reformation.

[xxx. 432]

KENNEDY, RANN (1772-1851), scholar and poet; intimate with Coleridge at St. John's College, Cambridge; M.A., 1798; second master at King Edward's School, Birmingham, 1807-36, and incumbent of St. Paul's Church, 1817-47; published 'The Reign of Youth' (1840) and other poems; assisted his younger son Charles Rann Kennedy [q. v.] in his translation of Virgil; examples of his work in 'Between Whiles,' by his elder son Dr. Benjamin Hall Kennedy [q. v.]

[xxx. 433]

KENNEDY, THOMAS (*d.* 1754), judge of the Scottish exchequer, 1714-54.

[xxx. 434]

KENNEDY, THOMAS (1784-1870?), violin and violoncello-maker; son of John Kennedy (1730?-1816) [q. v.]

[xxx. 413]

KENNEDY, THOMAS FRANCIS (1788-1879), politician; grand-nephew of Thomas Kennedy (*d.* 1754) [q. v.]; educated at Harrow and Edinburgh; whig M.P. for Ayr, 1818-34; carried bill of 1825 reforming the selection of Scottish juries in criminal cases; chairman of salmon fisheries committee, 1824; prepared Scottish reform bill; a lord of the treasury, 1832-4; paymaster of Irish civil service, 1837-50; a commissioner of woods and forests, 1850-4; friend of Cockburn and Jeffrey.

[xxx. 434]

KENNEDY, VANS (1784-1846), major-general, Sanskrit and Persian scholar; served as cadet, 2nd grenadiers, in Malabar district, 1800; Persian interpreter to the Peshwa's subsidiary force at Sirur, 1807; judge advocate-general to Bombay army, 1817-35; oriental translator to government, 1835-46; published philological writings.

[Suppl. iii. 58]

KENNEDY, WALTER (1460 ?–1508 ?), Scottish poet; nephew of James Kennedy (1406 ?–1465) [q. v.]; M.A. Glasgow, 1478, and an examiner, 1481 ; probably provost of Maybole, c. 1494 ; a rival of Dunbar ; wrote part of the ' Flyting,' 1508 ; most of his poems lost.					[xxx. 435]

KENNEDY, WILLIAM (1799–1871), poet; secretary to Lord Durham in Canada, 1838–9 ; British consul at Galveston, Texas, 1841–7 ; works include ' The Arrow and the Rose,' 1830, and a book on Texas, 1841 ; died in Paris.					[xxx. 436]

KENNEDY, WILLIAM DENHOLM (1813–1865), painter and friend of Etty; exhibited at the Academy from 1833.					[xxx. 437]

KENNETH I, MACALPINE (d. 860), founder of the Scottish dynasty ; succeeded Alpin in Galloway, 834, and as king of the Dalriad Scots, c. 844 ; finally defeated the Picts and became king of Alban, 846 ; removed the seat of government from Argyll to Scone, and made Dunkeld the ecclesiastical capital ; invaded ' Saxony ' (Lothian).					[xxx. 437]

KENNETH II (d. 995), son of Malcolm I ; succeeded Culen [q. v.] in Scottish Pictish monarchy, 971 ; extended his kingdom north of the Tay and made raids into Northumbria ; ' gave the great city of Brechin to the Lord ' ; probably secured Edinburgh ; consolidated central Scotland ; said to have been treacherously slain by Fenella. It is improbable that he received Lothian as a fief from Edgar.					[xxx. 439]

KENNETH III (d. 1005 ?), nephew of Kenneth II [q. v.]; succeeded Constantine in Scottish Pictish monarchy, 997 ; killed in battle, perhaps by Malcolm II.					[xxx. 440]

KENNETT, BASIL (1674–1715), miscellaneous writer; brother of White Kennett [q. v.], entered St. Edmund Hall, Oxford, 1689 ; scholar, Corpus Christi College, Oxford, 1690 ; M.A., 1696 ; fellow and tutor of Corpus Christi College, 1697 ; chaplain to the British factory at Leghorn, 1706–13 ; D.D. and president of Corpus, 1714 ; published antiquarian and religious works, of which the most important are : ' Romæ Antiquæ Notitia, or the Antiquities of Rome,' 1696, and ' A Brief Exposition of the Apostles' Creed,' 1705. He also translated many French works, among them Pascal's ' Thoughts upon Religion,' 1704.					[xxxi. 1]

KENNETT, WHITE (1660–1728), bishop of Peterborough; entered St. Edmund Hall, Oxford, 1678 ; began his career as a writer while an undergraduate, and employed by Anthony à Wood ; B.A., 1682 ; M.A., 1684 ; disliked James II's ecclesiastical policy ; openly supported the revolution ; tutor and vice-principal, St. Edmund Hall, 1691 ; D.D., 1700 ; prebendary of Salisbury, 1701 ; acquired reputation as historian and antiquarian, topographer, and philologist ; one of the original members of the Society for Propagating the Gospel in Foreign Parts, 1701 ; published the ' Compleat History of England,' his best-known work, 1706 ; chaplain in ordinary to Queen Anne ; dean of Peterborough, 1708 ; presented the books and documents collected for a projected history of the propagation of Christianity in the English-American colonies to the Society for Propagating the Gospel ; bishop of Peterborough, 1718–28.					[xxxi. 2]

KENNEY, ARTHUR HENRY (1776 ?–1855), controversialist; educated at Dublin University, 1793 ; M.A., 1800 ; B.D., 1806 ; D.D. and dean of Achonry, 1812 ; on account of pecuniary difficulties spent last ten years of his life abroad ; died at Boulogne-sur-Mer ; edited the fifth edition of Archbishop Magee's sermons, 1834 ; wrote a memoir of him for the ' Works ' (1842), and several religious and historical works.					[xxxi. 6]

KENNEY, CHARLES LAMB (1821–1881), journalist and author; born at Bellevue, near Paris ; son of James Kenney [q. v.], and godson of Charles Lamb ; educated at Merchant Taylors' School ; clerk in General Post Office, 1837 ; wrote for ' The Times ' and aided in promoting the exhibition of 1851 ; secretary to Sir Joseph Paxton during his organisation of transport service for Crimea, 1855 ; barrister, Inner Temple, 1856 ; secretary to M. de Lesseps, 1856–8 ; advocated Suez Canal in his book ' The Gates of the East,' 1857 ; joined staff of ' Standard,' 1858 ; supported International Exhibition at South Kensington, 1862 ; noted for his impromptu satirical rhyming skits on contemporary celebrities ; wrote libretti for some of Offenbach's opera-bouffes.					[xxxi. 7]

KENNEY, JAMES (1780–1849), dramatist; his successful farce, ' Raising the Wind,' produced 1803, and ' Turn him out,' 1812 ; wrote the popular drama, ' Sweethearts and Wives,' 1823 ; author of many successful and popular farces and comedies ; friend of Lamb and Rogers.					[xxxi. 8]

KENNEY, PETER JAMES (1779–1841), Irish jesuit; first apprenticed to a coach-builder, then educated at Carlow College and Stonyhurst College ; entered Society of Jesus, 1804 ; catholic chaplain to the English troops in Sicily ; returned to Ireland, 1811 ; became an eminent preacher and theologian ; vice-president of Maynooth College, 1812 ; mainly instrumental in reviving the jesuit mission in Ireland ; opened Clongowes Wood College, co. Kildare, since the leading catholic lay school in Ireland, 1814 ; assisted in establishing St. Stanislaus College, Tullabeg, and the jesuit residence of St. Francis Xavier, Dublin ; assisted Mary Aikenhead [q. v.], the foundress of the Irish sisters of charity ; visitor to the jesuit mission in the United States, 1819 and 1830 ; died at Rome.					[xxxi. 9]

KENNICOTT, BENJAMIN (1718–1783), biblical scholar ; educated at Wadham College, Oxford ; B.A. (by decree) and fellow of Exeter College, 1747 ; M.A., 1750 ; Whitehall preacher, 1753 ; D.D., 1761 ; F.R.S., 1764 ; Radcliffe librarian, 1767–83 ; canon of Christ Church, Oxford, 1770 ; spent much time in the collation of Hebrew manuscripts ; his great work, the ' Vetus Testamentum Hebraicum, cum variis lectionibus ' (vol. i. 1776, vol. ii. 1780).					[xxxi. 10]

KENNION, CHARLES JOHN (1789–1853), watercolour painter ; son of Edward Kennion [q. v.]; exhibited landscapes at Royal Academy, 1804 and 1853. [xxxi. 13]

KENNION, EDWARD (1744–1809), artist; commissary in expedition against Havannah, 1762 ; in Jamaica, 1765–9 ; engaged in trade in London, 1769 ; retired to Malvern, 1782 ; settled in London as teacher of drawing and artist, 1789 ; exhibited at Royal Academy, 1790–1807 ; published, as No. 1 of ' Elements of Landscape and Picturesque Beauty,' eight etchings of the oak-tree, 1790 ; died before the whole four volumes were completed, but ' An Essay on Trees in Landscape ' was issued, 1815.					[xxxi. 12]

KENNISH or **KINNISH**, WILLIAM (1799–1862), Manx poet ; entered navy as seaman, 1821 ; rose to be warrant-officer. and left navy, c. 1841 ; published ' Mona's Isle and other Poems,' 1844 ; went to America and became attached to United States admiralty.					[Suppl. iii. 59]

KENNY, SAINT (d. 598 ?). [See CAINNECH or CANNICUS, SAINT.]

KENNY, WILLIAM STOPFORD (1788–1867), compiler of educational works ; kept ' classical establishment ' in London ; an accomplished chess-player ; wrote two books on chess.					[xxxi. 13]

KENRICK or **KENDRICK**, DANIEL (fl. 1685), physician and poet ; M.A. Christ Church, Oxford, 1674 ; author of several poems, printed in ' The Grove,' 1721.					[xxxi. 14]

KENRICK, GEORGE (1792–1874), unitarian minister ; son of John Kenrick [q. v.]; educated at Glasgow College and Manchester College, York ; published sermons and contributed to the ' Monthly Repository.' [xxxi. 16]

KENRICK, JOHN (1788–1877), classical scholar and historian ; son of Timothy Kenrick [q. v.] ; entered Glasgow University, 1807 ; M.A., 1810 ; tutor in classics, history, and literature at Manchester College, York (now Manchester New College, Oxford) ; professor of history, 1840–50 ; the greatest scholar among the unitarians ; wrote historical and philological works.					[xxxi. 14]

KENRICK, TIMOTHY (1759–1804), unitarian commentator ; ordained, 1785 ; opened nonconformist academy, 1799 ; his ' Exposition of the Historical Writings of the New Testament ' (published 1807) typical of the older unitarian exegesis.					[xxxi. 16]

KENRICK, WILLIAM (1725 ?–1779), miscellaneous writer ; libelled almost every successful author and actor ; attacked Goldsmith in the ' Monthly Review,' 1759, but recanted with a favourable review of the ' Citizen of the World,' 1762 ; made LL.D. of St. Andrews for his translation of Rousseau's ' Eloisa ' ; attacked Garrick, Fielding, Johnson, and Colman.					[xxxi. 16]

KENT, KINGS OF. [See HENGIST, d. 488; HORSA, d. 455; ÆSC, d. 512?; OCTA, d. 532?; ETHELBERT, 552?–616; EADBALD, d. 640; WIHTRED, d. 725; SIGERED fl. 762; EADBERT, fl. 796; BALDRED, fl. 823–825.]

KENT, DUKE OF (1664?–1740). [See GREY, HENRY.]

KENT AND **STRATHERN**, EDWARD AUGUSTUS, DUKE OF (1767–1820), fourth son of George III by Queen Charlotte, and the father of Queen Victoria; educated in England under John Fisher [q. v.], successively bishop of Exeter and Salisbury, at Luneburg, Hanover, and Geneva under Baron Wangenheim; brevet-colonel, 1786; ordered to Gibraltar in command of the regiment of foot (royal fusiliers); sent to Canada, 1791; major-general, 1793; joined Sir Charles (afterwards Lord) Grey's force in the West Indies, 1794; took part in the subjection of Martinique and St. Lucia, 1794; returned to Canada; lieutenant-general, 1796; granted 12,000l. a year by parliament, 1799; made Duke of Kent and Strathern and Earl of Dublin, 1799; general, 1799; commander-in-chief of the forces in British North America, 1799–1800; governor of Gibraltar, 1802–3; field-marshal, 1805; keeper of Hampton Court, 1806; the first to abandon flogging in the army, and to establish a regimental school; married in 1818 Victoria Mary Louisa [see below], widow of Emich Charles, prince of Leiningen, by whom a daughter (afterwards Queen Victoria) was born to him, 1819. [xxxi. 19]

KENT, VICTORIA MARY LOUISA, DUCHESS OF (1786–1861), daughter of Francis Frederic Antony, hereditary prince (afterwards duke) of Saxe-Saalfeld-Coburg, by Augusta Carolina Sophia, daughter of Henry, count Reuss-Eberstadt; born at Coburg, 17 Aug. 1786; married firstly Emich Charles, hereditary prince (afterwards duke) of Saxe-Saalfeld-Coburg (d. 1814), 1803; married secondly Edward Augustus, duke of Kent [q. v.], 1818, her only child by him becoming Queen Victoria; granted an annuity of 6,000l. by parliament towards support of her daughter, 1825, and a further annuity of 10,000l. in 1831; appointed regent in event of her daughter succeeding as a minor, 1830. [xxxi. 20]

KENT, EARLS OF. [See ODO, d. 1097; BURGH, HUBERT DE, d. 1243; EDMUND 'of Woodstock,' 1301–1330; GREY, EDMUND, first EARL (of the Grey line), 1420?–1489; GREY, GEORGE, second EARL, d. 1503; GREY, HENRY, ninth EARL, 1594–1651; HOLLAND, SIR THOMAS, first EARL (of the Holland line), d. 1360; HOLLAND, THOMAS, second EARL, 1350–1397; HOLLAND, THOMAS, third EARL, and DUKE OF SURREY, 1374–1400; HOLLAND, EDMUND, fourth EARL (of the Holland line), d. 1408; NEVILLE, WILLIAM, d. 1463.]

KENT, EARL OF. [See WILLIAM OF YPRES, d. 1165?, erroneously styled EARL OF KENT.]

KENT, COUNTESS OF (1581–1651). [See GREY, ELIZABETH.]

KENT, MAID OF (1506?–1534). [See BARTON, ELIZABETH.]

KENT, JAMES (1700–1776), organist and composer; chorister of the Chapel Royal, 1714; organist to Trinity College, Cambridge, 1731, to Winchester Cathedral and College, 1737–74; published a collection of anthems, 1773 (republished, 1844). [xxxi. 21]

KENT or **GWENT**, JOHN (fl. 1348), twentieth provincial of the Franciscans in England; doctor of theology at Oxford; reputed miracle-worker; author of commentary on Peter Lombard's 'Sentences.' [xxxi. 22]

KENT, JOHN, or SION CENT (fl. 1400), also called JOHN OF KENTCHURCH, Welsh bard; went to Oxford; parish priest at Kentchurch; said to have lived till the age of a hundred and twenty; perhaps sympathised with Oldcastle; one of the best of the Welsh poets. [xxxi. 21]

KENT, NATHANIEL (fl. 1730), scholar; at Eton and King's College, Cambridge; M.A. and fellow of King's College, Cambridge, 1733; head-master of Wisbech school, 1748; his 'Excerpta quædam ex Luciani Samosatensis Operibus' published, 1730 (3rd ed. 1757; another ed. 1788). [xxxi. 23]

KENT, NATHANIEL (1737–1810), land valuer and agriculturist; secretary to Sir James Porter at Brussels; studied husbandry of Austrian Netherlands; quitted diplomacy, and returned to England, 1766; published 'Hints to Gentlemen of Landed Property,' 1775 (3rd ed. 1793); employed as an estate agent and land valuer; did much to improve land management in England. [xxxi. 22]

KENT, ODO OF (d. 1200). [See ODO.]

KENT, THOMAS (fl. 1460), clerk to the privy council, 1444; ambassador to various countries; sub-constable of England, 1445. [xxxi. 23]

KENT, THOMAS (d. 1489), mathematician; fellow of Merton College, Oxford, 1480; reputed as an astronomer and as author of a treatise on astronomy. [xxxi. 23]

KENT, WILLIAM (1684–1748), painter, sculptor, architect, and landscape-gardener; apprenticed to coach-maker, 1698; made attempt at painting in London, 1703; went to Rome, where he met several patrons; brought to England by the Earl of Burlington, with whom he lived for the rest of his life; employed in portrait-painting and decoration of walls and ceilings; severely criticised by Hogarth; excelled only as an architect; published the 'Designs of Inigo Jones,' 1727; built the Horse Guards and treasury buildings, and Devonshire House, Piccadilly; executed the statue of Shakespeare in Poet's Corner; principal painter to the crown, 1739. [xxxi. 23]

KENT, WILLIAM (1751–1812), captain in the navy; nephew of Vice-Admiral John Hunter (1738–1821) [q. v.]; lieutenant, 1781; sailed for New South Wales, 1795; returned to England, 1800; revisited Sydney, 1801; commander, 1802; discovered and named Port St. Vincent in New Caledonia, 1802; advanced to post rank, 1806; died off Toulon. [xxxi. 25]

KENTEN (d. 685). [See CENTWINE.]

KENTIGERN or ST. MUNGO (518?–603), the apostle of the Strathclyde Britons; grandson of Loth, a British prince, after whom the Lothians are named; trained in the monastic school of Culross; became a missionary; chosen bishop at Cathures (now Glasgow); driven by persecution to Wales; founded monastery of Llanelwy (afterwards St. Asaph's); returned to the north of England, and after reclaiming the Picts of Galloway from idolatry settled at Glasgow, where he died, and was buried in the crypt of Glasgow Cathedral, called after him St. Mungo's; many miracles attributed to him. [xxxi. 26]

KENTISH, JOHN (1768–1853), unitarian divine; minister at various places, 1790–4; at London, 1795; at Birmingham, 1803–44; conservative in religion, but whig in politics; published memoirs and religious treatises. [xxxi. 27]

KENTON, BENJAMIN (1719–1800), vintner and philanthropist; educated at a Whitechapel charity school; became a successful tavern-keeper; master of the Vintners' Company, 1776; a liberal benefactor to his old school, to Sir John Cass's School, to the Vintners' Company, and to St. Bartholomew's Hospital. [xxxi. 28]

KENTON, NICHOLAS (d. 1468), Carmelite; studied at Cambridge; priest, 1420; chosen provincial, 1444; credited with a commentary on the 'Song of Songs' and theological treatises. [xxxi. 28]

KENULF or **CYNEWULF** (fl. 750). [See KYNE-WULF.]

KENULF (d. 1006). [See CENWULF.]

KENWEALH (d. 672). [See CENWALH.]

KENYON, JOHN (1784–1856), poet and philanthropist; born in Jamaica; educated at Peterhouse, Cambridge; a friend and benefactor to the Brownings and other men and women of letters; spent his life in society, travel, dilettantism, and dispensing charity; published 'A Rhymed Plea for Tolerance,' 1833, 'Poems,' 1838, and 'A Day at Tivoli,' 1849. [xxxi. 29]

KENYON, LLOYD, first BARON KENYON (1732–1802), lord chief-justice; articled to a Nantwich solicitor, 1749; barrister, Middle Temple, 1756; K.C., 1780; chief-justice of Chester, 1780; M.P., Hendon, 1780; attorney-general, 1782; master of the rolls, 1784–8; privy councillor, 1784; knighted and created baronet, 1784; chief-justice, 1788–1802; raised to the peerage, 1788; lord-lieutenant of Flintshire, 1797. [xxxi. 30]

KEOGH, JOHN (1650 ?-1725), Irish divine; M.A. Trinity College, Dublin, 1678; led a scholar's life in country livings; left works in manuscript. [xxxi. 32]

KEOGH, JOHN (1681 ?-1754), divine; second son of John Keogh (1650 ?-1725) [q. v.]; D.D.; wrote on antiquities and medicinal plants of Ireland. [xxxi. 33]

KEOGH, JOHN (1740-1817), Irish catholic leader; instrumental in bringing about Catholic Relief Act of 1793; arrested as one of the United Irishmen, 1796; released; withdrew from public affairs after 1798.
[xxxi. 33]

KEOGH, WILLIAM NICHOLAS (1817-1878), Irish judge; educated at Trinity College, Dublin; called to the Irish bar, 1840; M.P., Athlone, 1847; Q.C., 1849; solicitor-general for Ireland, 1852; warmly denounced for joining the government after showing sympathy with popular party in Ireland; attorney-general and privy councillor for Ireland, 1855; judge of the court of common pleas in Ireland, 1856; on the commission for trial of Fenian prisoners, 1865; hon. LL.D. Dublin, 1867; died at Bingen-on-the-Rhine. [xxxi. 34]

KEON, MILES GERALD (1821-1875), novelist and colonial secretary; editor of 'Dolman's Magazine,' 1846; joined staff of 'Morning Post,' 1848; its representative at St. Petersburg, 1850 and 1856; sent to Calcutta to edit the 'Bengal Hurkaru,' 1858; colonial secretary at Bermuda, 1859-75; published novels. [xxxi. 35]

KEPER, JOHN (*fl.* 1580), poet; educated at Hart Hall, Oxford; M.A., 1569; author of complimentary poems. [xxxi. 36]

KEPPEL, ARNOLD JOOST VAN, first EARL OF ALBEMARLE (1669-1718), born in Holland; came to England with William of Orange, 1688; created Earl of Albemarle, 1696; major-general, 1697; K.G., 1700; confidant of William III, at whose death he returned to Holland; fought at Ramillies, 1706, and Oudenarde, 1708; governor of Tournay, 1709. [xxxi. 36]

KEPPEL, AUGUSTUS, first VISCOUNT KEPPEL (1725-1786), admiral; son of William Anne Keppel, second earl of Albemarle [q. v.]; educated at Westminster School; entered navy, 1735; accompanied Anson on a voyage round the world, 1740; commander, 1744; sent to treat with the dey of Algiers, 1748-51; commodore and commander of the ships on the North American station, 1754; a member of the court-martial on Byng, 1757; rear-admiral, 1762; one of the lord commissioners of the admiralty, 1766; vice-admiral, 1770; admiral of the blue, 1778; commander-in-chief of the grand fleet, 1778; court-martialled for conduct in the operations off Brest, 1779, the charge being pronounced 'malicious and ill-founded'; first lord of the admiralty, 1782; created Viscount Keppel and Baron Elden, 1782. [xxxi. 37]

KEPPEL, FREDERICK (1729-1777), bishop of Exeter; son of William Anne Keppel, second earl of Albemarle [q. v.]; educated at Westminster School and Christ Church, Oxford; M.A., 1754; D.D., 1762; chaplain in ordinary to George II and George III; canon of Windsor, 1754-62; bishop of Exeter, 1762; dean of Windsor, 1765; registrar of the Garter, 1765. [xxxi. 42]

KEPPEL, GEORGE, third EARL OF ALBEMARLE (1724-1772), general; colonel, 3rd dragoons (now hussars); eldest son of William Anne Keppel, second earl of Albemarle [q. v.]; ensign in Coldstream guards, 1738; captain and lieutenant-colonel, 1745; at Fontenoy, 1745, and Culloden, 1746; M.P., Chichester, 1746-54; succeeded to the earldom, 1754; major-general, 1756; lieutenant-general, 1759; privy councillor, 1761; governor of Jersey, 1761; assisted in attack on Havana 1762; K.B., 1764; K.G., 1771. [xxxi. 42]

KEPPEL, GEORGE THOMAS, sixth EARL OF ALBE-MARLE (1799-1891), grandson of George Keppel, third earl of Albemarle [q. v.]; educated at Westminster School; ensign in the 14th foot (now Yorkshire regiment), 1815; present at Waterloo; served in the Ionian islands, Mauritius, the Cape, and in India; returned home overland, 1823; M.P., East Norfolk, 1832; private secretary to Lord John Russell, 1846; succeeded to earldom, 1851.
[xxxi. 43]

KEPPEL, WILLIAM ANNE, second EARL OF ALBE-MARLE (1702-1754), lieutenant-general; colonel, Coldstream guards; son of Arnold Joost van Keppel, first earl of Albemarle [q. v.]; educated in Holland; succeeded as

earl, 1718; K.B., 1725; governor of Virginia, 1737; brigadier-general, 1739; major-general, 1742; general on the staff at Dettingen, 1743; colonel, Coldstream guards, 1744; wounded at Fontenoy, 1745; present at Culloden, 1746; ambassador-extraordinary to Paris, and commander-in-chief in North Britain, 1748; K.G., 1749; privy councillor, 1750; died in Paris. [xxxi. 44]

KEPPEL, WILLIAM COUTTS. seventh EARL OF ALBEMARLE and VISCOUNT BURY (1832-1894), son of George Thomas Keppel, sixth earl of Albemarle [q. v.]; educated at Eton; lieutenant in Scots guards, 1849; aide-de-camp to Lord Frederick Fitzclarence in India, 1852-3; retired from army; superintendent of Indian affairs in Canada, 1854-7; M.P. for Norwich, 1857 and 1859, Wick burghs, 1860-5, and Berwick, 1868-74; treasurer of household, 1859-66; K.C.M.G., 1870; raised to peerage as Baron Ashford, 1876; under-secretary at war, 1878-80 and 1885-6; succeeded to earldom, 1891; published writings relating to Canada and other subjects.
[Suppl. iii. 59]

KER. [See also KERR.]

KER, SIR ANDREW (*d.* 1526), of Cessford or Cess-ford; Scottish borderer; fought at Flodden, 1513; warden of the Middle marches, 1515; defeated Scott of Buccleuch in a skirmish, but was slain. [xxxi. 45]

KER, ANDREW (1471 ?-1545), of Ferniehirst; border chieftain; succeeded as laird, 1499; captured, 1523; escaped; undertook to serve England, 1544. [xxxi. 46]

KER, CHARLES HENRY BELLENDEN (1785 ?-1871), legal reformer; son of John Bellenden Ker [q. v.]; barrister, Lincoln's Inn, 1814; promoted legal reforms; conveyancing counsel to the courts of chancery; recorder of Andover; retired from practice, 1860; died at Cannes.
[xxxi. 47]

KER, JAMES INNES-, fifth DUKE OF ROXBURGH (1738-1823), second son of Sir Harry Innes, fifth baronet; captain of foot, 88th regiment, 1759, and 58th, 1779; succeeded to baronetcy, 1764; on death of William Ker, fourth duke of Roxburgh (1805), claimed the dukedom; his claims disputed; obtained title, 1812. [xxxi. 47]

KER, JOHN (1673-1726), of Kersland, Ayrshire; government spy; in the pay both of the government and the Jacobites; declared himself instrumental in securing the Hanoverian succession, 1714; died in King's Bench debtors' prison; his memoirs published by Edmund Curll [q. v.], 1726. [xxxi. 48]

KER, JOHN, fifth EARL and first DUKE OF ROXBURGH (*d.* 1741), brother of the fourth earl and second son of the third earl; succeeded his brother, 1696; secretary of state for Scotland, 1704; created duke, 1707; Scots representative peer, 1707, 1708, 1715, and 1722; a member of the council of regency; keeper of the privy seal of Scotland, 1714; lord-lieutenant of Roxburgh and Selkirk, 1714; privy councillor, 1714; distinguished himself at Sheriff-muir, 1715; one of the lords justices during George I's absence from England, 1716, 1720, 1723, and 1725.
[xxxi. 50]

KER, JOHN (*d.* 1741), Latin poet; master in Royal High School, Edinburgh, *c.* 1710; professor of Greek, King's College, Aberdeen, 1717, and of Latin at Edinburgh University, 1734; published 'Donaides,' 1725, and other Latin poems. [Suppl. iii. 60]

KER, JOHN, third DUKE OF ROXBURGH (1740-1804), book collector; succeeded to dukedom, 1755; lord of the bedchamber, 1767; K.T., 1768; groom of the stole and privy councillor, 1796; K.G., 1801; his splendid library, including an unrivalled collection of Caxtons, sold for 23,341*l.* in 1812. The Roxburghe Club was inaugurated by the leading bibliophiles on the day of the sale.
[xxxi. 51]

KER, JOHN (1819-1886), divine; educated at Edinburgh University, at Halle, and Berlin; ordained, 1845; preacher and platform orator; D.D. Edinburgh, 1869; published sermons and pamphlets. [xxxi. 52]

KER, JOHN BELLENDEN (1765 ?-1842), botanist, wit, and man of fashion; captain, second regiment of life guards, 1790; senior captain, 1793; forced to quit the army in consequence of his sympathy with the French revolution; claimed unsuccessfully the dukedom of Roxburgh, 1805-12; published many botanical works and first editor of 'Botanical Register,' 1812. [xxxi. 52]

KER, PATRICK (*fl.* 1691), poet; probably a Scottish episcopalian who migrated to London during the reign of Charles II; wrote ultra-loyalist verse; chief work, 'The Grand Politician,' 1691. [xxxi. 53]

KER, ROBERT, EARL OF SOMERSET (*d.* 1645). [See CARR.]

KER, ROBERT, first EARL OF ROXBURGH (1570 ?– 1650), helped James VI against Bothwell, 1594–9; member of the privy council of Scotland, 1599; created Baron Roxburgh, 1600; accompanied King James to London, 1603; succeeded to his father's estates, 1606; created Earl of Roxburgh, 1616; lord privy seal of Scotland, 1637; subscribed the king's covenant at Holyrood, 1638; sat in the general assembly at Glasgow, 1638; joined the king's party in the civil war, 1639; kept the door of the house open at Charles's attempted arrest of the five members, 1642; supported the 'engagement' for the king's rescue, 1648; consequently deprived of the office of privy seal, 1649. [xxxi. 53]

KER, ROBERT, first EARL OF ANCRUM (1578–1654), grandson of Andrew Ker of Ferniehirst [q. v.]; succeeded to the family estates on the assassination of his father, 1590; groom of the bedchamber to Prince Henry and knighted, 1603; gentleman of the bedchamber to Prince Charles in Spain, 1623; lord of the bedchamber, master of the privy purse, 1625–39; created Earl of Ancrum at the coronation of Charles in Scotland, 1633; retired from office, 1639; a faithful royalist, but lived in retirement, 1641–50; died at Amsterdam. [xxxi. 56]

KER, SIR THOMAS (*d.* 1586), of Ferniehirst; succeeded his father, the second son of Andrew Ker of Ferniehirst [q. v.], 1562; became a member of the privy council at the time of the Darnley marriage, 1565; joined Mary Queen of Scots after her escape from Lochleven, 1568; provost of Edinburgh, 1570; believed to have been directly implicated in the murder of Darnley, but pardoned, 1583; warden of the middle marches, 1584; suspected of a plot against the English, 1585; committed to ward in Aberdeen, where he died. [xxxi. 57]

KER, SIR WALTER (*d.* 1584 ?) of Cessfurd; eldest son of Sir Andrew Ker of Cessfurd [q. v.]; implicated in murder of Sir Walter Scott of Buccleuch; banished to France, 1552; pardoned, 1553; a leading opponent of Mary Queen of Scots. [xxxi. 58]

KERCKHOVEN, CATHERINE, LADY STANHOPE and COUNTESS OF CHESTERFIELD (*d.* 1667). [See KIRKHOVEN.]

KERNE, SIR EDWARD (*d.* 1561). [See CARNE.]

KEROUALLE, LOUISE RENÉE DE, DUCHESS OF PORTSMOUTH AND AUBIGNY (1649–1734), accompanied Henrietta, duchess of Orleans, the sister of Charles II, to England as maid of honour, 1670; established as Charles II's mistress *en titre,* 1671; naturalised and created Duchess of Portsmouth, 1673; granted by Louis XIV, at Charles II's persuasion, the fief of Aubigny, 1674; exerted her influence to keep Charles dependent on France; died at Paris. Her descendants, the Dukes of Richmond and Gordon, still bear her motto. [xxxi. 59]

KERR or **KER**, MARK (*d.* 1584), abbot of Newbattle; abbot, 1546; renounced Roman catholicism, 1560, but continued to hold his benefice; privy councillor, 1569; member of the council to carry on the government after Morton's retirement, 1578. [xxxi. 62]

KERR or **KER**, MARK, first EARL OF LOTHIAN (*d.* 1609), master of requests; eldest son of Mark Kerr (*d.* 1584) [q. v.]; master of requests, 1577; made a baron and privy councillor, 1587; created a lord of parliament, 1591; acted as interim chancellor, 1604; created Earl of Lothian, 1606, and resigned the office of master of requests, 1606. [xxxi. 62]

KERR, LORD MARK (*d.* 1752), general; son of Robert Kerr, fourth earl and first marquis of Lothian [q. v.]; wounded at Almanza, 1707; governor of Guernsey, 1740; general, 1743. [xxxi. 64]

KERR, NORMAN (1834–1899), physician; M.D. and C.M., Glasgow, 1861; practised in London from 1874; published works relating to temperance, in the advancement of which he was actively interested. [Suppl. iii. 60]

KERR, ROBERT, fourth EARL and first MARQUIS OF LOTHIAN (1636–1703), eldest son of William Kerr, third earl of Lothian [q. v.]; volunteer in the Dutch war, 1673; succeeded his father, 1675; a supporter of the revolution; privy councillor to William III, and justice-general, 1688; united earldom of Ancrum to his other titles, 1690; commissioner of the king to the general assembly of the kirk of Scotland, 1692; created marquis, 1701. [xxxi. 63]

KERR, ROBERT (1755–1813), scientific writer and translator; descendant of Sir Thomas Ker of Redden, brother of Robert Ker, first earl of Ancrum [q. v.]; studied medicine at Edinburgh University; surgeon to the Edinburgh Foundling Hospital; relinquished medical career for the management of a subsequently unsuccessful paper-mill; F.R.S. Edinburgh, 1805; translated from Lavoisier and Linnæus. [xxxi. 64]

KERR, SCHOMBERG HENRY, ninth MARQUIS OF LOTHIAN (1833–1900), diplomatist and secretary of state for Scotland; educated at New College, Oxford; attaché at Lisbon, Teheran (1854), Bagdad (1855), and Athens (*c.* 1857); second secretary at Frankfort (1862), Madrid (1865), and Vienna (1865); succeeded as Marquis of Lothian and fourth Baron Ker of Kersheugh, 1870; lord privy seal of Scotland, 1874–1900; privy councillor, 1886; secretary of state for Scotland in Lord Salisbury's administration, 1886–92; LL.D. Edinburgh, 1882; K.T., 1878. [Suppl. iii. 61]

KERR or **KER**, WILLIAM, third EARL OF LOTHIAN (1605 ?–1675), eldest son of Robert Ker, first earl of Ancrum [q. v.]; educated at Cambridge and Paris; accompanied Buckingham to the Isle of Rhé, 1627; served in expedition against Spain, 1629; succeeded as third Earl of Lothian, 1631; signed the national covenant, 1638; governor of Newcastle, 1641; subsequently one of the four commissioners of the treasury; lieutenant-general of the Scots army in Ireland; privy councillor; falsely accused of treachery while abroad and imprisoned on his return; released, 1643; in parliament, 1644; joined Argyll in expedition against Montrose, 1644; one of the commissioners sent to treat with the king at Newcastle, 1647; accompanied the king to Holmby House, 1647; secretary of state, 1648; one of the commissioners sent by the Scottish parliament to protest against proceeding to extremities against the king, 1649; general of the Scottish forces, 1650; refused to take the abjuration oath, 1662. [xxxi. 64]

KERR, WILLIAM, second MARQUIS OF LOTHIAN (1662 ?–1722), eldest son of Robert Kerr, first marquis of Lothian [q. v.]; succeeded to title of Lord Jedburgh, and sat in Scottish parliament, 1692; colonel of dragoons, 1696; succeeded his father, 1703; supporter of the English revolution and of the union of England and Scotland; Scots representative peer, 1708 and 1715; major-general on the North British staff after 1713. [xxxi. 66]

KERR, WILLIAM HENRY, fourth MARQUIS OF LOTHIAN (*d.* 1775), captain in the first regiment of footguards, 1741; present at Fontenoy, 1745, and Culloden, 1746; lieutenant-general, 1758; M.P., Richmond, 1747, 1754, 1761–3; succeeded his father, 1767; Scots representative peer, 1768; general, 1770. [xxxi. 67]

KERRICH, THOMAS (1748–1828), librarian of the university of Cambridge; educated at Magdalene College, Cambridge; M.A. and fellow, 1775; university taxor, 1793; principal librarian, 1797; prebendary of Lincoln, 1798, and of Wells, 1812; an antiquarian, painter, draughtsman, and one of the earliest lithographers; bequeathed his collections to the Society of Antiquaries, the British Museum, and the Fitzwilliam Museum, Cambridge. [xxxi. 67]

KERRISON, SIR EDWARD (1774–1853), general; cornet, 6th dragoons, 1796; captain, 1798; served in 7th hussars in Helder expedition, 1799; lieutenant-colonel in campaign of 1808; present at Waterloo, 1815; knighted, 1816; M.P., Shaftesbury, 1812–18, Northampton, 1818–24, Eye, 1824–52; general, 1851. [xxxi. 68]

KERRY, KNIGHTS OF. [See FITZGERALD, MAURICE, 1774–1849; FITZGERALD, SIR PETER GEORGE, 1808–1880.]

KERRY, BARONS. [See FITZMAURICE, THOMAS, sixteenth BARON, 1502–1590; FITZMAURICE, PATRICK, seventeenth BARON, 1551 ?–1600; FITZMAURICE, THOMAS, eighteenth BARON, 1574–1630.]

KERSEBOOM, FREDERICK (1632–1690), painter; born at Solingen; studied painting at Amsterdam; lived at Paris and Rome; settled in England as a portrait-painter; painted portraits of Robert Boyle [q. v.] and of Sophia Dorothea, George I's queen.   [xxxi. 69]

KERSEY, JOHN, the elder (1616–1690 ?), teacher of mathematics in London; published work on algebra at instigation of John Collins (1625–1683) [q. v.], 1673–4; edited the 'Arithmetic' of Edmund Wingate [q. v.], 1650–1683.   [xxxi. 69]

KERSEY, JOHN, the younger (*fl.* 1720), lexicographer; son of John Kersey the elder [q. v.]; his 'Dictionarium Anglo-Britannicum,' 1708, used by Chatterton.   [xxxi. 69]

KERSHAW, ARTHUR (*fl.* 1800), apparently son of James Kershaw [q. v.]; employed in enlargement of Walker's 'Gazetteer.'   [xxxi. 70]

KERSHAW, JAMES (1730 ?–1797), methodist preacher; converted by Henry Venn [q. v.]; his poem 'The Methodist attempted in Plain Metre' (1780), a sort of Wesleyan epic, determined Wesley to exercise a censorship over methodist publications.   [xxxi. 70]

KERSLAKE, THOMAS (1812–1891), bookseller; a second-hand bookseller at Bristol, 1828–70; wrote articles on antiquarian subjects.   [xxxi. 70]

KETCH, JOHN, commonly known as JACK KETCH (*d.* 1686), executioner; took office probably in 1663; executed Lord Russell, 1683, and Monmouth, 1685; notorious for his excessive barbarity; the office of executioner identified with his name by 1702.   [xxxi. 71]

KETEL, CORNELIS (1548–1616), portrait-painter; born at Gouda; worked in London, 1573–81; through Sir Christopher Hatton [q. v.] obtained a reputation among the nobility; settled at Amsterdam (1581), where he died.   [xxxi. 72]

KETEL or **CHETTLE**, WILLIAM (*fl.* 1150), hagiographer; a canon of Beverley; wrote a narrative, 'De Miraculis Sancti Joannis Beverlacensis,' given in the 'Acta Sanctorum.'   [xxxi. 73]

KETHE, WILLIAM (*d.* 1608 ?), protestant divine; accompanied Ambrose Dudley, earl of Warwick [q. v.], to Havre as minister to the English army, 1563; preacher to the troops in the north, 1569; remembered chiefly for his metrical psalms, first printed in the English psalter of 1561.   [xxxi. 73]

KETT or **KET**, FRANCIS (*d.* 1589), clergyman; educated at Corpus Christi College, Cambridge; M.A. and fellow, 1573; condemned for heresy, 1588; burned alive, 1589.   [xxxi. 74]

KETT, HENRY (1761–1825), miscellaneous writer; entered Trinity College, Oxford, 1777; M.A., 1783; fellow, 1784; Bampton lecturer, 1790; B.D., 1793; select preacher, 1801–2; classical examiner, 1803–4; drowned himself in a fit of depression.   [xxxi. 75]

KETT, ROBERT (*d.* 1549), rebel; took the popular side in a local quarrel, and, with sixteen thousand men, blockaded Norwich, 1549; defeated and executed.   [xxxi. 76]

KETTELL, RALPH (1563–1643), third president of Trinity College, Oxford; scholar of Trinity College, Oxford, 1579; fellow, 1583; M.A., 1586; D.D., 1597; president, 1599; vigilant in dealing with college estates and discipline; rebuilt Trinity College Hall. [xxxi. 77]

KETTERICH or **CATRIK**, JOHN (*d.* 1419), successively bishop of St. David's, Lichfield and Coventry, and Exeter; his name also spelt Catryk, Catterich, and Catrik, the latter appearing on his tomb; educated probably at one of the universities; employed on missions abroad, 1406–11; archdeacon of Surrey, 1410–14; king's proctor at the papal court, 1413; bishop of St. David's, 1414–15; one of the English representatives at council of Constance, 1414; bishop of Lichfield and Coventry, 1415; postulated to see of Exeter, 1419; died at Florence.   [xxxi. 78]

KETTLE or **KYTELER**, DAME ALICE (*fl.* 1324), reputed witch of Kilkenny; summoned before the dean of St. Patrick's at Dublin; escaped to England.   [xxxi. 79]

KETTLE, SIR RUPERT ALFRED (1817–1894), 'Prince of Arbitrators'; articled as attorney in Wolver-hampton; barrister, Middle Temple, 1845; bencher, 1882; judge of Worcestershire county courts, 1859–92; advocated arbitration in trade disputes; knighted, 1880, for his public services in establishing a system of arbitration between employers and employed; published works on trade questions.   [Suppl. iii. 62]

KETTLE, TILLY (1740 ?–1786), portrait-painter; exhibited at the Free Society of Artists, 1761; at the Society of Artists, 1765; in India, 1770–7; exhibited at Royal Academy, 1779–83; became bankrupt; died at Aleppo on his way to India; his portraits sometimes mistaken for the work of Sir Joshua Reynolds.   [xxxi. 79]

KETTLEWELL, JOHN (1653–1695), nonjuror and devotional writer; educated at St. Edmund Hall, Oxford; B.A., 1674; fellow and tutor of Lincoln College, Oxford, 1675; M.A., 1677; published 'The Measures of Christian Obedience,' 1681; vicar of Coleshill, 1682 (deprived, 1690); wrote several devotional works.   [xxxi. 80]

KETTLEWELL, SAMUEL (1822–1893), theological writer; licentiate of theology, Durham, 1848; ordained priest, 1849; vicar of St. Mark's, Leeds, 1851–70; M.A., 1860, and D.D., 1892, Lambeth; published works on Thomas à Kempis and other theological writings.   [Suppl. iii. 62]

KEUGH, MATTHEW (1744 ?–1798), governor of Wexford; rose during the American war from private to ensign; gazetted, 1763; lieutenant, 1769; retired from the army, 1774; chosen military governor of Wexford by the insurgents, 1798; court-martialled and executed.   [xxxi. 82]

KEUX, JOHN HENRY LE (1812–1896). [See LE KEUX.]

KEVIN, SAINT (498–618). [See COEMGEN.]

KEY. [See also CAIUS.]

KEY, SIR ASTLEY COOPER (1821–1888), admiral; son of Charles Aston Key [q. v.]; entered navy, 1833; lieutenant, 1842; wounded at Obligado, 1845; promoted commander, 1845; served in the Russian war, 1854–5; commanded battalion of the naval brigade at capture of Canton, 1857; rear-admiral, 1866; director of the new department of naval ordnance, 1866–9; superintendent of Portsmouth dockyard, 1869; subsequently of Malta dockyard and second in command in Mediterranean; president of the newly organised Royal Naval College, 1873; vice-admiral and K.C.B., 1873; commander-in-chief on the North American and West Indian station, 1876; admiral, 1878; first naval lord of the admiralty, 1879; F.R.S., F.R.G.S., and D.C.L.; G.C.B., 1882; privy councillor, 1884.   [xxxi. 82]

KEY, CHARLES ASTON (1793–1849), surgeon; half-brother of Thomas Hewitt Key [q. v.]; pupil at Guy's Hospital, London, 1814; pupil of Astley Cooper, 1815; demonstrator of anatomy at St. Thomas's Hospital, London; surgeon at Guy's, 1824; gained reputation by successful operations for lithotomy; lecturer on surgery at Guy's, 1825–44; F.R.S.; member of council of Royal College of Surgeons, 1845; surgeon to Prince Albert, 1847; famous operator, and one of the first to use ether as an anæsthetic.   [xxxi. 83]

KEY, SIR JOHN, first baronet (1794–1858), lord mayor of London; alderman of London, 1823; sheriff, 1824; master of the Stationers' Company, 1830; lord mayor, 1830–1; created baronet, 1831; M.P. for the city of London, 1833, and chamberlain, 1853.   [xxxi. 84]

KEY, THOMAS HEWITT (1799–1875), Latin scholar; half-brother of Charles Aston Key [q. v.], the surgeon; of St. John's and Trinity Colleges, Cambridge; M.A., 1824; studied medicine, 1821–4; professor of pure mathematics in university of Virginia, 1825–7; professor of Latin in the London University, and joint head-master of the school attached, 1828; resigned Latin professorship for that of comparative grammar, 1842; sole head-master, 1842–75; F.R.S., 1860; his best-known work, his 'Latin Grammar,' 1846.   [xxxi. 84]

KEYES or **KEYS**, ROGER (*d.* 1477), architect (1437), and warden of All Souls College, Oxford; one of the original fellows of All Souls; warden, 1442–5; clerk of the works of Eton College, 1448; archdeacon of Barnstaple, 1450; precentor of Exeter Cathedral, 1467 and 1469.   [xxxi. 86]

KEYL, FREDERICK WILLIAM (FRIEDRICH WILHELM) (1823–1873), animal-painter; born at Frankfort-on-the-Maine; came to London as pupil of Sir Edwin Henry Landseer [q. v.]; exhibited at the Royal Academy. [xxxi. 86]

KEYMER or **KEYMOR**, JOHN (*fl.* 1610–1620), economic writer; his 'Observations upon the Dutch Fishing' first published, 1664. [Suppl. iii. 63]

KEYMIS, LAWRENCE (*d.* 1618). [See KEMYS.]

KEYNES, GEORGE, *alias* BRETT (1630–1659), jesuit; entered his novitiate at Rome, 1649; studied at St. Omer; sailed for China mission, 1654; died in the Philippines; translated the 'Roman Martyrology' (2nd ed., 1667). [xxxi. 86]

KEYNES, JOHN (1625?–1697), jesuit; probably brother of George Keynes [q. v.]; studied at St. Omer and Valladolid; joined jesuits, 1645; taught philosophy and theology at Spanish universities; as prefect of the higher studies at Liège devoted himself to the plaguestricken English soldiers in the Netherlands; in England till 1679; rector of the college of Liège, 1680; English provincial, 1683–9; established jesuit college at Savoy Hospital, 1687; died at Watten, near St. Omer; author of a pamphlet intended to bring schismatics to the 'true religion,' which was translated into Latin, 1684, French, 1688, and answered by Burnet, 1675. [xxxi. 86]

KEYS, LADY MARY (1540?–1578), third surviving daughter of Henry Grey, third marquis of Dorset [q. v.]; sister of Lady Jane Grey [see DUDLEY, JANE]; secretly married Thomas Keys, Queen Elizabeth's serjeant-porter, 1565; detained in private custody through Queen Elizabeth's anger; released, 1573. [xxxi. 87]

KEYS, SAMUEL (1771–1850), china-painter; in the old Derby china factory under William Duesbury (1725–1786) [q. v.]; quitted Derby before the closing of the factory; worked under Minton at Stoke-upon-Trent; collected materials for the history of the Derby factory, to which his three sons were apprenticed. [xxxi. 87]

KEYSE, THOMAS (1722–1800), still-life painter and proprietor of the Bermondsey Spa; self-taught; member of the Free Society of Artists; exhibited at the Royal Academy, 1765–8; opened (*c.* 1770) a tea-garden in Bermondsey near a chalybeate spring. [xxxi. 88]

KEYSER, WILLIAM DE (1647–1692?). [See DE KEYSER.]

KEYWORTH, THOMAS (1782–1852), divine and hebraist; converted from unitarianism and became a congregational minister; interested himself in missionary work; his chief book, 'Principia Hebraica,' 1817. [xxxi. 88]

KIALLMARK or **KILMARK**, GEORGE (1781–1835), musical composer; leader of the music at Sadler's Wells; a successful teacher and composer. [xxxi. 88]

KIALLMARK, GEORGE FREDERICK (1804–1887), musician; son of George Kiallmark [q. v.]; studied under Zimmermann, Kalkbrenner, and Moscheles; distinguished for his rendering of Chopin; opened an academy for the study of the piano in London, 1842. [xxxi. 89]

KIARAN, SAINT (516–549). [See CIARAN.]

KICKHAM, CHARLES JOSEPH (1826–1882), journalist; took part in 'Young Ireland movement,' 1848; became a Fenian, 1860; arrested, 1865, and sentenced to fourteen years' penal servitude, but released, 1869; wrote nationalist poems and stories on Irish subjects. [xxxi. 89]

KIDD, JAMES (1761–1834), presbyterian divine; of humble origin; emigrated to America, 1784; usher to Pennsylvania College; learnt Hebrew and studied at Edinburgh; professor of oriental languages, Marischal College, Aberdeen, 1793; hon. D.D. New Jersey, 1818; author of religious works. [xxxi. 90]

KIDD, JOHN (1775–1851), physician: student, Christ Church, Oxford, 1793; M.A., 1800; M.D., 1804: studied at Guy's Hospital, London, 1797–1801; pupil of Sir Astley Paston Cooper [q. v.]; chemical reader, Oxford, 1801; first Aldrichian professor of chemistry, 1803–32; physician to the Radcliffe Infirmary, 1808–26; gave lectures on mineralogy and geology (published, 1809); Lee's reader in anatomy, 1816; F.R.C.P., 1818; regius professor of physic, Oxford, 1822–51; author of Bridgewater treatise 'On the Adaptation of External Nature to the Physical Condition of Man,' 1833; keeper of the Radcliffe Library, 1834–51; Harveian orator, 1836. [xxxi. 91]

KIDD, JOSEPH BARTHOLOMEW (1808–1889), painter; academician, Royal Scottish Academy, 1829–38; painted Scottish landscapes. [xxxi. 92]

KIDD, SAMUEL (1804–1843), missionary at Malacca and professor of Chinese at University College, London; entered London Missionary Society's training college at Gosport, 1820; sailed under the auspices of the society to Madras, and thence to Malacca, 1824; published tracts in Chinese, 1826; professor of Chinese in the Anglo-Chinese College, Malacca, 1827, and at University College, London, 1837; author of works on China. [xxxi. 92]

KIDD, THOMAS (1770–1850), Greek scholar and schoolmaster; entered Trinity College, Cambridge, 1789; M.A., 1797; held various livings; successively headmaster of schools of Lynn, Wymondham, and Norwich; edited tracts on classical scholarship. [xxxi. 93]

KIDD, WILLIAM (*d.* 1701), pirate; native of Greenock; lived at Boston, Massachusetts; given the command of a privateer to suppress piracy, 1696; imprisoned for piracy, 1699; sent to England under arrest, 1700; hanged, 1701. [xxxi. 93]

KIDD, WILLIAM (1790?–1863), painter; exhibitor at Royal Academy, 1817, and at British Institution, 1818. [xxxi. 95]

KIDD, WILLIAM (1803–1867), naturalist; bookseller in London; published various journals dealing with natural history, 1852–64. [xxxi. 95]

KIDDER, RICHARD (1633–1703), bishop of Bath and Wells; entered Emmanuel College, Cambridge, 1649; B.A., 1652; fellow, 1655; vicar of Stanground, 1659; ejected by the Bartholomew Act, 1662; 'conformed'; rector of Raine, 1664; preacher at the Rolls, 1674; a royal chaplain, 1689; bishop of Bath and Wells, 1691–1703; continually in difficulties with the cathedral chapter and censured by high churchmen; wrote on theological questions. [xxxi. 96]

KIDDERMINSTER, RICHARD (*d.* 1531?). [See KEDERMYSTER.]

KIDGELL, JOHN (*fl.* 1766), divine; entered Hertford College, Oxford, 1741; M.A., 1747; fellow, 1747; fraudulently obtained the proof-sheets of the 'Essay on Woman' (probably printed by Wilkes and written by Thomas Potter [q. v.]), and then published 'A genuine and succinct Narrative of a scandalous, obscene, and exceedingly profane Libel entitled "An Essay on Woman,"' 1763. [xxxi. 98]

KIDLEY, WILLIAM (*fl.* 1624), poet; B.A. Exeter College, Oxford, 1627; composed 'A Poetical Relation of the Voyage of Sr Richard Hawkins' and 'History of the year 1588, wth other Historical Passages of these Tymes,' 1624 (neither printed). [xxxi. 98]

KIFFIN or **KIFFEN**, WILLIAM (1616–1701), merchant and baptist minister; said to be apprenticed to John Lilburne [q. v.]; joined separatist congregation, 1638; baptist, 1642; arrested at a conventicle and imprisoned, 1641; parliamentary assessor of taxes for Middlesex, 1647; permitted to preach in Suffolk, 1649; M.P., Middlesex, 1656–8; arrested on suspicion of plotting against Charles II; released, 1664; alderman of London, 1687. [xxxi. 98]

KILBURN, WILLIAM (1745–1818), artist and calicoprinter; executed the plates for 'Flora Londinensis' of William Curtis [q. v.]; owned calico-printing factory in Surrey; eminent in Europe as a designer. [xxxi. 101]

KILBURNE, RICHARD (1605–1678), author of works on the topography of Kent. [xxxi. 101]

KILBYE, RICHARD (1561?–1620), biblical scholar; B.A. and fellow, Lincoln College, Oxford, 1578; M.A., 1582; rector of Lincoln College, 1590–1620; D.D., 1596; prebendary of Lincoln, 1601; regius professor of Hebrew, 1610; and one of the translators of the authorised version. [xxxi. 101]

KILDARE, EARLS OF. [See FITZTHOMAS, JOHN, first EARL, *d.* 1316; FITZGERALD, THOMAS, second EARL. *d.* 1328; FITZGERALD, MAURICE, fourth EARL, 1318–1390; FITZGERALD, THOMAS, seventh EARL, *d.* 1477; FITZGERALD,

GERALD, eighth EARL, *d.* 1513; FITZGERALD, GERALD, ninth EARL, 1487–1534; FITZGERALD, THOMAS, tenth EARL, 1513–1537; FITZGERALD, GERALD, eleventh EARL, 1525–1585.]

KILDELITH, ROBERT (*d.* 1273). [See KELDELETH.]

KILHAM, ALEXANDER (1762–1798), founder of the 'methodist new connexion'; maintained, against the Hull circular (1791), the right of Wesleyan methodist preachers to administer all Christian ordinances; wrote many pamphlets between 1792 and 1796; 'expelled from the connexion,' 1796; formed a 'new methodist connexion,' 1798. [xxxi. 102]

KILHAM, MRS. HANNAH (1774–1832), missionary and student of unwritten African languages; *née* Spurr; joined the Wesleyans, 1794; married Alexander Kilham [q. v.], 1798; joined the quakers, 1802; printed anonymously 'First lessons in Jaloof,' 1820; sailed for Africa, 1823; taught at St. Mary's in the Gambia and at Sierra Leone, 1824 and 1832; died at sea. [xxxi. 103]

KILIAN, SAINT (*d.* 697). [See CILIAN.]

KILKENNY, WILLIAM DE (*d.* 1256), bishop of Ely and keeper of the seal; archdeacon of Coventry, 1248; keeper of the seal, 1250–5; bishop of Ely, 1255; died at Surgho in Spain. [xxxi. 104]

KILKERRAN, LORD (1688–1759). [See FERGUSSON, SIR JAMES.]

KILLEN, JOHN (*d.* 1803), Irish rebel; arrested for participation in Emmet's movement, 1803; tried, unjustly condemned, and executed. [xxxi. 105]

KILLEN, THOMAS YOUNG (1826–1886), Irish presbyterian divine; entered old Belfast College, 1842; licensed to preach, 1848; ordained, 1850; a leader in the Ulster revival, 1859; moderator of the Irish general assembly, 1882; made D.D. by the presbyterian theological faculty of Ireland, 1883; published a 'Sacramental Catechism,' 1874. [xxxi. 105]

KILLIGREW, ANNE (1660–1685), poetess and painter; daughter of Henry Killigrew (1613–1700) [q. v.]; maid of honour to Mary of Modena, duchess of York; her 'Poems' published, 1686. [xxxi. 106]

KILLIGREW, CATHERINE or KATHERINE, LADY (1530?–1583), a learned lady; fourth daughter of Sir Anthony Cooke [q. v.]; said to have been proficient in Hebrew, Greek, and Latin; married Sir Henry Killigrew [q. v.], 1565. [xxxi. 106]

KILLIGREW, CHARLES (1655–1725), master of the revels; born at Maestricht; son of Thomas Killigrew the elder [q. v.]; gentleman of the privy chamber to Charles II, 1670, to James II, 1685, to William and Mary, 1689; master of the revels, 1680; patentee of Drury Lane Theatre, London, 1682. [xxxi. 106]

KILLIGREW, SIR HENRY (*d.* 1603), diplomatist and ambassador; educated probably at Cambridge; M.P., Launceston, 1553; in exile, 1554–8; employed by Queen Elizabeth on various missions, notably to Scotland, 1558–1566, and 1572–91; M.P., Truro, 1572; knighted, 1591. [xxxi. 107]

KILLIGREW, HENRY (1613–1700), divine; son of Sir Robert Killigrew [q. v.]; educated under Thomas Farnaby [q. v.]; of Christ Church, Oxford; M.A., 1638; chaplain to the king's army, 1642; D.D., 1642; chaplain and almoner to the Duke of York, 1660; master of the Savoy, 1663; published sermons and Latin verses, and 'The Conspiracy' (play), 1638. [xxxi. 108]

KILLIGREW, HENRY (*d.* 1712), admiral; son of Henry Killigrew (1613–1700) [q. v.]; brother of James Killigrew [q. v.]; commodore of squadron for suppression of piracy, 1686; vice-admiral of the blue, 1689; commander-in-chief against the French in the Mediterranean, 1689–90; joint-admiral with Sir Clowdisley Shovell [q. v.] and Sir Ralph Delavall [q. v.], and a lord commissioner of the admiralty, 1693; dismissed after the Smyrna disaster, 1693. [xxxi. 109]

KILLIGREW, JAMES (*d.* 1695), captain in the navy; son of Henry Killigrew (1613–1700) [q. v.]; lieutenant, 1688; captain, 1690; killed in action, 1695. [xxxi. 110]

KILLIGREW, SIR ROBERT (1579–1633), courtier; of Christ Church, Oxford; M.P. for various Cornish boroughs, 1601–28; knighted, 1603; famous for his concoctions of drugs and cordials; exonerated (1615) from suspicion of being implicated in Sir Thomas Overbury's death; prothonotary of chancery, 1618; ambassador to the States-General, 1626; vice-chamberlain to Queen Henrietta Maria, 1630. [xxxi. 110]

KILLIGREW, THOMAS, the elder (1612–1683), dramatist; son of Sir Robert Killigrew [q. v.]; page to Charles I, 1633; his best-known comedy, the 'Parson's Wedding,' played between 1637 and 1642; arrested for royalism, 1642; released, 1644; joined Prince Charles at Paris, 1647; appointed resident at Venice, 1651; groom of the bedchamber to Charles II, 1660; built playhouse on site of present Drury Lane Theatre, London, 1663; master of the revels, 1679; folio edition of his 'Works,' 1664; three of his plays acted; well known as a wit; painted by Vandyck with Thomas Carew. [xxxi. 111]

KILLIGREW, THOMAS, the younger (1657–1719), dramatist; son of Thomas Killigrew the elder [q. v.]; gentleman of the bedchamber to George II when Prince of Wales; author of 'Chit Chat' (comedy), performed, 1719. [xxxi. 115]

KILLIGREW, SIR WILLIAM (1579?–1622), chamberlain of the exchequer; groom of the privy chamber to Queen Elizabeth; M.P., Helston, 1572, Penryn, 1584 and 1614, Cornwall, 1597, Liskeard, 1604; knighted, 1603; chamberlain of the exchequer, 1605–6. [xxxi. 115]

KILLIGREW, SIR WILLIAM (1606–1695), dramatist; eldest son of Sir Robert Killigrew [q. v.]; entered St. John's College, Oxford, 1623; knighted, 1626; M.P., Penryn, Cornwall, 1628–9; gentleman usher to Charles I; commander in the king's body-guard during civil war; D.C.L. Oxford, 1642; vice-chamberlain to Charles I's queen, 1660–82; M.P., Richmond, Yorkshire, 1664–78; disappeared from court after 1682; published 'Three Plays,' 1665 (reprinted, 1674), and pamphlets in connection with the quarrels concerning the draining of the Lincolnshire fens, 1647–61. [xxxi. 116]

KILLINGWORTH, GRANTHAM (1699–1778), baptist controversialist; grandson of Thomas Grantham (1634–1692) [q. v.]; published controversial pamphlets. [xxxi. 117]

KILMAINE, BARON (1690–1773). [See O'HARA, JAMES.]

KILMAINE, CHARLES EDWARD SAUL JENNINGS (1751–1799), general in the French army; went to France, 1762; entered French army, 1774, and arrested American insurgents; lieutenant-general, 1793; served in Italy under Bonaparte, 1796; died at Paris. [xxxi. 117]

KILMARNOCK, fourth EARL OF (1704–1746). [See BOYD, WILLIAM.]

KILMOREY, first EARL OF (1748–1832). [See NEEDHAM, FRANCIS JACK.]

KILMOREY, fourth VISCOUNT (*d.* 1660). [See NEEDHAM, CHARLES.]

KILSYTH, first VISCOUNT (1616–1661). [See LIVINGSTONE, JAMES.]

KILVERT, FRANCIS (1793–1863), antiquary; entered Worcester College, Oxford, 1811; ordained, 1817; M.A., 1824; published sermons, memoirs, and papers on the literary associations of Bath. [xxxi. 118]

KILVERT, RICHARD (*d.* 1649), lawyer; concerned in the impeachment of Sir John Bennet [q. v.], 1621, and in the proceedings of the Star-chamber against Bishop Williams, 1634. [xxxi. 119]

KILWARDBY, ROBERT (*d.* 1279), archbishop of Canterbury and cardinal-bishop of Porto; studied, and afterwards taught, at Paris; entered the order of St. Dominic; teacher of Thomas of Cantelupe [q. v.]; provincial prior of the Dominicans in England, 1261; archbishop of Canterbury, 1272; crowned Edward I and Queen Eleanor, 1274; cardinal-bishop of Porto and Santo Rufina, 1278; on going to Italy took away all the registers and judicial records of Canterbury, which were never recovered; died at Viterbo; a voluminous writer on grammatical, philosophical, and theological subjects. [xxxi. 120]

KILWARDEN, VISCOUNT (1739-1803). [See WOLFE, ARTHUR.]

KIMBER, EDWARD (1719-1769), novelist and compiler; son of Isaac Kimber [q. v.] [xxxi. 122]

KIMBER, ISAAC (1692-1755), general baptist minister; conducted 'The Morning Chronicle,' 1728-32; edited Ainsworth's 'Latin Dictionary,' 1751; published 'Life of Oliver Cromwell,' 1724. [xxxi. 122]

KINASTON. [See KYNASTON.]

KINCAID, MRS. JEAN (1579-1600), murderess; daughter of John Livingstone of Dunipace; wife of John Kincaid of Warriston, an influential man in Edinburgh; procured his murder, 1600; condemned and beheaded. [xxxi. 123]

KINCAID, SIR JOHN (1787-1862), of the rifle brigade; joined 95th rifles, 1809; served in Peninsula, 1811-15; severely wounded at Waterloo; captain, 1826; retired, 1831; inspector of factories and prisons for Scotland, 1850; senior exon of the royal bodyguard of yeomen of the guard and knighted, 1852; published 'Adventures in the Rifle Brigade,' 1830, 'Random Shots of a Rifleman,' 1835. [xxxi. 123]

KINCARDINE, EARLS OF. [See BRUCE, ALEXANDER, second EARL, d. 1681; BRUCE, THOMAS, eleventh EARL, 1766-1841; BRUCE, JAMES, twelfth EARL, 1811-1863.]

KINDERSLEY, SIR RICHARD TORIN (1792-1879), vice-chancellor; born at Madras; of Haileybury and Trinity College, Cambridge; fellow, 1815; M.A., 1817; barrister, Lincoln's Inn, 1818; K.C., 1825; chancellor of county palatine of Durham, 1847; master in chancery, 1848; vice-chancellor, 1851; knighted, 1851; retired from the bench and privy councillor, 1866. [xxxi. 124]

KINDLEMARSH. [See KINWELMERSH.]

KING, CHARLES (fl. 1721), writer on economics; wrote articles in the 'British Merchant' respecting the proposed treaty of commerce with France in 1713; issued the chief numbers as 'The British Merchant, or Commerce preserved,' 1721, the volume enjoying high authority for forty years. [xxxi. 124]

KING, CHARLES (1687-1748), musical composer; Mus.Bac. Oxford; almoner and 'master of the children' of St. Paul's Cathedral, London, 1707; organist of St. Benet Finck, Royal Exchange, 1708; vicar-choral of St. Paul's, 1730; composed church music. [xxxi. 125]

KING, CHARLES WILLIAM (1818-1888), author of works on engraved gems; entered Trinity College, Cambridge, 1836; B.A., 1840; fellow, 1842; took holy orders; formed in Italy a notable collection of antique gems; sold his collection, 1878; published six works on gems between 1860 and 1872. [xxxi. 125]

KING, DANIEL (d. 1664?), engraver; executed the engravings in 'The Vale Royall of England, or the County Palatine of Chester,' 1656; etched some plates of Dugdale's 'Monasticon.' [xxxi. 126]

KING, DAVID (1806-1883), Scottish divine; educated at the Aberdeen and Edinburgh universities; studied theology at Glasgow; minister of Greyfriars secession church, Glasgow, 1833-55; made LL.D. Glasgow University, 1840; active in Evangelical Alliance, 1845; helped to form united presbyterian church, 1847; visited Jamaica and United States, 1848; founded presbyterian congregation in Bayswater, London, 1860; wrote chiefly on religious subjects. [xxxi. 126]

KING, SIR EDMUND (1629-1709), physician; published results of his researches and experiments in the 'Philosophical Transactions,' 1667, 1670, 1686, and 1688; incorporated at Cambridge, 1671; knighted, 1676; physician to Charles II, 1676; F.R.C.P., 1687; attended Charles II in his last illness. [xxxi. 127]

KING, EDWARD (1612-1637), friend of Milton; younger son of Sir John King (d. 1637) [q. v.]; educated at Christ's College, Cambridge; fellow, 1630; prælector and tutor, 1633-4; perished in a shipwreck off the Welsh coast when on the way to Ireland, 1637; commemorated by Milton in 'Lycidas.' [xxxi. 128]

KING, EDWARD (1735?-1807), miscellaneous writer; studied at Clare College, Cambridge; barrister, Lincoln's Inn, 1763; F.R.S., 1767; F.S.A., 1770; contributed papers to the 'Archæologia' (reprinted separately, 1774 and 1782); interim P.S.A., 1784; his most important work, 'Munimenta Antiqua, or Observations on ancient Castles,' 1799-1806. [xxxi. 129]

KING, EDWARD, VISCOUNT KINGSBOROUGH (1795-1837), educated at Exeter College, Oxford; M.P., co. Cork, 1818 and 1820-6; promoted and edited 'Antiquities of Mexico,' a magnificent work in nine volumes, published, 1830-48. [xxxi. 130]

KING, MRS. FRANCES ELIZABETH (1757-1821), author; married Richard King (1748-1810) [q. v.], 1782; assisted Hannah More in charitable work; chief work, 'Female Scripture Characters,' 1813 (10th ed. 1826). [xxxi. 151]

KING, SIR GEORGE ST. VINCENT DUCKWORTH (d. 1891), admiral; son of Sir Richard King the younger [q. v.]; succeeded to baronetcy, 1847; in the Crimean war, 1854-5; rear-admiral, 1863; commander-in-chief in China, 1863-7; vice-admiral, 1867, and admiral, 1875; K.C.B. [xxxi. 151]

KING, GREGORY (1648-1712), herald, genealogist, engraver, and statesman; educated at Lichfield grammar school; became clerk to Sir William Dugdale [q. v.], 1662; Rouge Dragon pursuivant, 1677; registrar of the College of Arms, 1684-94; published heraldic and genealogical works; his 'Natural and Political Observations and Conclusions upon the State and Condition of England,' published, 1696. [xxxi. 131]

KING, HENRY (1592-1669), bishop of Chichester; son of John King (1559?-1621) [q. v.]; educated at Westminster; M.A. Christ Church, Oxford, 1614; prebendary of St. Paul's, London, 1616; archdeacon of Colchester, 1617; a royal chaplain, 1617; canon of Christ Church, Oxford, 1624; D.D., 1625; dean of Rochester, 1639; bishop of Chichester, 1642; friend of Izaak Walton, Jonson, and Donne; published poems and sermons. [xxxi. 133]

KING, HUMPHREY (fl. 1613), verse-writer; author of 'An Halfe-penny-worth of Wit, in a Pennyworth of Paper. Or, the Hermites Tale. The third impression,' 1613. [xxxi. 134]

KING, JAMES, first BARON EYTHIN (1589?-1652), entered service of king of Sweden and was 'general-major' by 1632; joined Rupert and the Prince Palatine, 1638; recalled to England, 1640; created peer of Scotland as Baron Eythin and Kerrey, 1643; lieutenant-general, 1650; died in Sweden. [xxxi. 135]

KING, JAMES (1750-1784), captain in the navy; entered navy, 1762; lieutenant, 1771; accompanied Cook as astronomer and second lieutenant, 1776; captain, 1779; advanced to post rank, 1780; sent to West Indies with convoy of merchant ships, 1781; prepared Cook's journal of the third voyage for the press; F.R.S., and his 'Astronomical Observations,' published, 1782; died at Nice. [xxxi. 136]

KING, JOHN (1559?-1621), bishop of London; of Westminster and Christ Church, Oxford; M.A., 1583; B.D., 1591; prebendary of St. Paul's and one of Elizabeth's chaplains, 1599; D.D., 1601; dean of Christ Church, Oxford, 1605; vice-chancellor of Oxford, 1607-10; bishop of London, 1611-21; contributed to Oxford collections of poems and printed sermons. [xxxi. 136]

KING, SIR JOHN (d. 1637), Irish administrator; secretary to Sir Richard Bingham [q. v.], governor of Connaught, 1585; deputy vice-treasurer, 1605; muster-master-general and clerk of the cheque for Ireland, 1609; privy councillor and knighted, 1609; M.P., co. Roscommon, 1613. [xxxi. 138]

KING, JOHN (1595-1639), divine; son of John King (1559?-1621) [q. v.]; of Westminster and Christ Church, Oxford; M.A., 1614; prebendary of St. Paul's, 1616; public orator of Oxford, 1622; canon of Christ Church, 1624; D.D., 1625; archdeacon of Colchester, 1625; canon of Windsor, 1625; published Latin orations, 1623 and 1625, and poems in the university collections of 1613 and 1619. [xxxi. 137]

KING, JOHN, first BARON KINGSTON (d. 1676), eldest son of Sir Robert King [q. v.]; engaged in behalf of parliament in Irish war; knighted, 1658; created an Irish peer, 1660; privy councillor of Ireland, 1660; commissary-general of the horse, 1661; governor of Connaught, 1666. [xxxi. 139]

KING, SIR JOHN (1639–1677), lawyer; educated at Eton; of Queens' College, Cambridge; barrister, Inner Temple, 1667; bencher and knighted, 1674; treasurer, 1675; king's counsel and attorney-general to the Duke of York.   [xxxi. 139]

KING, JOHN (d. 1679), covenanting preacher; tried for holding conventicles, 1674; outlawed, 1675; executed, 1679.   [xxxi. 139]

KING, JOHN (1696–1728), classical writer; eldest son of John King (1652–1732) [q. v.]; of Eton and King's College, Cambridge; M.A., 1722, and fellow; published 'Euripidis Hecuba, Orestes et Phœnissæ,' 1726.
                [xxxi. 140]

KING, JOHN (1652–1732), miscellaneous writer; of Exeter College, Oxford; M.A., 1680; ordained; D.D. Cambridge, 1698; prebendary of York, 1718; published controversial pamphlets.   [xxxi. 140]

KING, JOHN (1788–1847), painter; entered the Royal Academy schools, 1810; exhibited at the British Institution, 1814, Royal Academy, 1817.   [xxxi. 141]

KING, JOHN DUNCAN (1789–1863), captain (1830) in the army and landscape-painter; served in the Walcheren expedition, 1809, and the Peninsular war; exhibited at the Royal Academy and British Institution between 1824 and 1858.   [xxxi. 141]

KING, JOHN GLEN (1732–1787), divine; educated at Caius College, Cambridge; M.A., 1763; chaplain to the English factory at St. Petersburg; F.S.A., F.R.S., and incorporated M.A. Oxford, 1771; D.D. Oxford, 1771; published verses in the Cambridge collection of 1752 and antiquarian works.   [xxxi. 141]

KING, MATTHEW PETER (1773–1823), musical composer; composed glees, ballads, pianoforte pieces, and one oratorio; wrote treatise on music, 1800.   [xxxi. 142]

KING, OLIVER (d. 1503), bishop of Bath and Wells; of Eton and King's College, Cambridge; French secretary to Edward IV, 1476; canon of Windsor, 1480; archdeacon of Oxford, 1482; deprived of secretaryship by Richard III, and imprisoned, 1483; reinstated by Henry VII, 1485; bishop of Exeter, 1493, and of Bath and Wells, 1495.
                [xxxi. 142]

KING, PAUL (d. 1655), Irish Franciscan; in early life captive among the Moors; taught moral theology at Brindisi, 1641; guardian of Kilkenny convent, 1644; unsuccessfully attempted to betray it to Owen Roe O'Neill [q. v.] and fled; guardian of St. Isidore's, Rome, 1649; published Latin writings; died probably at Rome.
                [xxxi. 143]

KING, PETER, first BARON KING of Ockham in Surrey (1669–1734), lord chancellor; published anonymously 'An Enquiry into the Constitution, Discipline, Unity and Worship of the Primitive Church,' &c., 1691; barrister, Middle Temple, 1698; M.P., Beeralston, Devonshire, 1701; recorder of London and knighted, 1708; assisted at the impeachment of Sacheverell, 1710; defended William Whiston [q. v.] on his trial for heresy, 1713; chief-justice of common pleas, 1714; privy councillor, 1715; raised to the peerage, 1725; lord chancellor, 1725–33; procured substitution of English for Latin in writs and similar documents. His 'History of the Apostles' Creed' (1702) was the first attempt to trace the evolution of the creed.   [xxxi. 144]

KING, PETER, seventh BARON KING of Ockham in Surrey (1776–1833), great-grandson of Peter King, first baron King [q. v.]; educated at Eton and Trinity College, Cambridge; succeeded to the title, 1793; published pamphlet on the currency question, 1803, enlarged, 1804, and reprinted, 1844; published 'Life of John Locke,' 1829.   [xxxi. 147]

KING, PETER JOHN LOCKE (1811–1885), politician; second son of Peter King, seventh baron King [q. v.]; of Harrow and Trinity College, Cambridge; M.A., 1833; M.P., East Surrey, 1847–74; passed the Real Estate Charges Act, 1854; advocated ballot and abolition of church rates; published works on legal reforms.
                [xxxi. 148]

KING, PHILIP GIDLEY (1758–1808), first governor of Norfolk island, and governor of New South Wales; served in the East Indies and Virginia; lieutenant, 1778;

served with Captain Philip in the famous 'first fleet' which sailed for Australia, 1787; commandant of Norfolk island, 1788; lieutenant-governor, 1790; governor of New South Wales, 1800–6.   [xxxi. 148]

KING, PHILIP PARKER (1793–1856), rear-admiral; son of Philip Gidley King [q. v.]; born at Norfolk island; entered navy, 1807; lieutenant, 1814; conducted survey of coast of Australia, 1817–22; commander, 1821; F.R.S., 1824; surveyed the southern coast of South America, 1825; published narrative and charts of the survey of the western coasts of Australia, 1827; advanced to post rank, 1830; published 'Sailing Directions to the Coasts of Eastern and Western Patagonia,' &c., 1831; settled in Sydney; rear-admiral on retired list, 1855. [xxxi. 149]

KING, SIR RICHARD, the elder, first baronet (1730–1806), admiral; nephew of Commodore Curtis Barnett [q. v.]; entered navy, 1738; served in the Mediterranean and the East Indies; lieutenant, 1746; in command of the landing party at the capture of Calcutta and Hoogly, 1757; distinguished in action off Sadras, 1782; knighted; rear-admiral, 1787; created baronet and appointed governor and commander-in-chief at Newfoundland, 1792; vice-admiral, 1793; M.P., Rochester, 1793; admiral, 1795.   [xxxi. 150]

KING, RICHARD (1748–1810), divine; of Winchester and Queen's College, Oxford; fellow of New College, 1768; M.A., 1776; held livings in Cambridgeshire; wrote, among other things, 'Brother Abraham's Answer to Peter Plymley,' 1808.   [xxxi. 151]

KING, SIR RICHARD, the younger, second baronet (1774–1834), vice-admiral; son of Sir Richard King the elder [q. v.]; entered navy, 1788; lieutenant, 1791; commander, 1793; captain, 1794; present at Trafalgar, 1805; succeeded to baronetcy, 1806; rear-admiral, 1812; K.C.B., 1815; commander-in-chief in East Indies, 1816–20; vice-admiral, 1821.   [xxxi. 151]

KING, RICHARD (1811 ?–1876), arctic traveller and ethnologist; educated at Guy's and St. Thomas's hospitals, London; M.R.C.S. and L.S.A., 1832; surgeon and naturalist to expedition of Sir George Back [q. v.] to Great Fish River, 1833–5; published 'Narrative of a Journey to the Shore of the Arctic Ocean,' 1836; originated the Ethnological Society, 1842; its first secretary, 1844; assistant-surgeon to the Resolute in expedition to find Franklin, 1850; received the Arctic medal, 1857; published summary of his correspondence with the admiralty concerning the Franklin expedition, 1855; author of works on the Esquimaux, Laplanders, and natives of Vancouver's island.   [xxxi. 152]

KING, RICHARD JOHN (1818–1879), antiquary; B.A. Exeter College, Oxford, 1841; expert in the literature and history of the west country; contributed to Murray's handbooks to the English counties and cathedrals, to 'Saturday Review,' 'Quarterly Review,' and 'Fraser's Magazine'; a selection from his articles published, 1874.
                [xxxi. 152]

KING, ROBERT (d. 1557), bishop of Oxford; joined the Cistercians; B.D., 1507; D.D., 1519; prebendary of Lincoln, 1535; bishop of Oseney and Thame, c. 1541; bishop of Oxford, 1545–57; sat at Cranmer's trial.
                [xxxi. 153]

KING, SIR ROBERT (1599 ?–1657), Irish soldier and statesman; eldest son of Sir John King (d. 1637) [q. v.]; mustermaster-general and clerk of the cheque in Ireland; knighted, 1621; M.P., Boyle, 1634, 1639; M.P., co. Roscommon, 1640; sent to manage the parliament's affairs in Ulster, 1645; member of the council of state, 1653; sat in Cromwell's parliament for cos. Sligo, Roscommon, and Leitrim, 1654.   [xxxi. 154]

KING, ROBERT (1600–1676), master of Trinity Hall, Cambridge; entered Christ's College, Cambridge, 1617; M.A., 1624; fellow of Trinity Hall, 1625; LL.D., 1630; master of Trinity Hall, 1660.   [xxxi. 155]

KING, ROBERT, second BARON KINGSTON (d. 1693), eldest son of John King, first baron Kingston [q. v.]; M.A. Brasenose College, Oxford, 1670; endowed a college in co. Roscommon to be called Kingston College.
                [xxxi. 155]

KING, ROBERT (fl. 1684–1711), composer; member of the band of music to William and Mary, and afterwards to Queen Anne; Mus.Bac. Cambridge, 1696; composed songs.   [xxxi. 156]

KING, ROBERT, second EARL OF KINGSTON (1754–1799), as Viscount Kingsborough was M.P. for co. Cork, 1783, 1790, and 1798; shot dead (1797) Henry Gerard Fitzgerald, an illegitimate son of his wife's brother, with whom his daughter had eloped; tried and acquitted by House of Lords, 1798. [xxxi. 156]

KING, SAMUEL WILLIAM (1821–1868), traveller and man of science; M.A. St. Catharine's College, Cambridge, 1853; entomologist and geologist; published 'The Italian Valleys of the Pennine Alps,' 1858; died at Pontresina. [xxxi. 157]

KING, THOMAS (d. 1769), portrait-painter; pupil of George Knapton [q. v.] [xxxi. 157]

KING, THOMAS (1730–1805), actor and dramatist; educated at Westminster; bred to the law, which he abandoned for the stage; engaged by Garrick for Drury Lane Theatre, 1748; acted under Sheridan at Smock Alley Theatre, Dublin, 1750–8; again at Drury Lane, 1759–1802; the original Sir Peter Teazle in the first representation of the 'School for Scandal,' 1777; played Puff in the first performance of the 'Critic,' 1779; connected with the management of Drury Lane and Sadler's Wells theatres; played Touchstone, 1789, and Falstaff, 1792; ruined himself by gambling and died in poverty; excellent in parts embracing the whole range of comedy. [xxxi. 157]

KING, THOMAS (1835–1888), prizefighter; served as seaman in navy and merchant service; coached by the ex-champion, Jem Ward; defeated Tommy Truckle of Portsmouth, 1860; defeated William Evans, 1861; defeated by Jem Mace, but won a return match, 1862; defeated American champion John Camel Heenan, the 'Benicia Boy,' 1863; retired from prize-ring and set up successfully as bookmaker. [Suppl. iii. 63]

KING, THOMAS CHISWELL (1818–1893), actor; apprenticed as painter and paperhanger at Cheltenham; entered theatrical profession; appeared first in London at Princess's, 1850, as Bassanio (in 'Merchant of Venice'); leading actor at Theatre Royal, Dublin, 1851–6; played successfully at Birmingham, 1856, Manchester, 1857, Queen's Theatre, Dublin, 1859, City of London Theatre, 1860, and in various provincial towns, 1861–8; at Drury Lane Theatre, 1869–70, and Adelphi, 1871; appeared at Lyceum Theatre, New York, 1873; toured with success in Canada, giving exclusively Shakespearean plays, 1873–4; lessee of Worcester Theatre, 1878–80; exponent of the school of tragedians which subordinated intelligence to precept and tradition. [Suppl. iii. 64]

KING, WILLIAM (1624–1680), musician; entered Magdalen College, Oxford, 1684; B.A., 1649; probationer-fellow of All Souls College, 1654; incorporated M.A. at Cambridge, 1655; organist at New College, Oxford, 1664–1680; composed church music; set to music Cowley's 'Mistress' (1668). [xxxi. 161]

KING, WILLIAM (1663–1712), miscellaneous writer; of Westminster and Christ Church, Oxford; M.A., 1688; D.C.L. and admitted advocate at Doctors' Commons, 1692; published 'Dialogues of the Dead' (attack on Bentley), 1699; judge of the admiralty court in Ireland, 1701–7; gazetteer, 1711. [xxxi. 161]

KING, WILLIAM (1650–1729), archbishop of Dublin; M.A. Trinity College, Dublin, 1673; D.D., 1689; dean of St. Patrick's, 1689; became an ardent whig; bishop of Derry, 1691; published his 'State of the Protestants of Ireland under the late King James's Government,' a powerful vindication of the principles of the revolution, 1691; his *magnum opus*, 'De Origine Mali,' published, 1702; archbishop of Dublin, 1703; founded Archbishop King's lectureship in divinity at Trinity College, Dublin, 1718. [xxxi. 163]

KING, WILLIAM (1685–1763), principal of St. Mary Hall, Oxford; entered Balliol College, Oxford, 1701; D.C.L., 1715; principal of St. Mary Hall, 1719; wrote several satires highly praised by Swift, as well as 'The Toast,' a mock-heroic poem (Dublin, 1732); supported Jacobitism; collected editions of his writings published, 1760. [xxxi. 167]

KING, WILLIAM (1701–1769), independent minister; educated at Utrecht University; returned to England, 1724; ordained, 1725; Merchants' lecturer at Pinners' Hall, 1748. [xxxi. 170]

KING, WILLIAM (1786–1865), promoter of co-operation; of Peterhouse, Cambridge; M.A., 1812; M.D. Cambridge, 1819; F.R.C.S., 1820; wrote a monthly magazine, 'The Co-operator,' 1828–30, unequalled by any publication of the kind; Harveian orator, 1843; friend and adviser of Lady Byron. [xxxi. 170]

KING, WILLIAM (1809–1886), geologist and lecturer on geology in the School of Medicine; curator of the Museum of Natural History at Newcastle-on-Tyne, 1841; professor of geology at Queen's College, Galway, 1849; and of natural history, 1882–3; D.Sc. of the Queen's University of Ireland, 1870; his chief published work, 'Monograph of the Permian Fossils' (1850). [xxxi. 170]

KINGHORN, JOSEPH (1766–1832), particular baptist minister; apprenticed to watch and clock making, 1779; clerk in white-lead works at Elswick, 1781; baptised, 1783; entered baptist academy at Bristol, 1784; minister at Norwich, 1789; published theological works. [xxxi. 171]

KINGHORNE, third EARL OF (1642–1695). [See LYON, PATRICK.]

KINGLAKE, ALEXANDER WILLIAM (1809–1891), historian of the Crimean war; educated at Eton; entered Trinity College, Cambridge, 1828; made the Eastern tour described in 'Eōthen' (published, 1844), 1835; M.A., 1836; barrister, Lincoln's Inn, 1837; went to Algiers and accompanied flying column of St. Arnaud, 1845; followed the English expedition to the Crimea; present at the battle of the Alma, 1854; was invited to undertake the history of the campaign by Lady Raglan, 1856; vols. i. and ii. of the 'Invasion of the Crimea' published, 1863; vols. iii. and iv., 1868; vol. v., 1875; vol. vi., 1880; vols. vii. and viii., 1887; M.P., Bridgewater, 1857–65; his history marked by literary ability and skill in dealing with technical details. [xxxi. 171]

KINGLAKE, ROBERT (1765–1842), medical writer; M.D. Göttingen; also studied at Edinburgh; advocated the cooling treatment in his writings on gout. [xxxi. 173]

KINGSBOROUGH, VISCOUNT (1795–1837). [See KING, EDWARD.]

KINGSBURY, WILLIAM (1744–1818), dissenting minister; educated at Merchant Taylors' School and Christ's Hospital, London; 'converted,' 1760; preached his first sermon, 1763; published his one controversial work, 'The Manner in which Protestant Dissenters perform Prayer in Public Worship vindicated,' 1796; a friend of John Howard (1726?–1790) [q. v.] and John Newton (1725–1807) [q. v.]; published several funeral sermons. [xxxi. 173]

KINGSCOTE, HENRY ROBERT (1802–1882), philanthropist; educated at Harrow; president of the M.C.C., 1827; instrumental in founding Church of England Scripture Readers' Association and Metropolitan Visiting and Relief Association; published pamphlet letter to the archbishop of Canterbury on the needs of the church, 1846; helped in alleviating Irish distress, 1847; sent out supplies to troops in the Crimea, 1854; one of the founders of the British and Colonial Emigration Society, 1868. [xxxi. 174]

KINGSDOWN, first BARON (1793–1867). [See PEMBERTON-LEIGH, THOMAS.]

KINGSFORD, MRS. ANNA (1846–1888), doctor of medicine and religious writer; *née* Bonus; married Algernon Godfrey Kingsford, vicar of Atcham, Shropshire, 1867; wrote stories in the 'Penny Post,' 1868–1872; turned Roman catholic, 1870; purchased the 'Lady's Own Paper,' 1872; edited it, 1872–3; studied medicine at Paris, 1874; M.D., 1880; practised in London; president of the Theosophical Society, 1883; founded Hermetic Society, 1884; published miscellaneous works between 1863 and 1881. [xxxi. 174]

KINGSFORD, WILLIAM (1819–1898), historian of Canada; articled as architect; enlisted in 1st dragoon guards, 1836; served in Canada; obtained discharge, 1840; qualified as civil engineer at Montreal; obtained post of deputy city surveyor; worked in connection with Grand Trunk and other railways; dominion engineer in charge of harbours of the lakes and the St. Lawrence, 1872–9; summarily cashiered by Sir Hector

Langevin, 1879 ; devoted himself to writing ' History of
Canada,' published, 1887-98 ; LL.D. Queen's University,
Kingston and Dalhousie ; F.R.S. Canada.
[Suppl. iii. 65]

KINGSLAND, VISCOUNTS. [See BARNEWALL,
NICHOLAS, first VISCOUNT, 1592-1663 ; BARNEWALL,
NICHOLAS, third VISCOUNT, 1668-1725.]

KINGSLEY, CHARLES (1819-1875), author ; student at King's College, London, 1836 ; entered Magdalene
College, Cambridge, 1838 ; curate of Eversley, Hampshire,
1842 ; married Fanny Grenfell and accepted living of
Eversley, 1844 ; published 'St. Elizabeth of Hungary,' a
drama, 1848 ; joined with Maurice and his friends in their
attempt at Christian socialism, 1848 ; lecturer on English
literature at Queen's College, London, 1848-9 ; contributed,
over the signature of 'Parson Lot,' to 'Politics for the
People,' 1848, and to the 'Christian Socialist,' 1850-1 ;
his 'Yeast' published, 1848, 'Alton Locke,' 1850 ; never
sympathised with the distinctively revolutionary movement ; published 'Hypatia,' 1853 ; 'Westward Ho !'
1855 ; 'Two Years Ago,' 1857 ; one of the queen's
chaplains in ordinary, 1859 ; professor of modern history
at Cambridge, 1860-9 ; published 'Water Babies,' 1863 ; engaged in a controversy with John Henry Newman [q. v.],
which led Newman to write his ' Apologia,' 1864 ; canon
of Chester, 1869 ; visited the West Indies, 1869 ; published
'At Last,' 1870 ; canon of Westminster, 1873 ; visited
America, 1874 ; his enthusiasm for natural history
shown by 'Glaucus, or the Wonders of the Shore'
(1855), and similar works ; a believer in the possibility of
reconciling religion and science.   [xxxi. 175]

KINGSLEY, GEORGE HENRY (1827-1892), traveller and author ; brother of Charles Kingsley [q. v.]
and of Henry Kingsley [q. v.] ; educated at King's
College school, London, and Edinburgh University ; M.D.
Edinburgh, 1846 ; graduated also at Paris, 1845 ; his
activity during the outbreak of cholera in England in
1848 commemorated by his brother Charles in the character of Tom Thurnall in ' Two Years Ago' ; adopting
foreign travel as his method of treatment of individual
patients, explored most of the countries of the world ;
his most successful book, 'South Sea Bubbles by the Earl
[of Pembroke] and the Doctor,' appeared, 1872 ; edited
from a manuscript at Bridgewater House, Francis
Thynne's 'Animadversions upon the Annotacions and
Corrections of some Imperfections of Impressiones of
Chaucer's Workes,' 1865.   [xxxi. 181]

KINGSLEY, HENRY (1830-1876), novelist ; brother
of Charles Kingsley [q. v.] and of George Henry Kingsley
[q. v.] ; educated at King's College, London ; entered
Worcester College, Oxford, 1850 ; at the Australian goldfields, 1853-8 ; published 'Geoffrey Hamlyn,' 1859, ' Ravens-
hoe,' 1861 ; edited 'Edinburgh Daily Review' after 1864 ;
correspondent for his paper in the Franco-German war ;
present at Sedan, 1870 ; wrote sixteen novels and tales
between 1863 and 1876.   [xxxi. 181]

KINGSLEY, MARY HENRIETTA (1862-1900),
traveller and writer ; daughter of George Henry Kingsley [q. v.] ; lived successively at Highgate and Bexley
in Kent (1879), Cambridge (1886), and Addison Road,
London ; educated at home ; made journeys to West
Coast of Africa, visiting Ambriz, the Congo river, and
Old Calabar, 1893-4, and to Old Calabar, Congo Français,
the Ogowé river, Agonjo and Lake Ncovi, ascending
the mountain of Mungo Mah Lobeh, 1894-5 ; formed
valuable zoological collections and made careful notes
and observations, which she subsequently utilised in
published works and lectures ; visited Cape Town during
Boer war, 1900 ; attached as nurse to Simon's Town
Palace Hospital for sick Boer prisoners ; died of enteric
fever. Her publications include ' Travels in West
Africa,' 1897.   [Suppl. iii. 67]

KINGSLEY, WILLIAM (1698?-1769), lieutenant-
general ; cornet, 1721 ; lieutenant and captain, 1721 ;
captain-lieutenant, 1743 ; captain and lieutenant-colonel,
1745 ; present at the battles of Dettingen, 1743 and Fontenoy, 1745, and took part in the 'march to Finchley,'
1745 ; brevet-colonel, 1750 ; regimental major with the
rank of colonel of foot, 1751 ; colonel, 1756 ; distinguished
himself at Minden, 1759 ; lieutenant-general, 1760 ; his
portrait painted by Reynolds.   [xxxi. 182]

KINGSMILL, ANDREW (1538-1569), puritan divine ;
of Corpus Christi College, Oxford ; fellow of All Souls,
1558 ; B.C.L., 1563 ; left the study of civil law for the
ministry ; died at Lausanne ; wrote devotional works.
[xxxi. 183]

KINGSMILL, SIR ROBERT BRICE, first baronet
(1730-1805), admiral ; son of Charles Brice ; lieutenant,
1756 ; commander, 1761 ; took part in the reduction of
Martinique and St. Lucia, 1762 ; his wife succeeding to
the estates of her grandfather, William Kingsmill, assumed the name of Kingsmill, 1766 ; fought off Ushant,
1778 ; M.P., Tregony, 1784 ; rear-admiral, 1793 ; commander-in-chief on coast of Ireland, 1793-1800 ; vice-
admiral, 1794 ; admiral, 1799 ; created baronet, 1800.
[xxxi. 183]

KINGSMILL, THOMAS (fl. 1605), regius professor
of Hebrew at Oxford ; educated at Magdalen College,
Oxford ; probationer-fellow, 1559-68 ; M.A., 1564 ; natural
philosophy lecturer, 1563 ; Hebrew lecturer and public
orator, 1565 ; junior dean of arts, 1567 ; regius professor
of Hebrew, 1570-91 ; B.D., 1572 ; published pamphlets and
sermons.   [xxxi. 184]

KINGSNORTH, RICHARD (d. 1677), baptist
minister ; a Kentish farmer.   [xxxi. 184]

KINGSTHORPE, RICHARD (fl. 1224). [See ING-
WORTH.]

KINGSTON, DUKES OF. [See PIERREPONT, EVELYN,
first DUKE, 1665?-1726 ; PIERREPONT, EVELYN, second
DUKE, 1711-1773.]

KINGSTON, self-styled DUCHESS OF (1720-1788).
[See CHUDLEIGH, ELIZABETH.]

KINGSTON, EARLS OF, in the peerage of England.
[See PIERREPONT, ROBERT, first EARL, 1584-1643 ;
PIERREPONT, HENRY, second EARL, 1606-1680 ; PIERRE-
PONT, EVELYN, fifth EARL, 1665 ?-1726.]

KINGSTON, EARL OF, in the peerage of Ireland
(1754-1799). [See KING, ROBERT, second EARL.]

KINGSTON, VISCOUNT, in the peerage of Scotland.
[See SETON, ALEXANDER, first VISCOUNT, 1621 ?-1691.]

KINGSTON, BARONS. [See KING, JOHN, first
BARON, d. 1676 ; KING, ROBERT, second BARON, d. 1693.]

KINGSTON, SIR ANTHONY (1519-1556), provost-
marshal in Cornwall ; son of Sir William Kingston
[q. v.] ; served in Pilgrimage of Grace, 1536-7 ; knighted,
1537 ; M.P., Gloucestershire, 1545, 1552-3, and 1555 ;
provost-marshal of the king's army in Cornwall, 1549 ;
sent to the Tower on charge of conspiring to put Elizabeth on the throne, but soon discharged, 1555 ; concerned
in plot to rob the exchequer for the same purpose, 1556 ;
died on his way to trial in London.   [xxxi. 185]

KINGSTON, RICHARD (fl. 1700), political pamphleteer ; chaplain in ordinary to Charles II, 1682 ; author
of controversial pamphlets.   [xxxi. 185]

KINGSTON, SIR WILLIAM (d. 1540), constable of
the Tower ; fought at Flodden, 1513 ; knighted, 1513 ;
took part in the Field of the Cloth of Gold ; captain of
the guard, 1523 ; constable of the Tower, 1524 ; brought
Wolsey to London, 1530 ; received Anne Boleyn in the
Tower, 1536 ; controller of the household, 1539 ; K.G.,
1539.   [xxxi. 186]

KINGSTON, WILLIAM HENRY GILES (1814-1880),
novelist ; grandson of Sir Giles Rooke [q. v.] ; spent
much of his youth in sports ; wrote newspaper articles
which assisted the conclusion of the commercial treaty
with Portugal, 1842 ; received order of Portuguese
knighthood and a pension from Donna Maria de Gloria ;
his first story, 'The Circassian Chief,' published, 1844 ;
edited ' The Colonist,' 1844, and ' The Colonial Magazine
and East India Review,' 1844 ; published 'How to
Emigrate,' 1850 ; wrote many books for boys, and edited
boys' annuals and weekly periodicals.   [xxxi. 187]

KINLOCH, GEORGE RITCHIE (1796 ?-1877), editor
of 'Ancient Scottish Ballads' ; became a lawyer ; his
'Ancient Scottish Ballads, recovered from Tradition, and
never before published,' issued, 1827 ; keeper of the register of deeds in Edinburgh Register House, 1851-69.
[xxxi. 188]

KINLOCH, LORD (1801-1872). [See PENNEY, WIL-
LIAM.]

KINLOSS, LORD (1549 ?–1611). [See BRUCE, EDWARD.]

KINMONT, WILLIE (*fl.* 1596). [See ARMSTRONG, WILLIAM.]

KINNAIRD, ARTHUR FITZGERALD, tenth BARON KINNAIRD (1814–1887), philanthropist; son of Charles Kinnaird, eighth baron Kinnaird [q. v.]; at Eton; attached to English embassy at St. Petersburg, 1835–7; partner in banking house of Ransom & Co. in succession to his uncle, Douglas James William Kinnaird [q. v.], 1837; M.P., Perth, 1837–9 and 1852–78; succeeded his brother, George William Fox Kinnaird [q. v.], as Baron Kinnaird, 1878; keenly interested in the well-being of the working classes. [xxxi. 188]

KINNAIRD, CHARLES, eighth BARON KINNAIRD (1780–1826), educated at Edinburgh, Cambridge, and Glasgow universities; M.P., Leominster, 1802–5; succeeded to the title, 1805; Scottish representative peer, 1806. [xxxi. 189]

KINNAIRD, DOUGLAS JAMES WILLIAM (1788–1830), friend of Byron; younger brother of Charles Kinnaird, eighth baron Kinnaird [q. v.]; educated at Eton, Göttingen, and Trinity College, Cambridge; M.A., 1811; travelled with John Cam Hobhouse [q. v.] and William Jerdan [q. v.], 1813–14; visited Byron at Venice, 1817; assumed chief management of Ransom's bank, 1819; M.P., Bishops Castle, Shropshire, 1819; author of a comedy and a pamphlet on Indian affairs. [xxxi. 189]

KINNAIRD, GEORGE PATRICK, first BARON KINNAIRD (*d.* 1689), supporter of Charles II; knighted, 1661; represented Perthshire in Scottish parliament, 1662–3; privy councillor; raised to peerage, 1682. [xxxi. 190]

KINNAIRD, GEORGE WILLIAM FOX, ninth BARON KINNAIRD (1807–1878), eldest son of Charles Kinnaird, eighth baron Kinnaird [q. v.]; at Eton; entered the army; resigned and succeeded to the Scottish peerage, 1826; created peer of the United Kingdom, 1831; privy councillor, 1840; K.T., 1857; lord-lieutenant of Perthshire, 1866; introduced agricultural reforms on his estate; did much to ameliorate condition of the labouring classes. [xxxi. 191]

KINNAIRD, MARY JANE, LADY (1816–1888), philanthropist; *née* Hoare; wife of Arthur Fitzgerald Kinnaird, tenth Baron Kinnaird [q. v.]; edited 'Servants' Prayers,' 1848; associated with Lady Canning in sending aid to the wounded in the Crimea; one of the founders of the Young Women's Christian Association. [xxxi. 189]

KINNEDER, LORD (1769–1822). [See ERSKINE, WILLIAM.]

KINNEIR, SIR JOHN MACDONALD (1782–1830), lieutenant-colonel H.E.I.C.S., traveller, and diplomatist; son of John Macdonald; ensign in Madras infantry, 1804; lieutenant, 1807; travelled in Persia, Armenia, and Kurdistan, 1813–14; published narrative of his travels; captain, 1818; took his mother's surname of Kinneir; envoy to Persia, 1824–30, and took part in the hostilities with Russia; knighted, 1829. [xxxi. 192]

KINNOULL, EARLS OF. [See HAY, SIR GEORGE, first EARL, 1572–1634; HAY, GEORGE, seventh EARL, *d.* 1758; HAY, THOMAS, eighth EARL, 1710–1787.]

KINSEY, WILLIAM MORGAN (1788–1851), divine and traveller; scholar of Trinity College, Oxford, 1805; M.A., 1813; fellow, 1815; dean of file and B.D., 1822; vice-president, 1823; bursar, 1824; travelled in Portugal, 1827; published 'Portugal Illustrated,' 1828 (2nd edit. 1829); witnessed outbreak of revolution at Brussels, 1830. [xxxi. 193]

KINSIUS (*d.* 1060). [See KYNSIGE.]

KINTORE, first EARL OF (*d.* 1714). [See KEITH, SIR JOHN.]

KINWELMERSH, KYNWELMERSH, or KINDLEMARSH, FRANCIS (*d.* 1580 ?), poet; produced, with the poet George Gascoigne [q. v.], a blank-verse rendering of Euripides's 'Phœnissæ,' entitled 'Jocasta,' 1566 (published, 1572); M.P., Bossiney, Cornwall, 1572; contributed to the 'Paradyse of Daynty Devises,' 1576. [xxxi. 193]

KIP, JOHANNES (1653–1722), draughtsman and engraver; born at Amsterdam; came to London shortly after 1686; employed in engraving portraits; most important work, 'Britannia Illustrata,' a series of etchings from drawings by Leonard Knyff [q. v.], 1708, of little artistic merit, but great archæological interest; published a 'Prospect of the City of London,' 1710 (2nd edit. 1726). [xxxi. 194]

KIPLING, THOMAS (*d.* 1822), dean of Peterborough; fellow of St. John's College, Cambridge, 1770; M.A., 1771; Lady Margaret's preacher, 1782; D.D., 1784; deputy regius professor of divinity, 1787; Boyle lecturer, 1792; promoted prosecution of the Rev. William Frend [q. v.], 1792; dean of Peterborough, 1798–1802; principal work, an edition of the 'Codex Bezæ,' 1793. [xxxi. 194]

KIPPIS, ANDREW (1725–1795), nonconformist divine and biographer; classical and philological tutor, Coward Academy, Hoxton, 1763–84; D.D. Edinburgh, 1767; F.S.A., 1778; F.R.S., 1779; tutor in new dissenting college at Hackney, 1786; his chief literary work, the preparation of the second edition of the 'Biographia Britannica' (five volumes published between 1778 and 1793, first part of a sixth volume printed, 1795); contributed to the 'Gentleman's Magazine,' 'Monthly Review,' and 'New Annual Register.' [xxxi. 195]

KIPPIST, RICHARD (1812–1882), botanist; helped to compile the 'Tourist's Flora'; librarian of the Linnean Society, 1842–81; specialist in Australian plants. [xxxi. 197]

KIRBY, ELIZABETH (1823–1873), authoress, with her sister Mrs. Gregg, of stories for children. [xxxi. 198]

KIRBY, JOHN (1690–1753), Suffolk topographer; published 'The Suffolk Traveller,' a road book with antiquarian notices, 1735 (new edition, 1764; reprint, 1800; fourth edition, 1829); issued a 'Map of the County of Suffolk,' 1736; an improved edition published by his sons, 1766; his portrait painted by Gainsborough. [xxxi. 198]

KIRBY, JOHN JOSHUA (1716–1774), clerk of the works at Kew Palace; eldest son of John Kirby [q. v.]; coach and house painter at Ipswich, 1738; published twelve drawings for projected history of Suffolk, 1748; lectured on linear perspective; published 'Dr. Brook Taylor's Method of Perspective made easy,' 1754 (reissued, 1755, 1765, and 1768); teacher of perspective to the Prince of Wales, afterwards George III; published 'The Perspective of Architecture,' 1761; secretary to the Incorporated Society of Artists; exhibited with them, 1765–70; president, 1768; portraits of him painted by Gainsborough and Hogarth. [xxxi. 198]

KIRBY, SARAH (1741–1810). [See TRIMMER.]

KIRBY, WILLIAM (1759–1850), entomologist; nephew of John Joshua Kirby [q. v.]; educated at Caius College, Cambridge; B.A., 1781; an original F.L.S., 1788; published monograph on bees, 1802; founded new insect order of *Strepsiptera*, 1811; M.A., 1815; his famous 'Introduction to Entomology' published in conjunction with William Spence [q. v.], 1815–26; F.R.S., 1818; honorary president of the Entomological Society, 1837, to which he bequeathed his collection of insects. [xxxi. 199]

KIRBYE, GEORGE (*d.* 1634), musician; employed by Thomas East [q. v.] to write new settings for his 'Whole Book of Psalms,' 1592; published 'The First Set of English Madrigalls,' 1597 (new edition, ed. Arkwright, 1891–2). [xxxi. 200]

KIRK. [See also KIRKE.]

KIRK, JOHN (1724 ?–1778 ?), medallist; produced medals of moderate excellence, 1740–76; member of the Incorporated Society of Artists. [xxxi. 201]

KIRK, JOHN (1760–1851), catholic divine and antiquary; admitted into the English college at Rome, 1773; priest, 1784; president of Sedgley Park school, 1793; chaplain and private secretary to Dr. Charles Berington [q. v.], vicar-apostolic of the midland district, 1797; received D.D. from Pope Gregory XVI, 1841; prepared materials for a continuation of Dodd's 'Church History of England'; finally handed work to the Rev. Mark Aloysius Tierney [q. v.]; published historical and theological works. [xxxi. 201]

KIRK, ROBERT (1641 ?–1692), Gaelic scholar; studied at Edinburgh University (M.A., 1661) and St. Andrews; made first complete translation of the Scottish metrical psalms into Gaelic, 1684; superintended printing of Bedell's Gaelic bible in London, and added Gaelic vocabulary, 1690. [xxxi. 202]

KIRK, THOMAS (1765 ?–1797), painter and engraver; pupil of Richard Cosway [q. v.]; painter of historical subjects and of miniatures; exhibited at Royal Academy, 1765–96. [xxxi. 203]

KIRK, THOMAS (1777–1845), sculptor; noted for his fine busts and work in relief on mantelpieces, monuments, &c.; member of the Royal Hibernian Academy, 1822; executed statue of Nelson for memorial column, Dublin; his most important work, the statue of Sir Sidney Smith at Greenwich Hospital. [xxxi. 203]

KIRKALL, ELISHA (1682 ?–1742), mezzotint-engraver; introduced new method of chiaroscuro engraving, 1722. [xxxi. 204]

KIRKBY, JOHN (d. 1290), bishop of Ely and treasurer; kept great seal in absence of chancellor, 1272, 1278–1279, 1281–3; member of royal council, 1276; treasurer, 1284; bishop of Ely, 1286; described unfavourably by contemporary chroniclers. [xxxi. 204]

KIRKBY, JOHN DE (d. 1352), bishop of Carlisle; Augustinian canon at Carlisle and afterwards prior of the house; bishop of Carlisle, 1332. [xxxi. 206]

KIRKBY, JOHN (1705–1754), divine; B.A. St. John's College, Cambridge, 1726; tutor to Edward Gibbon, who thought highly of him, 1744; M.A., 1745; author of philosophical and theological works, and of a Latin and English grammar. [xxxi. 207]

KIRKBY, RICHARD (d. 1703), captain in the navy; lieutenant, 1689; went to West Indies, 1696; tried for embezzling, plunder, and cruelty, and acquitted, 1698; second in command in the West Indies, when he disobeyed his superior's signals to engage the French, 1701; court-martialled and shot. [xxxi. 207]

KIRKCALDY or **KIRKALDY**, SIR JAMES (d. 1556), of Grange, lord high treasurer of Scotland; chief opponent of Cardinal Beaton; mainly procured Beaton's assassination, 1546. [xxxi. 208]

KIRKCALDY, SIR WILLIAM (d. 1573), of Grange, eldest son of Sir James Kirkcaldy [q. v.]; assisted in the murder of Cardinal Beaton, 1546; on accession of Mary entered French service; took part in peace negotiations, 1559; supported the protestants; opposed marriage of Mary to Darnley, 1565; privy to plot against Rizzio, 1566; hostile to Bothwell, but after his escape joined the queen's party; held Edinburgh town and castle for Queen Mary, 1568–73, when he surrendered it and was executed; an inconsistent politician, but a man of chivalrous honour. [xxxi. 209]

KIRKCUDBRIGHT, first BARON (d. 1641). [See MAC LELLAN, SIR ROBERT.]

KIRKE. [See also KIRK.]

KIRKE, EDWARD (1553–1613), friend of Edmund Spenser; entered Pembroke Hall, Cambridge, 1569; removed to Caius College; M.A., 1578; wrote the preface, the arguments, and a verbal commentary to Spenser's 'Shepheardes Calender,' under the initials 'E. K.,' 1579. Modern critics have, on insufficient grounds, endeavoured to prove that 'E. K.' was Spenser himself. [xxxi. 213]

KIRKE, GEORGE (d. 1675 ?), gentleman of the robes to Charles I and groom of the bedchamber, and keeper of Whitehall Palace to Charles II. [xxxi. 214]

KIRKE, JOHN (fl. 1638), dramatist; author of a popular tragi-comedy of small literary merit, 'The Seven Champions of Christendome,' published, 1638. [xxxi. 214]

KIRKE, PERCY (1646 ?–1691), lieutenant-general, colonel of 'Kirke's Lambs'; son of George Kirke [q. v.]; served under Duke of Monmouth in France, 1673; under Turenne, Luxembourg, and de Creci, 1676–7; lieutenant-colonel, 1680; governor of Tangier, 1682–4; transferred to colonelcy of the old Tangier regiment, the badge of which was a Paschal Lamb, whence the appellation 'Kirke's Lambs'; brigadier-general, 1685; present at

Sedgmoor, 1685, and notorious for his cruelty to the rebels; major-general, 1688; relieved Derry, 1689; lieutenant-general, 1690; died at Brussels. [xxxi. 214]

KIRKE, PERCY (1684–1741), eldest son of Lieutenant-general Percy Kirke [q. v.], lieutenant-general and colonel of the 'Lambs,' 1710–41; keeper of Whitehall Palace; taken prisoner at Almanza, 1708. [xxxi. 216]

KIRKE, THOMAS (1650–1706), virtuoso; distant relative and intimate friend of Ralph Thoresby [q. v.]; formed a fine library and museum; published 'A Modern Account of Scotland' (satire), 1679; the 'Journal' of the Scottish journey (made in 1677), printed in 'Letters addressed to R. Thoresby'; F.R.S., 1693. [xxxi. 216]

KIRKES, WILLIAM SENHOUSE (1823–1864), physician; studied at St. Bartholomew's Hospital, London; M.D. Berlin, 1846; F.R.C.P. London, 1855; demonstrator of morbid anatomy at St. Bartholomew's, 1848, assistant-physician, 1854, and physician, 1864; published, 1848, with Sir James Paget [q. v.], 'Handbook of Physiology.' [Suppl. iii. 69]

KIRKHAM, WALTER DE (d. 1260), bishop of Durham; of humble parentage; one of the royal clerks; bishop of Durham, 1241; took part in the excommunication of the violators of the charters, 1253. [xxxi. 217]

KIRKHOVEN or **KERCKHOVEN**, CATHERINE, LADY STANHOPE and COUNTESS OF CHESTERFIELD (d. 1667), governess to Mary, princess royal, daughter of Charles I; married Henry, lord Stanhope (d. 1634), son and heir to Philip Stanhope, first earl of Chesterfield, 1628; after refusing Vandyck, married John Polyander à Kerckhoven, lord of Heenvliet in Sassenheim, and one of the ambassadors from the States-General to negotiate the marriage between William of Orange and the princess royal, 1641; confidential adviser to the princess; privy to royalist plots hatched on the continent; arrested in England, 1651; was acquitted and returned to Holland, 1652; created Countess of Chesterfield for life, 1660; on the princess's death entered the service of the Duchess of York and married Daniel O'Neill (d. 1664); lady of the bedchamber to the queen, 1663. [xxxi. 217]

KIRKHOVEN, CHARLES HENRY, first BARON WOTTON and EARL OF BELLOMONT (d. 1683), son of Catherine Kirkhoven [q. v.] and John Polyander à Kerckhoven, lord of Heenvliet; created Baron Wotton of Wotton in Kent, 1650; favourite of the princess royal; chief magistrate of Breda, 1659–74; created Earl of Bellomont in peerage of Ireland, 1680. [xxxi. 218]

KIRKLAND, THOMAS (1722–1798), medical writer; M.D. St. Andrews, 1769; member of royal medical societies of Edinburgh and London; published medical treatises between 1754 and 1792. [xxxi. 219]

KIRKMAN, FRANCIS (fl. 1674), bookseller and author; printed 'Catalogue of all the English Stage-playes,' 1661 (revised edition, 1671); issued Webster and Rowley's comedies, 'A Cure for a Cuckold' (1661) and 'The Thracian Wonder' (1661); a collection of drolls and farces, 'The Wits, or Sport upon Sport,' 1673; published translations from the French and romances. [xxxi. 219]

KIRKMAN, JACOB (fl. 1800), musical composer; esteemed by contemporaries as pianist and composer of pianoforte works. [xxxi. 220]

KIRKPATRICK, JAMES (d. 1743), Irish presbyterian divine; educated at Glasgow University; one of the earliest members of the Belfast Society (founded, 1705); minister of the presbyterian congregation in Belfast, 1706; moderator of synod of Ulster, 1712; a leader of the non-subscribing party in the north of Ireland, 1720; subsequently M.D.; public sentiment in Ireland in the time of Queen Anne reflected in his 'Historical Essay upon the Loyalty of Presbyterians in Great-Britain and Ireland from the Reformation to this Present Year, 1713.' [xxxi. 220]

KIRKPATRICK, JOHN (1686 ?–1728), antiquary; a Norwich linen-merchant; accumulated material for the history of Norwich, but his manuscripts never published, and now dispersed; issued a large north-east prospect of Norwich, 1723. [xxxi. 221]

KIRKPATRICK, WILLIAM (1754–1812), orientalist; ensign, Bengal infantry, 1773; lieutenant, 1777; Persian interpreter to the commander-in-chief in Bengal, 1777–9

and 1780–5; in Mysore war, 1790–1; resident with the nizam of Hyderabad, 1795; military secretary to Marquis Wellesley; resident of Poona; translated Persian works; expert in oriental tongues and the manners, customs, and laws of India. [xxxi. 222]

KIRKPATRICK, WILLIAM BAILLIE (1802–1882), Irish presbyterian divine; M.A. Glasgow College; studied theology at the old Belfast College; moderator of the general assembly, 1850; published 'Chapters in Irish History,' 1875. [xxxi. 222]

KIRKSTALL, HUGH OF (*fl.* 1200), historian; received as Cistercian monk at Kirkstall, Yorkshire, between 1181 and 1191; his history of Fountains Abbey printed in Dugdale's 'Monasticon.' [xxxi. 223]

KIRKTON, JAMES (1620?–1699), Scottish divine and historian; M.A. Edinburgh, 1647; deprived of his living, 1662; denounced as a rebel for holding conventicles, 1674; in Holland till proclamation of Toleration Act, 1687; minister of the Tolbooth parish, Edinburgh, 1691; published sermons, and left in manuscript 'The Secret and True History of the Church of Scotland from the Restoration to the Year 1678,' printed, 1817. [xxxi. 223]

KIRKUP, SEYMOUR STOOKER (1788–1880), artist; admitted student of Royal Academy, 1809; acquainted with William Blake (1757–1827) [q. v.] and Benjamin Robert Haydon [q. v.]; present at funeral of Keats at Rome, 1821, and of Shelley, 1822; leader of a literary circle at Florence; died at Leghorn. [xxxi. 224]

KIRKWOOD, JAMES (*fl.* 1698), Scottish teacher and grammarian; master of the school in Linlithgow burgh, 1675–90; his dismissal (1690) followed by litigation decided in his favour; published account of it, 1711; master of Kelso school; again involved in difficulties, of which he published an account, 1698; edited Despauter's Latin grammar for use in Scottish schools, 1695 (2nd edit. 1700; 3rd, 1711; 4th, 1720). [xxxi. 226]

KIRKWOOD, JAMES (1650?–1708), advocate of parochial libraries; M.A. Edinburgh, 1670; deprived of living of Minto for refusing to take the test, 1683; migrated to England; rector of Astwick, Bedfordshire, 1685; ejected for not abjuring, 1702; his tract, 'An Overture for founding and maintaining Bibliothecks in every Paroch throughout the Kingdom,' printed, 1699. [xxxi. 225]

KIRTON, EDMUND (*d.* 1466), abbot of Westminster; monk of Westminster, 1403; B.D. Gloucester Hall (Worcester College), Oxford; prior of the Benedictine scholars at Gloucester Hall, 1423; present at Council of Basle, 1437; abbot of Westminster, 1440–62; a famous orator. [xxxi. 227]

KIRWAN, FRANCIS (1589–1661), bishop of Killala; educated at Galway and Lisbon; ordained, 1614; consecrated bishop of Killala against his will at St. Lazaire, 1645; took part in Irish struggles in Connaught; fled, 1652; surrendered, 1654; imprisoned, but (1655) allowed to retire to France; died at Rennes. [xxxi. 227]

KIRWAN, OWEN (*d.* 1803), Irish rebel; a tailor who joined Emmet's conspiracy and was employed in the manufacture of ammunition; arrested, found guilty, and shot. [xxxi. 228]

KIRWAN, RICHARD (1733–1812), chemist and natural philosopher; entered jesuit noviciate at St. Omer, 1754; called to the Irish bar, 1766; abandoned law to study science in London; F.R.S., 1780; Copley medallist, 1782; published 'Elements of Mineralogy,' the first English systematic treatise on the subject, 1784 (3rd edit. 1810); settled in Dublin, 1787; hon. LL.D. Dublin University, 1794; president of Royal Irish Academy, 1799; the 'Nestor of English chemistry.' [xxxi. 228]

KIRWAN, STEPHEN (*d.* 1602?), bishop of Clonfert; educated at Oxford and Paris; conformed to the protestant religion; archdeacon of Annaghdown, 1558; first protestant bishop of Kilmacduagh, 1573–82; bishop of Clonfert, 1582. [xxxi. 230]

KIRWAN, WALTER BLAKE (1754–1805), dean of Killala; educated at the jesuit college at St. Omer; studied at Louvain; professor of natural and moral philosophy at Louvain, 1777; chaplain to the Neapolitan ambassador at the British court, 1778; became a protestant dean of Killala, 1800. [xxxi. 230]

KITCHIN, *alias* DUNSTAN, ANTHONY (1477–1563), bishop of Llandaff; a Benedictine monk of Westminster; of Gloucester Hall (now Worcester College), Oxford; B.D., 1525; prior of his college, 1526; abbot of Eynsham, Oxford, 1530; surrendered his abbacy on dissolution of monasteries, and was appointed king's chaplain; bishop of Llandaff, 1545; was included by Queen Elizabeth in two commissions which she drew for the consecration of Parker, but refused to act; called Dunstan up to his election as bishop. [xxxi. 230]

KITCHINER, WILLIAM (1775?–1827), miscellaneous writer; educated at Eton; M.D. Glasgow; devoted himself to science; published 'Apicius Redivivus, or the Cook's Oracle,' 1817 (7th edit. 1827); wrote also on optics and music. [xxxi. 231]

KITCHINGMAN, JOHN (1740?–1781), painter; exhibited at Royal Academy from 1770; painted, among other portraits, one of Macklin as Shylock. [xxxi. 232]

KITE, CHARLES (*d.* 1811), medical writer; author of essays on the 'recovery of the apparently dead' (1788), and on the 'Submersion of Animals' (1795). [xxxi. 232]

KITE, JOHN (*d.* 1537), successively archbishop of Armagh and bishop of Carlisle; educated at Eton and King's College, Cambridge; prebendary of Exeter and sub-dean of the King's Chapel, Westminster, 1510; archbishop of Armagh, 1513–21; accompanied John Bourchier, second baron Berners [q. v.], on embassy to Charles V, 1518; present at the Field of the Cloth of Gold, 1520; bishop of Carlisle, 1521–37; owed his preferments to Wolsey's influence; renounced the pope's supremacy, 1534. [xxxi. 232]

KITTO, JOHN (1804–1854), author of the 'Pictorial Bible'; son of a Cornish stonemason; became deaf, 1817; sent to the workhouse, where he learnt shoemaking, 1819; apprenticed to a Plymouth shoemaker, 1821; entered missionary college, 1825; employed by the Church Missionary Society at Malta, 1827–9; with a private mission party in Persia, 1829–33; wrote for periodicals; at suggestion of Charles Knight (1791–1873) [q. v.] wrote narratives illustrative of life of the deaf and blind, collected as 'The Lost Senses,' 1845, 'Pictorial Bible' completed, 1838, and 'Pictorial History of Palestine,' 1840; D.D. Giessen, 1844; published 'Cyclopædia of Biblical Literature,' 1845; F.S.A., 1845; edited 'Journal of Sacred Literature,' 1848–53; his 'Daily Bible Illustrations' published, 1849–54; died at Cannstatt. [xxxi. 233]

KLITZ, PHILIP (1805–1854), pianist, violinist, and author; printed 'Songs of the Mid-watch,' 1838, and 'Sketches of Life, Character, and Scenery in the New Forest,' 1850. [xxxi. 235]

KLOSE, FRANCIS JOSEPH (1784–1830), musical composer; pianoforte-player and teacher; author of ballads and pianoforte pieces. [xxxi. 235]

KNAPP, JOHN LEONARD (1767–1845), botanist; F.L.S., 1796; F.S.A.; published 'Gramina Britannica, or Representations of the British Grasses,' 1804; reissued, 1842; contributed to 'Time's Telescope,' 1820–30 (reprinted as the 'Journal of a Naturalist,' 1829). [xxxi. 235]

KNAPP, WILLIAM (1698–1768), musical composer; parish clerk of Poole, Dorset, for thirty-nine years; published 'A Sett of New Psalm Tunes and Anthems,' 1738 (7th edit. 1762); originator of the psalm-tune called 'Wareham.' [xxxi. 236]

KNAPTON, CHARLES (1700–1760), brother of George Knapton [q. v.]; assisted in production of volume of imitations of original drawings by old masters, published, 1735. [xxxi. 237]

KNAPTON, GEORGE (1698–1778), portrait-painter; member of and first portrait-painter to the Society of Dilettanti, 1750–63; surveyor and keeper of the king's pictures, 1765; a skilful painter of the formal school. [xxxi. 236]

KNAPTON, PHILIP (1788–1833), musical composer; received his musical education at Cambridge; composer of works for orchestra, piano, and harp. [xxxi. 237]

KNAPWELL, RICHARD (*fl.* 1286). [See CLAPWELL.]

KNATCHBULL, SIR EDWARD, ninth baronet (1781-1849), statesman; succeeded to the baronetcy, 1819; M.P., Kent, 1819-30 and 1832; opposed corn-law reform and catholic emancipation; paymaster of the forces and privy councillor, 1834-45. [xxxi. 237]

KNATCHBULL, SIR NORTON, first baronet (1602-1685), scholar; B.A. St. John's College, Cambridge, 1620; M.P., Kent, 1639; knighted, 1639; sat in Long parliament as a loyalist, and made a baronet, 1641; published his critical 'Animadversiones in Libros Novi Testamenti,' 1659 (4th edit. in English, 1692); M.P. for New Romney, 1661. [xxxi. 238]

KNATCHBULL-HUGESSEN, EDWARD HUGESSEN, first BARON BRABOURNE (1829-1893), son of Sir Edward Knatchbull, ninth baronet [q. v.]; educated at Eton and Magdalen College, Oxford; M.A., 1854; took additional surname of Hugessen, 1849; liberal M.P. for Sandwich, 1857; lord of treasury 1859-60 and 1860-6; under-secretary for home affairs, 1860 and 1866; under-secretary for colonies, 1871-4; privy councillor, 1873; raised to peerage, 1880; adopted conservative views; published stories for children. [Suppl. iii. 69]

KNELL — (*fl.* 1586), actor; mentioned by Nashe and Heywood, and confused by Collier with Thomas Knell the younger [q. v.] [xxxi. 240]

KNELL, PAUL (1615?-1664), divine; B.A. Clare Hall, Cambridge, 1635; D.D. Oxford, 1643; chaplain in the king's army; published sermons. [xxxi. 239]

KNELL, THOMAS (*fl.* 1570), divine and verse-writer; chaplain to Walter Devereux, first earl of Essex [q. v.]. [xxxi. 239]

KNELL, THOMAS, the younger (*fl.* 1560-1581), clergyman; son of Thomas Knell (*fl.* 1570) [q. v.]; often confused with his father; author of theological treatises. [xxxi. 239]

KNELL, WILLIAM ADOLPHUS (*d.* 1875), marine-painter; exhibited (1826-66) at Royal Academy and British Institution; his 'Landing of Prince Albert' purchased for the royal collection. [xxxi. 240]

KNELLER, SIR GODFREY, first baronet (original name GOTTFRIED KNILLER) (1646-1723), painter; born at Lübeck; studied under Ferdinand Bol at Amsterdam; came to England, 1675; painted portrait of Charles II, 1678; sent by Charles II to paint portrait of Louis XIV; principal painter to William III, and knighted, 1691; painted Peter the Great during his visit to England; his equestrian portrait of William III, one of his best-known works, painted, 1697; retained his dignities under Anne and George I; created baronet, 1715; his monument by Rysbrack, with inscription by Pope, erected in Westminster Abbey, 1729. Ten reigning sovereigns sat to Kneller, and almost all persons of importance in his day. [xxxi. 240]

KNELLER or **KNILLER**, JOHN ZACHARIAS (1644-1702), painter; brother of Sir Godfrey Kneller, first baronet [q. v.]; born at Lübeck; travelled with his brother and settled with him in England; painted portraits and scenes containing architecture and ruins. [xxxi. 243]

KNEVET. [See also KNYVET and KNYVETT.]

KNEVET, RALPH (1600-1671), poet; probably rector of Lyng, Norfolk, 1652-71; published poems between 1628 and 1637. [xxxi. 243]

KNEWSTUBS or **KNEWSTUB**, JOHN (1544-1624), divine; fellow, St. John's College, Cambridge, 1567; M.A., 1568; B.D., 1576; preached against the teaching of the Family of Love sect; supporter of puritan doctrines; took part in the Hampton Court conference, 1604; published sermons and controversial works. [xxxi. 244]

KNIBB, WILLIAM (1803-1845), missionary and abolitionist; in printing business at Bristol; master of Baptist Missionary Society's free school at Kingston, Jamaica, 1824; undertook mission of Savannah la Mar, 1828; settled at Falmouth, near Montego Bay, 1830; visited England to advocate abolition of slavery and increased missionary activity, 1832-4, 1840, and 1845; died in Jamaica. [Suppl. iii. 70]

KNIGHT, CHARLES (1743-1827?), engraver; stated to have been a pupil of Francesco Bartolozzi [q, v.], but practised independently; his works often erroneously ascribed to Bartolozzi. [xxxi. 244]

KNIGHT, CHARLES (1791-1873), author and publisher; apprenticed to his father, a bookseller of Windsor, 1805; reported, 1812, for the 'Globe' and 'British Press'; started with his father the 'Windsor and Eton Express,' 1812; produced, in conjunction with Edward Hawke Locker [q. v.], the 'Plain Englishman,' 1820-2; editor and part proprietor of 'The Guardian,' a literary and political weekly, 1820-2; publisher in London, 1823; projected a cheap series of books to condense the information contained in voluminous works; published for the Society for the Diffusion of Useful Knowledge; produced 'Penny Magazine,' 1832-45, 'Penny Cyclopædia,' 1833-44; published 'Pictorial History of England,' in parts, 1837-1844; edited and published 'Pictorial Shakespere,' 1838-1841; began 'Weekly Volumes' series, 1844; began 'Half Hours with the Best Authors,' and 'The Land we live in,' 1847; his 'History of the Thirty Years' Peace,' completed by Harriet Martineau, published, 1851, and 'Passages of a Working Life' (autobiography), 1864-5. [xxxi. 245]

KNIGHT, EDWARD (1774-1826), actor; commonly known as 'LITTLE KNIGHT'; unequalled in the parts of pert footmen, cunning rustics, country boys, and decrepit old men. [xxxi. 248]

KNIGHT, ELLIS CORNELIA (1757-1837), authoress; companion to Queen Charlotte, 1805; companion to Princess Charlotte, 1813-14; her autobiography (published, 1861) valuable as throwing light on court history; wrote romantic tales; published 'A Description of Latium, or La Campagna di Roma,' 1805; died in Paris. [xxxi. 249]

KNIGHT, FRANCIS (*d.* 1589). [See KETT.]

KNIGHT, GOWIN (1713-1772), man of science; first principal librarian of the British Museum; held demyship of Magdalen College, Oxford, 1735-46; M.A., 1739; M.B., 1742; F.R.S., 1747; Copley medallist, 1747; his improved compass adopted in royal navy, 1752; principal librarian, British Museum, 1756; his papers on magnetism collected and published, 1758; rendered important, if unrecognised, services to navigation. [xxxi. 250]

KNIGHT, HENRIETTA, LADY LUXBOROUGH (*d.* 1756), friend of Shenstone; half-sister of Henry St. John, first viscount Bolingbroke [q.v.]; married in 1727 Robert Knight of Barrells, Warwickshire, who was created baron Luxborough in the Irish peerage in 1746; visited Shenstone at Leasowes; corresponded with him (correspondence published, 1775); friend also of the poet William Somerville [q. v.]; wrote verses. [xxxi. 252]

KNIGHT, HENRY GALLY (1786-1846), writer on architecture; great-grandson of Henry Gally [q. v.]; of Eton and Trinity College, Cambridge; travelled in Europe, Egypt, and Palestine, 1810-11; his first publications, verses on Greek and oriental themes, 1816-30; M.P., Aldborough, 1824-8, Malton, 1830, north Nottinghamshire, 1835 and 1837; works include 'Architectural Tour in Normandy,' 1836, and 'The Ecclesiastical Architecture of Italy,' 1842-1844. [xxxi. 253]

KNIGHT, JAMES (*d.* 1719?), arctic voyager and agent of the Hudson's Bay Company; governor of Fort Albany, 1693; governor of Nelson River settlement, 1714; established Prince of Wales's fort at mouth of Churchill River, 1717 or 1718; perished in an expedition to discover gold in the far north. [xxxi. 254]

KNIGHT, JAMES (1793-1863), divine; son of Samuel Knight (1759-1827) [q. v.]; scholar of Lincoln College, Oxford, 1812-15; M.A., 1817; perpetual curate of St. Paul's, Sheffield, 1824 (resigned, 1860); published theological works. [xxxi. 262]

KNIGHT, JOHN (*d.* 1606), mariner; commanded Danish expedition to coast of Greenland, 1605; employed by East India merchants to discover the north-west passage, 1606; went ashore after a gale at Labrador and was never again heard of. [xxxi. 254]

KNIGHT, JOHN (*fl.* 1670), mayor of Bristol, 1670; apparently no relation of his namesakes. [xxxi. 256]

KNIGHT, SIR JOHN, 'the elder' (1612-1683), mayor of Bristol; a provision merchant; member of Bristol common council till 1680; knighted, 1663; elected mayor, 1663; persecuted nonconformists and Roman catholics; M.P., Bristol, 1661, 1678, and 1679. [xxxi. 255]

KNIGHT, SIR JOHN, 'the younger' (d. 1718), Jacobite; probably a kinsman of Sir John 'the elder' [q. v.]; sheriff of Bristol, 1681; zealous against dissenters; knighted, 1682; mayor of Bristol, 1690; M.P., Bristol, 1691; arrested as a suspected Jacobite, 1696; released, 1696. [xxxi. 255]

KNIGHT, SIR JOHN (1748 ?-1831), admiral; entered navy, 1758; lieutenant, 1770; taken prisoner and exchanged, 1776; sent to West Indies, 1780; took part in action off Martinique, 1781; captain, 1781; present at Camperdown, 1797, and blockade of Brest, 1799-1800; vice-admiral, 1805; admiral, 1813; K.C.B., 1815. [xxxi. 256]

KNIGHT, JOHN BAVERSTOCK (1785-1859), painter; exhibited at Royal Academy; published etchings of old buildings, 1816. [xxxi. 257]

KNIGHT, JOHN PRESCOTT (1803-1881), portrait-painter; son of Edward Knight [q. v.]; student of Royal Academy, 1823; exhibited portraits of his father and Alfred Bunn [q. v.], 1824; A.R.A., 1836; professor of perspective, Royal Academy, 1839-60; exhibited 'The Waterloo Banquet,' 1842; R.A., 1844; secretary to the Academy, 1848-73; many of his works presentation portraits. [xxxi. 257]

KNIGHT, JOSEPH PHILIP (1812-1887), composer of songs; published set of six songs under name of 'Philip Mortimer,' 1832; composed his famous song, 'Rocked in the cradle of the deep,' 1839; took holy orders after 1841; was appointed to the charge of St. Agnes, Scilly Isles; composed numerous songs, duets, and trios. [xxxi. 258]

KNIGHT, MARY ANNE (1776-1831), miniature-painter; pupil of Andrew Plimer [q. v.]; exhibited at Royal Academy from 1807. [xxxi. 258]

KNIGHT, RICHARD PAYNE (1750-1824), numismatist; elder brother of Thomas Andrew Knight [q. v.]; visited Sicily with the German painter, Philipp Hackert, 1777; his diary translated and published by Goethe in his biography of Hackert; began to form collection of bronzes, 1785; M.P., Leominster, 1780, Ludlow, 1784-1806; wrote on ancient art; vice-president, Society of Antiquaries; bequeathed his magnificent collection to the British Museum. [xxxi. 259]

KNIGHT, SAMUEL (1675-1746), biographer; educated at St. Paul's School and Trinity College, Cambridge; M.A., 1706; fellow and one of the founders of the Society of Antiquaries, 1717; D.D., 1717; chaplain to George II, 1731; archdeacon of Berkshire, 1735; prebendary of Lincoln, 1742; published 'Life of Dr. John Colet, Dean of St. Paul's,' 1724 (2nd edit. 1823), and 'Life of Erasmus,' 1726. [xxxi. 261]

KNIGHT, SAMUEL (1759-1827), vicar of Halifax; entered Magdalene College, Cambridge, 1779; B.A. and fellow, 1783; M.A., 1786; published highly popular devotional manuals. [xxxi. 261]

KNIGHT, THOMAS (d. 1820), actor and dramatist; intended for the bar; studied elocution under the actor Charles Macklin [q. v.], and adopted the stage as profession; married Margaret Farren, sister of the Countess of Derby [see FARREN, ELIZABETH], an actress, 1787; lessee and manager of Liverpool Theatre, 1803-20; wrote many pieces, the best being 'Turnpike Gate' (farce), 1799; an admirable comic actor, with a repertory similar to that of Edward Knight [q. v.] [xxxi. 262]

KNIGHT, THOMAS ANDREW (1759-1838), vegetable physiologist and horticulturist; brother of Richard Payne Knight [q. v.]; entered Balliol College, Oxford, 1778; F.R.S., 1805; Copley medallist, 1806; F.L.S., 1807; president of the Horticultural Society, 1811-38; awarded first Knightian medal founded in his honour, 1836; author of 'A Treatise on the Culture of the Apple and Pear' (1797), 'Pomona Herefordiensis' (1811); a selection of his papers published, 1841. [xxxi. 263]

KNIGHT, WILLIAM (1476-1547), bishop of Bath and Wells; of Winchester School and New College, Oxford; fellow of New College, 1493; sent by Henry VIII on missions to Spain, Italy, and the Low Countries, 1512-1532; chaplain to Henry VIII, 1515; archdeacon of Chester, 1522, of Huntingdon, 1523; canon of Westminster, 1527; archdeacon of Richmond, 1529; bishop of Bath and Wells, 1541. [xxxi. 264]

KNIGHT, WILLIAM (fl. 1612), divine; fellow of Christ's College, Cambridge; M.A., 1586; incorporated at Oxford, 1603; rector of Barley, afterwards of Little Gransden; published theological 'Concordance Axiomatical,' 1610. [xxxi. 266]

KNIGHT, WILLIAM (1786-1844), natural philosopher; M.A. Aberdeen, 1802; professor of natural philosophy, Academical Institution, Belfast, 1816-22; LL.D., 1817; published 'Facts and Observations towards forming a new Theory of the Earth,' 1818; professor, natural philosophy, Aberdeen, 1822-44. [xxxi. 266]

KNIGHT, WILLIAM HENRY (1823-1863), painter; educated for the law, but abandoned it for painting; exhibited pictures of everyday life at the Royal Academy and the Society of British Artists. [xxxi. 267]

KNIGHT-BRUCE, GEORGE WYNDHAM HAMILTON (1852-1896). [See BRUCE.]

KNIGHT-BRUCE, SIR JAMES LEWIS (1791-1866). [See BRUCE.]

KNIGHTBRIDGE, JOHN (d. 1677), divine; B.A. Wadham College, Oxford, 1642; translated to Peterhouse, Cambridge, and admitted fellow, 1645; D.D., 1673; founded by will the Knightbridge professorship in moral theology at Cambridge. [xxxi. 267]

KNIGHTLEY, SIR EDMUND (d. 1542), serjeant-at-law; uncle of Sir Richard Knightley (1533-1615) [q. v.]; one of the chief commissioners for the suppression of religious property. [xxxi. 268]

KNIGHTLEY, SIR RICHARD (1533-1615), patron of puritans; knighted, 1566; sheriff of Northamptonshire, 1568-9, 1581-2, and 1589; officially attended execution of Mary Queen of Scots, 1589; M.P., Northampton, 1584 and 1585, Northamptonshire, 1589 and 1598; the press at which the Martin Mar-Prelate tracts were printed concealed in his house, 1588; arraigned and released, 1589; fined by Star-chamber and deprived of lieutenancy of Northamptonshire and commission of the peace. [xxxi. 268]

KNIGHTLEY, RICHARD (d. 1639), member of parliament; grandson of Sir Richard Knightley (1533-1615) [q. v.]; M.P., Northamptonshire, 1621, 1624, and 1625; sheriff of Northamptonshire, 1626; refused to subscribe to the forced loan, 1627; acted with Eliot and Hampden in Commons, 1628. [xxxi. 269]

KNIGHTLEY, SIR RICHARD (1617-1661), member of parliament; great-nephew of Sir Richard Knightley (1533-1615) [q. v.]; of Gray's Inn; married Elizabeth, eldest daughter of John Hampden, c. 1637; sat in Short parliament for Northampton; in the Long parliament, 1640, acted with the opposition; in Richard Cromwell's parliament, 1659; a member of the council which arranged the recall of Charles II, 1660; K.B., 1661. [xxxi. 269]

KNIGHTON or **CNITTHON**, HENRY (fl. 1363), historical compiler; author of 'Compilatio de eventibus Angliæ' in four books from Edgar to 1366 (based on the seventh book of Cestrensis, i.e. Higden, and Walter of Hemingburgh). Books iii. and iv. may be original; a fifth book, clearly the work of another hand, is added in the manuscripts, carrying the history down to 1395. [xxxi. 270]

KNIGHTON, SIR WILLIAM, first baronet (1776-1836), keeper of the privy purse to George IV; studied medicine; assistant-surgeon at the Royal Naval Hospital, Plymouth; studied at Edinburgh, 1803-6; M.D. Aberdeen; physician to George IV when Prince of Wales, 1810; created baronet, 1812; materially assisted George IV while prince on matters of business; private secretary to George IV and keeper of the privy purse, 1822; employed on confidential missions abroad, 1823-6; attended George IV during his last illness. [xxxi. 270]

KNILL, RICHARD (1787-1857), dissenting minister; volunteered for missionary work, and was in Madras, 1816-19; travelled through the United Kingdom to advocate the claims of foreign missions, 1833-41; published religious works. [xxxi. 272]

KNIPE, THOMAS (1638-1711), head-master of Westminster School; educated at Westminster School and Christ Church, Oxford; M.A., 1663; second master at Westminster, 1663; head-master, 1695; prebendary of Westminster, 1707; compiled two grammars for Westminster scholars. [xxxi. 272]

KNIPP or **KNEP**, Mrs. (fl. 1670), actress ; intimate with Pepys ; probably made her début as Epicœne in Jonson's 'Silent Woman' 1664 ; acted in plays by Jacobean and Restoration dramatists.   [xxxi. 273]

KNIVET. [See KNYVET.]

KNOLLES. [See also KNOLLYS and KNOWLES.]

KNOLLES, RICHARD (1550 ?-1610), historian of the Turks ; M.A. and fellow, Lincoln College, Oxford, 1570 ; his 'Generall Historie of the Turkes ' (valuable for its prose style) published, 1604 (2nd edit. 1610 ; 3rd, 1621 ; 4th, 1631 ; 5th, 1638 ; final and extended edition in three folio vols. 1687-1700).   [xxxi. 273]

KNOLLES, THOMAS (d. 1537), president of Magdalen College, Oxford ; a secular priest, educated at Magdalen College, Oxford ; fellow, 1495 ; sub-dean of York, 1507-1529 ; D.D., 1518 ; president of Magdalen, 1527-35.   [xxxi. 274]

KNOLLYS, CHARLES, called fourth EARL OF BANBURY (1662-1740), son of Nicholas Knollys, called third earl of Banbury [q. v.] ; twice unsuccessfully petitioned for a writ of summons ; killed his brother-in-law in a duel, 1692 ; imprisoned, but subsequently set free in name of Earl of Banbury.   [xxxi. 288]

KNOLLYS, SIR FRANCIS (1514 ?-1596), statesman ; educated at Oxford ; attended Anne of Cleves on her arrival in England, 1539 ; M.P., Horsham, 1542 ; knighted, 1547 ; favoured by Edward VI and Princess Elizabeth ; withdrew to Germany on Mary's accession, 1553 ; privy councillor, 1558 ; vice-chamberlain of the household and captain of the halberdiers ; M.P., Arundel, 1559, Oxford, 1562, Oxfordshire, 1572-96 ; governor of Portsmouth, 1563 ; in charge of the fugitive Queen of Scots, 1568-9 ; treasurer of the royal household, 1572-96 ; supported the puritans ; K.G., 1593.   [xxxi. 275]

KNOLLYS, HANSERD (1599 ?-1691), particular baptist divine ; educated at Cambridge ; became a separatist and renounced his orders, 1636 ; fled to New England ; returned to London, 1641 ; gathered a church of his own, 1645 ; held offices under Cromwell ; fled to Germany at the Restoration ; returned to London and resumed his preaching ; arrested under the second Conventicle Act, 1670 ; discharged ; author of religious works, and of an autobiography (to 1672).   [xxxi. 279]

KNOLLYS, NICHOLAS, called third EARL OF BANBURY (1631-1674), reputed son of William Knollys, earl of Banbury [q. v.], sat in House of Lords in Convention parliament, 1660 ; his right to sit as peer disputed, 1660 ; a bill declaring him illegitimate read, 1661, but never carried beyond the initial stage.   [xxxi. 287]

KNOLLYS or **KNOLLES**, SIR ROBERT (d. 1407), military commander ; knighted, 1351 ; served under Henry of Lancaster, 1357 ; captured Bertrand du Guesclin, 1359 ; joined the Black Prince in his Spanish expedition, 1367 ; commander of an expedition to France, 1370 ; took part in the great expedition under Thomas, earl of Buckingham [see THOMAS OF WOODSTOCK, DUKE OF GLOUCESTER], 1380 ; active against Wat Tyler, 1381 ; amassed 'regal wealth ' in the wars.   [xxxi. 285]

KNOLLYS, ROBERT (d. 1521), usher of the chamber to Henry VII and Henry VIII.   [xxxi. 275]

KNOLLYS, WILLIAM, EARL OF BANBURY (1547-1632), second but eldest surviving son of Sir Francis Knollys [q. v.] ; M.P., Tregony, 1572, Oxfordshire, 1584, 1593, 1597, and 1601 ; accompanied expedition to Low Countries under Leicester, 1586 ; knighted, 1586 ; colonel of foot regiments enrolled to assist the Armada, 1588 ; M.A. Oxford, 1592 ; a comptroller of the royal household, 1596, and privy councillor, 1596 ; treasurer of the royal household, 1602 ; created Baron Knollys of Rotherfield Greys, 1603 ; commissioner of the treasury and master of the court of wards, 1614 ; K.G., 1615 ; promoted to viscountcy of Wallingford, 1616 ; took leading part in the Lords in the case of Bacon, 1621 ; made Earl of Banbury by Charles I, 1626 ; declined to collect ship-money, 1628 ; left will making no mention of children.   [xxxi. 286]

KNOLLYS, WILLIAM, called eighth EARL OF BANBURY (1763-1834), general : lieutenant-governor of St. John's, 1818 ; general, 1819 ; governor of Limerick ;

petitioned the crown for his writ as a peer, 1806 ; declared by the House of Lords, 1813, to be not entitled to the title of earl of Banbury.   [xxxi. 289]

KNOLLYS, SIR WILLIAM THOMAS (1797-1883), general ; son of William Knollys, called eighth earl of Banbury [q. v.] ; held courtesy title of Viscount Wallingford until 1813 ; educated at Harrow and Sandhurst ; received his first commission, 1813 ; despatched to the Peninsula ; adjutant, 1821 ; lieutenant-colonel, 1844 ; regimental colonel, 1850 ; initiated Prince Albert into the art of soldiering ; major-general, 1854 ; governor of Guernsey, 1854 ; organiser of the newly formed camp at Aldershot, 1855 ; president of the council of military education, 1861 ; treasurer and comptroller of the household to the Prince of Wales, 1862-77 ; hon. LL.D. Oxford, 1863, and hon. D.C.L. Cambridge, 1864 ; K.C.B., 1867 ; privy councillor, 1871 ; gentleman usher of the black rod, 1877 ; published 'Some Remarks on the claim to the Earldom of Banbury,' 1835, and a translation of the Duc de Fezensac's 'Journal of the Russian Campaign of 1812,' 1852.   [xxxi. 289]

KNOTT, EDWARD (1582-1656), jesuit ; his real name MATTHEW WILSON ; entered Society of Jesus, 1606 ; penitentiary in Rome, 1608 ; professed father, 1618 ; missioner in Suffolk district, 1625 ; imprisoned, 1629 ; released and banished, 1633 ; English provincial, 1643 ; author of controversial works.   [xxxi. 291]

KNOWLER, WILLIAM (1699-1773), divine ; educated at St. John's College, Cambridge ; M.A., 1724 ; LL.D., 1728 ; published, at the request of Thomas Watson Wentworth, afterwards Marquis of Rockingham, a selection from the papers of his great-grandfather, Thomas Wentworth, first earl of Strafford [q. v.], 1739.   [xxxi. 292]

KNOWLES. [See also KNOLLYS.]

KNOWLES, SIR CHARLES, first baronet (d. 1777), admiral ; reputed son of Charles Knollys, called fourth earl of Banbury [q. v.] ; entered navy as captain's servant, 1718 ; rated as 'able seaman,' 1723-6 ; lieutenant, 1730 ; commander, 1732 ; surveyor and engineer of the fleet against Cartagena, 1741 ; generally supposed author of 'An Account of the Expedition to Carthagena,' 1743 ; governor of Louisbourg, 1746 ; rear-admiral of the white, 1747 ; commander-in-chief at Jamaica, 1747 ; involved in difficulties with those under his command in an engagement off Havana ; governor of Jamaica, 1752-6 ; vice-admiral, 1755 ; offended the government by his share in the miscarriage of the expedition against Rochefort, 1757 ; superseded from his command ; admiral, 1760 ; created baronet and nominated rear-admiral of Great Britain, 1765 ; accepted command in the Russian navy, 1770 ; translated De la Croix's ' Abstract on the Mechanism of the Motions of Floating Bodies,' 1775.   [xxxi. 292]

KNOWLES, SIR CHARLES HENRY, second baronet (1754-1831), admiral ; only surviving son of Sir Charles Knowles [q. v.] ; entered navy, 1768 ; lieutenant, 1776 ; succeeded to baronetcy, 1777 ; fought in action of St. Lucia, 1778, off Grenada, 1779 ; captain, 1780 ; present at battle of Cape St. Vincent, 1797 ; vice-admiral, 1804 ; admiral, 1810 ; nominated an extra G.C.B., 1820 ; author of pamphlets on technical subjects.   [xxxi. 295]

KNOWLES, GILBERT (fl. 1723), botanist and poet ; known only for his 'Materia Medica Botanica,' 1723.   [xxxi. 296]

KNOWLES, HERBERT (1798-1817), poet ; with Southey's help, to whom he sent some poems, was elected a sizar at St. John's College, Cambridge, 1817, but died a few weeks later. His reputation rests on 'The Three Tabernacles ' (better known as 'Stanzas in Richmond Churchyard ').   [xxxi. 296]

KNOWLES, JAMES (1759-1840), lexicographer ; head-master of English department of Belfast Academical Institution, 1813-16 ; compiled ' A Pronouncing and Explanatory Dictionary of the English Language,' 1835.   [xxxi. 297]

KNOWLES, JAMES SHERIDAN (1784-1862), dramatist ; son of James Knowles [q. v.] the lexicographer ; tried the army, medicine, the stage, and schoolmastering ; his tragedy of ' Caius Gracchus ' produced at Belfast, 1815, and ' Virginius ' at Covent Garden, 1820 ; his comedy, 'The Hunchback,' produced at Covent Garden, 1832, 'The Love Chase,' 1837 ; continued to act till 1843 ; visited United States, 1834 ; published also verses, adaptations, novels, and lectures on oratory.   [xxxi. 297]

KNOWLES, JOHN (*fl.* 1646–1668), antitrinitarian; adopted Arianism; joined parliamentarian army, 1648; apprehended on charge of heresy, 1665; released, 1666; author of controversial pamphlets. [xxxi. 300]

KNOWLES, JOHN (1600 ?–1685), nonconformist divine; educated at Magdalene College, Cambridge; fellow of Catharine Hall, Cambridge, 1625; went to New England, and was lecturer at Watertown, Massachusetts, 1639–49; lecturer in the cathedral at Bristol, 1650–60; his preaching made illegal by Act of Uniformity, 1662; given charge of a presbyterian congregation at the indulgence of 1672. [xxxi. 301]

KNOWLES, JOHN (1781–1841), biographer of Henry Fuseli [q. v.]; chief clerk in the surveyor's department of the navy office, 1806–32; published naval works, an edition of Fuseli's 'Lectures on Painting,' 1830, and a 'Life of Fuseli,' 1831; F.R.S. [xxxi. 302]

KNOWLES, MRS. MARY (1733–1807), quakeress; *née* Morris; married Dr. Thomas Knowles and travelled abroad; the authenticity of her account of a 'Dialogue between Dr. Johnson and Mrs. Knowles' respecting the conversion to quakerism of Miss Jane Harry doubted by Boswell, but established by Miss Seward (printed in the 'Gentleman's Magazine,' 1791). [xxxi. 302]

KNOWLES, RICHARD BRINSLEY (1820–1882), journalist; son of James Sheridan Knowles [q. v.]; barrister, Middle Temple, 1843; produced 'The Maiden Aunt' (comedy) at the Haymarket, 1845; converted to Roman catholicism; became (1849) editor of the 'Catholic Standard,' afterwards renamed the 'Weekly Register'; edited the 'Illustrated London Magazine,' 1853–5; on the staff of the 'Standard,' 1857–60; published the 'Chronicles of John of Oxenedes' in the 'Rolls Series,' 1859; engaged under the royal commission on historical manuscripts, 1871. [xxxi. 302]

KNOWLES, THOMAS (1723–1802), divine; educated at Pembroke Hall, Cambridge; M.A., 1747; D.D., 1753; prebendary of Ely, 1779; author of religious and controversial works. [xxxi. 303]

KNOWLTON, THOMAS (1692–1782), gardener and botanist; entered service of Richard Boyle, third earl of Burlington [q. v.], 1728; discoverer of the 'moor-ball,' a species of fresh-water algæ of the conferva family. [xxxi. 303]

KNOX, ALEXANDER (1757–1831), theological writer; descended from the family to which John Knox the reformer belonged; shown by his correspondence with Bishop Jebb to have anticipated the Oxford movement; advocated catholic emancipation. [xxxi. 304]

KNOX, ALEXANDER ANDREW (1818–1891), journalist and police magistrate; educated at Trinity College, Cambridge; B.A. and barrister, Lincoln's Inn, 1844; on staff of the 'Times,' 1846–60; M.A., 1847; police magistrate at Worship Street, 1860–2; at Marlborough Street, 1862–78. [xxxi. 306]

KNOX, ANDREW (1559–1633), bishop of Raphoe; educated at Glasgow University; M.A., 1579; ordained, 1581; helped to frustrate the conspiracy of Huntly, Errol, and Angus, 1592; bishop of the isles, 1600–19; bishop of Raphoe, 1610–33; privy councillor, 1612. [xxxi. 306]

KNOX, JOHN (1505–1572), Scottish reformer and historian; educated at Haddington school; at Glasgow University, 1522; notary in Haddington and the neighbourhood, 1540–3; called to the ministry and began preaching for the reformed religion, 1547; taken prisoner at capitulation of the castle of St. Andrews and sent to France, 1548; released, 1549; appointed a royal chaplain, 1551; fled to Dieppe at accession of Mary Tudor, 1553; met Calvin at Geneva, 1554; pastor of the English congregation at Frankfort-on-Maine, 1554–5; at Geneva 1556–8; published six tracts dealing with the controversy in Scotland, one of them the 'Blast of the Trumpet against the monstrous regiment of Women,' 1558, a work that gave great offence to Queen Elizabeth, and permanently affected her attitude to the Scottish reformation; published 'Treatise on Predestination,' 1560; had first interview with Mary Stuart, 1561; issued the Book of Common Order (service-book), 1564; obtained confirmation of presbyterian reformation in Scottish parliament, 1567; appointed minister at Edinburgh, 1572,

where he died; his influence as guiding spirit of the reformation in Scotland largely due to his power as an orator; his 'History of the Reformation of Religioun within the realme of Scotland' first printed, 1584 (best edition in the first two volumes of Laing's edition of Knox's 'Works,' 1846–8). [xxxi. 308]

KNOX, JOHN (1555 ?–1623), Scottish presbyterian divine; kinsman and adherent of John Knox (1505–1572) [q. v.]; M.A. St. Andrews, 1575; leader of the resistance to the re-establishment of episcopacy, 1617. [xxxi. 328]

KNOX, JOHN (*fl.* 1621–1654), Scottish divine; said to have been son of John Knox (1555 ?–1623) [q. v.]; member of the assembly, 1638; minister of Bowden, 1621–54. [xxxi. 328]

KNOX, JOHN (*d.* 1688), presbyterian divine; grandson of John Knox (1555 ?–1623) [q. v.]; M.A. Edinburgh, 1641; joined royalist army; ordained, 1653; deprived of his charge in consequence of his adherence to presbyterianism, 1662; indulged, 1672; convicted of offences and imprisoned, 1684–5. [xxxi. 328]

KNOX, JOHN (1720–1790), Scottish philanthropist; bookseller in London; improved the fisheries and manufactures of Scotland, 1764–90; published works on Scottish fisheries. [xxxi. 329]

KNOX, ROBERT (1640 ?–1720), writer on Ceylon; went to Fort George, 1657; on homeward voyage made prisoner at Ceylon, 1659; escaped, 1679; in the service of the East India Company, 1680–94; published 'An Historical Relation of the Island of Ceylon in the East Indies,' the first account of Ceylon in the English language, 1681. [xxxi. 330]

KNOX, ROBERT (1791–1862), anatomist and ethnologist; educated at Edinburgh High School; M.D. Edinburgh, 1814; assistant-surgeon in the army, 1815–32; made scientific researches at the Cape, 1817–20; conservator of the museum of comparative anatomy and pathology, Edinburgh College of Surgeons, 1825–31; anatomical lecturer at Edinburgh, 1826; unpopular after 1836 for heterodoxy and for procuring from the 'resurrectionists' his 'subjects' for dissection; fellow of the London Ethnological Society, 1860; honorary curator of its museum, 1862; distinguished anatomical teacher; author of medical works. [xxxi. 331]

KNOX, ROBERT (1815–1883), Irish presbyterian divine; M.A. Glasgow, 1837; established and edited the 'Irish Presbyterian,' and published many sermons; founder of the Sabbath School Society for Ireland, and of the presbyterian alliance. [xxxi. 333]

KNOX, ROBERT BENT (1808–1893), archbishop of Armagh; ordained, 1832; M.A. Trinity College, Dublin, 1834; chancellor of Ardfert, 1834; prebendary of Limerick, 1841; bishop of Down, Connor, and Dromore, 1849; D.D., 1858; archbishop of Armagh, 1886–93; LL.D. Cambridge, 1888; chief work, 'Ecclesiastical Index (of Ireland),' 1839. [Suppl. iii. 71]

KNOX, THOMAS FRANCIS (1822–1882), superior of the London Oratory; educated at Trinity College, Cambridge; B.A., 1845; entered the Roman catholic church, 1845; helped to found the London Oratory, 1849; became its superior; created D.D. by Pius IX, 1875; published religious and historical works. [xxxi. 333]

KNOX, SIR THOMAS GEORGE (1824–1887), consul-general in Siam; grandson of William Knox (1762–1831) [q. v.]; ensign, 1840; lieutenant, 1842; interpreter at Bangkok consulate, 1857; acting consul, 1859–60; consul, 1864; consul-general in Siam, 1868; agent and consul-general, 1875–9; K.C.M.G., 1880. [xxxi. 334]

KNOX, VICESIMUS (1752–1821), miscellaneous writer; entered St. John's College, Oxford, 1771; B.A. and fellow, 1775; ordained, 1777; published 'Essays Moral and Literary,' 1778; master of Tunbridge School, 1778–1812; M.A., 1779; D.D. Philadelphia; remembered as the compiler of the 'Elegant Extracts,' 1789. [xxxi. 334]

KNOX, WILLIAM (1732–1810), official and controversialist; provost-marshal of Georgia, 1757–61; agent in Great Britain for Georgia and East Florida; dismissed on account of pamphlets written to defend Stamp Act, 1765; under-secretary of state for America, 1770–82; published pamphlets on colonial matters. [xxxi. 336]

KNOX, WILLIAM (1789–1825), Scottish poet; became a journalist, 1820; befriended by Scott and Wilson; published poems between 1818 and 1825, complete edition, 1847. [xxxi. 337]

KNOX, WILLIAM (1762–1831), bishop of Derry; entered Trinity College, Dublin, 1778; B.A., 1781; chaplain to the Irish House of Commons; bishop of Killaloe, 1794–1803; bishop of Derry, 1803–31; published sermons. [xxxi. 338]

KNYFF, LEONARD (1650–1721), painter; born at Haarlem; settled in London, 1690; devoted himself to topographical drawing and painting; known principally by his series of bird's-eye views of palaces and gentlemen's seats in Great Britain. [xxxi. 338]

KNYVET or **KNEVET,** Sir EDMUND (d. 1546), sergeant-porter to Henry VIII; younger brother of Sir Thomas Knyvet [q. v.]; sergeant of the king's gates, 1524; keeper of the king's woods in Rockingham Forest, 1536. [xxxi. 338]

KNYVET or **KNIVETT,** Sir JOHN (d. 1381), chancellor of England; serjeant-at-law, 1357; justice of the court of common pleas, 1361; chief-justice of the king's bench, 1365; chancellor, 1372–7. [xxxi. 339]

KNYVET, Sir THOMAS (d. 1512), officer in the navy; brother of Sir Edmund Knyvet [q. v.]; knighted, 1509; master of the horse, 1510; killed in an engagement with the French. [xxxi. 339]

KNYVET, THOMAS, Baron Knyvet of Escrick (d. 1622), grand-nephew of Sir Edmund Knyvet [q. v.]; sergeant-porter to Henry VIII; educated at Jesus College, Cambridge; gentleman of the privy chamber to Queen Elizabeth; created M.A. on her visit to Oxford, 1592; M.P., Thetford, 1601; knighted, 1604; as justice of the peace for Westminster discovered Guy Fawkes plot, 1605; privy councillor, member of the council of Queen Anne, and warden of the mint; created Baron Knyvet of Escrick, 1607. [xxxi. 340]

KNYVETT, CHARLES (1752–1822), musician; member of the Royal Society of Musicians from 1778; one of the chief singers at the Handel commemoration, 1784; directed series of oratorio performances at Covent Garden, 1789; established Willis's Rooms concerts, 1791; organist of the Chapel Royal, 1796. [xxxi. 340]

KNYVETT, CHARLES (1773–1852), musician; eldest son of Charles Knyvett (1752–1822) [q. v.]; educated at Westminster School; organist of St. George's, Hanover Square; edited a 'Collection of Favourite Glees,' 1800; published harmonised airs. [xxxi. 341]

KNYVETT, WILLIAM (1779–1856), musical composer; third son of Charles Knyvett (1752–1822) [q. v.]; gentleman of the Chapel Royal, 1797; composer of the Chapel Royal, 1802; a fashionable singer in London; conductor of the Concerts of Antient Music, 1832–40; conductor of the Birmingham festivals, 1834–43; of the York Festival, 1835; author of popular vocal works, and of the anthems for the coronations of George IV and Queen Victoria. [xxxi. 341]

KŒHLER, GEORGE FREDERIC (d. 1800), brigadier-general, captain of royal artillery; of German birth; second lieutenant in royal artillery during siege of Gibraltar, 1780; first lieutenant, 1782; invented a gun-carriage; member of the staff of George Augustus Eliott, baron Heathfield [q. v.]; employed in Belgium against the Austrians, 1790; captain-lieutenant, 1793; brevet lieutenant-colonel, 1794; captain, 1796; on service in Egypt, 1798; died at Jaffa. [xxxi. 341]

KOLLMAN, AUGUST FRIEDRICH CHRISTOPH (1756–1829), organist and composer; born at Engelbostel near Hanover; chapel-keeper and schoolmaster at the German Chapel, St. James's Palace, London, 1784; author of pianoforte compositions and works on the theory of music. [xxxi. 343]

KONIG or **KÖNIG,** CHARLES DIETRICH EBERHARD (1774–1851), mineralogist; born in Brunswick; educated at Göttingen; keeper of department of natural history in British Museum, 1813; subsequently keeper of the mineralogical department. [xxxi. 343]

KOTZWARA or **KOCSWARA,** FRANZ (1750?–1793), musician; born in Prague; assisted in Handel commemoration, 1784; composer of the popular sonata 'Battle of Prague,' for piano, violin, and violoncello, hanged himself accidentally. [xxxi. 344]

KRABTREE. [See Crabtree.]

KRATZER, NICHOLAS (1487–1550?), mathematician; born at Munich; studied at Cologne and Wittemberg; fellow of Corpus Christi College, Oxford, 1517; M.A., 1523; skilled constructor of sundials; friend of Erasmus and Hans Holbein [q. v.], who painted his portrait, 1528; left in manuscript 'Canones Horopti' and 'De Compositione Horologiorum.' [xxxi. 344]

KRAUSE, WILLIAM HENRY (1796–1852), Irish divine; born in the West Indies; entered the army, 1814; present at Waterloo, 1815; entered Trinity College, Dublin; a noted evangelical clergyman of Dublin. [xxxi. 345]

KUERDEN, RICHARD (1623–1690?). [See Jackson.]

KUPER, Sir AUGUSTUS LEOPOLD (1809–1885), admiral; entered the navy, 1823; lieutenant, 1830; assisted his father-in-law, Captain Sir James John Gordon Bremer [q. v.], in forming settlement of Port Essington in North Australia, 1837; commander, 1839; employed in Chinese war, 1840–1; rear-admiral, 1861; commander-in-chief in China, 1862; K.C.B., 1864; admiral, 1872. [xxxi. 345]

KURZ, SULPIZ (1833?–1878), botanist; born in Munich; entered Dutch service in Java; curator of Calcutta herbarium; explored Burmah, Pegu, and the Andaman islands; published 'Forest Flora of Burmah,' 1877; died at Penang. [xxxi. 346]

KYAN, ESMOND (d. 1798), Irish rebel; commanded rebel artillery at battle of Arklow, 1798; arrested and executed. [xxxi. 346]

KYAN, JOHN HOWARD (1774–1850), inventor of the 'Kyanising' process for preserving wood; began experiments to prevent decay of wood, 1812; patented his invention, 1832; his process superseded, c. 1835; died at New York. [xxxi. 347]

KYD, ROBERT (d. 1793), founder of the Botanical Gardens, Calcutta; obtained cadetship, 1764; lieutenant Bengal infantry, 1765; major, 1780; lieutenant-colonel, 1782; secretary to military department of inspection, Bengal; laid out Botanical Garden, near Calcutta, 1786; died at Calcutta. [xxxi. 348]

KYD, STEWART (d. 1811), politician and legal writer; educated at King's College, Aberdeen; barrister, Middle Temple, London; friend of Thomas Hardy (1752–1832) [q. v.]; arrested for high treason and discharged, 1794; defended the publisher of Paine's 'Age of Reason,' 1797; wrote legal treatises. [xxxi. 348]

KYD or **KID,** THOMAS (1557?–1595?), dramatist; educated at Merchant Taylors' School, London; originally a scrivener; 'Spanish Tragedy' printed, 1594; his 'First Part of Ieronimo' published, 1605; his 'Cornelia' licensed for publication, 1594; often credited with 'The rare Triumphs of Love and Fortune' (acted, 1582) and 'The Tragedye of Solyman and Perseda' (printed, 1599); perhaps the author of a pre-Shakespearean play (now lost) on the subject of Hamlet; one of the best-known tragic poets of his time. [xxxi. 349]

KYDERMYNSTER. [See Kedermyster.]

KYFFIN, MAURICE (d. 1599), poet and translator; published 'The Blessednes of Brytaine, or a Celebration of the Queenes Holyday,' a poetical eulogy on the government of Elizabeth, 1587 (2nd edit. 1588); translated in prose the 'Andria' of Terence, 1588; issued his Welsh translation of Bishop Jewel's 'Apologia pro Ecclesia Anglicana,' 1594 or 1595. [xxxi. 352]

KYLE, JAMES FRANCIS (1788–1869), Scottish catholic prelate; ordained, 1812; D.D.; bishop of Germanicia in partibus, and vicar-apostolic of the northern district of Scotland, 1827; collected documents for history of catholicism in Scotland. [xxxi. 353]

KYLMINGTON or **KYLMETON,** RICHARD (d. 1361), dean of St. Paul's and theologian; educated at Oxford; D.D. before 1339; archdeacon of London, 1348–1350; dean of St. Paul's, 1353–61. [xxxi. 353]

KYME, titular EARLS OF. [See UMFRAVILLE, GILBERT DE, 1390–1421; TALBOYS or TAILBOYS, SIR WILLIAM, d. 1464.]

KYMER, GILBERT (d. 1463), dean of Salisbury and chancellor of the university of Oxford; educated at Oxford; proctor, 1412–13; principal of Hart Hall, Oxford, 1412–14; dean of Wimborne Minster, 1427; chancellor of Oxford University, 1431–3 and 1446–53; dean of Salisbury, 1449; physician in household of Humphrey, duke of Gloucester; attended Henry VI, 1455; wrote 'Diætarium de Sanitatis Custodia.' [xxxi. 353]

KYNASTON, EDWARD (1640?–1706), actor; first appeared at the Cockpit, Drury Lane, 1659; played Epicœne in the 'Silent Woman,' 1661; his first important male part, Peregrine in the 'Fox,' 1665; played Cassio in 'Othello,' 1682; acted with Betterton, 1682–99; one of the last male actors of female parts. [xxxi. 354]

KYNASTON or **KINASTON**, SIR FRANCIS (1587–1642), poet and scholar; entered Oriel College, Oxford, 1601; B.A., 1604; removed to Trinity College, Cambridge, where he graduated M.A., 1609; M.A. Oxford, 1611; barrister, Lincoln's Inn, 1611; knighted, 1618; M.P., Shropshire, 1621–2; the centre of a brilliant literary coterie at court; founded an academy of learning called the Musæum Minervæ, 1635; published poems and translations. [xxxi. 355]

KYNASTON, HERBERT (1809–1878), high-master of St. Paul's School; educated at Westminster School; entered Christ Church, Oxford, 1827; M.A., 1833; ordained, 1834; tutor and Greek reader of his college, 1836; high-master of St. Paul's School, London, 1838–76; D.D., 1849; well known as a schoolmaster and writer and translator of hymns. [xxxi. 356]

KYNASTON, JOHN (1728–1783), author; fellow of Brasenose College, Oxford, 1751; M.A., 1752; author of controversial pamphlets; contributor to the 'Gentleman's Magazine.' [xxxi. 357]

KYNDER, PHILIP (fl. 1665), miscellaneous writer; educated at Pembroke Hall, Cambridge; B.A., 1616; agent for court affairs, 1640–3; published 'The Surfeit. To A. B. C.' 1656; many of his works preserved in manuscript in the Bodleian. [xxxi. 358]

KYNEWULF (fl. 750). [See CYNEWULF.]

KYNGESBURY or **KYNBURY**, THOMAS (fl. 1390), Franciscan and D.D. of Oxford; twenty-sixth provincial minister of English Minorites, 1380–90; encouraged study of science. [xxxi. 360]

KYNNESMAN, ARTHUR (1682–1770), schoolmaster; entered Trinity College, Cambridge, 1702; M.A. 1709; master of Bury St. Edmunds grammar school, 1715–65; published 'A Short Introduction to Grammar,' 1768. [xxxi. 360]

KYNSIGE, KINSIUS, KINSI, or CYNESIGE (d. 1060), archbishop of York; monk of Peterborough; a chaplain of Edward the Confessor; archbishop of York, 1051–60. [xxxi. 361]

KYNTON, JOHN (d. 1536), divinity professor at Oxford; Franciscan friar; D.D., 1500; vice-chancellor and Senior Theologus, Oxford, at intervals between 1503 and 1513; one of the four doctors of divinity to consult with Wolsey about the Lutheran doctrines, 1521; Margaret professor of theology (resigned, 1530). [xxxi. 361]

KYNWELMARSH, FRANCIS (d. 1580). [See KINWELMERSH.]

KYNYNGHAM or **CUNNINGHAM**, JOHN (d. 1399), Carmelite; studied at Oxford; twenty-first provincial of his order, 1393; vigorously opposed Wycliffe. [xxxi. 361]

KYRLE, JOHN (1637–1724), the Man of Ross; educated at the Ross grammar school and Balliol College, Oxford; student of the Middle Temple, 1657; lived very simply on his estates at Ross; devoted his surplus income to works of charity; eulogised by Pope, 1732. The Kyrle Society was inaugurated in 1877 as a memorial of him. [xxxi. 362]

KYRTON, EDMUND (d. 1466). [See KIRTON.]

KYTE, FRANCIS (fl. 1710–1745), mezzotint-engraver and portrait-painter; published mezzotint-engravings after Kneller; subsequently devoted himself to portrait-painting. [xxxi. 363]

KYTE, JOHN (d. 1537). [See KITE.]

KYTELER, DAME ALICE (fl. 1324). [See KETTLE.]

KYTSON, SIR THOMAS (1485–1540), sheriff of London; master of the Mercers' Company, 1535; engaged in extensive mercantile transactions; member of Merchant Adventurers' Company; sheriff of London, 1533; knighted, 1533. [xxxi. 364]

L

LABELYE, CHARLES (1705–1781?), architect of the first Westminster Bridge; born at Vevey; came to England, c. 1725; employed in building Westminster Bridge, 1738–1750; naturalised, 1746; published 'A Description of Westminster Bridge,' 1751; died at Paris. [xxxi. 365]

LABLACHE, FANNY WYNDHAM (d. 1877), vocalist; née Wilton; wife of Frederick Lablache [q. v.]; died at Paris. [xxxi. 367]

LABLACHE, FREDERICK (1815–1887), vocalist; eldest son of Luigi Lablache [q. v.]; appeared in London in Italian opera, c. 1837; sang at Manchester with Mario, Grisi, and Jenny Lind; withdrew from the stage and devoted himself to teaching, c. 1865. [xxxi. 366]

LABLACHE, LUIGI (1794–1858), vocalist; born at Naples; sang the solos in Mozart's requiem on the death of Haydn, 1809; engaged at the San Carlo Theatre, Naples, 1812; at La Scala, Milan, 1817; in London, 1830; a magnificent bass singer and an excellent actor; taught singing to Queen Victoria; died at Naples; buried at Paris. [xxxi. 367]

LABOUCHERE, HENRY, first BARON TAUNTON (1798–1869), educated at Winchester; B.A. Christ Church, Oxford, 1821; liberal M.P., Michael Borough, 1826; M.A., 1828; M.P., Taunton, 1830; a lord of the admiralty, 1832; master of the mint, privy councillor, and vice-president of the board of trade, 1839; under-secretary of war and the colonies, February 1839; president of the board of trade and admitted to Lord Melbourne's cabinet, August 1839–1841; again president of the board of trade under Lord John Russell, 1847–52; secretary of state for the colonies under Lord Palmerston, 1855–8; raised to peerage, 1859; some of his speeches published separately. [xxxi. 367]

LACAITA, SIR JAMES PHILIP (1813–1895), Italian scholar and politician; born at Manduria, Italy; graduated in law at Naples; advocate, 1836; legal adviser to British legation, Naples; assisted Gladstone to collect information about Bourbon misrule, 1850; came to London, 1852; professor of Italian, Queen's College, London, 1853–6; naturalised in England, 1855; secretary to Gladstone's mission to Ionian islands, 1858; K.C.M.G., 1859; deputy to first Italian legislature, 1861–5; senator, 1876; completed Lord Vernon's edition of Dante, 1865. [Suppl. iii. 73]

LACEY, WILLIAM (1584–1673), jesuit; his real name WOLFE; entered Magdalen College, Oxford, 1600; B.A., 1606; became a Roman catholic; admitted to the English college, Rome, 1608; missioner in England, 1625–1673; published controversial pamphlets. [xxxi. 369]

LACHTAIN, LAICHTIN, LACHTNAIN, LACHTOC, or MOLACHTOC (d. 622), Irish saint; claimed descent from a king of Ireland in the second century; a disciple of Comgall [q. v.], of Beannchair; founded two churches in Ireland; his day, 19 March. [xxxi. 369]

LACKINGTON, GEORGE (1768–1844), bookseller; entered the bookselling business of his relative, James Lackington [q. v.], 1779, and became its head, 1798; official assignee of bankrupts. [xxxi. 369]

B b

LACKINGTON, JAMES (1746–1815), bookseller; his shop in Finsbury Square known as the 'Temple of the Muses' and one of the sights of London; published his 'Memoirs,' 1791, his 'Confessions,' 1804. [xxxi. 370]

LA CLOCHE, JAMES (*fl.* 1668), natural son of Charles II; born in Jersey; his mother's name unknown; brought up as a protestant in France and Holland; entered novitiate of jesuits at Rome; employed by Charles II as a means of secret communication with Rome, 1668. [xxxi. 371]

LACROIX, ALPHONSE FRANÇOIS (1799–1859), missionary; born in the canton of Neuchâtel; became a missionary; agent of the Netherlands Missionary Society at Chinsurah, near Calcutta; transferred his services to the London Missionary Society and became a British subject; removed to Calcutta, 1827; learned Bengali and preached with great success; revised the Bengali scriptures; trained native preachers. [xxxi. 372]

LACY, EDMUND (1370?–1455), bishop of Exeter; D.D. Oxford; master of University College, Oxford, 1398; prebendary of Hereford, 1412, and of Lincoln, 1414; dean of Chapel Royal under Henry V; bishop of Hereford, 1417, and of Exeter, 1420–55. [Suppl. iii. 74]

LACY, FRANCES DALTON (1819–1872), actress; first appeared in London at the Haymarket, 1838; joined Madame Vestris's company at Covent Garden, 1840; married the actor Thomas Hailes Lacy [q. v.], 1842. [xxxi. 388]

LACY, FRANCIS ANTONY (1731–1792), Spanish general and diplomatist; of Irish birth; commenced his military career in the Spanish service, 1747; commanded Spanish artillery at siege of Gibraltar; Spanish minister plenipotentiary at Stockholm and St. Petersburg; commandant-general of coast of Grenada; member of supreme council of war and commandant-general and sole inspector-general of artillery and of all ordnance-manufacturing establishments in Spain and the Indies; governor and captain-general of Catalonia, 1789. [xxxi. 372]

LACY, GILBERT DE, fourth BARON LACY (*fl.* 1150), grandson of Walter de Lacy, first baron Lacy [q. v.]; supported the Empress Matilda, 1138, but joined Stephen before 1146; joined the knights of the Temple and went to the Holy Land; preceptor of his order in the county of Tripoli. [xxxi. 375]

LACY, HARRIETTE DEBORAH (1807–1874), actress; *née* Taylor; made her début as Julia in the 'Rivals,' 1827; joined Macready's company and married Walter Lacy [q. v.], 1838; among her best performances were Nell Gwynne in Jerrold's play and Ophelia; retired from the stage, 1848. [xxxi. 373]

LACY, HENRY DE, third EARL OF LINCOLN of the Lacy family (1249?–1311), grandson of John de Lacy, first earl of Lincoln [q. v.]; succeeded his father, 1257; knighted, 1272; commanded division in Welsh war, 1276; joint-lieutenant of England in Edward I's absence, 1279; accompanied Edward I to Gascony, 1286–9; assisted in the deliberations respecting Scottish succession, 1291 and 1292; in command of the army in France, 1296–8; accompanied Edward I to Scotland and was present at his death, 1307; one of the lords ordainers and guardian of the kingdom in Edward II's absence, 1310. [xxxi. 373]

LACY, HUGH DE, fifth BARON LACY by tenure and first LORD OF MEATH (*d.* 1186), one of the conquerors of Ireland; doubtless the son of Gilbert de Lacy, fourth baron Lacy [q. v.]; went to Ireland with Henry II, 1171; procurator-general of Ireland, 1177–81 and 1185–6; accused of aspiring to the crown of Ireland; assassinated, 1186. [xxxi. 375]

LACY, HUGH DE, first EARL OF ULSTER (*d.* 1242?), earliest Anglo-Norman peer of Ireland; second son of Hugh de Lacy, fifth baron Lacy (*d.* 1186) [q. v.]; took part in the fighting in Ireland; created Earl of Ulster, 1205; fled to Scotland, and thence to France, 1210; returned to England, 1221; joined Llywelyn ab Iorwerth [q. v.] in Wales; engaged again in warfare in Ireland. [xxxi. 377]

LACY, JOHN DE (*d.* 1190), crusader; son of Richard FitzEustace, constable of Chester; assumed cousin's name as heir to the Lacy estates; died at Tyre. [xxxi. 388]

LACY, JOHN DE, first EARL OF LINCOLN of the Lacy family (*d.* 1240), son of Roger de Lacy [q. v.]; one of the twenty-five barons appointed to see to the maintenance of the Great Charter, 1215; crusader, 1218; created Earl of Lincoln, 1232; one of the witnesses of the confirmation of the charters, 1236. [xxxi. 380]

LACY, JOHN (*d.* 1681), dramatist and comedian; attached to Charles II's (Killigrew's) company of actors; his acting commended by Pepys and Evelyn; his best play 'The Old Troop, or Monsieur Raggou,' written before 1665 (printed, 1672); the original Bayes of the 'Rehearsal,' 1671. [xxxi. 380]

LACY, JOHN (*fl.* 1737), pseudo-prophet; camisard; published 'The Prophetical Warnings of John Lacy,' 1707; claimed the power of working miracles; committed to Bridewell, 1737. [xxxi. 382]

LACY or **DE LACY**, MAURICE (1740–1820), of Grodno; Russian general; born at Limerick; of the family of Peter Lacy, count Lacy [q. v.]; attained general's rank in Russian army; held command under Suwarrow in campaigns against the French in Switzerland and Italy; governor of Grodno. [xxxi. 384]

LACY, MICHAEL ROPHINO (1795–1867), violinist and composer; born at Bilbao; studied violin at Paris and in England, 1805; an actor of 'genteel comedy parts,' 1808–18; composed ballet-music for Italian opera, London, 1820–3; adapted foreign libretti; composed an oratorio (1833) and minor pieces. [xxxi. 385]

LACY, PETER, COUNT LACY (1678–1751), Russian field-marshal; entered Russian service, 1697; fought against Danes, Swedes, and Turks, 1705–21; commander-in-chief at St. Petersburg and other places, 1725; aided in establishing Augustus of Saxony on the throne of Poland, 1733–5; field-marshal, 1736; called by Frederick the Great the 'Prince Eugene of Muscovy.' [xxxi. 385]

LACY, ROGER DE (*d.* 1212), justiciar and constable of Chester; son of John de Lacy (*d.* 1190) [q. v.]; nephew of William de Mandeville, earl of Essex [q. v.]; constable of Chester, 1190; justiciar, 1209. [xxxi. 388]

LACY, THOMAS HAILES (1809–1873), actor and theatrical publisher; first appeared on the London stage, 1828; with Phelps at Sadler's Wells, 1844–9; theatrical bookseller, 1849; published acting editions of 1,485 dramas between 1848 and 1873; author of several plays. [xxxi. 389]

LACY, WALTER DE, first BARON LACY by tenure (*d.* 1085), said to have fought for the Conqueror at Hastings, 1066. [xxxi. 389]

LACY, WALTER DE, sixth BARON LACY by tenure, and second LORD OF MEATH (*d.* 1241), elder son of Hugh de Lacy, fifth baron Lacy (*d.* 1186) [q. v.]; elder brother of Hugh de Lacy, first earl of Ulster [q. v.]; took part in John's expedition to France, 1214; sheriff of Herefordshire, 1216–23; one of the chief supporters of the young king Henry III. [xxxi. 390]

LACY, WALTER (1809–1898), actor; his real name Williams; first appeared on stage in Edinburgh, 1829; played Charles Surface at Haymarket, London, 1838; with Charles Kean at Princess's, 1852. His parts included Edmund ('Lear'), Benedick, Comus, Faulconbridge, Malvolio, Touchstone, Henry VIII, and Ghost ('Hamlet'). [Suppl. iii. 74]

LACY, WILLIAM (1610?–1671), royalist divine; educated at St. John's College, Cambridge; M.A. and fellow, 1636; B.D., 1642; associated with John Barwick (1612–1664) [q. v.] in writing 'Certain Disquisitions' against the covenant; ejected from his fellowship, 1644; became chaplain to Prince Rupert; taken prisoner, 1645; restored to his fellowship, 1660; D.D., 1662. [xxxi. 392]

LACY, WILLIAM (1788–1871), bass-singer; appeared at concerts in London, 1798–1810; in Calcutta, 1818–25. [xxxi. 383]

LADBROOKE, HENRY (1800–1870), landscape-painter; second son of Robert Ladbrooke [q. v.], landscape-painter; acquired reputation for his moonlight scenes; exhibited at various institutions. [xxxi. 393]

LADBROOKE, JOHN BERNEY (1803–1879), landscape-painter; third son of Robert Ladbrooke [q. v.], landscape-painter; a pupil of John Crome [q. v.], whose manner he followed; exhibited at the Royal Academy, 1821–2, at the British Institution and the Suffolk Street Gallery up to 1873. [xxxi. 393]

LADBROOKE, ROBERT (1768–1842), landscape-painter; worked with John Crome [q. v.]; took a leading part in the establishment of the celebrated Norwich Society of Artists, 1803; vice-president, 1808; exhibitor at Royal Academy between 1804 and 1815; painted chiefly Norfolk scenery. [xxxi. 392]

LADYMAN, SAMUEL (1625–1684), divine; fellow, Corpus Christi College, Oxford, 1648; M.A., 1649; became an independent; conformed at the Restoration; prebendary of Cashel, 1677; archdeacon of Limerick; D.D.; published sermons, 1658. [xxxi. 393]

LAEGHAIRE or **LOEGHAIRE** (d. 458), king of Ireland; succeeded to the throne, 428; baptised by St. Patrick, 432; at war with the Leinster men, 453–7; defeated and slain by them. [xxxi. 393]

LAEGHAIRE LORC, mythical king of Ireland; assigned by chroniclers to B.C. 595–3. [xxxi. 394]

LAFFAN, SIR JOSEPH DE COURCY, first baronet (1786–1848), physician; educated at Edinburgh; M.D. Edinburgh, 1808; L.R.C.P., 1808; physician to the forces, 1812; served in Spain and Portugal during the latter part of the Peninsular war; physician in ordinary to the Duke of Kent; created baronet, 1828; K.H., 1836.
[xxxi. 394]

LAFFAN, SIR ROBERT MICHAEL (1821–1882), governor of Bermuda; educated at the college of Pont Levoy, near Blois; entered Royal Military Academy, Woolwich, 1835; second lieutenant in royal engineers, 1837; first lieutenant, 1839; organised engineering arrangements of expedition for relief of garrison of Natal besieged by the Boer Pretorius; captain, 1846; inspector of railways under the board of trade, 1847–52; M.P., St. Ives, Cornwall, 1852–7; deputy inspector-general of fortifications at the war office, 1855; brevet major, 1858; regimental lieutenant-colonel, 1859; commanding royal engineer at Malta, 1860–5; brevet-colonel, 1864; sent to Ceylon as member of commission to report on military expenditure of colony and on its defences, 1865; regimental colonel, 1870; commanding royal engineer at Gibraltar, 1872–7; governor and commander-in-chief of the Bermudas as brigadier-general, 1877; K.C.M.G., 1877; major-general, 1877; lieutenant-general, 1881; died at Mount Langton, Bermuda. [xxxi. 395]

LAFONTAINE, SIR LOUIS HYPOLITE, first baronet (1807–1864), Canadian statesman; born at Boucherville, Lower Canada; educated at Montreal; called to bar; member for county of Terrebonne in legislative assembly of Lower Canada, 1830–7; became leader of the *parti prêtre*, c. 1839; opposed union of Upper and Lower Canada, 1840; member of parliament of united provinces for fourth riding of York county, Upper Canada, 1841; leader of French Canadians; attorney-general for lower province in Baldwin-Lafontaine administration, 1842–3; member for Terrebonne, 1844, and for Montreal city, 1848; premier and attorney-general for Lower Canada, 1848; introduced (1849) rebellion losses bill, which met with extraordinary opposition; retired, 1851; chief-justice of Lower Canada, 1853, till death; created baronet, 1854.
[Suppl. iii. 75]

LAFOREY, SIR FRANCIS (1767–1835), son of Sir John Laforey [q. v.], admiral; present at the battle of Trafalgar, 1805; commander-in-chief at the Leeward islands, 1811–14; K.C.B., 1815; admiral of the blue, 1835.
[xxxi. 396]

LAFOREY, SIR JOHN, first baronet (1729?–1796), admiral; his ancestors Huguenot refugees; lieutenant, 1748; commander, 1755; present at reduction of Martinique, 1762; took part in action off Ushant, 1778; commissioner of the navy at Barbados, with instructions to act as commander-in-chief under special circumstances, 1779; rear-admiral of the red; created baronet, 1789; commander-in-chief at the Leeward islands, 1789–93 and 1795–6; vice-admiral, 1793; admiral, 1795; Demerara, Essequibo, and Berbice captured during his command; died on the passage home. [xxxi. 396]

LAGUERRE, JOHN (d. 1748), painter and actor; son of Louis Laguerre [q. v.]; educated for a painter, but became an actor; scene painter; best known by a series of drawings, 'Hob in the Well,' which were engraved.
[xxxi. 397]

LAGUERRE, LOUIS (1663–1721), painter; born at Paris; of Spanish origin; educated at the Jesuits' College, Paris; studied drawing at the school of the French Academy; employed in England as assistant by Verrio; painted halls, staircases, or ceilings at Burleigh House, Blenheim, Chatsworth, Marlborough House, and elsewhere; employed by William III at Hampton Court; his figure-drawing widely imitated. [xxxi. 397]

LAIDLAW, WILLIAM (1780–1845), friend of Sir Walter Scott; steward to Sir Walter Scott at Abbotsford, 1817; Scott's amanuensis; author of lyrics; compiled, under Scott's direction, part of the 'Edinburgh Annual Register' after 1817. [xxxi. 397]

LAING, ALEXANDER (1778–1838), antiquary; published the 'Caledonian Itinerary,' 1819, and 'Scarce Ancient Ballads never before published,' 1822; chief work, the 'Donean Tourist, interspersed with Anecdotes and Ancient National Ballads,' 1828. [xxxi. 398]

LAING, ALEXANDER (1787–1857), the Brechin poet; son of an agricultural labourer; contributed to local newspapers and poetical miscellanies : 'Wayside Flowers,' a collection of his poetry, published, 1846 (second edition, 1850); wrote in lowland Scotch. [xxxi. 398]

LAING, ALEXANDER GORDON (1793 – 1826), African traveller; educated at Edinburgh University; ensign in the Edinburgh volunteers, 1810; went to Barbados, 1811; lieutenant, 1815; deputy-assistant quartermaster-general in Jamaica; adjutant, 1820; despatched by the governor of Sierra Leone to the Kambian and Mandingo countries to ascertain the native sentiment regarding the slave trade, 1822; frequently engaged with and defeated the Ashantees, 1823; published 'Travels in Timmannee, Kooranko, and Soolima, Countries of Western Africa,' 1825; undertook expedition to ascertain source and course of Niger, 1825; murdered by Arabs on reaching Timbuctoo. [xxxi. 399]

LAING, DAVID (1774–1856), architect; articled to Sir John Soane [q. v.], c. 1790; surveyor of buildings at the custom house, London, 1811; designed a new custom house (built 1813–17), the front of which fell down, 1825, much litigation ensuing; wrote on practical architecture. [xxxi. 400]

LAING, DAVID (1793–1878), Scottish antiquary; second son of William Laing [q. v.], bookseller; educated at Edinburgh University; became partner in his father's business, 1821, and employed abroad in search of rare books; edited old Scottish ballads and metrical romances; secretary of the Bannatyne Club, 1823–61; fellow of the Society of Antiquaries of Scotland, 1826; issued first collected edition of the poems of William Dunbar [q. v.], 1834; librarian to the Signet Library, 1837; edited antiquarian works, 1840–78; hon. professor of antiquities to the Royal Scottish Academy, 1854. [xxxi. 401]

LAING, JAMES (1502–1594), doctor of theology, Paris; educated first in Scotland and then at the university of Paris; procurator of the Scots nation, 1556, 1558, 1560, 1568, 1571; doctor of theology, 1571; a violent enemy of the Reformation; wrote polemical treatises in Latin, 1581 and 1585; died at Paris. [xxxi. 402]

LAING, JOHN (d. 1483), bishop of Glasgow and chancellor of Scotland; king's treasurer, 1470; clerk of the king's rolls and register, 1472; bishop of Glasgow, 1474; founded the 'Greyfriars' of Glasgow, 1476; lord high chancellor, 1482; wrote the oldest extant rolls of the treasury. [xxxi. 403]

LAING, JOHN (1809–1880), bibliographer; educated at Edinburgh; chaplain to the presbyterian soldiers at Gibraltar, 1846; afterwards at Malta; librarian of New College, Edinburgh, 1850; completed 'A Dictionary of Anonymous and Pseudonymous Literature of Great Britain,' which Samuel Halkett [q. v.] began. The work was published 1882–8. [xxxi. 403]

LAING, MALCOLM (1762–1818), Scottish historian; brother of Samuel Laing (1780–1868) [q. v.]; educated at Edinburgh University; called to the Scottish bar, 1785; published 'A History of Scotland from the Union of the Crowns, on the Accession of King James VI to the Throne of England, to the Union of the Kingdoms,' 1802 (second edition, 1804); published 'Poems of Ossian, with Notes and Illustrations,' 1805; M.P., Orkney and Shetland, 1807–1812. [xxxi. 404]

LAING, SAMUEL (1780–1868), author and traveller; brother of Malcolm Laing [q. v.]; educated at Edinburgh; in the army and served in Peninsular war, 1805–9; travelled in Norway and Sweden, 1834; wrote on the economic and social condition of Scandinavia; his most considerable work, 'The Heimskringla, or Chronicle of the Kings of Norway, translated from the Icelandic,' 1844; published three series of 'Notes of a Traveller,' 1850–2. [xxxi. 404]

LAING, SAMUEL (1812–1897), politician and author; son of Samuel Laing (1780–1868) [q. v.]; B.A.; second wrangler and second Smith's prizeman, St. John's College, Cambridge, 1831; fellow, 1834; barrister, Lincoln's Inn, 1837; secretary to railway department of board of trade, 1842–6; member of railway commission, 1845; chairman and managing director of London, Brighton, and South Coast Railway, 1848–52 and 1867–94; liberal M.P. for Wick district, 1852–7, 1859, and 1865–8; financial secretary to treasury, 1859–60; financial minister in India, 1860; M.P., Orkney and Shetland, 1872–85; published 'Modern Science and Modern Thought' and anthropological works. [Suppl. iii. 76]

LAING, WILLIAM (1764–1832), bookseller; collector of and authority on best editions and valuable books, both English and foreign; published editions of Thucydides, Herodotus, and Xenophon, as part of a scheme for a worthy edition of the Greek classics. [xxxi. 406]

LAIRD, JOHN (1805–1874), shipbuilder; brother of Macgregor Laird [q. v.]; managing partner in firm of William Laird & Son till 1861; built a lighter for use on Irish lakes and canals, one of the first iron vessels ever constructed, 1829; the famous Birkenhead among the many iron vessels built by him; M.P., Birkenhead, 1861–74. [xxxi. 406]

LAIRD, MACGREGOR (1808–1861), African explorer; brother of John Laird [q. v.]; joined the company for African exploration; published narrative of the expedition made by him to the Niger, 1832–4; F.R.G.S.; one of the promoters of the British and North American Steam Navigation Company, 1837; fitted out private expedition to Africa, 1854; established trading depots on the Niger. [xxxi. 407]

LAKE, ARTHUR (1569–1626), bishop of Bath and Wells; brother of Sir Thomas Lake [q. v.]; educated at Winchester; fellow of New College, Oxford, 1589; M.A., 1595; master of St. Cross Hospital, Winchester, 1603; D.D., 1605; dean of Worcester, 1608; warden of New College, 1613; vice-chancellor of Oxford and bishop of Bath and Wells, 1616–26; his sermons published in 1629 and 1640. [xxxi. 408]

LAKE, Sir EDWARD, first baronet (1600?–1674), royalist; B.A. Cambridge; B.A. Oxford, 1627; B.C.L., 1628; advocate-general for Ireland; fought and wrote on the king's side; chancellor of diocese of Lincoln at the Restoration; assumed the title of baronet after 1662; account of his interviews with Charles I edited from the original manuscript, 1858. [xxxi. 409]

LAKE, EDWARD (1641–1704), archdeacon of Exeter; entered Wadham College, Oxford, 1658; removed to Cambridge before graduating; chaplain and tutor to the Princesses Mary and Anne; archdeacon of Exeter, 1676; D.D. Cambridge, 1676; author of 'Officium Eucharisticum,' a popular manual for his royal pupils, published in 1673 (30th ed. 1753), republished, 1843; his 'Diary' in 1677–8, published, 1846. [xxxi. 409]

LAKE, EDWARD JOHN (1823–1877), major-general in the royal engineers; born at Madras; second lieutenant, Bengal engineers, 1840; lieutenant, 1844; fought in Sikh wars, 1845 and 1848–9; assistant of John Lawrence in trans-Sutlej territory, 1846; captain and brevet-major, 1854; commissioner of the Jalundhur Doab, 1855; secured Kangra in the mutiny, 1857; lieutenant-colonel, 1861; financial commissioner of the Punjaub, 1865; C.S.I., 1866; colonel, 1868; retired with honorary rank of major-general, 1870; honorary lay secretary of the Church Missionary Society, 1869–76; edited 'Church Missionary Record,' 1871–4. [xxxi. 410]

LAKE, GERARD, first VISCOUNT LAKE of Delhi and Leswarree (1744–1808), general; descendant of Sir Thomas Lake [q. v.]; nephew of George Colman the elder [q. v.]; ensign, 1758; lieutenant and captain, 1762; captain-lieutenant, captain, and lieutenant-colonel, 1776;

served in North Carolina, 1781; regimental-major, 1784; major-general, 1790; M.P., Aylesbury, 1790–1802; regimental lieutenant-colonel, 1792; served in French war, 1793–4; lieutenant-general, 1797; commander-in-chief and second member of council in India, 1800; developed military resources of East India Company; assisted Wellesley to break up Mahratta confederacy, 1803; raised to peerage, 1804; advanced to a viscountcy, 1807. [xxxi. 411]

LAKE, Sir HENRY ATWELL (1808–1881), colonel of the royal engineers; educated at Harrow and Addiscombe military college; second lieutenant; went to India, 1826; lieutenant, 1831; brevet-captain, 1840; regimental captain, 1852; brevet-major, 1840; employed principally upon irrigation works; chief engineer at Kars, 1854; lieutenant-colonel, 1855; on the capitulation of Kars sent as prisoner of war to Russia; released, 1856; colonel, 1856; subsequently chief commissioner of police in Dublin; K.C.B., 1875; author of works on the defence of Kars, published, 1856–7. [xxxi. 415]

LAKE, JOHN (1624–1689), bishop of Chichester; educated at St. John's College, Cambridge; a royalist; received holy orders, 1647; vicar of Leeds, 1660; D.D. Cambridge, 1661; prebendary of York, 1671; bishop of Sodor and Man, 1684; bishop of Chichester, 1685; refused to take the oath of allegiance to William and Mary, 1688; active in the suppression of abuses; wrote life of John Cleveland [q. v.] the poet (published, 1677). [xxxi. 416]

LAKE, Sir THOMAS (1567?–1630), secretary of state; brother of Arthur Lake [q. v.]; educated probably at Cambridge; a member of the Elizabethan Society of Antiquaries; M.A. Oxford, 1592; clerk of the signet, c. 1600; Latin secretary to James I, 1603; knighted, 1603; keeper of the records at Whitehall, 1604; M.P., Launceston, 1604; privy councillor, 1614; M.P., Middlesex, 1614; secretary of state, 1616; charged with defamation of character by the Countess of Exeter and found guilty, 1619; fined, imprisoned, and dismissed from his office; M.P., Wells, 1625, Wootton Bassett, 1626. [xxxi. 417]

LAKE, WILLIAM CHARLES (1817–1897), dean of Durham; educated at Rugby and Balliol College, Oxford; fellow, 1838; took holy orders, 1842; prebendary of Wells, 1860; dean of Durham, 1869–94; greatly assisted in foundation of College of Science, Newcastle, 1871. [Suppl. iii. 78]

LAKINGHETH, JOHN DE (d. 1381), chronicler; monk of Bury St. Edmunds; surrendered to the insurgents in the peasant rising of 1381, and was beheaded by them; compiled 'Kalendare Maneriorum Terrarum . . . ad Monasterium S. Edmundi Buriensis spectantium.' [xxxi. 419]

LALOR, JAMES FINTON (d. 1849), politician; brother of Peter Lalor [q. v.]; contributed to the 'Nation,' 1847; prominent in revolutionary circles, 1847–8; edited the 'Irish Felon,' 1848. [xxxi. 419]

LALOR, JOHN (1814–1856), journalist and author; entered Trinity College, Dublin, 1831; B.A., 1837; one of the principal editors of the London 'Morning Chronicle'; joined unitarians, 1844; edited the 'Enquirer' (unitarian weekly). [xxxi. 420]

LALOR, PETER (1823–1889), colonial legislator; younger brother of James Finton Lalor [q. v.]; educated at Trinity College, Dublin; went to the Australian gold mines, 1852; leader among the insurgent miners, 1854; member for Ballarat in the legislative council of Victoria, 1855, and soon afterwards inspector of railways; member for South Grant in the parliament of Victoria, 1856–71 and 1875–7; chairman of committees, 1856; commissioner for customs, 1875; postmaster-general, 1878; speaker, 1880–8; died at Melbourne. [xxxi. 420]

LAMB. [See also LAMBE.]

LAMB, ANDREW (1565?–1634), bishop of Galloway; titular bishop of Brechin, 1607; bishop of Galloway, 1619; supported introduction of episcopacy into Scotland. [xxxi. 421]

LAMB, BENJAMIN (fl. 1715), organist of Eton College and verger of St. George's Chapel, Windsor, c. 1715; wrote church music and songs. [xxxi. 421]

LAMB, LADY CAROLINE (1785–1828), novelist; only daughter of the third Earl of Bessborough; married William Lamb, afterwards second Viscount Melbourne [q. v.], 1805; became passionately infatuated with Byron; 'Glenarvon,' her first novel, containing a caricature portrait of Byron, published anonymously, 1816 (reprinted as 'The Fatal Passion,' 1865); published 'A New Canto,' 1819; her second novel, Graham Hamilton,' published, 1822, and ' Ada Reis; a Tale,' 1823; never really recovered from the shock of meeting Byron's funeral procession; separated from her husband, 1825.   [xxxi. 421]

LAMB, CHARLES (1775–1834), essayist and humorist; educated at Christ's Hospital (1782–9), where he formed an enduring friendship with Coleridge; employed in the South Sea House, 1789–92; a clerk in the India House, 1792–1825; his mother killed by his sister Mary [see LAMB, MARY ANN] in a fit of insanity, 1796; undertook to be his sister's guardian, an office he discharged throughout his life; was himself in an asylum as deranged, 1795–6; contributed four sonnets to Coleridge's first volume, 'Poems on Various Subjects,' 1796; visited Coleridge at Nether Stowey and met Wordsworth and others, 1797; with Charles Lloyd published 'Blank Verse,' 1798; added to his scanty income by writing for the newspapers; published 'John Woodvil,' a blank-verse play of the Restoration period, 1802; his farce 'Mr. H.' damned at Drury Lane, 1805; 'Tales from Shakespeare,' by himself and his sister, published, 1807; published a child's version of the adventures of Ulysses, 1808, and 'Specimens of English Dramatic Poets contemporary with Shakespeare,' 1808; a collection of his miscellaneous writings in prose and verse in two volumes published, 1818; contributed to the 'London Magazine' between August 1820 and December 1822 twenty-five essays, signed Elia, which showed his literary gifts at their best (reprinted in a volume, 1823); buried in Edmonton churchyard.
    [xxxi. 423]

LAMB, EDWARD BUCKTON (1806–1869), architect; exhibited at Royal Academy from 1824; published 'Etchings of Gothic Ornament,' 1830, and 'Studies of Ancient Domestic Architecture,' 1846.   [xxxi. 429]

LAMB, FREDERICK JAMES, third VISCOUNT MELBOURNE and BARON BEAUVALE (1782–1853), third son of first Viscount Melbourne; educated at Eton, Glasgow University, and Trinity College, Cambridge; M.A. Trinity College, Cambridge, 1803; entered the diplomatic service; secretary of legation at the court of the Two Sicilies, 1811; minister plenipotentiary *ad interim*, 1812; secretary of legation at Vienna, 1813; minister plenipotentiary at the court of Bavaria, 1815–20; privy councillor, 1822; minister plenipotentiary to the court of Spain, 1825–7; civil grand cross of the Bath and ambassador at Lisbon, 1827; ambassador to the court of Vienna, 1831–41; created a peer of the United Kingdom with the title of Baron Beauvale, 1839; succeeded as Viscount Melbourne, 1848.
    [xxxi. 429]

LAMB, GEORGE (1784–1834), politician and writer, youngest son of the first Viscount Melbourne; educated at Eton and Trinity College, Cambridge; M.A., 1805; barrister, Lincoln's Inn; his comic opera, 'Whistle for it,' produced, 1807; his adaptations of 'Timon of Athens' produced, 1816; his most important work, a translation of the poems of Catullus, 1821 (republished, 1854); M.P., Westminster, 1819, Dungarvan, 1826; under-secretary of state in the home department, 1830.   [xxxi. 430]

LAMB, JAMES (1599–1664), orientalist; educated at Brasenose College, Oxford; M.A., 1620; D.D. and prebendary of Westminster, 1661; bequeathed many of his books to the library of Westminster Abbey; manuscripts by him on oriental subjects in the Bodleian.
    [xxxi. 431]

LAMB, SIR JAMES BLAND (1752–1824). [See BURGES.]

LAMB, JOHN (1789–1850), master of Corpus Christi College, Cambridge, and dean of Bristol; educated at Corpus Christi College, Cambridge; M.A., 1814; master of his college, 1822–50; D.D., 1827; dean of Bristol, 1837–50; chief works, a continuation of 'Masters's History of Corpus Christi College, Cambridge,' 1831, and 'A Collection of Letters, Statutes, and other Documents from the MS. Library of Corpus Christi College illustrative of the History of the University of Cambridge during the Time of the Reformation,' 1838.   [xxxi. 431]

LAMB, MARY ANN (1764–1847), sister of Charles Lamb [q. v.]; stabbed her mother in a fit of temporary insanity, 1796; assisted her brother in 'Tales from Shakespeare,' herself dealing with the comedies, 1807; lived with

her brother and with him brought up Emma Isola, an orphan, who married Edward Moxon [q. v.]
    [xxxi. 423]

LAMB, SIR MATTHEW, first baronet (1705–1768), politician; M.P., Stockbridge, 1741, Peterborough, 1741–1768; created baronet, 1755.   [xxxi. 432]

LAMB, WILLIAM, second VISCOUNT MELBOURNE (1779–1848), statesman; of Eton and Trinity College, Cambridge; B.A., 1799; barrister, Lincoln's Inn, 1804; married Lady Caroline Ponsonby [see LAMB, LADY CAROLINE], 1805; whig M.P. for Leominster, 1806; M.P., Portarlington, 1807; lost his seat for his support of catholic emancipation, 1812; out of parliament for four years; M.P., Northampton, 1816, Hertfordshire, 1819; Irish secretary under Canning, 1827, and under Wellington, 1828; succeeded his father, 1829; home secretary under Grey, 1830–4, being thus the cabinet minister responsible for Ireland; advocated Coercion Bill of 1833; summoned by the king to form a ministry on resignation of Grey, 1834; resigned at the bidding of the king, 1834; again summoned to form a ministry, 1835; remained prime minister for six years; acted as adviser to the young Queen Victoria, 1837–41; resigned office, 1841; universally approved as the political instructor of his young sovereign.   [xxxi. 432]

LAMBARDE, WILLIAM (1536–1601), historian of Kent; his first work a collection and paraphrase of Anglo-Saxon laws (published, 1568, republished with Bede's 'Historia Ecclesiastica,' 1644); completed first draft of his 'Perambulation of Kent,' 1570; printed, 1574 and 1576, the earliest county history known, and one considered a model of arrangement and style (second edition, 1596, reprinted, 1826); collected materials for a general account of England, but abandoned the design on learning that Camden was engaged on a similar work; his materials published from the original manuscript, 1730; bencher of Lincoln's Inn, 1579; his 'Eirenarcha; or of the Office of the Justices of Peace,' 1581, long a standard authority (reprinted seven times between 1582 and 1610); keeper of the records at the Rolls Chapel, 1597; keeper of the records in the Tower, 1601.   [xxxi. 438]

LAMBART. [See also LAMBERT.]

LAMBART, CHARLES, first EARL OF CAVAN (1600–1660), eldest son of Sir Oliver Lambart, first baron Lambart in the Irish peerage [q. v.]; succeeded his father, 1618; represented Bossiney, Cornwall, in the English parliaments of 1625 and 1627; created Earl of Cavan and Viscount Kilcoursie, 1647.   [xxxi. 439]

LAMBART, SIR OLIVER, first BARON LAMBART OF CAVAN (*d.* 1618), Irish administrator; distinguished himself as a soldier in the Netherlands, 1585–92; took part in the expedition against Cadiz and was knighted, 1596; supported the Earl of Essex in Ireland, 1599; privy councillor, 1603; created Baron Lambart of Cavan in the Irish peerage, 1618.   [xxxi. 440]

LAMBART, RICHARD FORD WILLIAM, seventh EARL OF CAVAN (1763–1836), general; succeeded to the title, 1778; ensign, 1779; lieutenant, 1781; captain-lieutenant, 1790; captain and lieutenant-colonel, 1793; major-general, 1798; commanded a brigade in the Ferrol expedition and before Cadiz, 1800; present at the attack on Alexandria, 1801; commander of the whole army in Egypt; commander in the eastern counties during the invasion alarms of 1803–4; knight of the Crescent and one of the six officers besides Nelson who received the diamond aigrette; general, 1814.   [xxxi. 441]

LAMBE. [See also LAMB.]

LAMBE, JOHN (*d.* 1628), astrologer; indicted for the practice of 'execrable arts,' 1608–23; imprisoned for fifteen years; protected by the Duke of Buckingham, 1623; fatally injured by a mob of apprentices, who denounced him as 'the duke's devil.'   [xxxii. 1]

LAMBE, SIR JOHN (1566?–1647), civilian; M.A. St. John's College, Cambridge, 1590; registrar of diocese of Ely, 1600; chancellor of the diocese of Peterborough; vicar, official, and commissary-general to the bishop of Peterborough, 1615; LL.D., 1616; commissary to the dean and chapter of Lincoln, 1617; knighted, 1621; member of the high commission court and an active supporter of Laud; dean of the arches court of Canterbury, 1633; chancellor and keeper of the great seal to Queen Henrietta Maria, 1640.   [xxxii. 2]

LAMBE, ROBERT (1712–1795), author; B.A. St. John's College, Cambridge, 1734; his chief work, 'An Exact and Circumstantial History of the Battle of Flodden, in verse, written about the time of Queen Elizabeth,' 1774. [xxxii. 3]

LAMBE or **LAMB**, THOMAS (*d.* 1686), philanthropist and sometime nonconformist; preached in London, 1641–1661; returned to the established church, 1658; remarkable for his philanthropic work; published religious works, 1642–56. [xxxii. 3]

LAMBE, WILLIAM (1495–1580), London merchant and benefactor; gentleman of the Chapel Royal to Henry VIII; master of the Clothworkers' Company, 1569–70; established a free grammar school and almshouses at Sutton Valence, Kent, his native town; an adherent of the reformed religion. [xxxii. 5]

LAMBE, WILLIAM (1765–1847), physician; educated at St. John's College Cambridge; B.D., 1786; fellow, 1788; M.D., 1802; F.R.C.P., 1804; censor and frequently Croonian lecturer between 1806 and 1828; Harveian orator, 1818; published medical works. [xxxii. 6]

LAMBERT. [See also LAMBART.]

LAMBERT or **LANBRIHT** (*d.* 791). [See JAENBERT.]

LAMBERT, AYLMER BOURKE (1761–1842), botanist; educated at St. Mary Hall, Oxford; an original F.L.S., 1788, and vice-president, 1796–1842; contributed papers on zoology and botany to its 'Transactions'; F.R.S., 1791; 'A Description of the genus Cinchona,' his first independent work, 1797; chief work, a monograph of the genus Pinus (vol. i. 1803, vol. ii. 1824, vol. iii. 1837). [xxxii. 6]

LAMBERT, DANIEL (1770–1809), the most corpulent man of whom authentic record exists; keeper of Leicester gaol, 1791–1805; weighed thirty-two stone in 1793; 'received company' daily in London, 1806–7; weighed at death fifty-two and three-quarters stone. [xxxii. 7]

LAMBERT, GEORGE (1710–1765), landscape and scene painter; studied under Warner Hassells [q. v.] and John Wootton [q. v.]; had a painting loft at Covent Garden Theatre, where distinguished men resorted to sup with him, the Beefsteak Club arising out of these meetings; a friend of Hogarth, who painted his portrait; exhibited with the Society of Artists of Great Britain, 1761–4. [xxxii. 8]

LAMBERT, GEORGE JACKSON (1794–1880), organist and composer; organist of Beverley Minster, 1818–75; a fine violoncello and violin player; composed overtures, instrumental chamber music, organ fugues, and other works. [xxxii. 8]

LAMBERT, HENRY (*d.* 1813), naval captain; entered navy, 1795; lieutenant, 1801; commander, 1803; captain, 1804; employed in the blockade of Mauritius and in the attack on the French squadron in Grand Port, when he surrendered and was detained as prisoner, 1810; mortally wounded in action off Brazil, 1812; buried at San Salvador. [xxxii. 9]

LAMBERT, JAMES (1725–1788), musician and painter; first painted inn-signs; best known by a series of water-colour drawings illustrating the antiquities of Sussex; exhibited at the Royal Academy and (1761–88) at the Society of Artists; organist of the Church of St. Thomas-at-Cliffe, Lewes. [xxxii. 9]

LAMBERT, JAMES (1741–1823), Greek professor at Cambridge; entered Trinity College, Cambridge, 1760; fellow, 1765; M.A., 1767; regius professor of Greek, 1771–1780; bursar of his college, 1789–99. [xxxii. 10]

LAMBERT, JOHN (*d.* 1538), martyr; his real name NICHOLSON; educated at Cambridge; B.A. and fellow of Queens' College, 1521; converted to protestantism and ordained; suffered persecution and took name of Lambert; chaplain to the English factory at Antwerp; imprisoned, 1532; released on the death of Archbishop Warham, 1532; condemned to death by Cromwell for denying the real presence, and burnt at the stake. [xxxii. 10]

LAMBERT, JOHN (1619–1683), soldier; took up arms for the parliament at the beginning of the civil war; commissary-general of Fairfax's army, 1644; in command of a regiment in the new model, 1646; assisted Ireton in drawing up the 'Heads of the Proposals of Army,' 1647; commander of the army in the north, 1647; engaged against the royalist Scottish army, 1648; took part in the battle of Dunbar, 1650, of Worcester, 1651; deputy lord-lieutenant of Ireland, 1652; president of the council appointed by the officers of the army, 1653; was the leading spirit in the council of officers who offered the post of protector to Cromwell, and a member of the Protector's council of state; major-general of the army; a lord of the Cinque ports; retired on account of a breach with Cromwell about the regal title; M.P., Pontefract, 1659; supported Richard Cromwell and recovered his old position; member of the committee of safety and of the council of state, 1659; major-general of the army sent to oppose Monck's advance into England; deprived of his commands, 1660; arrested and committed to the Tower, 1660; escaped and collected troops, but without success, 1660; again committed to the Tower, 1661; sent to Guernsey, 1661; tried for high treason and condemned to death, 1662; sent back to Guernsey; imprisoned till death, 1664–1683. [xxxii. 11]

LAMBERT, JOHN (*fl.* 1811), traveller; visited North America with a view to fostering the cultivation of hemp in Canada, 1806; published 'Travels through Lower Canada and the United States of North America, 1806–1808,' 1810. [xxxii. 18]

LAMBERT, SIR JOHN (1772–1847), general; ensign, 1st foot guards, 1791; captain, 1793; lieutenant-colonel, 1801; served in Portugal and Spain, 1808, and in Walcheren expedition, 1809; brevet colonel, 1810; in Spain, 1811–14; major-general, 1813; K.C.B., 1815; served with Sir Edward Michael Pakenham [q. v.] in America, 1815; at Waterloo, 1815; lieutenant-general, 1825; general, 1841; colonel of 10th regiment, 1824; G.C.B., 1838. [Suppl. iii. 78]

LAMBERT, SIR JOHN (1815–1892), civil servant; mayor of Salisbury, 1854; poor law inspector, 1857; superintended administration of the Public Works Act, 1865; receiver of the metropolitan common poor fund, 1867; permanent secretary to the local government board, 1871–82; K.C.B., 1879; privy councillor, 1885; author of 'The Modern Domesday Book,' 1872, and of several musical publications. [xxxii. 18]

LAMBERT, MARK (*d.* 1601). [See BARKWORTH.]

LAMBERTON, WILLIAM DE (*d.* 1328), bishop of St. Andrews; chancellor of Glasgow Cathedral, 1292; bishop of St. Andrews, 1297; a supporter of William Wallace; although swearing fealty to Edward I, 1304, assisted at coronation of Robert the Bruce, 1306; imprisoned for treason, 1306–8; subsequently worked in the interests of both parties at once. [xxxii. 19]

LAMBORN, PETER SPENDELOWE (1722–1774), engraver and miniature-painter; studied under Isaac Basire (1704–1768) [q. v.]; member of and (1764–74) exhibitor with the Incorporated Society of Artists; executed architectural drawings and etchings. [xxxii. 21]

LAMBORN, REGINALD (*fl.* 1363), astronomer; D.D. Merton College, Oxford, 1367; entered the Franciscan order at Oxford; two letters (1364 and 1367) of his on astronomical subjects extant in manuscript. [xxxii. 21]

LAMBTON, JOHN (1710–1794), general; ensign, 1732; lieutenant, 1739; regimental quartermaster, 1742–1745; captain and lieutenant-colonel, 1746; colonel, 1758; M.P., Durham, 1761–87. [xxxii. 21]

LAMBTON, JOHN GEORGE, first EARL OF DURHAM (1792–1840), grandson of John Lambton [q. v.]; educated at Eton; cornet in the dragoons, 1809; lieutenant, 1810; retired from the army, 1811; M.P. for Durham county, 1813–28; created Baron Durham of the city of Durham and of Lambton Castle; privy councillor and lord privy seal, 1830; assisted in preparation of first Reform Bill; ambassador extraordinary to St. Petersburg, Berlin, and Vienna, 1832; created Viscount Lambton and Earl of Durham, 1833; headed the advanced section of the whigs; ambassador extraordinary and minister plenipotentiary to St. Petersburg, 1835–7; G.C.B., 1837; high commissioner for the adjustment of important questions in Lower and Upper Canada and governor-general of the British provinces in North America, 1838; his high-handed proceedings denounced and disallowed in England; resigned and returned to England, 1838; the policy of all his successors guided by his 'Report on the Affairs of British North America' (1839), which is said to have been mostly written by Charles Buller. [xxxii. 22]

LAMBTON, WILLIAM (1756–1823), lieutenant-colonel, and geodesist; studied mathematics under Dr. Charles Hutton [q. v.]; ensign, 1781–3; lieutenant, 1794; barrack-master at St. John's, New Brunswick, till 1795; took part in the capture of Seringapatam, 1799; conducted a survey connecting Malabar and Coromandel coasts, 1800–15; F.R.S. and R.A.S.; died at Hinganghat, near Nagpoor; author of papers on geodesy. [xxxii. 25]

LAMINGTON, BARON (1816–1890). [See COCHRANE-BAILLIE, ALEXANDER DUNDAS ROSS WISHART.]

LAMONT, DAVID (1752–1837), Scottish divine; D.D. Edinburgh, 1780; chaplain to the Prince of Wales, 1785; moderator of the general assembly, 1822; chaplain-in-ordinary for Scotland, 1824; popular preacher; published sermons. [xxxii. 26]

LAMONT, JOHANN VON (1805–1879), astronomer and magnetician; born at Braemar; educated in mathematics by the prior of the Scottish Benedictine monastery at Ratisbon; extraordinary member of the Munich Academy of Sciences, 1827; director of the observatory of Bogenhausen near Munich, 1835; executed magnetic surveys of Bavaria (1849–52), France and Spain (1856–7), and North Germany and Denmark (1858); professor of astronomy in the university of Munich, 1852; died at Munich; author of important works on terrestrial magnetism. [xxxii. 26]

LAMONT, JOHN (fl. 1671), chronicler; his 'Diary,' 1649–71 (first published under the title of the 'Chronicle of Fife,' 1810), of great value to the Scottish genealogist. [xxxii. 28]

LA MOTHE, CLAUDE GROSTÊTE DE (1647–1713), theologian; born at Orleans; educated at Orleans University; joined the Paris bar, 1665; abandoned law for theology, and became a protestant pastor; on revocation of the edict of Nantes came to London, 1685; naturalised, 1688; minister of Savoy Church, 1694–1713. [xxxii. 28]

LA MOTTE, JOHN (1570?–1655), merchant of London; educated at Ghent and probably at Heidelberg University; established a foreign church at Sandtoft, 1636. [xxxii. 28]

LAMPE, JOHN FREDERICK (1703?–1751), musical composer; born probably in Saxony; came to London, 1725; one of the finest bassoonists of his time; composer of comic operas and songs; published two works on the theory of music. [xxxii. 29]

LAMPHIRE, JOHN (1614–1688), principal of Hart Hall, Oxford; educated at Winchester and New College, Oxford; fellow of New College, 1636–48; M.A., 1642; Camden professor of history, 1660; M.D., 1660; principal of New Inn Hall, 1662; of Hart Hall, 1663; owner of many manuscripts, some of which he published. [xxxii. 30]

LAMPLUGH, THOMAS (1615–1691), bishop of Exeter and archbishop of York; educated at Queen's College, Oxford; M.A., 1642; D.D., 1660; archdeacon of London, 1664; dean of Rochester, 1673; bishop of Exeter, 1676–1688; archbishop of York, 1688–91; assisted at the coronation of William III, 1689. [xxxii. 31]

LAMPSON, SIR CURTIS MIRANDA, first baronet (1806–1885), advocate of the Atlantic cable; born in Vermont; came to England and set up business as a merchant, 1830; naturalised, 1849; vice-chairman of the company for laying the Atlantic telegraph, 1856–66; created baronet, 1866. [xxxii. 32]

LANARK, EARL OF. [See HAMILTON, WILLIAM, second DUKE OF HAMILTON, 1616–1651.]

LANCASTER, DUKES OF. [See HENRY OF LANCASTER, 1299?–1361; JOHN OF GAUNT, 1340–1399; HENRY IV, KING OF ENGLAND, 1367–1413.]

LANCASTER, EARLS OF. [See THOMAS, 1277?–1322; LANCASTER, EDMUND, 1245–1296; HENRY, 1281?–1345.]

LANCASTER, CHARLES WILLIAM (1820–1878), improver of rifles and cannon; constructed a model rifle which had great success in 1846; elected associate of the Institution of Civil Engineers, 1852; his carbine adopted for the royal engineers, 1855; invented the oval-bored rifle cannon. [xxxii. 35]

LANCASTER, EDMUND, EARL OF (1245–1296), called CROUCHBACK; second son of Henry III [q. v.] and Eleanor of Provence; styled king of Sicily by the pope, 1255; renounced all claim to the kingdom of Sicily, 1263; crusader, 1271; married Blanche, daughter of the Count of Artois, younger son of Louis VIII of France and widow of Henry of Navarre, 1275; took part in the Welsh war, 1277–82; unsuccessfully commanded the English army in Gascony, 1296; buried in Westminster Abbey. [xxxii. 33]

LANCASTER, HENRY HILL (1829–1875), essayist; educated at the high school and university of Glasgow and at Balliol College, Oxford; M.A., 1872; passed as an advocate in Edinburgh, 1858; advocate-depute, 1868–74; took active interest in education and contributed to the North British and Edinburgh reviews; his articles published in a single volume entitled, 'Essays and Reviews' (with prefatory notice by Professor Jowett), 1876. [xxxii. 36]

LANCASTER, HUME (d. 1850), marine-painter; exhibited, 1836–49, at the Royal Academy, the Society of British Artists, and the British Institution. [xxxii. 36]

LANCASTER, SIR JAMES (d. 1618), pioneer of the English trade with the East Indies; took part in the Armada, 1588; sailed in the first English voyage to the East Indies, 1591; returned with a rich booty, 1594; appointed to command the first fleet of the East India Company, 1600; knighted, 1603. [xxxii. 36]

LANCASTER, JOHN OF, DUKE OF BEDFORD (1389–1435). [See JOHN.]

LANCASTER, JOHN (d. 1619), bishop of Waterford and Lismore; bishop of Waterford and Lismore, 1608–19. [xxxii. 38]

LANCASTER, JOSEPH (1778–1838), founder of the Lancasterian system of education; joined the Society of Friends; began teaching poor children before 1801, and soon had a free school of a thousand boys; set forth the results of his experience in a pamphlet, 'Improvements in Education,' 1803; opposed by members of the established church; published 'Report of Joseph Lancaster's progress from 1798,' 1810; suffered from pecuniary difficulties and went to America, 1818; established a school, which failed, at Montreal; his last pamphlet, 'Epitome of some of the chief Events and Transactions in the Life of J. Lancaster, containing an Account of the Rise and Progress of the Lancasterian system of Education,' &c., published, 1833; public interest in education aroused by his work. [xxxii. 39]

LANCASTER, NATHANIEL (1701–1775), author; chaplain to Frederick, Prince of Wales, 1733; D.D. Lambeth, 1733; wrote several books on manners between 1746 and 1767. [xxxii. 42]

LANCASTER, THOMAS (d. 1583), archbishop of Armagh; probably educated at Oxford; an enthusiastic protestant; bishop of Kildare, 1549–68; dean of Ossory, 1552; treasurer of Salisbury Cathedral, 1559; a royal chaplain, 1559; accompanied Sir Henry Sidney to Ireland, 1565; archbishop of Armagh, 1568–83. [xxxii. 43]

LANCASTER, THOMAS WILLIAM (1787–1859), Bampton lecturer; entered Oriel College, Oxford, 1804; fellow of Queen's College, 1809; M.A., 1810; ordained priest, 1812; preached Bampton lectures on 'The Popular Evidence of Christianity,' 1831; select preacher to the university, 1832; under-master of Magdalen College school, Oxford, 1840–9; published his Bampton lectures and theological works. [xxxii. 44]

LANCASTER, WILLIAM (1650–1717), divine; of Queen's College, Oxford; M.A., 1678; fellow, 1679; bursar, 1686–90; D.D., 1692; archdeacon of Middlesex, 1705–17; vice-chancellor of Oxford, 1706–10. [xxxii. 44]

LANCE, GEORGE (1802–1864), painter; pupil of Haydon; exhibited from 1824 at the British Institution, the Society of British Artists, and the Royal Academy; a painter of still-life. [xxxii. 45]

LANCEY. [See DE LANCEY.]

LANCRINCK, PROSPER HENRI (1628-1692). [See LANKRINK.]

LAND, EDWARD (1815-1876), vocalist and composer of popular songs. [xxxii. 46]

LANDEL, WILLIAM (d. 1385), bishop of St. Andrews, 1342-85; visited the shrine of St. James at Compostella, 1361, Rome, 1362 ; crowned Robert II, 1370. [xxxii. 47]

LANDELLS, EBENEZER (1808-1860), wood-engraver and projector of 'Punch'; apprenticed to Thomas Bewick [q. v.], wood-engraver ; superintended the fine-art engraving department of the firm of Branston & Vizetelly ; contributed chiefly to illustrated periodical literature ; conceived the idea of 'Punch,' the first number of which appeared 17 July 1841; contributed to the early numbers of the 'Illustrated London News'; started the 'Lady's Newspaper' (now incorporated with the 'Queen'), 1847 ; Birket Foster and the Dalziels among his pupils. [xxxii. 47]

LANDELLS, ROBERT THOMAS (1833-1877), artist and special war correspondent : eldest son of Ebenezer Landells [q. v.]; educated principally in France; studied drawing and painting in London ; special artist for the 'Illustrated London News' in the Crimea, 1856, in the war between Germany and Denmark, 1863, in the war between Prussia and Austria, 1866, and in the Franco-German war, 1870; employed by Queen Victoria to paint memorial pictures of several ceremonials attended by her. [xxxii. 48]

LANDEN, JOHN (1719-1790), mathematician ; published 'Mathematical Lucubrations,' 1755 ; F.R.S., 1766 ; discovered a theorem known by his name expressing a hyperbolic arc in terms of two elliptic arcs, 1775 ; failed to develop and combine his discoveries. [xxxii. 48]

LANDER, JOHN (1807-1839), African traveller ; younger brother of Richard Lemon Lander [q. v.]; accompanied his brother in his exploration of the Niger, 1830-1 ; his journal incorporated with that of his brother, published, 1832. [xxxii. 49]

LANDER, RICHARD LEMON (1804-1834), African traveller ; went to Cape Colony, 1823 ; accompanied Lieutenant Hugh Clapperton [q. v.] to Western Africa ; published journal and records of Clapperton's last expedition to Africa, 1830 ; made an expedition to explore the Niger, 1830-1 ; published 'Journal of an Expedition to explore the Course and Termination of the Niger,' 1832 ; conducted a second expedition to the Niger, 1832 ; mortally wounded in a fight with natives at Ingiamma ; died at Fernando Po ; the question of the course and outlet of the river Niger settled by his exploration. [xxxii. 49]

LANDMANN, GEORGE THOMAS (1779-1854), lieutenant-colonel, royal engineers ; son of Isaac Landmann [q. v.]; entered the Royal Military Academy, Woolwich, 1793 ; first lieutenant, 1797 ; employed in construction of fortifications in Canada, 1797-1802 ; captain, 1806 ; on active service in the Peninsular war, 1808-12 ; brevet-major, 1813 ; lieutenant-colonel, 1814 ; retired, 1824 ; author of books on Portugal and on his own adventures and recollections. [xxxii. 51]

LANDMANN, ISAAC (1741-1826 ?), professor of artillery and fortification ; held an appointment at the Royal Military School in Paris ; professor of artillery and fortification at the Royal Military Academy at Woolwich, 1777-1815 ; wrote on tactics and fortification. [xxxii. 52]

LANDON, LETITIA ELIZABETH, afterwards MRS. MACLEAN (1802-1838), poetess under the initials 'L. E. L.'; her first poem, 'Rome,' published in the 'Literary Gazette,' 1820 ; her 'Fate of Adelaide,' published, 1821 ; published poems between 1824 and 1829 ; contributed to albums and annuals, and edited the 'Drawing Scrap Book,' from 1832 ; published novels, 1831 and 1834 ; her 'Traits and Trials of Early Life' (supposed to be autobiographical) brought out, 1836, and her best novel, 'Ethel Churchill,' 1837 ; married George Maclean, governor of Cape Coast Castle, 1838 ; arrived at Cape Coast in August ; died mysteriously, probably from an accidental overdose of prussic acid, in October. Collected editions of her poems published, 1850 and 1873. [xxxii. 52]

LANDOR, ROBERT EYRES (1781-1869), author; youngest brother of Walter Savage Landor [q. v.]; scholar and fellow of Worcester College, Oxford;

author of a tragedy, 'Count Arezzi' (1823), which only sold while it was mistaken for a work of Byron ; published other tragedies between 1841 and 1848. [xxxii. 61]

LANDOR, WALTER SAVAGE (1775-1864), author of 'Imaginary Conversations'; educated at Rugby; entered Trinity College, Oxford, 1793 ; rusticated, 1794 ; lived for three years at Tenby and Swansea ; his 'Gebir' published, 1798; visited Paris, 1802; lived in Bath, Bristol, and Wells, with occasional visits to London : saw some fighting as a volunteer in Spain ; published 'Tragedy of Count Julian,' 1811; bought Llanthony Abbey, Monmouthshire, and married Julia Thuillier, 1811 ; quarrelled with the authorities at Llanthony ; went to Jersey and thence to France, 1814 ; started for Italy, 1815 ; lived for three years at Como ; insulted the authorities in a Latin poem and was ordered to leave, 1818 ; at Pisa, 1818-21 ; at Florence, 1821-35 ; first two volumes of 'Imaginary Conversations' published, 1824 (second edition, 1826), third volume, 1828, fourth and fifth, 1829 ; bought a villa at Fiesole; visited England, 1832 ; published 'Citation and Examination of William Shakespeare . . . touching Deer-stealing,' 1834 ; quarrelled with his wife and left Italy, 1835 ; published 'The Pentameron,' 1837 ; lived at Bath, 1838-58 ; his collected works published, 1846 ; returned to Florence, 1858 ; transferred his English estates to his son, and so became entirely dependent on his family ; assisted by Robert Browning, the poet ; visited by Mr. A. C. Swinburne, 1864 ; a classical enthusiast and an admirable writer of English prose ; died at Florence. [xxxii. 54]

LANDSBOROUGH, DAVID (1779-1854), naturalist ; educated at Edinburgh University ; ordained minister of the church of Scotland, 1811; studied natural history; discovered *Ectocarpus Landsburgii* (alga), and contributed to the 'Phycologia Britannica' of William Henry Harvey [q. v.]; joined the free kirk and became minister of Saltcoats, 1843 ; published 'Excursions to Arran, Ailsa Craig, and the two Cumbraes,' 1847 (second series, 1852), 'Popular History of British Sea-weeds,' 1849 (3rd edit. 1857) ; published 'Popular History of British Zoophytes or Corallines'; said to have discovered nearly seventy species of plants and animals new to Scotland. [xxxii. 62]

LANDSBOROUGH, WILLIAM (d. 1886), Australian explorer ; son of David Landsborough [q. v.]; an Australian squatter ; made explorations chiefly in Queensland between 1856 and 1862 ; member of the Queensland parliament, 1864 ; government resident in Burke district, 1865-9 ; explored the Gulf of Carpentaria ; died at Brisbane. [xxxii. 63]

LANDSEER, CHARLES (1799 - 1879), historical painter ; second son of John Landseer [q. v.]; entered the Royal Academy schools, 1816 ; first exhibited at Royal Academy, 1828 ; R.A., 1845 ; keeper of Royal Academy, 1851-73 ; gave 10,000l. to Royal Academy for the foundation of Landseer scholarships. [xxxii. 63]

LANDSEER, SIR EDWIN HENRY (1802-1873), animal-painter ; youngest son of John Landseer [q. v.]; entered the Royal Academy schools, 1816 ; began to exhibit, 1817 ; visited Sir Walter Scott at Abbotsford and drew the poet and his dogs, 1824 ; R.A., 1831 ; excelled in painting portraits of children ; frequently painted Queen Victoria and the Prince Consort and their children between 1839 and 1866 ; his most famous pictures painted between 1842 and 1850 ; knighted, 1850 ; the only English artist who received the large gold medal at the Paris Universal Exhibition, 1855 ; declined presidency of the Royal Academy, 1865 ; completed the lions for the Nelson monument, Trafalgar Square, 1866 ; buried in St. Paul's Cathedral. He struck out a new path by treating pictorially the analogy between the characters of animals and men ; 434 etchings and engravings were made from his works up to 1875. [xxxii. 64]

LANDSEER, JESSICA (1810-1880), landscape and miniature painter ; daughter of John Landseer [q. v.]; exhibited at the Royal Academy and the British Institution between 1816 and 1866. [xxxii. 68]

LANDSEER, JOHN (1769-1852), painter, engraver, and author ; apprenticed to William Byrne [q. v.]; delivered lectures on engraving at the Royal Institution, 1806 ; tried, but without success, to induce the Royal

Academy to place engraving on the same footing as in academies abroad; turned his attention to archæology and published a work on engraved views, 1817; made engravings after drawings and pictures by his son, Sir Edwin Henry Landseer [q. v.]; F.S.A.; engraver to William IV. [xxxii. 68]

LANDSEER, THOMAS (1795–1880), engraver; eldest son of John Landseer [q. v.]; his life mainly devoted to etching and engraving the drawings and pictures of his brother Sir Edwin Henry Landseer [q. v.]; A.R.A., 1868; published 'The Life and Letters of William Bewick,' 1871. [xxxii. 70]

LANE, CHARLES EDWARD WILLIAM (1786–1872), general in the Indian army; ensign, 1807; lieutenant, 1812; captain, 1824; major, 1835; lieutenant-colonel, 1841; commanded the garrison of Candahar, and repulsed an attack of the Afghans, 1842; C.B., 1842; colonel, 1852; major-general, 1854; lieutenant-general, 1866; general, 1870. [xxxii. 70]

LANE, EDWARD (1605–1685), theological writer; educated at St. Paul's School, London and St. John's College, Cambridge; M.A., 1629; incumbent of Sparsholt for fifty years; M.A. Oxford, 1639; published 'Look unto Jesus,' 1663, and 'Mercy Triumphant,' 1680. [xxxii. 71]

LANE, EDWARD WILLIAM (1801–1876), Arabic scholar; went to Egypt for the sake of his health, 1825; made voyages up the Nile, 1826 and 1827; studied the people of Cairo, 1833–5; spoke Arabic fluently and adopted the dress and manners of the Egyptian man of learning; published in two volumes 'Account of the Manners and Customs of the Modern Egyptians,' 1836 (still the standard authority on the subject); published a translation of the 'Thousand and one Nights' (the first accurate version), 1838–40; again in Egypt, 1842–9; compiled an exhaustive thesaurus of the Arabic language from native lexicons, published at intervals, 1863–92; the acknowledged chief of Arabic scholars in Europe. [xxxii. 71]

LANE, HUNTER (d. 1853), medical writer; licentiate of the Royal College of Surgeons, Edinburgh, 1829; M.D. Edinburgh, 1830; published his 'Compendium of Materia Medica and Pharmacy,' 1840; president of the Royal Medical Society of Edinburgh. [xxxii. 74]

LANE, JANE, afterwards LADY FISHER (d. 1689), heroine; distinguished herself by her courage and devotion in the service of Charles II after the battle of Worcester, 1651; helped Charles to escape his enemies in the disguise of her man-servant; fled to France and finally entered the service of the Princess of Orange; rewarded by Charles at the Restoration and her pension continued by William III; married Sir Clement Fisher, baronet, of Packington Magna, Warwickshire. [xxxii. 74]

LANE, JOHN (fl. 1620), verse-writer; friend of Milton's father; left many poems in manuscript, but only published a poem denouncing the vices of Elizabethan society, 1600, and an elegy upon the death of Queen Elizabeth, 1603; completed in manuscript Chaucer's unfinished 'Squire's Tale.' [xxxii. 75]

LANE, JOHN BRYANT (1788–1868), painter; exhibited at Royal Academy, 1808–13; lived at Rome, 1817–27; devoted himself to portrait-painting; exhibited at the Royal Academy till 1864. [xxxii. 76]

LANE, SIR RALPH (d. 1603), first governor of Virginia; sailed for North America in the expedition under Sir Richard Grenville [q. v.], 1583; governor of colony established at Wokokan, 1585; moved to Roanoke; brought home by Sir Francis Drake [q. v.] with all the colonists, 1586, the settlement being a failure; employed in carrying out measures for the defence of the coast, 1587–8; muster-master in Drake's Portuguese expedition, 1589; served under Hawkyns, 1590; fought in Ireland, 1592–4; knighted, 1593. [xxxii. 77]

LANE, SIR RICHARD (1584–1650), lord keeper; barrister, Middle Temple; practised in the court of exchequer; deputy-recorder of Northampton, 1615; reader to the Middle Temple, 1630; attorney-general to the Prince of Wales, 1634; treasurer of the Middle Temple, 1637; defended Strafford, 1641; knighted, 1644; lord chief baron, 1644; D.C.L. Oxford, 1644; lord keeper, 1645; followed Charles II into exile; died at Jersey; author of 'Reports in the Court of Exchequer from 1605 to 1612' (first published, 1657). [xxxii. 78]

LANE, RICHARD JAMES (1800–1872), line-engraver and lithographer; elder brother of Edward William Lane [q. v.]; famous for his pencil and chalk sketches, specially for his portrait of Princess Victoria, 1829; the best examples of his work in lithography, the 'Sketches from Gainsborough'; lithographer to Queen Victoria, 1837, and to the prince consort, 1840; helped to obtain the admission of engravers to the honour of full academician in 1865. [xxxii. 79]

LANE, SAMUEL (1780–1859), portrait-painter; studied under Joseph Farington [q. v.] and under Sir Thomas Lawrence [q. v.]; contributed to the Royal Academy, 1804–54. [xxxii. 79]

LANE, THEODORE (1800–1828), painter; came into notice as a painter of water-colour portraits and miniatures; etched pieces of sporting and social life with delicate finish; took up oil-painting, 1825. [xxxii. 80]

LANE, THOMAS (fl. 1695), civilian; entered St. John's College, Cambridge, 1674; B.A., 1677; B.A. Oxford, 1678; entered Merton College, Oxford, 1680; M.A., 1683; LL.D., 1686; bursar of Merton, 1688; left suddenly, carrying with him a large sum of money; wounded and taken prisoner at the battle of the Boyne, 1689; released, 1690; practised as an advocate in Doctors' Commons, 1695. [xxxii. 80]

LANE, WILLIAM (1746–1819), portrait draughtsman; engraver of gems in the manner of the antique; engraved small copperplates after Reynolds and Cosway, 1788–92; became a successful artist in crayon portraits; contributed to the exhibitions, 1797–1815. [xxxii. 81]

LANEHAM, ROBERT (fl. 1575), writer on the Kenilworth festivities of 1575; educated at St. Paul's School, London; apprenticed to a London mercer; travelled abroad for trade purposes and became efficient linguist; door-keeper of the council chamber; present in this capacity at the entertainment given by Leicester to Queen Elizabeth, 1575; published anonymously a description of the festivities in a letter dated 1575 (copies in the British Museum and Bodleian libraries). The work was reissued in 1784 and again in 1821. [xxxii. 81]

LANEY, BENJAMIN (1591–1675), bishop successively of Peterborough, Lincoln, and Ely; educated at Christ's College, Cambridge; B.A., 1611; entered Pembroke Hall; M.A., 1615; M.A. of Oxford, 1617; B.D., 1622; D.D. and master of Pembroke Hall, 1630; vice-chancellor, 1632–3; chaplain to Charles I; deprived of his preferments as a royalist and high churchman; ejected from Cambridge, 1643–4; at Restoration recovered his mastership and other preferments; bishop of Peterborough, 1660, of Lincoln, 1663, of Ely, 1667–75. His sermons were published in 1668–9, and 'Observations' upon a letter of Hobbes of Malmesbury (anonymous, 1677). [xxxii. 82]

LANFRANC (1005?–1089), archbishop of Canterbury; born at Pavia; educated in the secular learning of the time and in Greek; studied law; set up a school at Avranches, in Normandy, 1039; gained a great reputation as a teacher; became a monk and entered the convent of Herlwin at Bec; prior, 1045; opened school in the monastery, to which scholars flocked from all parts of Europe; took part in the controversy with Berengar on the question of transubstantiation before Pope Leo IX, 1050; confuted Berengar at the council of Tours, 1055, and in the Lateran council held by Pope Nicholas II, 1059; abbot of St. Stephen's, Caen, 1066; archbishop of Canterbury, 1070–89; worked in full accord with William the Conqueror; rebuilt Canterbury Cathedral after the fire of 1067 in Norman style; crowned William II, 1087; buried in Canterbury Cathedral; his collected works first published by Luc d'Achéry, 1648. [xxxii. 83]

LANG, JOHN DUNMORE (1799–1878), writer on Australia; M.A. Glasgow, 1820; ordained, 1822; went to New South Wales, 1823; D.D. Glasgow, 1825; formed a church at Sydney in connection with the established church of Scotland; founded the 'Colonist,' a weekly journal which lasted from 1835–40; edited first number of the 'Colonial Journal,' 1841; edited the 'Press,' 1851–2; encouraged emigration; New Zealand taken possession of for Queen Victoria in consequence of his representations, 1840; one of the six members for Port Phillip district to the legislative council which then ruled New South Wales, 1843–6; lectured in England on the advantages of

Australia, 1846-9; represented various constituencies in the parliament of New South Wales, 1850-64; wrote largely on emigration and colonisation; died in Sydney. [xxxii. 89]

LANGBAINE, GERARD, the elder (1609-1658), provost of Queen's College, Oxford; entered Queen's College, Oxford, 1625; M.A. and fellow, 1633; keeper of the archives of the university, 1644; provost of Queen's College and D.D. 1646; wrote literary and political pamphlets; a zealous royalist and supporter of episcopacy; left twenty-one volumes of collections of notes in manuscript to the Bodleian Library. [xxxii. 91]

LANGBAINE, GERARD, the younger (1656-1692), dramatic biographer and critic; son of Gerard Langbaine the elder [q. v.]; of University College, Oxford; married young and settled in London, where he led a gay and idle life; retired to Oxfordshire; published his best-known work, 'An Account of the English Dramatic Poets, or some Observations and Remarks on the Lives and Writings of all those that have published either Comedies, Tragedies, Tragicomedies, Pastorals, Masques, Interludes, Farces, or Operas, in the English tongue,' valuable as a work of reference, but weak in bibliographical details, 1691. [xxxii. 93]

LANGDAILE or **LANGDALE,** ALBAN (*fl.* 1584), Roman catholic divine; educated at St. John's College, Cambridge; fellow of St. John's, 1534; M.A., 1535; proctor, 1539; B.D., 1544; took part in disputations concerning transubstantiation, 1549; D.D., 1554; archdeacon of Chichester, 1555; chancellor of Lichfield Cathedral, 1559; refused to take oath of supremacy and was deprived of preferments; included in a list of popish recusants, 1561; retired to the continent; published controversial works. [xxxii. 94]

LANGDALE, BARON (1783-1851). [See BICKERSTETH, HENRY.]

LANGDALE, CHARLES (1787-1868), Roman catholic layman and biographer of Mrs. Fitzherbert; third son of Charles Philip Stourton, sixteenth Lord Stourton; assumed his mother's maiden name of Langdale, 1815; one of the first English Roman catholics to enter parliament; M.P., Beverley, 1834, Knaresborough, 1837-1841; published 'Memoirs of Mrs. Fitzherbert,' 1856, to vindicate her character [see FITZHERBERT, MARIA ANNE.] [xxxii. 95]

LANGDALE, MARMADUKE, first BARON LANGDALE (1598?-1661), knighted, 1628; opposed ship-money, 1639, but adopted the king's cause, 1642; raised regiment of foot, 1643; distinguished as a cavalry commander in the civil war; routed at Preston and captured, 1648; escaped to the continent and entered the Venetian service; created Baron Langdale by Charles II, 1658. [xxxii. 95]

LANGDON, JOHN (*d.* 1434), bishop of Rochester; monk of Christ Church, Canterbury, 1398; studied at Oxford; B.D., 1400; one of the twelve Oxford scholars appointed to inquire into Wycliffe's doctrines, 1411; bishop of Rochester, 1421; engaged on an embassy to France, 1432; died and was buried at Basle. [xxxii. 97]

LANGDON, RICHARD (1730-1803), organist and composer; organist of Exeter Cathedral, 1753; Mus. Bac. Oxford, 1761; organist of Bristol Cathedral, 1767, of Armagh Cathedral, 1782-94; composed anthems and songs. [xxxii. 98]

LANGFORD, ABRAHAM (1711-1774), auctioneer and playwright; produced a ballad-opera, 'The Lover his own Rival,' 1736; auctioneer in Covent Garden, 1748; the foremost auctioneer of the period. [xxxii. 98]

LANGFORD, THOMAS (*fl.* 1420), historian; a Dominican friar; said to have written a chronicle and other works. [xxxii. 99]

LANGHAM, SIMON (*d.* 1376), archbishop of Canterbury, chancellor of England, and cardinal; became monk of St. Peter's, Westminster, c. 1335; abbot, 1349; treasurer of England, 1360; bishop of Ely, 1361; chancellor of England, 1363; the first to deliver speeches in parliament in English; archbishop of Canterbury, 1366; removed Wycliffe from the headship of Canterbury Hall; created cardinal-priest, 1368, and forced to resign his archbishopric, 1368; cardinal-bishop of Praeneste, 1373; died at Avignon; buried first at Avignon, but his body transferred to Westminster Abbey, 1379. [xxxii. 99]

LANGHORNE, DANIEL (*d.* 1681), antiquary; M.A. Trinity College, Cambridge, 1657; fellow of Corpus Christi College, Cambridge, 1663; B.D., 1664; university preacher, 1664; wrote antiquarian works in Latin and English. [xxxii. 100]

LANGHORNE, JOHN (1735-1779), poet; entered Clare Hall, Cambridge, 1760; commenced writing for the 'Monthly Review,' 1764; assistant-preacher at Lincoln's Inn, 1765; published 'Poetical Works,' 1766; translated 'Plutarch's Lives' in collaboration with his brother William, 1770 (fifth edition, 1792); prebendary of Wells Cathedral, 1777; best remembered as the translator of Plutarch. [xxxii. 100]

LANGHORNE, RICHARD (*d.* 1679), one of Titus Oates's victims; barrister, Inner Temple, 1654; accused by Oates of being a ringleader in the 'Popish plot' of 1678; tried, condemned, and executed next year. [xxxii. 102]

LANGHORNE, SIR WILLIAM, first baronet (1629-1715), governor of Madras; of the Inner Temple; succeeded to his father's East India trade; created baronet, 1668; governor of Madras, 1670-7. [xxxii. 103]

LANGHORNE, WILLIAM (1721-1772), poet and translator; brother of John Langhorne [q. v.]; assisted him in his translation of Plutarch, and published sermons and poetical paraphrases of some books of the bible. [xxxii. 102]

LANGLAND, JOHN (1473-1547). [See LONGLAND.]

LANGLAND, WILLIAM (1330?-1400?), poet; details of his life chiefly supplied from his one work, 'The Vision of Piers the Plowman'; native of the Western Midlands; probably educated at the monastery of Great Malvern; went to London; engaged on his great poem, 1362-92; produced it in at least three versions (first, 1362, second, 1377, third, 1392), treating in them philosophical and social questions in the unrhymed alliterative line of the old English metre; possibly the author of 'Richard the Redeless,' a poem written to remonstrate with Richard II. [xxxii. 104]

LANGLEY, BATTY (1696-1751), architectural writer; attempted to remodel Gothic architecture by the invention of five orders for that style in imitation of classical architecture; did good work in the mechanical branches of his art; wrote twenty-one works on architecture. [xxxii. 108]

LANGLEY, EDMUND DE, first DUKE OF YORK (1341-1402), fifth son of Edward III; accompanied his father to the French wars, 1359; K.G., 1361; created Earl of Cambridge, 1362; accompanied the Black Prince to Spain, 1367; sent to France, 1369; shared in sack of Limoges, 1370; married Isabel of Castile, daughter of Pedro the Cruel, 1372; king's lieutenant in Brittany, 1374; constable of Dover, 1376-81; member of the council of regency to Richard II, 1377; took part in the king's expedition to Scotland, 1385; created Duke of York, 1385; regent during the king's absences, 1394-9; went over to the side of Henry of Lancaster (afterwards Henry IV); retired from the court after Henry IV's coronation, 1399. [xxxii. 109]

LANGLEY, HENRY (1611-1679), puritan divine; of Pembroke College, Oxford; M.A., 1635; master of Pembroke College, Oxford, 1647-60; canon of Christ Church, 1648; D.D., 1649. [xxxii. 111]

LANGLEY, JOHN (*d.* 1657), grammarian; entered Magdalen Hall, Oxford; M.A., 1619; high-master of the College School, Gloucester, 1617-27 and 1628-35; of St. Paul's School, 1640; a licenser of the press, 1643; published a work on rhetoric for St. Paul's School, 1644, and an 'Introduction to Grammar.' [xxxii. 111]

LANGLEY, THOMAS (*fl.* 1320?), writer on poetry; monk of St. Benet's Hulme, Norfolk; author of 'Liber de Varietate Carminum in capitulis xviii distinctus cum prologo,' of which ten chapters are preserved in manuscript at the Bodleian. [xxxii. 112]

LANGLEY or **LONGLEY,** THOMAS (*d.* 1437), bishop of Durham, cardinal, and chancellor; educated at Cambridge; in his youth attached to the family of John of Gaunt; canon of York, 1400; dean, 1401; keeper of the privy seal, 1403; chancellor, 1405-7; bishop of Durham, 1406; sent on embassies by the king, 1409, 1410, 1414; cardinal, 1411; again chancellor, 1417 (retiring, 1424); assisted at Henry VI's coronation, 1429; statesman and canonist. [xxxii. 112]

LANGLEY, THOMAS (d. 1581), canon of Winchester; B.A. Cambridge, 1538; chaplain to Cranmer, 1548; canon of Winchester, 1557; B.D. Oxford, 1560; chief work, an abridged English edition of Polydore Vergil's 'De Inventoribus Rerum,' published, 1546. [xxxii. 114]

LANGLEY, THOMAS (fl. 1745), engraver of antiquities, &c.; brother of Batty Langley [q. v.]; drew and engraved for his brother's books. [xxxii. 108]

LANGLEY, THOMAS (1769-1801), topographer; of Eton and Hertford College, Oxford; M.A., 1794; held livings in Northamptonshire and Buckinghamshire; published 'The History and Antiquities of the Hundred of Desborough and Deanery of Wycombe in Buckinghamshire,' 1797. [xxxii. 114]

LANGMEAD, afterwards **TASWELL-LANGMEAD**, THOMAS PITT (1840-1882), writer on constitutional law and history; educated at King's College, London; barrister, Lincoln's Inn, 1863; B.A. St. Mary Hall, Oxford, 1866; practised as a conveyancer; tutor in constitutional law and legal history at the Inns of Court; joint-editor of the 'Law Magazine and Review,' 1875-82; professor of constitutional law and legal history at University College, London, 1882; edited for Camden Society, 1858, 'Sir Edward Lake's Account of his Interviews with Charles I, on being created a Baronet'; published a pamphlet, 'Parish Registers: a Plea for their Preservation,' 1872, and 'English Constitutional History,' 1875. [xxxii. 115]

LANGRISH, BROWNE (d. 1759), physician; extra licentiate of the College of Physicians; F.R.S., 1734; published 'The Modern Theory and Practice of Physic,' 1735; delivered the Croonian lectures; graduated M.D., 1747. [xxxii. 115]

LANGRISHE, SIR HERCULES, first baronet (1731-1811), Irish politician; B.A. Trinity College, Dublin, 1753; M.P. for Knocktopher in the Irish parliament, 1760-1801; commissioner of barracks, 1766-74; supervisor of accounts, 1767-75; commissioner of revenue, 1774-1801; commissioner of excise, 1780-1801; opposed every effort to reform the Irish parliament; created baronet, 1777; privy councillor, 1777; introduced his Catholic Relief Bill, 1792; supported the union scheme, 1799; some of his speeches published. [xxxii. 115]

LANGSHAW, JOHN (1718-1798), organist; employed in London by the Earl of Bute, c. 1761; organist of Lancaster parish church, 1772. [xxxii. 117]

LANGSHAW, JOHN (fl. 1798), organist; son of John Langshaw (1718-1798) [q. v.]; succeeded his father as organist at Lancaster, 1798; published hymns, chants, songs, and pianoforte concertos. [xxxii. 117]

LANGSTON, JOHN (1641?-1704), independent divine; entered Pembroke College, Oxford, 1655; took out licence to preach, 1672; ministered in Ipswich, 1686-1704; author of two schoolbooks. [xxxii. 117]

LANGTOFT, PETER OF (d. 1307?), rhyming chronicler; author of a history of England up to the death of Edward I in French verse, the latter part of which was translated into English by Robert of Brunne (first published in the Rolls Series, 1866 and 1868). [xxxii. 117]

LANGTON, BENNET (1737-1801), friend of Dr. Johnson; as a lad obtained an introduction to the doctor, who visited him at Trinity College, Oxford, 1759; member of the Literary Club, 1764; M.A., 1769; famous for his Greek scholarship; professor of ancient literature at the Royal Academy, 1788; D.C.L. Oxford, 1790. [xxxii. 118]

LANGTON, CHRISTOPHER (1521-1578), physician; educated at Eton and King's College, Cambridge; B.A., 1542; published treatises in English on medicine, 1547, 1550, and 1552; M.D. Cambridge, 1552; F.R.C.P., 1552-8; expelled for profligate conduct, 1558. [xxxii. 119]

LANGTON, JOHN DE (d. 1337), bishop of Chichester and chancellor of England; clerk in the royal chancery and keeper of the rolls; chancellor, 1292-1302; treasurer of Wells, 1294; bishop of Chichester, 1305; chancellor, 1307-9; built the chapter-house at Chichester. [xxxii. 120]

LANGTON, JOHN (fl. 1390), Carmelite; studied at Oxford, and was bachelor of theology; took part in the trial (1392) of the lollard Henry Crump, and wrote an account of it. [xxxii. 121]

LANGTON, ROBERT (d. 1524), divine and traveller; nephew of Thomas Langton [q. v.]; educated at Queen's College, Oxford; prebendary of Lincoln, 1483-1517; archdeacon of Dorset, 1486-1514; D.C.L., 1501; treasurer of York Minster, 1509-14; prebendary of York, 1514-24. [xxxii. 121]

LANGTON, SIMON (d. 1248), archdeacon of Canterbury; brother of Stephen Langton [q. v.]; shared his brother's exile; returned to England, 1213; adopted the barons' cause; chancellor to Louis of France when he came to claim the English crown, 1216; exiled, 1217-27; archdeacon of Canterbury, 1227; rose into high favour with the king and pope; author of a treatise on the Book of Canticles. [xxxii. 121]

LANGTON, STEPHEN (d. 1228), archbishop of Canterbury and cardinal; studied at Paris University; became a doctor in arts and theology; went to Rome and was made cardinal-priest, 1206; archbishop of Canterbury, 1207-28; at first rejected by King John, 1207; remained at Pontigny for the next five years after the interdict of 1208; tried to act as peacemaker between John and the pope (Innocent III); visited Dover in the hope of making terms, but had to return into exile, 1209; received by John, 1213; acted as mediator during the business of the Great Charter, which he supported, 1215; held at Osney a church council, which is to the ecclesiastical history of England what the assembly at Runnymede (1215) is to her secular history, 1222; occupied in political affairs during the earlier years of Henry III's reign; a famous theologian, historian, and poet. [xxxii. 122]

LANGTON, THOMAS (d. 1501), bishop of Winchester and archbishop-elect of Canterbury; fellow of Pembroke Hall, Cambridge, 1461; took degrees in canon law at Cambridge; chaplain to Edward IV before 1476; sent on embassies to France, 1467, 1476, 1477, 1478, and 1480; treasurer of Exeter, 1478; prebendary of Wells, 1478; prebendary of Lincoln, 1483; bishop of St. David's, 1483; bishop of Salisbury, 1485; provost of Queen's College, Oxford, 1487-95; bishop of Winchester, 1493-1500; elected archbishop of Canterbury, 22 Jan. 1501; died of the plague, 27 Jan. [xxxii. 128]

LANGTON, WALTER (d. 1321), bishop of Lichfield and treasurer; clerk of the king's chancery; keeper of the king's wardrobe, 1292; a favourite councillor of Edward I; treasurer, 1295; bishop of Lichfield, 1297; accused of various crimes, 1301; formally absolved, 1303; accompanied Edward I to Scotland, and was present at his death, 1307; arrested by Edward II for misdemeanors as treasurer; imprisoned, 1308-12; liberated and restored to office of treasurer, 1312; in the king's council, 1315-18. [xxxii. 129]

LANGTON, WILLIAM (1803-1881), antiquary and financier; engaged in business in Liverpool, 1821-9; in Messrs. Heywood's bank, Manchester, 1829-54; managing director, Manchester and Salford bank, 1854-76; member of the Chetham Society, editing for it three volumes of miscellanies; an accurate genealogist, herald, and antiquary, philologist, and writer of English and Italian verse. [xxxii. 132]

LANGTON, ZACHARY (1698-1786), divine; of Magdalen Hall, Oxford; M.A., 1724; published anonymously 'An Essay Concerning the Human Rational Soul,' 1753 [xxxii. 133]

LANGWITH, BENJAMIN (1684?-1743), antiquary and natural philosopher; educated at Queens' College, Cambridge; M.A., 1708; D.D., 1717; prebendary of Chichester, 1725; assisted Francis Drake with his 'Eboracum'; published scientific dissertations. [xxxii. 133]

LANIER, SIR JOHN (d. 1692), military commander; governor of Jersey under Charles II; knighted; lieutenant-general, 1688; served in Ireland under William III, 1689-91; one of the king's generals of horse in Flanders, 1692; mortally wounded at battle of Steinkirk. [xxxii. 134]

LANIER, NICHOLAS (1568-1646?), etcher; possibly cousin of Nicholas Lanier (1588-1666) [q. v.]. [xxxii. 135]

LANIER (**LANIERE**), NICHOLAS (1588-1666), musician and amateur of art; a musician in the royal household; composed music for masque by Campion, 1613, for Ben Jonson's 'Lovers made Men,' and the 'Vision of Delight,' 1617; master of the king's music, 1625; sent by Charles I to Italy to collect pictures and statues for the royal collection; followed the royal family into exile; reinstated as master of the king's music, 1660. [xxxii. 134]

LANIGAN, JOHN (1758–1828), Irish ecclesiastical historian; ordained at Rome; appointed to the chairs of Hebrew ecclesiastical history and divinity in the university of Pavia; published the first part of his 'Institutiones Biblicæ,' 1793; D.D. Pavia, 1794; returned to Ireland, 1796; assistant-librarian, foreign correspondent, and general literary supervisor to the Royal Dublin Society, 1799; assisted to found Gaelic Society of Dublin, 1808; principal work, 'An Ecclesiastical History of Ireland, from the first Introduction of Christianity among the Irish to the beginning of the thirteenth Century,' 1822. [xxxii. 135]

LANKESTER, EDWIN (1814–1874), man of science; articled to a surgeon; studied at London University, 1834–7; M.R.C.S. and L.S.A., 1837; M.D. Heidelberg, 1839; secretary of the Ray Society, 1844; F.R.S., 1845; professor of natural history in New College, London, 1850; joint-editor of the 'Quarterly Journal of Microscopical Science,' 1853–71; president of the Microscopical Society of London, 1859; examiner in botany to the science and art department, 1862; engaged in important sanitary investigations; medical officer of health for the parish of St. James's, Westminster, 1856–74; coroner for Central Middlesex, 1862–74; published works on physiology and sanitary science. [xxxii. 137]

LANKRINK, PROSPER HENRICUS (1628–1692), painter; born in Germany; studied at Antwerp; visited Italy; came to England and was employed by Lely to paint the accessories in his portraits. [xxxii. 139]

LANQUET or **LANKET**, THOMAS (1521–1545), chronicler; studied at Oxford and devoted himself to historical research; at his death was engaged on a useful general history, completed by Thomas Cooper (1517 ?–1594) [q. v.] [xxxii. 139]

LANSDOWNE, MARQUISES OF. [See PETTY, WILLIAM, first MARQUIS, 1737–1805; PETTY-FITZMAURICE, HENRY, third MARQUIS, 1780–1863; PETTY-FITZMAURICE, HENRY THOMAS, fourth MARQUIS, 1816–1866.]

LANSDOWNE, first BARON (1667–1735). [See GRANVILLE or GRENVILLE, GEORGE.]

LANT, THOMAS (1556 ?–1600), herald and draughtsman; originally servant to Sir Philip Sidney [q. v.]; entered College of Arms as Portcullis pursuivant, 1588; Windsor herald, 1597; wrote on heraldry. [xxxii. 139]

LANTFRED or **LAMFRID** (*fl.* 980), hagiographer; author of 'De Miraculis Swithuni,' printed partly in the 'Acta Sanctorum,' the whole work being contained in the Cotton MSS. [xxxii. 140]

LANYON, SIR CHARLES (1813–1889), civil engineer; surveyor of co. Antrim, 1836–60; architect of some of the principal buildings in Belfast; mayor of Belfast, 1862; president of the Royal Institute of Architects of Ireland, 1862–8; M.P., Belfast, 1866; knighted, 1868; high sheriff of co. Antrim, 1876. [xxxii. 140]

LANYON, SIR WILLIAM OWEN (1842–1887), colonel and colonial administrator; son of Sir Charles Lanyon [q. v.]; served in Jamaica during native disturbances, 1865; C.M.G., 1874; administrator of Griqualand West, 1885–8, of the Transvaal, 1879–81; K.C.M.G., 1880; served in Egyptian campaign, 1882, with Nile expedition, 1884–5; died at New York. [xxxii. 141]

LANZA, GESUALDO (1779–1859), teacher of music; born in Naples; became known in London as a singing-master; delivered lectures and wrote various works on the art of singing. [xxxii. 141]

LAPIDGE, EDWARD (*d.* 1860), architect; sent various drawings to the Royal Academy; built a bridge over the Thames at Kingston, 1825–8, and altered and built several churches; F.R.I.B.A.; surveyor of bridges and public works for Surrey. [xxxii. 141]

LAPORTE, GEORGE HENRY (*d.* 1873), animal-painter; son of John Laporte [q. v.]; exhibited sporting subjects at the Academy, British Institution, and Suffolk Street Gallery from 1818; foundation member of the Institute of Painters in Water-colours. [xxxii. 142]

LAPORTE, JOHN (1761–1839), water-colour painter; drawing-master at the military academy at Addiscombe; exhibited landscapes at the Royal Academy and British Institution from 1785; in conjunction with William Frederick Wells [q. v.] executed a set of seventy-two etchings from Gainsborough, 1819; published works on art. [xxxii. 142]

LAPRAIK, JOHN (1727–1807), confined for a time as debtor after the collapse of the Ayr bank, 1772; conducted a public-house and the village post-office at Muirkirk after 1796; published 'Poems on Several Occasions,' 1788; three famous 'Epistles' addressed to him by Burns. [xxxii. 142]

LAPWORTH, EDWARD (1574–1636), physician and Latin poet; M.A. Exeter College, Oxford, 1595; master of Magdalen College school, Oxford, 1598–1610; licensed to practise medicine, 1605; M.D., 1611; first Sedleian reader in natural philosophy, 1618; Linacre physic lecturer, 1619–35. [xxxii. 143]

LARCOM, SIR THOMAS AISKEW (1801–1879), Irish official; educated Royal Military Academy, Woolwich; employed on ordnance survey of England and Wales, 1824–6, of Ireland, 1828–46; published admirable maps of Ireland; census commissioner, 1841; commissioner of public works, 1846; deputy-chairman of the board of works, 1850; under-secretary for Ireland, 1853; K.C.B., 1860; his administration marked by a steady increase of prosperity. [xxxii. 143]

LARDNER, DIONYSIUS (1793–1859), scientific writer; of Trinity College, Dublin; M.A., 1819; LL.D., 1827; took holy orders, but devoted himself to literary and scientific work; professor of natural philosophy and astronomy in London University, now University College, 1827; his principal work, the 'Cabinet Cyclopædia,' completed in 133 volumes, 1849; edited the 'Edinburgh Cabinet Library,' 1830–44; lectured in the United States and Cuba, 1840–5; settled at Paris, 1845; wrote at Paris works on railway economy and natural philosophy; died at Naples. [xxxii. 145]

LARDNER, NATHANIEL (1684–1768), biblical and patristic scholar; preached his first sermon, 1709; lectured on the 'Credibility of the Gospel History,' out of which grew his great work, 1723; first two volumes of part i. of his 'Credibility' published, 1727; part ii. vols. i–xii., 1733–55; founder of the modern school of critical research in the field of early Christian literature, and remains the leading authority on the conservative side; D.D. Marischal College, Aberdeen, 1745. [xxxii. 147]

LARKHAM, THOMAS (1602–1669), puritan divine; M.A. Trinity Hall, Cambridge, 1626; in trouble through his puritan proclivities; fled to New England before 1641; returned, 1642; vicar of Tavistock before 1649; resigned his benefice, 1660; wrote controversial pamphlets. [xxxii. 151]

LARKING, LAMBERT BLACKWELL (1797–1868), antiquary; educated at Eton and Brasenose College, Oxford; M.A., 1823; founder of the university lodge of Freemasons; hon. sec. Kent Archæological Society, 1857–1861; vice-president, 1861; edited volumes for the Camden Society, 1849, 1857, and 1861; the 'Domesday Book of Kent,' published, 1869; made extensive preparations for a revision of Hasted's 'History of Kent,' the first instalment of which—the Hundred of Blackheath—appeared in 1886. [xxxii. 153]

LAROCHE, JAMES (*fl.* 1696–1713), singer; appeared while a boy as Cupid in Motteux's 'Loves of Mars and Venus,' 1697; in a musical interlude, 'The Raree Show,' 1713. [xxxii. 153]

LAROON or **LAURON**, MARCELLUS, the elder (1653–1702), painter and engraver; born at the Hague; migrated to England; best known by his drawings, 'The Cryes of London'; painted draperies for Sir Godfrey Kneller [q. v.] [xxxii. 153]

LAROON, MARCELLUS, the younger (1679–1772), painter and captain in the army; second son of Marcellus Laroon the elder [q. v.]; studied painting and music; actor and singer at Drury Lane Theatre, London; joined the footguards, 1707; fought at Oudenarde, 1708; deputy quarter-master-general of the English troops in Spain; returned to England, 1712; captain, 1732; a friend and imitator of William Hogarth [q. v.]; best known for his conversation pieces. [xxxii. 154]

LARPENT, FRANCIS SEYMOUR (1776-1845), civil servant; eldest son of John Larpent [q. v.]; educated at St. John's College, Cambridge; fellow, 1799; M.A., 1802; called to the bar; deputy judge-advocate-general to the forces in the Peninsula, 1812-14; commissioner of customs, 1814; civil and admiralty judge for Gibraltar; employed in secret service with reference to the Princess Caroline, 1815 and 1820; chairman of the board of audit of the public accounts, 1826-43; his 'Private Journals' published, 1853. [xxxii. 154]

LARPENT, SIR GEORGE GERARD DE HOCHEPIED, first baronet (1786-1855), politician; son of John Larpent [q. v.]; entered East India House of Cockerell & Larpent; chairman of the Oriental and China Association; deputy-chairman of St. Katharine's Docks Company; M.P., Nottingham, 1841; created baronet, 1841; wrote pamphlets and edited works by his grandfather and his half-brother, Francis Seymour Larpent [q. v.] [xxxii. 155]

LARPENT, JOHN (1741-1824), inspector of plays; educated at Westminster; entered the foreign office; secretary to the Duke of Bedford at the peace of Paris, 1763; inspector of plays, 1778. [xxxii. 155]

LASCELLES, MRS. ANN (1745-1789). [See CATLEY, ANN.]

LASCELLES, HENRY, second EARL OF HAREWOOD (1767-1841), M.P., Yorkshire, 1796, 1802, and 1812, Westbury, 1807, Northallerton, 1818; styled Viscount Lascelles after death of his elder brother (1814), and succeeded his father, the first earl, 1820. [xxxii. 156]

LASCELLES, ROWLEY (1771-1841), antiquary and miscellaneous writer; educated at Harrow; barrister, Middle Temple, 1797; practised at the Irish bar for twenty years; selected by the record commissioners for Ireland (1813) to edit lists of all public officers recorded in Irish court of chancery from 1540 to 1774, the work appearing as 'Liber Munerum Publicorum Hiberniæ, ab an. 1152 usque ad 1827' (vol. i. 1824, vol. ii. 1830); prefixed to it a history of Ireland which gave so much offence that the book was suppressed (reissued, 1852); author of works on miscellaneous subjects. [xxxii. 156]

LASCELLES, THOMAS (1670-1751), colonel; chief engineer of Great Britain and deputy quartermaster-general of the forces; served as volunteer in Ireland, 1689-91; in the expedition to Cadiz, 1702; joined regular army, 1704; present at nearly all Marlborough's battles; wounded at Blenheim, 1704; employed in the demolition of the fortifications, &c., of Dunkirk, 1713-16, 1720-5, and 1729-32; deputy quartermaster-general of the forces, 1715; director of engineers, 1722; master-surveyor of the ordnance and chief engineer of Great Britain, 1742. [xxxii. 157]

LASKI or **À LASCO**, JOHN (1499-1560), reformer; born in Poland; mistakenly claimed descent from Henry de Lacy, third earl of Lincoln [q. v.]; at Bologna University, 1514-18; canon of Leczyc, 1517, of Cracow and Plock, 1518, and dean of Gnesen, 1521; lived at Basle in Erasmus's house, 1524-5; bishop of Vesprim, 1529; archdeacon of Warsaw, 1538; pastor of a congregation of reformers at Emden in East Frisia, 1542-8; superintendent of the London church of foreign protestants, 1550; had great influence at Edward VI's court; promoted the reformation in Poland, 1556-60; an austere Calvinist; published tracts advocating the reformation. [xxxii. 158]

LASSELL, WILLIAM (1799-1880), astronomer; educated at a school at Rochdale; apprenticed in a merchant's office at Liverpool, 1814-21; brewer at Liverpool, 1825; built observatory at Starfield, near Liverpool, and erected a nine-inch Newtonian, the first example of the adaptation to reflectors of the equatoreal plan of mounting, and with it followed the course of comets further than was possible at any public observatory; invented a new machine mounted at Starfield, 1846; verified discovery of Neptune by its aid, 1847; gold medallist, Royal Astronomical Society, 1849, and F.R.S., 1849; the first to ascertain clearly the composition of the Uranian system, 1851; removed his observatory to Bradstones, 1854; royal medallist, 1858; constructed a reflecting telescope of four feet aperture, 1859-60; mounted and worked with it at Valetta, 1861-4; set up an observatory near Maidenhead on his return to England; hon. LL.D. Cambridge, 1874. [xxxii. 160]

LASSELS, RICHARD (1603?-1668), Roman catholic divine; educated probably at Oxford; student of the English college at Douay, 1623; professor of classics at Douay, 1629; ordained priest, 1632; published account of travels in Italy, 1670; died at Montpellier. [xxxii. 161]

LATES, CHARLES (*fl.* 1794), organist and musical composer; son of John James Lates [q. v.]; pupil of Dr. Philip Hayes [q. v.]; entered Magdalen College, Oxford, 1793; Mus. Bac., 1794, composed an anthem, and sonatas for the pianoforte. [xxxii. 162]

LATES, JOHN JAMES (*d.* 1777?), organist; violinist and teacher of the violin at Oxford; probably organist of St. John's College, Oxford; composed solos and duets for the violin and violoncello. [xxxii. 162]

LATEWAR, RICHARD (1560-1601), scholar; educated at Merchant Taylors' School, London; scholar, 1580, and later fellow of St. John's College, Oxford; M.A., 1588; D.D., 1597; accompanied Charles Blount, eighth baron Mountjoy [q. v.], to Ireland, and died of a wound received at Benburb, co. Tyrone; wrote Latin poems. [xxxii. 162]

LATEY, GILBERT (1626-1705), quaker; joined the Society of Friends, 1654; suffered imprisonment for his belief; exerted his influence successfully on behalf of the quakers with James II and William and Mary; by persistently petitioning the king obtained act of 1697 (made perpetual, 1715), by which the quaker affirmation became equivalent to an oath; author of several religious tracts. [xxxii. 163]

LATHAM, HENRY (1794-1866), poetical writer; third son of John Latham (1761-1843) [q. v.]; educated at Brasenose College, Oxford; entered the church; published 'Sertum Shakesperianum, subnexis aliquot inferioris notæ floribus,' 1863. [xxxii. 166]

LATHAM, JAMES (*d.* 1750?), portrait-painter; called the 'Irish Vandyck.' Among his sitters were Margaret Woffington and Bishop Berkeley. [xxxii. 164]

LATHAM, JOHN (1740-1837), ornithologist; educated at Merchant Taylors' School, London; studied anatomy under Hunter; M.D. Erlangen, 1796; studied archæology; F.S.A., 1774; F.R.S., 1775; assisted to form the Linnean Society, 1788; chief work, 'A General History of Birds,' 1821-8. [xxxii. 164]

LATHAM, JOHN (1761-1843), physician; entered Brasenose College, Oxford, 1778; B.A., 1782; studied at St. Bartholomew's Hospital, London, 1782-4; M.A., 1784; M.B., 1786; physician to the Radcliffe Infirmary, Oxford, 1787; M.D., 1788; F.R.C.P., 1789; physician to the Middlesex Hospital, 1789-93, to St. Bartholomew's Hospital, 1793-1802; Gulstonian lecturer, 1793; Harveian orator, 1794; Croonian lecturer, 1795; physician extraordinary to the Prince of Wales, 1795; published pamphlet on rheumatism and gout, 1796, and works on clinical medicine. [xxxii. 165]

LATHAM, JOHN (1787-1853), poetical writer; eldest son of John Latham (1761-1843) [q. v.]; educated at Brasenose College, Oxford; elected fellow of All Souls' College while an undergraduate, 1806; published anonymously a volume of poems, 1836; English and Latin poems by him published posthumously, 1853. [xxxii. 166]

LATHAM, PETER MERE (1789-1875), physician; second son of John Latham (1761-1843) [q. v.]; educated at Brasenose College, Oxford; B.A., 1810; commenced studying at St. Bartholomew's Hospital, London, 1810; M.A., 1813; M.B., 1814; physician to the Middlesex Hospital, 1815-24; M.D., 1816; F.R.C.P., 1818; Gulstonian lecturer, 1819; physician to St. Bartholomew's Hospital, 1824-41; joint-lecturer on medicine in the school of St. Bartholomew's Hospital, 1836; physician extraordinary to Queen Victoria, 1837; Harveian orator, 1839; chief work, 'Lectures on Clinical Medicine, comprising Diseases of the Heart,' 1845. [xxxii. 167]

LATHAM, ROBERT GORDON (1812-1888), ethnologist and philologist; of Eton and King's College, Cambridge; B.A., 1832; studied in Germany, Denmark, and Norway; professor of English language and literature in University College, London, 1839; produced his well-known text-book on the English language, 1841; studied medicine; L.R.C.P., 1842; M.D. London; director of the ethnological department of the Crystal Palace, 1852; made protest against the Central Asian theory of the origin of the Aryans, 1862; completed his revision of Johnson's dictionary, 1870; published philological and ethnological works, 1840-78.   [xxxii. 168]

LATHAM, SIMON (*fl.* 1618), falconer; published 'Lathams Falconry or the Faulcons Lure and Cure, in two Bookes,' 1615-18.   [xxxii. 169]

LATHBERY, JOHN (*fl.* 1350), Franciscan; famous as a theologian throughout the later Middle Ages; D.D. Oxford, after 1350; his best-known work, 'Commentary on Lamentations,' one of the earliest books issued by the university press, printed at Oxford, 1482.
                    [xxxii. 169]

LATHBURY, THOMAS (1798-1865), ecclesiastical historian; of St. Edmund Hall, Oxford; M.A., 1827; vicar of St. Simon's, Baptist Mills, Bristol, 1848. His works include a history of convocation and 'A History of the Nonjurors,' 1845.   [xxxii. 169]

LATHOM, FRANCIS (1777-1832), novelist and dramatist; acted at and wrote for the Norwich Theatre before 1801; wrote several successful comedies and novels between 1795 and 1830.   [xxxii. 170]

LATHROP, JOHN (*d.* 1653). [See LOTHROPP.]

LATHY, THOMAS PIKE (*fl.* 1820), novelist; published 'Memoirs of the Court of Louis XIV,' 1819; perpetrated a successful plagiaristic fraud in the 'Angler, a poem in ten cantos,' 1819 (copied from 'The Anglers. Eight Dialogues in Verse,' 1758); author of 'Reparation, or the School for Libertines,' performed at the Boston Theatre, United States, 1800.   [xxxii. 171]

LATIMER, BARONS. [See LATIMER, WILLIAM, first BARON of the second creation, *d.* 1304; LATIMER, WILLIAM, fourth BARON, 1329?-1381; NEVILLE, RICHARD, second BARON of the third creation, 1468-1530; NEVILLE, JOHN, third BARON, 1490?-1543.]

LATIMER, HUGH (1485?-1555), bishop of Worcester; sent to Cambridge; fellow of Clare Hall and B.A., 1510; M.A., 1514; took priest's orders; refused to refute Luther's doctrines, 1525; compelled to explain himself before Wolsey and dismissed, with liberty to preach throughout England; preached his famous sermons 'on the card,' 1529; master in theology, Oxford, by 1530; preached before Henry VIII at Windsor, 1530; accused of heresy and brought before convocation by the bishop of London, and absolved on a complete submission, 1532; bishop of Worcester, 1535; preached Jane Seymour's funeral sermon, 1537; encouraged puritanism in his diocese; resigned his bishopric because he could not support the Act of the Six Articles, 1539; kept in custody for nearly a year; resumed preaching after eight years' silence and preached his famous sermon 'of the plough,' 1548; committed to the Tower on Mary's accession, 1553; sent to Oxford with Ridley and Cranmer to defend his views before the leading divines of the university, 1554; condemned as a heretic and burnt at Oxford with Ridley, 1555; his extant writings edited for the Parker Society, 1844-5.   [xxxii. 171]

LATIMER, WILLIAM, first BARON LATIMER (*d.* 1304), served in Wales, 1276 and 1282; took part in the expedition to Gascony, 1292; employed in Scotland; present at the battle of Stirling, 1297, at the battle of Falkirk, 1298.   [xxxii. 179]

LATIMER, WILLIAM, second BARON LATIMER (1276?-1327), son of William Latimer, first baron Latimer [q. v.]; employed in Scotland, 1297-1303; taken prisoner at Bannockburn, 1314; released, 1315; a supporter of Thomas of Lancaster, but afterwards of Edward II.
                    [xxxii. 180]

LATIMER, WILLIAM, fourth BARON LATIMER (1329?-1381), son of William, third baron; served in Gascony, 1359; governor of Bécherel in Brittany, 1360; K.G., 1361; chamberlain of the king's household, 1369; constable of Dover Castle and warden of the Cinque ports, 1374; in great favour with John of Gaunt; impeached by the Commons as a bad adviser (this being the earliest record of the impeachment of a minister of the crown by the Commons), 1376; the attempt to bring him to justice unsuccessful; governor of Calais, 1377; served in France, 1380-1.   [xxxii. 180]

LATIMER, WILLIAM (1460?-1545), classical scholar; fellow of All Souls' College, Oxford, 1489; studied at

Padua; M.A. Oxford, 1513; tutor to Reginald Cardinal Pole; prebendary of Salisbury; a great friend of Sir Thomas More; his 'Epistolæ ad Erasmum' alone extant.
                    [xxxii. 181]

LA TOUCHE, WILLIAM GEORGE DIGGES (1747-1803), resident at Bassorah; entered St. Paul's School, London, 1757; proceeded to Bassorah, 1764; became British resident there; gained the goodwill of the natives and showed kindness to the principal citizens during the siege, 1775; returned to England, 1784; partner in La Touche's bank in Dublin.   [xxxii. 182]

LATROBE, CHARLES JOSEPH (1801-1875), Australian governor and traveller; son of Christian Ignatius Latrobe [q. v.]; educated for the Moravian ministry, but abandoned the design; travelled in Switzerland, ascending mountains and unexplored passes, 1824-6; travelled in America, 1832-4; superintendent at the time of the gold fever of the Port Phillip district of New South Wales, 1839 (the post converted into the lieutenant-governorship of Victoria, 1851); retired, 1854; C.B., 1858; published descriptions of his travels.   [xxxii. 182]

LATROBE, CHRISTIAN IGNATIUS (1758-1836), musical composer; studied at the Moravian College, Niesky, Upper Lusatia, 1771; teacher in the high school there; returned to England, 1784; secretary to the Society for the Furtherance of the Gospel, 1787, of the Unity of the Brethren in England, 1795; the last to hold the office of 'senior civilis' at the Herrnhut synod, 1801; undertook a visitation in South Africa in connection with his church, 1815-16; published an account of his travels, 1818; composed anthems, chorales, and some instrumental works; editor of the first English edition of the 'Moravian Hymn Tune Book'; chiefly remembered for his 'Selection of Sacred Music from the works of the most eminent Composers of Germany and Italy,' 1806-25. [xxxii. 183]

LATROBE, JOHN ANTES (1799-1878), writer on music; son of Christian Ignatius Latrobe [q. v.]; educated at St. Edmund Hall, Oxford; M.A., 1829; took orders; honorary canon of Carlisle Cathedral, 1858; author of 'The Music of the Church considered in its various branches, Congregational and Choral' (1831), and of two volumes of hymns.   [xxxii. 183]

LATROBE, PETER (1795-1863), Moravian; son of Christian Ignatius Latrobe [q. v.]; took orders in the Moravian church and became secretary of the Moravian mission; wrote an 'Introduction on the Progress of the Church Psalmody,' for an edition of the 'Moravian Hymn Tunes.'   [xxxii. 184]

LATTER, MARY (1725-1777), authoress; published 'Miscellaneous Works in Prose and Verse,' 1759; published tragedy, 'The Siege of Jerusalem by Titus Vespasian,' in 1763 (accepted for Covent Garden by Rich, who died before it could be produced; proved unsuccessful at Reading, 1768).   [xxxii. 184]

LATTER, THOMAS (1816-1853), soldier and Burmese scholar; born in India; published a Burmese grammar, the first scholarly treatise on the subject, 1845; chief interpreter in second Burmese war, and shared in the fighting, 1852; resident deputy-commissioner at Prome, where he was murdered, 1853.   [xxxii. 184]

LAUD, WILLIAM (1573-1645), archbishop of Canterbury; entered St. John's College, Oxford, 1589; fellow, 1593; M.A., 1598; ordained, 1601; B.D., 1604; D.D., 1608; president of St. John's College, Oxford, 1611; archdeacon of Huntingdon, 1615; dean of Gloucester, 1616; bishop of St. David's, 1621-6; became predominant in the church of England at Charles I's accession, 1625; supported the king in his struggle with the Commons; dean of the Chapel Royal, 1626; bishop of Bath and Wells, 1626-8; privy councillor, 1627; bishop of London, 1628-33; chancellor of the university of Oxford, 1629; archbishop of Canterbury, 1633; adopted the policy of compelling compulsory uniformity of action on the part of churchmen; interfered disastrously with the Scottish church; impeached of high treason by the Long parliament, 1640; committed to the Tower, 1641; tried, 1644; condemned and beheaded, 1645. In his ecclesiastical policy he failed to allow for the diversity of the elements which made up the national church. His sermons were published, 1651, and a collected edition of his works appeared, 1695-1700.
                    [xxxii. 185]

LAUDER, GEORGE (*fl.* 1677), Scottish poet; grandson of Sir Richard Maitland, Lord Lethington [q. v.]; M.A. Edinburgh, *c.* 1620; entered the English army and became a colonel; as a royalist spent many years on the continent and probably joined the army of the Prince of Orange; his poems mainly patriotic and military. [xxxii. 195]

LAUDER, JAMES ECKFORD (1811–1869), painter; younger brother of Robert Scott Lauder [q. v.]; studied at the Trustees' Academy, Edinburgh, 1830–3; contributed to the exhibitions of the Royal Scottish Academy from 1832; studied in Italy, 1834–8; member R.S.A., 1846; exhibited at the Royal Academy, 1841–53. [xxxii. 195]

LAUDER, Sir JOHN, of Fountainhall, LORD FOUNTAINHALL (1646–1722), M.A. Edinburgh, 1664; travelled and studied on the continent, 1665–6; passed advocate at the Scottish bar, 1668; member of the Scottish parliament for Haddingtonshire, 1685, 1690–1702, and 1702–7; a protestant and supporter of the revolution; a lord of session with the title of Lord Fountainhall, 1689; opposed the union; chronicler and diarist; a portion of his diary, entitled 'Chronological Notes of Scottish Affairs from 1680 till 1701,' published by Sir Walter Scott, 1822, the full diary printed by the Bannatyne Club, 1840. [xxxii. 196]

LAUDER, ROBERT SCOTT (1803–1869), subject-painter; brother of James Eckford Lauder [q. v.]; studied at Edinburgh and London, 1822–9; member of the Scottish Academy, 1829; exhibited there and at Royal Academy and British Institution, London, 1827–49; studied in Italy, 1833–8; principal teacher in the Drawing Academy of the Board of Trustees, Edinburgh, 1852–61; his greatest picture the 'Trial of Effie Deans.' [xxxii. 197]

LAUDER, THOMAS (1395–1481), bishop of Dunkeld; master of the hospital of Soltre or Soltry, Midlothian, 1437; preceptor to James II; bishop of Dunkeld, 1452; finished the church of Dunkeld (begun by his predecessor, James Kennedy (1406 ?–1465) [q. v.]), 1464; built bridge over the Tay, 1461; wrote life of Bishop John Scott, one of his predecessors, and a volume of sermons. [xxxii. 197]

LAUDER, Sir THOMAS DICK, seventh baronet (1784–1848), author; son of the sixth baronet of Fountainhall, and a descendant of Sir John Lauder of Fountainhall [q. v.]; contributed scientific papers to the 'Annals of Philosophy' from 1815; succeeded to baronetcy, 1820; his most popular work, 'Account of the great Moray Floods of 1829,' published, 1830; secretary to the board of Scottish manufactures, 1839; encouraged the foundation of technical and art schools; published works on Scotland, 1837–48. [xxxii. 198]

LAUDER, WILLIAM (*d.* 1425), lord chancellor of Scotland and bishop of Glasgow; archdeacon of Lothian; bishop of Glasgow, 1408; lord chancellor, 1423–5. [xxxii. 199]

LAUDER, WILLIAM (1520 ?–1573), Scottish poet; educated at St. Andrews University; took priest's orders; celebrated as a deviser of court pageants, 1549–58; joined the reformers, 1560; appointed minister, *c.* 1563. His published verse, of which there are five separate volumes, consists mainly of denunciation of the immoral practices current in Scotland in his time. [xxxii. 199]

LAUDER, WILLIAM (*d.* 1771), literary forger; educated at Edinburgh University; M.A., 1695; a good classical scholar and student of modern Latin verse; published (1739) 'Poetarum Scotorum Musæ Sacræ'; published articles in the 'Gentleman's Magazine' to prove that 'Paradise Lost' was largely plagiarised from seventeenth-century Latin poets, 1747 (reprinted as 'An Essay on Milton's Use and Imitation of the Moderns in his "Paradise Lost,"' with a preface by Dr. Johnson, 1750). It was proved by John Douglas [q. v.], afterwards bishop of Salisbury, that Lauder had himself interpolated in the works of Masenius and Staphorstius (seventeenth-century Latin poets) extracts from a Latin verse rendering of 'Paradise Lost.' He confessed and apologised in 'A Letter to the Reverend Mr. Douglas,' 1751, and emigrated to Barbados, where he died. Incidentally he proved that Milton had deeply studied the works of modern Latin poets. [xxxii. 200]

LAUDERDALE, DUKE OF (1616–1682). [See MAITLAND, JOHN.]

LAUDERDALE, DUCHESS OF (*d.* 1697). [See MURRAY, ELIZABETH.]

LAUDERDALE, EARLS OF. [See MAITLAND, JOHN, second EARL, 1616–1682; MAITLAND, CHARLES, third EARL, *d.* 1691; MAITLAND, RICHARD, fourth EARL, 1653–1695; MAITLAND, JOHN, fifth EARL, 1650 ?–1710; MAITLAND, JAMES, eighth EARL, 1759–1839; MAITLAND, ANTHONY, tenth EARL, 1785–1863; MAITLAND, THOMAS, eleventh EARL, 1803–1878.]

LAUGHARNE, ROWLAND (*fl.* 1648), soldier; took up arms for the parliament, 1642; commander-in-chief of the forces in Pembrokeshire; appointed commander-in-chief of the counties of Glamorgan, Cardigan, Carmarthen, and Pembroke, 1646; deserted to the king, 1648; forced to surrender to Cromwell, 1648; court-martialled; was condemned to death with two others, but escaped through being, with his companions, allowed to cast lots for his life, 1649; pensioned by Charles II, 1660. [xxxii. 203]

LAUGHTON, GEORGE (1736–1800), divine; educated at Wadham College, Oxford; M.A., 1771; D.D., 1771; chief works, 'The History of Ancient Egypt,' 1774, and 'The Progress and Establishment of Christianity, in reply to . . . Mr. Gibbon,' 1780. [xxxii. 203]

LAUGHTON, RICHARD (1668 ?–1723), prebendary of Worcester; M.A. Clare College, Cambridge, 1691; ardently supported the Newtonian philosophy; prebendary of Worcester, 1717. [xxxii. 204]

LAURENCE. [See also LAWRENCE.]

LAURENCE or **LAWRENCE**, EDWARD (*d.* 1740 ?), land surveyor; brother of John Laurence [q. v.]; an expert on agricultural subjects, and famous for his books of maps; wrote on surveying and farming. [xxxii. 204]

LAURENCE, FRENCH (1757–1809), civilian; brother of Richard Laurence [q. v.]; educated at Winchester School and Corpus Christi College, Oxford; M.A., 1781; devoted himself to civil law; D.C.L., 1787; contributed to the 'Rolliad'; helped Burke in preparing the preliminary case against Warren Hastings, and was retained as counsel, 1788; friend and literary executor of Burke [see under BURKE, EDMUND]; regius professor of civil law at Oxford, 1796; M.P., Peterborough, 1796; chancellor of the diocese of Oxford; a judge of the court of admiralty of the Cinque ports; his 'Poetical Remains' published with those of his brother, Richard Laurence [q. v.], 1872. [xxxii. 205]

LAURENCE, JOHN (*d.* 1732), writer on gardening; entered Clare Hall, Cambridge, 1685; B.A., 1668; fellow of Clare Hall; prebendary of Sarum; published sermons, and works on gardening. [xxxii. 206]

LAURENCE, RICHARD (1760–1838), archbishop of Cashel; brother of French Laurence [q. v.]; educated at Corpus Christi College, Oxford; M.A., 1785; entered holy orders; D.C.L., 1794; deputy professor of civil law, Oxford, 1796; Bampton lecturer, 1804; regius professor of Hebrew and canon of Christ Church, Oxford, 1814; archbishop of Cashel, Ireland, 1822. His writings include Latin and English translations of Ethiopic versions of apocryphal books of the bible. [xxxii. 206]

LAURENCE, ROGER (1670–1736), nonjuror; educated at Christ's Hospital; studied divinity; ordained, 1714; headed a new party among the nonjurors, who objected to lay baptism; author of controversial pamphlets on lay baptism. [xxxii. 207]

LAURENCE, SAMUEL (1812–1884), portrait-painter; executed oil or crayon portraits of contemporary celebrities; exhibited at the Society of British Artists, 1834–1853, at the Royal Academy, 1836–82. [xxxii. 208]

LAURENCE, THOMAS (1598–1657), master of Balliol College, Oxford; educated at Balliol; fellow of All Souls' College before 1618, M.A., 1621; M.A. Cambridge, 1627; B.D., 1629; chaplain to Charles I; master of Balliol, 1637–48; Margaret professor of divinity, 1638–48; received certificate, 1648, attesting that he engaged to preach only practical divinity; appointed to an Irish bishopric by Charles II, but died before he could be consecrated; published three sermons. [xxxii. 209]

LAURENCE O'TOOLE, SAINT (1130 ?–1180). [See O'TOOLE.]

LAURENT, PETER EDMUND (1796-1837), classical scholar; born in Picardy; educated at the Polytechnic School, Paris; taught modern languages at Oxford University; French master at the Royal Naval College, Portsmouth; visited Italy and Greece, 1818-19; published 'Recollections of a Classical Tour,' 1821. [xxxii. 210]

LAURENTIUS (*d.* 619). [See LAWRENCE.]

LAURIE, SIR PETER (1779?-1861), lord mayor of London; saddler in London, becoming contractor for the Indian army; sheriff, 1823; knighted, 1824; alderman, 1826; lord mayor, 1832; master of the Saddlers' Company, 1833; chairman of the Union Bank, 1839-61; published two works on prison reform. [xxxii. 210]

LAURIE, ROBERT (1755?-1836), mezzotint engraver; his earliest portraits in mezzotint, 1771; acted as publisher of engravings, maps, charts, and nautical works, 1794-1812. His plates include both subject-pictures and portraits. [xxxii. 211]

LAVENHAM or **LAVYNGHAM**, RICHARD (*fl.* 1380), Carmelite; Carmelite friar at Ipswich; studied at Oxford; prior of the Carmelite house at Bristol; confessor to Richard II; more than sixty treatises ascribed to him. [xxxii. 211]

LAVINGTON, BARON (1738?-1807). [See PAYNE, SIR RALPH.]

LAVINGTON, GEORGE (1684-1762), bishop of Exeter; educated at Winchester and New College, Oxford; fellow of New College, Oxford, 1708; B.C.L., 1713; D.C.L., 1732; bishop of Exeter, 1747-62; opponent of methodism. [xxxii. 212]

LAVINGTON, JOHN (1690?-1759), presbyterian divine; ordained, 1715; drew up the formula of orthodoxy (1718) that was for thirty-five years the condition of ordination by the Exeter assembly; instituted a 'Western academy' at Ottery St. Mary, 1752; his pamphlets dealing with the Exeter controversy published anonymously, 1719-20. [xxxii. 214]

LAVINGTON, JOHN (*d.* 1764), nonconformist tutor; son of John Lavington (1690?-1759) [q. v.]; ordained, 1739; principal tutor at the 'Western academy'; published sermons, 1743-59. [xxxii. 214]

LAW, AUGUSTUS HENRY (1833-1880), jesuit; eldest son of William Towry Law [q. v.]; joined jesuits, 1854; with the mission in Demerara, 1866-71; joined first missionary staff to the Zambesi, 1879; died at King Umzila's kraal. [xxxii. 221]

LAW, CHARLES EWAN (1792-1850), recorder of London; second son of Edward Law, first baron Ellenborough [q. v.]; educated at St. John's College, Cambridge; M.A., 1812; barrister, Inner Temple, 1817; a judge of the sheriff's court, 1828; K.C., 1829; common serjeant, 1830; recorder of London, 1833-50; M.P. for Cambridge University, 1835-50; treasurer, Inner Temple, 1839; LL.D. Cambridge, 1847. [xxxii. 214]

LAW, EDMUND (1703-1787), bishop of Carlisle; educated at St. John's College, Cambridge; fellow of Christ's College, Cambridge; M.A., 1727; published 'Essay on the Origin of Evil,' 1731, 'Enquiry into the Ideas of Space and Time,' 1734, 'Considerations on the State of the World with regard to the Theory of Religion,' 1745; a disciple of Locke in his philosophical opinions and a whig in politics; master of Peterhouse, Cambridge, 1756-68; librarian of the university of Cambridge, 1760; Knightbridge professor of moral philosophy, 1764; bishop of Carlisle, 1768-87; published anonymously a pamphlet, 'Considerations on the Propriety of requiring Subscription to Articles of Faith,' advocating religious tolerance, 1774; edited Locke's 'Works,' 1777. [xxxii. 215]

LAW, EDWARD, first BARON ELLENBOROUGH (1750-1818), lord chief-justice of England; fourth son of Edmund Law [q. v.]; educated at the Charterhouse (1761-7) and Peterhouse, Cambridge; fellow, 1771; M.A., 1774; commenced practice as a special pleader, 1775; barrister, Lincoln's Inn, 1780; K.C., 1787; retained as leading counsel for Warren Hastings, 1788; opened the defence, 1792; attorney-general, 1793; serjeant of the county palatine of Lancaster, 1793; counsel for the crown at various state trials, 1794-1802; knighted, 1801; M.P. for Newtown, Isle of Wight, 1801; lord chief-justice of England, created Baron Ellenborough and privy councillor, 1802; speaker of the House of Lords, 1805; admitted to the cabinet of 'All the Talents' without office, 1806; councillor to George III's queen during the regency, 1811; resigned office, 1818. [xxxii. 216]

LAW, EDWARD, first EARL OF ELLENBOROUGH (1790-1871), governor-general of India; eldest son of Edward Law, first baron Ellenborough [q. v.]; educated at Eton and St. John's College, Cambridge; M.A., 1809; tory M.P., St. Michael's, Cornwall, 1813; succeeded his father as second baron, 1818; lord privy seal, 1828; member of the board of control, whence began his connection with Indian affairs, 1828-30; governor-general of India, 1841; successfully contended with great difficulties in China and Afghanistan, 1842; responsible for the annexation of Scinde, 1842; unpopular with the civilians; subjugated Gwalior, 1844; recalled and created Earl of Ellenborough, 1844; first lord of the admiralty in Sir Robert Peel's reconstituted ministry, 1846; president of the board of control under Lord Derby, 1858. [xxxii. 221]

LAW, GEORGE HENRY (1761-1845), bishop successively of Chester and of Bath and Wells; son of Edmund Law [q. v.]; educated at Charterhouse and Queens' College, Cambridge; fellow, 1781; M.A., 1784; D.D., 1804; bishop of Chester, 1812-24; bishop of Bath and Wells, 1824-45; F.R.S. and F.S.A.; published sermons, charges, and addresses. [xxxii. 227]

LAW, HENRY (1797-1884), dean of Gloucester; son of George Henry Law [q. v.]; educated at Eton and St. John's College, Cambridge; fellow, 1821; M.A., 1823; one of the first examiners in the classical tripos, 1824-5; archdeacon of Richmond, 1824, of Wells, 1826; residentiary canon of Wells, 1828; dean of Gloucester, 1862-84; one of the leaders of the evangelical party in the church; author of 'Christ is All,' vols. i-iv., 'The Gospel in the Pentateuch,' 1854-8, other theological works, and numerous tracts. [xxxii. 228]

LAW, HUGH (1818-1883), lord chancellor of Ireland; educated at Trinity College, Dublin; B.A., 1839; called to the bar, 1840; Q.C., 1860; drafted the Irish Church Act; legal adviser to lord-lieutenant of Ireland, 1868; bencher of the King's Inns, Dublin, 1870; solicitor-general for Ireland, 1872; Irish privy councillor and attorney-general for Ireland, 1873; M.P., Londonderry, 1874; attorney-general again under Gladstone, 1880; lord-chancellor for Ireland, 1881; LL.D. [xxxii. 229]

LAW, JAMES (1560?-1632), archbishop of Glasgow; graduated at St. Andrews, 1581; minister of Kirkliston, 1585; a royal chaplain, 1601; titular bishop of Orkney, 1605; moderator of the general assembly, 1608; bishop of St. Andrews, 1611-15; archbishop of Glasgow, 1615; zealously supported James I's ecclesiastical policy. [xxxii. 229]

LAW, JAMES A. B. (1768-1828), general in the French army; grandnephew of John Law (1671-1729) [q. v.]; a distinguished general in the French army, a favourite aide-de-camp of Napoleon I; made a marshal of France by Louis XVIII; created Comte de Lauriston. [xxxii. 233]

LAW, JAMES THOMAS (1790-1876), chancellor of Lichfield; eldest son of George Henry Law [q. v.]; educated at Christ's College, Cambridge; fellow, 1812; took orders, 1814; M.A., 1815; prebendary of Lichfield, 1818; chancellor of Lichfield, 1821; commissary of archdeaconry of Richmond, 1824; special commissary of diocese of Bath and Wells, 1840; published works on ecclesiastical law. [xxxii. 230]

LAW, JOHN (1671-1729), of Lauriston; controller-general of French finance; son of the great-grandnephew of James Law [q. v.]; educated at Edinburgh; migrated to London; killed Edward Wilson, known as 'Beau' Wilson [q. v.], in a duel, 1694, and was sentenced to death for murder; escaped from prison and fled to the continent; issued anonymously pamphlets dealing with Scottish finance, 1701 and 1709; established the Banque Générale, the first bank of any kind in France, 1716; his 'Mississippi scheme' incorporated as the 'Western Company,' 1717; enlarged its sphere of action, 1718-20; entered the Roman catholic church; appointed controller-general of the finances, 1720; fled from France on the fall of the company, 1720; died and was buried at

Venice; allowed by French historians to have furthered French industry and commercial enterprise.

LAW, JOHN (1745–1810), bishop of Elphin; eldest son of Edmund Law [q. v.]; of Charterhouse and Christ's College, Cambridge; M.A., 1769; fellow of his college; prebendary of Carlisle, 1773; archdeacon of Carlisle, 1777; D.D., 1785; bishop of Clonfert, 1785–7, of Killala, 1787–95, of Elphin, 1795–1810; published two sermons.
[xxxii. 230]

LAW, ROBERT (d. 1690?), covenanting preacher; grandson of James Law (1560?–1632) [q. v.]; M.A. Glasgow, 1646; sided with the protesters against episcopacy, and was deprived of his benefice, 1662; arrested on charge of preaching at conventicles, 1674; accepted the indulgence of 1679; author of 'Memorialls, or the Memorable Things that fell out within this Island of Brittain from 1638 to 1684' (edited, 1818).
[xxxii. 235]

LAW, THOMAS (1759–1834), of Washington; son of Edmund Law [q. v.]; in the service of the East India Company, 1773–91; went to America, 1793; tried to establish a national currency there; died at Washington; published works on finance.
[xxxii. 235]

LAW, WILLIAM (1686–1761), author of the 'Serious Call'; entered Emmanuel College, Cambridge, 1705; ordained and elected fellow, 1711; M.A., 1712; declined to take the oaths of allegiance to George I; attacked Mandeville's 'Fable of the Bees,' 1723; published the first of his practical treatises on 'Christian Perfection,' 1726; founded school for fourteen girls at Kings Cliffe, 1727; entered family of Edward Gibbon (1666–1736) as tutor to his son, afterwards father of the historian; published the 'Serious Call,' a work of much logical power, 1728; became an ardent disciple of the mystic, Jacob Behmen, 1737; retired to Kings Cliffe, 1740; joined by Mrs. Hutcheson and Miss Hester Gibbon (the historian's aunt), who wished to carry out literally the precepts of the 'Serious Call,' 1743–4. His works were collected in nine volumes, 1762.
[xxxii. 236]

LAW, WILLIAM JOHN (1786–1869), commissioner of insolvent court; grandson of Edmund Law [q. v.]; educated at Westminster School and Christ Church, Oxford, where he held a studentship, 1804–14; M.A., 1810; barrister, Lincoln's Inn, 1813; a commissioner of bankruptcy, 1825; chief commissioner of the insolvent court, 1853–61; published works on the bankruptcy law, also a treatise 'On the Passage of Hannibal over the Alps,' 1866.
[xxxii. 240]

LAW, WILLIAM TOWRY (1809–1886), youngest son of Edward Law, first baron Ellenborough [q. v.]; entered the army, but subsequently took holy orders; chancellor of the diocese of Bath and Wells; joined the church of Rome, 1851.
[xxxii. 221]

LAWDER. [See LAUDER.]

LAWERN, JOHN (fl. 1448), theologian; Benedictine monk of Worcester; student at Gloucester Hall (now Worcester College, Oxford). A manuscript volume of sermons and letters by him is in the Bodleian.
[xxxii. 240]

LAWES, HENRY (1596–1662), musician; received his early musical education from Giovanni Coperario (Cooper) [q. v.]; gentleman of the Chapel Royal, 1626; connected with the household of the Earl of Bridgewater, probably before 1633; suggested to Milton the composition of 'Comus' (performed, 1634), for which he wrote the music; his edition of 'Comus' published, 1637; published 'Choice Psalmes put into Musick for Three Voices,' 1648, 'Ayres and Dialogues for One, Two, and Three Voyces,' 1653; lost his appointments at outbreak of the civil wars; his third book of 'Ayres,' brought out, 1658; restored to his offices in the Chapel Royal, 1660; the first Englishman who studied and practised with success the proper accentuation of words, and made the sense of the poem of paramount importance.
[xxxii. 240]

LAWES, SIR JOHN BENNET, first baronet (1814–1900), agriculturist; educated at Eton and Brasenose College, Oxford; studied chemistry; resided on family estate at Rothamsted from 1834; conducted important agricultural experiments and started, 1843, on a regular basis the Rothamsted agricultural experiment station; patented, 1842, and started at Deptford, 1843, manufacture

of mineral superphosphate for manure; published independently and with his coadjutor and technical adviser, Dr. (Sir) Joseph Henry Gilbert, numerous reports on experiments; joined Royal Agricultural Society, 1846; vice-president, 1878; F.R.S., 1854, and gold medallist, 1867; received Albert medal from Society of Arts, 1877; LL.D. Edinburgh, 1877; D.C.L. Oxford, 1892; Sc.D. Cambridge, 1894; created baronet, 1882; acted on various commissions and committees.
[Suppl. iii. 79]

LAWES, WILLIAM (d. 1645), musical composer; elder brother of Henry Lawes [q. v.]; gentleman of the Chapel Royal, 1603; wrote the music for Shirley's masque, 'The Triumph of Peace,' performed, 1634; lost his life fighting for the royalists at the siege of Chester.
[xxxii. 242]

LAWLESS, JOHN (1773–1837), Irish agitator; commonly known as 'Honest Jack Lawless'; a distant cousin of Valentine Browne Lawless, second baron Cloncurry [q. v.]; refused admission to the bar in consequence of his intimacy with the leaders of the United Irish movement; editor of the 'Ulster Register,' a political and literary magazine,' and subsequently of the 'Belfast Magazine'; energetic member of the committee of the Catholic Association; strong opponent of O'Connell; chief work, 'A Compendium of the History of Ireland from the earliest period to the Reign of George I,' 1814.
[xxxii. 244]

LAWLESS, MATTHEW JAMES (1837–1864), artist; drew illustrations for 'Once a Week,' the 'Cornhill,' and 'Punch'; his best-known oil-painting, 'The Sick Call,' exhibited at the Royal Academy, 1863.
[xxxii. 245]

LAWLESS, VALENTINE BROWNE, second BARON CLONCURRY (1773–1853), B.A. Trinity College, Dublin, 1792; sworn a United Irishman; entered the Middle Temple, 1795; published his first pamphlet on the projected union of Great Britain and Ireland, 1797; arrested on a charge of suspicion of high treason and discharged, 1798; arrested a second time and committed to the Tower, 1799–1801; for several years took no active part in politics; opponent of O'Connell during the viceroyalties of Henry William Paget, marquis of Anglesey [q. v.], 1828 and 1830–4; published his 'Personal Reminiscences,' 1849.
[xxxii. 245]

LAWLESS, WILLIAM (1772–1824), French general; born at Dublin; joined the United Irishmen; outlawed; entered the French army; captain of the Irish legion, 1803; distinguished himself at Flushing, 1806; decorated by Napoleon with the legion of honour and made a lieutenant-colonel; colonel, 1812; wounded at Löwenberg, 1813; placed on half-pay with rank of brigadier-general, 1814; died at Paris.
[xxxii. 247]

LAWRANCE, MARY, afterwards MRS. KEARSE (fl. 1794–1830), flower-painter; exhibited at Royal Academy, 1795–1830; published plates illustrating 'The Various Kinds of Roses cultivated in England,' 1796–9; married Mr. Kearse, 1813.
[xxxii. 248]

LAWRENCE. [See also LAURENCE.]

LAWRENCE or **LAURENTIUS** (d. 619), second archbishop of Canterbury; landed in Thanet with Augustine [q. v.], 597; archbishop of Canterbury, 604.
[xxxii. 248]

LAWRENCE (d. 1154), prior of Durham and Latin poet; a Benedictine monk at Durham; prior, 1147; bishop of Durham, 1153; went to Rome for consecration and died in France on his return journey; wrote Latin poems.
[xxxii. 248]

LAWRENCE (d. 1175), abbot of Westminster; a monk of St. Albans; abbot of Westminster, c. 1159; obtained the canonisation of Edward the Confessor from the pope, 1163.
[xxxii. 250]

LAWRENCE, ANDREW (1708–1747), engraver; known in France as ANDRÉ LAURENT; studied engraving at Paris, where he died. His etchings are mostly after the Flemish seventeenth-century painters. [xxxii. 251]

LAWRENCE, CHARLES (d. 1760), governor of Nova Scotia; ensign, 1727; captain-lieutenant, 1741; captain, 1742; major, 1747; accompanied his regiment to Nova Scotia; appointed a member of council, 1749; commanded expedition which built Fort Lawrence at the head of the bay of Fundy, 1750; governor, 1753; brigadier-general 1757; died at Halifax, Nova Scotia. [xxxii. 251]

LAWRENCE, CHARLES (1794–1881), agriculturist; brother of Sir William Lawrence [q. v.]; took leading part in founding and organising Royal Agricultural College at Cirencester, 1842–5; published his 'Handy Book for Young Farmers,' 1859; contributed papers to the 'Transactions' of the Royal Agricultural Society. [xxxii. 252]

LAWRENCE or **LAURENCE**, EDWARD (1623–1695), nonconformist minister; educated at Magdalene College, Cambridge; B.A., 1648; M.A., 1654; ejected from his living of Baschurch, Shropshire, 1662; arrested for preaching under the Conventicle Act, 1670; published sermons. [xxxii. 252]

LAWRENCE, FREDERICK (1821–1867), barrister and journalist; employed in the printed book department of British Museum, 1846–9; barrister, Middle Temple, 1849; practised at the Middlesex sessions and the Old Bailey; contributed to the periodical press; published 'The Life of Henry Fielding,' 1855. [xxxii. 253]

LAWRENCE, GEORGE (1615–1695?), puritan divine; educated at St. Paul's School and New Inn Hall, Oxford; M.A., 1639; took the covenant; minister of the hospital of St. Cross, Winchester, before 1650; ejected, 1660; published sermons and pamphlets against the royalists. [xxxii. 254]

LAWRENCE, GEORGE ALFRED (1827–1876), author of 'Guy Livingstone'; entered Rugby, 1841, Balliol College, Oxford, 1845; B.A. from New Inn Hall, 1850; barrister, Inner Temple, 1852; abandoned law for literature; published 'Guy Livingstone, or Thorough,' 1857, and 'Sword and Gown,' 1859; went to the United States with the intention of joining the confederate army, but was imprisoned before he reached the confederate lines; released on condition of returning to England; recorded the adventure in 'Border and Bastile,' 1863. [xxxii. 254]

LAWRENCE, SIR GEORGE ST. PATRICK (1804–1884), general; brother of Sir Henry Montgomery Lawrence [q. v.] and of John Laird Mair Lawrence, first baron Lawrence [q. v.]; born at Trincomalee; entered Addiscombe College, 1819; joined the 2nd regiment of light cavalry in Bengal, 1822; adjutant, 1825–34; took part in the Afghan war, 1838–9; political assistant and (1839–41) military secretary to Sir William Hay Macnaghten, the envoy of Afghanistan; in charge of the ladies and children in the retreat from Cabul, 1842; assistant political agent in the Punjab, 1846; taken prisoner during the second Sikh war, 1848; released, 1849; brevet lieutenant-colonel, 1849; deputy-commissioner of Peshawur, 1849; political agent in Méwar, 1850–7; resident for the Rajputana states, 1857–64; held chief command of the forces there, 1857; C.B. (civil), 1860; major-general, 1861; K.C.S.I. and retired from the army, 1866; honorary lieutenant-general, 1867; published 'Forty-three Years in India,' 1874. [xxxii. 255]

LAWRENCE, GILES (fl. 1539–1584), professor of Greek at Oxford; member of Corpus Christi College, Oxford, 1539; became fellow of All Souls', c. 1542; regius professor of Greek, 1550–4 and 1559–84; D.C.L., 1556; archdeacon of Wiltshire, 1564–78, of St. Albans, 1581. [xxxii. 256]

LAWRENCE, HENRY (1600–1664), puritan statesman; of Emmanuel College, Cambridge; M.A., 1627; commissioner of plantations, 1648; commissioner for Ireland, 1652; M.P., Hertfordshire, and keeper of the library at St. James's House, 1653; lord president of the council of state, 1654–9; M.P., Carnarvonshire, 1654–7; published pamphlets on the doctrine of baptism. [xxxii. 256]

LAWRENCE, SIR HENRY MONTGOMERY (1806–1857), brigadier-general, chief commissioner in Oudh; brother of Sir George St. Patrick Lawrence [q. v.] and of John Laird Mair Lawrence, first baron Lawrence [q. v.]; born at Matura, Ceylon; educated at schools at Londonderry and Bristol; entered Addiscombe College, 1820; second lieutenant in the Bengal artillery, 1822; reached Calcutta, 1823; first lieutenant and adjutant, 1825; deputy commissary of ordnance at Akyab, 1826; posted to the foot artillery at Kurnaul, 1830; transferred to the horse artillery at Meerut, 1831; assistant revenue surveyor in the north-west provinces, 1833–5, full surveyor, 1835; captain, 1837; appointed to take civil charge of Ferozepore, 1839; took part in Cabul expedition, 1842; promoted brevet-major; resident of Nepaul, 1843–6;

founded the Lawrence Asylum for the Children of European Soldiers; governor-general's agent for foreign relations and the affairs of the Punjaub and the north-west frontier, and promoted brevet lieutenant-colonel, 1846; resident at Lahore, 1847; K.C.B., 1848; president of the board of administration for the affairs of the Punjaub and agent to the governor-general, 1849–53; agent to the governor-general in Rajpootana, 1853; colonel, 1854; chief commissioner and agent to the governor-general in Oudh, 1856; at breaking out of mutiny promoted brigadier-general, with military command over all troops in Oudh, 1857; killed while holding Lucknow successfully against the mutineers; a voluminous contributor to the Indian press. [xxxii. 258]

LAWRENCE, JAMES HENRY (1773–1840), miscellaneous writer; a descendant of Henry Lawrence [q. v.]; educated at Eton and in Germany; published a romance dealing with the Nair caste in Malabar in German, 1800; subsequently wrote a French version (an English version published, 1811); arrested in France and detained several years at Verdun, 1803; published 'A Picture of Verdun, or the English detained in France,' 1810, and a work ' On the Nobility of the British Gentry,' 1834 (4th edit. 1840). [xxxii. 265]

LAWRENCE, JOHN (1753–1839), writer on horses; began to write for the press, 1787; published his 'Philosophical and Practical Treatise on Horses,' 1796–8 (3rd edit. 1810); insisted on the duty of humanity to animals. [xxxii. 265]

LAWRENCE, JOHN LAIRD MAIR, first BARON LAWRENCE (1811–1879), governor-general of India; brother of Sir George St. Patrick Lawrence [q. v.] and of Sir Henry Montgomery Lawrence [q. v.]; educated at Bristol, Londonderry, Bath, and Haileybury; took up his appointment under the East India Company first at Calcutta, 1830; assistant-magistrate and collector at Delhi, 1830–4; in charge of the northern or Paniput division of the Delhi territory, 1834, of the southern or Gurgaon division, 1837; magistrate and collector of the districts of Paniput and Delhi, 1844; administrator of the newly constituted district, the Jullundur Doab, 1846–1848; member of the board of administration for the Punjaub, 1848–52; chief commissioner for the Punjaub, 1853–7; K.C.B., 1856; the capture of Delhi from the mutineers due to his advice and action, 1857; created baronet, 1858; privy councillor, 1858; in England at the India office, 1859–62; viceroy of India, 1863–9; sanitation, irrigation, railway extension, and peace the chief aims of his administration; created Baron Lawrence of the Punjaub and of Grately, 1869; chairman of the London school board, 1870–3; opposed the proceedings (by a series of letters in the 'Times') that led to tne Afghan war of 1878–9; buried in Westminster Abbey. [xxxii. 267]

LAWRENCE, RICHARD (fl. 1657), author of 'Gospel Separation separated from its Abuses,' 1657; of Magdalen Hall, Oxford. [xxxii. 274]

LAWRENCE, RICHARD (fl. 1643–1682), parliamentarian colonel; marshal-general of the horse in Cromwell's new model, 1645; published pamphlet on ecclesiastical abuses, 1647; employed in Ireland, 1651–9; member of the council of trade, 1660–80; published 'The Interest of Ireland in its Trade and Wealth stated,' 1682. [xxxii. 273]

LAWRENCE, SAMUEL (1661–1712), nonconformist divine; nephew of Edward Lawrence [q. v.]; minister of the presbyterian congregation of Nantwich, Cheshire, 1688–1712. [xxxii. 274]

LAWRENCE, SIR SOULDEN (1751–1814), judge; son of Thomas Lawrence (1711–1783) [q. v.]; educated at St. Paul's School and St. John's College, Cambridge; M.A. and fellow, 1774; barrister, Inner Temple, 1784; serjeant-at-law, 1787; justice of the common pleas and knighted, 1794; transferred to the court of king's bench; resigned the king's bench and returned to the common pleas, 1808; retired, 1812. [xxxii. 274]

LAWRENCE, STRINGER (1697–1775), major-general; 'father of the Indian army'; served at Gibraltar, 1727; lieutenant, 1736; served in Flanders, after Fontenoy, 1745, and fought at Culloden, 1746; went to India as ' major in the East Indies only ' to command all the company's troops there, 1748; taken prisoner by the French, but released at peace of Aix-la-Chapelle; civil

LEADBETTER, CHARLES (*fl.* 1728), astronomer ; gauger in the royal excise ; author of treatises on astronomy and mathematics ; one of the first commentators on Newton. [xxxii. 314]

LEAHY, ARTHUR (1830–1878), colonel, royal engineers ; educated at the Royal Military Academy, Woolwich ; lieutenant, 1848 ; fought through the Crimean war ; second captain, 1857 ; assistant-director of the works in the fortifications branch of the war office, 1864 ; brevet lieutenant-colonel, 1868 ; instructor of field works at the school of military engineering at Chatham, 1871 ; regimental lieutenant-colonel, 1873 ; brevet-colonel, 1877. [xxxii. 315]

LEAHY, EDWARD DANIEL (1797–1875), portrait and subject painter ; exhibited at the Royal Academy and British Institution, 1820–53 ; resided in Italy, 1837–43 ; painted portraits of many leading Irishmen. [xxxii. 315]

LEAHY, PATRICK (1806–1875), archbishop of Cashel ; educated at Maynooth ; vice-rector of the catholic university of Dublin, 1854 ; archbishop of Cashel, 1857–75 ; strong advocate of temperance. [xxxii. 316]

LEAKE. [See also LEEKE.]

LEAKE, SIR ANDREW (*d.* 1704), captain in the navy ; took part in Dutch war, 1690 ; commodore on the Newfoundland station, 1699–1700 ; flag-captain during the campaign of 1702 ; knighted, 1702 ; mortally wounded in attack on Gibraltar. [xxxii. 316]

LEAKE, SIR JOHN (1656–1720), admiral of the fleet ; son of Richard Leake [q. v.] ; governor and commander-in-chief at Newfoundland, 1702 ; knighted, 1704 ; took part in reduction of Gibraltar, 1704 ; employed on coast of Spain, 1704–6 ; admiral of the white, 1708 ; admiral and commander-in-chief in the Mediterranean, 1708 ; M.P., Rochester, 1708–14 ; rear-admiral of Great Britain ; a lord of the admiralty, 1709. [xxxii. 317]

LEAKE, JOHN (1729–1792), man-midwife ; M.D. Rheims, 1763 ; L.R.C.P., 1766 ; author of medical works, addressed rather to women than to physicians, the chief being 'The Chronic Diseases of Women,' 1777. [xxxii. 321]

LEAKE, RICHARD (1629–1696), master-gunner of England ; served in the navy under the parliament, in the Dutch army, and as commander of an English merchant-ship ; a master-gunner of England, 1677. [xxxii. 321]

LEAKE, STEPHEN MARTIN (1702–1773), herald and numismatist ; son of Captain Martin ; assumed surname of Leake on being adopted as the heir of Admiral Leake, 1721 ; of the Middle Temple ; F.S.A., 1727 ; F.R.S. ; Lancaster herald, 1727, Norroy, 1729, Clarenceux, 1741, Garter, 1754 ; consistently maintained the rights and privileges of the College of Arms. [xxxii. 322]

LEAKE, WILLIAM MARTIN (1777–1860), classical topographer and numismatist ; grandson of Stephen Martin Leake [q. v.] ; with his regiment in the West Indies, 1794–8 ; employed in instructing Turkish troops at Constantinople, 1799 ; travelled in Asia Minor (his 'Journal of a Tour in Asia Minor' published, 1824), 1800 ; engaged in general survey of Egypt, 1801–2, of European Turkey and Greece, 1804–7 ; resided in Greece, 1808–10 ; published 'Researches in Greece,' 1814 ; his collection of marbles presented to the British Museum, 1839 ; his vases, gems, and coins purchased by the university of Cambridge. His reputation rests chiefly on the topographical researches embodied in his 'Athens,' 1821, 'Morea,' 1830, and 'Northern Greece,' 1835. [xxxii. 323]

LEAKEY, CAROLINE WOOLMER (1827–1881), religious writer ; daughter of James Leakey [q. v.] ; resided in Tasmania ; published 'Lyra Australis,' 1854, and 'The Broad Arrow,' 1859. [xxxii. 325]

LEAKEY, JAMES (1775–1865), artist and miniaturist ; exhibited portraits, landscapes, and interiors at the Royal Academy. [xxxii. 325]

LEANDER A SANCTO MARTINO (1575–1636). [See JONES, JOHN.]

LEANERD, JOHN (*fl.* 1679), author of comedies published 1677 and 1678, and perhaps of 'The Counterfeits,' 1679 ; described as 'a confident plagiary.' [xxxii. 325]

LEAPOR, MARY (1722–1746), poet ; her 'Poems on Several Occasions' published in 1748 (vol. i.), and 1751 (vol. ii.) [xxxii. 325]

LEAR, EDWARD (1812–1888), artist and author ; his 'Family of the Psittacidæ,' one of the earliest volumes of coloured plates of birds on a large scale published in England ; gave lessons in drawing to Queen Victoria, 1845 ; invented 'Book of Nonsense' (published, 1846) for the grandchildren of his patron, the Earl of Derby, a book of which there have been twenty-six editions ; exhibited landscapes at the Suffolk Street Gallery and the Royal Academy ; published journals of his travels ; died at San Remo. [xxxii. 325]

LEARED, ARTHUR (1822–1879), traveller ; educated at Trinity College, Dublin ; B.A., 1845 ; M.D., 1860 ; visited India, 1851, Smyrna and the Holy Land, 1854, Iceland (four times between 1862 and 1874), America, 1870, Morocco, 1872, 1877, and 1879 ; published 'Morocco and the Moors,' 1876, and 'A Visit to the Court of Morocco,' 1879, and some medical treatises. [xxxii. 326]

LEARMONT or **LEIRMOND**, THOMAS (*fl.* 1220?–1297?). [See ERCELDOUNE, THOMAS OF.]

LEASK, WILLIAM (1812–1884), dissenting divine ; entered congregational ministry, and held several charges from 1839 ; edited the 'Christian World,' and other nonconformist journals ; author of sermons, lectures, and works on theological and moral questions. [xxxii. 327]

LEATE, NICHOLAS (*d.* 1631), a London merchant ; member of the Levant Company ; as the leading merchant in the Turkey trade furnished the government with news from abroad, obtained through his agents and correspondents ; master of the Company of Ironmongers, 1616, 1626, and 1627 ; introduced rare exotics for cultivation in England. [xxxii. 327]

LEATHAM, WILLIAM HENRY (1815–1889), verse-writer and member of parliament ; entered his father's bank at Wakefield, 1834 ; toured on the continent, 1835 ; published 'A Traveller's Thoughts, or Lines suggested by a Tour on the Continent,' 1841 ; M.P. for Wakefield, 1865–8 ; for the South-west Riding of Yorkshire, 1880–5 ; published several volumes of poems, 1841–79. [xxxii. 329]

LEATHES, STANLEY (1830–1900), hebraist ; B.A. Jesus College, Cambridge, 1852 ; first Tyrwhitt's Hebrew scholar, 1853 ; M.A., 1855 ; honorary fellow, 1885 ; ordained priest, 1857 ; professor of Hebrew at King's College, London, 1863 ; member of Old Testament revision committee, 1870–85 ; prebendary of St. Paul's Cathedral, 1876 ; rector of Cliffe-at-Hoo, Kent, 1880–9, and of Much Hadham, Hertfordshire, 1889–1900 ; published lectures, and theological and other writings. [Suppl. iii. 85]

LE BAS, CHARLES WEBB (1779–1861), principal of the East India College, Haileybury ; of Trinity College, Cambridge ; fellow, 1800 ; barrister, Lincoln's Inn, 1806 ; abandoned the law and entered holy orders, 1809 ; prebendary of Lincoln, 1812 ; mathematical professor and dean of Haileybury, 1813 ; principal, 1837–43 ; the Le Bas prize at Cambridge for an historical essay founded by his friends, 1848 ; contributed to the 'British Critic,' 1827–1838 ; wrote sermons and biographies of divines. [xxxii. 329]

LE BLANC, SIR SIMON (*d.* 1816), judge ; entered Trinity Hall, Cambridge, 1766 ; LL.B., 1773 ; barrister, Inner Temple, 1773 ; fellow of his college, 1779 ; serjeant-at-law, 1787 ; counsel to his university, 1791 ; puisne judge of the king's bench, 1799 ; knighted, 1799. [xxxii. 330]

LE BLON (LE BLOND), JACQUES CHRISTOPHE (1670–1741), painter, engraver, and printer in colours ; born at Frankfort-on-the-Maine ; studied at Zurich, Paris, and Rome ; lived for a time at Amsterdam ; came to London ; his invention of painting engravings in colour to imitate painting pecuniarily unsuccessful ; published an account of his process, 1730 ; the inventor of the modern system of chromolithography. [xxxii. 331]

LE BRETON, ANNA LETITIA (1808–1885), author ; daughter of Charles Rochemont Aikin [q. v.] ; married Philip Hemery le Breton, 1833 ; assisted her husband in his memoirs of Lucy Aikin [q. v.], 1864 ; edited Miss Aikin's correspondence with Dr. Channing, 1874 ; published a memoir of Mrs. Barbauld, and 'Memories of Seventy Years,' 1883. [xxxii. 332]

LE BRUN, JOHN (*d.* 1865), independent missionary in Mauritius ; born in Switzerland ; ordained for the congregational ministry, 1813 ; began to work at Port Louis, Mauritius, under the auspices of the London Missionary Society, 1814 : returned to England, 1833, the society subsequently abandoning its efforts in Mauritius in consequence of official opposition ; returned on his own account, 1834 ; reappointed agent of the Society, 1841 ; died at Port Louis. [xxxii. 332]

LEBWIN, LEBUINUS, or **LIAFWINE**, SAINT (*fl.* 755); of English parentage; went as missionary to the Germans ; dwelt by the river Yssel and built two churches ; opposed by the heathen Saxons ; the collegiate church at Deventer dedicated to him. [xxxii. 333]

LE CAPELAIN, JOHN (1814 ?–1848), painter ; native of Jersey ; presented drawings of the scenery of Jersey to Queen Victoria ; commissioned by her to paint pictures of the Isle of Wight. [xxxii. 333]

LE CARON, MAJOR HENRI (1841–1894). [See BEACH, THOMAS.]

LE CÈNE, CHARLES (1647 ?–1703), Huguenot refugee ; born at Caen, Normandy ; studied at Sedan, 1667–9, at Geneva, 1669–70, at Saumur, 1770–2 ; ordained protestant minister, 1672 ; came to England at the revocation of the edict of Nantes, 1685, and retired to Holland, 1691 ; returned to England, 1699 ; author of French theological works. [xxxii. 333]

LECHMERE, EDMUND (*d.* 1640 ?). [See STRATFORD.]

LECHMERE, SIR NICHOLAS (1613–1701), judge ; nephew of Sir Thomas Overbury [q. v.]; B.A. Wadham College, Oxford ; barrister, Middle Temple, 1641 ; bencher, 1655 ; sided with the parliament on outbreak of the civil war ; M.P., Bewdley, 1648 ; present at the battle of Worcester, 1651 ; M.P., Worcester, 1654, 1656, 1658–9 ; attorney-general to the duchy of Lancaster, 1654 ; reader at his inn, 1669 ; serjeant-at-law, 1689 ; knighted, 1689 ; judge of the exchequer bench, 1689–1700. [xxxii. 335]

LECHMERE, NICHOLAS, first BARON LECHMERE (1675–1727), educated at Merton College, Oxford; barrister, Middle Temple, 1698; M.P., Appleby, 1708, for Cockermouth, 1710, 1713, and 1715, and for Tewkesbury, 1717–20 ; Q.C., 1708 ; a collaborator of Steele in 'The Crisis,' 1714; solicitor-general, 1714–18 ; privy councillor, 1718 ; attorney-general, 1718–20, and chancellor of the duchy of Lancaster, 1718–27; raised to the peerage, 1721. [xxxii. 335]

LECLERCQ, CARLOTTA (1840 ?–1893), actress ; Ariel (' Tempest '), Nerissa (' Merchant of Venice '), Mrs. Ford, Mrs. Page (' Merry Wives '), and Rosalind (' As You Like It '), among her parts ; acted with Charles Albert Fechter [q. v.] in England and America. [Suppl. iii. 86]

LECLERCQ, ROSE (1845 ?–1899), actress ; sister of Carlotta Leclercq [q. v.]; Mrs. Page, and the queen in ' La Tosca ' among her parts ; the best representative of the grand style in comedy. [Suppl. iii. 87]

LE COUTEUR, JOHN (1761–1835), lieutenant-general ; of a Jersey family ; ensign, 1780 ; lieutenant and went to India, 1781 ; taken prisoner by Tippoo Sahib, 1783 ; released, 1784 ; captain, 1785 ; major, 1797 ; lieutenant-colonel, 1798 ; inspecting officer of militia and assistant quartermaster-general in Jersey, 1799 ; lieutenant-governor of Curacoa, 1813 ; lieutenant-general, 1821 ; author of two works in French relating his military experiences. [xxxii. 336]

LE DAVIS, EDWARD (1640 ?–1684 ?), engraver ; practised his art first in Paris and afterwards in London. [xxxii. 337]

LEDDRA, WILLIAM (*d.* 1661), quaker ; emigrated to Rhode island, 1658 ; passed to Connecticut, where he was arrested and banished ; proceeded to Salem ; imprisoned at Boston ; condemned and executed on Boston Common ; the last quaker executed in New England. [xxxii. 337]

LEDEREDE or **LEDRED**, RICHARD DE (*fl.* 1350), bishop of Ossory ; English Franciscan ; appointed to see of Ossory, 1316 ; conducted prosecutions for heresy and sorcery ; Latin verses ascribed to him extant in the ' Red Book of Ossory.' [xxxii. 338]

LE DESPENCER, BARON (1708–1781). [See DASHWOOD, SIR FRANCIS.]

LEDIARD, THOMAS (1685–1743), miscellaneous writer ; attached to the staff of the Duke of Marlborough, accompanying him on his visit to Charles XII of Sweden, 1707 ; returned to England before 1732 ; produced various historical and biographical works, 1735–6 ; author of a pamphlet dealing with a scheme for building bridge at Westminster, 1738 ; F.R.S., 1742 ; 'agent and surveyor of Westminster Bridge,' 1738–43 ; author of several works in German and an English opera, ' Britannia.' [xxxii. 339]

LEDWARD, RICHARD ARTHUR (1857–1890), sculptor ; studied at South Kensington art school ; exhibited busts at the Royal Academy, 1882. [xxxii. 339]

LEDWICH, EDWARD (1738–1823), antiquary ; entered Trinity College, Dublin, 1755 ; B.A., 1760 ; LL.B., 1763 ; became a priest in the established church ; published ' Antiquities of Ireland,' 1790 ; his best work ' A Statistical Account of the Parish of Aghaboe,' published, 1796 ; not identical with the Edward Ledwich (*d.* 1782) who was dean of Kildare, 1772. [xxxii. 340]

LEDWICH, THOMAS HAWKESWORTH (1823–1858), anatomist and surgeon ; grandson of Edward Ledwich [q. v.]; studied medicine in Dublin ; member, Irish College of Surgeons, 1845 ; a successful lecturer on Anatomy ; his great work ' The Anatomy of the Human Body,' published, 1852. [xxxii. 340]

LEDYARD, JOHN (1751–1788), traveller ; born at Groton in Connecticut, U.S.A. ; made his way to New York, worked his passage to Plymouth in England, and tramped to London, *c.* 1771 ; enlisted in the marines, and (1776) accompanied Captain Cook in the Resolution ; published account of the voyage, 1783 ; resolved to travel on foot to the east of Asia, as a preliminary to open up trade to the north-west coast of America ; reached St. Petersburg, 1787 ; made his way to Yakutsk ; returned to London, undertook a journey of exploration in Africa on behalf of the African Association ,but died at Cairo. [xxxii. 341]

LEE. [See also LEGH, LEIGH, LEY.]

LEE, LORD (*d.* 1674). [See LOCKHART, SIR JAMES.]

LEE, ALFRED THEOPHILUS (1829–1883), miscellaneous writer ; of Christ's College, Cambridge ; B.A., 1853 ; held various livings, 1853–68 ; M.A., 1856 ; honorary LL.D. Trinity College, Dublin, 1866 ; D.C.L. Oxford, 1867 ; held various clerical offices in Ireland, 1869–71 ; preacher at Gray's Inn, 1879 ; published articles on the church defence question, sermons, and pamphlets. [xxxii. 342]

LEE, ANN (1736–1784), foundress of the American Society of Shakers ; factory-hand and afterwards cook in Manchester ; joined a band of seceders from the Society of Friends, 1758, who were nicknamed the ' Shaking Quakers ' or ' Shakers'; married Abraham Standerin, 1762 ; discovered celibacy to be the holy state ; was sent to prison as a Sabbath-breaker, 1770 ; resumed preaching on her release ; acknowledged by the shakers as spiritual head ; sailed for America, 1774 ; founded first American Shaker Society, 1776 ; claimed the power of discerning spirits and working miracles ; died at Watervliet, near Albany. [xxxii. 343]

LEE, CHARLES (1731–1782), American major-general ; ensign, 1746 ; went to America as lieutenant ; present at the disaster at Fort Duquesne ; wounded at Ticonderoga, 1758 ; present at the capture of Montreal ; attached to staff of Portuguese army, 1762 ; accompanied the Polish embassy to Constantinople, 1766 ; went to New York, 1773 ; supported the revolutionary plans ; appointed second major-general, 1775 ; appointed second in command to Washington ; taken prisoner by the English, 1776 ; exchanged, 1778 ; blamed for disaster and court-martialled, 1778 ; retired, 1779 ; died at Philadelphia ; buried at Washington. [xxxii. 343]

LEE, CROMWELL (*d.* 1601), compiler of an Italian dictionary ; brother of Sir Henry Lee [q. v.]; educated at Oxford, where, after travelling in Italy, he settled and compiled part of an Italian-English dictionary, never printed (manuscript in St. John's College library). [xxxii. 347]

LEE, EDWARD (1482 ?–1544), archbishop of York ; fellow of Magdalen College, Oxford, 1500 ; M.A. Cambridge, 1504 ; ordained, 1504 ; B.D., 1515 ; opposed Erasmus, 1519–20 ; sent on various embassies, 1523–30 ; prebendary of York and Westminster, 1530 ; D.D. Oxford, 1530 ; archbishop of York, 1531 ; while anxious to avoid displeasing the king, was opposed to the party of the new learning and inclined to Roman usages; author of theological works in Latin and English. [xxxii. 347]

LEE, EDWIN (*d.* 1870), medical writer; M.R.C.S., 1829; awarded the Jacksonian prize for his dissertation on lithotrity, 1838; M.D. Göttingen, 1846; best known by his handbooks to continental health resorts. [xxxii. 349]

LEE, FITZROY HENRY (1699–1750), vice-admiral; entered navy, 1717; lieutenant, 1721; captain, 1728; governor of Newfoundland, 1735–8; commodore and commander-in-chief on the Leeward islands station, 1746; rear-admiral, 1747; vice-admiral of the white, 1748; probably the original of Smollett's Commodore Trunnion. [xxxii. 350]

LEE, FRANCIS (1661–1719), miscellaneous writer; entered St. John's College, Oxford, 1679; B.A., 1683; M.A., 1687; studied medicine at Leyden, 1692; became a disciple of Jane Lead [q. v.], 1694; M.D.; one of the founders of the Philadelphian Society, 1697; L.C.P. London, 1708; died at Gravelines, Flanders; his works (all unclaimed) said to have been very numerous. [xxxii. 351]

LEE, FREDERICK RICHARD (1799–1879), painter and royal academician; student of the Royal Academy, 1818; exhibitor at the British Institution from 1822, and at the Royal Academy, 1824–70; painted Devonshire, Scottish, and French landscape; R.A., 1838; died in South Africa. [xxxii. 352]

LEE, SIR GEORGE (1700–1758), lawyer and politician; brother of Sir William Lee [q. v.]; entered Christ Church, Oxford, 1720; B.C.L., 1724; D.C.L., 1729; M.P., Brackley, Northamptonshire, 1733–42; lord of admiralty, 1742; M.P., Devizes, 1742–7, Liskeard, 1747–54; dean of arches, 1751–8; judge of the prerogative court of Canterbury, 1751–8; privy councillor, 1752; knighted, 1752; M.P., Launceston, 1754–8. [xxxii. 353]

LEE, GEORGE ALEXANDER (1802–1851), musical composer; tenor at the Dublin Theatre, 1825; musical conductor at various London theatres, 1827–51; composed the music to several dramatic pieces, songs, and ballads. [xxxii. 354]

LEE, GEORGE AUGUSTUS (1761–1826), Manchester cotton-spinner; son of John Lee (*d.* 1781) [q. v.]; distinguished for his readiness to adopt new inventions in his factories. [xxxii. 360]

LEE, GEORGE HENRY, third EARL OF LICHFIELD (1718–1772), chancellor of Oxford University; created M.A. St. John's College, Oxford, 1737; M.P., Oxfordshire, 1740 and 1741–3; succeeded to the earldom, 1743; privy councillor, 1762; chancellor of Oxford, 1762–72; D.C.L., 1762; founded by bequest Lichfield clinical professorship at Oxford. [xxxii. 354]

LEE, HARRIET (1757–1851), novelist and dramatist; daughter of John Lee (*d.* 1781) [q. v.], and sister of Sophia Lee [q. v.]; published 'The Errors of Innocence' (a novel), 1786; her comedy, 'The New Peerage,' performed at Drury Lane, 1787; published another novel, 'Clara Lennox,' 1797; the first two volumes of her chief work, in which her sister Sophia assisted her, 'The Canterbury Tales,' was published, 1797–8, and the remaining three volumes, 1805; refused offer of marriage from William Godwin the elder [q. v.], 1798; a version of her story, 'Kruitzner,' dramatised by herself as 'The Three Strangers,' performed at Covent Garden, 1825, published, 1826, the story being dramatised by Byron in 'Werner,' 1822. [xxxii. 355]

LEE, SIR HENRY (1530–1610), master of the ordnance; educated by his uncle, Sir Thomas Wyatt; entered service of Henry VIII, 1545; clerk of the armoury, 1549–50; knighted, 1553; M.P., Buckinghamshire, 1558 and 1572; personal champion to Queen Elizabeth, 1559–90; master of the ordnance, 1590; visited by Queen Elizabeth at his country house, 1592; K.G., 1597; a great sheep-farmer and builder. [xxxii. 356]

LEE, HENRY (1765–1836), author of 'Caleb Quotem'; became an actor; his farce, 'Caleb Quotem,' written 1789, brought out at the Haymarket as 'Throw Physic to the Dogs,' 1789; charged George Colman the younger [q. v.] with plagiarising it in 'The Review,' 1800; author of some poems, and a volume of desultory reminiscences. [xxxii. 357]

LEE, HENRY (1826–1888), naturalist; naturalist to the Brighton Aquarium, 1872; wrote popular account of the octopus, 1874. [xxxii. 357]

LEE, HOLME (pseudonym). [See PARR, HARRIET, 1828–1900.]

LEE, JAMES (1715–1795), nurseryman; introduced cultivation of the fuchsia in England; translated part of Linnæus's works into English, 1760. [xxxii. 357]

LEE, JAMES PRINCE (1804–1869), bishop of Manchester; educated at St. Paul's School, London, and Trinity College, Cambridge; fellow, 1829; ordained, 1830; a master at Rugby, 1830–8; M.A., 1831; head-master of King Edward's School, Birmingham, 1838–47; bishop of Manchester, 1847. [xxxii. 358]

LEE, JOHN (*d.* 1781), actor and adapter of plays; acted in London under Garrick (with a short break in 1749–50), 1747–51; manager at Edinburgh, 1752–6; again in London under Garrick, 1761–6; manager of the Bath Theatre, 1778–9; tampered with many of Shakespeare's plays and other dramatic masterpieces. [xxxii. 359]

LEE, JOHN (1733–1793), lawyer and politician; barrister, Lincoln's Inn; attorney-general for county palatine of Lancaster; recorder of Doncaster, 1769; K.C., 1780; solicitor-general and M.P. for Higham Ferrers, Northamptonshire; attorney-general, 1783. [xxxii. 361]

LEE, JOHN (*d.* 1804), wood-engraver; engraved the cuts for 'The Cheap Repository,' 1794–8, and part of the designs by William Marshall Craig [q. v.] in 'Scripture Illustrated.' [xxxii. 361]

LEE, JOHN (1779–1859), principal of Edinburgh University; entered Edinburgh University, 1794; M.D., 1801; licensed as a preacher, 1807; professor of church history at St. Mary's College, St. Andrews, 1812–21; minister of the Canongate Church, Edinburgh, 1821; D.D. St. Andrews, 1821; chaplain in ordinary to the king, 1830; principal of Edinburgh University, 1840–59; professor of divinity, 1843–59; especially learned in Scottish literary and ecclesiastical history. [xxxii. 361]

LEE, JOHN (1783–1866), collector of antiquities and man of science; son of John Fiott; educated at St. John's College, Cambridge; made a tour through Europe and the East collecting objects of antiquity, 1807–10; M.A., 1809; assumed name of Lee by royal license, 1815; F.S.A., 1828; built observatory on his estate, 1830; F.R.S., 1831; practising member of the ecclesiastical courts till 1858; Q.C., 1864; published scientific and antiquarian works. [xxxii. 362]

LEE, JOHN EDWARD (1808–1887), antiquary and geologist; his chief work, 'Isca Silurum,' or an Illustrated Catalogue of the Museum of Antiquities at Caerleon,' published, 1862; translated foreign works on prehistoric archæology; presented his fine collection of fossils to the British Museum, 1885. [xxxii. 363]

LEE, JOSEPH (1780–1859), enamel-painter; enamel-painter to Princess Charlotte of Wales, 1818; occasionally exhibited at the Royal Academy till 1853. [xxxii. 363]

LEE, MATTHEW (1694–1755), benefactor to Christ Church, Oxford; educated at Westminster School and Christ Church; M.A., 1720; M.D., 1726; F.R.C.P., 1732; Harveian orator, 1736; physician to Frederick, prince of Wales, 1739; founded an anatomical lectureship at Christ Church, 1750. [xxxii. 364]

LEE, NATHANIEL (1653?–1692), dramatist; educated at Westminster School and Trinity College, Cambridge; B.A., 1668; drew the plots of his tragedies mainly from classical history; 'Nero,' his earliest effort, produced, 1675; wrote 'Gloriana' and 'Sophonisba,' two rhyming plays, 1676; his best-known tragedy, 'The Rival Queens,' produced, 1677; collaborated with Dryden in 'Œdipus,' 1679, and 'The Duke of Guise,' 1682; his last tragedy, 'Constantine the Great,' produced, 1684; lost his reason through intemperance, 1684, and confined in Bethlehem till 1689. Many of his plays (a collected edition appeared in 2 vols. in 1713) long kept the stage, and great actors performed the chief parts. [xxxii. 364]

LEE, MRS. RACHEL FANNY ANTONINA (1774?–1829), heroine of a criminal trial, and the subject of chap. iv. of De Quincey's 'Autobiographic Sketches'; a natural daughter of Francis Dashwood, lord le Despenser; married Matthew Lee, 1794, but soon separated from him;

eloped with Loudoun Gordon, accompanied by his brother Lockhart, 1804 ; appeared as a witness against the brothers when they were brought to trial for her abduction which resulted in their acquittal, 1804 ; published 'Essay on Government,' 1808.   [xxxii. 368]

LEE, SIR RICHARD (1513 ?–1575), military engineer ; surveyor of the king's works, 1540 ; knighted for services in Scotland, 1544 ; employed intermittently in improving the fortifications of Berwick and the Scottish border, 1557–65 ; received part of the domain of the monastery of St. Albans from Henry VIII.   [xxxii. 369]

LEE, RICHARD NELSON (1806–1872), actor and dramatist ; acted at the Surrey Theatre, 1827–34 ; became proprietor of 'Richardson's Show,' 1836 ; author of pantomimes and plays.   [xxxii. 371]

LEE, ROBERT (1804–1868), professor at Edinburgh ; educated at St. Andrews University ; minister of the old Greyfriars Church, Edinburgh, 1843–68 ; D.D. St. Andrews, 1844 ; professor of biblical criticism in Edinburgh University, 1847 ; dean of the Chapel Royal, Edinburgh, 1847 ; endeavoured to liberalise the church of Scotland ; introduced stained-glass windows, 1857, and an organ, 1864 ; published 'The Reform of the Church in Worship, Government, and Doctrine,' 1864 ; often censured by the Edinburgh presbytery for his innovations ; author of theological works and books of prayers.   [xxxii. 371]

LEE, ROBERT (1793–1877), obstetric physician ; educated at Edinburgh University ; M.D., 1814 ; physician to Prince Woronzow, governor-general of the Crimea, 1824–1826 ; F.R.S., 1830 ; lecturer on midwifery and diseases of women at St. George's Hospital, 1835–66 ; F.R.C.P., 1841 ; Lumleian lecturer, 1856–7 ; Croonian lecturer, 1862 ; Harveian orator, 1864 ; retired, 1875 ; made discoveries of permanent value ; unfairly treated by the Royal Society ; published works on the diseases of women. [xxxii. 372]

LEE or LEGH, ROWLAND (d. 1543), bishop of Coventry and Lichfield and lord president of the council in the marches of Wales ; educated at Cambridge ; ordained priest, 1512 ; doctor of decrees, 1520 ; prebendary of Lichfield, 1527 ; employed under Wolsey in the suppression of the monasteries, 1528–9 ; royal chaplain and master in chancery ; bishop of Coventry and Lichfield, 1534–43, and president of the king's council in the marches of Wales, 1534 ; devoted his energies to suppressing Welsh disorder, 1534–40.   [xxxii. 373]

LEE, SAMUEL (1625–1691), puritan divine ; educated at St. Paul's School, London, and Magdalen Hall, Oxford ; M.A., 1648 ; fellow of All Souls, 1650 ; dean of Wadham College, 1653–6 ; minister of various congregations in London, 1655–60 ; migrated to New England, 1686 ; sailed for home from Boston, 1691 ; taken by the French, his ship being seized, to St. Malo, where he died ; author of theological works.   [xxxii. 377]

LEE, SAMUEL (1783–1852), orientalist ; of humble origin ; taught himself Greek, Hebrew, Persian, Hindustani, and other Eastern languages ; entered Queens' College, Cambridge, 1813 ; M.A., 1819 ; professor of Arabic at Cambridge, 1819–31 ; B.D., 1827 ; regius professor of Hebrew, Cambridge, 1831–48 ; D.D., 1833. His chief works were his editions of the New Testament in Syriac, 1816, and of the Old Testament, 1823, and a translation of the book of Job from the original Hebrew, 1837. [xxxii. 378]

LEE, MRS. SARAH (1791–1856), artist and authoress ; daughter of John Eglinton Wallis ; married Thomas Edward Bowdich [q. v.], 1813 ; shared her husband's tastes and travelled with him in Africa, 1814, 1815, and 1823 ; married Robert Lee as her second husband, 1829 ; devoted the rest of her life to popularising natural science ; published books on natural history, many illustrated by herself, and 'Memoirs of Baron Cuvier,' 1833. [xxxii. 379]

LEE, SOPHIA (1750–1824), novelist and dramatist ; daughter of John Lee (d. 1781) [q. v.] ; her comedy, 'The Chapter of Accidents,' produced, 1780 ; conducted a girls' school at Bath, 1781–1803 ; published 'The Recess,' an historical romance, 1785, and 'Almeyda, Queen of Grenada,' a tragedy in blank verse, produced, 1796 ; helped her sister, Harriet Lee [q. v.], in the 'Canterbury Tales,' 1797.   [xxxii. 379]

LEE, THOMAS (d. 1601), captain in Ireland and supporter of Robert, earl of Essex ; went to Ireland before 1576 ; assisted in suppressing rebellions in Ireland, 1581–

1599 ; arrested for attempting to procure the release of Essex, 1601 ; tried and executed, 1601 ; wrote an historically valuable tract on the government of Ireland (first published, 1772).   [xxxii. 380]

LEE, SIR THOMAS, first baronet (d. 1691), politician ; created baronet, 1660 ; M.P. for Aylesbury, 1661–81 and 1689–91, and for Buckinghamshire in the Convention parliament.   [xxxii. 383]

LEE, WILLIAM (d. 1610 ?), inventor of the stocking-frame ; educated at Christ's and St. John's Colleges, Cambridge ; B.A. St. John's College, 1583 ; invented the stocking-frame, 1589 ; his invention discouraged by Elizabeth and James I ; settled at Rouen by invitation of Henry IV of France ; died at Paris.   [xxxii. 382]

LEE, SIR WILLIAM (1688–1754), judge ; brother of Sir George Lee [q. v.] ; entered the Middle Temple, 1703 ; barrister, Middle Temple ; Latin secretary to George I and George II, 1718–30 ; recorder of Buckingham, 1722 ; bencher of the Inner Temple, 1725 ; M.P., Chipping Wycombe, 1727 ; K.C., 1728 ; attorney-general to Frederick, prince of Wales, c. 1728 ; puisne judge of the king's bench, 1730 ; chief-justice of king's bench, 1737 ; knighted, 1737 ; privy councillor, 1737.   [xxxii. 383]

LEE, WILLIAM (1809–1865), water-colour painter ; member of the Institute of Painters in Water-colours, 1848 ; painter of English rustic figures and scenes on the French coast.   [xxxii. 385]

LEE, WILLIAM (1815–1883), archdeacon of Dublin ; educated at Trinity College, Dublin ; junior fellow, 1839 ; entered holy orders, 1841 ; D.D., 1857 ; professor of ecclesiastical history in the university of Dublin, 1857 ; Archbishop King's lecturer in divinity, 1852 ; archdeacon of Dublin, 1864 ; member of the New Testament revision company, 1870 ; author of theological works written from the conservative point of view.   [xxxii. 385]

LEECH, LEICH, or LEITCH, DAVID (fl. 1628–1653), poet ; brother of John Leech (fl. 1623) [q. v.] ; sub-principal of King's College, Aberdeen, 1632 ; chaplain to Charles II ; D.D. Aberdeen, 1653 ; left paraphrases of some of the Psalms in manuscript.   [xxxii. 385]

LEECH, HUMPHREY (1571–1629), jesuit ; educated at Brasenose College, Oxford, and Cambridge ; M.A. Cambridge (incorporated at Oxford, 1602) ; entered the English college at Rome, 1609 ; ordained priest, 1612 ; joined jesuits, 1618 ; missioner in England, 1622–9.
[xxxii. 386]

LEECH or LEITCH ('LEOCHÆUS '), JOHN (fl. 1623), epigrammatist ; brother of David Leech [q. v.] ; probably related to John Leech (1565–1650 ?) [q. v.] ; M.A. Aberdeen, 1614 ; published Latin epigrams, 1620 and 1623.
[xxxii. 386]

LEECH or LEACHE, JOHN (1565–1650 ?), schoolmaster ; educated at Brasenose College, Oxford ; M.A., 1589 ; published a book of grammar questions, c. 1622.
[xxxii. 387]

LEECH, JOHN (1817–1864), humorous artist ; educated at Charterhouse, where he made the acquaintance of Thackeray ; studied medicine by his father's desire ; adopted art as a profession ; his first work, 'Etchings and Sketchings, by A. Pen, Esq.,' published, 1835 ; his first popular hit, a caricature of Mulready's design for a universal envelope, 1840 ; contributed to 'Punch,' 1841–64 ; executed for it some three thousand drawings, six hundred being cartoons ; illustrated several books, and supplied cuts to a number of magazines ; his sporting sketches traceable to his love for hunting.   [xxxii. 387]

LEECHMAN, WILLIAM (1706–1785), divine ; studied at Edinburgh University ; licensed to preach, 1731 ; professor of divinity at Glasgow University, 1743 ; principal, 1761 ; prefixed a life of the author to Hutcheson's 'System of Moral Philosophy,' 1755 ; published a few sermons.
[xxxii. 391]

LEEDES, EDWARD (1599 ?–1677). [See COURTNEY, EDWARD.]

LEEDES, EDWARD (1627–1707), schoolmaster ; educated at Christ's College, Cambridge ; M.A. ; master of Bury St. Edmund's grammar school, 1663–1707 ; author of school-books.   [xxxii. 391]

LEEDS, DUKES OF. [See OSBORNE, SIR THOMAS, first DUKE, 1631–1712 ; OSBORNE, PEREGRINE, second DUKE, 1658–1729 ; OSBORNE, FRANCIS, fifth DUKE. 1751–1799.]

LEEDS, EDWARD (*d.* 1590), civilian; educated at Cambridge; M.A., 1545; prebendary of Ely, 1548-80; advocate of Doctors' Commons, 1560; master of Clare Hall, Cambridge, 1560-71; LL.D., 1569.   [xxxii. 392]

LEEDS, EDWARD (1695?-1758), serjeant-at-law; barrister, Inner Temple, 1718; took the coif, 1742; king's serjeant, 1748-55.   [xxxii. 392]

LEEDS, EDWARD (1728-1803), master in chancery; son of Edward Leeds (1695?-1758) [q. v.]; barrister, Inner Temple; sheriff of Cambridgeshire, 1768; master in chancery, 1773; M.P., Reigate, 1784-7.   [xxxii. 393]

LEEKE. [See also LEAKE.]

LEEKE, SIR HENRY JOHN (1790?-1870), admiral; entered navy, 1803; lieutenant, 1810; commander, 1814; knighted, 1835; flag-captain, 1845-8; superintendent and commander-in-chief of the Indian navy, 1852; rear-admiral, 1854; K.C.B., 1858; vice-admiral, 1860; admiral, 1864.   [xxxii. 393]

LEEKE, LAURENCE (*d.* 1357), prior of Norwich; appointed prior, 1352; author of 'Historiola de Vita et Morte Reverendi domini Willelmi Bateman Norwicensis episcopi.'   [xxxii. 393]

LEEMPUT, REMIGIUS VAN (1609?-1675). [See VAN LEEMPUT.]

LEES, CHARLES (1800-1880), painter; fellow of the Royal Scottish Academy and a regular contributor to its exhibitions; painted portraits, historical and domestic subjects, and landscape.   [xxxii. 394]

LEES, EDWIN (1800-1887), botanist; began to publish 'The Worcestershire Miscellany,' 1829; issued his 'Botany of the Malvern Hills,' 1843, and 'Botany of Worcestershire,' 1867; one of the first in England to pay regard to the forms of brambles.   [xxxii. 394]

LEES, SIR HARCOURT, second baronet (1776-1852), political pamphleteer; M.A. Trinity College, Cambridge, 1802; took holy orders; published pamphlets in support of protestant ascendency.   [xxxii. 394]

LEES, WILLIAM NASSAU (1825-1889), major-general in the Indian army and orientalist; son of Sir Harcourt Lees, second baronet [q. v.]; educated at Trinity College, Dublin; ensign, Bengal native infantry, 1846; edited Arabic and Persian works between 1853 and 1864; lieutenant, 1853; hon. LL.D. Dublin, 1857; captain, 1858; major, 1865; lieutenant-colonel, 1872; member of Royal Asiatic Society, 1872; colonel, 1876; major-general, 1885.   [xxxii. 395]

LEEVES, WILLIAM (1748-1828), poet and composer; entered the army, 1769; lieutenant, 1772; took holy orders, 1779; wrote the music to the song 'Auld Robin Gray,' by Lady Anne Barnard [q. v.]; author of other musical compositions, and of occasional poems.   [xxxii. 396]

LE FANU, MRS. ALICIA (1753-1817), playwright; sister of the dramatist Richard Brinsley Sheridan [q. v.]; married Joseph Le Fanu, brother of Philip Le Fanu [q. v.], divine, 1776; author of a comedy, 'Sons of Erin,' performed in London, 1812.   [xxxii. 398]

LE FANU, ALICIA (*fl.* 1812-1826), daughter of Henry Le Fanu, a brother of Philip Le Fanu [q. v.]; published 'Memoirs of Mrs. Frances Sheridan,' 1824.
    [xxxii. 398]

LE FANU, JOSEPH SHERIDAN (1814-1873), novelist and journalist; entered Trinity College, Dublin, 1833; devoted himself to journalism from 1839, when he began to issue 'The Evening Mail,' a Dublin paper; published 'Uncle Silas,' 1864, and twelve other novels, 1865-75; edited the 'Dublin University Magazine,' 1869-72; stands next to Lever among modern Irish novelists.
    [xxxii. 396]

LE FANU, PETER (*fl.* 1778), playwright; brother of Philip Le Fanu [q. v.]; his 'Smock Alley Secrets' produced at Dublin, 1778.   [xxxii. 398]

LE FANU, PHILIP (*fl.* 1790), divine; M.A. Trinity College, Dublin, 1755; D.D., 1776; published translation of the Abbé Guenée's 'Lettres de certaines Juives à Monsieur Voltaire,' 1777.   [xxxii. 397]

LEFEBURE, NICASIUS or NICOLAS (*d.* 1669). [See LE FEVRE.]

LEFEBVRE, ROLAND (1608-1677), painter; born at Anjou; resided at Venice; came to England, 1665; painted mediocre portraits and small history pictures under the patronage of Prince Rupert.   [xxxii. 398]

LEFEVRE, CHARLES SHAW, first VISCOUNT EVERSLEY (1794-1888). [See SHAW-LEFEVRE.]

LEFEVRE, SIR GEORGE WILLIAM (1798-1846), physician; studied at Edinburgh and at Guy's and St. Thomas's hospitals, London; M.D. Aberdeen, 1819; travelled in France, Austria, Poland, and Russia as physician to a Polish nobleman; published 'The Life of a Travelling Physician,' 1843; afterwards practised at St. Petersburg, and became physician to the embassy; knighted; settled in London, 1842; F.R.C.P., 1842; Lumleian lecturer, 1845; committed suicide.
    [xxxii. 398]

LEFEVRE, SIR JOHN GEORGE SHAW (1797-1879). [See SHAW-LEFEVRE.]

LE FEVRE, NICASIUS or NICOLAS (*d.* 1669), chemist; studied at Sedan; professor of chemistry to Charles II, and apothecary in ordinary to the royal household, 1660; F.R.S., 1663; published chemical works.
    [xxxii. 399]

LEFROY, SIR JOHN HENRY (1817-1890), governor of Bermuda and of Tasmania; educated at Royal Military Academy, Woolwich; lieutenant, royal artillery, 1837; engaged in a magnetical survey, chiefly at St. Helena, 1839-42; transferred to observatory at Toronto, 1842; engaged in magnetical survey of extreme north of America, 1843-4; worked at Toronto, 1844-53; captain, 1845; F.R.S., 1848; founded the Canadian Institute, 1849; compiled 'The Handbook of Field Artillery for the use of Officers,' 1854; lieutenant-colonel, 1855; inspector-general of army schools, 1857; brevet-colonel, 1858; director-general of ordnance, 1868; retired from the army, 1870; governor and commander-in-chief of the Bermudas, 1871-1877; K.C.M.G., 1877; governor of Tasmania, 1880-2; published the diary of his Canadian magnetic survey, 1883.   [xxxii. 399]

LEFROY, THOMAS LANGLOIS (1776-1869), Irish judge; educated at Trinity College, Dublin; B.A., 1795; called to the Irish bar, 1797; K.C., 1806; king's serjeant, 1808; bencher of the King's Inns, 1819; LL.D., 1827; M.P., university of Dublin, 1830-41; baron of the Irish court of exchequer, 1841-52; lord chief-justice of the queen's bench, 1852-66.   [xxxii. 404]

LEGAT, FRANCIS (1755-1809), engraver; historical engraver to the Prince of Wales; engraved several pictures in Boydell's Shakespeare Gallery. [xxxii. 404]

LEGAT, HUGH (*fl.* 1400), Benedictine; studied at Oxford; of St. Albans Abbey; studied history, and prepared a commentary on John de Hauteville's [q. v.] 'Architrenius.'   [xxxii. 405]

LEGATE, BARTHOLOMEW (1575?-1612), the last heretic burned at Smithfield; preacher among the 'Seekers'; denied divinity of Christ, 1604; proceedings taken against him in consistory court of London, 1611; committed to Newgate on charge of heresy; burned at Smithfield.   [xxxii. 405]

LEGATE, JOHN, the elder (*d.* 1620?), printer to Cambridge University; freeman of Stationers' Company, 1586; printer to Cambridge University, 1588-1609; afterwards carried on business in London.   [xxxii. 406]

LEGATE, JOHN, the younger (1600-1658), printer to Cambridge University; eldest son of John Legate the elder [q. v.]; freeman of the Stationers' Company, 1619; succeeded to his father's business, 1620; one of the Cambridge University printers, 1650-5.
    [xxxii. 406]

LE GEYT, PHILIP (1635-1716), writer on the laws of Jersey; born at St. Helier; educated at Saumur, Caen, and Paris; greffier of the royal court, 1660; jurat, 1665-1710; lieutenant-bailiff, 1676-94; his manuscript collections on the constitution and laws of Jersey published, 1846-7.   [xxxii. 407]

LEGGE, EDWARD (1710-1747), commodore; fifth son of William Legge, first earl of Dartmouth [q. v.]; entered navy, 1726; lieutenant, 1734; captain, 1738; accompanied Anson's voyage to the Pacific, 1740-2; commodore and commander-in-chief at the Leeward islands, 1747.   [xxxii. 407]

LEGGE, GEORGE, first BARON DARTMOUTH (1648-1691), admiral and commander-in-chief; eldest son of William Legge (1609?-1670) [q. v.]; of Westminster and King's College, Cambridge: lieutenant in Dutch war, 1665-7; captain, 1667; in intervals of war by sea held appointments on land; groom of the bedchamber, 1668; lieutenant-governor of Portsmouth, 1670-83; lieutenant-general of the ordnance, 1672; master of the horse to the Duke of York, 1673; commanded in Flanders, 1678; master-general of ordnance, 1682; created Baron Dartmouth, 1682; master of Trinity House, 1683; engaged in Tangier expedition, 1683-4; governor of the Tower, 1685; admiral and commander-in-chief of the fleet, 1688-9; accused of conspiring against William III and committed to the Tower, 1691. [xxxii. 408]

LEGGE, GEORGE, third EARL OF DARTMOUTH (1755-1810), statesman; son of William Legge, second earl [q. v.]; educated at Eton and Christ Church, Oxford; M.A., 1775; D.C.L., 1778; M.P., Plymouth, 1778, Staffordshire, 1780; privy councillor, 1801; president of the board of control, 1801; succeeded his father, 1801; lord chamberlain, 1804. [xxxii. 410]

LEGGE, JAMES (1815-1897), professor of Chinese at Oxford University; M.A. King's College, Aberdeen, 1835; appointed by London Missionary Society to Chinese mission at Malacca, 1839; principal of Anglo-Chinese College at Malacca, 1840, and later at Hong Kong; D.D. New York University, 1841; returned to England, 1873; LL.D. Aberdeen, 1870, and Edinburgh, 1884; first professor of Chinese at Oxford University and fellow of Corpus Christi College, Oxford, 1875; published numerous writings in Chinese and English, including an edition of Chinese classics. [Suppl. iii. 87]

LEGGE, HENEAGE (1704-1759), judge; second son of William Legge, first earl of Dartmouth [q. v.]; barrister, Inner Temple, 1728; raised to the exchequer bench, 1747. [xxxii. 410]

LEGGE, HENRY BILSON- (1708-1764), chancellor of the exchequer; fourth son of William Legge, first earl of Dartmouth [q. v.]; M.P., East Looe, 1740, Orford, 1741-3; a lord of the admiralty, 1745-7; a lord of the treasury, 1746; envoy-extraordinary to the king of Prussia, 1748; chancellor of the exchequer, 1754-5, 1756-7, 1757-61; M.P., Hampshire, 1759-64; had a great reputation as a financier. [xxxii. 411]

LEGGE, THOMAS (1535-1607), master of Caius College, Cambridge, and Latin dramatist; educated at Trinity College, Cambridge; M.A., 1560; fellow of Jesus College, Cambridge, 1568; master of Caius College, 1573-1607; LL.D., 1575; regius professor of civil law, Cambridge; vice-chancellor of Cambridge University, 1587-8 and 1592-3; master in chancery, 1593; his Latin tragedy of 'Richard III' acted, 1579. [xxxii. 413]

LEGGE, WILLIAM (1609?-1670), royalist; a leader in second army plot, 1641; joined the king's army, 1642; governor of Oxford, 1645; imprisoned for high treason, 1649-53; lieutenant-general of the ordnance, 1660. [xxxii. 414]

LEGGE, WILLIAM, first EARL OF DARTMOUTH (1672-1750), son of George Legge, first baron Dartmouth [q. v.]; of Westminster and King's College, Cambridge; M.A., 1689; succeeded his father in the Dartmouth barony, 1691; a commissioner of the board of trade and foreign plantations, 1702; privy councillor, 1702; secretary of state, 1710-13; created Earl of Dartmouth, 1711; lord keeper of the privy seal, 1713-14. [xxxii. 416]

LEGGE, WILLIAM, second EARL OF DARTMOUTH (1731-1801), grandson of William Legge, first earl of Dartmouth [q. v.]; educated at Westminster and Trinity College, Oxford; succeeded to earldom, 1750; M.A., 1751; F.S.A., 1754; D.C.L., 1756; privy councillor, 1765; president of the board of trade and foreign plantations, 1765-1766; colonial secretary, 1772-5; lord privy seal, 1775-82; high steward of Oxford University, 1786; strongly attached to the methodists; Dartmouth College in the United States (incorporated, 1769) named in his honour. [xxxii. 417]

LEGH. [See also LEE, LEIGH, and LEY.]

LEGH, ALEXANDER (d. 1501), ambassador; of Eton and King's College, Cambridge; M.A.; canon of Windsor, 1469; employed on embassies to Scotland, 1474, and later years; temporal chancellor of Durham Cathedral, 1490. [xxxii. 419]

LEGH, GERARD (d. 1563), writer on heraldry; published 'The Accedens of Armory,' 1562. [xxxii. 419]

LEGH, SIR THOMAS (d. 1545), visitor of the monasteries; B.C.L. (perhaps of King's College) Cambridge, 1527; D.C.L., 1531; ambassador to the king of Denmark, 1532-3; 'visited' monasteries, 1535; master in chancery, 1537; employed in suppressing religious houses, 1538-40; knighted, 1544. [xxxii. 420]

LEGLÆUS, GILBERTUS (fl. 1250). [See GILBERT THE ENGLISHMAN.]

LE GRAND, ANTOINE (d. 1699), Cartesian philosopher; native of Douay; Franciscan Recollect friar; as member of the English mission resided many years in Oxfordshire; provincial of his order, 1698-9; chief work, 'Institutio Philosophiæ, secundum principia Renati Descartes,' 1672 (Eng. trans., 1694). [xxxii. 421]

LEGREW, JAMES (1803-1857), sculptor; studied under Sir Francis Legatt Chantrey [q. v.] and at the Royal Academy schools; exhibited at the Royal Academy from 1826. [xxxii. 422]

LE GRICE, CHARLES VALENTINE (1773-1858), friend of Coleridge and Lamb; educated at Christ's Hospital, London, and Trinity College, Cambridge; B.A., 1796; ordained, 1798; M.A., 1805; conversationalist and author of small pieces in verse and prose. [xxxii. 422]

LE GRYS, SIR ROBERT (d. 1635), courtier and translator; published 'John Barclay his Argenis translated out of Latine into English,' 1629; knighted, 1629; his translation of 'Velleius Paterculus, his Romaine Historie' published, 1632; captain of the castle of St. Mawes, 1633-4. [xxxii. 423]

LEGUAT, FRANÇOIS (1638-1735), voyager and author; born at Bresse, Savoy; Huguenot refugee in Holland, 1689; founded colony of French protestants in Mascarene islands, 1691; sailed to Mauritius (1693), where he was imprisoned; transferred to Batavia, 1696; came to England on being released, 1698; published account of his travels, 1708. [xxxii. 424]

LE HART, WALTER (d. 1472). [See LYHERT.]

LEICESTER, EARLS OF. [See BEAUMONT, ROBERT DE, first EARL, 1104-1168; BEAUMONT, ROBERT DE, second EARL, d. 1190; MONTFORT, SIMON OF, second EARL of the second creation, 1208?-1265; DUDLEY, ROBERT, first EARL of the fourth creation, 1532?-1588; SIDNEY, ROBERT, first EARL of the fifth creation, 1563-1626; SIDNEY, ROBERT, second EARL, 1595-1677; SIDNEY, PHILIP, third EARL, 1619-1698; TOWNSHEND, GEORGE, first EARL of the seventh creation, 1755-1811.]

LEICESTER OF HOLKHAM, EARL OF (1752-1842). [See COKE, THOMAS WILLIAM.]

LEICESTER, SIR JOHN FLEMING, first BARON DE TABLEY (1762-1827), art patron; succeeded as sixth baronet, 1770; M.A. Trinity College, Cambridge, 1784; collected examples of British art; M.P., Yarmouth, Isle of Wight, 1791, Heytesbury, 1796, Stockbridge, 1807; created Baron de Tabley, 1826. [xxxii. 425]

LEICESTER, LETTICE, COUNTESS OF (d. 1634). [See DUDLEY, LETTICE.]

LEICESTER, ROBERT OF (fl. 1320), Franciscan; D.D. Oxford, 1325; author of works on Hebrew chronology, written in 1294 and 1295. [xxxii. 426]

LEICESTER, WILLIAM DE, or WILLIAM DU MONT (d. 1213). [See WILLIAM.]

LEICHHARDT, FRIEDRICH WILHELM LUDWIG (1813-1848), Australian explorer; born at Trebatsch, Prussia; studied at Göttingen and Berlin; went to New South Wales, 1841; crossed the Australian continent from east to north, 1844-5; published account of the expedition, 1847; explored Sturt's desert in the interior, 1847; started to cross the continent from east to west, 1848, and was never again heard of. [xxxii. 426]

LEIFCHILD, HENRY STORMONTH (1823-1884), sculptor; studied at the British Museum, the Royal Academy, and (1848-51) at Rome; exhibited at the Royal Academy from 1846. [xxxii. 427]

LEIFCHILD, JOHN (1780–1862), independent minister; student in Hoxton Academy, 1804–8; minister of several chapels between 1808 and 1854; published religious works. [xxxii. 427]

LEIGH. [See also LEE, LEGH, and LEY.]

LEIGH, ANTHONY (d. 1692), comedian; first appeared on the stage, 1672; played many original parts of importance in plays by Dryden, Otway, and Mrs. Behn. [xxxii. 428]

LEIGH, CHANDOS, first BARON LEIGH of the second creation (1791–1850), poet and author; descendant of Sir Thomas Leigh, first baron Leigh of a former creation [q. v.]; educated at Harrow and Christ Church, Oxford; wrote verses prized by the scholarly few, and took interest in social and political questions; created Baron Leigh of Stoneleigh, 1839; died at Bonn. [xxxii. 429]

LEIGH, CHARLES (d. 1605), merchant and voyager; made a voyage to the St. Lawrence, partly for fishing and trade, and partly for plundering Spanish ships, 1597; sailed for Guiana with a view to establishing a colony to look for gold, 1604–5; died in Guiana. [xxxii. 430]

LEIGH, CHARLES (1662–1701?), physician and naturalist; great-grandson of William Leigh [q. v.]; educated at Brasenose College, Oxford; B.A., 1683; F.R.S., 1685; M.A. and M.D. Cambridge, 1689; published an unimportant 'Natural History of Lancashire, Cheshire, and the Peak in Derbyshire,' 1700. [xxxii. 431]

LEIGH, EDWARD (1602–1671), miscellaneous writer; M.A. Magdalen Hall, Oxford, 1623; his writings mostly compilations, the best-known being 'Critica Sacra, or Philologicall and Theologicall Observations upon all the Greek Words of the New Testament,' 1639; M.P., Stafford, 1644–8, when he was expelled the house for voting that the king's concessions were satisfactory. [xxxii. 432]

LEIGH, EGERTON (1815–1876), writer on dialect; educated at Eton; entered the army, 1833; captain, 1840; edited 'Ballads and Legends of Cheshire,' 1867; M.P. for Mid-Cheshire, 1873 and 1874. His 'Glossary of Words used in the Dialect of Cheshire' published, 1877. [xxxii. 433]

LEIGH, EVAN (1811–1876), inventor; became a manufacturer of machinery, 1851; patented nineteen inventions between 1849 and 1870, the most useful for the improvement of the machinery of cotton manufacture; published 'The Science of Modern Cotton Spinning,' 1871. [xxxii. 433]

LEIGH, SIR FERDINAND (1585?–1654), governor of the Isle of Man; knighted, 1617; deputy-governor of Man, 1625; fought in the war on the royalist side. [xxxii. 434]

LEIGH, FRANCIS, first EARL OF CHICHESTER (d. 1653), great-grandson of Sir Thomas Leigh (1504?–1571) [q. v]; created baronet, 1618; M.P., Warwick, 1625; created Baron Dunsmore, 1628; privy councillor, 1641; created Earl of Chichester, 1644. [xxxii. 434]

LEIGH, HENRY SAMBROOKE (1837–1883), dramatist; son of James Mathews Leigh [q. v.]; engaged early in literary pursuits; published 'Carols of Cockayne,' 1869; translated and adapted French comic operas for the English stage, 1871. [xxxii. 435]

LEIGH, JAMES MATHEWS (1808–1860), painter and author; nephew of Charles Mathews the elder [q. v.]; exhibited at Royal Academy, 1830–49; published 'Cromwell,' historical play, 1838. [xxxii. 435]

LEIGH, JARED (1724–1769), amateur artist; painted chiefly sea-pieces and landscapes; exhibited with the Free Society of Artists, 1761–7. [xxxii. 435]

LEIGH, JOHN (1689–1726), dramatist and actor; played important parts in London, 1714–26; author of a comedy, 'The Pretenders,' 1720. [xxxii. 436]

LEIGH, SIR OLIPH or OLYFF (1560–1612), encourager of maritime enterprise; brother of Charles Leigh (d. 1605) [q. v.]; keeper of the great park at Eltham; sold the surrender of it, 1609. [xxxii. 430]

LEIGH, PERCIVAL (1813–1889), comic writer; studied medicine at St. Bartholomew's Hospital; L.S.A., 1834; M.R.C.S., 1835; abandoned medicine for literature;

joined the staff of 'Punch,' 1841, to which he contributed till his death; satirised prevailing fashions in 'Ye Manners and Customs of ye Englyshe,' 1849. [xxxii. 436]

LEIGH, RICHARD (b. 1649), poet; educated at Queen's College, Oxford; B.A., 1669; actor in London; attacked Dryden in pamphlets published, 1673; author of 'Poems upon Several Occasions,' published, 1675. [xxxii. 437]

LEIGH, SAMUEL (fl. 1686), author of a metrical version of the Psalms; born about 1635; educated at Merton College, Oxford; author of 'Samuelis Primitiæ, or an Essay towards a Metrical Version of the whole Book of Psalms,' 1661. [xxxii. 437]

LEIGH or **LEE**, SIR THOMAS (1504?–1571), lord mayor of London; warden of the Mercers' Company, 1544 and 1552; master, 1544, 1558, and 1564; alderman, 1552–1571; sheriff, 1555; lord mayor and knighted, 1558. [xxxii. 437]

LEIGH, SIR THOMAS, first BARON LEIGH of the first creation (d. 1671), second son of Sir Thomas Leigh (1504?–1571) [q. v.]; created baron Leigh of Stoneleigh, 1643; royalist. The barony became extinct, 1786. [xxxii. 438]

LEIGH, THOMAS PEMBERTON, first BARON KINGSDOWN (1793–1867). [See PEMBERTON-LEIGH.]

LEIGH, VALENTINE (fl. 1562), miscellaneous writer; published 'Death's Generall Proclamation,' 1561, and 'The most Profitable and Commendable Science of Lands, Tenements, Hereditaments,' 1562. [xxxii. 438]

LEIGH, WILLIAM (1550–1639), divine; educated at Brasenose College, Oxford; fellow, 1573; M.A., 1578; a popular preacher; B.D., 1586; tutor to Prince Henry, eldest son of James I; published sermons and religious pieces between 1602 and 1613. [xxxii. 439]

LEIGHTON, ALEXANDER (1568–1649), physician and divine; studied at St. Andrews and Leyden universities; M.A. St. Andrews; published 'Speculum Belli sacri, or the Looking Glass of the Holy War,' 1624, and 'An Appeal to the Parliament, or Sion's Plea against the Prelacie,' 1628; arrested and condemned by Star-chamber to mutilation and life-long imprisonment, 1630; released by Long parliament, 1640; keeper of Lambeth House, 1642. [xxxiii. 1]

LEIGHTON, ALEXANDER (1800–1874), editor of 'Tales of the Borders'; edited and helped to write 'Tales of the Borders,' 1835–40; re-edited the complete 'Tales of the Borders,' 1857; published 'Romance of the Old Town of Edinburgh,' 1867. [xxxiii. 2]

LEIGHTON, CHARLES BLAIR (1823–1855), artist; painted portraits and figure-pieces; occasionally exhibited at the Royal Academy. [xxxiii. 2]

LEIGHTON, SIR ELISHA (d. 1685), courtier; son of Alexander Leighton (1568–1649) [q. v.]; colonel in the royalist army; joined royalist party abroad after Charles I's execution; appointed by Charles secretary for English affairs in Scotland, 1650; knighted, 1659; F.R.S., 1663–77; one of the secretaries of the prize office, 1664; LL.D. Cambridge, 1665; secretary to the lord-lieutenant of Ireland, 1670; recorder of Dublin, 1672. [xxxiii. 2]

LEIGHTON, FREDERIC, BARON LEIGHTON OF STRETTON (1830–1896), painter and president of the Royal Academy; educated at London and various continental towns; studied art at Florence, Frankfort, at Paris, again at Frankfort under Johann Eduard Steinle (1810–86), and at Rome; exhibited 'Cimabue's "Madonna" carried through Streets of Florence' at Royal Academy, 1855; A.R.A., 1866; exhibited 'Venus disrobing for the Bath,' 1866; lived in Holland Park Road from 1866; R.A., 1869; made journey, 1873, to the East, which resulted in several oriental pictures; P.R.A., 1878–96; knighted, 1878; painted two wall-pictures in Victoria and Albert Museum, and wall-decoration on canvas on Royal Exchange (finished, 1895); raised to peerage by patent dated 24 Jan. 1896, the day before his death; hon. D.C.L. Oxford, LL.D. Cambridge and Edinburgh, 1879; buried in St. Paul's Cathedral, where an elaborate monument was erected. His 'Addresses delivered to students of the Royal Academy' appeared, 1896. Among his best works are 'Hercules wrestling with Death' and 'The Summer Moon' (1871–2), 'Athlete struggling with a Python' (1877, sculpture),

'The Bath of Psyche' (1890), 'Perseus and Andromeda' (1891), 'The Garden of the Hesperides' (1892), and 'Wedded' (1882). [Suppl. iii. 88]

LEIGHTON, LICHTON, or **LYCHTON,** HENRY (*d.* 1440), bishop successively of Moray and Aberdeen; bishop of Moray, 1415, of Aberdeen, 1423; built a great part of Aberdeen Cathedral; employed on diplomatic missions. [xxxii. 3]

LEIGHTON, HENRY (*d.* 1669), French scholar; educated in France; obtained Oxford M.A. by fraud, 1642; taught French at Oxford; published 'Linguæ Gallicæ addiscendæ Regulæ,' 1659. [xxxiii. 4]

LEIGHTON, ROBERT (1611–1684), archbishop of Glasgow; son of Alexander Leighton (1568–1649) [q. v.]; student at Edinburgh University, 1627; M.A., 1631; travelled on the continent; licensed priest, 1641; a famous preacher; principal of Edinburgh University, 1653, and professor of divinity at Edinburgh; bishop of Dunblane, 1661; archbishop of Glasgow, 1669–74; his sermons published, 1692–1708. [xxxiii. 4]

LEIGHTON, ROBERT (1822–1869), Scottish poet; entered the office of his brother, a shipowner, 1837; went round the world as a supercargo, 1842–3; managed the business of a firm of seed-merchants, 1854–67; published poems in 1855, 1861, 1866; other poems by him, some in the vernacular, posthumously published. [xxxiii. 7]

LEIGHTON, SIR WILLIAM (*fl.* 1603–1614), poet and composer; published a poem in praise of James I, 1603; knighted, 1603; published the 'Teares or Lamentations of a sorrowful Soule,' 1613, and 'Musicall Ayres,' 1614. [xxxiii. 7]

LEIGHTON, WILLIAM (1841–1869), Scottish poet, nephew of Robert Leighton (1822–1869) [q. v.]; employed in a Brazilian business house, 1864–9. 'Poems by the late William Leighton' appeared, 1870; and other volumes in 1872 and 1875. [xxxiii. 8]

LEIGHTON, WILLIAM ALLPORT (1805–1889), botanist; educated at St. John's College, Cambridge; B.A., 1833; published 'Flora of Shropshire,' 1841, and other works, including 'Lichen Flora of Great Britain,' 1871. [xxxiii. 8]

LEINSTER, DUKES OF. [See SCHOMBERG, MEINHARD, first DUKE of the first creation, 1641–1719; FITZGERALD, JAMES, first DUKE of the second creation, 1722–1773.]

LEINSTER, EARL OF (1584?–1659). [See CHOLMONDELEY, ROBERT.]

LEINTWARDEN or **LEYNTWARDYN,** THOMAS (*d.* 1421), chancellor of St. Paul's Cathedral, London; educated at Oxford; D.D. Oxford; chancellor of St. Paul's, 1401; provost of Oriel College, Oxford, 1417–21; wrote commentary on St. Paul's Epistles. [xxxiii. 9]

LEITCH, WILLIAM LEIGHTON (1804–1883), watercolour painter; scene-painter at the Theatre Royal, Glasgow, 1824, and later at the Queen's Theatre, London; a successful teacher of drawing and water-colours; drawing-master to Queen Victoria and the royal family for twenty-two years; member of the Institute of Painters in Water-colours, 1862; the last of the great English teachers of landscape-painting. [xxxiii. 9]

LEITH, ALEXANDER (1758–1838). [See HAY, ALEXANDER LEITH.]

LEITH, SIR JAMES (1763–1816), lieutenant-general; educated at Aberdeen and Lille; served in Toulon operations, 1793; colonel, 1794; brigadier-general, 1804; present at the battle of Coruña, 1809; with Peninsular army, 1810–12; K.B., 1813; lieutenant-general, 1813; commander of forces in West Indies and governor of the Leeward islands, 1814; G.C.B., 1815; died at Barbados. [xxxiii. 10]

LEITH, THEODORE FORBES (1746–1819), physician; studied at Edinburgh University; M.D., 1768; F.R.S., 1781; L.R.C.P., 1786. [xxxiii. 11]

LE KEUX, HENRY (1787–1868), engraver; brother of John Le Keux [q. v.]; apprenticed to James Basire (1730–1802) [q. v.]; engraved for fashionable annuals, 1820–40. [xxxiii. 12]

LE KEUX, JOHN (1783–1846), engraver; apprenticed to James Basire (1730–1802) [q. v.]; engraved plates for the architectural publications of John Britton [q. v.], Augustus Welby Northmore Pugin [q. v.], John Preston Neale [q. v.], and similar works. [xxxiii. 11]

LE KEUX, JOHN HENRY (1812–1896), architectural engraver and draughtsman; son of John Le Keux [q. v.]; exhibited at Royal Academy, 1853–65; engraved plates for Ruskin's 'Modern Painters' and 'Stones of Venice.' [Suppl. iii. 91]

LEKPREVICK, ROBERT (*fl.* 1561–1588), Scottish printer; principal printer for the reform party in Scotland; king's printer, 1568–88; imprisoned for printing a pamphlet which reflected on the Regent Morton, 1574. [xxxiii. 12]

LELAND or **LEYLOND,** JOHN, the elder (*d.* 1428), grammarian; taught as a grammarian at Oxford; wrote grammatical works in Latin. [xxxiii. 13]

LELAND or **LEYLAND,** JOHN (1506?–1552), the earliest of modern English antiquaries; educated at St. Paul's School, London, and Christ's College, Cambridge; B.A., 1522; studied at Paris; took holy orders; library-keeper to Henry VIII before 1530; king's antiquary, 1533; made an antiquarian tour through England, 1534–43; intended his researches to be the basis of a great work on the 'History and Antiquities of this Nation'; in 'A New Year's Gift,' 1545, described to the king the manner and aims of his researches; became insane, 1550. 'Leland's Itinerary' was first published at Oxford in nine volumes, 1710, and his 'Collectanea' in six, 1715. [xxxiii. 13]

LELAND, JOHN (1691–1766), divine; a nonconformist minister; D.D. Aberdeen, 1739; attacked the deists in 'A View of the principal Deistical Writers that have appeared in England during the last and present Century,' 1754–6, and other works. [xxxiii. 17]

LELAND, THOMAS (1722–1785), historian; entered Trinity College, Dublin, 1737; B.A., 1741; fellow, 1746; published Latin translation of the Philippics of Demosthenes, 1754, and English translation, 1754–61; published the 'History of Philip, King of Macedon,' 1758; presented the Irish manuscript chronicle, 'Annals of Loch Cé,' to Trinity College Library, 1766; vicar of St. Anne's, Dublin, 1773; D.D.; published 'History of Ireland from the Invasion of Henry II, with a preliminary Discourse on the ancient State of that Kingdom,' 1773. [xxxiii. 18]

LELY, SIR PETER (1618–1680), portrait-painter; born at Soest by Amersfoort, near Utrecht; studied at Haarlem; came to England, 1641; introduced to Charles I, 1647; painted Charles I's portrait during his captivity at Hampton Court; painted Cromwell and enjoyed considerable private practice under him; in high favour with Charles II; painted portraits of the beauties of Charles II's court, and of the admirals and commanders in the naval victory at Solebay, 1665; knighted, 1679. [xxxiii. 19]

LEMAN, SIR JOHN (1544–1632), lord mayor of London; alderman, 1605; sheriff, 1606; lord mayor, 1616–17, and knighted, 1617. [xxxiii. 21]

LEMAN, THOMAS (1751–1826), antiquary; educated at Emmanuel College, Cambridge; B.A., 1774; fellow of Clare Hall, Cambridge; M.A., 1778; Dixie (bye) fellow of Emmanuel College, 1783; chancellor of Cloyne, 1796–1802; visited every Roman and British road and station in Great Britain, and communicated his observations to county historians; F.S.A., 1788. [xxxiii. 22]

LE MARCHANT, SIR DENIS, first baronet (1795–1874), politician; son of John Gaspard le Marchant [q. v.]; educated at Eton and Trinity College, Cambridge; barrister, Lincoln's Inn, 1823; clerk of the crown in chancery, 1834; edited a highly successful pamphlet, 'The Reform Ministry and the Reform Parliament,' 1834; secretary to the board of trade, 1836–41; created baronet, 1841; liberal M.P., Worcester, 1846–7; under-secretary for the home department, 1847; secretary of the board of trade, 1848; chief clerk to the House of Commons, 1850–71; edited Walpole's 'Memoirs of the reign of George III,' 1845. [xxxiii. 22]

LE MARCHANT, JOHN GASPARD (1766–1812), major-general; ensign, 1781; intimate with George III; in Flemish campaigns, 1793–4; major, 1795; devised a system of cavalry sword-exercise, and suggested pattern for improved sword; lieutenant-colonel, 1797; projected schools of instruction for officers, which were the beginnings of Sandhurst; lieutenant-governor of the schools, 1801-10; major-general in the Peninsula, 1810-12; mortally wounded at Salamanca, 1812; wrote on military subjects. [xxxiii. 23]

LE MARCHANT, SIR JOHN GASPARD (1803-1874), lieutenant-general, colonial administrator; son of John Gaspard le Marchant [q. v.]; ensign, 1820; major in the new 98th foot, 1832; served at the Cape, 1832; as brigadier-general in the Carlist war, 1835-7; lieutenant-governor of Newfoundland, 1847-52, of Nova Scotia, 1852-7; governor of Malta, 1859-64; G.C.M.G., 1860; commander-in-chief at Madras, 1865-8; K.C.B., 1865. [xxxiii. 25]

LEMENS, BALTHAZAR VAN (1637-1704). [See VAN LEMENS.]

LE MESURIER, HAVILLAND (1758-1806), commissary-general; son of John Le Mesurier [q. v.]; 'adjutant commissary-general of stores, supplies, and storage' to the forces on the continent, 1793; with the army during winter retreat through Holland, 1794-5; served later in Egypt, Malta, Naples, and elsewhere; published pamphlets on commissariat matters. [xxxiii. 25]

LE MESURIER, HAVILLAND (1783-1813), lieutenant-colonel; son of Havilland Le Mesurier (1758-1806) [q. v.]; educated at Westminster; ensign, 1801; served under Sir John Moore in Sweden and at Coruña, 1809; brevet lieutenant-colonel, 1811; commandant of Almeida, 1811; shot in the battle of the Pyrenees; translated French military works. [xxxiii. 26]

LE MESURIER, JOHN (1781-1843), major-general, last hereditary governor of Alderney; nephew of Havilland Le Mesurier (1783-1813) [q.v.]; ensign, 1794; served in Ireland, 1798; at the occupation of Messina, 1799-1800; in Egypt, 1801; governor of Alderney, 1803-24. [xxxiii. 27]

LE MESURIER, PAUL (1755-1805), lord mayor of London; brother of Havilland Le Mesurier (1758-1806) [q.v.]; as a proprietor of the East India Company opposed Fox's India bill, 1783; M.P., Southwark, 1783; sheriff, 1787; colonel of the honourable artillery company, 1794; lord mayor, 1794. [xxxiii. 26]

LE MOINE, ABRAHAM (d. 1757), theological controversialist; probably son of a Huguenot refugee; chaplain to the French hospital in London, 1723-49, the Duke of Portland, 1729; chief work, a 'Treatise on Miracles' (reply to Thomas Chubb [q. v.]), 1747; also published French translations of theological works. [xxxiii. 27]

LEMOINE, HENRY (1756-1812), author and bookseller; son of a French protestant refugee; purchased a bookstall in the Little Minories, 1777; contributed to the magazines; published miscellaneous works; started and edited various periodicals; published anonymous books and pamphlets; contributed to the 'Gentleman's Magazine'; described as one of the best judges of old books in England, and an authority on foreign and Jewish literature. [xxxiii. 27]

LEMON, GEORGE WILLIAM (1726-1797), master of Norwich school; B.A. Queens' College, Cambridge, 1747; took holy orders and held several livings; master of Norwich free grammar school, 1769-78; published educational works, 1774-92. [xxxiii. 29]

LEMON, MARK (1809-1870), editor of 'Punch'; began his career as a playwright, 1835; published farces, melodramas, and operas; contributed to 'Household Words,' the 'Illustrated London News' and other periodicals, and edited the 'Family Herald' and 'Once a Week'; best known as one of the founders and the first editor of 'Punch' (first number published 17 July 1841); edited 'Punch,' 1841-70; began writing novels late in life with indifferent success; known among his friends as 'Uncle Mark.' [xxxiii. 30]

LEMON, ROBERT (1779-1835), archivist; educated at Norwich Grammar school; under his uncle, George William Lemon [q. v.], helped to compile appendix to the 'Report on Internal Defence,' 1798; deputy-keeper of the state paper office, 1818; F.S.A., 1824. [xxxiii. 31]

LEMON, ROBERT (1800-1867), archivist; son of Robert Lemon (1779-1835) [q. v.]; employed under his

father in the state paper office; interpreted a certain cypher found in some state papers; F.S.A., 1836, rearranging society's library, 1846. [xxxiii. 32]

LEMPRIÈRE, JOHN (1765? - 1824), classical scholar; educated at Winchester College and Pembroke College, Oxford; M.A., 1792; master of grammar school at Bolton, Lancashire, 1791; of grammar school at Abingdon, 1792-1808 (or 1809); D.D. Oxford, 1803; master of Exeter free grammar school, 1809-c. 1823; chief works, 'A Classical Dictionary' (1788) and a 'Universal Biography ... of Eminent Persons in all Ages and Countries' (1808 and 1812). [xxxiii. 32]

LEMPRIÈRE, MICHAEL (fl. 1640-1660), seigneur of Maufant, and one of the leaders of the parliamentary party in Jersey; as a jurat of the royal court actively opposed the bailiff of the island, Sir Philip de Carteret [q. v.]; succeeded De Carteret as bailiff, 1643; royal warrant issued for his arrest, 1643; in exile, 1643-51; on return of parliamentary party to power resumed his office of bailiff, 1651; removed from the bench of jurats, but allowed to retain his estates, 1660; highly esteemed by Cromwell. [xxxiii. 33]

LEMPRIÈRE, WILLIAM (d. 1834), traveller and medical writer; entered the army medical service; went to Morocco to attend the emperor's son, 1789, and also attended the ladies of the harem; published account of his travels, 1791; army surgeon in Jamaica, 1794-9; published medical pamphlets. [xxxiii. 34]

LEMPUT, REMIGIUS VAN (1609?-1675). [See VAN LEEMPUT.]

LENDY, AUGUSTE FREDERICK (1826 - 1889), military tutor and author; set up a private military college at Sunbury-on-Thames, c. 1854; held a commission in the army, 1859-79; published works on military subjects. [xxxiii. 34]

LE NEVE, JOHN (1679-1741), antiquary; of Eton and Trinity College, Cambridge; his greatest work, 'Fasti Ecclesiæ Anglicanæ, or an Essay towards a regular Succession of all the principal Dignitaries,' &c., published, 1716; took holy orders; imprisoned for insolvency, 1722. [xxxiii. 35]

LE NEVE, PETER (1661-1729), Norfolk antiquary; entered Merchant Taylors' School, London, 1673; president of the Antiquarian Society, 1687-1724; F.R.S.; Rouge Croix pursuivant, 1689-90; Richmond herald and Norroy king-at-arms, 1704; collected much material, but printed nothing; many of his manuscripts preserved in Bodleian, British Museum, Heralds' College, and elsewhere. His copious notes form the backbone of the history of Norfolk, begun by Blomefield and completed by Parkin. [xxxiii. 36]

LE NEVE, SIR WILLIAM (1600?-1661), herald and genealogist; Mowbray herald extraordinary, 1622; York herald and Norroy king, 1633; knighted, 1634; Clarenceux, 1635; sent by Charles I with proclamation to parliamentarians before battle of Edgehill, 1642; became insane, 1658. [xxxiii. 38]

LENEY, WILLIAM S. (fl. 1790-1810), engraver; articled to Peltro William Tomkins [q. v.]; executed five plates for Boydell's edition of Shakespeare; emigrated to America, 1806; engraved portraits of American celebrities. [xxxiii. 38]

LENG, JOHN (1665-1727), bishop of Norwich; educated at St. Paul's School, London, and Catharine Hall, Cambridge; fellow, 1688; M.A., 1690; a distinguished Latin scholar; D.D., 1716; Boyle lecturer, 1717-18; chaplain in ordinary to George I; bishop of Norwich, 1723-7; published sermons, his Boyle lectures, and translations from the classics. [xxxiii. 38]

LENIHAN, MAURICE (1811-1895), historian of Limerick; educated at Carlow College; engaged in journalism; editor of 'Limerick Reporter,' 1841-3, and of 'Tipperary Vindicator,' a paper started in the interests of the repeal movement at Nenagh, 1843; incorporated 'Limerick Reporter' with 'Tipperary Vindicator,' 1849, and conducted it on moderate nationalist lines; published 'Limerick, its History and Antiquities,' 1866. [Suppl. iii. 91]

LENNARD, FRANCIS, fourteenth BARON DACRE (1619-1662), succeeded to barony, 1630; sided with the parliament against Charles I; lord-lieutenant of

Herefordshire, 1641–2 ; retired from active support of parliament when the supremacy of the army became evident ; one of the twelve peers who rejected the bill for Charles I's trial, 1648–9 ; went abroad, 1655.

[xxxiii. 39]

LENNARD, SAMSON (*d.* 1633), genealogist and translator ; accompanied Sidney to the Netherlands, 1586 ; entered the College of Arms ; Rouge-rose pursuivant extraordinary, 1615 ; Bluemantle pursuivant, 1616 ; author of translations and a devotional work ; some of his heraldic visitations printed between 1619 and 1623.

[xxxiii. 40]

LENNIE, WILLIAM (1779–1852), grammarian ; founded bursaries at Edinburgh University ; published ' Principles of English Grammar,' 1816. [xxxiii. 40]

LENNON, JOHN (1768–1842 ?), master-mariner ; served in the navy during the American war ; traded from St. Thomas ; brought his vessel safely without convoy into the English Channel, 1812. [xxxiii. 40]

LENNOX, DUKES OF. [See STUART, ESMÉ, first DUKE, 1542 ?–1583 ; STUART, LUDOVICK, second DUKE, 1574–1624 ; STUART, JAMES, fourth DUKE, 1612–1655 ; STUART, CHARLES, sixth DUKE, 1640–1672.]

LENNOX, DUCHESS OF (1648–1702). [See STUART, FRANCES TERESA.]

LENNOX, EARLS OF. [See LENNOX, MALCOLM, fifth EARL, 1255 ?–1333 ; STEWART, Sir JOHN, first or ninth EARL, *d.* 1495 ; STEWART, MATTHEW, second or tenth EARL, *d.* 1513 ; STEWART, JOHN, third or eleventh EARL, *d.* 1526 ; STEWART, MATTHEW, fourth or twelfth EARL, 1516–1571.]

LENNOX, COUNTESS OF (1515–1578). [See DOUGLAS, LADY MARGARET.]

LENNOX, CHARLES, first DUKE OF RICHMOND (1672–1723), natural son of Charles II by Louise de Keroualle, duchess of Portsmouth [q. v.] ; created Baron of Settrington, Yorkshire, Earl of March, and Duke of Richmond, Yorkshire, in the peerage of England, and Baron Methuen of Tarbolton, Earl of Darnley, and Duke of Lennox in the peerage of Scotland, 1675 ; K.G., 1681, and governor of Dumbarton Castle, 1681 ; master of the horse, 1682–5 ; aide-de-camp in Flanders, 1693–1702 ; lord of the bedchamber to George I, 1714 ; Irish privy councillor, 1715. [xxxiii. 41]

LENNOX, CHARLES, second DUKE OF RICHMOND, LENNOX, and AUBIGNY (1701–1750), only son of Charles Lennox, first duke [q. v.] ; grandson of Charles II ; captain in royal regiment of horse-guards, 1722 ; M.P., Chichester, 1722–3 ; succeeded to the dukedom, 1723 ; F.R.S., 1724 ; K.B., 1725 ; K.G., 1726 ; lord of the bedchamber, 1727 ; LL.D. Cambridge, 1728 ; succeeded to dukedom of Aubigny in France on the death of his grandmother, the Duchess of Portsmouth [see KEROUALLE, LOUISE DE] ; master of the horse, 1735 ; privy councillor, 1735 ; present at Dettingen, 1743 ; lieutenant-general, 1745 ; M.D. Cambridge, 1749 ; P.S.A., 1750. [xxxiii. 42]

LENNOX, CHARLES, third DUKE OF RICHMOND and LENNOX (1735–1806), third son of Charles Lennox, second duke of Richmond, Lennox, and Aubigny [q. v.] ; educated at Westminster School and Leyden University ; graduated at Leyden, 1753 ; entered the army ; F.R.S., 1755 ; colonel, 1758 ; distinguished himself at Minden, 1759 ; succeeded to the title, 1750 ; lord-lieutenant of Sussex, 1763 ; ambassador extraordinary and minister plenipotentiary at Paris, 1765 ; secretary of state for the southern department, 1766–7 ; denounced ministerial policy with reference to the American colonies ; K.G., 1782 ; master-general of the ordnance, with a seat in the cabinet, 1782–95 ; strongly urged appointment of committee (never formed) upon parliamentary reform, 1782 ; member of Pitt's cabinet, 1783 ; became, in spite of former declarations, strongly opposed to all reform, and consequently extremely unpopular ; F.S.A., 1793. His letter ' On the Subject of a Parliamentary Reform,' demanding universal suffrage, together with annual elections, was published, 1783, and passed through a number of editions.

[xxxiii. 44]

LENNOX, CHARLES, fourth DUKE OF RICHMOND and LENNOX (1764–1819), eldest son of George Henry Lennox [q. v.] ; fought a duel with the Duke of York [see FREDERICK AUGUSTUS, DUKE OF YORK AND ALBANY], 1789 ; served in the Leeward islands ; M.P., Sussex, 1790 ; colonel, 1795 ; lieutenant-general, 1805 ;

succeeded to the title, 1806 ; privy councillor, 1807 ; lord-lieutenant of Ireland, 1807–13 ; general, 1814 ; gave a ball at Brussels, where he was residing, on the eve of Quatre Bras, 1815 ; present at Waterloo ; governor-general of British North America, 1818 ; died near Richmond, Canada. [xxxiii. 48]

LENNOX, CHARLES GORDON-, fifth DUKE OF RICHMOND (1791–1860), eldest son of Charles Lennox, fourth duke [q. v.] ; educated at Westminster School ; lieutenant, 1810 ; assistant military secretary to Wellington in Portugal, 1810–14 ; lieutenant-colonel, 1816 ; M.P., Chichester, 1812–19 ; succeeded his father, 1819 ; K.G., 1828 ; postmaster-general, 1830–4 ; president, Royal Agricultural Society, 1845–60. [xxxiii. 48]

LENNOX, CHARLOTTE (1720–1804), miscellaneous writer ; daughter of Colonel James Ramsay, lieutenant-governor of New York, where she was born ; sent to England, 1735 ; married one Lennox, *c.* 1748 ; befriended and flattered by Dr. Johnson ; author of ' The Female Quixote ' (novel), 1752 ; conducted ' The Ladies' Museum Magazine,' 1760–1 ; her comedy, ' The Sister,' acted once, 1769 ; published novels, poems, and translations from the French. [xxxiii. 50]

LENNOX, GEORGE HENRY (1737–1805), general ; son of Charles Lennox, second duke of Richmond [q. v.] ; ensign, 1754 ; saw service abroad, 1757–63 ; lieutenant-colonel, 1758 ; colonel, 1762 ; brigadier, 1763 ; secretary of legation to the court of France, 1765 ; major-general, 1772 ; constable of the Tower of London, 1783 ; privy councillor, 1784 ; general, 1793. [xxxiii. 51]

LENNOX, Lord HENRY CHARLES GEORGE GORDON- (1821–1886), son of Charles Gordon-Lennox, fifth duke of Richmond [q v.] ; M.P., Chichester, 1846–1885 ; a lord of the treasury, 1852 and 1858–9 ; secretary to the admiralty, 1866–8 ; first commissioner of public works, 1874–6. [xxxiii. 50]

LENNOX, MALCOLM, fifth EARL OF LENNOX (1255 ?–1333), succeeded to the earldom, 1292 ; a supporter of Bruce ; killed at battle of Halidon Hill. [xxxiii. 51]

LENNOX, Sir WILBRAHAM OATES (1830–1897), general, royal engineers ; studied at Woolwich ; lieutenant, royal engineers, 1854 ; brevet major, 1858 ; brevet lieutenant-colonel, 1859 ; first captain, 1863 ; major, 1872 ; lieutenant-colonel, 1873 ; major-general, 1881 ; lieutenant-general, 1888 ; general, 1893 ; served in Crimea, 1854–6 ; V.C. (Inkermann), 1854 ; took conspicuous part in second relief, 1857, and final siege of Lucknow, 1858 ; and in subsequent campaigns ; C.B. (military), 1867 ; instructor in field fortification at Chatham, 1866–71 ; attached officially to German armies in France during Franco-German war, 1870–1 ; second in command of royal engineers at Portsmouth, 1873–6 ; military attaché at Constantinople, 1876–8 ; commanded garrison of Alexandria, 1884–7 ; commanded troops in Ceylon, 1887–8 ; K.C.B., 1891 ; director-general of military education at war office, 1893–5 ; published writings on military subjects.

[Suppl. iii. 92]

LENNOX, Lord WILLIAM PITT (1799–1881), miscellaneous writer ; son of Charles Lennox, fourth duke of Richmond [q. v.] ; at Westminster School, 1808–14 ; cornet, 1813 ; present as spectator at Waterloo, 1815 ; captain, 1822 ; M.P., King's Lynn, 1832–4 ; published novels of little merit ; contributed to the annuals, ' Once a Week,' and the ' Court Journal ' ; edited the ' Review,' newspaper, 1858. [xxxiii. 52]

LE NOIR, ELIZABETH ANNE (1755 ?–1841), poet and novelist ; daughter of Christopher Smart [q. v.], the poet ; married Jean Baptiste le Noir de la Brosse, 1795 ; author of novels praised by Dr. Burney and Miss Mitford, and books of poems. [xxxiii. 52]

LENS, ANDREW BENJAMIN (*fl.* 1765–1770), miniature-painter ; son of Bernard Lens (1682–1740) [q. v.] ; re-engraved and published his father's ' Granadier's Exercise,' 1744 ; exhibited miniatures with the Incorporated Society of Artists, 1765–70. [xxxiii. 54]

LENS, BERNARD (1631–1708), enamel-painter ; of Netherlandish origin ; practised in London.

[xxxiii. 53]

LENS, BERNARD (1659–1725), mezzotint-engraver and drawing-master ; son of Bernard Lens (1631–1708) [q. v.] ; kept a drawing-school with John Sturt [q. v.]

[xxxiii. 53]

LENS, BERNARD (1682–1740), miniature-painter and drawing-master ; son of Bernard Lens (1659–1725) [q. v.] ; esteemed the best miniature-painter in water-colours of his time ; limner to George I and George II ; taught drawing at Christ's Hospital, London, and drew and engraved plates illustrating 'A New and Compleat Drawing-Book,' published posthumously ; published etchings illustrating 'The Granadier's Exercise,' 1735. [xxxiii. 53]

LENS, JOHN (1756–1825), serjeant-at-law ; barrister, Lincoln's Inn, 1784 ; M.A. St. John's College, Cambridge, 1782 ; serjeant-at-law, 1799 ; king's serjeant, 1806 ; counsel to the university of Cambridge, 1807. [xxxiii. 54]

LENTHALL, Sir JOHN (1625–1681), son of William Lenthall [q. v.], speaker of the House of Commons ; educated at Corpus Christi College, Oxford ; M.P. for Gloucester, 1645 ; knighted by Cromwell, 1658 ; governor of Windsor, 1660 ; high sheriff of Oxfordshire, 1672 ; knighted by Charles II, 1677. [xxxiii. 59]

LENTHALL, WILLIAM (1591–1662), speaker of the House of Commons ; entered St. Alban Hall, Oxford, 1607 ; barrister, Lincoln's Inn, 1616 ; bencher, 1633 ; reader, 1638 ; speaker of the Long parliament, 1640 ; behaved with discretion and dignity on the occasion of the king's attempt to arrest the five members, 1642 ; master of the rolls, 1643 ; one of the two commissioners of the great seal, 1646–8 ; chancellor of the duchy of Lancaster, 1647 ; abandoned his post of speaker, and left London, fearing mob violence, 1647 ; M.P., Oxfordshire, and speaker, 1653 ; speaker in the restored Long parliament, 1659 ; supported Monck and the Restoration. [xxxiii. 55]

LENTON, FRANCIS (*fl.* 1630–1640), court poet and anagrammatist ; said to have studied at Lincoln's Inn ; styled himself 'Queen's poet' ; author of 'The Young Gallants Whirligigg, or Youth's Reakes,' 1629 ; 'Characterismi, or Lenton's Leasures,' 1631 ; 'The Innes of Court Anagrammatist, or the Masquers masqued in Epigrammes,' 1666, and other works. [xxxiii. 60]

LENTON, JOHN (*fl.* 1682–1718), musician ; gentleman of the Chapel Royal extraordinary, 1685 ; member of the royal band, 1692–1718 ; composed music for 'Venice Preserved,' 1682, songs, catches, airs, and 'The Useful Instructor for the Violin' (1694, 1702). [xxxiii. 61]

LEOFRIC (Lat. LEURICUS), EARL OF MERCIA (*d.* 1057), witnessed charters as 'minister' or thegn, 1005–1026 ; succeeded his father in the earldom between 1024 and 1032 ; ranked with Godwine and Siward as one of the three great earls among whom the government of the kingdom was divided ; his wife Godgifu the Godiva [q. v.] of legend. [xxxiii. 61]

LEOFRIC (Lat. LEFRICUS) (*d.* 1072), first bishop of Exeter ; educated in Lotharingia ; chancellor to Edward the Confessor [q. v.], being the first to be so designated ; bishop of the united dioceses of Devonshire and Cornwall, 1046 ; had seat of bishopric removed from Crediton to Exeter, 1050 ; bestowed lands, money, and books, including the collection of poetry known as the 'Liber Exoniensis,' on the church. [xxxiii. 63]

LEOFRIC OF BOURNE (*fl.* 1100), monk ; said to have written a life of Hereward [q. v.] [xxxiii. 64]

LEOFWINE (*d.* 1066), son of Earl Godwine [q. v.] ; acted as governor of Kent, 1049 ; outlawed ; fled to Ireland, 1051 ; earl of Kent, Surrey, Essex, Middlesex (except London), Hertfordshire, and probably Buckinghamshire, 1057–66 ; killed at Hastings. [xxxiii. 64]

LEOMINSTER, first BARON (*d.* 1711). [See FERMOR, WILLIAM.]

LEONI, GIACOMO (1686–1746), architect ; Venetian, and architect to the elector palatine ; settled in England at beginning of eighteenth century ; prepared plates for the English editions of Palladio's 'Architecture,' 1715 ; translated Alberti's 'De re Ædificatoria,' 1726 ; built various country seats. [xxxiii. 64]

LEOPOLD, GEORGE DUNCAN ALBERT, DUKE OF ALBANY (1853–1884), fourth and youngest son of Queen Victoria ; entered Christ Church, Oxford, 1872 ; granted an annuity of 15,000*l.*, 1874 ; left Oxford with an honorary D.C.L., 1876 ; travelled in Europe and America ; president, Royal Society of Literature, 1878 ; vice-president, Society of Arts, 1879 ; created Duke of Albany, Earl of Clarence,

and Baron Arklow, 1881 ; married Princess Helen Frederica Augusta, daughter of H.S.H. George Victor, prince of Waldeck-Pyrmont, 1882 ; died at Cannes ; buried in St. George's Chapel, Windsor. [xxxiii. 65]

LEPIPRE (**LE PIPER**), FRANCIS (*d.* 1698), artist ; drew landscapes, humorous compositions, and caricatures, and etched subjects on silver plates ; painted twelve small pictures of scenes in 'Hudibras.' [xxxiii. 66]

LE QUESNE, CHARLES (1811–1856), writer on the constitutional history of Jersey ; contributed articles on commercial questions relating to the Channel islands to the 'Guernsey Magazine,' 1836–8 ; published 'Ireland and the Channel Islands, or a Remedy for Ireland,' 1848 ; jurat of the Royal Court of Jersey, 1850 ; his 'Constitutional History of Jersey' published, 1856. [xxxiii. 66]

LE ROMEYN, JOHN (*d.* 1296). [See ROMANUS.]

LERPINIERE, DANIEL (1745 ?–1785), engraver ; exhibited with the Free Society of Artists, 1773–83 ; engraved plates, chiefly landscapes, for Messrs. Boydell, 1776–85. [xxxiii. 67]

LESIEUR, Sir STEPHEN (*fl.* 1586–1627), ambassador ; a Frenchman ; secretary to the French ambassador to England, 1586 ; naturalised, *c.* 1589 ; taken into the public service, *c.* 1598 ; sent on embassy to Denmark, 1602, to the Emperor Rudolph II, 1603 and 1612–13, to Florence, 1608 and 1609. [xxxiii. 67]

LESLEY. [See also LESLIE and LESLY.]

LESLEY, ALEXANDER (1693–1758), jesuit ; studied at Douay and Rome ; joined jesuits, 1712 ; taught in the Illyrian College of Loreto, 1728 ; missioner in Aberdeenshire, 1729 ; taught in colleges of Ancona and Tivoli, 1734 ; again in England, 1738–44 ; prefect of studies in the Scots College, Rome, 1744–6 ; professor of moral theology in the English college, 1746–8 ; edited a fragment of the 'Thesaurus Liturgicus' entitled 'Missale mixtum secundum Regulam Beati Isidori dictum Mozarabes,' 1755. [xxxiii. 67]

LESLEY, WILLIAM ALOYSIUS (1641–1704), jesuit ; joined jesuits, 1656 ; superior of the Scots College at Rome, 1674–83 ; D.D. ; published 'Vita di S. Margherita, Regina di Scozia,' 1675 ; missioner in Scotland, 1694–1704. [xxxiii. 68]

LESLIE. [See also LESLEY and LESLY.]

LESLIE, ALEXANDER, first EARL OF LEVEN (1580 ?–1661), general ; served in the Swedish army for thirty years ; knighted by Gustavus Adolphus, 1626 ; compelled Wallenstein to raise the siege of Stralsund, 1628 ; governor of the Baltic district, 1628–30 ; engaged with the British contingent that aided Gustavus, 1630–2 ; fought at Lutzen, 1632 ; besieged and took Brandenburg, 1634 ; field-marshal, 1636 ; identified himself with the covenanters ; directed the military preparations in Scotland, 1638 ; lord-general of all the Scottish forces, 1639 ; victorious at battle of Newburn, 1640 ; created Earl of Leven and Lord Balgonie, 1641 ; general of the Scottish army in Ireland, 1642 ; sent to the assistance of the English parliament, 1643 ; present at Marston Moor, 1644 ; in charge of Charles I at Newcastle, 1645–7 ; fought for the royalists at Dunbar, 1650 ; prisoner of the English parliament, 1651–4. [xxxiii. 68]

LESLIE, ANDREW, properly fifth, but sometimes called fourth EARL OF ROTHES (*d.* 1611), eldest son of George, fourth earl [q. v.] ; succeeded to peerage, 1558 ; stedfastly supported Mary Queen of Scots from 1566. [xxxiii. 76]

LESLIE, CHARLES (1650–1722), nonjuror and controversialist ; son of John Leslie (1571–1671) [q. v.] ; M.A. Trinity College, Dublin, 1673 ; took holy orders, 1680 ; chancellor of Connor, 1686 ; refused to take the oaths at the revolution, and was deprived of his office ; commenced his series of controversial pamphlets with 'An Answer to a Book intituled the State of the Protestants in Ireland under the late King James's Government,' 1692 ; published attack on William III, 'Gallienus Redivivus, or Murther will out,' &c., 1695 ; attacked in various pamphlets the whig divines, Burnet, Tillotson, Sherlock, as well as the quakers, deists, and Jews, and defended the sacraments ; brought out 'The Rehearsal' in opposition to Defoe's 'Review,' 1704–9, carrying on at the same time his ecclesiastico-political pamphlet warfare ; warrant issued for his apprehension, 1710 ; escaped to St. Germains, 1711 ;

returned to England, but (1713) accepted a place in the household of the Pretender at Bar-le-duc. A collective edition of his 'Theological Works' was published in 1721. [xxxiii. 77]

LESLIE, CHARLES ROBERT (1794–1859), painter; son of American parents; born in London; taken to Philadelphia, 1799; educated at Pennsylvania University; apprenticed to publishers in Philadelphia, 1808; student at the Royal Academy schools, London, 1811; exhibited at the Royal Academy between 1813 and 1839; R.A., 1826; taught drawing at the Military Academy at West Point, America, 1833; summoned to Windsor to paint 'The Queen receiving the Sacrament at her Coronation,' 1838, and 'The Christening of the Princess Royal,' 1841; published 'The Memoirs of John Constable, R.A.,' 1845; professor of painting at the Royal Academy, 1848–52; published his lectures as 'Handbook for Young Painters,' 1855; excelled in depicting quiet humour. His 'Autobiographical Recollections,' edited by Tom Taylor [q. v.], and his 'Life of Reynolds,' completed by the same author, were published in 1865. [xxxiii. 84]

LESLIE, DAVID, first BARON NEWARK (d. 1682), military commander; entered service of Gustavus Adolphus; major-general in the Scottish army under Alexander Leslie, first earl of Leven [q. v.], 1643; at battle of Marston Moor, 1644; defeated Montrose at Philiphaugh, 1645; commander of the army raised on behalf of Charles II in Scotland in 1651; taken prisoner after Worcester, 1651; imprisoned in the Tower till 1660; created Baron Newark, 1661. [xxxiii. 86]

LESLIE, FRANK (1821–1880). [See CARTER, HENRY.]

LESLIE, FREDERICK (1855–1892), actor; his real name FREDERICK HOBSON; appeared first in London as Colonel Hardy ('Paul Pry') at the Royalty, 1878, and subsequently took numerous parts in light opera, and, with Miss Ellen Farren at the Gaiety, in burlesque.
[Suppl. iii. 94]

LESLIE, GEORGE, usually called third, but properly fourth, EARL OF ROTHES (d. 1558), sheriff of Fife, 1529–1540; a lord of session, 1541; a lord of the articles, 1544; tried for the murder of Cardinal Beaton and acquitted, 1547; ambassador to Denmark, 1550; died at Dieppe.
[xxxiii. 89]

LESLIE or **LESLEY**, GEORGE (d. 1637), Capuchin friar, known as FATHER ARCHANGEL; scholar in the Scots College, Rome, 1608; preached in Scotland, c. 1624–5; fled to France from persecution; returned to Scotland, 1631.
[xxxiii. 90]

LESLIE, GEORGE (d. 1701), divine and poet; works include 'Fire and Brimstone, or the Destruction of Sodom,' 1675, 'Abraham's Faith' (morality play), 1676.
[xxxiii. 111]

LESLIE, HENRY (1580–1661), bishop of Down and Connor; educated at Aberdeen; went to Ireland, 1614; ordained priest, 1617; prebendary of Connor, 1619; dean of Down, 1627; precentor of St. Patrick's, Dublin, 1628; prolocutor of lower house in Irish convocation, 1634; bishop of Down and Connor, 1635; a champion of Laudian episcopacy; withdrew to England after the loss of his property in the Irish rebellion, 1643; went abroad about the time of Charles I's execution; bishop of Meath, 1661.
[xxxiii. 91]

LESLIE or **LESLEY**, JOHN (1527–1596), bishop of Ross; M.A. Aberdeen; canon of Aberdeen Cathedral, 1547; studied at Paris and Poictiers, 1549–54; took holy orders, 1558; had a disputation with Knox and other reformers, 1561; employed in France about the person of Queen Mary; professor of canon law, Aberdeen, 1562; judge of session, 1565; privy councillor, 1565; bishop of Ross, 1566; chief adviser of Mary Queen of Scots in her ecclesiastical policy; appointed her ambassador to Queen Elizabeth, 1569; sent to the Tower in connection with the Ridolfi plot, 1571; set at liberty on condition of leaving England, 1573; went to Paris, 1574, and to Rome to represent Mary's interests, 1575; published there his Latin history of Scotland, 1578; suffragan and vicar-general of the diocese of Rouen, 1579; nominated to the bishopric of Coutances by Clement VIII; died at the Augustinian monastery at Guirtenburg, near Brussels. [xxxiii. 93]

LESLIE, JOHN, sixth EARL OF ROTHES (1600–1641), one of the leaders of the covenanting party; served heir to his grandfather, Andrew Leslie, fifth (or fourth) earl [q. v.], 1621; opposed Charles I's ecclesiastical policy in Scotland;

chief organiser of the movement against episcopacy, 1638; after pacification of 1640 remained in England at the court of Charles I; author of a 'Short Relation of Proceedings concerning the Affairs of Scotland from August 1637 to July 1638,' first published, 1830. [xxxiii. 99]

LESLIE, JOHN (1571–1671), bishop of Clogher; known as 'the fighting bishop'; educated at Aberdeen and in France; with Buckingham at Rhé, 1627; bishop of the Scottish isles, 1628–33, of Raphoe, 1633–61; a leader in the rebellion of 1641; after the king's execution defended Raphoe against the Cromwellians, and was one of the last royalists to submit; the only Anglican bishop who remained at his post during the interregnum; bishop of Clogher, 1661; left manuscript treatise on 'Memory.'
[xxxiii. 101]

LESLIE, JOHN, seventh EARL and first DUKE OF ROTHES (1630–1681), eldest son of John Leslie, sixth earl; [q. v.]; succeeded his father, 1641; entered the army; taken prisoner at Worcester, 1651; released, 1658; lord of session, 1661; commissioner of the exchequer, 1661; lord high treasurer, 1663; privy councillor of England, 1663; keeper of the privy seal, 1664; lord chancellor, 1667; created Duke of Rothes, 1680. [xxxiii. 102]

LESLIE, JOHN, eighth EARL OF ROTHES (1679–1722), eldest son of Charles (Hamilton), fifth earl of Haddington, and Margaret Leslie, elder daughter of John Leslie, duke of Rothes [q. v.], who succeeded her father as Countess of Rothes, the earldom surname of Leslie passing to her son; privy seal, 1704; aided the union of 1707; Scots representative peer, 1707–22; vice-admiral of Scotland, 1714; fought against James Edward, the Old Pretender, in 1715; governor of Stirling Castle, 1716–22. [xxxiii. 103]

LESLIE, JOHN, ninth EARL OF ROTHES (1698 ?–1767), eldest son of John Leslie, eighth earl [q. v.]; lieutenant-colonel, 1719; succeeded his father, 1722; Scots representative peer, 1723, 1727, 1747, 1754, and 1761; major-general, 1743; present at Dettingen, 1743; lieutenant-general, 1750; K.T., 1763; general, 1765; commander-in-chief of the forces in Ireland. [xxxiii. 104]

LESLIE, SIR JOHN (1766–1832), mathematician and natural philosopher; educated at St. Andrews and Edinburgh universities; his paper 'On the Resolution of Indeterminate Problems' communicated to the Royal Society of Edinburgh, 1788; superintended studies of the Wedgwoods, 1790–2; published, as outcome of his researches, 'Experimental Inquiry into the Nature and Properties of Heat,' 1804, a work of great scientific value; Rumford medallist, 1805; appointed professor of mathematics at Edinburgh, 1805; published 'Elements of Geometry, Geometrical Analysis, and Plane Trigonometry,' 1809, 'Geometry of Curve Lines,' 1813, and 'Philosophy of Arithmetic,' 1817; the first to achieve artificial congelation; contributed to the 'Edinburgh Review' and the 'Encyclopædia Britannica'; professor of natural philosophy, Edinburgh, 1819; published 'Elements of Natural Philosophy' (vol. i.), 1823; knighted, 1832. [xxxiii. 105]

LESLIE, NORMAN, MASTER OF ROTHES (d. 1554), leader of the party who assassinated Cardinal Beaton; eldest son of George Leslie, fourth earl of Rothes [q. v.]; sheriff of Fife, 1541; led the conspirators against Beaton, but took no personal part in the act of assassination, 1546; was carried captive to France, but escaped to England and was pensioned by Edward VI; on accession of Mary entered service of Henry II of France; mortally wounded in action near Cambray. [xxxiii. 107]

LESLIE, THOMAS EDWARD CLIFFE (1827 ?–1882), political economist; descended from Charles Leslie (1650–1722) [q. v.]; educated at Trinity College, Dublin; B.A., 1847; LL.B., 1851; later hon. LL.D.; professor of jurisprudence and political economy, Queen's College, Belfast, 1853; contributed articles on economic subjects to various periodicals, most of which were reprinted in 'Essays on Political and Moral Philosophy,' 1879, and 'Essays in Political Philosophy,' 1888; wrote on land systems and industrial economy. [xxxiii. 108]

LESLIE, WALTER, COUNT LESLIE (1606–1667), soldier of fortune and diplomatist; entered the imperial service and took part in war of Mantuan succession, 1630; served in Germany, 1632–45; instrumental in bringing about the assassination of Wallenstein, 1634; master of the ordnance, 1646; vice-president of the council of war, warden of the Sclavonian marches, and field-marshal,1650 ; privy councillor, 1655 ; invested with order of Golden Fleece, and ambassador extraordinary to the Ottoman Porte, 1665 ; died at Vienna. [xxxiii. 109]

LESLIE, WILLIAM (*d.* 1654 ?), principal of King's College, Aberdeen ; educated at Aberdeen ; regent, 1617 ; sub-principal, 1623 ; principal, 1632 ; with other Aberdeen doctors refused the covenant, 1639. [xxxiii. 110]

LESLIE, WILLIAM (1657-1727), bishop of Laybach in Styria : educated at Aberdeen ; studied at Padua, 1684 ; converted to Roman catholicism ; professor of theology, Padua ; bishop of Waitzen, Hungary, 1716, of Laybach, in Styria, 1718. [xxxiii. 111]

LESPEC, WALTER (*d.* 1153). [See Espec.]

LESSE, NICHOLAS (*fl.* 1550), religious writer ; author of 'The Apologie of the Worde of God,' 1547, and several translations. [xxxiii. 112]

LESTER, FREDERICK PARKINSON (1795-1858), major-general, Bombay artillery ; educated at Addiscombe ; lieutenant, 1815 ; captain, 1818 ; lieutenant-colonel, 1840 ; major-general, 1854 ; commander of the southern division of the Bombay army, 1857-8 ; instrumental in preventing the mutiny from extending to Western India, 1857-8. [xxxiii. 112]

LESTOCK, RICHARD (1679 ?-1746), admiral ; served with Sir Clowdisley Shovell [q. v.], 1704-5 ; with Sir George Byng, 1717-18 : took part in the operations against Cartagena, 1741 ; vice-admiral, 1743 ; court-martialled and acquitted (1746) for refusal to obey his superior, Mathews [see MATHEWS, THOMAS] in the action (1744) off Toulon, and admiral of the blue, 1746. [xxxiii. 113]

L'ESTRANGE, HAMON (1605-1660), theologian and historian ; brother of Sir Nicholas L'Estrange, first baronet [q. v.], and of Sir Roger L'Estrange [q. v.] ; published theological works, 1641-59. [xxxiii. 115]

L'ESTRANGE, HAMON (1674-1767), grandson of Hamon L'Estrange (1605-1660) [q. v.] ; on the commission of the peace for sixty-five years ; published legal and religious works. [xxxiii. 116]

LE STRANGE, HENRY L'ESTRANGE STYLEMAN (1815-1862), art amateur and decorative painter ; educated at Eton and Christ Church, Oxford ; B.A., 1837 ; employed in designing and carrying out the decoration of Ely Cathedral, 1853-62. [xxxiii. 117]

LE STRANGE, JOHN (*d.* 1269), lord marcher ; served under King John in Poitou, 1214 ; defended the Welsh border as a lord marcher. [xxxiii. 117]

L'ESTRANGE, JOHN (1836-1877), Norfolk antiquary ; clerk in the stamp office at Norwich ; made large collections for the history of the county of Norfolk, and the city of Norwich ; published 'The Church Bells of Norfolk,' 1874. [xxxiii. 117]

LE STRANGE, SIR NICHOLAS (1515-1580), steward of the manors of the Duchess of Richmond, 1547-80 ; son of Sir Thomas Le Strange [q. v.] ; knighted, 1547 ; M.P., Norfolk, 1547, King's Lynn, 1555, Castle Rising, 1571. [xxxiii. 129]

L'ESTRANGE, SIR NICHOLAS, first baronet (*d.* 1655), collector of anecdotes ; brother of Hamon L'Estrange (1605-1660) [q. v.] ; created baronet, 1629 ; compiled 'Merry Passages and Jests,' some of which were printed in 1839. [xxxiii. 118]

L'ESTRANGE, SIR ROGER (1616-1704), tory journalist and pamphleteer ; probably studied at Cambridge ; formed a plan to recapture Lynn ; seized by the parliament and imprisoned, 1644-8 ; projected a royalist rising in Kent ; had to flee to Holland ; employed while abroad by Hyde in service of Charles II ; returned to England, 1653 ; published broadsides attacking Lambert and the leaders of the army, 1659 ; wrote pamphlets in favour of monarchy, 1660, and to show that the presbyterians were responsible for the wars and the king's death, 1661-2 ; advocated a more stringent censorship of the press, 1663 ; appointed surveyor of printing presses and a licenser of the press, 1663 ; issued the ' Intelligencer' and 'The News,' 1663-6 ; encouraged, perhaps projected, 'The City Mercury, or Advertisements concerning trade,' 1675 ; published pamphlets to meet Shaftesbury's attack on

Charles II and his government, 1679.; adversely criticised the evidence for a supposed popish plot, 1680 ; J.P. for Middlesex, 1680 ; had to flee the country owing to the hostility of the promoters of the alleged popish plot ; returned to England, 1681 ; attacked dissenters and whigs in his periodical 'The Observator,' 1681-7 ; M.P., Winchester, 1685 ; knighted, 1685 ; deprived of his office of surveyor and licenser of the press at the revolution and imprisoned in 1688, 1691, and 1695-6. Besides his pamphlets and periodicals, he issued, among other things, 'The Fables of Æsop and other eminent Mythologists, with Moral Reflections,' 1692 (the most extensive collection of fables in existence), and 'The Works of Flavius Josephus compared with the Original Greek,' 1702, also translating 'Quevedo's Visions,' 1667. [xxxiii. 118]

LE STRANGE, SIR THOMAS (1494-1545), of Hunstanton, Norfolk : attended Henry VIII to the Field of the Cloth of Gold, 1520 ; knighted, 1529 ; high sheriff of Norfolk, 1532. [xxxiii. 128]

LE SUEUR, HUBERT (1595 ?-1650 ?), sculptor ; born probably in Paris ; came to England, 1628 ; received commission for an equestrian statue of Charles I, 1630, which was not set up at Charing Cross until 1674. [xxxiii. 129]

LETCHWORTH, THOMAS (1739-1784), quaker ; began preaching, 1758 ; published verse, 1765, 'The Monthly Ledger, or Literary Repository,' an unsectarian periodical, 1766-9 ; his 'Life and Writings of John Woolman' [q. v.], published, 1775, and a posthumous volume of his sermons, 1787. [xxxiii. 130]

LETHBRIDGE, JOSEPH WATTS (1817-1885), dissenting divine ; entered Lady Huntingdon's connexion, 1846 ; migrated to the independents ; published moral and religious works. [xxxiii. 131]

LETHBRIDGE, WALTER STEPHENS (1772-1831 ?), miniature-painter ; studied at the Royal Academy schools ; exhibited miniatures at the Academy, 1801-29. [xxxiii. 131]

LETHEBY, HENRY (1816-1876), analytical chemist ; M.B. London, 1842 ; lecturer on chemistry at the London Hospital ; for some years medical officer of health and analyst of foods for the city of London ; chief work, 'Food, its Varieties, Chemical Composition, etc.,' 1870. [xxxiii. 131]

LETHERLAND, JOSEPH (1699-1764), physician ; M.D. Leyden, 1724 ; M.D. Cambridge, by royal mandate, 1736 ; physician to St. Thomas's Hospital, 1736-58 ; F.R.C.P., 1737 ; physician to George III's queen, 1761 ; credited with being the first to draw attention in 1739 to the disease of diphtheria. [xxxiii. 131]

LETHIEULLIER, SMART (1701-1760), antiquary ; M.A. Trinity College, Oxford, 1723 ; formed collections and drawings of antiquities and English fossils ; F.R.S. and F.S.A. [xxxiii. 132]

LETHINGTON, LORD (1496-1586). [See MAITLAND, SIR RICHARD.]

LETHLOBOR (*d.* 871), Irish king ; defeated the Danes, 826 ; repulsed an invasion made by greater Ulster. 853 ; became king of all lesser Ulster or Ulidia. [xxxiii. 133]

LETTICE, JOHN (1737-1832), poet and divine : of Sidney Sussex College, Cambridge ; M.A., 1764 ; Seatonian prizeman, 1764 ; chaplain and secretary to British embassy at Copenhagen, 1768-72 ; published 'Letters on a Tour through various parts of Scotland in 1792,' 1794, and translations from the Italian and Latin. [xxxiii. 133]

LETTOU, JOHN (*fl.* 1480), printer ; the first to set up a printing press in the city of London. [xxxiii. 133]

LETTS, THOMAS (1803-1873), inventor of 'Letts's Diaries' ; bookbinder from 1835, devoting himself to the manufacture of diaries ; sold several hundred thousands annually. The diary business was purchased by Messrs. Cassell & Co. in 1885. [xxxiii. 134]

LETTSOM, JOHN COAKLEY (1744-1815), physician ; born in West Indies ; brought to England, 1750 ; studied at St. Thomas's Hospital, London ; returned to the West Indies, 1767 ; practised at Tortola ; studied at Edinburgh (1768) and at Leyden (1769) ; commenced practice in London, 1770 ; L.R.C.P., 1770 ; F.S.A., 1770 ; F.R.S., 1771 ; a

C c

successful quaker physician and philanthropist ; author of medical, biographical, and philanthropic works. [xxxiii. 134]

LETTSOM, WILLIAM NANSON (1796–1865), man of letters ; grandson of John Coakley Lettsom [q. v.] ; educated at Eton and Trinity College, Cambridge ; M.A., 1822 ; published 'The Fall of the Nebelungers,' 1850 ; edited William Sidney Walker's 'Shakespeare's Versification' (1854), and his 'Critical Examination of the Text of Shakespeare' (1860) ; aided Alexander Dyce [q. v.] in the preparation of his edition of Shakespeare. [xxxiii. 136]

LEVEN, EARLS OF. [See LESLIE, ALEXANDER, first EARL, 1580 ?–1661 ; MELVILLE, DAVID, third EARL, 1660–1728.]

LEVENS, PETER (*fl.* 1587), scholar and medical writer ; educated probably at Magdalen College, Oxford ; B.A., 1556 ; fellow, 1559 ; author of 'Manipulus Vocabulorum. A Dictionarie of English and Latine Wordes,' 1570, valuable as evidence of contemporary pronunciation. [xxxiii. 136]

LEVENS, ROBERT (1615–1650). [See LEVINZ.]

LEVER, SIR ASHTON (1729–1788), collector of the Leverian Museum ; educated at Corpus Christi College, Oxford ; first collected live birds, then shells, fossils, stuffed birds, all kinds of natural objects, savage costumes and weapons ; removed his museum to London, 1774 ; knighted, 1778 ; disposed of his museum by lottery in 1788. [xxxiii. 137]

LEVER, CHARLES JAMES (1806–1872), novelist ; nephew of Sir Ashton Lever [q. v.] ; entered Trinity College, Dublin, 1822 ; graduated, 1827 ; travelled in Holland and Germany, 1828, in Canada, 1829 ; studied medicine at Dublin ; M.B. Trinity College, Dublin, 1831 ; first instalment of 'Harry Lorrequer' produced in 'Dublin University Magazine,' 1837 ; practised medicine in Brussels, 1840–42 ; published 'Charles O'Malley,' first in 'Dublin University Magazine,' 1840, and 'Jack Hinton the Guardsman,' 1843 ; returned to Dublin and edited the 'Dublin University Magazine,' 1842–5 ; contributed to that magazine 'Tom Burke of Ours' and 'Arthur O'Leary,' 1844 ; published 'The O'Donoghue,' 1845, and the 'Knight of Gwynne,' 1847 ; settled at Florence and produced there 'Roland Cashel,' 1850, and 'The Dodd Family Abroad,' 1853–4 ; British consul at Spezzia, 1857 ; consul at Trieste, 1867–72 ; his last novel, 'Lord Kilgobbin,' 1872 (first issued in 'Cornhill Magazine') ; died at Trieste ; collected edition of his works was issued, 1876–8. [xxxiii. 138]

LEVER, CHRISTOPHER (*fl.* 1627), protestant writer and poet ; of Christ's College, Cambridge ; published religious poems and prose works, 1607–27. [xxxiii. 140]

LEVER, DARCY (1760 ?–1837), writer on seamanship ; nephew of Sir Ashton Lever [q. v.] ; published 'The Young Sea Officer's Sheet Anchor, or a Key to the Leading of Rigging and to Practical Seamanship,' 1808, for forty years the navy text-book. [xxxiii. 140]

LEVER or **LEAVER**, RALPH (*d.* 1585), master of Sherburn Hospital, Durham ; brother of Thomas Lever [q. v.] ; of St. John's College, Cambridge ; fellow, 1549 ; M.A., 1551 ; incorporated M.A. Oxford, 1560 ; archdeacon of Northumberland, 1566–73 ; canon of Durham, 1567 ; master of Sherburn Hospital, 1577 ; D.D. Cambridge, 1578 ; his work on chess published without his consent, 1563 ; published 'The Arte of Reason,' 1573, one of the rarest of early English treatises on logic. [xxxiii. 141]

LEVER or **LEAVER**, THOMAS (1521–1577), puritan divine ; brother of Ralph Lever [q. v.] ; M.A. St. John's College, Cambridge, 1545 ; fellow and college preacher, 1548 ; a leader of the extreme protestant reformers at Cambridge ; preached at court before Edward VI, 1550 ; master of St. John's College, Cambridge, 1551 ; B.D., 1552 ; at Mary's accession fled to Zurich, 1553 ; a hearer of Calvin at Geneva, 1554 ; minister of the English congregation at Aarau, 1556–9 ; returned to England, 1559 ; master of Sherburn Hospital, Durham, 1563 ; canon of Durham, 1564–7 ; published sermons and a religious treatise. [xxxiii. 142]

LEVERIDGE, RICHARD (1670 ?–1758), vocalist, song-writer, and composer ; sang at Drury Lane Theatre, 1703–8, at the Haymarket, London, 1708–13, at Lincoln's Inn Fields, 1715–32, at Covent Garden, 1732–51 ; said to have composed the music to Macbeth for the revival of 1702 ; his best-known songs 'All in the Downs' and 'The Roast Beef of Old England.' [xxxiii. 143]

LEVERTON, THOMAS (1743–1824), architect ; employed in the erection of dwelling-houses in London and the country ; exhibited designs at the Royal Academy, 1771–1803. [xxxiii. 144]

LEVESON, SIR RICHARD (1570–1605), vice-admiral of England ; volunteer against the Armada, 1588 ; had command in expedition against Cadiz, 1596 ; knighted, 1596 ; destroyed the Spanish fleet off Ireland, 1601 ; vice-admiral of England, 1604 ; marshal of the embassy to Spain to conclude the peace, 1605. [xxxiii. 145]

LEVESON-GOWER, LORD FRANCIS (1800–1857). [See EGERTON, FRANCIS, first EARL OF ELLESMERE.]

LEVESON-GOWER, GEORGE GRANVILLE, first DUKE OF SUTHERLAND (1758–1833), educated at Westminster and Christ Church, Oxford ; M.P., Newcastle-under-Lyme, 1778 and 1780 ; travelled in Europe, 1780–6 ; M.P., Staffordshire, 1787–98 ; ambassador to Paris, 1790–2 ; summoned as Baron Gower of Stittenham, Yorkshire, the original barony of his family, 1798 ; joint postmaster-general, 1799–1810 ; K.G., 1806 ; became possessed of the greater part of Sutherlandshire through his wife, Countess of Sutherland in her own right, 1785 ; inherited the Bridgewater estates from his uncle, the last Duke of Bridgewater, and by the death of his father, Marquis of Stafford, the estates of Stittenham (Yorkshire), Trentham (Staffordshire), Wolverhampton and Lilleshall (Shropshire), 1803 ; made 450 miles of roads and built 134 bridges in Sutherlandshire between 1812 and 1832 ; purchased Stafford House, London, 1827 ; created Duke of Sutherland, 1833. [xxxiii. 146]

LEVESON-GOWER, GEORGE GRANVILLE WILLIAM SUTHERLAND, third DUKE OF SUTHERLAND (1828–1892), succeeded to the dukedom, 1861 ; M.P., Sutherlandshire, 1852–61 ; improved his highland estates ; attended coronation of Czar Alexander II as member of the special mission, 1856 ; K.G., 1864 ; present at the opening of the Suez Canal, 1869 ; accompanied Edward VII, when Prince of Wales, to India, 1876. [xxxiii. 147]

LEVESON-GOWER, GRANVILLE, first MARQUIS OF STAFFORD (1721–1803), son of John Leveson-Gower, first earl Gower [q. v.] ; educated at Westminster and Christ Church, Oxford ; M.P., Bishop's Castle, 1744, Westminster, 1747 and 1749 ; lord of the admiralty, 1749–51 ; M.P., Lichfield, 1754 ; succeeded to the Upper House, 1754 ; lord privy seal, 1755–7 and 1785–94 ; master of the horse, 1757–60 ; keeper of the great wardrobe, 1760–3 ; lord chamberlain of the household, 1763–5 ; president of the council, 1767–79 and 1783–4 ; K.G., 1771 ; F.S.A., 1784 ; created marquis of the county of Stafford, 1786. [xxxiii. 148]

LEVESON-GOWER, LORD GRANVILLE, first EARL GRANVILLE (1773–1846), diplomatist ; youngest son of Granville Leveson-Gower, first marquis of Stafford [q. v.] ; entered Christ Church, Oxford, 1789 ; M.P., Lichfield, 1795–9 ; D.C.L., 1799 ; M.P., Staffordshire, 1799–1815 ; a lord of the treasury, 1800 ; privy councillor, 1804 ; ambassador extraordinary at St. Petersburg, 1804–5 ; created Viscount Granville, 1815 ; minister at Brussels ; ambassador at Paris, 1824–41 ; created Earl Granville and Baron Leveson of Stone, 1833. [xxxiii. 149]

LEVESON-GOWER, GRANVILLE GEORGE, second EARL GRANVILLE (1815–1891), statesman ; eldest son of Lord Granville Leveson-Gower, first earl Granville [q. v.] ; of Eton and Christ Church, Oxford ; attaché at the British embassy, Paris, 1835 ; Whig M.P., Morpeth, 1836 and 1837 ; B.A., 1839 ; under-secretary of state for foreign affairs, 1840–1 ; M.P., Lichfield, 1841 ; succeeded to peerage, 1846 ; vice-president of board of trade in Lord John Russell's ministry, 1848 ; paymaster of the forces, 1848 ; minister for foreign affairs, 1851–2 (under Lord John Russell), 1870–4, and 1880–5 (under William Ewart Gladstone) ; president of the council, 1852–4 ; chancellor of the duchy of Lancaster, 1854 ; leader of the House of Lords, when the liberals were in office, from 1855 ; chancellor of the university of London, 1856–91 ; K.G., 1857 ; president of the council, 1859 ; lord warden of the Cinque ports and hon. D.C.L., Oxford, 1865 ; secretary of state for the colonies, 1868–70 and 1886. [xxxiii. 150]

LEVESON-GOWER, HARRIET ELIZABETH GEORGIANA, DUCHESS OF SUTHERLAND (1806–1868), daughter of George Howard, sixth earl of Carlisle ; married (1823) George Granville Leveson-Gower, earl Gower, who succeeded his father as second Duke of Sutherland in

1833 ; mistress of the robes under liberal administrations, 1837–41, 1846–52, 1853–8, and 1859–61 ; a great friend of Queen Victoria. [xxxiii. 152]

LEVESON-GOWER, JOHN, first BARON GOWER (1675–1709) ; M.P., Newcastle-under-Lyme, Staffordshire, 1691–1703 ; created Baron Gower of Stittenham, 1703 ; privy councillor, 1703 ; chancellor of the duchy of Lancaster, 1703–6. [xxxiii. 153]

LEVESON-GOWER, JOHN, first EARL GOWER (d. 1754), eldest son of John Leveson-Gower, first baron Gower [q. v.] ; D.C.L. Oxford, 1732 ; one of the lords justices of the kingdom, 1740, 1743, 1745, 1748, 1750, and 1752 ; lord privy seal, 1742–3 and 1744 ; created Viscount Trentham and Earl Gower, 1746. [xxxiii. 153]

LEVESON-GOWER, JOHN (1740–1792), rear-admiral ; son of John Leveson-Gower, first earl Gower [q. v.] ; captain in the navy, 1760 ; commanded in Mediterranean, on coast of Guinea, in West Indies, and on the home and Newfoundland stations between 1760 and 1777 ; took part in action off Ushant, 1778 ; a junior lord of the admiralty, 1783–90 ; rear-admiral, 1787. [xxxiii. 153]

LEVETT, HENRY (1668–1725), physician ; educated at Charterhouse and Magdalen College, Oxford ; fellow of Exeter College, Oxford, 1688 ; M.A., 1694 ; M.D., 1699 ; F.R.C.P., 1708 ; physician to the Charterhouse, 1713–25 ; author of a letter in Latin on the treatment of small-pox, printed in the works of Dr. John Freind [q. v.], 1733. [xxxiii. 154]

LEVETT or **LEVET,** ROBERT (1701 ?–1782), 'that odd old surgeon whom Johnson kept in his house to tend the out-pensioners' ; made Johnson's acquaintance, c. 1746 ; became a regular inmate of Johnson's house, 1763 ; had some practice as a surgeon in London. [xxxiii. 154]

LEVI, DAVID (1740–1799), Jewish controversialist ; published 'A Succinct Account of the Rites and Ceremonies of the Jews . . . and the Opinion of Dr. Humphrey Prideaux . . . refuted,' 1783 ; published 'Lingua Sacra,' a Hebrew grammar, in weekly parts, 1785–7 ; replied (1787 and 1789) to Joseph Priestley's 'Letters to the Jews' ; replied to a fresh antagonist in 'Letters to Nathaniel Brassey Halhed, M.P.,' 1795 ; his 'Defence of the Old Testament in a Series of Letters addressed to Thomas Paine,' first published in New York, 1797. He also published the Pentateuch in Hebrew and English, and an English translation of the prayers used by the London congregations of Jews (1789–93), and 'Dissertations of the Prophecies of the Old Testament,' 3 vols., published, 1793–1800. [xxxiii. 155]

LEVI, LEONE (1821–1888), jurist and statistician ; born in Ancona ; settled at Liverpool as a merchant and was naturalised ; published pamphlets advocating the establishment in commercial centres of general representative chambers of commerce, 1849–50 ; hon. secretary, Liverpool chamber of commerce ; published his great work on commercial law, 1850–2 ; appointed to the newly created chair of commerce at King's College, London, 1852 ; F.S.A. and published his lectures as 'Manual of the Mercantile Law of Great Britain and Ireland,' 1854 ; his chief work on statistics, a periodical summary of parliamentary papers, published in eighteen volumes, 1856–68 ; his 'History of British Commerce and of the Economic Progress of the British Nation, 1763–1870,' published, 1872 ; vice-president of the Statistical Society, 1885. [xxxiii. 156]

LÉVIGNAC, ABBÉ DE (1769–1833). [See MACCARTHY, NICHOLAS TUITE.]

LEVINGE, SIR RICHARD, first baronet (d. 1724), Irish judge ; barrister, Inner Temple, 1678 ; recorder of Chester, 1686 ; M.P., Chester, 1690–2 ; solicitor-general for Ireland, 1690–4 and 1704–11 ; knighted, 1692 ; M.P. for Blessington in Irish House of Commons and speaker of the house, 1692–5 ; M.P. for Longford, 1695–1700 and 1703 ; created baronet, 1704 ; M.P., Derby, 1710 ; attorney-general for Ireland, 1711 ; M.P., Kilkenny, 1713 ; lord chief-justice of Irish common pleas, 1720–4 ; his correspondence on 'Various Points of State and Domestic Policy,' privately printed, 1877. [xxxiii. 158]

LEVINGE, SIR RICHARD GEORGE AUGUSTUS, seventh baronet (1811–1884), soldier and writer ; entered the army, 1828 ; lieutenant, 1834 ; served in the Canadian rebellion of 1837–8 ; lieutenant-colonel in the militia, 1846 ; succeeded to baronetcy, 1848 ; high sheriff for Westmeath, 1851 ; M.P. for co. Westmeath, 1857 and 1859 ; author of 'Echoes from the Backwoods,' 1846, 'Historical Notices of the Levinge Family,' 1853, 'Historical Records of the Forty-third Regiment, Monmouthshire Light Infantry,' 1868, and other works. [xxxiii. 159]

LEVINZ, BAPTIST (1644–1693), bishop of Sodor and Man ; brother of Sir Creswell Levinz [q. v.] ; educated at Magdalen Hall and College, Oxford ; M.A., 1666 ; Whyte's professor of moral philosophy, Oxford, 1677–82 ; bishop of Sodor and Man, 1685 ; prebendary of Winchester, 1691 ; contributed to 'Epicædia Universitatis Oxoniensis in obitum Georgii Ducis Albemarliæ,' 1670. [xxxiii. 159]

LEVINZ, SIR CRESWELL (1627–1701), judge ; brother of Baptist Levinz [q. v.] ; of Trinity College, Cambridge ; barrister, Gray's Inn, 1661 ; knighted, 1678 ; king's counsel, 1678 ; attorney-general, 1679 ; sat on the bench of common pleas, 1680–6 ; one of the counsel for the seven bishops, 1688. From manuscripts left by him was published in 1722 'The Reports of Sir Creswell Levinz, Knight.' [xxxiii. 160]

LEVINZ, LEVENS, or **LEVINGE,** ROBERT (1615–1650), royalist ; uncle of Sir Creswell Levinz [q. v.], Baptist Levinz [q. v.], and William Levinz [q. v.] ; educated at Lincoln College, Oxford ; B.A., 1634 ; D.C.L., 1642 ; fought for Charles I ; employed by Charles II to raise troops in England, 1650 ; arrested, condemned by court-martial, and hanged. [xxxiii. 161]

LEVINZ, WILLIAM (1625–1698), president of St. John's College, Oxford ; brother of Sir Creswell Levinz [q. v.] ; educated at Merchant Taylors' School, London, and St. John's College, Oxford, 1645 ; M.A., 1649 ; regius professor of Greek, 1665–98 ; president of his college, 1673 ; sub-dean of Wells, 1678 ; canon, 1682. [xxxiii. 161]

LEVIZAC, JEAN PONS VICTOR LECOUTZ DE (d. 1813), writer on the French language ; born in Languedoc ; canon in the cathedral of Vabres, and probably vicar-general of the diocese of St. Omer ; at the revolution fled to London, where he taught French and published books on the French language, 1797–1808. [xxxiii. 161]

LEVY, AMY (1861–1889), poetess and novelist ; educated at Newnham College, Cambridge ; her 'Xantippe and other Poems,' published, 1881, 'A Minor Poet and other Verse,' 1884, 'A London Plane Tree and other Poems,' and 'Reuben Sachs,' a novel, 1889 ; committed suicide. [xxxiii. 162]

LEVY, JOSEPH MOSES (1812–1888), founder of the 'Daily Telegraph' ; purchased a printing establishment ; took over the 'Daily Telegraph and Courier' and issued it as the 'Daily Telegraph,' the first London daily penny paper, 1855. [xxxiii. 162]

LEWES. [See also LEWIS.]

LEWES, CHARLES LEE (1740–1803), actor ; his first recorded appearance at Covent Garden, 1763 ; played young Marlow in first performance of 'She Stoops to Conquer,' 1773 ; at Covent Garden as leading comedian till 1783 ; at Drury Lane, 1783–5 ; at Edinburgh, 1787 ; played in Dublin in low comedy, 1792–3 ; published theatrical compilations. [xxxiii. 163]

LEWES, GEORGE HENRY (1817–1878), miscellaneous writer ; grandson of Charles Lee Lewes [q. v.] ; tried various employments, among them that of actor ; contributed to the quarterlies (1840–9) and wrote a play and two novels ; published 'Biographical History of Philosophy,' 1845–6 ; co-operated with Thornton Leigh Hunt [q. v.] in the 'Leader,' 1850 ; made the acquaintance of Miss Evans [see CROSS, MARY ANN], 1851, and went to Germany with her in 1854, and for the rest of his life lived with her as her husband ; his 'Life of Goethe,' the standard English work on the subject, published, 1855 ; studied physiology, and published 'Seaside Studies,' 1858, 'Physiology of Common Life,' 1859, 'Studies in Animal Life,' 1862, and 'Aristotle,' the first instalment of a projected history of science, 1864 ; edited 'Fortnightly Review,' 1865–6 ; his 'Problems of Life and Mind' published at intervals, 1873–9 ; his criticisms on the drama contributed to the 'Pall Mall Gazette' published, 1875. [xxxiii. 164]

LEWGAR, JOHN (1602–1665), Roman catholic controversialist ; M.A. Trinity College, Oxford, 1622 ; published controversial works. [xxxiii. 167]

LEWICKE, EDWARD (*fl.* 1562), poet; author of 'The most wonderfull and pleasaunt History of Titus and Gisippus,' 1562, a rhymed paraphrase of Sir Thomas Eliot's prose version of a tale of Boccaccio.
[xxxiii. 168]

LEWIN, JOHN WILLIAM (*fl.* 1805), naturalist; brother of William Lewin (*d.* 1795) [q. v.]; settled in Paramatta, New South Wales; published 'The Birds of New Holland,' 1808-22, and 'Prodromus (*sic*) Entomology,' 1805, a history of the lepidoptera of New South Wales.
[xxxiii. 170]

LEWIN, SIR JUSTINIAN (1613-1673), master in chancery; grandson of William Lewin (*d.* 1598) [q. v.]; of Pembroke College, Oxford; D.C.L., 1637; official to the archdeacon of Norfolk, 1631; judge marshal of the army in the Scottish expedition, 1639; a master in chancery, 1641; promoted Charles II's interest in Norfolk; knighted, 1661.
[xxxiii. 169]

LEWIN, THOMAS (1805-1877), miscellaneous writer; educated at Merchant Taylors' School and Worcester and Trinity Colleges, Oxford; M.A., 1831; conveyancing counsel to the court of chancery, 1852-77; F.S.A., 1863; chief works, 'Practical Treatise on the Law of Trusts and Trustees,' 1837, an authoritative text-book, 'The Life and Epistles of St. Paul,' 1851, and archæological pamphlets.
[xxxiii. 168]

LEWIN, WILLIAM (*d.* 1598), civilian; of Christ's College, Cambridge; M.A., 1565; public orator, 1570-1; LL.D., 1576; judge of the prerogative court of Canterbury, 1576-98; chancellor of the diocese of Rochester and commissary of the faculties; M.P., Rochester, 1586, 1589, and 1593; a master of chancery, 1593; friend of Gabriel Harvey [q. v.]; author of the Latin epistle to the jesuits before Harvey's 'Ciceronianus,' 1577.
[xxxiii. 168]

LEWIN, WILLIAM (*d.* 1795), naturalist; F.L.S., 1791; published an unscientific book, 'The Birds of Great Britain accurately figured,' 7 vols., 1789-95, of which he executed the drawings; and published vol. i. of 'The Insects of Great Britain systematically arranged, accurately engraved, and painted from Nature,' 1795.
[xxxiii. 170]

LEWINS or **LEWENS**, EDWARD JOHN (1756-1828), United Irishman; educated in France; envoy of the Society of United Irishmen at Hamburg, 1797; confidential agent at Paris; banished from Ireland by act of parliament at the union; inspector of studies at the university of Paris; exercised great influence in France during reign of Charles X.
[xxxiii. 170]

LEWIS. [See also LEWES.]

LEWIS OF CAERLEON (15th cent.) [See CAERLEON, LEWIS OF.]

LEWIS GLYN COTHI (*fl.* 1450-1486), Welsh bard; also sometimes called LEWIS Y GLYN or LLYWELYN GLYN COTHI; took the Lancastrian side in the wars of the roses; his poems, about 150 of which were published for the Cymmrodorion Society (1837), valuable as illustrating the part played by the Welsh in the wars of the roses.
[xxxiii. 183]

LEWIS, ANDREW (1720 ?-1781), soldier; volunteer in the Ohio expedition, 1754; major in Washington's Virginia regiment, 1755; commanded Sandy Creek expedition, 1756; taken prisoner at Fort Duquesne, 1758; brigadier-general, 1774; delegate to the Virginia conventions, 1775; took popular side in the war of independence and was brigadier-general of the continental army, 1776-1777; died in Virginia.
[xxxiii. 171]

LEWIS, CHARLES (1753-1795), painter of still-life; exhibited at the Society of Artists and Royal Academy, 1772-91.
[xxxiii. 171]

LEWIS, CHARLES (1786-1836), bookbinder; brother of Frederick Christian Lewis (1779-1856) [q. v.] and of George Robert Lewis [q. v.]; employed by Beckford on the Fonthill library.
[xxxiii. 172]

LEWIS, CHARLES GEORGE (1808-1880), engraver; son of Frederick Christian Lewis (1779-1856) [q. v.]; instructed by his father; his best-known plates engraved between 1830 and 1873.
[xxxiii. 172]

LEWIS, CHARLES JAMES (1830-1892), painter; his best work in water-colour; painted small domestic subjects and landscapes; member of the Royal Institute of Painters in Water-colours, 1882.
[xxxiii. 173]

LEWIS or **LEWES**, DAVID (1520 ?-1584), civilian; educated at All Souls College, Oxford; B.C.L., 1540; fellow, 1541; principal of New Inn Hall, Oxford, 1545-8; D.C.L., and admitted at Doctors' Commons, 1548; a master in chancery, 1553; M.P., Steyning, 1553; M.P., Monmouthshire, 1554-5; judge of the high court of admiralty, 1558-75; first principal of Jesus College, Oxford, 1571-2; joint commissioner of the admiralty, 1575.
[xxxiii. 173]

LEWIS, DAVID (1617-1679). [See BAKER, CHARLES.]

LEWIS, DAVID (1683 ?-1760), poet; probably educated at Westminster and Jesus College, Oxford; B.A., 1702; published 'Miscellaneous Poems by Several Hands,' 1726, 'Philip of Macedon' (tragedy), 1727, acted three times, and 'Collection of Miscellany Poems,' 1730.
[xxxiii. 174]

LEWIS, EDWARD (1701-1784), miscellaneous writer; M.A. St. John's College, Cambridge, 1726; held several livings and wrote and preached against Roman catholicism.
[xxxiii. 174]

LEWIS, ERASMUS (1670-1754), the friend of Swift and Pope; educated at Westminster and Trinity College, Cambridge; B.A., 1693; wrote news-letters from Berlin, 1698; secretary to the English ambassador at Paris, 1701, to Robert Harley, 1704, and secretary at Brussels, 1708; came to London, 1710; M.P., Lostwithiel, Cornwall, 1713; intimate with Prior, Arbuthnot, Pope, Gay, and Swift.
[xxxiii. 175]

LEWIS, EVAN (1828-1869), independent minister; B.A. London; served various independent chapels; F.R.G.S.; fellow of the Ethnological Society; published religious works.
[xxxiii. 176]

LEWIS, FREDERICK CHRISTIAN (1779-1856), engraver and landscape-painter; brother of Charles Lewis (1786-1836) [q. v.]; studied under J. C. Stadler and in the schools of the Royal Academy; aquatinted most of Girtin's etchings of Paris, 1803; made transcripts of drawings by the great masters for Ottley's 'Italian School of Design,' 1808-12; executed plates for Chamberlaine's 'Original Designs of the most celebrated Masters in the Royal Collection,' 1812; engraved Sir Thomas Lawrence's crayon portraits; engraver of drawings to Princess Charlotte, Prince Leopold, George IV, William IV, and Queen Victoria; painted landscapes, chiefly of Devonshire scenery; published several volumes of plates illustrating the Devonshire rivers between 1821 and 1843, and also etchings of the 'Scenery of the Rivers of England and Wales,' 1845-7.
[xxxiii. 177]

LEWIS, FREDERICK CHRISTIAN (1813-1875), painter; son of Frederick Christian Lewis (1779-1856) [q. v.]; studied under Sir Thomas Lawrence [q. v.]; went to India, 1834, and painted pictures of durbars for native princes, engraved by his father, and published in England; died at Genoa.
[xxxiii. 177]

LEWIS, GEORGE (1763-1822), dissenting divine; issued a manual of divinity in Welsh which became very popular, 1796, and a valuable Welsh commentary on the New Testament, 1802; head of Abergavenny Theological College, 1812-22.
[xxxiii. 178]

LEWIS, SIR GEORGE CORNEWALL, second baronet (1806-1863), statesman and author; son of Sir Thomas Frankland Lewis [q. v.]; of Eton and Christ Church, Oxford; M.A., 1831; assistant-commissioner to inquire into the condition of the poorer classes in Ireland, 1833, and into the state of religious and other instruction, 1834; joint-commissioner to inquire into the affairs of Malta, 1836-8; a poor-law commissioner for England and Wales, 1839-47; liberal M.P., Herefordshire, 1847; secretary to board of control, 1847; under-secretary for the home department, 1848; financial secretary to the treasury, 1850-2; editor of the 'Edinburgh Review,' to which he contributed eighteen articles, 1852-5; succeeded to baronetcy, 1855; M.P. for Radnor boroughs, 1855-63; published 'Enquiry into the Credibility of the Early Roman History,' 1855; chancellor of the exchequer, 1855-1858; home secretary, 1859-61; secretary for war, 1861-3; published, among other works on politics, 'A Treatise on the Methods of Observation and Reasoning in Politics' (1852).
[xxxiii. 178]

LEWIS, GEORGE ROBERT (1782–1871), painter of landscapes and portraits; brother of Charles Lewis (1786–1836) [q. v.]; studied at the Royal Academy schools; exhibited landscapes, 1805–7; accompanied Thomas Frognall Dibdin [q. v.] as draughtsman on his continental journey, and illustrated Dibdin's 'Bibliographical and Picturesque Tour through France and Germany' (published, 1821); etched 'Groups illustrating the Physiognomy, Manners, and Character of the People of France and Germany,' 1823; exhibited portraits and landscapes and figure-subjects, 1820–59. [xxxiii. 183]

LEWIS, GRIFFITH GEORGE (1784–1859), lieutenant-general; colonel-commandant, royal engineers; educated at Royal Military Academy, Woolwich; lieutenant, 1803; fought at Maida, 1806; captain, 1807; served in Spanish campaign under Wellington, 1813; served in Newfoundland, 1819–27; lieutenant-colonel, 1825; commanded royal engineers at Jersey, 1830–6; at the Cape of Good Hope, 1836–42; in Ireland, 1842–7; at Portsmouth, 1847–51; joint-editor of the 'Professional Papers of the Corps of Royal Engineers,' and of the 'Corps Papers,' 1847–54; governor of the Royal Military Academy, Woolwich, 1851–6; lieutenant-general, 1858. [xxxiii. 184]

LEWIS, HUBERT (1825–1884), jurist; educated at Emmanuel College, Cambridge; B.A., 1848; barrister, Middle Temple, 1854; published 'Principles of Conveyancing,' 1863, 'Principles of Equity Drafting,' 1865; his 'Ancient Laws of Wales' published, 1889. [xxxiii. 185]

LEWIS, JAMES HENRY (1786–1853), stenographer; taught and lectured on writing and stenography in the principal towns of the United Kingdom; his system of shorthand, 'The Art of Writing with the Velocity of Speech,' issued anonymously, 1814; his 'Historical Account of the Rise and Progress of Shorthand,' 1816, still the best history of the subject. [xxxiii. 185]

LEWIS, JOHN (1675–1747), author; educated at Exeter College, Oxford; B.A., 1697; ordained, 1698; vicar of Minster, Kent, 1709–47; M.A., 1712; master of Eastbridge Hospital, Canterbury, 1717; chiefly known by his biographies of Wycliffe (1720 and 1723), Caxton (1737), Pecock (1744), and Bishop Fisher (first printed, 1855); published valuable topographical works dealing mainly with Kent; made important contributions to religious history and bibliography. [xxxiii. 186]

LEWIS, JOHN DELAWARE (1828–1884), miscellaneous writer; born in St. Petersburg; educated at Eton and Trinity College, Cambridge; published 'Sketches of Cantabs,' 1849; M.A., 1853; barrister, Lincoln's Inn, 1858; M.P., Devonport, 1868–74; wrote miscellaneous works in French and English. [xxxiii. 188]

LEWIS, JOHN FREDERICK (1805–1876), painter of Italian, Spanish, and Oriental subjects; son of Frederick Christian Lewis (1779–1856) [q.v.]; painted and exhibited animal subjects, 1820–32; member of the Water-colour Society, 1829; visited Spain, 1832–4; painted Spanish subjects until about 1841; travelled in the East, 1839–51; painted oriental subjects, 1850–76, based on sketches made during his travels; R.A., 1865. [xxxiii. 188]

LEWIS, JOYCE or JOCASTA (d. 1557), martyr; daughter of Thomas Curzon of Croxall, Staffordshire; married, first, Sir George Appleby, and, secondly, Thomas Lewis; became a protestant, was imprisoned, 1556, and burned. [xxxiii. 190]

LEWIS, LEOPOLD DAVID (1828–1890), dramatist; dramatised 'The Bells' from Erckmann-Chatrian's 'Le Juif Polonais,' produced 1871; author of 'The Wandering Jew,' 1873, 'Give a Dog a bad Name,' 1876, and 'The Foundlings,' 1881; conducted 'The Mask,' 1868, and published 'A Peal of Merry Bells' (tales), 1880. [xxxiii. 191]

LEWIS, LADY MARIA THERESA (1803–1865), biographer; granddaughter of Thomas Villiers, first earl of Clarendon [q. v.], and sister of George William Frederick Villiers, fourth earl of Clarendon [q. v.]; married, first, Thomas Henry Lister [q. v.], 1830; and, secondly, Sir George Cornewall Lewis [q. v.], 1844; published 'The Lives of the Friends and Contemporaries of Lord Chancellor Clarendon,' 1852; edited 'Extracts of the Journals of Miss Berry,' 1865. [xxxiii. 191]

LEWIS, MARK (fl. 1678), financial and miscellaneous writer; invented a new method of teaching (patented), and published works expounding it between 1670? and 1675?; proposed quack schemes of financial reforms in pamphlets, issued, 1676–8. [xxxiii. 191]

LEWIS, MATTHEW GREGORY (1775–1818), author of the 'Monk'; of Westminster and Christ Church, Oxford; attaché to the British embassy at the Hague, 1794; published 'The Monk,' 1795, and immediately became famous; M.P., Hindon, 1796–1802; brought out the 'Castle Spectre' at Drury Lane, 1798; made Walter Scott's acquaintance (1798), and procured the publication of his translation of 'Goetz von Berlichingen,' 1799; visited his West Indian property in order to arrange for the proper treatment of the slaves, 1815–16 and 1817–18; died at sea on his way home. His writings are memorable on account of their influence on Scott's early poetical efforts; some of his numerous dramas and tales were translated from the German. His 'Journal of a West Indian Proprietor,' 1834, is interesting as showing the condition of the negroes in Jamaica at the time. [xxxiii. 192]

LEWIS MORGANWG, i.e. of Glamorganshire (fl. 1500–1540), Welsh bard; author of a poem on St. Iltutus [see ILLTYD or ILTUTUS], entitled 'Cowydd St. Illtyd,' printed with an English translation in the Iolo MSS. [xxxiii. 194]

LEWIS, OWEN, also known as LEWIS OWEN (1532–1594), bishop of Cassano; of Winchester and New College, Oxford; B.C.L., 1559; went to Douay University, 1561; appointed regius professor of law at Douay; canon of Cambray Cathedral and archdeacon of Hainault; bishop of Cassano, 1588; died at Rome. [xxxiii. 194]

LEWIS, SAMUEL, the younger (d. 1862), topographer; son of Samuel Lewis the elder [q. v.]; author of 'Islington as it was and as it is,' 1854, and other works. [xxxiii. 195]

LEWIS, SAMUEL, the elder (d. 1865), publisher; his best-known publications, topographical dictionaries, edited by Joseph Haydn [q. v.], and atlases, 1831–42. [xxxiii. 195]

LEWIS, SAMUEL SAVAGE (1836–1891), librarian of Corpus Christi College, Cambridge; grandson of George Lewis [q. v.]; educated at the City of London School and St. John's College, Cambridge; studied farming in Canada, 1857–60; migrated to Corpus Christi College, Cambridge, 1865, and fellow, 1869; librarian of Corpus Christi College, 1870–91; M.A., 1872; F.S.A., 1872; ordained, 1872; a diligent antiquary; bequeathed his collections of coins, gems, and vases to his college. [xxxiii. 195]

LEWIS, STUART (1756?–1818), Scottish poet; roamed over Scotland as 'the mendicant bard'; produced his poem, 'Fair Helen of Kirkconnell,' 1796, with an interesting preface on the history of the ballad on the same theme; 'O'er the Muir' the most noteworthy of his lyrics. [xxxiii. 196]

LEWIS, THOMAS (1689–1749?), controversialist; of Corpus Christi College, Oxford; B.A., 1711; ordained, 1713; forced to hide on account of the libellous nature of his periodical publication, 'The Scourge, in Vindication of the Church of England,' 1717; continued to issue controversial writings, 1719–35. [xxxiii. 196]

LEWIS, SIR THOMAS FRANKLAND, first baronet (1780–1855), politician; grandson of Sir Thomas Frankland [q. v.]; of Eton and Christ Church, Oxford; lieutenant-colonel of the Radnorshire militia, 1806–15; M.P., Beaumaris, 1812–26, Ennis, 1826–8; Radnorshire, 1828–34, Radnor boroughs, 1847–55; member of commission to inquire into Irish revenue, 1821, of commission to inquire into revenue of Great Britain and Ireland, 1822, and of commission on Irish education, 1825–8; joint-secretary to the treasury, 1827; vice-president of the board of trade and privy councillor, 1828; treasurer of the navy, 1830; chairman of the poor-law commission, 1834–9; created baronet, 1846. [xxxiii. 197]

LEWIS, THOMAS TAYLOR (1801–1858), geologist and antiquary; M.A. St. John's College, Cambridge, 1828; investigated the Silurian system; edited for the Camden Society the 'Letters of Lady Brilliana Harley,' 1853. [xxxiii. 198]

LEWIS, TITUS (1773–1811), baptist minister; in charge of baptist church at Carmarthen; published Welsh theological works, 1802–11. [xxxiii. 198]

LEWIS, WILLIAM (1592–1667), master of the hospital of St. Cross, Winchester, and canon of Winchester; educated at Hart Hall, Oxford; B.A. and fellow of Oriel, 1608; M.A., 1612; chaplain to Lord Chancellor Bacon; provost of Oriel, 1618–21; in the service of George Villiers, duke of Buckingham, 1627–8; canon of Winchester, 1627; D.D. Oxford, 1627; chaplain to Charles I and master of the hospital of St. Cross, 1628; D.D. Cambridge, 1629; ejected under the Commonwealth; reinstated, 1660. [xxxiii. 198]

LEWIS, WILLIAM (1714–1781), chemist; M.A. Christ Church, Oxford, 1737; M.B., 1741; M.D., 1745; delivered the oration at opening of Radcliffe Library, 1749; chief works, 'The New Dispensatory,' 1753, and 'Experimental History of the Materia Medica,' 1761. [xxxiii. 199]

LEWIS, WILLIAM (1787–1870), writer on chess and chess-player, also a teacher of chess; published elementary works on chess between 1814 and 1835. [xxxiii. 199]

LEWIS, WILLIAM GARRETT (1821–1885), baptist minister; obtained clerkship in post office, 1840; became a baptist, and was chosen minister; secretary of the London Baptist Association, which he helped to found, 1865–9, and president, 1870; editor of the 'Baptist Magazine' for twenty years. [xxxiii. 200]

LEWIS, WILLIAM THOMAS (1748 ?–1811), called 'Gentleman' Lewis, actor; great-grandson of Erasmus Lewis [q. v.]; appeared at Dublin, 1770–2, at Covent Garden, London, 1773–1809; played more characters, original and established, than almost any other English comedian; created, among other parts, Faulkland in the 'Rivals,' Doricourt in the 'Belle's Stratagem,' and Jeremy Diddler in 'Raising the Wind'; deputy-manager of Covent Garden, 1782–1804; lessee of the Liverpool Theatre, 1803–1811. [xxxiii. 200]

LEWSON, JANE (1700 ?–1816), commonly called LADY LEWSON; eccentric centenarian; her maiden name Vaughan; after the death of her husband (1726) lived in close retirement. Her peculiarities possibly suggested Dickens's character of Miss Havisham. [xxxiii. 202]

LEWYS AP RHYS AP OWAIN (d. 1616 ?). [See DWNN, LEWYS.]

LEXINGTON, BARONS. [See SUTTON, ROBERT, first BARON, 1594–1668; SUTTON, ROBERT, second BARON, 1661–1723.]

LEXINTON, HENRY DE (d. 1258), bishop of Lincoln; brother of John de Lexinton [q. v.]; dean of Lincoln, 1245; bishop of Lincoln, 1253–8. [xxxiii. 203]

LEXINTON or **LESSINGTON**, JOHN DE (d. 1257), baron, judge, and often described as keeper of the great seal; a clerk in chancery; had custody of great seal for short periods in 1238, 1242, 1247, 1249, 1253; king's seneschal, 1247; chief-justice of the forests north of the Trent, and governor of several northern castles, 1255; put in fetters the Jew Copin, supposed murderer, with his co-religionists, of Hugh of Lincoln [q. v.], 1255. [xxxiii. 202]

LEXINTON, OLIVER DE (d. 1299). [See SUTTON.]

LEXINTON or **LESSINGTON**, ROBERT DE (d. 1250), judge; prebendary of Southwell; senior of the justices, 1234; chief of the itinerant justices for the northern division, 1240. [xxxiii. 203]

LEXINTON or **LESSINGTON**, STEPHEN DE (fl. 1250), abbot of Clairvaux; studied at Paris and Oxford; prebendary of Southwell, 1214; abbot of Savigny, Normandy, 1229; abbot of Clairvaux, 1243–55; founded house in Paris for scholars of his order, 1244. [xxxiii. 204]

LEY, HUGH (1790–1837), physician; M.D. Edinburgh, 1813; L.R.C.P., 1818; published 'An Essay on Laryngismus Stridulus, or Crouplike Inspiration of Infants,' the first work containing a full pathological description of the malady, 1836. [xxxiii. 204]

LEY, JAMES, first EARL OF MARLBOROUGH (1550–1629), judge; of Brasenose College, Oxford; B.A., 1574; barrister, Lincoln's Inn, 1584; M.P., Westbury, 1597–8, 1604–5, and 1609–11; bencher of Lincoln's Inn, 1600; reader, 1602; serjeant-at-law and knighted, 1603; lord chief-justice of king's bench in Ireland, 1604; commissioner of the great seal at Dublin, 1605; commissioner

for the plantation of Ulster, 1608; attorney of the court of wards and liveries in England, 1608; governor of Lincoln's Inn, 1609–22; M.P., Bath, 1614; created baronet, 1619; lord chief-justice of king's bench, 1622–4; lord high treasurer and privy councillor, 1624, and created Baron Ley of Ley in Devonshire, 1624; Earl of Marlborough, 1626; president of the council, 1628; member of Elizabethan Society of Antiquaries. [xxxiii. 205]

LEY, JAMES, third EARL OF MARLBOROUGH (1618–1665), naval captain; grandson of James Ley, first earl of Marlborough [q. v.]; succeeded to the title, 1638; royalist commander, 1643; established a colony, which soon failed, at Santa Cruz, West Indies, 1645; commanded the squadron which went to the East Indies to receive Bombay from the Portuguese, 1661; nominated governor of Jamaica, 1664; killed in naval action with Dutch, 1665. [xxxiii. 207]

LEY, JOHN (1583–1662), puritan divine; M.A. Christ Church, Oxford, 1608; prebendary of Chester, 1627; took the solemn league and covenant, 1643; president of Sion College, 1645; a 'trier,' 1653; held various rectories, and wrote religious works. [xxxiii. 207]

LEYBOURN, THOMAS (1770–1840), mathematician; edited the 'Mathematical Repository,' 1799–1835; published 'A Synopsis of Data for the Construction of Triangles,' 1802; teacher of mathematics at the Military College, Sandhurst, 1802–39. [xxxiii. 208]

LEYBOURN, WILLIAM (1626–1700 ?), mathematician; teacher of mathematics and professional land surveyor; joint-author of the first book on astronomy written in English, 'Urania Practica,' 1648; published 'The Compleat Surveyor,' 1653, 'Arithmetick, Vulgar, Decimal, and Instrumental,' 1657, 'The Line of Proportion or [of] Numbers, commonly called Gunter's Line, made easie,' 1667; 'Cursus Mathematicus,' 1690, and 'Panarithmologia,' 1693 (the earliest ready-reckoner known in English). [xxxiii. 208]

LEYBOURNE, **LEYBURN**, **LEMBURN**, or **LEEBURN**, ROGER DE (d. 1271), warden of the Cinque ports; accompanied Henry III to Gascony, 1253; served against Llywelyn of Wales, 1256; sided with the barons, 1258, and was consequently deprived of all his revenues, c. 1260; took to marauding; associated himself with Simon de Montfort, 1263; reconciled to the king, 1264; took the king's side in the battle of Evesham, 1265. [xxxiii. 209]

LEYBOURNE, WILLIAM DE (d. 1309), baron; son of Roger de Leybourne [q. v.]; served in Wales, 1277; constable of Pevensey, 1282; described as 'admiral of the sea of the king of England,' 1297; served in Scotland, 1299–1300 and 1304. [xxxiii. 211]

LEYBURN, GEORGE (1593–1677), Roman catholic divine; studied at Douay, 1617–25; missioner in England, 1630; chaplain to Queen Henrietta Maria; forced to retire to Douay, where he taught philosophy and divinity; D.D. Rheims; returned to England, but during the civil war retired to France and rendered services to the royalist party; president of the English college at Douay, 1652–70; died at Châlon-sur-Saône; author of religious works. [xxxiii. 212]

LEYBURN, JOHN (1620–1702), Roman catholic prelate; nephew of George Leyburn [q. v.]; educated at the English college, Douay; taught classics there; president, 1670–6; D.D.; vicar-apostolic of all England, 1685–8, and first vicar-apostolic of the London district, 1688; translated Kenelm Digby's treatise on the soul into Latin (Paris, 1651). [xxxiii. 213]

LEYCESTER, JOHN (fl. 1639), miscellaneous writer; B.A. Brasenose College, Oxford, 1622; works include 'A Manual of the Choicest Adagies,' 1623, and two poems, one on the death of Hampden, 1641, and another entitled 'England's Miraculous Preservation,' 1646. [xxxiii. 214]

LEYCESTER, SIR PETER, first baronet (1614–1678), antiquary; of Brasenose College, Oxford; entered Gray's Inn, 1632; took royalist side in the civil war; rewarded with a baronetcy, 1660; author of 'Historical Antiquities in two Books,' 1673; contributed to the controversy concerning the legitimacy of Amicia, wife of Ralph Mainwaring, his ancestor. [xxxiii. 214]

LEYDEN, JOHN (1775–1811), physician and poet; studied at Edinburgh University, 1790–7; contributed to the 'Edinburgh Literary Magazine'; contributed to Lewis's 'Tales of Wonder,' 1801; assisted Scott with earlier volumes of the 'Border Minstrelsy,' 1802; published 'Scottish Descriptive Poems,' 1802; M.D. St. Andrews; assistant-surgeon at Madras, 1803–5; settled at Calcutta, 1806; published his essay on the Indo-Persian, Indo-Chinese, and Dekkan languages, 1807; commissioner of the court of requests, Calcutta, 1809; assay-master of the mint, Calcutta, 1810; accompanied Lord Minto to Java, 1811; translated into English the 'Sejárah Maláyu' ('Malay Annals'), published 1821, and 'Commentaries of Baber,' published 1826; died at Cornelis, Java. [xxxii. 215]

LEYLAND, JOSEPH BENTLEY (1811–1851), sculptor; his most important works a statue of Dr. Beckwith of York, in York Minster, and a group of African bloodhounds. [xxxiii. 216]

LEYSON, THOMAS (1549–1608 ?), poet and physician; of Winchester and New College, Oxford; fellow, 1509–86; M.A., 1576; M.B. and proctor, 1583; practised physic at Bath; wrote Latin verses. [xxxiii. 217]

LHUYD. [See also LLOYD, LLWYD, and LOYD.]

LHUYD, EDWARD (1660–1709), Celtic scholar and naturalist; entered Jesus College, Oxford, 1682; keeper of the Ashmolean Museum, 1690–1709; published catalogue of the figured fossils in the Ashmolean, 1699; M.A., 1701; vol. i. of his 'Archæologia Britannica' published, 1707; F.R.S., 1708; superior beadle of divinity in Oxford University, 1709. [xxxiii. 217]

LIAFWINE, SAINT (fl. 755). [See LEBWIN.]

LIARDET, FRANCIS (1798–1863), captain in the navy; entered navy, 1809; served on the coast of Africa and on the North American station, 1810–14; lieutenant, 1824; on the South American station, 1833–8; commander and serving in the Mediterranean, 1838–40; obtained post rank, 1840; New Zealand Company's agent at Taranaki, 1841–2; published 'Professional Recollections on Points of Seamanship, Discipline,' &c., 1849, and 'The Midshipman's Companion,' 1851; one of the captains of Greenwich Hospital, 1856; published 'Friendly Hints to the Young Naval Lieutenant,' 1858. [xxxiii. 219]

LIART, MATTHEW (1736–1782 ?), engraver; apprenticed to Simon François Ravenet [q. v.]; published engravings after Benjamin West, P.R.A. [xxxiii. 220]

LIBBERTOUN, LORD (d. 1650). [See WINRAM, GEORGE.]

LICHFIELD. [See also LITCHFIELD.]

LICHFIELD, EARLS OF. [See STUART, BERNARD, titular earl, 1623 ?–1646; LEE, GEORGE HENRY, third EARL of the Lee family, 1718–1772.]

LICHFIELD, LEONARD (1604–1657), printer and author; printer to the university of Oxford; printed public papers for Charles I, 1642–6. [xxxiii. 220]

LICHFIELD, LEONARD (d. 1686), printer; son of Leonard Lichfield (1604–1657) [q. v.]; printed at Oxford 'The Oxford Gazette,' a folio half-sheet, containing the government's official notices, the earliest English periodical of the kind (1665–6), which was continued in London as 'The London Gazette.' [xxxiii. 221]

LICHFIELD, WILLIAM (d. 1447), divine and poet; D.D.; rector of All Hallows the Great, London; a famous preacher; left 3,083 sermons written in English with his own hand. [xxxiii. 221]

LIDDEL, DUNCAN (1561–1613), mathematician and physician; educated at Aberdeen; studied mathematics and physic at Frankfort-on-Oder; professor of mathematics at Helmstadt, 1591–1603; M.D. Helmstadt, 1596, and dean of the faculty of philosophy, 1599; prorector, 1604; returned to Scotland, 1607; endowed a professorship of mathematics in the Marischal College, Aberdeen, 1613; published medical works. [xxxiii. 221]

LIDDELL, HENRY GEORGE (1811–1898), dean of Christ Church, Oxford; of Charterhouse and Christ Church, Oxford; M.A., 1835; D.D., 1855; tutor, 1836, and censor, 1845, of Christ Church, Oxford; White's professor of moral philosophy, 1845; domestic chaplain to Prince Albert, 1846; head-master of Westminster School, 1846–55;

published (1843), with Robert Scott (1811–1887) [q. v.], 'Greek-English Lexicon,' which he revised alone for 7th edit., 1883; member of first Oxford University commission, 1852; dean of Christ Church, 1855–91; took prominent part in administrative reforms at Christ Church; vice-chancellor, 1870–4; hon. LL.D. Edinburgh, 1884; hon. D.C.L. Oxford, 1893; his publications include 'A History of Ancient Rome,' 1855. [Suppl. iii. 94]

LIDDELL, HENRY THOMAS, first EARL OF RAVENSWORTH (1797–1878), educated at Eton and St. John's College, Cambridge; M.P., Northumberland, 1826; North Durham, 1837–47; Liverpool, 1853–5; succeeded his father as second Baron Ravensworth (of a second creation), 1855; created Earl of Ravensworth and Baron Eslington, 1874; published original poems, and translations from Horace and Virgil. [xxxiii. 222]

LIDDELL, SIR JOHN (1794–1868), director-general of the medical department of the royal navy, 1854–64; M.D. Edinburgh; entered the navy as assistant-surgeon, 1812; L.R.C.S., 1821; director of the hospital at Malta, 1831; inspector of fleets and hospitals, 1844; F.R.S., 1846; deputy inspector-general of Haslar Hospital; inspector-general of Royal Hospital, Greenwich; knighted, 1848; honorary physician to Queen Victoria, 1859; K.C.B., 1864. [xxxiii. 223]

LIDDESDALE, KNIGHT OF (1300 ?–1353). [See DOUGLAS, SIR WILLIAM.]

LIDDIARD, WILLIAM (1773–1841), miscellaneous writer; entered University College, Oxford, 1792; in the army, 1794–6; B.A. Trinity College, Dublin, 1803; author of poems and a book of travels. [xxxiii. 223]

LIDDON, HENRY PARRY (1829–1890), canon of St. Paul's Cathedral, London, and preacher; of King's College School, London, and Christ Church, Oxford; B.A., 1850; ordained, 1853; joined Pusey and Keble; vice-principal of Bishop Wilberforce's Theological College, Cuddesdon, 1854–1859; vice-principal of St. Edmund's Hall, Oxford, 1859; on the hebdomadal board three times between 1864 and 1875; Bampton lecturer, 1866; B.D., D.D., and D.C.L., 1870; Ireland professor of exegesis, 1870–82; canon of St. Paul's Cathedral, 1870; chancellor of St. Paul's Cathedral, 1886; his sermons at St. Paul's for twenty years a central fact of London life; most of his sermons published; left ready for publication three volumes of a 'Life of Pusey.' [xxxiii. 223]

LIFARD, GILBERT OF ST. (d. 1305). [See GILBERT.]

LIFFORD, first VISCOUNT (1709–1789). [See HEWITT, JAMES.]

LIGHT, EDWARD (1747–1832), professor of music and inventor of musical instruments; organist of St. George's, Hanover Square, 1794; invented the harp-guitar and the lute-harp, 1798, and the harp-lyre, lute-harp, and dital-harp, 1816; published 'A First Book on Music,' 1794; 'Lessons and Songs for the Guitar' in 1795 and 1800, and instructions for lute-playing, 1800 and 1817. [xxxiii. 228]

LIGHT, WILLIAM (1784–1838), colonel; surveyor-general of South Australia and founder of the city of Adelaide; lieutenant, 1809; served in the Peninsula; captain, 1821; employed in navy of Mehemet Ali, pasha of Egypt; surveyor-general of South Australia, 1836; selected site for city of Adelaide, 1836; died at Port Adelaide; author of 'A Trigonometrical Survey of Adelaide.' [xxxiii. 228]

LIGHTFOOT, HANNAH (fl. 1768), the beautiful quakeress; said by scandal to have been secretly married to George, prince of Wales, afterwards George III. [xxxiii. 229]

LIGHTFOOT, JOHN (1602–1675), biblical critic; entered Christ's College, Cambridge, 1617; took holy orders and held various cures; his first work, 'Erubhim, or Miscellanies, Christian and Judaical,' 1629; master of Catharine Hall, Cambridge, 1650; D.D., 1652; vice-chancellor of his university, 1654; prebendary of Ely, 1668; aided in Walton's Polyglot Bible, 1657; the first collected edition of his works published, 1684. [xxxiii. 229]

LIGHTFOOT, JOHN (1735–1788), naturalist; M.A. Pembroke College, Oxford, 1766; in holy orders, holding several cures; published the 'Flora Scotica,' 1778; F.R.S., 1781; member of the Linnean Society. [xxxiii. 231]

LIGHTFOOT, JOSEPH BARBER (1828 – 1889), bishop of Durham, divine and scholar; educated at King Edward's School, Birmingham, and Trinity College, Cambridge; B.A., 1851; fellow of Trinity College, 1852–79; edited 'Journal of Classical and Sacred Philology,' 1854–9; ordained, 1858; member of the 'council of senate,' 1860; Hulsean professor of divinity, 1861; chaplain to Queen Victoria, 1862; member of the New Testament Company of Revisers, 1870–80; Lady Margaret professor of divinity, 1875; bishop of Durham, 1879–89; published many valuable works on biblical criticism and early post-biblical Christian history and literature. [xxxiii. 232]

LIGONIER, EDWARD, first EARL LIGONIER in the peerage of Ireland (d. 1782), lieutenant-general; son of Francis Ligonier [q. v.]; entered the army, 1752; present at Minden, 1759; succeeded his uncle, Earl Ligonier, in the Irish viscounty, 1770; created Earl Ligonier, 1776; lieutenant-general, 1777; K.B., 1781. [xxxiii. 242]

LIGONIER, FRANCIS, otherwise FRANÇOIS AUGUSTE (d. 1746), colonel in the British army; brother of John Ligonier, first earl Ligonier [q. v.]; entered the army, 1720; present at Dettingen, 1743; colonel, 1745. [xxxiii. 242]

LIGONIER, JOHN, otherwise JEAN LOUIS, first EARL LIGONIER (1680–1770), field-marshal in the British army; born at Castres, France; educated in France and Switzerland; came to Dublin, 1697; fought under Marlborough at Blenheim, 1704, Ramillies, 1706, Oudenarde, 1708, Malplaquet, 1709; governor of Fort St. Philip, Minorca, 1712; adjutant-general of the Vigo expedition, 1718; colonel of the black horse (now 7th dragoons), 1720–49; major-general and governor of Kinsale, 1739; present at Dettingen, 1743; K.B. and lieutenant-general, 1743; commanded the British foot at Fontenoy, 1745; commander-in-chief in the Austrian Netherlands, 1746–7; M.P., Bath, 1748; governor of Jersey, 1750, of Plymouth, 1752; commander-in-chief and created Viscount Ligonier of Enniskillen, co. Fermanagh, 1757; master-general of the ordnance, 1759–62; his title altered to Viscount Ligonier of Clonmell, 1762; created Baron Ligonier in peerage of Great Britain, 1763; created Earl Ligonier of Ripley, Surrey, 1766; field-marshal, 1766. [xxxiii. 240]

LILBURNE, JOHN (1614?–1657), political agitator; accused before the Star-chamber of printing and circulating unlicensed books, 1637; imprisoned, 1638–40; fought for the parliament, 1642–5; left the service, because he would not take the covenant, 1645; expressed his distrust of the army leaders in pamphlets, 1648–9; sent to the Tower, tried and acquitted, 1649; advocated release of trade from the restrictions of chartered companies and monopolists, 1650; exiled for supporting his uncle, George Lilburne, in his quarrel with Sir Arthur Hesilrige [q. v.], 1652–3; allowed to return to England, but on refusing to promise compliance with the government was confined in Jersey and Guernsey, and at Dover Castle till 1655; joined the quakers. [xxxiii. 243]

LILBURNE, ROBERT (1613–1665), regicide; brother of John Lilburne [q. v.]; entered the parliamentarian army; signed Charles I's death-warrant, 1649; served in Cromwell's Scottish campaigns, 1651–2; M.P. for the East Riding of Yorkshire, 1656; acted with Lambert, 1659; condemned to life-long imprisonment, 1660. [xxxiii. 250]

LILFORD, fourth BARON (1833–1896). [See POWYS, THOMAS LITTLETON.]

LILLINGSTON, LUKE (1653–1713), brigadier-general; served in Ireland under William III; in the Martinique expedition, 1693; in Jamaica, 1695; brigadier-general, 1704; ordered to Antigua, 1707, whither his regiment had been sent in 1706; deprived of command for unreadiness, 1708. [xxxiii. 251]

LILLO, GEORGE (1693–1739), dramatist; his famous tragedy, 'The London Merchant, or the History of George Barnwell,' first acted, 1731; his 'Christian Hero' acted, 1735; his 'Fatal Curiosity' produced, 1736, and 'Elmerick, or Justice Triumphant,' after his death, 1740; helped to popularise the 'domestic drama' in England. [xxxiii. 252]

LILLY. [See also LILY and LYLY.]

LILLY, CHRISTIAN (d. 1738), military engineer; commenced his military career in service of the Dukes of Zelle and Hanover, 1685; entered service of William III, 1688; engineer of the office of ordnance, 1692; employed in the West Indies as engineer, 1693 and 1694–5; chief engineer at Jamaica, 1696; third engineer of England, 1701–15; chief engineer in West Indies, 1704–38. [xxxiii. 255]

LILLY, EDMOND (d. 1716), portrait-painter; executed indifferent portraits of enormous dimensions; his best-known work a portrait of Queen Anne, 1703. [xxxiii. 257]

LILLY, HENRY (d. 1638), Rouge-dragon pursuivant; educated at Christ's Hospital; Rouge-rose pursuivant, 1634; Rouge-dragon pursuivant, 1638; left in manuscript 'Pedigrees of Nobility' and 'The Genealogie of the Princelie Familie of the Howards.' [xxxiii. 257]

LILLY, JOHN (1554?–1606). [See LYLY.]

LILLY, WILLIAM (1602–1681), astrologer; wrote a treatise on 'The Eclipse of the Sun in the eleventh Degree of Gemini, 22 May 1639,' 1639; published his first almanac. 'Merlinus Anglicus Junior, the English Merlin revived,' 1644, and henceforth prepared one every year till his death; began to issue pamphlets of prophecy, 1644; published 'Christian Astrology modestly treated in three Books,' long an authority in astrological literature, 1647; while ostensibly serving the parliament endeavoured to aid Charles I, 1647–8; claimed scientific value for his 'Annus Tenebrosus, or the dark Year, together with a short Method how to judge the Effects of Eclipses,' 1652; studied medicine; granted a licence to practise, 1670. His published writings consist mainly of astrological predictions and vindications of their correctness; his chief non-professional work is his 'True History of King James I and King Charles I,' 1651. [xxxiii. 258]

LILLYWHITE, FREDERICK WILLIAM (1792–1854), cricketer; a bricklayer by trade; in middle life took a foremost place among professional cricketers; played his first match at Lord's, 1827; known as the 'Nonpareil Bowler'; bowler to the M.C.C., 1844–54. [xxxiii. 262]

LILY, GEORGE (d. 1559), Roman catholic divine; son of William Lily [q. v.]; educated at Magdalen College, Oxford; domestic chaplain to Cardinal Pole; canon of Canterbury, 1558; author of some Latin historical works. [xxxiii. 263]

LILY or **LILLY**, PETER (d. 1615), archdeacon of Taunton; grandson of William Lily [q. v.]; educated at Jesus College, Cambridge; fellow; M.A. and D.D.; prebendary of St. Paul's, 1599; archdeacon of Taunton, 1613; 'Conciones Duæ' and 'Two Sermons' published in 1619. [xxxiii. 263]

LILY, WILLIAM (1468?–1522), grammarian; probably entered Magdalen College, Oxford, 1486; graduated; made a pilgrimage to Jerusalem; studied Greek and Latin and classical antiquities in Italy; engaged in teaching in London; high-master of St. Paul's School, London, 1512–22; contributed a short Latin syntax, with the rules in English, under the title of 'Grammatices Rudimenta,' to Colet's 'Æditio,' first printed, 1527. [xxxiii. 264]

LIMERICK, first EARL of the second creation (1758–1845). [See PERY, EDMUND HENRY.]

LIMPUS, RICHARD (1824–1875), founder of the College of Organists, 1864; secretary, 1864–75; composed sacred and secular music. [xxxiii. 266]

LINACRE, THOMAS (1460?–1524), physician and classical scholar; educated at Oxford; fellow of All Souls College, Oxford, 1484; went to Italy, c. 1485–6; M D. Padua; returned to England about 1492; one of Henry VIII's physicians, 1509; lectured at Oxford, 1510; received many ecclesiastical preferments, 1509–20; mainly instrumental in founding College of Physicians, 1518; Latin tutor to the Princess Mary, 1523, for whom he composed a Latin grammar, 'Rudimenta Grammatices'; founded lectureships in medicine at Oxford and Cambridge; wrote grammatical and medical works, and translated from the Greek, especially from Galen. [xxxiii. 266]

LINCHE or **LYNCHE**, RICHARD (fl. 1596–1601), poet; author of 'The Fountaine of English Fiction,' 1599, and 'An Historical Treatise of the Travels of Noah into Europe,' 1601, both so-called translations from the Italian; supposed to be the 'R. L. gentleman' who published in 1596 a volume of sonnets entitled 'Diella.' [xxxiii. 271]

LINCOLN, EARLS OF. [See ROUMARE, WILLIAM DE, *fl.* 1140; LACY, JOHN DE, first EARL of the Lacy family, *d.* 1240; LACY, HENRY DE, third EARL, 1249 ?-1311; POLE, JOHN DE LA, 1464 ?-1487; CLINTON, EDWARD FIENNES DE, first EARL. of the Clinton family, 1512-1585; CLINTON, HENRY FIENNES, ninth EARL, 1720-1794.]

LINCOLN, HUGH OF, SAINT (1246 ?-1255). [See HUGH.]

LIND, JAMES (1716-1794), physician; surgeon in the navy; served at Minorca (1739) and in the West Indies, Mediterranean, and Channel; M.D. Edinburgh, 1748; fellow of the College of Physicians of Edinburgh, 1750; physician to the Naval Hospital, Haslar, 1758-94; published 'An Essay on Diseases incidental to Europeans in Hot Climates,' 1768, and other medical works; discovered lemon-juice to be a specific for scurvy at sea.
[xxxiii. 271]

LIND, JAMES (1736-1812), physician; M.D. Edinburgh, 1768; fellow of the Edinburgh College of Physicians, 1770; made a voyage to Iceland, 1772; F.R.S., 1777; settled at Windsor and became physician in the royal household; interested in astronomy and science; had a private press at which he printed mysterious little books, and (1795) Sir Robert Douglas's 'Genealogy of the Families of Lind and the Montgomeries of Smithson.'
[xxxiii. 272]

LIND, JOHANNA MARIA, known as JENNY LIND, and afterwards as MADAME JENNY LIND-GOLDSCHMIDT (1820-1887), vocalist; born at Stockholm; began to study singing at the Royal Theatre, Stockholm, 1830; first appearance at the theatre, 1838; appointed court singer, 1840; studied in Paris under Garcia; visited professionally Finland and Copenhagen, 1843, Dresden and Berlin, and other German cities, 1844-5, and Vienna, 1846-7; first appeared in London, 1847; retired from the operatic stage, but continued to sing at concerts, 1849; made tours in America, 1850-2; married Mr. Otto Goldschmidt of Hamburg, 1852, and lived at Dresden, 1852-5; made tours in Germany, Austria, and Holland, 1854-5, in Great Britain, 1855-6; became a naturalised British subject, 1859; made her last appearance in public, 1883; professor of singing at the Royal College of Music, 1883-6. [xxxiii. 273]

LIND, JOHN (1737-1781), political writer; M.A. Balliol College, Oxford, 1761; went to Warsaw and became tutor to Prince Stanislaus Poniatowski; appointed governor of an institution for educating four hundred cadets; F.S.A.; returned to England, 1773; published his 'Letters concerning the Present State of Poland,' 1773; F.R.S., 1773; barrister, Lincoln's Inn, 1776; wrote also on the American war. [xxxiii. 276]

LINDESAY, THOMAS (1656-1724), archbishop of Armagh; of Wadham College, Oxford; M.A., 1678; fellow, 1679; D.D., 1693; dean of St. Patrick's, Dublin, 1693; bishop of Killaloe, 1693-1713, and of Raphoe, 1713-14; archbishop of Armagh, 1714. [xxxiii. 277]

LINDEWOOD, WILLIAM (1375 ?-1446). [See LYNDWOOD.]

LINDLEY, JOHN (1799-1865), botanist and horticulturist; published his first book, a translation of Richard's 'Analyse du Fruit,' 1819; assistant-librarian to Sir Joseph Banks; published 'Rosarum Monographia,' 1820; F.L.S. and F.G.S., 1820; assistant-secretary to the Horticultural Society, 1822-41; F.R.S., 1828; professor of botany in the University of London, 1829-60; lecturer on botany to the Apothecaries' Company, 1836-53; vice-secretary, 1841-58; honorary secretary and member of the council, 1858-62; helped to found the 'Gardeners' Chronicle,' 1841. His chief work was 'The Vegetable Kingdom,' 1846. [xxxiii. 277]

LINDLEY, ROBERT (1776-1855), violoncellist; principal violoncello at the opera, 1794-1851; professor of the Royal Academy of Music, 1822; the greatest violoncellist of his time. [xxxiii. 279]

LINDLEY, WILLIAM (1808-1900), civil engineer; engineer-in-chief to Hamburg and Bergedorf railway, 1838-60; designed Hamburg sewerage and water works, and drainage and reclamation of the 'Hammerbrook' district; consulting engineer to city of Frankfort-on-Main, 1865-79. [Suppl. iii. 96]

LINDON, PATRICK (*d.* 1734), Irish poet; some of his songs, which were very popular while Irish was spoken in the district of the Fews, co. Armagh, are extant in manuscript. [xxxiii. 279]

LINDSAY, ALEXANDER, fourth EARL OF CRAWFORD (*d.* 1454), surnamed the TIGER EARL, and also EARL BEARDIE; hereditary sheriff of Aberdeen, 1446; warden of the marches, 1451; engaged in quarrels with other Scottish nobles, 1445-52; received king's pardon, 1453. [xxxiii. 279]

LINDSAY, ALEXANDER, first BARON SPYNIE (*d.* 1607), fourth son of the tenth Earl of Crawford; brother of David Lindsay, eleventh earl of Crawford [q. v.]; vice-chamberlain to James VI; created Baron Spynie, 1590; accused of harbouring the Earl of Bothwell, 1592; tried and acquitted; slain 'by a pitiful mistake,' in a brawl in his own house. [xxxiii. 280]

LINDSAY, ALEXANDER (*d.* 1639), bishop of Dunkeld; bishopric bestowed on him, 1607; deposed, 1638.
[xxxiii. 281]

LINDSAY, ALEXANDER, second BARON SPYNIE (*d.* 1646), eldest son of Alexander, first baron Spynie [q. v.]; commander-in-chief in Scotland, 1626-46; served under Gustavus Adolphus, 1628-33; supported Charles I against the covenanters. [xxxiii. 282]

LINDSAY, ALEXANDER, second BARON BALCARRES and first EARL OF BALCARRES (1618-1659), eldest son of David Lindsay, first baron Balcarres, and grandson of John Lindsay, lord Menmuir [q. v.]; succeeded his father, 1641; present at Marston Moor, 1644; declared for the king, severing his connection with the covenanting party, 1648; admitted to parliament, 1649; a commissioner of the exchequer, 1650; created Earl of Balcarres and hereditary governor of Edinburgh Castle, 1651; visited France to advise the king, 1653 and 1654; finally resided at the court of Charles II; died at Breda. [xxxiii. 282]

LINDSAY, ALEXANDER, sixth EARL OF BALCARRES (1752-1825), eldest son of James Lindsay, fifth earl of Balcarres, and grandson of Colin Lindsay, third earl [q. v.]; succeeded to peerage, 1768; studied at Göttingen, 1768-70; captain, 1771; major, 1775; present at Ticonderoga, 1777; compelled to surrender and a prisoner till 1779; lieutenant-colonel, 1782; Scots representative peer, 1784-1825; colonel, 1789; major-general and commander of the forces in Jersey, 1793; governor of Jamaica, 1794-1801; lieutenant-general, 1798; general, 1803; completed the 'Memoirs of the Lindsays' begun by his father, and left manuscript 'Anecdotes of a Soldier's Life.'
[xxxiii. 284]

LINDSAY, SIR ALEXANDER (1785-1872), general; colonel-commandant, royal (late Bengal) artillery; educated at the Royal Military Academy, Woolwich; received his first Indian commission as first lieutenant, 1804; on active service, 1806-18; captain, 1813; major, 1820; lieutenant-colonel, 1824; colonel and colonel-commandant, 1835; superintendent of telegraphs and agent for the manufacture of gunpowder; served in first Burmese war; major-general, 1838; lieutenant-general, 1851; general, 1859; K.C.B., 1862. [xxxiii. 285]

LINDSAY OF LUFFNESS, SIR ALEXANDER DE (*fl.* 1283-1309), high chamberlain of Scotland under Alexander III; wavered in his allegiance, sometimes supporting the English, sometimes the Scottish sovereign.
[xxxiii. 300]

LINDSAY, ALEXANDER WILLIAM CRAWFORD, twenty-fifth EARL OF CRAWFORD and eighth EARL OF BALCARRES (1812-1880), of Eton and Trinity College, Cambridge; M.A., 1833; travelled and collected books; succeeded to the earldoms, 1869; died at Florence; chief works, 'Lives of the Lindsays,' 1840, and 'Sketches of the History of Christian Art,' 1847. [xxxiii. 285]

LINDSAY, LADY ANNE (1750-1825). [See BARNARD.]

LINDSAY, COLIN, third EARL OF BALCARRES (1654 ?-1722), second son of Alexander Lindsay, second baron Balcarres and first earl of Balcarres [q. v.]; succeeded his brother in the earldom, 1662; went to sea with the Duke of York and distinguished himself at Solebay, 1672; privy councillor, 1680; a commissioner of the treasury, 1686; was connected with the Montgomery plot for James II's restoration; left the country, 1690; settled at Utrecht; returned to Scotland, 1700; privy councillor, 1705; supported the union, 1707; published his 'Memoirs touching the Revolution in Scotland,' 1714, a valuable narrative of proceedings and negotiations of 1688-90; joined Prince Charles Edward, 1715. [xxxiii. 286]

LINDSAY, COLIN (1819-1892), founder of English Church Union; fourth son of James Lindsay, twenty-fourth earl of Crawford; educated at Trinity College, Cambridge; founder and president of Manchester Church Society, which developed (1860) into English Church Union; president, 1860-7; joined Roman catholic church, 1868; published theological writings. [Suppl. iii. 97]

LINDSAY, SIR DAVID, first EARL OF CRAWFORD (1365 ?-1407), chiefly celebrated for his successful tournament with Lord Welles at London Bridge, 1390; succeeded as tenth Baron Crawford, 1397; created Earl of Crawford. 1398; deputy-chamberlain north of the Forth, 1406. [xxxiii. 288]

LINDSAY, DAVID, fifth EARL OF CRAWFORD and first DUKE OF MONTROSE (1440 ?-1495), eldest son of Alexander Lindsay, fourth earl of Crawford [q. v.]; succeeded to the earldom, 1454; ward of Sir James Hamilton of Cadzow, first baron Hamilton [q. v.], whose daughter he married, 1459; sheriff of Forfar, 1466; lord high admiral, 1476; master of the household, 1480; lord chamberlain, 1483; joint high justiciary of the north of Scotland, 1488; created Duke of Montrose, 1488, the first time such a dignity was conferred on a Scotsman not a member of the royal family; privy councillor, 1490. [xxxiii. 288]

LINDSAY or **LYNDSAY,** SIR DAVID (1490-1555), Scottish poet and Lyon king of arms; entered the royal service as equerry; usher to Prince James (afterwards James V), 1512-22; his first poem, 'The Dreme,' written 1528, not printed till after his death; Lyon king of arms, 1529; circulated 'The Complaynt to the King,' 1529, and 'The Testament and Complaynt of our Soverane Lordis Papyngo,' 1530; his first embassy as Lyon king to the court of the Emperor Charles V, 1531; his principal poem, 'Ane Satyre of the Three Estaits,' a drama, produced, 1540; his 'Register of Arms of the Scottish Nobility and Gentry' (unpublished till 1821), the best source for early Scottish heraldry, completed 1542; printed 'Ane Dialog betuix Experience and ane Courteour,' 1552, and 'The Monarchy,' 1554; a satirist of abuses in church and state and the poet of the Scottish Reformation. Repeated editions of the poems have been published from 1558 to 1870. [xxxiii. 289]

LINDSAY, DAVID, tenth EARL OF CRAWFORD (d. 1574), succeeded to earldom, 1558; supporter of Mary Queen of Scots, joining the association for her defence, 1568. [xxxiii. 295]

LINDSAY, DAVID, eleventh EARL OF CRAWFORD (1547 ?-1607), eldest son of David Lindsay, tenth earl of Crawford; lived abroad, 1579-82; master stabler to the king and provost of Dundee, 1582; converted to Roman catholicism and associated himself with the schemes of the Romanist nobles; convicted of treason and condemned to confinement, 1589. [xxxiii. 295]

LINDSAY, SIR DAVID, of Edzell, BARON EDZELL (1551 ?-1610), eldest son of the ninth Earl of Crawford; succeeded to the Edzell estates on death of his father, 1558, the earldom of Crawford passing to David Lindsay, tenth earl [q. v.], son of Alexander Lindsay the 'wicked master,' son of David Lindsay, eighth earl; educated on the continent with his brother, John Lindsay, lord Menmuir [q. v.], under care of John Lawson [q. v.]; knighted, 1581; lord of session as Lord Edzell, 1593; privy councillor, 1598; in seeking to avenge the murder of Sir Walter Lindsay of Balgavie [q. v.] indirectly occasioned the death of Alexander Lindsay, first baron Spynie [q. v.], 1607. [xxxiii. 297]

LINDSAY, DAVID (1531 ?-1613), bishop of Ross; one of the twelve original ministers nominated to the 'chief places in Scotland,' 1560; one of the recognised leaders of the kirk; as chaplain of James VI of Scotland accompanied him to Norway to fetch home his bride, 1589; bishop of Ross, 1600; privy councillor, 1600. [xxxiii. 297]

LINDSAY, DAVID, twelfth EARL OF CRAWFORD (d. 1621), slew his kinsman, Sir Walter Lindsay of Balgavie [q. v.], 1605; ultimately placed under surveillance in Edinburgh Castle. [xxxiii. 296]

LINDSAY, DAVID (1566 ?-1627), presbyterian divine; possibly son of David Lindsay (1531 ?-1613) [q. v.]; M.A. St. Andrews 1586; published theological works. [xxxiii. 298]

LINDSAY, DAVID (d. 1641 ?), bishop of Edinburgh; graduated at St. Andrews, 1593; master of Dundee grammar school, 1597-1606; member of the high commission, 1616; supported the 'king's articles' at Perth assembly, 1618; rewarded with the bishopric of Brechin, 1619; crowned Charles I at Holyrood, 1633; bishop of Edinburgh and one of the lords of exchequer, 1634; deposed by the Glasgow assembly, 1638. [xxxiii. 299]

LINDSAY, GEORGE, third BARON SPYNIE (d. 1671), second son of Alexander Lindsay, second baron Spynie [q. v.]; succeeded to the estates, 1646; supporter of Charles I; taken prisoner at the battle of Worcester, 1651, and committed to the Tower; reinstated in his possessions, 1660; became chief representative of the Lindsays on the death of Ludovic Lindsay, sixteenth earl of Crawford [q. v.] [xxxiii. 299]

LINDSAY, SIR JAMES, ninth BARON CRAWFORD, Lanarkshire (d. 1396), son of Sir James Lindsay, eighth baron Crawford; probably succeeded his father, 1357; fought at Otterburn, 1388; founded a convent of Trinity friars, Dundee, 1392; at feud with other Scottish nobles. [xxxiii. 299]

LINDSAY, JAMES, seventh BARON LINDSAY (d. 1601), son of Patrick Lindsay, sixth baron Lindsay of the Byres [q. v.]; chiefly responsible for the protestant tumult in the Tolbooth, 1596. [xxxiii. 312]

LINDSAY, JAMES BOWMAN (1799-1862), electrician and philologist; apprenticed as hand-loom weaver at Carmyllie, Forfarshire; studied at St. Andrews University; lecturer on mathematics and physical science at Watt Institution, Dundee, 1829; patented, 1854, a wireless system of telegraphy by which water was to be utilised as conductor of the electric current; devoted much time to compiling a Pentecontaglossal dictionary, which he left in MS. incomplete. [Suppl. iii. 97]

LINDSAY, JOHN (d. 1335), bishop of Glasgow; probably appointed, 1321; held office till 1329; a supporter of the house of Bruce; the year and manner of his death a matter of dispute. [xxxiii. 301]

LINDSAY, JOHN, fifth BARON LINDSAY OF THE BYRES, Haddingtonshire (d. 1563); descended from William, son of Sir David Lindsay of Crawford (d. 1355 ?); succeeded to the title on death of his grandfather, Patrick, fourth lord Lindsay, 1526; present at the death of James V, 1542; one of the four noblemen entrusted with the custody of the infant Princess Mary, 1543; subscribed the 'Book of Discipline,' 1561. [xxxiii. 301]

LINDSAY, JOHN, LORD MENMUIR (1552-1598), secretary of state in Scotland; brother of Sir David Lindsay, baron Edzell [q. v.]; studied at Paris and Cambridge; adopted the profession of the law; lord of session as Lord Menmuir, 1581; privy councillor, 1589; lord keeper of the privy seal and secretary of state, 1595; advised the king to establish episcopacy, 1596. [xxxiii. 302]

LINDSAY, JOHN, tenth BARON LINDSAY OF THE BYRES, first EARL OF LINDSAY, and afterwards known as JOHN CRAWFORD-LINDSAY, seventeenth EARL OF CRAWFORD (1596-1678), created Earl of Lindsay, 1633; leader of the covenanters; lord of session and commissioner of the treasury, 1641; distinguished himself at Marston Moor, and title and dignities of Earl of Crawford ratified on him, 1644; president of the parliament, 1645; took part in attempt to rescue Charles from Carisbrook, 1646; joined the coalition for Charles II's restoration, 1650; taken prisoner, 1652; released, 1660; lord high treasurer, 1661; refusing to abjure the covenant resigned his offices and retired from public life, 1663. [xxxiii. 304]

LINDSAY, JOHN, twentieth EARL OF CRAWFORD (1702-1749), military commander; educated at the universities of Glasgow and Edinburgh and the military academy of Vaudeuil, Paris; entered the army, 1726; Scots representative peer, 1733; captain, 1734; joined the imperial army under Prince Eugène, 1735; served in the Russian army, 1738-41; adjutant-general at Dettingen, 1743; brigadier-general at Fontenoy, 1745; engaged in suppressing the rebellion of 1745; lieutenant-general, 1747. [xxxiii. 305]

LINDSAY, JOHN (*fl.* 1758), chaplain of the Fougueux with Keppel at the Goree expedition; published 'A Voyage to the Coast of Africa in 1758,' 1759. [xxxiii. 307]

LINDSAY, JOHN (1686–1768), nonjuror; published historical and religious works. [xxxiii. 306]

LINDSAY, SIR JOHN (1737–1788), rear-admiral; served in Rochefort expedition, 1757, in expedition against Havana, 1762; knighted, 1763; in West Indies, 1764–5; commodore and commander-in-chief in East Indies, 1769–72; K.B., 1771; took part in engagement off Ushant, 1778; commodore and commander-in-chief in the Mediterranean, 1783; rear-admiral, 1787. [xxxiii. 307]

LINDSAY, LUDOVIC, sixteenth EARL OF CRAWFORD (1600–1652?), succeeded his brother Alexander Lindsay, fifteenth earl, 1639; entered Spanish service; connected with the 'Incident' plot, 1641; joined Charles I's standard, 1642; fought at Newbury, 1643, at Marston Moor, 1644; exiled, 1646; subsequently served in Spain and France; died probably in France. [xxxiii. 308]

LINDSAY, PATRICK, sixth BARON LINDSAY OF THE BYRES (d. 1589), supporter of the reformers in Scotland; eldest son of John Lindsay, fifth baron of the Byres [q. v.]; succeeded to title, 1563; supporter of the plot to murder David Riccio or Rizzio, 1566; supported the king's party, 1570–2; concerned in Ruthven raid, 1582, and in Gowrie conspiracy, 1584. [xxxiii. 309]

LINDSAY, PATRICK (1566–1644), archbishop of Glasgow; educated at St. Andrews; supported the episcopalian schemes of James I; bishop of Ross, 1613–33; privy councillor of Scotland, 1615; archbishop of Glasgow, 1633; deposed by the general assembly, 1638. [xxxiii. 312]

LINDSAY, PATRICK (d. 1753), lord provost of Edinburgh; served in Spain until peace of Utrecht, 1713; lord provost of Edinburgh, 1729 and 1733; published work on the economic resources of Scotland, 1733; M.P., Edinburgh, 1734–41; governor of the Isle of Man, 1741. [xxxiii. 312]

LINDSAY, ROBERT (1500?–1565?), of Pitscottie, Scottish historian; his 'History,' covering a period of Scottish history about the earlier part of which, from the death of James I to that of James III, very little is known, first published, 1728. [xxxiii. 313]

LINDSAY, SIR WALTER of Balgavie, Forfarshire (d. 1605), Roman catholic intriguer; acquired property of Balgavie, 1584; converted to Roman catholicism, and constantly charged with conspiring against presbyterianism; escaped the vengeance of the kirk by fleeing to Spain; there published 'An Account of the present State of the Catholic Religion in the Realm of Scotland,' 1594; returned to Scotland, 1598; took part in all the feuds of the Lindsays; barbarously murdered by his kinsman, David Lindsay, twelfth earl of Crawford [q. v.] [xxxiii. 314]

LINDSAY, WILLIAM, eighteenth EARL OF CRAWFORD and second EARL OF LINDSAY (d. 1698), eldest son of John Lindsay, tenth baron Lindsay of the Byres, seventeenth earl of Crawford, and first earl of Lindsay [q. v.]; succeeded to the earldoms, 1678; a zealous presbyterian; president of the Convention parliament, 1689; a commissioner of the treasury, 1690; one of the commissioners for settling the government of the church. [xxxiii. 315]

LINDSAY, WILLIAM (1802–1866), united presbyterian minister; studied at Glasgow University and the theological hall at Paisley; ordained, 1830; appointed professor of exegetical theology and biblical criticism by the relief synod; D.D. Glasgow, 1844; professor of sacred languages and biblical criticism on the staff of the United Presbyterian Hall, Glasgow, 1847, and professor of exegetical theology, 1858; published 'The Law of Marriage,' 1855, 'Exposition of Epistle to the Hebrews' (edited, 1867), and other works. [xxxiii. 315]

LINDSAY, WILLIAM LAUDER (1829–1880), botanist; educated at Edinburgh High School and University; M.D. Edinburgh, 1852; combined geological and botanical studies with his practice of medicine; published 'The History of British Lichens,' 1856; visited New Zealand, 1861–2; published 'Contributions to New Zealand Botany,' 1868, and 'Memoirs on the Spermogenes and Pycnides of Lichens,' 1870. Of his works on medi-

cal subjects, the chief is 'Mind in the Lower Animals in Health and Disease,' 1879. [xxxiii. 316]

LINDSAY, WILLIAM SCHAW (1816–1877), merchant and shipowner; began a seafaring life, 1831; captain in the merchant service, 1830–40; fitter to the Castle Eden Coal Company, Hartlepool, 1841; established firm of W. S. Lindsay & Co., one of the largest shipowning concerns in the world; M.P., Tynemouth and North Shields, 1854–9, Sunderland, 1859–65; published a valuable 'History of Merchant Shipping and Ancient Commerce,' 1874–6; author of other works on kindred subjects, and of 'Log of my Leisure Hours.' [xxxiii. 316]

LINDSELL, AUGUSTINE (d. 1634), bishop of Hereford; M.A. Clare Hall, Cambridge; fellow of Clare Hall, 1599; D.D., 1621; dean of Lichfield, 1628; bishop of Peterborough, 1633, of Hereford, 1634; his edition of Theophylact's 'Commentaries on St. Paul's Epistles,' published, 1636. [xxxiii. 317]

LINDSEY, EARLS OF. [See BERTIE, ROBERT, first EARL, 1582–1642; BERTIE, MONTAGUE, second EARL, 1608?–1666.]

LINDSEY, THEOPHILUS (1723–1808), unitarian; educated at St. John's College, Cambridge; fellow, 1747; held several livings, but his views becoming unitarian, resigned, 1773; opened a temporary chapel (established permanently, 1778) in London, 1774, and issued his 'Apology'; 'A Sequel to the Apology', 1776, his most valuable contribution to dogmatic theology; his 'Historical View of the State of the Unitarian Doctrine and Worship from the Reformation to our own Time', published, 1783; took leave of his pulpit, 1793; published 'Conversations on the Divine Government,' 1802, and a liturgy adapted for unitarian congregations. [xxxiii. 317]

LINE, *alias* HALL, FRANCIS (1595–1675), jesuit and scientific writer; joined jesuits, 1623; ordained, 1628; professor of the four vows, 1640; professor of Hebrew and mathematics in the jesuit college, Liège; missioner in England, 1656–69; constructed a sun-dial set up in the king's private garden at Whitehall, 1669; returned to Liège, 1672, where he died; author of several scientific works written between 1660 and 1675 on such subjects as squaring the circle, sundials, and the barometer. [xxxiii. 319]

LINES, SAMUEL (1778–1863), painter, designer, and art instructor; worked as designer to a clock-dial enameller, papier-mâché maker, and die engraver; began to teach drawing at Birmingham, 1807; set up in conjunction with others a life academy there, 1809; helped to found Birmingham School of Art, 1821; treasurer and curator of the Birmingham Society of Artists. [xxxiii. 319]

LINES, SAMUEL RESTELL (1804–1833), painter; son of Samuel Lines (1778–1863) [q. v.]; studied under his father; occasionally exhibited at the Royal Academy. [xxxiii. 320]

LINFORD, THOMAS (1650–1724). [See LYNFORD.]

LINGARD, FREDERICK (1811–1847), musician; organist, choirmaster, teacher of music, and composer; lay-vicar of Durham Cathedral, 1835; published 'Antiphonal Chants for the Psalter,' 1843, and a 'Series of Anthems.' [xxxiii. 320]

LINGARD, JOHN (1771–1851), Roman catholic historian of England; studied at the English college at Douay, 1782–93; ordained and appointed vice-president of Crookhall College, near Durham, 1795–1811; published 'The Antiquities of the Anglo-Saxon Church,' 1806; began his 'History of England' when missioner at Hornby, near Lancaster, 1811; D.D.; visited Rome, 1817 and 1825; took part in the jurisdiction of the Roman church in Great Britain; created doctor of divinity and of the canon and civil law by Pius VII, 1821; vols. i. ii. and iii. of the 'History' were published, 1819; the remainder followed at intervals, 1820–30. It had five editions before 1851, and remains the authority for the reformation from the side of the enlightened Roman catholic priesthood. [xxxiii. 320]

LINGARD or **LYNGARD**, RICHARD (1598?–1670), dean of Lismore; ordained, 1622; archdeacon of Clonmacnoise, 1639; professor of divinity, Dublin University, 1660; vice-provost, 1662; D.D., 1664; dean of Lismore, 1666. [xxxiii. 323]

LINGEN, SIR HENRY (1612–1662), royalist; raised troops and fought for Charles I, 1643–8; knighted, 1645; temporarily imprisoned, 1648; M.P., Hereford, 1660 and 1661. [xxxiii. 324]

LINLEY, ELIZABETH ANN, afterwards MRS. SHERIDAN (1754–1792). [See SHERIDAN.]

LINLEY, FRANCIS (1774–1800), organist and composer; blind from birth; organist at St. James's Chapel, Pentonville, London, c. 1790; carried on business as a music-seller, 1796; composed sonatas and airs for pianoforte and flute, and wrote a practical introduction to the organ (12th ed. c. 1810). [xxxiii. 325]

LINLEY, GEORGE (1798–1865), verse-writer and musical composer; composed fashionable and popular ballads, 1830–47; author of farces and satirical poems, including 'Musical Cynics of London, a satire,' 1862, a savage onslaught on Chorley; his operetta, 'The Toymakers,' performed, 1861, and 'Law versus Love' (comedietta), 1862. [xxxiii. 325]

LINLEY, GEORGE (d. 1869), son of George Linley [q. v.]; published 'The Goldseeker and other poems,' 1860, 'Old Saws newly set,' 1864. [xxxiii. 325]

LINLEY, MARIA (d. 1784), singer at the Bath concerts and in oratorio; daughter of Thomas Linley the elder [q. v.] [xxxiii. 327]

LINLEY, MARY, afterwards MRS. TICKELL (1756?–1787), vocalist; daughter of Thomas Linley the elder [q. v.], musician; first appeared in public, 1771; married Richard Tickell, pamphleteer and commissioner of stamps, 1780. [xxxiii. 325]

LINLEY, OZIAS THURSTON (1766–1831), organist; son of Thomas Linley the elder [q. v.]; educated at Corpus Christi College, Oxford; B.A., 1789; minor canon of Norwich, 1790; organist, Dulwich College, 1816. [xxxiii. 327]

LINLEY, THOMAS, the younger (1756–1778), violinist and composer; son of Thomas Linley the elder [q. v.]; studied violin under his father, and at Florence under Nardini; leader of the orchestra and solo-player at his father's concerts at Bath, 1773, and at the Drury Lane oratorios, 1774; drowned through the capsizing of a pleasure boat off the Lincolnshire coast; his compositions include songs for the 'Duenna' (1775), songs for the 'Tempest' (1776), and a short oratorio, 'The Song of Moses.' [xxxiii. 326]

LINLEY, THOMAS, the elder (1732–1795), musical composer; set up in Bath as a singing-master and carried on the concerts in the Bath Assembly Rooms; became joint-manager of the Drury Lane oratorios, 1774; composed with his son Thomas the music for Sheridan's 'Duenna,' 1775; directed the music at Drury Lane, 1776–1781; member of the Royal Society of Musicians, 1777. His compositions include the music to various dramatic pieces, and separate songs, glees, and canzonets. [xxxiii. 326]

LINLEY, WILLIAM (1771–1835), author and musical composer; son of Thomas Linley the elder [q. v.]; educated at St. Paul's School, London, and Harrow; writer under the East India Company, sailing for Madras, 1790; deputy-secretary to the military board, 1793; returned to England, and brought out at Drury Lane 'Harlequin Captive, or Magic Fire,' 1796; produced 'The Honeymoon' (comic opera), 1797, and 'The Pavilion' (entertainment), 1799; returned to Madras, 1800; paymaster at Nellore, 1801; sub-treasurer and mint-master to the presidency, Fort St. George, 1805; settled in London, 1806; collected Shakespeare's dramatic lyrics, with music by various composers and himself, in 2 vols., 1816; composed songs and wrote novels and verses. [xxxiii. 328]

LINLITHGOW, EARLS OF. [See LIVINGSTONE, ALEXANDER, first EARL, d. 1622; LIVINGSTONE, GEORGE, third EARL, 1616–1690; LIVINGSTONE, GEORGE, fourth EARL, 1652?–1695.]

LINNECAR, RICHARD (1722–1800), dramatist; postmaster at Wakefield; coroner for the West Riding of Yorkshire, 1763; published 'Miscellaneous Works,' containing two insipid comedies and other efforts, 1789. [xxxiii. 329]

LINNELL, JOHN (1792–1882), portrait and landscape painter; entered the Royal Academy schools, 1805; first exhibited at the Academy, 1807; member of the Society of Painters in Oil and Water-colours, 1812, exhibiting, 1813–20; treasurer, 1817; became intimate with William Blake (1757–1827) [q. v.], 1818; drew, painted, and engraved portraits; exhibited over a hundred portraits and ten or twelve landscapes at the Royal Academy, 1821–47; subsequently exhibited landscapes; put down his name for the A.R.A., 1821; withdrew it in disgust, 1842; declined membership when offered in later life. [xxxiii. 329]

LINSKILL, MARY (1840–1891), novelist; contributed, under pseudonym of Stephen Yorke, 'Tales of the North Riding' to 'Good Words' (published, 1871); author of four other novels, 1876–87, and of some short stories. [xxxiii. 331]

LINTON, ELIZA LYNN (1822–1898), novelist and miscellaneous writer; daughter of the Rev. James Lynn, and granddaughter of Samuel Goodenough [q. v.]; established herself in London, 1845, as a woman of letters; published 'Azeth the Egyptian,' 1846, 'Amymone,' 1848, and 'Realities,' 1851, none of which were very successful; member of staff of 'Morning Chronicle,' 1848–51; newspaper correspondent at Paris, 1851–4; contributed to 'All the Year Round'; married, 1858, William James Linton [q. v.], from whom she subsequently separated amicably; returned to fiction and achieved considerable success, two of her works, 'Joshua Davidson,' 1872, and 'Autobiography of Christopher Kirkland,' 1885 (the latter in a large measure her own autobiography), being especially notable; contributed to 'Saturday Review' from 1866. Her works include, 'The Girl of the Period, and other Essays' (1883), and 'George Eliot' (1897). [Suppl. iii. 98]

LINTON, WILLIAM (1791–1876), landscape-painter; first exhibited at Royal Academy, 1817; helped to found the Society of British Artists, 1824; visited the continent, 1828; published in two folio volumes, 'Sketches in Italy,' drawn on stone, with descriptive text, 1832; resigned membership of the Society of British Artists, 1842; well versed in chemistry of colours; published 'Ancient and Modern Colours, from the earliest periods to the present time; with their Chemical and Artistical Properties,' 1852; ceased to exhibit at Royal Academy after 1859, at Society of British Artists after 1871. [xxxiii. 331]

LINTON, SIR WILLIAM (1801–1880), army physician; educated at Edinburgh University; L.R.C.S. and entered army medical department, 1826; M.D. Glasgow, 1834; staff surgeon of the first class, 1848; served in Canada, the Mediterranean, and the West Indies; deputy-inspector of hospitals in the Crimea; present in every action up to Balaclava; in charge of barrack hospital, Scutari, from 1854 till return of British forces; proceeded to India as inspector-general of hospitals, 1857; held offices throughout the mutiny; retired from the active list, 1863; K.C.B., 1865. [xxxiii. 333]

LINTON, WILLIAM JAMES (1812–1898), engraver, poet, and political reformer; apprenticed as wood-engraver; became associated with John Orrin Smith [q. v.]; adopted advanced views in religion and politics; established, 1839, 'The National'; designed as a vehicle for reprints from publications inaccessible to working men; editor of 'The Illuminated Magazine,' 1845; formed intimate friendship with Mazzini; took part in founding 'International League' of patriots of all nations, 1847; supported 'The Friends of Italy'; founded and conducted, 1850–5, 'The English Republic' periodical; gained wide reputation as wood-engraver; married Eliza Lynn [see LINTON, ELIZA LYNN], 1858; engraved covers of 'Cornhill' and 'Macmillan's' magazines; went to America (1866) and established himself at Appledore, near New Haven, Connecticut, where he engaged privately in printing and engraving, and issued several books; died at New Haven. His publications include 'A History of Wood Engraving in America,' 1882, 'Masters of Wood Engraving,' 1890, some volumes of verse, and 'Memories,' an autobiography, 1895. [Suppl. iii. 100]

LINTOT, BARNABY BERNARD (1675–1736), publisher; apprentice at Stationers' Hall, 1690; free of the company, 1699; published poems and plays for Pope, Gay, Farquhar, Parnell, Steele, and Rowe, 1702–8; published Fenton's 'Oxford and Cambridge Miscellany Poems,' 1709, and 'Miscellaneous Poems and Translations' (containing Pope's 'Rape of the Lock' in its first form), 1712; published Pope's 'Iliad,' 1715–20, 'Odyssey,' 1725–6; under-warden of the Stationers' Company, 1729–30. [xxxiii. 333]

LINTOT, HENRY (1703–1758), publisher and, from 1730, partner with his father, Barnaby Bernard Lintot [q. v.] [xxxiii. 334]

LINWOOD, MARY (1755–1845), musical composer and artist in needlework; imitated pictures in worsted embroidery; exhibited at the Society of Artists, 1776 and 1778, and in London and the chief provincial towns, 1798–1835; composed an oratorio and some songs; published ' Leicestershire Tales,' 1808. [xxxiii. 335]

LINWOOD, WILLIAM (1817–1878), classical scholar; entered Christ Church, Oxford, 1835 ; M.A., 1842 ; public examiner at Oxford, 1850–1 ; his best-known works, ' A Lexicon to Æschylus,' 1843, and ' Sophoclis Tragœdiæ,' 1846. [xxxiii. 335]

LIONEL OF ANTWERP, EARL OF ULSTER and first DUKE OF CLARENCE (1338–1368), third son of Edward III ; born at Antwerp ; guardian and lieutenant of England during his father's absence, 1345 and 1346 ; created Earl of Ulster, 1347 ; married Elizabeth (d. 1362), daughter of William de Burgh, third earl of Ulster [q. v.], 1352 ; knighted, 1355 ; king's lieutenant in Ireland, 1361 ; created Duke of Clarence, 1362 ; met the parliament which drew up statute of Kilkenny, 1367 ; married at Milan, as his second wife, Violante, daughter of Galeazzo Visconti, lord of Pavia, 1368 ; died at Alba. [xxxiii. 335]

LIPSCOMB, CHRISTOPHER (1781–1843), first bishop of Jamaica, 1824 ; son of William Lipscomb [q. v.] [xxxiii. 339]

LIPSCOMB, GEORGE (1773–1846), historian of Buckinghamshire: studied surgery; house-surgeon of St. Bartholomew's Hospital, London, 1792 ; captain commandant of the Warwickshire volunteer infantry, and deputy-recorder of Warwick, 1798 ; M.D. Aberdeen, 1801 ; joint-editor of the ' National Adviser,' 1811 ; contributed to the ' Gentleman's Magazine '; his great work, ' The History and Antiquities of the County of Buckingham,' published in eight parts, 1831–47 ; published medical works. [xxxiii. 338]

LIPSCOMB, WILLIAM (1754–1842), miscellaneous writer : cousin of George Lipscomb [q. v.] ; educated at Winchester and Corpus Christi College, Oxford ; M.A., 1784 ; published ' Poems ' (including translations of Italian sonnets), 1784, and ' The Canterbury Tales of Chaucer completed in a Modern Version,' 1795. [xxxiii. 339]

LISGAR, first BARON (1807–1876). [See YOUNG ,SIR JOHN.]

LISLE, VISCOUNTS. [See PLANTAGENET, ARTHUR, 1480?–1542 ; DUDLEY, JOHN, 1502 ?–1553 ; SIDNEY, ROBERT, first VISCOUNT of the Sidney family, 1563–1626 ; SIDNEY, ROBERT, second VISCOUNT, 1595–1677 ; SIDNEY, PHILIP, third VISCOUNT, 1619–1698.]

LISLE, ALICE (1614 ?–1685), victim of a judicial murder ; daughter of Sir White Beckenshaw ; married John Lisle [q. v.], 1630 ; tried before Jeffreys for sheltering Monmouth's supporters at her house at Moyles Court ; found guilty and beheaded at Winchester. [xxxiii. 339]

LISLE, SIR GEORGE (d. 1648), royalist ; received his military education in the Netherlands; fought for Charles I in battles of Newbury, 1643 and 1644, Cheriton, 1644, and Naseby, 1645 ; governor of Faringdon, 1644–5 ; hon. D.C.L. Oxford, 1645 ; knighted, 1645 ; defended Colchester, but was forced to surrender and shot as a rebel, 1648. [xxxiii. 340]

LISLE, JAMES GEORGE SEMPLE (fl. 1799). [See SEMPLE.]

LISLE, JOHN (1610 ?–1664), regicide; educated at Magdalen Hall, Oxford ; B.A., 1626 ; barrister, Middle Temple, 1633 : bencher, 1649 ; M.P., Winchester, 1640 ; master of St. Cross Hospital, Winchester, 1644–9 ; one of the managers in Charles I's trial; appointed one of the commissioners of the great seal, and placed on the council of state, 1649 ; M.P., Southampton, 1654 ; held various offices in parliaments of 1654–9 ; commissioner of the admiralty and navy, 1660 ; at Restoration fled to Switzerland ; murdered at Lausanne by an Irishman known as Thomas Macdonnell, really named Sir James Fitz Edmond Cotter. Alice Lisle [q. v.] was his second wife. [xxxiii. 341]

LISLE, SAMUEL (1683–1749), successively bishop of St. Asaph and of Norwich; M.A. Wadham College, Oxford, 1706 ; received holy orders, 1707 ; chaplain to the Levant Company, 1710–19 ; archdeacon of Canterbury, 1724 ; prebendary of Canterbury, 1728 ; prolocutor of the lower house of convocation, 1734 and 1741 ; warden of Wadham College, Oxford, 1739–44 ; D.D., 1739 ; bishop of St. Asaph, 1744–8, of Norwich, 1748–9 ; printed a few sermons and collected inscriptions during his Levant chaplaincy, printed in the ' Antiquitates Asiaticæ ' of Edmund Chishull [q. v.], 1728. [xxxiii. 342]

LISLE, THOMAS (d. 1361), bishop of Ely ; called LYLE, LYLDE, and LYLDUS ; educated in the Dominican house, Cambridge ; joined the order of Predicant friars, and acquired celebrity as a preacher : bishop of Ely, 1345 ; built churches in his diocese, and rendered material services to the University of Cambridge ; at feud with Blanche, daughter of Henry, earl of Lancaster, and compelled to flee; died a refugee at Avignon. [xxxiii. 343]

LISLE or **L'ISLE**, WILLIAM (1569?–1637), Anglo-Saxon scholar ; of Eton and King's College, Cambridge ; M.A., 1592 ; lived at Cambridge ; a pioneer in the study of Anglo-Saxon ; printed for the first time, with an English translation, the ' Treatise on the Old and New Testament,' by Ælfric Grammaticus [q. v.]; published a rhymed version of Heliodorus's ' Æthiopica,' 1631. [xxxiii. 345]

LISTER, EDWARD (1556–1620), physician ; brother of Sir Matthew Lister [q. v.] ; of Eton and King's College, Cambridge ; M.A., 1583 ; M.D., 1590 ; F.R.C.P., 1594, and treasurer, 1612–18 ; physician in ordinary to Queen Elizabeth and to James I. [xxxiii. 346]

LISTER, JOSEPH (1627–1709), puritan autobiographer ; by turns trader, man-servant, and small farmer ; his autobiography edited by Thomas Wright, 1842. [xxxiii. 346]

LISTER, JOSEPH JACKSON (1786–1869), discoverer of the principle of the modern microscope ; occupied in the wine trade ; attempted to improve the object-glass, 1824 ; continued his investigations, 1826–7 ; discovered principle of construction of modern microscope, 1830 ; the first to ascertain the true form of the red corpuscle of mammalian blood, 1834 ; aided opticians in the construction of the microscope. His law of the aplanatic foci remains the guiding principle of microscopy. [xxxiii. 347]

LISTER, MARTIN (1638 ?–1712), zoologist ; nephew of Sir Matthew Lister [q. v.] ; of St. John's College, Cambridge ; fellow, 1660 ; M.A., 1662 ; F.R.S., 1671 ; practised medicine at York till 1683 ; removed to London, 1684 ; M.D. Oxford, 1684 ; published ' Historia sive Synopsis Methodica Conchyliorum,' 1685–92 ; F.R.C.P., 1687 ; censor, 1694 ; accompanied Earl of Portland on his embassy to Paris, and published an account of his journey, 1698. His contributions to the ' Philosophical Transactions ' (extending over Nos. 25–585) treat of plants, spiders, meteorology, minerals, molluscs, medicine, and antiquities. [xxxiii. 350]

LISTER, SIR MATTHEW (1571 ?–1656), physician ; M.A. Oriel College, Oxford ; 1595 ; M.D. Basle, incorporated at Oxford, 1605, at Cambridge, 1608 ; F.R.C.P., 1607 ; physician to Anne, queen of James I, and to Charles I ; knighted, 1636. [xxxiii. 351]

LISTER, THOMAS, alias BUTLER (1559–1626 ?), jesuit ; entered the English college at Rome, 1579 ; joined jesuits, 1583 ; D.D. Pont-à-Mousson, 1592 ; missioner in England, 1596 ; imprisoned at time of Gunpowder plot; banished, 1606 ; again in England, and professed of the four vows, 1610 ; superior of the Oxford district, 1621 ; author of a ' Treatise of Schism,' widely circulated in manuscript. [xxxiii. 351]

LISTER, THOMAS (1597–1668), parliamentarian colonel ; admitted to Gray's Inn, 1616 ; lieutenant-colonel in the parliamentary army and deputy-governor of Lincoln ; M.P., Lincoln, 1647–56, and in 1659 ; member of the council of state, 1651 ; forbidden to hold office from 1660. [xxxiii. 351]

LISTER, THOMAS (1810–1888), poet and naturalist ; assisted his father, a quaker gardener and small farmer ; published ' Rustic Wreath,' a collection of fugitive verses, 1834 : visited the continent, 1838 ; postmaster of Barnsley, 1839–70 ; an enthusiastic naturalist, and constant attendant and contributor of papers at the British Association meetings. [xxxiii. 352]

LISTER, THOMAS HENRY (1800-1842), novelist and dramatist; of Westminster and Trinity College, Cambridge; commissioner for inquiring into state of religious and other instruction in Ireland, 1834, into the opportunities of religious worship and means of religious instruction in Scotland, 1835; the first registrar-general of England and Wales, 1836; works include 'Granby' (novel), 1826, 'Epicharis' (a tragedy performed at Drury Lane, 1829), and 'The Life and Administration of Edward, first Earl of Clarendon,' 1837-8.   [xxxiii. 352]

LISTON, HENRY (1771-1836), writer on music; studied for the ministry at Edinburgh University; minister of Ecclesmachan, Linlithgowshire, 1793-1836; inventor of the 'Eucharmonic' organ, 1811; published 'Essay on Perfect Intonation,' 1812; conjunct clerk of the synod of Lothian and Tweeddale, 1820.
[xxxiii. 353]

LISTON, JOHN (1776?-1846), actor; master at the grammar school of St. Martin's, Leicester Square, London, 1799; his first efforts as an actor made in company with Stephen Kemble in north of England; played comic parts at Haymarket Theatre, London, 1805, at Covent Garden, London, 1808-22, at Drury Lane, London, 1823, subsequently at Olympic, London; retired from the stage, 1837; played, among other parts, Polonius, Slender, Sir Andrew Aguecheek, Bottom, and Oloten.   [xxxiii. 354]

LISTON, SIR ROBERT (1742-1836), diplomatist; educated at Edinburgh University; tutor to the sons of Sir Gilbert Elliot (1722-1777) [q. v.]; minister plenipotentiary at Madrid, 1783-8; LL.D. Edinburgh, 1785; envoy extraordinary at Stockholm, 1788-93; ambassador extraordinary and plenipotentiary, Constantinople, 1793-1796; ambassador extraordinary and minister plenipotentiary, Washington, 1796-1802; envoy extraordinary and plenipotentiary to the Batavian republic, 1802-4; ambassador extraordinary and plenipotentiary, Constantinople, 1811-21; privy councillor, 1812; G.C.B. (civil), 1816.   [xxxiii. 356]

LISTON, ROBERT (1794-1847), surgeon; son of Henry Liston [q. v.]; entered Edinburgh University, 1808; assistant to Dr. John Barclay (1758-1826) [q. v.]; house-surgeon at Royal Infirmary, Edinburgh, 1814-16; M.R.C.S., 1816; worked in Edinburgh as teacher of anatomy and operating surgeon, 1818-28; surgeon to the hospital attached to the London University, 1834; professor of clinical surgery, University College, London, 1835; F.R.S., 1841; a skilful operator; best known in connection with the 'Liston splint'; chief works, 'The Elements of Surgery,' 1831-2, and 'Practical Surgery,' 1837.   [xxxiii. 357]

LITCHFIELD. [See also LICHFIELD.]

LITCHFIELD, MRS. HARRIETT (1777-1854), actress; née Hay; made her first appearance on the stage, 1792; married John Litchfield (d. 1858) of the privy council office, 1794; acted at Covent Garden from 1797; retired after 1812; her best part Emilia in Othello.
[xxxiii. 358]

LITHGOW, WILLIAM (1582-1645?), traveller; made voyages to the Orkneys and Shetlands; travelled in Germany, Bohemia, Helvetia, and the Low Countries; claimed to have tramped over 36,000 miles in Europe, Asia, Africa, 1610-13; made other journeys, 1614-19 and 1620-2; walked from London to Edinburgh, 1627; journeyed in England, Scotland, and Holland, 1628-44; chief work, 'The Totall Discourse of the Rare Aduentures and painfull Peregrinations of long nineteene Yeares,' 1614.
[xxxiii. 359]

LITTLINGTON or **LITTLINGTON**, NICHOLAS (1316?-1386), successively prior and abbot of Westminster Abbey; prior of Westminster, 1352; abbot, 1362; built the Jerusalem Chamber; assisted at the coronation of Richard II, 1377.   [xxxiii. 361]

LITSTER or **LE LITESTER**, JOHN (d. 1381), 'king of the commons'; led the 'rustics and ribalds' of Norfolk, 1381; assumed the royal title as 'king of the commons,' 1381; taken at the battle of North Walsham and hanged, beheaded, and quartered at the command of Henry le Despenser [q. v.], bishop of Norwich.
[xxxiii. 362]

LITTLEDALE, SIR JOSEPH (1767-1842), judge; M.A. St. John's College, Cambridge, 1790; barrister, Gray's Inn, 1798; counsel to the University of Cambridge,

1813; edited Skelton's 'Magnyfycence, an Interlude,' 1821; judge in the court of king's bench, 1824-41; knighted, 1824; privy councillor, 1841.   [xxxiii. 363]

LITTLEDALE, RICHARD FREDERICK (1833-1890), Anglican controversialist; M.A. Trinity College, Dublin, 1858; LL.D., 1862; held curacies in England, but devoted himself mainly to literary work; published works in support of Anglicanism in opposition to Roman catholicism, 1857-89.   [xxxiii. 364]

LITTLER, SIR JOHN HUNTER (1783-1856), lieutenant-general, Indian army; lieutenant, 10th Bengal infantry, 1800; served in the campaigns under Lord Lake, 1804-5; in Java, 1811-16; captain, 1812; commissary-general in the Marquis of Hastings's army, 1816-24; major, 1824; colonel, 36th Bengal native infantry, 1839-1856; major-general, 1841; commander of the Agra division of the Bengal army, 1843; K.C.B., 1844; served in the Sikh war, 1845; G.C.B. and deputy governor of Bengal, 1849; lieutenant-general, 1851.   [xxxiii. 365]

LITTLETON. [See also LYTTELTON.]

LITTLETON, ADAM (1627-1694), lexicographer; educated at Westminster and Christ Church, Oxford; second master at Westminster, 1658; rector of Chelsea, 1669; chaplain to Charles II, 1670; published 'A Latin Dictionary in four parts,' 1673; prebendary of Westminster, 1674.   [xxxiii. 365]

LITTLETON, SIR EDWARD, first BARON LITTLETON (1589-1645), educated at Christ Church, Oxford; B.A., 1609; barrister, Inner Temple, 1617; chief-justice of North Wales, 1621; M.P., Leominster, 1625-6 and 1627-8; helped to frame the Petition of Right, 1628; bencher of his inn, 1629; recorder of London, 1631; reader to the Inner Temple, 1632; solicitor-general, 1634; knighted, 1635; chief-justice of the common pleas, 1640; lord keeper, 1641; created Baron Littleton, 1641; D.C.L. Oxford, 1643.   [xxxiii. 366]

LITTLETON, EDWARD (fl. 1694), agent for the island of Barbados; educated at Westminster and St. Mary Hall, Oxford; B.A., 1644; fellow of All Souls College, Oxford, 1647; M.A., 1648; senior proctor, 1656; barrister, Lincoln's Inn, 1664; went to Barbados as secretary to Lord Willoughby of Parham, 1666; judge, 1670-1683; elected member of the assembly, 1674; agent for Barbados, 1683; published tracts on the colonies, finance, and general politics, 1664-94.   [xxxiii. 368]

LITTLETON, EDWARD (d. 1733), divine and poet; educated at Eton and King's College, Cambridge; B.A., 1720; LL.D. comitiis regiis, 1728; assistant-master at Eton, 1720; M.A., 1724; a royal chaplain, 1730; his poems published in Dodsley's 'Collection' (edited 1782), the most celebrated being 'On a Spider'; two volumes of sermons published, 1735.   [xxxiii. 369]

LITTLETON, EDWARD JOHN, first BARON HATHERTON (1791-1863), of Rugby and Brasenose College, Oxford; M.P., Staffordshire, 1812-32; created D.C.L. Oxford, 1817; supported Reform Bill; M.P., South Staffordshire, 1832 and 1835; chief secretary to the lord-lieutenant of Ireland, 1833; privy councillor, 1833; supported new Coercion Bill, 1834, but resigned office in consequence of having made indiscreet communications to O'Connell, 1834; created Baron Hatherton of Hatherton, 1835; began his political career as member of the independent country party, and ended it as a whig.
[xxxiii. 369]

LITTLETON, HENRY (1823-1888), music publisher; entered music publishing house of Novello, 1841; manager, 1846; partner, 1861; sole proprietor, 1866; retired, leaving largest business of the kind in the world, 1887.
[xxxiii. 372]

LITTLETON, JAMES (d. 1723), vice-admiral; grand-nephew of Sir Thomas Littleton (1647?-1710) [q. v.]; present as first lieutenant at the battle of La Hogue, 1692; captain, 1693; on the Newfoundland station, 1696-1697; in the East Indies acting against pirates, 1699; present at Alicante, 1706; in the West Indies, 1709-12; resident commissioner and commander-in-chief at Chatham, 1715; rear-admiral of the red, 1716; vice-admiral of the blue, 1717; M.P., Queensborough, 1722.
[xxxiii. 372]

LITTLETON, SIR THOMAS (1422-1481), judge and legal author; sheriff of Worcestershire, 1447; serjeant-at-law, 1453; king's serjeant, 1455; justice of the common pleas, 1466 ; K.B., 1475. His fame rests on his treatise on 'Tenures,' written in law-French, and his text, with Coke's comment [see COKE, SIR EDWARD], long remained the principal authority on English real property law ; the *editio princeps* is a folio published in London without date or title. [xxxiii. 373]

LITTLETON, SIR THOMAS, third baronet (1647 ?–1710), speaker of the House of Commons and treasurer of the navy ; educated at St. Edmund Hall, Oxford ; entered Inner Temple, 1671 ; succeeded to his father's baronetcy, 1681 ; M.P., Woodstock, 1609–1702 ; an active whig ; a lord of the admiralty, 1697 ; speaker of the House of Commons, 1698–1700 ; treasurer of the navy, 1701–10 ; M.P., Castle Rising, Norfolk, 1702, Chichester, 1707, Portsmouth, 1708–10. [xxxiii. 376]

LITTLEWOOD, WILLIAM EDENSOR (1831–1886), miscellaneous writer ; of Merchant Taylors' School and Pembroke College, Cambridge ; B.A., 1854 ; ordained, 1858 ; M.A., 1860 ; published theological and historical works. [xxxiii. 377]

LITTLINGTON, WILLIAM OF (d. 1312). [See WILLIAM.]

LITTON, MARIE (1847–1884), actress ; her real name Lowe ; first appeared on the stage, 1868 ; managed the Court Theatre, 1871–4, the Imperial Theatre, 1878, and the Theatre Royal, Glasgow, 1880 ; made her reputation in old comedy in such parts as Lady Teazle, Lydia Languish, and Miss Hardcastle. [xxxiii. 377]

LIULF or **LIGULF** (d. 1080), Anglo-Saxon nobleman ; friend of Walcher, bishop of Durham ; excited envy of bishop's chaplain, Leobwine, by whom he was murdered. [xxxiii. 378]

LIVELY, EDWARD (1545 ?–1605), Hebrew professor at Cambridge ; M.A. Trinity College, Cambridge, 1572 ; regius professor of Hebrew, 1575 ; prebendary of Peterborough, 1602 ; one of the translators of the authorised version, 1604 ; published 'A true Chronologie of the . . . Persian Monarchie,' 1597, and other works. [xxxiii. 378]

LIVERPOOL, EARLS OF. [See JENKINSON, CHARLES, first EARL, 1727–1808 ; JENKINSON, ROBERT BANKS, second EARL, 1770–1828 ; JENKINSON, CHARLES CECIL COPE, third EARL, 1784–1851.]

LIVERSEEGE, HENRY (1803–1832), painter ; lived chiefly in Manchester ; painted subject-pictures. [xxxiii. 379]

LIVESAY, RICHARD (d. 1823 ?), portrait and landscape painter ; exhibited portraits and domestic subjects at Royal Academy, 1776–1821 ; copied pictures at Windsor for Benjamin West, and taught some of the royal children drawing, 1790 ; drawing-master to the Royal Naval College, Portsmouth, 1796. [xxxiii. 379]

LIVESEY, JAMES (1625 ?–1682), divine ; vicar of Great Budworth, Cheshire, 1657–82 ; published some scholarly sermons. [xxxiii. 380]

LIVESEY, JOSEPH (1794–1884), temperance advocate and philanthropist ; brought out 'The Moral Reformer,' a magazine, 1831–3 and 1838–9 ; issued the 'Preston Temperance Advocate,' the first teetotal publication in England, 1834 ; managed the 'Preston Guardian,' 1844–59 ; the 'Teetotal Progressionist,' 1851–2, 'The Staunch Teetotaler,' 1867–9 ; published an autobiography, 1881. [xxxiii. 380]

LIVESEY, SIR MICHAEL, first baronet (1611–1663 ?), regicide ; created baronet, 1627 ; M.P., Queensborough, Kent, 1645 ; signed Charles I's death-warrant ; commissioner of the admiralty and navy, 1660 ; escaped to the Low Countries at the Restoration. [xxxiii. 381]

LIVING, LYFING, ELFSTAN, or **ETHELSTAN** (d. 1020), archbishop of Canterbury ; bishop of Wells, 999 ; appointed to Canterbury by Ethelred the Unready [q. v.], 1013 ; crowned Edmund Ironside [q. v.], 1016, and Canute [q. v.], 1017. [xxxiii. 382]

LIVING or **LYFING** (d. 1046), bishop of Crediton ; abbot of Tavistock, Devonshire ; accompanied Canute [q. v.] to Rome, and brought back his famous letter to the English people ; bishop of Crediton, 1027 ; bishop of Worcester, holding the see in plurality, 1038, the see of Cornwall being merged with that of Crediton, c. 1043. [xxxiii. 382]

LIVINGSTONE, SIR ALEXANDER (d. 1450 ?), of Callendar ; guardian of James II of Scotland ; aided James I of Scotland's widow in foiling Sir William Crichton [q. v.], 1439 and 1443 ; justiciary of Scotland, 1449 ; fell into disgrace and was imprisoned. [xxxiii. 382]

LIVINGSTONE, ALEXANDER, seventh BARON LIVINGSTONE and first EARL OF LINLITHGOW (d. 1622), eldest son of William Livingstone, sixth baron [q. v.] ; supported Mary Queen of Scots ; lord of the bedchamber, 1580 ; succeeded his father, 1592 ; commissioner of taxation, 1594 ; guardian of Princess Elizabeth, 1596–1603 ; privy councillor, 1598 ; created Earl of Linlithgow, Lord Livingstone and Callendar, 1600. [xxxiii. 383]

LIVINGSTONE, CHARLES (1821–1873), missionary and traveller ; brother of David Livingstone [q. v.] ; emigrated to America and became a missionary, 1840 ; joined his brother in his African expeditions, 1857–63 ; appointed English consul at Fernando Po, 1864 ; the Bights of Benin and Biafra added to his district, 1867 ; died near Lagos. [xxxiii. 384]

LIVINGSTONE, CHARLOTTE MARIA, COUNTESS OF NEWBURGH (d. 1755). [See RADCLIFFE or RADCLYFFE, CHARLOTTE MARIA.]

LIVINGSTONE, DAVID (1813–1873), African missionary and explorer ; educated himself while working at a cotton factory near Glasgow ; attended the medical class at Anderson College and lectures at Glasgow University, 1832 ; entered the service of the London Missionary Society, studied medicine and science in London ; embarked as a missionary for the Cape of Good Hope, 1840 ; made journeys into the interior, 1841, 1842, and 1843 ; discovered Lake Ngami, 1849, and the Zambesi in the centre of the continent, 1851 ; made great exploring expedition from Cape Town northwards through Westcentral Africa to Loanda and back to Quilimane 1852–1856 ; visited England, 1856 ; D.C.L. Oxford and F.R.S. ; published his missionary travels, and severed his connection with the London Missionary Society, 1857 ; consul at Quilimane, 1858–64 ; commanded expedition to explore Eastern and Central Africa, 1858 ; discovered lakes Shirwa and Nyasa, 1859 ; lost his wife at Shupanga, 1862 ; visited England, 1864 ; published 'The Zambesi and its Tributaries,' 1865 ; started on expedition to solve the question of the Nile basin, 1865 ; discovered Lake Bangweolo, 1868 ; reached Ujiji, 1869 ; explored the cannibal country, enduring great sufferings, and returned, almost dying, to Ujiji, where he was rescued by Stanley, 1871 ; reached Unyanyembe, 1872 ; made further explorations to discover the sources of the Nile, and died at a village in the country of Ilala ; buried in Westminster Abbey, 1874. [xxxiii. 384]

LIVINGSTONE, GEORGE, third EARL OF LINLITHGOW (1616–1690), eldest son of Alexander Livingstone, second earl of Linlithgow ; M.P., Perthshire, 1654–5 ; privy councillor, 1660 ; major-general of the forces in Scotland, 1677–9 ; justice-general, 1684 ; deprived of the justice-generalship at the Revolution. [xxxiii. 396]

LIVINGSTONE, GEORGE, fourth EARL OF LINLITHGOW (1652 ?–1695), eldest son of George Livingstone, third earl of Linlithgow [q. v.] ; supported his father against the covenanters ; attempted to support King James, 1689 ; succeeded his father, 1690 ; privy councillor and commissioner of the treasury, 1692. [xxxiii. 397]

LIVINGSTONE, SIR JAMES, of Barncloich, first VISCOUNT KILSYTH (1616–1661), a devoted loyalist ; raised to the peerage of Scotland as Viscount Kilsyth and Lord Campsie, 1661. [xxxiii. 397]

LIVINGSTONE, SIR JAMES, of Kinnaird, first EARL OF NEWBURGH (d. 1670), gentleman of the bedchamber to Charles I, and created Viscount Newburgh, 1647 ; joined Charles II at the Hague, 1650 ; accompanied Charles's expedition to England, 1651 ; escaped to France after the battle of Worcester, 1651 ; captain of the guards, 1660 ; created Earl of Newburgh, Viscount Kinnaird, and Baron Livingstone of Flacraig, 1660. [xxxiii. 398]

LIVINGSTONE, JAMES, first EARL OF CALLANDER (d. 1674), third son of Alexander Livingstone, first earl of Linlithgow [q. v.] ; saw military service abroad ; knighted before 1629 ; created Baron Livingstone of Almond, 1633 ; accepted office from the covenanters, but secretly favoured Charles I, who created him Earl of Callander, Baron Livingstone and Almond, 1641 ; appointed lieutenant-general of the 'Engagement' army raised to liberate the king; escaped to Holland on its failure; took an active part in parliament, 1661-72. [xxxiii. 398]

LIVINGSTONE, JOHN (1603-1672), Scottish divine; educated at Glasgow University; licensed to preach, 1625; banished at the Restoration, 1660; died at Rotterdam; his 'Life' first published, 1754. [xxxiii. 401]

LIVINGSTONE, SIR THOMAS, first VISCOUNT OF TEVIOT (1652 ?-1711), lieutenant-general; born in Holland; succeeded as second baronet; came to England with William of Orange, 1688; appointed colonel of the (present) royal Scots greys, 1688; commander-in-chief in Scotland and privy councillor, 1690; major-general on the English establishment, 1696; created Viscount of Teviot in the peerage of Scotland, 1696; lieutenant-general, 1704. [xxxiii. 403]

LIVINGSTONE, WILLIAM, sixth BARON LIVINGSTONE (d. 1592), partisan of Queen Mary; succeeded to barony, 1553; fought for Mary Queen of Scots at Langside, and accompanied her in her flight, 1568; Mary's agent in England, 1570; advised the king to abolish the regency, 1577. [xxxiii. 403]

LIVINGUS (d. 1046). [See LIVING.]

LIVINUS, SAINT (d. 656 ?), known as the 'Apostle of Brabant'; the proof of his existence rests on an epistle and epitaph which he is said to have written; according to late authorities he was of Scottish or Irish race, and an archbishop of Ireland, who went to Ghent, 633, and was martyred at Escha. [xxxiii. 404]

LIVIUS, TITUS (fl. 1437), historian; called himself Titus Livius de Frulovisiis, of Ferrara; came to England and found a patron in Humphrey, duke of Gloucester [q. v.]; naturalised, 1437; his 'Vita Henrici Quinti, Regis Invictissimi,' edited by Hearne, 1716. [xxxiii. 405]

LIXNAW, BARONS. [See FITZMAURICE, PATRICK, 1551 ?-1600; FITZMAURICE, THOMAS, 1502-1590; FITZMAURICE, THOMAS, 1574-1630.]

LIZARS, JOHN (1787 ?-1860), surgeon; educated at Edinburgh University; his best-known work, 'A System of Anatomical Plates of the Human Body, with Descriptions,' 1822; professor of surgery in the Royal College of Surgeons, Edinburgh, 1831. [xxxiii. 405]

LIZARS, WILLIAM HOME (1788-1859), painter and engraver; brother of John Lizars [q. v.]; learnt engraving from his father; studied painting at Trustees' Academy, Edinburgh; carried on the engraving business after his father's death, 1812; perfected method of etching for book illustration. [xxxiii. 406]

LLANOVER, first BARON (1802-1867). [See HALL, SIR BENJAMIN.]

LLEWELYN. [See also LLUELYN and LLYWELYN.]

LLEWELYN, DAVID (d. 1415). [See GAM.]

LLEWELYN, THOMAS (1720 ?-1793), baptist minister; published an 'Historical Account of the British or Welsh Versions and Editions of the Bible,' 1768; prominent in establishment of baptist mission in North Wales, 1776. [xxxiii. 407]

LLEYN, SION (1749-1817). [See SION.]

LLEYN, WILLIAM (1530 ?-1587). [See OWEN.]

LLOYD. [See also LHUYD, LLWYD, and LOYD.]

LLOYD, BARTHOLOMEW (1772-1837), provost of Trinity College, Dublin; educated at Trinity College, Dublin; M.A., 1796; D.D., 1808; Erasmus Smith's professor of mathematics, 1813; regius professor of Greek, 1821, 1823, and 1825; Erasmus Smith's professor of natural and experimental philosophy, 1822; king's lecturer in divinity, 1823 and 1827; provost, 1831-7; president of the Royal Irish Academy, 1835; 'Lloyd Exhibitions' founded in his memory, 1839. [xxxiii. 407]

LLOYD or FLOYD, SIR CHARLES (d. 1661), royalist; brother of Sir Godfrey Lloyd or Floyd [q. v.]; quartermaster-general of the king's army, 1644; knighted, 1644. [xxxiii. 408]

LLOYD, CHARLES (1735-1773), secretary to George Grenville [q. v.]; of Westminster and Christ Church, Oxford; M.A., 1761; secretary to George Grenville, 1763; deputy-teller of the exchequer, 1767; published political pamphlets in Grenville's interest, 1763-7. [xxxiii. 408]

LLOYD, CHARLES (1748-1828), quaker; philanthropist; banker of Birmingham; a pioneer in the movement for the emancipation of slaves; published translations from Homer and Horace. [xxxiii. 409]

LLOYD, CHARLES (1766-1829), dissenting minister and schoolmaster; held ministries in England till 1793; pastor in Cardiganshire and Suffolk; LL.D. Glasgow, 1809; opened school in London, 1811; chief work, 'Particulars in the Life of a Dissenting Minister' (autobiography), 1813. [xxxiii. 410]

LLOYD, CHARLES (1784-1829), bishop of Oxford; of Eton and Christ Church, Oxford; M.A., 1809; mathematical lecturer, tutor, and censor, Christ Church, Oxford; preacher of Lincoln's Inn, 1819-22; regius professor of divinity, Oxford, 1822-9; bishop of Oxford, 1827-9; the first to publish the 'Book of Common Prayer' with red-lettered rubrics, 1829. [xxxiii. 411]

LLOYD, CHARLES (1775-1839), poet; son of Charles Lloyd (1748-1828) [q. v.]; published poems, 1795; lived with Coleridge, 1796-7; his poems appended to an edition of Coleridge's poems, along with verses by Charles Lamb, 1797; cultivated Lamb's society; his 'Desultory Thoughts in London,' published, 1821; became insane; died at Chaillot near Versailles. [xxxiii. 412]

LLOYD, CHARLES DALTON CLIFFORD (1844-1891), servant of the crown; grandson of Bartholomew Lloyd [q. v.]; educated at Sandhurst; in police force in British Burmah, 1862-72; resident magistrate for co. Down, 1874; employed to restore order in co. Longford, 1881; concerted scheme (1881) for vigorous administration of Protection of Person and Property Act; inspector-general of reforms to khedive of Egypt, 1883; under-secretary at the home office in Egypt; resigned (1884) because his schemes for prison reform were not supported; again resident magistrate in Ireland, 1885; lieutenant-governor of Mauritius, 1885-7; consul for Kurdistan, 1889; died at Erzeroum, 1891; his 'Ireland under the Land League, a Narrative of Personal Experiences,' published, 1892. [xxxiii. 414]

LLOYD, DAVID (1597-1663), author of the 'Legend of Captain Jones'; educated at Hart Hall, Oxford; B.A., 1615; fellow of All Souls College, Oxford, 1618; D.C.L., 1628; canon of Chester, 1639; remembered by his popular jeu d'esprit, 'The Legend of Captain Jones,' a burlesque on the adventures of an Elizabethan sea-rover named Jones, 1631. [xxxiii. 415]

LLOYD, DAVID (1635-1692), biographer; M.A. Merton College, Oxford, 1659; reader in the Charterhouse, London, 1659; chaplain to Isaac Barrow, bishop of St. Asaph [q. v.]; published 'The Statesmen and Favourites of England since the Reformation,' 1665 and 1670; his memoirs of royalist sufferers published, 1668. [xxxiii. 416]

LLOYD, DAVID (d. 1714 ?), captain in the navy, 1677; employed by James II as agent and emissary during the reign of William III; retired into private life after James's death. [xxxiii. 417]

LLOYD, DAVID (1752-1838), divine and poet; took holy orders, 1778; his 'Characteristics of Men, Manners, and Sentiments, on the Voyage of Life,' 1812, an imitation of Young; published 'Horæ Theologicæ,' 1823. [xxxiii. 417]

LLOYD, EDWARD (d. 1648 ?). [See FLOYD.]

LLOYD, EDWARD (fl. 1688-1726), coffee-house keeper, from whom the great commercial corporation known as 'Lloyd's' derives its name; his coffee-house in Lombard Street the centre of shipbroking and marine insurance business, 1692; issued 'Lloyd's News,' a shipping and commercial chronicle, 1696-7, revived as 'Lloyd's Lists,' 1726, and still continued. [xxxiii. 418]

LLOYD, EDWARD (d. 1847), captain of the Gambia River; captain in the royal African corps, 1804-12; regarded as the founder of the Gambia River settlement, where he died. [xxxiii. 419]

LLOYD, EDWARD (1815-1890), founder of 'Lloyd's Weekly London Newspaper'; sold books and published cheap literature in London; issued 'Lloyd's Penny Weekly Miscellany,' 1842-4, continued as 'Lloyd's Entertaining

Journal' till 1847; first issued 'Lloyd's Weekly London Newspaper,' 1842; bought the 'Daily Chronicle,' 1876. [xxxiii. 419]

LLOYD, EVAN (1734–1776), poet; M.A. Jesus College, Oxford, 1757; published 'The Powers of the Pen,' an attack on Warburton and Johnson, 1765, 'The Curate,' 1766, and 'The Methodist,' for which latter satire he underwent imprisonment for libel; friend of Wilkes and Garrick. [xxxiii. 419]

LLOYD, GEORGE (1560–1615), bishop of Chester; fellow of Magdalene College, Cambridge; rector of Heswell-in-Wirrall, Cheshire, and divinity reader in Chester Cathedral; bishop of Sodor and Man, 1600, of Chester, 1604; held livings in addition to his sees. [xxxiii. 420]

LLOYD or FLOYD, SIR GODFREY (*fl.* 1667), military engineer; brother of Sir Charles Lloyd or Floyd [q. v.]; captain in the Dutch service; knighted by Charles II, 1657; chief engineer of ports, castles, and fortifications in England, 1661–7. [xxxiii. 420]

LLOYD, HANNIBAL EVANS (1771–1847), philologist and translator; son of Henry Humphrey Evans Lloyd [q. v.]; settled at Hamburg, 1800; held appointment in London foreign office, 1813–47; published annals of Hamburg for 1813, 1813; his 'Theoretisch-praktische Englische Sprachlehre für Deutsche' (1833) long the standard grammar in several German universities; published translations from various European languages. [xxxiii. 421]

LLOYD, HENRY, or HENRY HUMPHREY EVANS (1720 ?–1783), historian and soldier; engineer in the Young Pretender's expedition to Scotland, 1745; distinguished himself at the siege of Bergen-op-Zoom, 1747, and was made major in the French army, 1747; served first on Austrian side, and afterwards on Prussian side, in the seven years' war; in the Russian service, 1774; occupied himself with literary work, 1779–83; died at Hay, Belgium; chief works, 'History of the War between the King of Prussia and the Empress of Germany and her Allies' (vol. i. 1766, vols. ii. and iii. 1782), and 'A Political and Military Rhapsody on the Defence of Great Britain,' 1779. [xxxiii. 422]

LLOYD, HUGH (1546–1601), master of Winchester College; educated at Winchester and New College, Oxford; B.A., 1566; chancellor of Rochester, 1578; master of Winchester, 1580–7; D.C.L., 1588; Latin phrase-book by him published, 1654. [xxxiii. 423]

LLOYD, HUGH (1586–1667), bishop of Llandaff; M.A. Oriel College, Oxford, 1614; held various livings in Wales, 1617–44; D.D., 1638; a staunch royalist; his benefices sequestered during the civil wars; canon and archdeacon of St. David's, 1644; bishop of Llandaff, 1660–7. [xxxiii. 424]

LLOYD, HUMPHREY (1610–1689), bishop of Bangor; educated at Jesus and Oriel Colleges, Oxford; M.A., 1635; prebendary of York, 1660; dean of St. Asaph, 1663–74; bishop of Bangor, 1674–89. [xxxiii. 424]

LLOYD, HUMPHREY (1800–1881), provost of Trinity College, Dublin, and man of science: son of Bartholomew Lloyd [q. v.]; B.A. Trinity College, Dublin, 1819; junior fellow, 1824; M.A., 1827; Erasmus Smith's professor of natural and experimental philosophy, 1831–43; president of Royal Irish Academy, 1846–51; D C.L. Oxford, 1855; vice-provost, 1862; provost, 1867; published treatises on optics and magnetism, embodying his discoveries. [xxxiii. 425]

LLOYD, JACOB YOUDE WILLIAM (1816–1887), genealogist; son of Jacob William Hinde, but assumed name of Lloyd on succeeding to estates, 1857; M.A. Wadham College, Oxford, 1874; convert to Roman catholicism; served in the pontifical Zouaves; published genealogical works. [xxxiii. 426]

LLOYD, FLOYD, or FLUD, JOHN (*d.* 1523), composer; took a musical degree at Oxford; attended Henry VIII at the Field of the Cloth of Gold, 1520; his extant compositions in the British Museum Addit. MSS. [xxxiii. 426]

LLOYD, JOHN (1558–1603), classical scholar; brother of Hugh Lloyd (1546–1601) [q. v.]; of Winchester and New College, Oxford; perpetual fellow, 1579–96; M.A., 1585; edited, with Latin translation and notes, 'Flavii Josephi de Maccabæis liber,' 1590; D.D., 1595; vicar of Writtle, Essex, 1598–1603. [xxxiii. 427]

LLOYD, JOHN (*d.* 1682), poet; brother of Nicholas Lloyd [q. v.]; M.A. Wadham College, Oxford, 1669; published a 'Paraphrase' of the Song of Solomon, 1682. [xxxiii. 427]

LLOYD, JOHN (1638–1687), bishop of St. David's; of Merton College, Oxford; M.A., 1662; precentor of Llandaff, 1672; principal of Jesus College, Oxford, 1673; D.D., 1674; vice-chancellor of Oxford 1682–5; bishop of St. David's, 1686. [xxxiii. 427]

LLOYD, JOHN AUGUSTUS (1800–1854), engineer and surveyor; served on the staff of Simon Bolivar, the liberator of Colombia, as a captain of engineers; surveyed Isthmus of Panama, 1827; F.R.S., 1830; colonial civil engineer and surveyor-general in Mauritius, 1831–49; British chargé d'affaires, Bolivia, 1851; died at Therapia. [xxxiii. 427]

LLOYD, JULIUS (1830–1892), divine and author: M.A. Trinity College, Cambridge, 1855; canon of Manchester, 1891; author of sermons and essays. [xxxiii. 428]

LLOYD, LUDOVIC, LODOWICK, or LEWIS (*fl.* 1573–1610), poet and compiler; 'Seargeant at Armes' to Queen Elizabeth and James I; author of 'The Pilgrimage of Princes,' compiled from Greek and Latin authors, 1573, and other compilations and poems, mainly treating of 'Collectanea Curiosa.' [xxxiii. 429]

LLOYD, SIR NATHANIEL (1669–1745), master of Trinity Hall, Cambridge; son of Sir Richard Lloyd (1634–1686) [q. v.]; of St. Paul's School, London, and Trinity College, Oxford; fellow of All Souls College, Oxford, 1689; D.C.L., 1696; member of the College of Advocates, 1696; knighted, 1710; master of Trinity Hall, Cambridge, 1710–35; king's advocate, 1715–27. [xxxiii. 430]

LLOYD, NICHOLAS (1630–1680), historical compiler; educated at Winchester and Hart Hall and Wadham College, Oxford; M.A., 1658; university rhetoric reader, 1665; sub-warden of Wadham College, 1666 and 1670; published a 'Dictionarium Historicum,' 1670. [xxxiii. 430]

LLOYD, RICHARD (1595–1659), royalist divine; educated at Oriel College, Oxford; B.D., 1628; on outbreak of civil law deprived of his preferments and imprisoned. [xxxiii. 431]

LLOYD, SIR RICHARD (1606–1676), royalist; entered Inner Temple, 1631; attended Charles I in the north, 1639; attorney-general for North Wales and knighted, 1642; justice of Glamorganshire, Brecknockshire, and Radnorshire, 1660; M.P., Radnorshire, 1661. [xxxiii. 431]

LLOYD, SIR RICHARD (1634–1686), judge; fellow of All Souls College, Oxford; D.C.L., 1662; advocate at Doctors' Commons, 1664; admiralty advocate, 1674–85; chancellor of the dioceses of Llandaff and Durham; knighted, 1677; M.P., Durham, 1679–81 and 1685; dean of the arches, 1684–6; judge of the high court of admiralty, 1685–6. [xxxiii. 430]

LLOYD, RICHARD (*d.* 1834), divine; educated at Magdalene College, Cambridge; M.A. and fellow, 1790; published theological works. [xxxiii. 432]

LLOYD, RIDGWAY ROBERT SYERS CHRISTIAN CODNER (1842–1884), physician and antiquary; M.R.C.S. and L.S.A., 1866; published 'An Account of the Altars, Monuments, and Tombs in St. Albans Abbey,' 1873, and wrote many archæological papers. [xxxiii. 432]

LLOYD, ROBERT (1733–1764), poet; of Westminster and Trinity College, Cambridge; M.A., 1758; published 'The Actor,' 1760, and a collection of poems, 1762; edited the 'St. James's Magazine,' 1762–3; imprisoned for debt; drudged for the booksellers; his comic opera, 'The Capricious Lovers,' performed, 1764; friend of Churchill, Garrick, and Wilkes. [xxxiii. 432]

LLOYD, SIMON (1756–1836), Welsh methodist; M.A. Jesus College, Oxford, 1779; associated himself with the Calvinistic methodist movement after 1785; edited the Welsh magazine 'Y Drysorfa,' 1814; published a biblical chronology, 1816, and a commentary on the Apocalypse, 1828, both in Welsh. [xxxiii. 434]

LLOYD, THOMAS (1784–1813), colonel; served in the Egyptian campaign, 1801; at Gibraltar, 1802; captain,

1803 ; served at Copenhagen and throughout the Peninsular campaigns, 1808-10 ; major, 1810 ; killed at battle of Nivelle. [xxxiii. 435]

LLOYD, WILLIAM (1637-1710), nonjuring bishop of Norwich ; M.A. St. John's College, Cambridge ; D.D. *per literas regias*, 1670 ; chaplain to the English Merchants' Factory, Portugal ; D.D., 1670 ; prebendary of St. Paul's, 1672-6 ; bishop of Llandaff, 1675-9, of Peterborough, 1679-85, of Norwich, 1685-91 ; deprived of his office for refusing the oath of allegiance to William III, 1691. [xxxiii. 435]

LLOYD, WILLIAM (1627-1717), successively bishop of St. Asaph, of Lichfield and Coventry, and of Worcester ; son of Richard Lloyd (1595-1659) [q. v.] ; of Oriel and Jesus Colleges, Oxford ; M.A., 1646 ; M.A. Cambridge, 1660 ; prebendary of Ripon, 1663 ; D.D., 1667 ; prebendary of Salisbury, 1667 ; archdeacon of Merioneth, 1668-72 ; dean of Bangor and prebendary of St. Paul's, 1672 ; bishop of St. Asaph, 1680 ; tried with the six other bishops on the charge of publishing a seditious libel against the king and acquitted, 1688 ; bishop of Lichfield and Coventry, 1692, of Worcester, 1700 ; being half crazed by excessive study of the apocalyptic visions prophesied to Queen Anne, Harley, Evelyn, and Whiston ; a staunch supporter of the revolution and an excellent scholar ; engaged Burnet to undertake 'The History of the Reformation of the Church of England' and gave him valuable assistance ; published sermons and controversial pamphlets. [xxxiii. 436]

LLOYD, WILLIAM FORSTER (1794-1852), mathematician ; of Westminster and Christ Church, Oxford ; M.A., 1818 ; Greek reader, 1823 ; mathematical lecturer at Christ Church, Oxford, 1824 ; Drummond professor of political economy, 1832-7 ; F.R.S., 1834 ; published professorial lectures. [xxxiii. 440]

LLOYD, WILLIAM WATKISS (1813-1893), classical and Shakespearean scholar ; partner in tobacco manufacturing business in London ; retired, 1864 ; member of Society of Dilettanti, 1854 ; published 'History of Sicily, to the Athenian War,' 1872, 'The Age of Pericles,' 1875, 'The Moses of Michael Angelo,' 1863, 'Homer, his Art and Age,' 1848, 'Shakespeare's "Much Ado about Nothing" ... in fully recovered Metrical Form,' 1884 (he contended that Shakespeare's prose was disguised blank verse), and other miscellaneous works. [Suppl. iii. 102]

LLUELYN. [See also LLEWELYN and LLYWELYN.]

LLUELYN or **LLUELLYN**, MARTIN (1616-1682), poet, physician, and principal of St. Mary Hall, Oxford ; of Westminster and Christ Church, Oxford ; M.A., 1643 ; joined the royal army ; published 'Men Miracles, with other Poems,' 1646 ; ejected from Oxford, 1648 ; physician in London ; M.D. Oxford, 1653 ; F.R.C.P., 1659 ; principal of St. Mary Hall, 1660-4 ; physician at High Wycombe after 1664 ; mayor of High Wycombe, 1671. [xxxiii. 440]

LLWYD. [See also LHUYD, LLOYD, and LOYD.]

LLWYD, EDWARD (*fl.* 1328-1405). [See IOLO GOCH.]

LLWYD, SIR GRUFFYDD (*fl.* 1322), Welsh hero ; grandson of Ednyved Vychan [q. v.] ; knighted, 1284 ; rebelled against the English and was defeated and imprisoned. [xxxiv. 1]

LLWYD, GRUFFYDD (*fl.* 1370-1420), Welsh poet ; family bard to Owen Glendower. Two poems by him published. [xxxiv. 1]

LLWYD, HUGH or HUW (1533 ?-1620), Welsh poet ; held commission in the English army and saw service abroad ; his best-known production, a 'Poem on the Fox,' printed in 'Cymru Fu,' i. 357. [xxxiv. 1]

LLWYD, HUMPHREY (1527-1568), physician and antiquary ; of Brasenose College, Oxford ; M.A., 1551 ; M.P., East Grinstead, 1559, Denbigh boroughs, 1563-7 ; author of antiquarian works, among them, 'Commentarioli Descriptionis Britannicæ Fragmentum,' published at Cologne, 1572 (an English translation, 'The Breviary of Britain,' published in London, 1573), and 'Cambriæ Typus,' one of the earliest known maps of Wales. [xxxiv. 2]

LLWYD or **LLOYD**, JOHN (1558 ?-1603), of Winchester and New College, Oxford ; fellow of New College,

1579 ; M.A., 1585 ; D.D., 1595 ; author of an edition of Josephus's 'De Maccabæis,' 1590 ; edited Barlaamus's 'De Papæ Principatu,' 1592. [xxxiv. 3]

LLWYD, MORGAN (1619-1659), Welsh puritan divine and mystic writer ; grandson or nephew of Hugh Llwyd [q. v.] ; served with the parliamentary army in England ; founded a nonconformist church at Wrexham, and became its first minister, *c.* 1646. His published works rank among the Welsh prose classics. [xxxiv. 3]

LLWYD, RICHARD (1752-1835), poet ; known as 'the Bard of Snowdon' ; 'Beaumaris Bay,' his best-known poem, published, 1800 ; published other poems, 1804. [xxxiv. 4]

LLYWARCH AB **LLYWELYN**, otherwise known as PRYDYDD Y MOCH (*fl.* 1160-1220), Welsh bard ; the most illustrious Welsh bard of the middle ages ; some of his poems, all of which are historically valuable, printed in the 'Myvyrian Archaiology of Wales.' [xxxiv. 5]

LLYWARCH HEN, or the AGED (496 ?-646 ?), British chieftain and bard ; not mentioned till several centuries after his death ; ancient form of his name Loumarc ; probably spent some time at Arthur's court. Twelve poems, six of an historical character and the remainder on moral subjects, are ascribed to him, and were first published with an English translation in 1792. [xxxiv. 5]

LLYWELYN. [See also LLEWELYN and LLUELYN.]

LLYWELYN AB **SEISYLL** or **SEISYLLT** (*d.* 1023 ?), king of Gwynedd ; took possession of the throne of North Wales, *c.* 1018. [xxxiv. 6]

LLYWELYN AB **IORWERTH**, called LLYWELYN THE GREAT (*d.* 1240), prince of North Wales, afterwards called Prince of Wales ; son of Owain Gwynedd [q. v.] ; brought up in exile, probably in England ; drove his uncle Davydd ab Owain [see DAVYDD I] from his territory, 1194 ; made peace with Gwenwynwyn [q. v.], 1202 ; married Joan (*d.* 1237) [q. v.], King John's illegitimate daughter, 1206 ; with John's help extended his power to South Wales, 1207 ; opposed by John with some success, 1208-11 ; regained his possessions and conquered South Wales, 1212-15 ; prince of all Wales not ruled by the Normans, 1216 ; did homage to Henry III, 1218 ; fought against the English, 1228 ; submitted to Henry III, 1237 ; the greatest of the native rulers of Wales. [xxxiv. 7]

LLYWELYN AB **GRUFFYDD** (*d.* 1282), prince of Wales ; son of Gruffydd ab Llywelyn (*d.* 1244) [q. v.] ; succeeded (with his elder brother, Owain the Red) his uncle, Davydd ab Llywelyn [see DAVYDD II], as ruler of Wales, 1246 ; did homage to Henry III, and gave up to him all lands east of the Conway, 1247 ; allied himself with Simon de Montfort, 1262 ; took the offensive against Prince Edward and forced him to a truce, 1263 ; after renewal of hostilities (1265) agreed to hold the principality of Wales subject to the crown of England, 1267 ; neglected to do homage to Edward I, 1272 ; quarrelled with Gruffydd ab Gwenwynwyn [q. v.] and Davydd III [q. v.] and drove them to England, 1274 ; signed treaty of Conway, 1277 ; married to Eleanor de Montfort (*d.* 1282), 1278 ; revolted against the English rule and was slain in a skirmish, 1282 ; the last champion of Welsh liberty. [xxxiv. 13]

LLYWELYN AB **RHYS**, commonly called LLYWELYN BREN (*d.* 1317), Welsh rebel ; held high office under Gilbert de Clare (1291-1314) [q. v.] ; revolted against one of the English overlords, 1314 ; surrendered, 1316 ; tried, condemned, and hung. [xxxiv. 21]

LLYWELYN OF LLANGEWYDD (or LLEWELYN SION) (1520 ?-1616), Welsh bard ; disciple of Thomas Llewelyn of Rhegoes ; gained his living by transcribing Welsh manuscripts ; several of his compositions published in the Iolo MSS. [xxxiv. 22]

LOBB, EMMANUEL (1594-1671). [See SIMEON, JOSEPH.]

LOBB, STEPHEN (*d.* 1699), nonconformist divine ; imprisoned for complicity in the Rye House plot, 1683 ; published controversial pamphlets. [xxxiv. 23]

LOBB, THEOPHILUS (1678-1763), physician ; son of Stephen Lobb [q. v.] ; educated for the ministry ;

studied medicine and practised while acting as nonconformist minister; M.D. Glasgow, 1722; F.R.S., 1729; applied himself wholly to medicine from 1736; L.R.C.P., 1740; published religious and medical works. [xxxiv. 24]

LÖBEL, HIRSCH (1721-1800). [See LYON, HART.]

LOCH, DAVID (d. 1780), writer on commerce; inspector-general of the woollen manufactures of Scotland, 1776, and afterwards of the fisheries; author of pamphlets advocating the abolition of the wool duties, 1774, and of 'Essays on the Trade, Commerce, Manufactures, and Fisheries of Scotland,' 1775. [xxxiv. 25]

LOCH, GRANVILLE GOWER (1813-1853), captain in the navy; son of James Loch [q. v.]; entered the navy, 1826; commander, 1837; attained post rank and went to China as a volunteer, 1841; published 'The Closing Events of the Campaign in China,' 1843; employed at Nicaragua, 1848; C.B., 1848; took prominent part in the second Burmese war, 1852-3; shot while attacking Donabew; buried at Rangoon. [xxxiv. 25]

LOCH, HENRY BROUGHAM, first BARON LOCH OF DRYLAW (1827-1900), gazetted to 3rd Bengal cavalry, 1844; aide-de-camp to Lord Gough in Sutlej campaign, 1845; adjutant of Skinner's (irregular) horse, 1850; served in Crimean war; attached to staff of embassy to China, 1857; private secretary to Lord Elgin when plenipotentiary in China, 1860; seized by Chinese officials, imprisoned and tortured; returned to England in charge of treaty of Tientsin, 1860; private secretary to Sir George Grey (1799-1882) [q. v.]; governor of Isle of Man, 1863-82; K.C.B., 1880; commissioner of woods and forests and land revenue, 1882-4; governor of Victoria, 1884-9; governor of the Cape and high commissioner in South Africa, 1889-1895; raised to peerage, 1895; took leading share in raising and equipping 'Loch's Horse' for service in South Africa, 1899; published 'Personal Narrative of ... Lord Elgin's second Embassy to China,' 1869. [Suppl. iii. 103]

LOCH, JAMES (1780-1855), economist; admitted an advocate in Scotland, 1801; barrister, Lincoln's Inn, 1806; abandoned law and assumed management of several noblemen's estates; M.P. for St. Germains, Cornwall, 1827-30, for Wick burghs, 1830-52. [xxxiv. 26]

LOCHINVAR, first BARON (1599?-1634). [See GORDON, SIR JOHN, first VISCOUNT KENMURE.]

LOCHORE, ROBERT (1762-1852), Scottish poet; published poems in Scottish vernacular, 1795-6 and 1815; edited the 'Kilmarnock Mirror,' c. 1817. [xxxiv. 26]

LOCK. [See also LOCKE and LOK.]

LOCKE. [See also LOK.]

LOCKE, JOHN (1632-1704), philosopher; educated at Westminster and Christ Church, Oxford; M.A., 1658; Greek lecturer at Oxford, 1660; lecturer on rhetoric, 1662; censor of moral philosophy, 1663; wrote 'An Essay concerning Toleration,' which contains his views on religion, 1667; became physician to Anthony Ashley Cooper (afterwards the first Earl of Shaftesbury) and settled in his house, 1667; F.R.S., 1668; M.B., 1675; secretary to the 'lords' proprietors of Carolina, 1669-72; secretary of presentations under Shaftesbury as lord chancellor, 1672; secretary to the reconstructed council of trade, 1673-5; in France, 1675-9; subsequently resided in Oxford until expelled for supposed complicity in Shaftesbury's plots, 1684; lived in Holland, where he became known to the Prince of Orange, 1679; commissioner of appeals, 1689-1704; his first letter on 'Toleration' published in Latin and then in English, 1689; published 'An Essay concerning Human Understanding,' 1690 (2nd edit. 1694; 3rd, 1695); his second letter on 'Toleration' published, 1690 (a third in 1692, a fourth left unpublished at his death); lived with the Masham family at Oates, Essex, 1691; published treatise 'On Education,' 1693, on the 'Reasonableness of Christianity,' 1695, and on the currency question, 1695; member of the new council of trade, 1696-1700; his 'Paraphrases of St. Paul's Epistles' published, 1705-7; first edition of his collected works, 1714; called by John Stuart Mill the 'unquestioned founder of the analytic philosophy of mind.' [xxxiv. 37]

LOCKE, JOHN (1805-1880), legal writer and politician; of Dulwich College and Trinity College, Cambridge; M.A., 1832; barrister, Inner Temple, 1833; bencher, 1857;

Q.C., 1857; M.P., Southwark, 1857-80; introduced and passed bill (1861) for the admission of witnesses in criminal cases to the same right of substituting an affirmation for an oath as in civil cases; published two legal works. [xxxiv. 37]

LOCKE, JOSEPH (1805-1860), civil engineer; aided George Stephenson in construction of the railway between Manchester and Liverpool (opened, 1830); constructed various lines on his own account in Great Britain, France, Spain, and Germany, 1835-52; F.R.S., 1838; M.P., Honiton, 1847-60; president of the Institution of Civil Engineers, 1858 and 1859; designer of the 'Crewe engine.' [xxxiv. 37]

LOCKE, MATTHEW (1630?-1677), musical composer; assisted in the composition of the music for Shirley's masque, 'Cupid and Death,' 1653, and D'Avenant's 'Siege of Rhodes,' 1656; created 'composer in ordinary to his majesty' (Charles II), 1661; organist to Queen Catherine's Roman catholic establishment at Somerset House; composed music for 'Macbeth,' 1666 and 1669, and for the 'Tempest'; published 'Melothesia, or Certain General Rules for Playing on a Continued Bass, with a choice collection of Lessons for the Harpsichord or Organ of all sorts,' 1673. [xxxiv. 38]

LOCKE or **LOCK,** WILLIAM, the elder (1732-1810), art amateur and collector of works of art. [xxxiv. 39]

LOCKE, WILLIAM (1804-1832), captain in the lifeguards and amateur artist; published illustrations to Byron's works; drowned in the lake of Como. [xxxiv. 40]

LOCKE, WILLIAM, the younger (1767-1847), amateur artist; son of William Locke the elder [q. v.]; painted historical and allegorical subjects. [xxxiv. 40]

LOCKER, ARTHUR (1828-1893), novelist and journalist; son of Edward Hawke Locker [q. v.]; educated at Charterhouse School and Pembroke College, Oxford; B.A., 1851; journalist in Victoria, 1852; returned to England, 1861; editor of the 'Graphic,' 1870-91. [Suppl. iii. 105]

LOCKER, EDWARD HAWKE (1777-1849), commissioner of Greenwich Hospital; son of William Locker [q. v.]; educated at Eton; entered the navy pay office, 1795; civil secretary to Sir Edward Pellew (afterwards Viscount Exmouth) [q. v.], 1804-14; secretary to Greenwich Hospital, 1819; civil commissioner, 1824-44; joint-editor of 'The Plain Englishman,' 1820-3; published 'Views in Spain,' 1824, and 'Memoirs of celebrated Naval Commanders,' 1832. He established the gallery of naval pictures at Greenwich, 1823. [xxxiv. 40]

LOCKER, JOHN (1693-1760), miscellaneous writer; educated at Merchant Taylors' School, London, and Merton College, Oxford; admitted of Gray's Inn, 1719; translated the last two books of Voltaire's 'Charles XII,' and wrote the preface, 1731; collected original or authentic manuscripts of Bacon's works, now in the British Museum; F.S.A., 1737. [xxxiv. 41]

LOCKER, WILLIAM (1731-1800), captain in the navy; son of John Locker [q. v.]; educated at Merchant Taylors' School, London; entered the navy, 1746; fought at Quiberon Bay, 1759; commander, 1762; served at Goree and in West Indies, 1763-6; advanced to post rank, 1768; lieutenant-governor of Greenwich Hospital, 1793-1800; compiled materials for a naval history, which he handed over to John Charnock [q. v.]. [xxxiv. 41]

LOCKER-LAMPSON, FREDERICK (1821-1895), poet; more commonly known as FREDERICK LOCKER; son of Edward Hawke Locker [q. v.]; clerk in Somerset House (1841) and the admiralty (1842), where he became deputy-reader and précis writer; left government service, c. 1850; published (1857) 'London Lyrics,' which he extended and rearranged in subsequent editions, of which the last is dated 1893; took name of Lampson, 1885 (his second wife's maiden name). He compiled 'Lyra Elegantiarum,' a collection of light verse, 1867, 'Patchwork,' a volume of prose extracts, 1879, and a catalogue of his choice library at Rowfant, 1886. His 'Confidences' appeared posthumously, 1896. [Suppl. iii. 105]

LOCKEY, ROWLAND (fl. 1590-1610), painter; mentioned in Francis Meres's 'Wit's Commonwealth,' 1598. [xxxiv. 43]

LOCKEY, THOMAS (1602-1679), librarian of the Bodleian and canon of Christ Church, Oxford; educated at Westminster School and Christ Church, Oxford; M.A., 1625; prebendary of Chichester, 1633–60; D.D.; librarian of the Bodleian, 1660–5; designed the catalogue of Selden's books; canon of Christ Church Cathedral, Oxford, 1665–79. [xxxiv. 43]

LOCKHART, DAVID (d. 1846, botanist: assistant-naturalist in Tuckey's Congo expedition, 1816; in charge of the gardens at Trinidad, 1818–46; died at Trinidad. [xxxiv. 44]

LOCKHART or **LOKERT**, GEORGE (fl. 1520), professor of arts at the college of Montaigu, Paris, 1516; a Scotsman; author of 'De Proportione et Proportionalitate,' 1518, and of 'Termini Georgii Lokert,' 1524. [xxxiv. 44]

LOCKHART, Sir GEORGE (1630?–1689), of Carnwath, lord president of the court of session; son of Sir James Lockhart, lord Lee [q. v.]; admitted advocate, 1656; M.P. Lanarkshire (in the English parliament), 1658–9; knighted, 1663; dean of the Faculty of Advocates, 1672; M.P. Lanarkshire (Scottish parliament), 1681–2, and 1685–1686; lord president of the court of session, 1685; privy councillor, 1686; commissioner of the exchequer, 1686; shot in Edinburgh by a man in favour of whose wife's claim for aliment he had decided. [xxxiv. 44]

LOCKHART, GEORGE (1673–1731), of Carnwath; Jacobite and author; son of Sir George Lockhart [q. v.]; M.P. for Edinburgh, 1702–7, and 1708–10, for Wigton burghs, 1710–13, and 1713–15; arrested during the rebellion of 1715; imprisoned, but liberated without a trial; confidential agent to Prince James Edward in Scotland, 1718–27; detected and forced to flee to Holland; permitted to return to Scotland, 1728; killed in a duel. His 'Memoirs of the Affairs of Scotland from Queen Anne's Accession . . . to the commencement of the Union . . . 1707,' was published anonymously, 1714. His 'Papers on the Affairs of Scotland,' the most valuable sources of the history of the Jacobite movement, appeared 1817. [xxxiv. 45]

LOCKHART, Sir JAMES, LORD LEE (d. 1674), Scottish judge; gentleman of the privy chamber to Charles I, by whom he was knighted; commissioner for Lanarkshire in parliaments of 1630, 1633, 1645, 1661, 1665, and 1669; lord of the articles, 1633; ordinary lord of session, 1646; fought for Charles I, 1648; deprived of his office, 1649; superintended levy for Charles II's invasion of England; imprisoned in the Tower, 1651; restored to his offices, 1661; lord justice clerk, 1671–4. [xxxiv. 47]

LOCKHART, JOHN GIBSON (1794–1854), biographer of Scott; educated at the high school and university of Glasgow, and Balliol College, Oxford; advocate, 1816; began to contribute to 'Blackwood's Magazine,' 1817; met Sir Walter Scott, 1818; published 'Peter's Letters to his Kinsfolk,' a description of Edinburgh society, 1819; married Scott's daughter Sophia, 1820; edited the 'Quarterly Review,' 1825–53; published his 'Life of Burns,' 1828; published his famous 'Life of Scott,' 1838; wrote several novels, the most notable being 'Some Passages in the Life of Adam Blair,' 1822; edited Motteux's 'Don Quixote,' 1822; translated 'Ancient Spanish Ballads,' 1823. [xxxiv. 47]

LOCKHART, LAURENCE WILLIAM MAXWELL (1831–1882), novelist; nephew of John Gibson Lockhart [q. v.]; educated at Glasgow University and Caius College, Cambridge; B.A., 1855; entered the army, 1855; served before Sebastopol, 1856; M.A., 1861; captain, 1864; retired, 1865; published three novels, 'Doubles and Quits,' 'Fair to See,' and 'Mine is Thine,' in 'Blackwood's Magazine'; 'Times' correspondent for the Franco-German war, 1870; died at Mentone. [xxxiv. 49]

LOCKHART, PHILIP (1690?–1715), Jacobite; brother of George Lockhart [q. v.]; taken prisoner at the battle of Preston, 1715; condemned to death as a deserter, having been previously a half-pay officer in Lord Mark Ker's regiment [xxxiv. 50]

LOCKHART, Sir WILLIAM (1621–1676), of Lee; soldier and diplomatist; son of Sir James Lockhart, lord Lee [q. v.]; entered the French army and rose to be captain; lieutenant-colonel of Lanark's regiment during the civil war; knighted, 1646; went over to Cromwell's side; a commissioner for the administration of justice in Scotland, 1652; M.P., Lanark, 1653, 1654–5, and 1656–8; English ambassador in Paris, 1656–8, 1673–6; commanded the English forces at Dunkirk and was made governor after the town's surrender, 1658; deprived of the office, 1660. [xxxiv. 50]

LOCKHART, WILLIAM (1820–1892), Roman catholic divine; B.A. Exeter College, Oxford, 1842; follower of John Henry Newman [q. v.]; received into the Roman communion, 1843; entered the Rosminian Order of Charity at Rome, 1845, and became its procurator-general; edited 'Outline of the Life of Rosmini,' 1856; wrote second volume of a 'Life of Antonio Rosmini-Serbati,' 1886; edited the 'Lamp.' [xxxiv. 52]

LOCKHART, WILLIAM EWART (1846–1900), subject and portrait painter; studied art in Edinburgh; R.S.A., 1878; commissioned by Queen Victoria to paint 'Jubilee Celebration in Westminster,' 1887; subsequently devoted himself principally to portraiture. His best works are Spanish and Majorca subjects. [Suppl. iii. 107]

LOCKHART, Sir WILLIAM STEPHEN ALEXANDER (1841–1900), general; nephew of Sir John Gibson Lockhart [q. v.]; lieutenant, 44th Bengal native infantry, 1859; major, 1877; brevet-colonel, 1883; lieutenant-general, 1894; general, 1896; served in Indian mutiny, 1858–1859, Bhutan campaigns, 1864–6, Abyssinian expedition, 1867–8, expedition to Hazara Black Mountains, 1868–9; quartermaster-general in Northern Afghanistan, 1878–80; C.B. (military), 1880; deputy quartermaster-general in intelligence branch at headquarters in India, 1880–5; brigadier-general in Burmese war, 1886–7; K.C.B. and C.S.I., 1887; assistant military secretary for Indian affairs at Horse Guards, London, 1889–90; commanded Punjab frontier force, 1890–5; K.C.S.I., 1895; commanded force sent to quell rising of tribes of the Tirah, 1897; G.C.B.; commander-in-chief in India, 1898. [Suppl. iii. 108]

LOCKHART-ROSS, Sir JOHN, sixth baronet (1721–1790). [See ROSS.]

LOCKIER, FRANCIS (1667–1740), dean of Peterborough and friend of Dryden and Pope; entered Trinity College, Cambridge, 1683; M.A., 1690; chaplain to the English factory at Hamburg; D.D., 1717; dean of Peterborough, 1725; his reminiscences of Dryden and Pope in Spence's 'Anecdotes,' ed. 1820. [xxxiv. 53]

LOCKMAN, JOHN (1698–1771), miscellaneous writer; author of occasional verses intended to be set to music for Vauxhall; wrote for the 'General Dictionary,' 1734–1741; translated French works; contributed to the 'Gentleman's Magazine.' [xxxiv. 53]

LOCKWOOD, Sir FRANK (1846–1897), solicitor-general; graduated at Caius College, Cambridge, 1869; barrister, Lincoln's Inn, 1872; joined old midland circuit; defended the burglar and murderer Charles Peace, 1879; Q.C., 1882; recorder of Sheffield, 1884; liberal M.P. for York, 1885–97; solicitor-general, 1894–5; several of his sketches reproduced in 'The Frank Lockwood Sketch-Book,' 1898. [Suppl. iii. 109]

LOCKYER, NICHOLAS (1611–1685), puritan divine; B.A. New Inn Hall, Oxford, 1633; incorporated at Cambridge, 1635; M.A. Emmanuel College, Cambridge, 1636; took the covenant and became a powerful preacher; B.D. Oxford, 1654; provost of Eton, 1659–60; compelled to leave the country for disregarding Uniformity Act, 1666 and 1670; published theological works. [xxxiv. 54]

LOCOCK, Sir CHARLES, first baronet (1799–1875), obstetric physician; M.D. Edinburgh, 1821; F.R.C.P. 1836; first physician-accoucheur to Queen Victoria, 1840; discovered the efficacy of bromide of potassium in epilepsy; created baronet, 1857; F.R.S.; D.C.L. Oxford, 1864. [xxxiv. 55]

LODER, EDWARD JAMES (1813–1865), musical composer; son of John David Loder [q. v.]; studied in Germany; his opera 'Nourjahad' produced, 1834; author of musical compositions, including operas and a cantata and 'Modern Pianoforte Tutor.' [xxxiv. 56]

LODER, GEORGE (1816?–1868), musician; nephew of John David Loder [q. v.]; went to America, 1836; principal of the New York Vocal Institute, 1844; published 'Pets of the Parterre,' a comic operetta, 1861, and 'The Old House at Home,' a musical entertainment, 1862; died at Adelaide. [xxxiv. 56]

LODER, JOHN DAVID (1788–1846), violinist; professor of the Royal Academy of Music, London, 1840; leader at the Ancient Concerts, 1845; author of a standard work of instruction for the violin, 1814. [xxxiv. 56]

LODER, JOHN FAWCETT (1812–1853), violinist; played the viola in Dando's quartet, 1842–53.
[xxxiv. 57]

LODGE, EDMUND (1756–1839), biographer; Blue-mantle pursuivant-at-arms at the College of Arms, 1782; F.S.A., 1787; Lancaster herald, 1793, Norroy, 1822, Clarenceux, 1838. His chief work is the series of 'biographical and historical memoirs,' attached to 'Portraits of Illustrious Personages of Great Britain, engraved from authentic pictures,' 1821–34.
[xxxiv. 57]

LODGE, JOHN (d. 1774), archivist; entered St. John's College, Cambridge, 1716; M.A., 1730; deputy-clerk and keeper of the rolls, 1759; chief work, 'The Peerage of Ireland,' 1754.
[xxxiv. 58]

LODGE, JOHN (1801–1873). [See ELLERTON, JOHN LODGE.]

LODGE, SIR THOMAS (d. 1584), lord mayor of London; alderman, 1553; sheriff of London, 1556; master of the Grocers' Company, 1559; chartered ships to 'sail and traffic in the ports of Africa and Ethiopia,' a voyage said to have inaugurated the traffic in slaves countenanced by Elizabeth, 1562; lord mayor and knighted, 1562.
[xxxiv. 59]

LODGE, THOMAS (1558?–1625), author; son of Sir Thomas Lodge [q. v.], lord mayor of London; educated at Merchant Taylors' School, London, and Trinity College, Oxford; B.A., 1577; student of Lincoln's Inn, 1578; M.A., 1581; abandoned law for literature; published 'A Defence of Plays,' a reply to 'School of Abuse' of Stephen Gosson [q. v.], 1580; published 'An Alarum against Usurers,' 1584, and his first romance, 'The Delectable Historie of Forbonius and Priseeria,' 1584; sailed to the islands of Terceras and the Canaries, 1588, and to South America, 1591; issued 'Scillaes Metamorphosis' (verse), 1589 (re-issued as 'A most pleasant Historie of Glaucus and Scilla,' 1610); issued his second and best-known romance 'Rosalynde. Euphues Golden Legacie,' 1590 (written during his voyage to the Canaries); his work praised by Spenser and Greene; his chief volume of verse, 'Phillis: honoured with Pastorall Sonnets, Elegies, and amorous Delights,' issued, 1593; published 'A Fig for Momus,' 1595, 'The Divel Conjured,' 1596, 'A Margarite of America' (romance of the Euphues pattern), 1596, 'Wits Miserie and Worlds Madnesse,' 1596; converted to Roman catholicism; studied medicine; M.D. at Oxford, 1603; published a laborious volume, 'The Famous and Memorable Workes of Josephus,' 1602; issued 'A Treatise of the Plague,' 1603; published 'The Workes, both Morrall and Natural, of Lucius Annæus Seneca,' 1614; his last literary undertaking, 'A learned Summary upon the famous Poeme of William of Saluste, lord of Bartas, translated out of the French,' published, 1625; excelled as a lyric poet.
[xxxiv. 60]

LODGE, WILLIAM (1649–1689), amateur artist and engraver; of Jesus College, Cambridge, and Lincoln's Inn; translated Giacomo Barri's 'Viaggio Pittoresco d'Italia,' 1679; a prolific draughtsman and etcher mainly of topography; painted a portrait of Oliver Cromwell.
[xxxiv. 66]

LODVILL or **LUDVILLE**, PHILIP (d. 1767), divine; published 'The Orthodox Confession of the Catholic and Apostolic Eastern Church,' 1762, the first authoritative work in English on the subject.
[xxxiv. 67]

LOE, WILLIAM (fl. 1639), compiler; son of William Loe (d. 1645) [q. v.]; of Westminster School and Trinity College, Cambridge; D.D.; contributed to the university collections of Latin and Greek verses on the birth of Princess Elizabeth, 1685, and of Princess Anne, 1637; compiled from his father's papers 'The Merchants Manuell,' &c., 1628.
[xxxiv. 68]

LOE, WILLIAM (d. 1645), divine; M.A. St. Alban Hall, Oxford, 1600; prebendary of Gloucester, 1602; D.D., 1618; pastor of the English Church at Hamburg; published 'Songs of Sion' (religious verse), 1620, and quaint prose writings, 1609–23.
[xxxiv. 67]

LOEGHAIRE (d. 458). [See LAEGHAIRE.]

LOEWE, LOUIS (1809–1888), linguist; born at Zülz, Prussian Silesia; educated at Berlin, where he graduated Ph.D.; accompanied Sir Moses Montefiore as his secretary to the Holy Land and other places thirteen times between 1839 and 1874; first principal of Jews' College, 1856; examiner in oriental languages to Royal College of

Preceptors, 1858; principal and director, Judith Theological College, Ramsgate, 1868–88; published English translation of J. B. Levinsohn's 'Efés Dammim,' conversations between a patriarch of the Greek church and a chief rabbi of the Jews, 1841; translated first two conversations in David Nieto's 'Matteh Dan,' 1842; edited the 'Diaries of Sir Moses and Lady Montefiore' (published, 1890).
[xxxiv. 68]

LOEWENTHAL or **LÖWENTHAL**, JOHANN JACOB (1810–1876), chess-player; born at Buda-Pesth; expelled from Austro-Hungary as a follower of Kossuth, 1849; settled in London, 1851; chess editor of the 'Illustrated News of the World' and of the 'Era'; published 'Morphy's Games of Chess,' 1860; edited 'Chess Player's Magazine,' 1863–7; manager of the British Chess Association, 1865–9; became a naturalised Englishman.
[xxxiv. 69]

LOFFT, CAPELL, the elder (1751–1824), miscellaneous writer; educated at Eton and Peterhouse, Cambridge; barrister, Lincoln's Inn, 1775; settled at Turin, 1822; died at Moncalieri; author of poems and works on miscellaneous subjects and translations from Virgil and Petrarch, published between 1775 and 1814.
[xxxiv. 69]

LOFFT, CAPELL, the younger (1806–1873), classical scholar, poet, and miscellaneous writer; son of Capell Lofft the elder [q. v.]; of Eton and King's College, Cambridge; M.A., 1832; barrister, Middle Temple, 1834; published an ethical 'Self-Formation, or the History of an Individual Mind,' 1837; published 'Ernest,' an epic poem, 1839, representing the growth, struggles, and triumphs of chartism; died at Millmead, Virginia, U.S.A.
[xxxiv. 71]

LOFTHOUSE, MARY (1853–1885), water-colour painter; née Forster; associate of the Royal Society of Painters in Water-colours, 1884; married Samuel H. S. Lofthouse, 1884.
[xxxiv. 72]

LOFTING or **LOFTINGH**, JOHN (1659?–1742), inventor; native of Holland; naturalised in England, 1688; patented a fire-engine, 1690; engaged in the manufacture of fire-engines.
[xxxiv. 72]

LOFTUS, ADAM (1533?–1605), archbishop of Armagh and Dublin; educated at Cambridge, probably at Trinity College; archbishop of Armagh, 1563; dean of St. Patrick's, 1565; D.D. Cambridge, 1566; archbishop of Dublin, 1567; lord keeper, 1573–6, 1579, and 1581; lord chancellor, 1581–1605; lord justice, 1582–4, 1597–9, and 1600; assisted in foundation of Trinity College, Dublin; appointed first provost, 1590.
[xxxiv. 73]

LOFTUS, ADAM, first VISCOUNT LOFTUS OF ELY (1568?–1643), lord chancellor of Ireland; nephew of Adam Loftus (1533?–1605) [q. v.]; prebendary of St. Patrick's, Dublin, 1592; judge of the Irish marshal court, 1597; master of chancery, 1598; knighted, c. 1604; Irish privy councillor, 1608; M.P., King's County, 1613; lord chancellor, 1619; created Viscount Loftus of Ely, 1622; lord justice, 1629.
[xxxiv. 77]

LOFTUS, DUDLEY (1619–1695), jurist and orientalist; great-grandson of Adam Loftus (1533?–1605) [q. v.]; educated at Trinity College, Dublin; B.A., 1638; incorporated B.A. at Oxford, 1639; M.A. University College, Oxford, 1640; M.P. for Naas in Irish House of Commons, 1642–8; deputy-judge advocate, 1651; commissioner of revenue and judge of admiralty, 1654; master in chancery, 1655; M.P., co. Kildare and co. Wicklow, 1659, Bannow, 1661, Fethard, 1692; supplied the Ethiopic version of the New Testament in Walton's Polyglott Bible (1657) and published several translations from the Armenian and Greek, 1657–95.
[xxxiv. 79]

LOFTUS, WILLIAM KENNETT (1821?–1858), archæologist and traveller; educated at Cambridge; geologist to the Turco-Persian Frontier Commission, 1849–52; at Babylon and Nineveh on behalf of the Assyrian Excavation Fund, 1853–5; published 'Travels and Researches in Chaldæa and Susiana,' 1857; died on the voyage home from India, where he had been appointed to the geological survey.
[xxxiv. 80]

LOGAN, GEORGE (1678–1755), controversialist; M.A. Glasgow, 1696; moderator of the general assembly, 1740; published ecclesiastical and political works.
[xxxiv. 81]

LOGAN, JAMES (1674–1751), man of science and Penn's agent in America; accompanied Penn to Pennsylvania as secretary, 1699; secretary to the province, commissioner of property, receiver-general and business agent for the proprietor, 1701; member of the provincial council, 1702–47; a justice of common pleas, 1715; presiding judge in court of common pleas and mayor of Philadelphia, 1723; published 'The Antidote,' 1725, and 'A Memorial from James Logan in behalf of the Proprietor's family and of himself,' 1726; chief-justice and president of the council, 1731–9; governor, 1836–8; published scientific works and translations from the classics; died at Philadelphia.   [xxxiv. 81]

LOGAN, JAMES (1794?–1872), author of the 'Scottish Gael'; studied at Marischal College, Aberdeen; published his 'Scottish Gael, or Celtic Manners as preserved among the Highlanders,' 1831.   [xxxiv. 83]

LOGAN, JAMES RICHARDSON (d. 1869), scientific writer; settled at Penang; rendered important services to the struggling settlement; contributed geological papers to 'Journal of the Asiatic Society of Bengal.' 1846; started and edited the 'Journal of the Indian Archipelago and Eastern Asia,' 1847–57; published his articles as 'The Languages [and Ethnology] of the Indian Archipelago,' 1857; started and edited the 'Penang Gazette'; died at Penang.   [xxxiv. 83]

LOGAN, JOHN (1748–1788), divine and poet; entered Edinburgh University, 1762; ordained, 1773; member of the committee for the revision of paraphrases and hymns in use in public worship, 1775; lectured on history in Edinburgh, 1779–80 and 1780–1; published analysis of lectures as 'Elements of the Philosophy of History,' 1781; his tragedy 'Runnamede' acted, 1783; his chief poem, the 'Ode to the Cuckoo,' pronounced by Burke the most beautiful lyric in the language.   [xxxiv. 84]

LOGAN, SIR ROBERT (d. 1606), of Restalrig; supposed Gowrie conspirator; supported the cause of Mary Queen of Scots. After his death, George Sprott [q. v.] confessed knowledge of letters written by Logan in connection with the Gowrie plot, and on that evidence his bones were exhumed (1609) and sentence of forfeiture for high treason passed against him.   [xxxiv. 85]

LOGAN, SIR WILLIAM EDMOND (1798–1875), Canadian geologist; born in Montreal; graduated at Edinburgh, 1817; head of the geological survey of Canada, 1842–70; F.R.S., 1851; knighted, 1856; his 'Geology of Canada' published, 1863.   [xxxiv. 86]

LOGGAN, DAVID (1635–1700?), artist and engraver; born at Danzig; came to England before 1653; engraver to Oxford University, 1669, naturalised and published his 'Oxonia Illustrata,' 1675, 'Cantabrigia Illustrata,' 1676–1690; engraver to Cambridge University, 1690.   [xxxiv. 87]

LOGGON, SAMUEL (1712–1778?), writer; M.A. Balliol College, Oxford, 1736; author of a popular schoolbook, 'M. Corderii Colloquia' (21st edit. 1830).   [xxxiv. 89]

LOGIER, JOHN BERNARD (1780–1846), musician; born at Kaiserslautern in the Palatinate; came to England, c. 1790; invented the 'chiroplast,' an apparatus to facilitate the position of the hands on the pianoforte; established chiroplast school at Berlin by invitation of the Prussian government, 1821.   [xxxiv. 90]

LOINGSECH (d. 704), king of Ireland; first mentioned in the annals, 672; slain in battle.   [xxxiv. 91]

LOK, LOCK, or LOCKE, HENRY (1553?–1608?), poet; grandson of Sir William Lok [q. v.]; educated probably at Oxford; contributed sonnet to the 'Essayes of a Prentice' by James VI of Scotland, 1591; his 'Ecclesiasticus . . . paraphristically dilated in English Poesie . . . whereunto are annexed sundrie Sonets of Christian Passions,' printed by Richard Field, 1597.   [xxxiv. 91]

LOK, MICHAEL (fl. 1615), traveller; son of Sir William Lok [q. v.]; 'travelled through almost all the countries of Christianity'; governor of the Cathay Company, 1577; consul for the Levant Company at Aleppo, 1592–4; translated into English part of Peter Martyr's 'Historie of the West Indies,' 1613.   [xxxiv. 92]

LOK, SIR WILLIAM (1480–1550), London merchant; sent Henry VIII and Cromwell letters of intelligence from Bergen-op-Zoom and Antwerp, 1532–7; sheriff of London, 1548; knighted, 1548.   [xxxiv. 93]

LOLA MONTEZ, COUNTESS VON LANDSFELD (d. 1861). [See GILBERT, MARIE DOLORES ELIZA ROSANNA.]

LOMBARD, DANIEL (1678–1746), divine; born at Angers; naturalised in England, 1688; of Merchant Taylors' School, London, and St. John's College, Oxford; fellow, 1697–1718; B.A., 1698; chaplain at Hanover to the Princess Sophia and the embassy, 1701; D.D., 1714; chaplain to Caroline, princess of Wales, 1714; chief work, 'Succinct History of Ancient and Modern Persecutions,' published 1747.   [xxxiv. 93]

LOMBARD, PETER (d. 1625), Irish Roman catholic prelate; educated at Westminster and Louvain University; D.D., 1594; provost of Cambrai Cathedral; archbishop of Armagh and primate of all Ireland, 1601; died at Rome; author of 'De Regno Hiberniæ, Sanctorum Insulâ Commentarius,' published, 1632.   [xxxiv. 94]

LOMBART, PIERRE (1620?–1681), engraver and portrait-painter; born in Paris; came to England, c. 1640; returned to France after 1660; died at Paris.   [xxxiv. 94]

LOMBE, JOHN (1693?–1722), half-brother of Sir Thomas Lombe [q. v.]; sent by his brother to Italy to make himself acquainted with the processes of silk-throwing; said to have been poisoned by jealous Italian workmen.   [xxxiv. 96]

LOMBE, SIR THOMAS (1685–1739), introducer of silk-throwing machinery into England; patented his new invention, 1718; sheriff of London and knighted, 1727.   [xxxiv. 95]

LONDESBOROUGH, first BARON (1805–1860). [See DENISON, ALBERT.]

LONDON, HENRY OF (d. 1228). [See LOUNDRES, HENRY DE.]

LONDON, JOHN OF (fl. 1267). [See JOHN.]

LONDON, JOHN OF (d. 1311). [See JOHN OF LONDON.]

LONDON, JOHN (1486?–1543), visitor of monasteries; educated at Winchester and New College, Oxford; fellow of New College, 1505–18; D.C.L. and prebendary of York, 1519; treasurer of Lincoln Cathedral, 1522; warden of New College, 1526; attached himself to Cromwell; a commissioner for the visitation of monasteries, 1535–8; after Cromwell's death (1540) attached himself to Stephen Gardiner [q. v.], and became canon of Windsor; convicted of perjury, stripped of his dignities, and committed to prison, where he died.   [xxxiv. 97]

LONDON, RICHARD OF (fl. 1190–1229). [See RICHARD DE TEMPLO.]

LONDON, WILLIAM (fl. 1658), bibliographer; his 'Catalogue of the most vendible Books in England,' 1658, and 'Catalogue of New Books by way of Supplement to the former,' 1660, the earliest bibliographical catalogues of value.   [xxxiv. 98]

LONDONDERRY, MARQUISES OF. [See STEWART, ROBERT, first MARQUIS, 1739–1821; STEWART, ROBERT, second MARQUIS, 1769–1822; STEWART, CHARLES WILLIAM, third MARQUIS, 1778–1854.]

LONDONDERRY, EARLS OF. [See RIDGEWAY, SIR THOMAS, first EARL, 1565?–1631; PITT, THOMAS, first EARL of the second creation, 1688?–1729.]

LONG, AMELIA, LADY FARNBOROUGH (1762–1837), daughter of Sir Abraham Hume [q. v.] of Wormleybury, Hertfordshire; married Charles Long, afterwards first baron Farnborough, 1793; art connoisseur and horticulturist.   [xxxiv. 99]

LONG, ANN (1681?–1711), granddaughter of Sir James Long [q. v.]; a celebrated beauty; acquainted with Swift.   [xxxiv. 105]

LONG, LADY CATHARINE (d. 1867), novelist and religious writer; daughter of Horatio Walpole, third earl of Orford; married Henry Lawes Long, 1822; her novel 'Sir Roland Ashton,' directed against the tractarian movement, 1833; published religious works, 1846–63.   [xxxiv. 99]

LONG, CHARLES, first BARON FARNBOROUGH 1761–1838), politician; of Emmanuel College, Cambridge; M.P., Rye, 1789–96, Midhurst, 1796, Wendover, 1802, and Haslemere, 1806–26; joint-secretary to the treasury, 1791–801; F.R.S., 1792; a lord commissioner of the treasury, 804; privy councillor, 1805; secretary of state for Ireland, 1806; joint-paymaster-general, and subsequently sole occupant of the office, 1810–26; G.C.B. (civil), 1820; created Baron Farnborough, 1820; assisted George III and George IV in the decoration of the royal palaces. [xxxiv. 99]

LONG, CHARLES EDWARD (1796–1861), genealogist and antiquary; grandson of Edward Long [q. v.]; of Harrow and Trinity College, Cambridge; M.A., 1822; published works, including 'Royal Descents,' 1845. [xxxiv. 100]

LONG, DUDLEY (1748–1829). [See NORTH.]

LONG, EDWARD (1734–1813), author; of Gray's Inn; in Jamaica as private secretary to Sir Henry Moore, the lieutenant-governor, and subsequently judge of the vice-admiralty court, 1757–69; his chief work, 'The History of Jamaica,' issued anonymously, 1774. [xxxiv. 100]

LONG, EDWIN LONGSDEN (1829–1891), painter and royal academician; R.A., 1881; excelled as a painter of oriental scenes. [xxxiv. 101]

LONG, GEORGE (1780–1868), police magistrate; barrister, Gray's Inn, 1811; magistrate at Great Marlborough street police court, 1839–41; recorder of Coventry, 1841–842; magistrate at Marylebone police court, 1841–59; published legal works. [xxxiv. 102]

LONG, GEORGE (1800–1879), classical scholar; B.A. Trinity College, Cambridge, 1822; fellow of Trinity College, Cambridge, 1823; professor of ancient languages in the university of Virginia at Charlottesville, 1824–8; professor of Greek, University College, London, 1828–31; edited 'Quarterly Journal of Education,' 1831–5; honorary secretary of the Royal Geographical Society (which he helped to found in 1830), 1846–8; edited 'Penny Cyclopædia,' 1833–46; professor of Latin, University College, London, 1842–6; published 'Two Discourses on Roman Law,' in which subject he surpassed all his English contemporaries, 1847; established and edited the 'Bibliotheca Classica,' 1851–8; published his translation of Marcus Aurelius, 1862, of the 'Discourses of Epictetus,' 877. [xxxiv. 102]

LONG, SIR JAMES, second baronet (1617–1692), royalist; nephew of Sir Robert Long [q. v.]; served in the royalist army; succeeded to baronetcy, 1673. [xxxiv. 104]

LONG, JAMES (1814–1887), missionary; went to India in the service of the Church Missionary Society, 846; wrote a preface, adversely criticising the English press at Calcutta, to an English version of 'Niladarpana Nataka,' a sort of oriental 'Uncle Tom's Cabin,' 1861; indicted for libel and imprisoned; author of various books, pamphlets, and contributions to periodical literature dealing with Anglo-Indian questions. [xxxiv. 105]

LONG, JOHN (1548–1589), archbishop of Armagh; of Eton and King's College, Cambridge; archbishop of Armagh and primate of all Ireland, 1584; Irish privy councillor, 1585. [xxxiv. 106]

LONG, JOHN ST. JOHN (1798–1834), empiric; studied drawing and painting at Dublin, 1816–22; set up practice in London and became fashionable, 1827; twice tried for manslaughter through the deaths of his patients; chief work, 'A Critical Exposure of the Ignorance and Malpractice of Certain Medical Practitioners in their Theory and Treatment of Disease,' 1831. [xxxiv. 106]

LONG, SIR LISLEBONE (1613–1659), speaker of the House of Commons; educated at Magdalen Hall, Oxford; B.A., 1631; barrister, Lincoln's Inn, 1640; M.P. (parliamentarian), Wells, 1645–53, 1654–5, and 1659, Somerset, 656–8; knighted, 1655; recorder of London, a master of requests, and treasurer of Lincoln's Inn, 1656; appointed speaker, 9 March 1659, but died 16 March. [xxxiv. 107]

LONG, SIR ROBERT (d. 1673), auditor of the exchequer; M.P., Devizes, 1625, Midhurst, 1640; knighted, 660; chancellor of the exchequer, 1660–7; M.P., Boroughbridge, 1661; auditor of the exchequer, 1662; privy councillor, 1672. [xxxiv. 107]

LONG, ROBERT BALLARD (1771–1825), lieutenant-general; son of Edward Long (1734–1813) [q. v.]; educated at Harrow and Göttingen University; captain, serving in Flanders, 1793–4; deputy adjutant-general, 1794–5; lieutenant-colonel, 1798; colonel on the staff in Spain, 1808, present at Coruña, 1809; brigadier-general in Wellington's army in Portugal, 1810–11; lieutenant-general, 1821. [xxxiv. 108]

LONG, ROGER (1680–1770), divine and astronomer; of Pembroke Hall, Cambridge; fellow, 1703; M.A., 1704; D.D., 1728; F.R.S., 1729; master of Pembroke Hall, 1733; vice-chancellor of the university, 1733 and 1769; published instalments of an important work on astronomy, 1742–64 (completed by Richard Dunthorne [q. v.], 1784); first Lowndean professor of astronomy and geometry, 1750. [xxxiv. 109]

LONG, SAMUEL (1638–1683), speaker of the Jamaica House of Assembly; served in the expedition which conquered Jamaica, 1655; clerk of the House of Assembly, 1661; speaker, 1672–4; chief-justice, 1674; died at St. Katherine, Jamaica. [xxxiv. 109]

LONG, THOMAS, the elder (1621–1707), divine; educated at Exeter College, Oxford; B.A., 1642; B.D., 1660; prebendary of Exeter, 1661–1701; a voluminous controversial writer. [xxxiv. 110]

LONG, THOMAS, the younger (1649–1707), son of Thomas Long the elder [q. v.]; educated at Corpus Christi College, Oxford; M.A., 1670; prebendary of Exeter, 1681; deprived at the revolution. [xxxiv. 111]

LONG, WILLIAM (1817–1886), antiquary; educated at Balliol College, Oxford; M.A., 1844; F.S.A.; published 'Stonehenge and its Burrows,' 1876. [xxxiv. 111]

LONGBEARD, WILLIAM (d. 1196). [See FITZOSBERT, WILLIAM.]

LONGCHAMP, WILLIAM OF (d. 1197), bishop of Ely and chancellor to Richard I; chancellor of the kingdom, 1189; bishop of Ely, 1189; justiciar, 1190; joined Richard I while in prison in Germany, 1193; Richard I's intermediary in England, France, Germany, and at home, 1194–5; a faithful servant to Richard I; died at Poitiers. [xxxiv. 111]

LONGDEN, SIR HENRY ERRINGTON (1819–1890), general; educated at Eton and the Royal Military College, Sandhurst; entered the army, 1836; captain, 1843; served in the Sikh wars, 1845–6 and 1848–9, in the Indian mutiny, 1857–8; colonel, 1859; adjutant-general in India, 1866–9; major-general, 1872; lieutenant-general, 1877; retired with honorary rank of general, 1880; K.C.B. and C.S.I. [xxxiv. 114]

LONGDEN, SIR JAMES ROBERT (1827–1891), colonial administrator; acting colonial secretary in the Falkland islands, 1845; president of the Virgin islands, 1861; governor of Dominica, 1865; governor of British Honduras, 1867; governor of Trinidad, 1870; K.C.M.G., 1876; governor of Ceylon, 1876–83; G.C.M.G., 1883. [xxxiv. 115]

LONGESPÉE or **LUNGESPÉE** (LONGSWORD), WILLIAM DE, third EARL OF SALISBURY (d. 1226), natural son of Henry II by an unknown mother; according to a late tradition by Rosamond Clifford ('Fair Rosamond') [q. v.]; received earldom of Salisbury, 1198; lieutenant of Gascony, 1202; warden of the Cinque ports, 1204–6; warden of the Welsh marches, 1208; counselled King John to grant the Great Charter, 1215; joined the dauphin Louis, 1216, but returned to the English allegiance, 1217; faithfully served his nephew, Henry III, 1218–26. [xxxiv. 115]

LONGESPÉE or **LUNGESPÉE**, **LUNGESPEYE**, or **LUNGESPERE**, WILLIAM DE, called EARL OF SALISBURY (1212?–1250), son of William de Longespée (d. 1226) [q. v.]; knighted, 1233; witnessed the confirmation of the Great Charter, 1236; accompanied Earl Richard of Cornwall to the crusade, 1240; accompanied Henry III to Gascony, 1242; went again to the crusades, 1247; killed at the battle near Mansourah, 1250. [xxxiv. 118]

LONGFIELD, MOUNTIFORT (1802–1884), Irish judge; M.A. Trinity College, Dublin, 1828; LL.D., 1831; professor of political economy at Trinity College, 1832–4; regius professor of feudal and English law, Dublin University, 1834–84; Q.C., 1841; judge of the landed estates court, 1858–67; Irish privy councillor, 1867. [xxxiv. 119]

LONGLAND, JOHN (1473–1547), bishop of Lincoln ; educated at Magdalen College, Oxford ; principal of Magdalen Hall, Oxford, 1505 ; D.D., 1511 ; dean of Salisbury, 1514 ; canon of Windsor, 1519 ; bishop of Lincoln, 1521 ; chancellor of the university of Oxford, 1532–47 ; printed sermons (1517, 1536, and 1538) and 'Tres Conciones' (1527). [xxxiv. 120]

LONGLAND, WILLIAM (1330 ?–1400 ?). [See LANGLAND.]

LONGLEY, CHARLES THOMAS (1794–1868), archbishop of Canterbury ; educated at Westminster School and Christ Church, Oxford ; student, 1812 ; M.A., 1818 ; D.D., 1829 ; head-master of Harrow, 1829–36 ; bishop of Ripon, 1836–56, of Durham, 1856–60 ; archbishop of York, 1860–2, of Canterbury, 1862–8 ; published sermons and addresses. [xxxiv. 121]

LONGLEY, THOMAS (d. 1437). [See LANGLEY.]

LONGMAN, THOMAS (1699–1755), founder of the publishing house of Longman ; bought a bookseller's business, 1724 ; increased his business by the purchase of shares in sound literary properties. [xxxiv. 122]

LONGMAN, THOMAS (1730 – 1797), publisher ; nephew of Thomas Longman (1699–1755) [q. v.] ; taken into partnership, 1753 ; succeeded to the business, 1755. [xxxiv. 122]

LONGMAN, THOMAS (1804–1879), publisher ; son of Thomas Norton Longman [q. v.] ; educated at Glasgow ; became partner in the firm, 1834, and its head, 1842 ; published for Macaulay and Disraeli. [xxxiv. 124]

LONGMAN, THOMAS NORTON (1771–1842), publisher ; son of Thomas Longman (1730–1797) [q. v.] ; succeeded to the business, 1797 ; took Owen Rees [q. v.] into partnership, on which the firm became one of the greatest in London : published for Wordsworth, Southey, Scott ('Lay of the Last Minstrel '), and Moore ; became sole proprietor of 'Edinburgh Review,' 1826. [xxxiv. 123]

LONGMAN, WILLIAM (1813–1877), publisher ; son of Thomas Norton Longman [q. v.] ; became a partner in the business, 1839 ; compiled 'A Catalogue of Works in all Departments of English Literature, classified, with a general Alphabetical Index ' (2nd edit. 1848) ; promoted the publication of 'Peaks, Passes, and Glaciers,' 1859–62 ; published his 'History of the Life and Times of Edward III,' 1869 ; president of the Alpine Club, 1871–4 ; published 'A History of the three Cathedrals dedicated to St. Paul in London,' 1873. [xxxiv. 123]

LONGMATE, BARAK (1738–1793), genealogist and heraldic engraver ; published fifth edition of Collins's 'Peerage,' 1779, and a 'Supplement,' 1784 ; edited 'Pocket Peerage of England, Scotland, and Ireland,' 1788. [xxxiv. 124]

LONGMATE, BARAK (1768–1836), compiler ; son of Barak Longmate (1738–1793) [q. v.] ; edited 'Pocket Peerage,' 1813 ; assisted John Nichols and other antiquaries in their researches. [xxxiv. 125]

LONGMUIR, JOHN (1803–1883), Scottish antiquary ; studied at Marischal College, Aberdeen ; M.A. ; LL.D., 1859 ; his most important work, a revised edition of Jamieson's 'Scottish Dictionary,' 1879–82 ; published verses and two guide-books. [xxxiv. 125]

LONGSTROTHER, JOHN (d. 1471), lord treasurer of England ; a knight of the order of St. John of Jerusalem ; castellan of Rhodes, 1453 ; English prior of the order of St. John, 1460 ; lord treasurer to Henry VI, 1470 ; tried and beheaded after the battle of Tewkesbury. [xxxiv. 125]

LONGSWORD. [See LONGESPÉE.]

LONGUEVILLE, WILLIAM (1639–1721), friend of the poet Samuel Butler [q. v.] ; barrister, Inner Temple, 1660, and treasurer, 1695 ; a six-clerk in chancery, 1660–1678 ; Farquhar indebted to him for part of his 'Twin Rivals.' [xxxiv. 126]

LONGWORTH, MARIA THERESA (1832 ?–1881), authoress and plaintiff in the Yelverton case ; married to William Charles Yelverton, afterwards the fourth Viscount Avonmore, by a priest at the Roman catholic chapel, Rostrevor, Ireland, 1857 ; the marriage repudiated by Yelverton (who afterwards married the widow of Pro-

fessor Edward Forbes [q. v.], 1858) ; the validity of Mi⟨s⟩ Longworth's marriage established in the Irish court, 186⟨0⟩ but annulled in the Scottish court, 1862 ; the Scottish jud⟨g⟩ ment confirmed in the House of Lords, 1864 ; publishe⟨d⟩ several novels, 1861–75, and 'The Yelverton Correspond⟨ence,' &c., 1863. [xxxiv. 126]

LONSDALE, EARLS OF. [See LOWTHER, JAME⟨S⟩ first EARL, 1736–1802 ; LOWTHER, WILLIAM, second EAR⟨L⟩ 1757–1844 ; LOWTHER, WILLIAM, third EARL, 1787–1872⟨.⟩]

LONSDALE, first VISCOUNT (1635 – 1700). [S⟨ee⟩ LOWTHER, SIR JOHN.]

LONSDALE, HENRY (1816 – 1876), biographe⟨r⟩ studied medicine at Edinburgh, 1834 ; became partner ⟨with⟩ Dr. Robert Knox (1791–1862) [q. v.], 1840 ; fellow ⟨of⟩ the Royal College of Physicians, Edinburgh, 184⟨1⟩ published biographies, including 'The Worthies of Cum⟨-⟩ berland,' 1867–75, 'A Sketch of the Life and Writings ⟨of⟩ Robert Knox, the Anatomist,' 1870. [xxxiv. 127]

LONSDALE, JAMES (1777–1839), portrait-painte⟨r⟩ first exhibited at Royal Academy, 1802 ; helped to foun⟨d⟩ Society of British Artists ; portrait-painter in ordina⟨ry⟩ to Queen Caroline. [xxxiv. 128]

LONSDALE, JAMES GYLBY (1816–1892), son ⟨of⟩ John Lonsdale (1788–1867) [q. v.] ; educated at Eton an⟨d⟩ Balliol College, Oxford ; fellow, 1838–64 ; took holy orde⟨r⟩ 1842 ; professor of classical literature, King's Colleg⟨e,⟩ London, 1865–70 ; published with Samuel Lee pro⟨se⟩ translation of Virgil, 1871, and of Horace, 1893. [xxxiv. 130]

LONSDALE, JOHN (1788–1867), bishop of Lichfiel⟨d⟩ educated at Eton and King's College, Cambridge ; fello⟨w⟩ of King's College, 1809 ; prebendary of Lincoln, 182⟨8,⟩ of St. Paul's, 1828, principal of King's College, Londo⟨n⟩ 1839 ; archdeacon of Middlesex, 1842 ; bishop of Lichfiel⟨d,⟩ 1843 ; prepared for press, in conjunction with Archdeaco⟨n⟩ Hale, 'The Four Gospels, with Annotations,' 1849. [xxxiv. 129]

LONSDALE, WILLIAM (1794 – 1871), geologis⟨t⟩ entered the army, 1812 ; fought at Waterloo, 1815 ; r⟨e-⟩ tired soon after 1815 and studied geology : curator a⟨nd⟩ librarian to the Geological Society, 1829–42 ; joint orig⟨i-⟩ nator with Murchison and Sedgwick of the theory of t⟨he⟩ independence of the devonian system. [xxxiv. 130]

LOOKUP, JOHN (fl. 1740), theologian ; a discip⟨le⟩ of John Hutchinson (1674–1737) [q. v.] ; published a⟨n⟩ essay on the Trinity, 1739, and a translation of Genesi⟨s⟩ 1740. [xxxiv. 130]

LOOSEMORE, GEORGE (fl. 1660), organist an⟨d⟩ composer ; son of Henry Loosemore [q. v.] ; organist ⟨of⟩ Trinity College, Cambridge ; Mus. Doc., 1665 ; compose⟨d⟩ anthems. [xxxiv. 131]

LOOSEMORE, HENRY (1600 ?–1670), organist an⟨d⟩ composer ; Mus. Bac. Cambridge, 1640 ; organist of Exet⟨er⟩ Cathedral, 1660 ; composed litanies and anthems. [xxxiv. 131]

LOOSEMORE, JOHN (1613 ?–1681), organ-builde⟨r⟩ brother of Henry Loosemore [q. v.] ; designed organ f⟨or⟩ Exeter Cathedral ; also made virginals. [xxxiv. 131]

LOOTEN (LOTEN), JAN (1618–1681), landscap⟨e⟩ painter ; native of Amsterdam ; came to London early ⟨in⟩ Charles II's reign. [xxxiv. 132]

LOPES, HENRY CHARLES, first BARON LUDLO⟨W⟩ (1828–1899), judge ; educated at Winchester and Ball⟨iol⟩ College, Oxford ; B.A., 1849 ; barrister, Inner Templ⟨e⟩ 1852 ; bencher, 1870 ; treasurer, 1890 ; Q.C., 1869 ; co⟨n-⟩ servative M.P. for Launceston, 1868–74, and Frome⟨,⟩ 1874 ; justice in high court, 1876 ; knighted, 187⟨6;⟩ sat successively in common pleas and queen's benc⟨h⟩ divisions, and was advanced to court of appeal, 188⟨5;⟩ privy councillor, 1885 ; raised to peerage, 1897. [Suppl. iii. 110]

LOPES, SIR MANASSEH MASSEH, first baron⟨et⟩ (1755–1831), politician ; descended from a family ⟨of⟩ Spanish Jews ; born in Jamaica ; conformed to church ⟨of⟩ England ; M.P., Romney, 1802 ; created baronet, 180⟨2;⟩ M.P., Barnstaple, 1812 ; imprisoned for bribery and co⟨r-⟩ ruption, 1819 ; M.P., Westbury, 1823 and 1826–9. [xxxiv. 132]

LOPEZ, RODERIGO (d. 1594), Jewish physicia⟨n;⟩ native of Portugal ; settled in England, 1559 ; first hou⟨se⟩ physician at St. Bartholomew's Hospital ; member ⟨of⟩

oyal College of Physicians before 1569 ; chief physician
o Queen Elizabeth, 1586 ; implicated in the plot to
murder Antonio Perez and Queen Elizabeth ; tried, found
guilty, and executed at Tyburn, 1594 ; possibly the
original of Shakespeare's Shylock.   [xxxiv. 132]

LORD, HENRY (*fl.* 1630), traveller ; of Magdalen
Hall, Oxford ; English chaplain at Surat, 1624 ; pub-
lished 'A Display of two forraigne Sects in the East
Indies,' &c., 1630.   [xxxiv. 134]

LORD, JOHN KEAST (1818 - 1872), naturalist ;
entered the Royal Veterinary College, London, 1842 ;
received his diploma, 1844 ; served in the Crimea as
veterinary surgeon to the artillery of the Turkish contingent, 1855-6 ; naturalist to the boundary commission
sent to British Columbia, 1858 ; employed in archæological and scientific researches in Egypt ; first manager of
the Brighton Aquarium, 1872 ; author of 'The Naturalist
in Vancouver's Island,' 1866, and a 'Handbook of Sea-
fishing.'   [xxxiv. 136]

LORD, PERCIVAL BARTON (1808-1840), diplomatic agent ; B.A. Dublin, 1829 ; M.B., 1832 ; studied medicine at Edinburgh ; assistant-surgeon under East India
company, 1834 ; accompanied the 'commercial mission'
under Sir Alexander Burnes to Cabul, penetrated into
Tartary, 1837 ; political assistant to William Hay Macnaghten [q. v.], 1838 ; killed in action at Purwan, 1840 ;
author of 'Popular Physiology,' 1834, and 'Algiers,
with Notices of the neighbouring States of Barbary,'
1835.   [xxxiv. 135]

LORD, THOMAS (*fl.* 1796), ornithologist ; published
'Lord's Entire New System of Ornithology,' 1791-6.
                                             [xxxiv. 135]

LORIMER, JAMES (1818-1890), jurist and political
philosopher ; educated at the universities of Edinburgh,
Berlin, Bonn, and the academy of Geneva ; member of
the Faculty of Advocates of Scotland, 1845 ; published
'Political Progress not necessarily Democratic,' 1857,
and the sequel 'Constitutionalism of the Future,' 1865 ;
appointed to the chair of 'The Law of Nature and of
Nations,' Edinburgh, 1865 ; published 'The Institutes of
Law,' 1872, and 'The Institutes of the Law of Nations,'
1883-4.   [xxxiv. 136]

LORIMER, PETER (1812-1879), presbyterian divine ;
entered Edinburgh University, 1827 ; professor of theology in the English presbyterian college, London,
1844, and principal, 1878 ; chief work, 'John Knox and
the Church of England,' 1875.   [xxxiv. 138]

LORING, SIR JOHN WENTWORTH (1775-1852),
admiral ; born in America ; entered the navy, 1789 ;
lieutenant, 1794 ; present in actions off Toulon, 1795 ;
employed off France, 1805-13 ; C.B., 1815 ; lieutenant-
governor of the Royal Naval College, Portsmouth, 1819-
37 ; K.C.B., 1840 ; vice-admiral, 1840 ; admiral, 1851.
                                             [xxxiv. 138]

LORKIN, THOMAS (1528 ?-1591), regius professor
of physic at Cambridge ; educated at Pembroke Hall,
Cambridge ; M.A., 1555 ; M.D., 1560 ; fellow of Queens'
College, of Peterhouse, 1554-62 ; published 'Recta
regula et Victus ratio pro studiosis et literatis,' 1562 ;
regius professor of physic, 1564.   [xxxiv. 139]

LORKYN, THOMAS (*d.* 1625), M.A. Emmanuel
College, Cambridge, 1604 ; secretary to the embassy at
Paris, 1623 ; drowned at sea, 1625.   [xxxiv. 140]

LORRAIN, PAUL (*d.* 1719), ordinary of Newgate,
1698-1719 ; compiled the official accounts of the dying
speeches of criminals ; published 'The Dying Man's
Assistant,' 1702, and a translation of Muret's 'Rites of
Funeral,' 1683.   [xxxiv. 140]

LORT, MICHAEL (1725-1790), antiquary ; M.A.
Trinity College, Cambridge, 1750 ; senior fellow, 1768 ;
B.S.A., 1755 ; regius professor of Greek at Cambridge,
1759-71 ; F.R.S., 1766 ; D.D. and prebendary of St. Paul's,
1780. The results of his antiquarian researches appeared
in works like Chalmers's 'Biographical Dictionary' and
Nichols's 'Literary Anecdotes.'   [xxxiv. 140]

LORTE, SIR ROGER, first baronet (1608-1664),
Latin poet ; B.A. Wadham College, Oxford, 1627 ; published 'Epigrammatum liber primus,' 1646 ; created
baronet, 1662.   [xxxiv. 142]

LORYNG, SIR NIGEL or **NELE** (*d.* 1386), soldier ;
knighted for bravery at Sluys, 1340 ; one of the original
knights of the Garter, 1344 ; present at Poitiers, 1356 ;
served in France and Spain, 1364-9.   [xxxiv. 142]

LOSINGA, HERBERT DE (1054 ?-1119), first bishop
of Norwich and founder of the cathedral church ; his
native place and the signification of his surname a matter
of dispute ; educated in the monastery at Fécamp, Normandy ; Benedictine monk, *c.* 1075 ; prior of Fécamp,
1088 ; abbot of Ramsey, 1088 ; bishop of Thetford, 1091 ;
removed the see from Thetford to Norwich, 1094 ; his
sermons and letters edited and translated by Goulburn and
Symonds, 1878.   [xxxiv. 143]

LOSINGA or **DE LOTHARINGIA, ROBERT** (*d.*
1095), bishop of Hereford : a native of Lotharingia or the
southern Netherlands : doubtless a relative of Herbert de
Losinga [q. v.] ; wrote astronomical works ; crossed to
England and became one of the royal clerks : bishop of
Hereford, 1079.   [xxxiv. 146]

LOTHIAN, MARQUISES OF. [See KERR, ROBERT,
first MARQUIS, 1636-1703 ; KERR, WILLIAM, second
MARQUIS, 1662-1722 ; KERR, WILLIAM HENRY, fourth
MARQUIS, *d.* 1775.]

LOTHIAN, EARLS OF. [See KERR, MARK, first EARL,
d. 1609 ; KERR, WILLIAM, third EARL, 1605 ?-1675 ; KERR,
ROBERT, fourth EARL, 1636-1703.]

LOTHIAN, ninth MARQUIS OF (1833-1900). [See
KERR, SCHOMBERG HENRY.]

LOTHIAN, WILLIAM (1740-1783), divine and
historian ; D.D. Edinburgh, 1779 ; published a history of
the Netherlands, 1780.   [xxxiv. 147]

LOTHROPP, LATHROP, or **LOTHROP, JOHN** (*d.*
1653), independent divine ; sailed for Boston, 1634 ; died
at Barnstaple, Massachusetts, where he ministered, 1639-
1653.   [xxxiv. 147]

LOUDON, EARLS OF. [See LOUDOUN.]

LOUDON, CHARLES (1801-1844), medical writer ;
M.R.C.S., 1826 ; M.D. Glasgow, 1827 ; published medical
works, 1826-42.   [xxxiv. 148]

LOUDON, JANE (1807-1858), horticultural and miscellaneous writer ; *née* Webb ; published 'The Mummy,
a Tale of the Twenty-second Century,' which may have
furnished some of the ideas of Lytton's 'Coming Race,'
1827 ; married John Claudius Loudon [q. v.], 1830 ; published 'The Ladies' Companion to the Flower Garden,'
1841, and other horticultural works.   [xxxiv. 148]

LOUDON, JOHN CLAUDIUS (1783-1843), landscape-
gardener and horticultural writer ; F.L.S., 1806 ; his
'Encyclopædia of Gardening' published, 1822, 'Encyclopædia of Agriculture,' 1825, 'Encyclopædia of Plants,'
1829 ; edited 'Gardener's Magazine,' 1826-43 ; began to
compile the 'Encyclopædia of Cottage, Farm, and Villa
Architecture,' 1832 ; began to publish his 'Arboretum
et Fruticetum Britannicum,' 1833 ; established 'Architectural Magazine,' 1834 ; 'Suburban Gardener and
Villa Companion,' 1836 ; published 'Encyclopædia of
Trees and Shrubs,' 1842.   [xxxiv. 149]

LOUDOUN, EARLS OF. [See CAMPBELL, JOHN, first
EARL, 1598-1663 ; CAMPBELL, HUGH, third EARL, *d.*
1731 ; CAMPBELL, JOHN, fourth EARL, 1705-1782.]

LOUGH, JOHN GRAHAM (1806-1876), sculptor ; first
exhibited at Royal Academy, 1826.   [xxxiv. 151]

LOUGHBOROUGH, first BARON HASTINGS OF. [See
HASTINGS, SIR EDWARD, *d.* 1573.]

LOUGHBOROUGH, BARONS. [See HASTINGS, HENRY,
d. 1667 ; WEDDERBURN, ALEXANDER, EARL OF ROSSLYN,
1733-1805.]

LOUGHER, ROBERT (*d.* 1585), civilian ; fellow of
All Souls College, Oxford, 1553 ; B.C.L., 1558 ; principal
of New Inn Hall, 1564-70 and 1575-80 ; D.C.L. and regius
professor of civil law, 1565 ; M.P., Pembroke, 1572 ; master
in chancery, 1574.   [xxxiv. 151]

LOUIS, SIR THOMAS, first baronet (1759-1807), rear-
admiral : entered the navy, 1770 ; in active service, 1778-
1780 ; advanced to post rank, 1783 ; present at the battle

of the Nile, 1798; acted under Nelson, 1799-1802; rear-admiral, 1804; performed brilliant service at battle of St. Domingo, 1806; rewarded with a baronetcy; died off the coast of Egypt. [xxxiv. 151]

LOUND, THOMAS (1802-1861), amateur painter; occasionally exhibited at the Royal Academy.
[xxxiv. 153]

LOUNDRES, HENRY DE (d. 1228), archbishop of Dublin from 1212; papal legate to Ireland, 1217-20; justiciary in Ireland, 1219-24. [xxxiv. 153]

LOUTH, first EARL OF (d. 1328). [See BERMINGHAM, SIR JOHN.]

LOUTH, GILBERT OF (d. 1153?). [See GILBERT.]

LOUTHERBOURGH (LOUTHERBOURG), PHILIP JAMES (PHILIPPE JACQUES) DE (1740-1812), painter and royal academician; born at Fulda, Germany; studied at Paris under Francis Casanova [q. v.]; exhibited at the Salon, 1763; member of the Académie Royale, 1767; came to England, 1771; assisted Garrick as designer of scenery and costume: exhibited at Royal Academy, 1772; R.A., 1781; painted landscapes, marine subjects, and battle pieces. [xxxiv. 154]

LOVAT, twelfth BARON (1667?-1747). [See FRASER, SIMON.]

LOVE, CHRISTOPHER (1618-1651), puritan minister; of New Inn Hall, Oxford; M.A., 1642; tried, condemned, and executed for plotting against the Commonwealth, 1651; published controversial pamphlets and sermons.
[xxxiv. 155]

LOVE, DAVID (1750-1827), pedlar-poet; issued verses in single sheets and chap-books; wrote the 'Life, Adventures, and Experience of David Love' (3rd edit. 1823).
[xxxiv. 157]

LOVE, JAMES (1722-1774). [See DANCE.]

LOVE, SIR JAMES FREDERICK (1789-1866), general; entered the army, 1804; served in the Coruña retreat, 1809; captain, 1811; present at Ciudad Rodrigo, 1812; wounded at Waterloo, 1815; saved Bristol during the riots of 1831; lieutenant-colonel, 1834; British resident at Zante, 1835-8; colonel, 1838; governor of Jersey, 1852-6; inspector-general of infantry, 1857-62; general, 1864; G.C.B. and K.H. [xxxiv. 157]

LOVE, JOHN (1695-1750), grammarian and controversialist; educated at Glasgow University; master of Dumbarton grammar school, 1721; issued 'Two Grammatical Treatises,' 1733; published, in conjunction with others, an edition of Buchanan's Latin version of the 'Psalms,' 1737; rector of Dalkeith grammar school, 1739.
[xxxiv. 158]

LOVE, JOHN (1757-1825), presbyterian divine; educated at Glasgow University; founded the London Missionary Society, 1795; D.D. Aberdeen, 1816; letters, sermons, and addresses by him published posthumously.
[xxxiv. 158]

LOVE, NICHOLAS (1608-1682), regicide; educated at Wadham College, Oxford; M.A., 1636; barrister, Lincoln's Inn, 1636; M.P., Winchester, 1645; one of the judges at Charles I's trial, but did not sign the death-warrant; M.P., Winchester, in the Rump Parliament of 1659; escaped to Switzerland at the Restoration; died at Vevey. [xxxiv. 159]

LOVE, RICHARD (1596-1661), dean of Ely; fellow of Clare Hall, Cambridge, before 1628; D.D. and prebendary of Lichfield, 1634; master of Corpus Christi College, Cambridge, 1632; vice-chancellor, 1633-4; Lady Margaret professor of divinity, 1649; dean of Ely, 1660; contributed commendatory verses to Quarles's 'Emblems.'
[xxxiv. 160]

LOVE, WILLIAM EDWARD (1806-1867), polyphonist; mimicked sounds made by musical instruments, beasts, birds, and insects; gave public performances in England, Scotland, France, United States, West Indies, and South America, 1826-56. [xxxiv. 161]

LOVEDAY, JOHN (1711-1789), philologist and antiquary; M.A. Magdalen College, Oxford, 1734; collected pictures, books, and antiquities, and assisted in literary researches. [xxxiv. 161]

LOVEDAY, JOHN (1742-1809), scholar; son of John Loveday (1711-1789) [q. v.]; educated at Magdalen

College, Oxford; assisted Dr. Chandler in the preparation of 'Marmora Oxoniensia,' 1763; D.C.L., 1771.
[xxxiv. 162]

LOVEDAY, ROBERT (fl. 1655), translator; studied at Cambridge; translated into English the first three parts of La Calprenède's 'Cleopatra,' as 'Hymen's Præludia, or Love's Master-Piece,' 1652-4-5.
[xxxiv. 162]

LOVEDAY, SAMUEL (1619-1677), baptist minister and author of religious pamphlets. [xxxiv. 162]

LOVEGROVE, WILLIAM (1778-1816), actor; first appeared in London, 1810. [xxxiv. 163]

LOVEKYN, JOHN (d. 1368), lord mayor of London; traded in salted fish; sheriff of London, 1342; M.P. for the city, 1347-8 and 1365; lord mayor, 1348, 1358, 1365 and 1366. [xxxiv. 164]

LOVEL. [See also LOVELL.]

LOVEL, PHILIP (d. 1259), treasurer and justice; treasurer, 1252; justice itinerant, 1255; prebendary of St. Paul's. [xxxiv. 164]

LOVELACE, FRANCIS (1618?-1675?), governor of New York; deputy-governor of Long island, 1664 or 1665; governor of New York and New Jersey, 1668; his paternal, but autocratic government not relished by the Dutch, and city surrendered to the Dutch fleet in his absence, 1673; arrested at Long island, sent back to England, and examined; died shortly afterwards.
[xxxiv. 165]

LOVELACE, JOHN, third BARON LOVELACE of Hurley (1638?-1693), M.A. Wadham College, Oxford, 1661; M.P., Berkshire, 1661-70; succeeded to barony, 1670; arrested on account of the Rye House plot, 1683; embraced the cause of William III; overpowered and imprisoned by James II's supporters, 1688; captain of the gentlemen pensioners, 1689. [xxxiv. 166]

LOVELACE, JOHN, fourth BARON LOVELACE of Hurley (d. 1709), cousin of John Lovelace, third baron [q. v.]; entered House of Lords, 1693; guidon of the horse guards, 1699; governor of New York and New Jersey, 1709; died at New York. [xxxiv. 167]

LOVELACE, RICHARD (1618-1658), cavalier and poet; educated at Charterhouse School and Gloucester Hall, Oxford; M.A., 1636 (incorporated at Cambridge, 1637); wrote 'The Scholar, a comedy,' 1636; contributed to 'Musarum Oxoniensium Charisteria,' 1638; repaired to court, and served in the Scottish expeditions, 1639; wrote his famous song, 'Stone walls do not a prison make' when imprisoned (1642) for supporting the 'Kentish Petition'; rejoined Charles I, 1645; served with the French king, 1646; again imprisoned, 1648; while in prison prepared for press his 'Lucasta: Epodes, Odes, Sonnets, Songs, &c.,' published, 1649; known almost exclusively by a few lyrics. [xxxiv. 168]

LOVELL. [See also LOVEL.]

LOVELL, DANIEL (d. 1818), journalist; proprietor and editor of the 'Statesman,' 1806-18; imprisoned for libel, 1811-15; heavily fined, 1817, for traducing the ministerial journal, the 'Courier.' [xxxiv. 172]

LOVELL, FRANCIS, first VISCOUNT LOVELL (1454-1487?), descended from Philip Lovel [q. v.]; son of John, eighth baron Lovell of Tichmarsh, Northamptonshire; knighted, 1480; summoned to parliament as ninth Baron Lovell of Tichmarsh, 1482; supporter of Richard III; created Viscount Lovell, privy councillor, and K.G., 1483; lord chamberlain, 1483-5; attainted, 1485; fought for Lambert Simnel, 1487, and seems to have escaped to his own house, where he died of starvation. [xxxiv. 172]

LOVELL, GEORGE WILLIAM (1804-1878), dramatic author; his first play, 'The Avenger,' produced, 1835; his most famous play, 'The Wife's Secret,' originally produced at New York, 1846, brought out in London, 1848.
[xxxiv. 173]

LOVELL, SIR LOVELL BENJAMIN BADCOCK (formerly BADCOCK) (1786-1861), major-general; descended from Sir Salathiel Lovell [q. v.]; educated at Eton; entered the army, 1805; served in the Monte Video expedition, 1807, in the Peninsular campaign, 1809-14; captain, 1811; lieutenant-colonel, 1826; one of the military reporters at the siege of Oporto and in the Migueli

war in Portugal ; published 'Rough Leaves from a Journal
n Spain and Portugal,' 1835 ; K.H., 1835 ; assumed surname of Lovell, 1840 ; major-general, 1854 ; K.C.B., 1856.
[xxxiv. 174]

LOVELL, MARIA ANNE (1803–1877), actress and
dramatist, *née* Lacy ; first appeared on the stage, 1818 ;
represented Belvidera at Covent Garden, London, 1822 ;
married George William Lovell [q. v.], 1830 ; retired
from the stage ; her 'Ingomar the Barbarian' produced
at Drury Lane, 1851, and 'The Beginning and the End' at
the Haymarket, 1855.   [xxxiv. 173]

LOVELL or **LOVEL**, ROBERT (1630?–1690), naturalist;
brother of Sir Salathiel Lovell [q.v.] ; M.A. Christ Church,
Oxford, 1659 ; published his 'Enchiridion Botanicum,'
1659, and 'A Compleat History of Animals and Minerals,'
1661.   [xxxiv. 174]

LOVELL, ROBERT (1770?–1796), poet ; son of a
quaker ; probably engaged in business at Bristol ; made
acquaintance of Southey (with whom he published 'Poems
by Bion and Moschus,' 1794) and Coleridge, and participated in their project for a pantisocratic colony on the
banks of the Susquehanna.   [Suppl. iii. 111]

LOVELL, SIR SALATHIEL (1619–1713), judge ;
brother of Robert Lovell (1630?–1690) [q. v.] ; barrister,
Gray's Inn, 1656 ; ancient, 1671 ; serjeant-at-law, 1688 ;
recorder of London, 1692–1708 ; knighted, 1692 ; king's
serjeant, 1695 ; judge on the Welsh circuit, 1696 ; fifth
baron of the exchequer, 1708.   [xxxiv. 175]

LOVELL, SIR THOMAS (d. 1524), speaker of the House
of Commons ; probably related to Francis, first viscount
Lovell [q.v.] ; fought at Bosworth on side of Henry Tudor,
afterwards Henry VII, 1485 ; created chancellor of the
exchequer for life, 1485 ; M.P., Northamptonshire, 1485 ;
speaker, 1485–8 ; knighted, 1487 ; president of the council,
1502 ; K.G., 1503 ; constable of the Tower, 1509 ; abandoned
public life, 1516.   [xxxiv. 175]

LOVER, SAMUEL (1797–1868), song-writer, novelist,
and painter ; applied himself to portraiture, especially
miniature-painting ; secretary to Royal Hibernian Aca-
emy, 1830 ; produced the best-known of his ballads,
Rory o' More,' 1826 ; published 'Legends and Stories of
Ireland,' illustrated by himself, 1831 ; helped to found the
Dublin University Magazine,' 1833 ; miniature-painter in
London, 1835 ; associated with Dickens in founding
Bentley's Magazine ' ; published 'Rory o' More, a National
Romance,' 1837 ; dramatised it and wrote other plays ;
published 'Songs and Ballads,' 1839, and his second and
best-known novel, 'Handy Andy,' 1842 ; gave an entertainment called 'Irish Evenings' in England, Canada,
and (1846) United States; produced selection of Irish
lyrics, 1858 ; produced parodies entitled 'Rival Rhymes,'
1859 ; 'Volunteer Songs,' 1859.   [xxxiv. 176]

LOVETT, RICHARD (1692–1780), author of works
on electricity ; declared himself able to cure disease by
the aid of electricity (1758).   [xxxiv. 178]

LOVETT, WILLIAM (1800–1877), chartist ; secretary of the British Association for Promoting Co-operative Knowledge, 1830 ; arrested and tried for rioting,
1832 ; assisted in drafting parliamentary petitions and
bills, 1836–8 ; arrested for his manifesto against the
police, tried and imprisoned, 1839–40 ; opened a bookseller's shop, and published 'Chartism : a new Organisation of the People,' the best book on the organisation of
the chartist party, 1841 ; member of the council of the
anti-Slavery League, 1846 ; published school-books on
elementary science.   [xxxiv. 178]

LOVIBOND, EDWARD (1724–1775), poet ; entered
Magdalen College, Oxford, 1739 ; contributed well-known
articles to the 'World,' a weekly newspaper started by
Edward Moore [q. v.] ; his best-known piece, 'The Tears
of Old May-day,' published, 1754 ; his 'Poems on several
occasions,' published by his brother, 1785. [xxxiv. 180]

LOW, DAVID (1768–1855), bishop of Ross, Moray,
and Argyll ; educated at Marischal College, Aberdeen ;
bishop of the united dioceses of Ross, Argyle, and the
Isles, to which Moray was added (1838), 1819–50 ; LL.D.,
1820 ; effected separation of Argyll and the Isles from

Ross and Moray, 1847 ; D.D. Hartford College, Connecticut, and Geneva College, New York, 1848.
[xxxiv. 181]

LOW, DAVID (1786–1859), professor of agriculture ;
educated at Edinburgh University ; published 'Observations on the Present State of Landed Property and on
the Prospects of the Landholder and the Farmer,' 1817 ;
established 'Quarterly Journal of Agriculture,' 1826,
editing it, 1828–72 ; professor of agriculture in Edinburgh
University, 1831–54 ; formed an agricultural museum ;
published 'The Breeds of the Domestic Animals of the
British Islands,' 1842, and works on agriculture.
[xxxiv. 182]

LOW, GEORGE (1747–1795), naturalist ; educated at
Aberdeen and St. Andrews Universities ; studied the
natural history and antiquities of the Orkney isles ; his
manuscripts never printed, but freely used by other
antiquaries.   [xxxiv. 182]

LOW, JAMES (d. 1852), lieutenant-colonel, Madras
army ; Siamese scholar ; captain, 1826 ; retired as lieutenant-colonel, 1845 ; in civil charge of Province Wellesley ; published 'A Dissertation on the Soil and Agriculture of Penang,' 1828, a grammar of the Siamese language,
and treatises on Siamese literature.   [xxxiv. 183]

LOW, SIR JOHN (1788–1880), general in the Indian
army and political administrator ; educated at St. Andrews University ; lieutenant, Madras native infantry,
1805 ; captain, 1820 ; resident of Cawnpore ; political
agent at Jeypore, 1825, at Gwalior, 1830, at Lucknow,
1831 ; governor-general's agent in Rajpootana and commissioner at Ajmere and Mhairwar, 1848–52 ; resident to
the nizam at Hyderabad, 1852 ; member of the council,
1853 ; major-general, 1854 ; gave valuable assistance in
Indian mutiny, 1857–8 ; K.C.B., 1862 ; general, 1867 ;
G.C.S.I., 1873.   [xxxiv. 184]

LOW, SAMPSON (1797–1886), publisher ; brought out
first number of 'Publishers' Circular,' 1837 (his sole property, 1867) ; issued the 'English Catalogue,' 1753–82 ;
retired from business, 1875.   [xxxiv. 185]

LOW, WILLIAM (1814–1886), civil engineer ; engaged
under Brunel in construction of Great Western Railway ;
colliery engineer ; M.I.C.E., 1867.   [xxxiv. 186]

LOWDER, CHARLES FUGE (1820–1880), vicar of
St. Peter's, London Docks ; educated at Exeter College,
Oxford ; M.A., 1845 ; joined the mission at St. George's-
in-the-East, 1856 ; riots in the congregation being pro-
duced by his high church views, built a new church, St.
Peter's, London Docks (consecrated, 1866) ; known as
'Father Lowder' ; published accounts of his ministry at
St. George's ; died at Zell-am-See, Salzburg, Austria.
[xxxiv. 187]

LOWE, EDWARD (d. 1682), composer and organist ;
organist of Christ Church, Oxford, 1630–56 ; one of the
organists at the Chapel Royal, London, 1660–82 ; published
'A Short Direction for the performance of Cathedrall Service,' &c., 1661 ; professor of music at Oxford, 1661 ; composed anthems.   [xxxiv. 187]

LOWE, EDWARD WILLIAM HOWE DE LANCY
(1820–1880), major-general ; son of Sir Hudson Lowe
[q. v.] ; educated at Royal Military College, Sandhurst ;
entered the army, 1837 ; captain, 1845 ; served in second
Sikh war, 1848–9 ; in Indian mutiny, 1857–8 ; lieutenant-
colonel, 1858 ; C.B., 1859 ; major-general, 1877.
[xxxiv. 189]

LOWE, SIR HUDSON (1769–1844), lieutenant-general
and governor of St. Helena ; gazetted ensign, 1787 ;
captain, 1795 ; served at Toulon and in Corsica, Elba,
Portugal, Minorca, and Egypt ; served in Italy, 1805–12 ;
served with Blücher ; knighted, 1817 ; major-general,
1814 ; served in Italy, 1815 ; while governor of St. Helena
(1815–21) had custody of Napoleon ; K.C.B., 1816 ; his
treatment of Napoleon the subject of an attack by Barry
Edward O'Meara [q. v.], at one time Napoleon's medical
attendant at St. Helena, 1822 ; governor of Antigua, 1823 ;
on the staff in Ceylon, 1825–30 ; lieutenant-general, 1830.
The 'Lowe Papers,' which supplied the materials for
Forsyth's 'Captivity of Napoleon at St. Helena' (1853),
are in the British Museum.   [xxxiv. 189]

LOWE, JAMES (d. 1865), journalist and translator ;
edited 'The Critic of Literature, Science, and the Drama,'
1843–63 ; projected a 'Selected Series of French Literature' (one volume issued, 1853).   [xxxiv. 193]

LOWE, JAMES (d. 1866), a claimant to the invention of the screw-propeller; patented 'improvements in propelling vessels,' 1838 and 1852. His propeller was used in the navy, but he never obtained any compensation for it. [xxxiv. 194]

LOWE, JOHN (d. 1467), bishop successively of St. Asaph and Rochester; prior of Augustinian eremites at London and provincial for England, 1428; bishop of St. Asaph, 1433, of Rochester, 1444. [xxxiv. 194]

LOWE, JOHN (1750-1798), Scottish poet; entered Edinburgh University, 1771; went to the United States, 1773; took orders and obtained a living as a clergyman of the church of England; his chief lyric, 'Mary's Dream.' [xxxiv. 195]

LOWE, MAURITIUS (1746-1793), painter; one of the first students in the school of the Royal Academy; gold medallist, 1769; obtained the travelling allowance for study at Rome, 1771; exhibited at Royal Academy and Society of Artists; befriended by Dr. Johnson. [xxxiv. 195]

LOWE, PETER (1550 ?-1612 ?), founder of the Faculty of Physicians and Surgeons of Glasgow; studied at Paris; published the 'Whole Covrse of Chirurgerie,' 1597; settled in Glasgow, 1598; founded the Glasgow Faculty, 1599. [xxxiv. 196]

LOWE, RICHARD THOMAS (1802-1874), naturalist; educated at Christ's College, Cambridge; B.A., 1825; English chaplain at Madeira, 1832-54; published 'A Manual Flora of Madeira,' 1857-72; drowned in the wreck of the Liberia, in which he was returning to Madeira. [xxxiv. 196]

LOWE, ROBERT, first VISCOUNT SHERBROOKE (1811-1892), politician; educated at Winchester and University College, Oxford; M.A., 1836; barrister, Lincoln's Inn, 1842; went to Sydney, where he practised, 1842; in the legislative council for New South Wales, 1843-50; returned to England and became leader-writer in the 'Times,' 1850; M.P., Kidderminster, 1852-9; joint-secretary of the board of control, 1852-5; vice-president of board of trade and paymaster-general, 1855-8; privy councillor, 1855; M.P., Calne, 1859-67; vice-president of the committee of council on education, 1859-64; his best speeches made during the reform debates, 1866-7; first M.P. for London University, 1868-80; chancellor of the exchequer, 1868-73; D.C.L. Oxford, 1870; home secretary, 1873-4; created Viscount Sherbrooke of Sherbrooke in Warlingham, Surrey, 1880; published 'Poems of a Life,' 1884; G.C.B., 1885. [xxxiv. 197]

LOWE, THOMAS (d. 1783), vocalist and actor; first appeared at Drury Lane, London, 1740; associated with the production of Handel's oratorios, 1742-50; lessee and manager of Marylebone Gardens, London, 1763-8; at Sadler's Wells, 1772-83. [xxxiv. 201]

LOWER, MARK ANTHONY (1813-1876), antiquary; son of Richard Lower (1782-1865) [q. v.]; mainly instrumental in founding the Sussex Archæological Society, 1846; author of 'Patronymica Britannica. A Dictionary of Family Names of the United Kingdom,' 1860, and antiquarian works on Sussex. [xxxiv. 202]

LOWER, RICHARD (1631-1691), physician and physiologist; brother of Thomas Lower [q. v.]; educated at Westminster School and Christ Church, Oxford; student, 1649; M.A., 1655; M.D., 1665; F.R.S., 1667; F.R.C.P., 1675; the most noted physician of his time in London; the first to perform the operation of direct transfusion of blood from one animal into the veins of another; author of three medical treatises, the chief being 'Tractatus de Corde,' 1669. [xxxiv. 203]

LOWER, RICHARD (1782-1865), Sussex poet; his best-known production, 'Tom Cladpole's Jurney to Lunnon,' printed as a sixpenny pamphlet, 1830; published 'Stray Leaves from an Old Tree,' 1862. [xxxiv. 204]

LOWER, THOMAS (1633-1720), quaker sufferer; brother of Richard Lower (1631-1691) [q. v.]; educated at Winchester College; became a quaker; imprisoned, with occasional periods of liberty, 1673-86; married a step-daughter of George Fox (1624-1691) [q. v.]. [xxxiv. 204]

LOWER, SIR WILLIAM (1600 ?-1662), dramatist; published 'The Phœnix in her Flames. A Tragedy,' 1639; fought for Charles I, 1640-5; knighted, 1645; lived in

Cologne and Holland, 1655-61; published 'The Enchanted Lovers; a Pastoral,' 1658; published a sumptuous 'Relation . . . of the Voyage and Residence which the most mighty . . . Prince Charles II . . . hath made in Holland,' 1660. [xxxiv. 205]

LOWICK, ROBERT (d. 1696), conspirator; fought for James II, 1689; implicated in the 'Assassination plot,' tried and executed. [xxxiv. 206]

LOWIN, JOHN (1576-1659), actor; his name spelt Lowine, Lowen, Lowyn, and Lewen; joined the king's company, 1603; acted with Shakespeare, Burbage, John Heming, Condell, &c., 1603-11; shared with Taylor the management of the king's players, 1623-42; acted in the chief plays of Shakespeare, Jonson, Beaumont and Fletcher, and Massinger. [xxxiv. 206]

LOWMAN, MOSES (1680-1752), nonconformist divine; studied at Leyden and Utrecht; chief work, 'Dissertation on the Civil Government of the Hebrews,' 1740. [xxxiv. 208]

LOWNDES, THOMAS (1692-1748), founder of the Lowndes chair of astronomy in Cambridge; provostmarshal of South Carolina, 1725-7, 1730-3; entrusted his duties to a deputy and never visited the colony, but advanced schemes for its improvement; published pamphlet advocating a project for supplying the navy with salt, 1746; left his property to found a chair of astronomy in Cambridge University. [xxxiv. 208]

LOWNDES, WILLIAM (1652-1724), secretary to the treasury; first connected with the treasury, 1679; secretary, 1695; M.P., Seaford, 1695-1714, St. Mawes, 1714, East Looe, 1722-4; credited with originating the phrase, 'ways and means.' [xxxiv. 210]

LOWNDES, WILLIAM THOMAS (d. 1843), bibliographer; published 'The Bibliographer's Manual,' the first systematic work of the kind in England, 1834, and 'The British Librarian,' 1839-42. [xxxiv. 212]

LOWRIE, alias WEIR, WILLIAM (d. 1700 ?). [See LAWRIE.]

LOWRY, JOHN (1769-1850), mathematician; contributed to Thomas Leybourn's 'Mathematical Repository' (1799-1819); his tract on spherical trigonometry appended to vol. ii. of Dalby's 'Course of Mathematics.' [xxxiv. 212]

LOWRY, JOSEPH WILSON (1803-1879), engraver; son of Wilson Lowry [q. v.]; illustrator of scientific works; engraver to the Geological Survey of Great Britain and Ireland; F.R.G.S. [xxxiv. 212]

LOWRY, WILSON (1762-1824), engraver; studied in the Royal Academy schools; engraver of architecture and mechanism, devising ingenious instruments for the work; discovered the secret of biting in steel successfully; the first to use diamond points for ruling; executed the plates for Dr. Rees's 'Cyclopædia'; F.R.S., 1812. [xxxiv. 213]

LOWTH or **LOUTH**, ROBERT (1710-1787), bishop of London; son of William Lowth [q. v.]; educated at Winchester College and New College, Oxford; M.A., 1737; professor of poetry at Oxford, 1741-50; archdeacon of Winchester, 1750; published his lectures on Hebrew poetry, 1753; created D.D. Oxford, 1753; prebendary of Durham, 1755; F.R.S., 1765; bishop of Oxford, 1766-77; bishop of London, 1777; dean of the Chapel Royal, 1777; privy councillor, 1777; wrote a life of William Wykeham, 1758; a short introduction to English grammar, 1762, and a new translation of Isaiah, 1778. [xxxiv. 214]

LOWTH, SIMON (1630 ?-1720), nonjuring clergyman; M.A. Clare Hall, Cambridge, 1660; D.D., 1689; deprived of his livings, 1690; wrote in defence of the nonjuring schism and an episcopal succession against any right of deposition by a civil magistrate. [xxxiv. 216]

LOWTH, WILLIAM (1660-1732), theologian; educated at Merchant Taylors' School, London, and St. John's College, Oxford; fellow; M.A., 1683; B.D., 1688; prebendary of Winchester, 1696; best-known work, 'Commentary on the Prophets,' 1714-25. [xxxiv. 216]

LOWTHER, SIR GERARD (d. 1624), Irish judge; third son of Sir Richard Lowther (1529-1607) [q. v.]; judge of the common pleas in Ireland from 1610 till death; knighted, 1618. [xxxiv. 223]

LOWTHER, Sir GERARD (1589–1660), Irish judge; godson of the elder Sir Gerard Lowther [q. v.], being natural son of the elder Sir Gerard's brother, Sir Christopher Gerard; educated at Queen's College, Oxford; barrister, Gray's Inn, 1614; baron of the Irish exchequer, 1628; knighted, 1631; chief-justice of the common pleas in Ireland, 1634; at first on Charles I's side, but subsequently joined the parliament; commissioner of the great seal in Ireland, 1654. [xxxiv. 223]

LOWTHER, HENRY, third VISCOUNT LONSDALE (d. 1751), son of Sir John Lowther, first viscount Lonsdale [q. v.]; lord of the bedchamber; constable of the Tower, 1726; lord privy seal, 1733–5. [xxxiv. 222]

LOWTHER, JAMES, EARL OF LONSDALE (1736–1802), M.P., Cumberland, 1757–61, 1762, 1768, 1774–84, Westmoreland, 1761, Cockermouth, 1769; created Earl of Lonsdale, 1784, and Viscount and Baron Lowther of Whitehaven, 1797; unrivalled in the art of electioneering. [xxxiv. 217]

LOWTHER, Sir JOHN, first VISCOUNT LONSDALE (1655–1700), educated at Queen's College, Oxford; succeeded to baronetcy, 1675; barrister, Inner Temple, 1677; M.P., Westmoreland, 1676–96; actively supported William of Orange; vice-chancellor and privy councillor, 1689; first lord of the treasury, 1690–2; created Baron Lowther and Viscount Lonsdale, 1636; lord privy seal, 1699; his 'Memoirs of the Reign of James II' privately printed, 1808. [xxxiv. 220]

LOWTHER, Sir RICHARD (1529–1607), lord warden of the west marches; knighted, 1566; assisted Mary Queen of Scots, 1568–72; lord warden of the west marches, 1591. [xxxiv. 222]

LOWTHER, WILLIAM, first EARL OF LONSDALE of the second creation (1757–1844), succeeded his third cousin, James Lowther, earl of Lonsdale [q. v.], as Viscount Lowther by special patent, 1802, and created Earl of Lonsdale, 1807; patron of Wordsworth. [xxxiv. 223]

LOWTHER, WILLIAM, second EARL OF LONSDALE of the second creation (1787–1872), of Harrow and Trinity College, Cambridge; M.A., 1808; M.P., Cockermouth, 1808–13, Westmoreland, 1813, 1818, 1820, 1826, and 1832; junior lord of the admiralty, 1809; on the treasury board, 1813–26; first commissioner of woods and forests, 1828; president of board of trade, 1834–5; postmaster-general, 1841; summoned to the House of Lords in his father's barony, 1841; succeeded to the earldom, 1844; president of council, 1852. [xxxiv. 223]

LOYD. [See also LHUYD, LLOYD, and LLWYD.]

LOYD, SAMUEL JONES, first BARON OVERSTONE (1796–1883), of Eton and Trinity College, Cambridge; M.P., Hythe, 1819–26; M.A., 1822; succeeded to his father's banking business (London and Westminster Bank, founded 1834), 1844; D.C.L. Oxford, 1854; created Baron Overstone of Overstone and Fotheringay, 1860; authority on banking and finance; the Bank Act of 1844 substantially based on his principles; influenced current politics on the financial side. [xxxiv. 224]

LUARD, HENRY RICHARDS (1825–1891), registrary of the university of Cambridge; fellow of Trinity College, 1849; M.A., 1850; vicar of Great St. Mary's, Cambridge, 1860–87; registrary of the university, 1862; contributed a 'Life of Porson' to the 'Cambridge Essays,' 1856, and to the ninth edition of the 'Encyclopædia Britannica'; contributed to the master of the rolls series; a frequent contributor of articles on mediæval and classical scholars to the 'Dictionary of National Biography' (vols. i–xxxii.) [xxxiv. 225]

LUARD, JOHN (1790–1875), lieutenant-colonel; author of the 'History of the Dress of the British Soldier'; served in the navy, 1802–7; in the army through the Peninsular campaigns, 1810–14; as lieutenant fought at Waterloo, 1815; retired as major, 1834; published 'Views in India, St. Helena, and bar Nicobar,' 1835, and 'History of the Dress of the British Soldier,' 1852. [xxxiv. 226]

LUARD, JOHN DALBIAC (1830–1860), artist; son of John Luard [q. v.]; educated at Sandhurst; in the army, 1848–53; studied art, and exhibited paintings at Royal Academy, 1855–8. [xxxiv. 226]

LUBBOCK, Sir JOHN WILLIAM, third baronet (1803–1865), astronomer and mathematician; of Eton and Trinity College, Cambridge; partner in his father's bank, 1825; F.R.S., 1829; treasurer and vice-president of the Royal Society, 1830–5 and 1838–47; Bakerian lecturer, 1836; first vice-chancellor of London University, 1837–1842; succeeded to baronetcy, 1840; compared in detail tidal observations with theory; mainly directed his researches in physical astronomy towards the simplification of methods; foremost among English mathematicians in adopting Laplace's doctrine of probability. [xxxiv. 227]

LUBY, THOMAS (1800–1870), mathematician; educated at Trinity College, Dublin; M.A., 1825; D.D., 1840; senior fellow, 1867; filled various college offices; wrote mathematical text-books. [xxxiv. 228]

LUCAN, titular EARL OF (d. 1693). [See SARSFIELD, PATRICK.]

LUCAN, COUNTESS OF (d. 1814). [See BINGHAM, MARGARET.]

LUCAN, third EARL OF (1800–1888). [See BINGHAM, GEORGE CHARLES.]

LUCAR, CYPRIAN (fl. 1590), mechanician and author; of Winchester and New College, Oxford; fellow of New College before 1564; entered Lincoln's Inn, 1568; issued work on artillery, 1588, and 'A Treatise named Lucar Solace,' dealing with mensuration, geometry, and practical mechanics, 1590. [xxxiv. 228]

LUCAS, ANTHONY (1633–1693), jesuit; studied at St. Omer; joined jesuits, 1662; professor of theology in the college at Liège, 1672; rector of the English College at Rome, 1687; provincial of his order, 1693; involved in a controversy with Sir Isaac Newton respecting the prismatic spectrum. [xxxiv. 229]

LUCAS, Sir CHARLES (d. 1648), royalist; knighted, 1638; taken prisoner at Marston Moor, 1644; lieutenant-general of the cavalry, 1645; played foremost part in defence of Colchester, and on its capitulation was condemned to death by court-martial, 1648. [xxxiv. 229]

LUCAS, CHARLES (1713–1771), Irish patriot; published 'Pharmacomastix,' 1741; interested himself in municipal reform in Dublin and issued 'Divelina Libera: an Apology for the Civil Rights and Liberties of the Commons and Citizens of Dublin,' 1744; behaved during his candidature for the parliamentary representation of Dublin city in such a way as to cause the government to prevent his going to the poll, to declare him an enemy of his country, and to condemn him to imprisonment, 1748; escaped to London; studied medicine at Paris, Rheims, and Leyden; M.D. Leyden, 1752; published a successful 'Essay on Waters,' 1756; L.R.C.P., 1760; M.P., Dublin, 1761–71; contributed to the 'Freeman's Journal' from 1763; 'the Wilkes of Ireland.' [xxxiv. 231]

LUCAS, CHARLES (1769–1854), miscellaneous writer and divine; educated at Oriel College, Oxford; published novels and poems between 1795 and 1810. [xxxiv. 234]

LUCAS, CHARLES (1808–1869), musical composer; principal of the Royal Academy of Music, 1859–66; composed an opera, symphonies, string quartets, anthems, and songs. [xxxiv. 235]

LUCAS, FREDERICK (1812–1855), Roman catholic journalist and politician; brother of Samuel Lucas (1811–1865) [q. v.]; brought up as a quaker; student at University College, London; barrister, Middle Temple, 1835; became a Roman catholic, 1830, and published 'Reasons for becoming a Roman Catholic'; started the 'Tablet,' 1840; M.P., co. Meath, 1852; identified himself with the nationalist party; at the suggestion of Pope Pius IX began to write a 'Statement' of the condition of affairs in Ireland (1854), which appears in the second volume of Lucas's 'Life' by his brother. [xxxiv. 235]

LUCAS, HENRY (d. 1663), founder of the Lucasian professorship; M.A. St. John's College, Cambridge, 1636; M.P., Cambridge University, 1640; left money to endow a professorship of the mathematical sciences at Cambridge. [xxxiv. 236]

LUCAS, HENRY (fl. 1795), poet; son of Charles Lucas (1713–1771) [q. v.]; educated at Trinity College, Dublin; M.A., 1762; wrote occasional verse. [xxxiv. 236]

LUCAS, HORATIO JOSEPH (1839-1873), artist; exhibited at the Royal Academy and the Salon, Paris; excelled in the art of etching.   [xxxiv. 237]

LUCAS, JAMES (1813-1874), 'the Hertfordshire hermit'; led an eccentric life at his house near Hitchin, abjured washing, slept on cinders, associated mainly with tramps, but was visited out of curiosity by many well-known persons.   [xxxiv. 237]

LUCAS, JOHN (1807-1874), portrait-painter; apprenticed to Samuel William Reynolds (1773-1835) [q. v.]; began to exhibit at Royal Academy, 1828; painted contemporary celebrities and court beauties. [xxxiv. 238]

LUCAS, JOHN TEMPLETON (1836-1880), artist; son of John Lucas (1807-1874) [q. v.]; exhibited landscapes at the Royal Academy, the British Institution, and the Suffolk Street Gallery, 1859-76; published a farce and (1871) a volume of fairy tales.   [xxxiv. 238]

LUCAS, LOUIS ARTHUR (1851-1876), African traveller; educated at University College, London; started to explore the Congo, 1875; reached Khartoum, 1876; arrived at Lardo; not permitted by Gordon to undertake so difficult an expedition, which was likely to be certain destruction; navigated the northern portion of Lake Albert Nyanza; died on the steamboat voyage from Suakim to Suez; buried at Jeddah. [xxxiv. 239]

LUCAS, MARGARET BRIGHT (1818-1890), sister of John Bright (1811-1889) [q. v.]; married Samuel Lucas (1811-1865) [q. v.], 1839; aided her husband in his public projects; visited America and began to take interest in temperance reform and women's suffrage, 1870; president of the British Women's Temperance Association.
                [xxxiv. 241]

LUCAS, RICHARD (1648-1715), prebendary of Westminster; M.A. Jesus College, Oxford, 1672; D.D., 1691; prebendary of Westminster, 1697; published his 'Enquiry after Happiness,' a popular devotional work, 1685, and other religious works.   [xxxiv. 239]

LUCAS, RICHARD COCKLE (1800-1883), sculptor; exhibitor at the Royal Academy, 1829-59; his best works medallion portraits, executed in marble, wax, and ivory; published 'An Essay on Art, especially that of Painting,' 1870.   [xxxiv. 240]

LUCAS, ROBERT (1748 ?-1812), divine and poet; of Trinity College, Cambridge; D.D., 1793; held a living in Worcestershire, and others in Northamptonshire; published 'Poems on Various Subjects,' 1810, containing a translation of the Homeric hymn to Ceres (Demeter).
                [xxxiv. 240]

LUCAS, SAMUEL (1811-1865), journalist and politician; brother of Frederick Lucas [q.v.]; married Margaret Bright [see LUCAS, MARGARET BRIGHT], sister of John Bright, 1839; member of the Anti-Cornlaw League; published 'Plan for the Establishment of a General System of Secular Education in the County of Lancaster,' 1847; edited the 'Morning Star,' 1856-65.   [xxxiv. 241]

LUCAS, SAMUEL (1818-1868), journalist and author; educated at Queen's College, Oxford; M.A. and barrister, Inner Temple, 1846; started the 'Shilling Magazine,' 1865; published essays and poems.   [xxxiv. 241]

LUCAS, SAMUEL (1805-1870), amateur painter; exhibited at the Royal Academy, 1830.   [xxxiv. 242]

LUCAS, THEOPHILUS (*fl.* 1714), biographer; author of an entertaining work entitled 'Memoirs of the Lives, Intrigues, and Comical Adventures' of famous gamblers and sharpers from Charles II to Anne, published, 1714.
                [xxxiv. 242]

LUCAS, SIR THOMAS (*d.* 1649), brother of Sir Charles Lucas (*d.* 1648) [q. v.]; distinguished himself on the king's side in Ireland in the civil war; knighted, 1628; Irish privy councillor, 1642.   [xxxiv. 231]

LUCAS, WILLIAM ? (*fl.* 1789), African explorer; three years a slave at Morocco, having been captured when a boy; vice-consul at Morocco till 1785; travelled in Africa in the service of the newly formed Association for Promoting African Exploration, 1788-9; published his account of Africa in the 'Reports' of the African Association.   [xxxiv. 242]

LUCIUS, a legendary hero; called the first Christian king in Britain; supposed to have lived in the second century. No record of his existence appears till three or four centuries after his supposed death. His legend owes its detail to Geoffrey of Monmouth.   [xxxiv. 243]

LUCKOMBE, PHILIP (*d.* 1803), miscellaneous writer and conchologist; edited dictionaries and cyclopædias, and wrote on printing.   [xxxiv. 243]

LUCY, CHARLES (1814-1873), historical painter; studied at Paris and at the Royal Academy, London; exhibited his first historical painting, 'The Interview between Milton and Galileo,' 1840; painted historical subjects and some portraits, frequently engraved.
                [xxxiv. 244]

LUCY, GODFREY DE (*d.* 1204), bishop of Winchester; son of Richard de Lucy [q. v.]; became a royal clerk and received many ecclesiastical preferments; archdeacon of Derby, 1182; canon of York and archdeacon of Richmond; justice itinerant for the district beyond the Trent and the Mersey, 1179; bishop of Winchester, 1189-1204.
                [xxxiv. 244]

LUCY, RICHARD DE (*d.* 1179), chief justiciary; maintained the cause of Stephen in Normandy against Geoffrey of Anjou; recalled to England, 1140; chief justiciary jointly with Robert de Beaumont, earl of Leicester (1104-1168) [q. v.], 1153-66; sole chief justiciary, 1166-79; excommunicated by Thomas Becket in 1166 and 1169 for his share in drawing up the constitutions of Clarendon (1164); commanded for Henry II in the insurrection of 1173.
                [xxxiv. 246]

LUCY, SIR RICHARD, first baronet (1592-1667), son of Sir Thomas Lucy (1532-1600) [q. v.]; B.A. Exeter College, Oxford, 1611; created baronet, 1618; M.P. for Old Sarum in the Long parliament, 1647, for Hertfordshire in Cromwell's parliament, 1654 and 1656.
                [xxxiv. 250]

LUCY, SIR THOMAS (1532-1600), owner of Charlecote, Warwickshire; educated by John Foxe [q. v.], the martyrologist, whose puritan sentiments he adopted; inherited the great Warwickshire estate, 1552; rebuilt his manor-house at Charlecote, 1558-9; knighted, 1565; M.P., Warwick, 1571 and 1584; alleged to have prosecuted Shakespeare for deer-stealing, 1585; Shakespeare's Justice Shallow.   [xxxiv. 248]

LUCY, SIR THOMAS (1585-1640), grandson of Sir Thomas Lucy (1532-1600) [q. v.]; of Magdalen College, Oxford; student of Lincoln's Inn, 1602; knighted, 1614; M.P., Warwickshire, 1614, 1621, 1624, 1625, 1626, 1628, and 1640; friend of Lord Herbert of Cherbury [see HERBERT, EDWARD, first BARON HERBERT OF CHERBURY].
                [xxxiv. 250]

LUCY, WILLIAM (1594-1677), bishop of St. David's; of the Charlecote family; educated at Trinity College, Oxford; B.A., 1613; entered Caius College, Cambridge, 1615; B.D., 1623; bishop of St. David's, 1660; inhibited the archdeacon of Brecon from holding visitations in his diocese; published controversial works.   [xxxiv. 251]

LUDERS, ALEXANDER (*d.* 1819), legal writer; probably of German extraction; barrister, Inner Temple, 1778; bencher, 1811; author of historico-legal writings, published, 1785-1818.   [xxxiv. 252]

LUDFORD, SIMON (*d.* 1574), physician; Franciscan; at dissolution of the monasteries became an apothecary; M.D. Oxford, 1560; F.R.C.P., 1563.   [xxxiv. 253]

LUDLAM, HENRY (1824-1880), mineralogist; bequeathed his fine collection of minerals to the Geological Museum, Jermyn Street, London.   [xxxiv. 253]

LUDLAM, ISAAC (*d.* 1817), rebel; prominent in the 'Derbyshire insurrection' promoted by Jeremiah Brandreth [q. v.], 1817; arrested, tried, and executed.
                [xxxiv. 253]

LUDLAM, THOMAS (1775-1810), governor of Sierra Leone; son of William Ludlam [q. v.]; retired, 1807; died at Sierra Leone.   [xxxiv. 255]

LUDLAM, THOMAS (1727-1811), theologian and essayist; brother of William Ludlam [q. v.]; M.A. St. John's College, Cambridge, 1752; attacked Calvinistic writers in the 'Orthodox Churchman's Review'; most of his essays included in 'Essays, Scriptural, Moral, and Logical,' by William and Thomas Ludlam, 1807.
                [xxxiv. 254]

LUDLAM, WILLIAM (1717-1788), mathematician; brother of Thomas Ludlam (1727-1811) [q. v.]; M.A. St. John's College, Cambridge, 1742; B.D., 1749;

Linacre lecturer in physic, 1767–9; published mathematical and theological works; his 'Rudiments of Mathematics' (1785) still used at Cambridge in 1815. [xxxiv. 254]

LUDLOW, BARON (1828–1899). [See LOPES, HENRY CHARLES.]

LUDLOW, EDMUND (1617?–1692), regicide; B.A. Trinity College, Oxford, 1636; fought at Edgehill, 1642; M.P., Wiltshire, 1646; one of the chief promoters of Pride's Purge, 1648; one of the king's judges who signed the death-warrant; member of council of state, 1649 and 1650; lieutenant-general of the horse in Ireland and a commissioner for the civil government of Ireland, 1650–5; after the proclamation of Cromwell as Protector refused to acknowledge his authority or to give security for peaceable behaviour, 1656; allowed to retire to Essex; M.P., Hindon, 1659; on the recall of the Long parliament (7 May 1659) made member of the committee of safety, of the council of state, and commander-in-chief of the Irish army; impeached by the restored parliament, 1660; surrendered to proclamation summoning all Charles I's judges to surrender, 1660; allowed his liberty by providing sureties; escaped to Switzerland; came to England in hope of being employed by William III, 1689; proclamation published by William III for his arrest; escaped abroad and died at Vevey. Ludlow's 'Memoirs,' the composition of his exile, were first printed, 1698–9. Their chief value lies in their account of the republican party's opposition to Cromwell and of the factions which caused the overthrow of the republic after its restoration in 1659. [xxxiv. 255]

LUDLOW, GEORGE (1596–1655), younger brother of Roger Ludlow [q. v.]; a prominent and influential colonist; held large grants of land in Massachusetts; member of the council, 1642–55. [xxxiv. 260]

LUDLOW, GEORGE JAMES, third and last EARL LUDLOW (1758–1842), general; entered the army, 1778; captain, serving in America, 1781–2; served in Flanders, where he lost his left arm, 1793–4; in the Vigo expedition (1801), the Egyptian campaign (1801), the Hanover expedition (1805), and the Copenhagen expedition (1807); succeeded his brother in the peerage (of Ireland), 1811; general, 1814; G.C.B., 1815; created Baron Ludlow (peerage of United Kingdom), 1831. [xxxiv. 261]

LUDLOW, ROGER (fl. 1640), deputy-governor of Connecticut; of Balliol College, Oxford; assistant of the Massachusetts colony, 1630–4; deputy-governor, 1634–5; deputy-governor of Connecticut, 1639; appointed to codify the laws of Connecticut, 1646; his code established, 1650; commissioner in the congress of the United Colonies of New England, 1651, 1652, and 1653; said to have finally settled in Ireland. [xxxiv. 262]

LUGHAIDH (d. 507), king of Ireland; ardrigh after the battle of Ocha, 484. [xxxiv. 263]

LUGID or **MOLUA**, SAINT (554?–608?), first abbot of Clonfertmulloe, alias Kyle, in Queen's County; his name also spelt Lua, Luaid, Luanus, Lugdach, Lugdaigh, Lughaidh, Lugidus, Lugeth, and Moluanus; trained under St. Comgall [q. v.] at Bangor; the Bollandists' and Fleming's life of him both untrustworthy. [xxxiv. 263]

LUKE, SIR SAMUEL (d. 1670), parliamentarian; knighted, 1624; M.P., Bedford, 1640; belonged to the presbyterian section of the popular party; present at Edgehill, 1642, and Chalgrove Field, 1643; scoutmaster-general of the army of the Earl of Essex, 1643–5; took no part in public affairs during the Commonwealth and protectorate; the supposed original of Butler's Sir Hudibras. [xxxiv. 264]

LUKE, STEPHEN (1763–1829), physician; studied medicine in London and Paris; M.D. Aberdeen, 1792; mayor of Falmouth, where he practised, 1797; L.R.C.P., 1815; M.D. Cambridge, 1821; physician extraordinary to George IV, 1828; contributed to Thomas Beddoes's 'Contributions to Physical and Medical Knowledge,' 1799. [xxxiv. 266]

LUKIN, HENRY (1628–1719), nonconformist divine; published religious works. [xxxiv. 266]

LUKIN, LIONEL (1742–1834), inventor of lifeboats; invented an 'unsubmergible' boat, 1785; his boat in little demand; published a description of his lifeboat, 1790. [xxxiv. 266]

LULACH, LUTHLACH, LULAG, LAHOULAN, DULACH, or **GULAK** (d. 1058), king of Scots; son of Gilcomgan, mormaer of Moray; his mother probably Gruoch, the wife, after Gilcomgan's death, of Macbeth [q. v.]; succeeded to the mormaership of Moray, 1057; set up as king by the people of Alban; slain by treachery; buried at Iona. [xxxiv. 268]

LUMBY, JOSEPH RAWSON (1831–1895), author and divine; M.A. Magdalen College, Cambridge, 1861; D.D., 1879; ordained priest, 1860; Tyrwhitt Hebrew scholar, 1861; classical lecturer at Queens' College, Cambridge, 1861; member of Old Testament Revision Company, 1873; fellow and dean of St. Catharine's College, Cambridge, 1874; vicar of St. Edward's, Cambridge, 1875; Norrisian professor of divinity, 1879; prebendary of York, 1887; Lady Margaret professor of divinity, 1892; helped to found Early English Text Society; edited literary, historical, and religious works. [Suppl. iii. 111]

LUMISDEN. [See also LUMSDEN.]

LUMISDEN or **LUMSDEN**, ANDREW (1720–1801), Jacobite; private secretary to Prince Charles Edward, 1745; present at Culloden, 1746; included in the Act of Attainder; escaped to France; under-secretary to the Chevalier de St. George at Rome, 1757; principal secretary, 1762–6; allowed to return to England, 1773; pardoned, 1778; published work on the antiquities of Rome, 1797. [xxxiv. 268]

LUMLEY, BENJAMIN (1811–1875), author and manager of the opera in London; solicitor, 1832; superintended the finances of Her Majesty's Theatre, 1836–41; took over the management, 1842; his position shaken by the opening of the Royal Italian Opera House, Covent Garden, 1847; saved for a time from disaster by the engagement of Jenny Lind [see LIND, JOHANNA MARIA], 1847–9; his theatre closed, 1853–5, reopened, 1856, closed, 1858; returned to the practice of the law; published a standard book, 'Parliamentary Practice on Passing Private Bills,' 1838, and 'Sirenia,' 1862, and 'Another World, or Fragments from the Star City of Montallayah by Hermes,' 1873, romances; published 'Reminiscences,' 1864. [xxxiv. 269]

LUMLEY, GEORGE, fourth BARON LUMLEY (d. 1508), grand-nephew of Marmaduke Lumley [q. v.]; fought on the Yorkist side; knighted, 1462; M.P., Northumberland, 1467; knight-banneret, 1481; submitted to Henry VII, 1485. [xxxiv. 271]

LUMLEY, GEORGE (d. 1537), son of John Lumley, fifth (or sixth) baron Lumley [q. v.]; took part with his father in the northern insurrection of 1536; surrendered, arraigned, and executed. [xxxiv. 272]

LUMLEY, HENRY (1660–1722), general and governor of Jersey; brother of Richard Lumley, first earl of Scarborough [q. v.]; entered the army, 1685; colonel, 1692; brigadier-general, 1693; at siege of Namur, 1695; major-general, 1696; M.P., Sussex, 1701 and 1702; lieutenant-general and governor of Jersey, 1703; fought at Blenheim, 1704, Ramillies, 1706, Oudenarde, 1708, and Malplaquet, 1709; general, 1711; M.P., Arundel, 1715; resigned his command, 1717. [xxxiv. 271]

LUMLEY, JOHN, fifth (or sixth) BARON LUMLEY (1493–1544), fought at Flodden, 1513; summoned to parliament, 1514; present at the Field of the Cloth of Gold, 1520; a leader in the Pilgrimage of Grace, 1536. [xxxiv. 272]

LUMLEY, JOHN, first BARON LUMLEY of the second creation (1534?–1609), son of George Lumley (d. 1537) [q. v.]; of Queens' College, Cambridge; K.B., 1553; high steward of Oxford University, 1559; implicated in the Ridolfi plot; imprisoned, 1569–73; founded a surgery lecture in the Royal College of Physicians, 1583; member of the Elizabethan Society of Antiquaries; collected portraits and books. [xxxiv. 272]

LUMLEY, MARMADUKE (d. 1450), bishop successively of Carlisle and Lincoln; LL.B. Cambridge; precentor of Lincoln, 1425; archdeacon of Northumberland, 1425; chancellor of Cambridge University, 1427; master of Trinity Hall, 1429–43; bishop of Carlisle, 1429–50; lord high treasurer of England, 1447; bishop of Lincoln, 1450. [xxxiv. 274]

LUMLEY, RICHARD, first VISCOUNT LUMLEY OF WATERFORD (d. 1661?), grandson of Anthony Lumley, brother of John Lumley, fifth (or sixth) baron Lumley [q. v.]; knighted, 1616; created Viscount Lumley of Waterford (peerage of Ireland), 1628; royalist in the civil war. [xxxiv. 275]

LUMLEY, RICHARD, first EARL OF SCARBOROUGH (d. 1721), grandson of Richard Lumley, first viscount Lumley of Waterford [q. v.]; educated as a Roman catholic: master of the horse to Queen Catherine, 1680-2; created Baron Lumley of Lumley Castle, 1681; treasurer to Charles II's queen, 1684; Monmouth captured by his troop of horse, 1685; became a protestant, 1687; signed the invitation to William of Orange, 1688; privy councillor, 1689; created Viscount Lumley, 1689, and Earl of Scarborough, 1690; fought at the Boyne, 1692; major-general, 1692; lieutenant-general, 1694; retired from active service, 1697; chancellor of the duchy of Lancaster, 1716-17; joint vice-treasurer of Ireland, 1717. [xxxiv. 275]

LUMLEY, SIR WILLIAM (1769-1850), general; educated at Eton; entered the army, 1787; lieutenant-colonel, 1795; served during the Irish rebellion, 1798, and in Egypt, 1801; major-general, 1805; took part in recapture of Cape of Good Hope, 1806, in the operations in South America, 1806-7; joined Wellington's army in the Peninsula, 1810; lieutenant-general, 1814; governor and commander-in-chief at Bermuda, 1819-25; G.C.B., 1831; general, 1837. [xxxiv. 276]

LUMSDEN. [See also LUMISDEN.]

LUMSDEN, SIR HARRY BURNETT (1821-1896), lieutenant-general; ensign, 1838; interpreter and quartermaster to 33rd Bengal native infantry, 1842; lieutenant, 59th, 1842; served in Sutlej campaign, 1845; assistant to (Sir) Henry Montgomery Lawrence [q. v.], then resident at Lahore, 1846; charged with formation of corps of guides for frontier service; introduced khaki uniform into Indian army; captain, 1853; went on mission to Candahar, 1857-8; lieutenant-colonel, 1858; C.B. (civil), 1859; severed connection with guides, and as brigadier-general commanded Hyderabad contingent, 1862; colonel, 1862; left India, 1869; major-general, 1868; K.C.S.I., 1873; retired as honorary lieutenant-general, 1875. [Suppl. iii. 112]

LUMSDEN, SIR JAMES (1598?-1660?), military commander; entered the service of Gustavus Adolphus; in England soon after 1639; taken prisoner at Dunbar, 1650; set free, 1652. [xxxiv. 277]

LUMSDEN, MATTHEW (1777-1835), orientalist; professor of Persian and Arabic in Fort William College, India, 1808; published 'A Grammar of the Persian Language,' 1810; secretary to the Calcutta Madressa, 1812; published 'A Grammar of the Arabic Language,' vol. i. 1813; in charge of the company's press at Calcutta, 1814-1817; secretary to the stationery committee, 1818; travelled through Persia, Georgia, and Russia to England, 1830. [xxxiv. 278]

LUMSDEN, ROBERT (d. 1651), brother of Sir James Lumsden [q. v.]; served under Gustavus Adolphus and in the civil war; killed at storming of Dundee. [xxxiv. 277]

LUMSDEN, WILLIAM (fl. 1651), brother of Sir James Lumsden [q. v.]; served under Gustavus Adolphus and in the civil war; present at Marston Moor, 1644, and at Dunbar, 1650. [xxxiv. 277]

LUNARDI, VINCENZO (1759-1806), 'first aerial traveller in the English atmosphere'; born probably at Lucca; secretary to the Neapolitan ambassador in England; made his first balloon ascent, 1784; published 'An Account of Five Aerial Voyages in Scotland,' 1786. [xxxiv. 278]

LUND, JOHN (fl. 1785), humorous poet. [xxxiv. 279]

LUNDGREN, EGRON SELLIF (1815-1875), water-colour painter; born at Stockholm; studied at Stockholm and Paris; accompanied Sir Colin Campbell's relief expedition on the campaign in Oudh, and made sketches on the spot, 1857; member of the Society of Painters in Water-colours, 1865; settled in Sweden; published 'Letters from Spain and Italy,' and 'Letters from India,' 1870; died at Stockholm. [xxxiv. 279]

LUNDIE, JOHN (d. 1652?), poet; professor of humanity, Aberdeen, 1631; author of Latin poems. [xxxiv. 279]

LUNDIN, SIR ALAN, EARL OF ATHOLL (d. 1268). [See DURWARD, ALAN.]

LUNDY, ROBERT (fl. 1689), governor of Londonderry; supported William III, 1689, yet advised the surrender of Londonderry to James II; turned out by the citizens who undertook their historic defence under George Walker (1618-1690) [q. v.]; his conduct found 'faulty' by the House of Commons; excepted from William's Act of Indemnity, 1690. [xxxiv. 280]

LUNN, JOSEPH (1784-1863), dramatic author; his burlesque, 'The Sorrows of Werther,' produced at Covent Garden, 1818; his 'Family Jars,' 'Fish out of Water,' 'Hide and Seek,' and 'Roses and Thorns,' produced at the Haymarket between 1822 and 1825; adapted other plays from the French. [xxxiv. 281]

LUNSFORD, HENRY (1611-1643), brother of Sir Thomas Lunsford [q. v.]; lieutenant-colonel, 1640; killed at the siege of Bristol. [xxxiv. 283]

LUNSFORD, SIR HERBERT (fl. 1640-1665), brother of Sir Thomas Lunsford [q. v.]; captain, 1640; present at Edgehill, 1642; knighted, 1645. [xxxiv. 283]

LUNSFORD, SIR THOMAS (1610?-1653?), royalist colonel; committed a murderous assault upon Sir Thomas Pelham, 1633; outlawed for failing to appear to receive judgment, 1637; pardoned, 1639; joined Charles I's army, 1639; lieutenant of the Tower, 1641; removed on petition from the Commons; knighted, 1641; made prisoner at Edgehill, 1642; released, 1644; went to Virginia, 1649, where he died. [xxxiv. 281]

LUNY, THOMAS (1759-1837), marine painter; studied under Francis Holman [q. v.]; exhibited at the Society of Artists, 1777-8, at the Royal Academy, 1780-93. [xxxiv. 283]

LUPO or LUPUS, THOMAS, the elder (d. 1628?), musician; member of the royal band, 1579. [xxxiv. 284]

LUPO, THOMAS, the younger (fl. 1598-1641), probably first cousin of Thomas Lupo the elder [q. v.]; one of her majesty's violins, 1598; in Prince Henry's band of musicians, 1610; many compositions assigned to him, some possibly by the elder Thomas Lupo. [xxxiv. 284]

LUPSET, THOMAS (1498?-1530), divine; of St. Paul's School, London, and Pembroke Hall, Cambridge; B.A. Paris; read the rhetoric and humanity lecture founded by Wolsey at Corpus Christi College, Oxford, 1520; M.A. Oxford, 1521; helped More, Erasmus, and Linacre to prepare their works for the press, and himself produced religious works and translations. [xxxiv. 285]

LUPTON, DONALD (d. 1676), miscellaneous writer; chaplain to the English forces in the Low Countries and Germany; hack author in London, 1632; puolished 'Emblems of Rarieties,' 1636, and biographical and other works, 1632-58. [xxxiv. 285]

LUPTON, ROGER (d. 1540), provost of Eton and founder of Sedbergh school in Yorkshire; B.A Cambridge, 1483; canon of Windsor, 1500; provost of Eton, 1504-35; founded a free school in his native town of Sedbergh, 1528, and scholarships and fellowships at St. John's College, Cambridge, 1528 and 1536. [xxxiv. 286]

LUPTON, THOMAS (fl. 1583), miscellaneous writer; best-known work, 'A Thousand Notable Things of Sundry Sortes,' a variety of enigmatic and grotesque recipes and nostrums, 1579. [xxxiv. 287]

LUPTON, THOMAS GOFF (1791-1873), engraver; studied mezzotint-engraving under George Clint [q. v.]; exhibited crayon portraits at Royal Academy, 1811-20; mainly responsible for the introduction of steel for mezzotint-engraving; employed by Turner on the 'Liber Studiorum'; engraved the plates for 'The Harbours of England,' with text by Ruskin, published, 1856. [xxxiv. 288]

LUPTON, WILLIAM (1676-1726), divine; fellow of Lincoln College, Oxford, 1698; M.A. Queen's College, Oxford, 1700; D.D., 1712; preacher of Lincoln's Inn and afternoon preacher at the Temple, 1714; prebendary of Durham, 1715; published single sermons. [xxxiv. 289]

LUPUS, HUGH, EARL OF CHESTER (d. 1101). [See HUGH OF AVRANCHES.]

LUSCOMBE, MICHAEL HENRY THORNHILL (1776-1846), bishop; of Catharine Hall, Cambridge; M.A., 1805; incorporated at Oxford and D.C.L., 1810; consecrated to a continental bishopric by the bishops of the Scottish episcopal church, and appointed embassy chaplain at Paris, 1825; helped to found the 'Christian Remembrancer,' 1841; published 'The Church of Rome Compared with the Bible, the Fathers of the Church and the Church of England,' 1839, and sermons; died at Lausanne. [xxxiv. 289]

LUSH, SIR ROBERT (1807-1881), lord justice; entered Gray's Inn, 1836; published an edition of 'The Act for the Abolition of Arrest on Mesne Process,' 1838; barrister, Gray's Inn, 1840; published 'The Practice of the Superior Courts of Common Law at Westminster in Actions and Proceedings over which they have a common Jurisdiction,' which became the standard book on common law practice, 1840; Q.C. and bencher, 1857; succeeded to the court of queen's bench, 1865; privy councillor, 1879; succeeded to the court of appeal, 1880. [xxxiv. 289]

LUSHINGTON, CHARLES (1785-1866), brother of Stephen Lushington [q. v.]; in the service of the East India Company in Bengal, 1800-27; M.P., Ashburton, 1833-41, Westminster, 1847-52; published a 'History of Calcutta's Religious Institutions,' 1824, and 'Dilemmas of a Churchman,' 1838. [xxxiv. 293]

LUSHINGTON, EDMUND LAW (1811-1893), Greek scholar; of Charterhouse and Trinity College, Cambridge; senior classic and senior chancellor's medallist, 1832; professor of Greek at Glasgow, 1838-75; hon. LL.D. Glasgow, 1875; lord rector of Glasgow University, 1884; he married (1842) Cecilia Tennyson, sister of Lord Tennyson, the epilogue to whose 'In Memoriam' is an epithalamium on the marriage. [Suppl. iii. 114]

LUSHINGTON, HENRY (1812-1855), chief secretary to the government of Malta; of Charterhouse and Trinity College, Cambridge; fellow, 1836; M.A., 1837; barrister, Inner Temple, 1840; chief secretary to the government of Malta, 1847-55; published verse and prose works, 1828-55; died at Paris. [xxxiv. 290]

LUSHINGTON, SIR JAMES LAW (1779-1859), general; brother of Stephen Rumbold Lushington [q. v.]; entered the Madras army, 1797; rose to be general; chairman of the East India Company, 1838-9; M.P. successively for Petersfield, Hastings, and Carlisle. [xxxiv. 294]

LUSHINGTON, STEPHEN (1782-1873), civilian; educated at Eton and Christ Church, Oxford; B.A. and fellow of All Souls College, Oxford, 1802; M.A.; barrister, Inner Temple, 1806; M.P., Great Yarmouth, 1806-8, Ilchester, 1820-6, Tregony, Cornwall, 1826-30, Winchelsea, 1830-1, Tower Hamlets, 1832-41; judge of the consistory court of London, 1828, of the high court of admiralty, 1838-67; privy councillor, 1838; dean of arches, 1858-67; reformer and abolitionist; some of his speeches and judgments published separately. [xxxiv. 291]

LUSHINGTON, SIR STEPHEN (1803-1877), admiral; nephew of Stephen Lushington (1782-1873) [q. v.]; entered navy, 1816; present at Navarino, 1827; distinguished at the reduction of Kastro Morea, 1828; superintendent of the Indian navy, 1848-52; commanded naval brigade at Sebastopol, 1854; K.C.B. and rear-admiral, 1855; lieutenant-governor of Greenwich Hospital, 1862-5; admiral, 1865; G.C.B., 1867. [xxxiv. 293]

LUSHINGTON, STEPHEN RUMBOLD (1776-1868), Indian official; educated at Rugby; assistant in military, political, and secret department, Madras, 1792; translator to board of revenue, 1793; deputy Persian translator to government, and Persian translator to revenue board, 1794; secretary to board of revenue, 1798; left the service, 1807; M.P., Rye, 1807-12, Canterbury, 1812-1830 and 1835-7; privy councillor, 1827; governor of Madras, 1827-35; hon. D.C.L. Oxford, 1839; published life of his father-in-law, Lord Harris, 1840. [xxxiv. 294]

LUSHINGTON, THOMAS (1590-1661), divine; educated at Oxford; M.A. Lincoln College, Oxford, 1618; prebendary of Salisbury, 1631; D.D., 1632; published a commentary on the Epistle to the Hebrews, 1646; 'Logica Analytica de Principiis,' 1650. [xxxiv. 294]

LUTTERELL, JOHN (d. 1335), theologian; D.D. Oxford; chancellor of Oxford University, 1317-22; pre-bendary of Salisbury, 1319, of York, 1334; said to have written theological, philosophical, and mathematical works; died at Avignon. [xxxiv. 296]

LUTTICHUYS, ISAAC (1616-1673), painter; brother of Simon Luttichuys [q. v.]; removed from London to Amsterdam before 1643, where he died. [xxxiv. 296]

LUTTICHUYS, SIMON (1610-1663?), painter of portraits and still-life; removed before 1650 from London to Amsterdam, where he died. [xxxiv. 296]

LUTTREL or **LUTTEREL**, EDWARD (fl. 1670-1710), crayon painter and mezzotint-engraver; invented a method of laying a ground on copper on which to draw in crayons; one of the earliest of English mezzotint-engravers. [xxxiv. 296]

LUTTRELL, HENRY (1655?-1717), colonel; brother of Simon Luttrell [q. v.]; assisted James II, but subsequently joined William III; enlisted Irish papists for the Venetian republic, 1693; shot dead in Dublin. [xxxiv. 297]

LUTTRELL, HENRY (1765?-1851), wit and poet of society; a natural son of Henry Lawes Luttrell, second earl of Carhampton [q. v.]; M.P., Clonmines, co. Wexford, in the Irish parliament, 1798; introduced to London society through the Duchess of Devonshire; famous as a conversationalist and diner-out; published 'Advice to Julia, a Letter in Rhyme,' 1820 (third and improved edition as 'Letters to Julia in Rhyme,' 1822), and 'Crockford House,' a satire on high play, 1827. [xxxiv. 298]

LUTTRELL, HENRY LAWES, second EARL OF CARHAMPTON (1743-1821), soldier and politician, entered the army, 1757; deputy adjutant-general to the forces in Portugal, 1762; M.P., Bossiney, 1768-9, and 1774-84, Middlesex, 1769-74; major-general, 1782; M.P., Old Leighton, in the Irish parliament, 1783; succeeded his father in the (Irish) peerage, 1787; lieutenant-general of the ordnance in Ireland, 1789; M.P., Plympton Earls, 1790-4; commander of the forces in Ireland, 1796-7; master-general of the ordnance, 1797-1800; M.P., Ludgershall, 1817-21. [xxxiv. 299]

LUTTRELL, JAMES (1751?-1788), captain in the navy; brother of Henry Lawes Luttrell, second earl of Carhampton [q. v.]; M.P. for Stockbridge, Hampshire, 1775-84; engaged in active service, 1782; surveyor-general of the ordnance, 1783-8; M.P., Dover, 1784. [xxxiv. 300]

LUTTRELL, JOHN, afterwards LUTTRELL-OLMIUS, third earl of Carhampton (d. 1829); brother of Henry Lawes Luttrell, second earl of Carhampton [q. v.]; captain in the navy, 1762; a commissioner of the excise, 1784; took the name and arms of Olmius, 1787; succeeded to peerage, 1821. [xxxiv. 300]

LUTTRELL, NARCISSUS (1657-1732), annalist and bibliographer; educated at St. John's College, Cambridge; M.A., 1675; collected valuable manuscripts and fugitive poetical tracts, broadsides, and slips relative to his own time; compiled in manuscript 'A Brief Historicall Relation of State Affairs from September 1678 to April 1714,' printed, 1857. [xxxiv. 300]

LUTTRELL, SIMON (d. 1698), colonel; brother of Henry Luttrell (1655?-1717) [q. v.]; an adherent of James II; M.P., co. Dublin, in Irish parliament, 1689; served in Italy as brigadier under Catinat, and in Catalonia under the Duke de Vendôme. [xxxiv. 301]

LUTTRELL, TEMPLE SIMON (d. 1803), third son of Simon Luttrell, first earl of Carhampton; M.P., Milborne Port, Somerset, 1774-80; arrested at Boulogne, 1793; imprisoned in Paris, 1793-5; died in Paris. [xxxiv. 297]

LUTWYCHE, SIR EDWARD (d. 1709), judge; barrister, Gray's Inn, 1661; ancient, 1671; king's serjeant, 1684; knighted, 1684; judge of the common pleas, 1686-8; prepared 'Reports of Cases in the Common Pleas,' 1704 (published, 1718). [xxxiv. 302]

LUTWYCHE, THOMAS (1675-1734), lawyer; son of Sir Edward Lutwyche [q. v.]; of Westminster School and Christ Church, Oxford; barrister, Inner Temple, 1697; treasurer, 1722; M.P., Appleby, 1710-15, Callington, 1722-7 Agmondesham, 1728-34. [xxxiv. 302]

LUXBOROUGH, HENRIETTA, LADY (d. 1756). [See KNIGHT, HENRIETTA.]

D d

LUXFORD, GEORGE (1807-1854), botanist; published 'Flora of Reigate,' 1838; sub-editor of the 'Westminster Review'; edited the 'Phytologist,' 1841-54; lecturer on botany in St. Thomas's Hospital, 1846-51. [xxxiv. 302]

LUXMOORE, CHARLES SCOTT (1794?-1854), dean of St. Asaph; son of John Luxmoore (1756-1830) [q. v.]; M.A. St. John's College, Cambridge, 1818; a notable pluralist; dean of St. Asaph and chancellor of the diocese; prebendary of Hereford, and holder of three rectories at the same time. [xxxiv. 303]

LUXMOORE, JOHN (1756-1830), bishop successively of Bristol, Hereford, and St. Asaph; of Eton and King's College, Cambridge; M.A., 1783; D.D. Lambeth, 1795; dean of Gloucester, 1799-1808; bishop of Bristol, 1807, of Hereford, 1808, of St. Asaph, 1815. [xxxiv. 303]

LYALL. [See also LYELL and LYLE.]

LYALL, ALFRED (1795-1865), philosopher and traveller; brother of George Lyall [q. v.]; educated at Eton and Trinity College, Cambridge; B.A., 1818; edited the 'Annual Register,' 1822-7; published 'Rambles in Madeira and Portugal,' 1827, and 'Principles of Necessity and Contingent Truth,' 1830; vicar of Godmersham, 1837; rector of Harbledown, 1848; criticised John Stuart Mill in 'Agonistes,' 1856; contributed to the 'History of the Mediæval Church' in vol. xi. of the 'Encyclopædia Metropolitana.' [xxxiv. 303]

LYALL, GEORGE (d. 1853), politician and merchant; succeeded to his father's shipowning and merchant's business, 1805; assisted to reform 'Lloyd's Register' of shipping, 1834; M.P. for the city of London, 1833-5 and 1841-7; chairman of the East India Company, 1841. [xxxiv. 304]

LYALL, ROBERT (1790-1831), botanist and traveller; M.D. Edinburgh; spent many years in Russia; published 'The Character of the Russians and a detailed History of Moscow,' 1823, and narrative of travel, 1825; British agent in Madagascar, 1826-8; collected plants and specimens; died at Mauritius. [xxxiv. 304]

LYALL, WILLIAM ROWE (1788-1857), dean of Canterbury; educated at Trinity College, Cambridge; M.A., 1816; conducted the 'British Critic,' 1816-17; reorganised the 'Encyclopædia Metropolitana,' 1820; Warburtonian lecturer, 1826; helped to edit the 'Theological Library,' vols. i-xiv., 1832-46; archdeacon of Maidstone, 1841; dean of Canterbury, 1845. [xxxiv. 305]

LYDE, WILLIAM (1622-1706). [See JOYNER.]

LYDGATE, JOHN (1370?-1451?), poet; ordained priest, 1397; celebrated civic ceremonies in verse at the request of the corporation of London; began his 'Troy Book' (finished, 1420) at request of the Prince of Wales (afterwards Henry V), 1412; acted as court poet, and found a patron in Humphrey, duke of Gloucester, from 1422; rewarded with lands and money; spent the later part of his life at Bury monastery; describes himself as Chaucer's disciple; shows to best advantage in his shorter poems on social subjects. His chief poems are 'Falls of Princes,' written between 1430 and 1438, first printed, 1494, 'Troy Book,' written between 1412 and 1420, first printed, 1513, 'The Story of Thebes,' written, c. 1420, first printed, c. 1500. He wrote also devotional, philosophical, scientific, historical, and occasional poems, besides allegories, fables, and moral romances. One prose work, 'The Damage and Destruccyon in Realmes,' written in 1400, is assigned to him. [xxxiv. 306]

LYDIAT, THOMAS (1572-1646), divine and chronologer; educated at Winchester and New College, Oxford; fellow of New College, 1593; M.A., 1599; chronographer and cosmographer to Henry, prince of Wales, to whom he dedicated his 'Emendatio Temporum,' 1609; in Dublin, becoming fellow of Trinity College and M.A., 1609-11; first contrived the octodesexcentenary period; published chronological works in Latin, 1605-21; some of his manuscripts printed after his death. [xxxiv. 316]

LYE, EDWARD (1694-1767), Anglo-Saxon and Gothic scholar; educated at Hertford College, Oxford; B.A., 1716; ordained, 1717; published, with additions, the 'Etymologicum Anglicanum' of Francis Junius [q. v.], and prefixed to it an Anglo-Saxon grammar, 1743; published 'Sacrorum Evangeliorum Versio Gothica,' with a Latin translation and a Gothic grammar, 1750; his Anglo-Saxon and Gothic dictionary published, 1772. [xxxiv. 318]

LYE, LEE, or LEIGH, THOMAS (1621-1684), nonconformist minister; B.A. Wadham College, Oxford, 1641; migrated to Emmanuel College, Cambridge; M.A., 1646; refused to sign the engagement, 1651; ejected from All Hallows, Lombard Street, London, 1662; a popular and successful instructor of children; wrote educational works for children. [xxxiv. 318]

LYELL. [See also LYALL and LYLE.]

LYELL, CHARLES (1767-1849), botanist and student of Dante; educated at St. Andrews and Peterhouse, Cambridge; M.A., 1794; studied mosses; published translations of Dante, 1835, 1842, and 1845. [xxxiv. 319]

LYELL, SIR CHARLES, first baronet (1797-1875), geologist; son of Charles Lyell (1767-1849) [q. v.]; M.A. Exeter College, Oxford, 1821; studied geology under Dr. Buckland; began the series of continental tours which formed the foundation of his best-known works, 1818; entered Lincoln's Inn, 1819; secretary of the Geological Society, 1823-6; F.R.S., 1826; published vol. i. of his 'Principles of Geology,' 1830 (vol. ii. 1832, vol. iii. 1833, whole work in four smaller volumes, 1834), finally discrediting the catastrophic school of geologists; professor of geology, King's College, London, 1831-3; president of the Geological Society, 1835-6 and 1849-50; published 'Elements of Geology,' supplementary to the 'Principles,' and more a descriptive text-book, 1838 (6th edit. 1865); lectured in the United States, 1841 and 1852; published 'Travels in North America, with Geological Observations,' 1845; knighted, 1848; published 'A Second Visit to the United States of North America,' 1849; D.C.L. Oxford, 1854; published 'The Antiquity of Man,' 1863; created baronet, 1864; published 'The Student's Elements of Geology,' 1871. [xxxiv. 319]

LYFORD, WILLIAM (1598-1653), nonconformist divine; educated at Magdalen College, Oxford; B.A., 1618; B.D., 1631; held Calvinistic views; author of theological works. [xxxiv. 324]

LYGON, FREDERICK, sixth EARL BEAUCHAMP (1830-1891), of Eton and Christ Church, Oxford; M.A., 1856; fellow of All Souls College, Oxford, 1852-6; M.P., Tewkesbury, 1857-63; a lord of the admiralty, 1859; M.P., Worcestershire, 1863-6; succeeded to earldom, 1866; D.C.L. Oxford, 1870; lord steward of the household, 1874-80; privy councillor, 1874; paymaster of the forces, 1885-6 and 1886-7; helped to found Keble College, Oxford. [xxxiv. 324]

LYGON, WILLIAM, first EARL BEAUCHAMP (1747-1816), of Christ Church, Oxford; M.P., Worcester, 1775-1806; created Baron Beauchamp of Powycke, Worcestershire, 1806, and Viscount Elmley and Earl Beauchamp, 1816. [xxxiv. 325]

LYHERT, otherwise LYART, LE HERT, or LE HART, WALTER (d. 1472), bishop of Norwich; fellow of Exeter and Oriel Colleges, Oxford; provost of Oriel College, Oxford, 1444; bishop of Norwich, 1446; when English ambassador to Savoy prevailed on the antipope, Felix V, to resign his claim to the papacy, 1449. [xxxiv. 325]

LYLE. [See also LYALL and LYELL.]

LYLE, DAVID (fl. 1762), stenographer; his 'The Art of Short-hand improved,' 1762, of little practical value. [xxxiv. 326]

LYLE, ROBERT, second BARON LYLE (d. 1497?), justiciary of Scotland; engaged on embassies to England, 1472, 1484, and 1485; a lord in council, 1485; great justiciary of Scotland, 1488; ambassador to Spain, 1491; an auditor of the exchequer, 1492. [xxxiv. 326]

LYLE, THOMAS (1792-1859), Scottish poet; educated at Glasgow University; took the diploma of surgeon, 1816; remembered solely for the song, 'Let us haste to Kelvin Grove,' first published, 1820. [xxxiv. 327]

LYLY, JOHN (1554?-1606), dramatist and author of 'Euphues'; of Magdalen College, Oxford; M.A., 1575; studied also at Cambridge, being incorporated M.A., 1579; published, in London, the first part of his 'Euphues, the Anatomy of Wit,' 1579, and the second part, 'Euphues and his England,' 1580; wrote light plays to be performed at court by the children's acting companies of the Chapel Royal and St. Paul's, London, including 'Campaspe' and 'Sapho and Phao,' produced, 1584 ; championed the cause of the bishops in the Martin Mar-Prelate controversy in a pamphlet, 'Pappe with an Hatchet,' 1589 ; M.P., Hindon, 1589, Aylesbury, 1593 and 1601, Appleby, 1597 ; his 'Euphues' interesting for its prose style, which is characterised by a continuous straining after antithesis and epigram, and received the name of 'Euphuism.' Lyly's style became popular and influenced some writers, while it was ridiculed by others, Shakespeare among them. His best plays are 'Alexander and Campaspe,' 1584, 'Midas,' 1592, and 'Endymion,' 1591 ; they contain attractive lyrics, which were first printed in Blount's collected edition of the plays, 1632.   [xxxiv. 327]

LYNAM, ROBERT (1796–1845), miscellaneous writer ; of Christ's Hospital and Trinity College, Cambridge ; M.A., 1821 ; assistant-chaplain and secretary to the Magdalene Hospital, London, 1832 ; wrote a history of the reign of George III and of the Roman emperors, but is chiefly remembered as an editor of such authors as Rollin, Skelton, Paley, and Johnson. His most complete compilation was 'The British Essayist,' 30 vols. 1827.
          [xxxiv. 332]

LYNCH, DOMINIC (d. 1697 ?), Dominican friar ; joined the order of St. Dominic ; lived for many years in the convent of St. Paul at Seville ; professor of theology in the College of St. Thomas, 1674 ; published a scholastic work in Latin, 1666–86.   [xxxiv. 333]

LYNCH, HENRY BLOSSE (1807–1873), Mesopotamian explorer ; brother of Thomas Kerr Lynch [q. v.] ; volunteer in the Indian navy, 1823 ; employed on the survey of the Persian Gulf ; Persian and Arabic interpreter to the gulf squadron, 1829–32 ; second in command of the expedition under Francis Rawdon Chesney [q. v.] to explore the Euphrates route to India, 1834 ; in full command of it, 1837 ; decorated by the shah, 1837 ; assistant to the superintendent of the Indian navy, 1843–51 ; captain, 1847 ; master attendant in Bombay dockyard, 1849 ; distinguished himself in second Burmese war, 1851–3 ; C.B., 1853 ; retired and settled in Paris, 1856 ; conducted the negotiations with Persia that led to the treaty of Paris, 1857 ; died at Paris.   [xxxiv. 333]

LYNCH, JAMES (1608 ?–1713), Roman catholic archbishop of Tuam ; educated at the English College, Rome ; archbishop of Tuam, 1669 ; accused of violating the statute of præmunire and forced to retire to Spain ; returned to Ireland, 1685 ; settled at Paris, 1691 ; died at the Irish college, Paris.   [xxxiv. 334]

LYNCH, JOHN (1599 ?–1673 ?), Irish historian ; educated by the jesuits ; secular priest, 1622 ; archdeacon of Tuam ; died probably at St. Malo ; author of Latin works on Irish history, including 'Cambrensis Eversus,' trans. 1795 and 1848–52.   [xxxiv. 335]

LYNCH, PATRICK EDWARD (d. 1884), lieutenant-general in the English army ; brother of Thomas Kerr Lynch [q. v.] ; entered the Indian army, 1826 ; employed in Persia and Afghanistan, 1840–1 and 1858 ; lieutenant-general and retired, 1878.   [xxxiv. 336]

LYNCH, RICHARD (1611–1676), jesuit ; educated in Irish college of Compostella ; joined jesuits, 1630 ; rector of the Irish college of Seville, 1637 ; published 'Universa Philosophia Scholastica,' 1654, and Latin sermons.
          [xxxiv. 336]

LYNCH, THEODORA ELIZABETH (1812–1885), poetical and prose writer ; daughter of Arthur Foulks ; married, in Jamaica, Henry Mark Lynch, 1835 ; returned to England after her husband's death and wrote seventeen volumes (1846–65) of poems and fiction for young people, frequently with a West Indian setting.   [xxxiv. 336]

LYNCH, SIR THOMAS (d. 1684 ?), governor of Jamaica ; grandson of John Aylmer [q. v.], bishop of London ; served in Jamaica expedition, 1655 ; provost-marshal of Jamaica, 1661 ; member of council, 1663 ; president, 1664 ; lieutenant-governor and knighted, 1670 ; recalled, 1676 ; sent out again, 1682 ; died in Jamaica.
          [xxxiv. 337]

LYNCH, THOMAS KERR (1818–1891), Mesopotamian explorer ; educated at Trinity College, Dublin ; accompanied his brother, Henry Blosse Lynch [q. v.], in second Euphrates expedition, 1837–42 ; travelled extensively in Mesopotamia and Persia ; consul-general for Persia in London ; published 'A Visit to the Suez Canal,' 1866.   [xxxiv. 338]

LYNCH, THOMAS TOKE (1818–1871), hymn-writer ; his 'Hymns for Heart and Voice : the Rivulet,' 1855, attacked as pantheistic ; composed several tunes for them, and other works both in prose and verse.
          [xxxiv. 338]

LYNCHE, RICHARD (fl. 1596 ? – 1601). [See LINCHE.]

LYNDE, SIR HUMPHREY (1579–1636), puritan controversialist ; of Westminster School and Christ Church, Oxford ; B.A., 1600 ; knighted, 1613 ; M.P., Brecknock, 1626 ; wrote numerous controversial works, including 'Via Tuta, the Safe Way,' 1628.   [xxxiv. 339]

LYNDHURST, first BARON (1772–1863). [See COPLEY, JOHN SINGLETON.]

LYNDSAY, SIR DAVID (1490–1555). [See LINDSAY.]

LYNDWOOD, WILLIAM (1375 ?–1446), civilian, canonist, and bishop of St. David's ; his name is variously spelt Lyndewode, Lindewood, Lyndwood, and Lindwood ; educated at Gonville Hall, Cambridge ; fellow of Pembroke Hall ; removed to Oxford, where he took LL.D. degree ; prebendary of Salisbury, 1412, of Hereford, 1422 ; dean of the arches, 1426 ; archdeacon of Oxford, 1433 ; keeper of the privy seal, 1433 ; bishop of Hereford, 1442 ; completed his 'Provinciale,' a digest of the synodal constitutions of the province of Canterbury from Stephen Langton to Henry Chichele, the principal authority for English canon law, 1433 (first printed, c. 1470–80).
          [xxxiv. 340]

LYNE, RICHARD (fl. 1570–1600), painter and engraver ; one of the earliest native artists in England whose works have been preserved ; employed by Matthew Parker [q. v.] ; drew and engraved map of the university of Cambridge, published, 1574 ; mentioned by Meres in 'Palladis Tamia' (1598) as among the leading painters of the time.   [xxxiv. 342]

LYNEDOCH, first BARON (1748–1843). [See GRAHAM, THOMAS.]

LYNFORD or **LINFORD**, THOMAS (1650–1724), divine ; of Christ's College, Cambridge ; M.A., 1674 ; fellow of Christ's College, 1675 ; canon of Westminster, 1700 ; archdeacon of Barnstaple, 1709–24 ; published sermons and 'Some Dialogues between Mr. Godden and others,' &c., 1687.   [xxxiv. 342]

LYNGARD, RICHARD (1598 ?–1670). [See LINGARD.]

LYNN, GEORGE, the elder (1676–1742), astronomer and antiquary ; communicated his astronomical observations and meteorological registers to the Royal Society, 1724–40.   [xxxiv. 343]

LYNN, GEORGE, the younger (1707–1758), barrister, Inner Temple ; son of George Lynn the elder [q. v.] ; F.S.A., 1726.   [xxxiv. 343]

LYNN, SAMUEL FERRIS (1836–1876), sculptor ; exhibited at the Royal Academy, 1856–75 ; member of the Institute of Sculptors, 1861 ; associate of the Royal Hibernian Academy.   [xxxiv. 343]

LYNN, THOMAS (1774–1847), writer on astronomy ; in the naval service of the East India Company ; examiner in nautical astronomy to the company's officers ; author of 'Solar Tables,' 'Star Tables,' 'Astronomical Tables,' 'A new Method of finding the Longitude,' 1826, and 'Practical Methods for finding the Latitude,' 1833.
          [xxxiv. 343]

LYNN, WALTER (1677–1763), medical writer and inventor ; brother of George Lynn the elder [q. v.] ; B.A. Peterhouse, Cambridge, 1698 ; M.B., 1704 ; published medical works ; chiefly remembered by his proposed improvements of the steam-engine, described in 'The Case of Walter Lynn, M.B.,' 1726.   [xxxiv. 343]

LYNNE, NICHOLAS OF (fl. 1360). [See NICHOLAS.]

LYNNE, WALTER (fl. 1550), printer and translator ; an ardent reformer ; printed and translated about nineteen religious works ; patronised by Cranmer.
          [xxxiv. 344]

LYON, Mrs. AGNES (1762-1840), Scottish poetess; *née* L'Amy; married the Rev. Dr. James Lyon, 1786; solely remembered by the song, 'You've surely heard of famous Niel.' [xxxiv. 345]

LYON, GEORGE FRANCIS (1795-1832), captain in the navy and traveller; entered the navy, 1808; travelled in Africa in the interests of the government, 1818-20; published 'A Narrative of Travels in North Africa,' 1821; took part in Parry's arctic expedition, 1821-3, publishing a narrative, 1824; unsuccessfully attempted to reach Repulse Bay, 1824; hon. D.C.L. Oxford, 1825; went to Mexico and South America; died at sea. [xxxiv. 345]

LYON, HART (more correctly HIRSCH LÖBEL or LEWIN) (1721-1800), chief rabbi; born at Resha, Poland; chief rabbi of the London congregation of German and Polish Jews, 1757-63; subsequently rabbi of Halberstadt, Mannheim, and Berlin; died at Berlin. [xxxiv. 346]

LYON, Sir JAMES FREDERICK (1775 - 1842), lieutenant-general; born on a homeward bound transport from America after Bunker's Hill, where his father was killed; entered the army, 1791; lieutenant, 1794; in Egypt as major, 1801; as lieutenant-colonel in the Peninsula, 1808-11; K.C.B., 1815; G.C.H., 1817; commander of the troops in the Windward and Leeward islands, 1828-33; lieutenant-general, 1830. [xxxiv. 347]

LYON, JANET, LADY GLAMMIS (d. 1537). [See DOUGLAS, JANET.]

LYON, JOHN, seventh BARON GLAMMIS (1510?-1558), son of John, sixth lord Glammis, by Janet Douglas [q. v.]; tried for conspiring to effect the death of James V, 1537; imprisoned, 1537-40; held a command in the Scottish army, 1545. [xxxiv. 347]

LYON, JOHN, eighth BARON GLAMMIS (d. 1578), lord high chancellor of Scotland; son of John, seventh baron Glammis [q. v.]; partisan and kinsman of Morton; lord chancellor of Scotland, 1573; accidentally slain in a street brawl. [xxxiv. 348]

LYON, JOHN (1514?-1592), founder of Harrow School; obtained charter for the foundation of a free grammar school for boys in Harrow, 1572; drew up statutes and course of study for the school, 1590. [xxxiv. 348]

LYON or **LYOUN**, JOHN (*fl.* 1608-1622), of Auldbar, the supposed author of 'Teares for the Death of Alexander, Earle of Dunfermeling' (first printed, 1622); son of Sir Thomas Lyon (d. 1608) [q. v.] [xxxiv. 349]

LYON, JOHN, ninth EARL OF STRATHMORE (1737-1776), married Mary Eleanor Bowes [q. v.], a member of a distinguished border family, 1767; took his wife's surname; Scots representative peer. [vi. 60]

LYON, JOHN (1702-1790), antiquary; M.A. Trinity College, Dublin, 1732; minor canon of St. Patrick's, Dublin, 1740; published nothing; reputed a learned ecclesiologist; took care of Swift in his last illness. [xxxiv. 349]

LYON, JOHN (1734-1817), historian of Dover; took holy orders; his principal work is a 'History of the Town and Port of Dover,' 1813-14; published works on electricity, 1780-96. [xxxiv. 350]

LYON, Sir PATRICK OF CARSE (d. 1695?), lord of session; second cousin of Patrick Lyon, first earl of Strathmore [q. v.]; professor of philosophy at St. Andrews; member of the Faculty of Advocates, 1671; lord of session as Lord Carse, 1683-8; a lord justiciary, 1684-8; deprived of both offices at the revolution, 1688. [xxxiv. 350]

LYON, PATRICK, first EARL OF STRATHMORE and third EARL OF KINGHORNE (1642-1695), succeeded to his estates, 1660; restored the fortunes of his family by a course of self-denial; privy councillor, 1682; lord of session, 1686-9; took the oath to King William III, 1690. [xxxiv. 351]

LYON, Sir THOMAS OF BALDUCKIE and AULDBAR, MASTER OF GLAMMIS (d. 1608), lord high treasurer of Scotland; son of John Lyon, seventh baron Glammis [q. v.]; a main contriver of the raid of Ruthven of 1582; escaped to Ireland, 1583; pardoned, 1585; lord high treasurer, 1585-96; lord of session, 1586; knighted, 1590; deprived of his office for favouring Bothwell, 1591; reappointed, 1593. [xxxiv. 351]

LYON, WILLIAM (d. 1617), bishop of Cork, Cloyne, and Ross; educated at Oxford; first protestant bishop of Ross, 1582; bishop of Cork and Cloyne, 1584 (three sees united, 1587); foiled machinations of jesuits and friars; recommended the strict exclusion of foreign priests. [xxxiv. 353]

LYONS, EDMUND, first BARON LYONS (1790-1858), admiral; entered the navy, 1803; present at the passing of the Dardanelles, 1807; saw active service in East Indies, 1810-11; commander, 1812; employed in the Mediterranean, 1828-33; K.C.H. and minister plenipotentiary at Athens, 1835; created baronet, 1840; minister to the Swiss confederation, 1849-51; rear-admiral, 1850; minister at Stockholm, 1851-3; second in command of the Mediterranean fleet, 1853-55; commander-in-chief, 1855-8; military G.C.B., 1855; created Baron Lyons of Christchurch, 1856; rear-admiral, with temporary rank of admiral, while in command in the Mediterranean, 1857. [xxxiv. 355]

LYONS, ISRAEL, the elder (d. 1770), hebraist; a Polish Jew settled at Cambridge; instructed members of the university in Hebrew; author of 'The Scholar's Instructor: an Hebrew Grammar, with Points,' 1735. [xxxiv. 357]

LYONS, ISRAEL, the younger (1739-1775), mathematician and botanist; son of Israel Lyons the elder [q. v.]; published 'A Treatise of Fluxions,' 1758, and 'Fasciculus Plantarum circa Cantabrigiam,' 1763; lectured on botany at Oxford, 1764; appointed by the board of longitude to accompany Captain Phipps as principal astronomer in his arctic expedition, 1773. [xxxiv. 357]

LYONS, JOHN CHARLES (1792-1874), antiquary and writer on gardening; educated at Pembroke College, Oxford; published a 'Treatise on the Management of Orchidaceous Plants,' 2nd ed. 1845; interested in local antiquities and literature, publishing 'The Grand Juries of Westmeath from 1727 to 1853, with an Historical Appendix,' 1853. [xxxiv. 358]

LYONS, RICHARD BICKERTON PEMELL, second BARON and first EARL LYONS (1817-1887), diplomatist; son of Edmund Lyons, first baron Lyons [q. v.]; of Winchester College and Christ Church, Oxford; M.A., 1843; unpaid attaché at Athens, 1839; paid attaché, 1844; transferred to Dresden, 1852; appointed to Florence, 1853; secretary of that legation, 1856; British minister at Washington, 1858-65; K.C.B., 1860; G.C.B., 1862; ambassador at Constantinople, and privy councillor, 1865-7, at Paris, 1867-87; created Viscount Lyons of Christchurch, 1881, and Earl Lyons, 1887. [xxxiv. 358]

LYONS, ROBERT SPENCER DYER (1826-1886), physician; educated at Trinity College, Dublin; M.B., 1848; licentiate, Royal College of Surgeons in Ireland, 1849; chief pathological commissioner to the army in the Crimea, 1855; investigated pathological anatomy of Lisbon yellow fever, 1857; joined St. George's Hospital, Dublin; professor of medicine in the Roman catholic university medical school; M.P., Dublin, 1880-5; published two medical works and a book on forestry. [xxxiv. 359]

LYSAGHT, EDWARD (1763-1811), Irish songwriter; educated at Trinity College, Dublin, and St. Edmund Hall, Oxford; M.A., 1788; called to the English and Irish bars, 1788; practised first in England and afterwards in Ireland; commissioner of bankruptcy in Ireland and police magistrate for Dublin; wrote poems (published posthumously, 1811), political squibs, and pamphlets. [xxxiv. 360]

LYSARDE, NICHOLAS (d. 1570). [See LYZARDE.]

LYSONS, DANIEL (1727-1800), physician; M.A. Magdalen College, Oxford, 1751; fellow and B.C.L. of All Souls College, Oxford, 1755; M.D., 1769; published medical works. [xxxiv. 360]

LYSONS, DANIEL (1762-1834), topographer; nephew of Daniel Lysons (1727-1800) [q. v.]; of St. Mary Hall, Oxford; M.A., 1785; his principal work, 'The Environs of London,' 1792-6; held family living of Rodmarton, 1804-33; in conjunction with his brother Samuel Lysons (1763-1819) [q. v.] began a 'Magna Britannia . . . Account of the . . . Counties of Great Britain,' dealing with ten counties from Bedfordshire to Devonshire, in alphabetical order, 1806-22. [xxxiv. 361]

LYSONS, SIR DANIEL (1816–1898), general ; son of Daniel Lysons (1762–1834) [q. v.] ; ensign, 1834 ; lieutenant, 1837 ; served in Canada ; received company in 3rd West India regiment, 1843 ; brigade-major of 23rd Welsh fusiliers in Barbados, 1845–7, and in Halifax, Nova Scotia, 1847–8 ; major, 1849 ; in Crimea, 1854 – 5 ; lieutenant-colonel, 1854 ; brevet-colonel and C.B., 1855 ; assistant adjutant-general at headquarters in England, 1856 ; in Canada in connection with the 'Trent' affair, 1861 ; major-general, 1868 ; quartermaster-general at headquarters, 1876 ; lieutenant-general and K.C.B., 1877 ; general, 1879 ; commanded Aldershot division, 1880–3 ; G.C.B., 1886 ; constable of the Tower, 1890 ; published 'Instructions for Mounted Rifle Volunteers,' 1860.   [Suppl. iii. 115]

LYSONS, SAMUEL (1763–1819), antiquary ; F.S.A., 1786 ; F.R.S., 1797 ; barrister, Inner Temple, 1798 ; keeper of the Tower of London records, 1803 ; vice-president and treasurer of the Royal Society, 1810 ; antiquary professor in the Royal Academy, 1818 ; assisted his brother, Daniel Lysons (1762–1834) [q. v.], on the 'Magna Britannia.' His greatest work, 'Reliquiæ Britannico-Romanæ, containing Figures of Roman Antiquities discovered in England,' with plates, was published,|1801–17.   [xxxiv. 362]

LYSONS, SAMUEL (1806–1877), antiquary ; son of Daniel Lysons (1762–1834) [q. v.] ; B.A. Exeter College, Oxford, 1830 ; honorary canon of Gloucester Cathedral, 1867 ; published antiquarian works connected with Gloucestershire, 1832–68.   [xxxiv. 363]

LYSTER, SIR RICHARD (d. 1554), chief-justice of the court of king's bench ; reader at the Middle Temple, 1515 ; solicitor-general, 1522–6 ; chief-baron of the exchequer, 1529 ; knighted, 1529 ; chief-justice of the king's bench, 1546–52.   [xxxiv. 363]

LYTE, HENRY (1529 ?–1607), botanist and antiquary ; student at Oxford, c. 1546 ; published a translation through the French of the 'Cruydeboeck' of Rembert Dodoens, with the title, 'A niewe Herball or Historie of Plantes,' 1578 ; published 'The Light of Britayne ; a Recorde of the honorable Originall and Antiquitie of Britaine,' 1588.   [xxxiv. 364]

LYTE, HENRY FRANCIS (1793 – 1847), hymnwriter ; lineal descendant of Henry Lyte [q. v.] ; educated at Trinity College, Dublin ; took holy orders ; published 'Poems, chiefly Religious,' 1833, and other works ; chiefly remembered for his hymns, the best of which appear in most hymnals ; died at Nice.   [xxxiv. 365]

LYTE, THOMAS (1568 ?–1638), genealogist ; educated at Sherborne School ; drew up the 'most royally ennobled Genealogy' of James I, now lost, which he presented to the king, 1610 ; compiled Lyte pedigrees.   [xxxiv. 366]

LYTTELTON or LITTLETON, SIR CHARLES, second baronet (1629–1716), governor of Jamaica ; son of Sir Thomas Lyttelton (1596–1650) [q. v.] ; fought in the royalist army ; escaped to France, 1648 ; cupbearer to Charles II, 1650 ; knighted, 1662 ; governor of Jamaica, 1662–4 ; founded first town of Port Royal ; summoned the first legislative assembly, 1664 ; major of the yellow-coated 'maritime' regiment, the precursor of the marine forces ; governor of Harwich and Landguard Fort at time of great sea-fight with the Dutch, 1672 ; M.P., Bewdley, 1685–9 ; succeeded his brother as second baronet, 1693.   [xxxiv. 367]

LYTTELTON, CHARLES (1714–1768), antiquary and bishop of Carlisle ; grandson of Sir Charles Lyttelton [q. v.] ; of Eton and University College, Oxford ; barrister, Middle Temple, 1738 ; ordained, 1742 ; F.R.S., 1743 ; D.C.L., 1745 ; F.S.A., 1746 ; dean of Exeter, 1747 ; bishop of Exeter, 1762 ; president of the Society of Antiquaries, 1765 ; contributed to the 'Philosophical Transactions' (1748 and 1750), and to 'Archæologia' (vols. i–iii.).
                [xxxiv. 368]

LYTTELTON, SIR EDWARD, first BARON LYTTELTON of Munslow (1589–1645). [See LITTLETON.]

LYTTELTON, GEORGE, first BARON LYTTELTON (1709–1773), descended from William, son of Sir Thomas Littleton (1402–1481) [q. v.] ; educated at Eton and Christ Church, Oxford ; M.P., Okehampton, 1735–56 ; opposed Walpole ; a lord of the treasury, 1744–54 ; with his con-

nections, Pitt and the Grenvilles, composed 'Cobhamite' party ; succeeded to baronetcy, 1751 ; privy councillor, 1754 ; chancellor of the exchequer for a short period, 1756 ; created Baron Lyttelton of Frankley, 1756 ; opposed the repeal of the Stamp Act, 1766 ; friend of Pope and a liberal patron of literature ; his best poem, the monody on the death of his wife, 1747 ; published, among numerous other works, 'Dialogues of the Dead,' 1760, and 'The History of the Life of Henry the Second, and of the Age in which he lived,' 1767–71.   [xxxiv. 369]

LYTTELTON, GEORGE WILLIAM, fourth BARON LYTTELTON of Frankley of the second creation (1817–1876), son of William Henry Lyttelton, third baron Lyttelton [q. v.] ; educated at Eton and Trinity College, Cambridge ; succeeded to peerage, 1837 ; M.A., 1838 ; LL.D., 1862 ; D.C.L., 1870 ; the centre of the intellectual life of Worcestershire from 1839 ; F.R.S., 1840 ; principal of Queen's College, Birmingham, 1845 ; under-secretary of state for the colonies, 1846 ; chairman of the Canterbury Association, a church of England corporation which established Canterbury, New Zealand, 1850 ; first president of the Birmingham and Midland Institute, 1853 ; chief commissioner of endowed schools, 1869 ; privy councillor, 1869 ; K.C.M.G., 1869 ; killed himself in an attack of constitutional melancholia ; published, together with Mr. Gladstone, a volume of translations, 1839.   [xxxiv. 374]

LYTTELTON, SIR HENRY, second baronet (1624–1693), son of Sir Thomas Lyttelton (1596–1650) [q. v.] ; educated at Balliol College, Oxford ; taken prisoner at the battle of Worcester, 1651 ; M.P., Lichfield, 1678–9.
                [xxxiv. 375]

LYTTELTON, JAMES (d. 1723). [See LITTLETON.]

LYTTELTON, SIR THOMAS (1402–1481). [See LITTLETON.]

LYTTELTON, SIR THOMAS, first baronet (1596–1650), royalist ; educated at Balliol College, Oxford ; B.A., 1614 ; created baronet, 1618 ; M.P., Worcester, 1621–2, 1624–5, 1625, 1626, 1640 ; colonel of the Worcestershire horse and foot, 1642 ; imprisoned, 1644–6. [xxxiv. 375]

LYTTELTON, SIR THOMAS (1647 ?–1710). [See LITTLETON.]

LYTTELTON, THOMAS, second BARON LYTTELTON (1744–1779), commonly called the wicked Lord Lyttelton ; son of George, first baron Lyttelton [q. v.] ; educated at Eton and Christ Church, Oxford ; M.P. Bewdley, 1768–9 ; took his seat in the House of Lords, 1774 ; prominent in debates on American affairs, 1774–8 ; warned in a dream (24 Nov. 1779), which was exactly fulfilled, that he would die in three days ; a notorious profligate.   [xxxiv. 375]

LYTTELTON, WILLIAM HENRY, first BARON LYTTELTON of Frankley of the second creation (1724–1808), educated at Eton College and St. Mary Hall, Oxford ; barrister, Middle Temple, 1748 ; M.P., Bewdley, 1748–55, and 1774–6 ; governor of South Carolina, 1755–62, of Jamaica, 1762–6 ; ambassador to Portugal, 1766–71 ; created Baron Westcote of Balamare, co. Longford (Irish peerage), 1776 ; a commissioner of the treasury, 1776–82 ; hon. D.C.L., 1781 ; created Baron Lyttelton of Frankley (peerage of Great Britain), 1794 ; chief published work 'An Historical Account of the Constitution of Jamaica,' 1792.   [xxxiv. 378]

LYTTELTON, WILLIAM HENRY, third BARON LYTTELTON of Frankley of the second creation (1782–1837), son of William Henry Lyttelton, first baron Lyttelton of the second creation [q. v.] ; educated at Christ Church, Oxford ; M.A., 1805 ; M.P., Worcestershire, 1807–1820 ; D.C.L., 1810 ; succeeded to the title on death of his half-brother, George Fulke, second baron, 1828 ; a whig and an eloquent orator.   [xxxiv. 378]

LYTTELTON, WILLIAM HENRY (1820–1884), canon of Gloucester ; son of William Henry Lyttelton, third baron Lyttelton [q. v.] ; of Winchester College and Trinity College, Cambridge ; M.A., 1841 ; honorary canon of Worcester, 1847 ; canon of Gloucester, 1880 ; published religious works.   [xxxiv. 379]

LYTTON, EDWARD GEORGE EARLE LYTTON BULWER-, first BARON LYTTON (1803–1873), novelist ; educated at private schools under a tutor, and then successively at Trinity College and Trinity Hall, Cambridge ; published a small volume of poems ; chancellor's medallist,

1825 ; B.A., 1826 ; frequented the fashionable circles of London and Paris ; married Rosina Wheeler, 1827 [see LYTTON, ROSINA BULWER-LYTTON, LADY] ; supported himself by energetic literary labour ; wrote for all kinds of periodicals, from 'Quarterly Reviews' to 'Keepsakes' ; published 'Falkland,' 1827, 'Pelham,' one of his best novels, 1828, and 'The Disowned,' 1828 ; published 'Devereux,' 1829, 'Paul Clifford,' 1830 ; edited the 'New Monthly,' 1831–2 ; M.P., St. Ives, Huntingdonshire, 1831, Lincoln, 1832–41 ; a reformer in politics and a steady supporter of authors' copyrights and the removal of taxes upon literature ; published 'Eugene Aram,' 1832, 'Godolphin,' 1833, 'The Last Days of Pompeii,' 1834, and 'Rienzi,' 1835 ; separated from his wife (legal separation, 1836), who spent her remaining years (d. 1882) in lawsuits directed against her husband, and in publishing a long series of attacks upon him ; the 'Lady of Lyons' produced at Covent Garden, 1838, and 'Richelieu,' 1839 ; produced 'Money' at the Haymarket, 1840 ; undertook, in conjunction with others, 'The Monthly Chronicle,' 1841 ; published 'The Last of the Barons,' 1843, and 'The New Timon,' a romantic story in heroic couplets, 1846 ; brought out 'Harold,' 1848 ; joined the conservatives and returned to politics ; M.P., Hertfordshire, 1852–66 ; published 'My Novel,' 1853 ; lord rector of Glasgow University, 1856 and 1858 ; secretary for the colonies, 1858–9 ; created Baron Lytton of Knebworth, 1866 ; published anonymously 'The Coming Race,' an ingenious prophecy of the society of the future, 1871, and 'The Parisians,' 1873.

[xxxiv. 380]

LYTTON, EDWARD ROBERT BULWER, first EARL OF LYTTON (1831–1891), statesman and poet, son of Edward George Earle Lytton Bulwer-Lytton, first baron Lytton [q. v.] ; educated at Harrow and Bonn ; private secretary to his uncle, Lord Dalling, at Washington and Florence ; paid attaché at the Hague and Vienna ; published 'Clytemnestra,' 'The Earl's Return,' and other poems,

under the pseudonym of Owen Meredith, 1855 ; published 'The Wanderer,' a volume of lyrics, 1857, and 'Lucile' (a poem), 1860 ; consul-general at Belgrade ; second secretary at Vienna, 1862 ; secretary of legation at Copenhagen, 1863 ; transferred to Athens, 1864, and to Lisbon, 1865 ; employed successively at Madrid and Vienna, 1868–72 ; published 'Chronicles and Characters,' 1868 ; 'Orval, or the Fool of Time,' the sole representative in English literature of the great Polish school of mystical poetry, 1869 ; secretary to the embassy at Paris, 1872–4 ; British minister at Lisbon, 1872 ; succeeded to his father's title, 1873 ; published 'Fables in Song,' 1874 ; viceroy of India, 1876–80 ; proclaimed Queen Victoria empress of India at Delhi, 1877 ; did admirable work in famine of 1877–8 ; responsible for the Afghan war, 1879 ; effected memorable internal reforms, but his administration regarded at home as a failure ; ambassador at Paris, an office in which he won great popularity, 1887–91 ; 'King Poppy,' his most original and best poem, published, 1892 ; takes high rank as a prose writer in his minutes and despatches.

[xxxiv. 387]

LYTTON, ROSINA BULWER-LYTTON, LADY (1802–1882), novelist ; née Wheeler ; married by Edward George Earle Lytton Bulwer-Lytton, first baron Lytton [q. v.], against his mother's wishes, 1827 ; a woman of excitable temperament ; became estranged from her husband (1836) and was legally separated from him ; wrote a long series of attacks upon him, publishing (1839), 'Cheveley, or the Man of Honour,' a novel in which she made her husband the villain. [xxxiv. 381]

LYVEDEN, first BARON (1800–1873). [See SMITH, ROBERT VERNON.]

LYZARDE, NICHOLAS (d. 1570), sergeant-painter ; painter to the court in time of Henry VIII and Edward VI ; sergeant-painter to queens Mary and Elizabeth.

[xxxiv. 392]

M

MAAS, JOSEPH (1847–1886), vocalist ; studied at Milan, 1869–71 ; public singer in London, 1871 ; principal tenor at her majesty's opera ; created the part of the Chevalier des Grieux in Massenet's 'Manon' at Drury Lane, 1885. [xxxiv. 392]

MAB or MABBE, JAMES (1572–1642?), Spanish scholar ; grandson of John Mab [q. v.] ; fellow of Magdalen College, Oxford, 1594–1633 ; M.A., 1598 ; secretary to Sir John Digby, ambassador at Madrid, 1611–13 ; published translations from the Spanish, including 'The Rogue, or the Life of Guzman de Alfarache,' 1622, and some 'Devout Contemplations, by Fr. Ch. de Fonseca,' 1629. [xxxiv. 392]

MAB or MABBE, JOHN (d. 1582), chamberlain of London ; freeman of the Goldsmiths' Company ; chamberlain of London, 1577–82 ; wrote 'Remembrances, faithfullie printed out of his own hand writing, etc.,' licensed, 1583. [xxxiv. 393]

MABERLY, CATHERINE CHARLOTTE (1805–1875), novelist ; née Prittie ; married William Leader Maberly [q. v.], 1830 ; wrote eight novels, published between 1840 and 1856. [xxxiv. 394]

MABERLY, FREDERICK HERBERT (1781–1860), politician ; of Westminster School and Trinity College, Cambridge ; M.A., 1809 ; led by his fanatical zeal against catholic emancipation into eccentric and violent conduct, which caused the magistrates and the home secretary anxiety about the public peace, 1812–35. [xxxiv. 393]

MABERLY, WILLIAM LEADER (1798–1885), secretary of the general post office ; entered the army, 1815 ; lieutenant-colonel ; M.P., Westbury, 1819–20, Northampton, 1820–30, Shaftesbury, 1831–2, Chatham, 1832–4 ; joint secretary of the general post office, 1836–54 ; opposed all Rowland Hill's schemes of reform ; transferred to the board of audit, 1854, where he remained till 1866 ; retired from the army, 1881. [xxxiv. 394]

MABS. [See MAB, JOHN.]

MACADAM, JOHN (1827–1865), chemist ; studied medicine at Glasgow University and chemistry at Edinburgh ; M.D. Glasgow ; lecturer on chemistry and natural science in the Scottish College, Melbourne, 1855 ; member of the legislative assembly of Victoria, 1859–64 ; postmaster-general, 1861 ; lecturer in chemistry in Melbourne University, 1861–2 ; died at sea on his way to New Zealand. [xxxiv. 395]

McADAM, JOHN LOUDON (1756–1836), the 'macadamiser' of roads ; began experiments in roadmaking in Ayrshire ; continued them at Falmouth, where he resided after 1798 as agent for revictualling the navy in the western ports ; arrived at the conclusion that roads should be constructed of broken stone ; surveyor-general of the Bristol roads, 1815 ; published 'Present State of Road-making,' 1820 ; general surveyor of roads, 1827 ; his process adopted in all parts of the civilised world, his name becoming the synonym for the invention.

[xxxiv. 395]

MACALISTER, ARTHUR (1818–1883), Australian politician ; emigrated to Australia, 1850 ; represented Ipswich in the first Queensland parliament, 1860 ; secretary for lands and works, 1862 ; premier and colonial secretary, 1866–7, 1874–6 ; speaker, 1870–1 ; agent-general for Queensland in London, 1876–81. [xxxiv. 397]

McALL, ROBERT STEPHENS (1792–1838), congregational minister ; ordained, 1823 ; a brilliant preacher ; published sermons and poems. [xxxiv. 397]

MACALLUM, HAMILTON (1841–1896), painter ; studied at Royal Academy, where he exhibited between 1876 and 1896. [Suppl. iii. 116]

MACALPINE, MACCABEUS, MACHABEUS, MACCABE, or MACHABE, JOHN (d. 1557), Scottish reformer and professor of theology at Copenhagen ; prior of Dominicans at Perth, 1532–4 ; imbibed reformation principles and fled to England ; passed to the continent ; professor in Copenhagen, 1542 ; assisted to translate Luther's bible into Danish, 1550 ; author of Latin theological works ; died at Copenhagen. [xxxiv. 398]

MACANWARD, HUGH BOY (1580?-1635), Irish historian; belonged to a clan, eight of whom, flourishing between 1587 and 1696, were poets; studied at the Franciscan convent of Donegal, at Salamanca, and in Paris; first professor of theology in the Irish college of St. Anthony at Louvain, 1616; made collections for a complete Irish martyrology and hagiology, which John Colgan [q. v.] used for his 'Acta Sanctorum Hiberniæ'; died at Louvain. [xxxiv. 398]

MACARDELL, JAMES (1729?-1765), mezzotint-engraver; studied under John Brooks [q. v.]; engraved over forty plates after Sir Joshua Reynolds and twenty-five after Hudson. [xxxiv. 399]

MACARIUS, called SCOTUS (d. 1153), abbot; migrated to Germany from Scotland, 1139; abbot of the Benedictine monastery of St. James, near Würzburg; author of 'De Laude Martyrum.' [xxxiv. 400]

MACARTHUR or **McARTHUR**, SIR EDWARD (1789-1872), lieutenant-general; son of John Macarthur (1767-1834) [q. v.]; born in England; lived as a boy at Parramatta, near Sydney; entered the army, 1803; saw action in the Peninsula, 1812-14, in Canada, 1814; captain, 1821; assistant adjutant-general in Ireland, 1837; deputy adjutant-general in the Australian colonies, 1841-1855; commander of the troops in Australia, with rank of major-general, 1855-60; acting governor of Victoria, 1856; K.C.B., 1862; lieutenant-general, 1866. [xxxiv. 400]

MACARTHUR, HANNIBAL HAWKINS (1788-1861), nephew of John Macarthur (1767-1834) [q. v.]; born in England; emigrated to New South Wales, 1805; engaged in the wool trade; police magistrate at Parramatta; member of the legislative council, 1843. [xxxiv. 402]

MACARTHUR, JAMES (1798-1867), son of John Macarthur (1767-1834) [q. v.]; born at Camden, New South Wales; published 'New South Wales, its Present State and Future Prospects,' 1838; member of the legislative council of New South Wales, 1839, 1848, and 1851; engaged in the exploration of Gippsland, 1840. [xxxiv. 402]

MACARTHUR, JOHN (1794-1831), son of John Macarthur (1767-1834) [q. v.]; of Caius College, Cambridge; appointed chief-justice of New South Wales; died before assuming office. [xxxiv. 402]

MACARTHUR, JOHN (1767-1834), 'the father' of New South Wales; born in England; entered the army, 1788; accompanied the New South Wales corps to Sydney, 1790; commandant at Parramatta, 1793-1804; turned his attention to agriculture and to improving the colonial breed of sheep; tried at Sydney for high misdemeanors in connection with the liquor traffic and acquitted, 1808; planted the first vineyard in the colony, 1817; member of the first legislative council of New South Wales, 1825-31; created the Australian wool and wine trade. [xxxiv. 401]

McARTHUR, JOHN (1755-1840), author; entered navy, 1778; secretary to Lord Hood, 1791; published 'A Treatise of the Principles and Practice of Naval Courts-Martial,' 1792 (the second edition, 1805, entitled 'Principles and Practice of Naval and Military Courts-Martial,' long the standard work); commenced publication, in conjunction with James Stanier Clarke [q. v.], of the 'Naval Chronicle,' 1799; chief work, 'Life of Lord Nelson,' also in conjunction with Clarke, 1809. [xxxiv. 402]

MACARTHUR, SIR WILLIAM (1800-1882), son of John Macarthur (1767-1834) [q. v.]; born at Parramatta; member of New South Wales legislative council, 1849 and 1864; knighted, 1855. [xxxiv. 402]

McARTHUR, SIR WILLIAM (1809-1887), lord mayor of London; a woollen draper of Londonderry; commenced exporting woollen goods to his brother in Sydney; transferred headquarters of his business to London, 1857; M.P., Lambeth, 1868-85; sheriff of London, 1867; alderman, 1872; lord mayor, 1880; one of the founders of the London Chamber of Commerce, 1881; K.C.M.G., 1882. [xxxiv. 404]

MACARTNEY, GEORGE (1660?-1730). [See MACARTNEY.]

MACARTNEY, GEORGE, first EARL MACARTNEY (1737-1806), diplomatist and colonial governor; M.A. Trinity College, Dublin, 1759; envoy extraordinary at St. Petersburg, 1764-7; M.P., Antrim, in Irish House of Commons; chief secretary for Ireland, 1769-72; captain-general and governor of the Caribbee islands, 1775-9; created Baron Macartney of Lissanoure (Irish peerage), 1776; governor and president of Fort St. George (Madras), 1780-6; Irish privy councillor, 1788; created Earl Macartney and Viscount Macartney of Dervock in the Irish peerage, 1792; ambassador extraordinary and plenipotentiary to Pekin, 1792-4; governor of the Cape of Good Hope, 1796-8; wrote 'An Account of an Embassy to Russia,' 'A Political Account of Ireland,' and 'Journal of the Embassy to China,' all published in Barrow's 'Memoir' of him (vol. ii.) [xxxiv. 404]

MACARTNEY, JAMES (1770-1843), anatomist; apprenticed as surgeon in Dublin; studied at Hunterian school of medicine, London, and at Guy's, St. Thomas's, and St. Bartholomew's hospitals; M.R.C.S., 1800; F.R.S., 1811; M.D. St. Andrews, 1813; professor of anatomy and surgery, Dublin University, 1813-37; hon. F.R.C.P. Ireland, 1818; hon. M.D. Cambridge, 1833; published anatomical works. [Suppl. iii. 116]

MACAULAY, AULAY (1758-1819), miscellaneous writer; brother of Zachary Macaulay [q. v.]; M.A. Glasgow, 1778; took orders; published sermons and miscellaneous essays, 1780. [xxxiv. 406]

MACAULAY, MRS. CATHARINE, after her second marriage known as CATHARINE MACAULAY GRAHAM (1731-1791), historian and controversialist; née Sawbridge; married George Macaulay, M.D. (d. 1766), 1760; published vol. i. of her 'History of England,' 1763; settled at Bath, 1774; married William Graham, brother of James Graham (1745-1794) [q. v.], the quack doctor, 1778; visited North America, 1784; stopped ten days with Washington, 1785; her most famous production, 'The History of England from the Accession of James I to that of the Brunswick Line' (i. 1763, ii. 1766, iii. 1767, iv. 1768, v. 1771, vi. and vii. 1781, viii. 1783), now almost forgotten. [xxxiv. 407]

MACAULAY, COLIN CAMPBELL (1799-1853), son of Aulay Macaulay [q. v.]; educated at Rugby; contributed to the transactions of the Leicester Literary and Philosophical Society. [xxxiv. 407]

MACAULAY, SIR JAMES BUCHANAN (1793-1859), Canadian judge; born at Niagara, Ontario; lieutenant, Glengarry fencibles, 1812, serving during the American war; admitted to the Canadian bar, 1822; judge of the court of king's bench, Canada, 1829; chief-justice of court of common pleas, 1849-56; subsequently judge of the court of error and appeal; chairman of commission to revise and consolidate statutes of Canada and Upper Canada; C.B., 1858; knighted, 1859. [xxxiv. 409]

MACAULAY, JOHN (d. 1789), divine; minister successively of South Uist, 1746, Lismore, 1756, Inverary, 1765, and Cardross, 1775; mentioned in Boswell's account of Johnson's 'Tour to the Hebrides in 1773.' [xxxiv. 418]

MACAULAY, KENNETH (1723-1779), alleged author of a 'History of St. Kilda'; M.A. Aberdeen, 1742; minister of Harris in the Hebrides and other places in Scotland; sent by the kirk on a special mission to St. Kilda, 1759; published 'History of St. Kilda' as his own composition, 1764; doubts thrown on his authorship by Dr. Johnson; probably did no more than supply the materials to Dr. John Macpherson of Skye, the real author. [xxxiv. 409]

MACAULAY, THOMAS BABINGTON, first BARON MACAULAY (1800-1859), historian; son of Zachary Macaulay [q. v.]; educated at private schools and Trinity College, Cambridge; fellow of Trinity College, 1824; barrister, Gray's Inn, 1826; his first article (on Milton) published in the 'Edinburgh Review,' 1825; became a mainstay of the 'Edinburgh Review'; a commissioner in bankruptcy, 1828; liberal M.P., Calne, 1830, Leeds, 1831; a commissioner of the board of control, 1832, secretary, 1833; member of the supreme council of India, 1834-8; president of the commission for composing a criminal code for India, 1835 (published 1837, becoming law 1860); returned to London and engaged in literature and politics, 1838; began his 'History of England,' 1839; M.P., Edinburgh, 1839-47, and 1852-6; secretary of war, 1839-41; published 'Lays of Ancient Rome,' 1842; a collective edition of the 'Edinburgh' essays published, 1843; proposed and carried the copyright bill of forty-two years, which is still law;

paymaster of the forces, 1846–7 ; published vols. i. and ii. of the 'History,' 1848, vols. iii. and iv. 1855; lord rector of Glasgow University, 1849 ; created Baron Macaulay of Rothley, 1857 ; buried in Westminster Abbey. His writings were largely coloured by his whig sympathies and dislike of speculation. His complete works appeared in eight volumes, 1866. [xxxiv. 410]

MACAULAY, ZACHARY (1768–1838), philanthropist; son of John Macaulay [q. v.] ; when manager of an estate in Jamaica, became deeply impressed with the miseries of the slave population ; governor of Sierra Leone, 1793–9 ; secretary to the Sierra Leone Company, 1799–1808; edited the 'Christian Observer,' an organ specially devoted to the abolition of the British slave-trade, and to the destruction of the slave-trade abroad, 1802–16 ; secretary to the African Institute, 1807–12 ; helped to form Anti-Slavery Society, 1823 ; did much for the abolitionist cause. His works, consisting chiefly of papers issued by the societies to which he belonged, are anonymous. [xxxiv. 418]

McAULEY, CATHARINE (1787–1841), foundress of the Order of Mercy ; founded the 'House of our Blessed Lady of Mercy' in Dublin, 1827, which became a flourishing (Roman catholic) order of Sisters of Mercy, and spread to England, 1839, Newfoundland, 1842, United States, 1843, Australia, 1845, Scotland and New Zealand, 1849, and South America, 1856. [xxxiv. 420]

M'AVOY, MARGARET (1800–1820), blind lady ; became blind, 1816 ; could distinguish colours and decipher printed or clearly written manuscript forms of letters by her touch. [xxxiv. 421]

MACBAIN, SIR JAMES (1828–1892), Australian statesman ; born in Scotland ; migrated to Melbourne, 1853 ; partner in Gibbs, Ronald & Co., a firm of mercantile and squatting agents which was bought by the Australian Mortgage Land and Finance Company ; of that company Macbain was chairman of Australian directorate, 1865–90 ; member of the legislative assembly, 1864 : member of the cabinet, without portfolio, 1881–3 : president of the legislative council, 1884 ; knighted, 1886 ; K.C.M.G., 1889 ; died at Toorak. [xxxiv. 421]

MACBEAN, ALEXANDER (d. 1784), one of the six amanuenses whom Johnson employed on the 'Dictionary' ; assisted when starving by Johnson, who wrote a preface for his 'Dictionary of Ancient Geography,' 1773 ; admitted to the Charterhouse, 1780. [xxxiv. 422]

MACBEAN, FORBES (1725–1800), lieutenant-general, royal artillery ; educated at Royal Military Academy, Woolwich ; present at Fontenoy, 1745 ; adjutant at Woolwich, 1755–9 ; distinguished himself at Minden, 1759, at Warburg, 1760, and at Fritzlar, 1761 ; inspector-general of Portuguese artillery, 1765–9 ; served in Canada, 1769–1773, and 1778–80 ; lieutenant-general, 1798 ; left valuable manuscript notes relating to the earlier history of the royal artillery. [xxxiv. 422]

MACBETH (d. 1057), king of Scotland ; commander of the forces of Duncan, king of Scotland, whom he slew, and whose kingdom he took, 1040 ; defeated by Siward, earl of Northumbria, 1054 ; defeated and slain by Malcolm III, Canmore [q. v.], 1057. [xxxiv. 423]

MACBETH, NORMAN (1821–1888), portrait-painter ; studied in the Royal Academy schools, London, and in Paris ; exhibited at the Royal Scottish Academy from 1845 ; R.S.A., 1880. [xxxiv. 424]

MACBRADY, FIACHRA (fl. 1712), Irish poet ; author of poems in Irish, printed in the 'Anthologia Hibernica.' [xxxiv. 424]

MACBRADY, PHILIP (fl. 1710), Irish scholar ; a protestant clergyman and famous wit ; translated sermons into Irish and wrote Irish poems. [xxxiv. 424]

MACBRIDE, DAVID (1726–1778), medical writer ; son of Robert McBride [q. v.] ; studied in Edinburgh and London ; secretary to the Medico-Philosophical Society, Dublin, 1762 ; published 'Experimental Essays,' 1764 ; suggested a method for treating scurvy by an infusion of malt, and advocated the use of lime-water in certain parts of the process of tanning ; published 'Introduction to the Theory and Practice of Physic' (Dublin lectures), 1772. [xxxiv. 424]

McBRIDE, JOHN (1651?–1718), Irish presbyterian divine ; graduated at Glasgow, 1673 ; received presbyterian ordination, 1680 ; minister of Belfast, 1694–1718 ; moderator of general synod of Ulster, 1697 ; refused oath of abjuration, 1703, in consequence of which his ministry was often interrupted ; an able preacher ; published controversial tracts. [xxxiv. 425]

MACBRIDE, JOHN (d. 1800), admiral ; son of Robert McBride [q. v.] ; entered the navy, 1754 ; lieutenant, 1761 ; took part in the action off Ushant, 1776, off Cape St. Vincent, 1780 ; M.P., Plymouth, 1784 ; rear-admiral and commander-in-chief in the Downs, 1793 ; admiral, 1799. [xxxiv. 427]

MACBRIDE, JOHN ALEXANDER PATERSON, (1819–1890), sculptor ; worked in the studio of Samuel Joseph [q. v.] ; exhibited at the Liverpool Academy from 1836 ; executed chiefly portrait busts and monuments for Liverpool Institution. [xxxiv. 428]

MACBRIDE, JOHN DAVID (1778–1868), principal of Magdalen Hall, Oxford ; son of John Macbride (d. 1800) [q. v.] ; educated at Exeter College, Oxford ; fellow, 1800 ; M.A., 1802 ; interested in oriental literature ; both principal of Magdalen Hall (named Hertford College, 1874) and lord almoner's reader in Arabic, 1813–68 ; his principal literary work, 'The Mohammedan Religion explained,' 1857. [xxxiv. 429]

McBRIDE, ROBERT (1687–1759), son of John McBride (1651?–1718) [q. v.] ; ordained minister of Ballymoney, 1716 ; took the side of subscription in the synodical controversies of 1720–6. [xxxiv. 427]

MACBRUAIDEDH, MAOILIN (d. 1602), Irish historian and poet, commonly called MAOILIN the younger; belonged to a family of hereditary historians ; ollamh (chief chronicler) to the chiefs of the O'Gradys and the O'Gormans ; author of a number of Irish poems, some in a very difficult metre called dan direch. [xxxiv. 430]

MACBRUAIDEDH, TADHG (1570–1652), Irish poet ; called by Irish writers Tadhg MacDaire ; ollamh to Donogh O'Brien, fourth earl of Thomond [q. v.], 1603 ; president of Munster, 1605 ; author of numerous Irish poems, some of them in defence of the northern Irish poetry against southern ; flung over a cliff and killed by a Cromwellian, to whom his estate had been granted. [xxxiv. 430]

MACCABE, CATHAOIR (d. 1740), Irish poet and harper ; name written MacCaba in Irish ; friend of the poet O'Carolan [q. v.] ; author of Irish poems. [xxxiv. 431]

M'CABE, EDWARD (1816–1885), cardinal and Roman catholic archbishop of Dublin ; educated at Maynooth ; ordained, 1839 ; bishop of Gadara as assistant to Cardinal Cullen [q. v.], 1877 ; archbishop of Dublin, 1879 ; created cardinal, 1882 ; denounced agrarian agitation. [xxxiv. 432]

MACCABE, WILLIAM BERNARD (1801–1891), author and historian ; connected with the Irish press from 1823 ; became member of the staff of the London 'Morning Chronicle,' 1833 ; published 'A Catholic History of England,' 3 vols. (closing with the Norman Conquest), 1847–54 : wrote historical romances ; edited Dublin 'Telegraph,' 1852. [xxxiv. 432]

M'CABE, WILLIAM PUTNAM (1776?–1821), United Irishman ; went about Ireland as an organiser ; joined French invaders, and on their capitulation escaped to Wales ; assumed name of Lee (his real name having been inserted in the Irish Banishment Act), and started cotton mill near Rouen ; encouraged by Napoleon ; visited England and Ireland on business, and is said to have had hairbreadth escapes from arrest. [xxxiv. 433]

MACCAGHWELL, HUGH (1571–1626), sometimes known as Aodh mac aingil, Roman catholic archbishop of Armagh ; went to Salamanca, where he was famous as a reader in theology ; taught at the Irish Franciscan College of St. Anthony of Padua at Louvain, 1616 ; reader in theology at the convent of Ara Cœli, Rome, 1623 ; consecrated archbishop of Armagh at Rome, 1626 ; died just as he was prepared to go to Ireland ; published Latin theological works. [xxxiv. 433]

MACCALL, WILLIAM (1812–1888), author ; M.A. Glasgow, 1833 ; joined the unitarian ministry ; wrote for the press and published works of individualist ethics. [xxxiv. 434]

MACCARTAIN, WILLIAM (*fl.* 1703), Irish poet; Roman catholic and royalist; wrote a poetical address to Sir James FitzEdmond Cotter, the real murderer of John Lisle [q. v.]; author of Irish poems. [xxxiv. 434]

M'CARTHY, SIR CHARLES (1770?-1824), governor of Sierra Leone; served in the West Indies with the Irish brigade, 1794-6; lieutenant-colonel, royal African corps, 1811; governor of Sierra Leone, 1812-24; knighted, 1820; mortally wounded in a battle with the Ashantees. [xxxiv. 435]

MACCARTHY, CORMAC LAIDHIR OGE (*d.* 1536), Irish chieftain and lord of Muskerry. [xxxiv. 435]

MACCARTHY, DENIS FLORENCE (1817-1882), poet; a descendant of the Irish sept of Maccauras; espoused the repeal movement and contributed political verse to the 'Nation'; published admirable translations of Calderon's plays, 1848-73, 'Ballads, Poems, and Lyrics,' 1850, and 'The Bell-founder,' and 'Under-glimpses,' 1857. [xxxiv. 436]

MACCARTHY or **MACCARTY**, DONOUGH, fourth EARL OF CLANCARTY (1668-1734), sent by his mother, his guardian after his father's death, to Christ Church, Oxford, 1676; decoyed to London by his uncle, Justin MacCarthy, titular viscount Mountcashel [q. v.]; married at the age of sixteen; became a Roman catholic, 1685; espoused James II's cause in Ireland; member of the Irish House of Lords, 1689; made prisoner at the capitulation of Cork, 1690; escaped from the Tower of London, 1694; went to St. Germains; arrested in London, and committed to Newgate, 1698; pardoned; resided on an island in the Elbe, near Altona; died at Praals-Hoff. [xxxiv. 436]

MACCARTHY, JOHN GEORGE (1829-1892), Irish land commissioner and author; M.P., Mallow, 1874-80; one of the two commissioners for carrying out the Land Purchase Act, 1885; published legal pamphlets and works dealing with Irish questions. [xxxiv. 438]

MACCARTHY, JUSTIN, titular VISCOUNT MOUNT-CASHEL (*d.* 1694), uncle of Donough MacCarthy, fourth earl of Clancarty [q. v.]; served under Tyrconnel in Ireland, 1687; took Bandon, disarmed the protestants in Cork, and was created Viscount Mountcashel by James II, 1689; taken prisoner at the battle of Newtown Butler, 1689; escaped to France though on parole; commanded with distinction the Irish regiments sent to France at the demand of Louis XIV; died at Barèges. [xxxiv. 439]

MACCARTHY, NICHOLAS TUITE, called the ABBÉ DE LÉVIGNAC (1769-1833), jesuit preacher; born in Dublin; taken to Toulouse, 1773; studied at Paris and received the tonsure; ordained, 1814; joined jesuits, 1820; one of the most eloquent of French preachers; died at Annécy. [xxxiv. 441]

MACCARTHY, ROBERT, VISCOUNT MUSKERRY and titular EARL OF CLANCARTY (*d.* 1769). son of Donough MacCarthy, fourth earl of Clancarty [q. v.]; entered the navy; governor of Newfoundland, 1733-5; unsuccessfully attempted to recover the family estates (forfeited by his father's attainder); left the navy; went over to France and devoted himself to the Stuart cause, 1741; excluded from the Act of Indemnity, 1747; died at Boulogne. [xxxiv. 438]

MACCARTHY REAGH, FLORENCE (FINEEN) (1562?-1640?), Irish chieftain; served on the side of the crown during Desmond's rebellion; suspected of intriguing with Spain, and committed to the Tower, 1589; liberated, 1591; returned to Ireland, 1593; again charged with disloyalty and plotting, arrested, sent to England and imprisoned, 1601-14, 1617-19, and 1624-6; wrote during his imprisonment a treatise on the history of Ireland in prehistoric times (published, 1858). [xxxiv. 441]

MACCARTNEY or **MACARTNEY**, GEORGE (1660?-1730), general; accompanied his regiment to Flanders, 1706, and afterwards to Spain, commanding a brigade at Almanza, 1707; distinguished himself at Malplaquet, 1709; major-general and acting engineer at the siege of Douay, 1710; dismissed from his appointments on Marlborough's fall; second to Charles Mohun, fifth baron [q. v.], in his duel with James Douglas, fourth duke of Hamilton [q. v.]; accused of giving the murderous thrust which caused the duke's death, 1712; escaped to Holland; surrendered and arraigned for murder, and found guilty as an accessory, 1716; immediately restored to his military rank and promoted lieutenant-general. [xxxiv. 443]

MACCARWELL or **MACCERBHAILL**, DAVID (*d.* 1289), archbishop of Cashel; dean of Cashel; elected archbishop, 1253; involved in disputes with the crown, 1266-81; founded the Cistercian abbey of the Rock of Cashel, *c.* 1270. [xxxv. 1]

M'CAUL, ALEXANDER (1799-1863), divine; B.A. Trinity College, Dublin, 1819; M.A., 1831; D.D., 1837; missionary in Poland under the London Society for promoting Christianity among the Jews, 1821-32; settled in London; published 'Old Paths,' a weekly pamphlet on Jewish ritual, 1837-8; principal of the Hebrew College, 1840; professor of Hebrew and rabbinical literature at King's College, London, 1841, and of divinity also, 1846; prebendary of St. Paul's, 1845; published a 'Hebrew Primer,' 1844, and religious works. [xxxv. 1]

McCAUSLAND, DOMINICK (1806-1873), religious writer; B.A. Trinity College, Dublin; called to the Irish bar, 1835; LL.D., 1859; Q.C., 1860; published religious works, the most popular being 'Sermons in Stones,' 1856. [xxxv. 2]

McCHEYNE, ROBERT MURRAY (1813-1843), Scottish divine; educated at Edinburgh University; licensed as a preacher, 1835; a member of the committee sent to Palestine by the church of Scotland to collect information about the Jews, 1839; published (jointly with Dr. Andrew Bonar) 'Narrative of a Mission of Inquiry to the Jews,' 1842; a fine preacher; several of his hymns constantly used in the Scottish churches. [xxxv. 3]

MACCLESFIELD, EARLS OF. [See GERARD, CHARLES, first EARL, *d.* 1694; GERARD, CHARLES, second EARL, 1659?-1701; PARKER, THOMAS, first EARL of the second creation, 1666?-1732; PARKER, GEORGE, second EARL, 1697-1764.]

McCLUER, JOHN (*d.* 1794?), commander in the Bombay marine and hydrographer; surveyed Persian Gulf, the bank of soundings off Bombay, the Pelew islands, the Sulu Archipelago, and part of the New Guinea coast, 1785-93; settled in the Pelew islands, 1793; sailed for China, taken ill at Macao, eventually sailed for Calcutta, and was never again heard of. [xxxv. 3]

McCLURE, SIR ROBERT JOHN LE MESURIER (1807-1873), vice-admiral; educated at Eton and Sandhurst; entered navy, 1824; made an Arctic voyage, 1836-1837; lieutenant, 1837; served in Canada, 1838-9, the West Indies, 1839-48; commander in the search for Sir John Franklin [q. v.], 1850-4; discovered the North-West passage, but had to abandon his ship, 1854; courtmartialled and honourably acquitted; knighted and made captain; served in China and the Straits of Malacca, 1856-61; C.B., 1859; vice-admiral on the retired list, 1873. [xxxv. 4]

MACCODRUM, JOHN (*fl.* 1750), Gaelic poet; last bard of the Macdonalds; his satirical and political verses, the most popular being 'Old Age' and 'Whisky,' never collected. [xxxv. 5]

MACCOISSE, ERARD, or URARD (*d.* 1023), Irish chronicler; poet to Maelsechlainn or Malachy II (*d.* 1022); five poems and one prose composition in Irish, partly historical, attributed to him; sometimes confused with another MacCoisse, who wrote a poem preserved in the 'Book of Leinster.' [xxxv. 6]

McCOMB, WILLIAM (1793-1873), poet; bookseller in Belfast, 1828-64; established 'McComb's Presbyterian Almanac,' 1840; his 'Poetical Works' collected, 1864. [xxxv. 7]

McCOMBIE, WILLIAM (1809-1870), journalist; began to write while a farm labourer, 1835; joined 'North of Scotland Gazette,' 1849; edited 'Aberdeen Daily Free Press,' 1853-70; published miscellaneous works, 1838-69. [xxxv. 7]

McCOMBIE, WILLIAM (1805-1880), cattle-breeder; educated at Aberdeen University; reformed cattle-breeding, and was one of the largest farmers in Aberdeenshire; M.P., West Aberdeen, 1868-76; published 'Cattle and Cattle-Breeders,' 1867. [xxxv. 8]

MACCONMIDHE, GILLABRIGHDE (*fl.* 1260), historian and poet; hereditary poet to the O'Neills; his chief work a lament on the death of Brian O'Neill, first printed with an English translation, 1849. Other literary members of the family lived between 1420 and 1583. [xxxv. 8]

McCONNELL, WILLIAM (1833–1867), humorous book-illustrator. [xxxv. 9]

MACCORMAC, HENRY (1800–1886), physician; studied at Dublin, Paris, and Edinburgh; M.D. Edinburgh, 1824; in charge of the Belfast hospitals during the cholera, 1832; retired from practice, 1866; author of medical works, many of which advocate the fresh-air treatment of consumption. [xxxv. 9]

McCORMICK, CHARLES (1755?–1807), historian and biographer; educated at St. Mary Hall, Oxford; B.C.L., 1794; abandoned law for literature; continued Hume and Smollett's histories to 1783, and wrote a 'Memoir of Edmund Burke,' famous for its party virulence, 1797. [xxxv. 10]

MACCORMICK, JOSEPH (1733–1799), Scottish divine; M.A. St. Andrews University, 1750; ordained, 1758; D.D., 1760; edited the 'State Papers and Letters addressed to William Carstares, to which is prefixed the Life of William Carstares,' 1774; moderator to the general assembly, 1782; principal of the United College of St. Andrews, 1783; dean of the Chapel Royal, London, 1788. [xxxv. 10]

McCORMICK, ROBERT (1800–1890), naval surgeon, explorer and naturalist; entered the navy as assistant-surgeon, 1823; served on various stations; accompanied the Antarctic expedition commanded by Captain Sir James Clark Ross [q. v.], 1839–43; conducted a search for Sir John Franklin [q. v.], 1852; published 'Narrative of a Boat Expedition up the Wellington Channel,' 1854; deputy-inspector of hospitals, 1859; published 'Voyages of Discovery in the Arctic and Antarctic Seas and round the World,' 2 vols. 1884. [xxxv. 11]

McCOSH, JAMES (1811–1894), philosopher; educated at Glasgow and Edinburgh; M.A. Edinburgh, 1834; licensed by presbytery of Ayrshire; officiated at Arbroath, 1835–8, and Brechin, 1838–50; adopted 'free-kirk' principles; published 'Method of the Divine Government,' 1850; professor of logic at Queen's College, Belfast, 1851–1868; president of Princeton College, New Jersey, 1868–1888, and professor of philosophy, 1868, till death; LL.D. Aberdeen, 1850, and Harvard, 1868; D.Lit. Royal University of Ireland, and D.D. His publications include 'Intuitions of the Mind inductively investigated,' 1860, 'Laws of Discursive Thought,' 1870, 'Scottish Philosophy,' 1874, and 'Psychology,' 1886–7. [Suppl. iii. 117]

McCOY, SIR FREDERICK (1823–1899), naturalist and geologist; studied medicine at Dublin and Cambridge; employed by Sir Richard John Griffith [q. v.] to make palæontological investigations required for the 'Geological Map of Ireland'; professor of mineralogy and geology, Queen's College, Belfast, 1852; of natural science in new university of Melbourne, 1854; founded National Museum of Natural History and Geology, Melbourne; F.G.S., 1852; F.R.S., 1880; hon. D.Sc. Cambridge, 1880; K.C.M.G., 1891. He arranged and issued, 1854, description of fossils in Woodwardian Museum, Cambridge, and published zoological and palæontological works. [Suppl. iii. 119]

McCRACKEN, HENRY JOY (1767–1798), united Irishman; helped to form the first society of United Irishmen in Belfast, 1791; commanded the rebels in co. Antrim, 1798; tried and executed. [xxxv. 11]

MACCREERY, JOHN (1768–1832), printer and poet; wrote and printed in Liverpool 'The Press: a poem published as a specimen of Typography,' 1803 (second part published in London, 1827); removed to London, where he printed the 'Bibliomania' for Dibdin; died in Paris. [xxxv. 12]

McCRIE, THOMAS, the elder (1772–1835), Scottish seceding divine and ecclesiastical historian; entered Edinburgh University, 1788; ordained, 1796; ejected from his pastorate, 1809; published his 'Life of John Knox,' 1812, a work of genius and erudition; D.D., 1813; professor of divinity, Edinburgh, 1816–18; published a history of the reformation in Italy, 1827, in Spain, 1829; and other biographical and historical works. [xxxv. 12]

McCRIE, THOMAS, the younger (1797–1875), Scottish divine and author; son of Thomas McCrie the elder [q. v.]; educated at Edinburgh University; ordained, 1820; D.D. Aberdeen, and LL.D. Glasgow before 1850; professor of church history and systematic theology at the London College of the English Presbyterian Church,

1856–66; published historical and religious works, 1840–1872. [xxxv. 14]

MACCUAIRT, JAMES (fl. 1712), Irish poet; became blind early; composed Irish poems and songs. [xxxv. 14]

McCULLAGH, JAMES (1809–1847), mathematician; educated at Trinity College, Dublin; professor of mathematics, Dublin University, 1836; secretary of council to the Royal Irish Academy, 1840–2, and secretary to the Academy, 1842–6; professor of natural philosophy, 1843; committed suicide. The most important of his scanty remains is the memoir on surfaces of the second order, read to the Royal Irish Academy, 1843. [xxxv. 15]

MACCULLOCH, HORATIO (1805–1867), landscape-painter; pupil of William Home Lizars [q. v.]; associate of the Scottish Academy, 1834; academician, 1838; the most popular landscape-painter of his day in Scotland; exhibited only once at Royal Academy, London, 1844. [xxxv. 15]

McCULLOCH, SIR JAMES (1819–1893), Australian politician; opened a branch of Messrs. Dennistoun & Co's business in Melbourne, 1853; nominee member of the Victoria chamber, 1854; member of the first elective legislative assembly, 1857; formed a government, of which he held the portfolio of trades and customs, 1857; resigned, and was elected member for East Melbourne, 1858; treasurer, 1859–60; member for Mornington, 1862; premier, 1863–8, 1868–9, 1870–1, 1875–7; knighted, 1869; agent-general in London, 1872–3; K.C.M.G., 1874; settled finally in England, 1877. [xxxv. 16]

MACCULLOCH, JOHN (1773–1835), geologist; studied medicine at Edinburgh; M.D., 1793; chemist to the board of ordnance, 1803; L.R.C.P., 1808; gave up practice as a physician, 1811; geologist to the trigonometrical survey, 1814; president of the Geological Society, 1816–17; F.R.S., 1820; commissioned to prepare a geological map of Scotland (published shortly after his death), 1826; chief works, 'A Description of the Western Isles of Scotland, including the Isle of Man,' still a classic in geology, 1819, 'A Geological Classification of Rocks,' 1821, and 'Highlands and Western Isles of Scotland,' 1824. [xxxv. 17]

McCULLOCH, JOHN RAMSAY (1789–1864), statistician and political economist; educated at Edinburgh University; devoted himself to the study of economics and wrote the articles on that subject for the 'Scotsman,' 1817–27; edited the 'Scotsman,' 1818–20; contributed to the 'Edinburgh Review,' 1818–37; delivered the Ricardo memorial lectures in London, 1824; published 'Principles of Political Economy,' 1825; professor of political economy, London University, 1828–32; expounded the celebrated 'wages' fund theory in an 'Essay on the Circumstances which determine the Rate of Wages and the Condition of the Labouring Classes,' 1826; published 'A Dictionary, Practical, Theoretical, and Historical, of Commerce and Commercial Navigation,' 1832, and a number of statistical and economical works between 1841 and 1860; comptroller of the stationery office, 1838–64. [xxxv. 19]

McCULLOCH, WILLIAM (1816–1885), resident at Manipur; son of John Ramsay McCulloch [q. v.]; entered the army, 1834; employed in India, 1835–67; political agent at Manipur, 1845–63, and 1864–7; retired from the army as lieutenant-colonel, 1861; published 'Account of the Valley of [Manipur or] Munnipore and the Hill Tribes,' 1859. [xxxv. 21]

MACCURTIN, ANDREW (in Irish MacCruitin) (d. 1749), Irish poet; hereditary ollamh to the O'Briens; two of his poems, one in praise of Sorley MacDonnell (written, c. 1720), the other an address to a fairy chief, still remembered in Clare. [xxxv. 21]

MACCURTIN, HUGH (1680?–1755), Irish antiquary; succeeded his cousin, Andrew MacCurtin [q. v.], as ollamh to the O'Briens; studied in France; tutor for seven years to the dauphin; returned to Ireland, 1714; works include 'The Elements of the Irish Language,' 1728, and an English-Irish Dictionary, a valuable record of the vernacular of its day, 1732. [xxxv. 22]

MACDIARMID, JOHN (1779–1808), journalist and author; studied at Edinburgh and St. Andrews Universities; settled in London, 1801; edited the 'St. James's Chronicle'; author of two works on military topics, published in 1805 and 1806. [xxxv. 23]

M'DIARMID, JOHN (1790–1852), Scottish journalist; editor of the 'Dumfries and Galloway Courier,' 1817; published his 'Scrap-Book,' 1820; started the 'Dumfries Magazine,' 1825; became owner of the 'Courier,' 1837; edited, with memoirs, Cowper's 'Poems,' 1817, and Goldsmith's 'Vicar of Wakefield,' 1823. [xxxv. 23]

MACDONALD, ALEXANDER, third LORD OF THE ISLES and tenth EARL OF ROSS (d. 1449), eldest son of Donald Macdonald, second lord of the Isles [q. v.]; imprisoned as a rebel, 1427–9; destroyed Inverness, but was eventually defeated by James I of Scotland and again imprisoned, 1429; later gave loyal obedience to the king; justiciar of Scotland north of the Forth, 1438. [xxxv. 24]

MACDONALD or **MACDONNELL**, ALEXANDER or ALASTER or ALASTAIR (d. 1647), general; joined the insurgents, 1641; with Montrose in Scotland, 1644–5; being defeated, escaped to Ireland, 1647; killed by treachery. [xxxv. 25]

MACDONALD, ALEXANDER or MacIAN OF GLENCOE (d. 1692), chief of his clan; joined Claverhouse, 1689; took part in the rising of the northern highlands; bidden to take the oath of allegiance within a stipulated time; when that period had almost elapsed, made a vain effort to find a magistrate to administer the oath; finally persuaded Sir Colin Campbell to administer the oath five days later; his tardy action ignored and the clan destroyed in their home in the valley of Glencoe, 1692. An inquiry was made, but, although the massacre of Glencoe was condemned, none of the agents were brought to justice. [xxxv. 26]

MACDONALD, ALEXANDER or ALESTAIR OF GLENGARRY (d. 1724). [See MACDONELL.]

MACDONALD, ALEXANDER, ALASDAIR MACMHAIGHSTIR ALASDAIR (1700 ?–1780 ?), Gaelic poet; educated at Glasgow University; assisted the Society for Propagating Christian Knowledge in the Highlands; published an 'English and Gaelic Vocabulary,' 1741; became a Roman catholic and joined the Chevalier, 1745; became the 'sacer vates' of the rebellion of 1745; served through the campaign, 1745–6; his collected poems, a fine contribution to martial literature, published as 'Ais-eiridh na Sean Chanoin Albannaich,' 1751. [xxxv. 27]

MACDONALD, ALEXANDER (1736–1791), Scottish catholic prelate; entered the Scots College, Rome, 1754; ordained, 1764; joined the mission in Scotland and was stationed at Barra, 1765–80; vicar-apostolic of the highland district, 1780. [xxxv. 29]

MACDONALD, ALEXANDER (1755–1837), Gaelic scholar; educated at the Roman catholic seminary of Bourblach and at the Scots College, Rome; ordained, 1778; returned to Scotland, 1782; published 'Phingateis, sive Hibernia Liberata,' 1820; contributed to the Gaelic dictionary published under the direction of the Highland Society of Scotland, 1828. [xxxv. 29]

MACDONALD, ALEXANDER (1791 ?–1850), Scottish antiquary; employed in the Register House, Edinburgh; principal keeper of the register of deeds and probate writs, 1836; supplied notes for the 'Waverley Novels'; editor of the Maitland Club publications. [xxxv. 29]

MACDONALD, ANDREW (1755 ?–1790), dramatist and verse-writer; educated at Edinburgh University; ordained to the Scottish episcopal church, 1775; resigned his charge and came to London; his most successful tragedy, 'Vimonda,' produced 1787, published 1788. His 'Miscellaneous Works' appeared, 1791. [xxxv. 30]

MACDONALD, ANGUS (1834–1886), medical writer; M.D. Edinburgh, 1864; practised and lectured in Edinburgh; published medical works. [xxxv. 30]

MACDONALD, ARCHIBALD (1736–1814), author; a Benedictine monk and Roman catholic pastor; published defence of the authenticity of Macpherson's 'Ossian,' 1805. [xxxv. 30]

MACDONALD, SIR ARCHIBALD, first baronet (1747–1826), judge; lineal descendant of the old Lords of the Isles; student of Christ Church, Oxford, 1764; B.A., 1768; barrister, Lincoln's Inn, 1770; M.A., 1772; K.C., 1778; M.P., Hindon, 1777, Newcastle-under-Lyme, 1780–1793; solicitor-general, 1784–8; knighted, 1788; attorney-general, 1788–92; lord chief baron of the exchequer, 1793–1813; privy councillor, 1793; created baronet, 1813. [xxxv. 30]

MACDONALD, DONALD, second LORD OF THE ISLES and ninth EARL OF ROSS (d. 1420 ?), eldest son of John Macdonald, first lord of the Isles [q. v.]; made permanent alliance with Henry IV, 1405; claimed the earldom of Ross, but after the battle of Harlaw (1411) surrendered his claim and became vassal to the Scottish throne, 1412. [xxxv. 32]

MACDONALD, DUNCAN GEORGE FORBES (1823 ?–1884), agricultural engineer and miscellaneous writer; son of John Macdonald (1779–1849) [q. v.]; published 'What Farmers may do with the Land,' 1852; member of the government survey staff in British North America; published 'British Columbia and Vancouver's Island,' 1862; drainage engineer of improvements to the enclosure commissioners for England and Wales; engineer-in-chief to the inspector-general of highland destitution. [xxxv. 33]

MACDONALD, FLORA (1722–1790), Jacobite heroine; daughter of Ranald Macdonald, farmer at Milton, South Uist (Hebrides); while in 1746 on a visit to the Clanranalds in Benbecula (Hebrides), met Prince Charles Edward in flight after Culloden; helped the prince to reach Skye; imprisoned in the Tower of London after Prince Charles Edward's escape; released by the Act of Indemnity, 1747; married Allan Macdonald, 1750; emigrated to North Carolina, 1774; returned to Scotland, 1779. [xxxv. 33]

MACDONALD, HUGH (1701–1773), Scottish catholic prelate; ordained, 1725; vicar of the highland district and bishop of Diana in Numidia, 1731; escaped to Paris after the rebellion of 1745; returned to Scotland, 1749; apprehended, 1755; sentenced to banishment, but sentence not carried out, 1756. [xxxv. 35]

MACDONALD, HUGH (1817–1860), Scottish poet; wrote verses in the 'Glasgow Citizen,' joining its staff, 1849; joined the 'Glasgow Sentinel,' 1855; edited the 'Glasgow Times'; wrote, for those journals, 'Rambles round Glasgow' and 'Days at the Coast,' afterwards published in book form; literary editor of the 'Morning Journal' (Glasgow), 1858–60. [xxxv. 35]

MACDONALD, JOHN, OF ISLA, first LORD OF THE ISLES (d. 1386 ?), joined Edward Baliol, 1335; transferred his allegiance to David II, 1341; joined Baliol again when the king objected to his assumption of the title of Lord of the Isles; persuaded to take an oath of obedience, 1369. [xxxv. 36]

MACDONALD, JOHN, fourth and last LORD OF THE ISLES and eleventh EARL OF ROSS (d. 1498 ?), son of Alexander, third lord of the Isles [q. v.]; rebelled against King James II of Scotland, but came to terms, and was made one of the wardens of the marches, 1457; one of the ambassadors who helped to bring about the treaty with the English signed at Westminster, 1463; summoned to answer for treasonable acts, and sentence of attainder passed against him, 1475; pardoned, 1476; finally retired to the monastery of Paisley. [xxxv. 37]

MACDONALD, JOHN (1620 ?–1716 ?), known in the highlands as Ian Lom, Gaelic poet and warrior; assisted Montrose, 1645–50; composed a 'Lament' in his honour, 1650; became absorbed in local politics; pensioned by the government, 1660; present at Killiecrankie, 1689; celebrated the triumph of the highlanders in his poem, 'Rinrory.' [xxxv. 39]

MACDONALD, JOHN (fl. 1778), gentleman's servant; became known as Beau Macdonald; spent some years in Bombay, and travelled in India and Europe with his employers, 1768–78; settled at Toledo, 1778; published 'Travels in Various Parts,' 1790. [xxxv. 40]

MACDONALD, JOHN (1727–1779), Scottish catholic prelate; nephew of Hugh Macdonald (1701–1773) [q. v.]; entered the Scots College, Rome, 1743; ordained, 1752; returned to Scotland, 1753; vicar-apostolic of the highland district of Scotland, 1773–9. [xxxv. 40]

MACDONALD, SIR JOHN (1782–1830). [See KINNEIR.]

MACDONALD, JOHN (1759–1831), lieutenant-colonel and military engineer; son of Flora Macdonald [q. v.]; as ensign, Bengal engineers, surveyed the Dutch settlements in Sumatra, 1783; remained there as military and civil engineer until 1796; employed in England during the French wars; F.R.S., 1800; author of military and technical engineering works, and of a book on Anglo-Indian administration. [xxxv. 40]

MACDONALD, JOHN (1779–1849), called the ' Apostle of the North' ; M.A. King's College, Aberdeen, 1801 ; ordained missionary minister, 1806 ; visited Ireland, 1824 ; joined the secession party, 1843 ; author of sermons, published 1830, and a volume of Gaelic verse, 1848.
[xxxv. 41]

MACDONALD, SIR JOHN (d. 1850), adjutant-general at the Horse Guards ; a connection of Flora Macdonald [q. v.] ; entered the army, 1795 ; served in Ireland and Egypt and on the continent ; held important staff appointments during the Peninsular campaign ; deputy adjutant-general at the Horse Guards, 1820–30 ; adjutant-general, 1830–50 ; G.C.B., 1847. [xxxv. 42]

MACDONALD, JOHN (1818–1889), Scottish catholic prelate ; at the Scots seminary, Ratisbon, 1830–7 ; at the Scots College, Rome, 1837–40 ; vicar-apostolic of the northern district of Scotland, 1869 ; bishop of Aberdeen, 1878. [xxxv. 43]

MACDONALD, SIR JOHN ALEXANDER (1815–1891), the organiser of the dominion of Canada ; born in Glasgow ; settled in Kingston, Canada, 1820 ; admitted to the bar, 1836 ; member for Kingston in the House of Assembly, 1844–54 ; commissioner for crown lands, 1847 ; attorney-general for Upper Canada, 1854 ; leader of the House of Assembly, 1856–91 ; premier, 1857 ; succeeded, despite strong opposition, in making Ottawa the capital, 1859 ; led the federation movement, and went to England as a delegate, 1866 ; mainly responsible for the British North America Act, 1867 ; C.B., 1867 ; first prime minister of the Dominion, 1867 ; one of the commissioners of the treaty of Washington, 1871 ; privy councillor of the United Kingdom, 1872 ; premier and minister of the interior, 1878–91 ; also president of the council and superintendent of Indian affairs, 1883 ; G.C.B., 1884. [xxxv. 43]

MACDONALD, LAWRENCE (1799–1878), sculptor ; entered the Trustees' Academy, Edinburgh, 1822 ; went to Rome, and helped to found the British Academy of Arts there, 1823 ; returned to Edinburgh, 1827 ; exhibited at the Royal Academy from 1829 ; member of the Scottish Academy, 1829–58 ; died at Rome ; noted for his portrait busts. [xxxv. 46]

MACDONALD, PATRICK (1729–1824), amateur musician ; educated at Aberdeen University ; ordained missionary, 1756 ; chief work, 'A Collection of Highland Vocal Airs never hitherto published,' 1784. [xxxv. 47]

MACDONALD, RANALD (1756–1832), Scottish catholic prelate ; educated at the Scots College, Douay ; returned to Scotland, 1782 ; D.D. ; vicar-apostolic of the highland district, 1819, and of the western district, 1827.
[xxxv. 47]

MACDONALD, WILLIAM BELL (1807–1862), linguist ; educated at Glasgow University ; graduated, 1827 ; surgeon on a flag-ship in the Mediterranean, 1828–31 ; famous linguist ; published miscellaneous works.
[xxxv. 47]

MACDONALD, WILLIAM RUSSELL (1787–1854), miscellaneous writer ; editor of, part proprietor of, and contributor to, various periodicals ; later wrote books for the young. [xxxv. 48]

MACDONELL, ALASTAIR RUADH, known as PICKLE THE SPY (1725 ?–1761), thirteenth chief of Glengarry ; went to France, 1738, and joined Lord Drummond's regiment of royal Scots guards, 1743 ; employed by highland chiefs on secret mission to Prince Charles, 1745 ; captured by English and imprisoned in Tower of London, 1745–7 ; acted, under pseudonym of 'Pickle,' as spy on Charles, 1749–54 ; succeeded as chief of clan, 1754.
[Suppl. iii. 119]

MACDONELL or **MACDONALD**, ALEXANDER or ALESTAIR OF (ГLENGARRY (d. 1724), Jacobite ; surnamed 'Dubh' from his dark complexion ; joined Claverhouse, 1689 ; one of the leaders at Killiecrankie, 1689 ; reluctantly took the oath to William III, 1691 ; joined Mar and fought at Sheriffmuir, 1715 ; a trustee for managing the Chevalier's affairs in Scotland, 1720.
[xxxv. 48]

MACDONELL, ALEXANDER (1762–1840), first Roman catholic bishop of Upper Canada ; educated at the Scots College, Valladolid ; ordained, 1787 ; while missionary priest, helped to form Romanist peasants into the 1st Glengarry fencibles (disbanded, 1801) ; obtained a

grant of land in Canada for the men ; again raised a regiment of Glengarry fencibles, which did good service for Upper Canada in the United States war, 1812 ; organised the colony, and devoted himself to missionary work in Upper Canada ; vicar-apostolic of Upper Canada, 1819 ; bishop of Regiopolis or Kingston, 1826 ; died at Dumfries ; was buried in Kingston Cathedral, Canada. [xxxv. 49]

MACDONELL or **MACDONNELL**, ALEXANDER RANALDSON, OF GLENGARRY (d. 1828), colonel, highland chieftain ; brother of Sir James Macdonell [q. v.] ; major in the Glengarry fencibles infantry, 1795–1801 ; lived in feudal style ; the original, to some extent, of Scott's Fergus MacIvor in 'Waverley' ; perished by shipwreck. [xxxv. 50]

MACDONELL, SIR JAMES (d. 1857), general ; brother of Alexander Ranaldson Macdonell of Glengarry [q. v.] ; fought in Naples, Sicily, and Egypt, 1804–7 ; lieutenant-colonel, 1809 ; in the Peninsula, 1812–14 ; present at Waterloo, and K.C.B., 1815 ; commanded in Canada, 1838–1841 ; lieutenant-general, 1841 ; general, 1854 ; G.C.B., 1855.
[xxxv. 51]

MACDONELL, JAMES (1842–1879), journalist ; on the staff of the 'Daily Review' in Edinburgh, 1862 ; editor of the Newcastle 'Northern Daily Express' ; on the staff of the 'Daily Telegraph,' 1865–75 ; special correspondent in France, 1870–1 ; leader-writer on the 'Times,' 1875 ; made a special study of French politics ; his 'France since the First Empire' published, 1880.
[xxxv. 51]

MACDONLEVY, CORMAC (fl. 1459), physician ; called in Irish MacDuinntshleibhe ; translated 'Gualterus' and other medical works into Irish ; hereditary physician to the O'Donnells, like other members of the family (1200–1586). [xxxv. 52]

MACDONNELL, ALEXANDER or ALASTER (d. 1647). [See MACDONALD.]

MACDONNELL, ALEXANDER, third EARL OF ANTRIM (d. 1696 ?), brother of Randal Macdonnell, second earl of Antrim [q. v.] ; joined the rebellion in Ireland ; represented Wigan at intervals, 1660–83 ; succeeded to the earldom, 1683 ; marched to the relief of Londonderry, but was mistaken for the enemy, 1689. [xxxv. 58]

MACDONNELL, ALEXANDER (1798–1835), chess-player ; merchant at Demerara, 1820–30 ; secretary to the West India Committee of Merchants, 1830 ; studied chess under William Lewis (1787–1870) [q. v.] ; admitted the best English player from 1833 ; beaten by the French player, Labourdonnais, 1834. [xxxv. 52]

McDONNELL, SIR ALEXANDER (1794–1875), commissioner of national education in Ireland ; educated at Westminster and Christ Church, Oxford ; student till 1826 ; M.A., 1820 ; barrister, Lincoln's Inn, 1824 ; renounced the bar and became chief clerk in the chief secretary's office, Ireland ; resident commissioner of the board of education, Ireland, 1839–71 ; privy councillor of Ireland, 1846 ; created baronet, 1872.
[xxxv. 52]

MACDONNELL, JOHN (1691–1754), Irish poet ; began a translation of Homer into Irish and a 'History of Ireland' ; some of his Irish poems printed. [xxxv. 53]

MACDONNELL, SIR RANDAL, first VISCOUNT DUNLUCE and first EARL OF ANTRIM (d. 1636), called 'Arranach' ; son of Sorley Boy MacDonnell [q. v.] ; joined O'Neill's rebellion, 1600 ; submitted to Mountjoy, the lord-deputy, 1602 ; created Viscount Dunluce, 1618, and Earl of Antrim, 1620. [xxxv. 54]

MACDONNELL, RANDAL, second VISCOUNT DUNLUCE, second EARL and first MARQUIS OF ANTRIM (1609–1683), son of Sir Randal MacDonnell, first viscount Dunluce and first earl of Antrim [q. v.] ; introduced at court, 1634 ; married the Duke of Buckingham's widow, 1635 ; sent by the king to raise forces in Scotland, 1639 ; took his seat in the Irish House of Lords, 1640 ; frequently imprisoned as a suspect, 1642–5 ; ordered to lay down his arms, 1646 ; retired to Ireland ; allowed to return to England, 1650 ; pardoned, 1663. [xxxv. 55]

MACDONNELL, SIR RICHARD GRAVES (1814–1881), colonial governor ; educated at Trinity College, Dublin ; M.A., 1836 ; called to the Irish bar, 1838 ; barrister, Lincoln's Inn, 1841 ; chief-justice of the Gambia, 1843 ; LL.B., 1845 ; governor of the British settlements on the Gambia, 1847–52; governor of St. Lucia, 1852–3; C.B., 1852; administrator and captain-general of St. Vincent, 1853–5; governor of South Australia, 1855–62; knighted, 1856; lieutenant-governor of Nova Scotia, 1864–5; governor of Hong Kong, 1865–72; K.C.M.G., 1871; died at Hyères. [xxxv. 58]

McDONNELL, ROBERT (1828–1889), surgeon; B.A. and M.B. Trinity College, Dublin, 1850; volunteered as civil surgeon in Crimean war, 1855; medical superintendent of Mountjoy government prison, 1857–67; F.R.S., 1865; president of Academy of Medicine in Ireland, 1885–8. [xxxv. 59]

MACDONNELL, SORLEY BOY (CAROLUS FLAVUS) (1505 ?–1590), Scoto-Irish chieftain, lord of the Route and constable of Dunluce Castle; appointed to lordship of Route district, 1558; made overtures to Elizabeth regarding the Scottish settlement on the Antrim coast, 1560; worsted by Shane O'Neill, 1564–7; defeated by Earl of Essex, 1575; after some success was forced to escape to Scotland, 1585; admitted his lack of legal right in Ulster, 1586, and submitted to government. [xxxv. 59]

MACDOUGALL, ALLAN (1750 ?–1829), Gaelic poet; published Gaelic verses, 1798; family bard to Colonel MacDonald, laird of Glengarry. [xxxv. 62]

MACDOUGALL, SIR DUNCAN (1787–1862), lieutenant-colonel, 79th Cameron highlanders; ensign, 1804; served at the Cape of Good Hope, in the Peninsula; and in the American war, 1814–15; entrusted, as commander of 79th foot at Halifax, Nova Scotia, with organisation of colonial militia, 1825; quartermaster-general and second in command of British auxiliary legion of Spain, 1835; a prominent figure in the volunteer movement; buried in St. Paul's Cathedral. [Suppl. iii. 120]

McDOUGALL, FRANCIS THOMAS (1817–1886), bishop of Labuan and Sarawak; studied medicine at Malta university, King's College, London, and London University; subsequently entered Magdalen College, Oxford; B.A., 1842; ordained, 1845; missionary in Borneo, 1847–67; bishop of Labuan, 1855–68; archdeacon of Huntingdon, 1870; canon of Ely, 1871, of Winchester, 1873; archdeacon of the Isle of Wight, 1874.
[xxxv. 62]

MACDOUGALL, SIR JOHN (1790–1865), vice-admiral; entered the navy, 1802; repeatedly in boat actions, 1803–1809; lieutenant, 1809; commander, 1820; captured the Bogue ports, Canton, 1847; K.C.B., 1862; vice-admiral, 1863. [xxxv. 64]

MACDOUGALL, SIR PATRICK LEONARD (1819–1894), general; educated at Military Academy, Edinburgh, and at Sandhurst; lieutenant, 36th foot, 1839; major, 1849; major-general, 1868; lieutenant-general, 1877; colonel, 2nd battalion West India regiment, 1881; and of Leinster regiment, 1891; general, 1883; served in Canada, 1844–54; superintendent of studies at Sandhurst 1854–8, but served in Crimea, 1854–5; adjutant-general of Canadian militia, 1865–9; deputy-inspector-general of auxiliary forces at headquarters, 1871; head of intelligence branch of war office, 1873–8; K.C.M.G., 1877; commander in North America, 1877–83; retired, 1885; principal work, 'The Theory of War,' 1856.
[Suppl. iii. 121]

MACDOWALL, ANDREW, LORD BANKTON (1685–1760), Scottish judge; educated at Edinburgh University; admitted advocate, 1708; became judge, with the title Lord Bankton, 1755; author of 'An Institute of the Laws of Scotland in Civil Rights,' 1751–3. [xxxv. 64]

M'DOWALL, WILLIAM (1815–1888), journalist and antiquary; appointed to the editorial staff of the 'Scottish Herald,' 1843; edited 'Dumfries and Galloway Standard,' 1846–88; published 'History of Dumfries,' 1867, 'The Man of the Woods and other Poems,' 1844, and 'Mind in the Face,' 1882. [xxxv. 64]

McDOWELL, BENJAMIN (1739–1824), presbyterian divine; born at Elizabethtown, New Jersey; educated at Princeton and Glasgow universities; joined the established church of Scotland; ordained, 1766; influential in Dublin presbyterianism; D.D. Edinburgh, 1789; author of controversial works. [xxxv. 65]

MACDOWELL, PATRICK (1799–1870), sculptor; exhibited at the Royal Academy, 1822 and 1826–9; entered the Academy Schools, 1830; R.A., 1846; executed,

among other works, 'Girl going to the Bath,' 1841, and 'Europa' for the Albert Memorial, 1870. [xxxv. 66]

MACDOWELL, WILLIAM (1590–1666), diplomatist; educated at St. Andrews University; professor of philosophy at Groningen, 1614; LL.D. Groningen, 1625; president of the council of war in Groningen and Friesland, 1627; ambassador to England, 1629, 1630, and 1636; Charles II's resident agent at the Hague, 1650; defeated the proposals of the envoys of the English parliament to the assembly of the States-General, 1651; his 'Answer to English envoys' published, 1651. [xxxv. 67]

MACDUFF, THANE or EARL OF FIFE (*fl.* 1056 ?), a half or wholly mythical personage; advanced the cause of Malcolm Canmore [q. v.] against the usurper Macbeth [q. v.], 1057. [xxxv. 67]

MACE, DANIEL (*d.* 1753), textual critic; presbyterian minister; published anonymously 'The New Testament in Greek and English . . . corrected from the Authority of the most authentic Manuscripts,' a precursor of the modern critical texts, 1729. [xxxv. 68]

MACE, THOMAS (1619 ?–1709 ?), musician; an accomplished lutenist, though deaf; devised a lute of fifty strings, 1672; published 'Music's Monument,' 1676.
[xxxv. 68]

MACEACHEN, EVAN (1769–1849), Gaelic scholar; entered the Scots College, Valladolid, 1788; ordained there, 1798; missioner in Scotland, 1798–1838; his most important work, 'Gaelic Translation of the New Testament' (unpublished). [xxxv. 69]

MACEGAN, MACEGGAN, MACEOGAN, or **MACKEGAN,** OWEN or EUGENIUS (*d.* 1603), bishop-designate of Ross, co. Cork; probably educated at an Irish Roman catholic seminary in Spain; encouraged rebellion in Ireland, 1600; went to Spain again and gained influence with Philip III, persuading him to assist Tyrone's rebellion, 1601; as a reward for this made vicar-apostolic by the pope; prevented Charles Blount, eighth baron Mountjoy [q. v.], from entirely crushing the rebellion, 1602; exercised great power, but was slain in an encounter with the English at Cladach. [xxxv. 69]

MACERONI, FRANCIS (1788–1846), aide-de-camp to Murat and mechanical inventor; aide-de-camp to Murat, king of Naples, 1814; Murat's envoy in England, 1815; settled in England, 1816; published a biography of Joachim Murat, king of Naples, 1817; meddled in American, Spanish, and Neapolitan politics, 1819–25. A 'steam-coach,' his most important invention, experimented with, 1833. [xxxv. 70]

M'EWEN, WILLIAM (1735–1762), Scottish secessionist; ordained, 1754; published religious works.
[xxxv. 72]

MACFAIT, EBENEZER (*d.* 1786), Greek scholar, mathematician, physician, and miscellaneous writer.
[xxxv. 72]

MACFARLAN, JAMES (1832–1862), poet; a professional pedlar; walked from Glasgow to London to publish a volume of lyrics, 1853; published other volumes of poems, 1854, 1855, and 1856; contributed to 'Household Words.' [xxxv. 72]

MACFARLAN, JAMES (1800–1871), presbyterian minister; son of John Macfarlan (*d.* 1846) [q. v.]; licensed, 1831; published an English version of the 'Prophecies of Ezekiel,' 1845. [xxxv. 73]

MACFARLAN, JAMES (1845–1889), presbyterian minister; son of James Macfarlan (1800–1871) [q. v.]; educated at Edinburgh Academy and University, 1858–64; minister of Ruthwell, 1871–89. [xxxv. 73]

MACFARLAN, JOHN (*d.* 1846), Scottish advocate; brother of Patrick Macfarlan [q. v.]; friend of Sir Walter Scott; author of two religious pamphlets. [xxxv. 73]

MACFARLAN, PATRICK (1780–1849), Scottish divine; brother of John Macfarlan [q. v.]; licensed, 1803; joined secessionists, 1843; moderator of the free general assembly, 1845; published religious works. [xxxv. 73]

MACFARLAN, WALTER (*d.* 1767), antiquary; devoted himself to Scottish antiquarian research; his materials used by Douglas in his 'Peerage of Scotland.'
[xxxv. 74]

MACFARLANE, MRS. (*fl.* 1716–1719), murderess; *née* Straiton; married John Macfarlane, writer to the signet; for some unknown reason shot Captain Cayley at her house in Edinburgh, 1716; not appearing to stand her trial (1717), was outlawed and remained in hiding, probably till her death.   [xxxv. 74]

MACFARLANE, CHARLES (*d.* 1858), miscellaneous writer; travelled in Italy, 1816–27; in Turkey, 1827–9; settled in London and supported himself by literary work, 1829; again travelled abroad, 1847–8; nominated a poor brother of the Charterhouse, 1857; his best works 'Civil and Military History of England' (8 vols.), 1838–44, and 'The Book of Table Talk,' 1836.   [xxxv. 74]

MACFARLANE, DUNCAN (1771–1857), principal of Glasgow University; educated at Glasgow University; ordained, 1792; D.D., 1806; principal of Glasgow University, 1824; as moderator, defended the established church in the disruption year, 1843.   [xxxv. 75]

MACFARLANE, JOHN (1807–1874), Scottish divine; educated at Edinburgh and Glasgow Universities; ordained, 1831; LL.D., 1842; promoted presbyterian church extension in England; published religious works.
                [xxxv. 76]

MACFARLANE, PATRICK (1758–1832), Gaelic scholar; translated religious books into Gaelic for the Society in Scotland for the Propagation of Christian Knowledge; published a collection of Gaelic poems, 1813, and a vocabulary of Gaelic and English, 1815.
                [xxxv. 76]

MACFARLANE, ROBERT (1734–1804), miscellaneous writer; M.A. Edinburgh; editor of the 'Morning Chronicle' and 'London Packet'; accidentally run over and killed; author of a Latin translation of the first book of Ossian's 'Temora,' 1769, and of vols. i. and iv. of a 'History of George III,' 1770 and 1796.   [xxxv. 76]

MACFARLANE, ROBERT, LORD ORMIDALE (1802–1880), senator of the College of Justice; educated at Glasgow and Edinburgh; writer to the signet, 1827; advocate at Edinburgh, 1838; sheriff of Renfrewshire, 1853; lord of session as Lord Ormidale, 1862; wrote on procedure of court of session.   [xxxv. 77]

MACFARREN, GEORGE (1788–1843), dramatist and theatrical manager; his first play performed, 1818; produced a play almost every year after 1818; took the Queen's Theatre, London, 1831; stage-manager of the Surrey Theatre, and then of the Strand Theatre, London; first suggested the Handel Society; editor and proprietor of the 'Musical World,' 1841.   [xxxv. 77]

MACFARREN, SIR GEORGE ALEXANDER (1813–1887), musical composer; son of George Macfarren [q. v.]; studied at the Royal Academy of Music, 1829–36; his symphony in C performed, 1830; other compositions performed, 1830–7; professor of harmony and composition at the Royal Academy of Music, 1837–46 and 1851–75; the 'Devil's Opera,' one of his best dramatic works, produced, 1838; founded the Handel Society, 1844; conductor at Covent Garden, 1845; became blind, 1860; composed operas, 1860–73; his first oratorio, 'St. John the Baptist,' performed, 1873; principal of the Royal Academy of Music, and professor of music, Cambridge, 1875–87; knighted, 1883.   [xxxv. 78]

MACFIE, ROBERT ANDREW (1811–1893), free-trade advocate; educated at Leith and Edinburgh; engaged in business as sugar refiner at Edinburgh and Liverpool, where he assisted in founding chamber of commerce; M.P., Leith Burghs, 1868–74; F.R.C.I. and F.R.S.E.; published works dealing with patents, copyright, and political questions.   [Suppl. iii. 122]

MACFIRBIS, DUALD (1585–1670), Irish historian; composed a treatise on Irish genealogy, finished, 1650; in Dublin translating Irish manuscripts for Sir James Ware [q. v.], 1655–66; stabbed at Dunfin while on his way to Dublin; the last of the hereditary sennachies of Ireland.
                [xxxv. 82]

MACFLYNN, FLORENCE or FLANN (*d.* 1256), archbishop of Tuam; also called FIACHA O'FLYN; consecrated archbishop, 1250; went to England to plead the cause of the Irish church, 1255.   [xxxv. 83]

M'GAULEY, JAMES WILLIAM (*d.* 1867), professor of natural philosophy to the board of national education in Ireland, 1836–56; in Canada, 1856–65; on the council of the Inventors' Institute, and editor of the 'Scientific Review'; published scientific works.   [xxxv. 84]

M'GAVIN, WILLIAM (1773–1832), controversialist; partner in a firm of cotton merchants, 1813; Glasgow agent for the British Linen Company's bank, 1822; belonged to the anti-burgher communion; contributed controversial letters to the 'Glasgow Chronicle' under the title of the 'Protestant,' 1818–22, afterwards issued in book form; author of other controversial works. [xxxv. 84]

McGEE, THOMAS D'ARCY (1825–1868), Irish-Canadian statesman and poet; emigrated to America, 1842; edited 'Boston Pilot'; London correspondent for the 'Nation'; secretary to the committee of the Irish Confederation, 1847; escaped to America on the rout of the 'Young Ireland' party, 1848; founded the 'American Celt,' and conducted it, 1850–7; started the 'New Era' at Montreal; member for Montreal in legislative assembly, 1858–62; president of the council, 1864; a warm advocate of federation; member for Montreal West, and minister of agriculture and emigration, 1867; openly denounced Irish disloyalty, and was shot in Ottawa; chief work, 'Popular History of Ireland,' 1862.   [xxxv. 85]

MACGEOGHEGAN, CONALL (*fl.* 1635). [See MACGEOGHEGAN.]

MACGEOGHEGAN, JAMES (1702–1763), historian; related to Conall Macgeoghegan [q. v.]; educated in France, becoming an abbé; published 'Histoire de l'Irlande,' vol. i. 1758, vol. ii. 1762, vol. iii. 1763; died at Paris.
                [xxxv. 86]

MACGEOGHEGAN, ROCHE, also called ROCHUS DE CRUCE (1580–1644), Irish Dominican and bishop of Kildare; studied at the Irish College, Lisbon; Dominican provincial of Ireland, 1622; bishop of Kildare, 1629–44; constantly persecuted and forced to live in hiding.
                [xxxv. 87]

MACGEORGE, ANDREW (1810–1891), antiquarian writer and historian; educated at Glasgow University; practised as an ecclesiastical lawyer, 1836–89; caricaturist and author of works on heraldry and antiquarian subjects.   [xxxv. 87]

MACGILL, HAMILTON MONTGOMERY (1807–1880), united presbyterian divine, educated at Glasgow University; ordained, 1837; home mission secretary of the united presbyterian church, 1865–8; foreign mission secretary, 1868–80; D.D. Glasgow, 1870; author of 'Songs of the Christian Creed and Life,' 1876.
                [xxxv. 88]

MACGILL, STEVENSON (1765–1840), professor of theology at Glasgow; educated at Glasgow University; ordained, 1796; D.D. Aberdeen and Marischal College, 1803; professor of theology, Glasgow, 1814; moderator of the general assembly, 1828; dean of the Chapel Royal, London, 1835.   [xxxv. 88]

M'GILL, WILLIAM (1732–1807), Scottish divine; M.A. Glasgow College; ordained, 1761; published essay on 'The Death of Christ,' 1786; the discussion of his supposed heterodoxy by the presbytery gave rise to Burns's satire, 'The Kirk's Alarm.'   [xxxv. 89]

MACGILLIVRAY, CHARLES R. (1804 ?–1867), M.D., 1853; lecturer in Gaelic at the Glasgow Institution, 1859; translated the 'Pilgrim's Progress' into Gaelic (translation published, 1869).   [xxxv. 90]

MACGILLIVRAY, JOHN (1822–1867), naturalist; son of William MacGillivray [q. v.]; studied medicine at Edinburgh; naturalist on various government surveying expeditions, 1842–55; after 1855 studied natural history in Australasian islands; died at Sydney.   [xxxv. 91]

MACGILLIVRAY, WILLIAM (1796–1852), naturalist; M.A. Aberdeen, 1815; dissector to the lecturer on comparative anatomy, Aberdeen; assistant and secretary to the regius professor (Robert Jameson [q. v.]) of natural history, Edinburgh, 1823; conservator of the Royal College of Surgeons' Museum, Edinburgh, 1831–41; professor of natural history, Aberdeen, 1841; best-known work, 'A History of British Birds,' 1837–52.
                [xxxv. 90]

MAC GIOLLA CUDDY (1618–1693). [See ARCHDEKIN, RICHARD.]

McGLASHAN, ALEXANDER (*d.* 1797), Scottish violinist; edited 'A Collection of Scots Measures, Hornpipes, Jigs,' &c., 1781.   [xxxv. 92]

McGLASHAN, JOHN (*d.* 1866), legal author; an Edinburgh solicitor; went to New Zealand, 1855, where he died; published legal works, 1831–44.   [xxxv. 92]

MACGOWAN, JOHN (1726–1780), baptist minister; pastor of the meeting-house, Devonshire Square, 1766–80; chief work, 'Infernal Conferences, or Dialogues of Devils, by the Listener,' 1772.   [xxxv. 92]

MACGRADOIGH, AUGUSTIN (1349–1405), also called MAGRAIDIN; Irish chronicler; canon-regular of St. Austin; continued the O'Brian annals to 1405.   [xxxv. 93]

MACGREGOR, SIR CHARLES METCALFE (1840–1887), major-general; educated at Marlborough; took part in the suppression of the Indian Mutiny, 1857–8; served in China, 1860–1; took part in the Abyssinian expedition, 1867–8; compiled the 'Gazetteer of Central Asia' for the Indian government, 1868–73; made expeditions to obtain information about the Afghan frontier, 1875; served in the second Afghan war, 1878–9; K.C.B., 1881; quartermaster-general of India, 1880; general officer commanding the Punjaub frontier force, 1885; major-general, 1887; published accounts of his travels in Afghanistan and Beloochistan, 1879 and 1882, and works suppressed by the Indian government, 1884 and 1885–6; died at Cairo.   [xxxv. 93]

MACGREGOR, SIR GREGOR (*fl.* 1817), calling himself His Highness Gregor, Cacique of Poyais, South American adventurer; said to have served in youth in British army; went to Caraccas to aid in the struggle for South American independence, 1811; general of brigade, Venezuelan army, 1812; distinguished himself in the campaign of 1813–21; general of division, 1817; assumed the title of cacique and settled among the Poyais Indians, 1821; failed in his schemes for colonising the mosquito territory; restored to the rank of general of division, Venezuelan army, 1839; died probably at Caraccas.   [xxxv. 95]

MACGREGOR, JAMES (*d.* 1551), dean of Lismore; notary public, 1511; dean of Lismore, 1514; collected Gaelic poetry (selection edited, 1862).   [xxxv. 96]

MACGREGOR, JOHN (1797–1857), statistician and historian; emigrated to Canada and settled in Prince Edward island; member of the House of Assembly; high sheriff, 1823; travelled over America collecting statistics; joint-secretary of the board of trade in London, 1840; M.P., Glasgow, 1847; promoter of the Royal British Bank, 1849; absconded shortly before it stopped payment; died at Boulogne; best-known works, 'My Note-book,' 1835, and 'The Resources and Statistics of Nations,' 1835.   [xxxv. 96]

MACGREGOR, JOHN, known as ROB ROY (1825–1892), philanthropist and traveller; entered Trinity College, Dublin, 1839; proceeded to Trinity College, Cambridge, 1844; B.A., 1847; M.A., 1850; barrister, Inner Temple, 1851; travelled widely, 1848–57; went for his first solitary cruise in his 'Rob Roy' canoe, 1865; published 'A Thousand Miles in the Rob Roy Canoe,' 1866; made other cruises, 1866, 1867, and 1868; member of the London school board, 1870 and 1873; actively promoted philanthropic schemes in London.   [xxxv. 97]

McGREGOR, JOHN JAMES (1775–1834), historian and topographer; edited 'Munster Telegraph,' and subsequently 'Church Methodist Magazine'; literary assistant to the Kildare Place Education Society, Dublin, 1829.   [xxxv. 99]

MACGREGOR or **CAMPBELL**, ROBERT, commonly called ROB ROY (1671–1734), highland freebooter; nominally a grazier, though deriving his principal income from cattle-lifting and exacting money for affording protection against thieves; a man of some education; penal acts enforced against him and his clan for their conduct at the revolution, 1693; accused of fraudulent bankruptcy, 1712; followed with his men in the wake of the rebel army, but did not join it, 1715; surrendered to the Duke of Atholl, 1717; escaped and continued his depredations; apprehended and sentenced to be transported to Barbados, but pardoned, 1727; eventually became a Roman catholic and a peaceful subject. Authentic particulars of his life are to be found in Scott's introduction to 'Rob Roy.'   [xxxv. 99]

McGRIGOR, SIR JAMES, first baronet (1771–1858), army surgeon; studied medicine at Aberdeen and Edin-

burgh Universities; M.A. Aberdeen, 1788; surgeon to de Burgh's regiment (Connaught rangers), 1793; saw service in Flanders, West Indies, and India; superintending surgeon to the European and Indian troops going to Egypt, 1801; M.D. Marischal College, Aberdeen, 1804; inspector-general of hospitals, 1809; chief of the medical staff of Wellington's army in the Peninsula, 1811; knighted, 1814; director-general of the army medical department, 1815–51; F.R.S., 1816; created baronet, 1830; hon. LL.D. Edinburgh; K.C.B., 1850; author of medical reports.   [xxxv. 102]

McGRIGOR, JAMES (1819–1863), lieutenant-colonel in the Indian army; nephew of Sir James McGrigor [q. v.]; distinguished himself in the Indian mutiny, 1857–8; major, 1858; lieutenant-colonel, 1862; drowned while bathing at Aden.   [xxxv. 105]

MACGUIRE. [See MAGUIRE.]

MACHABE, JOHN (*d.* 1557). [See MACALPINE.]

MACHADO, ROGER (*d.* 1511?), diplomatist and Clarenceux king-of-arms; present at Edward IV's funeral, 1483; Richmond herald and Norroy king-of-arms, 1485; Clarenceux king-of-arms, 1494; employed on diplomatic missions in France, 1494–6.   [xxxv. 105]

MACHALE, JOHN (1791–1881), archbishop of Tuam; educated at Maynooth; lecturer on theology there, 1814; coadjutor bishop of Killala, 1825; visited Rome, 1831; archbishop of Tuam, 1834; induced by his dislike of everything English to oppose Newman; quarrelled with Archbishop Cullen [q. v.]; translated the Pentateuch into Irish, 1801, also some of Moore's melodies and part of the Iliad, 1844–71.   [xxxv. 106]

MACHEN, THOMAS (1568–1614), M.A. Magdalen College, Oxford, 1592, and fellow; student of Lincoln's Inn, 1589; M.P., Gloucester, 1614.   [xxxv. 108]

McHENRY, JAMES (1785–1845), poet and novelist; emigrated to the United States, 1817; settled in Philadelphia, 1824; United States consul in Londonderry, 1842–5; best known by his novel, 'O'Halloran, or the Insurgent Chief,' 1824.   [xxxv. 108]

MACHIN or **MACHYN**, HENRY (1498?–1563?), diarist; kept a valuable diary of the years 1550–63 (published by the Camden Society, 1848).   [xxxv. 108]

MACHIN, JOHN (1624–1664), ejected nonconformist; converted after entering Jesus College, Cambridge, 1645; B.A., 1649; received presbyterian ordination, 1649; lectured at different towns, 1650–61; ejected from curacy of Whitley Chapel, Great Budworth, Cheshire, 1662.   [xxxv. 109]

MACHIN, JOHN (*d.* 1751), astronomer; F.R.S., 1710; professor of astronomy at Gresham College, London, 1713–51; left unpublished writings.   [xxxv. 110]

MACHIN, LEWIS (*fl.* 1608), author, in collaboration with Gervase Markham [q. v.], of a comedy, 'The Dumbe Knight,' 1608.   [xxxv. 109]

MACHIN or **MACHAM**, ROBERT (*fl.* 1344), legendary discoverer of Madeira; supposed to have fled from England with Anna Dorset, daughter of an English noble, and landed on an island at a port which he called Machico; Madeira was discovered by Genoese sailors in the Portuguese service prior to the date of Machin's voyage.   [xxxv. 110]

MACHLINIA, WILLIAM DE (*fl.* 1482–1490), printer; probably a native of Mechlin; printer in England after 1482; about twenty-two books assigned to his press.   [xxxv. 111]

MACHON, JOHN (1572–1640?), B.A. Magdalen College, Oxford, 1594; canon of Lichfield, 1631.   [xxxv. 109]

MACIAN OF GLENCOE (*d.* 1692). [See MACDONALD, ALEXANDER.]

M'IAN, ROBERT RONALD (1803–1856), historical painter; while studying art, was on the stage till 1839; exhibited at the Royal Academy from 1836; associate of the Royal Scottish Academy, 1852; painted chiefly pictures of highland life and history.   [xxxv. 111]

MACILWAIN, GEORGE (1797–1882), medical writer; studied under Abernethy at St. Bartholomew's Hospital, London; F.R.C.S., 1843; held various surgical appointments in London; published 'Memoirs of John Abernethy,' 1853, and medical treatises.   [xxxv. 111]

McILWRAITH, SIR THOMAS (1835–1900), premier of Queensland; educated as engineer at Glasgow University; went (1854) to Victoria, where he found employment on railways; engaged in pastoral pursuits in Queensland; member of legislative assembly for Maranoa, 1869; minister for works and mines, 1874; member for Mulgrave, 1878; premier, 1879–83; colonial treasurer, 1879–1881; colonial secretary, 1881–3; K.C.M.G., 1882; annexed New Guinea to Queensland, 1883; came to Great Britain; hon. LL.D. Glasgow, 1883; member for North Brisbane, 1888; premier, colonial secretary, and treasurer, 1888; resigned premiership, 1888, but retained seat in cabinet without portfolio; colonial treasurer, 1890; premier, 1893; returned (1893) to England, where he died. [Suppl. iii. 123]

MACINTOSH. [See also MACKINTOSH.]

MACINTOSH, CHARLES (1766–1843), chemist and inventor of waterproof fabrics; studied chemistry while a counting-house clerk; started the first alum works in Scotland, 1797; connected with the St. Rollox chemical works till 1814; patented his waterproof invention, 1823, and started works in Manchester (still continued); F.R.S., 1823. [xxxv. 112]

MACINTOSH, DONALD (1743–1808), Scottish nonjuring bishop; clerk for the Gaelic language to the Scottish Society of Antiquaries, 1785–9; ordained, 1789; acted as a missionary or untitled bishop of Jacobite episcopacy; Gaelic translator and keeper of Gaelic records to the Highland Society of Scotland, 1801; the last representative of the nonjuring Scottish episcopal church; compiled 'A Collection of Gaelic Proverbs,' the first ever made. [xxxv. 113]

MACINTYRE, DUNCAN BAN (1724–1812), Gaelic poet; joined the Hanoverian forces, 1745; present at the battle of Falkirk, 1746; published the first edition of his poems, 1786 (other editions, 1790 and 1804); some of his poems translated into English; vividly described highland scenery. [xxxv. 114]

MACKAIL, HUGH (1640?–1666), Scottish martyr; educated at Edinburgh University; ordained, 1661; apprehended for his preaching, 1662; escaped to Holland; joined a covenanters' rising in Scotland, 1666; tortured and hanged in Edinburgh. [xxxv. 115]

MACKAIL or **MACKAILLE**, MATTHEW (*fl.* 1657–1696), medical writer; M.D. Aberdeen, 1696; published medical works. [xxxv. 115]

MACKAIL, MATTHEW (*d.* 1734), son of Matthew Mackail (*fl.* 1657–1696) [q. v.]; studied medicine at Leyden; professor of medicine, Aberdeen, 1717. [xxxv. 116]

MACKARNESS, JOHN FIELDER (1820–1889), bishop of Oxford; educated at Eton and Merton College, Oxford; B.A., 1844; honorary canon of Worcester, 1854–8; prebendary of Exeter, 1858; bishop of Oxford, 1870–88; a liberal in politics. [xxxv. 116]

MACKARNESS, MRS. MATILDA ANNE (1826–1881), author; daughter of James Robinson Planché [q. v.]; published her best-known story, 'A Trap to Catch a Sunbeam,' 1849; married the Rev. Henry S. Mackarness (*d.* 1868), brother of John Fielder Mackarness [q. v.] [xxxv. 117]

MACKAY, ALEXANDER (1808–1852), journalist; barrister, Middle Temple, 1847; on the staff of the 'Morning Chronicle' till 1849; sent to India by the chambers of commerce of the big cities in the north to inquire into the cultivation of cotton, 1851; his 'Western World, or Travels in the United States in 1846–7,' 1849, long the most complete work on the subject. [xxxv. 117]

MACKAY, ALEXANDER (1815–1895), educational writer; M.A. King's College, Aberdeen, 1840; LL.D., 1866; first Free church minister of Rhynie, Aberdeenshire, 1844–67; studied local geology, and was F.R.G.S., 1859; published educational works, including 'Manual of Modern Geography,' 1861. [Suppl. iii. 124]

MACKAY, ALEXANDER MURDOCH (1849–1890), missionary; studied engineering subjects at Edinburgh University; draughtsman in an engineering firm at Berlin, 1873–5; joined the mission to Uganda, 1876, and gained great influence over the natives; died at Usambiro. [xxxv. 118]

MACKAY, ANDREW (1760–1809), mathematician; keeper of Aberdeen Observatory, 1781; LL.D. Aberdeen, 1786; mathematical examiner to the Trinity House (1805–9) and to the East India Company; chief works, 'The Theory and Practice of finding the Longitude at Sea or on Land,' 1793, 'A Collection of Mathematical Tables,' 1804, and 'The Complete Navigator,' 1804. [xxxv. 118]

MACKAY, ANGUS (1824–1886), colonial journalist and politician; taken by his parents to New South Wales, 1827; editor of the 'Atlas,' 1847; represented the 'Empire' at the goldfields, 1851; member for Sandhurst burghs, Victoria, 1868–79 and 1883–6; minister of mines, 1870; launched the 'Sydney Daily Telegraph,' 1879; died at Sandhurst burghs. [xxxv. 119]

McKAY, ARCHIBALD (1801–1883), poet and topographer; his most popular poems 'My First Bawbee,' 'My ain Couthie Wife,' and 'Drouthy Tam,' 1828; author of 'A History of Kilmarnock,' 1848. [xxxv. 120]

MACKAY, CHARLES (1814–1889), poet and journalist; educated at Brussels; private secretary to William Cockerill [q. v.], 1830–2; assistant sub-editor of the 'Morning Chronicle,' 1834–44; editor of the 'Glasgow Argus,' 1844–7, of the 'Illustrated London News,' 1852–9; special correspondent of 'The Times' at New York, 1862–5; wrote his song, 'The Good Time Coming,' 1846, of which 400,000 copies were circulated; published songs at intervals from 1834–90 (collected, 1859 and 1868), his 'Gossamer and Snowdrift,' being posthumous, 1890; LL.D. of Glasgow, 1846; published numerous prose works. [xxxv. 120]

MACKAY, SIR DONALD, of Far, first BARON REAY (1591–1649), succeeded to the headship of the clan, 1614; knighted, 1616; created baronet, 1627; served the King of Denmark with distinction, 1627–9; created Baron Reay, 1628; transferred his regiment to Gustavus Adolphus, 1629; present at the battles of Leipzig (1631) and Lutzen (1633); returned to Denmark, 1643; joined King Charles I, 1644; captured at Newcastle, 1644; set free, 1645; retired to Denmark (1648), where he died. [xxxv. 122]

MACKAY, HUGH (1640?–1692), of Scourie, general; served with his regiment abroad, 1660–73; transferred his services to the States-General, 1673; colonel of Scots Dutch regiments, 1680; summoned to England to aid against Monmouth, 1685; privy councillor of Scotland; returned to Holland, remaining there on the recall of the regiment by James II, 1687; in command of the English and Scots division in the expedition of William of Orange, 1688; commander-in-chief of the forces in Scotland, 1689; defeated by Claverhouse at Killiecrankie, 1689; induced the surrender of the forces of Cannon, Claverhouse's successor, 1689; led the attack at Steinkirk, where he was slain. [xxxv. 124]

MACKAY, JAMES TOWNSEND (1775?–1862), botanist; curator of the botanical garden, Trinity College, Dublin, 1806–62; published his 'Flora Hibernica,' 1836; LL.D. Dublin University, 1850; discovered plants new to the British isles. [xxxv. 127]

MACKAY, JOHN, second BARON REAY (*fl.* 1650), son of Sir Donald Mackay of Far, first baron Reay [q. v.]; took part in royalist insurrections in Scotland, 1649 and 1654. [xxxv. 123]

MACKAY, MACKINTOSH (1800–1873), Gaelic scholar; educated for the ministry; superintended the printing of the Gaelic dictionary of the Highland and Agricultural Society, 1828; published the 'Poems' of Robert Mackay, Rob Donn [q. v.], 1829; at the disruption joined the Free church; minister of the Gaelic church at Melbourne, 1854, and Sydney, 1856; returned to Scotland. [xxxv. 127]

MACKAY, ROBERT, commonly called ROB DONN (the Brown) (1714–1778), Gaelic poet; acted as herd, gamekeeper, and boman; in the Reay fencibles, 1759–67; wrote poems, chiefly elegies and satires, in the Sutherlandshire dialect. [xxxv. 127]

MACKAY, ROBERT WILLIAM (1803–1882), philosopher and scholar; educated at Winchester and Brasenose College, Oxford; M.A., 1828; published 'The Progress of the Intellect as exemplified in the Religious Development of the Greeks and Hebrews,' 1850, and other learned works. [xxxv. 129]

MACKELLAR, MARY (1834–1890), highland poetess; *née* Cameron; married John Mackellar, captain of a coasting vessel; obtained judicial separation from him; settled in Edinburgh, *c.* 1786; her 'Poems and Songs, Gaelic and English,' contributed to newspapers and periodicals, published, 1880; translated into Gaelic the second series of Queen Victoria's 'Leaves from our Journal in the Highlands.'   [xxxv. 129]

MACKELLAR, PATRICK (1717–1778), colonel, military engineer; clerk in the ordnance service, 1735; employed in Minorca, 1739–54 and 1763–78; engineer in ordinary, 1751; served in Braddock's campaign in North America, 1754; chief engineer of the frontier forts, 1756; taken prisoner and confined in Quebec and Montreal, 1756–7; second and then chief engineer at the capture of Louisburg, 1758; chief engineer to Wolfe, 1759; in the expedition against Martinique, 1761–2, and the attack on Havannah, 1762; director of engineering and colonel at Minorca, 1777.   [xxxv. 129]

MACKELVIE, WILLIAM (1800–1863), united presbyterian divine; studied for the ministry as a secessionist at Edinburgh University; ordained, 1829; promoted union of secession and relief churches; best-known work 'Annals and Statistics of the United Presbyterian Church' (published, 1873).   [xxxv. 131]

MACKEN, JOHN (1784?–1823), poet; merchant at Ballyconnell; joint-editor of the 'Enniskillen Chronicle,' 1808; in London, 1818; assisted in compiling 'Huntingdon Peerage,' 1821; returned to Ireland and resumed his joint-editorship of the 'Enniskillen Chronicle,' 1821; published verse.   [xxxv. 132]

MACKENNA, JOHN or JUAN (1771–1814), Chilian general; left Ireland and entered the Royal Academy of Mathematics at Barcelona, 1784; entered an Irish engineer corps in the Spanish army, 1787; served against the French, 1787–8 and 1794; went to Peru, 1796; governor of Osorno, 1797–1808; joined revolution, 1810; provisional governor of Valparaiso and commander-in-chief of artillery and engineers, 1811–14; brigadier-general, 1813; banished, 1814; killed in a duel at Buenos Ayres.   [xxxv. 132]

MACKENNA, NIAL (*fl.* 1700), Irish poet and harper; author of the celebrated song, 'Little Celia Connellan.'   [xxxv. 133]

MACKENNA, THEOBALD (*d.* 1808), Irish catholic writer; secretary to the catholic committee in Ireland; the mouthpiece of the seceders after 1791; opposed Wolfe Tone's views in a pamphlet, 1793; disappointed with the results of the union; suggested raising the Irish catholic church to an establishment, 1805; issued political pamphlets.   [xxxv. 133]

MACKENZIE, first BARON OF KINTAIL (1754–1815). [See HUMBERSTON, FRANCIS MACKENZIE, first BARON SEAFORTH and MACKENZIE.]

MACKENZIE, SIR ALEXANDER (1755?–1820), North American explorer; explored the then unknown north-west, 1789; started from Fort Chippewayan, a trading port at the head of Lake Athabasca, with the object of reaching the Pacific coast, 1792; published an account of his voyages, 1801; knighted, 1802; resided in Canada and represented Huntingdon county in the provincial parliament; returned to Scotland, where he died.   [xxxv. 134]

MACKENZIE, ALEXANDER (1822–1892), first liberal premier of the Canadian Dominion; emigrated to Canada, 1842; builder and contractor at Sarnia, 1848; edited 'Lambton Shield,' 1852; member for Lambton in the provincial parliament, 1861–7, and in the Dominion House of Commons, 1867; premier and minister of public works, 1873–8; resigned the leadership of the opposition, 1880; member for East York, 1882–92; died at Toronto; upheld the connection between Canada and Great Britain.   [xxxv. 135]

MACKENZIE, CHARLES FREDERICK (1825–1862), bishop of Central Africa; brother of William Forbes Mackenzie [q. v.]; educated at Caius College, Cambridge; M.A., 1851; fellow; accompanied John William Colenso [q. v.] to Natal as his archdeacon, 1855; chaplain to the troops round Durban, 1858; head of the universities' mission to Central Africa, 1860; consecrated bishop at Cape Town, 1861; settled at Magomero in the Manganja country; often resorted to force to help the Manganja; died at Malo.   [xxxv. 136]

MACKENZIE, COLIN (1753?–1821), colonel in the Madras engineers, Indian antiquary and topographer; served in the Madras engineers against Tippoo Sahib, 1790–2 and 1799; surveyed Mysore, 1799–1806; surveyor-general of Madras, 1807; commanding engineer in Java, 1811–15; C.B., 1815; surveyor-general of India, 1819; made valuable collections of Indian antiquities, inscriptions, and manuscripts.   [xxxv. 138]

MACKENZIE, COLIN (1806–1881), lieutenant-general in Indian army; cadet of infantry on Madras establishment, 1825; served in Coorg campaign, 1834, and in Straits of Malacca, 1836; assistant political agent at Peshawar, 1840; served with distinction at Kabul; brevet-captain; attended conference between Akbar Khan and Sir William Hay Macnaghten [q. v.] and was taken prisoner; on being released, chosen by Akbar Khan as one of the hostages to be given up to him; raised Sikh regiment during the last Sikh campaign; brigadier-general in command of Ellichpur division of Hyderabad contingent, 1853; dangerously wounded at Bolarum in mutiny of a cavalry regiment against orders which the government subsequently condemned as ill-judged, 1855; returned temporarily to England; agent to governor-general with Nawab Nazim of Bengal; C.B., 1867; failed to obtain divisional command owing to censure in Bolarum case, and finally left India, 1873.   [Suppl. iii. 125]

MACKENZIE, DUGAL (*d.* 1588?), Scottish author; educated at Aberdeen and Paris Universities; some Latin poems and epigrams attributed to him.   [xxxv. 139]

MACKENZIE, ENEAS (1778–1832), topographer; became baptist minister and ultimately printer and publisher; founded the Mechanics' Institution, Newcastle; published several topographical works.   [xxxv. 139]

MACKENZIE, FREDERICK (1788?–1854), water-colour painter and topographical draughtsman; employed in making topographical and architectural drawings; exhibited at the Royal Academy, 1804–28; member of the Society of Painters in Water-colours, 1823.   [xxxv. 140]

MACKENZIE, GEORGE, second EARL OF SEAFORTH (*d.* 1651), succeeded, 1633; of royalist inclination, but with the covenanters, 1639–40; sometimes supported and sometimes opposed Montrose, 1640–6; joined Charles II in Holland, 1649; died at Schiedam.   [xxxv. 140]

MACKENZIE, SIR GEORGE (1636–1691), of Rosehaugh, king's advocate; studied at St. Andrews, Aberdeen, and Bourges Universities; called to the bar at Edinburgh, 1659; distinguished himself in the trial of the Marquis of Argyll, 1661; knighted; M.P., Ross, 1669; king's advocate, 1677; privy councillor, 1677; called 'Bloody' from his severe treatment (1679–86) of the covenanters; resigned for a short time, 1686; again in office, 1688; opposed the dethronement of James II, and to escape the consequences retired from public life; founded the library of the Faculty of Advocates, opened 1689; author of moral essays and legal and historical works of a bigoted character.   [xxxv. 142]

MACKENZIE, GEORGE, first VISCOUNT TARBAT, first EARL OF CROMARTY (1630–1714), statesman; educated at St. Andrews and Aberdeen Universities; succeeded to the family estates, 1654; as a royalist had to remain in exile till 1660; lord of session as Lord Tarbat; planned Lauderdale's downfall by means of the 'act of billeting,' 1662; deprived of office, 1664; appointed lord justice-general of Scotland, 1678; chief minister of the king in Scotland, 1682–8; created Viscount Tarbat, 1685; joined the new government, 1689; secretary of state, 1702–4; created Earl of Cromarty, 1703; advocated the union; published miscellaneous pamphlets.   [xxxv. 145]

MACKENZIE, GEORGE (1669–1725), Scottish biographer; son of George Mackenzie, second earl of Seaforth [q. v.]; studied medicine at Aberdeen, Oxford, and Paris; M.D. Aberdeen; chief work, 'Lives and Characters of the most Eminent Writers of the Scots Nation,' vol. i. 1708, vol. ii. 1711, and vol. iii. 1722.   [xxxv. 148]

MACKENZIE, GEORGE, third EARL OF CROMARTY (*d.* 1766), succeeded, 1731; joined Prince Charles Edward, 1745; taken prisoner, tried, and sentenced to death, 1746; pardoned, 1749.   [xxxv. 148]

MACKENZIE, GEORGE (1741–1787), brother of John Mackenzie, baron Macleod [q. v.]; present at the defence of Gibraltar, 1780; lieutenant-colonel, 1783; died at Wallajabad. [xxxv. 156]

MACKENZIE, GEORGE (1777–1856), meteorologist; began a register of atmospheric changes, 1802; formed his 'primary cycle of the winds,' 1819; author of reports or 'Manuals' of the weather. [xxxv. 149]

MACKENZIE, SIR GEORGE STEUART, seventh baronet (1780–1848), of Coul, mineralogist; succeeded to baronetcy, 1796; discovered identity of diamond and carbon, 1800; F.R.S.; studied mineralogy and geology in Iceland, 1810; in the Faroe islands, 1812; joint author of 'Travels in Iceland,' 1811; wrote geological and miscellaneous works. [xxxv. 149]

MACKENZIE, HENRY (1745–1831), novelist and miscellaneous writer; educated at Edinburgh High School and University; attorney for the crown in Scotland; his novels, 'The Man of Feeling,' 1771, 'The Man of the World,' 1773, and 'Julia de Roubigné,' 1777, published anonymously; produced a successful tragedy, 'The Prince of Tunis,' 1773; superintended the periodicals, 'The Mirror,' 1779–80, and 'The Lounger,' 1785–7; wrote on contemporary politics, 1784–93; comptroller of taxes for Scotland, 1804–31; his 'Works' issued, 1807 and 1808; called by Scott the 'Northern Addison.' [xxxv. 150]

MACKENZIE, HENRY (1808–1878), bishop suffragan of Nottingham; educated at Merchant Taylors' School, London, and Pembroke College, Oxford; ordained, 1834; M.A.,1838; prebendary of Lincoln, 1858; sub-dean and canon-residentiary, 1864; archdeacon of Nottingham, 1866; D.D.,1869; bishop suffragan of Nottingham, 1870–8. [xxxv. 152]

MACKENZIE, JAMES (1680?–1761), physician; studied at Edinburgh and Leyden Universities; published 'The History of Health and the Art of preserving it,' 1758. [xxxv. 153]

MACKENZIE, JAMES ARCHIBALD STUART-WORTLEY-, first BARON WHARNCLIFFE (1776–1845). [See STUART-WORTLEY-MACKENZIE.]

MACKENZIE, JOHN (1648?–1696), Irish divine; ordained presbyterian minister, 1673; chaplain of Walker's regiment during the siege of Londonderry, 1689; wrote narrative of siege, 1690. [xxxv. 154]

MACKENZIE, JOHN, BARON MACLEOD, COUNT CROMARTY in the Swedish peerage (1727–1789), major-general in the British army; great-grandson of George Mackenzie, first viscount Tarbat and first earl of Cromarty [q. v.]; joined Prince Charles Edward, 1745; captured, 1746; pardoned, but deprived of his title and estates, 1748; joined a Swedish regiment, 1750; present at the battle of Prague as a volunteer of the Prussian army and aide-de-camp to Marshal Keith [see KEITH, JAMES FRANCIS EDWARD], 1757; returned to England, 1777; raised highland regiment, and as its colonel embarked with it for India, 1779; served in India till 1783; major-general, 1783; his estates restored, 1784. [xxxv. 154]

MACKENZIE, JOHN (1806–1848), Gaelic scholar; collected popular songs; book-keeper in Glasgow University printing-office, 1836; published 'Beauties of Gaelic Poetry,' 1841; translated theological works into Gaelic. [xxxv. 156]

MACKENZIE, JOHN KENNETH (1850–1888), medical missionary; obtained medical diplomas, London and Edinburgh, 1874; sent by the London Missionary Society to Hankow as a medical missionary, 1875; founded a medical school for native students at Tien-tsin; died at Tien-tsin. [xxxv. 157]

MACKENZIE, KENNETH, fourth EARL OF SEAFORTH (d. 1701), succeeded to the earldom, 1678; followed James II to France, 1689; served in the siege of Londonderry, 1689; created by James titular Marquis of Seaforth; failed to make terms with William III's government, 1690; imprisoned till 1697; died in Paris. [xxxv. 157]

MACKENZIE, KENNETH (1754–1833). [See DOUGLAS, SIR KENNETH.]

MACKENZIE, KENNETH DOUGLAS (1811–1873), colonel; ensign in the Gordon highlanders, 1831; captured William Smith O'Brien in the Irish insurrection, 1848; served in Crimea. 1854–6; went to India, 1857;

employed in the expedition to China, 1860; colonel, 1869; assistant quartermaster-general at the Horse Guards, 1870. [xxxv. 158]

MACKENZIE, MARIA ELIZABETH FREDERICA STEWART, LADY HOOD (1783–1862). [See STEWART.]

MACKENZIE, SIR MORELL (1837–1892), physician; studied medicine at the London Hospital, at Paris, Vienna, and Pesth; specialised on throat diseases; M.D. London, 1862; helped to found the Hospital for Diseases of the Throat, Golden Square, London, 1863; summoned to Berlin to attend the crown prince of Germany, afterwards the Emperor Frederick III, 1887; knighted, 1887; justified his conduct in regard to the German physicians and his general treatment of the case in 'Frederick the Noble,' 1888, an injudicious work, for which he was censured by the Royal College of Surgeons, 1889; published 'Manual of Diseases of the Throat and Nose,' vol. i. 1880, vol. ii. 1884. [xxxv. 159]

McKENZIE, MURDOCH, the elder (d. 1797), hydrographer; surveyed the Orkney and Shetland isles, 1749; admiralty surveyor till 1771; F.R.S., 1774; published 'A Treatise on Marine Surveying,' 1774, and the results of his work on the Scottish and Irish coasts, 1776. [xxxv. 160]

McKENZIE, MURDOCH, the younger (1743–1829), commander in the navy; nephew of Murdoch M'Kenzie the elder [q. v.]; admiralty surveyor, 1771–88; commander, 1814. [xxxv. 161]

MACKENZIE, ROBERT (1823–1881), miscellaneous writer; journalist and author of historical works. [xxxv. 161]

MACKENZIE, ROBERT SHELTON (1809–1880), miscellaneous writer; contributed poems to the 'Dublin and London Magazine,' published 'Lays of Palestine,' 1828; journalist in London after 1830; engaged in literary work in New York, 1852; settled at Philadelphia (1857), where he died; remembered chiefly for his compilations, including valuable editions of the 'Noctes Ambrosianæ,' 1861–3, and of Maginn's 'Miscellaneous Works,' 1855–7. [xxxv. 161]

MACKENZIE, SAMUEL (1785 - 1847), portrait-painter; studied in Raeburn's studio at Edinburgh; contributed to the exhibitions of Associated Artists, Edinburgh, 1812–16, and to the Royal Institution, Edinburgh, 1821–9; member of the Scottish Academy, and contributed to its exhibitions, 1829–46; especially successful in his female portraits. [xxxv. 162]

MACKENZIE, THOMAS, LORD MACKENZIE (1807–1869), Scottish judge; studied at St. Andrews and Edinburgh Universities; called to the Scottish bar, 1832; solicitor-general, 1851; raised to the bench with the title Lord Mackenzie, 1854; retired, 1864; author of 'Studies in Roman Law, with Comparative Views of the Laws of France, England, and Scotland,' 1862. [xxxv. 163]

MACKENZIE, WILLIAM, fifth EARL OF SEAFORTH (d. 1740), joined the Pretender, 1715; served throughout the war and escaped to France, 1716; accompanied George Keith, tenth earl Marischal [q. v.], in his expedition to the highlands, 1719; again escaped to France; pardoned and returned to Scotland, 1726. [xxxv. 163]

MACKENZIE, WILLIAM (1791–1868), ophthalmic surgeon; studied chiefly at Glasgow and Vienna; Waltonian lecturer, Glasgow University, 1828; surgeon-oculist to the queen in Scotland, 1838; helped to raise ophthalmic surgery to a high place among the special branches of medical science; his most important work, 'Practical Treatise on the Diseases of the Eye,' 1830. [xxxv. 164]

MACKENZIE, WILLIAM BELL (1806–1870), of Magdalen Hall, Oxford; M.A., 1837; published religious works. [xxxv. 165]

MACKENZIE, WILLIAM FORBES (1807 - 1862), of Portmore, Peeblesshire, politician; brother of Charles Frederick Mackenzie [q. v.]; called to the bar, 1827; M.P. Peeblesshire, 1837–52; lord of the treasury, 1845–6; author of the Forbes Mackenzie Act (for the regulation of public-houses in Scotland), 1852. [xxxv. 165]

MACKENZIE, WILLIAM LYON (1795 - 1861), leader of Canadian insurgents; a native of Dundee; emigrated to Canada, 1820; conducted the 'Colonial Advocate' at Toronto, 1824–34;.member of the Upper Canada legislative assembly for the county of York, 1828–30, and

1834-6; mayor of Toronto, 1834; led an insurrection (1837) which failed, and ended in his imprisonment for a year, but which drew the attention of the home government to colonial abuses; member of the united provinces legislature, 1850-8. [xxxv. 165]

MACKERELL, BENJAMIN (d. 1738), Norfolk antiquary; librarian of the Norwich public library, 1716-1732. [xxxv. 166]

McKERROW, JOHN (1789-1867), presbyterian divine; educated at Glasgow University; ordained by the secession church, 1813; published works on the history of his church. [xxxv. 167]

McKERROW, WILLIAM (1803-1878), presbyterian divine; educated at Glasgow University; ordained and ministered in Manchester, 1827-69; supported Manchester liberal movements; started the Manchester 'Examiner and Times,' 1846; member of the first Manchester school board, 1870. [xxxv. 167]

MACKESON, FREDERICK (1807-1853), lieutenant-colonel; in the East India Company's service; commissioner at Peshawur; received a Bengal cadetship, 1825; accompanied Sir Alexander Burnes [q. v.] to Cabul, 1837; distinguished himself in the Sikh wars; commissioner at Peshawur, 1851-3; employed in quieting the frontier tribes; assassinated by a native. [xxxv. 168]

McKEWAN, DAVID HALL (1816-1873), watercolour painter; studied under David Cox the elder [q. v.]; member of the Royal Institute of Painters in Water-colours, 1850; painted landscapes and interiors. [xxxv. 168]

MACKGILL or MACGILL, JAMES (d. 1579), of Nether Rankeillour, clerk register of Scotland; educated at St. Andrews University; admitted advocate, 1550; appointed clerk register and an ordinary lord of session, 1554; at first adhered to Queen Mary, but was concerned in Riccio's (Rizzio's) murder, 1565, and afterwards became her opponent; member of the new council, 1578. [xxxv. 169]

McKIE, JAMES (1816-1891), Burns collector; bookseller at Kilmarnock; started the 'Kilmarnock Journal' and the 'Kilmarnock Weekly Post'; collected rare editions of Burns, and published facsimiles; author of works connected with Burns. [xxxv. 170]

MACKIE, JOHN (1748-1831), physician; studied at Edinburgh University; spent much time abroad, where he occasionally practised; published a 'Sketch of a New Theory of Man,' 1819. [xxxv. 170]

McKINLAY, JOHN (1819-1872), Australian explorer; emigrated to New South Wales, 1836; left Adelaide to trace the fate of O'Hara Burke, and Wills, and to explore, 1861; proved that Lake Torrens did not exist; struck the coast at Gulf Carpentaria, 1862; headed another expedition to explore the northern territory, 1865. [xxxv. 171]

MACKINNON, DANIEL (1791-1836), colonel and historian of the Coldstream guards; brother of William Alexander Mackinnon [q. v.]; entered the guards, 1804; on the continent, 1805-14; wounded at Waterloo, 1815; colonel, 1830; published a famous 'Origin and History of the Coldstream Guards,' 1832. [xxxv. 171]

MACKINNON, DANIEL HENRY (1813-1884), soldier and author; B.A. Trinity College, Dublin; entered the army, 1836; served in Afghanistan, 1838-9; in the Sikh war, 1846; major-general, 1878; published 'Military Services and Adventures in the Far East,' 1849. [xxxv. 172]

MACKINNON, SIR WILLIAM, first baronet (1823-1893), founder of British East Africa Company; engaged in mercantile firm in Glasgow; went to India, 1847, and with a partner founded firm of Mackinnon, Mackenzie & Co. for coasting trade in Bay of Bengal; took great part in founding Calcutta and Burmah (after 1862, British India) Steam Navigation Company, 1856; negotiated with Sultan Seyyid Barghash, 1878, for lease of land now called German East Africa (sanction declined by British government); chairman of Imperial British East Africa Company, 1888-95; territory taken over by British government, 1895; shared largely in promoting Sir H. M. Stanley's expedition for relief of Emin Pasha, 1886; founded East African Scottish mission, 1891; C.I.E., 1882; created baronet, 1889. [Suppl. iii. 127]

MACKINNON, WILLIAM ALEXANDER (1789-1870), legislator; brother of Daniel Mackinnon [q. v.]; M.P., Dunwich, 1830-1, Lymington, 1831-52, Rye, 1853, 1857, and 1859-65; published 'On Public Opinion in Great Britain and other Parts of the World,' 1828; rewritten as 'History of Civilisation,' 1846. [xxxv. 172]

MACKINTOSH. [See also MACINTOSH.]

MACKINTOSH, SIR JAMES (1765-1832), philosopher; educated at Aberdeen University; studied medicine at Edinburgh; obtained his diploma, 1787; moved to London, 1788; became a regular contributor to the 'Oracle' belonging to John Bell (1745-1831) [q. v.]; published 'Vindiciæ Gallicæ,' 1791, in answer to Burke's 'Reflections on the French Revolution'; on becoming known to Burke, adopted his view of the French revolution; barrister, Lincoln's Inn, 1795; lectured on 'The Law of Nature and Nations,' 1799; recorder of Bombay, 1804-6; judge in the vice-admiralty court, Bombay, 1806-11; M.P., Nairn, 1813, Knaresborough, 1819; professor of 'law and general politics' at Haileybury, 1818-24; published 'Dissertation on the Progress of Ethical Philosophy,' 1830; commissioner of the board of control, 1830; wrote 'History of England' in Lardner's 'Cabinet Cyclopædia,' 1830, 'History of the Revolution in England in 1688,' published, 1834, and other historical works. [xxxv. 173]

MACKINTOSH, WILLIAM (1662-1743), of Borlum, Inverness-shire; brigadier in James Edward the Old Pretender's service; educated at King's College, Aberdeen; prominent in the Jacobite rising, 1714; confined in Newgate, 1715; escaped to France, 1716; returned to Scotland probably in 1719; again captured and imprisoned for life in Edinburgh Castle; published work on tillage in Scotland, 1729. [xxxv. 177]

MACKLIN, CHARLES (1697?-1797), actor and stage-manager; played in London at Lincoln's Inn Theatre, 1730, at Drury Lane, 1733-44, and 1744-8; made his reputation by his interpretation of the character of Shylock; appeared in Dublin (under Sheridan's auspices), 1748-50, and again, 1761 and 1763-70; at Covent Garden, London, 1750-3, 1761, 1772, 1775, 1781-9; retired from the stage, 1789. Of his dramatic productions, 'Love à la Mode,' a farce (1759) and 'The Man of the World' (1781), one of the best comedies of the century, are the most notable. [xxxv. 179]

MACKLIN, MARIA (d. 1781), actress; daughter of Charles Macklin [q. v.]; appeared first at Drury Lane in 'Richard III,' 1743; left the stage, 1777; Portia, Desdemona, and Rosalind among her parts. [xxxv. 183]

MACKNESS, JAMES (1804-1851), medical writer; passed the College of Surgeons, 1824; M.D. St. Andrews, 1840; member of the council of the British Medical Association, 1847; published medical works. [xxxv. 184]

MACKNIGHT, JAMES (1721-1800), biblical critic; educated at Glasgow and Leyden universities; ordained, 1753; published a 'Harmony of the Gospels,' 1756, which became celebrated; D.D. Edinburgh, 1759; main promoter of the declaratory act of assembly, 1782; issued a 'Translation of all the Apostolical Epistles,' 1795. [xxxv. 184]

MACKNIGHT, THOMAS (1829-1899), political writer; studied medicine at King's College, London; editor (1866-99) of Belfast 'Northern Whig,' which became mainstay of liberal party in Ireland, though it opposed home rule; published 'Life and Times of Edmund Burke,' 1858-1860, and other political and historical works. [Suppl. iii. 128]

MACKONOCHIE. [See also MACONOCHIE.]

MACKONOCHIE, ALEXANDER HERIOT (1825-1887), divine; of Wadham College, Oxford; ordained, 1849; M.A., 1851; adopted advanced ritualistic views, and was subjected to a series of lawsuits promoted by the Church Association, 1867-82. [xxxv. 185]

McKOWEN, JAMES (1814-1889), Ulster poet; employed in bleachworks at Belfast; contributed racy poems to various Irish newspapers; his 'Ould Irish Jig' known throughout Ireland. [xxxv. 186]

MACKRETH, SIR ROBERT (1726-1819), club proprietor; at first a billiard-marker, and then a waiter, at White's Club; proprietor of White's, 1761; bookmaker and usurer ; M.P. for Castle Rising through the nomination of the Earl of Orford, his debtor, 1774–1802 ; proceeded against and found guilty for taking advantage of a minor, 1786, and for assaulting John Scott (afterwards Lord Eldon), 1792 ; knighted for his services in parliament, 1795. [xxxv. 186]

MACKULLOCH, MAGNUS (*fl.* 1480), reputed continuator of Fordun's 'Scotichronicon' ; copied for the archbishop of St. Andrews the 'Scotichronicon,' 1483–84 ; probably wrote the additions at the end, which bring the narrative down to 1460. [xxxv. 187]

MACKWORTH, SIR HUMPHRY (1657–1727), politician and capitalist ; of Magdalen College, Oxford ; barrister, Middle Temple, 1682 ; knighted, 1683 ; M.P., Cardiganshire, 1701, 1702–5 and 1710–13 ; deputy-governor of a large mining company ; accused of peculation and found guilty by the House of Commons, 1710 ; one of the founders of the Society for Promoting Christian Knowledge ; author of political and financial pamphlets. [xxxv. 187]

MACKY, JOHN (*d.* 1726), government agent or spy ; discovered James II's intended expedition to England, 1692 ; inspector of the coast from Dover to Harwich, 1693 ; published 'A View of the Court of St. Germains from the Year 1690 to 1695,' 1696 ; directed the packet-boat service from Dover to France and Flanders, 1697–1702, and 1706–8 ; suspected by the government and imprisoned ; released at accession of George I ; died at Rotterdam. His 'Memoirs of the Secret Services of John Macky, Esq.,' published, 1733, is an important contribution to contemporary history. [xxxv. 189]

MACLACHLAN, EWEN (1775–1822), Gaelic poet and scholar ; educated at Aberdeen University ; head-master of Aberdeen grammar school, 1819–22 ; author of some Gaelic poems, also 'Attempts in Verse,' 1807, and 'Metrical Effusions,' 1816. [xxxv. 190]

MACLACHLAN, LAUCHLAN (*d.* 1746), fifteenth chief of the ancient Argyllshire clan ; succeeded his father, 1719 ; joined Prince Charles Edward, 1745 ; killed at Culloden, 1746. [xxxv. 190]

McLACHLAN, THOMAS HOPE (1845–1897), landscape-painter ; B.A. Trinity College, Cambridge, 1868 ; barrister, Lincoln's Inn, 1868 ; abandoned law for art, 1878. His picture, 'Ships that pass in the Night,' is in the National Gallery. [Suppl. iii. 128]

MACLAINE, ARCHIBALD (1722–1804), divine ; brother of James Maclaine [q. v.] ; co-pastor to the English church at the Hague, 1747–96 ; translated Mosheim's 'Ecclesiastical History,' 1765 (last reprint, 1825). [xxxv. 191]

MACLAINE or **MACLEAN**, JAMES (1724–1750), 'gentleman highwayman' ; spent his patrimony and took to the highway, 1748 ; arrested, 1750 ; tried and hanged. [xxxv. 191]

MACLAREN, ARCHIBALD (1755–1826), dramatist ; entered the army, 1755 ; served in the American war ; returned to Scotland ; on his discharge joined a troop of strolling players ; joined Dumbartonshire highlanders, 1794 ; discharged after serving in Guernsey and Ireland ; author of numerous dramatic pieces, two prose works describing the Irish rebellion, 1798–1800, and a few poems. [xxxv. 192]

MACLAREN, CHARLES (1782–1866), editor of the 'Scotsman' ; established the 'Scotsman,' 1817 ; editor, 1820–45 ; edited the sixth edition of the 'Encyclopædia Britannica,' 1823 ; published geological works. [xxxv. 194]

McLAREN, DUNCAN (1800–1886), politician ; member of the Edinburgh town council, 1833, provost, 1851–4 ; M.P., Edinburgh, 1865–81 ; wrote on political questions. [xxxv. 194]

McLAREN, WILLIAM (1772–1832), Scottish poet ; weaver, manufacturer, and tavern-keeper ; published verse, 1817 and 1827. [xxxv. 195]

MACLAUCHLAN, THOMAS (1816–1886), Scottish presbyterian divine, and Gaelic scholar ; M.A. Aberdeen, 1833 ; ordained, 1837 ; supported the non-intrusionists at the disruption, 1843 ; LL.D. Aberdeen, 1864 ; moderator of the Free Church Assembly, 1876 ; maintained the authenticity of Macpherson's Ossian ; edited the 'Book of the Dean of Lismore,' 1862. [xxxv. 195]

MACLAURIN, COLIN (1698–1746), mathematician and natural philosopher ; educated at Glasgow ; professor of mathematics in the Marischal College, Aberdeen, 1715–1726 ; F.R.S., 1719 ; deputy-professor at Edinburgh University, 1725 ; organised the defence of Edinburgh against the rebels, 1745 ; the one mathematician of first rank trained in Great Britain in the eighteenth century. His most noted works are ' Geometria Organica, sive Descriptio Linearum Curvarum Universalis,' 1720, 'A Treatise of Fluxions,' 1742, 'A Treatise of Algebra, with an Appendix De Linearum Geometricarum Proprietatibus Generalibus,' published, 1748, and 'An account of Sir Isaac Newton's Philosophy,' published, 1748. [xxxv. 196]

MACLAURIN, JOHN (1693–1754), presbyterian divine ; brother of Colin Maclaurin [q. v.] ; studied at Glasgow and Leyden ; ordained, 1719 ; a leader of the 'intrusionists' ; a famous preacher and controversialist ; his 'Sermons and Essays' published, 1755. [xxxv. 198]

MACLAURIN, JOHN, LORD DREGHORN (1734–1796), Scottish judge ; son of Colin Maclaurin [q. v.] ; educated at Edinburgh High School and University ; advocate, 1756 ; senator of the College of Justice, with the title Lord Dreghorn, 1788–96 ; published satirical poems and legal works. [xxxv. 198]

MACLEAN. [See also MACLAINE.]

MACLEAN, ALEXANDER (1840–1877), painter ; studied at Rome, Florence, and Antwerp ; exhibited at the Royal Academy, 1872–7. [xxxv. 199]

MACLEAN, ALLAN (1725–1784), colonel ; in the Scots brigade in the Dutch service ; taken prisoner, 1747 ; served in America, 1757–83 ; commanded the operations against Quebec, 1776–7 ; colonel, 1782. [xxxv. 199]

McLEAN, ARCHIBALD (1733–1812), baptist minister ; a printer and bookseller by trade ; successively a presbyterian and Sandemanian ; became a baptist minister, 1768 ; author of religious and controversial works (collected, 1823). [xxxv. 200]

MACLEAN, CHARLES (*fl.* 1788–1824), medical and political writer ; entered the service of the East India Company ; appointed surgeon to East Indiamen voyaging to Jamaica and India ; settled in Bengal, 1792 ; ordered to leave India for making an insinuation in an Indian newspaper against a magistrate, 1798 ; went to Hamburg and was forcibly detained by Napoleon, 1803 ; left the service on failing to obtain promotion ; travelled for the Levant Company, 1815–17 ; lecturer on the diseases of hot climates to the East India Company ; published medical works. [xxxv. 201]

McLEAN, SIR DONALD (1820–1877), New Zealand statesman ; emigrated to Sydney, *c.* 1837 ; went to New Zealand and devoted himself to the study of the Maori language ; local protector for the Taranaki district ; employed in difficult negotiations with the Maoris from 1844 ; resident magistrate for the Taranaki district, 1850 ; entered the legislative assembly, 1866 ; obtained the admittance of Maoris to the assembly, 1867 ; native minister and minister for colonial defence, 1869–76 ; brought about a final peace with the natives, 1870 ; K.C.M.G., 1874 ; died in New Zealand. [xxxv. 201]

MACLEAN, JOHN (1828–1886), first bishop of Saskatchewan ; M.A. Aberdeen, 1851 ; ordained, 1858, and went to Canada under the Colonial and Continental Church Society, 1858 ; archdeacon of Assiniboia, 1866 ; bishop of Saskatchewan, 1874 ; founder of the Alberta University. [xxxv. 202]

MACLEAN, JOHN (1835?–1890), actor ; first appeared on the stage at Plymouth, 1859 ; in London, 1861 ; thenceforth acted constantly at the Gaiety and other theatres. [xxxv. 203]

MACLEAN, SIR JOHN (1811–1895), archæologist ; entered ordnance department of war office, 1837 ; keeper of ordnance records in Tower of London, 1855–61, and deputy-chief auditor of army accounts, 1865–71 ; knighted, 1871 ; works include 'Parochial and Family History of Deanery of Trigg Minor,' 1868–79. [Suppl. iii. 129]

MACLEAN, MRS. LETITIA ELIZABETH (1802–1838). [See LANDON.]

MACLEAR, SIR THOMAS (1794–1879), astronomer; studied medicine in London; M.R.C.S., 1815; F.R.S., 1831; studied astronomy; royal astronomer at Cape of Good Hope, 1834–70; occupied with the re-measurement and extension of Lacaille's arc, 1837–47; made valuable astronomical, meteorological, magnetic, and tidal observations; knighted, 1860; became blind, 1876; his more important observations recorded in the 'Cape Catalogues'; died at Mowbray, Cape Town.   [xxxv. 204]

MACLEAY, ALEXANDER (1767–1848), entomologist and colonial statesman; chief clerk in the prisoners-of-war office, London, 1795; secretary of the transport board, 1806–18; F.R.S., 1809; colonial secretary for New South Wales, 1825–37; first speaker in the first legislative council, 1843–6; died at Sydney; possessed a fine collection of insects.   [xxxv. 205]

MACLEAY, SIR GEORGE (1809–1891), Australian explorer and statesman; son of Alexander Macleay [q. v.]; explored South Australia with Sturt; speaker of the legislative council of New South Wales, 1843–6; K.C.M.G., 1875.   [xxxv. 205]

MACLEAY, JAMES ROBERT (1811–1892), of the foreign office; son of Alexander Macleay [q. v.]; secretary and registrar to the British and Portuguese commission at the Cape of Good Hope for the suppression of the slave trade, 1843–58.   [xxxv. 205]

MACLEAY, KENNETH, the elder (*fl.* 1819), antiquary; physician in Glasgow; published 'Historical Memoirs of Rob Roy and the Clan MacGregor,' 1818.   [xxxv. 205]

MACLEAY, KENNETH, the younger (1802–1878), miniature-painter; son of Kenneth Macleay the elder [q. v.]; entered the Trustees' Academy, Edinburgh, 1822; one of the original members of the Royal Scottish Academy, founded, 1826; employed by Queen Victoria to paint figures illustrative of the highland clan costumes (selection published as 'Highlanders of Scotland,' 1870.)   [xxxv. 205]

MACLEAY, SIR WILLIAM (1820–1891), Australian statesman and naturalist; nephew of Alexander Macleay [q. v.]; emigrated to Australia, 1839; member of the legislative assembly, 1854–74; formed a valuable entomological museum, afterwards presented to the New South Wales University; member of the legislative council; knighted, 1889.   [xxxv. 206]

MACLEAY, WILLIAM SHARP (1792–1865), zoologist; son of Alexander Macleay [q. v.]; educated at Westminster and Trinity College, Cambridge; M.A., 1818; secretary to the board for liquidating British claims in France on the peace of 1815; commissary judge in Havana, 1830–7; went to New South Wales, 1839, where he enlarged his father's collection of insects; chief work, 'Horæ Entomologicæ,' propounding the circular or quinary system of classification, 2 vols., 1819 and 1821.   [xxxv. 206]

MACLEHOSE, MRS. AGNES (1759–1841), the 'Clarinda' of Robert Burns; *née* Craig; grandniece of Colin Maclaurin [q. v.]; married James Maclehose, a Glasgow lawyer, 1776; separated from him, 1780; moved to Edinburgh, 1782; first met Burns, 1787; entered into a familiar correspondence with him and sent him verses; her ambiguous relations with Burns were interrupted for a while by his marriage to Jean Armour, 1788, but were continued till 1791. Mrs. Maclehose went to Jamaica to join her husband, but soon returned, 1792; corresponded with Burns till 1794; the whole correspondence between Burns and herself published, 1843.   [xxxv. 207]

McLELLAN, ARCHIBALD (1797–1854), coach-builder and amateur of works of art; a leading Glasgow citizen. His collection of pictures forms the nucleus of the Corporation Galleries of Art at Glasgow.   [xxxv. 208]

MACLELLAN, JOHN (1609?–1651), of Kirkcudbright; covenanting minister; M.A. Glasgow, 1629; after ordination ministered in Ireland and Scotland; supposed to possess the gift of prophecy; prophesied the disaster of Hamilton's force in England, 1648; member of the assemblies' commissions, 1642, 1645, and 1649.   [xxxv. 209]

MACLELLAN, SIR ROBERT, of Bombie, first BARON KIRKCUDBRIGHT (*d.* 1641), succeeded his father as Baron of Bombie, 1608; gentleman of the bedchamber to James I

and Charles I; knighted by James I and created baronet by Charles I; created Baron Kirkcudbright (Scottish peerage), 1633; representative elder to the general assembly, 1638.   [xxxv. 209]

McLENNAN, JOHN FERGUSON (1827–1881), sociologist; educated at Aberdeen University and Trinity College, Cambridge; B.A., 1853; wrote for the 'Leader' for two years; called to the Scottish bar, 1857; contributed the article on 'Law' to the 'Encyclopædia Britannica' (8th edition), 1857; parliamentary draughtsman for Scotland, 1871; LL.D. Aberdeen, 1874; author of 'Primitive Marriage,' 1865, a book that gave immense impetus to research, and other works; originated theory that exogamy was the primitive form of marriage, polyandry and monandry being successive developments.   [xxxv. 210]

MACLEOD, ALEXANDER (1817–1891), presbyterian divine; educated at Glasgow University; ordained, 1844; D.D., 1865; moderator of the presbyterian church of England, 1889; author of articles and essays on religious subjects.   [xxxv. 211]

MACLEOD, ALLAN (*d.* 1805), political writer; editor and owner of the 'London Albion Journal'; author of virulent pamphlets.   [xxxv. 212]

McLEOD, SIR DONALD FRIELL (1810–1872), Indian administrator; son of Duncan Macleod [q. v.]; born at Calcutta; came to England, 1814; educated at Haileybury; returned to Calcutta, 1828; after holding subordinate posts became commissioner of the Trans-Sutlej states, 1849–54; at Lahore during the mutiny, 1857–8; lieutenant-governor of the Punjab, 1865–70; K.C.S.I., 1866.   [xxxv. 212]

McLEOD, DUNCAN (1780–1856), lieutenant-general; relative of Neil McLeod [q. v.]; second-lieutenant, Bengal engineers, 1795; chief engineer for Bengal; lieutenant-general, 1851.   [xxxv. 212]

MACLEOD, SIR GEORGE HUSBAND BAIRD (1828–1892), surgeon; son of Norman Macleod the elder [q. v.]; studied medicine at Glasgow (M.D., 1853), Paris, and Vienna; senior surgeon of the civil hospital at Smyrna during the Crimean war; regius professor of surgery, Glasgow, 1869; knighted, 1887.   [xxxv. 217]

McLEOD, JOHN (1777?–1820), naval surgeon and author; surgeon in the navy, 1801; on the Trusty, a slave trade boat, 1803; concerned in the capture of a French ship and tried for piracy; employed on foreign service till 1817; M.D. St. Andrews, 1818; surgeon to the Royal Sovereign yacht, 1818–20; published 'Narrative of a Voyage in His Majesty's late Ship Alceste to the Yellow Sea, along the coast of Corea,' 1817, and 'A Voyage to Africa, 1820.   [xxxv. 213]

MACLEOD, JOHN (1757–1841), presbyterian divine and Gaelic scholar; educated at Aberdeen University; ordained, 1779; D.D., 1795; superintended publication of Gaelic bible, 1826; general editor of the Gaelic dictionary, 1828.   [xxxv. 214]

MACLEOD, SIR JOHN MACPHERSON (1792–1881), Indian civilian; educated at Haileybury and Edinburgh University; writer in Madras civil service, 1811; commissioner (1832) for government of Mysore, of which province he organised the financial and political administration; K.C.S.I., 1866; privy councillor, 1871.   [Suppl. iii. 130]

MACLEOD, MARY (1569–1674), Gaelic poetess; called 'Poetess of the Isles'; her poems chiefly panegyrics of the Macleods.   [xxxv. 214]

MACLEOD, NEIL, eleventh of Assynt (1628?–1697?), betrayed Montrose to his enemies, 1650; imprisoned for having delivered up Montrose, 1660–6; pardoned, 1666; again imprisoned in consequence of a feud with the Mackenzies, 1672; tried on four charges, although acquitted on two; was deprived of his estates, 1690.   [xxxv. 214]

MACLEOD, SIR NORMAN (*fl.* 1650), founder of the Macleods of Bernera and Muiravonside; joined forces of Charles II, 1650; present at the battle of Worcester, 1651, and tried for high treason; escaped; was made lieutenant-colonel and employed by Charles II to carry information to his adherents; knighted at the Restoration.   [xxxv. 216]

MACLEOD, NORMAN, the elder (1783–1862), clergyman of the church of Scotland; ordained, 1806; D.D.

Glasgow, 1827; moderator of the general assembly, 1836; chaplain in ordinary to Queen Victoria, 1841; author of religious works in Gaelic and English.　　[xxxv. 216]

MACLEOD, NORMAN, the younger (1812–1872), Scottish divine; son of Norman Macleod the elder [q. v.]; studied divinity at Edinburgh, 1831; ordained, 1838; remained in the church at the disruption, 1843; one of the founders of the Evangelical Alliance, 1847; editor of the Edinburgh 'Christian Instructor,' 1849; chaplain to Queen Victoria, 1857–72; D.D. Glasgow, 1858; editor of 'Good Words,' 1860–72; made a tour in Palestine and published an account of it, entitled 'Eastward,' 1866; visited the mission stations in India, 1867; published 'Peeps at the Far East,' 1871.　　[xxxv. 217]

MACLEOD, RODERICK (d. 1852), physician; educated at Edinburgh University; M.D., 1816; F.R.C.P., 1836; Gulstonian lecturer, 1837; consiliarius, 1839; editor and proprietor of the 'London Medical and Physical Journal,' 1822.　　[xxxv. 219]

MACLIAC, MUIRCHEARTACH (d. 1015), Irish poet; chief poet to Brian (926–1014) [q. v.]; present at the battle of Clontarf, 1014; a legend of Carn Conaill in the 'Book of Leinster' is attributed to him and considered genuine.
　　[xxxv. 219]

MACLISE, DANIEL (1806–1870), historical painter; first studied art at the Cork Academy, 1822; unobserved made a clever drawing of Sir Walter Scott, while in a bookshop at Cork; opened a studio as a portrait-painter; went to London, 1827; came into notice in London by his portrait of Charles Kean, 1827; entered the Academy schools, 1828; exhibited at the Royal Academy, 1829–1870; contributed series of character portraits, including all the great literary men and women of the time, under the pseudonym of Alfred Croquis, to 'Fraser's Magazine,' 1830–8; R.A., 1840; occupied in painting the two frescoes in the Royal Gallery in the House of Lords, 'Wellington and Blücher at Waterloo' and 'The Death of Nelson,' 1857–66; refused presidency of Royal Academy; designed book illustrations for Tennyson (1860), and for some of his friend Dickens's Christmas books; his frescoes the greatest historical paintings of the English school.　　[xxxv. 219]

MACLONAN, FLANN (d. 896), Irish historian and poet; author of a poem contained in the 'Book of Leinster'; two other poems attributed to him.
　　[xxxv. 224]

MACMAHON, SIR CHARLES (1824–1891), captain; son of Sir William MacMahon [q. v.], in the army, 1842–1851; served in India and Canada, and (1851) attained a captaincy; entered the Melbourne police, 1853; chief commissioner till 1858; member of the legislative assembly at Melbourne, 1861–86; speaker, 1871–7 and 1880; knighted, 1875.　　[xxxv. 228]

MACMAHON, HEBER, EVER, or EMER, usually latinised as EMERUS MATTHEUS (1600–1650), bishop of Clogher and general in Ulster; educated at the Irish college, Douay, and at Louvain; ordained priest 1625; bishop of Clogher, 1643; a leader among the confederate catholics; general of the Ulster army against Cromwell, 1650; defeated at Scariffhollis, taken prisoner, and executed.　　[xxxv. 225]

MACMAHON, HUGH OGE (1606?–1644), Irish conspirator; joined the northern conspiracy, 1641; planned the assault on Dublin Castle, was betrayed by an accomplice, and arrested; imprisoned in Dublin and in the Tower of London; escaped, 1644; retaken, tried, and executed.　　[xxxv. 227]

MACMAHON, JOHN HENRY (1829–1900), scholar; M.A. Trinity College, Dublin, 1856; took holy orders, 1853; chaplain to lord-lieutenant, and, from 1890, to Mountjoy prison; published classical translations and other works.　　[Suppl. iii. 130]

McMAHON, THOMAS O'BRIEN (fl. 1777), Irish miscellaneous writer.　　[xxxv. 228]

MACMAHON, SIR THOMAS WESTROPP, third baronet (1813–1892), general; entered the army, 1829; served in the Sutlej campaign, 1846; major, 1847; served through the Crimean war; succeeded to baronetcy, 1860; general, 1880.　　[xxxv. 228]

MACMAHON, SIR WILLIAM, first baronet (1776–1837), Irish judge; called to the Irish bar, 1799; master of the rolls, 1814–37; received a baronetcy, 1814.
　　[xxxv. 228]

MACMANUS, TERENCE BELLEW (1823?–1860), Irish patriot; member of the '82 club, 1844; joined the 'physical force' movement, 1848; took part in the Tipperary civil war; arrested and transported to Van Diemen's Land, 1849; escaped (1852) to San Francisco, where he died.　　[xxxv. 229]

MACMICHAEL, WILLIAM (1784–1839), physician; of Christ Church, Oxford; M.A., 1807; Radcliffe travelling fellow, 1811; M.D., 1816; F.R.C.P., 1818; censor, 1822, registrar, 1824–9; published (1819) 'Journey from Moscow to Constantinople,' an account of his travels, 1814–17; published 'The Gold-headed Cane,' 1827; physician in ordinary to William IV, 1831; published also medical works.　　[xxxv. 229]

MACMILLAN, ANGUS (1810–1865), discoverer of Gippsland, Australia; emigrated to Australia, 1829; explored the country south-west of Sydney, afterwards called Gippsland, 1839–41; died in Australia.　[xxxv. 230]

MACMILLAN, DANIEL (1813–1857), bookseller and publisher; founder of the firm of Macmillan & Co., London; took service with a Cambridge bookseller, 1833–7, and with Messrs. Seeley of Fleet Street, London, 1837–43; set up for himself with his brother Alexander, at first in London, but soon re-settled at Cambridge, 1843; added publishing to the bookselling business at Cambridge, 1844; published Kingsley's 'Westward Ho!' 1855, and 'Tom Brown's School Days,' 1857.　　[xxxv. 230]

MACMILLAN, JOHN (1670–1753), founder of the reformed presbyterian church; studied at Edinburgh University; ordained, 1701; deposed for schismatical practices, 1703; retained his church and manse; resigned in order to terminate the insults to which his appointed successor was subjected, 1715; minister to the 'remnant' afterwards called Macmillanites, 1706–43; first pastor of the 'Reformed Presbyterians,' 1712; published controversial pamphlets.　　[xxxv. 231]

MACMOYER, FLORENCE (d. 1713), last keeper of the book of Armagh, written in 807; schoolmaster; pledged the 'Book of Armagh,' of which he was custodian, as a member of the Clan MacMoyre, to pay his expenses to London, 1680; a witness, probably perjured, at trial of Oliver Plunket [q. v.], 1681; imprisoned till after 1683; the 'Book of Armagh' was ultimately sold to Trinity College, Dublin.　　[xxxv. 233]

MACMURCHADA, DIARMAID (Dermod MacMurrough) (1110?–1171), king of Leinster, succeeding 1126; claimed the south of Ireland, 1134; ravaged the south with great cruelty and abducted Dervorgill, wife of the lord of Breifne, 1152; was defeated and banished by a combination of chieftains, 1166; his offer to become Henry II's vassal, if assisted in the restoration of his kingdom, accepted; returned to Ireland, 1167, having prevailed on Richard de Clare (Strongbow) to assist him, Henry II being unwilling to afford him direct help; took Waterford and Dublin with the aid of various Norman nobles; claimed to be king of all Ireland.　[xxxv. 233]

McMURDO, SIR WILLIAM MONTAGU SCOTT (1819–1894), general; studied at Sandhurst; lieutenant, 22nd foot, 1841; quartermaster-general in Scinde, 1842–1847; aide-de-camp to Sir Charles James Napier [q. v.], 1849; served against Afridis, 1851; brevet lieutenant-colonel, 1853; organised transport service in Crimea; aide-de-camp to Queen Victoria and brevet-colonel, 1855; C.B., 1857; colonel commandant of military train, 1857; lieutenant-general, 1876; general, 1878; K.C.B., 1881.　　[Suppl. iii. 130]

MACMURROGH or **MACMURCHAD**, ART (1357–1417), styled also CAVANAGH; Irish chief; descended from Donall, illegitimate son of Diarmaid or Dermod MacMurchada [q. v.]; frequently in arms against the English government for private reasons; a reward offered for his capture by Richard II.　　[xxxv. 236]

MACNAB, SIR ALLAN NAPIER, first baronet (1798–1862), Canadian soldier and politician; born at Newark, now Niagara, Ontario; joined the army and then the navy at the time of the American invasion, 1813–15; called to the Canadian bar, 1826; member of the House of Assembly, 1830, and speaker, 1837–41, 1844–8, and 1862; with the militia in the rebellion, 1837–8; knighted, 1838; created baronet, 1858.　　[xxxv. 236]

MACNAB, HENRY GRAY or GREY (1761–1823), publicist; studied medicine at Montpellier; prepared an educational scheme on Owenite lines, but died at Paris before it was put into practice; published works on education. [xxxv. 238]

McNAB, WILLIAM RAMSAY (1844–1889), botanist; M.D. Edinburgh, 1866; professor of botany, Dublin Royal College of Science, 1872–89; scientific superintendent of Royal Botanic Gardens, Glasnevin, and Swiney lecturer on geology at British Museum; author of botanical papers and text-books. [xxxv. 238]

MACNAGHTEN or **MACNAUGHTON**, JOHN (d. 1761), criminal; educated at Dublin University; sought to marry Miss Knox, an heiress of Prehen, Londonderry, and persuaded her to go through the ceremony with him; being forbidden to communicate with her by her family, he and his accomplices attacked the coach by which she was travelling to Dublin, and shot her; captured, tried, and hanged at Strabane. [xxxv. 238]

MACNAGHTEN, SIR WILLIAM HAY, first baronet (1793–1841), diplomatist; educated at Charterhouse School; went to India in the East India Company's service, 1809; studied Hindustani, Persian, and other Asiatic tongues; judge and magistrate of Shahabad, 1820; registrar of the Sudder Dewanny Adawlut for nine years; published works on Indian law, 1825–9; secretary to Lord William Bentinck, 1830–3; in charge of the secret and political departments of the secretariat, 1833–7; accompanied Lord Auckland to the north-west provinces, 1837; appointed envoy and minister to the Afghan court at Cabul, 1 Oct. 1838; accompanied expedition which placed Shah Soojah on Afghan throne; found difficulty in acting with the military authorities; created baronet and a provisional member of the council of India, 1840; nominated governor of Bombay, 1841; meanwhile rebellion broke out anew in Afghanistan, and Macnaghten unsuspectingly accepted the terms of the insurgents, which were not adhered to; he was shot at Cabul by Akbar Khan, the deposed ameer's son, at a meeting with the chiefs to discuss the situation. [xxxv. 239]

McNAIR, WILLIAM WATTS (1849–1889), traveller; joined Indian survey department, 1867; accompanied Aghan field force, 1879–80; attempted to visit Kafristan disguised as native doctor, but failed, 1883; continued his survey work; died at Mussooree. [xxxv. 243]

MACNALLY, LEONARD (1752–1820), playwright and political informer; called to the Irish bar, 1776; barrister, Middle Temple, 1783; edited 'The Public Ledger' and wrote plays; joined the United Irishmen, but secretly betrayed them to the government, 1794–1820; took briefs for the defence in government prosecutions, and disclosed their contents to the crown lawyers; his conduct only discovered after his death; author of dramatic pieces, legal works, and the song, 'Sweet Lass of Richmond Hill.' [xxxv. 243]

MACNAMARA, JAMES (1768–1826), rear-admiral; entered the navy, 1782; served on foreign stations; commander, 1793; served under Nelson, 1795–6; tried for manslaughter, having mortally wounded Colonel Montgomery in a duel, but was acquitted, 1803; served in the North Sea; rear-admiral, 1814. [xxxv. 244]

McNAMARA, THOMAS (1808–1892), Irish catholic divine; helped to establish Castleknock College, co. Dublin, 1834, and acted as its superior, 1804–8; rector of the Irish College in Paris, 1868–89; wrote works for the catholic clergy. [xxxv. 245]

MACNAUGHTON, JOHN (d. 1761). [See MACNAGHTEN.]

MACNEE, SIR DANIEL (1806–1882), portrait-painter; employed by William Home Lizars [q. v.]; an academician of the newly founded Royal Scottish Academy, 1830; portrait-painter at Glasgow, 1832; exhibited at the Royal Academy, 1840–81; president of the Royal Scottish Academy, 1876; knighted, 1877. [xxxv. 246]

McNEILE, HUGH (1795–1879), dean of Ripon; M.A. Trinity College, Dublin, 1821; D.D., 1847; ordained, 1820; canon of Chester, 1845–68; dean of Ripon, 1868–75; a strong evangelical; published sermons and religious works. [xxxv. 246]

McNEILL, DUNCAN, first BARON COLONSAY and ORONSAY (1793–1874), Scottish judge; educated at St.

Andrews and Edinburgh Universities; called to the Scottish bar, 1816; solicitor-general for Scotland, 1841–2; M.P., Argyllshire, 1843–51; lord advocate, 1842–1846; ordinary lord of session as Lord Colonsay and Oronsay, 1851; lord justice-general, 1852–67; created Baron Colonsay and Oronsay, 1867. [xxxv. 247]

MACNEILL, HECTOR (1746–1818), Scottish poet; filled a succession of subordinate posts with commercial firms in West Indies, 1761–76; assistant-secretary on board flagships in naval expeditions, 1780–6; subsequently failed to obtain remunerative employment; lived with friends, in Scotland and Jamaica; wrote, among other poems, 'Scotland's Scaith, or the History of Will and Jean,' 1795, and 'The Waes o' War, or the Upshot of the History of Will and Jean,' 1796. [xxxv. 248]

McNEILL, SIR JOHN (1795–1883), diplomatist; brother of Duncan McNeill, first baron Colonsay [q. v.]; M.D. Edinburgh, 1814; surgeon on the East India Company's Bombay establishment, 1816–36; envoy and minister plenipotentiary to the shah at Teheran, 1836; failed to prevent the shah from attacking the Afghans, 1838; eventually brought about treaty of commerce between Great Britain and Persia, 1841; chairman of the board of supervision of the working of the Scottish Poor Law Act, 1845–78; on commission of inquiry into the commissariat department and general organisation of troops in Crimea, 1855; privy councillor, 1857; died at Cannes. [xxxv. 249]

MACNEILL, SIR JOHN BENJAMIN (1793?–1880), civil engineer; one of Telford's chief assistants in road and bridge making; made known his plan of 'sectio-planography,' 1837; professor of civil engineering at Trinity College, Dublin, 1842–52; knighted, 1844; constructed railway lines in Scotland, and was surveyor to the Irish railway commission; on becoming blind withdrew from professional pursuits; author of works on engineering. [xxxv. 251]

MACNEVEN or **MACNEVIN**, WILLIAM JAMES (1763–1841), United Irishman; educated at Prague; studied medicine there and practised in Dublin, 1784; joined the United Irishmen, 1797; urged French intervention, and, his memorial falling into the hands of the English, was arrested, 1798; to allay the severity with which the government suppressed the rebellion, disclosed the conspiracy and offered to submit to banishment for life; eventually confined in Fort George, Scotland, till 1802; physician in New York, 1805; held various medical appointments in the College of Physicians and Surgeons there, 1808–39; champion of the Irish in America; died at New York. [xxxv. 252]

MACNICOL, DONALD (1735–1802), presbyterian divine and author; graduated at St. Andrews, 1756; published a defence of the highlands against Dr. Johnson's 'Journey to the Hebrides,' 1779. [xxxv. 253]

MACNISH, ROBERT (1802–1837), author and physician; M.D. Glasgow, 1825; contributed his one masterpiece in fiction, 'The Metempsychosis,' to 'Blackwood,' 1826; published 'The Philosophy of Sleep,' 1830. [xxxv. 253]

MACONOCHIE, afterwards **MACONOCHIE-WELWOOD**, ALEXANDER, LORD MEADOWBANK (1777–1861), Scottish judge; son of Allan Maconochie [q. v.]; admitted advocate, 1799; solicitor-general, 1813; lord-advocate, 1816; M.P., Yarmouth, Isle of Wight, 1817–18, Kilrenny district of burghs, 1818–19; raised to the Scottish bench as Lord Meadowbank, 1819; resigned, 1843; assumed the additional surname of Welwood on succeeding to his cousin's estates, 1854. [xxxv. 254]

MACONOCHIE, ALLAN, LORD MEADOWBANK (1748–1816), Scottish judge; educated at Edinburgh University; admitted advocate, 1770; professor of public law, Edinburgh, 1779–96; took his seat on the Scottish bench as Lord Meadowbank, 1796; author of legal and agricultural works. [xxxv. 256]

MACPHAIL, JAMES (fl. 1785–1805), gardener; invented a new method of growing cucumbers; published horticultural works. [xxxv. 257]

MACPHERSON, DAVID (1746–1816), historian and compiler; deputy-keeper in London of public records; edited Wyntoun's 'Orygynal Cronykil of Scotland,' 1795; assisted in preparing for publication 'Rotuli Scotiæ' (vol. i. and part of vol. ii.) [xxxv. 258]

MACPHERSON, DUNCAN (*d.* 1867), army surgeon and writer; surgeon to the army in Madras, 1836, in China, 1840-2, in Russia, 1855; inspector-general of the medical service of Madras, 1857; chief work, 'Antiquities of Kertch and Researches in the Cimmerian Bosphorus,' 1857; died at Merkára, Coorg. [xxxv. 258]

MACPHERSON, EWEN (*d.* 1756), of Cluny; Jacobite; before the outbreak of the rebellion supported the government, but on being pressed joined Prince Charles Edward, 1745; helped the prince to escape; fled to France, 1755; died at Dunkirk. [xxxv. 258]

MACPHERSON, EWEN (1804-1884), son of Ewen Macpherson (*d.* 1756) [q. v.]; captain in the 42nd highlanders; interested himself in the highland volunteer movement; C.B. [xxxv. 260]

MACPHERSON, SIR HERBERT TAYLOR (1827-1886), major-general, Bengal staff corps; served under Havelock at Lucknow, gaining the V.C., 1857; transferred to the Indian army, 1865; commanded a division in the Afghan war, 1878-9; K.C.B., 1879; major-general and present at Tel-el-Kebir, 1882; commander-in-chief at Madras, 1886; sent to organise the pacification of Burmah, 1886; fell ill and died on his way from Prome to Rangoon. [xxxv. 260]

MACPHERSON, JAMES (*d.* 1700), the Banff freebooter; of gipsy parentage; wandered about Scotland with his mother till captured, 1700; executed on the charge of 'going up and doune the country armed'; said to have played a 'rant' before his execution, the words of which are—probably wrongly—attributed to him. [xxxv. 261]

MACPHERSON, JAMES (1736-1796), the alleged translator of the Ossianic poems; studied at Aberdeen and Edinburgh Universities; said to have composed over four thousand verses while at college; published 'The Highlander,' 1758, and 'Fragments of Ancient Poetry collected in the Highlands,' 1760; issued two epic poems, 'Fingal,' 1762, and 'Temora,' 1763, which he alleged to be translated from the Gaelic of a poet called Ossian; was generally believed to have wholly invented the poems; never seriously rebutted the charge of forgery; attacked by Dr. Johnson in his 'Journey to the Western Islands of Scotland,' 1775; secretary to the governor of Pensacola, West Florida, 1764-6; published 'Original Papers containing the Secret History of Great Britain from the Restoration till the Accession of George I,' 1775; employed by North's ministry to defend their American policy, from 1766; M.P., Camelford, 1780-96; London agent to Mohammed Ali, nabob of Arcot, 1781. After Macpherson's death a committee was appointed by the Highland Society of Scotland to investigate the Ossianic poems, 1797. They reported that while a great legend of Fingal and Ossian existed in Scotland, Macpherson had liberally edited his originals and inserted passages of his own. Subsequent investigation has confirmed the committee's conclusions. [xxxv. 261]

MACPHERSON, JOHN (1710-1765), presbyterian minister; M.A. Aberdeen, 1728; D.D., 1761; work on the 'Ancient Caledonians,' published, 1768. [xxxv. 267]

MACPHERSON, SIR JOHN, first baronet (1745-1821), governor-general of India; educated at Edinburgh University; writer under the East India Company at Madras, 1770-6; dismissed in consequence of his conduct while on a secret mission to England for the nabob of the Carnatic in 1768, 1777; reinstated, 1781; M.P., Cricklade, 1779-82, Horsham, 1796-1802; member of the supreme council at Calcutta, 1782; governor-general of India, 1785-6; created baronet, 1786. [xxxv. 267]

MACPHERSON, JOHN (1817-1890), physician; brother of Samuel Charters Macpherson [q. v.] and of William Macpherson [q. v.]; M.A. and hon. M.D. Aberdeen; studied medicine in London and abroad, 1835-9; member Royal College of Surgeons, 1839; in the East India Company's service, 1839-64, becoming inspector-general of hospitals; published medical works. [xxxv. 269]

MACPHERSON, PAUL (1756-1846), Scottish abbé; studied at the Scots Colleges in Rome and Valladolid; procurator of the mission in Scotland, 1791; agent of the Scottish clergy at Rome, 1793-8 and 1800-11; first Scottish rector of the Scots College in Rome, 1820-6 and 1834-46; died at Rome. [xxxv. 269]

MACPHERSON, SAMUEL CHARTERS (1806-1860), political agent in India; brother of John Macpherson (1817-1890) [q. v.] and of William Macpherson [q. v.]; studied at Edinburgh University and at Trinity College, Cambridge; entered the Indian army, 1827; despatched to obtain information about the Khonds in Gumsur, 1837-9; principal assistant to the agent, completely reforming the tribe, 1842-4; governor-general's agent for suppression of human sacrifice in Orissa, 1845; agent at Gwalior; prevented Gwalior tribes from joining the mutiny, 1857; died in India. [xxxv. 270]

MACPHERSON, WILLIAM (1812-1893), legal writer; brother of John Macpherson (1817-1890) [q. v.], and of Samuel Charters Macpherson [q. v.]; of Charterhouse School and Trinity College, Cambridge; barrister, Inner Temple, 1837; M.A., 1838; master of equity in the supreme court, Calcutta, 1848-59; edited the 'Quarterly Review,' 1860-7; secretary to the Indian law commission, 1861-70; in the India office as legal adviser, 1874-9, and as secretary in the judicial department, 1879-82; chief work, 'Procedure of the Civil Courts of India,' 1850. [xxxv. 271]

MACQUARIE, LACHLAN (*d.* 1824), major-general and governor of New South Wales; entered the army, 1777; served in America and Jamaica, 1777-84, India, China, and Egypt, 1787-1807; governor of New South Wales, 1809-21; personally encouraged exploration in the colony; his administration attacked at home for his efforts on behalf of the convict population. [xxxv. 271]

MACQUEEN, JAMES (1778-1870), geographer; manager of a sugar plantation in the West Indies, 1796; a student of African geography; edited 'Glasgow Courier,' 1821; wrote in London on politics, geography, economics, and general literature. [xxxv. 273]

MACQUEEN, JOHN FRASER (1803-1881), lawyer; barrister, Lincoln's Inn, 1838; bencher, 1861; official reporter of Scottish and divorce appeals in the House of Lords, 1860-79; compiled 4 vols. of appellate reports, 1801-5; Q.C., 1861; published legal works. [xxxv. 274]

MACQUEEN, ROBERT, LORD BRAXFIELD (1722-1799), Scottish judge; educated at Edinburgh University; admitted advocate, 1744; ordinary lord of session as Lord Braxfield, 1776; lord of justiciary, 1780; lord justice clerk, 1788; expert in feudal law. [xxxv. 274]

MACQUIN, ANGE DENIS (1756-1823), abbé and miscellaneous writer; born at Meaux; professor of belles-lettres and rhetoric at Meaux; came to England, 1792; heraldic draughtsman to the College of Arms, 1793; published works on heraldry and other subjects. [xxxv. 275]

MACRAE, JAMES (1677?-1744), governor of Madras; went to sea, 1692; subsequently served under the East India Company; governor of Madras, 1725; effected reforms in the fiscal administration; settled in Scotland, 1731. [xxxv. 276]

MACREADY, WILLIAM CHARLES (1793-1873), actor; educated at Rugby; made his first appearance at Birmingham as Romeo, 1810; acted in the provinces with his father's company, at Newcastle playing with Mrs. Siddons; first appeared at Covent Garden, London, 1816; raised by his Richard III to the undisputed head of the theatre, 1819; quarrelled with the management of Covent Garden, and began to play at Drury Lane, 1823; acted in America, 1826-7, and in Paris, 1828; manager of Covent Garden, 1837-9; produced the 'Lady of Lyons,' 1838; at the Haymarket, 1839-41; manager of Drury Lane, 1841-3; visited America, 1843; played in Paris with Miss Helen Faucit; while in America (1848) was involved in an unfortunate quarrel with the actor Forrest, which caused a riot; obliged to leave the country in consequence; took leave of the stage as Macbeth at Drury Lane, 1851; called by Talfourd 'the most romantic of actors'; his impersonation of King Lear still held to be unrivalled. [xxxv. 277]

MACRO, COX (1683-1767), antiquary; educated at Christ's College, Cambridge (LL.B., 1710), and Leyden University; chaplain to George II; D.D. Cambridge, 1717; collected valuable antiquities, books, paintings, coins, and medals. [xxxv. 283]

MACSPARRAN, JAMES (*d.* 1757), writer on America; M.A. Glasgow, 1709; ordained, 1720; sent as a missionary to Narragansett, Rhode island, 1721, and ministered there till his death; visited England, 1736 and

1754–6; made D.D. Oxford as a recognition of his efforts against the dissenters, 1737; warned intending colonists against emigrating to America in 'America Dissected,' 1753. [xxxv. 284]

MACSWINNY, OWEN (*d.* 1754). [See SWINNY.]

MACTAGGART, JOHN (1791–1830), encyclopædist and versifier; studied at Edinburgh; clerk of works to Rideau canal, Canada, 1826–8; published 'Scottish Gallovidian Encyclopedia,' 1824, and 'Three Years in Canada,' 1829. [xxxv. 285]

MACVICAR, JOHN GIBSON (1800–1884), author; educated at St. Andrews and Edinburgh Universities; lecturer in natural history at St. Andrews, 1827; pastor of the Scottish Church in Ceylon, 1839–52; published scientific works. [xxxv. 285]

MACWARD or **MACUARD,** ROBERT (1633?–1687), covenanting minister; studied at St. Andrews University; ordained, 1654; preached in support of the covenant, 1661; banished to Holland; died at Rotterdam; published religious pamphlets. [xxxv. 286]

McWILLIAM, JAMES ORMISTON (1808–1862), medical officer to the Niger expedition; surgeon in the navy, 1830; M.D. Edinburgh, 1840; appointed senior surgeon (1840) on the Albert, one of the ships which joined the Niger expedition; practically saved his own ship when a fever broke out among the members of the expedition at the mouth of the Niger and their return was necessary, 1841; published his 'Medical History of the Niger Expedition,' 1843; sent to the Cape de Verde islands to study the yellow fever; medical officer to the custom house, 1847–62; F.R.S., 1848. [xxxv. 287]

MADAN, MARTIN (1726–1790), author of 'Thelyphthora'; educated at Westminster School and Christ Church, Oxford; B.A., 1746; barrister, 1748; adopted methodist principles after hearing a sermon by Wesley; ordained; became chaplain of the Lock Hospital, 1750–80; in close connection with Lady Huntingdon; corresponded with John Wesley; published 'Thelyphthora,' a book in favour of polygamy, 1780, which excited public indignation, the poet Cowper being among its assailants; author of religious works. [xxxv. 288]

MADAN, SPENCER (1729–1813), bishop successively of Bristol and Peterborough; younger brother of Martin Madan [q. v.]; of Westminster and Trinity College, Cambridge; M.A., 1753; fellow, 1753; D.D., 1756; chaplain in ordinary to the king, 1761–87; bishop of Bristol, 1792–1794, of Peterborough, 1794–1813. [xxxv. 290]

MADAN, SPENCER (1758–1836), translator of Grotius; son of Spencer Madan (1729–1813) [q. v.]; of Westminster School and Trinity College, Cambridge; M.A., 1778; chaplain in ordinary to the king, 1788; prebendary of Peterborough, 1800; D.D., 1809; published translation of Grotius's 'De Veritate,' 1782. [xxxv. 291]

MADDEN, SIR FREDERIC (1801–1873), antiquary and palæographer; nephew of Sir George Allan Madden [q. v.]; collated manuscripts of Cædmon for Oxford University, 1825; engaged on the British Museum 'Catalogue,' 1826–8; assistant-keeper of manuscripts, 1828; head of the department, 1837–66; F.R.S., 1830; an original member of the Athenæum Club, 1830; knighted, 1833; edited 'Layamon's Brut,' 1847, and 'Wyclif's Bible,' 1850. [xxxv. 291]

MADDEN, SIR GEORGE ALLAN (1771–1828), major-general in the British and Portuguese armies; entered the army, 1788; served in Italy, Corsica, and Portugal, 1793–5; in Egypt, 1801; tried by court-martial for perjury, 1801; had to resign his commission, 1802; brigadier-general in the Portuguese army, 1809; served with the Spanish troops, 1810–13; reinstated in the British army, 1813; knighted, 1816; major-general in the British army, 1819. [xxxv. 292]

MADDEN, RICHARD ROBERT (1798–1886), miscellaneous writer; studied medicine at Paris, Naples, and London; one of the special magistrates appointed to administer statute abolishing slavery in Jamaica plantations, 1833–41; superintendent of liberated Africans, and judge-arbitrator in the mixed court of commission, Havana, 1836–40; special commissioner on the west coast of Africa, 1841–3; special correspondent of the 'Morning Chronicle,' 1843–6; colonial secretary of Western Australia, 1847–50;

secretary to the Loan Fund Board, Dublin Castle, 1850–80; F.R.C.S., 1855; best-known work, 'The United Irishmen, their Lives and Times,' 7 vols. 1843–6. [xxxv. 295]

MADDEN, SAMUEL (1686–1765), miscellaneous writer and philanthropist; B.A. Dublin, 1705; D.D., 1723; ordained and held cures; organised the system of premiums in Dublin University, 1730; chief work, 'Reflections and Resolutions proper for the Gentlemen of Ireland as to their conduct for the service of their country,' 1738. [xxxv. 296]

MADDISON or **MADDESTONE,** SIR RALPH (1571?–1655?), economic writer; knighted, 1603; member of the royal commission on the woollen trade, 1622; held office in the mint during the Commonwealth; author of 'England's Looking in and out: presented to the High Court of Parliament now assembled,' a clear statement of the theory of the balance of trade, 1640. [xxxv. 297]

MADDOCK, HENRY (*d.* 1824), legal author; educated at St. John's College, Cambridge; barrister, Lincoln's Inn, 1801; died at St. Lucia in the West Indies; chief work, 'A Treatise on the ... High Court of Chancery,' 2 vols. 1815. [xxxv. 298]

MADDOX, ISAAC (1697–1759), bishop of Worcester; M.A. Edinburgh, 1723; ordained, 1723; B.A. Queen's College, Oxford, 1724; M.A. Queens' College, Cambridge, 1728; published his best-known work, a 'Vindication' of the Elizabethan settlement of the church of England, 1733; dean of Wells, 1734; bishop of St. Asaph, 1736, of Worcester, 1743. [xxxv. 298]

MADDOX, WILLIS (1813–1853), painter; exhibited at the Royal Academy, 1844–52; invited to Constantinople to paint the sultan; died at Pera. [xxxv. 299]

MADDY, WATKIN (*d.* 1857), astronomer; of St. John's College, Cambridge; M.A., 1823; fellow, 1823; B.D., 1830; joined Cambridge Astronomical Society; published 'The Elements of the Theory of Plane Astronomy,' 1826. [xxxv. 299]

MADERTY, first BARON (1540?–1623). [See DRUMMOND, JAMES.]

MADGETT or **MADGET,** NICHOLAS (*fl.* 1799), Irish adventurer; in the French foreign office, 1794; supported scheme for French expedition to Ireland, 1796; member of a 'secret committee for managing the affairs of Ireland and Scotland,' 1798; wrongly identified with another Maget, an Irish priest. [xxxv. 300]

MADOCKS, WILLIAM ALEXANDER (1774–1828), philanthropist; M.A. Christ Church, Oxford, 1799; reclaimed marsh land in Carnarvonshire and founded the town of Tremadoc; M.P., Boston, Lincolnshire, 1802–20, Chippenham, 1820–8; died in Paris. [xxxv. 300]

MADOG AP **MAREDUDD** (*d.* 1160), prince of Powys; nephew of Iorwerth ab Bleddyn [q. v.]; prince of Powys during the reign of Stephen; allied himself with the English to protect his own domains; defeated in battle by the Prince of Gwynedd; probably had a secret understanding with Henry II. [xxxv. 301]

MADOG AB **OWAIN GWYNEDD** (1150–1180?), supposed discoverer of America; said in a Welsh poem of the fifteenth century to have gone to sea in ten ships and never returned. Dr. David Powel, who published Llwyd's translation of the 'Brut y Tywysogion,' 1584, with additions of his own, declared that Madog, after leaving Ireland to the north, came to a land which must have been Florida or New Spain. The story, which is unsupported by evidence, is the subject of Southey's poem of 'Madoc.' [xxxv. 302]

MADOG AP **GRUFFYDD MAELOR** (*d.* 1236), prince of Northern Powys; ruler of Northern Powys, 1197; an ally of Llywelyn ab Iorwerth [q. v.]; founded Valle Crucis Abbey, 1200. [xxxv. 303]

MADOG (*fl.* 1294–1295), leader of the North Welsh rebellion; in consequence of heavy taxation rose in rebellion with many of the Welsh, 1294; forced to submit by Edward I, 1295. [xxxv. 304]

MADOG BENFRAS (i.e. GREATHEAD) (*fl.* 1350), Welsh poet; prominent with his brothers in the revival of Welsh poetry. [xxxv. 304]

MADOX, THOMAS (1666–1727), legal antiquary; sworn clerk in the lord-treasurer's office; joint-clerk in the augmentation office, and published his 'Formulare Anglicanum,' 1702, his 'History and Antiquities of the Exchequer of the Kings of England,' 1711, one of his best-known works; historiographer royal, 1714. [xxxv. 305]

MAEL, SAINT (d. 487). [See MEL.]

MAEL-DUBH (d. 675 ?). [See MAILDULF.]

MAELGARBH (d. 544). [See TUATHAL.]

MAELGWN GWYNEDD (d. 550 ?), British king; possibly the 'Maglocune' of Gildas; according to tradition succeeded to the throne by overthrowing an uncle; probably died of the 'yellow pestilence.' [xxxv. 305]

MAELMURA (d. 886), Irish historian; monk of Fahan; one of his historical poems preserved in the 'Book of Leinster.' [xxxv. 306]

MAELSECHLAINN I (d. 863), king of Ireland; succeeded his father, 842; defeated the Danes, 844 and 847; thrice invaded Munster; again defeated the Danes, 859. [xxxv. 307]

MAELSECHLAINN II (949–1022), king of Ireland; chief of his clan, 979; became king of all Ireland, 980; defeated the Danes, 980 and 1000; recognised the superiority of Brian (926–1014) [q. v.] as king, 1002; regained his kingship on Brian's death in the battle of Cluantarbh (Clontarf), in which the Danes were finally overthrown, 1014. [xxxv. 308]

MAGAN, FRANCIS (1772 ?–1843), Irish informer; graduated at Trinity College, Dublin, 1794; admitted to the Irish bar, 1793; acted as government spy on Lord Edward Fitzgerald (1763–1798) [q. v.], 1798; elected member of the committee of United Irishmen on the night of Fitzgerald's arrest; commissioner for enclosing waste lands and commons, 1821; had a secret pension from government until 1834. [xxxv. 309]

MAGAURAN, EDMUND (1548–1593), Roman catholic archbishop of Armagh; educated abroad; sent on a mission to the pope by the Irish chiefs, 1581; bishop of Ardagh, 1581; archbishop of Armagh and primate of all Ireland, 1587; went to Spain and obtained from Philip II a promise of help for the Irish against Queen Elizabeth, 1592; instigated a rebellion; killed in an engagement with Elizabeth's troops. [xxxv. 310]

MAGEE, JAMES (d. 1866), Irish journalist; son of John Magee (d. 1809) [q. v.]; conducted the 'Dublin Evening Post' from 1815; was subsequently a Dublin police magistrate. [xxxv. 313]

MAGEE, JOHN (d. 1809), Irish journalist and colliery broker; proprietor and printer of 'Magee's Weekly Packet,' 1777, of the 'Dublin Evening Post,' 1779; opposed government measures in his paper; tried for libel on Francis Higgins (1746–1802) [q. v.] and found guilty, 1789; imprisoned in Newgate, Dublin. [xxxv. 311]

MAGEE, JOHN (fl. 1814), son of John Magee (d. 1809) [q. v.]; carried on the 'Dublin Evening Post'; convicted of libel and imprisoned, 1813 and 1814; defended by Daniel O'Connell. [xxxv. 312]

MAGEE, MARTHA MARIA (d. 1846), foundress of the Magee College, Londonderry; daughter of Mr. Stewart of Lurgan, co. Armagh; married (1780) William Magee (d. 1800), presbyterian minister; inherited a fortune from her brothers; left 20,000l. to erect and endow a college for the education of the Irish presbyterian ministry (Magee College, opened, 1865). [xxxv. 313]

MAGEE, WILLIAM (1766–1831), archbishop of Dublin; educated at Trinity College, Dublin; B.A., 1785; fellow, 1788; ordained, 1790; Donellan lecturer, 1795; professor of mathematics, Trinity College, Dublin, 1800; published sermons, delivered (1798 and 1799) in Trinity College Chapel as 'Discourses on the Scriptural Doctrines of Atonement and Sacrifice,' 1801; dean of Cork, 1813–19; bishop of Raphoe, 1819–22; archbishop of Dublin, 1822–31; rendered considerable services to the Irish church; his 'Works published, 1842. [xxxv. 313]

MAGEE, WILLIAM CONNOR (1821–1891), successively bishop of Peterborough and archbishop of York; grandson of William Magee [q. v.]; entered Trinity College, Dublin, 1835; M.A., 1854; ordained, 1845; held various livings in England and Ireland, 1845–64; D.D. Dublin, 1860; dean of Cork, 1864–8; Donnellan lecturer at Trinity College, Dublin, 1865; dean of the Chapel Royal,

Dublin, 1866–8; bishop of Peterborough, 1868–91; opposed Irish disestablishment; honorary D.C.L. Oxford, 1870; archbishop of York, 1891; one of the greatest orators and most brilliant controversialists of his day; published speeches, addresses, and sermons. [xxxv. 315]

MAGELLAN or **MAGALHAENS**, JEAN HYACINTHE DE (1723–1790), scientific investigator; descendant of the Portuguese navigator who discovered Magellan Straits in 1520; born probably at Talavera; Augustinian monk; abandoned monastic life for scientific research, 1763; reached England, 1764; F.R.S., 1774; published work on English reflecting instruments, 1775; engaged in perfecting the construction of scientific instruments; published descriptions of them, and the memoirs of his friend the Hungarian Count de Benyowsky (posthumous, 1791). [xxxv. 317]

MAGEOGHEGAN, CONALL (fl. 1635), Irish historian; translated 'The Annals of Clonmacnois,' 1627. [xxxv. 318]

MAGHERAMORNE, first BARON (1823–1890). [See HOGG, SIR JAMES MACNAGHTEN McGAREL.]

MAGILL, ROBERT (1788–1839), Irish presbyterian clergyman; M.A. Glasgow, 1817; licensed to preach, 1818; his best-known work, 'The Thinking Few,' 1828. [xxxv. 319]

MAGINN, EDWARD (1802–1849), Irish catholic prelate; educated at the Irish College, Paris; ordained priest, 1825; agitated for the repeal of the union, 1829; coadjutor to the bishop of Derry and nominated bishop of Ortosia in the archbishopric of Tyre, in partibus infidelium, 1845; D.D. [xxxv. 319]

MAGINN, WILLIAM (1793–1842), poet, journalist, and miscellaneous writer; educated at Trinity College, Dublin; B.A., 1811; LL.D., 1819; contributed to 'Blackwood's Magazine,' 1819–28 and 1834–42; in Edinburgh, 1821–3; settled in London, 1823; joint-editor of the 'Standard'; contributed to the 'Age'; established 'Fraser's Magazine,' 1830, his 'Gallery of Literary Characters' being its most popular feature; his masterpiece in humorous fiction, 'Bob Burke's Duel with Ensign Brady,' 1834; published his 'Homeric Ballads' in 'Fraser,' 1838; published reproductions of Lucian's dialogues in the form of blank-verse comedies, 1839; his health ruined after imprisonment for debt; the original of Thackeray's 'Captain Shandon.' [xxxv. 320]

MAGLORIUS, SAINT (495 ?–575), second bishop of Dol in Brittany; educated in the college of St. Illtyd at Llantwit Major; placed at the head of one of the religious communities of St. Sampson [q. v.], near Dol; ordained priest and bishop; episcopal abbot there; retired to Jersey, where his hermitage grew into a monastery; his relics removed to Paris in the tenth century. [xxxv. 323]

MAGNUS, THOMAS (d. 1550), ambassador; archdeacon of the East Riding of Yorkshire, 1504; employed on diplomatic missions, 1509–19 and 1524–7; present at the Field of the Cloth of Gold, 1520; privy councillor, c. 1520; incorporated in a doctor's degree at Oxford, 1520; canon of Windsor. 1520–49; prebendary of Lincoln, 1522–1548; paymaster of the forces and treasurer of the wars in the north, 1523; custodian of St. Leonard's Hospital, York, 1529. [xxxv. 324]

MAGRAIDAN, AUGUSTIN (1349–1405). [See MACGRADOIGH.]

MAGRATH, JOHN MACRORY, in Irish Eoghan MacRuadhri MacCraith (fl. 1459), Irish historian; one of a family of hereditary men of letters; chief historian to the Dal Cais in Thomond; author of 'Cathreim Thoirdhealbhaigh,' a history of the wars of Thomond, of which the best existing copy is by Andrew MacCuirtin [q. v.] [xxxv. 325]

MAGRATH, MEILER (1523 ?–1622), archbishop of Cashel; became a Franciscan friar; lived, when young, in Rome; bishop of Clogher, 1570–1; archbishop of Cashel and bishop of Emly, 1571; attacked by James Fitzmaurice Fitzgerald (d. 1579) [q. v.] for imprisoning friars, 1571–80; continued to serve the government, though intriguing with rebels; bishop of Waterford and Lismore, 1582–1607; received sees of Killala and Achonry, 1611; according to Sir John Davies, 'a notable example of pluralities.' [xxxv. 325]

MAGUIRE, CATHAL MACMAGHNUSA (1439–1498), Irish historian; archdeacon of Clogher, 1483; collected a fine library of manuscripts, and compiled 'The Historical Book of Ballymacmanus' ('Annals of Ulster,' 60–1498); according to Paul Harris [q. v.], author of additions to the 'Felire' of Oengus and annotations to the 'Register of Clogher.' [xxxv. 327]

MAGUIRE, CONNOR or CORNELIUS, second BARON OF ENNISKILLEN (1616–1645), succeeded to peerage, 1634; inveigled by Roger More [q. v.] into taking part in catholic conspiracy, 1641, which was discovered through the folly of Hugh Oge MacMahon [q. v.]; imprisoned in the Tower of London and subsequently in Newgate; tried and sentenced to be hanged, drawn, and quartered.
[xxxv. 328]

MAGUIRE, HUGH, LORD OF FERMANAGH (d. 1600), implicated in a plot with Hugh O'Neill, second earl of Tyrone [q. v.]; succeeded to estates of Fermanagh, 1589; declared by the lord-deputy of Ireland to be a traitor; invaded Connaught; driven back by Sir Richard Bingham [q. v.]; slain in Tyrone's expedition into Munster and Leinster. [xxxv. 329]

MAGUIRE, JOHN FRANCIS (1815–1872), Irish politician; called to the Irish bar, 1843; journalist; founded (1841) and conducted 'Cork Examiner'; M.P., Dungarvan, 1852, Cork, 1865–72; acted with the Independent Irishmen; took prominent part in debates on the Irish land question; upheld the papacy and published 'Rome and its Ruler,' for which the pope named him knight commander of St. Gregory, 1856; issued third edition as 'The Pontificate of Pius IX,' 1870; published also miscellaneous works. [xxxv. 330]

MAGUIRE, NICHOLAS (1460?–1512), bishop of Leighlin; educated at Oxford; bishop of Leighlin, 1490; completed the 'Chronicon Hiberniæ' and 'Vita Milonis Episcopi Leighlinensis.' [xxxv. 331]

MAGUIRE, ROBERT (1826–1890), controversialist; educated at Trinity College, Dublin; clerical secretary to the Islington Protestant Institute, 1852; M.A., 1855; D.D., 1877; a popular preacher and lecturer; published addresses and sermons. [xxxv. 332]

MAGUIRE, THOMAS (1792–1847), Roman catholic controversialist; educated at Maynooth College; ordained, 1816; held various livings; engaged in platform discussions, of which 'Authenticated Reports' appeared in 1827 and 1839. [xxxv. 332]

MAGUIRE, THOMAS (1831–1889), classical scholar and metaphysician; first Roman catholic fellow of Trinity College, Dublin; educated at Trinity College; B.A., 1855; obtained law studentship at Lincoln's Inn, 1861; barrister, Lincoln's Inn, 1862; LL.D. Dublin, 1868; after 'Fawcett's Act' of 1873 was elected to a fellowship at Trinity College, Dublin, 1880; professor, classical composition (chair specially created), till 1882; professor of moral philosophy, 1882–9; took part in discussion concerning the 'Pigott letters' [see PIGOTT, RICHARD]; published philosophical works, including 'Essays on the Platonic Idea,' 1866, and translations. [xxxv. 333]

MAHOMED, FREDERICK HENRY HORATIO AKBAR (1849–1884), physician; son of the keeper of a Turkish bath; studied at Guy's Hospital, London; M.R.C.S., 1872; resident medical officer at the London Fever Hospital; medical tutor at St. Mary's Hospital, London, 1875; M.D. Brussels; medical registrar at Guy's, London; entered Caius College, Cambridge, going up to Cambridge every night to keep his term; F.R.C.P., 1880; M.B. Cambridge and assistant-physician to Guy's Hospital, London, 1881; contributed to medical periodicals.
[xxxv. 333]

MAHON, VISCOUNT (1805–1875). [See STANHOPE, PHILIP HENRY, fifth EARL STANHOPE.]

MAHON, CHARLES JAMES PATRICK, better known as THE O'GORMAN MAHON (1800–1891), Irish politician; educated at Trinity College, Dublin; M.A., 1826; urged O'Connell to wrest Clare from William Vesey Fitzgerald [q. v.] when Fitzgerald became president of the board of trade in 1828; failed to gain the seat himself in 1831, quarrelling with O'Connell in consequence; M.P., Ennis, 1847–52; lived a life of adventure under many flags 1852–71; as a supporter of Charles Stewart Parnell [q. v.] was M.P. for Clare, 1879–85; sat for Carlow, 1887–91, repudiating Parnell in 1890. [xxxv. 334]

MAHONY, CONNOR, CORNELIUS, or CONSTANTINE, called also CORNELIUS À SANCTO PATRICIO (fl. 1650), Irish jesuit; author of 'Disputatio Apologetica de Jure Regni Hiberniæ pro Catholicis Hibernis adversus hæreticos Anglos,' urging the Irish to elect a Roman catholic king for themselves, 1645. [xxxv. 335]

MAHONY, FRANCIS SYLVESTER, best known by his pseudonym of FATHER PROUT (1804–1866), humorist; educated at the jesuit colleges of Clongoweswood, co. Kildare, and of St. Acheul, Amiens, and at Rome; admitted jesuit; master of rhetoric at the Clongoweswood jesuits' college, August 1830; dismissed from the order, November 1830; abandoned the priesthood for literary life in London; befriended by William Maginn [q. v.]; contributed entertaining papers, over signature 'Father Prout,' to 'Fraser's Magazine,' 1834–6 (published collectively, 1836); contributed poems to 'Bentley's Miscellany,' 1837; correspondent at Rome to the 'Daily News,' 1846; Paris correspondent to the 'Globe,' 1858–66; died in Paris. [xxxv. 336]

MAIDMENT, JAMES (1795?–1879), Scottish antiquary; called to the Scottish bar, 1817; advocate; much engaged in disputed peerage cases; interested in historical and antiquarian research; edited works for the Bannatyne, Maitland, Abbotsford, and Hunterian Clubs, and for the Spottiswoode Society. One of his most valuable works is the 'Dramatists of the Restoration,' 1877.
[xxxv. 338]

MAIDSTONE or **MAYDESTONE**, CLEMENT (fl. 1410), theologian and historical writer; probably a Trinitarian friar; author of ecclesiastical works.
[xxxv. 339]

MAIDSTONE, RALPH OF (d. 1246). [See RALPH.]

MAIDSTONE or **MAYDESTONE**, RICHARD (d. 1396), Carmelite; educated at Oxford; D.D., and confessor to John of Gaunt; prominent opponent of Wyclif; manuscripts by him preserved in the Bodleian Library, British Museum, and elsewhere. [xxxv. 339]

MAIHEW, EDWARD (1570–1625), Benedictine; educated in the English College at Douay, and subsequently at Rome; took orders; secular priest in England; Benedictine in the abbey of Westminster, 1607; prior of the monastery of St. Laurence at Dieulwart in Lorraine, 1614–20; died at Cambray; author of some religious treatises. [xxxv. 340]

MAILDULF or **MAILDUF** (d. 675?), Scottish or Irish teacher; gave his name to the town of Malmesbury; according to William of Malmesbury, opened a school in 'the spot now called Malmesbury,' which Aldhelm [q. v.] attended, and where he took the tonsure later. [xxxv. 341]

MAIMBRAY or **MAINBRAY**, STEPHEN CHARLES TRIBOUDET (1710–1782). [See DEMAINBRAY.]

MAIN, JAMES (1700?–1761). [See MAN.]

MAIN, ROBERT (1808–1878), astronomer; brother of Thomas John Main [q. v.]; fellow of Queens' College, Cambridge; took orders; M.A., 1837; chief assistant at the Royal Observatory, 1835; gold medallist, Astronomical Society, 1858; F.R.S., 1860; Radcliffe observer, 1860; edited first Radcliffe catalogue and compiled second, 1860; collected materials for a third, with the Redhill transit circle purchased (1861) from Richard Christopher Carrington [q. v.]; published astronomical treatises and addresses. [xxxv. 342]

MAIN, THOMAS JOHN (1818–1885), mathematician; younger brother of Robert Main [q. v.]; senior wrangler, St. John's College, Cambridge, 1838; took orders; M.A., 1841; naval chaplain; placed on retired list, 1869; for thirty-four years professor of mathematics at the Royal Naval College, Portsmouth; published works on applied mathematics. [xxxv. 343]

MAINE, SIR HENRY JAMES SUMNER (1822–1888), jurist; of Christ's Hospital, London, and Pembroke College, Cambridge; senior classic, 1844; junior tutor at Trinity Hall, Cambridge, 1845–7; regius professor of civil law, 1847–54; called to the bar, 1850; reader in Roman law and jurisprudence at the Inns of Court, 1852; contributed to the 'Saturday Review' from its start in 1855; published 'Ancient Law: its Connection with the Early History of Society and its Relations to Modern Ideas,'

1861 ; legal member of the council of India, 1862-9 ; Corpus professor of jurisprudence, Oxford, 1869-78 ; published lectures as 'Village Communities,' 1871, 'Early History of Institutions,' 1875, and 'Dissertations on Early Law and Customs,' 1883 ; K.C.S.I. and appointed to a seat on the Indian council, 1871 ; master of Trinity Hall, Cambridge, 1877-88 ; Whewell professor of international law, Cambridge, 1887-8 ; died at Cannes ; one of the earliest to apply the historical method to the study of political institutions. [xxxv. 343]

MAINE, JASPER (1604-1672). [See MAYNE.]

MAINWARING or **MAYNWARING**, ARTHUR (1668-1712), auditor of imprests : entered Christ Church, Oxford, 1683, and the Inner Temple, 1687 ; at first opposed, but subsequently served the revolution government ; auditor of imprests, 1705-12 ; M.P., Preston, 1706-10, West Looe, 1710-12 ; started the 'Medley,' 1710 ; in his writings attacked Sacheverell, defended Marlborough, and arraigned the French policy. [xxxv. 346]

MAINWARING, EVERARD (1628-1699 ?). [See MAYNWARING.]

MAINWARING, MATTHEW (1561-1652), romancist ; published 'Vienna,' an adaptation of a romance of Catalonian origin, c. 1618. [xxxv. 348]

MAINWARING, SIR PHILIP (1589-1661), secretary for Ireland : B.A. Brasenose College, Oxford, 1613 ; M.P., Boroughbridge, 1624-6, Derby, 1628-9, Morpeth, 1640, Newton, Lancashire, 1661 ; knighted, 1634 ; secretary to the lord-lieutenant of Ireland, the Earl of Strafford, 1634 ; returned to London and was imprisoned as a delinquent, 1650-1. [xxxv. 348]

MAINWARING, ROGER (1590-1653). [See MANWARING.]

MAINWARING, ROWLAND (1783-1862), naval commander and author ; present at the battle of the Nile, 1798, at the blockade of Copenhagen, 1801 ; captain, 1830 ; author of 'Instructive Gleanings .. on Painting and Drawing,' 1832, and 'Annals of Bath,' 1838. [xxxv. 348]

MAINWARING, SIR THOMAS, first baronet (1623-1689), author of the 'Defence of Amicia' ; entered Brasenose College, Oxford, 1637, and Gray's Inn, 1640 ; took parliamentary side in civil war, but at the Restoration gained favour at court ; created baronet, 1660. His 'Defence of Amicia,' to prove that his ancestor Amicia was the lawful daughter of Earl Hugh of Cyveiliog [see HUGH, d. 1181] (published, 1673), led to a controversy with his relative Sir Peter Leycester [q. v.] [xxxv. 349]

MAINZER, JOSEPH (1801-1851), teacher of music ; born at Trèves ; ordained, 1826 ; singing-master to the college at Trèves ; being compelled to leave Germany on account of his political opinions, went to Brussels, 1833 ; proceeded to Paris and came to England, 1839 ; best-known work, 'Singing for the Million,' 1841. [xxxv. 349]

MAIR, JOHN (1469-1550). [See MAJOR, JOHN.]

MAIRE, CHRISTOPHER (1697-1767), jesuit ; educated at St. Omer ; joined jesuits, 1715 ; professed, 1733 ; rector of the English College at Rome, 1744-50 ; died at Ghent ; author of Latin theological and astronomical works. [xxxv. 350]

MAIRE, WILLIAM (d. 1769), Roman catholic prelate ; educated at the English College, Douay ; ordained priest, 1730 ; served the Durham mission, 1742-67 ; coadjutor to the vicar-apostolic of the northern district of England, 1767-9. [xxxv. 350]

MAITLAND, ANTHONY, tenth EARL OF LAUDERDALE (1785-1863), admiral of the red ; son of James Maitland, eighth earl of Lauderdale [q. v.] ; served under Nelson, 1801, and Lord Exmouth, 1826 ; G.C.B. and G.C.M.G. ; last baron Lauderdale. [xxxv. 357]

MAITLAND, CHARLES, third EARL OF LAUDERDALE (d. 1691), brother of John Maitland, first duke of Lauderdale [q. v.] ; master-general of the Scottish mint ; privy councillor, 1661 ; commissioner to parliament for the shire of Edinburgh, and lord of the articles, 1669 ; treasurer-depute, 1671 ; created baronet, 1672 ; assisted his brother in the management of Scottish affairs, 1674-1681 ; accused of perjury and deprived of his position, 1681 ; succeeded as Earl of Lauderdale, 1682. [xxxv. 350]

MAITLAND, CHARLES (1815-1866), author ; nephew of Sir Peregrine Maitland [q. v.] ; M.D. Edinburgh, 1838 ; studied theology and graduated B.A. Magdalen Hall, Oxford, 1852 ; held various curacies ; author of the first popular book on the 'Catacombs of Rome,' 1846. [xxxv. 351]

MAITLAND, EDWARD (1824-1897), mystical writer ; B.A. Caius College, Cambridge, 1847 ; went to California, 1849, became a commissioner of crown lands in Australia, and returned to England, 1857 ; published romances, including 'The Pilgrim and the Shrine' (largely autobiographical), 1867 ; collaborated with Anna Kingsford [q. v.] in 'Keys of the Creeds' (1875), and joined her in crusade against materialism, animal food, and vivisection ; declared (1876) that he had acquired a new sense, that of 'spiritual sensitiveness,' which enabled him to see the spiritual condition of people ; published, with Anna Kingsford, 'The Perfect Way ; or the Finding of Christ,' 1882, and founded with her the Hermetic Society, 1884 ; founded Esoteric Christian Union, 1891. His publications include 'Anna Kingsford. Her Life, Letters, Diary, and Work,' 1896. [Suppl. iii. 131]

MAITLAND, EDWARD FRANCIS, LORD BARCAPLE (1803-1870), Scottish judge ; brother of Thomas Maitland, lord Dundrennan [q. v.] ; LL.D. Edinburgh ; advocate, 1831 ; solicitor-general for Scotland, 1855-8 and 1859-62 ; lord of session as Lord Barcaple, 1802-70. [xxxv. 376]

MAITLAND, FREDERICK (1763-1848), general ; grandson of Charles Maitland, sixth earl of Lauderdale ; entered the army, 1779 ; present as lieutenant at the relief of Gibraltar, 1782 ; served chiefly in the West Indies ; lieutenant-colonel, 1795 ; major-general, 1805 ; lieutenant-governor of Grenada, 1805-10 ; lieutenant-general, 1811 ; second in command in the Mediterranean, 1812 ; lieutenant-governor of Dominica, 1813 ; general, 1825. [xxxv. 352]

MAITLAND, FREDERICK LEWIS (d. 1786), captain of the royal navy ; son of Charles Maitland, sixth earl of Lauderdale : commanded the royal yacht, 1763-75 ; served under Rodney, 1782 ; rear-admiral, 1786. [xxxv. 353]

MAITLAND, SIR FREDERICK LEWIS (1777-1839), rear-admiral ; son of Frederick Lewis Maitland (d. 1786) [q. v.] ; served in the Mediterranean and off the French and Spanish coasts ; commanded on the Halifax and West India stations, 1813-14 ; as commander of the Bellerophon took Napoleon to England, 1815 ; C.B., 1815 ; K.C.B. and rear-admiral, 1830 ; admiral superintendent of Portsmouth dockyard, 1832-7 ; commander-in-chief in the East Indies and China, 1837-9 ; died at sea. [xxxv. 353]

MAITLAND, JAMES, eighth EARL OF LAUDERDALE (1759-1839), studied at Edinburgh High School and University, Trinity College, Oxford (1775), and Glasgow University ; admitted to Lincoln's Inn, 1777 ; member of the Faculty of Advocates, 1780 ; M.P., Newport, Cornwall, 1780, Malmesbury, 1784 ; succeeded to the title, 1789 ; Scots representative peer, 1790 ; strenuously opposed Pitt's government ; published his 'Inquiry into the Nature and Origin of Public Wealth,' 1804 ; created Baron Lauderdale of Thirlestane in the county of Berwick (peerage of Great Britain and Ireland, 1806) ; lord high keeper of the great seal of Scotland, 1806 ; privy councillor, 1806 ; resigned, 1807 ; turned tory after 1821 ; retired from public life after 1830. [xxxv. 355]

MAITLAND, SIR JOHN, first BARON MAITLAND OF THIRLESTANE (1545 ?-1595), lord high chancellor of Scotland ; son of Sir Richard Maitland, lord Lethington [q. v.] ; brother of William Maitland of Lethington [q. v.] ; lord privy seal, 1567 ; favoured the queen and was rigorously treated by Morton, 1569-78 ; privy councillor, 1583 ; secretary of state, 1584 ; vice-chancellor, 1586 ; acquired great influence over the king ; created Baron Maitland of Thirlestane, 1590 ; responsible for the act which established the kirk on a strictly presbyterian basis ; wrote verse. [xxxv. 357]

MAITLAND, JOHN, second EARL and first DUKE OF LAUDERDALE (1616-1682), grandson of Sir John Maitland [q. v.] ; grand-nephew of William Maitland of Lethington [q. v.] ; regarded as a rising hope of the ultra-covenanting party ; commissioner for the Solemn League and Covenant, 1643-6 ; one of the commissioners who obtained the famous 'Engagement' ; with Charles II in

Holland, 1649 ; followed him to Worcester and was taken prisoner, 1651 ; kept a prisoner till 1660 ; secretary for Scottish affairs, 1660–80 ; aimed at making the crown absolute in Scotland both in state and church; had complete influence over Charles ; created Duke of Lauderdale and Marquis of March in the Scottish peerage, 1672 ; placed upon the commission for the admiralty, 1673 ; made a privy councillor and a peer of England as Earl of Guildford and Baron Petersham, 1674 ; supported by Charles II against attacks from the English parliament. [xxxv. 360]

MAITLAND, JOHN, LORD RAVELRIG, and fifth EARL OF LAUDERDALE (1650 ?–1710), brother of Richard Maitland, fourth earl of Lauderdale [q. v.]; passed advocate at the Scottish bar, 1680 ; concurred in the revolution, a lord of session as Lord Ravelrig, 1689 ; succeeded to the earldom of Lauderdale, 1695 ; supported the union. [xxxv. 367]

MAITLAND, JOHN GORHAM (1818–1863), civil servant; son of Samuel Roffey Maitland [q. v.]; fellow of Trinity College, Cambridge ; secretary to the civil service commission ; published pamphlets. [xxxv. 367]

MAITLAND, SIR PEREGRINE (1777–1854), general and colonial governor; entered the army, 1792 ; served in Flanders, 1794–8 ; in Spain, 1809 and 1812 ; major-general, 1814; present at Waterloo, 1815 ; K.C.B., 1815 ; lieutenant-governor of Upper Canada, 1818–28, of Nova Scotia, 1828–34 ; commander-in-chief of the Madras army, 1836–8, and at the Cape of Good Hope, 1844–7 ; general, 1846; resigned governorship of Cape of Good Hope, 1847 ; G.C.B., 1852. [xxxv. 367]

MAITLAND, SIR RICHARD, LORD LETHINGTON (1496–1586), poet, lawyer, and collector of early Scottish poetry ; educated at St. Andrews University ; studied law at Paris; employed by James V and Queen Mary ; an ordinary lord of session and privy councillor, 1561 ; keeper of the great seal, 1562–7 ; a selection from his collection of early Scottish poems, with additions by himself, published, 1786. [xxxv. 368]

MAITLAND, RICHARD, fourth EARL OF LAUDERDALE (1653–1695), Jacobite; son of Charles Maitland, third earl of Lauderdale [q. v.]; privy councillor and joint general of the mint with his father, 1678 ; lord-justice general, 1681–4 ; declined to agree to the revolution settlement ; for a time in exile at the court of St. Germains; outlawed, 1694; died at Paris ; author of a verse translation of Virgil, published, 1737. [xxxv. 370]

MAITLAND, RICHARD (1714 ?–1763), captor of Surat; enlisted in royal artillery, 1732 ; lieutenant-fire-worker, 1742 ; fought at Fontenoy as first lieutenant, 1745; served under Clive in India; commanded the expedition for capturing Surat, 1759 ; major, 1762 ; died at Bombay. [xxxv. 370]

MAITLAND, SAMUEL ROFFEY (1792–1866), historian and miscellaneous writer; educated at St. John's and Trinity Colleges, Cambridge ; barrister, Inner Temple, 1816 ; entered holy orders, 1821 ; published his elaborate monograph on the Albigenses and Waldenses, 1832 ; commenced contributing to the 'British Magazine,' 1835, the remarkable papers afterwards published as 'The Dark Ages,' 1844, and 'Essays on Subjects connected with the Reformation in England,' 1849 ; librarian and keeper of the manuscripts at Lambeth, 1838 ; F.R.S., 1839 ; editor of the 'British Magazine,' 1839–49 ; contributed to 'Notes and Queries'; author of thirty-seven works, mainly historical and ecclesiastical. [xxxv. 371]

MAITLAND, SIR THOMAS (1759 ?–1824), lieutenant-general; commander-in-chief in the Mediterranean ; served in India, both ashore and afloat, till 1790 ; in San Domingo, 1794–8 ; M.P., Haddington burghs, 1794–6 and 1800–6 ; brigadier-general, 1797 ; employed in the secret expedition against Belle Isle, 1799 ; major-general, 1805 ; lieutenant-general and commander-in-chief in Ceylon, 1806–11 ; major-general, 1811 ; governor of Malta, 1813 ; lord high commissioner of the Ionian islands and commander-in-chief in the Mediterranean, 1815 ; died at Malta ; an able administrator, though nicknamed ' King Tom' from his eccentricities and arbitrary conduct. [xxxv. 374]

MAITLAND, THOMAS, LORD DUNDRENNAN (1792–1851), Scottish judge ; studied at Edinburgh ; called to the Scottish bar, 1813 ; solicitor-general, 1840–1 and 1846–50 ; M.P., Kirkcudbrightshire, 1845–50 ; lord of session as Lord Dundrennan, 1850 ; studied antiquarian literature ; his fine library sold in 1851. [xxxv. 376]

MAITLAND, THOMAS, eleventh EARL OF LAUDERDALE (1803–1878), admiral of the fleet ; entered the navy, 1816 ; served on the South American station, 1826, the West Indian, 1832–3, the north coast of Spain, 1835–7 ; advanced to post rank, 1837 ; shared in the operations in the Persian Gulf, 1839 ; served during the first Chinese war, 1840–1 ; knighted, 1843 ; rear-admiral, 1857 ; commander-in-chief in the Pacific, 1860–3 ; succeeded to earldom on the death of his cousin, 1863 ; admiral, 1868 ; admiral of the fleet on the retired list, 1877. [xxxv. 376]

MAITLAND, WILLIAM (1528 ?–1573), of Lethington, known as the 'Secretary Lethington'; son of Sir Richard Maitland [q. v.]; educated at St. Andrews and on the continent ; in the service of the queen-regent of Scotland, 1554–9 ; entered into close relations with Cecil, 1560 ; secretary and entrusted with Mary's foreign policy, 1561 ; pursued a conciliatory policy towards England ; supported the Darnley marriage, 1564–5 ; said to have been a party to Darnley's murder, 1567 ; tried to reconcile the two Scottish factions, 1570 ; surrendered Edinburgh Castle to the English commander, 1573 ; died in prison at Leith. [xxxv. 377]

MAITLAND, WILLIAM (1693 ?–1757), topographer ; published topographical compilations, 1739–57, of ephemeral reputation. [xxxv. 383]

MAITLAND, WILLIAM FULLER (1813–1876), picture collector : of Trinity College, Cambridge ; M.A., 1839 ; formed a fine collection of early Italian masters and of English landscape paintings, some of which were bought after his death by the National Gallery. [xxxv. 383]

MAITTAIRE, MICHAEL (1668–1747), classical scholar and writer on typography ; born in France ; educated at Westminster School ; 'canoneer' student of Christ Church, Oxford ; M.A., 1696 ; second master of Westminster, 1695–9 ; began to publish, c. 1706, works consisting principally of editions of the Latin classics ; published 'Annales Typographici,' 5 vols. 1719–41. [xxxv. 384]

MAJENDIE, HENRY WILLIAM (1754–1830), bishop of Chester and Bangor ; of Charterhouse and Christ's College, Cambridge ; B.A., 1776 ; fellow, 1776 ; preceptor to Prince William, afterwards William IV ; canon of Windsor, 1785–98 ; D.D., 1791 ; canon of St. Paul's Cathedral, 1798 ; bishop of Chester, 1800–9, of Bangor, 1809–30. [xxxv. 385]

MAJOR or MAIR, JOHN (1469–1550), historian and scholastic divine ; studied at Cambridge and Paris ; M.A., 1496 ; taught at Paris in arts and scholastic philosophy ; published his first work on logic, 1503 ; D.D., 1505 ; began to lecture on scholastic divinity at the Sorbonæ, Paris, 1505 ; published 'A Commentary on the Four Books of Peter the Lombard's "Sentences,"' at intervals, 1509–17 ; professor of philosophy and divinity, Glasgow, 1518 ; published 'History of Greater Britain, both England and Scotland,' 1521 ; taught philosophy and logic in St. Andrews University, 1522 ; taught again at Paris University, 1525–31 ; returned to St. Andrews, 1531 ; provost of St. Salvator's College there, 1533–50 ; with William Manderston [q. v.] founded and endowed chaplaincy at St. Andrews, 1539 ; championed the doctrinal system of Rome ; wrote entirely in Latin. [xxxv. 386]

MAJOR, JOHN (1782–1849), bookseller and publisher ; a supporter of Dibdin's publications ; failed in business through becoming entangled in Dibdin's speculations ; well-known by his beautiful edition of Walton and Cotton's 'Complete Angler,' first published, 1823 ; published verse, including squibs on current politics. [xxxv. 388]

MAJOR, JOHN HENNIKER-, second BARON HENNIKER (1752–1821). [See HENNIKER-MAJOR.]

MAJOR, JOSHUA (1787–1866), landscape-gardener ; author of important works on gardening, published, 1829–1861. [xxxv. 388]

MAJOR, RICHARD HENRY (1818–1891), geographer ; keeper of the department of maps and plans, British Museum, 1867–80 ; his chief work, 'The Life of Prince Henry of Portugal, surnamed the Navigator,' 1868 ; edited ten works for the Hakluyt Society (hon. secretary, 1849–58), 1847–73. [xxxv. 389]

MAJOR, THOMAS (1720–1799), engraver: resided and worked for some time in Paris; returned to England, 1753; issued a series of his prints, 1754 (2nd edit. 1768); first English engraver to be elected A.R.A., 1770; engraver to the king and to the stamp office.   [xxxv. 389]

MAKELSFELD, WILLIAM (d. 1304). [See MYKELS-FELD.]

MAKEMIE, FRANCIS (1658–1708), Irish divine; studied at Glasgow University; missionary to America, 1682; worked in Virginia, Maryland, and Barbados; formed at Philadelphia the first presbytery in America, 1706, and the father of presbyterianism in America; died in Accomac, Virginia.   [xxxv. 390]

MAKIN, BATHSUA (fl. 1673), the most learned Englishwoman of her time; sister of John Pell (1611–1685) [q. v.]; tutoress to Charles I's daughters; probably kept a school at Putney, 1649; wrote on female education, 1673.   [xxxv. 391]

MAKITTRICK, JAMES (1728–1802). [See ADAIR, JAMES MAKITTRICK.]

MAKKARELL or **MACKARELL**, MATTHEW (d. 1537), abbot of Barlings, Lincolnshire; D.D. Paris (incorporated at Cambridge, 1516); abbot of Gilbertines or Premonstratensians at Alnwick; subsequently of Barlings or Oxeney, Lincolnshire; suffragan bishop of Lincoln, 1535; a leader in Lincolnshire rebellion, 1536; taken prisoner and executed, 1537.   [xxxv. 391]

MAKYN, DAVID (d. 1588?). [See MACKENZIE, DUGAL.]

MALACHY I (d. 863). [See MAELSECHLAINN I.]

MALACHY MOR (949–1022). [See MAELSECH-LAINN II.]

MALACHY OF IRELAND (fl. 1310), Franciscan; probably author of 'Libellus septem peccatorum mortalium' (Paris, 1518), remarkable for its denunciation of the government of Ireland.   [xxxv. 392]

MALACHY MACAEDH (d. 1348), archbishop of Tuam; bishop of Elphin, 1307–12; archbishop of Tuam, 1312–48; often confused with Malachy (fl. 1310) [q. v.].   [xxxv. 392]

MALACHY O'MORGAIR, SAINT (in Irish, MAEL-MAEDHOIG UA MORGAIR) (1094?–1148), archbishop of Armagh; gained a great reputation for sanctity and learning; head of the abbey of Bangor, co. Down; bishop of Connor, 1124; established monastery of Ibrach in south of Ireland after the destruction of the seat of his bishopric by a northern chieftain; archbishop of Armagh, 1132–6; bishop of Down, 1136; visited St. Bernard, his future biographer, at Clairvaux; died at Clairvaux on his way to Rome.   [xxxv. 392]

MALAN, CÉSAR JEAN SALOMON, calling himself later, SOLOMON CÆSAR MALAN (1812–1894), oriental linguist and biblical scholar; born at Geneva; educated at St. Edmund Hall, Oxford; Boden (Sanskrit) scholar, 1834; Pusey and Ellerton (Hebrew) scholar, 1837; B.A., 1837; classical lecturer at Bishop's College, Calcutta, 1838; deacon, 1838; returned to England, 1840; priest and M.A. Balliol College, 1843; held living of Broadwindsor, Dorset, 1845–85; travelled in the East, and published numerous translations from oriental literature; joined John William Burgon [q. v.] in attacking revised version of New Testament, 1881. His works include 'Notes on Proverbs,' 1892–3.   [Suppl. iii. 133]

MALARD, MICHAEL (fl. 1717–1720), French protestant divine; born at Vaurenard; educated for the Roman catholic priesthood; came to England, c. 1700; embraced protestantism, 1705; published pamphlets against the French committee for the distribution of the money charged upon the civil list for the benefit of the French protestants, 1717–20; author of manuals of French accidence.   [xxxv. 394]

MALBY, SIR NICHOLAS (1530?–1584), president of Connaught; served in France, Spain, and Ireland; stationed at Carrickfergus, 1567–9; collector of customs of Strangford, Ardglass, and Dundrum, 1571; made unsuccessful efforts to colonise part of Down, 1571–4; knighted and appointed military governor of Connaught, 1576; president of Connaught, 1579; engaged in

suppressing rebellions, 1579–81; his services ignored by Queen Elizabeth.   [xxxv. 395]

MALCOLM I (MACDONALD) (d. 954), king of Scotland; succeeded, 943; made treaty with Edmund, the West-Saxon king, 945; lost Northumbria, 954; slain in a border skirmish.   [xxxv. 398]

MALCOLM II (MACKENNETH) (d. 1034), king of Scotland; son of Kenneth II [q. v.]; succeeded, 1005, by defeating and killing Kenneth III [q. v.]; defeated Eadulf Cudel, 1018, thereby causing the cession of Lothian to the Scottish kingdom, Cambria north of the Solway becoming also an appanage of the same; did homage to Canute, 1031.   [xxxv. 399]

MALCOLM III, called CANMORE (d. 1093), king of Scotland; succeeded his father Duncan I in consequence of the defeat of Macbeth [q. v.] by Earl Edward of Northumbria, 1054; defeated and slew Macbeth at Lumphanan; crowned at Scone, 1057; married Margaret (d. 1093) [q. v.], sister of Edgar Atheling [q. v.]; did homage to the English kings, 1072 and 1091; treacherously slain while invading Northumberland.   [xxxv. 400]

MALCOLM IV (the MAIDEN) (1141–1165), king of Scotland; grandson of David I [q. v.]; succeeded his grandfather, 1153; surrendered Northumberland and Cumberland to Henry II, 1157; served as English baron in the expedition against Toulouse, 1159; engaged in suppressing rebellions in Scotland, 1160–4.   [xxxv. 401]

MALCOLM, SIR CHARLES (1782–1851), vice-admiral; brother of Sir Pulteney Malcolm [q. v.]; entered the navy, 1795; employed in the East Indies till 1802; on the coast of France and Portugal, 1806–9; chiefly in the West Indies, 1809–19; knighted while in attendance on the Marquis Wellesley, lord-lieutenant of Ireland, 1822–7; superintendent of the Bombay marine (name afterwards changed to the Indian navy), 1827–1837; rear-admiral, 1837; vice-admiral, 1847.   [xxxv. 402]

MALCOLM, SIR GEORGE (1818–1897), general; born at Bombay; ensign in East India Company's service, 1836; lieutenant, 1840; served in Scinde, and second Sikh war; lieutenant-colonel, 1854; in Persian war, 1856–7, and Indian mutiny, 1857–8; C.B., 1859; brevet-colonel, 1860; major-general, 1867; in Abyssinian expedition, 1868; general, 1877; G.C.B., 1886.   [Suppl. iii. 134]

MALCOLM, JAMES PELLER (1767–1815), topographer and engraver; born in Philadelphia; came to London and studied in the Royal Academy; chief work, 'Londinium Redivivum' (history and description), with forty-seven plates, published, 1802–7.   [xxxv. 403]

MALCOLM, SIR JOHN (1769–1833), Indian administrator and diplomatist; entered the service of the East India Company, 1782; preferring diplomacy to fighting, studied Persian, and was appointed Persian interpreter to the nizam of the Deccan, 1792; secretary to Sir Alured Clarke [q. v.], commander-in-chief, 1795–7, and to his successor, General George, lord Harris [q. v.], 1797–8; assistant to the resident of Hyderabad, 1798; chosen by Lord Wellesley, the governor-general, as envoy to Persia, 1799–1801; private secretary to Wellesley, 1801–2; political agent to General Wellesley during the Mahratta war, 1803–4; sent on a mission to Teheran, 1808–9, and 1810; published his 'Political History of India,' 1811, his 'History of Persia,' 1818; K.C.B., 1815; as brigadier in the army of the Deccan took part in the new Mahratta war, 1817–18; after assisting in the reclamation of Malwah, returned to England and occupied himself with literary work, 1822; governor of Bombay, 1826–30; M.P., Launceston, 1831–2; his 'Administration of India' published, 1833, and his life of Clive (completed by another hand), posthumously published, 1836.   [xxxv. 404]

MALCOLM, SIR PULTENEY (1768–1838), admiral; entered the navy, 1778; served in West Indies, Quebec, East Indies, and China seas; under Nelson in the Mediterranean, 1804–5; rear-admiral, 1813; K.C.B., 1815; commander-in-chief on the St. Helena station, 1816–17; vice-admiral, 1821; commander-in-chief in the Mediterranean, 1828–31 and 1833–4.   [xxxv. 412]

MALCOLM, SARAH (1710?–1733), criminal; charwoman in the Temple, London; murdered Mrs. Duncomb, her employer, and her two servants, 1733 ; condemned to death and executed ; painted by Hogarth while in the condemned cell.   [xxxv. 414]

MALCOLME, DAVID (d. 1748), philologist ; ordained as presbyterian minister, 1705 ; deposed for deserting his charge, 1742 : specialised in Celtic philology ; chief work, 'Letters, Essays, and other Tracts illustrating the Antiquities of Great Britain and Ireland . . . Also Specimens of the Celtic, Welsh, Irish, Saxon, and American Languages,' 1744.   [xxxv. 414]

MALCOM, ANDREW GEORGE (1782–1823), Irish presbyterian divine and hymn-writer ; M.A., Glasgow ; ordained, 1807 ; ministered at Newry, co. Down ; D.D., Glasgow, 1820 ; composed hymns.   [xxxv. 415]

MALCOME, JOHN (1662 ?–1729), presbyterian polemic ; M.A. Glasgow ; ordained, 1687 ; adhered to the subscription and invented the phrase 'new light,' 1720 ; published theological works.   [xxxv. 415]

MALDEN, DANIEL (d. 1736), prison-breaker ; adopted street-robbery as a profession ; condemned and ordered to be executed, 1736 ; escaped from prison twice, but was retaken and hanged.   [xxxv. 416]

MALDEN, HENRY (1800–1876), classical scholar ; of Trinity College, Cambridge ; fellow, 1824 ; M.A., 1825 ; professor of Greek at University College, London, 1831–1876 ; head-master of University College school with Thomas Hewitt Key [q. v.], 1833–42.   [xxxv. 417]

MALDON, THOMAS (d. 1404), Carmelite ; prior of the convent at Maldon : Latin works, now lost, ascribed to him by Leland and Bale.   [xxxv. 417]

MALEBYSSE, RICHARD (d. 1209), justiciar ; one of the leaders in an attack on and massacre of the Jews at York, 1190 ; justice itinerant for Yorkshire, 1201 ; sat to acknowledge fines at Westminster, 1202 ; employed in enforcing payment of aids, 1204.   [xxxv. 418]

MALET, SIR ALEXANDER, second baronet (1800–1886), diplomatist ; son of Sir Charles Warre Malet [q. v.]; educated at Winchester and Christ Church, Oxford ; B.A., 1822 ; entered diplomatic service, 1824 ; minister plenipotentiary to the Germanic confederation at Frankfort, 1849–66 ; K.C.B., 1866 ; published 'The Overthrow of the Germanic Confederation by Prussia in 1866,' 1870.   [xxxv. 418]

MALET, ARTHUR (1806–1888), Indian civilian ; son of Sir Charles Warre Malet [q. v.]; educated at Winchester, Addiscombe, and Haileybury ; appointed to the Bombay civil service, 1824 ; chief secretary for the political and secret departments of the Bombay government, 1847 ; member of the legislative council of India, 1854 ; of the government council of Bombay, 1855–60 ; published ' Notices of an English Branch of the Malet Family,' 1885.   [xxxv. 419]

MALET, SIR CHARLES WARRE, first baronet (1753 ?–1815), Indian administrator and diplomatist ; descendant of William Malet (d. 1071) [q. v.] of Graville ; resident minister at Poonah, 1785–91 ; created baronet for his services, 1791 ; acting governor at Bombay till 1798 ; retired and returned to England, 1798.   [xxxv. 419]

MALET, GEORGE GRENVILLE (1804 – 1856), lieutenant-colonel ; son of Sir Charles Warre Malet [q. v.]; entered the Indian army, 1822 ; political superintendent of Mellanee, Rájputána, 1839 ; engaged in the Afghan war, 1842, and in the war with Persia, 1856 ; superintendent of the Guicowar horse, 1856 ; killed in action.   [xxxv. 419]

MALET or **MALLET**, ROBERT (d. 1106 ?), baron of Eye ; son of William Malet (d. 1071) [q. v.] of Graville ; endowed a Benedictine monastery at Eye ; supported Robert against Henry I ; supposed to have been killed at the battle of Tinchebrai.   [xxxv. 420]

MALET or **MALLETT**, SIR THOMAS (1582–1665), judge ; descendant of William Malet (d. 1071) [q. v.] of Graville ; barrister, Middle Temple, 1606 ; reader, 1626 ; sat in the first two parliaments of Charles I ; serjeant, 1635 ; raised to the king's bench, 1641 ; knighted, 1641 ; supported the royal policy and prerogative ; imprisoned in the Tower, 1642–4 ; again on the bench, 1660–3.   [xxxv. 420]

MALET or **MALLET**, WILLIAM (d. 1071), of Graville in Normandy ; companion of the Conqueror ; his

exploits at Hastings celebrated by Wace in his 'Roman de Rou' (ll. 13472–84) ; sheriff of York, 1068 ; taken prisoner at capture of York, 1069, but subsequently released.   [xxxv. 421]

MALET or **MALLET**, WILLIAM (fl. 1195–1215), baron of Curry Mallet and Shepton Mallet, Somerset ; descended from Gilbert, son of William Malet (d. 1071) [q. v.] of Graville ; in Normandy with Richard I, 1195 ; sheriff of Dorset and Somerset, 1211 ; joined barons in their struggle with King John, 1215.   [xxxv. 421]

MALGER (d. 1212). [See MAUGER.]

MALHAM, JOHN (1747–1821), miscellaneous writer ; Northamptonshire curate ; acted as schoolmaster ; employed by London booksellers in the issue of a number of illustrated bibles, prayer-books, and popular historical works, 1782–1812.   [xxxv. 422]

MALIM, WILLIAM (1533–1594), schoolmaster ; educated at Eton and King's College, Cambridge ; fellow, 1551 ; M.A., 1556: head-master of Eton, 1561–71 ; prebendary of Lincoln, 1569 ; high-master of St. Paul's, 1573–81 ; his extant pieces chiefly commendary Latin verses and letters prefixed to the works of friends.   [xxxv. 422]

MALINS, SIR RICHARD (1805–1882), judge ; educated at Caius College, Cambridge ; B.A., 1827 ; barrister, Inner Temple, 1830 ; Q.C., 1849 ; M.P., Wallingford, 1852–65 ; a vice-chancellor, 1866–81 ; knighted, 1867 ; privy councillor, 1881.   [xxxv. 423]

MALKIN, BENJAMIN HEATH (1769–1842), miscellaneous writer ; of Harrow and Trinity College, Cambridge ; M.A., 1802 ; head-master of Bury St. Edmunds grammar school, 1809–28 ; D.C.L. St. Mary Hall, Oxford, 1810 ; professor of history, ancient and modern, London University, 1830 ; F.S.A. ; author of some antiquarian and historical works, 1795–1825, and of a translation of 'Gil Blas,' 1809.   [xxxv. 424]

MALLESON, GEORGE BRUCE (1825–1898), colonel and military writer ; educated at Winchester ; ensign, 1842 ; lieutenant, 33rd B.N.I., 1847 ; assistant military auditor-general, 1856 ; captain, 1861 ; major, Bengal staff corps, 1863 ; lieutenant-colonel, 1868 ; colonel in army, 1873 ; guardian of young Maharajah of Mysore, 1869–77 ; C.S.I., 1872 ; wrote on military history.   [Suppl. iii. 135]

MALLESON, JOHN PHILIP (1796–1869), unitarian minister and schoolmaster ; graduated at Glasgow, 1819 ; became minister of a presbyterian congregation ; adopted Arian views and resigned, 1822 ; unitarian minister at Brighton, 1829 ; conducted a school at Brighton.   [xxxv. 424]

MALLET, originally **MALLOCH**, DAVID (1705 ?–1765), poet and miscellaneous writer ; studied at Edinburgh University (1721–2, 1722–3) and formed a friendship with James Thomson, author of 'The Seasons' ; composed a number of short poems, 1720–4 ; produced 'Eurydice' (tragedy) at Drury Lane, London, 1731 ; studied at St. Mary Hall, Oxford ; M.A., 1734 ; produced 'Mustapha' (tragedy) at Drury Lane, London, 1739 ; with Thomson wrote the masque of 'Alfred,' 1740 ; under-secretary to Frederick, prince of Wales, 1742 ; received inspectorship of exchequer-book in the outports of London for his political writings, 1763 ; author of ' William and Margaret,' 1723, a famous ballad. The national ode, 'Rule Britannia,' sometimes ascribed to him, was more probably written by Thomson.   [xxxv. 425]

MALLET, SIR LOUIS (1823–1890), civil servant and economist ; of Huguenot origin ; clerk in the audit office from 1839 ; transferred to the board of trade, 1847 ; private secretary to the president, 1848–52 and 1855–7 ; employed chiefly in the work of extension of commercial treaties, 1860–5 ; C.B., 1866 ; knighted, 1868 ; nominated to the council of India in London, 1872 ; permanent under-secretary of state for India, 1874–83 ; privy councillor, 1883 ; after Cobden's death (1865) the principal authority on questions of commercial policy, and the chief official representative of free trade opinion ; his occasional writings, which set forth the 'free-trade' doctrine, published as 'Free Exchange,' 1891. [xxxv. 426]

MALLET, ROBERT (1810–1881), civil engineer and scientific investigator ; B.A. Trinity College, Dublin, 1830 ; M.A., 1862 ; assumed charge of the Victoria foundry, Dublin, 1831 ; conducted many engineering works in Ireland, among them the building of the Fastnet Rock lighthouse, 1848–9; F.R.S., 1854; consulting engineer in London, 1861; edited the 'Practical Mechanic's Journal,' 1865–9; contributed to 'Philosophical Transactions,' and published works on engineering subjects.   [xxxv. 429]

MALLETT, FRANCIS (d. 1570), dean of Lincoln; B.A. Cambridge, 1522; M.A., 1525; D.D., 1535; vice-chancellor, 1536 and 1540; chaplain to Thomas Cromwell, 1538; canon of Windsor, 1543; prebendary of Wells, 1544; chaplain to the Princess Mary, 1544; prebendary of Westminster and dean of Lincoln, 1554–70; master of the Hospital of St. Katherine by the Tower, London, 1555–8.   [xxxv. 430]

MALLOCH, DAVID (1705?–1765).   [See MALLET.]

MALLORY or **MALLERY**, THOMAS (fl. 1662), ejected minister; vicar of St. Nicholas, Deptford, 1644; ejected from lectureship of St. Michael's, Crooked Lane, London, 1662; mentioned by Evelyn.   [xxxv. 432]

MALLORY or **MALLORIE**, THOMAS (1605?–1666?), divine; of New College, Oxford; M.A., 1632; incumbent of Northenden, 1635; ejected as a loyalist, 1642; canon of Chester and D.D., 1660.   [xxxv. 431]

MALMESBURY, EARLS OF. [See HARRIS, JAMES, first EARL, 1746–1820; HARRIS, JAMES HOWARD, third EARL, 1807–1889.]

MALMESBURY, GODFREY OF (fl. 1081). [See GODFREY.]

MALMESBURY, OLIVER OF (fl. 1066). [See OLIVER.]

MALMESBURY, WILLIAM OF (d. 1143?). [See WILLIAM.]

MALONE, ANTHONY (1700–1776), Irish politician; educated at Christ Church, Oxford; called to the Irish bar, 1726; M.P., co. Westmeath, 1727–60 and 1769–76, Castlemartyr, 1761–8, in the Irish parliament; LL.D. Trinity College, Dublin, 1737; prime serjeant-at-law, 1740–64; chancellor of the exchequer, 1757–61.   [xxxv. 432]

MALONE, EDMUND (1704–1774), judge; called to the English bar, 1730; practised in the Irish courts after 1740; M.P. for Granard in the Irish parliament, 1760–6; judge of the court of common pleas, 1766.   [xxxv. 433]

MALONE, EDMUND (1741–1812), critic and author; son of Edmund Malone (1704–1774) [q. v.]; B.A. Trinity College, Dublin; entered the Inner Temple, 1763; called to the Irish bar soon after 1767; settled permanently in London as a man of letters, 1777; joined the Literary Club, 1782; intimate with Johnson, Reynolds, Bishop Percy, Burke, and Boswell; a supporter of the union with Ireland; published 'Attempt to ascertain the Order in which the Plays of Shakespeare were written,' 1778; edited Shakespeare, 1790; collected materials for a new edition, which he left to James Boswell the younger, who published it in 21 vols. in 1821 (the 'third variorum' edition of works of Shakespeare, and generally acknowledged to be the best); edited works of Dryden, 1800.   [xxxv. 433]

MALONE, RICHARD, LORD SUNDERLIN (1738–1816), elder brother of Edmund Malone (1741–1812) [q. v.]; B.A. Trinity College, Dublin, 1759; M.P. in Irish House of Commons, 1768–85; raised to Irish peerage, 1785.   [xxxv. 433]

MALONE, WILLIAM (1586–1656), jesuit; joined jesuits at Rome, 1606; joined the mission of the society in Ireland; issued 'The Jesuits' Challenge,' c. 1623 (answered by Ussher), protestant bishop of Armagh, 1624); issued 'A Reply to Mr. James Ussher, his answere,' 1627; president of the Irish College at Rome, 1635–47; superior of the jesuits in Ireland, 1647; taken prisoner by the parliamentarians and banished, 1648; rector of the jesuit college at Seville, where he died.   [xxxv. 438]

MALORY, SIR THOMAS (fl. 1470), author of 'Le Morte Arthur'; Malory translated, 'from the Frensshe,' 'a most pleasant jumble and summary of the legends about Arthur,' in 21 books, finished between March 1469 and March 1470. The translation was printed by Caxton in 1485. Malory's 'Le Morte Arthur' greatly influenced the English prose of the sixteenth century.   [xxxv. 439]

MALTBY, EDWARD (1770–1859), bishop of Durham; educated at Winchester and Pembroke Hall, Cambridge; M.A., 1794; D.D., 1806; preacher at Lincoln's Inn, 1824–1833; bishop of Chichester, 1831, of Durham, 1836–56 F.R.S. and F.S.A.; published a useful 'Lexicon Græco-prosodiacum,' 1815, and some sermons.   [xxxv. 440]

MALTBY, WILLIAM (1763–1854), bibliographer; cousin of Edward Maltby (1770–1859) [q. v.]; educated at Gonville and Caius College, Cambridge; principal librarian of the London Institution, 1809–34.
    [xxxv. 442]

MALTHUS, THOMAS ROBERT (1766–1834), political economist; was educated by his father, at Warrington dissenting academy and Jesus College, Cambridge; M.A., 1791; fellow, 1793; curate at Albury, Surrey, 1798; published 'Essay on Population,' 1798, in which he laid down that population increases in geometrical, and subsistence in arithmetical proportion only, and argued necessity of 'checks' on population in order to reduce vice and misery; travelled abroad, 1799 and 1802; professor of history and political economy at Haileybury College, 1805; published 'The Nature and Progress of Rent,' 1815, in which he laid down doctrines generally accepted by later economists; F.R.S., 1819, and member of foreign academies; supported factory acts and national education; disapproved of the poor laws; as exponent of new doctrine had great influence on development of political economy.
    [xxxvi. 1]

MALTON, JAMES (d. 1803), architectural draughtsman and author; son of Thomas Malton the elder [q. v.]   [xxxvi. 5]

MALTON, THOMAS, the elder (1726–1801), architectural draughtsman and writer on geometry. [xxxvi. 5]

MALTON, THOMAS, the younger (1748–1804), architectural draughtsman; son of Thomas Malton the elder [q. v.]; exhibited at Academy chiefly architectural views of great accuracy of execution; published' A Picturesque Tour through . . . London and Westminster,' 1792.
    [xxxvi. 5]

MALTRAVERS, SIR JOHN (1266–1343?), knighted, 1306; conservator of the peace for Dorset, 1307, 1308, and 1314; served in Scotland between 1314 and 1322, 1327 and 1331; sent to serve in Ireland, 1317, in Guienne, 1325.
    [xxxvi. 6]

MALTRAVERS, JOHN, BARON MALTRAVERS (1290?–1365), knighted, 1306; knight of the shire for Dorset, 1318; sided with Thomas of Lancaster [q. v.] and Roger Mortimer [q. v.]; fled abroad after battle of Boroughbridge, 1322; keeper of Edward II, 1327, whom he is said to have harshly treated; justice in eyre and keeper of the forests; accompanied Edward III to France as steward, 1329; concerned in death of Edmund, earl of Kent [q. v.], 1330; summoned to parliament as Baron Maltravers, 1330; constable of Corfe Castle, 1330; on fall of Mortimer was condemned to death for his share in the murder of the Earl of Kent, and fled abroad; allowed to return, 1345; subsequently employed by the king.   [xxxvi. 6]

MALVERN, WILLIAM OF, alias PARKER (fl. 1535), last abbot of St. Peter's, Gloucester, 1514; D.C.L., 1508, and D.D., 1515, Gloucester Hall, Oxford; attended parliament; added largely to the Abbey buildings.
    [xxxvi. 7]

MALVERNE, JOHN (d. 1414?), historian; prior of Worcester; author of continuation of Higden's 'Polychronicon,' 1346–94.   [xxxvi. 8]

MALVERNE, JOHN (d. 1422?), physician and priest; prebendary of St. Paul's Cathedral, 1405; wrote 'De Remediis Spiritualibus et Corporalibus. . . .' [xxxvi. 8]

MALVOISIN, WILLIAM (d. 1238), chancellor of Scotland and archbishop of St. Andrews; chancellor, 1199–1211; bishop of Glasgow, 1200; corresponded with archbishop of Lyons; archbishop of St. Andrews, 1202; energetically vindicated rights of his see; founded hospitals and continued building of cathedral; visited Rome; treated with King John in England, 1215.
    [xxxvi. 8]

MALYNES, MALINES, or DE MALINES, GERARD (fl. 1586–1641), merchant and economic writer; commissioner of trade in Netherlands, c. 1586, for establishing par of exchange, 1600, and on mint affairs, 1609; consulted by council on mercantile questions; attempted unsuccessfully development of English lead and silver mines; ruined by undertaking farthing coinage; proposed system of pawnbroking under government control to relieve poor from usurers; published 'A Treatise of the Canker of England's Commonwealth . . .,' 1601, 'Consuetudo vel Lex Mercatoria . . .,' 1622, and other important works; one of the first English writers to apply natural law to economic science.   [xxxvi. 9]

MAN, HENRY (1747-1799), author; deputy-secretary of the South Sea House and colleague of Charles Lamb [q. v.]; contributed essays to 'Morning Chronicle'; his works collected, 1802.   [xxxvi. 11]

MAN or **MAIN**, JAMES (1700?-1761), philologist; M.A. King's College, Aberdeen, 1721; exposed errors in Ruddiman's edition of Buchanan in 'A Censure,' 1753.
[xxxvi. 12]

MAN, JOHN (1512-1569), dean of Gloucester: of Winchester College and New College, Oxford; fellow, 1531; M.A., 1538; expelled for heresy, but (1547) made president of White Hall, Oxford; warden of Merton College, Oxford, 1562; dean of Gloucester, 1566-9; ambassador to Spain, 1567; published 'Common places of Christian Religion,' 1563.   [xxxvi. 12]

MANASSEH BEN ISRAEL (1604-1657), Jewish theologian and chief advocate of readmission of Jews into England; studied at Amsterdam; became minister of the synagogue there; formed friendships with Isaac Vossius and Grotius; established press for Hebrew printing, 1626; published 'Spes Israelis,' 1650; sent petition to the Long parliament for return of Jews into England; was encouraged by sympathy of Cromwell, but his request was refused by council of state, 1652; subsequently he petitioned Cromwell again and wrote in defence of his cause, 1655, after which Jews were tacitly allowed to settle in London and opened a synagogue; received pension of 100*l*. from Cromwell; published theological works.   [xxxvi. 13]

MANBY, AARON (1776-1850), engineer; ironmaster at Wolverhampton and founder of Horseley ironworks, Tipton; took out patent for (but did not invent) 'oscillating engine,' 1821; built the Aaron Manby, 1822, first iron steamship to go to sea and first vessel to make voyage from London to Paris; founded Charenton works, 1819; obtained concession with others for lighting Paris with gas, 1822; bought Creusot ironworks, 1826.
[xxxvi. 14]

MANBY, CHARLES (1804-1884), civil engineer; son of Aaron Manby [q. v.]; assisted his father in England and France; manager of Beaufort ironworks, South Wales, 1829; civil engineer in London, 1835; secretary to Institution of Civil Engineers, 1839-56; F.R.S., 1853.
[xxxvi. 16]

MANBY, GEORGE WILLIAM (1765-1854), inventor of apparatus for saving life from shipwreck; brother of Thomas Manby [q. v.]; schoolfellow of Nelson at Durham; joined Cambridgeshire militia; barrack-master at Yarmouth, 1803; invented apparatus for firing line from mortar to wreck, successfully used, 1808, and afterwards extensively employed; invented other life-saving apparatus; F.R.S., 1831; published miscellaneous works.
[xxxvi. 16]

MANBY, PETER (*d.* 1697), dean of Derry; M.A. Trinity College, Dublin; chancellor of St. Patrick's, 1666; dean of Derry, 1672; turned Roman catholic, but was authorised by James II to retain deanery, 1686; retired to France after battle of the Boyne; published controversial religious works.   [xxxvi. 18]

MANBY, PETER (*fl.* 1724), son of Peter Manby (*d.* 1697)[q. v.]; jesuit.   [xxxvi. 18]

MANBY, THOMAS (*fl.* 1670-1690), landscape-painter.   [xxxvi. 18]

MANBY, THOMAS (1769-1834), rear-admiral; brother of George William Manby [q. v.]; entered navy, 1783, and served on various ships and stations; convoyed ships to West Indies, on the Bordelais, 1799, and engaged in small successful fight with French ships, 1801; convoyed ships again to West Indies, 1802, on the Africaine, a third of the crew dying from yellow fever on the voyage home; commanded small squadron on voyage to Davis Straits, 1808; rear-admiral, 1825.   [xxxvi. 18]

MANCHESTER, DUKES OF. [See MONTAGU, CHARLES, first DUKE, 1660?-1722; MONTAGU, GEORGE, fourth DUKE, 1737-1788; MONTAGU, WILLIAM, fifth DUKE, 1768-1843.]

MANCHESTER, EARLS OF. [See MONTAGU, SIR HENRY, first EARL, 1563?-1642; MONTAGU, EDWARD, second EARL, 1602-1671; MONTAGU, ROBERT, third EARL, 1634-1683; MONTAGU, CHARLES, fourth EARL, 1660?-1722.]

MANDERSTOWN, WILLIAM (*fl.* 1515-1540), philosopher; studied at Paris University; rector, 1525; published philosophical works.   [xxxvi. 20]

MANDEVIL, ROBERT (1578-1618), puritan divine; M.A. St. Edmund's Hall, Oxford, 1603; wrote 'Timothies Taske,' published, 1619.   [xxxvi. 20]

MANDEVILLE, BERNARD (1670?-1733), author of the 'Fable of the Bees'; native of Dort, Holland; M.D. Leyden, 1691; settled in England, where he was known for his wit and advocacy of 'dram drinking'; published 'The Grumbling Hive' (poem), 1705, republished with 'Inquiry into the Origin of Moral Virtue' and 'The Fable of the Bees, or Private Vices Public Benefits,' 1714, and again with 'Essay on Charity and Charity Schools,' and a 'Search into the Nature of Society,' 1723. His 'Fable,' maintaining the essential vileness of human nature, was widely controverted.   [xxxvi. 21]

MANDEVILLE, GEOFFREY DE, first EARL OF ESSEX (*d.* 1144), rebel; constable of the Tower of London; detained there Constance of France after her betrothal to Eustace, son of King Stephen; created Earl of Essex, before 1141; got possession of vast lands and enormous power by giving treacherous support to the king and the Empress Maud and betraying both; arrested by Stephen, 1143, and deprived of the Tower and other castles; raised rebellion in the fens, but was fatally wounded in fighting against Stephen at Burwell.   [xxxvi. 22]

MANDEVILLE, SIR JOHN, was the ostensible author of a book of travels bearing his name, composed soon after middle of the fourteenth century, purporting to be an account of his own journeys in the east, including Turkey, Tartary, Persia, Egypt, India, and Holy Land, but really a mere compilation, especially from William of Boldensele and Friar Odoric of Pordenone, and from the 'Speculum' of Vincent de Beauvais; his work written originally in French, from which English, Latin, German, and other translatoins were made. The author of this book of travels certainly died 1372, and was buried in the church of the Guillemins at Liège in the name of John Mandeville. Probably this name was fictitious, and its bearer is to be identified with Jean de Bourgogne or Burgoyne, chamberlain to John, baron de Mowbray, who took part in insurrection against Despensers, and on Mowbray's execution (1322) fled from England.   [xxxvi. 23]

MANDEVILLE or **MAGNAVILLA**, WILLIAM DE, third EARL OF ESSEX and EARL or COUNT OF AUMÂLE (*d.* 1189), son of Geoffrey de Mandeville, first earl of Essex [q. v.]; knighted by Philip of Flanders and brought up at Philip's court; became Earl of Essex on death of his brother, 1166; came over to England, 1166; accompanied Henry II abroad and remained faithful during rebellion, 1173-5; took part in crusade with Philip of Flanders, 1177-8; married heiress of Aumâle, 1180, and received lands and title; ambassador to Emperor Frederic I, 1182; took part with Henry II in his French wars; remained with Henry till the last; made a chief justiciar by Richard I, 1189; died at Rouen; founded several religious houses.   [xxxvi. 29]

MANDUIT, JOHN (*fl.* 1310). [See MAUDUITH.]

MANFIELD, SIR JAMES (1733-1821). [See MANSFIELD.]

MANGAN, JAMES, commonly called JAMES CLARENCE MANGAN (1803-1849), Irish poet; lawyer's clerk; later employed in library of Trinity College, Dublin, and Irish ordnance survey office; contributed prose and verse translations and original poems to various Irish journals and magazines; wrote for the 'Nation' and 'United Irishman,' but was prevented from keeping regular employment by his indulgence in drink; probably the greatest of the poets of Irish birth; published 'German Anthology,' 1845, and other volumes.   [xxxvi. 30]

MANGEY, THOMAS (1688-1755), divine and controversialist; M.A. St. John's College, Cambridge, 1711; fellow, 1715, and D.D.; held livings of St. Nicholas, Guildford, Ealing, and St. Mildred's, Bread Street, London; canon of Durham, 1721; edited 'Philonis Judæi Opera,' 1742.   [xxxvi. 32]

E e

MANGIN, EDWARD (1772–1852), miscellaneous writer; of Huguenot descent; M.A. Balliol College, Oxford. 1795; prebendary of Killaloe; lived at Bath and devoted his time to literary study; published, among other works, 'An Essay on Light Reading,' 1808.   [xxxvi. 32]

MANGLES, JAMES (1786–1867), captain R.N. and traveller; saw much service abroad; travelled with Charles Leonard Irby [q. v.], 1816, their letters being published in Murray's 'Home and Colonial Library,' 1844; published a few miscellaneous works.   [xxxvi. 33]

MANGLES, ROSS DONNELLY (1801–1877), chairman of East India Company; educated at Eton and East India Company's College at Haileybury; writer in Bengal civil service, 1819; deputy-secretary in general department, 1832; secretary to government of Bengal in judicial and revenue departments, 1835–9; liberal M.P. for Guildford, 1841–58; director of East India Company, 1847–57; chairman, 1857–8; member of council of India, 1858–66; published writings on Indian affairs.   [Suppl. iii. 136]

MANGNALL, RICHMAL (1769–1820), schoolmistress of Crofton Hall, Yorkshire; works include 'Historical and Miscellaneous Questions,' 1800.   [xxxvi. 34]

MANING, FREDERICK EDWARD (1812–1883), the Pākĕhā Maori; his father an emigrant to Van Diemen's Land, 1824; went to New Zealand, 1833; married Maori wife and settled among the natives; a judge of the native lands court, 1865–81; author of 'Old New Zealand,' 1863, and 'History of the War . . . in 1845.'   [xxxvi. 34]

MANINI, ANTONY (1750–1786), violinist; played and taught in provinces and at Cambridge as leading violinist; taught Charles Hague [q. v.]   [xxxvi. 34]

MANISTY, SIR HENRY (1808–1890), judge; solicitor, 1830; barrister, Gray's Inn, 1845; Q.C., 1857; judge, 1876; knighted, 1876.   [xxxvi. 35]

MANLEY, MRS. MARY DE LA RIVIERE (1663–1724), author of the 'New Atalantis'; daughter of Sir Roger Manley [q. v.]; drawn into false marriage with her cousin, John Manley, his wife being then alive; lived with Duchess of Cleveland; subsequently brought out 'Letters,' 1696, several plays, some of which were acted with success, and fell into disreputable course of life; published 'The New Atalantis,' 1709, in which whigs and persons of note were slandered, and was arrested, but escaped punishment; published 'Memoirs of Europe . . . written by Eginardus,' 1710, and 'Court Intrigues,' 1711; attacked by Swift in the 'Tatler' (No. 63); succeeded Swift as editor of the 'Examiner,' 1711, and was assisted by him; wrote several political pamphlets and defended herself from attacks by Steele in the 'Guardian'; brought out 'Lucius' at Drury Lane,' 1717; published works, including 'The Power of Love,' 1720; mistress for some years of Alderman Barber.   [xxxvi. 35]

MANLEY, SIR ROGER (1626?–1688), cavalier; fought for the king, but was exiled to Holland, 1646–60; lieutenant-governor of Jersey, 1667–74; subsequently governor of Landguard Fort; published 'History of Late Warres in Denmark,' 1670, and 'De Rebellione,' 1686.   [xxxvi. 38]

MANLEY, THOMAS (1628–1690), author; barrister, Middle Temple, c. 1650; K.C., 1672; published several legal works and a pamphlet, 'Usury at Six per cent.,' against Culpeper's tract, 'Usury,' 1669, as well as 'The Present State of Europe . . . found languishing, occasioned by the greatness of the French Monarchy,' 1689.   [xxxvi. 38]

MANLOVE, EDWARD (*fl.* 1667), poet and lawyer; wrote 'Liberties and Customs of the Lead Mines,' 1653 (in verse), and other works.   [xxxvi. 39]

MANLOVE, TIMOTHY (*d.* 1699), presbyterian divine and physician; probably grandson of Edward Manlove [q. v.]; minister at Leeds; published religious works.   [xxxvi. 39]

MANN, GOTHER (1747–1830), general, inspector-general of fortifications, colonel-commandant, R.E.; served in Dominica, 1775–8; employed in tour of survey of north-east coast of England, 1781; commanding R.E. in Canada, 1785–91 and 1794–1804; served under Duke of York in Holland, 1793; colonel-commandant, R.E., 1805, and general, 1821; inspector-general of fortifications, 1811; several of his plans for fortifying Canada still preserved.   [xxxvi. 40]

MANN, SIR HORACE, first baronet (1701–1786), British envoy at Florence; friend of Horace Walpole and made by Sir Robert Walpole assistant to Fane, envoy at Florence. 1737, becoming Fane's successor, 1740–86; communicated with government principally on subject of Young Pretender, who resided at Florence; kept up artificial correspondence, extending to thousands of letters, with Horace Walpole, 1741–85, valuable as illustrating Florentine society; created baronet, 1755; K.B., 1768.   [xxxvi. 41]

MANN, NICHOLAS (*d.* 1753), master of the Charterhouse, 1737; M.A. King's College, Cambridge, 1707, and fellow; scholar, antiquarian, and author.   [xxxvi. 43]

MANN, ROBERT JAMES (1817–1886), scientific writer; educated for the medical profession at University College, London; practised in Norfolk, but soon devoted himself more especially to literature; published series of scientific text-books which had large circulation; contributed to various publications; M.D. St. Andrews, 1854; superintendent of education in Natal, 1859; emigration agent for Natal in London, 1866; member of numerous learned societies.   [xxxvi. 43]

MANN, THEODORE AUGUSTUS, called the ABBÉ MANN (1735–1809), man of science, historian, and antiquary; sent to London to study for legal profession, 1753; proceeded, unknown to his parents, to Paris, 1754, read Bossuet and turned Roman catholic; on outbreak of war went to Spain, 1756, and was given commission in O'Mahony's dragoons; became monk in the English Chartreuse, Nieuport, 1759, and prior, 1764; appointed imperial minister of public instruction at Brussels, 1776; wrote memoirs on various practical projects for imperial government and numerous educational primers; travelled; secretary and treasurer of Brussels Academy, 1786; F.R.S., 1788; retired to England, 1792, during French irruption; at Prague, 1794; published works in French and English, miscellaneous papers, and catalogues, reports, and letters.   [xxxvi. 44]

MANN, WILLIAM (1817–1873), astronomer; grandson of Gother Mann [q. v.]; assistant at Royal Observatory, Cape of Good Hope; erected transit-circle with native aid, 1855, and made valuable observations.   [xxxvi. 46]

MANNERS, MRS. CATHERINE, afterwards LADY STEPNEY (*d.* 1845). [See STEPNEY.]

MANNERS, CHARLES, fourth DUKE OF RUTLAND (1754–1787), eldest son of John Manners, marquis of Granby [q. v.]; M.A. Trinity College, Cambridge, 1774; M.P., Cambridge, 1774; opposed government policy in America; succeeded to dukedom, 1779; lord-lieutenant of Leicestershire, 1779; K.G., 1782; lord-steward, 1783; privy councillor, 1783; resigned on formation of coalition government, but lord privy seal in Pitt's ministry; lord-lieutenant of Ireland, 1784, advocated union and passed, with some concessions, Pitt's commercial propositions through Irish parliament; gave magnificent entertainments and made a tour through the country, 1787; died at Phœnix Lodge, Dublin, from fever.   [xxxvi. 46]

MANNERS, CHARLES CECIL JOHN, sixth DUKE OF RUTLAND (1815–1868), M.P.; strong protectionist, and supporter of George Bentinck; succeeded to title, 1857; K.G., 1867.   [xxxvi. 48]

MANNERS, EDWARD, third EARL OF RUTLAND (1549–1587), son of Henry Manners, second earl of Rutland [q. v.]; displayed great devotion to Elizabeth; filled numerous offices; lord-lieutenant of Nottinghamshire and Lincolnshire; K.G., 1584; commissioner to try Mary Queen of Scots, 1586; lord-chancellor designate, April 1587, dying the same month.   [xxxvi. 48]

MANNERS, FRANCIS, sixth EARL OF RUTLAND (1578–1632), brother of Roger Manners, fifth earl [q. v.]; travelled abroad; took part in Essex's plot, 1601; succeeded to earldom, 1612; lord-lieutenant of Lincolnshire and Northamptonshire; held several offices; K.G., 1616; privy councillor, 1617; admiral of the fleet to bring home Prince Charles from Spain, 1623.   [xxxvi. 49]

MANNERS, GEORGE (1778–1853), editor and founder of the 'Satirist,' 1807, a scurrilous periodical; consul at Boston, U.S.A., 1819–39; published miscellaneous works.   [xxxvi. 50]

MANNERS, HENRY, second EARL OF RUTLAND (*d.* 1563), son of Thomas Manners, first earl of Rutland [q. v.] ; succeeded to earldom, 1543 ; knighted, 1544 ; made chief-justice of Sherwood Forest, 1547 ; took part in Scottish operations ; attended embassy to France, 1551 ; belonged to the extreme reformers' party ; lord-lieutenant of Nottinghamshire, 1552, of Rutland, 1559 ; imprisoned at Mary's accession, 1553 ; admiral, 1556 ; general in French war, 1557 ; favourite of Elizabeth ; K.G., 1559 ; lord president of the north, 1561, and ecclesiastical commissioner for York. [xxxvi. 50]

MANNERS, JOHN, eighth EARL OF RUTLAND (1604–1679), descended from Thomas Manners, first earl of Rutland [q. v.] ; succeeded to earldom, 1642 ; moderate parliamentarian ; took covenant, 1643 ; filled various offices ; at the Restoration rebuilt Belvoir, which had been dismantled ; lord-lieutenant of Leicestershire, 1667. [xxxvi. 51]

MANNERS, JOHN (1609–1695). [See SIMCOCKS.]

MANNERS, JOHN, ninth EARL and first DUKE OF RUTLAND (1638–1711), son of John Manners, eighth earl of Rutland [q. v.] ; succeeded to earldom, 1679 ; lord-lieutenant of Leicestershire, 1677, dismissed, 1687, and restored, 1689 ; assisted in raising forces for William of Orange in Nottinghamshire ; created Marquis of Granby and Duke of Rutland, 1703. [xxxvi. 51]

MANNERS, JOHN, MARQUIS OF GRANBY (1721–1770), lieutenant-general ; colonel of royal horse guards (blues) ; eldest son of John Manners, third duke of Rutland (1696–1779) ; of Eton and Trinity College, Cambridge ; travelled with his tutor, John Ewer [q. v.] ; M.P. for Grantham and subsequently for Cambridge ; colonel of ' Leicester blues' at Jacobite invasion, 1745 ; served in Flanders, 1747 ; colonel of the blues, 1758 ; lieutenant-general, 1759 ; commanded blues at Minden, 1759, where his advance was stayed by orders of Lord George Sackville [see GERMAIN] ; succeeded latter as commander-in-chief of British contingent, 1759 ; performed brilliant services at Warburg, 1760, Fellinghausen, 1761, Gravenstein, Wilhelmstahl, heights of Homburg, and Cassel, 1762 ; master-general of the ordnance, 1763 ; twelfth commander-in-chief, 1766 ; savagely assailed by Junius ; retired from office, 1770 ; lord-lieutenant of Derbyshire. [xxxvi. 52]

MANNERS, SIR ROBERT (*d.* 1355 ?) ; M.P., Northumberland, 1340 ; constable of Norham before 1345 ; fought at Neville's Cross, 1346. [xxxvi. 54]

MANNERS, SIR ROBERT (1408–1461), sheriff, 1454, and M.P. for Northumberland, 1459. [xxxvi. 54]

MANNERS, LORD ROBERT (1758–1782), captain, R.N. ; son of John Manners, marquis of Granby [q. v.] ; served under Rodney and Hood and took part in actions off Ushant, 1778, Cape St. Vincent, 1779, Cape Henry, 1781, and Dominica, 1782, where he was fatally wounded. [xxxvi. 54]

MANNERS, ROGER, fifth EARL OF RUTLAND (1576–1612), son of fourth earl ; educated at Queens' and Corpus Christi Colleges, Cambridge ; M.A., 1595 ; travelled abroad, ' Profitable Instructions' being written for him, probably by Bacon ; knighted by Essex in Ireland, 1599 ; steward of Sherwood Forest, 1600 ; took part in Essex's conspiracy, 1601, and was heavily fined ; K.B., 1603 ; lord-lieutenant of Lincolnshire, 1603. [xxxvi. 55]

MANNERS, THOMAS, first EARL OF RUTLAND and thirteenth BARON ROS (*d.* 1543), became Baron Ros on his father's death, 1513 ; took part in French expedition, 1513 ; present at Field of the Cloth of Gold, 1520 ; favourite of Henry VIII, receiving numerous grants and offices ; warden of the east marches and of Sherwood Forest ; K.G., 1525 ; created Earl of Rutland, 1525 ; took active part against northern rebels, 1536 ; constable of Nottingham Castle, 1542. [xxxvi. 56]

MANNERS-SUTTON, CHARLES (1755–1828), archbishop of Canterbury ; brother of Thomas Manners-Sutton, first baron Manners [q. v.] ; fifteenth wrangler, 1777, and M.A. Emmanuel College, Cambridge, 1780 ; D.D., 1792 ; rector of Averham-with-Kelham and Whitwell, 1785 ; dean of Peterborough, 1791 ; bishop of Norwich, 1792–1805 ; dean of Windsor, 1794 ; favourite of royal family ; archbishop of Canterbury, 1805–28 ; active in church revival. [xxxvi. 57]

MANNERS-SUTTON, CHARLES, first VISCOUNT CANTERBURY (1780–1845), speaker of the House of Commons ; son of Charles Manners-Sutton [q. v.], archbishop of Canterbury ; of Eton and Trinity College, Cambridge ; M.A., 1805 ; LL.D., 1824 ; barrister, Lincoln's Inn, 1806 ; tory M.P. for Scarborough and subsequently for Cambridge University ; judge advocate-general, 1809 ; privy councillor, 1809 ; opposed inquiry into state of Ireland, 1812, and catholic claims, 1813 ; passed Clergy Residence Bill, 1817 ; speaker, 1817–35, when he was accused of partisanship and his candidature defeated ; refused office several times ; G.C.B. and received pension, 1833 ; created Baron Bottesford and Viscount Canterbury, 1835. [xxxvi. 58]

MANNERS-SUTTON, JOHN HENRY THOMAS, third VISCOUNT CANTERBURY (1814–1877), son of Charles Manners-Sutton, first Viscount Canterbury [q. v.] ; M.A. Trinity College, Cambridge, 1835 ; M.P., Cambridge 1841–7 ; under home secretary (1841–6) in Peel's administration ; lieutenant-governor of New Brunswick, 1854–61 ; governor of Trinidad, 1864–6, and Victoria, 1866–1873 ; K.C.B., 1866 ; succeeded to title, 1869 ; K.C.M.G., 1873 ; published 'Lexington Papers,' 1851. [xxxvi. 59]

MANNERS-SUTTON, THOMAS, first BARON MANNERS (1756–1842), lord chancellor of Ireland ; grandson of the third Duke of Rutland ; fifth wrangler, Emmanuel College, Cambridge, 1777 ; M.A., 1780 ; barrister, Lincoln's Inn, 1780 ; obtained large chancery practice ; M.P., Newark-upon-Trent, 1796–1805 ; Welsh judge, 1797 ; K.C., 1800, and solicitor-general to Prince of Wales, 1800 ; solicitor-general, 1802 ; knighted, 1802 ; serjeant-at-law and baron of exchequer, 1805 ; created Baron Manners and privy councillor, 1807 ; lord chancellor of Ireland, 1807–27 ; removed O'Hanlon from bench for supporting catholic claims ; took active part in proceedings against Queen Caroline, 1820 ; opposed catholic claims, 1828. [xxxvi. 60]

MANNIN, JAMES (*d.* 1779), flower-painter. [xxxvi. 62]

MANNING, ANNE (1807–1879), miscellaneous writer ; sister of William Oke Manning [q. v.] ; contributed to 'Sharpe's Magazine,' 1849, 'The Maiden and Married Life of Mistress Mary Powell' (frequently reprinted) ; was known thenceforward as the 'author of Mary Powell' ; her best works are historical tales of the sixteenth century. [Suppl. iii. 137]

MANNING, HENRY EDWARD (1808–1892), cardinal-priest ; educated at Balliol College, Oxford, under Charles Wordsworth, and with William Ewart Gladstone [q. v.] ; M.A., 1833 ; obtained post in colonial office, 1830 ; fellow, Merton College, 1832 ; curate of Woollavington-cum-Graffham, 1832, and rector, 1833 ; rural dean, 1832 ; archdeacon of Chichester, 1840 ; select preacher at Oxford, 1842 ; published 'The Unity of the Church,' an able exposition of Anglo-catholic principles, and 'Sermons,' 1844 ; disapproved of 'Tract XC.' and preached anti-papal sermon at Oxford on Guy Fawkes' day, 1843 ; voted against William George Ward's degradation by the Oxford convocation, 1845 ; travelled abroad and (1848) visited Pius IX ; supported resistance to government grants in aid of elementary schools, 1849 ; protested against Gorham judgment, 1850, and wrote 'The Appellate Jurisdiction of the Crown in Matters Spiritual' denying the jurisdiction ; resigned archdeaconry and became Roman catholic, 1851 ; published 'The Grounds of Faith,' 1852 ; superior of 'Congregation of the Oblates of St. Charles,' at Bayswater, 1857 ; occupied himself in preaching, education, mission work, and literary defence of papal temporal power ; appointed at Rome domestic prelate and monsignore, 1860 ; published letters 'To an Anglican Friend,' 1864, and on 'The Workings of the Holy Spirit in the Church of England,' addressed to Pusey ; nominated Roman catholic archbishop of Westminster, 1865 ; published 'The Temporal Mission of the Holy Ghost,' 1865 and 1875 ; as archbishop was autocratic and a thorough ultramontane ; established Westminster Education Fund, 1866 ; supported infallibility of the pope, and published 'Petri Privilegium,' 1871, and 'National Education,' 1872, in favour of voluntary teaching ; contributed articles to various papers defending his orthodoxy and ultramontane theory ; published 'The Vatican Decrees,' 1875, in answer to William Ewart Gladstone ; published in the 'Daily Telegraph' letters on the infallibility of the Roman church, in answer to Lord Redesdale, 1875 (reprinted, 1875) ; cardinal, 1875 ; carried on crusade against drink ; a zealous philanthropist ; sat on royal commissions on housing of the poor, 1884–5, and Education Acts, 1886–1887, and published articles on those topics ; favoured

Gladstone's domestic politics in later life; great preacher and ecclesiastical statesman; of ascetic temper; a subtle but unspeculative controversialist; published in late years 'The Eternal Priesthood,' 1883, sermons, and other works.
[xxxvi. 62]

MANNING, JAMES (1781–1866), serjeant-at-law; barrister, Lincoln's Inn, 1817; leader of western circuit; learned especially in copyright law; recorder of Sudbury, 1835–66, and Oxford and Banbury, 1857–66; serjeant-at-law, 1840, and queen's ancient serjeant, 1846; judge of Whitechapel County Court, 1847; published legal works.
[xxxvi. 68]

MANNING, MARIE (1821–1849), murderess; née de Roux; native of Lausanne; married Frederick George Manning, publican, 1847, and with him murdered O'Connor at Bermondsey, 1849, both being condemned and executed.
[xxxvi. 69]

MANNING, OWEN (1721–1801), historian of Surrey; M.A. Queens' College, Cambridge, 1744; B.D., 1753; fellow and incumbent of St. Botolph, Cambridge, 1741; obtained several other preferments; rector of Godalming, 1763–1801; prebendary of Lincoln, 1757 and 1760; collected materials for history of Surrey, afterwards published with additions by William Bray (1736–1832) [q. v.], 1804–9–14; completed Lye's Saxon dictionary, 1772, and annotated 'The Will of King Alfred,' 1788.
[xxxvi. 69]

MANNING, ROBERT (d. 1731), Roman catholic controversialist; professor at Douay English college; missioner in England; works include 'The Shortest Way to end disputes about religion,' 1716.
[xxxvi. 70]

MANNING, SAMUEL, the younger (fl. 1846), sculptor; son of Samuel Manning (d. 1847) [q. v.]
[xxxvi. 71]

MANNING, SAMUEL (d. 1847), sculptor; executed bust of Warren Hastings's statue in Westminster Abbey; exhibited statuary at Royal Academy.
[xxxvi. 71]

MANNING, SAMUEL (1822–1881), baptist minister at Sheppard's Barton, Somerset, 1846–61; editor of the 'Baptist Magazine'; general book editor of Religious Tract Society, 1863, and joint-secretary, 1876.
[xxxvi. 71]

MANNING, THOMAS (1772–1840), traveller and friend of Charles Lamb; scholar of Caius College, Cambridge, and private tutor; studied mathematics and made acquaintance with Porson and Lamb; studied Chinese at Paris, 1800–3; studied medicine and left for Canton, 1807, but failed to penetrate into China; went to Calcutta, 1810, and travelled from Rangpur to Lhasa, 1811, the first Englishman to enter Lhasa; returned to Canton, 1812; accompanied Lord Amherst to Pekin as interpreter, 1816; returned to England, 1817; considered first Chinese scholar in Europe; wrote mathematical works.
[xxxvi. 71]

MANNING, WILLIAM (1630?–1711), ejected minister; perpetual curate of Middleton, Suffolk; ejected, 1662; took out licence as 'congregational teacher' at Peasenhall, 1672; became Socinian; published sermons.
[xxxvi. 73]

MANNING, WILLIAM OKE (1809–1878), legal writer; nephew of James Manning (1781–1866) [q. v.]; published 'Commentaries on Law of Nations,' 1839.
[xxxvi. 74]

MANNINGHAM, JOHN (d. 1622), diarist; student of Middle Temple and utter barrister, 1605; his diary (1602–1603), of considerable value, was first printed by the Camden Society in 1868.
[xxxvi. 74]

MANNINGHAM, SIR RICHARD (1690–1759), man-midwife; son of Thomas Manningham [q. v]; LL.B. Cambridge, 1717; M.D.; F.R.S., 1720; knighted, 1721; chief man-midwife of the day; attended Mary Toft [q. v.], and published 'Exact Diary' on the case, 1726; published 'Artis Obstetricariæ Compendium,' 1740, and other works.
[xxxvi. 74]

MANNINGHAM, THOMAS (1651?–1722), bishop of Chichester; scholar of Winchester College and New College, Oxford; fellow, 1671–81; M.A., 1677; D.D. Lambeth, 1691; obtained various preferments; dean of Windsor, 1709; bishop of Chichester, 1709; published sermons.
[xxxvi. 75]

MANNOCK, JOHN (1677–1764), Benedictine monk; made profession at Douay, 1700; chaplain to Canning family; procurator of southern province, 1729; published religious works.
[xxxvi. 76]

MANNY or MAUNY, SIR WALTER DE, afterwards BARON DE MANNY (d. 1372), military commander and founder of the Charterhouse, London; native of Hainault; esquire to Queen Philippa; knighted, 1331; distinguished himself in Scottish wars; was rewarded with lands and governorship of Merioneth (1332) and Harlech Castle (1334); admiral of northern fleet, 1337, capturing Guy de Rickenburg in the Scheldt; according to Froissart took French castle of Thun l'Evêque with only forty lances on defiance of French king, 1339; served throughout campaign and won distinction at Sluys, 1340; sent by Edward III to assist Countess of Montfort against Charles of Blois, 1342; accompanied Earl of Derby in successful Gascony campaigns; according to Froissart conducted siege of Calais, and was summoned to parliament as baron, 1345; sent to negotiate in France, 1348, and in Netherlands, 1351; received grants of land; accompanied Edward III to Artois, 1355; present at siege of Berwick, 1355; took part in Edward's French campaigns, 1359–60, and negotiated in his name; a guarantor of treaty of Bretigni and guardian of King John of France at Calais, 1360; K.G., 1359; ordered to Ireland, 1368; accompanied John of Gaunt in invasion of France, 1369; obtained licence to found house of Carthusian monks, i.e. the Charterhouse in London, 1371; one of the ablest of Edward III's soldiers.
[xxxvi. 76]

MANNYNG, ROBERT, or ROBERT DE BRUNNE (fl. 1288–1338), poet; native of Bourne, Lincolnshire; entered Sempringham priory, 1288; wrote 'Handlyng Synne' (edited, 1862), the 'Chronicle of England' (first part edited by Dr. Furnivall, second part by Hearne), neither original works, but of great literary value; also probable author of 'Meditacyuns' (edited, 1875).
[xxxvi. 80]

MANSEL, CHARLES GRENVILLE (1806–1886), Indian official; filled various posts at Agra; member of Punjáb administration, 1849, resident of Nagpur, 1850.
[xxxvi. 81]

MANSEL, HENRY LONGUEVILLE (1820–1871), metaphysician; educated at Merchant Taylors' School, London, where he wrote verses; scholar, St. John's College, Oxford; obtained 'double first,' 1843; tutor, and ordained, 1844; strong tory and high churchman; 'professor fellow,' 1864; reader in theology at Magdalen College, Oxford, from 1855; wrote article on metaphysics in 'Encyclopædia Britannica,' 1857; Bampton lecturer, 1858; engaged in controversy with Maurice, Goldwin Smith, and Mill; select preacher, 1860–2, and 1869–71; professor of ecclesiastical history, 1866–8; lectured on 'The Gnostic Heresies,' 1868; dean of St. Paul's, 1868–71; published 'Phrontisterion,' 1850, 'Prolegomena Logica,' 1851, 'The Limits of Demonstrative Science,' 1853, 'Man's Conception of Eternity,' 1854, and other metaphysical works; contributed to 'The Speaker's Commentary,' and to 'Aids to Faith'; follower of Sir William Hamilton, and, with Veitch, edited his lectures, 1859. [xxxvi. 81]

MANSEL or MAUNSELL, JOHN (d. 1265), keeper of the seal and counsellor of Henry III; son of a country priest; obtained post at exchequer, 1234; accompanied Henry III on expedition to France, 1242–3, and greatly distinguished himself; keeper of the great seal, 1246–7, and subsequently; ambassador to Brabant, 1247; had considerable influence with Henry III; sent on missions to Scotland, Brabant, France, Germany, and Brittany; concerned in Edward's marriage to Eleanor of Castile, 1254, in the election of Richard, king of the Romans, 1257, and in the abandonment of English claims on Normandy, 1258; member of the committee of twenty-four and council of fifteen, 1258; followed Henry III to France; the king compelled to dismiss him, 1261; obtained papal bull releasing Henry III from his obligations, 1262; accompanied Henry III to France, 1262; on civil war breaking out, escaped to Boulogne, 1263; present at mise of Amiens, 1264; died in France in great poverty; said to have held three hundred benefices; by supporting the king's measures acquired much odium, but was a capable and diligent administrator.
[xxxvi. 84]

MANSEL, WILLIAM LORT (1753–1820), bishop of Bristol; M.A. Trinity College, Cambridge, 1777; fellow, 1777; D.D., 1778; tutor; master, 1798; vice-chancellor, 1799–1800; held livings of Bottisham and Chesterton; appointed bishop of Bristol by Perceval, a former pupil, 1808; well-known wit and writer of epigrams; author of sermons.
[xxxvi. 86]

MANSELL, FRANCIS (1579–1665), principal of Jesus College, Oxford; M.A. Jesus College, Oxford, 1611; fellow of All Souls College, Oxford, 1613; D.D., 1624; principal of Jesus College, 1620; after expelling several fellows retired from office; again principal, 1630–47; treasurer of Llandaff and prebendary of St. David's, 1631; benefactor of the college; assisted royalists in Wales, 1643–7; ejected from Jesus College, 1647; reinstated, 1660. [xxxvi. 87]

MANSELL, SIR ROBERT (1573–1656), admiral; served in Cadiz expedition and was knighted, 1596; took part in 'The Islands' Voyage,' 1597; held commands off Irish coast, 1599–1600; active in arresting accomplices of Essex and captured Hansa ships, 1601; M.P., King's Lynn, 1601, Carmarthen, 1603, Carmarthenshire, 1614, Glamorganshire, 1623–5, Lostwithiel, 1626, and Glamorganshire, 1628; intercepted Portuguese galleys, 1602; 'vice-admiral of the Narrow Seas, 1603; treasurer of the navy, 1604; accompanied Earl of Nottingham on Spanish mission, 1605; imprisoned in the Marshalsea for alleged political disaffection, 1613; vice-admiral of England, 1618; commanded unsuccessful expeditions against Algiers, 1620–1; obtained glass monopoly, 1615. [xxxvi. 88]

MANSELL, SIR THOMAS (1777–1858), rear-admiral; present at actions off Lorient, 1795, Cape St. Vincent, 1797, and battle of the Nile, 1798; promoted lieutenant by Nelson; held various commands and captured 170 ships; K.C.H., 1837; rear-admiral, 1849. [xxxvi. 89]

MANSFIELD, EARLS OF. [See MURRAY, WILLIAM, first EARL, 1705–1793; MURRAY, DAVID, second EARL, 1727–1796.]

MANSFIELD, CHARLES BLACKFORD (1819–1855), chemist and author; M.A. Clare Hall, Cambridge, 1849; discovered method of extracting benzol from coal-tar, 1848, and published pamphlet; joined Maurice and Kingsley in efforts for social reform (1848–9), and contributed to 'Politics for the People' and 'Christian Socialist'; published 'Aerial Navigation,' 1850, and delivered lectures at Royal Institution on chemistry of metals, 1851–2; visited Buenos Ayres and Paraguay, 1852–3; published 'Theory of Salts,' 1855; died from accident by burning. [xxxvi. 90]

MANSFIELD, HENRY DE (d. 1328). [See MAUNSFIELD.]

MANSFIELD (originally **MANFIELD**), SIR JAMES (1733–1821), lord chief-justice of common pleas; fellow, King's College, Cambridge, 1754; M.A., 1758; barrister, Middle Temple, 1758; adviser of Wilkes, 1768, Duchess of Kingston, and others; K.C., 1772; M.P., Cambridge University, 1779–84; solicitor-general, 1780–2, and in coalition ministry, 1783; chief-justice of common pleas and knighted, 1804. [xxxvi. 91]

MANSFIELD, SIR WILLIAM ROSE, first BARON SANDHURST (1819–1876), general; grandson of Sir James Mansfield [q. v.]; joined 53rd foot, 1835; distinguished himself in first Sikh war, Punjab war, 1849, and under Sir Colin Campbell on Peshawur frontier; military adviser to British ambassador at Constantinople, 1855; consul-general at Warsaw, 1856; chief of the staff to Sir Colin Campbell in Indian mutiny, 1857; present at relief and siege of Lucknow and fight at Cawnpore, when his conduct was much criticised; served in campaigns in Rohilcund, Oude, and other operations; commander of Bombay presidency, 1860; commander-in-chief in India, 1865; in Ireland, 1870; general, 1872; K.C.B., 1857; created Baron Sandhurst, 1871; G.C.S.I., 1866; G.C.B., 1870; D.C.L. Oxford, 1870; Irish privy councillor, 1870. [xxxvi. 92]

MANSHIP, HENRY (fl. 1562), topographer; directed construction of Yarmouth harbour; his 'Greate Yermouthe' printed, 1847. [xxxvi. 94]

MANSHIP, HENRY (d. 1625), topographer; son of Henry Manship [q. v.]; town clerk of Yarmouth, 1579–85; dismissed from corporation, 1604; managed Yarmouth affairs in London, again falling into disgrace, 1616; published 'History of Great Yarmouth,' 1619; died in poverty. [xxxvi. 94]

MANSON, DAVID (1726–1792), schoolmaster; began life as farmer's boy at Cairncastle, co. Antrim; opened school there and afterwards (1755) one at Belfast and also a brewery; published school-books. [xxxvi. 95]

MANSON, GEORGE (1850–1876), Scottish artist; executed woodcuts for 'Chambers's Miscellany'; disciple of Bewick and painter of homely subjects. [xxxvi. 96]

MANT, RICHARD (1776–1848), bishop of Down, Connor, and Dromore; scholar of Winchester College and Trinity College, Oxford; fellow of Oriel College, Oxford, 1798; gained chancellor's prize with essay 'On Commerce,' 1799; M.A., 1801; D.D., 1815; vicar of Coggeshall, Essex, 1810; Bampton lecturer, 1811; chaplain to the archbishop of Canterbury, 1813; rector of St. Botolph's, 1815, and East Horsley, 1818; bishop of Killaloe and Kilfenoragh, 1820; translated to Down and Connor, 1823, Dromore being added, 1842; built many new churches; published poetical, theological, miscellaneous, and historical works, including 'History of the Church of Ireland,' 1840. [xxxvi. 96]

MANT, WALTER BISHOP (1807–1869), divine; son of Richard Mant [q. v.]; archdeacon of Down, antiquarian, and author of works in prose and verse. [xxxvi. 98]

MANTE, THOMAS (fl. 1772), military writer; author of 'History of the late War in America,' 1772, and other works. [xxxvi. 98]

MANTELL, GIDEON ALGERNON (1790–1852), geologist; son of a shoemaker; articled to, and finally partner of Lewes surgeon; devoted himself to natural history and geology and made noted collection; removed to Brighton, 1835, and lectured; published 'The Wonders of Geology,' 1838, and other geological works, besides papers published by Royal and Geological Societies, setting forth his extensive investigations and discoveries; F.R.S., 1825; hon. F.R.C.S., 1844. [xxxvi. 99]

MANTELL, JOSHUA (1795–1865), surgeon and horticultural writer; brother of Gideon Algernon Mantell [q. v.] [xxxvi. 100]

MANTELL, SIR THOMAS (1751–1831), antiquary; F.S.A., 1810; surgeon at Dover and mayor; knighted, 1820; published 'Cinque Ports,' 1828, and other works. [xxxvi. 100]

MANTON, JOHN (d. 1834), gunmaker; brother of Joseph Manton [q. v.] [xxxvi. 101]

MANTON, JOSEPH (1766?–1835), gunmaker; took out several patents for improvements in guns, 1792–1825, and other inventions; bankrupt, 1826. [xxxvi. 101]

MANTON, THOMAS (1620–1677), presbyterian divine; B.A. Hart Hall, Oxford, 1639; ordained, 1640; lecturer at Cullompton and (c. 1645) obtained living of Stoke Newington; one of the scribes to Westminster Assembly; disapproved of Charles I's execution; attended Christopher Love [q. v.] on the scaffold and preached funeral sermon, 1651; rector of St. Paul's, Covent Garden, London, 1656; drew up with Baxter and others 'Fundamentals of Religion,' 1658; one of the deputies to Breda, and chaplain to Charles II; took part in religious conferences and was created D.D. Oxford, 1660; left St. Paul's, Covent Garden, 1662, and held meetings elsewhere in London; arrested, 1670; preacher at Pinners' Hall, London, 1672; discussed 'accommodation' with Tillotson and Stillingfleet, 1674; the most popular of the presbyterians; published religious works. [xxxvi. 101]

MANUCHE or **MANUCCI**, COSMO (fl. 1652), dramatist; of Italian origin; probably member of household of James Compton, third earl of Northampton; captain and major of foot in king's army during civil war; subsequently obtained employment under the Protector. Twelve plays have been assigned to him, three of which were published, 'The Just General,' 1652, 'The Loyal Lovers,' 1652, and 'The Bastard' (issued anonymously), 1652; of the remaining nine plays which were formerly in manuscript at Castle Ashby only one is still known there. [Suppl. iii. 138]

MANWARING or **MAYNWARING**, ROGER (1590–1653), bishop of St. David's; D.D. All Souls College, Oxford; rector of St. Giles's-in-the-Fields, London, 1616; chaplain to Charles I; preached sermons before Charles I on 'Religion' and 'Allegiance,' 1627, asserting 'peril of damnation' of those who resisted taxation levied by royal authority; on being sentenced to imprisonment, fine, and suspension, made retractation; received several preferments; dean of Worcester, 1633; bishop of St. David's, 1635; was deprived of vote in House of Lords by Short parliament, 1640; imprisoned and persecuted by Long parliament. [xxxvi. 104]

MANWOOD, JOHN (d. 1610), legal author; relative of Sir Roger Manwood [q. v.]; barrister, Lincoln's Inn; justice of the New Forest; published 'A Brefe Collection of the Lawes of the Forest,' 1592 (enlarged, 1615).
[xxxvi. 105]

MANWOOD, SIR PETER (d. 1625), antiquary; son of Sir Roger Manwood [q. v.]; student of the Inner Temple, 1583; represented between 1588 and 1621 Sandwich, Saltash, Kent, and New Romney; sheriff of Kent, 1602; K.B., 1603; patron of learned men at St. Stephen's, near Canterbury, and mentioned with great respect by Camden; published part of Williams's 'Actions of the Lowe Countries,' 1618. [xxxvi. 105]

MANWOOD, SIR ROGER (1525–1592), judge; barrister, Inner Temple, 1555; recorder of Sandwich, 1555–66, and steward of chancery and admiralty courts, Dover; M.P., Hastings, 1555, Sandwich, 1558; granted by Elizabeth manor of St. Stephen's, Kent; friend of Sir Thomas Gresham and Archbishop Parker, and founded with the latter grammar school at Sandwich; supported treason bill, 1571; judge of common pleas, 1572–8; with bishops of London and Rochester convicted of anabaptism two Flemings, who were burnt, 1575; showed himself severe towards enemies of the government; knighted, 1578; chief baron of the exchequer, 1578–92; member of Starchamber, which sentenced Lord Vaux of Harrowden, 1581; member of commission at Fotheringay, 1586; rebuked by Elizabeth for sale of office, 1591; accused of various malpractices and arraigned before privy council, 1592. [xxxvi. 106]

MAP or MAPES, WALTER (fl. 1200), mediæval author and wit; probably native of Herefordshire; studied in Paris under Girard la Pucelle; clerk of royal household and justice itinerant; accompanied Henry II abroad, 1173 and 1183; sent to Rome, 1179; canon of St. Paul's Cathedral, Lincoln, and Hereford; precentor, and, later, chancellor of Oxford; archdeacon of Oxford from 1197; author of 'De Nugis Curialium,' a collection of anecdotes and legends of considerable interest and of satirical purport (edited, 1850); probably also author, or largely author, of 'Lancelot,' and perhaps of some of the satirical Goliardic verse; specimens of his wit preserved by Giraldus. [xxxvi. 109]

MAPLET, JOHN (d. 1592), miscellaneous writer; fellow of Catharine Hall, Cambridge, 1564; M.A., 1567; vicar of Northolt, Middlesex, 1576; wrote 'A Greene Forest' (natural history), 1567, and 'The Diall of Destinie,' 1581. [xxxvi. 112]

MAPLET, JOHN (1612?–1670), physician; M.A., 1638, and M.D., 1647, Christ Church, Oxford; principal of Gloucester Hall, Oxford, 1647; travelled in France with third Viscount Falkland and went to Holland; ejected from Oxford appointments; practised medicine at Bath; reinstated at Oxford, 1660; author of miscellaneous works in Latin, prose and verse. [xxxvi. 113]

MAPLETOFT, JOHN (1631–1721), physician and divine; nephew of Robert Mapletoft [q. v.]; educated at Westminster School; scholar and fellow (1653) of Trinity College, Cambridge; M.A., 1655, and M.D., 1667 (incorporated at Oxford, 1669); tutor to Earl of Northumberland's son; practised medicine in London with Sydenham and became intimate with John Locke; travelled abroad; Gresham professor of physic, 1675–9; successively rector of Braybrooke and St. Lawrence Jewry, London; lecturer at Ipswich, 1685, and St. Christopher's, London, 1685; D.D. Cambridge, 1690; F.R.S., 1676; works include 'The Principles and Duties of the Christian Religion,' 1710.
[xxxvi. 113]

MAPLETOFT, ROBERT (1609–1677), dean of Ely; M.A. Queens' College, Cambridge, 1632; fellow of Pembroke College, 1631; chaplain to Bishop Wren; rector of Bartlow, 1639; ejected, 1644; officiated privately at Lincoln; D.D. at Restoration by royal mandate; sub-dean of Lincoln, 1660; master of Spital Hospital, 1660, reviving the charity; rector successively of Clayworth and Soham; master of Pembroke, 1664–77; vice-chancellor, 1671–2; dean of Ely, 1667–77; founded educational institutions.
[xxxvi. 115]

MAR, EARLS OF. [See ERSKINE, JOHN, first or sixth EARL of the Erskine line, d. 1572; ERSKINE, JOHN, second or seventh EARL, 1558–1634; ERSKINE, JOHN, sixth or eleventh EARL, 1675–1732; STEWART, ALEXANDER, EARL OF MAR, 1375?–1435; STEWART, JOHN, EARL OF MAR,

1457?–1479?; COCHRANE, ROBERT, EARL OF MAR, d. 1482; STEWART, LORD JAMES, EARL OF MAR, 1531?–1570.]

MAR, DONALD, tenth EARL OF (d. 1297), son of William Mar, ninth earl of Mar [q. v.]; supported Edward I's suzerainty over Scotland; revolted, 1294, but returned to allegiance after battle of Dunbar, 1296.
[xxxvi. 116]

MAR, DONALD, twelfth EARL OF (1293?–1332), grandson of Donald Mar, tenth earl of Mar [q. v.], and nephew of Robert Bruce; brought to England, 1306; was exchanged, 1314, after Bannockburn, but returned, preferring England; received grants; keeper of Newark Castle, 1321; joined Scots in raid, 1327; regent of Scotland, 1332; defeated by Baliol at Dupplin Moor and slain.
[xxxvi. 117]

MAR, THOMAS, thirteenth EARL OF (d. 1377), son of Donald Mar, twelfth earl of Mar [q. v.]; Scottish commissioner to treat for peace with England, 1351, and hostage chamberlain of Scotland, 1358; entered service of Edward III, 1359; his castle seized by David II, 1361, and himself imprisoned, 1370; present at coronation of Robert II, 1371. [xxxvi. 117]

MAR, WILLIAM, ninth EARL OF (d. 1281?), one of the regents of Scotland, 1249, and great chamberlain, 1252–5; commanded expedition to reduce chiefs of Western Isles, 1263. [xxxvi. 118]

MARA, MRS. GERTRUDE ELIZABETH (1749–1833), vocalist; née Schmeling; native of Cassel; violinist, but became singer; studied under Paradisi and Hiller; a better vocalist than actress; engaged by Frederick II at Berlin, 1771; married Johann Mara, who ill-treated her; escaped from Berlin, 1778, and toured on the continent; did not please Mozart; sang in London, 1784–7 and 1790–1802, chiefly in Handel's music; settled at Moscow till 1812; ruined by the burning of Moscow, 1812; sang again in London, 1816; died at Revel; Goethe sent her a poem for her birthday, 1831. [xxxvi. 118]

MARA, WILLIAM DE (fl. 1280), Franciscan; studied at Paris under Bonaventura and Roger Bacon; wrote 'Correctorium' (criticism of Thomas Aquinas), first printed at Strasburg, 1501, and other works.
[xxxvi. 119]

MARBECK or MERBECK, JOHN (d. 1585?), musician and theologian; lay-clerk and afterwards organist of St. George's Chapel, Windsor, 1541; Calvinist; arrested for possessing heretical writings, 1543; sentenced to be burnt, but pardoned through Gardiner's instrumentality, 1544; published his 'Concordance,' 1550 (the earliest concordance of whole English bible), 'The Boke of Common Praier noted,' 1550, adaptation of plain chant to liturgy of 1549, and several other works, besides musical compositions. [xxxvi. 120]

MARBECK, MARKBEEKE, or MERBECK, ROGER (1536–1605), provost of Oriel College, Oxford, and physician; son of John Marbeck [q. v.]; student of Christ Church, Oxford; M.A., 1558; senior proctor and public orator; elegant latinist, and twice pronounced oration before Elizabeth; prebendary of Hereford and canon of Christ Church; provost of Oriel, 1565; resigned all Oxford offices on account of discreditable marriage; M.D., 1573; fellow and registrar of London College of Physicians and physician to Queen Elizabeth; accompanied Howard in Cadiz expedition, 1596, and wrote account.
[xxxvi. 121]

MARCET, ALEXANDER JOHN GASPARD (1770–1822), physician; M.D. Edinburgh, 1797; physician and chemical lecturer at Guy's Hospital, London; professor of chemistry at Geneva, 1819; F.R.S., 1815; published medical and chemical papers. [xxxvi. 122]

MARCET, MRS. JANE (1769–1858), writer for the young; formerly Haldimand; of Swiss birth; married Alexander John Gaspard Marcet [q. v.], 1799; wrote popular scientific text-books, which obtained large circulation; her 'Conversations on Political Economy,' 1816, praised by Macaulay. [xxxvi. 122]

MARCH, EARLS OF, in the English peerage. [See MORTIMER, ROGER (IV) DE, first EARL, 1287?–1330; MORTIMER, ROGER (V) DE, second EARL, 1327?–1360; MORTIMER, EDMUND (II) DE, third EARL, 1351–1381; MORTIMER, ROGER (VI) DE, fourth EARL, 1374–1398; MORTIMER, EDMUND (IV) DE, fifth EARL, 1391–1425.]

MARCH, EARLS OF, in the Scottish peerage. [See DUNBAR, PATRICK, second EARL, 1285-1369; STEWART, ALEXANDER, 1454?-1485; DOUGLAS, WILLIAM, third EARL of the Douglas family, 1724-1810.]

MARCH, MRS. (1825-1877). [See GABRIEL, MARY ANN VIRGINIA.]

MARCH, JOHN (1612-1657), legal writer; employed by council of state during Commonwealth in various capacities; justice in Scotland, 1652; wrote 'Actions for Slander,' 1648, 'Reports,' 1648, 'Amicus Reipublicæ,' 1651, and other works. [xxxvi. 123]

MARCH, JOHN (1640-1692), vicar of Newcastle; educated at Queen's College and St. Edmund Hall, Oxford; M.A., 1664; B.D., 1674; tutor and (1664-72) vice-president of St. Edmund Hall; vicar successively of Embleton, 1672-9, and Newcastle-on-Tyne, 1679-92, and proctor for Durham; strong churchman and defended passive obedience; published sermons and a 'Vindication,' 1689. [xxxvi. 125]

MARCH, DE LA MARCHE, or **DE MARCHIA**, WILLIAM (d. 1302), treasurer, and bishop of Bath and Wells; clerk of the chancery, clerk of the king's wardrobe, c. 1285; treasurer, 1290-5; prominent official during Edward I's absence; received various preferments; bishop of Bath and Wells, 1293; became unpopular through Edward I's exactions; removed from treasury, 1295; built chapter-house at Wells; much venerated, 'miracles' being wrought at his tomb. [xxxvi. 125]

MARCHANT, NATHANIEL (1739-1816), gem-engraver and medallist; studied under Edward Burch [q. v.] and at Rome; exhibited at Royal Academy; R.A., 1809; F.S.A.; assistant-engraver at the mint, 1797; produced intaglios of great merit and delicacy; published catalogue, 1792. [xxxvi. 127]

MARCHI, GIUSEPPE FILIPPO LIBERATI (1735?-1808), painter and engraver; assistant to Sir Joshua Reynolds; excelled as a mezzotint-engraver and copyist. [xxxvi. 127]

MARCHILEY, JOHN (d. 1386?). [See MARDISLEY.]

MARCHMONT, EARLS OF. [See HUME, SIR PATRICK, first EARL, 1641-1724; CAMPBELL, ALEXANDER, second EARL, 1675-1740; HUME, HUGH, third EARL, 1708-1794.]

MARCKANT, JOHN (fl. 1562), contributor to Sternhold and Hopkins's 'Metrical Psalter,' 1562; vicar of Clacton-Magna, 1559, and Shopland, 1563-8; wrote other works. [xxxvi. 128]

MARCUARD, ROBERT SAMUEL (1751-1792?), engraver. [xxxvi. 128]

MARDELEY, JOHN (fl. 1548), clerk of the mint and author. [xxxvi. 128]

MARDISLEY, JOHN (d. 1386?), Franciscan; provincial minister; D.D. Oxford before 1355; denied pope's temporal power in council at Westminster, 1374. [xxxvi. 128]

MARE, SIR PETER DE LA (fl. 1370). [See DE LA MARE.]

MARE, THOMAS DE LA (1309-1396), abbot of St. Albans; entered St. Albans, 1326; prior of Tynemouth, 1340; abbot of St. Albans, 1349; skilful administrator; member of Edward III's council; zealous defender of rights of abbey against exactions of the pope and of powerful courtiers, including Alice Perrers [q. v.], as well as against recalcitrant tenants; his abbey threatened in peasant rising, 1381, when tenants extorted privileges, afterwards withdrawn; benefactor of the abbey; spent much on the maintenance of scholars at Oxford. [xxxvi. 129]

MAREDUDD AB OWAIN (d. 999?), Welsh prince; son of Owain ap Hywel Dda, whom he succeeded, 988. [xxxvi. 130]

MAREDUDD AB BLEDDYN (d. 1132), prince of Powys; brother of Iorwerth [q. v.] and Cadwgan [q. v.]; led resistance to invasion of Henry I, 1121; eventually became lord of all Powys. [xxxvi. 130]

MARETT or **MARET**, PHILIP (1568?-1637), attorney-general of Jersey, 1609; became involved in complicated feud with John Herault, the bailiff, ordered to make submission by privy council, and imprisoned on refusal; lieutenant-governor, 1632. [xxxvi. 131]

MARETT, SIR ROBERT PIPON (1820-1884), attorney-general and bailiff of Jersey; descendant of Philip Marett [q. v.]; distinguished judge; edited manuscripts of Philip Le Geyt [q. v.], 1847; wrote poems in Jersey patois. [xxxvi. 131]

MARFELD, JOHN (fl. 1393). [See MIRFELD.]

MARGARET, ST. (d. 1093), queen of Scotland and sister of Edgar Atheling [q. v.]; went to Scotland with him soon after Conquest, and married Malcolm III, c. 1067; had Roman use introduced into Scotland; reformed manners and customs; educated her sons with great care; died after hearing of slaughter of Malcolm her husband, and her eldest son; canonised, 1250. [xxxvi. 132]

MARGARET (1240-1275), queen of Scots; eldest daughter of Henry III of England; married Alexander III of Scotland, 1251; was treated unkindly, but eventually was provided with proper household; her tyrannical guardians, Robert de Ros and John Baliol, punished, English influence being restored, 1255; visited England with her husband, 1256 and 1260; gave birth to eldest child, Margaret, 1261, to Alexander, 1264, and David, 1270; visited Henry III, 1268, and attended Edward I's coronation, 1274. [xxxvi. 134]

MARGARET (1282?-1318), queen of Edward I; daughter of Philip III of France; married Edward, as his second wife, 1299; gave birth to three children: Thomas, 1300, Edmund, 1301, and Margaret, 1306; crossed to Boulogne to be present at Edward II's marriage, 1308. [xxxvi. 136]

MARGARET OF SCOTLAND (1425?-1445), wife of the dauphin Louis (afterwards Louis XI of France); daughter of James I of Scotland; married Louis at Tours, 1436, and was treated badly by him; wrote poetry. [xxxvi. 136]

MARGARET, the MAID OF NORWAY (1283-1290), queen of Scotland; daughter of Eric II of Norway and Margaret, daughter of Alexander III of Scotland (1241-1285) [q. v.], by his queen Margaret, daughter of Henry III [q. v.]; acknowledged by nobles as heir of kingdom of Scotland, 1284; affianced to Prince Edward, son of Edward I, 1287; died in the Orkneys while on voyage from Bergen to England. A woman declaring herself to be Margaret was burned at Bergen, 1301, by King Hakon V, and was reverenced as a saint by many who believed her story. [Suppl. iii. 139]

MARGARET OF ANJOU (1430-1482), queen consort of Henry VI; daughter of René of Anjou; brought up by her grandmother, Yolande of Aragon in Anjou; truce of Tours confirming her betrothal to Henry VI signed, 1444; married by proxy at Nancy, 1445, these events being brought about by Beaufort and the peace party; entered London and crowned at Westminster Abbey in same year, 1445; devoted her abilities towards identifying herself and Henry VI with one faction, the Beaufort-Suffolk party; brought about Henry's surrender of possessions in Maine, 1445; appropriated greedily part of Duke Humphrey's estates on his death, 1447; on fall of Suffolk (1449) transferred her confidence to Somerset, who incurred unpopularity by his loss of Normandy and Guienne; liberated Somerset from prison, 1450, and drove Richard, duke of York, into violent courses; displayed covetousness and high-handedness; founded, with Andrew Doket [q. v.], Queens' College, Cambridge, 1448; gave birth to son Edward, 1453; failed to secure regency on Henry's prostration, but on his recovery (1455) tried to crush York; defeated at St. Albans, 1455, when Somerset was killed, on which York again became protector; left Henry in disgust, 1456; was seemingly reconciled to York, 1458, but forthwith stirred up country against his party; communicated secretly with Brezé, seneschal of Normandy; on Henry's defeat at Northampton, 1460, fled with the prince into Cheshire, and after many adventures took refuge successively at Harlech Castle, at Denbigh, and in Scotland; signed treaty at Lincluden consenting to Edward's marriage with Mary of Scotland and surrendering Berwick, 1461; after victory at Wakefield (1460) marched to London and defeated Warwick at St. Albans, 1461; showed great brutality in execution of her enemies; after defeat at Towton (March 1461) retired again to Scotland with Henry, surrendering Berwick to the Scots; went to Brittany and Anjou and appealed to Louis XI, 1462; invaded Northumberland with Brezé and French troops, but failed, 1462; protected by a robber; landed at Sluys, 1463, almost destitute; took refuge in

Flanders and finally with her father; sent Jasper Tudor to raise revolt in Wales, 1468; made treaty with Warwick at Angers, 1470; landed at Weymouth with forces, 1471, though meanwhile Warwick had been killed at Barnet (1471) and Henry was again a prisoner; marched north gathering contingents, but being blocked by Edward IV turned towards Wales; defeated at Tewkesbury and captured, her son being slain on the field and her husband being murdered soon after, 1471; remained imprisoned till released by treaty of Pecquigny, 1476; was conveyed abroad and pensioned by Louis XI, but compelled to surrender all rights of succession to French territory; lived in extreme poverty and isolation in Anjou, and was buried at Angers; commemorated by Chastellain and Drayton. Shakespeare probably little responsible for the portrait of her in 'King Henry VI.' [xxxvi. 138]

MARGARET OF DENMARK (1457?-1486), queen of James III of Scotland; daughter of Christian I of Denmark, Norway, and Sweden; married James III, 1469; part of her dowry being the Orkney and Shetland Isles; gave birth to heir (afterwards James IV of Scotland), 1472. [xxxvi. 148]

MARGARET, DUCHESS OF BURGUNDY (1446-1503), sister of Edward IV; married Charles, duke of Burgundy, at Damme, 1468, thus cementing alliance between houses of York and Burgundy; reconciled Clarence to his brother, Edward IV, the latter having been compelled to take refuge in Burgundy, 1470; patroness of Caxton; visited England, 1480; on Henry VII's accession received discontented Yorkists at her court, and encouraged the pretenders, Lambert Simnel and Perkin Warbeck; apologised to Henry VII, 1498; died at Mechlin. [xxxvi. 148]

MARGARET BEAUFORT, COUNTESS OF RICHMOND AND DERBY (1443-1509). [See BEAUFORT.]

MARGARET TUDOR (1489-1541), queen of Scotland; eldest daughter of Henry VII; married James IV of Scotland at Holyrood, 1503; crowned, 1504; gave birth to six children, two of whom survived, James (afterwards James V) and Alexander; supported English party against the French; on James IV's death at Flodden, 1513, became regent and guardian of young king, but met with great opposition; secured peace with England, 1514; married Archibald Douglas, sixth earl of Angus [q. v.], 1514, whereby she strengthened French party; was besieged in Stirling and compelled to give up regency and young king to John Stewart, duke of Albany [q. v.], 1515; escaped to England and gave birth to Margaret, afterwards Countess of Lennox [q. v.]; returned to Edinburgh, 1517, but the promise made her of dower, rents, and access to her son never fulfilled; quarrelled with her husband, Angus, 1518; joined French party; was allowed access to the king, but constantly changed sides; allied herself with Albany, 1521; was accused of 'over-tenderness' for him, and caused withdrawal of her husband, Angus, to France; played with both parties; carried off her son James to Edinburgh, and abrogated Albany's regency, but alienated support by rash actions, 1524; fired on Angus when he broke into Edinburgh, but admitted him to the regency, 1525; regained influence over her son James, but retired to Stirling on his refusal to allow return of Henry Stewart, first lord Methven [q. v.], her favourite; obtained divorce from Angus, 1527, and married Stewart, and together with him became James's chief adviser on fall of Angus, 1528; helped to bring about peace with England, 1534; accused by James of taking bribes from England, and treated with coldness by Henry VIII; interceded with Henry VIII for her daughter, Lady Margaret Douglas; endeavoured unsuccessfully to procure divorce from Henry Stewart; attempted to escape into England, but was overtaken, 1537; troubled Henry VIII with various complaints; died at Methven Castle; buried in the church of St. John at Perth. [xxxvi. 150]

MARGARY, AUGUSTUS RAYMOND (1846-1875), traveller; interpreter in Chinese consular establishment; filled various appointments in China; travelled through south western provinces to Yunnan to meet Colonel Browne, 1875, being the first Englishman to accomplish the journey; murdered at Manwein; obtained medals for saving life at Formosa, 1872. [xxxvi. 157]

MARGETSON, JAMES (1600-1678), archbishop of Armagh; educated at Peterhouse, Cambridge; chaplain

to Wentworth in Ireland, 1633; dean of Waterford, 1635; successively rector of Armagh and Galloon or Dartry; prebendary of Cork and dean of Derry, 1637; dean of Christ Church, Dublin, 1639; refused to use directory instead of prayer-book, 1647; fled to England, and was imprisoned; archbishop of Dublin, 1661-3; privy councillor, 1661; archbishop of Armagh, 1663-78, and vice-chancellor of Dublin University, 1667; rebuilt Armagh Cathedral. [xxxvi. 157]

MARGOLIOUTH, MOSES (1820-1881), divine; Jewish native of Suwalki, Poland; entered church of England, 1838; taught Hebrew and other subjects; entered Trinity College, Dublin, 1840; ordained to curacy of St. Augustine, Liverpool, 1844; incumbent of Glasnevin, 1844; examining chaplain to bishop of Kildare, 1844; served several curacies; visited the Holy Land, 1847; vicar of Little Linford, 1877-81; published 'The Fundamental Principles of Modern Judaism,' 1843, and other works. [xxxvi. 159]

MARHAM, RALPH (fl. 1380), historian; D.D. Cambridge; prior of King's Lynn; wrote 'Manipulus Chronicorum.' [xxxvi. 159]

MARIANUS SCOTUS (1028-1082?), chronicler; native of Ireland; his true name Moelbrigte; pupil of Tigernach; entered Cologne monastery, 1056; 'recluse' successively at Fulda and Mentz; wrote universal chronicle. [xxxvi. 160]

MARIANUS SCOTUS or **MUIREDACH** (d. 1088), first abbot of St. Peter's, Ratisbon; famous for his calligraphy. [xxxvi. 160]

MARINER, WILLIAM (fl. 1800-1860), traveller; detained in friendly captivity in the Tonga islands, 1805-1810; communicated to John Martin (1789-1869) [q. v.] materials for his 'Account . . . of the Tonga Islands,' 1817. [xxxvi. 285]

MARISCHAL, EARLS OF. [See KEITH, WILLIAM, fourth EARL, d. 1581; KEITH, GEORGE, fifth EARL, 1553?-1623, KEITH, WILLIAM, sixth EARL, d. 1635; KEITH, WILLIAM, seventh EARL, 1617?-1661; KEITH, GEORGE, tenth EARL, 1693?-1778.]

MARISCO, ADAM DE (d. 1257?). [See ADAM.]

MARISCO, MARISCIS, MAREYS, or **MARES**, GEOFFREY DE (d. 1245), justiciar or viceroy of Ireland; nephew of John Comyn [q. v.], archbishop of Dublin; powerful in South Munster and Leinster; received large grants of land in Ireland; defeated Hugh de Lacy (d. 1242?) [q. v.] at Thurles; conquered Connaught, 1210; made protestation of loyalty to King John, 1211; justiciar of Ireland, 1215-21, 1226-8, and 1230-2; visited Henry III at Oxford and made agreement with him, leaving one of his sons as hostage, 1220; carried on private wars; treacherously brought about death of Richard Marshal, 1234; being suspected of having plotted assassination of Henry III, 1238, fled to Alexander II of Scotland; expelled from Scotland, 1244; died in poverty in France. [xxxvi. 161]

MARISCO, HERVEY DE (fl. 1169). [See MOUNT-MAURICE.]

MARISCO or **MARSH**, RICHARD DE (d. 1226), bishop of Durham and chancellor; clerk of the exchequer; held various preferments; advised King John's persecution of Cistercians, 1210; archdeacon of Northumberland before 1212, and Richmond, 1213; sheriff of Dorset and Somerset, 1212; suspended for officiating during interdict, 1212; visited Rome; justiciar, 1213-14; accompanied King John abroad, 1214; chancellor, 1214; sent on missions abroad, 1215; bishop of Durham, 1217-26; justice itinerant, 1219; engaged in violent dispute with his monks; one of John's worst advisers. [xxxvi. 163]

MARKAUNT, THOMAS (d. 1439), antiquary; B.D.; fellow of Corpus Christi College, Cambridge; proctor, 1417; said to have first collected the privileges, statutes, and laws of Cambridge University. [xxxvi. 164]

MARKHAM, MRS. (1780-1837). [See PENROSE, ELIZABETH.]

MARKHAM, FRANCIS (1565-1627), soldier and author; brother of Gervase Markham [q. v.]; fought in several campaigns abroad; muster-master at Nottingham; works include 'Five Decades of Epistles of War,' 1622. [xxxvi. 165]

MARKHAM, FREDERICK (1805-1855), lieutenant-general, son of John Markham (1761-1827) [q. v.]; joined 32nd foot, 1824; imprisoned for acting as second in fatal duel, 1830; served in Canada and was wounded, 1837; commanded divisions in Punjab campaign, 1848-9, including victory at Goojerat; C.B. and aide-de-camp to the queen; adjutant-general in India, 1854; commanded division at attack on the Redan, 1855; published 'Shooting in the Himalayas,' 1854. [xxxvi. 165]

MARKHAM, GERVASE or JERVIS (1568?-1637), author; brother of Francis Markham [q. v.]; fought in the Netherlands; a scholar acquainted with various languages; agricultural writer and reformer; said to have imported first Arab horse into England; 'earliest English hackney writer'; author of works and compilations, including 'The most Honorable Tragedie of Sir Richard Grinvile,' 1595, 'The English Arcadia,' 1607, 'Discourse on Horsemanshippe,' 1593, 'Country Contentments,' 1611, 'The Souldier's Accidence,' 1625, and 'The Faithfull Farrier,' 1635; collaborated in writing plays; styled 'a base fellow' by Ben Jonson. [xxxvi. 166]

MARKHAM, SIR GRIFFIN (1564?-1644?), soldier and conspirator; cousin of Francis and Gervase Markham [q. v.]; served in Netherlands; with Essex in France, where he was knighted, and in Ireland; concerned in the 'Bye' plot, 1603, convicted of high treason, but respited at moment of execution; banished with his estates confiscated; retired abroad. [xxxvi. 168]

MARKHAM, JOHN (d. 1409), judge of common pleas, 1396; member of commission which carried out change of dynasty, 1399. [xxxvi. 169]

MARKHAM, SIR JOHN (d. 1479), chief-justice of England; son of John Markham (d. 1409) [q. v.]; serjeant-at-law, 1440; judge, 1444; K.B. and chief-justice of king's bench, 1461; deprived, 1469; famous for his impartiality. [xxxvi. 170]

MARKHAM, JOHN (1761-1827), admiral; son of William Markham [q. v.]; entered navy, 1775; served on North America and West Indies stations; nearly wrecked and murdered when in charge of prize-ship, 1777; cashiered for firing upon a French cartel, 1782, but reinstated by Rodney and promoted post-captain, 1783; commanded Sphynx in Mediterranean, 1783-6; travelled, 1786-93; served under Lord St. Vincent at reduction of Martinique, 1793, off Cadiz, 1797, in Mediterranean, 1799, and off Brest, 1800; colleague of St. Vincent at admiralty board, 1801-4, and of Howick and Grenville, 1806-7; M.P., Portsmouth, 1807-26 (except 1818-20). [xxxvi. 171]

MARKHAM, PETER (fl. 1758), writer on adulteration of bread, 1758; M.D. [xxxvi. 172]

MARKHAM, WILLIAM (1719-1807), archbishop of York; descended from John Markham (d. 1409) [q. v.]; educated at Westminster School; student of Christ Church, Oxford; B.A., 1742; M.A., 1745; D.C.L., 1752; one of the best scholars of the day; published Latin verse; headmaster of Westminster School, 1753-65; chaplain to George II, 1756; prebendary of Durham, 1759; dean of Rochester, 1765; vicar of Boxley, 1765; dean of Christ Church, Oxford, 1767; bishop of Chester, 1771; preceptor to George, prince of Wales and Prince Frederick, 1771, but dismissed, 1776; archbishop of York, 1777; lord high almoner and privy councillor, 1777; denounced by Chatham and others for preaching 'pernicious' doctrines; attacked by Gordon rioters, 1780; used intemperate language in defence of Warren Hastings, which was brought under notice of parliament, 1793; at one time intimate friend of Burke. [xxxvi. 172]

MARKLAND, ABRAHAM (1645-1728), master of St. Cross Hospital, Winchester; scholar and fellow of St. John's College, Oxford; M.A., 1689; D.D., 1692; master of St. Cross, Winchester, 1694-1728; held several livings, and Winchester prebend; published poems and sermons. [xxxvi. 175]

MARKLAND, JAMES HEYWOOD (1788-1864), antiquary; London solicitor, 1808 and 1839; F.S.A., 1809; parliamentary agent to West Indian planters, 1814; student, Inner Temple, 1814; F.R.S., 1816; edited for Roxburghe Club, which (1813) he joined, 'Chester Mysteries,' 1818; assisted and contributed to various publications, including papers for the 'Archæologia'; wrote 'On the Reverence due to Holy Places,' 1845, and several other works. [xxxvi. 175]

MARKLAND, JEREMIAH (1693-1776), classical scholar; of Christ's Hospital, London, and St. Peter's College, Cambridge; M.A., 1717; fellow and tutor, 1717; contributed poetry to 'Cambridge Gratulations,' 1724; engaged in private tuition; settled finally at Milton Court, near Dorking; published 'Epistola Critica' (on Horace), 1723, 'Remarks on the Epistles of Cicero,' 1745, and other works. [xxxvi. 176]

MARKS, HENRY STACY (1829-1898), artist; employed in his father's coach-building business to paint heraldic devices on carriages; studied art under James Mathews Leigh [q. v.]; entered Royal Academy schools, 1851; exhibited at Royal Academy from 1853; executed wall-paintings, representing the Canterbury pilgrims, in Eaton Hall, Cheshire, 1876-8; R.A., 1878; member of Royal Water-colour Society, 1883. His earlier pictures were largely humorous Shakespearean subjects; in later years he specialised in natural-history subjects (principally birds), but produced also land and sea scapes. [Suppl. iii. 140]

MARKWICK or **MARKWICKE**, NATHANIEL (1664-1735), divine; M.A. St. John's College, Oxford, 1690; B.D. (as Markwith), 1696; prebendary of Bath and Wells, 1699; works include 'Stricturæ Lucis,' 1728. [xxxvi. 177]

MARLBOROUGH, DUKES OF. [See CHURCHILL, JOHN, first DUKE, 1650-1722; SPENCER, CHARLES, third DUKE, 1706-1758; SPENCER, GEORGE, fourth DUKE, 1739-1817; SPENCER, GEORGE, fifth DUKE, 1766-1840; CHURCHILL, JOHN WINSTON SPENCER, seventh DUKE, 1822-1883.]

MARLBOROUGH, SARAH, DUCHESS OF (1660-1744). [See CHURCHILL, SARAH.]

MARLBOROUGH, EARLS OF. [See LEY, JAMES, first EARL, 1550-1629; LEY, JAMES, third EARL, 1618-1665.]

MARLBOROUGH, HENRY OF (fl. 1420). [See HENRY.]

MARLEBERGE, THOMAS DE (d. 1236), abbot of Evesham; learned in canon and civil law; taught at Oxford; monk of Evesham, 1199 or 1200; engaged in dispute with bishop of Worcester concerning right of visitation of monastery; went to Rome and obtained verdict of exemption, 1205; quarrelled with Abbot Norreys; expelled and attacked with his companions, 1206, but beat off assailants; effected deposition of Norreys, 1213; made abbot, 1229; paid off the abbey's debts and carried out numerous and important restorations and adornments; architect, mechanical workman, painter, and embroiderer; wrote 'Chronicon Abbatiæ de Evesham' and other works. [xxxvi. 178]

MARLOW, WILLIAM (1740-1813), water-colour painter; member of Society of Artists; exhibited there and at Academy; painted mostly English country seats and scenes; worked also in oil. [xxxvi. 180]

MARLOWE, CHRISTOPHER (1564-1593), dramatist; son of a Canterbury shoemaker; educated at King's School, Canterbury, and Corpus Christi College, Cambridge; M.A., 1587; attached himself to Earl of Nottingham's theatrical company, which produced most of his plays; acquainted with leading men of letters, including Raleigh; wrote, not later than 1587, 'Tamburlaine' (published, 1590), in which he gave new development to blank verse; wrote 'The Tragedy of Dr. Faustus' (first entered on 'Stationers' Register,' 1601, but not apparently published till 1604), which was well received; produced after 1588, 'The Jew of Malta' (first published, 1633), 'Edward II,' the best-constructed of his plays, 1593 (first published, 1594), and two inferior pieces, the 'Massacre at Paris' (probably published, 1600), and 'Tragedy of Dido' (joint work of Marlowe and Nash), published, 1594; pointed to as part author of Shakespeare's 'Titus Andronicus,' by internal evidence; wrote much of the second and third parts of 'Henry VI,' which Shakespeare revised and completed, and of 'Edward III'; translated Ovid's 'Amores' (published with Sir John Davies's 'Epigrammes and Elegies,' c. 1597); paraphrased part of Musæus's 'Hero and Leander' (completed by George Chapman and published, 1598); translated 'The First Book of Lucan's Pharsalia' (published, 1600); wrote the song 'Come live with me and be my love' (published in 'The Passionate Pilgrim,' 1599, and in 'England's Helicon'); held and propagated atheistical opinions, and a warrant issued for his arrest, 1593; killed in a drunken brawl at Deptford; probably not guilty of the blasphemy and gross immorality often ascribed to him; spoken of with affection by Edward Blount, Nashe, and Chapman; his 'mighty line' spoken of by Ben Jonson; quoted and apostrophised by Shakespeare in 'As you like it.' Marlowe excelled in portraying human ambition and exerted much influence over Shakespeare. His collected works were first published, 1826. [xxxvi. 180]

MARMION, PHILIP (d. 1291), grandson of Robert Marmion (d. 1218); sheriff of Warwickshire and Leicestershire, 1249, of Norfolk and Suffolk, 1261; taken prisoner fighting for the king at Lewes, 1264. [xxxvi. 191]

MARMION, ROBERT (d. 1143), carried on war during anarchy in Stephen's reign; killed in fight with Earl of Chester at Coventry. [xxxvi. 190]

MARMION, ROBERT (d. 1218), justice itinerant and reputed king's champion; descended from lords of Fontenay le Marmion in Normandy, grandson of Robert Marmion (d. 1143); sheriff of Worcester, 1186; attended Richard I and King John in Normandy; sided with barons against King John; benefactor of Kirkstead Abbey, Lincolnshire. [xxxvi. 190]

MARMION, SHACKERLEY (1603–1639), dramatist; M.A. Wadham College, Oxford, 1624; soldier for a short time in the Netherlands; settled in London and was patronised by Ben Jonson, whose dramatic work he imitated; convicted of stabbing, 1629; joined Suckling's expedition to Scotland, 1638; wrote 'A Morall Poem intituled the Legend of Cupid and Psyche,' 1637 (in heroic couplets); contributed poetry to 'Annalia Dubrensia,' 1636, and to 'Jonsonus Virbius,' 1638; produced the comedies 'Hollands Leaguer,' 1632, 'A Fine Companion,' 1633, and 'The Antiquary,' published, 1641. [xxxvi. 191]

MARNOCK, ROBERT (1800–1889), landscape gardener; laid out botanical gardens in Sheffield and Regent's Park, London, becoming curator; carried out designs at Greenlands, Henley-on-Thames, Taplow Court, San Donato, near Florence, and Alexandra Park, Hastings; his designs distinguished by good taste and 'picturesqueness'; edited 'Floricultural Magazine' (1836–42) and other gardening publications, and wrote with Deakin first volume of 'Florigraphia Britannica,' 1837. [xxxvi. 192]

MAROCHETTI, CARLO (1805–1867), sculptor, baron of Italy; studied at Paris and Rome; executed statue of Emmanuel Philibert of Savoy for Turin, and other work; made baron by Carlo Alberto, later patronised by Louis-Philippe; executed at Paris statue of Duke of Orleans, relief of 'Assumption' in the Madeleine, and other sculptures; given Legion of Honour, 1839; patronised by Queen Victoria and Prince Albert after 1848; exhibited 'Sappho' and other work at Academy, and statue of Richard Cœur de Lion at Great Exhibition, 1851; executed statues of Queen Victoria, the Duke of Wellington, and others, the Inkerman monument in St. Paul's Cathedral, and other monuments and busts; R.A., 1866; advocate of polychromy in sculpture. [xxxvi. 193]

MARRABLE, FREDERICK (1818–1872), architect; superintending architect to metropolitan board of works, 1856–62; constructed offices in Spring Gardens, besides other important London buildings. [xxxvi. 194]

MARRAS, GIACINTO (1810–1883), singer and musical composer; born at Naples and studied music there; came to England, 1835; sang at, and gave, concerts with Grisi, Lablache, Balfe, and others; visited Russia, 1842, and Vienna and Naples later; was in Paris, 1844; settled in England, 1846; published songs and other works; sang in public; instituted 'après-midis musicales' at his own house; visited India, 1870–3, and the Riviera, 1879; possessed immense repertoire of oratorio, opera, and chamber music; as composer belongs to Italian school; published also 'Lezioni di Canto' and 'Elementi Vocali,' 1850, valuable treatises on singing. [xxxvi. 194]

MARRAT, WILLIAM (1772–1852), mathematician and topographer; contributed to mathematical serials; printer and publisher at Boston, Lincolnshire, and teacher of mathematics; works include 'An Introduction to the Theory and Practice of Mechanics,' 1810, and 'The History of Lincolnshire,' 1814–16. [xxxvi. 196]

MARREY or **MARRE**, JOHN (d. 1407), Carmelite; scholastic theologian, disputant, and preacher; head of Doncaster convent; wrote scholastic treatises and other works. [xxxvi. 196]

MARRIOTT, CHARLES (1811–1858), divine; son of John Marriott (1780–1825) [q. v.]; scholar of Balliol College, Oxford; B.A., 1832; fellow, mathematical lecturer, and tutor of Oriel, College, Oxford, 1833; principal of Theological College, Chichester, 1839; sub-dean of Oriel College, Oxford, 1841; disciple of Newman till Newman went over to Rome; had great influence among younger men at Oxford; vicar of St. Mary the Virgin, 1850–8; member of hebdomadal council; published sermons and pamphlets, and edited with Pusey and Keble 'The Library of the Fathers,' 1841–55, also 'The Literary Churchman' from 1855, and other publications. [xxxvi. 196]

MARRIOTT, SIR JAMES (1730?–1803), lawyer and politician; scholar and (1756) fellow of Trinity Hall, Cambridge; LL.D., 1757; patronised by Duke of Newcastle; advocate-general, 1764; master of Trinity Hall, 1764; vice-chancellor, 1767; judge of admiralty court, 1778; knighted, 1778; M.P., Sudbury, 1781–4 and 1796–1802; declared America to be represented in the English parliament by the member for Kent, the thirteen provinces being described in their charters as part and parcel of the manor of Greenwich, 1782; published poems and legal and political works. [xxxvi. 198]

MARRIOTT, JOHN (d. 1653), 'the great eater,' known as 'Ben Marriott'; celebrated in 'The Great Eater of Graye's Inn' (pasquinade), 1652, where his insatiable appetite is described in detail. [xxxvi. 199]

MARRIOTT, JOHN (1780–1825), poet and divine; student, Christ Church, Oxford; M.A., 1806; tutor to Lord Scott, 1804–8, and intimate with Sir Walter Scott, who addressed to him the second canto of 'Marmion'; rector of Church Lawford, Warwickshire, 1807; held curacies in Devonshire; contributed poems to Scott's 'Minstrelsy of the Scottish Border' and author of several others, including 'Marriage is like a Devonshire Lane,' and hymns, also of sermons. [xxxvi. 199]

MARRIOTT, WHARTON BOOTH (1823–1871), divine; scholar of Trinity College, Oxford, 1843–6; fellow of Exeter College, Oxford, 1846–51; B.C.L., 1851; M.A., 1856; B.D., 1870; university preacher, 1868; Grinfield lecturer, 1871; assistant-master at Eton, 1850–60; F.S.A., 1857; published 'Vestiarium Christianum,' 1868, and other works. [xxxvi. 200]

MARROWE, GEORGE (fl. 1437), alchemist. [xxxvi. 201]

MARRYAT, FLORENCE, successively MRS. CHURCH and MRS. LEAN (1838–1899), novelist; daughter of Frederick Marryat [q. v.]; married, firstly, T. Ross Church, afterwards colonel in Madras staff corps, 1854, and secondly, Colonel Francis Lean of royal marine light infantry, 1890; published from 1865 many novels, works dealing with spiritualism, and 'Life and Letters of Captain Marryat,' 1872. [Suppl. iii. 141]

MARRYAT, FREDERICK (1792–1848), captain R.N. and novelist; grandson of Thomas Marryat [q. v.]; served under Lord Cochrane in the Impérieuse, which performed several brilliant actions, including attack on French fleet in Aix Roads, 1809; took part in Walcheren expedition, 1809; served on Mediterranean, West Indies, North America, and St. Helena stations; commanded the Larne in first Burmese war, 1823; senior naval officer at Rangoon, 1824; commanded successful expedition up Bassein river, 1825; appointed to the Tees, 1825, and Ariadne, 1828; C.B., 1826; gold medallist, Royal Humane Society, for saving life at sea; adapted Popham's signalling system to mercantile marine; F.R.S., 1819; member of Legion of Honour, 1833; published 'The Naval Officer,' 1829, and series of well-known novels of sea-life, including 'Peter Simple,' 1834, and 'Mr. Midshipman Easy,' 1836, largely autobiographical; published children's books and other works, and (1832–5) edited 'Metropolitan Magazine'; lived for some time at Brussels and in Canada and the United States. [xxxvi. 201]

MARRYAT, THOMAS (1730–1792), physician and wit; belonged to poetical club which met at the Robin Hood, Butcher Row, Strand; was educated for presbyterian ministry; M.D. Edinburgh; practised in London, America, Ireland, and elsewhere, finally settling at

Bristol; administered strange remedies; published 'The Philosophy of Masons,' 'Therapeutics,' 1758, and verses, and other works. [xxxvi. 203]

MARSDEN, JOHN BUXTON (1803–1870), historical writer; M.A. St. John's College, Cambridge, 1830; vicar of Great Missenden, Buckinghamshire, 1844; perpetual curate of St. Peter, Dale End, Birmingham, 1851; works include 'The History of the Early Puritans,' 1850, 'The History of the Later Puritans,' 1852, 'History of Christian Churches,' 1856. [xxxvi. 204]

MARSDEN, JOHN HOWARD (1803–1891), antiquary; scholar of St. John's College, Cambridge, and Bell scholar; Seatonian prizeman, 1829; M.A., 1829; B.D., 1836; select preacher, 1834, 1837, and 1847; Hulsean lecturer, 1843 and 1844, and Disney professor of archæology, 1851–65; rector of Great Oakley, Essex, 1840–89, and rural dean; published religious, archæological, and historical works, and verses. [xxxvi. 205]

MARSDEN, SAMUEL (1764–1838), apostle of New Zealand; tradesman's son; studied at St. John's College, Cambridge; chaplain in New South Wales, 1793; had charge of convicts; while on visit to London in 1807 obtained audience of George III, who presented him with five Spanish sheep, the progenitors of extensive Australian flocks; made several visits to New Zealand, and was one of the chief settlers of that country; endeavoured to improve the standard of morals; was attacked by authorities, but defended himself successfully before commission, 1820; died at Parramatta. [xxxvi. 205]

MARSDEN, WILLIAM (1754–1836), orientalist and numismatist; entered East India Company's service, 1770; secretary to government at Sumatra; established agency business in London, 1785; second secretary, 1795, and secretary, 1804, to admiralty; F.R.S., 1783; subsequently treasurer and vice-president; member of various learned societies; D.C.L. Oxford, 1786; published 'History of Sumatra,' 1783, 'Dictionary and Grammar of the Malayan Language,' 1812, 'Numismata Orientalia,' 1823–5, and other works; presented his collection of oriental coins to British Museum, 1834. [xxxvi. 206]

MARSDEN, WILLIAM (1796–1867), surgeon; worked under Abernethy at St. Bartholomew's Hospital; M.R.C.P., 1827; founded Royal Free Hospital, London, where poor were admitted immediately without formalities, and Brompton Cancer Hospital; M.D. Erlangen, 1838; published 'Symptoms and Treatment of . . . Asiatic . . . Cholera,' 1834. [xxxvi. 207]

MARSH. [See also MARISCO.]

MARSH, ALPHONSO, the elder (1627–1681), musician to Charles I; gentleman of the Chapel Royal, c. 1661; composed songs. [xxxvi. 208]

MARSH, ALPHONSO, the younger (1648?–1692), musician; son of Alphonso Marsh the elder [q. v.]; gentleman of the Chapel Royal, 1676. [xxxvi. 208]

MARSH, CHARLES (1735–1812), clerk in war office; fellow of Trinity College, Cambridge; M.A., 1760; F.S.A., 1784; buried in Westminster Abbey. [xxxvi. 209]

MARSH, CHARLES (1774?–1835?), barrister, Lincoln's Inn; practised at Madras; M.P., East Retford, 1812; distinguished himself by knowledge of Indian affairs and denounced Wilberforce's attempt to force Christianity on natives; contributed to various publications and wrote able pamphlets. [xxxvi. 209]

MARSH, FRANCIS (1627–1693), archbishop of Dublin; M.A. Emmanuel College, Cambridge, 1650; fellow of Caius College, Cambridge, 1651; prælector rhetoricus, 1651–2 and 1654–7; dean of Connor, 1660; dean of Armagh and archdeacon of Dromore, 1661; bishop of Limerick, Ardfert, and Aghadoe, 1667; translated to Kilmore and Ardagh, 1672; archbishop of Dublin, 1682; opposed Tyrconnel; withdrew to England, 1689, and was included in act of attainder; returned after battle of the Boyne, 1690. [xxxvi. 209]

MARSH, GEORGE (1515–1555), protestant martyr; farmer; subsequently M.A. Cambridge, 1542; lived at Cambridge and also acted as curate in Leicestershire and Loudon; preached in Lancashire and was imprisoned at Lancaster, 1554, and Chester; burnt at Spital Boughton, his character and sufferings giving rise to marvellous traditions. [xxxvi. 210]

MARSH, SIR HENRY, first baronet (1790–1860), physician; descended from Francis Marsh [q. v.]; B.A., 1812, and M.D., 1840, Dublin; professor of medicine at Dublin College of Surgeons, 1827; president of the Irish College of Physicians, 1841, 1842, 1845, and 1846; physician to the queen, 1837; created baronet, 1839; clinical teacher and medical author. [xxxvi. 211]

MARSH, HERBERT (1757–1839), successively bishop of Llandaff and Peterborough; educated at King's School, Canterbury; scholar of St. John's College, Cambridge, 1775; second wrangler and second Smith's prizeman, 1779; fellow, 1779; M.A., 1782; D.D. (by royal mandate), 1808; studied at Leipzig; returned to Leipzig after prosecution of William Frend [q. v.]; published translation of Michaelis's 'Introduction to the New Testament,' with original notes, 1793–1801, which aroused a great controversy; supported English national credit by publishing translation of an essay by Patje (president of the board of finance at Hanover), 1797; his 'History of the Politics of Great Britain and France' widely read, 1799; given pension by Pitt and proscribed by Napoleon; Lady Margaret professor at Cambridge, 1807; gave several courses on biblical criticism, which were attended by crowded audiences; preached anti-Calvinistic sermons before university, 1805; opposed establishment of Bible Society in Cambridge; wrote various pamphlets and was answered by Simeon and Milner; published 'Comparative View of the Churches of England and Rome,' 1814, and 'Horæ Pelasgicæ,' 1815; bishop of Llandaff, 1816, of Peterborough, 1819; endeavoured to exclude evangelical clergy from diocese by his notorious 'eighty-seven questions'; successfully defended himself in House of Lords; denounced by Sydney Smith; opposed hymns in services and catholic emancipation; foremost divine at Cambridge; a vigorous but often coarse pamphleteer; introduced German methods of research into biblical study. [xxxvi. 211]

MARSH, JAMES (1794–1846), chemist; practical chemist at Woolwich Arsenal and assistant to Faraday at Military Academy, 1829; invented electro-magnetic apparatus and Marsh arsenic test; gained gold and silver medals from Society of Arts; wrote papers. [xxxvi. 215]

MARSH, JOHN (1750–1828), musical composer; wrote works on musical theory; compiled chart-books; composed various pieces. [xxxvi. 215]

MARSH, JOHN FITCHETT (1818–1880), antiquary; solicitor and town-clerk of Warrington; contributed to various societies papers on Milton and other subjects; his 'Annals of Chepstow Castle' printed, 1883. [xxxvi. 216]

MARSH, NARCISSUS (1638–1713), archbishop of Armagh; B.A. Magdalen Hall, Oxford, 1658; fellow of Exeter, 1658; D.D., 1671; incumbent of Swindon, 1662–3; preached at Oxford; chaplain to bishop of Exeter and Clarendon; principal of St. Alban Hall, Oxford, 1673; provost of Trinity College, Dublin, 1679; encouraged maintenance of Irish language, and prepared, with Robert Boyle [q. v.], Irish translation of Old Testament; enthusiastic mathematician; joined in founding Royal Dublin Society, contributing essay on sound, 1683; learned orientalist; built new hall and chapel; bishop of Ferns and Leighlin and rector of Killeban, 1683; fled to England, 1689, and obtained preferment; returned, 1690; archbishop of Cashel, 1691; gave Swift prebend of Dunlavin, 1700; established library at St. Sepulchre's, for which he purchased Stillingfleet's books; several times lord justice of Ireland; translated to Armagh, 1703; benefactor of Armagh diocese; published miscellaneous works. [xxxvi. 216]

MARSH, WILLIAM (1775–1864), divine; M.A. St. Edmund Hall, Oxford, 1807; D.D., 1839; curate of St. Lawrence, Reading, 1800; impressive evangelical preacher; friend and correspondent of Charles Simeon [q. v.]; held livings successively of Nettlebed, Basildon, and Ashampstead, St. Peter's, Colchester, St. Thomas, Birmingham, St. Mary, Leamington, and Beddington, Surrey; canon of Worcester, 1848; published religious works. [xxxvi. 218]

MARSH-CALDWELL, MRS. ANNE (1791–1874), novelist; née Caldwell; married Arthur Cuthbert Marsh, 1817; published 'Two Old Men's Tales,' 1834, followed by 'Emilia Wyndham,' 1846, and other novels. [xxxvi. 219]

MARSHAL, ANDREW (1742–1813), physician and anatomist; private tutor; later studied medicine in London; surgeon at Jersey to 83rd regiment, 1778–83; M.D. Edinburgh, 1782; successful teacher of anatomy in London; devoted himself to medical practice, 1800; wrote papers on madness. [xxxvi. 219]

MARSHAL, ANSELM, sixth and last EARL OF PEMBROKE and STRIGUIL (d. 1245), son of William Marshal, first earl of Pembroke and Striguil [q. v.] [xxxvi. 232]

MARSHAL, EBENEZER (d. 1813), historian; presbyterian minister; published 'The History of the Union of Scotland and England,' 1799, and other works.
[xxxvi. 220]

MARSHAL, GILBERT, iourth EARL OF PEMBROKE and STRIGUIL (d. 1241), son of William Marshal, first earl of Pembroke and Striguil [q. v.]; took minor orders; joined opposition to Henry III's foreign favourites; received fatal injuries in a tournament. [xxxvi. 231]

MARSHAL, JOHN (d. 1164?), warrior; was besieged by Stephen at Marlborough, 1139; supported Empress Maud; present at siege of Winchester, 1141; took refuge in Wherwell Abbey; with the empress Matilda at Oxford, 1142; given lands by Henry II on his accession; present at council of Clarendon, 1164; appealed to the king for justice against Becket, 1164. [xxxvi. 221]

MARSHAL, JOHN, first BARON MARSHAL of Hingham (1170?–1235), nephew of William Marshal, first earl of Pembroke and Striguil [q. v.]; accompanied his uncle on Flanders campaign, 1197–8; had charge of Falaise, 1203; received grant of lands; steward for his uncle in Ireland, 1204; marshal of Ireland, 1207; given charge of various counties and castles; received large grants of land; supported King John against the barons; went to Rome on mission for John, 1215; accompanied him north, 1216; fought against the French at Lincoln, 1217, and prepared for arrival of French fleet; sheriff of Hampshire, 1217; justice of the forest and justice itinerant, and for assize of arms, 1230; sent on various missions to Ireland; sent abroad, 1225. [xxxvi. 221]

MARSHAL, RICHARD, third EARL OF PEMBROKE and STRIGUIL (d. 1234), son of William Marshal, first earl [q. v.]; lived at first in France; on death of elder brother came to England and obtained possession of earldom, 1231; defended Hubert de Burgh, 1232, and opposed Peter des Roches; as head of baronage appealed in vain to Henry III to dismiss foreigners, 1233; engaged in war with Llywelyn ab Iorwerth [q. v.], 1233; being warned of intended treachery refused to come to council, 1233; proclaimed traitor and deprived of marshalship, 1233; made alliance with Llywelyn and captured several castles; defeated foreign mercenaries and royal army, 1234, and secured dismissal of Peter des Roches and Poitevins, 1234; went to Ireland to make war against enemies stirred up by Peter des Roches; treacherously betrayed and fatally wounded in Kildare. [xxxvi. 223]

MARSHAL, WALTER, fifth EARL OF PEMBROKE AND STRIGUIL (d. 1245), son of William Marshal, first earl of Pembroke and Striguil [q. v.] [xxxvi. 232]

MARSHAL, WILLIAM, first EARL OF PEMBROKE and STRIGUIL (d. 1219), regent of England; son of John Marshal (d. 1164?) [q. v.]; hostage in Stephen's hands, 1152; trained in Normandy; accompanied his uncle, Earl Patrick, to Poitou, 1168, but was wounded and captured; ransomed by Queen Eleanor; guardian of Prince Henry, 1170; sided with the prince in his rebellion against his father; left the court, 1182; went to France; recalled, 1183; on death of young Henry started for the Holy Land to bear Henry II's cross to the holy sepulchre and performed great exploits there; returned, c. 1187; became member of king's household; present at conference of Gisors, 1188, and volunteered to fight as champion; promised the hand of the heiress of Pembroke and Striguil; failed in mission to King Philip of France at Paris, 1189; took part in engagements; spared Prince Richard's life in battle; remained faithful to Henry II to the last at Chinon; joint-marshal at Richard I's coronation, 1189; subordinate justiciar under Longchamp; subsequently joined in opposition to Longchamp; received Nottingham Castle to hold for Richard I, 1191; associated in government with Walter de Coutances and excommunicated by Longchamp; retained Richard I's favour; took up arms against Earl John, brother of Richard I, 1193; accompanied Richard to Normandy, 1194, and took part in

fighting; made treaties with counts of Boulogne and Flanders, 1196; appointed custodian of Rouen by Richard before his death, 1199; declared for King John, and with Hubert secured his peaceful succession in England, 1199; invaded Wales, 1204; with John's consent did homage to King Philip of France for his Norman lands, 1204; refused to accompany John's projected expedition to Poitou, 1205; entrusted with defence of England in John's absence, 1206; visited his estates in Ireland, 1207; recalled to England, and his Irish lands ravaged by John's direction; returned to Ireland, 1208, and obtained full possession; received William de Braose [q. v.], 1208; compelled to give hostages to John; protested against papal encroachments, 1212; returned to England, 1213; became John's chief adviser, 1213; witnessed charter of resignation to pope, 1213; made guardian of John's eldest son, and guardian of England, 1214, during John's absence abroad; one of John's envoys to the barons, but also one of the counsellers of Magna Carta, 1215; sent to France to avert threatened invasion, end of 1215; executor of John's will, 1216; regent, 1216; republished Great Charter with omissions, 1216; took Lincoln, 1217, when Hubert defeated French fleet; effected treaty of Lambeth (1217) with Louis, and made himself responsible for payment of 10,000 marks; established order in the kingdom; took habit of a Templar before his death at Caversham, near Reading; possessed lands in Ireland, England, Wales, and Normandy. [xxxvi. 225]

MARSHAL, WILLIAM, second EARL OF PEMBROKE and STRIGUIL (d. 1231), son of William, first earl [q. v.]; hostage in King John's hands, 1205–12; joined barons and was one of twenty-five executors of Magna Carta, 1215; excommunicated by the pope; joined Louis of France, 1216, but abandoned him later; fought with his father at Lincoln, 1217; succeeded to earldom and estates, 1219, and surrendered Norman lands to his brother Richard [q. v.]; forced Llywelyn of Wales to make terms, 1223; justiciar in Ireland (1224), where he compelled submission of Hugh de Lacy, 1224; lived alternately in England and Ireland; married as second wife Henry III's sister Eleanor, 1224; high in Henry III's favour, though supporting Richard of Cornwall [q. v.], 1227; accompanied Henry III into Brittany, 1230, and fought in Normandy and Anjou. [xxxvi. 233]

MARSHALL, ARTHUR MILNES (1852–1893), naturalist; B.A. London, 1870, and St. John's College, Cambridge, 1874; lectured with Francis Maitland Balfour [q. v.] on zoology at Cambridge, 1875; M.B. Cambridge, D.Sc. London, and fellow of St. John's College, Cambridge, 1877; M.A., 1878; M.D., 1882; professor of zoology, Owens College, Manchester, 1879–93; secretary, and subsequently chairman of board of studies of the Victoria University; killed accidentally while on Scafell; F.R.S., 1885; published important memoirs on origin and development of nervous system in higher animals and other subjects.
[Suppl. iii. 142]

MARSHALL, BENJAMIN (1767?–1835), animal painter; exhibited thirteen pictures, chiefly portraits of racehorses and their owners, at Royal Academy, 1801–12 and 1818–19. [Suppl. iii. 143]

MARSHALL, CHARLES (1637–1698), quaker; 'chymist' and 'medical practitioner'; devoted his life to preaching throughout the country; was frequently imprisoned, fined, and prosecuted for non-payment of tithes; worked hard to counteract divisions; published 'The Way of Life Revealed,' 1674, 'A Plain and Candid Account of . . . certain experienced Medicines,' c. 1681, and a journal, and other works. [xxxvi. 234]

MARSHALL, CHARLES (1806–1890), scene-painter; executed very successful work under Macready at Covent Garden and Drury Lane, London, especially in some of Shakespeare's plays; employed also at the opera; painted landscapes and other pictures. [xxxvi. 235]

MARSHALL, CHARLES WARD (1808–1876), tenor singer; brother of William Marshall (1806–1875) [q. v.]
[xxxvi. 253]

MARSHALL, EDWARD (1578–1675), statuary and master-mason; master-mason to Charles II; executed monuments. [xxxvi. 236]

MARSHALL, EMMA (1830–1899), novelist; daughter of Simon Martin, banker at Norwich; married Hugh

George Marshall, 1854 ; settled at Clifton ; published numerous novels, the stories of which are generally woven round some historical character. [Suppl. iii. 144]

MARSHALL, FRANCIS ALBERT (1840–1889), dramatist ; of Harrow and Exeter College, Oxford ; clerk in audit office and later contributor to the press and dramatic critic ; wrote several plays and some other works ; edited the 'Henry Irving Edition' of Shakespeare, 8 vols., 1888–90. [xxxvi. 236]

MARSHALL, GEORGE (*fl.* 1554), poet ; wrote 'A Compendious Treatise in metre' describing growth of Christianity till Mary's reign from catholic point of view (reprinted, 1875). [xxxvi. 237]

MARSHALL, HENRY (1775–1851), inspector-general of army hospitals ; surgeon's mate in navy, 1803 ; served with army later ; served in South America, Cape, and Ceylon ; M.D. ; held various posts in England ; drew up valuable report with Tulloch concerning health of West Indian troops, 1836 ; hon. M.D. New York, 1847 ; founder of military medical statistics ; wrote on military and medical topics. [xxxvi. 237]

MARSHALL, JAMES (1796–1855), divine ; presbyterian minister, but subsequently joined English church ; held livings successively of St. Mary-le-Port, Bristol, 1842, and Christ Church, Clifton, 1847–55 ; published sermons and other works. [xxxvi. 238]

MARSHALL, SIR JAMES (1829–1889), colonial judge ; son of James Marshall [q. v.], vicar of Christ Church, Clifton ; graduated from Exeter College, Oxford ; was ordained, but turned Roman catholic, 1857 ; barrister, Lincoln's Inn, 1866 ; chief magistrate of Gold Coast, 1873 ; chief-justice, 1877–82 ; knighted, 1882 ; C.M.G., 1886 [xxxvi. 238]

MARSHALL or **MARISHALL,** JANE (*fl.* 1765), novelist and dramatist ; imitator of Richardson. [xxxvi. 239]

MARSHALL, JOHN (1534–1597). [See MARTIALL.]

MARSHALL, JOHN (1757–1825), village pedagogue ; educated at Newcastle-on-Tyne grammar school ; schoolmaster successively in Lake district and Freeman's Hospital, Newcastle ; published 'The Village Pedagogue, a poem,' 1817. [xxxvi. 239]

MARSHALL, JOHN (1784?–1837), lieutenant R.N. (1815) and author ; published the 'Royal Naval Biography,' 1823–35. [xxxvi. 240]

MARSHALL, JOHN (1783–1841), statistical writer ; employed at the home office ; chief work, 'A Digest of all the Accounts relating to . . . the United Kingdom,' 1833. [xxxvi. 240]

MARSHALL, JOHN, LORD CURRIEHILL (1794–1868), judge of the court of session as Lord Curriehill, 1852–68. [xxxvi. 240]

MARSHALL, JOHN (1818–1891), anatomist and surgeon ; entered University College, London, 1838 ; F.R.C.S., 1849 ; assisted Robert Liston [q. v.] and practised ; demonstrator of anatomy at University College, London, 1845 ; professor of surgery, 1866, subsequently professor of clinical surgery ; consulting surgeon, University College Hospital, 1884 ; Hunterian (1885) and Morton (1889) lecturer ; F.R.S., 1857 ; president of several medical societies ; LL.D. Edinburgh ; hon. M.D. Dublin, 1890 ; professor of anatomy at Royal Academy, 1873–91 ; Fullerian professor of physiology at Royal Institution ; introduced galvano-cautery and excision of varicose veins ; published 'The Outlines of Physiology,' 1867, and several valuable works. [xxxvi. 241]

MARSHALL, JOSHUA (1629–1678), statuary and master-mason ; son of Edward Marshall [q. v.] [xxxvi. 236]

MARSHALL, NATHANIEL (*d.* 1730), divine ; LL.B. Emmanuel College, Cambridge, 1702 ; took orders ; preacher in London and George I's chaplain, 1715 ; rector of St. Vedast and St. Michael-le-Querne, London, 1715 ; D.D. Cambridge, by royal mandate, 1717 ; canon of Windsor, 1722 ; works include 'A Defence of the Constitution,' &c., 1717. [xxxvi. 242]

MARSHALL, STEPHEN (1594?–1655), presbyterian divine ; son of a poor Huntingdonshire glover ; M.A. Emmanuel College, Cambridge, 1622 ; B.D., 1629 ; vicar of Finchingfield, Essex ; reported for 'want of

conformity,' 1636 ; a great preacher ; influenced elections for Short parliament, 1640, and delivered series of eloquent sermons before the Commons of great political influence ; advocated liturgical and episcopal reform ; supported ministers' 'petition' and 'remonstrance,' 1641, and wrote with other divines 'Smectymnuus,' 1641 ; supported bill for abolishing episcopacy, 1641 ; appointed preacher at St. Margaret's, Westminster, 1642 ; chaplain to regiment of third Earl of Essex, 1642 ; summoned to Westminster Assembly, 1643 ; sent to Scotland and took part in discussions with Scottish delegates ; waited on Laud before execution, 1645 ; attended Uxbridge conference, 1645 ; parliamentary commissioner at Newcastle-on-Tyne, 1647 ; chaplain to the king · at Holmby House and in the Isle of Wight ; prepared with others the 'shorter catechism,' 1647 ; town preacher at Ipswich, 1651 ; commissioner to draw up 'fundamentals of religion,' 1653 ; a 'trier,' 1654 ; buried in Westminster Abbey, but exhumed at Restoration. His sermons, especially the funeral sermon for Pym, 1643, helped to guide the course of events, and his influence was esteemed by Clarendon greater than that of Laud's on the other side. [xxxvi. 243]

MARSHALL, THOMAS (1621–1685), dean of Gloucester ; B.A. Lincoln College, Oxford, 1645 ; served in king's army ; preacher in Holland to merchant adventurers, 1650–76 ; published 'Observations' on Anglo-Saxon and Gothic versions of the gospel, 1665, and other works ; D.D. Oxford, 1659 ; rector of Lincoln College, 1672 ; chaplain to the king ; rector of Bladon, 1680–2 ; dean of Gloucester, 1681–5 ; left estate for maintenance of scholars at his college, and books and manuscripts to university library. [xxxvi. 247]

MARSHALL, THOMAS FALCON (1818–1878), portrait, landscape, genre and history painter. [xxxvi. 248]

MARSHALL, THOMAS WILLIAM (1818–1877), catholic controversialist ; B.A. Trinity College, Cambridge, 1840 ; took orders, but (1845) turned Roman catholic ; inspector of schools ; lectured in United States, 1873 ; published 'Christian Missions,' 1862, and controversial works. [xxxvi. 249]

MARSHALL, WALTER (1628–1680), presbyterian divine ; scholar of Winchester ; M.A. and fellow, New College, Oxford, 1650 ; fellow of Winchester, 1657–61 ; incumbent of Hursley, but ejected, 1662 ; later, minister at Gosport ; his 'Gospel Mystery of Sanctification,' published, 1692. [xxxvi. 249]

MARSHALL, WILLIAM (*fl.* 1535), reformer, printer, and translator ; enthusiastic protestant reformer, and Cromwell's agent ; published several anti-catholic works, including translation of Erasmus's 'Maner and Forme of Confession' ; 'The Defence of Peace' (translation from Marsilio of Padua), 1535, and 'Pyctures and Ymages,' 1535. [xxxvi. 251]

MARSHALL, WILLIAM (*fl.* 1630–1650), early English engraver ; illustrated books, and executed portraits of historical interest. [xxxvi. 251]

MARSHALL, WILLIAM (1745–1818), agriculturist and philologist ; traded in West Indies ; subsequently took farm near Croydon, 1774 ; agent in Norfolk to Sir Harbord Harbord, 1780 ; published 'Minutes of Agriculture,' 1778 (submitted to Dr. Johnson), 'General Survey of the Rural Economy of England,' 1787–98 ; originated board of agriculture, 1793 ; published vocabulary of Yorkshire dialect in his 'Economy of Yorkshire.' [xxxvi. 251]

MARSHALL, WILLIAM (1748–1833), violinist and composer, and factor (1790) to the Duke of Richmond and Gordon ; published 'Marshall's Scottish Airs,' 1821. [xxxvi. 252]

MARSHALL, WILLIAM (1806–1875), organist at Christ Church, Oxford, and St. John's College, Oxford, 1825, and St. Mary's, Kidderminster, 1846 ; Mus. Doc. Oxford, 1840 ; composer and compiler. [xxxvi. 252]

MARSHALL, WILLIAM (1807–1880), Scottish divine and controversialist ; studied at Glasgow and Edinburgh Universities ; secessionist minister at Coupar-Angus, Perthshire, 1830 ; champion of 'the voluntary principle' ; zealous advocate of free trade and abolitionism ; instrumental in effecting union between relief and secession churches, 1847 ; moderator of presbyterian synod, 1865 ; published historical and other works. [xxxvi. 253]

MARSHALL, WILLIAM CALDER (1813-1894), sculptor; studied at Trustees' Academy, Edinburgh, and at Royal Academy, London; A.R.S.A., 1840; R.A., 1852; retired, 1890; his works include the group symbolic of 'Agriculture' on the Albert Memorial, Hyde Park. [Suppl. iii. 144]

MARSHAM, SIR JOHN, first baronet (1602-1685), writer on chronology; M.A. St. John's College, Oxford, 1625; travelled abroad; chancery clerk, 1638; followed Charles I to Oxford; compounded, 1646, and retired to his seat at Cuxton, Kent; M.P., Rochester, 1660; reinstated in chancery and knighted, 1660; created baronet, 1663; published 'Chronicus Canon . . .,' 1672, and other works; according to Wotton, the first to make the Egyptian antiquities intelligible. [xxxvi. 254]

MARSHAM, THOMAS (d. 1819), entomologist; published 'Coleoptera Britannica,' 1802. [xxxvi. 254]

MARSHE, GEORGE (1515-1555). [See MARSH.]

MARSHMAN, JOHN CLARK (1794-1877), author of 'History of India'; son of Joshua Marshman [q. v.]; accompanied his father to Serampur, 1800, and directed mission; subsequently undertook secular work; started first paper-mill in India, and, (1818) first paper in Bengali, and first English weekly, the 'Friend of India,' 1821; published 'Guide to the Civil Law,' long the civil code of India; established Serampur College for education of natives; official Bengali translator; published his 'History of India,' 1842, the 'History of Bengal,' 1848, and other works; C.I.E., 1868. [xxxvi. 255]

MARSHMAN, JOSHUA (1768-1837), orientalist and missionary; weaver; master of baptist school at Broadmead, Bristol, 1794; baptist missionary to Serampur, 1799; took prominent part in translating scriptures into various dialects, and with his son, John Clark Marshman [q. v.], established newspapers and Serampur College; published first complete Chinese bible and other works, including translation of Confucius, 1809. [xxxvi. 255]

MARSTON, BARONS. [See BOYLE, CHARLES, first BARON, 1676-1731; BOYLE, JOHN, second BARON, 1707-1762.]

MARSTON, JOHN (1575?-1634), dramatist and divine; belonged to Shropshire Marstons; B.A. Brasenose College, Oxford, 1594; incumbent of Christchurch, Hampshire, 1616-31; published 'The Metamorphosis of Pigmalion's Image,' 1598, and 'The Scourge of Villanie,' 1598 and 1599 (satires); issued 'History of Antonio and Mellida,' a tragedy, 1602, which was ridiculed by Ben Jonson; wrote a series of comedies: 'The Malcontent,' with additions by Webster, 1604, 'Eastward Ho' (comedy), 1605 (with Jonson and Chapman), for which latter they were imprisoned, 'The Dutch Courtezan,' 1605, and 'Parasitaster,' 1606; finally published a tragedy on Sophonisba, 1606, 'What You will' (comedy), 1607, and 'The Insatiate Countess' (tragedy), 1613, the last sometimes assigned to William Barksteed. [xxxvi. 256]

MARSTON, JOHN WESTLAND (1819-1890), dramatic poet; solicitor's clerk; joined mystical society of James Pierrepont Greaves [q. v.]; edited 'Psyche,' a mystical periodical; wrote 'Gerald . . . and other Poems,' 1842, and several plays, including the 'Patrician's Daughter,' 1841, 'Strathmore' (historical drama), 1849, 'Marie de Méranie,' 1850, 'a stirring tragedy'; his 'Hard Struggle,' 1858, much praised by Dickens, and the most successful of all his pieces; 'Donna Diana,' 1863, his best play; from about 1863 contributed poetical criticism to the 'Athenæum,' including celebrated review of 'Atalanta in Calydon'; published 'Our Recent Actors . . .,' 1888; contributed to the 'Dictionary of National Biography'; chief upholder of poetical drama on English stage; praised for his elegant diction and well-constructed plots. [xxxvi. 258]

MARSTON, PHILIP BOURKE (1850-1887), poet; son of John Westland Marston [q. v.]; lost his sight at early age; wrote 'Song-Tide and other Poems,' 1871, 'All in All,' 1875, and 'Wind Voices,' 1883; the subject of an elegy by Mr. Swinburne. There were published posthumously, 'For a Song's Sake,' 1887 (a collection of short stories), 'Garden Secrets,' 1887, and 'A Last Harvest,' 1891. [xxxvi. 260]

MARTEN. [See also MARTIN, MARTINE, and MARTYN.]

MARTEN, SIR HENRY (1562?-1641), civilian; fellow of New College, Oxford, 1582; D.C.L., 1592; king's advocate, 1609; sent on mission to Palatinate, 1613; chancellor of London diocese, 1616; knighted, 1617; judge of admiralty court, 1617-41; member of high commission, 1620-41; dean of arches and judge of Canterbury prerogative court, 1624; was superseded as dean of arches in 1633 by Sir John Lambe [q. v.]; M.P., St Germans, 1625 and 1626, Oxford University, 1628, and St. Ives, Cornwall (Short parliament), 1640; supported attack on Buckingham; prominent in debates on Petition of Right, 1628; unsuccessfully appealed to king against writs impeding his administration of admiralty court, 1630; argued before privy council against 'new canons,' 1640. [xxxvi. 261]

MARTEN, HENRY or HARRY (1602-1680), regicide; son of Sir Henry Marten [q. v.]; B.A. University College, Oxford, 1619; admitted to Gray's Inn, 1618; lived a dissipated life; refused to subscribe to loan for Scottish war, 1639; M.P. Berkshire, 1640; supported Strafford's attainder and supremacy of parliament; raised regiment of horse; served on committee of safety; specially excepted from pardon by Charles I, 1642; governor of Reading, which he soon evacuated; conducted himself with great violence; seized the king's private property, and was expelled the house and imprisoned for advocating destruction of royal family, 1643; governor of Aylesbury, 1644; commanded at siege of Dennington Castle, 1645-6; re-admitted to parliament, 1646; leader of extreme party; opposed Scottish influence and claims; proposed motion that no more addresses should be sent to Charles I, 1647; sided with army against parliament, and was supported by the levellers; said to have desired Cromwell's assassination; raised troop of horse on his own authority to prevent restoration of Charles I, 1648; extremely active in bringing king to trial and in establishing republic; signed death-warrant, 1649; member of first, second, and fourth councils of state, and granted lands, 1649; influential speaker in parliament; became hostile to Cromwell and Bradshaw; gave offence by his immorality and lost support of army; disappeared from political life at expulsion of Long parliament; outlawed and imprisoned for debt, 1655-7; resumed seat in Long parliament, 1659; surrendered at Restoration and conducted his defence with great courage and ability; escaped death and was imprisoned for life; published speech and pamphlets, including 'The Independency of England . . . Maintained,' 1647. [xxxvi. 263]

MARTEN, MARIA (d. 1827); murdered by her lover, William Corder [q. v.]. [xii. 214]

MARTIAL or **MARSHALL**, RICHARD (d. 1563), dean of Christ Church, Oxford; M.A. Corpus Christi College, Oxford, 1540; D.D., 1552; Roman catholic and protestant alternately in reigns of Henry VIII, Edward VI, Mary, and Elizabeth; witness against Cranmer; vice-chancellor of Oxford University, 1552; dean of Christ Church, 1553-63. [xxxvi. 269]

MARTIALL or **MARSHALL**, JOHN (1534-1597), Roman catholic divine; perpetual fellow of New College, Oxford, 1551; B.C.L., 1556; usher of Winchester School, but being Roman catholic left England at Elizabeth's accession; one of the founders of English College, Douay; B.D. Douay, 1568; canon of St. Peter at Lille; published theological treatises. [xxxvi. 269]

MARTIN. [See also MARTEN, MARTINE, and MARTYN.]

MARTIN (d. 1241). [See CADWGAN.]

MARTIN, LADY (1817-1898). [See FAUCIT, HELENA SAVILLE.]

MARTIN OF ALNWICK (d. 1336), Franciscan; member of minorite convent at Oxford; D.D.; took part at Avignon in controversy between conventual and spiritual Franciscans, 1311. [xxxvi. 270]

MARTIN, ANTHONY (d. 1597), miscellaneous writer; gentleman sewer, c. 1570, and cup-bearer to Queen Elizabeth; keeper of royal library at Westminster, 1588-97; published translations and other works. [xxxvi. 270]

MARTIN or **MARTYN**, BENDAL (1700–1761), son of Henry Martin or Martyn [q. v.]; M.A. King's College, Cambridge, 1726; fellow, 1722; entered of the Temple; treasurer of excise, 1738–61. [xxxvi. 270]

MARTIN, BENJAMIN (1704–1782), mathematician, instrument maker, and general compiler; schoolmaster and travelling lecturer; published 'Philosophical Grammar,' 1735, 'Bibliotheca Technologica,' 1737; invented and made optical and scientific instruments; settled in Fleet Street, 1740; published 'An English Dictionary,' 1749, 'Martin's Magazine,' 1755–64, and some not very original works; became bankrupt and hastened his death by attempted suicide. [xxxvi. 271]

MARTIN, DAVID (1737–1798), painter and engraver; studied under Allan Ramsay (1713–1784) [q. v.]; successful engraver in mezzotint and in line and portrait-painter in Ramsay's style. [xxxvi. 272]

MARTIN, EDWARD (d. 1662), dean of Ely; M.A. Queens' College, Cambridge, 1612; M.A., 1617; chaplain to Laud, 1627; preached at St. Paul's Cross, London, against presbyterianism; received several livings; president of Queens' College, Cambridge, 1631; D.D. by royal mandate, 1631; sent college plate to Charles I, 1642, and thereupon was imprisoned in the Tower and ejected; drew up famous mock petition, 'Submission to the Covenant'; escaped to Suffolk, 1648, but was again imprisoned; released, 1650; reinstated, 1660; a manager at Savoy conference; dean of Ely, 1662; published controversial works. [xxxvi. 273]

MARTIN, ELIAS (1740?–1811), painter and engraver; born in Sweden; exhibited at Academy landscapes, views of country seats, engravings, and other work; A.R.A., 1771; court painter to king of Sweden, 1780. [xxxvi. 274]

MARTIN, FRANCIS (1652–1722), Augustinian divine; studied at Louvain; lector in theology at convent of St. Martin; professor of Greek at Collegium Buslidianum; supported ultramontane party; visited England, 1687 or 1688, and suggested to papal nuncio assassination of William of Orange, 1688; doctor of theology at Louvain, 1688; involved in various controversies; regius professor of holy scripture and canon of St. Peter's at Louvain, 1694; works include 'Scutum Fidei contra Hæreses hodiernas,' 1714, in answer to Tillotson. [xxxvi. 274]

MARTIN, FREDERICK (1830–1883), miscellaneous writer; secretary to Thomas Carlyle after 1856; inaugurated the 'Statesman's Year-Book,' 1864; given pension by Lord Beaconsfield, 1879. [xxxvi. 275]

MARTIN, SIR GEORGE (1764–1847), admiral of the fleet; great-nephew of William Martin (1696?–1756) [q. v.]; present under his uncle, Joshua Rowley [q. v.], at actions off Ushant, 1778, and Martinique, 1780, and battle of Grenada, 1779; served in Jamaica and commanded ships in various stations; present in the Irresistible at battle of Cape St. Vincent, 1797; captured the Ninfa and was warmly commended by Lord St. Vincent, 1797; assisted in capture of the Généreux, 1800; took part in action off Cape Finisterre, 1805; rear-admiral, 1805; held important commands; knighted, 1814; G.C.B., 1821; G.C.M.G., 1836; admiral of the fleet, 1846. [xxxvi. 276]

MARTIN, GEORGE WILLIAM (1828–1881), musical composer; chorister at St. Paul's Cathedral; first organist of Christ Church, Battersea; established National Choral Society, 1860; composed glees and hymns. [xxxvi. 277]

MARTIN, GREGORY (d. 1582), biblical translator; scholar of St. John's College, Oxford; M.A., 1565; tutor to sons of Thomas Howard, fourth duke of Norfolk [q.v.]; escaped to Douay, 1570; ordained priest, 1573; lectured on Hebrew and the scriptures; went to Rome to help organise the new English college there, 1577; returned to Douay and removed with the Douay college to Rheims, 1578; translated the bible (the 'Douay version') with some assistance from Richard Bristow [q. v.] and other theologians, the New Testament being published, 1582, and the Old Testament, 1610. Martin's translation was revised by Bishop Challoner, 1749–50. Martin also published religious works. [xxxvi. 277]

MARTIN, HARRIET LETITIA (1801–1891), writer of tales; daughter of Richard ('Humanity') Martin [q. v.] [xxxvi. 293]

MARTIN or **MARTYN**, HENRY (d. 1721), essayist; lawyer; wrote in 'Spectator' and 'Guardian'; praised by Steele; largely caused by his writings rejection of commercial treaty with France, 1714; inspector-general of imports and exports of customs. [xxxvi. 279]

MARTIN, HUGH (1822–1885), minister of Scottish free church; M.A. Aberdeen, 1839; minister at Panbride, 1844–58, at Free Greyfriars, Edinburgh, 1858–65; mathematical examiner at Edinburgh University, 1866–8; D.D. Edinburgh, 1872; his works mostly religious. [xxxvi. 279]

MARTIN, JAMES (fl. 1577), philosophical writer; professor of philosophy at Paris; published 'De prima simplicium & concretorum corporum Generatione . . . disputatio,' 1577, and other treatises. [xxxvi. 280]

MARTIN, SIR JAMES (1815–1886), chief-justice of New South Wales; taken by his parents to New South Wales, 1821; member of legislative council, 1848, and of first parliament under responsible government, 1856; attorney-general, 1856 and 1857; premier, 1863, 1866–8, and 1870–2; knighted, 1869; chief-justice, 1873–86; published 'The Australian Sketch-book,' 1838. [xxxvi. 280]

MARTIN, SIR JAMES RANALD (1793–1874), surgeon; surgeon on Bengal medical establishment, 1817; served in first Burmese war; presidency surgeon, 1830, and surgeon to Calcutta Hospital; wrote with Dr. James Johnson 'On the Influence of Tropical Climates on European Constitutions,' 1841, and published memoirs and pamphlets; F.R.C.S., 1843; F.R.S., 1845; inspector-general of army hospitals; C.B., 1860; knighted, 1860. [xxxvi. 280]

MARTIN, JOHN (1619–1693), divine; B.A. Oriel College, Oxford, 1640; M.A.; obtained living of Compton Chamberlayne, Wiltshire, seat of the Penruddockes, 1645, but was ejected; arrested after Penruddocke's rising, 1654; given living of Melcombe Horsey, Dorset, at Restoration; prebendary of Salisbury, 1668 and 1677; nonjuror; published religious works. [xxxvi. 281]

MARTIN, JOHN (1741–1820), baptist minister; called to various places, finally (1795) to Keppel Street, London; offended his congregation by his opinions, and was ejected from communion of particular baptists; published various works, including autobiography, 1797. [xxxvi. 282]

MARTIN, JOHN (1789–1854), historical and landscape painter; apprenticed to coach-painter and subsequently to china-painter; exhibited at the Royal Academy, 1812; exhibited 'Joshua,' 1816, which obtained prize from British Institution; sent other pictures to British Institution, including 'The Fall of Babylon,' 1819, and 'Belshazzar's Feast,' 1821, considered his finest work, which obtained premium of 200l.; exhibited 'The Fall of Nineveh' at Brussels, 1833; elected member of Belgian Academy and given order of Leopold; died while engaged on a series of three large pictures of Apocalypse, 1853; his artistic work marked by wild imaginative power. [xxxvi. 282]

MARTIN, JOHN (1791–1855), bibliographer; London bookseller; librarian at Woburn, 1836; wrote description of Bedfordshire churches in local papers; published 'Bibliographical Catalogue of Books privately printed,' 1834, 'History . . . of Woburn,' 1845, and other works; F.S.A. and F.L.S. [xxxvi. 284]

MARTIN, JOHN (1789–1869), meteorologist; M.D. London physician; made meteorological charts; published 'An Account of the Natives of the Tonga Islands,' 1817; died at Lisbon. [xxxvi. 285]

MARTIN, JOHN (1812–1875), Irish nationalist; B.A. Trinity College, Dublin, 1834; travelled abroad; member of Repeal Association; subsequently joined secession of Young Ireland party; took prominent part in meetings of Irish confederation, and contributed to Mitchel's 'United Irishman'; on arrest of Mitchel, 1848, issued 'The Irish Felon' and was arrested; exhorted people from Newgate to retain arms in spite of proclamation, 1848; convicted of treason-felony and transported to Van Diemen's Land, 1849; allowed to return, 1856; prosecuted for violent speech at funeral at Dublin of 'Manchester Martyrs,' 1867; home rule M.P., co. Meath, 1871–5; secretary to Home Rule League; known in Ireland as 'Honest John Martin.' [xxxvi. 285]

MARTIN, JOHN FREDERICK (1745–1808), engraver; brother of Elias Martin [q. v.] [xxxvi. 274]

MARTIN, JONATHAN (1715–1737), organist to Chapel Royal, London, 1736, and once chorister : composed 'To thee, O gentle sleep,' in ' Tamerlane.' [xxxvi. 287]

MARTIN, JONATHAN (1782–1838), incendiary ; brother of John Martin (1789–1854) [q. v.], the painter ; apprentice to a tanner ; pressed for the navy, 1804 ; subsequently farm labourer, Wesleyan, and disturber of church services ; confined in asylum for threatening to shoot bishop of Oxford, 1817 ; escaped, and was excluded from methodist societies ; wrote his biography, 1826 ; set fire to York Minster, 1829 ; tried and confined as a lunatic. [xxxvi. 287]

MARTIN, JOSIAH (1683–1747), quaker ; classical scholar ; published 'A Letter from one of the People called Quakers to Francis de Voltaire,' 1741, and other works. [xxxvi. 288]

MARTIN, LEOPOLD CHARLES (1817–1889), miscellaneous writer ; son of John Martin (1789–1854) [q. v.], the painter ; published with his brother ' Civil Costumes of England,' 1842, and other works ; skilful artist and authority on costume and numismatics. [xxxvi. 288]

MARTIN, MARTIN (d. 1719), author ; visited western islands of Scotland ; published 'Voyage to St. Kilda,' 1698, and ' A Description of the Western Islands of Scotland,' 1703. [xxxvi. 288]

MARTIN, MARY LETITIA (1815–1850), novelist ; 'Mrs. Bell Martin' of Ballinahinch Castle, co. Galway ; married Arthur Gonne Bell, 1847 ; became impoverished ; published 'Julia Howard' 1850, and other works ; died at New York. [xxxvi. 289]

MARTIN, MATTHEW (1748–1838), naturalist and philanthropist : Exeter tradesman ; member of Bath Philosophical Society ; published works on natural history ; investigated and wrote report on London mendicity, 1803. [xxxvi. 289]

MARTIN, PETER JOHN (1786–1860), geologist ; received medical education at London hospitals and Edinburgh ; M.R.C.S. ; joined his father in practice at Pulborough ; wrote ' Geological Memoir on a part of Western Sussex,' 1828, and contributed geological, archæological, and gardening articles to various publications. [xxxvi. 290]

MARTIN, Sir RICHARD (1534–1617), master of the mint and lord mayor of London ; goldsmith to Queen Elizabeth ; warden, 1560–95, and (1581–1617) master of the mint : as master of the mint, issued report, 1601 ; lord mayor, 1581, 1589, and 1594 ; removed from aldermanship for debt, 1602 ; knighted by Queen Elizabeth ; president of Christ's Hospital, London, 1593–1602. [xxxvi. 290]

MARTIN, RICHARD (1570–1618), recorder of London ; commoner of Broadgates Hall, Oxford ; expelled from Middle Temple for riot, 1591 ; M.P., Barnstaple, 1601 ; barrister, 1602 ; recorder of London, 1618 ; celebrated as a wit. [xxxvi. 291]

MARTIN, RICHARD (1754–1834), ' Humanity Martin ' ; of Harrow and Trinity College, Cambridge ; Irish M.P. for Jamestown, 1776–83, Lanesborough, 1798–1800, Galway (first united parliament), 1801–26 ; owned extensive estates at Connemara ; supported union ; friend of George IV ; supported catholic emancipation ; succeeded in carrying ' first modern legislation for protecting animals,' 1822 ; a founder of Royal Society for Prevention of Cruelty to Animals, 1824 ; worked to abolish death penalty for forgery, and to secure counsel for prisoners charged with capital crimes ; declined peerage ; elected to parliament, 1826, but his name erased, 1827 ; withdrew to Boulogne, where he died. [xxxvi. 292]

MARTIN, ROBERT MONTGOMERY (1803?–1868), historical writer and statistician ; travelled as botanist and naturalist in Ceylon, Africa, Australia, and India ; took part in naval expedition as surgeon ' off coasts of Africa, Madagascar, and South-Eastern Islands,' 1823 ; energetic member of court of East India Company ; treasurer of Hongkong, 1844–5 ; on mission to Jamaica, 1851 ; published 'The History of the British Colonies,' 1834, and other important works. [xxxvi. 293]

MARTIN, SAMUEL (1817–1878), congregational minister ; architect ; subsequently minister at Cheltenham and afterwards at Westminster ; attracted enormous congregations and worked successfully for improvement

of bad neighbourhood ; took active part in management of Westminster Hospital, London ; chairman of Congregational Union, 1862 ; published sermons and other works. [xxxvi. 294]

MARTIN, Sir SAMUEL (1801–1883), baron of the exchequer ; M.A. Trinity College, Dublin, 1832 ; hon. LL.D., 1857 ; barrister, Middle Temple, 1830 ; Q.C., 1843 ; liberal M.P. for Pontefract, 1847 ; baron of exchequer, 1850–74 ; knighted, 1850. [xxxvi. 295]

MARTIN, SARAH (1791–1843), prison visitor ; dressmaker and Sunday school teacher ; visited the notorious Yarmouth gaol and workhouse ; preached and gave instruction, 1819–41 ; exerted great influence over the criminals ; wrote poems and journals. [xxxvi. 296]

MARTIN, THOMAS (1697–1771), antiquary ; ' Honest Tom Martin of Palgrave' ; clerk to his brother Robert, attorney ; settled at Palgrave, Suffolk, 1723 ; F.S.A. 1720 ; his collections afterwards published by Richard Gough [q. v.] as ' The History of Thetford,' 1779. [xxxvi. 297]

MARTIN, THOMAS BARNEWALL (d. 1847), M.P., co. Galway, 1832–47 ; son of Richard ('Humanity') Martin [q. v.] [xxxvi. 293]

MARTIN, Sir THOMAS BYAM (1773–1854), admiral of the fleet ; ' captain's servant' in the Pegasus, 1786 ; captured the Tamise, 1796, and while commanding various ships off Irish and French coasts, and in West Indies, the Immortalité, 1798, and large number of privateers and other ships ; had large share in capture of Russian ship Sewolod, 1808 ; received Swedish order of the Sword ; rear-admiral, 1811 ; took part in defence of Riga, 1812 ; comptroller of the navy, 1816–31 ; M.P., Plymouth, 1818–1831 ; G.C.B., 1830 ; admiral of the fleet, 1849. [xxxvi. 298]

MARTIN, WILLIAM (1696?–1756), admiral ; entered navy, 1708 ; served on various ships and stations ; commanded squadron which enforced neutrality of Naples, 1742, and protected Italy against Spaniards ; vice-admiral, 1744 ; commanded fleet at Lisbon and in North Sea ; retired, 1747 ; linguist and classical scholar. [xxxvi. 299]

MARTIN, WILLIAM (1767–1810), naturalist ; actor and, later, drawing-master ; F.L.S., 1796 ; published ' Figures and Descriptions of Petrifications collected in Derbyshire,' 1793, and other works. [xxxvi. 300]

MARTIN, WILLIAM (fl. 1765–1821), painter ; assistant to Cipriani ; exhibited Shakespearean and classical subjects and portraits at the Royal Academy. [xxxvi. 301]

MARTIN, WILLIAM (1772–1851), 'natural philosopher and poet' ; brother of John Martin (1789–1854) [q. v.] and of Jonathan Martin (1782–1838) [q. v.] ; ropemaker ; announced discovery of perpetual motion and collapse of Newtonian system ; gained medal from Society of Arts for spring weighing machine, 1814, and exhibited other inventions ; affected great singularity of dress and founded ' Martinean Society,' 1814, in opposition to Royal Society ; works include ' W. M.'s Challenge to the whole Terrestrial Globe,' 1829. [xxxvi. 301]

MARTIN, WILLIAM (1801–1867), writer for the young ; woollen-draper's assistant at Woodbridge and subsequently schoolmaster at Uxbridge ; returned to Woodbridge, 1836, and gained livelihood by writing and lecturing ; author of ' Peter Parley's Annual,' 1840–67, various books of simple instruction, and household tracts. [xxxvi. 302]

MARTIN, Sir WILLIAM (1807–1880), scholar and first chief-justice of New Zealand ; fellow of St. John's College, Cambridge, 1831 ; M.A., 1832 ; gained classical and mathematical distinctions ; barrister, 1836 ; chief-justice of New Zealand, 1841 ; supported rights of natives and protested against Lord Grey's instructions, 1847 ; D.C.L. Oxford, 1861 ; knighted, 1861. [xxxvi. 303]

MARTIN, WILLIAM CHARLES LINNÆUS (1798–1864), writer on natural history ; son of William Martin (1767–1810) [q. v.] ; superintendent of museum of Zoological Society, 1830–8 ; wrote several volumes in ' Farmer's Library.' [xxxvi. 304]

MARTIN, Sir WILLIAM FANSHAWE, fourth baronet (1801–1895), admiral ; son of Sir Thomas Byam Martin [q. v.] ; entered navy, 1813 ; lieutenant, 1820 ; commander, 1823 ; served with distinction at Callao at time of civil war ; post captain, 1824 ; in Mediterranean, 1826–31 ; commodore in command of Lisbon squadron,

1849-52; rear-admiral, 1853; superintendent of Portsmouth dockyard, 1853-8; vice-admiral, 1858; lord of admiralty, 1859; commanded with great rigour on Mediterranean station, 1860-3; admiral, 1863; succeeded to baronetcy on a cousin's death, 1863; commander-in-chief at Portsmouth, 1866-9; G.C.B., 1873; rear-admiral of United Kingdom, 1878. [Suppl. iii. 145]

MARTINDALE, ADAM (1623-1686), presbyterian divine; tutor and schoolmaster; later deputy quartermaster; took 'covenant,' 1643; became preacher at Manchester and vicar of Rostherne, Cheshire, 1648; sympathised with rising of George Booth (1622-1684) [q. v.]; deprived, 1662; preached and taught mathematics; chaplain to Lord Delamer (Sir George Booth) at Dunham, 1671; took out licence, 1672; imprisoned on groundless suspicions, 1685; works include controversial publications and an autobiography. [xxxvi. 304]

MARTINDALE, MILES (1756-1824), Wesleyan minister; preacher in Cheshire; governor of Woodhouse Grove school, 1816; published sermons, poems, and other works. [xxxvi. 307]

MARTINDELL or **MARTINDALL**, SIR GABRIEL (1756?-1831), major-general in East India Company's service; ensign in Bengal native infantry, 1776; distinguished himself in Mahratta war, 1804-5; held commands in India; major-general, 1813; K.C.B., 1815; commander of field army, 1820. [xxxvi. 307]

MARTINE. [See also MARTEN, MARTIN, and MARTYN.]

MARTINE, GEORGE, the elder (1635-1712), historian of St. Andrews; commissary clerk, but deprived for refusing to take oath, 1690; secretary to Archbishop Sharp; his 'Reliquiæ divi Andreæ' published, 1797. [xxxvi. 308]

MARTINE, GEORGE, the younger (1702-1741), physician; son of George Martine the elder [q. v.]; M.D. Leyden, 1725; accompanied Cathcart's American expedition, 1740, and various expeditions against Carthagena; published scientific works. [xxxvi. 308]

MARTINEAU, HARRIET (1802-1876), miscellaneous writer; daughter of Norwich manufacturer and sister of James Martineau [q. v.]; of Huguenot origin; unitarian; suffered from feeble health and deafness; attracted by philosophical books; contributed article on 'Female Writers on Practical Divinity' to the 'Monthly Repository,' 1821, followed by other papers, and published short tales; went through long illness and was left penniless, 1829; published successful works, 'Illustrations of Political Economy,' 1832-4, 'Poor Law and Paupers Illustrated,' 1833, and 'Illustrations of Taxation,' 1834; came to London; became acquainted with literary celebrities, and was consulted by cabinet ministers; visited America, 1834-6, and wrote 'Society in America,' 1837, and a 'Retrospect of Western Travel,' 1838; published 'Deerbrook,' a novel, 1839; visited Venice and returned seriously ill; published 'The Playfellow' series and other books; tried mesmerism and recovered, 1844; friend of Wordsworth; travelled in Egypt and Palestine, and published 'Eastern Life,' 1848, and 'History of England during the Thirty Years' Peace,' 1849; published Atkinson's 'Letters on the Laws of Man's Social Nature and Development,' 1851, containing anti-theological views; brought out condensed translation of Comte's 'Philosophie Positive,' 1853; contributed to the 'Daily News' and 'Edinburgh Review,' and wrote, among other works, an autobiography, which was published posthumously. [xxxvi. 309]

MARTINEAU, JAMES (1805-1900), unitarian divine; educated at Norwich grammar school under Edward Valpy [q. v.], and at Bristol under Lant Carpenter [q. v.]; apprenticed as civil engineer, 1821; studied divinity at Manchester College, York, 1822-7; assistant in Lant Carpenter's school at Bristol, 1827; assistant pastor of Eustace Street congregation, Dublin, 1828; ordained, 1828; chief promoter and first secretary of 'Irish Unitarian Christian Society,' 1830; colleague with John Grundy (1782-1843) [q. v.] at Paradise Street Chapel, Liverpool, 1832, and sole pastor, 1835, continuing in that office despite other appointments elsewhere till 1857 (the chapel removed to Hope Street, 1849); published 'Rationale of Religious Enquiry,' 1836; professor of mental and moral philosophy and political economy from 1840 to 1857 at Manchester New College (removed from Manchester, 1853, to University Hall, Gordon Square, London); joint-

editor with John James Tayler [q. v.] and Charles Wicksteed of 'Prospective Review,' 1845-54, and contributed (1855-64) much to 'National Review,' which R. H. Hutton [q. v.] and Walter Bagehot [q. v.] edited; professor of mental, moral, and religious philosophy at Manchester New College, 1857-69; colleague with Tayler in charge of Little Portland Street Chapel, London, 1859, and sole pastor, 1860-72; principal of Manchester New College, 1869-85; D.D. Edinburgh, 1884; D.C.L. Oxford, 1888; Litt.D. Dublin, 1892. His publications include 'Ideal Substitutes for God,' 1879, 'Study of Spinoza,' 1882, 'Types of Ethical Theory,' 1885, 'Study of Religion,' 1888; 'Seat of Authority in Religion,' 1890, and two volumes of hymns. [Suppl. iii. 146]

MARTINEAU, ROBERT BRAITHWAITE (1826-1869), painter; educated at University College, London; first exhibited at Royal Academy, 1852. [xxxvi. 314]

MARTINEAU, RUSSELL (1831-1898), orientalist; son of James Martineau [q. v.]; educated at Heidelberg and University College, London; M.A. London, 1854; joined staff of British Museum Library, 1857, and was assistant-keeper, 1884-98; lecturer on Hebrew language and literature at Manchester New College, London, 1857-1866, and professor, 1866-74; published philosophical and other writings. [Suppl. iii. 150]

MARTYN. [See also MARTEN, MARTIN, and MARTINE.]

MARTYN, BENJAMIN (1699-1763), miscellaneous writer; nephew of Henry Martin [q. v.]; examiner at the custom house, secretary to Society for Colony of Georgia, and (1733) published account; original member of Society for Encouragement of Learning, 1736; instrumental in erecting Shakespeare's monument in Westminster Abbey; composed life of first Earl of Shaftesbury, unsatisfactory and suppressed; produced 'Timoleon' (tragedy) at Drury Lane, 1730. [xxxvi. 314]

MARTYN, ELIZABETH (1813-1846). [See INVERARITY.]

MARTYN, FRANCIS (1782-1838), Roman catholic divine; published 'Homilies on the Book of Tobias,' 1817, and other works. [xxxvi. 315]

MARTYN, HENRY (1781-1812), missionary; senior wrangler and Smith's prizeman, St. John's College, Cambridge; fellow, 1802; M.A., 1804; curate to Simeon at Holy Trinity, Cambridge, 1803; chaplain on Bengal establishment, 1805; opened church at Cawnpore for natives; translated New Testament and Prayer Book into Hindustani, New Testament and Psalms into Persian, and Gospels into Judæo-Persic; visited Persia, and died at Tokat from fever; left 'Journals and Letters,' edited, 1837. [xxxvi. 315]

MARTYN, JOHN (1699-1768), botanist; translated Tournefort's works, 'The Compleat Herbal' and 'History of Plants growing about Paris'; made excursions in country and collected botanical specimens; became secretary to botanical society meeting at Rainbow Coffeehouse; F.R.S., 1724; contributed to Bailey's 'Dictionary,' 1725, and lectured in London and at Cambridge, and practised as apothecary; published 'Historia Plantarum rariorum,' 1728-37, and, with Dr. Alexander Russel [q. v.], 'The Grub Street Journal' (styling himself 'Bavius'), 1730-7; entered Emmanuel College, Cambridge, 1730; Cambridge professor of botany, 1732-68; corresponded with Sloane, Linnæus, and others; collected material for an English dictionary; contributed to 'Philosophical Transactions'; published editions of Virgil's 'Georgicks,' 1741, and 'Bucolicks,' 1749, and other works. [xxxvi. 317]

MARTYN or **MARTIN**, RICHARD (d. 1483), bishop of St. David's; LL.D. Cambridge; archdeacon of London, 1469, and member of king's council before 1471; prebendary of St. Paul's Cathedral, 1471, and Hereford, 1472; chancellor of the marches, 1471; served on commissions; master in chancery, 1472-7; perhaps bishop of Waterford and Lismore, 1472; archdeacon of Hereford and king's chaplain, 1476; chancellor of Ireland and ambassador to Castile, 1477; bishop of St. David's, 1482-3. [xxxvi. 319]

MARTYN or **MARTIN**, THOMAS (d. 1597?), civilian and controversialist; fellow of New College, Oxford, 1538-53; member of College of Advocates, 1555; chancellor to Gardiner, bishop of Winchester and master in chancery, 1553; took active part against Cranmer, Hooper, and others; went to Calais, 1555; master of requests, 1556;

sent on mission to King Philip at Ghent, 1556 ; member of council of the north, 1557 ; commissioner to settle matters between England and Scotland, 1557 ; miscellaneous writer. [xxxvi. 320]

MARTYN, THOMAS (*fl.* 1760-1816), natural history draughtsman and pamphleteer ; established academy in Great Marlborough Street, London, where his books on natural history were prepared ; published also political pamphlets. [xxxvi. 321]

MARTYN, THOMAS (1735-1825), botanist ; son of John Martyn [q. v.] ; studied at Emmanuel College, Cambridge, and gained scholarships ; fellow of Sidney Sussex College, Cambridge ; M.A., 1758 ; tutor, 1760-74 ; Cambridge professor of botany, 1762-1825 ; lectured and introduced Linnæan system ; published ' Plantæ Cantabrigienses,' 1763, and travelled abroad ; B.D., 1766 ; incumbent of Ludgershall, Buckinghamshire, 1774, and Little Marlow, 1776 ; travelled abroad with a ward, 1778-1780 ; purchased Charlotte Street Chapel, Pimlico ; published translation and continuation of Rousseau's ' Letters on the Elements of Botany,' 1785 ; edited Miller's ' Gardener's Dictionary ' on Linnæan system, 1807, and other works ; rector of Pertenhall, 1804 ; F.R.S., 1786 ; F.L.S., 1785. [xxxvi. 321]

MARTYN, WILLIAM (1562-1617), lawyer and historian ; barrister, Middle Temple, 1589 ; M.P., Exeter, 1597-8 ; recorder of Exeter, 1605-17 ; published 'The Historie and Lives of the Kings of England,' 1615 and 1638, and ' Youth's Instruction,' 1612. [xxxvi. 323]

MARVELL, ANDREW, the elder (1586 ?-1641), divine ; M.A. Emmanuel College, Cambridge, 1608 ; ' minister ' of Flamborough, 1610 ; incumbent of Winestead, 1614-24 ; master of grammar school, Hull, 1624 ; master of the Charterhouse and lecturer at Holy Trinity Church, *c.* 1624 ; drowned in the Humber ; described by Fuller as excellent preacher. [xxxvi. 324]

MARVELL, ANDREW, the younger (1621-1678), poet and satirist ; son of Andrew Marvell the elder [q. v.] ; educated under his father at Hull grammar school ; scholar of Trinity College, Cambridge ; B.A., 1638 ; contributed verses to ' Musa Cantabrigiensis,' 1637 ; travelled abroad ; wrote poems, including satire on death of Thomas May [q. v.] ; tutor to Mary, daughter of Lord Fairfax, *c.* 1650 ; wrote poems in praise of gardens and country life, and became ardent republican ; recommended unsuccessfully to council of state by Milton to be his assistant in the secretaryship for foreign tongues, 1653 ; resided at Eton, in house of John Oxenbridge, as tutor of William Dutton, Cromwell's ward, 1653 ; became Milton's colleague in Latin secretaryship, 1657 ; wrote several poems in the Protector's honour, including ' Horatian Ode upon Cromwell's Return from Ireland,' 1650, his greatest achievement (first printed, 1776) and elegy upon his death ; thrice elected M.P., Hull, 1660 and 1661 ; guarded vigilantly interests of his constituents and corresponded with corporation ; went to Holland, 1663 ; accompanied Earl of Carlisle, ambassador to northern powers, as secretary, 1663-5, publishing an account of the mission, 1669 ; vigorously defended Milton ; opposed Bill for Securing the Protestant Religion, 1677 ; became disgusted at management of public affairs, and wrote, for private circulation, bitter satires, first attacking ministers, but afterwards Charles II himself, and advocating republic ; wrote the ' Rehearsal Transprosed,' 1672 and 1673, against Samuel Parker [q. v.], afterwards bishop of Oxford, a leading champion of intolerance ; took part also in controversy about predestination, 1678 ; wrote, anonymously, ' Account of the Growth of Popery and Arbitrary Government in England,' 1677, which produced great sensation ; according to his biographer, Cooke, refused court favours ; intimate with James Harrington and Milton ; wrote prefatory lines extolling the ' mighty poet ' to second edition of ' Paradise Lost,' and rebuked Dryden for attempting to convert it into a rhyming opera ; as pamphleteer was admired by Swift ; his work as poet belongs to pre-Restoration period. [xxxvi. 324]

MARVIN, CHARLES THOMAS (1854-1890), writer on Russia ; resided in Russia, 1870-6 ; while writer at foreign office disclosed secret treaty with Russia to the ' Globe,' 1878, and published an account of the secret treaty of 1878 ; sent to Russia by Joseph Cowen, 1882 ; wrote several books on Russia, including ' The Russians at the Gates of Herat,' 1885. [xxxvi. 332]

MARWOOD, WILLIAM (1820-1883), public executioner ; introduced the ' long drop.' [xxxvi. 333]

MARY I (1516-1558), queen of England and Ireland ; third but only surviving child of Henry VIII and Catherine of Arragon ; tentatively betrothed to son of Francis I, and subsequently to the Emperor Charles V ; made princess or governor of Wales at Ludlow Castle, 1525 ; studied Greek, Latin, French, Italian, science, and music, and read Erasmus's ' Paraphrases ' and More's ' Utopia ' ; attended by Countess of Salisbury, mother of Reginald Pole ; was separated from her mother on Queen Catherine's divorce, 1532, but boldly avowed sympathy with her ; was declared illegitimate, 1533, but refused to give up title of princess ; sent to Hatfield to reside there with her half-sister Princess Elizabeth, under care of Lady Shelton, aunt of Anne Boleyn ; ill-treated, denounced by Henry, and her life threatened ; received much public sympathy and had a protector in the Emperor Charles V ; after Queen Anne Boleyn's execution was reconciled with Henry VIII on acknowledging her illegitimacy and the king's ecclesiastical supremacy ; chief mourner at funeral of Queen Jane Seymour, 1537 ; proposed in marriage to Duke Philip of Bavaria, 1539 ; declared capable of inheriting crown after Henry's legitimate children, 1544 ; translated Erasmus's Latin paraphrase of St. John ; on friendly terms with her half-brother Edward and her half-sister Elizabeth after her father's death and Edward's succession to the throne, 1547 ; received proposal of marriage from Lord Seymour ; refused to give up mass on passing of Act of Uniformity, 1549 ; was supported by Charles V, who prepared for her escape to the continent ; on Edward VI's death and proclamation as queen of Lady Jane Grey, took refuge at Framlingham Castle, Suffolk, 1553 ; on country declaring for her accession to the throne, journeyed to London, and was proclaimed queen 16 July ; released Duke of Norfolk, Stephen Gardiner, and other prisoners in the Tower of London ; first queen regnant of England ; announced her intention abroad to re-introduce Roman catholicism, but promised in England that religion should be settled by common consent ; restored Gardiner and Bonner to their sees and made Gardiner chancellor and chief adviser, 1553 ; executed the Duke of Northumberland, but for the time spared Lady Jane Grey ; crowned with great splendour, 1 Oct. 1553 ; in first parliament abolished new treasons and felonies and Edward VI's religious laws ; had her legitimacy declared ; announced (contrary to Gardiner's and to the French ambassador's wishes) intention of marrying her cousin Philip of Spain, a suitor agreeable to her on account of his fanatical Roman catholicism ; evoked by her steadfast pursuit of this project three insurrections, 1554 ; showed courage in rebellion of Sir Thomas Wyatt, who marched into London but was defeated in the city ; executed Wyatt, Duke of Suffolk, Lady Jane Grey and her husband, and many others, and imprisoned Princess Elizabeth ; began campaign against protestantism and expelled married clergy ; married Philip of Spain at Winchester, 25 July, 1554, and pardoned Elizabeth ; with Philip opened parliament which reversed Cardinal Pole's attainder and passed acts restoring papal power ; imagined herself to be pregnant ; gave consent to re-enactment of statute against lollardy and set on foot great persecution, ninety-six protestants suffering death, including Bishop Hooper, during 1555, and three hundred before end of the reign ; restored some of the property taken by the crown from the church and re-established many monasteries ; had disputes with her husband, who left the country (Aug. 1555) ; suffered from continued ill-health and grief caused by Philip's absence ; received Philip at Greenwich, 1557 ; agreed to join in his schemes of war with France ; said farewell to Philip, July 1557 ; successfully resisted appointment by the pope of new legate in place of Pole, 1557 ; demanded forced loans to support war against France and Scotland ; lost Calais, Jan. 1558 ; took measures during her last days to secure accession of Elizabeth ; buried in Westminster Abbey. Religious devotion to the catholic faith was the central feature of Mary's life, inducing her to marry Philip, one of the great errors of her reign, and to persecute her protestant subjects. Owing mainly to her persecution of the protestants, her personal character has been assailed with fanatical animosity. [xxxvi. 333]

MARY II (1662-1694), queen of England, Scotland, and Ireland ; eldest child of James II and Anne Hyde [q. v.], lived with her grandfather, Clarendon, at Twickenham, and later at Richmond Palace; brought up a protestant; received religious instruction from Compton, bishop of London; married William of Orange, the marriage being part of Danby's policy for pacifying parliament; left with her husband for Holland, 1677; at first neglected by William; received visits from the Duke and Duchess of York and from Monmouth, 1679; received the latter again, 1685; obtained great popularity among the Dutch by her noble and amiable character; became estranged from English court on expedition of Monmouth; promised William that he should always bear rule, 1686; obliged to dismiss Burnet, 1687; joined with William in protesting against Declaration of Indulgence; received proselytising letters from her father, James II, 1687-8; identified herself completely with William in subsequent events; believed birth of Prince of Wales a fraud, 1688; repudiated idea of reigning as sole sovereign (suggested by Danby); arrived in England, 1689; accepted crown with William and assented to Declaration of Rights; interfered little in public affairs, but was very popular; settled at Hampton Court and Kensington Palace; endeavoured to improve social morals, and in accordance with her puritan opinions abolished singing of prayers at the Chapel Royal, Whitehall; became estranged from her sister, Princess Anne; governed England during William's absence, and in a time of great crisis, 1690-1; exercised wise patronage in church matters, and endeavoured to obtain lenient treatment for nonjuring bishops; alarmed by conspiracy of Anne and the Marlboroughs, 1692; administered government, 1692; disturbed by fears of a French invasion, conspiracies against her life and that of William, and William's defeats in Holland; addressed letter of confidence to the navy; issued orders to magistrates for enforcing law against vice; resumed regency, 1693 and 1694; requested and obtained loan from city of London of 300,000l.; died of small-pox, to the great grief of William and England and Holland, her scheme of Greenwich Hospital being carried out by William in memory of her; buried in Henry VII's chapel, Westminster Abbey. Obliged by fate to choose between father and husband, she chose the latter, making devotion to William III's interests almost a religious duty, but retaining kindly feelings for James II till his connivance in Grandvaal's attempt on William's life, 1692. She endowed William and Mary Missionary College, Virginia, and supported S.P.C.K.

[xxxvi. 354]

MARY OF MODENA (1658–1718), queen of James II of England; only daughter of Alfonso IV, duke of Modena; brought up religiously and strictly; intended becoming a nun; married James, duke of York, through influence of Louis XIV, who aimed at England's conversion and subservience to French policy, 1673; received with great honours on her way to England at Versailles and elsewhere; found favour at court and was attached to her husband's daughters, Mary and Anne, but shared unpopularity of James with the public; gave birth to five children, 1675–1682, who all died young; visited Mary in Holland, 1678; her secretary, Edward Coleman (d. 1678) [q. v.], fatally involved in the 'Popish plot,' though she herself was innocent; accompanied James, on his withdrawal from England, to the Netherlands, 1679, and to Scotland; returned with him to England, 1680, and again to Scotland; finally came to London with him, 1682; on accession of James II to the throne became identified with aggressive Roman catholic faction; became ill and distressed by the king's infidelities, 1685; announced her pregnancy, 1687; gave birth to Prince of Wales, 1688, an event beyond question, but then commonly disbelieved, suspicion being greatly increased by absence of the proper witnesses; fled to France, followed soon afterwards by James; in contrast with James made very favourable impression on French court; supported schemes for invasion of England and for exciting religious war; corresponded with Jacobites; resided at St. Germains Palace, retiring frequently to nunnery at Chaillot; gave birth to Princess Louisa, 1692; received with James pension of fifty thousand crowns a month from Louis, and after his death, 1701, annuity of a hundred thousand francs; buried at Chaillot; was praised by St. Simon and Madame de Sévigné, but was always unpopular in England.

[xxxvi. 365]

MARY QUEEN OF SCOTS (1542–1587), third child and only daughter of James V of Scotland [q. v.] and Mary of Guise [q. v.]; queen in infancy on her father's death,

1542; sent to France, 1548, the agreement for her marriage with the dauphin of France (Francis II) being ratified by the estates; educated with royal children of France; brought up strict Roman catholic, and taught various accomplishments, but not English; famous for her beauty and grace; the great hope of catholicism; married Francis, 1558, and made secret treaty delivering Scotland to France in case of her death without heir; laid claim to English throne on death of Mary I, 1558, as great-granddaughter of Henry VII; styled herself queen of England; was prostrated by her husband Francis II's death, 1560; entertained various proposals of marriage which were brought forward by the Guises, but obstructed by Catherine de Medici; determined to return to Scotland; arrived, 1561, accompanied by Brantôme, Chastelard, and others; heard mass in her chapel; had stormy interview with Knox, who had denounced the 'idolatry'; informed the pope of her determination to restore catholicism; carried on negotiations with Elizabeth for a reconciliation, 1562; entered into sports of the nobles and life of the people, and disarmed hostility; conferred on the protestant Lord James Stewart, afterwards earl of Moray (1531?–1570) [q. v.], the title of Earl of Mar, and sanctioned expedition against George Gordon, fourth earl of Huntly [q. v.], 1562; sent Maitland to England to claim right of succession to Elizabeth, 1563; showed imprudent partiality for Chastelard, who was executed, after being found concealed in her bedroom, 1563; her project of marriage with Don Carlos of Spain thwarted by the French; pretended to be guided in choice of a husband by Elizabeth, who proposed the Earl of Leicester, 1563; married in 1565 Henry Stewart, earl of Darnley [q. v.], thus strengthening her claims as heir-presumptive and defying Elizabeth; marched with a force to Glasgow to capture Moray and rebellious lords, on which Moray took refuge in England; determined to make herself absolute and to impose Roman catholicism on the country; quarrelled with Darnley, who was supported by the nobles; her favourite, Rizzio, murdered, 1566; determined on revenge, but for the time was reconciled to her husband; fled to Dunbar with Darnley and entered Edinburgh with a powerful force; gave birth to a prince (afterwards James I of England), 1566; became finally estranged from Darnley and showed more marked favour to James Hepburn, fourth earl of Bothwell [q. v.]; visited Darnley at Glasgow, 1567; persuaded him to accompany her to Edinburgh, and was met by Bothwell, who conveyed them to a house in Kirk-o'-Field, which was blown up in her temporary absence, Darnley being killed; was probably actuated, in conniving at the murder, by motives of revenge and love for Bothwell; co-operated with Bothwell and others in making trial of murderers a fiasco, and left for Seton with Bothwell and others implicated; was carried off to Dunbar, probably at her own instigation; refused offer of a rescue; married to Bothwell at Edinburgh with protestant rites, 1567; consented to prohibition of cathedral services throughout Scotland, 1567; joined Bothwell, who had escaped from Borthwick Castle, and rode with him to Dunbar; delivered herself to the lords at Carberry Hill, and was imprisoned at Lochleven, 1567; was allowed to choose between a divorce, a trial at which the Casket letters were to be adduced as evidence, and abdication; chose the last and nominated Moray regent; escaped from Lochleven (1568) with George Douglas to Hamilton Palace, where she was joined by nobles and six thousand men; watched the battle of Langside, and seeing all was lost escaped to England, 1568; guarded closely at Carlisle and denied interview by Elizabeth till she had cleared herself of Darnley's murder; refused to allow Elizabeth's jurisdiction when conferences meeting at York and Westminster finally reached a formal verdict that nothing had been proved against either party; was nevertheless kept for life a prisoner by Elizabeth; removed to care of Earl of Shrewsbury, 1569, to Tutbury, and to Wingfield; accepted proposal of marriage with Norfolk, and joined plot formed for her escape and for a catholic rising, 1569; on advance of Northumberland and Westmorland to Tutbury was removed to Coventry; approved of Moray's assassination, 1570; obtained papal bull dissolving marriage with Bothwell, 1570; was transferred to Chatsworth and then to Sheffield; her death contemplated by Elizabeth after Ridolfi plot, 1572, and the massacre of St. Bartholomew; made plans for escape, but achieved nothing by treating with both parties; proposed to pope and Philip conquest of England, and superintended details of projected invasion under the Duke of Guise; was accused unjustly by Countess of Shrewsbury of criminal intrigues with Shrewsbury, and removed once more to Wingfield; was ignored by her son James VI in negotiations between England and Scotland, 1584, on which she bequeathed her crown to Philip II of Spain; was removed to Tutbury and then to Chartley, 1586; involved herself, through facilities afforded her by Walsingham, in the Babington conspiracy; was removed to Fotheringay; put on her trial there, 1586, condemned to death, and was at length executed, 1587, Elizabeth maintaining that she had never intended the execution to take place. A woman of much cultivation, she wrote verse of no great merit. 'Adieu plaisant pays de France,' sometimes ascribed to her, was really written by Meusnier de Querlon. [xxxvi. 373]

MARY OF GUELDRES (d. 1463), queen of James II of Scotland; daughter of Arnold, duke of Gueldres; brought up by Philip the Good of Burgundy; married James II, 1449; on death of James at Roxburgh, 1460, set out for the camp with the infant king and took the castle; regent of Scotland during James III's minority; received Margaret and Henry VI after defeat at Towton, 1461. [xxxvi. 390]

MARY OF GUISE (1515-1560), queen of James V of Scotland [q. v.], and mother of Mary Queen of Scots [q. v.]; daughter of Claude, count of Guise; married Louis of Orleans, 1534, and gave birth to a son, Francis, 1535; sought in marriage by Henry VIII on death of her husband, 1537; married James V of Scotland at Paris, 1538, and brought him as dower 150,000 livres; after giving birth to two princes, who died, became mother of a daughter, Mary, 1542; almost at the same time received news of disaster of Solway Moor and death of James; failed in preventing nomination to regency of James Hamilton, second earl of Arran and duke of Châtelherault [q. v.], who as next heir after the infant princess was regent according to constitutional precedent, but being a protestant and supporter of English interests came under her displeasure; carried off by David Beaton [q. v.], her chief adviser, with her daughter to Stirling, 1543; accused of too great familiarity with Beaton; accepted French offers of help against England, on which war was declared; desired to marry her daughter in France, but was opposed by Arran and Beaton; secured support of the Douglases, 1544, and was left leading figure in Scotland by murder of Beaton, 1546; resisted Somerset's attempts to force Mary's marriage with Edward VI; showed great courage in subsequent disasters; obtained consent of nobles and parliament to Mary's marriage with the dauphin, 1548; sent the princess to France; made peace, 1550; went to France and was received with great honour; on her way back to Scotland visited Edward VI, 1551; became regent of Scotland, 1554; bent on bringing Scotland into line with policy of her family, the Guises; but in order to promote French marriage was obliged to temporise with protestant party; provoked war with England, 1557, but failed to raise force for invasion; succeeded in bringing about marriage of Mary and dauphin, 1558, and subsequently (1559) treated reformers with severity, with the result that civil war broke out; received help from France, while the protestants were encouraged by Cecil, by English money, and the aid of Arran; fortified Leith with French help; on approach of English force to besiege Leith, took refuge in Edinburgh Castle and died there. [xxxvi. 391]

MARY OF FRANCE (1496-1533), queen of Louis XII, king of France; daughter of Henry VII by Elizabeth of York; betrothed to Charles, prince of Castile (afterwards Emperor Charles V), 1508, but contract subsequently broken off, 1514; married by Henry VIII to Louis XII at Abbeville, 1514; on his death (1515) married in France Charles Brandon, first duke of Suffolk [q. v.], to the annoyance of Henry VIII, who was, however, pacified by large gifts of money; gave birth to a son, 1516, and to two daughters, one, Frances, being mother of Lady Jane Grey; present at Field of the Cloth of Gold, 1520; disliked Anne Boleyn, and refused to go with her and Henry to meeting with Francis I, 1532. [xxxvi. 397]

MARY, PRINCESS ROYAL OF ENGLAND and PRINCESS OF ORANGE (1631-1660), eldest daughter of Charles I and Queen Henrietta Maria; celebrated for her beauty and intelligence; married William, son of Frederick Henry, prince of Orange, 1641; went to Holland, 1642, and welcomed Charles and James, 1648; gave birth to son, afterwards William III of England, after death of her husband,

1650; made guardian of young prince, 1651; disliked by the Dutch, whose sympathies were with Cromwell; received Charles II secretly, 1651, and helped her brothers and their adherents liberally; finally forbidden by the Dutch States to receive them on outbreak of war between England and Holland, 1652; her son William formally elected stadtholder by Zealand and several northern provinces, but excluded from his father's military dignities; visited Charles II at Cologne and Paris, 1656; courted by Buckingham and others; became sole regent, 1658, opposed by Dona, governor of town of Orange; invoked help of Louis XIV of France, who took Orange, 1660; took part in festivities at the Hague on Charles's restoration; visited England and died there of small-pox. [xxxvi. 400]

MARY (1723-1772), princess of Hesse; daughter of George II and Queen Caroline; married Frederic, hereditary prince, afterwards landgrave of Hesse-Cassel, 1740; separated from him on his turning Roman catholic, 1754, and resided with her children at Hanau. [xxxvi. 404]

MARY, PRINCESS, DUCHESS OF GLOUCESTER AND EDINBURGH (1776-1857), fourth daughter of George III; mentioned by Miss Burney; married William Frederick, second duke of Gloucester [q. v.], 1816. [lxi. 349]

MARY OF BUTTERMERE (fl. 1802). [See ROBINSON, MARY.]

MARYBOROUGH, VISCOUNTS. [See MOLYNEUX, SIR RICHARD, first VISCOUNT, 1593-1636; MOLYNEUX, SIR RICHARD, second VISCOUNT, 1617?-1654?; MOLYNEUX, CARYLL, third VISCOUNT, 1621-1699.]

MARYBOROUGH, first BARONET. [See WELLESLEY-POLE, WILLIAM, 1763-1845.]

MARZAI, STEPHEN DE (d. 1193). [See STEPHEN.]

MASCALL, EDWARD JAMES (d. 1832), collector of customs for port of London, 1816; published works on the customs. [xxxvi. 404]

MASCALL, LEONARD (d. 1589), author and translator; clerk of the kitchen to Archbishop Parker [q. v.]; possibly author of 'A Booke of the Arte . . . howe to plant and graffe all sortes of trees,' 1572, and works on poultry, cattle, fishing, and 'remedies'; drew up 'Registrum parochiæ de Farnham,' 1573. [xxxvi. 404]

MASCALL, ROBERT (d. 1416), bishop of Hereford; distinguished himself at Oxford in philosophy and theology; confessor to Henry IV, c. 1400; bishop of Hereford, 1404; took part in condemnation of Cobham, 1413; delegate to council of Constance, 1415; 'De Legationibus suis lib. i.' and sermons attributed to him. [xxxvi. 405]

MASCARENE, PAUL (1684-1760), lieutenant-governor of Nova Scotia; of Huguenot family; educated at Geneva; nationalised in England, 1706; commanded grenadiers at storming of Port Royal; brevet major; lieutenant-governor of Annapolis, 1740, and of province, 1744; defended fort against Indians and French, 1744, in spite of state of garrison and neglect by authorities; sent on mission to New England by Cornwallis, 1751; major-general, 1758; his services inadequately recompensed. [xxxvi. 406]

MASCHIART, MICHAEL (1544-1598), Latin poet; perpetual fellow of New College, Oxford, 1562; D.C.L., 1573; vicar of Writtle, Essex, 1572-98; reputed author of 'Poemata Varia.' [xxxvi. 407]

MASERES, FRANCIS (1731-1824), mathematician, historian, and reformer; of Huguenot family; B.A. Clare College, Cambridge, 1752; first Newcastle medallist, 1752; M.A., 1755; fellow, 1756-9; barrister, Inner Temple, 1750, and later, bencher and treasurer; attorney-general of Quebec, 1766-9; cursitor baron of exchequer, 1773-1824; senior judge of London sheriffs' court, 1780; zealous protestant and whig; unitarian; inherited great wealth, which he generously employed; F.R.S., 1771; published several mathematical works, and rejected negative quantities; wrote several books on Quebec, and on social and political questions, including translations from French writers; edited reprints of historical works, and supplied funds for other publications. [xxxvi. 407]

MASHAM, ABIGAIL, LADY MASHAM (d. 1734), daughter of Francis Hill, first cousin of Sarah, duchess of Marlborough [see CHURCHILL, SARAH], and related to Harley; entered service of Lady Rivers, and subsequently lived with the Duchess of Marlborough; made bedchamber woman to Queen Anne by the latter's influence; sympathised with Anne's opinions on church and state matters, and gradually supplanted the duchess in Anne's favour; married privately Samuel Masham (1679?-1758) [q. v.], groom of the bedchamber to Prince George of Denmark [q. v.], 1707; kept queen's favour in spite of the duchess's indignation; medium of Harley's communications with Anne after his fall, 1708; given care of privy purse on dismissal of the duchess, 1711, and her husband made peer; procured Harley's dismissal, and sided with Bolingbroke and the Jacobites, 1714; lived in retirement after death of Anne; much esteemed by Swift. [xxxvi. 410]

MASHAM, DAMARIS, LADY MASHAM (1658-1708), theological writer; daughter of Ralph Cudworth [q. v.]; studied under her father and Locke; married Sir Francis Masham, third baronet, of Oates, Essex, 1685; gave birth to a son, 1686; adopted the views of John Locke, who resided at Oates from 1691 till his death in 1704; published 'A Discourse concerning the Love of God,' 1696, 'Occasional Thoughts,' c. 1700, and account of Locke in 'Great Historical Dictionary.' [xxxvi. 412]

MASHAM, SAMUEL, first BARON MASHAM (1679?-1758), son of Sir Francis Masham, third baronet; successively page, equerry, and groom of the bedchamber to Prince George of Denmark; married Abigail Hill, 1707 [see MASHAM, ABIGAIL, LADY]; brigadier-general, 1710; M.P., Ilchester, 1710, Windsor, 1711; cofferer of household to Queen Anne, 1711; one of twelve tory peers created, 1712; remembrancer of the exchequer, 1716; belonged to famous Society of Brothers. [xxxvi. 411]

MASHAM, SAMUEL, second BARON MASHAM (1712-1776), son of Samuel Masham, first baron Masham [q. v.]; auditor-general of household of George, prince of Wales; given pension by George III, 1761; lord of the bedchamber, 1762; hated by Swift. [xxxvi. 412]

MASKELL, WILLIAM (1814?-1890), mediævalist; M.A. University College, Oxford, 1838; extreme high churchman; attacked Bishop Stanley of Norwich for his support of relaxation of subscription, 1840; rector of Corscombe, Dorset, 1842-7; vicar of St. Mary Church, near Torquay, 1847-50; published 'Ancient Liturgy of the Church of England,' 1844, and other works, which placed him in front rank of English ecclesiastical historians; chaplain to Bishop of Exeter; published 'Holy Baptism,' 1848, and other works; questioned jurisdiction of privy council in Gorham case [see GORHAM, GEORGE CORNELIUS]; became Roman catholic, 1850; acquiesced unwillingly in dogma of papal infallibility; lived in retirement and devoted himself to literature and collecting mediæval service books and objects; J.P. and deputy-lieutenant for Cornwall. [xxxvi. 413]

MASKELYNE, NEVIL (1732-1811), astronomer royal; wrangler, Trinity College, Cambridge, 1754; fellow, 1757; M.A., 1757; D.D., 1777; obtained livings of Shrawardine, 1775, and North Runcton, 1782; assisted Bradley; sent by Royal Society to observe transit of Venus at St. Helena, 1761; was unsuccessful, but made other useful observations; astronomer royal, 1765; established the 'Nautical Almanac,' 1766; made about ninety thousand observations, published, 1776-1811, with one assistant only; perfected method of transit-observation, 1772; obviated effects of parallax; invented prismatic micrometer (in part anticipated); Copley medallist for 'Observations on the Attraction of Mountains,' 1775; edited Mason's correction of Mayer's 'Lunar Tables,' 1787, and other works; wrote essay on 'Equation of Time'; member of French Institute, 1802; F.R.S., 1758. [xxxvi. 414]

MASON, CHARLES (1616-1677), royalist divine; of Eton and King's College, Cambridge; B.A., 1635; fellow, 1635-44; D.D. Oxford, 1642, Cambridge, 1660; deprived of fellowship, 1644; rector of Stower Provost, Dorset, 1647; rector of St. Mary Woolchurch, London, 1660-6, and of St. Peter-le-Poor, London, 1669-77, and prebendary of St. Paul's, London, 1663, and of Salisbury, 1671; published sermons and verse. [xxxvi. 416]

MASON, CHARLES (1730-1787), astronomer; assistant to Bradley at Greenwich; with Dixon observed transit of Venus at Cape of Good Hope, 1761; settled boundary between Pennsylvania and Maryland, 1763-7; measured an arc of the meridian, 1764; employed by Royal Society on mission at Cavan, Ireland, 1769; ob-

served second transit of Venus and other phenomena; corrected Mayer's 'Lunar Tables'; died at Philadelphia. [xxxvi. 417]

MASON, FRANCIS (1566?-1621), archdeacon of Norfolk; fellow of Merton College, Oxford, 1586; B.A. Brasenose College, Oxford, 1587; M.A. Merton College, Oxford, 1590; B.D., 1597; obtained rectory of Sudbourn, with chapel of Orford in Suffolk, 1599; wrote 'Of the Consecration of the Bishops in the Church of England,' 1613, proving validity of their consecration, and exciting several answers from Roman catholics; published Latin and enlarged editions, and other works. [xxxvi. 417]

MASON, FRANCIS (1837-1886), surgeon; F.R.C.S., 1862; filled posts of surgeon and lecturer at Westminster and St. Thomas's hospitals and elsewhere; president of Medical Society, 1882; published medical works. [xxxvi. 419]

MASON, GEORGE (1735-1806), miscellaneous writer; of Corpus Christi College, Oxford; barrister, Inner Temple, 1761; collector of scarce books; published 'A Supplement to Johnson's "English Dictionary,"' 1801, 'Life of Richard Earl Howe,' 1803, and other works. [xxxvi. 419]

MASON, GEORGE HEMING (1818-1872), painter; travelled to Rome through France and Switzerland with his brother, mostly on foot, 1843-5, and earned livelihood by painting portraits of English settlers and their pet animals; tended the wounded during Italian war; painted cattle in the Campagna; formed friendships with Frederic Lord Leighton and Costa; painted 'Ploughing in the Campagna,' 1856, and similar pictures; visited Paris exhibition, 1855; returned to England, married, and settled in family mansion at Whitby Abbey, 1858; painted 'Wind on the Wolds,' followed by series of English idylls; exhibited at Academy and Dudley Gallery several fine pictures, including 'The Cast Shoe,' 1865, and the 'Harvest Moon' (his last), 1872; A.R.A., 1869. [xxxvi. 420]

MASON, GEORGE HENRY MONCK (1825-1857), British resident at Jodhpore; nephew of Henry Joseph Monck Mason [q. v.]; distinguished himself as assistant to agent at Rajpootana from 1847, and as political agent at Kerowlee; resident at Jodhpore, 1857; provided for safety of Europeans on mutiny of the Jodhpore legion; accompanied troops to meet Sir George St. Patrick Lawrence [q. v.], and was murdered by the rebels. [xxxvi. 422]

MASON, HENRY (1573?-1647), divine; brother of Francis Mason (1566?-1621) [q. v.]; M.A. Corpus Christi College, Oxford, 1603; B.D., 1610; obtained several livings, including (1613) that of St. Andrew Undershaft, London; chaplain to bishop of London; prebendary of St. Paul's, London, 1616; works include 'The New Art of Lying,' covered by Jesuits,' 1624. [xxxvi. 422]

MASON, HENRY JOSEPH MONCK (1778-1858), miscellaneous writer; brother of William Monck [q. v.]; scholar and gold medallist, Trinity College, Dublin; B.A., 1798; Irish barrister, 1800; examiner to prerogative court; subsequently librarian of King's Inns, 1815; corresponded with Robert Southey; organised societies for giving religious instruction to the Irish-speaking population, and for improvement of prisons; instrumental in founding Irish professorship and scholarships at Dublin University; LL.D. Dublin, 1817; works include 'Essay on the Antiquity and Constitution of Parliaments in Ireland,' 1820. [xxxvi. 423]

MASON, JAMES (fl. 1743-1783), landscape engraver; executed plates from pictures by Claude, Poussin, and contemporary English artists. [xxxvi. 424]

MASON, JAMES (1779-1827), miscellaneous writer; supporter of Fox; advocated abolition of slavery and catholic emancipation; published political pamphlets and 'The Natural Son' (tragedy), 1805, 'Literary Miscellanies,' 1809, and other works. [xxxvi. 424]

MASON, SIR JOHN (1503-1566), statesman; son of a cowherd at Abingdon; fellow of All Souls College, Oxford; M.A., 1525; king's scholar at Paris; obtained living of Kyngeston, 1532; travelled abroad on the king's service for several years; secretary to Sir Thomas Wyatt (1503?-1542) [q. v.]; gained reputation as diplomatist; clerk to privy council, 1542; master of the posts, 1544, and French secretary; knighted by Edward VI, 1547; searched registers to establish English suzerainty over Scotland, 1548; dean of Winchester, 1549; ambassador to France, 1550-1, and corresponded with council; master of requests and clerk of parliament, 1551; commissioner to collect 'church

stuff,' 1552; obtained some of Somerset's lands; M.P.,
Reading, 1551 and 1552, Taunton, 1552-3; chancellor of
Oxford University, 1552-6 and 1559-64; witness to
Edward VI's will, 1553; signed letter to Mary announcing proclamation of Jane, but soon afterwards arranged
with lord mayor proclamation of Mary, 1553; gave
up ecclesiastical offices, but, favoured by Mary, was made
treasurer of the chamber, 1554; ambassador to the Emperor Charles V at Brussels, 1553-6, and present at his
abdication; reinstated in chancellorship and deanery at
Elizabeth's accession; directed foreign policy and negotiated with France, 1559 and 1564.   [xxxvi. 425]

MASON, JOHN (*fl.* 1603), fellow of Corpus Christi
College, Oxford; M.A., 1603; B.D.; brother of Francis
Mason (1566 ?-1621) [q. v.]   [xxxvi. 419]

MASON, JOHN (1586-1635), founder of New Hampshire; matriculated from Magdalen College, Oxford,
1602; assisted in reclamation of the Hebrides, 1610;
governor of Newfoundland, 1615; completed first English
map of the island, 1625, and wrote ' A Briefe Discovrse of
the Newfoundland,' 1620; received various patents for
lands in New England; returned to England, 1624;
treasurer and paymaster of the army, 1627; received new
patents and sailed again, 1629; associated with Sir
Ferdinando Gorges [q. v.] and six London merchants,
obtained land on Piscataqua river, 1631 (colony afterwards known as New Hampshire); returned, 1634; was
appointed captain of Southsea Castle and inspector of
forts and castles on south coast; nominated to council for
New England, 1633, and ' vice-admiral of New England,'
1635; zealous churchman and royalist.   [xxxvi. 428]

MASON, JOHN (1600-1672), New England commander; served in Netherlands under Sir Thomas, afterwards Baron Fairfax (1612-1671) [q. v.]; went to
Dorchester, Massachusetts, 1630, and obtained military
command; assisted migration to Windsor, New Connecticut, 1635; with help of friendly Indians exterminated
the Pequots, 1637; major-general of colonial forces,
1638-70; deputy-governor of Connecticut, 1660, and chief
judge of colonial county court, 1664-70; prepared ' Brief
History of the Pequot War.'   [xxxvi. 429]

MASON, JOHN (1646 ?-1694), enthusiast and poet;
M.A. Clare Hall, Cambridge, 1668; vicar of Stantonbury,
1668-74, and rector of Water Stratford, 1674; Calvinist
and enthusiastic preacher on the millenium, which he
announced was beginning at Water Stratford; preached,
1690, and published sermon on the ten virgins, which made
some stir; attracted noisy encampment of followers to
the village, who remained unconvinced of his mortality
after his exhumed corpse had been shown to them; wrote
' A living stream as crystal clear,' and other familiar
hymns.   [xxxvi. 430]

MASON, JOHN (1706-1763), nonconformist divine
and author; grandson of John Mason (1646 ?-1694)
[q. v.]; tutor and chaplain in family of Governor Feaks;
presbyterian minister at Dorking, 1729, and at Cheshunt,
1746; published ' Plea for Christianity,' 1743, and other
works, and trained students for ministry. [xxxvi. 432]

MASON, JOHN CHARLES (1798-1881), marine
secretary to Indian government; solicitor's clerk; later
employed in important affairs in secretary's office at East
India House; compiled ' An Analysis of the Constitution
of the East India Company,' 1825-6; marine secretary,
1837; introduced great improvements; arranged for
transport of fifty thousand troops on outbreak of mutiny,
1857.   [xxxvi. 432]

MASON, JOHN MONCK (1726-1809), Shakespearean
commentator; M.A. Trinity College, Dublin, 1761; Irish
barrister, 1752; Irish M.P., Blessington, 1761 and 1769,
St. Canice, 1776, 1783, 1790, and 1798; made commissioner
of public works, 1771, and of revenue of Ireland, 1772;
became supporter of government in Ireland; Irish privy
councillor; voted for union in last Irish parliament;
works include ' Comments on the last Edition of Shakespeare's Plays,' 1785.   [xxxvi. 433]

MASON, SIR JOSIAH (1795-1881), pen manufacturer
and philanthropist; was successively fruit-seller in the
streets, shoemaker, carpenter, blacksmith, house-painter,
and manufacturer of imitation gold jewellery and split
rings; made split rings by machinery; manufactured
pens for Perry; joined the Elkingtons in electro-plate
business, 1844, and in smelting works; acquired great

wealth; founded almshouses and orphanage at Erdington
and the Mason College at Birmingham; knighted, 1872.
          [xxxvi. 434]

MASON, MARTIN (*fl.* 1650-1676), quaker; continually imprisoned for his opinions, 1650-71; concerned in
schism of John Perrot [q. v.]; wrote ' An Address' (to
Charles II), and another to parliament, 1660; liberated,
1672; published controversial tracts.   [xxxvi. 435]

MASON, RICHARD (1601-1678). [See ANGELUS À
SANCTO FRANCISCO.]

MASON, ROBERT (1571-1635), politician and author;
of Balliol College, Oxford, and Lincoln's Inn; M.P.
Ludgershall, Wiltshire, 1626, Winchester, 1628; opponent
of the court; assistant to managers of Buckingham's
impeachment, 1626; one of the framers of the Petition
of Right, 1628; defended Eliot, 1630; recorder of London,
1634; author of 'Reason's Monarchie,' 1602, and of other
writings.   [xxxvi. 435]

MASON, ROBERT (1589 ?-1662), secretary to Duke of
Buckingham; fellow of St. John's College, Cambridge, and
LL.D.   [xxxvi. 436]

MASON, THOMAS (1580-1619 ?), divine; of Magda-
len College, Oxford; vicar of Odiham, 1614-19; published
' Christ's Victorie over Sathan's Tyrannie,' 1615, and ' A
Revelation of the Revelation,' 1619.   [xxxvi. 436]

MASON, THOMAS (*d.* 1660), Latin poet; demy,
1596, and fellow, 1603-14; of Magdalen College, Oxford,
M.A., 1605; D.D., 1631; prebendary of Salisbury, 1624;
rector of North Waltham, 1623, and Weyhill, 1624;
ejected during rebellion; wrote Latin verses.
          [xxxvi. 436]

MASON, WILLIAM (*fl.* 1672-1709), stenographer;
London writing-master; published three treatises on
shorthand, 1672, 1682, and 1707, embodying three systems,
the last and best, with modifications, being still in use;
greatest stenographer of seventeenth century; celebrated
for his skill in minute handwriting.   [xxxvi. 437]

MASON, WILLIAM (1724-1797), poet; scholar of
St. John's College, Cambridge; M.A., 1749; wrote
' monody ' on Pope's death, published, 1747; elected fellow
of Pembroke College, Cambridge, through Gray's influence, 1749; composed ' Isis' (poem denouncing Oxford
Jacobitism), 1748, an ode upon Duke of Newcastle's installation, 1749, and ' Elfrida,' dramatic poem, 1752; became
acquainted with Hurd and Warburton; rector of Aston,
Yorkshire, 1754, and chaplain to Lord Holderness; visited
Germany, 1755; king's chaplain, 1757; canon of York,
1762; published odes, 1756, ' Caractacus,' 1759, and
' elegies,' 1762; maintained close friendship with Gray, and
was his literary executor; published ' An Heroic Epistle '
to Sir William Chambers, a sharp satire, 1773; published
Gray's ' Life and Letters,' 1774; corresponded with
Horace Walpole; prominent in political agitation for
retrenchment and reform, 1780, but later became follower
of Pitt; his ' Sappho ' (lyrical drama) first printed, 1797;
imitator of Gray, and, in satire, follower of Pope; composed church music, and invented an instrument, the
' Celestina'; his ' Works' collected, 1811.   [xxxvi. 438]

MASON, WILLIAM MONCK (1775-1859), historian;
brother of Henry Joseph Monck Mason [q. v.]; ' land
waiter for exports' at Dublin, 1796; published ' The
History and Antiquities of the ... Church of St. Patrick,'
1819 (portion of much larger projected work), and a
pamphlet, ' Suggestions relative to ... a Survey ... of
Ireland,' 1825.   [xxxvi. 441]

MASON, WILLIAM SHAW (1774-1853), statist;
B.A. Dublin, 1796; remembrancer, 1805, and secretary to
commissioners for public records in Ireland, 1810; published ' A Statistical Account ... of Ireland,' 1814, 1816,
1819, and other works.   [xxxvi. 442]

MASQUERIER, JOHN JAMES (1778-1855), painter;
studied at Paris and in London; exhibited a picture of
' Napoleon reviewing the Consular Guards,' 1801, which
caused him to be bitterly attacked as a spy by William
Cobbett; painted, among others, portraits of Emma, lady
Hamilton, Harriot Mellon, afterwards Duchess of St.
Albans, Miss O'Neil, and Warren Hastings; intimate with
Sir Francis Burdett, Baroness Burdett Coutts, John Wilkes,
Michael Faraday, and Thomas Campbell.   [xxxvii. 1]

MASSEREENE, second EARL OF. [See SKEFFING-
TON, CLOTWORTHY, 1742-1805.]

MASSEREENE, VISCOUNTS. [See CLOTWORTHY, SIR JOHN, first VISCOUNT, d. 1665; SKEFFINGTON, SIR JOHN, second VISCOUNT, d. 1695; SKEFFINGTON, JOHN SKEFFINGTON FOSTER, tenth VISCOUNT, 1812–1863.]

MASSEY, SIR EDWARD (1619?–1674?), major-general; royalist, 1642; joined parliamentarians; general of the Western Association, 1645; co-operated with Fairfax in reducing the west, 1645–6; M.P., Gloucester, 1646; commander-in-chief of the London forces; impeached by the army, 1647; fled to Holland; returned, 1648; excluded from the House of Commons by Pride's Purge, 1648, and imprisoned with Waller; again escaped to Holland and joined the king, 1649; lieutenant-general, 1651; wounded at Worcester, taken prisoner, and lodged in the Tower, 1651; again escaped to Holland; negotiated with English presbyterians, 1654, 1655, and 1660; appointed governor of Gloucester by Charles and knighted, 1660; M.P., Gloucester, 1661–74. [xxxvii. 2]

MASSEY, EYRE, first BARON CLARINA (1719–1804), general; served in West Indies, 1739; ensign, 1741; commanded Niagara expedition, 1759; routed the French at La Belle Famille and gained possession of all the Upper Ohio; commanded grenadiers at Montreal, 1760, Martinique, 1761, Havana, 1762, New York and Quebec, 1763–1769; Halifax, 1776–80, and Cork, 1794–6; raised to peerage of Ireland, 1800. [xxxvii. 5]

MASSEY, JOHN (1651–1715), Roman catholic divine; fellow of Merton College, Oxford, 1672; M.A. Magdalen Hall, Oxford, 1676; senior proctor, 1684; became a Roman catholic, 1685; dean of Christ Church, Oxford, 1686; one of the founders of the Oxford Chemical Society, 1683; fled to France, 1688; died in Paris. [xxxvii. 6]

MASSEY, WILLIAM (1691–1764?), miscellaneous writer and translator; published 'Origin and Progress of Letters,' 1763, and translations. [xxxvii. 6]

MASSEY, WILLIAM NATHANIEL (1809–1881), politician and historian; recorder of Portsmouth, 1852, Plymouth, 1855; M.P., Newport, Isle of Wight, 1855–7, Salford, 1857–63; financial member of government of India, 1863–8; M.P., Tiverton, 1872–81; published history of George III's reign, 1855–63. [xxxvii. 7]

MASSIE, JAMES WILLIAM (1799–1869), independent minister; missionary in India, 1822–39; secretary to Home Missionary Society; advocated free trade and emancipation of slaves. [xxxvii. 7]

MASSIE, JOSEPH (d. 1784), writer on trade and finance; formed collection of fifteen hundred treatises on economics, 1557–1763; compiled statistics to illustrate the growth of British trade and published works on political economy. [xxxvii. 8]

MASSIE, THOMAS LEEKE (1802–1898), admiral; entered navy, 1818; lieutenant, 1827; commander, 1838; captain, 1841; served in Burmese war, 1849; on North American station, 1855–6; rear-admiral, 1860; admiral, 1872. [Suppl. iii. 151]

MASSINGBERD, FRANCIS CHARLES (1800–1872), chancellor of Lincoln; went to Italy with Dr. Arnold and William Ralph Churton [q. v.], 1824; M.A. Magdalen College, Oxford, 1825; prebendary of Lincoln, 1847; chancellor and canon, 1862; active member of convocation; proctor for parochial clergy, 1857, for the chapter, 1868; published 'English History of the Leaders of the Reformation,' 1842. [xxxvii. 9]

MASSINGER, PHILIP (1583–1640), dramatist; entered at St. Alban Hall, Oxford, 1602; came to London, 1606; soon became a famous playwright; collaborated with Nathaniel Field, Robert Daborne, Cyril Tourneur, and Dekker; wrote regularly in conjunction with Fletcher, 1613–25; associated with the king's company of actors, 1616–23 and 1625–40; with the Cockpit company, 1623–1625; remarkable for his skill in the working out of plots and his insight into stage requirements. Among his patrons were the Herbert family, the Earl of Carnarvon, Sir Warham St. Leger, Sir Francis Foljambe, Sir Thomas Bland, Sir Aston Cokayne, and Lord Mohun; the fifteen plays entirely written by him are 'The Duke of Milan,' 1623, 'The Unnatural Combat,' 1639, 'The Bondman,' 1624, 'The Renegado,' 1630, 'The Parliament of Love' (licensed for the Cockpit, 1624), 'A New Way to pay Old Debts,' 1632, 'The Roman Actor,' 1629, 'The Maid of Honour,'

1632, 'The Picture,' 1630, 'The Great Duke of Florence,' 1635, 'The Emperor of the East,' 1631, 'Believe as you list' ('Stationers' Registers,' 1653), 'The City Madam,' 1658, 'The Guardian,' 1655, and 'The Bashful Lover,' 1655. In collaboration with Fletcher he wrote, among others, portions of 'Henry VIII,' 1617, and of 'Two Noble Kinsmen,' 1634, in both of which a large share is attributed to Shakespeare. His political views inclined to the popular party; in 'The Bondman' he supported the Herberts in their quarrel with Buckingham, whom he denounced under the guise of Gisco. Thinly veiled reflections on current politics figure in other plays. [xxxvii. 10]

MASSON, FRANCIS (1741–1805), gardener and botanist; sent, by the authorities at Kew Gardens, to collect plants and bulbs at the Cape, 1772; in 1776 to the Canaries, Azores, Madeira, and the West Indies, and to Portugal and Madeira, 1783; again sent to the Cape, 1786–95, and to North America, 1798; genus Massonia named after him by Linnæus. [xxxvii. 16]

MASSON, GEORGE JOSEPH GUSTAVE (1819–1888), educational writer; educated at Tours; B. ès L. Université de France, 1837; came to England as private tutor, 1847; French master at Harrow, 1855–88; Vaughan librarian from 1869; published works on French literature and history, and edited French classics. [xxxvii. 16]

MASSUE DE RUVIGNY, HENRI DE, second MARQUIS DE RUVIGNY, first EARL OF GALWAY (1648–1720), born in Paris; entered the army and served in Portugal; aide-de-camp to Marshal Turenne, 1672–5; sent by Louis XIV to England to detach Charles II from the Dutch alliance and elected deputy-general of the Huguenots, 1678; endeavoured unsuccessfully to avert their persecution; retired to England, 1688; as major-general of horse in the English service served in Ireland under William III, 1691; commander-in-chief of the forces in Ireland, 1692; created Viscount Galway and Baron Portarlington, 1692; joined the army in Flanders, 1693; envoy extraordinary to Turin, 1694; created Earl of Galway, 1697; appointed one of the lords justices of Ireland, 1697; retired from government of Ireland, 1701; sent on a mission to the elector of Cologne, 1701; commander of the English forces in Portugal, 1704; badly wounded while besieging Badajoz, 1705; reduced fortresses of Alcantara and Ciudad Rodrigo, and entered Madrid, 1706; compelled to retreat to Valentia, 1706; defeated at Almanza through the cowardice of the Portuguese, 1707; collected 14,600 troops in less than five months; envoy extraordinary to Lisbon, 1708; displayed great personal bravery at the battle on the Caya, 1709; recalled, 1710; appointed lord justice in Ireland, in view of Jacobite rising, 1715; retired, 1716. [xxxvii. 17]

MASTER, JOHN (fl. 1654–1680), physician; B.A. Christ Church, Oxford, 1657, and M.D., 1672; M.A. St. Mary Hall, Oxford, 1659; honorary F.R.C.P., 1680, and assisted Dr. Thomas Willis (1621–1675) [q. v.] in his medical publications. [xxxvii. 24]

MASTER, RICHARD (d. 1588), physician; fellow of All Souls, Oxford, 1533; M.A., 1537; F.C.P., 1553; M.D. Christ Church, Oxford, 1555; physician to Queen Elizabeth, 1559; president, College of Physicians, 1561; prebendary of York, 1563. [xxxvii. 22]

MASTER, STREYNSHAM (1682–1724), naval captain; brother-in-law of George Byng [q. v.]; captain, 1709; as captain of the Superbe at the battle of Cape Passaro, 1718, captured the Spanish commander-in-chief. [xxxvii. 22]

MASTER, THOMAS (1603–1643), divine; fellow of New College, Oxford, 1624; M.A., 1629; B.D., 1641; rector of Wykeham, 1637; assisted Edward Herbert, baron Herbert of Cherbury [q. v.], in his 'Life of Henry VIII,' and translated Herbert's work into Latin. [xxxvii. 23]

MASTER, SIR WILLIAM (d. 1662), high sheriff of Gloucestershire; grandson of Richard Master [q. v.]; member of the Inner Temple, 1612; knighted, 1622; M.P., Cirencester, 1624; high sheriff of Gloucestershire, 1627; at first a parliamentarian, but (1642) forced to contribute to the royal garrison of Cirencester; submitted to parliament, 1644, but his estate sequestered for entertaining Charles I, 1644. [xxxvii. 23]

MASTER, WILLIAM (1627–1684), divine; son of Sir William Master [q. v.]; bachelor-fellow of Merton College, Oxford, 1651; M.A., 1652; vicar of Preston,

near Cirencester, 1658 ; rector of Woodford, Essex, 1661 ;
prebendary of St. Paul's, London, 1663 ; rector of South-
church, 1666, for a year ; prebendary of Cadington Major,
1667 ; rector of St. Vedast, Foster Lane, London, 1671 ;
published moral essays.   [xxxvii. 23]

MASTERS, Mrs. MARY (*d.* 1759 ?), poetess ; acquainted with Dr. Johnson ; wrote hymns. [xxxvii. 25]

MASTERS, ROBERT (1713–1798), historian ; grandson of Sir William Master [q. v.] ; fellow of Corpus
Christi College, Cambridge, 1736–50 ; M.A., 1738 ; B.D.,
1746 ; F.S.A., 1752 ; rector of Landbeach, 1756, and of
Waterbeach, 1759 ; resigned his rectories in favour of
relations ; published 'History of Corpus Christi College,'
1753 (with appendix of lives of its members), 1755.
                                               [xxxvii. 25]

MASTERTOWN, CHARLES (1679–1750), presbyte-
rian divine ; M.A. Edinburgh, 1697 ; ministered at Connor,
co. Antrim, 1704–23 ; moderator of the general synod at
Dungannon, and installed at Third Belfast, 1723, where
the non-subscription controversy was in active progress ;
established an orthodox congregation ; published expository and polemical works.   [xxxvii. 26]

MATCHAM, GEORGE (1753–1833), traveller and
Indian civil servant ; wrote account of part of his overland journey home from India in 1783 ; patented apparatus for preserving vessels from shipwreck, 1802.
                                               [xxxvii. 27]

MATCHAM, GEORGE (1789–1877), civil lawyer ; son of
George Matcham (1753–1833) [q. v.] ; advocate in Doctors'
Commons, 1820 ; contributed to Hoare's 'History of Wilts,'
1825.   [xxxvii. 27]

MATHER, COTTON (1663–1728), New England divine ;
son of Increase Mather [q. v.] ; minister at Boston, Mass.,
1684–1728 ; D.D. Glasgow, 1710 ; F.R.S., 1714 ; linguist and
author of ' Magnalia Christi Americana,' 1702.
                                               [xxxvii. 28]

MATHER, INCREASE (1639–1723), president of Har-
vard College ; son of Richard Mather [q. v.] ; M.A. and
fellow of Harvard, 1656 ; came to England, 1657 ; M.A.
Trinity College, Dublin, 1658 ; ordained at Boston, Massa-
chusetts, 1664 ; presided at Boston synod, 1680 ; procured
refusal to give up Boston charter, 1683 ; president of
Harvard, 1684–1701 ; conveyed (1688) thanks of colony to
James II for declaration of liberty of conscience, 1687 ;
D.D. ; gained an enlarged charter from William III for
Massachusetts ; published religious writings.
                                               [xxxvii. 27]

MATHER, NATHANAEL (1631–1697), congrega-
tional divine ; son of Richard Mather [q. v.] ; M.A. Harvard, 1647 ; vicar of Harberton, 1655, of Barnstaple, 1656 ;
pastor of English church, Rotterdam, 1660, and at New
Row, Dublin, 1671, and Paved Alley, Lime Street, London,
1688 ; joined the 'happy union,' 1691, but aided in its
disruption ; Pinners' Hall lecturer, 1694.   [xxxvii. 28]

MATHER, RICHARD (1596–1669), congregational
divine ; originally a schoolmaster ; ordained minister at
Toxteth, 1618 ; suspended, 1633, for not using ceremonies ;
emigrated to New England, 1635 ; accepted call from
Dorchester, Massachusetts ; his plan to check presbyterianism (the ' Cambridge platform ') adopted by the Cambridge synod, 1648 ; wrote principally on church government.   [xxxvii. 29]

MATHER, ROBERT COTTON (1808–1877), mission-
ary ; went to India, 1833 ; built schools and churches at
Mirzapore, 1838–73 ; revised and edited the bible in Hindustani ; LL.D. Glasgow, 1862 ; returned to England, 1873 ;
published a New Testament commentary in Hindustani.
                                               [xxxvii. 30]

MATHER, SAMUEL (1626–1671), congregational
divine ; son of Richard Mather [q. v.] ; M.A. and fellow,
Harvard, 1643 ; chaplain of Magdalen College, Oxford,
1650 ; attended parliamentary commissioners to Scotland,
1653 ; incorporated M.A. Cambridge and (1654) Dublin ;
senior fellow of Trinity College, Dublin, 1654 ; ordained,
1656 ; curate of Burtonwood, 1660 ; ejected, 1662 ; erected
meeting house in New Row, Dublin, 1662 ; published
religious works.   [xxxvii. 31]

MATHER, WILLIAM (*fl.* 1695), author ; quaker
from 1661 ; schoolmaster and surveyor of highways at Bedford ; chief work, ' Young Man's Companion,' 1681, reaching twenty-four editions.   [xxxvii. 31]

MATHETES (1821 ?–1878). [See JONES, JOHN.]

MATHEW. [See also MATTHEW.]

MATHEW, THEOBALD (1790–1856), apostle of temperance ; Roman catholic priest, 1841 ; sent to small
chapel in Cork ; opened free school for boys and another
for girls ; signed total abstinence pledge, 1838 ; visited
the principal cities of Ireland with wonderful effect ;
his preaching in London described by Mrs. Carlyle, 1843 ;
worked energetically during the Irish famine ; preached
in the United States, 1849 ; returned to Ireland, 1851.
                                               [xxxvii. 32]

MATHEWS. [See also MATTHEWS.]

MATHEWS, CHARLES (1776–1835), comedian ; went
to Ireland, 1794 ; played at Dublin, Cork, and Limerick ;
left Ireland, 1795 ; played in Wales, 1795-7 ; joined Tate
Wilkinson, and became a popular actor on the York circuit ; appeared at the Haymarket, 1803, 1805-7, and 1812-
1817 ; at Drury Lane, London, 1804 and 1807 ; accompanied the burnt-out actors of Drury Lane to the Lyceum,
London, 1809-11 ; instituted at entertainments, called ' At
Homes,' a series of sketches, the first called ' The Mail
Coach,' 1808 ; produced numerous other ' At Homes ' ; went
on tour in America, 1822-3 ; undertook with Frederick
Henry Yates [q. v.] the management of the Adelphi, 1828 ;
played with Yates in Paris, 1829 ; again visited America,
1834 ; compelled to return by the failure of his voice ;
played four hundred different parts ; praised by Leigh
Hunt, Horace Smith, and Lord Byron ; intimate with
Coleridge and the Lambs ; his collection of pictures,
largely consisting of theatrical portraits, bought for the
Garrick Club, 1836.   [xxxvii. 34]

MATHEWS, CHARLES JAMES (1803–1878), actor
and dramatist ; son of Charles Mathews [q. v.] ; articled
to Augustus Charles Pugin [q. v.], 1819 ; visited with
Pugin, York, Oxford, and Paris ; amateur actor, 1822 ;
went to Ireland to build a house for Lord Blessington,
1823, whom he accompanied to Italy ; entered the employ
of John Nash in Italy, 1827, where he acted at a
private theatre built by Lord Normanby ; returned home,
1830 ; district surveyor at Bow, London ; took to the stage,
1835 ; joined Yates in management of the Adelphi, London ;
appeared at the Olympic, London, 1835, after the failure
of the Adelphi ; married his manageress, Lucia Elizabeth
Vestris [see below], 1838 ; unsuccessful in American tour,
1838, and management of Covent Garden, London, 1839-
1842 ; produced over a hundred pieces at Covent Garden,
London ; opened the Lyceum, London, 1847 ; resigned, in
consequence of heavy debts, though his management was
remunerative ; bankrupt, 1856 ; revisited America, 1856 ;
played in London, 1858-63, in Paris, 1863 and 1865 ;
appeared at Melbourne, 1870, leaving Australia, 1871 ;
visited Auckland, Honolulu, San Francisco, and New
York ; took Wallack's Theatre, New York, 1872 ; acted
in London, 1872-7, except for a season in Calcutta (1875) ;
successful chiefly in comedy and farce ; wrote various
light pieces, mostly adaptations.   [xxxvii. 37]

MATHEWS, LUCIA ELIZABETH or ELIZA-
BETTA, also known as MADAME VESTRIS [q. v.], 1856),
actress ; daughter of Gaetano Stefano Bartolozzi [q. v.] ;
first appeared in Italian opera, 1815 ; acted at Paris, 1816 ;
appeared frequently at Drury Lane, Covent Garden, and
the Haymarket, London, as well as in Ireland and the
provinces, 1820-31 ; opened the Olympic, London, with
Maria Foote, 1831 ; married Charles James Mathews
[q. v.], 1835, and went with him to America ; aided him in
his management of Covent Garden, London, 1839-42, and
the Lyceum, 1847-54 ; unrivalled as a stage singer.
                                               [xxxvii. 41]

MATHEWS, THOMAS (1676–1751), admiral ; entered
the navy, 1690 ; lieutenant, 1699 ; captain, 1703 ; assisted
in capture of Spanish flagship at Cape Passaro, 1718 ;
blockaded Messina unsuccessfully ; commanded squadron
in East Indies against pirates, 1722-4 ; virtually retired,
1724 ; but was appointed commissioner of the navy at
Chatham, 1736 ; vice-admiral of the red, 1742 ; commander-in-chief in the Mediterranean, and plenipotentiary to the king of Sardinia and the States of Italy,
1742 ; to prevent the allies slipping away to the south
fought without waiting for the rear division to close up,
on which a panic seized the English fleet and the blockade
off Toulon was fairly broken ; resigned, 1744 ; charged
by Richard Lestock [q. v.] with having neglected to give
necessary orders, and having fled from the enemy and
given up the chase, though there was every chance of
success ; dismissed, after a trial of unprecedented length,
1747 ; regarded the sentence as merely the outcome of
parliamentary faction.   [xxxvii. 43]

MATHIAS, BENJAMIN WILLIAMS (1772–1841), divine; M.A. Trinity College, Dublin, 1799; ordained to the curacy of Rathfryland, 1797; chaplain of Bethesda Chapel, Dorset Street, Dublin, 1805–35; published theological works. [xxxvii. 46]

MATHIAS, THOMAS JAMES (1754 ?–1835), satirist and Italian scholar; major-fellow, Trinity College, Cambridge, 1776; M.A., 1777; sub-treasurer to George III's queen, 1782; afterwards treasurer; F.S.A. and F.R.S., 1795; librarian at Buckingham Palace, 1812; lost heavily over his edition of Gray's works, 1814; went to Italy, 1817; published the 'Pursuits of Literature,' 1794, a reckless satire on authors, which went through sixteen editions and provoked many replies; the best English scholar in Italian since Milton; translated English poets into Italian and Italian works into English; published 'Poesie Liriche,' 1810, and 'Canzoni Toscane.' [xxxvii. 47]

MATILDA (d. 1083), queen of William the Conqueror; daughter of Baldwin V of Flanders, descendant of Alfred [q. v.]; forbidden to marry Duke William of Normandy by the council of Rheims, 1049; married at Eu, 1053, dispensation being granted by Nicolas II, 1059; built abbey at Caen as a penance; ruled Normandy in William's absence; crowned at Westminster, 1067; resided much in Normandy superintending the affairs of the duchy; sent quantities of valuables to her son Robert, 1079, during his quarrel with her father; founded the abbey of St. Mary de Pré at Rouen; benefactor of French religious houses. [xxxvii. 49]

MATILDA, MAUD, MAHALDE, MOLD (1080–1118), first wife of Henry I of England; daughter of Malcolm III of Scotland and granddaughter of Edmund Ironside; educated at Romsey; left Scotland on her father's death; went to her uncle Edgar Ætheling, 1094; married Henry I, 1100; crowned at Westminster, 1100; corresponded with Bishop Hildebert of Le Mans, and Anselm [q. v.], whose return she welcomed, 1106; built a leper hospital at St. Giles-in-the-Fields, London, and a bridge over the Lea at Stratford; founded Austin priory, Aldgate, 1108. [xxxvii. 52]

MATILDA OF BOULOGNE (1103 ?–1152), wife of Stephen, king of England; daughter of Eustace III of Boulogne; married, before 1125, Stephen of Blois, who seized the crown on Henry I's death, 1135; crowned at Westminster, 1136; made treaty with David of Scotland, 1139; secured alliance of France, 1140; her husband a prisoner, 1141; regained London for her husband; besieged the Empress Matilda (1102–1167) [q. v.], who was besieging Winchester, and compelled her to withdraw, soon effecting Stephen's release, 1141. [xxxvii. 53]

MATILDA, MAUD, MOLD, ÆTHELIC, AALIZ (1102–1167), empress; daughter of Henry I; married to Henry V of Germany, and crowned at Mainz, 1114; after her husband's death (1125) returned to England, 1126; recognised as Henry I's successor by the barons and bishops, 1126, 1131, and 1133; on her father's death (1135) entered Normandy, which, as well as England, chose her cousin Stephen for its king; gained nothing by an appeal to Rome, 1136; landed in England, 1139; Stephen brought captive to her at Gloucester, 1141; acknowledged by a council at Winchester as 'Lady of England and Normandy,' 1141; went to London, but, her confiscations and demands for money irritating the citizens, was driven from the city; besieged Winchester, but, being in turn besieged by Stephen's wife, Matilda (1103 ?–1152) [q. v.], cut her way out and fled to Gloucester; besieged by Stephen in Oxford Castle, 1142; escaped from Oxford, but had no further hope of success, 1142; conjointly with her husband, who held Normandy as a conqueror, ceded the duchy to her son Henry (afterwards Henry II), 1150; induced Henry II not to invade Ireland, 1155; founded several religious houses. [xxxvii. 54]

MATILDA, DUCHESS OF SAXONY (1156–1189), daughter of Henry II of England; married Henry the Lion, duke of Saxony, at Minden, 1168; Brunswick besieged by the emperor in consequence of her husband's refusal to submit to the forfeiture of his lands, 1180, but the siege raised on her appeal to his chivalry; sought refuge in England with her husband, who, however (1181), had submitted, returning to Brunswick, 1185; her husband again exiled, 1189. [xxxvii. 58]

MATON, ROBERT (1607–1653 ?), divine; M.A. Wadham College, Oxford, 1630; took orders; 'millenary' and believer in the literal meaning of scriptural prophecy; published 'Israel's Redemption,' 1642; replied to controversy thereby excited, in 'Israel's Redemption Redeemed,' 1646. [xxxvii. 59]

MATON, WILLIAM GEORGE (1774–1835), physician; M.A. Queen's College, Oxford, 1797; F.L.S., 1794, subsequently vice-president; physician to Westminster Hospital, London, 1800–8; M.D. Oxford, 1801; F.R.C.P., 1802; Gulstonian lecturer, 1803; Harveian orator, 1815; physician extraordinary to Queen Charlotte, 1816, to the Duchess of Kent, and the infant Princess Victoria, 1820; published (1797) account of tour in Dorset, Devonshire, Cornwall, and Somerset. [xxxvii. 60]

MATTHEW. [See also MATHEW.]

MATTHEW PARIS (d. 1259). [See PARIS.]

MATTHEW WESTMINSTER. [See WESTMINSTER.]

MATTHEW, TOBIE or TOBIAS (1546–1628), archbishop of York; B.A. University College, Oxford, 1564; M.A. Christ Church, Oxford, 1566, and student; D.D., 1574; ordained, 1566; attracted Queen Elizabeth's notice at Oxford, 1566; public orator, 1569–72; canon of Christ Church, 1570; prebendary of Salisbury, 1572; president of St. John's College, Oxford, 1572–7; dean of Christ Church, 1576; vice-chancellor, 1579; preached a Latin sermon defending the reformation, 1581; dean of Durham, 1584; vicar of Bishop's Wearmouth, 1590; acted as political agent in the north; bishop of Durham, 1595; active against recusants; prominent in the Hampton Court conference, 1604; archbishop of York, 1606; entrusted with the detention of Lady Arabella Stuart, who, however, escaped, 1611; frequently opposed the royal policy. [xxxvii. 60]

MATTHEW, SIR TOBIE (1577–1655), courtier, diplomatist, and writer; son of Tobie or Tobias Matthew [q. v.]; M.A. Christ Church, Oxford, 1597; admitted of Gray's Inn, 1599; M.P., Newport, Cornwall, 1601, St. Albans, 1604; travelled in Italy, 1604–6; converted to Roman catholicism at Florence, 1606; returned to England and was committed to the Fleet on account of his religion; allowed to leave prison on parole in consequence of the plague, 1608; obtained leave to go abroad, 1608; ordained priest at Rome, 1614; returned to London, 1617; exiled on refusing to take the oath of allegiance, 1619; allowed to return, 1621; acquainted government with a scheme for erecting titular Roman catholic bishoprics in England, 1622; sent to Madrid to advise Charles and Buckingham, 1623; knighted on his return, 1623; member of abortive Academy Royal, 1624; in Paris and Brussels, 1625–33; secretary to Strafford in Ireland, 1633; soon returned to court, where the puritans suspected him of being a papal spy; retired to Ghent, both houses of parliament having petitioned for his banishment, 1640; Bacon's later work submitted by the author to his criticism; translated Bacon's 'Essays' into Italian, 1618; wrote an account of his conversion (never printed); died at Ghent; a collection of letters made by him, published, 1660. [xxxvii. 63]

MATTHEWS. [See also MATHEWS.]

MATTHEWS, HENRY (1789–1828), judge and traveller; son of John Matthews [q. v.]; of Eton and King's College, Cambridge; fellow of King's College; M.A., 1815; advocate-fiscal of Ceylon, 1821–7; judge, 1827; published 'Diary' of continental travels, 1820 (5th edit. 1835); died in Ceylon. [xxxvii. 68]

MATTHEWS, JOHN (1755–1826), physician and poet; M.A. Merton College, Oxford, 1779; M.D., 1782; physician to St. George's Hospital, London, 1781–3; F.R.C.P., 1783; Gulstonian lecturer, 1784; mayor of Hereford, 1793; M.P., Herefordshire, 1803–6; composed prose and verse; parodied Pope's 'Eloisa,' 1780. [xxxvii. 68]

MATTHEWS or **MATHEWS**, LEMUEL (fl. 1661–1705), archdeacon of Down; son of Marmaduke Matthews [q. v.]; M.A. Lincoln College, Oxford, before 1667; rector of Lenavy and chaplain to Jeremy Taylor, bishop of Down [q. v.]; prebendary of Carncastle, 1667; archdeacon of Down, 1674; chancellor of Down and Connor, 1690; held nine livings; attainted by Irish parliament, 1689; found guilty and suspended by the Lisburn visitation,

1694, for maintenance, non-residence, and neglect of duties; agitated in a series of fourteen appeals; restored only to his prebend. [xxxvii. 69]

MATTHEWS, MARMADUKE (1606–1683?), Welsh nonconformist; M.A. All Souls, Oxford, 1627; inhibited by the bishop of St. David's; fled to West Indies; 'teaching-elder' at Maldon, New England; appointed to St. John's, Swansea, 1658; ejected, 1662; licensed to preach, 1672. [xxxvii. 70]

MATTHEWS, THOMAS (pseudonym) (1500?–1555). [See ROGERS, JOHN.]

MATTHEWS, THOMAS (1805–1889), actor and pantomimist; coached by Grimaldi; clown at Sadler's Wells, Theatre, 1829; in pantomimes in London, Paris, and Edinburgh; retired, 1865. [xxxvii. 70]

MATTHIAS. [See MATHIAS.]

MATTHIESSEN, AUGUSTUS (1831–1870), chemist and physicist; studied at Giessen, 1852, and at Heidelberg, 1853; returned to London and studied with Hofmann, 1857; F.R.S., 1861; lecturer on chemistry at St. Mary's Hospital, London, 1862–8, at St. Bartholomew's, London, 1868; worked chiefly on the constitution of alloys and opium alkaloids. [xxxvii. 71]

MATTOCKS, ISABELLA (1746–1826), actress; daughter of Lewis Hallam, a comedian; played children's parts, 1753; chief support of Covent Garden, at which she played an immense variety of parts, 1761 till her retirement, 1808; also appeared at Portsmouth and Liverpool, where her husband became manager; especially shone in the rôle of chambermaid. [xxxvii. 72]

MATURIN, CHARLES ROBERT (1782–1824), novelist and dramatist; B.A. Trinity College, Dublin, 1800; curate of St. Peter's, Dublin; set up a school and took to literature, 1807; compelled to give up the school, 1813; his manuscript tragedy 'Bertram,' recommended by Scott to Kemble, who declined it; produced by Kean, on Byron's recommendation, at Drury Lane, 1816, with great success; produced two unsuccessful tragedies; published, besides other novels, 'Montorio,' 1807, which Scott reviewed with appreciation, 'The Milesian Chief,' 1812, imitated by Scott in 'The Bride of Lammermoor,' and 'Melmoth,' 1820, his masterpiece; had great influence on the rising romantic school of France. [xxxvii. 74]

MATURIN, WILLIAM (1803–1887), divine; son of Charles Robert Maturin [q. v.]; M.A. and D.D. Dublin, 1866; was made perpetual curate of Grangegorman, 1844; librarian in Archbishop Marsh's library, Dublin, 1860; tractarian. [xxxvii. 76]

MATY, MATTHEW (1718–1776), physician, writer, and principal librarian of the British Museum, born near Utrecht; Ph.D. and M.D. Leyden, 1740; physician in London, 1741; published 'Journal Britannique,' 1750–5, which reviewed English publications in French; F.R.S., 1751; appointed under-librarian on the establishment of the British Museum, 1753; foreign secretary, Royal Society, 1762; principal secretary, 1765; L.R.C.P., 1765; principal librarian of the British Museum, 1772; disliked by Dr. Johnson, but intimate with other literary men of the day. [xxxvii. 76]

MATY, PAUL HENRY (1745–1787), assistant-librarian of the British Museum; son of Matthew Maty [q. v.]; of Westminster School and Trinity College, Cambridge; M.A., 1770, and travelling fellow; F.R.S., 1772; chaplain to Lord Stormont, English ambassador at Paris; assistant-librarian at the British Museum, 1776; foreign secretary, Royal Society, 1776 (principal secretary, 1778); protested strongly against Dr. Charles Hutton's dismissal and resigned his secretaryship, 1784; started the 'New Review,' 1782. [xxxvii. 78]

MAUCLERK, WALTER (d. 1248), bishop of Carlisle; sent to Ireland, 1210, and to Rome, to urge the royal complaints, 1215; justice of the northern counties, 1221; sheriff of Cumberland and constable of Carlisle, 1222; bishop of Carlisle, 1223; employed on diplomatic missions; treasurer, 1227–33; councillor during Henry III's absences, 1243 and 1245; resigned bishopric, 1248. [xxxvii. 79]

MAUD. [See MATILDA.]

MAUDE, THOMAS (1718–1798), minor poet and essayist; surgeon on board the Barfleur, 1755; steward of

the Yorkshire estates of his commander, Lord Harry Paulet [q. v.], at whose court-martial (1755) he had given favourable evidence, 1765–94; wrote verses descriptive of Yorkshire dales; contributed to Grose's 'Antiquities.' [xxxvii. 80]

MAUDSLAY, HENRY (1771–1831), engineer; entered Woolwich arsenal; employed by Bramah, 1789–98; set up business in London and made improvements in the lathe and marine engines; Sir Joseph Whitworth and James Nasmyth among his pupils. [xxxvii. 81]

MAUDSLAY, JOSEPH (1801–1861), engineer, son of Henry Maudslay [q. v.]; originally a shipbuilder; patented marine engines, which were extensively used; built the engines of the first admiralty screw steamship, 1841. [xxxvii. 82]

MAUDSLAY, THOMAS HENRY (1792–1864), engineer; son of Henry Maudslay [q. v.]; greatly contributed to the success of his father's firm, which constructed engines for royal navy for over twenty-five years; gave evidence before a House of Commons committee on steam navigation, 1831. [xxxvii. 82]

MAUDUIT, ISRAEL (1708–1787), political pamphleteer; preached at the Hague and other protestant chapels; partner in a woollen-draper's business, London; F.R.S., 1751; appointed customer of Southampton and agent in England for Massachusetts, 1763; witness for the defence at Governor Hutchinson's trial; declared for American independence, 1778; published pamphlets on the American war, and 'Considerations on the present German War,' 1760, the latter, according to Walpole, having enormous influence. [xxxvii. 82]

MAUDUIT, WILLIAM, EARL OF WARWICK (1220–1268), became Earl of Warwick, in right of his mother, 1263; sided with the barons, but afterwards joined Henry III; surprised and taken prisoner at Warwick Castle, 1264. [xxxvii. 83]

MAUDUITH or **MANDUIT**, JOHN (fl. 1310), astronomer; fellow of Merton College, Oxford, c. 1305; famous as physician, astronomer, and theologian; his mathematical tables well known in Leland's time. [xxxvii. 84]

MAUGER (d. 1212), bishop of Worcester; physician to Richard I and archdeacon of Evreux; bishop of Worcester, 1199; urged King John to submit to the pope; pronounced the interdict, 1208; fled to France; attempted reconciliation with King John, 1208 and 1209; died at Pontigny. [xxxvii. 84]

MAUGHAM, ROBERT (d. 1862), first secretary to the Incorporated Law Society, of which he urged the formation, 1825, establishment, 1827, and incorporation, 1831; sole proprietor and editor of the 'Legal Observer,' 1830–56; promoted Attorneys Act, 1843, and Solicitors Act, 1860; published legal works. [xxxvii. 85]

MAULE, FOX, second BARON PANMURE of the United Kingdom, and eventually eleventh EARL OF DALHOUSIE in the peerage of Scotland (1801–1874); in the army, 1820–32; M.P., Perthshire, 1835–7, Elgin burghs, 1838–41, and Perth, 1841–52; under-secretary of state, 1835–41; secretary at war, 1846–52 and 1855–8; succeeded to earldom, 1860. [xxxvii. 85]

MAULE, HARRY, titular EARL OF PANMURE (d. 1734), joined Jacobite rising, 1715; fought at Sheriffmuir, rescuing his brother, James Maule, fourth earl of Panmure [q. v.], under perilous circumstances, 1715; fled to Holland, 1716; corresponded with leading Jacobites; collected at Kelly Castle, chronicles, chartularies, and historical documents of Scotland; compiled a family history, 1733. [xxxvii. 85]

MAULE, JAMES, fourth EARL OF PANMURE (1659?–1723), Jacobite; privy councillor to James II, 1686–7; proclaimed the Old Pretender king at Brechin, 1715; taken prisoner at Sheriffmuir and rescued by his brother, Harry Maule, titular earl of Panmure [q. v.]; escaped to the continent, 1716; his estates confiscated, 1716; twice declined their restoration at the price of swearing allegiance to George I; died at Paris. [xxxvii. 86]

MAULE, PATRICK, first EARL OF PANMURE (d. 1661); gentleman of the bedchamber, 1603; keeper of Eltham and sheriff of Forfarshire, 1625; endeavoured to reconcile the king and the covenanters; created Baron Maule of Brechin and Man and Earl of Panmure, 1646; fined by Cromwell. [xxxvii. 87]

MAULE, SIR WILLIAM HENRY (1788–1858), judge; senior wrangler, Trinity College, Cambridge, 1810; fellow, 1811; barrister, Lincoln's Inn, 1814; joined Oxford circuit; K.C., 1833; counsel to Bank of England, 1835; M.P., Carlow, 1837; baron of the exchequer and knighted, 1839; transferred to court of common pleas, 1839; member of judicial committee of privy council. [xxxvii. 88]

MAULE, WILLIAM RAMSAY, BARON PANMURE (1771–1852), cornet, 11th dragoons, 1789; whig M.P., Forfarshire, 1796 and 1805–31; created Baron Panmure (peerage of Great Britain), 1831. [xxxvii. 88]

MAULEVERER, JOHN (d. 1650), colonel; parliamentary governor of Hull, 1646; colonel of foot regiment in Scots war, 1650. [xxxvii. 90]

MAULEVERER, SIR RICHARD (1623? – 1675), royalist; son of Sir Thomas Mauleverer (d. 1655) [q. v.]; admitted of Gray's Inn, 1641; knighted, 1645; fined by parliament, 1649; his estates sequestered, 1650; declared outlaw, 1654; taken prisoner, 1655; escaped to the Hague; gentleman of the privy chamber, 1660; M.P., Boroughbridge, 1661. [xxxvii. 89]

MAULEVERER, SIR THOMAS, first baronet (d. 1655), regicide; admitted of Gray's Inn, 1617; M.P., Boroughbridge, 1640; created baronet, 1641; raised two foot regiments and a troop of horse for parliament; fought at Atherton Moor, 1643; attended the king's trial and signed the death-warrant. [xxxvii. 89]

MAULEVERER, SIR THOMAS (1643? – 1687), eldest son of Sir Richard Mauleverer [q. v.]; M.P., Boroughbridge, 1679; commanded a troop of horse in Monmouth's rebellion, 1685. [xxxvii. 90]

MAULEY, PETER DE (d. 1241), favourite of King John; took charge of treasure and prisoners at Corfe Castle, 1215; sheriff of Somerset and Dorset, 1216; summoned to bring regalia to coronation, 1220; arrested for treason, 1221; given charge of Sherborne Castle, 1221; died a crusader in the Holy Land. [xxxvii. 90]

MAUND, BENJAMIN (1790 – 1863), botanical writer; at once chemist, bookseller, printer, and publisher; F.L.S., 1827; on committee of Worcestershire Natural History Society; started monthly botanical publications. [xxxvii. 91]

MAUNDER, SAMUEL (1785–1849), compiler; assisted his partner, William Pinnock [q. v.], in the 'Catechisms,' 1837–49; published the 'Literary Gazette'; compiled educational dictionaries. [xxxvii. 91]

MAUNDRELL, HENRY (1665–1701), oriental traveller; M.A. Exeter College, Oxford, 1688; B.D., 1697; fellow, 1697; chaplain to the Levant merchants at Aleppo, 1695; travelled in the Holy Land, spending Easter at Jerusalem, 1697; his narrative of the expedition (published, 1703) frequently reprinted, and translated into French, Dutch, and German. [xxxvii. 92]

MAUNSELL, ANDREW (d. 1595), bibliographer and publisher; brought out Martin's translation of Peter Martyr's 'Commonplaces,' 1583; designed a classified catalogue of English books, the first two parts (divinity and science) published, 1595. [xxxvii. 93]

MAUNSELL, JOHN (d. 1265). [See MANSEL.]

MAUNSFIELD, MAUNNESFELD, MAMMESFELD, or **MAYMYSFELD**, HENRY DE (d. 1328), dean of Lincoln; chancellor of Oxford University, 1309 and 1311; dean of Lincoln, 1314; declined bishopric of Lincoln, 1319; canon of Carlisle, 1324. [xxxvii. 94]

MAUNY, SIR WALTER, afterwards BARON DE MANNY (d. 1372). [See MANNY.]

MAURICE (d. 1107), bishop of London, chaplain and chancellor to William the Conqueror; bishop of London, 1086; controversy with Anselm as to the right to consecrate Harrow church decided against him, 1094; crowned Henry I in Anselm's absence, 1100; commenced building St. Paul's Cathedral. [xxxvii. 94]

MAURICE (fl. 1210), called MORGANENSIS, and MORGANIUS, epigrammatist; wrote a volume of epigrams; probably identical with Meyrig (fl. 1250) [q. v.], treasurer of Llandaff. [xxxvii. 95]

MAURICE, PRINCE (1620–1652), son of the elector palatine Frederick V and Elizabeth, daughter of James I; landed in England, 1642, to aid the royalist cause; commissioned to protect Gloucestershire, 1643; forced his way to Oxford for reinforcements, 1643; Exeter and Dartmouth surrendered to him, 1643; abandoned the siege of Plymouth in consequence of illness, 1643; lieutenant-general of the southern counties, 1644; present at the second battle of Newbury, 1644; unable to keep order in Wales, 1645; relieved by his brother, Prince Rupert [q. v.], at Chester, 1645; fought on the right wing at Naseby, 14 June 1645; besieged in Oxford, 1646; banished by parliament, 26 June 1646; joined Rupert in his piracy, 1648; lost at sea off the Anagadas. [xxxvii. 95]

MAURICE, FREDERICK DENISON (1805–1872), divine; went up to Cambridge, 1823; with Sterling founded the 'Apostles' Club'; with Whitmore edited the 'Metropolitan Quarterly Magazine' for a year, 1825; first-class in 'civil law classes,' Trinity Hall, Cambridge, 1827; edited the 'London Literary Chronicle' until 1830; went up to Oxford to take orders, 1830; joined the 'Essay Society' and met William Ewart Gladstone [q. v.]; curate of Bubbenhall, 1834; published 'Subscription no Bondage,' against abolishing subscription to the Thirty-nine Articles; chaplain at Guy's Hospital, London, 1836–46, lecturing on moral philosophy; married Anna, sister-in-law of John Sterling [q. v.], 1837; published 'Letters to a Quaker,' 1837; edited the 'Education Magazine,' 1839–1841; professor of English literature and history at King's College, London, 1840; Boyle lecturer and Warburton lecturer, 1845; chaplain of Lincoln's Inn, 1846; resigned chaplaincy of Guy's Hospital, London, 1846; helped to found Queen's College, London, 1848; married Julius Hare's half-sister, 1849; edited for a few weeks the paper of the 'Christian Socialists,' and had his attention drawn to co-operation and trade associations; called upon by the principal of King's College to clear himself of charges of heterodoxy brought against him in the 'Quarterly Review,' 1851; cleared by a committee of inquiry, 1852; asked to retire by the council of King's College after the publication of his 'Theological Essays,' 1853; strongly advocated abolition of university tests, 1853; inaugurated (1854) the Working Men's College in Red Lion Square, London (afterwards removed to Great Ormond Street), of which he was chosen principal; accepted the chapel of St. Peter's, Vere Street, London, 1860–9; professor of moral philosophy at Cambridge, 1866; incumbent of St. Edward's, Cambridge, 1870–2; Cambridge preacher at Whitehall, 1871. [xxxvii. 97]

MAURICE, GODFREY (d. 1598). [See JONES, JOHN.]

MAURICE, HENRY (1648–1691), divine; M.A. Jesus College, Oxford, 1671; D.D., 1683; fellow; gained, as curate of Cheltenham, 1669, great reputation in a controversy with the Socinians; chaplain to Sir Leoline Jenkins [q. v.] at Cologne, 1673–6; domestic chaplain to Sancroft, 1680–91; treasurer of Chichester, 1681; rector of Newington, Oxfordshire, 1685; represented Oxford at Westminster convocation, 1689; Margaret professor of divinity at Oxford, 1691; published controversial works; well versed in canon law. [xxxvii. 105]

MAURICE, JAMES WILKES (1775–1857), rear-admiral; entered navy, 1789; lieutenant, 1797; went to West Indies, 1802; commander, 1804; held Diamond Rock, Martinique, for more than a year, 1805; governor of Marie Galante, 1808; advanced to post rank, 1809; governor of Anholt, 1810–12, where he defeated the Danes, 1811; retired rear-admiral, 1846. [xxxvii. 106]

MAURICE, THOMAS (1754–1824), oriental scholar and historian; M.A. University College, Oxford, 1808; while at Oxford translated 'Œdipus Tyrannus,' for which Dr. Johnson wrote the preface; vicar of Wormleighton, 1798; assistant-keeper of manuscripts in the British Museum, 1798; obtained pension, 1800; vicar of Cudham, 1804; a voluminous author, and the first to popularise Eastern history and religions. [xxxvii. 107]

MAURICE, WILLIAM (fl. 1640–1680), collector and transcriber of Welsh manuscripts; his collection preserved at Wynnstay. [xxxvii. 108]

MAVOR, WILLIAM FORDYCE (1758–1837), compiler of educational works; schoolmaster at Woodstock; ordained, 1781; vicar of Hurley and LL.D. Aberdeen, 1789; rector of Stonesfield, Oxfordshire, which he exchanged (1810) for Bladon-with-Woodstock; chief compilation, 'English Spelling Book,' 1801. [xxxvii. 108]

MAWBEY, SIR JOSEPH, first baronet (1730–1798), politician; inherited property in Surrey, 1754; sheriff, 1757; M.P., Southwark, 1761–74; created baronet, 1765; M.P., Surrey, 1775–90; chairman of Surrey quarter sessions for twenty-seven years; contributed to the 'Gentleman's Magazine.' [xxxvii. 109]

MAWE, JOHN (1764–1829), mineralogist; a sailor for fifteen years; collected minerals in England and Scotland for the King of Spain; blockaded in Cadiz, 1804; imprisoned at Monte Video, 1805–6; visited the interior of Brazil, 1809–10; opened a shop in the Strand, 1811; wrote books on mineralogy and his South American travels. [xxxvii. 110]

MAWE or **MAW,** LEONARD (d. 1629), bishop of Bath and Wells; fellow of Peterhouse, Cambridge, 1595; M.A. (incorporated at Oxford, 1599); master of Peterhouse, Cambridge, 1617; vice-chancellor of Cambridge University, 1621; prebendary of Wells, and chaplain to Charles, prince of Wales; joined him in Spain, 1623; master of Trinity College, Cambridge, 1625; bishop of Bath and Wells, 1628. [xxxvii. 111]

MAWSON, MATTHIAS (1683–1770), bishop of Ely; of St. Paul's School, London, and Corpus Christi College, Cambridge; fellow, 1707; M.A., 1708; D.D., 1725; master of Corpus Christi College, Cambridge, 1724–44; vice-chancellor, 1730; bishop of Llandaff, 1738; transferred to Chichester, 1740; bishop of Ely, 1754; founded twelve scholarships at Corpus Christi College, Cambridge, 1754. [xxxvii. 111]

MAX MÜLLER, FRIEDRICH (1823–1900), orientalist and philologist; son of the poet Wilhelm Müller (1794–1827); born at Dessau; educated at Leipzig; Ph.D., 1843; studied under Franz Bopp and Schelling at Berlin and under Eugène Burnouf at Paris; obtained introduction to Baron Bunsen, then Prussian minister in London; came to England, 1846, and was commissioned by board of directors of East India Company to bring out edition of the Sanskrit classic 'Rigveda,' with Sāyana's commentary (published, 1849–73); settled at Oxford, 1848; deputy Taylorian professor of modern European languages, 1850; hon. M.A. and member of Christ Church, 1851; full M.A. and Taylorian professor, 1854–68; curator of Bodleian Library, 1856–63 and 1881–94; fellow of All Souls College, Oxford, 1858; unsuccessfully opposed (Sir) Monier Monier-Williams [q. v.] as candidate for professorship of Sanskrit at Oxford, 1860; studied comparative philology and was first professor of that subject at Oxford, 1868 till death, though he retired from the active duties of the chair, 1875; devoted much attention to comparative mythology and the comparative study of religions; edited, from 1875, 'Sacred Books of the East,' a series of English translations of oriental works of a religious character. He was a privy councillor and obtained numerous honours from British and foreign courts and learned bodies. Though much in his works and methods may already be superseded, his writings exercised an extraordinarily stimulating influence in many fields. They fall under the heads of Sanskrit, Pāli, science of religion, comparative mythology, comparative philology, philosophy, biography, and writings in German. A collected edition of his essays entitled 'Chips from a German Workshop' appeared, 1867–75. A full collected edition of his works began to appear in 1898. [Suppl. iii. 151]

MAXEY, ANTHONY (d. 1618), dean of Windsor; M.A. Trinity College, Cambridge, 1585; D.D., 1608; chaplain to James I; dean of Windsor and registrar of the order of the Garter, 1612; made the highest bid for the vacant see of Norwich, 1618. [xxxvii. 112]

MAXFIELD, THOMAS (d. 1616), Roman catholic priest; educated at Douay; missioner in England, 1615; arrested; refused the oath of allegiance, and was executed. [xxxvii. 112]

MAXFIELD, THOMAS (d. 1784), Wesleyan; converted by John Wesley, 1739; travelled with Charles Wesley, 1740; left in charge of the Foundery Society by John Wesley, 1742; seized by the press-gang, 1745;

transferred to the army; on his discharge, became one of Wesley's chief assistants and chaplain to the Countess of Huntingdon; separated from the Wesleys, 1763; preached in Moorfields, 1767; at his secession became Wesley's enemy; unsuccessfully negotiated for a reunion, 1772 and 1779. [xxxvii. 113]

MAXSE, FREDERICK AUGUSTUS (1833–1900), admiral and political writer; brother of Sir Henry Berkeley Fitzhardinge Maxse [q. v.]; lieutenant R.N., 1852; captain, 1855; retired as admiral, 1867; wrote on social questions. Mr. George Meredith's novel, 'Beauchamp's Career,' is largely a study of his character. [Suppl. iii. 157]

MAXSE, SIR HENRY BERKELEY FITZHARDINGE (1832–1883), governor of Heligoland; army captain, 1854; served through Crimean war (medals); lieutenant-colonel, 1863; governor of Heligoland, 1864–81, during which time the constitution was reformed, 1868, the gaming-tables abolished, 1870, and telegraphic communication established; governor of Newfoundland, 1881–3; died at St. John's, Newfoundland. [xxxvii. 114]

MAXWELL, CAROLINE ELIZABETH SARAH, LADY STIRLING (1808–1877). [See NORTON.]

MAXWELL, SIR GEORGE CLERK (1715–1784). [See CLERK-MAXWELL.]

MAXWELL, JAMES (fl. 1600–1640), author; M.A. Edinburgh, 1600; went abroad; returned to England and published numerous works, including poems on Charles I and Prince Henry, and works in defence of the English church; nicknamed by Laud 'Mountebank Maxwell.' [xxxvii. 115]

MAXWELL, JAMES (1708?–1762), of Kirkconnel; Jacobite; joined the rebellion of 1745; escaped to France after Culloden; published 'Narrative of Charles Prince of Wales's Expedition in 1745.' [xxxvii. 117]

MAXWELL, JAMES (1720–1800), 'Poet in Paisley'; followed numerous trades; received assistance from Paisley town council, 1787; author of doggerel religious publications. [xxxvii. 117]

MAXWELL, JAMES CLERK (1831–1879). [See CLERK-MAXWELL.]

MAXWELL, SIR JOHN of Terregles, MASTER OF MAXWELL, and afterwards fourth BARON HERRIES (1512?–1583), partisan of Mary Queen of Scots; held Lochmaben Castle, 1545; warden of the west marches, 1552–3; reappointed warden of the west marches, 1561; endeavoured to mediate between Mary and Moray, 1565; after Rizzio's murder joined Mary with a strong force at Dunbar, 1566; became Baron Herries, 1566; one of the assize who acquitted Bothwell; entreated Mary not to marry Bothwell; submitted to Moray's regency, 1567; commanded Mary's horse at Langside, 1568; commissioner to England, 1568; joined a revolt against Moray, 1569; submitted to the regent on finding that Elizabeth would not aid Mary; assisted in depriving Morton, 1578; member of the new privy council; on Morton's return to power sent to Stirling to maintain quiet; subsequently supported Lennox. [xxxvii. 121]

MAXWELL, JOHN, seventh or eighth BARON MAXWELL and EARL OF MORTON (1553–1593), attended Perth convention, 1569; voted for Mary's divorce from Bothwell, 1569; his territories invaded and castles demolished by Lord Scrope, 1570; came to terms with Morton, 1573; imprisoned at Edinburgh on claiming (1577) the earldom of Morton, which he obtained on Morton's execution, 1581; denounced as rebel after Lennox's overthrow, 1582 and 1585, when the earldom of Morton and its adjuncts were revoked; assisted in the capture of Stirling Castle, 1585; granted indemnity, 1585; imprisoned for causing mass to be celebrated; exiled; returned without permission, was again exiled, the earldom of Morton being ratified by parliament to the Earl of Angus, 1587; assembled his followers to help Spanish invasion, 1588; captured and brought prisoner to Edinburgh; appointed, under title of Earl of Morton, warden of the west marches, 1592; subscribed presbyterian confession of faith, 1593; slain in an encounter with the laird of Johnstone's followers. [xxxvii. 124]

MAXWELL, JOHN, eighth or ninth BARON MAXWELL (1586?–1612), son of John Maxwell, seventh or eighth baron Maxwell [q. v.]; at feud with Johnstone on account of his father's death, and with the Douglases regarding the earldom of Morton; constantly called before the council to answer for his plots against Johnstone, 1598–1603; reconciled, 1605; committed to Edinburgh Castle for his feud with the Earl of Morton, 1607; escaped, 1607; denounced as rebel; shot Johnstone and escaped to the continent, 1608; in his absence found guilty of acts of treason, including Johnstone's murder, 1608; condemned to death; on his return, 1612, apprehended and beheaded at Edinburgh. [xxxvii. 126]

MAXWELL, JOHN (1590?–1647), archbishop of Tuam; M.A. St. Andrews, 1611; advocated the restoration of liturgical forms in Scotland; bishop of Ross, 1633; privy councillor and extraordinary lord of session, 1636; assisted in compilation of new service-book, using it at Fortrose, 1637–8; deposed and excommunicated by the assembly, 1638; appealed, 1639; D.D. Trinity College, Dublin, 1640; bishop of Killala and Achonry, 1640; left for dead in the rebellion, 1641; finally went to Oxford and acted as royal chaplain; appointed archbishop of Tuam, 1643. [xxxvii. 128]

MAXWELL, JOHN HALL (1812–1866), agriculturist; called to Scottish bar, 1835; secretary to Highland Agricultural Society; collected stock and crop statistics; C.B., 1856. [xxxvii. 130]

MAXWELL, SIR MURRAY (1775–1831), naval captain; entered navy, 1790; lieutenant, 1796; commander, 1802; took part in capture of Tobago, Demerara, and Essequibo, 1803, of Berbice and Surinam, 1804; C.B., 1815; after landing Lord Amherst at Pei-ho, 1816, explored the Gulf of Pechili, the west coast of Corea, and the Loo-Choo islands, an account of which was published (1818) by Captain Basil Hall; wrecked in the Straits of Gaspar, with Lord Amherst on board, 1817, and was in charge of the crew (all saved) on Pulo Leat; acquitted by court-martial, 1817; knighted, 1818; F.R.S., 1819; lieutenant-governor of Prince Edward's island, 1831. [xxxvii. 130]

MAXWELL, SIR PETER BENSON (1817–1893), chief-justice of Straits Settlements; B.A. Trinity College, Dublin, 1839; barrister, Middle Temple, 1841; recorder of Penang, 1856–66, and of Singapore, 1866–71; chief-justice of Straits Settlements, 1867–71; knighted, 1856. [Suppl. iii. 158]

MAXWELL, ROBERT, fifth BARON MAXWELL (d. 1546); warden of the west marches, 1517; lord provost of Edinburgh on the removal of the king there, 1524; councillor, 1526; extraordinary lord of session, 1533; one of the regents, 1536; taken prisoner at Solway Moss, 1542; sent to London, but released on James V's death; intrigued with Henry VIII; taken prisoner at Glasgow, 1544; set free on approach of the English; imprisoned in the Tower of London for supposed treachery; released, 1545; taken prisoner by Beaton, but granted remission on stating he only made terms with Henry VIII under compulsion; chief-justice of Annandale and warden of the west marches, 1546. [xxxvii. 132]

MAXWELL, ROBERT (1695–1765), writer on agriculture; experimented in farming; member of the Society of Improvers in the Knowledge of Agriculture in Scotland, 1723; insolvent, 1749; land-valuer; published agricultural works. [xxxvii. 134]

MAXWELL, WILLIAM, fifth BARON HERRIES (d. 1603), son of Sir John Maxwell, fourth baron Herries [q. v.]; gentleman of the chamber, 1580; privy councillor, 1583; warden of the west marches, 1587; called before the council to answer for his feud with the Johnstones, whom he attacked unsuccessfully (1595) with three hundred men; submitted the feud to arbitration, 1599. [xxxvii. 135]

MAXWELL, WILLIAM, fifth EARL OF NITHSDALE (1676–1744), Jacobite; joined the English Jacobites, 1715; taken prisoner at Preston, 1715; sent to the Tower of London; condemned to death; escaped by the aid of his wife Winifred Maxwell [q. v.]; joined the Chevalier James Edward at Rome, where he died. [xxxvii. 136]

MAXWELL, WILLIAM (1732–1818), friend of Dr. Johnson; M.A. Trinity College, Dublin, 1755; D.D., 1777; first met Dr. Johnson, c. 1755; assistant-preacher at the Temple, London; rector of Mount Temple, co. Westmeath, 1775–1808; copied Dr. Johnson's appearance and manner; furnished Boswell with collectanea. [xxxvii. 137]

MAXWELL, SIR WILLIAM EDWARD (1846–1897), governor of the Gold Coast; son of Sir Peter Benson Maxwell [q. v.]; educated at Repton; qualified at local bar in Singapore and Penang, 1867; assistant resident of Perak and member of state council, 1878; barrister, Inner Temple, 1881; C.M.G., 1884; British resident of Selangor, 1889; colonial secretary of Straits Settlements, 1892, and acting governor, 1893–5; governor of Gold Coast, 1895; K.C.M.G., 1896; died at sea. [Suppl. iii. 158]

MAXWELL, WILLIAM HAMILTON (1792–1850), Irish novelist; graduate, Trinity College, Dublin; served in Peninsular campaign and at Waterloo; rector of Ballagh, 1820–44; originated a rollicking style of fiction, which culminated in Lever. [xxxvii. 137]

MAXWELL, SIR WILLIAM STIRLING-, ninth baronet (1818–1878). [See STIRLING-MAXWELL.]

MAXWELL, WINIFRED, COUNTESS OF NITHSDALE (d. 1749), daughter of William Herbert, first marquis of Powis; married William Maxwell, fifth earl of Nithsdale [q. v.], 1699; fruitlessly petitioned George I (1716) for the life of her husband, who had been sentenced to death for his share in the rebellion of 1715; enabled him to escape from the Tower of London, 1716, and joined him at Rome; wrote a narrative of his escape, first published in the 'Transactions of the Society of Antiquaries of Scotland,' vol. i. [xxxvii. 136]

MAXWELL-INGLIS, MRS. MARGARET (1774–1843). [See INGLIS.]

MAY. [See also MEY.]

MAY, BAPTIST (1629–1698), keeper of the privy purse to Charles II; registrar in chancery court, 1660; keeper of the privy purse, 1665; M.P., Midhurst, 1670; clerk of the works at Windsor Castle, 1671; with Lely and Evelyn recommended Grinling Gibbons to Charles II, 1671; M.P., Thetford, 1690. [xxxvii. 138]

MAY, GEORGE AUGUSTUS CHICHESTER (1815–1892), Irish judge; of Shrewsbury School and Magdalene College, Cambridge; M.A., 1841; fellow; called to Irish bar, 1844; Q.C., 1865; legal adviser at Dublin Castle, 1874; attorney-general, 1875; lord chief-justice of Ireland and privy councillor, 1877; president of the queen's bench division, 1878, retaining title or lord chief-justice of Ireland; withdrew from presiding at Parnell's trial on being accused of partiality, 1881; resigned, 1887. [xxxvii. 140]

MAY, SIR HUMPHREY (1573–1630), statesman; of St. John's College, Oxford, and the Middle Temple; B.A., 1592; groom of the king's privy chamber, 1604; M.P., Beeralston, 1605–11, Westminster, 1614, Lancaster, 1621–2, Leicester, 1624–5, Lancaster, 1625, and Leicester, 1626 and 1628–9; pensioned and knighted, 1613; surveyor of the court of wards, 1618; chancellor of the duchy of Lancaster, 1618; privy councillor, 1625; defended Charles and Buckingham in the House of Commons against the attacks of the opposition; attempted to rescue Speaker Finch from violence, 1629. [xxxvii. 140]

MAY, JOHN (d. 1598), bishop of Carlisle; brother of William May [q. v.]; fellow of Queens' College, Cambridge, 1550; M.A., 1553; master of Catharine Hall, Cambridge, 1559; held various rectories; canon of Ely, 1564–82; Lent preacher at court, 1565; archdeacon of East Riding of Yorkshire, 1569; vice-chancellor of Cambridge, 1570; bishop of Carlisle, 1577. [xxxvii. 141]

MAY, JOHN (fl. 1613), economic writer; deputy-aulnager, c. 1606; published (1613) an account of the means by which woollen manufacturers evaded the statutes. [xxxvii. 142]

MAY, THOMAS (1595–1650), author; B.A. Sidney Sussex College, Cambridge, 1612; admitted to Gray's Inn, 1615; prevented by defective utterance from practising law; unsuccessful as a playwright; his translations of the classics praised by Ben Jonson; wrote two narrative poems, one on Henry II, 1633, the other on Edward III, 1635, by the king's command; unsuccessful candidate for laureateship, 1637; adopted parliamentary cause; secretary for the parliament, 1646; his 'History of the Long Parliament,' 1647, considered by Chatham 'honester and more instructive than Clarendon's.' [xxxvii. 142]

MAY, SIR THOMAS ERSKINE, first BARON FARNBOROUGH (1815–1886), constitutional jurist; assistant-librarian of the House of Commons, 1831; barrister, Middle

Temple, 1838; examiner of petitions for private bills and taxing-master for both houses of parliament, 1847–56; clerk of the House of Commons, 1871–86; K.C.B., 1866; president of the Statute Law Revision Committee, 1866–84; privy councillor, 1885; created Baron Farnborough, 1886; wrote historical works and on parliamentary procedure. [xxxvii. 145]

MAY, MEY, or **MEYE,** WILLIAM (*d.* 1560), archbishop-elect of York; brother of John May (*d.* 1598) [q. v.], bishop of Carlisle; LL.D. Cambridge, 1531; fellow of Trinity Hall; energetically supported the Reformation; chancellor of Ely, 1532; vicar-general of Ely, 1533; signed the Ten Articles, 1536; assisted in the 'Institution of a Christian Man,' 1537; president of Queens' College, Cambridge, 1537; prebendary of Ely, 1541; prebendary of St. Paul's, London, 1545; saved the Cambridge colleges from dissolution by his favourable report, 1546; dean of St. Paul's, 1546; a prominent ecclesiastic in Edward VI's reign; dispossessed on Queen Mary's, restored on Queen Elizabeth's, accession; died on the day of his election to the archbishopric of York. [xxxvii. 146]

MAYART, SIR SAMUEL (*d.* 1660?), Irish judge; appointed justice of Irish common pleas, having offered 300*l.* to anyone who should procure him the office, 1625; knighted, 1631; wrote on constitutional relations between England and Ireland, 1643. [xxxvii. 148]

MAYDESTONE, RICHARD (*d.* 1396). [See MAIDSTONE.]

MAYER, JOHN (1583–1664), biblical commentator; M.A. Emmanuel College, Cambridge, 1605; D.D., 1627; published a biblical commentary, 1627–59, and other theological works. [xxxvii. 148]

MAYER, JOSEPH (1803–1886), antiquary and collector; first studied Greek coins; sold his cabinet of Greek coins to the French government, 1844; presented his collection, which included Egyptian antiquities and Saxon remains (valued at 80,000*l.*), to the corporation of Liverpool, 1867; purchased some spurious papyri of the scriptures from Simonides (published, 1861); acquired many thousands of drawings, engravings, and autograph letters on the history of art in England, including the collections of William Upcott [q. v.] and Thomas Dodd [q. v.]; founded the Historic Society of Lancashire and Cheshire; president, 1866–9; established a free library at Bebington, 1866. [xxxvii. 149]

MAYER, SAMUEL RALPH TOWNSHEND (1840–1880), miscellaneous writer; secretary of the Free and Open Church Association, 1866–72; one of the founders of the Junior Conservative Club, 1870; editor of various magazines. [xxxvii. 150]

MAYERNE, SIR THEODORE TURQUET DE (1573–1655), physician; M.D. Montpellier, 1597; royal district physician at Paris, 1600; his treatise on chemical remedies condemned by the College of Physicians at Paris, 1603; came to England, 1603; physician to James I's queen; returned to Paris, but after 1611 resided entirely in England, attending the royal family and nobility; knighted, 1624; made chemical and physical experiments; drew up a series of precautions against plague, 1644; wrote an historically valuable account of the typhoid fever, of which Prince Henry died, 1612; twenty-three volumes of his notes on cases in the British Museum. [xxxvii. 150]

MAYERS, WILLIAM FREDERICK (1831–1878), Chinese scholar; went to China as student-interpreter, 1859; secretary of legation at Pekin, 1872; F.R.G.S., 1861; F.R.A.S., 1861; wrote on Chinese subjects. [xxxvii. 152]

MAYHEW, AUGUSTUS SEPTIMUS (1826–1875), author; brother of Henry Mayhew [q. v.] and Horace Mayhew [q. v.]; wrote popular fiction with his brother Henry Mayhew [q. v.]; with Henry Sutherland Edwards wrote six plays. [xxxvii. 153]

MAYHEW, EDWARD (1570–1625). [See MAIHEW.]

MAYHEW, HENRY (1812–1887), author; brother of Augustus Septimus Mayhew [q. v.] and Horace Mayhew [q. v.]; educated at Westminster; started 'Figaro in London,' 1831–9; collaborated with Augustus Septimus Mayhew [q. v.]; an originator of 'Punch,' 1841; started philanthropic journalism on the subject of the London poor, 1862; published 'German Life and Manners in Saxony,' 1864, humorous works, and plays. [xxxvii. 153]

MAYHEW, HORACE (1816–1872), author; brother of Augustus Septimus Mayhew [q. v.] and Henry Mayhew [q. v.]; wrote farces and tales; contributed to Cruikshank's 'Table-book,' 1845, and 'Lloyd's Weekly News,' 1852; sub-editor of 'Punch'; many of his books illustrated by Cruikshank. [xxxvii. 154]

MAYMYSFELD, MAUNNESFELD, or **MAUNSFIELD,** HENRY DE (*d.* 1328). [See MAUNSFIELD.]

MAYNARD, EDWARD (1654–1740), antiquary; fellow of Magdalen College, Oxford, 1678–94; M.A., 1677; D.D., 1691; canon and precentor of Lichfield, 1700; edited Dugdale's 'History of St. Paul's Cathedral,' 1716. [xxxvii. 154]

MAYNARD, JOHN (*fl.* 1611), lutenist; one of the first to use the lyra-viol; wrote 'The Twelve Wonders' (songs), 1611. [xxxvii. 155]

MAYNARD, SIR JOHN (1592–1658), courtier, presbyterian, and royalist; entered the Inner Temple, 1610; partisan of Buckingham; M.P., Chippenham, 1624; K.B. and servant of the privy chamber, 1625; M.P., Calne, 1628; raised troops in Surrey for parliament, 1642; M.P., Lostwithiel, 1647; leader of the presbyterian party and charged with disaffection by Fairfax, 1647; readmitted to the house and placed on the committee of safety, 1647; committed to the Tower and impeached, 1648; protested against the Lords' jurisdiction over the Commons, 1648; resumed his seat, 1648. [xxxvii. 155]

MAYNARD, JOHN (1600–1665), divine; B.A. Queen's College, Oxford, 1620; M.A. Magdalen Hall, 1622; incumbent of Mayfield, 1624; became a puritan; chosen one of the Westminster Assembly; preached before the Long parliament, 1644, 1646, and 1648; Sussex commissioner for ejecting scandalous ministers and schoolmasters, 1654; ejected, 1662; published sermons. [xxxvii. 157]

MAYNARD, SIR JOHN (1602–1690), judge; barrister, Middle Temple, 1626; M.P., Totnes, in Short and Long parliaments; framed Strafford's impeachment; deputy-lieutenant of militia under parliament, 1642; member of the Westminster Assembly; advocated abolition of feudal wardships; protested against the king's deposition, 1648; serjeant-at-law, 1654; imprisoned for hinting Cromwell's government a usurpation, 1655; M.P., Plymouth, 1656–8; Protector's serjeant, 1658; solicitor-general on Richard Cromwell's accession; one of the first serjeants called at the Restoration; king's serjeant and knighted, 1660; appeared for the crown at most of the state trials at the Restoration, and at most of the popish plot prosecutions; M.P., Plymouth, in the convention, 1689; lord commissioner of the great seal, 1689; left such an obscure will that a private act of parliament was passed, 1694, to settle the disputes to which it gave rise; his legal manuscript collections preserved in Lincoln's Inn Library. [xxxvii. 158]

MAYNARD, WALTER (pseudonym) (1828–1894). [See BEALE, THOMAS WILLERT.]

MAYNE, CUTHBERT (*d.* 1577), first seminary priest executed in England; chaplain of St. John's College, Oxford; M.A., 1570; went to Douay, 1573; ordained Roman catholic priest, 1575; chaplain to Francis Tregian, 1576; discovered and imprisoned, 1577; executed. [xxxvii. 161]

MAYNE, JASPER (1604–1672), archdeacon of Chichester and dramatist; student of Christ Church, Oxford, 1627; M.A., 1631; D.D., 1646; wrote 'City Match' (comedy), 1639, and 'The Amorous War' (tragi-comedy), 1648; in middle life abandoned poetry and (1639) became rector of Cassington; preached before Charles I at Oxford and wrote controversial pamphlets; ejected from his studentship and from Cassington, but made rector of Pyrton, 1648; ejected from Pyrton, 1656; reinstated in his benefices at the Restoration and appointed canon of Christ Church, Oxford, archdeacon of Chichester, and chaplain in ordinary to the king. [xxxvii. 162]

MAYNE, JOHN (1759–1836), Scottish poet; printer; subsequently proprietor and joint-editor of the 'Star'; wrote poems for magazines; praised by Scott and Burns. [xxxvii. 164]

MAYNE, PERRY (1700?–1761), vice-admiral; entered navy, 1712; captain, 1725; present at reduction of Portobello, 1739; unsuccessfully attacked Cartagena, 1741; rear-admiral, 1745; presided at the trials of Vice-admiral Richard Lestock [q. v.], 1747, and Admiral Thomas Mathews [q. v.]; vice-admiral, 1747.   [xxxvii. 164]

MAYNE, SIR RICHARD (1796-1868), police commissioner; B.A. Trinity College, Dublin, 1818; M.A. Trinity College, Cambridge, 1821; barrister, Lincoln's Inn, 1822; commissioner to institute metropolitan police, 1850; K.C.B., 1851.   [xxxvii. 165]

MAYNE, RICHARD CHARLES (1835-1892), admiral; educated at Eton; entered navy, 1847; commanded survey expedition to the Straits of Magellan, 1866-9, the results of which he published, 1871; rear-admiral, 1879; C.B., 1879; vice-admiral, 1885; M.P., Pembroke and Haverfordwest, 1886.   [xxxvii. 166]

MAYNE, SIMON (1612-1661), regicide; student at Inner Temple, 1630; M.P., Aylesbury, 1645; judge at Charles I's trial, signing the warrant; attainted, 1660; died in the Tower of London.   [xxxvii. 166]

MAYNE, WILLIAM (1818-1855), colonel and brigadier of the Hyderabad contingent; ensign in East India Company's service, 1837; lieutenant, 1841; distinguished himself at Julgar, 1840, Jellalabad, and Istiliff, 1842; suppressed disturbances in the Deccan, 1851-4; brevet-colonel and aide-de-camp to Queen Victoria, 1854. [xxxvii. 167]

MAYNE, ZACHARY (1631-1694), religious writer; fellow of Magdalen College, Oxford, 1652; M.A., 1654; convened before the vice-chancellor for a sermon preached in St. Mary's Church, Oxford, 1660; expelled from his fellowship, 1660; schoolmaster at Dalwood, 1671-90; master of Exeter grammar school, 1690-4; published religious treatises.   [xxxvii. 167]

MAYNWARING.   [See also MAINWARING and MANWARING.]

MAYNWARING, ARTHUR (1668-1712).   [See MAINWARING.]

MAYNWARING, EVERARD (1628-1699?), medical writer; M.B. St. John's College, Cambridge, 1652; visited America; M.D. Dublin, 1655; began to practise in London, 1663; condemned violent purgatives and bloodletting; had charge of Middlesex pest-house during the plague, 1665; published medical works. [xxxvii. 168]

MAYO, sixth EARL OF (1822-1872). [See BOURKE, RICHARD SOUTHWELL.]

MAYO, CHARLES (1750-1829), historian; M.A. Queen's College, Oxford, 1774; B.C.L., 1779; incumbent of Huish, 1775, Beechingstoke, 1779; wrote a European, 1793, and a universal, history, 1804; founded two scholarships at Oxford.   [xxxvii. 169]

MAYO, CHARLES (1792-1846), educational reformer; of Merchant Taylors' School, London, and St. John's College, Oxford; D.C.L., 1822; head-master of Bridgnorth grammar school, 1817-19; English chaplain to Pestalozzi's establishment at Yverdun, 1819; introduced Pestalozzi's system at Epsom, 1822, and at Cheam, 1826; published school-books and 'Memoirs of Pestalozzi,' 1828.
            [xxxvii. 169]

MAYO, CHARLES (1767-1858), professor of Anglo-Saxon at Oxford; son of Herbert Mayo (1720-1802) [q. v.]; of Merchant Taylors' School, London; fellow of St. John's College, Oxford, 1788; M.A., 1793; professor of Anglo-Saxon, 1795-1800; B.D., 1796; Whitehall preacher, 1799; F.S.A., 1820; F.R.S., 1827.   [xxxvii. 170]

MAYO, CHARLES (1837-1877), army surgeon; of Winchester School; fellow of New College, Oxford, 1856; M.A., 1863; M.D., 1871; M.R.C.S., 1861; L.R.C.P., 1869; university coroner, 1865-9; in medical service corps under Grant, 1862; with the German army, 1870; with the Dutch in Sumatra, 1873-4; published 'History of Wimborne Minster,' 1860; died at sea. [xxxvii. 170]

MAYO, DANIEL (1672?-1733), presbyterian minister; son of Richard Mayo [q. v.]; educated at Glasgow (M.A.) and Leyden; presbyterian minister at Kingston-on-Thames, where he kept a school, 1698; presbyterian pastor in London; published sermons. [xxxvii. 171]

MAYO, ELIZABETH (1793-1865), educational reformer; with her brother, Charles Mayo (1792-1846) [q. v.], at Epsom and Cheam; published school-books.
            [xxxvii. 172]

MAYO, HENRY (1733-1793), dissenting minister; pastor of independent church, Wapping, 1762; D.D. and LL.D.; acquainted with Dr. Johnson, and known as the 'Literary Anvil.'   [xxxvii. 172]

MAYO, HERBERT (1720-1802), divine; fellow of Brasenose College, Oxford, 1740; M.A., 1745; D.D., 1763; rector of Middleton Cheney, 1764, of St. George's, London, 1764-1802; J.P. for Middlesex.   [xxxvii. 170]

MAYO, HERBERT (1796-1852), physiologist; son of John Mayo [q. v.]; pupil of Sir Charles Bell, 1812-15; M.D. Leyden; M.R.C.S., 1819; discovered the real function of the nerves of the face, 1822; surgeon of Middlesex Hospital, 1827-42; professor of anatomy and surgery to Royal College of Surgeons, 1828-9; F.R.S., 1828; professor of anatomy at King's College, London, 1830-6; F.G.S., 1832; founded medical school at the Middlesex Hospital, 1836; physician to hydropathic establishment at Boppart, 1843, afterwards at Bad Weilbach; published medical works.   [xxxvii. 172]

MAYO, JOHN (1761-1818), physician; fellow of Oriel College, Oxford, 1784; M.A., 1785; M.D., 1788; F.R.C.P., 1788; censor, 1790, 1795, 1804, and 1808; Harveian orator, 1795; physician to Foundling Hospital, London, 1787-1809, Middlesex Hospital, 1788-1803; physician in ordinary to Caroline, princess of Wales.   [xxxvii. 173]

MAYO, PAGGEN WILLIAM (1766-1836), physician; son of Herbert Mayo (1720-1802) [q. v.]; medical fellow, St. John's College, Oxford, 1792; M.D., 1795; physician to Middlesex Hospital, 1793-1801; F.R.C.P., 1796; censor, 1797; Gulstonian lecturer, 1798; Harveian orator, 1807.
            [xxxvii. 170]

MAYO, RICHARD (1631?-1695), ejected divine; vicar of Kingston-on-Thames, 1648; ejected, 1662; presbyterian minister in London; merchants' lecturer, 1694; published theological works.   [xxxvii. 174]

MAYO, THOMAS (1790-1871), president of the Royal College of Physicians; son of John Mayo [q. v.]; fellow of Oriel College, Oxford, 1813; M.A., 1814; M.D., 1818; F.R.C.P., 1819; censor, 1835, 1839, 1850; F.R.S., 1835; Lumleian lecturer, 1839, 1842; physician to Marylebone Infirmary, 1841; Harveian orator, 1841; Croonian lecturer, 1853; president, R.C.P., 1857-62; wrote on mental diseases.   [xxxvii. 174]

MAYOW, MAYOUWE, or MAYO, JOHN (1640-1679), physiologist and chemist; fellow of All Souls, Oxford, 1660; D.C.L., 1670; published tract on respiration, 1668 (republished at Leyden, 1671), in which he discovered the double articulation of the ribs with the spine, and put forward views (still discussed) on the internal intercostals, developed in 'Tractatus quinque,' 1674 (translated into French, German, and Dutch); discussed the chemistry of combustion, and described muscular action; F.R.S., 1678.   [xxxvii. 175]

MAZZINGHI, JOSEPH, COUNT (1765-1844), composer; pupil of John Christian Bach, Bertolini, Sacchini, and Anfossi; organist at the Portuguese Chapel, London, 1775; composer and director of music at the Italian opera, 1785-92; arranged Carlton House and Nobility concerts, 1791; partner in Goulding, D'Almaine & Co., 1790; composed stage pieces, pianoforte sonatas, and other works.
            [xxxvii. 177]

MEAD or **MEDE**, JOSEPH (1586-1638), biblical scholar; M.A. Christ's College, Cambridge, 1610; fellow, 1613; appointed to the Greek lectureship, 1619; philologist, historian, mathematician, and physicist; botanist and practical anatomist; studied astrology, egyptology, and the origin of Semitic religions; chief work, 'Clavis Apocalyptica,' 1627.   [xxxvii. 178]

MEAD or **MEADE**, MATTHEW (1630?-1699), independent divine; fellow of King's College, Cambridge, 1649-51; contested the rectorship of Great Brickhill, 1653; appointed by Cromwell to St. Paul's, Shadwell, 1658; ejected, 1662; went to Holland, 1664; in London during the plague, 1665; minister at Stepney, 1671; guardian of James Peirce [q. v.], the Exeter heretic, 1680; suspected of complicity in the Rye House plot, but discharged, 1683; assisted in amalgamation of the presbyterian and congregationalist bodies, 1690; published sermons.   [xxxvii. 180]

MEAD, RICHARD (1673-1754), physician; son of Matthew Mead [q. v.]; educated at Utrecht under

Grævius, and at Leyden under Paul Herman and Archibald Pitcairne [q. v.]; travelled in Italy, 1695; M.D. Padua, 1695; began practice at Stepney, 1696; published 'Mechanical Account of Poisons' (an account of venomous snakes), 1702; F.R.S., 1703; physician to St. Thomas's Hospital, 1703-15; published a treatise on the influence of the sun and moon on human bodies, 1704; on the council of the Royal Society, 1705 and 1707-54; vice-president, 1717; M.D. Oxford, 1707; F.R.C.P., 1716; censor, 1716, 1719, and 1724; anatomy lecturer to the Barber-Surgeons, 1711-15; collected objects of vertu; procured the release of Dr. Freind from the Tower; attended Sir Isaac Newton [q. v.], Bishop Burnet [q. v.], George I, and Sir Robert Walpole [q. v.]; friend of Richard Bentley (1662-1742) [q. v.]; drew up a statement concerning the prevention of the plague, 1720; successfully inoculated seven condemned criminals, 1721; Harveian orator, 1723; physician to George II, 1727; financially assisted various literary projects. [xxxvii. 181]

MEAD, ROBERT (1616-1653), poet; contributed, while at Westminster School, to Cowley's 'Poetical Blossomes,' 1633; as an undergraduate of Christ Church, Oxford, wrote a comedy, 'The Combat of Love and Friendship'; contributed to 'Jonsonus Virbius,' 1638; M.A., 1641; royalist captain at the siege of Oxford and assault on Abingdon, 1646; Charles II's envoy to Sweden, 1649-51. [xxxvii. 186]

MEAD, WILLIAM (1628-1713), quaker; originally captain of a train-band; joined the quakers, 1670; imprisoned with William Penn, 1670; jury committed to Newgate for acquitting him and Penn, 1670; wrote in defence of the quakers. [xxxvii. 187]

MEADE, JOHN (1572-1653). [See ALMEIDA.]

MEADE, RICHARD CHARLES FRANCIS, third EARL OF CLANWILLIAM (Irish peerage) and first BARON CLANWILLIAM (peerage of United Kingdom) (1795-1879), educated at Eton; succeeded to earldom, 1805; attended Lord Castlereagh at Vienna congress, 1814; Castlereagh's private secretary, 1817-19; foreign under-secretary, 1822; with Wellington at Verona congress, 1822; minister at Berlin, 1823-7; G.C.H., 1826; created Baron Clanwilliam, 1828. [xxxvii. 187]

MEADE, SIR ROBERT HENRY (1835-1898), civil servant; second son of Richard Charles Francis Meade, third earl of Clanwilliam [q. v.]; of Eton and Exeter College, Oxford; M.A., 1860; entered foreign office, 1859; accompanied Prince of Wales (now Edward VII) on tour in Palestine and Eastern Europe, 1861-2; groom of bedchamber to Prince of Wales (now Edward VII), 1862; private secretary to Earl Granville as president of council, 1864-6, and in colonial office, 1868; assistant under-secretary of state in colonial office, 1871-92, and permanent under-secretary, 1892-6; G.C.B., 1897. [Suppl. iii. 158]

MEADLEY, GEORGE WILSON (1774-1818), biographer; banker's apprentice, 1788-93; founded Sunderland subscription library, 1795; met Paley, whose 'Memoirs' he wrote, 1809; made mercantile voyages to the Levant, 1796, to Danzig, 1801, and to Hamburg, 1803; became a unitarian; published biographies of Algernon Sidney, 1813, and others. [xxxvii. 188]

MEADOWBANK, LORDS. [See MACONOCHIE, ALLAN, 1748-1816; MACONOCHIE, afterwards MACONOCHIE-WELWOOD, ALEXANDER, 1777-1861.]

MEADOWCOURT, RICHARD (1695-1760), divine and author; fellow of Merton College, Oxford, 1718; M.A., 1718; controversy caused by his sermon on calumny in religious polemics, 1722; vicar of Oakley, 1727; canon of Worcester, 1734; incumbent of Quinton, 1738, of Lindridge, 1751; published 'Critique on Paradise Regained,' 1732, and similar works. [xxxvii. 189]

MEADOWE, JOHN (1622-1697). [See MEADOWS.]

MEADOWS. [See also MEDOWS.]

MEADOWS, ALFRED (1833-1887), obstetric physician; entered King's College medical school, 1853; M.D. London, 1858; F.R.C.P., 1873; house-physician, 1856, and assistant-physician, 1860, at King's College Hospital, London; physician to Hospital for Women, Soho Square, London, 1863-74; physician accoucheur and lecturer to

St. Mary's Hospital, London, 1871-87; first president of British Gynæcological Society, 1884; his 'Manual of Midwifery' (3rd edit. 1876), translated into Japanese. [xxxvii. 189]

MEADOWS, DRINKWATER (1799-1869), actor; acted at Covent Garden, 1821-44; at the Lyceum, London, under the Keeley management, 1844-7; joined Kean and Keeley in the management of the Princess's, London, where he remained under Harris until his retirement, 1862; most successful in eccentric comedy. [xxxvii. 190]

MEADOWS or MEADOWE, JOHN (1622-1697), ejected minister; fellow of Christ's College, Cambridge, 1644; M.A., 1646; rector of Ousden, 1653; ejected, 1662; licensed as a presbyterian, 1672. [xxxvii. 191]

MEADOWS, JOHN (1676-1757), divine; son of John Meadows (1622-1697) [q. v.]; presbyterian minister at Needham Market, 1701; published 'Apostolic Rule of Ordination,' 1738. [xxxvii. 191]

MEADOWS, JOSEPH KENNY (1790-1874), draughtsman; produced an illustrated edition of Shakespeare, 1839-43; exhibited occasionally at the Royal Academy and 'the Society of British Artists; received civil list pension, 1864. [xxxvii. 192]

MEADOWS, SIR PHILIP, the elder (1626-1718), diplomatist; M.A. Queens' College, Cambridge; appointed Latin secretary to Cromwell's council to relieve Milton, 1653; represented Cromwell at Lisbon, 1656; envoy to Frederick III of Denmark at the treaty of Roskild, 1658; knighted, 1658; ambassador to Sweden, 1658; published in retirement an account of the wars between Sweden and Denmark, 1675, also a book on naval supremacy and marine jurisdiction, 1689; commissioner of public accounts, 1692; member of the council of trade, 1696; commissioner of trade, 1708. [xxxvii. 192]

MEADOWS, SIR PHILIP, the younger (d. 1757), son of Sir Philip Meadows the elder [q. v.]; commissioner of excise, 1698-1700; knight-marshal of the king's household and knighted, 1700; envoy to Holland, 1706; sent on a mission to the emperor, 1707; controller of army accounts, 1707. [xxxvii. 194]

MEAGER, LEONARD (1624 ?-1704 ?), gardener; published 'English Gardener,' 1670 (11th edit. c. 1710). [xxxvii. 194]

MEAGHER, THADDEUS or THADÉE DE (1670-1765), soldier of fortune; left Ireland and served in the French army; chamberlain to Frederick Augustus II, king of Poland and elector of Saxony, 1739; lieutenant-general in the Polish army, 1752; despatched to negotiate with Frederick the Great, 1756 died at Dresden. [xxxvii. 194]

MEAGHER, THOMAS FRANCIS (1823-1867), Irish nationalist; studied at Dublin for the bar, 1844; made a brilliant speech against peace with England, 1846, which led Thackeray to dub him 'Meagher of the Sword'; founded the Irish Confederation, 1847; arrested for sedition, 1848; found guilty of high treason for endeavouring to raise an insurrection in Ireland, 1848; transported to Van Diemen's Land, 1849; escaped to America, 1852; admitted to the New York bar, 1855; founded the 'Citizen,' 1854, and 'Irish News,' 1856; volunteer in the civil war, becoming brigadier-general, 1862; secretary of Montana territory, 1865; temporary governor, 1866; drowned in the Missouri. [xxxvii. 194]

MEANS, JOSEPH CALROW (1801-1879), general baptist minister; on general baptist assembly committee, 1823; entered University College, London, 1828; afternoon preacher at Worship Street, London, 1829-39; secretary to general baptist assembly, 1831; edited 'General Baptist Advocate,' 1831-6; minister at Chatham, 1843-55; headmaster of Chatham proprietary school; returned to Worship Street, London, 1855. [xxxvii. 196]

MEARA, DERMOD or DERMITIUS (fl. 1610), author and physician; studied at Oxford; physician in Ireland; published Latin poem on the Earl of Ormonde, 1615, and treatise on hereditary diseases, 1619. [xxxvii. 197]

MEARA or O'MEARA, EDMUND (d. 1680), physician; son of Dermod Meara [q. v.]; M.D. Rheims, 1636; honorary F.R.C.P., 1664; defended in his 'Examen,' 1665, Thomas Willis (1621-1675) [q. v.], and was attacked by Richard Lower (1631-1691) [q. v.] [xxxvii. 197]

MEARES. [See also MERES.]

MEARES, JOHN (1756 ?-1809), naval commander and voyager; entered navy, 1771; lieutenant, 1778; went to India, 1783; formed a company for trading with North-west America, and (1786) explored Prince William Sound; obtained promise of monopoly of Nootka Sound trade, 1788; returned to India, 1788, leaving at Nootka Sound the Iphigenia, which was seized by the Spaniards; appealed to government, 1790, war being only averted by Spain acceding to the British demands; his accounts of his voyages disputed by George Dixon (*d.* 1800 ?) [q. v.] [xxxvii. 198]

MEARNS, DUNCAN (1779-1852), professor of theology; M.A. Aberdeen, 1795; minister of Tarves, 1799; professor of divinity, Aberdeen, 1816; moderator of the general assembly, 1821; one of George IV's chaplains for Scotland, 1823. [xxxvii. 199]

MEARS or **MAIRS,** JOHN (1695 ?-1767), Irish presbyterian divine; studied divinity, Glasgow; M.A., 1713; licensed to Newtownards, 1720; non-subscriber; formed a separate congregation, 1723; minister at Clonmel, 1735-1740, at Stafford Street, Dublin, 1740-67; his 'Catechism,' 1732, long in use. [xxxvii. 199]

MEARS, WILLIAM (*fl.* 1722), publisher; foreman of the Stationers' Company, 1707; issued in 1722 editions of Holinshed, Defoe's 'Moll Flanders' (3rd edit.) and Ludlow's 'Memoirs'; imprisoned for publishing 'Philosophical Dissertation on Death' by de Passereau and Morgan, 1732; mentioned in the 'Dunciad.' [xxxvii. 275]

MEATH, LORDS OF. [See LACY, HUGH DE, first LORD, *d.* 1186; LACY, WALTER, second LORD, *fl.* 1241.]

MECHI, JOHN JOSEPH (1802-1880), agriculturist; clerk in the Newfoundland trade, 1818; cutler; made a fortune by his 'magic razor strop'; purchased a farm, 1841; effected improvements in agriculture; sheriff of London, 1856; alderman, 1857; published agricultural works. [xxxvii. 200]

MEDBOURNE, MATTHEW (*d.* 1679), actor and dramatist; of the Duke's Theatre company; imprisoned on Oates's information, 1678; wrote and translated plays. [xxxvii. 201]

MEDE, JOSEPH (1586-1638). [See MEAD.]

MEDHURST, GEORGE (1759-1827), projector of the atmospheric railway; clockmaker; subsequently engineer; patented windmill for compressing air, 1799, 'Æolian engine,' 1800, and compound crank, 1801; machinist and ironfounder in London; invented balance scales; suggested 'pneumatic dispatch' for conveying letters and goods in tubes by compressed air, 1810; extended his suggestion to passengers, 1812, developing it into a project for a carriage on rails in the open air, 1827. [xxxvii. 201]

MEDHURST, WALTER HENRY (1796-1857), missionary, of St. Paul's School, London; went to China as missionary printer, 1816; learnt Malay and Chinese; ordained, 1819; translated the bible into Chinese, and published English and Japanese (1830) and Chinese and English (1842-3) dictionaries. [xxxvii. 202]

MEDHURST, SIR WALTER HENRY (1822-1885), British consul in China; son of Walter Henry Medhurst [q. v.]; entered office of Chinese secretary, 1840; sent to Hong Kong, 1841; present at Amoy and Chusan (gaining medal), 1841; consular interpreter at Shanghai, 1843; vice-consul at Amoy and (1854) at Foo-chow-foo, also at Tang-chow and Shanghai; mentioned in war despatches, 1861; consul at Hankow, 1864; defended British treaty rights, 1868; removed to Shanghai, 1868-77; knighted, 1877; promoted formation of British North Borneo Company, 1881. [xxxvii. 203]

MEDINA, JOHN (1721-1796), painter; grandson of Sir John Baptist Medina [q. v.]; restored the Holyrood pictures; made copies of the 'Ailsa' portrait of Mary Queen of Scots; exhibited at Royal Academy, 1772 and 1773. [xxxvii. 204]

MEDINA, SIR JOHN BAPTIST (1659-1710), portrait-painter; born at Brussels; went to Scotland, 1688, where he was known as 'the Kneller of the North'; last knight made in Scotland before the union, 1707. [xxxvii. 203]

MEDLAND, THOMAS (*d.* 1833), engraver and draughtsman; drawing-master at Haileybury College, 1806; exhibited at Royal Academy; illustrated various works. [xxxvii. 204]

MEDLEY, HENRY (*d.* 1747), vice-admiral; entered navy, 1703; lieutenant, 1710; captain, 1720; rear-admiral of the white, 1744; vice-admiral, 1745; commander-in-chief in the Mediterranean, 1745; vice-admiral of the red, 1747. [xxxvii. 204]

MEDLEY, JOHN (1804-1892), first bishop of Fredericton, New Brunswick; M.A. Wadham College, Oxford, 1830; vicar of St. John's, Truro, 1831; prebendary of Exeter, 1842; D.D., 1845; bishop of Fredericton, 1845; metropolitan of Canada, 1879; hon. LL.D. Cambridge and D.D. Durham, 1889; published theological works. [xxxvii. 205]

MEDLEY, SAMUEL (1738-1799), baptist minister and hymn-writer; wounded off Cape Lagos and discharged from the navy, 1759; schoolmaster, 1762-6; baptist minister at Watford, 1767, at Byrom Street, Liverpool, 1772; worked among the seamen; wrote hymns and devotional works. [xxxvii. 205]

MEDLEY, SAMUEL (1769-1857), painter; son of Samuel Medley (1738-1799) [q. v.]; painted portraits, 1792-1805; assisted in founding University College, London, 1826. [xxxvii. 206]

MEDOWS. [See also MEADOWS.]

MEDOWS, SIR WILLIAM (1738-1813), general; grandson of Sir Philip Meadows (*d.* 1757) [q. v.]; entered the army, 1756; served in Germany, 1760-4; lieutenant-colonel, 1764; distinguished himself at Brandywine, 1776, and against Santa Lucia, 1778; colonel, 1780; sent to Cape of Good Hope, 1781; commander-in-chief and governor of Bombay, 1788; led unsuccessful campaign against Tippoo, sultan of Mysore, 1790; distinguished himself at Nandidrug, 1791, and Seringapatam, 1792; K.B., 1792; lieutenant-general, 1793; general and governor of the Isle of Wight, 1798; commander-in-chief in Ireland, 1801. [xxxvii. 206]

MEDWALL, HENRY (*fl.* 1486), writer of interludes; chaplain to Morton, archbishop of Canterbury; his extant interlude, 'Nature' (printed, *c.* 1515), performed before Morton in Henry VII's reign. [xxxvii. 207]

MEDWIN, THOMAS (1788-1869), biographer of Shelley and author of 'Conversations of Lord Byron'; lieutenant, 24th dragoon guards, 1813; served in India; introduced by his cousin Shelley to Byron at Pisa, 1821; took notes of his conversation, which he published on Byron's death, 1824; expanded his memoir of Shelley, issued in 'Shelley Papers' (1833), into a life, 1847. [xxxvii. 208]

MEDWYN, LORD (1776-1854). [See FORBES, JOHN HAY.]

MEE, ANNE (1775 ?-1851), miniature-painter; eldest child of John Foldsone [q. v.]; received much royal and aristocratic patronage; exhibited at the Royal Academy, 1815-37. [xxxvii. 208]

MEEHAN, CHARLES PATRICK (1812-1890), author and translator; educated at Ballymahon and Rome; Roman catholic curate of Rathdrum, 1834; member of Royal Irish Academy; published translations and historical compilations in connection with Irish Roman catholic subjects. [xxxvii. 209]

MEEK, SIR JAMES (1778-1856), public servant; entered commissariat department, 1798; collected supplies for Egyptian expedition, 1800; comptroller of the victualling and transport services, 1830; collected information (1841) for Peel's free-trade measures; knighted, 1851. [xxxvii. 209]

MEEKE, MRS. MARY (*d.* 1816 ?), novelist; published novels, from 1795, in her own name and under the pseudonym 'Gabrielli.' [xxxvii. 210]

MEEN, HENRY (*d.* 1817), classical scholar; fellow of Emmanuel College, Cambridge; M.A., 1769; B.D., 1776; minor canon of St. Paul's, London, 1792; prebendary of St. Paul's, London, 1795; published 'Remarks on the Cassandra of Lycophron,' 1800. [xxxvii. 210]

MEESON, ALFRED (1808-1885), architect and surveyor; superintended construction of houses of parliament under Sir Charles Barry [q. v.], 1842, and other public buildings. [xxxvii. 211]

MEETKERKE, EDWARD (1590-1657), divine; of Westminster School; student and tutor of Christ Church, Oxford, 1610; M.A., 1613 (incorporated at Cambridge,

1617); regius professor of Hebrew, 1620–6; D.D., 1625; prebendary of Winchester, 1631; deprived of his stall under parliament; wrote poems in Hebrew and Latin. [xxxvii. 211]

MEGGOT or **MEGGOTT**, RICHARD (*d*. 1692), dean of Winchester; M.A. Queens' College, Cambridge, 1657; D.D., 1669; incumbent of Twickenham and St. Olave's, Southwark, 1668–86; canon of Windsor, 1677; dean of Winchester, 1679; entertained James II at Winchester, 1685. [xxxvii. 212]

MEGGOTT, JOHN (1714–1789). [See ELWES.]

MEIDEL, CHRISTOPHER (*fl.* 1687–1708), quaker; of Norwegian birth; chaplain to Prince George of Denmark in England, *c*. 1683; minister of Danish congregation, 1687; joined quakers, 1699; accompanied Claridge, preaching in Herefordshire and Buckinghamshire, 1705; imprisoned, 1706; visited Holstein; arrested in France, 1608; published Danish translations of quaker books. [xxxvii. 212]

MEIGANT, MAUGANTIUS, MEUGAN, MEUGANT (*fl.* 6th cent.), Welsh saint or druid; president of the college of St. Illtyd at Llantwit; subsequently moved to the establishment of St. Dubricius. [xxxviii. 173]

MEIKLE, ANDREW (1719–1811), millwright and inventor of the thrashing-machine; millwright near Dunbar; patented machine for dressing grain, 1768; unsuccessful with first thrashing-machine, 1778; invented drum thrashing-machine, 1784; manufactured thrashing-machines, 1789; subscription raised for his benefit, 1809. [xxxvii. 213]

MEIKLE, GEORGE (*d*. 1811), millwright; son of Andrew Meikle [q. v.]; invented a water-raising wheel, used to drain Kincardine Moss, 1787. [xxxvii. 214]

MEIKLE, JAMES (1730–1799), surgeon and devotional writer; passed at Surgeons' Hall, London; second surgeon's mate to the Portland, 1758; present at Cape Lagos, 1759; promoted first mate, 1759; obtained discharge, 1762; published religious meditations. [xxxvii. 214]

MEILAN, MARK ANTHONY (*fl.* 1812), miscellaneous writer; resigned situation in post-office; schoolmaster at Hoxton, 1776; curate of St. John, Wapping, 1809; published dramatic works and religious books for children. [xxxvii. 215]

MEILYR BRYDYDD (i.e. THE POET) (*d*. 1140?), Welsh bard; chief bard of Gruffydd ab Cynan; once acted as envoy; three poems by him preserved in 'Myvyrian Archaiology.' [xxxvii. 215]

MEL (*d*. 487), Irish saint; nephew of St. Patrick [q. v.]; founded see of Ardagh, *c*. 454. [xxxvii. 216]

MELBANCKE, BRIAN (*fl.* 1583), euphuistic writer; B.A. St. John's College, Cambridge, 1579; imitated Lyly's 'Euphues' in 'Philotimus,' 1583; alludes to story of Romeo and Juliet as well known. [xxxvii. 216]

MELBOURNE, VISCOUNTS. [See LAMB, WILLIAM, second VISCOUNT, 1779–1848; LAMB, FREDERICK JAMES, BARON BEAUVALE, third VISCOUNT, 1782–1853.]

MELCOMBE, first BARON (1691–1762). [See DODINGTON, GEORGE BUBB.]

MELDOLA, RAPHAEL (1754–1828), Jewish theologian; born at Leghorn; 'rabbi' of the Spanish and Portuguese Jews in London, 1804; restored synagogue, 1824; endeavoured to maintain sanctity of Sabbath; wrote devotional books in Hebrew. [xxxvii. 216]

MELDRUM, GEORGE (1635?–1709), rector of Marischal College, Aberdeen, and professor of divinity at Edinburgh; minister of Aberdeen, 1658; M.A. Aberdeen; suspended, 1662–3; elected rector of Marischal College ten times; deprived, 1681, for refusing the test; minister of Kilwinning, 1688, of Tron Church, Edinburgh, 1692; moderator of the general assembly, 1698 and 1703; professor of divinity, Edinburgh, 1702; published sermons and treatises on church matters. [xxxvii. 217]

MELDRUM, SIR JOHN (*d*. 1645), soldier; assisted in plantation of Ulster, 1610–17; served in the Low Countries; knighted, 1622; took part in Rochelle expedition and French war; patentee for erecting lighthouses on north and south Foreland, 1635; wrote to the king justifying his conduct in joining the parliament; fought at Edgehill, 1642, and the siege of Reading, 1643; raised

siege of Hull, 1643; captured Gainsborough, Cawood Castle, and the fort of Airemouth, 1643; forced to a disadvantageous capitulation at Newark by Rupert, 1644; mortally wounded at Scarborough. [xxxvii. 218]

MELFORT, first EARL and titular DUKE OF (1649–1714). [See DRUMMOND, JOHN.]

MELIA, PIUS (1800–1883), Roman catholic divine; professor of literature in the jesuits' college, Rome; missioner in England, 1848; almoner of the Italian Benevolent Society, 1862; published doctrinal works. [xxxvii. 219]

MELITON, MILITON, or **MILTON**, WILLIAM OF (*d*. 1261), Franciscan; fifth master of the Friars Minors, Cambridge, 1250; D.D.; finished Alexander of Hales's 'Summa Theologiæ,' 1252; died in Paris; his commentaries extant among the National Library manuscripts, Paris. [xxxvii. 219]

MELL, DAVIS (*fl.* 1650), violinist; musician to Charles I; considered the first violinist in England; entertained at Oxford, 1658; leader of Charles II's band, 1660; some of his compositions contained in Simpson's 'Division Violin,' 1684. [xxxvii. 220]

MELLENT, COUNT OF (1104–1166). [See BEAUMONT, WALERAN DE.]

MELLIS, HUGH (*fl.* 1588), mathematician; Southwark schoolmaster; published works on arithmetic and book-keeping. [xxxvii. 220]

MELLISH, SIR GEORGE (1814–1877), lord justice of appeal; educated at Eton and University College, Oxford; M.A., 1839; honorary fellow, 1872; barrister, Inner Temple, 1848; Q.C., 1861; lord justice of appeal, 1870; knighted and privy councillor, 1870; hon. D.C.L. Oxford, 1874. [xxxvii. 220]

MELLITUS (*d*. 624), first bishop of London and third archbishop of Canterbury; sent from Rome by Pope Gregory to reinforce Augustine, 601; consecrated bishop by Augustine, and sent to preach to the East Saxons; won the support of Æthelbert, king of Kent, who built St. Paul's Church, London; attended a council at Rome, 610; brought back decrees and letters from the pope; banished, 616; returned to Kent, 617, on Eadbald's conversion; archbishop of Canterbury, 619–24. [xxxvii. 221]

MELLON, ALFRED (1820–1867), musician; leading violinist of the Royal Italian Opera, London; musical director at the Haymarket and Adelphi Theatres; his opera 'Victorine' produced at Covent Garden, London, 1859. [xxxvii. 222]

MELLON, HARRIOT, DUCHESS OF ST. ALBANS (1777?–1837), actress; first appeared, 1787; at Drury Lane, 1795–1815, playing an extensive round of characters; married Thomas Coutts [q. v.], the banker, 1815, and after his death, William Aubrey de Vere, ninth duke of St. Albans, 1827. [xxxvii. 223]

MELLOR, SIR JOHN (1809–1887), judge; barrister, Inner Temple, 1833; Q.C., 1851; recorder of Warwick, 1849–52, of Leicester, 1855–61; M.P., Great Yarmouth, 1857, Nottingham, 1859; justice of the queen's bench and knighted, 1861; tried the Fenians at Manchester, 1867, and Arthur Orton [q. v.] for perjury, 1873; privy councillor, 1879; published a life of Selden. [xxxvii. 224]

MELMOTH, COURTNEY (1749–1814). [See PRATT, SAMUEL JACKSON.]

MELMOTH, WILLIAM, the elder (1666–1743), religious writer and lawyer; barrister, 1693; member of Lincoln's Inn, 1699; corresponded anonymously with Archbishop Tenison, 1705; bencher, 1719; treasurer (1730) of Lincoln's Inn; published anonymously the 'Great Importance of a Religious Life,' 1711, which was generally assigned to John Perceval, first earl of Egmont [q. v.]. [xxxvii. 224]

MELMOTH, WILLIAM, the younger (1710–1799), author and commissioner of bankrupts; son of William Melmoth the elder [q. v.]; abandoned law, 1739; commissioner of bankrupts, 1756; derided by Dr. Johnson; knew Mrs. Thrale at Bath, 1780; wrote 'Letters on Several Subjects,' 1742, under the pseudonym Sir Thomas Fitzosborne; translated Pliny's 'Letters,' 1746, Cicero's 'Ad Familiares,' 1753, and 'De Senectute,' 1773. [xxxvii. 225]

MELROSE, first EARL OF (1563-1637). [See HAMILTON, THOMAS.]

MELTON, SIR JOHN (d. 1640), politician and author; read law; knighted, 1632; traded in saltpetre and coal; secretary to the council of the north, 1635; M.P., Newcastle-on-Tyne, 1640; published 'Sixefolde Politician,' 1609, and 'Astrologaster,' 1620. [xxxvii. 226]

MELTON, WILLIAM DE (d. 1340), archbishop of York; held posts in the king's household; received ecclesiastical preferments; keeper of the privy seal, 1307; accompanied Edward II to France as secretary, 1308; commissioner to the Cinque ports, 1312; archbishop of York, 1316; commissioner to treat with Scotland, 1318, 1321, and 1323; routed by the Scots at Myton-on-Swale ('Chaptour of Mytoun'), 1319; treasurer of England, 1325-7; officiated at Edward III's marriage, 1328; acquitted of complicity in the Earl of Kent's plot, 1329; treasurer, 1330; empowered to open parliament at York, 1332; keeper of the great seal, 1333-4; asserted his right to bear the cross in the southern province. [xxxvii. 227]

MELTON, WILLIAM DE (d. 1528), chancellor of York; M.A. Cambridge, 1479; D.D., 1496; master of Michaelhouse, Cambridge, 1495; chancellor of York, 1496; author of 'Sermo Exhortatorius,' published by Wynkyn de Worde, 1494; sometimes confounded with three namesakes. [xxxvii. 229]

MELUN, ROBERT DE (d. 1167). [See ROBERT.]

MELVILL, HENRY (1798-1871), canon of St. Paul's Cathedral; sizar of St. John's College, Cambridge, 1817; migrated to St. Peter's College, Cambridge; second wrangler, 1821; fellow and tutor, 1822-32; M.A., 1824; B.D., 1836; chaplain at the Tower of London, 1840; principal of Haileybury College, 1843-57; chaplain to Queen Victoria, 1853; canon of St. Paul's, 1856-71; rector of Barnes, 1863-71; published numerous sermons. [xxxvii. 229]

MELVILL, SIR JAMES COSMO (1792-1861), brother of Henry Melvill [q. v.]; entered home service of East India Company, 1808, became financial secretary, 1834, and was chief secretary, 1836, till termination of company's existence as governing body, 1858; government director of Indian railways, 1858; F.R.S., 1841; K.C.B., 1853. [Suppl. iii. 159]

MELVILL, THOMAS (1726-1753), experimental philosopher; divinity student at Glasgow, 1748-9; read before Edinburgh Medical Society 'Observations on Light and Colours,' containing fundamental experiments in spectrum analysis, 1752, 'Refrangibility of the Rays of Light' before Royal Society, 1753. [xxxvii. 230]

MELVILLE, VISCOUNTS. [See DUNDAS, HENRY, first VISCOUNT, 1742-1811; DUNDAS, ROBERT SAUNDERS, second VISCOUNT, 1771-1851; DUNDAS, HENRY, third VISCOUNT, 1801-1876.]

MELVILLE or **MELVILL**, ANDREW (1545-1622), Scottish presbyterian leader and scholar; educated at Montrose grammar school under Pierre de Marsiliers, 1557-9, and St. Mary's College, St. Andrews; went to Paris, 1564; studied Greek, oriental languages, mathematics, and law; influenced by Peter Ramus; went to Poitiers, 1566; helped to defend Poitiers during the siege, 1568; professor of humanity, Geneva, 1568; met Beza, Joseph Scaliger, and Francis Hottoman; returned to Scotland, 1573; appointed head of Glasgow College, 1574; introduced an enlarged curriculum and established chairs in languages, science, philosophy, and divinity, confirmed by royal charter, 1577; assisted in the organisation of the Scottish church in the presbyterian mould, which was set forth in the 'second book of discipline,' sanctioned, 1581; assisted in the reconstitution of Aberdeen University, 1575, and the re-formation of St. Andrews, 1579; became principal of St. Mary's College, St. Andrews, 1580, where he promoted the study of Aristotle, and created a taste for Greek letters; moderator of the general assembly at St. Andrews, 1582, at which the order for the excommunication of Montgomery (whom he prosecuted as a 'tulchan' bishop) caused open war between the assembly and the court; his party placed in power by the 'raid of Ruthven,' 1582; charged with treason, 1584; escaped to England, and was well received in Oxford, Cambridge, and London; returned to Scotland on Arran's fall, 1585; effected a compromise, 1586; rector of St. Andrews University, 1590; unsuccessfully claimed the right to sit in

the assembly at Dundee, 1598, and at Montrose, 1600; deprived of the rectorship in a visitation of St. Andrews, but made dean of the faculty of theology, 1599; protested on behalf of the leaders of a general assembly constituted at Aberdeen, 1605, in defiance of the king's messenger; summoned to London, 1606, where he made two long uncompromising speeches on behalf of the freedom of assemblies; confined in the Tower for a bitter epigram on Anglican ritual, 1607; his release at last obtained, 1611, by Henri de la Tour, duc de Bouillon, who wished him to become professor of biblical theology in the university of Sédan; wrote controversial prose works; ranked by Isaac Walton next to Buchanan as a Latin poet; died at Sédan. [xxxvii. 230]

MELVILLE, ANDREW (1624-1706), soldier of fortune; studied languages at Königsberg; joined presbyterian troops, 1647; joined Charles II at Breda; escaped after Worcester (1651) to Holland; fought for France, Sweden, and Brandenburg; sent by the Duke of Celle to congratulate Charles II, 1660; appointed commandant of Gifhorn, 1677; published an autobiography, 1704; died at Gifhorn. [xxxvii. 237]

MELVILLE, DAVID, third EARL OF LEVEN, second EARL OF MELVILLE (1660-1728), son of George Melville, first earl of Melville [q. v.]; military commander; became Earl of Leven, 1681; confidential agent to the Prince of Orange; raised regiment of Scottish refugees, 1688; distinguished himself at Killiecrankie (1689) and in the Irish campaign; served in Flanders, 1692; major-general of the Scottish forces, 1703; master of ordnance, 1705; commander-in-chief of the Scots forces, 1706; suppressed Jacobite rising, 1708; deprived of all offices by tory administration, 1712. [xxxvii. 237]

MELVILLE, ELIZABETH (fl. 1603). [See COLVILLE.]

MELVILLE, GEORGE, fourth BARON and first EARL OF MELVILLE (1634?-1707), welcomed Charles II in London, 1660; joined Monmouth against the covenanters, 1679, and endeavoured to avoid a conflict; fled on discovery of the Rye House plot and joined the Prince of Orange, 1683; secretary of state for Scotland, 1689; commissioner to the parliament (1690) which established presbyterianism; trusted by the king to propitiate the presbyterians; created Earl of Melville, Viscount Kirkcaldy, 1690; lord privy seal, 1691; president of the privy council and member of the committee for the security of the kingdom, 1696; deprived of his offices, 1702. [xxxvii. 238]

MELVILLE, CAPTAIN GEORGE JOHN WHYTE-(1821-1878). [See WHYTE-MELVILLE.]

MELVILLE or **MELVILL**, JAMES (1556-1614), Scottish reformer; nephew of Andrew Melville (1545-1622) [q. v.]; educated at St. Andrews (B.A. St. Leonard's College, 1571) and Glasgow; professor of Hebrew and oriental languages at St. Mary's College, St. Andrews, 1580; seconded his uncle in his views on presbyterianism; fled to Berwick, 1584; prohibited from preaching; attacked Bishop Adamson at the synod of Fife, 1586; ordained to a charge in Fifeshire, 1586; moderator of the general assembly, 1589; presented petitions on ecclesiastical matters to James VI of Scotland, who sent him to collect subscriptions from the presbyterians to pay for the expedition against Bothwell; opposed James VI's proposal of a parliamentary vote for ministers, 1598; summoned to London on ecclesiastical affairs, 1606; ordered to confine himself within ten miles of Newcastle, 1607; died at Berwick on his way back to Scotland; published numerous poems; 'Diary' printed, 1829. [xxxvii. 241]

MELVILLE, SIR JAMES (1535-1617), of Hallhill; autobiographer; son of Sir John Melville [q. v.]; page to Mary Queen of Scots, 1549; wounded at St. Quentin, 1557; sent to discover the designs of Lord James Stewart, earl of Moray [q. v.], 1557; endeavoured to win Queen Elizabeth's approval of Mary Stuart's marriage to Darnley; sent to offer the regency to Moray; entrusted with diplomatic missions throughout James VI's minority; knighted; privy councillor; manuscript of his autobiography first discovered, 1660, last edited, 1827. [xxxvii. 240]

MELVILLE, SIR JOHN (d. 1548), laird of Raith; engaged in the disputes of the regency during James V's minority; master of artillery, 1526; followed James V in his border expeditions; assisted in the trial of Janet

Douglas, lady Glamis [q. v.], 1537; captain of Dunbar Castle, 1540; a reformer, supporting the 'English' party in Scotland; convicted of treason and executed. [xxxvii. 244]

MELVILLE, ROBERT, first BARON MELVILLE (1527–1621), son of Sir John Melville [q. v.]; in the French service; returned to Scotland, 1559; opposed Mary Stuart's marriage to Darnley; visited Mary Stuart in Lochleven Castle, 1567; taken prisoner at Langside, but released as a non-combatant, 1568; declared traitor, 1573; his forfeiture rescinded, 1580; knighted, 1581; clerk and treasurer depute, 1581; privy councillor, 1582; entreated Queen Elizabeth for Mary Stuart's life: acted as chancellor, 1589; sent to negotiate with Queen Elizabeth, 1593; extraordinary lord of session as Lord Murdocairnie, 1594; resigned his offices, 1600; accompanied James VI to England, 1603; commissioner for the union, 1605; created Baron Melville of Monimail, 1616. [xxxvii. 245]

MELVILLE, ROBERT (1723–1809), general and antiquary; studied at Glasgow and Edinburgh Universities; ensign, 1744; served in Flanders: captain, 1751; major, 1756; lieutenant-governor of Guadeloupe, 1759, governor, 1760; governor of the ceded islands, 1763–70; sent to France to solicit certain indulgences for the British in Tobago; suggested a new theory of Hannibal's route across the Alps; invented a naval gun, 1759 (used until the middle of this century); F.R.S.; F.S.A. [xxxvii. 246]

MELVIN, JAMES (1795–1853), Latin scholar; educated at Aberdeen grammar school and Marischal College, Aberdeen; M.A., 1816; LL.D., 1834; master at Aberdeen grammar school, 1822, rector, 1826; 'lecturer on humanity' at Marischal College; published Latin grammar, 1822, exercises, posthumous, 1857; collected classical and mediæval Latin literature. [xxxvii. 247]

MENASSEH BEN ISRAEL (1604–1657). [See MANASSEH.]

MENDES, FERNANDO (d. 1724), physician: born in Portugal; M.D. Montpellier, 1667; attended Catherine of Braganza to England; physician in ordinary to Catherine of Braganza, 1669; attended Charles II; F.R.C.P., 1687. [xxxvii. 247]

MENDES, MOSES (d. 1758), poet and dramatist; grandson of Fernando Mendes [q. v.]; successful stock-broker; bon-vivant and wit; wrote dramatic pieces set to music by Boyce and Burney, and poems and songs in imitation of Spenser. [xxxvii. 248]

MENDHAM, JOSEPH (1769–1856), controversialist: M.A. St. Edmund Hall, Oxford, 1795; incumbent of Hill Chapel in Arden, 1836; wrote against Romish doctrine and organisation; his library presented to the Incorporated Law Society. [xxxvii. 249]

MENDIP, first BARON (1713–1802). [See ELLIS WELBORE.]

MENDOZA, DANIEL (1764–1836), pugilist: successfully united sparring with boxing; encountered 'the Bath butcher,' 1787; at times acted as officer of the sheriff of Middlesex; made tours in Ireland, 1791, and England; retired, 1820; published the 'Art of Boxing,' 1789. [xxxvii. 250]

MENDOZA Y RIOS, JOSEPH DE (1762–1816), astronomer; born at Seville; educated at the Royal College of Nobles, Madrid; served in the Spanish navy with distinction; commissioned by government to form a maritime library at Madrid; travelled in France; made his home in England after being elected F.R.S., 1793; published works on nautical astronomy, which revolutionised that science, and on navigation. [xxxvii. 251]

MENDS, SIR ROBERT (1767?–1823), commodore: entered navy, 1779; lost right arm at the defence of York town, 1781; wounded at battle of Dominica; lieutenant, 1789; severely burnt by an explosion in action off Lorient, 1795; captain, 1800; distinguished himself on Spanish coast, 1810; superintendent of Portsmouth harbour, 1811–14; knighted, 1815; appointed commodore and commander-in-chief on the west coast of Africa, 1821; died on board his ship at Cape Coast, 1823. [xxxvii. 251]

MENDS, SIR WILLIAM ROBERT (1812–1897), admiral; nephew of Sir Robert Mends [q. v.]; studied at Royal Naval College, Portsmouth; served under Captain Henry John Rous [q. v.] on the Pique, 1835; lieutenant,

1835; commander, 1846; post-captain, 1852; in Mediterranean, 1853; distinguished at bombardment of Odessa, 1854; flag-captain to Sir Edmund (afterwards Lord) Lyons [q. v.], 1854–7; C.B., 1855; deputy controller-general of coastguard at admiralty, 1861–2; director of transports, 1862–83; rear-admiral, 1869; vice-admiral, 1874; admiral, 1879; G.C.B., 1882; his 'Life' published by his son, Bowen Stilon Mends, 1899. [Suppl. iii. 159]

MENKEN, ADAH ISAACS, formerly ADELAIDE McCORD (1835–1868), actress and writer; acted at New Orleans and in Texas; journalist; taught French, Greek, and Latin in a school at New Orleans; married Alexander Isaac Menken, 1856; became a Jewess; acted in the States, New York, and (1864) London; became acquainted with Dickens, Charles Reade, and Swinburne; met the elder Dumas and Gautier in Paris, 1866; published 'Infelicia' (poems), 1868; was married four and divorced three times; died in Paris. [xxxvii. 252]

MENMUIR, LORD (1552–1598). [See LINDSAY, JOHN.]

MENNES, SIR JOHN (1599–1671), admiral; recommended by Sir Alexander Brett for command, 1626; served in the Narrow Seas; raised troop of carabineers, 1640; knighted, 1642; governor of North Wales for Charles I, 1644; commander of the king's navy, 1645; comptroller of the navy, 1661, 'though not fit for business,' according to Pepys; commander-in-chief in the Downs and admiral, 1662; published, with Dr. James Smith, 'Wits Recreations,' 1640, and 'Musarum Deliciæ,' 1655. [xxxvii. 253]

MENTEITH, EARLS OF. [See COMYN, WALTER, d. 1258; GRAHAM, WILLIAM, seventh EARL, 1591–1661.]

MENTEITH, SIR JOHN DE (d. after 1329), Scottish knight: imprisoned for resistance to Edward I, 1296; released, 1297; warden of castle, town, and sheriffdom of Dumbarton, 1304; captured Wallace at Glasgow and took him to London; nominated one of the Scots barons in the united parliament; on the Scottish council and created Earl of Lennox; joined Bruce in his revolt, 1307; commissioned to treat for truce, 1316 and 1323; present at Arbroath parliament, 1320; last recorded grants to him, 1329. [xxxvii. 255]

MENTEITH, MENTET, or MONTEITH, ROBERT (fl. 1621–1660), author of 'Histoire des Troubles de la Grande Bretagne'; M.A. Edinburgh, 1621; professor of philosophy at Saumur; presented to the kirk of Duddingston, 1630; fled to Paris, 1633; denounced as rebel; became Roman catholic and secretary to De Retz till (1652) the cardinal's arrest; canon of Notre-Dame; his 'Histoire' published, 1660. [xxxvii. 257]

MENZIES, ARCHIBALD (1754–1842), botanical collector; studied at Edinburgh; naval surgeon; accompanied fur-trading voyage of discovery to North-west coast of America and China, 1786–9; as naturalist and surgeon went with Vancouver to the Cape, New Zealand, and North-west America, 1790–5; ascended Wha-ra-rai and Mauna Loa in Hawaii, determining their altitude by the barometer; brought back various plants, cryptogams, and natural-history objects; F.L.S., 1790. [xxxvii. 258]

MENZIES, JOHN (1624–1684), Scottish divine and professor; graduate and regent, Marischal College, Aberdeen; professor of divinity, Marischal College, Aberdeen, and pastor of Greyfriars Church, Aberdeen, 1649; became an independent, 1651; 'trier' in Scotland, 1654; returned to presbyterianism; reluctantly conformed to episcopacy; engaged in controversy with Roman catholics and quakers; professor of divinity, King's College, Old Aberdeen, 1679, but soon resigned; reinstated professor at Marischal College, Aberdeen, 1679; deprived on refusing the test, 1681; gave way, and was reinstated, 1682; published theological works. [xxxvii. 258]

MENZIES, JOHN (1756–1834), founder of Blairs College, Kincardineshire; educated at Dinant; conveyed to Bishop Paterson his estate of Blairs for the education of secular priests, 1827; benefactor of St. Margaret's Convent, Edinburgh, opened, 1835; acquainted with Scott. [xxxvii. 259]

MENZIES, MICHAEL (d. 1766), advocate and inventor; advocate, 1719; invented a thrashing-machine, 1734, a machine for conveying coal to the shaft, 1750, and a machine for draining coal-mines, 1761, which came into partial use. [xxxvii. 259]

MEOPHAM or **MEPEHAM**, SIMON (d. 1333), archbishop of Canterbury; fellow of Merton College, Oxford; D.D.; prebendary of Llandaff, 1295; canon of Chichester; archbishop of Canterbury, 1327; consecrated at Avignon; mediated between Henry, earl of Lancaster, and Mortimer, 1328; enthroned at Canterbury, 1329; crowned Queen Philippa, 1329; held several church councils; irritated his suffragans by a series of systematic visitations; contested right of Archbishop of York to have his cross borne erect before him in the southern province; called on the monks of St. Augustine's Abbey to justify their rights to their Kentish churches, 1329; refused to appear before the papal nuncio on the monks' appeal, 1332; pronounced contumacious, fined 700l., and excommunicated for non-payment. [xxxvii. 260]

MERBECKE, JOHN (fl. 1583). [See MARBECK.]

MERBURY or **MARBURY**, CHARLES (fl. 1581), author; B.A. Oxford, 1570; entered Gray's Inn, 1571; went to Italy; entered household of Earl of Sussex; in France on official business, 1583; corresponded with Anthony Bacon [q. v.] and Walsingham; published defence of absolute monarchy, 1581. [xxxvii. 263]

MERCER, ANDREW (1775–1842), poet and topographer; gave up theology for miniature-painting; wrote for magazines in Edinburgh; settled at Dunfermline and taught drawing; wrote poems and 'History of Dunfermline,' 1828. [xxxvii. 264]

MERCER, HUGH (1726?–1777), American brigadier-general; medical student at Aberdeen; surgeon's mate in the Pretender's army; went to America, 1747; lieutenant-colonel of provincials, 1758; in command at the new Fort Du Quesne; doctor at Fredericksburg; drilled the Virginian militia; colonel, 1775; brigadier-general, 1776; died of wounds received at Princetown. [xxxvii. 264]

MERCER, JAMES (1734–1804), poet and soldier; second cousin to Hugh Mercer [q. v.]; M.A. Aberdeen, 1754; went to Paris; joined a British regiment, 1756; distinguished himself at Minden, 1759, and in Ireland; major, 1770; sold out of the army, 1772; major in the 'Gordon Fencibles,' 1777; intimate with Beattie, Dr. Reid, Sir William Forbes, and Robert Arbuthnot; his 'Lyric Poems,' 1797, republished 1804 and 1806. [xxxvii. 265]

MERCER, JOHN (1791–1866), calico-printer and chemist; bobbin-winder and hand-loom weaver; experimented in dyeing; studied mathematics and chemistry; discovered dyes suitable for printing calico in orange, yellow, and bronze; chemist at Messrs. Fort Brothers' print-works, 1818; partner, 1825; propounded theory of 'catalytic' action at British Association meeting, 1842; joined Chemical Society, 1847; discovered process of 'Mercerising,' 1850; F.R.S., 1852; read paper on ferrocyanides at British Association, 1858; made other discoveries connected with dyeing processes. [xxxvii. 265]

MERCER, WILLIAM (1605?–1675?), lieutenant-colonel and poet; served in Denmark and Sweden; granted prebend of Glenholme, 1630; officer in Ireland, 1638; lieutenant-colonel in parliamentarian army, 1646; swore allegiance at the Restoration; published poems, including 'Angliæ Speculum,' 1646, and 'News from Parnassus,' 1682. [xxxvii. 267]

MERCHISTON, LORDS OF. [See NAPIER, ARCHIBALD, first LORD, 1574–1645; NAPIER, ARCHIBALD, second LORD, d. 1660.]

MERCIA, EARL OF (d. 1057). [See LEOFRIC.]

MERCIANS, KINGS OF. [See PENDA, 577?–655; PEADA, under-king of the South Mercians, d. 656; WULFHERE, d. 675; COENRED, fl. 704–709; CEOLRED, d. 716; ETHELBALD, d. 757; OFFA, d. 796; BEORNWULF, d. 826; WIGLAF, d. 838; BEORHTWULF, d. 852; BURHRED, fl. 852–874.]

MERCIER, HONORÉ (1840–1894), premier of Quebec; born at Ste.-Athanase, Lower Canada; educated at jesuit college, Montreal; edited 'Le Courier'; called to Montreal bar, 1867; member of House of Commons for Rouville in province of Quebec, 1872; solicitor-general, 1878–9; member for Ste.-Hyacinthe and liberal leader in provincial house, 1883; premier of Quebec, 1887–92. His measures included the consolidation of provincial statutes and the establishment of an agricultural department. In 1891 investigations, begun in the senate, traced to Mercier or his agents sums which the provincial house had voted

to the Baie des Chaleurs railway; a royal commission was issued and the ministry dismissed; a prosecution against him, 1892, on an indictment of conspiracy to defraud the province, failed. Subsequently he again took an active part in politics. [Suppl. iii. 161]

MERCIER, PHILIP (1689–1760), portrait-painter; born at Berlin; studied under Antoine Pesne; visited Italy, France, and Hanover; painted the then Prince of Wales's portrait; settled in London, 1716; appointed principal painter (1727) and librarian to Frederick, prince of Wales. [xxxvii. 269]

MERDDIN, WYLLT (fl. 580?). [See MYRDDIN.]

MEREDITH, EDWARD (1648–1689?), Roman catholic controversialist; educated at Westminster School and Christ Church, Oxford; accompanied Sir William Godolphin to Spain as secretary; became Roman catholic; went abroad, 1688; published controversial works; died in Italy. [xxxvii. 270]

MEREDITH, RICHARD (1550?–1597), bishop of Leighlin and Ferns; M.A. Jesus College, Oxford, 1575; held several ecclesiastical appointments in Wales; chaplain to Sir John Perrot [q. v.], lord deputy of Ireland, 1584; dean of St. Patrick's, Dublin, 1584; bishop of Leighlin, 1589; accused of complicity in Perrot's treasonable designs; tried in the Star-chamber, 1590; imprisoned and fined, 1591 and again, 1594; died in Dublin. [xxxvii. 270]

MEREDITH, RICHARD (1559–1621), dean of Wells; educated at Westminster School and New College, Oxford (fellow, 1578); B.C.L., 1584; B.D., 1606; royal chaplain and dean of Wells, 1607. [xxxvii. 271]

MEREDITH, SIR WILLIAM, third baronet (d. 1790), politician; D.C.L. Christ Church, Oxford, 1749; M.P., Wigan, 1754–61; Liverpool, 1761–80; a whig and follower of Lord Rockingham; admiralty lord, 1765; protected Lord North from the mob, 1771; his bill for repealing a clause in the Nullum Tempus Act rejected, 1771; failed in attempt to abolish subscription for members of the universities, 1773; comptroller of the household and privy councillor, 1774; resigned, 1777; sold his property, 1779; wrote on political subjects; died at Lyons. [xxxvii. 271]

MEREDYDD (d. 999?). [See MAREDUDD AB OWAIN.]

MEREDYDD AB BLEDDYN, PRINCE OF POWYS (d. 1132). [See MAREDUDD.]

MEREDYTH, first BARON. [See SOMERVILLE, SIR WILLIAM MEREDYTH, 1802–1873.]

MERES, FRANCIS (1565–1647), divine and author; M.A. Pembroke College, Cambridge, 1591; incorporated at Oxford, 1593; rector and schoolmaster at Wing, 1602; author of 'Gods Arithmeticke,' 1597, 'Palladis Tamia,' 1598, and 'Wits Treasury,' 1598; translated works by Luis de Granada. [xxxvii. 272]

MERES or **MEERES**, JOHN (1698–1761), printer and journalist; printer's apprentice, 1712; partner and manager with Richard Nutt; owner of the 'London Evening Post' and 'Daily Post'; imprisoned, 1740, for remarks on an act of parliament; compiled a catalogue of English plays, 1713 (with continuation, 1715) and 1734. [xxxvii. 274]

MERES, SIR THOMAS (1635–1715), knighted, 1660; whig M.P., Lincoln, 1659–1710; commissioner of the admiralty, 1679–84; tried to pass a bill compelling foreigners in England to adopt the English liturgy, 1685. [xxxvii. 274]

MEREWETHER, HENRY ALWORTH (1780–1864), serjeant-at-law; barrister, 1809; serjeant-at-law, 1827; D.C.L. Oxford, 1839; town clerk of London, 1842–59; Q.C., 1853; recorder of Reading; attorney-general to Adelaide, queen-dowager; chief work, 'History of Boroughs and Municipal Corporations,' 1835. [xxxvii. 275]

MEREWETHER, JOHN (1797–1850), dean of Hereford; B.A. Queen's College, Oxford, 1818; D.D., 1832; incumbent of New Radnor, 1828; dean of Hereford, 1832; deputy clerk of the closet to William IV, 1833; opposed election of Hampden to see of Hereford, 1847; F.S.A., 1836; assisted in the restoration of Hereford Cathedral. [xxxvii. 275]

MEREWETHER, SIR WILLIAM LOCKYER (1825–1880), Indian military officer and administrator; son of Henry Alworth Merewether [q. v.]; educated at

Westminster School; entered Bombay army, 1841; distinguished himself during Sindh campaign, 1843; commandant of the frontier force, 1859; C.B., 1860; political agent at Aden, 1865; commanded the pioneer force in Abyssinia, 1867; K.C.S.I., 1868; chief commissioner in Sindh, 1867; member of the council of India, 1876. [xxxvii. 276]

MERFYN FRYCH, i.e. FRECKLED (*d.* 844), Welsh prince; became lord of Anglesey, 825. His descendants became princes of North and South Wales. [xxxvii. 277]

MERICK. [See MERRICK and MEYRICK.]

MERITON or **MERYTON**, GEORGE (*d.* 1624), dean of York; graduated M.A. from St. John's College, 1588; fellow of Queens' College, Cambridge, 1589; rector of Hadleigh, 1599; dean of Peterborough, 1612; chaplain to James I's queen; dean of York, 1617; published sermons. [xxxvii. 277]

MERITON or **MERRITON**, GEORGE (1634–1711), author; grandson of George Meriton (*d.* 1624) [q. v.]; lawyer at Northallerton; went to Ireland, 1684; LL.D. of Dublin, 1700; published legal works and a curious poem in 'Praise of Yorkshire Ale,' 1683. [xxxvii. 278]

MERITON, JOHN (1636–1704), divine; sizar of St. John's College, Cambridge; recommended by Cromwell to St. Nicholas Acons, London, 1656; M.A. Cambridge, by royal mandate, 1660, and D.D., 1669; rector of St. Michael's, Cornhill, 1663; remained at his post during the plague, 1665; assisted in uniting and rebuilding churches after the fire, 1666; published devotional works. [xxxvii. 279]

MERITON, THOMAS (*fl.* 1658), dramatist; grandson of George Meriton (*d.* 1624) [q. v.]; M.A. St. John's College, Cambridge, 1669; published 'Love and War,' 1658, and 'The Wandring Lover,' 1658, two tragedies. [xxxvii. 280]

MERIVALE, CHARLES (1808–1893), dean of Ely; son of John Herman Merivale [q. v.]; of Harrow and St. John's College, Cambridge; M.A., 1833; B.D., 1840; rowed for university in first contest with Oxford at Henley, 1829; fellow of St. John's College, Cambridge, 1833; rector of Lawford, Essex, 1848; chaplain to speaker of House of Commons (John Evelyn Denison), 1863–9; Hulsean lecturer, 1862; Boyle lecturer, 1864–5; dean of Ely, 1863; hon. D.C.L. Oxford, 1866; published 'History of the Romans under the Empire,' 1850–64, and other historical writings, sermons, and lectures, besides numerous Latin poems, including a translation of Keats's 'Hyperion.' [Suppl. iii. 163]

MERIVALE, HERMAN (1806–1874), under-secretary for India; son of John Herman Merivale [q. v.]; was educated at Harrow and Oxford; B.A. Trinity College, Oxford, 1827; fellow of Balliol College, 1828; barrister, Inner Temple, 1832; professor of political economy at Oxford, 1837; assistant under-secretary of state for the colonies, 1847; permanent under-secretary, 1848; transferred to the India office and C.B., 1859; D.C.L. Oxford, 1870; principal works, 'Lectures on Colonisation,' 1841, 'Historical Studies,' 1865, and 'Life of Sir Henry Lawrence,' 1872. [xxxvii. 280]

MERIVALE, JOHN HERMAN (1779–1844), scholar and minor poet; grandson of Samuel Merivale [q. v.]; of St. John's College, Cambridge; barrister, Lincoln's Inn, 1804; practised in chancery and bankruptcy; chancery commissioner, 1824; bankruptcy commissioner, 1831; published law reports and translations from Greek and Italian poetry. [xxxvii. 281]

MERIVALE, SAMUEL (1715–1771), presbyterian minister at Sleaford, 1737, and Tavistock, 1743; tutor at Exeter Presbyterian Theological Seminary, 1761; published devotional works. [xxxvii. 281]

MERKE, THOMAS (*d.* 1409), bishop of Carlisle; educated at Oxford; D.D.; monk of Westminster; appointed bishop of Carlisle, 1397; ambassador to the German princes, 1397; present in parliament, 1397; commissioner for Queen Isabella's dowry, 1398; accompanied Richard II to Ireland, 1399; protested against Henry IV's treatment of Richard; committed to the Tower of London, 1400; found guilty and deprived of his bishopric; received conditional pardon, 1401; acted occasionally as deputy to Wykeham; commissioned to perform episcopal functions in the diocese of Winchester during its vacancy; sided against the pope at Lucca, 1408. [xxxvii. 282]

MERLAC, DANIEL OF (*fl.* 1170–1190). [See MORLEY.]

MERLE or **MORLEY**, WILLIAM (*d.* 1347), meteorologist; rector of Driby, 1331; kept systematic record of the weather for seven years, preserved in Digby MS., Merton College, Oxford. [xxxvii. 285]

MERLIN AMBROSIUS, or **MYRDDIN EMRYS**, legendary enchanter and bard; brought before Vortigern as a child; foretold the king's death and the triumph of Aurelius Ambrosius; made ruler of the western part of Britain by Vortigern; advised Aurelius, as a memorial of his triumph, to send for the stones called 'Giants' Dance' from Ireland; defeated the Irish by his art, and the 'Dance' was set up (Stonehenge). One legend represents Merlin to have gone to sea in a glass vessel and disappeared. Welsh tradition recognises another Merlin, Merlin Silvester, or Myrddin Wyllt, who lived *c.* 570, was connected with the fatal battle of Arderydd, 573, and subsequently became insane and lived in the forest. The Merlin legend is common to Scotland, Wales, Cornwall, and Brittany. The popular French romance of 'Merlin,' by Robert de Borron (thirteenth century), was founded on Geoffrey of Monmouth. Sir Thomas Malory borrowed much from Borron's 'Merlin' in his 'Morte d'Arthur.' [xxxvii. 285]

MERLIN CELIDONIUS or **SILVESTER**. [See MYRDDIN, WILT.]

MERRET or **MERRETT**, CHRISTOPHER (1614–1695), physician; M.D. Gloucester Hall, Oxford, 1643; F.R.C.P., 1651; Gulstonian lecturer, 1654; censor seven times between 1657 and 1670; first librarian at Royal College of Physicians, which was destroyed, 1666, and his services dispensed with; expelled from his fellowship for non-attendance, 1681; published works on natural history and medicine. [xxxvii. 288]

MERREY, WALTER (1723–1799), numismatist; Nottingham manufacturer; published a history of English coinage, 1789. [xxxvii. 289]

MERRICK, JAMES (1720–1769), poet and scholar; M.A. Trinity College, Oxford, 1742; fellow, 1745; ordained, but lived in college; published poems, including 'The Chameleon'; translated from the Greek and advocated the compilation and amalgamation of indexes to the principal Greek authors; versified the Psalms, several editions of which were set to music. [xxxvii. 289]

MERRICK, RICE (*d.* 1587), historian of Glamorgan; clerk of the peace; his history printed, 1825 and 1887. [xxxvii. 291]

MERRIFIELD, CHARLES WATKINS (1827–1884), mathematician; entered the education department, 1847; barrister, 1851; F.R.S., 1863; held offices in the London Mathematical Society and the Royal Institution of Naval Architects; principal of Royal School of Naval Architecture and Marine Engineering, 1867–73; served on royal commissions; wrote books and papers in periodicals on mathematics and hydraulics. [xxxvii. 291]

MERRIMAN, BRIAN (1757–1808), Irish poet; schoolmaster at Kilclerin; wrote a poem, 'Midnight Court,' 1780; composed songs. [xxxvii. 292]

MERRIMAN, JOHN (1774–1839), surgeon; first cousin to Samuel Merriman (1771–1852) [q. v.]; M.R.C.S. and M.S.A.; general medical attendant on the Duchess of Kent; apothecary extraordinary to Queen Victoria, 1837. [xxxvii. 294]

MERRIMAN, NATHANIEL JAMES (1810–1882), bishop of Grahamstown, South Africa; educated at Winchester College and Oxford; M.A. Brasenose College, Oxford, 1834; archdeacon of Grahamstown, 1848; undertook a Kaffir mission, 1850; one of Bishop Colenso's accusers, 1863; bishop of Grahamstown, 1871; wrote on South Africa. [xxxvii. 292]

MERRIMAN, SAMUEL (1731–1818), physician; M.D. Edinburgh, 1753; settled in London, 1757; specialised in midwifery. [xxxvii. 293]

MERRIMAN, SAMUEL (1771–1852), physician; studied medicine under his uncle, Samuel Merriman (1731–1818) [q. v.]; hon. M.D. Marischal College, Aberdeen; physician-accoucheur, Westminster General Dispensary, London, 1808–15, to Middlesex Hospital, London, 1809–26, where he lectured on midwifery, 1810–25; published medical works, some on obstetrics. [xxxvii. 293]

MERRIOT, THOMAS (1589–1662), grammarian; fellow of New College, Oxford, 1610–24; B.C.L., 1615; vicar of Swalcliffe, 1624, where he taught grammar; sequestered, 1646; published grammatical works in Latin. [xxxvii. 294]

MERRITT, HENRY (1822–1877), picture-cleaner and art-critic; came to London, 1846; cleaned pictures for the National Portrait Gallery, London, Hampton Court, and Marlborough House; acquainted with Gladstone and Ruskin, with whom he corresponded; published 'Robert Dalby' (autobiographical romance), 1865; art-critic to the 'Standard,' 1866. [xxxvii. 295]

MERRY, ROBERT (1755–1798), dilettante; educated at Harrow; left Christ's College, Cambridge, without graduating; entered Lincoln's Inn; purchased a commission in the horse guards, which he sold on account of gambling debts; settled at Florence, 1784; wrote for the 'Arno' and 'Florence Miscellany,' 1785; member of the Della Cruscan Academy; left for London, 1787; carried on a sentimental correspondence in verse in the 'World' with Mrs. Hannah Cowley [q. v.], 1787; sympathised with the French revolution; visited Paris, 1789, 1791, and 1792; went to America, 1796, where his wife, Elizabeth Brunton, acted in the chief cities in the States; wrote several unsuccessful plays; died at Baltimore. [xxxvii. 295]

MERRYFELLOW, DICK (1723–1781). [See GARDINER, RICHARD.]

MERSINGTON, LORD (1625?–1700). [See SWINTON, ALEXANDER.]

MERTON, WALTER DE (d. 1277), bishop of Rochester and founder of Merton College, Oxford; probably a pupil of Adam de Marisco, at Manger Hall, Oxford; founded a hospital at Basingstoke in memory of his parents; protonotary of chancery; negotiated with the pope about the grant of Sicily to Edmund, the king's son, 1258; chancellor, 1261–3; justiciar, 1271; again chancellor, 1272–4; bishop of Rochester, 1274. He obtained charters, 1261, 1263, 1264, 1270, 1274, to assign various manors for the support of scholars at Oxford who should form a corporate body under a warden. [xxxvii. 297]

MERVIN or **MERVYN**, SIR AUDLEY (d. 1675), soldier, lawyer, and politician; acquired lands in Ulster; M.P., Tyrone, 1640; lieutenant-colonel against the rebels, 1641; governor of Derry, 1644; taken prisoner by parliamentarians, 1648; co-operated against Sir Charles Coote, but afterwards withdrew from the royalist party, 1649; admitted to King's Inns in Dublin, 1658; assisted in the restoration of Charles II in Ireland; knighted, 1660; serjeant-at-law in Ireland, 1660; commissioner of lands and for the settlement of Ireland, 1661; speaker of the Irish House of Commons, 1661–6. [xxxvii. 299]

MERYCK, SIR WILLIAM (d. 1668). [See MEYRICK.]

MERYON, CHARLES LEWIS (1783–1877), physician and biographer of Lady Hester Stanhope [q. v.]; educated at Merchant Taylors' School, London, St. John's College, Oxford, and St. Thomas's Hospital, London; M.A., 1809; M.D., 1817; accompanied Lady Hester Stanhope as medical attendant, 1810; revisited her in Syria; F.R.C.P., 1821; published 'Memoirs,' 1845, and 'Travels,' 1846, of Lady Hester Stanhope. [xxxvii. 301]

MESSING, RICHARD (d. 1462?). [See MISYN.]

MESTON, WILLIAM (1688?–1745), burlesque poet; educated at Marischal College, Aberdeen, and (1715) regent; governor of Dunnottar Castle during Jacobite rising, 1715; schoolmaster at Elgin and Turriff; published 'The Knight of the Kirk' (imitation of Hudibras), 1723. [xxxvii. 301]

METCALF, JOHN (1717–1810), commonly known as 'Blind Jack of Knaresborough'; became blind when six years old; distinguished athlete and dealer in horses; rode several races successfully; walked from Knaresborough to London and back; recruiting-serjeant, 1745; fought at Falkirk, 1746, and Culloden, 1746; set up a stage-coach between York and Knaresborough, 1754; a pioneer road-maker and bridge-builder; constructed about 180 miles of turnpike road; retired to a small farm, 1792. [xxxvii. 302]

METCALFE, CHARLES THEOPHILUS, first BARON METCALFE (1785–1846), provisional governor-general of India; educated at Eton; appointed to a Bengal writership, 1800; political agent successively to generals Lake, Smith, and Dowdeswell; sent on a mission to Lahore, 1808; resident of Delhi, 1811–20; developed the industrial resources of Delhi territory; resident of Hyderabad, 1820–7; member of the supreme council, 1827; provisional governor-general, 1835–6; G.C.B. and lieutenant-governor of the North-west Provinces, 1836–8; as governor of Jamaica, 1839–42, smoothed matters between proprietors and negroes; governor-general of Canada, 1843–5, where his tact won the general election, 1844, for the government; created Baron Metcalfe, 1845; retired, 1845. [xxxvii. 303]

METCALFE, FREDERICK (1815–1885), Scandinavian scholar; B.A. St. John's College, Cambridge, 1838; fellow of Lincoln College, Oxford, 1844–85; M.A., 1845; published works on Norway, Sweden, and Iceland. [xxxvii. 306]

METCALFE, JAMES (1817–1888), lieutenant-colonel, Indian army; natural son of Charles Theophilus Metcalfe, first baron Metcalfe [q. v.]; entered Bengal regiment, 1836; adjutant, 1839–46; aide-de-camp to the Marquis of Dalhousie, 1848–53; interpreter to Sir Colin Campbell during the mutiny; C.B., 1860. [xxxvii. 306]

METCALFE, NICHOLAS (1475?–1539), archdeacon of Rochester; B.A. Michaelhouse, Cambridge, 1494; D.D., 1507; archdeacon, 1515; master of St. John's College, Cambridge, 1516–37; opposed Henry VIII's divorce from Catherine and royal supremacy in doctrinal matters; founded scholarships at Cambridge. [xxxvii. 306]

METCALFE, ROBERT (1590?–1652), fellow of Trinity College, Cambridge; fellow of St. John's College, Cambridge, 1606; regius professor of Hebrew, Cambridge, till 1648; fellow and vice-master of Trinity College, Cambridge, 1648; benefactor of Beverley school. [xxxvii. 307]

METCALFE, THEOPHILUS (fl. 1649), stenographer; teacher of shorthand; published stenographic system, 1635; on lines of Shelton's 'Tachygraphy' (frequently reprinted and used by Isaac Watts). [xxxvii. 307]

METCALFE, SIR THEOPHILUS JOHN (1828–1883), joint-magistrate at Meerut; nephew of Charles Theophilus Metcalfe, first baron Metcalfe [q. v.]; entered Bengal civil service, 1848; joint-magistrate at Meerut and deputy-collector at Futtepur, 1857; joined army before Delhi; C.B., 1864. [xxxvii. 308]

METEYARD, ELIZA (1816–1879), author; contributed to periodicals, published novels, 'Life of Josiah Wedgwood,' 1865–6, besides other works on Wedgwood's friends and ware. [xxxvii. 308]

METFORD, WILLIAM ELLIS (1824–1899), inventor; apprenticed as engineer; employed on Wilts, Somerset, and Weymouth railway, 1846–50; associate of Institution of Civil Engineers, 1856; held appointment on East India railway, 1857–8; an explosive rifle bullet invented by him adopted by government, 1863; the pioneer of substitution of shallow grooving and a hardened cylindrical bullet expanding into it for deep grooving and soft bullets of lead; produced his first match rifle, 1865, and his first breech-loading rifle, 1871. A rifle which combined the Metford bore with the bolt-action and detachable magazine invented by the American, James P. Lee, was selected for British use, 1888. [Suppl. iii. 165]

METHOLD, SIR WILLIAM (1560?–1620), chief baron of the exchequer in Ireland; entered Lincoln's Inn, 1581 (bencher, 1608); serjeant, 1611; chief baron of the exchequer in Ireland, 1612; privy councillor and knighted, 1612; lord chief-justice in Ireland and joint-keeper of the great seal, 1619. [xxxvii. 309]

METHOLD, WILLIAM (d. 1653), nephew of Sir William Methold [q. v.]; entered East India Company, 1615; visited Golconda, 1622; director, 1628; sent on a mission to Persia, 1633; deputy-governor of the East India Company, 1650; published travels. [xxxvii. 309]

METHUEN, JOHN (1650?–1706), lord chancellor of Ireland; son of Paul Methuen (d. 1667) [q. v.]; educated at St. Edmund Hall, Oxford; barrister, Inner Temple; master in chancery, 1685; M.P., Devizes, 1690; envoy to Portugal, 1691; lord chancellor of Ireland, 1697; again sent to Portugal, 1702; ambassador extraordinary to Portugal, 1703; concluded 'Methuen Treaty' (commercial treaty with Portugal), 1703; died at Lisbon; buried in Westminster Abbey. [xxxvii. 310]

METHUEN, PAUL (*fl.* 1566), Scottish reformer; a Dundee baker; converted to protestantism; escaped arrest and preached publicly during the war, 1556; found guilty of usurping ministerial office, 1559; nominated to Jedburgh Church, 1560; deposed and excommunicated for adultery, 1562; fled to England; commanded by the assembly to repent publicly at Edinburgh, Dundee, and Jedburgh, 1566; partly obeyed and returned to England. [xxxvii. 311]

METHUEN, PAUL (*d.* 1667), Bradford clothier; obtained spinners from Holland. [xxxvii. 310]

METHUEN, SIR PAUL (1672–1757), diplomatist; son of John Methuen [q. v.]; entered diplomatic service, 1690; envoy to king of Portugal, 1697–1705; minister at Turin, 1705; ambassador to Portugal, 1706–8; M.P., Devizes, 1708–10, Brackley, 1713–47; lord of the admiralty, 1714–1717; ambassador to Spain and Morocco and privy councillor, 1714; comptroller of the household, 1720; K.B., 1725; retired, 1730; collected pictures. [xxxvii. 312]

METHVEN, first BARON (1495 ?–1551 ?). [See STEWART, HENRY.]

METHVEN, LORD (1746–1801). [See SMYTHE, DAVID.]

MEUDWY MÔN (1806–1889). [See JONES, OWEN.]

MEULAN, COUNTS OF. [See BEAUMONT, ROBERT DE, *d.* 1118; BEAUMONT, WALERAN DE, 1104–1166.]

MEURYG (*fl.* 1250). [See MEYRIG.]

MEVERALL, OTHOWELL (1585–1648), physician; B.A. Christ's College, Cambridge; M.D. Leyden, 1613; F.R.C.P., 1618; censor for eight years, registrar, 1639–40, president, 1641–4; lecturer on anatomy, 1638; lecturer to the Barber-Surgeons, 1638; notes of his lectures still extant. [xxxvii. 313]

MEWS, PETER (1619–1706), bishop of Winchester; educated at Merchant Taylors' School, London, and St. John's College, Oxford; M.A., 1645; served in the king's army, 1642; retired to Holland, 1648; acted as royalist agent; went to Scotland as secretary to Middleton, 1654; served in Flanders; rewarded at the Restoration; president of St. John's College, Oxford, 1667–73; vice-chancellor of Oxford University, 1669–73; bishop of Bath and Wells, 1672, of Winchester, 1684; opposed Monmouth at Sedgmoor, 1685; upheld the fellows of Magdalen College, Oxford, in their contention with James II, 1687; took the oaths to William and Mary. [xxxvii. 314]

MEY, JOHN (*d.* 1456), archbishop of Armagh; official of the court of Meath; archbishop of Armagh, 1444; as deputy lord-lieutenant was unsuccessful in maintaining order. [xxxvii. 316]

MEY, WILLIAM (*d.* 1560). [See MAY.]

MEYER, HENRY (1782 ?–1847), portrait-painter and engraver; nephew of John Hoppner [q. v.]; pupil of Bartolozzi; worked in mezzotint and painted portraits in oil and water colours; foundation member of the Society of British Artists, 1824; president, 1828. [xxxvii. 316]

MEYER, JEREMIAH (1735–1789), miniature-painter; born at Tübingen; pupil of Zincke; his profile of George III used on the coinage, 1761; original director of Incorporated Society of Artists; foundation member of Royal Academy. [xxxvii. 316]

MEYER, PHILIP JAMES (1732–1820), musician; born at Strassburg; improved the harp; visited England, 1772; returned to Paris, but finally settled in England, 1784; composer and teacher of the harp. [xxxvii. 317]

MEYNELL, CHARLES (1828–1882), Roman catholic divine; professor of metaphysics at St. Mary's College, Oscott; missioner of Caverswall, 1873; published controversial works. [xxxvii. 317]

MEYRICK, SIR GELLY or GILLY (1556 ?–1601), conspirator; son of Rowland Meyrick [q. v.]; attended Essex to Flushing, 1585; steward in Essex's household; accompanied him to Portugal, 1589, Normandy, 1591, and Cadiz, 1596, where he was knighted; with Essex in the Islands Voyage, 1597, and accompanied him to Ireland, 1599; defended Essex House, 1601; surrendered at Essex's bidding; hanged at Tyburn. [xxxvii. 318]

MEYRICK, JOHN (1538–1599), bishop of Sodor and Man; scholar of Winchester College, 1550; scholar, 1555, and fellow, 1557, of New College, Oxford; M.A., 1562; vicar of Hornchurch, 1570; bishop of Sodor and Man, 1575. [xxxvii. 319]

MEYRICK, SIR JOHN (*d.* 1638), English ambassador to Russia; agent for the London Russia Company at Jaroslavl, 1584, and at Moscow, 1592; forwarded political intelligence from Russia, 1596–7; visited England, 1600; ambassador to the czar, 1602; secured protection for English merchants from successive Russian czars; reappointed ambassador and knighted, 1614; took part in peace negotiations between Russia and Sweden, 1615; obtained commercial treaty, 1623; governor of Russia Company, 1628. [xxxvii. 319]

MEYRICK, SIR JOHN (*d.* 1659), parliamentarian general; grandson of Rowland Meyrick [q. v.]; fought under Essex in Flanders, 1620; served in the United Provinces, 1624, and Spain, 1625; knighted; wounded before Maestricht, 1632; M.P., Newcastle-under-Lyme, 1640; president of the council of war; general of ordnance, 1643; after Lostwithiel fled with Essex to Plymouth, withdrew from public affairs, 1649. [xxxvii. 320]

MEYRICK, ROWLAND (1505–1566), bishop of Bangor; principal of New Inn Hall, Oxford, 1534–6; D.C.L. Oxford, 1538; precentor of Llandewy-Velfrey, 1541; chancellor of Wells, 1547; canon and chancellor of St. David's, 1550; led the struggle between the chapter and Bishop Robert Ferrar [q. v.]; ejected from St. David's on his marriage, 1554; bishop of Bangor, 1559. [xxxvii. 321]

MEYRICK, SIR SAMUEL RUSH (1783–1848), antiquary; M.A., 1810, D.C.L., 1811, Queen's College, Oxford; ecclesiastical and admiralty lawyer; F.S.A., 1810; consulted on the arrangement of the armour at the Tower of London and Windsor Castle, 1826; knighted, 1832; high sheriff of Herefordshire, 1834; principal works: a history of Cardiganshire, 1810, and of arms and armour, 1824, and an edition of Lewis Dwnn's ' Heraldic Visitations of Wales,' 1840. [xxxvii. 322]

MEYRICK or **MERICKE**, SIR WILLIAM (*d.* 1668), civilian; scholar of Winchester College, and fellow of New College, Oxford, 1616–26; D.C.L. New College, Oxford, 1627; advocate, 1628; judge of the prerogative court of Canterbury, 1641; joined the king; ejected, 1648; reinstated and knighted, 1660. [xxxvii. 323]

MEYRIG or **MEURYG** (*fl.* 1250), treasurer of Llandaff; probably identical with the epigrammatist Maurice (*fl.* 1210) [q. v.]; wrote various Welsh works (none traced), including ' Y Cwtta Cyfarwydd ' (existing copy, *c.* 1445, possibly borrowed from an older manuscript). [xxxvii. 95]

MIALL, EDWARD (1809–1881), politician; independent minister at Leicester, 1834; established and edited the 'Nonconformist' (weekly), 1841; endeavoured to amalgamate with the chartists, 1842; procured a conference on disestablishment in London, 1844, which founded the 'British Anti-State Church Association'; M.P., Rochdale, 1852–7; commissioner on education, 1858; M.P., Bradford, 1869–74; endeavoured to bring forward disestablishment, 1871 and 1872; retired from public life, 1874; published pamphlets on disestablishment. [xxxvii. 324]

MICHAEL, BLAUNPAYN (*fl.* 1250), also called MICHAEL THE CORNISHMAN and MICHAEL THE ENGLISHMAN, Latin poet; possibly studied at Oxford and Paris; traditionally dean of Utrecht; wrote a satirical Latin poem, *c.* 1250. [xxxvii. 326]

MICHEL, SIR JOHN (1804–1886), field-marshal; educated at Eton; entered the army, 1823; lieutenant, 1825; passed his examinations, 1832; major, 1840; lieutenant-colonel, 1842; served in the Kaffir wars, 1846–7 and 1852–1853 (medal and C.B.); brevet-colonel, 1854; chief of the staff of the Turkish contingent in the Crimean war (medals); sent to the Cape, 1856; transferred to China; wrecked and carried to Singapore, 1857; placed on the Bombay staff, 1858; major-general, 1858; defeated the rebels at Beorora, Mingrauli, and Sindwaha, 1858 (K.C.B. and medal); commanded at Sinho and Pekin, 1860 (G.C.B. and medal); lieutenant-general, 1866; general, 1874; Irish privy councillor and commander of the forces in Ireland, 1875–1880; field-marshal, 1885. [xxxvii. 326]

MICHELBORNE, Sir EDWARD (d. 1611 ?), adventurer; served in the Low Countries, 1591; M.P., Bramber, 1593; accompanied Essex on Islands voyage, 1597; served in Ireland and was knighted, 1599; subscriber to the East India Company, 1600; implicated in Essex's rebellion, 1601; sailed for the East, 1604, nominally to trade; returned, after plundering a Chinese ship, 1606.
[xxxvii. 328]

MICHELBORNE, EDWARD (1565–1626), Latin poet; of St. Mary and Gloucester Halls, Oxford; friend of Charles Fitzgeffrey and Thomas Campion, contributing to the works of both.
[xxxvii. 328]

MICHELBORNE, MITCHELBURN, or **MICHELBURNE,** JOHN (1647–1721), governor of Londonderry; served under Percy Kirke (1646 ?–1691) [q. v.] at Tangier, 1680–3; acted as military governor during the siege of Londonderry after Governor Baker's death, 1689; sole governor after the relief, 1689; petitioned for arrears of pay, 1691 (paid, 1703); his sword and saddle preserved at Londonderry.
[xxxvii. 329]

MICHELL. [See also MICHEL, MITCHEL, and MITCHELL.]

MICHELL, CHARLES CORNWALLIS (1793–1851), lieutenant-colonel; entered army, 1809; distinguished himself in Peninsular war; lieutenant, 1813; captain, 1817; on the staff of Marshal Beresford in Lisbon; accompanied Beresford to the Brazils, 1820; master at Sandhurst, 1824, and Woolwich, 1825; major, 1826; superintendent of works at the Cape, 1828–48; assistant quartermaster-general during Kaffir war, 1833–4; lieutenant-colonel, 1841.
[xxxvii. 330]

MICHELL, EDWARD THOMAS (1787–1841), brigadier-general; lieutenant, 1803; commanded artillery in Peninsular war; served in Holland, 1813–14; brevetmajor, 1814; lieutenant-colonel, 1838; C.B., 1838; British commissioner in Spain, 1839–40; sent as brigadier-general to Syria; present at Medjdel, 1841; died of fever at Jaffa.
[xxxvii. 331]

MICHELL, Sir FRANCIS (fl. 1621), commissioner for enforcing monopolies; educated at Magdalen Hall, Oxford; secured reversion of clerk of the market, 1603; commissioner for enforcing gold and silver thread patents, 1618; knighted, 1620; tried for corruption; sentenced to degradation from knighthood and imprisoned, 1621; released immediately; subsequently petitioned for financial assistance.
[xxxvii. 331]

MICHELL, HENRY (1714–1789), scholar; fellow of Clare Hall, Cambridge; M.A., 1739; vicar of Brighton, 1744; assisted in development of Brighton; wrote on classical antiquities.
[xxxvii. 332]

MICHELL, JOHN (1724–1793), astronomer; fellow of Queens' College, Cambridge, 1749–64; M.A., 1752; B.D., 1761; lectured on Hebrew, arithmetic, geometry, and Greek; F.R.S., 1760; Woodwardian professor of geology, 1762; rector of Thornhill, 1767; wrote on artificial magnets, 1750, earthquakes, 1760, longitude, 1767, and fixed stars, 1767; invented apparatus for weighing the earth with torsion-balance.
[xxxvii. 333]

MICHELL or **MITCHELL,** MATTHEW (d. 1752), commodore; lieutenant, 1729; commanded the Gloucester, the only ship besides Anson's which doubled Cape Horn, 1740; commodore of a squadron off Flanders coast; M.P., Westbury, 1747.
[xxxvii. 334]

MICHELL, NICHOLAS (1807–1880), miscellaneous writer; encouraged by Campbell; author of poems and novels in prose and verse.
[xxxvii. 334]

MICHELL, RICHARD (1805–1877), first principal of Hertford College, Oxford; educated at Wadham College, Oxford; M.A., 1827; D.D., 1868; fellow of Lincoln College, 1830; first prælector of logic, 1839; Bampton lecturer, 1849; public orator, 1849–77; vice-principal, 1848; principal, 1868, of Magdalen Hall, 1848; agitated for its formation into a college; the Hall endowed with fellowships and scholarships by T. C. Baring, M.P., and called Hertford College, 1874.
[xxxvii. 335]

MICKLE, WILLIAM JULIUS (1735–1788), poet; owner of a brewery in Edinburgh, 1757; failed, 1763; corrector to Clarendon Press, Oxford, 1765–71; author of 'The Concubine,' 1767, and 'Voltaire in the Shades,' 1770; translated the 'Lusiad' of Camoens, 1775 (reprinted, 1778, 1798, and 1807); as secretary to George Johnstone (1730–1787) [q. v.]; sailed to Portugal, 1779; received

share of naval prizes; wrote the ballad 'Cumnor Hall'; credited with the song 'There's na'e luck about the hoose.'
[xxxvii. 336]

MICKLETHWAITE, Sir JOHN (1612–1682), physician; studied at Leyden, Padua, and Oxford; physician at St. Bartholomew's Hospital, London, 1653; F.R.C.P., 1643; Gulstonian lecturer, 1644; censor seven times; president, 1676–81; attended Charles II; knighted, 1681.
[xxxvii. 337]

MIDDIMAN, SAMUEL (1750–1831), engraver; engraved Shakespearean scenes for Boydell. [xxxvii. 338]

MIDDLEMORE, GEORGE (d. 1850), lieutenant-general; entered the army, 1793; lieutenant, 1794; major, 1804; served at the Cape and in India, Egypt, and Portugal (Talavera medal); C.B., 1815; lieutenant-colonel, 1815; major-general, 1830; commanded in West Indies, 1830–5; governor of St. Helena, 1836; Napoleon's remains removed during his governorship; lieutenant-general, 1841.
[xxxvii. 338]

MIDDLESEX, EARLS OF. [See CRANFIELD, LIONEL, first EARL, 1575–1645; SACKVILLE, CHARLES, first EARL of the second creation, 1638–1706.]

MIDDLETON. [See also MYDDELTON.]

MIDDLETON, CHARLES, second EARL OF MIDDLETON and titular EARL OF MONMOUTH (1640 ?–1719), secretary of state to James II; eldest son of John Middleton, first earl of Middleton [q. v.]; accompanied his father abroad, 1653; envoy extraordinary at Vienna, 1660; privy councillor and joint-secretary of Scotland, 1682; privy councillor and secretary of state for England, 1684; M.P., Winchelsea, 1685; endeavoured to induce James to abandon his flight and summon parliament, 1688; remained in England; apprehended, 1692; released; chief adviser of the exiled king at St. Germain; created Earl of Monmouth by James Edward the Old Pretender, 1701; became a Roman catholic, 1703; responsible for the abortive expedition to Scotland, 1707; resigned office of secretary of state for England, 1713, and returned to St. Germain.
[xxxvii. 339]

MIDDLETON, CHARLES, first BARON BARHAM (1726–1813), admiral; on convoy service; cruised in West Indies, 1761; comptroller of the navy, 1778–90; created baronet, 1781; M.P., Rochester, 1784; rear-admiral, 1787; vice-admiral, 1793; admiral, 1795; lord commissioner of the admiralty, 1794; first lord of the admiralty, 1805, and created Baron Barham, 1805.
[xxxvii. 341]

MIDDLETON, CHRISTOPHER (1560 ?–1628), translator and poet; translated Digby's 'Art of Swimming,' 1595; published works, including 'The Famous Historie of Chinon,' 1597, and 'The Legend of Humphrey, Duke of Glocester,' 1600.
[xxxvii. 341]

MIDDLETON, CHRISTOPHER (d. 1770), naval commander and arctic voyager; employed by the Hudson's Bay Company, 1720; observed variation of magnetic needle, 1721; discovered how to obtain true time at sea with Hadley's quadrant, c. 1737; F.R.S., 1737; commander in the navy; set out to discover the north-west passage, 1741; arrived in Hudson's Bay too late in the season for discovery, 1741; examined the coast to the northward and entered a river inlet, 1742; returned to England, 1742; stationed off Scottish and Flemish coasts, 1745.
[xxxvii. 342]

MIDDLETON, CONYERS (1683–1750), divine; M.A. Trinity College, Cambridge, 1707; fellow of Trinity College, Cambridge, 1706; known for his musical tastes; one of thirty fellows who petitioned against Bentley, the master of Trinity, 1710; D.D. on George I's visit to Cambridge, 1717; involved in a bitter dispute with Bentley about the fees, 1717; an action for a libel contained in 'The Present State of Trinity College,' 1719, brought against him by Bentley, a compromise resulting; 'Protobibliothecarius' of the university library, 1721; in Italy, 1724–5; published 'Letter from Rome,' 1729; Woodwardian professor, 1731–4; engaged in a controversy with Waterland on the historical accuracy of the bible, for which he was threatened with the loss of his degrees; published a 'Life of Cicero,' 1741, mainly plagiarised from William Bellenden (d. 1633 ?) [q. v.]; excited much criticism by his latitudinarian treatise on 'Miracles,' 1748.
[xxxvii. 343]

MIDDLETON, DAVID (d. 1615), merchant and seacaptain; younger brother of John and Sir Henry Middleton [q. v.]; joint-commander in a voyage to West Indies

1601; made successful voyages to East Indies, 1604–6, 1607–8, and 1609–11; wrecked on the coast of Madagascar, 1615. [xxxvii. 348]

MIDDLETON, ERASMUS (1739–1805), author; of St. Edmund Hall, Oxford; expelled, 1768, for publicly praying and preaching; curate in London; rector of Turvey, 1804; published theological works.
[xxxvii. 349]

MIDDLETON, HENRY (d. 1587), printer; probably son of William Middleton (fl. 1541–1547) [q. v.]; admitted of the Stationers' Company, 1567; partner with Thomas East, 1567–72; under-warden of the Stationers' Company, 1587. [xxxvii. 349]

MIDDLETON, SIR HENRY (d. 1613), merchant and sea-captain; promoted captain during the first voyage of the East India Company, 1602; commanded the second voyage, 1604–6; knighted, 1606; commanded the sixth voyage, 1610–13; escaped from imprisonment at Mocha; attempted (1611–12) to trade at Surat and Dabul; died in Java. [xxxvii. 350]

MIDDLETON, SIR HUGH (1560?–1631). [See MYDDELTON.]

MIDDLETON, JANE (1645–1692). [See MYDDELTON.]

MIDDLETON, JOHN, first EARL OF MIDDLETON (1619–1674), pikeman in Hepburn's regiment in France; major in covenant army, 1639; lieutenant-general in parliamentary army; second in command at Philiphaugh, 1645; negotiated Montrose's submission, 1646, suppressed royalist rising, 1647; as lieutenant-general of the Scottish cavalry distinguished himself at Preston, 1648; wounded and taken prisoner at Worcester, 1651; escaped from the Tower to France; captain-general of a highland force, dispersed by Monck, 1654; joined the king at Cologne; created an earl by Charles II, 1656 (the creation confirmed at the Restoration); commander-in-chief, governor of Edinburgh Castle, and lord high commissioner to the Scottish parliament, 1660; urged restoration of episcopacy in Scotland, 1661; accused of withholding letters from the king, consenting to measures without authority, and taking bribes, 1663; deprived of his offices; subsequently became governor of Tangier, where he died.
[xxxvii. 352]

MIDDLETON, JOHN (1827–1856), landscape-painter.
[xxxvii. 354]

MIDDLETON, JOHN HENRY (1846–1896), archæologist and architect; educated at Cheltenham College and Exeter College, Oxford; studied art and archæology; travelled abroad; practised as architect at Westminster till 1885; F.S.A., 1879, vice-president, 1894; contributed to 'Encyclopædia Britannica' (9th edit.); Slade professor of fine art at Cambridge, 1886; hon. M.A., 1886, and Litt.D., 1892, Cambridge; M.A., 1887, and D.C.L., 1894, Oxford; director of Fitzwilliam Museum, Cambridge, 1889–92; art director at South Kensington Museum, London, 1892–6; published works on artistic and archæological subjects. [Suppl. iii. 166]

MIDDLETON, JOSHUA (1647–1721), quaker; early joined the quakers and travelled as a minister.
[xxxvii. 354]

MIDDLETON, MARMADUKE (d. 1593), bishop of Waterford and St. David's; left Oxford without a degree; obtained preferment in Ireland; bishop of Waterford, 1579; accused of plundering the cathedral, but acquitted; translated to St. David's, 1582; D.D. Oxford, 1583; fined by the Star-chamber, 1589, and handed over to the high commission court for degradation, which took place at Lambeth House. [xxxvii. 355]

MIDDLETON, PATRICK (1662–1736), Scottish nonjuring divine; M.A. St. Leonard's College, St. Andrews, 1680; summoned 1689, 1692, 1716, and 1717 for not praying for William III and George I; published theological works. [xxxvii. 356]

MIDDLETON, RICHARD (fl. 1280), Franciscan; B.D., 1283, and D.D. Paris; one of the fifteen chief doctors of his order; wrote works of theology and canon law.
[xxxvii. 356]

MIDDLETON, RICHARD (d. 1641), divine; B.A. Jesus College, Oxford, 1586; prebendary of Brecon, 1589; archdeacon of Cardigan, 1589–1629; published theological works. [xxxvii. 357]

MIDDLETON, THOMAS (1570?–1627), dramatist; entered at Gray's Inn, 1593; became connected with the stage, 1592; collaborated with Dekker, Rowley, Munday, Drayton, Webster, and others; turned his attention to satirical comedies of contemporary manners, 1607–8; wrote pageants and masques for city ceremonials; city chronologer, 1620; wrote a political drama, 'A Game at Chess,' 1624, for which he and the players were censured on the representations of the Spanish ambassador. His plays (which were very popular) include 'The Old Law,' 1656 (in collaboration with Massinger and Rowley); 'Michaelmas Terme,' 1607, 'A Trick to catch the Old-One,' 1608, 'The Familie of Love,' 1608, 'A Mad World, my Masters,' 1608, 'The Roaring Girle,' 1611 (with Dekker), 'A Faire Quarrell,' 1617 (with Rowley), 'More Dissemblers besides Women,' 1657, 'A Game at Chess,' 1624, 'A Chast Mayd in Cheape-side,' 1630, 'No Wit, no Help like a Woman's,' 1657, 'Women beware Women,' 1657; 'The Witch' (not published until 1778), 'Anything for a Quiet Life,' 1662, 'The Widow,' 1652 (with Ben Jonson and Fletcher). His pageants and masques include 'The Triumphs of Truth,' 1613, 'Civitatis Amor,' 1616, 'The Tryumphs of Honor and Industry,' 1617, 'The Inner Temple Masque,' 1619, 'The Triumphs of Love and Antiquity,' 1619, 'The World Tost at Tennis,' 1620, 'The Triumphs of Honor and Virtue,' 1622, 'The Triumphs of Integrity,' 1623, 'The Triumphs of Health and Prosperity,' 1626. He is supposed to have also written some miscellaneous verse and prose. [xxxvii. 357]

MIDDLETON, SIR THOMAS (1550–1631). [See MYDDELTON.]

MIDDLETON, SIR THOMAS (1586–1666). [See MYDDELTON.]

MIDDLETON, THOMAS FANSHAW (1769–1822), bishop of Calcutta; of Christ's Hospital and Pembroke College, Cambridge; M.A., 1795; D.D., 1808; curate of Gainsborough, 1792; edited 'The Country Spectator,' 1792–3; rector of Tansor, 1795, of Bytham, 1802; prebendary of Lincoln, 1809; edited 'British Critic,' 1811; F.R.S., 1814; bishop of Calcutta, 1814; organised schools, 1815, and established the Bishop's Mission College, Calcutta, 1820; died at Calcutta. [xxxvii. 363]

MIDDLETON, WILLIAM OF (d. 1261). [See MELITON.]

MIDDLETON or **MYDDYLTON**, WILLIAM (fl. 1541–1547), printer; succeeded to Pynson and Redman's press; printed legal, medical, and other learned works.
[xxxvii. 365]

MIDDLETON, WILLIAM (d. 1613), protestant controversialist; of Queens' College, Cambridge; B.A., 1571; fellow, 1572–90; denied Cambridge M.A.; M.A. Oxford; deprived of fellowship for not taking his M.A.; restored by Lord Burghley, chancellor of Cambridge University; incorporated M.A. Cambridge, 1576; B.D., 1582; elected master of Corpus Christi College, Cambridge, in place of John Jegon [q. v.], who was subsequently restored; published defence of protestantism, 1606. [xxxvii. 365]

MIDDLETON, WILLIAM (1556?–1621). [See MYDDELTON.]

MIDGLEY, ROBERT (1653–1723), alleged author of the 'Turkish Spy'; B.A. St. John's College, Cambridge, 1673; M.D. Christ's College, Cambridge, 1687; candidate of the College of Physicians, 1687; licenser of the press, 1686; remembered chiefly as the 'editor' of 'Letters writ by a Turkish Spy,' 1687–93 (probably written in French by a Genoese, Giovanni Paolo Marana, translated by Bradshaw and edited by Midgley). [xxxvii. 366]

MIDLETON, first VISCOUNT (1660?–1728). [See BRODRICK, ALAN.]

MIDNIGHT (MARY). [Pseudonym of NEWBERY, JOHN, q. v., and SMART, CHRISTOPHER, q. v.]

MIEGE, GUY (1644–1718?), miscellaneous writer; native of Lausanne; came to London, 1661; under-secretary to Charles Howard, first earl of Carlisle [q. v.]; ambassador extraordinary to Russia, Sweden, and Denmark, 1663; published account of the embassy, 1669; best-known work, the 'New State of England,' 1691, Scotland and Ireland being subsequently added; published also French and English dictionaries and grammars.
[xxxvii. 367]

MIERS, JOHN (1789–1879), engineer and botanist; accompanied Lord Cochrane to Chile, 1818; made collections of birds, insects, and plants; settled in London, 1836; F.L.S., 1839; F.R.S., 1843; published 'Travels in Chile and La Plata,' 1825, and botanical works.
[xxxvii. 369]

MILBANKE, MARK (1725?–1805), admiral; entered navy, 1737; lieutenant, 1744; promoted to command the Serpent, 1746; commissioner to Morocco, 1759; rear-admiral of the white, 1779; sat on the court-martial of Admiral Keppel; vice-admiral of the blue, 1780; port-admiral at Plymouth, 1783–6; commander-in-chief in Newfoundland, 1790–2; admiral, 1793; commander-in-chief at Portsmouth, 1799–1803. [xxxvii. 369]

MILBOURN, JOHN (fl. 1773–1790), portrait painter; exhibited at the Royal Academy, 1772–4. [xxxvii. 370]

MILBOURNE, LUKE (1622–1668), ejected non-conformist divine; M.A. Emmanuel College, Cambridge, 1646; perpetual curate of Honiley; royalist; in retirement at Kenilworth, 1645–60; ejected, 1662; schoolmaster at Coventry; compelled to leave by the Five Mile Act, 1666. [xxxvii. 370]

MILBOURNE, LUKE (1649–1720), poet; son of Luke Milbourne (1622–1668) [q. v.]; of Pembroke Hall, Cambridge; held chaplaincies at Hamburg, Rotterdam, and Harwich; rector of St. Ethelburga's, London, 1704; supported Dr. Sacheverell; attempted an English rendering of Virgil; chiefly remembered by his subsequent strictures on Dryden's translations of Virgil, and the retaliation made by Dryden and Pope. [xxxvii. 371]

MILBURG, MILDBURGA, or MILDBURH (d. 722?), saint and abbess; reputed miracle-worker; built nunnery at Winwick or Wenlock, 680, restored by the Earl of Shrewsbury, 1080; her day 23 Feb.
[xxxvii. 372]

MILDMAY, SIR ANTHONY (d. 1617), ambassador; son of Sir Walter Mildmay [q. v.]; was educated at Peterhouse, Cambridge; entered at Gray's Inn, 1579; knighted, 1596; ambassador to Henry IV of France, 1596–7. [xxxvii. 376]

MILDMAY, SIR HENRY (d. 1664?), master of the king's jewel-house; knighted, 1617; master of the king's jewel-house, 1620; M.P., Maldon, 1620, Westbury, 1624, Maldon again, 1625–60; attended Charles I to Scotland, 1639; deserted the king, 1641; revenue commissioner, 1645–52; left as hostage in Scotland, 1646; present at Charles I's trial; member of state councils, 1649–52; attempted escape when called on to account for the king's jewels, 1660; degraded and sentenced to imprisonment for life; warrant issued for his transportation to Tangier, 1664; died at Antwerp on the way. [xxxvii. 376]

MILDMAY, SIR WALTER (1520?–1589), chancellor of the exchequer and founder of Emmanuel College, Cambridge; educated at Christ's College, Cambridge; entered Gray's Inn, 1546; surveyor-general of the court of augmentation, 1545; knighted, and appointed revenue commissioner, 1547; examiner of the mint accounts, 1550; M.P., Maldon, 1553, Peterborough, 1553, Northamptonshire, 1557–89; after Elizabeth's accession directed the issue of a new coinage, 1560; chancellor of the exchequer and auditor of the duchy of Lancaster, 1566; a commissioner at the trial of Mary Queen of Scots, 1586; founded Emmanuel College, Cambridge, 1585; benefactor of Christ's Hospital, London, Christ's College, Cambridge, and other educational institutions. [xxxvii. 374]

MILDRED or MILDRYTH (d. 700?), saint and abbess; sister of Milburg [q. v.]; instructed in ecclesiastical learning at Chelles, near Paris; being persecuted by the abbess, escaped to England and succeeded her mother as abbess of Minster, St. Augustine's, and St. Gregory's, Canterbury. The two latter houses claimed possession of her body. [xxxvii. 376]

MILES. [See also MILLES.]

MILES DE GLOUCESTER, EARL OF HEREFORD (d. 1143). [See GLOUCESTER.]

MILES, CHARLES POPHAM (1810–1891), divine; son of William Augustus Miles [q. v.]; midshipman in the navy; M.A. Caius College, Cambridge, 1851; chaplain of the Sailors' Home, London Docks, 1838; principal of Malta Protestant College, 1858–67; rector of Monkwearmouth, 1867–83; edited his father's correspondence and published religious treatises. [xxxvii. 380]

MILES, EDWARD (d. 1798), miniature-painter; copied some of Reynolds's pictures; exhibited at the Royal Academy, 1775–97. [xxxvii. 377]

MILES, GEORGE FRANCIS, known as FRANK MILES (1852–1891), painter; known for a series of pretty female heads; student of Japanese art and botany.
[xxxvii. 377]

MILES, HENRY (1698–1763), dissenting minister and scientific writer; F.R.S., 1743; communicated scientific papers to 'Philosophical Transactions,' 1741–53.
[xxxvii. 378]

MILES, JOHN (1621–1684). [See MYLES.]

MILES, MRS. SIBELLA ELIZABETH (1800–1882), poetess; née Hatfield; kept boarding-school at Penzance; married Alfred Miles, 1833; published poems and prose works. [xxxvii. 378]

MILES, WILLIAM (d. 1860), major-general, Indian army; entered army, 1799; lieutenant, 1800; captain, 1815; concluded treaty with rajah of Rodanpur, 1820; major, 1821; lieutenant-colonel, 1824; captured Mergui; concluded treaty with Suigam chiefs, 1826; political resident at Pallampur, 1829; brevet-colonel, 1829; translated oriental works. [xxxvii. 379]

MILES, WILLIAM AUGUSTUS (1753?–1817), political writer; held appointment in ordnance office, 1770; served under Rodney in West Indies; prisoner of war in St. Lucia; settled at Seraing, near Liège, 1783; corresponded with Pitt; met all the leading French politicians at Paris, 1790; pensioned, 1791; suggested a Suez canal, 1791; author of political tracts and two comic operas; published pamphlet on the then Prince of Wales's debts, 1795, which went through thirteen editions; died at Paris, where he was collecting materials for a history of the French revolution. [xxxvii. 379]

MILEY, JOHN (1805?–1861), Roman catholic divine; educated at Maynooth and Rome; D.D.; endeavoured to reconcile the young Ireland party and Daniel O'Connell [q. v.], 1846; accompanied O'Connell to Italy, 1847; rector of the Irish College, Paris, 1849–59; vicar of Bray, 1859; wrote on ecclesiastical history. [xxxvii. 381]

MILL, HENRY (1683?–1771), engineer; engineer to the New River Company, 1720; carried out Houghton Hall water supply; possibly invented a type-writer, 1714.
[xxxvii. 381]

MILL or MILLE, HUMPHREY (fl. 1646), verse-writer. [xxxvii. 382]

MILL, JAMES (fl. 1744), Indian colonel; captain and second in command of the East India Company's military in Bengal, 1743; submitted project for the conquest of India to Francis, duke of Lorraine, 1744. [xxxvii. 382]

MILL, JAMES (1773–1836), utilitarian philosopher; educated at Edinburgh by Sir John Stuart of Fettercairn; licensed to preach, 1798; came to London, 1802; became editor of the 'Literary Journal,' 1803, and the 'St. James's Chronicle,' 1805; wrote for the 'Edinburgh Review,' 1808–1813; met Bentham, 1808; promulgator of Benthamism in England; supported his family by writing, at the same time working at his history of India; abandoned theology after his acquaintance with Bentham; took active part in Bell and Lancaster educational controversy, supporting the Lancastrian institution; formed an association to set up a 'Chrestomathic' school for superior education on the same lines, 1814, the outcome being the formation of the London University, 1825; published 'History of India,' 1818; assistant to the examiner of India correspondence, 1819; second assistant, 1821; assistant-examiner, 1823; examiner, 1830; encouraged Ricardo to publish his political economy; took part in meetings at Ricardo's house, which resulted in the 'Political Economy Club,' founded 1820; contributed utilitarian articles to the 'Encyclopædia Britannica,' 1816–23, and to the 'Westminster Review,' started (1824) as the official Benthamite organ; wrote in the 'London Review,' 1835. He published an essay on the export of grain, 1804, 'Commerce Defended,' 1808, 'History of India,' 1818, 'Elements of Political Economy,' 1821, 'Analysis of the Phenomena of the Human Mind,' 1829, and 'Fragment on Mackintosh,' 1835. [xxxvii. 382]

MILL, JOHN (1645–1707), principal of St. Edmund Hall, Oxford; M.A. Queen's College, Oxford, 1669; D.D., 1681; speaker of the 'Oratio Panegyrica' at the opening of the Sheldonian Theatre, 1669; prebendary of Exeter, 1677; rector of Bletchington and chaplain to Charles II, 1681; elected principal of St. Edmund Hall, Oxford, 1685; prebendary of Canterbury, 1704; collated all the readings of the principal manuscripts in England and on the continent in his edition of the New Testament in Greek, 1707.
[xxxvii. 388]

MILL, JOHN STUART (1806–1873), philosopher; son of James Mill (1773–1836) [q. v.]; educated entirely by his father; before he was fourteen had studied classical literature, logic, political economy, history, general literature, and mathematics; visited France, 1820; junior clerk in the India House, 1823; formed the Utilitarian Society, which met to read essays and discuss them, 1823–6; edited Bentham's 'Treatise upon Evidence,' 1825; assisted in the formation of the Speculative Society, 1826; visited Paris, 1830; contributed to the 'London Review,' started (1835) as an organ of philosophical radicalism; was its proprietor, 1837–40; published his 'Logic,' 1843, and 'Political Economy,' 1848; retired with a pension on the dissolution of the East India Company, 1858; M.P., Westminster, 1865–8; a follower of William Ewart Gladstone [q. v.]; rector of St. Andrews University, 1866; returned to literary pursuits, 1868. His works, devoted to the humanising and widening of utilitarian teaching, include 'A System of Logic,' 1843, essays on 'Political Economy,' 1844, 'Principles of Political Economy,' 1848, 'On Liberty,' 1859, 'Thoughts on Parliamentary Reform,' 1859, 'Representative Government,' 1861, 'Utilitarianism,' 1863, 'Examination of Sir William Hamilton's Philosophy,' 1865, 'Auguste Comte and Positivism,' 1865, 'The Subjection of Women,' 1869, 'Chapters and Speeches on the Irish Land Question,' 1870, 'Autobiography,' 1873, and 'Three Essays on Religion,' posthumously published, 1874.
[xxxvii. 390]

MILL, WALTER (d. 1558). [See MYLNE.]

MILL, WILLIAM HODGE (1792–1853), orientalist; sixth wrangler, Trinity College, Cambridge, 1813; fellow, 1814; M.A., 1816; first principal of Bishop's College, Calcutta, 1820; vice-president, Bengal Asiatic Society, 1833–7; regius professor of Hebrew at Cambridge, with canonry at Ely, 1848; chief work, 'Christa-Sangitā,' 1831 (the Gospel-story in Sanskrit). [xxxvii. 400]

MILLAIS, SIR JOHN EVERETT (1829 – 1896), painter, and president of Royal Academy; a native of Southampton; lived during various periods of early life in Jersey and Brittany; came to London, 1838; studied art under Henry Sass [q. v.]; entered Royal Academy schools, 1840, and obtained gold medal for painting 'The Young Men of Benjamin seizing their Brides,' 1846; first exhibited at Royal Academy 'Pizarro seizing the Inca of Peru,' 1846; originated (1848), with Mr. Holman Hunt, the pre-Raphaelite movement, soon joined by Dante Gabriel Rossetti [q. v.], who exerted influence on some of Millais's subsequent work; his most successful pre-Raphaelite picture, 'Isabella,' 1849; great hostility aroused by his 'Christ in the House of his Parents,' 1850, owing to the unconventional treatment of a scene in the life of the Holy Family; among the most notable of his works at this period are 'The Return of the Dove to the Ark' and 'Mariana of the Moated Grange,' 1851, 'The Huguenot' and 'Ophelia,' 1852, 'The Proscribed Royalist' and 'The Order of Release,' 1853; A.R.A., 1853; married, 1855, Euphemia Chalmers, daughter of George Gray, who had obtained a decree of the 'nullity' of her marriage with John Ruskin [q. v.]; exhibited 'Autumn Leaves' and 'Peace concluded,' 1856, 'Sir Isumbras at the Ford' and 'The Escape of a Heretic,' 1857, 'Apple Blossoms' and 'The Vale of Rest,' 1859; deviated from the pre-Raphaelite manner in his 'Black Brunswicker,' 1860; R.A., 1863; exhibited 'The Eve of St. Agnes,' 1863, 'Jephthah,' 1867, 'Rosalind and Celia,' 1868, 'The Boyhood of Ralegh,' 'The Knight Errant,' 1870, and 'Victory, O Lord,' 'Chill October' (his first exhibited pure landscape), 1871; after 1870 devoted himself mainly to portrait and landscape, and to single figures of children and pretty girls under fancy titles such as 'Cherry Ripe'; exhibited 'The North-West Passage,' 1874, 'A Yeoman of the Guard,' 1877, 'The Princes in the Tower,' 1878, and 'The Princess Elizabeth,' 1879; painted his own portrait for the Uffizi Gallery, Florence, 1880; created baronet, 1885;

the last subject picture exhibited by him, 'The Forerunner'; P.R.A., 1896. [Suppl. iii. 167]

MILLAR. [See also MILLER and MÜLLER.]

MILLAR, ANDREW (fl. 1503–1508). [See MYLLAR.]

MILLAR, ANDREW (1707–1768), publisher; published Johnson's 'Dictionary,' Thomson's 'Seasons,' Fielding's works, and the histories of Robertson and Hume.
[xxxvii. 400]

MILLAR, JAMES (1762–1827), physician and miscellaneous writer; educated at Glasgow; M.D. and F.R.C.P. Edinburgh; chaplain to Glasgow University; edited the fourth and part of the fifth editions of the 'Encyclopædia Britannica,' 1810–17, also the 'Encyclopædia Edinensis,' 1827. [xxxvii. 401]

MILLAR, JOHN (1735–1801), professor of law; educated under Adam Smith at Glasgow; intimate with James Watt; an advocate, 1760; professor of law at Glasgow, 1761; lectured on civil law, jurisprudence, Scottish and English law; member of the Literary Society; sympathised with the French revolution, and opposed the slave trade; published 'The Origin of the Distinction of Ranks,' 1771, and 'Historical View of the English Government,' 1787. [xxxvii. 401]

MILLAR, JOHN (1733–1805), medical writer; M.D. Edinburgh; physician, Westminster General Dispensary, London, 1774; published medical works. [xxxvii. 403]

MILLAR, WILLIAM (d. 1838), lieutenant-general; colonel commandant, royal artillery; son of John Millar (1735–1801) [q. v.]; second lieutenant, royal artillery, 1781; first lieutenant, 1787; captain lieutenant, 1794; captain, 1799; major, 1806; lieutenant-colonel, 1806; colonel, 1814; major-general, 1831; colonel commandant, 1834; lieutenant-general, 1837; originated the 10-inch and 8-inch shell-guns; inspector-general of artillery, 1827; director-general of the field-train department, 1833.
[xxxvii. 404]

MILLER. [See also MILLAR and MÜLLER.]

MILLER, ANDREW (d. 1763), mezzotint-engraver, mainly of portraits. [xxxvii. 404]

MILLER, ANNA, LADY (1741–1781), verse-writer; née Riggs; married John Miller of Ballicasey, 1765; travelled in Italy, 1770–1, publishing an account; her husband created an Irish baronet, 1778; instituted a literary salon at Batheaston, at which each guest was invited to contribute an original poem; four volumes of the compositions published. [xxxvii. 405]

MILLER, EDWARD (1731–1807), organist and historian of Doncaster; trained by Dr. Burney at King's Lynn; organist of Doncaster, 1756–1807; created Mus. Doc. Cambridge, 1786; set the psalms to music, 1774; published 'Thorough Bass and Composition,' 1787, 'History and Antiquities of Doncaster,' 1804; taught Francis Linley [q. v.]. [xxxvii. 406]

MILLER, GEORGE (1764 – 1848), divine; M.A. Trinity College, Dublin, 1789; fellow, 1789; D.D., 1799; assistant-professor of modern history, Dublin, 1799–1803; head-master of the royal school, Armagh, 1817; as vicar-general of the diocese of Armagh (1843) settled important points in law of marriage and divorce; member of the Royal Irish Academy; published two pamphlets on the Athanasian creed, 1825 and 1826, besides sermons and miscellanea; Newman's 'Tract XC.' partly elicited by his 'Letter' to Pusey, 1840. [xxxvii. 406]

MILLER, HUGH (1802–1856), man of letters and geologist; stonemason by trade; accountant in the Commercial Bank at Cromarty, 1834; contributed to Mackay Wilson's 'Tales of the Borders'; became editor of the 'Witness,' 1840, the non-intrusionists' organ; his 'Old Red Sandstone' (published serially in the 'Witness') republished, 1841; chief works, 'Footprints of the Creator,' 1847, 'My Schools and Schoolmasters,' 1852, and 'The Testimony of the Rocks,' published, 1857. [xxxvii. 408]

MILLER, JAMES (1706–1744), playwright; of Wadham College, Oxford; lecturer at Trinity Chapel, Conduit Street, London; took to dramatic writing to enlarge his income; but by his supposed representation of the keepers of Temple coffee-house caused the templars to ruin his subsequent pieces; his principal plays, 'Humours of

Oxford,' 1730, ' The Man of Taste,' 1735 (an adaptation of Molière, to be distinguished from a like-named piece attacking Pope), 'Universal Passion,' 1737, 'The Coffee-house,' 1737, and 'Mahomet the Impostor,' 1744. [xxxvii. 410]

MILLER, JAMES (1812–1864), surgeon; educated at St. Andrews and Edinburgh Universities; L.R.C.S., 1832; assistant to Robert Liston [q. v.]; 1842; surgeon in ordinary to Queen Victoria, 1848; published surgical works. [xxxvii. 411]

MILLER, JOHN (fl. 1780), architect; studied in Italy; practised in London; published books on architecture, with designs. [xxxvii. 412]

MILLER, JOHN, otherwise JOHANN SEBASTIAN MÜLLER (1715?–1790?), draughtsman and engraver; born at Nuremberg; came to England, 1744; published ' Illustration of the Sexual System in Plants,' 1777 (arranged according to the system of Dr. Linnæus); also executed other plates, including those for Lord Bute's ' Botanical Tables,' 1785. [xxxvii. 412]

MILLER, JOHN CALE (1814–1880), evangelical divine; M.A. Lincoln College, Oxford, 1838; D.D., 1857; curate of Park Chapel, Chelsea; incumbent of St. Martin's, Birmingham, 1846; most successful among the working classes; canon of Rochester, 1873; published theological works. The Miller Hospital of Greenwich was opened (1884) as a memorial to him. [xxxvii. 414]

MILLER, JOHN FREDERICK (fl. 1785), draughtsman; son of John Miller (1715?–1790?) [q. v.]; accompanied Sir Joseph Banks to Ireland, 1772; published ' Various Subjects of Natural History,' 1785. [xxxvii. 414]

MILLER, JOSEPH or JOSIAS, commonly called JOE MILLER (1684–1738), actor and reputed humorist; joined Drury Lane Company, 1709; a prominent member of the company; temporarily engaged at Goodman's Fields, London, 1731; returned to Drury Lane, London, 1732; described as a natural spirited comedian. After his death a collection of jests by John Mottley [q. v.] was published, unwarrantably entitled 'Joe Miller's Jests,' 1739, which became a standard book. [xxxvii. 415]

MILLER, JOSIAH (1832–1880), hymnologist; M.A. London, 1855; independent minister and missionary secretary; wrote biographical sketches of hymn-writers and hymns. [xxxvii. 417]

MILLER, MRS. LYDIA FALCONER (1811?–1876), authoress; née Fraser; married Hugh Miller [q. v.], 1837; assisted him in the management of the 'Witness' and edited his works after his death; published stories for the young under the pseudonym of Harriet Myrtle. [xxxvii. 417]

MILLER, PATRICK (1731–1815), projector of steam navigation; brother of Sir Thomas Miller [q. v.]; Edinburgh merchant, 1760; a director of the Bank of Scotland, 1767; deputy-governor, 1790; shareholder in Carron Iron Company; purchased estate of Dalswinton, 1785; devoted himself to agricultural improvements and shipbuilding experiments; his first idea, a ship with two or three hulls propelled by paddle-wheels placed between the hulls and worked by men from capstans on deck; subsequently experimented with a double boat fitted with a steam engine made by Symington, 1788 and 1789; lost heart at not meeting with James Watt's approval; introduced fiorin grass into Scotland, 1810; numbered among his friends Burns and the Nasmyths. [xxxvii. 417]

MILLER, PHILIP (1691–1771), gardener; began business as a florist; appointed gardener of the Chelsea Botanical Garden on Sir Hans Sloane's recommendation, 1722; discovered the method of flowering bulbous plants in bottles filled with water, 1730; visited Holland between 1723 and 1730; experimented in fertilisation, 1751; grew rare plants; chief works, ' The Gardener's and Florist's Dictionary,' 1724 (translated into German, Dutch, and French), 'Gardener's Kalendar,' 1732, and ' Method of cultivating Madder,' 1758. [xxxvii. 420]

MILLER, RALPH WILLETT (1762–1799), naval captain; born in New York; came to England and entered the navy; promoted lieutenant by Rodney, 1781; posted to command the Mignonne, 1796; became flag-captain to Nelson, 1796; with Nelson at Cape St. Vincent (1797) and the Nile (1798); served under Sir Sidney Smith off the coast of Egypt and Syria; killed during the defence of St. Jean d'Acre by the accidental bursting of some shells. [xxxvii. 422]

MILLER, SIR THOMAS, LORD GLENLEE, first baronet (1717–1789), lord-president of the College of Justice; educated at Glasgow University; advocate, 1742; solicitor of the excise in Scotland, 1755; solicitor-general, 1759; lord advocate, 1760; M.P., Dumfries, 1761; rector of Glasgow University, 1762; lord justice clerk, 1766, as Lord Glenlee; lord president of the College of Justice, 1788; created baronet, 1789. [xxxvii. 423]

MILLER, THOMAS (1731–1804), bookseller; brother of Edward Miller [q. v.]; combined grocery and bookselling, 1755; formed collections which comprised a nearly complete series of Roman and English silver and brass coins. [xxxvii. 423]

MILLER, THOMAS (1807–1874), poet and novelist; apprenticed to a basket-maker; encouraged by Thomas Bailey [q. v.] to publish ' Songs of the Sea Nymphs,' 1832; bookseller in London, 1841; noticed by W. H. Harrison; granted a pension by Disraeli; published novels, poems, and children's books. [xxxvii. 424]

MILLER, WILLIAM (1740?–1810?), painter; exhibited at the Society of Artists, 1780–3, and the Royal Academy, 1788–1803. [xxxvii. 425]

MILLER, WILLIAM (d. 1815), lieutenant-colonel; second son of Sir William Miller, lord Glenlee [q. v.]; mortally wounded at Quatre-Bras; referred to by Scott. [xxxvii. 426]

MILLER, WILLIAM (1769–1844), publisher; son of Thomas Miller (1731–1804) [q. v.]; placed in Hookham's publishing house, 1787; commenced publishing on his own account, 1790; succeeded by John Murray, 1812; Fox's ' James II ' and Scott's edition of Dryden among his publications. [xxxvii. 425]

MILLER, SIR WILLIAM, LORD GLENLEE, second baronet (1755–1846), Scottish judge; son of Sir Thomas Miller, lord Glenlee [q. v.]; advocate, 1777; principal clerk in the high court of justiciary; M.P., Edinburgh, 1780; unseated, 1781; succeeded to baronetcy, 1789; lord of session as Lord Glenlee, 1795–1840. [xxxvii. 426]

MILLER, WILLIAM (1795–1861), general in Peruvian army; assistant-commissary in (British) royal artillery, 1811; served in the Peninsula and North America; went out to La Plata and repeatedly distinguished himself in Chili and Peru; governor of Potosi, 1825; became grand marshal; left Chili owing to political changes, 1839; British consul-general in the Pacific, 1843; died at Callao. [xxxvii. 426]

MILLER, WILLIAM (1810–1872), Scottish poet; contributed to ' Whistle Binkie,' 1832–53; wrote ' Wee Willie Winkie' and other nursery lyrics. [xxxvii. 427]

MILLER, WILLIAM (1796–1882), line-engraver; educated in England and Edinburgh; landscape-engraver in Edinburgh, 1821; acquired fame as an interpreter of the works of Turner; engraved plates after Clarkson, Stanfield, and other artists. [xxxvii. 428]

MILLER, WILLIAM ALLEN (1817–1870), chemist; studied at Birmingham General Hospital and King's College, London; worked in Liebig's laboratory, 1840; chemical demonstrator, King's College, London; M.D. London, 1842; professor of chemistry at King's College, London, 1845; F.R.S., 1845; experimented in spectrum analysis, on which he read papers at the British Association, 1845 and 1861; with Dr. (Sir William) Huggins investigated the spectra of heavenly bodies and procured the first trustworthy information on stellar chemistry, 1862; assayer to the mint and Bank of England; LL.D. Edinburgh, 1860; D.C.L. Oxford, 1868; LL.D. Cambridge, 1869; published 'Elements of Chemistry,' 1855–7. [xxxvii. 429]

MILLER, WILLIAM HALLOWES (1801–1880), mineralogist; of St. John's College, Cambridge; fifth wrangler, 1826; fellow, 1829; M.D., 1841; professor of mineralogy, 1832–70; developed system of crystallography adapted to mathematical calculation, 1838; commissioner for standard weights and measures; member of the international commission, 1870; LL.D. Dublin, 1865; D.C.L. Oxford, 1876; foreign secretary, Royal Society, 1856–73; royal medallist, 1870; published scientific works. [xxxvii. 430]

MILLER, WILLIAM HENRY (1789-1848), book collector ; M.P., Newcastle-under-Lyme, 1830-7 ; formed a library at Britwell Court, unrivalled among private collections for its examples of early English and Scottish literature. [xxxvii. 431]

MILLES, ISAAC, the elder (1638-1720), divine ; of St. John's College, Cambridge ; vicar of Chipping Wycombe, 1674, of Highclere, 1680 ; taught the sons of Thomas Herbert, eighth earl of Pembroke [q. v.]. [xxxvii. 432]

MILLES, ISAAC, the younger (*fl.* 1701-1727), son of Isaac Milles the elder [q. v.] ; B.A. Balliol College, Oxford, 1696 ; M.A. Sidney Sussex College, Cambridge, 1701 ; treasurer of the diocese of Waterford, 1714 ; prebendary of Lismore, 1716. [xxxvii. 432]

MILLES, JEREMIAH (1675-1746), son of Isaac Milles the elder [q. v.] ; fellow and tutor of Balliol College, Oxford, 1696-1705 ; rector of Duloe, 1704-46.
[xxxvii. 432]

MILLES, JEREMIAH (1714-1784), antiquary ; son of Jeremiah Milles (1675-1746) [q. v.] ; of Eton and Corpus Christi College, Oxford ; M.A., 1735 ; D.D., 1747 ; travelled through Europe, 1733-7 ; treasurer of Lismore, 1735-45 ; precentor of Waterford, 1737-44 ; F.S.A., 1741 ; F.R.S., 1742 ; member of the Egyptian Club ; son-in-law of Archbishop Potter ; precentor and prebendary of Exeter, 1747, dean, 1762 ; P.S.A., 1768 ; collected materials for a history of Devonshire ; maintained the antiquity of Chatterton's Rowley poems ; his library sold, 1843. [xxxvii. 432]

MILLES, THOMAS (*d.* 1627 ?), customer of Sandwich ; bailiff of Sandwich, 1579 ; accompanied Randolph on his mission to Edinburgh, 1586 ; customer of Sandwich, 1587 ; sent to Brittany to report on the forces there, 1591 ; prize commissioner at Plymouth, 1596 ; secretary to Lord Cobham, lord warden of the Cinque ports, 1598 ; obtained reversion of keepership of Rochester Castle, 1598 ; wrote books on economics in support of the staple system ; edited the manuscripts of his brother-in-law, Robert Glover, Somerset herald. [xxxvii. 434]

MILLES, THOMAS (1671-1740), bishop of Waterford and Lismore ; eldest son of Isaac Milles (1638-1720) [q. v.] ; M.A. Wadham College, Oxford, 1695 ; B.D., 1704 ; chaplain of Christ Church, Oxford, 1694 ; vice-principal of St. Edmund Hall, Oxford, 1695-1707 ; regius professor of Greek, 1707 ; bishop of Waterford and Lismore, 1708 ; published tracts and sermons and edited the works of St. Cyril of Jerusalem, 1703. [xxxvii. 436]

MILLHOUSE, ROBERT (1788-1839), weaver and poet ; wrote his first verses, 1810 ; received grant from the Royal Literary Fund, 1822 ; assistant at a savings bank, 1832 ; published poems. [xxxvii. 436]

MILLIGAN, WILLIAM (1821-1893), Scottish divine ; M.A. St. Andrews, 1839 ; ordained minister of Cameron, Fifeshire, and of Kilconquhar, 1850 ; first professor of biblical criticism, Aberdeen University, 1860-93 ; member of company formed for revision of English New Testament, 1870 ; moderator of general assembly, 1882 ; principal clerk of general assembly, 1886 ; took prominent part in formation of Scottish Church Society, 1892 (first president) ; published theological and other writings, including article on ' Epistle to Ephesians ' in ' Encyclopædia Britannica,' 1879. [Suppl. iii. 174]

MILLIKEN or **MILLIKIN**, RICHARD ALFRED (1767-1815), poet ; admitted attorney ; volunteered on the outbreak of the Irish rebellion ; chiefly remembered for ' The Groves of Blarney ' and other lyrics, sung by the elder Charles Mathews on the stage. [xxxvii. 437]

MILLINGEN, JAMES (1774-1845), archæologist ; brother of John Gideon Millingen [q. v.] ; educated at Westminster School ; banker's clerk, 1790 ; obtained post in French mint ; arrested as a British subject, 1792 ; partner in Sir Robert Smith & Co., 1794 ; resided in Italy ; granted civil list pension ; F.S.A. and member of many learned societies in Europe ; compiled valuable works on coins, medals, Etruscan vases, and kindred subjects in English, French, and Italian ; died in Florence.
[xxxvii. 437]

MILLINGEN, JOHN GIDEON (1782-1862), physician and writer ; brother of James Millingen [q. v.] ; obtained a medical degree in Paris ; assistant-surgeon in the British army, 1802 ; served in the Peninsular campaigns

and at Waterloo (medal) and the surrender of Paris ; retired, 1823 ; physician to the military asylum at Chatham and Hanwell, 1837 ; published medical and other works.
[xxxvii. 439]

MILLINGEN, JULIUS MICHAEL (1800-1878), physician and writer ; son of James Millingen [q. v.] ; studied at Rome and Edinburgh, 1817 ; M.R.C.S. Edinburgh, 1821 ; went to Corfu, 1823 ; attended Byron in his last illness ; surgeon in Greek army, 1824 ; settled in Constantinople, 1827 ; court physician to five successive sultans ; instrumental in introducing Turkish baths into England ; discovered ruins of Aczani and excavated site of temple of Jupiter Urius on the Bosphorus ; published memoirs ; died in Constantinople. [xxxvii. 439]

MILLINGTON, GILBERT (*d.* 1666), regicide ; member of Lincoln's Inn, 1614 ; M.P., Nottingham, in Long parliament ; deputy-lieutenant for Nottingham, 1642 ; agent of communication between the governor, John Hutchinson (1615-1664) [q. v.], and parliament ; energetic at Charles I's trial ; signed the king's death-warrant, 1649 ; condemned to death, 1660 ; his sentence commuted to life imprisonment ; died in Jersey. [xxxvii. 440]

MILLINGTON, JAMES HEATH (*d.* 1873), painter ; curator of the Royal Academy School of Painting.
[xxxvii. 441]

MILLINGTON, JOHN (1779-1868), engineer ; professor of mechanics at the Royal Institution, London, 1817-29 ; engineer of some Mexican mines, 1829 ; professor of chemistry at Williamsburg, 1837, where he died ; wrote on scientific subjects. [xxxvii. 441]

MILLINGTON, SIR THOMAS (1628-1704), physician ; of Westminster School and Trinity College, Cambridge ; M.A., 1657 ; M.D. Oxford, 1659 ; fellow of All Souls College, Oxford ; original member of the Royal Society ; Sedleian professor of natural philosophy, Oxford, 1675 ; court physician and knighted, 1680 ; alleged discoverer of sexuality in plants. [xxxvii. 442]

MILLINGTON, WILLIAM (*d.* 1466 ?), first provost of King's College, Cambridge ; probably educated at Clare Hall, Cambridge ; rector, 1440 ; provost, 1443, of King's College ; deprived by royal commissioners ; assisted in drawing up Queens' College statutes, 1448 ; vice-chancellor, 1457. [xxxvii. 442]

MILLNER. [See also MILNER.]

MILLNER, JOHN (*fl.* 1712), captain in the Scots royal ; served under Marlborough ; published journal of Marlborough's marches (1702-12), 1733. [xxxvii. 443]

MILLS, ALFRED (1776-1833), draughtsman.
[xxxvii. 443]

MILLS, CHARLES (1788-1826), historical writer ; abandoned law for literature ; published ' History of Muhammedanism,' 1817, ' History of the Crusades,' 1820, and other works. [xxxvii. 444]

MILLS, SIR CHARLES (1825-1895), first agent-general for Cape Colony ; born at Ischl, Hungary ; private in 98th regiment, 1843 ; with his regiment in China ; staff clerk in adjutant-general's office ; served in Punjab, 1849 ; ensign and adjutant, 1851 ; lieutenant, 1854 ; brigade major in Crimea, 1855 ; in charge of military settlement of Germans on east border of British Kaffraria, 1858 ; retired on its incorporation with Cape Colony, 1865 ; member of Cape parliament for Kingwilliamstown, 1866 ; chief clerk for finance, 1867 ; permanent under-secretary, 1872 ; in colonial secretary's office ; agent-general in London for Cape Colony, 1882 ; K.C.M.G., 1885 ; C.B., 1886.
[Suppl. iii. 175]

MILLS, GEORGE (1792 ?-1824), medallist ; gained three gold medals from the Society of Arts ; exhibited at the Royal Academy, 1816-23 ; engraved for Mudie's ' National Medals.' [xxxvii. 444]

MILLS, GEORGE (1808-1881), shipbuilder, journalist, and novelist ; as shipbuilder began to build iron steamers, 1838 ; stockbroker, 1848-50 ; started ' Glasgow Advertiser and Shipping Gazette,' 1857 ; started the Milton chemical works, 1866 ; started ' The Northern Star ' in Aberdeen, 1869 ; literary critic of the ' Glasgow Mail ' ; wrote three novels. [xxxvii. 444]

MILLS, JOHN (*d.* 1736), actor ; acted at Drury Lane Theatre, London, for forty years, and occasionally at the Haymarket, London. [xxxvii. 445]

MILLS, JOHN (*d.* 1784?), writer on agriculture; translated French agricultural works; F.R.S.,1766; first foreign associate of the French Agricultural Society, 1767–84; author of 'System of Practical Husbandry,' 1767. [xxxvii. 446]

MILLS, JOHN (1812–1873), author and Calvinistic methodist minister; extended musical culture in Wales; visited the Holy Land, 1855 and 1859; published Welsh miscellaneous works. [xxxvii. 447]

MILLS, RICHARD (1809–1844), Welsh musician; published congregational tunes. [xxxvii. 447]

MILLWARD. [See MILWARD.]

MILLYNG, THOMAS (*d.* 1492), bishop of Hereford; D.D. Gloucester Hall, Oxford; prior of Westminster, 1465, abbot, 1469; received (1470) Elizabeth, queen of Edward IV, into sanctuary at Westminster, where her son Edward was born; bishop of Hereford, 1474. [xxxvii. 447]

MILMAN, SIR FRANCIS, first baronet (1746–1821), physician; M.A. Exeter College, Oxford, 1767; M.D., 1776; Radcliffe fellow, 1771; physician to Middlesex Hospital, 1771–9; F.C.P., 1778; Gulstonian lecturer, 1780; Croonian lecturer, 1781; Harveian orator, 1782; president, 1811 and 1812; created baronet, 1800; physician to George III, 1806; published medical works. [xxxvii. 1]

MILMAN, HENRY HART (1791–1868), dean of St. Paul's; son of Sir Francis Milman [q. v.]; of Eton and Brasenose College, Oxford; M.A., 1816; D.D., 1849; Newdigate prizeman, 1812; chancellor's English essay prizeman, 1816; fellow of Brasenose, 1814; incumbent of St. Mary's, Reading, 1818; professor of poetry at Oxford, 1821–31; Bampton lecturer, 1827; rector of St. Margaret's, Westminster, 1835; dean of St. Paul's, 1849; published 'Fazio,' 1815 (acted in London, 1818), 'Samor' (epic), 1818, 'The Fall of Jerusalem,' 1820, 'The Martyr of Antioch,' 1822, 'Belshazzar,' 1822, and 'Anne Boleyn,' 1826; 'History of the Jews,' 1830, 'History of Christianity under the Empire,' 1840, and 'Latin Christianity,' 1855; edited Gibbon, 1838; a history of St. Paul's Cathedral, published by his son, 1868. [xxxviii. 1]

MILMAN, ROBERT (1816–1876), bishop of Calcutta; grandson of Sir Francis Milman [q. v.]; educated at Westminster School, and Exeter College, Oxford; M.A. and D.D., 1867; vicar of Chaddleworth, 1840, of Lambourn, 1851, of Great Marlow, 1862; bishop of Calcutta, 1867; published devotional works and a life of Tasso, 1850. [xxxviii. 4]

MILN, JAMES (1819–1881), archæologist; entered navy, 1842; merchant in China and India; interested in astronomy, archæology, and small arms; excavated at Carnac and Kermario, accounts of which he published. [xxxviii. 5]

MILN, WALTER (*d.* 1558). [See MYLNE.]

MILNE, SIR ALEXANDER, first baronet (1806–1896), admiral of the fleet; son of Sir David Milne [q. v.]; lieutenant, 1827; commander, 1830; served in West Indies, North America, and Newfoundland, 1836–41; flag-captain to his father at Devonport, 1842–5; junior lord of admiralty, 1847–59; rear-admiral and civil K.C.B., 1858; commanded in West Indies and North American station, 1860; military K.C.B., 1864; junior naval lord of admiralty, 1866–8 and 1872–6; commander-in-chief in Mediterranean, 1869–70; G.C.B., 1871; created baronet, 1876. [Suppl. iii. 176]

MILNE, COLIN (1743?–1815), divine and botanist; educated at Marischal College, Aberdeen; LL.D. Aberdeen; rector of North Chapel, Sussex; founded Kent Dispensary (Miller Hospital), Greenwich, 1783; promoted the Royal Humane Society; published botanical works. [xxxviii. 6]

MILNE, SIR DAVID (1763–1845), admiral; entered navy, 1779; in the East India service until 1793; lieutenant, 1794; commander, 1795; served on various stations abroad; in command of Forth district of Sea Fencibles, 1803–11; captain, 1814; served with distinction against Algiers, 1816; K.C.B., 1816; commander-in-chief in North American waters; M.P., Berwick, 1820; vice-admiral, 1825; G.C.B., 1840; admiral, 1841; commander-in-chief at Plymouth, 1845. [xxxviii. 6]

MILNE, JOSHUA (1776–1851), actuary to the Sun Life Assurance Society, 1810; compiled 'Treatise on the Valuation of Annuities . . . the Probabilities and Expectations of Life,' 1815, which revolutionised actuarial science. [xxxviii. 8]

MILNE, WILLIAM (1785–1822), missionary; ordained, 1812; settled at Malacca; founded and became principal of an Anglo-Chinese college; D.D. Glasgow, 1818. [xxxviii. 9]

MILNE, WILLIAM CHARLES (1815–1863), Chinese missionary at Macao, Canton, and Shanghai; son of William Milne [q. v.]; assistant Chinese secretary to the Pekin legation; wrote books on China. [xxxviii. 9]

MILNE-HOME, DAVID (1805–1890), founder of Scottish Meteorological Society; son of Sir David Milne [q. v.]; proposed Ben Nevis as an observatory, 1877. [xxxviii. 8]

MILNER. [See also MILLNER.]

MILNER, ISAAC (1750–1820), mathematician and divine; brother of Joseph Milner [q. v.]; sizar of Queens' College, Cambridge, 1770; B.A., 1774; fellow, 1776; F.R.S., 1776; rector of St. Botolph's, Cambridge, 1778–92; first professor of natural philosophy at Cambridge, 1783–92; president of Queens' College, Cambridge, 1788–1820; dean of Carlisle, 1791; vice-chancellor, 1792 and 1809; Lucasian professor of mathematics, 1798–1820; intimate with William Wilberforce [q. v.]; wrote on chemistry and mathematics; edited his brother's theological works. [xxxvii. 9]

MILNER, JAMES (*d.* 1721), merchant of London; traded extensively with Portugal; wrote several articles on the Methuen treaty and Portuguese trade, 1713, and on the South Sea Company, 1720; M.P., Minehead, 1717. [xxxviii. 12]

MILNER, JOHN (1628–1702), nonjuring divine; of Christ's College, Cambridge; curate of Beeston, 1660; B.D., 1662; vicar of Leeds, 1673; prebendary of Ripon, 1681; joined nonjurors, 1688; retired to St. John's College, Cambridge; published theological and controversial works. [xxxviii. 13]

MILNER, JOHN (1752–1826), bishop of Castabala and vicar-apostolic of the western district of England; educated at the English College, Douay, 1766–77; ordained Roman catholic priest, 1777; missioner in England; established at Winchester the Benedictine nuns who fled from Brussels during the French revolution; F.S.A., 1790; successfully opposed the suggested oath of allegiance in the Catholic Relief Bill, 1791; bishop of Castabala, 1803; steadily opposed the right of English government to 'veto' appointment of Roman catholic bishops. He published 'The History, Civil and Ecclesiastical, and Survey of the Antiquities of Winchester,' 1798–1801, 'The End of Religious Controversy,' 1818, and other theological works. [xxxviii. 14]

MILNER, JOSEPH (1744–1797), evangelical divine; brother of Isaac Milner [q. v.]; third senior optime, Catharine Hall, Cambridge; head-master at Hull grammar school; afternoon lecturer at Holy Trinity, Hull, 1768; subsequently vicar of North Ferriby; his chief work, 'The History of the Church of Christ,' 1794–7, edited and continued by his brother Isaac. [xxxviii. 17]

MILNER, THOMAS (1719–1797), physician; M.D. St. Andrews, 1740; physician to St. Thomas's Hospital, London, 1759–62; wrote on electricity. [xxxviii. 18]

MILNER-GIBSON, THOMAS (1806–1884). [See GIBSON, THOMAS MILNER-.]

MILNES, RICHARD MONCKTON, first BARON HOUGHTON (1809–1885), son of Robert Pemberton Milnes [q. v.]; educated at Trinity College, Cambridge, where he was an 'Apostle' and intimate with Tennyson, Hallam, and Thackeray; M.A., 1831; travelled, 1832–6; conservative M.P., Pontefract, 1837; did much to secure the Copyright Act; became a liberal on Peel's conversion to free trade; assisted in preparation of 'The Tribune,' 1836; visited Egypt and the Levant, 1842–3; established Philobiblon Society, 1853; interested himself in Miss Nightingale's fund during the Crimean war; advocated mechanics' institutes and penny banks; created Baron Houghton, 1863; supported reform of franchise; visited Canada and United States, 1875; trustee of the British

Museum; president of the London Library, 1882-5; hon.
D.C.L. Oxford; published poems of a meditative kind,
and political and social writings; died at Vichy.
[xxxviii. 18]

MILNES, ROBERT PEMBERTON (1784-1858), graduated from Trinity College, Cambridge, 1804; M.P.,
Pontefract, 1806; resided chiefly in Milan and Rome after
1829. [xxxviii. 19]

MILO OF GLOUCESTER. [See GLOUCESTER, MILES DE,
EARL OF HEREFORD, *d.* 1143.]

MILRED or **MILRET** (*d.* 775), bishop of the Hwiccas
(Worcester); succeeded Wilfrith, 743; visited Boniface
and Lullus in Germany, 754. [xxxviii. 21]

MILROY, GAVIN (1805-1886), medical writer and
founder of the 'Milroy lectureship' at the Royal College
of Physicians; M.D. Edinburgh, 1828; assisted in founding Hunterian Society; co-editor of Johnson's 'Medico-
Chirurgical Review,' 1844-7; superintendent medical inspector of the general board of health, 1849-50; inspected
sanitary condition of Jamaica, 1852; sanitary commissioner to the army during the Crimean war, 1855-6; left
2,000*l.* to the London College of Physicians to found a
lectureship. [xxxviii. 22]

MILTON, LORD. [See FLETCHER, ANDREW, 1692-
1766.]

MILTON, SIR CHRISTOPHER (1615-1693), judge;
brother of the poet John Milton [q. v.]; of St. Paul's
School and Christ's College, Cambridge; barrister, Inner
Temple, 1639; deputy recorder of Ipswich, 1674; invested
with the coif, knighted, and raised to exchequer bench,
1686; transferred to common pleas, 1687. [xxxviii. 23]

MILTON, JOHN, the elder (1563?-1647), musician;
of Christ Church, Oxford; scrivener in London, 1595;
admitted to Scriveners' Company, 1600; composed motets,
madrigals, and melodies. [xxxviii. 23]

MILTON, JOHN (1608-1674), poet; son of John
Milton the elder [q. v.]; of St. Paul's School and Christ's
College, Cambridge, 1625; B.A., 1629; M.A., 1632; at
Cambridge wrote Latin poems on university events, an
'Ode on the Nativity,' 1629, the sonnet to Shakespeare,
1630, and English poems; lived at Horton with his
father, reading classics, 1632-8; wrote 'L'Allegro' and
'Il Penseroso,' 1632, and 'Arcades,' 1633, and 'Comus,'
1634, two masques, for which Lawes wrote the music;
wrote 'Lycidas,' 1637 (published, 1638); travelled abroad,
chiefly in Italy, 1637-9; on his return became tutor to
his two nephews, Edward and John Phillips [q. v.];
published three pamphlets against episcopacy, 1641, to
which Bishop Hall replied acrimoniously; defended himself in his 'Apology,' 1642, bitterly abusing Hall;
abandoned intention of taking orders, and married
Mary Powell, 1643, who returned to her father's house
after a month; immediately published pamphlet on
'doctrine and discipline of divorce,' which made him
notorious; published 'The Judgment of Martin Bucer on
Divorce,' 1644, being attacked by the Stationers' Company for publishing these two pamphlets without licence;
wrote 'Areopagitica,' 1644; reconciled to his wife, 1645;
gave up pupils, 1647, and employed himself on the
'History of Britain'; published, after Charles I's execution, 'Tenure of Kings and Magistrates,' 1649; Latin
secretary to the newly formed council of state, 1649,
officially replying to 'Eikon Basilike' with 'Eikono-
klastes,' 1649, and to Salmasius with 'Pro Populo
Anglicano Defensio,' 1650, also to du Moulin's 'Clamor'
with 'Defensio Secunda,' 1654, which contains autobiographical passages; being blind, was assisted in his
secretarial duties successively by G. R. Weckherlin [q. v.],
Philip Meadows [q. v.], and Andrew Marvell (1621-1678)
[q. v.]; retained his post until the Restoration; married,
as his second wife, Catharine Woodcock, 1656 (died, 1658);
concealed himself at the Restoration; arrested during the
summer, but fined and released; married his third wife,
Elizabeth Minshull, 1662; his 'Paradise Lost' said by
Aubrey to have been finished, 1663 (begun, 1650), but
agreement for his copyright not signed till 1667; received
10*l.* for it, his widow afterwards settling all subsequent
claims for 8*l.*; sold thirteen hundred copies by 1688; his
last poems, 'Paradise Regained' and 'Samson Agonistes,'
published together, 1671; published his Latin grammar
and 'History of Great Britain,' 1669 (written long before),
a compendium of Ramus's 'Logic,' 1672, a tract on 'True
Religion,' 1673, 'Familiar Letters,' 1674, and 'College

Exercises,' 1674; died from 'gout struck in'; buried, beside his father, in St. Giles's, Cripplegate, London.
[xxxviii. 24]

MILTON, JOHN (*fl.* 1770), painter; descendant of Sir
Christopher Milton [q. v.] [xxxviii. 41]

MILTON, JOHN (*d.* 1805), medallist; assistant engraver at the Royal Mint, 1789-98; exhibited at the
Royal Academy, 1785-1802; F.S.A., 1792; executed the
Isle of Man penny, 1786, and the Barbados penny and
halfpenny. [xxxviii. 41]

MILTON, THOMAS (1743-1827), engraver; son of
John Milton (*fl.* 1770) [q. v.]; engraved 'Views of Seats
in Ireland,' 1783-93, and 'Views in Egypt,' 1801; unique
in his power of distinguishing the foliage of trees.
[xxxviii. 42]

MILTON, WILLIAM OF (*d.* 1261). [See MELITON.]

MILVERLEY, WILLIAM (*fl.* 1350), Oxford schoolman; wrote scholastic works in Latin. [xxxviii. 42]

MILVERTON, JOHN (*d.* 1487), Carmelite; studied
at Oxford, where he became prior; English provincial,
1456-65 and 1469-82; opposed by William Ive or Ivy
[q. v.]; excommunicated and imprisoned by the bishop,
1464; went to Rome; possibly chosen bishop of St.
David's; imprisoned by Paul II for three years; acquitted
of heresy. [xxxviii. 42]

MILWARD, EDWARD (1712?-1757), physician; of
Trinity College, Cambridge; created M.D. Cambridge,
1741; F.R.S., 1742; F.R.C.P., 1748; censor and Harveian
orator, 1752; published essay on Alexander Trallianus,
1733; collected materials for a history of British medical
writers and for a treatise on gangrene. [xxxviii. 43]

MILWARD, JOHN (1556-1609), divine; B.A. St.
John's College, Cambridge, subsequently of Christ Church,
Oxford, 1582; M.A. and D.D. Oxford, 1584; vicar of
Bovey Tracey, 1596; rector of Passenham, 1605, of St.
Margaret Pattens, Billingsgate, London, 1608; chaplain
to James I, *c.* 1603; sent to Scotland to aid the establish-
ment of episcopacy, 1609. [xxxviii. 44]

MILWARD, JOHN (1619-1683), nonconformist divine;
B.A. New Inn Hall, Oxford, 1641; fellow of Corpus
Christi College, Oxford, and M.A., 1648; ejected from
living of Darfield, Yorkshire, 1660. [xxxviii. 44]

MILWARD, MATTHIAS (*fl.* 1603-1641), divine;
brother of John Milward (1556-1609) [q. v.]; scholar of
St. John's College, Cambridge; rector of East Barnet,
1603; member of Gray's Inn, 1624; rector of St. Helen's,
Bishopsgate, London. [xxxviii. 44]

MILWARD, RICHARD (1609-1680), editor of Selden's
'Table Talk'; sizar of Trinity College, Cambridge, 1625;
B.A., 1628; M.A., 1632; D.D. by royal mandate, 1662;
rector of Great Braxted in Essex, 1643-80; canon of
Windsor, 1666; vicar of Isleworth, 1678-80; amanuensis
to John Selden; arranged Selden's 'Table Talk' for publication (published, 1689). [xxxviii. 45]

MIMPRISS, ROBERT (1797-1875), Sunday school
worker; went to sea; became a merchant's clerk; studied
art; devised system of instruction for Sunday schools
based on Greswell's 'Harmony of the Gospels,' and published devotional works. [xxxviii. 45]

MINIFIE, SUSANNAH (1740?-1800). [See GUN-
NING.]

MINNAN, SAINT (*d.* 875?). [See MONAN.]

MINNES, SIR JOHN (1599-1671). [See MENNES.]

MINNS or **MINGH,** SIR CHRISTOPHER (1625-1666).
[See MYNGS.]

MINOT, LAURENCE (1300?-1352?), lyric poet;
probably a soldier; his poems (terminating abruptly
in 1352) remarkable for their personal devotion to
Edward III and savage triumph in the national successes.
[xxxviii. 46]

MINSHEU, JOHN (*fl.* 1617), lexicographer; taught
languages in London; published Spanish dictionaries and
a grammar (1599), also a 'Guide into Tongues,' 1617 (the
first book published by subscription), which contained
equivalents in eleven languages. [xxxviii. 47]

MINSHULL or **MYNSHUL,** GEFFRAY (1594?-
1668), author; admitted at Gray's Inn, 1612; occupied
himself, when imprisoned for debt, by writing a series of
prison 'characters,' published, 1618. [xxxviii. 48]

MINTO, EARLS OF. [See ELLIOT, SIR GILBERT, first EARL, 1751-1814; ELLIOT, GILBERT, second EARL, 1782-1859.]

MINTO, LORD [See ELLIOT, SIR GILBERT, 1651-1718; ELLIOT, SIR GILBERT, 1693-1766.]

MINTO, WILLIAM (1845-1893), critic; M.A. Aberdeen, 1865; assistant to Dr. Alexander Bain at Aberdeen; edited the 'Examiner' in London, 1874-8; leader-writer to the 'Daily News' and 'Pall Mall Gazette'; professor of logic and literature, Aberdeen, 1880-93; wrote three novels, books on logic, and works on literature; edited Scott's works. [xxxviii. 48]

MINTON, HERBERT (1793-1858), manufacturer of pottery and porcelain; partner with his father, 1817-36; sole proprietor from 1836; manufactured, among other things, majolica and Palissy ware. [xxxviii. 49]

MIRFIELD, JOHN (*fl.* 1393), writer on medicine; Augustinian canon of St. Bartholomew's, Smithfield; wrote 'Breviarium Bartholomæi.' [xxxviii. 50]

MIRK, JOHN (*fl.* 1403?), prior of Lilleshall in Shropshire; wrote 'Liber ffestialis,' 'Manuale Sacerdotum,' and 'Instructions to Parish Priests.' [xxxviii. 50]

MISAUBIN, JOHN (*d.* 1734), physician; born in France; M.D. Cahors, 1687; L.R.C.P., 1719; mentioned in 'Tom Jones.' [xxxviii. 51]

MISSELDEN, EDWARD (*fl.* 1608-1654), merchant and economic writer; deputy-governor of the Merchant Adventurers' Company at Delft, 1623-33; commissioner at Amsterdam for the East India Company to negotiate a Dutch treaty, 1624, and to obtain satisfaction for the Amboyna outrages, 1624-8; endeavoured to thrust the prayer-book on the Merchant Adventurers at Delft, 1633; published 'Free Trade,' 1622, and 'The Circle of Commerce,' 1623. [xxxviii. 51]

MISSON, FRANCIS MAXIMILIAN (1650?-1722), traveller and author; French refugee; became tutor to Charles Butler, afterwards Earl of Arran, 1685; published 'Voyage d'Italie,' 1691, 'Mémoires et Observations,' 1698, and 'Théâtre Sacré des Cevennes,' 1707. His 'Observations' form a humorous descriptive dictionary of London in Queen Anne's reign. [xxxviii. 52]

MIST, NATHANIEL (*d.* 1737), printer; originally a sailor; became a printer and started the 'Weekly Journal,' 1716, afterwards the organ of the Jacobites; twice arrested for libel, 1717, but discharged; assisted by Daniel Defoe [q. v.], a secret agent of the whig government, who became 'translator of foreign news' for the 'Journal,' 1717; twice examined, 1718, but discharged through Defoe's intervention; found guilty of scandalously reflecting on George I's interposition in favour of protestants abroad, 1720; was sentenced to the pillory and three months' imprisonment; arrested and fined for printing libels on the government, 1723, 1724, 1727; retired to France, 1728; died at Boulogne. [xxxviii. 53]

MISYN, RICHARD (*d.* 1462?), Carmelite; probably bishop of Dromore, 1457, and suffragan of York; translated Hampole's 'De Emendatione Vitæ' and 'Incendium Amoris' into English. [xxxviii. 57]

MITAN, JAMES (1776-1822), line-engraver; exhibited at Royal Academy, 1802-5 and 1818. [xxxviii. 57]

MITAN, SAMUEL (1786-1843), line-engraver; brother of James Mitan [q. v.]; engraved plates of French scenery, 1822. [xxxviii. 58]

MITAND, LOUIS HUGUENIN DU (*fl.* 1816), educational writer; born in Paris; taught languages in London, 1777; published 'New Method of Teaching Languages,' 1778, and Greek and French grammars; edited Boyer's 'French Dictionary,' 1816. [xxxviii. 58]

MITCH, RICHARD (*fl.* 1557), lawyer; educated at Cambridge; fellow of St. John's College, Cambridge, 1543; M.A., 1544; subsequently of Trinity Hall, Cambridge; advocate of Doctors' Commons, 1559; active opponent at Cambridge of the reformed religion in Mary's reign; subsequently went abroad. [xxxviii. 58]

MITCHEL. [See also MICHELL and MITCHELL.]

MITCHEL, JOHN (1815-1875), Irish nationalist; matriculated at Trinity College, Dublin, 1830; solicitor,

1840; aided Repeal Association, 1843-6; employed on staff of the 'Nation,' 1845-7; started the 'Weekly Irishman,' 1848; tried for sedition and transported, 1848; escaped to San Francisco, 1853; started the 'Citizen' at New York, 1854; farmer and lecturer, 1855; edited the 'Southern Citizens,' 1857-9; strenuously opposed abolition; edited the New York 'Daily News,' 1864-5; financial agent of the Fenians in Paris, 1865-6; started and conducted 'Irish Citizen,' 1867-72; elected M.P. for Tipperary, 1875, but a new writ ordered on the ground that Mitchel was a convicted felon; was again returned by a large majority, but died soon after. [xxxviii. 58]

MITCHEL, JONATHAN (1624?-1668), New England divine; went to America, 1635; graduated at Harvard, 1647; fellow, 1650; pastor of Cambridge, Massachusetts, 1662; drew up petition to Charles II respecting the colony's charter, 1664; published theological works. [xxxviii. 60]

MITCHEL, WILLIAM (1672-1740?), pamphleteer; the 'Tinklarian Doctor'; tinsmith in West Bow, Edinburgh, and town lamplighter, 1695-1707; issued from 1712 illiterate pamphlets dealing with religion and church politics. [xxxviii. 61]

MITCHELBURN. [See MICHELBORNE.]

MITCHELL. [See also MICHELL and MITCHEL.]

MITCHELL, ALEXANDER (1780-1868), civil engineer; invented in 1842 the Mitchell screw-pile and mooring, a simple means of constructing durable lighthouses in deep water on shifting sands, extensively used in India and the breakwater at Portland. [xxxviii. 62]

MITCHELL, ALEXANDER FERRIER (1822-1899), Scottish ecclesiastical historian; M.A. St. Mary's College, St. Andrews, 1841; D.D., 1862; ordained to presbyterian ministry of Dunnichen, 1847; member of general assembly, 1848; professor of Hebrew, St. Mary's College, 1848, and of divinity and ecclesiastical history, 1868-94; moderator of church of Scotland, 1885; hon. LL.D. Glasgow, 1892; published works on Scottish ecclesiastical history. [Suppl. iii. 177]

MITCHELL, SIR ANDREW (1708-1771), diplomatist; educated at Edinburgh and Leyden; barrister, Middle Temple, 1738; under-secretary of state for Scotland, 1741-7; M.P., Aberdeenshire, 1747, Elgin burghs, 1755 and 1761; British envoy to Frederick the Great, 1756; accompanied Frederick during the seven years' war; K.B., 1765; died at Berlin. [xxxviii. 63]

MITCHELL, SIR ANDREW (1757-1806), admiral; entered navy, 1771; lieutenant, 1777; rear-admiral, 1795; vice-admiral, 1799; served in expedition to Holland, 1799; K.B., 1800; commanded in Channel fleet, 1800 and 1801; president of the court-martial for mutiny in the Channel fleet, 1801; commander-in-chief on the North American station, 1802; died at Bermuda. [xxxviii. 64]

MITCHELL, CORNELIUS (*d.* 1749?), naval captain; entered navy, 1709; lieutenant, 1720; captain, 1731; met convoy off Cape Nicolas and failed to engage it, 1746; court-martialled, 1747, and cashiered. [xxxviii. 65]

MITCHELL, SIR DAVID (1650?-1710), vice-admiral; pressed into the navy, 1672; lieutenant, 1678; commander, 1683; captain of the fleet, 1691; groom of the bedchamber; convoyed William III to Holland, 1693; rear-admiral of the blue, 1693; knighted, 1694; vice-admiral, 1695; convoyed Peter the Great to England, 1698; lord commissioner of the admiralty, 1699-1701; visited Holland, 'to negotiate matters relating to the sea,' 1709. [xxxviii. 66]

MITCHELL, HUGH HENRY (1770-1817), colonel; ensign, 1782; lieutenant, 1783; lieutenant-colonel, 1805; colonel, 1815; C.B., 1815; served with distinction at Waterloo. [xxxviii. 67]

MITCHELL or **MITCHEL**, JAMES (*d.* 1678), fanatic; graduated at Edinburgh, 1656; joined covenanter rising, 1666; escaped to Holland, 1667; returned to Edinburgh, 1668; fired at James Sharp, archbishop of St. Andrews, 1668, but again escaped; returned, 1673; confessed on receiving promise of his life, but denied his guilt before the justiciary court, 1674; imprisoned, and, in 1677, tortured, but persisted in his denial; tried and executed. [xxxviii. 67]

MITCHELL, JAMES (1786?-1844), scientific writer; M.A. University and King's College, Aberdeen, 1804;

created LL.D. Aberdeen; secretary to insurance companies; served on factory, weaving, and colliery commissions; collected Scottish antiquities and published scientific works. [xxxviii. 69]

MITCHELL, JAMES (1791-1852), line-engraver. [xxxviii. 69]

MITCHELL or MYCHELL, JOHN (*fl.* 1556), printer; at Canterbury, compiled 'A breviat Cronicle' of the kings from Brut to the year 1551; printed other works. [xxxviii. 69]

MITCHELL, JOHN (*d.* 1768), botanist; emigrated to Virginia, *c.* 1700, and discovered several new species of plants; returned to England, 1748; F.R.S., 1748; published, besides botanical works, 'A Map of the British and French Dominions in North America,' 1755. [xxxviii. 70]

MITCHELL, JOHN (1785-1859), major-general; ensign, 1803; captain, 1807; served in the Peninsula and Holland; major, 1821; colonel, 1851; major-general, 1855; published works, including 'The Life of Wallenstein,' 1837, and 'The Fall of Napoleon,' 1845. [xxxviii. 70]

MITCHELL, JOHN (1806-1874), theatrical manager; introduced various foreign plays, actors, and musicians into England. [xxxviii. 71]

MITCHELL, SIR JOHN (1804-1886). [See MICHEL.]

MITCHELL, JOHN MITCHELL (1789-1865), antiquary; brother of Sir Thomas Livingstone Mitchell [q. v.]; Leith merchant; acted as consul-general for Belgium; published miscellaneous works, including 'Mesehowe: Illustrations of the Runic Literature of Scandinavia,' 1863. [xxxviii. 71]

MITCHELL, JOSEPH (1684-1738), dramatist; settled in London under the patronage of Sir Robert Walpole; published dramas and lyrics. [xxxviii. 72]

MITCHELL, PETER (1821-1899), Canadian politician; born at Newcastle, New Brunswick; called to New Brunswick bar, 1848; member of provincial assembly for Northumberland, 1858; member of New Brunswick legislative council, 1860; delegate to meeting at Quebec for union of British America, 1864; provincial premier and president of council, 1866; strongly advocated federation, and on proclamation of the dominion (1867) became privy councillor of Canada and dominion minister of marine and fisheries; member of senate, 1867-72; conducted fisheries negotiations with United States, 1869-71; edited 'Herald' newspaper, Montreal, 1873; inspector of fisheries, 1897. [Suppl. iii. 178]

MITCHELL, ROBERT (*fl.* 1800), architect; exhibited at the Royal Academy, 1782-98; wrote on perspective, 1801. [xxxviii. 72]

MITCHELL, ROBERT (1820-1873), mezzotint engraver; son of James Mitchell (1791-1852) [q. v.]; etched plates after Landseer. [xxxviii. 69]

MITCHELL, THOMAS (*fl.* 1735-1790), marine-painter and naval official; assistant-surveyor of the navy; exhibited at the Royal Academy, 1774-89. [xxxviii. 73]

MITCHELL, THOMAS (1783-1845), classical scholar; of Christ's Hospital and Pembroke College, Cambridge; M.A., 1809; fellow of Sidney Sussex College, Cambridge, 1809-12; translated plays of Aristophanes into English verse, 1820-2; edited plays of Aristophanes, 1834-8, and Sophocles. [xxxviii. 73]

MITCHELL, SIR THOMAS LIVINGSTONE (1792-1855), Australian explorer; brother of John Mitchell Mitchell [q. v.]; served as a volunteer in the Peninsula; lieutenant, 1813; captain, 1822; major, 1826; surveyor-general to New South Wales, 1828; surveyed road to western plains and Bathurst, 1830; made four explorations into the interior of Australia, in the third of which he proved the junction of the Murray with the Darling and struck the Glenelg, which he followed to the sea, 1836; knighted, 1839; endeavoured to find an overland route to the Gulf of Carpentaria and discovered sources of Barcoo, 1845-7; D.C.L. of Oxford and F.R.S.; published accounts of his explorations; died at Darling Point. [xxxviii. 74]

MITCHELL, SIR WILLIAM (1811-1878), maritime writer; chief proprietor and editor of the 'Shipping and Mercantile Gazette,' 1836; introduced international code of signals for ships; knighted, 1867. [xxxviii. 76]

MITCHELL, SIR WILLIAM HENRY FANCOURT (1811-1884), Australian politician; became writer in the colonial secretary's office in Tasmania, 1833, and assistant-colonial secretary, 1839; head of the police in the gold districts of Victoria, 1853; postmaster-general of Victoria, 1857-8; commissioner of railways, 1861-3, and president of the council, 1870-84; knighted, 1875. [xxxviii. 76]

MITFORD, JOHN (1782-1831), miscellaneous writer; entered navy, 1795; commanded revenue cutter on Irish coast, 1804-6; employed by Lady Perceval, who had promised to secure him a lucrative appointment in the civil service, to write in the 'Star' and 'News' in support of Caroline, princess of Wales; placed in a private lunatic asylum, 1812-13; falsely accused of perjury and acquitted, 1814; took to journalism; became a drunkard and fell into poverty. [xxxviii. 77]

MITFORD, JOHN (1781-1859), miscellaneous writer; B.A. Oriel College, Oxford, 1804; combined the livings of Benhall, Weston St. Mary's, and Stratford St. Andrew; formed an extensive library, principally of English poetry, at Benhall; devoted to landscape gardening; edited the 'Gentleman's Magazine,' 1834-50, Gray's 'Works,' 1814, and many of the Aldine editions of the poets; published original poems; his collections sold, 1859. [xxxviii. 78]

MITFORD, JOHN FREEMAN-, first BARON REDESDALE (1748-1830), brother of William Mitford [q. v.]; barrister, Inner Temple, 1777; practised at the chancery bar; M.P., Beeralston, 1788; K.C., 1789; Welsh judge, 1789; solicitor-general and knighted, 1793; attorney-general, 1799; speaker of the House of Commons, 1801; privy councillor, 1801; lord chancellor of Ireland, 1802; created Baron Redesdale, 1802; unpopular in Ireland through his opposition to catholic emancipation; dismissed from the chancellorship, 1806; opposed repeal of Test and Corporation Acts; supported restrictions on corn; F.S.A., 1794; F.R.S., 1794; published treatise on pleadings in chancery, 1780, and other works, chiefly on catholic emancipation. [xxxviii. 80]

MITFORD, JOHN THOMAS FREEMAN-, first EARL OF REDESDALE (1805-1886), son of John Freeman-Mitford, first baron Redesdale [q. v.]; educated at Eton and New College, Oxford; M.A., 1828; D.C.L., 1853; interested himself in the detail of parliamentary bills; chairman of committees, 1851; carried on a controversy in the press with Cardinal Manning, 1875; opposed the divorce laws and Irish disestablishment; created Earl of Redesdale, 1877. [xxxviii. 83]

MITFORD, MARY RUSSELL (1787-1855), novelist and dramatist; published 'Miscellaneous Poems,' 1810; wrote much for magazines; contributed 'Our Village' (sketches of country life) to the 'Lady's Magazine,' 1819, thereby originating a new branch of literature; published 'Rienzi,' a tragedy, 1828; published 'Belford Regis,' 1835, and 'Recollections of a Literary Life,' 1852; 'Atherton,' 1854; won high praise from Ruskin; conversationalist and letter-writer. [xxxviii. 84]

MITFORD, WILLIAM (1744-1827), historian; brother of John Freeman-Mitford, first baron Redesdale [q. v.]; matriculated from Queen's College, Oxford, 1761; colonel of the South Hampshire militia with Gibbon; wrote at Gibbon's suggestion 'History of Greece' (published, 1784-1810), which became very popular; M.P., Newport, Cornwall, 1785-90; Beeralston, 1796-1806, New Romney, 1812-18; published some miscellaneous works. [xxxviii. 86]

MIVART, ST. GEORGE JACKSON (1827-1900), biologist; studied at King's College, London; joined Roman catholic church and proceeded to St. Mary's College, Oscott; barrister, Lincoln's Inn, 1851; member of Royal Institution, 1849; F.R.S., 1858; lecturer on comparative anatomy in St. Mary's Hospital, London, 1862; F.L.S., 1862; secretary, 1874-80, and vice-president, 1892; F.R.S., 1869; professor of biology at Roman catholic university college, Kensington, 1874; received degree of Ph.D. from the pope, 1876; M.D. Louvain, 1884; professor of philosophy at Louvain, 1890-3; excommunicated by Cardinal Vaughan in consequence of several articles contributed to the 'Nineteenth Century' and 'Fortnightly Review' (1885-1900) in which he repudiated ecclesiastical authority; published biological, philosophical, and other works. [Suppl. iii. 179]

MOBERLY, GEORGE (1803-1885), bishop of Salisbury; of Winchester College and Balliol College, Oxford; gained the English essay prize, 1826; fellow and tutor at Balliol, 1826; M.A., 1828; D.C.L., 1836; select preacher, 1833, 1858, and 1863; Bampton lecturer, 1868; headmaster of Winchester College, 1835-66; canon of Chester, 1868; bishop of Salisbury, 1869; objected to the damnatory clauses in the Athanasian creed, 1872; opposed confession, 1877; published sermons and charges.
[xxxviii. 87]

MOCHAEI (d. 497), saint and bishop of Aendruim; known also as Cailan; baptised and ordained by St. Patrick; built a church of wattles on Mahee island; his monastery also a school. [xxxviii. 88]

MOCHAEMOG or **PULCHERIUS**, SAINT (d. 655), studied under St. Comgall, and was sent as a missionary to Tipperary; granted site for a monastery on Lake Lurgan; had great influence over local chieftains; credited with curing blindness. [xxxviii. 89]

MOCHUA or **CRONAN**, SAINT (580?-637), educated by St. Comgall; travelled through Armagh and Westmeath into Galway; effected many cures during the yellow plague; miraculously created a road connecting Inishlee with the mainland. [xxxviii. 90]

MOCHUDA (d. 636). [See CARTHACH, SAINT, the younger.]

MOCKET, MOKET, or **MOQUET**, RICHARD (1577-1618), warden of All Souls College, Oxford; B.A. Brasenose College, Oxford, 1595; fellow of All Souls College, Oxford, 1599; M.A., 1600; D.D., 1609; held several livings; licensed books for entry at Stationers' Hall, 1610-14; warden of All Souls College, Oxford, 1614; said to have written a tract, 'God and the King,' 1615, which was ordered to be bought by every householder in England and Scotland; published a volume of theological tracts (including one on ecclesiastical jurisdiction), 1616, which was condemned to be burnt, 1617. [xxxviii. 91]

MOCKET, THOMAS (1602-1670?), puritan divine; M.A. Queens' College, Cambridge, 1631; incorporated M.A. Oxford, 1639; chaplain to John Egerton, first earl of Bridgewater [q. v.]; rector of Gilston, 1648-60; resigned Gilston to the sequestered rector, 1660; published theological works. [xxxviii. 91]

MODESTUS, SAINT (fl. 777), missionary to the Carinthians and regionary bishop; of Irish birth; disciple of St. Fergil of Salzburg; founded three churches in Carinthia; said to have baptised St. Domitian; his day 5 Dec. [xxxviii. 92]

MODWENNA or **MONINNE**, SAINT (d. 518), an Irish princess baptised by St. Patrick; travelled with other maidens to England and Scotland, founding churches; died at Dundee; buried at Burton-on-Trent.
[xxxviii. 92]

MODYFORD, SIR JAMES, baronet (d. 1673), merchant; colonial agent and deputy-governor of Jamaica; brother of Sir Thomas Modyford [q. v.]; served the Turkey Company; knighted, 1660; created baronet, 1661; visited Jamaica and sent home a survey and description of the island, 1663; agent for the colony, 1664-6; deputy-governor and chief judge of the admiralty court of Jamaica, 1667; died in Jamaica. [xxxviii. 93]

MODYFORD, SIR THOMAS, baronet (1620?-1679), governor of Jamaica; brother of Sir James Modyford [q. v.]; barrister, Lincoln's Inn; went to Barbados, 1647; a zealous royalist, afterwards going over to the parliamentarians; governor of Barbados, 1660; resigned to become speaker of the assembly; created baronet, 1664; governor of Jamaica, 1664, this island prospering under his rule; accused of encouraging piracy and sent home under arrest, 1671; he returned to Jamaica, where he died. [xxxviii. 94]

MOELES, BALDWIN OF (d. 1100?). [See BALDWIN.]

MOELMUD, DYFNWAL (fl. 500), Northern British prince; in legend the primitive legislator of the Britons; probably a mythical personage. [xxxviii. 95]

MOELS or **MOLIS**, NICHOLAS DE (fl. 1250), seneschal of Gascony; constantly sent abroad as a royal messenger, 1215-28; sheriff of Hampshire and custos of Winchester Castle, 1228-32; sheriff of Yorkshire, 1239-41; seneschal of Gascony, 1243-5; when warden, established the Carmelites in Oxford Castle, 1254; warden of Cinque ports, 1258; had charge of Sherborne Castle, 1261, and of Corfe Castle, 1263. [xxxviii. 96]

MOETHEU, THOMAS (1530-1620?). [See JONES, THOMAS.]

MOFFAT, ROBERT (1795-1883), missionary; was accepted by the London Missionary Society, 1816; sent to Namaqualand, he converted the chief, Afrikaner; married Mary Smith, 1819; appointed superintendent at Lattakoo, 1820; discovered that the Mantatees were on their way to take Lattakoo, and secured assistance from the Griquas; compelled by the restlessness of the natives to seek refuge at Griquatown, 1824, the mission station being moved to Kuruman, 1825; commenced learning the Sechwana language; gained many converts; completed his translation of the New Testament, 1839, and visited England, 1839-1843; met, and secured for the Bakwana mission, David Livingstone, who (1844) married his daughter, Mary Moffat; established (1859) a mission station among the Matabeles, but was obliged by failing health to leave Africa, 1870; translated into Sechwana the Old and New testaments and 'Pilgrim's Progress,' and compiled a Sechwana hymn-book, besides writing books on South African mission work, of which he was the pioneer.
[xxxviii. 97]

MOFFATT, JOHN MARKS (d. 1802), antiquary and dissenting minister; published a history of Malmesbury, 1805. [xxxviii. 97]

MOFFETT, PETER (d. 1617), divine; brother of Thomas Moffett [q. v.]; rector of Fobbing, 1592-1617; published scripture commentaries. [xxxviii. 101]

MOFFETT, MOUFET, or **MUFFET**, THOMAS (1553-1604), physician and author; brother of Peter Moffett [q. v.]; educated at Merchant Taylors' School, London; matriculated at Trinity College, Cambridge, 1569, but B.A. Caius College, 1572; M.A. Trinity College, Cambridge, 1576, and expelled from Caius College, Cambridge; studied medicine at Cambridge and Basle; M.D. Basle, 1578; visited Italy, Spain, and Germany, 1579-82; published 'De Jure et Præstantia Chemicorum Medicamentorum Dialogus Apologeticus,' 1584; practised at Ipswich and afterwards in London; F.R.C.P., 1588; attended Anne, duchess of Somerset, widow of the Protector, 1586, and attested her will; patronised by Henry Herbert, second earl of Pembroke [q. v.], who induced him to settle at Wilton; M.P., Wilton, 1597; published an interesting poem on the silkworm, 1599; two scientific works by him published, 1634 and 1655. [xxxviii. 101]

MOGFORD, THOMAS (1809-1868), portrait and landscape painter; exhibited at the Royal Academy, 1838-46.
[xxxviii. 103]

MOGRIDGE, GEORGE (1787-1854), miscellaneous writer; published, under his own name and various pseudonyms, tales and religious books for children, and religious tracts and ballads. [xxxviii. 104]

MOHL, MADAME MARY (1793-1883), née Clarke; educated in a convent school; visited Madame Récamier, 1831-49, and Chateaubriand; married Julius Mohl, the orientalist, 1847; her receptions in Paris attended by most literary and other celebrities for nearly forty years.
[xxxviii. 104]

MOHUN, CHARLES, fifth BARON MOHUN (1675?-1712), duellist; fought his first recorded duel, 1692; arrested for being concerned in the death of William Mountfort [q. v.], but acquitted before his peers, 1693; volunteered for the Brest expedition, 1694; made captain of horse, 1694; distinguished himself in Flanders; fought a duel with Captain Richard Cook, 1699; became a staunch supporter of the whigs; attended Charles Gerard, second earl of Macclesfield [q. v.], as envoy extraordinary to Hanover, 1701; entered on a complicated dispute with James Douglas, fourth duke of Hamilton [q. v.], concerning Macclesfield's real estate, and challenged the duke to a duel, in which both combatants were mortally wounded, 1712. This duel forms an incident in Thackeray's 'Esmond.' [xxxviii. 105]

MOHUN, JOHN DE (1270?-1330), baron; lord of Dunster in Somerset; great-grandson of Reginald de Mohun [q. v.]; a prominent figure in the reigns of Edward I and II; granted charters to Dunster and Bruton priories. [xxxviii. 107]

MOHUN, JOHN DE (1320–1376), baron; lord of Dunster; grandson of John de Mohun (1270?–1330) [q. v.]; served in Scotland and France; an original K.G.; gave a charter to the monks of Dunster. [xxxviii. 108]

MOHUN, JOHN, first BARON MOHUN (1592?–1640), royalist and politician; B.A. Exeter College, Oxford, 1608; student at the Middle Temple, 1610; M.P., Grampound, 1623–4 and 1625; created Baron Mohun, 1628. [xxxviii. 108]

MOHUN, MICHAEL (1620?–1684), actor; performed under Beeston at the Cockpit; entered the royalist army; went to Flanders and attained the rank of major; resumed acting at the Restoration, joining Killigrew's company; many of his parts original; played second to Hart. [xxxviii. 109]

MOHUN, **MOUN**, or **MOYUN**, REGINALD DE (d. 1257), sometimes called Earl of Somerset; great-grandson of William de Mohun (fl. 1141) [q. v.]; sat among the king's justices, 1234; founded Newnham Abbey, 1246; said to have received his title Earl of Somerset from the pope; benefactor of Cleeve Abbey and other religious houses. [xxxviii. 111]

MOHUN or **MOION**, WILLIAM DE (fl. 1066), baron and sheriff of Somerset; a Norman who followed William the Conqueror to England, 1066; received manors in the west of England, was sheriff of Somerset, and (c. 1095) founded Dunster priory. [xxxviii. 112]

MOHUN, **MOION**, or **MOYNE**, WILLIAM DE, EARL OF SOMERSET or DORSET (fl. 1141), son of William de Mohun [q. v.]; rose against Stephen, 1138; marched to the siege of Winchester, 1141, with Matilda, who created him Earl of Dorset or Somerset; founded Bruton priory, 1142. [xxxviii. 112]

MOINENNO, SAINT (d. 570), suffragan bishop of Clonfert; a disciple of St. Brendan. [xxxviii. 113]

MOIR, DAVID MACBETH (1798–1851), physician and author; known as Delta (Δ); obtained his surgeon's diploma, 1816; practised in Musselburgh; became a regular writer of essays and serious verse for a number of magazines and of jeux d'esprit for 'Blackwood's,' for which he wrote 'The Autobiography of Mansie Wauch' (republished, 1828); published works, including 'Outlines of the Ancient History of Medicine,' 1831. [xxxviii. 113]

MOIR, GEORGE (1800–1870), advocate and author; advocate, 1825; became acquainted with Sir William Hamilton, 1788–1856 [q. v.] and Thomas Carlyle [q. v.]; professor of rhetoric and belles lettres at Edinburgh, 1835–1840; sheriff of Ross and Cromarty, 1855–9; sheriff of Stirlingshire, 1859; professor of Scots law, 1864; wrote on Scots law and translated Schiller's 'Piccolomini' and 'Wallenstein,' 1827, and 'Thirty Years' War,' 1828. [xxxviii. 114]

MOIRA, EARL OF. [See HASTINGS, FRANCIS RAWDON-, second EARL, 1754–1826.]

MOISES, HUGH (1722–1806), schoolmaster; B.A. Trinity College, Cambridge, 1745; fellow of Peterhouse, Cambridge; M.A., 1749; head-master (1749–87) of Newcastle-on-Tyne grammar school, which he raised to a high state of efficiency; rector of Greystoke, 1787. [xxxviii. 115]

MOIVRE, ABRAHAM DE (1667–1754), mathematician; born at Vitry; educated at Sedan and Namur; devoted himself to mathematics in Paris under Ozanam; came to London, 1688; F.R.S., 1697; commissioner to arbitrate on the claims of Newton and Leibnitz to the invention of the infinitesimal calculus, 1712; wrote on fluxions, 1695, on the doctrine of chances, 1711 and 1718, and on life annuities, 1725; published 'Miscellanea Analytica,' 1730, in which his method of recurring series created 'imaginary trigonometry.' [xxxviii. 116]

MOLAGA or **MOLACA** (fl. 650), Irish saint; baptised by St. Cuimin; travelled through Ulster, Scotland, and Wales; cured the king of Dublin, who gave him a town in Fingal, where he erected a church; confessor to the king of Tulachmin, at which place he founded a sanctuary and arrested the yellow plague. [xxxviii. 117]

MOLAISSI (533–563), Irish saint; founded a church on an island in Loch Erne; made pilgrimage to Rome. [xxxviii. 118]

MOLE, JOHN (1743–1827), mathematician; farm labourer; opened school at Nacton, 1773; removed to Witnesham, 1793; wrote books on algebra, 1788 and 1809. [xxxviii. 118]

MOLE, JOHN HENRY (1814–1886), water-colour painter; vice-president of the Royal Institute of Painters in Water-colours, 1879. [xxxviii. 118]

MOLESWORTH, JOHN, second VISCOUNT MOLESWORTH (1679–1726), ambassador in Tuscany and Turin; son of Robert Molesworth, first viscount [q. v.]; commissioner of trade and plantations, 1715. [xxxviii. 122]

MOLESWORTH, JOHN EDWARD NASSAU (1790–1877), vicar of Rochdale; great-grandson of Robert Molesworth, first viscount [q. v.]; graduated M.A. Trinity College, Oxford, 1817; D.D., 1838; curate of Millbrook, 1812–28; vicar of Rochdale, 1840; started and edited 'Penny Sunday Reader'; opposed Bright on the abolition of church rates; promoted the Rochdale Vicarage Act, 1866; which converted thirteen chapels of ease into parish churches; had a misunderstanding with Bishop Prince Lee of Manchester; published pamphlets and sermons. [xxxviii. 119]

MOLESWORTH, HON. MARY (d. 1715). [See MONCK.]

MOLESWORTH, RICHARD, third VISCOUNT MOLESWORTH (1680–1758), field-marshal; son of Robert Molesworth, first viscount [q. v.]; abandoned law to join the army in Holland; present at Blenheim, 1704; saved Marlborough's life at Ramillies, 1706; lieutenant-colonel, 1707; colonel, 1710; lieutenant of the ordnance in Ireland, 1714; M.P., Swords, 1714; served against the Jacobites, 1715; succeeded as Viscount Molesworth, 1731; Irish privy councillor, 1735; major-general, 1735; lieutenant-general, 1742; general of horse, 1746; commander-in-chief in Ireland, 1751; field-marshal, 1757. [xxxviii. 120]

MOLESWORTH, ROBERT, first VISCOUNT MOLESWORTH (1656–1725), educated at Dublin; supported the Prince of Orange in Ireland, 1688; sent on missions to Denmark, 1689 and 1692, where he gave serious offence; returned to Ireland, 1695; M.P., Dublin, 1695, Swords (Irish parliament), 1703–5, Lostwithiel and East Retford (English parliament), 1705–8; Irish P.C., 1697; after George I's accession sat for St. Michael's; created Baron Molesworth of Philipstown and Viscount Molesworth of Swords, 1719; published pamphlets and an 'Account of Denmark,' 1692. [xxxviii. 121]

MOLESWORTH, SIR WILLIAM, eighth baronet (1810–1855), politician; educated at Offenbach near Frankfort; entered at Trinity College, Cambridge, but, offering to fight a duel with his tutor, was expelled; finished his education at Edinburgh; travelled in the south of Europe; M.P., East Cornwall, 1832 and 1835; started 'London Review,' 1835; supported all measures for colonial self-government; M.P., Leeds, 1837; Southwark, 1845; first commissioner of the board of works in Lord Aberdeen's government, 1853; colonial secretary in Lord Palmerston's government, 1855; first opened Kew Gardens on Sunday; edited Hobbes's 'Works,' 1839–45. [xxxviii. 123]

MOLESWORTH, WILLIAM NASSAU (1816–1890), historian; son of John Edward Nassau Molesworth [q. v.]; B.A. Pembroke College, Cambridge, 1839; M.A., 1842; incumbent of St. Clement's, Spotland, near Rochdale, 1844–89; honorary canon of Manchester, 1881; LL.D. Glasgow, 1883; chief work, 'History of England from 1830' (published, 1871–3). [xxxviii. 125]

MOLEYNS, BARON. [See HUNGERFORD, ROBERT, 1431–1464.]

MOLEYNS, ADAM (d. 1450). [See MOLYNEUX.]

MOLINES or **MULLEN**, ALLAN (d. 1690), anatomist; M.D. Dublin, 1686; F.R.S., 1683; went to Barbados, 1690; wrote on human and comparative anatomy; made discoveries in connection with the eye; died in Barbados. [xxxviii. 125]

MOLINES, EDWARD (d. 1663), surgeon; son of James Molines (d. 1639) [q. v.]; surgeon to St. Thomas's and St. Bartholomew's hospitals, London; fought in the royalist army and was expelled from his offices; restored, 1660. [xxxviii. 126]

MOLINES, **MOLEYNS**, or **MULLINS**, JAMES (d. 1639), surgeon; warden of the Barber-Surgeons' Company, 1625; master, 1632; surgeon to St. Bartholomew and St. Thomas's hospitals, London. [xxxviii. 126]

MOLINES, JAMES (*fl.* 1675), surgeon; cousin of James Molines (1628–1686) [q. v.]; left manuscript notes on the surgical practice at St. Thomas's Hospital, London. [xxxviii. 126]

MOLINES, JAMES (1628–1686), surgeon; son of Edward Molines [q. v.]; surgeon to St. Thomas's Hospital, London, 1663; surgeon-in-ordinary to Charles II and James II; M.D. Oxford, 1681. [xxxviii. 126]

MOLINES, MOLYNS, or **MOLEYNS,** SIR JOHN DE (*d.* 1362 ?), soldier; assisted William de Montacute [q. v.] to arrest Mortimer, 1330; received grants of land from Edward III; served in the Scottish wars, 1336–8; apprehended, 1340; escaped from the Tower of London; pardoned, 1345; served against the French, 1346–7; steward to Queen Philippa, 1352; probably died in Cambridge gaol; benefactor of St. Mary Overy, Southwark, and St. Frideswide's, Oxford. [xxxviii. 127]

MOLINES, WILLIAM (*fl.* 1680), author of 'Myotomia,' a manual of dissection, 1680. [xxxviii. 126]

MOLINEUX, THOMAS (1759–1850), stenographer; writing-master at Macclesfield grammar school, 1776; published works on Byrom's shorthand. [xxxviii. 128]

MOLINS, LEWIS DU (1606–1680). [See MOULIN.]

MOLL, HERMAN (*d.* 1732), geographer; of Dutch nationality; came to London, 1698; published works on geography and maps of all parts of the world. [xxxviii. 128]

MOLLINEUX, HENRY (*d.* 1719), quaker; imprisoned in Lancaster Castle, 1684 and 1690; wrote in defence of quaker principles. [xxxviii. 130]

MOLLING (*d.* 696). [See DAIRCELL or TAIRCELL.]

MOLLOY, CHARLES (1646–1690), legal writer; entered Lincoln's Inn, 1663; migrated to Gray's Inn, 1669; published treatise on maritime law and commerce, 1676. [xxxviii. 130]

MOLLOY, CHARLES (*d.* 1767), journalist and dramatist; author of three comedies; adopted whig journalism and contributed to 'Fog's Weekly Journal' and 'Common Sense,' 1737–9. [xxxviii. 130]

MOLLOY or **O'MAOLMHUAIDH**, FRANCIS (*fl.*1660), theologian and grammarian; appointed theological professor at St. Isidore's College, Rome; acted as Irish agent at the papal court; wrote on theology and compiled a grammar of the Irish language in Latin, 1677. [xxxviii. 131]

MOLTENO, SIR JOHN CHARLES (1814–1886), South African statesman; went to Cape Town, where he was employed in public library, 1831; started commercial business, 1837; engaged in wool trade in the great Karoo, 1841–52; burgher and commandant in Kaffir war, 1846; returned to mercantile pursuits, 1852; first member for Beaufort in Cape legislative assembly, 1854; advocated responsible government and became first Cape premier, 1872; came into conflict on questions of policy and administration with Sir Henry Bartle Edward Frere [q. v.], who dismissed him from office, 1878; colonial secretary, 1881–2; K.C.M.G., 1882. [Suppl. iii. 181]

MOLUA, SAINT (554 ?–608 ?). [See LUGID.]

MOLYNEUX, MOLEYNS, or **MOLINS,** ADAM DE (*d.* 1450), bishop of Chichester; clerk of the council, 1436–41; archdeacon of Taunton, 1440; prebendary of St. Paul's Cathedral, 1440; archdeacon of Salisbury, 1441; employed on diplomatic missions abroad; keeper of the privy seal, 1444; bishop of Chichester, 1446–50; considered responsible for the unpopular peace negotiations which led to the surrender of Maine and Anjou; mortally wounded in a riot over the payment of the sailors at Portsmouth. [xxxviii. 131]

MOLYNEUX, CARYLL, third VISCOUNT MARYBOROUGH (1621–1699), son of Sir Richard Molyneux, second viscount Maryborough [q. v.]; royalist in civil war; lord-lieutenant of Lancashire; arrested on charge of treason, 1694, but acquitted. [xxxviii. 135]

MOLYNEUX, SIR EDMUND (*d.* 1552), judge; B.A. Oxford, 1510; entered Gray's Inn, 1510; serjeant-at-law, 1542; K.B., 1547; on the council of the north, 1549; justice of common pleas, 1550. [xxxviii. 133]

MOLYNEUX, EDMUND (*fl.*1587), biographer; son of Sir Edmund Molyneux [q. v.]; accompanied Sir Henry Sidney [q. v.] to Ireland; acted as clerk to the council there; reported on state of Ireland, 1578; contributed biographies of the Sidneys to Holinshed's 'Chronicles' (ed. 1587). [xxxviii. 133]

MOLYNEUX, SIR RICHARD (*d.* 1459), soldier; chief forester of West Derbyshire, 1446; constable of Liverpool, 1446; sided with Henry VI in the wars of the Roses; fell at Bloore Heath. [xxxviii. 134]

MOLYNEUX, SIR RICHARD, first VISCOUNT MARYBOROUGH (1593–1636), receiver-general of the duchy of Lancaster; created Viscount Molyneux of Maryborough (Irish peerage), 1628. [xxxviii. 135]

MOLYNEUX, SIR RICHARD, second VISCOUNT MARYBOROUGH (1617 ?–1654 ?), son of Sir Richard Molyneux, first viscount Maryborough [q. v.]; raised two royalist regiments; defeated at Whalley, 1643, and at Ormskirk, 1644; escaped after battle of Worcester, 1651. [xxxviii. 135]

MOLYNEUX, SAMUEL (1689–1728), astronomer and politician; son of William Molyneux [q. v.]; M.A. Trinity College, Dublin, 1710; visited England and Holland; sent to Hanover, 1712; secretary to George, prince of Wales; M.P., Bossiney, 1715, St. Mawes, 1726, and Exeter (British parliament), 1727; M.P., Dublin University (Irish parliament), 1727; successfully experimented on construction of reflecting telescopes, 1724; endeavoured to determine stellar annular parallax; lord of the admiralty, 1727; privy councillor of England and Ireland. [xxxviii. 136]

MOLYNEUX or **MOLINEL,** SIR THOMAS (1531–1597), chancellor of the exchequer in Ireland; born at Calais; surveyor of victuals for the army in Ireland, 1578; chancellor of the Irish exchequer, 1590. [xxxviii. 137]

MOLYNEUX, SIR THOMAS, first baronet (1661–1733), physician; brother of William Molyneux [q. v.]; M.A. and M.B. Trinity College, Dublin, 1683; visited London, Cambridge, and Oxford; corresponded with Locke; entered Leyden University, 1683; M.D. Dublin, 1687; F.R.S., 1687; practised in Dublin; president, Irish College of Physicians, 1702, 1709, 1713, and 1720; professor of medicine, Dublin, 1717; created baronet, 1730; several of his zoological papers the first upon their subjects. [xxxviii. 137]

MOLYNEUX, SIR WILLIAM (1483–1548), soldier; a leader at Flodden Field, 1513, where he took two Scottish banners; joined Derby's Sallee expedition, 1536. [xxxviii. 134]

MOLYNEUX, WILLIAM (1656–1698), philosopher; brother of Sir Thomas Molyneux (1661–1733) [q. v.]; B.A. Trinity College, Dublin; entered Middle Temple, 1675; studied philosophy and applied mathematics; surveyor-general of the king's buildings, 1684–8; F.R.S., 1685; commissioner for army accounts, 1690; M.P., Dublin University, 1692 and 1695; wrote on philosophy and optics; best known as the author of 'The Case of Ireland's being bound by Acts of Parliament in England stated,' 1698. [xxxviii. 138]

MOLYNS, JOHN (*d.* 1591), divine; M.A. Magdalen College, Oxford, 1545; D.D., 1566; reader in Greek at Frankfort during Queen Mary's reign; canon of St. Paul's Cathedral, 1559; archdeacon of London, 1559; endowed two scholarships at his college, Oxford. [xxxviii. 141]

MOMERIE, ALFRED WILLIAMS (1848–1900), divine; educated at City of London School and Edinburgh University; M.A., 1875; D.Sc., 1876; entered St. John's College, Cambridge, 1875; B.A., 1878; M.A., 1881; ordained priest, 1879; fellow of his college, 1880; professor of logic and mental philosophy, King's College, London, 1880–91; published sermons and works on philosophy of Christianity. [Suppl. iii. 183]

MOMPESSON, SIR GILES (1584–1651 ?), politician; M.P., Great Bedwin, 1614; suggested creation of licensing commission, 1616; made one of the commissioners and knighted, 1617; charged exorbitant fees and exacted heavy fines; gold and silver thread commissioner, 1618; surveyor of the New River Company profits, 1619; received charcoal licence, 1620; committed to the care of the serjeant-at-arms, the House of Commons having ordered an investigation of the licensing patent, 1621; escaped to France; his sentence, degradation from knighthood, imprisonment for life, and a fine of 10,000*l.* ; permitted to return to England on private business, 1623, and lived in retirement in Wiltshire ; possibly the original of Massinger's Sir Giles Overreach.   [xxxviii. 141]

MOMPESSON, WILLIAM (1639–1709), hero of the 'plague at Eyam' ; M.A. Peterhouse, Cambridge, 1662 ; rector at Eyam, Derbyshire, 1664 ; persuaded the people to confine themselves to the village, plague infection having reached Eyam, 1665, receiving necessaries in exchange for money placed in running water ; rector of Eaking, 1669 ; prebendary of Southwell (1676) and York.   [xxxviii. 143]

MONAHAN, JAMES HENRY (1804–1878), Irish judge ; B.A. Trinity College, Dublin, 1823 ; called to the Irish bar, 1828 ; Q.C., 1840 ; solicitor-general for Ireland, 1846 ; attorney-general, 1847 ; Irish privy councillor, 1848 ; conducted revolutionary prosecutions, 1848 ; chief-justice of common pleas, 1850 ; LL.D. Dublin, 1860 ; commissioner of national education, 1861.   [xxxviii. 144]

MONAMY, PETER (1670?–1749), marine-painter ; native of Jersey ; devoted himself in London to drawing shipping ; painted parts of the decorative paintings at Vauxhall, London.   [xxxviii. 145]

MONAN, SAINT (*d.* 875 ?), missionary in Fifeshire ; is said to have preached in Fifeshire, and been martyred by the Danes in the Isle of May in the Firth of Forth.   [xxxviii. 145]

MONBODDO, LORD (1714–1799). [See BURNETT, JAMES.]

MONCK. [See also MONK.]

MONCK, SIR CHARLES STANLEY, fourth VISCOUNT MONCK in Irish peerage and first BARON MONCK in peerage of United Kingdom (1819–1894), B.A. Trinity College, Dublin, 1841 ; LL.D., 1870 ; called to Irish bar at King's Inn, Dublin, 1841 ; succeeded as viscount, 1849 ; liberal M.P. for Portsmouth, 1852 ; lord of treasury, 1855–8 ; captain-general and governor-in-chief of Canada and governor-general of British North America, 1861 ; received renewal of appointment, with title of governor-general of Dominion of Canada, 1866 ; privy councillor of Canada, 1867 ; resigned office, 1868, after inaugurating the federation ; created Baron Monck of Ballytrammon, 1866 ; G.C.M.G. and privy councillor, 1869 ; on commission to carry out provisions of new Irish Land Acts, 1882–4.   [Suppl. iii. 183]

MONCK, CHRISTOPHER, second DUKE OF ALBEMARLE (1653–1688), son of George Monck, first duke of Albemarle [q. v.] ; succeeded to title, 1670 ; K.G., 1670 ; colonel of foot regiment, 1673 ; lord-lieutenant of Devonshire and joint lord-lieutenant of Essex, 1675, and Wiltshire, 1681 ; colonel of the 1st horse guards and captain of all king's guards of horse, 1679 ; chancellor of Cambridge University, 1682 ; raised Devon and Cornwall militia against Monmouth, 1685 ; governor-general of Jamaica, 1687 ; died in Jamaica.   [xxxviii. 146]

MONCK or **MONK**, GEORGE, first DUKE OF ALBEMARLE (1608–1670), volunteered for Cadiz expedition, 1625 ; distinguished himself at Breda, 1637, and in the Scottish troubles, 1640 ; served against the Irish rebels in command of a foot regiment ; returned with Irish troops to help Charles I ; taken prisoner by Fairfax at Nantwich, 1644, and imprisoned in the Tower of London ; offered command in Ireland by the parliament on condition of taking the negative oath, after which he became adjutant-general and governor of Ulster, 1647 ; captured Robert Monro [q. v.], commander of the royalist Scots in Ireland, 1648 ; as governor of Carrickfergus, concluded a cessation of arms with O'Neill, 1649 ; thereupon forced by his discontented soldiers to surrender Dundalk, 1649 ; proceeded to England and was censured by parliament, 1649 ; went with Cromwell to Scotland, a new regiment having been formed (which became the Coldstream guards), 1650 ; appointed lieutenant-general of the ordnance and left commander-in-chief in Scotland, 1651 ; completed conquest of Scotland, 1652 ; admiral (1652), fighting in the three great battles which practically ended the Dutch war ; resumed command of army in Scotland, 1654 ; extended powers of civil government granted him and his council, 1655 ; much trusted by Oliver Cromwell ; sent Richard Cromwell a letter of valuable advice on Oliver's death ; received royalist overtures, 1659 ; promised support to the parliament, a breach with the army seem-

ing imminent, and, on hearing of the parliament's expulsion, expostulated with Lambert and Fleetwood ; after parliament had again resumed its place at Westminster, marched slowly towards London, besieged by addresses from all parts of England ; ordered to make the city of London indefensible ; the quarrel between the city and parliament having come to a head, roused the indignation of the soldiers against the parliament by obeying this order, February 1660 ; demanded the issue of writs for a new parliament, and ordered the guards to admit the secluded members ; elected head of a new council, February 1660 ; general-in-chief of the land forces and joint-commander of the navy ; refused to listen to the suggestions offered by Heselrige and others of supreme power ; had entered into direct communication with Charles II, but the precise date at which he resolved to restore the king much disputed ; his suggestions practically adopted by the king in the declaration of Breda, 4 April 1660 ; received from the king a commission as captain-general, authority to appoint a secretary of state, and letters for the city, the council, and parliament, the king's letters being presented to parliament, 1 May, and the restoration of the monarchy voted the same day ; knighted on the king's arrival, made K.G., and (July 1660) created Baron Monck, Earl of Torrington, and Duke of Albemarle ; had much influence in military affairs, his own regiments being retained as king's guards ; had less influence in purely political and none in ecclesiastical questions ; his advice of weight in the settlement of Scotland, but the withdrawal of English garrisons carried out against his wishes ; lord-lieutenant of Ireland, but (1661) withdrew in favour of Ormonde ; remained in London throughout the plague, 1665, maintaining order and superintending preventive measures ; largely responsible for the conduct of the Dutch war ; put to sea with Rupert as his colleague, 1666 ; defeated by the Dutch off the North Foreland, 1666, but later in the same year gained a victory, facilitated by the jealousy between Tromp and De Ruyter ; called to restore order in the city after the great fire, 1666, the large ships being subsequently harboured ; his orders on the appearance of the Dutch, 1667, in the Thames being neglected, eight great ships burnt in the Medway and the Royal Charles captured ; first lord of the treasury, 1667 ; retired, 1668.   [xxxviii. 147]

MONCK, MARY (*d.* 1715), poetess ; daughter of Robert Molesworth, first viscount Molesworth [q. v.] ; married George Monck of Dublin ; her 'Marinda, Poems, and Translations,' published, 1716.   [xxxviii. 162]

MONCK or **MONK**, NICHOLAS (1610–1661), provost of Eton and bishop of Hereford ; brother of George Monck, first duke of Albemarle [q. v.] ; M.A. Wadham College, Oxford, 1633 ; rector of Plymtree, 1646 ; incumbent of Kilhampton, Cornwall, 1653 ; sent to Scotland to discover his brother's intentions, 1659, but failed to do so ; made provost of Eton after the Restoration ; D.D. Oxford, 1660 ; bishop of Hereford, 1660.   [xxxviii. 162]

MONCKTON, MARY, afterwards COUNTESS OF CORK AND ORRERY (1746–1840), daughter of John Monckton, first viscount Galway ; became known as a 'blue-stocking' ; her mother's house a rendezvous of persons of genius and talent ; married Edmund Boyle, seventh earl of Cork and Orrery, 1786 ; as Lady Cork entertained, among many notable people, including the prince regent, Canning, Byron, Scott, Sheridan, Lord John Russell, and Sir Robert Peel ; possibly the 'Lady Bellair' of Beaconsfield's 'Henrietta Temple' and 'Mrs. Leo Hunter' of Pickwick.   [xxxviii. 163]

MONCKTON, SIR PHILIP (1620?–1679), royalist ; distinguished himself at Atherton Moor, 1643, and Naseby, 1645 ; wounded at Rowton Heath ; knighted, 1644 ; shared command of the Yorkshire cavaliers ; defeated and taken prisoner at Willoughby Field, 1648 ; after five months' imprisonment received a pass to the continent ; controller of the excise and customs of Dunkirk, 1661 ; M.P., Scarborough, 1670 ; sheriff of Yorkshire, 1675 ; committed to the Tower for writing defamatory letters, 1676 ; held various military appointments.   [xxxviii. 164]

MONCKTON, ROBERT (1726–1782), lieutenant-general ; commissioned to serve in Flanders, 1742 ; captain, 1744 ; major, 1747 ; lieutenant-colonel, 1751 ; M.P., Pontefract, 1752 ; sent to Nova Scotia, 1752, and appointed lieutenant-governor of Annapolis Royal, 1754 ; reduced forts Beauséjour and Gaspereau in the 1755 campaign ; second in command of Wolfe's expedition to Quebec, 1759, where he was wounded ; major-general, 1761 ; governor of New York, 1761 ; sailed with Rodney, 1762 ; after surrender of Martinique, Grenada, St. Lucia, and St. Vincent returned to England, 1763 ; governor of Berwick-on-Tweed, 1765 ; lieutenant-general, 1770 ; governor of Portsmouth, 1778 ; M.P., Portsmouth, 1779-1782. [xxxviii. 165]

MONCREIFF, SIR HENRY, eighth baronet, afterwards SIR HENRY MONCREIFF WELLWOOD of Tulliebole (1750–1827), Scottish divine ; educated at Glasgow and Edinburgh Universities ; ordained minister at Blackford, 1771 ; appointed to one of the charges of St. Cuthbert's, Edinburgh, 1775 ; moderator of the assembly and D.D. of Glasgow, 1785 ; chaplain to George III, 1793 ; published sermons and religious biographies. [xxxviii. 167]

MONCREIFF, SIR HENRY WELLWOOD, tenth baronet (1809–1883), Scottish divine ; son of Sir James Wellwood Moncreiff, afterwards Lord Moncreiff [q. v.] ; B.A. New College, Oxford, 1831 ; studied divinity under Dr. Chalmers, minister of East Kilbride, 1837–52 ; joined free church at disruption, 1843 ; succeeded to baronetcy, 1851 ; minister of Free St. Cuthbert's, Edinburgh, 1852 ; joint principal clerk (1855) and moderator (1869) of the free general assembly ; D.D. Glasgow, 1860 ; wrote vindications of the free church. [xxxviii. 168]

MONCREIFF, JAMES, first BARON MONCREIFF of Tulliebole (1811–1895), lord justice-clerk of Scotland ; son of Sir James Wellwood Moncreiff [q. v.] ; educated at Edinburgh ; called to Scottish bar, 1833 ; M.P. for Leith Burghs, 1851–9, Edinburgh, 1859–68, and Glasgow and Aberdeen Universities, 1868 ; solicitor-general for Scotland, 1850 ; lord advocate, 1851–2, 1852–8, 1859–66, and 1868–9 ; lord justice-clerk, 1869–88 ; dean of Faculty of Advocates, 1858–69 ; LL.D. Edinburgh, 1858 ; rector of Glasgow University, 1868–71, and LL.D., 1879 ; privy councillor, 1869 ; created baronet, 1871, and baron of United Kingdom, 1874 ; succeeded as eleventh baronet of Tulliebole, 1883. [Suppl. iii. 184]

MONCREIFF, SIR JAMES WELLWOOD, LORD MONCREIFF (1776–1851), Scottish judge ; son of Sir Henry Wellwood Moncreiff of Tulliebole [q. v.] ; called to the Scottish bar, 1799 ; B.C.L. Balliol College, Oxford, 1800 ; sheriff of Clackmannan and Kinross, 1807 ; dean of the Faculty of Advocates, 1826 ; judge of the session, 1829 ; favoured catholic emancipation and strongly opposed patronage ; joined free church at disruption. [xxxviii. 168]

MONCRIEFF, ALEXANDER (1695–1761), presbyterian minister ; studied at St. Andrews and Leyden ; minister of Abernethy, 1720 ; agitated against patronage ; being suspended by the assembly, helped to form the secession church of Scotland, 1733 ; professor of divinity, 1742 ; published vindication of secession church, 1750. [xxxviii. 169]

MONCRIEFF, JAMES (1744–1793), military engineer ; entered Woolwich, 1759 ; practitioner engineer and ensign, 1762 ; served in West Indies ; sub-engineer and lieutenant, 1770 ; engineer extraordinary and captain-lieutenant, 1776 ; distinguished himself at the defence of Savannah, 1779 (promoted brevet-major), and at the capture of Charlestown, 1780 (promoted brevet lieutenant-colonel) ; quartermaster-general to the allies in Holland, 1793 ; chief engineer at Valenciennes, 1793 ; promoted lieutenant-colonel of the royal engineers, 1793 ; mortally wounded at the siege of Dunkirk and buried at Ostend with military honours. [xxxviii. 170]

MONCRIEFF, WILLIAM THOMAS (1794–1857), dramatist ; clerk in a solicitor's office, 1804 ; associated with Robert William Elliston, 1815, William Oxberry, 1824, and Charles Mathews the elder [q. v.], whom he assisted in his entertainments ; opened a music shop in Regent Street, 1828 ; gradually became blind, and on Queen Victoria's presentation became a Charterhouse brother, 1844 ; 'Tom and Jerry,' dramatisation of Egan's 'Life in London,' 1821, the most successful of his numerous dramatic pieces. [xxxviii. 171]

MO-NENNIUS (*fl.* 500), bishop of Whithorn ; *protégé* of St. Ninian: bishop of Whithorn before 497; master or abbat of a celebrated school at Whithorn called Monasterium Rosnatense ; fell a victim to his own plot for the death of Finian, one of his pupils ; author of

'Hymn of Mugint' (parts of which are embodied in the Anglican church service). [xxxviii. 173]

MONEY, JOHN (1752–1817), aeronaut and general ; entered army, 1762 ; captain, 1770 ; brevet lieutenant-colonel, 1790 ; colonel, 1795 ; major-general, 1798 ; lieutenant-general, 1805 ; general, 1814 ; one of the earliest English aeronauts, making two ascents, 1785. [xxxviii. 173]

MONGRÉDIEN, AUGUSTUS (1807–1888), political economist and miscellaneous writer ; born in London of French parents ; gradually withdrew from business and devoted himself to literary pursuits ; joined National Political Union, 1831 ; member of Cobden Club, 1872 ; received a civil list pension ; wrote on free trade and botanical subjects. [xxxviii. 174]

MONIER-WILLIAMS, SIR MONIER (1819–1899), orientalist ; born at Bombay ; came to England, 1822 ; educated at King's College School, London, and Balliol College, Oxford ; received writership in East India Company's civil service, 1839 ; studied at Haileybury, 1840, but abandoned intention of going to India and entered University College, Oxford ; studied Sanskrit ; Boden scholar, 1843 ; B.A., 1844 ; professor of Sanskrit, Persian, and Hindūstānī at Haileybury, 1844–58 ; Boden professor of Sanskrit at Oxford, 1860 ; conceived plan of Indian Institute, which was founded at Oxford largely owing to his exertions, 1883 ; fellow of Balliol College, 1882–8 ; hon. fellow of University College, Oxford, 1892 ; keeper and perpetual curator of Indian Institute ; hon. D.C.L. Oxford, 1875 ; knighted, 1886 ; K.C.I.E., 1887, when he assumed additional surname of Monier ; published Sanskrit texts and translations and other works, including a 'Sanskrit-English Dictionary,' 1872. [Suppl. iii. 186]

MONK. [See also MONCK.]

MONK, JAMES HENRY (1784–1856), bishop of Gloucester and Bristol, educated at Charterhouse School and Trinity College, Cambridge ; M.A., 1807 ; D.D. *per literas regias*, 1822 ; fellow of Trinity College, Cambridge, 1805 ; regius professor of Greek, 1809–23 ; dean of Peterborough, 1822 ; assisted in restoration of Peterborough Cathedral ; canon of Westminster, 1830 ; consecrated bishop of Gloucester, 1830, the see of Bristol being amalgamated with Gloucester, 1836 ; wrote on classical subjects. [xxxviii. 174]

MONK, RICHARD (*fl.* 1434), chronologer ; an Oxford chaplain who compiled chronological tables. [xxxviii. 176]

MONK, WILLIAM HENRY (1823–1889), composer ; organist and professor of music at King's College, London, 1874, and Bedford College, 1878 ; lectured at London Institute, Manchester, and Edinburgh ; musical editor of 'Hymns Ancient and Modern,' and many other collections. [xxxviii. 176]

MONK-BRETTON, first BARON. [See DODSON, JOHN GEORGE, 1825–1897.]

MONKSWELL, first BARON (1817–1886). [See COLLIER, ROBERT PORRETT.]

MONMOUTH, DUKE OF (1649–1685). [See SCOTT, JAMES.]

MONMOUTH, EARLS OF. [See CAREY, ROBERT, first EARL, 1560 ?–1639 ; CAREY, HENRY, second EARL, 1596–1661 ; MORDAUNT, CHARLES, first EARL of the second creation, 1658–1735.]

MONMOUTH, titular EARL OF. [See MIDDLETON, CHARLES, 1640 ?–1719.]

MONMOUTH, GEOFFREY OF (1100 ?–1154). [See GEOFFREY.]

MONMOUTH or **MONEMUE**, JOHN DE (1182 ?–1247 ?), lord marcher ; actively supported King John against the barons ; negotiated with the barons, 1215 ; justice itinerant in Gloucestershire, 1221 ; built Cistercian abbey of Grace Dieu in Wales, 1226 ; negotiated truce with Llywelyn, 1231 ; justiciar and commander of the foreign mercenaries in South Wales ; defeated by Richard Marshal, 1233 ; witnessed confirmation of Magna Charta and rebuilt abbey of Grace Dieu, 1236 ; chief bailiff of Cardigan, Carmarthen, and South Wales, 1242 ; defeated Davydd, 1244. [xxxviii. 177]

MONMOUTH, JOHN DE (*fl.* 1320), partisan of Roger Mortimer, first earl of March [q. v.]
[xxxviii. 178]

MONNOYER, ANTOINE (*d.* 1747), flower-painter; called 'Young Baptiste'; son of Jean Baptiste Monnoyer [q. v.]; died at St. Germain-en-Laye. [xxxviii. 178]

MONNOYER, JEAN BAPTISTE, better known by the surname BAPTISTE (1634–1699), flower-painter; born at Lille; decorated the French royal palaces; accompanied Ralph Montagu, afterwards duke of Montagu [q.v.], to England, 1678; painted panels at Hampton Court, Kensington Palace, London, and elsewhere.
[xxxviii. 178]

MONRO. [See also MUNRO.]

MONRO, ALEXANDER (*d.* 1715?), principal of Edinburgh University; educated at St. Andrews University; D.D. and professor of divinity, St. Andrews, 1682; principal of Edinburgh University, 1685; forced to demit his office at the revolution. [xxxviii. 179]

MONRO, ALEXANDER, primus (1697–1767), physician; M.D. Edinburgh; studied at London, Paris, and (1718) Leyden; professor of anatomy and surgery to the Surgeons' Company, Edinburgh, 1719; first professor of anatomy, Edinburgh University, 1720; attended the wounded at Prestonpans, 1745; published 'Osteology,' 1726; edited 'Transactions' of the Medico-Chirurgical Society, 1732. [xxxviii. 179]

MONRO, ALEXANDER, secundus (1733–1817), anatomist; son of Alexander Monro primus [q. v.], entered Edinburgh University, 1752; coadjutor to his father as professor of anatomy and surgery; M.D. Edinburgh, 1755; studied at London, Paris, Leyden, and Berlin; lectured in Edinburgh, 1759–1808; the communication between the lateral ventricles of the brain called the 'foramen of Monro' from his description, 1783; described accurately the bursæ mucosæ, 1788, and wrote other medical works.
[xxxviii. 180]

MONRO, ALEXANDER, tertius (1773–1859), anatomist; son of Alexander Monro secundus [q. v.]; M.D. Edinburgh, 1797; studied at London and Paris; joint-professor with his father, 1800; published no works of permanent value. [xxxviii. 181]

MONRO, SIR DAVID (1813–1877), colonial politician; son of Alexander Monro tertius [q. v.]; member of first general assembly in New Zealand, 1854; speaker, 1861, 1862–70; knighted, 1862. [xxxviii. 182]

MONRO, DONALD (*fl.* 1550), known as HIGH DEAN OF THE ISLES; parson of Kiltearn; transferred on account of his ignorance of Gaelic to Lymlair, 1574; published narrative of travels through the western isles, 1549. [xxxviii. 182]

MONRO, DONALD (1727–1802), medical writer; son of Alexander Monro primus [q. v.]; M.D. Edinburgh, 1753; army physician; L.R.C.P., 1756; physician to St. George's Hospital, London, 1758–86; F.R.S., 1766; F.R.C.P., 1771; censor, 1772, 1781, 1785, and 1789; Croonian lecturer, 1774–5; Harveian orator, 1775; published works on medicine and soldiers' health.
[xxxviii. 182]

MONRO, EDWARD (1815–1866), divine and author; brother of Henry Monro (1817–1891) [q. v.]; educated at Harrow and Oriel College, Oxford; B.A., 1836; perpetual curate of Harrow Weald, 1842–60; established college for poor boys at Harrow Weald, which was pecuniarily unsuccessful; vicar of St. John's, Leeds, 1860–6; published stories, allegories, and religious works. [xxxviii. 183]

MONRO or **MUNRO**, SIR GEORGE (*d.* 1693), of Culrain and Newmore; royalist general; served under Gustavus Adolphus; commanded troops in Ireland, 1644; recalled to Scotland, 1648; followed Hamilton into England, 1648, but was not present at Preston; disbanded his troops and went to Holland; appointed lieutenant-general under John Middleton, first earl of Middleton [q. v.] to promote a rising on behalf of Prince Charles, 1654; M.P., Ross-shire, 1661–3, 1680–6, and 1689–93, and Sutherland, 1669–74; K.B.; supported the revolution.
[xxxviii. 184]

MONRO, MONROE, or **MUNRO**, HENRY (1768–1798), United Irishman; entered the linen business, 1788; joined the United Irishmen, 1795; chosen to command the rebels, 1798; routed at Ballinahinch; tried by court-martial and hanged. [xxxviii. 185]

MONRO, HENRY (1791–1814), portrait and subject painter; son of Thomas Monro (1759–1833) [q. v.]; exhibited at the Royal Academy and British Institution.
[xxxviii. 186]

MONRO, HENRY (1817–1891), physician and philanthropist; brother of Edward Monro [q. v.]; B.A. Oriel College, Oxford, 1839; M.D., 1863; F.R.C.P., 1848; president of the Medical Psychological Society, 1864; physician of Bethlehem Hospital, London, 1848; chief work, 'Remarks on Insanity,' 1851. [xxxviii. 186]

MONRO, JAMES (1680–1752), physician; son of Alexander Monro (*d.* 1715?) [q.v.]; M.A. Balliol College, Oxford, 1708; M.D., 1722; F.R.C.P., 1729; studied insanity; physician to Bethlehem Hospital, London, 1728–1752. [xxxviii. 186]

MONRO, JOHN (1715–1791), physician; son of James Monro [q. v.]; of Merchant Taylors' School, London, and St. John's College, Oxford; M.A., 1740; Radcliffe travelling fellow, 1741; studied insanity at Edinburgh and on the continent; physician to Bethlehem Hospital, 1751; F.R.C.P., 1752. [xxxviii. 187]

MONRO or **MUNRO**, ROBERT (*d.* 1633), styled the BLACK BARON; joined the Scottish corps in the German wars, 1626; colonel under Gustavus Adolphus; died at Ulm of a wound. [xxxviii. 187]

MONRO or **MUNRO**, ROBERT (*d.* 1680?), general; cousin of Robert Monro, the 'Black Baron' [q. v.]; served for seven years on the continent; sided with the Scots against Charles I; sent to Ireland as major-general on the outbreak of the Irish rebellion; dispersed Lord Iveagh's forces near Moira, 1642, sacked Newry, 1642, and (1642) captured Randal Macdonnell, second earl of Antrim [q. v.], who subsequently escaped; relieved Sir John Clotworthy, gained a dubious advantage over Owen Roe O'Neill [q. v.], and recaptured Antrim, 1643; surprised Belfast, 1644; defended Ulster against Castlehaven, 1644; defeated by O'Neill at Benburb, 1646; came to an understanding with the royalist party, but was taken prisoner by Monck and sent to England, 1648, where he was imprisoned till 1654; he thenceforth lived in Ireland. [xxxviii. 188]

MONRO or **MUNRO**, SIR ROBERT, twenty-seventh BARON and sixth BARONET OF FOULIS (*d.* 1746), served in Flanders; M.P., Wick, 1710–41; assisted Sutherland against Jacobites, 1715; commissioner for forfeited estates of highland chiefs, 1716; lieutenant-colonel of the 'Black Watch,' 1739; distinguished at Fontenoy, 1745; ordered to Scotland at the outbreak of the rebellion; killed at Falkirk. [xxxviii. 190]

MONRO, THOMAS (1764–1815), miscellaneous writer; educated under Dr. Samuel Parr [q. v.] and at Magdalen College, Oxford; M.A., 1791; rector of Little Easton, 1800–15; projector and editor of 'Olla Podrida,' 1787; with William Beloe [q. v.] translated 'Alciphron's Epistles,' 1791. [xxxviii. 191]

MONRO, THOMAS (1759–1833), physician and connoisseur; son of John Monro [q. v.]; educated under Dr. Samuel Parr [q. v.] and at Oriel College, Oxford; M.A., 1783; M.D., 1787; F.R.C.P., 1791, censor, 1792, 1799, and 1812; Harveian orator, 1799; physician at Bethlehem Hospital, London, 1792–1816; a patron of young artists, including Joseph Mallord William Turner [q. v.] and John Linnell [q. v.] [xxxviii. 192]

MONSELL, JOHN SAMUEL BEWLEY (1811–1875), hymn-writer; B.A. Trinity College, Dublin, 1832; LL.D., 1856; successively chancellor of the diocese of Connor, vicar of Egham, and rector of St. Nicholas, Guildford; a popular writer of hymns and religious verse.
[xxxviii. 192]

MONSELL, WILLIAM, BARON EMLY (1812–1894), politician; of Winchester College and Oriel College, Oxford; moderate liberal M.P., Limerick, 1847–74; clerk of ordnance, 1852–7; president of board of health, 1857; privy councillor, 1855; vice-president of board of trade and paymaster-general, 1866; under-secretary for colonies, 1868–70; postmaster-general, 1871–3; raised to peerage, 1874; vice-chancellor of Royal University of Ireland, 1885.
[Suppl. III. 187]

MONSEY, MESSENGER (1693–1788), physician; B.A. Pembroke College, Cambridge, 1714; L.R.C.P., 1723; physician to Chelsea Hospital and chief medical adviser of the whigs; eccentric and rough in his manner.
[xxxviii. 193]

MONSON, GEORGE (1730–1776), Indian officer and opponent of Warren Hastings; son of Sir John Monson, first baron Monson [q. v.] ; entered the army, 1750 ; lieutenant, 1754 ; M.P., Lincoln, 1754–68 ; groom of the bedchamber to George, prince of Wales, 1756 ; major, 1757 ; went to India, 1758 ; distinguished himself at Pondicherry, 1760, and Manila, 1762 ; brigadier-general, 1763 ; colonel and aide-de-camp to George III, 1769 ; one of the supreme council of Bengal, 1773 ; united with Clavering and Francis against Warren Hastings ; died in India. [xxxviii. 194]

MONSON, Sir JOHN, second baronet (1600–1683), royalist ; son of Sir Thomas Monson [q. v.] ; studied law ; M.P., Lincoln, 1625 ; K.B., 1626 ; undertook to reclaim some of the fens, 1638 ; succeeded to baronetcy, 1641 ; D.C.L. Oxford, 1642 ; negotiated surrender of Oxford to Fairfax, 1646 ; signed the engagement to the Commonwealth, 1652 ; refused to pay decimation tax, 1655 ; imprisoned in his own house, 1655–7 ; endowed a free school in South Carlton, and a hospital in Burton ; published religious works. [xxxviii. 195]

MONSON, Sir JOHN, first BARON MONSON (1693–1748), educated at Christ Church, Oxford ; M.P. for Lincoln, 1722 and 1727 ; K.B., 1725 ; succeeded to baronetcy, 1727 ; created Baron Monson of Burton, 1728 ; commissioner of trade and plantations and privy councillor, 1737. [xxxviii. 196]

MONSON, JOHN, second BARON MONSON (1727–1774), son of Sir John Monson, first baron Monson [q. v.] ; created LL.D. Cambridge, 1749 ; warden and chief-justice in eyre of the forests south of the Trent, 1765 ; resigned with Portland. [xxxviii. 197]

MONSON, ROBERT (d. 1583), judge ; educated at Cambridge ; barrister, Lincoln's Inn, 1550 ; M.P., Dunheved, 1553 and 1557, Looe, 1554, Newport-juxta-Launceston, 1554, Lincoln, 1558 and 1566, Totnes, 1572 ; serjeant-at-law and justice of the common pleas, 1572 ; a commissioner for examination of anabaptists, 1575. [xxxviii. 197]

MONSON, Sir THOMAS, first baronet (1564–1641), master of the armoury at the Tower of London ; brother of Sir William Monson (1569–1643) [q. v.] ; educated at Magdalen College, Oxford ; knighted, 1588 ; M.P., Lincolnshire, 1597, Castle Rising, 1603, Cricklade, 1614 ; created M.A. Oxford, 1605 ; master falconer ; keeper of the armoury at Greenwich ; master of the armoury at the Tower of London, 1611 ; created baronet, 1611 ; accused of complicity in the Overbury poisoning case, 1615 ; remained in the Tower of London till 1617 ; clerk for the king's bills before the council of the north, 1625. [xxxviii. 198]

MONSON, Sir WILLIAM (1569–1643), admiral ; brother of Sir Thomas Monson [q. v.] ; matriculated from Balliol College, Oxford, 1581 ; went to sea, 1585 ; lieutenant, 1588 ; commanded the Margaret in the voyage to the Azores and the Canaries, 1589 ; prisoner in Spain, 1591–3 ; distinguished himself in Cadiz expedition and was knighted by Essex, 1596 ; commanded in the narrow seas and the Downs ; vice-admiral of squadron sent to intercept a Spanish treasure fleet, 1602 ; admiral of the narrow seas, 1604 ; enforced proclamation prohibiting nations from offering violence one to another within the compass of a line drawn from headland to headland, 1605 ; arrested Lady Arabella Stuart as she was escaping to France, 1611 ; suppressed the pirates of Broad Haven in Ireland, 1614 ; suspected of complicity in the Overbury murder, 1615, and in consequence deprived of his command ; vice-admiral of the fleet under Lindsey, which restored the sovereignty of the narrow seas to the English, 1635 ; author of 'Naval Tracts.' [xxxviii. 199]

MONSON, Sir WILLIAM, first VISCOUNT MONSON OF CASTLEMAINE (d. 1672 ?), regicide ; son of Sir Thomas Monson [q. v.] ; created Viscount Monson of Castlemaine (Irish peerage), 1628 ; knighted, 1633 ; M.P., Reigate, 1640 ; nominated one of the king's judges, but only attended three sittings ; sentenced by Parliament to degradation from his honours and titles and to be imprisoned for life, 1661 ; died in the Fleet. [xxxviii. 202]

MONSON, WILLIAM (1760–1807), Indian officer ; son of John Monson, second baron Monson [q. v.] ; went to India with his regiment, 1780 ; captain, 1785 ; served against Tippoo, sultan of Mysore ; major, 1795 ; lieutenant-colonel, 1797 ; obliged to retreat before the Mahratta chief, 1804, but employed in the final operations against him ; M.P., Lincoln, 1806. [xxxviii. 203]

MONT, MOUNT, MUNDT, or **MONTABORINUS**, CHRISTOPHER (d. 1572), English agent in Germany ; entered Cromwell's service, 1531 ; sent to Germany to report on the political situation, 1533 ; continued to act as agent in Germany during Edward VI's reign ; recalled under Queen Mary ; regained his position on Queen Elizabeth's accession ; died at Strasbourg. [xxxviii. 204]

MONT, WILLIAM DU (d. 1213). [See WILLIAM.]

MONTACUTE, BARON (1492 ?–1539). [See POLE, HENRY.]

MONTACUTE or **MONTAGU**, JOHN DE, third EARL OF SALISBURY (1350 ?–1400), nephew of William de Montacute, second earl of Salisbury [q. v.] ; knighted before Bourdeille, 1369 ; held a command in Ireland, 1394–5 ; privy councillor ; advocated Richard II's marriage with Isabella of France, 1396 ; succeeded as Earl of Salisbury, 1397 ; K.G. ; commissioner for discharging the functions of parliament, 1398 ; deputy-marshal of England for three years, 1398 ; joint-ambassador to France, 1398 ; accompanied Richard II to Ireland, 1399 ; accused on Henry IV's accession of complicity in Gloucester's death ; entered into a conspiracy, 1400, and beheaded at Cirencester by the anti-lollard mob ; author of ballads and songs, not now extant. [xxxviii. 205]

MONTACUTE, NICHOLAS (fl. 1466), historian ; wrote accounts in verse of the popes, and of the kings and bishops of England, the first only extant. [xxxviii. 207]

MONTACUTE, SIMON DE, first BARON MONTACUTE (d. 1317), served in the Welsh wars, 1277 and 1282 ; broke through the French fleet blockading Bordeaux, 1296 ; summoned to an assembly of the lay estates at York, 1298 ; served in the Scottish wars ; signed the barons' letter to the pope, 1301 ; governor of Beaumaris Castle, 1308 ; admiral of the fleet, 1310 ; employed against the Scots, 1310 ; guarded the northern frontier, 1315–16. [xxxviii. 207]

MONTACUTE, SIMON DE (d. 1345), son of William de Montacute, second baron Montacute [q. v.] ; studied at Oxford ; archdeacon of Canterbury ; bishop of Worcester, 1334, of Ely, 1337. [xxxviii. 211]

MONTACUTE or **MONTAGUE**, THOMAS DE, fourth EARL OF SALISBURY (1388–1428), son of John de Montacute, third earl of Salisbury [q. v.] ; K.G., 1414 ; joint-commissioner to treat with France concerning Henry V's rights, 1414 ; served against France in command of the rear division of Henry V's army, and was appointed lieutenant-general of Normandy and created Earl of Perche, 1419 ; besieged Meulan, Frénay, and Melun, 1420 ; marched into Maine and Anjou, 1421 ; governor of Champagne and Brie, 1422 ; distinguished himself in the relief of Crevant, 1423, and the siege of Montaguillon, which latter surrendered, 1424 ; completed the subjugation of Champagne and Maine, 1425 ; went to England to obtain reinforcements and petition for the payment of arrears, 1427 ; returned to France, 1428 ; after gaining many victories besieged Orleans, 1428 ; died at Meung of injuries received from a cannon ball at Tourelles. [xxxviii. 208]

MONTACUTE, WILLIAM DE, second BARON MONTACUTE (d. 1319), son of Simon de Montacute, first baron Montacute [q. v.] ; served continually against the Scots ; commanded an expedition into Wales, 1316 ; seneschal of Aquitaine and Gascony, 1318 ; died in Gascony. [xxxviii. 211]

MONTACUTE or **MONTAGU**, WILLIAM DE, third BARON MONTACUTE and first EARL OF SALISBURY (1301–1344), son of William de Montacute, second baron Montacute [q. v.] ; knighted, 1325 ; accompanied Edward III to Scotland, 1327, and abroad, 1329 ; assisted in arrest of Mortimer, 1330 ; rewarded with some of Mortimer's forfeited lands ; present at the siege of Berwick and battle of Halidon Hill, 1333 ; left in command with Arundel, 1335 ; blockaded Dunbar Castle and concluded a truce in Scotland, 1336 ; created Earl of Salisbury, 1337 ; sent to declare Edward III's claim to the French crown and to organise a league against France, 1337 ; marshal of England, 1338 ; served in Flanders and taken prisoner to Paris, 1340 ; conquered and was crowned king of the Isle of Man, 1341 ; sent on an embassy to Carlisle, 1343 ; benefactor of the church. [xxxviii. 212]

MONTACUTE or **MONTAGU**, WILLIAM DE, second EARL OF SALISBURY (1328–1397), son of William de

Montacute, first earl of Salisbury [q. v.]; served in France and was knighted, 1346; K.G., 1350; constable of Edward III's army in France, 1354; distinguished himself at Poitiers, 1356; served in France, 1357, 1359, 1360, and 1369; commander to guard the coast, 1373; joint-commissioner to treat for peace with France, 1375; captain against the rebels in Somerset and Dorset, 1381; commissioner to treat with France, 1389 and 1392.
[xxxviii. 214]

MONTAGU, MARQUIS OF (d. 1471). [See NEVILLE, JOHN.]

MONTAGU or MONTAGUE, first VISCOUNT (1526-1592). [See BROWNE, ANTHONY.]

MONTAGU, BARON (1492?-1538). [See POLE, HENRY.]

MONTAGU, BASIL (1770-1851), legal and miscellaneous writer; of Charterhouse and Christ's College, Cambridge; M.A., 1793; intimate with Coleridge and Wordsworth at Cambridge; barrister, Gray's Inn, 1798; commissioner in bankruptcy, 1806; K.C., 1835; accountant-general in bankruptcy, 1835; suggested radical reform in the existing bankruptcy procedure, and wrote on bankruptcy; published 'Essays' and pamphlets; edited Bacon, 1825-37; died at Boulogne. [xxxviii. 215]

MONTAGU, CHARLES, first EARL OF HALIFAX (1661-1715), brother of Sir James Montagu [q. v.]; educated at Westminster School and Trinity College, Cambridge, where he formed friendship with Sir Isaac Newton [q. v.]; M.A. and fellow of Trinity College, Cambridge; M.P., Maldon, 1689-95; clerk of the privy council, 1689; a lord of the treasury, 1692; the national debt originated by his proposal (1692) to raise a million by life annuities; introduced bill establishing the Bank of England, which became law, 1694; chancellor of the exchequer and privy councillor, 1694; M.P., Westminster, 1695; supported bill for regulating trials in cases of high treason; introduced Recoinage Bill, 1695; issued the first exchequer bills to provide credit for the government when the old coins had been withdrawn; carried his scheme for the formation of a consolidated fund to meet the interest on the various government loans, 1696; first lord of the treasury, 1697; resigned his offices of chancellor of the exchequer and first lord of the treasury, 1699; auditor of the exchequer, 1700; created Baron Halifax of Halifax, 1700; impeached by the House of Commons, 1701, on account of grants obtained from William III in the names of Railton, Seager, and Montagu, in trust for himself, and for advising and promoting the conclusion of the second Partition Treaty, but his impeachment dismissed for want of prosecution; resisted Occasional Conformity Bill, 1703; next charged (1703) with neglect of his duties as auditor of the exchequer; continued out of office uring Anne's reign; first lord of the treasury on George I's accession; created K.G. and Viscount Sunbury and Earl of Halifax, 1714; lord-lieutenant of Surrey. [xxxviii. 218]

MONTAGU, CHARLES, first DUKE OF MANCHESTER (1660?-1722), diplomatist; son of Robert Montagu, third earl of Manchester [q. v.]; educated at Trinity College, Cambridge, and abroad; succeeded to title and estates, 1683; raised troop for Prince of Orange; fought in Ireland, 1690; ambassador extraordinary at Venice, 1697, Paris, 1699, Venice again, 1707. [xxxviii. 223]

MONTAGU, SIR EDWARD (d. 1557), judge; educated at Cambridge; barrister, Middle Temple; serjeant-at-law, 1531; knighted, 1537; chief-justice of the king's bench, 1539; assisted in the examination of the Duchess of Norfolk, 1541; transferred to the common pleas, 1545; member of the council of regency appointed by Henry VIII's will; drafted the clauses in Edward VI's will in favour of Lady Jane Grey, for which he was fined 1,000l. on Queen Mary's accession. [xxxviii. 223]

MONTAGU, EDWARD, first BARON MONTAGU of Boughton (1562-1644), grandson of Sir Edward Montagu [q. v.]; B.A. Christ Church, Oxford, 1579; student of the Middle Temple, 1580; M.P., Brackley, 1601, Northamptonshire, 1603-4, 1614, 1620-1-2; K.B., 1603; created Baron Montagu of Boughton, 1621; imprisoned as a royalist in the Tower of London, 1642; died in the Tower of London. [xxxviii. 225]

MONTAGU, EDWARD (1635-1665), son of Edward Montagu, second baron Montagu [q. v.]; of Westminster School, Christ Church, Oxford, and Sidney Sussex College

Cambridge; created M.A. Oxford, 1661; M.P., Sandwich, 1661-5; killed at Bergen. [xxxviii. 226]

MONTAGU, EDWARD, second EARL OF MANCHESTER (1602-1671), son of Sir Henry Montagu, first earl of Manchester [q. v.]; of Sidney Sussex College, Cambridge; M.P., Huntingdon, 1623 and 1625; K.B. and created Baron Montagu of Kimbolton, but known as Viscount Mandeville on his father being created Earl of Manchester, 1626; took command of a foot regiment in Essex's army, 1642; lord-lieutenant of Huntingdonshire and Northamptonshire, 1642; succeeded as Earl of Manchester, 1642; major-general of the associated counties, 1643; joined Cromwell and Fairfax in winning Horncastle fight and Lincoln, 1643; directed to 'regulate' the university of Cambridge, 1644; secured Lincolnshire for the parliament, 1644; marched to Fairfax's assistance at York, 1644; palpably negligent at the second battle of Newbury, 1644; charged by Cromwell in the House of Commons with neglect and incompetency in the prosecution of the war, 1644; resigned his commission, 1645; opposed the ordinance for the king's trial, 1649; retired from public life when the formation of a commonwealth became inevitable; chancellor of the university of Cambridge, 1649-51; welcomed Charles II; one of the commissioners of the great seal, 1660; restored to his lord-lieutenancy and chancellorship, 1660; privy councillor and lord chamberlain, 1660; inclined to leniency on the trial of the regicides, 1660; K.G., 1661; made a general when the Dutch appeared in the Channel, 1667. [xxxviii. 227]

MONTAGU, or more properly MONTAGU, ED-WARD, first EARL OF SANDWICH (1625-1672), admiral and general at sea; raised foot regiment in Cambridgeshire and joined parliamentarian army, 1643; distinguished himself at Naseby, 1645, and the storming of Bristol, 1645; member of the council of state, 1653; conjoint general at sea with Blake, 1656; commanded in the Downs, 1657; supported Richard Cromwell, but on his fall listened to overtures from Charles II; resigned his command, 1659, but was re-appointed jointly with Monck, 1660; sailed to Holland to convey Charles II to England; nominated K.G. and created Viscount Hinchinbroke and Earl of Sandwich, 1660; admiral of the narrow seas, lieutenant-admiral to the Duke of York and master of the wardrobe, 1660; negotiated the marriage between Charles II and Catherine of Braganza, receiving the surrender of Tangier and conducting the queen to England, 1661; distinguished himself in a battle with the Dutch fleet off Lowestoft, 1664; captured some Dutch East Indiamen, 1665, and fell into general disfavour by his manner of dealing with the cargo; ambassador extraordinary to Madrid, concluding a treaty with Spain, 1666; president of the council of trade and plantations, 1670; second in command of the English fleet on the outbreak of the Dutch war, 1672; blown up in his ship when the fleet were surprised by the Dutch in Solebay, 1672; his body found near Harwich and buried in Westminster Abbey; Samuel Pepys [q. v.] was his secretary. [xxxviii. 232]

MONTAGU, EDWARD, second BARON MONTAGU of Boughton (1616-1684), son of Edward Montagu, first baron Montagu [q. v.]; of Sidney Sussex College, Cambridge; M.P., Huntingdon, 1640; treated for the surrender of Newark, 1646; conducted Charles I to Holmby House and attended him till his escape, 1647. [xxxviii. 226]

MONTAGU, EDWARD (1755-1799), Indian officer; son of John Montagu (1719-1795) [q. v.]; went out to Bengal, 1770; lieutenant-fireworker, 1772; first lieutenant, 1777; served in the Mahratta campaign, 1781, and in the Carnatic, 1782; captain, 1784; took prominent part in invasion of Mysore, 1791; lieutenant-colonel, 1794; commanded the Bengal artillery at Seringapatam, where he was shot. [xxxviii. 237]

MONTAGU, EDWARD WORTLEY (1713-1776), author and traveller; son of Lady Mary Wortley Montagu [q. v.]; was sent to Westminster School, from which he ran away several times, and then to the continent in charge of a keeper; studied Arabic and European languages; held a commission in the army of the allies, 1745; M.P., Huntingdon, 1747; secretary at the congress of Aix-la-Chapelle, 1748; M.P., Bossiney, 1754-62; travelled in Italy, 1762, and Egypt and the Holy Land; returned to Italy, 1775, and died at Padua; published 'Reflections on the Rise and Fall of the Antient Republics,' 1759, an historical didactical essay. [xxxviii. 237]

MONTAGU, MRS. ELIZABETH (1720–1800), authoress and leader of society; née Robinson; married Edward Montagu, grandson of the first Earl of Sandwich, 1742; sought to make her husband's house 'the central point of union' for all the intellect and fashion of the metropolis, 1750; held evening assemblies, at which literary topics were discussed; the epithet 'blue stocking' applied to her; lost her husband, 1775; built a mansion at Sandleford after plans by Wyatt, 1781, and Montagu House at the corner of Portman Square, London, designed by James ('Athenian') Stuart, where she entertained George III and his queen, 1791; she contributed three dialogues to Lyttleton's 'Dialogues of the Dead,' 1760, and attacked Voltaire in 'An Essay on the Writings and Genius of Shakespear,' 1769; four volumes of her letters published by her nephew, 1809 and 1813.　　[xxxviii. 240]

MONTAGU, FREDERICK (1733–1800), politician; of Eton and Trinity College, Cambridge; barrister, Lincoln's Inn, 1757; bencher, 1782; M.P., Northampton, 1759–67, Higham Ferrers, 1768–90; lord of the treasury, 1782 and 1783; member of the committee which prepared the articles of Warren Hastings's impeachment, 1787; privy councillor, 1790; retired from public life, 1790.
　　[xxxviii. 244]

MONTAGU, GEORGE, second EARL OF HALIFAX (1716–1771). [See DUNK.]

MONTAGU, GEORGE, fourth DUKE OF MANCHESTER (1737–1788), M.P., Huntingdonshire, 1761; succeeded to dukedom, 1762; appointed lord-lieutenant of the county and collector of the subsidies of tonnage and poundage in London, 1762; lord of the bedchamber, 1763–70; sided with the colonies in the disputes preceding the American war of independence, but opposed the Roman catholic relief bill of 1778; lord chamberlain and privy councillor, 1782; named ambassador to France to treat for peace, 1783; resisted Pitt's commercial treaty, 1786.
　　[xxxviii. 244]

MONTAGU, GEORGE (1751–1815), writer on natural history; captain in the army during the war with the American colonies; devoted himself at Easton Grey to scientific study; chief works, 'The Sportsman's Directory,' 1792, 'Ornithological Dictionary,' 1802, and 'Testacea Britannica,' 1803.　　[xxxviii. 246]

MONTAGU, SIR GEORGE (1750–1829), admiral; son of John Montagu (1719–1795) [q. v.]; lieutenant in navy, 1771; commander, 1773; served with distinction on the North American station; rear-admiral, 1794; unsuccessfully attempted to intercept the French provision convoy, 1794; vice-admiral, 1795; admiral, 1801; commander-in-chief at Portsmouth, 1803; G.C.B., 1815. [xxxviii. 247]

MONTAGU (formerly **BRUDENELL**), GEORGE BRUDENELL, DUKE OF MONTAGU of a new creation, and fourth EARL OF CARDIGAN (1712–1790), succeeded his father as fourth Earl of Cardigan, 1732; on the death of his father-in-law, John Montagu, second duke of Montagu [q. v.], 1749, took name and arms of Montagu; K.G., 1762; received dukedom of Montagu, 1766; appointed governor to the Prince of Wales, 1776; master of the horse, 1778; governor of Windsor Castle; privy councillor and lord-lieutenant of Huntingdon.　　[xxxviii. 248]

MONTAGU, SIR HENRY, first EARL OF MANCHESTER (1563?–1642), judge and statesman; of Christ's College, Cambridge; barrister, Middle Temple; M.P., Higham Ferrers, 1601, London, 1604 and 1614; recorder of London and knighted, 1603; K.C., 1607; serjeant-at-law and king's serjeant, 1611; opened case against Earl and Countess of Somerset [see CARR, ROBERT, EARL OF SOMERSET], 1616; as chief-justice of the king's bench condemned Sir Walter Ralegh, 1618; lord high treasurer of England, 1620; created Baron Montagu of Kimbolton and Viscount Mandeville, 1620; appointed master of the court of wards and placed at the head of the Virginian commission, 1624; created Earl of Manchester, 1626; on the legislative council for the colonies, 1634; a commissioner of the treasury, 1635; one of the guardians of the realm during Charles I's absence, 1641; published 'Contemplatio Mortis et Immortalitatis,' 1631.　　[xxxviii. 249]

MONTAGU or **MOUNTAGUE**, JAMES (1568?–1618), bishop of Winchester; brother of Sir Henry Montagu, first earl of Manchester [q. v.]; of Christ's College, Cambridge; first master of Sidney Sussex College, Cambridge, 1595; dean of Lichfield, 1603; dean of Worcester, 1604; bishop of Bath and Wells, 1608–16; bishop of Winchester, 1616; edited and translated the works of James I, 1616.　　[xxxviii. 251]

MONTAGU, SIR JAMES (1666–1723), judge; barrister, Middle Temple; M.P., Tregony, 1695, Beeralston, 1698; knighted, 1705; Q.C., 1705; solicitor-general, 1707; attorney-general, 1708–10; first baron of the exchequer, 1722.　　[xxxviii. 252]

MONTAGU, JAMES (1752–1794), navy captain; son of John Montagu (1719–1795) [q. v.]; lieutenant, 1771; commander, 1773; carried home despatches announcing capture of Rhode island, 1776; served in Channel and East Indies, 1782, and with the grand fleet, 1793–4; killed in the battle off Ushant.　　[xxxviii. 252]

MONTAGU, JOHN (1655?–1728), divine; son of Edward Montagu, first earl of Sandwich [q. v.]; educated at Trinity College, Cambridge; M.A. jure natalium, 1673; D.D. per literas regias, 1686; fellow, 1674; master of Sherburn Hospital, Durham, 1680; prebendary of Durham, 1683; master of Trinity College, Cambridge, 1683; vice-chancellor of Cambridge University, 1687; dean of Durham, 1699.　　[xxxviii. 253]

MONTAGU, JOHN, second DUKE OF MONTAGU (1688?–1749), courtier; son of Ralph Montagu, first duke of Montagu [q. v.]; succeeded as second duke, 1709; K.G., 1719; was granted the islands of St. Vincent and St. Lucia, 1722, but failed in his attempt to establish a footing; grand master of the order of the Bath, 1725; master-general of the ordnance, 1740; raised regiment of horse ('Montagu's Carabineers'), 1745 (disbanded after Culloden).　　[xxxviii. 253]

MONTAGU, JOHN, fourth EARL OF SANDWICH (1718–1792), educated at Eton and Trinity College, Cambridge; toured on the continent and in the East, 1737–9; F.R.S., 1740; lord commissioner of the admiralty, 1744; appointed captain in the Duke of Bedford's foot regiment; aide-de-camp and colonel in the army, 1745; plenipotentiary at Breda, 1746, and at Aix-la-Chapelle, 1748; first lord of the admiralty, 1748; with Anson's help detected abuses and instituted stringent reforms; dismissed, 1751; again nominated first lord of the admiralty and one of the principal secretaries of state, 1763; his reputation permanently sullied by the part he took in the prosecution of Wilkes; postmaster-general, 1768; returned to his post at the admiralty, 1771, and began to employ the vast patronage of the office as an engine for bribery and political jobbery, in consequence of which, when war broke out, 1778, the navy was found inadequate and the naval storehouses empty; Sandwich islands named after him; retired from public life on the fall of the North administration, 1782.　　[xxxviii. 254]

MONTAGU, JOHN (1719–1795), admiral; lieutenant in the navy, 1741; commander, 1745; rear-admiral, 1770; commander-in-chief on the North American station, 1771–4; vice-admiral and commander-in-chief at Newfoundland, 1776; admiral of the blue, 1782; commander-in-chief at Portsmouth, 1783–6; admiral of the red, 1787.　　[xxxviii. 258]

MONTAGU, JOHN (1797–1853), colonial official; son of Edward Montagu (1755–1799) [q. v.]; ensign, 1814; lieutenant, 1815; captain, 1822; private secretary, 1824–7, to (Sir) George Arthur [q. v.] when lieutenant-governor of Van Diemen's Land; was clerk of excise and legislative councils, 1827–9; colonial treasurer, 1832; colonial secretary, 1834; suspended from office owing to difference with the governor, Sir John Franklin [q. v.], 1842; colonial secretary at Cape of Good Hope, 1843 till death; left colony owing to ill-health, 1851; died in London. He greatly improved the financial condition of Cape Colony.　　[Suppl. iii. 188]

MONTAGU, LADY MARY WORTLEY (1689–1762), writer of 'Letters'; daughter of Evelyn Pierrepont, afterwards fifth earl and first duke of Kingston; taught herself Latin at an early age; married (1712) Edward Wortley Montagu, M.P. for Huntingdon, commissioner (1714–15) of the treasury, and ambassador to Constantinople, 1716; went to Constantinople with her husband, and on her return to England (1718) introduced the practice of inoculation for small-pox; became a leader of society; quarrelled with Pope, who had professed a

special admiration for her ; her favour courted by Young ; on good terms with Sarah, duchess of Marlborough ; went to Italy, 1739 ; settled in Avignon, 1742 ; moved to Brescia, 1746 ; finally settled at Venice ; returned to England on her husband's death, 1761 ; author of 'Town Eclogues,' privately published as 'Court Poems,' 1716, and 'Letters from the East,' posthumously published.
[xxxviii. 259]

MONTAGU, RALPH, first DUKE OF MONTAGU (1638?–1709), son of Edward Montagu, second baron Montagu of Boughton [q. v.] ; master of the horse to the Duchess of York ; ambassador extraordinary to Louis XIV, 1669 ; purchased the mastership of the great wardrobe, 1671 ; privy councillor, 1672 ; again ambassador extraordinary to Louis XIV, 1676 ; unsuccessfully intrigued for the post of secretary of state ; being denounced by the Duchess of Cleveland, returned to England without permission, to find himself struck out of the privy council (1678) and superseded as ambassador ; negotiated with the French ambassador, offering to procure Danby's fall within six months ; his papers seized ; produced two letters, which were voted as sufficient ground for Danby's impeachment, 1678 ; escaped arrest after the dissolution of parliament, 1678 ; unsuccessfully endeavoured to get Monmouth declared Prince of Wales ; retired to France, 1680 ; succeeded as Baron Montagu, 1684, and returned to England on the accession of James II ; took up William's cause at the revolution ; privy councillor and created Viscount Monthermer and Earl of Montagu, 1689 ; the mastership of the wardrobe restored to him ; several lawsuits concerning the Albemarle property caused by his marriage with Elizabeth Cavendish, widow of Christopher Monck, second duke of Albemarle [q. v.], 1692 ; became Marquis of Monthermer and Duke of Montagu, 1705.
[xxxviii. 263]

MONTAGU or MOUNTAGUE, RICHARD (1577–1641), controversialist and bishop ; of Eton and King's College, Cambridge ; M.A., 1602 ; B.D., 1609 ; assisted Sir Henry Savile [q. v.] in his literary work ; fellow of Eton, 1613 ; dean of Hereford, 1616 ; exchanged deanery for a canonry of Windsor, 1617 ; archdeacon of Hereford and chaplain to James I, 1617 ; prepared an answer to Baronius, issued as 'Analecta Ecclesiasticarum Exercitationum,' 1622 ; published 'Diatribæ upon the first part of the late History of Tithes,' 1621 ; answered Matthew Kellison's 'Gag for the New Gospel' with 'A New Gagg,' 1624, in 'Appello Cæsarem,' 1625 ; vindicated his teaching from the charge of Arminianism and popery ; committed to the custody of the serjeant-at-arms in consequence of a hot debate in the House of Commons ; his punishment petitioned for by the House of Commons ; appointed by Charles I bishop of Chichester, 1628 ; a bitter pamphlet against him addressed to the House of Commons, 1629 ; endeavoured to recover the alienated estates of his diocese ; diligent in procuring obedience to church discipline ; published a book on the Eucharistic Sacrifice, 1638 ; according to Panzani, considered reunion with the Roman church quite possible ; bishop of Norwich, 1638.   [xxxviii. 266]

MONTAGU, ROBERT, third EARL OF MANCHESTER (1634–1683), son of Edward Montagu, second earl of Manchester [q. v.] ; M.P., Huntingdonshire, 1660 and 1661 ; sent on a mission to France, 1663 ; gentleman of the bedchamber, 1666 ; died at Montpellier.
[xxxviii. 231]

MONTAGU, WALTER (1603?–1677), abbot of St. Martin near Pontoise ; son of Sir Henry Montagu, first earl of Manchester [q. v.] ; educated at Sidney Sussex College, Cambridge, and on the continent ; employed by Buckingham on a secret mission to France, 1624 and 1625 ; continued in secret service in France, 1627–33 ; became Roman catholic, 1635 ; collected catholic contributions to the royalist army ; imprisoned in the Tower of London, 1643–7 ; exiled, 1649 ; became abbot of St. Martin near Pontoise ; resigned in favour of Cardinal Bouillon at the request of the French government, 1670, but continued to enjoy the revenues ; published a comedy, verses, and theological and political works.
[xxxviii. 270]

MONTAGU, SIR WILLIAM (1619?–1706), judge ; son of Edward Montagu, first baron Montagu of Boughton [q. v.] ; educated at Sidney Sussex College, Cambridge ; barrister, Middle Temple, 1641 ; M.P., Huntingdon, 1640 ; Cambridge University, 1660 ; attorney-general to Charles II's queen, 1662 ; serjeant-at-

law and lord chief baron of the exchequer, 1676 ; removed from the bench on his refusal to give an unqualified opinion in favour of the prerogative of dispensation, 1686 ; assessor to the convention, 1689.
[xxxviii. 272]

MONTAGU, WILLIAM (1720?–1757), naval captain ; brother of John Montagu, fourth earl of Sandwich [q. v.] ; lieutenant, 1740 ; commander, 1744 ; distinguished in the action of 3 May 1747 ; M.P., Huntingdon, 1745, Bossiney, 1752.   [xxxviii. 273]

MONTAGU, WILLIAM, fifth DUKE OF MANCHESTER (1768–1843), governor of Jamaica ; son of George Montagu, fourth duke of Manchester [q. v.] ; gazetted lieutenant, 1787 ; colonel in the army, 1794 ; lord-lieutenant of Huntingdonshire, 1793 ; governor of Jamaica, 1808 ; reforms made in the law courts and post office during his governorship, 1814 ; alleviated the distress caused by the hurricane and floods, 1815 ; the Jamaica slaves pacified by his personal influence during the insurrection of the slaves in Barbados ; returned to England, 1827 ; post-master-general, 1827–30 ; voted against the Reform Bill ; died in Rome.   [xxxviii. 274]

MONTAGUE. [See also MONTAGU.]

MONTAGUE, BARON (1492?–1539). [See POLE, HENRY.]

MONTAGUE, HENRY JAMES (1843?–1878), actor ; his real name MANN ; held an appointment in the Sun Fire office ; appeared in London at Astley's Theatre, 1863, the St. James's, 1864, the Prince of Wales's, 1867, and the Princess's, 1868 ; partner in the Vaudeville, 1870–1 ; sole lessee of the Globe, 1871–4 ; excelled in juvenile parts ; went to America and died at San Francisco.   [xxxviii. 275]

MONTAIGNE or MOUNTAIN, GEORGE (1569–1628), archbishop of York ; M.A. Queens' College, Cambridge, 1593 ; fellow, 1591 ; attended Essex as chaplain to Cadiz, 1596 ; professor of divinity at Gresham College, London, 1607 ; master of the Savoy and chaplain to James I, 1608 ; incumbent of Cheam, 1609 ; dean of Westminster, 1610 ; bishop of Lincoln, 1617 ; lord high almoner, 1619 ; bishop of London, 1621 ; enthusiastic supporter of Laud ; bishop of Durham, 1627 ; said to have secured the primacy of York by a witty remark, 1628. He founded two scholarships at Queens' College, Cambridge.   [xxxviii. 276]

MONTALBA, HENRIETTA SKERRETT (1856–1893), sculptor ; first exhibited at the Royal Academy, 1876 ; devoted herself mainly to portrait or fancy busts ; worked mostly in terracotta ; died at Venice.
[xxxviii. 277]

MONTE, ROBERT DE (1110?–1186). [See ROBERT.]

MONTEAGE, STEPHEN (1623?–1687), merchant and accountant ; agent to Christopher Hatton, first viscount Hatton [q. v.] ; did much to bring double entry into general use ; published books on double entry.
[xxxviii. 278]

MONTEAGLE, BARONS. [See STANLEY, EDWARD, first BARON, 1460?–1523 ; PARKER, WILLIAM, fourth BARON, 1575–1622.]

MONTEAGLE OF BRANDON, first BARON. [See SPRING-RICE, THOMAS, 1790–1866.]

MONTEATH, GEORGE CUNNINGHAM (1788–1828), physician and oculist ; studied in Glasgow ; licensed by the R.C.S. ; surgeon to Northumberland militia, 1809–13 ; physician and oculist in Glasgow ; published 'Manual of the Diseases of the Human Eye,' 1821.   [xxxviii. 278]

MONTEATH, SIR THOMAS (1787–1868). [See DOUGLAS, SIR THOMAS MONTEATH.]

MONTEFIORE, SIR MOSES HAIM, first baronet (1784–1885), philanthropist and centenarian ; amassed a fortune as a stockbroker and retired, 1824 ; sheriff of London and knighted, 1837 ; secured a firman from the sultan placing Jews on the same footing as all other aliens, 1840 ; obtained abrogation of ukase for removal of Jews into the interior of Russia, 1846 ; received baronetcy, 1846 ; collected and distributed fund for relief of sufferers by Syrian famine, 1855 ; founded girls' school and hospital at Jerusalem, 1855 ; raised funds for the Jewish and Christian refugees at Gibraltar, 1860 ; obtained from the sultan of Morocco an edict giving equality to the Jews,

1864; interceded on behalf of the Moldavian Jews, 1867; visited Jerusalem for the seventh time, 1875; wrote a narrative of his visit for private circulation.

[xxxviii. 278]

MONTEITH, ROBERT (*fl.* 1621-1660). [See MENTEITH.]

MONTEITH, WILLIAM (1790-1864), lieutenant-general, Indian army, diplomatist, and historian; lieutenant in Madras engineers, 1809; captain, 1817; colonel, 1839; accompanied Sir John Malcolm's embassy to Persia, 1810; commanded against Russians, 1810-13; employed to ascertain the boundary between Persia and Turkey, 1821, and between Persia and Russia, 1828; left Persia, 1829; chief engineer at Madras, 1832; major-general, 1841; retired from service, 1847; lieutenant-general, 1854; wrote books on geography and the Russian campaigns of 1808-9 and 1826-8. [xxxviii. 280]

MONTEZ, LOLA (1818-1861). [See GILBERT, MARIE DOLORES ELIZA ROSANNA.]

MONTFICHET, RICHARD DE (*d.* 1268), justiciar; one of the twenty-five barons appointed to enforce Magna Charta; justice itinerant for Essex and Hertfordshire, 1225; baron of the exchequer, 1234; justice of the forest for nineteen counties, 1237; sheriff of Essex and Hertfordshire, 1242-6. [xxxviii. 281]

MONTFORT, ALMERIC OF (*d.* 1292 ?), son of Simon of Montfort, earl of Leicester [q. v.]; canon and treasurer of York, 1265; lost these preferments on his father's fall, 1265; went to Italy, 1268; chaplain to the pope; assumed title of Earl of Leicester, his brother Guy being an outlaw, 1272; refused permission to return to England, 1273; sued Edmund Mortimer, the treasurer of York, before the official of Paris, 1274; captured at Bristol, 1276; imprisoned for six years and liberated on condition of abjuring the realm, 1282. [xxxviii. 282]

MONTFORT, ELEANOR OF (1252-1282), daughter of Simon of Montfort, earl of Leicester [q. v.]; exiled to France, 1265; married by proxy to Llywelyn ab Gruffydd, prince of Wales, 1275; captured and imprisoned till 1278; married to Llywelyn on his submission to Edward I, 1278. [xxxviii. 282]

MONTFORT, GUY OF (1243 ?-1288 ?), son of Simon of Montfort, earl of Leicester [q. v.]; shared command at Lewes, 1264; wounded and taken prisoner at Evesham, 1265; escaped to France, 1266; governor of Tuscany, 1268; with his brother Simon murdered Henry of Cornwall at Viterbo, 1271, in revenge for his father's death; excommunicated and outlawed, 1273; bought his freedom, 1274; captain-general of the papal forces, 1283; captured at Catania, 1287; died in a Sicilian prison. [xxxviii. 283]

MONTFORT, HENRY OF (1238-1265), son of Simon of Montfort, earl of Leicester [q. v.]; accompanied his father to Gascony, 1252; knighted by Prince Edward, 1260; represented barons at Mise of Amiens, 1264; commanded on Welsh border, 1264; seized Worcester, 1264; led van at Lewes, 1264; constable of Dover Castle, governor of the Cinque ports, and treasurer of Sandwich, 1264; fought and fell at Evesham. [xxxviii. 283]

MONTFORT, SIMON OF, EARL OF LEICESTER (1208 ?-1265), son of Simon IV of Montfort l'Amaury (Normandy); born in Normandy; agreed with his elder brother Almeric to exchange his share in their continental patrimony for the earldom of Leicester, the heritage of their English grandmother; went to England, 1229; found that the estates had been given to the Earl of Chester, who, however, acknowledged Simon's right to them and petitioned the king to restore them, 1231; unable to support the rank and dignity of an earl, although he officiated as grand seneschal at the queen's coronation, 1236, an office belonging to the earldom of Leicester; married Eleanor, sister of Henry III, 1238; went to Rome to obtain the pope's dispensation, the marriage being an ecclesiastical offence, as Eleanor had taken a vow of perpetual widowhood; formally invested with the earldom of Leicester, 1239; quarrelled with Henry III concerning a debt, 1239; crusader, 1240; returned to Europe, 1242, and helped Henry III in Poitou; commissioner to answer the king's demand for money, 1244; induced (1248) to undertake the government of Gascony on condition of having absolute control; his high-handed severity, at first successful, followed by a rising in Gascony, 1251; besieged chief malcontents at Castillon and took the town,

forcing the rebel leaders one by one to make their peace; after a second rising Henry III heard complaints against Simon at Westminster; he was accused of all sorts of oppression and violence; denied some of the charges and claimed that his severity was justified by the utter lawlessness of the Gascons; the accusers agreeing to no settlement, Simon was acquitted; returned to Gascony to find the truce broken and prepared to fight Gaston de Béarn, 1252; yielded to Henry III's demand that he should resign his governorship, 1252; withdrew to France; his help in quelling the revolt requested by Henry III, 1253; envoy to Scotland, 1254, to France, 1255, 1257, and 1258, and to Italy, 1257; one of the commissioners of administrative reform, who drew up the 'Provisions of Oxford,' 1258; attacked by Henry III in council, 1260; withdrew to France, 1261, Henry having proclaimed his intention of ruling as he pleased; summoned to England as its leader by the parliament, which had denounced the king as false to his oath and proclaimed war on all violators of the 'Provisions,' 1263; agreed with the other barons to refer the dispute to the arbitration of St. Louis of France, whose decision, the 'Mise of Amiens' (1264), quashed the 'Provisions,' but recognised popular rights; defeated the royalists and captured the king at the battle of Lewes (14 May 1264); being by the 'Mise of Lewes' virtually governor of the king and kingdom summoned (1264) a parliament (January 1265), not only of churchmen, barons, and knights, but also two citizens from every borough in England; quarrelled with Gilbert de Clare, the young (ninth) earl of Gloucester [q. v.], who thereupon joined Prince Edward and the marcher lords; killed in the resulting battle at Evesham, 4 Aug. 1265. He was not the inventor of the representative system, nor the creator of the House of Commons, but a champion of righteousness rather than a reformer of government, a hero rather than a statesman. [xxxviii. 284]

MONTFORT, SIMON OF, the younger (1240-1271), son of Simon of Montfort, earl of Leicester [q. v.]; knighted by Prince Edward, 1260; defended Northampton, 1264, but was captured by Henry III; released after Lewes (1264), but reached Evesham after the battle and withdrew to Kenilworth, 1265, where he was forced to submit; escaped over sea, 1266; took part with his brother Guy of Montfort [q. v.] in the murder of Henry of Cornwall at Viterbo, 1271; died at Siena. [xxxviii. 295]

MONTGOMERIE. [See also MONTGOMERY.]

MONTGOMERIE, SIR ALEXANDER DE, of Ardrossan, first BARON MONTGOMERIE (*d.* 1470 ?), grandson of Sir John Montgomerie [q. v.]; privy councillor, 1425; joint-governor of Cantyre and Knapdale, 1430; commissioner to England and sent on various important embassies; keeper of Brodick Castle, 1444; lord of parliament, 1445. [xxxviii. 296]

MONTGOMERIE, ALEXANDER (1556 ?-1610 ?), Scottish poet; brother of Robert Montgomerie (*d.* 1609) [q. v.]; held office in the Scottish court, 1577; styled captain; became laureate of the court; travelled on the continent, 1586; imprisoned abroad and his pension withheld, a protracted lawsuit resulting; wrote, besides miscellaneous poems, 'The Cherrie and the Slae,' (first edition printed, 1597), which has long been popular; his 'Flyting betwixt Montgomery and Polwart,' published by Andro Hart, 1621. [xxxviii. 297]

MONTGOMERIE or **SETON**, ALEXANDER, sixth EARL OF EGLINTON (1588-1661), originally known as Sir Alexander Seton; succeeded his cousin Hugh, fifth earl of Eglinton, who, having no issue, made a resignation and settlement of the earldom and entail on him, provided he took the name and arms of Montgomerie, 1612 (confirmed by the king, 1615); petitioned against the prayer-book and assisted in the preparations of the national covenant; privy councillor of Scotland, 1641; commanded Scottish regiment of horse at Marston Moor, 1644; on the execution of Charles I supported the recall of Charles II and the policy of Argyll; betrayed to Cromwell, 1651; detained in Edinburgh Castle, but afterwards allowed the liberty of Berwick; his estates sequestered for two years; included in Cromwell's Act of Grace. [xxxviii. 298]

MONTGOMERIE, ALEXANDER, ninth EARL OF EGLINTON (1660 ?-1729), grandson of Hugh Montgomerie, seventh earl of Eglinton [q. v.]; educated at St. Andrews University; privy councillor and a lord of the treasury under William III; succeeded as ninth earl, 1701; Scottish representative peer, 1710 and 1713; supported bill for resuming bishops' revenues in Scotland and applying them to the episcopal clergy; raised and disciplined the Ayrshire fencibles, 1715. [xxxviii. 300]

MONTGOMERIE, ALEXANDER, tenth EARL OF EGLINTON (1723–1769), son of Alexander Montgomerie, ninth earl of Eglinton [q. v.]; purchased the sheriffship of Renfrew, 1748; governor of Dumbarton Castle, 1759; lord of the bedchamber to George III; strongly opposed to the optional clause in the Scottish Bank Act and to the accumulation of the public debt; published 'Inquiry into the Origin and Consequences of the Public Debt,' 1754; representative peer for Scotland, 1761 and 1768; shot by Mungo Campbell, an excise officer, perhaps accidentally. [xxxviii. 301]

MONTGOMERIE, ARCHIBALD, eleventh EARL OF EGLINTON (1726–1796), son of Alexander Montgomerie, ninth earl of Eglinton [q. v.]; raised regiment of highlanders and was appointed lieutenant-colonel commandant, 1757; served in America; colonel, 1769; succeeded to earldom, 1769; lieutenant-general, 1777.
 [xxxviii. 302]

MONTGOMERIE, ARCHIBALD WILLIAM, thirteenth EARL OF EGLINTON and first EARL OF WINTON in the peerage of the United Kingdom (1812–1861), born at Palermo; succeeded his grandfather, Hugh Montgomerie, twelfth earl of Eglinton [q. v.], 1819; lord-lieutenant of Ayrshire, 1842; one of the whips of the protection party, 1846; lord-lieutenant of Ireland, 1852; privy councillor, 1852 (February to December) and 1858–9; K.T., 1853; created Earl of Winton, 1859; held tournament at Eglinton Castle, 1839, described in Disraeli's 'Endymion'; lord rector of Aberdeen and Glasgow, 1852; president of the Burns commemoration, 1844; D.C.L. Oxford, 1853. [xxxviii. 303]

MONTGOMERIE, HUGH, third BARON MONTGOMERIE and first EARL OF EGLINTON (1460 ?–1545), grandson of Sir Alexander Montgomerie, first baron Montgomerie [q. v.]; was privy councillor, 1489; created Earl of Eglinton, 1506; guardian of the infant James V, 1513; justice-general of the northern parts of Scotland, 1527; one of the council of regency, 1536. [xxxviii. 304]

MONTGOMERIE, HUGH, third EARL OF EGLINTON (1531 ?–1585), great-grandson of Hugh Montgomerie, first earl of Eglinton [q. v.]; student of St. Mary's College, St. Andrews, 1552; visited Mary Stuart in France and returned in her train, 1560; supported Mary's Roman catholic policy; had no connection with Darnley's murder; opposed Mary's marriage to Bothwell; joined her after her escape from Lochleven; fought for her at Langside, 1568; subscribed his obedience to the regent, 1571; endeavoured to secure toleration for Romanists, 1573; privy councillor, 1578; subscribed order for prosecution of the Hamiltons, 1579; one of the assize for Morton's trial, 1581; formally approved Ruthven raid, 1582. [xxxviii. 305]

MONTGOMERIE, HUGH, seventh EARL OF EGLINTON (1613–1669), son of Alexander Montgomerie, sixth earl of Eglinton [q. v.]; student of Glasgow University, 1628; opposed Charles I's ecclesiastical policy; colonel under Leslie at Newburn; failed to seize Tynemouth, 1640; engaged in northern campaign under Middleton, 1646; defeated by Huntly at Aberdeen, 1646; disqualified for public service until 1650 for being accessory to the 'engagement'; taken prisoner, 1651; excepted from Cromwell's Act of Grace, 1654. [xxxviii. 306]

MONTGOMERIE, HUGH, twelfth EARL OF EGLINTON (1739–1819), captain in the army during the American war; major in the western fencibles, 1788; M.P., Ayrshire, 1780–1789; inspector of military roads in Scotland, 1789; colonel of west lowland fencibles, 1793; succeeded to earldom, 1796; representative peer of Scotland, 1798 and 1802; created Baron Ardrossan of Ardrossan in the United Kingdom, 1806; K.T.; lord-lieutenant of Ayrshire; commenced a harbour for Ardrossan, 1806; composed popular airs. [xxxviii. 307]

MONTGOMERIE, SIR JOHN, ninth of Eaglesham and first of Eglinton and Ardrossan (d. 1398 ?), succeeded his father, c. 1380; obtained baronies of Eglinton and Ardrossan by his marriage; distinguished himself at Otterburn, 1388. [xxxviii. 308]

MONTGOMERIE, ROBERT (d. 1609), titular archbishop of Glasgow; brother of Alexander Montgomerie (1556 ?–1610 ?) [q. v.]; minister at Cupar, 1562, Dunblane, 1567, and Stirling, 1572; presented to the archbishopric of Glasgow, 1581; censured and interdicted from taking the office by the general assembly; having entered Glasgow church with an armed force, was excommunicated by the presbytery of Edinburgh; his excommunication was declared void by parliament, 1584; resigned bishopric, 1587; pastor of Symington, 1588, of Ayr, 1589. [xxxviii. 309]

MONTGOMERIE, ROBERT (d. 1684), parliamentary and afterwards royalist officer; son of Alexander Montgomerie, sixth earl of Eglinton [q. v.]; educated at Glasgow University; fought at Marston Moor, 1644; commanded under Middleton, 1646; joined western whigamores in march on Edinburgh, 1648; after the recall of Charles II, 1650, was employed on the royalist side; fought as major-general and captured at Worcester, 1651; escaped from the Tower of London, 1654; arrested and confined in Edinburgh Castle; again escaped, 1657; lord of the bedchamber to Charles II; imprisoned for his presbyterian sympathies, 1665–8. [xxxviii. 310]

MONTGOMERIE, THOMAS GEORGE (1830–1878), colonel, royal engineers, and geographer; second lieutenant, Bengal engineers, 1849; assisted in surveying plain of Chach, 1853, and Karachi, 1854–5; first lieutenant, 1854; given charge of the trigo-topographical survey of Janin and Kashmir, 1855–64; captain, 1858; appointed to the Himalaya survey in Kumaon and Gurhwal, 1867; trained natives, who passed freely to and fro as traders, it being impossible for European officers to extend the survey without the risk of political complications; responsible for the survey of the route to Yarkand, 1863, and the discovery of the upper valley and source of the Brahmaputra; officiated as superintendent of the great trigonometrical survey of India, 1870–3; major, 1872; lieutenant-colonel, 1874; retired as colonel, 1876; F.R.S.; contributed to scientific periodicals papers on the native explorers' travels and the geography of India. [xxxviii. 311]

MONTGOMERY, EARLS OF. [See HERBERT, PHILIP, first EARL, 1584–1650; HERBERT, HENRY, sixth EARL, 1693–1751; HERBERT, HENRY, seventh EARL, 1734–1794; HERBERT, GEORGE AUGUSTUS, eighth EARL, 1759–1827.]

MONTGOMERY, COUNTESS OF. [See CLIFFORD, ANNE, 1590–1676.]

MONTGOMERY, HENRY (1788–1865), founder of the remonstrant synod of Ulster; M.A. Glasgow, 1807; pastor of Dunmurry, near Belfast, 1809; head-master of Belfast Academical Institution, 1817–39; moderator of the synod, 1818; strongly opposed Henry Cooke's attempt to render presbyterian discipline more stringent; adopted a 'remonstrance,' 1829, the first meeting of the remonstrance synod being held, 1830; advocated catholic emancipation and Irish disestablishment; elected by the combined remonstrance synod, Antrim presbytery, and Munster synod professor of ecclesiastical history and pastoral theology, 1838; an original editor of the 'Bible Christian'; contributed 'Outlines of the History of Presbyterianism in Ireland' to the 'Irish Unitarian Magazine,' 1846–7.
 [xxxviii. 313]

MONTGOMERY, SIR HENRY CONYNGHAM, second baronet (1803–1878), Madras civil servant; educated at Eton and Haileybury; went to India, 1825; succeeded to baronetcy, 1830; sent on special commission to Rájahmundry district, 1843, and recommended utilisation of waters of the Godávery for irrigation [see COTTON, SIR ARTHUR THOMAS]; secretary to government in revenue and public works department, 1843–50; chief secretary, 1850; member of governor's council, 1855–7; original member of new council of India in London, 1858–76; privy councillor, 1876. [Suppl. iii. 189]

MONTGOMERY, HUGH OF, second EARL OF SHREWSBURY (d. 1098). [See HUGH.]

MONTGOMERY, HUGH, third VISCOUNT MONTGOMERY of the Ards and first EARL OF MOUNT ALEXANDER (1623 ?–1663), succeeded his father as viscount, and was appointed to command his father's regiment, 1642; commander-in-chief of the royalist army in Ulster, 1649; seized successively Belfast, Antrim, and Carrickfergus; surrendered to Cromwell, and was banished to Holland; life master of ordnance in Ireland, 1660; created Earl of Mount Alexander, 1661. [xxxviii. 315]

MONTGOMERY or **MONTGOMERIE**, SIR JAMES, tenth BARONET OF SKELMORLIE (*d.* 1694), politician; imprisoned for harbouring covenanters, 1684; visited Holland in connection with the invitation to William, prince of Orange; M.P., Ayrshire, 1689; organised 'The Club' political society; went to London with his confederates, but William III having declined to listen to their complaints, joined the Jacobites in the Montgomery plot; confessed on promise of indemnity; was imprisoned for writing against the government, but escaped to Paris, 1694; died at St. Germain. [xxxviii. 316]

MONTGOMERY, JAMES (1771–1854), poet; clerk and book-keeper to the 'Sheffield Register,' 1792, becoming a contributor to and finally editor of the paper, which was renamed the 'Sheffield Iris,' and became Montgomery's property, 1795; imprisoned for libel, 1795 and 1796; sold his paper, 1825; lectured on poetry at the Royal Institution, 1830 and 1831. His best-known hymns include 'For ever with the Lord,' 'Songs of praise the Angels sang,' and 'Go to dark Gethsemane,' and among his poems are 'The Wanderer of Switzerland,' 1806, 'The West Indies,' 1809, 'The World before the Flood,' 1812, 'Greenland,' 1819, and 'The Pelican Island,' 1826. [xxxviii. 317]

MONTGOMERY, SIR JAMES WILLIAM, first baronet (1721–1803), Scottish judge; called to the Scottish bar, 1743; sheriff of Peeblesshire, 1748; joint solicitorgeneral, 1760; sole solicitor-general, 1764; lord advocate, 1766; M.P., Dumfries burghs, 1766, Peeblesshire, 1768; introduced measure for reform of entails, 1770; created lord chief baron of the Scottish exchequer, 1775; resigned his judgeship and was created baronet, 1801. [xxxviii. 320]

MONTGOMERY, JEMIMA (1807–1893). [See TAUTPHOEUS, BARONESS VON.]

MONTGOMERY, PHILIP OF (*d.* 1099). [See PHILIP.]

MONTGOMERY, RICHARD (1736–1775), majorgeneral; of St. Andrews and Trinity College, Dublin; entered the army, 1756; captain, 1762; served in Canada, 1759, and Cuba, 1762; sold out of the army, 1772; settled on the Hudson river; became brigadier-general in the American army, 1775; took (1775) Fort Chamblai and St. John's, but was killed in an attack on Quebec. [xxxviii. 320]

MONTGOMERY, SIR ROBERT, eleventh BARONET OF SKELMORLIE (1680–1731), projector of a scheme for colonisation in America; served in war of Spanish succession, 1702–13; granted land in South Carolina, 1717; recommended as governor, 1718. [xxxviii. 321]

MONTGOMERY, ROBERT (1807–1855), poetaster; wrote religious poems (including 'The Omnipresence of the Deity,' 1828, and 'Satan,' 1830) which were extravagantly praised in the press, and severely criticised by Macaulay in the 'Edinburgh Review,' 1830; B.A. Lincoln College, Oxford, 1833; M.A., 1838; curate of Whittington, 1835; incumbent of St. Jude's, Glasgow, 1836; minister of Percy Chapel, St. Pancras, London, 1843. [xxxviii. 322]

MONTGOMERY, SIR ROBERT (1809–1887), Indian administrator; appointed to the Bengal civil service, 1827; transferred to the Punjáb; commissioner of the Lahore division, 1849; disarmed the sepoys at Lahore and Mean Meer, 12 May 1857, and warned Ferozepore, Mooltan, and Kangra of the mutiny; chief commissioner of Oudh, 1858; lieutenant-governor of the Punjáb, 1859–65; K.C.B., 1859; G.C.S.I., 1866; member of the council of state for India, 1868. [xxxviii. 323]

MONTGOMERY, ROGER OF, EARL OF SHREWSBURY (*d.* 1093?). [See ROGER.]

MONTGOMERY, WALTER (1827–1871), actor; his real name RICHARD TOMLINSON; born at Long Island, America; acted in London, 1863; acted with Helen Faucit [q. v.] and Mrs. Kendal; made some reputation in America and Australia; committed suicide. [xxxviii. 324]

MONTGOMERY, WILLIAM (1633–1707), historian; educated at Glasgow and Leyden Universities; M.P., Newtownards, 1661; high sheriff of Down, 1670; chief works, 'Incidentall Remembrances of the two Ancient Families of the Savadges,' first printed, 1830, 'The Narrative of Gransheogh,' 'Memoires of William Montgomery of Rose-

mount, co. Down,' and 'Memoirs of the Montgomerys of England and Scotland,' first printed, 1869. [xxxviii. 325]

MONTHERMER, RALPH DE, EARL OF GLOUCESTER AND HERTFORD (*d.* 1325?), a squire of Gilbert de Clare, earl of Gloucester, whose widow he married, 1297, and whose titles he bore in right of his wife; served in Scotland, 1298, 1303, 1304, and 1306; received earldom of Athol, 1306, but surrendered it, 1307; keeper of castles in Wales, 1307; warden and lieutenant for Edward II in Scotland, 1311 and 1312; taken prisoner at Bannockburn, 1314; warden of the royal forest south of the Trent, 1320. [xxxviii. 326]

MONTJOY. [See MOUNTJOY.]

MONTMORENCY, HERVEY DE (*fl.* 1169). [See MOUNT-MAURICE.]

MONTRESOR, JAMES GABRIEL (1702–1776), director and colonel, royal engineers; matross, 1727; practitioner-engineer, 1731; ensign, 1732; lieutenant, 1737; engineer extraordinary, 1742; engineer at Port Mahon, 1743–7; chief engineer at Gibraltar, 1747–54; chief engineer of the expedition to North America under Majorgeneral Braddock, 1754; prepared roads over the Alleghany mountains, 1755; surveyed Lake Champlain and strategic vicinity, 1756; major, 1757; director and lieutenant-colonel, 1758; designed and constructed Fort George, 1759; superintended erection of new powder magazines at Purfleet, 1763–5; chief engineer at Chatham, 1769; colonel, 1772. [xxxviii. 327]

MONTRESOR, JOHN (1736–1788?), major, royal engineers; son of James Gabriel Montresor [q. v.]; born at Gibraltar; accompanied his father to North America, 1754; wounded at battle of Du Quesne, 1755; sub-engineer, 1759; took part in reduction of Canada; captainlieutenant, 1765; chief engineer in America, 1775; captain and engineer in ordinary, 1776; constructed Philadelphia lines of defence; retired, 1779. [xxxviii. 328]

MONTROSE, DUKES OF. [See LINDSAY, DAVID, first DUKE, 1440?–1495; GRAHAM, JAMES, first DUKE of the second creation, *d.* 1742; GRAHAM, JAMES, third DUKE, 1755–1836; GRAHAM, JAMES, fourth DUKE, 1799–1874.]

MONTROSE, MARQUISES OF. [See GRAHAM, JAMES, first MARQUIS, 1612–1650; GRAHAM, JAMES, second MARQUIS, 1631?–1669; GRAHAM, JAMES, fourth MARQUIS, *d.* 1742.]

MONTROSE, EARLS OF. [See GRAHAM, JOHN, third EARL, 1547?–1608; GRAHAM, JAMES, fifth EARL, 1612–1650.]

MOODIE, DONALD (*d.* 1861), commander, royal navy, and colonial secretary in Natal; entered navy, 1808; lieutenant, 1816; emigrated to Cape Colony, 1816; resident magistrate at Fort Francis, 1825, at Graham's Town, 1828; protector of slaves in the eastern district, 1830–4; superintendent of the government bank, Cape Town, 1840; secretary and colonial treasurer of Natal, 1845–51; published works on the history of the Cape; died at Pietermaritzburg. [xxxviii. 329]

MOODIE, JOHN WEDDERBURN DUNBAR (1797–1869), soldier; brother of Donald Moodie [q. v.]; second lieutenant, 1813; first lieutenant, 1814; wounded at Bergen-op-Zoom, 1814; joined his brothers James and Donald in South Africa, 1814–24; emigrated to Upper Canada; captain of militia on the Niagara frontier, 1837; sheriff of Vittoria, Ontario, 1839; wrote on the wars in Holland, 1814; published descriptions of sports and life in the Bush, 1835 and 1852. [xxxviii. 330]

MOODIE, MRS. SUSANNAH (1803–1885), authoress; sister of Agnes Strickland [q. v.]; married John Wedderburn Dunbar Moodie [q. v.]; published poems and stories. [xxxviii. 330]

MOODY, JOHN (1727?–1812), actor; his real name Cochran; first acted in Jamaica; in London, 1759; acted chiefly at Drury Lane; retired, 1796; excelled in comic characters. [xxxviii. 331]

MOODY, RICHARD CLEMENT (1813–1887), colonial governor; born in Barbados; entered Woolwich, 1827; second lieutenant in the royal engineers, 1830; for some years at St. Vincent; first lieutenant, 1835; professor of fortification at Woolwich, 1838; first governor of the Falkland islands, 1841; captain, R.E., 1847; returned to

England, 1849; lieutenant-colonel, 1855; brevet-colonel, 1858; lieutenant-governor of British Columbia, 1858; colonel, 1863; returned home, 1863, retired as major-general, 1866. [xxxviii. 332]

MOON, SIR FRANCIS GRAHAM, first baronet (1796–1871), printseller and publisher; placed with the book and print seller Tugwell, whose business he subsequently purchased; joined the firm Moon, Boys & Graves in Pall Mall, 1825; reproduced some of the finest works of Wilkie, Eastlake, Landseer, and others; sheriff of London, 1843; alderman, 1844; lord mayor, 1854; created baronet, 1855. [xxxviii. 333]

MOON, WILLIAM (1818–1894), inventor of Moon's embossed type for the blind; became totally blind, 1840; taught blind children, and constructed (1845) a system of embossed type differing from former systems in almost entirely discarding contractions; issued several publications, including the bible, in his system, which he extended to foreign languages, beginning with Irish and Chinese; F.R.G.S., 1852; fellow of Society of Arts, 1859; LL.D. Philadelphia, 1871; advocated and assisted in forming home teaching societies and lending libraries for the blind. [Suppl. iii. 190]

MOONE, PETER (*fl.* 1548), poet; author of 'A short Treatise of certayne Thinges abused in the Popysh Church.' [xxxviii. 334]

MOOR. [See also MOORE and MORE.]

MOOR, EDWARD (1771–1848), writer on Hindoo mythology; cadet under the East India Company, 1782; lieutenant, 1788; served with the Mahratta army, 1790–1; wounded at Doridroog and Gadjmoor, 1791; brevet-captain, 1796; garrison storekeeper at Bombay, 1799–1805; member of the Asiatic Society of Calcutta, 1796; F.R.S., 1806; F.S.A., 1818; wrote principally on Hindoo mythology and other Indian subjects. [xxxviii. 334]

MOOR, JAMES (1712–1779), professor of Greek; distinguished himself in classics and mathematics at Glasgow University; private tutor; librarian of Glasgow University, 1742; professor of Greek, Glasgow, 1745–74; vice-rector, 1761; LL.D., 1763; edited classical authors for the Foulis press, and wrote on classical subjects. [xxxviii. 335]

MOOR, MICHAEL (1640–1726), provost of Trinity College, Dublin; studied at Nantes and Paris; prebendary of Tymothan, 1685; provost of Trinity College, Dublin, 1689; his deposition procured by the jesuits; censor of books at Rome; rector of Paris University, 1702; principal of the Collège de Navarre; professor of Greek and Latin philosophy at the Collège de France; helped to remodel the university, and to found the college, of Cambray; wrote against the Cartesian philosophy; died in Paris. [xxxviii. 336]

MOOR, ROBERT (1568–1640), chronographer; of Winchester College and New College Oxford; M.A., 1595; D.D., 1614; perpetual fellow of New College, 1589–97; rector of West Meon and vicar of East Meon, 1597; prebendary of Winchester, 1613; published a long Latin poem intended as a universal chronology, 1595. [xxxviii. 336]

MOOR, SIR THOMAS DE LA (*fl.* 1327–1347). [See MORE.]

MOORCROFT, WILLIAM (1765 ?–1825), veterinary surgeon and traveller; studied veterinary science in France; settled in London, where he realised an ample fortune, but lost it over patents; veterinary surgeon to the Bengal army, 1808; crossed the Himalaya and examined the sources of the Sutlej and Indus, 1811–12; explored Lahore and Cashmere, 1819–22; visited Bokhara, 1825; died at Andekhui; a summary of his travels published, 1841; wrote also on veterinary surgery. [xxxviii. 337]

MOORE. [See also MOOR and MORE.]

MOORE, ALBERT JOSEPH (1841–1893), painter; son of William Moore (1790–1851) [q. v.]; exhibited natural-history subjects at the Royal Academy, 1857–9, and sacred subjects, 1861–5; devoted himself entirely to decorative pictures from 1865; noted for his diaphanous draperies. [xxxviii. 338]

MOORE, ANN (*fl.* 1813), the 'fasting woman of Tutbury'; *née* Pegg; married a farm servant, James Moore, who deserted her; arrived at Tutbury, c. 1800; originally

compelled to fast by poverty, she afterwards traded on her fame as a 'fasting woman'; confessed the fraudulence of her fasts in 1813. [xxxviii. 339]

MOORE, ARTHUR (1666 ?–1730), economist and politician; born in Ireland; studied trade questions; M.P., Grimsby, 1695–1715; high steward of Grimsby, 1714–30; director of the South Sea Company; comptroller of army accounts, 1704; lord commissioner of trade and plantations, 1710; responsible for the reciprocal tariff clauses in the treaty of commerce, 1712, which were eventually cancelled; charged before the South Sea Company with being privy to clandestine trade, 1714; censured and declared incapable of further employment, 1714; held advanced views on trade questions. [xxxviii. 340]

MOORE, AUBREY LACKINGTON (1848–1890), writer on theology; of St. Paul's School, London, and Exeter College, Oxford; M.A., 1874; fellow of St. John's College, Oxford, 1872–6; rector of Frenchay, 1876–81; tutor of Keble College, Oxford, 1881; select preacher at Oxford, 1885–6, Whitehall, 1887–8; hon. canon of Christ Church, Oxford, 1887; contributed to 'Lux Mundi,' 1889; published scientific and philosophical works. [xxxviii. 342]

MOORE, SIR CHARLES, second VISCOUNT MOORE of Drogheda (1603–1643), son of Sir Garret Moore, viscount Moore of Drogheda [q. v.]; succeeded his father, 1627; energetically set about repairing the fortifications of Drogheda, and endeavoured to procure assistance from government against the rebels, 1641; distinguished himself at the siege and was active in suppressing the Meath rebellion, 1642; commissioner to hear the grievances of the confederate catholics, 1643; advanced against Owen O'Neill at Portlester, where he was killed.
[xxxviii. 342]

MOORE, CHARLES, sixth EARL and first MARQUIS OF DROGHEDA (1730–1822), entered the army, 1755; M.P., St. Canice, 1756–8; succeeded as earl, 1758; governor of Meath, 1759; lieutenant-colonel, 1759; colonel, 1762; secretary to the lord-lieutenant, 1763; lord justice, 1766; governor of Queen's County, 1767; lieutenant-general, 1777; general, 1793; field-marshal, 1821; M.P., Horsham, 1776–80; K.P., 1783; created Marquis of Drogheda, 1791; joint postmaster-general, 1797–1806.
[xxxviii. 344]

MOORE, CHARLES (1815–1881), geologist; F.G.S., 1854; discovered the Rhaetic beds and founded the Museum at Bath Institute; contributed papers to geological and scientific societies. [xxxviii. 344]

MOORE, DAVID (1807–1879), botanist; migrated to Ireland, 1828; assistant in Dublin University botanic garden; director of Glasnevin botanic garden, 1838; published botanical papers. [xxxviii. 345]

MOORE, DUGALD (1805–1841), Scottish poet; bookseller in Glasgow; published lyrical poems, including 'The African,' 1829, and 'The Bard of the North,' 1833.
[xxxviii. 345]

MOORE, SIR EDWARD (1530 ?–1602), constable of Philipstown; went to Ireland, c. 1559; sheriff of Louth, 1571; constable of Philipstown, 1576; commissioner for concealed lands and ecclesiastical causes, 1577; knighted, 1579; Irish privy councillor, 1589; negotiated with the Earl of Tyrone and acted as commissioner for the preservation of the peace of Leinster, 1599 and 1601.
[xxxviii. 346]

MOORE, EDWARD (1712–1757), fabulist and dramatist; failed as a linendraper; patronised by George Lyttelton, first baron Lyttelton [q. v.], and Henry Pelham [q. v.]; editor of 'The World,' a satirical periodical, 1753–7; published 'Fables for the Female Sex,' 1744, 'The Trial of Selim the Persian,' 1748, 'The Foundling,' 1748, 'Gil Blas,' 1751, and 'The Gamester,' 1753; probably assisted by Garrick. [xxxviii. 347]

MOORE, EDWIN (1813–1893), water-colour painter; son of William Moore (1790–1851) [q. v.]; taught painting at York. [xxxviii. 386]

MOORE, ELEANORA, otherwise NELLY (*d.* 1869), actress; most successful at the Haymarket Theatre, London, with Sothern. [xxxviii. 348]

MOORE, SIR FRANCIS (1558–1621), law reporter; commoner of St. John's College, Oxford, 1574; member of New Inn; entered Middle Temple, 1580; autumn reader, 1607; counsel and under-steward of Oxford University, 1612; created M.A. Oxford, 1612; serjeant-at-law, 1614; knighted, 1616; M.P., Boroughbridge, 1588-9, Reading, 1597-8, 1601, 1604-11, and 1614; invented the conveyance known as lease and release. His law reports (1663) extend from 1512 to 1621. [xxxviii. 348]

MOORE, FRANCIS (1657-1715?), astrologer and almanac-maker; physician, astrologer, and schoolmaster in Lambeth; published an almanac prophesying the weather, 1699, to advertise his pills; published the 'Vox Stellarum' ('Old Moore's Almanac'), 1700.
[xxxviii. 349]

MOORE, FRANCIS (*fl.* 1744), traveller; entered service of Royal African Company, 1730; factor at Joar, 1732; assisted in establishing the colony of Georgia, 1735-6 and 1738-43; wrote descriptions of the interior of Africa and Georgia. [xxxviii. 349]

MOORE, Sir GARRET, first BARON MOORE of Mellifont, first VISCOUNT MOORE of Drogheda (1560?-1627), son of Sir Edward Moore [q. v.]; commissioner for arranging matters with Tyrone, 1594, 1596, and 1598; constable of Philipstown, 1602; Irish privy councillor, 1604; accused of complicity in Tyrone's schemes by Howth, 1607; fully acquitted, 1609; undertaker in the Ulster plantation; M.P., Dungannon, 1613; created Baron Moore, 1615, and Viscount Moore, 1621.
[xxxviii. 350]

MOORE, Sir GEORGE (1563-1632), lieutenant of the Tower of London. [See MORE.]

MOORE, GEORGE (1806-1876), philanthropist; came to London, 1825; traveller for a lace house; partner in Groucock, Copestake & Moore, 1829; devoted himself to philanthropic work; died from the effects of an accident at Carlisle. [xxxviii. 351]

MOORE, GEORGE (1803-1880), physician and author; studied at Paris with Erasmus Wilson; M.R.C.S., 1829; M.D. St. Andrews, 1841; M.R.C.P., 1859; physician in London; published 'The Lost Tribes and the Saxons,' 1861, and other works of religious and medical character.
[xxxviii. 352]

MOORE, GEORGE BELTON (1806-1875), painter; drawing-master at the Royal Military Academy, Woolwich; wrote on perspective. [xxxviii. 352]

MOORE, GEORGE HENRY (1811-1870), Irish politician; educated at Oscott College, Birmingham, and Christ's College, Cambridge; M.P., co. Mayo, 1847; a leader of the tenant-right movement; unseated, 1857; elected unopposed, 1868. [xxxviii. 352]

MOORE, Sir GRAHAM (1764-1843), admiral; son of John Moore (1729-1802) [q. v.]; entered navy, 1777; lieutenant, 1782; commander, 1790; seized four treasure ships off Spanish coast, 1803; escorted Portuguese royal family to Brazil, 1807; served in Walcheren expedition, 1809; rear-admiral, 1812; K.C.B., 1815; lord of the admiralty, 1816-20; vice-admiral, 1819; commander-in-chief in the Mediterranean and G.C.M.G., 1820; G.C.B., 1836; admiral, 1837; commander-in-chief at Plymouth, 1839-42. [xxxviii. 353]

MOORE, Sir HENRY, first baronet (1713-1769), colonial governor; born in Vere, Jamaica; studied at Leyden; trained in the militia; lieutenant-governor of Jamaica, 1755-62; allayed quarrels between the two houses of legislature; suppressed slave rising, 1760; created baronet, 1762; governor of New York, 1765; suspended the Stamp Act; tried unsuccessfully to determine the question of boundary with Massachusetts, 1767; died at New York. [xxxviii. 354]

MOORE, HENRY (1732-1802), unitarian minister and hymn-writer; became minister successively of Dulverton, 1756; Modbury, 1757, and Liskeard, 1787; secured by Priestley as a contributor to his 'Commentaries and Essays'; wrote essays, lyrical poems, and hymns.
[xxxviii. 355]

MOORE, HENRY (1751-1844), Wesleyan minister and biographer; originally a wood-carver; converted to methodism, 1777; John Wesley's assistant, travelling companion, and amanuensis, 1784-6 and 1788-90; one of John Wesley's literary executors, and entrusted by him with joint-authority at City Road Chapel; with Thomas Coke wrote a life of John Wesley, 1792; after obtaining

access to Wesley's private papers published a more valuable biography, 1824-5. [xxxviii. 355]

MOORE, HENRY (1831-1896), marine-painter; son of William Moore (1790-1851) [q. v.], by whom he was taught painting; exhibited at Royal Academy from 1853, British Institution, 1855-65, and at Suffolk Street gallery from 1855; R.A., 1893. [Suppl. iii. 192]

MOORE, JAMES (1702-1734). [See SMYTHE, JAMES MOORE.]

MOORE, JAMES or JAMES CARRICK (1763-1834), surgeon; son of John Moore (1729-1802) [q. v.]; studied medicine in Edinburgh and London; M.C.S., 1792; director of the national vaccine establishment, 1809; wrote two accounts of his brother, Sir John Moore (1761-1809) [q. v.], and medical works. [xxxviii. 357]

MOORE, JOHN (*d.* 1619), divine; of University College, Oxford; rector of Knaptoft, 1586, of Shearsby, 1615; published 'A Target for Tillage,' 1612, and a theological work. [xxxviii. 357]

MOORE, JOHN (1595?-1657), son of John Moore (*d.* 1619) [q. v.]; of Exeter College, Oxford; rector of Knaptoft, 1638, of Lutterworth, 1647; preached and wrote against enclosures. [xxxviii. 357]

MOORE, JOHN (*fl.* 1669), author of 'Moses Revived,' 1669. [xxxviii. 362]

MOORE, JOHN (*fl.* 1696), curate of Brislington; published episcopalian sermons. [xxxviii. 362]

MOORE, Sir JOHN (1620-1702), lord mayor of London; gained wealth in East India trade; alderman, 1671; sheriff of London and knighted, 1672; lord mayor, 1681; supported the court party in London; M.P. city of London, 1685; benefactor to city charities and to Christ's Hospital (president, 1681); founded and endowed Appleby grammar school, 1697; rebuilt Grocers' Company's Hall, London, 1682, of which company he was master. [xxxviii. 358]

MOORE, JOHN (1646-1714), bishop successively of Norwich and Ely; grandson of John Moore (1595?-1657) [q. v.]; M.A. Clare College, Cambridge, 1669; D.D., 1681; incorporated D.D. Oxford, 1673; fellow of Clare College, 1667-77; canon of Ely, 1679; held two rectories in London; bishop of Norwich, 1691-1707, of Ely, 1707; presided, as visitor of Trinity College, Cambridge, at Bentley's trial, a draft sentence of deprivation being found among his papers. His library, which was famous throughout Europe, was bought by George I and presented to Cambridge University. He was a munificent patron of Clare College Library. [xxxviii. 359]

MOORE, JOHN (1642?-1717), dissenting minister; of Brasenose College, Oxford; curate of Long Burton, Dorset, 1662; became a dissenter, 1667; pastor of Christ Church Chapel, Bridgwater, 1676. [xxxviii. 361]

MOORE, JOHN (*fl.* 1721), dissenting minister; kept a seminary at Bridgwater and wrote a defence of the 'Deity of Christ,' 1721. [xxxviii. 362]

MOORE, Sir JOHN, first baronet (1718-1779), admiral; entered navy, 1729; lieutenant, 1738; commander, 1743; distinguished himself in the action with L'Etenduère, 1747; commodore and commander-in-chief on the Leeward islands station, 1756; convoyed General Hopton to Martinique, 1759; assisted in the reduction of Guadeloupe, 1759; rear-admiral, 1762; commander-in-chief in the Downs; created baronet, 1766; K.B., 1772; admiral, 1778. [xxxviii. 362]

MOORE, JOHN (1729-1802), physician and man of letters; studied at Glasgow; surgeon's mate in the Duke of Argyll's regiment serving in Holland, 1747; studied at Paris and London; practised in Glasgow, 1751; M.D. Glasgow, 1770; travelled with Douglas, eighth duke of Hamilton, 1772-8; published 'A View of Society and Manners in France, Switzerland, and Germany,' 1779, and 'A View of . . . Italy,' 1781; published 'Zeluco,' 1786, 'Edward,' 1796, and 'Mordaunt,' 1800, three novels; in France, 1792; published journal of Paris disturbances, 1793 and 1794; published an account of the French revolution, 1795; edited the works of his friend and patient, Smollett, with memoir, 1797. [xxxviii. 363]

MOORE, JOHN (1730-1805), archbishop of Canterbury; M.A. Pembroke College, Oxford, 1751; private

G g

tutor to the sons of the second Duke of Marlborough ; prebendary of Durham, 1761 ; canon of Christ Church, Oxford, 1763 ; dean of Canterbury, 1771 ; bishop of Bangor, 1775–83 ; archbishop of Canterbury, 1783–1805.

[xxxviii. 365]

MOORE, Sir JOHN (1761–1809), lieutenant-general ; son of John Moore (1729–1802) [q. v.] ; ensign, 1776 ; captain-lieutenant, 1778 ; served in the American war, 1779 ; M.P. Linlithgow, Selkirk, Lanark, and Peebles burghs, 1784–90 ; major, 1785 ; lieutenant-colonel, 1790 ; sent to Corsica to interview General Paoli ; assisted in the reduction of the French garrisons there ; adjutant-general, 1794 ; recalled to England by reason of disputes between the military and naval forces, 1795 ; brevet-colonel, with local rank of brigadier-general ; sent to the West Indies, 1796 ; under Sir Ralph Abercromby attacked St. Lucia, 1796 ; left in command of the island ; re-established order and security ; major-general, 1798 ; ordered to Holland, 1799 ; wounded at Egmont-op-Zee, 1799 ; colonel-commandant, second battalion 52nd foot, 1799 ; served in Mediterranean, 1800, and Egypt, 1801 ; distinguished himself before Alexandria and Cairo, 1801 ; colonel, 1801 ; introduced a new system of drill and manœuvre in the Shorncliffe camp ; K.B., 1804 ; lieutenant-general, 1805 ; held Mediterranean command, 1806 ; sent under Sir Harry Burrard to Portugal, 1808 ; commander-in-chief on Burrard's recall ; decided to transport his troops by land from Lisbon to Coruña, 1808 ; decided, partly in consequence of want of supplies, to retreat into Portugal, when he was requested by Sir Charles Stuart (1808) to come to the defence of Madrid ; effected junction with Baird at Majorga, 20 Dec. 1808, and had advanced to within a march of the enemy when an intercepted letter brought news that Napoleon had already entered Madrid and cut off his own retreat into Portugal ; commenced his historic retreat over difficult country in midwinter to Coruña, arriving there on 13 Jan. 1809, and began the embarkation 16 Jan. ; mortally wounded, on the arrival of the French, who soon appeared ; lived to hear that the French were defeated ; buried at midnight in the citadel of Coruña, 16 Jan. 1809. A temporary monument placed over his grave by the Spanish commander, Marquis de la Romana, was converted into a permanent one by the prince regent, 1811.   [xxxviii. 366]

MOORE, JOHN (1742–1821), biblical scholar ; of Merchant Taylors' School, London, and St. John's College, Oxford ; B.A., 1763 ; LL.B. ; prebendary of St. Paul's, London, 1766 ; rector of Langdon Hill, Essex, 1798 ; assisted Kennicott in collating Hebrew manuscripts of the Old Testament ; published works on the Old Testament.

[xxxviii. 372]

MOORE, JOHN BRAMLEY (1800–1886). [See BRAMLEY-MOORE.]

MOORE, JOHN COLLINGHAM (1829 – 1880), painter ; son of William Moore (1790–1851) [q. v.] ; exhibited at the Royal Academy Italian scenes and portraits of children.   [xxxviii. 386]

MOORE, JOHN FRANCIS (d. 1809), sculptor ; native of Hanover ; executed monuments to Mrs. Catherine Macaulay, Earl Ligonier, Robert, earl Ferrers, and others.

[xxxviii. 372]

MOORE, Sir JOHN HENRY, second baronet (1756–1780), poet ; son of Sir Henry Moore [q. v.] ; born in Jamaica ; of Eton and Emmanuel College, Cambridge ; M.A., 1776 ; acquainted with Edward Jerningham and Lady Miller of Bath Easton ; published ' The New Paradise of Dainty Devices,' 1777.   [xxxviii. 372]

MOORE, Sir JONAS (1617–1679), mathematician ; clerk to Dr. Burghill, chancellor of Durham ; mathematical tutor to the Duke of York, 1647 ; surveyor of Fen drainage system, 1649, publishing an account, 1685 ; sent to report on fortifications of Tangier, 1663 ; knighted ; surveyor-general of the ordnance, 1663 ; published ' Arithmetick,' 1650, a ' New System of the Mathematicks,' (posthumous, 1681), and other works.   [xxxviii. 373]

MOORE, JONAS (1691 ?–1741), military engineer ; probably grandson of Sir Jonas Moore [q. v.] ; probationer-engineer, 1709 ; sub-engineer at Gibraltar, 1711 ; chief engineer and commander-in-chief of artillery train, 1720 ; sub-director of engineers and major, 1722 ; distinguished himself at siege of Gibraltar, 1727 ; chief engineer of

expedition to Spanish America, 1740 ; mortally wounded during attack on Carthagena.   [xxxviii. 374]

MOORE, JOSEPH (1766–1851), Birmingham benefactor ; acquired wealth in the button trade at Birmingham ; founded a dispensary ; established Birmingham Oratorio Choral Society, 1808 ; agitated for erection of the town hall (1832–4) ; induced Mendelssohn to compose ' St. Paul ' (given at the festival, 1837) and ' Elijah ' (performed, 1846).   [xxxviii. 375]

MOORE, JOSEPH (1817–1892), medallist and die-sinker ; die-sinker's apprentice in Birmingham ; partner in a business which manufactured papier-mâché and metal articles, 1844–56 ; executed numerous prize and commemoration medals ; his medal, bearing ' Salvator Mundi ' of Da Vinci on the obverse and ' Christus Consolator ' of Scheffer as the reverse, 1846, much praised by Scheffer.   [xxxviii. 375]

MOORE, PETER (1753–1828), politician ; amassed a fortune in the East India Company ; radical M.P., Coventry, 1803 ; known as the most adroit manager of private bills ; lent his name as director to companies with such freedom that he was obliged to fly to Dieppe to escape arrest, 1825 ; gave up nearly all his property ; died at Abbeville.

[xxxviii. 376]

MOORE, PHILIP (fl. 1573), medical writer ; practised physic and chirurgery ; wrote on medicinal herbs ; published 'Almanack and Prognostication for xxxiiii. yeares,' 1573.   [xxxviii. 377]

MOORE, PHILIP (1705–1783), Manx scholar ; rector of Kirk Bride and master of Douglas school ; revised the Manx translation of the bible and prayer-book and religious pieces.   [xxxviii. 377]

MOORE, RICHARD (1619–1683), nonconformist divine ; B.A. Magdalen Hall, Oxford, 1640 ; preached at Worcester and Alvechurch ; published sermons.

[xxxviii. 377]

MOORE, RICHARD (1810–1878), politician ; originally a wood-carver, began young to take part in radical politics ; acquainted with and assisted Robert Owen, Sir Francis Burdett, Lovett, Collins, Henry Hetherington, and James Watson ; worked for the promotion of electoral purity, the chartist cause, and the abolition of newspaper stamps.   [xxxviii. 378]

MOORE, ROBERT ROSS ROWAN (1811–1864), political economist ; B.A. Trinity College, Dublin, 1835 ; barrister, Gray's Inn, 1837 ; intimate with Cobden and Bright ; joined the Anti-cornlaw League ; a valuable speaker in favour of free trade in England, Scotland, and Ireland ; unsuccessfully contested Hastings, 1844.

[xxxviii. 378]

MOORE, SAMUEL (fl. 1680–1720), draughtsman and engraver ; drew plates of the coronation of James II and of William and Mary.   [xxxviii. 379]

MOORE, Sir THOMAS (d. 1735), playwright ; admitted at Gray's Inn, 1670 ; of Corpus Christi College, Oxford, 1674 ; knighted, 1716 ; his tragedy, ' Mangora, King of the Timbusians,' acted, 1717.   [xxxviii. 379]

MOORE, THOMAS (d. 1792), teacher of psalmody ; taught music at Manchester, 1750 ; precentor and psalmody teacher at Glasgow, 1755–87 ; kept a bookseller's shop in Glasgow ; edited collections of psalms.

[xxxviii. 380]

MOORE, THOMAS (1779–1852), poet ; entered at Trinity College, Dublin, 1794, and Middle Temple, 1799 ; admiralty registrar at Bermuda, 1803 ; discovered the office to be a sinecure, and travelled through the States on his way back to London ; became the national lyrist of Ireland by his publication of ' Irish Melodies,' 1807–34 (with music by Sir John Stevenson) ; inspired by the failure of the Prince of Wales as regent to support catholic emancipation to write airily malicious lampoons in verse, which were collected into a volume called ' The Twopenny Post Bag,' 1813 ; acquainted with Byron and Leigh Hunt ; acquired a European reputation by his 'Lalla Rookh,' 1817 ; rendered liable for 6,000l. by the defalcations of his deputy at Bermuda ; took refuge abroad, visiting Italy with Lord John Russell ; given his memoirs by Byron at Venice ; returned to England, the debt to the admiralty being paid, 1822 ; excited much reprehension by his ' Loves of the Angels,' 1823 ; destroyed Byron's memoirs, and on his death wrote a graceful life of Byron

(1830); edited Byron's works; received a literary pension, 1835, to which a civil list pension was added, 1850; his last work, 'The History of Ireland' for Lardner's 'Cabinet Cyclopædia,' 1846. Moore also wrote 'Poems by the late Thomas Little,' 1801, 'Odes and Epistles,' 1806, 'National Airs,' 1815, 'Sacred Song,' 1816, 'The Fudge Family in Paris,' 1818, 'The Fudges in England' (published, 1835), and 'Rhymes on the Road' and 'Fables for the Holy Alliance,' 1823 (the last four under the pseudonym of Thomas Brown the younger); first collective edition, 1840-1. [xxxviii. 380]

MOORE, THOMAS (1821-1887), gardener and botanist; assisted in laying out Regent's Park gardens, London; curator of the Apothecaries' Company's garden, Chelsea, 1840; edited numerous botanical publications; F.L.S., 1851; wrote chiefly on British ferns. [xxxviii. 385]

MOORE, WILLIAM (1590-1659), librarian; M.A., Gonville and Caius College, Cambridge, 1613; fellow, 1613; university librarian, 1653; contributed to the 'Obsequies to the Memorie of Mr. Edward King,' 1638.
[xxxviii. 386]

MOORE, WILLIAM (1790-1851), portrait-painter; successful as a portrait-painter in oils, water-colour, and pastel. [xxxviii. 386]

MOOREHEAD, JOHN (d. 1804), violinist and composer; brought to London by Thomas Dibdin, 1794; engaged at Sadler's Wells; at Covent Garden Theatre, 1798; became insane; was sailor, afterwards bandmaster, on board H.M.S. Monarch; with Attwood, Reeve, and Braham composed theatre music; committed suicide.
[xxxviii. 387]

MOORSOM, CONSTANTINE RICHARD (1792-1861), vice-admiral; brother of William Scarth Moorsom [q. v.]; entered navy, 1809; lieutenant, 1812; commander, 1814; devised a new mortar for bombs, first used in the bombardment of Algiers (1816); received post rank, 1818; senior officer at Mauritius; flag-captain to his father, then commander-in-chief at Chatham, 1825-7; rear-admiral, 1851; vice-admiral, 1857; director and chairman of London and North Western Railway; published 'Principles of Naval Tactics,' 1843. [xxxviii. 387]

MOORSOM, WILLIAM (1817-1860), cousin of Constantine Richard Moorsom [q. v.]; served as lieutenant in the first China war, as captain in the Black Sea and Crimea; C.B.; inventor of the Moorsom shell with percussion fuse, and of the 'director' for concentrating a ship's broadside; published two naval works.
[xxxviii. 388]

MOORSOM, WILLIAM ROBERT (1834-1858), son of William Scarth Moorsom [q. v.]; ensign, 1852; lieutenant, 1853; served in the siege of Lucknow as aide-de-camp to Havelock; helped forward the relief of Lucknow by his skilful plans; killed at Lucknow. [xxxviii. 389]

MOORSOM, WILLIAM SCARTH (1804-1863), captain; civil engineer; brother of Constantine Richard Moorsom [q. v.]; ensign, 1821; lieutenant, 1825; captain, 1826; served in Nova Scotia; deputy quartermaster-general; sold out of the army, 1832; employed in laying out many railway systems in England and Ireland; his plans for the railway bridge over the Rhine at Cologne adopted, 1850; sent to Ceylon to report on the feasibility of a railway to the highlands of Kandy, 1856; published an account of Nova Scotia and papers on engineering.
[xxxviii. 388]

MORANT, PHILIP (1700-1770), historian of Essex; born in Jersey; B.A. Pembroke College, Oxford, 1721; curate of Great Waltham, Essex, 1724; M.A. Sidney Sussex College, Cambridge, 1729; chaplain to the English church at Amsterdam, 1732-4; patronage conferred on him by the bishop of London; held cures of Colchester and Aldham conjointly; F.S.A., 1755; prepared for the press the ancient records of parliament (1278-1413); chief works, 'The History and Antiquities of Colchester,' 1748, and 'History and Antiquities of the County of Essex,' 1760-8; published also theological and historical works. [xxxviii. 390]

MORAY. [See MURRAY.]

MORAY or MURRAY, EARLS OF. [See RANDOLPH, SIR THOMAS, first EARL of the Randolph family, d. 1332; RANDOLPH, JOHN, third EARL, d. 1346; STEWART, JAMES, first EARL of the Stewart family, 1499 ?-1544; STEWART,

JAMES, first EARL of a new creation, 1531 ?-1570; STEWART, JAMES, second EARL, d. 1592; STEWART, ALEXANDER, fourth EARL, d. 1701.]

MORAY, GILBERT OF (d. 1245). [See GILBERT.]

MORCAR or MORKERE (fl. 1066), earl of the Northumbrians; son of Ælfgar [q. v.]; stirred up a revolt against Earl Tostig, 1065; chosen earl by the Northumbrians, an election which Harold eventually recognised, 1065; defeated, with his brother Edwin, by the Norsemen at the battle of Fulford Gate, near York, the invaders being soon defeated by Harold at Stamford Bridge; submitted to William the Conqueror and remained at court; joined in a rebellion against William the Conqueror, 1068; made submission and was pardoned; joined insurgents in Isle of Ely; on its surrender committed to the custody of Roger de Beaumont in Normandy; transferred to Winchester prison, 1087. [xxxviii. 391]

MORDAF HAEL (i.e. THE GENEROUS) (fl. 550 ?), North British prince; one of the three princes who went to avenge upon Arfon the death of Elidyr Mwynfawr.
[xxxviii. 392]

MORDAUNT, CHARLES, third EARL OF PETERBOROUGH and first EARL OF MONMOUTH of the second creation (1658-1735), admiral, general, and diplomatist; son of John Mordaunt, viscount Mordaunt (1627-1675) [q. v.]; served in the Mediterranean, 1674-7 and 1678-9, and on shore at Tangier, 1680; active member of the parliamentary opposition, 1680-6; went to Holland and intrigued against James II; commanded Dutch squadron in West Indies, 1687; privy councillor on William III's accession, 1689; made lord of the bedchamber, 1689, and first lord of the treasury, 1689; created Earl of Monmouth, 1689; one of the queen's 'council of nine,' 1689; accompanied William III to Holland, 1691 and 1692; endeavoured to incriminate Marlborough, Russell, and Shrewsbury in Sir John Fenwick's plot, 1696; ordered to the Tower of London for three months; succeeded his uncle as third Earl of Peterborough, 1697; advocated the impeachment of Somers; declined command of an inadequate expedition to Jamaica, 1702; helped Somers (1702) to translate the 'Olynthiacs' and 'Philippics' of Demosthenes; appointed joint-commander with Sir Clowdisley Shovell [q. v.] of the expeditionary force to Spain, 1705; surprised Montjuich and compelled the surrender of Barcelona, deemed impregnable, 1705, on which the Archduke Charles made a formal entry and was proclaimed king of Spain, 12 Oct. 1705; proceeded to Valencia, leaving Barcelona at the mercy of the French Marshal de Tessé, who was, however, obliged to abandon the siege on the arrival (1706) of the English fleet; remained at Valencia; ordered by King Charles, who had turned aside towards Aragon, to join him with every available man; having no means of transport, arrived with only four hundred dragoons; decided to go to Italy to arrange with the Duke of Savoy for a combined attack on Toulon, September 1706; negotiated a loan at ruinous interest without authority; returned to Spain, but was recalled to England to explain his conduct, 1707; charges against him at the official inquiry not adopted by the House of Lords, 1708; ordered to render an account of money received and expended; inquiry into his conduct renewed without effect, 1711; sent on special embassies to Vienna, Frankfort, and Italy, 1712; K.G., 1713; ambassador extraordinary to Italian princes, 1713; recalled on the accession of George I, 1714; travelled for the sake of his health; said to have married Anastasia Robinson [q. v.], the singer, 1722; corresponded with and addressed verses to Mrs. Howard; patron of letters and science; numbered among his friends Swift, Pope, Arbuthnot, and Gay; died at Lisbon.
[xxxviii. 393]

MORDAUNT, HENRY, second EARL OF PETERBOROUGH (1624 ?-1697), cavalier; educated at Eton; served in the parliamentary army; deserted to Charles I, 1643; raised the royal standard at Dorking, 1647, but was defeated and wounded; escaped to Antwerp, 1647; governor of Tangier, 1661; resigned, 1662; escorted Mary of Modena to England, 1673; privy councillor, 1674; suspected of complicity in the Popish plot; K.G., 1685; became a Roman catholic, 1687; impeached, 1689, but released on bail, 1690; published a book on the genealogies of his family under the pseudonym 'Robert Halstead,' 1685. [xxxviii. 403]

MORDAUNT, HENRY (1681 ?-1710), navy captain; son of Charles Mordaunt, third earl of Peterborough [q. v.];

captain, 1703; ran his ship ashore, landed his men, and burnt the ship on being attacked between Barcelona and Genoa by the French, 1707; tried by court-martial and honourably acquitted, 1709; M.P., Malmesbury, 1705. [xxxviii. 405]

MORDAUNT, SIR JOHN (d. 1504), speaker of the House of Commons; chosen speaker, 1487, being M.P. for Bedfordshire; serjeant-at-law and king's serjeant, 1495; chief-justice of Chester, 1499; knighted, 1503; high steward of Cambridge University, 1504; chancellor of the duchy of Lancaster, 1504; privy councillor; benefactor of the church. [xxxviii. 405]

MORDAUNT, JOHN, first BARON MORDAUNT OF TURVEY (1490?-1562), courtier; son of Sir John Mordaunt (d. 1504) [q. v.]; sheriff of Bedfordshire and Buckinghamshire, 1509; knighted, 1520; privy councillor, 1526; general surveyor of the king's woods, 1526; supported the Reformation; made Baron Mordaunt of Turvey, 1532; engaged in trial of Lord Dacre, 1534, of Anne Boleyn, 1536. [xxxviii. 406]

MORDAUNT, JOHN, afterwards first EARL OF PETERBOROUGH (d. 1642), ward of Archbishop Abbot; educated at Oxford; K.B., 1616; created Earl of Peterborough, 1628; general of the ordnance under Essex in the parliamentary army. [xxxviii. 403]

MORDAUNT, JOHN, first BARON MORDAUNT of Reigate in Surrey, and VISCOUNT MORDAUNT of Avalon in Somerset (1627-1675), cavalier and conspirator; son of John Mordaunt, first earl of Peterborough [q. v.]; educated in France and Italy; planned an insurrection in Sussex; arrested and committed to the Tower, 1658; acquitted; raised to the peerage in anticipation of another insurrection in the king's favour, 1659; escaped to Calais on its suppression; messenger of King Charles II to the city of London, April 1660; constable of Windsor Castle, 1660; lord-lieutenant of Surrey, 1660; impeached for arbitrary acts, 1667, but pardoned. [xxxviii. 406]

MORDAUNT, SIR JOHN (1697-1780), general; nephew of Charles Mordaunt, third earl of Peterborough [q. v.]; entered the army, 1721; colonel, 1741; brigadier-general, 1745; served in Scotland and Holland; major-general and colonel, 1747; M.P., Cockermouth, 1754-67; lieutenant-general, 1754; commanded the futile expedition against Rochefort, 1757; censured by a court of inquiry, but acquitted by court-martial; general, 1770; K.B. and governor of Berwick. [xxxviii. 408]

MORDEN, SIR JOHN (1623-1708), founder of Morden's College, Blackheath; acquired wealth as a Levant merchant; created baronet, 1688; on the committee of the East India Company; excise commissioner, 1691; M.P., Colchester, 1695-8; founded a 'college' at Blackheath for twelve decayed merchants (the number increased after his death to forty). [xxxviii. 409]

MORDEN, ROBERT (d. 1703), geographer; commenced business as a map and globe maker in London, 1668; went into partnership with Thomas Cockerill at the Atlas in Cornhill, 1688; published astronomical, navigation, and geographical maps and terrestrial and celestial globes. [xxxviii. 410]

MORDINGTON, fourth BARON. [See DOUGLAS, GEORGE, d. 1741.]

MORE, ALEXANDER (1616-1670), protestant divine and antagonist of Milton; born of Scots parents at Castres; educated at Castres and Geneva; professor of Greek at Geneva, 1639, and of theology at Geneva, 1642-8, at Middelburg, 1649; professor of ecclesiastical history, Amsterdam, 1652-9; pastor of Charenton, 1659; violently attacked by Milton as the supposed author of 'Regii Sanguinis Clamor ad Cœlum adversus Parricidas Anglicanos' (1652); a reply to his rejoinder published by Milton. [xxxviii. 411]

MORE, SIR ANTHONY, who is also known as ANTONIO MORO, but whose name was properly ANTHONIS MOR (1512?-1576?), portrait-painter; was born in Utrecht; admitted to the guild of St. Luke in Antwerp, 1547; in Italy, 1550 and 1551; employed at the court at Madrid, 1552; sent to England, 1553, to paint Queen Mary's portrait for Philip of Spain; knighted; remained in England until 1555; went to the Netherlands; visited Madrid, 1559; settled at Antwerp, 1568; one of the chief portrait-painters of the world; Sir Thomas Gresham and Sir Henry Lee are probably his only genuine portraits of English patrons. [xxxviii. 411]

MORE, CRESACRE (1572-1649), biographer (1631) and grandson of Sir Thomas More [q. v.] [xxxviii. 448]

MORE, EDWARD (1479-1541), divine; scholar of Winchester College, 1492; fellow, 1498-1502; B.D. New College, Oxford, 1518; head-master of Winchester, 1508-17; canon of Chichester; rector of Cranford, 1521-41; eighth warden of Winchester, 1526. [xxxviii. 413]

MORE, EDWARD (1537?-1620), grandson of Sir Thomas More [q. v.]; wrote a poem in defence of women, 1560. [xxxviii. 413]

MORE or **MOORE**, SIR GEORGE (1553-1632), lieutenant of the Tower of London; of Corpus Christi College, Oxford; entered the Inner Temple, 1574; M.P., Guildford, 1584-5, 1586-7, 1593, 1604-11, and 1624-5, Surrey, 1597-8, 1614, and 1621-2; knighted, 1597; sheriff of Surrey and Sussex, 1598; chamberlain of receipt of the exchequer, 1603; visited by James I, 1603 and 1606; created M.A. Oxford, 1605; chancellor of the order of the Garter, 1611-1629; lieutenant of the Tower of London, 1615-17; induced Robert Carr, earl of Somerset [q. v.], to appear for trial; collector of loans in Surrey, 1625. [xxxviii. 413]

MORE, GERTRUDE (1606-1633), daughter of Cresacre More [q. v.]; originally Helen, took the veil as Gertrude, and became a nun of Cambray, 1623. [xxxviii. 448]

MORE, HANNAH (1745-1833), religious writer; acquired Italian, Spanish, and Latin at her sister's boarding-school in Bristol, 1757; published a pastoral drama, 'The Search after Happiness,' 1762 (intended for school children); engaged to a Mr. Turner of Belmont, but the match was broken off; visited London, 1774; intimate with Garrick and his wife; met Burke, Reynolds, Dr. Johnson, Mrs. Montagu, Mrs. Delany, Mrs. Carter, Mrs. Chapone, and Mrs. Boscawen; her tragedy 'Percy', produced by Garrick, 1777; her 'Fatal Falsehood' produced, 1779; came to think playgoing wrong after Garrick's death; published 'Sacred Dramas,' 1782; became acquainted with Dr. Kennicott, Dr. Horne, Bishop Porteus, John Newton, and Wilberforce, and published 'Thoughts on the Importance of the Manners of the Great to General Society,' 1788, which met with great success; induced by the general ignorance and distress in Cheddar to institute Sunday schools in the neighbourhood, 1789; involved (1800-2), in the 'Blagdon controversy,' which originated in a complaint of the curate of Blagdon that the master of the school she had started there (1795) was holding a kind of conventicle; wrote, during the excitement caused by the French revolution, a tract called 'Village Politics,' 1792; emboldened by its success, she issued series of cheap tracts called 'Cheap Repository Tracts,' which appeared regularly, and the venture being supported by committees all over the kingdom, led (1799) to the formation of the Religious Tract Society; published her most popular work, 'Cœlebs in Search of a Wife,' 1809; continued writing her moral and religious treatises until 1819; during illness compiled her 'Spirit of Prayer,' 1825; left about 30,000l. in legacies to charitable institutions and religious societies. [xxxviii. 414]

MORE, HENRY (1586-1661), jesuit; son of Edward More (1537?-1620) [q. v.]; studied at St. Omer and Louvain; professed of the four vows, 1622; missioner in London; vice-provincial of his order; author of 'Historia Missionis Anglicanæ Societatis Jesu,' 1649, and other theological works; died at Watten, Belgium. [xxxviii. 420]

MORE, HENRY (1614-1687), theologian; of Eton and Christ's College, Cambridge; M.A., 1639; fellow, 1639; received holy orders, but refused all preferment, including two bishoprics, and shrank from theological and political disputes; benevolent to the poor; one of the Cambridge Platonists; published theological and philosophical works in verse and prose, including 'Psychozoia Platonica' (verse), 1642, 'Philosophical Poems,' 1647, 'Enthusiasmus Triumphatus' (prose), 1656, and 'Divine Dialogues' (prose), 1668; believed to have written 'Philosophiæ Teutonicæ Censura,' 1670; supposed to have edited Glanvill's 'Saducismus Triumphatus,' 1681; his writings valued by John Wesley and Coleridge. [xxxviii. 421]

MORE, JACOB (1740-1793), landscape-painter, known as 'More of Rome'; born in Edinburgh; went to Italy, 1773; employed by Prince Borghese; sent views of Italian scenery to English exhibitions; his paintings praised by Goethe; died in Rome. [xxxviii. 423]

MORE, Sir JOHN (1453?-1530), judge; butler of Lincoln's Inn and subsequently barrister; serjeant-at-law, 1503; mentioned as judge of the common pleas, 1518, and judge of the king's bench, 1523.   [xxxviii. 424]

MORE, JOHN (d. 1592), the 'Apostle of Norwich'; B.A. Christ's College, Cambridge, 1562; fellow; incumbent of St. Andrew's, Norwich, till death; refused to wear a surplice, 1573; entered into a controversy with Andrew Perne [q. v.], 1573; suspended (1576-8) for objecting to the imposition of ceremonies; his works (theological and chronological) published by Nicholas Bownde [q. v.]
                                                          [xxxviii. 425]

MORE, JOHN (1630-1689). [See CROSS.]

MORE, RICHARD (d. 1643), puritan; burgess of Bishop's Castle, 1610; J.P. and M.P. for Bishop's Castle, in the Short and Long parliaments; supported parliamentary cause in Shropshire; published 'A true Relation of the Murders of Enoch ap Evan' (printed, 1641, though a licence had been refused before) and a translation of Mede's 'Clavis Apocalyptica,' 1641.   [xxxviii. 426]

MORE, RICHARD (1627-1698), lawyer; son of Samuel More [q. v.]; admitted of Gray's Inn, 1646; commissioner for compounding, 1646-59; serjeant of Gray's Inn; M.P., Bishop's Castle, 1680-98.   [xxxviii. 428]

MORE, ROBERT (1671-1727?), writing-master; master of Colonel John Ayres's school at St. Paul's Churchyard, London; published 'The Writing Master's Assistant,' 1696, and similar works.   [xxxviii. 427]

MORE, ROBERT (1703-1780), botanist; grandson of Samuel More [q. v.]; F.R.S.   [xxxviii. 428]

MORE, ROGER (fl. 1620-1652). [See O'MORE, RORY.]

MORE, SAMUEL (1594-1662), parliamentarian; son of Richard More (d. 1643) [q. v.]; member of the 'committee of parliament for Shropshire'; governor of Montgomery Castle, 1645-7, Monmouth, 1645, Ludlow Castle, 1646, and Hereford Castle, 1647; accused of complicity in an attempt to depose Cromwell; M.P., Bishop's Castle, 1658.   [xxxviii. 427]

MORE or **MOORE**, Sir THOMAS DE LA (fl. 1327-1351), alleged chronicler; passed for three centuries as the author of 'Vita et Mors Edwardi Secundi,' which is really nothing but an extract from the chronicle of Geoffrey Baker [q. v.]; M.P., Oxfordshire, 1340, 1343, and 1351; possibly constable or vice-warden of Porchester Castle, 1370.   [xxxviii. 428]

MORE, Sir THOMAS (1478-1535), lord chancellor of England and author; son of Sir John More [q. v.]; educated at St. Anthony's School, Threadneedle Street, London; placed, 1491, in the household of John Morton [q. v.], archbishop of Canterbury, on whose recommendation he entered Canterbury Hall, Oxford, 1492; pupil of Linacre and Grocyn; entered at New Inn, 1494; removed to Lincoln's Inn, 1496, and was called to the outer bar; appointed reader at Furnival's Inn; devoted his leisure to literature and became intimate (1497) with Colet, Lily, and Erasmus, who afterwards stayed frequently at his house; contemplated becoming a priest, but at the end of four years returned to secular affairs; brilliantly successful at the bar; began to study politics; member of parliament, 1504; successfully opposed Henry VII's demand for an aid of three-fifteenths on his daughter Margaret's marriage, 1503; visited Louvain and Paris, 1508; bencher of Lincoln's Inn, 1509; reader, 1511 and 1516; undersheriff of London, 1510; nominated one of the envoys to Flanders to secure by treaty fuller protection of English commerce, 1515; during his absence sketched his description of the imaginary island of 'Utopia,' which he completed and published, 1516; included in the commission of the peace for Hampshire, 1515 and 1528; a member of a new embassy to Calais to arrange disputes with French envoys, 1516; impressed Henry VIII with the necessity of making him an officer of the crown by the adroitness of his arguments in a Star-chamber case against the claim of the crown to seize a ship belonging to the pope; master of requests and privy councillor, 1518; treated by Henry VIII with exceptional familiarity, affability, and courtesy during his residence at court; frequently chosen as spokesman of the court at ceremonial functions; welcomed Campeggio, 1518; present at the Field of the Cloth of Gold, 1520, when he met William Budée or Budæus, the greatest Greek scholar of

the age; knighted, 1521; sub-treasurer to the king, 1521; accompanied Wolsey to Calais and Bruges, 1521; received grants of land in Oxfordshire and Kent, 1522 and 1525; as speaker of the House of Commons pleaded privilege of the House against Wolsey, 1523; high steward of Cambridge University, 1525; chancellor of the duchy of Lancaster, 1525; took part in important negotiations with Wolsey at Amiens, 1527, and with Tunstall at Cambray, 1529; completed his 'Dialogue,' his first controversial book in English (directed mainly against Tyndale's writings), 1528; succeeded Wolsey as lord chancellor, 1529; unrivalled in the rapidity with which he despatched chancery business; vexed the king by his opposition to the relaxation of the heresy laws, and (1532) resigned the chancellorship; attacked by protestants for having used undue severity to persons charged with heresy; lived for some time after his resignation in complete retirement, mainly engaged in religious controversy with Tyndale and Frith; on the arrest of the 'Holy Maid of Kent,' 1533, was included as guilty of misprision of treason in the bill of attainder aimed at the nun's friends, 1534; summoned before four members of the council (1534) to explain why he declined to acknowledge the wisdom of Henry VIII's attitude to the pope; his name struck out of the bill in consequence of his personal popularity; although willing to swear fidelity to the new Act of Succession, refused to take any oath that should impugn the pope's authority, or assume the justice of the king's divorce from Queen Catherine, 1534, and was committed to the Tower of London with John Fisher, bishop of Rochester, who had assumed a like attitude; during the first days of his imprisonment prepared a 'Dialogue of Comfort against Tribulation' and treatises on Christ's passion; examined from time to time, but without result; indicted of high treason in Westminster Hall, 1 July 1535; denied that he had maliciously opposed the king's second marriage, or advised Fisher to disobey the Act of Supremacy; found guilty and sentenced to be hanged at Tyburn; executed, 6 July 1535, the sentence having been commuted to decapitation; his body buried in St. Peter's in the Tower, London, and his head exhibited on London Bridge. Catholic Europe was shocked by the news, and English ambassadors abroad were instructed to declare that More and Fisher had been found traitors by due course of law.

More was a critic and a patron of art, and Holbein is said to have stayed three years in his house at Chelsea; he painted portraits of him and his family. For two centuries he was regarded in catholic Europe as one of the glories of English literature; his Latin verse and prose are scholarly and fluent, while his epigrams embody much shrewd satire. The English prose in his controversial tracts is simple and direct, and his devotional works are noticeable for their sincerity. The 'Utopia,' his greatest literary effort, was written in Latin in two books, the second in 1515 and the first in 1516. It describes the social defects of England, and suggests remedies in the account of the social and political constitution of the imaginary island of 'Utopia,' where communism is the law of the land, a national system of education is extended to men and women alike, and the freest toleration in religion is recognised. The 'Utopia,' however, does not contain his own personal and practical opinions on religion and politics. The book at once became popular and was translated into French, 1530, into English, 1551, into German, 1524, into Italian, 1548, and into Spanish, 1790. More's other chief English works are his 'Life of John Picus, Earl of Mirandula' (printed by Wynkyn de Worde, 1510), his 'History of Richard III' (printed imperfectly in Grafton's 'Chronicle,' 1543, used by Hall, and printed fully by Rastell in 1557), 'A Dyaloge of Syr Thomas More,' 1528, 'Supplycacyon of Soulys,' 1529, 'Confutacyon of Tyndale's Answere,' 1532, and 'An Apologye of Syr Thomas More,' 1533. His English works were collected in 1557. His Latin publications included two dialogues of Lucian, epigrammata, and controversial tracts in divinity. Collections of his Latin works are dated 1563, 1565, 1566, and 1689.
                                                          [xxxviii. 429]

MORE, THOMAS (1587-1623?), jesuit; son of Edward More (1537?-1620) [q. v.]; translated into Latin, 1620, 'God and the King,' by John Floyd [q. v.]
                                                          [xxxviii. 420]

MORE, THOMAS (d. 1685), author; of Merton College and St. Alban Hall, Oxford; barrister, Gray's Inn, 1642; joined the parliamentary army and afterwards took Anglican orders; published 'The English Catholic Christian' and 'True old News,' both in 1649; died of drink. [xxxviii. 449]

MORE, THOMAS (1722–1795), jesuit; descendant of Cresacre More [q. v.]; provincial of the English jesuits, 1769–73. [xxxviii. 448]

MORE, WILLIAM (d. 1540), suffragan bishop of Colchester; studied at Oxford and Cambridge; B.D.; rector of Bradwell and of West Tilbury, 1534, prebendary of Lincoln, 1535, bishop of Colchester, 1536 (suffragan to Ely); master in chancery and archdeacon of Leicester. [xxxviii. 450]

MORE, WILLIAM (1472–1559 ?), prior of Worcester; entered Worcester priory, 1488, sub-prior, 1507, prior, 1518; spent much on repairs, books, and plate for the monastery and on churches on its estates; J.P., Worcestershire, 1532; resigned the priory, 1535. [xxxviii. 450]

MOREHEAD, CHARLES (1807–1882), Bombay medical officer; brother of William Ambrose Morehead [q. v.]; studied at Edinburgh and Paris; M.D. Edinburgh; went to India, 1829; first principal and professor of medicine, Grant Medical College, Bombay; retired, 1862; C.I.E., 1881; F.R.C.P.; published 'Researches on the Diseases of India,' 1856. [xxxix. 1]

MOREHEAD, WILLIAM (1637–1692), divine; of Winchester College and New College, Oxford; M.A., 1663; fellow, 1658–72; incumbent of Bucknell, 1670; published 'Lachrymæ Scotiæ,' 1660, on the departure from Scotland of his uncle, General Monck. [xxxix. 1]

MOREHEAD, WILLIAM AMBROSE (1805–1863), Indian official; brother of Charles Morehead [q. v.]; entered Madras civil service, 1825; as sub-collector of Cuddapah, 1832, restored order and brought to justice the murderers of Macdonald, the head assistant-collector; judge of the court of Sadr Adálut, 1846; member of the council of the governor of Madras, 1857–1862. [xxxix. 2]

MORELL, SIR CHARLES (pseudonym). [See RIDLEY, JAMES, 1736–1765.]

MORELL, JOHN DANIEL (1816–1891), philosopher and inspector of schools; M.A. Glasgow, 1841; studied at Bonn, 1841; congregational minister at Gosport, 1842–5; inspector of schools, 1848–76; published works dealing with English grammar and spelling, and a 'Historical and Critical View of the Speculative Philosophy of Europe in the Nineteenth Century,' 1846. [xxxix. 2]

MORELL, THOMAS (1703–1784), classical scholar; of Eton and King's College, Cambridge; M.A., 1730; D.D., 1743; incorporated M.A. at Oxford, 1733; rector of Buckland, 1737; F.S.A., 1737; chaplain to Portsmouth garrison, 1775; compiled 'Thesaurus Græcæ Poeseωs,' 1762; supplied libretti for Handel's oratorios, including the well-known lines, 'See the Conquering Hero comes'; edited Chaucer, 1737, and Spenser, 1747, and published miscellaneous writings. [xxxix. 4]

MOREMAN, JOHN (1490 ?–1554), divine; fellow of Exeter College, Oxford, 1510–22; M.A., 1513; D.D., 1530; principal of Hart Hall, Oxford, 1522–7; vicar of Menheniot, 1529; canon of Exeter, 1544; opposed Henry VIII's divorce from Catherine of Arragon; imprisoned during Edward VI's reign. [xxxix. 5]

MORES, EDWARD ROWE (1731–1778), antiquary; of Merchant Taylors' School, London, and Queen's College, Oxford; F.S.A., 1752; M.A., 1753; started Society for Equitable Assurances, 1761; purchased John James's collection of printing materials, 1772; composed a valuable 'Dissertation upon English Typographical Founders and Foundries' (published, 1778); collected materials for histories of Merchant Taylors' School, London, and Oxford; his books, manuscripts, engravings, and printing types now in the Bodleian and the British Museum. [xxxix. 6]

MORESBY, SIR FAIRFAX (1786–1877), admiral of the fleet; entered navy, 1799; lieutenant, 1806; commander, 1811; received post rank, 1814; C.B., 1815; suppressed slave trade at Mauritius, 1821–3; rear-admiral, 1849; D.C.L. Oxford, 1854; vice-admiral, 1856; admiral, 1864; G.C.B., 1865; admiral of the fleet, 1870. [xxxix. 7]

MORESIN, THOMAS (1558 ?–1603 ?). [See MORISON.]

MORET, HUBERT (fl. 1530–1550), goldsmith and jeweller; a Paris merchant; friend of Holbein; visited London and sold jewels to Henry VIII. [xxxix. 8]

MORETON, EDWARD (1599–1665), royalist divine; educated at Eton and Cambridge; prebendary of Chester, 1637; his property sequestered, 1645, but restored, 1660. [xxxix. 9]

MORETON, HENRY GEORGE FRANCIS, second EARL OF DUCIE (1802–1853), educated at Eton; M.P., Gloucestershire, 1831, East Gloucestershire, 1832–4; succeeded his father, 1840; lord-in-waiting to the queen, 1846–7; charity commissioner, 1847; advocated free trade; agriculturist and breeder of shorthorns. [xxxix. 8]

MORETON, WILLIAM (1641–1715), bishop successively of Kildare and Meath; son of Edward Moreton [q. v.]; M.A. Christ Church, Oxford, 1667; B.D., 1674; accompanied the Duke of Ormonde (lord-lieutenant) to Ireland as chaplain, 1677; dean of Christ Church, Dublin, 1677; bishop of Kildare, 1682; Irish privy councillor, 1682; translated to Meath, 1705. [xxxix. 9]

MOREVILLE, HUGH DE (d. 1204). [See MORVILLE.]

MORGAN (fl. 400 ?). [See PELAGIUS.]

MORGAN MWYNFAWR (d. 665 ?), regulus of Glamorgan; owned lands in Gower, Glamorgan, and Gwent; granted lands to the church of Llandaff, and was proceeded against by Oudoceus for murdering his uncle, Ffriog. [xxxix. 10]

MORGAN HEN (i.e. the AGED) (d. 973), regulus of Glamorgan; chief prince of the region between the Towy and the Wye; attended the courts of Edgar, Athelstan, Edred, and Edwy. [xxxix. 10]

MORGAN (fl. 1294–1295), leader of rebels in Glamorgan, 1294; submitted to Edward I, 1295. [xxxix. 11]

MORGAN, ABEL (1673–1722), baptist minister; pastor of Blaenau Gwent, 1700–11; emigrated to Pennsylvania; compiled the first 'Concordance of the Welsh Bible' (published, 1730). [xxxix. 11]

MORGAN, MRS. ALICE MARY (1850–1890), painter; née Havers; studied at South Kensington; married Mr. Frederick Morgan, 1872; exhibited (1873–89) at the Society of British Artists, the Royal Academy, and the Salon. [xxxix. 11]

MORGAN, ANTHONY (fl. 1652), royalist; served the Earl of Worcester, 1642; his estates sequestered. [xxxix. 13]

MORGAN, ANTHONY (d. 1665), royalist; knighted, 1642; fought at Edgehill, 1642; succeeded to his half-brother's estates, which were sequestered, 1646; being a 'papist delinquent' was unable to compound, 1650. [xxxix. 13]

MORGAN, SIR ANTHONY (1621–1668), soldier; B.A. Magdalen College, Oxford, 1641; first a royalist captain; then a parliamentarian, 1645; captain in Ireton's horse in Ireland, 1649; major, 1652; M.P., Wicklow and Kildare, 1654, Meath and Louth, 1659, in Cromwell's united parliament; knighted, 1656, and again by Charles II, 1660; commissioner of the English auxiliaries in France; an original F.R.S., 1663. [xxxix. 12]

MORGAN, AUGUSTUS DE (1806–1871). [See DE MORGAN.]

MORGAN, SIR CHARLES (1575 ?–1642), soldier; served in the Netherlands; knighted, 1603; commanded the English at Bergen, 1622, and Breda, 1625; compelled through want and disease to surrender Stade, 1628; helped to besiege Breda, 1637; governor of Bergen; died at Bergen. [xxxix. 13]

MORGAN, SIR CHARLES (1726–1806). [See GOULD.]

MORGAN, CHARLES OCTAVIUS SWINNERTON (1803–1888), antiquary; grandson of Sir Charles Gould [q. v.]; of Westminster School and Christ Church, Oxford; M.A., 1832; M.P., Monmouthshire, 1841–74; deputy-lieutenant and J.P., Monmouthshire; president of Caerleon Antiquarian Association, to whose papers he contributed, as also to the Society of Antiquaries. [xxxix. 14]

MORGAN, DANIEL (1828 ?–1865), or SAMUEL MORAN, Australian bushranger; a stockrider for whose apprehension 500l. reward was offered, 1864; increased to 1,500l., 1865, in consequence of murders; captured and shot at Peechalba Station. [xxxix. 14]

MORGAN, GEORGE CADOGAN (1754–1798), scientific writer; brother of William Morgan (1750–1833) [q. v.]; was educated at Jesus College, Oxford; unitarian minister at Norwich, 1776; tutor at Hackney College, 1787–91; took private pupils at Southgate, Middlesex, 1791; wrote on electricity and chemistry. [xxxix. 15]

MORGAN, Sir GEORGE OSBORNE, first baronet (1826–1897), lawyer and politician; born at Gothenburg, Sweden; educated at Shrewsbury School and Balliol College, Oxford; gained Craven scholarship while at school, 1844; scholar of Worcester College, Oxford, 1847; B.A., 1848; Eldon law scholar, 1851; barrister, Lincoln's Inn, 1853; joint-editor of the 'New Reports'; liberal M.P. for Denbighshire, 1868; introduced burials bill, 1870, and places of worship (sites) bill, which became law, 1873; Q.C. and bencher of Lincoln's Inn, 1869, and treasurer, 1890; chairman of select committee on land titles and transfer, 1878–9; judge advocate-general, 1880–5; privy councillor, 1880; introduced successfully annual army discipline bill, 1881; took charge of married women's property bill, 1882; M.P., East Denbighshire, 1885, 1886, and 1892; parliamentary under-secretary for colonies, 1886; founded emigration inquiry office; created baronet, 1892; published translation of Virgil's 'Eclogues' in English hexameters, and other writings. [Suppl. iii. 192]

MORGAN, HECTOR DAVIES (1785–1850), theological writer; assumed the name of Morgan in addition to Davies, 1800; M.A. Trinity College, Oxford, 1815; curate of Castle Hedingham, 1809–46; opened savings-bank there, 1817; chief work, 'The Doctrine and Law of Marriage, Adultery, and Divorce,' 1826. [xxxix. 16]

MORGAN, HENRY (d. 1559), bishop of St. David's; became an Oxford student, 1515; D.C.L., 1525; principal of St. Edward's Hall, Oxford, c. 1525; admitted at Doctors' Commons, 1528; obtained much clerical preferment, 1530–51; bishop of St. David's, 1554–9. [xxxix. 16]

MORGAN, Sir HENRY (1635?–1688), buccaneer; lieutenant-governor of Jamaica; commanded a privateer, 1663; sailed with Edward Mansfield, and was elected 'admiral' of the buccaneers on Mansfield's death, 1666; on a rumoured Spanish invasion of Jamaica (1668) received commission to sail towards the mainland, where he attacked Porto Bello and utterly sacked it; unsuccessfully attacked by the president of Panama; reproved on his return for exceeding his commission; forced the entrance to Lake Maracaybo, 1669, sacked the town and proceeded to the head of the lake and sacked Gibraltar; after ravaging the coast of Cuba and the mainland of America, resolved to take Panama, 1670; the castle of Chagre being successfully stormed, proceeded over the ridge on foot, dispersed the Spaniards after two hours' fighting, and took possession of the city of Panama; received the formal thanks of Jamaica, but was sent to England to answer for his conduct, 1672; in disgrace for a short time; knighted, 1675, and appointed lieutenant-governor of Jamaica, senior member of the council, and commander-in-chief of the forces; died at Port Royal. [xxxix. 17]

MORGAN, J. (fl. 1739), historical compiler; projected and edited 'Phœnix Britannicus,' 1732 (discontinued after six months); compiled oriental biographies, 1739. [xxxix. 21]

MORGAN, JAMES (1799–1873), Irish presbyterian divine; studied at Glasgow and Belfast; minister of Carlow, 1820, Lisburn, 1824, Fisherwick Place, Belfast, 1828; moderator of the general assembly, 1846; D.D. Glasgow, 1847; published devotional works. [xxxix. 21]

MORGAN or YONG, JOHN (d. 1504), bishop of St. David's; doctor of laws at Oxford; a counsellor of Sir Rhys ap Thomas; bishop of St. David's, 1496. [xxxix. 22]

MORGAN, JOHN MINTER (1782–1854), miscellaneous writer; devoted himself to philanthropy; founded National Orphan Home, 1849; tried to form a self-supporting village, 1850; wrote principally on the education and condition of the lower classes. [xxxix. 22]

MORGAN, MACNAMARA (d. 1762), dramatist; his 'Philoclea' (based on Sidney's 'Arcadia'), acted, 1754, and 'Florizel and Perdita' (based on 'Winter's Tale'), 1754; possibly wrote (1742) 'The Causidicade' and (1746) 'The Processionade,' satires on William Murray, afterwards earl of Mansfield [q. v.] [xxxix. 23]

MORGAN, MATTHEW (1652–1703), verse-writer; M.A. St. John's College, Oxford, 1674; D.C.L., 1685; vicar of Wear, 1693; translated Plutarch's 'Morals,' 1684; wrote biographies and elegies. [xxxix. 23]

MORGAN, PHILIP (d. 1435), bishop successively of Worcester and Ely; doctor of laws before 1413; continually sent on foreign missions, 1414–18; prebendary of Lincoln, 1416; bishop of Worcester, 1419; privy councillor, 1419; constantly attended the council during Henry VI's minority; unanimously elected archbishop by the chapter at York, 1423, but was instead translated by the pope to Ely, 1426; arbitrator between Gloucester and Beaufort, 1426; vigilant in putting down clerical abuses. [xxxix. 24]

MORGAN, PHILIP (d. 1570). [See PHILIPPS, MORGAN.]

MORGAN, Sir RICHARD (d. 1556), judge; barrister, Lincoln's Inn, 1529; reader, 1542 and 1546; serjeant-at-law, 1546; recorder and M.P. for Gloucester, 1545–7 and 1553; chief-justice of common pleas, 1553; knighted, 1553. [xxxix. 26]

MORGAN, ROBERT (1608–1673), bishop of Bangor; M.A. Jesus College, Cambridge, 1630; incumbent of Llanwnol, 1632, Llangynhafal, Llanfair, 1637, and Efenechtyd, 1638; B.D., 1642; bought the lease of the tithes of Llandyvnan, 1642, but was ejected from his other preferments; archdeacon of Merioneth, 1660; bishop of Bangor, 1666; gave an organ to, and effected considerable restorations in, Bangor Cathedral. [xxxix. 26]

MORGAN, SYDNEY, LADY MORGAN (1783?–1859), novelist; daughter of Robert Owenson [q. v.]; published sentimental verse, 1801; took to fiction, 1804; made her reputation by 'The Wild Irish Girl,' 1806; married Sir Thomas Charles Morgan [q. v.], 1812; attacked in the 'Quarterly Review' for her patriotic novels 'O'Donnel,' 1814, and 'Florence M'Carthy,' 1816; induced by the popularity of her 'France,' 1817, to publish a similar book on Italy, 1821, and the 'Life of Salvator Rosa,' 1823; published 'The O'Briens and the O'Flaherties,' 1827; visited France a second time, 1829, and Belgium, 1835; received a government pension, 1837; came to live in London, 1839; subsequently gave her whole attention to society. [xxxix. 27]

MORGAN, SYLVANUS (1620–1693), arms-painter and author; published 'London,' a poem, 1648, 'Horologiographia Optica,' 1652, and two books on heraldry, 1661 and 1666. [xxxix. 29]

MORGAN, Sir THOMAS (d. 1595), 'the warrior'; appointed captain of a band of English volunteers under William of Orange, 1572; served in Holland, 1572–3, in Ireland, 1574; returned to the Low Countries, 1578; conspicuous for his bravery at Kowenstyn Dyke, 1585; governor of Flushing for a short time, then commander of the fortress of Rheinberg; ousted as governor of Bergen-op-Zoom, 1586, by Peregrine Bertie, baron Willoughby de Eresby [q. v.]; decision given in his favour by Elizabeth and the States-General; knighted, 1587; deprived of his governorship, 1593; returned to England. [xxxix. 29]

MORGAN, THOMAS (1543–1606?), Roman catholic conspirator; became secretary to the Earl of Shrewsbury, 1569, in order to serve Mary Queen of Scots; dismissed unpunished after ten months' imprisonment on a charge of conspiracy, 1572; secretary to James Beaton, Mary Stuart's ambassador in Paris, 1573; Queen Elizabeth having applied for his extradition, he was sent to the Bastille, 1583; corresponded with Mary Stuart through Gilbert Gifford [q. v.], who betrayed him; helped to organise the Babington plot, 1586, and advised Mary Stuart to send Babington a letter of approval; released, 1590, and again imprisoned for three years in Flanders; visited Italy and returned to Paris. [xxxix. 31]

MORGAN, Sir THOMAS (d. 1679?), soldier; served in the Low Countries, and under Fairfax in the thirty years' war; parliamentary governor of Gloucester, 1645; took Chepstow Castle and Monmouth, 1645; besieged Raglan Castle, 1646; assisted Monck in Scotland, 1651–7, becoming major-general; second in command in Flanders, 1657; knighted on his return, 1658; rejoined Monck in Scotland, and played a conspicuous part in the Restoration in Edinburgh; governor of Jersey, 1665; repaired Jersey forts and reorganised militia; a pamphlet narrating his acts in France and Flanders (1657 and 1658), said to be by himself, published, 1699. [xxxix. 33]

MORGAN, THOMAS (*d.* 1743), deist; of humble origin; independent minister of Burton, 1716, and Marlborough; dismissed for heterodoxy, 1720; studied medicine; M.D.; described himself as a 'Christian deist'; published pamphlets in opposition to Samuel Chandler, John Chapman, Thomas Chubb, Samuel Fancourt, and John Leland.   [xxxix. 35]

MORGAN, SIR THOMAS CHARLES (1783–1843), philosophical and miscellaneous writer; of Eton and Peterhouse, Cambridge: M.D., 1809; F.R.C.P., 1810; knighted in Ireland, 1811; physician to the Marshalsea prison; a commissioner of Irish fisheries, 1835, supplying an appendix to the first report; published 'Sketches of the Philosophy of Life,' 1818, and 'Sketches of the Philosophy of Morals,' 1822.   [xxxix. 36]

MORGAN, SIR WILLIAM (*d.* 1584), soldier; volunteered in the Huguenot army, 1569; assisted in capture of Valenciennes, 1572, and defence of Mons, 1572; took part in the colonisation of Ireland under Essex, 1573; knighted, 1574; governor of Dungarvan, 1579–82; displayed great activity against the rebels in South Munster.
                                                [xxxix. 36]

MORGAN, WILLIAM (1540?–1604), bishop of St. Asaph; sizar of St. John's College, Cambridge; M.A., 1571; D.D., 1583; university preacher, 1578; incumbent of Llanrhaiadr Mochnant, 1578, of Llanfyllin, 1579; summoned before Archbishop Whitgift to justify his pretensions to translate the bible into Welsh, 1587; bishop of Llandaff, 1595–1604, and of St. Asaph, 1601. [xxxix. 38]

MORGAN, WILLIAM (1623–1689), jesuit; of Westminster School and Trinity College, Cambridge; exiled after Naseby; professed of the four vows, 1666; missioner in Wales, 1670; rector of the English college at Rome, 1683; provincial of his order, 1689.   [xxxix. 39]

MORGAN, WILLIAM (1750–1833), actuary; brother of George Cadogan Morgan [q. v.]; assistant (1774), afterwards chief (1775–1830) actuary to the Equitable Assurance Society; published 'Doctrine of Annuities,' 1779, upon the basis of which new tables of mortality were constructed; vigorously denounced the accumulation of the National Debt in many pamphlets; wrote life of his uncle, Richard Price (1723–1791) [q. v.], 1816; intimate with Horne Tooke, Sir Francis Burdett, Samuel Rogers, and Tom Paine.   [xxxix. 40]

MORGAN, SIR WILLIAM (1829–1883), South Australian statesman; emigrated to Australia, 1848, and became head of a leading mercantile house; member of the legislative council, 1869; intercolonial delegate, 1871, and chief secretary of the legislative council, 1875–6 and 1877–8; premier, 1878–81; K.C.M.G., 1883.   [xxxix. 41]

MORGANENSIS (*fl.* 1210). [See MAURICE.]

MORGANN, MAURICE (1726–1802), commentator on the character of Sir John Falstaff; under-secretary of state, 1782; secretary to the embassy for peace with America, 1782; chief work, 'Essay on the Dramatic Character of Sir John Falstaff' (vindication of Falstaff's courage), 1777.   [xxxix. 42]

MORGANWG, IOLO (1746–1826). [See WILLIAMS, EDWARD.]

MORGANWG, LEWIS (*fl.* 1500–1540). [See LEWIS.]

MORI, FRANCIS (1820–1873), composer; son of Nicolas Mori [q. v.]; composed 'Fridolin' and 'The River Sprite,' 1865; died at Chamant.   [xxxix. 43]

MORI, NICOLAS (1797–1839), violinist; born in London; pupil of Barthélemon and Viotti; leader of the Philharmonic orchestra, 1816; published 'The Musical Gem' (annual); member of the first board of professors of the new Academy of Music, 1823; principal orchestral leader of festivals.   [xxxix. 42]

MORIARTY, DAVID (1814–1877), bishop of Kerry; educated at Boulogne-sur-Mer and Maynooth; bishop of Kerry, 1856; opposed treasonable movements and home rule.   [xxxix. 43]

MORICE. [See also MORRIS.]

MORICE, HUMPHRY (1640?–1696), son of Sir William Morice [q. v.]; auditor of the exchequer; probably secretary to the embassy to the Dutch, 1667.
                                                [xxxix. 49]

MORICE, HUMPHRY (1671?–1731), governor of the Bank of England; son of Humphry Morice (1640?–1696) [q. v.]; a Turkey merchant; M.P., Newport, 1713–22, Grampound, 1722–31; steadily supported Walpole; director of the Bank of England, 1716; deputy-governor, 1725–6; governor, 1727–8; discovered, after his death, to have drawn fictitious bills and to have appropriated trust funds.   [xxxix. 44]

MORICE, SIR HUMPHRY, fourth baronet (1723–1785), politician; son of Humphry Morice (1671?–1731) [q. v.]; succeeded to his cousin's baronetcy and estates, 1750; M.P., Launceston, 1754 and 1757; clerk-comptroller of the household of George II, 1757; went abroad, 1760; his household appointment not renewed till 1761; privy councillor, 1763; lord warden of the stannaries, 1763; high steward of the duchy of Cornwall, 1763; recorder of Launceston, 1771; retired from parliament, 1780; resigned the recordership, 1782; ousted from the stannaries, 1783; died at Naples.
                                                [xxxix. 44]

MORICE, RALPH (*fl.* 1523–1570), secretary to Archbishop Cranmer; M.A. Cambridge, 1523; Cranmer's secretary, 1528; bailiff for some crown lands, 1537; registrar to the commissioners for Rochester, Canterbury, Chichester, and Winchester, 1547; was imprisoned in Queen Mary's reign, but escaped; supplied information to Foxe and others.   [xxxix. 46]

MORICE, WILLIAM (*fl.* 1547), brother of Ralph Morice [q. v.]; gentleman-usher to Henry VIII; imprisoned for heresy, but released on Henry's death; M.P.
                                                [xxxix. 46]

MORICE, SIR WILLIAM (1602–1676), secretary of state and theologian; B.A. Exeter College, Oxford, 1622; J.P., 1640; M.P., 1648, 1654, and 1656; excluded in Pride's Purge; high sheriff of Devonshire, 1651; M.P., Newport, 1658, Plymouth, 1660; related to Monck; assisted in the Restoration; secretary of state, 1660; knighted, 1660; privy councillor, 1660; resigned secretaryship, 1668; published treatise on the administration of the sacrament to all church members, 1657.   [xxxix. 47]

MORIER, DAVID (1705?–1770), painter; born at Berne; came to England, 1743; exhibited equestrian portraits at the Society of Artists, 1760, 1762, 1765, and 1768; died in the Fleet.   [xxxix. 49]

MORIER, DAVID RICHARD (1784–1877), diplomatist; son of Isaac Morier [q. v.]; born at Smyrna; entered the diplomatic service, 1804; served in South-east Europe, Egypt, Dardanelles, and Constantinople, till 1812; assisted in the 'settlement of Europe,' 1813–15; consul-general for France, 1815–32; minister plenipotentiary to the Swiss States, 1832–47; published two religious pamphlets and 'Photo,' a tale of modern Greece, 1857.
                                                [xxxix. 49]

MORIER, ISAAC (1750–1817), consul-general of the Levant Company; born at Smyrna; naturalised in England, 1803; consul-general of the Levant Company at Constantinople, 1804; his post converted into a British consulship, 1806; died of plague at Constantinople.
                                                [xxxix. 50]

MORIER, JAMES JUSTINIAN (1780?–1849), diplomatist, traveller, and novelist; son of Isaac Morier [q. v.]; born at Smyrna; entered Persian diplomatic service, 1807; travelled home by Turkey in Asia, 1809, publishing an account, 1812; returned from Tehrán through Asia Minor, 1815, and published a second book, 1818; published oriental romances, 'Hajji Baba,' 1824, being the best.
                                                [xxxix. 51]

MORIER, JOHN PHILIP (1776–1853), diplomatist; son of Isaac Morier [q. v.]; born at Smyrna; became attached to Constantinople embassy, 1799; sent to Egypt, 1799; published account of the Egyptian campaign, 1800; consul-general in Albania, 1803; secretary of legation at Washington, 1810; under-secretary for foreign affairs, 1815; envoy extraordinary to court of Saxony, 1816–25.
                                                [xxxix. 52]

MORIER, SIR ROBERT BURNETT DAVID (1826–1893), diplomatist; son of David Richard Morier [q. v.]; born in Paris; B.A. Balliol College, Oxford, 1849; entered diplomatic service, 1851; held various appointments at German courts, 1853–76, and acquired an unrivalled intimacy with German politics; minister at Lisbon, 1876–1881, Madrid, 1881–4; ambassador at St. Petersburg, 1884–93; K.C.B., 1882; privy councillor, 1885; G.C.M.G., 1886; G.C.B., 1887; D.C.L. Oxford, 1889; displayed exceptional ability in the conduct of British relations with Russia, especially in 1885; died at Montreux. [xxxix. 52]

MORIER, WILLIAM (1790–1864), admiral; son of Isaac Morier [q. v.]; born at Smyrna; entered navy, 1803; served in Mediterranean and North Sea, 1825; post captain, 1830; rear-admiral, 1855; vice-admiral, 1862. [xxxix. 54]

MORINS, RICHARD DE (d. 1242), historian; canon of Merton; became prior of Dunstable, 1202; went to Rome, 1203 and 1215; arbitrated between the bishop of London and the abbey of Westminster, 1222; compiled the early portion of the 'Dunstable Annals' (Rolls Ser., 1866). [xxxix. 54]

MORISON. [See also MORRISON and MORYSON.]

MORISON, SIR ALEXANDER (1779–1866), physician; M.D. Edinburgh, 1799; F.R.C.P., 1841; knighted, 1838; wrote on mental diseases. [xxxix. 55]

MORISON, DOUGLAS (1814–1847), painter and lithographer; associate of the New Society of Painters in Water-colours, 1836–8. [xxxix. 55]

MORISON, GEORGE (1757–1845), son of James Morison (1708–1786) [q. v.]; graduated at Aberdeen; minister of Banchory-Devenick, 1785; D.D. Aberdeen, 1824; wrote on the Scottish church. [xxxix. 56]

MORISON, JAMES (1708–1786), of Elsick; elected provost of Aberdeen, 1744; forced by John Hamilton to hear the Pretender proclaimed king, but declined to drink his health, 1745. [xxxix. 55]

MORISON, JAMES (1762–1809), theologian; Perth bookseller; seceded from the Glassites; founded a new sect, and published theological works. [xxxix. 56]

MORISON, JAMES (1770–1840), self-styled 'the Hygeist'; merchant; cured himself of ill-health and became a vendor of 'Morison's pills,' 1825, of which he wrote puffs; died in Paris. [xxxix. 56]

MORISON, JAMES (1816–1893), founder of the evangelical union; educated at Edinburgh University; embodied his views of the atonement being for all mankind in a tract, 1840; minister of Kilmarnock, 1840; suspended by the presbytery, 1841; being joined by other suspended ministers formed 'evangelical union,' 1843; established a theological college, 1843, of which he was first principal; left Kilmarnock for Glasgow, 1853; D.D. Michigan, 1862, Glasgow, 1883; retired from the ministry, 1884; published New Testament commentaries. [xxxix. 56]

MORISON, JAMES AUGUSTUS COTTER (1832–1888), author; son of James Morison (1770–1840) [q. v.]; lived in Paris, 1834–40; M.A. Lincoln College, Oxford, 1859; contributed to 'Saturday Review'; wrote 'Life of St. Bernard,' 1863, 'Gibbon,' 1878, and 'Macaulay,' 1882, in 'Men of Letters' series; published 'Service of Man' (positivist essay), 1887; contemplated a history of Louis XIV's reign. [xxxix. 58]

MORISON, JOHN (1750–1798), Scottish divine and poet; M.A. King's College, Aberdeen, 1771; minister of Canisbay, 1780; contributed to 'Scottish Paraphrases,' 1781, and Chalmers's 'Caledonia.' [xxxix. 59]

MORISON, JOHN (1791–1859), congregational minister; pastor at Chelsea, 1815–16, at Trevor Chapel, London, 1816–59; edited 'Evangelical Magazine,' 1827–57; D.D. Glasgow, 1830; published devotional works. [xxxix. 60]

MORISON, SIR RICHARD (d. 1556), ambassador; B.A. Oxford, 1528; visited Italy; prebendary of Salisbury, 1537; ambassador to the Hanse towns, 1546; commissioner to visit Oxford, 1549; knighted before 1550; ambassador to Charles V, 1550–3, with Ascham as his secretary; studied with Peter Martyr at Strasburg, 1554–1556; published a defence of Henry VIII against Cochlæus, 1537, and other works; died at Strasburg. [xxxix. 60]

MORISON, ROBERT (1620–1683), botanist; M.A. and Ph.D. Aberdeen, 1638; studied science at Paris; M.D. Angers, 1648; physician to Gaston, duke of Orleans, 1649; senior physician and king's botanist to Charles II, 1660; professor of botany at Oxford, 1669; published 'Præludia Botanica,' 1669, and 'Historia Plantarum Oxoniensis,' 1680, containing a clear conception of genus, species, and family; his name perpetuated by the genus Morisonia; died from the effects of an accident. [xxxix. 61]

MORISON or **MORESIN,** THOMAS (1558?–1603?), physician and diplomatist; born in Scotland; M.D. Montpellier; visited Frankfort; after his return to Scotland (1593) became one of Essex's intelligencers; wrote against alchemists and astrologers, 1593; published a history of the papacy, 1594. [xxxix. 63]

MORISON, THOMAS (d. 1824), army surgeon; son of James Morison (1708–1786) [q. v.]; brought into notice the medicinal properties of Strathpeffer springs. [xxxix. 56]

MORLAND, GEORGE (1763–1804), painter; son of Henry Robert Morland [q. v.]; exhibited when ten years old at the Royal Academy; copied Flemish and Dutch pictures; early developed a taste for dissipation; his original picture, 'The Angler's Repast,' was engraved by William Ward and published by John Raphael Smith, 1780; married Anne sister of William Ward (1766–1826) [q. v.], 1786, his marriage having for a time a steadying effect; again fell into bad habits, and was arrested for debt, 1799; released, 1802; died in a sponging-house, his own epitaph on himself being 'Here lies a drunken dog.' He was a master of genre and animal painting, and his most characteristic pictures are faithful reflections of lowly life in England. His total production is estimated at four thousand pictures. [xxxix. 66]

MORLAND, GEORGE HENRY (d. 1789?), genre painter; assisted by the Incorporated Society of Artists, 1760; his works engraved by Watson and Philip Dawe. [xxxix. 67]

MORLAND, SIR HENRY (1837–1891), Indian official; entered Indian navy, 1852; fourth lieutenant, 1857; lieutenant, 1859; transferred to the marines, 1863; transport officer at Bombay, 1865; superintended Abyssinian expedition, 1867; organised commissariat and transport of Afghan war; conservator of the port of Bombay and registrar of shipping, 1873; knighted, 1887; died in Bombay. [xxxix. 67]

MORLAND, HENRY ROBERT (1730?–1797), portrait-painter; son of George Henry Morland [q. v.]; picture-dealer; exhibited (1760–91) portraits and domestic subjects at the Royal Academy and Society of Artists. [xxxix. 68]

MORLAND, SIR SAMUEL, first baronet (1625–1695), diplomatist, mathematician and inventor; of Winchester School and Magdalene College, Cambridge; fellow and tutor, 1649; supported parliamentarians; accompanied Whitelocke's embassy to Sweden, 1653; assistant to Secretary Thurloe, 1654; sent to remonstrate with the Duke of Saxony on the Waldensian cruelties, 1655; published history of Waldensian church, 1658; became acquainted with Sir Richard Willis's plot, and from that time endeavoured to promote the Restoration; joined Charles II at Breda, May 1660; created baronet and gentleman of the privy chamber, 1660; visited France 'about the king's waterworks,' 1682; became blind, 1692. He invented two arithmetical machines and a speaking trumpet, and by the 'plunger-pump' raised water to the top of Windsor Castle, 1675. Besides this, he endeavoured to use high-pressed steam as a power, and suggested it for the propulsion of vessels. He wrote on mathematics and hydrostatics. One of Morland's calculating machines is now at South Kensington, and a speaking trumpet is preserved at Cambridge. [xxxix. 68]

MORLEY, EARLS OF. [See PARKER, JOHN, first EARL, 1772–1840; PARKER, EDMUND, second EARL, 1810–1864.]

MORLEY, BARONS. [See PARKER, HENRY, eighth BARON, 1476–1556; PARKER, HENRY, ninth BARON, d. 1577.]

MORLEY, CHRISTOPHER LOVE (fl. 1700), physician; M.D. Leyden, 1679; studied under Schacht, Drelincourt, Maëts, Marggraff, and Le Mort; honorary F.C.P., 1680; published 'De Morbo Epidemico,' 1679, and 'Collectanea Chemica Leydensia,' 1684. [xxxix. 73]

MORLEY, MERLAI, MERLAC, or MARLACH, DANIEL OF (fl. 1170–1190), astronomer; said to have studied at Oxford, Paris, and Toledo; author of 'Philosophia Magistri Danielis de Merlac,' or 'Liber de Naturis inferiorum et superiorum.' [xxxix. 74]

MORLEY, GEORGE (1597–1684), bishop of Winchester; of Westminster School and Christ Church, Oxford; M.A., 1621; D.D., 1642; met at Oxford Robert Sanderson, Gilbert Sheldon, Edward Hyde, afterwards earl of Clarendon, and subsequently Edmund Waller and John Hampden; canon of Christ Church, 1641; rector of Mildenhall, 1641; preached before the House of Commons, 1642; ejected, 1648; went abroad and performed service for the English royalists wherever he stayed; sent to England to win over the presbyterians to the Restoration; regained his canonry, became dean of Christ Church, Oxford, and in October bishop of Worcester, 1660; preacher of the coronation sermon, 1661; translated to Winchester, 1662; frequently entertained the Duke of York at Farnham Castle; signified to Clarendon the king's wish that he should leave the country, 1667; of Calvinistic leanings; benefactor of Winchester diocese, St. Paul's Cathedral, and Christ Church and Pembroke College, Oxford; published controversial works. [xxxix. 74]

MORLEY, HENRY (1822–1894), author; educated at King's College, London; editor of Dickens's periodicals, 1850–65, and the 'Examiner'; evening lecturer at King's College, London, 1857; professor of literature at University College, London, 1865, and Queen's College, London, 1878; principal of University Hall, Gordon Square, London, 1882–90; edited 'Morley's Universal Library' and 'Cassell's National Library'; wrote on English literature and biographies. [xxxix. 78]

MORLEY, HERBERT (1616–1667), colonel; educated at Lewes with John Evelyn; entered the Inner Temple, 1634; M.P., Lewes, 1640; colonel in the parliamentary army; put Sussex in a state of defence, 1642; assisted in the recapture of Arundel and at Basing House, 1644; refused to act as one of the king's judges; opposed Cromwell as long as possible and (1653) withdrew into private life; M.P., Sussex, 1659; elected one of the council of state and admiralty commissioner, 1659; collected troops and opposed Lambert, October 1659; restored parliament, December 1659; refused to negotiate for the king's return; purchased pardon, 1660; was elected M.P. for Rye, but probably did not sit. [xxxix. 79]

MORLEY, JOHN (1656–1732), known as 'Merchant Morley'; agent and landjobber of Halstead, Essex; a butcher who became agent to Edward Harley, afterwards second earl of Oxford [q. v.], and negotiated his marriage (1713) with Lady Henrietta Holles. [xxxix. 80]

MORLEY, JOHN (d. 1776?), medical writer; grandson of John Morley (1656–1732) [q. v.]; published an essay on scrofula, 1767. [xxxix. 81]

MORLEY, ROBERT DE, second BARON MORLEY (1296?–1360), summoned to parliament, 1317; served in Ireland, 1331; admiral of the fleet; gained the victory of Sluys, 1340; commanded the fleet, 1341, 1348, and 1354; served in the French wars, 1341, 1346, 1347, and 1359. [xxxix. 81]

MORLEY, SAMUEL (1809–1886), politician; amassed a fortune in the hosiery business; active in religious, philanthropic, and temperance movements; M.P., Nottingham, 1865; unseated on petition, 1866; became proprietor of the 'Daily News'; M.P., Bristol, 1868–85; consistently followed Gladstone; supported Irish disestablishment, and was converted to state education; on the London School Board, 1870–6; took part in all movements for the abolition of tests and dissenters' burial grievances; munificent builder of chapels; pensioned his employés at a cost of 2,000l. annually. [xxxix. 82]

MORLEY, THOMAS (1557–1604?), musician; pupil of William Byrd [q. v.]; Mus. Bac. Oxford, 1588; organist of St. Paul's Cathedral, 1591–2; gentleman of the Chapel Royal, 1592; wrote 'Plaine and Easie Introduction to Practicall Musicke,' 1597; composed graceful madrigals (including the well-known ' It was a Lover and his Lass ') and church music. [xxxix. 84]

MORLEY, WILLIAM (d. 1347). [See MERLE.]

MORLEY, WILLIAM HOOK (1815–1860), orientalist; barrister, Middle Temple, 1840; discovered (1838) a missing manuscript of Rashīdudīn Jām'ia Tawārīkh; librarian of Royal Asiatic Society. [Suppl. iii. 195]

MORNINGTON, EARLS OF. [See WELLESLEY, GARRETT, first EARL, 1735–1781; WELLESLEY, RICHARD COLLEY, second EARL, 1760–1842; WELLESLEY-POLE, WILLIAM, third EARL, 1763–1845; WELLESLEY, WILLIAM POLE TYLNEY LONG-, fourth EARL, 1788–1857.]

MORNINGTON, BARONS. [See WELLESLEY, RICHARD COLLEY, first BARON, 1690?–1758; WELLESLEY, GARRETT, second BARON, 1735–1781.]

MORPETH, VISCOUNT (1773–1848). [See HOWARD, GEORGE, sixth EARL OF CARLISLE.]

MORPHETT, SIR JOHN (1809–1892), pioneer and politician of South Australia; emigrated, 1836; general merchant; nominated for the legislative assembly, 1843; speaker, 1851–5; chief secretary, 1861; president of the council, 1865–73; knighted, 1870; died in Australia. [xxxix. 85]

MORRELL, HUGH (d. 1664?), woollen merchant; was engaged in export trade between Exeter and France; obtained patents to regulate manufactures in Herefordshire, 1624, and Devonshire, 1626; having had his goods at Rouen seized by the French, petitioned the king for satisfaction, 1627; made efforts to improve trade, 1633, 1638, 1647; surveyor of customs at Dover, 1642; employed by government in commercial negotiations with France, 1650. [xxxix. 86]

MORRELL, WILLIAM (fl. 1625), New England poet; an Anglican clergyman who remained a year in Massachusetts, 1623; wrote Latin hexameters and English verse on New England, 1625. [xxxix. 87]

MORREN, NATHANIEL (1798–1847), Scottish divine; M.A. Marischal College, Aberdeen, 1814; minister at Greenock, 1823, and Brechin, 1843; wrote 'Annals of the General Assembly' and other ecclesiastical works. [xxxix. 87]

MORRES, HERVEY MONTMORENCY (1767–1839), United Irishman; entered the Austrian service; returned to Ireland, 1795; became a United Irishman, 1796; chosen county representative for Tipperary, 1797; adjutant-general of Munster; escaped to Hamburg after the capitulation of the French at Ballinamuck, 1798; arrested and extradited, 1799; prosecuted, but without result; released, 1801; entered the French service, c. 1811, and became adjutant-commandant, with the rank of colonel, 1812; obtained letters of naturalisation, 1816; wrote on Irish topography and the Montmorency genealogy; died at St. Germain-en-Laye. [xxxix. 87]

MORRES, HERVEY REDMOND, second VISCOUNT MOUNTMORRES (1746?–1797), B.A. Christ Church, Oxford, 1766; created M.A., 1766; D.C.L., 1773; supported Pitt strongly in Ireland, 1788; wrote on political questions; shot himself in a fit of insanity. [xxxix. 89]

MORRICE. [See MORICE and MORRIS.]

MORRIS. [See also MORICE.]

MORRIS, CHARLES (1745–1838), song-writer; entered 17th foot, 1764; served in America; exchanged into the 2nd life-guards; punch-maker and bard of the Beefsteak Society, 1785, at which he sang many of his wittiest songs; visited frequently at Carlton House; his songs published as 'Lyra Urbanica,' 1840. [xxxix. 90]

MORRIS, MORES, or MORICE, SIR CHRISTOPHER (1490?–1544), master of ordnance; gunner in the Tower, 1513; served on the coast of France, 1522–4; master of ordnance, 1537; master-gunner of England, and knighted, 1537; with Hertford in Scotland, 1544; mortally wounded at Boulogne. [xxxix. 91]

MORRIS, CORBYN (d. 1779), commissioner of customs; provoked controversy on the national income by a 'Letter from a Bystander,' 1742; made proposals for regulating the highlands, 1745; secretary of the customs in Scotland, 1751; suggested a census to the Duke of Newcastle, 1753; F.R.S., 1757; commissioner of customs in England, 1763; published economic works. [xxxix. 92]

MORRIS, EDWARD (d. 1689), Welsh poet; wrote carols, ballads, and 'englynion'; translated an English ecclesiastical work into Welsh. [xxxix. 94]

MORRIS, FRANCIS ORPEN (1810–1893), naturalist; grandson of Roger Morris [q. v.]; B.A. Worcester College, Oxford, 1833; incumbent of Nafferton, 1844, of Nunburnholme, 1854; anti-vivisectionist; wrote against Darwinianism and on religion and natural history; chief work, 'History of British Birds,' 1851–7. [xxxix. 94]

MORRIS or **MORUS**, HUW (1622–1709), Welsh poet; composed carols, ballads, and occasional verse; royalist; wrote satires on the parliamentary party; collected edition of his poems, published, 1823. [xxxix. 95]

MORRIS, SIR JAMES NICOLL (1763?–1830), vice-admiral; joined navy before 1778; lieutenant, 1780; commander, 1790; served in the Channel and Mediterranean, and with Nelson off Cadiz; wounded at Trafalgar, 1805; rear-admiral, 1811; third in command in the Baltic, 1812; K.C.B., 1815; vice-admiral, 1819.   [xxxix. 96]

MORRIS, JOHN (1617?–1649), soldier; brought up in the household of Thomas Wentworth, first earl of Strafford [q. v.]; after Strafford's death became major, 1643; threw up his commission, 1644; colonel in the parliamentary army; ousted from command by the New Model; took Pontefract Castle by stratagem, 1645 (castle retaken by parliamentarians, 1649); imprisoned in Lancaster Castle; escaped, but was retaken and executed.   [xxxix. 96]

MORRIS, JOHN (1810–1886), geologist; originally a pharmaceutical chemist; professor of geology, University College, London, 1854–77; F.G.S., 1845; published 'Catalogue of British Fossils,' 1845, and, in conjunction with John Lycett, 'Great Oolite Mollusca.'   [xxxix. 98]

MORRIS, JOHN (1826–1893), jesuit; son of John Carnac Morris [q. v.]; born at Ootacamund; entered Trinity College, Cambridge, 1845; became a Roman catholic, 1846; ordained to the English mission, 1849; vice-rector of the English College, Rome, 1852–5; secretary to Cardinal Wiseman; professed of the four vows, 1877; rector at Roehampton, 1880–6; F.S.A., 1889; published works on ecclesiastical history.   [xxxix. 98]

MORRIS, JOHN BRANDE (1812–1880), theological writer; M.A. Balliol College, Oxford, 1837; fellow and Hebrew lecturer, Exeter College, Oxford, 1837; joined church of Rome, 1846; priest, 1849; held various charges; published mystic and devotional works.   [xxxix. 99]

MORRIS, JOHN CARNAC (1798–1858), Telugu scholar; midshipman, 1813–15; entered Madras civil service, 1818; F.R.S., 1831; Telugu translator to government, 1832; accountant-general, 1834; established bank in Madras, 1834; returned to England, 1846, and engaged in commercial enterprise; published an 'English-Telugu Dictionary,' 1835; died at St. Heliers.   [xxxix. 100]

MORRIS, JOHN WEBSTER (1763–1836), baptist minister and author; pastor of Clipstone, 1785, of Dunstable, 1803–9; set up as a printer, and published the works of Sutcliffe, Fuller, and Hall; chief works, 'Sacred Biography' and 'Memoirs of . . . Andrew Fuller,' 1816.   [xxxix. 101]

MORRIS or **MORYS**, LEWIS (1700–1765), Welsh poet; philologist and antiquary; originally a land surveyor; collector of customs at Holyhead, 1729; surveyed the Welsh coast, 1737–48; superintendent of crown lands and mines in Wales, 1750; retired to Penbryn, 1761; published poetry and works on Welsh history and antiquities; author of a dictionary of Celtic mythology, history, and geography, completed, 1760, published, 1878.   [xxxix. 101]

MORRIS, MORRIS DRAKE (*fl.* 1717), biographer; of Trinity College, Cambridge; assumed surname Morris, 1717; compiled biographies of famous men, 1715–16.   [xxxix. 104]

MORRIS or **MORYS**, RICHARD (*d.* 1779), Welsh scholar; brother of Lewis Morris [q. v.]; clerk of foreign accounts in navy office; supervised editions of the Welsh bible, 1746 and 1752, and of the prayer-book.   [xxxix. 104]

MORRIS, RICHARD (1833–1894), philologist; Winchester lecturer on English language and literature at King's College school, 1869; ordained, 1871; head-master of Royal Masonic Institution for Boys, Wood Green, London, 1875–88; LL.D. Lambeth, 1870; hon. M.A. Oxford, 1874; published educational works on English grammar, besides editions of texts for the Early English Text Society and Pali Text Society.   [Suppl. iii. 196]

MORRIS, ROBERT (*fl.* 1754), architect; supervised building of Inverary Castle, 1745–61, Richmond Park Lodge, Brandenburgh House, c. 1750, Wimbledon House, and Kirby Hall, c. 1750; published architectural works.   [xxxix. 104]

MORRIS, ROGER (1727–1794), lieutenant-colonel; American loyalist; captain in 48th foot, 1745; went to America, 1755; aide-de-camp to Major-general Braddock and major, 1758; wounded at Quebec; lieutenant-colonel,

1760; retired, 1764; returned to England, 1776, after his wife's property on the Hudson River was confiscated and she was attainted.   [xxxix. 105]

MORRIS, THOMAS (1660–1748), nonjuror; minor canon of Worcester and vicar of Claines; M.A. King's College, Cambridge, 1688; deprived, 1689; buried in Worcester Cathedral as 'Miserimus' (*sic*), without name or date, a fact which called forth poems from Wordsworth and others, and a novel by Frederic Mansel Reynolds [q. v.], 1832. The epitaph was nearly obliterated in 1829, but renewed as 'Miserrimus.'   [xxxix. 106]

MORRIS, THOMAS (*fl.* 1780–1800), engraver; pupil of Woollett; confined himself to line-engravings of landscapes after Gilpin and Garrard.   [xxxix. 106]

MORRIS, CAPTAIN THOMAS (*fl.* 1806), song-writer; brother of Charles Morris [q. v.]; of Winchester College and Jesus College, Oxford; B.A., 1753; served with 17th foot in America; published songs and verses.   [xxxix. 91]

MORRIS, SIR WILLIAM (1602–1676). [See MORICE.]

MORRIS, WILLIAM (1834–1896), poet, artist, manufacturer, and socialist; of Marlborough School and Exeter College, Oxford; formed friendship with (Sir) Edward Coley Burne-Jones [q. v.]; B.A., 1856; articled as architect to George Edmund Street [q. v.], 1856; followed profession of painter, 1857–62; one of originators of 'Oxford and Cambridge Magazine,' to which he contributed tales, essays, and poems; assisted in painting frescoes in Oxford Union, 1857; published 'Defence of Guenevere and other Poems,' 1858; helped to found manufacturing and decorating firm of Morris, Marshall, Faulkner & Co. (dissolved, 1874), in which Rossetti, Burne-Jones, Madox Brown, and Philip Webb were also partners; published 'Life and Death of Jason,' 1867, and 'Earthly Paradise,' 1868–70; travelled in Iceland, 1871; acquired Kelmscott Manor House, near Lechlade; published 'Love is Enough,' 1872; produced numerous illuminated manuscripts, including two of Fitzgerald's 'Omar Kháyyám'; published 'Æneids of Virgil' (an English verse translation), 1875, 'Three Northern Love Stories,' 1875, and the epic, 'Sigurd the Volsung and the Fall of the Niblungs,' 1876; studied practical arts of dyeing and carpet weaving; founded Society for the Protection of Ancient Buildings, 1877; treasurer of National Liberal League, 1879; joined, 1883, Democratic Federation, the doctrine of which, largely under his leadership, developed into socialism, and on its disruption, 1884, became head of the seceders, who organised themselves as the Socialist league; published English verse translation of 'Odyssey,' 1887, 'Dream of John Ball,' 1888, 'House of the Wolfings,' 1889, 'The Roots of the Mountains,' 1890, 'Story of the Glittering Plain,' 1890, 'News from Nowhere,' 1891, 'The Wood beyond the World,' 1894, 'Child Christopher,' 1895, 'The Well at the World's End,' 1896, and 'The Water of the Wondrous Isles' and 'Story of the Sundering Flood,' posthumously, 1897 and 1898 respectively; started, 1890, at Hammersmith, the Kelmscott Press, for which he designed founts of type and ornamental letters and borders, and from which were issued fifty-three books, comprising (1) Morris's own works, (2) reprints of English classics, and (3) various smaller books, originals or translations.   [Suppl. iii. 197]

MORRISON, ALFRED (1821–1897), collector of works of art; son of James Morrison [q. v.]; made at his houses at Fonthill and Carlton House Terrace, London, collections of works of art and autographs. The autographs comprised many valuable manuscripts, including the papers of Sir Richard Bulstrode [q. v.], which he printed for the first time.   [Suppl. iii. 203]

MORRISON, CHARLES (*fl.* 1753), first projector of the electric telegraph; a Greenock surgeon who emigrated to Virginia; in a letter to the 'Scots Magazine,' 1753, he suggested conveying messages by electricity; died in Virginia.   [xxxix. 107]

MORRISON, GEORGE (1704?–1799), general; gunner, 1722; served in Flanders, 1747; employed in surveying and constructing roads in the highlands, 1745–50; captain and engineer in ordinary, 1758; engaged in descents on the French coast, 1758; lieutenant-colonel, 1761; quartermaster-general, 1763; equerry to the Duke of York, 1764; colonel, 1777; lieutenant-general, 1782; general, 1796.   [xxxix. 107]

MORRISON, JAMES (1790–1857), merchant and politician; amassed a fortune as a draper; M.P., St. Ives, 1830; voted for the Reform Bill; M.P., Ipswich, 1831–7, Inverness burghs, 1840–7; endeavoured to improve railway legislation, and published pamphlets on the subject. [xxxix. 108]

MORRISON, JOHN ROBERT (1814–1843), officiating colonial secretary of Hongkong; son of Robert Morrison [q. v.]; born at Macao; translator to the Canton merchants, 1830; secretary and interpreter to the British government, 1834–42; officiating colonial secretary of Hongkong; published the 'Chinese Commercial Guide,' 1833; died at Hongkong. [xxxix. 111]

MORRISON, SIR RICHARD (1767–1849), architect; knighted, 1841; built, among other public works, the Roman catholic cathedral at Dublin. [xxxix. 109]

MORRISON, RICHARD JAMES (1795–1874), inventor and astrologer; known by his pseudonym of 'Zadkiel'; entered navy, 1806; served in the Adriatic and on the North Sea, Baltic, and Cork stations; lieutenant, 1815; coastguard, 1827–9; presented plan to the admiralty (1824) for registering merchant seamen, and another (1835) for providing seamen without impressment; brought out the 'Herald of Astrology,' 1831 (continued as 'Zadkiel's Almanac'); wrote on astrology and astronomy. [xxxix. 109]

MORRISON, ROBERT (1782–1834), Chinese missionary; originally a shoemaker; studied in England, 1801–7; went to China, 1807; translator to the East India Company, 1809; interpreter to Lord Amherst, 1817; D.D. Glasgow, 1817; established the Anglo-Chinese College at Malacca, 1818; F.R.S., 1824; published 'Dictionary of the Chinese Language,' 1815–23, and translated the bible into Chinese; died at Macao. [xxxix. 111]

MORRISON, THOMAS (d. 1835?), medical writer; M.R.C.S.; practised in Chelsea, 1798; moved to Dublin, 1806. His medical works include 'An Examination into the . . . Brunonian System,' 1806. [xxxix. 112]

MORRISON, WILLIAM VITRUVIUS (1794–1838), architect; son of Sir Richard Morrison [q. v.]; made tour through Europe, 1821; assisted his father. [xxxix. 109]

MORRITT, JOHN BACON SAWREY (1772?–1843), traveller and classical scholar; M.A. St. John's College, Cambridge, 1798; travelled in Greece and Asia Minor, 1794–6; surveyed the scene of the Iliad; maintained historical existence of Troy against Jacob Bryant; M.P., Beverley, 1799–1802, Northallerton, 1814–18, Shaftesbury, 1818–20; exchanged visits with Scott; 'arch-master' of the Dilettanti Society; a founder of the Travellers' Club, 1819. [xxxix. 112]

MORS, RODERICK (d. 1546). [See BRINKELOW, HENRY.]

MORSE, HENRY (1595–1645), jesuit; known as CLAXTON and WARDE; studied at Douay and Rome; missioner in England, 1624; jesuit, 1625; three times arrested and imprisoned in England, and finally executed at Tyburn; his diary in the British Museum. [xxxix. 113]

MORSE, ROBERT (1743–1818), general; employed in descents on the French coast, 1758; served in the West Indies, 1759, and in the expedition against Belleisle, 1761; in Germany, 1762–3; captain-lieutenant and engineer extraordinary, 1763; commanded in the West Indies; chief engineer in America, 1782; lieutenant-colonel, 1783; colonel, 1788; commanding engineer at Gibraltar, 1791; major-general, 1793; lieutenant-general, 1799; inspector-general of fortifications, 1802; general, 1808; author of report on Nova Scotia and plans. [xxxix. 114]

MORSE, WILLIAM (d. 1649), jesuit; brother of Henry Morse [q. v.]; missioner in England. [xxxix. 114]

MORSHEAD, HENRY ANDERSON (1774?–1831), colonel, royal engineers; entered artillery, 1790; served in Flanders; transferred to the engineers, 1794; first lieutenant, 1796; captain-lieutenant, 1801; captain, 1805; assumed name of Morshead, 1805; served in Madeira, 1808–12; lieutenant-colonel, 1813; commanding royal engineer of western district, 1815; colonel, 1825; commanding engineer at Malta, 1829; died at Valetta. [xxxix. 115]

MORT, THOMAS SUTCLIFFE (1816–1878), a pioneer of commerce in New South Wales; went to Australia, 1838; promoted steam navigation, 1841; started public wool sales, 1843; promoted first railway in New South Wales, 1849; encouraged pastoral development; commenced dock at Port Jackson, 1863; originated frozen meat trade, 1875; died in Australia. [xxxix. 116]

MORTAIN, ROBERT OF, COUNT OF MORTAIN, in the diocese of Avranches (d. 1091?), brother of Odo of Bayeux; uterine brother of William the Conqueror; received from William the county of Mortain, 1049; accompanied William to England and received many grants; held Pevensey Castle against Rufus, 1088. [xxxix. 117]

MORTEN, THOMAS (1836–1866), painter and book-illustrator; occasionally exhibited at the Royal Academy; illustrated works, including 'Gulliver's Travels,' 1846. [xxxix. 117]

MORTIMER, CROMWELL (d. 1752), physician; son of John Mortimer [q. v.]; M.A. Cambridge *comitiis regiis*, 1728; studied under Boerhaave at Leyden; M.D. Leyden, 1724; L.R.C.P., 1725; assistant to Sir Hans Sloane, 1729–40; issued account of his system of payments, 1744; F.R.S., 1728 (secretary, 1730–52); promoted incorporation of Society of Antiquaries 1750; edited Royal Society's 'Transactions'; wrote on chemistry. [xxxix. 118]

MORTIMER, EDMUND (II) DE, third EARL OF MARCH (1351–1381), son of Roger de Mortimer (V), second earl of March [q. v.]; succeeded to earldom, 1360; married Philippa, daughter of Lionel, second son of Edward III, 1368, and handed on to the house of York the claim to the throne, which resulted in the Wars of the Roses; marshal of England, 1369–77; ambassador to France and Scotland, 1373; led the constitutional and popular party in opposition to the court and John of Gaunt in the Good parliament, 1376; bore the sword and spurs at Richard II's coronation, 1377; elected on the king's new council; commissioner to treat with Scotland and inspect the fortifications in the north, 1378; lieutenant of Ireland, 1379; established himself in eastern Ulster; attempted to gain possession of Connaught and Munster; died at Cork. [xxxix. 119]

MORTIMER, SIR EDMUND (III) DE (1376–1409?), son of Edmund de Mortimer (II), third earl of March [q. v.]; adhered to Henry of Lancaster's rising fortunes, 1399; assisted to put down revolt of Owen Glendower [q. v.], but, on being taken prisoner at Brynglas, 1402, joined with Glendower, married his daughter, and possibly assisted in the triple partition treaty, 1405; perished during the siege of Harlech. [xxxix. 121]

MORTIMER, EDMUND (IV) DE, fifth EARL OF MARCH and third EARL OF ULSTER (1391–1425), son of Roger de Mortimer (VI), fourth earl of March [q. v.]; succeeded his father and was recognised as heir-presumptive by Richard II, 1398; honourably treated, but strictly guarded on the Lancastrian revolution; his estates restored, 1413; K.B. and summoned to parliament, 1413; founded college of secular canons at Stoke-by-Clare, 1414; retained Henry V's friendship, divulging a plot formed in his favour against the king, and served with him in France, 1415–21; lieutenant of Ireland, 1423, sending a deputy there; obliged by the unsettled state of Ireland to go there in person, 1424, and negotiate with the native septs, but he died suddenly of plague. [xxxix. 123]

MORTIMER, MRS. FAVELL LEE (1802–1878), authoress; *née* Bevan; corresponded with Henry Edward Manning [q. v.]; married Thomas Mortimer, 1841; wrote educational works for the young, including 'Peep of Day' (last edit. 1891), 'Line upon Line,' 1837, and 'Reading without Tears,' 1857. [xxxix. 125]

MORTIMER, GEORGE FERRIS WHIDBORNE (1805–1871), schoolmaster and divine; B.A. Queen's College, Oxford, 1826; headmaster of Newcastle grammar school, 1828, Brompton proprietary school, 1833, and the City of London school, 1840–65; honorary prebendary of St. Paul's Cathedral, 1864. [xxxix. 126]

MORTIMER, HUGH (I) DE (d. 1181), lord of Wigmore and founder of Wigmore Priory; son of Ralph de Mortimer (I) [q. v.]; during Stephen's reign devoted himself to strengthening his local position and fortifying Bridgnorth, Cleobury, and Wigmore castles; resisted

Henry II, 1155; his castles taken; subsequently allowed to retain his castles and lands, which he held free from military service, aids, and scutages; established Wigmore Priory (consecrated, 1174). [xxxix. 126]

MORTIMER, JOHN (1656?-1736), writer on agriculture and merchant; chief work, 'The whole Art of Husbandry,' 1707 (sixth edition, 1761). [xxxix. 128]

MORTIMER, JOHN HAMILTON (1741-1779), historical painter; studied under Cipriani, Robert Edge Pine, and Reynolds; won, in competition with Romney, the prize for an historical picture, with 'St. Paul converting the Britons,' 1763; vice-president of the Incorporated Society of Arts, 1773; R.A., 1779; painted historical and allegorical pictures. [xxxix. 129]

MORTIMER, RALPH (I) DE (d. 1104?), Norman baron; son of Roger de Mortimer (fl. 1054) [q. v.]; received forfeited estates, including Wigmore, in the middle marches of Wales, 1074; probably seneschal of the Earl of Shrewsbury; joined in the rising of 1088; as a partisan of Rufus joined the barons of Caux in repelling the French, 1089; received fresh estates, 1102; upheld Henry I in Normandy against Robert, 1104. [xxxix. 130]

MORTIMER, ROGER DE (fl. 1054-1074), son of Hugh, bishop of Coutances; assumed the name of Mortimer from Mortemer-en-Brai, where he won a victory, 1054; transferred his chief seat to Saint-Victor-en-Caux and erected an abbey there, 1074. [xxxix. 130]

MORTIMER, ROGER (II) DE, sixth BARON OF WIGMORE (1231?-1282), succeeded to his father's estates and married Matilda de Braose, 1247; knighted, 1253; on the outbreak of the struggle between Henry III and the barons, 1258, sided with the barons and was elected to various councils; after the compromise of 1261 became a strong royalist; fought against Llywelyn with varying success, 1262 and 1263; returned to Wales after the battle of Lewes, 1264, and was exiled to Ireland, when de Montfort marched to subdue the marcher lords, who were obliged to surrender; did not leave England, but prepared for fresh resistance; assisted Prince Edward in his escape from de Montfort, 1265, commanded the rear-guard at Evesham, 1265, and assisted in the siege of Kenilworth, 1266; remained Prince Edward's close friend, and was one of the guardians of his children, 1270 and 1271, and of the realm, 1272; he took a conspicuous part in Edward I's early struggles with Llywelyn. [xxxix. 131]

MORTIMER, ROGER (III) DE, LORD OF CHIRK (1256?-1326), son of Roger de Mortimer (II) [q. v.]; assisted his brothers to entice Llywelyn of Wales to his doom, 1282; granted the lordship of Chirk, 1282; raised troops of Welsh infantry for Edward I's wars in Gascony, 1294 and 1297, and in Scotland, 1300, 1301, and 1303; king's lieutenant and justice of Wales, 1307-21; served in the Bannockburn campaign and in those of 1319-20; joined in the attack on the Despensers, 1321, and finally surrendered to Edward II at Shrewsbury, 1322; remained in the Tower of London until his death. [xxxix. 135]

MORTIMER, ROGER (IV) DE, eighth BARON OF WIGMORE and first EARL OF MARCH (1287?-1330), succeeded his father, Edmund de Mortimer, seventh baron, c. 1304; knighted, 1306; acquired large estates in Ireland through his wife, Joan de Genville; went to Ireland, 1308, and defeated his kinsfolk, the Lacys; defeated at Kells, 1316, by Edward Bruce, whom the Lacys had invited to assist them; appointed lieutenant of Ireland, 1316; drove Bruce to Carrickfergus, 1317; defeated the Lacys and the Leinster clans, 1317; justiciar of Ireland, 1319; helped his uncle Roger (of Chirk) to establish in Wales the independent position of house of Mortimer, which was threatened by the Despensers, 1320; obliged, on the appearance of Edward II in the west, to submit, and was sent to the Tower of London, 1322; escaped, after two years' imprisonment, with the help of Orleton, bishop of Hereford, to Paris, 1324; became chief adviser to Queen Isabella, his paramour, and with her and her son Edward landed at Orwell, 1326; employed his agent, Orleton, to obtain Edward II's deposition in parliament, 1327; after Edward III's election as king virtually ruled the realm for four years through his influence over Queen Isabella; appointed justiciar of Wales and the border counties, 1327; became Earl of March, 1328, and received palatine jurisdiction in Trim, Meath, and Louth; popularly regarded as responsible for Edward II's murder, the failure

of the Scots expedition, 1327, and the 'Shameful Peace' with Scotland, 1328; his position assailed by Henry of Lancaster (1328), who was, however, ultimately obliged to accept mediation; formed a plot, which resulted in the execution for treason of the king's uncle, Edmund, earl of Kent, 1330; seized by William de Montacute, who had been joined by Edward III, and taken to the Tower of London; accused before parliament of causing dissension between Edward II and his queen, of usurping royal power, procuring Edward II's murder, and the execution of Edmund, earl of Kent; hanged, drawn, and quartered like a common malefactor at Tyburn. [xxxix. 136]

MORTIMER, ROGER (V) DE, second EARL OF MARCH (1327?-1360), grandson of Roger Mortimer (IV), first earl of March [q. v.]; was gradually restored to the family estates and honours; accompanied Edward III to France, 1346; knighted, 1346; K.G. and summoned to parliament, 1348; obtained the reversal of his grandfather's sentence and the remainder of the Mortimer inheritance, 1354; received various offices; fought in France, 1355 and 1359; died suddenly at Rouvray. [xxxix. 144]

MORTIMER, ROGER (VI) DE, fourth EARL OF MARCH and ULSTER (1374-1398), son of Edmund Mortimer (II), third earl of March [q. v.]; succeeded his father, 1381; brought up as a royal ward and proclaimed heir-presumptive, 1385; married Eleanor Holland, the king's niece, 1388; knighted, 1390; accompanied Richard II to Ireland, 1394; lieutenant of Ulster, Connaught, and Meath, 1395, and of Ireland, 1397; waged war against native septs without notable result; summoned to attend parliament, his growing popularity having aroused Richard II's suspicions; by his caution or duplicity deprived Richard of any opportunity of attacking him; returned to Ireland and was slain in battle at Kells. [xxxix. 145]

MORTIMER, THOMAS (1730-1810), author; grandson of John Mortimer [q. v.]; vice-consul of the Austrian Netherlands, 1762-8; man of letters and private tutor in England; wrote on economic subjects, and published 'The British Plutarch,' 1762. [xxxix. 146]

MORTON, EARLS OF. [See DOUGLAS, JAMES, fourth EARL, d. 1581; DOUGLAS, SIR WILLIAM, of Lochleven, sixth or seventh EARL, d. 1606; DOUGLAS, WILLIAM, seventh or eighth EARL, 1582-1650; DOUGLAS, JAMES, fourteenth EARL, 1702-1768; and MAXWELL, JOHN, 1553-1593.]

MORTON, SIR ALBERTUS (1584?-1625), secretary of state; of Eton and King's College, Cambridge; accompanied his half-uncle, Sir Henry Wotton [q. v.], to Venice as secretary, 1604; minister to Savoy, 1612; clerk of the council, 1615; secretary to the electress palatine, 1616; knighted, 1617; clerk of the council, 1619-23; ambassador to France, 1624; secretary of state, 1625; M.P., Kent. [xxxix. 148]

MORTON, ANDREW (1802-1845), portrait-painter; brother of Thomas Morton (1813-1849) [q. v.]; exhibited portraits of distinguished people at the Royal Academy and the British Institution, 1821-45. [xxxix. 148]

MORTON, CHARLES (1627-1698), puritan divine; M.A. Wadham College, Oxford, 1652 (incorporated at Cambridge, 1653); rector of Blisland, 1655; ejected, 1662; master of the dissenters' school at Stoke Newington; went to New England and became minister of the first church at Charlestown, 1686; prosecuted for seditious sermon, but acquitted, 1687; wrote on social and theological questions; approved the prosecutions for witchcraft at Salem; died at Charlestown. [xxxix. 149]

MORTON, CHARLES (1716-1799), principal librarian of the British Museum; M.D. Leyden, 1748; practised in London; under-librarian of the British Museum, 1756; secretary to the trustees and principal librarian, 1776; F.R.S., 1752; secretary to the Royal Society, 1760-74; F.S.A.; edited Whitelocke. [xxxix. 150]

MORTON, GEORGE HIGHFIELD (1826-1900), geologist; house decorator at Liverpool; formed valuable collection of fossils; F.G.S., 1858, and Lyell medallist, 1892; lecturer on geology, Queen's College, Liverpool; chief work, 'Geology of Country round Liverpool,' 1863. [Suppl. iii. 204]

MORTON, JOHN (1420?-1500), archbishop of Canterbury and cardinal; D.C.L. Balliol College, Oxford;

practised as a canon lawyer in the court of arches; given much ecclesiastical preferment and the principalship of Peckwater Inn, Oxford; followed the Lancastrian party in their wanderings and was attainted; submitted after the battle of Tewkesbury, on which his attainder was reversed; prebendary of St. Paul's Cathedral, 1472; master of the rolls, 1473; went on an embassy to Hungary, 1474; helped to negotiate the treaty of Pecquigny, 1475; elected bishop of Ely, 1479; present at Edward IV's death and funeral, 1483; arrested, 1483, and imprisoned, first in the Tower of London, and afterwards at Brecknock Castle, where he encouraged Buckingham to revolt; escaped to Ely and thence to Flanders, where he remained till summoned home (1485) by Henry VII; privy councillor; archbishop of Canterbury, 1486-1500; lord chancellor, 1487; cardinal, 1493; chancellor of Oxford, 1495. He was a great builder and repairer, and Morton's Dyke in the Fens perpetuates his memory. It was probably he who wrote the Latin version of the 'History of Richard III' usually ascribed to Sir Thomas More. [xxxix. 151]

MORTON, JOHN (1671 ?-1726), naturalist; M.A. Emmanuel College, Cambridge, 1695; rector of Great Oxendon, 1706; F.R.S., 1703; published 'The Natural History of Northamptonshire, with some Account of the Antiquities,' 1712. [xxxix. 153]

MORTON, JOHN (1781-1864), agriculturist; agent on Lord Ducie's Gloucestershire estates, where he conducted the 'Whitfield Example Farm'; invented the 'Uley cultivator' and other agricultural appliances; wrote 'On Soils,' 1838. [xxxix. 154]

MORTON, JOHN CHALMERS (1821-1888), agriculturist; son of John Morton (1781-1864) [q. v.]; editor of the 'Agricultural Gazette,' 1844; commissioner for inquiry into the pollution of rivers, 1868-74; wrote and edited works on agriculture. [xxxix. 154]

MORTON, JOHN MADDISON (1811-1891), dramatist; son of Thomas Morton (1764 ?-1838) [q. v.]; educated in France; held clerkship in Chelsea Hospital, London, 1832-40; Charterhouse brother, 1881; wrote farces and showed exceptional facility in suiting French dialogues to English tastes; his most popular piece, 'Box and Cox,' 1847. [xxxix. 155]

MORTON, NICHOLAS (*fl.* 1586), papal agent; M.A. Cambridge, 1545; fellow of Trinity College, Cambridge, 1546; B.D., 1554; withdrew to Rome on Queen Elizabeth's accession, 1558; D.D. Rome; came to England and promoted the northern rebellion of 1569; again intrigued against Queen Elizabeth at Rheims, 1580. [xxxix. 156]

MORTON, RICHARD (1637-1698), ejected minister and physician; M.A. New College, Oxford, 1659; vicar of Kinver, 1659; ejected, 1662; M.D. Oxford, 1670; F.R.C.P., 1679; incorporated M.D. Cambridge, 1680; censor of the College of Physicians, 1690, 1691, and 1697; physician to the king; published 'Phthisiologia,' 1689, and 'Pyretologia,' 1692. [xxxix. 157]

MORTON, RICHARD (1669-1730), physician; son of Richard Morton (1637-1698) [q. v.]; B.A. Catharine Hall, Cambridge, 1691; M.D., 1695; F.R.C.P., 1707; physician to Greenwich Hospital, 1716 [xxxix. 158]

MORTON, ROBERT (*d.* 1497), bishop of Worcester; nephew of John Morton (1420 ?-1500) [q. v.]; master of the rolls, 1479; deprived during Richard III's reign, but reinstated by Henry VII; canon of Windsor, 1481-6; collated archdeacon of Gloucester, 1482; bishop of Worcester, 1487. [xxxix. 158]

MORTON, THOMAS (*d.* 1646), author of 'New English Canaan'; an attorney of Clifford's Inn; landed in New England, 1622; established himself at Merry Mount, Massachusetts Bay, 1626; traded with the Indians; arrested and sent home, 1628; returned to New England as Isaac Allerton's secretary, 1629; again banished, 1630; successfully prosecuted a suit at law repealing the Massachusetts Company's patent, 1635; returned to New England, 1643, and died in poverty at Acomenticus, 1646; published 'New English Canaan,' a descriptive work, 1637. [xxxix. 158]

MORTON, THOMAS (1564-1659), bishop successively of Chester, Lichfield, and Durham; M.A. St. John's College, Cambridge, 1590; D.D., 1606; fellow; university lecturer in logic; rector of Long Marston, 1598; devoted himself to the plague-stricken sufferers at York, 1602; accompanied Lord Eure, ambassador extraordinary to

Germany and Denmark, 1602; one of James I's chaplains and dean of Gloucester, 1606; transferred to deanery of Winchester, 1609, and collated to canony at York, 1610; bishop of Chester, 1616; on his translation to Lichfield and Coventry, 1618, continued his endeavours to win over nonconformists and recusants; appointed, 1632, to the see of Durham, which he held canonically until his death, although parliament claimed to deprive him of it, 1647; impeached, 1641, but released after four months' imprisonment without trial; imprisoned, 1645, for refusing to surrender the seal of Durham; driven from Durham House, Strand, 1648; resided ultimately at Easton-Mauduit with Sir Christopher Yelverton; patron and friend of learned men. The larger portion of his writings were devoted to the exposure of Romish fallacies; his three chief works are 'Apologia Catholica,' 1605, 'Catholic Appeal,' 1609, and 'Causa Regia,' 1620. [xxxix. 160]

MORTON, THOMAS (1781-1832), inventor of the 'patent slip' for docking vessels; shipwright; invented a cheap substitute for a dry dock, 1819, which is now used in nearly all harbours (extension of patent refused, 1832). [xxxix. 165]

MORTON, THOMAS (1764 ?-1838), dramatist; entered Lincoln's Inn, 1784; wrote a considerable number of comedies, in which John Emery, Charles and John Kemble, and Macready appeared; honorary member of the Garrick Club, 1837. [xxxix. 166]

MORTON, THOMAS (1813-1849), surgeon; brother of Andrew Morton [q. v.]; studied at University College Hospital, London, 1832; M.R.C.S., 1835; demonstrator of anatomy, 1836; surgeon, 1848, at University College Hospital, London; wrote on surgical anatomy; committed suicide. [xxxix. 167]

MORTON, SIR WILLIAM (*d.* 1672), judge; M.A. Sidney Sussex College, Cambridge, 1625; barrister, Inner Temple, 1630; fought on the royalist side; knighted; imprisoned in the Tower of London, 1644; serjeant-at-law, 1660; king's serjeant, 1663; justice of the king's bench, 1665. [xxxix. 167]

MORVILLE, HUGH DE (*d.* 1162), constable of Scotland under David I; assisted in making William Cumin bishop of Durham, 1140; founded Kilwinning Abbey, 1140, and Melrose Abbey, 1150. [xxxix. 169]

MORVILLE, HUGH DE (*d.* 1204), one of the murderers of St. Thomas of Canterbury; attached to the court from the beginning of the reign of Henry II; itinerant justice for Cumberland and Northumberland, 1170; kept back the crowd with his sword while St. Thomas was murdered; did penance in the Holy Land, and soon regained royal favour. [xxxix. 168]

MORVILLE, RICHARD DE (*d.* 1189), son of Hugh de Morville (*d.* 1162) [q. v.]; constable of Scotland, 1162; adviser of William the Lion; commanded part of the Scottish army before Alnwick, 1174; benefactor of Melrose Abbey. [xxxix. 169]

MORWEN, MORING, or MORVEN, JOHN (1518 ?-1561 ?), divine; was placed under a relative, Robert Morwen [q. v.]; president of Corpus Christi College, Oxford; M.A., 1543; B.D., 1552; secretary to Bishop Bonner; prebendary of St. Paul's Cathedral, 1558; deprived on Queen Elizabeth's accession; charged with scattering libel, 1561; a famous Greek scholar. [xxxix. 170]

MORWEN, MORWENT, or MORWINGE, PETER (1530 ?-1573 ?), translator; B.A. Magdalen College, Oxford, 1550; fellow, 1552; M.A., 1560; went to Germany, 1553; received various livings; prebendary of Lichfield, 1567; translated Joseph Ben Gorion's 'History of the Jews,' 1558, and two medical works. [xxxix. 170]

MORWEN, MORWENT, or MORWYN, ROBERT (1486 ?-1558), president of Corpus Christi College, Oxford; B.A. Oxford, 1507; fellow of Magdalen College, Oxford, 1510; M.A., 1511; vice-president of the newly founded Corpus Christi College, 1517; president, 1537; conformed outwardly during Edward VI's reign, but carefully preserved the Roman catholic vessels and vestments; on Pole's commission for visiting the university, 1556. [xxxix. 171]

MORYS or **MORIZ**, SIR JOHN (*fl.* 1346), deputy of Ireland; M.P., Bedford, 1322-40; commissioner of array for Bedfordshire and Buckinghamshire, 1322 and 1324; knighted and acting deputy in Ireland, 1341; held parliament in Dublin, 1341; again deputy, 1346. [xxxix. 171]

MORYSINE, SIR RICHARD (d. 1556). [See MORI-SON.]

MORYSON, FYNES (1566–1630), traveller ; B.A. Peterhouse, Cambridge fellow, c. 1584 ; M.A., 1587 ; obtained licence to travel, 1589 ; visited Germany, the Low Countries, Denmark, Poland, Italy, Switzerland, and France, 1591–5 ; visited the Holy Land, Constantinople, and Scotland, 1598 ; went to Ireland, 1600 ; became chief secretary to Sir Charles Blount [q. v.], 1600, and helped to suppress Tyrone's rebellion ; published an account of his travels and a history of Tyrone's rebellion, 1617.
[xxxix. 172]

MORYSON, SIR RICHARD (1571 ?–1628), vice-president of Munster ; brother of Fynes Moryson [q. v.] ; sailed in the Islands Voyage, 1597 ; colonel with Essex in Ireland, 1599 ; knighted by Essex, 1599 ; governor of Waterford and Wexford, 1604 ; vice-president of Munster, 1609 ; M.P., Bandon (Irish parliament), 1613 ; lieutenant-general of the ordnance in England, 1616–28 ; M.P., Leicester, 1621.
[xxxix. 174]

MOSELEY. [See also MOSLEY.]

MOSELEY, BENJAMIN (1742–1819), physician ; studied at London, Paris, and Leyden ; practised in West Indies ; returned to England, 1784 ; M.D. St. Andrews, 1784 ; visited continental hospitals ; L.R.C.P., 1787 ; physician to the Royal Hospital, Chelsea, 1788 ; wrote chiefly on tropical diseases.
[xxxix. 174]

MOSELEY, HENRY (1801–1872), mathematician ; M.A. St. John's College, Cambridge, 1836 ; LL.D. hon. causa, 1870 ; professor of natural and experimental philosophy and astronomy, King's College, London, 1831–44 ; F.R.S., 1839 ; one of the first inspectors of schools, 1844 ; canon of Bristol, 1853 ; published works on mechanics.
[xxxix. 175]

MOSELEY, HENRY NOTTIDGE (1844–1891), naturalist ; son of Henry Moseley [q. v.] ; of Harrow and Exeter College, Oxford ; B.A., 1868 ; Radcliffe travelling fellow, 1869 ; joined government expedition to Ceylon, 1871, and Challenger expedition, 1872–6 ; fellow of Exeter College, Oxford, 1876 ; went to California and Oregon, 1877 ; F.R.S. ; F.Z.S., 1879 ; assistant-registrar to the University of London, 1879 ; Linacre professor of human and comparative anatomy at Oxford, 1881 ; published 'Notes by a Naturalist on the Challenger,' 1879, and other scientific works.
[xxxix. 176]

MOSELEY, HUMPHREY (d. 1661), bookseller ; warden of the Stationers' Company, 1659 ; published the first collected edition of Milton's 'Poems,' 1645, and early editions of Crashaw, D'Avenant, and others, also translations of Spanish, Italian, and French romances.
[xxxix. 177]

MOSER, GEORGE MICHAEL (1704–1783), chaser and enameller ; born at Schaffhausen ; came to England ; distinguished for compositions in enamel on watches and bracelets ; drawing-master to George III ; engraved George III's first great seal ; assisted in establishing the Royal Academy, 1767 ; elected the first keeper.
[xxxix. 177]

MOSER, JOSEPH (1748–1819), artist, author, and magistrate ; nephew of George Michael Moser [q. v.] ; exhibited at the Royal Academy, 1774–82 ; magistrate for Westminster, 1794 ; published political pamphlets, dramas, and fiction.
[xxxix. 178]

MOSER, MARY (d. 1819), flower-painter ; daughter of George Michael Moser [q. v.] ; foundation member of the Royal Academy, contributing to its exhibitions till 1802 ; married Captain Hugh Lloyd of Chelsea, 1793.
[xxxix. 178]

MOSES, HENRY (1782 ?–1870), engraver ; obtained great reputation for his outline plates.
[xxxix. 179]

MOSES, WILLIAM (1623?–1688), serjeant-at-law ; of Christ's Hospital, London, and Pembroke College, Cambridge ; M.A. ; master, 1655–60 ; counsel to the East India Company ; serjeant-at-law, 1688.
[xxxix. 179]

MOSES, WILLIAM STAINTON (1840–1892), spiritualist ; M.A. Exeter College, Oxford, 1865 ; English master at University College School, London, 1872–90 ; a 'medium,' writing and editing spiritualistic literature.
[xxxix. 180]

MOSLEY. [See also MOSELEY.]

MOSLEY, CHARLES (d. 1770 ?), engraver ; employed by Hogarth.
[xxxix. 180]

MOSLEY, NICHOLAS (1611–1672), author and royalist ; his estates sequestered, 1643, but restored, 1646 ; headed the Manchester procession on coronation day, 1661 ; published 'The Soul of Man,' 1653. [xxxix. 180]

MOSLEY, SAMUEL (fl. 1675–1676), New England settler ; served in the war against the Indian chief 'King Philip,' and distinguished himself in the capture and destruction of Canonicut, 1675.
[xxxix. 181]

MOSS, CHARLES (1711–1802), bishop successively of St. David's and of Bath and Wells ; nephew of Robert Moss [q. v.] ; M.A. Caius College, Cambridge, 1735 ; fellow, 1735 ; received much preferment from Sherlock, bishop of Salisbury ; bishop of St. David's, 1766–74, of Bath and Wells, 1774.
[xxxix. 181]

MOSS, CHARLES (1763–1811), bishop of Oxford ; son of Charles Moss (1711–1802) [q. v.] ; B.A. Christ Church, Oxford, 1783 ; D.D., 1797, received preferment from his father ; bishop of Oxford, 1807–11.
[xxxix. 182]

MOSS, JOSEPH WILLIAM (1803–1862), bibliographer ; M.A. Magdalen Hall, Oxford, 1827 ; M.B., 1829 ; practised in Dudley ; F.R.S., 1830 ; published 'Manual of Classical Bibliography,' 1825. [xxxix. 182]

MOSS, ROBERT (1666–1729), dean of Ely ; M.A. Corpus Christi College, Cambridge, 1688 ; fellow, c. 1685 ; D.D., 1705 ; chaplain in ordinary to William III, Anne, and George I ; dean of Ely, 1713 ; his sermons collected and published, 1736.
[xxxix. 183]

MOSS, THOMAS (d. 1808), poet ; B.A. Emmanuel College, Cambridge, 1761 ; perpetual curate of Brinley Hill Chapel ; published 'Poems on several Occasions,' 1769, including the well-known 'Beggar's Petition.'
[xxxix. 183]

MOSSE, BARTHOLOMEW (1712–1759), philanthropist ; travelled through England, France, and Holland to perfect himself in midwifery and surgery ; rented a house in Dublin for poor lying-in women, 1745 ; erected the Rotunda Hospital (incorporated, 1756, opened, 1757).
[xxxix. 184]

MOSSE or **MOSES**, MILES (fl. 1580–1614), divine ; educated at Cambridge (D.D., c. 1600) ; minister at Norwich, 1580 ; published 'A Catechism,' 1590, and various sermons with a Calvinistic tendency. [xxxix. 184]

MOSSES, ALEXANDER (1793–1837), artist ; taught drawing at Liverpool Royal Institution ; exhibited portraits at the Liverpool Academy, 1811–36. [xxxix. 185]

MOSSMAN, GEORGE (fl. 1800), medical writer ; physician at Bradford ; wrote on the use of digitalis in consumption and scrofula.
[xxxix. 185]

MOSSMAN, THOMAS WIMBERLEY (1826–1885), divine ; B.A. St. Edmund Hall, Oxford, 1845 ; held several livings ; became a Roman catholic during his last illness ; published controversial works.
[xxxix. 185]

MOSSOM, ROBERT (d. 1679), bishop of Derry ; M.A. Peterhouse, Cambridge, 1638 ; used the prayer-book, notwithstanding its prohibition, at St. Peter's, Paul's Wharf, London, 1650–5 ; dean of Christ Church, Dublin, 1660 ; bishop of Derry, 1666 ; published religious works.
[xxxix. 186]

MOSSOP, HENRY (1729 ?–1774 ?), actor ; appeared in Dublin, 1749 ; acted with Garrick in London, 1751–9, where he was most successful as Richard III ; returned to Dublin, 1759 ; acted with Barry at Crow Street, Dublin ; opened Smock Alley Theatre, Dublin, in opposition to Barry, 1760, Barry being ruined, 1768 ; tried to manage both theatres, but broke down under troubles, vexations, and debt ; arrested for debt, 1771 ; became bankrupt ; admirable in heroic parts.
[xxxix. 187]

MOSSOP, WILLIAM (1751–1804), medallist ; a die-sinker who prepared numerous seals for public bodies in Ireland, and engraved a large number of portraits on medals.
[xxxix. 189]

MOSSOP, WILLIAM STEPHEN (1788–1827), medallist ; son of William Mossop [q. v.] ; studied under Francis West ; followed his father's method of making a wax model before cutting the steel die ; made dies for the stamp office, Dublin ; projected a series of portrait-medals of distinguished Irishmen.
[xxxix. 189]

MOSTYN, JOHN (1710–1779), general; son of Sir Roger Mostyn (1675–1739) [q. v.]; of Westminster School and Christ Church, Oxford; captain, 2nd foot guards, 1743; major-general, 1757; governor and commander-in-chief of Minorca, 1758; M.P., Malton, 1747, 1754, and 1761; governor of Chelsea Hospital, 1768; general, 1772. [xxxix. 192]

MOSTYN, SIR ROGER, first baronet (1625 ?–1690), royalist; took up arms for Charles I; sacked the houses of parliamentarians in Chester, 1642 and 1643; governor of Flint Castle, but (1643) forced to surrender it; captured Hawarden Castle and went to Chester; raised recruits in Ireland, 1645; arrested, 1658, but immediately released on parole; created baronet, 1660. [xxxix. 190]

MOSTYN, SIR ROGER, third baronet (1675–1739), politician; grandson of Sir Roger Mostyn, first baronet [q. v.]; tory M.P. for Cheshire, 1701, for Fintshire, 1705–1734, except 1713, when he sat for Flint borough; paymaster of the marines, 1711; teller of the exchequer, 1714–16. [xxxix. 191]

MOSTYN, SAVAGE (d. 1757), vice-admiral; son of Sir Roger Mostyn (1675–1739) [q. v.]; lieutenant in navy, 1734; commander, 1739; post-captain, 1739; failed to engage two French ships off Ushant, 1745; acquitted by court-martial, but his conduct unfavourably commented on; M.P., Weobley, 1747; comptroller of the navy, 1749; vice-admiral and second in command on the North American station, 1755; junior lord of the admiralty, 1757. [xxxix. 192]

MOTHERBY, GEORGE (1732–1793), medical writer; a Highgate physician; compiled a 'New Medical Dictionary,' 1776. [xxxix. 193]

MOTHERWELL, WILLIAM (1797–1835), poet; sheriff-clerk depute of Renfrewshire, 1819–29; editor of 'Paisley Advertiser,' 1828–30, and 'Glasgow Courier,' 1830; issued 'Poems, Narrative and Lyrical,' 1832; collaborated with Hogg in an edition of Burns, 1835. [xxxix. 193]

MOTTE, ANDREW (d. 1730), mathematician; lecturer in geometry at Gresham College, London, before 1727; published treatise on 'Motion,' 1727; translated Newton's 'Principia,' 1729. [xxxix. 194]

MOTTE, BENJAMIN (d. 1738), bookseller and publisher; brother of Andrew Motte [q. v.]; edited an abridgment of the Royal Society's 'Transactions,' 1700–1721; succeeded to Benjamin Tooke's business with the tories; published 'Gulliver's Travels,' 1726; acted as London agent to Swift. [xxxix. 194]

MOTTERSHEAD, JOSEPH (1688–1771), dissenting minister; studied under Timothy Jollie [q. v.] and Matthew Henry [q. v.]; minister at Cross Street, Manchester, 1717; published religious discourses. [xxxix. 195]

MOTTEUX, PETER ANTHONY (1660–1718), translator and dramatist; born at Rouen; came to England, 1685; edited 'Gentleman's Journal,' 1692–3; collaborated with Sir Thomas Urquhart [q. v.] in bringing out an edition of Rabelais, 1693–1708; wrote comedies and masques; clerk in the foreign department of the post office, 1703–11; published a free translation of 'Don Quixote,' 1712; became an East India merchant, 1712. [xxxix. 195]

MOTTLEY, JOHN (1692–1750), dramatist and biographer; clerk in the excise office, 1708–20; wrote two dull pseudo-classical tragedies, but was more successful with comedies; published 'Joe Miller's Jest-book,' 1739; wrote the life of Peter I of Russia, 1739, of Catherine of Russia, 1744. [xxxix. 197]

MOTTRAM, CHARLES (1807–1876), engraver; exhibited at the Royal Academy from 1861; engraved after Landseer, Rosa Bonheur, and Holman Hunt. [xxxix. 198]

MOUFET, THOMAS (1553–1604). [See MOFFETT.]

MOULE, HENRY (1801–1880), divine and inventor; M.A. St. John's College, Cambridge, 1826; vicar of Fordington, 1829; exerted himself unweariedly during the cholera, 1849–54; invented dry-earth system, 1860; wrote on sanitary science, gardening, and religious topics. [xxxix. 198]

MOULE, THOMAS (1784–1851), writer on heraldry and antiquities; bookseller, 1816–23; clerk in the post-office and chamber-keeper in the lord-chamberlain's department and member of the Westminster Society; published 'Bibliotheca Heraldica Magnæ Britanniæ,' 1822, and antiquarian works. [xxxix. 199]

MOULIN, LEWIS DU (1606–1680), nonconformist controversialist; son of Pierre du Moulin [q. v.]; born at Paris; M.D. Leyden; graduated at Cambridge, 1634, and Oxford, 1649; L.R.C.P., 1640; Camden professor of ancient history, Oxford, 1648–60; published violent attacks on Anglican theologians. [xxxix. 200]

MOULIN, PETER DU (1601–1684), Anglican divine; son of Pierre du Moulin [q. v.]; born at Paris; studied at Sedan, Leyden, and Cambridge; D.D. Cambridge; incumbent of St. John's, Chester, 1625; published 'Regii Sanguinis Clamor' anonymously; D.D. Oxford, 1656; chaplain to Charles II, 1660; prebendary of Canterbury, 1660. [xxxix. 200]

MOULIN, PIERRE DU (1568–1658), French protestant divine; born at Buhy; studied at Sedan and Cambridge, 1588–92; professor of philosophy, Leyden, 1592–8; protestant minister at Charenton, 1599; assisted James I in his 'Regis Declaratio pro Jure Regio,' and received prebend at Canterbury, 1615; professor of theology at Sedan, 1620–8; died at Sedan. [xxxix. 201]

MOULTON, THOMAS (fl. 1540?), Dominican; called himself 'Doctor of Divinity of the order of Friar Preachers'; his 'Myrour or Glasse of Helthe,' published c. 1539. [xxxix. 202]

MOULTON, WILLIAM FIDDIAN (1835–1898), biblical scholar; M.A. London, 1856; entered Wesleyan ministry, 1858; classical tutor at Wesley College, Richmond, Surrey, 1858–74; published (1870) translation of Winer's 'Grammar of New Testament Greek'; member of committee of revisers of New Testament, 1870; first head-master of the Leys school, Cambridge, 1874–98; D.D. Edinburgh, 1874; hon. M.A. Cambridge, 1877; published 'History of the English Bible,' and other writings relating to the bible. [Suppl. iii. 204]

MOULTRIE, GERARD (1829–1885), devotional writer; son of John Moultrie [q. v.]; B.A. Exeter College, Oxford, 1851; vicar of Southleigh and warden of St. John's College there, 1873; wrote hymns and religious verse. [xxxix. 203]

MOULTRIE, JOHN (1799–1874), poet; educated at Eton under Dr. Keate, and at Trinity College, Cambridge; M.A., 1822; abandoned law for the church; went to reside at Rugby as rector, 1828, Thomas Arnold being head-master at the school; 'My Brother's Grave,' 1820, and 'Godiva,' 1820, his best work, which he never afterwards surpassed; collected works published, 1876. [xxxix. 202]

MOUNDEFORD, THOMAS (1550–1630), physician; fellow of King's College, Cambridge, 1571; M.A., 1576; M.D.; studied medicine; censor seven times and president of the Royal College of Physicians, 1612, 1613, 1614, 1619, 1621, 1622, and 1623; published 'Vir Bonus,' 1622. [xxxix. 204]

MOUNSEY, MESSENGER (1693–1788). [See MONSEY.]

MOUNSLOW, BARON LITTLETON OF (1589–1645). [See LITTLETON, SIR EDWARD.]

MOUNSTEVEN, JOHN (1644–1706), politician; B.A. Christ Church, Oxford, 1671; secretary to the Earl of Sunderland and under-secretary of state; M.P. Bossiney, 1685–8, West Looe, 1695, 1701, and 1705–6; committed suicide. [xxxix. 204]

MOUNT, CHRISTOPHER (d. 1572). [See MONT.]

MOUNT, WILLIAM (1545–1602), master of the Savoy; B.A. King's College, Cambridge, 1567; fellow, 1566; master of the Savoy, 1594; wrote on distilled waters. [xxxix. 205]

MOUNTAGU. [See MONTAGU.]

MOUNTAGUE, FREDERICK WILLIAM (d. 1841), architect; son of William Mountague [q. v.]; made many architectural improvements in London. [xxxix. 205]

MOUNTAGUE, WILLIAM (1773–1843), architect and surveyor; clerk of works to city of London, 1816. [xxxix. 205]

MOUNTAIGNE or **MOUNTAIN**, GEORGE (1569-1628). [See MONTAIGNE.]

MOUNTAIN, ARMINE SIMCOE HENRY (1797-1854), adjutant-general in India ; son of Jacob Mountain [q. v.] ; born at Quebec ; entered army, 1815 ; lieutenant, 1818 ; captain, 1825 ; major, 1826 ; went to India, 1829 ; military secretary to Sir Colin Halkett, 1832 ; served throughout the China war as deputy adjutant-general ; C.B. ; colonel and aide-de-camp to Queen Victoria, 1845 ; military secretary to Lord Dalhousie, 1847 ; brigadier-general ; served in the second Sikh war ; adjutant-general, 1849 ; died at Futtyghur.   [xxxix. 205]

MOUNTAIN, DIDYMUS (pseudonym). [See HILL, THOMAS, *fl.* 1590.]

MOUNTAIN, GEORGE JEHOSHAPHAT (1789-1863), protestant bishop of Quebec ; son of Jacob Mountain [q. v.] ; B.A. Trinity College, Cambridge, 1810 ; D.D., 1819 ; rector of Quebec and bishop's official, 1817 ; suffragan bishop of Montreal, 1836 ; bishop of Quebec, 1850 ; published sermons and journals.   [xxxix. 207]

MOUNTAIN, JACOB (1749-1825), protestant bishop of Quebec ; M.A. Caius College, Cambridge, 1777 ; fellow, 1779 ; D.D., 1793 ; prebendary of Lincoln, 1788 ; first bishop of Quebec, 1793.   [xxxix. 208]

MOUNTAIN, Mrs. ROSOMAN (1768 ?-1841), vocalist and actress ; *née* Wilkinson ; taught by Dibdin ; performed at Hull, York, Leeds, Liverpool, and Doncaster, 1784 ; appeared at Covent Garden, London, 1786-1798, chiefly in musical pieces ; married John Mountain, violinist, 1787 ; one of the first vocalists of the day ; retired, 1815.   [xxxix. 208]

MOUNTAIN, THOMAS (*d.* 1561 ?), divine ; M.A. Cambridge ; partisan of Lady Jane Grey ; imprisoned, 1553 ; went abroad, but returned on Queen Elizabeth's accession ; rector of St. Pancras, Soper Lane, London ; his narrative used by Strype and Froude.   [xxxix. 210]

MOUNT ALEXANDER, first EARL OF. [See MONTGOMERY, HUGH, 1623 ?-1663.]

MOUNTCASHEL, VISCOUNT. [See MACCARTHY, JUSTIN, *d.* 1694.]

MOUNT-EDGCUMBE, EARLS OF. [See EDGCUMBE, GEORGE, first EARL, 1721-1795 ; EDGCUMBE, RICHARD, second EARL, 1764-1839.]

MOUNTENEY or **MOUNTNEY**, RICHARD (1707-1768), Irish judge and classical scholar ; fellow, King's College, Cambridge, 1729 ; M.A., 1735 ; barrister, Inner Temple ; baron of the Irish exchequer, 1737 ; edited Demosthenes, 1731.   [xxxix. 210]

MOUNTFORT, Mrs. SUSANNA (1667 ?-1703). [See VERBRUGGEN.]

MOUNTFORT, WILLIAM (1664 ?-1692), actor and dramatist ; joined Dorset Garden company, 1678 ; married Mrs. Susanna Verbruggen [q. v.], 1686 ; wrote an unsuccessful tragedy, 'The Injur'd Lovers,' 1688 ; his comedies, 'Successful Strangers,' 1690, 'King Edward the Third,' 1691, and 'Greenwich Park,' 1691, well received ; intimate with Judge Jeffreys ; stabbed by Captain Richard Hill ; praised by Cibber as an affecting lover in tragedy.   [xxxix. 211]

MOUNTGARRET, third VISCOUNT. [See BUTLER, RICHARD, 1578-1651.]

MOUNTIER, THOMAS (*fl.* 1719-1733), vocalist ; lay vicar and preceptor of Chichester, 1719-32 ; sang in London, 1732 ; joined Italian opera troupe, 1733.   [xxxix. 213]

MOUNTJOY, first VISCOUNT. [See STEWART, SIR WILLIAM, 1653-1692.]

MOUNTJOY, BARONS. [See BLOUNT, WALTER, first BARON, *d.* 1474 ; BLOUNT, WILLIAM, fourth BARON, *d.* 1534 ; BLOUNT, CHARLES, fifth BARON, *d.* 1545 ; BLOUNT, CHARLES, eighth BARON, 1563-1606 ; BLOUNT, MOUNTJOY, ninth BARON, 1597 ?-1665.]

MOUNT-MAURICE, HERVEY DE (*fl.* 1169-1176), invader of Ireland ; probably served in France ; sent by his nephew, Earl Richard, called Strongbow [see CLARE, RICHARD DE, *d.* 1176], to Ireland, 1169, to report on affairs there ; was victorious at Wexford, and received

grants of land ; shared in Raymond FitzGerald's victory at Waterford ; arranged matters between Earl Richard and Henry II, 1171 ; commanded in Ireland, 1173 ; constable of Leinster ; probably advised the disastrous expedition into Munster, 1174 ; returned to England after Earl Richard's death, 1176, and became a monk ; benefactor of the church and one of the four principal conquerors of the Irish.   [xxxix. 213]

MOUNTMORRES, second VISCOUNT. [See MORRES, HERVEY REDMOND, 1746 ?-1797.]

MOUNTNEY, RICHARD. [See MOUNTENEY, RICHARD, 1707-1768.]

MOUNTNORRIS, first BARON. [See ANNESLEY, SIR FRANCIS, 1585-1660.]

MOUNTRATH, first EARL OF. [See COOTE, SIR CHARLES, *d.* 1661.]

MOUNT-TEMPLE, first BARON. [See COWPER (afterwards COWPER-TEMPLE), WILLIAM FRANCIS, 1811-1888.]

MOUTRAY, JOHN (*d.* 1785), naval captain ; lieutenant, 1744 ; commander, 1759 ; advanced to post rank, 1758 ; convoyed a valuable fleet for the East and West Indies, 1780, nearly the whole of which was captured by the Franco-Spanish fleet ; tried by court-martial and censured ; resident commissioner of the navy at Antigua, 1783 ; recalled, 1785.   [xxxix. 216]

MOWBRAY, JOHN (I) DE, eighth BARON MOWBRAY (1286-1322), great-grandson of William de Mowbray, fourth baron Mowbray [q. v.] ; succeeded his father, 1298 ; knighted, 1306 ; ordered to arrest Percy for permitting Gaveston's death, 1312 ; involved in a dispute with the Despensers (1320) about the lordship of Gower, which his father-in-law, William de Brewes, had granted him ; joined by the other lords-marchers, who harried Glamorgan, 1321 ; pardoned with them on the fall of the Despensers, 1321 ; taken prisoner at Boroughbridge, 1322, Edward II having recourse to arms, and executed at Pontefract.   [xxxix. 217]

MOWBRAY, JOHN (II) DE, ninth BARON MOWBRAY (*d.* 1361), son of John (I) de Mowbray [q. v.] ; released from the Tower of London and his father's lands restored to him, 1327 ; involved in litigation through the De Brewes's inheritance, 1338-47 ; served frequently against the Scots, 1327-37 and 1347-55 ; justiciar of Lothian and governor of Berwick, 1340 ; fought at Neville's Cross, 1346 ; J.P., 1359 ; commissioner of array at Leicester, 1360.   [xxxix. 219]

MOWBRAY, JOHN (III) DE (1328 ?-1368), son of John (II) de Mowbray [q. v.] ; killed by the Turks near Constantinople on his way to the Holy Land.   [xxxix. 220]

MOWBRAY, JOHN (V), second DUKE OF NORFOLK (1389-1432), son of Thomas Mowbray (I) first duke of Norfolk [q. v.] ; earl-marshal and fourth Earl of Nottingham on the execution of his brother, Thomas Mowbray (II) [q. v.], 1405 ; commissioner to investigate the Earl of Cambridge's plot, 1415 ; prominent in the French wars, 1417-21, 1423-4, and 1430 ; K.G., 1421 ; nominated one of the Protector's council, 1422 ; restored to the dukedom of Norfolk, 1425 ; assisted in the arbitration between Gloucester and Beaufort, 1426 ; marshal at Henry VI's coronation, 1429 ; attended parliament, 1432.   [xxxix. 221]

MOWBRAY, JOHN (VI), third DUKE OF NORFOLK, hereditary EARL MARSHAL OF ENGLAND, and fifth EARL OF NOTTINGHAM (1415-1461), son of John (V) Mowbray [q. v.] ; knighted, 1426 ; succeeded his father, 1432 ; summoned to the council, 1434 ; warden of the east march, 1437 ; inquired into the Norwich disturbances, 1441 ; went on a pilgrimage, 1446 ; supported Richard, duke of York (his uncle by marriage), in his struggle for the direction of the royal policy ; his influence with York overshadowed by that of the Nevilles ; took the oath to the Lancastrian succession, 1459 ; renewed his allegiance to the Yorkist cause, 1460 ; shared Warwick's defeat at St. Albans, 1461 ; accompanied Edward, duke of York, to his enthronement and fought at Towton, 1461 ; rewarded with the offices of steward and chief-justice of the royal forests south of Trent, and made constable of Scarborough Castle, 1461.   [xxxix. 222]

MOWBRAY, JOHN (VII), fourth DUKE OF NORFOLK (1444-1476), son of John (VI) Mowbray, third duke of Norfolk [q. v.] ; figures in the 'Paston Correspondence' ;

besieged and took Caistor Castle in support of his father's baseless claim, 1469 (recovered by the Pastons, 1476); transferred his Gower and Chepstow estates to William Herbert, first earl of Pembroke (d. 1469) [q. v.], in exchange for manors in Norfolk and Suffolk. [xxxix. 225]

MOWBRAY (formerly **CORNISH**), SIR JOHN ROBERT, first baronet (1815–1899), 'father of the House of Commons'; son of Robert Stribling Cornish; educated at Westminster School and Christ Church, Oxford; M.A., 1839; barrister, Inner Temple, 1841; married (1847) daughter of George Isaac Mowbray, whose name he assumed; conservative M.P. for Durham city, 1853–68, and for Oxford University, 1868–99; made baronet and privy councillor, 1880; chairman of House of Commons committee of selection and committee of standing orders, 1874–99; became 'father of the house' on death of Charles Pelham Villiers [q. v.], 1898; his 'Seventy Years at Westminster,' published posthumously, 1900.
[Suppl. iii. 205]

MOWBRAY, ROBERT DE, EARL OF NORTHUMBERLAND (d. 1125?), nephew of Geoffrey (d. 1093) [q. v.], bishop of Coutances; became Earl of Northumberland, c. 1080; sided with Robert against William Rufus, 1088; ejected a Durham monk from St. Oswine's and bestowed the church on the Benedictines, c. 1091; surprised and slew Malcolm of Scotland at Alnwick, 1093; joined a conspiracy to transfer the crown to Count Stephen of Aumâle, 1095; taken prisoner and deprived of his earldom and possessions; remained a prisoner at Windsor until his death, or possibly until he became a monk of St. Albans. [xxxix. 225]

MOWBRAY, ROGER (I) DE, second BARON (d. 1188?), ward of the crown; went on crusades, 1147 and 1164; joined the Scottish king in the rebellion of 1174, but surrendered on the collapse of the rising in the midlands; his Yorkshire castles demolished; went on a third crusade, 1186; according to one tradition buried at Tyre; according to another tradition he returned to England and was buried in Byland Abbey; benefactor of the church and credited with the foundation of thirty-five monasteries and nunneries, as well as the leper hospital at Burton. [xxxix. 227]

MOWBRAY, THOMAS (I), twelfth BARON MOWBRAY and first DUKE OF NORFOLK (1366?–1399), son of John de Mowbray (III) [q. v.]; succeeded his brother John (IV), 1383; K.G., 1383; summoned as Earl of Nottingham, 1383; served against the Scots, 1384, and shared with Arundel the glory of the naval victory, 1387; joined the revolted lords and assisted (1388) in the prosecution of Richard II's friends in the Merciless parliament; conciliated by Richard II after that king had thrown off the yoke of the appellants; made warden of the Scottish marches, 1389; exchanged wardenship for the captaincy of Calais, 1391; accompanied Richard II to Ireland, 1394; assisted in negotiating the marriage of Richard with Isabella of France, 1396; confirmed his ancestor's grants to various monasteries, and founded a Cistercian priory at Epworth, 1396; helped to arrest Gloucester, Arundel, and Warwick, and received Gloucester into his custody at Calais; present at the trial of Arundel, 1397; when called upon to produce Gloucester for trial asserted that he had died in prison; possibly responsible for Gloucester's death; received part of Arundel's estates, and was created Duke of Norfolk, 1397; being accused of treason by Hereford, 1398, denied the charges, but in the end was banished and his estates forfeited; reached Venice, 1399, and made preparations to visit Palestine, but died at Venice.
[xxxix. 230]

MOWBRAY, THOMAS (II), EARL MARSHAL and third EARL OF NOTTINGHAM (1386–1405), son of Thomas Mowbray, first duke of Norfolk [q. v.]; smarting under his exclusion from his father's honours, entered into the treasonable movements of 1405, and marched with Archbishop Scrope to join Northumberland; seized with Scrope at Shipton Moor, and along with him beheaded without trial. [xxxix. 236]

MOWBRAY, WILLIAM DE, fourth BARON MOWBRAY (d. 1222?), one of the executors of Magna Charta; grandson of Roger (I) de Mowbray, second baron Mowbray [q. v.]; prominent among John's opponents, 1215; executor of Magna Charta; assisted in driving William of Aumâle from Bytham, 1221; benefactor of the church.
[xxxix. 237]

MOWSE or **MOSSE**, WILLIAM (d. 1588), civilian; LL.D. Cambridge, 1552; master of Trinity Hall, Cambridge, 1552–3; deprived, 1553; reinstated, 1555; regius professor of civil law at Oxford, 1554; deprived on Queen Elizabeth's accession; prebendary of Southwell, 1559, of York, 1561; liberal donor to his college. [xxxix. 238]

MOXON, EDWARD (1801–1858), publisher and versewriter; came to London from Wakefield, 1817; entered the service of Messrs. Longman, 1821; published a volume of verse, 1826; set up as a publisher, 1830, his first publication being Lamb's 'Album Verses'; married Lamb's adopted daughter Emma Isola, 1833; published for Barry Cornwall, Southey, Wordsworth, Tennyson, Monckton Milnes, Landor, and Coventry Patmore; published 'Sordello,' 'Bells and Pomegranates,' and 'Cleon,' and 'The Statue and the Bust,' by Browning; accompanied Wordsworth and Crabb Robinson to Paris, 1837; visited Wordsworth at Rydal Mount, 1846; commenced a series of single-volume editions of poets, 1840. He wrote a second volume of sonnets, 1837, and the two were republished together, 1843 and 1871. [xxxix. 239]

MOXON, GEORGE (fl. 1650–1660), ejected minister; son of George Moxon (1603?–1687) [q. v.]; rector of Radwinter, 1650; ejected, 1660; chaplain to Samuel Shute, sheriff of London. [xxxix. 241]

MOXON, GEORGE (1603?–1687), congregational divine; of Sidney Sussex College, Cambridge; perpetual curate of St. Helens, Lancashire; pastor of Springfield, Massachusetts, 1637–53; returned to England, 1653; ejected from Rushton, 1662; licensed to preach, 1672.
[xxxix. 241]

MOXON, JOSEPH (1627–1700), hydrographer and mathematician; visited Holland; settled in London, 1657; sold mathematical and geographical instruments and maps; nominated hydrographer to the king, 1660; published 'Mechanick Exercises,' 1678, and works on astronomy, geography, architecture, mathematics, and typography. [xxxix. 242]

MOXON, WALTER (1836–1886), physician; gave up commerce to enter Guy's Hospital, London, 1854; M.D. London, 1864; F.R.C.P., 1868; physician, 1873; lecturer on medicine, 1882, at Guy's Hospital, London; Croonian lecturer, 1881; contributed to many medical papers; poisoned himself. [xxxix. 242]

MOYLAN, FRANCIS (1735–1815), bishop of Cork; educated at Paris, Montpellier, and Toulouse; bishop of Kerry, 1775; translated to Cork, 1786; actively engaged in the establishment of Maynooth College and in the 'veto' controversy. [xxxix. 243]

MOYLE, JOHN (1592?–1661), friend of Sir John Eliot [q. v.]; met Eliot at Exeter College, Oxford; wounded by him in a temporary fit of rage, caused by his having represented to Eliot's father his son's extravagance; sheriff of Cornwall, 1624; M.P., East Looe, 1649.
[xxxix. 243]

MOYLE, JOHN (d. 1714), naval surgeon; served in various naval engagements; wrote four works on his surgical experiences. [xxxix. 244]

MOYLE, MATTHEW PAUL (1788–1880), meteorologist; M.R.C.S., 1809; practised at Helston; wrote on the atmosphere and temperature of mines.
[xxxix. 244]

MOYLE, SIR THOMAS (d. 1560), speaker of the House of Commons; grandson of Sir Walter Moyle [q. v.]; Lent reader, Gray's Inn, 1533; knighted, 1537; receiver, afterwards chancellor of the court of augmentations, 1537; M.P., Kent, 1542, and chosen speaker; first speaker to claim privilege of freedom of speech; M.P., Rochester, 1544, 1553, and King's Lynn, 1554. [xxxix. 245]

MOYLE, SIR WALTER (d. 1470?), judge; reader at Gray's Inn and serjeant-at-law, 1443; king's serjeant and judge of the king's bench, 1454; knighted, 1465.
[xxxix. 245]

MOYLE, WALTER (1672–1721), politician and student; grandson of John Moyle (1592?–1661) [q. v.]; left Exeter College, Oxford, without taking a degree; studied constitutional law and history at the Middle Temple, 1691; frequented Will's coffee-house; became acquainted with Congreve, Wycherley, and others; M.P., Saltash, 1695–8; issued, with John Trenchard, a pamphlet against a standing army, 1697; contributed to Dryden's issue of Lucian, 1711; studied botany and ornithology; wrote on the forms and laws of government; his works edited, 1726; reprinted, 1727. [xxxix. 246]

MOYNE, WILLIAM DE, EARL OF SOMERSET or DORSET (*fl.* 1141). [See MOHUN.]

MOYSIE, MOISE, MOYSES, or **MOSEY,** DAVID (*fl.* 1582–1603), author of 'Memoirs of the Affairs of Scotland, 1577–1603,' the record of an eye-witness, since he was clerk of the privy council, 1582, and (1596) in the office of the king's secretary. [xxxix. 248]

MOYUN, REGINALD DE (*d.* 1257). [See MOHUN.]

MOZEEN, THOMAS (*d.* 1768), actor and dramatist; forsook the bar for the stage, and appeared at Drury Lane, London, 1745; acted in Dublin, 1748–9; wrote a farce, verses, and fables in verse; with one Owen Bray wrote the song 'Kilruddery.' [xxxix. 248]

MOZLEY, ANNE (1809–1891), author; sister of James Bowling Mozley [q. v.]; reviewed books; contributed to the 'Saturday Review' and 'Blackwood's Magazine'; edited her brother's 'Letters,' 1885, and those of Newman, 1891. [xxxix. 249]

MOZLEY, JAMES BOWLING (1813–1878), regius professor of divinity at Oxford; M.A. Oriel College, 1838; D.D., 1871; gained the English essay, 1835; fellow of Magdalen College, Oxford, 1840; took part in the Oxford movement; joint-editor of the 'Christian Remembrancer'; incumbent of Old Shoreham, 1856; agreed with the Gorham decision (1850), and wrote three works on the subject of dispute; his Bampton lectures on 'Miracles' published, 1865; canon of Worcester, 1869; regius professor of divinity, 1871; his lectures and collected works published after his death. [xxxix. 249]

MOZLEY, THOMAS (1806–1893), divine and journalist; B.A. Oriel College, Oxford, 1828; fellow, 1829; married Newman's sister, Harriet Elizabeth, 1836; rector of Cholderton, 1836–47; took part in the tractarian movement; editor of the 'British Critic,' 1841–3; wrote leaders for the 'Times' from 1844; rector of Plymtree, 1868–80; attended the œcumenical council at Rome as the 'Times' correspondent, 1869–70. His 'Reminiscences,' 1882, contain a valuable account of Oxford during the tractarian movement. [xxxix. 251]

MUCKLOW, WILLIAM (1631–1713), quaker controversialist; seceded from the quakers before 1673; carried on a controversy with William Penn and George Whitehead, but finally rejoined the connection. [xxxix. 252]

MUDD, THOMAS (*fl.* 1577–1590), musical composer; M.A. Peterhouse, Cambridge, 1584; fellow of Pembroke Hall, Cambridge; composed church music and pieces for four viols. [xxxix. 252]

MUDFORD, WILLIAM (1782–1848), author and journalist; originally assistant, then editor, of the 'Courier,' supporting Canning; editor and proprietor of the 'Kentish Observer'; succeeded Hook as editor of the 'John Bull,' 1841; published tales, essays, and translations, and an account of the Waterloo campaign, 1815. [xxxix. 253]

MUDGE, HENRY (1806–1874), temperance advocate; studied at St. Bartholomew's; M.R.C.S., 1828; practised in Bodmin, where he was twice mayor; published works advocating strict temperance. [xxxix. 254]

MUDGE, JOHN (1721–1793), physician; son of Zachariah Mudge [q. v.]; studied at Plymouth Hospital and practised at Plymouth; published 'Dissertation on Small-pox,' 1777; F.R.S. and Copley medallist, 1777; made two large telescopes, one of which passed from Count Bruhl to the Gotha observatory; intimate with Sir Joshua Reynolds, Dr. Johnson, John Smeaton, James Ferguson, and James Northcote. [xxxix. 254]

MUDGE, RICHARD ZACHARIAH (1790–1854), lieutenant-colonel, royal engineers; son of William Mudge (1762–1820) [q. v.]; second lieutenant, 1807; first lieutenant, 1807; fought at Talavera, 1809; second captain, 1813; employed on ordnance survey; went to Dunkirk, 1819, and the north of France, 1821; F.R.S., 1823; lieutenant-colonel, 1837; commissioner to report on the boundary between Maine and New Brunswick, 1838. [xxxix. 255]

MUDGE, THOMAS (1717–1794), horologist; son of Zachariah Mudge [q. v.]; apprenticed to a watchmaker, 1731; constructed an elaborate chronometer for Ferdinand VI of Spain; went into partnership with William Dutton, 1750; retired to Plymouth, 1771; devoted himself to improving maritime chronometers; king's watchmaker, 1776; completed his first maritime chronometer, and submitted it to Nevil Maskelyne [q. v.] to test for the government award, 1776–7; rewarded, after some discussion, by government, 1792. [xxxix. 256]

MUDGE, THOMAS (1760–1843), horologist; son of Thomas Mudge (1717–1794) [q. v.]; barrister, Lincoln's Inn; successfully advocated his father's claims to government award; wrote on the improvement of timekeepers. [xxxix. 258]

MUDGE, WILLIAM (1762–1820), major-general, royal artillery; son of John Mudge [q. v.]; a godson of Dr. Johnson; commissioned, 1779; first lieutenant, 1781; director of ordnance survey and F.R.S., 1798; major, 1801; lieutenant-colonel, 1804; lieutenant-governor of Woolwich, 1809; superintended the extension of the meridian line into Scotland, and was promoted colonel, 1813; commissioner of board of longitude, 1818; major-general, 1819; wrote geodetic works. [xxxix. 258]

MUDGE, WILLIAM (1796–1837), naval commander; son of William Mudge (1762–1820) [q. v.]; employed (1821–5) on survey of the east coast of Africa; conducted (1825–37) survey of the coast of Ireland; wrote on hydrography. [xxxix. 259]

MUDGE, ZACHARIAH (1694–1769), divine; second master in John (grandfather of Sir Joshua) Reynolds's school, becoming intimately acquainted with three generations of the Reynolds family; master of Bideford grammar school, 1718; left nonconformists and joined the church of England and became incumbent of Abbotsham, 1729, of St. Andrew's, Plymouth, 1732; prebendary of Exeter, 1736; acquainted with Dr. Johnson, John Smeaton, and Edmund Burke; author of sermons and a new version of the Psalms, 1744. [xxxix. 260]

MUDGE, ZACHARY (1770–1852), admiral; son of John Mudge [q. v.]; entered the navy, 1780; lieutenant, 1789; commander, 1797; advanced to post rank, 1800; his ship reduced to a wreck by a small French squadron, 1805; rear-admiral, 1830; vice-admiral, 1841; admiral, 1849. [xxxix. 261]

MUDIE, CHARLES EDWARD (1818–1890), founder of Mudie's Lending Library, London; stationer and bookseller, 1840; commenced lending books, 1842; published Lowell's poems in England, 1844; advertised extensively, and by his knowledge of public requirements made his library successful; published verse, 1872. [xxxix. 262]

MUDIE, CHARLES HENRY (1850–1879), philanthropist; son of Charles Edward Mudie [q. v.]; devoted himself to work among the poor. [xxxix. 262]

MUDIE, ROBERT (1777–1842), miscellaneous writer; professor of Gaelic and drawing, Inverness academy, 1802; master at Dundee High School, *c.* 1808; removed to London; reporter to the 'Morning Chronicle,' 1820; subsequently edited the 'Sunday Times'; wrote for a Winchester bookseller, 1838; described George IV's visit to Edinburgh in 'Modern Athens,' 1824; wrote mostly on natural history. [xxxix. 263]

MUDIE, THOMAS MOLLESON (1809–1876), composer; pianoforte professor at the Royal Academy of Music, 1832–44, and at Edinburgh, 1844–63. [xxxix. 264]

MUFFET, THOMAS (1553–1604). [See MOFFETT.]

MUGGLETON, LODOWICKE (1609–1698), heresiarch; apprenticed to a tailor; journeyman to his cousin William Reeve, a strong puritan, 1631; had inward revelations, 1651–2; declared by Reeve to have been appointed with himself messenger of a new dispensation, 1652; identified himself and Reeve as the 'two witnesses' and made some converts of position; imprisoned for blasphemy, 1653; his authority twice disputed, 1660 and 1670, the ringleaders returning to their allegiance; had controversies with the quakers; arrested for blasphemous writings and fined 500*l.*, 1677; prepared an autobiography and wrote an abundance of doctrinal letters, published after his death; in some respects anticipated Swedenborg. Reeve and Muggleton's 'commission book,' the 'Transcendent Spirituall Treatise,' was published, 1652. [xxxix. 264]

MUILMAN, RICHARD (1735 ?-1797). [See Chiswell, Trench.]

MUIR, JOHN (1810-1882), orientalist; entered service of East India Company, 1829, principal of Queen's College, Benares, 1844; judge at Fatehpur, 1845; retired, 1853; D.C.L. Oxford, 1855; LL.D. Edinburgh, 1861; wrote Sanskrit works dealing with Indian history, Christian apologetics, and biography; founded Sanskrit and comparative philology professorship, Edinburgh, 1862.
[xxxix. 267]

MUIR, THOMAS (1765-1798), parliamentary reformer; M.A. Edinburgh, 1782; advocate, 1787; assisted to found a society for obtaining parliamentary reform, 1792; arrested for sedition, 1793, and sentenced to fourteen years' transportation to Botany Bay; escaped, 1796, and after a variety of adventures was severely wounded on board a Spanish frigate at Cadiz; died at Chantilly.
[xxxix. 268]

MUIR, WILLIAM (1787-1869), divine; minister of St. George's, Glasgow, 1810; transferred to Edinburgh, 1822; moderator of the general assembly, 1838; at the disruption remained with the established church; dean of the Thistle, 1845, and chaplain to Queen Victoria.
[xxxix. 269]

MUIR, WILLIAM (1806-1888), engineer; apprenticed at Kilmarnock; came to London, 1831; became acquainted with James Nasmyth and Joseph Whitworth; worked for Maudslay, Holtzapffel, and Bramah, and at Manchester for Whitworth; started business at Manchester as a maker of lathes and machine-tools, 1842.
[xxxix. 270]

MUIRCHEARTACH (d. 533), king of Ireland; victorious in battles at Ocha, 482, Kellistown, 489, and Indemor, 497, and in the Curlieu Hills, 504; made king of Ireland, 517; he attacked and conquered the Oirghialla; fought against the Leinstermen and the Connaughtmen, 524.
[xxxix. 271]

MUIRCHEARTACH (d. 943), king of Ailech; won important battles over the Danes, 921 and 926, and (938) plundered their territory; made an expedition to the Hebrides, 941; his most famous campaign ('Moirthimchell Eireann,' or great circuit of Ireland) described in a poem by Cormacan, son of Maolbrighde; killed in battle at Ardee.
[xxxix. 271]

MUIRCHEARTACH (d. 1166). [See O'Lochlainn, Muircheartach.]

MUIRCHU MACCU MACHTHENI, SAINT (fl. 697), only known as the author of the life of St. Patrick in the 'Book of Armagh'; identified the author of the 'Confession' with the popular saint.
[xxxix. 272]

MUIRHEAD, GEORGE (1715-1773), M.A. Edinburgh, 1742; ordained, 1746; professor of oriental languages at Glasgow, 1752, and of humanity, 1754-73.
[Suppl. iii. 206]

MUIRHEAD, JAMES (1742-1808), song-writer; minister of Urr, 1770; replied to a satire of Burns, 1795; naturalist and mathematician; author of 'Bess the Gawkie,' 1776.
[xxxix. 273]

MUIRHEAD, JAMES (1831-1889), jurist; barrister, Inner Temple, 1857, and admitted advocate, 1857; professor of civil law, Edinburgh, 1862; sheriff in chancery, 1885; wrote on Roman law.
[xxxix. 273]

MUIRHEAD, JAMES PATRICK (1813-1898), biographer of James Watt; educated at Glasgow College and Balliol College, Oxford; B.A., 1835; M.A., 1838; admitted advocate, 1838; became acquainted with James Watt, son of the great engineer, who entrusted him with the task of writing his father's life; published 'Life of James Watt,' 1858, several works relating to Watt's inventions, and other writings.
[Suppl. iii. 206]

MULCASTER, SIR FREDERICK WILLIAM (1772-1846), lieutenant-general; second lieutenant, 1792; first lieutenant, 1793; captain-lieutenant, 1798; judge of the vice-admiralty court in the Mediterranean, 1799-1801; under-secretary to Chatham, 1801; major, 1810; lieutenant-colonel, 1811; colonel and K.C.H. 1817; major-general, 1825; inspector-general of fortifications, 1834; lieutenant-general, 1838.
[xxxix. 274]

MULCASTER, RICHARD (1530 ?-1611), schoolmaster and author; educated at Eton under Udall, and at Christ Church, Oxford; M.A., 1556; first head-master

of Merchant Taylors' School, London, 1561-86; vicar of Cranbrook, 1590; prebendary of Salisbury, 1594; high-master at St. Paul's School, London, 1596-1608; rector of Stanford Rivers, 1598; wrote chiefly on the training of children; masques frequently performed at court by his pupils.
[xxxix. 275]

MULGRAVE, EARLS OF. [See Sheffield, Edmund, first EARL, 1564 ?-1646; Sheffield, Edmund, second EARL, 1611 ?-1658; Sheffield, John, third EARL, 1648-1721; Phipps, Henry, first EARL of the second creation, 1755-1831.]

MULGRAVE, BARONS. [See Phipps, Constantine John, second BARON, 1744-1792; Phipps, Henry, third BARON, 1755-1831.]

MULHALL, MICHAEL GEORGE (1836-1900), statistical compiler; born in Dublin; educated at Irish College, Rome; went to South America; founded (1861) Buenos Ayres 'Standard,' with which he remained connected till 1894; published 'Dictionary of Statistics,' 1883, and other statistical works.
[Suppl. iii. 207]

MULHOLLAND, ANDREW (1791-1866), cotton and linen manufacturer; set up flax-spinning machinery in Belfast, 1828; mayor of Belfast, 1845; subsequently J.P., deputy-lieutenant, and high sheriff of Down and Antrim.
[xxxix. 276]

MULLEN, ALLAN (d. 1690). [See Molines.]

MULLENS, JOSEPH (1820-1879), missionary; B.A. London, 1841; worked at Bhowanipore in India, 1842-58; foreign secretary to the London Missionary Society, 1865; visited America, 1870, Madagascar, 1873, and Central Africa, 1879; wrote on missionary work; died at Chakombe.
[xxxix. 276]

MÜLLER, FRIEDRICH MAX (1823-1900). [See Max Müller.]

MÜLLER, GEORGE (1805-1898), preacher and philanthropist; born at Kroppenstadt, near Halberstadt; educated at Halle; came to London, 1829; pastor of congregation at Teignmouth, 1830; adopted (1830) principle that trust in God is sufficient for all purposes temporal and spiritual; and thenceforth depended for support on free-will offerings; lived (1832 till death) at Bristol, where he conducted philanthropic work, which gradually grew to immense proportions; published 'The Lord's Dealings with George Müller,' 1845.
[Suppl. iii. 208]

MÜLLER, JOHANN SEBASTIAN (fl. 1715 ?-1790 ?). [See Miller, John.]

MULLER, JOHN (1699-1784), mathematician; born in Germany; head-master and professor of fortification and mathematics at Woolwich, 1741; wrote on mathematics and fortification.
[xxxix. 277]

MÜLLER, WILLIAM (d. 1846), writer on military and engineering science; a Hanoverian officer; instructor in military science at Göttingen University; came to England, 1807; lieutenant of engineers in George III's German legion, 1807; captain of engineers in the reformed Hanoverian army, 1816; wrote military and engineering works in German and English; K.H.; died at Stade.
[xxxix. 277]

MÜLLER, WILLIAM JOHN (1812-1845), landscape painter; studied under Pyne at Bristol; travelled in Germany, Switzerland, and Italy, 1833; Greece and Egypt, 1838; and Lycia, 1841; painted in oil and water colour; exhibited at the Royal Academy, 1833-45, his best-known work, 'The Ammunition Waggon.'
[xxxix. 278]

MULLINER, THOMAS (fl. 1550 ?), musician; possibly master of St. Paul's (Cathedral) choir school before 1559; collected virginal music.
[xxxix. 279]

MULLINS, GEORGE (fl. 1760-1775), painter; an Irishman; exhibited landscapes at the Royal Academy, 1770-5.
[xxxix. 280]

MULLINS, JAMES (d. 1639). [See Molines.]

MULLINS, JOHN (d. 1591). [See Molyns.]

MULOCK, DINAH MARIA, afterwards MRS. CRAIK (1826-1887), authoress; came to London, c. 1846; at first wrote children's books; her chief novel, 'John Halifax, Gentleman,' 1857; published latterly didactic essays; married (1864) George Lillie Craik, a partner in the house of Macmillan & Co.
[xxxix. 280]

MULREADY, WILLIAM (1786–1863), genre painter; showed early a tendency towards art, and received tuition through the kindness of Thomas Banks; admitted as a student of the Royal Academy, 1800; entered the house of John Varley [q. v.] as pupil teacher, and married Varley's sister, 1803; taught drawing, illustrated children's books, and exhibited at the Royal Academy figure subjects and domestic scenes of the Wilkie type; R.A., 1816; illustrated 'The Vicar of Wakefield,' c. 1840; designed the first penny postage envelope issued by Rowland Hill, 1840 (caricatured by John Leech in 'Punch'); his 'Choosing the Wedding Gown,' 1846, celebrated for its technical merits in the representation of textures.
[xxxix. 281]

MULSO, HESTER (1727–1801). [See CHAPONE.]

MULTON or **MULETON**, THOMAS DE (d. 1240?), justiciar; sheriff of Lincolnshire, 1206–8; accompanied King John to Ireland, 1210; sided with the barons, 1215; imprisoned at Corfe, 1215–17; justice itinerant in the north, 1219; after 1224 sat continually at Westminster; witnessed confirmation of Magna Charta, 1225; endowed various religious foundations.
[xxxix. 284]

MULVANY, CHARLES PELHAM (1835–1885), minor poet and journalist; B.A. Trinity College, Dublin, 1856; naval surgeon; subsequently emigrated to Canada, 1868; curate in Ontario, contributing to newspapers and magazines.
[xxxix. 285]

MULVANY, GEORGE F. (1809–1869), painter; son of Thomas James Mulvany [q. v.]; keeper of the Royal Hibernian Academy, 1845; director of the Irish National Gallery, 1854.
[xxxix. 285]

MULVANY, THOMAS JAMES (d. 1845?), painter; advocated incorporation of Irish artists (charter obtained, 1823); academician on the foundation of the Royal Hibernian Academy, 1823; keeper, 1841.
[xxxix. 285]

MUMFORD, JAMES (1606–1666), jesuit; professed at St. Omer, 1641; remained abroad till 1650, when he was sent to Norwich, seized by parliamentary soldiers and imprisoned; his theological works frequently reprinted and translated.
[xxxix. 285]

MUMMERY, ALBERT FREDERICK (1855–1895), author of works relating to economical questions and to climbing in the Alps and Caucasus. [Suppl. iii. 209]

MUN, THOMAS (1571–1641), economic writer; engaged in mercantile affairs in Italy and the Levant; a director of the East India Company, 1615; declined the deputy-governorship, 1624; published 'A Discourse of Trade, from England unto the East Indies,' 1621, defending the East India Company from the complaints that the scarcity of specie was due to the company's exportation of it. His second book, 'England's Treasure by Forraign Trade' (written c. 1630, published 1664), defines the balance of trade, makes interesting reference to the customs revenue in relation to trade with India and other countries, and deplores the neglect of the English fishing trade.
[xxxix. 286]

MUNBY, GILES (1813–1876), botanist; studied medicine at Edinburgh, London, and Paris; travelled in the south of France, 1836; lived at Algiers, 1839–44, collecting plants; returned to England, 1860; wrote on the flora of Algeria.
[xxxix. 289]

MUNCASTER, BARONS. [See PENNINGTON, SIR JOHN, first BARON, 1737–1813; PENNINGTON, LOWTHER, second BARON, 1745–1818.]

MUNCASTER, RICHARD (1530?–1611). [See MULCASTER.]

MUNCHENSI, WARINE (II) DE (d. 1255), baron; served in Wales, 1223, and Poitou, 1225; distinguished himself at the battle of Saintes.
[xxxix. 290]

MUNCHENSI, WILLIAM DE (d. 1289), baronial leader; son of Warine (II) de Munchensi [q. v.]; taken prisoner with the younger Simon de Montfort at Kenilworth, 1265; made submission, 1267, but was not fully pardoned until 1279; served in Wales and was killed at the siege of Dyryslwyan Castle.
[xxxix. 290]

MUNDAY, ANTHONY (1553–1633), poet and playwright; apprenticed to John Allde, stationer, 1576; went to Rome, 1578; described the arrangements at the English College, the carnival, and matters likely to excite protestants, in 'The English Romayne Lyfe,' 1582; on his return, 1579, tried the stage; published an anti-catholic work narrating the circumstances of Campion's capture, 1581; employed for a short time in guarding and taking bonds of recusants; concerned in eighteen plays (1584–1602), of which only four are extant, 'John a Kent and John a Cumber,' 1595, 'The Downfall of Robert, Earl of Huntingdon,' produced, 1599, 'The Death of Robert Earle of Huntingdon' (with Chettle), and the 'True and Honourable History of the Life of Sir John Oldcastle, the good Lord Cobham,' 1600 (with Drayton, Hathway, and Wilson); accompanied Pembroke's players on a foreign tour to the exclusion of Ben Jonson, 1598; ridiculed by Ben Jonson as Antonio Balladino in the 'Case is Altered,' 1599; was also a ballad-writer, all his pieces being lost, unless 'Beauty sat bathing in a Springe,' by 'Shepherd Tonie,' in 'England's Helicon,' can be assigned to him; wrote (1592–1623) most of the city pageants, and was keeper of the properties of the show; best known for his voluminous translation of popular romances, including 'Palladino of England,' 1588, and 'Amadis de Gaule,' 1589–95; as literary executor produced Stow's 'Survey of London,' 1618. In some cases he uses the pseudonym 'Lazarus Piot' or 'L. P.,' and some miscellaneous pieces bear his motto, 'Honos alit artes.'
[xxxix. 290]

MUNDAY, HENRY (1623–1682), physician; B.A. Merton College, Oxford, 1647; head-master of Henley-on-Thames grammar-school, 1656; his Βιοχρησολογία, published, Oxford, 1680 and 1685, London, 1681, Frankfort, 1685, Leipzig, 1685, Leyden, 1715.
[xxxix. 297]

MUNDEFORD, OSBERT or OSBERN (d. 1460), treasurer of Normandy; English representative at various foreign conferences; treasurer of Normandy, 1448; taken prisoner at Pont Audemer, 1449; beheaded at Calais.
[xxxix. 297]

MUNDELLA, ANTHONY JOHN (1825–1897), statesman; entered partnership with Messrs. Hine & Co., hosiery manufacturers at Nottingham, 1848; took part in local politics; formed 'Nottingham board of conciliation in glove and hosiery trade,' 1866; radical M.P. for Sheffield, 1868–85, and for Brightside division of Sheffield, 1885–97; brought about the passing of Mr. (afterwards Viscount) Cross's Factories Act, 1874; largely responsible for procuring Education Act, 1870; privy councillor, 1880; vice-president of committee of council for education, 1880–5; introduced important educational reforms, including Compulsory Education Act, 1881; president of board of trade, 1886 and 1892–4; created labour department, 1886; chairman of departmental committee on poor-law schools, 1894–5.
[Suppl. iii. 209]

MUNDEN, SIR JOHN (d. 1719), rear-admiral; brother of Sir Richard Munden [q.v.]; lieutenant, 1677; commander, 1688; rear-admiral and knighted, 1701; fully acquitted by court-martial for failing to intercept a French squadron, 1702, but cashiered by government.
[xxxix. 298]

MUNDEN, JOSEPH SHEPHERD (1758–1832), actor; joined a company of strolling players; gradually became a leading comic actor in the northern towns; came to London, 1790; acted at Covent Garden, with occasional appearances at the Haymarket, till 1811, gradually becoming the most celebrated comedian of his day; acted at Drury Lane, 1813–24. His appearance and merits are described by Lamb, Hazlitt, Leigh Hunt, and Talfourd.
[xxxix. 298]

MUNDEN, SIR RICHARD (1640–1680), naval captain; brother of Sir John Munden [q. v.]; first appears as commander, 1666; captain, 1672; knighted for capturing St. Helena from the Dutch, 1673; convoyed the trade to the Mediterranean, 1677–80.
[xxxix. 301]

MUNDY, SIR GEORGE RODNEY (1805–1884), admiral of the fleet; grandson of George Brydges Rodney, first baron Rodney [q. v.]; lieutenant, 1826; commander, 1828; advanced to post rank, 1837; engaged against the Borneo pirates, 1846, publishing an account of his operations, 1848; rear-admiral, 1857; C.B., 1859; protected British interests at Palermo and Naples, 1859–60, and published a history of the revolution, 1863; K.C.B., 1862; vice-admiral, 1863; admiral, 1869; commander-in-chief at Portsmouth, 1872–5; G.C.B., 1877; admiral of the fleet, 1877.
[xxxix. 301]

MUNDY, JOHN (d. 1630), organist and composer; son of William Mundy [q. v.]; Mus. Bac. Oxford, 1586; Mus. Doc., 1624; organist of St. George's Chapel, Windsor, c. 1586–c. 1630; composed songs and church music.

[xxxix. 302]

MUNDY, PETER (fl. 1600–1667), traveller; went to Rouen, 1609; rose to independent circumstances after being cabin-boy on a merchant ship; kept journals of his voyages to India, China, and Japan, 1628–36; visited Denmark, Russia, and Prussia, 1639–48. [xxxix. 303]

MUNDY, SIR ROBERT MILLER (1813–1892), colonial governor; entered the army, 1833; joined the horse artillery, 1841; lieutenant-colonel, 1856; lieutenant-governor of Grenada, 1863, of British Honduras, 1874; K.C.M.G., 1877.

[xxxix. 303]

MUNDY, WILLIAM (fl. 1564), musical composer; member of St. Paul's (Cathedral) choir; gentleman of the Chapel Royal, 1564; composed church music, songs, and Latin motets in parts. [xxxix. 304]

MUNGO, SAINT (518?–603). [See KENTIGERN.]

MUNK, WILLIAM (1816–1898), physician; educated at University College, London; M.D. Leyden, 1837; F.R.C.P., 1854; Harveian librarian, 1857–98; published 'Roll of Royal College of Physicians of London,' 1861, and other works relating to eminent physicians.

[Suppl. iii. 212]

MUNN, PAUL SANDBY (1773–1845), water-colour painter; godson of Paul Sandby [q. v.]; exhibited at the Royal Academy and other exhibitions from 1798.

[xxxix. 304]

MUNNU, SAINT (d. 634). [See FINTAN.]

MUNRO. [See also MONRO.]

MUNRO, ALEXANDER (1825–1871), sculptor; employed on stone-carving at the Houses of Parliament, 1848; exhibited portrait-busts of celebrities at the Royal Academy from 1849; died at Cannes. [xxxix. 305]

MUNRO, SIR HECTOR (1726–1805), general; received his commission, 1747; lieutenant, 1754; captain, 1756; major, 1759; served in India; effectively suppressed mutiny at Patna, 1764; routed the confederated princes of Hindostan at Buxar, 1764; lieutenant-colonel, 1765; M.P., Inverness burghs, 1768–1801; local major-general to command the army in Madras, 1777; captured Pondicherry, 1778; K.B., 1779; commanded right division of Coote's army at Porto Novo, 1781; captured Negapatam, 1781; returned home; major-general, 1782; lieutenant-general, 1793; general, 1798. [xxxix. 305]

MUNRO, HUGH ANDREW JOHNSTONE (1819–1885), classical scholar and critic; of Shrewsbury School and Trinity College, Cambridge; B.A., 1842; fellow, 1843; collated Vatican and Laurentian manuscripts of Lucretius, examined those at Leyden, and in 1860 edited the text; published text of 'Aetna,' 1867, of Horace, 1868; first Kennedy professor of Latin, 1869 (resigned, 1872); published 'Criticisms and Elucidations of Catullus,' 1878; his translations into Latin and Greek verse privately printed, 1884; died at Rome. [xxxix. 307]

MUNRO, INNES (d. 1827), of Poyntzfield; lieutenant-colonel; fought (1780–4) against Hyder Ali, publishing an account of the campaigns, 1789; left the army, 1808; published 'A System of Farm Book-keeping,' 1821.

[xxxix. 309]

MUNRO, SIR THOMAS, first baronet (1761–1827), major-general; governor of Madras; educated at Glasgow; infantry cadet at Madras, 1780; served against Hyder Ali, 1780–4; assisted in forming the civil administration of the Baramahal, 1792–9; after Seringapatam, secretary to the commission for the administration of Mysore; contracted a lasting friendship with Colonel Wellesley, the future Duke of Wellington; in administrative charge of Canara, but soon transferred to the ceded districts south of the Tungabhadra, 1800, where he introduced and developed the ryotwár system of land tenure and revenue; left India for England, 1807, and informed the government on internal Indian administration, on trade questions, and on the organisation of the Indian army; returned to India, 1814, on a special commission to reorganise the judicial and police departments; brigadier-general during the second Mahratta war K.C.B.; nominated governor of Madras, 1819; created baronet for

services in connection with first Burmah war; died of cholera while on a farewell tour through the ceded districts. [xxxix. 309]

MUNRO, WILLIAM (1818–1880), general and botanist; entered the army, 1834; commanded 39th foot at Sebastopol; C.B.; served in India, the Crimea, Canada, and Bermuda; general, 1878; wrote on botany, specialising on grasses. [xxxix. 313]

MUNSON, LIONEL (d. 1680). [See ANDERSON.]

MUNSTER, KINGS OF. [See O'BRIEN, DONOUGH, d. 1064; O'BRIEN, TURLOUGH, 1009–1086; O'BRIEN, MURTOUGH, d. 1119; O'BRIEN, DOMHNALL, d. 1194; O'BRIEN, DONOGH CAIRBRECH, d. 1242; O'BRIEN, CONCHOBHAR, d. 1267; O'BRIEN, BRIAN RUADH, d. 1276.]

MUNSTER, first EARL OF. [See FITZCLARENCE, GEORGE AUGUSTUS FREDERICK, 1794–1842.]

MUNTZ, GEORGE FREDERICK (1794–1857), political reformer; went into his father's metal works; took out patents, 1832 and 1846, in connection with Muntz's metal; actively supported the repeal of the Test and Corporation Acts, catholic emancipation, and political reform; M.P., Birmingham, 1840–57; induced the adoption of perforated postage-stamps; opposed church rates.

[xxxix. 313]

MÜNTZ, JOHN HENRY (fl. 1755–1775), painter; of Swiss origin; employed by Horace Walpole as painter and engraver; published 'Encaustic,' 1760. [xxxix. 315]

MURA (d. 645?), Irish saint; founded Fahan Abbey, becoming the first abbot; received lands from Aodh Uairidhneach, king of Ireland; possibly wrote a poem on St. Columcille; founded church of Banagher; his staff and bell still preserved. [xxxix. 315]

MURCHISON, CHARLES (1830–1879), physician; born in Jamaica; studied at Aberdeen, Edinburgh (M.D. 1851), Turin, Dublin, and Paris; went to India, 1853; professor of chemistry at Calcutta; served in Burma, 1854; settled in London, 1855; attached to several London hospitals; a prominent figure in many scientific societies; wrote principally on 'Continued Fevers' and 'Diseases of the Liver'; F.R.C.P., 1859; Croonian lecturer, 1873; F.R.S., 1866; LL.D. Edinburgh, 1870.

[xxxix. 316]

MURCHISON, SIR RODERICK IMPEY, first baronet (1792–1871), geologist; entered the army, 1807; served in Portugal, Sicily, and Ireland; sold out of the army, 1814; became acquainted with Sir Humphry Davy, 1823; studied secondary rocks, making summer geological tours, 1825–31; F.R.S., 1826; subsequently devoted himself to the older masses underlying the old red sandstone, to which, in 1835, he assigned the name Silurian; published 'The Silurian System,' 1838; travelled extensively in Germany, Russia, Scandinavia, and Finland, and collaborated with Von Keyserling and De Verneuil in 'The Geology of Russia and the Ural Mountains,' 1845; director-general of the Geological Survey, 1855; attempted to unravel the complicated structure of the Scottish highlands; president of the Royal Geographical Society, 1843; received Russian orders; knighted, 1846; K.C.B., 1863; created baronet, 1866; D.C.L. Oxford; LL.D. Cambridge and Dublin. [xxxix. 317]

MURCOT, JOHN (1625–1654), puritan divine; B.A. Merton College, Oxford, 1647; went to Ireland, 1651; preacher to the lord-deputy and attached to Dr. Winter's independent congregation; wrote on religious topics.

[xxxix. 320]

MURDAC, HENRY (d. 1153), archbishop of York; Cistercian monk; first abbot of Vauclair, 1135, and third abbot of Fountains in Yorkshire, 1143; five daughter houses founded during his abbacy; elected archbishop of York, 1147, on the deprivation of William Fitzherbert, King Stephen's nephew, whom Stephen upheld; refused admission into the city of York by the citizens; interdicted the citizens and complained to the pope, on which a reconciliation followed, and he was magnificently received at York, 1151; refused to recognise the election of Hugh of Puiset, 1153, and excommunicated the offenders, but finally absolved them.

[xxxix. 321]

MURDAC or **MURDOCH**, second DUKE OF ALBANY (d. 1425). [See STEWART.]

MURDOCH, JOHN (1747–1824), miscellaneous writer; friend and fellow-pupil of Burns at Ayr school; visited Paris; taught languages in London; corresponded with Burns, and wrote on the pronunciation of French and English. [xxxix. 323]

MURDOCH, PATRICK (d. 1774), author; distinguished himself at Edinburgh in mathematics; after acting as travelling tutor became rector of Stradishall, 1738; published memoirs of Colin Maclaurin, 1748, and of Thomson, 1762; published 'Mercator's Sailing,' 1741, and geographical works. [xxxix. 323]

MURDOCH, SIR THOMAS WILLIAM CLINTON (1809–1891), civil servant; entered colonial office, 1826; in Canada, 1839–42; chairman of the Colonial Land and Emigration Commission, 1847; special commissioner to Canada, 1870; K.C.M.G., 1870. [xxxix. 324]

MURDOCK, WILLIAM (1754–1839), engineer and inventor of coal-gas lighting; obtained employment under Boulton & Watt at Soho, 1777; commenced making experiments on the illuminating properties of gases produced by distilling coal, wood, peat, &c., 1792; put up experimental gas apparatus at Soho, 1800, the foundry being regularly lighted with gas, 1803; Rumford gold medallist for paper which he read before the Royal Society, 1808; issued a 'Letter to a Member of Parliament . . . in Vindication of his Character and Claims,' answering the charge of plagiarism, 1809, gas-lighting having fallen into the hands of company promoters; sometimes supposed to have invented the steam locomotive, but wrongly, since, though he made three steam engines, his experiments led to no results; originated the 'sun and planet motion' and the 'bell-crank engine.' He took out a patent for making stone pipes, 1810, and the invention of 'iron cement' is also attributed to him. [xxxix. 324]

MURE, SIR WILLIAM (1594–1657), poet; probably educated at Glasgow; M.P., Edinburgh, 1643; wounded at Marston Moor, 1644; commanded his regiment at Newcastle, 1644; left numerous manuscript verses, some of which occur in Lyle's 'Ancient Ballads and Songs.' [xxxix. 328]

MURE, WILLIAM (1718–1776), baron of the Scots exchequer; studied at Edinburgh and Leyden; M.P., Renfrewshire, 1742–1761; baron of the Scots exchequer, 1761; lord rector of Glasgow, 1764 and 1765; the friend of John Stuart, third earl of Bute [q. v.], and of David Hume (1711–1766) [q. v.]. [xxxix. 329]

MURE, WILLIAM (1799–1860), classical scholar; grandson of William Mure (1718–1776) [q. v.]; educated at Edinburgh and Bonn; travelled in Greece, 1838; M.P., Renfrewshire, 1846–55; rector of Glasgow, 1847–8; chief work, 'A critical History of the Language and Literature of Ancient Greece,' 1850–7. [xxxix. 330]

MURFORD, NICHOLAS (fl. 1638–1652), poet; salt merchant at Lynn; travelled widely for business purposes; petitioned parliament, 1638, on the infringement of his patent method of manufacture; imprisoned for debt, 1652; produced two volumes of pedestrian verse. [xxxix. 330]

MURGATROID, MICHAEL (1551–1609), author; fellow, Jesus College, Cambridge, 1577–1600; M.A., 1580; secretary to Archbishop Whitgift and commissary of the faculties; wrote on Greek scholarship and on Whitgift's archiepiscopate. [xxxix. 331]

MURIMUTH, ADAM (1275 ?–1347), historian; D.C.L. Oxford before 1312; agent at Avignon for Oxford University, for the chapter of Canterbury, and Edward II, 1312–1317; and again for Edward II, 1319 and 1323; sent on a mission to Sicily, 1323; prebendary of St. Paul's Cathedral and vicar-general for Archbishop Reynolds, 1325; exchanged precentorship of Exeter for rectory of Wraysbury, 1331; author of 'Continuatio Chronicarum' (from 1303 to 1347); the continuation of the 'Flores Historiarum' sometimes ascribed to him. [xxxix. 331]

MURLIN, JOHN (1722–1799), methodist preacher; converted to methodism, 1749; itinerant preacher in England and Ireland; resided at Bristol and (1784) at Manchester; published religious verse and doctrinal letters. [xxxix. 333]

MURPHY, ARTHUR (1727–1805), author and actor; educated at St. Omer; became a merchant's clerk; published the 'Gray's Inn Journal,' 1752–4; took to the stage, 1754; refused admission to the Middle Temple, 1757, because he was an actor, but admitted at Lincoln's Inn; a commissioner of bankrupts and granted a pension, 1803; invariably took his plots from previous writers; edited Fielding's works, 1762, and wrote an 'Essay on the Life and Genius of Samuel Johnson,' 1792, a 'Life of David Garrick,' 1801, and miscellaneous works. [xxxix. 334]

MURPHY, DENIS (1833–1896), historical writer; trained in various jesuit colleges in England, Germany, and Spain; entered Society of Jesus; professor of history and literature at University College, Dublin; published 'Cromwell in Ireland,' 1883, and other historical writings; vice-president of Royal Irish Academy. [Suppl. iii. 213]

MURPHY, DENIS BROWNELL (d. 1842), miniature-painter; settled in London, 1803; commanded by Princess Charlotte to copy in miniature Lely's 'Beauties' (purchased by Sir Gerard Noel and published as 'Beauties of the Court of King Charles II,' 1833). [xxxix. 337]

MURPHY or **MORPHY**, EDWARD or DOMINIC EDWARD (d. 1728), bishop of Kildare and Leighlin, 1715–1724; archbishop of Dublin, 1724–8. [xxxix. 337]

MURPHY, FRANCIS (1795–1858), first Roman catholic bishop of Adelaide; educated at Maynooth; went to New South Wales, 1838; bishop of Adelaide, 1844; established twenty-one churches and commenced a cathedral. [xxxix. 337]

MURPHY, SIR FRANCIS (1809–1891), first speaker of the legislative assembly of Victoria; studied medicine at Trinity College, Dublin; district surgeon for Bungonia, Argyle county, 1837–40; on the separation of Victoria became member for Murray and chairman of committees, 1851; speaker, 1856–60; knighted, 1860. [xxxix. 338]

MURPHY, FRANCIS STACK (1810 ?–1860), serjeant-at-law; M.A. Trinity College, Dublin, 1832; called to the English bar; contributed to 'Fraser's Magazine,' 1834; M.P., co. Cork, 1837–53; serjeant-at-law, 1842; commissioner of bankruptcy, 1853. [xxxix. 339]

MURPHY, JAMES (1725–1759), dramatic writer; brother of Arthur Murphy [q. v.]; barrister, Middle Temple; adopted the surname French; wrote a comedy and a farce; died at Kingston, Jamaica. [xxxix. 336]

MURPHY, JAMES CAVANAH (1760–1814), architect and antiquary; consulted as to additions to the House of Commons, 1786; made drawings of Batalha church and monastery, 1788; studied Moorish architecture at Cadiz, 1802; wrote on Portugal and on Arabian antiquities. [xxxix. 339]

MURPHY, JEREMIAH DANIEL (1806–1824), boy linguist; cousin of Francis Stack Murphy [q. v.]. [xxxix. 339]

MURPHY, JOHN (1753 ?–1798), Irish rebel; D.D. Seville; assistant priest at Boulavogue, 1785; raised the standard of revolt, 1798; established a camp on Vinegar Hill, 1798; failed to take Arklow, and after the battle of Vinegar Hill escaped to Wexford; attacked and routed by Sir Charles Asgill at Kilcomney Hill; beheaded and his body burnt. [xxxix. 340]

MURPHY, JOHN (fl. 1780–1820), engraver; engraved historical subjects after contemporary painters and old masters. [xxxix. 341]

MURPHY, MARIE LOUISE (1737–1814), mistress of Louis XV; an Irish shoemaker's daughter; born at Rouen; first occupant of the Parc aux Cerfs, 1753; dismissed for aiming at supplanting Madame de Pompadour; married Major Beaufranchet d'Ayat, 1755, François-Nicolas Le Normant, 1757, and Louis Philippe Dumont, who obtained a divorce in 1799. [xxxix. 341]

MURPHY, MICHAEL (1767 ?–1798), Irish rebel; officiating priest of Ballycanew; joined the rebellion, 1798; shot while leading the attack at Arklow. [xxxix. 342]

MURPHY, PATRICK (1782–1847), weather prophet; accurately predicted in the 'Weather Almanack' that 20 Jan. 1838 would be the coldest day of winter; wrote also on natural science. [xxxix. 342]

MURPHY, ROBERT (1806–1843), mathematician; B.A. Gonville and Caius College, Cambridge; fellow, 1829; dean, 1831; examiner in mathematics in London University, 1838; wrote on the theory of equations and electricity. [xxxix. 343]

MURRAY or **MORAY**, EARLS OF. [See RANDOLPH, THOMAS, first EARL of the Randolph family, *d.* 1332; RANDOLPH, JOHN, third EARL, *d.* 1346; STEWART, JAMES, first EARL of the Stewart family, 1499 ?–1544; STEWART, JAMES, first EARL of a new creation, 1531 ?–1570, the regent; STEWART, JAMES, second EARL, *d.* 1592; STEWART, ALEXANDER, fourth EARL, *d.* 1701.]

MURRAY, ADAM (*d.* 1700), defender of Londonderry; raised troop of horse against Tyrconnel, 1688; leader of the no-surrender party, and chosen to command the horse; distinguished by his bravery and was badly wounded.
[xxxix. 343]

MURRAY, ALEXANDER (*d.* 1777), Jacobite; actively supported Sir George Vandeput, the anti-ministerial candidate at the Westminster election, 1750; tried by the House of Commons as the ringleader of a mob, and committed to Newgate, 1751; released after five months' imprisonment; went to France; recalled from exile, 1771.
[xxxix. 344]

MURRAY, ALEXANDER, LORD HENDERLAND (1736–1795), Scottish judge: called to the Scottish bar, 1758; solicitor-general for Scotland, 1775; lord of session and a commissioner of the court of justiciary, 1783.
[xxxix. 345]

MURRAY, ALEXANDER (1775–1813), linguist; taught himself Latin, Greek, Hebrew, French, German, and some Abyssinian; translated Drackenburg's German lectures on Roman authors; student at Edinburgh; studied the languages of Western Asia and North-east Africa and Lappish; wrote the biography and edited the works of Bruce the Abyssinian traveller; minister of Urr, 1806; translated an Ethiopic letter for George III, 1811; professor of oriental languages at Edinburgh, 1812; wrote 'History of European Languages,' edited by Dr. Scott, 1823.
[xxxix. 346]

MURRAY, AMELIA MATILDA (1795–1884), writer; daughter of Lord George Murray (1761–1803) [q. v.]; maid of honour to Queen Victoria, 1837–56; abolitionist; published 'Letters from the United States,' 1856, and 'Recollections from 1803–37,' 1868.
[xxxix. 347]

MURRAY or **MORAY**, SIR ANDREW (*d.* 1338), of Bothwell; warden of Scotland; led a rising, 1297; joined with Wallace in command of the Scottish raiders, 1297; elected warden by David II's adherents, 1332; opposed the English, 1334; relieved Kildrummie, 1335; again made warden, 1335; captured and sacked St. Andrews and marched to Carlisle, 1337; returned to invest Edinburgh; claimed the victory at Crichton, but raised the siege.
[xxxix. 348]

MURRAY, SIR ANDREW, first BARON BALVAIRD (1597 ?–1644), minister of Abdie; M.A. St. Andrews, 1618; presented to Abdie, 1622; knighted, 1633; created peer, 1641.
[xxxix. 349]

MURRAY, ANDREW (1812–1878), naturalist; abandoned law and took up natural science; F.R.S. Edinburgh, 1857; president of Edinburgh Botanical Society, 1858; secretary of the Royal Horticultural Society, 1860; F.L.S., 1861, and its scientific director, 1877; wrote on botany and entomology.
[xxxix. 349]

MURRAY, LORD CHARLES, first EARL OF DUNMORE (1660–1710), son of John Murray, first marquis of Atholl [q. v.]; lieutenant-colonel of Dalyell's regiment of horse, 1681; served in Flanders, 1684; created Earl of Dunmore, 1686; imprisoned at the revolution; privy councillor, 1703; examiner of public accounts, 1704; supported the union; governor of Blackness Castle, 1707.
[xxxix. 350]

MURRAY, LORD CHARLES (*d.* 1720), Jacobite; son of John Murray, first duke of Atholl [q. v.]; taken prisoner at Preston in the 1715 rebellion, but ultimately pardoned.
[xxxix. 351]

MURRAY, CHARLES (1754–1821), actor and dramatist; son of Sir John Murray of Broughton (1718–1777) [q. v.]; abandoned surgery and acted in York, Bath, Norwich, and elsewhere; came to Covent Garden, London, 1796; commended in *rôle* of dignified old man; wrote 'The Experiment,' 1779, and possibly the 'New Maid of the Oaks,' 1778.
[xxxix. 351]

MURRAY, SIR CHARLES AUGUSTUS (1806–1895), diplomatist and author; second son of George Murray, fifth earl of Dunmore (1762–1836); of Eton and Oriel College, Oxford; B.A. and fellow of All Souls College, Oxford, 1827; M.A., 1832; entered Lincoln's Inn, 1827; travelled in America, 1834, and published 'Travels in North America,' 1839; groom-in-waiting to Queen Victoria, 1838; master of household, 1838–44; secretary of legation at Naples, 1844; consul-general in Egypt, 1846–53; minister to Swiss confederation at Berne, 1853; envoy and minister plenipotentiary to court of Persia, 1854–9; charged by the grand vizier, Sadr Azim, with odious offences, on which, the charges not being withdrawn, war was declared by Great Britain, 1856; minister at court of Saxony, 1859; C.B., 1848; K.C.B., 1866; minister at Copenhagen, 1866, and subsequently at Lisbon till 1874; privy councillor, 1875.
[Suppl. iii. 213]

MURRAY, DANIEL (1768–1852), archbishop of Dublin; studied at Dublin and Salamanca; coadjutor to the archbishop of Dublin, 1809; succeeded to the see, 1823; corresponded with John Henry Newman [q. v.]
[xxxix. 352]

MURRAY, SIR DAVID (1567–1629), of Gorthy, poet; held various court appointments, 1600–15; received the estate of Gorthy from Charles I; published 'The Tragicall Death of Sophonisba,' and 'Cœlia,' 1611.
[xxxix. 352]

MURRAY, SIR DAVID, of Gospertie, BARON SCONE and afterwards VISCOUNT STORMONT (*d.* 1631), comptroller of Scotland and captain of the king's guard; brought up at the court of James VI; knighted and admitted privy councillor, 1599; comptroller of the royal revenues, 1599; provost of Perth, 1600; attended James VI of Scotland to England, 1603; invested with the lordship of Scone, 1605; James I's commissioner at the synods of Perth and Fife, 1607, and the conference at Falkland, 1609; re-chosen privy councillor and appointed justice of Fife, Kinross, and Perth, 1610; James I's commissioner at the general assembly at Perth, 1618, when sanction was given to the 'five articles'; created Viscount Stormont, 1621.
[xxxix. 353]

MURRAY, DAVID, second EARL OF MANSFIELD (1727–1796), diplomatist and statesman; succeeded his father as Viscount Stormont, 1748; attaché at the British embassy, Paris, 1751; envoy extraordinary to Saxony, 1756–9; privy councillor, 1763; envoy extraordinary to Austria, 1763–72; transferred to Paris, 1772; recalled, 1778; entered the cabinet as secretary of state for the southern department, 1779–82; succeeded his uncle William Murray [q. v.] as second Earl of Mansfield, 1793; president of the council in the coalition ministry, 1783, and again from 1794 to 1796.
[xxxix. 355]

MURRAY, ELIZABETH, COUNTESS OF DYSART and afterwards DUCHESS OF LAUDERDALE (*d.* 1697), succeeded her father, William Murray, first earl of Dysart [q. v.], 1650; her title confirmed by Charles II, 1670; married Sir Lionel Tollemache, 1647; married John Maitland, duke of Lauderdale [q. v.], 1672; a prominent beauty in the court of Charles II.
[xxxix. 356]

MURRAY, MRS. ELIZABETH LEIGH (*d.* 1892), daughter of Henry Lee (1765–1836) [q. v.]; married Henry Leigh Murray [q. v.], 1841; accompanied him to London, 1845, and became famous as a singer in domestic comedy.
[xxxix. 368]

MURRAY, GASTON (1826–1889), his real name Garstin Parker Wilson; brother of Henry Leigh Murray [q. v.]; essayed his brother's parts.
[xxxix. 368]

MURRAY, MRS. GASTON (*d.* 1891), actress; *née* Hughes; married Gaston Murray [q. v.], the actor.
[xxxix. 368]

MURRAY, LORD GEORGE (1700 ?–1760), Jacobite general; son of John Murray, first duke of Atholl [q. v.]; fought in the rebellion of 1715 and the highland expedition, 1719; acquired a high reputation in the Sardinian army; joined Prince Charles Edward, 1745; made lieutenant-general; advanced from Edinburgh and defeated Sir John Cope [q. v.] at Prestonpans, September 1745; marched into England and besieged Carlisle, which surrendered 18 Nov.; during the retreat from Derby attacked Cumberland's dragoons and successfully checked his pursuit of Prince Charles Edward; led the right wing at Falkirk and completely routed Hawley's forces, 17 Jan. 1746; after the highlanders' retreat to Inverness, attempted to free the Atholl country and Blair Castle from the royal troops, but was recalled to Inverness; averse to making a stand at Culloden; commanded the right wing at the battle, 1746; retired to France, failing to persuade Prince Charles Edward to remain in Scotland; travelled on the continent and died at Medenblik in Holland.
[xxxix. 357]

MURRAY, LORD GEORGE (1761–1803), bishop of St. David's; son of John Murray, third duke of Atholl [q. v.]; B.A. New College, Oxford, 1782; D.D. by diploma, 1800; archdeacon of Man, 1787; director of the telegraph at the admiralty, 1796; consecrated bishop of St. David's, 1801. [xxxix. 361]

MURRAY, SIR GEORGE (1759–1819), vice-admiral; entered navy, 1772; lieutenant, 1778; wrecked on the Breton coast; prisoner in France till 1781; served in East Indies; took part in battle off Cape St. Vincent, 1797; wrecked off the Scilly islands, 1798, but acquitted by court-martial; distinguished himself at Copenhagen, 1801; captain of the fleet to Nelson, 1803–5; vice-admiral, 1809; K.C.B., 1815. [xxxix. 361]

MURRAY, SIR GEORGE (1772–1846), general and statesman; of Edinburgh University; entered the army, 1789; served in Flanders; lieutenant-colonel, 1799; served in Egypt, the West Indies, 1802, and Ireland, 1804; quartermaster-general in the Peninsular war; major-general, 1812; K.C.B., 1813; lieutenant-general and governor of Canada, 1814; with the army of Flanders after Waterloo, 1815–18; governor of the Royal Military College at Sandhurst, 1819–24; M.P., Perth, 1823; commander-in-chief in Ireland, 1825–8; privy councillor and colonial secretary, 1828–30; master-general of the ordnance; general, 1841; edited Marlborough's despatches, 1845. [xxxix. 363]

MURRAY, GEORGE (1784–1860), bishop; son of Lord George Murray (1761–1803) [q. v.]; M.A. Christ Church, Oxford, 1810; D.D. by diploma, 1814; archdeacon of Man, 1808; bishop of Sodor and Man, 1814; bishop of Rochester, 1827–54; dean of Worcester, 1828–54. [xxxix. 361]

MURRAY, SIR GIDEON, LORD ELIBANK (d. 1621), deputy-treasurer and lord of session; imprisoned for killing a man in a quarrel, 1586; justiciary for the borders, 1603; knighted, 1605; commissioner for establishing peace on the borders, 1607; privy councillor and commissioner of the exchequer, 1610; M.P. Selkirkshire, 1612; treasurer depute, 1612; lord of session as Lord Elibank, 1613; held in high esteem by James I; committed suicide in a fit of insanity caused by an accusation of malversation as treasurer depute. [xxxix. 364]

MURRAY, GRENVILLE (1824–1881), journalist; his full name Eustace Clare Grenville Murray; sent as attaché to Vienna, 1851; correspondent to the 'Morning Post,' 1851; vice-consul at Mitylene, 1852; consul-general at Odessa, 1855–68; publicly horsewhipped by Lord Carrington, 1869; published several novels, but was more successful in satirical essays and sketches for the London and American press; died at Passy. [xxxix. 366]

MURRAY, HENRY LEIGH (1820–1870), actor; his original name Wilson; made his début under Hooper on the York circuit, 1839; acted in Scotland; appeared in London at the Princess's Theatre, 1845; acted with Macready, 1846, and Miss Faucit (Lady Martin), 1848; became stage-manager at the Olympic Theatre, London, under Spicer, Davidson, and William Farren; a painstaking and natural actor. [xxxix. 367]

MURRAY, HUGH (1779–1846), geographer; clerk in the Edinburgh excise office; F.R.S. Edinburgh, 1814; editor of the 'Scots Magazine'; F.R.G.S.; brought out 'Encyclopædia of Geography,' 1834, to which Hooker, Wallace, and Swainston contributed. [xxxix. 368]

MURRAY, JAMES (d. 1596), of Pardovis; opponent of the Earl of Bothwell (d. 1583); brother of Sir William Murray of Tullibardine [q. v.]; helped Bothwell to return to Scotland, 1564, but accused him of Darnley's murder by placards affixed on the Tolbooth, Edinburgh; escaped arrest, offered proofs of Bothwell's guilt and challenged him. [xxxix. 369]

MURRAY, SIR JAMES, LORD PHILIPHAUGH (1655–1708), lord register of Scotland; succeeded his father as sheriff of Selkirk; accused of remissness in proceeding against conventicles and deprived, 1681; concerned in the Rye House plot, 1683; confessed and witnessed against the chief contrivers, 1684 and 1685; lord of session as Lord Philiphaugh, 1689; political associate of Queensberry; clerk-register, 1702–4 and 1705–8. [xxxix. 370]

MURRAY, JAMES (1702–1758), presbyterian divine; published 'Alethia,' an ethical work, 1747. [xxxix. 371]

MURRAY, JAMES, second DUKE OF ATHOLL (1690?–1764), lord privy seal; son of John Murray, first duke of Atholl [q. v.]; succeeded his father, 1724, in consequence of the attainder of his elder brother William, marquis of Tullibardine [q. v.]; lord privy seal, 1733–63; keeper of the great seal and lord justice general, 1763. [xxxix. 371]

MURRAY, JAMES (1732–1782), author of 'Sermons to Asses'; studied at Edinburgh; minister at Alnwick, 1761; removed to Newcastle-on-Tyne, 1764; opposed the catholic relief bill and the American war, of which he wrote a history, 1778; published, besides his 'Sermons to Asses,' 1768, various theological works. [xxxix. 372]

MURRAY, JAMES (1719?–1794), general; governor of Quebec and Minorca; brother of Alexander Murray (d. 1777) [q. v.]; entered the army, c. 1728; served in West Indies, Flanders, and Brittany; major, 1749; lieutenant-colonel, 1751; distinguished himself at Louisburg, 1758, and in the expedition against Quebec, 1759; left in command of Quebec after its surrender, 1759; defended Quebec against the French, who retired disheartened to Montreal, 1760; governor of Quebec, 1760; major-general, 1762; governor of Canada, 1763–6, where his efforts to alleviate discontent met with only partial success; lieutenant-general, 1772; governor of Minorca, 1774; Sir William Draper [q. v.] sent as his lieutenant-governor when war broke out with Spain, 1779; was obliged to capitulate (1782) after Minorca was blockaded by De Crillon, and sickness broke out in the garrison; acquitted by court-martial (1783) of charges brought against him by Sir William Draper; general, 1783. [xxxix. 373]

MURRAY (afterwards **MURRAY - PULTENEY**), SIR JAMES, seventh baronet of Clermont, Fifeshire (1751?–1811), general; entered the army, 1771; succeeded to baronetcy, 1771; served in America and the West Indies; lieutenant-colonel, 1780; aide-de-camp to the king, 1789; major-general, 1790; assumed the name Pulteney on his marriage with Henrietta Laura Pulteney, baroness Bath, 1794; major-general, 1798; lieutenant-general, 1799; accompanied Abercromby to Holland; temporarily occupied the heights of Ferrol, 1800; M.P. Weymouth, 1790–1811; died from the effects of the bursting of a powder-flask. [xxxix. 376]

MURRAY, JAMES (1831–1863), architect; executed several works with Edward Welby Pugin [q. v.]; published two works on architecture. [xxxix. 377]

MURRAY, SIR JAMES (1788–1871), discoverer of fluid magnesia; M.D. Edinburgh, 1829; published 'Heat and Humidity,' 1829; resident physician to the lord-lieutenant of Ireland; knighted; hon. M.D. Dublin, 1832; inspector of anatomy in Dublin; established manufactory for fluid magnesia; suggested electricity as a curative agent; published 'Observations on Fluid Magnesia,' 1840. [xxxix. 378]

MURRAY, JOHN (d. 1510), laird of Falahill; sheriff of Selkirk, 1501; according to the ballad held possession of Ettrick Forest, but finally swore fealty on being made hereditary sheriff; slain by Andrew Ker. [xxxix. 378]

MURRAY or **MORAY**, JOHN (1575?–1632), Scottish divine; brother of Sir David Murray of Gorthy [q. v.]; M.A. Edinburgh, 1595; opposed episcopacy, and in consequence of an 'impertinent sermon' on Galatians iii. 1 was imprisoned at Edinburgh, 1608–9; minister at Dunfermline, 1614; summoned to answer for nonconformity, 1621; ordered to confine himself within his native parish of Fowlis Wester, 1624. [xxxix. 379]

MURRAY, JOHN, first EARL OF ANNANDALE (d. 1640), accompanied James VI to England, 1603; keeper of the privy purse, received many grants of land, those in Scotland being erected into the earldom of Annandale, 1625; frequently engaged on judicial border commission. [xxxix. 380]

MURRAY, JOHN, second EARL and first MARQUIS OF ATHOLL (1635?–1703), royalist; supported a highland rising, 1653; exempted from the Act of Grace, 1654; privy councillor, 1660; sheriff of Fifeshire, 1660; justice-general of Scotland, 1670–8; succeeded as Earl of Tullibardine, 1670; created Marquis of Atholl, 1676; severed himself from Lauderdale on account of the excesses committed in the western raid, 1678; lord-lieutenant of Argyll, 1684; captured the Earl of Argyll, 1685; irresolute at the revolution, but probably had no desire to further the interests of William of Orange, and his clan declared for Dundee during his absence at Bath ; concerned in intrigues, 1691 ; subsequently appointed to negotiate the pacification of the highlands. [xxxix. 380]

MURRAY, JOHN, second MARQUIS and first DUKE OF ATHOLL (1659/60–1724), son of John Murray, first marquis of Atholl [q. v.]; unsuccessfully endeavoured to prevent clan joining Dundee during his father's absence, 1689 ; a secretary of state for Scotland, 1696–8 ; created Earl of Tullibardine, 1696 ; became privy councillor, lord privy seal, and Duke of Atholl, 1703 ; exasperated at his treatment by the whigs in connection with the Queensberry plot ; strongly opposed the union, 1705, and was suspected of Jacobite sympathies ; proclaimed George I at Perth, 1714, but was deprived nevertheless of his office of lord privy seal ; sided with the government in the 1715 rebellion, and displayed great activity in collecting arms from the rebels ; captured Rob Roy Macgregor, 1717. [xxxix. 383]

MURRAY, JOHN, third DUKE OF ATHOLL (1729–1774), son of Lord George Murray (1700 ?–1760) [q. v.]; successfully claimed the dukedom on the death of his uncle, second Duke of Atholl, 1764, whose daughter he had married ; representative peer, 1764 and 1768 ; sold the sovereignty of the Isle of Man to the treasury, 1765 ; K.T., 1767. [xxxix. 385]

MURRAY, SIR JOHN, baronet (1718–1777), of Broughton, secretary to Prince Charles Edward during the rebellion of 1745 ; educated at Edinburgh University ; visited Prince Charles Edward in Rome, 1742, and Paris, 1743 ; joined Prince Charles Edward on his arrival and acted as his secretary ; too ill to be present at Culloden, but was arrested at Polmood and sent to London, where he turned king's evidence, and was one of the chief witnesses against Simon Fraser, twelfth lord Lovat ; succeeded to baronetcy, 1770 ; a client of Sir Walter Scott's father. [xxxix. 386]

MURRAY, LORD JOHN (1711–1787), of Banner Cross, Yorkshire, general ; son of John Murray, first duke of Atholl [q. v.]; entered army, 1727 ; colonel of Black Watch, 1745–87 ; major-general, 1755 ; lieutenant-general, 1758 ; general, 1770 ; M.P., Perth, 1741, 1747, and 1754 ; died in Paris. [xxxix. 387]

MURRAY, JOHN, fourth EARL OF DUNMORE (1732–1809), succeeded to peerage, 1756 ; governor of New York and Virginia, 1770 ; nearly provoked armed resistance by his removal of some powder to a man-of-war, 1775 ; withdrew to a warship during a riot, 1775 ; returned to England, 1776 ; governor of the Bahama islands, 1787. [xxxix. 388]

MURRAY, JOHN (d. 1820), chemist and physicist ; M.D. St. Andrews, 1814 ; lectured at Edinburgh on chemistry, materia medica, and pharmacy, on which he wrote ; F.R.C.P. Edinburgh ; F.R.S. Edinburgh ; F.G.S. [xxxix. 388]

MURRAY, SIR JOHN, eighth baronet of Clermont (1768 ?–1827), general ; half-brother of Sir James Murray (1751 ?–1811) [q. v.]; entered the army, 1788 ; captain, 1793 ; lieutenant-colonel, 1794 ; commanded in the Red Sea, 1798–1800 ; quartermaster-general of the Indian army, 1801–5 ; major-general, 1805 ; served in Sweden and Portugal ; succeeded to baronetcy, 1811 ; lieutenant-general, 1812 ; appointed to the army in Sicily, 1812 ; court-martialled, after long delay (1815), for sacrificing stores and guns at Tarragona, 1813, and neglecting Wellington's instructions ; acquitted with an admonition ; general, 1825 ; died at Frankfort-on-Maine. [xxxix. 389]

MURRAY, JOHN (1778–1843), publisher ; London agent for Constable of Edinburgh, 1803, sharing in 'Marmion' and other joint publications (business relations broken off, 1808, and though resumed, 1810, finally terminated, 1813) ; started 'Quarterly Review' on tory principles, with Gifford as editor, 1809, Scott and Southey being among the contributors ; moved to Albemarle Street, 1812, and became acquainted with Byron ; published for Jane Austen, Crabbe, Lyell, Borrow, and many others ; published Mrs. Mariana Starke's 'Guide for Travellers on the Continent,' 1820, which led to the publication of Murray's guide-books ; involved in the controversy about Byron's 'Memoirs' which resulted in their destruction in 1824 ; Murray's project of 'The Representative,' a daily newspaper, suggested by Disraeli, proved a failure, and was discontinued after six months, 1826. His

chief literary advisers were Lockhart, who became editor of the 'Quarterly' in 1824, Milman, Barrow, and Lady Calcott. [xxxix. 390]

MURRAY, JOHN (1786 ?–1851), scientific writer and lecturer ; became well known as a scientific lecturer at mechanics' institutions ; exhibited at his lectures an experimental safety-lamp ; F.L.S., 1819 ; F.S.A., 1822 ; F.G.S., 1823 ; F.H.S., 1824 ; contributed to scientific journals and periodicals. [xxxix. 394]

MURRAY, JOHN (1798–1873), man of science ; son of John Murray (d. 1820) [q. v.]; edited his father's works ; died in Melbourne. [xxxix. 389]

MURRAY, JOHN (1808–1892), publisher ; son of John Murray (1778–1843) [q v.]; of Charterhouse School and Edinburgh University ; M.A., 1827 ; present when Scott acknowledged the authorship of the 'Waverley Novels,' 1827 ; travelled on the continent, 1829–32 ; wrote guide-books on Holland, France, South Germany, and Switzerland ; published for Layard, Grote, Dr. (Sir William) Smith, Milman, Darwin, Dean Stanley, Dr. Smiles, and many others ; inaugurated series of illustrated books of travel by Mrs. Bird, Mr. Whymper, and others. [xxxix. 394]

MURRAY, SIR JOHN ARCHIBALD, LORD MURRAY (1779–1859), Scottish judge ; son of Alexander Murray, lord Henderland [q. v.]; contributed to the 'Edinburgh Review' from its commencement ; promoted the (1832) reform bill ; M.P., Leith, 1832 ; lord advocate, 1835 ; knighted and appointed judge as Lord Murray, 1839. [xxxix. 396]

MURRAY, JOHN FISHER (1811–1865), Irish poet and humorist ; son of Sir James Murray (1788–1871) [q. v.]; M.A. Trinity College, Dublin, 1832 ; contributed satirical sketches to 'Blackwood's Magazine,' the 'Nation,' and the 'United Irishman.' [xxxix. 397]

MURRAY, MRS. LEIGH (d. 1892). [See MURRAY, MRS. ELIZABETH LEIGH.]

MURRAY, LINDLEY (1745–1826), grammarian ; born in Pennsylvania ; called to the bar at New York, where he practised ; settled in England, 1784 ; published religious works and an 'English Grammar,' 1795, 'Reader,' 1799, and 'Spelling Book,' 1804, which went through many editions, and were used in schools to the exclusion of any others ; introduced system into grammar ; styled the 'father of English grammar.' [xxxix. 397]

MURRAY, MATTHEW (1765–1826), engineer ; worked at Marshall's, Leeds, 1789–95, and made many improvements in flax-spinning ; set up in partnership with Fenton and Wood at Leeds, 1795 ; patented improvements in the steam-engine, notably the 'short D-slide valve' ; built four railway engines, 1812–13, and fitted up a steamboat, 1813. [xxxix. 398]

MURRAY, MUNGO (d. 1770), author of a treatise on shipbuilding, 1754 ; appointed to the Magnanime as schoolmaster, 1758–62 ; published 'Rudiments of Navigation,' 1760. [xxxix. 399]

MURRAY, PATRICK, fifth BARON ELIBANK (1703–1778), brother of James Murray (1719–1794) [q. v.]; advocate, 1722 ; lieutenant-colonel in the army ; succeeded his father, 1736 ; wrote on the currency, entails, and the state of the Scottish peerage. [xxxix. 400]

MURRAY, PATRICK ALOYSIUS (1811–1882), Roman catholic theologian ; professor of belles-lettres at Maynooth, 1838, of theology, 1841–82 ; published 'Tractatus de Ecclesiâ Christi,' 1860–6. [xxxix. 400]

MURRAY or **MORAY**, SIR ROBERT (d. 1673), one of the founders of the Royal Society ; served in the French army ; knighted by Charles I, 1643 ; negotiated between France and Scotland on Charles's behalf, and unsuccessfully planned his escape from Newcastle, 1646 ; joined Charles II in Paris, 1654, after the collapse of the highland rising ; lord of exchequer for Scotland and deputy-secretary, 1663 ; assisted in the foundation of the Royal Society, 1661 ; learned in geology, chemistry, and natural history. [xxxix. 401]

MURRAY, ROBERT (1635–1725 ?), writer on trade ; took up his freedom in the Clothworkers' Company, 1660 ; invented ruled copybooks ; originated the idea of penny post in London, 1681 ; possibly clerk to the Irish revenue commissioners ; appointed paymaster of the 1714 lottery ; published various proposals for the advancement and improvement of trade and raising of revenue. [xxxix. 402]

MURRAY, the HON. MRS. SARAH (1744-1811). [See AUST.]

MURRAY, SIR TERENCE AUBREY (1810-1873), Australian politician; went to New South Wales, 1827; represented Murray in the legislature, 1843-56, and Argyle, 1856-62; appointed to the upper house, 1862; secretary for lands and works, 1856 and 1857-8; speaker, 1860-73; knighted, 1869. [xxxix. 403]

MURRAY, THOMAS (1564-1623), provost of Eton; tutor to Charles, duke of York, afterwards Charles I; secretary to Charles when Prince of Wales, 1617; provost of Eton, 1622. [xxxix. 404]

MURRAY, SIR THOMAS (1630?-1684), of Glendoick, clerk-register; advocate, 1661; lord clerk-register, 1662-81; senator, with the title of Lord Glendoick, 1674; created baronet, 1676; received licence to print the statutes, 1679. [xxxix. 404]

MURRAY or **MURREY**, THOMAS (1663-1734), portrait-painter; painted faces only, others supplying the accessories. [xxxix. 405]

MURRAY, THOMAS (1792-1872), printer and miscellaneous writer; intimate with Carlyle and Alexander Murray at Edinburgh; established a printing business in Edinburgh, 1841; published biographical works; contributed to 'Brewster's Cyclopædia.' [xxxix. 405]

MURRAY, SIR WILLIAM (d. 1583), of Tullibardine, comptroller of Scotland; supported the marriage of Mary Queen of Scots with Darnley; comptroller and privy councillor, 1565; joined the confederate lords after the queen's marriage to Bothwell; attended the coronation of the young king James VI; was ready to help the queen after Bothwell's flight, and (1569) voted for her divorce; joint-governor of the young king James VI, 1572; joined conspiracy against Morton, 1578. [xxxix. 406]

MURRAY, WILLIAM, first EARL OF DYSART (1600?-1651), nephew of Thomas Murray (1564-1623) [q. v.]; educated with Charles, prince of Wales; gentleman of his bedchamber, 1626; negotiated between Charles I and the leading covenanters; created Earl of Dysart, 1643; on the outbreak of civil war negotiated for the king with Scotland, foreign powers, and the pope; arrested as a spy, 1646; joined Charles at Newcastle on his release; went to Charles II at the Hague, 1649; accused by Burnet of duplicity. [xxxix. 407]

MURRAY, LORD WILLIAM, second BARON NAIRNE (d. 1724). [See NAIRNE, WILLIAM.]

MURRAY, WILLIAM, MARQUIS OF TULLIBARDINE (d. 1746), son of John Murray, first duke of Atholl [q. v.]; attainted for taking part in the 1715 rebellion; commanded in the highland expedition, 1719, and in 1745; gained a large number of Atholl men and accompanied the Pretender into England; delivered himself up after the defeat at Culloden, 1746; died in the Tower of London. [xxxix. 408]

MURRAY, WILLIAM, first EARL OF MANSFIELD (1705-1793), judge; M.A. Christ Church, Oxford, 1730; barrister, Lincoln's Inn, 1730; K.C., 1742; M.P., Boroughbridge, 1742; solicitor-general, 1742; proved himself an able defender of the government; attorney-general, 1754; serjeant-at-law, 1756; privy councillor, 1756; lord chief-justice, 1756; created Baron Mansfield of Mansfield, 1756; reversed Wilkes's outlawry on account of a technical flaw, discovered by himself, and substituted a sentence of fine and imprisonment, 1768; gained more and more unpopularity over the cases of seditious libel arising out of Junius's 'Letter to the King,' 1770, and the case of the dean of St. Asaph, 1784, holding in both cases that if the jury were satisfied of the fact of publication or sale they ought to find for the crown, as the question of libel or no libel was matter of law for the court to decide (this view was technically correct until Fox's Libel Act, 1792); created Earl of Mansfield, 1776; his house sacked and burned during the Gordon riots, 1780; he resigned office, 1788; instrumental in the improvement of mercantile law, the law of evidence, and the procedure of courts; termed by Macaulay 'the father of modern toryism.' As a parliamentary debater he was second only to Chatham, but as a statesman his fame is tarnished by his adhesion to the policy of coercing America. [xxxix. 409]

MURRAY, WILLIAM HENRY (1790-1852), actor and manager; son of Charles Murray [q. v.]; played minor parts at Covent Garden, London, 1803-4; appeared in Edinburgh, 1809; took up the management of the Theatre Royal, Edinburgh, on the death of his brother-in-law, Henry Siddons, 1815, after which Mrs. Siddons reappeared, and Miss O'Neill, Kemble, Charles Mathews, Kean, Yates, and Mackay were engaged; acquired both theatres in Edinburgh, and was for one year in partnership with Yates; retired, 1848; a good actor in comedy and 'character' parts; wrote many dramas for a temporary purpose and without literary aim. [xxxix. 415]

MURRELL, JOHN (fl. 1630), writer on cookery; improved his knowledge of his art by foreign travel; published two books on cookery, which passed through seven editions. [xxxix. 417]

MUSCHAMP, GEOFFREY DE (d. 1208). [See GEOFFREY.]

MUSGRAVE, SIR ANTHONY (1828-1888), administrator; student at the Inner Temple, 1851; governor of Newfoundland, 1864, of British Columbia, 1869; lieutenant-governor of Natal, 1872; governor of South Australia, 1873, of Jamaica, 1877, of Queensland, 1888; K.C.M.G., 1875; published 'Studies in Political Economy,' 1875. [xxxix. 418]

MUSGRAVE, SIR CHRISTOPHER, fourth baronet (1632?-1704), politician; son of Sir Philip Musgrave [q. v.]; B.A. Queen's College, Oxford, 1651; student of Gray's Inn, 1654; a captain in Carlisle garrison; mayor of Carlisle, 1672; governor of Carlisle Castle, 1677; lieutenant-general of ordnance, 1681-7; M.P., Carlisle, 1661-90, Westmoreland, 1690-5, 1700-1, and 1702-4, Appleby, 1695-8, Oxford University, 1698-1700, Totnes, 1701-2; fiercely opposed Sir John Lowther in parliamentary contest and was well rewarded for supporting the crown; a teller of the exchequer, 1702. [xxxix. 418]

MUSGRAVE, GEORGE MUSGRAVE (1798-1883), divine and topographer; M.A. Brasenose College, Oxford, 1822; incumbent of Bexwell, 1835-8, of Borden, 1838-54; travelled, principally in France; author of 'Cautions to Travellers,' 1863, and of seven volumes narrating his rambles; published instructive books for his parishioners. [xxxix. 419]

MUSGRAVE, JOHN (fl. 1654), pamphleteer; captain in parliamentary army; wrote three virulent pamphlets during his imprisonment for contempt of court, 1644-7; made various attempts to induce parliament to redress his grievances, and charged the Cumberland commissioners with disaffection; published apologetic pamphlets. [xxxix. 420]

MUSGRAVE, SIR PHILIP, second baronet (1607-1678), royalist; M.P., Westmoreland, 1640; governor of Carlisle, 1642; taken prisoner at Rowton Heath, 1644; intrigued for the king with the Scots; capitulated at Appleby, 1648; withdrew to the Isle of Man, 1649; engaged in royalist conspiracies, 1653, 1655, and 1659; again governor of Carlisle, 1660; M.P. for Westmoreland in Charles II's Long parliament. [xxxix. 421]

MUSGRAVE, SIR RICHARD, first baronet (1757?-1818), Irish political writer; M.P., Lismore, 1778; created baronet, 1782; wrote on contemporary political events; attached to the English connection, but opposed to the Act of Union. [xxxix. 422]

MUSGRAVE, SAMUEL (1732-1780), physician and classical scholar; B.A. Corpus Christi College, Oxford, 1754; M.A., 1756; Radcliffe travelling fellow, 1754; went to Holland and France; F.R.S., 1760; M.D. Leyden, 1763; published pamphlets accusing three persons of rank of having sold the peace of 1763 to the French; M.D. Oxford, 1775; F.R.C.P., 1777; Gulstonian lecturer and censor, 1779; had few superiors as a Greek scholar; published medical works and edited and collated various plays of Euripides; his notes on Sophocles bought by Oxford University after his death and inserted in the 1800 edition. [xxxix. 423]

MUSGRAVE, THOMAS, BARON MUSGRAVE (d. 1384), summoned to parliament, 1341-4 and 1350-73; warden of Berwick, 1373-8; taken prisoner at Melrose, 1377; released, 1378, and his ransom paid, 1382. [xxxix. 425]

MUSGRAVE, SIR THOMAS (1737-1812), general; entered the army, 1754; lieutenant, 1756; major, 1775; lieutenant-colonel, 1776; distinguished himself at Philadelphia, 1777; appointed colonel of the 'Hindostan' regiment, 1787; served on the staff at Madras; lieutenant-general, 1797; general, 1802. [xxxix. 425]

MUSGRAVE, THOMAS (1788–1860), successively bishop of Hereford and archbishop of York; fellow, Trinity College, Cambridge, 1812; M.A., 1813; professor of Arabic, 1821; dean of Bristol and bishop of Hereford, 1837–47; archbishop of York, 1847–60.   [xxxix. 426]

MUSGRAVE, WILLIAM (1655 ?–1721), physician and antiquary; fellow of New College, Oxford, 1677–92; B.C.L., 1682; M.D., 1689; F.R.S., 1684; secretary of the Royal Society, 1685; F.R.C.P., 1692; practised at Exeter; published three treatises on arthritis, 1703, 1707, 1776, and four volumes of 'Antiquitates Britanno-Belgicæ,' 1719–1720.   [xxxix. 427]

MUSH, JOHN (1552–1617), Roman catholic divine; educated at Douay and Rome; opposed George Blackwell's appointment as archpriest, and urged the grievances of the secular clergy at Rome, 1602; assistant to the archpriest; spiritual director of Mrs. Margaret Clitheroe, whose biography he wrote, 1586; published defence of the secular clergy in their conflicts with the jesuits and Blackwell, 1601.   [xxxix. 428]

MUSHET, DAVID (1772–1847), metallurgist; authority on iron and steel; discovered the economic value of black-band ironstone, 1801; his chief invention the preparation of steel from bar-iron by a direct process, 1800; wrote papers on iron and steel.   [xxxix. 429]

MUSHET, ROBERT (1782–1828), officer of the royal mint, brother of David Mushet [q. v.]; entered the mint, 1804; wrote and gave evidence to a parliamentary committee on currency questions, 1819.   [xxxix. 430]

MUSHET, ROBERT (1811–1871), officer of the royal mint, nephew of David and Robert Mushet (1782–1828) [q. v.]; senior clerk and melter at the mint, 1851; wrote on symbols and coinage.   [xxxix. 430]

MUSHET, ROBERT FORESTER (1811–1891), metallurgist; son of David Mushet [q. v.]; discovered the value of spiegeleisen in restoring the quality of 'burnt iron,' which discovery he applied to the Bessemer process and produced cast steel, but neglected to secure his patent rights; invented 'special steel' for engineers' tools, 1870; Sir Henry Bessemer [q. v.] paid Mushet an annuity, but steadily refused him any royalty; Mushet stated his own case in the 'Bessemer-Mushet Process,' 1883.
   [xxxix. 430]

MUSHET, WILLIAM (1716–1792), physician; M.D. King's College, Cambridge, 1746; F.R.C.P., 1749; Gulstonian lecturer, 1751; physician in chief to the forces; fought at Minden, 1759.   [xxxix. 432]

MUSKERRY, VISCOUNT. [See MACCARTHY, ROBERT, d. 1769.]

MUSKERRY, LORD OF. [See MACCARTHY, CORMAC LAIDHIR OGE, d. 1536.]

MUSKET, alias FISHER, GEORGE (1583–1645), Roman catholic divine; converted to Roman catholicism, 1597; educated at Douay and Rome; missioner in England, 1608; held a disputation with Dr. Daniel Featley and Dr. Thomas Goad, 1621; imprisoned under Charles I; chosen president of the English College at Douay, 1640; released and banished, 1641; took up duties at Douay, 1641; possibly wrote 'The Bishop of London, his Legacy,' 1624.   [xxxix. 432]

MUSPRATT, JAMES (1793–1886), founder of the alkali industry in Lancashire; apprenticed to a wholesale chemist; went to Spain; enlisted as a midshipman, 1812, but deserted, 1814; started Leblanc soda works in Liverpool, 1823, opening other works in St. Helens, Widnes, and Flint; helped to found the Liverpool Institute.   [xxxix. 433]

MUSPRATT, JAMES SHERIDAN (1821–1871), chemist; son of James Muspratt [q. v.]; entered Liebig's laboratory, 1843; founded the Liverpool College of Chemistry, 1848; partner in his father's business, 1857; edited a dictionary of chemistry, 1854–60. [xxxix. 434]

MUSS, CHARLES (1779–1824), enamel and glass painter; copied the works of the old masters.
   [xxxix. 434]

MUSTERS, GEORGE CHAWORTH (1841–1879), 'King of Patagonia,' commander, royal navy; born at Naples; entered navy, 1854; lieutenant, 1861; travelled from Magellan Straits to the Rio Negro with a horde of Patagonian aborigines; published an account of the

experience, 1873; visited Vancouver's Island, British Columbia, and Bolivia.   [xxxix. 435]

MUTFORD, JOHN DE (d. 1329), judge; justice for ten counties, 1306; a justice of common pleas, 1316.   [xxxix. 436]

MUTRIE, ANNIE FERAY (1826–1893), artist; sister of Martha Darley Mutrie [q. v.]; exhibited paintings of flowers and fruit at the Royal Academy, 1851–82.   [xxxix. 436]

MUTRIE, MARTHA DARLEY (1824–1885), artist; sister of Annie Feray Mutrie [q. v.]; exhibited paintings of flowers and fruit at Manchester and the Royal Academy, 1853–78.   [xxxix. 436]

MWYNFAWR (d. 665 ?). [See MORGAN MWYNFAWR.]

MYCHELBOURNE. [See MICHELBORNE.]

MYCHELL, JOHN (fl. 1556). [See MITCHELL.]

MYDDELTON. [See also MIDDLETON.]

MYDDELTON or **MIDDLETON**, SIR HUGH, first baronet (1560 ?–1631), projector of New River; brother of Sir Thomas Myddelton (1550–1631) [q. v.] and of William Myddelton [q. v.]; traded as a goldsmith, banker, and clothmaker; alderman of Denbigh, 1597; M.P., Denbigh, 1603, 1614, 1620, 1623, 1625, and 1628; the London corporation having obtained authority from parliament to bring in a stream from Chadwell and Amwell, offered to execute the work; compelled by the opposition and demands of the landlords to apply to James I for money, on which James paid half the cost on condition of receiving half the profits (the canal, which was about thirty-eight miles long, ten feet wide, and four feet deep, completed, 1613); obtained large profits from some lead and silver mines in Cardiganshire, 1617; began reclaiming Brading harbour, 1620; created baronet, 1622.   [xxxix. 436]

MYDDELTON or **MIDDLETON**, JANE (1645–1692), 'the great beauty of Charles II's time'; daughter of Sir Robert Needham; married to Charles Myddelton, 1660; attracted many lovers, including the Chevalier de Grammont, Ralph, duke of Montagu, the Duke of York, and Edmund Waller; menaced the supremacy of the Countess of Castlemaine, 1665; received pension from James II.   [xxxix. 439]

MYDDELTON or **MIDDLETON**, SIR THOMAS (1550–1631), lord mayor of London; brother of Sir Hugh Myddelton [q. v.]; admitted to the Grocers' Company, 1582; M.P. for Merionethshire, 1597–8, for the city of London, 1624–6; original member of the East India Company, 1600, the New River Company, 1613, and member of the Virginia Company, 1623; alderman, sheriff, and knighted, 1603; lord mayor, 1613.   [xxxix. 440]

MYDDELTON, SIR THOMAS (1586–1666), parliamentarian; son of Sir Thomas Myddelton [q. v.]; of Queen's College, Oxford; student of Gray's Inn, 1607; knighted, 1617; M.P., Weymouth, 1624–5, and Denbigh, 1625 and 1640–8; was appointed (1643) sergeant-major-general for North Wales, but after taking several strongholds hastily retreated before Irish reinforcements; finally crushed the royalists of North Wales at Montgomery, 1644; took up arms in behalf of Charles II, 1659, but was defeated by Lambert.   [xxxix. 441]

MYDDELTON, WILLIAM (1556 ?–1621), Welsh poet and seaman; brother of Sir Hugh Myddelton [q. v.]; served under Cumberland off Portugal, 1591; sent to the Azores to warn Lord Thomas Howard of the impending Spanish attack, 1591; wrote on Welsh prosody, 1593, and published a metrical version of the Psalms, 1603; died in Antwerp.   [xxxix. 443]

MYERS, FREDERIC (1811–1851), author and divine; son of Thomas Myers [q. v.]; B.A. Clare Hall, Cambridge, 1833; fellow; perpetual curate of St. John's, Keswick, 1838; published 'Catholic Thoughts,' 1834–48, and sermons and 'Lectures on Great Men,' 1848.   [xxxix. 444]

MYERS, FREDERIC WILLIAM HENRY (1843–1901), poet and essayist; son of Frederic Myers [q. v.]; educated at Cheltenham, where he displayed a remarkable taste for poetry; first minor scholar of Trinity College, Cambridge, 1860; B.A., 1864; fellow, 1865; classical lecturer, 1865–9; on education department's permanent staff of school inspectors, 1872–1900; published, 1867–82, several volumes of poems including 'St. Paul,' 1867;

his 'Essays Classical and Modern,' published, 1883; contributed monograph (1881) on Wordsworth to the 'English Men of Letters' series, and wrote on Shelley, 1880, for Ward's 'English Poets'; began to give much attention to the phenomena of mesmerism and spiritualism, c. 1870; one of the founders of the Society for Psychical Research, 1882; joint-author of 'Phantasms of the Living.' 1886, which embodied the first considerable results of the society's labours; contributed to the society's Proceedings' on the 'Subliminal Self.'   [Suppl. iii. 215]

MYERS, THOMAS (1774–1834), mathematician and geographer; professor at Woolwich, 1806; wrote on geography, mathematics, and astronomy. [xxxix. 445]

MYKELFELD, MAKELSFELD, MACLESFELD, or MASSLT, WILLIAM (d. 1304), cardinal; B.D. Paris; fellow of Merton College, Oxford, 1291; D.D. Oxford; cardinal, 1303; wrote theological works. [xxxix. 445]

MYLES or MILES, JOHN (1621–1684), founder of Welsh baptist churches; of Brasenose College, Oxford; formed the first baptist church, 1649; obtained the sequestered rectory of Ilston; emigrated to New England, 1663, and was preacher at Rehoboth, Barrington, and Swansea, Massachusetts; died at Swansea, Massachusetts. [xxxix. 445]

MYLLAR, ANDROW (fl. 1503–1508), the first Scottish printer; a bookseller, who published Joannes de Garlandia's 'Multorum vocabulorum equiuocorum interpretatio,' 1505, and 'Expositio Sequentiarum,' 1506, both of which were printed abroad; in partnership with Walter Chepman set up a printing press in Edinburgh, 1507; issued 'The Maying or Disport of Chaucer,' 1508. [xl. 1]

MYLNE or MYLN, ALEXANDER (1474–1548?), abbot of Cambuskenneth and president of the court of session in Scotland; graduated from St. Andrews, 1494; canon of Aberdeen; dean of Angus; abbot of Cambuskenneth, 1517; lord of the articles, 1532–42; president of the court of session, 1532–48; wrote a history of the bishops of Dunkeld, and collected the records of Cambuskenneth. [xl. 2]

MYLNE, ALEXANDER (1613–1643), sculptor; son of John Mylne (d. 1657) [q. v.]; assisted his brother, John Mylne (1611–1667) [q. v.]. [xl. 4]

MYLNE, JAMES (d. 1788), poet; his 'Poems, consisting of Miscellaneous Pieces and two Tragedies,' published, 1790. [xl. 3]

MYLNE or MYLN, JOHN (d. 1621), mason; greatnephew of Alexander Mylne (1474–1548?) [q. v.]; mastermason in Scotland before 1584; repaired the Dundee harbour works; built bridge over the Tay, 1604–17 (destroyed, 1621). [xl. 3]

MYLNE, JOHN (d. 1657), mason; son of John Mylne (d. 1621) [q. v.]; engaged on the present steeple of the Tolbooth at Aberdeen, 1622–9, on fortifications at Dundee, 1643–51; master-mason, 1631–6. [xl. 3]

MYLNE, JOHN (1611–1667), mason; son of John Mylne (d. 1657) [q. v.]; principal master-mason, 1636; designed Tron Church (opened, 1647), partly built Heriot's Hospital, 1643–59, and Edinburgh College, 1646–7; served with the covenanters, 1640; master-gunner of Scotland, 1646; sat on Edinburgh town council, 1655–64; M.P., Edinburgh, 1662–3. [xl. 4]

MYLNE, ROBERT (1633–1710), mason; son of Alexander Mylne (1613–1643) [q. v.]; master-mason, 1668; reclaimed the foreshore and constructed the sea-wall at Leith, 1669–85; superintended building of Holyrood Palace, 1670–9; erected many stone buildings in the principal streets of Edinburgh, and built 'Mylne's Mount,' one of the bastions in Edinburgh Castle. [xl. 5]

MYLNE, ROBERT (1643?–1747), writer of pasquils and antiquary; collected public records; notorious for his bitter political squibs against the whigs. [xl. 6]

MYLNE, ROBERT (1734–1811), architect and engineer; son of Thomas Mylne [q. v.]; studied at Rome, 1754–8; travelled through Switzerland and Holland,

1759; constructed Blackfriars Bridge, 1760–9; engaged in many architectural and engineering works in England and Scotland; designed the Gloucester and Berkeley Canal, and an improvement to the fen level drainage by the Eau Brink Cut; surveyor of St. Paul's Cathedral, 1766; engineer to the New River Company, 1770–1811; F.R.S., 1767; original member of the Architects' Club, 1791. [xl. 6]

MYLNE, ROBERT WILLIAM (1817–1890), architect, engineer, and geologist; son of William Chadwell Mylne [q. v.]; engineer to the Limerick water works; wrote on artesian wells and the geology of London. [xl. 10]

MYLNE, THOMAS (d. 1763), city surveyor of Edinburgh; son of William Mylne (1662–1728) [q. v.] [xl. 6]

MYLNE or MILN, WALTER (d. 1558), martyr; imbibed protestant doctrines in Germany, and was condemned as a heretic before 1546; fled abroad, but in 1558 was burnt as a heretic at St. Andrews. [xl. 9]

MYLNE, WILLIAM (1662–1728), master-mason; son of Robert Mylne (1633–1710) [q. v.] [xl. 5]

MYLNE, WILLIAM (d. 1790), architect; son of Thomas Mylne [q. v.]; architect to city of Edinburgh, 1765; built the North Bridge, Edinburgh, 1765–72. [xl. 8]

MYLNE, WILLIAM CHADWELL (1781–1863), engineer and architect; son of Robert Mylne (1734–1811) [q. v.]; engineer to the New River Company, 1811–61; much engaged in engineering projects in connection with water-supply and drainage; F.R.A.S., 1821; F.R.S., 1826; F.R.I.B.A., 1834; M.I.C.E., 1842. [xl. 9]

MYNGS, SIR CHRISTOPHER (1625–1666), vice-admiral; entered the navy when young; captain, 1653; captured a fleet of Dutch merchant-vessels, 1653; served in Jamaica, 1655–64; knighted, 1665; led the van on the fourth day of the battle off the North Foreland, 1–4 June 1666, and was mortally wounded. [xl. 10]

MYNN, ALFRED (1807–1861), cricketer; originally a hop merchant; became a cricketer, 1832; played for the Gentlemen, Kent, and All England; the first fast round-arm bowler of eminence. [xl. 13]

MYNORS, ROBERT (1739–1806), surgeon; practised at Birmingham; wrote on surgery. [xl. 13]

MYNSHUL, GEFFRAY (1594?–1668). [See MINSHULL.]

MYRDDIN EMRYS. [See MERLIN AMBROSIUS.]

MYRDDIN WYLLT, i.e. THE MAD (fl. 580?), legendary Welsh poet; erroneously credited with six poems printed in the 'Myvyrian Archaiology'; has been improbably identified with Merlin Ambrosius and Merlin 'Silvester' or 'Celidonius' [see MERLIN]. [xl. 13]

MYTENS, DANIEL (1590?–1642), portrait-painter; born at the Hague; member of the Guild of St. Luke, 1610; came to England before 1618; became 'king's painter' on Charles I's accession; painted portraits of the court and nobility and copied old masters; returned to Holland, 1630, and died there. [xl. 14]

MYTTON, JOHN (1796–1834), sportsman and eccentric; of Westminster School; served in the army, 1816–17; M.P., Shrewsbury, 1818–20; high sheriff for Shropshire and Merionethshire; a great sportsman; ran through a fortune and died of delirium tremens in the King's Bench prison. [xl. 15]

MYTTON, THOMAS (1597?–1656), parliamentarian; of Balliol College, Oxford; student of Lincoln's Inn, 1616; a prominent parliamentarian in Shropshire; seized, and became governor of, Wem, 1643, and Oswestry, 1644, and captured Shrewsbury, 1645; commander-in-chief and vice-admiral in North Wales, 1645; recovered Anglesea from the royalists, 1648–9; member of the court-martial which condemned the Earl of Derby, 1651; represented Shropshire in Cromwell's first parliament. [xl. 16]

MYVYR, OWAIN (1741–1814). [See JONES, OWEN.]

N

NAAS, BARON. [See BOURKE, RICHARD SOUTHWELL, sixth EARL OF MAYO (1822–1872).]

NABBES, THOMAS (*fl.* 1638), dramatist; matriculated from Exeter College, Oxford, 1621, but left without a degree; settled in London, *c.* 1630; wrote passable comedies censuring the foibles of middle-class society; excelled as a writer of masques, two of which, with some occasional verse, were published (1639) as 'The Spring's Glory'; his collected works, excepting his continuation of Richard Knolles's 'Generall Historie of the Turkes' from 1628 to 1637, privately printed by Mr. A. H. Bullen, 1887 (2 vols.). [xl. 17]

NADEN, CONSTANCE CAROLINE WOODHILL (1858–1889), poetess; disciple of Robert Lewins from 1876; studied at Mason College, Birmingham, 1881–7; won prizes for geology, 1885, and for an essay on 'Induction and Deduction,' 1887; sympathised with Herbert Spencer's philosophy; adopted a system of 'Hylo-Idealism.' Her poems were published in 1881 and 1887. [xl. 18]

NADIN, JOSEPH (1765–1848), deputy-constable of Manchester; a successful cotton-spinner; when deputy-constable (1801–21) became very unpopular through his endeavours to repress popular claims. [xl. 19]

NAESMITH. [See NASMITH and NASMYTH.]

NAFTEL, MAUD (1856–1890), daughter of Paul Jacob Naftel [q. v.]; painted flowers in water-colour. [xl. 20]

NAFTEL, PAUL JACOB (1817–1891), painter; native of Guernsey; came to London, 1870; exhibited scenery at the 'Old' Society of Painters in Water-colours, 1856–91 (member, 1859). [xl. 20]

NAGLE, SIR EDMUND (1757–1830), admiral; relative of Edmund Burke; entered navy, 1770; commander, 1782; knighted, 1794; vice-admiral, 1810; governor of Newfoundland, 1813; K.C.B., 1815; admiral, 1819; intimate with the prince regent (George IV). [xl. 20]

NAGLE, NANO or HONORA (1728–1784), foundress of the Presentation order of nuns; devoted herself to the poor of Ireland from 1750, and started schools for Roman catholic girls of the poorer classes in Cork, 1771, founding the Order of the Presentation of the Blessed Virgin Mary, 1775; the rules were approved by Pope Pius VI, 1791, and confirmed, 1805. [xl. 21]

NAGLE, SIR RICHARD (*fl.* 1689–1691), attorney-general; regarded by Lord-deputy Clarendon as the authorised representative of the Irish Roman catholics; privy councillor, knighted, and attorney-general for Ireland, 1686; active in destroying protestant corporations and churches; speaker of the 1689 parliament; took part in repealing the Act of Settlement and passing the great Act of Attainder; became secretary to James II, and after the battle of the Boyne (1690) urged the defeated king's flight to France; followed him after the surrender of Limerick, 1691, and probably died abroad. [xl. 22]

NAIRNE, BARONESS. [See ELPHINSTONE, MARGARET MERCER (1788–1867).]

NAIRNE, CAROLINA, BARONESS NAIRNE (1766–1845), Scottish ballad-writer; *née* Oliphant; began to write, 1792; married Major William Murray Nairne, 1806, who became fifth Baron Nairne, 1824; travelled on the continent, 1834–7 and 1838–44; ranks with Hogg in her Jacobite songs, and approaches Burns in her humorous ballads and pathetic songs; her poems, anonymous in her lifetime, were collected and published as 'Lays from Strathearn,' 1846. The best known are 'Land o' the Leal,' 'Caller Herrin',' and 'Charlie is my darling.' [xl. 23]

NAIRNE, SIR CHARLES EDWARD (1836–1899), lieutenant-general; lieutenant, Bengal artillery, 1858; second captain, royal artillery, 1865; major, 1872; lieutenant-colonel, 1880; commanded horse artillery in Egypt, 1882; C.B., 1882; inspector-general of artillery in India, 1887–92; major-general, 1890; held chief command in Bombay, 1893; lieutenant-general, 1895; K.C.B., 1897; acting commander-in-chief in India, 1898. [Suppl. iii. 218]

NAIRNE, EDWARD (1742?–1799), attorney and supervisor of customs at Sandwich; published humorous poetry. [xl. 25]

NAIRNE, EDWARD (1726–1806), electrician; an instrument-maker in Cornhill, who constructed and patented, on plans supplied by Priestley, 'Nairne's electrical machine,' 1782; F.R.S., 1776; contributed scientific papers to the 'Philosophical Transactions.' [xl. 25]

NAIRNE, JOHN, third BARON NAIRNE (*d.* 1770), Jacobite; son of William Nairne, second baron Nairne [q. v.]; taken prisoner at Preston, 1715; held a command in the 1745 rebellion; escaped after Culloden and died in France. [xl. 26]

NAIRNE, SIR ROBERT, of Strathord, first BARON NAIRNE (1600–1683), imprisoned in the Tower of London, 1651–60; lord of session and knighted, 1661; appointed a criminal judge, 1671; created Baron Nairne, 1681. [xl. 27]

NAIRNE, WILLIAM, second BARON NAIRNE (*d.* 1724), son of John Murray, first marquis of Atholl [q. v.]; succeeded his father-in-law, Sir Robert Nairne, first baron Nairne [q. v.], 1683, and assumed his name; opposed the union, 1707; taken prisoner at Preston, 1715; death sentence passed on him but remitted. [xl. 26]

NAIRNE, SIR WILLIAM, LORD DUNSINANE (1731?–1811), Scottish judge; admitted advocate, 1755; joint commissary clerk of Edinburgh, 1758; lord of session, 1786; lord of the justiciary court, 1792. [xl. 27]

NAISH, JOHN (1841–1890), lord chancellor of Ireland; B.A. Dublin University; called to the Irish bar, 1865; Q.C., 1880; solicitor-general for Ireland, 1883; attorney-general, 1884; Irish privy councillor and lord chancellor of Ireland, May to July 1885 and February to June 1886; died at Ems. [xl. 28]

NAISH, WILLIAM (*d.* 1800), miniature-painter; exhibited at the Royal Academy, 1783–1800. [xl. 28]

NAISH, WILLIAM (1785–1860), quaker writer; haberdasher in Gracechurch Street, London; published anti-slavery tracts and pamphlets. [xl. 28]

NALSON, JOHN (1638?–1686), historian and royalist pamphleteer; LL.D. Cambridge, 1678; rector of Doddington, Isle of Ely; prebendary of Ely, 1684; an active polemical writer on the side of the government, 1677–83; published two volumes (extending only to January 1642) of his only important work, 'Impartial Collection of the Great Affairs of State, from the beginning of the Scotch Rebellion in the year 1639 to the Murder of Charles I,' 1682 and 1683. His valuable collections of manuscripts were gradually broken up. [xl. 29]

NALTON, JAMES (1600?–1662), 'the weeping prophet'; M.A. Trinity College, Cambridge, 1623; incumbent of Rugby, 1632–42, of St. Leonard's, Foster Lane, London, 1644–62; concerned in Love's plot, 1651. [xl. 31]

NANFAN, JOHN (*d.* 1716), captain; a descendant of Sir Richard Nanfan [q. v.]; lieutenant-governor of New York, 1697–1702; returned to England, 1705. [xl. 32]

NANFAN or **NANPHANT,** SIR RICHARD (*d.* 1507), deputy of Calais; J.P. for Cornwall, 1485; received frequent grants; knighted, 1488; sent on a mission to Portugal, 1489; deputy at Calais; patron of Thomas Wolsey [q. v.] [xl. 31]

NANGLE, RICHARD (*d.* 1541?), bishop of Clonfert; D.D. and provincial of the Augustinians in Ireland; was made bishop of Clonfert by Henry VIII, 1536, but never occupied the see. [xl. 32]

NANMOR, DAFYDD (*fl.* 1400), Welsh bard; sang the honour of the house of Gogerddan (Cardiganshire). [xl. 32]

NANMOR, DAFYDD (*fl.* 1480), bard; son of Rhys Nanmor [q. v.] [xl. 32]

NANMOR, RHYS (*fl.* 1440), Welsh bard; probably son of Dafydd Nanmor (*fl.* 1400) [q. v.] [xl. 32]

NANTGLYN, BARDD. [See DAVIES, ROBERT (1769 ?-1835).]

NAPIER, SIR ALEXANDER (*d.* 1473 ?), second of Merchiston, comptroller of Scotland; belonged to the household of the queen-mother, Joan Beaufort; comptroller of the household, 1449-61; ambassador to England, 1451-61; knighted and made vice-admiral before 1461; negotiated a marriage between James III and Margaret of Denmark, 1468; sent on special embassies to Bruges, 1472, and Burgundy, 1473. [xl. 33]

NAPIER, ALEXANDER (1814-1887), editor; of Trinity College, Cambridge; son of Macvey Napier [q. v.]; vicar of Holkham, 1847-87; edited Barrow's works, 1859, and Boswell's 'Johnson,' 1885. [xl. 69]

NAPIER, SIR ARCHIBALD (1534-1608), seventh of Merchiston, master of the Scottish mint; knighted, 1565; master of the mint, 1576; frequently acted on religious commissions; commissioner 'anent the cunzie' in London, 1604; interested in the mining industry. [xl. 34]

NAPIER, SIR ARCHIBALD, first BARON NAPIER (1576-1645), ninth of Merchiston, treasurer-depute of Scotland; son of John Napier [q. v.]; educated at Glasgow University; devoted special attention to agriculture; accompanied James VI to England, 1603; privy councillor, 1615; treasurer-depute of Scotland, 1622-31; created baronet, 1625, and a peer of Scotland, 1627; subscribed Charles I's confession at Holyrood, 1638; assisted Montrose to draw up the band of Cumbernauld, 1640, for which he was imprisoned, 1641, but released with a caution, 1641; confined at Edinburgh and Linlithgow, 1644, on account of his sympathies with Montrose, who liberated him after the victory of Kilsyth, 1645; fled to Atholl after the defeat of Montrose at Philiphaugh. [xl. 35]

NAPIER, ARCHIBALD, second BARON NAPIER (*d.* 1658), tenth of Merchiston; son of Sir Archibald Napier, first baron [q. v.]; left his confinement in Holyrood to join Montrose, 1645; distinguished himself at battles of Auldearn and Alford, 1645; succeeded his father, 1645; subsequently communicated with Montrose from the continent; excluded from Scotland, 1650, and from Cromwell's Act of Grace, 1654; died in Holland. [xl. 37]

NAPIER, SIR CHARLES (1786-1860), admiral; entered navy, 1799; lieutenant, 1805; commander, 1807; captain, 1809; actively engaged (1811-13) in stopping the coasting-trade on the west coast of Italy; distinguished himself in the expeditions against Alexandria and Baltimore, 1814; C.B., 1815; travelled over the continent, and (1819) endeavoured to promote iron steamers on the Seine; appointed to the Galatea frigate, 1829; sent to watch over British interests in the Azores, 1831, being brought thereby into close connection with Portuguese affairs; accepted command of Portuguese fleet to serve Dona Maria, 1833; sighted the squadron of Dom Miguel off Cape St. Vincent, and, in spite of disparity of forces, won a very creditable victory (1833), for which he was ennobled in the Portuguese peerage as Viscount Cape St. Vincent; obtained leave after the surrender of Lisbon to attack the northern ports, where he raised the siege of Oporto and secured the Entre-Douro-e-Minho, 1834; received in triumph at Oporto and created Count Cape St. Vincent; obtained the surrender of Figuera and Ourem, on which the civil war ended; resigned on account of the rejection of his scheme for the government of the navy, and returned to England, 1835; published an account of the war, 1836; sent to reinforce Sir Robert Stopford [q. v.] in the Mediterranean as commodore, 1839; at Beyrout (1840) given command of the land forces; when prepared for attack received orders to retire and hand over the command, but, judging a retreat to be disastrous, fought and won a victory, which resulted in the immediate evacuation of Beyrout; caused general dissatisfaction by his disregard of orders; signed a convention with Mohammed Ali without authority and without consulting the admiral, 1840, the convention being repudiated, but adopted as the basis of negotiations; K.C.B. and decorated by the European powers, 1840; M.P., Marylebone, 1841; published a somewhat inaccurate 'History of the War in Syria,' 1842; rear-admiral and commander of the Channel fleet, 1846; vice-admiral, 1853; commanded in the Baltic, 1854; declined the G.C.B., 1855; M.P., Southwark, 1855; admiral, 1858. [xl. 38]

NAPIER, SIR CHARLES JAMES (1782-1853), conqueror of Sind (Scinde); son of George Napier [q. v.]; obtained commission and was promoted lieutenant, 1794; aide-de-camp to Sir James Duff [q. v.], 1799, and to General Edward Fox, 1803; as captain in the staff corps came under the notice of Sir John Moore, 1805; major, 1806; commanded battalion under Moore in Spain, 1808; was severely wounded and taken prisoner at Coruña, 1809; exchanged, 1810; distinguished himself at Coa and Busaco; lieutenant-colonel, 1811; served against the United States, 1813; volunteered on Napoleon's escape from Elba and made C.B., 1815; resident of Cephalonia, 1822; became acquainted with Byron and sympathised with the Greeks, but finally declined to become their commander; returned to England, after quarrelling with the new high commissioner, 1830; major-general, 1837; K.C.B., 1838; appointed to command the northern district of England, 1839, where chartism was rife; accepted an Indian commission, 1841; ordered to take command of Upper and Lower Sind, which he found in a state bordering on war; offered the amirs a fresh treaty as an ultimatum, and occupied the fortress of Imamghar, their impregnable refuge, after which, the amirs being unable to restrain their followers, hostilities commenced; with a force of 2,800 men discovered an enemy of 22,000 entrenched in the bed of the Falaili River, near Miani (Meanee), 17 Feb. 1843, and after a desperate conflict won the battle, after which Haidarabad surrendered and six amirs submitted; victorious over Shir Muhammad, the Lion of Mirpur, at Dubba, 24 March, who, however, escaped to the hills, and was not finally defeated until 14 June at Shah-dal-pur; set about receiving the submission of the chiefs and organising the military occupation; established a civil government, in its social, financial, and judicial branches, and organised an effective police force; warmly congratulated by Wellington and made G.C.B., 1843; began his campaign against the northern hill tribes, 1844, finally capturing Beja and his followers at Traki, 9 March 1845; assembled an army and siege train at Rohri, but took no further part in the first Sikh war; lieutenant-general, 1846; resigned the government of Sind, 1847; in response to popular demand was given command against the Sikhs, 1849, but arrived in India after the war was over; suppressed the 66th regiment, which showed a mutinous spirit, but on being reprimanded for suspending a regulation pending a reference to the supreme council, resigned, 1850, and returned to England; published works on the roads of Cephalonia, the administration of the colonies, the defects of Indian government, and on military subjects. [xl. 45]

NAPIER, DAVID (1790-1869), marine engineer; cousin of Robert Napier (1791-1876) [q. v.]; introduced (1818) steam packets for post-office service; established regular steam communication between Greenock and Belfast, and between Liverpool, Greenock, and Glasgow, 1822; invented the steeple engine. [xl. 54]

NAPIER, EDWARD DELAVAL HUNGERFORD ELERS (1808-1870), lieutenant-general and author; stepson of Sir Charles Napier [q. v.]; received his commission, 1825; lieutenant, 1826; captain, 1831; major, 1839; served with distinction in Syria and Egypt; brevet lieutenant-colonel, 1841; brevet colonel, 1854; major-general, 1858; lieutenant-general, 1864; published a life of his stepfather, 1862, and works on sport in foreign countries. [xl. 54]

NAPIER, FRANCIS, seventh BARON NAPIER (1758-1823), succeeded his father, 1775; entered the army, 1774; major, 1784; representative peer of Scotland, 1796-1807; prepared a genealogical account of his family. [xl. 55]

NAPIER, SIR FRANCIS, ninth BARON NAPIER in Scottish peerage, first BARON ETTRICK of ETTRICK in peerage of United Kingdom, eleventh (Nova Scotia) baronet of Scott of Thirlestane (1819-1898), diplomatist and Indian governor; son of William John Napier, eighth baron Napier [q. v.]; educated at Trinity College, Cambridge; joined diplomatic service, 1840; ambassador at St. Petersburg, 1860-4, and Berlin, 1864-6; governor of Madras, 1866; devoted particular attention to questions of public health and the development of public works, and especially works of irrigation; temporarily governor-general of India on assassination of Richard Southwell Bourke, sixth earl of Mayo [q. v.], 1872; returned to

England and was created Baron Ettrick, 1872 ; LL.D. Edinburgh, Glasgow, and Harvard ; resided in Scotland, where he took an active interest in condition of the poor. [Suppl. iii. 218]

NAPIER, GEORGE (1751–1804), colonel ; educated under David Hume ; entered the army, 1767 ; lieutenant, 1771 ; served in America ; captain, 1778 ; re-entered the army, 1782 ; superintendent of Woolwich laboratory, c. 1788 ; major and deputy quartermaster-general under the Earl of Moira, 1793 ; fortified his house at Celbridge during the Irish rebellion, 1798 ; wrote on the composition of gunpowder, 1788. [xl. 56]

NAPIER, SIR GEORGE THOMAS (1784–1855), general and governor of the Cape of Good Hope ; son of George Napier [q. v.] ; entered the army, 1800 ; captain, 1804 ; served under Sir John Moore in Sicily, Sweden, and Portugal ; major, 1811 ; C.B., 1815 ; major-general, 1837 ; governor at the Cape, 1837–43 ; K.C.B., 1838 ; lieutenant-general, 1846 ; general, 1854 ; wrote an account of his early life. [xl. 57]

NAPIER, SIR GERARD, first baronet (1606–1673), royalist ; grandson of Sir Robert Napier (d. 1615) [q. v.] ; M.P., Melcombe Regis, 1640 ; created baronet, 1641 ; commissioner for Charles I, 1643 ; submitted to parliament, 1644 ; sent money to Charles I ; commissioner for waste lands, 1662. [xl. 58]

NAPIER, HENRY EDWARD (1789–1853), historian ; son of George Napier [q. v.] ; entered the navy, 1803 ; lieutenant, 1810 ; commander, 1814 ; captain, 1830 ; author of a Florentine history, 1846–7 ; F.R.S., 1820. [xl. 59]

NAPIER, JAMES (1810–1884), dyer and antiquary ; published ‘ Folklore, or Superstitious Beliefs in the West of Scotland within this Century,’ 1879, and works on metallurgy and dyeing. [xl. 59]

NAPIER or **NEPER,** JOHN (1550–1617), laird of Merchiston ; inventor of logarithms ; son of Sir Archibald Napier (1534–1608) [q. v.] ; educated at St. Andrews ; infefted in the baronies of Edenbellie-Napier and Merchiston, 1571 ; entered into a bond for the loyalty of his father-in-law, Sir James Chisholm, 1593 ; had constant trouble in connection with the disputes between his tenants and those of his neighbours, 1591 and 1611–13 ; succeeded his father, 1608, some family litigation being caused thereby ; made valuable experiments in the use of manures, and invented an hydraulic screw for clearing coal-pits of water, for which he was granted a monopoly, 1597 ; published ‘ A plaine Discovery of the whole Revelation of St. John,’ 1593 ; invented the present notation of decimal fractions, and in his work, ‘ Constructio’ (published, 1619), explained the method of the construction of logarithms, which were there called artificial numbers ; published in his ‘ Mirifici Logarithmorum Canonis Descriptio,’ 1614, the canon or table, and an explanation of the nature of logarithms and their use in numeration and trigonometry ; subsequently in conjunction with Henry Briggs [q. v.] determined that 0 should become the logarithm of unity, and 10 000 000 000 the logarithm of the whole sine, Briggs computing the new canon ; in his last work, ‘ Rabdologiæ seu numerationis per virgulas libri duo,’ 1615, explained enumeration by little rods (termed Napier’s bones) and multiplication and division by metal plates (the earliest attempt at the invention of a calculating machine). [xl. 59]

NAPIER, SIR JOSEPH, first baronet (1804–1882), lord chancellor of Ireland ; educated at Belfast under James Sheridan Knowles ; M.A. Trinity College, Dublin, 1828 ; barrister, Gray’s Inn, 1830 ; called to the Irish bar, 1831 ; Q.C., 1844, and much employed in appeals before the House of Lords ; M.P., Dublin University, 1848–58 ; spoke in the interests of protestantism and Ireland ; prepared and carried through the House ‘ Napier’s Ecclesiastical Code,’ 1849 ; appointed Irish attorney-general and privy councillor, 1852 ; failed to pass his measures for the reform of the land laws, 1852 ; D.C.L. Oxford 1853 ; lord chancellor of Ireland, 1858–9 ; devoted himself to evangelical religious work, and endeavoured to avert the disestablishment of the Irish church ; vice-chancellor of Dublin University, 1867–1882 ; created baronet, 1867 ; nominated to a vacancy in the judicial committee of the privy council, 1868 ; actively engaged in the reconstruction of the Irish church ; chief commissioner of the great seal of Ireland, 1874 ; published legal works and others on church questions. [xl. 65]

NAPIER, MACVEY (1776–1847), editor of the ‘ Edinburgh Review’ ; originally Napier Macvey, the name being changed to Macvey Napier at his grandfather’s wish ; studied at Edinburgh and Glasgow ; became acquainted with Archibald Constable, 1798 ; librarian to the writers to the signet, 1805 ; edited a supplement to the sixth edition of the ‘ Encyclopædia Britannica,’ 1814–24, and the seventh edition, 1827–42 ; first professor of conveyancing at Edinburgh, 1824 ; editor of the ‘ Edinburgh Review,’ 1829 ; clerk of session in Edinburgh, 1837 ; F.R.S. [xl. 68]

NAPIER, MARK (1798–1879), Scottish historical biographer ; was educated at Edinburgh ; advocate, 1820 ; sheriff-depute of Dumfriesshire, 1844 ; published ‘ The Law of Prescription in Scotland,’ 1839, and historical works on the earldom of Lennox, the Napiers, Montrose, and Graham of Claverhouse. [xl. 69]

NAPIER, SIR NATHANIEL, second baronet (1636–1709), dilettante ; son of Sir Gerard Napier, first baronet [q. v.] ; matriculated as fellow-commoner of Oriel College, Oxford, 1654 ; knighted, 1662 ; travelled in Holland, 1667, and France, 1672 and 1697 ; succeeded to baronetcy, 1673 ; M.P., Dorset, 1677–8, Corfe Castle, 1679, 1681, and 1685–7. [xl. 70]

NAPIER or **NAPPER,** RICHARD (1559–1634), astrologer ; matriculated from Exeter College, Oxford, 1577 ; rector of Great Linford, 1590 ; studied astrology under Simon Forman [q. v.] ; legatee of Forman’s manuscripts, 1611 ; licensed to practise medicine, 1604. [xl. 71]

NAPIER, SIR RICHARD (1607–1676), physician ; son of Sir Robert Napier (1560–1637) [q. v.] ; nephew and heir of Richard Napier [q. v.] ; student at Gray’s Inn, 1622 ; B.A. Wadham College, Oxford, 1626 ; created M.A., 1627 ; fellow of All Souls College, Oxford, 1628 ; B.C.L., 1630 ; licensed to practise medicine, 1633 ; M.D. Oxford, 1642 ; incorporated at Cambridge, 1663 ; knighted, 1647 ; F.R.C.P., 1664. [xl. 72]

NAPIER, SIR ROBERT (d. 1615), judge ; joined the Middle Temple ; M.P., Dorchester, 1586 ; knighted before 1593 ; chief baron of the exchequer in Ireland, 1593–1602 ; M.P., Bridport, 1601, Wareham, 1603–4. [xl. 73]

NAPIER, SIR ROBERT, first baronet (1560–1637), brother of Richard Napier [q. v.] ; a Turkey merchant ; high sheriff of Bedfordshire, 1611 ; knighted and created baronet, 1612. [xl. 72]

NAPIER, ROBERT (1611–1686), royalist ; grandson of Sir Robert Napier (d. 1615) [q. v.] ; of Queen’s College, Oxford ; barrister, Middle Temple, 1637 ; receiver-general and auditor of the duchy of Cornwall ; compounded, 1649 ; granted renewal of receiver-generalship, 1663. [xl. 73]

NAPIER, SIR ROBERT, first baronet (1642?–1700), son of Robert Napier (1611–1686) [q. v.] ; of Trinity College, Oxford ; high sheriff of Dorset, and knighted, 1681 ; created baronet, 1682 ; M.P., Weymouth, 1689–90, Dorchester, 1698. [xl. 74]

NAPIER, ROBERT (1791–1876), marine engineer ; constructed his first marine engine, 1823, and supplied engines for the East India Company and the Cunard Company ; took to shipbuilding, 1841 ; constructed iron ships for the Peninsular and Oriental Company and for the British, French, Turkish, Danish, and Dutch governments ; took out patents for improvements in warships ; president of the Institution of Mechanical Engineers, 1863–5. [xl. 74]

NAPIER, ROBERT CORNELIS, first BARON NAPIER OF MAGDALA (1810–1890), field-marshal ; born at Colombo, Ceylon ; received his commission in the Bengal engineers, 1826 ; first lieutenant, 1828 ; sailed for India, 1828 ; employed in irrigation works on the Eastern Jamna Canal, 1831 ; visited European engineering works, 1836 ; laid out the settlement of Darjiling, 1838, and established communication with the plain below, for which he organised a local corps of workmen called ‘ Sebundy sappers’ ; second captain, 1841 ; laid out a cantonment at Sirhind in échelon on the slopes, 1842, an arrangement which became known as ‘ Napier’s system’ ; distinguished himself in the first Sikh war and was promoted brevet major, 1846 ; showed special engineering skill in the reduction of Kote Kangra, 1846 ; took part in the second Sikh war and became brevet lieutenant-colonel, 1849 ; civil engineer to the

Punjab board of administration, 1849; constructed the high road from Lahore to Peshawar and the Bári-Doab canal, and strengthened the frontier defences; brevet colonel, 1854; relinquished his post, 1856; at the relief of Lucknow, 1857, successfully effected the union of the rear guard and was wounded with the main relieving force; undertook the general direction of the mining operations during the second siege; commanded a brigade of engineers during the third attack on Lucknow; C.B.; joined Sir Hugh Rose at Gwalior and gained a signal victory over Tantia Topi on the plains of Jaora Alipúr, 1858; routed Feroze-shah (who had joined Tantia Topi), December 1858, by means of destroying the forts of Parone, and cutting clearings through the jungle succeeded in capturing both rebel leaders, 1859; K.C.B.; appointed to command the second division in the Chinese expedition, 1860; assisted (1860) in taking Pehtang-ho and Peiho, and maintained communications and pushed supplies to the front; promoted major-general for his distinguished services, 1861; military member of the governor-general's council, 1861–5; commander-in-chief of the Bombay army, 1865; promoted lieutenant-general of the Bombay army, 1865; appointed to command the Abyssinian expedition, 1867; organised his base, provided for his communications, defeated his enemy, and attained the object of his mission; pensioned, made G.C.S.I. and G.C.B., and created Baron Napier of Magdala, 1868; commander-in-chief in India, 1870; general, 1874; governor of Gibraltar, 1876; field-marshal, 1883. [xl. 75]

NAPIER, Sir THOMAS ERSKINE (1790–1863), general; brother of Sir Charles Napier [q. v.]; entered the army, 1805; lieutenant, 1806; served in Sweden, 1808, and the Peninsula (medals); C.B., 1838; general, 1861; K.C.B., 1860. [xl. 81]

NAPIER, Sir WILLIAM FRANCIS PATRICK (1785–1860), general and historian of the Peninsular war; son of George Napier [q. v.]; entered the army, 1800; lieutenant, 1801; joined Sir John Moore's brigade at Shorncliffe, 1803, and took part in Moore's campaign in Spain, 1808; served in Portugal, 1809, and specially distinguished himself in the fight on the Coa, 1810; badly wounded at Casal Novo, 1811; major, 1812; brevet lieutenant-colonel, 1813; retired on half-pay, 1819; C.B.; began to collect materials in 1823 for his 'History of the Peninsular War' (published, 1828–40), which placed Napier high among historical writers, and was translated into French, Spanish, Italian, German, and Persian; colonel, 1830; major-general, 1841; lieutenant-governor of Guernsey, 1842–7; published a history of the 'Conquest of Scinde,' 1844–6, in reality a defence of his brother Charles; published, 1851, 'History of the Administration of Scinde' and a 'Life' of his brother, 1857; K.C.B., 1848; general, 1859. [xl. 82]

NAPIER, WILLIAM JOHN, eighth BARON NAPIER (1786–1834), naval captain; son of Francis Napier, seventh baron Napier [q. v.]; entered navy, 1803; lieutenant, 1809; commander, 1812; promoted to post rank, 1814; published treatise on sheep-farming, 1822; succeeded his father, 1823; chief superintendent of trade in China, 1833; died at Macao. [xl. 87]

NAPLETON, JOHN (1738?–1817), divine and educational reformer; M.A. Brasenose College, Oxford, 1761; D.D., 1789; fellow, 1760; rector of Wold, 1777; became golden prebendary in Hereford Cathedral, 1789, and received much preferment in the diocese; wrote a book on logic in Latin, 1770, and on Oxford examinations, 1773; published also sermons. [xl. 88]

NAPPER. [See NAPIER.]

NAPPER - TANDY, JAMES (1747 – 1803). [See TANDY.]

NARBONNE, PETER REMI (1806–1839), Canadian insurgent; born at St. Remi; took an active part in the rebellions of 1837 and 1838; hanged at Montreal. [xl. 89]

NARBROUGH, Sir JOHN (1640–1688), admiral; lieutenant, 1664; commander, 1666; captain of the Duke of York's flagship in the battle of Solebay, 1672; rear-admiral of the red, 1673; knighted, 1673; admiral and commander-in-chief of a squadron sent against the Tripoli corsairs, 1674, and the Algerine corsairs, 1677; commis-sioner of the navy, 1680–7; sent to St. Domingo to recover treasure from a wreck, where he caught fever and died. [xl. 89]

NARES, EDWARD (1762 – 1841), miscellaneous writer; son of Sir George Nares [q. v.]; of Westminster School and Christ Church, Oxford; fellow, 1788–97; M.A., 1789; vicar of St. Peter-in-the-East, Oxford, 1792; rector of Biddenden, 1798; Bampton lecturer, 1805; regius professor of modern history at Oxford, 1813–41; published memoirs of Lord Burghley, 1828–31, also two novels satirising fashionable society, and theological works. [xl. 91]

NARES, Sir GEORGE (1716–1786), judge; brother of James Nares [q. v.]; barrister, Inner Temple, 1741; king's serjeant, 1759; M.P. for Oxford city, 1768; justice of the common pleas, 1771; knighted, 1771; D.C.L. Oxford, 1773. [xl. 91]

NARES, JAMES (1715–1783), composer; brother of Sir George Nares [q. v.]; organist of York Cathedral, 1734; Mus. Doc. Cambridge, 1757; organist, Chapel Royal, London, 1757; composed church music. [xl. 92]

NARES, ROBERT (1753–1829), philologist; son of James Nares [q. v.]; educated at Westminster School and Christ Church, Oxford; M.A., 1778; tutor to Sir Watkin Wynn, 1779–83; usher at Westminster School, 1786–8; assistant-librarian at the British Museum, 1795; canon of Lichfield, 1798; prebendary of St. Paul's, London, 1798; archdeacon of Stafford, 1801; published a 'Glossary' of Elizabethan literature, 1822; revised 'General Biographical Dictionary,' 1789, and assisted in Bridges's 'History of Northamptonshire,' 1790. [xl. 93]

NARFORD, NERFORD, or **NEREFORD**, ROBERT (d. 1225), constable of Dover Castle; received grants, 1216; became chief constable of Dover; present at the defeat of Eustace the Monk, 1217; founded the priory of St. Mary de Pratis. [xl. 94]

NARRIEN, JOHN (1782–1860), astronomical writer; optician; mathematical professor at Sandhurst, 1820; F.R.S., 1840; wrote on astronomy and mathematics. [xl. 94]

NARY, CORNELIUS (1660–1738), Irish catholic divine; belonged to the Irish College in Paris, 1682–96; D.D. Paris, 1694; imprisoned in Dublin on account of his religion, 1702; published theological works and some controversial pamphlets. [xl. 95]

NASH, FREDERICK (1782–1856), water - colour painter; studied at the Royal Academy, and with Thomas Malton the younger [q. v.]; architectural draftsman to the Society of Antiquaries, 1807; contributed to the Royal Academy, 1800–47, and to the Society of Painters in Water-colours, 1810–56; declared by Turner to be the finest architectural painter of the day. [xl. 95]

NASH, GAWEN (1605–1658), royalist divine; sizar of Pembroke Hall, Cambridge, 1620; fellow, 1627; rector of St. Matthew's, Ipswich, 1638; vicar of Waresley, 1642; ejected, 1646. [xl. 110]

NASH, JOHN (1752–1835), architect; pupil of Sir Robert Taylor [q. v.]; began to practise, c. 1793; laid out Regent's Park, London, and designed most of the terraces near it, 1811; also planned Regent Street, London, between Carlton House and Regent's Park, 1813–20; repaired and enlarged Buckingham House, from which its large entrance gateway, known as the Marble Arch, was removed to Cumberland Gate, Hyde Park, 1851. His style lacks grandeur, and great monotony is produced by his persistent use of stucco. [xl. 96]

NASH, JOSEPH (1809–1878), water-colour painter and lithographer; studied under the elder Pugin; drew figure subjects illustrating poets and novelists; earned celebrity by his picturesque views of Gothic buildings, English and foreign. [xl. 98]

NASH, MICHAEL (fl. 1796), protestant controversialist; collector of subscriptions for the Societas Evangelica, 1791–4; secretary of the Society for the Promotion of the French protestant bible; attacked Dr. William Romaine [q. v.] and William Huntington [q. v.]. [xl. 98]

NASH, RICHARD, BEAU NASH (1674–1762), 'king of Bath'; educated at Carmarthen grammar school; matriculated from Jesus College, Oxford, 1692; after

H h

trying the army entered the Inner Temple, 1693; derived an income from accepting extravagant wagers and gambling; went to Bath, 1705; established the Assembly Rooms and a code of etiquette and of dress, and became unquestioned autocrat of Bath; evaded the gambling laws of 1740, by inventing new games, but after 1745 gradually lost his popularity, and in 1758 was allowed 10*l.* a month by the corporation; assisted in establishing the mineral-water hospital at Bath.   [xl. 99]

NASH or **NASHE**, THOMAS (1567–1601), author; sizar of St. John's College, Cambridge, 1582; B.A., 1586; made a hasty tour through France and Italy, and before 1588 settled in London; his promise recognised by Sir George Carey [q. v.]; endeavoured to secure the patronage of the Earls of Southampton and Derby; but did not retain the favour of any patron long; his first publication an acrid review of recent literature prefixed to Greene's 'Menaphon,' 1589, which he discussed at greater length in 'Anatomie of Absurdities,' 1589; attracted to the Martin Marprelate controversy by his hatred of puritanism; under the pseudonym of 'Pasquil' wrote 'A Countercuffe given to Martin Junior,' 1589, 'The Returne of the renouned Cavaliero Pasquil of England,' 1589, and 'The First Parte of Pasquils Apologie,' 1590; possibly the author of other attacks on the Martinists; replied to the savage denunciations of Richard Harvey [q. v.] with 'A wonderful, strange, and miraculous Astrologicall Prognostication,' 1591, and 'Pierce Pennilesse his Supplication to the Divell,' 1592, which was translated into French and six times reprinted, and the second edition of which was called 'The Apologie of Pierce Pennilesse'; avenged Gabriel Harvey's attack on Greene with 'Strange Newes of the Intercepting certaine Letters,' 1593; being subsequently troubled with religious doubts published his repentant reflections under the title 'Christes Teares over Jerusalem,' 1593, but, Harvey being deaf to his appeal for peace, repeated his attacks in a second edition of 'Christes Teares'; published (1594) 'The Terrors of the Night,' notable for the praise of Daniel's 'Delia'; published the 'Unfortunate Traveller, or the Life of Jack Wilton,' a romance of reckless adventure, dedicated to the Earl of Southampton, 1594; further satirised Harvey in 'Haue with you to Saffron-Walden,' 1596, to which Harvey replied, the government subsequently ordering the two authors to desist; attacked so many current abuses in the state in his lost comedy 'The Isle of Dogs,' 1597, that he was sent to the Fleet prison for some months; published (1599) 'Lenten Stuffe,' a burlesque panegyric of the red herring, and a comedy, still extant, called 'Summers Last Will,' 1600. Nash's original personality gives him a unique place in Elizabethan literature, and his writings have something of the fascination of Rabelais. His romance of 'Jack Wilton' inaugurated the novel of adventure in England.   [xl. 101]

NASH, THOMAS (1593–1647), entered Lincoln's Inn, 1619; intimate with Shakespeare's family; married Shakespeare's granddaughter, Elizabeth Hall, 1626; became, with his wife, owner of New Place, Stratford, 1635.   [xl. 110]

NASH, THOMAS (1588–1648), author; matriculated from St. Edmund Hall, Oxford, 1605; entered the Inner Temple, 1607; royalist; his death said to have been caused by the misfortunes of Charles I; published 'Quaternio, or a Fourfold Way,' 1633.   [xl. 109]

NASH, TREADWAY RUSSELL (1725–1811), historian of Worcestershire; matriculated from Worcester College, Oxford, 1740; M.A., 1747; vicar of Eynsham, *c.* 1751; tutor of Worcester College, Oxford, *c.* 1751–7; F.R.S., 1773; vicar of Leigh, 1773; published 'Collections for the History of Worcestershire,' 1781–2; edited Butler's 'Hudibras,' 1793.   [xl. 110]

NASMITH. [See also NASMYTH.]

NASMITH, DAVID (1799–1839), originator of town and city missions; became secretary to twenty-three charitable societies in Glasgow, 1813–28; founded Glasgow City Mission, 1826, and similar institutions in Ireland, United States, France, and London.   [xl. 111]

NASMITH, JAMES (1740–1808), antiquary; M.A. Corpus Christi College, Cambridge, 1767; D.D., 1797; fellow, 1765; F.S.A., 1769; rector of Snailwell, 1773, of Leverington, 1796; arranged and catalogued the manuscripts which Archbishop Parker gave to Corpus Christi

College, Cambridge; edited (1787) Tanner's 'Notitia Monastica,' and wrote antiquarian pamphlets.   [xl. 112]

NASMITH or **NAYSMITH**, JOHN (*d.* 1619?), surgeon to James VI of Scotland and I of England; present in Holyrood Palace when Bothwell attempted to capture the young king James VI 1591, and imprisoned in consequence; accompanied James to London, 1603; bought the lands of Cowdenknowes, 1612; devoted special attention to botany.   [xl. 112]

NASMYTH, ALEXANDER (1758–1840), portrait and landscape painter; at first employed to paint the panels of carriages, but after studying under Allan Ramsay in London set up as portrait-painter in Edinburgh, 1778; travelled on the continent, 1782–4; intimate with Robert Burns; finally restricted himself chiefly to landscape; belonged to many artistic societies, and was interested in science; designed the 'bow-and-string bridge' used at Charing Cross and Birmingham stations.   [xl. 113]

NASMYTH, CHARLES (1826–1861), major, 'defender of Silistria'; entered the East India Company, 1843; sent as 'The Times' correspondent to Omar Pasha's camp at Shumla; instrumental in checking the Russians at Silistria, 1854; transferred to the royal army as major, 1854; present at the Alma and Sebastopol; brigade-major at Sydney; died at Pau.   [xl. 115]

NASMYTH or **NAESMITH**, SIR JAMES, first baronet (*d.* 1720), lawyer; admitted advocate, 1684; created baronet, 1706.   [xl. 115]

NASMYTH, JAMES (*d.* 1779), botanist; son of Sir James Nasmyth [q. v.]; introduced the birch and silver fir into Scotland; genus *Nasmythia* named after him.   [xl. 116]

NASMYTH, JAMES (1808–1890), engineer; son of Alexander Nasmyth [q. v.]; constructed a six-inch diameter reflecting telescope, 1827; constructed (1827) a steam-engine capable of carrying six people; became assistant to Maudslay, 1829; started in business at Manchester, 1834, as a maker of machine-tools; invented the steam hammer, 1839, and patented it, 1842; the first to observe a mottled appearance of the sun's surface called 'willow leaves' or 'rice grains,' 1860; invented a nut-shaping machine, a flexible shaft for driving small drills, and an hydraulic punching-machine; proposed the use of chilled cast-iron shot, 1862; published, in conjunction with James Carpenter, an elaborate work on the moon, 1874.   [xl. 116]

NASMYTH, PATRICK (1787–1831), landscape-painter; son of Alexander Nasmyth [q. v.]; studied art under his father; contributed to Scottish and English art institutions; styled, from the character of his works, 'the English Hobbema.'   [xl. 118]

NASSAU, GEORGE RICHARD SAVAGE (1756–1823), bibliophile; formed a library, which was especially rich in early English books; made extensive collections on the history of Suffolk, most of which were sold, 1824.   [xl. 119]

NASSAU, HENRY, COUNT and LORD OF AUVERQUERQUE (1641–1708), general; accompanied William, prince of Orange, on his visit to Oxford, 1670, and was made D.C.L.; attended William of Orange to England, 1688; promoted major-general, 1691; appointed deputy stadtholder, 1693; with the rank of field-marshal cooperated with Marlborough and died in camp at Lille.   [xl. 119]

NASSYNGTON, WILLIAM OF (*fl.* 1375?), translator; translated from Latin into English verse 'Treatise on the Trinity and Unity, with a Declaration of God's Works and of the Passion of Jesus Christ,' written by John of Waldeby or Waldly.   [xl. 120]

NATARES or **NATURES**, EDMUND (*d.* 1549), master of Clare Hall, Cambridge; fellow of Catharine Hall, Cambridge; M.A. by special grace, 1502; D.D., 1516; was master of Clare Hall, Cambridge, 1514–30; vice-chancellor, 1518, 1521, and 1526–7; rector of Middleton-upon-Tees, 1522.   [xl. 120]

NATHALAN or **NAUCHLAN** (*d.* 452?), Scottish saint; devoted himself to contemplation and practised agriculture; went, partially bound, to Rome as a penance, and was made bishop by the pope; founded the churches of Meldrum, Cowie, and Tullich.   [xl. 121]

NATHAN, ISAAC (1791?-1864), musical composer and author; abandoned theology for music and studied under Domenico Corri; became intimate with Byron, 1812, who wrote 'Hebrew Melodies' for Nathan to set to music; emigrated to Australia, 1841· published 'Musurgia Vocalis,' 1823, on musical theory, Fugitive Pieces and Reminiscences of Lord Byron . . . . also . . . . Recollections of Lady Caroline Lamb,' 1829, the 'Life of Madame Malibran de Beriot,' 1836, and 'The Southern Euphrosyne,' 1846; killed in Sydney by accident. [xl. 121]

NATTER, LORENZ (1705-1763), gem-engraver and medallist; born in Suabia; taught by Johann Rudolph Ochs at Berne; studied in Italy; copied ancient gems, which he frequently signed; came to England, c. 1741; visited the northern capitals of Europe, 1743, returning to England, c. 1754; patronised by the royal family and employed at the royal mint; published a treatise on ancient and modern methods of engraving, 1754, and a catalogue of the Bessborough gems, 1761; died of asthma at St. Petersburg. [xl. 123]

NATTES, JOHN CLAUDE (1765?-1822), topographical draughtsman; travelled in Great Britain, Ireland, and France, working as a topographical draughtsman and colouring his drawings. [xl. 124]

NAU, CLAUDE DE LA BOISSELIERE (fl. 1574-1605), secretary to Mary Queen of Scots; a lawyer, who acted as secretary to the Cardinal of Lorraine; became secretary to Mary Queen of Scots, 1574; managed her accounts and advised her in matters of policy; went on missions to Scotland, 1579 and 1581; supposed agent in the Babington plot, 1586; defended himself against the accusation of betraying Mary Queen of Scots and was liberated, 1587; returned to France; ennobled by Henry IV, 1605; wrote a 'History of Mary Stewart' (published, 1883). [xl. 125]

NAUCHLAN (d. 452?). [See NATHALAN.]

NAUNTON, SIR ROBERT (1563-1635), politician; B.A. Trinity College, Cambridge, 1582; M.A.; major fellow, 1586; accompanied his uncle, William Ashby, on a diplomatic mission to Scotland, 1589; fellow of Trinity Hall, Cambridge, 1592; acted as travelling tutor, and regularly communicated to the Earl of Essex any political news he could learn; returned to Cambridge, c. 1600; M.P., Helston, 1606, Camelford, 1614, and Cambridge University, 1621, 1624, and 1625; knighted, 1614, and made master of requests, 1616; secretary of state, 1618, exercising what influence he possessed in behalf of the Elector Frederick in Bohemia; retired from the secretaryship, 1623; master of the court of wards, 1623-35; his manuscript account of Queen Elizabeth's courtiers (compiled c. 1630) frequently printed after his death. [xl. 126]

NAVARRE, JOAN OF (1370?-1437). [See JOAN.]

NAYLER, SIR GEORGE (1764?-1831), garter king-of-arms; became Blanc Coursier herald, 1792; bluemantle pursuivant and member of the College of Arms, 1793; York herald, 1794; F.S.A., 1794; knighted, 1813; first king-of-arms of the Hanoverian Guelphic order, 1815, and of the order of St. Michael and St. George, 1818; Clarenceux king-of-arms, 1818; Garter king-of-arms, 1822; formed a collection of private acts of parliament (1733-1830), and commenced a history of George IV's coronation. [xl. 129]

NAYLER, JAMES (1617?-1660), quaker; joined parliamentary army, 1642, and was quartermaster in Lambert's horse; became a quaker, 1651; being convinced of a call to the travelling ministry, left home, 1652, and preached in the north; imprisoned for a short time at Appleby, 1653, for alleging that 'Christ was in him'; went to London, 1655; gained many devoted followers, and was attended by a 'company' when he set out for Launceston, where Fox was imprisoned; created a disturbance at Exeter and was imprisoned with his 'company'; gained more followers, who displayed great extravagance; arrested with seven of his following at Bristol and sent to London, 1656; adjudged guilty of 'horrid blasphemy' and sentenced to be pilloried in New Palace Yard, London, and the Exchange, London, his tongue to be pierced with a hot iron, his forehead to be branded with 'B' (for blasphemer), and he himself to be whipped through the city of Bristol and imprisoned at Bridewell, London; released, 1659; for a short time in

Westmoreland with George Whitehead [q. v.]; published controversial pamphlets distinguished by depth of thought, beauty of expression, and moderation in tone. [xl. 130]

NAYLOR, FRANCIS HARE (1753-1815). [See HARE-NAYLOR.]

NEADE, WILLIAM (fl. 1625), archer and inventor; invented a combined bow and pike, exhibited before James I, 1624, on which he wrote a pamphlet, 1625; failed to get his invention generally adopted. [xl. 134]

NEAGLE, JAMES (1760?-1822), line-engraver; illustrated books; emigrated to America and died there. [xl. 134]

NEAL. [See also NEALE, NEELE, NEILE, and NEILL.]

NEAL, DANIEL (1678-1743), historian of the puritans; educated at Merchant Taylors' School, London; studied at Utrecht and Leyden; became pastor to a congregation in Aldersgate Street, London, which subsequently removed to Jewin Street, London; published the 'History of New England,' 1720, and became honorary M.A. of Harvard, 1721; wrote an introduction to a treatise on small-pox, 1722. His 'History of the Puritans' down to 1689, in four volumes, 1732, 1733, 1736, 1738 (subsequently translated into Dutch), was somewhat severely criticised by Isaac Maddox [q. v.] and Zachary Grey [q. v.] [xl. 134]

NEAL or **NEALE**, THOMAS (1519-1590?), professor of Hebrew at Oxford; of Winchester College; admitted perpetual fellow of New College, Oxford, 1540; M.A., 1546; B.D., 1556; became chaplain to Bishop Bonner; regius professor of Hebrew, 1559-69; wrote account of Queen Elizabeth's entertainment at Oxford, 1566; translated the 'Prophets' from Hebrew into Latin. [xl. 136]

NEALE. [See also NEAL, NEELE, NEILE, and NEILL.]

NEALE, ADAM (d. 1832), army physician and author; M.D. Edinburgh, 1802; published an account of the Peninsular war, 1808, continental travels, 1818, and medical works; died at Dunkirk. [xl. 137]

NEALE, EDWARD VANSITTART (1810-1892), Christian socialist and co-operator; M.A. Oriel College, Oxford, 1836; barrister, Lincoln's Inn, 1837; founded two building societies and the Central Co-operative Agency, and purchased the Atlas Ironworks, all of which failed; frequently acted as legal adviser to co-operative societies, and published a handbook on limited liability laws, 1860; assisted in founding the North of England Co-operative Society, 1863, the Cobden Mills, 1866, and the Agricultural Association, 1867; promoted the annual co-operative congress, 1869, of which he was secretary (1875-91). He became a member of the Christian Social Union on its formation, and wrote pamphlets on co-operation and socialism. [xl. 138]

NEALE, ERSKINE (1804-1883), divine and author; son of Adam Neale [q. v.]; M.A. Emmanuel College, Cambridge, 1832; vicar of Exning, 1854; published theological works and religious novels. [xl. 141]

NEALE, SIR HARRY BURRARD, second baronet (1765-1840), admiral; originally named Burrard; entered the navy, 1778; lieutenant, 1787; commander, 1790; succeeded his uncle as baronet, 1791; assumed his wife's name, Neale, 1795; a lord of the admiralty, 1804; rear-admiral, 1810; vice-admiral, 1814; K.C.B., 1815; G.C.B., 1822; G.C.M.G. and commander-in-chief in the Mediterranean, 1823-6; admiral, 1830; M.P. for Lymington for forty years. [xl. 141]

NEALE, JAMES (1722-1792), biblical scholar; M.A. Pembroke College, Cambridge, 1746; schoolmaster at Henley-on-Thames, 1747-62; translated 'Hosea,' 1771. [xl. 142]

NEALE, JOHN MASON (1818-1866), divine and author; graduated B.A. from Trinity College, Cambridge, 1840; tutor of Downing College, Cambridge; espoused high church views and was one of the founders of the Cambridge Camden Society, 1839, afterwards called the Ecclesiological Society; became warden of Sackville College, East Grinstead, 1846, where he founded the nursing sisterhood of St. Margaret's; leader-writer for the 'Morning Chronicle,' 1851-3; published works on theological and ecclesiastical subjects and tales and books for the young. One-eighth of the 'Hymns Ancient and Modern' are by Neale. [xl. 143]

NEALE, JOHN PRESTON (1780–1847), architectural draughtsman; executed architectural drawings with a pen and tinted them with water-colour; exhibited at the Royal Academy and other exhibitions. [xl. 146]

NEALE, SAMUEL (1729–1792), quaker; became a minister, 1752; influenced by Mary Peisley, whom he married, 1757; preached in Holland, Germany, and America. [xl. 147]

NEALE, THOMAS (*fl.* 1643), author; nephew of Walter Neale [q. v.]; published a travelling guide to 'forraigne countries,' 1643. [xl. 148]

NEALE, THOMAS (*fl.* 1657), engraver. [xl. 149]

NEALE, THOMAS (*d.* 1699?), master of the royal mint and groom-porter; master and worker of the royal mint, 1678–99; groom-porter to Charles II, *c.* 1684; as master of the transfer office conducted public lotteries; engaged in banking and building and mining schemes, and in East India trade. [xl. 147]

NEALE, WALTER (*fl.* 1639), New England explorer; fought in Bohemia, 1618; governor of part of New Hampshire, 1630–3; appointed lieutenant-governor of Portsmouth, 1639. [xl. 149]

NEALE, SIR WILLIAM (1609–1691), royalist; scout-master-general in Prince Rupert's army; knighted, 1643; fought at Newark, 1644; taken prisoner, 1659. [xl. 149]

NEALE, WILLIAM HENRY (1785–1855), grandson of James Neale [q. v.]; schoolmaster at Beverley, 1808–1815; nominated a Charterhouse brother, 1853; published theological works. [xl. 143]

NEALE, WILLIAM JOHNSON (1812–1893), lawyer and novelist; son of Adam Neale [q. v.]; quitted the navy; barrister, Middle Temple, 1836; recorder of Walsall, 1859; wrote sea stories. [xl. 150]

NEATE, CHARLES (1784–1877), pianist and composer; an original member of the Philharmonic Society, 1813; became intimate with Beethoven in Vienna, 1815; composed pianoforte pieces. [xl. 150]

NEATE, CHARLES (1806–1879), economist and political writer; educated in Paris and at Lincoln College, Oxford; B.A., 1828; fellow of Oriel College, Oxford, 1828; barrister, Lincoln's Inn, 1832; examiner in law and history at Oxford, 1853–6; Drummond professor of political economy, 1857; M.P., Oxford city, 1863–8; published pamphlets mainly on political subjects. [xl. 150]

NEAVES, CHARLES, LORD NEAVES (1800–1876), Scottish judge; called to the bar at Edinburgh, 1822; solicitor-general, 1852; judge of the court of session as Lord Neaves, 1853; rector of St. Andrew's, 1872; published 'The Greek Anthology,' 1870, and contributed to periodicals. [xl. 152]

NECHTAN (*d.* 732), son of Derelei or Dergard, king of the Picts; conformed to the Roman date for Easter; applied to Bede for arguments to confute heresy, 710; supplanted to Bede for arguments to confute heresy, 710; his kingdom, 728. [xl. 153]

NECHTAN MORBET (*d.* 481?), king of the Picts; said to have dedicated Abernethy to St. Brigit in the presence of Darlugdach, the exiled abbess of Kildare. [xl. 153]

NECKAM or **NECHAM**, ALEXANDER (1157–1217), scholar; went to Paris University; was a distinguished teacher there, 1180; returned to England, 1186; Augustinian canon; abbot of Cirencester, 1213; wrote 'De naturis rerum,' 'De Laudibus Divinæ Sapientiæ,' 'De Contemptu Mundi,' and some treatises on grammar. [xl. 154]

NECTON or **NECHODUN**, HUMPHREY (*d.* 1303), an early Carmelite, who preached against heretics at Cambridge; his works lost. [xl. 155]

NEEDHAM, CHARLES, fourth VISCOUNT KILMOREY (*d.* 1660), succeeded to the title, 1657; his estates subjected to sequestration; failed in a plot to restore Charles (II), 1659; died in prison. [xl. 155]

NEEDHAM, ELIZABETH, known as 'MOTHER NEEDHAM' (*d.* 1731), a procuress employed by Colonel Charteris, 1731; died from the effects of being pilloried. [xl. 155]

NEEDHAM, FRANCIS JACK, twelfth VISCOUNT and first EARL OF KILMOREY (1748–1832), entered the army, 1762; lieutenant, 1773; captain, 1774; distinguished himself at the battle of Arklow, 1798; colonel, 1810; general, 1812; M.P., Newry, 1806; succeeded to peerage, 1818; created Earl of Kilmorey, 1822. [xl. 156]

NEEDHAM or **NEDEHAM**, JAMES (*fl.* 1530–1533), architect and master-carpenter; appointed clerk of the king's works, 1530, and overseer, 1533. [xl. 156]

NEEDHAM, SIR JOHN (*d.* 1480), judge; M.P., Newcastle-under-Lyme, 1441, 1446, 1448, and London, 1449; common serjeant, 1449; king's serjeant, 1453, and justice of the common pleas, 1457; knighted, 1470. [xl. 157]

NEEDHAM, JOHN TURBERVILLE (1713–1781), Roman catholic divine and man of science; educated at Douay; ordained priest, 1732; taught rhetoric in the college, 1736–40; ordered to the English mission, 1740; did much scientific work with Buffon; F.R.S., 1747; F.S.A., 1761; travelled as a tutor, 1751–67; director of the Imperial Academy, Brussels, 1768–80; belonged to many foreign societies; endeavoured by means of the Chinese characters to interpret an Egyptian inscription on a bust at Turin; published miscellaneous scientific treatises, some embodying his theory that every organised substance is formed by vegetation. [xl. 157]

NEEDHAM or **NEDHAM**, MARCHAMONT (1620–1678), journalist; chorister at All Souls, Oxford; B.A. All Souls, Oxford, 1637; member of Gray's Inn, 1652; studied medicine; chief author of 'Mercurius Britanicus,' 1643–6 a satirical weekly commentary on the news of the day; twice arrested for the scurrilous character of his paper; took up medicine for a time; became a royalist, obtained pardon, and published in Charles I's defence 'Mercurius Pragmaticus,' 1647, the royalism of which was combined with hostility to the Scots; his paper suppressed by government and himself committed to Newgate, 1649; again engaged to support the Commonwealth, and published the first-fruits of his conversion in a pamphlet, 'The Case of the Commonwealth,' 1650, and a new weekly paper, 'Mercurius Politicus,' in which he championed Cromwell's foreign and ecclesiastical policy; translated Selden's 'Mare Clausum,' 1652; also edited the official journal, the 'Public Intelligencer,' 1653–60; on Cromwell's death wrote against the restoration of the monarchy and fled to Holland, May 1660; obtained a pardon, returned to England, and lived by practising physic; in 'Schools and Schoolmasters' (1663) suggested various educational reforms, and complained of the neglect of chemistry for anatomy in 'Medela Medicinæ,' 1665; employed by government to attack the opposition and its leaders in 'Pacquet of Advices to the men of Shaftesbury,' 1676; was attacked in numerous verse and prose satires. [xl. 159]

NEEDHAM, PETER (1680–1731), classical scholar; M.A. St. John's College, Cambridge, 1700; D.D., 1717; fellow, 1698–1716; prebendary of St. Florence, Pembrokeshire, 1714, and rector of Stanwick, 1717; edited Greek and Latin texts. [xl. 164]

NEEDHAM, WALTER (1631?–1691?), physician and anatomist; of Westminster School and Trinity College, Cambridge; B.A., 1654; fellow of Queens' College, Cambridge, 1655; honorary F.R.C.P., 1664; F.R.S., 1671; physician to the Charterhouse, London, 1672; published 'Disquisitio anatomica de formato Fœtu,' 1667. [xl. 165]

NEEDLER, BENJAMIN (1620–1682), ejected minister; of Merchant Taylors' School, London, and St. John's College, Oxford; fellow, 1645–51; B.C.L., 1648; rector of St. Margaret Moses, Friday Street, London, 1648; ejected, 1662; preached privately at North Warnborough; published sermons. [xl. 165]

NEEDLER, CULVERWELL (*fl.* 1710), son of Benjamin Needler [q. v.]; clerk-assistant of the House of Commons; published 'Debates of the House of Commons in January 1704,' 1721 (2nd ed.) [xl. 166]

NEEDLER, HENRY (1685–1760), musical amateur; accountant for the candle duty, 1710; studied under Purcell and Bannister; performed at private concerts; intimate with Handel. [xl. 166]

NEELE. [See also NEAL, NEALE, NEILE, and NEILL.]

NEELE, HENRY (1798–1828), poet and miscellaneous writer; solicitor; published poems, 1817 and 1823 (collected, 1827); contributed tales to periodicals, and published 'Romance of English History,' 1827; committed suicide. [xl. 166]

NEELE or **NEALE**, SIR RICHARD (d. 1486), judge; member of Gray's Inn, 1463; serjeant, 1463; king's serjeant, 1466; judge of common pleas, 1470; knighted before 1483. [xl. 167]

NEGRETTI, ENRICO ANGELO LUDOVICO (1817–1879), optician; born in Como; came to London, 1829; took Joseph Warren Zambra into partnership, 1850, with whom he obtained a reputation as maker of scientific and mathematical instruments; intimate with Garibaldi. [xl. 167]

NEGUS, FRANCIS (d. 1732), reputed inventor of negus; secretary to the Duke of Norfolk, 1685–8; lieutenant-colonel under Marlborough; held various court appointments; M.P., Ipswich, 1717–32; invented negus to avert a political fracas, attention being diverted from political matters at a party in Queen Anne's reign to a discussion of the merits of wine and water. [xl. 168]

NEGUS, SAMUEL (fl. 1724), author of a list of English printers, 1724. [xl. 168]

NEGUS, WILLIAM (1559?–1616), puritan minister; B.A. Trinity College, Cambridge, 1578; beneficed in Essex; suspended, 1584; restored, 1585; went to Leigh, 1586, and was suspended for a short time, 1587; deprived, 1609. [xl. 169]

NEILD, JAMES (1744–1814), philanthropist; a jeweller who became interested in prisons, 1762; treasurer of a society for helping debtors, 1773; visited prisons in England, Scotland, Flanders, and Germany; published an account of his work, 1800; public interest roused by his 'Prison Remarks' in the 'Gentleman's Magazine'; exposed system of imprisonment for debt, 1812. [xl. 169]

NEILD, JOHN CAMDEN (1780?–1852), eccentric; son of James Neild [q. v.]; of Eton and Trinity College, Cambridge; M.A., 1804; barrister, Lincoln's Inn, 1808; a confirmed miser; left 500,000l. to Queen Victoria; his servants provided for by Queen Victoria after his death. [xl. 170]

NEILE. [See also NEAL, NEALE, NEELE, and NEILL.]

NEILE, RICHARD (1562–1640), archbishop of York; of Westminster School and St. John's College, Cambridge; installed dean of Westminster, 1605; bishop of Rochester, 1608–10; appointed Laud his chaplain and gave him valuable preferments; elected bishop of Lichfield, 1610; translated to Lincoln, 1614, and to Durham, 1617; politically active in the northern province; privy councillor, 1627; bishop of Winchester, 1628–31; sat regularly on the high commission and in the Star-chamber; archbishop of York, 1631–40; reported on the state of his diocese and province, 1634; kept up a political and ecclesiastical correspondence with Laud, Windebank, and Sir Dudley Carleton. [xl. 171]

NEILE, WILLIAM (1637–1670), mathematician; grandson of Richard Neile [q. v.]; discovered an exact rectification of the cubical parabola, 1657; F.R.S., 1663. [xl. 173]

NEILL. [See also NEAL, NEALE, NEELE, and NEILE.]

NEILL, JAMES GEORGE SMITH (1810–1857), colonel and brigadier-general; entered East India Company's service, 1826; lieutenant, 1828; brevet-captain, 1842; major, 1850; deputy assistant adjutant-general in the second Burmese war; promoted brevet lieutenant-colonel, 1853; appointed second in command of the Turkish contingent in the war with Russia; organised and reformed the Turkish contingent; on the news of the mutiny was sent up to Banáras, where he completely routed the mutineers and succeeded in reinforcing Allahabad and clearing the adjacent villages; colonel and aide-de-camp to Queen Victoria; disappointed at being superseded by Havelock, but after some friction joined Havelock as second in command at Cawnpore, where he was left in command, and punished the mutineers with great severity; kept open communications with Havelock, who was advancing on Lucknow; accompanied Havelock as brigadier-general in the final advance on Lucknow, and while fighting bravely was shot dead. [xl. 174]

NEILL or **NEIL**, PATRICK (d. 1705?), first printer in Belfast; came from Scotland, c. 1694; his books, which are very rare, consist of religious works printed between 1699 and 1702. [xl. 178]

NEILL, PATRICK (1776–1851), naturalist; a publisher who devoted himself to botany and horticulture; fellow of Linnean and Edinburgh Royal societies; published 'The Flower, Fruit, and Kitchen Garden,' and other works. [xl. 178]

NEILSON, JAMES BEAUMONT (1792–1865), inventor of the hot blast in iron manufacture; enginewright of a colliery at Irvine, 1814; foreman of the Glasgow Gasworks, 1817; introduced important improvements in the manufacture of gas, and exerted himself for the mental and technical improvement of the workmen under him; led by the inefficiency of a particular engine to his discovery that the substitution of a hot blast, instead of a refrigerated one, produced three times as much iron with the same amount of fuel; tested its effects at the Clyde Ironworks, and patented it in England, Scotland, and Ireland, 1828. The validity of the patent was tested in the law courts, 1840, 1841, and 1842, but the verdict in each case was given in Neilson's favour. [xl. 179]

NEILSON, JOHN (1778–1839), benefactor of Paisley; amassed a considerable fortune as a grocer, and founded a school for boys in Paisley. [xl. 181]

NEILSON, JOHN (1776–1848), Canadian journalist; a Scotsman who went to Canada, 1790; edited the 'Quebec Gazette,' 1796; member for Quebec County in the assembly of Lower Canada, 1818–34; delegate to England, 1823, 1828, and 1835; member for Quebec county in the united legislature, 1841; speaker, 1844. [xl. 182]

NEILSON, LAURENCE CORNELIUS (1760?–1830), organist at Chesterfield, 1808–30. [xl. 183]

NEILSON, LILIAN ADELAIDE (1848–1880), actress; her real name ELIZABETH ANN BROWN; successively a mill hand at Guiseley, a nursemaid, and a barmaid; first appeared as Juliet in London, 1865; visited America, where she was very popular, 1872, 1874, 1876, and 1879; had no English rival as a tragedian; died suddenly in Paris. [xl. 183]

NEILSON, PETER (1795–1861), poet and mechanical inventor; exporter of cotton goods to America, where he lived, 1822–8; proposed improvements to the lifebuoy, 1846; suggested iron-plated warships, 1848; wrote on slavery, 1846; his poems published, 1870. [xl. 184]

NEILSON, SAMUEL (1761–1803), United Irishman; a woollendraper interested in politics; suggested the idea of a united Irish society, which Theobald Wolfe Tone organised, 1791; to propagate it a bi-weekly newspaper was started (the 'Northern Star'), 1792, with Neilson as editor; arrested for seditious libel, 1796, and his paper violently suppressed, 1797; released on condition of abstaining from conspiracy, February 1798; again took part in politics, and was re-arrested in May; included in the arrangement of July 1798 and banished; revisited Ireland, 1802, and, eluding the authorities, sailed for America, where he died. [xl. 185]

NEILSON, WILLIAM (1760?–1821), grammarian; presbyterian minister and schoolmaster at Dundalk; professor of Greek and Hebrew in Belfast College, 1817; published 'Greek Exercises,' 1804 (eighth edition, 1846), an Irish grammar, 1808, 'Greek Idioms,' 1810, and 'Elementa Linguæ Græcæ,' 1820. [xl. 187]

NELIGAN, JOHN MOORE (1815–1863), physician; M.D. Edinburgh, 1836; lectured on materia medica and botany at Cork and Dublin; published compilations on medicines, 1844, scalp diseases, 1848, and skin diseases, 1852. [xl. 187]

NELSON, SIR ALEXANDER ABERCROMBY (1816–1893), lieutenant-general; entered the army, 1835; lieutenant, 1839; served at Kandahar and in Afghanistan, 1841–2; brigade-major at Portsmouth; major, 1856; colonel, 1869; lieutenant-governor of Guernsey, 1870–83; major-general, 1880; lieutenant-general, 1883; K.C.B., 1891. [xl. 188]

NELSON, FRANCES HERBERT, VISCOUNTESS NELSON (1761–1831), née Woodward; widow of Josiah Nisbet; married Horatio Nelson [q. v.] at Nevis in the West Indies, 1787, and lived with him at Burnham Thorpe; corresponded affectionately with her husband till 1798, when she heard of his intimacy with Lady

Hamilton; on his return to England, 1800, they had frequent altercations, and separated early in 1801, Nelson settling 1,200*l.* a year on her. [xl. 188]

NELSON, HORATIO, VISCOUNT NELSON (1758–1805), vice-admiral; entered the navy, 1770; served in the West Indies; commander, 1778; posted, 1779; compelled to return to England on account of ill-health, 1780; took a convoy to America, 1782; returned to the West Indies; placed on half-pay, 1783; went to St. Omer to learn French; appointed to the Boreas, 1784, and sent again to the West Indies, where he seized five American ships for irregular trading, and married Mrs. Nisbet, 1787; ordered home; remained unemployed from 1787 to 1793, when he sailed in the Agamemnon for the Mediterranean; at Naples first met Sir William and Lady Hamilton, August 1793; Lord Hood having resolved on capturing Corsica, 1794, Nelson was landed in command of the seamen and marines and successfully built and armed the batteries at Bastia; again with the land forces at the surrender of Calvi, where he had the sight of his right eye destroyed, 1794, after which battle the reduction of Corsica was complete; appointed commodore, 1796, and employed in harassing the French on shore and preventing their coasting trade; his share in the battle of Cape St. Vincent against the combined French and Spanish fleets, 13 Feb. 1797, a main cause of the victory; made K.B. and promoted rear-admiral; resumed his command of the inshore squadron, and in July 1797 failed to capture a treasure-ship at Santa Cruz, losing his right arm; rejoined the fleet, April 1798, and was sent to watch the French at Toulon; sent to discover the whereabouts of the French fleet. which had succeeded in putting to sea, and take or destroy it; arrived at Alexandria without getting any news of the French, but at last (1 Aug. 1798) discovered them in Aboukir Bay, lying at anchor. close in shore; found the French only prepared for an attack from the sea; Nelson put his fleet between them and the shore, and brought such overwhelming fire to bear on them, that only two frigates escaped; rewards bestowed on him from all the courts of Europe; created Baron Nelson of the Nile; returned to Naples, 1798; instructed to co-operate with the Austrians, with whom the Neapolitan government, declaring war on France, had made an alliance; left for Leghorn, 22 Nov. 1798; Naples, unprotected on the land side, was taken by the French, aided by the Neapolitan Jacobins, January 1799, and a capitulation with the rebels was agreed on by Ruffo, the commander of the royal forces; Nelson, on his return, annulled the capitulation and insisted on the absolute surrender of Neapolitan Jacobins; court-martialled and hanged Caracciolo, a commodore of the Neapolitan navy who had deserted, restored the civil power in Naples, and was made Duke of Bronté in Sicily; was infatuated with Lady Hamilton, and remained in close attendance on the Neapolitan court, regulating the blockade of Egypt and Malta from Palermo; obtained permission to return home on account of ill-health, 1800; travelled back overland in company with the Hamiltons; joined his wife in London, which resulted, after a few weeks' acrimonious intercourse, in a separation; vice-admiral, 1801; sent to command the attack on Copenhagen, 1801; returned to England, an armistice being agreed on, and was created Viscount Nelson, 1801; shared houses with the Hamiltons in London and at Merton in Surrey, the arrangement continuing after Sir W. Hamilton's death (April 1803). On the imminence of war, 1803, Nelson was appointed to the Mediterranean, and for two years kept a watch on the French fleet at Toulon under very adverse circumstances. In January 1805 Napoleon proposed to form a junction of the French and Spanish fleets in the West Indies, whence they were to return in overwhelming force to Europe; Villeneuve eluded Nelson at Toulon and reached Martinique; Nelson was delayed by contrary winds and false intelligence, while Villeneuve returned to Europe and was met off Cape Finisterre by Sir Robert Calder; resumed command of Cadiz, and on 9 Oct. issued his celebrated memorandum with instructions to form in two columns; on the appearance of the enemy (21 Oct.) off Cape Trafalgar, reserved for himself the task of restraining the enemy's van; struck by a musket shot from the mizentop of the Redoubtable, of which his ship, the Victory, had run foul; died three hours later, just as the victory was complete; accorded a public funeral and buried in St. Paul's Cathedral. [xl. 189]

NELSON, JAMES (1710–1794), author of moral works, and apothecary. [xl. 207]

NELSON, JOHN (1660–1721), New England statesman; went to Boston, c. 1680; commanded Boston militia, 1689; captured by the French on his way to Accadia, 1691; gave information of the French designs on Boston; sent to the Bastille; while still in prison (1698), contrived to send further information to England; released soon after. [xl. 207]

NELSON, JOHN (1707–1774), methodist; stonemason; converted by John Wesley, 1739; pressed for a soldier; had considerable influence over the poor and ignorant; his journal subsequently published. [xl. 209]

NELSON, JOHN (1726–1812), sculptor. [xl. 209]

NELSON, RICHARD JOHN (1803–1877), major-general, royal engineers, and geologist; entered the army, 1826; superintended work in the Bermudas and studied their coral formation; captain, 1841; regimental colonel, 1854; commanding royal engineer at Halifax, Nova Scotia, 1858–61; major-general, 1864; chief work, 'Geology of the Bermudas.' [xl. 209]

NELSON, ROBERT (1665–1715), religious writer; of St. Paul's School, London; entered Trinity College, Cambridge, 1678, but never resided; F.R.S., 1680; lived chiefly on the continent until 1691; became intimate with John Kettlewell, and joined the nonjurors before 1694; took an active part in the various charitable enterprises of the day, especially schools and parochial libraries; published a life of Dr. George Bull (1713) and other religious works. [xl. 210]

NELSON, SYDNEY (1800–1862), composer; pupil of Sir George Smart; visited America, Canada, and Australia; a prolific writer. [xl. 212]

NELSON, THOMAS (*fl.* 1580), printer and ballad-writer; obtained the freedom of the Stationers' Company, 1580; chiefly published short tracts or ballads, most of which were by himself. [xl. 213]

NELSON, THOMAS (1822–1892), publisher; entered his father's business at Edinburgh, 1839; established a London branch, 1844; invented a rotary press, 1850, now used for newspapers; children's books and school books produced by his firm; entered into partnership with Bartholomew & Co., map engravers. [xl. 214]

NELSON, WILLIAM (*fl.* 1720), legal writer; of Trinity College, Oxford; barrister, Middle Temple, 1684; practised in chancery; wrote chiefly reports of chancery cases. [xl. 215]

NELSON, WILLIAM, first EARL NELSON (1757–1835), brother of Horatio, viscount Nelson [q. v.]; M.A. Christ's College, Cambridge, 1781; rector of Brandon Parva, 1784; chaplain to the Boreas, 1784–6; D.D. Cambridge and Oxford, 1802; prebendary of Canterbury, 1803; succeeded his brother as second Baron Nelson, 1805; created Viscount Merton and Earl Nelson, 1805; on good terms with Lady Hamilton; succeeded in the title by his nephew. [xl. 215]

NELSON, WILLIAM (1816–1887), publisher; brother of Thomas Nelson (1822–1892) [q. v.]; entered the publishing business, 1835; travelled and collected china and bronzes; interested himself in the improvement of Edinburgh. [xl. 214]

NELSON, WOLFRED (1792–1863), Canadian insurgent; became doctor, brewer, and distiller at St. Denis; allied himself with Papineau and was imprisoned, 1837–8; elected to the Canadian assembly, 1845; chairman of the board of health, 1847; inspector of prisons, 1851; chairman of prison inspectors, 1859. [xl. 216]

NELTHORPE, RICHARD (*d.* 1685), conspirator; admitted of Gray's Inn, 1669; concerned in Rye House plot; escaped to Switzerland; landed with Monmouth, 1685; betrayed and executed. [xl. 217]

NENNIUS (*fl.* 796), historian; the traditional author of the 'Historia Britonum'; lived on the borders of Mercia, in Brecknock or Radnor, and was a pupil of Elbod, bishop of Bangor. There are several versions of the 'Historia,' the North-Welsh, the South-Welsh, the Irish, and the English. The principal manuscripts are the Cambridge, the Harleian, and the Vatican. The 'Historia' was first printed by Gale, 1691, in 'Scriptores Quindecim.' [xl. 217]

NEOT, SAINT (d. 877 ?), Saxon anchoret ; said to have been ordained by Bishop Ælfheah, to have visited Rome seven times, to have preached much near Bodmin, and to have reproved Ælfred, whose kinsman he was. [xl. 221]

NEPEAN, SIR EVAN, first baronet (1751-1822), administrator ; clerk in the navy ; became under-secretary of state in the Shelburne ministry ; secretary of the admiralty, 1795 ; created baronet, 1802 ; chief secretary for Ireland for a few months, 1804 ; governor of Bombay, 1812-19. [xl. 222]

NEPER. [See NAPIER.]

NEQUAM, ALEXANDER (1157-1217). [See NECKAM.]

NESBIT. [See also NISBET.]

NESBIT, ALFRED ANTHONY (1854-1894), analytical chemist ; son of John Collis Nesbit [q. v.] ; invented an ink for preventing fraudulent alteration of cheques and postage stamps. [xl. 225]

NESBIT, ANTHONY (1778-1859), schoolmaster ; started a school at Bradford, 1814 ; removed to Manchester, 1821, and to London, 1841 ; published works on land surveying, also ' English Parsing,' 1817, and ' Arithmetic,' 1826. [xl. 223]

NESBIT, CHARLTON (1775-1838), wood-engraver ; apprenticed to Thomas Bewick [q. v.] ; moved to London, 1799 ; silver medallist of the Society of Arts, 1802 : illustrated books. [xl. 223]

NESBIT, JOHN COLLIS (1818-1862), agricultural chemist ; son of Anthony Nesbit [q. v.] ; introduced natural science teaching into his father's school, which he converted into a chemical and agricultural college ; F.G.S. ; fellow of the Chemical Society, 1845 ; wrote chiefly on chemical manures. [xl. 224]

NESBITT, JOHN (1661-1727), independent minister ; displayed excessive protestant zeal and fled from Edinburgh, 1681 ; became a classical scholar in Holland ; came to London, 1690 ; pastor in Hare Court, Aldersgate Street, London, 1691 ; published sermons. [xl. 225]

NESBITT, LOUISA CRANSTOUN (1812 ?-1858). [See NISBETT.]

NESBITT or **NISBET**, ROBERT (d. 1761), physician ; son of John Nesbitt [q. v.] ; M.D. Leyden, 1721 ; created M.D. at Cambridge, 1728 ; F.R.C.P., 1729 ; filled many offices at the College of Physicians ; wrote on osteology. [xl. 225]

NESFIELD, WILLIAM ANDREWS (1793-1881), artist ; entered the army, 1809 ; served in the Peninsular war and in Canada ; retired lieutenant, 1816 ; famous as a painter of cascades ; exhibited at the Society of Painters in Water-colours, 1820-50 ; frequently consulted as a landscape gardener. [xl. 226]

NESFIELD, WILLIAM EDEN (1835-1888), architect ; son of William Andrews Nesfield [q. v.] ; studied under William Burn and Anthony Salvin ; wrote on ' Mediæval Architecture,' 1862. [xl. 226]

NESHAM, CHRISTOPHER JOHN WILLIAMS (1771-1853), admiral ; entered the navy, 1782 ; in Normandy at the outbreak of the revolution, 1789 ; lieutenant, 1790 ; commander, 1798 ; advanced to post rank, 1802 ; took part in the capture of Martinique, 1809 ; rear-admiral, 1837 ; vice-admiral, 1846 ; admiral, 1852. [xl. 227]

NESS or **NESSE**, CHRISTOPHER (1621-1705), divine and author ; M.A. St. John's College, Cambridge ; schoolmaster and preacher in various parts of Yorkshire ; moved to London, c. 1674 ; excommunicated four times ; wrote on election and predestination. [xl. 228]

NEST or **NESTA** (c. 1095-c. 1114), mistress of Henry I ; married (c. 1095) to Gerald of Windsor, constable of Pembroke Castle : abducted by Owen, son of Cadwgan, c. 1106 ; wife or mistress of Stephen, constable of Cardigan ; mistress of Henry I, c. 1114. [xl. 228]

NETHERSOLE, SIR FRANCIS (1587-1659), secretary to the Electress Elizabeth ; scholar, fellow, and tutor of Trinity College, Cambridge ; M.A., 1610 ; became secretary to James Hay, viscount Doncaster, afterwards earl of Carlisle [q. v.], 1619 ; accompanied him on his mission to the Elector Palatine ; knighted, 1619 ; secretary to the Electress Palatine, 1620-3 ; M.P., Corfe Castle, 1624, 1625, and 1628 ; endeavoured unsuccessfully to raise money for the electress, 1633 ; imprisoned for a few months for too zealously supporting her, 1634 ; took no part in the civil wars and compounded for his estates, 1653 ; wrote political pamphlets advocating peace under the signature ' P. D.' ; endowed school at Polesworth. [xl. 229]

NETTER or **WALDEN**, THOMAS (d. 1430), Carmelite ; entered the Carmelite order at London ; D.D. Oxford ; attended the Paris council, 1409 ; inquisitor in England ; took prominent part in the persecution of the Wycliffites ; confessor to Henry V and one of the English representatives at Constance, 1415 ; sent on a mission to Wladislaw, king of Poland, 1419, to prevent the failure of the papal army against the Hussites ; confessor to Henry VI, accompanying him to France, 1430 ; died at Rouen. He instituted the Carmelite nuns in England and defended the Roman catholic faith against Wycliffe and Huss. His chief work was ' Doctrinale Fidei Ecclesiæ Catholicæ contra Wiclevistas et Hussitas,' and he probably wrote part of ' Fasciculi Zizaniorum, Johannis Wyclif.' [xl. 231]

NETTERVILLE, SIR JOHN, second VISCOUNT NETTERVILLE of Dowth (d. 1659), joined Lord Moore at Drogheda on the outbreak of the Irish rebellion, 1641 ; sent to Dublin, being distrusted, and was imprisoned for about a year, 1642-3 ; on his release joined Preston's Leinster army, but afterwards adhered to Ormonde and Clanricarde, 1648 ; retired to England, 1653. [xl. 234]

NETTERVILLE or **NUTREVILLA**, LUCAS DE (d. 1227), archbishop of Armagh ; archdeacon of Armagh, 1207 ; archbishop, 1216 ; commenced a Dominican monastery, 1224. [xl. 235]

NETTERVILLE, RICHARD (1545 ?-1607), Irish lawyer ; imprisoned when sent (1576) on a mission to Queen Elizabeth for the abolition of the cess ; released on account of the plague, 1577 ; M.P., co. Dublin, 1585. [xl. 235]

NETTLES, STEPHEN (fl. 1644), controversialist ; fellow Queens' College, Cambridge, 1599 ; M.A., 1602 ; B.D. Corpus Christi College, Cambridge, 1611 ; held preferments in Essex, 1610 ; ejected, 1644. [xl. 236]

NETTLESHIP, HENRY (1839-1893), Latin scholar ; educated at Charterhouse School ; scholar of Corpus Christi College, Oxford, 1857 ; won the Hertford scholarship and the Gaisford prize, 1859, and a Craven scholarship, 1861 ; B.A., 1861 ; fellow and tutor of Lincoln College, Oxford, 1862 ; assistant-master at Harrow, 1868 ; fellow of Corpus Christi College, Oxford, 1873 ; Corpus professor of Latin, 1878-93 ; spent many years on the study of Latin lexicography ; wrote on the classics. [xl. 236]

NETTLESHIP, RICHARD LEWIS (1846-1892), fellow and tutor of Balliol College, Oxford ; brother of Henry Nettleship [q. v.] ; scholar of Balliol College, Oxford, 1864 ; Hertford scholar, 1866 ; Ireland scholar, 1867 ; Gaisford prizeman, 1868 ; Craven scholar, 1870 ; Arnold prizeman, 1873 ; fellow of Balliol, 1869-92 ; died from exposure attempting to ascend Mont Blanc ; published an essay on ' The Theory of Education in Plato's Republic ' in ' Hellenica,' 1880 ; formed collections for a history of ' The Normans in Italy and Sicily.' [xl. 238]

NEUHOFF, FREDERICK DE (1725 ?-1797). [See FREDERICK, COLONEL.]

NEVAY, JOHN (d. 1672), covenanter ; nephew of Andrew Cant [q. v.] ; M.A. Aberdeen, 1626 ; strongly opposed to all set forms of prayer ; joined the whigamores, 1648, and the extreme covenanters, 1650 ; banished, 1660 ; died in Holland. [xl. 238]

NEVAY, JOHN (1792-1870), poet ; a handloom weaver ; gained repute as a lyric poet. [xl. 239]

NEVE. [See LE NEVE.]

NEVE, CORNELIUS (fl. 1637-1664), portrait-painter ; of Netherlandish origin ; painted portraits now at Petworth, Knole, and Oxford. [xl. 239]

NEVE or **LE NEVE**, JEFFERY (1579-1654), astrologer ; merchant and alderman of Great Yarmouth ; bailiff of Yarmouth, 1620 ; deputy water-bailiff of Dover, 1626 ; commissioned to encourage archery, 1628-31 ; M.D. Franeker ; established himself in London ; author of ' An Almanacke and Prognostication,' 1607-24, and a manuscript ' Vindicta Astrologiæ Judiciariæ,' [xl. 240]

NEVE, TIMOTHY (1694–1757), divine and antiquary; B.A. St. John's College, Cambridge, 1714; schoolmaster at Spalding, 1716–29; minor canon of Peterborough, 1729–1745; founded at Peterborough a Gentleman's Society; prebendary of Lincoln, 1744; archdeacon of Huntingdon, 1747.   [xl. 241]

NEVE, TIMOTHY (1724–1798), divine; son of Timothy Neve (1694–1757) [q. v.]; M.A. Corpus Christi College, Oxford, 1744; D.D., 1758; rector of Middleton Stoney, 1759; Lady Margaret professor of divinity at Oxford, 1783; prebendary of Worcester, 1783; published a vindication of the Protestant reformation, 1766.   [xl. 241]

NEVELL, JOHN (d. 1697), vice-admiral; lieutenant, 1673; commander, 1682; posted, 1682; rear-admiral, 1693; commanded off Dunkirk, 1693; commander-in-chief in the Mediterranean, 1696; vice-admiral and ordered to the West Indies, 1697; endeavoured unsuccessfully to intercept the French fleet after the attack on Cartagena; died of fever on the coast of Virginia.   [xl. 242]

NEVILE, NEVYLE, and **NEVILL**. [See NEVILLE.]

NEVILLE, ALAN DE (d. 1191?), judge of the exchequer, 1165; justice of the forests, 1166; excommunicated for supporting Henry II against Becket, 1166; went to Jerusalem, but was again excommunicated, 1168.   [xl. 243]

NEVILLE, ALEXANDER (d. 1392), archbishop of York; son of Ralph, brother Neville [q. v.]; prebendary of York, 1361; archdeacon of Durham, 1369–71; succeeded Thoresby as archbishop of York, 1373; engaged in various ecclesiastical quarrels, and was a conspicuous member of the court party; appealed of treason, 1388, and deprived; died at Louvain.   [xl. 243]

NEVILLE, ALEXANDER (1544–1614), scholar; brother of Thomas Neville [q. v.]; M.A. Cambridge, 1581; studied law and became secretary to Archbishop Parker, and edited for him 'Tabula Heptarchiæ Saxonicæ'; wrote a Latin account of Kett's rebellion, 1575, with a description of Norwich and its antiquities; translated Seneca's 'Œdipus' into ballad metre, 1563; published 'Academiæ Cantabrigiensis lacrymæ tumulo . . . P. Sidneij sacratæ per A. Nevillum,' 1587.   [xl. 244]

NEVILLE, ANNE (1456–1485). [See ANNE.]

NEVILLE, CHARLES, sixth EARL OF WESTMORLAND (1543–1601), son of Henry, fifth earl of Westmorland [q. v.]; succeeded his father, 1563; endeavoured with the Earl of Northumberland to release Mary Queen of Scots, 1569, and marched towards Tutbury; after the removal of Mary to Coventry and retreat of the rebels went to Louvain; was attainted, 1571, losing his estates; lived at Maestricht, c. 1577; went to Rome, 1581; died at Nieuport.   [xl. 245]

NEVILLE, CHRISTOPHER (fl. 1569), rebel; son of Ralph, fourth earl of Westmorland [q. v.]; a leader in the northern rebellion of 1569; fled to Scotland and then to the Low Countries, where he died.   [xl. 246]

NEVILLE, CUTHBERT (fl. 1569), son of Ralph, fourth earl of Westmorland [q. v.]; took part in the 1569 rebellion, fled to the Low Countries, and died there.   [xl. 247]

NEVILLE, EDMUND (1560?–1618), conspirator; claimed to be heir to his grand-uncle, fourth Baron Latimer, c. 1584; implicated in Parry's plot, 1584; imprisoned in the Tower of London, 1584–95; died in Brussels.   [xl. 247]

NEVILLE, EDMUND (1605–1647), jesuit; studied at St. Omer and Rome; professed of the four vows, 1640; missioner in England; wrote on Christian fortitude, 1630.   [xl. 248]

NEVILLE, EDWARD (d. 1476), first BARON OF BERGAVENNY or ABERGAVENNY (the form finally adopted 1730), son of Ralph Neville, first earl of Westmorland [q. v.]; married Elizabeth Beauchamp, heiress of Richard, earl of Worcester, who had inherited the castle and lands of Bergavenny; obtained possession of his father-in-law's lands, 1436, but did not definitely acquire the castle and lordship of Bergavenny till 1450; served in Normandy, 1449, and followed the heads of his family in the civil strife; sat regularly in the privy council and served in the north, 1462; commissioner of array for Kent.   [xl. 248]

NEVILLE, SIR EDWARD (d. 1538), courtier; brother of George Neville, third baron Bergavenny; held many court offices; knighted at Tournay, 1513; held command in the army in France, 1523; assisted at Anne Boleyn's coronation, 1533, and Prince Edward's baptism, 1537; found guilty of conspiring with the Poles and beheaded.   [xl. 250]

NEVILLE, verè SCARISBRICK, EDWARD (1639–1709), jesuit; assumed the name Neville, 1660; professed of the four vows, 1677; English missioner and royal chaplain, 1686; on the continent, 1688–93; published sermons.   [xl. 250]

NEVILLE, GEOFFREY DE (d. 1225), baron; son of Alan de Neville [q. v.]; king's chamberlain, 1207; his fidelity to John rewarded with grants of land and the shrievalty of Yorkshire, 1214; seneschal of Poitou and Gascony, 1215–19; reappointed, 1223; died in Gascony.   [xl. 251]

NEVILLE, GEOFFREY DE (d. 1285), baron; brother of Robert de Neville (d. 1282) [q. v.]; sided with the king in the barons' war; constable of Dover Castle, 1265, of Scarborough, 1270; served against Llywelyn, 1276 and 1282.   [xl. 252]

NEVILLE, GEORGE (1433?–1476), bishop of Exeter, archbishop of York, and chancellor of England; son of Richard Neville, first earl of Salisbury [q. v.], prebendary of York, 1446; B.A. Balliol College, Oxford, 1450; M.A., 1452; chancellor of Oxford University, 1453–7; received much ecclesiastical preferment; bishop-elect of Exeter, 1455; consecrated, 1458; avoided being compromised in the rebellion of his family, 1459, and on their successful return to London became chancellor, 1460; succeeded in detaching Louis XI of France from the Lancastrians and obtaining a commercial truce with Flanders at a conference at Hesdin, 1463; arranged a peace with Scotland, 1464; celebrated his installation (1465) in the archbishopric of York with great extravagance; deprived of the seal, 1467; was apparently reconciled to Edward IV, 1468, but performed the marriage (1469) between Warwick's elder daughter Isabel and the Duke of Clarence, and, on Edward's flight to Holland, 1470, became chancellor to Henry VI; surrendered Henry VI and himself to Edward IV when Edward entered London as victor, 1471; was imprisoned for two months only, and thought himself restored to favour, but (1472) was seized secretly and imprisoned in France till 1475, and his lands and see forfeited. He was a benefactor of Balliol College, Oxford, and saved Lincoln College, Oxford, from confiscation, 1462.   [xl. 252]

NEVILLE, GEORGE, third BARON OF BERGAVENNY (1461?–1535), brother of Sir Edward Neville [q. v.]; K.B., 1483; succeeded his father, 1492; warden of the Cinque ports and K.G., 1513; arrested on account of his knowledge of the schemes of his father-in-law, Edward Stafford, third duke of Buckingham [q. v.], 1521; released, 1522; commanded in the army in France, 1523.   [xl. 257]

NEVILLE, GEORGE (1509–1567), divine; son of Richard, second baron Latimer; B.A. Cambridge, 1524; D.D.; held many livings and (c. 1558) became archdeacon of Carlisle.   [xl. 296]

NEVILLE, GEORGE, afterwards GRENVILLE (1789–1854), son of Richard Aldworth Griffin-Neville [q. v.]; of Eton and Trinity College, Cambridge; M.A., 1810; nominated master of Magdalene College, Cambridge, 1813, inherited the property and assumed the surname of his uncle Thomas Grenville (1755–1846) [q. v.], 1825; dean of Windsor, 1846.   [xl. 297]

NEVILLE, GREY (1681–1723), politician; M.P. Abingdon, 1705, Wallingford, 1708, Berwick-on-Tweed, 1715; joined the Walpole section of the whigs. [xl. 258]

NEVILLE, HENRY, fifth EARL OF WESTMORLAND (1525?–1563), son of Ralph Neville, fourth earl of Westmorland [q. v.]; knighted, 1544; succeeded as earl, 1550; K.G., 1552; supported Queen Mary on Edward VI's death; lieutenant-general of the north, 1558–9.   [xl. 278]

NEVILLE, SIR HENRY (1564?–1615), courtier and diplomatist; matriculated from Merton College, Oxford, 1577; created M.A., 1605; sat in parliament from coming of age till his death; knighted and sent as ambassador to France, 1599; imprisoned in the Tower of London for complicity in Essex's plot, 1600–3; identified himself with the popular party.   [xl. 258]

NEVILLE, HENRY (1620–1694), political and miscellaneous writer; grandson of Sir Henry Neville (1564?–1615) [q. v.]; educated at Merton and University Colleges, Oxford; visited Italy; M.P., Reading, 1658; arrested on suspicion of implication in the Yorkshire rising, 1663; released, 1664; author of some coarse lampoons and of a successful story, 'The Isle of Pines,' 1668; translated Macchiavelli's works. [xl. 259]

NEVILLE, HUGH DE (d. 1222), baron; accompanied Richard I to Palestine, 1190; present at the siege of Joppa, 1192; chief-justice of forests, 1198; one of King John's chief advisers, but on his death joined the barons; a benefactor of Waltham Abbey. [xl. 260]

NEVILLE, HUGH DE (d. 1234), son of Hugh de Neville (d. 1222) [q. v.]; chief-justice and warden of forests, 1223. [xl. 261]

NEVILLE, SIR HUMPHREY (1439?–1469), insurgent; imprisoned in the Tower for joining Henry VI, 1461; escaped and was pardoned and knighted, 1463; again joined the Lancastrians, 1464; raised a fresh revolt, 1469, which was suppressed by Warwick; beheaded at York. [xl. 262]

NEVILLE, JOHN DE, fifth BARON NEVILLE OF RABY (d. 1388), son of Ralph Neville, fourth baron Neville [q. v.]; fought in Gascony, 1345, 1349, and 1360; knighted, 1360; succeeded his father, 1367; K.G., 1369; admiral of the fleet, 1370; negotiated an offensive and defensive alliance with John de Montfort, duke of Brittany, 1372; commanded at the siege of Brest; impeached, 1376, but his impeachment was reversed, 1377; as lieutenant of Aquitaine, 1378, recovered many towns and forts; constantly employed on the Scottish border after 1381. He founded a chantry in the Charterhouse at Coventry, erected a screen in Durham Cathedral, and built a great part of Raby Castle. [xl. 262]

NEVILLE, JOHN, MARQUIS OF MONTAGU and EARL OF NORTHUMBERLAND (d. 1471), son of Richard Neville, first earl of Salisbury [q. v.]; knighted, 1449; took part in the northern conflicts, 1453 and 1457; taken prisoner and confined in Chester Castle, 1459; released after the battle of Northampton, 1460, raised to the peerage as Baron Montagu, 1465; imprisoned at York after the second battle of St. Albans, 1461, but liberated by Edward after Towton, 1461; kept employed in the north; K.G., 1462; commissioner to arrange definite peace with the Scots, 1463; avoided Humphrey Neville's ambush; utterly defeated the Lancastrians at Hexham, 1464, for which he was rewarded with the estates and earldom of Northumberland, 1464; joined the Lancastrians in anger that the estates and earldom of Northumberland were restored to Henry Percy (1446–1489) [q. v.]; allowed Edward IV to land in Yorkshire, but fought on the Lancastrian side at Barnet, where he was slain; his body exposed for two days at St. Paul's and then interred at Bisham Abbey. [xl. 265]

NEVILLE, JOHN, third BARON LATIMER (1490?–1543), son of Richard Neville, second baron Latimer [q. v.]; secured valuable grants of land; succeeded his father, 1531; implicated in the Pilgrimage of Grace, 1536; second husband of Catherine Parr, afterwards sixth wife of Henry VIII. [xl. 269]

NEVILLE, JOLLAN DE (d. 1246), judge; justice in eyre in Yorkshire and Northumberland, 1234–41; sat at Westminster, 1241–5; possibly author or part author of the 'Testa de Nevill.' [xl. 269]

NEVILLE, RALPH (d. 1244), bishop of Chichester and chancellor; clerk of the seal under Peter des Roches, [q. v.], 1213; held many preferments; became vice-chancellor, c. 1220; chancellor and bishop of Chichester, 1222; justiciar in Shropshire, 1224; lord chancellor, 1226; his election as archbishop of Canterbury (1231) quashed by Gregory IX; granted the Irish chancellorship for life, 1232; assent to Neville's election as bishop of Winchester (1238) refused by Henry III; forcibly deprived of the seal, 1238, but restored to office, 1242. [xl. 270]

NEVILLE, RALPH DE, fourth BARON NEVILLE OF RABY (1291?–1367), seneschal of the household; succeeded his father, 1331; with Henry Percy, lord Percy (1299?–1352) [q. v.], made warden of the marches, 1334; assisted in the victory of Neville's Cross, near Durham, 1346; made David Bruce prisoner and was much occupied with negotiations for Bruce's release; for a time governor of Berwick, 1355. [xl. 271]

NEVILLE, RALPH, sixth BARON NEVILLE OF RABY and first EARL OF WESTMORLAND (1364–1425), son of John de Neville, fifth baron Neville [q. v.]; knighted, 1380; succeeded his father, 1388; joint-warden of the marches and constantly employed in peace negotiations with Scotland; closely connected with the court party; assisted at the trial of the lords appellant, 1397; created Earl of Westmorland, 1397; took part against Richard II, 1399, and conveyed his resignation to convocation; assisted at Henry IV's coronation; marshal of England, 1399; captain of Roxburgh Castle and K.G., 1402; warden of the west marches after the battle of Shrewsbury, 1403, where Hotspur was slain; in the revolt, 1405, threw himself between the two main bodies of the rebels, routed the Cleveland force, and took Scrope and Mowbray prisoners; constantly occupied in negotiations with Scotland; assisted the regent Bedford, and was one of the executors of Henry V's will; benefactor of Staindrop and a great builder. [xl. 273]

NEVILLE, RALPH, second EARL OF WESTMORLAND (d. 1484), grandson of Ralph Neville, first earl [q. v.]; married a daughter of Hotspur (Sir Henry Percy (1364–1403) [q. v.]). [xl. 277]

NEVILLE, RALPH, fourth EARL OF WESTMORLAND (1499–1550), great-nephew of Ralph Neville, second earl of Westmorland [q. v.]; received livery of his lands, 1520; knighted, 1523; K.G., 1525; vice-warden of the east and middle marches; chief commissioner to treat with Scotland, 1525; privy councillor, 1526; remained loyal during the Pilgrimage of Grace, 1536; member of the council of the north, 1545. [xl. 278]

NEVILLE, RICHARD, first EARL OF SALISBURY (1400–1460), son of Ralph Neville, first earl of Westmorland [q. v.]; warden of the west march, 1420; married Alice, only child of Thomas de Montacute, fourth earl of Salisbury [q. v.], 1425; became Earl of Salisbury in right of his wife, 1429; joined Henry VI in France, 1431; warden of both marches, 1434; helped to arrest Humphrey, duke of Gloucester, 1447; persuaded York to lay down his arms, 1452; chancellor during the Duke of York's protectorate, 1453–5; by a victory at Blore Heath effected a junction with York at Ludlow, 1459, with whom, when defeated at Ludford, he fled to France and was attainted in his absence; returned with Warwick, 1460, and remained in charge of London while Warwick went to meet the Lancastrians at Northampton; his attainder removed and himself made chamberlain, 1460; captured the night after the battle of Wakefield, taken to Pontefract Castle, and murdered there. [xl. 279]

NEVILLE, RICHARD, EARL OF WARWICK and SALISBURY (1428–1471), the 'king-maker'; son of Richard Neville, first earl of Salisbury [q. v.]; married Anne, only daughter of Richard de Beauchamp, earl of Warwick [q.v.]; succeeded to the title and estates in right of his wife, 1449; when Richard, duke of York, claimed the regency, 1453, sided with York, took up arms with him, 1455, and distinguished himself in the first battle of St. Albans, 1455, rewarded with the captaincy of Calais, where he entered into negotiations with Philip of Burgundy, 1457; took part in the 'love-day' procession, 1458; made a popular hero in England by his attack on a fleet of Spanish ships off Calais, 1458; brought into Calais five great carracks of Spain and Genoa, 1459; with York at Ludlow, but returned to Calais in time to close its gates against Somerset, who had been appointed to succeed him by Queen Margaret; landed at Sandwich, June 1460, and marched to London, which was friendly; gained an easy victory at Northampton, 1460, and brought the captive King Henry VI to London, after which matters were compromised by making York heir-presumptive, an arrangement which came to nothing, since the Lancastrians rallied in December at Wakefield, 1460, and York and Salisbury, the 'king-maker's' father, were both killed; became Earl of Salisbury, K.G., and great chamberlain, 1461; lost control of King Henry VI by the victory of Queen Margaret at the second battle of St. Albans, 1461; joined Edward, the young duke of York (afterwards Edward IV), who had been victorious at Mortimer's Cross, 1461, and assisted in declaring him king; with Edward followed the Lancastrians and defeated them at Towton, March 1461; confirmed in all his offices by Edward IV at his coronation; the real ruler of England during the first three years of Edward's reign; secured ascendency for Edward IV at home and honour abroad; annoyed at Edward IV's marriage with Elizabeth Woodville, 1464, and at having to negotiate with foreign powers according to the dictates of the Woodvilles; withdrew from court, 1467; married his daughter Isabel to the Duke of Clarence early in 1469 at Calais, and instigated the revolt of Robin of Redesdale, arriving himself just after the victory of Northampton, July 1469; kept Edward IV prisoner, but was obliged to release him to suppress a rising in Yorkshire; with Clarence fomented fresh disturbances. February 1470; was defeated at Stamford by Edward IV, 1470, but escaped to Honfleur; joined the Lancastrians, and after some difficulty persuaded Queen Margaret to accept his aid: landed in England, September 1470, advanced on London, and proclaimed Henry VI king, Edward IV being compelled to flee to Flanders; maintained his position with difficulty, and when (March 1471) Edward IV landed in Yorkshire, allowed him to pass and proclaim himself king; defeated and slain by Edward IV at Barnet, 14 April 1471; his body exposed for two days in St. Paul's Cathedral and buried at Bisham Abbey. Warwick devoted himself to the acquisition of power for himself and his family; he was singularly energetic, and his genuine diplomatic talent, favoured by opportunity, enabled him to grasp and utilise almost royal power. His title of the 'king-maker' is not traceable further back than the Latin history of Scotland of John Major (1469–1550) [q. v.]   [xl. 283]

NEVILLE, RICHARD, second BARON LATIMER (1468–1530), succeeded his father, 1469; served on the northern border; made lieutenant-general, 1522; commissioner for the north, 1525.   [xl. 296]

NEVILLE, RICHARD ALDWORTH GRIFFIN-, second BARON BRAYBROOKE (1750–1825), son of Richard Neville Aldworth Neville [q. v.]; M.P. for Grampound, 1774, for Reading, 1782–96; succeeded his father's maternal uncle as Baron Braybrooke and assumed the name Griffin, 1797; lord-lieutenant of Essex, 1798.   [xl. 296]

NEVILLE, RICHARD CORNWALLIS, fourth BARON BRAYBROOKE (1820–1861), archæologist; son of Richard Griffin Neville, third baron Braybrooke [q. v.]; entered the army, 1837; served in Canada, 1842; F.S.A., 1847; brought to light the Roman station at Great Chesterford, and the Saxon cemeteries near Little Wilbraham and Linton; wrote about his discoveries; succeeded his father, 1858.   [xl. 297]

NEVILLE, RICHARD GRIFFIN, third BARON BRAYBROOKE (1783–1858), son of Richard Aldworth Griffin-Neville, second baron [q. v.]; was educated at Eton and Oxford; M.P. from 1805 until his succession to the peerage, 1825; was first editor of Pepys's 'Diary,' 1825.
[xl. 298]

NEVILLE, RICHARD NEVILLE ALDWORTH (1717–1793), statesman; originally Aldworth, assumed name of Neville on succeeding to his maternal uncle's widow's property, 1762; educated at Eton and Merton College, Oxford; travelled in Switzerland and Italy; M.P., Reading, 1747, Wallingford, 1754–61, Tavistock, 1761–74; under-secretary of state under Bedford, 1748; secretary to the embassy at Paris, 1762–3.   [xl. 298]

NEVILLE, ROBERT DE, second BARON NEVILLE OF RABY (d. 1282), brother of Geoffrey de Neville (d. 1285) [q. v.]; succeeded his father, 1254; governor of northern castles; chief-justice of forests, 1264; reinstated on the final defeat of the barons and made chief assessor in the northern counties, 1275.   [xl. 299]

NEVILLE, ROBERT (1404–1457), bishop of Salisbury and Durham; son of Ralph Neville, first earl of Westmorland [q. v.]; received much ecclesiastical preferment and (1427) became bishop of Salisbury; founded Sherborne almshouses; translated to Durham, 1438; built the 'Exchequer' near Durham Castle; visited by Henry VI, 1448; commissioner in the truces with Scotland, 1449 and 1457.   [xl. 300]

NEVILLE or NEVILE, ROBERT (d. 1694), dramatist and divine; educated at Eton and King's College, Cambridge; M.A., 1664; B.D. by royal mandate, 1671; rector of Anstie, 1671; published 'The Poor Scholar,' 1673.
[xl. 302]

NEVILLE, SIR THOMAS (d. 1542), speaker of the House of Commons; brother of George Neville, third baron of Bergavenny [q. v.]; member of Henry VIII's household, and privy councillor; M.P., Kent, and speaker, 1514; commissioner for enclosures, 1517; member of the Star chamber, 1519.   [xl. 302]

NEVILLE, THOMAS (d. 1615), dean of Canterbury; brother of Alexander Neville (1544–1614) [q. v.]; fellow, Pembroke College, Cambridge, 1570; master of Magdalene College, Cambridge, 1582; prebendary of Ely, 1587; D.D., 1588; vice-chancellor of Cambridge, 1588; dean of Peterborough, 1590; master of Trinity College, Cambridge, 1593–1615; dean of Canterbury, 1597; assisted largely in rebuilding Trinity College, and contributed to the library; benefactor of Eastbridge Hospital, Canterbury.
[xl. 302]

NEVILLE, SIR WILLIAM DE (d. 1389?), lollard; son of Ralph de Neville, fourth baron Neville of Raby [q. v.]; admiral of the fleet north of the Thames, 1372; a member of the king's household; supported the lollard movement.
[xl. 303]

NEVILLE, WILLIAM, BARON FAUCONBERG and afterwards EARL OF KENT (d. 1463), son of Ralph Neville, first earl of Westmorland [q. v.]; knighted, 1426; became Baron Fauconberg in right of his wife Joan, 1424; served in Normandy, 1436 and 1439–40; K.G., 1439; taken prisoner at Pont de l'Arche, 1449; keeper of Roxburgh Castle, 1452; remained as Warwick's lieutenant at Calais, 1459; took prominent part at Towton, 1461; raised to the earldom of Kent, 1460; when admiral of the Channel fleet (1462) failed to intercept Queen Margaret.   [xl. 304]

NEVILLE, WILLIAM (fl. 1518), poet; son of Richard Neville, second baron Latimer [q. v.]: author of 'The Castell of Pleasure,' printed by Hary Pepwell, 1518, and Wynkyn de Worde.   [xl. 306]

NEVILLE-PAYNE, HENRY (fl. 1672–1710). [See PAYNE.]

NEVIN, THOMAS (1686?–1744), Irish presbyterian minister; M.A., Glasgow; ordained minister of Downpatrick, 1711; charged with Arianism by Charles Echlin, 1724, when the civil courts dismissed the case, but the general synod struck him off the roll; readmitted, 1726.
[xl. 306]

NEVISON, JOHN (1639–1684), highwayman; served in Holland; took to highway robbery, c. 1660; convicted and imprisoned at York, 1676; escaped; a reward offered for his apprehension, which was effected at Thorp, 1685; hanged at York.   [xl. 307]

NEVOY, SIR DAVID, LORD REIDIE, afterwards LORD NEVOY (d. 1683), Scottish judge; appointed lord of session and knighted, 1661.   [xl. 308]

NEVYLE, ALEXANDER (1544–1614). [See NEVILLE.]

NEVYNSON, CHRISTOPHER (d. 1551), lawyer; cousin of Stephen Nevynson [q. v.]; admitted advocate, 1539; commissioner for diocesan visitations and heresy trials, 1547.   [xl. 308]

NEVYNSON, STEPHEN (d. 1581?), prebendary of Canterbury; fellow and tutor of Trinity College, Cambridge, 1544; M.A. Christ's College, Cambridge, 1548; LL.D., 1553; commissioner for diocesan visitations, 1559; commissary-general of Canterbury, 1560; canon of Canterbury before 1563; vicar-general of Norwich, 1566.
[xl. 309]

NEWABBEY, LORD (1596–1646). [See SPOTTISWOOD, SIR ROBERT.]

NEWALL, ROBERT STIRLING (1812–1889), engineer and astronomer; invented wire-ropes, 1840; laid many submarine telegraph cables; invented the 'brakedrum' and cone for laying cables in deep seas, 1853; made a series of drawings of the sun, 1848–52; had a large telescope made, 1871; wrote on submarine cables; F.R.A.S., 1864; F.R.S., 1875; M.I.M.E., 1879.
[xl. 309]

NEWARK, first LORD (d. 1682). [See LESLIE, DAVID.]

NEWARK or NEWERK, HENRY DE (d. 1299), archbishop of York; received much preferment; prebendary of St. Paul's Cathedral, 1271; archdeacon of Richmond, 1281; prebendary of York before 1283; commissioner to arrange services due to Edward I, 1283; dean of York, 1290; present at Norham, at the process between the claimants to the Scottish crown, 1291; archbishop of York, 1296–9.   [xl. 310]

NEWBALD or NEWBAUD, GEOFFREY DE (d. 1283), judge; assessor of the fifteenth in Norfolk and Suffolk, 1275; justice, 1276; chancellor of the exchequer, 1277.   [xl. 311]

NEWBERY, FRANCIS (1743–1818), publisher; son of John Newbery [q. v.]; succeeded to his father's business, 1767; wrote a voluminous account of Goldsmith's death; scholar, poet, and lover of music; his classical translations published as 'Donum Amicis,' 1815. [xl. 312]

NEWBERY, JOHN (1713–1767), publisher and originator of children's books; assistant-editor of the 'Reading Mercury,' 1730; combined patent medicine selling and publishing in London, 1744; identified himself with newspaper enterprise; first to issue books specially for children; planned, if he did not write, 'Giles Gingerbread,' 'Mrs. Margery Two Shoes,' and 'Tommy Trip and his Dog Jowler'; Dr. Johnson, Oliver Goldsmith, Christopher Smart, and Dr. Dodd among his literary clients. [xl. 312]

NEWBERY, RALPH or RAFE (*fl.* 1590), publisher; made free of the Stationers' Company, 1567; published 'Hakluyt's Voyages,' 'Holinshed's Chronicles,' 1574, Barnabe Googe's 'Ecloges,' 1563, and Stow's 'Annals,' 1580, 1592, and 1600. [xl. 314]

NEWBERY, THOMAS (*fl.* 1563), author of 'Dives Pragmaticus,' 1563, a work to teach children to read and write. [xl. 314]

NEWBERY, THOMAS (*fl.* 1656), printer; published 'Rules for the Government of the Tongue,' 1656. [xl. 314]

NEWBOLD, THOMAS JOHN (1807–1850), traveller; obtained commission under the East India Company, 1828; lieutenant, 1834; aide-de-camp to brigadier-general Wilson, 1835–40; collected in his constant intercourse with Malayan chiefs materials for his book on the Straits of Malacca, 1839; studied the geology of Southern India; R.A.S., 1841; captain, 1842; assistant at Kurnool, 1843–1848, at Hyderabad, 1848; died at Mahabuleshwar. [xl. 314]

NEWBOULD, WILLIAM WILLIAMSON (1819–1886), botanist; M.A. Trinity College, Cambridge, 1845; was ordained, 1844, but did not officiate regularly; fellow of the Botanical Society of Edinburgh, 1841; an original member of the Ray Society, 1844; F.L.S., 1863; devoted himself to helping scientific workers; *Newbouldia* (Bignoniaceæ) named after him. [xl. 315]

NEWBURGH, first EARL OF (*d.* 1670). [See LIVINGSTONE, SIR JAMES.]

NEWBURGH, COUNTESS OF (*d.* 1755). [See RADCLIFFE, CHARLOTTE MARIA.]

NEWBURGH, NEUBOURG, or **BEAUMONT**, HENRY DE, first EARL OF WARWICK (*d.* 1123), lord of Neubourg in Normandy; keeper of Warwick Castle, 1068; created Earl of Warwick by William II; friend of Henry I; benefactor of Préaux abbey and the monks of Warwick. [xl. 316]

NEWBURGH, WILLIAM OF (1136–1198?). [See WILLIAM.]

NEWBYTH, LORD (1620–1698). [See BAIRD, SIR JOHN.]

NEWCASTLE, HUGH OF (*fl.* 1322), Franciscan; pupil of Duns Scotus; attended the chapter of Perugia, 1322; wrote on Antichrist; buried at Paris. [xl. 317]

NEWCASTLE-ON-TYNE, DUKES OF. [See CAVENDISH, WILLIAM, first DUKE, 1592–1676; HOLLES, JOHN, first duke of the second creation, 1662–1711.]

NEWCASTLE-ON-TYNE, DUCHESS OF (1624?–1674). [See CAVENDISH, MARGARET.]

NEWCASTLE-UNDER-LYME, DUKES OF. [See PELHAM-HOLLES, THOMAS, first DUKE, 1693–1768; CLINTON, HENRY FIENNES, second DUKE, 1720–1794; CLINTON, HENRY PELHAM FIENNES PELHAM, fourth DUKE, 1785–1851; CLINTON, HENRY PELHAM FIENNES PELHAM, fifth DUKE, 1811–1864.]

NEWCOMB, THOMAS (1682?–1762), poet; B.A. Corpus Christi College, Oxford, 1704; chaplain to the Duke of Richmond and rector of Stopham, 1705; published 'Bibliotheca' (satire), 1712, and, by subscription, 'The Last Judgment of Men and Angels,' 1723; suffered in old age from poverty, gout, and rheumatism; wrote much, chiefly odes. [xl. 318]

NEWCOMBE, THOMAS, the elder (1627–1681), king's printer to Charles II; was proprietor and printer of 'Mercurius Publicus' and other newspapers; granted the patent of king's printer for thirty years, 1675. [xl. 319]

NEWCOMBE, THOMAS, the younger (*d.* 1691), son of Thomas Newcombe the elder [q. v.]; king's printer to Charles II, James II, and William III. [xl. 319]

NEWCOME, HENRY (1627–1695), nonconformist minister; M.A. St. John's College, Cambridge, 1651; schoolmaster at Congleton, 1647; received presbyterian ordination; curate of Goostrey, 1648; rector of Gawsworth, 1650; elected preacher at the collegiate church, Manchester, 1656, but not retained on its reconstitution, 1660; continued to preach till 1662; took out a licence, 1672, and performed such ministrations as he could in and near Manchester; moderator of a meeting of the United Brethren, 1693; kept a 'diary' (part published) and wrote devotional works. [xl. 319]

NEWCOME, HENRY (1650–1713), divine; of St. Edmund Hall, Oxford; son of Henry Newcome (1627–1695) [q. v.]; rector of Tattenhall, 1675, of Middleton, 1701. [xl. 321]

NEWCOME, PETER (1656–1738), divine; of Magdalene College, Cambridge, St. Edmund Hall, Oxford, and Brasenose College, Oxford; son of Henry Newcome (1627–1695) [q. v.]; vicar of Aldenham, 1683, of Hackney, 1703. [xl. 321]

NEWCOME, PETER (1727–1797), antiquary; grandson of Peter Newcome (1656–1738) [q. v.]; prebendary of Llandaff, 1757; wrote a history of St. Albans Abbey, 1793–5. [xl. 322]

NEWCOME, WILLIAM (1729–1800), archbishop of Armagh; grand-nephew of Henry Newcome (1627–1695) [q. v.]; scholar of Pembroke College, Oxford, 1745; removed to Hertford College and became fellow (1753), tutor, and vice-principal; M.A., 1753; D.D., 1765; bishop of Dromore, 1766; translated to Ossory, 1775, to Waterford and Lismore, 1779; finally became archbishop of Armagh, 1795; worked at the revision of the whole bible; his works chiefly exegetical. [xl. 322]

NEWCOMEN, ELIAS (1550?–1614), schoolmaster; second cousin of Matthew Newcomen [q. v.]; M.A. Magdalene College, Cambridge, 1572; fellow; set up a school near London; incumbent of Stoke-Fleming, 1600; translated from the Dutch an account of the events in the Netherlands, *c.* 1575. [xl. 323]

NEWCOMEN, MATTHEW (1610?–1669), ejected minister, and one of the authors of 'Smectymnuus'; M.A. St. John's College, Cambridge, 1633; lecturer at Dedham, 1636; headed the church reform party in Essex; assisted Edmund Calamy the elder [q. v.], whose sister-in-law he had married, to write 'Smectymnuus' (published 1641); preached before parliament, 1643; protested against the 'agreement,' 1649; became pastor of the English church at Leyden, 1662; died of the plague at Leyden. [xl. 324]

NEWCOMEN, THOMAS (1603?–1665), royalist divine; brother of Matthew Newcomen [q. v.]; M.A. St. John's College, Cambridge, 1629; incumbent of Holy Trinity, Colchester, 1628; a strong royalist; rector of Clothall, 1653; D.D. by mandamus; prebendary of Lincoln, 1660. [xl. 325]

NEWCOMEN, THOMAS (1663–1729), inventor of the atmospheric steam-engine; great-grandson of Elias Newcomen [q. v.]; an ironmonger or blacksmith of Dartmouth; corresponded with Dr. Hooke on Papin's proposals to obtain motive power by exhausting the air from a cylinder furnished with a piston (John Calley or Cawley, a glazier, was associated with him in this invention); entered into partnership with Thomas Savery [q. v.], who had taken out a patent for raising water from mines, 1698; so greatly improved Savery's patent, which had been up to that time rather unsuccessful, that it furnished the model for pumping-engines for three-quarters of a century; there are two prints extant of Newcomen's engine, which was a beam engine of familiar type, of five and a-half horse-power, raising fifty gallons of water per minute from a depth of a hundred and fifty-six feet. [xl. 326]

NEWCOURT, RICHARD, the elder (*d.* 1679), topographical draughtsman; executed a map of London and the suburbs (published by William Faithorne, 1658), only two copies of which are extant. [xl. 329]

NEWCOURT, RICHARD, the younger (*d.* 1716), author of 'Repertorium Ecclesiasticum'; son of Richard Newcourt the elder [q. v.]; principal registrar of London, 1669–96; published the 'Repertorium Ecclesiasticum,' 1708–10. [xl. 329]

NEWDEGATE, CHARLES NEWDIGATE (1816–1887), politician; of Eton and Christ Church, Oxford; M.A., 1859; created D.C.L., 1863; conservative M.P. for North Warwickshire, 1843–85; privy councillor, 1886; published letters on trade, 1849–51. [xl. 329]

NEWDEGATE or **NEWDIGATE**, JOHN (1541–1592), scholar and country gentleman; of Eton and King's College, Cambridge; B.A., 1563; M.A. Prague; wrote verses in the University Collection on Bucer; M.P. for Middlesex in Queen Elizabeth's second and third parliaments. [xl. 330]

NEWDIGATE, SIR RICHARD, first baronet (1602–1678), grandson of John Newdegate [q. v.]; barrister, Gray's Inn, 1628; serjeant, 1654; justice of the king's bench, 1654; returned to the bar, 1655; chief-justice, 1660; received a baronetcy, 1677. [xl. 331]

NEWDIGATE, SIR ROGER, fifth baronet (1719–1806), antiquary; great-grandson of Sir Richard Newdigate [q. v.]; succeeded his brother as baronet, 1734; educated at Westminster School and University College, Oxford; created M.A., 1738; D.C.L., 1749; M.P., Middlesex, 1741–7, for Oxford University, 1750–80; travelled and collected ancient marbles; a benefactor of University College and the Radcliffe Library, Oxford; founded the Newdigate prize for English verse, 1805. [xl. 331]

NEWELL, EDWARD JOHN (1771–1798), Irish informer; practised miniature-painting at Belfast, 1796; joined United Irishmen and betrayed them, 1797, in revenge for their distrust of him; published some confessions and was assassinated. [xl. 332]

NEWELL, ROBERT HASELL (1778–1852), amateur artist and author; fourth wrangler, St. John's College, Cambridge, 1799; M.A., 1802; B.D., 1810; rector of Little Hormead, 1813; illustrated an edition of Goldsmith, 1811–20, and wrote and illustrated letters on North Wales, 1821. [xl. 333]

NEWENHAM, SIR EDWARD (1732–1814), Irish politician; collector of the excise of Dublin, 1764–72; M.P. Enniscorthy, 1769–76, co. Dublin, 1776–97; anxious to reform parliamentary abuses on a strictly protestant basis; advocated protective duties. [xl. 333]

NEWENHAM, FREDERICK (1807–1859), a fashionable painter of ladies' portraits; exhibited at the Royal Academy and British Institution. [xl. 334]

NEWENHAM, JOHN DE (*d.* 1382?), chamberlain of the exchequer; received much ecclesiastical preferment; prebendary of Lichfield, 1359, of Lincoln, 1360; chamberlain of the exchequer, 1364. [xl. 334]

NEWENHAM, THOMAS DE (*fl.* 1393), clerk in chancery; receiver of parliamentary petitions, 1371–91; had custody of the great seal, 1377 and 1386. [xl. 335]

NEWENHAM, THOMAS (1762–1831), writer on Ireland; nephew of Sir Edward Newenham [q. v.]; M.P., Clonmel, 1798; opposed the union; wrote on the resources and capabilities of Ireland. [xl. 335]

NEWHALL, LORD (1664?–1736). [See PRINGLE, SIR WALTER.]

NEWHAVEN, first VISCOUNT (1624?–1698). [See CHEYNE or CHIENE, CHARLES.]

NEWLAND, ABRAHAM (1730–1807), chief cashier of the Bank of England; entered the bank, 1748; became chief cashier, 1782; bank-notes being long known as 'Abraham Newlands' from bearing his signature; resigned his position, 1807; amassed a fortune by economy and speculation in Pitt's loans. [xl. 336]

NEWLAND, HENRY GARRETT (1804–1860), divine; M.A. Corpus Christi College, Cambridge, 1830; rector of Westbourne, 1829; vicar of St. Mary-Church, 1855; supported the tractarian movement, and published pamphlets on it. [xl. 336]

NEWLAND, JOHN (*d.* 1515), abbot of St. Augustine's, Bristol, 1481; superseded, 1483; reinstated, 1485. [xl. 337]

NEWLIN, THOMAS (1688–1743), divine; M.A. Magdalen College, Oxford, 1713; fellow, 1717–21; B.D., 1727; incumbent of Upper Beeding, 1720; translated Parker's 'History,' 1727, and published sermons. [xl. 337]

NEWMAN, ARTHUR (*fl.* 1619), poet and essayist; of Trinity College, Oxford; student of the Middle Temple, 1616; published 'The Bible-bearer' (satire), 1607, and 'Pleasvres Vision,' 1619. [xl. 337]

NEWMAN, ARTHUR SHEAN (1828–1873), architect; son of John Newman (1786–1859) [q. v.]; built chiefly churches. [xl. 340]

NEWMAN, EDWARD (1801–1876), naturalist; one of the founders of the Entomological Club, 1826; an all-round naturalist; M.L.S., 1833; wrote on 'British Ferns,' 1840, 'Birds-nesting,' 1861, 'Moths,' 1869, and 'Butterflies,' 1871. [xl. 338]

NEWMAN, FRANCIS (*d.* 1660), New England statesman; emigrated to America, 1638; held many public offices in Connecticut; became governor of Newhaven, 1658. [xl. 339]

NEWMAN, FRANCIS WILLIAM (1805–1897), scholar and man of letters; brother of John Henry Newman [q. v.]; B.A. Worcester College, Oxford, 1826; fellow of Balliol College, Oxford, 1826–30; classical tutor at Bristol College (unsectarian), 1834; professor of classical literature, Manchester New College, 1840, and of Latin, University College, London, 1846–69; principal of University Hall, London, 1848; acquired repute by his writings on religion, among the most important of which were 'History of Hebrew Monarchy,' 1847, 'The Soul,' 1849, and 'Phases of Faith' (an autobiographical account of his religious changes, which excited much controversy), 1850; joined British and Foreign Unitarian Association, 1876, and was vice-president, 1879; took keen interest in political questions bearing on social problems; published numerous educational, political, social, and religious works and pamphlets. [Suppl. iii. 221]

NEWMAN, JEREMIAH WHITAKER (1759–1839), medical and miscellaneous writer; practised at Ringwood and Dover; published 'The Lounger's Commonplace Book,' 1805, and medical essays. [xl. 339]

NEWMAN, JOHN (1677?–1741), presbyterian minister; became assistant to Taylor at Salters' Hall, 1696, and co-pastor, 1716; trustee of Daniel Williams's foundations, 1728. [xl. 339]

NEWMAN, JOHN (1786–1859), architect and antiquary; pupil of Sir Robert Smirke [q. v.]; commissioner of sewers, 1815; clerk of the Bridge House estates; his collection of antiquities exhibited before the Archæological Association, 1847; F.S.A., 1830; F.R.I.B.A.; died at Passy. [xl. 340]

NEWMAN, JOHN HENRY (1801–1890), cardinal; educated at Dr. Nicholas's school at Ealing; matriculated from Trinity College, Oxford, 1816, where he gained a scholarship, 1818; B.A., 1820; fellow of Oriel, 1822; curate of St. Clement's, Oxford, 1824; vice-principal of Alban Hall, Oxford, 1825; assisted the principal, Dr. Whately, in his 'Logic'; tutor of Oriel College, Oxford, 1826, Richard Hurrell Froude [q. v.] being elected in the same year; Whitehall preacher, 1827; examiner in *literæ humaniores*, 1827–8; influential in Hawkins's election to the provostship of Oriel College, Oxford, and was himself presented to the vicarage of St. Mary's, Oxford, vacated by Hawkins, 1828; resigned his tutorship, 1832, and went to the south of Europe with Hurrell Froude; wrote most of the 'Lyra Apostolica' in Rome (1834); published 'Lead kindly light,' composed during his passage in an orange boat from Palermo to Marseilles, 1833; on his return, 1833, met William Palmer, Hurrell Froude, and Arthur Philip Perceval at Hugh James Rose's rectory at Hadleigh, and with them resolved to fight for the doctrine of apostolical succession and the integrity of the prayer-book; preached four o'clock sermons at St. Mary's, Oxford; commenced 'Tracts for the Times' and published his book on 'Arians of the fourth Century,' 1833; found an ally in Dr. Pusey, who joined the 'Oxford movement,' 1835; published in defence of Anglo-catholicism 'Romanism and Popular Protestantism,' 1837, and 'Justification,' 'Disquisition on the Canon of Scripture,' and 'Tractate on Antichrist,' 1838, and became editor of the 'British Critic'; began to doubt the

Anglican view, 1839; maintained in 'Tract XC.,' 1841, that the articles were opposed to Roman dogma and errors, but not to catholic teaching, a view which raised a storm of indignation. and brought the tractarians under the official ban ; retired to Littlemore, 1842, and passed the next three years in prayer, fasting, and seclusion; formally retracted all he had said against the Romish church and resigned the living of St. Mary's, Oxford, 1843 ; received into the Roman church, 1845 ; published 'An Essay on the Development of Christian Doctrine,' 1845 ; went to Rome, 1846, and was ordained priest and created D.D. ; returned to England to establish the oratory at Birmingham, 1847, and London, 1850 ; published 'Twelve Lectures,' 1850 ; in 'Lectures on the present Position of Catholics,' 1851, exposed the moral turpitude of Achilli, an apostate monk, which led to prosecution for libel, when Newman was fined 100l., although he established his facts, 1853 ; rector of the Dublin Catholic University, 1854–8 ; laid down the aims and principles of education in 'Idea of a University' ; published 'Apologia pro Vita sua,' 1864, in answer to Charles Kingsley, who in 'Macmillan's Magazine' had remarked that Newman did not consider truth a necessary virtue ; asserted that papal prerogatives cannot touch the civil allegiance of catholics in his 'Letter to the Duke of Norfolk'; honorary fellow of Trinity College, Oxford, 1877 ; formally created cardinal of St. George in Velabro, 1879. His guiding motive was the conception of an infallible church. [xl. 340]

NEWMAN, SAMUEL (1600?–1663), B.A. St. Edmund Hall, Oxford, 1620 ; prosecuted for nonconformity ; went to Massachusetts, 1636 ; published a concordance, 1643 ; died in Massachusetts. [xl. 351]

NEWMAN, THOMAS (fl. 1578–1593), stationer ; freeman of Stationers' Company, 1586 ; printed a faulty issue of Sidney's 'Astrophel and Stella,' 1591. [xl. 351]

NEWMAN, THOMAS (1692–1758), dissenting minister ; matriculated at Glasgow University, 1710 ; ordained, 1721 ; assisted Dr. Wright at Blackfriars, London, and succeeded him as pastor, 1746 ; published theological works. [xl. 351]

NEWMARCH or **NEUFMARCHÉ**, BERNARD OF (fl. 1093). [See BERNARD.]

NEWMARCH, WILLIAM (1820–1882), economist and statistician ; clerk in a banking house in Wakefield, 1843–6 ; appointed to the London branch of the Agra bank, 1846 ; appointed manager of Glyn, Mills & Co., 1862 ; president of the Statistical Society, 1869 ; gave evidence in committee on the Bank Acts, 1857 ; F.R.S. The Newmarch professorship of economic science at University College, London, and the Newmarch memorial essay were founded in his memory. His chief works are 'The New Supplies of Gold,' 1853, a work on Pitt's financial operations, 1855, and (with Thomas Tooke) 'A History of Prices and of the State of the Circulation during the Nine Years, 1848–56,' 1857. [xl. 352]

NEWMARKET, ADAM DE (fl. 1220), justiciar ; an adherent of the baronial party ; justiciar in Yorkshire, 1215 ; justice itinerant, 1219–20. [xl. 354]

NEWMARKET, ADAM DE (fl. 1265), baronial leader ; grandson of Adam de Newmarket (fl. 1220) [q. v.] ; taken prisoner at Northampton, 1264, and again at Kenilworth, 1265. [xl. 354]

NEWMARKET, THOMAS OF (fl. 1410?). [See THOMAS.]

NEWNHAM, WILLIAM (1790–1865), medical and religious writer ; studied at Guy's Hospital, London, and in Paris ; practised at Farnham ; an active member of the British Medical Association ; published works on medical subjects and on mental and spiritual phenomena. [xl. 354]

NEWPORT, first EARL OF (1597?–1665). [See BLOUNT, MOUNTJOY, BARON MOUNTJOY.]

NEWPORT, ANDREW (1623–1699), royalist ; son of Richard Newport, first baron Newport [q. v.] ; of Christ Church, Oxford ; actively engaged in the rising of 1659 ; commissioner of customs, 1662 ; M.P., Montgomeryshire, 1661–78, Preston, 1685, and Shrewsbury, 1689–98 ; wrongly identified with the hero of Defoe's 'Memoirs of a Cavalier.' [xl. 355]

NEWPORT, CHRISTOPHER (1565?–1617), sea captain ; sailed as captain, 1592 ; made five voyages to

Virginia, and was wrecked on the Bermudas, 1609 ; made two successful voyages for the East India Company, 1612 and 1615 ; died at Bantam on his third voyage. [xl. 356]

NEWPORT, FRANCIS, first EARL OF BRADFORD (1619–1708), son of Richard Newport, first baron Newport [q. v.] : of Gray's Inn, 1633, the Inner Temple, 1634, and of Christ Church, Oxford, 1635 ; M.P. for Shrewsbury in the Short and Long parliaments ; engaged in royalist plots, 1655 and 1657 ; created Viscount Newport, 1675, and Earl of Bradford, 1694. [xl. 356]

NEWPORT, GEORGE (1803–1854), naturalist ; M.R.C.S., 1835 ; house surgeon to the Chichester Infirmary, 1835–7 ; made anatomical researches on insect structure and the generative system, on which he wrote ; president of the Entomological Society, 1844–5 ; F.R.C.P., 1843 ; F.R.S., 1846 ; F.L.S., 1847. [xl. 357]

NEWPORT, SIR JOHN, first baronet (1756–1843), politician ; banker ; created baronet, 1789 ; M.P., Waterford, 1803–32 ; appointed chancellor of the Irish exchequer and English privy councillor, 1806 ; comptroller-general of the exchequer, 1834–9. [xl. 358]

NEWPORT, verè EWENS, MAURICE (1611–1687), jesuit ; assumed the name Newport, 1635 ; professed of the four vows, 1643 ; missioner in England, 1644 ; resided in Belgium for some years ; published 'Votum Candidum' (panegyric in Latin verse on Charles II), 1665. [xl. 359]

NEWPORT, RICHARD DE (d. 1318), bishop of London ; was archdeacon of Middlesex in 1303 ; dean of St. Paul's, London, 1314 ; bishop of London, 1317. [xl. 359]

NEWPORT, RICHARD, first BARON NEWPORT (1587–1651), B.A. Brasenose College, Oxford, 1607 ; knighted, 1615 ; M.P., Shropshire, 1614–29 ; created Baron Newport, 1642 ; escaped to France before 1646 ; died at Moulins. [xl. 359]

NEWPORT, SIR THOMAS (d. 1522), knight of St. John of Jerusalem ; became receiver-general of the order in England ; went to Rhodes, 1513 ; drowned off the coast of Spain. [xl. 360]

NEWSAM, BARTHOLOMEW (d. 1593), clockmaker to Queen Elizabeth before 1582 ; received numerous grants of land. A striking clock by Newsam is in the British Museum. [xl. 360]

NEWSHAM, RICHARD (d. 1743), fire-engine maker ; patented improvements, 1721 and 1725 ; supplied engines to the chief provincial towns ; one of his fire-engines preserved in South Kensington Museum. [xl. 361]

NEWSTEAD, CHRISTOPHER (1597–1662), divine ; of St. Alban Hall, Oxford ; chaplain to Sir Thomas Roe [q. v.] at Constantinople, 1621–8 ; rector of Stisted, 1643 ; sequestered, 1645 ; appointed to Maidenhead, 1650 ; prebendary of St. Paul's, London, 1660 ; published 'Apology for Women,' 1620. [xl. 362]

NEWTE, JOHN (1655?–1716), divine ; son of Richard Newte [q. v.], educated at Blundell's school and Balliol College, Oxford ; M.A., 1679 (incorporated at Cambridge, 1681) ; rector of Tidcombe Portion, 1679, and Pitt's Portion, Tiverton, 1680 ; made numerous gifts to Tiverton, and defended the lawfulness of church music. [xl. 362]

NEWTE, RICHARD (1613–1678), divine ; of Blundell's school and Exeter College, Oxford ; fellow, 1635–1642 ; M.A., 1636 ; rector of Tidcombe and Clare portions, Tiverton, 1641 ; dispossessed of his benefices, 1654 ; reinstated, 1660. [xl. 363]

NEWTH, SAMUEL (1821–1898), principal of New College, London ; B.A. and M.A. London ; minister of congregational chapel at Broseley, 1842–5 ; professor of classics and mathematics at Western College, Plymouth, 1845 ; professor of mathematics and ecclesiastical history at New College, St. John's Wood, 1855–89, and of classics from 1867 ; principal of the college, 1872–89 ; member of company of New Testament revisers, 1870–80 ; D.D. Glasgow, 1875 ; chairman of congregational union of England and Wales, 1880 ; published religious and educational scientific works. [Suppl. iii. 223]

NEWTON, LORD. [See HAY, ALEXANDER (d. 1616); OLIPHANT, SIR WILLIAM (1537–1628) ; FALCONER, SIR DAVID (1640–1686).]

NEWTON, SIR ADAM, first baronet (*d.* 1630), dean of Durham; tutor to Prince Henry (afterwards prince of Wales), 1600; dean of Durham, 1605; tutor to Prince Charles, 1612; created baronet, 1620; translated into Latin James I's 'Discourse against Vorstius.' [xl. 364]

NEWTON, ALFRED PIZZI (1830-1883), water-colour painter; attracted Queen Victoria's notice; exhibited landscapes at the Royal Academy. [xl. 364]

NEWTON, ANN MARY (1832-1866), portrait-painter; daughter of Joseph Severn [q. v.]; born at Rome; studied under Richmond and Scheffer; married Sir Charles Thomas Newton [q. v.], 1861. [xl. 365]

NEWTON, BENJAMIN (1677-1735), divine; M.A. Clare Hall, Cambridge, 1702; held numerous preferments; published sermons. [xl. 365]

NEWTON, BENJAMIN (*d.* 1787), divine; son of Benjamin Newton (1677-1735) [q. v.]; M.A. Jesus College, Cambridge, 1747, and dean of his college; wrote on civil liberty and morals. [xl. 366]

NEWTON, SIR CHARLES THOMAS (1816-1894), archæologist; educated at Shrewsbury School and Christ Church, Oxford; M.A., 1840; assistant in department of antiquities at British Museum, 1840; vice-consul at Mytilene, 1852; consul at Rhodes, 1853-4; superintended excavations in Calymnos, 1854-5, and identified site and recovered chief remains of mausoleum at Halicarnassus; consul at Rome, 1860; keeper of Greek and Roman antiquities at British Museum, 1861-85; Yates professor of archæology at University College, London, 1880-8; D.C.L. Oxford, 1875; LL.D. Cambridge, 1879; C.B., 1875; K.C.B., 1877; published archæological writings. [Suppl. iii. 224]

NEWTON, FRANCIS (*d.* 1572), dean of Winchester; fellow of Jesus College, Cambridge, 1555; M.A., 1553; D.D., 1563; prebendary of North Newbold, 1560; vice-chancellor of Cambridge University, 1563; dean of Winchester, 1565. [xl. 366]

NEWTON, FRANCIS MILNER (1720-1794), portrait-painter and royal academician, whose efforts to establish a national academy of art resulted in the Royal Academy, 1768 (secretary, 1768-88); exhibited portraits. [xl. 367]

NEWTON, GEORGE (1602-1681), nonconformist divine; M.A. Exeter College, Oxford, 1624; vicar of Taunton, 1631; deprived, 1662; imprisoned for unlawful preaching; published sermons. [xl. 367]

NEWTON, GILBERT STUART (1794-1835), painter; born in Nova Scotia; studied at Florence, Paris, and the Royal Academy; exhibited humorous subject-pictures and some portraits; R.A. 1832; became insane, *c.* 1832. [xl. 368]

NEWTON, HARRY ROBERT (*d.* 1889), collector of manuscripts; son of Sir William John Newton [q. v.]; collected drawings and manuscripts, now in the possession of the Institute of British Architects. [xl. 407]

NEWTON, afterwards **PUCKERING**, SIR HENRY, third baronet (1618-1701), royalist; son of Sir Adam Newton [q. v.]; raised a troop of horse; fought at Edgehill, 1642; compounded, 1646; assumed the name Puckering on inheriting his uncle's estates, 1654; paymaster-general of the forces, 1660; M.P., Warwick, 1661-79. [xl. 369]

NEWTON, SIR HENRY (1651-1715), British envoy in Tuscany; M.A. St. Mary Hall, Oxford, 1671; D.C.L. Merton College, Oxford, 1678; advocate, 1678; judge-advocate to the admiralty, 1694; envoy extraordinary to Florence, 1704-9; judge of the high court of admiralty, 1714; knighted, 1715; published some Latin letters, verses, and speeches, 1710. [xl. 370]

NEWTON, SIR ISAAC (1642-1727), natural philosopher; born at Woolsthorpe; attended Grantham grammar school, 1654-6; matriculated as a sub-sizar at Trinity College, Cambridge, 1661; scholar, 1664; B.A., 1665; while absent from Cambridge during the plague (1665-6) discovered the binomial theorem, differential calculus, integral calculus, computed the area of the hyperbola, and conceived the idea of universal gravitation; returned to Cambridge, 1667, as fellow of Trinity College, and turned his attention to optics; made a reflecting telescope, 1668; elected Lucasian professor, 1669; his second reflecting telescope sent to the Royal Society, 1671; F.R.S., 1672;

his first communication, which contained his 'New Theory about Light and Colours,' read 6 Feb. 1672, and handed over for report to Robert Hooke [q. v.], who did not accept Newton's reasoning; founder of the emission theory of light, but did not accept it as entirely satisfactory; his researches summed up in 'Optics,' 1704. In 1679 Hooke's letter to Newton on the laws of motion started the train of thought which resulted in the first book of Newton's 'Principia.' The idea of universal gravitation had presented itself to Newton in 1665, and early in 1680 he discovered how to calculate the orbit of a body moving under a central force, but published no account of his discoveries, possibly in consequence of his inability to solve the question of the mutual attraction of two spheres; first book of his 'Principia' exhibited at the Royal Society, 1686, and the whole published about midsummer, 1687, the completion and publication of the work being entirely due to Halley, who smoothed over difficulties between Hooke and the author, paid all expenses of publication, and corrected the proofs; M.P., Cambridge University, 1689 and 1701-2; appointed warden of the mint, 1696, and master, 1699; elected president of the Royal Society, 1703, and annually re-elected for twenty-five years; as president was involved in the difficulties relating to the publication of Flamsteed's observations, which lasted from 1705 to 1712; his method of fluxions, which he brought out as an appendix to the 'Optics,' 1704, the cause of a bitter controversy between himself and Leibnitz as to priority of discovery, which lasted from 1705 until 1724; knighted by Queen Anne on occasion of her visit to Cambridge, 1705; one of Bishop Moore's assessors at the trial of Richard Bentley [q. v.], 1714; presented reports on the coinage, 1717 and 1718. Died at Kensington. There are portraits of him by Kneller and Vanderbank. He attempted to amend ancient chronology by astronomy, corresponded with Locke, and wrote on theological subjects, objecting to the manner in which certain texts were treated with the view of supporting Trinitarian doctrine. Many anecdotes are told of his absence of mind and his modesty. His body lay in state in the Jerusalem Chamber and was buried in Westminster Abbey, 28 March 1727. The only collected edition of his works is an incomplete one by Samuel Horsley in five volumes, 1779-85. [xl. 370]

NEWTON, JAMES (1670?-1750), botanist; M.D.; kept a private lunatic asylum and studied botany to divert his attention; his 'Compleat Herbal' published, 1752. [xl. 393]

NEWTON, JOHN (1622-1678), mathematician and astronomer; M.A. St. Edmund Hall, Oxford, 1642; D.D., 1660; a loyalist; became king's chaplain and rector of Ross, 1661; canon of Hereford, 1673; wrote on arithmetic, geometry, astronomy, logic, and rhetoric. [xl. 394]

NEWTON, JOHN (1725-1807), divine and friend of Cowper; led a wandering life at sea, 1736-55; began to have strong religious experiences, 1748, which were increased under the influence of Whitefield and Wesley; ordained deacon in the church of England, 1764, with the curacy of Olney, where Cowper and Mrs. Unwin settled in 1767; with Cowper published the 'Olney Hymns,' 1779; became incumbent of St. Mary Woolnoth, London, 1780, where he soon collected a very large congregation and proved a strong evangelical influence; D.D. New Jersey, 1792; published 'Review of Ecclesiastical History,' 1770, and 'Cardiphonia,' 1781, and aided Wilberforce with a ghastly recital of facts from his own experience of the slave trade. [xl. 395]

NEWTON, SIR RICHARD (1370?-1448?), judge; serjeant-at-law, 1424; justice itinerant, 1427; king's serjeant, 1429; recorder of Bristol, 1430; justice of the common bench, 1438; knighted, 1439. [xl. 398]

NEWTON, RICHARD (1676-1753), educational reformer; of Westminster School and Christ Church, Oxford; M.A., 1701; D.D. Hart Hall, Oxford, 1710; tutor at Christ Church; rector of Sudborough, 1704; appointed principal of Hart Hall, Oxford, 1710; endeavoured to establish it as a college for poor students; built part of a quadrangle for Hart Hall, and obtaining a charter, 1740, became the first principal of Hertford College (dissolved through insufficiency of endowments, 1805, reconstituted, 1874); canon of Christ Church, 1753; wrote on university education and in explanation and defence of his schemes for Hertford College. [xl. 399]

NEWTON, RICHARD (1777–1798), caricaturist and miniature-painter. [xl. 401]

NEWTON, ROBERT (1780–1854), Wesleyan minister; entered the Wesleyan ministry, c. 1800; preached at London, Liverpool, Manchester, Leeds, and Stockport; president of the Wesleyan conference, 1824, 1832, 1840, and 1848. [xl. 401]

NEWTON, SAMUEL (1628–1718), notary public; notary public and burgess of Cambridge, 1661; alderman, 1668; registrar of Pembroke Hall and (1673) Trinity College, Cambridge; mayor of Cambridge, 1671 and 1687; his diary (1662–1717) printed, 1890. [xl. 402]

NEWTON, THEODORE (d. 1569), brother of Francis Newton [q. v.]; M.A. Christ Church, Oxford, 1552; prebendary of Canterbury, 1559; rector of Ringwould, 1565; rector of St. Dionis Backchurch, London, 1567. [xl. 366]

NEWTON, THOMAS (1542?–1607), poet, physician, and divine; of Trinity College, Oxford, and Queens' College, Cambridge; probably practised as a physician at Butley; rector of Little Ilford, c. 1583; published works on historical, medical, and theological subjects; translated from Latin; a skilled writer of Latin and English verse. [xl. 402]

NEWTON, THOMAS (1704–1782), bishop of Bristol; educated at Westminster School and Trinity College, Cambridge; M.A., 1730; fellow of Trinity College, Cambridge; rector of St. Mary-le-Bow, 1744; D.D., 1745; Boyle lecturer, 1754; chaplain to George II, 1756; prebendary of Westminster, 1757; precentor of York, 1759; bishop of Bristol, 1761–82; became dean of St. Paul's, London, 1768; wrote an autobiography, a work on the prophecies, and sermons (collected edition, 1782); edited Milton's 'Paradise Lost,' 1749. [xl. 403]

NEWTON, WILLIAM (1735–1790), architect; travelled in Italy, 1766; designed residences in London and the vicinity; became assistant to James Stuart, 'The Athenian,' and clerk of the works to Greenwich Hospital, 1782; completed Stuart's 'Antiquities of Athens' (published, 1787); translated Vitruvius (published, 1791). [xl. 405]

NEWTON, WILLIAM (1750–1830), the Peak Minstrel; a machinery carpenter whose verses and sonnets attracted the notice of Peter Cunningham (d. 1805) [q. v.] and Anna Seward, who procured him a mill-partnership. [xl. 406]

NEWTON, SIR WILLIAM JOHN (1785–1869), miniature-painter; nephew of William Newton (1735–1790) [q. v.]; became one of the most fashionable miniaturists of his day; appointed miniature-painter to William IV and Queen Victoria; exhibited at the Royal Academy, 1808–63; knighted, 1837. [xl. 406]

NIAL, AOD or HUGH (1540?–1616). [See O'NEILL, HUGH.]

NIALL (d. 405), king of Ireland; known in Irish as Naighiallach; made war on the Leinstermen and Munstermen, and fought in Britain and Gaul; his importance due to the fame of his descendants. [xl. 407]

NIALL (715–778), king of Ireland; surnamed Frassach; descended from Niall (d. 405) [q. v.]; became king, 763; exacted tribute from Connaught, Munster, and Leinster; resigned, 770, and became a monk. [xl. 407]

NIALL (791–845), king of Ireland; surnamed Caille; grandson of Niall (715–778) [q. v.]; raised the clans of Tyrone and Tyrconnell to avenge the primate of Armagh, 825; became king, 833; fought successfully in Leinster, Meath, and Munster, and defeated the Danes, 843; drowned near Armagh. [xl. 408]

NIALL (870?–919), king of Ireland; surnamed Glundubh; grandson of Niall (791–845) [q. v.]; made forays into Connaught, 905 and 909; became king of Ailech, 911; king of Ireland, 915; marched against the Danes and was defeated and mortally wounded at Kilmashoge. [xl. 408]

NIALL (d. 1061), king of Ailech; succeeded his brother, whom he killed in battle; made forays into Louth (1044) and Monaghan, in revenge for the violation of an oath sworn upon St. Patrick's bell. [xl. 409]

NIALL (d. 1062), king of Ulidia or Lesser Ulster; defeated, deposed, and succeeded his nephew, 1011; defeated a Danish fleet, 1022; was himself defeated, 1027; a

great famine, 1047, in his reign followed by a deep snow, frequently mentioned by Irish chroniclers. [xl. 409]

NIALL (d. 1139), anti-primate of Armagh; unsuccessfully seized the staff and book of Armagh, 1131; reasserted his claim, 1137. [xl. 410]

NIAS, SIR JOSEPH (1793–1879), admiral; entered the navy, 1807; appointed to the Arctic expedition, 1818; lieutenant, 1820; commander, 1827; advanced to post rank, 1835; employed in the capture of Canton; C.B., 1841; rear-admiral, 1857; vice-admiral, 1863; K.C.B., 1867; admiral, 1867. [xl. 410]

NICCOLS, RICHARD (1584–1616), poet; accompanied Charles Howard, earl of Nottingham, on his voyage to Cadiz, 1596; B.A. Magdalen Hall, Oxford, 1606; his chief patrons the Earl of Nottingham, James Hay, earl of Carlisle, and Sir Thomas Wroth; wrote, besides several funeral orations, 'The Cuckoo,' 1607, a narrative poem; revised the 'Mirror for Magistrates,' 1610, in which he omitted some poems and added 'A Winter Night's Vision' and 'England's Eliza'; published a poetical account of Overbury's murder, 1616, and (1627) 'The Beggar's Ape.' His play, 'The Twynnes Tragedie,' entered on the 'Stationers' Registers,' 1612, is not otherwise known. [xl. 411]

NICHOL, JOHN (1833–1894), man of letters; son of John Pringle Nichol [q. v.]; educated at Glasgow University and Balliol College, Oxford; M.A., 1874; entered Gray's Inn, 1859; appointed by the crown professor of English language and literature at Glasgow, 1862; resigned, 1889; founded, with Professor Knight, the New Speculative Society, 1867. His publications include 'Fragments of Criticism,' 1860, 'Hannibal' (historical drama), 1873, 'Death of Themistocles and other Poems,' 1881, 'Byron,' 1880, and 'Carlyle,' 1892 ('English Men of Letters' series), 'Robert Burns,' 1882, and 'Francis Bacon,' 1888–9. [Suppl. iii. 225]

NICHOL, JOHN PRINGLE (1804–1859), astronomer; educated at King's College, Aberdeen; rector of Montrose Academy, 1827; regius professor of astronomy at Glasgow University, 1836; instrumental in transferring the observatory to Downhill, 1840; lectured in the United States, 1848–9; wrote on astronomy and contributed to current literature. [xl. 412]

NICHOLAS. [See also NICOLAS.]

NICHOLAS (d. 1124), prior of Worcester; educated by Bishop Wulfstan II of Worcester and by Lanfranc; prior of Worcester, 1113; corresponded with Eadmer [q. v.] [xl. 413]

NICHOLAS AP GWRGANT (d. 1183), bishop of Llandaff; elected to the see, 1148; supported Henry II and was twice suspended. [xl. 414]

NICHOLAS DE WALKINGTON (fl. 1193?), mediæval writer; wrote a short account of the battle between Henry I and Louis the Great of France. [xl. 414]

NICHOLAS OF MEAUX (d. 1227?), called KOLUS, KOLIUS, or KOLAS, bishop of the Isles; an Augustinian canon of Wartre; entered the Cistercian order and became ultimately de facto abbot of Furness; nominated bishop of Man and the Sudreys (c. 1207) by Olaf, king of the Isles, although the monks of Furness claimed the right of election to the see; consecrated by the archbishop of Trondjem, 1210; driven into exile, c. 1217; became attached to the church of Kelloe. c. 1225. [xl. 415]

NICHOLAS DE GUILDFORD (fl. 1250). [See GUILDFORD.]

NICHOLAS DE FARNHAM (d. 1257), bishop of Durham; professor of medicine in the universities of Paris and Bologna; began his studies at Oxford and proceeded to Paris, where, in addition to medical studies, he directed courses of dialectics, physics, and theology; went for a short time to Bologna as professor of medicine; returned to England, 1229; taught logic and natural philosophy at Oxford and became physician to Henry III; received much ecclesiastical preferment; elected bishop of Durham, 1241; had cathedral rebuilt; resigned, 1248. Two treatises, 'Practica Medicinæ' and 'De Viribus Herbarum,' mentioned as his by Pits, have not been traced. There are three medical treatises extant in manuscript in the Bibliothèque Nationale in Paris written by Nicholas de Anglia, who is probably identical with Nicholas de Farnham. [xl. 416]

NICHOLAS OF ELY (*d.* 1280). [See ELY.]

NICHOLAS OF OCCAM (*fl.* 1280). [See OCCAM.]

NICHOLAS LE BLUND (*d.* 1304), bishop of Down; treasurer of Ulster and prior of St. Patrick's, Down; elected bishop, 1277; administered his diocese in accordance with Irish customs, which led to litigation. [xl. 417]

NICHOLAS (1316?-1386). [See LITLINGTON or LITTLINGTON.]

NICHOLAS OF LYNNE (*fl.* 1386), Carmelite; lecturer in theology at Oxford; in 1386 composed a calendar for the period from 1387 to 1462; conjectured to have made an arctic voyage. [xl. 418]

NICHOLAS OF HEREFORD or NICHOLAS HERFORD (*fl.* 1390), lollard; student and fellow of Queen's College, Oxford; D.D. Oxford, 1382; preached constantly in support of Wycliffe, 1382, and was suspended and excommunicated; at once set out for Rome, but was ordered by the pope to be imprisoned for life; escaped to England, 1385, and was imprisoned for a time; was chief leader of the lollards after Wycliffe's death, but in 1391 recanted, and was appointed chancellor of Hereford Cathedral; treasurer of Hereford, 1397-1417; became a Carthusian monk at St. Anne's, Coventry. Very little of Hereford's work has survived except his translation of the Old Testament, which stops short in the book of Baruch, chap. iii. [xl. 418]

NICHOLAS OF FAKENHAM (*fl.* 1402), Franciscan; D.D. Oxford, 1395; provincial minister of his order, 1395-1402; examined into the charges against his successor, and reappointed him. His 'Determinatio' (1395) is extant. [xl. 420]

NICHOLAS DE BURGO (*fl.* 1517-1537), divinity lecturer at Oxford; was a Florentine Franciscan friar who studied at Paris, and began to lecture at Oxford, 1517; was joint-author of a book advocating Henry VIII's divorce from Catherine of Aragon, and was appointed public reader in divinity at Cardinal College (afterwards Christ Church, Oxford), and at Magdalen College, Oxford; acted as vice-chancellor, 1534; returned to Italy, 1535. [xl. 421]

NICHOLAS, ABRAHAM (1692-1744?), schoolmaster; published three copybooks; emigrated to Virginia, *c.* 1722. [xl. 421]

NICHOLAS, DAVID (1705?-1769), Welsh ballad-writer; a day schoolmaster in Glamorgan; admitted to the 'congress of bards,' 1730; wrote a letter containing the rules of Welsh prosody, 1754. [xl. 422]

NICHOLAS, SIR EDWARD (1593-1669), secretary of state to Charles I and Charles II; matriculated from Queen's College, Oxford, 1611; entered the Middle Temple, 1612; became secretary to Edward, baron Zouch [q. v.], warden of the Cinque ports, 1618, and to his successor, George, duke of Buckingham, 1624; M.P., Winchelsea, 1620-4, Dover, 1627-8; secretary to the admiralty, 1625, and to the admiralty commissioners after Buckingham's death; clerk of the council in ordinary, 1635; knighted and appointed secretary of state, 1641; conducted the treaty of Uxbridge and the surrender of Oxford, 1646; retired to Caen in Normandy; remained in name Charles I's secretary of state till the king's execution, and subsequently made vigorous efforts to serve his son in a like capacity, but was disliked by Queen Henrietta Maria and practically excluded from Prince Charles's counsels; directed to attend the Duke of York, 1650, and from 1650 to 1654 resided at the Hague; joined Charles at Aix-la-Chapelle, 1654, and was formally reappointed secretary of state, but was set aside and pensioned with 10,000*l.* on account of age and sickness, 1662. [xl. 422]

NICHOLAS, HENRY, or **NICLAES**, HENRIK (*fl.* 1502-1580), founder of the religious sect known as the 'Family of Love'; born in Westphalia; imprisoned on a suspicion of heresy, 1529; began to see visions, 1540, and represented that he had received a divine summons to become a prophet and founder of a new sect, to be called 'Familia Caritatis,' with three elders to aid him; lived at Embden (1540-60), writing the divine revelations he had received; made many converts in Holland, Brabant, and Paris; his books prohibited, 1570, 1582, and 1590; visited England, *c.* 1552 or 1553; probably died at Cologne. He taught an anabaptist mysticism, and regarded love of humanity as the essential rule of life. The constitution of the sect consisted of the highest bishop, twenty-four elders, seraphim or archbishops, and three orders of priests. The sect did not attract much attention in England until 1574, when its numbers had grown large, chiefly in Norfolk, Suffolk, Cambridgeshire, and Essex. It endured some persecution between 1574 and 1604, but before 1700 familists had become extremely rare. Nearly all of his books were translated into English. [xl. 427]

NICHOLAS, MATTHEW (1594-1661), dean of St. Paul's; brother of Sir Edward Nicholas [q. v.]; scholar of Winchester College and New College, Oxford; D.C.L., 1627; canon of Salisbury and dean of Bristol, 1639; canon of Westminster, 1642; deprived at the rebellion; canon and dean of St. Paul's, London, 1660. [xl. 426]

NICHOLAS, ROBERT (1595-1667), judge; M.P., Devizes, 1640; assisted in prosecuting Laud, 1643; serjeant-at-law, 1648; judge of the upper bench, 1649; baron of the exchequer, 1655; pardoned, 1660; commissioner for raising money in Wiltshire, 1660. [xl. 431]

NICHOLAS, THOMAS (*fl.* 1560-1596), translator; employed by the Levant Company in the Canary isles; imprisoned for heresy, 1560-2 and 1562-4; brought to Spain and finally released, 1565; translated Spanish histories of the conquest of Mexico and Peru. [xl. 432]

NICHOLAS, THOMAS (1820-1879), Welsh antiquary; educated at Manchester and in Germany; professor of biblical literature at the Presbyterian College, Carmarthen, 1856; settled in London, 1863; promoted the University College of Wales at Aberystwith, and became a governor of it; wrote on education and Welsh antiquities. [xl. 433]

NICHOLAS, WILLIAM (1785-1812), major in the royal engineers; entered the army, 1801; promoted second captain, 1806; distinguished himself at Rosetta, 1807; succeeded to the command of the engineers at Cadiz, 1810; signally distinguished himself at Barossa, 1811, and at Badajos, 1812, where he was mortally wounded. [xl. 433]

NICHOLL. [See also NICHOL, NICOL, and NICOLL.]

NICHOLL, JOHN (*fl.* 1607), traveller and author; started with a band of Englishmen to Guiana, 1605; wrecked, rescued by Spaniards, and imprisoned as a spy; finally reached England, 1607, and published an account of his adventures, 1607. [xl. 434]

NICHOLL, SIR JOHN (1759-1838), judge; fellow of St. John's College, Oxford; D.C.L., 1785; admitted an advocate at Doctors' Commons, 1785; knighted, 1798; king's advocate, 1798; M.P., Penryn, 1802, Hastings, 1806, and Great Bedwin, 1807-32; strongly opposed to parliamentary reform and catholic emancipation; dean of arches and judge of the prerogative court of Canterbury, 1809-34; judge of the high court of admiralty, 1833; vicar-general to the archbishop of Canterbury, 1834; F.S.A. and F.R.S. [xl. 435]

NICHOLL, JOHN (1790-1871), antiquary; F.S.A., 1843; served as master of the Ironmongers' Company, 1859; made extensive researches in heraldry and the genealogy of Essex families and that of the various families of Nicholl, Nicholls, or Nichol; compiled a history of the Ironmongers' Company. [xl. 436]

NICHOLLS. [See also NICCOLS, NICHOLS, NICKOLLS, and NICOLLS.]

NICHOLLS, DEGORY (*d.* 1591), divine; fellow of Peterhouse, Cambridge, 1566; M.A., 1567; incorporated at Oxford, 1567; was 'contentious' and 'verye disorderlie'; B.D. university preacher, 1574; master of Magdalene College, Cambridge, 1577-82; canon of Exeter, 1579; D.D., 1581. [xl. 436]

NICHOLLS, EDWARD (*fl.* 1617), sea-captain of the Dolphin, 1617; was attacked by five Turkish men-of-war when returning from the Levant, and forced the Turks to retire. [xl. 437]

NICHOLLS, FRANK (1699-1778), physician; of Westminster School and Exeter College, Oxford; M.A., 1721; M.D., 1729; lectured at Oxford on anatomy; demonstrated the minute structure of blood-vessels, and was the first to use corroded preparations; F.R.S., 1728; F.R.C.P., 1732; Gulstonian lecturer, 1734 and 1736; Harveian orator, 1739, and Lumleian lecturer, 1748-9; published a compendium of his lectures, 1732. [xl. 437]

NICHOLLS, SIR GEORGE (1781–1865), poor-law reformer and administrator; became midshipman on board an East India Company's ship, 1797; obtained command of a ship, 1809; left the service in consequence of the ship under his command being burnt in harbour, 1815, although the company attached no blame to him; started the first savings bank at Farndon, and at Southwell became (1821) overseer of the poor; in three years reduced the amount of relief to almost a quarter without injury to the poor, his leading idea being to abolish outdoor relief; became practically the controller of the Gloucester and Berkeley Ship Canal, 1823; appointed superintendent of the branch of the Bank of England at Birmingham, 1826; became a director of the Birmingham Canal Navigations; consulted by the poor-law commissioners, and on the passing of the act (1834) made one of three commissioners; visited Ireland to observe poor-law legislation there, 1836 and 1837, and visited Holland and Belgium (1838) to examine their methods of administering relief; resided in Ireland to direct the working of the Irish Poor-law Act, 1838–42; appointed permanent secretary of the poor-law board, 1847; K.C.B., 1851; wrote on the poor and the poor-laws.   [xl. 438]

NICHOLLS, JAMES FAWCKNER (1818–1883), antiquary and librarian; tried various occupations, and finally was appointed city librarian of Bristol, 1868; brought the libraries into a high state of efficiency; F.S.A., 1878; published 'The Life and Discoveries of Sebastian Cabot,' 1869, and a number of antiquarian books, the chief of which was 'Bristol Past and Present,' 1881–2.   [xl. 441]

NICHOLLS, JOHN (1555–1584?) controversialist; left Oxford without a degree; became a curate in Somerset; in 1577 went to Rome by way of Antwerp, Douay, Grenoble, and Milan; voluntarily gave himself up to the inquisition and publicly abjured protestantism, 1578; left Rome, on the plea of ill-health, 1580, and proceeded to England, where he was committed to the Tower of London; he wrote during his imprisonment an account of the English seminaries and the popes, and a recantation of Romanism, 1581; employed to preach to the Roman catholics in the Tower of London; went to the Low Countries and Germany and again turned Roman catholic, 1582, expressed penitence, and withdrew all his accusations against Rome and Roman institutions, a report of it being published, 1583.   [xl. 441]

NICHOLLS, JOHN ASHTON (1823–1859), philanthropist; interested in physical science; life member of the British Association, 1842; F.R.A.S., 1849; entered his father's cotton manufactory, and gave much time to improving the education and condition of the working classes; organised classes and delivered lectures in Manchester and the neighbourhood.   [xl. 443]

NICHOLLS, NORTON (1742?–1809), friend of the poet Gray; was educated at Eton and Trinity Hall, Cambridge; LL.B., 1766; met Gray about 1761; visited the continent by Gray's advice; became rector of Lound and Bradwell, 1767; travelled with Gray through the midland counties, 1770; his full correspondence with Gray and his 'Reminiscences of Gray' were published in the fifth volume of Mitford's edition of Gray.   [xl. 443]

NICHOLLS, RICHARD (1584–1616). [See NICCOLS.]

NICHOLLS, SUTTON (*fl.* 1700–1740), draughtsman and engraver; drew and engraved views of London, 1725.   [xl. 445]

NICHOLLS, WILLIAM (1664–1712), author and divine; educated at St. Paul's School, London; B.A. Wadham College, Oxford, 1683; probationary fellow of Merton College, Oxford, 1684; M.A., 1688; D.D., 1695; rector of Selsey, 1691; said to have been rector of Bushy, 1691–3, and canon of Chichester, 1707; published theological works, his 'Defensio Ecclesiæ Anglicanæ,' 1707 and 1708, resulting in an interesting foreign correspondence; chief work, 'Comment on the Book of Common Prayer,' 1710.   [xl. 445]

NICHOLS. [See also NICOLLS.]

NICHOLS, JAMES (1785–1861), printer and theological writer; became a printer and bookseller; edited the 'Leeds Literary Observer' (1819, 1 vol.); removing to London published 'Calvinism and Arminianism compared,' 1824; translated two volumes of Arminius's 'Works,' 1825; printed and edited Thomson's 'Works,' 1849, and Young's 'Complete Works,' 1855.   [xli. 1]

NICHOLS or **NICHOLSON**, JOHN (*d.* 1538). [See LAMBERT.]

NICHOLS, JOHN (1745–1826), printer and author; educated at Islington and apprenticed to William Bowyer the younger [q. v.], whose partner he became, 1766; edited three additional volumes of Swift's 'Works,' 1775, 1776 and 1779, and William King's 'Works,' 1776; joined David Henry in the management of the 'Gentleman's Magazine,' 1778, for which he was solely responsible from 1792 to 1826; published his 'Royal Wills,' 1780, a 'Collection of Miscellaneous Poems,' 1780–2; and between 1780 and 1800 his 'Bibliotheca Topographica' (10 vols.); published 'Biographical Anecdotes of Hogarth,' 1781, and between 1808 and 1817 edited, with Steevens, Hogarth's 'Genuine Works'; edited Bowyer's 'Anecdotes,' and 'Miscellaneous Tracts,' 1785, Atterbury's 'Correspondence,' 1783–99, the 'Biographical Dictionary,' 1784, the 'Tatler,' 1786, Steele's 'Correspondence,' 1788–91, 'The Progresses of Queen Elizabeth,' 1788–1821, and 'Shakespeare's Plays,' 1790; published between 1795 and 1815 'The History and Antiquities of Leicester' (8 vols.), his most important work, and, in 1801, his edition of Swift's works (19 vols.)   [xli. 2]

NICHOLS, JOHN BOWYER (1779–1863), printer and antiquary; son of John Nichols [q. v.]; educated at St. Paul's School, London; entered his father's printing office, 1796; became part editor of the 'Gentleman's Magazine,' and subsequently, in 1833, sole proprietor; printer of parliamentary proceedings and published important county histories; wrote and edited antiquarian and topographical works.   [xli. 5]

NICHOLS, JOHN GOUGH (1806–1873), printer and antiquary; son of John Bowyer Nichols [q. v.]; educated at Merchant Taylors' School, London; entered the printing offices of his father and grandfather, 1824; joint-editor of the 'Gentleman's Magazine,' 1828–51; sole editor, 1851–6; a founder of the Camden Society, whose volumes he printed, and many of which he edited; edited 'Literary Remains of Edward VI,' and 'Sir Nicholas Throckmorton' for the Roxburghe Club; edited the periodicals 'Collectanea Topographica et Genealogica,' 1834–43, 'The Topographer and Genealogist,' 1846–58, and 'The Herald and Genealogist,' 1863–73; published heraldic and genealogical works.   [xli. 6]

NICHOLS, JOSIAS (1555?–1639), puritan divine; B.A. Oxford, 1574; rector of Eastwell, 1580; described as a ringleader of puritan ministers and suspended, 1584, but soon restored; deprived in consequence of his puritan writings, 1603.   [xli. 8]

NICHOLS, PHILIP (*fl.* 1547–1559), protestant writer; published a very protestant and outspoken 'Letter' to Canon Crispyn, 1547, and other works in the same spirit.   [xli. 9]

NICHOLS, THOMAS (*fl.* 1550), translator of Thucydides; a goldsmith; translated Thucydides from Seyssel's French version, 1550.   [xli. 10]

NICHOLS, THOMAS (*fl.* 1554), merchant; lived in the Canary islands, c. 1554–61; his description of the Canary islands and Madeira included in Hakluyt's 'Principall Navigations,' 1589.   [xli. 10]

NICHOLS, WILLIAM (1655–1716), Latin poet; M.A. Christ Church, Oxford, 1677; rector of Stockport, 1694–1716; wrote elegant Latin elegiacs, 1711, and translated portions of the prayer-book into Latin verse.   [xli. 10]

NICHOLS, WILLIAM LUKE (1802–1889), antiquary; M.A. Queen's College, Oxford, 1829; held various charges in the English church; published 'Horæ Romanæ,' 1838.   [xli. 10]

NICHOLSON. [See also NICOLSON.]

NICHOLSON, ALFRED (1788–1833), landscape-painter; son of Francis Nicholson (1753–1844) [q. v.]   [xli. 15]

NICHOLSON, BRINSLEY (1824–1892), scholar; studied medicine at Edinburgh and Paris; M.D. Edinburgh; army surgeon; served in Africa, China, and New Zealand; edited the first quarto of 'Henry the Fifth,' 1875, 'The Best Plays of Ben Jonson,' published, 1893, and Donne's poems, published, 1895.   [xli. 11]

NICHOLSON, CHARLES (1795–1837), flautist and composer; appointed professor of the flute at the Royal Academy of Music, 1822; improved the instrument and possessed some talent for composition.   [xli. 12]

NICHOLSON, SIR FRANCIS (1660–1728), colonial governor; entered the army, 1678; lieutenant-governor of the colonies north of Chesapeake Bay, 1686; fled to England when the colonists rose, 1689; lieutenant-governor of Virginia, 1690–4; successfully established schools, improved the condition of the clergy, and urged a vigorous policy against Canada; governor of Maryland, 1694, of Virginia, 1698; served against Canada, 1705; governor of Acadia, 1713, of South Carolina, 1719; knighted, 1720; lieutenant-general, 1725; though in England, held nominal governorship of South Carolina till 1728. [xli. 12]

NICHOLSON, FRANCIS (1650–1731), theologian; M.A. University College, Oxford, 1673; avowed himself a Roman catholic, 1685; joined the English Carthusians at Nieuport, 1688; subsequently lived at Lisbon and died at the Lisbon College; wrote on the eucharist, 1688. [xli. 13]

NICHOLSON, FRANCIS (1753–1844), water-colour painter; at first painted portraits, but finally devoted himself to landscapes; left Yorkshire for London, 1800; an original member of the Society of Painters in Water-colours, 1804; wrote on drawing and painting in water-colours, 1820; changed the art from mere paper-staining with light tints to the production of depth of tone and variety of shade and colour. [xli. 14]

NICHOLSON, GEORGE (1760–1825), printer and author; commenced publishing chap-books at Bradford, c. 1784; published his 'Literary Miscellany' at Manchester, c. 1797; possessed great taste and originality as a typographer; wrote on vegetarianism, education, and stenography. [xli. 15]

NICHOLSON, GEORGE (1795?–1839?), artist; exhibited at Liverpool Academy exhibitions, chiefly water-colour landscapes, 1827–38. [xli. 16]

NICHOLSON, GEORGE (1787–1878), painter; nephew of Francis Nicholson (1753–1844) [q. v.] [xli. 15]

NICHOLSON, HENRY ALLEYNE (1844–1899), biologist; Ph.D. Göttingen; B.Sc. Edinburgh, 1866; D.Sc., 1867; M.D., 1869; professor of natural history, Toronto, 1871–4, of physical science in Durham College of Physical Science, 1874–5, and of natural history at St. Andrews, 1875–82; regius professor of natural history at Aberdeen, 1882–99; fellow of Geological Society, 1867; F.L.S.; F.R.S., 1897; published zoological and palæontological text-books and numerous scientific papers. [Suppl. iii. 227]

NICHOLSON, ISAAC (1789–1848), wood-engraver; apprenticed to John Bewick [q. v.], whose style he successfully copied. [xli. 16]

NICHOLSON, JOHN (d. 1538). [See LAMBERT.]

NICHOLSON, JOHN (1730–1796), Cambridge bookseller; married Anne Watts, daughter of a Cambridge bookseller, to whose business he succeeded, 1752; nicknamed 'Maps'; supplied undergraduates with their class-books by subscription. [xli. 16]

NICHOLSON, JOHN (1781–1822), author; grandson of John Nicholson (1730–1796) [q. v.]; published anonymously 'Pætus and Arria,' 1809, and 'Right and Wrong,' 1812. [xli. 17]

NICHOLSON, JOHN (1790–1843), 'the Airedale poet'; a wool-sorter, who published 'Airedale in Ancient Times,' 1825; his separate poems collected in a complete edition, with biography, 1844. [xli. 17]

NICHOLSON, JOHN (1821–1857), brigadier-general; born in Dublin; obtained cadetship in Bengal infantry, 1839; served in Afghanistan and (1842) took a prominent part in the defence of Ghazni; made prisoner, but ultimately rescued by Major-general (afterward Sir) George Pollock [q. v.], 1842; promoted adjutant of his regiment, 1843; accompanied the Maharajah Guláb Singh to Kashmir, 1846; captain, 1848; regarded as a demi-god by the natives, a brotherhood of fakirs in Hazara originating the worship of Nikkul Seyn, 1848; when in charge of the Sind Ságar Doab, secured Attak and scoured the country on the rebellion of Mulraj, performing almost incredible marches and prodigies of valour; distinguished himself during the second Sikh war, especially at Gujrat, 1849, and was promoted brevet-major, 1849; administrative officer at Bannú, 1851–6; brevet lieutenant-general, 1854; was promoted brigadier-general on the outbreak of the

mutiny, and commander of the Punjab movable column; disarmed suspected sepoy regiments; intercepted the mutineers who were hastening to Delhi, and destroyed them at Trimmu Ghaut and at the Ravi river; he arrived at Delhi 14 Aug. 1857; captured thirteen guns and the camp equipment of the enemy, who were manœuvring to get at the British rear, 25 Aug. 1857; commanded the main storming party in the assault on Delhi, 14 Sept. 1857; was shot through the chest and died a few days later. [xli. 17]

NICHOLSON, JOHN (1777–1866), publisher, of Kirkcudbright; brother of William Nicholson (1782?–1849) [q. v.]; antiquary and local historian. [xli. 32]

NICHOLSON, JOSHUA (1812–1885), silk manufacturer and philanthropist; partner in J. & J. Brough, Nicholson & Co.; built the Nicholson Institute at Leek, 1884, and endowed it for ten years. [xli. 21]

NICHOLSON, SIR LOTHIAN (1827–1893), general; entered Woolwich, 1844; first lieutenant, 1847; second captain, 1855; served in the Crimea; brevet major, 1855; present at the final siege of Lucknow; promoted brevet lieutenant-colonel, 1858; C.B., 1859; brevet colonel, 1866; major-general, 1877; lieutenant-governor of Jersey, 1878–1883; lieutenant-general, 1881; K.C.B., 1887; appointed governor of Gibraltar, 1891; died at Gibraltar. [xli. 21]

NICHOLSON, MARGARET (1750?–1828), assailant of George III; a housemaid who (1786) attempted to stab George III with a dessert-knife; certified insane and sent to Bedlam; burlesque verses written on her by Percy Bysshe Shelley [q. v.] and Thomas Jefferson Hogg [q. v.], 1810. [xli. 22]

NICHOLSON, MICHAEL ANGELO (d. 1842), architectural draughtsman; son of Peter Nicholson [q. v.]; invented the inverted trammel for drawing ellipses; published professional works and exhibited at the Royal Academy. [xli. 25]

NICHOLSON, PETER (1765–1844), mathematician and architect; opened an evening school for mechanics in Soho; set up as an architect at Glasgow, 1800; removed to Carlisle, 1805, and to Newcastle, 1829; devoted his life to improving the mechanical processes of building; formulated rules for finding sections of prisms, cylinders, or cylindroids, invented the centrolinead, and claimed to have invented a method for obtaining rational roots and approximating to the irrational roots of an equation of any order; published many useful works on architecture and mathematics. [xli. 23]

NICHOLSON, RENTON (1809–1861), known as the Lord Chief Baron; finally became editor of a society journal and a sporting paper; opened the Garrick's Head, London, 1841, and there established the Judge and Jury Society, where he presided as lord chief baron over humorous trials; subsequently removed his 'court' to 103 Strand; wrote on boxing, and was proprietor and editor of 'Illustrated London Life,' 1843. [xli. 25]

NICHOLSON, RICHARD (d. 1639), musician; Mus. Bac. Oxford, 1596; organist, Magdalen College, Oxford, c. 1596; first professor of music at Oxford, 1626; composed madrigals. [xli. 26]

NICHOLSON, SAMUEL (fl. 1600–1602), poet and divine; M.A. Catharine Hall, Cambridge, 1602; his 'Acolastus his After-Witte,' 1600, interesting from its plagiarisms from Shakespeare's and other works; published a devotional treatise, 1602. [xli. 26]

NICHOLSON, THOMAS JOSEPH (1645–1718), first vicar-apostolic of Scotland; regent, Glasgow University; became a Roman catholic, 1682; missionary to Scotland, 1687; imprisoned for a short time, 1688 and 1697; consecrated bishop of Peristachium and first vicar-general of Scotland, 1695. [xli. 26]

NICHOLSON, WILLIAM (1591–1672), bishop of Gloucester; M.A. Magdalen College, Oxford, 1615; master of Croydon free school, 1616–29; rector of Llandilo-Vawr, 1626; archdeacon of Brecon, 1644; kept a school in Carmarthenshire in partnership with Jeremy Taylor [q. v.] and William Wyatt [q. v.]; bishop of Gloucester, 1661–72; published expositions of the catechism and apostles' creed, and an analysis of the Psalms; published 'Apology for the Discipline of the Ancient Church,' 1659. [xli. 27]

NICHOLSON, WILLIAM (1753-1815), man of science and inventor; sailed under the East India Company, 1769-76; settled in London and engaged in scientific studies; invented (c. 1789) an ingenious aerometer, which bore his name, and was long used in laboratories; acted as a patent agent, and himself patented a cylindrical machine for printing on linen and other articles, 1790, which was never used; sketched arrangements for the water supply of Portsmouth and Gosport, and became engineer to the company; brought out a 'Dictionary of Practical and Theoretical Chemistry,' 1808; edited Nicholson's 'Journal of Natural Philosophy,' 1797-1815, and wrote and translated many books on chemistry and natural philosophy. [xli. 28]

NICHOLSON, WILLIAM (1781-1844), portrait-painter and etcher; exhibited portraits at the Royal Academy, 1808-22; removed to Edinburgh, 1814; minia-turist and painter in oils, but chiefly successful with water-colour portraits; etched a few of his own and other painters' portraits, and exhibited at Scottish exhibitions; instrumental in the formation of the Scottish Academy of Painting, Sculpture, and Architecture, 1826. [xli. 30]

NICHOLSON, WILLIAM (1782?-1849), the Galloway poet; a pedlar who was encouraged by Hogg and Dr. Alexander Murray (1775-1813) [q. v.]; published 'Tales in Verse and Miscellaneous Poems,' 1814; visited London to preach universal redemption, 1826. [xli. 31]

NICHOLSON, WILLIAM (1816-1865), Australian statesman and 'father of the ballot'; went out from England to Melbourne, 1841; elected to the city council, 1848; alderman and mayor, 1850; elected to the mixed legislative council for North Bourke, 1852; moved a resolu-tion in favour of the ballot, 1855; unsuccessful in con-structing a cabinet, but his scheme, ultimately the 'Australian ballot,' accepted; visited England, 1856; premier of Victoria, 1859; endeavoured to settle the Victoria land question. [xli. 32]

NICHOLSON, WILLIAM ADAMS (1803-1853), architect; articled to John Buonarotti Papworth [q. v.]; established himself at Lincoln, 1828, and acquired exten-sive practice; original F.R.I.B.A. [xli. 33]

NICKLE, SIR ROBERT (1786-1855), major-general; entered the army, 1799; lieutenant, 1802; captain, 1809; served through the Peninsular war; in America, 1814; entered Paris, 1815; brevet major, 1819; lieutenant-colonel, 1825; served in Canada, 1838; K.H.; brevet colonel, 1848; major-general, 1851; appointed commander of the Australian forces, 1853; died at Melbourne. [xli. 34]

NICKOLLS, JOHN (1710?-1745), antiquary; mer-chant; collected prints of heads; acquired original letters formerly possessed by Milton, which he published, 1743; F.S.A., 1740. [xli. 35]

NICOL. [See also NICHOLL, NICHOL, and NICOLL.]

NICOL, MRS. (d. 1834?), actress; a housekeeper who became an actress; appeared first at Edinburgh, 1806; retired, 1834; excelled in old-women rôles. [xli. 35]

NICOL, ALEXANDER (fl. 1739-1766), Scottish poet; teacher of English at Abernyte; his poems collected, 1766. [xli. 36]

NICOL, EMMA (1801-1877), actress; daughter of Mrs. Nicol [q. v.]; played at Edinburgh, 1808-24; ap-peared in London and the smaller Scottish towns after 1824; in Edinburgh, 1834-62, devoting herself to old-women rôles. [xli. 36]

NICOL, JAMES (1769-1819), poet; was minister of Traquair, 1802; contributed to magazines; published two volumes of poems, 1805. [xli. 37]

NICOL, JAMES (1810-1879), geologist; son of James Nicol (1769-1819) [q. v.]; studied at Edinburgh, Bonn, and Berlin; professor of geology, Queen's College, Cork, 1849, and at Aberdeen, 1853-78; F.G.S. and F.R.S.E., 1847; published handbooks on mineralogy, 1849 and 1858, and wrote on the geology of Scotland, 1844 and 1866; discovered the true relations of the rock-masses in the complicated region of the highlands. [xli. 38]

NICOL or **NICOLL**, JOHN (fl. 1590-1667), diarist; writer to the signet; compiled a diary in two vols. from 1637 to 1649 and 1650 to 1657, prefixing an intro-duction on earlier Scottish history. Vol. i. has been lost,

but vol. ii. (1650-7) was printed by the Bannatyne Club, 1836. [xli. 39]

NICOL, WILLIAM (1744?-1797), friend of Burns; studied theology and medicine at Edinburgh; classical master at Edinburgh High School; Burns was his guest, 1787 and 1789, and they visited the highlands together. [xli. 39]

NICOLAS. [See also NICHOLAS.]

NICOLAS BREAKSPEAR, POPE ADRIAN IV (d. 1159). [See ADRIAN.]

NICOLAS, GRANVILLE TOUP (d. 1894), navy captain; son of John Toup Nicolas [q. v.]; entered navy, 1848; engaged in suppression of Tae-ping insurrec-tion; retired as captain, 1882. [xli. 41]

NICOLAS, JOHN TOUP (1788-1851), rear-admiral; brother of Sir Nicholas Harris Nicolas [q. v.]; entered navy, 1799; lieutenant, 1804; commander, 1809; served in the Mediterranean; C.B. and post captain, 1815; K.H., 1834; rear-admiral, 1850. [xli. 40]

NICOLAS, SIR NICHOLAS HARRIS (1799-1848), antiquary; entered navy, 1808; lieutenant, 1815; put on half-pay, 1816; F.S.A., 1824-8; barrister, Inner Temple, 1825; many desirable reforms produced by his attacks on the record commission, the Society of Antiquaries, and the British Museum; K.H., 1831; G.C.M.G., 1840; died at Boulogne. He compiled or edited many valuable works, amongst others, 'The Life of William Davison,' 1823, 'Notitia Historica,' 1824 (improved edition, 'Chron-ology of History,' 1833), 'Synopsis of the Peerage of England,' 1825, 'Testamenta Vetusta,' 1826, 'Literary Remains of Lady Jane Grey,' 1825, 'The Battle of Agin-court,' 1827, 'The Scrope and Grosvenor Controversy,' 1832, 'Proceedings and Ordinances of the Privy Council, 1386-1542,' 'Despatches and Letters of Lord Nelson,' 1844-6, 'History of Royal Navy,' 1847, and 'Memoirs of Sir Christopher Hatton,' 1847. [xli. 41]

NICOLAY, SIR WILLIAM (1771-1842), colonial ad-ministrator; second lieutenant, 1785; present at Seringa-patam, 1792, and Pondicherry, 1793; captain, 1798; major, 1801; served at Waterloo; C.B., 1815; governor of Dominica, 1824-31, of Antigua, 1831-2, of Mauritius, 1832-40; lieutenant-general, 1837; K.C.H. [xli. 44]

NICOLL. [See also NICHOL and NICOL.]

NICOLL, ALEXANDER (1793-1828), orientalist; M.A. Balliol College, Oxford, 1814; regius professor of Hebrew and canon of Christ Church, Oxford, 1822-8; D.C.L., 1822; made catalogues of the oriental manu-scripts at the Bodleian Library, of which he was a sub-librarian. [xli. 44]

NICOLL or **NICOLLS**, ANTHONY (1611-1659), par-liamentarian; nephew of John Pym [q. v.]; M.P. for Bodmin in the Long parliament; joined the presbyterian members; several charges being preferred against him, was ordered into restraint, 1647; escaped; the orders against him revoked by the presbyterians, 1647; master of the armouries, 1648; M.P., Cornwall, 1654-5, Bossiney, 1659; sheriff of Cornwall, 1657. [xli. 45]

NICOLL, FRANCIS (1770-1835), Scottish divine; M.A. Aberdeen, 1789; minister of Mains, 1799-1819; D.D. St. Andrews, 1807; minister of St. Leonard's, Fife, 1819-24; principal of St. Leonard's and St. Salvator's, St. Andrews, 1819, and rector of the university, 1822. [xli. 46]

NICOLL, ROBERT (1814-1837), poet; wrote for 'Tait's Magazine'; opened a circulating library at Dundee; became editor of the 'Leeds Times,' 1836; a strong radical; published poems, 1835, the best being his lyrics in the Scottish dialect. [xli. 46]

NICOLL, WHITLOCK (1786-1838), physician; M.R.C.S., 1809; M.D. Aberdeen, 1816; chief work, 'Cere-bral Structures in Infants,' 1821; wrote also on theology. [xli. 47]

NICOLLS or **NICHOLLS**, SIR AUGUSTINE (1559-1616), judge; reader at the Middle Temple, 1602; ser-jeant-at-law, 1603; justice of common pleas, 1612; knighted, 1612; chancellor to Charles, prince of Wales, 1616. [xli. 48]

NICOLLS, BENEDICT (d. 1433), bishop of St. David's; bishop of Bangor, 1408-18; a trier of petitions, 1414 and 1429; bishop of St. David's, 1418-33; founded a chantry at St. David's. [xli. 49]

NICOLLS, FERDINANDO (1598–1662), presbyterian divine; M.A. Magdalen College, Oxford, 1621; rector of St. Mary Arches, Exeter, 1634; Devonshire commissioner for the ejection of scandalous ministers, 1654; ejected, 1662; published 'Life of Ignatius Jourdain,' 1654.
[xli. 49]

NICOLLS, Sir FRANCIS, first baronet (1585–1642), nephew of Sir Augustine Nicolls [q. v.]; entered the Middle Temple, 1602; M.P., Northamptonshire, 1629; high sheriff of the county, 1631; secretary to the elector palatine, 1640; created baronet, 1641.
[xli. 49]

NICOLLS, Sir JASPER (1778–1849), lieutenant-general; gazetted, 1793; lieutenant, 1794; captain, 1799; went to India, 1802; major, 1804; distinguished himself at the assault of Buenos Ayres, 1807; lieutenant-colonel, 1807; present at Coruña (medal); quartermaster-general, 1812; colonel, 1814; distinguished himself in the conquest of Camoan, 1814–16; major-general, 1821; created K.C.B. for his brilliant services at Bhurtpore, 1825; lieutenant-general, 1837; commander-in-chief in Madras, 1838; transferred to Bengal, 1839; resigned, 1843.
[xli. 50]

NICOLLS, MATHIAS (1630?–1687), jurist; barrister; secretary of the province of New Netherlands, 1664, compiling 'the Duke's Laws,' the first code of laws in New York; mayor of New York, 1672; first judge of the common pleas, New York; died in America.
[xli. 52]

NICOLLS, RICHARD (1624–1672), first English governor of New York; fought as a royalist in the civil war; sent as commissioner to organise the seaboard from the Kennebec to the Hudson, 1664; on the surrender of New Netherlands, 1664, retained Dutch officials where possible, and established courts of law; returned to England, 1667; killed at Solebay.
[xli. 52]

NICOLLS, WILLIAM (1657–1723), jurist; son of Mathias Nicolls [q. v.]; went to America and became clerk of Queen's County, New York, 1683; imprisoned for opposing Jacob Leisler's usurpation in New York; member for Suffolk County, New York, 1702, and speaker, 1702–18.
[xli. 52]

NICOLS, THOMAS (*fl.* 1659), writer on gems; studied at Jesus College, Cambridge; wrote a curious work on precious stones, published thrice, each time with a different title.
[xli. 54]

NICOLSON. [See also NICHOLSON.]

NICOLSON, ALEXANDER (1827–1893), Gaelic scholar; B.A. Edinburgh, 1850; hon. M.A., 1859; took to journalism; called to the Scottish bar, 1860; assistant-commissioner of Scottish education, 1865; sheriff-substitute of Kirkcudbright, 1872, of Greenock, 1885; LL.D. Edinburgh, 1880; revised the Gaelic bible and collected Gaelic proverbs.
[xli. 54]

NICOLSON, WILLIAM (1655–1727), divine and antiquary; M.A. Queen's College, Oxford, 1679; fellow, 1679–1682; visited Leipzig to learn German and the northern languages of Europe; prebendary of Carlisle, 1681; archdeacon of Carlisle, 1682; bishop of Carlisle, 1702; involved by his impetuosity as bishop in perpetual strife; formed a collection of manuscripts and contributed to antiquarian works; translated to the bishopric of Derry, 1718, to the archbishopric of Cashel and Emly, 1727; did not live to take charge of the archbishopric. He showed great zeal for the preservation of official documents, for which purpose he built special rooms at Derry. His chief work consists of the 'Historical Library' (English part published, 1696, 1697, and 1699, Scottish, 1702, Irish, 1724; entire work republished, 1732 and 1776). In 1705 he brought out 'Leges Marchiarum, or Border Laws' (republished, 1747).
[xli. 55]

NIELD, JAMES (1744–1814). [See NEILD.]

NIEMANN, EDMUND JOHN (1813–1876), landscape-painter; exhibited in London and the provinces.
[xli. 58]

NIETO, DAVID (1654–1728), Jewish theologian; born at Venice; came to London, 1701, as rabbi to the Spanish and Portuguese Jews; published theological works in Spanish and Latin.
[xli. 58]

NIGEL, called the DANE (*d.* 921?), reputed king of Deira; said by the English chroniclers to have ruled in Northumbria and to have been slain by his brother Sitric; the Irish chroniclers do not mention him.
[xli. 59]

NIGEL (*d.* 1169), bishop of Ely and statesman; nephew of Roger [q. v.], bishop of Salisbury; educated by Anselm at Laon; prebendary of St. Paul's, London; consecrated bishop of Ely, 1133, and was then 'the king's treasurer'; restored several estates to the see; raised Stephen's suspicions and fortified Ely, which was taken (1139) by Stephen; fled to Matilda, but, realising the hopelessness of her cause, submitted, and was restored, 1142; accused of connivance in Geoffrey de Mandeville's revolt, and obliged to purchase his peace. On Henry II's accession Nigel was called upon to reinstate Henry I's official system, and was also presiding justiciar in the curia regis.
[xli. 60]

NIGEL, called WIREKER (*fl.* 1190), satirist; monk of Christ Church, Canterbury; best-known work, 'Speculum Stultorum,' in which the vices and corruption of society and the religious orders are satirised; wrote also 'Contra Curiales et Officiales Clericos.'
[xli. 62]

NIGER, RALPH (*fl.* 1170), historian and theologian; educated at Paris; supported Thomas à Becket; accused before Henry II and fled into exile; in addition to theological works wrote two chronicles, which contain only borrowed notices of English affairs.
[xli. 63]

NIGER or **LE NOIR**, ROGER (*d.* 1241), bishop of London; prebendary of St. Paul's, London, 1192; archdeacon of Colchester, 1218; elected bishop of London, 1228; threatened to excommunicate all concerned in dragging Hubert de Burgh from Boisars Chapel, 1232; cleared himself at Rome, at great cost, of the charge of pillaging the Romans, 1232; dedicated the choir of St. Paul's Cathedral, 1240.
[xli. 64]

NIGHTINGALE, JOSEPH (1775–1824), miscellaneous writer; became a Wesleyan methodist, 1796; was a schoolmaster and became a unitarian, 1804; exposed to criticism by his 'Portraiture of Methodism,' 1807; returned to methodism, 1824; wrote on history, religion, stenography, and topography.
[xli. 65]

NIGHTINGALL, Sir MILES (1768–1829), lieutenant-general; entered the army, 1787; present at Seringapatam, 1792, and Pondicherry, 1793; captain, 1794; major and lieutenant-colonel before 1797; quartermaster-general in Bengal, 1803; present (1808) at Roleia and Vimeiro, and (1811) at Fuentes d'Onoro (medals); major-general, 1810; commander-in-chief in Java, 1813–15; lieutenant-general, 1814; K.C.B., 1815.
[xli. 66]

NIMMO, ALEXANDER (1783–1832), civil engineer; of St. Andrews and Edinburgh Universities; originally a schoolmaster; commissioner to fix the county boundaries of Scotland; engineer of the western district of Ireland, where he reclaimed waste land and built bridges and harbours; F.R.S.; member of the Institute of British Architects.
[xli. 67]

NIMMO, JAMES (1654–1709), covenanter; was among the defeated at Bothwell Bridge, 1679; ultimately fled to Holland, but (1688) returned to Scotland, and was appointed to the customs.
[xli. 67]

NIMROD (pseudonym). [See APPERLEY, CHARLES JAMES, 1779–1843.]

NINIAN or **NINIAS**, SAINT (*d.* 432?), apostle of Christianity in North Britain; a Briton who made a pilgrimage to Rome; trained at Rome; consecrated bishop, establishing his episcopal seat at Whithorn, where he built a stone church dedicated to St. Martin of Tours, and commonly called Candida Casa; evangelised the southern Picts; Bæda and Ailred of Rievaulx give accounts of him.
[xli. 68]

NISBET. [See also NESBIT, NESBITT, NISBETT.]

NISBET, ALEXANDER (1657–1725), heraldic writer; educated at Edinburgh for the law; devoted himself to heraldry and antiquities; chief work, 'System of Heraldry,' 1722.
[xli. 69]

NISBET, CHARLES (1736–1804), Scottish divine; educated at Edinburgh University; called to the charge of Montrose, 1764; advocated the cause of the American colonies; appointed (1785) principal of Dickinson College, Carlisle, Pennsylvania, where he died.
[xli. 70]

NISBET, JOHN (1627 ?–1685), covenanter ; took an active and prominent part in the struggles of the covenanters for civil and religious liberty ; wounded and left for dead at Pentland, 1666 ; fought as captain at Bothwell Bridge, 1679 ; seized and executed as a rebel. [xli. 70]

NISBET, SIR JOHN (1609 ?–1687), lord-advocate ; admitted advocate, 1633 ; sheriff-depute of the county of Edinburgh, 1639 ; defended Montrose, 1641 ; appointed lord-advocate and raised to the bench as Lord Dirleton, 1664 ; severely persecuted the covenanters ; commissioner for the union of the two kingdoms, 1670 ; forced to resign position of lord advocate, 1677. [xli. 70]

NISBET, WILLIAM (*fl.* 1787–1805), medical writer ; F.R.C.S. of Edinburgh ; wrote on venereal diseases, 1787, on scrofula and cancer, 1795 ; published ' The Clinical Guide,' 1793, and a 'General Dictionary of Chemistry,' 1805. [xli. 71]

NISBETT, LOUISA CRANSTOUN (1812 ?–1858), actress : the daughter of one Macnamara, who acted under the name Mordaunt ; began to act as Miss Mordaunt at Greenwich, 1826 ; played in the provinces till 1829 ; married John Alexander Nisbett, 1831, but returned to the stage (1832) in consequence of her husband's sudden death and his affairs being put into chancery ; acted in various London theatres ; married Sir William Boothby, 1844 ; again returned to the stage after his death, 1846 ; retired, 1851 ; a charming actress in comedy. [xli. 72]

NITHSDALE, fifth EARL OF (1676–1744). [See MAXWELL, WILLIAM.]

NITHSDALE, COUNTESS OF (*d.* 1749). [See MAXWELL, WINIFRED.]

NITHSDALE, LORD OF (*d.* 1392 ?). [See DOUGLAS, SIR WILLIAM.]

NIX or **NYKKE**, RICHARD (1447 ?–1535), bishop of Norwich ; studied at Trinity Hall, Cambridge (LL.D.), Oxford, and Bologna ; prebendary of Wells, 1489 ; archdeacon of Exeter, 1492 ; archdeacon of Wells, 1494 ; prebendary of York, 1494 ; canon of Windsor, 1497 ; dean of the Chapel Royal, London, 1497 ; bishop of Norwich, 1501–5 ; belonged to the old catholic party ; opposed to Henry VIII's divorce, and to the reformers ; fined for infringing the Act of Præmunire, 1534 ; swore to recognise royal supremacy, 1534. [xli. 74]

NIXON, ANTHONY (*fl.* 1602), pamphleteer and poet ; was the author of miscellaneous prose pamphlets, with scraps of original and translated verse interspersed. [xli. 75]

NIXON, FRANCIS RUSSELL (1803–1879), bishop of Tasmania ; son of Robert Nixon (1759–1837) [q. v.] ; of Merchant Taylors' School, London ; probationary fellow St. John's College, Oxford, 1827 ; M.A., 1841 ; D.D., 1842 ; held various preferments ; consecrated first bishop of Tasmania, 1842 ; returned to England, 1863 ; rector of Bolton-Percy, 1863–6 ; died at Lago Maggiore ; published miscellaneous works. [xli. 76]

NIXON, JAMES (1741 ?–1812), miniature-painter ; limner to the Prince of Wales and miniature-painter to the Duchess of York ; exhibited in London (1765–1805) portraits of theatrical and other celebrities ; A.R.A., 1778. [xli. 76]

NIXON, JOHN (*d.* 1818), amateur artist and merchant ; exhibited landscapes and caricatures, 1784–1815. [xli. 76]

NIXON, JOHN (1815–1899), pioneer of steam-coal trade in South Wales ; apprenticed as mining engineer at Garesfield ; employed on coal and iron field at Languin, near Nantes ; perceived advantages of Welsh coal for furnaces, and induced French government to make trial of it ; sank mine at Werfa, and gradually, in association with others, acquired and made many collieries in South Wales ; introduced important improvements in mining methods. [Suppl. iii. 229]

NIXON, ROBERT (*fl.* 1620 ?), the ' Cheshire prophet ' ; an idiot inspired at intervals to deliver oracular prophecies (first published by John Oldmixon, 1714). [xli. 77]

NIXON, ROBERT (1759–1837), painter, brother of John Nixon (*d.* 1818) [q. v.] ; graduated at Christ Church, Oxford, 1780 ; B.D., 1790 ; curate of Foot's Cray, 1784–1804 ; exhibited paintings at the Royal Academy, 1790–1818. [xli. 77]

NIXON, SAMUEL (1803–1854), sculptor ; exhibited at the Royal Academy, 1826 ; executed the sculptural decorations of the Goldsmiths' Hall, London ; his principal work the statue of William IV in King William Street, London. [xli. 77]

NOAD, HENRY MINCHIN (1815–1877), electrician ; studied chemistry and electricity under Hofmann ; professor of chemistry at St. George's Hospital, London, 1847 ; gained the Astley Cooper prize, 1852 ; consulting chemist to Welsh ironworks ; F.R.S., 1856 ; wrote on electricity and chemistry. [xli. 77]

NOAKE, JOHN (1816–1894), antiquary ; edited Worcester newspapers ; sheriff, 1878, mayor and alderman, 1879, and magistrate, 1882, of Worcester, wrote on the history and antiquities of Worcester. [xli. 78]

NOBBES, ROBERT (1652–1706 ?), writer on angling ; M.A. Sidney Sussex College, Cambridge, 1675 ; vicar of Apethorpe, 1676–90, of Sausthorpe, 1702–6 ; his ' Compleat Troller,' 1682, frequently reprinted. [xli. 79]

NOBBS, GEORGE HUNN (1799–1884), missionary and chaplain of Pitcairn island ; entered the navy, 1811 ; joined the patriots of South America, 1816 ; captured by Spaniards, 1817 ; made several voyages to Sierra Leone, 1823 ; settled on Pitcairn island, 1828 ; ordained, 1852 ; subsequently removed with the islanders to Norfolk island, where he died. [xli. 79]

NOBLE, GEORGE (*fl.* 1795–1806), line-engraver ; brother of William Bonneau Noble [q. v.] ; engraved for Boydell's 'Shakespeare,' 1802, and Bowyer's 'Hume,' 1806. [xli. 80]

NOBLE, JAMES (1774–1851), vice-admiral ; entered navy, 1787 ; served in Mediterranean ; lieutenant, 1796 ; distinguished himself at Loano, 1796, and St. Vincent, 1797 ; promoted commander, 1796 ; post-captain, 1802 ; rear-admiral, 1837 ; vice-admiral, 1846. [xli. 80]

NOBLE, JOHN (1827–1892), politician and writer on public finance ; supported the Anti-Cornlaw league, manhood suffrage, and municipal reform in London ; secretary of the County Council Union, 1889 ; wrote on financial reform. [xli. 81]

NOBLE, MARK (1754–1827), biographer ; abandoned the law for the church ; incumbent of Baddesley Clinton and Packwood, 1781 ; rector of Barming, 1786 ; F.S.A., 1781 ; produced, among other works, ' Memoirs of the Protectoral House of Cromwell,' 1784, 'The Lives of the English Regicides,' 1798, and continued James Granger's ' Biographical History of England,' 1806 ; his numerous manuscripts sold, 1827. [xli. 81]

NOBLE, MATTHEW (1818–1876), sculptor ; studied under John Francis (1780–1861) [q. v.] ; exhibited at the Royal Academy, 1845–76 ; executed chiefly busts. [xli. 83]

NOBLE, RICHARD (1684–1713), criminal ; an attorney who became intimate with Mary, daughter of Admiral John Nevell [q. v.] and wife of one John Sayer ; subsequently killed Sayer, the husband, and was executed. [xli. 83]

NOBLE, SAMUEL (1779–1853), engraver and minister of the ' new church ' ; brother of William Bonneau Noble [q. v.] ; a skilful architectural engraver ; minister of Cross Street congregation, London, 1819 ; his view that Christ's body was not resuscitated, but dissipated in the grave and replaced by a new divine frame, controverted by John Clowes and Robert Hindmarsh ; published an ' Appeal on behalf of the … Doctrines … held by the … New Church,' 1826, and other theological works. [xli. 84]

NOBLE, WILLIAM BONNEAU (1780–1831), landscape-painter in water-colours ; brother of Samuel Noble [q. v.] ; taught drawing and exhibited water-colour paintings of Welsh scenery, 1809 and 1811. [xli. 85]

NOBLE, WILLIAM HENRY (1834–1892), major-general, royal artillery ; M.A. Trinity College, Dublin, 1859 ; lieutenant, 1856 ; captain, 1866 ; major, 1875 ; lieutenant-colonel, 1882 ; brevet-colonel, 1886 ; served as associate-member of the ordnance select committee for carrying out balistic and other experiments in scientific gunnery ; the manufacture of cordite largely due to his researches ; served in the Afghan war, 1876–8 ; major-general, 1889 ; F.R.S. [xli. 85]

NOBYS, PETER (*fl.* 1520–1523), master of Corpus Christi College, Cambridge ; M.A. Cambridge, 1504 ; fellow of Christ's College, Cambridge, 1503 : rector of Landbeach, 1516 ; master of Corpus Christi College, Cambridge, 1517 ; visited Rome, 1519 ; resigned his mastership and benefice, 1523. [xli. 86]

NODDER, FREDERICK P. (*d.* 1800 ?), botanic painter and engraver ; supplied illustrations to various botanical works ; exhibited, 1786–1800. [xli. 86]

NOEL, SIR ANDREW (*d.* 1607), sheriff of Rutland ; brother of Henry Noel [q. v.] ; sheriff of Rutland, 1587, 1595, and 1600 ; M.P., Rutland, 1586, 1588, and 1593 ; knighted, 1585. [xli. 87]

NOEL, BAPTIST, second BARON NOEL OF RIDLINGTON, and third VISCOUNT CAMPDEN and BARON HICKS OF ILMINGTON (1611–1682), son of Edward Noel, second viscount Campden [q. v.] ; knight of the shire for Rutland in both Short and Long parliaments ; captain, and promoted colonel in the royal troops, 1643 ; taken prisoner, 1645 ; released, 1646 ; his estates sequestered, but his fine reduced from 19,558*l.* to 11,078*l.* 17*s.* ; lord-lieutenant of Rutland, 1660, and J.P., 1661. [xli. 88]

NOEL, BAPTIST WRIOTHESLEY (1798–1873), divine ; brother of Gerard Thomas Noel [q. v.] ; of Westminster School and Trinity College, Cambridge ; M.A., 1821 ; took orders and became evangelical minister of St. John's Chapel, Bedford Row, London ; became a baptist, 1848 ; minister of John Street Baptist Chapel, London, 1849–68 ; published controversial pamphlets and devotional works. [xli. 89]

NOEL, EDWARD, first BARON NOEL OF RIDLINGTON, and second VISCOUNT CAMPDEN (1582–1643), son of Sir Andrew Noel [q. v.] ; knighted when serving in the Irish wars, 1602 ; created baronet, 1611 ; master of the game in Lyfield Forest, 1614 ; created Baron Noel of Ridlington, 1617 ; commissioner for collecting subsidies, 1624 ; succeeded his father-in-law as second Baron Hicks and Viscount Campden, 1629 ; assisted the attempts to levy shipmoney, 1636 ; one of the council of peers at York, 1639 ; raised a regiment of horse for Charles I. [xli. 90]

NOEL, GERARD THOMAS (1782–1851), divine ; brother of Baptist Wriothesley Noel [q. v.] ; M.A. Trinity College, Cambridge, 1808 ; vicar of Romsey, 1840, where he restored the abbey church ; honorary canon of Winchester, 1834 ; published sermons and hymns. [xli. 91]

NOEL, HENRY (*d.* 1597), courtier ; brother of Sir Andrew Noel [q. v.] ; a gentleman-pensioner of Queen Elizabeth ; admitted M.A. Oxford, 1592 ; notorious for his extravagance. [xli. 87]

NOEL, RODEN BERKELEY WRIOTHESLEY (1834–1894), poet ; M.A. Trinity College, Cambridge, 1858 ; groom of the privy chamber to Queen Victoria, 1867–71 ; published poetry and miscellaneous works ; died at Mainz. [xli. 92]

NOEL, THOMAS (1799–1861), poet ; B.A. Merton College, Oxford, 1824 ; corresponded with Miss Mitford ; wrote the song, 'Rocked in the Cradle of the Deep,' and other verses. [xli. 92]

NOEL, WILLIAM (1695–1762), judge ; barrister, the Inner Temple, 1721 ; M.P., Stamford, 1722–47, West Looe, 1747–57 ; K.C., 1738 ; chief-justice of Chester, 1749 ; justice of the common pleas, 1757. [xli. 93]

NOEL-FEARN, HENRY (1811–1868). [See CHRISTMAS.]

NOEL-HILL, WILLIAM, third BARON BERWICK (*d.* 1842). [See HILL.]

NOKE or **NOKES**, JAMES (*d.* 1692 ?), actor ; became an actor, 1659 ; represented the Duke of Norfolk in 'Henry VIII,' to Charles II's admiration, *c.* 1663 ; acted the Nurse so successfully in Nevil Payne's 'Fatal Jealousy' that he was known as 'Nurse Nokes.' [xli. 93]

NOLAN, FREDERICK (1784–1864), divine ; studied at Dublin and Exeter College, Oxford (D.C.L., 1828) ; ordained, 1806 ; vicar of Prittlewell, 1822 ; Boyle lecturer, 1814 ; Bampton lecturer, 1833 ; Warburtonian lecturer, 1833–6 ; F.R.S., 1832 ; published theological works and a 'Harmonical Grammar of the Principal Ancient and Modern Languages,' 1822. [xli. 95]

NOLAN, LEWIS EDWARD (1820 ?–1854), captain, 15th hussars, and writer on cavalry ; entered the army, 1839 ; purchased his lieutenancy, 1841, and his troop, 1850 ; served in India, and at Balaclava, 1854, carried the order which, owing to a misunderstanding, resulted in the charge of the light brigade, and was shot while endeavouring to divert the brigade. He wrote on 'Cavalry,' 1851, and 'Cavalry Horses,' 1861 (published posthumously). [xli. 96]

NOLAN, MICHAEL (*d.* 1827), legal author ; barrister, Lincoln's Inn ,1792 ; M.P., Barnstaple, 1820–6 ; introduced Poor Law Reform bills, 1822–3–4 ; justice of Brecon, Glamorgan, and Radnor, 1824 ; wrote on poor laws and edited 'reports.' [xli. 97]

NOLLEKENS, JOSEPH (1737–1823), sculptor ; son of Joseph Francis Nollekens [q. v.] ; placed in the studio of Peter Scheemakers [q. v.] ; gained three prizes for clay-modelling ; started for Rome, 1760 ; met Garrick and Sterne at Rome and executed busts of both ; employed as an agent in the collection of antiques ; subsequently speculated successfully on the Stock Exchange ; returned to England, 1770 ; contributed to the Royal Academy, 1771–1816 : R.A., 1772 ; married (1772) Mary, daughter of Saunders Welch, a friend of Dr. Johnson, who seconded her husband's economies ; became partially paralysed and sank into a state of senile imbecility during his later years. Besides busts of all the important people of the day, his work as sculptor of monuments was considerable, and his 'Venuses' were greatly admired. [xli. 97]

NOLLEKENS, JOSEPH FRANCIS (1702–1748), painter ; commonly called 'Old Nollekens' ; born at Antwerp ; studied under Watteau and Panini, whose works he copied on coming to London, 1733 ; painted conversation pieces. [xli. 100]

NON FENDIGAID, i.e. the BLESSED (*fl.* 550 ?), mother of St. David ; was, according to Ricemarchus, a nun violated by Sant, king of Cardiganshire. [xli. 100]

NONANT, HUGH DE (*d.* 1198), bishop of Lichfield and Coventry, or Chester ; brought up by his maternal uncle, Arnulf, bishop of Lisieux, who gave him preferment ; entered the service of Thomas Becket before 1164, but by 1170 became clerk and friend of Henry II ; successfully carried out a mission to the pope, 1184, and was made bishop of Lichfield and Coventry or Chester, as it was then styled, 1185 ; sent on a second mission to the pope, 1186 ; abroad with Henry II, 1188 ; involved in a quarrel with his monks at Coventry ; expelled his monks, 1190, who were, however, restored, 1198 : sheriff of Warwickshire and Leicestershire, 1189, though Archbishop Baldwin objected to a bishop holding such a post ; continued to hold the post of sheriff in the interest of Earl John ; one of Longchamp's opponents, writing an account of his fall ; made his way to Germany during Richard I's captivity, 1193 ; retired to Normandy, and died at Bec. [xli. 100]

NOORTHOUCK, JOHN (1746 ?–1816), author ; index-maker and press-corrector ; published 'History of London,' 1773, and 'An Historical and Classical Dictionary,' 1776. [xli. 103]

NORBURY, first EARL OF (1745–1831). [See TOLER, JOHN.]

NORCOME, DANIEL (1576–1647 ?), musician ; instrumentalist at Brussels ; wrote a madrigal. [xli. 103]

NORCOTT, WILLIAM (1770 ?–1820 ?), Irish satirist ; B.A. Trinity College, Dublin, 1795 ; LL.D., 1806 ; called to the Irish bar, 1797 ; wrote poetical satires which appeared in Dublin after the union ; given an appointment in Malta, *c.* 1815 ; fled from Malta and lived in destitution at Constantinople, becoming a Mohammedan ; recanted his Mohammedanism, and was captured while attempting to escape and beheaded. [xli. 104]

NORDEN, FREDERICK LEWIS (1708–1742), traveller and artist ; born at Glückstadt ; lieutenant in the Danish navy, 1732 ; sent to study shipbuilding in Holland, Italy, and Egypt ; came to London, 1740 ; present at siege of Carthagena, 1741 ; F.R.S., 1741 ; published accounts of Egypt and Nubia ; died at Paris. [xli. 104]

NORDEN, JOHN (*fl.* 1600), devotional author ; M.A. Hart Hall, Oxford, 1572 ; published devotional works. [xli. 108]

NORDEN, JOHN (1548–1625 ?), topographer ; the first to design a complete series of county histories ; prevented by pecuniary difficulties from carrying out his design; published 'Middlesex,' 1593, and 'Hertfordshire,' 1598; finished in manuscript Essex, Northampton, Cornwall, Kent, and Surrey; surveyor of crown woods, 1600; surveyor to the duchy of Cornwall, 1605; surveyed Windsor and neighbourhood, 1607; published 'Observations concerning Crown Lands and Woods,' 1613; engraved a number of maps, in which roads were indicated for the first time; one of his maps depicts London in Shakespeare's time.   [xli. 105]

NORFOLK, DUKES OF. [See MOWBRAY, THOMAS I, first DUKE, 1366–1399; MOWBRAY, JOHN, second DUKE, 1389–1432; MOWBRAY, JOHN, third DUKE, 1415–1461; RICHARD, first DUKE of the second creation, 1472–1483; HOWARD, JOHN, first DUKE (of the Howard line), 1430 ?–1485; HOWARD, THOMAS, second DUKE, 1443–1524; HOWARD, THOMAS, third DUKE, 1473–1554; HOWARD, THOMAS, fourth DUKE, 1536–1572; HOWARD, HENRY, sixth DUKE, 1628–1684; HOWARD, HENRY, seventh DUKE, 1655–1701; HOWARD, CHARLES, tenth DUKE, 1720–1786; HOWARD, CHARLES, eleventh DUKE, 1746–1815; HOWARD, BERNARD EDWARD, twelfth DUKE, 1765–1842; HOWARD, HENRY CHARLES, thirteenth DUKE, 1791–1856; HOWARD, HENRY GRANVILLE FITZALAN-, fourteenth DUKE, 1815–1860.]

NORFOLK, ELIZABETH, DUCHESS OF (1494–1558). [See HOWARD, ELIZABETH.]

NORFOLK, EARLS OF. [See GUADER or WADER, RALPH, fl. 1070; BIGOD, HUGH, first EARL, d. 1176 or 1177; BIGOD, ROGER, second EARL, d. 1221; BIGOD, ROGER, fourth EARL, d. 1270; BIGOD, ROGER, fifth EARL, 1245–1306; THOMAS OF BROTHERTON, 1300–1338.]

NORFORD, WILLIAM (1715–1793), medical writer; surgeon at Halesworth and Bury St. Edmunds; wrote on cancer, intestinal obstruction, and intermittent fevers.   [xli. 108]

NORGATE, EDWARD (d. 1650), illuminer and herald-painter; son of Robert Norgate [q. v.]; Blue-mantle pursuivant, 1616; illumined royal patents and wrote letters to foreign sovereigns; Windsor herald, 1633; clerk of the signet, 1638; attended Charles I to Scotland, 1639 and 1640; employed as an art connoisseur to purchase pictures.   [xli. 109]

NORGATE, ROBERT (d. 1587), master of Corpus Christi College, Cambridge; B.A. St. John's College, Cambridge, 1565; fellow of Corpus Christi College, Cambridge; M.A., 1568; D.D., 1581; master of Corpus Christi College, Cambridge 1573–87, vice-chancellor, 1584; received preferment from Archbishop Parker, whose library he preserved for the college.   [xli. 110]

NORGATE, THOMAS STARLING (1772–1859), miscellaneous writer; entered at Lincoln's Inn; established (1830) the 'East Anglian' (weekly newspaper). [xli. 111]

NORGATE, THOMAS STARLING (1807–1893), translator; son of Thomas Starling Norgate (1772–1859) [q. v.]; B.A. Gonville and Caius College, Cambridge, 1832; rector of Sparham, 1840; published blank-verse translations of Homer.   [xli. 111]

NORIE, JOHN WILLIAM (1772–1843), writer on navigation; published naval books and charts. 'Navigation House,' the business in which he succeeded William Heather, is mentioned in Charles Dickens's 'Dombey and Son.'   [xli. 111]

NORMAN, GEORGE WARDE (1793–1882), writer on finance; merchant in the Norway timber trade till 1830; a director of the Bank of England, 1821–72; a member of the committee of the treasury at the bank, 1840; an exchequer bill commissioner, 1831–76; an original member of the Political Economy Club; wrote on currency and taxation.   [xli. 112]

NORMAN, JOHN (1491 ?–1553 ?), Cistercian; B.A. Cambridge, 1514; abbot of Bindon, c. 1523–38. [xli. 113]

NORMAN, JOHN (1622–1669), presbyterian divine; B.A. Exeter College, Oxford, 1641; presbyterian vicar of Bridgwater, 1647; ejected, 1662; imprisoned for preaching; published 'Cases of Conscience practically resolved,' posthumous, 1673.   [xli. 113]

NORMAN, ROBERT (fl. 1590), mathematical instrument maker; wrote on the compass.   [xli. 114]

NORMANBY, first DUKE OF (1648–1721). [See SHEFFIELD, JOHN.]

NORMANBY, MARQUISES OF. [See SHEFFIELD, JOHN, first MARQUIS, 1648–1721; PHIPPS, CONSTANTINE HENRY, first MARQUIS of the second creation, 1797–1863; PHIPPS, GEORGE AUGUSTUS CONSTANTINE, second MARQUIS, 1819–1890.]

NORMANDY, ALPHONSE RENÉ LE MIRE DE (1809–1864), chemist; born at Rouen; studied medicine, but devoted himself to chemistry; patentee for indelible inks and dyes, 1839, and for hardening soap, 1841; came to England, c. 1843; patented (1851) an apparatus for distilling sea-water for drinking, which is still used; wrote on chemical analysis.   [xli. 114]

NORMANNUS, SIMON (d. 1249). [See CANTELUPE, SIMON.]

NORMANVILLE, THOMAS DE (1256–1295), judge; governor of Bamborough Castle and king's escheator beyond the Trent, 1276; justice in eyre in Nottinghamshire and Lancashire, 1286; summoned to council at Westminster, 1288; held pleas 'de quo warranto,' 1292.   [xli. 115]

NORREYS. [See NORRIS.]

NORRIS, ANTONY (1711–1786), antiquary; of Gonville and Caius College, Cambridge; barrister, Middle Temple, 1735; compiled a history of the eastern part of Norfolk, and Norfolk pedigrees.   [xli. 115]

NORRIS, CATHERINE MARIA (d. 1767). [See FISHER.]

NORRIS, CHARLES (1779–1858), artist; of Eton and Christ Church, Oxford; issued three numbers of 'Architectural Antiquities of Wales,' 1810–11, and 'An Historical Account of Tenby,' 1818, with plates by himself.   [xli. 116]

NORRIS, SIR EDWARD (d. 1603), governor of Ostend; son of Sir Henry Norris, baron Norris of Rycote [q. v.]; lieutenant to Sir Philip Sidney in Holland; knighted at Utrecht by Leicester, 1586; quarrelled with Count Hohenlohe, 1586; deputy-governor of Ostend, 1588; accompanied Drake to Portugal, and wounded at Burgos, 1589; governor of Ostend, 1590–9; entertained Queen Elizabeth at Englefield, 1601.   [xli. 117]

NORRIS, EDWARD (1584–1659), New England divine; M.A. Magdalen Hall, Oxford, 1609; an uncompromising opponent of John Traske [q. v.]; went to America, 1639, and (1640) became pastor of Salem Church. [xli. 118]

NORRIS, EDWARD (1663–1726), physician; brother of Sir William Norris, first baronet [q. v.]; M.A. Brasenose College, Oxford, 1689; M.D., 1695; F.R.S., 1698; went to the Deccan with his brother, 1699; F.R.C.P., 1716. [xli. 118]

NORRIS, EDWIN (1795–1872), orientalist and Cornish scholar; clerk to the East India Company, 1818–37; assistant-secretary of the Royal Asiatic Society, 1837, and secretary, 1859; edited the society's 'Journal'; compiled grammars of eastern languages, and published 'The Ancient Cornish Drama,' with a Cornish grammar, 1859; one of the earliest decipherers of cuneiform; produced an 'Assyrian Dictionary' from Aleph to Nun, 1868–72.   [xli. 119]

NORRIS, FRANCIS, EARL OF BERKSHIRE (1579–1623), grandson of Sir Henry Norris, first baron Norris of Rycote [q. v.]; succeeded to the title, 1600; K.B., 1605; in attendance on Earl of Nottingham in Spain, 1605; created Viscount Thame and Earl of Berkshire, 1621; imprisoned in the Fleet in consequence of an encounter with Lord Scrope in the House of Lords, 1621; shot himself with a cross-bow from mortification. His descendants became Earls of Abingdon.   [xli. 120]

NORRIS, SIR FRANCIS (1609–1669), illegitimate son of Francis Norris, earl of Berkshire [q. v.]; knighted, 1633; sheriff of Oxfordshire, 1636; M.P., Oxfordshire, 1656 and 1658.   [xli. 120]

NORRIS, HENRY (d. 1536), courtier; came early to court; gentleman of the king's chamber; became a friend of Henry VIII, and received many grants and offices; adhered to Anne Boleyn; took part in the Greenwich tournament, 1536, after which he was arrested on suspicion of an intrigue with Anne; found guilty and executed, though probably innocent.   [xli. 121]

NORRIS, Sir HENRY, first BARON NORRIS OF RYCOTE (1525 ?-1601), son of Henry Norris (d. 1536) [q. v.]; restored to much of his father's confiscated estate by Henry VIII, and held office under Edward VI; shown exceptional favour by Queen Elizabeth; sheriff of Oxfordshire and Berkshire, 1561; entertained Queen Elizabeth at Rycote, 1566 and 1592; knighted and appointed ambassador to France, 1566; recalled, 1570; created Baron Norris of Rycote, 1572. [xli. 122]

NORRIS, HENRY (1665-1730 ?), known as JUBILEE DICKY; actor; played in Dublin, 1695; became known as Jubilee Dicky from his remarkable success as Dicky in the 'Constant Couple, or a Trip to the Jubilee,' at Drury Lane, London, 1699; disqualified by his short stature for important parts. [xli. 124]

NORRIS, HENRY HANDLEY (1771-1850), theologian; graduated M.A. Peterhouse, Cambridge, 1806 (ad eundem, Oxford, 1817); perpetual curate, subsequently rector, of St. John of Jerusalem at Hackney; prebendary of Llandaff, 1816; prebendary of St. Paul's, London, 1825; on the committee of the S.P.C.K., 1793-1834; wrote on missions and published devotional works. [xli. 126]

NORRIS, ISAAC (1671-1735), mayor of Philadelphia; born in London; taken to Jamaica, 1678; settled in Philadelphia, 1690; elected to the Philadelphia council and assembly, 1708; speaker, 1712; J.P., 1717; mayor of Philadelphia, 1724. [xli. 127]

NORRIS, Sir JOHN (1547 ?-1597), military commander; son of Sir Henry Norris, first baron Norris of Rycote [q. v.]; volunteer under Admiral Coligny, 1571; captain under Essex in Ireland, 1573; crossed to the Low Countries, 1577; distinguished himself at Rymenant, 1578, and Steenwyk, 1580; was made lord-president of Munster, 1584, but left his brother, Sir Thomas Norris [q. v.], as deputy and again served in the Low Countries, 1585; knighted for his victory at Grave, 1586; the campaign rendered futile, 1586, by his dissensions with Leicester, who was in command; recalled to England; returned to Holland under Lord Willoughby, 1587, for a short time; assisted in preparations to resist the Armada, and acted as ambassador to the States-General, 1588; took command with Drake of the expedition to the coast of Spain, 1589; served in Brittany against the forces of the League, 1591 and 1593; returned to Ireland, 1595, to assist in reducing Tyrone; patched up a hollow peace at Dundalk, 1596, and made a futile effort to pacify Connaught; retired to Munster, his health failing, and died at Mallow. [xli. 127]

NORRIS, JOHN (1657-1711), divine; of Winchester College and Exeter College, Oxford; B.A., 1680; M.A., 1684; fellow of All Souls, Oxford; incumbent of Newton St. Loe, 1689; rector of Bemerton, 1692; published devotional works; entered into controversies with the quakers; chiefly remarkable as a solitary representative of Malebranche's theories in England; principal work, 'Essay towards the Theory of an Ideal and Intelligible World' (pt. i. 1701, pt. ii. 1704). [xli. 132]

NORRIS, Sir JOHN (1660 ?-1749), admiral of the fleet; brother of Sir William Norris (1657-1702) [q. v.]; was in 1689 lieutenant of the Edgar with Sir Clowdisley Shovell [q. v.]; commander, 1690, and posted, 1693; served with credit off Lagos, 1693; sent to Hudson's Bay, 1697; distinguished himself at Malaga, 1704, and Barcelona, 1705; knighted, 1705; rear-admiral of the blue, 1707; vice-admiral of the white, 1708; M.P., Rye, 1708-22 and 1734-1749, Portsmouth, 1722-34; admiral of the blue, 1709; commander-in-chief in the Mediterranean, 1710-11; employed in the Baltic, 1715-27, at first to give effect to the treaty with Denmark, afterwards to secure the independence of Sweden; a lord of the admiralty, 1718-30 admiral and commander-in-chief, 1734; commanded the Channel fleet, 1739-44. [xli. 134]

NORRIS, JOHN (1734-1777), founder of the Norrisian professorship at Cambridge; of Eton and Caius College. Cambridge; B.A., 1760; contributed towards the education of Richard Porson [q. v.]; founded by will a professorship of divinity at Cambridge and a theological prize essay; endowed small schools at Witton and Witchingham. [xli. 137]

NORRIS, JOHN PILKINGTON (1823-1891), divine; of Rugby and Trinity College, Cambridge; M.A., 1849; D.D., 1881; fellow of Trinity College, Cambridge, 1848;

inspector of schools, 1849-64; canon of Bristol, 1864; vicar of St. George's, Bristol, 1870, and of St. Mary Redcliffe, Bristol, 1877; held various offices in connection with the cathedral and assisted in its restoration; wrote on theology and education. [xli. 137]

NORRIS, PHILIP (d. 1465), dean of St. Patrick's, Dublin; vicar of St. Nicholas, Dundalk, 1427; entered University College, Oxford; became proficient in learning and advocated the reform or suppression of mendicant friars; bulls promulgated against him, 1440 and 1458, but not enforced; dean of St. Patrick's, Dublin, 1457. [xli. 138]

NORRIS, ROBERT (d. 1791), African trader; brother of William Norris (1719-1791) [q. v.]; visited the king of Dahomey, 1772, and published an account of him, 1789. [xli. 139]

NORRIS, NORREYS, or NOREIS, ROGER (d. 1223), abbot of Evesham; one of the monks of Christchurch, Canterbury, deputed to appeal to Henry II against Archbishop Baldwin, 1187, but acknowledged the archbishop's sway; consecrated abbot of Evesham, 1191, and in 1195 and 1198 hushed up complaints of the monks; pleaded Evesham's exemption from episcopal visitation at Rome, 1205; ordered to resign on charges of misconduct, 1213; made prior of Penwortham, 1213. [xli. 139]

NORRIS, SYLVESTER (1572-1630), Roman catholic controversialist; educated at Rheims and Rome; English missioner, 1596; banished, 1605; D.D.; professed of the four vows, 1618; superior of the Hampshire district, 1621; published controversial works. [xli. 140]

NORRIS, Sir THOMAS (1556-1599), president of Munster; son of Sir Henry Norris, first baron Norris of Rycote [q. v.]; captain of a troop of horse in Ireland, 1579; served against Gerald Fitzgerald, fifteenth earl of Desmond [q. v.], 1580; acted as governor of Connaught, 1580-1; colonel of the forces in Munster, 1582; M.P., Limerick, 1585-6; appointed vice-president of Munster, 1585; unable to do much for the plantation of Munster; knighted, 1588; served under his brother, Sir John Norris [q. v.], 1595-6, and succeeded him as president of Munster, 1597; relieved Kilmallock, 1598; died of a jaw-wound received in a skirmish with Thomas Burke. [xli. 141]

NORRIS, THOMAS (1653-1700), brother of Sir William Norris (1657-1702) [q. v.]; M.P., Liverpool, 1688-1695; high sheriff of Lancashire, 1696. [xli. 144]

NORRIS, THOMAS (1741-1790), singer; chorister in Salisbury Cathedral; Mus. Bac. and organist of Christ Church and St. John's College, Oxford, 1765; sang at festivals. [xli. 143]

NORRIS, Sir WILLIAM (1523-1591), of Fyfield; M.P., Windsor, 1554-7; as herald declared war against Henri II of France, 1557; held various offices under Queen Elizabeth. [xli. 124]

NORRIS, WILLIAM (1670 ?-1700 ?), composer; lay vicar of the choir of Lincoln Cathedral, 1686; steward of the choristers, 1693; left manuscript compositions. [xli. 143]

NORRIS, Sir WILLIAM, first baronet (1657-1702), British envoy to India; brother of Thomas Norris (1653-1700) [q. v.]; M.P., Liverpool, 1695-1701; created baronet, 1698; sent out as king's commissioner to obtain trading privileges from the mogul emperor for the new General Society or English Company, a task which was almost hopeless in face of the determined opposition of the old East India Company, and was further complicated by the English Company's representative at Surat, who offered to suppress piracy on the Indian Seas; finally received an audience of the emperor at Aurangzib, near Panalla, but failed in his mission through being unable honestly to promise to suppress piracy; died on his return voyage and was buried at sea. [xli. 144]

NORRIS, WILLIAM (1719-1791), secretary to the Society of Antiquaries; brother of Robert Norris [q. v.]; secretary S.A., 1759-86. [xli. 146]

NORTH, BROWNLOW (1741-1820), bishop of Winchester; son of Francis North, first earl of Guilford [q. v.]; of Eton and Trinity College, Oxford; B.A., 1762; fellow of All Souls College, Oxford, 1763; M.A., 1766; D.C.L., 1770; canon of Christ Church, Oxford, 1768; dean of Canterbury, 1770; bishop of Coventry and

Lichfield, 1771 ; translated to Worcester, 1774, and to Winchester, 1781 ; organised clerical charities and was generous to literary men ; published sermons. [xli. 146]

NORTH, BROWNLOW (1810–1875), lay preacher ; grandson of Brownlow North (1741–1820) [q. v.] ; registrar of Winchester, 1817 ; became notorious for his irregular life ; served with Don Pedro, 1832–3 ; converted by a sudden illness, 1854 ; conducted evangelical meetings, principally in Scotland. [xli. 147]

NORTH, CHARLES NAPIER (1817–1869), colonel ; entered the army, 1836 ; lieutenant, 1838 ; captain, 1848 ; major, 1857 ; served in the relief of Lucknow (medals and clasp) ; lieutenant-colonel, 1858 ; colonel, 1865 ; published a ' Journal,' 1858. [xli. 148]

NORTH, CHRISTOPHER (pseudonym). [See WILSON, JOHN, 1785–1854.]

NORTH, DUDLEY, third BARON NORTH (1581–1666), son of Sir John North [q. v.] ; succeeded his grandfather as third baron, 1600 ; served in the Low Countries, 1602 ; discovered the springs at Tunbridge Wells, 1606 ; a conspicuous figure at court and in court entertainments ; in opposition in the House of Lords, 1626 ; attended Charles I in his expedition to Scotland, 1639 ; took no part in the civil war, but was commissioner of the admiralty, 1645, and lord-lieutenant of Cambridgeshire ; an accomplished musician ; a collection of his essays published, 1657. [xli. 149]

NORTH, DUDLEY, fourth BARON NORTH (1602–1677), son of Dudley North, third baron North (1581–1666) [q. v.], K.B., 1616 ; volunteered for the relief of the palatinate, 1620 ; M.P., Cambridgeshire, 1640–53 ; wrote on economic and religious subjects. [xli. 151]

NORTH, SIR DUDLEY (1641–1691), financier and economist ; son of Dudley North, fourth baron North [q. v.] ; apprenticed to a Turkey merchant ; became agent at Smyrna and, in 1662, at Constantinople ; realised a fortune and returned to England, 1680 ; sheriff of London and knighted, 1682 ; commissioner for the customs, 1683, and afterwards for the treasury ; carried out reforms in both departments ; wrote on ' Currency,' and advocated free-trade. [xli. 152]

NORTH, DUDLEY LONG (1748–1829), politician ; great-grandson of Sir Dudley North [q. v.] ; M.A. Emmanuel College, Cambridge, 1774 ; M.P., St. Germans, 1780–4, Great Grimsby, 1784–90 and 1793–6, Banbury, 1790–1812, Richmond, Yorkshire, 1812–18, Jedburgh boroughs, 1818–20 ; a prominent whig. [xli. 153]

NORTH, DUDLEYA (1675–1712), granddaughter of Dudley North, fourth baron North [q. v.] ; mastered Latin, Greek, Hebrew, and some eastern languages ; bequeathed her collection of oriental literature to her uncle's parochial library at Rougham. [xli. 182]

NORTH, EDWARD, first BARON NORTH (1496 ?–1564), chancellor of the court of augmentations ; of St. Paul's School, London, and Peterhouse, Cambridge ; barrister ; clerk of the parliament, 1531 ; treasurer of the court of augmentations and knighted, 1541 ; promoted to the chancellorship, 1545 ; privy councillor, 1546 ; resigned chancellorship under Edward VI ; supported ' Queen Jane,' but was employed by Queen Mary ; again privy councillor ; created Baron North, 1554 ; his house twice visited by Queen Elizabeth, 1558 and 1561. [xli. 154]

NORTH, FRANCIS, first BARON GUILFORD (1637–1685), lord chancellor ; son of Dudley North, fourth baron North [q. v.] ; barrister, Middle Temple, 1661 ; K.C., 1668 ; solicitor-general and knighted, 1671 ; M.P., King's Lynn, 1673 ; attorney-general, 1673 ; chief-justice of common pleas, 1675–82 ; greatly increased the popularity of that court ; included in the government, 1679 ; lord chancellor, 1682, and created Baron Guilford, 1683 ; took part in James II's coronation, 1685 ; a patron of art, music, and science. [xli. 155]

NORTH, FRANCIS, first EARL OF GUILFORD (1704–1790), grandson of Francis North, first baron Guilford [q. v.] ; M.P., Banbury, 1727 ; succeeded his father as third baron, 1729, and his kinsman William North, baron North and Grey [q. v.], as seventh Baron North of Kirtling, 1734 ; held court appointments ; created Earl of Guilford, 1753 ; treasurer to Queen Charlotte, 1773. [xli. 158]

NORTH, FRANCIS, fourth EARL OF GUILFORD (1761–1817), son of Frederick North, second earl of Guilford [q. v.] ; entered the army, 1777 ; quitted it as lieutenant-colonel, 1794 ; succeeded to the earldom, 1802 ; his drama, the ' Kentish Baron,' produced, 1791 ; died at Pisa. [xli. 164]

NORTH, FREDERICK, second EARL OF GUILFORD, better known as LORD NORTH (1732–1792), son of Francis North, first earl of Guilford [q. v.] ; of Eton and Trinity College, Oxford ; M.A., 1750 ; M.P., Banbury, 1754 ; junior lord of the treasury, 1759 ; retired, 1766 ; took a leading part against Wilkes ; joint-paymaster of the forces, 1766 ; privy councillor, 1766 ; chancellor of the exchequer and leader of the House of Commons, 1767 ; first lord of the treasury, 1770 ; met with considerable opposition, he himself being the agent of George III who entirely directed the policy of the ministry ; K.G., 1772 ; gained considerable reputation by his earlier budgets, but lost popularity as a financier through the extravagant terms of the 1781 loan ; continued in office against his better judgment after the outbreak of war with America, but resigned, 1782 ; combined with Fox and overthrew Shelburne's ministry, 1783 ; after the dissolution of the coalition, which lasted only nine months, he acted with the opposition against Pitt ; succeeded his father as second Earl of Guilford, 1790. [xli. 159]

NORTH, FREDERICK, fifth EARL OF GUILFORD (1766–1827), philhellene ; younger son of Frederick North, second earl of Guilford [q. v.] ; educated mostly abroad and at Eton and Christ Church, Oxford ; travelled in Greece and entered the Greek church, 1791 ; created D.C.L., 1793 ; M.P., Banbury, 1792 ; comptroller of the customs in the port of London, 1794 ; governor of Ceylon, 1798–1805 ; improved Ceylon revenues and education ; succeeded his brother as fifth earl, 1817 ; G.C.M.G., 1819 ; largely promoted the Ionian university at Corfu, and became first chancellor, 1824. [xli. 164]

NORTH, GEORGE (*fl.* 1580), translator ; translated three books into English, two of which he dedicated to Sir Christopher Hatton [q. v.] [xli. 166]

NORTH, GEORGE (1710–1772), numismatist ; of St. Paul's School, London, and Corpus Christi College, Cambridge ; M.A., 1744 ; vicar of Codicote, 1743 ; F.S.A., 1741 ; wrote and corresponded on English numismatics and antiquities. [xli. 166]

NORTH, GEORGE AUGUSTUS, third EARL OF GUILFORD (1757–1802), son of Frederick North, second earl of Guilford [q. v.] ; M.A. Trinity College, Oxford, 1777 ; M.P., Harwich, 1778–84, Wootton Basset, 1784–90, Petersfield, 1790, and Banbury, 1790–2 ; supported his father's ministry, and was his under-secretary, 1783 ; succeeded as earl, 1792. [xli. 163]

NORTH, SIR JOHN (1551 ? – 1597), scholar and soldier ; son of Roger North, second baron North [q. v.] ; M.A. Trinity College, Cambridge, 1572 ; travelled, 1576 ; fought in the Netherlands, 1579, 1585, and 1597 ; M.P., Cambridgeshire, 1584, 1586, and 1587 ; died in Flanders. [xli. 167]

NORTH, JOHN (1645–1683), professor of Greek and master of Trinity College, Cambridge ; son of Dudley North, fourth baron North [q. v.] ; fellow of Jesus College, Cambridge, 1666 ; preached before Charles II at Newmarket, 1668 ; migrated to Trinity College, Cambridge, attracted by Isaac Barrow and Newton ; professor of Greek, 1672 ; clerk of the closet and prebendary of Westminster, 1673 ; master of Trinity College, Cambridge, 1677–83. [xli. 167]

NORTH, MARIANNE (1830–1890), flower-painter ; took painting-lessons from Valentine Bartholomew ; travelled in Syria and Egypt, 1865, with her father, and after his death travelled all round the world, painting the flora ; presented her paintings to Kew Gardens, building the gallery for them at her own expense (opened, 1882). [xli. 168]

NORTH, ROGER, second BARON NORTH (1530–1600), son of Edward North, first baron North [q. v.] ; appeared early at court ; M.P., Cambridgeshire, 1555, 1558, and 1563 ; K.B., 1559 ; succeeded his father as second Baron North, 1564 ; alderman and free burgess of Cambridge, 1568 ; went as joint-ambassador to Vienna, 1568 ; appointed lord-lieutenant of Cambridgeshire, 1569, and high steward of Cambridge, 1572 ; sent as ambassador to congratulate Henri III on his accession, 1574; visited by Queen Elizabeth at Kirtling, 1578; intimate with Leicester and accompanied him to Holland, 1585, where he greatly distinguished himself; returned, 1588, to prepare Cambridgeshire against Spanish invasion; treasurer of queen's household and privy councillor, 1596; keeper of the royal parks at Eltham and Horne, 1597. [xli. 169]

NORTH, ROGER (1585?-1652?), colonial projector; son of Sir John North [q. v.]; accompanied Ralegh on his last voyage to Guiana, 1617; went up the Orinoco, and assisted in routing the Spaniards settled there; forced to return by the disaffection of soldiers and sailors; broke the tidings to James I; his petition for the right to plant and trade on the Amazon (1619) opposed by Gondomar; finally sailed without permission and made a most successful voyage, but was imprisoned for six months on his return, 1621; obtained letters patent to plant Guiana, 1627; returned to England, 1632.
[xli. 173]

NORTH, ROGER (1653-1734), lawyer and historian; son of Dudley North, fourth baron North [q. v.]; entered Jesus College, Cambridge, 1667; barrister, Middle Temple, 1675; steward to the see of Canterbury, 1678; K.C., 1682; solicitor-general to the Duke of York, 1684; attorney-general to James II's queen, 1686; M.P., Dunwich, 1685; quitted political life at the revolution; a nonjuror; executor to Sir Peter Lely [q. v.] and his brothers; his 'Memoires of Musick' edited by Rimbault, 1846; his 'Apology' for Charles II and a 'Vindication' of his brother Francis, in reply to White Kennett, published, 1742, and his 'Lives' of Sir Dudley North and Dr. John North, 1744; a complete edition, with his autobiography and some correspondence, 1890. [xli. 176]

NORTH, SIR THOMAS (1535?-1601?), translator; son of Edward North, first baron North [q. v.]; perhaps studied at Peterhouse, Cambridge; entered Lincoln's Inn, 1557; accompanied his brother to France, 1574; knighted, 1591; J.P. for Cambridgeshire, 1592; pensioned by Queen Elizabeth, 1601; translated 'Marcus Aurelius' from French and Spanish editions, 1557, 'The Morall Philosophie of Doni,' from Italian, 1570, and Plutarch's 'Lives' from the French of Amyot, 1579, to which he made additions from other authors, 1595. His Plutarch formed Shakespeare's chief storehouse of classical learning, and exerted a powerful influence on Elizabethan prose. [xli. 179]

NORTH, THOMAS (1830-1884), antiquary and campanologist; employed in a bank at Leicester; F.S.A., 1875; secretary of the Leicestershire Architectural and Archaeological Society, and edited its 'Transactions'; wrote on the church of St. Martin, Leicester, 1866, and the church bells of various counties. [xli. 181]

NORTH, WILLIAM, sixth BARON NORTH (1678-1734), grandson of Dudley North, fourth baron North [q. v.]; succeeded his father as sixth baron, 1690; left Magdalene College, Cambridge, for Foubert's military academy, London, 1694; commissioned as captain, 1702; colonel, 1703; lost his right arm at Blenheim, 1704; brigadier-general, 1705; lieutenant-general, 1710; lord-lieutenant of Cambridgeshire, 1711; privy councillor and governor of Portsmouth, 1711; defended the Pretender in the Lords, 1713; committed to the Tower of London for complicity in Atterbury's plot, 1722, but admitted to bail; travelled abroad; died at Madrid. [xli. 181]

NORTHALIS, RICHARD (d. 1397), archbishop of Dublin; a Carmelite friar; became bishop of Ossory, 1386; was absent on Richard II's business, 1387, 1389, and 1391; lord chancellor of Ireland, 1393; translated to the archbishopric of Dublin, 1396. [xli. 183]

NORTHALL, JOHN (1723?-1759), captain in the royal artillery; entered the service, 1741; lieutenant, 1742; captain-lieutenant, 1752; captain, 1755; his 'Travels through Italy' published, 1766. [xli. 183]

NORTHALL, WILLIAM OF (d. 1190), bishop of Worcester; canon of St. Paul's, London; archdeacon of Gloucester, 1177; had custody of the temporalities of the sees of Rochester, 1184, and Worcester, 1185; bishop of Worcester, 1186; negotiated with the monks of Canterbury in their dispute with Archbishop Baldwin, 1187.
[xli. 184]

NORTHAMPTON, MARQUISES OF. [See PARR, WILLIAM, first MARQUIS, 1513-1571; COMPTON, SPENCER

JOSHUA ALWYNE, second MARQUIS of the second creation, 1790-1851.]

NORTHAMPTON, EARLS OF. [See SENLIS, SIMON DE, d. 1109; SENLIS, SIMON DE, d. 1153; BOHUN, WILLIAM DE, d. 1360; HOWARD, HENRY, 1540-1614; COMPTON, SPENCER, 1601-1643.]

NORTHAMPTON or **FITZPETER,** HENRY DE (fl. 1189-1207), judge; an officer of the exchequer and a canon of St. Paul's; justice itinerant, 1189; king's justice at Westminster and in the country, 1202; joined the baronial party. [xli. 184]

NORTHAMPTON or **COMBERTON,** JOHN DE (fl. 1376-1390), lord mayor of London; prominent member of the Drapers' Company; alderman, 1376; sheriff, 1377; member for the city, 1378; mayor, 1381; head of John of Gaunt's party; sought the favour of the populace at the expense of the greater companies; reduced the price of fish under violent opposition; his decision reversed by his successor and himself arrested on a charge of sedition; condemned to be hanged, but his sentence commuted; released, 1387, but not restored to his former position till 1390. [xli. 185]

NORTHBROOK, first BARON (1796-1866). [See BARING, SIR FRANCIS THORNHILL.]

NORTHBROOKE, JOHN (fl. 1568-1579), preacher and writer against plays; preached at St. Mary de Redcliffe, Bristol, 1568; procurator for the Bristol clergy in the synod at London, 1571; published theological works and in 'Spiritus est Vicarius Christi in Terra,' 1579, made the earliest attack upon dramatic performances.
[xli. 186]

NORTHBURGH, MICHAEL DE (d. 1361), bishop of London; entered the royal service and received considerable preferment; went on a mission to the pope, 1345; accompanied Edward III on his French expedition, 1346; commissioner to negotiate alliances with foreign powers, 1346; when secretary to Edward III frequently treated with France; elected bishop of London, 1354; conducted negotiations for peace with France, 1354 and 1355; died of plague; left bequests for students of civil and canon law at Oxford and the Carthusian house at Newchurchhaw. [xli. 187]

NORTHBURGH, ROGER DE (d. 1359?), bishop of Lichfield and Coventry; educated at Cambridge; a royal clerk in 1310, and royal messenger; comptroller of the wardrobe, 1315; held temporary charge of the great seal, 1321, and was papally provided to the bishopric of Lichfield and Coventry, 1322; swore to support Queen Isabella, January 1327; treasurer for three months, 1328, and occasionally employed in public business; again treasurer for a short time, 1340. [xli. 188]

NORTHCOTE, JAMES (1746-1831), painter and author; apprenticed as a watchmaker at Plymouth; spent his leisure in drawing and painting; came to London, 1771; worked as an assistant in the studio of Sir Joshua Reynolds, and studied in the Royal Academy schools; travelled in Italy, 1777-80; regularly contributed portraits to the Royal Academy; R.A., 1787; commissioned by Boydell to paint nine pictures for his Shakespeare gallery, 1786; attained his chief excellence as a portrait-painter; published a 'Memoir' of Sir Joshua Reynolds, 1813, 'One Hundred Fables' (illustrated by himself), 1828, and a 'Life of Titian,' 1830; William Hazlitt published some of his 'Conversations,' 1830.
[xli. 190]

NORTHCOTE, SIR JOHN, first baronet (1599-1676), politician; matriculated from Exeter College, Oxford, 1617; entered at the Inner Temple, 1618; was sheriff of Devonshire, 1626-7; created baronet, 1641; M.P., Ashburton, 1641; acted with the presbyterians and aided the parliamentary cause by his influence and wealth; taken prisoner by the royalists, 1643; released, 1645; excluded from parliament, 1648-54; sat for Barnstaple, 1667-76. His 'Note Book' was published, 1887. [xli. 193]

NORTHCOTE, SIR STAFFORD HENRY, first EARL OF IDDESLEIGH (1818-1887); educated at Eton and Balliol College, Oxford; M.A., 1840; D.C.L., 1863; barrister, Inner Temple, 1847; private secretary to William Ewart Gladstone [q. v.], 1842; assisted William Ewart Gladstone in his Oxford elections of 1847, 1852, and 1853; succeeded his grandfather as eighth baronet, 1851; C.B., 1851; conservative M.P., Dudley, 1855, Stamford, 1858; became a recognised opposition speaker and was greatly in Disraeli's confidence; appointed president of the board of trade, 1866, and secretary for India, 1867; M.P. for North Devon, 1866; governor of the Hudson's Bay Company, 1869–74; commissioner for the settlement of the Alabama claims, 1871; chancellor of the exchequer, 1874–80; pointed out that the income tax had lost its temporary character and increased exemptions by which he eased pressure of the tax on smaller incomes; made a serious attempt, by an annual sinking fund, to reduce the national debt; leader of the house, 1876, and much hampered by parliamentary obstruction; leader of the opposition to Gladstone's government in the House of Commons, 1880–5, and defeated the ministry on the Affirmation Bill, 1883, but assisted in the compromise on the Franchise Bill, 1884; created Earl of Iddesleigh and Viscount St. Cyres, 1885; became foreign secretary, 1886, but resigned six months later, dying suddenly on the day of his resignation. He published 'A Short Review of the Navigation Laws,' 1849, 'Twenty Years of Financial Policy,' 1862, and (for the Roxburghe Club) 'The Triumphes of Petrarch,' 1887. [xli. 194]

NORTHCOTE, WILLIAM (d. 1783?), naval surgeon; passed at the Surgeons' Company as second mate, 1757; first mate, 1759; surgeon, 1771; published medical works for naval surgeons, devoting special attention to tropical diseases. [xli. 199]

NORTHESK, seventh EARL OF (1758–1831). [See CARNEGIE, WILLIAM.]

NORTHEY, SIR EDWARD (1652–1723), attorney-general; of St. Paul's School, London, and Queen's College, Oxford; barrister, Middle Temple, 1674; attorney-general, 1701–7 and 1710–18; knighted, 1702; M.P., Tiverton, 1710. [xli. 200]

NORTHINGTON, EARLS OF. [See HENLEY, ROBERT, first EARL, 1708?–1772; HENLEY, ROBERT, second EARL, 1747–1786.]

NORTHLEIGH, JOHN (1657–1705), physician; B.C.L. Exeter College, Oxford, 1681; student, Middle Temple, 1682; incorporated LL.B. Magdalene College, Cambridge, 1682; subsequently fellow of King's College, Cambridge; LL.D., 1687; M.D.; practised medicine at Exeter; wrote in defence of James II and on polemical theology. [xli. 200]

NORTHMORE, THOMAS (1766–1851), miscellaneous writer and inventor; M.A. Emmanuel College, Cambridge, 1792; F.S.A., 1791; divided his time between mechanics, literature, and science; discovered the ossiferous nature of Kent's cavern at Torquay, 1824. [xli. 201]

NORTHUMBERLAND, DUKES OF. [See DUDLEY, JOHN, first DUKE, 1502?–1553; FITZROY, GEORGE, first DUKE of the second creation, 1665–1716; PERCY, HUGH, first DUKE of the third creation, 1715–1786; PERCY, HUGH, second DUKE, 1742–1817; PERCY, HUGH, third DUKE, 1785–1847; PERCY, ALGERNON, fourth DUKE, 1792–1865.]

NORTHUMBERLAND, titular DUKE OF (1573–1649). [See DUDLEY, SIR ROBERT.]

NORTHUMBERLAND, EARLS OF. [See MORCAR, fl. 1066; COPSI, d. 1067; GOSPATRIC, fl. 1067; COMIN, ROBERT DE, d. 1069; WALTHEOF, d. 1076; WALCHER, d. 1080; MOWBRAY, ROBERT DE, d. 1125?; PUISET or PUDSEY, HUGH DE, 1125?–1195; PERCY, HENRY, first EARL of the Percy family, 1342–1408; PERCY, HENRY, second EARL, 1394–1455; PERCY, HENRY, third EARL, 1421–1461; NEVILLE, JOHN, d. 1471; PERCY, HENRY, fourth EARL, 1446–1489; PERCY, HENRY ALGERNON, fifth EARL, 1478–1527; PERCY, HENRY ALGERNON, sixth EARL, 1502?–1537; PERCY, THOMAS, seventh EARL, 1528–1572; PERCY, HENRY, eighth EARL, 1532?–1585; PERCY, HENRY, ninth EARL, 1564–1632; PERCY, ALGERNON, tenth EARL, 1602–1668.]

NORTHUMBRIANS, KINGS OF THE. [See ETHEL-FRID, d. 617; EDWIN, 585?–633; OSWALD, 605?–642; OSWY, 612?–670; ALDFRITH, d. 705; OSRED, 697?–716; OSRIC, d. 729; OSWULF, d. 758; CEOLWULF, d. 764; EADBERT, d. 768; OSRED, d. 792; EARDWULF, d. 810; OSBERHT, d. 867; ÆLLA, d. 867.]

NORTHWELL or **NORWELL**, WILLIAM DE (d. 1363), baron of the exchequer; clerk of the kitchen, 1313; received preferment, including a prebend of Southwell;

keeper of Edward III's wardrobe, 1335, resigning the post, 1340, but soon reappointed; baron of the exchequer for a short time, 1340; kept the accounts during the Crecy expedition, 1346. [xli. 202]

NORTHWOLD, HUGH OF (d. 1254), bishop of Ely; a monk of the Benedictine Abbey of Bury St. Edmunds; re-elected abbot, 1213, in opposition to the king's party in the abbey; after a long series of complications obtained King John's assent, 1215; itinerant justice for Norfolk, 1227; bishop of Ely, 1220–54; escorted Eleanor of Provence to England, 1235; attended parliament, 1248; offended Henry III by refusing the benefice of Dereham to Henry's half-brother; present at the confirmation of Magna Charta, 1253. [xli. 203]

NORTHWOOD, JOHN DE (d. 1317), son of John de Northwood, baron Northwood [q. v.]; died before his father, leaving six sons, the eldest, Roger, succeeding his grandfather in the barony. [xli. 205]

NORTHWOOD or **NORTHWODE**, JOHN DE, BARON NORTHWOOD (1254–1319), succeeded his father, 1285; served constantly in official capacities for Kent; served in the French war, 1294, in Flanders, 1297, and in Scotland, 1298, 1309, 1311, 1314, and 1318; summoned to parliament as a baron, 1313. [xli. 205]

NORTHWOOD or **NORTHWODE**, ROGER DE (d. 1285), baron of the exchequer; employed in the exchequer; warden of the Cinque ports, 1257; baron of the exchequer before 1274; acted on various judicial commissions. [xli. 205]

NORTON, BONHAM (1565–1635), printer, son of William Norton [q. v.]; became a freeman of the Stationers' Company and held various offices in the company; king's printer; served as sheriff of Shropshire, 1611. [xli. 225]

NORTON, CAROLINE ELIZABETH SARAH, known as the HON. MRS. NORTON, afterwards LADY STIRLING-MAXWELL (1808–1877), poetess; daughter of Thomas Sheridan (1775–1817) [q. v.]; distinguished for her beauty and wit; married the Hon. George Chapple Norton, 1827; definitely entered upon a literary career, her husband having no independent means and only a small legal appointment; published 'The Sorrows of Rosalie .... with other Poems,' 1829, which was enthusiastically received; became a popular writer in periodicals; published 'The Undying One,' 1830, and 'The Dream,' 1840; attacked social conditions in 'A Voice from the Factories,' 1836, and 'The Child of the Islands,' 1845; her best poem, 'The Lady of La Garaye,' 1862; wrote also three novels, 'Stuart of Dunleath,' 1851, 'Lost and Saved,' 1863, and 'Old Sir Douglas,' 1867. Mrs. Norton led an unhappy life with her husband, from whom she separated in 1836; a crim. con. action was unsuccessfully brought against Lord Melbourne by her husband, but the evidence was so manifestly weak that the trial was considered by some as a political attempt to discredit him. In 1853 she endeavoured to obtain legal protection from her husband, and her pamphlets on the custody of offspring and female earnings contributed to the amelioration of the laws affecting the social condition of women. In 1877 she married Sir William Stirling-Maxwell [q. v.], her first husband having died in 1875. [xli. 206]

NORTON, CHAPPLE (1746–1818), general; son of Fletcher Norton, first baron Grantley [q. v.]; captain of the 19th foot, 1763; distinguished himself in America, 1780; general, 1802; M.P., Guildford, 1784–1812. [xli. 208]

NORTON, CHRISTIAN (fl. 1740–1760), engraver; studied under Pierre Charles Canot at Paris, and accompanied him to England. [xli. 209]

NORTON, FLETCHER, first BARON GRANTLEY (1716–1789), barrister, Middle Temple, 1739; K.C., 1754; M.P., Appleby, 1756, Wigan, 1761; solicitor-general, 1762; knighted, 1762; attorney-general, 1763, but dismissed on the formation of the Rockingham administration, 1765; M.P., Guildford, 1768; elected speaker of the House of Commons, 1770; supported Burke in carrying the Establishment Bill (civil list expenditure), 1780; not re-elected speaker, 1780; created Baron Grantley of Markenfield, 1782. He was usually nicknamed 'Sir Bull-face Double Fee' in satires and caricatures, and was attacked by Junius in Letter 39. [xli. 209]

NORTON, FRANCES, LADY (1640–1731), authoress; née Freke; married, first, Sir George Norton, 1672, secondly, Colonel Ambrose Norton, a cousin of her first husband, 1718, and, thirdly, William Jones, 1724; she published 'The Applause of Virtue,' 1705. [xli. 212]

NORTON, HUMPHREY (*fl.* 1655-1659), quaker; London agent for the assistance of Friends, 1655-6; preached in Ireland and was arrested at Galway and at Wexford, 1656; went to Boston, 1657; arrested and banished from Rhode island, 1657; again arrested at Newhaven and branded with H at Plymouth and again at Boston; imprisoned, 1658; went to Barbados, 1659, and wrote an account of his sufferings ('New England's Ensigne '), 1659. [xli. 212]

NORTON, JOHN (*fl.* 1485), sixth prior of the Carthusian monastery of Mountgrace; wrote three works, still extant in Lincoln Cathedral MS., 'De Musica Monachorum,' 'Thesaurus cordium amantium,' and 'Devota Lamentacio.' [xli. 213]

NORTON, SIR JOHN (*d.* 1534), soldier; served under Poynings in Guelderland; knighted, 1511; sheriff of Kent, 1522, of Yorkshire, 1514; knight of the body to Henry VIII; in France, 1514 and 1532. [xli. 214]

NORTON, JOHN (*d.* 1612), printer; nephew of William Norton [q. v.]; printed Gerard's 'Herbal,' 1597; became printer of Latin, Greek, and Hebrew to Queen Elizabeth; printed Savile's edition of the Greek text of Chrysostom's works, 1610-12; master of the Stationers' Company, bequeathing it 1,000*l*. [xli. 226]

NORTON, JOHN (1606-1663), divine; B.A. Peterhouse, Cambridge, 1627; landed in New England, 1635, and was 'called' to Ipswich; wrote 'Responsio ad totam quæstionum syllogen' (the first Latin book composed in the colonies), 1648; helped to draw up the 'Platform of Church Discipline' at the Cambridge synod, 1646; 'called to Boston,' 1652; instigated the persecution of the quakers; went to England to obtain a confirmation of the Boston charter, 1662; published Calvinistic works. [xli. 214]

NORTON, JOHN (*fl.* 1674), a youthful prodigy; made a paraphrase translation of Marcus Antonius Flaminius (published as 'The Scholar's Vade Mecum' 1674). [xli. 215]

NORTON, JOHN BRUCE (1815-1883), advocategeneral at Madras; of Harrow and Merton College, Oxford; B.A., 1838; barrister, Lincoln's Inn, 1841; sheriff of Madras, 1843-5; clerk of the crown in the supreme court, 1845-62; advocate-general, 1863-71; returned to England and was first lecturer on Indian law at the Temple, 1873; wrote on Indian law and administration. [xli. 216]

NORTON, MATTHEW THOMAS (1732-1800), Dominican; professed as a Dominican, 1754; English missioner, 1759; elected prior of Bornhem, 1767; appointed vicar-provincial of Belgium, 1774-8; returned to England, 1780; won three medals at Brussels for dissertations on agriculture. [xli. 216]

NORTON, RICHARD (*d.* 1420), chief-justice of the court of common pleas; serjeant-at-law before 1403; justice of assize for the county palatine of Durham; chief-justice of the court of common pleas, 1413; trier of petitions in parliament, 1414-20. [xli. 217]

NORTON, RICHARD (1488?-1588), rebel; took part in the Pilgrimage of Grace, but was pardoned; one of the council of the north, 1545 and 1556; governor of Norham Castle, 1555-7; sheriff of Yorkshire, 1568; joined the rebellion of 1569; his estates confiscated and himself attainted; fled to Flanders and was pensioned by Philip of Spain; known as 'Old Norton'; died abroad. [xli. 217]

NORTON, ROBERT (1540?-1587?), divine; M.A. Caius College, Cambridge, 1563; B.D., 1570; vicar of Aldborough, 1572; preacher in Ipswich, 1576-85; translated Rodolph Gualter's sermons, 1573. [xli. 218]

NORTON, ROBERT (*d.* 1635), engineer and gunner; son of Thomas Norton (1532-1584) [q. v.]; entered the royal service; sent as engineer to Plymouth, 1627; engineer of the Tower of London, 1627; wrote on mathematics and artillery, and translated Camden's 'Annals of Elizabeth,' 1630. [xli. 219]

NORTON, SIR SAMPSON (*d.* 1517), surveyor of the ordnance and marshal of Tournay; knighted in Brittany,

c. 1483; commissioner to inquire into the exportation of wool, 1486; constable of Flint Castle, 1495; chamberlain of North Wales, 1509; served in France as surveyor of the ordnance; marshal of Tournay, 1515; chamberlain of the exchequer, 1516. [xli. 219]

NORTON, SAMUEL (1548-1604?), alchemist; studied at St. John's College, Cambridge; J.P. and sheriff of Somerset, 1589; muster-master of Somerset and Wiltshire, 1604; wrote several alchemistic tracts, which were edited and published in Latin by Edmund Deane at Frankfort, 1630. [xli. 220]

NORTON, THOMAS (*fl.* 1477), alchemist; M.P. Bristol, 1436; member of Edward IV's privy chamber and employed on embassies; studied alchemy under George Ripley [q. v.], and wrote chemical tracts in English verse. His 'Ordinal of Alchimy' was several times published. [xli. 220]

NORTON, THOMAS (1532-1584), lawyer and poet; admitted to the Grocers' Company; entered the service of Protector Somerset as amanuensis; admitted at the Inner Temple, 1555; M.P., Galton, 1558, Berwick, 1562, and London, 1571, 1572, and 1580; created M.A. Cambridge, 1570; appointed remembrancer of the city of London, 1571; in parliament strongly supported all active measures against the Roman catholics, and in 1579 went to Rome to procure information against them; kept diary (still extant) of his journey; became an official censor of Queen Elizabeth's Roman catholic subjects, 1581, and conducted the examination of many Roman catholic prisoners under torture; involved through his dissatisfaction with episcopacy in a charge of treason, and committed to the Tower of London for a short time, 1584. He devoted much time to literature, and in early life his sonnets and verses attracted attention. Among his translations were Calvin's 'Institutions of the Christian religion,' 1559, and Nowell's 'Middle Catechism,' 1570; but he owes his place in literature to his joint-authorship with Sackville of the earliest tragedy in English and in blank verse, 'The Tragedie of Gorboduc,' of which he wrote three acts. 'Gorboduc' was performed on Twelfth Night at the Inner Temple, 1561. A corrupt edition of the play was published, 1565, and an authorised version, undated, a few years later. [xli. 221]

NORTON, WILLIAM DE (*fl.* 1346-1363). [See NOTTON.]

NORTON, WILLIAM (1527-1593), printer and publisher; an original freeman of the Stationers' Company, 1555; filled various offices; published Guicciardini's 'Historie,' 1579, two editions of Horace, 1574 and 1585, and the 'Bishops' Bible,' 1575. [xli. 225]

NORWELL, WILLIAM DE (*d.* 1363). [See NORTHWELL.]

NORWICH, first EARL of the second creation (1583?-1663). [See GORING, GEORGE.]

NORWICH, JOHN DE. BARON NORWICH (*d.* 1362), son of Sir Walter de Norwich [q. v.]; admiral of the fleet north of the Thames, 1336; went to France, 1338; summoned to parliament as a baron, 1342; served in France, 1344, and specially distinguished himself there, 1346; founded a chantry of eight priests and a warden at Raveningham, 1350. [xli. 226]

NORWICH, RALPH DE (*fl.* 1256), chancellor of Ireland; acted frequently as king's messenger, 1216-21; employed on exchequer business in Ireland. 1218 and 1221; received considerable ecclesiastical preferment; justice of the king's bench, 1229; chancellor of Ireland, 1249; resigned chancellorship, 1256; his election as archbishop of Dublin (1256) quashed by the pope. [xli. 227]

NORWICH, ROBERT (*d.* 1535), judge; member of Lincoln's Inn, 1503, reader, 1518, and subsequently governor; sat on various commissions; king's serjeant, 1523; justice of common pleas, 1530; chief-justice, 1531. [xli. 229]

NORWICH, SIR WALTER DE (*d.* 1329), chief baron of the exchequer; remembrancer by 1308; appointed a baron of the exchequer, 1311; chief baron, 1312; resigned his office of chief baron, 1314, on being appointed treasurer; resigned treasurership, 1317, and probably returned to the exchequer; keeper of the treasury, 1321; reappointed chief baron, 1327. [xli. 229]

NORWICH, WILLIAM OF (1298?-1355). [See BATE-MAN.]

NORWOLD, HUGH OF (d. 1254). [See NORTHWOLD.]

NORWOOD, RICHARD (1590?-1675), teacher of mathematics and surveyor ; surveyed the islands of Bermuda for the Bermuda Company, 1616 ; taught mathematics in London and measured the distance between London and York, 1633-5 ; calculated the length of a degree of the meridian ; returned to Bermuda, where he died ; wrote on mathematics.   [xli. 230]

NORWYCH, GEORGE (d. 1469), abbot of Westminster ; succeeded Abbot Keyton, 1462 ; mismanaged affairs and (1467) had to resign the management to the prior, he himself receiving a pension.   [xli. 230]

NOTARY, JULIAN (fl. 1498-1520), printer ; produced a missal for Wynkyn de Worde, 1498 ; his best-known production is the fifth edition of ' The Kalender of Shepardes,' c. 1518.   [xli. 231]

NOTHELM (d. 739), tenth archbishop of Canterbury ; supplied Bede with information for his 'Ecclesiastical History' ; visited Rome ; consecrated archbishop, 735 ; held a synod, c. 736.   [xli. 231]

NOTT, GEORGE FREDERICK (1767-1841), divine and author ; nephew of John Nott [q. v.] ; B.A. Christ Church, Oxford, 1788 ; fellow of All Souls', Oxford ; M.A., 1792 ; D.D., 1807 ; Bampton lecturer, 1802 ; prebendary of Winchester, 1810, of Salisbury, 1814 ; produced an exhaustive edition of the works of Surrey and Sir Thomas Wyatt the elder, 1815-16, containing biographies.   [xli. 232]

NOTT, JOHN (1751-1865), physician and classical scholar ; studied at London and Paris ; surgeon in an East India vessel sailing to China, 1783 ; went as travelling physician on the continent, 1789-93 ; settled at Bristol ; wrote on medicine ; translated Catullus, 1794, Propertius, 1782, the 'Basia of Joannes Secundus Nicolaius,' 1775, and Petrarch's sonnets and odes, 1777 ; wrote original poems and tales ; edited Dekker's ' Gulls Hornbook,' 1812.   [xli. 233]

NOTT, SIR THOMAS (1606-1681), royalist ; educated at Merchant Taylors' School, London ; M.A. Pembroke College, Cambridge, 1628 ; knighted, 1639 ; in constant attendance on Charles I during the civil war ; gentleman-usher, 1660.   [xli. 234]

NOTT, SIR WILLIAM (1782-1845), major-general ; commander of the army of Kandahar ; obtained a Bengal cadetship, 1800 ; lieutenant, 1801 ; distinguished himself at Moko, 1804 ; captain, 1814 ; major, 1823 ; lieutenant-colonel, 1824 ; colonel, 1829 ; promoted major-general, 1838, on the outbreak of the Afghan war, and given command of the second brigade, first division, at Quetta, 1839 ; successfully defeated the Ghilzais and destroyed their forts, while the enemy evacuated Kalát on his approach, 1840 ; made commander of all troops in Lower Afghanistan and Sindh, 1842 ; repulsed the chiefs near Kandahar, January and June, 1842 ; on receiving orders to withdraw from Afghanistan, sent General England by Quetta and Sakhar, while he himself arranged to meet General Pollock at Kabul ; completely defeated the enemy near Ghazni, which he entered without opposition, 1842 ; after a series of successful engagements joined Pollock at Kabul ; appointed resident at the court of Lucknow ; G.C.B., 1843.   [xli. 234]

NOTTINGHAM, EARLS OF. [See MOWBRAY, THOMAS, first EARL of the second creation, 1366?-1399 ; HOWARD, CHARLES, first EARL of the sixth creation, 1536-1624 ; FINCH, HENEAGE, first EARL of the seventh creation, 1621-1682 ; FINCH, DANIEL, second EARL, 1647-1730 ; FINCH-HATTON, GEORGE WILLIAM, fifth EARL, 1791-1858.]

NOTTINGHAM, WILLIAM OF (d. 1251), Franciscan ; elected fourth provincial minister, 1240 ; went to Rome, 1244, and obtained a letter restraining the Dominicans ; wrote a commentary on the gospels ; died at Genoa of the plague.   [xli. 239]

NOTTON or **NORTON**, WILLIAM DE (fl. 1346-1361), judge ; king's serjeant by 1346 ; judge of the king's bench, 1355 ; excommunicated, 1358 ; judge of assize, 1361 ; chief-justice in Ireland, 1361.   [xli. 239]

NOURSE, EDWARD (1701-1761), surgeon ; received his diploma from the Barber-Surgeons' Company, 1725 ;

assistant-surgeon to St. Bartholomew's Hospital, London, 1731, surgeon, 1745 ; demonstrator of anatomy to the Barber-Surgeons, 1731-4 ; published lectures. [xli. 240]

NOURSE, TIMOTHY (d. 1699), miscellaneous writer ; fellow of University College, Oxford, 1659 ; M.A., 1660 ; became a Roman catholic, 1672 ; bequeathed his collection of coins to the Bodleian Library ; wrote on religion, husbandry, and various other subjects.   [xli. 240]

NOVELLO, VINCENT (1781-1861), organist, musical composer, editor, and arranger ; born in London ; his father an Italian ; at school for a time in France ; chorister at the Sardinian embassy chapel, London, 1793 ; organist at the Portuguese embassy chapel, 1797 till 1822 ; arranged two volumes of sacred music (1811), which proved the foundation of the publishing house of Novello & Co. ; original member (1813) and subsequently conductor of the Philharmonic Society ; examined and reported on the musical manuscripts in the Fitzwilliam Museum at Cambridge, 1824 ; organist at the Westminster Abbey festival, 1834 ; organist of the Roman catholic chapel at Moorfields, 1840-3 ; went to Nice, 1850, where he subsequently died.   [xli. 241]

NOWELL, **NOWEL**, or **NOEL**, ALEXANDER (1507?-1602), dean of St. Paul's ; elder brother of Laurence Nowell [q. v.] ; fellow of Brasenose College, Oxford, 1526 ; M.A., 1540 ; master of Westminster School, 1543 ; prebendary of Westminster Abbey, 1551 ; during Queen Mary's reign resided principally at Frankfort ; archdeacon of Middlesex, 1558 ; dean of St. Paul's, London, 1560 ; did much for the restoration of the reformed religion ; prolocutor of the lower house of convocation, and presented a catechism for its approval ; attended the Duke of Norfolk at his execution, 1572 ; sat on ecclesiastical commissions, 1573, 1576, and 1590 ; successful in making converts from Romanism ; twice visited Lancashire, preaching, 1570 and 1580 ; appointed to hold conferences with papists, 1582 ; elected principal of Brasenose College, Oxford, 1595, but resigned it three months later ; loyally complied with Queen Elizabeth's ecclesiastical settlement, though inclined to Calvinism ; a liberal benefactor of Middleton School and Brasenose College. Apart from his controversial and theological works, Nowell was the author of three catechisms, the 'Large Catechism,' which he sent to Cecil, 1563, the 'Middle Catechism,' and the 'Small Catechism,' which is practically that of the Book of Common Prayer. The three were written by Nowell in Latin and translated into Greek by William Whitaker and into English by Thomas Norton.   [xli. 243]

NOWELL, INCREASE (1590-1655), New England settler ; arrived in America, 1630 ; commissioner of military affairs, 1634 ; secretary of Massachusetts colony, 1644-9 ; a founder of the church in Charlestown.
                                                       [xli. 250]

NOWELL or **NOWEL**, LAURENCE (d. 1576), dean of Lichfield ; brother of Alexander Nowell [q. v.] ; matriculated from Brasenose College, Oxford, but migrated to Cambridge to study logic ; B.A., 1542 (incorporated at Oxford, 1542) ; M.A., 1544 ; master of Sutton Coldfield grammar school, 1546 ; went abroad during Queen Mary's reign, but received preferment under Elizabeth ; dean of Lichfield, 1560. He was a diligent antiquary and left manuscripts on Anglo-Saxon.   [xli. 250]

NOWELL, RALPH (d. 1144?). [See RALPH.]

NOWELL, SAMUEL (1634-1688), New England settler ; son of Increase Nowell [q. v.] ; distinguished himself in Philip's war ; assistant of the colony of Massachusetts, 1680, and treasurer, 1685.   [xli. 250]

NOWELL, THOMAS (1730-1801), divine ; M.A. Oriel College, Oxford, 1753 ; fellow, 1753 ; principal of St. Mary Hall, Oxford, 1764-1801 ; regius professor of modern history, 1771-1801 ; public orator, 1760-76 ; criticised for some expressions in his sermon on Charles I preached before the House of Commons, 1772.   [xli. 251]

NOWER or **NOWERS**, FRANCIS (d. 1670), heraldpainter ; edited Guillim's ' Display of Heraldry,' 1660 ; perished in a fire at his house.   [xli. 252]

NOYE or **NOY**, WILLIAM (1577-1634), attorney-general ; of Exeter College, Oxford ; barrister, Lincoln's Inn, 1602 ; autumn reader, 1622 ; bencher from 1618 ; treasurer, 1632 ; represented various boroughs in Cornwall from 1604 ; led the attack on monopolies, 1621 ; attorney-general, 1631 ; revised the 'Declaration of Sports,' 1633 ; prosecuted William Prynne [q. v.] in the Star-chamber, 1634; incurred much popular odium by his revival of the forest laws, the soap monopoly, and the writ of ship-money; satirised in 'A Projector lately Dead,' 1634. He wrote on the 'Rights of the Crown,' the tenure of property, and reports of cases.   [xli. 253]

NUCE, THOMAS (d. 1617), translator; fellow of Pembroke Hall, Cambridge, 1562; prebendary of Ely, 1585; translated Seneca's 'Octavia,' 1561.   [xli. 255]

NUGENT, BARON (1788–1850). [See GRENVILLE, GEORGE NUGENT]

NUGENT, SIR CHARLES EDMUND (1759?–1844), admiral of the fleet; entered navy, 1771; commander, 1778; posted, 1779; rear-admiral, 1797; vice-admiral, 1801; admiral, 1808; admiral of the fleet, 1833; G.C.H., 1834.   [xli. 256]

NUGENT, SIR CHRISTOPHER, fourteenth BARON DELVIN (1544–1602), succeeded to the title, 1559; fellow-commoner of Clare Hall, Cambridge; went to Ireland, 1565; distinguished himself against Shane O'Neill, 1565; knighted, 1566; protested against provisioning the army at a fixed price, and (1577) was imprisoned; commanded the forces of the Pale, 1579; again imprisoned on a suspicion of treason, 1580, and sent to England for trial, 1582; allowed to return to Ireland to transact business with regard to his property, 1585, and in 1588 to remain there; leader of the forces of Westmeath, 1593; commissioner to inquire into abuses, 1597; arrested after the outbreak of Tyrone's rebellion on suspicion of treason; died in Dublin Castle. He wrote 'A Primer of the Irish Language' and a 'Plot for the Reformation of Ireland.'   [xli. 256]

NUGENT, CHRISTOPHER (d. 1731), soldier; went to France after the capitulation of Limerick, 1691; served in Flanders, Germany, and Italy; succeeded to the command of Sheldon's regiment and changed its name to Nugent's, 1706; commanded his regiment at Ramillies, Oudenarde, and Malplaquet; promoted maréchal-de-camp, 1718.   [xli. 259]

NUGENT, CHRISTOPHER (fl. 1775), physician; graduated M.D. in France; practised in Bath; wrote on hydrophobia, 1753; removed to London, 1764; an original member of the Literary Club; F.R.S., 1765.   [xli. 259]

NUGENT, SIR GEORGE, first baronet (1757–1849), field-marshal; entered the army, 1773; lieutenant, 1777; served in America; captain, 1778; major, 1782; lieutenant-colonel, 1783; accompanied the guards to Holland, 1793; raised a corps from Buckinghamshire; M.P., Buckinghamshire, 1790–1800; lieutenant-governor of Jamaica, 1801–6; created baronet, 1806; commander-in-chief in India, 1811–13; general, 1813; G.C.B., 1815.   [xli. 260]

NUGENT, JOHN, fifth EARL OF WESTMEATH (1672–1754), brother of Thomas Nugent, fourth earl of Westmeath [q. v.]; present at the battle of the Boyne and at Limerick; went to France, 1691; served with the army of Flanders till 1705; subsequently served under the French standard; major in the German army, 1720; brigadier, 1740; maréchal-de-camp, 1744; succeeded to the earldom, 1752; died at Nivelles.   [xli. 261]

NUGENT, LAVALL, COUNT NUGENT (1777–1862), prince of the Holy Roman Empire and Austrian field-marshal; entered the Austrian engineer corps, 1793; lieutenant-colonel, 1805; came to England, 1812; visited Wellington in Spain, 1813; fought in the north of Italy, 1813, and became lieutenant-general, 1814; hon. K.C.B. of England, 1815; fought in the south of Italy, 1815–16, becoming a prince of the Holy Roman Empire, 1816; commanded the Neapolitan army, 1817–20; created a magnate of Hungary, 1826; organised two reserve corps during the revolts of 1848–9, captured Essigg, secured control of the Danube, but unsuccessfully besieged Comorn; became a field-marshal, 1849; died at Bosiljevo, near Karlstadt.   [xli. 261]

NUGENT, NICHOLAS (d. 1582), chief-justice of the common bench in Ireland; uncle of Sir Christopher Nugent, fourteenth baron Delvin [q. v.]; chief solicitor to the crown, 1566; served on several commissions; on Sir Henry Sidney's retirement from the lord-deputyship became chief-justice of the common pleas, but (1582) was arrested on a charge of treason; condemned and hanged, popular opinion attributing his death to the private malice of Sir Robert Dillon (d. 1597) [q. v.]   [xli. 263]

NUGENT, SIR RICHARD, tenth BARON DELVIN (d. 1460?), lord-deputy of Ireland; succeeded his father, 1415; sheriff of Meath, 1424; distinguished himself in the wars against the native Irish; lord-deputy, 1444 and 1449; seneschal of Meath, 1452.   [xli. 264]

NUGENT, RICHARD, twelfth BARON DELVIN (d. 1538?), succeeded his father, 1493; assisted the lord-deputy against the Irish chiefs, 1504; J.P., 1515; joined the council, 1522; acted as vice-deputy of Ireland, 1527; seized by stratagem, 1528, and detained a prisoner at O'Conor's house till 1529; continued to fight actively against the rebels, and probably died on an expedition against O'Conor, 1538.   [xli. 265]

NUGENT, RICHARD (fl. 1604), poet; son of Nicholas Nugent [q. v.]; probably the author of 'Ric. Nugent's Cynthia' (sonnets and madrigals), 1604.   [xli. 264]

NUGENT, SIR RICHARD, fifteenth BARON DELVIN, first EARL OF WESTMEATH (1583–1642), son of Sir Christopher Nugent, fourteenth baron Delvin [q. v.]; succeeded his father, 1602; knighted, 1603; being exasperated by the revocation of a grant, joined a conspiracy, for which he was arrested, 1607; escaped from Dublin Castle, but submitted, 1608; summoned to England on account of parliamentary obstruction, 1614, but recovered favour and was created Earl of Westmeath, 1621; refused to join the rebels, 1641.   [xli. 266]

NUGENT, RICHARD, second EARL OF WESTMEATH (d. 1684), succeeded his grandfather, Sir Richard Nugent, first earl of Westmeath [q. v.], 1642; raised a troop of horse and a regiment of foot for Charles I, 1645; field-marshal, 1648; submitted to the parliamentary commissioners, 1652; raised a regiment for the Spanish service, 1653; arrested on suspicion, 1659; recovered his liberty and estates, 1660.   [xli. 268]

NUGENT, ROBERT, EARL NUGENT (1702–1788), who afterwards assumed the surname CRAGGS, politician and poet; M.P., St. Mawes, 1741–54, Bristol, 1754–74, and St. Mawes, 1774–84; became controller to Frederick, prince of Wales, 1747, and lent him money; created lord of the treasury, 1754; vice-treasurer for Ireland, 1760–5 and 1768–82; president of the board of trade, 1766–8; became Viscount Clare and Baron Nugent, 1766, and Earl Nugent, 1776; three times married, twice to rich widows, on which Horace Walpole invented the word 'Nugentize' to describe this practice; wrote various odes and poems, his ode to William Pulteney being so good that he was suspected of paying Mallet to write it.   [xli. 269]

NUGENT, THOMAS, titular BARON OF RIVERSTON (d. 1715), chief-justice of Ireland; son of Richard Nugent, second earl of Westmeath [q. v.]; one of James II's council, 1685; judge of the king's bench, 1686; privy councillor and lord chief-justice, 1687; furthered James II's anti-protestant policy; on James's landing in Ireland became Baron Riverston and commissioner of the empty Irish treasury, 1689.   [xli. 271]

NUGENT, THOMAS, fourth EARL OF WESTMEATH (1656–1752), served with James II at the Boyne, 1690, and at Limerick, 1691; succeeded his brother as fourth earl, 1714.   [xli. 272]

NUGENT, THOMAS (1700?–1772), miscellaneous writer; honorary LL.D. Aberdeen, 1765; F.S.A., 1767; wrote on travels and history and translated a great number of books, mostly from the French, including Voltaire, Rousseau, and Montesquieu.   [xli. 273]

NUGENT, WILLIAM (d. 1625), Irish rebel; brother of Sir Christopher Nugent, fourteenth baron Delvin [q. v.]; driven to rebellion by the unwise severity of Lord Grey; escaped to Rome, 1582, and, returning by Paris and Scotland, formally submitted; accused Sir Robert Dillon (d. 1597) [q. v.] of maladministration, 1591.   [xli. 273]

NUNN, MARIANNE (1778–1847), hymn-writer; wrote sacred pieces and hymns.   [xli. 274]

NUNN, WILLIAM (1786–1840), brother of Marianne Nunn [q. v.]; wrote several hymns.   [xli. 274]

NUNNA or **NUN** (fl. 710), king of the South-Saxons; confirmed a charter of Nothelm, 692. His three charters in the Chichester register are of doubtful antiquity.   [xli. 274]

NUNNELEY, THOMAS (1809–1870), surgeon ; L.S.A., 1832 ; M.R.C.S., 1832 ; studied in Paris ; practised in Leeds ; surgeon to the Leeds Eye and Ear Hospital and the General Infirmary ; studied and wrote on ophthalmic surgery in its scientific aspects. [xli. 275]

NUTHALL, THOMAS (d. 1775), politician and public official ; registrar of warrants in the excise office, 1740 ; receiver-general for hackney coaches, 1749 ; solicitor to the treasury, 1765 ; secretary of bankrupts, 1766 ; intimate with William Pitt, afterwards earl of Chatham, whose marriage settlements he drew up. [xli. 275]

NUTT, JOSEPH (1700–1775), surveyor of highways ; introduced at Hinckley a system of flooding the highways to render them firm. [xli. 276]

NUTTALL, JOSIAH (1771–1849), naturalist ; an expert taxidermist ; published 'Belshazzar' (epic poem), 1845. [xli. 276]

NUTTALL, THOMAS (1786–1859), naturalist ; went to America, 1807 ; professor of natural history at Harvard, 1822–34 ; wrote on the botany, geology, and ornithology of North America. [xli. 276]

NUTTALL, THOMAS (1828–1890), lieutenant-general, Indian army ; entered the army, 1845 ; lieutenant, 1847 ; captain, 1856 ; suppressed the Bheel rebels, 1857 ; major, 1865 ; served in the Abyssinian expedition, 1867 ; lieutenant-colonel, 1871 ; colonel, 1873 ; brigadier-general in the Afghan expedition, 1878 ; specially distinguished himself at Maiwand and Kandahar, 1880 ; lieutenant-general, 1887. [xli. 277]

NUTTALL, WILLIAM (d. 1840), author and schoolmaster ; wrote, in doggerel verse, the first attempt at a history of Rochdale, 1810. [xli. 278]

NUTTER, WILLIAM (1759 ?–1802), engraver and draughtsman ; executed plates after leading English artists, 1780–1800, in Bartolozzi's stipple manner. [xli. 278]

NUTTING, JOSEPH (fl. 1700), engraver. [xli. 278]

NYE, JOHN (d. 1688), theological writer ; son of Philip Nye [q. v.] ; B.A. Magdalen College, Oxford 1654 ;

clerk to the 'triers,' 1654 ; conformed, 1660 ; rector of Quendon, 1662 ; published controversial works. [xli. 279]

NYE, NATHANIEL (fl. 1648), author ; wrote 'The Art of Gunnery,' 1647, for the help of gunners and others 'not well versed in arithmetic' ; published an almanac for 1642, and two others for 1645. [xli. 279]

NYE, PHILIP (1596 ?–1672), independent divine ; M.A. Magdalen Hall, Oxford, 1622 ; his retirement to Holland (1633–40) necessitated by his nonconformity ; vicar of Kimbolton ; summoned to the Westminster Assembly of Divines, 1643, where he took decided part with the 'dissenting brethren' who objected to the assembly's propositions on church government ; desired 'uniformity, but only in institutions,' and proposed to tolerate all peaceable preachers ; on the commission of 'triers,' 1654, of 'expurgators,' 1654 ; took part in the Savoy conference, 1655 ; lost his preferments, 1660 ; preached in London, 1666, and ministered in Queen Street, 1672 ; published theological works, separately and with other dissenters. [xli. 279]

NYE, STEPHEN (1648 ?–1719), theological writer ; son of John Nye [q. v.] ; B.A. Magdalene College, Cambridge, 1665 ; rector of Little Hormead, 1679 ; intimate with Thomas Firmin [q. v.], and took part in the current controversies on the Trinity ; believed to have invented the term 'unitarian.' [xli. 282]

NYNDGE, ALEXANDER (fl. 1573), demoniac ; lived at Lyeringswell, Suffolk ; suffered from epileptic or hysterical attacks, 1573 ; an account of his condition written by his brother Edward. [xli. 283]

NYREN, JOHN (fl. 1830), cousin of John Nyren (1764–1837) [q. v.] ; author of 'Tables of the Duties, Bounties, and Drawbacks of Customs,' 1830. [xli. 284]

NYREN, JOHN (1764–1837), cricket chronicler ; interested himself in cricket from an early age ; belonged to the Hambledon Club ; a left-handed batsman of average ability and a fine field at point and middle wicket. His recollections were published in 'The Young Cricketer's Tutor' (edited by Charles Cowden Clark, 1833). [xli. 283]

O

OAKELEY, SIR CHARLES, first baronet (1751–1826), governor of Madras ; nominated to a writership in the East India Company, 1766 ; became secretary, 1773 ; judge-advocate-general and translator, 1777–80 ; president of the committee of assigned revenue of the nabob of Arcot, 1781–4 ; president of the Madras board of revenue, 1786–8 ; named governor of Madras, 1790 ; created baronet, 1790 ; improved the administration, retrenched expenses, resumed cash payments, and was able to supply Lord Cornwallis with money, grain, and cattle, 1791 ; in sole charge of Madras as governor, 1792 ; converted the company's floating debt and equipped the Pondicherry expedition, 1793, without disturbing government credit ; retired, 1795. [xli. 284]

OAKELEY, FREDERICK (1802–1880), tractarian ; son of Sir Charles Oakeley [q. v.] ; B.A. Christ Church, Oxford, 1824 ; chaplain-fellow of Balliol College, Oxford, 1827 ; joined the tractarian movement ; prebendary of Lichfield, 1830 ; appointed Whitehall preacher, 1837, and incumbent of Margaret Chapel, London, 1839, where he introduced ritualism ; joined the Roman communion, 1845, and was an original canon of the Roman catholic diocese of Westminster, 1852 ; published theological works before and after his secession. [xli. 286]

OAKELEY, SIR HERBERT, third baronet (1791–1845), archdeacon of Colchester ; son of Sir Charles Oakeley [q. v.] ; of Westminster School and Christ Church, Oxford (senior student) ; M.A., 1813 ; domestic chaplain to Dr. Howley, bishop of London, 1814–22 ; prebendary of St. Paul's, London, 1822 ; succeeded his brother as baronet, 1830 ; rector of Bocking, 1834 ; archdeacon of Colchester, 1841 ; one of the first to institute district visitors and Sunday schools. [xli. 287]

OAKES, SIR HENRY, second baronet (1756–1827), lieutenant-general, East India Company's service ; brother

of Sir Hildebrand Oakes [q. v.] ; second lieutenant, 1775 ; taken prisoner by Tippoo Sultan, 1783 ; served at Seringapatam and in Malabar ; major, 1795 ; colonel, 1802 ; major-general, 1810 ; lieutenant-general, 1814 ; succeeded his brother as baronet, 1822 ; committed suicide. [xli. 288]

OAKES, SIR HILDEBRAND, first baronet (1754–1822), lieutenant-general ; entered the army, 1767 ; served in America, 1775, in Corsica, 1794–6, in Egypt, 1801 ; brigadier-general at Malta, 1802–4 ; major, 1791 ; lieutenant-colonel, 1795 ; colonel, 1798 ; major-general, 1805 ; lieutenant-general, 1811 ; created baronet, 1813 ; G.C.B., 1820. [xli. 288]

OAKES, JOHN WRIGHT (1820–1887), landscape-painter ; painted landscapes, chiefly of Welsh mountains, from 1843 ; A.R.A., 1876. [xli. 289]

OAKES, THOMAS (1644–1719), speaker of the Massachusetts House of Representatives ; born at Cambridge, Massachusetts ; brother of Urian Oakes [q. v.] ; graduated at Harvard, 1662 ; was elected representative and (1689 and 1705) chosen speaker ; represented Massachusetts in England, 1689. [xli. 290]

OAKES, URIAN (1631 ?–1681), New England divine ; went as a boy to America ; graduated at Harvard, 1649 ; incumbent of Titchfield, England, during the Commonwealth ; ejected, 1662 ; pastor of Cambridge, Massachusetts, 1671 ; president of Harvard, 1675 ; published sermons. [xli. 289]

OAKLEY, EDWARD (fl. 1732), architect ; published works on architecture and building. [xli. 290]

OAKLEY, JOHN (1834–1890), dean of Manchester ; M.A. Brasenose College, Oxford, 1859 ; vicar of St. Saviour's,

Hoxton, 1867–81 ; high churchman and friend of the working classes ; dean of Carlisle, 1881 ; dean of Manchester, 1883. [xli. 291]

OAKLEY, OCTAVIUS (1800–1867), water-colour painter ; exhibited at the Royal Academy, 1826–60 ; frequently painted groups of gipsies, and was nicknamed 'Gipsy Oakley'; member of the Society of Painters in Water-colours, 1844. [xli. 292]

OAKMAN, JOHN (1748?–1793), engraver and author; wrote worthless novels, popular songs and burlettas, and engraved wood illustrations for cheap literature. [xli. 292]

OASLAND or **OSLAND**, HENRY (1625–1703), ejected minister ; M.A. Trinity College, Cambridge, 1653 ; pastor of Bewdley, 1650 ; arrested on suspicion of complicity in Pakington's plot, 1661 ; released, 1662 ; associated with Baxter ; ejected, 1662 ; preached regularly after 1688. [xli. 292]

OASTLER, RICHARD (1789–1861), 'the factory king'; articled to an architect ; steward of the Fixby estates, Huddersfield, 1820 ; advocated the abolition of slavery and opposed catholic emancipation ; his attention drawn to the evils of children's employment in factories, 1830 ; continually wrote and spoke for the improvement of factory legislation ; objected to the new poor law and resisted the commissioners at Fixby, an action which ultimately resulted in his dismissal from his stewardship, 1838, and imprisonment in the Fleet for debt, 1840–4 ; constantly wrote in periodicals on factory legislation ; joint-editor of the 'Ashton Chronicle.' [xli. 293]

OATES, FRANCIS (1840–1875), traveller and naturalist ; travelled in Central America and explored the Zambesi ; amassed large collections ; died near the Makalaka kraal ; his journals edited by his brother, Charles George Oates, 1881. [xli. 295]

OATES, TITUS (1649–1705), perjurer; expelled from Merchant Taylors' School, London, 1665, during his first year there ; entered Gonville and Caius College, Cambridge, 1667 ; migrated to St. John's College, Cambridge, 1669, but took no degree ; vicar of Bobbing, 1673 ; imprisoned at Dover in consequence of his making a disgraceful charge against a Hastings schoolmaster ; escaped before the trial and became a naval chaplain: expelled from the navy ; as chaplain to the protestants in the Duke of Norfolk's household first came in contact with papists ; met Israel Tonge [q. v.], who employed him to produce diatribes against the jesuits, 1676 ; became a Roman catholic, 1677, to procure further information, and entered the Jesuit College at Valladolid, whence he was expelled after five months' residence ; expelled also from St. Omer ; fabricated the 'popish plot', which he and Tonge affirmed before Sir Edmund Berry Godfrey [q. v.], 1678, his revelations being in effect that Charles II was to be killed and the country administered by the jesuits ; alleged that the details had been settled at a 'general consult' held at the White Horse Tavern, Fleet Street, in April 1678 ; summoned to repeat his story before the privy council and lodged in Whitehall, with a salary of 40l. monthly ; implicitly trusted, in consequence of Godfrey's murder ; his evidence corroborated by William Bedloe and others, the result being that about thirty-five men were judicially murdered ; lost prestige by the acquittal of Queen Catherine of Braganza's physician, Wakeman, July 1679, and Scroggs's successful defence of himself, January 1680 ; his pension reduced, April 1682, and in August stopped altogether: tried for perjury, May 1685, and condemned to stand in the pillory annually and to be flogged and imprisoned for life ; his sentence reversed and himself (1689) set at liberty ; married a rich widow, 1693, but was allowed 500l. to pay his debts and a pension of 300l. a year, 1698 ; joined the Wapping baptists and frequently preached, but was expelled, 1701, 'as a disorderly person and a hypocrite'; published many pamphlets on the popish plot and against the jesuits. [xli. 296]

OATLANDS, HENRY OF (1639–1660). [See HENRY, DUKE OF GLOUCESTER.]

O'BEIRNE, THOMAS LEWIS (1748?–1823), divine and pamphleteer ; educated as a Roman catholic at St. Omer ; adopted protestant views; chaplain in the navy ; wrote in periodicals in the whig interest ; chaplain and private secretary to the Duke of Portland, viceroy of Ireland, 1782; retired to Aubigny, 1783–5 ; chaplain and

secretary to Lord Fitzwilliam in Ireland, 1794 ; bishop of Ossory, 1795 ; translated to Meath, 1798; wrote controversial tracts and whig pamphlets. [xli. 303]

O'BRAEIN, TIGHEARNACH (d. 1088), Irish annalist ; abbot of Clonmacnoise and of Roscommon ; wrote annals, in which Irish events are synchronised with those of Europe. [xli. 305]

O'BRIEN, BARNABAS, sixth EARL OF THOMOND (d. 1657), son of Donough O'Brien, fourth earl of Thomond [q. v.]; succeeded his brother, 1639 ; lord-lieutenant of Clare, 1640–1 ; his rents seized, 1644 ; admitted a parliamentary garrison to Bunratty Castle and went to England ; joined Charles I ; successfully petitioned parliament for 2,000l. spent in the parliamentary cause. [xli. 305]

O'BRIEN, BRIAN RUADH (d. 1276), king of Thomond ; son of Conchobbar O'Brien [q. v.] ; inaugurated king, 1267 ; allied himself with De Clare, to defend himself against the rebellious Turlough O'Brien ; defeated with his ally ; hanged by De Clare in mortification at his defeat. [xli. 306]

O'BRIEN, CHARLES, fifth VISCOUNT CLARE (d. 1706), son of Daniel O'Brien, third viscount Clare [q. v.]; served in James II's army in Ireland, 1689–91 ; went to France, 1692 ; succeeded his brother, 1693 ; colonel of the Clare regiment, 1696 ; maréchal-de-camp, 1704 ; mortally wounded at Ramillies, 1706. [xli. 307]

O'BRIEN, CHARLES, sixth VISCOUNT CLARE (1699–1761), son of Charles O'Brien, fifth viscount Clare [q. v.]; succeeded his father, 1706 ; visited England, 1715 ; officer in the French army; distinguished himself at Dettingen, 1743, and Fontenoy, 1745 ; created maréchal, 1757 ; died at Montpellier. [xli. 307]

O'BRIEN, CONCHOBHAR (d. 1267), king of Thomond ; succeeded his father, Donogh Cairbrech O'Brien [q. v.], 1242 ; had some success against the English, 1257 ; mustered an army and fought in King's County, Tipperary, and Clare ; defeated and slain at Belaclugga. [xli. 307]

O'BRIEN, CONOR (d. 1539), prince of Thomond ; succeeded to Thomond, 1528 ; with his sons by his second marriage supported Fitzgerald, earl of Kildare, his son by his first marriage siding with the Butlers; defeated at O'Brien's Bridge, 1536 ; made peace, 1537. [xli. 308]

O'BRIEN, CONOR, third EARL OF THOMOND (1534?–1581), called Groibleach, or 'Long-nailed'; grandson of Conor O'Brien (d. 1539) [q. v.]; succeeded to the earldom, 1553 ; his right to the lordship of Thomond disputed by his uncle, Donnell ; confirmed in his possessions by the Earl of Sussex, 1558, who proclaimed his uncles traitors, though peace was not established till 1565 ; intrigued with the 'arch-rebel' Fitzgerald, 1569, and fled to France ; returned to Ireland and received pardon, 1571, with the restoration of his lands, 1573. [xli. 309]

O'BRIEN, DANIEL, first VISCOUNT CLARE (1577?–1663), called of Moyarta and Carrigaholt ; grandson of Conor O'Brien, third earl of Thomond [q. v.]; wounded and made prisoner by Tyrone, 1599 ; knighted, 1604 ; became a Roman catholic ; prominent in the disturbances in the Irish parliament as member for co. Clare ; joined the Kilkenny confederation, 1641 ; fled abroad to Charles II, 1651 ; created Viscount Clare, 1663. [xli. 310]

O'BRIEN, DANIEL, third VISCOUNT CLARE (d. 1690), followed Charles II into exile; lord-lieutenant of Clare under James II : Irish privy councillor ; sat among the peers, 1689 ; raised regiments for James II's service. [xli. 311]

O'BRIEN, DOMHNALL (d. 1194), king of Munster; son of Turlough O'Brien (1009–1086) [q. v.]; became king, 1168 ; engaged in plundering wars and blinded rival chiefs ; frequently successful against the English, but submitted to Henry II, 1171. [xli. 311]

O'BRIEN, DONAT HENCHY (1785–1857), rear-admiral; entered navy, 1796 ; wrecked and taken prisoner to Verdun, 1804; escaped, 1808 ; commander, 1813 ; rear-admiral, 1852 ; published an account of his imprisonment and escape. [xli. 311]

O'BRIEN, DONOGH CAIRBRECH (d. 1242), king of Thomond ; son of Domhnall O'Brien [q. v.]; betrayed his brother Murtogh to the English and succeeded him, 1208 ; successfully ravaged the south of Ireland. [xli. 312]

O'BRIEN, DONOUGH (*d.* 1064), king of Munster; son of Brian (926–1014) [q. v.]; obtained supremacy over Meath, Ossory, and Leinster; deposed, 1064, went to Rome, and died there. [xli. 312]

O'BRIEN, DONOUGH, BARON OF IBRICKAN and fourth EARL OF THOMOND (*d.* 1624), son of Conor O'Brien, third earl of Thomond [q. v.]; succeeded his father, 1581; assisted in suppressing Tyrone's rebellion, 1595; governor of Clare and privy councillor, 1599; constantly employed in the war, 1600; visited England and, on his return, took part in the siege of Kinsale, 1601; obtained the transfer of Clare from the jurisdiction of Connaught to Munster, 1602; president of Munster, 1605; governor of Clare, 1619. [xli. 312]

O'BRIEN, EDWARD (1808–1840), author; brother of William Smith O'Brien [q. v.]; M.A. Trinity College, Cambridge, 1832; published 'The Lawyer,' 1842, a work depicting a lawyer of ideal holiness. [xli. 314]

O'BRIEN, HENRY (1808–1835), antiquary; B.A. Trinity College, Dublin, 1831; published 'The Round Towers of Ireland,' 1834, with the object of proving them Buddhistic remains. [xli. 314]

O'BRIEN, JAMES, third MARQUIS OF THOMOND and seventh EARL OF INCHIQUIN (1769–1855), admiral; entered the navy, 1783; commander, 1796; rear-admiral, 1825; vice-admiral, 1837; admiral, 1847; lord of the bedchamber, 1830; G.C.H., 1831; succeeded his brother, 1846. [xli. 315]

O'BRIEN, JAMES [BRONTERRE] (1805–1864), chartist; B.A. Dublin, 1829; entered Gray's Inn; became practically editor of the 'Poor Man's Guardian,' 1831, signing himself 'Bronterre'; steadily developed revolutionary views; was a prominent chartist, and at first advocated physical force, contributing violent articles to the 'Northern Star'; imprisoned for seditious speaking, 1840; quarrelled with Feargus O'Connor [q. v.]; edited various newspapers and lectured on the nationalisation of the land and other topics. [xli. 315]

O'BRIEN, JAMES THOMAS (1792–1874), bishop of Ossory, Ferns, and Leighlin; B.A. Trinity College, Dublin, 1815; fellow, 1820; D.D., 1832; instituted dean of Cork, 1842; bishop of Ossory, 1842; wrote on justification by faith and the evidences of religion, and opposed the Oxford movement. [xli. 316]

O'BRIEN, JOHN (*d.* 1767), Irish catholic prelate; vicar-general of Cork, Cloyne, and Ross; on the separation of Cork and Cloyne (1747) was appointed bishop of Cloyne and Ross; said to have compiled an Irish-English dictionary, published, 1768; edited the statutes of Cloyne and Ross, 1756; his work on gavelkind and tanistry in Ireland, published, 1774–5. [xli. 317]

O'BRIEN, SIR LUCIUS HENRY, third baronet (*d.* 1795), Irish politician; entered parliament as member for Ennis, 1763; prominent member of the popular party; endeavoured to remove trade restrictions between England and Ireland, and agitated for Irish legislative independence; succeeded as baronet, 1765; M.P., co. Clare, 1768–76, Ennis, 1776–83, Tuam, 1783–90, Ennis, again, 1790–5; privy councillor, 1787; clerk of the crown and hanaper in the high court of chancery, 1787. [xli. 318]

O'BRIEN, MATTHEW (1814–1855), mathematician; M.A. Caius College, Cambridge, 1841; lecturer at Woolwich, 1849–55, and at King's College, London, 1844–54; wrote on mathematics. [xli. 319]

O'BRIEN, MURROUGH, first EARL OF THOMOND and BARON INCHIQUIN (*d.* 1551), succeeded his brother, Conor O'Brien (*d.* 1539) [q. v.], in the lordship of Thomond, 1539; agreed to conditions of peace and submission, 1541; created Earl of Thomond with reversion to his nephew, his son being created Baron Inchiquin, 1543; visited England for his installation, 1543. [xli. 319]

O'BRIEN, MURROUGH, first EARL OF INCHIQUIN and sixth BARON INCHIQUIN (1614–1674), known as 'Murchadh na atoithean' or ' of the conflagrations'; studied war in the Spanish service; accompanied Strafford into Leinster on the outbreak of the Irish rebellion, 1641; governor of Munster, 1642; had some small success, but was hampered by lack of funds; outwitted the Irish leader, Muskerry, at Cappoquin and Lismore; his forces dispersed at the truce, 1643; visited Charles I at

Oxford, 1644; forced to submit to parliament, 1644, the parliamentarians being masters of the sea, and therefore the only people who could help the Munster protestants; made president of Munster; supplies having been brought him by Philip Sidney, lord Lisle (afterwards third earl of Leicester) [q. v.], 1647, he became gradually master of the south of Ireland; declared for Charles I, 1648; fortified the southern ports against parliament; made a truce with the confederate catholics, 1648; joined by Ormonde, with whom he got possession of Drogheda and Dundalk; lost influence in Munster, which revolted after Cromwell's landing, 1649; made some stand at Kilmallock, 1649, but after retiring west of the Shannon left Ireland for France, 1650; made one of the royal council and created earl of Inchiquin, 1654; served under the French in Catalonia, 1654; engaged in the Sexby plot, 1656, and became a Roman catholic; taken prisoner by the Algerines, 1660, but ransomed the same year; became high steward of Queen Henrietta Maria's household; lived quietly in Ireland after 1663. [xli. 320]

O'BRIEN, MURTOGH (*d.* 1119), king of Munster; son of Turlough O'Brien [q. v.]; constantly at war with his neighbours; became king, 1086; made a circuit of Ireland in six weeks, 1101. [xli. 327]

O'BRIEN, PATRICK (1761 ?–1806). [See COTTER.]

O'BRIEN, PAUL (1750 ?–1820), professor of Irish at Maynooth, 1802; published a 'Practical Grammar of the Irish Language,' 1809. [xli. 327]

O'BRIEN, TERENCE or TOIRDHELBHACH (*d.* 1460), bishop of Killaloe; treacherously slain. [xli. 328]

O'BRIEN, TERENCE ALBERT (1600–1651), bishop of Emly; educated at Limerick and Toledo; became prior of the Limerick Dominicans; provincial of the Irish Dominicans, 1643; bishop of Emly, 1647; joined Rinuccini's party; exhorted resistance against the Cromwellians at Limerick, 1651, and nursed the sufferers; hanged by Ireton. [xli. 328]

O'BRIEN, TURLOUGH (1009–1086), king of Munster; relative of Brian (926–1014) [q. v.]; disputed the chieftainship of the Dal Cais with his kinsman, Murchadh, 1055–64; became king of Munster, 1067; robbed Clonmacnoise, 1073, and attacked his neighbours with moderate success. [xli. 329]

O'BRIEN, WILLIAM, second EARL OF INCHIQUIN (1638 ?–1692), son of Murrough O'Brien, first earl of Inchiquin [q. v.]; taken prisoner by the Algerines, 1660; governor of Tangier, 1674–80; succeeded as second earl, 1674; welcomed William of Orange, 1688; attainted by the Irish parliament, 1689; successfully headed the Munster protestants against the Roman catholics; appointed governor of Jamaica, 1690, where his troubles with the French and the negroes finally caused his death. [xli. 330]

O'BRIEN, WILLIAM (*d.* 1815), actor and dramatist; engaged by Garrick to replace Woodward, 1758; left the stage on his marriage to Lady Susan Fox-Strangways, 1764; lived for a time in America; subsequently became receiver-general of Dorset; produced 'Cross Purposes,' 1772, and 'The Duel,' 1773. [xli. 331]

O'BRIEN, WILLIAM SMITH (1803–1864), Irish nationalist; brother of Edward O'Brien [q. v.]; of Harrow and Trinity College, Cambridge; B.A., 1826; M.P., Ennis, 1828–31; as a supporter of Peel approved of catholic emancipation, and brought in an Irish poor-law bill, 1831; M.P., co. Limerick, 1835–49; made repeated efforts to improve the poor relief and education in Ireland; joined the Repeal Association, 1843; in the custody of the serjeant-at-arms, April–May 1846, for refusing to serve on a railway committee; seceded from the Repeal Association and founded the Irish confederation to attain an Irish parliament by force of opinion only, 1846; urged the formation of a national guard in Ireland, 1848, for which he was tried, the jury being discharged as unable to agree; failing to raise the towns, made an abortive insurrection in the rural districts, was arrested on a charge of high treason, and sentenced to be hanged, drawn, and quartered, 1848, his sentence being commuted to transportation for life; refused a ticket-of-leave and was confined on Maria island, Tasmania; pardon, except for the United Kingdom, granted him, 1854; settled at Brussels; received an unconditional pardon, 1856; visited America, 1859, and Poland, 1863; wrote during his exile the greater part of his 'Principles of Government' (published, 1856). [xli. 332]

O'BROLCHAIN, FLAIBHERTACH (*d.* 1175), first bishop of Derry; abbot of Derry, 1150, and chief of the Columban churches; obtained grants of cattle from Oinel Eoghain; attended a convocation at Bric Mic Taidhg, 1158, when the papal legate made him bishop of Derry; obtained grant of cattle from the king of Lesser Ulster, and built his cathedral, 1164. [xli. 337]

O'BRUADAIR, DAVID (*fl.* 1650–1694), Irish poet; a violent opponent of protestantism and everything English; wrote the difficult Irish metre, Dan direch, correctly; a Jacobite; evidence of the feelings of the Irish-speaking gentry of Munster supplied by his writings; about twenty of his poems extant. [xli. 338]

O'BRYAN, WILLIAM (1778–1868), founder of the Bible Christian sect; was converted to Wesleyanism, 1795; expelled from the society in consequence of differences about discipline, 1810; gradually formed a sect, the 'Arminian Bible Christians,' 1816, part of which seceded, 1829; went to America, 1831; published 'Rules of Society,' 1812; died at Brooklyn. [xli. 339]

O'BRYEN, DENNIS (1755–1832), dramatist and political pamphleteer; wrote 'A Friend in Need is a Friend indeed' (comedy), 1783; supported Fox in various political pamphlets. [xli. 340]

O'BRYEN, EDWARD (1754?–1808), rear-admiral; entered the navy, *c.* 1767; commander, 1783; distinguished himself at Camperdown, 1797; rear-admiral, 1805. [xli. 340]

O'BYRNE, FIAGH MacHUGH (1544?–1597), in Irish FIACHA MAC AODHA UA BROIN, chief of the O'Byrnes of Wicklow; combined with Rory Oge O'More, 1571; was implicated in the murder of Robert Browne, 1572, and defeated the seneschal, but was pardoned, 1573; invaded Wexford, 1580, and, joining Baltinglas, advanced within ten miles of Dublin, plundering and burning, but after some negotiations submitted and was pardoned, 1581; renewed his submission, 1584, 1586, and 1588; held responsible (1594) for his son's outrage on the sheriff of Kildare, and proclaimed traitor; again submitted, 1595, and appealed to Queen Elizabeth, 1596, but immediately joined Tyrone; captured and beheaded. [xli. 341]

O'BYRNE, WILLIAM RICHARD (1823–1896), author of 'Naval Biographical Dictionary,' which was begun 1845, and published 1849; succeeded to Cabinteely estate, co. Wicklow; M.P., co. Wicklow, 1874–80; died in distressed circumstances owing to depreciation of Irish land. [Suppl. iii. 230]

O'CAHAN or **O'KANE**, SIR DONNELL BALLAGH or THE FRECKLED (*d.* 1617?), Irish chieftain; chief vassal of Tyrone; rebelled under Tyrone, 1598, but submitted after siege of Kinsale on the promise of holding his lands direct from the crown, and he proceeded at law (1606) against Tyrone, who claimed his submission; knighted, 1607; surrendered for trial and was imprisoned in Dublin, 1609; transferred to London, dying in the Tower without being tried. [xli. 344]

O'CALLAGHAN, EDMUND BAILEY (1797–1880), historian; studied medicine at Paris; emigrated to Canada, 1823; fled to the States when the 1837 rising in Canada failed; attached to the secretary of state's office; published 'History of New Netherland,' 1846, and 'State Records,' 1849–51. [xli. 345]

O'CALLAGHAN, JOHN CORNELIUS (1805–1883), Irish historical writer; called to the Irish bar, 1829; wrote for periodicals, including the 'Nation'; published a 'History of the Irish Brigades in the Service of France,' 1869. [xli. 346]

O'CALLAGHAN, SIR ROBERT WILLIAM (1777–1840), general; entered the army, 1794; captain, 1795; lieutenant-colonel, 1803; distinguished himself in the Peninsula; major-general, 1814; appointed commander at Madras, 1830–6; G.C.B., 1838. [xli. 346]

O'CARAN, GILLA-AN-CHOIMHDEDH (*d.* 1180), archbishop of Armagh; bishop of Cinel Conaill; archbishop of Armagh, 1175; held office during Cardinal Vivianus's visitation. [xli. 347]

O'CAROLAN or **CAROLAN**, TORLOGH (1670–1738), Irish bard; became blind from small-pox, 1684; began wandering as a bard, 1692; repaid hospitality in songs

named after his entertainers, such as 'Gracey Nugent,' 'Bridget Cruise,' and the famous 'Receipt for Drinking' or 'Planxty Stafford.' About fifty of his pieces survive in Irish collections. [xli. 347]

O'CARROLL, MAOLSUTHAIN (*d.* 1031), confessor of Brian (926–1014) [q. v.], king of Ireland; accompanied Brian in his journey round Ireland, 1004; wrote a short chapter in the 'Book of Armagh.' [xli. 349]

O'CARROLL, MARGARET (*d.* 1451), hospitable lady; married Calbhach O'Connor Faly; but retained her maiden name; gave two great entertainments to learned men. [xli. 350]

OCCAM, NICHOLAS OF (*fl.* 1280), Franciscan; also called Nicholas de Hotham; disputed at Oxford and wrote sermons. [xli. 350]

OCCAM, WILLIAM (*d.* 1349?). [See OCKHAM.]

OCCLEVE, THOMAS (1370?–1450?). [See HOCCLEVE.]

O'CEARBHALL, LORD OF OSSORY (*d.* 888). [See CEARBHALL.]

O'CEARNAIDH, BRIAN (1567–1640). [See KEARNEY, BARNABAS.]

OCHILTREE, second BARON (*fl.* 1548–1593). [See STEWART, ANDREW.]

OCHILTREE, MICHAEL (*fl.* 1425–1445), bishop of Dunblane; dean of Dunblane before 1425; became bishop before 1430. [xli. 350]

OCHINO, BERNARDINO (1487–1564), reformer; born at Siena; quitted the Observantine Franciscans, 1534, for the Capuchins; became an extraordinarily eloquent preacher; chosen vicar-general of the Capuchins, 1538; fled to Geneva on the establishment of the inquisition, 1542; settled at Augsburg, 1545; migrated to England, 1547; prebendary of Canterbury, 1548; returned to Basle on Queen Mary's accession and was for a time pastor of Zürich; expelled from Switzerland in consequence of his 'Thirty Dialogues' on the Trinity, 1563; went to Poland, but was not allowed to remain there, and died at Slakow in Moravia; published theological works in Italian, most of which were translated into English. [xli. 350]

OCHS, JOHANN RUDOLPH (1673–1749), medallist; born at Bern; cut seals and engraved gems; came to England, 1719, and was employed at the royal mint. [xli. 353]

OCHS or **OCKS**, JOHN RALPH (1704–1788), medallist; son of Johann Rudolph Ochs [q. v.]; employed at the royal mint of England from 1741. [xli. 353]

OCHTERLONY, SIR DAVID, first baronet (1758–1825), conqueror of Nipál (Nepaul); born at Boston, Massachusetts; entered the Bengal army, 1777; lieutenant, 1778; served under Sir Eyre Coote against the French; major, 1800; lieutenant-colonel, 1803; appointed British resident at Delhi, 1803; defended Delhi against Holkar, 1804; colonel, 1812; major-general, 1814; his column the only one of the four invading Nipál which was successful; took Nalagur, 1814, and advanced to Biláspur, 1814; defeated Amar Singh after desperate fighting, May 1815; created baronet and K.C.B., 1815; negotiated a treaty with the Gúrkha government, 1815, which it subsequently refused to ratify; again took the field to march on Khátmándu; obliged the Gúrkhas to evacuate the Kourea Ghát pass and defeated them within twenty miles of Khátmándu, 1816, after which the treaty was duly ratified and faithfully kept; G.C.B., 1816; made a peaceable settlement with Amir Khán, 1818, and effected the disarmament of the Pathán forces; took a large part in the reconstruction of government in Central India, in the course of which Balwant Singh, a boy of six, was recognised as raja of Bhartpur, 1825; proceeded to uphold Balwant Singh against his rebellious cousin by force of arms; died at Mirat broken-hearted by the decision of the governor-general to investigate the matter before allowing him to carry out his intention. [xli. 353]

OCKHAM, BARONS OF. [See KING, PETER, first BARON KING, 1669–1734; KING, PETER, seventh BARON KING, 1776–1833.]

OCKHAM, NICHOLAS OF (*fl.* 1280). [See OCCAM.]

OCKHAM or **OCCAM**, WILLIAM (*d.* 1349 ?), 'Doctor invincibilis'; studied at Oxford, possibly under Duns Scotus; became a Franciscan; B.D. Oxford; went to Paris and associated with Marsiglio; D.D. Paris; entered into the Franciscan controversy concerning poverty, and defended (1323) against Pope John XXII, the doctrine of 'evangelical poverty,' accepted (1322) by the chapter at Perugia; was imprisoned at Avignon on a charge of heresy, 1328, but escaped to the emperor at Pisa; accompanied him back to Bavaria, 1330, and resided in the Franciscan house at Munich, where, with Michael da Cesena, he was a leader of the 'evangelical poverty' minority; refuted in 'Opus nonaginta Dierum' (*c.* 1330) the pope's treatise against it, 'Sentence by sentence,' and in 'Compendium errorum papæ' (*c.* 1338) made him answerable for seventy errors and seven heresies; defended the contention of Lewis of Bavaria that his election to the empire was valid without the pope's confirmation, and elaborated the general discussion of the nature of imperial and papal authority in a 'Dialogus,' which is incomplete as we have it now; was vicar of his order from 1342, but passed on the ring of office, 1349, and probably was reconciled to the pope upon the recantation of his more obnoxious doctrines; died and was buried at Munich. His eminence lies in his work in logic, philosophy, and political theory. He was the second founder of nominalism, and made the method of logic known as the 'Byzantine logic' his fundamental basis. The title 'Venerabilis Inceptor' is apparently older than the more familiar 'Doctor invincibilis.' [xli. 357]

OCKLAND, CHRISTOPHER (*d.* 1590 ?). [See OCLAND.]

OCKLEY, SIMON (1678–1720), orientalist; entered Queens' College, Cambridge, 1693, where he was made Hebrew lecturer; M.A. Cambridge (incorporated at Oxford, 1706); B.D. Cambridge, 1710; became curate and subsequently vicar of Swavesey, 1705; his 'History of the Saracens,' published 1708–57, the main source of the average notions of Mohammedan history for generations; frequently visited Oxford to consult Arabic manuscripts; appointed professor of Arabic at Cambridge, 1711; translated the Second Book of Esdras from the Arabic, 1716, and other Arabic works. [xli. 362]

OCKS, JOHN RALPH (1704–1788). [See OCHS.]

OCLAND, CHRISTOPHER (*d.* 1590 ?), Latin poet and controversialist; a schoolmaster at Cheltenham and Greenwich; his 'Anglorum Prælia,' 1580, ordered to be used in grammar schools; published also Latin poems on Queen Elizabeth. [xli. 365]

O'CLERY, CUCOIGCRICHE (*d.* 1664), Irish chronicler; son of Lughaidh O'Clery [q. v.]; assisted Michael O'Clery [q. v.] in compiling the 'Annals of the Four Masters' and wrote poems. [xli. 366]

O'CLERY, LUGHAIDH (*fl.* 1609), Irish historian; became chief of his sept, 1595; took part in the contention between the northern and southern Irish bards, 1600; dictated 'Life of Aodh Ruadh O'Donnell' (translated, 1820). [xli. 366]

O'CLERY, MICHAEL (1575–1643), Irish chronicler; third cousin of Cucoigcriche O'Clery [q. v.]; was baptised Tadhg, but entered the Franciscan order as Michael; studied Irish history and literature in East Munster; entered the Louvain convent and was sent (1620) to collect Irish manuscripts, especially historical and hagiological ones; assisted by other Irish scholars composed 'The Royal List' of Irish kings and their pedigrees, 1624–30, the 'Book of Invasions,' 1627–31, a digest of the 'Annals of Kingdom of Ireland' or 'Annals of the Four Masters,' 1632–6, and 'Martyrologium Sanctorum Hiberniæ,' 1636. [xli. 367]

O'COBHTHAIGH, DERMOT (*fl.* 1584), Irish poet; belonged to a family of hereditary poets; wrote a lament for a murdered kinsman and five theological poems. [xli. 369]

O'CONNELL, DANIEL or DANIEL CHARLES, COUNT (1745 ?–1833), French general; uncle of Daniel O'Connell (1775–1847) [q. v.], called the 'Liberator'; entered the French army, 1760; became adjutant of the Clare regiment; obtained the cross of St. Louis for a pamphlet on army discipline; wounded at Gibraltar; became colonel of the Salm-Salm regiment; accepted the revolution, but (1792) joined the Bourbons; suggested the formation of an Irish brigade to Pitt, 1796; became lieutenant-general under the Bourbons; died at Mâdon, in Blois. [xli. 370]

O'CONNELL, DANIEL (1775–1847), Irish politician, called the 'Liberator'; entered the English College of St. Omer, 1791; was transferred to Douay, 1792, which was suppressed, 1793; entered Lincoln's Inn, 1794; called to the Irish bar, 1798; joined the Munster circuit and soon gained a reputation for legal ability and unrivalled power of cross-examination; protested, in his first public speech (1800), against the insinuation that Roman catholics approved the Act of Union; signed a petition for catholic emancipation, 1805, and was chairman of a sub-committee for reporting on the laws affecting catholics, 1811; vigorously opposed Grattan's bill, 1813, as inadequate, 'restricted in principle,' and doubtful in its wording; leading counsel for Magee, proprietor and editor of the 'Dublin Evening Post,' 1813; powerfully vindicated the catholic policy, knowing the court to be hostile; challenged by a Dublin merchant named D'Esterre, whom he fatally wounded, 1815; arrested in London on his way to the continent, his projected duel with Peel having been frustrated in Ireland, and bound over to keep the peace; formed the Catholic Association to deal with practical questions and grievances which pressed on the catholic peasant, 1823; started (1824) the 'catholic rent,' which made all who paid one shilling a year to the Catholic Association members, by which a spirit of hope was infused into the peasantry; gained thereby a high place in the estimation of his countrymen; his work thwarted (February 1825) by a bill which suppressed the association, and by the rejection of the Catholic Relief Bill by the Lords; founded, August 1826, his 'Order of Liberators,' to which every man who had performed one real act of service to Ireland was entitled to belong, with the object of preventing feuds and riots at fairs, discountenancing secret societies, and making the franchise effective; elected M.P. for co. Clare at a bye-election, 1828; believed that in the absence of a direct prohibition in the Act of Union no legal obstacle could prevent a duly elected Roman catholic from taking his seat; found that before parliament reassembled it had been determined to admit Roman catholics to parliament, the bill passing April 1829; refused to take the oath of supremacy, on which his claim to sit was rejected; again returned unopposed, a national testimonial in the form of an annual tribute being provided for his expenses; published a series of letters giving his views on current political questions, 1830, and, after all the societies which he formed to prepare the way for the repeal of the union had been promptly suppressed, was finally arrested, 1831, for evading the proclamations; skilfully averted a riot in Dublin; the prosecution of him dropped through the influence of English reformers; considered parliamentary reform a necessary step to the repeal of the union, but failed to obtain the restoration of the forty-shilling freeholders; returned, unsolicited, for Dublin, 1832; moved for the appointment of a committee to inquire into and report on the union, 1834; was defeated, but created a more conciliatory disposition towards Ireland, which in 1835, when the balance of power lay in his hands, issued in the 'Lichfield House compact' and the impartial government of Thomas Drummond [q. v.]; denunciations and charges of corruption excited by his friendly relations with the ministry; rendered valuable assistance to the English Municipal Corporations Bill, and agitated for similar reform in Ireland; founded the Repeal Association, 1840, on the lines of the old Catholic Association, and addressed meetings on the subject in Ireland and England; elected lord mayor of Dublin, 1841; refrained from agitation during his year of office; his cause considerably strengthened by the establishment of the 'Nation' newspaper, 1842; countermanded the meeting at Clontarf, thereby averting the danger which would otherwise have arisen from the suppression of the existing agitation by parliament, 1843; arrested on a charge of creating discontent and disaffection, and sentenced to a fine of 2,000*l.* and a year's imprisonment, 1844, but liberated, judgment being reversed on appeal, 1844; wrote in favour of federalism, but withdrew his offer of co-operation with federalist advocates, as it was interpreted as an abandonment of repeal; called attention to the constant distress in Ireland, 1846, and made his last appeal to the house, February 1847 ; went abroad on account of his health and died at Genoa. The system of constitutional agitation by mass meetings, in his hands, reached a perfection never before attained, and he re-created national feeling in Ireland. [xli. 371]

O'CONNELL, JOHN (1810–1858), Irish politician ; son of Daniel O'Connell, the ' Liberator ' [q. v.] ; called to the Irish bar ; M.P., Youghal, 1832–7, Athlone, 1837–41, Kilkenny, 1841–7, Limerick, 1847–51, Clonmel, 1853–7 ; actively assisted his father in the repeal agitation, and shared his trial and imprisonment, 1844 ; succeeded his father as head of the Repeal Association, which failed (1848) for lack of funds ; joined the whigs and, as ' young Liberator,' tried to start agitation ; clerk of the Hanaper Office, Ireland, 1857 ; published ' Life and Speeches ' (1846) of his father and various reports for the Repeal Association. [xli. 389]

O'CONNELL, SIR MAURICE CHARLES (1812–1879), soldier and colonial statesman ; son of Sir Maurice Charles Philip O'Connell [q. v.] ; born at Sydney ; educated in England, Edinburgh, Dublin, and Paris ; entered the army, 1828 ; lieutenant, 1834 ; raised a regiment in Ireland for service in Spain, 1835 ; captain, 1838 ; went to New South Wales, where he was member of the legislative council for Port Philip, 1845–8, and appointed commissioner for crown lands, 1848 ; member of the legislative council of Queensland, 1859, and president of the council, 1861–79 ; knighted, 1868. [xli. 390]

O'CONNELL, SIR MAURICE CHARLES PHILIP (d. 1848), lieutenant-general ; educated in Paris by his kinsman, Daniel O'Connell (1745 ?–1833) [q. v.] ; a captain in the French service by 1792 ; came into the English service on the transfer of the Irish brigade, 1794 ; served with distinction in the West Indies ; lieutenant-colonel and lieutenant-governor of New South Wales, 1809–14 ; knighted and K.C.H., 1834 ; major-general commanding the forces in New South Wales, 1838–46 ; lieutenant-general, 1841 ; died at Sydney. [xli. 391]

O'CONNELL, MORGAN (1804–1885), politician ; son of Daniel O'Connell, the ' Liberator ' [q. v.] ; served in the Irish South American legion and the Austrian army ; M.P., Meath, 1832–40 ; assistant-registrar of deeds for Ireland, 1840–68 ; did not agree with his father on the repeal question, but fought a duel with William, second baron Alvanley, on his father's account. [xli. 392]

O'CONNELL, MORITZ, BARON O'CONNELL (1740 ?–1830), Austrian officer ; went abroad with Daniel, count O'Connell (1745 ?–1833) [q. v.], 1762, entered the Austrian army, was imperial chamberlain fifty-nine years, and became a baron ; died at Vienna. [xli. 393]

O'CONNELL, PETER (1746–1826),Irish lexicographer ; a schoolmaster who studied old Irish manuscripts and prepared an Irish dictionary, 1785–1819, but was unable to publish it. The manuscript was finally purchased by the British Museum. [xli. 393]

O'CONNOR. [See also O'CONOR.]

O'CONNOR, AEDH (d. 1067), king of Connaught ; called 'an gha bhearnaigh ' ('of the clipped spear ') ; contended with the O'Rourkes for the kingship throughout his life ; killed their chief, 1039 ; defeated by them, 1051 ; received the submission of the O'Briens, 1059, admitted the supremacy of the king of Ailech, 1063 ; killed fighting against the O'Rourkes near Oranmore.
[xli. 393]

O'CONNOR, ARTHUR (1763–1852), Irish rebel ; brother of Roger O'Connor [q. v.] ; B.A. Trinity College, Dublin, 1782 ; called to the Irish bar, 1788 ; sat in the Irish parliament for Philipstown, 1791–5 ; joined the ' United Irishmen,' 1796 ; imprisoned for seditious libel, 1797 ; editor of the ' Press '; was arrested in England, but, having given some information to the government, was despatched to Scotland, 1799 ; released and sent to France, 1803 ; appointed by Napoleon general of division, 1804 ; published books on political questions ; died at Bignon. [xli. 394]

O'CONNOR, BERNARD (1666 ?–1698). [See CONNOR.]

O'CONNOR, BRIAN or BERNARD (1490 ?–1560 ?), more properly known as BRIAN O'CONOR FALY ; succeeded to the lordship of Offaly, 1511 ; kept prisoner for nearly a year the vice-deputy, who had attempted (1528) to withhold his black-rents, but was pardoned on the liberation from detention of his kinsman, the earl of Kildare; took up arms, 1534, and through his brother

Cahir's treachery was compelled to submit, 1535 ; his country invaded by Lord Leonard Grey [q. v.], 1537, who appointed Cahir lord of Offaly ; forcibly expelled Cahir, and offered to submit, 1538 ; invaded the Pale, 1540, but submitted to St. Leger ; kept the peace till 1547, when he joined O'More in an attack on the Pale ; gave himself up, 1548, after St. Leger had made two inroads into Offaly, and was imprisoned in the Tower of London ; escaped, 1552, but was rearrested ; returned to Ireland, 1554, but was soon imprisoned in Dublin Castle, where he died. [xli. 395]

O'CONNOR, CALVACH (1584–1655), Irish commander ; rumoured that he was to be made king of Connaught and the centre of the confederate party, 1641 ; attacked and routed, 1642 ; excepted from pardon, 1652.
[xli. 398]

O'CONNOR, CATHAL (d. 1010), king of Connaught ; became king, 980 ; built a bridge over the Shannon, 1000 ; entered the monastery of Clonmacnoise, 1003. [xli. 398]

O'CONNOR, CATHAL (1150 ?–1224), king of Connaught ; called Croibhdheirg (red-handed), son, possibly illegitimate, of Turlough O'Connor [q. v.], king of Ireland ; opposed his brother and nephew, but succeeded as king, on the latter's death at Boyle, 1201 ; acknowledged King John's supremacy, 1215, but resisted Walter de Lacy, 1220 and 1224 ; founded three abbeys.
[xli. 398]

O'CONNOR or O'CONOR FALY, CATHAL or CHARLES, otherwise known as DON CARLOS (1540–1596), son of Brian O'Connor [q. v.], brought up in Scotland ; went to France, 1560 ; a spy in the service of Mary Queen of Scots ; fled to Spain for the murder of Captain Henry Mackworth, 1582 ; joined the Spanish army ; wrecked in the Spanish armada for the invasion of Ireland, 1596. [xli. 397]

O'CONNOR, FEARGUS (1794–1855), chartist leader ; son of Roger O'Connor [q. v.] ; of Trinity College, Dublin ; called to the Irish bar ; took part in the reform agitation, 1831, and organised the electorate registration in Cork ; returned as a repealer for co. Cork, 1832 ; associated with the extreme English radicals ; unseated, 1835 ; travelled through the northern and midland districts advocating radicalism and, afterwards, the ' six points of the charter,' his paper, the ' Northern Star,' being the official organ of chartism ; sentenced to eighteen months' imprisonment at York, for seditious libel, 1840 ; quarrelled with most of the other leaders, 1841 ; advocated peasant proprietorship, and founded the National Land Company to buy estates and let them to subscribers by ballot, 1846 ; M.P., Nottingham, 1847 ; averted disturbances at the mass meeting on Kennington Common, 1848 ; visited America ; pronounced insane, June 1852. [xli. 400]

O'CONNOR, HUGH (1617–1669), Irish chief ; captured and examined, 1642 ; entered into articles of surrender, 1652 ; served abroad ; succeeded his father, Calvach O'Connor [q. v.], as chief, 1655 ; applied to be reinstated after 1660, but died before his claim had been decided.
[xli. 398]

O'CONNOR, JAMES ARTHUR (1791–1841), painter ; was brought up as an engraver, but took to landscape-painting ; visited Brussels, 1826, Paris, 1832, Belgium and Rhenish Prussia, 1833 ; exhibited at the Royal Academy, 1822–40. [xli. 402]

O'CONNOR, JOHN (1824–1887), Canadian statesman ; born at Boston, Massachusetts ; worked on his father's land ; called to the Canadian bar, 1854 ; elected to the Canadian legislature for Essex, 1867 ; successively (1872–1873) president of the council, minister of inland revenue, and postmaster-general ; elected for Russell County, 1878 ; again became president of the council and postmaster-general ; secretary of state ; puisne judge at Ontario, 1884. [xli. 403]

O'CONNOR, JOHN (1830–1889), scene-painter and architectural painter ; came to London, 1848, and obtained work at the theatres ; after 1857 exhibited at the Royal Academy, chiefly architectural subjects ; visited Sedan, 1870, and Paris, during the Prussian occupation, 1871 ; made drawings of several court ceremonies ; designed and directed tableaux vivants. [xli. 403]

O'CONNOR, LUKE SMYTHE (1806–1873), major-general ; entered the army, 1827 ; captain, 1834 ; brevet lieutenant-colonel, 1853 ; major-general, 1866 ; served with special distinction in West Africa (C.B., 1855) and in Jamaica ; died at Dresden. [xli. 404]

O'CONNOR, RODERIC, or in Irish RUAIDHRI (*d.* 1118), king of Connaught; son of Aedh O'Connor [q. v.]; became king, 1076; won a great victory at Cunghill, 1087; treacherously seized and blinded, 1092; retired to Clonmacnoise. [xli. 405]

O'CONNOR, RODERIC, called in Irish RUAIDHRI UA CONCHOBHAIR (1116?–1198), king of Ireland; son of Turlough O'Connor [q. v.]; became king of Connaught, 1156; ravaged the plain of Teffia; suffered reverses at Athlone and Ardee, 1159; took advantage of the weakness of the north, went to Dublin, and was inaugurated king of all Ireland, 1166; called two important assemblies, 1167 and 1168, to adopt laws and determine justice; granted ten cows annually for teaching scholars at Armagh, 1169; besieged Strongbow in Dublin, 1171, but was routed by him; acknowledged Henry II as his liege lord, 1175; entered the abbey of Cong and died there. [xli. 405]

O'CONNOR, ROGER (1762–1834), Irish nationalist; brother of Arthur O'Connor [q. v.]; called to the English bar, 1784; joined the United Irishmen; arrested, 1797, but liberated, 1798; imprisoned for some years with his brother Arthur; rearrested for raiding the Galway coach, 1817, but acquitted; published 'Chronicles of Eri,' 1822, mainly imaginative. [xli. 407]

O'CONNOR, TURLOUGH (1088–1156), king of Ireland; called in Irish Toirdhealbhach mór ua Conchobhair; son of Roderic O'Connor (*d.* 1118) [q. v.]; became king of Connaught, 1106; made war on his neighbours with varying success; allied himself to Murchadh O'Maeleachlainn, 1118, but in 1120 drove him into the north and assumed the kingship of Ireland; divided the kingdom into three parts, under separate chiefs; deposed by Murchadh, 1135; regained the kingship, 1141; had to give hostages to O'Lochlainn, king of Ailech, 1149, who prevented him from becoming king of Ireland again. [xli. 408]

O'CONOR. [See also O'CONNOR.]

O'CONOR, CHARLES (1710–1791), Irish antiquary; educated in Ireland; published 'Dissertations on the Ancient History of Ireland,' 1753, and a preface and terminal essay to O'Flaherty's 'The Ogygia Vindicated,' and letters on Irish history in Vallancey's 'Collectanea'; collected ancient Irish manuscripts and published pamphlets on the abolition of the political disabilities of Roman catholics. [xli. 410]

O'CONOR, CHARLES (1764–1828), Irish antiquary and librarian; grandson of Charles O'Conor (1710–1791) [q. v.]; educated at Rome, 1779–91; chaplain and librarian at Stowe to Richard Grenville, afterwards duke of Buckingham and Chandos [q. v.]; wrote a memoir of his grandfather, 1796; supported the royal veto on catholic episcopal appointments in Ireland in 'Columbanus ad Hibernos,' 1810–13; published the annals of Tighearnach, of Ulster, and of the Four Masters, and other chronicles from the Stowe Library as 'Rerum Hibernicarum Scriptores Veteres,' 1814–26, an inaccurate work; became insane before his death. [xli. 412]

O'CONOR, MATTHEW (1773–1844), Irish historical writer; brother of Charles O'Conor (1764–1828) [q. v.]; studied at Rome; barrister; wrote on Irish military history. [xli. 413]

O'CONOR, WILLIAM ANDERSON (1820–1887), author; B.A. Trinity College, Dublin, 1864; Latin lecturer at St. Aidan's theological college, Birkenhead; attracted notice as an eloquent and original preacher when rector of St. Simon and St. Jude, Manchester, 1858–87; wrote on theology and Irish history. [xli. 414]

OCTA, OCGA, OHT, or **OIRIC** (*d.* 532?), king of Kent; son of Aesc or Oisc [q. v.]; succeeded his father, *c.* 512; reigned over the Jutish invaders in Kent. [xli. 414]

O'CULLANE, JOHN (1754–1816), Irish poet and schoolmaster; many of his poems extant in Munster. [xli. 415]

O'CURRY, EUGENE (1796–1862), Irish scholar; obtained employment in the topographical section of the Irish ordnance survey, 1834–7; copied and arranged Irish manuscripts; first professor of Irish history and archæology in the Catholic University of Ireland, 1855; gave an account of mediæval Irish manuscripts and their contents in his lectures (published, 1860 and 1873); his text

and translation of two mediæval Irish tales published by the Celtic Society, 1855. His facsimile copies in Irish character of manuscripts are preserved at Trinity College, Dublin, and the Royal Irish Academy. [xli. 415]

O'DALY, AENGUS (*d.* 1350), Irish poet. [xli. 416]

O'DALY, AENGUS (*d.* 1617), Irish poet; wrote an abusive poem on the Irish tribes; assassinated. [xli. 417]

O'DALY, DANIEL or DOMINIC (1595–1662). [See DALY.]

O'DALY, DONNCHADH (*d.* 1244), Irish poet; the most famous member of the greatest family of hereditary poets in Ireland; more than thirty poems, chiefly on devotional subjects, attributed to him. [xli. 417]

O'DALY, MUIREDHACH (*fl.* 1213), Irish poet; having killed O'Donnell's steward fled from place to place, followed by O'Donnell; wrote in Scotland three poems in praise of O'Donnell, which led to his being forgiven. [xli. 418]

ODDA. [See ODO.]

ODELL, THOMAS (1691–1749), playwright; wrote political lampoons for Walpole; built a theatre in Leman Street, London, 1729, which he sold to Giffard, 1731; deputy-licenser of the stage, 1738; composed 'The Chimera,' 1729, 'The Smugglers,' 1729, 'The Patron,' 1730, and 'The Prodigal,' 1744. [xli. 418]

O'DEMPSEY, DERMOT (*d.* 1193), Irish chief; became chief of the Clan Mailughra, 1162, and subsequently of the group of clans allied to his own; founded a Cistercian abbey at Rosglas, 1178. [xli. 419]

O'DEVANY or **O'DUANE**, CORNELIUS (1533–1612), called in Irish Conchobhar O'Duibheannaigh, Roman catholic bishop of Down and Connor; appointed to the bishopric, 1582, and consecrated at Rome; twice arrested for religious reasons; arrested for complicity in Tyrone's rebellion and executed. [xli. 419]

ODGER, GEORGE (1820–1877), trade unionist; a shoemaker, who became secretary to the London trades council, 1862; believed in the combination of trade-unionism with political action, and made five unsuccessful attempts to enter parliament; president of the international association of working men, 1870. [xli. 420]

ODINGSELLS, GABRIEL (1690–1734), playwright; author of three indifferent comedies; committed suicide while insane. [xli. 421]

ODINGTON, WALTER, or WALTER OF EVESHAM (*fl.* 1320). [See WALTER.]

ODO or **ODA** (*d.* 959), archbishop of Canterbury, called 'the Good'; was early converted to Christianity; adopted and educated by Æthelhelm, a noble, with whom he went to Rome; ordained at Rome; esteemed by Æthelstan, who gave him the bishopric of Ramsbury, 927, and the archbishopric of Canterbury, 942; restored Canterbury Cathedral and promoted the reformation of morals, the rights of the church, and the restoration of monastic discipline; published constitutions respecting these matters during Edmund's reign; accompanied Edred to the north, 947, and translated the Ripon relics to Canterbury; crowned Edwy, 956, and separated him from Ælfgifu. [xli. 421]

ODO or **ODDA**, EARL (*d.* 1056), a kinsman of Edward the Confessor; had an hereditary connection with Mercia; became, on the banishment of Godwine and Harold (1051) Earl of Somerset, Devon, Dorset, and 'the Wealas,' losing his earldom on their return; compensated with the earldom of the Hwiccas; built the minster at Deerhurst for his brother's soul. [xli. 423]

ODO (*d.* 1097), bishop of Bayeux and earl of Kent; half-brother of William the Conqueror, who made him bishop of Bayeux, 1049; accompanied the Normans to England, fought at Hastings (1066), and was rewarded with Dover Castle and the earldom of Kent, 1066; viceroy in William's absence, ruling harshly; second in power only to William himself; acquired vast wealth; built himself a palace at Rome and aspired to succeed Hildebrand as pope, but was arrested by William I and kept captive at Rouen till William's death; was unable to regain his old power under William II and became the

centre of conspiracy ; besieged at Pevensey and Rochester, and was obliged to leave England, 1088 ; held a prominent position under Robert in Normandy ; present at
the proclamation of the first crusade, 1095, and elected to
accompany Robert as crusader, 1096 ; died at Palermo in
Sicily ; a liberal patron of religion and learning.
[xli. 424]

ODO OF CANTERBURY (d. 1200), abbot of Battle ; also
called Odo Cantianus ; a monk of Christchurch, Canterbury ; sub-prior, 1163 ; represented Canterbury at Rome,
1163 ; vacillated between the king and Becket, but took
the ecclesiastical side on Becket's murder ; recommended
for the archbishopric, 1173, but not chosen ; became
abbot of Battle, 1175 ; chosen a second time as archbishop, but again refused by the king, 1184 ; commissioned by the pope to remonstrate with Archbishop Baldwin (d. 1190) [q. v.] on his quarrel with his monks, 1187.
There is some uncertainty as to his writings owing to
confusion with other writers of the same name.
[xli. 426]

ODO OF CHERITON, or, less familiarly, SHERSTON (d.
1247), fabulist and preacher ; completed his sermons on
the gospels, 1219 ; illustrated his arguments by quaint
extracts from the bestiaries and from older collections of
fables, some of which he formed into a separate collection
as 'Parabolæ.'   [xli. 428]

O'DOGHERTY, SIR CAHIR (1587-1608), lord of
Inishowen ; a minor at his father's death, but supported
as chief of Inishowen by Sir Henry Docwra [q. v.] ;
knighted on the field of Augher ; visited England, 1603 ;
insulted by Sir George Paulet [q. v.], 1608, and in revenge
seized Culmore Castle and sacked and burnt Derry, 1608 ;
shot during an engagement near Kilmacrenan.
[xli. 429]

O'DOHERTY, WILLIAM JAMES (1835-1868), sculptor ; studied at Dublin ; came to London, 1854, and
exhibited from 1857 ; visited Rome, 1865 ; died in hospital
in Berlin.   [xli. 431]

O'DOIRNIN, PETER (1682-1768), Irish poet and
schoolmaster ; composed poems, including one on the
ancient divisions of Ireland.   [xli. 431]

O'DOMHNUILL, WILLIAM (d. 1628). [See DANIEL.]

ODONE, WILLIAM OF (d. 1298). [See HOTHUM.]

O'DONNEL, JAMES LOUIS (1738-1811), ' the Apostle
of Newfoundland ' ; educated at Rome and ordained
priest at Prague ; prior of the Franciscan house at
Waterford, 1779 ; went as vicar-apostolic to Newfoundland, 1784 ; consecrated bishop of Thyatira, 1796 ; divided
the diocese into missions, 1801 ; resigned, 1807.
[xli. 432]

O'DONNELL, CALVAGH (d. 1566), lord of Tyrconnel ; son of Manus O'Donnell [q. v.] ; quarrelled with
his father and claimed the leadership of the clan, 1547 ;
reconciled to his father by the lord-deputy, 1549 ; being
again at feud with his father, went to Scotland, and returning with assistance, 1555, captured him and usurped
the government, which was acquiesced in by England,
1558 ; surprised and captured by Shane O'Neill, 1561 ;
released, 1564 ; went to England to solicit aid from
Queen Elizabeth ; returned with Sir Henry Sidney [q. v.],
and was restored by him, 1566, but died soon afterwards.
[xli 432]

O'DONNELL, DANIEL (1666-1735), brigadier-general
in the Irish brigade in the French service ; appointed
captain in James II's army, 1688 ; transferred to the
French service, 1691 ; served in Germany, Italy, and the
Netherlands, 1707-12 ; brigadier-general, 1719 ; died at
St. Germain-en-Laye.   [xli. 434]

O'DONNELL, GODFREY (d. 1258), Irish chief ;
made chief, 1248 ; made successful raids into Tyrone and
Lower Connaught ; was victorious but severely wounded
at Roscede, 1257 ; fought victoriously against O'Neill,
1258, but died from his old wounds.   [xli. 435]

O'DONNELL, HUGH BALLDEARG (d. 1704), Irish
soldier of fortune ; had property in Spain, went to Ireland without permission, 1690, raised ten thousand men
for Tyrconnel, with whom he quarrelled, joined the
Williamites, and contributed to the fall of Sligo ; subsequently fought for Austria ; returned to Spain, 1697 ;
became major-general in the Spanish army. [xli. 435]

O'DONNELL, HUGH ROE (1571 ?-1602), lord of
Tyrconnel ; grandson of Manus O'Donnell [q. v.] ; seized
by stratagem as a hostage for his father's loyalty, 1587,
escaped and was recaptured, but escaped again, 1591,
when his father surrendered the chieftaincy in his favour ;
formally submitted to government, 1592, but applied to
Spain for assistance, and secretly helped Hugh Maguire
[q. v.] against the English ; made a marauding expedition into Connaught, which he gained by the destruction
of Sligo Castle and other fortresses, 1595 ; invaded and
plundered Connaught, 1597 ; forced by O'Conor Sligo,
who had established himself at Sligo with English assistance, to retreat across the Erne ; assisted Tyrone in defeating the English at Yellow Ford and received O'Conor
Sligo's submission, 1598 ; lost Lifford and Donegal, his
cousin Niall Garv O'Donnell [q. v.] having deserted to
the English, 1600 ; on the arrival of the Spanish went
southwards and attacked the English besieging Kinsale ;
went to Spain, 1602, but gained no assistance ; died from
poison at Simancas.   [xli. 436]

O'DONNELL, JOHN FRANCIS (1837-1874), poet ;
journalist in Limerick, 1854, in London, 1856, in Dublin,
1862, in London again, 1864 ; contributed prose and
verse to the 'Nation,' and was one of the ablest fenian
propagandists in the press ; published two volumes of
poems.   [xli. 440]

O'DONNELL, MANUS (d. 1564), lord of Tyrconnel ;
deputy-governor of Tyrconnel, 1510 ; forced by his quarrels with his brothers into an alliance with O'Neill ; became
chief, 1537 ; with O'Neill invaded the Pale, 1539, but was
utterly routed ; submitted to the lord-deputy, 1541, and
released his brothers in deference to St. Leger's wishes,
1542 ; attacked by his son Calvagh O'Donnell [q. v.], 1548,
who was defeated, but (1555) succeeded in taking |his
father prisoner and usurping his authority ; built the castle
of Portnatrynod, where the 'Life of St. Columbkille' was
completed under his direction, 1532.   [xli. 441]

O'DONNELL, MARY STUART (fl. 1632), daughter
of Rory O'Donnell, first earl of Tyrconnel [q. v.] ;
escaped from her grandmother in male attire, 1626 ; was
suspected at Bristol, but succeeded in reaching Brussels ;
continued her adventures as a man and married an
O'Gallagher.   [xli. 446]

O'DONNELL, SIR NIALL GARV (1569-1626), grandson of Calvagh O'Donnell [q. v.] ; objected to the election
of his cousin Hugh Roe O'Donnell [q. v.] as chief of Tyrconnel ; promised the grant of Tyrconnel by Sir Henry
Docwra, 1600 ; wrested Lifford and Donegal from his
cousin ; resented the establishment of Sir Cahir O'Dogherty
[q. v.] as Lord of Inishowen ; caused himself to be inaugurated chief, 1602, and proceeded to London to receive
pardon for his insubordination ; arrested for complicity
in O'Dogherty's rebellion, 1608, the jury eventually refusing to convict him ; sent to the Tower of London,
1609, where he died.   [xli. 443]

O'DONNELL, RORY, first EARL OF TYRCONNEL
(1575-1608), grandson of Manus and brother of Hugh
Roe O'Donnell [q. v.] ; became acting chief on his
brother's flight to Spain, 1602 ; created Earl of Tyrconnel, 1603, and granted the greater part of Donegal, 1604 ;
with Tyrone aimed at tribal independence, and in 1606
divulged to Richard Nugent, lord Delvin, a plan to seize
Dublin and various other places ; finding his rash speeches
were known, left Ireland with the Earl of Tyrone and
various relatives, 1607 ; with them landed in France and
went to Brussels and Louvain and finally through
Switzerland to Rome, where he was well received ; died
of Roman fever ; in his formal statement of his grievances
he put religious disabilities in the foreground. His flight
cleared the way for the settlement of Ulster. [xli. 444]

O'DONOVAN, EDMUND (1844-1883), newspaper
correspondent ; son of John O'Donovan [q. v.] ; educated
by the jesuits ; studied medicine at Trinity College,
Dublin ; contributed to newspapers, 1866, joined the
French army, 1870, wrote letters on his experiences to
London and Dublin papers ; proceeded to Spain, 1873, and
represented the 'Daily News' in Asia Minor, 1876 ; accomplished a hazardous journey to Merv, 1879, an account of
which he published, 1882 ; perished with the army of Hicks
Pasha in the Soudan.   [xli. 447]

O'DONOVAN, JOHN (1809-1861), Irish scholar ;
obtained work in the Irish Record Office, 1826 ; appointed

to the historical department of the Irish ordnance survey, 1829; called to the Irish bar, 1847; employed to transcribe legal manuscripts by the commission for the publication of the ancient laws of Ireland, 1852; transcribed, translated, and edited the 'Annals of the Four Masters,' 1848-51; published, among other works, poems and tales and a 'Grammar of the Irish Language,' 1845.
[xli. 448]

O'DUANE, CORNELIUS (1533-1612). [See O'DEVANY.]

O'DUGAN, JOHN, THE GREAT (d. 1372), Irish historian and poet; belonged to a literary family, ollamhs to O'Kelly; made a pilgrimage to St. Columba's tomb and retired to a monastery on Lough Rea. He wrote valuable historical poems describing Ireland, the early kings of Ireland, and the kings of Leinster and Munster.
[xli. 450]

O'DUINN, GILLANANAEMH (1102-1160), Irish historian; chief poet of the king of Leinster; five of his historical poems extant. [xlii. 1]

O'FARRELLY, FEARDORCHA (*fl.* 1736), Irish poet; his works chiefly in manuscript books in farmhouses of Meath and Cavan. [xlii. 1]

O'FERRALL, RICHARD MORE (1797-1880), governor of Malta; M.P., co. Kildare, 1830-46 and 1859-65, co. Longford, 1850-1; a lord of the treasury, 1835; secretary to the admiralty, 1839, to the treasury, 1841; privy councillor, 1847; governor of Malta, 1847-51. [xlii. 2]

OFFA (*fl.* 709), king of the East-Saxons; died while on pilgrimage at Rome. [xlii. 2]

OFFA (d. 796), king of the Mercians from 757; subjugated the Hestingi, 771; defeated Kentishmen at Otford, 775; subjected the East-Saxons and gained London; defeated West-Saxons at Bensington, 779, and took territory beyond Severn from Welsh; made Offa's Dyke from mouth of Wye to mouth of Dee; allied himself with the West-Saxon house, 789; described as King of the English by Pope Hadrian I, who sanctioned formation of archbishopric of Lichfield, 788; made first yearly payments to Rome; traded and corresponded with Charlemagne; a liberal benefactor of some monasteries; made alliance with Northumbria in later years; caused Æthelbert (d. 794) [q. v.], king of East Anglia, to be beheaded, 794; again at war with Welsh and men of Kent. His laws are not extant, but were used by Alfred. [xlii. 2]

OFFALEY, BARONESS (1588?-1658). [See DIGBY, LETTICE, LADY.]

OFFALY, LORDS OR BARONS OF. [See FITZGERALD, GERALD, d. 1204; FITZGERALD, MAURICE, 1194?-1257; FITZTHOMAS, JOHN, first EARL OF KILDARE, d. 1316; FITZGERALD, THOMAS, tenth EARL OF KILDARE, 1513-1537.]

OFFLEY, SIR THOMAS (1505?-1582), lord mayor of London; educated under William Lily [q. v.] at St. Paul's School, London; master of Merchant Taylors' Company, London, 1547; alderman, 1549; sheriff, 1553; lord mayor of London, 1556; knighted, 1557; originated night bellmen; made many charitable bequests.
[xlii. 5]

OFFOR, GEORGE (1787-1864), editor and biographer of Bunyan, and collector of early English bibles, psalters, and testaments; most of his library burnt at Sotheby's, 1865. [xlii. 6]

OFFORD, ANDREW (d. 1358), clerk or master in chancery; brother of John de Offord [q. v.]; employed in negotiations with the pope, France, Castile, Flanders, and Bavaria; one of the council of regency, 1345; prebendary of Salisbury and York; provost of Wells, 1350; had charge of great seal, 1353. [xlii. 7]

OFFORD or **UFFORD**, JOHN DE (d. 1349), chancellor of England and archbishop-elect of Canterbury; educated probably at Cambridge; dean of arches; archdeacon of Ely, 1335; keeper of the privy seal, 1342; dean of Lincoln, 1344; chancellor of England, 1345-9; much employed in negotiations with European courts; archbishop-elect of Canterbury, 1348. [xlii. 7]

O'FIHELY, DOMHNALL (*fl.* 1505), author of lost 'Irish Annals.' [xlii. 9]

O'FIHELY, MAURICE (d. 1513), archbishop of Tuam; known as Mauritius de Portu; regent of Franciscan

schools at Milan, 1488; lectured on theology at Padua; archbishop of Tuam, 1506, but continued to reside in Italy; present at Lateran council, 1512; edited works by Duns Scotus. [xlii. 8]

O'FLAHERTY, RODERIC (1629-1718), historiographer; published 'Ogygia, seu rerum Hibernicarum chronologia,' 1685; his 'Chorographical Description of West or H-Iar Connaught,' edited by James Hardiman [q. v.], 1846. [xlii. 9]

O'FLYN, FIACHA (d. 1256). [See MacFLYNN, FLORENCE or FLANN.]

OFTFOR (d. 692), bishop of Worcester; consecrated, 692. [xlii. 10]

OGBORNE, DAVID (d. 1801), artist and author; best known by his picture representing the Dunmow 'flitch of bacon' ceremony. [xlii. 10]

OGBORNE, ELIZABETH (1763-1853), author of an unfinished 'History of Essex'; wife of John Ogborne [q. v.] [xlii. 11]

OGBORNE, JOHN (1755-1837), stipple-engraver; son of David Ogborne [q. v.] [xlii. 11]

OGDEN, JAMES (1718-1802), Manchester poet and author of 'A Description of Manchester' (1783).
[xlii. 11]

OGDEN, JONATHAN ROBERT (1806-1882), musical composer; pupil of Moscheles and August Friedrich Christoph Kollman [q. v.]; published 'Holy Songs and Musical Prayers,' 1842. [xlii. 12]

OGDEN, SAMUEL (1628?-1697), presbyterian divine; of Christ's College, Cambridge; B.A.; vicar of Mackworth, 1657-62; kept school there, and afterwards at Derby and Wirksworth. [xlii. 12]

OGDEN, SAMUEL (1716-1778), divine; of Manchester School and St. John's College, Cambridge; M.A., 1741, D.D., 1753, senior fellow, 1758; master of free school, Halifax, 1744-53; popular as preacher at round church of the Holy Sepulchre, Cambridge, 1753-71; Woodwardian professor of geology, 1764-78; incumbent of Lawford and Stansfield, 1766-78; classical scholar and orientalist.
[xlii. 13]

OGILBY, JOHN (1600-1676), author and printer; in early life taught dancing; employed by Strafford in Ireland, where he became deputy-master, and afterwards master of the revels; entrusted with 'poetical part' of Charles II's coronation, 1661; his house and booksellers' stock destroyed in fire of London, 1666; afterwards set up large printing establishment and became 'king's cosmographer'; published verse translations of Virgil, Æsop's 'Fables,' and Homer, with plates by Hollar, and printed an edition of the bible (Cambridge, 1660), a folio Virgil, 'Entertainment of Charles II,' and many geographical works. He was ridiculed by Dryden and Pope, but utilised by the latter. [xlii. 14]

OGILVIE. [See also OGILVY.]

OGILVIE, CHARLES ATMORE (1793-1873), theologian; fellow of Balliol College, Oxford, 1816-34; M.A., 1818, D.D., 1842, lecturer, 1836; rector and vicar of Ross from 1839; first regius professor of pastoral theology at Oxford, 1842-73; canon of Christ Church, 1849; friend of Routh and Blanco White. [xlii. 17]

OGILVIE, JAMES (1760-1820), claimant of earldom of Findlater; lectured in Virginia; published 'Philosophical Essays,' 1816. [xlii. 18]

OGILVIE or **OGILBY**, JOHN (1580?-1615), jesuit; admitted to the society at Olmütz and ordained at Paris; came to Scotland in disguise, 1613; visited London and Paris, 1614; arrested at Glasgow and examined by special commission at Edinburgh, where, being denied sleep and rest, he revealed names of accomplices; tried and executed for stirring up rebellion. [xlii. 18]

OGILVIE, JOHN (1733-1813), presbyterian divine and author; M.A. Aberdeen; minister of Midmar from 1759; D.D. Aberdeen, 1766; member of committee for revision of 'Scottish Translations and Paraphrases,' 1775; published poems and apologetic treatises. [xlii. 20]

OGILVIE, JOHN (1797-1867), lexicographer; a ploughman till twenty-one; M.A. Aberdeen, 1828; hon. LL.D. Aberdeen, 1848; mathematical master in Gordon's

Hospital, Aberdeen, 1831–59 ; compiled 'Imperial Dictionary,' 1850 (supplement, 1855), 'Comprehensive English Dictionary,' 1863, and 'Students' English Dictionary,' 1865. [xlii. 21]

OGILVIE, WILLIAM (1736–1819), professor of humanity and advocate of common property in land ; studied at Glasgow, Aberdeen, and Edinburgh ; professor of philosophy, King's College, Aberdeen, 1762–5, of humanity, 1765–1817 ; hon. D.D. Columbia College, 1793 ; advocated union of Marischal and King's Colleges ; published 'Essay on the Right of Property in Land' (1781), advocating common ownership ; classical scholar and numismatist. [xlii. 21]

OGILVY. [See also OGILVIE.]

OGILVY, ALEXANDER, second BARON OF INVERQUHARITY (d. 1456), sheriff of Kincardine ; excommunicated for raid on Bishop Kennedy's lands in Fife and Angus, 1444 ; died in Finhaven Castle after his defeat and capture by the master of Crawford. [xlii. 22]

OGILVY, SIR ALEXANDER, first baronet and LORD FORGLEN (d. 1727), Scottish judge ; created baronet, 1701 ; M.P. for Banff burgh in Scots parliament, 1702–7 ; lord of session, 1706 ; commissioner for the union. [xlii. 23]

OGILVY, DAVID, LORD OGILVY and titular EARL OF AIRLIE (1725–1803), Jacobite : of Aberdeen and Edinburgh Universities ; joined Prince Charles Edward with six hundred men, 1745 ; commanded cavalry during retreat from Derby ; fought at Falkirk, 1746, and Culloden, 1746 ; escaped to Norway ; lived in France till 1778, becoming lieutenant-general in French army ; returned to Scotland, being restored to full rights, 1782. [xlii. 23]

OGILVY, SIR GEORGE, of Dunlugas, first BARON BANFF (d. 1663), created baronet of Nova Scotia, 1627 ; slew his cousin James, 1628 ; supported the royal cause against the covenanters, whom he defeated in the Trot of Turriff, 1639 ; one of the accusers of Hamilton, 1634 ; created a Scots peer, 1642. [xlii. 24]

OGILVY, SIR GEORGE, of Barras, first baronet (fl. 1634–1679), created a Nova Scotia baronet at the Restoration for his defence of Dunottar Castle against Cromwell and preservation of the regalia of Scotland, 1651–2. [xlii. 25]

OGILVY or **OGILVIE**, JAMES, fifth or sixth BARON OGILVY OF AIRLIE (d. 1605), partisan of Mary Queen of Scots ; a lord of the articles, 1559 ; joined Mary's raid against Moray ; subscribed band for Bothwell marriage, 1567, and Hamilton band of 1568 ; declared a rebel, 1569 ; escaped Morton's attack, 1569, and went abroad ; employed by Mary Queen of Scots to negotiate with Mar and Morton, 1571 and 1577 ; member of the privy council and one of the eight 'notable men,' 1578 ; subscribed confession of faith, 1581 ; intermediary between Mary Queen of Scots and James VI ; helped to overthrow Morton, 1581, after whose death he obtained grants of land. [xlii. 26]

OGILVY, JAMES, first EARL OF AIRLIE (1593 ?– 1666), royalist ; grandson of James Ogilvy, fifth or sixth baron Ogilvy of Airlie [q. v.] ; created earl, 1639 ; joined Montrose, 1644 ; his forfeiture rescinded, 1647. [xlii. 27]

OGILVY, JAMES, second EARL OF AIRLIE (1615 ?– 1704 ?), aide-de-camp of Montrose ; son of James Ogilvy, first earl of Airlie [q. v.] ; held Airlie Castle against covenanters, and was allowed by Montrose to escape, 1640 ; accompanied Montrose to court of Charles I, 1643 ; captured in Lancashire carrying despatches to the king, 1644 ; released from prison after Kilsyth, 1645, but captured at Philiphaugh, 1645 ; was condemned to death, but escaped and secured pardon ; took part in Pluscarden's rising, 1649 ; again captured, 1651, and imprisoned in Tower of London till 1657 ; declared for William of Orange at the revolution. [xlii. 28]

OGILVY, JAMES, fourth EARL OF FINDLATER and first EARL OF SEAFIELD (1664–1730), lord chancellor of Scotland ; called to bar, 1685 ; M.P., Banffshire, 1681–2 and 1689–95 ; solicitor-general, 1693 ; secretary of state, 1696–1702, and joint-secretary, 1704–5 ; created Viscount Seafield and appointed president of the parliament, 1698 ; unpopular as opponent of the African Company ; commissioner to general assembly, 1700 ; created earl, 1701 ; commissioner for the union, 1702, and active as its promoter, 1706–7 ; lord chancellor of Scotland, 1702–4 and 1705–7 ; Scottish representative peer from 1707 ; privy

councillor of England, 1707 ; lord chief baron in the court of exchequer, 1707 ; succeeded as Earl of Findlater, 1711 ; moved repeal of the union, 1713, but soon afterwards became keeper of the great seal. [xlii. 29]

OGILVY, JAMES, sixth EARL OF FINDLATER and third EARL OF SEAFIELD (1714 ?–1770), agriculturist ; known as Lord Deskford till 1764 ; Scots commissioner of customs, 1754–61 ; a lord of police, 1765. [xlii. 31]

OGILVY, JOHN (fl. 1592–1601), political adventurer ('Powrie-Ogilvy') ; professed to be accredited agent of James VI in Flanders and at Rome, 1595, and in Spain, 1596 ; imprisoned at Barcelona ; employed by Cecil in Scotland as 'John Gibson,' 1600. [xlii. 31]

OGILVY or **OGILVIE**, SIR PATRICK, seventh BARON OF BOYNE (fl. 1707), a lord of session, 1681 ; knighted, 1681 ; M.P., Banffshire, 1669–93 ; signed the 'assurance' and entered into relations with the Pretender. [xlii. 32]

OGILVY or **OGILVIE**, SIR WALTER (d. 1440), of Lintrathen ; lord high treasurer of Scotland, 1425–31 ; commissioner to negotiate with England, 1430 ; treasurer of the household, 1431. [xlii. 32]

O'GLACAN, NIAL (fl. 1629–1655), physician ; native of Donegal ; treated patients for plague in France ; published 'Tractatus de Peste,' 1629 ; afterwards professor at Toulouse and physician to the king ; published, at Bologna, 'Cursus Medicus,' 1646–55. [xlii. 33]

OGLANDER, SIR JOHN (1585–1655), author of 'Diary' (ed. W. H. Long, 1888) : of Balliol College, Oxford, and the Middle Temple ; knighted, 1615 ; deputy-governor of the Isle of Wight, 1624–43 ; sheriff of Hampshire ; arrested for royalism, 1643 and 1651. [xlii. 34]

OGLE, SIR CHALONER (1681 ?–1750), admiral of the fleet ; entered the navy, 1697 ; when commander of the Tartar frigate made valuable prizes in the Mediterranean ; knighted (1723) for capture of pirates off Cape Lopez ; commander-in-chief in Jamaica, 1732 ; rear-admiral, 1739 ; with Vernon in attack on Carthagena, 1742, succeeding him in command ; vice-admiral, 1743 ; admiral, 1744 ; admiral and commander-in-chief, 1749. [xlii. 34]

OGLE, SIR CHARLES, second baronet (1775–1858), admiral of the fleet ; grand-nephew of Sir Chaloner Ogle [q. v.] ; entered the navy, 1787 ; posted, 1797 ; commander-in-chief in North America, 1827–30, at Portsmouth, 1845–8. [xlii. 36]

OGLE, CHARLES CHALONER (1851–1878), 'Times' correspondent in Montenegro and Thessaly, 1876–1878 ; probably assassinated by Turks at Katochori, near Volo, after second battle of Macrynitza. [xlii. 36]

OGLE, GEORGE (1704–1746), translator of Anacreon and Horace ; published 'Antiquities explained' (vol. i.), 1737 ; contributed to modernised versions of Chaucer, 1741. [xlii. 37]

OGLE, GEORGE (1742–1814), Irish politician and composer of 'Banna's Banks' and 'Molly Asthore' ; as M.P. for Wexford county, 1768–96, and Dublin, 1798–1800, in Irish parliament supported legislative independence, but opposed catholic emancipation ; colonel in the volunteers, 1782 ; Irish privy councillor, 1783 ; governor of Wexford, 1796 ; represented Dublin in imperial parliament, 1801–4. [xlii. 37]

OGLE, JAMES ADEY (1792–1857), physician ; of Eton and Trinity College, Oxford ; M.A., 1816 ; M.D., 1820 ; studied also at Edinburgh and on the continent ; practised at Oxford and became Aldrich professor of medicine, 1824, clinical, 1830, and regius professor, 1851 ; as mathematical tutor at Trinity College, Oxford, had John Henry Newman [q. v.] as pupil ; advocated establishment of science school at Oxford, 1841 ; F.R.C.P., 1822 ; F.R.S., 1826 ; Harveian orator, 1844. [xlii. 39]

OGLE, SIR JOHN (1569–1640), military commander ; sergeant-major-general under Sir Francis Vere in the Low Countries, 1591 ; as lieutenant-colonel rallied the English forces at Nieuport, 1600 ; knighted, 1603 ; helped to recover Sluys, 1604 ; governor of Utrecht for the stadtholder Maurice, 1610–18 ; granted coat-armour by James I, 1615 ; member of the council of war, 1624 ; active member of the Virginia Company ; employed in Ireland under Wentworth. [xlii. 39]

OGLE, JOHN (1647 ?–1685 ?), gamester and buffoon; mentioned in the 'Tatler' (No. 132). [xlii. 41]

OGLE, OWEN, second BARON OGLE (*fl.* 1483–1494), son of Robert Ogle, first baron Ogle [q. v.]; first summoned to parliament, 1483, last summoned, 1485; with Henry VII's army at Stoke, 1486, and Surrey's at relief of Norham, 1494. [xlii. 41]

OGLE, SIR ROBERT DE (*d.* 1362), soldier; captured five Scottish knights, and was allowed to castellate Ogle House, Northumberland, 1341; distinguished himself in resisting the foray into Cumberland of Sir William Douglas, 1345; fought at Neville's Cross, 1346; held Berwick Castle, 1355. [xlii. 42]

OGLE, ROBERT, first BARON OGLE (*d* 1469), Yorkist; descendant of Sir Robert de Ogle [q. v.]; sheriff of Northumberland, 1438; brought six hundred men to the Yorkists at first battle of St. Albans, 1455; summoned to parliament as baron, 1461, and made warden of the east marches; received grants of forfeited Percy and Talbots estates; distinguished himself in the dash upon Holy island, 1462; constable of Bamborough, 1464. [xlii. 42]

OGLETHORPE, JAMES EDWARD (1696–1785), colonist of Georgia; entered the army, 1710; of Corpus Christi College, Oxford; served as volunteer in eastern Europe with Prince Eugene; chairman of parliamentary committee on debtors' prisons, 1729; obtained charter for settlement of Georgia as a refuge for paupers and a barrier for British colonies against Spanish aggression, 1732; encountered during his administration of the new colony much opposition, owing to his prohibition of negro slavery and rum, and had difficulties with the Wesleys and Whitfield; successfully, and partly at his own expense, defended Georgia against the Spaniards, allying himself with the Indians, but failed in an attack on St. Augustine, 1740; named brigadier-general, 1743; returned to England, 1743; served in Lancashire against the Jacobites, 1745; was accused by Cumberland of misconduct, and, though acquitted, did not return to military life; as M.P., Haslemere, for thirty-two years acted at first with the Jacobite tories, and afterwards as an independent whig; friend of Dr. Johnson and his circle, and immortalised by Pope. [xlii. 43]

OGLETHORPE, OWEN (*d.* 1559), bishop of Carlisle; fellow of Magdalen College, Oxford, 1526; M.A., 1529; D.D., 1536; president of Magdalen, 1535–52; junior proctor, 1533, and vice-chancellor, 1551; held numerous livings and a canonry of Christ Church, Oxford; canon of Windsor and one of Cranmer's commissioners on the sacraments, 1540; entertained Peter Martyr, Bucer, and Coverdale at Magdalen College, Oxford, but was much attacked by the puritans, and obliged to retire from the presidency, 1552; reappointed by Queen Mary; one of the Oxford divines who disputed with Cranmer, Ridley, and Latimer; dean of Windsor, 1553; as bishop of Carlisle (1557–9) crowned Queen Elizabeth, but was deprived, 1559; founded a school at Tadcaster, his birthplace. [xlii. 48]

OGLETHORPE, SIR THEOPHILUS (1650–1702), brigadier-general; served in Charles II's lifeguards; as lieutenant-colonel of royal dragoons commanded advance guard of Monmouth at Bothwell Brigg, 1679; routed rebels at Keynsham and led charge at Sedgmoor, 1685; brigadier-general and principal equerry to James II; returned from France and took oaths to William and Mary, 1698; M.P., Haslemere, 1698–1702; his daughter Anne said to have been mistress of James Edward, the Old Pretender. [xlii. 50]

O'GORMAN, MAELMUIRE (*d.* 1181), martyrologist and abbot of Cnoc or Louth, known also as Marianus Gorman and Maelmuire O'Dunian; his 'Martyrology,' in Irish verse (composed, 1156–73), recently edited by Dr. Whitley Stokes for Bradshaw Society. [xlii. 51]

O'GORMAN MAHON, THE (1800–1891). [See MAHON, CHARLES JAMES PATRICK.]

O'GRADY, STANDISH, first VISCOUNT GUILLAMORE (1766–1840), lord chief baron of the Irish exchequer, 1805–1831; B.A. Trinity College, Dublin, 1784; attorney-general, 1803; a noted wit; created Irish peer, 1831. [xlii. 51]

O'GRADY, STANDISH, second VISCOUNT GUILLAMORE (1792–1848), soldier; son of Standish O'Grady, first viscount Guillamore [q. v.]; did good service as officer of the 7th hussars at Waterloo and on the preceding day; afterwards lieutenant-colonel. [xlii. 52]

OGSTON, FRANCIS (1803–1887), professor at Aberdeen; M.D. Edinburgh, 1824, hon. LL.D. Aberdeen; first professor of medical jurisprudence at Aberdeen, 1857–83; his 'Lectures' (1878) a standard work in England and Germany. [xlii. 52]

O'HAGAN, JOHN (1822–1890), judge; M.A. Trinity College, Dublin, 1865; called to Irish bar, 1842; Q.C., 1865; education commissioner, 1861; active member of the Young Ireland party, and counsel for Gavan Duffy, 1848; judicial commissioner under Irish Land Act of 1881, and patriotic song-writer. [xlii. 53]

O'HAGAN, THOMAS, first BARON O'HAGAN (1812–1885), lord chancellor of Ireland; called to Irish bar, 1836; edited 'Newry Examiner,' 1836–40; friend and supporter of Daniel O'Connell (1775–1847) [q. v.], but opposed his repeal policy and upheld the national system of education; defended Gavan Duffy in libel case, 1842, and acted under Whiteside in trials of 1843–4; offered retainers both by crown and repealers at trials of the agitators, 1848; Q.C., 1849; defended Father Petcherine, 1855; third serjeant and bencher of King's Inns, 1859; solicitor-general for Ireland, 1861, attorney-general, 1862; whig M.P. for Tralee, 1863; judge of common pleas in Ireland, 1865–8; lord chancellor of Ireland, 1868–74 and 1880–1; created peer, 1870, he carried bill for amending the Irish jury system; first vice-chairman of the intermediate education board (established, 1878), and first vice-chancellor of the Royal University of Ireland (founded, 1880). [xlii. 53]

O'HAINGLI, DONAT or DONNGUS (*d.* 1095), bishop of Dublin, 1084–95; a monk of Lanfranc's monastery at Canterbury. [xlii. 55]

O'HAINGLI, SAMUEL (*d.* 1121), last bishop of Dublin, 1096–1121; nephew of Donat O'Haingli [q. v.]; was consecrated by Anselm, but neglected canonical obedience. [xlii. 55]

O'HALLORAN, SIR JOSEPH (1763–1843), major-general in East India Company's service; son of Sylvester O'Halloran [q. v.]; entered Bengal army, 1782; adjutant at Midnapur, 1802; commanded irregulars against Raja Rām, 1805, and led attacks in Rogoulee and Adjeghur, 1809; C.B. for services in Nepaulese campaigns, 1815–16; commandant of 25th Bengal infantry in Straits Settlements, 1818–25; brigadier-general, 1828; knighted after return to England, 1835; major-general, 1837; G.C.B., 1841. [xlii. 56]

O'HALLORAN, LAWRENCE HYNES (1766–1831). [See HALLORAN.]

O'HALLORAN, SYLVESTER (1728–1807), surgeon and antiquary; studied at Paris and Leyden; practised at Limerick, specialising in ophthalmic surgery and treatment of injuries to the head; hon. M.R.C.S. of Ireland, 1786; published 'Ierne Defended,' 1774, and 'General History of Ireland to close of the 12th Century' (1774). [xlii. 57]

O'HALLORAN, THOMAS SHULDHAM (1797–1870), Australian administrator; second son of Sir Joseph O'Halloran [q. v.]; served with 17th foot in Nepaul, 1814–16, and Deccan, 1817–18; on Dunkin's staff in Burmese war, 1824–5; with 6th regiment at Saugor, 1829–34; retired, 1838; settled in South Australia and became commandant of the militia and police commissioner, 1840–3, member of the nominated council, 1843–51, and of the elected legislative council, 1857–63. [xlii. 58]

O'HALLORAN, WILLIAM LITTLEJOHN (1806–1885), auditor-general of South Australia; son of Sir Joseph O'Halloran [q. v.]; served with the 14th and 38th foot, 1824–32; retired, 1840, and went to Australia and became private secretary to the governor and clerk of the councils, 1843; auditor-general, 1851–68. [xlii. 57]

O'HANLON, REDMOND (*d.* 1681), Irish outlaw; having lost his estates during the civil wars became a leader of tories in Ulster, *c.* 1670, levying contributions in Armagh, Tyrone, and Down; left many traditions in Slieve Gullion; held out till treacherously shot by his foster-brother under Ormonde's commission. [xlii. 59]

O'HANLY, DONAT (*d.* 1095). [See O'HAINGLI.]

O'HARA, Sir CHARLES, first BARON TYRAWLEY (1640?–1724), general; lieutenant-colonel of 1st foot-guards, 1688; knighted, 1689; served under William III in Flanders and received colonelcy of royal fusiliers (7th foot); distinguished himself at capture of Vigo and burning of Spanish fleet, 1703, and at Guadalaxara, 1706; created an Irish peer, 1706; Galway's second-in-command in Spain, leading the left wing at Almanza, where he was wounded; privy councillor, 1710; supported Galway against Peterborough in debate on Spanish campaign; general, 1714; commander-in-chief in Ireland, 1714–21. [xlii. 60]

O'HARA, CHARLES (1740?–1802), general; grandson of Sir Charles O'Hara [q. v.]; entered Coldstream guards, of which his father was colonel, 1756; aide-de-camp to Granby after Minden; quartermaster-general under Tyrawley in Portugal, 1762; commandant at Goree, 1766; commanded brigade of guards in America, being wounded at Guilford Courthouse, 1781; and captured at Yorktown, 1781; major-general, and colonel of 22nd, 1782; lieutenant-general, 1793, when he was wounded and captured by the French at Toulon; governor of Gibraltar (where he died), 1795–1802; general, 1798; friend of Horace Walpole, and for some time engaged to Mary Berry [q. v.] [xlii. 61]

O'HARA, JAMES, BARON KILMAINE and second BARON TYRAWLEY (1690–1773), field-marshal and diplomatist; wounded at Almanza and Malplaquet; succeeded his father, Sir Charles O'Hara, first baron Tyrawley [q. v.], as colonel of the royal fusiliers, 1713; created Baron Kilmaine of Ireland, 1722; succeeded to English peerage, 1724; ambassador in Portugal, 1728–41 and 1752–6, and in Russia, 1743–5; major-general, 1739, lieutenant-general, 1743; governor of Minorca, 1752–6, and Gibraltar, 1756–7; general, 1761; field-marshal and governor of Portsmouth, 1763; plenipotentiary and general in Portugal, 1762–3. [xlii. 62]

O'HARA, KANE (1714?–1782), burlesque writer; M.A. Trinity College, Dublin, 1735; lived at Dublin; travestied Italian burletta in 'Midas'; produced also 'The Golden Pippin,' 1773, 'The Two Misers,' 1775, and other pieces. [xlii. 63]

O'HARTAGAIN, CINETH (d. 975), Irish poet. [xlii. 64]

O'HEARN, FRANCIS (1753–1801), divine and traveller; rector of the Irish College, Louvain; wrote poems in Flemish; travelled in Eastern Europe and Siberia; died parish priest in Waterford. [xlii. 64]

O'HELY, PATRICK (d. 1578), Roman catholic bishop of Mayo; Franciscan in Spain; afterwards went to Rome; bishop of Mayo, 1576–8; tried at Kilmallock and hanged. [xlii. 65]

O'HEMPSY, DENIS (1695?–1807), Irish harper; travelled all over Ireland; played before Prince Charles Edward at Holyrood, 1745; attended Belfast meeting of harpers, 1792. [xlii. 65]

O'HENEY, MATTHEW (d. 1206), archbishop of Cashel and (1192) papal legate for Ireland; died a Cistercian monk of Holy Cross (Tipperary); his works lost. [xlii. 66]

O'HIGGIN, CORMAC (fl. 1590), Irish poet. [xlii. 68]

O'HIGGIN, DOMHNALL (d. 1502), 'professor of poetry in the schools of Ireland'; wrote a poem in praise of Ian MacDonald. [xlii. 67]

O'HIGGIN, DOMHNALL (fl. 1600), Irish poet. [xlii. 68]

O'HIGGIN, MAOLMUIRE (d. 1591), poet and archbishop of Tuam; died at Antwerp. [xlii. 68]

O'HIGGIN, MATHGHAMHAIN (fl. 1584), bard to the O'Byrnes of Wicklow. [xlii. 67]

O'HIGGIN, TADHG MÓR (d. 1315), poet and tutor to Maghnus O'Connor Connacht. [xlii. 67]

O'HIGGIN, TADHG ÓG (d. 1448), poet; bard to Tadhg O'Connor Sligo and afterwards to the chief of Ui Maine. [xlii. 60]

O'HIGGIN, TEAGUE (d. 1617), blind poet (Tadhg dall Ua hUiginn), brother of Maolmuire O'Higgin [q. v.]; panegyrised the O'Neills and Burkes; urged Sir Brian O'Rourke (d. 1591) [q. v.] to attack the English, c. 1588; described the home-life of the Maguires. [xlii. 66]

O'HIGGINS (HIGGINS), DON AMBROSIO, MARQUIS DE OSORNO (1720?–1801), viceroy of Peru; of humble Irish parentage; as captain of cavalry in the Chilian service defeated the Indians and founded San Carlos, 1770; when intendant of Concepcion entertained La Pérouse, founded San Ambrosio de Ballenar, and made the road from Santiago to Valparaiso; major-general, 1789, and viceroy of Chili, 1789–96; rebuilt Osorno and was created marquis, 1792; lieutenant-general, 1794; viceroy of Peru, 1795–1801; father of Bernardo, liberator of Chili. [xlii. 68]

OHTHERE (fl. 880), Norse explorer in the service of Alfred the Great; sailed from Halogaland round the North Cape and along the north coast of Lapland to the mouth of the Dwina, and thence southwards to Schleswig. [xlii. 68]

O'HURLEY, DERMOT (1519?–1584), archbishop of Cashel; professor of philosophy at Louvain, c. 1559, and of canon law at Rheims; while at Rome plotted against the English government, which having been apprised of his coming to Ireland as archbishop of Cashel (1581), captured him at Carrick-on-Suir, discovered his correspondence with Desmond and Baltinglas, and, after causing him to be tortured, had him condemned by martial law and hanged at Dublin. [xlii. 69]

O'HUSSEY, EOCHAIDH (fl. 1630), Irish poet (Ua hEodhasa). [xlii. 70]

O'HUSSEY or **O'HEOGHUSA**, MAELBRIGHDE (d. 1614), Irish Franciscan (in religion Bonaventura); guardian of Louvain, where he died; author of devotional works and poems in the Irish language. [xlii. 71]

O'KANE, EACHMARCACH (1720–1790), Irish harper; sometimes known as Acland, played at Rome and Madrid, also in France and Scotland. [xlii. 71]

OKE, GEORGE COLWELL (1821–1874), legal writer; chief clerk to the lord mayor of London; published works including 'Oke's Magisterial Synopsis,' 1849, and 'Magisterial Formulist,' 1850. [xlii. 72]

O'KEARNEY or **CARNEY** (O'CEARNAIDH), JOHN (d. 1600?), Irish divine. [See KEARNEY.]

O'KEEFE, EOGHAN (1656–1726), Irish poet; parish priest of Doneraile. [xlii. 72]

O'KEEFFE, ADELAIDE (1776–1855?), poet and novelist; daughter of John O'Keeffe [q. v.] [xlii. 74]

O'KEEFFE, JOHN (1747–1833), dramatist; twelve years an actor in Henry Mossop's company at Dublin, but gradually became blind; his 'Tony Lumpkin in Town' produced at the Haymarket, 1778; lived in England from 1780 and wrote comic pieces for the Haymarket and Covent Garden, London, among which 'Wild Oats' is still played, and 'The Castle of Andalusia' was revived by Buckstone; author of the famous song 'I am a Friar of Orders Grey' (in his opera 'Merry Sherwood'); received a benefit at Covent Garden, 1800, and a royal pension, 1820; published 'Recollections,' 1826. [xlii. 72]

O'KELLY, CHARLES (1621–1695), Irish historian; served in the royal army in Ireland and France; afterwards in the Spanish service; sat in James II's Irish parliament, 1689; defended Connaught under Sarsfield; his 'Macariæ Excidium' (1692) edited by Crofton Croker, 1841, by John Cornelius O'Callaghan, 1850, and Count Plunket, 1894; author also of the lost 'O'Kelly Memoirs.' [xlii. 74]

O'KELLY, DENNIS (1720?–1787), owner of the racehorse Eclipse and of a famous talking parrot; made a fortune by gaming and horse-breeding. [xlii. 75]

O'KELLY, JOSEPH (1832–1883), geologist; M.A. Trinity College, Dublin, 1860; secretary to Irish Geological Survey, 1865. [xlii. 76]

O'KELLY, PATRICK (1754–1835?), 'Bard O'Kelly'; author of the 'Doneraile Litany' and other verses. [xlii. 76]

O'KELLY, RALPH (d. 1361). [See KELLY.]

OKELY, FRANCIS (1719?–1794), minister of the Unitas Fratrum at Bedford and Nottingham; of the Charterhouse School and St. John's College, Cambridge; B.A., 1739; translated and edited mystical works by Jacob Behmen and others. [xlii. 77]

OKEOVER, OKEVER, or **OKER,** JOHN (*fl.* 1619–1634), organist of Wells Cathedral, 1619; M.B. New College, Oxford, 1633; composer of 'fancies.' [xlii. 78]

OKES, RICHARD (1797–1888), provost of King's College, Cambridge; Browne's medallist, 1819 and 1820; scholar and fellow of King's College, Cambridge; provost, 1850–88; some time master at Eton; editor of 'Musæ Etonenses,' 1796–1833. [xlii. 78]

OKEY, JOHN (*d.* 1662), regicide; colonel of dragoons at Naseby, 1645; led storming party at Bath, but was captured at Bristol, 1645; present at battle of St. Fagan's, 1648; signed Charles I's death-warrant, 1649; created master of arts at Oxford, 1649; took part in and described storming of Dundee, 1651; sat in parliament, 1654; opposed the protectorate and was cashiered for circulating a petition against it; arrested for renewed opposition to Cromwell, 1658; represented Bedfordshire in Richard Cromwell's parliament, which restored him to command; again cashiered for resistance to Lambert, 1659, but regained his regiment the same year; being deprived by Monck, joined Lambert at Daventry, 1660; fled to Germany; arrested at Delft; executed in England. [xlii. 79]

OKEY, SAMUEL (*fl.* 1765–1780), mezzotint engraver after Reynolds; afterwards printseller at Newport, Rhode island, U.S.A. [xlii. 80]

OKHAM, JOHN DE (*fl.* 1317–1322), baron of the exchequer, 1317–22. [xlii. 81]

OKING, ROBERT (*fl.* 1525–1554), archdeacon; D.C.L. Trinity College, Cambridge, 1534; commissary of Cambridge University, 1529, Bangor, 1534; archdeacon of Salisbury, 1539–52; a moderate reformer. [xlii. 81]

OLAF GODFREYSON (*d.* 941), leader of the Ostmen, and king of Dublin (934) and Deira (940); took Lodore, 935; plundered Clonmacnoise abbey; fought at Brunanburh, 937, under Olaf Sitricson [q. v.]; killed near Dunbar. [xlii. 81]

OLAF SITRICSON (*d.* 981), leader of Ostmen, and king of Dublin and Deira (called in sagas 'Olaf the Red'); married daughter of Constantine II of Scotland; defeated, with Olaf Godfreyson [q. v.] and Constantine II, by Athelstan at Brunanburh, 937; shared kingship of Northumbrians with Olaf Godfreyson, 940–1, and afterwards with Reginald; driven out by Eadmund, 944; restored Dublin and established his rule in Ireland, 945; defeated at Slane by O'Cananain, 947; failed in last attempt on Northumbria, 952, having held Deira since 949; allied himself with Toole in Ireland; slew Congalach, 956; slew the heirs of both northern and southern O'Neill and won victory at Belan, 977; resigned Dublin after defeat of Tara, 980; died at Iona. [xlii. 82]

OLAF (1117?–1238), king of the Isles ('the Black'); set aside by his half-brother, Reginald, and imprisoned (*c.* 1208–14) by William the Lion of Scotland; driven, after second marriage, from the island of Lewis, the patrimony assigned him by Reginald; recovered the Isles, his paternal kingdom, allowing Reginald to remain king of Man, 1224; king of Man and the Isles, 1226–8; defeated Reginald at Dingwall, 1230; superseded after visit to Norway; shared Man with Godred Don and afterwards ruled alone; exchanged allegiance to Norway for subordination to England; visited Henry III, 1235. [xlii. 84]

OLD, JOHN (*fl.* 1545–1555), one of the translators of Erasmus's 'Paraphrase of the New Testament' (1548); commissioner for several dioceses; prebendary of Lincoln and Lichfield; vicar of Cubington, 1545, till accession of Queen Mary; published religious works. [xlii. 85]

OLDCASTLE, SIR JOHN, styled LORD COBHAM (*d.* 1417), lollard leader; of a Herefordshire family; his age much exaggerated; employed under Henry IV in Welsh marches, where he probably became acquainted with Henry IV's son, Prince Henry; knight of the shire for Herefordshire, 1404; sheriff, 1406–7; married, as second wife, Joan, lady Cobham, 1409; summoned to parliament as baron Cobham till 1413; a leader of troops sent to help Burgundy, 1411; perhaps attached to Prince Henry's household, but never his boon companion; said to have attempted his conversion; attacked by clergy for maintaining heresy in London, Rochester, and Herefordshire,

1413; arrested after vain attempts by Henry V to convert him; tried by Archbishop Arundel and other bishops, presented a confession of faith to the court; after heterodox declarations as to the eucharist and confession and denunciation of the pope as antichrist before an enlarged court, was declared heretic, and handed over to the secular arm; escaped mysteriously from the Tower of London after respite; concealed himself in London during lollard rising; outlawed, 1414; in hiding near Malvern, 1415; believed to have engaged deeply in intrigues with the Scots and to have instigated attack of Albany and Douglas, 1416; surprised and captured by Charlton at Cae'r Barwn, near Welshpool, 1417; condemned by parliament; 'hung and burnt hanging' in St. Giles's Fields. He was extravagantly execrated by contemporary writers, but described as a blessed martyr by Bale and Foxe in the next century. Contemporary calumnies revived in the Elizabethan stage, and were embodied in Shakespeare's Falstaff, who was originally called Oldcastle. A play of 1600 bore his name, and he is the hero of Weever's poem, 'The Mirror of Martyrs' (1601). [xlii. 86]

OLDCORNE, EDWARD (1561–1606), jesuit; ordained priest and admitted to society at Rome; missioner in England, 1588; arrested at Hindlip Hall, Worcestershire, with Garnett, after Gunpowder plot; tortured in the Tower of London, but denied complicity; was executed after trial. [xlii. 93]

OLDE, JOHN (*fl.* 1545–1555). [See OLD.]

OLDENBURG, HENRY (1615?–1677), first secretary of the Royal Society; born and educated at Bremen; lived in England, 1640–8; agent of Bremen in England, 1653; made the acquaintance of Milton, 1654, and of Robert Boyle while studying at Oxford, 1656–7; travelled as tutor to Richard Jones (Lord Ranelagh), 1657–60; first secretary of the Royal Society, 1663–77; published and edited the 'Transactions' of the society, 1664–77; corresponded with Spinoza; imprisoned on account of political correspondence, 1667; undertook many translations; Huyghens's watch patent assigned to him. [xlii. 94]

OLDFIELD, ANNE (1683–1730), actress; daughter of a guardsman named Oldfield; while living with her mother at the Mitre, St. James's Market, London, was introduced by Vanbrugh to John Rich [q. v.] and engaged at Drury Lane, 1692; appeared as Alinda in Vanbrugh's 'Pilgrim,' 1700, and many other parts, but made slow progress till she played Lady Betty Modish, 1704; appeared with seceders at Haymarket in pieces by Cibber and others, 1706–8 and 1709–10; returned finally to Drury Lane, 1711, playing there till 1730; excelled both in tragedy and comedy; Cleopatra and Calista her best tragic and Lady Townly her best comic parts; praised by Cibber, Steele, Walpole, and Thomson, but sneered at by Pope; buried in Westminster Abbey, beneath Congreve's monument. [xlii. 96]

OLDFIELD, HENRY GEORGE (*d.* 1791?), antiquary. [xlii. 100]

OLDFIELD or **OTEFIELD,** JOHN (1627?–1682), ejected minister; rector of Carsington, 1649–62; regular attendant of Wirksworth classis; settled at Alfreton; quoted in Mrs. Gaskell's 'North and South,' 1855. [xlii. 100]

OLDFIELD, JOHN (1789–1863), general; nominated to Woolwich by Cornwallis, in consideration of services of his uncle, Thomas Oldfield [q. v.]; entered royal engineers, 1806; directed inundation of country round Ypres, 1815; made sketch-plan of Waterloo for Wellington and took part in battle; K.H., 1830; commanding royal engineer in Canadian rebellion, 1839; colonel commandant of engineers, 1859; general, 1862. [xlii. 100]

OLDFIELD, JOSHUA (1656–1729), presbyterian minister; son of John Oldfield (1627?–1682) [q. v.]; studied at Lincoln College, Oxford, and Christ's College, Cambridge; minister successively at Tooting, Oxford, Coventry, and Globe Alley, Southwark; kept a training academy for presbyterians in Coventry and London; one of Daniel Williams's trustees; moderator at Salters' Hall conference, 1719; D.D.; intimate with Locke and Calamy. [xlii. 102]

OLDFIELD, THOMAS (1756–1799), major of royal marines; wounded when a volunteer at Bunker's Hill, 1775; served on Cornwallis's staff, 1778–81; distinguished as commander of marines in St. Domingo, 1794; wounded at bombardment of Cadiz, 1797; assisted in attack on Teneriffe; senior of marines at the Nile, 1798; captured mortally wounded in sortie from Acre. [xlii. 103]

OLDFIELD, THOMAS HINTON BURLEY (1755–1822), author of 'Representative History of Great Britain and Ireland,' 1816. [xlii. 104]

OLDHALL, SIR WILLIAM (1390?–1466?), soldier; won his spurs at Verneuil, 1424; distinguished as seneschal of Normandy in invasion of Maine and Anjou; commandant at La Ferté Bernard, 1449; chamberlain to Richard, duke of York, 1440; speaker, 1450; twice attainted as Yorkist. [xlii. 105]

OLDHAM, HUGH (d. 1519), founder of Manchester grammar school and bishop of Exeter; educated in household of Thomas Stanley, earl of Derby, and at Queens' College, Cambridge; chaplain to 'the Lady Margaret' (Countess of Richmond and Derby), from whom he received numerous benefices; as bishop of Exeter (1504–19) had disputes with Archbishop Warham and the abbot of Tavistock; contributed largely to the foundation of Corpus Christi College, Oxford. [xlii. 105]

OLDHAM, JOHN (1600?–1636), 'pilgrim father'; arrived at Plymouth, Massachusetts, in the Anne, 1623; being expelled for plotting against church and state, went to Nantasket (Hull), 1624; wrecked off Cape Cod, 1626; went to England, but returned, 1629; one of the first settlers in Watertown; projector of first Connecticut plantation; granted island in Narragansett Bay, 1634; murdered by Indians. [xlii. 107]

OLDHAM, JOHN (1653–1683), poet; B.A. St. Edmund Hall, Oxford, 1674; three years usher in Whitgift's school, Croydon; afterwards a tutor; befriended by Lord Kingston; eulogised by Waller and Dryden; published several Pindaric odes, the most important being that to the memory of Charles Morwent; chiefly celebrated for his ironical 'Satire against Virtue,' 'Satires upon the Jesuits,' and his imitations of Horace and other Latin writers, as well as of Bion, Moschus, and Boileau; his 'Poems and Translations' collected, 1683. [xlii. 108]

OLDHAM, JOHN (1779–1840), engineer; employed by Bank of Ireland and Bank of England, where his machinery for printing and numbering notes was in use till 1853; patented paddle-wheels for steamers; introduced system of warming buildings. [xlii. 110]

OLDHAM, NATHANIEL (fl. 1740), virtuoso; collected paintings and curiosities; died prisoner for debt in King's Bench. [xlii. 111]

OLDHAM, THOMAS (1801–1851), engineer to Bank of England; son of John Oldham (1779–1840) [q. v.]; died at Brussels. [xlii. 111]

OLDHAM, THOMAS (1816–1878), geologist; professor of geology, Trinity College, Dublin, 1845; M.A., 1846; president of Dublin Geological Society, 1846; director of Irish geological survey, 1846–50; discovered 'Oldhamia' fossils at Bray Head, 1849; superintendent of Indian survey, 1850–76; F.R.S., 1848; royal medallist, 1875. [xlii. 111]

OLDIS. [See OLDYS.]

OLDISWORTH, GILES (1619–1678), royalist divine; of Westminster School and Trinity College, Cambridge; B.A., 1643; created M.A. Oxford, 1646; incumbent of Bourton-on-the-Hill, 1645–78; published 'The Stone Rolled Away' (1663) and 'The Holy Royalist' (1664); left also poems in manuscript. [xlii. 112]

OLDISWORTH, MICHAEL (1591–1654?) parliamentarian politician; fellow of Magdalen College, Oxford, 1612; M.A., 1614; secretary to William Herbert, third earl of Pembroke, and his brother Philip, fourth earl; M.P., Old Sarum, 1624–9, Salisbury, 1640–50; witness against Laud, 1644; keeper of Windsor Great Park, 1650; master of the prerogative office; much satirised by royalist pamphleteers; eulogised by Herrick. [xlii. 113]

OLDISWORTH, WILLIAM (1680–1734), author and translator; of Hart Hall, Oxford; edited several volumes of the tory 'Examiner'; published 'Annotations on the "Tatler."' 1710, verse translations of the 'Odes and Epodes of Horace' (with 'Notes upon Notes'), 1712–13, and poems;

with the Jacobites at Preston, 1715; died a debtor in the King's Bench prison. [xlii. 114]

OLDMIXON, JOHN (1673–1742), whig historian and pamphleteer; published poems, 1696; produced at Drury Lane, London, his opera, 'The Grove, or Love's Paradise,' 1700, and at Lincoln's Inn Fields, London, his tragedy, 'The Governor of Cyprus,' 1703; published 'The British Empire in America,' 1708. 'History of Addresses,' 1709–10; contributed to 'The Medley,' 1711; answered Swift's 'Conduct of Allies' in 'The Dutch Barrier Ours,' 1712; published 'Secret History of Europe' (in parts, 1712, 1713, 1715) and other works against the Stuarts; collector of Bridgwater, 1716; attacked Clarendon's 'History of the Rebellion' in his 'Critical History,' 1724–6; placed in the 'Dunciad' and the 'Art of Sinking in Poetry' by Pope, in retaliation for reflections upon him; made unwarranted attacks upon Clarendon's editors in his 'History of England during the Reigns of the Royal House of Stuart,' 1729; published as a second volume, 'History of England during Reigns of William III, Anne, and George I,' 1735 (third volume, dealing with Tudor period, 1739); his 'Memoirs of the Press, 1710–40,' issued posthumously, 1742; perhaps author of 'History and Life of Robert Blake.' [xlii. 115]

OLDSWORTH. [See OLDISWORTH.]

OLDYS or **OLDIS**, VALENTINE (1620–1685), poet and patron of men of letters; M.A. Cambridge, *per literas regias*, 1671. [xlii. 119]

OLDYS, WILLIAM (1591?–1645), royalist; of Winchester College and New College, Oxford; M.A., 1618, D.D., 1643; vicar of Adderbury, 1627–45; shot by parliamentarians. [xlii. 119]

OLDYS, WILLIAM (1636–1708), admiralty advocate and chancellor of Lincoln diocese; fellow of New College, Oxford, 1655–71; D.C.L., 1667; son of William Oldys (1591?–1645) [q. v.] [xlii. 119]

OLDYS, WILLIAM (1696–1761), Norroy king-of-arms and antiquary; grandson of William Oldys (1591?–1645) [q. v.]; one of the sufferers in the South Sea Bubble, 1720; issued 'Essay on Epistolary Writings,' 1729; collected valuable library; published a 'Dissertation upon Pamphlets,' 1731; edited Ralegh's 'History of the World,' prefixing biography, 1736; issued anonymously 'British Librarian,' 1737; literary secretary to Earl of Oxford, 1738–41; joint-editor with Dr. Johnson of 'Harleian Miscellany,' 1744–6, and drew up and annotated catalogue of Harleian pamphlets; contributed to first edition of 'Biographia Britannica,' 1747–60; imprisoned for debt in the Fleet till released by Norfolk; Norroy king-of-arms, 1755–61; his notes for life of Shakespeare used by Reed in appendix to Rowe's 'Life'; wrote life of Cotton for Hawkins's edition of the 'Compleat Angler' (1760); transcripts of his notes to Langbaine's 'Dramatick Poets' made by Percy, Steevens, and Malone; left various works in manuscript. [xlii. 119]

O'LEARY, ARTHUR (1729–1802), Irish priest and politician; while a Capuchin friar at St. Malo acted as chaplain to prisoners in France, 1756–62; settled in Cork, 1771; wrote pamphlets exhorting Romanists to be loyal to British rule; defended them against Wesley, 1780; published 'Essay on Toleration,' c. 1781; chaplain to Irish national volunteers, 1782–4, but in receipt of pension from British government to reveal secrets of disaffected Roman catholics; published 'Addresses to the Common People of Ireland,' and exerted personal influence against Whiteboys in Munster, 1785–6; came to England as chaplain of Spanish embassy, 1789; attended meetings of catholic committee, but opposed its action; preached in Sutton Street, Soho, London. [xlii. 123]

O'LEARY, ELLEN (1831–1889), Fenian poet; contributed poems to the 'Irish People,' 1863–5; assisted James Stephens with his organisation. [xlii. 126]

O'LEARY, JOSEPH (fl. 1835), Irish barrister and writer on tithes. [xlii. 127]

O'LEARY, JOSEPH (d. 1845?), song-writer and journalist; contributed to the 'Freeholder' and other Cork papers, 1818–42; published the 'Tribute,' 1833; unsuccessful in London; drowned himself in Regent's Canal, London. [xlii. 126]

OLEY, BARNABAS (1602–1686), royalist divine; M.A. Clare College, Cambridge, 1625; B.D.; fellow (some time president) of Clare College, Cambridge, and vicar of Great Gransden, Huntingdonshire ; began the rebuilding of his college, 1638 ; brought college plate to Charles I at Nottingham, 1642 ; ejected from fellowship by the Earl of Manchester, 1644 ; restored, 1660 ; prebendary of Worcester, 1660–86 ; edited George Herbert's 'Remains,' 1652, and some works of Thomas Jackson (1579–1640) [q. v.], 1653–7 ; benefactor of Gransden, Worcester Cathedral, and Clare and King's Colleges, Cambridge.   [xlii. 127]

OLIFARD, SIR WILLIAM (d. 1329). [See OLIPHANT, SIR WILLIAM.]

OLIPHANT, CAROLINA, BARONESS NAIRNE (1766–1845). [See NAIRNE, CAROLINA.]

OLIPHANT, FRANCIS WILSON (1818–1859), painter and designer of stained glass ; educated at Edinburgh ; worked with Pugin at windows in houses of parliament ; exhibited historical pictures at Royal Academy ; designed windows in Ely Cathedral, King's College, Cambridge, and Aylesbury Church ; died at Rome.   [xlii. 129]

OLIPHANT, JAMES (1734–1818), Scottish divine ; M.A. Glasgow, 1756 ; lampooned, when minister of Kilmarnock, by Burns ; minister of Dumbarton, 1773 ; compiled 'The Mother's Catechism,' 1772, and 'Sacramental Catechism,' 1779.   [xlii. 130]

OLIPHANT, SIR LAURENCE, of Aberdalgie, first BARON OLIPHANT (d. 1500 ?), sat in parliament of 1467 ; sheriff of Perthshire, 1470 ; commissioner for treaty with England, 1484 ; lord of the articles, 1488 ; privy councillor, 1488 ; supported the king in rebellion of 1489 ; ambassador to France and Castile, 1491 ; keeper of Edinburgh Castle, 1493.   [xlii. 130]

OLIPHANT, LAURENCE, third BARON OLIPHANT (d. 1566), succeeded his grandfather, 1516 ; captured at Solway Moss, 1542 ; ransomed on conditions, 1543, but did not fulfil his pledges.   [xlii. 131]

OLIPHANT, LAURENCE, fourth BARON OLIPHANT (1529–1593), son of Laurence Oliphant, third baron Oliphant [q. v.] ; extraordinary member of privy council, 1565 ; member of assize for trial of Bothwell, but signed band for his marriage with Mary Queen of Scots ; fought for the queen at Langside, 1568, but signed 'band for the king,' 1569 ; voted against Mary's divorce from Bothwell ; joined anti-Marian party, 1572   [xlii. 131]

OLIPHANT, LAURENCE (1691–1767), Jacobite ; present at Sherriffmuir, 1715 ; laird of Gask (1732–46) ; joined Prince Charles Edward at Perth, 1745, and was made governor of the north ; present with his son at Falkirk and Culloden, 1746, after which they escaped to Sweden ; Gask estates (forfeited) purchased for him, 1753 ; allowed to return, 1763.   [xlii. 132]

OLIPHANT, LAURENCE (1829–1888), novelist, war correspondent and mystic ; born at Capetown ; received a desultory education ; travelled with his parents in France, Germany, Italy, and Greece, 1846–8 ; barrister in Ceylon ; published 'Journey to Khatmandu,' 1852, 'The Russian Shores of the Black Sea and a Tour through the Country of the Don Cossacks,' 1853 ; secretary to Lord Elgin at Washington and in Canada, 1853–4 ; accompanied Lord Stratford de Redcliffe to the Crimea and represented 'The Times' in Circassia ; issued 'Minnesota and the Far West,' 1855, 'The Trans-Caucasian Campaign,' 1856, 'Patriots and Filibusters,' 1860 (describing adventures in Southern States) ; private secretary to Elgin in China ; published 'Narrative of Mission to China and Japan in 1857–8–9,' 1859 ; plotted with Garibaldi in Italy, 1860 ; in Montenegro, 1861 ; when first secretary of legation in Japan visited Corea ; visited Corfu and the Herzegovina, 1862, and Poland, Moldavia, and Schleswig-Holstein, 1863 ; contributed to 'The Owl,' 1864 ; his satirical novel, 'Piccadilly,' which had appeared in 'Blackwood,' 1865, published, 1870 ; M.P., Stirling burghs, 1865–7 ; lived at Brocton or 'Salem-on-Erie' as Thomas Lake Harris's spiritual slave, 1867–70 ; 'Times' correspondent in the Franco-German war ; married Miss L'Estrange, 1872 ; commercially employed by Harris in America ; wrote 'Autobiography of a Joint Stock Company,' 1876 ; published 'The Land of Gilead,' 1880 (describing first journey to Palestine), and 'The Land of Khemi' (Egypt), 1882 ; freed himself from the 'prophet' Harris and recovered his land at Brocton, 1881 ; wrote 'Altiora Peto' at Haifa, 1883, where he formed a com-

munity of Jewish immigrants, and several mystical works ; on the death of his wife (1886) returned temporarily to England ; published 'Episodes of Adventure,' 1887 ; visited America and married Rosamond Dale Owen, 1888 ; died at York House, Twickenham, having finished 'Scientific Religion.'   [xlii. 133]

OLIPHANT, MARGARET OLIPHANT (1828–1897), novelist and historical writer ; née Wilson ; published 'Passages in Life of Mrs. Margaret Maitland,' 1849, and 'Merkland,' 1851 ; married her cousin, Francis Wilson Oliphant [q. v.], 1852 ; began connection with firm of Messrs. Blackwood, and from 1853 contributed to 'Blackwood's Magazine' many novels, including 'Salem Chapel,' 1863, one of the series of four entitled 'Chronicles of Carlingford' (issued anonymously, 1863–76) ; published 'Life of Edward Irving,' 1862 ; lived in perpetual embarrassment owing to her undertaking education and maintenance of her widowed brother's children in addition to her own two sons ; edited series of monographs on foreign classics, for which she wrote volumes on Dante (1877) and Cervantes (1880). Her works include 'Memoir of Laurence Oliphant (1829–1888) [q. v.] and Alice Oliphant,' 1892, and 'Literary History of England in end of Eighteenth and beginning of Nineteenth Century,' 1882.

[Suppl. iii. 230]

OLIPHANT, THOMAS (1799–1873), musical composer and writer ; president of Madrigal Society, 1871 ; sung in Handel festival, 1834 ; published 'Comments of a Chorus-singer' by 'Solomon Sackbut,' 1834 ; published works on madrigals, also versions of 'Fidelio,' 'Lohengrin,' and other compositions.   [xlii. 137]

OLIPHANT or **OLIFARD**, SIR WILLIAM (d. 1329), soldier ; captured at Dunbar, 1296 ; forced to serve Edward I in Flanders, 1297 ; held Stirling Castle against him for ninety days, 1304 ; prisoner in the Tower of London, 1305 ; released by Edward II, 1308 ; held Perth for Edward II during six weeks against Bruce, 1312 ; returned to England, 1313 ; received grants from Bruce, 1317 and 1326 ; present at Scots parliaments of 1320 and 1326.   [xlii. 138]

OLIPHANT, SIR WILLIAM, LORD NEWTON (1551–1628), lord (king's) advocate ; admitted, 1577 ; advocate-depute, 1604 ; gained favour of James VI by throwing up his brief for the six ministers, 1606 ; lord of session, 1611–1626 ; lord advocate, 1612–28 ; member of new high commission court, 1615 ; present procedure of examining witnesses originated by him.   [xlii. 139]

OLIVER OF MALMESBURY, otherwise EILMER, ELMER, or ÆTHELMÆR (fl. 1066), astrologer and mechanician ; monk of Malmesbury ; made himself wings and attempted to fly ; prophesied on the great comet of 1066. [xlii. 140]

OLIVER (d. 1219), bastard son of King John ; took part in defence of Dover, 1217 ; died on crusade at Damietta.   [xlii. 141]

OLIVER, ANDREW (1706–1774), lieutenant-governor of Massachusetts ; graduated at Harvard, 1724 ; secretary of Massachusetts, 1756 ; hanged in effigy when distributor of stamps, 1765, and compelled to renounce collection ; lieutenant-governor of Massachusetts, 1770–4 ; his letters to Thomas Whately, one of the secretaries of the English treasury, laid before assembly by Franklin, 1772.

[xlii. 141]

OLIVER, ARCHER JAMES (1774–1842), portrait-painter and curator of Academy painting-school ; A.R.A., 1807.   [xlii. 142]

OLIVER, EMMA SOPHIA (1819–1885), painter ; wife of William Oliver (1804 ?–1853) [q. v.]   [xlii. 155]

OLIVER, GEORGE (1781–1861), historian of Exeter ; taught for eleven years at Stonyhurst ; forty-four years jesuit missioner at St. Nicholas, Exeter ; created D.D. by Gregory XVI, 1844 ; published works, including 'History of Exeter,' 1821, 'Ecclesiastical Antiquities of Devon,' 3 vols., 1839, 1840, 1842, 'Lives of the Bishops of Exeter,' 1861, and biographical notices of jesuits.   [xlii. 142]

OLIVER, GEORGE (1782–1867), topographer and writer on freemasonry ; head-master of Grimsby grammar school, 1809 ; rector of Scopwick from 1831 ; perpetual curate of St. Peter's, Wolverhampton, 1834–46 ; rector of South Hyckham, 1846 ; deputy past grand master of Lincolnshire masons, 1832 ; D.D. Lambeth, 1835 ; published, among other books, topographical works on Great Grimsby, Beverley, and the collegiate church of Wolverhampton. His masonic works include 'Antiquities of

Free-Masonry,' 1823, 'History of Initiation,' 1829, 'Historical Landmarks of Freemasonry,' 1844-6, and 'Golden Remains of Early Masonic Writers,' 1847-50. [xlii. 143]

OLIVER, OLIVIER, or OLLIVIER, ISAAC (1556 ?-1617), miniature-painter ; perhaps native of Rouen ; pupil of Nicholas Hilliard [q. v.] ; mentioned in Francis Meres's 'Palladis Tamia,' 1598 ; painted portraits, among others, of James I and his family, Sir Philip Sidney, and the family of Sir Kenelm Digby ; drew portrait of Queen Elizabeth ; his 'Entombment of Christ' much admired by contemporaries. [xlii. 145]

OLIVER, JOHN (d. 1552), dean of Christ Church, Oxford, and master in chancery ; D.Can.L. and D.C.L. Oxford, 1522 ; Wolsey's commissary, 1527 ; held numerous preferments ; employed in divorce proceedings, 1531-3 ; took part in trials of James Bainham [q. v.] and of Bishops Gardiner, Day, and Heath. [xlii. 146]

OLIVER, JOHN (1601-1661), president of Magdalen College, Oxford, 1644-7 and 1660-1 ; fellow of Merton College, Oxford, 1620 ; M.A., 1622, D.D., 1639 ; dean of Worcester, 1660-1. [xlii. 147]

OLIVER, JOHN (1616-1701), glass-painter and master-mason ; one of the commissioners for rebuilding London after the fire. [xlii. 147]

OLIVER, JOHN (1838-1866), Welsh poet. [xlii. 148]

OLIVER, MARTHA CRANMER, 'PATTIE OLIVER' (1834-1880), actress ; performed children's parts at Salisbury and Southampton ; appeared at the Marylebone, London, 1847 ; with Madame Vestris at the Lyceum, London, 1849-55 ; played Helen in 'The Hunchback' at Drury Lane, London, 1856 ; in burlesques by Byron and Talfourd at the Strand, London, 1857-60 ; at the Haymarket, London, in 'Our American Cousin,' 1861 ; as manageress of the New Royalty, London, 1866-70, made a great hit with Burnand's parody of 'Black-eyed Susan.' [xlii. 148]

OLIVER or OLIVIER, PETER (1594-1648), miniature-painter ; son of Isaac Oliver [q. v.] ; finished his father's 'Entombment' ; his copy of Vandyck's portrait of Lady Southampton particularly fine. [xlii. 149]

OLIVER, RICHARD (1734 ?-1784), politician ; born in Antigua ; alderman of Billingsgate ward, London, 1770 ; sheriff, 1772 ; M.P. for the city, 1770-80 ; committed to Tower of London by commons, 1771 ; quarrelled with Wilkes ; proposed vote of censure on American policy of ministers, 1775 ; died at sea on return from Antigua, whither he had been to look after his estates. [xlii. 149]

OLIVER, ROBERT DUDLEY (1766-1850), admiral ; saw service in West Indies, 1782-3 ; promoted commander after capture of Révolutionnaire, 1794 ; posted, 1796 ; commanded Melpomene on French coast, 1803-5 ; towed prizes from Trafalgar ; served in second American war, 1813-14 ; admiral, 1841. [xlii. 150]

OLIVER or OLYUER, THOMAS (d. 1624), physician and mathematician ; published 'New Handling of the Planisphere,' 1601, and 'De Sophismatum Præstigiis cavendis Admonitio,' 1603. [xlii. 151]

OLIVER, THOMAS (1725-1799). [See OLIVERS.]

OLIVER, THOMAS (1734-1815), lieutenant-governor of Massachusetts ; graduated at Harvard ; erected Lowell's mansion near Cambridge, Massachusetts ; lieutenant-governor of Massachusetts, 1774 ; obliged to renounce his seat on council board after the seizure by the royal troops of the public stock of powder provided for the militia ; proscribed, 1778 ; died at Bristol, England. [xlii. 151]

OLIVER, TOM (1789-1864), pugilist, 'the Chelsea gardener' ; beat George Cooper, 1813, and Ned Painter, 1814 ; defeated by Jack Carter, 1816, and Bill Neat, 1818 ; defeated Hendrick the black, but was beaten by Dan Donnelly, 1819 ; beat Skelton, but was defeated by Ned Painter, 1820 ; imprisoned for presence at a fight, 1846. [xlii. 152]

OLIVER, WILLIAM (1659-1716), physician ; studied at Leyden University ; accompanied Monmouth's expedition as surgeon ; escaped to Holland and went to Poland ; came to England with William of Orange, 1688 ; physician with the fleet, 1693-1702, to Chatham Hospital, 1709-1714, Greenwich Hospital, 1714-16 ; published 'Practical Essay on Fevers,' 1704, and 'Dissertation on Bath Waters,' 1707. [xlii. 153]

OLIVER, WILLIAM (1695-1764), physician ; M.D. Pembroke College, Cambridge, 1725 ; F.R.S., 1730 ; introduced by Ralph Allen [q. v.] to Pope, Warburton, and Borlase ; physician to Bath Mineral Water Hospital, 1740-1761 ; invented the 'Bath Oliver' biscuit ; published 'Practical Essay on Use and Abuse of Warm Bathing in Gouty Cases,' 1751 ; his 'Faint Sketch of the Life, Character, and Manners of the late Mr. Nash' used by Goldsmith. [xlii. 153]

OLIVER, WILLIAM (1804 ?-1853), landscape-painter ; published 'Scenery of the Pyrenees,' 1842. [xlii. 155]

OLIVERS, THOMAS (1725-1799), methodist preacher and hymn-writer ; for twenty-two years itinerant preacher ; supervisor of Wesleyan press, 1775-89 ; published tracts and composed the tune 'Helmsley' and 'Hymn to the God of Abraham' ; buried in Wesley's tomb. [xlii. 156]

OLLIER, CHARLES (1788-1859), publisher of Shelley's works and first poems of Keats ; collected works of Lamb, and some by Leigh Hunt ; also issued romances by himself. [xlii. 156]

OLLIER, EDMUND (1827-1886), author ; son of Charles Ollier [q. v.] ; published 'Poems from the Greek Mythology,' 1867 ; edited works by Lamb and Leigh Hunt ; compiled for Cassell. [xlii. 157]

OLLIFFE, SIR JOSEPH FRANCIS (1808-1869), physician ; M.A. Paris, 1829 ; M.D., 1840 ; physician to British embassy, 1852 ; knighted, 1852 ; an assessor at exhibitions of 1855 and 1862 ; friend of Count de Morny. [xlii. 158]

OLLIVANT, ALFRED (1798-1882), bishop of Llandaff ; of St. Paul's School, London, and Trinity College, Cambridge ; Craven scholar, 1820, sixth wrangler, 1821, and senior chancellor's medallist ; fellow of Trinity College, Cambridge ; M.A., 1824, D.D., 1836 ; vice-principal of St. David's, Lampeter, 1827-43 ; regius professor of divinity at Cambridge University, 1843-9 ; bishop of Llandaff, 1849-1882 ; restored his cathedral and formed Church Extension Society ; an Old Testament reviser. [xlii. 158]

OLLYFFE, JOHN (1647-1717), divine ; B.C.L. New Inn Hall, Oxford, 1672 ; rector of West Almer, 1673-93, of Dunton, 1693-1717 ; published 'Essay towards a Comprehension,' 1701, 'Defence of Ministerial Conformity,' 1792 (against Calamy), and other works. [xlii. 159]

OLMIUS, JOHN LUTTRELL-, third EARL OF CARHAMPTON (d. 1829). [See LUTTRELL-OLMIUS, JOHN.]

O'LOCHLAINN, DOMHNALL (1048-1121), king of Ireland ; king of Oilech, 1082 ; received submission of Connaught, 1088, of Munster and Meath, 1090 ; king of Ireland, 1090-1121 ; ruled Donegal from 1093 ; drove Danes from Dublin, 1094 ; repelled attacks on Ulster ; defeated Leinstermen at Donaghmore, 1103. [xlii. 160]

O'LOCHLAINN, MUIRCHEARTACH (d. 1166), king of Ireland ; grandson of Domhnall O'Lochlainn [q. v.] ; defeated the O'Dubhdas of Ulster, 1139 ; as chief of Cinel Eoghain defeated Ulidians at Dundrum, 1147 ; received submission of Dublin Danes and of Leinster, 1149, of Connaught, 1150 ; restored Turlough O'Brien in Munster, 1153 ; received as king at Dublin by the Danes, 1154 ; king of Ireland, 1156-66 ; attended synod of Mellifont, 1157 ; granted charter to Cistercian abbey of Newry, 1158 ; deposed king of Meath and defeated Connaughtmen at Ardee, 1159 ; received submission of Roderic O'Connor and Diarmaid MacMurchadha, 1161 ; killed in battle with the Ulidians in Armagh. [xlii. 161]

O'LOGHLEN, SIR COLMAN MICHAEL, second baronet (1819-1877), judge-advocate-general ; son of Sir Michael O'Loghlen [q. v.] ; Q.C. in Ireland, 1852 ; M.P., Clare, 1863 ; judge-advocate-general, 1868-70 ; privy councillor, 1868 ; carried bill admitting catholics to Irish chancellorship. [xlii. 163]

O'LOGHLEN, SIR MICHAEL, first baronet (1789-1842), Irish judge ; B.A. Trinity College, Dublin, 1809 ; called to Irish bar, 1811 ; O'Connell's favourite junior ; K.C., 1830 ; bencher of King's Inn, 1832 ; Irish solicitor-general under Melbourne, 1834-5, attorney-general, 1835-1836 ; baron of the exchequer, 1836 ; master of the rolls in Ireland, 1837-42 ; first Roman catholic judge since James II's reign ; created baronet, 1838. [xlii. 163]

O'LOTHCHAIN, CUAN (d. 1024), chief man of learning (Primheices) to Maelsechlainn II [q. v.]; afterwards with Corcran Cleirech governed Ireland; wrote account of the kings of Tara.   [xlii. 164]

O'MAELCHONAIRE, FEARFEASA (fl. 1636), one of the authors of 'Annales Quatuor Magistrorum' (Annals of Kingdom of Ireland); recorded lives of more than forty of Connaught hereditary bards.   [xlii. 164]

O'MAHONY, CONNOR, CORNELIUS, or CONSTANTINE (fl. 1650). [See MAHONY.]

O'MAHONY, DANIEL (d. 1714), general in French and Spanish services; left Ireland, 1692; when commanding Dillon's regiment under Villeroy saved Cremona from the Austrians, 1702; promoted and pensioned by Louis XIV, and knighted by the Old Pretender; afterwards served under Vendôme; transferred to Spanish service, 1704; created maréchal-de-camp, 1706; defended Alicante against Sir John Leake, 1706; commanded in Valencia and distinguished himself at head of Irish brigade at Almanza; captured Alcoy, 1708; commanded Spanish in Sicily, 1709; commanded Gallo-Spanish cavalry at Saragossa and Villa Viciosa; created count of Castile and commander of Iago and ennobled by Louis XIV; died at Ocana.   [xlii. 165]

O'MAHONY, JOHN (1816–1877), Irish politician; of Trinity College, Dublin; translated Keating's Gaelic 'History of Ireland,' 1857; seceded from O'Connell, 1845; joined Smith O'Brien, 1848, and fought on borders of Waterford and Kilkenny; fled to France; helped to found Emmet Monument Association in New York, 1854; co-operated with Stephens in formation of Fenian brotherhood, 1858, and directed the movement in America till 1867; died in New York, but was buried at Glasnevin.   [xlii. 167]

O'MALLEY, GEORGE (d. 1843), major-general; volunteer in Castlebar yeomanry during Humbert's invasion, 1798; served with 13th foot at Ferrol and (1801) in Egypt; assisted in recruiting of 101st foot in Mayo, with which he served in New Brunswick and Jamaica, 1808–13; commanded second battalion 44th foot at Quatre Bras and Waterloo, being there wounded and created C.B.; major-general, 1841.   [xlii. 168]

O'MALLEY, GRACE (1530?–1600?), Irish chieftainess (Graine Ui Maille in Irish); in local traditions Graine Mhaol; married, first, the chieftain of Ballinahinch, secondly, the chief of the Burkes of Mayo; famous as leader of expeditions by sea; allied with Sir Henry Sidney, 1576; captured by Desmond and brought to Dublin, 1577–8; seized by Sir Richard Bingham for plundering Aran island, but was released; fled to Ulster; pardoned through Perrot's influence; died in great poverty.   [xlii. 169]

O'MALLEY, THADEUS (1796–1877), politician; as a priest several times suspended for advocating reforms in ecclesiastical discipline; supported Doyle's poor-law policy, and national education for Ireland; rector of catholic university, Malta; started 'The Social Economist,' 1845; disputed with O'Connell on repeal, and published the 'Federalist'; supported Butt's movement, 1870; issued 'Home Rule on the basis of Federalism,' 1873.   [xlii. 170]

O'MAOLMHUAIDH, FRANCIS (fl. 1660). [See MOLLOY.]

O'MEARA, BARRY EDWARD (1786–1836), surgeon to Napoleon in St. Helena; assistant-surgeon with the 62nd foot in Sicily, Calabria, and Egypt; dismissed the army for participation in a duel at Messina, 1807; naval surgeon on the Bellerophon and other ships; surgeon to Napoleon at St. Helena; dismissed (1818) for intrigues with Napoleon; eulogised by Byron in 'Age of Bronze'; partisan of Queen Caroline and O'Connell; wrote pamphlets against Sir Hudson Lowe [q. v.] and denounced his treatment of Napoleon in 'Napoleon in Exile,' 1822; published also 'Observations upon the Authenticity of Bourrienne's " Memoirs,"' 1831.   [xlii. 171]

O'MEARA, DERMOD or DERMITIUS (fl. 1610). [See MEARA.]

O'MEARA, EDMUND (d. 1680). [See MEARA.]

O'MEARA, KATHLEEN (1839–1888), novelist and biographer; granddaughter of Barry Edward O'Meara

[q. v.]; lived in Paris; published six novels, 1867–88, also lives of Frederick Ozanam, 1876, Madame Mohl, 1885, and others.   [xlii. 172]

OMMANNEY, SIR JOHN ACWORTH (1773–1855), admiral; present at Bridport's engagement off Lorient, 1795; caused Swedish merchant fleet to be searched for contraband of war, 1799; flag-captain on Newfoundland station, 1804–6; C.B. for services at Navarino, 1827; K.C.B., 1838; commander on Lisbon station, 1837–40, Malta, 1840–1, Devonport, 1851–4; admiral, 1849.   [xlii. 173]

O'MOLLOY, ALBIN or ALPIN O'MOELMHUAIDH (d. 1223), bishop of Ferns, 1187–1223; recommended by King John for archbishopric of Cashel, 1206; sent on mission to Connaught, 1208; attended council at Rome, 1215; excommunicated William Marshal, first earl of Pembroke [q. v.], 1216.   [xlii. 174]

O'MOLLOY, FRANCIS (fl. 1660). [See MOLLOY.]

O'MORAN, JAMES (1735–1794), lieutenant-general in French service; born at Elphin; served in Germany, 1760–1, and America, 1779–83; fought under Dumouriez, 1792; general of division (lieutenant-general), 1792; guillotined in the revolution.   [xlii. 174]

O'MORE, RORY (fl. 1554), Irish rebel (Ruaidhri og ua Mordha).   [xlii. 175]

O'MORE, RORY or RURY OGE (d. 1578), Irish rebel; son of Rory O'More (fl. 1554) [q. v.]; pardoned, 1566; fought Ormonde and Queen Elizabeth at the same time, 1566; protected Desmond, 1572; implicated with Kildare, 1574; pardoned on submission to Sidney, 1576; attacked the Pale, 1577; with the O'Connors burned Naas and captured Harrington, but was afterwards defeated; killed by the Fitzpatricks.   [xlii. 175]

O'MORE, RORY (fl. 1620–1652), Irish rebel (called ROGER MOORE or MORE); assisted in concerting rising of 1641; won victory at Julianstown, 1641; negotiated with gentry of the Pale at Crofty, 1641; outlawed, 1642; commanded confederate Irish in King's and Queen's counties, 1643; among Owen Roe O'Neill's followers, 1644; in arms against Kilkenny confederation, 1648; tried to effect arrangement between O'Neill and Ormonde, 1649; commanded foot in Connaught, 1650; had Clanricarde's commission as commander in Leinster; driven into island of Bofin; said to have escaped to Scotland, but perhaps perished in Ireland; the most humane of the Irish leaders.   [xlii. 176]

O'MULCONRY, FEARFEASA (fl. 1636). [See O'MAELCHONAIRE.]

O'MULLEN, THOMAS (fl. 1685–1708). [See TAAFFE, JOHN.]

O'NEAL or **O'NEALE**. [See also O'NEILL.]

O'NEAL, JEFFREY HAMET (fl. 1760–1772), miniature-painter.   [xlii. 178]

O'NEIL, **O'NEAL**, and **O'NEALE**. [See also O'NEILL.]

O'NEIL, HENRY NELSON (1817–1880), historical painter; exhibited at Royal Academy, British Institution, and Society of British Artists; his 'Boaz and Ruth' bought by Prince Albert, 1844; A.R.A., 1860; published 'Lectures on Painting,' 1866, 'Satirical Dialogues,' 1870, and other works.   [xlii. 178]

O'NEILL, SIR BRIAN MacPHELIM (d. 1574), chief of the O'Neills of Clandeboye; cousin of Shane O'Neill [q. v.], against whom and other rebellious chiefs he fought in interests of English government; knighted, 1567; served against Turlough Luineach O'Neill [q. v.], but joined with him in ravaging the Ards, 1572; on learning of the project of Sir Thomas Smith (1513–1577) [q. v.] to plant them with Englishmen; compelled by Walter Devereux, earl of Essex [q. v.], to submit, 1572, but was again in rebellion, 1573; proclaimed traitor, 1574, and, having been pardoned, was put to death at Essex's instigation.   [Suppl. iii. 234]

O'NEILL, CHARLES HENRY ST. JOHN, second VISCOUNT and first EARL O'NEILL (1779–1841), grand master of Irish Orangemen; son of John O'Neill, first viscount O'Neill [q. v.]; created earl, 1800; joint post-master-general of Ireland, 1807.   [xlii. 199]

O'NEILL, CON BACACH, first EARL OF TYRONE (1484?–1559?), grandson of Henry O'Neill (d. 1489) [q. v.]; invaded the Pale, 1520, but was conciliated by Surrey, the viceroy; defeated by O'Donnell, 1522; intrigued against Ormonde, 1528; supported rebellion of 'Silken Thomas,' 1534-5; attacked Ardglass, 1537; with Manus O'Donnell [q. v.] invaded the Pale, but was defeated by Lord Leonard Grey [q. v.] at Ballahoe, 1539; again invaded the Pale, 1541, but after three invasions of Tyrone submitted to St. Leger, went to England (1542), and was created earl; privy councillor of Ireland, 1543, his authority subsequently becoming diminished in Ireland; obliged to take refuge within the Pale. [xlii. 178]

O'NEILL, DANIEL (1612?-1664), royalist soldier; nephew of Owen Roe O'Neill [q. v.]; became a protestant and frequented court of Charles I; wounded at siege of Breda, 1636; an active enemy of Strafford; captured by the Scots at Newburn, 1640; implicated in army plots; was impeached, but escaped from the Tower of London, 1642; fought at two battles of Newbury, 1643 and 1644, and at Naseby, 1645, and commanded Rupert's foot at Marston Moor, 1644; accompanied Randal MacDonnell [q. v.] on mission to Ormonde, and became groom of the bedchamber to Charles I, 1644; went to Ireland and negotiated between Ormonde and Owen Roe, 1649; defended Trim, 1649; commanded Ulster army during Owen Roe's illness; made terms with Ireton; captured in Scotland but released, 1650; joined in Charles II's invasion of 1651; subsequently employed in royalist intrigues abroad, having great influence with Charles II; received pension and numerous grants of land at Restoration; postmaster-general, 1663; nicknamed 'Infallible Subtle.' [xlii. 181]

O'NEILL, ELIZA (1791-1872). [See BECHER, ELIZA, LADY.]

O'NEILL, SIR FELIM (1604?-1653). [See O'NEILL, SIR PHELIM.]

O'NEILL, FLAITHBHEARTACH (d. 1036), king of Ailech; son of Muircheartach [q. v.]; made war on Ulidians, Meath, and the O'Donnells; went on pilgrimage to Rome, 1030. [xlii. 184]

O'NEILL, GORDON (d. 1704), Irish Jacobite; son of Sir Phelim O'Neill [q. v.]; lord-lieutenant of Tyrone, 1689; fought at Derry, the Boyne, and Aughrim; afterwards colonel in French service. [xlii. 207]

O'NEILL, HENRY (d. 1392), Irish chief; known as Enri aimhreidh ('The Contentious'). [xlii. 185]

O'NEILL, HENRY (d. 1489), chief of Cinel Eoghain; son of Owen or Eoghan O'Neill [q. v.]; captured by Neachtan O'Donnell, 1431; defeated the O'Donnells in Donegal, 1435; mutilated Brian O'Neill's sons; obtained tribute of Inishowen, 1442; deposed his father and became chief of Cinel Eoghain, 1455; recognised by England, 1459; plundered Donegal; resigned chieftainship to his son, 1483. [xlii. 185]

O'NEILL, HENRY (1800-1880), Irish archæologist; published 'The Most Interesting of the Sculptured Crosses of Ancient Ireland,' 1857, and 'Fine Arts and Civilisation of Ancient Ireland,' 1863. [xlii. 186]

O'NEILL, HUGH (d. 1230), lord of Cinel Eoghain from 1197; defeated John de Courcy, 1199; deposed after defeat by Connaughtmen at Ballysadare, 1201, but soon restored; defeated English at Narrow-Water, 1211, and again, 1214; allied himself with Hugh de Lacy; aided sons of Roderic O'Connor (1116?-1198) [q. v.] against Hugh Croibhdhearg, 1225. [xlii. 187]

O'NEILL, HUGH, third BARON OF DUNGANNON and second EARL OF TYRONE (1540?-1616), grandson of Con Bacach O'Neill [q. v.]; as Baron of Dungannon lived in England, 1562-8; set up by government in Armagh as counterpoise to Turlough O'Neill; intrigued with him, but returned to allegiance, 1580; captured John Cusack the rebel, 1582; made defender of northern marches, 1583; admitted earl, 1585; was refused regrant of Con Bacach O'Neill's lands by the English government, 1587; submitted to Perrot, 1588; routed by Turlough O'Neill and his allies at Carricklea, 1588; placed under restraint in England for hanging Hugh Geimhleach, 1590; eloped with Mabel Bagenal, 1591; came to terms with Turlough O'Neill and was inaugurated O'Neill, 1593; unwillingly accompanied Sir Henry Bagenal against Hugh Maguire [q. v.], 1593; intrigued with Fiagh O'Byrne [q. v.]; anticipated English attack by invading Louth, 1594, and was outlawed;

signed treaty with the government, 1596, but negotiated with Spain, and was again attacked by the English, 1597; pardoned on submission to Ormonde, 1598; soon rebelled again, defeated Bagenal, 1598, and invaded Munster in support of the Sugan Earl; made truce with Essex, 1599, but invaded Munster, 1600; received supplies from Spain, but was obliged to act on the defensive in Ulster, 1601-2, a price being set on his head; compelled to retreat north, 1603; submitted on promise of pardon, liberty, and restoration of estates, 1603, abjuring title of O'Neill and all foreign relations; well received by James I at Hampton Court, 1603, but regarded with distrust on return to Ireland; on receipt of another summons to England fled with Tyrconnel to France, 1607; compelled to withdraw to Spanish Netherlands; entertained at Rome by Pope Paul V from 1608 till his death, permission to return being refused him. [xlii. 188]

O'NEILL, HUGH (fl. 1642-1660), major-general; nephew of Hugh O'Neill (1540?-1616) [q. v.]; served in Spanish army; came to Ireland with Owen O'Neill, 1642; captured by British, 1643; major-general of the Irish in Ulster ('Mac-Art'), 1646-9; as governor of Clonmel, 1650, repulsed Cromwell's attack; obliged to surrender Limerick to Ireton, 1651; condemned to death, but reprieved as Spanish subject; after release from the Tower of London, 1652, returned to Spain. [xlii. 197]

O'NEILL, HUGH (1784-1824), architectural draughtsman; made drawings of buildings at Oxford and Bristol. [xlii. 198]

O'NEILL, JOHN, first VISCOUNT O'NEILL in the peerage of Ireland (1740-1798), politician; created M.A. Christ Church, Oxford, 1762; M.P., Randalstown, 1761, 1769, and 1776, and afterwards for Antrim in Irish parliament, 1783 and 1790; one of the Ulster delegates to national convention, 1783; member of deputation of Irish parliament to offer regency in Ireland to George, prince of Wales, 1789; created baron, 1793, viscount, 1795; shot by rebels at Antrim in rebellion. [xlii. 198]

O'NEILL, JOHN (1777?-1860?), shoemaker poet; wrote temperance verses and other works; his 'Drunkard' (1840) illustrated by Cruikshank, 1842. [xlii. 200]

O'NEILL, JOHN BRUCE RICHARD, third VISCOUNT O'NEILL (1780-1855), general; second son of John O'Neill, first viscount O'Neill [q. v.]; M.P., Antrim, 1802-41; constable of Dublin Castle, 1811; representative peer, 1842. [xlii. 199]

O'NEILL, SIR NEILL or NIALL, second baronet (1658?-1690), Irish Jacobite; nephew of Richard Talbot, earl of Tyrconnel [q. v.]; raised regiment of dragoons for James II, 1687; present at siege of Derry, 1689; mortally wounded at the Boyne, 1690. [xlii. 200]

O'NEILL, OWEN or EOGHAN (1380?-1456), chief of Cinel Eoghain; imprisoned at Dublin, 1399; with the O'Donnells ravaged Tyrone and expelled the O'Neill, 1419; helped English to attack Connaught, 1422, but ravaged Louth, 1423; after capture by Sir John Talbot [q. v.] acknowledged English suzerainty, 1425, but attacked English settlers again, 1430; chief of Cinel Eoghain, 1432-1455; defeated Brian Oge O'Neill, 1435; levied blackmail on the Pale, 1436; deposed by eldest son, 1455. [xlii. 201]

O'NEILL, OWEN ROE (1590?-1649), Irish general; nephew of Hugh O'Neill, second earl of Tyrone [q. v.]; served in Spanish army thirty years; chosen general by Ulstermen, 1642; defeated Scottish army under Monro at Benburb 1646; checked parliamentarians in Leinster, 1647; supported Rinuccini's opposition to treaty with Ormonde, and was declared an enemy by Kilkenny confederates, 1648; was acting with confederate catholics at his death. [xlii. 201]

O'NEILL, SIR PHELIM (1604?-1653), Irish rebel (Feidlimidh ruadh); inherited property in Armagh and Tyrone; expelled from Irish parliament as rebel, 1641; concerted rebellion with Antrim and nobles of the Pale, 1641; captured Charlemont Castle, 1641; held responsible for outrages, but (1653) acquitted of Caulfeild's murder; chosen commander of northern forces of rebels; forged commission from Charles I, 1641; captured Lurgan and Strabane, but failed elsewhere, 1641; made governor of Meath and director of siege of Drogheda by lords of the Pale; proclaimed traitor, 1642; defeated (1642) at Glenmaquin and passage of the Blackwater; yielded command to Owen Roe O'Neill [q. v.], but intrigued with confederate catholics against him; supported Ormonde's pacific overtures, 1646; nominated commissioner of trust for government of Ireland and governor of Charlemont, 1648; capitulated to parliament, 1650; betrayed and captured by Caulfeild in Tyrone, 1653; tried and executed as traitor at Dublin. [xlii. 204]

O'NEILL, SHANE, second EARL OF TYRONE, 'The Proud' (1530?-1567), eldest son of Con Bacach O'Neill [q. v.]; refused to submit to supersession by his younger brother Matthew (Dungannon), and raised faction against him; intrigued with the Antrim Scots; expelled his father and Dungannon, 1556; defeated by the O'Donnells, 1556; murdered his brother, 1558; recognised by Queen Elizabeth on accession, but recognition revoked. 1560; captured Calvagh O'Donnell [q. v.] and harassed English army; attempts made to assassinate him by Sussex; signed treaty with Kildare and went to England, 1562, making public submission to Queen Elizabeth, but intrigued with Spanish; acknowledged as captain of Tyrone, 1562, but failed to keep conditions of restoration; made advantageous treaty with English at Drumcree, 1563; destroyed Scottish settlements in Antrim and captured chiefs of the MacDonnells, 1565; intrigued in support of Mary Queen of Scots; offered submission to France in exchange for help against England; invaded the Pale, but failed before Dundalk, 1566; burned Armagh, 1566; made overtures to Desmond and Argyll; defeated by the O'Donnells at Letterkenny, 1567; took refuge with the MacDonnells, taking back their chiefs with him; murdered by them at Cushendun, at instigation of governor of Carrickfergus, who obtained reward for his head.
[xlii. 208]

O'NEILL, SIR TURLOUGH LUINEACH (1530?-1595), lord of Tyrone; tried to supplant his cousin Shane O'Neill [q. v.], 1562; murdered Brian, baron of Dungannon, 1562; inaugurated O'Neill, 1567; protested loyalty, but allied himself with O'Donnell and MacQuillin; resisted colonisation of Antrim, 1572; signed treaty with Essex, 1575; a title proposed for him on recommendation of Sidney, but withdrawn in consequence of his ambiguous attitude; made another peace, 1580; but refused to surrender William Nugent [q. v.]; accompanied Perrot against the Scots, 1583, and agreed to surrender territory to Tyrone; defeated Tyrone when attacked by him at Carricklea, 1588; resigned chieftainship in his favour after some fighting, 1593; died when attempting to reach Dublin. [xlii. 213]

O'NEILL, WILLIAM CHICHESTER, first BARON O'NEILL (1813-1883), musical composer; of Shrewsbury School; graduated at Trinity College, Dublin; son of the Rev. Edward Chichester; assumed name of O'Neill on coming into possession of family estates, 1835; peerage restored, 1868. [xlii. 216]

ONSLOW, ARTHUR (1691-1768), speaker of the House of Commons; descendant of Sir Richard Onslow (1601-1664) [q. v.]; of Winchester College and Wadham College, Oxford; barrister, Middle Temple, 1713; recorder of Guildford, 1737; whig M.P., Guildford, 1720-7, Surrey, 1728-61; speaker of the House of Commons, 1728-61; privy councillor, 1728; chancellor to Queen Caroline, 1729; treasurer of the navy, 1734-42; opposed regency bill, 1751; received annuity for three lives and freedom of the city, 1761; a trustee of British Museum; appended notes to Burnet and Hatsell. [xlii. 216]

ONSLOW, GEORGE (1731-1792), politician; nephew of Arthur Onslow [q. v.]; lieutenant-colonel in foot guards, 1759; M.P., Guildford, 1760-84; opposed expulsion of Wilkes; took leading part in proceedings against printers of parliamentary debates and was hanged in effigy, 1771; at first a supporter of Rockingham, but afterwards of Grafton and North; in favour of giving up Gibraltar.
[xlii. 218]

ONSLOW, GEORGE, first EARL OF ONSLOW (1731-1814), politician; son of Arthur Onslow [q. v.]; of Westminster School and Peterhouse, Cambridge; M.A., 1766; M.P., Rye, 1754-61, Surrey, 1761-76; a lord of the treasury under Rockingham, 1765; privy councillor, 1767; moved invalidation of Wilkes's election for Middlesex, 1769; non-suited in action for libel against Horne Tooke, 1770; awarded damages in new trial but judgment arrested on technical grounds, 1771; introduced bill taking away privilege from members' servants, 1770, but generally supported parliamentary privilege; created Baron Cranley, 1776, succeeding to Onslow barony the same year;

comptroller of the household, 1777, and treasurer, 1779; lord of the bedchamber from 1780; present at marriage of George, prince of Wales with Mrs. Fitzherbert, 1785; lord-lieutenant of Surrey; created earl, 1801. [xlii. 219]

ONSLOW, GEORGE or GEORGES (1784-1853), musical composer; grandson of George Onslow, first earl of Onslow [q. v.]; lived and died at Clermont-Ferrand, Auvergne; studied under Hullmandel and J. B. Cramer in England, and afterwards in Paris; original honorary member of London Philharmonic Society, 1832; president of the Institut de France, 1842; composed quintets, symphonies, quartets, sonatas for pianoforte, and trios for piano, violin, and violoncello, besides three operas.
[xlii. 221]

ONSLOW, RICHARD (1528-1571), speaker of the House of Commons; barrister, Inner Temple; recorder of London, 1563; M.P., Steyning, 1557-71; solicitor-general, 1566; speaker of the House of Commons, 1566-71; probable author of 'Arguments relating to Sea Landes and Salt Shores' (edited, 1855). [xlii. 222]

ONSLOW, SIR RICHARD (1601-1664), parliamentarian; grandson of Richard Onslow (1528-1571) [q. v.]; knighted, 1624; M.P. for Surrey, 1628-9 and in Short and Long parliaments; raised a regiment for parliament, 1642; one of the colonels at siege of Basing House, 1644; libelled in Wither's 'Justiciarius Justificatus,' 1646; one of the secluded members, 1647, but sat in Cromwell's two parliaments; member of Cromwell's upper house, 1657, of Richard's parliament, 1659, and of the Convention parliament; intimate with Ashley Cooper (Shaftesbury).
[xlii. 223]

ONSLOW, RICHARD, first BARON ONSLOW (1654-1717), speaker of the House of Commons; grandson of Sir Richard Onslow (1601-1664) [q. v.]; M.P., Guildford, 1679-87, Surrey, 1689-1710 and 1713-16, and St. Mawes, 1710-13; speaker, 1708-10; a lord of the admiralty, 1690-1693; privy councillor, 1710; chancellor of the exchequer, 1714-15; created peer, 1716. [xlii. 224]

ONSLOW, SIR RICHARD, first baronet (1741-1817), admiral, brother of George Onslow (1731-1792) [q. v.]; took part in repulse of D'Estaing in the Cul-de-sac, 1778, and in reliefs of Gibraltar, 1781, 1782; second in command in North Sea, 1796; created baronet for his services at Camperdown and given freedom of the city, 1797; G.C.B., 1815. [xlii. 225]

ONSLOW, THOMAS, second EARL OF ONSLOW (1755-1827), M.P., Rye, 1775-84, Guildford, 1784-1806.
[xlii. 221]

ONWHYN, THOMAS (d. 1886), humorous draughtsman and engraver; executed 'illegitimate' illustrations to Dickens's works, 1837-8; illustrated works by Cockton and others. [xlii. 225]

OPICIUS, JOHANNES (fl. 1497), writer of poems in praise of Henry VII. [xlii. 226]

OPIE, MRS. AMELIA (1769-1853), novelist and poet; née Alderson; sought in marriage by Thomas Holcroft [q. v.]; married John Opie [q. v.], 1798; her tale 'Father and Daughter' well received, 1801, also her poems, 1802; met Fox and other celebrities in Paris; published 'Adeline Mowbray' (suggested by story of Mary Wollstonecraft), 1804, and 'Simple Tales,' 1806; wrote memoir of her husband, 1809; paid frequent visits to London and saw much good society; became a quaker under influence of the Gurneys, 1825; ceased writing stories after 1822, but issued 'Illustrations of Lying,' 1825, 'Detraction Displayed,' 1828, and 'Lays for the Dead,' 1833; much occupied in philanthropic movements; a street in Norwich named after her; intimate with Sydney Smith, Sheridan, Madame de Stael, and Lady Cork. [xlii. 226]

OPIE, JOHN (1761-1807), portrait and historical painter; son of a Cornish carpenter; when employed as a travelling portrait-painter met Dr. Wolcot ('Peter Pindar'); came with him to London, 1780; introduced to the court through Mrs. Boscawen, and became fashionable as 'the Cornish wonder'; received commission from George III and painted many court ladies, 1782, when he began to exhibit at the Academy; elected A.R.A. after exhibition of 'Assassination of Rizzio,' 1787; R.A., 1788; much employed in illustrating; having divorced first wife married Amelia Alderson [see OPIE, AMELIA], 1798; lectured as professor of painting at the Academy, 1807;

died chiefly of overwork; buried in St. Paul's. He painted Dr. Johnson three times, also Fox, Burke, Southey, Bartolozzi, Mrs. Inchbald, and Mrs. Shelley.   [xlii. 230]

O'QUINN, JEREMIAH (d. 1657), Irish presbyterian; M.A. Glasgow, 1644; as minister of Billy, co. Antrim, suspended for refusing to read the Belfast representation against execution of Charles I; after submission in presbytery, 1652, became intermediary between it and government.   [xlii. 233]

ORAM, EDWARD (fl. 1770–1800), landscape-painter; son of William Oram [q. v.]   [xlii. 234]

ORAM, WILLIAM (d. 1777), painter and architect; employed at Buckingham House and Hampton Court.   [xlii. 234]

ORANGE, PRINCESS OF (1631–1660). [See MARY.]

ORCHEYERD or **ORCHARD**, WILLIAM (d. 1504), mason and architect; employed by Wayneflete at Magdalen College, Oxford, and at Eton.   [xlii. 235]

ORD, CRAVEN (1756–1832), antiquary; nephew of Robert Ord [q. v.]; vice-president of Society of Antiquaries and F.R.S.; assisted Gough, Nichols, and others; formed fine collection of impressions of brasses and of historical manuscripts; his Suffolk collections in the British Museum.   [xlii. 235]

ORD, SIR HARRY ST. GEORGE (1819–1885), colonial governor and major-general; served with royal engineers at Bomarsund, 1854; reported on naval works at Ascension, 1850; employed on West African questions, 1856–7; lieutenant-governor of Dominica, 1857–60; governor of the Bermudas, 1860–6; first colonial governor of Straits Settlements, 1867–73, and of South Australia, 1877–9; major-general, 1869; G.C.M.G., 1881.   [xlii. 236]

ORD, JOHN (1729?–1814), lawyer and politician, son of Robert Ord [q. v.]; B.A. Trinity College, Cambridge, 1750, and lay fellow; barrister, Lincoln's Inn; master in chancery, 1778, and sometime chairman of committees in House of Commons; M.P. successively for Midhurst, Hastings, and Wendover (1774–90).   [xlii. 238]

ORD, JOHN WALKER (1811–1853), journalist and author; edited 'Metropolitan Literary Journal' and 'Britannia'; published poems and 'History and Antiquities of Cleveland,' 1846.   [xlii. 237]

ORD or **ORDE**, ROBERT (d. 1778), chief baron of Scottish exchequer.   [xlii. 238]

ORDE, SIR JOHN, first baronet (1751–1824), admiral; commanded Zebra at reduction of Philadelphia, 1778; present at reduction of Charleston, 1780; created baronet, 1790, for services as governor of Dominica (appointed 1783); when third in command under St. Vincent made complaints of supersession by Nelson and Curtis; commanded squadron off Finisterre, 1804–5; admiral, 1805; M.P., Yarmouth (Isle of Wight), 1807–24.   [xlii. 238]

ORDE, afterwards **ORDE-POWLETT**, THOMAS, first BARON BOLTON (1746–1807), chief secretary for Ireland; brother of Sir John Orde [q. v.]; while fellow of King's College, Cambridge, etched portraits of local celebrities; M.A., 1773; barrister, Lincoln's Inn; F.S.A., 1775; M.P., Aylesbury, 1780–4, Harwich, 1784–96, and in Irish parliament for Rathcormack, 1784–90; drew up fifth report of secret committee on Indian affairs, 1781; secretary to the treasury under Shelburne, 1782; as Irish secretary introduced propositions for commercial union with England, 1785, and carried scheme of Irish education, 1787; created peer, 1797; governor of Isle of Wight, 1791; lord-lieutenant of Hampshire, 1800; friend of Romney.   [xlii. 239]

ORDERICUS VITALIS or **ORDERIC VITAL** (1075–1143?), author of 'Historia Ecclesiastica'; born in England, but throughout his life a monk of St. Evroult, Normandy; visited Croyland and Worcester; his work completed, 1141 (valuable after period of Norman Conquest), first printed by Duchesne, 1619, translated into French, 1825, and into English, 1853–5 (Bohn).   [xlii. 241]

ORDGAR or **ORGAR** (d. 971), ealdorman of Devon.   [xlii. 242]

ORDGAR or **ORGAR** (fl. 1066), sheriff of Edward the Confessor.   [xlii. 243]

ORDGAR or **ORGAR** (d. 1097?), English noble; accused Edgar Atheling of treason, and was killed in combat with his champion.   [xlii. 243]

ORDISH, ROWLAND MASON (1824–1886), engineer; made drawings for buildings of exhibition of 1851, and was employed in their re-erection at Sydenham; patented 'straight chain suspension' system for bridges, 1858; designed roofs of St. Pancras and other stations and of the Albert Hall; president of Society of Engineers, 1860.   [xlii. 243]

O'REILLY, ALEXANDER (1722?–1794), Spanish general; born in Ireland; served against Austrians in Italy; in Austrian service against Prussians; joined French army, 1759, but soon re-entered Spanish service; served in Portuguese war, 1762; became governor of Havana and Louisiana; governor of Madrid during émeute of 1765; commanded disastrous expedition against Algiers, 1775; commander-in-chief in Andalusia and governor of Cadiz; died when about to lead army of Eastern Pyrenees against French.   [xlii. 244]

O'REILLY, ANDREW (1742–1832), Austrian general of cavalry; born in Ireland; served in Bavarian succession war, and against the Turks and in Flanders; captured by French, 1796; distinguished himself in Italy, 1800, and at Coldrerio, 1805; as governor of Vienna surrendered to Napoleon, 1809.   [xlii. 245]

O'REILLY, EDMUND (1606–1669), Roman catholic archbishop of Armagh; prefect of college of Irish secular ecclesiastics at Louvain; vicar-general of Dublin, 1642–9; governor of Wicklow, 1642; deprived of vicar-generalship on suspicion of treachery, 1649, but restored, 1650; convicted of murder, 1654, but pardoned; archbishop of Armagh, c. 1654; lived at Lille till 1657; ordered to withdraw from Ireland, 1660; remained at Rome five years; attended Dublin synod, 1666; again banished, 1666; died at Saumur.   [xlii. 246]

O'REILLY, EDMUND JOSEPH (1811–1878), Irish jesuit provincial; studied at Rome; professor of theology at Maynooth, 1838–50; teacher at St. Beuno's college and in the Roman catholic university of Ireland; superior of Milltown Port, Dublin, 1859–78; Irish jesuit provincial, 1863–70; his 'Relations of the Church to Society' issued, 1892.   [xlii. 247]

O'REILLY, EDWARD (d. 1829), compiler of 'Irish-English Dictionary' (1817); published also 'Chronological Account of nearly four hundred Irish Writers,' 1820, and prize essays on the Brehon laws, 1824, and the authenticity of Macpherson's 'Ossian,' 1829.   [xlii. 247]

O'REILLY, HUGH (1580–1653), Roman catholic bishop of Kilmore, 1625–8, and archbishop of Armagh, 1628–53.   [xlii. 246]

O'REILLY, HUGH (d. 1695?). [See REILLY.]

O'REILLY, JOHN BOYLE (1844–1890), Irish revolutionist and author; enlisted in 10th hussars, really as Fenian agent; sentenced to death by court-martial, but his sentence commuted to penal servitude, 1866; escaped from West Australia in American whaler, 1869; after cruising in Indian Ocean settled in Boston, Massachusetts; took part in O'Neill's invasion of Canada, 1870, and in organising rescue by the Catalpa of convicts in West Australia, 1876; edited the 'Pilot' and published four volumes of poems and the convict story 'Moondyne,' 1880; died at Boston, Massachusetts.   [xlii. 248]

O'REILLY, MILES (pseudonym). [See HALPIN or HALPINE, CHARLES GRAHAM, 1829–1868.]

O'REILLY, MYLES WILLIAM PATRICK (1825–1880), Irish politician; B.A. London, 1845; LL.D. London; commanded Irish brigade in papal service; as M.P. for Longford (1862–79) supported Butt; assistant-commissioner of intermediate education, 1879; compiler of a work on Irish catholic martyrs, 1868.   [xlii. 250]

O'REILLY, PHILIP MacHUGH (d. 1657?), Irish rebel; prominent in Irish parliament as member for Cavan, 1639–41; active promoter of rebellion in the county, though discouraging outrage; besieged Drogheda and captured other places, 1642; colonel under Owen Roe O'Neill [q. v.], his brother-in-law; commissioner in the confederate's treaty with royalists, 1646; captured, 1647; served under Hugh O'Neill (fl. 1642–1660) [q. v.] at Clonmel, 1650; laid down his arms and went abroad, 1653; died at Louvain in Spanish service.   [xlii. 250]

OREM, WILLIAM (*fl.* 1702), author of 'Description of the Chanonry, Cathedral, and King's College of Old Aberdeen,' printed, 1791.   [xlii. 252]

ORFORD, EARLS OF. [See RUSSELL, EDWARD, 1653–1727 ; WALPOLE, SIR ROBERT, first EARL of the second creation, 1676–1745 ; WALPOLE, HORATIO, fourth EARL, 1717–1797.]

ORFORD, ROBERT (*fl.* 1290), Dominican writer.   [xlii. 252]

ORFORD, ROBERT (*d.* 1310), bishop of Ely ; prior of Ely, 1299–1302 ; bishop, 1302–10 ; refused confirmation in see by Archbishop Winchelsea, but upheld by the pope after visit to Rome.   [xlii. 252]

ORGER, MRS. MARY ANN (1788–1849), actress ; *née* Ivers ; married George Orger, 1804 ; appeared as Lydia Languish at Drury Lane, London, 1808 ; afterwards acted at the Lyceum, London ; with Vestris at the Olympic and Covent Garden, London, but after 1816 usually seen at Drury Lane ; excelled in broad farce.   [xlii. 253]

ORIEL, first BARON (1740–1828). [See FOSTER, JOHN.]

ORIVALLE, HUGH DE (*d.* 1085), bishop of London, 1075–85 ; a leper.   [xlii. 254]

ORKNEY, EARLS OF. [See PAUL, *d.* 1099 ; SINCLAIR, SIR HENRY, first EARL, *d.* 1400 ? ; SINCLAIR, HENRY, second EARL, *d.* 1418 ; SINCLAIR, SIR WILLIAM, EARL OF CAITHNESS, 1404 ?–1480 ; STEWART, ROBERT, *d.* 1592 ; STEWART, PATRICK, *d.* 1614 ; HAMILTON, LORD GEORGE, 1666–1737.]

ORKNEY, COUNTESS OF (1657 ?–1733). [See VILLIERS, ELIZABETH.]

ORLEANS, DUCHESS OF, fifth daughter of Charles I. (1644–1670). [See HENRIETTA or HENRIETTE ANNE.]

ORLTON or **ORLETON**, ADAM OF (*d.* 1345). [See ADAM.]

ORM or **ORMIN** (*fl.* 1200 ?), author of 'Ormulum' (metrical paraphrases of the gospels of the year, with commentary) ; Augustinian monk of north-east Mercia ; unique manuscript of his 'Ormulum' in Bodleian, probably author's own copy (first printed by R. Meadows White, 1852).   [xlii. 254]

ORME, DANIEL (1766 ?–1832 ?), portrait-painter and engraver to George III ; exhibited at Royal Academy, 1797–1801, and at Manchester.   [xlii. 255]

ORME, ROBERT (1728–1801), author of 'History of the Military Transactions of the British Nation in Indostan from 1745' (vol. i. 1763, ii., iii. 1778) ; educated at Harrow ; entered service of East India Company, 1743 ; as member of Madras council, 1754–8, recommended appointment of Clive to command against Suráj-ud-Dowlah ; commissary-general, 1757–8 ; captured by French on voyage to England, 1759 ; historiographer to East India Company ; published 'Historical Fragments of the Mogul Empire, the Morattoes, and English Concerns in Indostan from 1659' (1782) ; intimate with Dr. Johnson ; his collections of Indian tracts and manuscripts preserved at India office.   [xlii. 256]

ORME, WILLIAM (1787–1830), nonconformist biographer ; aided in formation of Congregational Union of Scotland, 1813 ; pastor of Camberwell Green, London, 1824 ; foreign secretary of London Missionary Society, 1824 ; published memoirs of John Owen, 1820, William Kiffin, 1823, John Urquhart, 1827, and 'Life and Times of Baxter' (posthumously, 1830).   [xlii. 257]

ORMEROD, EDWARD LATHAM (1819–1873), physician ; sixth son of George Ormerod [q. v.] ; educated at Rugby and Caius College, Cambridge ; M.D., 1851 ; F.R.S., 1872 ; physician to Sussex County Hospital, 1853 ; author of pathological papers in St. Bartholomew's Hospital Reports, and 'British Social Wasps,' 1868.   [xlii. 258]

ORMEROD, GEORGE (1785–1873), author of 'History of the County Palatinate and City of Chester,' 1819 ; of Brasenose College, Oxford ; D.C.L., 1818 ; F.R.S., 1819 ; published genealogical works relating to Lancashire and Cheshire, and papers on Roman and British remains in Gloucestershire.   [xlii. 258]

ORMEROD, GEORGE WAREING (1810–1891), geologist ; son of George Ormerod [q. v.] ; M.A. Brasenose

College, Oxford, 1836 ; published papers on Devonshire and Cheshire formations ; indexed publication of the Geological Society.   [xlii. 260]

ORMEROD, OLIVER (1580 ?–1626), controversialist ; B.A. Emmanuel College, Cambridge, 1599 ; held livings in Somerset ; published treatises against puritans and Roman catholics.   [xlii. 260]

ORMEROD, WILLIAM PIERS (1818–1860), anatomist and surgeon ; son of George Ormerod [q. v.] ; friend of Sir James Paget ; demonstrator in anatomy at St. Bartholomew's, 1835–44 ; practised at Oxford ; published 'Clinical Collections and Observations in Surgery,' 1846.   [xlii. 261]

ORMESBY or **ORMSBY**, WILLIAM DE (*d.* 1317), judge ; justice in eyre for northern counties of England, 1292 ; justice of king's bench, 1296 ; as justice of Scotland carried out with some harshness Edward I's measures, and was attacked at Scone, 1297 ; chief of justices of trailbaston in Norfolk and Suffolk, 1305 ; continued to act under Edward II and to be summoned to parliament.   [xlii. 261]

ORMIDALE, LORD (1802–1880). [See MACFARLANE, ROBERT.]

ORMIN (*fl.* 1200 ?). [See ORM.]

ORMISTON, LORD (1656–1735). [See COCKBURN, ADAM.]

ORMOND, LORD (1530 ?–1592). [See CHAMBERS, DAVID.]

ORMONDE, DUKES OF. [See BUTLER, JAMES, first DUKE, 1610–1688 ; BUTLER, JAMES, second DUKE, 1665–1745.]

ORMONDE, first EARL OF (1609–1655). [See DOUGLAS, ARCHIBALD.]

ORMONDE, EARLS OF. [See BUTLER, JAMES, second EARL, 1331–1382 ; BUTLER, JAMES, fourth EARL, *d.* 1452 ; BUTLER, JAMES, fifth EARL, 1420–1461 ; BUTLER, JOHN, sixth EARL, *d.* 1478 ; BUTLER, SIR PIERCE, eighth EARL *d.* 1539 ; BUTLER, THOMAS, tenth EARL, 1532–1614 ; BUTLER, WALTER, eleventh EARL, 1569–1633 ; BUTLER, JAMES, twelfth EARL, 1610–1688.]

ORMONDE, SIR JAMES (*d.* 1497), lord-treasurer of Ireland ; natural son of James Butler, fifth earl of Ormonde [q. v.] ; called 'Black James' ; knighted for services in Ireland during Simnel's rising ; lord-treasurer of Ireland, 1492–4 ; as acting head of his family engaged in constant feuds with Kildare and the Geraldines ; served with Poynings against Warbeck, 1494 ; killed by Sir Piers Butler near Kilkenny.   [xlii. 262]

ORMSBY, JOHN (1829–1895), author ; B.A. Trinity College, Dublin, 1843 ; entered Middle Temple, 1848 ; published translations from Spanish, including 'Poema del Cid' (in English verse and prose), 1879, and 'Don Quixote,' 1885.   [Suppl. iii. 235]

ORMSBY, WILLIAM DE (*d.* 1317). [See ORMESBY.]

ORNSBY, GEORGE (1809–1886), antiquary ; vicar of Fishlake, 1850 ; hon. M.A. Durham, 1872 ; F.S.A., 1873 ; prebendary of York, 1879 ; published 'Sketches of Durham,' 1846, and 'Diocesan History of York,' 1882 ; edited Dean Granville's 'Remains' (vol. i. 1861, vol. ii. 1865), and Cosin's 'Correspondence' (two volumes), 1869–72.   [xlii. 263]

ORNSBY, ROBERT (1820–1889), classical scholar and biographer ; brother of George Ornsby [q. v.] ; B.A. Lincoln College, Oxford, 1840 ; fellow of Trinity College, Oxford, 1843 ; M.A. ; became a Romanist, 1847 ; some time professor of Greek and Latin in Irish Catholic University ; fellow of Royal University of Ireland, 1882 ; published lives of St. Francis de Sales, 1856, and of James Robert Hope-Scott, 1884 ; published 'The Greek Testament from Cardinal Mai's edition of the Vatican Bible,' 1860.   [xlii. 264]

ORONSAY, BARON (1793–1874). [See McNEILL, DUNCAN, BARON COLONSAY and ORONSAY.]

O'ROURKE, SIR BRIAN-NA-MURTHA (*d.* 1591), declared the O'Rourke, 1564 ; knighted and allowed to regain possession of Leitrim by the English, 1578, but rebelled, 1580 ; invaded Connaught, 1580 ; refused to acknowledge the governor and protected refugee

Spaniards, 1588; driven out by Sir Richard Bingham, 1589; fled to Scotland, but was given up by James VI and executed; generally identified with the proud Irish rebel of Bacon's essay 'Of Custom and Education.' [xlii. 264]

O'ROURKE, BRIAN OGE or BRIAN-NA-SAMH-THACH (d. 1604), natural son of Sir Brian-na-Murtha O'Rourke [q. v.], whom he succeeded as O'Rourke; made war on the English and the O'Donnells alternately. [xlii. 266]

O'ROURKE, EDMUND (1814–1879). [See FALCONER.]

O'ROURKE, TIERNAN (d. 1172), king of Breifne (Tighearnan Ua Ruairc); made war on Meath and Connaught; expelled from chieftainship, 1141, but soon restored; attacked O'Connor and (1148) invaded Ulidia; his wife carried off by O'Connor and Diarmait Mac Murchadha, 1152, but reparation made 1167; slain by Hugo de Lacy. [xlii. 266]

ORR, HUGH (1717–1798), inventor of machines for cleaning flax-seed and for the manufacture of cotton; emigrated from Scotland to Bridgewater, Massachusetts, where he introduced the first trip-hammer and the first muskets. [xlii. 267]

ORR, JAMES (1770–1816), United Irishman and poet of Ballycarry; fought at Antrim, 1798; his song, 'The Irishman,' erroneously attributed to Curran. [xlii. 267]

ORR, JOHN (1760?–1835), lieutenant-general of the Madras army; while governor of Pondicherry rendered important services to Sir Eyre Coote's army as commander of a flying column, 1780–4; afterwards commanded Lord Macartney's bodyguard; chief officer of 1st native cavalry in second Mysore war, 1790–2. [xlii. 267]

ORR, WILLIAM (1766–1797), United Irishman; charged with administering a treasonable oath to soldiers, 1796; tried at Carrickfergus, and though defended by Curran (who brought forward affidavits of improper influence on the jury) convicted and executed; his memory popularised in Drennan's poem. [xlii. 268]

ORRERY, EARLS OF. [See BOYLE, ROGER, first EARL, 1621–1679; BOYLE, CHARLES, fourth EARL, 1676–1731; BOYLE, JOHN, fifth EARL, 1707–1762.]

ORRERY, COUNTESS OF (1746–1840). [See MONCKTON, MARY.]

ORRIDGE, BENJAMIN BROGDEN (1814–1870), antiquary; member of court of common council of London, 1863–9; chief works, 'Account of Citizens of London and their Rulers, 1060 to 1867' (1867), and 'Illustrations of Jack Cade's Rebellion' (1869). [xlii. 269]

ORTELIANUS, JACOBUS COLIUS (1563–1628), nephew of Abraham Ortelius [q. v.]; a London silk-merchant; published 'De Statu Civitatis Londinensis peste laborantis,' 1604, and other works. [xlii. 270]

ORTELIUS, ABRAHAM (1527–1598), map-maker of Antwerp; became intimate with Camden in England; geographer to Philip II of Spain, 1573; helped Humphrey Llwyd with map of England and Wales; published 'Theatrum Orbis Terrarum,' 1570; died at Antwerp. [xlii. 269]

ORTON, ARTHUR (1834–1898), the Tichborne claimant; youngest son of a butcher at Wapping; went to sea, c. 1849; deserted at Valparaiso; lived eighteen months at Melipilla and returned to England, 1851; entered his father's business; emigrated to Australia, 1852, and ceased to correspond with his family, 1854; returned to England, 1866, at invitation of Lady Tichborne (d. 1868), widow of Sir James Francis Doughty Tichborne, tenth baronet (d. 1862), who had convinced herself from descriptions that he was her eldest son Roger Charles, who was reported to have been drowned at sea in 1854, and whose will was proved, 1855; was received by Lady Tichborne, who professed to recognise in him her long-lost son; brought ejectment action (1871–2) against Sir Henry Tichborne, twelfth baronet, and posthumous heir of Sir Alfred Tichborne, Sir James's younger son, who had succeeded as eleventh baronet, 1862, and died, 1866; at the trial, which lasted 102 days, Serjeant Ballantine led for the claimant, and Sir John (afterwards Lord chief-justice) Coleridge [q. v.] and Mr. Hawkins, Q.C. (afterwards Sir Henry Hawkins, lord Brampton), for the trustees of the Tichborne estates; finally Serjeant

Ballantine elected to be non-suited; the claimant was accordingly arrested for perjury, was tried, 1873–4 (188 days), and was sentenced to fourteen years' penal servitude, Mr. Hawkins leading for the crown and Edward Vaughan Hyde Kenealy [q. v.] representing the claimant. He was released, 1884, and subsequently died in poverty in Marylebone, after publishing (1895) in the 'People' newspaper, a signed confession of his imposture, which he is said afterwards to have recanted. [Suppl. iii. 236]

ORTON, JOB (1717–1783), dissenting minister; educated at Shrewsbury, where he was minister of a united congregation of presbyterians and independents, 1741–66; assistant to Doddridge at Northampton, 1739–41; afterwards retired to Kidderminster, where he kept up an extensive correspondence; published 'Memoirs of Doddridge,' 1766, and theological and devotional works. [xlii. 271]

ORTON, REGINALD (1810–1862), surgeon to Sunderland Eye Infirmary; instrumental in obtaining repeal of glass and window duties; patented a lifeboat and reel life-buoy, 1845. [xlii. 272]

ORUM, JOHN (d. 1436?), vice-chancellor of Oxford University, 1406 and 1408; D.D. University College, Oxford; canon of Wells, 1410; archdeacon of Cornwall, 1411; chancellor of Exeter, 1429–36; author of 'Lectures (Latin) on the Apocalypse.' [xlii. 273]

OSBALD (d. 799), king of Northumbria, 796; outlawed after twenty-seven days' reign; fled to Lindisfarne, but left on Alcuin's exhortation and became abbot among the Picts. [xlii. 273]

OSBALDESTON, GEORGE (1787–1866), sportsman; master of hounds while at Brasenose College, Oxford; master of Quorn hounds, 1817–21 and 1823–8, afterwards of Pytchley; rode two hundred miles in ten consecutive hours, and fought duel with Lord George Bentinck, 1831; M.P., East Retford, 1812–18. [xlii. 274]

OSBALDESTON or **OSBOLSTON**, LAMBERT (1594–1659), master of Westminster School; educated at Westminster School and Christ Church, Oxford; M.A., 1619 (incorporated M.A. Cambridge, 1628); had joint-patent of mastership, 1621; master of Westminster School, 1625–39; prebendary of Westminster, Lincoln, and Wells; sentenced to the pillory, fine, and forfeiture, for letters reflecting on Laud, 1639; restored to benefices by Long parliament. [xlii. 275]

OSBALDESTON, RICHARD (1690–1764), bishop of Carlisle and London; M.A. St. John's College, Cambridge, 1714; fellow of Peterhouse, 1714; D.D., 1726; chaplain to George II and tutor to George III; bishop of Carlisle, 1747–62, of London, 1762–4; neglected Carlisle diocese and prohibited introduction of statuary at St. Paul's, London; patronised John Jortin [q. v.] [xlii. 275]

OSBALDESTON or **OSBOLSTON**, WILLIAM (1577–1645), divinity professor at Gresham College, London; brother of Lambert Osbaldeston [q. v.]; professor, 1610–1611; deprived of benefices by parliament. [xlii. 276]

OSBERHT, OSBRITH, or **OSBYRHT** (d. 867), under-king of Northumbria; deposed, 866; defeated and slain by Danes at York, together with his rival, Ælla (d. 867) [q. v.] [xlii. 277]

OSBERN (fl. 1090), hagiographer; sub-prior and precentor of Christ Church, Canterbury; compiled lives of Dunstan, Alphege, and Archbishop Odo of Canterbury, under Lanfranc's direction; treatises on music also attributed to him. [xlii. 277]

OSBERN or **OSBERT** (d. 1103), bishop of Exeter, and chancellor in early years of William I; brother of William Fitzosbert [q. v.]; chaplain to Edward the Confessor; bishop of Exeter, 1072–1103. [xlii. 278]

OSBERN, CLAUDIANUS (fl. 1148), classical scholar; monk of Gloucester under Hamelin. [xlii. 278]

OSBERT OF STOKE (fl. 1136). [See CLARE, OSBERT DE.]

OSBOLSTON. [See OSBALDESTON.]

OSBORN WYDDEL (the IRISHMAN) (fl. 1280), founder of Merionethshire families; migrated from Ireland, and was perhaps a Geraldine. [xlii. 279]

OSBORN, ELIAS (1643–1720), quaker; imprisoned for non-payment of tithes, 1670; built meeting-house at

Ilminster; imprisoned, 1680; subsequently preached in western counties; his autobiography published, 1723.
[xlii. 279]

OSBORN, GEORGE (1808–1891), president of Wesleyan conference, 1863 and 1881; professor of divinity at Richmond College, 1868–85; published 'Poetical Works of J. and C. Wesley,' 1868, and 'Outlines of Wesleyan Bibliography,' 1869.
[xlii. 280]

OSBORN, JOHN (1584?–1634?), worker in pressed horn and whalebone; settled at Amsterdam, 1600.
[xlii. 281]

OSBORN, ROBERT DURIE (1835–1889), orientalist and soldier; saw service in the Indian mutiny, 1857–9, and served in Afghan campaign of 1879; retired as lieutenant-colonel, 1879; published 'Islam under the Arabs,' 1876, and 'Islam under the Khalifs of Baghdad,' 1877, also 'Lawn Tennis,' 1881, and other works; when editor of the 'Statesman,' 1879–80, opposed Lord Lytton's Indian policy.
[xlii. 281]

OSBORN, SHERARD (1822–1875), rear-admiral and author; commanded tender at blockade of Quedah, 1838–9; served in Chinese war, 1840–3; commanded the Pioneer steam-tender in Captain Austin's arctic expedition, 1850–1, and in Sir Edward Belcher's expedition, 1852–4; C.B. for services against Russia in Sea of Azov, 1855; escorted gunboats to Canton, 1857, and took Lord Elgin to Shanghai, Yedo, and up the Yangtze to Hankow, 1858; managing director of Telegraph Construction Company, 1867–73; rear-admiral, 1873; member of the Arctic Committee of 1874–5; published 'Last Voyage and Fate of Sir John Franklin,' and other works on Arctic exploration (collected, 1865).
[xlii. 282]

OSBORNE, DOROTHY, afterwards LADY TEMPLE (1627–1695). [See TEMPLE, DOROTHY, LADY.]

OSBORNE, SIR EDWARD (1530?–1591), lord mayor of London; said to have rescued infant daughter of Sir William Hewett [q. v.] from the Thames when apprentice, c. 1545; married her, and succeeded to Hewett's business and estates; traded with Spain and Turkey; obtained incorporation of Turkey company, and was its first governor; president of St. Thomas's Hospital, London, 1586–91; alderman of London, 1573, sheriff, 1575, lord mayor, 1583; knighted, 1584; M.P. for the city of London, 1586; ancestor of first Duke of Leeds.
[xlii. 284]

OSBORNE, FRANCIS (1593–1659), author of 'Advice to a Son,' 1656; master of horse to William Herbert, third earl of Pembroke [q. v.]; afterwards in office of lord-treasurer's remembrancer, and employed under Commonwealth at Oxford; friend of Hobbes; his 'Advice' ridiculed by John Heydon (fl. 1667) [q. v.], but one of the most popular contemporary works; published also 'Traditional Memoirs of Reigns of Queen Elizabeth and King James I,' 1658, and other works (first collected, 1673). [xlii. 285]

OSBORNE, FRANCIS, fifth DUKE OF LEEDS (1751–1799), politician; of Westminster School and Christ Church, Oxford; M.A., 1769; D.C.L., 1773; as Marquis of Carmarthen represented Eye and Helston, 1774–5; called to House of Lords as Baron Osborne of Kiveton, 1776, but known as Carmarthen till his succession to dukedom, 1789; lord chamberlain to George III's queen, and privy councillor, 1777; dismissed from lord-lieutenancy of East Riding of Yorkshire for opposition to Lord North, 1780; restored by second Rockingham ministry and named ambassador extraordinary to Paris, 1782; foreign secretary under Pitt, 1783–91, resigning on question of Russian armament; took part in negotiations for coalition between Pitt and Fox, 1791; his 'Political Memoranda' printed, 1884.
[xlii. 286]

OSBORNE, GEORGE ALEXANDER (1806–1893), pianist and composer; appointed instructor to eldest son of Prince of Orange by influence of Prince de Chimay; as chapel-master of Prince of Orange at Brussels gave successful concerts, and collaborated with De Bériot; captured by revolutionists, 1830; while in Paris (1831–44) intimate with Berlioz and Chopin; accompanied Chopin in F minor concerto, 1832; returned to England (1844) where he played, taught pupils, and composed chamber and violin music, overtures, and two operas; his 'Pluie de Perles' published in Paris.
[xlii. 289]

OSBORNE or **OSBORN**, HENRY (1698?–1771), admiral; present in action off Cape Passaro, 1718;

commanded the Princess Caroline in Toulon action, 1744; commander-in-chief on Leeward islands station, 1748; in Mediterranean, 1757–8, where he captured two French ships; admiral of the white and vice-admiral of England, 1763.
[xlii. 290]

OSBORNE, PEREGRINE, second DUKE OF LEEDS (1658–1729), vice-admiral; created Viscount Osborne in Scottish peerage, 1674; summoned to parliament as Baron Osborne of Kiveton, 1690, but known as Earl of Danby, 1689–94, and Marquis of Carmarthen, 1694–1712; captain of the Windsor Castle at Barfleur, 1692; led covering squadron at attempted landing in Camaret Bay, 1694; allowed valuable East Indiaman to be captured, 1695; vice-admiral of the white, 1702; succeeded to dukedom, 1712.
[xlii. 291]

OSBORNE, PETER (1521–1592), keeper of the privy purse to Edward VI; of Cambridge and Lincoln's Inn; barrister; friend of Sir John Cheke [q. v.] and other leading reformers; ecclesiastical commissioner, 1566; M.P., Horsham, 1562–3, Plympton, 1572, Aldeburgh, 1584–6, and Westminster, 1588; an authority on commercial matters; executor of Archbishop Parker; member of commission of oyer and terminer, 1570.
[xlii. 292]

OSBORNE, SIR PETER (1584–1653), governor of Guernsey; grandson of Peter Osborne [q. v.]; knighted, 1611; M.P., Corfe Castle, 1623–4 and 1625; held Castle Cornet (Guernsey) for Charles I till 1646.
[xlii. 293]

OSBORNE, RALPH BERNAL (1808–1882). [See BERNAL OSBORNE.]

OSBORNE, RUTH (1680–1751), reputed witch; died from effects of ducking by mob at Longmarstone, Buckinghamshire; a chimney-sweep hanged for her murder at Tring; last victim of English belief in witchcraft.
[xlii. 293]

OSBORNE, LORD SIDNEY GODOLPHIN (1808–1889), philanthropist; of Rugby and Brasenose College, Oxford; B.A., 1830; rector of Stoke Pogis, 1832, of Durweston, Dorset, 1841–75; visited the Nightingale hospitals at Scutari during Crimean war and western Ireland during the famine; as 'S. G. O.' addressed letters to 'The Times' on agricultural, social, educational, and other matters (selection issued, 1888); published various works.
[xlii. 294]

OSBORNE, SIR THOMAS, successively first EARL OF DANBY, MARQUIS OF CARMARTHEN, and DUKE OF LEEDS (1631–1712), statesman; great-grandson of Sir Edward Osborne [q. v.]; succeeded to baronetcy and Yorkshire estates, 1647; introduced at court by Buckingham; high sheriff of Yorkshire, 1661; M.P., York, 1665; attacked lord-chancellor Clarendon; treasurer of the navy, 1671; made privy councillor and a Scottish peer, 1673, and soon after lord high treasurer of England and a British peer; created earl and lord-lieutenant of the West Riding, 1674; managed the House of Commons during his five years' administration by corruption, and enriched himself, but tried to maintain national credit and to neutralise French influence; failed to pass proposal to make profession of passive obedience necessary qualification for office, 1675; K.G., 1677; made peace with Holland and promoted marriage of Mary, the Duke of York's daughter, with William of Orange, 1677; obliged to connive at secret treaty between Charles II and Louis XIV, 1676, and to demand Charles II's pension from France, 1678; impeached, 1678, after betrayal by Ralph Montagu [q. v.] of his letters to Louis XIV, being also charged with concealing the 'Popish plot'; received pardon from Charles II under great seal and promise of marquisate on resignation, 1679, but his impeachment being revived in new parliament, although the trial was not proceeded with, he was kept prisoner in the Tower of London; was accused by Oates of plotting murder of Godfrey; refused bail in 1682 and 1683, but granted it, 1684, and released from Tower; resumed seat in House of Lords, 1685; on the dismissal of Halifax (1685) joined the opposition to James II, became reconciled with the whigs, signed the invitation to William of Orange, and secured York for him, but supported the claim of the Princess Mary (Mary II) to the crown; lord-president of the council, 1689–99, being virtually prime minister, 1690–5; created marquis, 1689, and duke, 1694; lord-lieutenant of Yorkshire, 1692–9; bitterly attacked by whigs and accused of Jacobite intrigues; supported

Triennial bill, 1694 ; impeached for receiving bribe to procure East India charter, 1695, but proceedings not concluded ; created D.C.L. of Oxford and commissioner of trade, 1695 ; discouraged attainder of Fenwick ; attacked Halifax in House of Lords, 1702 ; granted pension, 1710 ; published defences of his conduct under Charles II, 1710 ; left large fortune ; his papers acquired by British Museum, 1869. [xlii. 295]

OSBORNE, THOMAS (d. 1767), bookseller ; at his shop in Gray's Inn Gateway issued Richardson's ' Pamela,' the catalogue (1743-5) of the Harleian Library purchased by him, and the ' Harleian Miscellany' (1744-6); satirised in the ' Dunciad ' ; principal bookseller of his time, but ignorant of books ; beaten by Dr. Johnson for impertinence. [xlii. 303]

OSBORNE, WILLIAM (1736-1808), man-midwife ; practised as surgeon and became M.D. of St. Andrews, 1777 ; lectured on obstetrics, and published ' Essay on Laborious Paturition,' 1783 ; opposed Cæsarian section. [xlii. 305]

OSBORNE MORGAN, SIR GEORGE (1826-1897). [See MORGAN.]

OSBRITH (d. 867). [See OSBERHT.]

OSBURGA or OSBURH (fl. 861), wife of Ethelwulf [q. v.], king of the West-Saxons, and mother of Alfred the Great and three other kings. [xlii. 305]

OSGAR, OSCAR, or ORDGAR (d. 984), abbot of Abingdon, 963-84 ; brought Benedictine rule from Fleury ; finished buildings begun by Ethelwold [q. v.] [xlii. 305]

OSGITH or OSYTH (fl. 7th cent. ?) [See OSYTH.]

OSGODBY, ADAM DE (d. 1316), keeper of the rolls of chancery, 1295-1316, and temporary keeper of great seal under Edward I and Edward II ; held numerous offices and attended Edward II's council in later years. [xlii. 306]

OSGOD CLAPA (d. 1054), thegn in the service of Cnut ; outlawed by Edward the Confessor, 1046 ; took service with Swegen Estrithson of Denmark, and harried Essex coast, 1049 ; died probably in England ; Clapham said to be named from his house there. [xlii. 307]

OSGOODE, WILLIAM (1754-1824), Canadian judge ; M.A. Christ Church, Oxford, 1777 ; barrister, Lincoln's Inn, 1779 ; published ' Remarks on Laws of Descent,' 1779 ; chief-justice of Upper Canada, 1792-4, of Lower Canada, 1794-1801 ; as president of committee of public lands carried on contest with Prescott (lieutenant-governor), who espoused cause of French Canadians ; member of royal commissions on courts of law. [xlii. 307]

O'SHANASSY, SIR JOHN (1818-1883), Australian statesman ; left Ireland, 1839 ; settled in Melbourne, 1846 ; agitated for separation from New South Wales, and against penal settlements ; member for Melbourne in legislative council, 1851 ; member of gold commission, 1855 ; elected for Melbourne and Kilmore to first legislative assembly of Victoria, 1856 ; premier of Victoria, 1857, 1858-9, and 1861-3 ; member of legislative council for central province, 1868-74 ; K.C.M.G., 1874 ; supported free trade, immigration, and Australian federation ; negotiated first Victorian loan and carried Crown Lands Act (1862) and Local Government Act. [xlii. 308]

O'SHAUGHNESSY, ARTHUR WILLIAM EDGAR (1844-1881), poet and herpetologist; assistant in zoological department, British Museum, from 1863 ; published ' Epic of Women,' 1870, ' Lays of France,' 1872, and ' Music and Moonlight,' 1874 ; collaborated with wife in ' Toyland,' 1875 ; English correspondent of ' Le Livre.' [xlii. 308]

O'SHAUGHNESSY, WILLIAM (1674-1744), major-general in French service ; of Gort, co. Galway ; went to France with Daniel O'Brien's Irish brigade, 1690 ; served in Italian campaign, 1692-6 ; in Germany, 1702-5, being present at Blenheim, 1704 ; fought at Ramillies, 1706, Oudenarde, 1708, and Malplaquet, 1709 ; at siege of Kehl, 1733 ; major-general (maréchal-de-camp, 1734) ; commanded at Cambray, 1743 ; died at Gravelines. [xlii. 309]

O'SHAUGHNESSY, SIR WILLIAM BROOKE (1809-1889), director-general of Indian telegraphs ; assumed name of Brooke, 1861 ; M.D. Edinburgh, 1830 ; F.R.S.,

1843 ; sometime surgeon in Bengal army and professor of chemistry at Calcutta ; laid down first Indian telegraphs as director-general, 1853 ; knighted, 1856 ; published works on chemistry. [xlii. 310]

OSHERE (fl. 680), under-king of the Hwiccii. [xlii. 311]

OSKYTEL (d. 971), bishop of Dorchester, 950, and archbishop of York, 956-71 ; invited Oswald (d. 992) [q. v.] to live with him, 958, and learnt from him Benedictine rule. [xlii. 311]

OSLAC (fl. 954-975), Northumbrian earl ; ruled Deira under Edgar, 954-75 ; styled ' the great earl ' in ' Saxon Chronicle ' ; banished, 975. [xlii. 311]

OSLER, EDWARD (1798-1863), author of ' Life of Admiral Viscount Exmouth ' (1835); house-surgeon at Swansea Infirmary, 1819-25 ; when naval surgeon visited West Indies and wrote ' The Voyage,' a poem ; collaborated with William John Hall in the ' Mitre Hymn-Book ' ; published ' Church and King ' ; edited ' Royal Cornwall Gazette ' from 1841. [xlii. 312]

OSMUND (fl. 758), king of the South-Saxons. [xlii. 313]

OSMUND (fl. 803), bishop of London. [xlii. 313]

OSMUND or OSMER, SAINT (d. 1099), bishop of Salisbury ; accompanied his uncle, William of Normandy, to England ; acted as chancellor, 1072-8, and was employed in Domesday survey ; bishop of Salisbury, 1078-99 ; consecrated Sarum Cathedral, 1092 ; founded chapter on Norman model and drew up an Ordinal and Consuetudinary for the diocese (' Use of Sarum '); canonised, 1457, when his bones were translated to Salisbury ; ' Register of St. Osmund ' printed, 1883-4. [xlii. 313]

OSRED (697 ?-716), king of Northumbria, 705-16, succeeding his father, Aldfrith [q. v.], after Eadwulf's short usurpation ; ruled with violence ; slain in battle with his kinsman, Cenred. [xlii. 315]

OSRED (d. 792), king of Northumbria ; succeeded Alfwold, 788, but was captured, tonsured, and banished to Man by Æthelred, 789 ; returned secretly, but was taken and put to death. [xlii. 315]

OSRIC (d. 634), king of Deira, 633-4 ; cousin of Edwin of Northumbria [q. v.] ; defeated and slain by Cædwalla (d. 634) [q. v.] [xlii. 315]

OSRIC (d. 729), king of Northumbria ; grandson of Oswy [q. v.] ; sometimes identified with Osric, king of the Hwiccii ; founded Gloucester Abbey. [xlii. 315]

OSSIAN or OISIN, legendary character in Gaelic literature ; said to have been associate of Fionn and other third-century warriors at court of Tara and to have related their exploits to St. Patrick ; Macpherson's ' translations ' inconsistent with accurate knowledge of Gaelic literature. [xlii. 316]

OSSINGTON, first VISCOUNT (1800-1873). [See DENISON, JOHN EVELYN.]

OSSORY, EARLS OF. [See BUTLER, SIR PIERCE or PIERS, first EARL, d. 1539 ; BUTLER, THOMAS, third EARL, 1532-1614 ; BUTLER, WALTER, fourth EARL, 1569-1633 ; BUTLER, JAMES, fifth EARL, 1610-1688.]

OSSORY, styled EARL OF (1634-1680). [See BUTLER, THOMAS.]

OSSORY, LORD OF (d. 888). [See CEARBHALL.]

OSTLER, WILLIAM (fl. 1601-1623), actor ; when one of the children of Queen Elizabeth's chapel, played in Jonson's ' Poetaster,' 1601 ; appeared also in the ' Alchemist,' 1610, and ' Catiline,' 1611 ; played Antonio in ' Duchess of Malfy,' c. 1616. [xlii. 317]

OSTRITH or OSTHRYTH (d. 697), queen of Mercia ; daughter of Oswy [q. v.] ; married Ethelred, son of Penda [q. v.] of Mercia, 675 ; removed bones of St. Oswald to Bardney Abbey ; murdered by Mercian nobles. [xlii. 317]

O'SULLIVAN or O'SULLIVAN-BEARE, DONALL (1560-1618), chief of the O'Sullivans of Beare, co. Cork ; held Dunboy Castle with Spanish garrison against Sir George Carew, 1602 ; after its capture retired to Glengariff and Ulster ; ennobled by Philip III of Spain ; killed by a refugee at Madrid. [xlii. 318]

O'SULLIVAN, (SIR) JOHN (*fl.* 1747), adjutant-general to the Young Pretender; served in French army during war of Austrian succession; assisted Lochiel in capture of Edinburgh, 1745, and drew up rebel army at Culloden, 1746; afterwards escaped to France; knighted by the Pretender, 1747. [xlii. 318]

O'SULLIVAN, MORTIMER (1791?–1859), Irish protestant divine; M.A. Trinity College, Dublin, 1832; Donellan lecturer, 1851; prebendary of St. Patrick's, 1827–30; chaplain to the earl of Carlisle when viceroy; published in answer to Moore 'Captain Rock Detected' (1824) and 'Guide to an Irish Gentleman in Search of a Religion' (1833), and to Newman, 'Theory of Developments in Christian Doctrine applied and tested' (1846), and with William Phelan 'Digest of Evidence on State of Ireland' (1826). [xlii. 319]

O'SULLIVAN or O'SULLIVAN-BEARE, PHILIP (1590?–1660?), author; nephew of Donall O'Sullivan or O'Sullivan-Beare [q. v.]; educated at Compostella; served with Spanish fleet; published 'Historiæ Catholicæ Iberniæ Compendium,' 1621, a life of St. Patrick, 1629, and other works. [xlii. 320]

O'SULLIVAN, SAMUEL (1790–1851), Irish divine and author; brother of Mortimer O'Sullivan [q. v.]; M.A. Trinity College, Dublin, 1825; chaplain to Royal Hibernian Military School, Dublin, 1827. [xlii. 320]

O'SULLIVAN, THOMAS HERBERT (*d.* 1824), soldier of fortune; son of (Sir) John O'Sullivan [q. v.]; served with John Paul Jones [q. v.], 1779, and in the British army; died a major in the Dutch service at the Hague. [xlii. 319]

OSWALD or OSUUALD, SAINT (605?–642), king of the Northumbrians; son of Ethelfrith [q. v.]; on his father's death fled to Iona and became Christian; defeated Cædwalla (*d.* 634) [q. v.] at Hefenfelth, near Hexham, 634, where he set up a cross; became king of all Northumbria, 634; helped Aidan [q. v.] to spread Christianity, adopting the Scottish rite; completed Edwine's church at York; said to have been over-lord of Strathclyde; exercised authority over the Trent Valley and in Lindsey; his supremacy acknowledged by West-Saxons and probably by Kent; called 'sixth Bretwalda' by Bede and 'emperor of all Britain' by Adamnan; defeated and slain by Penda [q. v.] of Mercia; his body translated from Bardney to monastery founded in his honour by Ethelfleda [q. v.] at Gloucester, 909; his head and hands carried to Bamborough, where they were venerated; the head taken to Lindisfarne and carried thence in St. Cuthbert's coffin to Durham, 1104. [xlii. 321]

OSWALD, SAINT (*d.* 992), archbishop of York; nephew of Archbishop Odo (*d.* 959) [q. v.]; when head of secular house at Winchester went to Fleury to learn the Benedictine rule; accompanied Oskytel [q. v.] to Rome, 959, and afterwards assisted him at York; bishop of Worcester, 961–92; co-operated with Dunstan and Ethelwold [q. v.] in replacing married clergy by monks, but showed moderation in reforms; founded monasteries at Westbury, Worcester, Winchcombe, and the Isle of Ramsey; archbishop of York, 972–92; took part in coronation of Eadgar, 973; removed bones of St. Wilfrid from Ripon to Worcester; encouraged learning. [xlii. 323]

OSWALD or OSWOLD (*fl.* 1010), monk of Ramsey; nephew of St. Oswald (*d.* 992) [q. v.]; studied at Fleury and visited abbeys in France; enjoyed great repute as scholar and was probably author of 'Vita S. Oswaldi' and of the Worcester manuscript at Corpus Christi College, Cambridge. [xlii. 325]

OSWALD (*d.* 1437), priest of the Charterhouse, Perth, 1429–37; friend of Gerson. [xlii. 326]

OSWALD, GEORGE (*d.* 1819), rector of Glasgow University, 1797; nephew of Richard Oswald [q. v.] [xlii. 330]

OSWALD, JAMES (1715–1769), politician and friend of Adam Smith; called to Scottish bar, 1740; M.P., Kirkcaldy burghs, 1741–7 and 1754–68, Fifeshire, 1747–54; Scottish commissioner of the navy, 1744; commissioner of trade, 1751–9; a lord of the treasury, 1759–63; privy councillor and joint vice-treasurer in Ireland, 1763. [xlii. 326]

OSWALD, JOHN (*d.* 1793), republican pamphleteer; served with the 42nd highlanders in America and India; joined the Jacobin Club at Paris; published poems and pamphlets, political and vegetarian; killed at head of his regiment at Ponts-de-Cée, La Vendée. [xlii. 326]

OSWALD, SIR JOHN (1771–1840), general; grandson of James Oswald [q. v.]; took part in capture of French West Indies, 1794; commanded 35th regiment in Holland, 1799, and at reduction of Malta, 1800; commanded brigade at Maida, 1806; captured Scylla Castle, 1806; led attack on Alexandria and defended Rosetta, 1807; commanded reserve in capture of Ischia and Procida, 1809; directed capture of Ionian islands, 1809; drove French from Santa Maura, 1810; held temporary command of the 5th division in the Peninsula, 1812–13; G.C.B., 1824; general, 1837; G.C.M.G., 1838. [xlii. 327]

OSWALD, RICHARD (1705–1784), merchant and politician; commissary to Brunswick's army in Seven years' war; introduced by Adam Smith to Shelburne; Shelburne's agent in negotiations with Franklin at Paris, 1782, and was chief negotiator of the treaty with United States. [xlii. 329]

OSWELL, WILLIAM COTTON (1818–1893), African explorer; educated at Rugby and the East Indian College, Haileybury; during his ten years in Madras civil service won reputation as linguist and elephant hunter; spent two years' furlough in hunting over unexplored South Africa; took part in Livingstone's discovery of Lake Ngami, 1849, and the Zambesi, 1851; during Crimean war carried secret-service money from Lord Raglan to Sir Lintorn Simmons at Shumla; contributed African chapter to C. P. Wolley's 'Big Game Shooting.' [xlii. 330]

OSWEN, JOHN (*fl.* 1548–1553), printer at Ipswich and Worcester; issued, among other publications, Cranmer's New Testament, 1550. [xlii. 331]

OSWESTRY, LORD OF (1223–1267). [See FITZALAN, JOHN II.]

OSWIN or OSWINI (*d.* 651), last king of Deira; son of Osric (*d.* 634) [q. v.]; recalled from exile in Wessex, 642, and ruled Deira under Penda [q. v.], but helped St. Aidan; betrayed by Hunvald to Oswy [q. v.], king of Bernicia, and murdered at Ingetlingum (Gilling); said to have been buried at Tynemouth, where he had a shrine. [xlii. 332]

OSWULF or OSULF (*d.* 758), king of Northumbria; succeeded his father, Eadberht, who resigned the kingdom to him, 758; assassinated by the men of his household. [xlii. 333]

OSWULF or OSULF (*d.* 1067), earl of Bernicia under Morcar [q. v.], 1065–7; slew Copsige [q. v.], his dispossessor, but was himself slain soon after. [xlii. 333]

OSWY, OSUIU, OSWIU, OSWIO, OSGUID, OSWEUS, OSWIUS (612?–670), king of Northumbria; younger son of Ethelfrith [q. v.]; baptised in Iona; became king of Bernicia, 643; had constant wars with Penda and the Britons; married daughter of Eadwine; invaded Deira, 651, and procured death of Oswin [q. v.], after whose death he ruled all Northumbria, 651–70; erected monastery at Gilling in expiation; gave Peada [q. v.], king of the Middle Angles, his daughter in marriage conditionally on his acceptance of Christianity, *c.* 653; assisted in reconversion of East-Saxons; defeated Penda [q. v.] by the river Winwæd, 655, and gained possession of Mercia, Lindsey, and the land of the South-Angles; his supremacy also acknowledged by East-Angles and East-Saxons; probably ruled Britons of Alclyde and Scots of Dalriada, and is said to have subjugated Picts; seventh Bretwalda of the 'Saxon Chronicle'; lost Southern Mercia, 658; presided at synod of Whitby, 664, and accepted Roman rite, but substituted Ceadda [q. v.] for Wilfrith to see of York after rebellion of Alchfrith. [xlii. 333]

OSWYN (*fl.* 803). [See OSMUND.]

OSYTH, OSITH, or OSGITH, SAINT (*fl.* 7th cent.?), said to have been a granddaughter of the Mercian king Penda [q. v.]; founded a nunnery at Chich, Essex; according to an unhistorical legend beheaded by Danes on her refusal to apostatise. [xlii. 337]

OTHERE (*fl.* 880). [See OHTHERE.]

O'TOOLE, ADAM DUFF (*d.* 1327), reputed heretic; burnt at Le Hogges, Dublin. [xlii. 337]

O'TOOLE, BRYAN (*d.* 1825), lieutenant-colonel; served with Hompesch's hussars in France and Belgium, 1792-3, in Holland, 1794-5, the West Indies, 1796-7; aide-de-camp to Sir Galbraith Lowry Cole [q. v.] at Maida, 1806; commanded Calabrian free corps, 1810; served with Portuguese in Peninsula; lieutenant-colonel, 1813; C.B., 1815. [xlii. 338]

O'TOOLE, LAURENCE (LORCÁN UA TUATHAIL) (1130 ?-1180), Irish saint and first archbishop of Dublin; coarb of Glendalough, 1155; archbishop of Dublin, 1162-1180; converted secular canons of Christ Church, Dublin, into canons regular of Aroasia; practised austerities: attended great meeting at Athboy, 1167; took leading part in rising against Anglo-Norman invaders, 1171; attended council of Cashel, 1172; ambassador of Roderic O'Connor (1116 ?-1198) [q. v.] to Henry II at Windsor, 1175; attended Lateran Council and obtained bull of confirmation for Dublin, 1179; again appealed to Henry II, 1180; followed him to France and died at Eu, being buried in the cathedral; canonised, 1226. [xlii. 338]

OTTEBY, JOHN (*d.* 1487). [See HOTHBY.]

OTTER, WILLIAM (1768-1840), bishop of Chichester; of Jesus College, Cambridge; fourth wrangler, 1790; M.A., 1793; fellow, 1796-1804; D.D., 1836; master of Helston grammar school, 1791-6; travelled with Malthus in northern Europe, 1799; rector of Colmworth, 1804, of Sturmer, 1810, of Chetwynd, 1811, of St. Mark's, Kennington, 1825; first principal of King's College, London, 1830-6; Chichester theological college founded during his episcopate (1836-40); training college erected in his memory, 1850; published 'Life and Remains of Edw. Daniel Clarke,' 1824, and wrote memoir of Malthus prefixed to 'Political Economy,' 1836. [xlii. 340]

OTTERBOURNE, NICHOLAS (*fl.* 1448-1459), clerk-registrar of Scotland and secretary to James II; M.A. Glasgow; reputed author of 'Epithalamium Jacobi II, Lib. I.' [xlii. 341]

OTTERBOURNE, THOMAS (*fl.* 1400), author of chronicle extending to 1420 (printed by Hearne with Whethamstede, 1732); probably not identical with the Franciscan of the same name. [xlii. 341]

OTTERBURNE, SIR ADAM (*d.* 1548), king's advocate of Scotland and ambassador; as provost of Edinburgh tried to stamp out the plague, 1529; much employed in negotiations with England, generally favouring the English against the French party; knighted, *c.* 1534; imprisoned for relations with the Douglases, 1538-9; pardoned and again diplomatically employed, 1542; opposed marriage of Edward, son of Henry VIII, with Mary, daughter of James V, and joined French party after Solway Moss; accredited to England by Mary of Guise, 1547; died from wound in campaign against English. [xlii. 342]

OTTHEN, D'OTTHEN, or D'OTHON, HIPPOCRATES (*d.* 1611), physician successively to the earls of Leicester and Essex, Mountjoy (in Ireland), and the earl of Hertford (in Austria); M.D. of Montpellier and Oxford; L.R.C.P., 1589. [xlii. 344]

OTTLEY, SIR FRANCIS (1601-1649), royalist; educated at Lincoln College, Oxford; entered Inner Temple, 1620; knighted, 1642; governor of Shrewsbury, 1643-4; nominated by royalists sheriff of Shropshire, 1644; surrendered to parliamentarians at Bridgenorth, 1646, being given option of banishment; left collections of papers relating to civil war. [Suppl. iii. 238]

OTTLEY, WILLIAM YOUNG (1771-1836), writer on art and amateur artist; sold fine collections of drawings to Sir Thomas Lawrence [q. v.]; published etchings and engravings and works on the history of engraving, besides 'Inquiry into Invention of Printing' (posthumous, 1863); keeper of prints in British Museum, 1833-6. [xlii. 344]

OTWAY, CÆSAR (1780-1842), author; B.A. Trinity College, Dublin, 1801; co-operated with Joseph Henderson Singer [q. v.] in establishment of 'Christian Examiner,' 1825, and with George Petrie [q. v.] in 'Dublin Penny Journal'; preached at Leeson Street Chapel, London; published miscellaneous works. [xlii. 345]

OTWAY, SIR ROBERT WALLER, first baronet (1770-1846), admiral; took distinguished part in action of 1 June 1794 on flagship of Rear-admiral Sir Benjamin

Caldwell [q. v.]; took leading part in capture of Grenada, 1796, and captured or destroyed two hundred privateers or merchantmen in West Indies, 1795-1800; as commander of Sir Hyde Parker's flagship at Copenhagen communicated message to Nelson during action, 1801; co-operated with Catalonians, 1808; employed in blockade of Toulon, 1809-10; co-operated in siege of St. Sebastian, 1813; commander-in-chief at Leith, 1818-21, on South American station, 1826-9; admiral, 1830; created baronet, 1831; G.C.B., 1845. [xlii. 345]

OTWAY, THOMAS (1652-1685), dramatist; educated at Winchester College and Christ Church, Oxford, but did not graduate; appeared unsuccessfully on the stage; his tragedy, 'Alcibiades,' acted at Dorset Garden Theatre, London, by the Bettertons and Mrs. Barry, 1675; gained great success with 'Don Carlos,' 1676; produced 'Titus and Berenice' and 'The Cheats of Scapin' (adaptations), 1677, 'Friendship in Fashion' (first comedy), 1678; patronised by the Duke of York and Lords Plymouth, Falkland, Middlesex, and Rochester; enlisted in the army in Holland, 1678, and received a commission, but soon returned; his first blank-verse tragedy, 'The Orphan,' produced successfully, 1680, 'Soldier's Fortune' (comedy), 1681; caricatured Shaftesbury as Antonio in 'Venice Preserved,' 1682, in which Betterton played Jaffier and Mrs. Barry Belvidera; his play, 'The Atheist' (comedy), performed 1684; also wrote prologues, epilogues, and a few poems; the manner of his death when in a state of destitution disputed. French, German, Dutch, Russian, and Italian versions of 'Venice Preserved' have been made, and the play has been commended by Dryden, Hazlitt, and Taine; parts also of 'The Orphan' have been highly praised. Both have been frequently revived, the former being seen at Drury Lane Theatre, London, in 1829. First published edition of Otway's collected plays, 1713. [xlii. 346]

OTWAY, THOMAS (1616-1693), bishop of Ossory; of Christ's College, Cambridge, and Trinity College, Dublin (D.D.); captured and banished to West Indies by parliamentarians when chaplain to Sir Ralph Hopton [q. v.]; chaplain to Lord Berkeley when viceroy of Ireland; bishop of Killaloe, 1670-80, of Ossory, 1680-93; adhered to James II; benefactor of Christ's College, Cambridge, and Trinity College, Dublin. [xlii. 352]

OUDART, NICHOLAS (*d.* 1681), Latin secretary to Charles II; brought to England from Brabant by Sir Henry Wotton; created M.A. Oxford, 1636 (incorporated at Cambridge, 1638); secretary to Sir William Boswell at the Hague, 1640; assistant-secretary to Sir Edward Nicholas [q. v.], 1641-51; amanuensis to Charles I; secretary to Princess Mary of Orange, 1651-61; Latin secretary to Charles II, 1666-81; a copy of 'Eikon Basilike' said to be in his handwriting. [xlii. 353]

OUDNEY, WALTER (1790-1824), naval surgeon and African traveller; friend of Abercrombie at Edinburgh; M.D. Edinburgh, 1817; joined Hugh Clapperton [q. v.] and Dixon Denham [q. v.] in expedition to trace sources of the Niger, 1821; died at Kouka, Soudan. [xlii. 354]

OUDOCEUS (*fl.* 630 ?), bishop of Llandaff; reputed successor of Teilo; church of Llandogo, Monmouthshire, dedicated to him. [xlii. 354]

OUGHTON, SIR JAMES ADOLPHUS DICKENSON (1720-1780), lieutenant-general; served at Culloden, 1746, and in Flanders, 1747-8; lieutenant-governor of Antigua; K.B. and commander-in-chief in North Britain, 1768-80; lieutenant-general, 1770; met Dr. Johnson at Boswell's house, 1773. [xlii. 355]

OUGHTRED, WILLIAM (1575-1660), mathematician; of Eton and King's College, Cambridge; fellow of King's College, 1595; held clerical preferment; composed 'Easy Method of Geometrical Dialling' while an undergraduate; invented horizontal instrument for delineating dials, which he showed to Gunter, 1618; published 'Clavis Mathematicæ,' 1631, 'Circles of Proportion,' 1632, and other works; invented trigonometrical abbreviations and introduced multiplication and proportion signs; correspondent of leading contemporary mathematicians. [xlii. 356]

OULD, SIR FIELDING (1710-1789), man-midwife and author of 'Treatise on Midwifery' (1742); master of Dublin Lying-in Hospital, 1759; knighted, 1759. [xlii. 358]

OULTON, WALLEY CHAMBERLAIN (1770?–1820?), author of compilations on the history of London theatres from 1771 to 1795 and 1795 to 1817 (1786, 1818); produced numerous plays at Dublin and in London; published works, including 'Beauties of Kotzebue,' 1800; as 'George Horne' attacked Richard Brothers [q. v.] and Nathaniel Brassey Halhed [q. v.]; defended authenticity of Ireland's 'Vortigern.' [xlii. 358]

OUSELEY, Sir FREDERICK ARTHUR GORE, second baronet (1825–1889), musician and composer; son of Sir Gore Ouseley [q. v.]; of Christ Church, Oxford; M.A., 1849; Mus.Doc. Oxford, 1854 (incorporated at Durham, 1856, Cambridge, 1862, Dublin, 1888); professor of music at Oxford and precentor of Hereford, 1855; canon of Hereford, 1886; composed an opera at eight; founded St. Michael's College, Tenbury, 1857; composed a sacred cantata, two oratorios, and much church and secular music; published three treatises on musical theory. [xlii. 359]

OUSELEY, GIDEON (1762–1839), methodist; cousin of Sir Gore Ouseley [q. v.]; preached in Irish, chiefly in Ulster, from 1799; published 'Short Defence of the Old Religion,' 1812 (reprinted as 'Old Christianity against Papal Novelties,' 1827), and other works. [xlii. 360]

OUSELEY, Sir GORE, first baronet (1770–1844), diplomatist and oriental scholar; while engaged in commerce in India was aide-de-camp to the nabob vizier of Oudh; created baronet, 1808, for his services to British government; as ambassador extraordinary in Persia concluded treaty with England, 1812, and mediated between Persia and Russia, 1813; privy councillor, 1820; G.C.H., 1831; chairman of Oriental Translation Committee and president of Society for Publication of Oriental Texts, 1842; his 'Biographical Notices of Persian Poets' published posthumously, 1846. [xlii. 361]

OUSELEY, (Sir) RALPH (1772–1842), major-general in Portuguese army; brother of Gideon Ouseley [q. v.]; served during French invasion of Ireland, 1798, and in Emmet's rising, 1803; entered Portuguese service under Beresford, 1809; commanded 18th Portuguese in Pyrenees, 1813; severely wounded in successful night attack on Urda; organised at Rio Janeiro and commanded regiment in reduction of Pernambuco, 1817; retired from British service as major, 1825; died at Lisbon as Portuguese knight and major-general. [xlii. 362]

OUSELEY, Sir WILLIAM (1767–1842), orientalist; brother of Sir Gore Ouseley [q. v.]; studied Persian at Paris and Leyden, and received honorary degrees from Dublin and Rostock; knighted by Cornwallis, 1800; accompanied his brother to Persia, 1810; published 'Persian Miscellanies,' 1795, 'Oriental Collections,' 1797–9, and other works. [xlii. 363]

OUSELEY, Sir WILLIAM GORE (1797–1866), diplomatist; son of Sir William Ouseley [q. v.]; while attaché at Washington issued a book on American institutions, 1832; chargé d'affaires in Brazil, 1838; minister to Argentine, 1844; secured evacuation of Uruguay by Argentine troops, 1847; K.C.B., 1852; D.C.L. Oxford, 1855; went on special mission in Central America, 1857; published 'Description of Views in South America, from original drawings,' 1852. [xlii. 364]

OUTRAM, BENJAMIN (1764–1805), civil engineer; introduced iron railways for colliery traffic; founded Butterley Ironworks. [xlii. 364]

OUTRAM, Sir BENJAMIN FONSECA (1774–1856), naval surgeon; in the Superb during Sir J. Saumarez's victory at Cadiz, 1801; M.D. Edinburgh, 1809; practised in London and became medical inspector of fleets and hospitals, 1841; F.R.S., 1838; K.C.B., 1850; F.R.C.P., 1852. [xlii. 365]

OUTRAM, GEORGE (1805–1856), author of 'Lyrics, Legal and Miscellaneous' (published, 1874); nephew of Benjamin Outram [q. v.]; edited 'Glasgow Herald,' 1837–1856; collaborated with Christopher North in 'Dies Boreales.' [xlii. 365]

OUTRAM, Sir JAMES, first baronet (1803–1863), lieutenant-general in Indian army; son of Benjamin Outram [q. v.]; educated at Aberdeen; entered Indian army, 1819; directed capture of Malegáon, 1825; subdued Dáng country, 1830; put down rising of Bhíls of Barwáni, 1833; performed great hunting exploits; reported on state of

Gujerat, 1835, and became political agent in the Máhi Kánta; employed by Sir John Keane on missions to Shah Shuja and McNaghten, 1839; led expeditions against Dost Muhammad and against Ghilzais; promoted for services at siege of Kalát, 1839; carried despatches in Afghan disguise from General Willshire to Bombay by Sonmiáni Bundar route; when political agent in Lower Sindh (1839–41) negotiated treaty with Mir Sher Muhammad, 1841; as agent in Upper Sindh assisted Nott and Sir Charles James Napier [q. v.] in Afghanistan and Baluchistan, 1842; described by Napier as the 'Bayard of India,' 1842; defended residency at Haidarabad against eight thousand Sikhs, 1843; C.B. and promoted for services in first Sikh war; espoused cause of amir of Sindh against Napier, 1843; head of intelligence department during campaign in southern Marátha country, 1844; resident of Baroda, 1847–51; dismissed in connection with his report (1851) on corruption (khatpat), but reinstated by Dalhousie, 1854; wrote 'Memorandum on the Invasion of India from the Westward,' 1853; as resident at Oudh recommended annexation, 1855; K.C.B., 1856; G.C.B. after successfully conducting war against Persia, 1857; at the outbreak of the Indian mutiny had command of two Bengal divisions between Calcutta and Cawnpore, being also chief commissioner of Oudh after Lawrence's death, but waived his military rank and acted as volunteer under Havelock during the first relief of Lucknow; commanded Lucknow garrison until the second relief under Sir Colin Campbell; conducted the evacuation and held the place in check till the third relief, defeating Ahmad Shah's troops in several engagements; co-operated with Campbell in the final capture, 1858; received a baronetcy, a pension, and the freedom of London; military member of Lord Canning's council, 1858–60; lieutenant-general, 1858; died at Pau and received public funeral in Westminster Abbey. He published works concerning the campaign in Sindh and Afghanistan, the conquest of Sindh, and his Baroda administration. [xlii. 366]

OUTRAM, WILLIAM (1626–1679). [See OWTRAM.]

OUVILLY, GEORGE GERBIER (fl. 1661). [See D'OUVILLY.]

OUVRY, FREDERIC (1814–1881), president of Society of Antiquaries, treasurer, 1854–74, president, 1876–8; friend of Dickens; made fine collections of manuscripts, ballads, and autograph letters. [xlii. 374]

OVERALL, JOHN (1560–1619), bishop successively of Coventry and Lichfield and of Norwich; educated at Cambridge; major fellow of Trinity College, Cambridge, 1582; M.A., 1582; regius professor of theology, 1596–1607; D.D., 1596; master of Catharine Hall, Cambridge, 1598–1607; opposed extreme Calvinists; dean of St. Paul's, London, 1602; took part in Hampton Court conference and enlargement of church catechism, 1604; prolocutor of Canterbury lower house, 1605 (his Convocation Book published by Sancroft, 1690); one of the Old Testament revisers, 1611; bishop of Coventry and Lichfield, 1614, of Norwich, 1618; correspondent of Voss and Grotius; wrote against Lambeth articles and on predestination. [xlii. 375]

OVERALL, WILLIAM HENRY (1829–1888), librarian of the Guildhall, 1865–88; F.S.A., 1868; with his cousin prepared analytical index to 'Remembrancia,' 1878; chief work, 'History of Clockmakers' Company,' 1881. [xlii. 377]

OVERBURY, Sir THOMAS (1581–1613), poet and victim of court intrigue; of Queen's College, Oxford (B.A., 1598), and the Middle Temple; made acquaintance of Robert Carr [q. v.] at Edinburgh, whose adviser at court he became; made sewer to the king and knighted, 1608; travelled in Netherlands, 1609, and is said to have written 'Observations upon the Seventeen Provinces'; encouraged Rochester's (Carr's) intrigue with Frances Howard, countess of Essex, and is said himself to have attempted intrigue with Lady Rutland; broke with Ben Jonson in consequence; opposed Rochester's marriage with Lady Essex and was supposed cognisant of some secret concerning him; after refusal of diplomatic employment was sent to the Tower, 1613, and there slowly poisoned by agents of Lady Essex, four of whom were hanged, 1615, Somerset (Carr) and his wife (Lady Essex) being convicted, but pardoned. Twenty writers (including Ford) contributed prefatory verses to his poem 'A Wife' (published, 1614), and Ben Jonson credited him with introducing culture into the court. Subsequent editions of 'A Wife' have additional compositions of the author, some of doubtful authenticity; his 'Miscellaneous Works in Verse and Prose' edited by Edward F. Rimbault, 1856. [xlii. 377]

OVERBURY, SIR THOMAS (d. 1684), author of curious tract in 'Harleian Miscellany' and controversial writer; nephew of Sir Thomas Overbury (1581–1613); knighted, 1660. [xliii. 382]

OVEREND, MARMADUKE (d. 1790), organist of Isleworth, Middlesex, 1760–90, and composer. [xlii. 382]

OVERSTONE, BARON (1796–1883). [See LOYD, SAMUEL JONES.]

OVERTON, CHARLES (1805–1889), evangelical divine; son of John Overton (1763–1838) [q. v.]; vicar of Clapham, Yorkshire, 1837, of Cottingham, 1841–89; published 'Cottage Lectures on Bunyan's "Pilgrim's Progress" practically explained' (1848, pt. i., pt. ii. 1849) and similar works, besides verse and a parochial history. [xlii. 382]

OVERTON, CONSTANTINE (d. 1687), quaker. [xliii. 383]

OVERTON, JOHN (1640–1708 ?), principal vendor of mezzotints of his day. [xliii. 384]

OVERTON, JOHN (1763–1838), evangelical divine; B.A. Magdalene College, Cambridge, 1790; incumbent of St. Crux and St. Margaret's, York, 1802–38; published 'The True Churchman Ascertained,' 1801. [xlii. 384]

OVERTON, JOHN (1764–1838), author of 'The Genealogy of Christ elucidated by Sacred History,' 1817, and works applying astronomical results to biblical chronology. [xlii. 385]

OVERTON, RICHARD (fl. 1642–1663), pamphleteer and satirist; attacked bishops in 'Lambeth Fayre,' 1642; his 'Man's Mortality,' 1643, followed by foundation of the sect called 'soul sleepers' and censured by parliament, together with Milton's tract concerning divorce; attacked Westminster Assembly of Divines in tracts signed 'Martin Marpriest,' 1646; sent to Newgate for defence of Lilburne, 1646, but released, 1647; imprisoned in the Tower of London with other leaders of the levellers for share in authorship of 'England's new Chains Discovered,' 1649; released, 1649; fled to Flanders with Sexby, 1655, and obtained commission from Charles II; again imprisoned, 1659 and 1663. [xlii. 385]

OVERTON, ROBERT (fl. 1640–1668), Fifth-monarchy man and friend of Milton; admitted to Gray's Inn, 1631; fought at Marston Moor, 1644; reduced Sandal Castle, 1645; made parliamentary governor of Hull, 1647; commanded brigade of foot at Dunbar, 1650; governor of Edinburgh, 1650; led reserve at Inverkeithing, 1651; reduced Orkney and Shetland; commander in Western Scotland, 1652–3; opposed Protectorate and was imprisoned on charge of intending to head military insurrection; released by Richard Cromwell, 1659, and restored to commands by revived Long parliament, 1659; refused obedience to Monck and tried to maintain independent position in Yorkshire; imprisoned as Fifth-monarchy leader, after Restoration, in the Tower of London and in Jersey; his exploits celebrated in Milton's 'Defensio Secunda.' [xliii. 387]

OVERTON, WILLIAM (1525 ?–1609), bishop of Coventry and Lichfield; fellow of Magdalen College, Oxford, 1551; M.A. (incorporated at Cambridge, 1562), D.D., 1566; rector of Balcombe and vicar of Eccleshall, 1553; canon of Chichester, 1563, treasurer, 1567; took prominent part in reception of Queen Elizabeth at Oxford, 1564; canon of Salisbury and rector of Stoke-on-Trent, 1570; bishop of Coventry and Lichfield, 1579–1609; unjustly attacked by 'Martin Marprelate' as an 'unlearned prelate.' [xliii. 389]

OWAIN AP EDWIN (d. 1104), Welsh chieftain, of Counsillt, called 'Fradwr' (Traitor) on account of his having assisted in the invasion of Anglesey, 1098. [xlii. 390]

OWAIN AP CADWGAN (d. 1116), prince of Powys; sent to Ireland in childhood; carried off Nest, wife of Gerald of Windsor, 1110; took refuge with Muircheartach in Ireland; on return allied himself with Madog ap Rhiryd, devastated much country, and murdered William of Brabant; prince of Powys, 1112–16; blinded and deprived Madog of his share of Powys, 1113; accompanied Henry I to Normandy, 1114; killed in battle with Gerald of Windsor. [xlii. 390]

OWAIN GWYNEDD or OWAIN AP GRUFFYDD (d. 1169), king of Gwynedd (North Wales), 1137–69; succeeded Gruffydd ab Cynan [q. v.]; thrice invaded Ceredigion and burnt Carmarthen, 1137; drove back Irish Danes, 1144; during reign of Stephen captured Mold (Gwyddgrug) and defeated Randulf of Chester and Madog ap Maredudd at Counsillt; after Henry II's invasion of 1157 did homage, gave hostages, and restored Cadwaladr (his own brother) to his territory; supported the English against Rhys ap Gruffydd [q. v.], 1159; successfully invaded Arwystli, 1162; induced Rhys to submit to Henry II, and with him did homage at Woodstock, 1164, but combined with him and the Prince of Powys in repelling the king's expedition against South Wales, 1165; joined Rhys against Powys and the Normans, 1167; kept see of Bangor vacant and opposed Norman nominees; excommunicated by Becket for marriage with his cousin Crisiant, but the sentence disregarded by the Welsh; praised by Giraldus Cambrensis as a wise and moderate ruler, and much celebrated by Welsh bards, but guilty of exceptional cruelties to kinsfolk. [xlii. 391]

OWAIN BROGYNTYN (fl. 1180), Welsh chieftain; natural son of Madog ap Maredudd [q. v.]; ruled in Dinmael and Edeyrnion. [xlii. 395]

OWAIN CYVEILIOG or OWAIN AB GRUFFYDD (d. 1197), Welsh poet and prince of Powys, 1160–1197; joined Gwynedd and South Wales in resisting Henry II, 1165; shared Mochnant with Owain Gwynedd [q. v.], but was afterwards attacked by him and Rhys of South Wales; cultivated good relations with Henry II; attended great council at Oxford, 1177; excommunicated for neglecting to meet Archbishop Baldwin, 1188, but founded Cistercian house of Strata Marcella (Ystrad Marchell), and there died a monk; praised by Giraldus Cambrensis as ruler. [xliii. 395]

OWAIN, GUTYN (fl. 1480), Welsh bard and genealogist (Gruffydd ap Huw ab Owain); consulted by Henry VII as to Tudor pedigree. [xlii. 396]

OWAIN MYVYR (1741–1814). [See JONES, OWEN.]

OWEN. [See also OWAIN.]

OWEN OF WALES (d. 1378), soldier in French service; claimed descent from Welsh princes; went to France in boyhood; fought under John II at Poitiers, 1356; won distinction in Lombardy, 1360; given command of French expedition against Wales, which made descent on Guernsey, 1372; captured Sir Thomas Percy [q. v.] and the Captal de Buch at Soubise, 1372; cooperated with Spanish in capture of La Rochelle, 1372; under Bertrand du Guesclin at Chizé, 1373; took part in Enguerrand de Coucy's expedition against Leopold of Austria, 1375; treacherously murdered by a Welshman before Mortagne; his invasion of Guernsey subject of a ballad. [xlii. 396]

OWEN GLENDOWER (1359 ?–1416 ?). [See GLENDOWER.]

OWEN TUDOR (d. 1461). [See TUDOR.]

OWEN, MRS. ALICE (d. 1613), philanthropist; née Wilkes; married, as her third husband, Thomas Owen (d. 1598) [q. v.]; founded school and almshouses at Islington; made bequests to Christ's Hospital, London, and Oxford and Cambridge Universities. [xlii. 398]

OWEN, ANEURIN (1792–1851), Welsh historical scholar; son of William Owen (afterwards Pughe) [q. v.]; assistant tithe commissioner, 1836; enclosure commissioner, 1845; edited for Record Office collection of ancient Welsh laws, 1841; edited part of 'Brut y Tywysogion' in 'Monumenta Historica Britannica,' 1848. [xlii. 399]

OWEN, CADWALLADER (1562–1617), rector of Llanfechain, 1601, and Llanbrynmair (sinecure), 1610; M.A. Jesus College, Oxford, 1588; fellow of Oriel College, Oxford, 1585; B.D., 1603; a great disputant. [xlii. 434]

OWEN, CHARLES (d. 1746), presbyterian minister and tutor at Warrington; hon. D.D. Edinburgh, 1728; indicted for sermon on 'Plain Dealing; or Separation without Schism,' 1715; influential supporter of Hanoverian dynasty; published controversial works. [xlii. 400]

OWEN, CORBET (1646–1671), Latin poet, of Westminster School and Christ Church, Oxford (M.A., 1670). [xlii. 401]

OWEN, DAVID (*fl.* 1642), controversialist, of Catharine Hall (B.A., 1598) and Clare Hall, Cambridge (M.A., 1602); incorporated M.A. Oxford, 1608; created D.D. Cambridge, 1618; defended divine right of kings. [xlii. 401]

OWEN, DAVID, or DAFYDD Y GARREG WEN (1720–1749), Welsh harper, to whom several airs are ascribed, for one of which Scott wrote words ('The Dying Bird'). [xlii. 402]

OWEN, DAVID (1784–1841), Welsh poet ('Dewi Wyn o Eifion'); awarded second prizes by Gwyneddigion Society of London, 1803 and 1805; awarded cup (which was withheld) at Tremadoc Eisteddfod for poem on 'Agriculture,' 1811; valued after his death; his chief works collected in 'Blodau Arfon,' 1842. [xlii. 402]

OWEN, DAVID (1794–1866), Welsh journalist ('Brutus'); made his reputation by an article in 'Seren Gomer' on the 'Poverty of the Welsh Language,' 1824; edited 'Lleuad yr Oes,' 1827–30, and 'Efengylydd,' 1831–5; afterwards joined church of England and edited the 'Haul.' [xlii. 403]

OWEN, EDWARD (1728–1807), translator of Juvenal and Persius (1785) and author of 'New Latin Accidence' (1770); M.A. Jesus College, Oxford, 1752; head-master (1757) and rector (1767–1807) of Warrington. [xlii. 404]

OWEN, SIR EDWARD CAMPBELL RICH (1771–1849), admiral; while in command of the Immortalité captured and destroyed many French gunboats and privateers, 1802–5; attached to Walcheren expedition, 1809; K.C.B., 1815; commander-in-chief in West Indies, 1822–5; surveyor-general of ordnance, 1827; commander in East Indies, 1828–32, in Mediterranean, 1841–5; G.C.H., 1832; G.C.B., 1845; admiral, 1846. [xlii. 405]

OWEN, EDWARD PRYCE (1788–1863), etcher; son of Hugh Owen (1761–1827) [q. v.]; M.A. St. John's College, Cambridge, 1816; vicar of Wellington and rector of Eyton-upon-Wildmoors, Shropshire, 1823–63. [xlii. 405]

OWEN, ELLIS (1789–1868), Welsh antiquary and poet; F.S.A., 1868; his 'Cell Meudwy' issued, 1897. [xlii. 406]

OWEN, SIR FRANCIS PHILIP CUNLIFFE- (1828–1894), director of South Kensington Museum; entered science and art department, South Kensington, 1854; assisted Sir Henry Cole [q. v.] in international exhibitions at Paris, 1855 and 1857, and Vienna, 1873; assistant-director at South Kensington, 1860–73; director, 1873–93; superintended British section at Paris exhibition, 1878; as director organised Fisheries, and succeeding exhibitions, 1883–6; C.B., 1873; K.C.M.G. and legion of honour, 1878; K.C.B., 1886. [xlii. 406]

OWEN, GEORGE (*d.* 1558), physician to Henry VIII, Edward VI, and Mary I; fellow of Merton College, Oxford, and M.D., 1528; received grants of property at and near Oxford; president Royal College of Physicians, 1553 and 1554; friend of Thomas Caius [q. v.]. [xlii. 407]

OWEN, GEORGE (*fl.* 1604). [See HARRY, GEORGE OWEN.]

OWEN, GEORGE (1552–1613), author of 'Description of Pembrokeshire' (1603); son of William Owen (1469 ?–1574) [q. v.]; vice-admiral of Pembroke and Cardigan and sheriff of Cardigan, 1589 and 1602; gave assistance to Camden; author also of descriptions of Wales and Milford Haven and 'Cataloge and Genelogie of the Lordes of Kemes,' and other treatises, printed in nineteenth century. [xlii. 408]

OWEN, GEORGE (*d.* 1665), York herald; son of George Owen (1552–1613) [q. v.]; Rouge Croix, 1626; York herald, 1633 (reappointed, 1660); D.C.L. Oxford, 1643; Norroy king-of-arms, 1658; frequently confounded with his father and George Owen Harry [q. v.]. [xlii. 410]

OWEN, GORONWY or GRONOW (1723–1769 ?), Welsh poet; son of a tinker in Anglesey; of Jesus College, Oxford; while master of Donnington school, corresponded with Lewis Morris [q. v.] and composed 'Cywydd y Farn Fawr'; secretary to Cymmrodorion Society of London, 1755; master of William and Mary College, Williamsburg, Virginia, 1758–60; died minister of St. Andrew's, Brunswick County; published 'Diddanwch Teuluaidd,' 1763; his complete works edited by Robert Jones, 1876. [xlii. 411]

OWEN, GRIFFITH (*d.* 1717), colonist and doctor; emigrated to Pennsylvania, 1684, and became member of executive council; died at Philadelphia. [xlii. 412]

OWEN, HENRY (1716–1795), divine and scholar; M.A. Jesus College, Oxford, 1743; M.D., 1753; vicar of Terling, 1752; rector of St. Olave's, Hart Street, 1760–1794; vicar of Edmonton, 1775–95; chaplain to Bishop Shute Barrington; Boyle lecturer, 1769–71; friend of Bowyer and Nichols; published theological works. [xlii. 412]

OWEN, HENRY CHARLES CUNLIFFE- (1821–1867), lieutenant-colonel of royal engineers; brother of Sir Francis Philip Cunliffe-Owen [q. v.]; served against Boers and Kaffirs, 1845–7; general superintendent of the exhibition of 1851; inspector of art schools; wounded before Sebastopol; C.B. and pensioned; deputy inspector-general of fortifications, 1856–60; commanding engineer of western district, 1860–7; friend of Pusey. [xlii. 413]

OWEN, HUGH, properly JOHN HUGHES (1615–1686), Welsh jesuit. [xlii. 414]

OWEN, HUGH (1639–1700), Welsh nonconformist preacher; of Jesus College, Oxford. [xlii. 414]

OWEN, HUGH (1761–1827), collaborator with John Brickdale Blakeway [q. v.] in 'History of Shrewsbury' (1825); M.A. St. John's College, Cambridge, 1807; archdeacon of Shropshire, 1821; published separate work on Shrewsbury, 1808. [xlii. 415]

OWEN, HUGH (1784–1861), colonel in Portuguese army; commanded cavalry skirmishers at Talavera; entered Portuguese service, 1810; received troop in 7th hussars for services at Vittoria, 1813, but sold out, 1817; organised and commanded 6th Portuguese regiment after 1815; accompanied Beresford to Brazil, 1820; published 'Civil War in Portugal' (English and Portuguese, 1836). [xlii. 415]

OWEN, SIR HUGH (1804–1881), promoter of Welsh education and philanthropist; chief clerk of poor law commission, 1853–72; circulated 'Letter to the Welsh People' on day-schools, 1843; hon. secretary to Cambrian Educational Society, 1846; took up cause of deaf and dumb; organised state-aided undenominational education; promoted establishment of training colleges for teachers; the virtual creator of Aberystwith University College (opened, 1872); chiefly instrumental in reform of Eisteddfod and revival (1873) of Cymmrodorion Society; prominent in foundation of London-Welsh Charitable Aid Society, 1873; connected with London Fever Hospital, National Thrift Society, and National Temperance League; member of London school board, 1872; knighted, 1881. [xlii. 416]

OWEN, HUMPHREY (1712–1768), Bodley's librarian and principal of Jesus College, Oxford; M.A. Jesus College, Oxford, 1725; fellow, 1726; D.D., 1763; rector of Tredington (second portion), 1744–63; Bodley's librarian, 1747–68; principal of Jesus College, Oxford, 1763–8. [xlii. 418]

OWEN, JACOB (1778–1870), architect and engineer to Irish board of works, 1832–56; erected Dundrum Asylum, 1848, and Mountjoy prison, Dublin, 1850. [xlii. 418]

OWEN, JAMES (1654–1706), presbyterian; brother of Charles Owen [q. v.]; took part in public disputation with William Lloyd (1627–1717) [q. v.] at Oswestry, 1681, where he established academy for training presbyterians, 1690; joint-pastor of High Street Chapel, Shrewsbury, 1700; carried on controversies with Benjamin Keach [q. v.], Thomas Gipps [q. v.], and William Lloyd [q. v.] [xlii. 419]

OWEN, JOHN (1560 ?–1622), epigrammatist; of Winchester College and New College, Oxford; fellow, 1584–91; B.C.L., 1590; head-master of King Henry VIII's school, Warwick, *c.* 1594; buried in St. Paul's Cathedral; his Latin epigrams collected, 1624, and translated into English, French, German, and Spanish. [xlii. 420]

OWEN, JOHN (1580–1651), bishop of St. Asaph; fellow of Jesus College, Cambridge; M.A., 1600, D.D., 1618; rector of Burton Latimer, 1608, of Carlton and Cottingham, 1625; chaplain to Prince Charles; bishop of

St. Asaph, 1629–41; instituted Welsh sermons in his diocese and improved the cathedral; impeached, imprisoned, and sequestrated, 1641.   [xlii. 421]

OWEN, SIR JOHN (1600–1666), royalist; his appointment as governor of Ruabon (1644) resisted by Archbishop Williams; knighted, 1644; surrendered to Mytton, 1646; attacked Carnarvon, but after a first victory was defeated and captured at Llandegai, 1648; imprisoned at Denbigh and Windsor; condemned to death with lords Goring, Holland, Cambridge, and Capel, but respited, 1649; attempted unsuccessfully to raise north Wales in concert with Sir George Booth, 1659, and was again sequestered.   [xlii. 422]

OWEN, JOHN (1616–1683), theologian: of Queen's College, Oxford; M.A., 1635; created D.D., 1653; left the university on account of Laud's statutes; private chaplain to Sir Robert Dormer and Lord Lovelace; published tracts against Arminianism and in favour of presbyterianism, and obtained rectory of Fordham, Essex, 1643; ejected by patron, but presented by House of Lords to Coggeshall, 16_6; adopted independent views and expanded them in 'Eshcol,' 1648; preached before parliament, 1649, and accompanied Cromwell to Ireland and Scotland, 1650, as chaplain; dean of Christ Church, Oxford, 1651–60; vice-chancellor, 1652–8; chairman of committee for composing differences in Scottish church, 1654; carried on controversies with John Goodwin [q. v.], Henry Hammond [q. v.], and William Sherlock (1641?–1707) [q. v.]; wrote 'Vindiciæ Evangelicæ' against John Biddle [q. v.], 1655; charged Grotius with Socinianism; published treatise 'On Schism,' 1657, with attack on quaker theory of inspiration; ejected from Christ Church, Oxford, 1660; wrote anonymous answer to the 'Fiat Lux' of Vincent Canes [q. v.], 1662; indicted for holding religious assemblies at Oxford, 1665; removed to London and published anonymous tracts in defence of religious liberty, and, with his name, other writings, including one book of the 'Exercitations on Epistle to the Hebrews,' 1668; attacked occasional conformity; discussed nonconformity with the Duke of York, 1674; received audience from Charles II and money for nonconformists; allowed to preach to independent congregation in Leadenhall Street, London, 1673; wrote against Romanism and rationalism, 1674–80; defended dissenters against Stillingfleet and contended for historical position of congregationalism, 1680–1; his 'Meditations and Discourse on the Glory of Christ,' and other treatises, published posthumously; collective editions of his works issued, 1721 (imperfect), 1826 and 1850.   [xlii. 424]

OWEN, JOHN (1766–1822), secretary of British and Foreign Bible Society; fellow of Corpus Christi College, Cambridge, 1789; M.A., 1791; curate of Fulham, 1795–1813; secretary of British and Foreign Bible Society, 1804–22; rector of Paglesham, 1808; minister of Park Chapel, Chelsea; chief work, 'History of the Origin and first ten years of the British and Foreign Bible Society,' 1816.   [xlii. 428]

OWEN, JOHN (1821–1883), Welsh musician ('Owain Alaw'); organist in Chester; won many prizes at eisteddfod, and composed cantatas, glees, songs, and anthems; edited 'Gems of Welsh Melody,' 1860.   [xlii. 429]

OWEN, JOSIAH (1711?–1755), presbyterian minister at Rochdale, 1740–52, and at Ellenthorp, 1752–5; nephew of Charles Owen [q. v.]; prominent as writer against Jacobites.   [xlii. 429]

OWEN, LEWIS (d. 1555), vice-chamberlain of North Wales and baron of the exchequer of Carnarvon ('Y Barwn Owen'); sheriff of Merionethshire, 1545–6 and 1554–5, and M.P. for county, 1547, 1553, and 1554; murdered by Mawddwy brigands.   [xlii. 430]

OWEN, LEWIS (1532–1594). [See LEWIS, OWEN.]

OWEN, LEWIS (1572–1633), anti-jesuit writer; sometime a jesuit in Spain; employed by government as spy at Rome, 1611, and afterwards in London; published 'Unmasking of all Popish Monks, Friers and Iesuits,' 1623, 'Speculum Jesuiticum,' 1629, and other works.   [xlii. 431]

OWEN, MORGAN (1585?–1645), bishop of Llandaff; of Jesus and New Colleges, Oxford (B.A., 1613); M.A. Hart Hall, 1616; created D.D., 1636; chaplain to Laud when bishop of St. David's; canon of St. David's, 1623; bishop of Llandaff, 1640–2; impeached and imprisoned

for promulgating Laud's canons and protesting against action of Long parliament, 1641–2; left bequest to Carmarthen school.   [xlii. 432]

OWEN, NICHOLAS (d. 1606), jesuit ('Little John'); was imprisoned, but escaped; said to have effected escape of John Gerard (1564–1637) [q. v.], 1597; travelled with Henry Garnett [q. v.]; designed hiding-places at Hindlip Hall for priests; captured there and taken to the Tower of London, where he died, probably from effects of torture.   [xlii. 433]

OWEN, NICHOLAS (1752–1811), Welsh antiquary; M.A. Jesus College, Oxford, 1776; rector of Llandyfrydog, and Meyllteyrn; published works, including 'British Remains,' 1777.   [xlii. 434]

OWEN, RICHARD (1606–1683), royalist divine; son of Cadwallader Owen [q. v.]; fellow of Oriel College, Oxford, 1628–38; M.A., 1630, B.D., 1638; rector of Llanfechain, 1634; vicar of Eltham, 1636; rector of St. Swithin, London Stone, 1639; ejected for royalism, 1643; regained St. Swithin at Restoration and was made prebendary of St. Paul's Cathedral; intimate with John Evelyn (1620–1706) [q. v.]; Latin version of George Bate's 'Royal Apologie' attributed to him.   [xlii. 434]

OWEN, SIR RICHARD (1804–1892), naturalist; educated at Lancaster school with Whewell; studied anatomy at Edinburgh under John Barclay (1758–1826) [q. v.]; prosector to Abernethy at St. Bartholomew's Hospital, 1825, and lecturer on anatomy, 1829; assistant-conservator of Hunterian Museum, 1827, joint-conservator, 1842, and afterwards sole conservator till 1856; attended Cuvier's lectures at Paris, 1831; made his name as anatomist with 'Memoir on the Pearly Nautilus,' 1832; F.R.S., 1834; first Hunterian professor of comparative anatomy and physiology, 1836–56; Wollaston medallist, 1838; first president of Microscopical Society, 1840; received civil list pension, 1842; elected to 'the club,' 1845; on royal commission on public health, 1847, and Smithfield market, 1809; while at the Hunterian museum prepared 'Descriptive and Illustrative Catalogue of Physiological Series of Comparative Anatomy' and catalogue of osteological collections; gave annual lectures, and wrote memoirs of animals dissected at Zoological Society, on marsupialia and monotremes, on bones and teeth, on cephalopoda, and parthenogenesis, 1849; chairman of jury on raw materials at exhibition of 1851, on 'Prepared and Preserved Alimentary Substances' at Paris, 1855; devised models of extinct animals at Crystal Palace; as superintendent of natural history collections of the British Museum (1856–83) obtained their separation from the library and removal to South Kensington (1881), where he designed the 'Index Museum,' but was overruled on the general scheme of arrangement; lectured on fossils at Jermyn Street Museum and Royal Institution, 1859–61; presided at Leeds meeting of British Association, 1858; gave Rede lecture at Cambridge, 1859; lectured to royal family, 1860 and 1864; helped Livingstone to write 'Missionary Travels,' 1857; visited Egypt with Albert Edward, prince of Wales, 1869; received the 'Prix Cuvier,' 1857; edited 'Posthumous Papers of John Hunter' (1861); attacked 'Origin of Species' in 'Edinburgh Review' (April 1860), taking up an ambiguous attitude on evolution; royal medallist, 1846; Copley medallist, 1851; Baley medallist for physiology, 1869, gold medallist, Linnean Society, 1888; received honorary degrees from Oxford, Cambridge, and Dublin, and was foreign associate of Institute of France; K.C.B., 1884; had many foreign orders. He received Sheen Lodge as a residence from Queen Victoria in 1852. He enjoyed the friendship of many leading contemporaries, but his acerbity as a controversialist isolated him in the scientific world. His chief larger works were, 'Odontography,' 1840–5, 'Lectures on Comparative Anatomy and Physiology of Invertebrates,' 1843, 'History of British Fossil Mammals and Birds,' 1846, 'On the Anatomy of Invertebrates,' vols. i. and ii. 1866, vol. iii. 1868, 'Researches on Fossil Remains of Extinct Mammals of Australia,' 1877–8, 'Memoirs on Extinct Wingless Birds of New Zealand,' 1879.   [xlii. 435]

OWEN, ROBERT (1771–1858), socialist and philanthropist; born and died at Newtown, Montgomeryshire; read widely when a boy; obtained knowledge of fabrics while assistant at a shop in Stamford, Northamptonshire; while employed in Manchester set up a small cotton-spinning establishment; afterwards very successful as manager of large mills, and became known in Manchester; had discussion with Coleridge and lent money to Robert Fulton; formed Chorlton Twist Company, 1794-5; bought for company New Lanark Mills from David Dale [q. v.] and married his daughter, 1799; in order to carry out his schemes bought out partners and, with William Allen (1770-1843) [q. v.], Bentham, and others, formed new company, 1814; became famous for his 'institution for the formation of character,' including infant and two other grades of schools (opened, 1816); his essays circulated by the British and American governments; consulted by Prussian and Austrian ambassadors; received offers in person from Grand Duke Nicholas for an establishment in Russia; propounded scheme of 'villages of unity and co-operation' to great meeting at City of London Tavern, 1817; made continental tour, attending Germanic diet and congress of Aix-la-Chapelle, 1818; largely instrumental in bringing about the Factory Act of 1819; obtained formation of committee to carry out his scheme under presidency of Duke of Kent, 1819, but alienated sympathy by declaration against religion; during a visit to Ireland, 1823, met with much opposition; a settlement on his communistic principles at Orbiston maintained for only about two years; gave addresses at Washington and took over Harmony Settlement, 1825; framed communistic constitution, 1826, and several times visited it, but being unable to enforce his principles, abandoned it, 1828; withdrew from New Lanark after disputes with partners, 1829; received an abortive offer from Mexican government, 1829; took part in co-operative and social congresses, lecturing, and publishing periodicals; carried on 'Equitable Labour Exchange,' 1832-4; took up case of Dorset labourers, 1834; conducted 'New Moral World,' 1834-41; was presented by Lord Normanby to Queen Victoria, 1840; again in America, 1844-7; published 'Revolution in Mind and Practice,' 1849; took up spiritualism; held 'millenial' meetings in St. Martin's Hall, London, 1855; published an 'Autobiography,' 1857-8; appeared at social science congresses at Birmingham and Liverpool, introduced by Brougham. He spent most of his fortune on the promotion of his schemes, and attempted to convert many public men. [xlii. 444]

OWEN, ROBERT DALE (1801-1877), publicist and author; son of Robert Owen [q. v.]; educated under Fellenberg at Hofwyl; joined New Harmony settlement, 1826; edited 'New Harmony Gazette' and commenced (1828) 'Free Inquirer'; published 'Moral Physiology,' 1831; as member of House of Representatives for Indiana supported annexation of Texas; U.S. minister at Naples, 1853-8; published 'Policy of Emancipation,' 1863, and 'The Wrong of Slavery,' &c., 1864; also 'Footfalls on the Boundary of another World,' 1859, and 'Debatable Land between this World and the next,' 1872; published 'Threading my Way' (autobiography, 1874). [xlii. 452]

OWEN, SIR ROGER (1573-1617), politician; son of Thomas Owen (d. 1598) [q. v.]; B.A. Christ Church, Oxford, 1592; M.P., Shrewsbury, 1597, and Shropshire, 1601-14; knighted, 1604; barrister and treasurer, Lincoln's Inn, 1613; dismissed from commission of peace for anti-royalist speeches. [xlii. 455]

OWEN, SAMUEL (1769?-1857), water-colour painter; exhibited battle-pieces at Royal Academy and marine subjects with Associated Artists in Water-colours.
 [xlii. 453]

OWEN, THANKFULL (1620-1681), independent divine; educated at St. Paul's School, London, and Exeter College, Oxford; fellow of Lincoln College, Oxford, 1642; M.A., 1646; senior proctor, 1649; president of St. John's College, Oxford, 1650-60; prominent in management of university during Commonwealth; published 'A true and lively Representation of Popery,' 1679. [xlii. 454]

OWEN, THOMAS (d. 1598), judge; graduated at Oxford, 1559; barrister, Lincoln's Inn, 1570; M.P., Shrewsbury, 1584-5; member of council of Welsh marches, 1590; queen's serjeant, 1593; judge of common pleas, 1594-8; his common pleas reports printed, 1656; buried in Westminster Abbey. [xlii. 455]

OWEN, THOMAS (1557-1618), rector of English jesuit college, Rome, 1610-18; published translation from French. [xlii. 455]

OWEN, THOMAS (1749-1812), translator of agricultural works; B.A. Jesus College, Oxford, 1770; M.A.

Queen's College, Oxford, 1773; incumbent of Upton Scudamore, Wiltshire, 1779. [xlii. 456]

OWEN, THOMAS ELLIS (1764-1814), author of 'Methodism Unmasked' (1802); of Westminster School and Christ Church, Oxford; B.A., 1789; incumbent of South Stoke, 1792, Llandyfrydog, Anglesey, 1794.
 [xlii. 456]

OWEN, WILLIAM (1469?-1574), compiler of 'Le Bregement de Statutis' (1521); of the Middle Temple; recovered barony of Kemes after nineteen years' suit; vice-admiral of Wales. [xlii. 456]

OWEN, WILLIAM (1530?-1587), Welsh poet (WILLIAM LLEYN); M.A.; vicar of Oswestry, 1583-7; made chief bard at Caerwys, 1568; some of his pieces printed in 'Gorchestion Beirdd Cymru' (1864) and 'Y Brython.'
 [xlii. 457]

OWEN, WILLIAM (1769-1825), portrait-painter; exhibited at Royal Academy from 1792; R.A., 1806; principal portrait-painter to George, prince regent, 1813; accidentally poisoned. [xlii. 457]

OWEN, WILLIAM (1759-1835). [See PUGH.]

OWEN, WILLIAM FITZWILLIAM (1774-1857), vice-admiral; brother of Sir Edward Campbell Rich Owen [q. v.]; midshipman in the Culloden in battle of 1 June 1794; explored Maldive islands, 1806, and discovered Seaflower Channel, Sumatra, 1806; served against Dutch in East Indies; taken by French, 1808; surveyed Canadian lakes, 1815-16, west and east African coasts, 1821-6; settled Fernando Po, 1827; published 'Narrative of Voyages to explore shores of Africa, Arabia, and Madagascar,' 1833; vice-admiral, 1854. [xlii. 458]

OWENS, JOHN (1790-1846), founder of Owens College, Manchester; a Manchester merchant who left about 100,000l. to found a college, which was to be free from religious tests. Owens College was opened, 1851, and incorporated by parliament, 1871. [xliii. 1.]

OWENS, JOHN LENNERGAN (fl. 1780), actor; succeeded Henry Mossop [q. v.] at Smock Alley Theatre, Dublin. [xliii. 2]

OWENS, OWEN (d. 1593), divine; M.A. Oxford, 1564; last archdeacon of Anglesey to hold it pleno jure, the bishops of Bangor subsequently holding it in commendam. [xliii. 421]

OWENSON, ROBERT (1744-1812), actor; introduced to Garrick by Goldsmith, c. 1771; made his London début at Covent Garden, 1774; opened Fishamble Street Theatre, Dublin, 1785; retired from the stage, 1798. [xliii. 2]

OWENSON, MISS SYDNEY (1783?-1859). [See MORGAN, SYDNEY, LADY.]

OWTRAM, WILLIAM (1626-1679), divine; B.A. Trinity College, Cambridge, 1645; fellow of Christ's College and (1649) M.A.; created D.D., 1660; rector of St. Mary Woolnoth, London, till 1666; archdeacon of Leicester, 1669; preacher and rabbinical scholar. [xliii. 2]

OWTRED (1315?-1396). [See UHTRED.]

OXBERRY, WILLIAM (1784-1824), actor; attracted the attention of Henry Siddons [q. v.], and first appeared at Covent Garden Theatre, London, in 1807; was for long manager of the Olympic; took the Craven's Head chophouse in 1821; said to have been unsurpassed in the rôles of Slender, Sir David Daw, and Petro; edited 'The New English Drama,' 1818-24, besides projecting 'Dramatic Biography,' 1825. [xliii. 3]

OXBERRY, WILLIAM HENRY (1808-1852), actor; son of William Oxberry [q. v.]; first appeared at the Olympic Theatre, London, 1825; unsuccessful as manager of the English Opera House (1833-7), and returned to the stage, acting at the Princess's, the Lyceum, Covent Garden, and many other theatres in London; author of burlesques and plays. [xliii. 5]

OXBURGH, HENRY (d. 1716), Jacobite; settled in Cheshire, 1700, after serving in the army in Ireland and France; joined Jacobite rising, 1715, and received colonel's commission under Thomas Forster (1675?-1738) [q. v.]; surrendered at Preston and was executed. His head was displayed on the top of Temple Bar, London. [xliii. 6]

OXENBRIDGE, JOHN (1603-1674), puritan divine; became tutor at Magdalen Hall, Oxford (M.A., 1631), but (1634) was deprived by Laud for drawing up a document for the better government of the society, which he persuaded his scholars to subscribe; after exercising his ministry in the Bermudas returned to England in 1641 and preached in various parts of the country: became a fellow of Eton, 1652, where he formed a friendship with Andrew Marvell (1621–1678) [q. v.]; being ejected, 1660, emigrated to Surinam, Barbados, and finally to Boston, where he became pastor; published sermons.   [xliii. 7]

OXENDEN, ASHTON (1808–1892), bishop of Montreal; of Harrow and University College, Oxford; M.A., 1859; D.D., 1869; rector of Pluckley, Kent, 1849–69; honorary canon of Canterbury, 1864; elected bishop of Montreal and metropolitan of Canada, May 1869; assiduously attended to his duties till ill-health caused him to resign the bishopric, 1878; vicar of St. Stephen's, near Canterbury, and rural dean, 1879–84; published minor theological works, which his plain and simple language made very popular.   [xliii. 9]

OXENDEN, SIR GEORGE (1620–1669), governor of Bombay; spent his youth in India; knighted, 1661; appointed by the East India Company president and chief director of their affairs at Surat, 1662; found the company's trade threatened by the hostility of the French and Dutch, but during his term of office established the company's affairs on a sound basis and prepared the way for the subsequent development of its power; repulsed an attack on Surat by the Mahrattas, 1663; on the cession of Bombay to the company by Charles II (1667) was nominated governor and commander-in-chief; died at Surat.   [xliii. 9]

OXENDEN, GEORGE (1651–1703), civil lawyer; nephew of Sir George Oxenden (1620–1669) [q. v.]; M.A. *per literas regias* Trinity Hall, Cambridge, 1675; LL.D., 1679; was appointed regius professor of civil law at Cambridge, 1684, vicar-general to the archbishop of Canterbury, 1688, and chancellor of the diocese of London; master of Trinity Hall, Cambridge, 1689–1703; represented the university in parliament (1695–8); author of several Latin poems.   [xliii. 10]

OXENDEN, SIR GEORGE, fifth baronet (1694–1775), son of George Oxenden [q. v.]; lord of the admiralty and of the treasury; M.P., Sandwich; noted for his profligate character.   [xliii. 11]

OXENDEN or **OXINDEN**, HENRY (1609–1670), poet; first cousin of Sir George Oxenden (1620–1669) [q. v.]; B.A. Corpus Christi College, Oxford, 1627; author of 'Jobus Triumphans,' 1651, and other poems. [xliii. 11]

OXENEDES or **OXNEAD**, JOHN DE (*d.* 1293?), chronicler; reputed author of a chronicle really written by a monk of St. Benet's, Hulme, Norfolk, covering the period from Alfred to 1293. There is a copy in the Cotton MSS. edited by Sir Henry Ellis (1777–1869) [q. v.] (1859) for the Rolls Series, and another in the Duke of Newcastle's MSS.   [xliii. 12]

OXENFORD, JOHN (1812–1877), dramatist; author of many plays and of translations from German, French, Spanish, and Italian; became dramatic critic to 'The Times,' *c.* 1850, and held that position for more than a quarter of a century. An essay by him on 'Iconoclasm in Philosophy' based on Schopenhauer's 'Parerga und Paralipomena' first called public attention to Schopenhauer's philosophy in England.   [xliii. 12]

OXENHAM, HENRY NUTCOMBE (1829–1888), Roman catholic writer; of Harrow and Balliol College, Oxford; M.A., 1854; took orders with English church, but in 1857 was received into the church of Rome; worked at the Brompton Oratory, and afterwards on the staff of St. Edmund's College, Ware; subsequently held a mastership at the Oratory School, Birmingham; published theological and historical books, including translations of works by Döllinger, under whom he had studied.   [xliii. 13]

OXENHAM, JOHN (*d.* 1575), sea-captain; with Drake in Central America, 1572; undertook (1574) a second expedition, which was destroyed by the Spaniards; captured and hanged at Lima. Kingsley has introduced a late and partly legendary account of his expedition into his novel 'Westward Ho!'   [xliii. 15]

OXFORD, EARLS OF. [See VERE, ROBERT DE, third EARL of the first creation, 1170?–1221; VERE, JOHN DE, seventh EARL, 1313–1360; VERE, ROBERT DE, ninth EARL, 1362–1392; VERE, AUBREY DE, tenth EARL, 1340?–1400; VERE, JOHN DE, thirteenth EARL, 1443–1513; VERE, JOHN DE, sixteenth EARL, 1512?–1562; VERE, EDWARD DE, seventeenth EARL, 1550–1604; VERE, HENRY DE, eighteenth EARL, 1593–1625; VERE, AUBREY DE, twentieth EARL, 1626–1703; HARLEY, ROBERT, first EARL of the second creation, 1661–1724; HARLEY, EDWARD, second EARL, 1689–1741.]

OXFORD, JOHN OF (*d.* 1200), bishop of Norwich; commissioned by Henry II (1164) to request Pope Alexander III to sanction the constitutions of Clarendon; subsequently employed on other important foreign missions; was excommunicated by Becket (1166) for recognising the anti-pope Paschal, but obtained absolution from Alexander; escorted Becket to England, 1170, and by his firmness prevented the prelate's enemies attacking him when he landed; consecrated bishop of Norwich, 1175; was with two other bishops appointed 'archijusticiarius' on the reconstruction of the judicial system, 1179.   [xliii. 15]

OXINDEN, HENRY (1609–1670) [See OXENDEN.]

OXLEE, JOHN (1779–1854), divine; rector of Scawton, 1815–26, Molesworth, 1836–54; was acquainted with 120 languages and dialects, and had an exceptional knowledge of Hebrew literature; author of 'The Christian Doctrine of the Trinity, the Incarnation, and the Atonement . . . maintained on the Principles of Judaism' (3 vols.), 1815–1850.   [xliii. 17]

OXLEY, JOHN (1781–1828), Australian explorer; surveyor-general of New South Wales, 1812; made explorations between 1817 and 1823 in the interior of New South Wales.   [xliii. 18]

OXLEY, JOSEPH (1715–1775), quaker; travelled much in the United States, and was the author of a series of autobiographical letters.   [xliii. 19]

OXNEAD, JOHN DE (*d.* 1293?). [See OXENEDES.]

OYLEY. [See D'OYLEY.]

OZELL, JOHN (*d.* 1743), translator; an accountant by trade; became auditor-general of the city of London and bridge accounts and of St. Paul's Cathedral and St. Thomas's Hospital, London; mentioned in the 'Dunciad'; published numerous translations of slight merit.   [xliii. 19]

P

PAAS, SIMON (1595?–1647). [See PASS.]

PABO (*fl.* 520?), Welsh king; one of the rulers of the northern Welsh of Strathclyde.   [xliii. 21]

PACE, JOHN (1523?–1590?), professional fool; nephew of Richard Pace [q. v.]; of Eton and King's College, Cambridge; became jester to the Duke of Norfolk and afterwards in Elizabeth's court.   [xliii. 21]

PACE, RICHARD (1482?–1536), diplomatist and dean of St. Paul's Cathedral; employed by Wolsey in 1515 to incite the Swiss against Francis I, in 1519 to promote Henry VIII's election as emperor, and in 1521 and 1523 to support Wolsey's candidature for the papacy; author of

the treatise 'De Fructu,' 1517, and of the oration 'De Pace,' 1518. From 1514 to 1524 his despatches form no inconsiderable portion of the state papers of this country.   [xliii. 22]

PACE, THOMAS (*d.* 1533). [See SKEVINGTON.]

PACIFICO, DAVID (1784–1854), Greek trader; a Portuguese Jew, but born a British subject at Gibraltar; his house in Athens burnt by a mob, 1847, compensation for which was delayed by the Greek government; a dispute followed between France and England and almost ended in war, owing to resolute action in Pacifico's behalf of Palmerston, foreign secretary of English government.   [xliii. 24]

PACK, Sir DENIS (1772 ?–1823), major-general; descendant of Sir Christopher Packe [q. v.]; saw service in Flanders, 1794, in the Quiberon expedition, 1795, and in Ireland, 1798 ; commanded the 71st foot at the capture of Cape of Good Hope, 1806, in the Peninsula, 1808, and in the Walcheren expedition, 1809 ; major-general, 1813 ; commanded (1810–14) a Portuguese brigade in Spain ; K.C.B., 1815 ; commanded in 1815 a brigade of Picton's division at Waterloo. [xliii. 25]

PACK, GEORGE (*fl.* 1700–1724), actor ; originally a singer ; acted at Lincoln's Inn Fields, London, 1700–5, at the Haymarket, London, 1705–7, and at Drury Lane, London ; retired, 1724. [xliii. 26]

PACK, RICHARDSON (1682–1728), miscellaneous writer ; of Merchant Taylors' School, London, and St. John's College, Oxford : barrister, Middle Temple ; entered the army ; saw service in Spain, 1710, and was promoted major. Edmund Curll [q. v.] printed several works by Pack in verse and prose between 1719 and 1729. [xliii. 27]

PACKE, Sir CHRISTOPHER (1593 ?–1682), lord mayor of London ; member of the Drapers' Company ; lord mayor, 1654 ; a prominent member of the Company of Merchant Adventurers ; knighted and appointed an admiralty commissioner, 1655 ; a strong partisan of Cromwell, proposing on 23 Feb. 1656, in the Protector's last parliament, that Cromwell should assume the title of king ; disqualified at the Restoration from holding any public office. [xliii. 28]

PACKE, CHRISTOPHER (*fl.* 1711), chemist : practised as a quack under the patronage of Edmund Dickinson [q. v.] and others ; author of chemical works of an empirical character. [xliii. 30]

PACKE, CHRISTOPHER (1686–1749), physician ; son of Christopher Packe (*fl.* 1711) [q. v.]; of Merchant Taylors' School, London ; created M.D. Cambridge (*comitiis regiis*), 1717 ; practised at Canterbury from 1726 ; published two 'philosophico-chorographical' dissertations on a chart of East Kent, 1736 and 1743. [xliii. 30]

PACKE or **PACK**, CHRISTOPHER (*fl.* 1796), portrait- and landscape-painter. [xliii. 31]

PACKE, EDMUND (*fl.* 1735), 'M.D. and chemist'; son of Christopher Packe (*fl.* 1711) [q. v.] [xliii. 30]

PACKER, JOHN (1570 ?–1649), clerk of the privy seal, 1604 ; of Cambridge and Trinity College, Oxford ; envoy to Denmark, 1610 ; received many favours from Charles I, but in 1640 refused him a loan and allied himself with parliament ; his property in Kent sequestered for a time by the royalist forces ; a visitor of the university of Oxford, 1647. [xliii. 31]

PACKER, JOHN HAYMAN (1730–1806), actor ; originally a saddler ; acted at Drury Lane Theatre, London, under Garrick ; retired, 1805. [xliii. 32]

PACKER, WILLIAM (*fl.* 1644–1660), soldier ; entered the parliamentary army early in the war and commanded Cromwell's regiment at Dunbar, 1650 ; promoted by Cromwell, but on becoming discontented at the restoration of the House of Lords, and opposing the Protector's policy, was deprived of his posts ; joined Lambert against parliament, 1659 ; his property confiscated at the Restoration. [xliii. 33]

PACKINGTON. [See PAKINGTON.]

PADARN (*fl.* 550), Welsh saint; born of Breton parents ; laboured in Britain and Ireland as a missionary ; spent his last days in Brittany, founding a monastery at Vannes. His Latin name, Paternus, has caused him to be wrongly identified with Paternus, bishop of Avranches. [xliii. 34]

PADDOCK, TOM (1823 ?–1863), pugilist; champion of England, 1855, but defeated (1856) by Bill Perry, the Tipton slasher. [xliii. 34]

PADDY, Sir WILLIAM (1554–1634), physician ; of Merchant Taylors' School, London, and St. John's College, Oxford (fellow); B.A., 1573 ; M.D. Leyden, 1589 (incorporated at Oxford, 1591); physician to James I, 1603 ; knighted, 1603 ; president of the College of Physicians, 1609, 1610, 1611, and 1618 ; friend of Laud and benefactor of St. John's College, Oxford. [xliii. 35]

PADRIG (373–463). [See PATRICK.]

PADUA, JOHN OF (*fl.* 1542–1549), architect ; employed in matters relating to architecture and music by Henry VIII and Edward VI ; doubtfully identified with Sir John Thynne [q. v.], John Thorpe (*fl.* 1570–1610) [q. v.], and John Caius (1510–1573) [q. v.] [xliii. 36]

PAGAN, ISOBEL (*d.* 1821), versifier ; author of 'A Collection of Songs and Poems' (published, *c.* 1805); credited by legend with the songs 'Ca' the Yowes to the Knowes' (revised by Burns) and the 'Crook and Plaid.' [xliii. 36]

PAGAN, JAMES (1811–1870), journalist ; editor of the 'Glasgow Herald' from 1856; published works on Glasgow antiquities. [xliii. 36]

PAGANEL, ADAM (*fl.* 1210), founder of a monastic house at Glandford Bridge in the time of King John. [xliii. 38]

PAGANEL, FULK (*d.* 1182), baron of Hambie in Normandy ; son of William Paganel [q. v.]; a constant attendant of Henry II when abroad. [xliii. 37]

PAGANEL, FULK (*d.* 1210 ?), second son of Fulk Paganel (*d.* 1182) [q. v.]; suspected of treachery to King John, 1203, but afterwards restored to favour. [xliii. 37]

PAGANEL, RALPH (*fl.* 1089), sheriff of Yorkshire; seized the lands of William de St. Carilef [q. v.], 1088, by the order of William II. [xliii. 37]

PAGANEL, WILLIAM (*fl.* 1136), soldier ; son of Ralph Paganel [q. v.]; defeated at Moutiers Hubert (1136) by Geoffrey Plantagenet. [xliii. 37]

PAGANELL or **PAINEL** (*fl.* 1189), baron, lord of Dudley Castle ; joined the rebellion of Prince Henry, 1173. [xliii. 38]

PAGE, BENJAMIN WILLIAM (1765–1845), admiral ; saw much service in the eastern seas, and piloted the squadron which captured the Moluccas in 1796. [xliii. 38]

PAGE, DAVID (1814–1879), geologist : educated at St. Andrews ; LL.D., 1867 ; became 'scientific editor' to W. & R. Chambers, 1843 ; F.G.S., 1853 ; professor of geology at Durham University College of Science, 1873. [xliii. 39]

PAGE, Sir FRANCIS (1661 ?–1741), judge ; barrister, Inner Temple, 1690 ; bencher, 1713 ; knighted, 1715 ; appointed a baron of the exchequer, 1718 ; transferred to the court of common pleas, 1726, and to the king's bench, 1727 ; known to his contemporaries as 'the hanging judge'; satirised by Pope, assailed by Dr. Johnson, and vituperated by Savage, whom he had condemned to death for killing a man in a tavern brawl. [xliii. 39]

PAGE, FREDERICK (1769–1834), writer on the poor laws ; of Oriel College, Oxford ; barrister, Inner Temple, 1792 ; bencher, 1826. [xliii. 41]

PAGE, JOHN (1760 ?–1812), vocalist and compiler of musical works ; vicar-choral of St. Paul's Cathedral, 1801. [xliii. 41]

PAGE, SAMUEL (1574–1630), poet and divine ; M.A. Christ Church, Oxford, 1594 ; fellow, 1591 ; D.D., 1611 ; naval chaplain in the expedition to Cadiz, 1595 ; vicar of St. Nicholas, Deptford, 1597 ; author of sermons and of 'The Love of Amos and Laura,' a poem which appeared in 'Alcilia,' 1613. [xliii. 42]

PAGE, THOMAS (1803–1877), civil engineer ; M.I.C.E., 1837 ; made designs for the embankment of the Thames, 1842 ; constructed the Chelsea suspension bridge, 1858, and Westminster Bridge, London, 1862 ; carried out the Albert Embankment, London, 1869. [xliii. 42]

PAGE, Sir THOMAS HYDE (1746–1821), military engineer ; served in the war of independence in North America, and was severely wounded at Bunker's Hill, 1775 ; constructed the ferry at Chatham ; F.R.S., 1783 ; knighted, 1783 ; consulting engineer to several Irish institutions. [xliii. 42]

PAGE, WILLIAM (1590–1663), divine ; M.A. Balliol College, Oxford, 1614 ; incorporated at Cambridge, 1615 ; fellow of All Souls College, Oxford, 1619 ; D.D., 1634 ; master of Reading grammar school, 1629–44, and rector of Hannington, Hampshire: sequestered from both preferments, but in 1647 made rector of East Lockinge ; translated Thomas à Kempis's 'Imitatio Christi,' 1639, and published religious treatises. [xliii. 44]

PAGEHAM or **PAGHAM**, JOHN DE (*d.* 1158), bishop of Worcester ; consecrated, 1151; assisted at Henry II's coronation, 1154 ; died at Rome. [xliii. 45]

PAGET, LORD ALFRED HENRY (1816–1888), son of Sir Henry William Paget, first marquis of Anglesey [q v.] ; of Westminster School ; liberal M.P. for Lichfield, 1837–65 ; was chief equerry, 1846–74, and clerk marshal of the royal household, 1846–88 ; general in the army, 1881. [xliii. 57]

PAGET, SIR ARTHUR (1771–1840), diplomatist ; brother of Sir Henry William Paget, first marquis of Anglesey [q. v.] ; of Westminster School and Christ Church, Oxford ; M.P., Anglesey, 1794–1807 ; represented England at Berlin, 1794 ; envoy extraordinary to elector palatine, 1798, to court of Naples, 1800, to Vienna, 1801–6, where he assisted to form the third coalition against France, 1805 ; privy councillor, 1804 ; G.C.B., 1815 ; ambassador to Turkey, 1807–9. [xliii. 45]

PAGET, SIR AUGUSTUS BERKELEY (1823–1896), diplomatist ; son of Sir Arthur Paget [q. v.] ; attaché at Madrid, 1843–6, and at Paris, 1846–52 ; secretary of legation at Athens, 1852, and at the Hague, 1854–5 ; chargé d'affaires at the Hague, 1855–6, Lisbon, 1857–8, and Berlin, 1858 ; minister at court of Denmark, 1859 ; envoy extraordinary and minister plenipotentiary to King Victor Emmanuel, 1867–76, and ambassador, 1876–83 ; ambassador at Vienna, 1884–93 ; K.C.B., 1863 ; privy councillor, 1876 ; G.C.B., 1883 ; published his father's memoirs under title of 'The Paget Papers,' 1895.

[Suppl. iii. 239]

PAGET, CHARLES (*d.* 1612), Roman catholic conspirator ; of Gonville and Caius College and Trinity Hall, Cambridge ; son of William Paget, first baron Paget [q. v.] ; retired to Paris in 1572 and became secretary to Mary Stuart's ambassador, James Beaton (1517–1603) [q. v.] ; secretly opposed Beaton and acted as an English spy ; visited England, 1583, but was justly suspected of treasonable plotting ; retired again to France ; his surrender demanded by the English ambassador, 1584 ; attainted, 1587 ; entered service of king of Spain, 1588 ; removed to Brussels, but perfidiously corresponded with Cecil ; advocated the claims of James VI to the English crown, opposing those of the infanta, and in 1599 threw up his Spanish employment ; his attainder reversed after James's accession and his estates restored. [xliii. 46]

PAGET, SIR CHARLES (1778–1839), vice-admiral ; brother of Sir Henry William Paget, first marquis of Anglesey [q. v.] ; entered the navy, 1790 ; commanded on the North American and West Indian stations, 1837–9 ; G.C.H., 1832 ; vice-admiral, 1837. [xliii. 49]

PAGET, LORD CLARENCE EDWARD (1811–1895), admiral ; son of Sir Henry William Paget, first marquis of Anglesey [q. v.] ; of Westminster School ; M.P., Sandwich, 1847–52 and 1857–66 ; secretary to the admiralty, 1859–66 ; commander-in-chief in the Mediterranean, 1866–1869 ; admiral, 1870 ; privy councillor ; G.C.B., 1886. [xliii. 57]

PAGET, SIR EDWARD (1775–1849), general ; brother of Sir Henry William Paget, first marquis of Anglesey [q. v.] ; cornet, 1792 ; commanded the reserve at Coruña, 1809 ; conducted the advance to Oporto, 1809 ; appointed second in command to Wellesley, 1811, but almost immediately taken prisoner ; G.C.B., 1812 ; conducted the Burmese campaigns of 1824–5 ; general, 1825. [xliii. 49]

PAGET, FRANCIS EDWARD (1806–1882), divine and author ; son of Sir Edward Paget [q. v.] ; of Westminster School and Christ Church, Oxford ; student, 1825–36 ; M.A., 1830 ; rector of Elford, 1835 ; published tales illustrating his views on church and social reforms. [xliii. 50]

PAGET, LORD GEORGE AUGUSTUS FREDERICK (1818–1880), general ; son of Sir Henry William Paget, first marquis of Anglesey [q. v.] ; of Westminster School ; served throughout the Crimean campaign ; commanded the third line in the charge of the light brigade at Balaclava ; his 'Crimean Journals' published, 1881. [xliii. 51]

PAGET, SIR GEORGE EDWARD (1809–1892), physician ; fellow of Caius College, Cambridge, 1832–51 ; M.D.,1838 ; physician to Addenbrooke's Hospital, 1839–84, and regius professor of physic at Cambridge, 1872–92 ; K.C.B., 1885. [xliii. 52]

PAGET, HENRY, first EARL OF UXBRIDGE (*d.* 1743), son of William, sixth baron Paget [q. v.] ; M.P., Staffordshire, 1695–1711, and lord of the treasury, 1711–15 ; privy councillor, 1711 ; created Baron Burton, 1711, and Earl of Uxbridge, 1714. [xliii. 53]

PAGET, HENRY, second EARL OF UXBRIDGE (1719–1769), son of Thomas Catesby Paget, baron Paget [q. v.] ; chiefly remarkable for an inordinate love of money. [xliii. 54]

PAGET, SIR HENRY WILLIAM, first MARQUIS OF ANGLESEY and second EARL OF UXBRIDGE of the second creation (1768–1854), descended from William Paget, fifth baron Paget [q. v.] ; of Westminster School and Christ Church, Oxford ; M.P., Carnarvon boroughs, 1790–6, for Milborne Port, 1796–1810 ; raised a regiment of infantry in 1793, chiefly from among his father's Staffordshire tenants, which on the outbreak of war became the 80th foot ; served in Flanders, 1794, and in Holland, 1799 ; commanded the cavalry with great distinction in Spain under Sir John Moore, and the cavalry and horse artillery at Waterloo, where he lost a leg ; created Marquis of Anglesey, 1815 ; lord-lieutenant of Ireland, 1828 ; favoured catholic emancipation ; adopted a conciliatory attitude to the catholics, and was recalled in January 1829 in consequence of differences with the prime minister, the Duke of Wellington ; re-appointed by Lord Grey (December 1830), found himself opposed by O'Connell, and retired in 1833, after establishing the board of education ; field-marshal, 1846. [xliii. 54]

PAGET, SIR JAMES, first baronet (1814–1899), surgeon ; brother of Sir George Edward Paget [q. v.] ; studied at St. Bartholomew's Hospital, London ; M.R.C.S., 1836 ; sub-editor of 'Medical Gazette,' 1837–42 ; demonstrator of morbid anatomy at St. Bartholomew's, 1839 ; lecturer on general anatomy and physiology, 1843 ; warden of the college for students, 1843–51 ; full surgeon, 1861–71 ; consulting surgeon, 1871 ; F.R.C.S., 1843 ; Arris and Gale professor of anatomy, 1847–52 ; vice-president, 1873–4 ; president, 1875 ; surgeon extraordinary to Queen Victoria, 1858, serjeant-surgeon extraordinary, 1867–77, and serjeant-surgeon, 1877 ; baronet, 1871 ; vice-chancellor of London University, 1883–95 ; F.R.S., 1851 ; D.C.L. Oxford ; LL.D. Cambridge ; M.D. Dublin, Bonn, and Würzburg ; published 'Lectures on Surgical Pathology,' 1853, and other writings. [Suppl. iii. 240]

PAGET, JOHN (*d.* 1640), nonconformist divine ; M.A. Trinity College, Cambridge, 1598 ; rector of Nantwich, 1598 ; ejected for nonconformity ; went to Holland (1604) and was minister of the English presbyterian church at Amsterdam, 1607–37 ; wrote on controversial subjects. [xliii. 58]

PAGET, JOHN (1808–1892), agriculturist and writer on Hungary ; M.D. Edinburgh ; married (1837) the Baroness Polyxena Wesselényi, and settled on her Hungarian estates. [xliii. 58]

PAGET, JOHN (1811–1898), police magistrate and author ; barrister, Middle Temple, 1838 ; secretary successively to lord chancellors Truro and Cranworth, 1850–1855 ; magistrate at Thames police court, 1864, and subsequently at the Hammersmith and Wandsworth, and the West London court ; resigned, 1889 ; published essays on literary, historical, and legal subjects. [Suppl. iii. 242]

PAGET, NATHAN (1615–1679), physician ; M.A. Edinburgh ; M.D. Leyden, 1639 ; son of Thomas Paget (*d.* 1660) [q. v.] ; nominated physician to the Tower of London in 1649 ; friend of Milton. [xliii. 59]

PAGET, THOMAS, third BARON PAGET (*d.* 1590), son of William, first baron Paget [q. v.] ; fellow-commoner of Gonville and Caius College, Cambridge, 1559 ; being a Roman catholic fled to the continent, 1583, on the discovery of Throgmorton's plot ; obtained a pension from Spain ; attainted, 1587 ; died at Brussels. [xliii. 59]

PAGET, THOMAS (*d.* 1660), divine ; brother of John Paget (*d.* 1640) [q. v.] ; M.A. Trinity College, Cambridge, 1612 ; succeeded his brother at Amsterdam ; obtained preferment in England, 1639. [xliii. 58]

PAGET, THOMAS CATESBY, BARON PAGET (*d.* 1742), son of Henry Paget, first earl of Uxbridge [q. v.] ; M.P., Staffordshire, 1715 and 1722 ; wrote several pieces in prose and verse. [xliii. 53]

PAGET, WILLIAM, first BARON PAGET OF BEAU-DESERT (1505–1563), educated at St. Paul's School, London, and Trinity Hall, Cambridge; employed on various diplomatic services by Henry VIII; sent as ambassador to France, 1541, to explain the fall of Catherine Howard; made a privy councillor and a secretary of state on his return; for the closing years of the reign was, with the first Earl of Hertford [see SEYMOUR, EDWARD (1506?–1552)], probably Henry's chief adviser; K.G. and comptroller of the king's household on the accession of Edward VI; played a prominent part in the plot to set aside Henry VIII's will, and proposed a protectorate in the council; created Baron Paget of Beaudesert, 1549; remained faithful to Somerset, was arrested (1551) on the charge of conspiring against Warwick's life, and (1552) degraded from the Garter on the ground of insufficient birth, and fined 6,000l. for using his offices for his private emolument; after Edward VI's death joined Queen Jane's council, but sanctioned the proclamation of Queen Mary, 1553; became a privy councillor, was restored to the Garter, and, in 1556, made lord privy seal; relinquished his offices on Queen Elizabeth's accession.   [xliii. 60]

PAGET, WILLIAM, fourth BARON PAGET (1572–1629), son of Thomas, third baron Paget [q. v.]; B.A. Christ Church, Oxford, 1590; a staunch protestant; restored by James I to the lands and honours forfeited by his father's attainder.   [xliii. 63]

PAGET, SIR WILLIAM, fifth BARON PAGET (1609–1678), son of William, fourth baron Paget [q. v.]; K.B., 1625; of Christ Church, Oxford; at first in sympathy with parliament against Charles I, but on the outbreak of war joined the king; his estates sequestered.   [xliii. 63] .

PAGET, WILLIAM, sixth BARON PAGET (1637–1713), son of Sir William, fifth baron Paget [q. v.]; ambassador at Vienna, 1689–93; ambassador to Turkey, 1693–1702, where he negotiated the treaty of Carlowitz, 1699.   [xliii. 64]

PAGIT or **PAGITT**, EPHRAIM (1575?–1647), heresiographer; son of Eusebius Pagit [q. v.]; matriculated from Christ Church, Oxford; author of 'Christianographie,' 1635, and 'Heresiographie,' 1645, a valuable account of contemporary sects.   [xliii. 65]

PAGIT, EUSEBIUS (1547?–1617), puritan divine; student of Christ Church, Oxford; B.A. Christ's College, Cambridge, 1567; rector of Lamport, 1572–4, and of Kilkhampton, of which he was deprived for nonconformity to parts of the Anglican ritual in 1585; rector of St. Anne and St. Agnes, London, 1604–17; remained without a charge from 1585 to the death of Whitgift; published theological treatises.   [xliii. 65]

PAGULA, WILLIAM (d. 1350?), theologian; vicar of Winkfield, near Windsor, 1330; devoted his time to study; wrote theological treatises.   [xliii. 66]

PAIN. [See also PAINE and PAYNE.]

PAIN, GEORGE RICHARD (1793?–1838), architect; practised with his brother, James Pain [q.v.]   [xliii. 67]

PAIN, JAMES (1779?–1877), architect and builder; grandson of William Pain [q. v.]; designed and built a number of churches and glebe houses in Munster.   [xliii. 66]

PAIN, WILLIAM (1730?–1790?), writer on architecture and joinery; wrote several treatises between 1759 and 1785.   [xliii. 67]

PAINE. [See also PAIN and PAYNE.]

PAINE or **PAYNE**, JAMES (1725–1789), architect; designed many large houses, described in his 'Plans of Noblemen and Gentlemen's Residences,' 1767–83; he held several government appointments, and (1771) was elected president of the Society of Artists of Great Britain.   [xliii. 67]

PAINE, JAMES (d. 1829?), architect; son of James Paine (1725–1789) [q. v.]; original member of the 'Architects' Club,' 1791.   [xliii. 69]

PAINE, THOMAS (1737–1809), author of the 'Rights of Man'; son of Joseph Paine, a staymaker and small farmer of Thetford, and a member of the Society of Friends; put to his father's business at the age of thirteen; joined a privateer when nineteen years old; became a supernumerary excise officer at Thetford, 1761; drew up, while stationed at Lewes, 1772, a statement of the excisemen's grievances, which was printed and distributed to members of parliament in promotion of a movement for increase of pay; dismissed after the failure of the agitation; separated from h s wife, 1774; sailed for America with an introduction from Franklin, 1774; published his pamphlet 'Common Sense,' 1776, a history of the transactions which had led to the war with England, which established his fame; joined the provincial army in the autumn and became a volunteer aide-de-camp to General Nathaniel Greene, animating the troops by his writings; appointed secretary to the committee of foreign affairs, April 1777, but lost his post, 1779, in consequence of making indiscreet revelations in regard to the French alliance; clerk to the Pennsylvania assembly, 1779; continued to write political pamphlets on public affairs; resigned position as clerk, 1780, and (1781) went to France on a political mission as secretary to Colonel Laurens, the American envoy, returning to Boston in August 1781; allowed a salary of eight hundred dollars on the conclusion of the war to enable him to continue his writings; became absorbed in an invention for an iron bridge, c. 1786, and sailed to Europe to promote his idea, 1787; published in London the first part of his 'Rights of Man,' in reply to Burke's 'Reflexions on the Revolution,' 1790; on the appearance of the second part (1792) was compelled to fly to France to avoid prosecution, the book having become a manifesto of the party in sympathy with the French revolution; given the title of French citizen 17 Aug. 1792; elected a member of the convention, September 1792; opposed the execution of Louis XVI, and was arrested in December 1793, just after the completion of the first part of the 'Age of Reason'; his life saved by the fall of Robespierre; released, November 1794, having written most of the second part of the 'Age of Reason' while in prison; published the 'Age of Reason,' 1793, which increased the odium in which he was held in England; returned to America, 1802; during his last sojourn there lived in easier circumstances, but found political and theological antipathies strong, and was more or less 'ostracised,' both as an opponent of Washington and the federalists and as the author of the 'Age of Reason'; died at New York. He is the only English writer who expresses with uncompromising sharpness the abstract doctrine of political rights held by the French revolutionists. His connection with the American struggle, and afterwards with the French movement, gave him a unique position, and his writings became a sort of text-book for the extreme radical party in England.   [xliii. 69]

PAINTER, EDWARD (1784–1852), pugilist; beat Thomas Winter Spring [q. v.], 1818, and Tom Oliver [q. v.], 1820.   [xliii. 79]

PAINTER, WILLIAM (1540?–1594), author; of St. John's College, Cambridge; head-master of Sevenoaks school; made clerk of the ordnance, 1561; acquired fortune by irregular practices with public money; author of 'The Palace of Pleasure' (1566) (last reprint, 1890), a work consisting of stories translated from Latin, Greek, French, and Italian, which made Italian novelists known in England, and was largely utilised by the Elizabethan dramatists.   [xliii. 80]

PAISIBLE, JAMES (1656?–1721), flautist and composer; native of France; came to England, c. 1680; performed for the Duchesse de Mazarin at Chelsea and before Queen Anne; published numerous works.   [xliii. 82]

PAISLEY, first BARON (1543?–1622). [See HAMILTON, CLAUD.]

PAKEMAN, THOMAS (1614?–1691), dissenting divine; M.A. Clare College, Cambridge, 1637; officiated from 1648 at Harrow-on-the-Hill; ejected, 1662; afterwards ministered at Brentford and Stratford.   [xliii. 82]

PAKENHAM, SIR EDWARD MICHAEL (1778–1815), major-general, brother of Sir Hercules Robert Pakenham [q. v.]; entered the army, 1794; commanded the 64th (1803) at the capture of St. Lucia, where he was wounded; brevet-colonel, 1805; joined Wellington in the Peninsula after Talavera; led the decisive movement of the third division at Salamanca, 1812, his conduct earning him a remarkable eulogy from Wellington; commanded the north division at Sauroren, 1813; major-general, 1812; G.C.B., 1815; killed in America while directing an assault on New Orleans.   [xliii. 83]

к k

PAKENHAM, Sir HERCULES ROBERT (1781–1850), lieutenant-general ; brother of Sir Edward Michael Pakenham [q. v.] ; entered the army, 1803 ; served throughout the Peninsular war, and was described by Wellington as 'one of the best officers of riflemen I have seen' ; major-general, 1837 ; K.C.B., 1838 ; lieutenant-general, 1846. [xliii. 84]

PAKENHAM, Sir RICHARD (1797–1868), diplomatist ; son of Sir Thomas Pakenham [q. v.] ; of Trinity College, Dublin ; minister plenipotentiary to Mexico (1835–43), the United States (1843–7), and at Lisbon (1851–5). [xliii. 85]

PAKENHAM, Sir THOMAS (1757–1836), admiral ; uncle of Sir Edward Michael Pakenham [q. v.] ; entered the navy, 1771 ; honourably acquitted by court-martial for the loss of his ship, 1781 ; his conduct in the battle of 1 June 1794 spoken of as particularly brilliant ; admiral, 1810 ; G.C.B., 1820. [xliii. 85]

PAKINGTON, DOROTHY, LADY (d. 1679), reputed author of 'The Whole Duty of Man' (1658) ; daughter of Thomas Coventry, first baron Coventry [q. v.], and wife of Sir John Pakington (1620–1680) [q. v.] ; probably only a copyist of the 'Duty.' The first public allusion to her as author was not made till 1697, while internal evidence shows that the author was a practised divine, and one acquainted with Hebrew, Syriac, and Arabic. It was probably written by Richard Allestree [q. v.], who in all likelihood was the author also of other works generally ascribed to Lady Dorothy Pakington. [xliii. 86]

PAKINGTON, Sir JOHN (d. 1560), serjeant-at-law ; treasurer, Inner Temple, 1529 ; granted licence to remain covered in the king's presence, 1529 ; serjeant-at-law, 1532 ; in later life lived in Wales, where he is often spoken of as a judge, and in Worcestershire. [xliii. 88]

PAKINGTON, Sir JOHN, first baronet (1600–1624), son of Sir John Pakington (1549–1625) [q. v.] ; created baronet, 1620 ; M.P., Aylesbury, 1623–4. [xliii. 89]

PAKINGTON, Sir JOHN (1549–1625), courtier ; great-nephew of Sir John Pakington (d. 1560) [q. v.] ; B.A. Christ Church, Oxford, 1569 ; student, Lincoln's Inn, 1570 ; remarkable for wit and personal beauty ; knighted, 1587 ; nicknamed 'Lusty Pakington' by Queen Elizabeth, who took great pleasure in his athletic achievements ; lived for a few years in great splendour in London, and outran his fortune, but retrieved it by the queen's favour, strict economy, and (1598) a wealthy marriage ; sheriff of Worcestershire, 1595 and 1607. [xliii. 88]

PAKINGTON, Sir JOHN, second baronet (1620–1680), royalist ; son of Sir John Pakington, first baronet [q. v.] ; fought at Kineton, 1642, but voluntarily surrendered himself to the speaker to compound, 1646 ; took part in the Worcester campaign (1651), and suffered considerable pecuniary losses under the Commonwealth ; his fortunes retrieved by the Restoration ; M.P., Worcestershire, 1661–79. [xliii. 89]

PAKINGTON, Sir JOHN, third baronet (1649–1688), Anglo-Saxon scholar ; of Christ Church, Oxford ; son of Sir John Pakington, second baronet [q. v.] ; a pupil of George Hickes [q. v.] ; under his tuition he became one of the finest Anglo-Saxon scholars of the time ; M.P., Worcestershire, 1685–7. [xliii. 91]

PAKINGTON, Sir JOHN, fourth baronet (1671–1727), politician and alleged original of Addison's 'Sir Roger de Coverley' ; only son of Sir John Pakington, third baronet [q. v.] ; M.P., Worcestershire, 1690–5 and 1698–1727 ; a pronounced tory ; proposed an address to William III requesting him to remove Burnet from the post of preceptor to the Duke of Gloucester, 1699 ; supported the bill for preventing occasional conformity, 1703 ; and opposed the union, 1707 ; warrant issued for his arrest on the outbreak of the 1715 rebellion ; managed to clear himself before the council. He was first identified with Sir Roger de Coverley in 1783 by Thomas Tyers [q. v.], but there is little resemblance beyond the fact that both were baronets of Worcestershire. Pakington was only thirty-nine when the 'Spectator' first appeared in 1711, while Sir Roger was fifty-five. He had been twice married, while Sir Roger was a bachelor, and he was an energetic politician, while Sir Roger visited London only occasionally. [xliii. 91]

PAKINGTON, Sir JOHN SOMERSET, first BARON HAMPTON and first baronet (1799–1880), was son of William Russell, taking the name of his maternal uncle, Sir John Pakington, eighth baronet, in 1831, on succeeding to his estates ; of Eton and Oriel College, Oxford ; conservative M.P. for Droitwich, 1837–74 ; created baronet, 1846 ; secretary for war and colonies under Lord Derby in 1852 ; twice first lord of the admiralty, under Lord Derby, 1858 and 1866 ; secretary for war, 1867, retaining office until Disraeli's resignation in December 1868 ; indiscreetly revealed (1867) the secret history of the ministerial Reform Bill, afterwards known as the 'Ten Minutes Bill' ; created Baron Hampton, 1874. [xliii. 94]

PAKINGTON, WILLIAM (d. 1390), chronicler ; clerk and treasurer of the household of Edward the Black Prince ; chancellor of the exchequer, 1381 ; dean of Lichfield, 1381–90 ; held several prebends ; wrote a chronicle in French, beginning with the ninth year of John ; only some extracts made by Leland from a French epitome are extant. [xliii. 95]

PALAIRET, ELIAS (1713–1765), philologer ; born at Rotterdam ; pastor of several foreign congregations in London ; published some useful treatises on the philology of the New Testament and kindred subjects. [xliii. 96]

PALAIRET, JOHN (1697–1774), author ; born at Montauban ; French teacher to three of George II's children ; wrote educational compendiums in French. [xliii. 96]

PALAVICINO, Sir HORATIO (d. 1600), merchant and political agent ; born at Genoa ; on his arrival in England was appointed by Queen Mary collector of the papal taxes ; according to tradition abjured Romanism on Queen Mary's death, and, appropriating the sums he had collected, laid the foundation of an enormous fortune, extending his business operations to most parts of the globe ; knighted, 1587 ; lent largely to Queen Elizabeth, Henry of Navarre, and the United Provinces ; of importance as a collector of political intelligence, his numerous commercial correspondents often enabling him to forestall other sources of information ; English envoy to various continental states. [xliii. 97]

PALEY, FREDERICK APTHORP (1815–1888), classical scholar ; grandson of William Paley [q. v.] ; of Shrewsbury School and St. John's College, Cambridge ; M.A., 1842 ; hon. LL.D. Aberdeen, 1883 ; became famous as a Greek scholar with 'Æschyli quæ supersunt omnia,' 1844–7 ; sympathised with the Oxford movement, and (1846) was forced to leave Cambridge in consequence of a suspicion that he had encouraged one of his pupils to join the Roman church ; became a Roman catholic, and (1847–56) acted as private tutor in various wealthy families ; returned to Cambridge on the partial removal of religious disabilities, 1860 ; private tutor till 1874 ; professor of classical literature of the new catholic university college at Kensington, 1874–7. His publications include 'The Tragedies of Euripides,' 1857, his introductions to the plays of Euripides being models of clearness, 'Manual of Gothic Mouldings,' 1845, 'The Epics of Hesiod,' 1861, editions and translations of other classical authors, and 'Bibliographia Græca,' 1881. He was a firm believer in theory of the 'Solar Myth,' and propounded the suggestion that the Iliad and Odyssey were put together out of a general stock of traditions in the time of Pericles. [xliii. 99]

PALEY, WILLIAM (1743–1805), archdeacon of Carlisle and author of the 'Evidences of Christianity' ; educated at Christ's College, Cambridge ; senior wrangler, 1763 ; fellow of Christ's College, Cambridge, 1766, and college lecturer ; presented to Musgrave in Cumberland, 1775, whence he removed to Appleby, 1777 ; installed a prebendary of Carlisle, 1780, and (1782) appointed archdeacon ; published 'Principles of Morals and Political Philosophy,' 1785, for which he received 1,000l., and which at once became a Cambridge text-book ; published his most original book, 'Horæ Paulinæ,' which was also the least successful, 1790 ; brought out 'Evidences of Christianity,' 1794, which succeeded brilliantly, and secured him ample preferment ; his last book, 'Natural Theology,' 1802 ; a good whist player and equestrian. His morality is one of the best statements of the utilitarianism of the eighteenth century, differing chiefly from Bentham by its introduction of the supernatural sanction. His book upon the 'Evidences' is a compendium of a whole library of arguments produced by the orthodox opponents of the deists of the eighteenth century, and his 'Natural Theology' an admirably clear account of the *a posteriori* argument. The accusation of plagiarism brought against Paley arises from a misconception of his purpose, which was rather inclusiveness and harmony than originality. The latest collections of his works were published, 1837 and 1851. [xliii. 101]

PALFREYMAN, THOMAS (*d.* 1589 ?), author ; gentleman of the Chapel Royal, London, till 1589 ; published four religious exhortations, besides editing a ' Treatise of Moral Philosophy,' 1567. [xliii. 107]

PALGRAVE, SIR FRANCIS (1788-1861), historian ; son of Meyer Cohen, a Jew ; embraced Christianity and adopted the surname Palgrave in 1823 ; barrister, Middle Temple, 1827 ; deputy-keeper of her majesty's records, 1838-61 ; author, among other works, of ' The Rise and Progress of the English Commonwealth,' 1832, and of ' The History of Normandy and England,' 1851-64 ; assisted in the publication of public records ; knighted, 1832 ; rendered great service in promoting the critical study of mediæval history in England. [xliii. 107]

PALGRAVE, FRANCIS TURNER (1824-1897), poet and critic ; son of Sir Francis Palgrave [q. v.] ; educated at Charterhouse School and Balliol College, Oxford ; fellow of Exeter College, Oxford, 1847 ; B.A. and M.A., 1856 ; assistant private secretary to William Ewart Gladstone [q. v.], 1846 ; entered education department, *c.* 1848 ; vice-principal, 1850-5, of Kneller Hall, Twickenham, where he became close friend of Tennyson ; successively examiner and assistant secretary of education department, 1855-84 ; art critic to ' Saturday Review ' : published, 1864, ' Golden Treasury of Songs and Lyrics,' and other anthologies, including a second series of ' The Golden Treasury,' 1896 ; professor of poetry at Oxford, 1885-95. His publications include lectures, critical essays, and several volumes of original poems. [Suppl. iii. 242]

PALGRAVE, WILLIAM GIFFORD (1826-1888), diplomatist ; son of Sir Francis Palgrave [q. v.] ; of Charterhouse School and Trinity College, Oxford (B.A.) ; became a jesuit missionary in Syria and Arabia, and often assumed the disguise of a Syrian doctor that he might visit parts of Arabia to which no European could penetrate ; severed his connection with the jesuits, 1865, and became an English diplomatist in Abyssinia (1865), Trebizond (1867), Turkish Georgia (1870), the Upper Euphrates (1872), the West Indies (1873), Manilla (1876), Bulgaria (1878), Bangkok (1879), and Uruguay (1884). His ' Narrative of a Year's Journey through Central and Eastern Arabia ' (1865) is well known. [xliii. 109]

PALIN, WILLIAM (1803-1882), divine ; matriculated from St. Alban Hall, Oxford ; B.A. Trinity College, Cambridge, 1833 ; M.A., 1851 ; rector of Stifford, 1834-82 ; author and hymn-writer. [xliii. 110]

PALK, SIR ROBERT, first baronet (1717-1798), governor of Madras ; became a member of the Madras council, 1753, and governor, 1763 ; concluded the pusillanimous treaty of Hyderabad (1766) with the nizam, by which he surrendered the sircar of Guntur, consented to pay tribute for the other sircars, and agreed to furnish the nizam with military assistance ; returned to England, 1767 ; M.P. Ashburton, 1767-84 and 1774-87 ; created baronet, 1772. Palk Strait, between Ceylon and India, was named after him. [xliii. 111]

PALLADIUS (*fl.* 431 ?), archdeacon and missionary to Ireland ; native of southern Gaul ; sent to Ireland by Pope Celestine, after Patrick's mission had begun, probably to introduce the Roman discipline, but met with no success, and crossed to Britain, where he died shortly after. [xliii. 112]

PALLADY, RICHARD (*fl.* 1533-1555), architect ; of Eton and King's College, Cambridge ; designed the original Somerset House, which was commenced in 1546. [xliii. 113]

PALLISER, FANNY BURY (1805-1878), writer on art ; sister of Frederick Marryat [q. v.] ; married Captain Richard Bury Palliser, 1832 ; published seven original works, chiefly on art subjects. [xliii. 114]

PALLISER, SIR HUGH, first baronet (1723-1796), admiral ; entered the navy, 1735 ; commander, 1746 ;

governor and commander-in-chief at Newfoundland, 1762-1766, and directed a survey of the coasts ; comptroller of the navy, 1770 ; created a baronet, 1773 ; rear-admiral, 1775 ; a lord of the admiralty, 1775 ; vice-admiral, 1778 ; while serving under Keppel in 1778 acted very insubordinately during action in the Channel, but was acquitted by a packed court-martial, in spite of popular indignation ; not reinstated in the offices which he had resigned in anticipation of his trial, but in 1782 was appointed governor of Greenwich Hospital ; admiral, 1787. [xliii. 114]

PALLISER, JOHN (1807-1887), geographer and explorer ; travelled in North America, in the unknown regions of the far west, between 1847 and 1861. [xliii. 116]

PALLISER, WILLIAM (1646-1726), archbishop of Cashel ; fellow of Trinity College, Dublin, 1668 ; professor of divinity, Dublin, 1678 ; appointed bishop of Cloyne, 1693 ; translated to Cashel, 1694 ; bequeathed the ' Bibliotheca Palliseriana ' to Trinity College, Dublin. [xliii. 117]

PALLISER, SIR WILLIAM (1830-1882), inventor of ' Palliser shot ' ; brother of John Palliser [q. v.] ; of Rugby, Trinity College, Dublin, and Trinity Hall, Cambridge ; author of numerous inventions, particularly in relation to projectiles, among the chief being his method of converting smooth bores into rifled guns (1862) and his patent for chilled cast-iron shot (1863), which for a time superseded steel projectiles ; C.B., 1868 ; knighted, 1873. [xliii. 117]

PALLISER, WRAY RICHARD GLEDSTANES (*d.* 1891), commander ; brother of John Palliser [q. v.] ; distinguished himself in 1854 in expeditions against Chinese pirates. [xliii. 119]

PALMARIUS, THOMAS (*fl.* 1410). [See PALMER.]

PALMER, ALICIA TINDAL (*fl.* 1809-1815), novelist ; author of three novels and of ' Authentic Memoirs of Sobieski,' 1815. [xliii. 119]

PALMER, ANTHONY (1618 ?-1679), independent ; fellow of Balliol College, Oxford, 1640 ; M.A., 1641 ; ejected from rectory of Bourton-on-the-Water, 1362 ; published six theological treatises. [xliii. 119]

PALMER, ANTHONY (*d.* 1693), divine ; rector of Bratton Fleming, *c.* 1645 ; ejected, 1662. [xliii. 120]

PALMER, ANTHONY (1675 ?-1749), New England pioneer ; probably born in England ; administered the government of Pennsylvania in 1747-8. [xliii. 120]

PALMER, ARTHUR (1841-1897), classical scholar and textual critic ; born at Gwelph, Ontario, Canada ; educated at Cheltenham College and Trinity College, Dublin ; fellow, 1867 ; professor of Latin, 1880 ; public orator, 1888 ; M.A., 1867 ; Litt.D. Dublin ; LL.D. Glasgow, 1890 ; D.C.L. Oxford, 1894 ; published several editions of classical texts. [Suppl. iii. 244]

PALMER, SIR ARTHUR HUNTER (1819-1898), colonial politician ; emigrated to New South Wales, 1838 ; member of legislative assembly of Queensland for Port Curtis, 1866 ; premier and colonial secretary, 1870-4, and secretary for lands, 1873-4 ; president of legislative council and K.C.M.G., 1881. [Suppl. iii. 245]

PALMER, BARBARA, COUNTESS OF CASTLEMAINE and DUCHESS OF CLEVELAND (1641-1709). [See VILLIERS.]

PALMER, CHARLES (1777-1851), major-general ; of Eton and Oriel College, Oxford ; son of John Palmer (1742-1818) [q. v.] ; whig M.P., Bath, 1808-26 and 1830-7 ; served through the Peninsular war with the 10th dragoons, and became, after his father, proprietor of the Bath Theatre ; major-general, 1825. [xliii. 142]

PALMER, CHARLES JOHN (1805-1882), historian of Great Yarmouth ; practised as an attorney there from 1827 ; edited the history of Yarmouth by Henry Manship (*d.* 1625) [q. v.] in 1854, and wrote a continuation in 1856, besides other works. [xliii. 120]

PALMER, CHARLOTTE (*fl.* 1780-1797), author ; engaged in the profession of teaching ; published several novels and letters. [xliii. 121]

PALMER, EDWARD (*fl.* 1572), antiquary ; of Magdalen Hall, Oxford ; made a collection of English antiquities, which was dispersed on his death. [xliii. 121]

PALMER, EDWARD HENRY (1840-1882), orientalist; son of a schoolmaster; learned Italian and French, while a junior clerk in London, from conversations in cafés; made the acquaintance of the teacher of Hindustani at Cambridge, 1860, and turned his attention to oriental tongues; gained admission to St. John's College, Cambridge, as a sizar, 1863; fellow, 1867; M.A., 1870; accompanied Henry Spencer Palmer [q. v.] and (Sir) Charles Wilson in their survey of Sinai; visited Palestine, and improved his knowledge of Arabic dialects, 1869-70; published 'The Desert of the Exodus' (a popular account of his travels), 1871; lord almoner's professor of Arabic at Cambridge, 1871; from that time did much literary work in Arabic, Hindustani, and Persian; went to London, 1881, and was employed on the staff of the 'Standard' as a leader-writer; despatched by Gladstone's government on a secret mission, the purport of which, so far as known, was to attempt to detach the Arab tribes from the side of the Egyptian rebels, 1882; succeeded, and was appointed interpreter-in-chief to the English forces in Egypt, but while engaged in further negotiations with tribes beyond Suez was murdered at Wady Sudr by Arab robbers. His remains were brought home and buried in St. Paul's Cathedral in April 1883.   [xliii. 122]

PALMER, ELEANOR, LADY (1720 ?-1818), daughter of Michael Ambrose, a brewer of Dublin; married, in 1752, Roger Palmer of Mayo and Dublin, created a baronet in 1777; celebrated for her beauty, in which she rivalled the Gunnings.   [xliii. 126]

PALMER, SIR GEOFFREY, first baronet (1598-1670), attorney-general; barrister, Middle Temple, 1623, treasurer, 1661; an original member of the Long parliament, but joined the king's party; nominated attorney-general and created baronet at the Restoration.   [xliii. 126]

PALMER, GEORGE (1772-1853), philanthropist; an East India merchant who designed a style of lifeboat which was in general use between 1826 and 1858; master of the Mercers' Company, 1821; conservative M.P., South Essex, 1836-1847.   [xliii. 127]

PALMER, GEORGE (1818-1897), biscuit manufacturer; apprenticed as miller and confectioner at Taunton, c. 1832; established at Reading (1841) with Thomas Huntley (d. 1857), biscuit business of Huntley & Palmer, which, on application of steam machinery to manufacture of biscuits, rapidly grew to large proportions; mayor of Reading, 1857; liberal M.P. for Reading, 1878-85.   [Suppl. iii. 245]

PALMER, SIR HENRY (d. 1559), soldier; brother of Sir Thomas Palmer (d. 1553) [q. v.]; took part in capture of Boulogne, 1544; master of ordnance at Boulogne, 1546; for many years held a subordinate command at Calais, at the fall of which in 1558 he was taken prisoner.   [xliii. 161]

PALMER, SIR HENRY (d. 1611), naval commander; on active service between 1576 and 1611; fought against the Spanish Armada, 1588; comptroller of the navy, 1598.   [xliii. 128]

PALMER, HENRY SPENCER (1838-1893), major-general, royal engineers; nephew of Sir Henry James [q. v.]; entered royal engineers, 1856; took part in the survey of British Columbia (1858-63), in the parliamentary boundaries commission under Disraeli's reform act (1867), and in the survey of Sinaitic Peninsula (1868-9); sent with the New Zealand party as chief astronomer to observe the transit of Venus, 1873; appointed engineer of the admiralty works at Hong Kong, 1878; became commanding royal engineer of the Manchester district, 1883; employed (1885-93) in designing waterworks for the Japanese government; retired as major-general, 1887.   [xliii. 128]

PALMER, HERBERT (1601-1647), puritan divine; grandson of Sir Thomas Palmer (1540-1626) [q. v.]; educated at St. John's College, Cambridge; M.A., 1622, and fellow, 1623, of Queens' College, Cambridge; resisted Laud's 'innovations,' and was articled for his puritanism, but without result; rector of Ashwell, 1632; lecturer at Westminster Abbey, 1643; a renowned catechist; assisted in preparing the 'Shorter Catechism' for the Westminster Assembly, of which he was an original member; became president of Queens' College, Cambridge, 1644; published theological works.   [xliii. 130]

PALMER, SIR JAMES (d. 1657), chancellor of the order of the Garter, 1645; third son of Sir Thomas Palmer (1540-1626) [q. v.]; personal friend of Charles I.   [xliii. 132]

PALMER, JAMES (1585-1660), divine; M.A. Magdalene College, Cambridge, 1605; incorporated at Oxford, 1611; B.D., 1613; showed puritan predilections in middle life, and preached frequently before both houses of parliament; surrendered his living, St. Bride's, Fleet Street, London, in 1645 on account of failing health. He founded several charities at Westminster.   [xliii. 132]

PALMER, SIR JAMES FREDERICK (1804-1871), Australian politician; great-nephew of Sir Joshua Reynolds [q. v.]; went to Australia, 1839, and became first president of the Victorian legislative assembly, 1856; knighted, 1857.   [xliii. 133]

PALMER, JOHN (d. 1607), dean of Peterborough; fellow of St. John's College, Cambridge, 1573; M.A, 1575 (incorporated at Oxford, 1580); master of Magdalene College, Cambridge, 1595-1604; D.D., 1595; dean of Peterborough in 1597.   [xliii. 134]

PALMER, JOHN (d. 1614), divine; of Westminster and Trinity College, Cambridge; fellow, 1582; M.A., 1583; B.D., 1592; archdeacon of Ely, 1592-1600.   [xliii. 134]

PALMER, JOHN (1650-1700 ?), colonial official; came from Barbados to New York, c. 1674; judge of oyer and terminer, New York, 1684; published 'An impartial Account of the State of New England,' 1689. [xliii. 134]

PALMER, JOHN, the elder (d. 1768), actor; known as GENTLEMAN PALMER; celebrated as Captain Plume, as Osric, as the Duke's servant in 'High Life Below Stairs,' and as Mercutio.   [xliii. 139]

PALMER, JOHN (1742-1786), unitarian divine; minister at Macclesfield and Birmingham; published various treatises.   [xliii. 135]

PALMER, JOHN (1729 ?-1790), unitarian divine; minister in New Broad Street, London, 1759-80; published several treatises.   [xliii. 135]

PALMER, JOHN (1742 ?-1798), actor; son of a billsticker and door-keeper at Drury Lane Theatre, London; his desire to go upon the stage discouraged by Garrick and Foote; gradually rose to high position in the London theatres, and for a time obtained control, all but undisputed, over the highest comedy; held unapproachable in the part of Joseph Surface; involved himself in an unsuccessful contest with the managers of the patent houses by commencing to build the Royalty Theatre in Wellclose Square, London, 1785; frequently insolvent; died on the stage at Liverpool while playing in 'The Stranger.' Except singing characters and old men, there was no character in which he did not achieve a high degree of excellence.   [xliii. 136]

PALMER, JOHN (1742-1818), projector of mail-coaches; son of the proprietor of the two Bath theatres, for whom he acted as agent in London; being struck with the slowness of the state post, prevailed on Pitt in 1784 to order a trial of the possibility of conveying the posts by stage-coach, in spite of the fact that the post office declared the project impracticable; his innovation established by 1785; in consequence post-office revenue increased from 51,000l. to 73,000l. between 1784 and 1787; nominated comptroller-general of the post office, 1786; compulsorily retired on a pension owing to quarrels with the postmaster-general, Lord Walsingham, 1793; obtained 50,000l. as compensation (1813), after a long controversy.   [xliii. 139]

PALMER, JOHN (fl. 1818), traveller; published a 'Journal of Travels in the United States and Lower Canada,' 1818.   [xliii. 143]

PALMER, JOHN (BERNARD) (1782-1852), mitred abbot; entered the Cistercian order, 1808; became superior of the monastery in Charnwood Forest, 1841; his house constituted an abbey, 1848.   [xliii. 143]

PALMER, JOHN HORSLEY (1779-1858), governor of the Bank of England; brother of George Palmer (1772-1853) [q. v.]; became a director of the Bank, 1811; governor of the Bank, 1830-2.   [xliii. 144]

PALMER, formerly BUDWORTH, JOSEPH (1756–1815), miscellaneous writer; nephew of William Budworth [q. v.]; adopted his wife's name in 1811; wrote under the pseudonym 'Rambler,' in the 'Gentleman's Magazine.' [xliii. 144]

PALMER, JULINS (d. 1556), martyr; B.A. Magdalen College, Oxford, 1548; master in Reading grammar school; burnt at Newbury for holding protestant opinions. [xliii. 145]

PALMER, MARY (1716–1794), author; sister of Sir Joshua Reynolds [q. v.]; married John Palmer of Torrington, 1740; her 'Devonshire Dialogue' (first complete edition, 1839) frequently reprinted. [xliii. 145]

PALMER, RICHARD (d. 1195), archbishop of Messina; born in England, settled in Sicily, and was a chief counsellor of William the Bad, one of the Norman kings of Sicily; elected bishop of Syracuse, c. 1155, and archbishop of Messina before 1183; one of the embassy who endeavoured to avert the wrath of Richard I against King Tancred, after the capture of Messina by the former in 1190; corresponded with Thomas Becket [q. v.] [xliii. 146]

PALMER, RICHARD (d. 1625), physician; B.A. Christ's College, Cambridge, 1579; M.A. Peterhouse, 1583; F.R.C.P., 1597, president, 1620; attended the deathbed of Henry, prince of Wales, 1612. [xliii. 148]

PALMER, ROBERT (1757–1805 ?), actor; brother of John Palmer (1742 ?–1798) [q. v.]; excelled in rustic roles. [xliii. 139]

PALMER, ROGER, EARL OF CASTLEMAINE (1634–1705), diplomatist and author; son of Sir James Palmer [q. v.]; of Eton and King's College, Cambridge; student, Inner Temple, 1656; married Barbara Villiers (afterwards Duchess of Cleveland) [q. v.], 1659, who became Charles II's mistress at the Restoration; M.P., New Windsor, 1660–1; forced by Charles II to become Earl of Castlemaine in order to propitiate Barbara's jealousy of the marriage of Charles II, 1661; accused of complicity in the Popish plot, but acquitted; as envoy to Rome, 1686, met with a cold reception, his excessive zeal for Petre and other of James II's favourites embarrassing Pope Innocent XI; privy councillor, 1687; at the revolution was exempted from the Act of Indemnity, and after imprisonment in the Tower of London escaped to the continent; indicted of high treason, 1695; on returning and surrendering himself was released without trial, on condition of going over-seas; linguist, mathematician, and political pamphleteer. [xliii. 148]

PALMER, SIR ROUNDELL, first EARL OF SELBORNE (1812–1895), lord chancellor; nephew of George Palmer (1772–1853) [q. v.]; was educated at Rugby, Winchester, and Christ Church and Trinity College, Oxford; Ireland scholar, 1832; Eldon law scholar, 1834; fellow of Magdalen College, Oxford, 1835; M.A., 1836; D.C.L., 1862; hon. LL.D. Cambridge; barrister, Lincoln's Inn, 1837; bencher, 1849; treasurer, 1864; Q.C., 1849; entered parliament in 1847 as a conservative (M.P., Plymouth), but from the first was extremely independent in his views, and gradually passed over to the liberal party; solicitor-general in Palmerston's ministry, 1861; knighted, 1861; M.P., Richmond, Yorkshire, 1861–72; attorney-general from 1863 to the fall of Lord Russell's administration, 1866; declined Gladstone's offer of the great seal and a peerage on account of his opposition to the disendowment of the Irish church, 1868; succeeded Lord Hatherley as lord chancellor, and was created Baron Selborne, 1872; took up the question of judicature reform, and although unable fully to carry out his wishes obtained the passage of a measure doing away with the multiplicity of courts of original jurisdiction, and providing for the gradual fusion of law and equity into a common system, 1873; retired from the woolsack on the return of the conservatives to power, 1874; again lord chancellor (1880–5) under Gladstone; created Earl of Selborne, 1882; refrained from entering Gladstone's third cabinet (1886), on account of his antipathy to granting Irish home rule; a high churchman and author of writings on ecclesiastical matters and of several hymns. As a judge of first instance and as lord chancellor he contributed largely to the extension and refinement of some of the leading doctrines of equitable jurisprudence. [xliii. 150]

PALMER, SAMUEL (d. 1724), pamphleteer; originally a presbyterian minister; wrote in defence of dissenters' academies; vicar of All Saints' and St. Peter's, Maldon, 1710–24. [xliii. 154]

PALMER, SAMUEL (d. 1732), printer; worked in Bartholomew Close; Benjamin Franklin among his employés, 1725; his 'History of Printing' completed by George Psalmanazar [q. v.], 1732, who in his 'Memoirs' claimed to have written the whole book. [xliii. 155]

PALMER, SAMUEL (1741–1813), nonconformist biographer; was minister of the independent congregation at Mare Street, Hackney, Middlesex, and St. Thomas's Square, London, 1766–1813; published 'The Protestant Dissenters' Catechism,' 1772, and 'The Nonconformist's Memorial,' 1775–8, the latter an abridgment and continuation of the 'Account of the Ministers . . . Ejected,' by Edmund Calamy (1671–1732) [q. v.] [xliii. 156]

PALMER, SAMUEL (1805–1881), poetical landscape-painter; began to exhibit at the Royal Academy, 1819; member of the Etching Society, 1853, of the Water-colour Society, 1854; almost the last of the ideal school of landscape-painters represented in England by Wilson, Turner, and others; much influenced by his intercourse with William Blake (1757–1827) [q. v.] Among his finest works are his drawings to illustrate Milton's 'L'Allegro' and 'Il Penseroso' (exhibited at the Water-colour Society between 1868 and 1882). [xliii. 157]

PALMER, SHIRLEY (1786–1852), medical writer; M.R.C.S., 1807; M.D. Glasgow, 1815; practised in Tamworth and Birmingham; chief work, 'Popular Illustrations of Medicine,' 1829. [xliii. 159]

PALMER or PALMARIUS, THOMAS (fl. 1410), theological writer; Dominican friar of London; wrote orthodox works to repair the schisms in the church. [xliii. 160]

PALMER, SIR THOMAS (d. 1553), soldier; knighted, 1532; held appointments at Calais and Guisnes under Henry VIII; disclosed Somerset's treason, 1550; executed as an adherent of Lady Jane Grey. [xliii. 160]

PALMER, SIR THOMAS, first baronet (1540–1626), 'the Travailer'; son of Sir Henry Palmer (d. 1559) [q. v.]; high sheriff of Kent, 1595; went on the expedition to Cadiz and was knighted, 1596; published 'An Essay on Foreign Travel,' 1606; created baronet, 1621; not identical with the Thomas Palmer or Palmar who was appointed principal of Gloucester Hall, Oxford, 1563. [xliii. 161]

PALMER, THOMAS (fl. 1644–1666), independent minister and agitator; chaplain to Skippon's regiment, 1644; rector of Aston-upon-Trent, 1646; ejected, 1660; wandered about the country preaching; went to Ireland 'to do mischief,' 1666; published four religious treatises. [xliii. 162]

PALMER, THOMAS FYSHE (1747–1802), unitarian minister; of Eton and Queens' College, Cambridge; M.A., 1772; B.D., 1781; fellow, 1781; pastor at Montrose, 1783–5, at Dundee, 1785–93; sympathised with political reform and, in 1793, corrected the proof of a handbill by George Mealmaker, a member of the Society of the Friends of Liberty at Dundee, for which (1793) he was sentenced to twelve years' transportation on the charge of treason, government at the time being in a state of panic on account of the French revolution; served his sentence at Botany Bay and died at the Ladrone islands while returning home. [xliii. 162]

PALMER, WILLIAM (1539 ?–1605), divine; B.A. Pembroke Hall, Cambridge, 1560; fellow, 1560; held several minor preferments; famous as a disputant. [xliii. 164]

PALMER, WILLIAM (1824–1856), the Rugeley poisoner; M.R.C.S., 1846; practised as a medical man at Rugeley after acting as a house-surgeon at St. Bartholomew's Hospital, London, in 1846; poisoned his wife in 1854, his brother Walter in August 1855, and his friend John Parsons Cook in December 1855 for the purpose of obtaining money; convicted of the last murder and hanged at Stafford on 14 June 1856, after a trial which excited extraordinary interest. He was convicted entirely upon circumstantial evidence, but no innocent explanation of his conduct has yet been suggested. [xliii. 165]

PALMER, WILLIAM (1802–1858), conveyancer and legal author; son of George Palmer (1772–1853) [q. v.];

M.A. St. Mary Hall, Oxford, 1828; barrister, Inner Temple, 1830; professor of law, Gresham College, London, 1836-8; published legal works. [xliii. 166]

PALMER, WILLIAM (1811–1879), theologian and archæologist; brother of Roundell Palmer, first earl of Selborne [q. v.]; fellow of Magdalen College, Oxford, 1832; M.A., 1833; an extreme high churchman and a devoted advocate of intercommunion with the Greek and Roman churches; made several unsuccessful attempts to obtain admission to the Greek church without declaring the English church heretical; entered the Roman communion without rebaptism, 1855, passing the rest of his life at Rome in retirement; published works, including 'An Introduction to Early Christian Symbolism,' 1859, and left voluminous manuscripts chiefly autobiographical. [xliii. 167]

PALMER, WILLIAM (1803–1885), theologian and ecclesiastical antiquary; B.A. Trinity College, Dublin, 1824; M.A. Magdalen Hall, Oxford, 1829; published 'Origines Liturgicæ,' 1832, and a 'Treatise on the Church of Christ,' 1838, and associated himself with the tractarians; subsequently published several controversial treatises; prebendary of Salisbury, 1849-58. He assumed the title of baronet in 1865. [xliii. 168]

PALMERANUS or **PALMERSTON** (*fl.* 1306–1316). [See THOMAS HIBERNICUS.]

PALMERSTON, VISCOUNTS. [See TEMPLE, HENRY, first VISCOUNT, 1673?–1757; TEMPLE, HENRY, second VISCOUNT, 1739–1802; TEMPLE, HENRY JOHN, third VISCOUNT, 1784–1865.]

PALMES, SIR BRYAN (1599–1654), royalist; of Trinity College, Oxford; M.P., Stamford, 1626, Aldborough, Yorkshire, 1640; knighted and created D.C.L. Oxford, 1642; raised a regiment on the outbreak of the civil war, but compounded for his estate in 1646. [xliii. 170]

PALSGRAVE, JOHN (*d.* 1554), chaplain to Henry VIII; B.A. Corpus Christi College, Cambridge; M.A. Paris; tutor to the Princess Mary, 1513–14, and Henry VIII's natural son, the Duke of Richmond, 1525–9; rector of St. Dunstan-in-the-East, London, 1538, of Wadenhoe, 1545; published 'Lesclarcissement de la Langue Francoyse,' 1530, and other works. [xliii. 170]

PALTOCK, ROBERT (1697–1767), romance-writer; an attorney at Clement's Inn; published 'The Life and Adventures of Peter Wilkins, a Cornish Man,' 1751, which was praised by Southey and Leigh Hunt, and admired by Coleridge, Scott, and Lamb. [xliii. 172]

PAMAN, HENRY (1626–1695), physician; of Emmanuel and St. John's Colleges, Cambridge; fellow of St. John's College; M.A., 1650 (incorporated at Oxford, 1655); M.D. Cambridge, 1658 (incorporated at Oxford, 1669); professor of physic at Gresham College, London, 1679–89; master of the faculties at Cambridge, 1684–90; a nonjuror. [xliii. 173]

PANDULF (*d.* 1226), papal legate and bishop of Norwich; a Roman by birth, but erroneously identified with Pandulfus Masca (made a cardinal in 1182); came to England, July 1211, to determine the succession to the see of Canterbury, and excommunicated King John for refusing to restore Langton; returned to the continent after King John had made repeated attempts to break his resolution; revisited England, John having made overtures for a reconciliation in 1213, and forbade Philip Augustus of France to invade the country until his mission was accomplished; remained in England after King John had made his submission, 15 May 1213; elected bishop of Norwich, 1216; appointed papal legate, 1218; exercised almost royal authority from the death of Pembroke in May 1219 till his recall in 1221, and acted with statesmanlike capacity; eventually found himself at enmity with Hubert de Burgh and Langton, and made his position untenable; died at Rome and was buried in Norwich Cathedral. [xliii. 174]

PANITER. [See PANTER.]

PANIZZI, SIR ANTHONY (1797–1879), principal librarian of the British Museum; born at Brescello in Modena; graduated in law at Parma, 1818; afterwards practising as an advocate; compelled to fly as a conspirator against the government, 1822, and was sentenced to death in his absence as contumacious; came to England and was befriended by William Roscoe [q. v.];

the chief patron of Italian literature in the country; became intimate with Henry Peter Brougham, baron Brougham and Vaux, who in 1831 procured his appointment as assistant-librarian at the British Museum; chief keeper of the printed books, 1837; chief librarian, 1856; resigned on account of ill-health, 1866; formed the plan of the catalogue of printed books, and obtained an annual grant of 10,000*l.* to repair literary specimens of the library; conceived the plan of the great reading-room and annexes in the central quadrangle; procured the recognition of the staff as civil servants; K.C.B., 1869. The bequest of the Grenville Library in 1846 was entirely due to his personal influence [see GRENVILLE, THOMAS (1755–1846)]. During the whole of his official career Panizzi was much occupied in political questions, especially as they affected the movement for the liberation of Italy. His influence with the English whigs was frequently used to assist the Italian patriots. [xliii. 179]

PANKE, JOHN (*fl.* 1608), divine; educated at Oxford; author of four works against Roman catholics. [xliii. 183]

PANMURE, EARLS OF. [See MAULE, PATRICK, first EARL, *d.* 1661; MAULE, JAMES, fourth EARL, 1659?–1723.]

PANMURE, titular EARL OF (*d.* 1734). [See MAULE, HARRY.]

PANMURE, BARONS. [See MAULE, WILLIAM RAMSAY, first BARON PANMURE, 1771–1852; MAULE, FOX, second BARON PANMURE, 1801–1874.]

PANMURE, LORD OF (*d.* 1215). [See VALOGNES, PHILIP DE.]

PANTER, DAVID (*d.* 1558), bishop of Ross; nephew of Patrick Panter [q. v.]; acted as secretary to James V; bishop of Ross, 1545. [xliii. 183]

PANTER, PANNITER, or **PANTHER,** PATRICK (1470?–1519), abbot of Cambuskenneth; studied at Paris; nominated royal secretary, 1505; abbot of Cambuskenneth, *c.* 1512. [xliii. 184]

PANTIN, THOMAS PINDAR (1792–1866), theological writer; M.A. Queen's College, Oxford, 1827; wrote against Roman catholicism. [xliii. 184]

PANTON, PAUL (1731–1797), Welsh antiquary; formed a large collection of Welsh manuscripts at Plâs Gwyn. [xliii. 184]

PANTON, THOMAS (*d.* 1685), gambler; held commission in Charles II's life-guards and captaincy in the foot-guards; made a fortune by card-playing at Charles II's court. [xliii. 185]

PANTON, THOMAS (1731–1808), sportsman; keeper of racehorses; won the Derby in 1786. [xliii. 185]

PANTULF, HUGH (*d.* 1224?), sheriff of Shropshire (1179–1189); son of Ivo Pantulf [q. v.] [xliii. 186]

PANTULF, IVO (*d.* 1176?), feudatory; probably son of Robert Pantulf [q. v.]; made grants to several abbeys. [xliii. 187]

PANTULF, ROBERT (*fl.* 1130), feudatory; son of William Pantulf (*d.* 1112?) [q. v.]; was accused of robbing the nuns of Caen. [xliii. 187]

PANTULF or **PANTOLIUM,** WILLIAM (*d.* 1112?), Norman knight; held land of Robert of Bellême, but supported Henry I when Robert rebelled, 1102. [xliii. 186]

PANTULF, WILLIAM (*d.* 1233), feudatory; son of Hugh Pantulf [q. v.]; probably served King John in Ireland, 1210. [xliii. 186]

PAOLI, PASCAL (1725–1807), Corsican general and patriot; son of Hyacinth Paoli, a Corsican leader in the revolt of 1734; brought up in exile at Naples, where he entered the army; offered the dictatorship by the Corsican insurgents against the Genoese yoke, 1755; expelled the Genoese from the greater part of the island, who, however, in 1764 obtained French assistance, and in 1768 yielded Corsica to France; commanded the Corsicans at Pontenuovo, where they were signally defeated, 1769; cut his way through the French troops and took refuge on board an English frigate, 1769; resided in England, receiving a pension and enjoying the society of the famous men of the time; elected a

member of the Club, and intimate with the Johnsonian group ; on the outbreak of the French revolution recalled by the French National Assembly to Corsica, where he became mayor of Bastia and commander-in-chief of the national guard, and was afterwards appointed by Louis XVI lieutenant-general and military commandant in Corsica ; on the execution of Louis XVI drove the French from Corsica and obtained an English protectorate, but was disappointed in his expectation of being nominated viceroy ; retired to a private estate in England in 1795 ; died and was buried in London.
[xliii. 187]

PAPILLON, DAVID (1581–1655 ?), architect and military engineer ; born in France of Huguenot parents ; brought up in England ; fortified Gloucester for parliament, 1646 ; published 'An Essay on Fortification,' 1645, and other works. [xliii. 190]

PAPILLON, PHILIP (1620–1641), writer of verses ; M.A. Exeter College, Oxford, 1641 ; son of David Papillon [q. v.] [xliii. 191]

PAPILLON, THOMAS (1623–1702), merchant and politician ; son of David Papillon [q. v.] ; M.P., Dover, 1673–81 ; a staunch member of the country party ; fled to Utrecht, 1684, to avoid payment of 10,000l. damages awarded against him by a packed jury [see MAYNARD, SIR JOHN (1602–1690)] ; returned at the revolution ; M.P., Dover, 1689–95 ; London, 1695–1700.
[xliii. 190]

PAPILON or **PAPYLION**, RALPH, called DE ARUNDEL (d. 1223), abbot of Westminster ; elected abbot, 1200, and deposed for incontinency, 1213. [xliii. 192]

PAPIN, DENIS (1647–1712 ?), natural philosopher ; born at Blois ; graduated in medicine at Angers, 1669 ; lived chiefly in England after 1675 ; F.R.S., 1680 ; professor of mathematics at Marburg, 1688–95. His claims to be regarded as inventor of the steam engine have been urged by French writers, but the evidence is inconclusive. He constructed a boat with paddle-wheels on the Weser, but there is nothing to show that it was to be driven by steam. [xliii. 192]

PAPIN, ISAAC (1657–1709), theologian ; born at Blois ; entered the English church, 1686, but became a Roman catholic, 1690 ; published theological works in French. [xliii. 193]

PAPINEAU, LOUIS JOSEPH (1786–1871), Canadian rebel ; regarded as head of the French Canadian party from the beginning of his career in 1809 ; speaker of the legislative assembly of Lower Canada, 1815–37 ; fled to the territory of the United States after a controversy with the home government concerning the constitution of the upper house had issued in rebellion in 1837, instead of joining the insurgents ; returned under the general amnesty of 1847, and entered the lower house of the united Canadian legislature ; retired into private life, 1854.
[xliii. 193]

PAPWORTH, EDGAR GEORGE (1809–1866), sculptor ; nephew of John Papworth [q. v.] ; travelling student of the Royal Academy, 1834 ; executed chiefly busts, statuettes, and sketch designs. [xliii. 194]

PAPWORTH, GEORGE (1781–1855), architect ; brother of John Papworth [q. v.] ; settled in Dublin and designed many public and private buildings in Ireland.
[xliii. 195]

PAPWORTH, JOHN, afterwards JOHN BUONAROTTI (1775–1847), architect and designer ; contributed to the Royal Academy exhibitions, 1794–1841 ; carried out a number of important works, including (1823–30) St. Bride's Avenue in Fleet Street, London ; original member of the Associated Artists in Water-colours (1807) and of the Institute of British Architects (1834) ; published treatises on architecture and landscape-gardening.
[xliii. 196]

PAPWORTH, JOHN THOMAS (1809–1841), honorary secretary to the Institute of Irish Architects ; son of George Papworth [q. v.] [xliii. 195]

PAPWORTH, JOHN WOODY (1820–1870), architect and antiquary ; son of John Papworth [q. v.] ; fellow of the Institute of British Architects, 1846 ; author of the 'Ordinary of British Armorials,' published, 1874, and other works. [xliii. 198]

PAPWORTH, WYATT ANGELICUS VAN SANDAU (1822–1894), architect and antiquary ; son of John

Papworth [q. v.] ; projector and editor of the 'Dictionary of Architecture' (1852–92), published by the Architectural Publication Society ; curator of Sir John Soane's Museum, 1893–4 ; published treatises and papers on various subjects, mainly architectural. [xliii. 198]

PARADISE, JOHN (1743–1795), linguist and friend of Dr. Johnson ; a Macedonian by birth ; grandson of Philip Lodvill [q. v.] ; created M.A. Oxford, 1769, and D.C.L., 1776 ; F.R.S., 1771 ; member of Dr. Johnson's evening club at the Essex Head, in London. [xliii. 200]

PARDOE, JULIA (1806–1862), author of a number of historical and descriptive works, as well as of several tales ; received a civil list pension, 1860. [xliii. 201]

PARDOE, WILLIAM (d. 1692), baptist divine ; suffered imprisonment for his belief, 1675 ; became pastor of a baptist church in Lichfield, c. 1688 ; author of two devotional works. [xliii. 202]

PARDON, GEORGE FREDERICK (1824–1884), miscellaneous writer ; editor of several minor periodicals ; published, besides other works, about twenty volumes on games, sports, and pastimes, under the pseudonym of 'Captain Crawley.' [xliii. 202]

PARE, WILLIAM (1805–1873), co-operator ; a Birmingham tobacconist ; one of the founders of the first Birmingham Co-operative Society, 1828 ; left Birmingham, 1842, and interested himself in the promotion of co-operation ; acting governor of Owen's community at Queenwood, Hampshire, 1842–4 ; published works on co-operation. [xliii. 203]

PARENT, ÉTIENNE (1801–1874), Canadian journalist ; called to the bar, 1828 ; editor of the 'Canadien' ; imprisoned (1837) for his attacks on the executive ; clerk to the executive, 1842 ; assistant-secretary for Lower Canada, 1847. [xliii. 204]

PAREPA-ROSA, EUPHROSYNE PAREPA DE BOYESKU (1836–1874), operatic singer ; daughter of a Wallachian, Baron Georgiades de Boyesku, and niece of Arthur Edward Shelden Seguin [q. v.] ; made her début at Malta, 1855 ; came to England, 1857 ; married (1864) Captain Henry de Wolfe Carvell (d. 1865), and in 1867 Carl August Nicholas Rosa [q. v.] Her voice was soprano in quality. [xliii. 204]

PARFEW or **PURFOY**, ROBERT (d. 1557). [See WARTON.]

PARFITT, EDWARD (1820–1893), naturalist ; left a manuscript work on the fungi of Devonshire in twelve volumes. [xliii. 205]

PARFRE, JHAN (fl. 1512), copyist ; generally reputed the author, but is in reality only the transcriber, of the mystery play, 'Candlemas Day' (printed in 1835 by the Abbotsford Club). [xliii. 205]

PARIS, JOHN AYRTON (1785–1856), physician ; studied at Caius College, Cambridge, and Edinburgh ; M.B. Cambridge 1808 ; M.D., 1813 ; Harveian orator, 1843, and president of the Royal College of Physicians, 1844–56 ; published medical works. [xliii. 206]

PARIS, MATTHEW (d. 1259), historian and monk ; entered monastery of St. Albans, 1217 ; became an expert in writing, in drawing and painting, and in working gold and silver ; succeeded Roger of Wendover [q. v.] in his office of chronicler to the monastery, 1236, and carried on the 'Chronica Majora' from the summer of 1235 ; expanded the scope of the chronicle, introducing narratives and accounts of events in foreign countries as well as in England, which he obtained from kings and all manner of great persons who came to St. Albans ; visited Norway, 1248, having received a commission from Innocent IV to reform the abbey of St. Benet Holm in the province of Trondhjem ; cordially received by King Hacon ; returned to England in 1249, after successfully accomplishing his mission ; favourite with Henry III, who frequently talked with him and listened to his views on ecclesiastical questions. He carried his greater chronicle down to May 1259, where he ends abruptly, and certainly died about that time. In vigour and brightness of expression he stands before every other English chronicler ; and his writing possesses peculiar historic value from the information he derived from leading actors in contemporary events, and from his bold and independent treatment of the history of his times, which led him to denounce the promotion of foreign ecclesiastics to English benefices and the expenditure of English wealth on schemes of no benefit to the country. Besides the great chronicle he wrote a summary of the chief events between 1200 and 1250, which is known as the 'Historia Minor,' or 'Historia Anglorum.' The 'Chronica Majora,' to the year 1253, is preserved in the library of Corpus Christi College, Cambridge, and the part from 1254 to 1259, which is not in his handwriting, is contained in the Arundel manuscript in the British Museum. The 'Chronica Majora' was first printed by Archbishop Parker in 1571. The standard edition is that by Henry Richards Luard [q. v.], published in seven volumes in the Rolls Series between 1869 and 1883. The manuscript of the 'Historia Minor' (edited by Sir Frederic Madden [q. v.] in the Rolls Series, 3 vols. 1866-9) is in the British Museum. Though essentially an abridgment, it contains a few matters not to be found in the 'Chronica Majora.' In the Cotton manuscripts will be found 'Vitæ duæ Offarum,' attributed to him, though probably spurious—printed in 1649 by William Watts (1590?-1649) [q. v.] These lives are followed by 'Vitæ Abbatum S. Albani,' being the lives of the first twenty-three abbots to 1255, of which all were certainly compiled, and the last two or three composed, by him. They were incorporated, with some alterations, by Thomas Walsingham [q. v.] in his 'Gesta Abbatum.' The whole of his writings, and the various questions relating to them, are carefully discussed by Luard in the prefaces to his edition of the 'Chronica Majora.' [xliii. 207]

PARISH, Sir WOODBINE (1796-1882), diplomatist; sent to Buenos Ayres as a special agent, 1823; concluded a treaty of amity with the new state, 1825; chargé d'affaires at Buenos Ayres, 1825-32; K.C.H., 1837; chief commissioner at Naples, 1840-5, where he concluded a commercial treaty with the king, 1845; published an elaborate work on Buenos Ayres, 1839. [xliii. 213]

PARISH-ALVARS, ELI or ELIAS (1808-1849), harpist and musical composer; performed in many European countries; one of the most distinguished harpists of any period; excelled in the production of novel effects, and was known at Vienna, where he died, as 'der Paganini der Harfe'; composed music for the harp. [xliii. 214]

PARK, ANDREW (1807-1863), poet; employed in trade in Paisley and Glasgow; unsuccessful in business; gained some fame by his poems, especially the 'Bridegroom and the Bride' (1834) and 'Silent Love' (1845). [xliii. 215]

PARK, HENRY (1745-1831), surgeon to Liverpool Infirmary, 1767-98; published a treatise on diseases of the joints, 1783. [xliii. 215]

PARK or **PARKES**, JAMES (1636-1696), quaker; joined the quakers before 1663 and suffered imprisonment in 1667 at Harwich for being present at a meeting; continued to preach till his death, in spite of fines and prohibitions; published religious works. [xliii. 215]

PARK, Sir JAMES ALAN (1763-1838), judge; barrister, Lincoln's Inn, 1784; appointed vice-chancellor of the Duchy of Lancaster, 1791; recorder of Durham, 1802; attorney-general of Lancaster, 1811; justice of the common pleas and knighted, 1816. [xliii. 216]

PARK, JOHN (1804-1865), divine and poet; studied at Aberdeen and Glasgow; D.D. St. Andrews; minister of the first charge of St. Andrews, 1854-65; song-writer and composer; his songs published, 1876. [xliii. 217]

PARK, JOHN JAMES (1795-1833), jurist and antiquary; son of Thomas Park [q. v.]; barrister, Lincoln's Inn, 1822; was appointed to the chair of English law at King's College, London, 1831; his 'Treatise on the Law of Dower,' 1819, long a standard work. [xliii. 217]

PARK, JOHN RANICAR (1778-1847), surgeon and theologian; son of Henry Park [q. v.]; M.D. Jesus College, Cambridge, 1818; F.R.C.S., 1819; Gulstonian lecturer, 1821; F.L.S.; published several treatises on the Apocalypse. [xliii. 218]

PARK, MUNGO (1771-1806), African explorer; born near Selkirk; studied at Edinburgh University and became a surgeon in the mercantile marine; visited Sumatra, 1792, and on his return attracted the attention of naturalists by his botanical and zoological investigations; went to Africa under the auspices of the African Association to explore the course of the Niger, 1795; proceeded up the Gambia, attended only by a negro servant and a boy; reached Sego in 1796, after incredible hardships, and was imprisoned by the Arabs there, but escaped and returned to England in 1799; made his fame by his 'Travels' (1799); acquired a good practice at Peebles, but though married and acquainted with many famous men, including Sir Walter Scott, was restless in Scotland, and eagerly accepted an invitation from government to organise a fresh expedition; departed on a second journey to the Niger, 1805; reached Bambakoo, but while proceeding thence down the Niger perished at Boussa, in a conflict with the natives, together with all his men. Particulars of his fate were not ascertained until 1812. [xliii. 218]

PARK, PATRIC (1811-1855), sculptor; began life as a stonecutter, but by the assistance of the Duke of Hamilton was enabled to study under Thorwaldsen, 1831-3; best known by his portrait busts; executed, among others, portraits of Campbell the poet, Charles Dickens, Sir Charles Napier, Lord Dundonald, and Macaulay. [xliii. 221]

PARK, THOMAS (1759-1834), antiquary and bibliographer; was brought up as an engraver, but (1797) abandoned the art and devoted himself entirely to literature and the study of antiquities; F.S.A., 1802; published several volumes of verse and edited many works of importance; had a unique knowledge of poetical literature and biography. [xliii. 223]

PARKE, DANIEL (1669-1710), governor of, the Leeward islands; murdered at Antigua during an insurrection occasioned by his attempts at internal reform. A tory government succeeding to office at the time no steps were taken to bring his assassins to justice until 1715, when one Henry Smith was tried, but acquitted for want of proof. [xliii. 225]

PARKE, HENRY (1792?-1835), architect; son of John Parke [q. v.]; made an extensive collection of drawings of antique remains, which is now in the possession of the R.I.B.A. [xliii. 225]

PARKE, Sir JAMES, BARON WENSLEYDALE (1782-1868), judge; Craven scholar (Cambridge), 1799; fifth wrangler, Trinity College, Cambridge, 1803; fellow, 1804; M.A., 1806; LL.D., 1835; barrister, Inner Temple, 1813; knighted and raised to the king's bench, 1828; transferred to the exchequer, 1834; created baron, 1856. His patent was at first only for a life peerage, but the committee of privileges decided that the crown had by disuse lost the power of creating life peerages. [xliii. 226]

PARKE, JOHN (1745-1829), oboist; taken into the Duke of Cumberland's band, 1783, being at that time the principal oboist in England. [xliii. 226]

PARKE, MARIA HESTER, afterwards MRS. BEARDMORE (1775-1822), vocalist; daughter of John Parke [q. v.]; came out in 1790 as second singer, and in 1794 as principal soprano in the Three Choirs festival; married John Beardmore, 1815, and retired from her profession. [xliii. 227]

PARKE, ROBERT (*fl.* 1588), translator of the Chinese 'History' of Gonzales de Mendoza, 1588. His work was republished by the Hakluyt Society, 1853. [xliii. 227]

PARKE, ROBERT (1600-1668), nonconformist divine; of Emmanuel College, Cambridge; vicar of Bolton, 1625; fled to Holland, 1630; returned, 1644, and became lecturer at Bolton; ejected, 1662. [xliii. 227]

PARKE, ROBERT (*fl.* 1787-1816), architect and builder; designed many public buildings in Dublin. [xliii. 228]

PARKE, THOMAS HEAZLE (1857-1893), African traveller; entered the army medical service and (1893) became surgeon-major; saw service in Egypt between 1882 and 1885, and accompanied Stanley's expedition in 1887 as an unpaid volunteer, and throughout the expedition commanded a company, besides acting as medical officer. He contributed to periodicals articles on his travels and on professional subjects. [xliii. 228]

PARKE, WILLIAM THOMAS (1762-1847), oboist, composer, and author; brother of John Parke [q. v.]; a famous oboist and member of the Duke of Cumberland's band; extended the compass of the instrument a third higher, to G in alt. [xliii. 230]

PARKER, ALEXANDER (1628–1689), quaker; friend of George Fox, whom he joined in 1654, and with whom he frequently travelled; imprisoned for his principles on several occasions; published religious treatises.
[xliii. 230]

PARKER, BENJAMIN (d. 1747), author; was unsuccessful as a quack, and afterwards failed to gain appreciation as theologian and philosopher; wrote much and died poor. Lord Chesterfield was among his patrons.
[xliii. 232]

PARKER, CHARLES (1800–1881), architect; F.R.I.B.A., 1834; published 'Villa Rustica,' an important work on domestic dwellings near Rome and Florence, 1832.
[xliii. 232]

PARKER, SIR CHARLES CHRISTOPHER, fifth baronet (1792–1869), admiral; son of Christopher Parker [q. v.]; saw service in the Mediterranean and the Baltic between 1806 and 1815; admiral, 1863.
[xliii. 233]

PARKER, CHRISTOPHER (1761–1804), vice-admiral; son of Sir Peter Parker (1721–1811) [q. v.]; served in the West Indies under Jarvis, in the Channel under Howe; vice-admiral, 1804.
[xliii. 266]

PARKER, EDMUND, second EARL OF MORLEY (1810–1864), son of John Parker, first earl of Morley [q. v.]; B.A. Christ Church, Oxford, 1830; lord-in-waiting to Queen Victoria, 1846; special deputy-warden of the Stannaries, 1852.
[xliii. 250]

PARKER, EMMA (fl. 1811–1817), author of four novels published between 1811 and 1816.
[xliii. 233]

PARKER, GEORGE (1651–1743), almanac maker; a man of disreputable character; set up as an astrologer and quack at the Ball and Star in Salisbury Court, Strand, London; rival of John Partridge (1644–1715) [q. v.], who attacked him with great bitterness in his 'Defectio Geniturarum' (1697–8, p. 331).
[xliii. 233]

PARKER, GEORGE, second EARL OF MACCLESFIELD (1697–1764), astronomer; son of Sir Thomas Parker, first earl of Macclesfield [q. v.]; F.R.S., 1722; M.P., Wallingford, 1722–7; erected a fine observatory (1739) at Shirburn Castle, Oxfordshire; patron of James Bradley [q. v.] and Thomas Phelps [q. v.]; mainly instrumental in procuring the change of style in the computation of current chronology in 1752; president of the Royal Society, 1752; hon. D.C.L. Oxford, 1759.
[xliii. 234]

PARKER, GEORGE (1732–1800), soldier, actor, and lecturer; attained the rank of sergeant during the Seven Years' war; afterwards made unsuccessful essays as an actor and lecturer, and in spite of the patronage of Goldsmith, Dr. Johnson, and Reynolds sank into poverty; published an untrustworthy autobiography, 1781, and other works.
[xliii. 235]

PARKER, SIR GEORGE (1767–1847), admiral; nephew of Sir Peter Parker (1721–1811) [q. v.]; saw service during French war; admiral, 1837; K.C.B., 1837.
[xliii. 236]

PARKER, SIR GEORGE, fourth baronet (d. 1857), major; grandson of Sir William Parker (1743–1802) [q. v.]; entered the East India Company's service, 1833; succeeded as baronet, 1852; major, 1857; died in Cawnpore during the siege.
[xliii. 237]

PARKER, GEORGE LANE (1724–1791), lieutenant-general; son of George Parker, second earl of Macclesfield [q. v.]; M.P., Tregony; lieutenant-general, 1777.
[xliii. 235]

PARKER, HENRY (d. 1470), Carmelite; an inmate of the Carmelite house at Doncaster; D.D. Cambridge; author, among other works, of 'Dives and Pauper' (printed, 1493, by Richard Pynson [q. v.]).
[xliii. 237]

PARKER, HENRY, eighth BARON MORLEY (1476–1556), courtier and author; descended from Robert de Morley, second baron Morley [q. v.]; educated at Oxford; gentleman-usher to Henry VIII, 1516; published a translation of Petrarch's 'Trionfi,' c. 1553, and left many manuscripts, which display his robust faith as a catholic and his appreciation of classical and modern Italian literature.
[xliii. 238]

PARKER, SIR HENRY, ninth BARON MORLEY (d. 1577), son of Henry Parker, eighth baron Morley [q. v.]; of Gonville Hall, Cambridge; K.B., 1553; left England,

c. 1569, owing to his attachment to Roman catholicism; lived under Spanish protection and was regarded as a dangerous traitor.
[xliii. 240]

PARKER, HENRY (1604–1652), political writer; M.A. St. Edmund Hall, Oxford, 1628; barrister, Lincoln's Inn, 1637; secretary to the parliamentary army, 1642; secretary to the House of Commons, 1645; published numerous pamphlets.
[xliii. 240]

PARKER, HENRY PERLEE (1795–1873), artist; exhibited eighty-six pictures—portraits and historical and marine subjects—in London between 1817 and 1863.
[xliii. 241]

PARKER, SIR HENRY WATSON (1808–1881), premier of New South Wales; went out as private secretary to Governor Sir George Gipps, 1838; premier, 1856–7; knighted, 1858; K.C.M.G., 1877.
[xliii. 242]

PARKER, SIR HYDE, third baronet (1714–1782), vice-admiral; great-grandson of Alexander Hyde [q. v.]; entered navy as an able seaman, 1728; appointed lieutenant, 1745; served on the Indian coast, 1760–4, in West Indies, 1779–80 (vice-admiral, 1780), and in the North Sea, 1781; fought with the Dutch on the Doggerbank, 5 Aug. 1781; succeeded as baronet, 1782; lost in the Cato off South America.
[xliii. 242]

PARKER, SIR HYDE (1739–1807), admiral; second son of Sir Hyde Parker (1714–1782) [q. v.]; served in North America during the war of independence; knighted, 1779; commander-in-chief at Jamaica, 1796–1800; commanded fleet despatched to coerce Denmark, but showed some irresolution both before and after the battle of Copenhagen, 1801, and was recalled.
[xliii. 244]

PARKER, HYDE (1784?–1854), vice-admiral; son of Sir Hyde Parker (1739–1807) [q. v.], C.B., 1839; vice-admiral, 1852; first sea lord of the admiralty, 1853.
[xliii. 245]

PARKER, JAMES (1750–1805), engraver; executed his early plates in the stipple type, but afterwards became an excellent line-engraver; much employed on book illustrations.
[xliii. 245]

PARKER, SIR JAMES (1803–1852), vice-chancellor; seventh wrangler, Trinity College, Cambridge, 1825; M.A., 1828; barrister, Lincoln's Inn, 1829; Q.C., 1844; vice-chancellor, 1851; knighted, 1851.
[xliii. 246]

PARKER, JOHN (1534–1592), divine; M.A. Christ Church, Oxford, 1558 (incorporated at Cambridge, 1564); D.D. Cambridge, 1583; prebendary, 1565, and archdeacon of Ely, 1568; declined bishopric of Ely, 1581; author of 'A Pattern of Pietie,' 1592.
[xliii. 246]

PARKER, JOHN (fl. 1611–1660), judge; barrister, Gray's Inn, 1617; appointed a Welsh judge, 1647; a baron of the exchequer, 1655; lost his post at the Restoration, but was made a serjeant.
[xliii. 247]

PARKER, JOHN (d. 1681), archbishop of Dublin; D.D. Trinity College, Dublin; bishop of Elphin, 1660; archbishop of Tuam, 1667; archbishop of Dublin, 1678.
[xliii. 247]

PARKER, JOHN (fl. 1676–1705), colonel and Jacobite conspirator; entered the army, followed James to St. Germain and Ireland, and was concerned in the assassination plot of 1693; escaped from the Tower of London, 1694; confined in the Bastille for offending Mary of Modena, 1702; on his return made overtures to the English government.
[xliii. 247]

PARKER, JOHN (1730?–1765?), painter; made copies of antiquities at Rome for English amateurs.
[xliii. 248]

PARKER, JOHN (fl. 1762–1776), painter; exhibited landscapes at the Free Society of Artists and the Royal Academy in 1765 and 1766.
[xliii. 248]

PARKER, JOHN, second BARON BORINGDON and first EARL OF MORLEY (1772–1840), succeeded his father in the barony, 1788; created D.C.L. Christ Church, Oxford, 1799; supported Pitt and Canning in the House of Lords; created Earl of Morley, 1815; after Canning's death became a whig, supporting parliamentary reform; F.R.S., 1795.
[xliii. 248]

PARKER, JOHN (1798–1860), amateur architect; of Eton and Christ Church, Oxford; M.A., 1825; designed several ecclesiastical structures, including the church of Llan-y-Blodwell, of which he was vicar.
[xliii. 250]

PARKER, JOHN (1799–1881), politician ; M.A. Brasenose College, Oxford, 1823 ; barrister, Lincoln's Inn, 1824 ;
whig M.P. for Sheffield, 1832–52 ; secretary of the admiralty, 1841 and 1849–52, holding also other offices ; privy
councillor, 1854.   [xliii. 250]

PARKER, JOHN HENRY (1806–1884), writer on
architecture ; succeeded his uncle, Joseph Parker, as
bookseller, and published at Oxford in 1832 ; published for
Pusey, and brought out libraries of the fathers and of
Anglo-catholic theology ; F.S.A., 1849 ; first keeper of the
Ashmolean, Oxford, 1870–84 ; C.B., 1871 ; published works
on architecture, including ' The Archæology of Rome,'
1874–6, and ' An Introduction to the Study of Gothic
Architecture,' 1849.   [xliii. 250]

PARKER, JOHN WILLIAM (1792–1870), publisher
and printer ; set up business, London ; printer to Cambridge University, 1836 ; his London business sold to
Longmans, 1863.   [xliii. 251]

PARKER, MARTIN (d. 1656 ?), ballad-monger ;
native of London and a royalist ; commended by Dryden
as the best ballad-maker of his day ; produced ' When
the king enjoyes his owne again,' 1643 ; produced also a
number of small books of poetry, often mere chap-books,
and some romances.   [xliii. 252]

PARKER, MATTHEW (1504–1575), archbishop of
Canterbury ; son of William Parker, a calenderer of
stuffs ; educated at St. Mary's Hostel, Cambridge, and
Corpus Christi College, Cambridge ; fellow, 1527 ; ordained
priest, 1527 ; M.A., 1528 ; became associated with the
group of students known as the ' Cambridge reformers' ;
friend of Thomas Bilney [q. v.] and Hugh Latimer [q. v.],
but studied patristic literature, and throughout life
showed great moderation in doctrine ; licensed by Cranmer to preach throughout the southern province, 1533 ;
appointed chaplain to Anne Boleyn and dean of Stoke-by-
Clare, 1535, where he spent much of the next ten years ;
elected master of Corpus Christi College, Cambridge, 1544 ;
during the last three years of Henry VIII's reign manfully
opposed the spoliation with which the colleges generally
were threatened ; continued to grow rapidly in favour
with the reformers, and (1552) was installed dean of
Lincoln ; espoused the cause of Lady Jane Grey and was
deprived of his preferments by Queen Mary, after which
he lived in concealment ; reluctantly accepted the archbishopric of Canterbury on the accession of Queen Elizabeth, and was consecrated at Lambeth on 17 Dec. 1559 ;
identified himself with the great party, afterwards known
as the Anglican party, which sought to establish a *media
via* between Romanism and puritanism ; revived the
powers of convocation, and with its assent revised the
articles in 1562, reducing them from forty-two to thirty-
nine, and substantially bringing them to the form they
finally assumed in 1571 ; occupied in publishing the
' Bishops' Bible,' 1563–8, his most distinguished service to
the theological studies of his day, with respect to which
he informed Cecil that, besides the prefaces, he contemplated undertaking Genesis, Exodus, Matthew, Mark,
and the Pauline epistles, except Romans and 1 Corinthians ; involved, by the publication of his celebrated
' Advertisements,' 1565, in a controversy with the puritans concerning vestments ; during his later years made
his exercise of church patronage, hitherto impartial
and judicious, serve as an instrument for checking the
spread of obnoxious puritan doctrines ; withdrew more
and more from society, being conscious of the strength of
the opposing current, headed by the all-powerful Leicester,
and went but seldom to court ; died, 17 May 1575, and
was buried in his private chapel at Lambeth. In 1648 his
remains were disinterred and buried under a dunghill, but
after the Restoration they were restored to their original
resting-place. He was a great benefactor to his college
and to the university of Cambridge, where he constructed
a handsome new street, which he named University
Street, leading from the schools to Great St. Mary's. To
his efforts we are indebted for the earliest editions of
Gildas, Asser, Ælfric, the ' Flores Historiarum,' Matthew
Paris, and other important early chroniclers. In spite of
Queen Elizabeth's dislike of clerical matrimony, he was
married, and left one son. His ' De Antiquitate Ecclesiæ
et Privilegiis Ecclesiæ Cantuariensis cum Archiepiscopis
ejusdem 70' (1572) is said to be the first book privately
printed in England. The copies differed materially. A
new edition appeared in 1605 and a third in 1729, edited

by Samuel Drake (1686 ?–1753) [q. v.] Numerous tractates by him have been printed in various collections.
                                                 [xliii. 254]

PARKER, Sir NICHOLAS (1547–1619), military commander ; served in the Low Countries ; knighted by Lord
Willoughby, 1588 ; commander of the ordnance for the
forces in France under Willoughby, 1589 ; accompanied
Essex in the Islands' voyage, 1597 ; governor of Plymouth,
1601–3 ; governor of Pendennis Castle, 1598–1619.
                                                 [xliii. 264]

PARKER, Sir PETER, first baronet (1721–1811),
admiral of the fleet ; commanded a squadron which
attacked Charlestown, 1775, and was repulsed with the
loss of three frigates ; took part in the reduction of Long
island and Rhode island, 1775 ; rear-admiral and commander-in-chief at Jamaica, 1777 ; became a baronet,
1782 ; admiral of the fleet, 1799 ; the early patron of
Nelson.   [xliii. 265]

PARKER, Sir PETER, second baronet (1785–1814),
captain in the navy ; grandson of Sir Peter Parker (1721–
1811) [q. v.] ; performed much meritorious service during
the French war ; fell in a skirmish on the Chesapeake
during the war with the United States.   [xliii. 266]

PARKER, Sir PHILIP (*fl.* 1578–1580), country
gentleman ; son of Sir Henry Parker, ninth baron Morley
[q. v.] ; played a large part in the local affairs of the
eastern counties.   [xliii. 240]

PARKER, RICHARD (1572–1629), historian of Cambridge University ; son of John Parker (1534–1592)
[q. v.] ; fellow of Caius College, Cambridge ; M.A., 1597 ;
B.D., 1610 ; held clerical preferment in Essex ; wrote
'Σκελετὸς Cantabrigiensis,' 1622 (first printed by Hearne,
1715), and several other treatises.   [xliii. 267]

PARKER, RICHARD (1767 ?–1797), mutineer ; married the daughter of a farmer in Braemar, ran through
her money, and was imprisoned for debt in Perth ;
obtained his release by volunteering for the navy in 1797 ;
became an able seaman on the Sandwich ; chosen president
by the mutineers at the Nore on 23 May 1797, who
blockaded the Thames and made the most extravagant
demands ; hanged after the collapse of the mutiny.
                                                 [xliii. 268]

PARKER, ROBERT (1564 ?–1614), puritan divine ;
fellow of Magdalen College, Oxford, 1585–93 ; M.A., 1587 ;
rector of Patney, Devizes, 1592–3 ; vicar of Stanton St.
Bernard, 1594–1605 ; crossed to Holland (1607) to avoid
prosecution before the court of high commission and
settled in Leyden ; removed to Antwerp, 1611, but was
compelled to leave the congregation there (1613) owing to
doctrinal differences ; published theological works ; died
at Doesburg.   [xliii. 269]

PARKER, ROBERT (*fl.* 1683–1718), soldier ; saw
much service in Ireland and the Low Countries ; wrote
' Memoirs of the most Remarkable Military Transactions
from . . . 1683 to 1718' (Dublin, 1746), in which Marlborough is the hero, while Ormonde is vigorously denounced.   [xliii. 271]

PARKER, SAMUEL (1640–1688), bishop of Oxford ;
son of John Parker (*fl.* 1611–1660) [q. v.] ; educated at
Oxford, at Wadham and Trinity colleges ; M.A. Trinity
College, Oxford, 1663 ; appointed chaplain to Archbishop
Sheldon, 1667 ; archdeacon of Canterbury, 1676 ; wrote
voluminously on ecclesiastical history and political
science, criticised Plato, Aristotle, Descartes, and
Hobbes, and attacked the puritans ; strongly supported the power of the crown and desired to restrict
church authority to purely spiritual questions ; published ' Ecclesiastical Politie' (1670), which became a
popular work and provoked much controversy ; D.D.
Cambridge, *per literas regias*, 1671 ; attracted the attention of James II by his advocacy of erastian views ; made
bishop of Oxford, 1686 ; nominated president of Magdalen
College, 1687, where he admitted many Roman catholic
fellows on the royal mandate ; his patience was exhausted
by a command from the king to admit nine more catholic
fellows, and a burst of anger led to a convulsive fit, in
which he died. Although universally regarded by contemporaries as merely a time-server, an examination of
his writings leads to the conclusion that he held views
on religious toleration in advance of his age.
                                                 [xliii. 272]

PARKER, SAMUEL (1681–1730), nonjuror and
theological writer ; son of Samuel Parker (1640–1688)

[q. v.] ; of Trinity College, Oxford : refused the oaths of allegiance and lived in retirement at Oxford ; conformed, 1711 ; issued 'Censura Temporum' (1708–10), a monthly periodical, in the interest of the high-church school of Queen Anne's reign, and wrote a number of treatises. [xliii. 275]

PARKER, SAMUEL WILLIAM LANGSTON (1803–1871), surgeon ; F.R.C.S. in 1843 ; devoted his energies to the treatment of syphilis, in which department he obtained a world-wide reputation, though he did not advance the scientific knowledge of the disease. [xliii. 276]

PARKER, THOMAS (*fl.* 1536–1581), Roman catholic divine ; M.A. and fellow, Trinity College, Cambridge, 1541 ; B.D., 1548 ; became vicar of Mildenhall, 1556 ; went abroad after Queen Elizabeth's accession, becoming D.D. [xliii. 277]

PARKER, THOMAS (1595–1677), New England divine : son of Robert Parker (1564 ?–1614) [q. v.] ; of Magdalen College, Oxford ; M.A. Leyden, 1617 ; driven by his puritan opinions to embark for New England, 1634 ; first pastor at Newbury in Massachusetts ; devoted himself to the study of prophecy and wrote several works, only one of which was published, 'The Visions and Prophecies of Daniel Expounded' (1646). [xliii. 277]

PARKER, Sir THOMAS, first EARL OF MACCLES-FIELD (1666 ?–1732), lord chancellor ; son of an attorney at Leek ; of Trinity College, Cambridge ; barrister, Inner Temple, 1691, bencher, 1705 ; attended the midland circuit, where he became known as the ' silver-tongued counsel ' ; whig M.P. for Derby, 1705, continuing to sit until his elevation to the bench ; knighted, 1705 ; appointed one of the committee to draw up articles of impeachment against Sacheverell, 1709 ; distinguished himself at Sacheverell's trial in 1710 by his vehemence ; lord chief-justice of England, 1710 ; refused the offer of the seals, 1711, being opposed to the peace ; a favourite of George I, who was delighted with his activity against the Jacobites at the time of Queen Anne's death, and in 1716 was created Baron Macclesfield ; appointed lord chancellor, 1718 ; received the tellership of the exchequer, 1719 ; created Earl of Macclesfield, 1721. In 1724 a committee of the privy council was appointed to inquire into the funds of the suitors in the hands of the masters in chancery. They reported not only that there were considerable defalcations in some of the masters' offices, but that there was a case of grave suspicion against the lord chancellor. In consequence he resigned the seals in January 1725, though he still continued in favour at court. In May he was impeached, found guilty, and fined 30,000*l.* He took no further part in public affairs. He was an able judge, both in common law and equity. Though a member of the cabinet and a great personal favourite of George I, he did not possess much political influence. [xliii. 278]

PARKER, Sir THOMAS (1695 ?–1784), judge ; barrister, Middle Temple, 1724 ; king's serjeant, 1736 ; baron of the exchequer, 1738 ; knighted, 1742 ; removed to the common pleas, 1740 ; returned to the exchequer as chief baron, 1742, retiring, 1772. [xliii. 282]

PARKER, THOMAS LISTER (1779–1858), antiquary ; of Christ's College, Cambridge ; displayed a collection of antiquities and pictures at Browsholme Hall, Yorkshire, partly formed by himself. His manuscripts were used by Thomas Dunham Whitaker [q. v.]. [xliii. 283]

PARKER, WILLIAM (*fl.* 1535). [See MALVERN.]

PARKER, WILLIAM (*d.* 1618), sea-captain ; made successful expeditions against the Spanish Indies in 1597 and 1600–1, when he sacked St. Vincent in the Cape Verd Islands and captured Porto Bello ; died on a voyage to the East Indies. [xliii. 283]

PARKER, WILLIAM, fourth BARON MONTEAGLE and eleventh BARON MORLEY (1575–1622), grandson of Sir Henry Parker, ninth baron Morley [q. v.] ; related to the chief Roman catholic families of the country ; after being involved in Essex's rebellion became protestant in 1605 ; rewarded by a writ of summons to the House of Lords as Baron Monteagle, 1605 ; received a warning from his brother-in-law, Francis Tresham [q. v.], which led to the detection of the Gunpowder plot ; sat in parliament till his death ; summoned to the Lords, 1621, as Baron Morley and Monteagle. [xliii. 284]

PARKER, WILLIAM (1714–1802), divine ; M.A. Balliol College, Oxford, 1738 ; D.D., 1754 ; F.R.S., 1746 ; eminent as a pulpit orator ; chaplain in ordinary to George II and George III. His works consist, for the most part, of single sermons, in which he defends the Mosaic history against the attacks of Bolingbroke, Morgan, and Conyers Middleton. [xliii. 286]

PARKER, Sir WILLIAM, first baronet (1743–1802), vice-admiral ; entered navy, 1756 ; fought a gallant action (28 May 1794) in the Audacious against the French ship Révolutionnaire ; third in command at the battle of Cape St. Vincent, where he betrayed some resentment at Nelson's account of the battle, 1797 ; created baronet, 1797 ; commander on the Halifax station, 1800, but recalled in 1801. [xliii. 287]

PARKER, Sir WILLIAM, first baronet (1781–1866), admiral of the fleet ; grandson of Sir Thomas Parker (1695 ?–1784) [q. v.] ; entered navy, 1793, and saw much service ; settled down in Staffordshire as a country gentleman, 1812 ; returned to service, 1827 ; acted as senior officer on the coast of Greece, 1828 ; protected British interests on the Tagus during the civil war of 1834 ; lord of the admiralty, 1834, and from 1835–41 ; commander in China, 1841, capturing Amoy, Ningpo, Woosung, and Shanghai, and bringing the war to a successful conclusion by capturing Chin-kiang-foo ; G.C.B., 1843 ; created baronet, 1844 ; nominated to the command of the Channel fleet, 1846, retiring, 1852 ; commander-in-chief at Devonport, 1854–7 ; admiral of the fleet, 1863. [xliii. 288]

PARKER, WILLIAM KITCHEN (1823–1890), comparative anatomist : Hunterian professor of comparative anatomy, Royal College of Surgeons, 1873. His most extensive work is that upon the skull, embodied in a series of monographs and smaller papers reduced into book form in 1877. [xliii. 290]

PARKES, ALEXANDER (1813–1890), chemist and inventor ; took out forty-six patents extending over forty-six years, most of them connected with the deposition of metals by electricity ; discovered the method of using zinc for the desilverisation of lead (1850) and invented celluloid. [xliii. 292]

PARKES, DAVID (1763–1833), schoolmaster, draughtsman, and antiquary ; established a mercantile school at Shrewsbury ; collected books, and made innumerable drawings of antiquities. [xliii. 293]

PARKES, EDMUND ALEXANDER (1819–1876), professor of hygiene and physician ; nephew of Anthony Todd Thomson [q. v.] ; M.D. London, 1846 ; professor of clinical medicine, University College, London, 1849 ; superintended the large civil hospital in the Dardanelles during the Crimean war ; founder of the science of modern hygiene, and famous throughout Europe in the field of military hygiene. [xliii. 294]

PARKES, Sir HARRY SMITH (1828–1885), diplomatist ; went to China, 1841, and entered government service ; assisted in concluding the first European treaty with Siam, 1855 ; took an important part in the hostilities at Canton, 1856 ; one of the three commissioners appointed (1858) to control the government of Canton ; arrested while carrying on negotiations for the termination of the third Chinese war, 1860, and kept in heavy chains at Peking for eleven days ; constantly threatened with death and was kept in close confinement for three weeks before his release ; consul at Shanghai ; appointed minister to Japan, 1865 ; associated with every forward movement in Japan, in spite of several attempts to assassinate him, till 1872 ; G.C.M.G., 1882 ; gazetted minister to China, and concluded a treaty with Korea opening the country to British trade, 1883. [xliii. 296]

PARKES, Sir HENRY (1815–1896), Australian statesman ; born of humble parents at Stoneleigh, Warwickshire ; apprenticed as ivory turner at Birmingham ; emigrated to Sydney, 1839 ; worked as farm labourer ; opened shop as ivory and bone turner in Hunter Street, Sydney ; became known as a working-class agitator, 1848 ; founded and edited (1850–7) the 'Empire' newspaper as organ of liberalism in New South Wales ; member for Sydney in legislative council ; strongly advocated responsible government, and on its establishment (1858) was member for East Sydney, 1858–61 ; colonial secretary, 1866–8 ; member for Mudgee, 1871 ; prime minister of New South Wales, 1872–5, 1878–82, and 1887–9 ; K.C.M.G., 1877 ; G.C.M.G., 1888 ;

strongly advocated federation, and presided (1891) over Sydney convention, which practically laid foundations of the Australian commonwealth; published works on Australian history and politics and several volumes of poems. [Suppl. iii. 246]

PARKES, JAMES (1794–1828), artist; son of David Parkes [q. v.]; assisted his father in his archæological drawings. [xliii. 294]

PARKES, JOSEPH (1796–1865), politician; brother of Josiah Parkes [q. v.]; a Birmingham solicitor; after acting as an intermediary between the whigs and radicals on the question of parliamentary reform, became a member of the Birmingham political union in 1832, and prepared for armed rebellion if the Reform Bill was again rejected; subsequently built up a considerable business as a parliamentary solicitor. [xliii. 304]

PARKES, JOSIAH (1793–1871), inventor of the deep-drainage system; became a civil engineer and discovered the advantages of deep drains while engaged in draining a part of Chat Moss, Lancashire. [xliii. 305]

PARKES, RICHARD (fl. 1574–1607), divine; M.A. Brasenose College, Oxford, 1585; wrote against Andrew Willet [q. v.] in support of Augustinian doctrines. [xliii. 306]

PARKES, SAMUEL (1761–1825), chemist; manufacturing chemist in London, 1803; published manuals of chemistry between 1806 and 1815, which brought him many honours from learned societies. [xliii. 307]

PARKES, WILLIAM (fl. 1612), satirist; author of 'The Curtaine-Drawer of the World' (a tract in prose and verse), 1612. [xliii. 307]

PARKHOUSE, HANNAH (1743–1809). [See COWLEY.]

PARKHURST, FERDINANDO (fl. 1653–1662), translator; rendered several works from Latin into English. [xliii. 310]

PARKHURST, JOHN (1512?–1575), bishop of Norwich; fellow of Merton College, Oxford, 1529; M.A., 1533; created D.D. Oxford, 1566; supported the Reformation and went to Zurich on Queen Mary's accession; became bishop of Norwich, 1560; published a collection of Latin epigrams, 1574. [xliii. 308]

PARKHURST, JOHN (1564–1639), master of Balliol College, Oxford; a fellow of Magdalen College, Oxford, 1581; M.A., 1590; D.D., 1610; secretary to Sir Henry Wotton [q. v.] at Turin, 1613, and was sent by the Duke of Savoy to negotiate with the protestants of Geneva; elected master of Balliol College, Oxford, in 1617; resigned mastership, 1637. [xliii. 309]

PARKHURST, JOHN (1728–1797), biblical lexicographer; grandson of Sir Robert Dormer [q. v.]; M.A. Clare Hall, Cambridge, 1752, and fellow; published 'An Hebrew and English Lexicon,' 1762, 'A Greek and English Lexicon to the New Testament,' 1769. [xliii. 310]

PARKHURST, NATHANIEL (1643–1707), divine; M.A. Queens' College, Cambridge, 1664; vicar of Yoxford, 1665–1707; published religious works. [xliii. 310]

PARKHURST, THOMAS (1629?–1707?), London bookseller; eminent as a publisher of presbyterian works. [xliii. 311]

PARKIN, CHARLES (1689–1765), antiquary; M.A. Pembroke Hall, Cambridge, 1717; rector of Oxburgh, 1717; completed Francis Blomefield's 'History of Norfolk,' published 1775. [xliii. 311]

PARKINS. [See PARKYNS and PERKINS.]

PARKINSON, ANTHONY, in religion CUTHBERT (1667–1728), Franciscan friar; missioner in England; provincial, 1713; author of 'Collectanea Anglo-Minoritica,' 1726. [xliii. 312]

PARKINSON, JAMES (1653–1722), polemical writer; B.A. Gloucester Hall, Oxford, 1674; fellow of Lincoln College, Oxford, 1674; M.A., 1675; took orders; as an extreme whig was expelled from the university in 1683, but re-admitted, 1689, without regaining his fellowship; head-master of King Edward's School, Birmingham, from 1694 to 1722. [xliii. 312]

PARKINSON, JAMES (1730?–1813), museum proprietor; won the museum of Sir Ashton Lever [q. v.] in a lottery in 1784, and exhibited it near Blackfriars Bridge until 1806, when he sold it by auction. [xliii. 313]

PARKINSON, JAMES (d. 1824), surgeon and palæontologist; published numerous small medical works, 1799–1807, besides issuing 'Organic Remains of a Former World,' 1804–11 (3 vols.) [xliii. 314]

PARKINSON, JOHN (1567–1650), apothecary and herbalist; apothecary to James I; published botanical works. [xliii. 315]

PARKINSON, JOSEPH (1783–1855), architect; son of James Parkinson (1730?–1813) [q. v.]; designed many alterations and additions at Magdalen College, Oxford, 1822–30. [xliii. 314]

PARKINSON, RICHARD (1748–1815), agricultural writer; employed as agriculturist by George Washington at Mount Vernon, c. 1798. [xliii. 315]

PARKINSON, RICHARD (1797–1858), canon of Manchester; M.A. St. John's College, Cambridge, 1824; D.D., 1851; principal of St. Bees College, 1846; one of the founders of the Chetham Society and its vice-president from its commencement in 1843. [xliii. 316]

PARKINSON, STEPHEN (1823–1889), mathematician; senior wrangler, St. John's College, Cambridge, 1845; tutor of St. John's College, Cambridge, 1864–82; took a leading part in university affairs. [xliii. 317]

PARKINSON, SYDNEY (1745?–1771), draughtsman; accompanied Captain Cook to the South Seas in 1768, dying at sea. Owing to a dispute with his brother, Stanfield Parkinson, concerning his papers, his name was excluded from the official account of the voyage made by John Hawkesworth [q. v.] [xliii. 317]

PARKINSON, THOMAS (fl. 1769–1789), portrait-painter, chiefly known as a painter of theatrical portraits and groups. [xliii. 318]

PARKINSON, THOMAS (1745–1830), mathematician; fellow of Christ's College, Cambridge, 1771–91; M.A., 1772; D.D., 1795; F.R.S., 1786; archdeacon of Huntingdon, 1794, of Leicester, 1812; published 'A System of Mechanics and Hydrostatics,' 1789. [xliii. 318]

PARKYNS, MANSFIELD (1823–1894), traveller; great-grandson of Sir Thomas Parkyns, second baronet [q. v.]; travelled in Abyssinia between 1843 and 1846, publishing an account, 1853. [xliii. 319]

PARKYNS, SIR THOMAS, second baronet (1664–1741), 'Luctator'; of Westminster School and Trinity College, Cambridge; student, Gray's Inn, 1682; J.P., Leicestershire and Nottinghamshire, 1684–1741; owed his celebrity to his extraordinary passion for wrestling, establishing an annual competition at his residence, Bunny Hall, which lasted till 1810; embodied his theories in 'Προγυμνάσματα' (1713, latest edit. 1810). [xliii. 319]

PARKYNS or PERKINS, SIR WILLIAM (1649?–1696), conspirator; barrister, Inner Temple, 1675; knighted, 1681; clerk of the court of chancery and Jacobite; associated in the plot of Sir George Barclay [q. v.] to assassinate William III, 1696; executed on Tower Hill, London. [xliii. 321]

PARLEY, PETER (pseudonym). [See MARTIN, WILLIAM, 1801–1867; MOGRIDGE, GEORGE, 1787–1854.]

PARMENTIER, JAMES (JACQUES) (1658–1730), painter; born in France; resided intermittently in England from 1676; employed as a decorative painter by William III. [xliii. 322]

PARNELL, CHARLES STEWART (1846–1891), political leader; born at Avondale, co. Wicklow; grandson of William Parnell [q. v.]; of Magdalene College, Cambridge; offered his services to Isaac Butt [q. v.], leader of the Irish parliamentary party, 1874; M.P., co. Meath, 1875, a seat which he exchanged for Cork city, 1880; attracted attention by his extreme attitude, and won the confidence of the Fenians, which Butt had lost; from 1877 rapidly fulfilled, by his tactics of obstruction, his object of bringing discredit upon the House of Commons; his action at first disapproved by Butt, but countenanced, January 1878, at a conference in Dublin; resolved to consolidate and dominate all the scattered forces inside and outside parliament which aimed at securing legislative independence for Ireland; courted the support of the Fenians, and in December 1878, after a visit to America, obtained an alliance with the Clan-na-Gael, or new Fenians, who had hitherto despised parliamentary agitation, one of the conditions of the treaty being that the land question should be vigorously agitated on a basis of peasant proprietorship, to carry which stipulation into effect the National Land League of Ireland was formed in October 1879 for the reduction of rack-rents and the transfer of the ownership of the land to the occupiers ; president of the Land League ; elected chairman of the home-rule party in the House of Commons, May 1880 ; exerted over his parliamentary supporters a sway unparalleled in parliamentary annals, and wielded enormous influence outside the house ; though at first disliked by the Irish clergy, was soon supported by the Irish bishops ; kept together for nearly ten years a heterogeneous crowd of supporters, many of them having mutually strong antipathies ; he initiated, in a speech at Ennis, September 1880, the system of ' boycotting ' those who took the farms of evicted tenants, a move by which government in Ireland was paralysed throughout the autumn ; bitterly opposed William Edward Forster's Coercion Bill early in 1881 ; founded, July 1881, 'The Irish National Newspaper and Publishing Company,' which issued the 'Irishman' and ' United Ireland,' under the editorship of William O'Brien ; arrested for incendiary speeches and imprisoned in Kilmainham gaol with several of his supporters, October 1881, the Land League being declared an illegal association at the same time ; gained great popularity by his imprisonment, the duration of which was marked by an increase in the number of outrages ; generally known to his followers as 'the uncrowned king of Ireland ' ; given the freedom of Dublin ; released, 2 May 1882, soon after the accommodation with Gladstone's government known as the 'Kilmainham treaty' had been effected, contrary to the advice of Forster, who resigned the office of Irish secretary in consequence ; disavowed all sympathy with the perpetrators of the murder in Phœnix Park (6 May 1882) of Lord Frederick Charles Cavendish [q. v.], the new chief secretary, and the permanent under-secretary, Thomas Henry Burke [q. v.] ; resumed his attitude of implacable hostility on fresh coercive legislation being announced by government ; attended a national conference at Dublin, October 1882, at which the Land League was avowedly revived as the 'Irish National League,' for the purpose of attaining national self-government, landlaw reform, and the development of Irish industry ; accused by Forster, February 1883, in the House of Commons of planning outrage and assassination ; met the charge with a blunt denial ; on the defeat of the liberal government by the Irish vote, June 1885, received overtures from the succeeding tory government, which he welcomed, as he probably desired to employ them to induce William Ewart Gladstone [q. v.] to outbid the tory offers ; left master of the situation by the balance of parties after the general election of December ; with the help of the liberal party overthrew the tory government, January 1886, which had announced its intention of introducing a bill for the suppression of the National League ; on Gladstone's return to power, was seen to have converted Gladstone to his home-rule scheme ; on the conservative triumph at the election (July 1886) which followed Gladstone's appeal to the country after the defeat of his bill for the establishment of an Irish parliament, made a complete change of front in his treatment of the English parties, and, instead of holding aloof from both, formed an alliance with the liberals for all parliamentary purposes, and sought rather 'to win than to force his way' by the ordinary rules of parliamentary warfare ; attended parliament irregularly, his health being bad between 1885 and 1890 ; spoke rarely at public meetings in Ireland, and lost influence in consequence ; charged, along with many of his colleagues, with connivance with crime and outrage in the days of the Land League in a series of articles entitled ' Parnellism and Crime,' which appeared in ' The Times ' in the earlier months of 1887 ; denied in the House of Commons the authenticity of a fac-simile letter printed in ' The Times ' purporting to have been written by himself on 15 May 1882 in extenuation of the Phœnix Park murders ; declared in the house that similar letters read in court à propos of a libel action unsuccessfully brought against ' The Times ' in July 1888 by Mr. Frank Hugh O'Donnell were all forgeries ; was ultimately vindicated, after the government constituted a special commission to inquire into all the charges brought against the Irish members by ' The Times ; ' this trial commenced October 1888, and during its course, in February 1889, Richard Pigott [q. v.], who had sold the incriminating letters to 'The Times,' broke down under cross-examination, and the counsel for ' The Times ' withdrew from the case the charges founded on the letters which Pigott had supplied ; the commission reported that Parnell had failed to denounce agrarian outrage ; report of the trial entered in the journals, an amendment by Gladstone in the House of Commons in reprobation of the charges against Parnell being rejected, March 1890. Parnell's career was ruined in November 1890 by his appearance as co-respondent in a suit for divorce brought by Captain O'Shea against his wife, Parnell's adultery with her being legally proved. Parnell gradually lost the support of the liberal nonconformists in consequence, Gladstone in an open letter to Mr. John Morley declaring his continuance as leader of the Irish party undesirable. Parnell summoned the Irish party, December 1890, in committee room No. 15 at the House of Commons to consider the situation, and, on refusing to put the question of his deposition to the vote, was abandoned by the majority of the party ; endeavoured to re-establish his position, and was supported by the Fenians and more extreme home-rulers, but had against him the influence of the Roman catholic church ; spoke in public for the last time at Creggs in Galway, 27 Sept. 1891 ; died at Brighton of inflammation of the lungs on 6 Oct. and was buried in Glasnevin cemetery, Dublin. On 25 June 1891 he married Katherine, the divorced wife of Captain O'Shea and the daughter of Sir John Page Wood [q. v.] His influence on the course of English and Irish history may be estimated by the fact that when he entered public life home-rule for Ireland was viewed by English politicians as a wild impracticable dream, while within eleven years he had induced a majority of one of the two great English political parties to treat it as an urgent necessity.

[xliii. 322]

PARNELL, FANNY (1854-1882), poetess and politician ; sister of Charles Stewart Parnell [q. v.] ; wrote many patriotic poems for the nationalist press, and assisted in organising the Land League and the Ladies' Land League. [xliii. 342]

PARNELL, SIR HENRY BROOKE, fourth baronet and first BARON CONGLETON (1776-1842), son of Sir John Parnell, second baronet [q. v.] ; M.P., Maryborough, Irish House of Commons, 1797, and Queen's County (united parliament), 1802 ; appointed a commissioner of the treasury for Ireland in the ministry of ' all the talents,' 1806, retiring from office, March 1807 ; conspicuous as an advocate of catholic emancipation from 1810, supporting the second reading of the Catholic Emancipation Act, 1829 ; secretary at war in Lord Grey's administration, 1831, but dismissed from office (1832) for refusing to support the ministry on the question of the Russian-Dutch war ; treasurer of the navy in Lord Melbourne's ministry, 1835 ; paymaster of the forces, 1835 ; obtained the new office of paymaster-general, 1836, which he held until his death ; created Baron Congleton, 1841 ; published numerous works, mainly in the field of economics ; committed suicide after suffering for some time from ill-health. He was an active and useful member of the most liberal section of the whig party, and achieved a high reputation as a political economist and a writer on finance.

[xliii. 342]

PARNELL, JAMES (1637 ?-1656), quaker and pamphleteer ; a convert of George Fox [q. v.], whom he visited in prison at Carlisle ; imprisoned at Cambridge, c. 1654, for attacking the magistrates and priests, and in 1655 was confined in Colchester Castle ; died in consequence of his severe treatment ; considered the 'quaker protomartyr.' He wrote several works, of which the earliest, 'A Trial of Faith' (1654), was translated into Dutch and French.

[xliii. 346]

PARNELL, SIR JOHN, second baronet (1744-1801), chancellor of the Irish exchequer ; student of Lincoln's Inn, 1766 ; bencher, King's Inns, Dublin, 1786 ; M.P., Bangor, 1761-8 (Irish parliament), Inistioge, 1776-83 ; chancellor of the Irish exchequer, 1785 ; warmly opposed the liberal policy of the English government ; helped to dissuade Pitt and Dundas from measures of reform, 1792 ; removed from his post (1799) in consequence of his opposition to the union ; entered the first parliament of the United Kingdom (M.P., Queen's County), 1801.

[xliii. 347]

PARNELL, SIR JOHN VESEY, fifth baronet and second BARON CONGLETON (1805-1883), eldest son of Sir Henry Brooke Parnell, first baron [q. v.] ; educated in France and at Edinburgh University ; joined the Plymouth brethren, 1829, and spent his life in making preaching tours. [xliii. 345]

PARNELL, THOMAS (1679–1718), poet: born in Dublin; M.A. Trinity College, Dublin, 1700; installed a minor canon of St. Patrick's, Dublin, 1704; archdeacon of Clogher, 1706–16; presented to the vicarage of Finglas, 1716; on friendly terms with Swift and other members of the tory party by 1711; contributed (1712–13) occasional allegorical papers to the 'Spectator' and 'Guardian'; created D.D. Dublin, 1712; aided Pope in his translation of the 'Iliad,' also contributing to the work an introductory 'Essay on Homer'; vicar of Finglas, 1716; addicted to excessive drinking. As a poet his work is marked by fluent versification and high moral tone. His more important pieces, including 'The Hermit' and 'The Fairy Tale' were revised by Pope. The first collective edition of his poems appeared, 1721, the last Aldine edition, 1894.   [xliii. 349]

PARNELL, WILLIAM, afterwards **PARNELL-HAYES** (d. 1821), controversialist; the son of Sir John Parnell, second baronet [q. v.]; M.P., co. Wicklow, 1817, 1819, and 1820; opposed the union and, though a protestant, had a warm admiration for the Roman catholic clergy, whose influence he supported in his works.   [xliii. 351]

PARNING, SIR ROBERT (d. 1343), chancellor; knight of the shire for Cumberland, 1325, 1327, 1328, 1331, and 1332; chief-justice of the court of king's bench, 1340; chancellor, 1341.   [xliii. 352]

PARR, BARTHOLOMEW (1750–1810), medical writer; M.D. Edinburgh, 1773; physician to the Devon and Exeter Hospital, 1775; published the 'London Medical Dictionary' (1809, 2 vols.)   [xliii. 352]

PARR, CATHERINE (1512–1548). [See CATHERINE.]

PARR, ELNATHAN (d. 1632?), divine; of Eton and King's College, Cambridge; M.A., 1601; B.D., 1615; rector of Palgrave; author of four theological treatises.   [xliii. 353]

PARR, GEORGE (1826–1891), cricketer; represented Nottinghamshire, 1846–70; captain of the All England Eleven, 1857–70; succeeded Fuller Pilch [q. v.] as the finest batsman in England.   [xliii. 353]

PARR, HARRIET (1828–1900), novelist; published (1854–82) under pseudonym of HOLM LEE, numerous novels and, under her own name, 'Life of Joan of Arc,' 1866, and other works.   [Suppl. iii. 248]

PARR, JOHN (1633?–1716?), dissenting minister; M.A. Trinity College, Cambridge, 1662; ministered for a time to the Darwen nonconformists and also at Walton and Preston, enduring considerable persecution.   [xliii. 354]

PARR, NATHANIEL (fl. 1730–1760), engraver.   [xliii. 355]

PARR, REMIGIUS (fl. 1747), engraver; probably son or brother of Nathaniel Parr [q. v.]; his work difficult to distinguish from that of Nathaniel; some of his engravings of historical importance.   [xliii. 355]

PARR or **PARRE**, RICHARD (1592?–1644), bishop of Sodor and Man; fellow of Brasenose College, Oxford, 1614; M.A., 1616; D.D., 1634; consecrated, 1635.   [xliii. 355]

PARR, RICHARD (1617–1691), divine; M.A. Exeter College, Oxford, 1642; fellow; created D.D., 1660; vicar of Reigate, 1646–53, of Camberwell, 1653–91; published the life of James Ussher [q. v.], partly compiled by Thomas Marshall [q. v.]   [xliii. 356]

PARR, SAMUEL (1747–1825), pedagogue; son of a Harrow apothecary; educated at Harrow School and Emmanuel College, Cambridge; M.A. per literas regias, 1771; forced by the 'rapacity' of his step-mother to leave Cambridge on his father's death in 1766; became first assistant at Harrow under Robert Carey Sumner [q. v.]; on Sumner's death (1771) took offence at not being elected to succeed him, and started a rival school at Stanmore, which declined after the departure of the first set of boys; obtained the mastership of Colchester grammar school, 1776, which did not prosper under him; removed to Norwich as head-master of the grammar school, 1779; settled at Hatton in Warwickshire as perpetual curate and took in private pupils, 1785; lived there for the rest of his life, enlarging the parsonage and building a library, which finally contained over ten thousand volumes; prebendary of St. Paul's, 1783; exchanged (1789) his perpetual curacy for the rectory of Wadenhoe, but retained the parsonage and continued to serve the church at Hatton; prevented from obtaining high preferment by his strong whiggism; became conspicuous as a political writer in 1787; met Priestley at Warwick, 1790, and at once formed a friendship with him; nearly involved by this acquaintance in the Birmingham riots of 1791, the rioters being expected to attack Hatton after their outrages on Priestley and his supporters; continually involved in literary quarrels, and at different times was at variance with Richard Hurd [q. v.], bishop of Worcester, with Charles Combe [q. v.], and with William Godwin (1756–1836) [q. v.]; published his 'Characters of Fox' (a collection of articles and notes), 1809. He was regarded as the whig Johnson, but his conversation was apparently very inferior to that of his model. His mannerism and verbosity make his English writings in general unreadable. He was admittedly a fine Latin scholar, and excelled as a writer of Latin epitaphs. He knew Rogers and Moore, and met Byron. Among literary men who have warmly acknowledged his kindness to them were Landor and the first Lord Lytton. His works were collected in eight volumes in 1828.   [xliii. 356]

PARR, THOMAS (1483?–1635), 'Old Parr'; a native of Alberbury, near Shrewsbury, whose longevity was celebrated by Taylor the water-poet; said to have been born in 1483, to have gone into service in 1500, and to have done penance for incontinence at the age of 105; sent to court by the Earl of Arundel, 1635, where the change in his mode of life killed him. Sir George Cornewall Lewis and William John Thoms regard the story of his extraordinary age as unsupported by any trustworthy evidence.   [xliii. 364]

PARR, SIR WILLIAM (1434–1483?), courtier and soldier; K.G.; supported the revolt of the Nevilles and Clarence, 1469, but returned to Edward IV, 1471, and was made comptroller of the household; chief commissioner for exercising the office of constable of England, 1483.   [xliii. 366]

PARR, SIR WILLIAM, MARQUIS OF NORTHAMPTON, EARL OF ESSEX, and BARON PARR (1513–1571), brother of Catherine Parr [q. v.]; educated at Cambridge; created Baron Parr and Ross, 1539, Earl of Essex, 1543, and Marquis of Northampton, 1547; a supporter of Somerset and afterwards of Northumberland, whom he accompanied into the eastern counties on Edward VI's death to maintain the cause of Lady Jane Grey; condemned to death on Queen Mary's triumph, but pardoned, with forfeiture of his titles and part of his estates; again created marquis, 1559.   [xliii. 367]

PARRIS, EDMUND THOMAS (1793–1873), painter; constructed panoramas, and was for some years a fashionable portrait-painter; restored Thornhill's paintings in the cupola of St. Paul's Cathedral, London, completely repainting them and depriving them of all interest, between 1853 and 1856.   [xliii. 368]

PARRIS or **PARIS**, GEORGE VAN (d. 1551), heretic; an inhabitant of Mentz; naturalised, 1550; burnt at Smithfield, 1551, for denying the humanity of Christ.   [xliii. 369]

PARROT or **PERROT**, HENRY (fl. 1600–1626), epigrammatist; author of 'Springes for Woodcocks,' 1613, and six other little volumes of profligate epigrams and satires.   [xliii. 369]

PARRY, BENJAMIN (1634–1678), bishop of Ossory; M.A. Jesus College, Oxford, 1654; fellow of Corpus Christi College, Oxford, and Greek reader, 1660; D.D., 1670; son of Edward Parry (d. 1650) [q. v.]; appointed bishop in 1677 as his brother's successor; author of 'Chimia Cœlestis,' 1659.   [xliii. 370]

PARRY, CALEB HILLIER (1755–1822), physician; son of Joshua Parry [q. v.]; M.D. Edinburgh, 1778; L.R.C.P., 1778; settled as a physician in Bath, 1779; his medical researches of considerable importance, especially his tract on 'The Nature, Cause, and Varieties of the Arterial Pulse,' 1816.   [xliii. 371]

PARRY, CHARLES HENRY (1779–1860), physician; son of Caleb Hillier Parry [q. v.]; studied medicine at Göttingen; M.D. Edinburgh, 1804; L.R.C.P., 1806; F.R.S., 1812; practised for some years at Bath, and published treatises on miscellaneous subjects.   [xliii. 372]

PARRY, CHARLES JAMES (1824–1894), painter; son of David Henry Parry [q. v.]; executed landscapes in oil. [xliii. 381]

PARRY, DAVID HENRY (1793–1826), portrait-painter; son of Joshua Parry [q. v.]; painted portraits of Manchester worthies, both in oils and watercolours. [xliii. 380]

PARRY, EDWARD (d. 1650), bishop of Killaloe; B.A. Trinity College, Dublin, 1620; fellow, 1624; consecrated bishop, 1647; never visited Killaloe, where he would not have been safe, owing to the predominance of the catholics during the civil war; died of the plague in Dublin. [xliii. 372]

PARRY, EDWARD (1830–1890), bishop suffragan of Dover; son of Sir William Edward Parry [q. v.]; M.A. Balliol College, Oxford, 1855; D.D., 1870; domestic chaplain of Archibald Campbell Tait, bishop of London, 1857; archdeacon of Canterbury, 1869, and suffragan bishop of Dover, 1870; published memorials of his father and his brother, Charles Parry. [xliii. 373]

PARRY, HENRY (1561–1616), successively bishop of Gloucester and Worcester; M.A. Corpus Christi College, Oxford, 1585; fellow, 1586; D.D., 1596; chaplain to Queen Elizabeth, and present at her death; bishop of Gloucester, 1607, of Worcester, 1610; published several treatises. [xliii. 375]

PARRY, HENRY HUTTON (1827–1893), bishop of Western Australia; son of Thomas Parry [q. v.]; of Rugby and Balliol College, Oxford; B.A., 1851; was consecrated coadjutor to his father, 1868, and appointed to the see of Perth, 1876. [xliii. 386]

PARRY, JAMES (d. 1871?), artist; son of Joseph Parry [q. v.]; drew and engraved views of Manchester. [xliii. 380]

PARRY, JOHN (d. 1677), bishop of Ossory; son of Edward Parry (d. 1650) [q. v.]; of Trinity College, Dublin (B.A.), and Jesus College, Oxford (fellow); M.A., 1653; Ormonde's chaplain and consecrated bishop, 1672; benefactor of his see; published (1666) 'Tears well directed, or pious Reflections on our Saviour's Sufferings.' [xliii. 375]

PARRY, JOHN (d. 1782), musician; a blind harper of Ruabon; editor with Evan Williams [q. v.] of the earliest published collections of Welsh music. [xliii. 376]

PARRY, JOHN (1776–1851), musician and composer; wrote several plays and contributed to the musical press. His compositions include songs, glees, and pieces for the harp, piano, flageolet, flute, and violin. [xliii. 376]

PARRY, JOHN DOCWRA (d. 1833?), topographer; M.A. Peterhouse, Cambridge, 1827; took orders; published several treatises of small value. [xliii. 377]

PARRY, JOHN HUMFFREYS (1786–1825), Welsh antiquary; barrister, Temple, 1811; practised at the bar, but finally turned to literature for a livelihood; assisted in publishing the government edition of Welsh historians; active in the re-establishment of the Cymmrodorion Society, 1820; killed in the street at Pentonville in a quarrel. [xliii. 377]

PARRY, JOHN HUMFFREYS (1816–1880), serjeant-at-law; son of John Humffreys Parry (1786–1825) [q. v.]; barrister, Middle Temple, 1843; serjeant, 1856; bencher of the Middle Temple, 1878; practised at first in the criminal, but afterwards in the civil, courts. [xliii. 378]

PARRY, JOHN ORLANDO (1810–1879), actor and entertainer; son of John Parry (1776–1851) [q. v.]; made his début as a vocalist, 1830, and as an actor at St. James's Theatre, London, 1836; forsook the stage for the concert room, 1842; came out as an entertainer, 1850; joined Thomas German Reed [q. v.], 1860, retiring, 1869. [xliii. 379]

PARRY, JOSEPH (1744–1826), artist; often called the father of art in Manchester. His best pictures are familiar scenes in everyday life, but he was also a portrait and historical painter. [xliii. 380]

PARRY, JOSHUA (1719–1776), dissenting divine; presbyterian minister in Cirencester from 1742; possessed much literary ability, which he dissipated in fugitive pieces, political, metaphysical, and satirical. [xliii. 381]

PARRY, SIR LOVE PARRY JONES (1781–1853), lieutenant-general; of Westminster School and Christ Church, Oxford; M.A., 1811; student, Lincoln's Inn, 1802; commanded a brigade on the Canadian frontier during the war of 1812–14; whig M.P., Horsham, 1806–7, Carmarthen, 1835–40; K.H., 1835; high sheriff of Carmarthenshire, 1840; lieutenant-general, 1846. [xliii. 382]

PARRY, RICHARD (1560–1623), bishop of St. Asaph; of Westminster School and Christ Church, Oxford; M.A., 1586; D.D., 1597; dean of Bangor, 1599; consecrated bishop, 1604; revised the Welsh translation of the bible by his predecessor, William Morgan (1540?–1604) [q. v.] [xliii. 382]

PARRY, RICHARD (1722–1780), divine; of Westminster School and Christ Church, Oxford; student, 1740; preacher at Market Harborough, 1754; M.A., 1747; D.D., 1757; rector of Witchampton, 1757; author of theological works. [xliii. 383]

PARRY, ROBERT (fl. 1595), translator; author of 'Moderatus' (1595); perhaps the 'R. P.' who translated parts ii. iii. and iv. of the 'Myrrour of Princely Deeds' from the Spanish original. [xliii. 383]

PARRY, SEFTON HENRY (1822–1887), theatrical manager; built the London theatres, the Holborn in 1866, the Globe in 1868, and the Avenue in 1882. [xliii. 384]

PARRY, SIR THOMAS (d. 1560), controller of the household; steward of the Princess Elizabeth, and appointed controller at her accession; knighted and made privy councillor. [xliii. 384]

PARRY, SIR THOMAS (d. 1616), ambassador in France; son of Sir Thomas Parry (d. 1560) [q. v.]; M.P., Berkshire, 1586; ambassador, 1601–5; knighted, 1601; had the custody of Lady Arabella Stuart for a short time, 1610–11. [xliii. 385]

PARRY, THOMAS (1795–1870), bishop of Barbados; was fellow and tutor of Balliol College, Oxford, 1816; M.A., 1819; D.D., 1842; archdeacon of Antigua, 1824; archdeacon of Barbados, 1840; bishop of Barbados, 1842; retired, 1869. [xliii. 385]

PARRY, THOMAS GAMBIER (1816–1888), inventor of the 'spirit fresco' process; of Eton and Trinity College, Cambridge; M.A., 1848; published (1880) an account of his process, which ensured permanence for colours in fresco painting; painted frescoes in several English abbeys and cathedrals, and was recognised as the chief authority on decorative painting. [xliii. 386]

PARRY, WILLIAM (d. 1585), conspirator; after squandering his own and his wife's money became a spy of Burleigh on the continent; he secretly became a catholic, c. 1579, and a double traitor; accused (1585) of a plot to murder Queen Elizabeth by his accomplice Edmund Neville (1560?–1618) [q. v.] and executed. There is some doubt as to his guilt. [xliii. 387]

PARRY, WILLIAM (fl. 1601), traveller; accompanied Sir Anthony Shirley [q. v.] in his travels, and published an account of them in 1601, entitled 'A New and Large Discourse of the Travels of Anthony Sherley.' [xliii. 389]

PARRY, WILLIAM (1687–1756?), caligrapher and numismatist; M.A. Jesus College, Oxford, 1712; B.D., 1719; fellow; vicar of Shipston-on-Stour, 1739; wrote so elegant a hand that some of his manuscripts resemble typography. [xliii. 390]

PARRY, WILLIAM (1742?–1791), portrait-painter; son of John Parry (d. 1782) [q. v.]; A.R.A., 1776. [xliii. 390]

PARRY, WILLIAM (1754–1819), congregational minister and tutor; minister at Little Baddow and tutor of the academy of the Coward Trust at Wymondley in Hertfordshire; published theological works. [xliii. 390]

PARRY, WILLIAM (fl. 1823–1825), major of Lord Byron's brigade in Greece; originally a 'firemaster' in the navy; employed by Thomas Gordon (1788–1841) [q. v.] in 1823 to prepare a plan for supplying artillery to the Greeks; kept Byron's accounts, and was his favourite butt at Missolonghi; published 'The Last Days of Lord Byron,' 1825. According to Trelawny he subsequently became insane through drink. [xliii. 391]

PARRY, SIR WILLIAM EDWARD (1790–1855), rear-admiral and arctic explorer; son of Caleb Hillier Parry [q. v.]; commanded expeditions in search of the north-west passage, 1819–20, 1821–3, and 1824–5; attempted (1827) to reach the North Pole from Spitzbergen by travelling with sledge-boats over the ice; was finally stopped by the current which set the ice floes to the southwards almost as fast as the men could drag the sledges towards the north, but attained latitude 82° 45', the highest reached until 1876; hydrographer to the admiralty, 1825–9; knighted, 1829; rear-admiral, 1852. [xliii. 392]

PARS, HENRY (1734–1806), draughtsman and chaser; kept a drawing school in the Strand for over forty years. [xliii. 393]

PARS, WILLIAM (1742–1782), portrait-painter and draughtsman; brother of Henry Pars [q. v.]; illustrated 'Ionian Antiquities' for Dr. Richard Chandler (1738–1810) [q. v.] [xliii. 394]

PARSELL, THOMAS (1674–1720), head-master of Merchant Taylors' School, London; of Merchant Taylors' School, London, and St. John's College, Oxford; M.A., 1701; D.D., 1706; appointed head-master, 1707; translated the prayer-book into Latin, 1706. [xliii. 394]

PARSLEY or **PERSLEY**, OSBERT (1511–1585), musical composer; for fifty years singing-master at Norwich Cathedral. [xliii. 394]

PARSON, THOMAS (1631–1681?), dissenting divine; M.A. and nominated (1650) fellow of Pembroke College, Cambridge, by Oliver Cromwell; ejected from St. Michael's, Wood Street, London, 1662. [xliii. 395]

PARSONS, ABRAHAM (d. 1785), traveller and consul; made several journeys in Asia Minor, Persia, India, and Egypt, of which he left a journal, published in 1808, under the title, 'Account of Travels in Asia and Africa.' [xliii. 395]

PARSONS, ANDREW (1616–1684), dissenting minister; M.A. Christ Church, Oxford, 1638; rector of Wem, 1646; ejected at the Restoration; afterwards ministered in London. [xliii. 396]

PARSONS, BARTHOLOMEW (1574–1642), divine; M.A. Oriel College, Oxford, 1603; B.D., 1611; held several preferments; published eight sermons, 1616–37. [xliii. 396]

PARSONS, BENJAMIN (1797–1855), congregational minister; ordained to Ebley, 1826; wrote on the voluntary system of education, temperance, and the observance of the sabbath. [xliii. 397]

PARSONS, EDWARD (1762–1833), congregational minister; minister at Leeds, 1785–1832; published sermons and tracts. [xliii. 398]

PARSONS, EDWARD (1797–1844), congregational minister; son of Edward Parsons (1762–1833) [q. v.]; published several small historical works. [xliii. 398]

PARSONS, ELIZA (d. 1811), novelist and dramatist; was the daughter of a Plymouth wine merchant named Phelp; married a turpentine merchant named Parsons; wrote above sixty volumes of novels, all mediocre. [xliii. 399]

PARSONS, ELIZABETH (1749–1807), 'the Cock Lane ghost'; daughter of the deputy parish clerk at St. Sepulchre's, London; attracted attention, when a 'little artful girl about eleven years of age,' by making mysterious scratchings and noises supposed to proceed from a ghost; visited by the Duke of York and numerous leaders of fashion; but was detected in 1762; Dr. Johnson published an account of the investigations in the 'Gentleman's Magazine,' which gave the imposture its deathblow. [xliii. 399]

PARSONS, ELIZABETH (1812–1873), hymn-writer; née Rooker; married T. Edgecumbe Parsons, 1844; author of a number of hymns, including 'Jesus, we love to meet.' [xliii. 401]

PARSONS, FRANCIS (fl. 1763–1783), portrait-painter and picture-dealer. [xliii. 401]

PARSONS, Mrs. GERTRUDE (1812–1891), novelist; daughter of John Hext; married Daniel Parsons, 1845; from 1846 wrote a series of tales chiefly with the object of serving the church of Rome, which she and her husband joined in 1843–4. [xliii. 401]

PARSONS, HUMPHREY (1676?–1741), lord-mayor of London; a brewer by trade at Aldgate; twice lord-

mayor, 1730 and 1740; died during his second term of office. He was a favourite with Louis XV, who permitted him to import beer into France free of duty. [xliii. 402]

PARSONS, JAMES (1705–1770), physician and antiquary; M.D. Rheims, 1736; F.R.S., 1741 (foreign secretary, c. 1750); F.S.A.; L.R.C.P., 1751; practised in London; published medical treatises and one philological work. [xliii. 403]

PARSONS, JAMES (1762–1847), divine; vice-principal of St. Alban Hall, Oxford; of Trinity and Wadham Colleges, Oxford; M.A., 1786; B.D. St. Alban Hall, Oxford, 1815; completed the 'Oxford Septuagint,' 1827. [xliii. 404]

PARSONS, JAMES (1799–1877), preacher; son of Edward Parsons (1762–1833) [q. v.]; congregational minister at York, 1822–70; the most remarkable pulpit orator of his time. [xliii. 404]

PARSONS, JOHN (d. 1623), organist and composer; said to be the son of Robert Parsons (d. 1570) [q. v.]; became organist at Westminster Abbey, 1621. [xliii. 405]

PARSONS, JOHN (1742–1785), physician; M.A. Christ Church, Oxford, 1766; M.D., 1772; first professor of anatomy at Oxford, 1766. [xliii. 405]

PARSONS, JOHN (1761–1819) bishop of Peterborough; M.A. Wadham College, Oxford, 1785; D.D., 1799; fellow of Balliol College, Oxford, 1785, master, 1798–1819; vice-chancellor of Oxford, 1807–10; in conjunction with Dr. Eveleigh, the provost of Oriel College, gave the lead to the university in making the examinations, which had degenerated into a discreditable farce, a reality; elaborated the new examination statute of 1801, by which honours were for the first time awarded for real merit; dean of Bristol, 1810; bishop of Peterborough, 1813. [xliii. 405]

PARSONS, JOHN MEESON (1798–1870), picture collector; chairman of the London and Brighton Railway Company, 1843–4; amassed a valuable gallery, chiefly of the German and Dutch Schools, many of which he left to public institutions. [xliii. 407]

PARSONS, Sir LAWRENCE, first baronet (d. 1698), Irish protestant; grand-nephew of Sir William Parsons (1570?–1650) [q. v.]; created baronet, 1677; refusing to deliver Birr Castle to James II, was besieged, captured, and condemned for high treason, 1689, but liberated after the battle of the Boyne. [xliii. 407]

PARSONS, Sir LAWRENCE, second EARL OF ROSSE (1758–1841), B.A. Trinity College, Dublin, 1780; entered the Irish parliament (M.P., Dublin University, 1782), and disclaimed party politics, though influenced by Henry Flood [q. v.]; opposed the union; became Earl of Rosse, 1807; joint postmaster-general for Ireland in 1809. [xliii. 408]

PARSONS, PHILIP (1594–1653), principal of Hart Hall (now Hertford College), Oxford; of Merchant Taylors' School, London, and St. John's College, Oxford; fellow, 1613; M.A., 1618 (incorporated at Cambridge, 1622); M.D. Padua (incorporated at Oxford, 1628); principal of Hart Hall, 1633; wrote 'Atalanta' (Latin comedy). [xliii. 409]

PARSONS, PHILIP (1729–1812), divine; M.A. Sidney Sussex College, Cambridge, 1776; perpetual curate of Wye, 1761; published miscellaneous works. [xliii. 410]

PARSONS, RICHARD (1643–1711), divine and antiquary; of Winchester College and New College, Oxford; fellow, 1659; D.C.L., 1687; vicar of Driffield, 1674; made considerable collections for a history of the diocese of Gloucester (now in the Bodleian). [xliii. 410]

PARSONS, ROBERT (d. 1570), musical composer; gentleman of the Chapel Royal, 1563; composed church music. [xliii. 411]

PARSONS or **PERSONS**, ROBERT (1546–1610), jesuit missionary and controversialist; fellow of Balliol College, Oxford, 1568; M.A., 1572; tutor and for some time (1574) bursar and dean; being at enmity with the fellows, left, or was dismissed, the college, 1574; proceeded to Louvain and was received into the Roman catholic church; joined jesuits, 1575; returned to England with Edmund Campion [q. v.], 1580, on a religious mission; made many converts among the gentry; set up a secret printing press and also engaged in political intrigues in England and on the continent; in the Spanish peninsula, 1588–97; offended the patriotism of the majority of English catholics by his conduct in inciting Philip II to attack England, and by his violent treatises written from a place of safety; drew down on them suspicions of treason, which most of them did not deserve; appointed rector of the English College at Rome, 1597, where he died. His published works, chiefly controversial pamphlets, are over thirty in number.   [xliii. 411]

PARSONS, ROBERT (1647–1714), archdeacon of Gloucester; M.A. University College, Oxford, 1670; patronised by the family of John Wilmot, second earl of Rochester [q. v.], whose funeral sermon (frequently republished) he preached.   [xliii. 418]

PARSONS, SIR WILLIAM, first baronet (1570 ?–1650), lord justice of Ireland; came to Ireland as assistant to his uncle, Sir Geoffrey Fenton [q. v.], and in 1602 succeeded him as surveyor-general; obtained numerous grants of land; took an active part in the plantation of Ulster (1610), Wexford (1618), Longford (1619), and Leitrim (1620); privy councillor, 1623; M.P., co. Wicklow, 1639; appointed lord justice, 1640; has been accused of stimulating the rebellion to obtain 'a new crop of confiscations'; retired to England, where he met with a cold reception, 1648.   [xliii. 419]

PARSONS, WILLIAM (1658–1725 ?), chronologer; of Christ Church, Oxford; lieutenant-colonel in the English army, 1687; published valuable 'Chronological Tables of Europe,' 1707.   [xliii. 421]

PARSONS, WILLIAM (1736–1795), actor; first acted in the provinces, appearing in 1762 at Drury Lane Theatre, London, with which he was all his life associated; popularly known as the comic Roscius; excelled in the *rôle* of old man.   [xliii. 421]

PARSONS, WILLIAM (*fl.* 1785–1807), poet; was one of the 'knot of fantastic coxcombs' who wrote verse for the 'World'; published several volumes of bad poetry.
[xliii. 424]

PARSONS, SIR WILLIAM (1746 ?–1817), professor of music; Mus. Doc. Oxford, 1790; master of the king's band, 1786; knighted, 1795.   [xliii. 424]

PARSONS, WILLIAM, third EARL OF ROSSE (1800–1867), astronomer; son of Sir Lawrence Parsons, second earl of Rosse [q. v.]; of Trinity College, Dublin, and Magdalen College, B.A., 1822; M.P., King's County, 1823–34; commenced experiments for improving the reflecting telescope, 1827; began to make observations with his great telescope (1845) erected at Parsonstown in King's County; discovered spiral nebulæ and detected a complex annular structure in many of the 'planetary' kind; elected to the House of Lords, 1845.   [xliii. 425]

PARTINGTON, CHARLES FREDERICK (d. 1857 ?), scientific writer; wrote and edited popular manuals and lectures on scientific subjects.   [xliii. 427]

PARTRIDGE, JOHN (*fl.* 1566–1573), translator and poet; translated into English verse several well-known romances.   [xliii. 427]

PARTRIDGE, JOHN (1644–1715), astrologer and almanac-maker; originally a shoemaker; began to publish astrological calendars, 1678, his almanac, 'Merlinus Liberatus,' first appearing in 1680; an almanac predicting his death, and a pamphlet and epitaph chronicling the fulfilment of the prophecy issued by Swift under the name of Isaac Bickerstaff, 1708; spent the rest of his days attempting, without much success, to demonstrate that he was still alive.   [xliii. 428]

PARTRIDGE, JOHN (1790–1872), portrait-painter; settled in London, 1827; became, under the patronage of Queen Victoria and Prince Albert, a fashionable portrait-painter.   [xliii. 430]

PARTRIDGE, JOSEPH (1724–1796), author; master of the free grammar school at Acton, Cheshire; published miscellaneous works.   [xliii. 431]

PARTRIDGE, SIR MILES (d. 1552), courtier; a follower of Somerset; fought at Pinkie, 1547; knighted, 1547; accused of plotting against Northumberland and hanged.   [xliii. 431]

PARTRIDGE, PARTRICHE, or **PERTRICH**, PETER (d. 1451), chancellor of Lincoln Cathedral, 1424; B.D. Oxford; sent on an embassy to the king of Aragon and king of the Romans, 1428; represented the English clergy at Basle, 1432.   [xliii. 431]

PARTRIDGE, RICHARD (1805–1873), surgeon; brother of John Partridge (1790–1872) [q. v.]; F.R.S., 1837; held all the chief posts at the Royal College of Surgeons; surgeon at King's College Hospital, London, 1840–70.   [xliii. 432]

PARTRIDGE, SETH (1603–1686), mathematical writer; wrote a couple of practical works to assist surveyors.   [xliii. 433]

PARVUS, JOHN (d. 1180). [See JOHN OF SALISBURY.]

PARYS, WILLIAM (d. 1609), author; M.A. Peterhouse, Cambridge, 1589; master of St. Olave's grammar school, Southwark, 1595–1609; probably the 'W. P.' who wrote or translated between 1580 and 1598.
[xliii. 433]

PASCHAL, JOHN (d. 1361), bishop of Llandaff; D.D. Cambridge, 1333; bishop of Llandaff, 1347–61; wrote several homilies (a copy in the British Museum).
[xliii. 434]

PASCO, JOHN (1774–1853), rear-admiral; was Nelson's signal officer at Trafalgar, and made the famous signal ('England expects,' &c.) before the battle, 1805; promoted to flag rank, 1847.   [xliii. 434]

PASCOE, FRANCIS POLKINGHORNE (1813–1893), entomologist; M.R.C.S., 1835; formed a great collection, now in the Natural History Museum at South Kensington.
[xliii. 435]

PASFIELD or **PASHFIELD**, ROBERT (*fl.* 1590), servant of John Bruen [q. v.]; had a leathern girdle, which, being marked into portions for the several books of the bible, with points and knots for the smaller divisions, served him as a *memoria technica*.   [vii. 139]

PASHE or **PASCHE**, WILLIAM (*fl.* 1500 ?), musical composer; manuscript compositions by him at Cambridge.   [xliii. 435]

PASHLEY, ROBERT (1805–1859), barrister and traveller; fellow of Trinity College, Cambridge, 1830; M.A., 1832; barrister, 1837; published 'Travels in Crete' (1837), having toured in Asia Minor, Crete, and Greece, 1833.   [xliii. 436]

PASKE, THOMAS (d. 1662), royalist divine; fellow of Clare Hall, Cambridge, 1603–12; master, 1621; B.A., 1606; D.D., 1621; deprived by parliament of the mastership of Clare Hall, Cambridge, the archdeaconry of London, and other preferments, some of which (including the mastership) he recovered at the Restoration.
[xliii. 436]

PASLEY, CHARLES (1824–1890), major-general, royal engineers; eldest son of Sir Charles William Pasley [q. v.]; colonial engineer for Victoria, 1853; nominated to a seat in the legislative council of the colony of Victoria, 1854; helped to suppress the serious disturbances that broke out in the goldfields of Ballarat, 1854; took office in the ministry as commissioner of public works, Victoria having become a self-governing colony, 1855; served in New Zealand against the Maoris, 1860; director of engineering works and architecture to the admiralty, 1873–82; C.B., 1880; retired as major-general, 1881.
[xliii. 437]

PASLEY, SIR CHARLES WILLIAM (1780–1861), general; served in Minorca, Malta, Naples, Sicily, Spain, and Holland between 1799 and 1809; first captain, 1807; F.R.S., 1816; introduced (1811), while in command of the Plymouth company of military artificers, a course of instruction for non-commissioned officers in military engineering, which developed in 1812 into the formation of the establishment for field instruction at Chatham; director, 1812–41; organised, during his tenure of office, improved systems of telegraphing, sapping, mining, pontooning, and exploding gunpowder on land and in water; K.C.B., 1846; general, 1860; published treatises on subjects connected with military engineering.   [xliii. 439]

PASLEY, SIR THOMAS, first baronet (1734–1808), admiral; saw much service in North America and the West Indies; bore a distinguished part in the battle of 1 June 1794; created baronet, 1794; admiral, 1801.
[xliii. 442]

PASLEY, SIR THOMAS SABINE, second baronet (1804–1884), admiral; grandson of Sir Thomas Pasley, first baronet [q. v.], whom he succeeded by special provision; rear-admiral, 1856; vice-admiral, 1863; admiral, 1866; K.C.B., 1873. [xliii. 442]

PASOR, MATTHIAS (1599–1658), mathematician, linguist, and theologian; born in Nassau; M.A. Heidelberg, 1617, professor of philosophy there, 1619, and professor of mathematics, 1620; settled at Oxford, 1624; incorporated M.A.; reader of Arabic, Chaldee, and Syriac, Oxford, 1626; removed (1629) to Groningen, where he held two professorships; died at Groningen. [xliii. 443]

PASS (**VAN DE PAS** or **PASSE, PASSÆUS**), SIMON (1595?–1647), engraver; son of Crispin van de Pas, a famous engraver of Utrecht; practised in England, but (1622) removed to Copenhagen. [xliii. 443]

PASS, WILLIAM (1598?–1637?), engraver; brother of Simon Pass [q. v.]; settled in London, 1621.
[xliii. 444]

PASSELEWE or **PASSELE**, EDMUND DE (d. 1327), baron of the exchequer; a justice of assize from 1309; baron of the exchequer, 1323. [xliii. 444]

PASSELEWE or **PASSELEU**, ROBERT (d. 1252), deputy-treasurer; a clerk of Falkes de Breauté [q. v.]; became a favourite of Henry III and deputy-treasurer, 1232; was dismissed, 1234, but made his peace, 1235; elected bishop of Chichester, 1244, but rejected by Boniface of Savoy [q. v.], who declared the election void.
[xliii. 444]

PASSELEWE, SIMON (fl. 1237–1269), baron of the exchequer; probably brother of Robert Passelewe [q. v.]; employed by Henry III to raise money, nominally by way of loans, 1258; envoy in France, 1263, 1265, and 1268; baron of the exchequer, 1267–8. [xliii. 446]

PASTON, CLEMENT (1515?–1597), sea-captain; son of Sir William Paston (1479?–1554) [q. v.]; commanded the Pelican and captured Baron St. Blanchard in a French galley, 1546; sheriff of Norfolk, 1588. [xliv. 1]

PASTON, EDWARD (1641–1714), president of Douay College; entered Douay, 1651 (D.D., 1681); president, 1688.
[xliv. 2]

PASTON, JOHN (1421–1466), letter-writer and country gentleman; son of William Paston [q. v.]; of Peterhouse, Cambridge, and the Inner Temple; friend of Sir John Fastolf [q. v.], on whose death he produced a doubtful will, by which he inherited his estates; spent the rest of his life in maintaining his hold on the estates against the Dukes of Norfolk and Suffolk. [xliv. 2]

PASTON, SIR JOHN (1442–1479), courtier and letter-writer; eldest son of John Paston [q. v.]; possibly educated at Cambridge; knighted, 1463; obtained royal recognition of his rights to the Fastolf estates on his father's death, 1466; fought for the Nevilles at Barnet, but was pardoned and again taken into favour; subsequently became involved in financial difficulties, which ended in a sacrifice of part of his estates to satisfy rival claimants. [xliv. 3]

PASTON, SIR ROBERT, second baronet and first EARL OF YARMOUTH (1631–1683), descended from Sir William Paston (1528–1610) [q. v.]; of Westminster School and Trinity College, Cambridge; M.P., Castle Rising, 1661–1673; succeeded as baronet, 1663; a friend of Charles II, whom he entertained in 1676 at his seat, Oxnead; created Viscount Yarmouth, 1673, Earl of Yarmouth, 1679.
[xliv. 5]

PASTON, WILLIAM (1378–1444), judge; one of the small gentry of Norfolk; a serjeant-at-law, 1421; justice of common pleas, 1429. His conduct on the bench earned him the honourable title of the 'Good Judge,' and a place among Fuller's 'Worthies.' [xliv. 5]

PASTON, SIR WILLIAM (1479?–1554), lawyer and courtier; educated at Cambridge University; bred to the law, but chiefly known as a courtier; a commissioner of array for Norfolk, 1511; knighted before 1520; present at the reception of the Emperor Charles V and at the Field of the Cloth of Gold, 1520. [xliv. 7]

PASTON, SIR WILLIAM (1528–1610), founder of North Walsham grammar school; son of Sir William Paston (1479?–1554) [q. v.]; knighted, 1578; benefactor of Caius College, Cambridge. [xliv. 8]

PASTON, SIR WILLIAM, third baronet and second EARL OF YARMOUTH (1652–1732), son of Sir Robert Paston, first earl of Yarmouth [q. v.]; treasurer of the household, 1686–9. [xliv. 5]

PASTORINI, BENEDICT (BENEDETTO) (fl. 1775–1810), draughtsman and engraver; a native of Italy; obtained employment in England as a decorator of ceilings. [xliv. 8]

PASTORIUS, FRANCIS DANIEL (1651–1719?), New England settler; born at Sommerhausen, Franconia; doctor of law, Nuremberg, 1676; became a quaker, and (1683) conducted a colony of German and Dutch Mennonites and quakers to Pennsylvania, where they founded Germantown; drew up the first protest (1688) against negro slavery made by a religious body; published ecclesiological works, and left many manuscripts. [xliv. 8]

PATCH, RICHARD (1770?–1806), criminal; executed in Horsemonger Lane, London, for the murder of his employer, Isaac Blight, a ship-breaker; numerous accounts of his trial published. [xliv. 9]

PATCH, THOMAS (d. 1782), printer and engraver; famous for his work in connection with early Florentine art, publishing many valuable engravings of frescoes.
[xliv. 10]

PATE, **PATES**, or **PATYS**, RICHARD (d. 1565), bishop of Worcester; B.A. Corpus Christi College, Oxford, 1523; M.A. Paris; made archdeacon of Worcester in 1526 and received other preferments; ambassador to Charles V, 1533–6; 'provided' to the see of Worcester by Paul III, 1541; attended the council of Trent (1547, 1549, 1551); during Edward VI's reign remained in banishment, but was consecrated bishop, 1554; deprived and imprisoned, 1559; died at Louvain in exile. [xliv. 10]

PATE, RICHARD (1516–1588), educational benefactor; scholar of Corpus Christi College, Oxford; founded Cheltenham grammar school, 1586. [xliv. 12]

PATE, WILLIAM (1666–1746), 'the learned woollen-draper'; friend of Steele, Swift, and Arbuthnot, and a familiar figure in the literary society of his time; sheriff of the city, 1734. [xliv. 12]

PATER, WALTER HORATIO (1839–1894), critic and humanist; descended from a family of Dutch extraction; B.A. Queen's College, Oxford, 1862; fellow of Brasenose College, Oxford, 1864, and M.A., 1865; became associated with the pre-Raphaelites, particularly with Mr. Swinburne, 1869; published (1873) 'Studies in the History of the Renaissance' and (1885) 'Marius the Epicurean,' the latter written to illustrate the highest ideal of the æsthetic life. He possessed all the qualities of a humanist.
[xliv. 13]

PATERNUS (fl. 550). [See PADARN.]

PATERSON. [See also PATTERSON.]

PATERSON, ALEXANDER (1766–1831), Scottish catholic prelate; consecrated bishop of Cybistra in partibus, 1816; vicar-apostolic of the Lowland district, 1825. [xliv. 15]

PATERSON, CHARLES WILLIAM (1756–1841), admiral; saw much service in the West Indies; admiral, 1837. [xliv. 16]

PATERSON, DANIEL (1739–1825), author of 'The Road Book'; entered the army and (1798) became lieutenant-colonel; nominated lieutenant-governor of Quebec, 1812; published (1771) 'A New and Accurate Description of all the Direct and Principal Cross Roads in Great Britain' (eighteenth edition, 1829). [xliv. 16]

PATERSON, EMMA ANNE (1848–1886), organiser of trade unions among women; née Smith; married Thomas Paterson, 1873; founded the Women's Protective and Provident League, 1874, which promoted women's unions in London and elsewhere. She was (1875) the first woman admitted to the Trade Union Congress.
[xliv. 17]

PATERSON, JAMES (1805–1876), antiquary and miscellaneous writer; journalist; contributed most of the biographies to Kay's 'Edinburgh Portraits' (1837–9).
[xliv. 18]

PATERSON, JOHN (1604?–1679), bishop of Ross; graduated at Aberdeen, 1624; consecrated bishop, 1662.
[xliv. 18]

PATERSON, JOHN (1632–1708), last archbishop of Glasgow; eldest son of John Paterson (1604?–1679) [q. v.]; studied at St. Andrews and became minister of Ellon, 1660, of the Edinburgh Tron church, 1663, and of the Edinburgh High Kirk, 1672; appointed bishop of Galloway, 1674, through his patron, Lauderdale, and (1679) translated to Edinburgh; nominated to Glasgow, 1687; actively engaged in all the intolerant measures of the government, and opposed, until the accession of James II, the granting of all indulgences; adhering to James II, was banished from Scotland before 1695; restored in Queen Anne's reign. His character was painted by his opponents in the blackest colours. [xliv. 18]

PATERSON, JOHN (1776–1855), missionary; studied at Glasgow University; became a missionary in Denmark, 1804, removing to Stockholm, 1807, and to St. Petersburg, 1812; treated with great kindness and granted a pension for life by the Emperor of Russia; returning to Edinburgh, 1825, was many years Scottish secretary of the London Missionary Society. [xliv. 20]

PATERSON, NATHANIEL (1787–1871), author; grandson of Robert Paterson [q. v.]; of Edinburgh University; minister of Galashiels, 1821, went out at the disruption, removed to Free St. Andrews, Glasgow, and (1850) was moderator of the Free Church of Scotland; D.D.; friend of Sir Walter Scott. [xliv. 21]

PATERSON, ROBERT (1715–1801), 'Old Mortality,' Cameronian stone-cutter; for over forty years employed himself in repairing the memorials placed over covenanters' graves; the original of Scott's 'Old Mortality.' [xliv. 22]

PATERSON, SAMUEL (1728–1802), bookseller and auctioneer; carried on his business in Covent Garden and was one of the first in England to produce good catalogues for book sales; had a great acquaintance with literature, and published several books. Dr. Johnson was godfather to his son. [xliv. 22]

PATERSON, THOMAS (1780–1856), lieutenant-general; served in the Napoleonic wars; lieutenant-general, 1854. [xliv. 23]

PATERSON, WILLIAM (1658–1719), founder of the Bank of England; born in Dumfriesshire, but bred in England from infancy; made money by trade, and in 1681 became a member of the Merchant Taylors' Company; by 1691, having acquired great influence in the city and a considerable fortune, proposed to establish the Bank of England, pointing out at the same time the necessity of restoring the currency; became a director on the foundation of the bank, 1694; considered the scope of the bank's operations too narrow, and in 1695 withdrew on a difference with his colleagues and matured the scheme, which he first conceived in 1684, of establishing a colony at Darien; accompanied the Darien expedition, 1698, but had little influence in the conduct of affairs, which were entrusted to seven councillors, who quarrelled among themselves; returned in December, 1699; from 1701 urged upon government the financial measures which became the basis of 'Walpole's Sinking Fund,' and the great scheme of 1717 for the consolidation and conversion of the national debt; actively promoted the union, and assisted in framing the articles of the treaty; published political and economic treatises. [xliv. 23]

PATERSON, WILLIAM (1755–1810), traveller and lieutenant-governor of New South Wales; travelled in South Africa between 1777 and 1779, and published an account of his journeys, 1789; had entered the army at an early age, and (1789) was one of the lieutenants chosen to recruit and command a company of the corps formed to protect the new convict settlement at Botany Bay; proceeded to New South Wales, 1791; sent (1804) to Port Dalrymple in Tasmania as lieutenant-governor, and (1809) administered the government at Sydney after the deposition of William Bligh [q. v.]; died on the voyage home. [xliv. 26]

PATESHULL, HUGH DE (d. 1241), bishop of Coventry and Lichfield; son of Simon de Pateshull [q. v.]; treasurer of the kingdom, 1234; elected bishop, 1239. [xliv. 28]

PATESHULL, SIR JOHN DE (1291?–1349), knight; sat in the parliament of 1342. [xliv. 30]

PATESHULL, MARTIN DE (d. 1229), judge and dean of London; sat as a justice at Westminster, 1217; dean of London, 1228. [xliv. 28]

PATESHULL, PETER (fl. 1387), theological writer; an Augustinian friar, who attacked his order in a set of theses nailed to the door of St. Paul's, London, 1387. [xliv. 29]

PATESHULL or **PATTISHALL**, SIMON DE (d. 1217?), judge; chief-justice of the common pleas division of the king's court during King John's reign. [xliv. 29]

PATESHULL or **PATTISHALL**, SIR SIMON DE (d. 1274), judge and knight; son or grandson of Simon de Pateshull [q. v.]; a king's justice, 1257; joined the baronial party. [xliv. 30]

PATESHULL, WALTER DE (d. 1232), judge; itinerant justice for Bedfordshire, Buckinghamshire, and other counties, 1218. [xliv. 30]

PATEY, CHARLES GEORGE EDWARD (1813–1881), admiral; administrator of Lagos (1866) and governor of St. Helena (1869–73); C.M.G., 1874; admiral, 1877. [xliv. 30]

PATEY, JANET MONACH (1842–1894), contralto singer; née Whytock; married John George Patey, 1866; became the principal English contralto on the retirement of Madame Sainton-Dolby in 1870; known as the English Alboni. [xliv. 31]

PATIENT or **PATIENCE**, THOMAS (d. 1666), divine; proceeded to New England between 1630 and 1635, where he became a baptist; returned (1644) to England, and was chosen assistant to William Kiffin [q. v.]; appointed by parliament 'to dispense the gospel in the city of Dublin,' 1649, returning to England, 1660; died of the plague in London, 1666. [xliv. 31]

PATIN, WILLIAM (fl. 1548–1580). [See PATTEN.]

PATMORE, COVENTRY KERSEY DIGHTON (1823–1896), poet; son of Peter George Patmore [q. v.]; educated privately; published volume of poems, 1844; assistant in printed book department, British Museum, 1846; formed intimate relations with Tennyson and Ruskin, and (1849) made acquaintance of the pre-Raphaelite group, to whose organ, 'The Germ,' he contributed; promoted volunteer movement, 1851; published 'Tamerton Church Tower,' 1853; issued 'The Betrothal,' 1854, 'The Espousals,' 1856, 'Faithful for Ever,' 1860, and 'The Victories of Love,' 1862—the four poems forming parts of 'The Angel in the House,' a long poem designed to be the apotheosis of married love; became Roman catholic, 1864; published 'The Unknown Eros and other Odes,' 1877, 'Amelia,' 1878; his collected poetical works published, with an appendix on English metrical law, 1886; contributed to 'St. James's Gazette,' from c. 1885, articles subsequently published under titles 'Principle in Art,' 1889, and 'Religio Poetæ,' 1893; his 'Rod, Root, and Flower,' observations and meditations chiefly on religious subjects, published, 1895. [Suppl. iii. 249]

PATMORE, HENRY JOHN (1860–1883), poet; son of Coventry Kersey Dighton Patmore [q. v.]; educated at Ushaw College; a selection from his lyrics published privately. [Suppl. iii. 252]

PATMORE, PETER GEORGE (1786–1855), author; edited the 'New Monthly Magazine,' 1841–53; best known by his 'Imitations of Celebrated Authors' (1826) and his 'My Friends and Acquaintances' (1854). [xliv. 33]

PATON, ANDREW ARCHIBALD (1811–1874), author and diplomatist; employed in several minor diplomatic offices; consul at Ragusa and Bocca di Cattaro, 1862; published books of travel. [xliv. 33]

PATON, DAVID (fl. 1650–1700), painter; executed portraits and medallions. [xliv. 34]

PATON, GEORGE (1721–1807), bibliographer and antiquary; clerk in the custom-house; amassed an extensive antiquarian library and a valuable collection of antiquities by frugal living. Two volumes of his correspondence were privately printed (1829–30). [xliv. 34]

PATON, JAMES (d. 1596), bishop of Dunkeld; consecrated, 1572, and deprived for simony, c. 1581, after resisting the decrees of the general assembly for over five years; privy councillor, 1575. [xliv. 35]

PATON, JAMES (d. 1684), covenanter; fought against Montrose at Kilsyth, 1645, and for Charles II at Worcester, 1651; fought for the covenanters at Rullion Green, 1666, and Bothwell Bridge, 1679; taken, 1684, and hanged at Edinburgh. [xliv. 35]

PATON, JOHN STAFFORD (1821–1889), general in the Indian army; served against the Sikhs in 1845–6 and 1848–9, being severely wounded at Chillianwallah; fought against the Afridis, 1850, and (1857) commanded the field detachment from Lahore sent to aid in suppressing the Gogaira insurrection; C.B., 1873. [xliv. 36]

PATON, MARY ANN, afterwards MRS. WOOD (1802–1864), vocalist; appeared in public at the age of eight; joined the Haymarket company, 1822; married (1824) Lord William Pitt Lennox [q. v.], whom she divorced in 1831, marrying Joseph Wood in the same year; from 1826 she was considered first in her profession as a soprano. [xliv. 36]

PATON, RICHARD (1716?–1791), marine painter; executed numerous pictures of naval engagements. [xliv. 37]

PATON, WALLER HUGH (1828–1895), Scottish landscape-painter; member of the Royal Scottish Academy, 1857, contributing yearly to its exhibition from 1851. [xliv. 38]

PATRICK (373–463), saint and bishop, originally named Sucat; born in Ailclyde, now Dumbarton, and was captured in a raid of the Picts and Scots, 389; sold to Miliuc, a chieftain of Antrim; after six years of bondage proceeded to Gaul and studied under Martin of Tours; returned to his parents in Britain, and felt a supernatural call to go and preach to the heathen Irish; after episcopal consecration landed in Wicklow, 405, accompanied by a missionary party, but meeting with a hostile reception proceeded up the east coast to Strangford Lough; remained at Strangford Lough until he had converted all the Ulstermen; subsequently journeyed through Ireland, preaching Christianity; founded, near Armagh, his first mission settlement; probably died in 463, though there is much discussion as to the date; according to St. Bernard, was buried at Armagh, pilgrimages being afterwards made to the place. His extant works are the 'Epistles,' consisting of the 'Confession,' the letter to Coroticus, and an Irish hymn, all of which are considered genuine. At a later time these and the early life by Muirchu [q. v.] were all tampered with, chiefly by way of excision, to bring them into conformity with the elaborated life of the apostle, according to which legendary foreign experiences delayed his arrival in Ireland till he was sixty years old. When the Irish came in contact with Augustine of Canterbury it was felt that the learning and culture of the Roman missionaries contrasted too strongly with the Irish saint's absence of pretension. Hence a spirit of national pride ascribing to him a learning he never claimed and a Roman mission of which he knew nothing, protracted his stay in Gaul and extended his travels to Italy. [xliv. 38]

PATRICK (d. 1084), bishop of Dublin; consecrated in London by Lanfranc, 1074. [xliv. 43]

PATRICK, JOHN (1632–1695), protestant controversialist; grandson of Simon Patrick (d. 1613) [q. v.]; M.A. Peterhouse, Cambridge, 1671; preacher of the Charterhouse, London, from 1671–95; prebendary of Peterborough, 1685–95; distinguished himself as a champion of protestantism in the time of James II. His works, almost all anonymous, are noteworthy, and include, besides controversial treatises, 'A Century of Select Psalms,' 1679, which were in high repute among many dissenting congregations. [xliv. 43]

PATRICK, RICHARD (1769–1815), classical scholar and divine; M.A. Magdalene College, Cambridge, 1808; vicar of Sculcoates, Hull, from 1794. [xliv. 44]

PATRICK, ROBERT WILLIAM COCHRAN- (1842–1897). [See COCHRAN-PATRICK.]

PATRICK, SAMUEL (1684–1748), scholar; for some years usher at Charterhouse; edited several Latin works. [xliv. 44]

PATRICK, SIMON (d. 1613), translator; a landed proprietor of Caistor in Lincolnshire; translated two works from the French. [xliv. 45]

PATRICK, SIMON (1626–1707), successively bishop of Chichester and Ely, grandson of Simon Patrick (d. 1613) [q. v.]; M.A. Queens' College, Cambridge, 1651; D.D., 1666; vicar of Battersea, 1658–62; rector of St. Paul's, Covent Garden, London, 1662–89; elected (1661) president of Queens' College, Cambridge, but his appointment overridden by a royal mandate; made a royal chaplain, 1671, and, 1672, presented to a prebend at Westminster; dean of Peterborough, 1679; consecrated bishop of Chichester, 1689; translated to Ely, 1691; one of the chief instruments in the revival of church life which marked the late years of the seventeenth century; was one of the five original founders of the Society for the Promotion of Christian Knowledge, and took a warm interest in the Society for the Propagation of the Gospel; a voluminous writer in polemical theology, scriptural exegesis, and edificatory literature. In 1719 appeared a volume of 'Poems upon Divine and Moral Subjects,' to which he had contributed. [xliv. 45]

PATRINGTON, STEPHEN (d. 1417), bishop of Chichester; educated at Oxford; entered the Carmelite order, of which he was chosen provincial in 1399; a leading opponent of the lollards; consecrated bishop of St. David's, 1415; translated to Chichester, 1417. [xliv. 47]

PATTEN, GEORGE (1801–1865), portrait and historical painter; portrait-painter in ordinary to Prince Albert. [xliv. 48]

PATTEN, JOHN WILSON-, BARON WINMARLEIGH (1802–1892). [See WILSON-PATTEN.]

PATTEN, ROBERT (fl. 1715–1717), historian of the Jacobite rebellion of 1715; curate of Allendale; joined the insurgents and afterwards turned king's evidence. His history appeared in 1717. [xliv. 49]

PATTEN, THOMAS (1714–1790), divine; of Brasenose and Corpus Christi Colleges, Oxford; fellow of Corpus Christi College, Oxford; M.A., 1737; D.D., 1754; rector of Childrey; friend of Dr. Johnson. [xliv. 49]

PATTEN, WILLIAM (1395?–1486). [See WAYNFLETE.]

PATTEN, WILLIAM (fl. 1548–1580), historian and teller of the exchequer; accompanied the expedition into Scotland, 1548, and by Earl Warwick, lieutenant of the host, was made 'one of the judges of the Marshelsey'; published an account of the expedition in June, 1549, and subsequently held various offices, including that of receiver-general of Queen Elizabeth's revenues in the county of York. [xliv. 50]

PATTESON, MATTHEW (fl. 1623), Roman catholic controversialist; published 'The Image of Bothe Churches, Hiervsalem and Babel' (1623); physician in ordinary to Charles I. [xliv. 50]

PATTERSON. [See also PATERSON.]

PATTERSON, SIR JAMES BROWNE (1833–1895), Australian statesman; emigrated to Victoria, 1852; conducted business of slaughterman at Chewton, Castlemaine district; member of legislative assembly for Castlemaine, 1870, till death; commissioner of public works and president of board of land and works, 1875 and 1877–80; postmaster-general, 1877–80 and 1890; minister of railways, 1880–1, and of customs, 1889–90; minister of public works, 1890; premier and minister of railways, 1893–4; K.C.M.G., 1894. [Suppl. iii. 252]

PATTERSON, JOHN BROWN (1804–1835), divine; became minister of Falkirk, 1829; his discourses published in two volumes, 1837. [xliv. 51]

PATTERSON, ROBERT (1802–1872), naturalist; a Belfast merchant; founded the 'Natural History Society of Belfast,' 1821, being its president for many years. His zoological works had a wide circulation. [xliv. 51]

PATTERSON, ROBERT HOGARTH (1821–1886), journalist and miscellaneous writer; became editor of the 'Edinburgh Advertiser,' 1852, of the London 'Press,' 1858, of the 'Globe,' 1865, of the 'Glasgow News,' 1872. [xliv. 52]

PATTERSON, WILLIAM (1755–1810). [See PATERSON.]

PATTESON, SIR JOHN (1790–1861), judge; M.A. King's College, Cambridge, 1816; barrister, Middle Temple

1821 ; appointed judge in the court of king's bench and knighted, 1830 ; resigned, 1852 ; frequently chosen arbitrator in government questions. [xliv. 53]

PATTESON, JOHN COLERIDGE (1827–1871), first missionary bishop in Melanesia ; elder son of Sir John Patteson [q. v.] ; B.A. Balliol College, Oxford, 1849 ; fellow of Merton College, Oxford, 1852 ; became a missionary in Melanesia, 1855, under the influence of George Augustus Selwyn (1809–1878) [q. v.] ; consecrated bishop in 1861, fixing his residence at Mota ; greatly aided by linguistic powers, which enabled him to speak readily twenty-three languages ; reclaimed the natives from savagery ; killed at Nukapu in September 1871, in revenge for the kidnapping practised by the traders to supply labour in Fiji and Queensland. His death led to an attempt in England to regulate the labour traffic. [xliv. 53]

PATTI, CARLOTTA (1835–1889), vocalist ; born at Florence ; sister of Adelina Patti ; made her first appearance (1861) at New York ; attained great fame as singer, retiring (1879) on her marriage to M. Ernest de Munck ; possessed a voice of abnormal compass, extending to G in altissimo. [xliv. 56]

PATTINSON, HUGH LEE (1796–1858), metallurgical chemist ; patented a process for desilverising lead, 1833, which rendered it profitable to extract silver when only present in the proportion of two or three ounces to the ton, the previous limit being eight ounces. [xliv. 56]

PATTISON, DOROTHY WYNDLOW, known as SISTER DORA (1832–1878), philanthropist ; sister of Mark Pattison [q. v.] ; became a member of the sisterhood of the Good Samaritan at Coatham, 1864 ; was an excellent surgical nurse, and indefatigable in ministering to the sick and unfortunate ; left the sisterhood to take charge of a hospital at Walsall, 1877. [xliv. 57]

PATTISON, GRANVILLE SHARP (1791–1851), anatomist ; professor of anatomy in the University of London, and afterwards in the University of New York (1840–51). [xliv. 58]

PATTISON, MARK (1813–1884), rector of Lincoln College, Oxford ; B.A. Oriel College, Oxford, 1836 ; fellow of Lincoln College, Oxford, 1839 ; M.A., 1840 ; tutor, 1843 ; for a time an ardent follower of Newman and Pusey, and in 1838–9 lived with other young men in Newman's house in St. Aldate's, Oxford, and aided in the translation of Thomas Aquinas's 'Catena Aurea on the Gospels' ; acquired a high reputation as tutor and examiner ; gradually separated from his close connection with the high church party ; in 1851 failed to be elected rector of Lincoln College ; threw up his tutorship, 1855, on account of differences with the new rector, and for some years wrote largely, chiefly on educational subjects ; for three months Berlin correspondent of 'The Times,' 1858 ; appointed (1859) an assistant-commissioner to report upon continental education ; elected rector of Lincoln College, 1861, and continued his literary activity in a wider field ; took a less active part in college administration than might have been expected ; wrote for the 'Quarterly,' the 'North British,' and other reviews, and was an occasional contributor to 'The Times' ; dictated (1883) his 'Memoirs' reaching to 1860, comparable for their introspection only to Rousseau's 'Confessions.' He collected much material for a life of Joseph Scaliger, and published (1875) a life of Isaac Casaubon (2nd edit. 1892). [xliv. 58]

PATTISON, WILLIAM (1706–1727), poet ; commenced to work in London as an author in 1726 ; died of small-pox in great poverty in the house of Curll the bookseller. Pope accused Curll of starving him. His 'Poetical Works' appeared, 1728. [xliv. 63]

PATTON, CHARLES (1741–1837), post-captain ; brother of Philip Patton [q. v.] ; published two abstract political treatises on the nature of freedom and on a project for basing representation upon property.
[xliv. 66]

PATTON, GEORGE, LORD GLENALMOND (1803–1869), Scottish judge ; studied law at Edinburgh ; conservative M.P., Bridgewater, 1866 ; lord advocate, 1866 ; appointed himself lord justice clerk, 1867, partly to avoid an inquiry into charges of bribery in connection with his election to parliament ; committed suicide. [xliv. 64]

PATTON, PHILIP (1739–1815), admiral ; overcame by his firmness, while acting captain of the Prince George,

a mutiny of the ship's company, 1779 ; rear-admiral, 1795 ; vice-admiral, 1801 ; admiral, 1805. [xliv. 65]

PATTON, ROBERT (1742–1812), brother of Philip Patton ; entered the army of the East India Company ; governor of St. Helena ; wrote two elaborate historical treatises upon the 'Monarchy and Republic of Rome' (1797) and upon 'Principles of Asiatic Monarchies' (1803). [xliv. 66]

PATTRICK or **PATRICK**, GEORGE (1746–1800), divine ; of Sidney Sussex College, Cambridge ; LL.B., 1777 ; filled several small preferments ; popular as a preacher in London. [xliv. 66]

PATYS, RICHARD (d. 1565). [See PATE.]

PAUL or **POL** (d. 573), saint ; also called AURELIAN, bishop of Léon in Brittany ; said to have been born in Cornwall or Wales ; consecrated probably in 512 ; built several monasteries, and died in retirement as a hermit in the island of Batz. [xliv. 67]

PAUL (d. 1093), abbot of St. Albans ; according to tradition a son of Lanfranc [q. v.] ; appointed abbot, 1077 ; built the existing abbey ; despised the English monks, and destroyed the tombs of his English predecessors, declaring that they were ignorant and uncultivated ; neglected to translate the bones of the founder of his house, Offa, king of Mercia, to his new church ; died soon after taking possession of a church at Tynemouth granted to the abbey by Robert de Mowbray, earl of Northumberland [q. v.] ; his death regarded as a judgment by the monks of Durham, who claimed the church as their property. [xliv. 67]

PAUL, EARL OF ORKNEY (d. 1099), succeeded his father Torfinn, 1064, conjointly with his younger brother Erlend, but took the entire management of the earldom ; fought at Stamford Bridge on the side of Harald Hardradi ; sent by Magnus Barelegs a prisoner (1098) to Norway, where he died. [xliv. 68]

PAUL THE SILENT, EARL OF ORKNEY (fl. 1136), grandson of Paul, earl of Orkney [q. v.] ; ruled over the islands with his half-brother Harald, and afterwards alone ; forced by his second cousin Rognvald to divide his dominions with him, but immediately after (1136) was carried into captivity, from which he never returned, by Maddad, earl of Athole. [xliv. 69]

PAUL ANGLICUS (fl. 1404), canonist ; assailed the Roman church in the 'Aureum Speculum,' written in 1404, the work being well known in Germany prior to the Reformation (first published at Basle, 1555) ; described as 'Doctor Anglus.' [xliv. 70]

PAUL OF ST. MAGDALEN (1599–1643). [See HEATH, HENRY.]

PAUL, SIR GEORGE ONESIPHORUS, second baronet (1746–1820), philanthropist ; son of Sir Onesiphorus Paul, first baronet [q. v.] ; created M.A. St. John's College, Oxford, 1766 ; did much useful work in connection with the improvement of prisons in Gloucestershire.
[xliv. 70]

PAUL, HAMILTON (1773–1854), poet ; educated at Glasgow University ; minister of Broughton, Kilbucho, and Glenholm, 1813–54 ; wrote humorous poems, and edited the works of Burns, 1819. [xliv. 71]

PAUL, ISABELLA HOWARD (1833?–1879), actress and vocalist ; made her first appearance on the London stage as Isabella Featherstone, 1853 ; married Howard Paul, an actor, 1857 ; acted many parts, including Lady Macbeth, at Drury Lane, London, 1869. [xliv. 72]

PAUL, JOHN (1707–1787), legal author ; wrote several manuals of a popular type. [xliv. 72]

PAUL, JOHN (1777–1848), Irish divine ; of Glasgow University ; reformed presbyterian minister of Loughmourne from 1805 ; took a prominent part in the Arian controversy in the north of Ireland, defending the Calvinistic position. [xliv. 73]

PAUL, SIR JOHN DEAN, second baronet (1802–1868), banker ; belonged to the firm of William Strahan, Paul, and Robert Makin Bates, which suspended payment in 1855, on which the partners were severally sentenced to fourteen years' penal servitude, as they had fraudulently disposed of their clients' securities. [xliv. 73]

PAUL, LEWIS (*d.* 1759), inventor of spinning machinery; invented 'roller spinning,' for which he took out a patent, 1738; patented a carding-machine, 1748, and a spinning-machine, 1758.   [xliv. 74]

PAUL, Sir ONESIPHORUS, first baronet (1706–1774), woollen manufacturer at Woodchester, who introduced many improvements into the trade; created baronet, 1774.   [xliv. 70]

PAUL, ROBERT BATEMAN (1798–1877), miscellaneous writer; fellow of Exeter College, Oxford, 1817–1827; M.A., 1822; held various benefices; published miscellaneous works.   [xliv. 75]

PAUL, WILLIAM DE (*d.* 1349), bishop of Meath; D.D. Oxford; elected provincial of the Carmelites in England and Scotland, 1309; consecrated bishop of Meath, 1327, by John XXII at Avignon.   [xliv. 76]

PAUL, WILLIAM (1599–1665), bishop of Oxford; fellow, All Souls College, Oxford, 1618; M.A., 1621; D.D., 1632; became chaplain in ordinary to Charles I after the outbreak of the civil war, and lost his preferments; regained them at the Restoration; consecrated bishop of Oxford, 1663.   [xliv. 76]

PAUL, WILLIAM (1678–1716), Jacobite; M.A. St. John's College, Cambridge, 1705; vicar of Orton-on-the-Hill, 1709; joined the Pretender, 1715; taken in London and hanged.   [xliv. 77]

PAULDEN, THOMAS (1626–1710?), royalist; killed Thomas Rainborow [q. v.] at Doncaster, 1648, while attempting to take him prisoner by surprise; lived in poverty after the Restoration; published an account of his exploit at Doncaster, 1702.   [xliv. 78]

PAULE, Sir GEORGE (1563?–1637), registrar of the court of high commission; M.P., Downton, 1597, Hindon, 1601; for long a servant of Archbishop Whitgift, whose biography he published in 1612; knighted, 1607; became registrar of the court of high commission before 1625.   [xliv. 79]

PAULET or **POULET**, Sir AMIAS or AMYAS (*d.* 1538), soldier; attainted after Buckingham's rebellion in 1483; restored, 1485; knighted, 1487; served in France in Henry VIII's reign.   [xliv. 80]

PAULET or **POULET**, Sir AMIAS (1536?–1588), keeper of Mary Queen of Scots; son of Sir Hugh Paulet [q. v.]; lieutenant-governor of Jersey; knighted, 1576; ambassador to France, 1576–9; nominated keeper of Mary Queen of Scots, 1585, in spite of her protest against him on account of his puritanism and the dislike he had shown to her agents at Paris; had custody of Mary Queen of Scots at Tutbury, Chartley, and Fotheringay, repelled her attempts to gain him, and assisted in the inspection of her correspondence; acted as a commissioner on her trial, and after her condemnation vehemently urged her execution; declined, however, to act on Secretary Davison's suggestion that he might murder her privately; appointed chancellor of the order of the Garter, April 1587; sent as a commissioner to the Low Countries to discuss Queen Elizabeth's relations with the States-General, 1588.   [xliv. 81]

PAULET or **POWLETT**, CHARLES, first DUKE OF BOLTON and sixth MARQUIS OF WINCHESTER (1625?–1699), eldest son of John Paulet, fifth marquis of Winchester [q. v.]; strongly supported the whigs in the crisis of Charles II's reign; during the reign of James II counterfeited disorder of mind; actively supported William of Orange on his landing; created Duke of Bolton, 1689; considered by Burnet 'a very crafty politic man'; said to have caused Marlborough's disgrace, 1692, by revealing to William III a conversation he had had with him.   [xliv. 83]

PAULET or **POWLETT**, Sir CHARLES, second DUKE OF BOLTON and seventh MARQUIS OF WINCHESTER (1661–1722), son of Charles Paulet, first duke [q. v.]; joined William of Orange in Holland, 1688, took part in his English expedition, and filled several minor offices during the reigns of William III and Queen Anne; privy councillor, 1690; K.G., 1714; created lord chamberlain, 1715; lord-lieutenant of Ireland, 1717–22.   [xliv. 84]

PAULET or **POWLETT**, Sir CHARLES, third DUKE OF BOLTON, eighth MARQUIS OF WINCHESTER, and BARON

BASING (1685–1754), eldest son of Sir Charles Paulet, second duke of Bolton [q. v.]; was summoned to the House of Lords (1717) as Lord Basing; deprived of all his places (1733) on account of his persistent opposition to Walpole; married as his second wife (1751) Lavinia Fenton [q. v], the theatrical singer, who had previously been his mistress.   [xliv. 85]

PAULET, Sir GEORGE (*d.* 1608), governor of Derry; brother of Sir William Paulet, third marquis of Winchester [q. v.]; appointed governor, 1606; said to have insulted the Irish chieftain, Sir Cahir O'Dogherty [q. v.], and thereby driven him into rebellion; killed by O'Dogherty at the sack of Derry after a stormy administration.   [xliv. 86]

PAULET or **POWLETT**, HARRY, sixth DUKE OF BOLTON and eleventh MARQUIS OF WINCHESTER (1719–1794), admiral; nephew of Sir Charles Paulet, third duke of Bolton [q. v.]; served in the East Indies (1746–50), and on his return procured the suspension of Thomas Griffin (*d.* 1771) [q. v.] from the service on charges of misconduct; rear-admiral, 1756; vice-admiral, 1759; succeeded as Duke of Bolton, 1765; admiral, 1770; governor of the Isle of Wight, 1766–80 and 1782–94.   [xliv. 87]

PAULET, HARRY (*d.* 1804), master mariner; according to his own account brought information to England which led to Wolfe's expedition (1759) to Quebec, and afterwards gave Admiral Hawke news of the escape of Conflans. There is no evidence for his story.   [xliv. 88]

PAULET or **POULET**, Sir HUGH (*d.* 1572?), military commander and governor of Jersey; said to have been the eldest son of Sir Amias Paulet (*d.* 1538) [q. v]; captain of Jersey, 1550 till death; vice-president of the Welsh marches, 1559; present at the surrender of Havre to Queen Elizabeth, 1562, as adviser to the commander of the place, Ambrose Dudley, earl of Warwick [q. v.]; knight of the shire for Somerset, 1572.   [xliv. 89]

PAULET, Sir JOHN (*fl.* 1497–1501), soldier; a commander at the battle of Blackheath, 1497; K.B., 1501.   [xliv. 80]

PAULET, JOHN, fifth MARQUIS OF WINCHESTER (1598–1675), grandson of Sir William Paulet, third marquis of Winchester [q. v.]; kept terms at Exeter College, Oxford. His chief seat, Basing House, was the great resort of Queen Henrietta Maria's friends in south-west England. On the outbreak of the civil war he fortified and garrisoned Basing House and held it for Charles I during 1643 and 1644, until it was stormed by Cromwell in October 1645; thenceforth known as 'the great loyalist'; committed to the Tower of London on a charge of high treason, 1645, where he remained a long time; his property sequestered and partially sold; suffered to go unrecompensed at the Restoration, but regained his lands.   [xliv. 90]

PAULET, LAVINIA, DUCHESS OF BOLTON (1708–1760). [See FENTON.]

PAULET, PAWLET, or **POULET**, Sir WILLIAM, first MARQUIS OF WINCHESTER, first EARL OF WILTSHIRE, and first BARON ST. JOHN (1485?–1572), eldest son of Sir John Paulet [q. v.]; knighted before 1525; comptroller of the royal household, 1532; treasurer of the household, 1537 to March 1539, when the old St. John barony was revived in his favour; chamberlain of the household, 1543, and was great master (*i.e.* lord steward) of the same, 1545–50; became lord president of the council a year before Henry VIII's death, and was nominated by Henry VIII's will one of the council of regency; keeper of the great seal under Somerset (1547), but joined in overthrowing the Protector, and afterwards adhered to Northumberland's party; was, however, strongly opposed to the proclamation of Queen Jane, and on 19 July 1553 proclaimed Mary at Baynard's Castle; on Elizabeth's accession succeeded in obtaining her favour, and advocated a moderate foreign policy; disliked Cecil's projects, and was in sympathy with the intrigues of 1569 against the secretary; was treasurer from 1550 till his death; created earl, 1550, marquis, 1551.   [xliv. 92]

PAULET, Sir WILLIAM, third MARQUIS OF WINCHESTER (1535?–1598), grandson of Sir William Paulet, first marquis of Winchester [q. v.]; knighted before 1559; one of the commissioners to try Mary Queen of Scots, 1586, and lord steward of her funeral, 1587; published 'The Lord Marques Idlenes,' 1586 (2nd edit. 1587).   [xliv. 95]

PAULET, LORD WILLIAM (1804–1893), field-marshal; educated at Eton; commanded on the Bosphorus, at Gallipoli, and the Dardanelles during the Crimean war; field-marshal, 1886. [xliv. 95]

PAULINUS (*fl.* 500 ?), British ecclesiastic; a bishop who lived as an anchorite upon an island; St. David's early teacher. [xliv. 96]

PAULINUS (*d.* 644), archbishop or bishop of York; a Roman who joined Augustine [q. v.] in Kent in 601; was episcopally ordained, and in 625 accompanied Ethelburga, sister of Eadbald [q. v.], to Northumbria on her marriage to Edwin [q. v.]; converted Edwin and established his episcopal see at York, labouring incessantly and with great success to convert the Northumbrians; extended his journeys to Lindsey and Nottinghamshire; fled on the overthrow of Edwin (633) to Eadbald, and became bishop of Rochester. He did not receive the archiepiscopal pall until after his flight from Northumbria, and it is therefore doubtful whether he should be reckoned among the archbishops of York. [xliv. 96]

PAULL, JAMES (1770–1808), politician; established himself as a trader in Lucknow, *c.* 1790, returning to England with a fortune in 1804, where he assailed the Indian administration of Wellesley, with whom he had quarrelled in India; entered parliament as M.P. for Newtown in 1805, and at once pressed his charges of maladministration against Wellesley, but failed to obtain government support; was not re-elected after the dissolution of parliament in 1806, though he twice stood for Westminster; committed suicide while in pecuniary difficulties. [xliv. 98]

PAULTON, ABRAHAM WALTER (1812–1876), politician and journalist; lectured for the Anti-Cornlaw League, and edited its journal until the repeal of the corn laws in 1846; conducted the 'Manchester Examiner and Times,' 1848–54. [xliv. 100]

PAUPER, HERBERT (*d.* 1217). [See POOR.]

PAUPER, ROGER (*fl.* 1139). [See ROGER.]

PAVELEY, SIR WALTER (1319–1375), soldier; served in Brittany and Gascony in the French war; chosen one of the first knights-companions of the order of the Garter, 1350. [xliv. 100]

PAVER, WILLIAM (1802–1871), genealogist; made extensive manuscript genealogical collections for Yorkshire, now in the British Museum; published 'Pedigrees of Families of the City of York,' 1842. [xliv. 101]

PAXTON, GEORGE (1762–1837), Scottish secession divine; studied at Edinburgh; professor of divinity by appointment of the general associate synod, 1807–20, after which he seceded and became professor of divinity to the Associate Synod of Original Seceders. [xliv. 102]

PAXTON, JAMES (1786–1860), surgeon and medical writer; M.R.C.S., 1810; practised at Rugby, 1843–58; M.D. St. Andrews, 1845; published medical works. [xliv. 102]

PAXTON, JOHN (*d.* 1780), painter; an original member of the Incorporated Society of Artists, 1766; exhibited portraits at the Royal Academy, 1769 and 1770. [xliv. 103]

PAXTON, SIR JOSEPH (1801–1865), gardener and architect; was superintendent of the gardens at Chatsworth from 1826, and became an intimate friend of the Duke of Devonshire, whom he accompanied on his travels between 1838 and 1840; F.L.S., 1833; designed the plan of the Industrial Exhibition of 1850, after which he was knighted. His building, generally known as the Crystal Palace, was re-erected at Sydenham, 1853–4. [xliv. 103]

PAXTON, PETER (*d.* 1711), medical writer and pamphleteer; M.D., *per literas regias*, Pembroke College, Cambridge, 1687; compiled medical and political works. [xliv. 104]

PAXTON, STEPHEN (1735–1787), violoncellist and composer; a professional member of the Catch Club, 1780; published violoncello music. [xliv. 104]

PAXTON, WILLIAM (*fl.* 1780), violoncellist; brother of Stephen Paxton [q. v.] [xliv. 105]

PAYE, HENRY (*fl.* 1403–1414), sea-captain; ravaged the coasts of France and Castile. [xliv. 105]

PAYE, RICHARD MORTON (*d.* 1821), painter; executed portraits, miniatures, and small figure subjects. [xliv. 105]

PAYN, JAMES (1830–1898), novelist; educated at Eton and Woolwich; contributed article describing Woolwich Academy to 'Household Words,' then edited by Charles Dickens [q. v.]; entered Trinity College, Cambridge, 1847; president of the Union; B.A., 1852; contributed regularly to 'Household Words' and to 'Chambers's Journal,' of which he became co-editor with Leitch Ritchie [q. v.], 1858, and was sole editor, 1859–74; resided in London, 1861 till death; reader to Messrs. Smith, Elder & Co., 1874; editor of 'Cornhill Magazine,' 1883–96. He published, besides numerous novels, 'Poems,' 1853, 'Some Private Views,' 1882, 'Some Literary Recollections,' 1884, 'Gleams of Memory,' 1894, and 'The Backwater of Life' (posthumously, 1899). [Suppl. iii. 253]

PAYNE. [See also PAIN and PAINE.]

PAYNE, GEORGE (1781–1848), congregational divine; M.A. Glasgow, 1807; minister in Edinburgh (1812–1823) and theological tutor of the Blackburn academy (1823–9) and of the Western academy (1829–48). His writings, the most noteworthy of which is 'Elements of Mental and Moral Science' (1828), show a genuine gift for metaphysical speculation. [xliv. 106]

PAYNE, GEORGE (1803–1878), patron of the turf; of Eton and Christ Church, Oxford; dissipated three large fortunes in various forms of extravagance, including racing and gambling. [xliv. 107]

PAYNE, HENRY NEVILLE (*fl.* 1672–1700), conspirator and author; produced plays and pamphlets; became after the revolution 'the most active and determined of all King James's agents'; instigated the Montgomery plot, 1690, and was arrested on the discovery of the plot; was tortured, 1690, but confessed nothing; kept in prison till December 1700, when he seems to have been liberated. He was the last person tortured in Scotland. [xliv. 108]

PAYNE, JOHN (*d.* 1506), bishop of Meath; D.D. Oxford; elected provincial of the Dominicans in England; bishop of Meath, 1484; a strenuous Yorkist, supporting Lambert Simnel on his landing in Ireland in 1487, but after the battle of Stoke was one of the first to make his peace with Henry VII; afterwards on bad terms with Gerald Fitzgerald, eighth earl of Kildare [q. v.]; remained loyal during the rebellion of Perkin Warbeck; master of the rolls in Ireland, 1496. [xliv. 109]

PAYNE, JOHN (*d.* 1647 ?), engraver; an early exponent of line-engraving in England. [xliv. 110]

PAYNE, JOHN (*d.* 1787), publisher; a friend of Dr. Johnson; carried on a publishing business in Paternoster Row, London, and was employed from 1744 in the Bank of England, where he became accountant-general, 1780. [xliv. 110]

PAYNE, JOHN (*fl.* 1770–1800), compiler; originally a publisher; took to authorship on the consumption of his property by fire, and became an 'indefatigable manufacturer of books.' [xliv. 111]

PAYNE, JOHN WILLETT (1752–1803), rear-admiral; saw much service during the war of the American revolution, and at the peace became a boon companion of George, prince of Wales, who made him his private secretary; M.P., Huntingdon; strenuously urged the prince's claim to the regency, 1788; served till 1798 in the war of the French revolution, when ill-health compelled him to retire; rear-admiral, 1799; treasurer of Greenwich Hospital, 1803. [xliv. 111]

PAYNE, JOSEPH (1808–1876), professor of education in England; when a schoolmaster, introduced Jacotot's system into England, 1830; nominated first professor of education in England by the College of Preceptors, 1872. [xliv. 112]

PAYNE, PETER (*d.* 1455), lollard and Taborite; born in Lincolnshire; son of a Frenchman by an English wife; educated at Oxford; principal of St. Edmund's Hall, Oxford, 1410–14; adopted Wycliffe's views and fled to Bohemia to avoid persecution, *c.* 1416; protected by Elizabeth, widow of King Wenceslas, and soon attained a prominent position; joined the sect of the 'Orphans,' 1427; a Bohemian delegate at the council of Basle, 1433, where his unyielding temper contributed to the failure of the Bohemians to come to terms with the council; joined the Taborites, 1434, after the outbreak of civil war; narrowly escaped arrest as a heretic in subsequent years; died in Prague after the overthrow of the Taborites; several of his manuscripts are extant at Prague and Vienna. [xliv. 114]

PAYNE, SIR PETER, third baronet *de jure* (1763-1843), politician; the eldest son of Sir Gillies Payne born in wedlock: refused to register himself as baronet; M.A. Queens' College, Cambridge, 1787; attacked Pitt's foreign policy in several pamphlets, written from a whig standpoint; advocated the repeal of the corn laws, 1832. [xliv. 118]

PAYNE, SIR RALPH first BARON LAVINGTON (1738 ?-1807), M.P., Shaftesbury, 1768-71, supporting the ministry: was captain-general and governor-in-chief of the Leeward islands, 1771-5: M.P., Camelford, 1776-80, Plympton, 1780-4, and Woodstock, 1795-9; an ally of Fox till 1795: joined Pitt, 1795; created Baron Lavington (Irish peerage), 1795; reappointed governor of the Leeward islands, 1799, where he died. [xliv. 119]

PAYNE, ROBERT (*fl.* 1590), writer on agriculture; author of 'A Briefe Description of Ireland' (1590), edited for the Irish Archæological Society in 1841. [xliv. 120]

PAYNE, ROGER (1739-1797), bookbinder; set up his business near Leicester Square, London, and became famous for his bindings; considered by some to have originated a new style of bookbinding, but was undoubtedly influenced by the work of Samuel Mearn and other binders of the end of the seventeenth century: Earl Spencer, the Duke of Devonshire, and Colonel Stanley among his patrons. [xliv. 121]

PAYNE, THOMAS, the elder (1719-1799), bookseller: established himself in the Strand, London; published catalogues annually, 1755-90; retired in favour of his son, 1790; known as 'Honest Tom Payne.' [xliv. 122]

PAYNE, THOMAS, the younger (1752-1831), bookseller; eldest son of Thomas Payne the elder [q. v.]; succeeded his father in the business, 1790; transferred his business to Pall Mall, London, 1806; retired, 1825. [xliv. 123]

PAYNE, WILLIAM (1650-1696), controversialist; fellow of Magdalene College, Cambridge, 1671-5; D.D., 1689; rector of Whitechapel, London, 1681; wrote against the Roman catholics during the agitation concerning the 'Popish plot,' and afterwards against the unitarians. [xliv. 123]

PAYNE, WILLIAM (*fl.* 1776-1809), water-colour-painter; became soon after 1790 the most popular drawing-master in London; increased the resources of water-colour art, especially in the rendering of sunlight and atmosphere; invented Payne's grey. [xliv. 124]

PAYNE, WILLIAM HENRY SCHOFIELD (1804-1878), actor and pantomimist; appeared at Covent Garden, London, 1831, as clown, and afterwards played many parts at Covent Garden, London, Manchester, and Sadler's Wells, London; pre-eminent as a mime. [xliv. 124]

PAYNE SMITH, ROBERT (1819-1895), dean of Canterbury, orientalist, and theologian; of Pembroke College, Oxford; fellow of Pembroke College, Oxford, 1843; was regius professor of divinity at Oxford, 1865-70; dean of Canterbury, 1870-95; left almost complete a 'Thesaurus Syriacus,' which occupied him for thirty-six years; conservative as a theological controversialist. [xliv. 125]

PAYNELL. [See also PAGANEL and PAGANELL.]

PAYNELL, MAURICE DE, BARON OF LEEDS (1184 ?-1230). [See GAUNT.]

PAYNELL, THOMAS (*fl.* 1528-1568), translator; an Austin friar and canon of Merton Abbey, Surrey; chaplain to Henry VIII; translated many books from the Latin from 1528 onwards; an intimate friend of Alexander Barclay [q. v.]; confused by Wood, Cooper, and others with a contemporary Thomas Paynell or Farnell, a companion of Robert Barnes [q. v.] [xliv. 127]

PAYNTER, DAVID WILLIAM (1791-1823), author; published mainly tragedies. [xliv. 129]

PAYNTER or CAMBOURNE, WILLIAM (1637-1716), rector of Exeter College, Oxford; fellow of Exeter College, Oxford, 1657; M.A., 1663 (incorporated at Cambridge, 1664); D.D., 1695; rector, 1690-1716. [xliv. 129]

PEABODY, GEORGE (1795-1869), philanthropist; born in Massachusetts; made a fortune in dry goods; came to England, 1827; began business in London as a banker and merchant, 1843; founded the 'Peabody dwellings' for workmen in various parts of London, and was a munificent benefactor of Harvard and Yale Universities; D.C.L. Oxford, 1867. [xliv. 130]

PEACH, CHARLES WILLIAM (1800-1886), naturalist and geologist; employed in the customs till 1861; made important researches in the study of marine invertebrates and in geology. [xliv. 131]

PEACHAM, EDMOND (*d.* 1616), reputed traitor; rector of Hinton St. George, 1587; a strong puritan; was arrested by the court of high commission, 1614, and, refusing to defend himself against the charge of uttering words of treasonable intent, tortured with the object of drawing a statement from him; condemned to death, 1615; died in gaol. [xliv. 131]

PEACHAM, HENRY (1576 ?-1643 ?), author; M.A. Trinity College, Cambridge, 1598; master of the free school at Wymondham; painted, drew, and engraved portraits and landscapes, and was besides a musical composer, a student of heraldry, and a mathematician; published 'Graphice,' 1606, a practical treatise on art, which passed through many editions under the new title of 'The Gentleman's Exercise,' given it in 1607; travelled widely (1613-14) as tutor to the sons of Thomas Howard, second earl of Arundel [q. v.], the great art collector; gained admission into literary society, and quickly made a reputation by his epigrams; published 'The Compleat Gentleman,' the work by which he is best known (1622) from the last edition of which (1661) Dr. Johnson drew all the heraldic definitions in his dictionary. [xliv. 133]

PEACHELL, JOHN (1630-1690), master of Magdalene College, Cambridge; M.A. Magdalene College, Cambridge, 1653; D.D., 1680; foundation fellow, 1656; a staunch toper and unswerving loyalist; elected master, 1679; suspended from his mastership, 1687, for refusing as vice-chancellor of the university to admit the Benedictine Alban Francis [q. v.] to the master's degree until he had taken the oaths; terrified by Jeffreys on his appearance before the council, when he showed great ignorance and timidity; restored by James II, 1688, and (1690) rebuked by Sancroft for drunkenness and ill-conduct; his death said to have been caused by a self-imposed penance of four days' abstinence. [xliv. 136]

PEACHI, JOHN (*fl.* 1683), physician; a doctor of medicine of Caen in Normandy; has been frequently confused with John Pechey [q. v.] [xliv. 184]

PEACOCK, SIR BARNES (1810-1890), judge; barrister, Inner Temple, 1836; became legal member of the supreme council of India, 1852; chief-justice at Calcutta, 1859-70; knighted, 1859; member of the judicial committee of the privy council, 1872. [xliv. 137]

PEACOCK, DMITRI RUDOLF (1842-1892), traveller and philologist; born in Russia of an English father; consul at Batoum, 1890; consul-general at Odessa, 1891; published original vocabularies of five west Caucasian languages. [xliv. 137]

PEACOCK, FREDERICK BARNES (1836-1894), Indian civilian; educated at Haileybury; chief secretary of Bengal, 1883; C.S.I., 1890. [xliv. 137]

PEACOCK, GEORGE (1791-1858), mathematician and dean of Ely; fellow of Trinity College, Cambridge, 1814; M.A., 1816; appointed lecturer in mathematics at Trinity College, Cambridge, 1815, and tutor, 1823; from 1835 till 1839 he was sole tutor; F.R.S., 1818; with Robert Woodhouse, Herschel, and Babbage had a great share in introducing analytical methods and the differential notation into the mathematical course; formed with them (1812) an analytical society, which held meetings, read papers, and published a volume of 'Transactions'; his reputation as a philosophic mathematician greatly increased by the publication of his 'Algebra,' 1830; Lowndean professor of astronomy, 1836-58; dean of Ely, 1839-58; persuaded the chapter of Ely to undertake a complete restoration of the cathedral, which was carried out by Sir George Gilbert Scott [q. v.] [xliv. 138]

PEACOCK, GEORGE (1805-1883), sea-captain and shipowner; served as a master in the navy (1828-40), and as a captain in the Pacific Steam Navigation Company (1840-6); published pamphlets. [xliv. 140]

PEACOCK, JAMES (*d.* 1653), vice-admiral; active in the parliamentary navy as a commodore and vice-admiral; killed in the concluding action of the Dutch war (29–31 July 1653). [xliv. 141]

PEACOCK, JAMES (1738 ?–1814), architect; practised in London; wrote on architecture and social problems, his main project being to find employment for the destitute. [xliv. 142]

PEACOCK, JOHN MACLEAY (1817–1877), verse-writer; a boiler-maker by trade; an active chartist and the author of several volumes of verse. [xliv. 142]

PEACOCK, LUCY (*fl.* 1785–1816), bookseller and author; kept a shop in Oxford Street, London; wrote tales for children, mainly anonymously. [xliv. 143]

PEACOCK, REGINALD (1395? – 1460?). [See Pecock.]

PEACOCK, THOMAS (1516 ?–1582 ?), president of Queens' College, Cambridge; fellow of St. John's College, Cambridge, 1534; M.A., 1537; B.D., 1554; president of Queens' College, Cambridge, 1558–9; after the accession of Queen Elizabeth lost all his preferments for adhering to the Roman catholic faith, resigning the presidency in order to avoid expulsion. [xliv. 143]

PEACOCK, THOMAS BEVILL (1812–1882), physician; M.D. Edinburgh, 1842; F.R.C.P., 1850; a founder of the Pathological Society (1846) and of the Victoria Park Hospital, London; published medical works. [xliv. 143]

PEACOCK, THOMAS LOVE (1785–1866), novelist, poet, and official of the East India Company; son of a London merchant; found mercantile occupation and employment as secretary to Sir Home Riggs Popham [q. v.] equally uncongenial, and was enabled by his private means to live mainly for study; friend of Shelley; entered the East India Company's service in London, 1819; chief examiner, 1837–56; published satirical novels interspersed with lyrics, among the most notable being 'Headlong Hall' (1816), 'Melincourt' (1817), 'Nightmare Abbey' (1818), 'The Misfortunes of Elphin' (1829), and 'Crotchet Castle' (1831); published 'Paper Money Lyrics and other Poems,' 1837. [xliv. 144]

PEADA (*d.* 656), under-king of the South Mercians; eldest son of Penda [q. v.]; ealdorman of the Middle Mercians, 653; baptised on his marriage with the daughter of Oswy [q. v.]; under-king of the South Mercians, 655; slain the following Easter. [xliv. 147]

PEAK or **PEAKE**, JAMES (1703 ?–1782 ?), engraver; engraved landscape in the manner of Thomas Vivares [q. v.] [xliv. 147]

PEAKE, RICHARD BRINSLEY (1792–1847), dramatist; wrote numerous farces and comedies between 1818 and 1847 for the London theatres. [xliv. 147]

PEAKE, ROBERT (*d.* 1626 ?), serjeant-painter to James I; extolled by Henry Peacham [q. v.] for his skill in oil-painting. [xliv. 148]

PEAKE, SIR ROBERT (1592 ?–1667), printseller and royalist; son of Robert Peake [q. v.]; knighted, 1645; one of the garrison of Basing House, 1645; exiled for refusing the oath of allegiance to Cromwell; appointed vice-president and leader of the Honourable Artillery Company after the Restoration; published a number of engravings by Faithorne. [xliv. 148]

PEAKE, THOMAS (1771–1838), serjeant-at-law and legal author; barrister, Lincoln's Inn, 1796; serjeant-at-law, 1820; published reports of proceedings in the king's bench. [xliv. 148]

PEARCE. [See also Pearse, Peirce, Pierce, and Piers.]

PEARCE, SIR EDWARD LOVET (*d.* 1733), architect; M.P., Ratoath (Irish parliament), 1727; designed Irish parliament house on College Green, Dublin (commenced, 1729). The building—now the bank of Ireland—was completed by Arthur Dobbs [q. v.], 1739. [xliv. 149]

PEARCE, NATHANIEL (1779–1820), traveller; lived at Tigré from 1806 to 1818; died at Alexandria; his journals published, 1831. [xliv. 149]

PEARCE, SAMUEL (1766–1799), hymn-writer; baptist minister in Birmingham. [xliv. 150]

PEARCE, THOMAS (*fl.* 1722–1756), legal author; M.P., Melcombe Regis, 1722–6; commissioner of the navy, 1727; published 'The Complete Justice of the Peace,' 1756, and other works. [xliv. 150]

PEARCE, SIR WILLIAM, first baronet (1833–1888), naval architect; founded the Fairfield Shipbuilding and Engineering Company (chairman, 1885); M.P., Govan, 1885–8; created baronet, 1887. [xliv. 150]

PEARCE, ZACHARY (1690–1774), successively bishop of Bangor and Rochester; fellow of Trinity College, Cambridge, 1716–20; obtained the patronage of Thomas Parker, first earl of Macclesfield [q. v.], and received rapid preferment; dean of Winchester, 1739; consecrated bishop of Bangor, 1748; translated to Rochester, 1756; refused the bishopric of London, 1761; published theological and classical works, including an edition of 'Longinus,' 1724 (9th edit. 1806). [xliv. 151]

PEARD, GEORGE (1594?–1644), parliamentarian; of the Middle Temple; sat in the two parliaments of 1640; took an active part in the proceedings against Strafford; assisted in the unsuccessful defence of Barnstaple against Rupert, 1643. [xliv. 152]

PEARD, JOHN WHITEHEAD (1811–1880), 'Garibaldi's Englishman,' a youth of 'great stature and extraordinary muscular strength'; son of Shuldham Peard [q. v.]; M.A. Exeter College, Oxford, 1836; barrister, Inner Temple, 1837; joined Garibaldi's forces, 1859, distinguished himself at the battle of Melazzo, 1860, and commanded the English legion during Garibaldi's advance on Naples; received from Victor Emmanuel the cross of the order of Valour. [xliv. 153]

PEARD, SHULDHAM (1761–1832), vice-admiral; saw much service during the French wars of the revolution; showed great courage in repressing a mutiny (1797) on the St. George, of which he was in command; vice-admiral, 1830. [xliv. 154]

PEARL, CORA (1842–1886), courtesan; her real name EMMA ELIZABETH CROUCH; from 1858 resided chiefly in Paris, where she was a prominent figure during the second empire; died in Paris in poverty after numerous wanderings. [xliv. 155]

PEARMAN, WILLIAM (*fl.* 1810–1824), vocalist; originally a seaman; made his début at the English Opera House, 1817. His tenor voice, veiled in tone, was unsuited for large houses. [xliv. 155]

PEARS, STEUART ADOLPHUS (1815–1875), schoolmaster and author; brother of Sir Thomas Townsend Pears [q. v.]; B.A. Corpus Christi College, Oxford, 1836; fellow; head-master of Repton, 1854–74, raising the number of pupils from fifty to three hundred; published Sir Philip Sidney's correspondence with Languet, 1845. [xliv. 156]

PEARS, SIR THOMAS TOWNSEND (1809–1892), major-general, royal engineers; entered the East India Company's service, 1823; served in the Chinese war (1840–2) as commanding engineer; consulting engineer for railways in Madras, 1851–7; retired with honorary rank of major-general, 1861; military secretary at the India office, 1861–77; K.C.B., 1871. [xliv. 156]

PEARSALL, RICHARD (1698–1762), dissenting divine; independent minister at Bromyard, at Warminster, 1731–47, Taunton, 1747–62; published religious works, feebly imitating James Hervey (1714–1758) [q. v.] [xliv. 157]

PEARSALL, ROBERT LUCAS (DE) (1795–1856), musical composer; wrote a cantata at the age of thirteen, entitled 'Saul and the Witch of Endor'; settled at Wartensee, on Lake Constance, 1842; his name chiefly identified with the composition of madrigals. [xliv. 158]

PEARSE. [See also Pearce, Peirce, Pierce, and Piers.]

PEARSE, EDWARD (1633 ?–1674 ?), nonconformist divine; B.A. St. John's College, Oxford, 1654; a prolific author; ejected from the post of preacher at St. Margaret's, Westminster, 1662. [xliv. 159]

PEARSE, EDWARD (1631–1694), divine; M.A. Jesus College, Oxford, 1657; a Northamptonshire vicar and a controversialist; confused by Wood with Edward Pearse (1633 ?–1674 ?) [q. v.] [xliv. 159]

PEARSE, THOMAS DEANE (1738 ?–1789), colonel ; colonel, 1779 ; commanded the Bengal sepoy corps serving in Madras, 1781–3. [xliv. 160]

PEARSE, WILLIAM (1625–1691), ejected minister ; of Exeter College, Oxford ; presented to living of Dunsford, 1655 ; ejected, 1662. [xliv. 159]

PEARSON. [See also PEERSON, PEIRSON, and PIERSON.]

PEARSON, ALEXANDER, LORD SOUTHALL (d. 1657), Scottish judge ; lord of session, 1649–51 ; a judge of the high court, 1654. [xliv. 160]

PEARSON, ANTHONY (1628–1670 ?), quaker ; became (1648) secretary to Sir Arthur Hesilrige [q. v.] ; acted as clerk and registrar of the committee for compounding from its appointment in 1649 ; became a quaker, c. 1653 ; wrote in reprobation of the persecution of the Friends ; enlarged on the same theme in a personal interview with Cromwell, 1654 ; published his well-known work, 'The Great Case of Tythes truly stated,' 1657 (latest edition, 1850) ; his loyalty suspected after the Restoration ; renounced his faith in his endeavour to stand well with government ; under-sheriff for Durham, 1665. [xliv. 161]

PEARSON, CHARLES BUCHANAN (1807–1881), divine ; eldest son of Hugh Nicholas Pearson [q. v.] ; B.A. Oriel College, Oxford, 1828 ; rector of Knebworth, 1838 ; published 'Latin Translations of English Hymns,' 1862. [xliv. 167]

PEARSON, CHARLES HENRY (1830–1894), colonial minister and historian ; son of John Norman Pearson [q. v.] ; was educated at King's College, London, and Oriel and Exeter Colleges, Oxford ; M.A. Oxford, 1856 ; professor of modern history at King's College, London, 1855–65 ; lectured on modern history at Trinity College, Cambridge, 1869–71 ; emigrated to South Australia (1871) on account of his health ; removed to Victoria, 1874 ; took a deep interest in the public affairs of that colony, and (1878) undertook an inquiry for its government into the state of education in Victoria ; minister of education in Victoria, 1886–90, completely reorganising the system in vogue, separating primary from secondary education, and raising the pay of certified teachers ; author of ' The History of England during the Early and Middle Ages,' 1867, which occasioned some controversy with Edward Augustus Freeman [q. v.] ; published (1893) ' National Life and Character, a Forecast,' containing very pessimistic conclusions respecting the future of mankind. [xliv. 162]

PEARSON, EDWARD (1756–1811), theologian ; M.A., 1785, B.D., 1792, and fellow of Sidney Sussex College, Cambridge ; master of Sidney Sussex College, Cambridge, 1808 ; D.D., 1808 ; vice-chancellor, 1808 ; published treatises on theological and ecclesiastical questions. [xliv. 164]

PEARSON, EGLINGTON MARGARET (d. 1823), glass-painter ; daughter of Samuel Paterson [q. v.] and wife of James Pearson [q. v.] ; assisted her husband in his art, and after his death (1805) practised independently. [xliv. 167]

PEARSON, GEORGE (1751–1828), physician and chemist ; physician to St. George's Hospital, London, 1787 ; F.R.S., 1791, and member of the council ; an early advocate of vaccination, and one of the first Englishmen to welcome the chemical theories of Lavoisier, which he did much to spread in England by translating (1794) the ' Nomenclature Chimique.' [xliv. 165]

PEARSON, HUGH (1817–1882), canon of Windsor ; son of Hugh Nicholas Pearson [q. v.] ; M.A. Balliol College, Oxford, 1841 ; installed canon of Windsor, 1876 ; a close friend of Arthur Penrhyn Stanley [q. v.] [xliv. 167]

PEARSON, HUGH NICHOLAS (1776–1856), dean of Salisbury ; M.A. St. John's College, Oxford, 1803 ; D.D., 1821 ; dean of Salisbury, 1823–46 ; author of biographies of the missionaries Claudius Buchanan [q. v.] and Christian Friedrich Schwartz [q. v.] [xliv. 166]

PEARSON, JAMES (d. 1805), glass-painter ; introduced some improvements into the colouring of glass ; married Eglinton Margaret Pearson [q. v.] [xliv. 167]

PEARSON, JOHN (1613–1686), bishop of Chester ; fellow of King's College, Cambridge, 1634–40 ; M.A., 1639 ; D.D., c. 1660 ; prebendary of Salisbury and rector of

Thorington, 1640 ; joined the last remnant of Charles I's party in the west, acting as chaplain (1645) to Goring's forces ; on the collapse of the royal cause withdrew to London, where he remained till the Restoration, devoting himself to study ; accepted (1654) post of weekly preacher at St. Clement's, Eastcheap, London, where he preached in substance the series of discourses which he published in 1659 as an 'Exposition of the Creed,' within its limits the most perfect and complete production of English dogmatic theology ; while debarred from the full exercise of his ministry, defended the church with his pen against both Romanist and puritan assailants, and interested himself in promoting the polyglot bible, which established his reputation as a scholar ; after the Restoration made prebendary of Ely and archdeacon of Surrey, and appointed a royal chaplain ; became master of Jesus College, Cambridge, 1660 ; chosen with John Earle by convocation, 1661, to superintend a translation into Latin of the Book of Common Prayer ; elected master of Trinity College, Cambridge, 1662, and during his tenure of office wrote ' Vindiciæ Epistolarum S. Ignatii' (1672), in defence of the authenticity of the letters ascribed to Ignatius of Antioch, a position which has been confirmed by the recent labours of Zahn and Lightfoot ; consecrated bishop of Chester, 1673, his elevation to the episcopate having been long delayed by the influence of the Cabal ministry ; careful and painstaking in discharging his episcopal duties, though Burnet gives another account of him ; a tomb was erected over his grave in Chester Cathedral (1860) by his admirers in England and America. The 'Exposition of the Creed,' on which his reputation still mainly rests, has long been a standard book in English divinity. The notes of the 'Exposition'—a rich mine of patristic and general learning—are at least as remarkable as the text, and form a complete catena of the best authorities upon doctrinal points. He was probably the ablest scholar and best systematic theologian among Englishmen of the seventeenth century. His learning and critical skill were greater than his originality. [xliv. 168]

PEARSON, JOHN (1758–1826), surgeon ; house-surgeon to the Lock Hospital, London, 1782–1818 ; F.R.S., 1803 ; published medical treatises. [xliv. 173]

PEARSON, SIR JOHN (1819–1886), judge ; son of John Norman Pearson [q. v.] ; M.A. Caius College, Cambridge, 1844 ; barrister, Lincoln's Inn, 1844 ; created judge, 1882 ; knighted, 1882. [xliv. 174]

PEARSON, JOHN LOUGHBOROUGH (1817–1897), architect ; worked with Anthony Salvin [q. v.] and Philip Hardwick [q. v.] in London ; began practice independently, 1843 ; F.S.A., 1853 ; F.R.I.B.A., 1860 ; engaged on restorations at Lincoln Cathedral, 1870 ; architect for new cathedral of Truro, 1879–87 ; gold medallist, R.I.B.A., 1880 ; R.A., 1880 ; he restored Westminster Hall, c. 1888, and north transept of Westminster Abbey, and was also engaged in restorations at Peterborough, Canterbury, Bristol, Rochester, Chichester, and Exeter cathedrals. He was a consummate master of building according to mediæval precedent. [Suppl. iii. 255]

PEARSON, JOHN NORMAN (1787–1865), divine ; son of John Pearson (1758–1826) [q. v.] ; Hulsean prizeman, Trinity College, Cambridge, 1807 ; principal of the missionary college at Islington, 1826 ; published theological works. [xliv. 174]

PEARSON, SIR RICHARD (1731–1806), captain in the navy ; captured by John Paul Jones [q. v.] (1779) while commanding the Serapis ; knighted for his brave resistance to superior force, which caused Jones to remark, ' Should I have the good fortune to fall in with him again, I'll make a lord of him.' [xliv. 174]

PEARSON, RICHARD (1765–1836), physician ; M.D. Edinburgh, 1786 ; physician to the General Hospital, Birmingham, 1792–1801 ; wrote a number of medical treatises. [xliv. 175]

PEARSON, THOMAS HOOKE (1806–1892), general ; educated at Eton ; saw much service in India ; general, 1877. [xliv. 176]

PEARSON, WILLIAM (1767–1847), astronomer ; F.R.S. and hon. LL.D., 1819 ; largely instrumental in founding the London Astronomical Society, 1820 ; published an 'Introduction to Practical Astronomy ' (vol. i. 1824, vol. ii. 1829). [xliv. 176]

PEARSON-JERVIS, WILLIAM HENLEY (1813–1883). [See JERVIS.]

PEART, CHARLES (*fl.* 1778–1798), sculptor; produced works of a monumental character; gold medallist, Royal Academy, 1782; last exhibited, 1798. [xliv. 177]

PEART, EDWARD (1756?–1824), physician; practised at Butterwick; chiefly remembered for his works on physical and chemical theory. [xliv. 178]

PEASE, EDWARD (1767–1858), railway projector; constructed the first railway line. It ran from Stockton to Darlington, and was opened in 1825. Pease was persuaded by George Stephenson [q. v.] to employ steam traction. He was a founder of the Peace Society. [xliv. 178]

PEASE, HENRY (1807–1881), railway projector; son of Edward Pease [q. v.]; constructed the line across Stainmoor, 1861. [xliv. 179]

PEASE, JOSEPH (1799–1872), railway projector; son of Edward Pease [q. v.]; persuaded the mine-owners of the utility of railways, to which they were opposed till c. 1830. [xliv. 179]

PEAT, THOMAS (1708–1780), almanac-maker; edited the 'Gentleman's Diary' from its foundation in 1741 till his death, and also 'Poor Robin's Almanac.' [xliv. 180]

PEABODY, CHARLES (1839–1890), journalist; edited the 'Yorkshire Post,' 1882–90. [xliv. 180]

PECHE, RICHARD (*d.* 1182), bishop of Lichfield; consecrated, 1161; excommunicated by Becket (1170) for his share in the coronation of Prince Henry. [xliv. 181]

PECHELL. [See also PEACHELL and PESHALL.]

PECHELL, SIR GEORGE RICHARD BROOKE, fourth baronet (1789–1860), vice-admiral; grandson of Sir Paul Pechell [q. v.]; entered the navy, 1803, served chiefly in American waters; whig M.P. for Brighton, 1835–60; vice-admiral, 1858. [xliv. 181]

PECHELL, SIR PAUL, first baronet (1724–1800), soldier; entered the army, 1744; served in Holland, 1747; lieutenant-colonel, 1762; created baronet, 1797. [xliv. 182]

PECHELL, SIR SAMUEL JOHN BROOKE, third baronet (1785–1849), rear-admiral; grandson of Sir Paul Pechell [q. v.]; entered the navy, 1796; took part in the reduction of Martinique (1810); M.P., Hallestone, 1830, Windsor, 1833; a lord of the admiralty, 1830–4, 1839–41; rear-admiral, 1846. [xliv. 183]

PECHEY, JOHN (1655–1716), medical writer; M.A. New Inn Hall, Oxford, 1678; practised in London; L.R.C.P., 1684; published medical treatises. His methods of advertisement were those of an apothecary rather than of a physician. He has often been confused with John Peachi [q. v.] [xliv. 184]

PECK, FRANCIS (1692–1743), antiquary; M.A. Trinity College, Cambridge, 1713; rector of Goadby-Marwood, 1723–43; prebendary of Lincoln, 1738–43; F.S.A., 1732; devoted himself to the study of antiquities from 1721; exhibited in his well-known 'Desiderata Curiosa' (1732–5) a remarkable faculty for the accumulation of out-of-the-way facts; his researches, which were mainly confined to the seventeenth century, not sufficiently concentrated to render him an expert in dealing with subjects of controversy; published, among other works, 'A Complete Catalogue of all Discourses written both for and against Popery in the time of James II,' 1735 (edited for the Chetham Society, 1859), 'Memoirs of Oliver Cromwell,' 1740, and 'New Memoirs of the Life and Poetical Works of Mr. John Milton,' 1740. [xliv. 184]

PECK, JAMES (1773–1810?), musician; composed songs, glees, and hymn-tunes. [xliv. 187]

PECKARD, PETER (1718?–1797), whig divine; M.A. Corpus Christi College, Oxford, 1742; probationary fellow, 1744; rector of Fletton, 1760–97; vicar of Yaxley, 1760–77; appointed master of Magdalene College, Cambridge, 1781; dean of Peterborough, 1792; published sermons and tracts of a liberal tendency, and in later life drew attention to the evils of the slave traffic. [xliv. 187]

PECKE, THOMAS (*fl.* 1655–1664), verse-writer; of Caius College, Cambridge; barrister, Inner Temple,

1664; published, besides other verses, 'Parnassi Puerperium,' a collection of epigrams, 1658. [xliv. 188]

PECKHAM, SIR EDMUND (1495?–1564), treasurer or master of the mint (appointed, 1546); M.P., Buckinghamshire, 1554; privy councillor; knighted, 1555; helped to carry into effect Queen Elizabeth's measures for the restoration of the coinage; voluntarily exiled himself (1564) on account of the final triumph of protestantism; died at Rome. [xliv. 189]

PECKHAM, SIR GEORGE (*d.* 1608), merchant venturer; son of Sir Edmund Peckham [q. v.]; knighted, 1570; associated with Gilbert, Grenville, and Carleill in American explorations. [xliv. 189]

PECKHAM, HENRY (*d.* 1556), conspirator; son of Sir Edmund Peckham [q. v.]; M.P., Chipping Wycombe, 1552–3, 1555; hanged for conspiring to rob the exchequer. [xliv. 189]

PECKHAM, JOHN (*d.* 1292), archbishop of Canterbury; studied at Oxford; proceeded, c. 1250, to Paris, where he enjoyed the favour of Margaret, wife of Louis IX, and defended the doctrine of St. Thomas Aquinas on the 'Unity of Form'; returned to Oxford, c. 1270; elected (c. 1276) ninth provincial minister of the Franciscans in England; summoned to Rome a year or two later by Pope Nicholas III, and made 'Lector sacri palatii,' or theological lecturer in the schools in the papal palace; nominated, 1279, by Nicholas III archbishop of Canterbury very much against his will; as a friar was naturally inclined to favour the pretensions of the papal see; his tenure of office marked by several bold though ineffectual attempts to magnify ecclesiastical authority at the expense of the temporal power; his attitude made by Edward I the occasion for passing the statute of Mortmain or De Religiosis; precipitated the overthrow of Llywelyn's power by his pretensions to authority over the Welsh church, and after the completion of the conquest took various measures intended to bring the church in Wales into conformity with English customs; in his ecclesiastical administration in England applied himself with much zeal to the correction of abuses in the church, passing statutes at the council of Reading (1279) and the council of Lambeth (1281) to check the growth of plurality; involved by his insistence on his visitorial rights (1280) in a dispute with Edward I; lost no opportunity of advancing the interests of the two great mendicant orders, denied the claim of his own order; appointed by Pope Nicholas III 'protector of the privileges of the order of minors in England'; interposed on the behalf of the Franciscans against the Cistercians of Scarborough, 1281, and denied the claim of the Dominicans to superiority over them; condemned (1284) at Oxford certain erroneous opinions in grammar, logic, and natural philosophy, and gave a decision on the vexed question of the 'form' of the body of Christ, involving the received doctrine of the eucharist, which brought him into conflict with the Dominicans. He was a voluminous writer of treatises on science and theology, as well as of poetry. Twenty-five of his treatises are extant, of which four have been printed, 'Perspectiva Communis' (Milan, 1482), 'Divinarū Sententiarū Librorū Biblie ad certos titulos redacte Collectariū' (Paris, 1513), 'De Summa Trinitate et Fide Catholica' (London, 1510), 'Philomela' (Paris, 1503), the last erroneously printed among the works of St. Bonaventure. [xliv. 190]

PECKITT, WILLIAM (1731–1795), glass-painter; was brought up as a carver and gilder, but adopted glass-painting as a profession; did much for English cathedrals, and for the colleges of Oxford and Cambridge. [xliv. 197]

PECKWELL, HENRY (1747–1787), divine; of St. Edmund Hall, Oxford; chaplain to the Countess of Huntingdon; his outspoken preaching in the chapel of the Magdalen Institution, Dublin, much resented; rector of Bloxholm-cum-Digby; published 'A Collection of Psalms and Hymns,' c. 1760. [xliv. 198]

PECKWELL, afterwards **BLOSSET**, SIR ROBERT HENRY (1776–1823), judge; only son of Henry Peckwell [q. v.]; M.A. Christ Church, Oxford, 1799; barrister, Lincoln's Inn, 1801; serjeant-at-law, 1809; chief-justice of Calcutta, 1822–3; knighted, 1822. [xliv. 198]

PECOCK, REGINALD (1395 ?–1460 ?), bishop successively of St. Asaph and Chichester ; a Welshman by birth ; fellow of Oriel College, Oxford, 1417 ; B.D., 1425 ; master (1431) of Whittington College, London, where he distinguished himself by his writings against the lollards ; promoted by papal provision to the bishopric of St. Asaph, 1444 ; excited indignation by preaching at St. Paul's Cross, London, against church reform, 1447 ; translated to Chichester, 1450 ; publicly attached to the house of Lancaster by his appointment, which was one of the last acts of William de la Pole, first duke of Suffolk [q. v.] ; subsequently became a privy councillor ; issued (1455) 'Repressor of over much Blaming for the Clergy,' a work directed against lollard teachings and a monument of fifteenth-century English, clear and pointed in style ; issued (1456) his ' Book of Faith,' also in English (the greater part printed in 1688) ; in another work, the 'Provoker,' not extant, denied the authenticity of the Apostles' Creed, of which he had already issued a revised version ; alienated by such writings every section of theological opinion in England ; cited with his accuser before Thomas Bouchier, Archbishop of Canterbury, 1457, and in November expelled from the privy council ; his creed condemned ; and after making a public abjuration at St. Paul's Cross, London, resigned his bishopric (1458) and was sent to Thorney Abbey in Cambridgeshire, where he probably lived in seclusion. His ' Repressor ' and the ' Book of Faith' have been printed, and a collection of excerpts from his works included in Foxe's ' Commentarii Rerum in Ecclesia Gestarum' (1554). [xliv. 198]

PECTHELM (d. 735), first bishop of Whithorn ; consecrated, 730 ; learned in ecclesiastical law ; friend of Boniface [q. v.] [xliv. 202]

PECTWIN (d. 776), bishop of Whithorn ; consecrated in 763. [xliv. 203]

PEDDER, JOHN (1520 ?–1571), dean of Worcester ; M.A. Cambridge, 1542 ; B.D., 1552 ; being a protestant went abroad on Queen Mary's accession ; returned, 1558 ; dean of Worcester, 1559–71. [xliv. 203]

PEDDIE, JAMES (1758–1845), presbyterian divine ; of Edinburgh University ; minister of the Bristo Street secession church in Edinburgh, 1782–1845 ; twice moderator ; took a leading part in the ' old ' and ' new light' controversy as a ' new light.' [xliv. 203]

PEDDIE, JOHN (d. 1840), lieutenant-colonel ; ensign, 1805 ; lieutenant-colonel 31st foot, 1830, 72nd highlanders, 1832 ; K.H., 1832 ; at Izolo Berg in Kaffraria defeated the Kaffirs in a night attack, 1835. [xliv. 204]

PEDDIE, WILLIAM (1805–1893), minister ; of Edinburgh University ; son of James Peddie [q. v.] ; appointed colleague and successor to his father at Bristo Street, Edinburgh, 1828 ; moderator 1855. [xliv. 204]

PEDEN, ALEXANDER (1626 ?–1686), covenanter ; of Glasgow University ; ordained minister of New Luce, 1660 ; ejected, 1663, for refusing to obtain episcopal collation ; by his power of speech and supposed prophetical gifts, as well as his extraordinary hardships, gained immense influence among the conventicles of southern Scotland ; imprisoned on the Bass Rock, 1673, but liberated, 1678 ; spent his last days in a cave near Sorn in Ayrshire. [xliv. 205]

PEDLEY, ROBERT (1760–1841). [See DEVERELL.]

PEDROG (fl. 550 ?), British saint ; was of royal birth, but declining a crown retired to a monastery and founded the ancient church of Bodmin. [xliv. 206]

PEEBLES or **PEBLIS**, DAVID (d. 1579), musician ; canon of St. Andrews before the Reformation ; wrote the music of the famous St. Andrews harmonised psalter, and probably the words also. [xliv. 207]

PEECKE, RICHARD (fl. 1620–1626). [See PIKE.]

PEEL, JOHN (1776–1854), Cumberland huntsman ; maintained a pack of hounds at his own expense at Caldbeck for fifty years. He is famous through the song ' D'ye ken John Peel,' written impromptu by his friend, John Woodcock Graves. [xliv. 207]

PEEL, JONATHAN (1799–1879), politician and patron of the turf ; son of Sir Robert Peel, first baronet [q. v.] ; entered the army, 1815 ; major-general, 1859 ;

tory M.P. for Norwich, 1826, for Huntingdon, 1831–68 ; surveyor-general of the ordnance, 1841–6, under his brother, Sir Robert Peel ; secretary for war under Lord Derby, 1858 and 1866, resigning office in 1867 rather than support Disraeli's scheme or reform ; noted for his devotion to horseracing and his extensive acquaintance with all matters connected with the turf. [xliv. 207]

PEEL, SIR LAWRENCE (1799–1884), chief-justice of Calcutta ; nephew of Sir Robert Peel, first baronet [q. v.] ; of Rugby and St. John's College, Oxford ; M.A., 1824 ; barrister, Middle Temple, 1824, bencher, 1856, treasurer, 1866 ; knighted, 1842 ; was chief-justice, 1842–55 ; created D.C.L. Oxford, 1858. [xliv. 209]

PEEL, PAUL (1861–1892), Canadian painter ; born in Ontario ; studied in Paris, where he settled ; his art entirely French in character. [xliv. 209]

PEEL, SIR ROBERT, first baronet (1750–1830), manufacturer ; son of Robert Peel, parent of the calicoprinting industry in Lancashire ; applied the discoveries of Arkwright and Hargreaves in his business ; M.P., Tamworth, 1790, and took an interest in industrial and financial measures ; carried an act (1802) for the preservation of the health of apprentices and others, which was the forerunner of all factory reform. [xliv. 209]

PEEL, SIR ROBERT, second baronet (1788–1850), statesman ; eldest son of Sir Robert Peel, first baronet [q. v.] ; educated at Harrow and Christ Church, Oxford ; double first class, 1807 ; tory M.P. for Cashel (seat bought for him by his father), 1809 ; under-secretary for war and the colonies under Lord Liverpool, 1810–12 ; chief secretary for Ireland, 1812–18 ; successfully opposed catholic emancipation, and established the peace preservation police, vulgarly called 'peelers' ; met with vehement opposition from O'Connell, with whom he declined a duel, 1815 ; M.P., Oxford University, 1817 ; carried ' Peel's Act' (1819) providing for the resumption of cash payments in 1823 ; began to distrust rigorously unchanging toryism as a political creed ; rejoined Lord Liverpool's ministry as home secretary, 1822 ; after effecting important reforms in criminal law, resigned office on account of his opposition to catholic emancipation (April 1827) ; after Canning's death (August 1827) laboured successfully to reunite the tory party, and in January 1828 joined Wellington's administration as home secretary and leader of the House of Commons ; abandoned his opposition on finding the country determined on catholic emancipation, and (March 1829) introduced a bill for granting the measure ; M.P., Westbury, 1829, Tamworth, 1830 and 1833 ; resigned office (November 1830) on the defeat of Wellington's government ; became premier (November 1834) at the instance of William IV, holding the offices of first lord of the treasury and chancellor of the exchequer ; confronted in the Commons by a hostile majority, and outvoted six times in six weeks ; resigned office (April 1835), and retiring to opposition gradually built up a great party, which became known as the conservative party, a name first used in 1831, its policy being to maintain intact the established constitution of church and state ; on the resignation of Melbourne, 1839, summoned to form a cabinet, but was unable to acquiesce in the retention of the whig ladies of the bedchamber, on which Melbourne resumed office ; the question of the household being decided in his favour, and the government having been defeated, Peel formed a ministry, Aug. 1841 ; seven past or future prime ministers and five future viceroys of India members of his party ; held no post beyond that of first lord of the treasury ; introduced (1842) his first budget, in which he began his task of lightening the burden of indirect taxation, and make good the temporary deficiency by the imposition of an incometax ; had repealed 605 duties by 1846, largely reducing 1,035 others ; increased consumption by this system of lightening imposts on trade ; ensured for English trade the first position in the world, and improved the credit of the country so much that the funds rose from 89 almost to par ; reorganised the Bank of England, and initiated a policy of reform in Ireland, which, however, he had not been able to carry very far before the downfall of his ministry ; the great work of his administration was the repeal of the corn laws ; steadily opposed the cry for repeal till 1845, although desirous of ameliorating the condition of consumers ; inclined to free trade by his experiments

in the relaxation of other duties; led by the failure of the
harvest in 1845, with its threat of imminent famine, to
introduce a measure 'involving the ultimate repeal of the
corn laws'; failed to carry his cabinet with him, and
resigned, 9 Dec. 1845; resumed office, 20 Dec. 1845, Lord
John Russell having failed to form a government, supported by all his former colleagues except Stanley (afterwards Lord Derby); introduced (January 1846) his corn
law and customs bill into the Commons, in which he proposed the total repeal of the corn duties, though the ports
were not to be completely opened till 1849; in spite of
the strenuous resistance of many of his former followers
succeeded in getting the bill passed through the Lords by
25 June 1846, but on the same night was defeated in the
Commons over the first reading of his Irish bill by a combination of whigs and protectionists; resigned office,
29 June 1846; refused the Garter; during the few succeeding years of opposition organised no party, but constituted himself the guardian of the policy of free trade
and the mainstay of the whig government; thrown from
his horse on Constitution Hill, 29 June 1850, and died
from his injuries on 2 July. In an age of revolution he
alone had the foresight and strength to form a conservative party, resting not on force or corruption, but
on administrative capacity and the more stable portion
of the public will. While always decided in his measures, when he had resolved on a line of action, no
statesman was more controlled by a sense of public duty.
Wellington said of him, 'I never knew a man in whose
truth and justice I had more lively confidence.'
                                        [xliv. 210]

PEEL, Sir ROBERT, third baronet (1822–1895),
politician; eldest son of Sir Robert Peel, second baronet
[q. v.]; of Harrow and Christ Church, Oxford; entered
the diplomatic service, 1844; M.P., Tamworth, 1850,
Huntingdon, 1884, Blackburn, 1885; became Irish secretary, 1861, in Palmerston's ministry, but in 1865, under
Russell, was succeeded by Chichester Fortescue; his
political career marred by his lack of dignity and his
inability to accept a fixed political creed; G.C.B., 1866.
                                        [xliv. 223]

PEEL, Sir WILLIAM (1824–1858), captain in the
navy; son of Sir Robert Peel, second baronet [q. v.];
entered the navy, 1838; captain, 1849; distinguished himself by his bravery at Sebastopol during the Crimean war
and by his services with the naval brigade during the
Indian mutiny; was severely wounded at the second
relief of Lucknow, and while still weak succumbed at
Cawnpore to an attack of confluent small-pox.
                                        [xliv. 224]

PEEL, WILLIAM YATES (1789–1858), politician;
son of Sir Robert Peel, first baronet [q. v.]; of Harrow
and St. John's College, Cambridge; M.A., 1815; barrister,
Lincoln's Inn, 1816; tory M.P. for Bossiney, 1817–18,
Tamworth, 1818–30, Yarmouth, Isle of Wight, 1830–1,
Cambridge University, 1831–5, Tamworth, 1835–7 and
1847–52; held office under Liverpool, Wellington, and his
brother, Sir Robert Peel [q. v.], being under-secretary
for the home department, 1828, and twice a lord of the
treasury, 1830 and 1834–5.   [xliv. 210]

PEELE, GEORGE (1558?–1597?), dramatist; son of
a London citizen and salter; educated at Christ's Hospital, London, and Broadgates Hall (Pembroke College)
and Christ Church, Oxford; M.A., 1579; esteemed as a
poet at Oxford; led a dissipated life, and in 1579 was
turned out of his father's dwelling, within the precincts
of Christ's Hospital, by the governors of the institution;
married before 1583, and acquired some land in his wife's
right; almost certainly a successful player as well as playwright; his lyrics popular in literary circles. His works,
which are very numerous, fall under three heads, plays,
pageants, and 'gratulatory' and miscellaneous verse.
Among his plays may be mentioned 'The Arraignment of
Paris' (presented to Queen Elizabeth by the chapel children,
c. 1581) and 'The Battle of Alcazar' (printed, 1594); among
his miscellaneous verse, 'Polyhymnia,' 1590, and 'The
Honours of the Garter,' 1593. His dramatic writings
show versatility of fancy and brilliancy of imagery, but
betray a lack of constructive power.   [xliv. 225]

PEEND or **DE LA PEEND**, THOMAS (*fl.* 1565),
translator and poet; of Oxford University; a London
barrister; translated 'The pleasant Fable of Hermaphro-
ditus and Salmacis,' 1565, from the 'Metamorphoses.'
                                        [xliv. 229]

PEER, WILLIAM (*d.* 1713), actor; became property
man at the Theatre Royal (Drury Lane), London; celebrated by Steele in the 'Guardian' (No. 82). [xliv. 230]

PEERIS, WILLIAM (*fl.* 1520), family chronicler;
secretary to Sir Henry (Algernon) Percy, fifth earl of
Northumberland [q. v.]; wrote a 'Metrical Chronicle'
of the Percies (now in the British Museum). [xliv. 230]

PEERS, RICHARD (1645–1690), translator and
author; of Westminster School and Christ Church, Oxford;
M.A., 1671; translated the 'History and Antiquities' of
Anthony Wood [q. v.] into Latin, 1674.   [xliv. 230]

PEERS, RICHARD (1685–1739), author; son of
Richard Peers [q. v.]; M.A. Trinity College, Oxford,
1708; vicar of Faringdon, 1711–39; published 'The
Character of an Honest Dissenter' (1717) and other
works.   [xliv. 231]

PEERSON or **PIERSON**, ANDREW (*d.* 1594), divine;
fellow of Corpus Christi College, Cambridge; M.A., 1544–5;
chaplain to Archbishop Parker; held livings in Kent;
prebendary of Canterbury, 1563; took part in preparing
for press the 'Bishops' Bible.'   [xliv. 231]

PEERSON, **PIERSON**, or **PEARSON**, MARTIN
(1590?–1651?), musical composer; Mus. Bac. Lincoln
College, Oxford, 1613; master of the choristers at St.
Paul's Cathedral, London; published songs, airs, and
madrigals.   [xliv. 232]

PEETERS, GERARD (*fl.* 1582–1592), author; of
Westminster School; fellow of Trinity College, Cambridge, 1587; M.A., 1590; probably author of two small
treatises on memory.   [xliv. 233]

PEETERS or **PIETERS**, JOHN (1667–1727), painter;
born at Antwerp; came to England, 1685; a skilled
copyist, and called Doctor Peeters from his success in repairing damaged pictures.   [xliv. 233]

PEGGE, Sir CHRISTOPHER (1765–1822), physician;
son of Samuel Pegge (1733–1800) [q. v.]; B.A. Christ
Church, Oxford, 1786; fellow of Oriel College, Oxford,
1788; M.A. and M.B., 1789; F.R.S., 1795; knighted, 1799;
regius professor of physic at Oxford, 1801–22.
                                        [xliv. 233]

PEGGE, SAMUEL, the elder (1704–1796), antiquary;
M.A. St. John's College, Cambridge, 1729, and held
various fellowships there; prebendary of Lichfield, 1757–
1796, of Lincoln, 1772–96; created LL.D. Oxford, 1791;
published works on English antiquities. [xliv. 233]

PEGGE, SAMUEL, the younger (1733–1800), antiquary, poet, and musical composer; of St. John's College,
Cambridge; barrister, Middle Temple; a groom of the
king's privy chamber; F.S.A., 1796; composed catches,
glees, and popular songs; wrote elegies and prologues,
and published works on antiquarian topics. [xliv. 235]

PEILE, THOMAS WILLIAMSON (1806–1882), author
and divine; fellow of Trinity College, Cambridge, 1829;
M.A., 1831; D.D., 1843; head-master of Repton, 1841–54;
vicar of Luton, 1857–60; vicar of St. Paul, South Hampstead, 1860–73; works include editions of the 'Agamemnon' of Æschylus, 1839, and of the 'Choephori,' 1840.
                                        [xliv. 235]

PEIRCE.   [See also PEARCE, PEARSE, PIERCE, and
PIERS.]

PEIRCE, JAMES (1674?–1726), dissenting divine;
independent minister at Cambridge, 1701–6; presbyterian
minister at Newbury, 1706–13; minister at Exeter, 1713–
1719; his theology originally Sabellian; claimed by his
correspondent Whiston as a unitarian, though he rejected
the 'distinctive opinion' of Arius; suspected (1716) of
Arianism, and, refusing to subscribe to any proposition
not in scripture, was ejected from his Exeter charge, 1719.
His published works were very numerous. [xliv. 235]

PEIRSON.   [See also PEARSON, PEERSON, and PIER-
SON.]

PEIRSON, FRANCIS (1757–1781), major, 1780;
stationed in Jersey in January 1781, when St. Heliers was
surprised by the French under Baron de Rullecour; at
the head of the regular troops and island militia worsted
the French and regained the town, but fell at the moment
of victory.   [xliv. 240]

PELAGIUS (*fl.* 400–418), heresiarch; born in Britain;
came to Rome early in the fifth century, and became prominent as a theological disputant; proceeded to Palestine,

c. 409; accused of heresy by Orosius on behalf of the African church, 415, and acquitted by a synod at Jerusalem; on an appeal to Rome was called on by Innocent I to abjure, but was declared cleared (417) by Pope Zosimus; Theodosius, the emperor, being influenced against him, he was finally condemned (418), after which his history is very obscure. He was opposed to the Augustinian doctrines of predestination and of original sin. [xliv. 240]

PELGRIM, JOYCE (*fl.* 1504–1514), stationer in London; conducted a business in St. Paul's Churchyard in partnership with Henry Jacobi. [xliv. 242]

PELHAM, SIR EDMUND (*d.* 1606), chief baron of the exchequer in Ireland; brother of Sir William Pelham [q. v.]; reader, Gray's Inn, 1588; M.P., Hastings, 1597; serjeant-at-law, 1601; appointed chief baron, 1602; knighted, 1604; first English judge to go on circuit in the north of Ireland. [xliv. 243]

PELHAM, FREDERICK THOMAS (1808–1861), rear-admiral; son of Thomas Pelham, second earl of Chichester [q. v.]; entered the navy, 1823; rear-admiral, 1858. [xliv. 254]

PELHAM, GEORGE (1766–1827), bishop successively of Bristol, Exeter, and Lincoln; son of Thomas Pelham, first earl of Chichester [q. v.]; B.A. Clare College, Cambridge, 1787; consecrated bishop of Bristol, 1803; D.C.L. Lambeth; translated to Exeter, 1807, to Lincoln, 1820; notorious for his greed of lucrative office. [xliv. 243]

PELHAM, HENRY (1695?–1754), statesman; son of Thomas Pelham, first baron Pelham [q. v.]; of Westminster School and Hart Hall, Oxford; served as a volunteer in the defeat of the Jacobites at Preston; entered parliament as M.P., Seaford, 1717, and consistently supported Walpole and Townshend; M.P., Sussex, 1722–1754; nominated secretary at war, 1724; paymaster of the forces, 1730; first lord of the treasury and chancellor of the exchequer, 1743; after 1746 was with his brother, the Duke of Newcastle, supreme in parliament, though nearly breaking up the party for a time by his quarrel (1749) with Newcastle. He was a timid, peace-loving politician, without any commanding abilities or much strength of character. He was, however, a good man of business, and both an able and an economical financier. His parliamentary influence was chiefly maintained by an elaborate system of corruption. [xliv. 244]

PELHAM, HENRY (1749–1806), painter; son of Peter Pelham [q. v.]; painted historical subjects and miniatures; exhibited at the Royal Academy, 1777 and 1778. [xliv. 251]

PELHAM, HENRY THOMAS, third EARL OF CHICHESTER (1804–1886), son of Thomas Pelham, second earl of Chichester [q. v.]; of Westminster School and Trinity College, Cambridge; major in the army, 1841, resigning, 1844; head of the church estates committee, 1850–78. To him were largely due the reforms carried out in the management and distribution of church revenues. [xliv. 247]

PELHAM, HERBERT (1600–1673), colonist; joined the Massachusetts Company, 1629, and went to Massachusetts, 1635; took an active part in the settlement of Sudbury; returned to England, 1647. [xliv. 248]

PELHAM, JOHN DE (*d.* 1429), treasurer of England; son of a Sussex knight; an early supporter of Henry IV in his successful attempt on the crown, 1399; made constable of Pevensey, 1400; keeper of the New Forest, and steward of the duchy of Lancaster, 1405; treasurer, 1412, but deprived of his office on Henry V's accession. [xliv. 248]

PELHAM, JOHN THOMAS (1811–1894), bishop of Norwich; son of Thomas Pelham, second earl of Chichester [q. v.]; of Westminster School and Christ Church, Oxford; M.A. and D.D., 1857; consecrated, 1857; resigned see, 1893; a life-long friend of Henry Edward Manning [q. v.], the cardinal. [xliv. 251]

PELHAM, SIR NICHOLAS (1517–1560), soldier and member of parliament; defended Seaford against a French invasion, 1545; M.P., Arundel, 1547–52, and Sussex, 1558; sheriff of Sussex and Surrey, 1549; knighted, 1549. [xliv. 243]

PELHAM, PETER (*d.* 1751), mezzotint-engraver; produced a number of excellent portraits in London between 1720 and 1726; emigrated to Boston, Massachusetts, 1726; first artist resident in New England, publishing first mezzotint plate executed there. [xliv. 250]

PELHAM, SIR THOMAS, fourth baronet and first BARON PELHAM OF LAUGHTON (1650?–1712), a member of the whig party; M.P., East Grinstead, 1678–9, Lewes, 1679–1702, Sussex, 1702; held various minor offices; created baron, 1706. [xliv. 251]

PELHAM, THOMAS, first EARL OF CHICHESTER and second BARON PELHAM OF STANMER (1728–1805), great-nephew of Sir Thomas Pelham, first baron Pelham [q. v.]; M.P., Rye, 1749, Sussex, 1754–68; a follower of his cousin, the Duke of Newcastle; created Earl of Chichester, 1801. He held several lucrative sinecures. [xliv. 252]

PELHAM, THOMAS, second EARL OF CHICHESTER (1756–1826), eldest son of Thomas Pelham, first earl of Chichester [q. v.]; of Westminster School and Clare Hall, Cambridge; M.A., 1775; M.P., Sussex, 1780; acted with the Rockingham whigs; appointed surveyor-general of the ordnance, 1782; from 1783 remained in opposition till 1794, when he joined the old whigs, who supported Pitt's foreign policy; Irish secretary, 1795–8; home secretary under Addington, 1801; removed by Addington to the chancellorship of the duchy of Lancaster, 1803; deprived of this office by Pitt, 1804; joint-postmaster-general, 1807–1823, and sole holder of the office, 1823–6. [xliv. 252]

PELHAM, SIR WILLIAM (*d.* 1587), lord-justice of Ireland; half-brother of Sir Nicholas Pelham [q. v.]; commanded the pioneers at the siege of Leith, 1560, and at Havre, 1562; subsequently lieutenant-general of the ordnance, being occupied for several years in strengthening the defences of the kingdom; knighted by Sir William Drury [q. v.]; chosen lord-justice, 1579, and in that year and 1580 carried on vigorous warfare in Munster; appointed marshal of Leicester's force in the Netherlands, 1581, serving in the Netherlands till 1587. [xliv. 255]

PELHAM-HOLLES, SIR THOMAS, fifth baronet, first DUKE OF NEWCASTLE-UPON-TYNE and of NEWCASTLE-UNDER-LYME, EARL OF CLARE, second BARON PELHAM OF LAUGHTON, and first BARON PELHAM OF STANMER (1693–1768), eldest son of Sir Thomas Pelham, first baron Pelham [q. v.]; of Westminster School and Clare Hall, Cambridge; created LL.D., 1728; chancellor of Cambridge University, 1748; assumed the name of Holles, 1711, on succeeding to the estates of his uncle, John Holles, duke of Newcastle [q. v.]; created Earl of Clare, 1714, Duke of Newcastle, 1715; adhered at first to Townshend, but on the schism of 1717 went over to Sunderland and was made lord chamberlain; became secretary of state for the southern department, 1724; as Walpole's power declined began to coquet with the opposition, and increased Walpole's difficulties by his high tone to the Spanish court on the occasion of the merchants' petition; on Walpole's resignation managed the negotiations which led to the formation of Lord Wilmington's administration, retaining the seals of the southern department for himself; took advantage of the Jacobite rebellion to force Pitt on George II as secretary of war, 1746; succeeded Pelham as first lord of the treasury, 1754, but was driven to resign, 1756, by the ill-success of the French war; formed a coalition with Pitt, 1757, but in 1762, having acquiesced in forcing Pitt out of office, found he had played into Bute's hands, and was driven to resign; pursued into retirement by Bute's hostility and deprived of his posts; lost his adherents in face of this proscription; was lord privy seal in Rockingham's administration (July 1765 to August 1766). Many stories are told of his ignorance of common things; though a master of political corruption, he was not himself corrupt, and died 300,000*l.* poorer for his half-century of official life. [xliv. 257]

PELL, JOHN (1611–1685), mathematician; M.A. Trinity College, Cambridge, 1630 (incorporated at Oxford, 1631); professor of mathematics (1643) at Amsterdam, whence he removed (1646) to Breda; returned to England (1652) and was employed by Cromwell as a diplomatist in Switzerland, 1654–8; rector of Fobbing, 1661–85; vicar of Laindon, 1663–85; D.D. Lambeth, 1663; died in poverty. His mathematical reputation was great, but he accomplished little, and left nothing of moment. [xliv. 261]

PELL, SIR WATKIN OWEN (1788–1869), admiral; entered the navy, 1799; employed in the defence of Cadiz, 1811–13; knighted, 1837; K.C.H., 1837; admiral, 1861. [xliv. 263]

PELL, WILLIAM (1634–1698), nonconformist divine: M.A. Magdalene College, Cambridge; fellow, 1656; ejected from the rectory of Great Stainton, 1662; subsequently pastor at Boston, 1687–94, and Newcastle-upon-Tyne, 1694–98. [xliv. 263]

PELLATT, APSLEY (1791–1863), glass manufacturer; possessed a glass warehouse in Southwark, and took out several patents for glass manufactures; published 'Curiosities of Glass Making,' 1849. [xliv. 264]

PELLEGRINI, CARLO (1839–1889), caricaturist; born at Capua; came to England, 1864; known by his caricatures in 'Vanity Fair' signed 'Ape,' from 1869 onwards. [xliv. 265]

PELLETT, THOMAS (1671 ?–1744), physician; M.B. Queens' College, Cambridge, 1694; M.D., 1705; Harveian orator, 1719; president of the Royal College of Physicians, 1735–9. [xliv. 265]

PELLEW, SIR EDWARD, first baronet and first VISCOUNT EXMOUTH (1757–1833), admiral; entered the navy, 1770; earned repeated promotion by his gallantry, and (1793) took the first frigate in the French war; under circumstances of great bravery saved the crew and passengers of a transport driven ashore at Plymouth Sound, 1796, and was created a baronet; while commanding a frigate (1797), with a companion frigate destroyed the French 74-gun ship, the Droits de l'Homme, in an action which became famous; prevented a general mutiny (1799) while in command of a squadron in Bantry Bay by throwing himself among the mutineers, seizing a ringleader and securing him with his own hands; M.P., Barnstaple, 1802; supported the admiralty in parliament against hostile criticism; rear-admiral, 1804; commander-in-chief in the East Indies, 1804, where in 1807 he destroyed the Dutch fleet; vice-admiral, 1808; returned to England, 1809; nominated commander-in-chief in the North Sea, 1810; commander-in-chief in the Mediterranean, 1811; admiral of the blue, 1814; G.C.B., 1815; bombarded Algiers (1816) on the refusal of the dey to abolish Christian slavery, for which feat he received honours from most of the states of Christendom, and was raised to the dignity of a viscount; commander-in-chief at Plymouth, 1817–21; vice-admiral of the United Kingdom, 1832. [xliv. 266]

PELLEW, SIR FLEETWOOD BROUGHTON REYNOLDS (1789–1861), admiral; son of Sir Edward Pellew, first viscount Exmouth [q. v.]; entered the navy, 1799; C.B., 1815; K.C.H., 1836; commander-in-chief on the East India and China station, 1852, where in 1853 his arbitrary severity provoked a mutiny, the third which had broken out under his command; summarily recalled in consequence; saw no further service; admiral, 1858; died at Marseilles. [xliv. 270]

PELLEW, GEORGE (1793–1866), theologian; son of Sir Edward Pellew, first viscount Exmouth [q. v.]; M.A. Corpus Christi College, Oxford, 1818; D.D., 1828; dean of Norwich, 1828–86, holding also other preferments; wrote sermons and tracts, and published (1847) the life of his father-in-law, Henry Addington, first viscount Sidmouth [q. v.] [xliv. 271]

PELLEW, SIR ISRAEL (1758–1832), admiral; brother of Sir Edward Pellew, first viscount Exmouth [q. v.]; entered the navy, 1771; captured the French flagship, the Bucentaure, at Trafalgar; K.C.B., 1815; admiral, 1830. [xliv. 272]

PELLEW or **PELLOW,** THOMAS (_fl._ 1715–1738), captive in Barbary; was captured off Finisterre in an English merchantman by two Sallee rovers, 1715; was converted to Islam and remained in captivity in the sultan's service till 1738, when he escaped and returned to Cornwall, his native county. In 1739 were published his experiences, which in regard to detail are more interesting than authentic. [xliv. 273]

PELLHAM, EDWARD (_fl._ 1630–1631), sailor; published (1631) a narrative of his residence in Greenland in the previous winter (frequently reprinted). [xliv. 274]

PELLING, EDWARD (_d._ 1718), divine; of Westminster School and Trinity College, Cambridge; fellow, 1664; M.A., 1665; D.D., 1689; prebendary of Westminster, 1683–91; rector of Petworth, 1691–1718; a stout defender of the Anglican church in his writings against both Roman catholics and dissenters. [xliv. 274]

PELLY, SIR JOHN HENRY, first baronet (1777–1852), governor of the Hudson's Bay Company; mainly instrumental (1835) in sending out the exploring parties which, under Peter Warren Dease and Thomas Simpson (1808–1840) [q. v.], did so much for the discovery of the north-west passage and the coast-line of North America; created baronet, 1840. [xliv. 275]

PELLY, SIR LEWIS (1825–1892), Indian official; nephew of Sir John Henry Pelly [q. v.]; educated at Rugby; entered the Bombay army, 1841; lieutenant-general, 1887; assistant resident at Baroda, 1851–2; served in the Persian war, 1857; secretary of the legation at Teheran; went on a special mission through Afghánistán and Belúchistán in 1860, riding from Persia to India without an escort; political agent and consul at Zanzibar, 1861–2, and on the Persian Gulf, 1862–71; K.C.S.I., 1874; despatched as special commissioner to Baroda to investigate the disordered condition of that state, 1874; was sent to Pesháwar as envoy extraordinary, 1877; K.C.B., 1877; returned to England, 1878; conservative M.P. for North Hackney, 1885–92. [xliv. 275]

PELLY, SAVILLE MARRIOTT (1819–1895), surgeon-general; brother of Sir Lewis Pelly [q. v.]; educated at Winchester College and Guy's Hospital, London; C.B.; saw service in India, retiring as inspector-general of hospitals in the Bombay presidency, 1870. [xliv. 277]

PEMBER, ROBERT (_d._ 1560), scholar; fellow of St. John's College, Cambridge, 1524; was one of the great group of scholars at St. John's College, Cambridge, in Henry VIII's reign who raised that college to the highest place among English centres of learning; taught Roger Ascham Greek; reader in Greek at Trinity College, Cambridge, 1546–60. [xliv. 277]

PEMBERTON, CHARLES REECE (1790–1840), actor and lecturer; seized by the press-gang, 1807; served in the navy seven years; acted in tragic parts, and in later life recited and lectured, chiefly at mechanics' institutes. [xliv. 278]

PEMBERTON, CHRISTOPHER ROBERT (1765–1822), physician; grandson of Sir Francis Pemberton [q. v.]; M.D. Caius College, Cambridge, 1794; F.R.C.P., 1796; censor, 1796, 1804, and 1811, and Harveian orator, 1806; published, 1806, 'A practical Treatise on various Diseases of the Abdominal Viscera.' [xliv. 279]

PEMBERTON, SIR FRANCIS (1625–1697), judge; B.A. Emmanuel College, Cambridge, 1644; barrister, Inner Temple, 1654, bencher, 1671, Lent reader, 1674; serjeant-at-law, 1675; was arrested (1675) by the House of Commons, in spite of the protection of the House of Lords, for appearing in the case of Crisp _v._ Dalmahoy; knighted, 1675; puisne judge on the king's bench, 1679; lord chief-justice, 1681; chief-justice of the common pleas, 1683; removed from the bench (September 1683) and privy council (October 1683) for want of zeal against Lord Russell; by his successful defence of the seven bishops helped to bring about the revolution; thrown into gaol (1689) for an attack on parliamentary privilege in 1682, and lay there until the prorogation. [xliv. 279]

PEMBERTON, HENRY (1694–1771), physician and writer; M.D. Leyden, 1719; employed by Newton to superintend the third edition of the 'Principia,' 1726; Gresham professor of physic, 1728; prepared the fifth 'London Pharmacopœia' for the Royal College of Physicians (published, 1746). [xliv. 280]

PEMBERTON (afterwards **PEMBERTON-LEIGH**), THOMAS, BARON KINGSDOWN (1793–1867), a descendant of Sir Francis Pemberton [q. v.]; barrister, Lincoln's Inn, 1816; achieved great success in equity; conservative M.P., Rye, 1831–2, Ripon, 1835–43; repeatedly refused honours, including the great seal; created a baron, 1858, and strengthened the appellate tribunal of the House of Lords. [xliv. 281]

PEMBLE, WILLIAM (1592 ?–1623), puritan divine; M.A. Magdalen Hall, Oxford, 1618; an able exponent of Calvinism in his numerous writings, besides being famous as a preacher. [xliv. 283]

PEMBRIDGE, CHRISTOPHER (_fl._ 1370 ?), Irish annalist; apparently the author of 'Annales Hiberniæ' (1162–1370). The original manuscript is in the Bodleian, and was first printed at the end of Camden's 'Britannia,' 1607. [xliv. 283]

PEMBRIDGE or **PEMBRUGGE**, SIR RICHARD DE (d. 1375), soldier; fought at Sluys, 1340, at Poitiers, 1356; K.G., 1368. [xliv. 284]

PEMBROKE, EARLS OF. [See ARNULF, *fl.* 1090–1110; CLARE, RICHARD DE, second EARL of the Clare line, *d.* 1176; MARSHAL, WILLIAM, first EARL of the Marshal line, *d.* 1219; MARSHAL, WILLIAM, second EARL, *d.* 1231; MARSHAL, RICHARD, third EARL, *d.* 1234; MARSHAL, GILBERT, fourth EARL, *d.* 1241; MARSHAL, WALTER, fifth EARL, *d.* 1245; MARSHAL, ANSELM, sixth EARL, *d.* 1245; AYMER DE VALENCE, *d.* 1324; HASTINGS, LAURENCE, first EARL of the Hastings line, 1318?–1348; HASTINGS, JOHN, second EARL, 1347–1375; TUDOR, JASPER, 1431?–1495; HERBERT, SIR WILLIAM, first EARL of the Herbert line of the first creation, *d.* 1469; HERBERT, WILLIAM, second EARL, 1460–1491; HERBERT, SIR WILLIAM, first EARL of the Herbert line of the second creation, 1501?–1570; HERBERT, HENRY, second EARL, 1534?–1601; HERBERT, WILLIAM, third EARL, 1580–1630; HERBERT, PHILIP, fourth EARL, 1584–1650; HERBERT, PHILIP, fifth EARL, 1619–1669; HERBERT, PHILIP, seventh EARL, 1653–1683; HERBERT, THOMAS, eighth EARL, 1656–1733; HERBERT, HENRY, ninth EARL, 1693–1751; HERBERT, HENRY, tenth EARL, 1734–1794; HERBERT, GEORGE AUGUSTUS, eleventh EARL, 1759–1827; HERBERT, GEORGE ROBERT CHARLES, thirteenth EARL, 1850–1895.]

PEMBROKE, titular EARL OF (d. 1296). [See WILLIAM DE VALENCE.]

PEMBROKE, COUNTESSES OF. [See HERBERT, MARY, 1555?–1621; CLIFFORD, ANNE, 1590–1676.]

PEMBROOKE, THOMAS (1662?–1690?), painter; painted small domestic or mythological pictures. [xliv. 285]

PENCESTER, **PENCHESTER**, or **PENSHURST**, STEPHEN DE (d. 1299), warden of the Cinque ports; appears as warden after 1271; was a conspicuous and successful figure among the minor agents of Edward I's policy, and superintended the laying out of the site and constructing the buildings of New Winchelsea, the port which Edward ordered to be constructed to replace Old Winchelsea, which was swallowed up by the sea. [xliv. 286]

PENDA (577?–655), king of the Mercians; came to the throne, 626, and raised the Mercians from a mere tribe to a powerful people; became the champion of heathenism against Christianity; delegate of the West-Saxons at Cirencester, 628, and (633) defeated the Northumbrians and slew Edwin [q. v.] at Heathfield; reduced the East-Saxons to dependence and (642) slew Oswald [q. v.], king of the Northumbrians; defeated and slain at Winwaed by Oswy [q. v.], Oswald's successor. [xliv. 287]

PENDARVES, JOHN (1622–1656), puritan controversialist; B.A. Exeter College, Oxford, 1642; anabaptist minister at Abingdon; subsequently a Fifth-monarchy man; published 'Arrowes against Babylon,' (1656), attacking the church of Rome, the English church, and the quakers. [xliv. 288]

PENDER, SIR JOHN (1815–1896), pioneer of submarine telegraphy; engaged as merchant in textile fabrics at Glasgow and Manchester; director of first Atlantic Cable Company, 1856; joint-founder of Anglo-American Company, 1865; chairman of Telegraph Construction and Maintenance Company, to which he personally guaranteed 250,000*l.*; liberal M.P. for Totnes, 1865–6 (unseated on petition), and Wick boroughs (liberal), 1872–85, and (liberal unionist) 1892–6; K.C.M.G., 1888; G.C.M.G., 1892. [Suppl. iii. 258]

PENDEREL, RICHARD (d. 1672), royalist; a Staffordshire yeoman; primarily instrumental with his four brothers in the escape of Charles II after Worcester; at the Restoration was with them rewarded and pensioned. [xliv. 289]

PENDERGRASS, SIR THOMAS (1660?–1709). [See PRENDERGAST.]

PENDLEBURY, HENRY (1626–1695), dissenting divine; M.A. Christ's College, Cambridge; ejected from Holcome, near Bury, 1662; one of the most learned nonconformists of his day. Most of his works were published posthumously. [xliv. 290]

PENDLEBURY, JAMES (d. 1758?), colonel; the last officer to bear the title of master-gunner of England, an office which he obtained in 1709. [xliv. 291]

PENDLETON, FREDERICK HENRY SNOW (1818–1888), divine; educated at Ghent and St. Aidan's College, Birkenhead; English chaplain in several foreign towns, and (1882) rector of St. Sampson's, Guernsey; published 'Lettres Pastorales,' 1851. [xliv. 291]

PENDLETON, HENRY (d. 1557), Roman catholic controversialist; M.A. Brasenose College, Oxford, 1544; D.D., 1552; a zealous protestant under Edward VI, and a zealous Romanist under Mary; published two homilies, 1555. [xliv. 292]

PENDRAGON, UTHER. [See UTHER.]

PENGELLY, SIR THOMAS (1675–1730), chief baron of the exchequer; barrister, Inner Temple, 1700, bencher, 1710; appointed king's prime serjeant, 1719; knighted, 1719; judge in 1726; M.P., Cockermouth, 1717 and 1722; died of gaol fever at Taunton. [xliv. 292]

PENGELLY, WILLIAM (1812–1894), geologist; lectured on mathematics and geology in various parts of Great Britain; F.G.S., 1850; F.R.S., 1863; the geology of Devonshire was his principal study. [xliv. 294]

PENINGTON. [See also PENNINGTON.]

PENINGTON, EDWARD (1667–1711), surveyor-general of Pennsylvania, 1700; son of Isaac Penington [q. v.] [xliv. 300]

PENINGTON or **PENNINGTON**, SIR ISAAC (1587?–1660), lord mayor of London; a fishmonger by trade; sheriff in 1638; a staunch puritan; represented the city of London in the Short and Long parliaments, and was chosen lord mayor in 1642 and 1643; his influence in the city of London invaluable to parliament on the outbreak of hostilities in raising loans and supplies for the army; member of the commission for the trial of Charles I, but declined to append his signature to the death-warrant; one of the council of state, 1648; knighted, 1649; died in the Tower of London after the Restoration. [xliv. 295]

PENINGTON or **PENNINGTON**, ISAAC (1616–1679), puritan and quaker; eldest son of Sir Isaac Penington [q. v.]; joined the Friends, 1657, to the indignation of his father; imprisoned (1660) for refusing the oath of allegiance; suffered several subsequent confinements; published religious treatises. [xliv. 297]

PENINGTON, SIR JOHN (1568?–1646), admiral; second cousin of Sir Isaac Penington [q. v.]; vice-admiral under Ralegh in the voyage to the Orinoco, 1617; served against Algiers, 1621, under Sir Robert Mansell [q. v.]; commanded (1625) a squadron placed at the disposal of the French king, and intended by Richelieu for service against the Huguenots; knighted, 1634; in command in the Downs (1639) when Tromp violated English neutrality by attacking the Spanish fleet there; superseded by parliament, 1642; remained attached to Charles I, with the nominal rank of lord high admiral, but without any fleet to command. [xliv. 300]

PENINGTON, JOHN (1655–1710), quaker; eldest son of Isaac Penington [q. v.]; engaged in controversy with George Keith (1639?–1716) [q. v.] [xliv. 299]

PENKETH, THOMAS (d. 1487), schoolman; famous as a theologian and philosopher; D.D. Oxford; teacher of theology at Padua, 1474; a pupil of Duns Scotus, whose works he edited. [xliv. 302]

PENKETHMAN, JOHN (*fl.* 1623–1638), accountant; published 'Artachthos, or a new booke declaring the Assise or Weight of Bread' (1638) and other works. [xliv. 302]

PENLEY, AARON EDWIN (1807–1870), water-colour-painter; exhibited at the Royal Academy, 1835–57; published various elaborate treatises on his art, some of them illustrated by chromolithography. [xliv. 302]

PENN, GRANVILLE (1761–1844), author; son of Thomas Penn [q. v.]; of Magdalen College, Oxford; clerk in the war department; published a number of competent translations from the Greek, and many theological and semi-scientific works. [xliv. 303]

PENN, JAMES (1727–1800), divine; M.A. Balliol College, Oxford, 1752; grammar master of Christ's Hospital, London, 1753–67; vicar of Clavering-cum-Langley, 1760–1800; published chiefly miscellaneous tracts and sermons. [xliv. 304]

PENN, JOHN (1729–1795), colonist; grandson of William Penn (1644–1718) [q. v.]; lieutenant-governor of Pennsylvania, 1763–71, and 1773–6; the predominance of his family in the state ended by the American revolution.
[xliv. 304]

PENN, JOHN (1760–1834), miscellaneous writer; son of Thomas Penn [q. v.]; created M.A. Clare Hall, Cambridge, 1779, and LL.D. 1811; went to Pennsylvania, 1782; settled in Buckinghamshire, 1789; published poems, plays, and pamphlets. [xliv. 305]

PENN, JOHN (1770–1843), engineer; improved the oscillating engine of Aaron Manby [q. v.] [xliv. 305]

PENN, JOHN (1805–1878), engineer; son of John Penn (1770–1843) [q. v.]; succeeded his father in the firm of John Penn & Sons at Greenwich. [xliv. 305]

PENN, RICHARD (1736–1811), colonist; grandson of William Penn (1644–1718) [q. v.]; deputy-governor of Pennsylvania, 1771–3. [xliv. 306]

PENN, RICHARD (1784–1863), humorist; son of Richard Penn (1736–1811) [q. v.]; entered the colonial office; F.R.S., 1824; published 'Maxims and Hints for an Angler,' 1833, and other works. [xliv. 307]

PENN, THOMAS (1702–1775), colonist; son of William Penn (1644–1718) [q. v.]; with his brother succeeded his father as joint-proprietor of Pennsylvania, 1718.
[xliv. 307]

PENN, SIR WILLIAM (1621–1670), admiral and general at sea; after some service on the Irish coast was engaged in the pursuit of Prince Rupert, 1651–2; served under Blake in the Dutch war, and at the battle off Portland (18 Feb. 1653); while in command of the blue squadron rescued Blake and redeemed the fortunes of the day; as commander of the white squadron had a very important share in the victories of 2–3 June and of 29–31 July, 1653; made one of the 'commissioners for ordering and managing the affairs of the admiralty and navy,' December 1653; appointed general and commander-in-chief of the fleet directed to act against the Spanish West Indies in conjunction with General Robert Venables [q. v.], 1654; failed in an attack on St. Domingo in April 1655, but captured Jamaica in May; on his return to England was committed to the Tower of London, ostensibly for returning home without leave; released after a few weeks on making an abject submission; retired to his estates in Munster, where he remained in secret correspondence with the royalists until the eve of the Restoration; knighted at the Restoration, and made a commissioner of the navy; as Pepys's superior officer came in for a good deal of abuse in Pepys's 'Diary'; accompanied the Duke of York (1665) to the fleet and served with him in the campaign against the Dutch, with title of great captain commander; probably drew up 'The Duke of York's Sailing and Fighting Instructions' (code of instructions); present at the battle of Lowestoft (3 June 1665), but incurring undeserved censure, was not employed again afloat, though he continued in the navy office till his death. [xliv. 308]

PENN, WILLIAM (1644–1718), quaker and founder of Pennsylvania; son of Sir William Penn [q. v.]; educated at Christ Church, Oxford; from early boyhood he united a taste for athletic sports with a strong bent towards mystical pietism; sent down from Oxford for nonconformity, 1661; after some time spent in travel and naval service was admitted a student at Lincoln's Inn, 1665; attached himself to the quakers, 1667; committed to the Tower of London, 1668, for publishing his once celebrated 'Sandy Foundation Shaken,' in which he assailed the Athanasian doctrine of the Trinity, the Anselmian rationale of the atonement, and the Calvinistic theory of justification; wrote in the Tower 'No Cross no Crown' (1669), an eloquent and learned dissertation upon the Christian duty of self-sacrifice (frequently reprinted); his release obtained by his father, July 1669, through the intercession of the Duke of York; suffered frequent persecutions and imprisonments and exerted himself to lighten the hardships of the quakers; turned his thoughts seriously to America as a refuge from persecution for his co-religionists, and (1682) obtained grants of East New Jersey and of Pennsylvania by letters patent, and as proprietor and governor was invested by the charter with executive and legislative power; formed a 'Free Society of Traders of Pennsylvania,' 1682, and framed, in concert with Algernon Sidney, a constitution and code of laws for the colony, by which all modes of religious worship compatible with monotheism and religious liberty were to be tolerated; sailed for America (September 1682) and concluded a treaty with the Lenni Lenape Indians; the population of his colony increased by a steady influx of immigrants from Germany, Holland, and Scandinavia, as well as from the British Isles; returned to England, 1684, hoping much from the accession of James II, whom he believed to be a sincere advocate of toleration, his hopes being flattered by James II from motives of policy; being frequently closeted for hours with the king, was denounced as a jesuit by some, and courted as a royal favourite by others; has been charged on insufficient evidence by Lord Macaulay with having accepted the odious office of extorting from the families of the 'Taunton Maids' the ransom assigned by James II's queen to her maids of honour; interceded with James II for the fellows of Magdalen, and endeavoured to procure the release of the seven bishops; was nevertheless summoned before the council on the Revolution as an adherent of the fugitive king, and was held to bail; remained, however, in London in constant communication with Lord Sidney and other friends at court until he obtained (1693) a formal assurance of William III's goodwill towards him; resumed the practice of itinerant preaching, 1693, and undertook literary work; returned to Pennsylvania (1699) with the intention of settling there for the rest of his life; came to England (1701) to oppose a bill for converting the province into a crown colony; he was well received by Queen Anne, and resided successively at Knightsbridge, at Brentford, and at Ruscomb, where he died. He was buried at Jordans, near Chalfont St. Giles. His piety was profound, and though he had little or no interest in humane learning for its own sake, his knowledge of the Christian and pre-Christian mystics was considerable, and enabled him to give to the doctrine of the 'light within' a certain philosophical breadth. His theological polemics, though for the most part occupied with questions of ephemeral importance, evince no small controversial power. His works were numerous; a collective edition appeared in 1726, with a life by Joseph Besse [q. v.].
[xliv. 311]

PENN, WILLIAM (1776–1845), author; elder son of Richard Penn (1736–1811) [q. v.]; of St. John's College, Cambridge; wrote for the 'Gentleman's Magazine,' and the 'Anti-Jacobin.' [xliv. 306]

PENNANT, RICHARD, BARON PENRHYN (1737?–1808), whig M.P. for Petersfield, 1761, Liverpool, 1767, 1768, 1774, and 1784; created baron, 1783; did much to develop the Welsh slate trade in Carnarvonshire.
[xliv. 320]

PENNANT, THOMAS (1726–1798), traveller and naturalist; of Queen's College, Oxford; travelled on the continent and in Ireland and Scotland; drew other tourists to the highlands by his 'Tour in Scotland' (1771). His name stands high among naturalists of the eighteenth century. His 'British Zoology,' 1766 (new edit. 1812) and his 'History of Quadrupeds,' 1781 (3rd edit., 1793), long remained classical works. Gilbert White [q. v.] published his 'Selborne' in the form of letters to Pennant and Daines Barrington [q. v.]. [xliv. 320]

PENNECUIK, ALEXANDER (1652–1722), physician and poet; M.D; possessed an estate in Tweeddale, where he practised as a physician; published satires and other pieces, often coarse, but full of humour; his works reprinted (1762). [xliv. 323]

PENNECUIK, ALEXANDER (d. 1730), poet; possibly nephew of Alexander Pennecuik (1652–1722) [q. v.]; author of several meritorious poems and satires; died in want after a life of dissipation. [xliv. 324]

PENNEFATHER, CATHERINE (1818–1893), hymnwriter; daughter of Rear-admiral James William King; married William Pennefather [q. v.], 1847; after her husband's death carried on his religious work at Mildmay Park, Islington. [xliv. 327]

PENNEFATHER, EDWARD (1774?–1847), Irish judge; brother of Richard Pennefather (1773–1859) [q. v.]; M.A. Dublin, 1832; called to the Irish bar, 1796; bencher of King's Inns, Dublin, 1829; solicitor-general for Ireland, 1835 and 1841; chief-justice of the queen's bench, 1841, retiring, 1846. [xliv. 325]

PENNEFATHER, SIR JOHN LYSAGHT (1800–1872), general; cousin of Richard Pennefather (1773–1859) [q. v.];

entered the army, 1818; commanded a brigade at Alma and a division at Inkerman, where he bore the brunt of the fight with great credit; G.C.B., 1867. [xliv. 325]

PENNEFATHER, RICHARD (1808–1849), politician; son of Richard Pennefather (1773–1859) [q. v.]; B.A. Balliol College, Oxford, 1828; entered at Lincoln's Inn, 1826; under-secretary for Ireland, 1845. [xliv. 327]

PENNEFATHER, RICHARD (1773–1859), Irish judge; B.A. Dublin, 1794; called to the Irish bar, 1795; appointed chief baron of the Irish exchequer, 1821; sat on the bench for thirty-eight years. [xliv. 326]

PENNEFATHER, WILLIAM (1816–1873), divine; son of Richard Pennefather (1773–1859) [q. v.]; B.A. Trinity College, Dublin, 1840; incumbent of Christ Church, Barnet, 1852, of St. Jude's, Mildmay Park, Islington, 1864; commenced at Barnet, and continued at Mildmay Park, conferences on missionary enterprise, which gave rise to many permanent organisations for home and foreign mission work. [xliv. 327]

PENNETHORNE, SIR JAMES (1801–1871), architect; employed by government from 1832 to prepare plans for improvements in the metropolis; his designs thought too extensive to be adopted in their entirety, but New Oxford Street and Endell Street carried into execution from them; knighted, 1870; did much important work in connection with government buildings. [xliv. 328]

PENNETHORNE, JOHN (1808–1888), architect and mathematician; brother of Sir James Pennethorne [q. v.]; first discovered (1832) the incorrectness of the general belief that the system of design in Greek architecture was absolutely rectilinear. [xliv. 329]

PENNEY, WILLIAM, LORD KINLOCH (1801–1872), Scottish judge; educated at Glasgow University; raised to the bench, 1858; author of religious works in prose and verse. [xliv. 330]

PENNIE, JOHN FITZGERALD (1782–1848), writer; wrote comedies, tragedies, and epic poems; published an autobiography, 'The Tale of a Modern Genius' (1827), under the pseudonym of 'Sylvaticus.' [xliv. 331]

PENNINGTON. [See also PENINGTON.]

PENNINGTON, SIR ISAAC (1745–1817), physician; fellow of St. John's College, Cambridge, 1768; M.A., 1770; M.D., 1777; appointed professor of chemistry at Cambridge, 1773; F.R.C.P., 1779; Harveian orator, 1783; regius professor of physic, 1793; knighted, 1796. [xliv. 331]

PENNINGTON, JAMES (1777–1862), writer on currency and banking; engaged by the treasury to regulate the West Indian currency, 1833; frequently consulted by government on questions of currency and finance. [xliv. 332]

PENNINGTON, SIR JOHN (d. 1470), soldier; fought in Scotland and for the Lancastrians during the civil war; presented by Henry VI with a cup, known as the 'luck of Muncaster' (still preserved at Muncaster Castle). [xliv. 332]

PENNINGTON, SIR JOHN, first BARON MUNCASTER in the peerage of Ireland and fifth baronet (1737–1813), descendant of Sir John Pennington (d. 1470) [q. v.]; entered the army, 1756; M.P., Milbourne Port, 1781, 1784, and 1790; follower of Lord North; M.P., Colchester, 1796, Westmorland, 1806, 1807, and 1812, supporting Pitt; created an Irish peer, 1783. [xliv. 332]

PENNINGTON, SIR LOWTHER, second BARON MUNCASTER and sixth baronet (1745–1818), brother of Sir John Pennington, first baron Muncaster [q. v.]; entered the army, 1764; general, 1808. [xliv. 334]

PENNINGTON, MONTAGU (1762–1849), biographer and editor; M.A. Trinity College, Oxford, 1784; vicar of Northbourne, 1806–49; perpetual curate of St. George's Chapel, Deal, 1814–49; wrote 'Memoirs' (1807) of his aunt, Elizabeth Carter [q. v.], and edited her letters and the 'Works' (1809) of Catherine Talbot [q. v.]. [xliv. 334]

PENNY, EDWARD (1714–1791), portrait and historical painter; foundation member of the Royal Academy of Arts, 1768, and its first professor of painting. [xliv. 335]

PENNY, JOHN (d. 1520?), successively bishop of Bangor and Carlisle; of Lincoln College, Oxford; LL.D.

Cambridge; consecrated bishop of Bangor in 1504; translated to Carlisle, 1508. [xliv. 335]

PENNY, JOHN (1803–1885), journalist; edited the 'Sherborne Journal,' 1828–58. [xliv. 336]

PENNY, NICHOLAS (1790–1858), brigadier-general; served with the utmost distinction throughout the siege of Bhurtpore (1825), the first Sikh war (1846–8), and the Indian mutiny; C.B., 1846; second class brigadier, 1851; killed by the mutineers while commanding the Meerut division. [xliv. 336]

PENNY, THOMAS (d. 1589), botanist and entomologist; M.A. Trinity College, Cambridge, 1559; prebendary of St. Paul's, London, 1560 (deprived for nonconformity, 1577). [xliv. 337]

PENNYCUICK, JOHN (d. 1849), brigadier-general; served in Java (1811), Afghanistan (1839), Aden (1841), and in the second Sikh war (1848–9); K.H., 1837; C.B., 1839; killed at Chillianwalla. [xliv. 338]

PENNYCUICK, JOHN FARRELL (1829–1888), general; eldest son of John Pennycuick [q. v.]; served in the Crimea (1854–6), in the Indian mutiny (1857), and in China (1860); C.B., 1861; general, 1886. [xliv. 338]

PENNYMAN, JOHN (1628–1706), pseudo-quaker; fought for Charles I in the civil war; joined the quakers, c. 1658; claimed a special portion of 'the inner light,' and (1670) was committed to prison for burning quaker books in the Royal Exchange; married Mary Boreman, his deceased wife's sister, 1671; wrote with her several works, including 'The Quakers Rejected,' 1676. [xliv. 338]

PENNYMAN, SIR WILLIAM, first baronet (1607–1643), royalist; of Christ Church, Oxford, and the Inner Temple, 1623; created baronet, 1628; bencher, Gray's Inn, 1639; sat in the Short and Long parliaments for Richmond, 1640; disabled from sitting, 1642; fought at Edgehill, 1642; appointed governor of Oxford, 1643. [xliv. 340]

PENRHYN, BARON (1737?–1808). [See PENNANT, RICHARD.]

PENROSE, SIR CHARLES VINICOMBE (1759–1830), vice-admiral; rear-admiral, 1813; placed in command of a squadron co-operating with the army in the Peninsula; chief in command in the Mediterranean, 1814 and 1816; K.C.B. and G.C.M.G., 1816; vice-admiral, 1821. [xliv. 341]

PENROSE, ELIZABETH (1780–1837), writer for the young; daughter of Edmund Cartwright [q. v.]; married John Penrose [q. v.], 1814. She wrote school histories of England (1823) and France (1828), under the pseudonym of 'Mrs. Markham,' taking that name from the village where her aunts resided. [xliv. 342]

PENROSE, FRANCIS (1718–1798), medical writer; practised surgery for many years at Bicester; a voluminous writer of pamphlets upon scientific subjects cognate to medicine. [xliv. 343]

PENROSE, JOHN (1778–1859), divine; of Exeter and Corpus Christi Colleges, Oxford; M.A., 1802; held several preferments, including the vicarage of Langton-by-Wragby, 1802–59; published theological and religious works. [xliv. 343]

PENROSE, THOMAS (1742–1779), poet; of Wadham College, Oxford; rector of Beckington-cum-Standerwick, 1777–9; wrote mainly imitations of Collins and Gray, but in several poems dealt in a natural vein with his disappointments in life. [xliv. 344]

PENRUDDOCK, JOHN (1619–1655), royalist; of Queen's College, Oxford, and Gray's Inn; a Wiltshire gentleman, who fought along with his father and brother for Charles I; joined the abortive insurrection of 1655, and was surprised and taken at South Molton and beheaded at Exeter. [xliv. 345]

PENRY, JOHN (1559–1593), Welsh puritan; B.A. Peterhouse, Cambridge, 1584; M.A. St. Alban Hall, Oxford, 1586; while at the university adopted puritanism in its most extreme Calvinistic form; was brought before the court of high commission (1587) for attacking the Welsh clergy, and sent to prison for twelve days; resolved, in conjunction with John Udall [q. v.], Job Throckmorton [q. v.], and the printer, Robert Waldegrave [q. v.], to pursue the attack against the bishops under the pseudonymous signature of Martin Mar-Prelate, and so became chief author and superintendent of a series of pamphlets in which the bishops' dignity was mercilessly outraged by means of coarse sarcasm and homely wit; fled to Scotland, being suspected of having written the Mar-Prelate tracts, 1590; returned to London, 1592, and was arrested and hanged on the charge of exciting rebellion by his publications while settled in Scotland. [xliv. 346]

PENSHURST, BARONS. [See SMYTHE, PERCY CLINTON SYDNEY, first BARON, 1780–1855; SMYTHE, GEORGE AUGUSTUS FREDERICK PERCY SYDNEY, second BARON, 1818–1857; SMYTHE, PERCY ELLEN FREDERICK WILLIAM, third BARON, 1826–1869.]

PENSHURST, STEPHEN DE (d. 1299). [See PENCESTER.]

PENTLAND, JOSEPH BARCLAY (1797–1873), traveller; educated at Armagh and Paris University; in company with (Sir) Woodbine Parish [q. v.] surveyed a large portion of the Bolivian Andes, 1826–7, and explored other South American districts. [xliv. 350]

PENTON, STEPHEN (1639–1706), divine; of Winchester College and New College, Oxford; fellow of New College, Oxford, 1659–72; M.A., 1667; principal of St. Edmund Hall, Oxford, 1676–84; rector of Glympton, 1684–93; rector of Worth-by-Ripon, 1693–1706; published miscellaneous works. [xliv. 351]

PENTREATH, DOLLY (1685–1777). [See JEFFERY, DOROTHY.]

PEPLOE, SAMUEL (1668–1752), bishop of Chester; M.A. Jesus College, Oxford, 1693; a strong whig in politics; according to tradition, won the favour of George I by refusing to cease praying for him while Preston was in the hands of the Jacobites, although threatened with instant death; nominated (1718) warden of the collegiate church of Manchester; bishop of Chester, 1726–52. [xliv. 352]

PEPPER, JOHN HENRY (1821–1900), exhibitor of 'Pepper's Ghost'; educated at King's College School, London; analytical chemist and lecturer to Royal Polytechnic, London, 1848, and 'honorary' director, c. 1852–1872; began to exhibit (1862) optical illusion known as 'Pepper's Ghost,' invented (1858) by Henry Dircks [q. v.]; published popular scientific works and other writings. [Suppl. iii. 259]

PEPPERELL, SIR WILLIAM, first baronet (1696–1759), the 'hero of Louisburg'; born in New England; distinguished himself in 1745 as commander of the colonial force which captured the strong fortress of Louisburg from the French; created baronet, 1746; promoted lieutenant-general, 1759. [xliv. 353]

PEPUSCH, JOHN CHRISTOPHER (1667–1752), professor of music and composer; born at Berlin; came to London, 1688; as a composer was overshadowed by Handel; famous as a teacher of the science of harmony, many notable musicians being among his pupils; Mus. Doc. Oxford, 1713; became organist to the Charterhouse, London, 1737, where he took up his abode. [xliv. 354]

PEPWELL, HENRY (d. 1540), printer and stationer; carried on business in St. Paul's Churchyard, London, 1518–40. [xliv. 356]

PEPYS, SIR CHARLES CHRISTOPHER, first EARL OF COTTENHAM and third baronet (1781–1851), lord chancellor; nephew of Sir Lucas Pepys [q. v.]; of Harrow and Trinity College, Cambridge; LL.B., 1803; barrister, Lincoln's Inn, 1804; bencher, 1826; whig M.P. for Higham Ferrars, 1831, for Malton, September 1831–6; solicitor-general, 1834; master of the rolls, 1834–6; privy councillor, 1834; lord-chancellor, 1836–41; created baron, 1836; resigned office, 1841; on the retirement of the Peel ministry in 1846, reappointed lord chancellor under Lord John Russell; created Earl of Cottenham, 1850. [xliv. 356]

PEPYS, HENRY (1783–1860), successively bishop of Sodor and Man and of Worcester; brother of Sir Charles Christopher Pepys, first earl of Cottenham [q. v.]; B.A. Trinity College, Cambridge, 1804; fellow of St. John's College, Cambridge; M.A., 1807; D.D., 1840; consecrated bishop of Sodor and Man, 1840; translated to Worcester, 1841. [xliv. 358]

PEPYS, SIR LUCAS, first baronet (1742–1830), physician; of Eton and Christ Church, Oxford; M.A., 1767; M.D., 1774; physician extraordinary to George III, 1777; created baronet, 1784; attended George III in his insanity, 1788–9 and 1804; physician in ordinary, 1792; physician-general of the army, 1794; president, Royal College of Physicians, 1804–10. [xliv. 359]

PEPYS, SIR RICHARD (1588?–1659), lord chief-justice of Ireland of the Middle Temple (treasurer, 1643); sat in the Short parliament for Sudbury, 1640; serjeant-at-law, 1654; baron of the exchequer, 1654; appointed lord chief-justice of Ireland, 1654. [xliv. 359]

PEPYS, SAMUEL (1633–1703), diarist; son of John Pepys, a London tailor, was educated at St. Paul's School, London, and Trinity Hall and Magdalene College, Cambridge; M.A., 1660; formed the family of his father's first cousin, Sir Edward Montagu (afterwards first Earl of Sandwich) [q. v.], 1656; 'clerk of the king's ships' and a clerk of the privy seal, 1660; surveyor-general of the victualling office, 1665, in which capacity he showed himself an energetic official and a zealous reformer of abuses; committed to the Tower of London on charge of complicity with the popish plot, and deprived of his offices, 1679, but released, 1680; secretary of the admiralty, 1686; deprived of the secretaryship of the admiralty at the revolution, after which he lived in retirement, chiefly at Clapham. Fifty volumes of his manuscripts are in the Bodleian Library, Oxford. His 'Diary' remained in cipher in Magdalene College, Cambridge, until 1825, when it was deciphered by John Smith and edited by Lord Braybrooke. An enlarged edition by Mynors Bright [q. v.] appeared in 1875–9, and the whole, except a few passages which cannot be printed, was published in eight volumes (1893, &c.) by Mr. Henry B. Wheatley. [xliv. 360]

PEPYS, WILLIAM HASLEDINE (1775–1856), man of science; descended from Sir Richard Pepys [q. v.]; an original manager of the London Institution (was honorary secretary, 1821–4). He invented many important devices in chemical apparatus, including the present forms of mercury gasometer and water gasholder. [xliv. 366]

PERBURN, JOHN (fl. 1316–1343), admiral; appointed admiral north of the Thames, 1317 and 1321; M.P. for Yarmouth, 1321 and 1324; probably fought at Sluys, 1340. [xliv. 367]

PERCEVAL, ALEXANDER (1787–1858), sergeant-at-arms of the House of Lords; of Trinity College, Dublin; conservative M.P. for Sligo, 1831–41; lord of the treasury, 1841; sergeant-at-arms, 1841–58. [xliv. 367]

PERCEVAL, ARTHUR PHILIP (1799–1853), divine; B.A. Oriel College, Oxford, 1820; B.C.L., 1824; fellow of All Souls College, Oxford, 1821–5; chaplain to George IV, William IV, and Victoria till his death; published slight theological works and 'Origines Hibernicæ,' 1849, in which he identified Ireland with the Patmos of Revelation. [xliv. 368]

PERCEVAL, SIR JOHN, first EARL OF EGMONT, first VISCOUNT PERCEVAL, first BARON PERCEVAL, and fifth baronet (1683–1748), great-grandson of Sir Philip Perceval [q. v.]; of Magdalen College, Oxford; F.R.S., 1702; sat in the Irish parliament for Cork, 1704–15; created a baron, 1715, viscount, 1723, and earl in the Irish peerage, 1733; M.P., Harwich, 1727–34; aided James Edward Oglethorpe [q. v.] in establishing the colony of Georgia (trustees incorporated by royal charter, 1732); his portrait painted by Kneller. [xliv. 368]

PERCEVAL, SIR JOHN, second EARL OF EGMONT, first BARON LOVEL AND HOLLAND, and sixth baronet (1711–1770), eldest son of Sir John Perceval, first earl of Egmont [q. v.]; sat in the Irish House of Commons as member for Dingle Icouch, 1731–48; M.P., Westminster, 1741, Weobley, 1747, Bridgwater, 1754 and 1761; joined Frederick, prince of Wales, and (1748–9), became the most prominent leader of opposition; created Baron Lovel and Holland of Enmore, 1762; first lord of the admiralty, 1763, resigning in 1766 on account of his dissatisfaction with Chatham; published political pamphlets. [xliv. 370]

PERCEVAL, SIR PHILIP (1605–1647), politician; son of Richard Perceval [q. v.]; knighted, 1636; lost an extensive property in Ireland owing to the rebellion of 1641; opposed Charles's intention of granting the demands of the insurgents in order to employ them in England; joined the parliamentary party in 1644, obtaining a

seat in the House of Commons as member for Newport, Cornwall, where he threw in his lot with the moderate presbyterians ; compelled to retire into the country owing to his opposition to the independents, September 1647.
[xliv. 373]

PERCEVAL, RICHARD (1550–1620), colonist and politician ; educated at St. Paul's School, London ; rewarded with a pension for deciphering (1586) packets containing the first sure news of the Spanish Armada; member of the Virginian Company ; author of the well-known Spanish-English dictionary, 'Bibliotheca Hispanica,' 1591.
[xliv. 374]

PERCEVAL, ROBERT (1756–1839), physician and chemist ; descended from Sir Philip Perceval [q. v.]; B.A. Trinity College, Dublin, 1777 ; M.D. Edinburgh, 1780 ; first professor of chemistry, Dublin University, 1785–1805 ; helped to found the Royal Irish Academy (becoming secretary); physician-general to the forces in Ireland, 1819 ; published a few contributions to chemistry.
[xliv. 375]

PERCEVAL, SPENCER (1762–1812), statesman ; second son of Sir John Perceval, second earl of Egmont [q. v.]; educated at Harrow and Trinity College, Cambridge ; M.A., 1781 ; called to the bar ; joined the midland circuit ; obtained crown briefs on the trial of Thomas Paine, 1792, and that of Horne Tooke, 1794 ; counsel to the board of admiralty, 1794 ; king's counsel, 1796 ; M.P. Northampton, 1796 ; supported Pitt in Parliament ; solicitor-general under Addington, 1801 ; attorney-general, 1802 ; during Addington's administration defended the ministry in the Commons, almost single-handed, against Pitt, Fox, and Windham ; retained office on Pitt's return to power ; resigned on Pitt's death, 1806 ; chancellor of the exchequer under the Duke of Portland, 1807 ; successful with his budget, his scheme to convert the three-per-cent. stock into terminable annuities being generally approved ; succeeded the Duke of Portland as prime minister, 1809, but found great difficulty in forming a ministry owing to the dissatisfaction of Canning and Castlereagh ; the government formed by him generally regarded as weak ; saved his position after the disastrous result of the Walcheren expedition (1809) by forcing its leader, Lord Chatham, to resign office ; framed a successful budget, and, in spite of strong opposition to the continuance of the war, insisted that it must go on ; though much disliked by George, prince of Wales, was retained in office by him when he became regent, 1811, on finding that he could not displace him (Perceval) without sacrificing his (the prince's) personal friends ; made banknotes legal tender, July 1811, on the ground that the value of gold had appreciated owing to the drain on it for military payments ; opposed in the cabinet by Lord Wellesley, who thought he was ruining the Peninsular army by his niggardliness ; assassinated, 11 May 1812, in the lobby of the House of Commons by one John Bellingham, a bankrupt, who had a grievance against government.
[xliv. 376]

PERCIVAL, JOHN (d. 1515 ?), provincial of the Franciscans in England ; D.D. Oxford, 1501 ; provincial, c. 1502.
[xliv. 382]

PERCIVAL, JOHN (fl. 1530–1550), Carthusian author; studied at Oxford and Cambridge ; published 'Compendium Divini Amoris,' 1530 ; prior of the Carthusian house at Paris, 1550.
[xliv. 382]

PERCIVAL, ROBERT (1765–1826), traveller and writer ; captain in the army ; fought at Cape of Good Hope, 1796–7, and published 'An Account' of that country, 1804 ; visited Ceylon, 1797, and published 'An Account of Ceylon,' 1803.
[xliv. 382]

PERCIVAL, THOMAS (1719–1762), antiquary ; a Lancashire country gentleman ; contributed papers on the antiquities of northern England to the Royal Society and the Society of Antiquaries.
[xliv. 383]

PERCIVAL, THOMAS (1740–1804), physician and author ; practised medicine in Manchester, and published 'Medical Ethics,' 1803 (new edit. 1849). His works were edited with a memoir. 1807.
[xliv. 383]

PERCY, ALAN (d. 1560), master of St. John's College, Cambridge ; son of Sir Henry Percy, fourth earl of Northumberland [q. v.]; chosen second master of St. John's College Cambridge, 1516, but resigned, 1518 ; given a house and garden at Stepney by Henry VIII, with various preferments.
[xliv. 384]

PERCY, SIR ALGERNON, tenth EARL OF NORTHUMBERLAND (1602–1668), elder son of Sir Henry Percy, ninth earl of Northumberland [q. v.] ; of St. John's College, Cambridge; K.B., 1616 ; M.P., Sussex, 1624, Chichester, 1625 and 1626 ; K.G., 1635 ; admiral of the fleet, 1636 ; lord high admiral, 1638 ; became (1639), on the eve of the Scottish war, general of all the forces south of the Trent, but was dissatisfied with Charles I's policy ; opposed the dissolution of the Short parliament, and in the Long parliament gradually drew to the side of the opposition ; accepted (1642) a place in the parliamentary committee of safety, and endeavoured to promote a reconciliation with Charles I ; appointed (1644) one of the committee of both kingdoms ; became guardian of Charles I's two youngest children, 1645 ; one of the commissioners appointed to negotiate with Charles I at Newport, 1648 ; subsequently headed the opposition in the House of Lords to Charles I's trial ; under the Commonwealth and protectorate remained rigidly aloof from public affairs ; privy councillor after the Restoration ; called by Clarendon 'the proudest man alive.'
[xliv. 385]

PERCY, SIR ALGERNON, fourth DUKE OF NORTHUMBERLAND and first BARON PRUDHOE (1792–1865), second son of Sir Hugh Percy, second duke of Northumberland [q. v.]; entered navy, 1805 ; created baron, 1816 ; travelled in the East; hon. D.C.L. Oxford, 1841 ; succeeded his brother as duke, 1847 ; first lord of the admiralty, 1852–3 ; K.G., 1853 ; admiral, 1862 ; F.R.S. and member of many other learned societies ; prompted by his love of learning to bear the expense of preparing and printing the gigantic 'Arabic Lexicon ' of Edward William Lane [q. v.] (first volume published, 1863). [xliv. 390]

PERCY, LADY ELIZABETH (1667–1722), only surviving daughter and sole heiress of Josceline Percy, eleventh and last earl of Northumberland ; was married (1679) to Henry Cavendish, earl of Ogle; married (1681) to Thomas Thynne [q. v.], but before the consummation of the marriage fled to Lady Temple at the Hague for protection, after which Thynne was assassinated by a rival suitor ; married (1682) to Sir Charles Seymour, sixth duke of Somerset [q. v.] [li. 297]

PERCY, GEORGE (1580–1632), author and colonist; son of Sir Henry Percy, eighth earl of Northumberland [q. v.]; took part in the colonisation of Virginia, 1606 ; deputy-governor, 1609–10 and 1611. He wrote (c. 1625) ' A true Relation ' of affairs in the colony in refutation of the account by John Smith (1580–1631) [q. v.]
[xliv. 391]

PERCY, HENRY, seventh BARON PERCY by tenure (1228 ?–1272), eldest son of Sir William de Percy, sixth baron Percy [q. v.]; fought for Henry III at Northampton and at Lewes.
[xliv. 392]

PERCY, SIR HENRY, first BARON PERCY OF ALNWICK by writ (1272 ?–1315), son of Henry Percy, seventh baron Percy by tenure [q. v.]; took an important part in the Scottish wars of Edward I ; knighted, 1296 ; present at Bannockburn, 1314.
[xliv. 392]

PERCY, HENRY, second BARON PERCY OF ALNWICK (1299 ?–1352), elder son of Sir Henry Percy, first baron Percy [q. v.]; appointed warden of the Scottish marches, 1328 ; along with his father made the Percies the hereditary guardians of the north ; largely helped to secure the victory of Neville's Cross, 1346.
[xliv. 393]

PERCY, HENRY, third BARON PERCY OF ALNWICK (1322–1368), eldest son of Henry Percy, second baron Percy [q. v.]; employed on several occasions as warden of the Scottish marches.
[xliv. 394]

PERCY, SIR HENRY, called HOTSPUR (1364–1403), eldest son of Sir Henry Percy, first earl of Northumberland [q. v.]; knighted, 1377 ; associated with his father as warden of the marches, 1384 ; invested with the Garter, 1387 ; taken prisoner (August 1388) by the Scots at Otterburn, but free and in command on the borders before July 1389 ; assisted (1399) in placing Henry IV on the throne, and as a reward was appointed justiciary of North Wales ; with his father and George Dunbar, earl of March, completely defeated the Scots at Humbledon Hill (Homildon Hill), 1402 ; being already discontented with Henry IV, was further annoyed by being forbidden to ransom his brother-in-law, Sir Edmund de Mortimer [q. v.], on which a quarrel ensued at the October parliament ; though an outward reconciliation was effected, revolted with his father, June 1403, and after giving out for a time that Richard II was in his camp, proclaimed king Edmund of March; was supported by his prisoner, Douglas (captured at Humbledon Hill), and by Owen Glendower [q. v.]; defeated (16 June) and slain by Henry IV at the battle of Shrewsbury.   [xliv. 395]

PERCY, Sir HENRY, first EARL OF NORTHUMBERLAND (1342–1408), elder son of Henry Percy, third baron Percy [q. v.]; K.G., 1366; took part in the French war, and acted as warden of the Scottish marches: in common with Lancaster took up the cause of Wycliffe, being attacked in consequence by the London populace, 1377; marshal of England, 1377; created earl, 1377, thus becoming earl-marshal; quarrelled with his ally, Lancaster, 1381, being offended by his making a truce with the Scots, the violent dispute which ensued being only composed by Richard II's order; supported Richard II's assumption of despotic power, 1397, but was alienated by his violence, and joined Henry of Lancaster with a large force on his landing in Yorkshire; made earl-constable by Henry, and given the Isle of Man in fief; revolted (1403) with his son, Sir Henry Percy, called Hotspur [q. v.]; differences, however, having arisen chiefly in regard to Scottish affairs, submitted after Hotspur's defeat and death at Shrewsbury, and (1404) was pardoned and restored to his offices, except the constableship, and to his possessions, with the exception of grants made by Henry IV; conspired with Owen Glendower [q. v.] and Sir Edmund de Mortimer [q. v.] and was declared a traitor, 1405; fled to Scotland, his revolt being crushed; again invaded England, 1408, and was defeated and slain, 20 Feb., on Bramham Moor.   [xliv. 399]

PERCY, Sir HENRY, second EARL OF NORTHUMBERLAND (1394–1455), only son of Sir Henry Percy, called Hotspur [q. v.]; restored to his dignities and estates (1416) by Henry V; appointed warden of the east marches, and on the death of Henry V became a member of the council of regency, 1422; his later years disquieted by the feud between the Percies and the Nevilles; fell at St. Albans fighting against the Duke of York.   [xliv. 405]

PERCY, Sir HENRY, third EARL OF NORTHUMBERLAND (1421–1461), son of Sir Henry Percy, second earl of Northumberland [q. v.]; appointed warden of the east marches, 1439; defeated and slew the Duke of York at Wakefield, 1460; with Queen Margaret defeated Warwick at St. Albans, 1461; slain at Towton.   [xliv. 407]

PERCY, Sir HENRY, fourth EARL OF NORTHUMBERLAND (1446–1489), only son of Sir Henry Percy, third earl of Northumberland [q. v.]; confined in the Fleet by Edward IV and afterwards in the Tower of London; restored to his earldom, 1469, and appointed warden of the eastern marches; received many favours from Richard III, but was not loyal to him, and, being taken at Bosworth, at once became an adherent of Henry VII; killed near Thirsk, in a contest with the commons of Yorkshire.   [xliv. 408]

PERCY, Sir HENRY (ALGERNON), fifth EARL OF NORTHUMBERLAND (1478–1527), eldest son of Sir Henry Percy, fourth earl of Northumberland [q. v.]; K.B., 1481; fought against the Cornish rebels at Blackheath, 1497; appointed warden-general of the eastern marches, 1503; served in France (1513) with a great retinue; member of the council of the north, 1522.   [xliv. 414]

PERCY, Sir HENRY (ALGERNON), sixth EARL OF NORTHUMBERLAND (1502?–1537), son of Sir Henry Percy, fifth earl of Northumberland [q. v.]; knighted, 1519; warden of the eastern and western marches, 1527; arrested Wolsey, 1530; K.G., 1531; lord president of the council of the north, 1536; unlike his mother and brothers, remained loyal during the Pilgrimage of Grace (1537). [xliv. 416]

PERCY, Sir HENRY, eighth EARL OF NORTHUMBERLAND (1532?–1585), brother of Sir Thomas Percy, seventh earl of Northumberland [q. v.]; M.P., Morpeth, 1554; knighted, 1557; took part in the war against the Scots (1559–60) and remained loyal during his brother's rebellion, 1569, but in 1571 began to intrigue with Mary Queen of Scots; arrested, 1571; released, 1573; commenced fresh intrigues, and (1584) was sent to the Tower of London, when he was found shot through the heart. A verdict of suicide was returned.   [xliv. 409]

PERCY, Sir HENRY, ninth EARL OF NORTHUMBERLAND (1564–1632), eldest son of Sir Henry Percy,

eighth earl of Northumberland [q. v.]; earned by his scientific experiments the sobriquet of 'The Wizard Earl'; served in the Low Countries under Leicester, 1585–6, and against the Spanish Armada, 1588; served at Ostend, 1600; although a protestant, was dissatisfied with James I's treatment of the Roman catholics; after the Gunpowder plot was tried for misprision of treason and condemned to imprisonment for life; was released, 1621, but took no further part in public affairs. George Peele [q. v.] dedicated to him his 'Honour of the Garter,' 1593.
                                              [xliv. 411]

PERCY, Sir HENRY, BARON PERCY OF ALNWICK (d. 1659), son of Sir Henry Percy, ninth earl of Northumberland [q. v.]; sat in the Short parliament as M.P. for Portsmouth, and in the Long parliament as M.P. for Northumberland; an originator of the 'first army plot' (1641), after which he retired to France; general of the ordnance of the king's army, 1643; created baron, 1643; fell in disgrace (1644) through his desire for peace; resigned his command; went to France (1645) and joined Queen Henrietta Maria's party.   [xliv. 413]

PERCY, HENRY (1785–1825), lieutenant-colonel; brother of Hugh Percy [q. v.]; educated at Eton; was aide-de-camp to Sir John Moore and to Wellington, and brought home the Waterloo despatches; C.B., 1815.
                                              [xliv. 414]

PERCY, Lord HENRY HUGH MANVERS (1817–1877), general; educated at Eton; entered the army, 1836; served with distinction in the Crimea, 1854–5; K.C.B., 1873; general, 1877.   [xliv. 417]

PERCY, originally **SMITHSON**, Sir HUGH, first DUKE OF NORTHUMBERLAND of the third creation, second EARL OF NORTHUMBERLAND and fourth baronet (1715–1786), of Christ Church, Oxford; F.R.S., 1736; married (1740) Elizabeth Seymour, heiress of the Percy property, being granddaughter of Charles Seymour, sixth duke of Somerset [q. v.], by his first wife, Elizabeth, heiress of Josceline Percy, eleventh earl of Northumberland; K.G., 1756; privy councillor, 1762; attached himself to Bute and was lord-lieutenant of Ireland under Grenville, 1763–5; made duke, 1766; master of the horse under Lord North, 1778–80; as lord-lieutenant of Middlesex opposed Wilkes's election, and in 1768 was forced by the mob to drink his health.   [xliv. 418]

PERCY, Sir HUGH, second DUKE OF NORTHUMBERLAND (1742–1817), eldest son of Sir Hugh Percy, first duke of Northumberland [q. v.]; served in the Seven Years' war under Ferdinand of Brunswick, and (1774–7) in the American war; M.P., Westminster, 1763–76; joined George, prince of Wales's circle of friends, c. 1790; general, 1793. His temper in politics was impracticable, and he was in perpetual opposition.   [xliv. 420]

PERCY, Sir HUGH, third DUKE OF NORTHUMBERLAND (1785–1847), eldest son of Sir Hugh Percy, second duke of Northumberland [q. v.]; created M.A. St. John's College, Cambridge, 1805; LL.D., 1809; K.G., 1819; ambassador extraordinary in Paris at the coronation of Charles X, 1825, bearing himself the whole cost of the mission; lord-lieutenant of Ireland, 1829–30. [xliv. 422]

PERCY, HUGH (1784–1856), successively bishop of Rochester and Carlisle; M.A. Trinity College, Cambridge, 1805; D.D., 1825; incorporated at Oxford, 1834; consecrated bishop of Rochester in 1827, and translated to Carlisle a few months later.   [xliv. 423]

PERCY, JAMES (1619–1690?), claimant to earldom of Northumberland; trunkmaker in Dublin; made his first claim in 1670, as great-great-grandson of Sir Richard Percy, fifth son of Henry Percy, eighth earl of Northumberland [q. v.]; prosecuted his suit till 1689, when final judgment was given against him in the Lords.
                                              [xliv. 424]

PERCY, JOHN (1569–1641). [See FISHER.]

PERCY, JOHN (1817–1889), metallurgist; M.D. Edinburgh, 1838; elected physician to the Queen's Hospital, Birmingham, 1839; F.R.S., 1847; invented (1848) a method of extracting silver from its ores, which has since been developed, and has suggested other important metallurgical processes; F.G.S., 1851.   [xliv. 425]

PERCY, JOSCELINE (1784–1856), vice-admiral; grandson of Sir Hugh Percy, first duke of Northumberland [q. v.]; entered the navy, 1797; M.P., Beeralston, 1806–20; C.B., 1831; became vice-admiral, 1851, after seeing much active service.   [xliv. 427]

PERCY, PETER (*fl.* 1486), writer of a treatise on the philosopher's stone (Ashmolean MSS.) ; canon of the collegiate church at Maidstone.   [xliv. 428]

PERCY, SIR RALPH (1425–1464), soldier ; son of Sir Henry Percy, second earl of Northumberland [q. v.] ; killed at Hedgely Moor, fighting for the Lancastrians.
[xliv. 428]

PERCY, REUBEN (pseudonym). [See BYERLEY, THOMAS, *d.* 1826.]

PERCY, RICHARD DE, fifth BARON PERCY (1170 ?–1244), one of the twenty-five executors of Magna Charta ; assisted to reduce Yorkshire for the dauphin Louis of France, 1216 ; submitted to Henry III, 1217. [xliv. 428]

PERCY, SHOLTO (pseudonym). [See ROBERTSON, JOSEPH CLINTON, 1788–1852.]

PERCY, SIDNEY RICHARD (1821 ?–1886), landscape-painter and founder of the 'School of Barnes,' ; son of Edward Williams ; painted chiefly English and Welsh scenery, especially views on the Thames ; exhibited at the Royal Academy and other institutions.
[xliv. 429]

PERCY, THOMAS (1333–1369), bishop of Norwich ; son of Henry Percy, second baron Percy [q. v.] ; consecrated, 1356.   [xliv. 395]

PERCY, SIR THOMAS, EARL OF WORCESTER (1344 ?–1403), son of Sir Henry Percy, third baron Percy [q. v.] ; served in France, 1369–73, and on a mission to Flanders with Geoffrey Chaucer, 1377 ; K.G. before 1376 ; took part in Buckingham's French expedition, 1380–1, and (1386) in John of Gaunt's Spanish enterprise ; steward of Richard II's household, 1394 ; created Earl of Worcester 1397, but deserted Richard II for Henry IV, 1399 ; joined his brother Northumberland's rebellion, 1403, and was taken prisoner at Shrewsbury and beheaded. [xliv. 429]

PERCY, SIR THOMAS, seventh EARL OF NORTHUMBERLAND (1528–1572), grandson of Sir Henry Percy, fifth earl of Northumberland [q. v.] ; favoured by Queen Mary as a Roman catholic and restored to his earldom, 1557, his father having been attainted ; rebelled in the interest of Mary Queen of Scots, 1569 ; on the failure of the revolt took refuge in Scotland, but (1572) was handed over to the English authorities and beheaded.
[xliv. 433]

PERCY, THOMAS (1560–1605), organiser of the 'Gunpowder plot' ; great-grandson of Sir Henry Percy, fourth earl of Northumberland [q. v.] ; received from James VI in 1602 assurances which were interpreted as a promise of toleration for Roman catholics on his accession to the English throne ; being disappointed in his hopes, took a most active part in the 'Gunpowder plot,' and was mortally wounded at Holbeach, while resisting capture.
[xliv. 436]

PERCY, THOMAS (1768–1808), editor of Percy's 'Reliques' ; nephew of Thomas Percy (1729–1811) [q. v.] ; of Merchant Taylors' School, London, and St. John's College, Oxford ; fellow, 1792 ; D.C.L., 1793 ; edited the fourth edition of the 'Reliques,' 1794, in which edition the assertion of Ritson that the original manuscripts were not genuine is assailed.   [xliv. 437]

PERCY, THOMAS (1729–1811), editor of the 'Reliques of Ancient English Poetry' and bishop of Dromore ; M.A. Christ Church, Oxford, 1753 ; D.D. Emmanuel College, Cambridge, 1770 ; published from a folio manuscript containing copies, in an early seventeenth-century handwriting, of ancient poems of various dates, the 'Reliques,' 1765, a book which promoted with lasting effect the revival of interest in older English poetry ; bishop of Dromore, 1782–1811 ; published works of antiquarian interest, including 'Northern Antiquities,' 1770.
[xliv. 437]

PERCY, SIR WILLIAM DE, first BARON PERCY (1030 ?–1096), belonged to a Norman family seated at Perci in the present department of La Manche ; came to England (1067) and obtained many lordships in Yorkshire and Lincolnshire.   [xliv. 439]

PERCY, SIR WILLIAM DE, sixth BARON PERCY (1183 ?–1245), nephew of Richard de Percy, fifth baron Percy [q. v.] ; opposed King John in 1215, but left the baronial party before the king's death.   [xliv. 440]

PERCY, WILLIAM (1575–1648), poet ; son of Sir Henry Percy, eighth earl of Northumberland [q. v.] ; of

Gloucester Hall, Oxford ; published a collection of 'Sonnets,' 1594, and left six plays in manuscript, now in the possession of the Duke of Devonshire.   [xliv. 441]

PERCY, WILLIAM HENRY (1788–1855), rear-admiral ; brother of Josceline Percy [q. v.] ; entered the navy, 1801 ; M.P., Stamford ; rear-admiral, 1846. [xliv. 427]

PEREIRA, JONATHAN (1804–1853), pharmacologist ; L.S.A. and apothecary to the dispensary of St. Bartholomew's Hospital, London, 1823 ; F.R.S., 1838 ; author of 'The Elements of Materia Medica,' 1839–40 ; became assistant-physician at London Hospital, 1840 ; M.D. Erlangen, c. 1840, and full physician, 1851.   [xlv. 1]

PERFORATUS, ANDREAS (1490 ?–1549). [See BOORDE, ANDREW.]

PERIGAL, ARTHUR, the elder (1784 ?–1847), historical painter ; began to exhibit in the Royal Academy and British Institution, 1810, and in the Royal Scottish Academy, 1833.   [xlv. 2]

PERIGAL, ARTHUR, the younger (1816–1884), landscape-painter ; son of Arthur Perigal the elder [q. v.] ; painted foreign scenery, but particularly studied the Scottish highlands ; Scottish academician, 1841.   [xlv. 2]

PERKINS. [See also PARKYNS.]

PERKINS, ANGIER MARCH (1799 ?–1881), engineer and inventor ; born in Massachusetts ; made improvements in warming buildings (1831–51), in the manufacture of iron (1843), and in railway axles and boxes (1851).
[xlv. 3]

PERKINS or **PARKINS**, SIR CHRISTOPHER (1543 ?–1622), diplomatist ; B.A. Oxford, 1565 ; joined jesuits, 1566 ; denounced by Edward Kelley [q. v.] as a conspirator, imprisoned, and shortly released, 1589–90 ; employed from 1590, when he became a protestant, as a diplomatic agent ; dean of Carlisle, 1595 ; knighted, 1604 ; master of requests, 1617.   [xlv. 3]

PERKINS, HENRY (1778–1855), book collector ; formed a library at Springfield, Surrey, which realised 26,000*l.* in 1873.   [xlv. 5]

PERKINS or **PARKINS**, JOHN (*d.* 1545), jurist ; educated at Oxford ; barrister, Inner Temple ; author of 'Perutilis Tractatus,' a popular text-book for law students (1st edit., Norman-French, 1530, English translation, 1642 ; 5th edit. 1827).   [xlv. 5]

PERKINS, JOSEPH (*fl.* 1675–1711), poet ; B.A. Oriel College, Oxford, 1679 ; wrote many Latin elegies, and published (1707) 'The Poet's Fancy' and 'Poematum Miscellaneorum Liber primus.'   [xlv. 5]

PERKINS, LOFTUS (1834–1891), engineer and inventor ; son of Angier March Perkins [q. v.] ; M.I.C.E., 1881 ; especially directed his attention to the use of very high pressure steam as a motive power, and to the production of cold, inventing the 'arktos' cold chamber.
[xlv. 6]

PERKINS, WILLIAM (1558–1602), theological writer ; fellow of Christ's College, Cambridge, 1584–92 ; M.A., 1584 ; distinguished for his strong Calvinism ; had great reputation as a teacher, and as a writer was esteemed in the seventeenth century little inferior to Hooker or Calvin ; his works rendered into Dutch, Spanish, Welsh, and Irish. The most famous, 'Armilla Aurea' (1590), reached fifteen editions in twenty years.
[xlv. 6]

PERLEY, MOSES HENRY (1804–1862), Canadian commercial pioneer and man of science ; made many journeys of exploration on behalf of his native state, New Brunswick.   [xlv. 9]

PERNE, ANDREW (1519 ?–1589), dean of Ely ; M.A. St. John's College, Cambridge, 1540 ; fellow, 1540 ; fellow of Queens' College, Cambridge ; vice-president from 1551 ; D.D., 1552 (incorporated at Oxford, 1553) ; vice-chancellor of Cambridge, 1551, 1556, 1559, 1574, and 1580 ; distinguished himself by his eagerness to adjust his theological opinions to his sovereign's pleasure ; made canon of Windsor by Edward VI, 1552 ; rewarded by Queen Mary with the mastership of Peterhouse, 1554, and the deanery of Ely, 1557 ; known as 'old Andrew Turncoat,' 'Andrew Ambo,' 'Old Father Palinode,' and Judas, and a cloak that had been turned was in common parlance said to have been Perned.   [xlv. 10]

PERNE, ANDREW (1596–1654), puritan; fellow of Catharine Hall, Cambridge, 1622–7; rector of Wilby in Northamptonshire, 1627–54; twice preached to the Long parliament. [xlv. 11]

PERRERS or DE **WINDSOR**, ALICE (d. 1400), mistress of Edward III; probably a member of the Hertfordshire family of Perrers, though said by her enemies to be of low birth; entered the service of Philippa of Hainault [q. v.] before October 1366, and became mistress of Edward III in the queen's lifetime; accused of influencing the judges in their determination of suits, and under an ordinance of the Good parliament was sentenced to banishment and forfeiture, 1376; returned to court on the death of Edward, prince of Wales, on which her sentence was reversed by the Bad parliament; her sentence confirmed by the first parliament of Richard II, but revoked (1379) at the instance of her husband, William de Windsor. [xlv. 12]

PERRIN, JEAN BAPTISTE (fl. 1786), teacher of French; born in Paris; migrated to Dublin and published a number of text-books. [xlv. 14]

PERRIN, LOUIS (1782–1864), Irish judge; son of Jean Baptiste Perrin [q. v.]; B.A. Trinity College, Dublin, 1801; justice of the king's bench in Ireland, 1835; privy councillor, 1835. [xlv. 14]

PERRINCHIEF, RICHARD (1623?–1673), royalist divine; M.A. Magdalene College, Cambridge, 1645; fellow; author of several controversial works; completed the edition of 'Βασιλικά' (1662) by William Fulman [q. v.] [xlv. 15]

PERRING, JOHN SHAE (1813–1869), civil engineer and explorer; went to Egypt, 1836, and afterwards became member of the board of public works there; assisted Richard William Howard Vyse [q. v.] in exploring the pyramids. [xlv. 15]

PERRONET, EDWARD (1721–1792), hymn-writer; son of Vincent Perronet [q. v.]; joined John and Charles Wesley and afterwards (1771) the Countess of Huntingdon; finally an independent minister at Canterbury; author of 'All hail the power of Jesu's Name,' 1780. [xlv. 18]

PERRONET, VINCENT (1693–1785), methodist; B.A. Queen's College, Oxford, 1718; vicar of Shoreham, 1728–85; intimate with John and Charles Wesley from 1746, and consulted by them in matters of organisation; styled 'the archbishop of methodism.' He persuaded John Wesley to marry in 1751, and in 1771 supported him against the Countess of Huntingdon [see HASTINGS, SELINA] and her party at the Bristol conference. [xlv. 16]

PERROT, GEORGE (1710–1780), baron of the exchequer; educated at Westminster School; barrister, Inner Temple, 1732; bencher, 1757; K.C., 1759; judge, 1763. [xlv. 19]

PERROT, HENRY (fl. 1600–1626). [See PARROT.]

PERROT, SIR JAMES (1571–1637), politician; son of Sir John Perrot [q. v.]; of Jesus College, Oxford, and the Middle Temple; knighted, 1603; M.P., Haverfordwest, 1597–8, 1604, 1614, and 1628, Pembrokeshire, 1624; author of various treatises. [xlv. 19]

PERROT, SIR JOHN (1527?–1592), lord-deputy of Ireland; commonly reputed to be a son of Henry VIII by Mary Berkley (afterwards wife of Thomas Perrot); K.B. at the coronation of Edward VI; appointed president of Munster (1570), where, until 1572, he was engaged with the rebel, James Fitzmaurice Fitzgerald (d. 1579) [q. v.]; forced Fitzmaurice to submit, and returned to England without leave, 1573; after holding several naval commands, was appointed lord-deputy of Ireland, 1584; defeated (1584) a large body of Hebridean Scots in Ulster, and attempted to expel the MacDonnells from settlements on the Antrim coast; his government efficient but indiscreet, his blundering hostility to Archbishop Adam Loftus [q. v.] being a chief cause of his downfall; returned in disgrace, 1588, and was committed to the Tower of London; found guilty of high treason, 1592; died in the Tower of London. [xlv. 20]

PERROT, JOHN (d. 1671?), quaker sectary; possibly an illegitimate descendant of Sir John Perrot [q. v.]; imprisoned at Rome for preaching against the Romish church, 1658–61; emigrated to the West Indies, 1662; published tracts. [xlv. 26]

PERROT, ROBERT (d. 1550), organist; appointed organist of Magdalen College, Oxford, c. 1515. [xlv. 28]

PERROTT, SIR RICHARD, second baronet (d. 1796), soldier and diplomatist; served under Frederick the Great; succeeded as baronet, 1759. The scandalous 'Life, Adventures, and Amours of Sir R[ichard] P[errott]' was probably due to the malice of an enemy. [xlv. 29]

PERRY, CHARLES (1698–1780), traveller and medical writer; published medical works, besides a valuable 'View of the Levant,' 1743. [xlv. 29]

PERRY, CHARLES (1807–1891), first bishop of Melbourne; senior wrangler, Trinity College, Cambridge, 1828; M.A. Trinity College, Cambridge, 1831; fellow and D.D., 1837; tutor, 1837–41; consecrated bishop, 1847; procured the passage through the parliament of Victoria of the Church Assembly Act (1854), which provided for lay representation; retired, 1876. [xlv. 29]

PERRY, FRANCIS (d. 1765), engraver; best known for his engravings of medals and coins. [xlv. 31]

PERRY, GEORGE (1793–1862), musician; composed several oratorios, operas, and cantatas. [xlv. 31]

PERRY, GEORGE GRESLEY (1820–1897), church historian; B.A. Corpus Christi College, Oxford, 1840; fellow of Lincoln College, Oxford; M.A., 1843; tutor at Lincoln College, Oxford, 1847–52; held college living of Waddington, 1852–97; non-residentiary canon and rural dean of Longoboby, 1861; proctor in convocation, 1867–1893; archdeacon of Stow, 1894. His writings include, 'History of Church of England,' 1860–4, 'Life of Bishop Grosseteste,' 1872, and 'Life of St. Hugh of Avalon, Bishop of Lincoln,' 1879, and contributions to 'Dictionary of National Biography.' [Suppl. iii. 260]

PERRY or **PARRY**, HENRY (1560?–1617?), Welsh scholar; M.A. Balliol College, Oxford, 1583; B.D. Jesus College, Oxford, 1597; canon of Bangor, 1613; published a Welsh treatise on rhetoric (1595), compiled from the notes of William Salisbury (1520?–1600?) [q. v.] [xlv. 32]

PERRY, JAMES (1756–1821), journalist; of Marischal College, Aberdeen; originally a provincial actor; founded the 'European Magazine,' 1782; edited the 'Morning Chronicle'; several times prosecuted for his radical opinions. [xlv. 32]

PERRY, JOHN (1670–1732), civil engineer and traveller; engaged in constructing waterways in Russia, 1698–1712. [xlv. 35]

PERRY, SAMPSON (1747–1823), publicist; editor of the 'Argus,' 1789–93; repeatedly convicted for political libels; finally fled to France, 1793; confined in Newgate (1794–1801) on his return; died an insolvent debtor. [xlv. 36]

PERRY, STEPHEN JOSEPH (1833–1889), astronomer and jesuit; observed several transits and solar eclipses, and (1880) set on foot the regular delineation by projection of the solar surface. [xlv. 36]

PERRY, SIR THOMAS ERSKINE (1806–1882), Indian judge; son of James Perry [q. v.]; B.A. Trinity College, Cambridge, 1829; barrister, Inner Temple, 1834; judge of the supreme court of Bombay, 1840; knighted, 1841; chief-justice, 1847; retired, 1852; M.P., Devonport, 1854–9; member of the council of India, 1859–82; published legal works and books on Indian subjects. [xlv. 38]

PERRYN, SIR RICHARD (1723–1803), baron of the exchequer; of Queen's College, Oxford; barrister, Inner Temple, 1747; was knighted and appointed judge, 1776; retired, 1799. [xlv. 40]

PERSALL, alias HARCOURT, JOHN (1633–1702), jesuit; professor of theology at Liège, 1672–9; preacher in ordinary to James II; rector of the college at Liège, 1694; missioner in the London district, 1701–2. [xlv. 41]

PERSE, STEPHEN (1548–1615), founder of the Perse grammar school at Cambridge; B.A. Caius College, Cambridge, 1569; M.D., 1582; fellow, 1571–1615. In 1888 the Perse grammar school, which he founded by will, was removed from Free School Lane, Cambridge, to Hills Road, Cambridge. [xlv. 41]

PERSONS, ROBERT (1546–1610). [See PARSONS.]

PERTH, EARLS and titular DUKES OF. [See DRUM-MOND, JAMES, fourth EARL and first titular DUKE, 1648-1716; DRUMMOND, JAMES, fifth EARL and second titular DUKE, 1675-1720; DRUMMOND, JAMES, sixth EARL and third titular DUKE, 1713-1747; DRUMMOND, JOHN, seventh EARL and fourth titular DUKE, d. 1747.]

PERTRICH, PETER (d. 1451). [See PARTRIDGE.]

PERUSINUS, PETRUS (1530?-1586?). [See BIZARI, PIETRO.]

PERY, EDMOND SEXTON, VISCOUNT PERY (1719-1806), called to the Irish bar, 1745: member of the Irish House of Commons for Wicklow (1751-60) and Limerick (1760-85), filling the office of speaker, 1771-85: created viscount on retiring, 1785.   [xlv. 42]

PERY, EDMUND HENRY, first EARL OF LIMERICK and second BARON GLENTWORTH (1758-1845), nephew of Edmond Sexton Pery, viscount Pery [q. v.]; of Trinity College, Dublin; politician, attached to the protestant ascendency party; succeeded his father as Baron Glentworth, 1794; created Earl of Limerick, 1803, Baron Foxford (United Kingdom), 1815.   [xlv. 44]

PERYAM, SIR WILLIAM (1534-1604), judge; fellow of Exeter College, Oxford, 1551; M.P., Plymouth, 1562-7; barrister, Middle Temple, 1565; serjeant-at-law, 1579; appointed judge of the common pleas, 1581; sat on various commissions, including that for the trial of Mary Queen of Scots.   [xlv. 44]

PERYN, WILLIAM (d. 1558), Dominican; author of three devotional treatises.   [xlv. 45]

PESHALL or **PECHELL**, SIR JOHN, baronet (1718-1778), historical writer; rector of Stoke Bliss; published 'The History of the University of Oxford to the Death of William the Conqueror,' 1772.   [xlv. 45]

PESTELL, THOMAS (1584?-1659?), divine; M.A. Queens' College, Cambridge, 1609; chaplain to the Earl of Essex; wrote several poems and sermons.   [xlv. 45]

PESTELL, THOMAS (1613-1701), divine; son of Thomas Pestell (1584?-1659?) [q. v.]; M.A. Queens' College, Cambridge, 1636; contributed verses to 'Lachrymæ Musarum' (1650) in memory of Henry, lord Hastings.   [xlv. 46]

PETER (d. 1085), bishop of Lichfield; chaplain to William I; consecrated, 1072; removed the see to Chester, 1075.   [xlv. 46]

PETER OF BLOIS (fl. 1160-1204), archdeacon of Bath and author; born at Blois; studied at Bologna, 1160; went to Sicily, 1167, and became tutor to William II of Sicily; returned to France (1170) and taught at Paris; became secretary to Rotrou, archbishop of Rouen, c. 1171; became cancellarius to the archbishop of Canterbury, c. 1173; archdeacon of Bath, c. 1175 (deprived, c. 1191); secretary to Queen Eleanor, 1190; archdeacon of London, c. 1192. His 'Epistolæ' are historically the most important of his works. A definite edition has yet to appear. He was also the author of over twenty extant 'Opuscula,' chiefly theological in character, of sixty-five sermons, and of several poems. His 'Opera Omnia' were edited by Pierre de Goussainville (1667) and his complete works by John Allen Giles (1848).   [xlv. 46]

PETER HIBERNICUS, DE HIBERNIA, or DE ISERNIA (fl. 1224), jurisconsult; probably of Irish birth; became a subject of the Emperor Frederic II, who sent him (1224) to teach law in the newly established university of Naples.   [xlv. 52]

PETER DES ROCHES (d. 1238), bishop of Winchester; a native of Poitou; served under Richard I as knight and clerk, and became one of his chamberlains; continued in King John's service as a clerk; consecrated bishop of Winchester, 1205; stood by King John in his struggle with Innocent III, and also in his differences with the barons; justiciar, 1213; excommunicated the dauphin Louis, then invading England, May 1216, and fled from Winchester with Henry III, to whom he was appointed guardian after the coronation, in October 1216; involved in controversy from 1223 with Hubert de Burgh [q. v.], and in 1227, when Henry III renounced his guardianship, joined the crusade under the Emperor Frederic II, employing himself as mediator between pope and emperor; after his return obtained Hubert's dismissal from the justiciarship, 1232, filled all offices with his adherents and countrymen,

and became involved in a struggle with the national party under Richard Marshal, third earl of Pembroke [q. v.]; lost his influence on the appointment of Edmund Rich [q. v.] to the see of Canterbury; assisted Gregory IX to defeat the Romans (1235) at Viterbo; died at Farnham.   [xlv. 52]

PETER OF AIGUEBLANCHE (d. 1268), bishop of Hereford; a Savoyard of high rank; accompanied Eleanor of Provence [q. v.] to England, 1236; became bishop of Hereford, c. 1240; assisted in Henry III's foreign transactions and in wringing money from English ecclesiastics: imprisoned and spoiled by the barons, 1263; retired to Savoy, c. 1264, where he died.   [xlv. 60]

PETER OF SAVOY, EARL OF RICHMOND (d. 1268), seventh son of Thomas I of Savoy; received (1234) some possessions in Bugei, which he afterwards enlarged by warfare; came to England, 1240, and was created Earl of Richmond; held various offices in England and Guienne; supported Simon de Montfort and the baronial party, 1258; passed over to Henry III on the breach between Richard de Clare and Simon; became ninth Count of Savoy and marquis in Italy, 1263; died in Bugei. The Savoy Palace in London derived its name from him.   [xlv. 56]

PETER OF ICKHAM (fl. 1290?). [See ICKHAM.]

PETER MARTYR (1500-1562). [See VERMIGLI, PIETRO MARTIRE.]

PETER THE WILD BOY (1712-1785), a protégé of George I; found in the woods near Hamelin, near Hanover, in 1725, 'climbing trees like a squirrel'; was maintained in England from 1726 till death. His story became a theme of satire for Swift and Arbuthnot, and of philosophic speculation for Monboddo.   [xlv. 65]

PETER, DAVID (1765-1837), independent minister; president of the college at Carmarthen, 1795-1837.   [xlv. 65]

PETER, WILLIAM (1788-1853), politician and poet; M.A. Christ Church, Oxford, 1809; barrister, Lincoln's Inn, 1813; an advocate of parliamentary reform; was M.P. for Bodmin (1832-4) and a voluminous author.   [xlv. 66]

PETERBOROUGH, EARLS OF. [See MORDAUNT, JOHN, first EARL, d. 1642; MORDAUNT, HENRY, second EARL, 1624?-1697; MORDAUNT, CHARLES, third EARL, 1658-1735.]

PETERBOROUGH, COUNTESS OF (d. 1755). [See ROBINSON, ANASTASIA.]

PETERBOROUGH, BENEDICT OF (d. 1193). [See BENEDICT.]

PETERBOROUGH, JOHN OF (fl. 1380). [See JOHN.]

PETERBOROUGH, WILLIAM OF (fl. 1188). [See WILLIAM.]

PETERKIN, ALEXANDER (1780-1846), miscellaneous writer; studied law at Edinburgh University; a writer to the signet and journalist; included among his friends Scott, Jeffrey, and Wilson.   [xlv. 67]

PETERKIN, ALEXANDER (1814-1889), journalist; son of Alexander Peterkin [q. v.]   [xlv. 67]

PETERS, CHARLES (1695-1746), physician; M.A. Christ Church, Oxford, 1724; M.D. Oxford, 1732; physician extraordinary to George II, 1733; physician-general to the army, 1739; censor, Royal College of Physicians, 1744; published an edition of the 'Syphilis sive Morbus Gallicus,' of Frascatorius, 1720.   [xlv. 67]

PETERS, CHARLES (1690-1774), Hebrew scholar; M.A. Exeter College, Oxford, 1713; engaged in controversy with Warburton concerning the book of Job.   [xlv. 68]

PETERS or **PETER**, HUGH (1598-1660), independent divine; son of Thomas Dyckwoode, alias Peters; M.A. Trinity College, Cambridge, 1622; lecturer at St. Sepulchre's, London, but (c. 1629) proceeded to Holland and (1635) became minister at Salem, Massachusetts; took a leading part in ecclesiastical matters; rebuked the governor, Henry Vane, for intervening in church matters; took a warm interest in the foundation of the colony of Connecticut, and intervened between the English settlers and the Dutch; returned to England (1641) and became prominent in controversy, war, and politics; his sermons were valuable in winning recruits to the parliamentary army, and his relations of battles and sieges are a semi-official supplement to the generals' reports; influential among the independents; regarded with aversion by the presbyterians; acted with the army during its quarrel with parliament; accompanied Cromwell to Ireland, 1649; present at the battle of Worcester, 1650; made a chaplain to the council of state, 1650, and during the protectorate acted as a regular preacher at Whitehall; endeavoured, 1652-3, to put an end to the war with the Dutch, but after the death of the Protector took little part in public affairs; executed at Charing Cross, 16 Oct. 1660, as an abettor of the execution of Charles I. [xlv. 69]

PETERS, MARY (1813-1856), hymn-writer; *née* Bowley; married John McWilliam Peters, afterwards vicar of Langford, Oxfordshire. [xlv. 77]

PETERS, MATTHEW WILLIAM (1742-1814), portrait and historical painter; a clever artist and pleasant colourist; exhibited at the Royal Academy, 1769-85; B.C.L. Exeter College, Oxford, 1788; held various rectories; became chaplain to George, the prince regent. [xlv. 78]

PETERS or **PETER**, THOMAS (d. 1654), puritan divine; brother of Hugh Peters [q. v.]; M.A. Brasenose College, Oxford, 1625; vicar of Mylor in Cornwall; emigrated to Connecticut, 1644; returned to Mylor, 1647. [xlv. 78]

PETERSDORFF, CHARLES ERDMAN (1800-1886), legal writer; barrister, Inner Temple, 1833; serjeant-at-law, 1858; nominated a judge of the county courts, 1863. [xlv. 79]

PETERSON, PETER (1847-1899), Sanskrit scholar; graduated at Edinburgh, 1867; studied Sanskrit at Lincoln College, Oxford; Boden Sanskrit scholar, 1870; graduated at Balliol College, Oxford, 1872; professor at Elphinstone College, Bombay, 1873; engaged (1882) in search for Sanskrit manuscripts, and discovered many of high literary value in Bombay presidency; published editions of Sanskrit texts. [Suppl. iii. 261]

PETERSON, ROBERT (*fl.* 1576-1606), translator of two treatises from the Italian, one being Giovanni della Casa's 'Galateo,' 1576; a member of Lincoln's Inn. [xlv. 79]

PETGORMO, LORD (1480?-1539). [See SCOTT, THOMAS.]

PETHER, ABRAHAM (1756-1812), landscape-painter; made a reputation by his moonlight subjects; known among dealers as 'Old' Pether. [xlv. 80]

PETHER, SEBASTIAN (1790-1844), landscape-painter; son of Abraham Pether [q. v.]; known to dealers as 'Young' Pether; painted chiefly moonlight views and nocturnal conflagrations. [xlv. 80]

PETHER, THOMAS (*fl.* 1781), wax-modeller; lived at one time with Abraham Pether [q. v.] [xlv. 80]

PETHER, WILLIAM (1738?-1821), mezzotint-engraver and miniaturist; fellow of the Incorporated Society of Artists; occasionally exhibited at the Royal Academy. [xlv. 81]

PETHERAM, JOHN (d. 1858), antiquary and publisher; edited the Mar-Prelate tracts, 1843-7; published 'Historical Sketch of Anglo-Saxon Literature,' 1840. [xlv. 81]

PETIT, JOHN LEWIS (1736-1780), physician; M.A. Queens' College, Cambridge, 1759; M.D., 1766; elected physician to St. Bartholomew's Hospital, London, 1774. [xlv. 81]

PETIT, JOHN LOUIS (1801-1868), divine and artist; descended from Lewis Petit des Etans [q. v.]; M.A. Trinity College, Cambridge, 1826 (incorporated at Oxford, 1850); published 'Architectural Studies in France,' 1854 (new edition by Edward Bell, 1890), and other works. [xlv. 81]

PETIT DES ETANS, LEWIS (1665?-1720), brigadier-general and military engineer; came to England on the revocation of the edict of Nantes, 1685; distinguished himself in the war of the Spanish succession. [xlv. 82]

PETIT, **PETYT**, or **PETYTE**, THOMAS (*fl.* 1536-1554), printer and publisher; issued books bearing his name, 1536-54. [xlv. 84]

PETIT, **PETYT**, or **PARVUS**, WILLIAM (1136-1198?). [See WILLIAM OF NEWBURGH.]

PETIT, WILLIAM (d. 1213), lord justice of Ireland; a follower of Hugh de Lacy, first lord of Meath [q. v.]; served as lord justice, 1191. [xlv. 85]

PETIVER, JAMES (1663-1718), botanist and entomologist; practised as an apothecary; made large collections, which were purchased by Sir Hans Sloane [q. v.], and published many treatises. [xlv. 85]

PETO, SIR SAMUEL MORTON, baronet (1809-1889), contractor and politician; partner in the firm of Grissell & Peto (1830-1847), which constructed many important works, including Nelson Column, 1843; engaged from 1840 in constructing railways in England and abroad; liberal M.P. for Norwich, 1847-54, for Finsbury, 1859-65, for Bristol, 1865-8; created baronet, 1855; with Brassey constructed the Balaclava railway during the Crimean war without commission; retired from public life after the failure of his firm, Peto & Betts, 1866. [xlv. 86]

PETO, WILLIAM (d. 1558), cardinal; provincial of the Grey Friars in England, and a strenuous opponent of Henry VIII's divorce; went abroad, 1533, remaining in the Low Countries till Queen Mary's accession; created cardinal, 1557, and was offered, but refused, the office of legate in England. [xlv. 88]

PETOWE, HENRY (*fl.* 1598-1612), poetaster; was marshal of the artillery guard in London from 1612; author of several unimportant pieces. [xlv. 89]

PETRE, BENJAMIN (1672-1758), Roman catholic prelate; nephew of William Petre (1602-1677) [q. v.]; consecrated bishop of Prusa *in partibus*, 1721. [xlv. 90]

PETRE, EDWARD (1631-1699), confessor of James II; joined jesuits, 1652; sent on the English mission, 1671; committed to Newgate, 1679; summoned to court by James II, 1683, where he allied himself with Richard Talbot and Henry Jermyn; privy councillor, 1687; fled to France at the revolution; rector of St. Omer, 1693-1697. [xlv. 91]

PETRE, SIR WILLIAM (1505?-1572), secretary of state; of Exeter College, Oxford; fellow of All Souls College, Oxford, 1523; D.C.L., 1533; clerk of chancery; knighted and appointed secretary, 1543, retaining office until 1566. [xlv. 93]

PETRE, WILLIAM (1602-1677), translator; of Exeter and Wadham Colleges, Oxford, and the Inner Temple; great-grandson of Sir William Petre [q. v.]; published at St. Omer an English translation of Ribadeneira's 'Flos Sanctorum,' 1669 (2nd edit. 1730). [xlv. 95]

PETRE, WILLIAM, fourth BARON PETRE (1622-1684), descendant of Sir William Petre [q. v.]; accused by Titus Oates (1678) of complicity in the Popish plot, and died in the Tower of London after five years' imprisonment. [xlv. 96]

PETRIE, ALEXANDER (1594?-1662), Scottish divine; M.A. St. Andrews, 1615; first minister of the Rotterdam church, 1643-62; author of 'A Compendious History of the Catholic Church, 600-1600,' 1662. [xlv. 97]

PETRIE, GEORGE (1789-1866), Irish antiquary; painted Irish landscapes, made sketches of Irish antiquarian remains, and wrote valuable articles on Irish antiquities. [xlv. 98]

PETRIE, HENRY (1768-1842), antiquary; appointed keeper of the records in the Tower of London, 1819; projected a 'corpus historicum' for early English history, one volume of which, edited by Sir Thomas Duffus Hardy [q. v.], appeared in 1848. [xlv. 99]

PETRIE, MARTIN (1823-1892), colonel; sixth in descent from Alexander Petrie [q. v.]; ensign, 1846, colonel, 1876; published military works. [xlv. 100]

PETROCUS or **PETROCK**, SAINT (*fl.* 550?). [See PEDROG.]

PETRONIUS (d. 654), fifth abbot of St. Augustine's, Canterbury (hallowed, 640); said to have been a Roman. [xlv. 101]

PETRUCCI, LUDOVICO (*fl.* 1603-1619), poet and soldier of fortune; born at Siena; entered the Venetian service, and afterwards the imperial; came to England, 1610, and became commoner of St. Edmund Hall, Oxford, and afterwards of Balliol College, Oxford; wrote in Latin and Italian. [xlv. 101]

PETRUS (*d.* 606 ?), first abbot of St. Augustine's Abbey, Canterbury; accompanied St. Augustine [q. v.] to England, 596–7; drowned at Ambleteuse.   [xlv. 102]

PETT, PETER (*d.* 1589), master-shipwright; master-shipwright at Deptford from some time in the reign of Edward VI till his death.   [xlv. 102]

PETT, PETER (1610–1670 ?), commissioner of the navy; son of Phineas Pett [q. v.]; commissioner at Chatham, 1648–67; was largely responsible for the efficiency of the ships during the Dutch wars; his supersession due to the disaster at Chatham, 1667.   [xlv. 103]

PETT, SIR PETER (1630–1699), lawyer and author; great-grandson of Peter Pett (*d.* 1589) [q. v.]; of St. Paul's School, London, and Sidney Sussex College, Cambridge; B.A.; migrated to Pembroke College, Oxford; fellow of All Souls College, Oxford, 1648; B.C.L., 1650; student of Gray's Inn; M.P., Askeaton (Irish parliament), 1661–6; barrister, Middle Temple, 1664; original F.R.S., 1663–75; knighted and appointed advocate-general for Ireland; published several treatises, generally polemic in character.   [xlv. 104]

PETT, PHINEAS (1570–1647), master-builder of the navy and naval commissioner; elder son of Peter Pett (*d.* 1589) [q. v.]; of Emmanuel College, Cambridge; master-shipwright at Deptford, 1605; was removed to Woolwich, 1607; appointed commissioner of the navy, 1630.   [xlv. 104]

PETTIE, GEORGE (1548–1589), writer of romances; B.A. Christ Church, Oxford, 1569; author of 'A Petite Pallace of Pettie his Pleasure,' 1576, on the model of 'The Palace of Pleasure' by William Painter [q. v.]; translated Guazzo's 'Civile Conversation,' 1581.   [xlv. 106]

PETTIE, JOHN (1839–1893), painter; pupil of Robert Scott Lauder [q. v.]; first exhibited at the Royal Academy with 'The Armourers,' 1860; R.A., 1873.   [xlv. 106]

PETTIGREW, THOMAS JOSEPH (1791–1865), surgeon and antiquary; made secretary of the Medical Society of London, 1811, of the Royal Humane Society, 1813; acted as surgeon to the Duke and Duchess of Kent; F.R.S., 1827; surgeon of the Charing Cross Hospital, London, from its foundation till 1835; made researches into medical history and biography, publishing several volumes on the subject; contributed to archæological journals.   [xlv. 108]

PETTINGALL or **PETTINGAL**, JOHN (1708–1781), antiquary; B.A. Jesus College, Oxford, 1728; M.A. Corpus Christi College, Cambridge, 1740; D.D.; F.S.A., 1752; prebendary of Lincoln, 1758; published antiquarian works.   [xlv. 109]

PETTINGALL, THOMAS (1745–1826), Whitehall preacher; son of John Pettingall [q. v.]; tutor and censor of Christ Church, Oxford, 1774–9.   [xlv. 109]

PETTITT, HENRY (1848–1893), dramatist; in earlier life a schoolmaster in Camden Town; wrote between 1872 and 1893 a great number of melodramas, musical farces, and other plays.   [xlv. 110]

PETTO, SAMUEL (1624?–1711), puritan divine; M.A. St. Catharine Hall, Cambridge; appointed, 1648, rector of Sandcroft, which cure he relinquished before the enforcement of the Act of Uniformity; published religious works.   [xlv. 111]

PETTUS, SIR JOHN (1613–1690), deputy-governor of the royal mines; knighted, 1641; fought for Charles I, but was appointed deputy-governor of the royal mines by Cromwell, 1655; M.P., Dunwich, 1670; published miscellaneous works.   [xlv. 111]

PETTY, SIR WILLIAM (1623–1687), political economist; studied on the continent and became the friend of Hobbes; Oxford professor of anatomy, 1651; executed for the Commonwealth the 'Down Survey' in Ireland, the first attempt on a large scale at carrying out a survey scientifically, and superintended the redistribution of lands in Ireland; acquiesced in the Restoration; knighted and made an original member of the Royal Society, 1662; published economic treatises, 1662–90, in which he rejected the old 'prohibitory' system, and showed the error of the supporters of the 'mercantile' system in regarding the abundance of the precious metals as the standard of prosperity; analysed the sources of wealth as being labour and land.   [xlv. 113]

PETTY, SIR WILLIAM, first MARQUIS OF LANSDOWNE and second EARL OF SHELBURNE (1737–1805), eldest son of John Petty, first earl of Shelburne; of Christ Church, Oxford; entered the army, 1757, and served in Germany under Lord Granby; took his seat in the House of Lords, 1761, and refused office under Bute; became president of the board of trade under Grenville, 1763, but resigned in September 1763, and soon afterwards attached himself to Pitt; dismissed from the post of aide-de-camp to George III for opposing the government in regard to Wilkes, 1763; attacked the policy of the Stamp Act, 1764; assisted Rockingham in repealing the Stamp Act, 1766, and was appointed secretary of state for the southern department upon Pitt's return to power, 1766; began a policy of conciliation towards the American colonies, but was denounced by his colleagues and hated by George III; found himself perpetually thwarted, and resigned his post, 1768; spent the next fourteen years in strong opposition, especially to the American policy of government; became, on Chatham's death (1778) the leader of that statesman's followers in opposition to Lord North, though he opposed the recognition of American independence; became home secretary under Rockingham, 1782; on Rockingham's death became first lord of the treasury; conceded independence to the United States and made peace with France and Spain; his administration was overthrown by Fox and North, 1783, after which he did not hold office again; created a marquis, 1784; one of the most unpopular statesmen of his time, possibly on account of his contempt for political parties; was generally credited with insincerity, and commonly known as 'Malagrida,' which occasioned Goldsmith's unfortunate remark to him, 'Do you know that I never could conceive the reason why they call you Malagrida, for Malagrida was a very good sort of man.' He was a munificent patron of the fine arts, and his collection of manuscripts was purchased for the British Museum in 1807.   [xlv. 119]

PETTY-FITZMAURICE, SIR HENRY, third MARQUIS OF LANSDOWNE (1780–1863), son of Sir William Petty, first marquis of Lansdowne [q. v.]; of Westminster School, Edinburgh University, and Trinity College, Cambridge; M.A. Cambridge, 1801; created LL.D., 1811; M.P., Calne, 1803, Cambridge, 1805; became chancellor of the exchequer under Grenville, 1806, raising the property tax from six and a-half to ten per cent.; on the resignation of the ministry (1807), became an active leader of opposition; succeeded his half-brother as third marquis, 1809; for the next twenty years supported the abolition of the slave trade and other liberal measures; brought about a coalition between a section of the whigs and the followers of Canning, and entered the cabinet without office, 1827; resigned, 1828; became president of the council (1830) under Lord Grey, retaining office intermittently until 1841; again president of the council (1846–52) under Lord John Russell; remained in the cabinet without office, 1852–63; throughout life he was 'a very moderate whig.'   [xlv. 127]

PETTY-FITZMAURICE, SIR HENRY THOMAS, fourth MARQUIS OF LANSDOWNE (1816–1866), son of Sir Henry Petty-Fitzmaurice, third marquis of Lansdowne [q. v.]; of Westminster School and Trinity College, Cambridge; M.P., Calne, 1847–56; junior lord of the treasury under Russell, 1847–9; under-secretary of state for foreign affairs under Palmerston, 1856–8; K.G., 1864.   [xlv. 131]

PETTYT, THOMAS (1510?–1558 ?), military engineer; distinguished himself in 1548 by his successful defence of Haddington against the Scots and French.   [xlv. 131]

PETYT, WILLIAM (1636–1707), archivist and antiquary; barrister, Middle Temple, 1670, autumn reader, 1694, treasurer, 1701; for many years keeper of the records in the Tower of London; drew up a list of the records, made a collection of parliamentary tracts, in above eighty volumes, and published three historical and legal treatises; his manuscripts in the Inner Temple library.   [xlv. 132]

PEVERELL, THOMAS (*d.* 1419), successively bishop of Ossory, Llandaff, and Worcester; educated at Oxford; became a Carmelite; consecrated bishop of Ossory, 1397; translated to Llandaff, 1398, to Worcester, 1407, where he was active against the lollards.   [xlv. 133]

PEVERELL, WILLIAM (*fl.* 1131–1155), a Nottinghamshire baron; leader in the battle of the Standard, 1138; supported Stephen; on Henry II's advance northwards (1155) took refuge in a monastery. [xlv. 134]

PEYTO, WILLIAM (*d.* 1558). [See PETO.]

PEYTON, SIR EDWARD, second baronet (1588?–1657), parliamentarian: educated at Cambridge; knighted, 1611; succeeded as baronet, 1616; M.P., Cambridgeshire, 1621–6; took an active part in the war of pamphlets in 1641–2 and fought for parliament. In the 'Divine Catastrophe' (1652) he showed sympathies with the Fifth-monarchy men. [xlv. 134]

PEYTON, EDWARD (*d.* 1749), commodore; entered the navy, 1707; being left by the death of Curtis Barnett [q. v.] in command of the East India squadron, avoided engaging La Bourdonnais, thinking his force inferior; put under arrest by his successor, Thomas Griffin (*d.* 1771) [q. v.], and sent to England, where he died. [xlv. 135]

PEYTON, SIR HENRY (*d.* 1622?), adventurer; knighted, 1606; commanded a Venetian fleet, 1618. [xlv. 136]

PEYTON, SIR JOHN (1544–1630), governor of Jersey; knighted, 1586; lieutenant of the Tower of London, 1597–1603; governor of Jersey, 1603–30. [xlv. 137]

PEYTON, SIR JOHN (1579–1635), governor of Jersey; only son of Sir John Peyton (1544–1630) [q. v.]; of Queens' College, Cambridge; knighted, 1603; lieutenant-governor of Jersey, 1628–30, and afterwards governor, 1630–5. [xlv. 138]

PEYTON, SIR JOHN STRUTT (1786–1838), captain in the navy; great-grandson of Edward Peyton [q. v.]; entered the navy in 1797, and saw much service; K.C.H., 1836. [xlv. 138]

PEYTON, THOMAS (1595–1626), poet; probably brother of Sir Edward Peyton [q. v.]; of Cambridge University and Lincoln's Inn; published 'The Glasse of Time,' 1620–3, a scriptural poem. [xlv. 139]

PFEIFFER, EMILY JANE (1827–1890), poetess; *née* Davis; married J. E. Pfeiffer, a German merchant, 1853; published several volumes of poetry in the style of Mrs. Browning. [xlv. 139]

PHAER or PHAYER, THOMAS (1510?–1560), lawyer, physician, and translator; M.D. Oxford, 1559; wrote two legal handbooks and several popular medical treatises, and translated nine books of Virgil's ' Æneid,' as well as part of the tenth, into English verse between 1555 and 1560. Thomas Twyne [q. v.] completed the translation in 1584. [xlv. 140]

PHALERIUS, GULLIELMUS (pseudonym). [See WHITE, WILLIAM, 1604–1678.]

PHAYRE, SIR ARTHUR PURVES (1812–1885), first commissioner of British Burma; educated at Shrewsbury School; entered the Bengal army, 1828; became commissioner of Arakan, 1849, of Pegu, 1852; chief commissioner of British Burma, 1862–7; G.C.M.G., 1878; published a 'History of Burma,' 1883. [xlv. 141]

PHAYRE or PHAIRE, ROBERT (1619?–1682), regicide; one of the three to whom the warrant for the execution of Charles I was addressed; escaped severe punishment at the Restoration through having married the daughter of Sir Thomas Herbert (1606–1682) [q. v.]; became a Muggletonian, 1662. [xlv. 142]

PHAYRE, SIR ROBERT (1820–1897), general; brother of Sir Arthur Purves Phayre [q. v.]; educated at Shrewsbury School; ensign in East India Company's service, 1839; captain, 1848; in Persian expedition, 1856–7; quartermaster-general to Bombay army, 1857–68; major, Bombay staff corps, 1861; colonel, 1868; in Abyssinian campaign, 1868; C.B. and aide-de-camp to Queen Victoria, 1868; commandant of Sind frontier force, 1868–72; resident (1873–4) of Baroda, where his life was attempted at the instigation of the gaekwar, Malhar Rao, who was in consequence deposed, 1875; major-general, 1880; commanded reserve division in second Afghan war, 1880; K.C.B. and lieutenant-general, 1881; commanded division of Bombay army, 1881–6; general, 1889; G.C.B., 1894. [Suppl. iii. 262]

PHELIPS. [See also PHILIPPS, PHILIPS, and PHILLIPS.]

PHELIPS, SIR EDWARD (1560?–1614), speaker of the House of Commons and master of the rolls; autumn reader, Middle Temple, 1596; entered parliament (1601) as knight of the shire for Somerset; king's serjeant and knighted, 1603; speaker, 1604; became master of the rolls, 1611. [xlv. 143]

PHELIPS, SIR ROBERT (1586?–1638), parliamentarian; eldest son of Sir Edward Phelips [q. v.]; knighted, 1603; M.P., East Looe, 1604–11; took a prominent part in opposition, 1621, attacking the Spanish marriage, for which he was imprisoned; assumed an attitude of hostility to Buckingham, 1625. [xlv. 144]

PHELPS, JOHN (*fl.* 1636–1666), regicide; of Corpus Christi College, Oxford; one of the clerks of the court which sat to try Charles I; was attainted on the Restoration, but escaped to the continent. [xlv. 145]

PHELPS, SAMUEL (1804–1878), actor; first appeared on the stage in 1826; after some years spent in the provinces, appeared at the Haymarket, London, as Shylock, 1837, and afterwards at Covent Garden, London, under Macready; joined in opening Sadler's Wells, Islington, 1844, where he succeeded in 'making Shakespeare pay' for nearly twenty years; became sole manager in the season, 1860–1, but gave up the enterprise (1862), after he had produced thirty-four of Shakespeare's plays; afterwards acted chiefly at Drury Lane, London; excelled in characters of rugged strength. [xlv. 146]

PHELPS, THOMAS (*fl.* 1718–1776), astronomer; the first in England to detect the great comet of 1743. [xlv. 150]

PHELPS, WILLIAM (1776–1856), topographer; of Balliol College, Oxford; B.A. St. Alban Hall, 1797; issued seven parts of an elaborate 'History and Antiquities of Somersetshire,' 1835–9. [xlv. 150]

PHERD, JOHN (*d.* 1225), erroneous name of JOHN OF FOUNTAINS. [See FONTIBUS, JOHN DE.]

PHESANT, PETER (1580?–1649), judge; barrister, Gray's Inn, 1608, ancient, 1622, bencher, 1623, reader, 1624; serjeant-at-law, 1640; voted a judge of common pleas by the House of Commons, 1645. [xlv. 150]

PHILALETHES, ALAZONOMASTIX (pseudonym). [See MORE, HENRY, 1614–1687.]

PHILALETHES, EIRENÆUS (pseudonym). [See EIRENÆUS, *b.* 1622?]

PHILALETHES, EUGENIUS (pseudonym). [See VAUGHAN, THOMAS, 1622–1666.]

PHILIDOR, FRANÇOIS ANDRÉ DANICAN (1726–1795), chess-player and composer; born at Dreux; son of a French musician; learned chess while in attendance as a musician at Versailles; his fame European from early youth; spent much of his time in England; published (1748) his 'Analyse du jeu des Echecs'; his skill commemorated among chess-players by 'Philidor's defence' and 'Philidor's legacy.' He was also celebrated as a composer, introducing several new modes. [xlv. 151]

PHILIP. [See also PHILLIP and PHYLIP.]

PHILIP II OF SPAIN (1527–1598), king of Spain and husband of Queen Mary of England; son of the emperor Charles V; married Queen Mary, who chose him against the wishes of parliament and the country, in Winchester Cathedral, 1554; K.G., 1554; became unpopular; advised Mary to pardon the Princess Elizabeth; resolved to leave England, in disappointment that an expected heir was not born to him, 1555; still continued to watch English politics, but was at variance with Queen Mary, urging her against her will to select a less bigoted man than Bishop Thirlby as chancellor; returned to England, 1557, desiring to draw England into his schemes upon the Low Countries; left for the Low Countries, and never saw Queen Mary again; made overtures to the Princess Elizabeth, but finally married (1559) the French king's daughter, Isabella; sent the Spanish Armada against England, 1588; died in Spain. [xxxvi. 343]

PHILIP OF MONTGOMERY, called GRAMMATICUS (*d.* 1099), crusader; son of Roger de Montgomery, earl of Shrewsbury and Arundel [q. v.]; rebelled with Robert de Mowbray [q. v.], 1095; died at Jerusalem, while accompanying Robert of Normandy in the first crusade. [xlix. 103]

PHILIP DE THAUN (*fl.* 1120), Anglo-Norman writer; wrote two poems of great value for the history of Anglo-Norman literature; perhaps the earliest poet in the *langue d'oïl* whose work has survived. [xlv. 153]

PHILIP DE BRAOSE (*fl.* 1172). [See BRAOSE.]

PHILIP OF POITIERS (*d.* 1208 ?), bishop of Durham; accompanied Richard I on his crusade; returned to England before Richard I, and (1195) was elected bishop; mentioned as one of King John's evil counsellors in the controversy with Pope Innocent III. [xlv. 154]

PHILIP DE VALOGNES (*d.* 1215). [See VALOGNES.]

PHILIP DE ULECOT (*d.* 1220). [See ULECOT.]

PHILIP or **PHILIPPE** DE RIM or DE REMI (1246 ?-1296), supposed Anglo-Norman poet; now generally identified with Philippe de Beaumanoir (1246 ?-1296), the French jurist and poet. [xlv. 154]

PHILIP, ALEXANDER PHILIP WILSON (1770 ?-1851 ?), physician and physiologist; M.D. Edinburgh, 1792; elected physician to the Worcester infirmary, 1802; removed to London, 1817; F.R.C.P., 1834; went to Boulogne (*c.* 1842) in consequence of financial difficulties; published medical works, several of which were translated into various languages. [xlv. 155]

PHILIP, JOHN (*fl.* 1566), author; produced (1566) three tracts, chiefly in verse, describing the trial of three witches at Chelmsford. [xlv. 156]

PHILIP, JOHN (1775-1851), South African missionary; went to South Africa (1819) with a deputation to visit the stations of the London Missionary Society; remained in Cape Town, and for the rest of his life constantly endeavoured to defend the natives against the treatment of the colonists; his views endorsed by a parliamentary committee, 1837, on which Governor D'Urban was dismissed; his policy of erecting independent native states wrecked by the Kaffir war of 1846. [xlv. 156]

PHILIP, JOHN BIRNIE (1824-1875), sculptor; executed portrait busts and statues; employed for eight years on the Albert Memorial in Hyde Park, London. [xlv. 158]

PHILIP, ROBERT (1791-1858), divine; independent minister at Maberley Chapel, London, 1826-55; published numerous works. [xlv. 158]

PHILIPHAUGH, LORD (1655-1708). [See MURRAY, SIR JAMES.]

PHILIPOT. [See also PHILPOT.]

PHILIPOT, **PHELIPOT**, or **PHILPOT**, SIR JOHN (*d.* 1384), mayor of London; a member of the Grocers' Company; M.P., London, 1371 and 1381; headed the opposition to John of Gaunt; appointed joint-treasurer for the French war (1377) at the request of the Commons; mayor, 1378; assisted Richard II during the peasants' revolt, 1381. [xlv. 159]

PHILIPOT, JOHN (1589 ?-1645), Somerset herald; Rouge Dragon, 1618; Somerset herald, 1624; accompanied Charles I to Oxford after the outbreak of the civil war; made many county visitations. [xlv. 161]

PHILIPOT, THOMAS (*d.* 1682), poet and miscellaneous writer; son of John Philipot [q. v.]; M.A. Clare Hall, Cambridge, *regiis literis*, 1636 (incorporated at Oxford, 1640); published miscellaneous works. [xlv. 163]

PHILIPPA OF HAINAULT (1314 ?-1369), queen of Edward III; daughter of William the Good, count of Holland and Hainault; married to her second cousin, Edward III, 1328, a papal dispensation being procured; said by Froissart to have harangued the English troops (1346) before the battle of Neville's Cross; before Christmas, 1346, joined Edward III before Calais, where she interceded for the six principal burgesses on the surrender of the town in August 1347; received Froissart on his arrival in England, 1361, and made him her clerk or secretary; died, and was buried at Windsor. [xlv. 164]

PHILIPPA OF LANCASTER (1359-1415), queen of John I of Portugal; daughter of John of Gaunt, duke of Lancaster [q. v.]; married, 1387; became the mother of five celebrated sons, Edward I, Don Pedro the great regent, Prince Henry the navigator, Ferdinand the saint, and John. [xlv. 167]

PHILIPPART, JOHN (1784 ?-1874), military writer; clerk in the war office, and for forty-three years chancellor of the order of St. John of Jerusalem; industriously compiled many books of reference relating to the army. [xlv. 168]

PHILIPPS. [See also PHELIPS, PHILIPS, and PHILLIPS.]

PHILIPPS, BAKER (1718 ?-1745), lieutenant in the navy; entered the navy, 1733; shot for neglect of duty in surrendering (after the death of the captain) the Anglesea to a French warship of superior force—an unjust sentence, since he only assumed command when the vessel was virtually lost. [xlv. 168]

PHILIPPS, SIR ERASMUS, fifth baronet (*d.* 1743), economic writer; of Pembroke College, Oxford, and Lincoln's Inn; M.P., Haverfordwest, 1726-43; succeeded to the baronetcy, 1736; wrote four economic treatises. [xlv. 169]

PHILIPPS, FABIAN (1601-1690), author; spent much money during the civil war in publishing books in support of the royal cause; became at the Restoration remembrancer of the court of the council and marches of Wales. [xlv. 169]

PHILIPPS, JENKIN THOMAS (*d.* 1755), translator; became tutor to the children of Prince George (George II) before 1726; published Latin dissertations and translations from the German. [xlv. 170]

PHILIPPS or **PHILIPPES**, MORGAN (*d.* 1570), Roman catholic divine; fellow of Oriel College, Oxford, 1538; M.A., 1542; principal of St. Mary Hall, Oxford, 1546-50; publicly disputed with Peter Martyr, 1549; retired to Louvain on the accession of Queen Elizabeth, dying at Douay. The 'Treatise concerning' Mary Queen of Scots' right to the English throne, by John Leslie (1527-1596) [q. v.] was republished in 1571 under his name. [xlv. 171]

PHILIPPS, THOMAS (1774-1841), vocalist and composer; first appeared at Covent Garden, London, 1796; made a tour in America; retired early from the stage; taught singing and composed ballads. [xlv. 171]

PHILIPS. [See also PHELIPS, PHILIPPS, and PHILLIPS.]

PHILIPS, AMBROSE (1675 ?-1749), poet; fellow of St. John's College, Cambridge, 1699-1708; M.A., 1700; joined the Addison circle, and had his 'Distressed Mother' (1712, an adaptation of Racine's 'Andromaque') lauded in the 'Spectator'; M.P., Armagh borough (Irish parliament), 1727; judge of the prerogative court, 1733. His pastorals excited Pope's jealousy, and gave rise to bitter attacks in Pope's satires. He brought out the 'Freethinker' (1718-19), an imitation of the 'Spectator.' [xlv. 172]

PHILIPS, CHARLES (1708-1747), portrait-painter; noted for his small whole-lengths and conversation pieces; patronised by Frederick, prince of Wales. [xlv. 173]

PHILIPS or **PHILLIPS**, GEORGE (1599 ?-1696), Irish writer and governor of Londonderry; warned the inhabitants of Londonderry in 1688 to be on their guard against Antrim's highlanders; became governor, December 1688, but resigned shortly in favour of Robert Lundy [q. v.]; published several political pamphlets on Irish matters. [xlv. 174]

PHILIPS, HUMPHREY (1633-1707), nonconformist minister; B.A. Wadham College, Oxford, 1654; M.A. Magdalen College, Oxford, 1656; elected fellow of Magdalen, 1656, but ejected, 1660, and imprisoned, 1662; went to Holland on his release, returning afterwards to England, where he was much persecuted. [xlv. 175]

PHILIPS, JOHN (1676-1709), poet; of Christ Church, Oxford; author of the 'Splendid Shilling,' a mock heroic poem in Miltonic blank verse, first published in 1701; employed by Harley and St. John to write verses on 'Blenheim' as a tory counterpart to Addison's 'Campaign'; wrote his most important work, 'Cyder' (1708), in imitation of Virgil's 'Georgics.' [xlv. 175]

PHILIPS, KATHERINE (1631-1664), verse-writer; daughter of John Fowler, a London merchant; married (1647) James Philips of Cardigan; adopted the pseudonym 'Orinda,' to which her contemporaries prefixed the epithet 'Matchless'; her earliest verses prefixed (1651) to the 'Poems' of Henry Vaughan (1622–1695) [q. v.]; her translation of Corneille's 'Pompée' acted in Dublin with great success. Her collected verses appeared, 1667. [xlv. 177]

PHILIPS, MILES (*fl.* 1568–1582), mariner; sailed with Captain John Hawkyns (1568) to the Indies, and became a prisoner in Mexico; eventually escaped and landed in England in 1582. He himself related his story to Hakluyt. [xlv. 178]

PHILIPS, NATHANIEL GEORGE (1795–1831), artist; exhibited landscapes in Liverpool and Manchester; executed engravings of old halls in Lancashire and Cheshire. [xlv. 179]

PHILIPS, PEREGRINE (1623–1691), nonconformist preacher; studied at Oxford; puritan incumbent of several livings in Pembroke, but ejected, 1662; suffered much persecution. [xlv. 179]

PHILIPS or **PHILIPPI,** PETER or PIETRO (*fl.* 1580–1621), musical composer; born in England; organist to the Archduke Albert and Archduchess Isabella in the Netherlands, 1596–1621; published many works at Antwerp. [xlv. 180]

PHILIPS or **PHILLIPS,** RICHARD (1661–1751), governor of Nova Scotia; was governor from 1720 to 1749, but after 1730 resided in England, neglecting his duties. [xlv. 181]

PHILIPS, ROBERT (*fl.* 1543–1559 ?), musician; said by Fox to have been a gentleman of the king's chapel at Windsor and 'a notable singing man.' [xlv. 180]

PHILIPS, ROBERT (*d.* 1650 ?), confessor to Queen Henrietta Maria; of Scottish origin; attached to Queen Henrietta Maria after the expulsion of her French attendants, 1626; commissioned by Queen Henrietta Maria to request aid from Pope Urban VIII against the Long parliament, for which he was summoned before parliament, the matter being eventually allowed to drop; accompanied Queen Henrietta Maria to the Hague, 1642. [xlv. 181]

PHILIPS, ROWLAND (*d.* 1538?), warden of Merton College, Oxford; educated at Oriel College, Oxford; elected warden of Merton College, 1521; resigning, 1525; D.D., 1522. [xlv. 182]

PHILIPS, WILLIAM (*d.* 1734), dramatist; son of George Philips [q. v.]; wrote several tragedies, produced in London and Dublin. [xlv. 182]

PHILLIMORE, GREVILLE (1821–1884), divine and author; son of Joseph Phillimore [q. v.]; of Westminster School, the Charterhouse, and Christ Church, Oxford; M.A., 1844; vicar of Down-Ampney, 1851–67; rector of Henley, 1867–83; rector of Ewelme, 1883–4; joint-editor of the 'Parish Hymn Book' (1863), to which he contributed eleven original hymns. [xlv. 182]

PHILLIMORE, SIR JOHN (1781–1840), captain in the navy; brother of Joseph Phillimore [q. v.]; entered the navy, 1795; advanced to post rank, 1807; fought a stubborn action with the French frigate Clorinde, 1814, and (*c.* 1819) thrashed William James (*d.* 1827) [q. v.] for his description of the action in his naval history; C.B., 1815; retired, 1826. [xlv. 183]

PHILLIMORE, JOHN GEORGE (1808–1865), jurist; eldest son of Joseph Phillimore [q. v.]; of Westminster School and Christ Church, Oxford; M.A., 1831; a clerk of the board of control of India, 1827–32; barrister, Lincoln's Inn, 1832; bencher, 1851; Q.C., 1851; published several works on Roman and canon law. [xlv. 185]

PHILLIMORE, JOSEPH (1775–1855), civilian; of Westminster School and Christ Church, Oxford; D.C.L., 1804; regius professor of civil law, Oxford, 1809–55; M.P., St. Mawes, 1817–26, Yarmouth, Isle of Wight, 1826–1830; advocating catholic emancipation; filled several important judicial posts, and edited two series of cases heard in the ecclesiastical courts. [xlv. 185]

PHILLIMORE, SIR ROBERT JOSEPH, first baronet (1810–1885), civilian and judge; son of Joseph Phillimore [q. v.]; of Westminster School and Christ Church, Oxford; D.C.L., 1838; barrister, Middle Temple, 1841; judge of the Cinque ports, 1855; admiralty advocate, 1855; liberal-conservative M.P., Tavistock, 1852–7; Q.C., 1858; became judge of the high court of admiralty, 1867; created baronet, 1883; a scholar both in the classical and modern languages, and a jurist of wide reading; his most important work, 'Commentaries on International Law,' 1854–61. [xlv. 186]

PHILLIP. [See also PHILIP and PHYLIP.]

PHILLIP, ARTHUR (1738–1814), vice-admiral and first governor of New South Wales; entered the navy, 1755; reached post rank, 1781; founded, January 1788, a convict settlement on the harbour of Port Jackson, which he named Sydney after Thomas Townshend, viscount Sydney [q. v.]; carried the settlement through many privations from lack of food and of free settlers; returned to England (1792) in bad health; rear-admiral, 1801; vice-admiral, 1810. [xlv. 188]

PHILLIP, JOHN (1817–1867), subject and portrait painter; began to execute likenesses while apprenticed to an Aberdeen glazier, and (1836) attracted the attention of Lord Panmure, who paid for his education in London; exhibited at the Royal Academy from 1838, painting chiefly portraits and Scottish subjects; the style of his painting changed by a visit to Seville, 1851; his later work influenced by Velasquez; 'La Bomba,' 1863, 'La Gloria,' 1864, and 'Il Cigarrillo,' 1864, among his masterpieces; A.R.A., 1857, and R.A., 1859. [xlv. 189]

PHILLIP, WILLIAM (*fl.* 1596–1619), translator; made several translations from the Dutch, chiefly of books of travel. [xlv. 191]

PHILLIPPS. [See also PHELIPS, PHILIPPS, PHILIPS, and PHILLIPS.]

PHILLIPPS, JAMES ORCHARD HALLIWELL- (1820–1889). [See HALLIWELL.]

PHILLIPPS, SAMUEL MARCH, formerly SAMUEL MARCH (1780–1862), legal writer; of the Charterhouse and Sidney Sussex College, Cambridge; M.A., 1805; assumed the surname Phillipps in 1796; barrister, Inner Temple, 1806; permanent under-secretary for home affairs, 1827–48. His 'Treatise on the Law of Evidence' (1814) was in its day a standard text-book. [xlv. 192]

PHILLIPPS, SIR THOMAS, first baronet (1792–1872), antiquary and bibliophile; of Rugby and University College, Oxford; M.A., 1820; showed from his earliest years a passion for collecting books and manuscripts; his collection rich in old Welsh poetry; possessed four hundred or five hundred volumes of oriental manuscripts; created baronet, 1821; established (*c.* 1822) a private printing press at his residence, Middle Hill, Broadway, Worcestershire; printed visitations, extracts from registers, genealogies, cartularies, and brief catalogues of collections of manuscripts in private and public libraries; removed in later life to Thirlestane House, Cheltenham. [xlv. 192]

PHILLIPS. [See also PHELIPS, PHILIPPS, and PHILIPS.]

PHILLIPS, ARTHUR (1605–1695), musician; of New College, Oxford; organist at Bristol, 1638, and at Magdalen College, Oxford, 1639; choragus and professor of music at Oxford, 1639–56; afterwards served Queen Henrietta Maria as organist in France. [xlv. 195]

PHILLIPS, CATHERINE (1727–1794), quakeress; daughter of Henry Payton; entered the ministry, 1748, and thenceforth went on annual preaching tours amongst the Friends; married William Phillips, 1772; a volume of 'Memoirs' appeared, 1797. [xlv. 195]

PHILLIPS, CHARLES (*fl.* 1766–1783), engraver; worked chiefly in mezzotint after the old masters. [xlv. 196]

PHILLIPS, CHARLES (1787 ?–1859), barrister and miscellaneous writer; B.A. Trinity College, Dublin, 1806; entered the Middle Temple, 1807; called to the Irish bar, 1812; joined the Connaught bar and speedily made a reputation by his florid oratory; called to the English bar, 1821, becoming shortly leader at the Old Bailey; appointed commissioner of the insolvent debtors' court of London, 1846; published miscellaneous works, including 'Napoleon III' (3rd edit. 1854). [xlv. 196]

PHILLIPS, EDWARD (1630–1696 ?), author; son of Edward Phillips and his wife Ann, only sister of the poet Milton, by whom he was educated and with whom he maintained affectionate relations until the poet's death; of Magdalen Hall, Oxford; became (1663) tutor to the son of John Evelyn the diarist, and (1665) to Philip Herbert (afterwards seventh Earl of Pembroke) [q. v.]; subsequently resumed his former occupation of hack-writer in London; chiefly remembered for his 'New World of Words,' 1658, a philological dictionary of doubtful originality, little merit, and great popularity, and by his 'Mysteries of Love and Eloquence,' 1658.   [xlv. 197]

PHILLIPS, EDWARD (*fl.* 1730–1739), dramatist; author of comic musical pieces produced in London theatres, 1730–9.   [xlv. 199]

PHILLIPS, GEORGE (*fl.* 1579–1597), divine; M.A. Trinity College, Cambridge, 1587; published sermons.
[xlv. 199]

PHILLIPS, GEORGE (1593–1644), nonconformist divine and colonist; B.A. Caius College, Cambridge, 1617; sailed for Massachusetts, 1630; pastor at Watertown till his death.   [xlv. 200]

PHILLIPS, GEORGE (1804–1892), oriental scholar; of Magdalen College, Oxford, and Queens' College, Cambridge; fellow of Queens' College, Cambridge, 1830; M.A., 1832; D.D., 1859; held the living of Sandon from 1846–1857; president of Queens' College, Cambridge, 1857–92; vice-chancellor of Cambridge University, 1861–2; published, with other works, a Syriac grammar, 1837, and an elaborate 'Commentary on the Psalms,' 1846. [xlv. 200]

PHILLIPS, GEORGE SEARLE (1815–1889), miscellaneous writer; said to have graduated B.A. Trinity College, Cambridge; edited several newspapers in England and the United States; became insane (1873) and was confined in the Trenton asylum; published mostly under the pseudonym of 'January Searle.'   [xlv. 201]

PHILLIPS, GILES FIRMAN (1780–1867), landscape-painter; published two treatises on his art. [xlv. 201]

PHILLIPS, HENRY (1775–1838), horticultural writer; a banker at Worthing; afterwards resident in London and Brighton; fellow of the Horticultural Society; F.L.S., 1825; published 'History of Cultivated Vegetables' (last edit. 1831), and other works. [xlv. 201]

PHILLIPS, HENRY (1801–1876), musician; appeared as a singing boy at the Haymarket and Drury Lane, London; successfully sang the music of Caspar at the production of 'Der Freischütz,' 1824, and thenceforth rose rapidly in public estimation as a bass singer; retired, 1863.
[xlv. 202]

PHILLIPS, HENRY WYNDHAM (1820–1868), portrait-painter; son of Thomas Phillips (1770–1845) [q. v.]; first exhibited at the Royal Academy, 1838. [xlv. 217]

PHILLIPS, PHILIPS, or PHILLYPS, JOHN (*fl.* 1570–1591), author; educated at Queens' College, Cambridge; became a puritan preacher; possibly never beneficed. Five edificatory treatises by him are extant, as well as four epitaphs and three longer poems commemorative of the Countess of Lennox (1578), Sir Philip Sidney (1587), and Sir Christopher Hatton (1591). [xlv. 202]

PHILLIPS, JOHN (1555 ?–1633), bishop of Sodor and Man; M.A. St. Mary Hall, Oxford, 1584; appointed archdeacon of Cleveland, 1601; consecrated bishop of Sodor and Man, 1605; introduced many reforms, and made a Manx translation of the Book of Common Prayer, 1610.
[xlv. 203]

PHILLIPS, JOHN (*d.* 1640), divine; M.A. and B.D. Cambridge; vicar of Faversham, 1606–40; published the 'Way to Heaven,' 1625.   [xlv. 203]

PHILLIPS, JOHN (1631–1706), author; brother of Edward Phillips (1630–1696 ?) [q. v.]; was brought up by his uncle, the poet Milton; made a scathing attack upon puritanism, 1655, in his 'Satyr against Hypocrites'; gained a living by his labours as a hack-writer and translator and a scurrilous controversialist; employed by Oates to write on behalf of the reality of the Popish plot; commenced (1690) the periodical 'Present State of Europe,' which he continued till his death.   [xlv. 205]

PHILLIPS, JOHN (*fl.* 1785–1792), writer on inland navigation; brought up as a builder and surveyor; published works containing schemes for the construction of canals.   [xlv. 207]

PHILLIPS, JOHN (1800–1874), geologist; intimately associated in his studies with his uncle, William Smith (1769–1839) [q. v.]; keeper of the York Museum, 1825–40;

assistant secretary of the British Association, 1832–59; F.R.S., 1834; professor of geology at Trinity College, Dublin, 1844–53; Wollaston medallist, Geological Society, 1845, president, 1859 and 1860; keeper of the Ashmolean Museum, 1854–70; hon. LL.D. Dublin, 1857, Cambridge, 1866; hon. M.A. Oxford, 1853, D.C.L., 1866; contributed over a hundred papers to scientific literature, and published works on geology.   [xlv. 207]

PHILLIPS, JOHN ARTHUR (1822–1887), geologist; professor of metallurgy at the college for civil engineers, Putney, 1848–50; practised in London as a mining engineer and consulting expert; F.R.S., 1881; vice-president of the Geological Society; one of the first to devote himself to the study of the microscopic structure of minerals and rocks; author of numerous scientific papers.
[xlv. 208]

PHILLIPS, JOHN ROLAND (1844–1887), lawyer and antiquary; won the prize offered at Cardigan eisteddfod for the best essay on the 'History of Cilgerran,' 1866; barrister, Lincoln's Inn, 1870; published (1874) 'Memoirs of the Civil War in Wales and the Marches.' [xlv. 209]

PHILLIPS, MOLESWORTH (1755–1832), lieutenant-colonel; second lieutenant, royal marines, 1776; accompanied James Cook (1728–1779) [q. v.] on his last voyage, 1776–9; captain, 1780; married (1782) Susanna Elizabeth, daughter of Charles Burney (1726–1814) [q. v.]; brevet-major, 1794; brevet lieutenant-colonel, 1798; resided at Boulogne (1784) till after French revolution, and on returning to France (1802) was seized by Napoleon and detained in France till 1814; became acquainted with Charles Lamb [q. v.] and his friends.   [Suppl. iii. 263]

PHILLIPS, SIR RICHARD (1767–1840), author, bookseller, and publisher; in turn a schoolmaster, a hosier, and a stationer, bookseller, and patent-medicine vendor in the town of Leicester; founded the 'Leicester Herald,' 1792, in which he expressed his republican opinions; came to London, 1795, and (1796) established the 'Monthly Magazine'; sheriff, 1807; knighted, 1808; friend of Priestley and Orator Hunt, and a patron of Bamford and other radicals; issued elementary class-books and cheap manuals under a variety of pseudonyms.   [xlv. 210]

PHILLIPS, RICHARD (1778–1851), chemist; brother of William Phillips (1775–1828) [q. v.]; F.R.S., 1822; president of the Chemical Society, 1849–50; chemist and curator of the Museum of Practical Geology, Jermyn Street, London, 1839–51; discovered (1823) the true nature of uranite; did useful work in mineralogical and pharmaceutical chemistry; author of four works and some seventy papers on chemical subjects. [xlv. 211]

PHILLIPS, SAMUEL (1814–1854), journalist; appeared on the stage in his youth; forced on his father's death to write for a living; author of 'Caleb Stukely,' 1844; placed on the staff of 'The Times,' 1845, as a writer of literary reviews; created LL.D. Göttingen, 1852; appointed literary director on the establishment of the Crystal Palace in 1853.   [xlv. 212]

PHILLIPS, TERESIA CONSTANTIA (1709–1765), courtesan; commenced a life of intrigue at a very early age; according to her own account had an intrigue with 'Thomas Grimes' (afterwards fourth Earl of Chesterfield), 1721; married a Dutch merchant named Muilman (1723), who obtained decree of nullity; continued to assume the name of Muilman; mentioned by Horace Walpole under the name 'Con Phillips' as being equally notorious with 'the czarina,' and in a similar manner in the first chapter of Fielding's 'Amelia'; determined, after many experiences in France, England, and the West Indies, to blackmail her friends by publishing 'An Apology,' which appeared in parts in 1748; removed to Jamaica (1754), where she died.
[xlv. 213]

PHILLIPS, THOMAS (1635 ?–1693), military engineer; appointed master-gunner of the Portsmouth, 1661; a gunner of the Tower of London, 1672, and master-gunner at Sheerness, 1673; became James II's second engineer, 1685; dismissed (1689) for refusing to join Schomberg in Ireland, but reinstated, 1691; present at the bombardment of St. Malo (1693), where he exploded a vessel filled with powder and carcases at the foot of the sea-wall.   [xlv. 214]

PHILLIPS, THOMAS (1708–1774), biographer of Cardinal Pole; great-nephew of William Joyner [q. v.];

brought up as a Roman catholic; joined jesuits, 1728, but left them, 1733; after studying at Liège and Rome returned to England, acting as chaplain to several noble families; principal work, 'The History of the Life of Cardinal Pole' (1764), a valuable piece of biography; died at Liège.   [xlv. 215]

PHILLIPS, THOMAS (d. 1815), historian of Shrewsbury; had a place in the customs; published 'History and Antiquities of Shrewsbury,' 1779, a second edition of which formed the first volume of the 'History of Salop' (1837) by Charles Hulbert [q. v.]   [xlv. 216]

PHILLIPS, THOMAS (1770–1845), portrait-painter; began to exhibit at the Royal Academy, 1792; R.A., 1808; painted many notable persons, including George, prince of Wales, Lord Byron, Crabbe, Scott, Southey, and Coleridge; professor of painting in the Royal Academy, 1825–32.
        [xlv. 216]

PHILLIPS, THOMAS (1760–1851), surgeon and benefactor of Welsh education; entered the service of the East India Company, 1782, and became finally a member of the Calcutta medical board, returning to England with a competent fortune in 1817; presented large quantities of books to Welsh town and college libraries, and established six scholarships and a Phillips professorship of natural science at St. David's, Lampeter.   [xlv. 217]

PHILLIPS, SIR THOMAS (1801–1867), mayor of Newport and lawyer; elected mayor, 1838, and knighted for his courage in repelling an attack by seven thousand chartists under John Frost (d. 1877) [q. v.]; acquired coal mines in Monmouthshire, and became a large landed proprietor in Wales; bestowed large sums in charities, particularly in assisting Brecon College.   [xlv. 218]

PHILLIPS, WATTS (1825–1874), dramatist and designer; became, according to the story, George Cruikshank's only pupil; resided for some years in Paris, where he acquired a knowledge of the French stage; settled in London, 1853–4; brought out 'Joseph Chavigny' at the Adelphi, London, 1857, and the 'Dead Heart,' 1859, the latter being a great success; gradually abandoned caricature and illustration for the novel and the drama; his plays were numerous and successful; his novels chiefly appeared in the 'Family Herald.'   [xlv. 218]

PHILLIPS, WILLIAM (1731?–1781), major-general of the royal artillery; commanded a company of miners raised for the defence of Minorca, 1756; served in Germany under Ferdinand of Brunswick, commanding the artillery at Minden (1759) with great ability, and at Warburg (1760), and other engagements; in Canada under Carleton and Burgoyne, 1776; took part (1777) in the campaign which ended in the capitulation of Saratoga; was exchanged, 1781, on which he joined Clinton at New York, proceeding thence to Virginia, where he died in the midst of the campaign.   [xlv. 220]

PHILLIPS, WILLIAM (1775–1828), mineralogist and geologist; grandson of Catherine Phillips [q. v.]; a London printer and bookseller, devoting his leisure to geology; F.G.S., 1807; F.R.S., 1827; F.L.S.: wrote with William Daniel Conybeare [q. v.] 'Outlines of the Geology of England and Wales,' 1822, and, among other works exclusively his own, published the well-known 'Elementary Introduction to the Knowledge of Mineralogy,' 1816.
        [xlv. 221]

PHILLPOTTS, HENRY (1778–1869), bishop of Exeter; B.A. Corpus Christi College, Oxford, 1795; fellow of Magdalen College, Oxford, 1795–1804; M.A., 1798; became chaplain to Shute Barrington [q. v.], bishop of Durham, 1806, and prebendary of Durham, 1809; began (c. 1819) to appear as a writer upon public questions by penning a defence of the existing poor-law and of the conduct of the government in regard to the Peterloo massacre; vehemently opposed catholic emancipation in his controversy with Charles Butler (1750–1832) [q. v.], 1825; shared the conversion of the tory ministry, 1829; bishop of Exeter, 1830–69; opposed the Reform Bill in the House of Lords and came into collision with Earl Grey in regard to the Tithes Bill, 1831; a strict disciplinarian in his diocese, having lawsuits with several of his clergy, including George Cornelius Gorham [q. v.] Although a high churchman he had no sympathy with the Oxford movement, and vehemently attacked Tract XC.   [xlv. 222]

PHILP, ROBERT KEMP (1819–1882), compiler: joined the chartist movement and lectured for it; ousted

from the committee by the more violent section (1842) for the moderation of his opinions; credited with having drawn up the monster petition, 1842; settled in Great New Street, Fetter Lane, London, as a publisher, 1845; sub-editor of the 'People's Journal,' 1846–8; published 'The Family Friend' (editor, 1849–52) and other cheap popular literature, including 'Enquire within upon Everything' (1856) of which over a million copies had been sold by 1888.   [xlv. 225]

PHILPOT. [See also PHILIPOT.]

PHILPOT, JOHN (1516–1555), protestant martyr; fellow of New College, Oxford, 1534–41, and B.C.L.; archdeacon of Winchester; constantly engaged in controversy, and after Mary's accession was imprisoned as a heretic; burned at Smithfield. Several of his works survive, some of them in Foxe's 'Actes and Monuments.'   [xlv. 226]

PHILPOTT, HENRY (1807–1892), bishop of Worcester; elected fellow of St. Catharine's Hall, Cambridge, 1829; M.A., 1832; master of St. Catharine's Hall, Cambridge, 1845–60; vice-chancellor, 1846, 1856, and 1857; D.D., 1847; bishop of Worcester, 1860–90. His episcopal career was uneventful.   [xlv. 227]

PHIPPS, SIR CHARLES BEAUMONT (1801–1866), court official; son of Sir Henry Phipps, first earl of Mulgrave [q. v.]; entered the army, 1820; steward of the viceregal household in Ireland, 1835–9; lieutenant-colonel, 1837; equerry to Queen Victoria, 1846; private secretary to Prince Albert, 1847; appointed keeper of the queen's purse and treasurer to the then Prince of Wales, 1849; K.C.B., 1858; receiver-general of the duchy of Cornwall, 1862.   [xlv. 228]

PHIPPS, CHARLES JOHN (1835–1897), architect; articled at Bath, where he began to practise, 1858; reconstructed Bath Theatre, 1862–3; removed to London, and became recognised authority on theatre construction, and was engaged on construction or alteration of more than twenty theatres in London, besides others in many provincial towns; F.R.I.B.A., 1866; F.S.A. His principal work was Her Majesty's Theatre, Haymarket, London, (completed, 1897).   [Suppl. iii. 264]

PHIPPS, SIR CONSTANTINE (1656–1723), lord chancellor of Ireland; barrister, Gray's Inn, 1684, bencher, 1706; his rise hindered by his Jacobite sympathies, though his practice among friends of the house of Stuart was considerable; defended Henry Sacheverell [q. v.], 1710, and gained such distinction that he was knighted and made lord chancellor of Ireland in the same year; extremely unpopular with the whig faction in Ireland, and on Queen Anne's death was removed from office; defended Francis Atterbury [q. v.], 1723.   [xlv. 228]

PHIPPS, SIR CONSTANTINE HENRY, first MARQUIS OF NORMANBY and second EARL OF MULGRAVE (1797–1863), eldest son of Sir Henry Phipps, first earl of Mulgrave [q. v.]; of Harrow and Trinity College, Cambridge; M.A., 1818; entered parliament, 1818 (M.P., Scarborough), and supported parliamentary reform; M.P., Higham Ferrers, 1822, Malton, 1826; governor of Jamaica, 1832–4; G.C.H., 1832; became lord privy seal, with a seat in the cabinet, under Lord Melbourne, 1834; sent to Ireland as lord-lieutenant, 1835; his friendly relations with O'Connell bitterly attacked at protestant meetings, but his administration (1835–9) beneficial to Ireland; created Marquis of Normanby, 1838; secretary of war and the colonies, 1839; transferred to the home office, 1839, where he remained till the fall of the ministry, 1841; ambassador at Paris, 1846–52, and minister at Florence, 1854–8, in which posts he mingled too much in the politics of foreign states. In early life he wrote a number of novels and tales.   [xlv. 230]

PHIPPS, CONSTANTINE JOHN, second BARON MULGRAVE (1744–1792), entered the navy, 1760; M.P., Lincoln, 1768, when he identified himself with the 'king's friends'; commanded the Racehorse in a polar expedition, 1773, of which he published an account, and in which Nelson took part as midshipman; succeeded his father as an Irish peer, 1775; M.P., Huntingdon, and appointed a lord of the admiralty, 1777; distinguished himself in the action off Ushant in 1778, while in command of the Courageux.   [xlv. 231]

PHIPPS, EDMUND (1808–1857), author; son of Sir Henry Phipps, first earl of Mulgrave [q. v.]; M.A.

Trinity College, Oxford, 1831; barrister, Inner Temple, 1832; published several financial pamphlets, as well as 'Memoirs of Robert Plumer Ward,' 1850.   [xlv. 235]

PHIPPS, SIR GEORGE AUGUSTUS CONSTANTINE, second MARQUIS OF NORMANBY (1819–1890), son of Sir Constantine Henry Phipps, first marquis of Normanby [q. v.]; entered the army, 1838, but retired, 1847, when he was returned (M.P., Scarborough) to parliament in the liberal interest; privy councillor, 1851; M.P., Scarborough, 1852 and 1857; liberal whip; treasurer of the household, 1853–8; lieutenant-governor of Nova Scotia, 1858–63; governor of Queensland, 1871–4; governor of New Zealand, 1874–9, where he was in constant collision with Sir George Grey; G.C.M.G., 1877; appointed governor of Victoria, 1879, retiring, 1884; G.C.B., 1885; joined the liberal unionist secession, 1886.   [xlv. 232]

PHIPPS, SIR HENRY, first EARL OF MULGRAVE, first VISCOUNT NORMANBY, and third BARON MULGRAVE (1755–1831), brother of Constantine John Phipps, second baron Mulgrave [q. v.]; educated at Eton; entered the army, 1775, and attained the rank of general, 1809; M.P., Totnes, 1784, Scarborough, 1790; a supporter of Pitt and one of his chief military advisers; made by Pitt chancellor of the duchy of Lancaster, with a seat in the cabinet, 1804, and (1805) secretary for foreign affairs, a post generally thought beyond his powers; resigned, with the bulk of Pitt's friends, after the death of Pitt (January 1806); became first lord of the admiralty in the Portland ministry, 1807, his tenure of office being marked by the seizure of the Danish fleet, the Walcheren expedition, and the operations of Collingwood in the Mediterranean; resigned, 1810, and became master of the ordnance, keeping his seat in the cabinet; created Earl of Mulgrave, 1812; master of the ordnance till 1818, when, at his own suggestion, he was replaced by Wellington; retired from the cabinet, 1820. He was a generous patron of art, befriending Jackson, the portrait-painter, Wilkie, and Haydon.   [xlv. 233]

PHIPPS, JOSEPH (1708–1787), quaker; undertook a street-preaching tour through the metropolis, 1753; published controversial works in defence of the quakers against Samuel Newton of Norwich, and others.   [xlv. 236]

PHIPPS, SIR WILLIAM (1651–1695), governor of Massachusetts; cousin of Sir Constantine Phipps [q. v.]; began life as a ship-carpenter, and in time became a merchant-captain of Boston; raised (1667) a Spanish treasure-ship, sunk near the Bahamas, and gained 16,000l.; knighted, and appointed provost-marshal of New England, 1687; commanded a colonial expedition, which captured Port Royal from the French, 1690, but failed in an attempt on Montreal and Quebec, 1690; nominated governor of Massachusetts, 1691; did little against the French and their Indian allies, and was summoned to England to answer for his undignified conduct, 1694, but died before proceedings were taken.   [xlv. 236]

PHISTON or **FISTON**, WILLIAM (fl. 1571–1609), translator and author; describes himself as 'a student of London'; made translations from the French, Latin, Italian, and Spanish.   [xlv. 237]

PHIZ (pseudonym). [See BROWNE, HABLOT KNIGHT, 1815–1882.]

PHREAS or **FREE**, JOHN (d. 1465), scholar; fellow of Balliol College, Oxford; M.A., 1454; went abroad after leaving Oxford; taught medicine at Ferrara, Florence, and Parma, and died at Rome. As a scholar he was distinguished for his knowledge of philosophy, medicine, and the civil law. Several of his manuscripts are preserved among the Balliol and Bodleian MSS.   [xlv. 238]

PHYLIP. [See also PHILIP and PHILLIP.]

PHYLIP, SION (1543–1620), Welsh poet; was drowned near Pwllheli while on a bardic tour; many of his poems preserved in the Cymrodorion MSS. (British Museum).   [xlv. 239]

PHYLIP, WILLIAM (1590?–1670), Welsh poet; wrote a Welsh elegy in 1649 on the death of Charles I; forced to go into hiding during the Commonwealth.   [xlv. 239]

PICKEN, ANDREW (1788–1833), Scottish author; son of a Paisley clothier; bookseller in Liverpool, and proceeded to London, where he speedily became popular as a man of letters; published miscellaneous works, including 'Tales and Sketches of the West Coast of Scotland,' 1824, and other stories of Scottish and Irish life and manners.   [xlv. 239]

PICKEN, ANDREW (1815–1845), draughtsman and lithographer; son of Andrew Picken (1788–1833) [q. v.]; executed on stone a large number of landscapes, chiefly illustrations of books of travel, and private commissions.   [xlv. 240]

PICKEN, ANDREW BELFRAGE (1802–1849), author; son of Ebenezer Picken [q. v.]; published 'The Bedouins and other Poems,' 1828.   [xlv. 241]

PICKEN, EBENEZER (1769–1816), minor poet; son of a Paisley weaver; studied at Glasgow University; opened a school at Falkirk, 1791; settled (1796) in Edinburgh, where he lived in straitened circumstances; published several volumes of poetry.   [xlv. 240]

PICKEN, JOANNA BELFRAGE (1798–1859), poetess; daughter of Ebenezer Picken [q. v.]; wrote satirical verses for various journals; went to Canada, 1842, and taught music at Montreal till her death.   [xlv. 240]

PICKERING, BASIL MONTAGU (1836–1878), publisher and dealer in rare books; son of William Pickering [q. v.]; began business (1858) in Piccadilly, London; continued his father's traditions as publisher. [xlv. 246]

PICKERING, DANBY (fl. 1737–1769), legal writer; barrister, Gray's Inn; edited the original four volumes of 'Modern Reports' with supplements (1757), and Sir Henry Finch's 'Law, or a Discourse thereof' (1759); published 'The Statutes at Large to the end of the Eleventh Parliament of Great Britain,' 24 vols. 1762–1769.   [xlv. 241]

PICKERING, ELLEN (d. 1843), novelist; published her first novel, 1826.   [xlv. 241]

PICKERING, GEORGE (d. 1857), artist; exhibited water-colours at the Liverpool Academy (non-resident member, 1827); succeeded George Cuitt (1779–1854) [q. v.] as a drawing-master at Chester; drew landscapes to illustrate Ormerod's 'History of Cheshire' and other works.   [xlv. 241]

PICKERING, SIR GILBERT, first baronet (1613–1668), parliamentarian; of Gray's Inn, 1629; M.P., Northamptonshire, in the Short and Long parliaments and in those of the Commonwealth; active at the beginning of the civil war in raising troops and money in his county; sided with the army, 1648, and was appointed one of Charles I's judges, but attended only at first, and did not sign the death-warrant; member of the councils of state under the Commonwealth; escaped punishment after the Restoration, but was declared incapable of holding office; was a baronet of Nova Scotia.   [xlv. 242]

PICKERING, SIR JAMES (fl. 1368–1397), speaker of the House of Commons; head of a Westmoreland family; knight of the shire for Westmoreland, 1362, 1365, 1377, 1378, 1379, and 1382, for Yorkshire, 1383, 1384, 1388, 1390, and 1397; elected speaker, 1378.   [xlv. 243]

PICKERING, JOHN (d. 1537), leader in the Pilgrimage of Grace; B.D. Cambridge, 1525; prior of the Dominican house at Cambridge, 1525; took part in organising the Pilgrimage of Grace, 1536; executed at Tyburn.   [xlv. 243]

PICKERING, JOHN (d. 1645), parliamentarian; brother of Sir Gilbert Pickering [q. v.]; of Gray's Inn, 1634; commanded a regiment in the Earl of Manchester's army and in the new model army.   [xlv. 242]

PICKERING, THOMAS (d. 1475), genealogist; abbot of St. Hilda's monastery at Whitby, 1462; compiled genealogies of a few Yorkshire families.   [xlv. 244]

PICKERING, SIR WILLIAM (1516–1575), courtier and diplomatist; educated at Cambridge; appointed ambassador in France, 1551, but after Queen Mary's accession recalled; joined the opponents of the Spanish marriage; involved in Wyatt's conspiracy, but eventually pardoned; one of the lieutenants of London, 1569.   [xlv. 244]

PICKERING, WILLIAM (1796–1854), publisher; commenced business (1820) in Lincoln's Inn Fields; published the 'Diamond Classics,' 1821–31; removed to

24 Chancery Lane, 1824, and (1830) adopted the trade mark of the Aldine press ; increased his reputation by his Aldine edition of the English poets in fifty-three volumes ; his last days troubled by pecuniary embarrassments, due to the failure of a friend for whom he had stood security. [xlv. 245]

PICKERSGILL, FREDERICK RICHARD (1820-1900), historical painter ; nephew of Henry William Pickersgill [q. v.] ; taught by his uncle, William Frederick Witherington [q. v.] ; studied at Royal Academy schools, and exhibited between 1839 and 1875 ; R.A., 1857 ; keeper and trustee of Royal Academy, 1873-87. His works include ' The Burial of Harold at Waltham Abbey,' which gained prize at Westminster Hall, 1847, and was purchased for the houses of parliament. [Suppl. iii. 265]

PICKERSGILL, HENRY HALL (d. 1861), painter ; son of Henry William Pickersgill [q. v.] ; exhibited at the Royal Academy from 1834. [xlv. 247]

PICKERSGILL, HENRY WILLIAM (1782-1875), painter ; first exhibited at the Royal Academy, 1806 ; subsequently devoted himself to portrait-painting ; R.A., 1826 ; obtained after the death of Thomas Phillips (1770-1845) [q. v.] almost a monopoly of painting the portraits of men and women of eminence. [xlv. 246]

PICKFORD, EDWARD (d. 1657). [See DANIEL, EDWARD.]

PICKLE THE SPY (pseudonym). [See MACDONELL, ALASTAIR RUADH, 1725 ?-1761.]

PICKWORTH, HENRY (1673 ?-1738 ?), writer against the quakers ; joined the quakers in Lincolnshire, but soon after holding an unsuccessful disputation with Francis Bugg [q. v.], 1701, renounced his beliefs, and began writing against his former opinions. [xlv. 247]

PICTON, SIR JAMES ALLANSON (1805-1889), antiquary and architect ; executed some important buildings about Liverpool, and became an authority on land arbitrations ; entered the Liverpool town council, 1849 ; originated the Liverpool public library and museum, and did much other useful work ; his principal literary work, ' Memorials of Liverpool,' 1873 ; knighted, 1881. [xlv. 248]

PICTON, SIR THOMAS (1758-1815), lieutenant-general ; younger son of Thomas Picton of Poyston, Pembrokeshire ; entered the 12th foot, 1771 ; lieutenant, 1777 ; captain, 75th foot, 1778 ; checked an incipient mutiny by his promptitude on the disbandment of his regiment, 1783 ; major, 68th foot, 1795 ; took a distinguished part in the capture of St. Lucia, 1796, and was nominated lieutenant-colonel ; appointed by Sir Ralph Abercromby [q. v.] commander and military governor after the capture of Trinidad, 1797 ; appointed (1801) to the civil government of the island ; his rule popular with the influential inhabitants, but serious charges of cruelty made against him in consequence of his permitting the use of tortures sanctioned by the Spanish law ; on the appointment (1802) by Addison of three commissioners, of whom he was one, to govern the island, indignantly tendered his resignation ; tried on one of the charges in the court of king's bench, but no judgment delivered against him ; became brigadier-general, 1801 ; major-general, 1808 ; took part (1809) in the siege and capture of Flushing, and was appointed governor of the town, but shortly afterwards was invalided home ; joined the army in Portugal, 1810, and was placed in command of the third division ; successfully checked Masséna's advance in the pass of San Antonio, 27 Sept. 1810 ; took a chief part in the pursuit, March 1811, when Masséna retreated from the lines of Torres Vedras ; prominent in the battle of Fuentes d'Onoro on 5 May 1811 ; saved his division from an overwhelming force by a brilliant retreat across six miles of level country, while harassed by artillery and cavalry, September 1811 ; conducted the siege of Badajoz, March 1812, led the successful assault in person, and was severely wounded ; nominated K.B. ; promoted lieutenant-general, 1813 ; at Vittoria forced the passage of the Douro and carried the heights in the centre, his division bearing the brunt of the battle ; thanked by the House of Commons seven times for his services in the Peninsula, but on the conclusion of peace was excluded by the ministry from the list of those honoured ; G.C.B., 1815 ; engaged at Quatre Bras in command of the fifth division (1815),

and was wounded ; shot while leading his second brigade to the charge at Waterloo. A monument was erected to him in St. Paul's Cathedral, London. [xlv. 248]

PIDDING, HENRY JAMES (1797-1864), humorous artist ; attained some note as a painter of humorous subjects from domestic life ; frequently exhibited at the Society of British Artists (member, 1843) ; exhibited at the Royal Academy. [xlv. 256]

PIDDINGTON, HENRY (1797-1858), meteorologist ; a commander in the mercantile marine ; retired from the sea, c. 1830, and was appointed curator of the Museum of Economic Geology in Calcutta ; accumulated important data for determining the course of storms at sea ; originated the term ' cyclone ' in his ' Sailor's Horn-Book for the Law of Storms,' 1848. [xlv. 256]

PIDGEON, HENRY CLARK (1807-1880), painter in water-colours and antiquary ; practised in London, and afterwards in Liverpool, as a teacher of drawing ; exhibited at the Liverpool Academy ; returned to London in 1851 ; president of the Sketching Club ; member of the Institute of Painters in Water-colours, 1861 ; contributed drawings and papers to various archæological journals. [xlv. 257]

PIERCE. [See also PEARCE, PEARSE, PEERS, PEIRCE, and PIERS.]

PIERCE or **PEARCE**, EDWARD (d. 1698), sculptor and mason ; practised in London. Among other works he rebuilt St. Clement Danes in 1680, and executed a marble bust of Oliver Cromwell. [xlv. 257]

PIERCE, ROBERT (1622-1710), physician ; of Winchester and Lincoln College, Oxford ; M.A., 1650 ; M.D., 1661 ; practised in Bath, many famous physicians sending their patients to him ; F.R.C.P., 1689 ; published ' Bath Memoirs,' 1697. [xlv. 258]

PIERCE, SAMUEL EYLES (1746-1829), Calvinist divine ; began his ministry as a preacher in Lady Huntingdon's connexion, 1776 ; became independent pastor at Truro, 1783, and subsequently a popular London preacher ; published theological works. [xlv. 259]

PIERCE or **PEIRSE**, THOMAS (1622-1691), controversialist ; fellow of Magdalen College, Oxford, 1643 (expelled by the parliamentary visitors, 1648) ; M.A., 1644 ; became tutor to Robert Spencer (afterwards second earl of Sunderland) [q. v.] ; carried on a bitter attack on the Calvinists, whose tenets he had abandoned in 1644 ; regained his fellowship at the Restoration, and became chaplain in ordinary to Charles II ; president of Magdalen College, Oxford, by Charles II's wish, 1661 ; his tenure of office stormy ; resigned the presidency, 1672 ; became dean of Salisbury, 1675 ; quarrelled vehemently with the bishop, Seth Ward [q. v.] His learning and controversial ability are undoubted, but his fierce temper provoked his opponents, and his works did more harm than good. [xlv. 260]

PIERREPONT, SIR EVELYN, first DUKE OF KINGSTON, first MARQUIS OF DORCHESTER of the second creation, and fifth EARL OF KINGSTON (1665 ?-1726), grandson of William Pierrepont [q. v.] ; M.P., East Retford, 1689 (Convention parliament) and 1690 ; succeeded his brother William as fifth earl, 1690 ; created Marquis of Dorchester, 1706 ; privy councillor, 1714 ; created Duke of Kingston, 1715 ; as a whig obtained the favour of George I ; lord-president of the council, 1719-20 ; K.G., 1719 ; one of the most prominent leaders of the fashionable world. [xlv. 262]

PIERREPONT, SIR EVELYN, second DUKE OF KINGSTON (1711-1773), grandson of Sir Evelyn Pierrepont, first duke of Kingston [q. v.] ; educated at Eton ; took his seat in the House of Lords, 1733 ; K.G., 1741 ; raised a regiment of horse to oppose the Jacobites, 1745, and was nominated lieutenant-general, 1759. [xlv. 263]

PIERREPONT, HENRY, first MARQUIS OF DORCHESTER, second EARL OF KINGSTON, and first BARON PIERREPONT (1606-1680), eldest son of Robert Pierrepont, first earl of Kingston [q. v.] ; educated at Emmanuel College, Cambridge ; M.P., Nottinghamshire, as Viscount Newark, 1628-9 ; summoned to the House of Lords as Baron Pierrepont, 1641 ; succeeded his father, 1643 ; created marquis of Dorchester, 1645 ; followed Charles I to

Oxford; compounded for his estate, 1647, and studied medicine and law; F.R.C.P., 1658; F.R.S., 1663; privy councillor, 1660–73; according to his biographer hastened his end by taking his own medicines. [xlv. 264]

PIERREPONT or **PIERREPOINT**, ROBERT, first EARL OF KINGSTON and first VISCOUNT NEWARK (1584–1643), of Oriel College, Oxford; created Viscount Newark, 1627, and Earl of Kingston-upon-Hull, 1628; endeavoured to remain neutral at the outbreak of the civil war, and refused to lend money to Charles I; joined Charles I, 1643, but was taken prisoner in July and killed by a chance shot from a royalist battery. [xlv. 266]

PIERREPONT, WILLIAM (1607?–1678), politician; son of Robert Pierrepont, first earl of Kingston [q. v.]; sat in the Long parliament as M.P., Great Wenlock, and was a leader of the peace party during the early stages of the war; became one of the committee of both kingdoms, 1644, and threw himself with vigour into the conduct of hostilities; associated himself with the moderate independents until Pride's Purge, when he withdrew from politics; remained friendly with Cromwell and his family, and (February 1660) was elected to the new council of state; sat in the Convention parliament for Nottinghamshire; retired into private life, 1661. [xlv. 267]

PIERS. [See also PEARCE, PEARSE, PEERS, PEIRCE, and PIERCE.]

PIERS, HENRY (d. 1623), author; son of William Piers (d. 1603) [q. v.]; visited Rome, became a Roman catholic, and wrote observations on Rome and other continental towns, which were published, 1896. [xlv. 269]

PIERS, SIR HENRY, first baronet (1628–1691), chorographer; son of Henry Piers [q. v.]; created baronet, 1660; wrote a description of West Meath (printed, 1774). [xlv. 269]

PIERS, JAMES (fl. 1631–1635), writer; probably a son of Henry Piers [q. v.]; professor of philosophy at Bordeaux; published two Latin treatises. [xlv. 269]

PIERS or **PEIRSE**, JOHN (1523?–1594), successively bishop of Rochester and Salisbury and archbishop of York; fellow of Magdalen College, Oxford, 1545 and 1549; senior student of Christ Church, Oxford, 1547; M.A., 1549; D.D., 1566; master of Balliol College, Oxford, 1570; bishop of Rochester, 1576; translated to Salisbury, 1577, to York, 1589. [xlv. 269]

PIERS, WILLIAM (d. 1603), constable of Carrickfergus; came from Yorkshire to Ireland, c. 1530, and (1556), with Richard Bethell, obtained a grant of the constableship of Carrickfergus Castle, an outpost which involved him in frequent hostilities with the Hebridean Scots and the O'Neills; defeated the Scots with great loss near Castlereagh, 1569; suspected (1573) of intriguing with Sir Brian MacPhelim, deprived of the constableship, and imprisoned for more than a year; subsequently occupied himself with unsuccessful projects for settling the northern parts of Ireland with the assistance of the native gentry. [xlv. 270]

PIERS, **PIERSE**, or **PIERCE**, WILLIAM (1580–1670), successively bishop of Peterborough and of Bath and Wells; M.A. Christ Church, Oxford, 1603; D.D., 1614; chaplain to John King (1559?–1621) [q. v.], bishop of London; became (1622) dean of Peterborough; consecrated bishop of Peterborough, 1630; translated to Bath and Wells, 1632; a zealous adherent of Laud; carried out various ceremonial changes in his diocese with a high hand, and discountenanced sabbatarianism; impeached, 1640, committed to the Tower of London, 1641, and deprived of his bishopric; restored, 1660. [xlv. 272]

PIERSON. [See also PEARSON and PEERSON.]

PIERSON, ABRAHAM (d. 1678), New England divine; B.A. Trinity College, Cambridge; went out to Boston between 1630 and 1640, and (1640) joined in forming a new settlement on Long Island called Southampton; removed to Branford, 1664, to Newark, 1666; published a pamphlet in the Indian tongue, with an English rendering. [xlv. 274]

PIERSON, originally **PEARSON**, HENRY HUGO (1815–1873), musician; son of Hugh Nicholas Pearson [q. v.]; B.A. Trinity College, Cambridge, 1830; elected Reid professor of music at Edinburgh University, 1844,

but soon afterwards retired to Germany; his greatest work, 'Jerusalem,' performed at the Norwich festival of 1852; died at Leipzig. The 'Jerusalem' gave rise to great controversy, its composer being denounced as a follower of Wagner, though in reality his music more resembled that of Schumann. His unfinished oratorio, 'Hezekiah,' occasioned the same difference of opinion. [xlv. 274]

PIERSON, WILLIAM HENRY (1839–1881), major (late Bengal) engineers; went to India, 1860, and did important engineering work in Sikhim (1861) and in Persia (1863–73) in connection with the Indo-European telegraph; appointed military secretary to Lord Ripon, 1880; nominated (March 1881) commanding royal engineer of the field force proceeding against the Mahsud Waziris; died of dysentery while on active service. [xlv. 276]

PIGG, OLIVER (fl. 1565–1591), puritan divine; B.A. St. John's College, Cambridge, 1569; imprisoned at Bury St. Edmunds (1578), for dispraising the Book of Common Prayer; published two devotional treatises and a sermon. [xlv. 277]

PIGOT, DAVID RICHARD (1797–1873), chief baron of the exchequer in Ireland; B.A. Trinity College, Dublin, 1819; called to the Irish bar, 1826; became solicitor-general for Ireland, 1839; M.P., Clonmel, 1839, 1840, and 1841; attorney-general, 1840–1; chief baron of the exchequer in Ireland, 1846–73. [xlv. 277]

PIGOT, ELIZABETH BRIDGET (1783–1866), friend and correspondent of Lord Byron; lived at Southwell on Burgage Green, where in 1804 Byron and his mother settled, occupying Burgage Manor; corresponded regularly with Byron till 1811, and during the rest of her long life amused herself and her friends with narrating the minute incidents of her intimacy with the poet. [xlv. 278]

PIGOT, SIR GEORGE, BARON PIGOT and first baronet (1719–1777), governor of Madras; arrived at Madras, 1737; became governor, 1755; conducted the defence of the city against Lally with skill and spirit, 1758–9; resigned office, 1763; created baronet, 1764, and an Irish baron, 1766; created LL.D. Cambridge, 1769; again nominated governor of Madras, 1775, but soon found himself at variance with his council in regard to the restoration of the raja of Tanjore, which he had been ordered by the directors to carry out; found that the majority were determined to overrule him in regard to the details of the restoration, and refused to sign the instructions drawn up by the council in regard to the matter; eventually regained a majority by preferring charges against two of the members, and thus debarring them from voting, to which step the council replied by a *coup de main*, and he was arrested by their order; died in confinement. In England opinion was nearly equally divided among the proprietors of the East India Company, but before the news of his death was known he was declared restored to his office and ordered to give up the government to his successor within a week. [xlv. 278]

PIGOT, SIR HENRY (1750–1840), general; son of Hugh Pigot (1721?–1792) [q. v.]; entered the army, 1769; commanded at the blockade of Malta, 1800; general, 1812; G.C.M.G., 1837. [xlv. 281]

PIGOT, HUGH (1721?–1792), admiral; brother of Sir George Pigot, baron Pigot [q. v.]; entered the navy as an 'able seaman'; lieutenant, 1742; commander, 1745; rear-admiral, 1775; lord of the admiralty, 1782; admiral of the blue, 1782; commander-in-chief in the West Indies (1782), superseding Rodney. [xlv. 281]

PIGOT, HUGH (1769–1797), captain in the navy; son of Hugh Pigot (1721?–1792) [q. v.]; entered the navy, 1782; nominated to command the Hermione, 1797, when his cruelty caused the crew to mutiny, kill nearly all the officers, and hand the ship over to the Spaniards. [xlv. 281]

PIGOT, SIR ROBERT, second baronet (1720–1796), lieutenant-general; colonel, 1772; fought at Lexington and Bunker's Hill, 1775; succeeded his brother, Sir George Pigot, baron Pigot [q. v.], in his baronetcy, 1778; lieutenant-general, 1782. [xlv. 282]

PIGOTT, SIR ARTHUR LEARY (1752–1819), attorney-general; barrister, Middle Temple, 1777; bencher, 1799; matriculated at University College, Oxford, 1778; commenced practice at Grenada, where he became attorney-general; K.C., 1783; became attorney-general (1806) under the administration of 'All the Talents,' retiring with the ministry in 1807; knighted, 1806; M.P., Steyning, 1806, Arundel, 1806–19.

[xlv. 282]

PIGOTT, CHARLES (*d.* 1794), author; brother of Robert Pigott [q. v.]; was, like Robert, an ardent champion of the French revolution, and published a reply to Burke (1791) and other works. [xlv. 286]

PIGOTT, EDWARD (*fl.* 1768–1807), astronomer; son of Nathaniel Pigott [q. v.]; aided his father's geodetic operations in Flanders, 1772; introduced John Goodricke [q. v.] to astronomy; made several important observations and discoveries. [xlv. 283]

PIGOTT, SIR FRANCIS (1508–1537). [See BIGOD.]

PIGOTT, SIR GILLERY (1813–1875), baron of the exchequer; barrister, Middle Temple, 1839; serjeant-at-law, 1856; M.P., Reading, 1860–3; baron of the exchequer, 1863; knighted, 1863. [xlv. 283]

PIGOTT, HARRIET (1766–1846), authoress; niece of Robert Pigott [q. v.]; published 'Records of Real Life,' 1839, and other works. [xlv. 286]

PIGOTT, NATHANIEL (*d.* 1804), astronomer; chiefly remembered for his geodetic work for the Austrian government in 1772 with a view to determining the geographical position of the chief towns in the Low Countries.

[xlv. 284]

PIGOTT, RICHARD (1828?–1889), Irish journalist and forger; errand-boy in the 'Nation' office, and afterwards manager of the 'Irishman' (proprietor, 1865); sold his journalistic property to the land league, 1879, and began to blackmail his political associates in order to support himself; began to traffic with 'The Times' newspaper in information connecting the leading Irish home rulers with murders and outrages, 1886; caused by the serious nature of the charges made in the articles entitled 'Parnellism and Crime' the appointment of a special judicial commission (1888) to investigate their truth; appeared as a witness, but broke down under cross-examination, February 1889; fled to Madrid, where he committed suicide. [xlv. 284]

PIGOTT, ROBERT (1736–1794), food and dress reformer; a gentleman of Shropshire; sold his estate, 1776, and retired to the continent, where he made the acquaintance of Voltaire, Franklin, and Brissot; condemned the use of bread, advocated putting prisoners on a vegetable diet to reclaim them, and maintained the superiority of caps over hats; died at Toulouse.

[xlv. 286]

PIKE, PIK, or **PYKE,** JOHN (*fl.* 1322?), chronicler; master of the schools at St. Martin-le-Grand, London; several of his compilations in the Harleian and Arundel MSS. [xlv. 287]

PIKE, JOHN BAXTER (1745–1811), writer on horticulture; doctor in London; contributed letters to the 'Monthly Magazine' on horticulture, poultry farming, and kindred subjects. [xlv. 287]

PIKE, JOHN DEODATUS GREGORY (1784–1854), baptist; pastor of the Baptist Church, Brook Street, Derby, 1810–54; editor of 'The General Baptist Repository,' 1822–54; his religious tracts widely circulated in England and America. [xlv. 287]

PIKE or **PEAKE,** RICHARD (*fl.* 1620–1626), adventurer; took part in the attack on Algiers (1620) made by Sir Robert Mansell [q. v.]; taken prisoner (1625) in the attack on Cadiz; published (1626) an account of his adventures on his return to England. [xlv. 288]

PIKE, RICHARD (1834–1893), master-mariner; was in command of the Proteus when she was nipped in the pack-ice off Cape Sabine; after extreme hardship reached Upernavik with his companions, where they were rescued. [xlv. 289]

PIKE, SAMUEL (1717?–1773), Sandemanian; became an independent minister, and (1757) adopted the views of Robert Sandeman [q. v.]; published theological and devotional works. [xlv. 289]

PILCH, FULLER (1803–1870), cricketer; a native of Norfolk; first appeared at Lord's at the age of seven-

teen, and continued to play till 1854; first bat of his day until the appearance of George Parr [q. v.] [xlv. 290]

PILCHER, GEORGE (1801–1855), aural surgeon; for many years consulting surgeon to the Surrey Dispensary; an honorary fellow, Royal College of Surgeons, 1843; published three treatises on aural surgery.

[xlv. 291]

PILFOLD, JOHN (1776?–1834), captain in the navy; entered the navy in 1788; commanded the Ajax at the battle of Trafalgar, when a first lieutenant, and was in consequence advanced to post rank, 1805. [xlv. 292]

PILKINGTON, SIR ANDREW (1767?–1853), lieutenant-general; entered the army, 1783; saw much service in all parts of the world; K.C.B., 1838; lieutenant-general, 1841. [xlv. 292]

PILKINGTON, FRANCIS (1560?–1625?), lutenist and musical composer; Mus. Bac. Lincoln College, Oxford, 1595; minor canon and chaunter of Chester Cathedral, 1623–4. His compositions were not marked by much originality. [xlv. 292]

PILKINGTON, GILBERT (*fl.* 1350), reputed author of 'The Tournament of Tottenham,' a burlesque in verse on 'the parade and fopperies of chivalry.' The earliest manuscript of the piece (in the Cambridge University library) bears his signature, but it is doubtful if he was more than copyist. [xlv. 293]

PILKINGTON, JAMES (1520?–1576), first protestant bishop of Durham; of Pembroke Hall and St. John's College, Cambridge; elected fellow of St. John's College, Cambridge, 1539; M.A., 1542; B.D., 1551; president, 1550; fled to the continent (1554), being a protestant, but returned on Queen Elizabeth's accession; was master of St. John's College (1559–61), and regius professor of divinity, 1559; bishop of Durham, 1561–76. He assisted in the revision of the Book of Common Prayer (1558–9), and in settling the Thirty-nine Articles promulgated in 1562. Several of his writings survive. [xlv. 293]

PILKINGTON, LÆTITIA (1712–1750), adventuress; daughter of Van Lewen, a man-midwife; married Matthew Pilkington (*fl.* 1729–1733) [q. v.], 1729; became acquainted with Swift, and rapidly gained his favour, her reminiscences being one of the chief authorities for Swift's later years; was subsequently separated from her husband, after which she set up a small bookshop in St. James's Street, London. Her 'Memoirs,' written by herself, appeared in 1748. [xlv. 295]

PILKINGTON, LEONARD (1527?–1599), master of St. John's College, Cambridge; brother of James Pilkington [q. v.]; B.A. St. John's College, Cambridge, 1544; admitted fellow, 1546, but ejected as a protestant on Mary's accession; fled to Frankfort, but on Queen Elizabeth's accession returned to Cambridge; was re-elected a senior fellow of St. John's College, Cambridge, subsequently being master, 1561–4. [xlv. 297]

PILKINGTON, LIONEL SCOTT, *alias* JACK HAWLEY (1828–1875), sportsman and eccentric; educated at Rugby; only son of Redmond William Pilkington [q. v.]; developed a strong love for stable life, and although a man of property served Sir Joseph Henry Hawley [q. v.] as a groom, and afterwards adopted the surname of Hawley and settled at Doncaster. [xlv. 302]

PILKINGTON, MARY (1766–1839), writer; *née* Hopkins; married (1786) a surgeon named Pilkington; published over fifty volumes of fiction, poetry, and biography. [xlv. 298]

PILKINGTON, MATTHEW (*fl.* 1729–1733), poet; a poor Irish parson; married Lætitia Pilkington [q. v.], 1729; attracted the attention of Swift by his servility, but afterwards forfeited it by his baseness; obtained by Swift's influence the post of chaplain to the lord mayor of London, 1732. [xlv. 296]

PILKINGTON, MATTHEW (1705–1765), author; LL.B. Jesus College, Cambridge, 1728; prebendary of Lichfield, 1748–65; published 'A Rational Concordance, or an Index to the Bible,' 1749. [xlv. 299]

PILKINGTON, MATTHEW (1700?–1784), divine and author of the 'Dictionary of Painters'; B.A. Trinity College, Dublin, 1722; vicar of Donabate and Portrahan; author of 'The Gentleman's and Connoisseur's Dictionary of Painters,' published 1770. [xlv. 299]

PILKINGTON, REDMOND WILLIAM (1789-1844), architect; son of William Pilkington [q. v.]; carried out the additions at the London Charterhouse commenced by his father.   [xlv. 302]

PILKINGTON, RICHARD (1568 ?-1631), protestant controversialist; probably a nephew of James Pilkington [q. v.]; M.A. Emmanuel College, Cambridge, 1593 (incorporated M.A. Oxford, 1599); D.D. Queen's College, Oxford, 1607; rector of Hambledon, Buckinghamshire, 1596-1631; wrote 'Parallela,' 1618, in reply to Anthony Champney [q. v.]   [xlv. 299]

PILKINGTON, ROBERT (1765-1834), major-general and inspector-general of fortifications; entered the royal artillery, 1787; transferred to the royal engineers, 1789; commanding royal engineer at Gibraltar, 1818-30; inspector-general, 1832.   [xlv. 299]

PILKINGTON, SIR THOMAS (d. 1691), lord mayor of London; a staunch whig; distinguished himself in the city of London by his opposition to the Duke of York; imprisoned for nearly four years (1682-6) for *scandalum magnatum* in consequence of rash speeches against the duke; thrice lord mayor, 1689, 1690, and 1691; M.P. for the city of London, 1689; knighted by William III, 1689.   [xlv. 300]

PILKINGTON, WILLIAM (1758-1848), architect; had a large practice in London, and was employed for a while at Salisbury as surveyor and architect by the Earl of Radnor.   [xlv. 302]

PILLANS, JAMES (1778-1864), Scottish educational reformer; M.A. Edinburgh, 1801; rector of the Edinburgh High School, 1810-20; professor of 'humanity and laws' at Edinburgh University, 1820-63; improved the system of education both at the high school and the university; highly successful as a disciplinarian and teacher of Latin literature.   [xlv. 302]

PILLEMENT, JEAN (1727-1808), painter; born at Lyons; came to England before 1757; painted landscapes, marine pieces, and genre subjects in a theatrical and artificial style; returned in later life to Lyons, where he died.   [xlv. 305]

PILON, FREDERICK (1750-1788), actor and dramatist; first appeared on the stage at Edinburgh and afterwards drifted to London, where from 1778 he wrote clever ephemeral plays for Covent Garden and Drury Lane.   [xlv. 305]

PIM, BEDFORD CLAPPERTON TREVELYAN (1826-1886), admiral; entered the navy, 1842; served under Sir Edward Belcher [q. v.] in Franklin search expedition, 1852, and rescued Sir Robert John Le Mesurier McClure [q. v.]; retired from active service, 1861, and (1873) commenced to practise at the bar in admiralty cases, being (1873) a barrister of Gray's Inn; published miscellaneous works.   [xlv. 306]

PINCHBECK, CHRISTOPHER (1670 ?-1732), clockmaker; invented the copper and zinc alloy called after him. No contemporary mention of the metal called after him has been discovered.   [xlv. 307]

PINCHBECK, CHRISTOPHER (1710 ?-1783), inventor; son of Christopher Pinchbeck (1670 ?-1732) [q. v.]. Among his patents was one for snuffers, which long held the market.   [xlv. 307]

PINCHBECK, EDWARD (fl. 1732-1738), clockmaker; eldest son of Christopher Pinchbeck (1670 ?-1732) [q. v.]; succeeded to his father's business in Fleet Street, London.   [xlv. 307]

PINCK or **PINK**, ROBERT (1573-1647), warden of New College, Oxford; of Winchester College and New College, Oxford; M.A., 1602; D.D., 1619; fellow of New College, Oxford, 1596; became warden, 1617; a close ally of Laud in his measures for the reorganisation of the university, assisting to draw up the new statutes; took measures for the defence of Oxford, 1642, and was arrested and sent to London, but contrived to get back to Oxford, where he died.   [xlv. 308]

PINCKARD, GEORGE (1768-1835), physician; M.D. Leyden, 1792; L.R.C.P., 1794; appointed a physician to the forces, 1795, visiting the West Indies with Sir Ralph Abercromby's expedition; published 'Notes on the West Indies,' 1806; physician of the Bloomsbury Dispensary for thirty years.   [xlv. 310]

PINDAR, SIR PAUL (1565 ?-1650), diplomatist; a factor in Venice, c. 1583-1602; consul at Aleppo, 1609-11;

sent as ambassador to Turkey, 1611; knighted in England, 1620; finally returned to England, 1623; brought home some remarkable jewels, several of which came into possession of the crown.   [xlv. 310]

PINDAR, PETER (pseudonym). [See WOLCOT, JOHN, 1738-1819.]

PINE, SIR BENJAMIN CHILLEY CAMPBELL (1809-1891), colonial governor; M.A. Trinity College, Cambridge, 1840; barrister, Gray's Inn, 1841; acted as temporary governor of Sierra Leone, 1848, displaying much military capacity, and was governor of Natal, 1849-1856; knighted, 1856; governor of the Gold Coast, 1856-9; lieutenant-governor of St. Christopher, 1859-69; governor-in-chief of the Leeward islands, 1869-73; K.C.M.G., 1871; governor of Natal, 1873-5.   [xlv. 312]

PINE, JOHN (1690-1756), engraver; practised in London; probably pupil of Bernard Picart, whom he resembled in style.   [xlv. 312]

PINE, ROBERT EDGE (1730-1788), painter; son of John Pine [q. v.]; devoted himself to history and portrait-painting, and obtained much success; painted numerous portraits of actors and actresses; also (1771) of Brass Crosby, Wilkes, and Richard Oliver, while they were in the Tower of London; settled in Philadelphia, 1783.   [xlv. 313]

PINGO, BENJAMIN (1749-1794), herald; son of Thomas Pingo [q. v.]; rougedragon pursuivant, 1780; York herald, 1786.   [xlv. 315]

PINGO, JOHN (fl. 1768-1786), medallist; son of Thomas Pingo [q. v.]; appointed assistant-engraver to the mint, c. 1786.   [xlv. 315]

PINGO, LEWIS (1743-1830), medallist; son of Thomas Pingo [q. v.]; succeeded his father as assistant-engraver at the mint, 1776; chief engraver, 1779-1815. [xlv. 314]

PINGO, THOMAS (1692-1776), medallist; born in Italy; came to England, c. 1742-5; assistant-engraver at the mint, 1771-6.   [xlv. 314]

PINK, CHARLES RICHARD (1853-1889), architect; designed a number of houses and schools and a few churches, especially in Hampshire; F.R.I.B.A., 1886.   [xlv. 315]

PINK, ROBERT (1573-1647). [See PINCK.]

PINKE, WILLIAM (1599 ?-1629), author; probably related to Robert Pinck [q. v.]; M.A. Magdalen Hall, Oxford, 1622; elected fellow of Magdalen College, Oxford, 1628; published a translation and a popular devotional work.   [xlv. 316]

PINKERTON, JOHN (1758-1826), Scottish antiquary and historian; published (1783) 'Select Scottish Ballads,' several of which he forged, and (1784) an 'Essay on Medals,' a valuable work, which introduced him to Horace Walpole and Gibbon; published, 1786, his important volumes of 'Ancient Scottish Poems,' in the preface of which he detailed his former forgeries; published, 1797, his 'History of Scotland from the Accession of the House of Stuart to that of Mary.' His powers of research were greater than his literary talent.   [xlv. 316]

PINKETHMAN, WILLIAM (d. 1725), actor; held originally a low rank at the Theatre Royal, London, but was established in the favour of the 'Groundlings' by a tendency to overact and to introduce vulgar and impertinent 'business,' and rose in time to be a competent performer; subsequently acted at Drury Lane, London, where he had many original parts, and though after the union with the Haymarket company in 1708 he obtained fewer original characters, was assigned important parts in standard plays; a clown rather than a comedian, imitating Anthony Leigh [q. v.]   [xlv. 318]

PINKNEY, MILES (1599-1674). [See CARRE, THOMAS.]

PINNEY, CHARLES (1793-1867), mayor of Bristol; held the office of mayor in 1831 during the riots caused by the rejection of the Reform Bill; thrice read the riot act, and ran the risk of losing his life, the mob being finally dispersed only by the military, who fired on the people; tried in the king's bench for neglect of duty, 1832, but acquitted by the jury.   [xlv. 320]

PINNOCK, WILLIAM (1782–1843), publisher and educational writer; began life as a Hampshire schoolmaster; went to London, 1817, and in conjunction with Samuel Maunder [q. v.] commenced shortly afterwards a series of manuals of popular instruction, which met with extraordinary success, and were collected in the 'Juvenile Cyclopædia'; still more successful in his abridgments of Goldsmith's histories of England, Greece, and Rome, and his series of county histories: lost much money by a mania for speculation. [xlv. 321]

PINNOCK, WILLIAM HENRY (1813–1885), divine and author; son of William Pinnock [q. v.]; LL.D. Corpus Christi College, Cambridge, 1855 (incorporated at Oxford, 1859); vicar of Pinner, 1879–85; in his early years compiled, like his father, elementary text-books, and was also the author of several works upon ecclesiastical laws and usages. [xlv. 322]

PINTO, CHARLOTTE (*d*. 1802). [See BRENT.]

PINTO, GEORGE FREDERIC (1787–1806), violinist and musical composer; grandson of Thomas Pinto [q. v.]; travelled with Johann Peter Salomon [q. v.] after 1800, playing with great success at Oxford, Cambridge, Bath, and Edinburgh. He wrote sonatas for pianoforte solos and with violin, as well as a large number of songs. [xlv. 322]

PINTO, THOMAS (1710?–1773), violinist; of Neapolitan origin; was at an early age a remarkable player, but became careless and neglected to practise; roused to greater efforts by the arrival in England (1750) and success of Giardini; recovered his position in part, but was unsuccessful in a theatrical venture. [xlv. 322]

PINWELL, GEORGE JOHN (1842–1875), water-colour painter; began his professional career (1863) by designing and drawing on wood, chiefly for the brothers Dalziel; member of the Water-colour Society, 1870. [xlv. 323]

PIOZZI, HESTER LYNCH (1741–1821), friend of Dr. Johnson; only child of John Salusbury of Bachycraig, Flintshire; was, after her father's death (1762), married against her inclinations to Henry Thrale, the son of a wealthy brewer, 1763; began an intimacy with Dr. Johnson, which became famous (1764), Johnson being (1765) almost domesticated at Thrale's house at Streatham Park, and accompanying the Thrales to Wales in 1774 and to France in 1775; lost her husband, 1781, and, though the mother of several daughters, married (1784) Gabriel Piozzi, an Italian Roman catholic musician; went with her husband to Italy, this marriage being naturally disapproved by the society of that time; wrote in Italy her 'Anecdotes of the late Samuel Johnson' (1786), a book which gives a very lively picture of Dr. Johnson, though frequently coloured by personal feelings; returned to England, 1787, and was well received; settled at Streatham Park; left Streatham (1795) for Bachycraig, where she passed the remainder of her days; after her husband's death (1809), adopted his nephew, John Piozzi, who took her maiden name, Salusbury; published (1788) her correspondence with Dr. Johnson, and other works. [xlv. 323]

PIPRE or **PIPER**, FRANCIS LE (*d*. 1698). [See LEPIPRE.]

PIRAN or **PIRANUS** (*fl*. 550), saint; usually identified with Saint Ciaran (*fl*. 500–560) [q. v.] The names are identical—*p* in Britain being identical with the Irish *k*. The history of the two saints is in its main features the same, though the Irish lives of St. Ciaran do not record his migration to Cornwall. He holds a foremost place in Cornish hagiology, being the patron saint of Cornwall, or, at least, of all miners. The ruins of his oratory at Perranzabuloe were laid bare in 1835 by the shifting of the sands. [xlv. 326]

PIRIE, ALEXANDER (1737–1804), Scottish divine; appointed teacher in philosophy in the anti-burgher divinity school at Abernethy; joined the burghers, 1763, but (1769) being suspended for heresy, joined the independents; held exceptionally liberal religious views for his time; published theological works. [xlv. 326]

PIRIE, WILLIAM ROBINSON (1804–1885), professor of divinity and principal of the university of Aberdeen; studied at University and King's College, Aberdeen; minister of Dyce, 1830–43; professor of divinity at Marischal College, Aberdeen, 1843–60; hon. D.D. Marischal

and King's Colleges, Aberdeen, 1844; professor of divinity and church history at Marischal and King's Colleges, 1860–85; moderator of the church of Scotland, 1864; principal of Aberdeen University, 1876–85; published theological works. [xlv. 327]

PIRRIE, WILLIAM (1807–1882), surgeon; M.A. Aberdeen, 1825; M.D. Edinburgh, 1829; became first regius professor of surgery at Marischal College, Aberdeen, 1839; and on the union of Marischal and King's College, Aberdeen, 1860, continued to teach as university professor; an intrepid and successful operator, and recognised in later life as the foremost surgeon in the north of Scotland. [xlv. 328]

PISTRUCCI, BENEDETTO (1784–1855), gem-engraver and medallist; born in Rome; son of a judge of the high criminal court in Rome; commenced work in Rome, proceeding to Paris in 1814, and to London in 1815; modelled the portrait of Sir Joseph Banks [q. v.], who sent him to the master of the mint, for whom he modelled the St. George and the Dragon on the reverse of the gold coinage; performed the duties of chief engraver from 1817, and (1828) was nominated chief medallist. As a gem-engraver his reputation stands high, and he imparted to the English coinage a distinction of style that had long been absent. [xlv. 328]

PITCAIRN. [See also PITCAIRNE and PITCARNE.]

PITCAIRN, DAVID (1749–1809), physician; brother of Robert Pitcairn (1747?–1770?) [q. v.]; M.D. Corpus Christi College, Cambridge, 1784; began to practise in London, 1779; succeeded his uncle, William Pitcairn [q. v.] as physician to St Bartholomew's Hospital, 1780; F.R.C.P., 1785. [xlv. 331]

PITCAIRN, ROBERT (1520?–1584), commendator of Dunfermline and Scottish secretary of state; became commendator of Dunfermline, 1561; chosen a lord of the articles, 1567, and an extraordinary lord of session, 1568; accompanied Moray to the conference at York (1568) in reference to the charges against Queen Mary; succeeded William Maitland (1528?–1573) [q. v.] as secretary of state, 1570; a party to the conspiracy against Morton, 1578, and, after the regent's fall, was one of the new council of twelve chosen to govern in the name of James VI; had a chief share in contriving the raid of Ruthven, 1582, and did his utmost to hinder the counter-revolution of 1583, which deprived him of most of his influence. [xlv. 332]

PITCAIRN, ROBERT (1747?–1770?), midshipman; is remembered as the first to sight Pitcairn's island (named after him), on 2 July, 1767, which was afterwards the home of the mutineers of the Bounty; lost at sea. [xlv. 333]

PITCAIRN, ROBERT (1793–1855), antiquary and miscellaneous writer; published 'Trials before the High Court in Scotland' (3 vols. 1833), which attracted the attention of Sir Walter Scott. [xlv. 334]

PITCAIRN, WILLIAM (1711–1791), physician; M.D. Rheims; M.D. Oxford, 1749; was physician to St. Bartholomew's Hospital, London, 1750–80, where a ward is named after him; president of the Royal College of Physicians, 1775–85. [xlv. 334]

PITCAIRNE, ARCHIBALD (1652–1713), physician and poet; studied law at Edinburgh and Paris; M.A. Edinburgh, 1671; turned his attention to medicine, and commenced to practise in Edinburgh, *c*. 1681; professor of physic at Leyden, 1692, resigning his chair, however (1693) and returning to Edinburgh; suspected of being at heart an atheist, chiefly on account of his mockery of the puritanical strictness of the presbyterian church; reputed author of two satirical works, 'The Assembly, a Scotch Reformation: a Comedy,' 1692, and 'Babel, a Satirical Poem,' 1692; wrote also a number of Latin verses, some of which appear in 'Selecta Poemata A. Pitcarnii et aliorum' (1727). He was one of the most celebrated physicians of his time. [xlv. 335]

PITCARNE, ALEXANDER (1622?–1695), Scottish presbyterian divine; M.A. St. Salvator's College, St. Andrews, 1643; regent of St. Salvator's College, St. Andrews, 1648–56; minister of Dron, 1656–62; deprived, 1662, but permitted by the bishop to discharge his duties; again deprived, 1681, and troops quartered on his parishioners;

restored, 1690 ; appointed principal of St. Mary's College, St. Andrews, 1693 ; published controversial works, the best known being ' The Spiritual Sacrifice,' 1664.

[xlv. 337]

PITMAN, SIR ISAAC (1813–1897), inventor of phonography ; master of school at Barton-on-Humber, Lincolnshire, 1832, and at Wootton-under-Edge, Gloucestershire, 1836–7 ; dismissed (1837) for joining the ' New Church,' founded by Emmanuel Swedenborg ; established and conducted (1839–43) school at Bath ; learned shorthand system of Samuel Taylor [q. v.], and, with object of popularising the art, published at fourpence ' Stenographic Sound-Hand,' 1837, substituting phonographic for the mainly orthographic methods adopted by former shorthand authors, a penny plate entitled ' Phonography ' appearing, in 1840, and fuller explanations of the system being published in 1840 and subsequent years ; issued numerous instruction books and standard works printed in shorthand characters ; with assistance of Alexander John Ellis [q. v.] advocated spelling reform ; knighted, 1894. His system, which has been adapted to several foreign languages, has to a very large extent superseded all others. [Suppl. iii. 266]

PITMAN, JOHN ROGERS (1782–1861), divine and author ; M.A. Pembroke College, Cambridge, 1815 ; well known in London as a preacher, prolific writer, compiler, and editor. [xlv. 338]

PITMEDDEN, LORD (1639?–1719). [See SETON, SIR ALEXANDER.]

PITS, ARTHUR (1557–1634 ?), Roman catholic priest ; studied at Oxford and Douay, and returned to England (1581) as one of a company of forty-seven priests sent from Douay during the year ; arrested, 1582, and banished, 1585 ; imprisoned for a time on a charge of disaffection to the French king, due to his patriotism ; made canon when Pope Urban VIII re-established the English hierarchy, 1623. [xlv. 339]

PITS or **PITSEUS**, JOHN (1560–1616), Roman catholic divine and biographer ; studied at Winchester College, New College, Oxford (probationer-fellow, 1578), and Rome, and passed most of his life in Germany and Lorraine ; principal work, ' Relationum Historicarum de Rebus Anglicis Tom. I.' (1619), the most valuable part being that dealing with the biographies of catholic writers after the Reformation. [xlv. 339]

PITSCOTTIE, ROBERT OF (1500?–1565 ?). [See LINDSAY.]

PITSLIGO, fourth and last BARON FORBES OF (1678–1762). [See FORBES, ALEXANDER.]

PITT, ANN (1720 ?–1799), actress ; appeared as Miss Pitt at Drury Lane, London, under Garrick in 1748, after some practice in the country ; first advertised as Mrs. Pitt, 3 Oct. 1755 ; among her most notable characters the nurse in ' Romeo and Juliet,' which she played to many famous Juliets, and Mrs. Croaker in the ' Good-natured Man ' ; continued on the stage until the age of seventy-two. [xlv. 340]

PITT, CHRISTOPHER (1699–1748), poet and translator ; of Winchester College and Wadham and New Colleges, Oxford ; fellow of New College, 1721 ; M.A., 1724 ; presented in 1722 to the rectory of Pimperne, where he resided till his death ; had some acquaintance with Pope, and published a translation of Virgil's ' Æneid ' in 1740, which has been included in many collected editions of English poets. [xlv. 342]

PITT, GEORGE, first BARON RIVERS (1722 ?–1803), M.A. Magdalen College, Oxford, 1739 ; D.C.L., 1745 ; whig M.P. for Shaftesbury, 1742, Dorset, 1747–74 ; created baron, 1776 ; filled several diplomatic posts ; published ' Letters to a Young Nobleman,' 1784, and other works.

[xlv. 343]

PITT, HARRIET (d. 1814), dancer ; daughter of Ann Pitt [q. v.] ; appeared chiefly at Covent Garden ; took the name of Mrs. Davenet, to distinguish her from her mother, 1783 ; mother of Thomas John Dibdin [q. v.] by Charles Dibdin [q. v.] [xlv. 341]

PITT, SIR JOHN, second EARL OF CHATHAM (1756–1835), eldest son of William Pitt, first earl of Chatham [q. v.] ; entered the army, 1778 ; first lord of the admiralty, 1788–94 ; privy councillor, 1789 ; K.G., 1790 ; lord privy seal, 1794–6 ; president of the council, 1796–

1801 ; master of the ordnance, 1801–6 ; was keenly disappointed by the appointment of Wellesley to command in the Peninsula, 1808, and as a consolation was placed in command of the Walcheren expedition, 1809 ; proved himself quite unequal to the task assigned him, and on failure of the expedition blamed the naval commander, Sir Richard John Strachan [q. v.], for the result ; his reputation ruined by the ensuing inquiry ; general, 1812 ; governor of Gibraltar, 1820–35. [xlv. 344]

PITT, MOSES (fl. 1654–1696), publisher and author ; chiefly known for his publication of ' The English Atlas,' a work formerly held in great estimation (maps based on Janssen's atlas). Of this work four volumes and part of a fifth appeared between 1680 and 1682, but it was not a pecuniary success, and in 1689–91 he was imprisoned for debt. [xlv. 345]

PITT, ROBERT (1653–1713), physician ; fellow of Wadham College, Oxford, 1674 ; M.A., 1675 ; M.D., 1682 ; F.R.S., 1682 ; censor, Royal College of Physicians, 1687 and 1702 ; physician to St. Bartholomew's Hospital, London, 1698–1707 ; published several pamphlets against the excessive use of drugs and against frauds common in medical practice. [xlv. 346]

PITT, THOMAS (1653–1726), East India merchant and governor of Madras ; often called ' Diamond Pitt ' ; engaged in the East India trade as an interloper, and settling at Balasore (1674) began a long struggle with the East India Company ; engaged (1683–7) in litigation in England on the question of his trading without authorisation from the East India Company, but (1693) he started on his last interloping voyage, and made terms with the company, 1694 ; president of Fort St. George, 1697–1709, building up a great reputation ; kept a constant look-out for large diamonds during his stay at Madras, obtaining (1701) the great Pitt diamond from an Indian merchant, which he sold (1717) to the French regent for 135,000l. (It was in 1791 valued at 480,000l., and is still among the state jewels of France). [xlv. 347]

PITT, THOMAS, first EARL OF LONDONDERRY (1688 ?–1729), son of Thomas Pitt (1653–1726) [q. v.] ; M.P., Wilton, 1713–27, Old Sarum, 1727–8 ; created Baron Londonderry, 1719, and Earl of Londonderry, 1726 ; governor of the Leeward islands, 1728–9. [xlv. 349]

PITT, THOMAS, first BARON CAMELFORD (1737–1793), nephew or William Pitt, first earl of Chatham [q. v.] ; M.A. Clare College, Cambridge, per literas regias, 1759 ; whig M.P. for Old Sarum, 1761–8, Okehampton, 1768–74, and again for Old Sarum, 1774–84 ; one of the strongest opponents of Lord North's ministry and a warm antagonist of the coalition ; declined the leadership of the House of Commons, 1783 ; raised to the peerage, 1784. From March 1762 he lived at Twickenham, where his skill in Gothic architecture was recognised by his neighbour, Horace Walpole. He was a friend of Mrs. Delany [q. v.] [xlv. 350]

PITT, THOMAS, second BARON CAMELFORD (1775–1804), only son of Thomas Pitt, first baron Camelford [q. v.] ; educated at the Charterhouse ; entered the navy, 1789 ; being put ashore for insubordination at Hawaii (1794) had to work his passage home, afterwards ineffectually challenging his commander, George Vancouver [q. v.], to a duel ; shot Charles Peterson, first lieutenant of the Perdrix, during a dispute concerning seniority (1798), for which he was acquitted by court-martial on the ground that Peterson had refused to obey his orders, and was therefore a mutineer, although, according to naval law, Peterson was the senior officer ; his name struck off the list of commanders at his own request, in consequence of an altercation with the admiralty, 1798 ; subsequently lived in London, where he achieved extraordinary notoriety by disorderly conduct ; killed in a duel near Holland House, London. [xlv. 352]

PITT, WILLIAM, first EARL OF CHATHAM (1708–1778), statesman ; born in Westminster ; younger son of Robert Pitt of Boconnoc in Cornwall, by his wife, Harriet, daughter of Edward Villiers of Dromana, co. Waterford, and grandson of Thomas Pitt (1653–1726) [q. v.] ; educated at Eton and Trinity College, Oxford ; from early life suffered severely from gout ; obtained a cornetcy in Lord Cobham's horse, 1731, and four years later entered parliament for Old Sarum ; dismissed from the army for his first speech—on the marriage of Frederick, prince of

Wales ; again M.P. for Old Sarum, 1741 ; distinguished himself by his opposition to the system of foreign subsidies, and by his attacks on the Hanoverian policy of the ministers ; was passed over on Granville's dismissal (November 1744), while several of his political associates obtained seats in the 'Broad-bottom' administration ; admitted (1746) to office as joint vice-treasurer of Ireland, in consequence of Pelham's bringing pressure to bear upon George II, tendering his resignation during the Jacobite rebellion ; promoted paymaster-general of the forces (May 1746), in which post he created a precedent by declining any of the emoluments of the office beyond the legal salary ; gained public confidence by his disinterested conduct, in spite of the fact that he supported a continental policy in the interest of Hanover, such as he had formerly denounced ; failed to conciliate George II by his change of sentiment ; being disappointed in his hope on Pelham's death (March 1754) of succeeding to the leadership of the House of Commons, joined Henry Fox (afterwards first Baron Holland) [q. v.] in ridiculing the actual leader, Sir Thomas Robinson (afterwards first Baron Grantham) [q. v.], and even proceeded to assail Newcastle, the prime minister, himself ; dismissed from office, November 1755 ; his accession to power made a necessity by the disasters of the French war, which completed the unpopularity of Newcastle's ministry ; refused to act with Newcastle or Fox, who had deserted him in the previous year and accepted a seat in the cabinet ; became actual premier and secretary of state for the southern department (4 Dec. 1756), as well as leader of the House of Commons, with the Duke of Devonshire as first lord of the treasury ; found that Newcastle's corrupt influence still dominated the House of Commons, and that he could not carry on the government with the aid of public opinion alone ; dismissed with Temple from office by George II, April 1757, but in consequence of the public discontent and the necessities of the time was recalled with him within a few weeks ; formed a coalition with Newcastle ; planned the expeditions and selected the commanders in the succession of victories all over the world which early in 1758 took the place of England's former reverses, and raised loans for war expenses with a profusion which appalled more timid financiers ; made England as much an object of jealousy and dread to Europe as Spain or France in earlier times ; became aware of the family compact, September 1761, and proposed to commence hostilities against Spain ; failed to convince the cabinet, and on 5 Oct. resigned office with Temple ; denounced the preliminary treaty with France and Spain in December 1762, maintaining that the peace was insecure and the terms inadequate ; refused (1763) to resume office unless the great whig families were restored, and (1766) supported the repeal of the Stamp Act ; on Rockingham's dismissal, July 1766, formed a heterogeneous administration, composed of 'patriots and courtiers, king's friends and republicans' ; accepted an earldom, 1766, and took the sinecure office of lord privy seal ; found his administration become gradually more distinctly tory in character as time went on ; mentally incapacitated by suppressed gout from all attention to business, 1767 ; resigned office, 1768, but (January 1770) was sufficiently recovered from his mental disease to reappear in the House of Lords and attack the American policy of the government ; allied himself from this time forward definitely with Rockingham and the whigs ; largely disabled by the infirmity of his health from attending the House of Lords, 1771–4 ; strenuously opposed the harsh measures taken in regard to the American colonies, 1774–5, and (May 1777) unsuccessfully moved an address to the crown for the stoppage of hostilities, though he was not willing to recognise the independence of the colonies ; some unavailing efforts made to induce him to join North's administration in 1778, when the hostility of France and Spain was manifest ; fell backwards in a fit while opposing the Duke of Richmond's motion for the withdrawal of the English forces from America, 7 April ; died at Hayes on 11 May, and was buried in Westminster Abbey on 9 June. As an orator he must be ranked with the greatest of ancient or modern times ; as a statesman, and especially as a war minister, he possessed ability of a high order. ' Il faut avouer,' said Frederick the Great, 'que l'Angleterre a été longtems en travail, et qu'elle a beaucoup soufferte pour produire M. Pitt ; mais enfin elle est accouchée d'un homme.'   [xlv. 354]

PITT, WILLIAM (1759–1806), statesman ; second son of William Pitt, first earl of Chatham [q. v.] ; born at Hayes ; educated at Pembroke Hall, Cambridge ; M.A., 1776 ; called to the bar at Lincoln's Inn, 1780 ; M.P., Appleby, 1781 ; joined Lord Shelburne, leader of the party that had followed his father, Chatham ; resolved not to accept a minor office, and (1782) declined Rockingham's offers, though giving the government independent support ; became chancellor of the exchequer under Shelburne on Rockingham's death, July 1782 ; refused the treasury on Shelburne being overthrown by the coalition of North and Fox (February 1783), in spite of George III's importunity and the solicitations of Shelburne himself ; on the dismissal of the ministry was made prime minister in his twenty-fifth year (December 1783), the announcement being received with laughter in the House of Commons, where the late ministers had a large majority ; had great difficulty in forming an administration, and was the only member of the Commons in his own cabinet ; although repeatedly defeated in parliament, refused to dissolve until certain that public feeling was strongly on his side, Fox unwittingly assisting him by his mistaken tactics in endeavouring to prevent a dissolution ; obtained an overwhelming majority at the general election of 1784, to the satisfaction of the House of Lords, which had consistently supported him, and of George III, who regarded him as his only hope of salvation from men whom he hated ; at once turned his attention to the finances, took measures for funding and reducing the national debt, and made great abatements in the customs duties ; instituted (1786) the sinking fund for paying off the national debt, which, although its continuance after the outbreak of war in 1793 was economically unsound, undoubtedly contributed to maintain public credit ; his position imperilled (November 1788) by the king's insanity, since, had George, prince of Wales, become regent, he would have been dismissed in favour of Fox and his followers ; maintained that the regent ought to be appointed by parliament, and was engaged in passing a bill limiting his authority, when the necessity was removed by George III's recovery ; formed (1788) an alliance with Holland and Prussia, and (1791) attempted to abate racial feeling in Canada by dividing the country into the provinces of Upper and Lower Canada ; his attention roused by the outbreak of the French revolution, which involved him in a conflict which occupied all his later life ; he viewed the outbreak of 1789 as a domestic quarrel, which did not concern him, but was disturbed by the spread of republican principles in England, and by his attitude towards the French demand for the opening of the Scheldt caused war to be declared in February 1793 ; his government strengthened by the accession of many leading whigs, 1794, only Fox and his small party maintaining a stedfast opposition ; issued large loans, and suspended the Habeas Corpus Act (May 1793), abandoning at the same time his former partiality for parliamentary reform ; formed between March and October a great coalition with Russia, Sardinia, Spain, Naples, Prussia, Austria, Portugal, and some German princes, and granted subsidies of 832,000l. for the hire of foreign troops ; England successful at sea under the coalition formed by him, which, however, on the continent met with reverses, so that in a short time Austria and Sardinia were the only active allies left to England ; made a triple alliance with Russia and Austria, which was equally fruitless, Russia remaining inactive, while Austria effected nothing of moment ; his dismissal demanded by the mob, October 1795, which met George III going to open parliament with cries of ' Bread,' ' Peace,' and ' No Pitt,' a consequence of bad harvests and financial distress ; unsuccessfully laid proposals of peace before the French directory, March 1796, in the year after which (October 1797) the war on the continent came to an end, and England, loaded with taxation and threatened with financial panic, seemed likely to bear the whole brunt of the French attack ; insulted by the mob, December 1797, and guarded with cavalry ; anxiously sought for peace, but on the outbreak of the Irish rebellion of 1798 renewed the suspension of the Habeas Corpus Act and passed other coercive measures ; aided by the victory of the Nile on 1 Aug. 1798 in forming his second great coalition against France, which included Portugal, Naples, Russia, The Porte, and Austria ; by this the French were driven back to the Rhine, and Masséna was penned up in Genoa, though Napoleon, returning from Egypt, broke the power of Austria at Marengo, and Moreau re-established the French in southern Germany ; made the land tax perpetual, April 1798, and (December 1798) introduced an income tax, levying ten per cent. on incomes of 200l. and upwards, besides a lesser rate on incomes exceeding 60*l.*; had the Irish parliament united to that of Great Britain, 1800, the passage of the bill in Ireland being procured by methods which show a low standard of political morality; though largely responsible for the corruption, was not the inventor of the system which had become an evil tradition in Ireland long before the union; desired to complete his Irish policy by introducing a measure of catholic emancipation, but found himself unable to overcome George III's opposition; found George III obdurate, and resigned office, 14 March 1801, but in view of the foreign perils threatening the country agreed to support Addington's administration; relaxed his attendance in parliament in 1802, but maintained constant communication with the prime minister, and advised him both on the budget in April and on the royal speech in June; approved the treaty of Amiens, but disliked many of the government's proceedings, particularly its system of finance; after the outbreak of war in May 1803, when the feebleness of government became apparent, at first maintained an attitude of neutrality, but gradually came into opposition; re-entered office on the resignation of Addington, May 1804, though without the support of most of his former allies among the whigs, who seceded with Grenville; desired to include Fox in his cabinet; opposed in the Commons by the parties of Addington, Windham, and Fox; inaugurated a more vigorous policy, and (April 1805) formed a third coalition with Russia, Austria, and Sweden, but incurred the hostility of Spain, which declared war against England, December 1804; personally reconciled to Addington, December 1804; increased the property tax by twenty-five per cent., February 1805, raising a loan of 20,000,000*l.*; his health, which had been declining for some time, seriously affected by the censure on his old friend Melville for conduct of the public funds while first lord of the admiralty, and the renewed disaffection of Addington, now lord Sidmouth; he was almost broken down by the news of the capitulation of Ulm, October 1805; his death caused by the battle of Austerlitz, which shattered the coalition he had built up; he died in January 1806, his last words being 'Oh, my country! how I leave my country!'; buried (22 Feb.) in Westminster Abbey. Eager by nature, Pitt trained himself to singular calmness and self-possession. His judgment on party matters was admirable, and by the destruction of the whig oligarchy he prepared for later parliamentary reform. He made some serious political mistakes, and was not his father's equal as a war minister. His policy of opposing France by means of European coalitions, while vigorous and daring, imposed on England a heavy financial burden, and, perhaps owing to the petty views and selfish character of his continental allies, it could never have attained much success. His administration covered a time of great difficulty and peril, which forced him to abandon most of his early schemes of internal reform, but he preserved England from serious disaster, established the reputation of her arms, and greatly increased her colonial possessions.   [xlv. 367]

PITT, WILLIAM (1749–1823), writer on agriculture; prepared reports on several English counties for the board of agriculture, besides publishing economic and agricultural treatises.   [xlv. 386]

PITT, Sir WILLIAM AUGUSTUS (1728–1809), general; brother of George Pitt, first baron Rivers [q. v.]; entered the army, 1744; distinguished himself in several actions; K.B., 1792; general, 1793; governor of Portsmouth, 1794–1809.   [xlv. 344]

PITT-RIVERS, AUGUSTUS HENRY LANE FOX (1827–1900), lieutenant-general, anthropologist, and archæologist; son of William Augustus Lane Fox; assumed name of Pitt-Rivers (1880) on eventually inheriting estates of his great-uncle, George Pitt, second baron Rivers (1751–1828); educated at Sandhurst; received commission in grenadier guards, 1845; captain, 1850; lieutenant-general, 1882; employed in investigations as to use and improvement of rifle, 1851–7; served in Crimea; collected weapons, and subsequently other articles illustrating the course of human invention; the collection was housed by government at Bethnal Green, London, and South Kensington, London, till 1883, when it was presented to Oxford University and placed in the Pitt-Rivers Museum; resided, from 1880, at Rushmore, Wiltshire, and explored local antiquities, accurately recording excavations, and causing models of sites to be placed in the museum of Farnham, Dorset, which he built; F.R.S., 1876; vice-

president of Society of Antiquaries; first inspector of ancient monuments, 1882; hon. D.C.L. Oxford, 1886; published scientific writings and accounts of excavations.   [Suppl. iii. 268]

PITTARROW, LORD (*d.* 1576). [See WISHART, SIR JOHN.]

PITTENDREICH, LORD (*d.* 1583). [See BALFOUR, SIR JAMES.]

PITTIS, THOMAS (1636–1687), divine; of Trinity and Lincoln Colleges, Oxford; M.A. Lincoln College, 1658; D.D., 1670; was expelled from the university, 1658; became a royal chaplain, *c.* 1670; rector of St. Botolph's, Bishopsgate, London, 1678–87.   [xlv. 386]

PITTIS, WILLIAM (1674–1724), pamphleteer; son of Thomas Pittis [q. v.]; of Winchester and New College, Oxford; fellow, 1692–5; B.A., 1694; member of the Inner Temple; ordered, in 1706, to stand in the pillory three hours and to pay a fine for writing 'A Memorial of the Church of England,' not now extant, and was taken into custody (1714) for his 'Reasons for a War with France.'   [xlv. 386]

PITTMAN, JOSIAH (1816–1886), musician and author; organist at Lincoln's Inn, 1852–64; accompanist at Her Majesty's Opera, London, 1865–8, and at Covent Garden, 1868–86; edited many works for Messrs. Boosey.   [xlv. 387]

PITTS, JOSEPH (1663–1731?), traveller; captured by an Algerine pirate (1678), and enslaved at Algiers; performed the pilgrimage to Mecca; escaped, 1693; published at Exeter (1704) the first authentic account by an Englishman of the pilgrimage to Mecca.   [xlv. 387]

PITTS, WILLIAM (1790–1840), silver-chaser and sculptor; gained a great reputation for models and reliefs in pure classical taste; was ambidextrous, drawing and modelling equally well with either hand.   [xlv. 388]

PIX, MARY (1666–1720?), dramatist; *née* Griffith; married George Pix, a merchant tailor of London, 1684; produced (1696) the blank-verse tragedy, 'Ibrahim,' at Dorset Garden, London, and published a novel and farce; devoted herself from this time to dramatic authorship, her plays appearing at several London theatres; devoid of learning and notorious for her fatness and love of good wine; left passable comedies and intolerable tragedies; travestied in 'The Female Wits,' a dramatic satire.   [xlv. 388]

PLACE, FRANCIS (1647–1728), amateur artist; modelled his style on his friend Wenceslaus Hollar [q. v.]; had considerable merit as a painter of animals and still-life, and also drew portraits in crayon; one of the first Englishmen to practise the newly discovered art of mezzotint engraving.   [xlv. 390]

PLACE, FRANCIS (1771–1854), radical reformer; apprenticed to a leather-breeches maker, and (1791) became a journeyman, but owing to the decay of the trade could hardly obtain work; studied when he had opportunity, and became secretary to the clubs of several trades, including his own; tailor in London, 1799; supported Sir Francis Burdett [q. v.] (1807 and 1810) in his political campaigns, and made the acquaintance of many leading politicians and political thinkers; carried on a campaign (1816–23) against the sinking fund, and (1824) succeeded in getting the laws against combinations of workmen repealed; eventually regarded as the source of radical inspiration; his power lessened after the passing of the Reform Bill. Seventy-one volumes of his manuscripts and materials, largely autobiographical, are in the British Museum.   [xlv. 390]

PLAMPIN, ROBERT (1762–1834), vice-admiral; entered the navy, 1775; possessed a good knowledge of French and Dutch, which greatly assisted him in his profession; saw much service during the French war, especially in European waters; commander-in-chief in Ireland, 1825–8; promoted vice-admiral, 1825.   [xlv. 393]

PLANCHÉ, JAMES ROBINSON (1796–1880), Somerset herald and dramatist; wrote 'Amoroso,' a burlesque, which was produced at Drury Lane, London, 1818; subsequently wrote numerous pieces for the London theatres; musical manager at Vauxhall Gardens, London, 1826–7; manager of the Adelphi, London, 1830; connected with the Olympic, London, Covent Garden, London, and the Lyceum, London, under Madame Vestris from 1831 to 1856; continued to write till 1872; antiquary and student of heraldry and costume; his 'History of British Costumes' (1834) the result of ten years' study. In 1866 he became Somerset herald, and he went on various foreign missions to invest continental princes with the order of the Garter. [xlv. 395]

PLANCHÉ, MATILDA ANNE (1826-1881). [See MACKARNESS.]

PLANT, THOMAS LIVESLEY (1819-1883), meteorologist; kept systematic meteorological records at Birmingham for forty-six years (1837-83), besides writing largely on the subject. [xlv. 397]

PLANTA, JOSEPH (1744-1827), librarian; born in the Grisons; came to London, 1752, with his father, whom he succeeded (1773) as assistant-librarian at the British Museum; promoted (1776) keeper of manuscripts, and (1799) principal librarian. During his term of office he granted many facilities to the public. [xlv. 397]

PLANTA, JOSEPH (1787-1847), diplomatist; son of Joseph Planta (1744-1827) [q. v.]; educated at Eton; Canning's private secretary, 1807-9, and afterwards secretary to Castlereagh, 1813-14, during his mission to the allied sovereigns. [xlv. 398]

PLANTAGENET, FAMILY OF. Though the surname has become attached by usage to the house which occupied the English throne from 1154 to 1485, the family did not assume it until the middle of the fifteenth century. It was originally a personal nickname of Geoffrey, count of Anjou, father of Henry II, and Richard, duke of York, desiring to express the superiority of his descent over the Lancastrian line, adopted Plantagenet as a surname. It first appeared in formal records in 1460.

The sovereigns of the Angevin dynasty appear in this index under their christian names. Other members of the family are noticed under the following headings; ARTHUR, VISCOUNT LISLE (1480?-1542), see PLANTAGENET, SIR ARTHUR; EDMUND, called CROUCHBACK (1245-1296), see LANCASTER; EDMUND, second EARL OF CORNWALL (1250-1300), see EDMUND; EDMUND OF WOODSTOCK, EARL OF KENT (1301-1330), see EDMUND; EDMUND OF LANGLEY, first DUKE OF YORK (1341-1402), see LANGLEY; EDWARD, 'THE BLACK PRINCE' (1330-1376), see EDWARD; EDWARD, second DUKE OF YORK (1373?-1415), see 'PLANTAGENET,' EDWARD; EDWARD, EARL OF WARWICK (1475-1499), see EDWARD; GEOFFREY, archbishop of York (d. 1212), see GEOFFREY; GEORGE, DUKE OF CLARENCE (1449-1478), see GEORGE; HENRY OF CORNWALL (1235-1271), see HENRY; HENRY, EARL OF LANCASTER (1281?-1345), see HENRY; HENRY, first DUKE OF LANCASTER (1299?-1361), see HENRY; HUMPHREY, DUKE OF GLOUCESTER (1391-1447), see HUMPHREY; JOHN OF ELTHAM, EARL OF CORNWALL (1316-1336), see JOHN; JOHN OF GAUNT, DUKE OF LANCASTER (1340-1399), see JOHN; JOHN OF LANCASTER, DUKE OF BEDFORD (1389-1435), see JOHN; LIONEL OF ANTWERP, DUKE OF CLARENCE (1338-1368), see LIONEL; MARGARET, COUNTESS OF SALISBURY (1473-1541), see POLE, MARGARET; RICHARD, EARL OF CORNWALL and KING OF THE ROMANS (1209-1272), see RICHARD; RICHARD, EARL OF CAMBRIDGE (d. 1415), see RICHARD; RICHARD, DUKE OF YORK (1411-1460), see RICHARD; RICHARD, DUKE OF YORK (1472-1483), see RICHARD; THOMAS, EARL OF LANCASTER (1277?-1322), see THOMAS; THOMAS OF BROTHERTON, EARL OF NORFOLK (1300-1338), see THOMAS; THOMAS OF WOODSTOCK, DUKE OF GLOUCESTER (1355-1397), see THOMAS; THOMAS, DUKE OF CLARENCE (1388?-1421), see THOMAS. [xlv. 398]

PLANTAGENET, ARTHUR, VISCOUNT LISLE (1480? 1542), natural son of Edward IV by Elizabeth Lucie; an esquire of Henry VIII's bodyguard; married (1511) Elizabeth, daughter of Edward Grey, viscount Lisle, obtaining a grant of the title, 1523; became deputy of Calais, 1533, and in 1540 was arrested on suspicion of being implicated in a plot; was declared innocent in 1542, but died in the Tower of London of excitement. [xlv. 399]

'PLANTAGENET,' EDWARD, more correctly EDWARD OF NORWICH, second DUKE OF YORK (1373?-1415), eldest son of Edmund de Langley, first duke of York [q. v.]; K.G., 1387; created Earl of Rutland, 1390; became admiral of the northern fleet, 1391, and sole admiral, 1392; created Earl of Cork, 1396; took a leading part in Richard II's attack upon the lords appellant, 1397, and was rewarded with large grants of land, the duchy of

Albemarle, and the office of constable; his fidelity to Richard II in 1399 much questioned, although perhaps without sufficient cause; deprived by Henry IV of the constableship, of the dignity of duke, and of his later grants of land, but was soon afterwards sitting in the privy council; the story of his complicity in the conspiracy of Christmas 1399 not supported by trustworthy evidence; succeeded as Duke of York, 1402; appointed lieutenant of South Wales, 1403; engaged in the abortive attempt to carry off the Mortimers from Windsor and was arrested, 1405, but released by the close of the year; commanded the right wing at Agincourt, and was killed in the battle. [xlv. 401]

PLANTAGENET, GEORGE, DUKE OF CLARENCE (1449-1478). [See GEORGE.]

PLAT or **PLATT,** SIR HUGH (1552-1611?), writer on agriculture and inventor; son of a London brewer; amply provided for by his father; B.A. St. John's College, Cambridge, 1572; developed an active interest in mechanical inventions and in agriculture, which he treated scientifically; published (1594) 'The Jewell House of Art and Nature,' which contained descriptions of a number of inventions and of experiments in agriculture; knighted, 1605; author of other curious works on such topics as household recipes for preserving fruits, distilling, cooking, and dyeing the hair; published his chief work on gardening, 'Floraes Paradise,' 1608. [xlv. 407]

PLATT, SIR THOMAS JOSHUA (1790?-1862), baron of the exchequer; of Harrow and Trinity College, Cambridge; M.A., 1814; barrister, Inner Temple, 1816; knighted, 1845; baron of the exchequer, 1845-56. [xlv. 409]

PLATT, THOMAS PELL (1798-1852), orientalist; fellow, Trinity College, Cambridge, 1820; M.A., 1823; acted for some years as librarian of the British and Foreign Bible Society, and (c. 1825) collated for the society the Æthiopic texts of the New Testament; also prepared an edition of the Syriac gospels, 1829, and an Amharic version of the bible, 1844. [xlv. 409]

PLATTES, GABRIEL (fl. 1638-1640), writer on agriculture; published his 'Treatise on Agriculture,' 1638, and subsequently other works; said to have died destitute during the Commonwealth. [xlv. 410]

PLATTS, JOHN (1775-1837), unitarian divine and compiler; unitarian minister at Boston, 1805-17, and Doncaster, 1817-37; published, besides other works, 'A new Universal Biography' (1825, 5 vols.), arranged chronologically, and extending to the end of the sixteenth century, and a 'New Self-interpreting Testament,' 1827. [xlv. 410]

PLAW, JOHN (1745?-1820), architect; architect and master-builder in Westminster; published several professional works. [xlv. 411]

PLAYER, SIR THOMAS (1608-1672), chamberlain of London; M.A. St. Alban Hall, Oxford, 1633; a member of the Haberdashers' Company; was elected chamberlain, 1651; knighted, 1660; became, as chamberlain, official collector of the hearth-tax, 1664. [xlv. 411]

PLAYER, SIR THOMAS (d. 1686), chamberlain of London; only son of Sir Thomas Player [q. v.]; knighted, 1660; succeeded his father as chamberlain, 1672, resigning in 1683. He is gibbeted as Rabshakeh by Dryden in 'Absalom and Achitophel.' [xlv. 411]

PLAYFAIR, SIR HUGH LYON (1786-1861), Indian officer and provost of St. Andrews; son of James Playfair [q. v.]; studied at St. Andrews University; entered the Bengal artillery, 1804, and saw much service in India, retiring, 1834; provost of St. Andrews, 1842-61; revived the Royal and Ancient Golf Club; LL.D. St. Andrews, 1856; knighted, 1856. [xlv. 412]

PLAYFAIR, JAMES (1738-1819), principal of St Andrews; D.D. St. Andrews, 1779; appointed principal of the United College, St. Andrews, and minister of the church of St. Leonard's, 1800; for many years historiographer to George, prince of Wales. [xlv. 413]

PLAYFAIR, JOHN (1748-1819), mathematician and geologist; graduated at St. Andrews, 1765; minister of Liff and Benvie, 1773-83, and joint-professor of mathematics at Edinburgh, 1785-1805; became professor of natural philosophy, 1805; F.R.S., 1807; published, besides other works, 'Elements of Geometry,' 1795 (11th edit.

1859), and 'Illustrations of the Huttonian Theory of the Earth,' 1802, which latter helped to create the modern science of geology. [xlv. 413]

PLAYFAIR, SIR LYON, first BARON PLAYFAIR OF ST. ANDREWS (1818–1898); brother of Sir Robert Lambert Playfair [q. v.]; educated at St. Andrews; studied chemistry under Thomas Graham [q. v.] at Glasgow; assistant to Graham at University College, London; Ph.D. Giessen; honorary professor of chemistry to Royal Institution, Manchester, 1842–5; chemist to Geological Survey and professor in new School of Mines, Jermyn Street, London, 1845; F.R.S., 1848; president of Chemical Society, 1857–9; took part in organising Great Exhibition, 1851; C.B., 1851; secretary for science to Department of Science and Art, 1853, and secretary for science and art, 1855–8; professor of chemistry at Edinburgh, 1858–69; liberal M.P. for universities of Edinburgh and St. Andrews, 1868–85; postmaster-general, 1873; chairman and deputy-speaker of House of Commons, 1880–3; K.C.B., 1883; liberal M.P. for South Leeds, 1885–92; vice-president of council, 1886; raised to peerage, 1892; lord-in-waiting to Queen Victoria, 1892; G.C.B., 1895. He made important investigations on the nitroprussides, a new class of salts which he discovered. [Suppl. iii. 270]

PLAYFAIR, SIR ROBERT LAMBERT (1828–1899), author and administrator; grandson of James Playfair [q. v.]; brother of Sir Lyon Playfair, baron Playfair [q. v.]; entered Madras artillery, 1846; captain, 1858; transferred to Madras staff corps, 1861; major, 1866; retired from army as lieutenant-colonel, 1867; assistant political resident at Aden, 1854–62; F.R.G.S., 1860; political agent at Zanzibar, 1862, and consul, 1863; consul-general for Algeria, 1867, for Algeria and Tunis, 1885, and for Algeria and northern coast of Africa, 1889–96; K.C.M.G., 1886. His publications include bibliographies of Algeria, 1851–87 (1888), of Tripoli and the Cyrenaica (1889), and of Morocco (1892), books of travel, handbooks for travellers, and other writings. [Suppl. iii. 272]

PLAYFAIR, WILLIAM (1759–1823), publicist; brother of John Playfair [q. v.]; apprenticed to Andrew Meikle [q. v.]; took out several patents, and opened a shop in London for their sale; removed to Paris, not being successful, but (c. 1793), after taking part in the French revolution, returned to London, where (1795) he began writing against the French revolution; became editor of 'Galignani's Messenger' in Paris after the battle of Waterloo, but fled to London (1818) to avoid imprisonment for libel; earned a precarious livelihood in London by pamphlets and translations; wrote over forty works. [xlv. 414]

PLAYFAIR, WILLIAM HENRY (1789–1857), architect; nephew of John Playfair [q. v.]; practised in Edinburgh, where between 1815 and 1820 he laid out part of the new town; engaged (1817–24) in rebuilding and enlarging the university buildings; executed other important works, including the Advocates' Library and the National Gallery of Scotland. His classical buildings are predominant in any view of Edinburgh, and have gained for it the sobriquet of the 'Modern Athens.' [xlv. 415]

PLAYFERE, THOMAS (1561?–1609), divine; M.A. St. John's College, Cambridge, 1583; fellow of St. John's College, Cambridge, 1584; D.D., 1596 (incorporated at Oxford, 1596); Lady Margaret professor of divinity, 1596–1609. He was chaplain to James I. [xlv. 416]

PLAYFORD, HENRY (1657–1706?), musical publisher; son of John Playford (1623–1686?) [q. v.]; carried on his father's business, and published a large number of collections of music; established in 1699 a concert of music, held three times a week in a coffee-house; instituted weekly clubs for the practice of music, c. 1701. [xlv. 418]

PLAYFORD, JOHN, the elder (1623–1686?), musician and publisher; became known as a musical publisher in London, c. 1648, and from 1652 until his retirement kept a shop in the Inner Temple, near the church door; almost monopolised the business of music publishing in England under the Commonwealth, and for some years of Charles II's reign; famous for his collected volumes of songs and catches. In typographical technique his most original improvement was the invention, in 1658, of 'the new-ty'd note.' His original compositions were few and slight. [xlv. 416]

PLAYFORD, JOHN, the younger (1656–1686), music printer; nephew of John Playford the elder [q. v.]; entered into partnership, in 1679, with Ann Godbid in the printing-house at Little Britain (also the chief printing-house for setting up mathematical works). [xlv. 419]

PLEASANTS, THOMAS (1728–1818), philanthropist; a gentleman of affluence who made many large contributions to philanthropic institutions in Dublin. [xlv. 419]

PLECHELM, SAINT (*fl.* 700), 'the apostle of Guelderland'; an Irishman of noble birth who received holy orders and made a pilgrimage to Rome; having been consecrated a bishop, went with St. Wiro, an Irish bishop, on a mission to Gaul; settled at Ruremund, whence many missions were sent to the provinces between the Rhine and the Meuse. He has been doubtfully identified with Pecthelm [q. v.] [xlv. 420]

PLEGMUND (*d.* 914), archbishop of Canterbury; a Mercian by birth; lived as a hermit on an island (Plemstall) near Chester; called to court by Alfred, where he instructed the king and helped him in his literary work; chosen archbishop, 890; visited Rome, 890 and 908. [xlv. 420]

PLESSIS or **PLESSETIS**, JOHN DE, EARL OF WARWICK (*d.* 1263), of Norman origin; first mentioned in 1227; accompanied Henry III to Poitou, 1242; married Margaret de Neubourg, countess of Warwick, 1242, assuming the title in 1245; one of the royal representatives on the committee of twenty-four at the parliament of Oxford, 1258, one of the royal electors of the council of fifteen, and a member of the latter body; member of the council selected to act when Henry III was out of England, 1259. [xlv. 421]

PLESSIS, JOSEPH OCTAVE (1762–1825), Roman catholic archbishop of Quebec; became bishop-coadjutor of Quebec, 1801, bishop, 1806, and archbishop, 1818; a powerful leader of the French national party; opposed (1822) the union of Upper and Lower Canada. [xlv. 422]

PLESYNGTON, SIR ROBERT DE (*d.* 1393), chief baron of the exchequer; was appointed chief baron in 1380, but removed in 1386 on account of his adhesion to the party of Thomas of Woodstock, duke of Gloucester [q. v.]. [xlv. 422]

PLEYDELL-BOUVERIE, EDWARD (1818–1889) [See BOUVERIE.]

PLEYDELL-BOUVERIE, WILLIAM, third EARL RADNOR (1779–1869). [See BOUVERIE.]

PLIMER, ANDREW (1763–1837), miniature-painter; practised in London; exhibited at the Royal Academy, 1786–1810 and 1819. His miniatures are of the finest quality, and much sought after by collectors. [xlv.424]

PLIMER, NATHANIEL (1751–1822), miniature-painter; brother of Andrew Plimer [q. v.]; exhibited at the Royal Academy, 1787–1815; his work much inferior to that of his brother. [xlv. 424]

PLIMSOLL, SAMUEL (1824–1898), 'the Sailors' Friend'; honorary secretary for Great Exhibition, 1851; established himself as coal merchant in London, 1853; radical M.P. for Derby, 1868–80; did much to expedite passing of Merchant Shipping Act, 1876, and in 1875 created a scene in the House of Commons by a violent protest against the obstruction of the ship-owning members; president of Sailors' and Firemen's Union, 1890; published pamphlets and contributed many articles to periodicals, chiefly on subjects of mercantile shipping. [Suppl. iii. 273]

PLOT, ROBERT (1640–1696), antiquary; a gentleman of property in Kent; author of 'The Natural History of Oxfordshire,' 1677, and 'The Natural History of Staffordshire,' 1686, works of some interest, but marked by great credulity; appointed first 'custos' of the Ashmolean Museum and professor of chemistry at Oxford, 1683, historiographer royal, 1688, and Mowbray herald extraordinary, 1695. [xlv. 424]

PLOTT, JOHN (1732–1803), miniature-painter; a pupil of Nathaniel Hone [q. v.]; practised miniature-painting with success, both at London and Winchester. [xlv. 426]

PLOUGH, JOHN (*d.* 1562), protestant controversialist; B.C.L. Oxford, 1544; became rector of St. Peter's,

Nottingham, but on Queen Mary's accession fled to Bâle; returned to England, 1559, and became rector of East Ham, 1560. His works are not extant. [xlv. 426]

PLOWDEN, CHARLES (1743–1821), rector of Stony-hurst College; entered the Society of Jesus, 1759, and after passing some years at Bruges and Liège returned to England; appointed master of the novices at Stony-hurst, 1803, and declared rector, 1817; a writer of great power and a good orator. [xlv. 426]

PLOWDEN, EDMUND (1518–1585), jurist; studied at Cambridge; barrister, Middle Temple; one of the council of the marches of Wales, 1553; sat in parliament during Queen Mary's reign as M.P., Wallingford, 1553, Reading, 1554, Wootton-Bassett, 1555, but after Queen Elizabeth's accession found public life closed to him on account of his being a Roman catholic; had such great fame as a jurist that his name was embodied in the proverb 'The case is altered, quoth Plowden'; regarded with great admiration by Sir Edward Coke; published several legal compilations. [xlv. 428]

PLOWDEN, FRANCIS PETER (1749–1829), writer; brother of Charles Plowden [q. v.]; entered the Society of Jesus, and was master of the college at Bruges, 1771–3; returned to a secular life on the suppression of the jesuits by papal bull in 1773, being only a novice; entered the Middle Temple and practised as a conveyancer; called to the bar, 1796, on the removal of catholic disabilities; became eminent as a legal and political writer, publishing several pamphlets against Pitt; fled to France, 1813, to avoid the consequences of a libel suit, and became a professor in the Scots College at Paris, where he died. His greatest work is 'An Historical Review of the State of Ireland,' 1803. [xlv. 429]

PLOWDEN, WALTER CHICHELE (1820–1860), consul in Abyssinia; joined Mr. J. T. Bell (1843) in an expedition into Abyssinia to explore the sources of the White Nile; appointed consul, 1848, remaining in the interior till 1860, when he died of injuries received during a conflict with a rebel chieftain. [xlv. 431]

PLUGENET, ALAN DE (d. 1299), baron; fought on Henry III's side in the barons' war, and in 1282 served in the Welsh war; provoked the rising under Rhys ap Meredith in 1287 by his oppressive conduct as king's steward in Wales; summoned to parliament as a baron from 1292 to 1297. [xlv. 431]

PLUGENET, ALAN DE (1277–1319), baron; served in the Scottish wars, 1309–11, 1313–17, and 1319; summoned to parliament as a baron, 1311. [xlv. 432]

PLUKENET, LEONARD (1642–1706), botanist; perhaps educated at Westminster School; practised as a physician in London, and published many works on botany at his own expense; appointed superintendent of the royal gardens at Hampton Court, with the title of 'Queen's Botanist,' after 1689. [xlv. 432]

PLUME, THOMAS (1630–1704), archdeacon of Rochester; M.A. Christ's College, Cambridge, 1649; B.D., per literas regias, 1661; D.D., 1673; vicar of Greenwich, 1658 till death; subscribed declaration under Act of Uniformity, 1662; archdeacon of Rochester, 1679–1704. He left considerable sums of money for charitable objects, including the erection of an observatory and maintenance of a professor of astronomy and experimental philosophy at Cambridge (the Plumian professorship). [Suppl. iii. 274]

PLUMER, SIR THOMAS (1753–1824), master of the rolls; was educated at Eton and University College, Oxford; fellow, 1780; Vinerian scholar, 1777; M.A., 1778; B.C.L., 1783; barrister, Lincoln's Inn, 1778; appointed a commissioner in bankruptcy, 1781; defended Sir Thomas Rumbold [q. v.], 1783, and (1787) was one of the three counsel returned to defend Warren Hastings; successfully defended Lord Melville on his impeachment, 1806, and assisted Eldon and Perceval in the defence of Caroline, princess of Wales against the charges brought against her, 1806; solicitor-general in the Duke of Portland's administration, 1807; knighted, 1807; became attorney-general, 1812; created first vice-chancellor of England, under the provisions of 53 George III, 1813; became master of the rolls, 1818. [xlv. 432]

PLUMPTON, SIR ROBERT (1453–1523), soldier; son of Sir William Plumpton [q. v.], by Joan Winteringham,

to whom he had been privately married (1451), according to his statement, before the ecclesiastical court of York, 1467–8; knighted by the Duke of Gloucester, 1482; supported Henry VII after he had secured the crown; though loyal, fell into the hands of Henry VII's minister, Empson, who raked up the old claims of the heirs-general of Sir William Plumpton (already referred to), and was thus reduced to poverty, being imprisoned in the Counter on Henry VIII's accession; soon after released and his estate restored. The 'Plumpton Correspondence,' consisting of letters from the time of Sir William Plumpton down to 1551, was edited for the Camden Society in 1838–9 by Thomas Stapleton (1805–1849) [q. v.]. [xlv. 435]

PLUMPTON, SIR WILLIAM (1404–1480), soldier; a gentleman of Plumpton in Yorkshire; fought in the French wars; was closely connected with the Percy family, and was thus drawn to support the house of Lancaster; fought at Towton, 1461; fell into Edward IV's hands, submitted, and received a pardon, 1462. In 1471, owing to some fresh move in the Lancastrian interest, he received a general pardon, but lost his offices. [xlv. 434]

PLUMPTRE, ANNA or ANNE (1760–1818), author; daughter of Robert Plumptre [q. v.]; a good linguist; was one of the first to make German plays known in London, translating many of Kotzebue's dramas in 1798 and 1799; intimate with Helen Maria Williams [q. v.]; published (1810) her 'Narrative of a Three Years' [1802–5] Residence in France,' and (1817) her 'Narrative of a Residence in Ireland'; published novels, and several translations of travels from the French and German. [xlv. 435]

PLUMPTRE, ANNABELLA (fl. 1795–1812), author; daughter of Robert Plumptre [q. v.]; wrote several novels and translations of German tales. [xlv. 435]

PLUMPTRE, CHARLES JOHN (1818–1887), barrister and writer on elocution; barrister, Gray's Inn, 1844; gradually withdrew from practice and devoted himself to lecturing on elocution; an official lecturer at Oxford and at King's College, London. [xlv. 436]

PLUMPTRE, EDWARD HAYES (1821–1891), dean of Wells and biographer of Bishop Ken; brother of Charles John Plumptre [q. v.]; was fellow of Brasenose College, Oxford, 1844–7; M.A., 1847; chaplain at King's College, London, 1847–68, professor of pastoral theology, 1853–63, and professor of exegesis, 1864–81; member of the Old Testament revision committee, 1869–74; Grinfield lecturer at Oxford University, 1872–4; dean of Wells, 1881–1891; wrote largely on the interpretation of scriptures and on theological topics; published also verse and (1888) his 'Life of Bishop Ken,' a work of much literary charm. [xlv. 437]

PLUMPTRE, HENRY (d. 1746) president of the Royal College of Physicians; M.A. Queens' College, Cambridge, 1705; M.D. per literas regias, 1706; fellow, Queens' College, Cambridge, 1703–7; F.R.C.P., 1708 (president, 1740–5); worked on the fifth 'Pharmacopœia Londinensis' (appeared, 1746). [xlv. 438]

PLUMPTRE, JAMES (1770–1832), dramatist and divine; son of Robert Plumptre [q. v.]; of Queens' College and Clare Hall, Cambridge; M.A. Clare Hall, 1795; B.D., 1808; fellow of Clare Hall, Cambridge, 1793; held the living of Great Gransden, 1812–32. He wrote plays, and advocated the claims of the stage as a moral educator, and endeavoured to improve its tone. [xlv. 438]

PLUMPTRE, JOHN (1753–1825), dean of Gloucester; cousin and brother-in-law of James Plumptre [q. v.]; of Eton and King's College, Cambridge; fellow of King's College, 1775; M.A., 1780; became dean of Gloucester, 1808; published 'The Elegies of C. Pedo Albinovanus . . . with an English version,' 1807, and was probably the author of 'The Principles of Natural and Revealed Religion,' 1795. [xlv. 439]

PLUMPTRE, ROBERT (1723–1788), president of Queens' College, Cambridge; grandson of Henry Plumptre [q. v.]; M.A. Queens' College, Cambridge, 1748; D.D., 1761; fellow of Queens' College, Cambridge, 1745; prebendary of Norwich, 1756; president of Queens' College, Cambridge, 1760–88; vice-chancellor, 1760–1 and 1777–8; left some manuscript collections on the history of the college, besides publishing pamphlets and Latin verses. [xlv. 439]

PLUMPTRE, RUSSELL (1709–1793), professor of physic; son of Henry Plumptre [q. v.]; M.D. Queens' College, Cambridge, 1738; F.R.C.P., 1739; appointed regius professor of physic at Cambridge University, 1741. [xlv. 438]

PLUMRIDGE, SIR JAMES HANWAY (1787–1863), vice-admiral; entered the navy, 1799; was present at Trafalgar, 1805; saw much service during the French war; K.C.B., 1855; vice-admiral, 1857. [xlv. 440]

PLUNKET, CHRISTOPHER, second EARL OF FINGALL (d. 1649), took his seat in the Irish parliament, 1639; endeavoured to preserve neutrality on the outbreak of the rebellion, 1641; was proclaimed an outlaw, November 1641; joined the Ulster party, and was subsequently appointed general of the horse for Meath; taken prisoner at the battle of Rathmines, 1649; died in Dublin Castle. [xlv. 440]

PLUNKET, JOHN (1664–1738), Jacobite agent; a Roman catholic layman, sometimes known under the alias of Rogers; for over twenty years in the employ of leading Jacobites as a spy or diplomatic agent; forged letters from Prince Eugène detailing whig plots against the government, in order to alarm public feeling; arrested (1723) for complicity in Layer's plot [see LAYER, CHRISTOPHER], and was confined in the Tower of London till 1738; died soon after his release. [xlv. 441]

PLUNKET, NICHOLAS (fl. 1641), compiler; known only as the author of a contemporary account of affairs in Ireland in 1641, which Carte frequently cites in his 'Life of Ormonde.' [xlv. 442]

PLUNKET, OLIVER (1629–1681), Roman catholic archbishop of Armagh and titular primate of Ireland; went to Rome in 1645 and entered the Irish College; filled the chair of theology at the Propaganda College from 1657 till his nomination as archbishop of Armagh in 1669; secretly tolerated by government until the passing of the Test Act, when he went into hiding for a time; committed to Dublin Castle, 1678, at the time of the panic concerning the 'Popish plot'; tried in London for treason, 1681, convicted on inadequate evidence, and hanged, drawn, and quartered. [xlv. 442]

PLUNKET, PATRICK, ninth BARON OF DUNSANY (d. 1668), succeeded to the title and estates, 1603; held aloof, though a Roman catholic, from the rebellion of 1641, but was driven into exile by the English parliament, and only restored in 1662. [xlv. 445]

PLUNKET, THOMAS, BARON PLUNKET of the Holy Roman Empire (1716–1779), general in the service of Austria; born in Ireland; entered the Austrian army and fought in Turkey and in the war of the Spanish succession; distinguished himself in Italy, 1746, and (1757) greatly contributed to the victory of Kollin; nominated a baron, 1758; governor of Antwerp, 1770–9. [xlv. 446]

PLUNKET, WILLIAM CONYNGHAM, first BARON PLUNKET (1764–1854), lord-chancellor of Ireland; son of a presbyterian minister of Enniskillen; called to the Irish bar, 1787; K.C., 1797; entered the Irish parliament as M.P. for Charlemont, 1798, and opposed the project of union; became solicitor-general, 1803, and attorney-general, 1805, and sat in the House of Commons in 1807 for two months as M.P. for Midhurst; re-entered parliament (1812) as a follower of Lord Grenville, having by that time a reputation and an income unequalled at the Irish bar; exerted himself in parliament on behalf of the Roman catholic claims; succeeded Grattan (1820) as foremost champion of catholic emancipation, and created a great impression by his speeches; appointed Irish attorney-general by Lord Liverpool, January 1822; his conduct assailed by the extremists of either party; held the position of master of the rolls for a few days, resigning on account of the feeling of the English bar against the appointment of an Irish barrister to an English judicial post, 1827; was then appointed chief-justice of the Irish common pleas and created Baron Plunket, 1827; laboured successfully in the House of Lords on behalf of the Catholic Relief Bill, which was passed in 1829; appointed by Lord Grey lord chancellor of Ireland, 1830, resigning (1841) in consequence of the desire of government to replace him by Sir John Campbell; passed the rest of his life in retirement. [xlv. 446]

PLUNKET, WILLIAM CONYNGHAM, fourth BARON PLUNKET (1828–1897), archbishop of Dublin; grandson of William Conyngham Plunket, first baron Plunket [q. v.]; of Cheltenham College and Trinity College, Dublin; B.A., 1853; ordained, 1857; rector of Kilmoylan and Cummer, 1858; active member of Irish Church Missions Society; married (1863) Anne, daughter of Sir Benjamin Lee Guinness [q. v.]; treasurer of St. Patrick's, Dublin, 1864, and precentor, 1869; succeeded to peerage, 1871; bishop of Meath, 1876–84; recognised as leader of evangelical party in Irish church; energetically resisted attack on Irish church establishment; assisted in reorganising Church of Ireland Training College; archbishop of Dublin, Glendalough, and Kildare, 1884; dean of Christ Church Cathedral, Dublin, 1884–7; actively assisted cause of protestant reformers in Spain, and conferred consecration on its leader, Señor Cabrera, 1894; president and chairman of Italian Reform Association, 1886. [Suppl. iii. 275]

PLUNKETT, MRS. ELIZABETH (1769–1823). [See GUNNING.]

PLUNKETT, JOHN HUBERT (1802–1869) Australian statesman; B.A. Trinity College, Dublin, 1824; called to the Irish bar, 1826; accepted the post of solicitor-general of New South Wales, 1831, to which in 1836 was added that of attorney-general; resigned his appointment and entered politics on the establishment of responsible government in 1856; joined the Martin ministry as leader in the upper chamber, 1863, and in 1865 joined the Cowper ministry as attorney-general. [xlv. 449]

PLYMOUTH, EARLS OF. [See FITZCHARLES, CHARLES, 1657?–1680; WINDSOR, THOMAS WINDSOR, first EARL of the second creation, 1627?–1687.]

POCAHONTAS or **MATOAKA** (1595–1617), American-Indian princess; daughter of Powhattan, an Indian chief in Virginia; according to the unreliable tale of Captain John Smith (1580–1631) [q. v.], interposed on his behalf when her father was about to slay him; became a frequent visitor at Jamestown from 1608, and (1612) was seized as a hostage for the good behaviour of the Indian tribes; became a Christian and was named Rebecca, 1613; married John Rolfe [q. v.], 1613; came to England, 1616, and died at Gravesend. [xlix. 157]

POCKLINGTON, JOHN (d. 1642), divine; M.A. Sidney Sussex College, Cambridge, 1603; B.D., 1610; fellow of Pembroke College, Cambridge, 1612–18; a chaplain of Charles I; enjoyed other preferments, of which he was deprived by the House of Lords (1641), on account of his high-church views; his 'Altare Christianum' and 'Sunday no Sabbath' sentenced to be burnt, 1641. [xlv. 450]

POCKRICH, **POKERIDGE**, or **PUCKERIDGE**, RICHARD (1690?–1759), inventor of the musical glasses; dissipated a large fortune in the pursuit of visionary projects; invented musical glasses, from which afterwards was developed the harmonica; gave concerts in later life in various parts of England; suffocated in a fire in his room at Hamlin's coffee-house, near the Royal Exchange. [xlv. 451]

POCOCK, SIR GEORGE (1706–1792), admiral; entered the navy, 1718; was in chief command in the Leeward islands, 1747–8; rear-admiral, 1755; vice-admiral, 1756; commanded on the East India station, 1758–9, and fought two indecisive actions with the French; admiral, 1761; K.B., 1761; captured Havana, 1762; retired, 1766. [xlvi. 1]

POCOCK, ISAAC (1782–1835), painter and dramatist; son of Nicholas Pocock (1741?–1821) [q. v.]; painted historical pictures and portraits from 1800 till 1818, when he inherited some property and turned his attention to the drama; wrote musical farces, comic operas, and operatic dramas, among other achievements converting some of the Waverley novels into plays. [xlvi. 3]

POCOCK, ISAAC JOHN INNES (1819–1886), barrister; only son of Isaac Pocock [q. v.]; of Eton and Merton College, Oxford; B.A., 1842; called to the bar, 1847; printed privately 'Franklin, and other Poems,' 1872. [xlvi. 5]

POCOCK, LEWIS (1808–1882), art amateur; took the leading part in founding the Art Union of London in 1837; published (1842) a work on life assurance, with a bibliography of the subject. [xlvi. 5]

POCOCK, NICHOLAS (1741 ?–1821), marine painter ; in early life a merchant captain ; commenced painting sea pieces in oils, 1780 ; settled (1789) in London, where he rose to distinction as a painter of naval engagements ; helped to found the Water-colour Society, 1804, and exhibited there and at the Royal Academy no fewer than 295 works. [xlvi. 5]

POCOCK, NICHOLAS (1814–1897), historical writer ; grandson of Nicholas Pocock (1741 ?–1821) [q.v.] ; M.A. Queen's College, Oxford, 1837 ; Michel fellow, 1838 ; mathematical lecturer ; ordained priest, 1855 ; published an edition of Gilbert Burnet's ' History of the Reformation,' 1864–5, and other writings relating to the Reformation, besides mathematical and theological works.
[Suppl. iii. 277]

POCOCK, ROBERT (1760–1830), printer and antiquary ; founded the first circulating library and printing office at Gravesend, 1786 ; published a history of Gravesend, 1797, and other works. [xlvi. 6]

POCOCK, WILLIAM FULLER (1779–1849), architect ; designed the hall of the Leathersellers' Company in London (1820–2) and other buildings. [xlvi. 7]

POCOCK, WILLIAM INNES (1783–1836), author ; son of Nicholas Pocock (1741 ?–1821) [q. v.] ; a lieutenant in the navy ; published ' Five Views of the Island of St. Helena,' 1815. [xlvi. 7]

POCOCKE, EDWARD (1604–1691), orientalist : of Magdalen Hall and Corpus Christi College, Oxford ; M.A., 1626 ; fellow of Corpus Christi College, Oxford, 1628 ; studied oriental languages under Matthias Pasor [q. v.] and William Bedwell [q. v.] ; discovered and edited the missing Syriac version of Peter ii., John ii., iii., and Jude, and published it at Leyden, 1630 ; chaplain to the 'Turkey Merchants' at Aleppo, 1630–6, where he collected manuscripts ; appointed by Laud first Oxford professor of Arabic, 1636 ; appointed Hebrew professor by the parliamentary visitors, 1648, which appointment was confirmed at the Restoration. His learning was the admiration of Europe. His two most notable works were an edition of the Arabic text with a Latin translation of Abu-l-Faraj's 'Historia compendiosa Dynastiarum,' 1663, and his 'Lexicon Heptaglotton,' 1669. [xlvi. 7]

POCOCKE, EDWARD (1648–1727), orientalist ; son of Edward Pococke (1604–1691) [q. v.] ; student at Christ Church, Oxford ; translated into Latin Ibn al Tufail, 1671, and began, in collaboration with his father, to edit ' Abdollatiphi Historiæ Ægypti Compendium,' which remained a fragment. [xlvi. 11]

POCOCKE, RICHARD (1704–1765), traveller ; B.A. Corpus Christi College, Oxford, 1725 ; D.C.L., 1733 ; visited Egypt, 1737–8, ascending the Nile to Philæ, and proceeded to Palestine, Cyprus, Asia Minor, and Greece, 1738–40 ; explored the Mer de Glace in the valley of Chamounix, 1741 ; regarded as the pioneer of Alpine travel ; published an account of his eastern travels, 1743–1745 ; bishop of Ossory, 1756–65 ; translated as bishop of Meath, 1765. His manuscript accounts of his tours in England, Scotland, and Ireland between 1747 and 1760 have been recently published (1888–91). [xlvi. 12]

POE, LEONARD (d. 1631 ?), physician ; originally in the service of the Earl of Essex ; a royal physician in ordinary, 1609 ; attended Lord-treasurer Salisbury on his deathbed, 1612 ; M.D. Cambridge by mandate, 1615.
[xlvi. 14]

POER.   [See also POOR and POWER.]

POER, RANULF LE (d. 1182), sheriff of Gloucestershire ; killed by the Welsh while sheriff. [xlvi. 15]

POER, ROBERT LE (fl. 1166–1190), marshal in the court of Henry II ; seized for ransom by Raymond of Toulouse (1188) while returning from a pilgrimage to the shrine of St. James of Compostella, thereby occasioning the invasion of Toulouse by Richard (afterwards Richard I of England). [xlvi. 15]

POER, ROGER LE (d. 1186), one of the conquerors of Ireland ; took part in the invasion of Ulster, 1177 ; subsequently settled in Ossory, where he was killed in battle.
[xlvi. 15]

POER, WALTER LE (fl. 1215–1227), official ; sheriff of Devonshire, 1222 ; justice itinerant, 1226 and 1227.
[xlvi. 15]

POGSON, NORMAN ROBERT (1829–1891), astronomer ; became in 1852 assistant-astronomer at the Radcliffe Observatory, Oxford, where he discovered four minor planets ; appointed (1859) director of the Hartwell Observatory, and (1860) government astronomer at Madras, where he discovered five minor planets.
[xlvi. 15]

POINGDESTRE, JEAN (1609–1691). writer on the laws and history of Jersey ; fellow of Exeter College, Oxford, 1636 ; chief work, ' Cæsarea, or a Discourse of the Island of Jersey,' written in 1682 and presented to James II. [xlvi. 16]

POINS.   [See POYNTZ.]

POINTER, JOHN (1668–1754), antiquary ; M.A. Merton College, Oxford, 1694 ; rector of Slapton, 1694–1754 ; wrote among other works a 'Chronological History of England,' 1714, and 'Oxoniensis Academia,' 1749.
[xlvi. 17]

POINTER, WILLIAM (fl. 1624).   [See KIDLEY.]

POITIERS, PHILIP OF (d. 1208 ?).   [See PHILIP.]

POKERIDGE, RICHARD (1690 ?–1759).   [See POCKRICH.]

POL (d. 573).   [See PAUL.]

POLACK, JOEL SAMUEL (1807–1882), trader and author of works on New Zealand ; emigrated to New Zealand, 1831 ; returned to London, 1837, and finally settled at San Francisco. [xlvi. 18]

POLDING, JOHN BEDE (1794–1877), first Roman catholic archbishop of Sydney ; consecrated bishop of Hiero-Cæsarea and vicar-apostolic of Australia, 1834, and archbishop of Sydney, 1842. [xlvi. 18]

POLE, ARTHUR (1531–1570 ?), conspirator ; eldest son of Sir Geoffrey Pole [q. v.] ; proposed himself to France and Spain as a claimant of the English crown, and imprisoned in the Tower of London from 1563.
[xlvi. 19]

POLE, SIR CHARLES MORICE (1757–1830), admiral of the fleet ; entered the navy, 1772 ; commanded at Newfoundland, 1800, and in the Baltic, 1801 ; G.C.B., 1818 ; admiral of the fleet, 1830. [xlvi. 19]

POLE, DAVID (d. 1568), bishop of Peterborough ; fellow of All Souls College, Oxford, 1520 ; D.Can.L., 1528 ; consecrated bishop, 1557, and deprived, 1559, for refusing to take the oath of supremacy. [xlvi. 20]

POLE, SIR EDMUND DE LA, EARL OF SUFFOLK (1472 ?–1513), son of John de la Pole, second duke of Suffolk [q. v.] ; created earl, 1493 ; led a company (1496) against the Cornish rebels at Blackheath ; became discontented (1499) and fled to Flanders, Henry VII being thereby alarmed ; persuaded by Henry VII to return, and received again into favour ; repaired to the Emperor Maximilian in the Tyrol, hearing that he would gladly help one of Edward IV's blood to gain the English throne, 1501 ; outlawed and his friends imprisoned ; seized by the Duke of Gueldres while on his way to Friesland (1504), and delivered to Henry VII by Philip, king of Castile, 1506 ; confined in the Tower of London ; exempted from the general pardon on Henry VIII's accession ; executed. [xlvi. 21]

POLE, SIR GEOFFREY (1502 ?–1558), a victim of Henry VIII's tyranny ; brother of Reginald Pole [q. v.] ; knighted, 1529 ; was opposed, like the rest of his family, to Henry VIII's divorce from Catherine of Arragon, and visited Chapuys, the Spanish ambassador, with a view to persuading Charles V to invade England ; resolved to desert to the northern rebels, 1536, but was prevented by circumstances and (1538) was sent to the Tower of London, Henry VIII having resolved to crush the whole family, chiefly on account of the action of Reginald Pole ; endeavoured to commit suicide, fearing the rack, but was obliged to undergo seven separate examinations ; his brother Sir Henry Pole, baron Montague [q. v.], and others condemned from his confessions ; received a pardon, 1539 ; escaped to Rome, 1540, where he obtained absolution for his brother's death ; returned to England after Queen Mary's accession. [xlvi. 23]

POLE, SIR HENRY, BARON MONTAGUE or MONTACUTE (1492 ?–1538), brother of Reginald Pole [q. v.] ; distinguished himself in the French campaign of 1513 ; knighted, 1513 ; took part in Suffolk's invasion of France, 1523 ; was deeply grieved at the overthrow of the monasteries and the abrogation of the pope's authority, though remaining loyal ; committed to the Tower of London in consequence of the confessions of his brother, Sir Geoffrey Pole [q. v.], 1538 ; found guilty of treason and executed on Tower Hill, London, on 9 Dec. with the Marquis of Exeter. In 1539 he was attainted. [xlvi. 25]

POLE, JOHN DE LA, EARL OF LINCOLN (1464 ?–1487), eldest son of John de la Pole, second duke of Suffolk [q. v.], by Elizabeth, sister of Edward IV ; created Earl of Lincoln, 1467 ; firmly attached to Richard III, and (1483) made president of the council of the north ; became lord-lieutenant of Ireland, 1484, and was recognised as heir-presumptive to the throne ; was not molested by Henry VII after Richard III's death, though he still cherished the ambition to succeed Richard ; promoted Lambert Simnel's plot, and was killed at Stoke. [xlvi. 26]

POLE, JOHN DE LA, second DUKE OF SUFFOLK (1442–1491), only son of William de la Pole, first duke of Suffolk [q. v.] ; was restored to the dukedom by Henry VI, 1455, but notwithstanding joined the Yorkists and married Edward IV's sister ; fought at the second battle of St. Albans, 1461 ; steward of England at the coronation of Edward IV, 1461 ; K.G., 1472 ; high steward of Oxford University, 1472 ; received many favours from Edward IV, but on the king's death immediately supported Richard III, and after Bosworth field (1485) swore fealty to Henry VII, who continued to trust him in spite of his eldest son's defection [see POLE, JOHN DE LA, EARL OF LINCOLN]. [xlvi. 27]

POLE, MARGARET, COUNTESS OF SALISBURY (1473–1541), daughter of George Plantagenet, duke of Clarence [q. v.] ; married, by Henry VII, to Sir Richard Pole (d. 1505), a gentleman of Buckinghamshire, probably c. 1491 ; given the family lands of the earldom of Salisbury in fee by Henry VIII, who was desirous to atone for the execution of her brother, Edward, earl of Warwick [q. v.], and (1513) created Countess of Salisbury ; governess to the Princess Mary ; refused, on the marriage of Henry VIII with Anne Boleyn, to give up the Princess Mary's jewels to the new queen, and was discharged from her office ; returned to court after Anne's fall in 1536 ; her position compromised (1536) by her son Reginald Pole's book, ' De Unitate Ecclesiastica,' for which, in spite of her condemnation of the work, Henry VIII resolved to destroy the whole family ; her son, Sir Henry Pole, baron Montague [q. v.], executed, 1538 ; included in an act of attainder, May 1539 ; beheaded, May 1541, within the precincts of the Tower of London on the news of Sir John Neville's rising in Yorkshire. [xlvi. 28]

POLE, MICHAEL DE LA, called in English MICHAEL ATTE POOL, first EARL OF SUFFOLK (1330 ?–1389), son of Sir William de la Pole (d. 1366) [q. v.] ; chiefly occupied from 1355 onward, for many years, with the war against the French ; first summoned to parliament as a baron, 1366 ; took part under the Black Prince in the famous siege of Limoges, 1370 ; attached himself to John of Gaunt, and in the Good parliament (1376) stood strongly on the side of the crown ; appointed admiral north of the Thames, 1376 ; superseded as admiral, December 1377 ; became the most trusted personal adviser of the young king Richard II on the retirement of John of Gaunt to Castile ; appointed chancellor of England, 1383 ; unsuccessfully advocated a policy of peace in his speech to parliament, 1384 ; incurred much odium on account of his great wealth ; created Earl of Suffolk, 1385 ; opposition to him formally organised (1386) under Richard II's uncle, Thomas, duke of Gloucester ; his dismissal demanded by both Lords and Commons, who were apprehensive of large pecuniary demands for the prosecution of the war ; dismissed, in spite of King Richard II's reluctance, and articles of impeachment drawn up against him, charging him with misappropriation of funds and remissness in carrying on the war, 1386 ; convicted on three charges, and sentenced to the loss of the lands and grants he had received contrary to his oath, and was committed to prison until he had paid an adequate fine ; released from custody by Richard II on the termination of the Wonderful parliament, his fine remitted, and himself reinstated as Richard II's adviser ; compelled (November 1387), by dread of the meeting of parliament, to flee the realm ; reached Paris after many difficulties ; died at Paris. During his absence he was condemned to death, and his title and estates forfeited. [xlvi. 29]

POLE, MICHAEL DE LA, second EARL OF SUFFOLK (1361 ?–1415), eldest son of Michael de la Pole, first earl of Suffolk [q. v.] ; restored to his father's earldom, 1397, the restoration being renewed after Henry IV's accession. He joined Henry V's expedition to France in 1415, and died during the siege of Harfleur. [xlvi. 33]

POLE, MICHAEL DE LA, third EARL OF SUFFOLK (1394–1415), eldest son of Michael de la Pole, second earl of Suffolk [q. v.] ; served with his father before Harfleur ; distinguished himself by his bravery at Agincourt, where he was killed. [xlvi. 34]

POLE or DE LA POLE, RALPH (fl. 1442–1459), judge ; serjeant-at-law, 1442 ; justice of the king's bench, 1452. His name occurs in the latter capacity until 1459. [xlvi. 34]

POLE, REGINALD (1500–1558), cardinal and archbishop of Canterbury ; son of Sir Richard Pole, by his wife Margaret [see POLE, MARGARET] ; educated at Charterhouse School and Magdalen College, Oxford ; B.A., 1515 ; received several preferments while a youth and still a layman ; sent by Henry VIII at his own wish to Italy, 1521, where he studied at Padua, and visited Rome ; returned, 1527, and was elected dean of Exeter ; studied at Paris, 1529–30 ; returned to England, soon after which Henry VIII, desirous to obtain his approbation of his divorce, pressed him to accept the archbishopric of York ; refused the offer, though genuinely fond of Henry VIII ; disapproved of the royal supremacy over the English church, and was allowed (January 1532) to return to Padua ; formulated at Henry VIII's request (1536) his views on Henry VIII's divorce and the divine institution of the papal supremacy in his treatise ' Pro Ecclesiasticæ Unitatis Defensione,' severely criticising Henry VIII's conduct ; declined an invitation to return to England ; summoned to Rome in November by Pope Paul III to act on a committee to draw up a scheme for reforming the discipline of the church ; took deacon's orders and was made a cardinal, December 1536 ; nominated papal legate to England, February 1537, and despatched thither by Pope Paul III ; travelled through France, where Francis I was summoned by Henry VIII to deliver him up as a rebel ; received an intimation from Francis I that he must leave France ; made his way to Cambray, and eventually to Liège, where he was safe from extradition ; returned to Rome, and (1538) heard of the arrest of his mother and eldest brother on charge of treason ; accepted a mission from Pope Paul III to form a league of Christian princes against Henry VIII, which, however, failed, chiefly on account of the jealousies between Francis I and Charles V ; returned to Rome in 1540, when Pope Paul III bestowed on him the legation of the patrimony ; one of the three legates appointed (1540) to open the council of Trent ; vainly endeavoured, on the death of Henry VIII in 1547, to reconcile England with the holy see, through the Protector Somerset and the Earl of Warwick ; just missed election as pope, though supported by the Spanish party, 1549 ; favoured by the new pontiff, Julius III ; nominated papal legate to the queen on Mary's accession, but hindered from coming to England by the Emperor Charles V's reluctance to allow him to influence Queen Mary before her marriage with his son Philip ; his attainder reversed in November 1554, after the marriage, and he himself permitted to return, Queen Mary praying him to come, not as legate, but only as cardinal and ambassador ; entrusted with the care of Queen Mary by her husband, Philip, on Philip's leaving England in October 1555 ; raised to the dignity of cardinal-priest, December 1555, Queen Mary designing him to succeed Cranmer as archbishop ; occupied with the proceedings in a synod of both convocations for the reform and settlement of the affairs of the English church and its reconciliation with Rome ; consecrated archbishop of Canterbury, March 1556 ; chancellor of Cambridge University, 1556 ; found that he had underestimated the difficulties of reconciling the realm with Rome, the question of the restoration of church property proving an especial stumbling-block, as no assurances of immunity to the lay proprietors could allay their disquiet ; his anxieties increased by the war between Pope Paul IV and Philip II, and by the violent personal animosity of Pope Paul IV, who cancelled his legation and stigmatised him privately as a heretic ; died at Lambeth Palace on 17 Nov. 1558, the evening of the day of Mary's death ; buried in St. Thomas's Chapel, Canterbury. His ' De Concilio ' was printed at Venice in 1562, his ' De Unitate' at Ingolstadt in 1587. His life was animated by a single purpose, the restoration of that ecclesiastical system which Henry VIII had shattered. [xlvi. 35]

POLE, SIR RICHARD DE LA (*d.* 1345), royal officer ; became collector of Edward II's customs at Hull, 1320 ; M.P., Hull, 1322 and 1327 ; Edward III's chief butler, 1327-1338 ; removed to London, 1333 ; knighted, 1340.
[xlvi. 48]

POLE, RICHARD DE LA (*d.* 1525), pretender to the crown, son of John de la Pole, second duke of Suffolk [q.v.] ; escaped abroad in 1501 with his brother, Sir Edmund de la Pole, earl of Suffolk [q. v.] ; attainted, 1504, and exempted (1509) from the general pardon at the accession of Henry VIII ; recognised as king of England by Louis XII, 1512 ; fought for France in Spain and the Netherlands ; compelled to leave France on the conclusion of peace in 1514 ; resided at Metz till 1519 ; made preparations to invade England, in concert with the Scots, 1523 ; killed at the battle of Pavia, by the side of Francis I. [xlvi. 46]

POLE, THOMAS (1753-1829), quaker and physician ; settled in London, 1781 ; published his ' Anatomical Instructor,' 1790 ; M.D. St. Andrews, 1801 ; removed to Bristol, 1802 ; devoted much time throughout life to ministerial work in the Society of Friends, travelling through England and Wales to visit their meetings. [xlvi. 48]

POLE, SIR WILLIAM DE LA, called in English WILLIAM ATTE POOL (*d.* 1366), baron of the exchequer and merchant ; younger brother of Sir Richard de la Pole [q. v.] ; was a merchant of Hull, who with his brother advanced large sums to the government during the regency of Isabella and Mortimer ; M.P., Hull, 1332, 1334, 1336, and 1338 ; received various offices from Edward III in return for loans of money ; knight-banneret, 1338 ; appointed baron of the exchequer, 1339 ; fell into temporary disgrace, 1340, and although eventually enjoying royal favour, for more than twenty years does not again appear in a prominent position. [xlvi. 48]

POLE, WILLIAM DE LA, fourth EARL and first DUKE OF SUFFOLK (1396-1450), son of Michael de la Pole, second earl of Suffolk [q. v.] ; served in Henry V's French wars, and after Henry V's death fought under the Duke of Bedford ; created Earl of Dreux, *c.* 1426, and on the death of the Earl of Salisbury in 1428 succeeded to the command of the English forces ; forced to surrender at Jargeau, soon after Jeanne d'Arc had raised the siege of Orleans, 1429 ; ransomed himself and (1430) again took part in the war ; occupied himself with home politics from 1431 ; admitted a member of the council, 1431, becoming an advocate of peace ; inclined, by his marriage to the widowed Countess of Salisbury, to connection with the Beauforts ; came forward as the chief opponent of Humphrey, duke of Gloucester, who after Bedford's death (1435) led the war party ; desired that Henry VI should marry Margaret of Anjou, and defeated Gloucester's project to unite him to a daughter of the Count of Armagnac, 1442 ; escorted Margaret to England, November 1444 ; peace negotiations continued under his influence without definite result through 1446 ; with Queen Margaret spared no pains to effect the overthrow of Gloucester, who was arrested at the parliament summoned at Bury, February 1447, and died five days later ; left without a rival by the death of Cardinal Beaufort six weeks after ; had Richard of York deprived of the command in France and sent into banishment as lieutenant of Ireland, thereby incurring his implacable enmity, which, however, troubled him little, as he had Henry VI's support ; became a duke, 1448, thereby reaching the summit of his power ; had become unpopular, in consequence of the cession of the English possessions in Anjou and Maine, to which he had agreed at the time of the royal marriage, and was finally discredited by the renewed outbreak of war in France and the English losses, 1449 ; accused by the Commons (1450) of having sold the realm to the French, and was committed to the Tower of London ; banished by Henry VI for five years (March 1450), a compromise by which Henry VI hoped to save him and satisfy the Commons as well ; intercepted when off Dover and beheaded at sea, possibly at the instigation of Richard of York. He married Alice, daughter of Thomas Chaucer [q. v.], probably a granddaughter of the poet. [xlvi. 50]

POLE, SIR WILLIAM (1561-1635), antiquary ; a Devonshire landowner ; entered the Inner Temple, 1578 ;

M.P., Bossiney, 1586 ; knighted, 1606 ; left large manuscript collections for the history and antiquities of Devonshire, the greater part of which perished during the civil war ; but two folio volumes, entitled ' The Description of Devonshire,' were printed in 1791. [xlvi. 56]

POLE, WILLIAM (1814-1900), engineer, musician' and authority on whist ; apprenticed as engineer at Birmingham, and subsequently worked in London ; M.I.C.E., 1840, and honorary secretary, 1885-96 ; first professor of engineering at Elphinstone College, Bombay, 1844-7 ; assistant (1852-7) to James Meadows Rendel [q. v.], under whom he was chiefly engaged in connection with railways ; assistant to Sir John Fowler [q. v.], 1857 ; established himself as consulting engineer at Westminster, 1858, and was thenceforth constantly employed on government work ; secretary to royal commission on London water supply, 1867 ; professor of civil engineering at University College, London, 1859-67 ; F.R.S., 1851, and vice-president, 1875 and 1888 ; Mus.Doc. Oxford, 1867 ; examiner for musical degrees in London University, 1878-1891 ; vice-president of Royal College of Organists ; published historical and technical works and papers relating to engineering and musical subjects, besides several successful treatises on whist. [Suppl. iii. 278]

POLE, WILLIAM WELLESLEY-, third EARL OF MORNINGTON (1763-1845). [See WELLESLEY-POLE.]

POLEHAMPTON, HENRY STEDMAN (1824-1857), Indian chaplain ; fellow of Pembroke College, Oxford, 1845 ; M.A., 1849 ; accepted an East Indian chaplaincy, 1855, and took part in the defence of the residency at Lucknow, dying of cholera during the siege. The value of his services is attested by Havelock's despatches.
[xlvi. 57]

POLENIUS, ROBERT (*d.* 1147 ?). [See PULLEN.]

POLHILL, EDWARD (1622-1694 ?), religious writer ; barrister, Gray's Inn ; divided his time between the care of his estates in Sussex and the compilation of religious tracts, somewhat Calvinistic in temper, but supporting the established church. [xlvi. 57]

POLIDORI, JOHN WILLIAM (1795-1821), physician and author ; M.D. Edinburgh, 1815 ; appointed physician and secretary to Lord Byron, 1816 ; returned to England, the engagement being dissolved (1817) parting on good terms with Byron ; published (1819) ' The Vampire,' which he attributed to Byron, and which, in spite of Byron's disclaimer, gained great celebrity on the continent ; wrote other tales in his own name ; committed suicide in consequence of a gaming debt. [xlvi. 58]

POLKEMMET, LORD (*d.* 1816). [See BAILLIE, WILLIAM.]

POLLARD, SIR HUGH, second baronet (*d.* 1666), royalist ; descended from Sir Lewis Pollard [q. v.] ; served against the Scots, 1640 ; M.P., Beeralston, 1640 ; implicated in the ' first army plot,' 1641 ; mainly employed in Devon and Cornwall during the civil war ; governor of Dartmouth, 1645 ; taken prisoner, 1646, and afterwards submitted ; became governor of Guernsey and comptroller of Charles II's household at the Restoration. [xlvi. 59]

POLLARD, SIR JOHN (*d.* 1557), speaker of the House of Commons ; serjeant-at-law, 1547-50 ; M.P., Oxfordshire, 1553 and 1554, Wiltshire, 1555 ; knighted, 1553 ; speaker, 1553-5. [xlvi. 59]

POLLARD, LEONARD (*d.* 1556), divine ; fellow of Peterhouse, Cambridge, 1546 ; M.A., 1547 ; D.D. ; prebendary of Worcester, 1551, of Peterborough, 1553 ; fellow of St. John's College, Cambridge, 1554. [xlvi. 60]

POLLARD, SIR LEWIS (1465 ?-1540), judge ; barrister, Middle Temple (reader, 1502) ; king's serjeant, 1507 ; a justice of common pleas, 1514-26 ; knighted, 1514. [xlvi. 60]

POLLARD, ROBERT (1755-1838), designer and engraver ; practised for a time as a landscape and marine painter, but (*c.* 1782) established himself in Spa Fields, London, as an engraver and printseller ; director of the Incorporated Society of Artists, 1789. [xlvi. 61]

POLLARD, WILLIAM (1828-1893), quaker ; wrote several school-books and works on quaker tenets ; secretary of the Manchester Peace and Arbitration Society, 1872-91. [xlvi. 61]

POLLARD-URQUHART, WILLIAM (1815–1871), miscellaneous writer; of Harrow and Trinity College, Cambridge; M.A., 1843; took the additional name of Urquhart, 1846; liberal M.P. for Westmeath, 1852–7, and 1859–71; wrote chiefly on currency and agriculture. [xlvi. 61]

POLLEXFEN, Sir HENRY (1632?–1691); judge; barrister, Inner Temple, 1658 (bencher, 1674); earned the reputation as a barrister of being the antagonist of court and crown, but in 1685 was crown prosecutor against Monmouth's followers in the west; defended the seven bishops, June 1688; knighted, 1689; became attorney-general, February 1689; chief-justice of the common pleas, May 1689. [xlvi. 62]

POLLEXFEN, JOHN (*fl.* 1675–1697), merchant and economic writer; was a member of the board of trade; published 'A Discourse of Trade' (1697), in which he treated labour as the sole source of wealth. [xlvi. 62]

POLLOCK, Sir CHARLES EDWARD (1823–1897), judge; son of chief-baron Sir Jonathan Frederick Pollock [q. v.]; educated at St. Paul's School, London; served as private secretary and marshal to his father; called to bar at Inner Temple, 1847; bencher, 1866; Q.C., 1866; raised to exchequer bench, invested with coif, and knighted, 1873; received status of justice of high court, 1875, but retained his old official designation, and on death of Baron Huddleston (1890) was left last baron of exchequer; published legal works. [Suppl. iii. 280]

POLLOCK, Sir DAVID (1780–1847), judge; of St. Paul's School, London, and Edinburgh University; barrister, Middle Temple, 1803; K.C., 1833; chief-justice of the supreme court of Bombay in 1846–7; knighted, 1846. [xlvi. 63]

POLLOCK, Sir GEORGE, first baronet (1786–1872), field-marshal; brother of Sir David Pollock [q. v.]; entered the East India Company artillery, 1803; took part in the campaign against Holkar, 1804–5, and served in Nipál, 1814, and in the first Burmese war, 1824–6; major-general, 1838; appointed (January 1842) to command the expedition for the relief of Jalálábád, which he reached after heavy fighting in April; with Brigadier-general (Sir) William Nott [q. v.], who was at Kandahar, was instructed by Lord Ellenborough, then governor-general, to make arrangements for withdrawing from Afghanistan; being, however, convinced of the practicability of advancing on Kábul, remonstrated strongly, and was allowed to advance at his own discretion; defeated the enemy at Jagdalak and Tezin, and arrived before Kábul in September 1842, and next day was joined by Nott; remained at Kábul till October, and returned to India in December 1842; created G.C.B. and thanked for his services by both houses of parliament; appointed military member of the supreme council of India, 1844; returned to England, 1846, and (1854) became senior government director of the East India Company; field-marshal, 1870; created baronet, 1872. [xlvi. 63]

POLLOCK, Sir JONATHAN FREDERICK, first baronet (1783–1870), judge; brother of Sir David Pollock [q. v.]; fellow of Trinity College, Cambridge, 1807; M.A., 1809; barrister, Middle Temple, 1809; K.C., 1827; tory M.P. for Huntingdon from 1831; knighted, 1834; attorney-general in Peel's first administration, 1834–5, and in his second administration, 1841–4; chief-baron of the exchequer, 1844–66; created baronet, 1866. [xlvi. 68]

POLLOCK, Sir WILLIAM FREDERICK, second baronet (1815–1888), queen's remembrancer and author; eldest son of Sir Jonathan Frederick Pollock [q. v.]; M.A., Trinity College, Cambridge, 1840; barrister, Inner Temple, 1838; queen's remembrancer, 1874–86; rendered Dante's 'Divine Comedy' into English blank verse, 1854; published 'Personal Remembrances,' 1887. [xlvi. 69]

POLLOK, ROBERT (1798–1827), poet; seventh son of a small farmer in Renfrewshire; wrote 'The Course of Time' (1827), a poem in ten books, the versification of which recalls Cowper and Young. [xlvi. 69]

POLTON, LORD (1660?–1733). [See CALDERWOOD, Sir WILLIAM.]

POLTON, THOMAS (d. 1433), successively bishop of Hereford, Chichester, and Worcester; papal prothonotary and head of the English 'nation' at the council of Constance, 1414–18; consecrated bishop of Hereford,

1420; translated to Chichester, 1421, to Worcester, 1426; died and was buried at Basle, having been sent to the council of Basle. [xlvi. 70]

POLWARTH, BARON (1641–1724). [See HUME, Sir PATRICK, first EARL OF MARCHMONT.]

POLWHELE, RICHARD (1760–1838), miscellaneous writer; was educated at Christ Church, Oxford; held several small livings in Cornwall, but was a man of independent means; commenced publishing poems at the age of seventeen, and became in turn poet, topographer, theologian, and literary chronicler. His topographical works included unsatisfactory histories of Devon and Cornwall, but his volumes of reminiscences and anecdotes were less worthless, including much interesting biographical matter. [xlvi. 71]

POLWHELE or **POLWHEILE**, THEOPHILUS (d. 1689), puritan divine; M.A. Emmanuel College, Cambridge, 1651; held a rectory at Tiverton from 1654 till 1660, when he was ejected; author of devotional works. [xlvi. 73]

POMFRET, fourth EARL OF (1770–1833). [See FERMOR, THOMAS WILLIAM.]

POMFRET, COUNTESS OF (d. 1761). [See FERMOR, HENRIETTA LOUISA.]

POMFRET, JOHN (1667–1702), poet; M.A. Queens' College, Cambridge, 1688; rector of Maulden, 1695–1702, of Millbrook, 1702; chiefly remembered by 'The Choice' (1700), which procured his inclusion in Johnson's 'Lives of the Poets.' [xlvi. 74]

POMFRET, SAMUEL (1650–1722), divine; minister at Sandwich for seven years, when he was arrested for nonconformity; subsequently became an itinerant preacher. [xlvi. 75]

PONCE, JOHN (d. 1660?), author; professor of theology at the Irish College at Rome; died at Paris, after publishing several works on the theology of the schoolmen. [xlvi. 75]

POND, ARTHUR (1705?–1758), painter and engraver; a successful portrait-painter in London and a prolific etcher. [xlvi. 76]

POND, EDWARD (d. 1629), almanac-maker; published an annual almanac from 1601, which was continued after his death till 1709. [xlvi. 76]

POND, JOHN (1767–1836), astronomer royal; of Trinity College, Cambridge; detected errors in the Greenwich observations when fifteen; settled at Westbury in Somerset, 1798, where he erected an altazimuth; appointed astronomer royal, 1811; substituted (1821) a mercury-horizon for the plumb-line and spirit-level, and (1825) introduced the system of observing the same objects alternately by direct and reflected vision; published (1833) a catalogue of 1,113 stars, determined with unexampled accuracy. His reform of the national observatory, by procuring for it a modern outfit, was of immense importance. [xlvi. 76]

PONET or **POYNET**, JOHN (1514?–1556), successively bishop of Rochester and Winchester; became fellow of Queens' College, Cambridge, 1532; D.D., 1547; a strong divine of the reforming school; became Cranmer's chaplain before 1547, receiving also other preferments; consecrated bishop of Rochester, 1550, and in 1551 translated to Winchester; deprived on the accession of Queen Mary, after which he fled to the continent; died at Strasburg. He wrote, besides other works, an exposition of the doctrine of tyrannicide in a 'Short Treatise of Politique Power,' 1556. [xlvi. 78]

PONSONBY, LADY EMILY CHARLOTTE MARY (1817–1877), daughter of John William Ponsonby, fourth earl of Bessborough [q. v.]; published a number of novels, some anonymously, between 1848 and 1873. [xlvi. 79]

PONSONBY, Sir FREDERIC CAVENDISH (1783–1837), major-general; grandson of William Ponsonby, second earl of Bessborough [q. v.]; entered the army, 1800, and went with his regiment to Spain in 1809, distinguishing himself as a cavalry officer at Talavera and Barosa; obtained command (1811) of the 11th light dragoons, whom he led for the rest of the war; wounded at Waterloo, 1815; went on half-pay in 1820; major-general, 1825; governor of Malta, 1826–35; G.O.M.G., 1828; K.C.B. and K.C.H., 1831. [xlvi. 80]

PONSONBY, FREDERICK GEORGE BRABAZON, sixth EARL OF BESSBOROUGH (1815–1895), son of John William Ponsonby, fourth earl of Bessborough [q. v.]; of Harrow and Trinity College, Cambridge; M.A., 1837; barrister, Lincoln's Inn, 1840; succeeded his brother as sixth earl, 1880. He was an enthusiastic cricketer, playing for Harrow and Cambridge, as well as in Gentlemen v. Players, and founding I Zingari Club in 1845. [xlvi. 81]

PONSONBY, GEORGE (1755–1817), lord chancellor of Ireland; son of John Ponsonby (1713–1789) [q. v.]; studied at Trinity College, Cambridge; M.P., Wicklow, 1776, Inistioge, 1783–97, Galway (in the last Irish parliament, dissolved 1800); called to the Irish bar, 1780; chancellor of the exchequer under the Duke of Portland, 1782; urged the claims of the Irish catholics, and in 1797, being disappointed in his attempts to settle the question and to purify political life, seceded from parliament; returned to political life and resisted the union in the last Irish parliament; M.P., co. Wicklow (United Kingdom), 1801, co. Cork, 1806–7, Tavistock, 1808; became lord chancellor of Ireland on the formation of the Fox-Grenville ministry, 1806, retiring within a year; leader of the opposition in the Commons from 1808. [xlvi. 82]

PONSONBY, HENRY (d. 1745), major-general; captain of foot, 1705; M.P., Fethard (Irish parliament), 1715; subsequently M.P. for Clonmeen, Inistioge, and Newtown; fought at Dettingen, 1743; major-general, 1743; killed at Fontenoy, while in the front of the famous charge of the British and Hanoverian infantry. [xlvi. 84]

PONSONBY, SIR HENRY FREDERICK (1825–1895), major-general; eldest son of Sir Frederic Cavendish Ponsonby [q. v.]; served in the Crimea; major-general, 1868; appointed private secretary to Queen Victoria, 1870; privy councillor, 1880; G.C.B., 1887. [xlvi. 81]

PONSONBY, JOHN (1713–1787), speaker of the Irish House of Commons; entered Irish parliament as M.P., Newtown, 1739; appointed secretary to the revenue board, 1742; first commissioner, 1744–71; elected speaker, 1756; possessed very great parliamentary influence, being eminent among the 'undertakers,' a few families who engrossed the emoluments of the county; the appointment of the Marquis of Townshend as resident viceroy a serious blow to his influence; dismissed from the board of revenue for opposition to government, 1771, resigning the speakership at the close of the session; gradually ceased to take an active part in politics after 1776. [xlvi. 84]

PONSONBY, SIR JOHN, VISCOUNT PONSONBY and second BARON PONSONBY (1770?–1855), eldest son of William Brabazon Ponsonby, first baron Ponsonby [q. v.]; minister plenipotentiary at Buenos Ayres, 1826–8, and at Rio de Janeiro, 1828–30; envoy extraordinary at Brussels, 1830–1; envoy at Naples, 1832; ambassador at Constantinople, 1832–7; G.C.B., 1834; created Viscount Ponsonby, 1839; ambassador at Vienna, 1846–50. [xlvi. 86]

PONSONBY, JOHN WILLIAM, fourth EARL OF BESSBOROUGH and VISCOUNT DUNCANNON (1781–1847), grandson of William Ponsonby, second earl of Bessborough [q. v.]; created M.A. Christ Church, Oxford, 1802; whig M.P. for Knaresborough, 1805, Higham Ferrers, 1806 and 1807, Malton, 1812–26, Kilkenny, 1826 and 1831, Nottingham, 1832–4; called to the House of Lords as Viscount Duncannon, 1834; home secretary under Lord Melbourne, 1834–5; succeeded to the earldom of Bessborough, 1844; lord-lieutenant of Ireland, 1846–7. [xlvi. 87]

PONSONBY, RICHARD (1772–1853), bishop of Derry; son of William Brabazon Ponsonby, first baron Ponsonby [q. v.]; M.A. Dublin, 1816; consecrated bishop of Killaloe and Kilfenora, 1828; translated to Derry, 1831, becoming also bishop of Raphoe in pursuance of the Church Temporalities Act, 1834. [xlvi. 86]

PONSONBY, SARAH (1745?–1831), recluse of Llangollen; grand-daughter of Henry Ponsonby [q. v.]; was the companion of Lady Eleanor Butler [q. v.] for fifty years in her retirement at Llangollen. [viii. 49]

PONSONBY, WILLIAM (1546?–1604), publisher; apprenticed (1560–70) to William Norton [q. v.]; began business on his own account (1577) in St. Paul's Churchyard. He owes his fame to his connection with Spenser from 1590, no less than ten volumes of Spenser's works appearing under his auspices. [xlvi. 87]

PONSONBY, WILLIAM, second EARL OF BESSBOROUGH (1704–1793), M.P., Newtown, 1725, co. Kilkenny, 1727–58; M.P., Derby, 1742–54, Saltash, 1754–6, Harwich, 1756–8; succeeded to his father's title, 1758; appointed secretary to the lord-lieutenant, 1739; became joint postmaster-general, 1759, resigning in 1762, on the dismissal of his brother-in-law, the Duke of Devonshire; reappointed, 1765; resigned, 1766. [xlvi. 88]

PONSONBY, SIR WILLIAM (1772–1815), major-general; son of William Brabazon Ponsonby, first baron Ponsonby [q. v.]; obtained command of the 5th dragoon guards, 1803; served in Spain, 1811–14; led his brigade at Vittoria, 1812; K.C.B., 1815; led the famous charge of the Union brigade on d'Erlon's shattered corps at Waterloo, and was killed by French lancers. [xlvi. 89]

PONSONBY, WILLIAM BRABAZON, first BARON PONSONBY (1744–1806), eldest son of John Ponsonby [q. v.]; M.P., Cork, 1764–76, Bandon Bridge, 1776–83, co. Kilkenny, 1783–1806; appointed joint postmaster-general of Ireland, 1784; removed, 1789; created Baron Ponsonby of Imokilly in co. Cork, 1806; he was a staunch whig, and a steady adherent of Charles James Fox [q. v.]. [xlvi. 90]

PONT, KYLPONT, or **KYNPONT**, ROBERT (1524–1606), Scottish reformer; studied at St. Andrews, where he was settled in 1559; appointed minister successively at Dunblane and Dunkeld, 1562, and 1563 commissioner of Moray, Inverness, and Banff; became minister of Birnie, 1567; appointed provost of Trinity College, near Edinburgh, 1571; nominated (1572) a lord of session by special permission of the assembly; translated (1573) to St. Cuthbert's, Edinburgh; became minister at St. Andrews, 1581; compelled to take refuge in England for protesting against the validity of acts of parliament regarding the jurisdiction of the church, 1584; returned to Scotland, 1586, and continued to take a leading part in ecclesiastical affairs until his death; published chronological and religious works. [xlvi. 91]

PONT, TIMOTHY (1560?–1614?), topographer; elder son of Robert Pont [q. v.]; M.A. St. Andrews, 1584; was an accomplished mathematician, and the first projector of a Scottish atlas. The originals of his maps are in the Advocates' Library, Edinburgh. [xlvi. 94]

PONT L'EVÊQUE, ROGER OF (d. 1181). [See ROGER.]

PONTACK, —— (1638?–1720?), tavern-keeper; son of Arnaud de Pontac, president of the parliament of Bordeaux; had some skill in rabbinical learning; opened a tavern in Abchurch Lane, called Pontack's Head, which became the most fashionable eating-house in London. It is frequently noticed in contemporary literature. [xlvi. 94]

PONTON, MUNGO (1802–1880), photographic inventor; was a writer to the signet; discovered (1839) that the action of the sun renders bichromate of mercury insoluble, the basis of permanent photography. [xlvi. 95]

POOLE, ARTHUR WILLIAM (1852–1885), missionary bishop; M.A. Worcester College, Oxford, 1876; D.D., 1883; went to Masulipatam as a missionary in 1877; made bishop of Japan, 1883. [xlvi. 96]

POOLE, EDWARD STANLEY (1830–1867), Arabic scholar; elder son of Sophia Poole [q. v.]; among other works, published (1850) a new edition of the translation of the 'Thousand and One Nights' by his uncle, Edward William Lane [q. v.]. [xlvi. 104]

POOLE, GEORGE AYLIFFE (1809–1883), divine and author; M.A. Emmanuel College, Cambridge, 1838; vicar of Welford, 1843–76; rector of Winwick, 1876–83; was a strong high churchman, and took part in ecclesiastical controversy; but the work of his life was to promote the revival of Gothic architecture. [xlvi. 96]

POOLE, JACOB (1774–1827), antiquary; studied the customs and language of the dwellers in the baronies of Bargy and Forth in Wexford, who spoke an English dialect dating from the English conquest. His collection of words and phrases was published by William Barnes, 1867. [xlvi. 97]

POOLE, JOHN (1786?–1872), dramatist and miscellaneous author; obtained pronounced success as a dramatist in early life; wrote comedies and farces for the London theatres; obtained a pension through Charles Dickens in later life. [xlvi. 97]

M m

POOLE, JONAS (*d.* 1612), mariner; made a voyage to Virginia in 1607 in the employment of Sir Thomas Smith (1558 ?–1625) [q. v.], and in 1610, 1611, and 1612 visited Spitzbergen.   [xlvi. 98]

POOLE, JOSHUA (*fl.* 1632–1646), writer of school-books; M.A. Clare Hall, Cambridge; published 'The English Accidence,' 1646, and 'The English Parnassus' (posthumous), 1657.   [xlvi. 98]

POOLE, MARIA (1770 ?–1833). [See DICKONS.]

POOLE or POLE, MATTHEW (1624–1679), biblical commentator; M.A. Emmanuel College, Cambridge, 1652 (incorporated at Oxford, 1657); rector of St. Michael-le-Querne, 1649–62, resigning on the passing of the Uniformity Act; engaged (1666–76) on the work of his life, his 'Synopsis' of the critical labours of biblical commentators, which ran to five folio volumes and had a large sale; died at Amsterdam in 1679.   [xlvi. 99]

POOLE, PAUL FALCONER (1807–1879), historical painter; was almost entirely self-taught; began to exhibit in the Royal Academy, 1830; attracted much notice by his picture of 'Solomon Eagle exhorting the People to Repentance during the Plague of the Year 1665,' 1843.   [xlvi. 100]

POOLE, REGINALD STUART (1832–1895), archæologist and orientalist; younger son of Sophia Poole [q. v.]; devoted himself in early life to the study of ancient Egypt; admitted assistant to the British Museum, 1852; became keeper of the coins and medals, 1870; initiated a system of scientific catalogues, editing and collating thirty-five volumes; lectured and wrote much on Egyptology.   [xlvi. 101]

POOLE, ROBERT (1708–1752), medical and theological writer; physician to the Middlesex infirmary, 1745–6, to the small-pox hospital, 1746–8; friend and follower of George Whitfield. Besides two books, recording his travels, issued in his own name, he wrote devotional and medical works under the pseudonym 'Theophilus Philanthropos.'   [xlvi. 103]

POOLE, SOPHIA (1804–1891), author of 'The Englishwoman in Egypt'; sister of Edward William Lane [q. v.]; married (1829) Edward Richard Poole, a well-known bibliophile; resided in Egypt with her brother, 1842–9; published 'The Englishwoman in Egypt,' 1844–6.   [xlvi. 104]

POOLE, THOMAS (1765–1837), friend of Coleridge; a tanner by trade; began an intimacy with Coleridge (*c.* 1794) which continued throughout life. He assisted Coleridge pecuniarily.   [xlvi. 104]

POOR or PAUPER, HERBERT (*d.* 1217), bishop of Salisbury; son of Richard of Ilchester (*d.* 1188) [q. v.], bishop of Winchester; appointed archdeacon of Canterbury, 1175; consecrated bishop of Salisbury, 1194; conceived the design of removing the see from Old Sarum to a more suitable site in the plain, a project which was afterwards carried out by his brother and successor, Richard Poor [q. v.]   [xlvi. 105]

POOR, POORE, POURE, or LE POOR, RICHARD (*d.* 1237), successively bishop of Chichester, Salisbury, and Durham; son of Richard of Ilchester (*d.* 1188) [q. v.], bishop of Winchester; elected bishop of Chichester, 1214, and translated to Salisbury, 1217; commenced (1220) the erection of the present Early-English cathedral of Salisbury, which was consecrated in 1225; bishop of Durham, 1228–37; perhaps author of the 'Ancren Riwle.' Panciroli's identification of him with Richard Anglicus [q. v.] the jurist and canonist is probably incorrect.   [xlvi. 106]

POOR, ROGER LE (*fl.* 1139). [See ROGER PAUPER.]

POPE, ALEXANDER (1688–1744), poet; son of Alexander Pope (1641 ?–1717), a Roman catholic linen-draper of London; a precocious child, and called 'the little nightingale' from the beauty of his voice; his health ruined and his figure distorted by a severe illness at the age of twelve, brought on by 'perpetual application'; began at an early age to imitate his favourite authors; became intimate (*c.* 1704) with William Wycherley [q. v.], who introduced him to town life; came into notice by the publication of the 'Pastorals,' in 1709, in Tonson's 'Poetic Miscellanies'; published anonymously (1711) the 'Essay on Criticism,' which was warmly praised by Addison in the 'Spectator'; became known to the Addison circle;

his 'Messiah' published in the 'Spectator,' 14 May 1712; published 'Rape of the Lock' in Lintot's 'Miscellanies,' 1712, and separately, 1714; published (1713) 'Windsor Forest,' which appealed to the tories by its references to the peace of Utrecht, and won him the friendship of Swift; drifted apart from Addison's 'little senate' and became a member of the 'Scriblerus Club,' an informal association, which included Swift, Gay, Arbuthnot, Atterbury, Oxford, and others; issued (1715) the first volume of his translation of the 'Iliad' (completed in 1720), which reflected with genuine rhetorical vigour the classicism of the time; bought (1719) the lease of a house at Twickenham, where he lived for the rest of his life; a close friend of Lady Mary Wortley Montagu [q. v.] and Martha Blount [q. v.], 1715–22; after the final publication of the 'Iliad' was engaged for a time on task work, editing the poems of Parnell in 1722, and beginning an edition of Shakespeare for Tonson, which appeared in 1825; assisted in his translation of the 'Odyssey,' by William Broome [q. v.] and Elijah Fenton [q. v.]; issued his translation of the 'Odyssey,' 1725–6, which brought an addition of fortune, though not much of fame; published the 'Dunciad' (anonymously), 1712, thereby making an unprecedented stir among authors; issued an enlarged edition, 1729, though the poem was not acknowledged till it appeared in Pope's 'Works' in 1735; his 'Dunciad' attacked in numerous rejoinders, which caused him some mortification; led by Bolingbroke's influence over him as a friend and philosopher into writing the 'Essay on Man' (1733) and the four 'Moral Essays,' which were the only parts completed of a series of poems intended to embrace a systematic survey of human nature; published (1733) his translation from Horace of the first satire of the second book, the first of a series of his most felicitous writings, continued intermittently until the close of his life; occupied himself in the meantime with the publication of his earlier correspondence, which he edited and amended in such a manner as to misrepresent totally the literary history of the time, and also employed a series of discreditable artifices to make it appear that it was published against his wish; assisted Edmund Curll [q. v.], the publisher, who had printed his 'Familiar Letters to Henry Cromwell' in 1726, to publish his 'Literary Correspondence' in 1735, and then endeavoured to disavow him; ungenerously took advantage of Swift's failing powers in 1741 in order to saddle him with the responsibility for a similar publication in 1741; lost his friend, Arbuthnot, by death, 1735; deprived of the society of Bolingbroke, who retired to France, 1735; undertook, by the advice of William Warburton, to complete the 'Dunciad' by a fourth book, which appeared in 1742, and contains some of his finest verses; his last literary quarrel the result of a reference in it to Colley Cibber [q. v.]; buried in Twickenham Church. His writings accurately reflect the tendencies of his age, and with reference to that age he was certainly a great poet. Satire and didactic poetry corresponded to the taste of such an epoch; and his scholarly sense of niceties of language led him to polish all his work with unwearied care. The first collective edition of his 'Works' appeared in 1751. The standard edition is that edited by Whitwell Elwin [q. v.] and Mr. W. J. Courthope, and published between 1871 and 1889.   [xlvi. 109]

POPE or PAIP, ALEXANDER (*d.* 1782), Scottish divine; M.A. King's College, Aberdeen, 1725; minister of Reay in Caithness, 1734–82; translated a large part of the 'Orcades' of Torfæus, and was acquainted with Alexander Pope (1688–1744) [q. v.]   [xlvi. 127]

POPE, ALEXANDER (1763–1835), actor and painter; practised portrait-painting for a time at Cork, but subsequently went on the stage, appearing at Covent Garden, London, in 1785; made an eminently favourable impression, and for many years played the principal tragic parts in the same house; also made occasional appearances in the country, especially at Edinburgh, where he was a favourite; exhibited fifty-nine miniatures at the Royal Academy between 1787 and 1821.   [xlvi. 127]

POPE, CLARA MARIA (*d.* 1838), painter; daughter of Jared Leigh [q. v.]; married at an early age Francis Wheatley [q. v.], and in 1807 became the third wife of Alexander Pope (1763–1835) [q. v.]; exhibited at the Royal Academy from 1796; in later life enjoyed a great reputation for her groups of flowers.   [xlvi. 130]

POPE, ELIZABETH (1744?-1797), actress; *née*
Younge; became the first wife of Alexander Pope (1763-
1835) [q. v.] in 1786; first appeared at Drury Lane, London
(1768) in the character of Imogen and obtained immediate recognition; removed from Drury Lane, London
(1778) to Covent Garden, London, where she remained for
the rest of her stage career; found Mrs. Siddons a for-
midable rival in tragedy and Miss Farren in comedy, but
while perhaps surpassed by each in her own province, had
a wider range than either. [xlvi. 130]

POPE, JANE (1742-1818), actress; first appeared at
Drury Lane, London, 1756; remained at Drury Lane till
her retirement from the stage, 1808; excelled in the role
of soubrette; praised by Lamb, Hazlitt, and Leigh Hunt.
[xlvi. 132]

POPE, MARIA ANN (1775-1803), actress; *née* Campion; first appeared at the Crow Street Theatre, Dublin,
1792, and was rapidly promoted to be the heroine of the
Irish stage; appeared at Covent Garden, London, under
the name of Mrs. Spenser, 1797; became the second wife
of Alexander Pope (1763-1835) [q. v.] in 1798; accompanied her husband to Drury Lane, London, 1801, when
she was taken ill on 10 June 1803, while playing Desdemona, and died on the 18th. [xlvi. 134]

POPE, SIR THOMAS (1507?-1559), founder of Trinity
College, Oxford; educated at Eton; held many offices
about the court, and was enriched by grants of monastic
lands; knighted, 1537; withdrew largely from public life
during Edward VI's reign, owing to lack of sympathy with
the Reformation; became privy councillor on Queen
Mary's accession, 1553; retained Queen Elizabeth's favour
on her accession. On 28 March 1555 he executed a deed
of erection for Trinity College, Oxford, which he endowed
with the site and buildings of Durham College, the Oxford
house of the abbey of Durham. [xlvi. 135]

POPE, SIR THOMAS, second EARL OF DOWNE (1622-
1660), of Christ Church, Oxford; succeeded his grandfather as earl, 1631; raised a troop of horse for Charles I,
when the civil war broke out, but compounded, 1645, and
took the solemn oath and covenant; left England, *c.* 1652,
and travelled in France and Italy. [xlvi. 138]

POPE, SIR THOMAS, third EARL OF DOWNE (1598-
1668), uncle of Sir Thomas Pope, second earl of Downe
[q. v.]; suffered severely from both sides during the civil
war; imprisoned by Charles I at Oxford, and arrested in
1656 on suspicion of complicity with the 'cavalier' plot.
[xlvi. 138]

POPE, WALTER (*d.* 1714), astronomer; of Trinity
College, Cambridge, and Wadham College, Oxford; fellow
of Wadham College, Oxford, 1651; M.A., 1651; became
professor of astronomy in Gresham College, London, 1660;
M.D. Oxford, 1661; published a 'Life of Seth Ward,' 1697,
besides other works. [xlvi. 138]

POPE-HENNESSY, SIR JOHN (1834-1891), colonial
governor; M.P., King's County, 1859, being the first
Roman catholic conservative who obtained a seat;
barrister, Inner Temple, 1861; governor of Labuan,
1867-71, of the Gold Coast, 1872-3, of the Windward
islands, 1875-6, of Hongkong, 1877-82, and of the
Mauritius, 1883-9; espoused the cause of the French
creoles in the Mauritius and was suspended from office in
1886; returned for Kilkenny as an anti-Parnellite home
ruler, 1890. [xlvi. 139]

POPHAM, ALEXANDER (1729-1810), prison reformer; of Balliol and All Souls Colleges, Oxford; M.A.,
1755; barrister, Middle Temple, 1755 (bencher, 1785);
M.P., Taunton, 1768, 1774-80, and 1784-96; was the
author of the bill passed in 1774 for the prevention of the
gaol distemper. [xlvi. 141]

POPHAM, EDWARD (1610?-1651), admiral and
general at sea; son of Sir Francis Popham [q. v.]; threw
in his lot with parliament in the civil war; M.P., Minehead, 1644; commanded a force in Somerset and Dorset;
appointed a commissioner for the immediate ordering of
the navy, 1648; commanded in the Downs and North
Sea, 1649; joined Blake at Lisbon in blockading Prince
Rupert, 1650. [xlvi. 141]

POPHAM, SIR FRANCIS (1573-1644), soldier and
politician; only son of Sir John Popham (1531?-1607)
[q. v.]; of Balliol College, Oxford, and the Middle Temple;
knighted, 1596; M.P., 1597-1644, for Somerset, Wiltshire,

Marlborough, Great Bedwin, Chippenham, and Minehead,
sitting in every parliament except the Short parliament,
1640; took an active interest in the settlement of Virginia
and New England. [xlvi. 143]

POPHAM, SIR HOME RIGGS (1762-1820), rear-
admiral; educated at Westminster School and Cambridge;
entered the navy, 1778; obtained leave from the admiralty
and engaged in the East India and China trade, 1787, but
was nearly ruined by the capture of his vessel, the Etrusco,
in 1793, and her condemnation for illegal trading in con-
travention of the charter of the East India Company, in
spite of the fact that he had obtained the sanction of the
governor-general in council; served in Flanders (1794)
under the Duke of York, who obtained his promotion to
the rank of post-captain; while in Kronstadt he received
marks of favour from the Russian emperor, 1799; commanded an expedition against the Cape of Good Hope
in conjunction with a land force under Sir David Baird
[q. v.], 1806; on the completion of this enterprise proceeded with William Carr Beresford (afterwards Viscount
Beresford) [q. v.] to Buenos Ayres, where Beresford and
his force were captured by the Spaniards; superseded,
January 1807, and (March 1807) reprimanded by a court-
martial; took part in the expedition against Copenhagen,
1808; K.C.B., 1815; commander-in-chief on the Jamaica
station, with the rank of rear-admiral, 1817-20; retired
in broken health, 1820. [xlvi. 143]

POPHAM, SIR JOHN (*d.* 1463?), military commander
and speaker-elect of the House of Commons; took part in
Henry V's invasion of France in 1415 and in the French
wars under the Duke of Bedford; elected speaker of the
House of Commons (M.P., Hampshire), 1449, but was permitted by Henry VI to decline the office on the ground of
infirmity. [xlvi. 146]

POPHAM, SIR JOHN (1531?-1607), chief-justice of
the king's bench; of Balliol College, Oxford, and the
Middle Temple (treasurer, 1580); M.P., Bristol, 1571 and
1572-83; privy councillor, 1571; solicitor-general, 1579;
elected speaker of the House of Commons, 1580; appointed
attorney-general, 1581; nominated lord chief justice, 1592;
knighted, 1592. [xlvi. 147]

POPPLE, WILLIAM (*d.* 1708), author; a London
merchant; appointed secretary to the board of trade,
1696; published 'A Rational Catechism,' 1687.
[xlvi. 149]

POPPLE, WILLIAM (1701-1764), dramatist; grandson of William Popple (*d.* 1708) [q. v.]; entered the
cofferer's office, *c.* 1730; promoted solicitor and clerk of
the report to the commissioners of trade and plantations, 1737; governor of the Bermudas from 1745 till
shortly before his death; author of mediocre plays and
pamphlets. [xlvi. 149]

PORCHESTER, third VISCOUNT (1800-1849). [See
HERBERT, HENRY JOHN GEORGE, third EARL OF CAR-
NARVON.]

PORDAGE, JOHN (1607-1681), astrologer and mystic;
rector of Bradfield, Berkshire; ejected as 'ignorant and
insufficient,' 1655, but restored, 1660; described by Baxter
as chief of the Behmenists; published a number of works,
partly astrological and partly devotional. [xlvi. 150]

PORDAGE, SAMUEL (1633-1691?), poet; eldest son
of John Pordage [q. v.]; of Merchant Taylors' School,
London, and Lincoln's Inn; published a translation of
Seneca, entitled 'Troades Englished,' 1660, and subse-
quently several poems and plays, including an answer to
Dryden's 'Absalom and Achitophel,' entitled 'Azaria and
Hushai,' 1682. [xlvi. 151]

PORDEN, ELEANOR ANNE (1797?-1825). [See
FRANKLIN.]

PORDEN, WILLIAM (1755-1822), architect; student
under James Wyatt [q. v.]; his most important work
Eaton Hall, Cheshire, 1804-12. [xlvi. 152]

PORRETT, ROBERT (1783-1868), chemist; was a
clerk in the war office from 1795 until 1850, when he
retired on a pension; discovered sulpho-cyanic acid
between 1808 and 1814, and ferro-cyanic acid, 1814; independently discovered electric endosmosis, 1816; F.S.A.,
1840; F.R.S., 1848. [xlvi. 153]

PORSON, RICHARD (1759-1808), Greek scholar; son
of the parish clerk at East Ruston, near North Walsham;
showed an extraordinary memory when a boy, and

attracted the attention of T. Hewett, the curate of the parish, who educated him with his own sons; placed at Eton by Mr. Norris of Witton Park, 1774; a fund started to maintain him at Cambridge by Sir George Baker [q. v.] on Norris's death; entered at Trinity College, 1778; scholar, 1780; Craven scholar, 1781; first chancellor's medallist and fellow, 1782; M.A., 1785; became widely known by his 'Letters to Travis' [see TRAVIS, GEORGE], 1788-9; lost his fellowship, which expired, 1792, owing to his refusal to take orders, and failed to obtain a lay fellowship, for which he applied; an annuity of 100*l*. purchased for him by his admirers, on which he took rooms at Essex Court in the Temple; was elected regius professor of Greek at Cambridge University, November 1792, but continued to live in London, absorbed in private study; his society much sought by literary men; married (1796) Mrs. Lunan (*d.* 1797), the sister of James Perry [q. v.], one of his intimate friends; edited four plays of Euripides, 'Hecuba' (1797 and 1802), 'Orestes' (1798), 'Phœnissæ' (1799), and 'Medea' (1801), his finest single piece of criticism being the 'Supplement' to the preface in the second edition of the 'Hecuba,' in which he states and illustrates certain rules of iambic and trochaic verse; died in London, and was buried in the chapel of Trinity College, Cambridge. His memory was remarkable, not only for its tenacity, but also for its readiness. In later life he gave way to intemperance. His transcripts of Photius from the Gale MS. and of the 'Medea' and 'Phœnissæ' are marvels of calligraphy. His literary remains were published after his death, between 1812 and 1834. His 'Correspondence' appeared in 1867. He definitely advanced Greek scholarship in three principal respects : (1) by remarks upon countless points of Greek idiom and usage ; (2) by adding to the knowledge of metre, and especially of the iambic trimeter ; (3) by emendation of texts. [xlvi. 154]

PORT or **PORZ**, ADAM DE (*d.* 1213 ?), baron ; accused (1172) of treason and plotting Henry II's death ; fled from England on being summoned to appear before Henry II's court and was outlawed ; joined William of Scotland during the barons' rebellion of 1174, but in 1180 made his peace with Henry II and received back his paternal lands ; warden of Southampton Castle, 1213. [xlvi. 163]

PORT, SIR JOHN (1480 ?-1541), judge ; studied law in the Middle Temple (governor, 1520) ; attorney to the earldom of Chester before 1512 ; serjeant-at-law, 1522 ; knighted, 1525 ; a judge of the king's bench, 1525. He was a benefactor to Brasenose College, Oxford, at the time of its foundation. [xlvi. 165]

PORT, SIR JOHN (*d.* 1557), founder of Repton School ; son of Sir John Port (1480 ?-1541) [q. v.] ; first scholar on his father's foundation at Brasenose College, Oxford ; knighted at the coronation of Edward VI ; knight of the shire for Derbyshire, 1553 ; sheriff of Derbyshire, 1554. By his will he left a bequest for the foundation of Repton school. [xlvi. 165]

PORTAL, ABRAHAM (*fl.* 1758-1796), dramatist ; wrote a number of plays between 1758 and 1796 ; published 'Poems,' 1781. [xlvi. 165]

PORTAL, SIR GERALD HERBERT (1858-1894), diplomatist ; entered the diplomatic service, 1879 ; stationed in Egypt between 1882 and 1887 ; went on a mission to Abyssinia, 1887 ; K.C.M.G., 1892 ; visited Uganda, 1892. Accounts of his missions to Abyssinia and Uganda were written by him and published in 1888 and 1894 respectively. [xlvi. 166]

PORTEN, SIR STANIER (*d.* 1789), government official ; entered the diplomatic service, and was undersecretary to Lord Rochford, 1768-82 ; knighted, 1772 ; appointed keeper of the state papers at Whitehall, 1774 ; uncle of Edward Gibbon [q. v.], the historian. [xlvi. 167]

PORTEOUS. [See also PORTEUS.]

PORTEOUS, JOHN (*d.* 1736), captain of the Edinburgh city guard ; enlisted in the army, and, after serving some time in Holland, was employed in 1715 to train the Edinburgh city guard ; promoted to be captain ; fired on the crowd and killed or wounded nearly thirty persons (1736) in a slight tumult at the execution of Andrew Wilson, an Edinburgh merchant, who had excited the admiration of the Edinburgh mob by contriving the escape of his accomplice in robbing the custom house ;

was brought to trial, found guilty, and sentenced to death, but reprieved ; taken out of prison and hanged by a number of persons (7 Sept. 1736), none of whom were captured, in spite of the most rigorous investigation. The plot of Sir Walter Scott's 'Heart of Midlothian' turns upon the incidents of the Porteous riot. [xlvi. 168]

PORTEOUS, WILLIAM (1735-1812), Scottish divine; minister of Whitburn, 1759-70, and of the Wynd Church, Glasgow, and the new St. George's Church, Glasgow, 1770-1812 ; strongly orthodox, writing against all innovations. [xlvi. 169]

PORTER, ANNA MARIA (1780-1832), novelist; sister of Sir Robert Ker Porter [q. v.] ; devoted herself to literature, and at thirteen began a series of 'Artless Tales,' published in 1795 ; published (1807) 'The Hungarian Brothers,' a tale of the French revolutionary war, besides other novels. [xlvi. 170]

PORTER, SIR CHARLES (*d.* 1696), Irish lord chancellor ; was concerned as a London apprentice in the riots of 1648 ; escaped to Holland, served as a common soldier, and kept an eating-house ; received among the chancery clerks on returning to London, and (1660) called to the bar at the Middle Temple ; taken into custody (June 1675) in the middle of an argument, by order of the House of Commons, for breach of privilege, in common with all parties engaged in the Dalmahoy case ; knighted, 1675 ; made Irish lord chancellor in 1686 by James II, who hoped he would prove a useful tool ; recalled at Tyrconnel's instance, January 1687 ; an active partisan of William III, returning to Ireland as lord chancellor in 1690. He was frequently assailed by the extreme protestants, but retained office till his death. [xlvi. 170]

PORTER, CLASSON EMMETT (1814-1885), ecclesiastical historian ; brother of John Scott Porter [q. v.] ; minister of the first presbyterian church at Larne, co. Antrim, 1834-85. His contributions to Irish presbyterian church history were numerous and important. [xlvi. 186]

PORTER, ENDYMION (1587-1649), royalist; brought up in Spain, and some time page in the household of Olivares ; after his return obtained a place in Buckingham's service, and became groom of the bedchamber to Prince Charles ; made use of by Buckingham to conduct his Spanish correspondence ; sent to Spain (October 1622) to prepare the way for Prince Charles's visit ; accompanied Prince Charles and Buckingham to Spain, 1623, and was again in that country in 1628 with proposals for peace ; rewarded with numerous promotions and grants ; wrote verses and was the friend and patron of poets, including D'Avenant, Dekker, Gervase Warmestry, and Edmund Bolton ; one of the agents employed by Charles I in forming his great collection of pictures ; sat in the Long parliament as M.P., Droitwich, and voted against Strafford's attainder ; attended Charles I from London ; expelled from parliament and exempted from pardon, on account of the unfounded belief that he was a chief instrument in a 'popish plot' against English liberties, 1643 ; left England, 1645, and after enduring great poverty compounded in 1649. [xlvi. 172]

PORTER, FRANCIS (*d.* 1702), Irish Franciscan ; passed most of his life at Rome, where he became president of the Irish college ; author of five rare Latin works. [xlvi. 175]

PORTER, GEORGE (1622 ?-1683), royalist ; eldest son of Endymion Porter [q. v.] ; major-general of Newcastle's foot at Marston Moor, where he was taken prisoner, 1644 ; was exchanged and subsequently became lieutenant-general and commander of the horse under his brother-in-law, Goring ; deserted Charles I's service and went to London, November 1645 ; engaged in plots for Charles II's restoration, 1659, and after Charles II's return became gentleman of the privy chamber to the queen-consort. [xlvi. 176]

PORTER, GEORGE (*fl.* 1684-1697), conspirator ; captain in Slingsby's horse, 1688 ; was proclaimed a dangerous Jacobite, 1692 ; engaged in the plot to assassinate William III, 1696 ; was captured, turned king's evidence, and was largely instrumental in the conviction of the other prisoners. [xlvi. 176]

PORTER, SIR GEORGE HORNIDGE, first baronet (1822-1895), surgeon ; only son of William Henry Porter [q. v.] ; M.D. Trinity College, Dublin ; elected surgeon to the Meath Hospital, Dublin, 1849 ; president of the College of Surgeons of Ireland, 1868–9 ; given a baronetcy, 1889 ; regius professor of surgery at Dublin University, 1891. [xlvi. 177]

PORTER, GEORGE RICHARDSON (1792–1852), statistician ; failed in business as a sugar-broker, and devoted himself to economics and statistics ; the statistical department of the board of trade established mainly under his supervision, 1834 ; became joint-secretary to the board, 1841 ; published ' The Progress of the Nation from the Beginning of the Nineteenth Century,' 1836–43, and other works. [xlvi. 178]

PORTER, HENRY (*fl.* 1596–1599), dramatist ; author of five plays mentioned in Henslowe's ' Diary,' of which the only one extant is ' The Pleasant Historie of the two Angrie Women of Abington ' (1599), which has been frequently edited, and was praised by Charles Lamb. [xlvi. 179]

PORTER, SIR JAMES (1710–1786), diplomatist ; employed at Vienna, 1741 and 1742 ; ambassador at Constantinople, 1746–62 ; minister plenipotentiary at Brussels, 1763–5 ; knighted, 1763 ; published ' Observations on the Religion, Law, Government and Manners of the Turks,' 1768. [xlvi. 179]

PORTER, JAMES (1753–1798), author of ' Billy Bluff ' ; presbyterian minister at Greyabbey, co. Down, 1787–98 ; joined the volunteer movement, 1778, and after its suppression (1793) became a prominent opponent of government ; contributed (1796) to the ' Northern Star ' a series of letters, forming an admirable satire on local tyranny in Ireland, which were at once reprinted with the title ' Billy Bluff and Squire Firebrand,' and made his name a household word in Ulster ; apprehended on the outbreak of the rebellion of 1798, convicted before a court-martial on the testimony of an informer, whom he was not even suffered to cross-examine, and hanged at Greyabbey. He was a well-known collector of books, and his scientific apparatus was unrivalled in the north of Ireland in his day. [xlvi. 180]

PORTER, JANE (1776–1850), novelist ; sister of Sir Robert Ker Porter [q. v.] ; published (1803) her first romance, ' Thaddeus of Warsaw,' which had a rapid success, and reached a ninth edition by 1810 ; published (1810) her most notable novel ' The Scottish Chiefs,' which had an immense success in Scotland and, being translated into German and Russian, won European fame ; attempted plays with less success, her tragedies of ' Switzerland,' 1819, and ' Owen, Prince of Powys,' 1822, being entire failures ; settled in London with her sister, Anna Maria Porter [q. v.], 1832 ; suffered from pecuniary difficulties in later life. [xlvi. 182]

PORTER or **NELSON,** JEROME (*d.* 1632), Benedictine monk ; an inmate of St. George's, Douay ; wrote biographies of English, Scottish, and Irish saints ; died at Douay. [xlvi. 184]

PORTER, JOHN SCOTT (1801–1880), Irish biblical scholar and unitarian divine ; minister of the presbyterian congregation in Carter Lane, London, 1826–31, and of the first presbyterian church at Belfast, 1831–8 ; was appointed (1838) joint-professor of theology to the ' Association of Irish non-subscribing presbyterians,' and (1851) became in addition professor of Hebrew ; published theological works. [xlvi. 185]

PORTER, JOSIAS LESLIE (1823–1889), traveller and promoter of Irish education ; M.A. Glasgow, 1842 ; studied theology at Edinburgh, 1842 ; presbyterian minister at Newcastle-on-Tyne, 1846–9 ; became missionary to the Jews at Damascus, 1849, and during the next ten years acquired an intimate knowledge of Syria and Palestine ; professor of biblical criticism in the presbyterian college, Belfast, 1860–78 ; nominated by government (1878) one of the two assistant-commissioners of the newly established board of intermediate education for Ireland ; president of Queen's College, Belfast, 1879–89. Among his works may be mentioned ' Five Years in Damascus,' 1855, and ' The Giant Cities of Bashan,' 1865. [xlvi. 187]

PORTER, MARY (*d.* 1765), actress ; at Lincoln's Inn Fields, London, 1699 ; acted at the new theatre (Opera House) in the Haymarket, London, 1705 ; migrated to Drury Lane, London, 1708, returning to the Haymarket, London, 1709 ; reappeared at Drury Lane, London, 1710 ; left without a rival on the retirement of Mrs. Oldfield, 1730 ; retired, 1743. [xlvi. 188]

PORTER, ROBERT (*d.* 1690), ejected divine ; educated at Cambridge ; became vicar of Pentrich, Derbyshire, 1650, but was ejected, 1662 ; on the passing of the Five Mile Act retired to Mansfield, where he was unmolested. A valuable collection of Derbyshire nonconformist biographies by him was posthumously published. [xlvi. 190]

PORTER, SIR ROBERT KER (1777–1842), painter and traveller ; was admitted an academy student at Somerset House, London, 1790 ; scene-painter at the Lyceum Theatre, London, 1800 ; executed (1800) the ' Storming of Seringapatam,' a sensational panorama 120 feet in length, subsequently producing a number of other battle-scenes of the same kind, besides painting easel-pictures, the majority of which were historical pieces or landscapes ; appointed historical painter to the czar of Russia, 1804 ; left Russia, 1806, and travelled in Finland, Sweden, and Germany ; accompanied Sir John Moore throughout the Coruña campaign, and published accounts of his journeys in 1809 ; married a Russian princess, 1812, and (1813), returning to England, published a graphic ' Narrative of the Campaign in Russia during 1812 ' ; knighted, 1813 ; visited (1817–20) Georgia, Persia, Armenia, and ancient Babylonia, publishing an account of his ' Travels ' in those countries, 1821 ; British consul in Venezuela, 1826–41 ; died at St. Petersburg. [xlvi. 191]

PORTER, SARAH (1791–1862), writer on education ; sister of David Ricardo [q. v.] ; married George Richardson Porter [q. v.] ; published ' On Infant Schools for the Upper and Middle Classes,' 1838, and similar works. [xlvi. 178]

PORTER, THOMAS (1636–1680), dramatist ; son of Endymion Porter [q. v.] ; imprisoned (1655) for abducting Anne, daughter of Mountjoy Blount, earl of Newport [q. v.] ; his tragedy, ' The Villain ' (acted 1662, published 1663), thought deficient in fancy by the diarist Pepys. [xlvi. 193]

PORTER, WALTER (1595 ?–1659), composer ; appointed master of the choristers of Westminster Abbey, 1639 ; composed chiefly madrigals and hymn-tunes. [xlvi. 193]

PORTER, WHITWORTH (1827–1892), major-general, royal engineers ; entered the royal engineers, 1845 ; served before Sebastopol, 1855 ; commanding royal engineer in the western district, 1877–81 ; retired, 1881 ; works include an elaborate ' History of the Corps of Royal Engineers,' 1889. [xlvi. 194]

PORTER, WILLIAM (1805–1880), attorney-general at the Cape of Good Hope ; brother of John Scott Porter [q. v.] ; called to the Irish bar, 1831 ; attorney-general at the Cape of Good Hope, 1839–65. [xlvi. 186]

PORTER, WILLIAM HENRY (1790–1861), surgeon ; president of the Irish College of Surgeons, 1838 ; professor of surgery in College of Surgeons school of medicine at Dublin. [xlvi. 177]

PORTEUS, BEILBY (1731–1808), successively bishop of Chester and London ; B.A. Christ's College, Cambridge, 1752 ; fellow, 1752 ; appointed (1762) domestic chaplain to Thomas Secker [q. v.], archbishop of Canterbury ; chaplain to George III, 1769 ; bishop of Chester, 1776–87, of London, 1787–1808 ; supported the rising evangelical party in both sees, although not identifying himself with their more decidedly Calvinistic doctrines ; was an early patron of the Church Missionary Society, and joined the British and Foreign Bible Society ; published several doctrinal treatises, besides collected sermons, charges, and hortatory letters. [xlvi. 195]

PORTLAND, DUKES OF. [See BENTINCK, WILLIAM HENRY CAVENDISH, third DUKE, 1738–1809 ; BENTINCK-SCOTT, WILLIAM JOHN CAVENDISH, fifth DUKE, 1800–1879.]

PORTLAND, EARLS OF. [See WESTON, SIR RICHARD, first EARL, 1577–1635 ; WESTON, JEROME, second EARL, 1605–1663 ; BENTINCK, WILLIAM, first EARL of the second creation, 1649–1709.]

PORTLAND, titular EARL OF. [See HERBERT, SIR EDWARD, 1648 ?–1698.]

PORTLESTER, BARON. [See EUSTACE, ROLAND FITZ, *d.* 1496.]

PORTLOCK, JOSEPH ELLISON (1794–1864), major-general, royal engineers; only son of Nathaniel Portlock [q. v.]; entered the royal engineers, 1813; took part in the Canadian campaign, 1814; engaged (1824–43) in the Irish survey, particularly on the geological and productive economical sections; retired from active service, 1857.   [xlvi. 197]

PORTLOCK, NATHANIEL (1748?–1817), captain in the navy; entered the navy (1772) as an 'able seaman,' but was placed on the quarterdeck by (Sir) Charles Douglas [q. v.]; sailed round the world (1785–8) in command of the King George, and published 'A Voyage round the World,' 1789; attained post rank, 1799.
[xlvi. 198]

PORTMAN, EDWARD BERKELEY, first VISCOUNT PORTMAN (1799–1888), of Eton and Christ Church, Oxford; M.A., 1826; liberal M.P. for Dorset, 1823–32, Marylebone, 1832–3; created Baron Portman of Orchard Portman, 1837, and Viscount Portman, 1873.   [xlvi. 199]

PORTMAN, SIR WILLIAM (d. 1557), judge; made a judge, 1547; knighted by Edward VI; made chief-justice, 1554.   [xlvi. 199]

PORTMAN, SIR WILLIAM, sixth baronet (1641?–1690), captor of the Duke of Monmouth; of All Souls College, Oxford; K.B. at the Restoration; M.P., Taunton, 1661–79 and 1685–90; was considered the most influential tory in the west of England, after Sir Edward Seymour (1633–1708) [q. v.]; F.R.S., 1664; with Lord Lumley captured Monmouth in the New Forest, 8 July 1685; joined the Prince of Orange at Exeter, 1688. [xlvi. 200]

PORTMORE, first EARL OF (d. 1730). [See COLYEAR, SIR DAVID.]

PORTSMOUTH, DUCHESS OF (1649–1734). [See KÉROUALLE, LOUISE RENÉE DE.]

PORTSMOUTH, first EARL OF (1690–1762). [See WALLOP, JOHN.]

PORTU, MAURITIUS DE (d. 1513). [See O'FIHELY, MAURICE.]

PORY, JOHN (d. 1573?), master of Corpus Christi College, Cambridge; M.A. Corpus Christi College, Cambridge, 1527; D.D., 1557; elected fellow of his college, c. 1534, and master, 1557; resigned mastership under pressure (1570) on account of infirmity; friend of Matthew Parker [q. v.]   [xlvi. 200]

PORY, JOHN (1570?–1635), traveller and geographer; M.A. Caius College, Cambridge, 1595 (incorporated at Oxford, 1610); M.P., Bridgwater, 1605; travelled in France and the Low Countries, 1607, in Turkey, 1613–16; went to America as secretary to Sir George Yeardley [q. v.], 1619; settled in London, 1624.   [xlvi. 201]

PORY or **POREY**, ROBERT (1608?–1669), archdeacon of Middlesex; educated at St. Paul's School, London, and Christ's College, Cambridge; M.A., 1632; D.D. per literas regias, 1660 (incorporated at Oxford, 1663); collated to the rectory of St. Margaret's, Fish Street, London, 1640; plundered and sequestered on the outbreak of the civil war; rector of St. Botolph, Bishopsgate Street, London, 1660–3; appointed archdeacon of Middlesex, 1660.
[xlvi. 202]

POST, JACOB (1774–1855), quaker; published popular expositions of the history and belief of the Society of Friends.   [xlvi. 202]

POSTE, BEALE (1793–1871), divine and antiquary; educated at Trinity College, Cambridge; LL.B., 1819; curate successively of High Halden and Milstead in Kent; his works mainly concerned with early British history.
[xlvi. 203]

POSTGATE, JOHN (1820–1881), initiator of the laws against adulteration; started life as a grocer's boy at Scarborough; began practice in Birmingham as a surgeon, 1851; F.R.C.S., 1854; he began (1854) his lifelong crusade against the adulteration of food substances, the result of which was that the Birmingham member, William Scholefield [q. v.], obtained a parliamentary committee of inquiry in 1855, and a restraining bill was passed in 1860; the Amendment Act introduced at his instance, and passed, to render the check more effective, 1872.   [xlvi. 203]

POSTLETHWAITE, THOMAS (1731–1798), master of Trinity College, Cambridge; M.A. Trinity College, Cambridge, 1756; D.D. (by royal mandate), 1789; elected fellow of his college, 1755; master of his college, 1789–98; when master passed over Richard Porson [q. v.], who was in 1792 a candidate for the lay fellowship. [xlvi. 204]

POSTLETHWAYT, JAMES (d. 1761), writer on revenue; probably a brother of Malachy Postlethwayt [q. v.]; published 'The History of the Public Revenue from 1688 to 1758,' 1759.   [xlvi. 205]

POSTLETHWAYT, JOHN (1650–1713), chief master of St. Paul's School, London; M.A. Merton College, Oxford, 1678; high master of St. Paul's School, 1697–1713; proved an eminent schoolmaster.   [xlvi. 205]

POSTLETHWAYT, MALACHY (1707?–1767), economic writer; devoted twenty years to the preparation of 'The Universal Dictionary of Trade and Commerce,' 1751 (4th ed. 1774), a translation, with large additions, from the French of J. Savary des Brulons; wrote, among other topics, on the African trade.   [xlvi. 205]

POSTLETHWAYT, MATTHEW (1679–1745), archdeacon of Norwich; nephew of John Postlethwayt [q. v.]; M.A. St. John's College, Cambridge, 1706; archdeacon of Norwich and rector of Redenhall, 1742.   [xlvi. 205]

POTE, JOSEPH (1703?–1787), bookseller; kept a boarding-house for Eton boys, and was well known as an editor and publisher in Eton.   [xlvi. 206]

POTENGER or **POTTINGER**, JOHN (1647–1733), master in chancery and author; of Winchester College and Corpus Christi College, Oxford; B.A., 1668; admitted to the Inner Temple, 1675; obtained the post of master in chancery after 1678, subsequently selling it; refused to support James II's religious policy; author of 'A Pastoral Reflection on Death,' 1691, and many unpublished poems.
[xlvi. 206]

POTT, JOSEPH HOLDEN (1759–1847), archdeacon of London; son of Percivall Pott [q. v.]; of Eton and St. John's College, Cambridge; M.A., 1783; was archdeacon of St. Albans, 1789–1813, of London, 1813–42; chancellor of Exeter, 1826; wrote works in prose and verse.
[xlvi. 207]

POTT, PERCIVALL (1714–1788), surgeon; was bound an apprentice to Edward Nourse [q. v.], 1729; became master of anatomy to the newly formed Corporation of Surgeons, 1753, and master of the corporation, 1765; became surgeon to St. Bartholomew's Hospital, London, 1749; introduced many improvements into the art of surgery during his long tenure of office, rendering its practice more humane; suffered a compound fracture of the leg (still known as 'Pott's fracture'), 1756, which, in spite of the opinion of the surgeons in favour of amputation, he and his friend and colleague Nourse succeeded in curing without it; resigned his office of surgeon, 1787. He was the teacher of John Hunter (1728–1793) [q. v.], whom he excelled in practical, but to whom he was much inferior in scientific, surgery. The spinal disease known as 'Pott's disease' obtained its name from his discussion of it in a medical work published in 1779. His works, which are numerous and important, were collected, 1775.
[xlvi. 207]

POTTER, BARNABY (1577–1642), provost of Queen's College, Oxford, and bishop of Carlisle; M.A. Queen's College, Oxford, 1602; D.D., 1615; fellow of his college, 1604; provost, 1616–26; liked by Charles I, in spite of his puritan leanings; chief almoner to Charles I, 1628; bishop of Carlisle, 1629–42.   [xlvi. 211]

POTTER, CHARLES (1634–1663), courtier; son of Christopher Potter (1591–1646) [q. v.]; educated at Queen's College, Oxford; student of Christ Church, Oxford, 1647; M.A., 1651; joined the exiled court of Charles II, and became a Roman catholic; made usher to Queen Henrietta Maria at the Restoration.   [xlvi. 213]

POTTER, CHRISTOPHER (1591–1646), provost of Queen's College, Oxford; nephew of Barnaby Potter [q. v.]; M.A. Queen's College, Oxford, 1613; D.D., 1627; fellow of Queen's College, Oxford, 1615; provost, 1626–46; he attached himself to Laud, and was made chaplain in ordinary to Charles I; dean of Worcester, 1636; vice-chancellor of Oxford University, 1640; suffered much in Charles I's cause during the civil war; was nominated dean of Durham, 1646, but died before his installation.
[xlvi. 212]

POTTER, CHRISTOPHER (d. 1817), introducer into France of printing on porcelain; settled in Paris in 1789, and received credit for the invention of printing on porcelain and glass, though it had been practised at Liverpool and Worcester from 1756-7. He reopened the Chantilly potteries. [xlvi. 214]

POTTER, FRANCIS (1594–1678), divine and mechanician; brother of Hannibal Potter [q. v.]; M.A. Trinity College, Oxford, 1616; B.D., 1625; rector of Kilmington, 1628–78; made quadrants with a graduated compass of his own invention, which he gave to John Aubrey [q. v.]; F.R.S., 1663. [xlvi. 214]

POTTER, GEORGE (1832–1893), trade-unionist; a carpenter by trade; first became prominent in the lockout in the building trades in 1859; headed the deputation of London workmen who welcomed Garibaldi, 1864; member of the London school board, 1873–82; contributed to 'The Times' and the 'Contemporary Review.' [xlvi. 215]

POTTER, HANNIBAL (1592–1664), president of Trinity College, Oxford; M.A. Trinity College, Oxford, 1614; D.D., 1630; fellow of his college, 1613; president in 1643; deprived of the presidentship by the parliamentary visitors, 1647, but restored, 1660. [xlvi. 215]

POTTER, JOHN (1674?–1747), archbishop of Canterbury; matriculated at University College, Oxford, 1688; M.A., 1694; D.D., 1706; fellow of Lincoln College, Oxford, 1694; became domestic chaplain to Archbishop Tenison, 1704; regius professor of divinity at Oxford, 1707–15; bishop of Oxford, 1715–37; archbishop of Canterbury, 1737–47; edited Lycophron, 1697, and Clement of Alexandria, 1715, and published 'Archæologia Græca,' vol. i. 1697, vol. ii. 1698. [xlvi. 216]

POTTER, JOHN (*fl.* 1754–1804), dramatic and miscellaneous author; resided chiefly in London, wrote plays and contributed theatrical criticism to the 'Public Ledger'; M.D. Edinburgh, 1784; L.R.C.P., 1785; practised medicine at Enniscorthy after 1785, but in 1798 returned to London and supported himself by literature. [xlvi. 217]

POTTER, JOHN PHILLIPS (1818–1847), anatomist; studied at University College, London; became house surgeon to Robert Liston [q. v.] in University College, Hospital, London, *c.* 1840; assistant-surgeon to University College Hospital, 1847; died of a poisoned wound received while dissecting. [xlvi. 218]

POTTER, PHILIP CIPRIANI HAMBL[E]Y (1792–1871), musician; ranked high among contemporary pianists and (1823) was appointed principal professor of the pianoforte at the Royal Academy of Music; principal of the academy, 1832–59. His published works extend to Opus 29, but are now rarely heard. [xlvi. 218]

POTTER, RICHARD (1778–1842), politician; known as 'Radical Dick'; brother of Sir Thomas Potter (1773–1845) [q. v.], with whom he was associated in business and politics at Manchester; M.P., Wigan, 1832, 1835, 1837. [Suppl. iii. 281]

POTTER, RICHARD (1799–1886), scientific writer; after engaging in mercantile life without success was elected a fellow of Queens' College, Cambridge, in 1839; M.A., 1841; professor of natural philosophy and astronomy, University College, London, 1841–3 and 1844–65. [xlvi. 219]

POTTER, ROBERT (1721–1804), poet and politician; M.A. Emmanuel College, Cambridge, 1788; master of Scarning school, 1761–89; occupied his spare time in translating the Greek tragedians; canon of Norwich, 1788; best known by his translation of Æschylus (1777), and in a less degree by his translation of Sophocles and Euripides; attacked the administration of the poor laws, 1785. [xlvi. 219]

POTTER, THOMAS (1718–1759), wit and politician; son of John Potter (1674?–1747) [q. v.]; M.A. Christ Church, Oxford, 1738; barrister, Middle Temple, 1740; secretary to Frederick, prince of Wales, 1748–51; M.P. St. Germans, 1747–54, Aylesbury, 1754–7, Okehampton, 1757–9; attacked the Duke of Newcastle in his first session in a speech, which was rebuked by Henry Pelham and published in the magazines, and (1756) allied himself with Pitt; appointed paymaster-general of the land forces, December 1756, and (July 1757) joint vice-treasurer of Ireland; was notorious at Medmenham and an associate of Wilkes, whom he introduced to Jewish moneylenders. To him has been attributed the infamous 'Essay on Woman.' [xlvi. 221]

POTTER, SIR THOMAS (1773–1845), politician; founded, with his brother, Richard Potter (1778–1842) [q. v.], the 'Manchester Guardian,' and afterwards 'Times' (Manchester), later called 'Examiner and Times'; first mayor of Manchester, 1838; knighted, 1839. He established with his brother the wholesale house in Manchester trade known as 'Potter's,' which became rendezvous for political and philanthropic reformers. [Suppl. iii. 281]

POTTER, THOMAS BAYLEY (1817–1898), politician; son of Sir Thomas Potter [q. v.]; educated at Rugby; entered his father's business house at Manchester and became a vigorous supporter of the Manchester school of liberals; espoused cause of North Americans in civil war, 1861; founded Union and Emancipation Society, 1863; succeeded his friend, Richard Cobden [q. v.], as M.P. for Rochdale, 1865, and held seat till 1895; consistently supported free trade; established Cobden Club, 1866, and acted as secretary. [Suppl. iii. 281]

POTTER, THOMAS JOSEPH (1828–1873), Roman catholic story-writer and professor; director of All Hallows' College, Dublin, and professor of sacred eloquence; his works chiefly passable religious poems or romances. [xlvi. 222]

POTTER, THOMAS ROSSELL (1799–1873), antiquary; kept a school at Wymeswold in Leicestershire; published 'The History and Antiquities of Charnwood Forest,' and other works. [xlvi. 222]

POTTER, WILLIAM (*fl.* 1650–1656), writer on banks; one of the earliest writers on paper currency; recommended the issue, by means of a land-bank, of bills payable at sight, under a guarantee of land mortgages. [xlvi. 223]

POTTINGER, ELDRED (1811–1843), soldier and diplomatist; nephew of Sir Henry Pottinger [q. v.]; entered the Bombay artillery, 1827; subsequently entered the political department and became assistant to his uncle; travelled in Afghanistan disguised as a horse-dealer, 1837, and, on the siege of Herát by the Russians, made himself known and conducted a successful defence; C.B.; made political officer in Kohistán, 1841, and on the revolt against Shah Shuja succeeded in escaping to Kábul, where he succeeded Sir William Hay Macnaghten [q. v.] as resident; detained as a hostage when the British troops agreed to evacuate the town, January 1842; returned to India, September 1842; died on a visit to Hongkong. [xlvi. 224]

POTTINGER, SIR HENRY, first baronet (1789–1856), soldier and diplomatist; obtained a cadetship in the Indian army, 1804; with a friend explored the country between Persia and India disguised as a native, 1809–11; served during the Mahratta war, and (1836–40) was political agent in Sindh; created baronet in recognition of his services, 1840; appointed envoy in China, 1840; distinguished himself during the opium war; G.C.B., 1842; made first British governor of Hongkong, 1843; returned to England, 1844, and was made a privy councillor; governor of the Cape of Good Hope, 1846–7; returned to India as governor of Madras, 1847; was an unsuccessful governor, and retired, 1854. [xlvi. 224]

POTTINGER, ISRAEL (*fl.* 1759–1761), dramatist; set up as a bookseller in Paternoster Row, London, and projected a variety of periodicals; subsequently suffered from a mental disorder, but supported himself in his lucid intervals by his pen, writing several plays of a farcical nature. [xlvi. 226]

POTTINGER, JOHN (1647–1733). [See POTENGER.]

POTTS, LAURENCE HOLKER (1789–1850), physician and inventor; educated at Westminster School; practised as a physician in Truro; M.D. Aberdeen, 1825; became superintendent of the county lunatic asylum at Bodmin, 1828, and (1837) established an institution at Blackheath for the treatment of spinal diseases; gave up this establishment (*c.* 1843) in order to have more time for his work in mechanics; took out a patent for sinking foundations under water by creating a partial vacuum (1843), an invention with which his name is closely connected, and which incidentally gave rise to the system of sinking foundations by means of compressed air. [xlvi. 226]

POTTS, ROBERT (1805–1885), mathematician ; M.A. Trinity College, Cambridge, 1835 ; a successful private tutor; acquired a wide reputation as editor of Euclid's 'Elements,' 1845. [xlvi. 228]

POTTS, THOMAS (*fl.* 1612), author of the 'Discoverie of Witches' ; clerk of the circuit at the trial of the Lancashire witches, 1612, compiling an account of the proceedings. [xlvi. 228]

POTTS, THOMAS (1778–1842), compiler ; a solicitor, at one time connected with Skinners' Hall ; published compilations on law, 1803, agriculture, 1806, and topography, 1810. [xlvi. 228]

POULETT. [See also PAULET.]

POULETT, SIR JOHN, first BARON POULETT (1586–1649), cavalier ; grandson of Sir Amias Paulet (1536 ?–1588) [q. v.] ; of University College, Oxford ; student of the Middle Temple, 1610 ; M.P., Somerset, 1610 and 1614, Lyme Regis, 1621–2 ; raised to the peerage, 1627 ; knighted, 1635 ; regarded as a 'popular' man until the passing of the militia ordinance in 1642, when he withdrew from parliament and assisted to put the commission of array into execution ; was taken prisoner near Bridgnorth, October 1642, but regained his liberty and served under Hopton ; again taken prisoner at Exeter, 1646, and was afterwards set free on payment of a fine. [xlvi. 229]

POULETT, SIR JOHN, second BARON POULETT (1615–1665), eldest son of Sir John Poulett, first baron Poulett [q. v.] ; knighted, 1635 ; M.P., Somerset, 1640–2 ; M.D. Exeter College, Oxford, 1643 ; fought on the royalist side ; compounded at the surrender of Exeter ; went abroad, 1658, but returned, 1660. [xlvi. 230]

POULETT, SIR JOHN, fourth BARON and first EARL POULETT (1663–1743), grandson of Sir John Poulett, second baron Poulett [q. v.] ; threw in his lot with the tories, but was always a lukewarm politician ; privy councillor, 1702 ; created Earl Poulett 1706 ; F.R.S., 1706 ; nominally first lord of the treasury, Harley in reality directing affairs, 1710–11 ; K.G., 1713 ; lost his places on the accession of George I. [xlvi. 230]

POULSON, GEORGE (1783–1858), topographer ; published the 'History and Antiquities of Holderness,' 1840–1, and other works. [xlvi. 231]

POUNCY, BENJAMIN THOMAS (*d.* 1799), draughtsman and engraver ; during the latter part of his life executed plates of landscape and marine subjects after popular artists. [xlvi. 231]

POUND, JAMES (1669–1724), astronomer ; B.A. Hart Hall, Oxford, 1694 ; M.A. Gloucester Hall, Oxford, 1694 ; M.B., 1697 ; went to Madras (1699) as chaplain to the merchants at Fort St. George, and thence proceeded to the settlement on the Cambodia, where he lost everything in an insurrection in 1705 ; afterwards held ecclesiastical preferments in England ; admitted F.R.S., 1713 ; distinguished himself by his observations of the satellites of Jupiter and Saturn. [xlvi. 232]

POUNDS, JOHN (1766–1839), gratuitous teacher of poor children ; crippled for life by an accident, 1781 ; started as a shoemaker at Portsmouth, 1803 ; from 1818 he became famous as teacher and friend of children, and was proclaimed by Dr. Guthrie to be the originator of the idea of ragged schools. [xlvi. 233]

POVEY, CHARLES (1652 ?–1743), miscellaneous writer and projector ; wrote in favour of the revolution, and from 1705 floated life and fire insurance schemes. [xlvi. 233]

POVEY, THOMAS (*fl.* 1633–1685), civil servant ; sat in the Long parliament as M.P., Liskeard, 1647 ; M.P., Bossiney, 1659 ; after the Restoration was much favoured at court ; held many offices and was a master of requests from 1662 till the accession of James II ; friend of Evelyn and Pepys. [xlvi. 235]

POWEL. [See POWELL and POWLE.]

POWELL, MRS. (*d.* 1831), actress ; previously known as MRS. FARMER and subsequently as MRS. RENAUD ; first appeared at the Haymarket as Mrs. Farmer, *c.* 1787 ; married (1789) a Liverpool prompter named Powell, and (1814) another husband named Renaud ; was generally cast for 'heavy' parts ; retired, 1829. [xlvi. 236]

POWELL, BADEN (1796–1860), Savilian professor of geometry ; M.A. Oriel College, Oxford, 1820 ; F.R.S., 1824 ; Savilian professor at Oxford, 1827–60 ; well known for his researches on optics and radiation, and was active in university reform ; engaged in theological controversy from a latitudinarian standpoint. [xlvi. 237]

POWELL or **POWEL**, DAVID (1552 ?–1598), Welsh historian ; B.A. Jesus College, Oxford, 1573 ; fellow of All Souls College, Oxford, 1573 ; M.A., 1576 ; held several Welsh benefices ; published (1584) 'The Historie of Cambria,' practically a new work, though founded on a manuscript translation by Humphrey Llwyd [q. v.] of the 'Chronicle of the Princes.' [xlvi. 238]

POWELL, EDWARD (1478 ?–1540), Roman catholic divine ; M.A. Oxford ; fellow of Oriel College, Oxford, 1495 ; D.D., 1506 ; opposed the spread of Luther's doctrines in England and pronounced against the royal divorce ; condemned for treason in refusing the oath of succession, 1534, and (1540) was executed at Smithfield, being drawn on the same hurdle as the protestant Robert Barnes [q. v.] [xlvi. 239]

POWELL, FOSTER (1734–1793), pedestrian ; clerk to an attorney in the Temple ; performed extraordinary pedestrian feats for small wagers ; walked (1792) from London to York and back, four hundred miles, in 5 days 15¼ hours. Most of his feats were afterwards eclipsed by Robert Barclay Allardice [q. v.] [xlvi. 240]

POWELL or **POWEL**, GABRIEL (1576–1611), polemical divine ; son of David Powell [q. v.] ; B.A. Jesus College, Oxford, 1596 ; became domestic chaplain to Richard Vaughan (1550 ?–1607) [q. v.], bishop of London ; wrote vigorously in support of Anglicanism. [xlvi. 240]

POWELL, GEORGE (1658 ?–1714), actor and dramatist ; is first heard of at the Theatre Royal, London, 1687 ; retired, *c.* 1713 ; praised by Addison as a tragedian ; lived a profligate life, and was in such constant dread of arrest as to menace with his sword sheriffs' officers when he saw them in the street. [xlvi. 241]

POWELL, SIR GEORGE SMYTH BADEN- (1847–1898), author and politician ; son of Baden Powell [q. v.] ; educated at St. Paul's School, London, and Marlborough College ; M.A. Balliol College, Oxford, 1878 ; entered Inner Temple, 1876 ; private secretary to Sir George Ferguson Bowen [q. v.], governor of Victoria ; joint-commissioner to inquire into administration of West India colonies, 1882 ; conservative M.P. for Kirkdale (Manchester), 1885–98 ; joint special commissioner to arrange details of new Maltese constitution, 1887 ; K.C.M.G., 1888 ; appointed to investigate subject of Behring Sea fisheries, 1891, and was British member of joint commission at Washington, 1892, and adviser on conduct of British case before arbitrators in Paris, 1893 ; published works and articles on political and economic questions. [Suppl. iii. 282]

POWELL or **POWEL**, GRIFFITH (1561–1620), principal of Jesus College, Oxford ; M.A. Jesus College, Oxford, 1589 ; D.C.L., 1599 ; principal, 1613–20 ; wrote on Aristotle and the sophists. [xlvi. 243]

POWELL, HUMPHREY (*fl.* 1548–1556), printer ; was in 1548 engaged in printing in Holborn Conduit, London, but in 1551 removed to Dublin, where he established the first printing-press in Ireland. [xlvi. 243]

POWELL, SIR JOHN (1633–1696), judge ; M.A. Jesus College, Oxford, 1664 ; barrister, Gray's Inn, 1657 (antient, 1676) ; knighted and appointed a judge of the common pleas, 1686 ; removed to the king's bench, 1687, but dismissed (July 1688) for stating, on the trial of the seven bishops, that the Declaration of Indulgence was a nullity ; restored to the common pleas, May 1689. [xlvi. 244]

POWELL, SIR JOHN (1645–1713), judge ; barrister, Inner Temple, 1671 ; appointed to the exchequer, 1691 ; knighted, 1691 ; transferred to the common pleas, 1695, and to the queen's bench, 1702. [xlvi. 244]

POWELL, JOHN (*fl.* 1770–1785), portrait-painter ; pupil and assistant of Sir Joshua Reynolds ; lived at Sir Joshua's house, and made reduced copies of many of his portraits. [xlvi. 245]

POWELL, JOHN (*fl.* 1796–1829), water-colour painter ; largely engaged as a teacher of painting in water-colours ; executed landscapes chiefly drawn from English scenery. [xlvi. 245]

POWELL, JOHN JOSEPH (1755 ?-1801), legal writer; practised as a conveyancer, and wrote on mortgages, contracts, and other legal subjects. [xlvi. 245]

POWELL, MARTIN (*fl.* 1709-1729), puppet showman: established (1710) his puppet-show in Covent Garden, London, where it became famous, and was frequently alluded to in the 'Tatler' and 'Spectator.' [xlvi. 245]

POWELL, NATHANIEL (*d.* 1622), navigator and colonist; settled in Virginia in 1607, when he made explorations and wrote, apparently, 'The Diarie of the Second Voyage in discovering the [Chesapeake] Bay,' 1608. [xlvi. 246]

POWELL, RICHARD (1767-1834), physician; of Pembroke and Merton Colleges, Oxford; M.A., 1791; M.D., 1795; physician to St. Bartholomew's Hospital, London, 1801-24; censor, R.C.P., 1798, 1807, 1820, and 1823; Lumleian lecturer, 1811-22; Harveian orator, 1808; one of the revisers of the 'Pharmacopœia Londinensis,' 1809. His medical writings were important. [xlvi. 246]

POWELL, ROBERT (*fl.* 1634-1652), legal writer; a solicitor in Gloucestershire; wrote on English legal antiquities. [xlvi. 247]

POWELL, THOMAS (1572 ?-1635 ?), attorney and author; solicitor-general in the marches of Wales, 1613-1622; published various works in poetry and prose, including 'A Welch Bayte to spare Prouender' (1603), a justification of Queen Elizabeth's treatment of papists and puritans, which was suppressed. [xlvi. 248]

POWELL, THOMAS (1766-1842 ?), musician; taught music in Dublin, Edinburgh, and London; a skilled artist on several instruments. His compositions are numerous. [xlvi. 249]

POWELL, VAVASOR (1617-1670), nonconformist divine; adopted the career of an itinerant evangelist in Wales, *c.* 1639, and on the outbreak of the civil war went to London; resumed his work in the principality, 1646, and created a band of missionary preachers, becoming known as the 'metropolitan of the itinerants'; drew up a protest against Cromwell's 'usurpation,' and by 1654 had joined the baptist section of independents, holding many Fifth-monarchy opinions; arrested at the Restoration, and on his refusal to abstain from preaching imprisoned, with some slight intervals, for the rest of his life. His use of travelling preachers anticipated, and probably suggested, George Fox's employment of the same agency. He published over twenty treatises. [xlvi. 249]

POWELL, WILLIAM (1735-1769), actor; made his first appearance on the stage at Drury Lane, London (1763) as Garrick's understudy, after being carefully coached by Garrick, who was anxious for foreign travel; made Garrick uneasy by the extent of his popularity; joined (1767) in the Covent Garden venture; the original Honeywood in the 'Good-natured Man,' 1768; his early death generally lamented. [xlvi. 253]

POWELL, WILLIAM SAMUEL (1717-1775), divine; fellow of St. John's College, Cambridge, 1740-63; M.A., 1742; D.D., 1757; left Cambridge, 1761, and took a house in London; master of St. John's College, Cambridge, 1765-75. [xlvi. 254]

POWER, HENRY (1623-1668), physician and naturalist; B.A. Christ's College, Cambridge, 1644; practised for a time as a physician at Halifax; F.R.S., 1663; published 'Experimental Philosophy,' 1664, and left a number of works in manuscript. [xlvi. 256]

POWER, JOSEPH (1798-1868), librarian of the university of Cambridge; fellow of Clare College, Cambridge, 1823, of Trinity Hall, Cambridge, 1829, and re-elected at Clare College, Cambridge, 1844; M.A. Clare College, Cambridge, 1824; librarian of the university, 1845-64; wrote on mathematical subjects. [xlvi. 256]

POWER, LIONEL (*fl.* 1450 ?), composer and writer on musical theory; author of extant compositions and a tract in the British Museum entitled 'Lionel Power of the Cordis of Musike.' [xlvi. 257]

POWER, SIR MANLEY (1773-1826), lieutenant-general; entered the army, 1783, and saw much active service between 1799 and 1802; took part in the Peninsular war from 1810, and (1813) was attached to the Portuguese army, commanding a brigade at Salamanca, Vittoria, Nivelle, and Orthes; K.C.B., 1815. [xlvi. 257]

POWER, MARGUERITE, afterwards COUNTESS OF BLESSINGTON (1789-1849). [See BLESSINGTON.]

POWER, MARGUERITE A. (1815 ?-1867), author; niece of Marguerite, countess of Blessington [q. v.]; wrote, besides other works, a poem entitled 'Virginia's Hand' (1860). [xlvi. 258]

POWER, RICHARD, first EARL OF TYRONE (1630-1690), was taken into Cromwell's 'special protection,' in consequence of his father, John, lord de la Power (*d.* 1661), having become insane; made governor of Waterford, 1661; created Earl of Tyrone, 1673; was charged with treason on unsubstantial evidence, 1679, and failed to gain his discharge till 1681; became a Roman catholic on the accession of James II; privy councillor, 1686; assisted in the defence of Cork against Marlborough, 1690, and after the capitulation was committed to the Tower of London, where he died. [xlvi. 258]

POWER, TYRONE (1797-1841), Irish comedian; joined a company of strolling players in his fourteenth year; obtained small engagements in the London theatres, 1821; succeeded Charles Connor [q. v.] as leading Irish comedian at Drury Lane, 1826; his last appearance in London at the Haymarket, 1840; went down in the President when returning from the United States. [xlvi. 260]

POWERSCOURT, VISCOUNT (*d.* 1634). [See WINGFIELD, SIR RICHARD.]

POWIS, titular DUKES OF. [See HERBERT, WILLIAM, first DUKE, 1617-1696; HERBERT, WILLIAM, second DUKE, *d.* 1745.]

POWIS, MARQUISES OF. [See HERBERT, WILLIAM, first MARQUIS, 1617-1696; HERBERT, WILLIAM, second MARQUIS, *d.* 1745.]

POWIS, second EARL OF. [See HERBERT, EDWARD, 1785-1848.]

POWIS, WILLIAM HENRY (1808-1836), wood-engraver; regarded as one of the best wood-engravers of his day. [xlvi. 261]

POWLE. [See also POWELL.]

POWLE, GEORGE (*fl.* 1764-1771), etcher and miniature-painter; pupil of Thomas Worlidge [q. v.], whose mode of etching he imitated. [xlvi. 261]

POWLE, HENRY (1630-1692), master of the rolls and speaker of the Convention parliament; of Christ Church, Oxford; barrister, Lincoln's Inn, 1654 (bencher, 1659); M.P., Cirencester, 1671 and 1679, East Grinstead, 1681, New Windsor, 1689; identified himself with the opponents of the court in Charles II's reign; advocated a Dutch alliance, 1677; led the attack on Danby, 1678; made a member of Temple's new composite privy council, but from the commencement of 1681 took little part in politics until the revolution; was immediately voted to the chair on the assemblage of the Convention parliament, and was William III's most trusted adviser while the parliament sat; made master of the rolls, 1690, on which he retired from parliament. His historical, legal, and antiquarian knowledge were highly esteemed. [xlvi. 262]

POWLETT. [See PAULET and POULETT.]

POWLETT, THOMAS ORDE-, first BARON BOLTON (1746-1807). [See ORDE.]

POWNALL, ROBERT (1520-1571), protestant divine; fled from England during Queen Mary's reign; and was afterwards rector of Harbledown (1562-71); published several treatises and translations from the French. [xlvi. 264]

POWNALL, THOMAS (1722-1805), known as 'Governor Pownall'; politician and antiquary; B.A. Trinity College, Cambridge, 1743; obtained a place in the office of the board of trade and plantations, *c.* 1744, and (*c.* 1753) was nominated lieutenant-governor of New Jersey, and in 1757 governor of Massachusetts; laboured zealously to drive the French from North America; commanded an expedition to the Penobscot River, 1759; transferred to South Carolina, 1759, his manners being unsuited to the gravity of the New England puritans; quitted America and resigned his post, 1760; published (1764) his famous work (6th ed. 1777) on 'The Administration of the Colonies,' in which he projected the union of all the American possessions in one dominion, and drew attention to the reluctance of colonists to be taxed without their own consent;

M.P., Tregony, 1767–74, Minehead, 1774–80; allied himself at first with the whigs, but supported Lord North when war broke out, insisting at the same time that England's sovereignty over the colonies was lost, and urging the government to treat. He was the author of twenty-five works on various subjects, chiefly political and economic. [xlvi. 264]

POWRIE-OGILVY, JOHN (*fl.* 1592–1601). [See OGILVY.]

POWYS, HORATIO (1805–1877), bishop of Sodor and Man; of Harrow and St. John's College, Cambridge; M.A., 1826; created D.D., 1854; consecrated, 1854; involved himself in much litigation on behalf of the rights of the see. [xlvi. 268]

POWYS, SIR LITTLETON (1648 ?–1732), judge; barrister, Lincoln's Inn, 1671; appointed a judge on the Chester circuit, 1689; serjeant and knighted, 1692; became a baron of the exchequer, 1695; transferred to the king's bench, 1700; retired, 1726. [xlvi. 269]

POWYS, SIR THOMAS (1649–1719), judge; brother of Sir Littleton Powys [q. v.]; barrister, Lincoln's Inn, 1673; solicitor-general and knighted, 1686; attorney-general, 1687; conducted the prosecution of the seven bishops, 1688, with much fairness; became a judge of the queen's bench, 1713 (removed, 1714). [xlvi. 269]

POWYS, THOMAS LITTLETON, fourth BARON LILFORD (1833–1896), ornithologist; educated at Harrow and Christ Church, Oxford; travelled abroad and made valuable ornithological collections; F.Z.S., 1852; F.L.S., 1862; one of the founders of the British Ornithologists' Union, 1858, and president from 1867; published 'Coloured Figures of Birds of British Islands,' 1885–97 (completed by Osbert Salvin [q. v.]), and various ornithological writings. [Suppl. iii. 284]

POYER, JOHN (*d.* 1649), royalist; mayor of Pembroke, 1642; became captain in the service of parliament; went over to Charles I's party in 1648, and raised an armed force; executed nine months after Cromwell's capture of Pembroke. [xlvi. 269]

POYNDER, JOHN (1779–1849), theological writer; for nearly forty years clerk and solicitor to the royal hospitals of Bridewell and Bethlehem, London; attacked the East India Company for encouraging idolatry, and obtained the abolition of the suttee and of the pilgrim tax. His works are numerous. [xlvi. 270]

POYNET, JOHN (1514 ?–1556). [See PONET.]

POYNINGS, SIR EDWARD (1459–1521), lord-deputy of Ireland; grandson of Robert de Poynings, fifth baron Poynings [q. v.]; a leader of the rising in Kent in 1483; planned to second Buckingham's insurrection against Richard III; escaped abroad and landed with Henry VII at Milford Haven; commanded an expedition sent to assist Maximilian in the reduction of Flanders, 1492; governor of Calais, 1493; sent to Ireland as deputy to the governor, Prince Henry, 1494; assembled a parliament (1494) which passed numerous important acts (repealed, 1782) restricting Irish independence, the most momentous of which was that (afterwards known as Poynings' law) providing that no act of parliament should be valid unless previously submitted to the English privy council, and another which enacted that all laws passed in England previous to 1494 should be valid in Ireland; compelled Perkin Warbeck, who invaded Ireland, 1495, to seek refuge in Scotland; succeeded in extirpating Yorkist cause in Ireland; was recalled, 1496, and some time before Henry VII's death became controller of the household and warden of the Cinque ports, offices which were continued to him in the next reign; K.G; negotiated a league of partition against France, 1513; took part in the capture of Térouenne and Tournai; took an important part in negotiations with the emperor Charles V. [xlvi. 271]

POYNINGS or **PONYNGS**, MICHAEL DE, second BARON POYNINGS (1317–1369), served in Flanders in 1339–40, in Scotland in 1341, and in France in 1345–6 and in 1355–6; summoned to parliament from 1342. [xlvi. 274]

POYNINGS, ROBERT DE, fifth BARON POYNINGS (1380–1446), grandson of Michael de Poynings, second baron Poynings [q. v.]; summoned to parliament, 1404; served in the French wars of Henry IV and Henry V. [xlvi. 274]

POYNINGS, THOMAS, BARON POYNINGS (*d.* 1545), illegitimate son of Sir Edward Poynings [q. v.]; took part in the French expedition of 1544, greatly distinguishing himself at the capture of Boulogne; created baron, 1545. [xlvi. 275]

POYNTER, AMBROSE (1796–1886), architect; set up as an architect in Westminster, 1821; foundation member of the R.I.B.A.; designed, besides other buildings, many government schools and several London churches. [xlvi. 275]

POYNTER, WILLIAM (1762–1827), Roman catholic prelate; prefect of studies at the English College at Douay; D.D. Douay; imprisoned by the French revolutionaries, 1793 and 1795; sent to England; became president of St. Edmund's College, near Ware, 1801; coadjutor bishop to John Douglass [q. v.], 1803; became vicar-apostolic of the London district, 1812. [xlvi. 276]

POYNTZ, SIR ANTHONY (1480 ?–1533), diplomatist; knighted, 1513; went on an embassy to Francis I, 1518; was present at the Field of the Cloth of Gold, 1520. [xlvi. 277]

POYNTZ, SIR FRANCIS (*d.* 1528), diplomatist; was sent as ambassador to Charles V, 1527; died of the plague. [xlvi. 277]

POYNTZ, JOHN (*fl.* 1658–1683), captain in the navy; fought for parliament in the civil war in Ireland and England; subsequently travelled in America; published a proposal (1683) for colonising Tobago. [xlvi. 281]

POYNTZ, ROBERT (*fl.* 1554–1566), Roman catholic writer; of Winchester College and New College, Oxford; was elected perpetual fellow of New College, 1554; M.A., 1560; settled in Louvain early in Queen Elizabeth's reign; published (1566) 'Testimonies for the Real Presence.' [xlvi. 278]

POYNTZ, SIR ROBERT (1589 ?–1665), royalist; descended from Sir Anthony Poyntz [q. v.]; of Brasenose College, Oxford; M.P., Gloucestershire, 1626 and 1628–9; knighted, 1627; published 'A Vindication of Monarchy,' 1661. [xlvi. 278]

POYNTZ, STEPHEN (1665–1750), diplomatist; fellow of King's College, Cambridge; M.A., 1711; envoy extraordinary to Sweden, 1724; governor to the Duke of Cumberland; privy councillor, 1735. [xlvi. 278]

POYNTZ, SYDENHAM (*fl.* 1645–1650), soldier; brother of John Poyntz [q. v.]; served in the Dutch and imperial armies, returning to England in 1645; became commander-in-chief of the northern association under parliament and governor of York, and gained the battle of Rowton Heath, 24 Sept. 1645; published (1646) a 'Vindication,' containing an account of his services; supposed by the presbyterians to be likely to oppose the new model, but in 1647 was sent by his soldiers a prisoner to Fairfax; fought for London against the army, 1647, and on the collapse of his cause fled to Holland; accompanied Lord Willoughby to the West Indies, 1650, and finally settled in Virginia. [xlvi. 280]

PRAED, WINTHROP MACKWORTH (1802–1839), poet; descended from Sir Humphry Mackworth [q. v.]; educated at Eton, where he founded the 'Etonian,' and at Trinity College, Cambridge; B.A., 1825; fellow, 1827; barrister, Middle Temple, 1829; conservative M.P. for St. Germans, 1830, Great Yarmouth, 1834, Aylesbury, 1837; appointed secretary to the board of control under Peel, 1834. The first collection of his poems appeared at New York in 1844, and an authorised edition by Derwent Coleridge [q. v.] was published in 1864. His prose essays were collected in a volume of Henry Morley's 'Universal Library' in 1887. [xlvi. 281]

PRANCE, MILES (*fl.* 1678–1689), perjurer; Roman catholic goldsmith of Covent Garden, London; arrested (1678) on suspicion of the murder of Sir Edmund Berry Godfrey [q. v.] and committed to Newgate; endeavoured to procure his release by a fabricated account of Godfrey's death, but his falsehood being detected was sent back to prison; procured his liberty and the death of three innocent men by a new story; subsequently gave evidence in support of Oates and Bedloe, was convicted of perjury (1686) and afterwards went abroad. [xlvi. 283]

PRATT, ANNE, afterwards MRS. PEARLESS (1806–1893), botanist; married John Pearless, 1866; published popular but useful botanical works, including 'The Flowering Plants and Ferns of Great Britain' (5 vols. 1855). [xlvi. 284]

PRATT, Sir CHARLES, first EARL CAMDEN and first BARON CAMDEN (1714–1794), lord chancellor; son of Sir John Pratt [q. v.]; educated at Eton and King's College, Cambridge; fellow, 1734; M.A., 1740; barrister, Middle Temple, 1738; failed at first, but eventually succeeded in gaining a reputation at the bar; became attorney-general under Pitt, 1757, and sat in parliament as whig M.P. for Downton; appointed chief-justice of the court of common pleas, 1761; knighted, 1761; decided in the case of John Wilkes (1763) that general warrants were illegal; became almost as great a popular idol as Wilkes himself and (1765) was created baron; opposed in the House of Lords the taxation of the American colonies, and declared the Stamp Act unconstitutional; became lord chancellor in Chatham's administration, 1766; although opposed to the American policy of the ministry, retained the great seal until it was taken from him, January 1770; threw himself into opposition until the death of Chatham, when he lost heart and (1781) withdrew from public life; entered the Rockingham ministry as president of the council, 1782, resigning during the negotiations for the formation of the coalition ministry in March 1783; resumed the presidency of the council, 1784, retaining it till his death; created Earl Camden, 1786. [xlvi. 285]

PRATT, Sir CHARLES (1768–1838), lieutenant-general; entered the army, 1794; served in the Peninsular war, 1812–14; K.C.B., 1830; lieutenant-general, 1834. [xlvi. 288]

PRATT, Sir JOHN (1657–1725), judge; of Magdalen Hall and Wadham College, Oxford; fellow of Wadham College, Oxford, 1678; M.A., 1679; barrister, Inner Temple, 1682; made a judge of the court of king's bench, 1714; M.P., Midhurst, 1711–15; knighted, 1714; became lord chief-justice, 1718. [xlvi. 288]

PRATT, JOHN (1772–1855), organist; became organist at King's College, Cambridge, and to Cambridge University, 1799; organist at Peterhouse, Cambridge, 1813; occupied himself with publications for the choirs of college chapels, and published (1810) a 'Psalmody,' which was widely used. [xlvi. 289]

PRATT, JOHN BURNETT (1799–1869), Scottish divine and antiquary; M.A. Aberdeen (hon. LL.D., 1865); minister of the Scottish episcopal church at Cruden, 1825–69; author of several publications on local antiquities and other topics. [xlvi. 290]

PRATT, JOHN HENRY (d. 1871), mathematician; son of Josiah Pratt [q. v.]; M.A. and fellow, Caius College, Cambridge, 1836; wrote several mathematical treatises. [xlvi. 294]

PRATT, Sir JOHN JEFFREYS, second EARL and first MARQUIS OF CAMDEN (1759–1840), only son of Sir Charles Pratt, first earl of Camden [q. v.]; M.A. Trinity College, Cambridge, 1779; M.P., Bath, 1780–94; lord of the admiralty (July 1782 to April 1783, and December 1783 to July 1788); a lord of the treasury, 1789–94; appointed lord-lieutenant of Ireland, 1794; unpopular with the Irish, who saw in his appointment the frustration of all remedial legislature; shared with the English cabinet the responsibility for the policy which terminated in the rebellion of 1798; placed Ulster under martial law (March 1797), but on the outbreak of the rebellion (May 1798) maintained a merely defensive attitude, and implored to be superseded by a military man, on which Lord Cornwallis was sent; secretary of war, 1804–5; president of the council, 1805–6 and 1807–12; created Marquis of Camden, 1812. [xlvi. 290]

PRATT, JOHN TIDD (1797–1870), registrar of friendly societies; barrister, Inner Temple, 1824; barrister to the commissioners for the reduction of the national debt, 1828–70; registrar of friendly societies, 1846–70; published legal works. [xlvi. 292]

PRATT, JOSIAH (1768–1844), evangelical divine; B.A. St. Edmund Hall, Oxford, 1792; secretary to the Church Missionary Society, 1802–24, devoting all his energies to the institution, and displaying great tact and business capacity; helped to form the British and Foreign Bible Society, 1804; became vicar of St. Stephen's, Coleman Street, London, in 1826; edited Bishop Hall's works, 1808. [xlvi. 293]

PRATT, Sir ROGER (1620–1684), architect; of Magdalen College, Oxford; student, Inner Temple, 1640; took a considerable part in designing and rebuilding London after the great fire of 1666; knighted, 1668. [xlvi. 295]

PRATT or **PRAT**, SAMUEL (1659?–1723), dean of Rochester; educated at Merchant Taylors' School, London; D.D. per literas regias, 1697; published, among other works, treatise on the problem of restoring the currency, 1696. [xlvi. 295]

PRATT, SAMUEL JACKSON (1749–1814), miscellaneous writer, mainly under the pseudonym of COURTNEY MELMOTH; was ordained in the English church, but soon abandoned the clerical profession, and appeared in 1773 on the stage at Dublin under the name of Courtney Melmoth; failed as an actor; adopted literature as a profession, 1774; traded in Bath for some years as a bookseller; several of his plays produced at Drury Lane, London; published miscellaneous works in prose and verse. [xlvi. 295]

PRATT, Sir THOMAS SIMSON (1797–1879), commander of the forces in Australia; educated at St. Andrews; entered the army, 1814; in command in Australia (1856–61), with the rank of major-general; conducted the war against the Maoris, 1860–1; K.C.B., 1861; general, 1873; retired from active service, 1877. [xlvi. 298]

PRATTEN, ROBERT SIDNEY (1824–1868), flautist; made his début at Clifton in 1835; went to London in 1846, and attained the front rank in his art. [xlvi. 298]

PRENCE, THOMAS (1600–1673), governor of Massachusetts; emigrated to New Plymouth, and (1634) was elected governor; resigned, 1635; did good service against the Pequot Indians, 1637; was a second time governor, 1638, and for a third time, 1657–73. [xlvi. 298]

PRENDERGAST, JOHN PATRICK (1808–1893), historian; B.A. Trinity College, Dublin, 1825; called to the Irish bar, 1830. He published 'The History of the Cromwellian Settlement of Ireland,' 1863, and other treatises. [xlvi. 299]

PRENDERGAST or **PENDERGRASS**, Sir THOMAS, first baronet (1660?–1709), soldier and Jacobite; gave information to government of the plot to assassinate William III at Turnham Green in February 1696, and gave evidence against the conspirators; created baronet, 1699; entered the army, and (1709) was promoted brigadier-general; mortally wounded at Malplaquet. [xlvi. 300]

PRENDERGAST, THOMAS (1806–1886), inventor of the 'mastery' system of learning languages; entered the East India Company's service, 1826, and retired, 1859. His system of learning languages, which was in some respects a development of the Ollendorffian, had considerable success. He published several handbooks on it, which went through numerous editions. [xlvi. 301]

PRENTICE, ARCHIBALD (1792–1857), journalist; helped to found the 'Manchester Gazette' in 1821, as the organ of radical opinion, which was incorporated (1828) with the 'Manchester Times' (sole manager of the new paper, 1828); obtained the transfer of the centre of anti-cornlaw agitation from London to Manchester, 1836, and (1838) assisted in forming the Anti-Cornlaw League; devoted his paper solely to the interests of free trade; compelled to relinquish his post in 1847 after the establishment (1845) of a rival radical journal, the 'Manchester Examiner,' which was started in the manufacturing interest, and proved a serious blow to the 'Times.' [xlvi. 301]

PRENTIS, EDWARD (1797–1854), painter; portrayed scenes from domestic life; exhibited (1823–50) chiefly at the Society of British Artists. [xlvi. 303]

PRENTIS, STEPHEN (1801–1862), poet; M.A. Christ's College, Cambridge, 1830; author of numerous short poems printed for private circulation. [xlvi. 303]

PRESCOTT, Sir HENRY (1783–1874), admiral; grandson of Richard Walter [q. v.]; entered the navy, 1796; promoted to post rank (1810) for gallantry while in command of the boat attack at Amantea; governor of Newfoundland, 1834–41; admiral, 1860; G.C.B., 1869. [xlvi. 303]

PRESCOTT, ROBERT (1725–1816), general; served at Rochefort, 1757, at Louisburg, 1758, at Martinique, 1761, and in several actions in the American war of independence; reduced Martinique and was appointed civil governor, 1794; governor of Canada, 1796–9; general, 1798. [xlvi. 304]

PRESTON, first VISCOUNT (1648–1695). [See GRAHAM, SIR RICHARD.]

PRESTON, SIR AMYAS DE (d. 1617?), naval commander; took part in an expedition to the Spanish main, 1595; knighted, 1596; took part in the Islands voyage, 1597; keeper of stores and ordnance at the Tower of London, 1603–17. [xlvi. 305]

PRESTON, GEORGE (1659?–1748), governor of Edinburgh Castle; was a captain in the service of the States-General in 1688, and accompanied William of Orange to England; colonel of the Cameronian regiment, 1706–20; made governor of Edinburgh Castle and commander-in-chief of the forces in Scotland on the outbreak of the rebellion of 1715; superseded by General Joshua Guest [q. v.], 1745, but is said to have prevented Guest from surrendering to the Jacobites. [xlvi. 305]

PRESTON, GILBERT DE (d. 1274), chief-justice of the court of common pleas; son of Walter de Preston [q. v.]; justice itinerant, 1240; appointed to the common pleas, 1242, retaining the post till his death; first to hold the title of chief-justice of the court of common pleas. [xlvi. 306]

PRESTON, SIR JOHN (fl. 1394–1428), judge; was recorder of London, 1406–15; a justice of common pleas, 1415–28. [xlvi. 306]

PRESTON, SIR JOHN, LORD FENTONBARNS (d. 1616), Scottish judge; appointed an ordinary judge of the court of session, 1595; became president, 1609; one of the new Octavians, 1611. [xlvi. 307]

PRESTON, JOHN (1587–1628), puritan divine; fellow of Queens' College, Cambridge, 1609; M.A., 1611; commenced, on becoming dean of Queens' College, Cambridge, a course of sermons, which drew large crowds; his appointment as chaplain in ordinary to Prince Charles (c. 1620) due to the influence of Buckingham, who desired to conciliate the puritans; became preacher at Lincoln's Inn, 1622, and master of Emmanuel College, Cambridge, 1622–8; D.D. by royal mandate, 1623; exerted all his influence on behalf of the puritans after the accession of Charles I, but found his plans counteracted by Laud, and failed to accomplish anything considerable. [xlvi. 308]

PRESTON, RICHARD (1768–1850), legal author; began life as an attorney, but was called to the bar at the Inner Temple, 1807 (bencher, 1834); K.C., 1834; conservative M.P., Ashburton, 1812–18; supported the corn duties; published an admirable 'Treatise on Conveyancing' (1806–9) and other works. [xlvi. 312]

PRESTON, SIR SIMON (fl. 1538–1570), provost of Edinburgh; provost, 1538–43 and 1544–5; one of the most trusted friends of Mary Queen of Scots after her arrival in Scotland; again made provost by her orders, 1565, becoming also a member of the privy council; by his hostile attitude compelled Moray to evacuate Edinburgh in September, 1565; abandoned the cause of Mary Queen of Scots after her marriage to Bothwell. [xlvi. 312]

PRESTON, THOMAS (1537–1598), master of Trinity Hall, Cambridge, and dramatist; fellow of King's College, Cambridge, 1556; M.A., 1561; LL.D., 1576; master of Trinity Hall, Cambridge, 1584–98; vice-chancellor of Cambridge University, 1589–90; wrote 'A Lamentable Tragedy mixed full of Mirth conteyning the Life of Cambises, King of Percia' (1569), which illustrates the transition from the morality play to historical drama. The bombastic grandiloquence of the piece became proverbial. [xlvi. 314]

PRESTON, THOMAS, first VISCOUNT TARA (1585–1655), son of the fourth Viscount Gormanston; educated in the Spanish Netherlands, where he took service with the archdukes; returned to Ireland and joined the rebellion, 1642; totally defeated by Ormonde near New Ross, 1643; captured Duncannon fort, 1645, and Roscommon, 1646; injured the Roman catholic cause by his persistent quarrels with Owen Roe O'Neill [q. v.] and with the papal nuncio; his army was almost annihilated by Michael Jones [q. v.] at Dangan Hill, 1647; allied himself with Ormonde and the royalists, 1648, and (1650) defended Waterford against Ireton; created Viscount Tara,

1650; escaped to the continent, 1652; exempted from pardon in the Cromwellian Act of Settlement. [xlvi. 314]

PRESTON, WALTER DE (d. 1230), sheriff of Northamptonshire, 1207 and 1208; also known as Walter Fitz Winemar; took part with the barons against King John. [xlvi. 306]

PRESTON, WILLIAM (1753–1807), poet and dramatist; M.A. Trinity College, Dublin, 1773; called to the Irish bar, 1777; wrote occasional poems for periodicals and several tragedies, of which the most successful, 'Democratic Rage,' was produced at Dublin in 1793. [xlvi. 318]

PRESTON, WILLIAM (1742–1818), printer and writer on freemasonry; became partner in Andrew Strahan's business, 1804, and published 'Illustrations of Masonry,' 1772. The first edition, which differs from all subsequent issues, was reprinted in 1887. [xlvi. 319]

PRESTONGRANGE, LORD (1701?–1764). [See GRANT, WILLIAM.]

PRESTWICH, JOHN, called SIR JOHN (d. 1795), antiquary; chiefly known by his heraldic work, 'Prestwich's Respublica,' 1787. [xlvi. 319]

PRESTWICH, SIR JOSEPH (1812–1896), geologist; studied science and chemistry at University College, London; entered his father's business of wine merchant in London; established reputation as geologist by two papers read to Geological Society of London on coalfield of Coalbrookdale, Shropshire; published work on water-bearing strata round London, 1851; on water commission, 1862; professor of geology at Oxford, 1874–88; M.A. and member of Christ Church, Oxford, 1874; D.C.L., 1888; knighted, 1896; fellow of Geological Society, 1833, and Wollaston medallist, 1849; F.R.S., 1853, and royal medallist, 1865. As a geologist his chief strength lay in stratigraphy, and he accepted on the whole the uniformitarian view. His writings include 'Geology, Chemical, Physical, and Stratigraphical,' 1886–8, ' The Tradition of the Flood,' 1895, and numerous pamphlets, reports, and contributions to scientific periodicals. [Suppl. iii. 284]

PRETYMAN, SIR GEORGE (1750–1827). [See TOMLINE.]

PREVOST, SIR GEORGE, first baronet (1767–1816), soldier and governor-general of Canada; nominated military governor of St. Lucia, 1798, and civil governor, 1801; appointed governor-in-chief in Dominica, 1802; created baronet, 1805; appointed lieutenant-governor in Nova Scotia, 1808; chosen governor of Lower Canada and governor-general of British North America, 1811; intervened, unfortunately for his reputation, in the military operations during the campaigns of 1812–14; left Canada to meet the charges against his conduct in the field, but died in London before the meeting of the court-martial. [xlvi. 320]

PREVOST, SIR GEORGE, second baronet (1804–1893), tractarian; only son of Sir George Prevost [q. v.]; M.A. Oriel College, Oxford, 1827; a pupil and disciple of John Keble [q. v.]; became perpetual curate of Stinchcombe (1834–93), archdeacon of Gloucester, 1865–81, and honorary canon of Gloucester, 1859–93; translated Chrysostom's homilies on St. Matthew for Pusey's 'Library of the Fathers,' 1843. [xlvi. 321]

PRÉVOST, LOUIS AUGUSTIN (1796–1858), linguist; born at Troyes; came to England, 1823; became acquainted with upwards of forty languages, and was employed (1843–55) in cataloguing the Chinese books at the British Museum. [xlvi. 322]

PRICE. [See also PRYCE.]

PRICE, ARTHUR (d. 1752), archbishop of Cashel; B.A. Trinity College, Dublin, 1700; D.D., 1724; consecrated bishop of Clonfert, 1724, and translated to Ferns and Leighlin, 1730, and to Meath, 1734; archbishop of Cashel, 1744–52; abandoned the old cathedral of Cashel. [xlvi. 322]

PRICE, BARTHOLOMEW (1818–1898), master of Pembroke College, Oxford; B.A. Pembroke College, Oxford, 1840; M.A., 1843; fellow of Pembroke College, Oxford, 1844; tutor and mathematical lecturer, 1845; proctor, 1858; F.R.S., 1852; F.R.A.S., 1856; Sedleian professor of natural philosophy at Oxford, 1853–98; as secretary of the Clarendon Press (1868–84) greatly improved its position and organisation; master of Pembroke College, 1891–8;

published 'Treatise on Infinitesimal Calculus' (4 vols.), 1852–60. [Suppl. iii. 287]

PRICE, BONAMY (1807–1888), economist; M.A. Worcester College, Oxford, 1832; became mathematical master at Rugby in 1832, resigning in 1850; Drummond professor of political economy at Oxford, 1868–88; wrote chiefly on currency and banking. [xlvi. 322]

PRICE, SIR CARBERY (d. 1695). [See PRYSE.]

PRICE, SIR CHARLES, first baronet (1708–1772), speaker of the house of assembly of Jamaica; born in Jamaica; studied at Trinity College, Oxford; elected to the assembly, 1732, and chosen speaker, 1745, holding office till 1763; created baronet, 1768. [xlvi. 323]

PRICE, SIR CHARLES, second baronet (1732–1788), speaker of the house of assembly in Jamaica; son of Sir Charles Price, first baronet [q. v.]; of Trinity College, Oxford; elected to the house of assembly, 1753; speaker in succession to his father, 1763–75. [xlvi. 324]

PRICE, DANIEL (1581–1631), divine; of St. Mary Hall and Exeter College, Oxford; M.A., 1604; joined the Middle Temple, 1609; D.D., 1613; chaplain to James I; published sermons. [xlvi. 324]

PRICE, DAVID (1762–1835), orientalist; for a time at Jesus College, Cambridge; enlisted in the East India Company's service; became major, 1804; retired, 1807; devoted himself to oriental studies, writing long, leisurely works on Arabian, Persian, and Indian history, the best known being the 'Chronological Retrospect . . . of Mahommedan History,' 1811–21, which is still for some branches of eastern history almost the only English work of reference. [xlvi. 325]

PRICE, DAVID (1790–1854), rear-admiral; entered the navy, 1801; commander-in-chief in the Pacific, 1853; committed suicide while about to attack the Russian port of Petropaulovski on 30 Aug. 1854. [xlvi. 326]

PRICE, EDMUND (1541?–1624). [See PRYS.]

PRICE, ELLEN (1814–1887). [See WOOD, ELLEN.]

PRICE, ELLIS (1505?–1599), Welsh administrator; LL.B. St. Nicholas's Hostel, Cambridge, 1533; D.C.L., 1534; became commissary-general of the diocese of St. Asaph, 1538; devoted himself mainly to civil administration, repeatedly acting as sheriff for various counties during the reigns of Mary and Elizabeth. [xlvi. 326]

PRICE, FRANCIS (d. 1753), architect; became surveyor to Salisbury Cathedral and clerk of the works to the dean and chapter, 1734; published 'The British Carpenter,' 1735 (4th ed. 1759), long the best text-book on carpentry. [xlvi. 327]

PRICE, HUGH (1495?–1574), founder of Jesus College, Oxford; B.C.L. Oxford, 1512; D.Can.L., 1526; prebendary of Rochester, 1541–74; treasurer of St. David's, 1571–4. Jesus College, Oxford, was established in 1571 on his petition. [xlvi. 328]

PRICE, JAMES (1752–1783), chemist; son of James Higginbotham; M.A. Magdalen Hall, Oxford, 1777; changed his name to Price, 1781; professed (1782) to be able to convert mercury into gold and silver, but in 1783 failed to repeat his experiments and committed suicide. [xlvi. 328]

PRICE, AP RICE, or AP RHYS, SIR JOHN (d. 1573?), visitor of the monasteries; acted with Sir Thomas Legh [q. v.] as a visitor of the greater monasteries, 1535; author of three historical treatises. [xlvi. 329]

PRICE (PRICÆUS), JOHN (1600–1676?), scholar; student of Christ Church, Oxford, 1617; made his mark in 1635 by an edition of the 'Apologia' of Apuleius, published at Paris; professor of Greek at Pisa; passed the greater part of his life on the continent and settled in Florence, 1652. [xlvi. 330]

PRICE, JOHN (1625?–1691), royalist; of Eton and King's College, Cambridge (fellow); M.A., 1653 (incorporated at Oxford, 1680); D.D. per literas regias, 1661; attended Monck as chaplain from 1654 to 1659, and was his confidant in the enterprise of the Restoration; his loyalty rewarded with several church preferments. [xlvi. 331]

PRICE, JOHN (d. 1736), architect; executed several buildings in London and the neighbourhood. [xlvi. 332]

PRICE, JOHN (1773–1801), topographer; published works on Leominster (1795), Hereford (1796), Ludlow (1797), and Worcester (1799). [xlvi. 332]

PRICE, JOHN (1734–1813), Bodley's librarian; M.A. Jesus College, Oxford, 1760; B.D., 1768; janitor of the Bodleian, 1757, sub-librarian, 1761, acting librarian, 1765, and Bodley's librarian, 1768, filling the last office for forty-five years. [xlvi. 332]

PRICE, JOSHUA (fl. 1715–1717), glass-painter; brother of William Price the elder (d. 1722) [q. v.], with whom he worked at Oxford. [xlvi. 343]

PRICE, LAURENCE (fl. 1625–1680?), writer of ballads and political squibs; compiled, between 1625 and 1680, numerous ballads, pamphlets, and broadsides in verse on political or social subjects. [xlvi. 333]

PRICE, OWEN (d. 1671), schoolmaster and author; of Jesus College, Oxford; head-master of Magdalen College School, Oxford, 1657 (ejected at Restoration); subsequently taught in Devonshire and near Abingdon; published two works on orthography. [xlvi. 333]

PRICE, RICHARD (1723–1791), nonconformist minister and writer on morals, politics, and economics; officiated in various dissenting congregations; published (1756) his best-known work, a 'Review of the Principal Questions in Morals' (professedly directed against Hutcheson); subsequently became known as a writer on financial and political questions, advocating the reduction of the national debt, 1771, and attacking the justice and policy of the American war, 1776; the intimate friend of Franklin and (1778) invited by congress to transfer himself to America; denounced by Burke for his approbation of the French revolution. [xlvi. 334]

PRICE, RICHARD (1790–1833), philologist and antiquary; barrister, Middle Temple, 1830; practised as a barrister and assisted Henry Petrie [q. v.] in his edition of the 'Saxon Chronicle.' [xlvi. 337]

PRICE, ROBERT (1655–1733), judge; of St. John's College, Cambridge; barrister, Lincoln's Inn, 1679; tory M.P. for Weobley, 1685–7, 1690–1700, and 1701–2; made a baron of the exchequer, 1702. [xlvi. 337]

PRICE, SAMPSON (1585–1630), divine; brother of Daniel Price [q. v.]; of Hart Hall and Exeter College, Oxford; M.A. Hart Hall, 1608; D.D. Exeter College, Oxford, 1617; became a noted preacher in Oxford and chaplain in ordinary to James I and Charles I. [xlvi. 324]

PRICE, THEODORE (1570?–1631), prebendary of Westminster; M.A. All Souls College, Oxford, 1591; fellow of Jesus College, Oxford; D.D. New College, Oxford, 1614; held many ecclesiastical preferments through the favour of Williams and Laud; denounced by Prynne as 'an unpreaching epicure and an Arminian.' [xlvi. 338]

PRICE or PRYS, THOMAS (fl. 1586–1632), captain and Welsh poet; eldest son of Ellis Price [q. v.]; though 'a gentleman of plentiful fortune,' followed a seafaring life for many years. His literary works in prose and verse are in manuscript in the British Museum. [xlvi. 339]

PRICE, THOMAS (1599–1685), archbishop of Cashel; fellow of Trinity College, Dublin, 1626; M.A., 1628; bishop of Kildare, 1660–7, of Cashel, 1667–85. [xlvi. 340]

PRICE, THOMAS (1787–1848), Welsh historian; best known as 'Carnhuanawc,' became vicar of Llanfihangel Cwmdu, 1825; commenced the great work of his life (1836), 'Hanes Cymru,' a compilation of Welsh history in Welsh, and for many years the most trustworthy history of Wales, which appeared in fourteen parts, and was completed in 1842. [xlvi. 340]

PRICE, SIR UVEDALE, first baronet (1747–1829), writer on 'the picturesque'; of Eton and Christ Church, Oxford; came into a considerable fortune on his father's death in 1761; developed his views on garden landscape in 'An Essay on the Picturesque,' 1794, in which he argued in favour of natural beauty; 'converted the age to his views,' according to Scott, who studied the work; created baronet, 1828; resided at Foxley in Herefordshire, and laid out his estate in accordance with his principles. [xlvi. 341]

PRICE, WILLIAM (1597–1646), divine; M.A. Christ Church, Oxford, 1619; B.D., 1628; first reader in moral philosophy at Oxford on Thomas White's foundation, 1621–1629; rector of Dolgelly, 1631–46. [xlvi. 342]

PRICE, WILLIAM (*d.* 1666), divine; one of the Westminster divines; pastor of the presbyterian church at Amsterdam, 1648-66. [xlvi. 342]

PRICE, WILLIAM, the elder (*d.* 1722), glass-painter; executed some work at Oxford, including (1700) the great east window of Merton Chapel. [xlvi. 343]

PRICE, WILLIAM, the younger (*d.* 1765), glass-painter; son of Joshua Price [q. v.]; filled several windows in Westminster Abbey, at Winchester College, and at New College, Oxford. [xlvi. 343]

PRICE, WILLIAM (1780-1830), orientalist; served in India as an interpreter; on his return to England devoted himself to literary pursuits; published several Persian translations and other works. [xlvi. 343]

PRICHARD, **RICHARDS**, or **RHISIART**, EVAN (1770-1832), Welsh poet; usually called IEUAN LLEYN; successively excise officer and schoolmaster; a versatile writer in all forms of Welsh verse. [xlvi. 344]

PRICHARD, JAMES COWLES (1786-1848), physician and ethnologist; studied at St. Thomas's Hospital, London; M.D. Edinburgh, 1808; possessed great knowledge of modern Greek and Spanish; began to practise medicine at Bristol, 1810; published 'Researches as to the Physical History of Man,' the fruit of his studies in ethnology, 1813, and 'Treatise on Insanity and other Disorders affecting the Mind,' 1835 (long the standard work on this branch of medicine), developing in it his theory of 'moral insanity' apart from serious intellectual derangement; M.D. by diploma, Oxford, 1835; in his 'Natural History of Man,' 1843, sustained the opinion that the races of man are varieties of one species; made a commissioner of lunacy, 1845; F.R.S. [xlvi. 344]

PRICHARD, RHYS or RICE (1579-1644), Welsh religious poet; M.A. Jesus College, Oxford, 1626; became vicar of Llandingad, 1602, prebendary of Brecon, 1614, and chancellor of St. David's, 1626. The last edition of his poems, none of which were published till after his death, appeared in 1867. [xlvi. 346]

PRICKE, ROBERT (*fl.* 1669-1698), engraver; kept a shop at Cripplegate, London; published architectural works, mostly translated from the French. [xlvi. 347]

PRICKET, ROBERT (*fl.* 1603-1645), poet; saw some military service, and afterwards worked as a verse-writer and pamphleteer; took holy orders (*c.* 1606) and obtained some preferment in Ireland, whence he was driven by the rebellion of 1641. [xlvi. 347]

PRIDDEN, JOHN (1758-1825), antiquary; of St. Paul's School, London, and Queen's College, Oxford; B.A., 1781; held a number of small ecclesiastical preferments at various times; was at once an antiquary, an amateur artist, an architect, and a philanthropist; F.S.A., 1785. [xlvi. 348]

PRIDE, THOMAS (*d.* 1658), soldier; entered the parliamentary army as captain, and commanded Harley's regiment at Naseby, 1645; active on behalf of the army against parliament, and in 1648, in order to frustrate the intended agreement with Charles I, prevented about 130 members from entering the House of Commons ('Pride's Purge'); a commissioner for the trial of Charles I, signing the death-warrant, 1649; commanded a brigade at Dunbar, 1650; fought at Worcester, 1651; opposed Cromwell's appointment as king, but accepted a seat in his upper house. [xlvi. 349]

PRIDEAUX, SIR EDMOND (*d.* 1659), lawyer and politician; M.A. Cambridge (incorporated at Oxford, 1625); barrister, Inner Temple, 1623, and was returned as M.P. for Lyme Regis to the Long parliament, when he opposed Charles I; solicitor-general, 1648-9; attorney-general, 1649-59; made important reforms in the postal service, with which he was connected for many years. [xlvi. 350]

PRIDEAUX, FREDERICK (1817-1891), conveyancer; barrister, Lincoln's Inn, 1840; author of the standard treatise, 'Precedents in Conveyancing,' 1852 (16th edit. 1895), and other works. [xlvi. 351]

PRIDEAUX, HUMPHREY (1648-1724), orientalist; of Westminster School and Christ Church, Oxford; M.A., 1675; D.D., 1686; became a canon of Norwich, 1681, archdeacon of Suffolk, 1688, dean of Norwich, 1702-1724. His literary reputation rests on his 'Life of Mahomet' (1697), written as a polemical tract against the deists, and worthless as a biography, and on his 'Old and New Testament connected, in the History of the Jews and Neighbouring Nations' (1716-18), a work of great value in the author's day. [xlvi. 352]

PRIDEAUX, JOHN (1578-1650), bishop of Worcester; fellow of Exeter College, Oxford, 1601; M.A., 1603; D.D., 1612; rector of Exeter College, Oxford, 1612-42; regius professor of divinity, 1615-41; vice-chancellor of Oxford University, 1619-21, 1624-6, and 1641-3; bishop of Worcester, 1641; maintained himself in his see until the end of the war, when he took refuge with his son-in-law, Henry Sutton, rector of Bredon; published logical and theological works, the latter showing a dislike of Arminianism. [xlvi. 354]

PRIDEAUX, JOHN (1718-1759), brigadier-general; entered the army, 1739; colonel, 55th foot, 1758; killed in Canada while conducting the siege of Fort Niagara, an outpost of the French. [xlvi. 356]

PRIDEAUX, MATTHIAS (1622-1646 ?), royalist; son of John Prideaux (1578-1650) [q. v.]; fellow of Exeter College, Oxford, 1641; M.A., 1645; obtained the rank of captain in Charles I's service. [xlvi 356]

PRIESTLEY, JOSEPH (1733-1804), theologian and man of science; eldest child of Jonas Priestley, a Yorkshire cloth-dresser; adopted by his father's sister, Sarah Keighley, a strong Calvinist; educated at Batley grammar school and at Heckmondwike, and (1751) entered Daventry academy under Caleb Ashworth [q. v.] to study for the presbyterian ministry; engaged (1755) as assistant and successor to John Meadows (1676-1757) [q. v.], presbyterian minister at Needham Market; after a little time rejected the atonement, the inspiration of the sacred text, and other doctrines; became minister at Nantwich, 1758, and (1761) tutor in languages and belles-lettres at Warrington academy; hon. LL.D. Edinburgh, 1764; F.R.S., 1766; became minister of Mill Hill Chapel, Leeds, 1767; published 'An Essay on Government,' 1768, containing the sentence to which Jeremy Bentham [q. v.] considered himself indebted for the phrase 'the greatest happiness of the greatest number'; librarian or literary companion of the Earl of Shelburne, 1772-80; published his 'Examination of Scottish Philosophy,' his first effort in psychology, 1774; began to enunciate (1775) his doctrine of the homogeneity of man, which brought on him the imputation of atheism; elected an associate of the French Academy of Sciences soon after 1772, member of the Imperial Academy of Sciences at St. Petersburg, 1780; elected junior minister of the New Meeting, Birmingham, 1780; published (1782) the best known, though not the best, of his theological writings, his 'History of the Corruptions of Christianity,' which was burned by the common hangman at Dort in 1785; ultimately rejected the doctrine of the infallibility of Christ, publishing his 'History of Early Opinions concerning Jesus Christ,' 1786; involved in a controversy with Samuel Horsley [q. v.], which lasted till 1790; produced (1790) the first instalment of his 'General History of the Christian Church'; intended (July 1791) to be present at a dinner of the 'Constitutional Society' of Birmingham to commemorate the fall of the Bastille; his house at Fairhill wrecked, and nearly all his books, papers, and apparatus destroyed in consequence by the crowd, which had assembled to molest the guests; received insufficient compensation; resolved to settle in London, and in November 1791 was elected morning preacher at the Gravel Pit, Hackney; found that his opinions rendered life in England uncomfortable, and emigrated to New York, 1794; settled at Northumberland, Pennsylvania, where he died; adopted in America a doctrine of 'universal restitution.' He is most generally remembered as a man of science, and chiefly as a chemist, the 'discoverer' of oxygen. In his 'History of Electricity' (1767) he anticipated the suggestion that the law of electric attraction is that of the inverse square, and explained the formation of rings (since known as Priestley's rings) when a discharge takes place on a metallic surface. He also attacked the problem of conduction, studied gases, and by the use of mercury in the pneumatic trough was able to deal for the first time with gases soluble in water. In 1774 he obtained what he termed 'dephlogisticated air,' afterwards named oxygen by Lavoisier, a discovery which was the germ of the modern science of chemistry, but owing to his blind faith in the phlogistic theory, its significance was lost on him. Cuvier has styled him a 'father of modern chemistry

. . . who never would acknowledge his daughter.' His 'Theological and Miscellaneous Works' were edited in twenty-six volumes (1817-32) by John Towil Rutt [q. v.] His scientific works and memoirs are numerous, but have never been collected. [xlvi. 357]

PRIESTLEY, TIMOTHY (1734-1814), independent minister; younger brother of Joseph Priestley [q. v.]; pastor at Kipping, Yorkshire, 1760-6, at Hunter's Croft, Manchester, 1766-84, at Dublin, 1784-6, and at Jewin Street, London, 1786-1814; published religious works.
[xlvi. 376]

PRIESTLEY, SIR WILLIAM OVEREND (1829-1900), physician; great nephew of Joseph Priestley [q. v.]; educated at King's College, London, Paris, and Edinburgh University; M.R.C.S. England, 1852; M.D. Edinburgh, 1853; lecturer on midwifery at Middlesex Hospital, 1858; F.R.C.S. Edinburgh, 1858; professor of obstetric medicine, King's College, London, and obstetric physician to King's College Hospital, London, 1862-72; F.R.C.P. London, 1864; Lumleian lecturer, 1887, and censor, 1891-2; knighted, 1893; conservative M.P. for universities of Edinburgh and St. Andrews, 1896; published medical works.
[Suppl. iii. 287]

PRIESTMAN, JOHN (1805-1866), quaker; entered business as a corn-miller, but commenced as a manufacturer of worsted goods; was active in philanthropic enterprise, his treatment of his mill-hands, chiefly women and girls, being so successful in elevating them, that his works became known as 'Lady Mills.' [xlvi. 377]

PRIME, JOHN (1550-1596), divine; of Winchester College; fellow of New College, Oxford, 1570-91; M.A., 1576; D.D., 1588; rector of Adderbury, 1587-96; published two treatises and some volumes of sermons. [xlvi. 378]

PRIMROSE, SIR ARCHIBALD, first baronet, LORD CARRINGTON (1616-1679), Scottish judge; son of James Primrose (d. 1641) [q. v.]; joined Montrose and (1646) was condemned for treason: after his release joined Charles II and was made a baronet in 1651 during the march to Worcester; his property sequestrated after the battle; appointed at the Restoration lord clerk register, and (1661) lord of session, a lord of exchequer, and a member of the privy council; principal author of the Rescissory Act; removed (1676) from the office of lord clerk register and appointed justice-general, of which office he was deprived in 1678. [xlvi. 378]

PRIMROSE, ARCHIBALD, first VISCOUNT ROSEBERY and first EARL OF ROSEBERY (1661-1723), son of Sir Archibald Primrose, lord Carrington [q. v.]; opposed the policy of James II; M.P., Edinburgh county (Scottish parliament), 1695; created Viscount Rosebery, 1700; created an earl on the accession of Queen Anne; Scottish representative peer, 1707, 1708, 1710, and 1713; a commissioner for the union with England. [xlvi. 379]

PRIMROSE, SIR ARCHIBALD JOHN, fourth EARL OF ROSEBERY and sixth baronet (1783-1868), great grandson of Archibald Primrose, first earl of Rosebery [q. v.]; M.A. Pembroke College, Cambridge, 1804; M.P., Helston, 1805-6, Cashel, 1806-7; succeeded to earldom, 1814; hon. D.C.L. Cambridge, 1819; created Baron Rosebery (British peerage), 1828; privy councillor, 1831; supported the Reform Bill of 1832; F.R.S.; K.T., 1840. He was grandfather of the present and fifth Lord Rosebery. [xlvi. 379]

PRIMROSE, GILBERT (1580 ?-1641), divine; M.A. St. Andrews; D.D. Oxford, 1625; became a minister of the French reformed church at Bordeaux, 1603; compelled to quit France on the prohibition to ministers of other nations to officiate, 1623; subsequently became a minister of the French church in London; canon of Windsor, 1629. [xlvi. 380]

PRIMROSE, JAMES (d. 1641), clerk of the privy council of Scotland; appointed clerk for life, 1599.
[xlvi. 381]

PRIMROSE or PRIMEROSE, JAMES (d. 1659), physician; son of Gilbert Primrose [q. v.]; born at St. Jean d'Angély; M.D. Montpellier, 1617 (incorporated at Oxford, 1628); settled in Hull; published medical treatises.
[xlvi. 381]

PRINCE, JOHN (1643-1723), author of 'Worthies of Devon'; B.A. Brasenose College, Oxford, 1664; M.A. Caius College, Cambridge, 1675; vicar of Berry Pomeroy, 1681-1723; remembered by his 'Damnonii Orientales Illustres,' better known as the 'Worthies of Devon,' 1701 (2nd edit. 1810). [xlvi. 382]

PRINCE, JOHN CRITCHLEY (1808-1866), poet; practised reed-making at Wigan; began to write verses in 1827; published (1840) 'Hours with the Muses' (6th edit., 1857); fell into dissipated habits. [xlvi. 383]

PRINCE, JOHN HENRY (fl. 1794-1818), author; started life as an errand-boy, and afterwards laboured as a solicitor's clerk and a methodist minister; published miscellaneous works. [xlvi. 384]

PRING, MARTIN (1580-1626 ?), sea-captain; after making three expeditions to America, entered the service of the East India Company, 1608; became general of the company's ships, 1619; fell under the displeasure of the company for fraternising with the Dutch, and joined the Virginia Company in 1622. [xlvi. 384]

PRINGLE, ANDREW, LORD ALEMOOR (d. 1776), Scottish judge; named Scottish solicitor-general, 1755; lord of session as Lord Alemoor, 1759. He had an unrivalled reputation as a lawyer and pleader. [xlvi. 385]

PRINGLE, GEORGE (1631-1689), covenanter; fought against Cromwell at Dunbar, 1650; made his peace with Cromwell, 1655, and in 1662 accepted Charles II's pardon; implicated in the Rye House plot, 1683, after which he fled to Holland; aided in Argyll's expedition and returned to Scotland after the revolution; member of the Convention parliament. [xlvi. 386]

PRINGLE, SIR JOHN, baronet (1707-1782), physician; nephew of Sir Walter Pringle [q. v.]; studied medicine at Leyden (M.D., 1730), and settled in Edinburgh as a physician; joint-professor of pneumatics (metaphysics) and moral philosophy at Edinburgh University, 1734-44; resigned his professorship on being appointed physician-general to the forces in Flanders, 1744; settled in London, 1748; F.R.C.P., 1763; given baronetcy, 1766; became physician to George III, 1774; attained a position of great influence in scientific circles, and (1772) was elected president of the Royal Society. His great work in life was the reform of military medicine and sanitation. His book, 'Observations on the Diseases of the Army' (1752), attained a European reputation, and has become a military classic. [xlvi. 386]

PRINGLE, ROBERT (d. 1736), politician; brother of Sir Walter Pringle [q. v.]; studied at Leyden; took service under William of Orange, and was appointed undersecretary of state for Scotland; secretary at war, 1718.
[xlvi. 388]

PRINGLE, THOMAS (1789-1834), Scottish poet; studied at Edinburgh University; was permanently lamed by an accident in infancy; gained the friendship of Scott by a contribution to Hogg's 'Poetic Mirror' (1816); obtained by Scott's influence a grant of land in South Africa for his father and brothers, 1819; became librarian at Cape Town, but ruined his prospects by publishing two violent political papers, which were suppressed by the governor; returned to London and became (1827) secretary to the Anti-Slavery Society; published 'Ephemerides,' 1828, and 'South African Sketches,' 1834.
[xlvi. 389]

PRINGLE, WALTER (1625-1667), covenanter; fought against Cromwell at Dunbar; imprisoned for refusing the oath of allegiance, 1664. [xlvi. 390]

PRINGLE, SIR WALTER, LORD NEWHALL (1664 ?-1736), Scottish judge; great-nephew of Walter Pringle [q. v.]; lord of session as Lord Newhall, 1718; knighted and made a lord of justiciary, 1718. [xlvi. 391]

PRINSEP, CHARLES ROBERT (1789-1864), economic writer; M.A. St. John's College, Cambridge, 1814; barrister, Inner Temple, 1817; was advocate-general of Bengal; created LL.D., 1824; author of an 'Essay on Money,' 1818. [xlvi. 394]

PRINSEP, HENRY THOBY (1792-1878), Indian civil servant; brother of Charles Robert Prinsep [q. v.]; entered the service of the East India Company in Bengal, 1807; published (1823) a 'History of Transactions in India during the Administration of the Marquis of Hastings,' the best narrative of the events of the time; appointed Persian secretary to the government, 1820; became a member of the council, 1835, retiring, 1843; nominated on the council of India, 1858, retaining his seat till 1874. His writings on Indian subjects were important; especial value attaches to his autobiographical sketch of his official life, written in 1865. [xlvi. 392]

PRINSEP, JAMES (1799–1840), architect and orientalist; brother of Charles Robert Prinsep [q. v.]; became assistant assay-master at the Calcutta mint, 1819, and assay-master, 1832; executed several important architectural works in India, besides completing the Hugli canal; unrivalled as an authority on Indian antiquities.   [xlvi. 395]

PRIOR, SIR JAMES (1790?–1869), miscellaneous writer; entered the navy as a surgeon, and wrote accounts of his voyages, which were published (1820) in the 'New Voyages and Travels' of Sir Richard Phillips [q. v.]; F.S.A., 1830; became deputy-inspector of hospitals, 1843; knighted, 1858; chief works, biographies of Burke (1824) and Goldsmith (1837).   [xlvi. 396]

PRIOR, MATTHEW (1664–1721), poet and diplomatist; educated at Westminster School, under the patronage of Lord Dorset (king's scholar, 1681); obtained a fellowship at St. John's College, Cambridge, 1688, having graduated B.A. 1686; appointed secretary to the ambassador at the Hague; was employed (1697) as secretary in the negotiations at the treaty of Ryswick; M.P., East Grinstead, 1701; joined the tories, 1702; made a commissioner of customs, 1711; proceeded to Paris to negotiate peace, 1711, the subsequent treaty of Utrecht (1713) being popularly known as 'Matt's peace'; became plenipotentiary at Paris, 1712; recalled on Queen Anne's death, and (1715) imprisoned; a folio edition of his poems (1719) brought out by his admirers after his release (1717), by which he gained four thousand guineas; given by Lord Harley 4,000*l.*, for the purchase of Down Hall in Essex, where he resided till his death. He is one of the neatest of English epigrammatists, and in occasional pieces and familiar verse has no rival in English. Among his poems may be mentioned 'The Town and Country Mouse,' an answer to Dryden's 'Hind and Panther,' 'Alma, or the Progress of the Mind,' 'The Secretary,' 'The Female Phaeton,' 'To a Child of Quality,' and 'The Conversation.' His prose works are of slight importance.   [xlvi. 397]

PRIOR, THOMAS (1682?–1751), founder of the Dublin Society and philanthropist; B.A. Trinity College, Dublin, 1703; devoted himself to the promotion of material and industrial works among the Irish protestants; established the Dublin Society for the promotion of agriculture, manufactures, arts, and sciences, 1731.   [xlvi. 401]

PRIOR, THOMAS ABIEL (1809–1886), line-engraver; executed a number of plates after Joseph Mallord William Turner [q. v.]; resided at Calais in later life. [xlvi. 402]

PRISOT, SIR JOHN (d. 1460), judge; serjeant-at-law, 1443; made chief-justice of the common bench, 1449; knighted; assisted Sir Thomas Littleton (1402–1481) [q. v.] in compiling his tenures.   [xlvi. 402]

PRITCHARD, ANDREW (1804–1882), microscopist; in business as a London optician till 1852; early turned his attention to microscopy and wrote extensively; his 'History of Infusoria' (1841) long a standard work.
          [xlvi. 402]

PRITCHARD, CHARLES (1808–1893), astronomer; of Merchant Taylors' School and Christ's Hospital, London; fellow of St. John's College, Cambridge, 1832; M.A., 1833; turned his attention to educational reform, on which the Clapham grammar school was founded to give him an opportunity, 1834; head-master of Clapham grammar school, 1834–62; had a small observatory at Clapham, where he did some useful astronomical work; Hulsean lecturer at Cambridge, 1867; became Savilian professor of astronomy at Oxford, 1870; a new observatory in the 'Parks,' where his chief work was accomplished, especially in stellar photometry, erected through his initiative; invented the wedge-photometer to obviate discordances in estimates of the brightness of various stars, 1881; fellow of New College, Oxford, 1883; member of the council of the Royal Society, 1885–7; wrote numerous astronomical papers and scientific articles, and also gave much attention to the relations of science and religion.
          [xlvi. 403]

PRITCHARD, EDWARD WILLIAM (1825–1865), poisoner; practised as a surgeon at Glasgow; M.D. Erlangen; poisoned his wife and mother-in-law with doses of antimony, 1865; tried, found guilty, and executed in front of Glasgow gaol. He published several works, besides many papers on medical subjects.   [xlvi. 406]

PRITCHARD, GEORGE (1796–1883), missionary and consul at Tahiti; settled in the Society islands, 1824, which were annexed by France in spite of his protests, 1843; compelled to leave the islands, 1844; subsequently lived in retirement in England.   [xlvi. 406]

PRITCHARD, HANNAH (1711–1768), actress; *née* Vaughan; married a poor actor in early life; appeared at Bartholomew Fair, London, and at the Haymarket, London, 1733; played at Drury Lane, London, 1734 to 1740-1, appearing in a wide range of characters, chiefly comic; afterwards appeared chiefly at Drury Lane, London, and Covent Garden, London; last appeared, April 1768. She was held the greatest Lady Macbeth of her day, and the Queen in Hamlet, Estifania, and Doll Common were also among her greatest parts.   [xlvi. 407]

PRITCHARD, HENRY BADEN (1841–1884), chemist and writer; son of Andrew Pritchard [q. v.]; conducted the photographic department at the Royal Arsenal, Woolwich; published novels and other works.   [xlvi. 403]

PRITCHARD, JOHN LANGFORD (1799–1850), actor; first appeared at Bath, 1820, as Captain Absolute; joined Murray's company at Edinburgh, 1823, and (1835) made his first appearance in London at Covent Garden.
          [xlvi. 409]

PRITCHARD or **PRICHARD**, SIR WILLIAM (1632?–1705), lord mayor of London; a 'merchant taylor'; became sheriff, 1672; knighted, 1672; elected mayor as court candidate, 1682; took active measures against the whig party; M.P. for the city of London, 1702.   [xlvi. 410]

PRITCHETT, JAMES PIGOTT (1789–1868), architect; practised in York, where he and his partner, Watson, had almost a monopoly of the architectural work in Yorkshire.   [xlvi. 411]

PRITZLER, SIR THEOPHILUS (d. 1839), Indian commander; entered the army, 1793; served in Holland, 1794-5; proceeded to India, c. 1814; took an important part in the third Mahratta war, 1817–18, with the rank of brigadier-general; K.C.B., 1822.   [xlvi. 411]

PROBERT, WILLIAM (1790–1870), unitarian minister; minister at Walmsley for over forty-eight years; an authority on Welsh laws and customs, and an orientalist of some ability.   [xlvi. 412]

PROBUS (d. 948?), biographer of St. Patrick; was the author of the first life of the saint to be printed (Basle, 1563). In it he falsified the earlier part of Patrick's life.   [xlvi. 413]

PROBY, GRANVILLE LEVESON, third EARL OF CARYSFORT (1781–1868), admiral; son of Sir John Joshua Proby, first earl of Carysfort [q. v.]; entered the navy, 1798; present at the battles of the Nile and Trafalgar; admiral, 1857.   [xlvi. 413]

PROBY, SIR JOHN, first BARON CARYSFORT (1720–1772), M.A. Jesus College, Cambridge, 1742; M.P., Stamford, 1747, Huntingdonshire, 1754–68; made an Irish baron, 1752; Irish privy councillor; K.B., 1761; a lord of the admiralty, 1757 and 1763-5.   [xlvi. 413]

PROBY, SIR JOHN JOSHUA, first EARL OF CARYSFORT and second BARON CARYSFORT (1751–1828), only son of Sir John Proby, first baron Carysfort [q. v.]; of Westminster School and Trinity College, Cambridge; M.A., 1770; F.R.S., 1779; appointed joint-guardian and keeper of the rolls in Ireland and created an Irish earl, 1789; M.P., East Looe, 1790, Stamford, June 1790–1801; supported Pitt; created an English baron, 1801, and (February 1806) appointed joint postmaster-general, a post which he resigned in the following year; created D.C.L. Oxford, 1810, and LL.D. Cambridge, 1811; author of several tragedies, poems, and essays.   [xlvi. 414]

PROBYN, SIR EDMUND (1678–1742), judge; of Christ Church, Oxford; barrister, Middle Temple, 1702; made a Welsh judge, 1721; defended the Earl of Macclesfield, 1725; became puisne judge of the king's bench, 1726; knighted, 1726; lord chief-baron of the exchequer, 1740.   [xlvi. 415]

PROCTER, ADELAIDE ANN (1825–1864), poetess; eldest child of Bryan Waller Procter [q. v.]; contributed to the 'Book of Beauty' in 1843, and afterwards to Dickens's periodicals, under the pseudonym Mary Berwick'; took great interest in social questions affecting women. Her poems were collected, 1858, under the title 'Legends and Lyrics' (10th edit. 1866). Many of her hymns are still in use. [xlvi. 416]

PROCTER, BRYAN WALLER (1787–1874), poet; practised as a solicitor in London, and ultimately obtained a large connection as a conveyancer; began to contribute to the 'Literary Gazette,' 1815; intimate with Leigh Hunt, Charles Lamb, and Dickens; barrister and (1832–1861) a metropolitan commissioner in lunacy; produced a successful tragedy, 'Mirandola,' at Covent Garden Theatre, London, under the pseudonym of 'Barry Cornwall,' 1821; songs published, 1832; published his biography of Charles Lamb, his last important work, 1864. [xlvi. 416]

PROCTER, RICHARD WRIGHT (1816–1881), author; a Manchester barber who published a number of works on Manchester. [xlvi. 419]

PROCTOR, JOHN (1521?–1584), divine and historian; of Corpus Christi and All Souls Colleges, Oxford; fellow of All Souls College, Oxford, 1540; M.A., 1544; presented to the rectory of St. Andrew, Holborn, London, 1578; published 'The Historie of Wyates Rebellion,' 1554, and two other works. [xlvi. 419]

PROCTOR, RICHARD ANTHONY (1837–1888), astronomer; twenty-third wrangler, St. John's, Cambridge, 1860; kept terms at the Temple, but abandoned law for science; devoted himself, 1863, to the study of astronomy and mathematics; published, 1865, his celebrated monograph on 'Saturn and his System,' and, 1866, his 'Handbook of the Stars,' which hardly paid expenses, but made his reputation; successfully lectured in America from 1873; founded 'Knowledge,' a weekly scientific periodical, 1881 (after 1885 a monthly periodical); removed to Florida, 1887, and died of yellow fever in New York. [xlvi. 419]

PROCTOR, THOMAS (fl. 1578–1584), poet; son of John Proctor [q. v.]; author or editor of several works, chiefly in verse, including 'A gorgious Gallery of gallant Inventions,' 1578. [xlvi. 421]

PROCTOR, THOMAS (1753–1794), historical painter and sculptor; exhibited at the Royal Academy from 1780; discovered by West subsisting in Clare Market, London, in great poverty; died of mental anguish and privation before measures could be taken for his relief. [xlvi. 421]

PROUD, JOSEPH (1745–1826), minister of the 'New Church'; became a general baptist minister, 1767, but (1788) accepted the opinions of Swedenborg and (1791) became a 'new church' minister at Birmingham; removed to Manchester, 1793, returning to Birmingham, 1794; went to London, 1797; again returned to Birmingham, 1814, and retired, 1821; published theological works. [xlvi. 422]

PROUT, FATHER (pseudonym). [See MAHONY, FRANCIS SYLVESTER, 1804–1866.]

PROUT, JOHN (1810–1894), agriculturist; brought up as a farmer; emigrated to Ontario, 1832; returned to England, 1842, and in 1861 bought Blount's farm, Sawbridgeworth, Hertfordshire, which he cultivated till his death. His scientific system of farming, based on his Canadian experience, was of great value to agriculturists. [xlvi. 423]

PROUT, JOHN SKINNER (1806–1876), water-colour painter; nephew of Samuel Prout [q. v.]; was a member of a little coterie of Bristol artists, and subsequently member of the Institute of Painters in Water-colours. [xlvi. 424]

PROUT, SAMUEL (1783–1852), water-colour painter; began to exhibit scenes in the south-western counties in 1805, and contributed to 'Beauties of England and Wales,' 1803–13; began in 1818 the series of paintings of continental streets which made his fame; highly esteemed by Ruskin. [xlvi. 424]

PROUT, WILLIAM (1785–1850), physician and chemist; M.D. Edinburgh, 1811; L.R.C.P., 1812; one of the pioneers of physiological chemistry; discovered free hydrochloric acid in the stomach, 1823. The view that the atomic weights of all the elements are multiples of the atomic weight of hydrogen is known as 'Prout's Law.' [xlvi. 426]

PROVAND, LORD (d. 1593). [See BAILLIE, WILLIAM.]

PROWSE, WILLIAM (1752?–1826), rear-admiral; entered the navy as an able seaman, 1771; rated a midshipman, 1778; became a commander, 1796, and saw much service in the French war; C.B., 1815; rear-admiral, 1821. [xlvi. 427]

PROWSE, WILLIAM JEFFERY (1836–1870), humorist; developed a remarkable talent for humorous verse before the age of twenty; contributed to various periodicals, including 'Fun.' [xlvi. 428]

PRUJEAN, SIR FRANCIS (1593–1666), physician; M.D. Caius College, Cambridge, 1625; practised in London from 1638; president R.C.P., 1650–4; knighted, 1661. [xlvi. 428]

PRYCE. [See also PRICE, PRYS, and PRYSE.]

PRYCE, GEORGE (1801–1868), historian of Bristol; an accountant in Bristol; F.S.A., 1857; published several historical works relating to that city, including a 'Popular History of Bristol,' 1861. [xlvi. 429]

PRYCE, WILLIAM (1725?–1790), antiquary; author of 'Mineralogia Cornubiensis,' 1778, and 'Archæologia Cornu-Britannica,' 1790. [xlvi. 429]

PRYDYDD Y BYCHAN (i.e. 'The Little Poet') (1200–1270?), Welsh bard; his real name unknown; wrote a number of compositions, twenty-one of which are printed in 'Myvyrian Archaiology.' [xlvi. 429]

PRYDYDD Y MOCH (fl. 1160–1220). [See LLYWARCH AB LLYWELYN.]

PRYME, ABRAHAM DE LA (1672–1704), antiquary; B.A. St. John's College, Cambridge, 1694; F.R.S., 1702; wrote on the antiquities of Lincolnshire and Yorkshire. His diary was published by the Surtees Society (vol. liv.) [xlvi. 430]

PRYME, GEORGE (1781–1868), political economist; sixth wrangler, 1803; fellow of Trinity College, Cambridge, 1805; barrister, Lincoln's Inn, 1806; began to lecture at Cambridge on political economy, 1816, and (1828) was recognised as professor by the senate; whig M.P. for Cambridge, 1832–41; published several pamphlets and treatises. [xlvi. 430]

PRYNNE, WILLIAM (1600–1669), puritan pamphleteer; educated at Bath grammar school and Oriel College, Oxford; B.A., 1621; barrister, Lincoln's Inn, 1628; studied law, theology, and ecclesiastical antiquities; wrote against Arminianism from 1627, and endeavoured to reform the manners of his age; published 'Histriomastix,' directed against stage-plays, 1632; for supposed aspersion on Charles I and his queen in 'Histriomastix' was sentenced by Star-chamber, in 1634, to be imprisoned during life, to be fined 5,000l., and to lose both his ears in the pillory; continued to write in the Tower of London, and (1637) was again fined 5,000l., deprived of the remainder of his ears, and branded on the cheeks; released by Long parliament, and his sentences declared illegal, November 1640; defended parliament in the press on the outbreak of war, and pursued Laud with great animosity; after Laud's execution published by order of the parliament the first part of an account of the trial, entitled 'Canterburies Doom,' 1646; devoted much attention to independency, which he detested as heartily as episcopacy; was equally opposed to the ascendency of the presbyterian clergy, his theory of ecclesiastical policy being thoroughly erastian; assailed the army in various pamphlets, 1647, and (1648) attacked it in the House of Commons; arrested by Pride, November 1648; retired to Swanswick, January 1649, and began a paper war against the government, demonstrating that he was bound to pay taxes to the Commonwealth neither in conscience, law, nor prudence, for which government imprisoned him for nearly three years without trial; on his release (1653) drew a parallel between Cromwell and Richard III, and (May 1658) forced his way into the House of Commons, which could only get rid of him by adjournment; walked into parliament at the head of the members; readmitted by Monck, 1660; asserted the rights of Charles II with such boldness as to be styled 'the Cato of the age' by a royalist, and was thanked by Charles II; M.P. for Bath in the Convention parliament, 1660; laboured zealously to restrict the Act of Indemnity and to disband the army; opposed the thirty-nine articles, and, in 1661, was reprimanded by the speaker for a speech against the Corporation Bill; appointed keeper of the records in the Tower of London; published his most valuable work, 'Brevia Parliamentaria Rediviva,' 1662. He published about two hundred books and pamphlets. [xlvi. 432]

PRYOR, ALFRED REGINALD (1839-1881), botanist ; B.A. University College, Oxford, 1862 ; projected a new flora in his native county, Hertfordshire, which occupied the remainder of his life. His 'Flora of Hertfordshire' appeared in 1887.   [xlvi. 437]

PRYS, EDMUND (1541 ?-1624), translator of the Psalms into Welsh verse ; of St. John's College, Cambridge ; became archdeacon of Merioneth, 1576, and canon of St. Asaph, 1602 ; his translation of the Psalms, appended to the Welsh version of the Book of Common Prayer, issued in 1621.   [xlvi. 438]

PRYSE, SIR CARBERY, fourth baronet (d. 1695), mine-owner ; formed a company to work mines discovered on his estate in Cardiganshire, which were afterwards exploited by Sir Humphry Mackworth [q. v.]
                                               [xlvi. 438]

PSALMANAZAR, GEORGE (1679 ?-1763), literary impostor ; a native of the south of France ; his real name unknown, his usual designation being fashioned by himself from the biblical character, Shalmaneser ; educated at a Dominican convent ; commenced life as a mendicant, and to insure alms styled himself a native Japanese Christian, but afterwards represented himself as still a pagan, living on raw flesh, roots, and herbs ; invented an elaborate alphabet and grammar and a worship of his own ; enlisted in a regiment of the Duke of Mecklenburg, and attracted the attention of William Innes, chaplain to the Scottish regiment at Sluys, who became a confederate in the imposture, baptized Psalmanazar as a protestant convert, and for security persuaded him to remove his birthplace to the obscurity of Formosa ; came to London at the end of 1703 and became a centre of interest, presenting Bishop Compton with the catechism in 'Formosan' (his invented language), and being voluble in Latin to Archbishop Tillotson ; silenced suspicion by never modifying a statement, and gained the sympathy of English churchmen by abuse of the jesuits ; published, 1704, a 'Description' of Formosa, with an introductory autobiography ; after the withdrawal of his mentor Innes, who was rewarded by being appointed chaplain-general of the forces in Portugal (c. 1707), was unable to sustain the imposture unaided, and passed from ridicule to obscurity, although he still found patrons ; renounced his past life after a serious illness in 1728 ; became an accomplished hebraist, wrote 'A General History of Printing,' and contributed to the 'Universal History'; was regarded with veneration by Dr. Johnson, who used to sit with him at an alehouse in Old Street, London. In 1764 appeared his autobiographical 'Memoirs,' containing an account of the imposture.   [xlvi. 439]

PUCCI, FRANCESCO (1540-1593 ?), theological writer ; born in Florence, embraced reformed opinions, and came to Oxford, 1572 (admitted M.A., 1574), but was expelled, 1575 ; being an extreme Pelagian, encountered persecution in most countries in Europe ; met John Dee [q. v.] and Edward Kelley [q. v.] at Cracow, 1585, and was initiated into their trade of magic, but re-entered the Roman communion shortly afterwards.   [xlvi. 442]

PUCKERIDGE, RICHARD (1690 ?-1759). [See POCKRICH.]

PUCKERING, SIR HENRY (1618-1701). [See NEWTON.]

PUCKERING, SIR JOHN (1544-1596), lord keeper of the great seal ; barrister, Lincoln's Inn, 1567 (governor, 1575) ; M.P., Carmarthen, 1584-6, Gatton, 1586-7 ; speaker of the House of Commons, 1584-5 and 1586-7 ; made lord keeper and knighted, 1592.   [xlvi. 443]

PUCKERING, SIR THOMAS, first baronet (1592-1636), politician ; son of Sir John Puckering ; M.P., Tamworth, 1621-8 ; created baronet, 1612 ; a companion of Henry, prince of Wales.   [xlvi. 444]

PUCKLE, JAMES (1667 ?-1724), author of 'The Club' ; notary public ; remembered as the author of 'The Club, or a Dialogue between Father and Son, in vino veritas,' 1711 (latest reprint, 1890), a collection of character sketches of the class which Earle brought to perfection in his 'Micro-Cosmographie.'   [xlvii. 1]

PUDSEY, HUGH DE (1125 ?-1195). [See PUISET.]

PUGH, ELLIS (1656-1721), Welsh quaker ; emigrated to Pennsylvania, 1686, and published 'Annerch i'r Cymry' (1721), probably the first Welsh book printed in America.
                                               [xlvii. 2]

PUGH, HERBERT (fl. 1758-1788), landscape-painter ; exhibited at the Society of Artists, 1766-76.   [xlvii. 2]

PUGH, PHILIP (1679-1760), dissenting minister ; for many years pastor at Cilgwyn.   [xlvii. 2]

PUGH, ROBERT (1609-1679), Roman catholic controversialist ; educated at the jesuits' college at St. Omer under the name of Robert Phillips ; served in the army of Charles I, and engaged in frequent controversy ; committed to Newgate, 1678, during the 'popish plot' panic ; died in prison.   [xlvii. 3]

PUGHE, WILLIAM OWEN, known in early life as WILLIAM OWEN (1759-1835), Welsh antiquary and lexicographer ; was occupied for twenty years (1783-1803) in preparing and publishing a Welsh-English dictionary (abridged, 1806 ; new editions, 1832 and 1857), which is still the most complete in existence ; F.S.A., 1793 ; given the Oxford D.C.L., 1822 ; published (1801-3) the 'Myvyrian Archaiology of Wales' (reprinted, 1870) ; assumed the surname of Pughe, 1806 ; published a Welsh version of 'Paradise Lost,' 1819.   [xlvii. 4]

PUGIN, AUGUSTUS CHARLES (1762-1832), architect, archæologist, and architectural artist ; born in France ; came to London, c. 1798 ; employed by John Nash [q. v.] in making drawings of Gothic buildings ; had little practice, but became famous as an educator of young architects, particularly his own son ; paved the way for the real revival of Gothic architecture which followed the 'Strawberry-Hill' enthusiasm.   [xlvii. 5]

PUGIN, AUGUSTUS WELBY NORTHMORE (1812-1852), architect, ecclesiologist, and writer ; son of Augustus Charles Pugin [q. v.] ; educated at Christ's Hospital, London, and trained by his father ; inherited a remarkable facility in draughtsmanship ; obtained a regular practice, partly through the patronage of the Earl of Shrewsbury ; published his 'Gothic Furniture,' 1835, and 'Contrasts,' 1836, the latter an attack on the 'Pagan' method of architecture ; employed (1836-43) by (Sir) Charles Barry [q. v.] in providing the detail drawings for the houses of parliament ; published 'True Principles of Pointed or Christian Architecture,' 1841, after which his ecclesiastical practice became very extensive ; lost his reason from excess of work, 1851, and, after confinement in Bedlam, died at Ramsgate. His reputation lies chiefly in his chronological position as a Gothic architect.   [xlvii. 6]

PUGIN, EDWARD WELBY (1834-1875), architect ; son of Augustus Welby Northmore Pugin [q. v.] ; found himself with the control of a large practice at the age of seventeen, owing to his father's failing health ; practised for fourteen years, a very large number of works, chiefly Roman catholic churches, being entrusted to him.
                                               [xlvii. 10]

PUISET or PUDSEY, HUGH DE (1125 ?-1195), bishop of Durham and earl of Northumberland ; probably came to England under the protection of his uncle, Henry of Blois [q. v.], bishop of Winchester ; became treasurer of York, 1143, and (1153) was chosen bishop of Durham ; excommunicated by Pope Alexander III for attending the coronation of Henry II's son, 1170 ; contrived on the whole to keep aloof from the quarrel between Henry II and Thomas Becket ; took a somewhat prominent part in public affairs during the latter part of Henry II's reign, and on the accession of Richard I purchased the earldom of Northumberland ; made justiciar as colleague of William de Mandeville, third earl of Essex [q. v.], 1189 ; his jurisdiction confined to north of the Humber after the chief justiciarship had been bestowed on William of Longchamp [q. v.], 1190 ; arrested by Longchamp and compelled to acknowledge his authority ; after Longchamp's deposition resisted the authority of Geoffrey (d. 1212) [q. v.], archbishop of York, but (1192) was compelled to make his submission ; fell under Richard I's displeasure, 1194, and was compelled to surrender his earldom ; still engaged in the endeavour to obtain its restoration at his death. Although not himself a man of learning, he was a munificent patron of learning in others.   [xlvii. 10]

PULCHERIUS (d. 655). [See MOCHAEMOG.]

PULESTON or **PULISTON**, HAMLET (1632-1662), political writer; nephew of John Puleston [q. v.]; M.A. Wadham College, Oxford, 1653; fellow of Jesus College, Oxford; published a royalist treatise, 'Monarchiæ Britannicæ singularis Protectio,' 1660. [xlvii. 16]

PULESTON, JOHN (d. 1659), judge; reader, Middle Temple, 1634; appointed by parliament a judge of common pleas, 1649; his patent not renewed in 1653. [xlvii. 16]

PULLAIN, **PULLAYNE**, or **PULLEYNE**, JOHN (1517-1565), divine and poet; M.A. New College, Oxford, 1544; senior student of Christ Church, Oxford, 1547; B.D., 1553; became rector of St. Peter's, Cornhill, London, 1553, but was deprived on Queen Mary's accession; went to Geneva, but regained his rectory on Queen Elizabeth's accession, holding it till 1560; archdeacon of Colchester, 1559; prebendary of St. Paul's Cathedral, 1561; author of metrical renderings of the 148th and 149th psalms. [xlvii. 17]

PULLAN, RICHARD POPPLEWELL (1825-1888), architect and archæologist; became an early convert to mediævalism, and was employed by (Sir) Charles Thomas Newton and by the Society of Dilettanti in making excavations at Halicarnassus, Cnidus, and other places, from 1857; completed all the unfinished works of William Burges [q. v.] [xlvii. 17]

PULLEIN. [See PULLEN.]

PULLEN, JOSIAH (1631-1714), vice-principal of Magdalen Hall, Oxford; M.A. Oxford, 1657; vice-principal of Magdalen Hall, Oxford, 1657-1714; long remembered for his eccentricities. [xlvii. 19]

PULLEN, ROBERT (d. 1147?), philosopher, theologian, and cardinal; studied at Oxford, and is the second master known to have taught in the schools there; subsequently taught at Paris; archdeacon of Rochester, 1134 and 1143; in his later years settled at Rome, where he was probably created a cardinal by Pope Cœlestine II; chancellor of the holy Roman church, 1145 and 1146; an upholder of the orthodox conservative cause against the Abelardian influence. His 'Sermones' are preserved in manuscript at Lambeth. [xlvii. 19]

PULLEN, **PULLEIN**, or **PULLEYNE**, SAMUEL (1598-1667), archbishop of Tuam; M.A. Pembroke Hall, Cambridge, 1623; accompanied Ormonde to Ireland as private chaplain, 1632, and soon obtained preferment; escaped to England on the outbreak of rebellion in 1641; archbishop of Tuam, 1661-7. [xlvii. 20]

PULLEN or **PULLEIN**, SAMUEL (fl. 1734-1760), writer on the silkworm; probably a grandson of Tobias Pullen [q. v.]; M.A. Trinity College, Dublin, 1738; interested himself in introducing the cultivation of silk into the American colonies, and published several treatises on the subject. [xlvii. 21]

PULLEN, TOBIAS (1648-1713), successively bishop of Cloyne and of Dromore; probably a nephew of Samuel Pullen (1598-1667) [q. v.]; D.D. Trinity College, Dublin, 1668; fellow, 1671-7; created bishop of Cloyne, 1694, and translated to Dromore, 1695; published one or two sermons and pamphlets. [xlvii. 21]

PULLEN, WILLIAM JOHN SAMUEL (1813-1887), vice-admiral; lieutenant, 1846; engaged in Arctic exploration; vice-admiral, 1879. [xlvii. 22]

PULLER, SIR CHRISTOPHER (1774-1824), barrister-at-law; of Eton and Christ Church, Oxford; B.A., 1795; fellow of Queen's College, Oxford; barrister, Inner Temple, 1800; bencher, Lincoln's Inn, 1822; became chief-justice of Bengal, 1823; knighted, 1823. [xlvii. 22]

PULLER, TIMOTHY (1638?-1693), divine; M.A. Jesus College, Cambridge, 1660 (incorporated at Oxford, 1661); D.D., 1673; fellow of Jesus College, Cambridge, 1657; student of Gray's Inn, 1658; author of 'The Moderation of the Church of England,' 1679 (reprinted, 1843). [xlvii. 22]

PULLING, ALEXANDER (1813-1895), serjeant-at-law and legal author; educated at Merchant Taylors' School, London; barrister, Inner Temple, 1843; one of the last surviving members of the Ancient Order of Serjeants-at-Law; published 'The Order of the Coif' (1884) and other works. [xlvii. 23]

PULMAN, GEORGE PHILIP RIGNEY (1819-1880), antiquary; published 'The Book of the Axe' (1841) and other works on local topography and antiquities. [xlvii. 24]

PULTENEY, DANIEL (d. 1731), politician; of Christ Church, Oxford; M.P., Tregony, March 1721, Hedon, November 1721, Preston, 1722-31; became a lord of the admiralty under Walpole, 1721; hated Walpole, and was a follower of Sunderland, having married the sister of Sunderland's third wife. [xlvii. 24]

PULTENEY, SIR JAMES MURRAY, seventh baronet (1751?-1811). [See MURRAY.]

PULTENEY or **POULTNEY**, SIR JOHN DE (d. 1349), mayor of London; a member of the Drapers' Company; served as mayor, 1331, 1332, 1334, and 1337; acquired great wealth, and frequently advanced money to Edward III. The parish of St. Lawrence Pountney owes its name to his connection with it. [xlvii. 25]

PULTENEY, RICHARD (1730-1801), botanist; was from 1750 a constant contributor to the 'Gentleman's Magazine,' chiefly on botanical topics; M.D. Edinburgh, 1764; physician to his kinsman, Sir William Pulteney, earl of Bath [q. v.], 1764; published botanical works. [xlvii. 26]

PULTENEY, SIR WILLIAM, EARL OF BATH (1684-1764), statesman; educated at Westminster School and Christ Church, Oxford; inherited a considerable property, and entered parliament (M.P., Hedon, 1705-34) as a whig; became secretary at war, 1714, and was one of 'the three grand allies,' the other two being Stanhope and Walpole; concurred with Walpole in resigning office, 1717, but in 1721, when Walpole became first lord of the treasury, was mortified at not being offered office; gradually became alienated from Walpole, and in 1725 openly broke with him; joined Bolingbroke in a journalistic war upon Walpole, and became a mainstay of 'The Craftsman' under the signature 'O'; joined Sir William Wyndham [q. v.] in forming a new party of malcontent whigs called 'the patriots,' of which the two originators were designated 'the consuls,' with the object of attacking the Hanoverian policy of the government; hoped much from George II, whose friend he had been when Prince of Wales, but on the death of George I was disappointed in his hope of superseding Walpole, and began to intrigue actively against him; his name struck off the list of privy councillors, 1731; was an important agent in the overthrow of Walpole's scheme of excise, 1733; M.P., Middlesex, 1734-42; did not support Frederick, prince of Wales, in his extreme opposition to George II, considering his proceedings too rash to be defensible; vigorously fanned the agitation against Spain (1739), which led to the downfall of Walpole's government; was requested to form a government, 1742, but refused office, merely stipulating that he should be a member of Wilmington's cabinet; created Earl of Bath, 1742; disappointed in his hope of becoming first lord of the treasury on the death of Wilmington, 1743; attempted to overthrow Pelham, 1746, when at the instance of George II he agreed to form an administration from which Pitt should be excluded; failed to accomplish his task, and from that time played no part of consequence in public affairs; buried in Westminster Abbey. He is chiefly to be remembered for his power as an orator, which made Walpole say that he feared Pulteney's tongue more than another man's sword. [xlvii. 28]

PULTON or **POULTON**, ANDREW (1654-1710), jesuit; probably great-nephew of Ferdinando Pulton [q. v.]; entered the Society of Jesus, 1674; became joint-master of the new jesuit college in the Savoy, Strand, London, 1687; gained a wide reputation by his conference with Thomas Tenison [q. v.], afterwards archbishop of Canterbury; imprisoned at the revolution, subsequently retiring to Liège and afterwards to St. Germain; accompanied James II to Ireland, 1690; author of controversial works. [xlvii. 35]

PULTON, FERDINANDO (1536-1618), legal author; fellow of Christ's College, Cambridge; B.A., 1556; member of Lincoln's Inn, 1559, but being a Roman catholic was never called to the bar; the first private person to edit the statutes. [xlvii. 36]

PUNSHON, WILLIAM MORLEY (1824-1881), Wesleyan preacher and lecturer; educated as a timber merchant ; joined the methodist society at Hull, 1838 ; ordained a Wesleyan minister, 1845 ; lived in London, 1858–1864 ; laboured in Canada, 1867–72, and thereafter resumed his residence in London ; published several works in prose and verse. [xlvii. 37]

PURBECK, VISCOUNT (1591 ?–1657). [See VILLIERS, JOHN.]

PURBECK, titular VISCOUNTS. [See DANVERS, ROBERT, 1621 ?–1674 ; VILLIERS, JOHN, 1677 ?–1723.]

PURCELL, DANIEL (1660 ?–1717), musical composer ; brother of Henry Purcell [q. v.] ; organist of Magdalen College, Oxford, 1688–95 ; subsequently resided in London, when, from 1713, he was organist of St. Andrew's, Holborn ; copied the style of his brother, displaying no originality. [xlvii. 38]

PURCELL, HENRY (1658 ?–1695), composer ; appointed a chorister of the Chapel Royal, London, 1664, where in 1672 he became a pupil of Pelham Humfrey [q. v.] ; began to write music for the stage when young, the most important of his early productions being the masque in Shadwell's 'Timon of Athens' ; produced, 1680, 'Dido and Eneas,' in some respects his most remarkable achievement ; became organist at Westminster Abbey, 1680, and (1682) was also nominated organist of the Chapel Royal, London ; buried beneath the organ in Westminster Abbey. He was a master of technical ingenuity, and gifted with a high power of expression, which finds its supreme utterance in the death song of Dido in his first opera. He anticipated Handel in the use of broad choral effect, while he rivalled him in the melodic beauty of his airs. Only a few of his compositions were published during his lifetime. His 'Sonatas for III Parts' appeared in 1683, and in 1696 and 1702 two books of 'Collections' were published. His sacred music was edited in four volumes by Vincent Novello (1829–32), and other of his works issued by the Musical Antiquarian Society. In 1878 the Purcell Society commenced a complete edition of his works. [xlvii. 39]

PURCELL, JOHN (1674 ?–1730), physician ; M.D. Montpellier, 1699 ; L.R.C.P., 1721 ; author of 'A Treatise of Vapours,' 1702, and 'A Treatise of the Cholick,' 1714. [xlvii. 44]

PURCELL, RICHARD (*fl.* 1750–1766), engraver ; worked for Sayer, a London printseller, who employed him in copying popular prints and in executing portraits and caricatures. [xlvii. 44]

PURCHAS, JOHN (1823–1872), divine and author ; M.A. Christ's College, Cambridge, 1847 ; became perpetual curate of St. James's College, Brighton, 1866 ; prosecuted before the court of arches and the privy council for ritualistic practices, 1870 ; was suspended by the privy council, 1872, but took no notice of the order, and continued his services at St. James's Chapel until his death. [xlvii. 44]

PURCHAS, SAMUEL (1575 ?–1626), author of the 'Pilgrimes' ; graduate of St. John's College, Cambridge ; rector of St. Martin's, Ludgate, London, 1614–26 ; chiefly known by his work, 'Hakluytus Posthumus, or Purchas his Pilgrimes,' 1625, a record of travel (never reprinted); published also 'Purchas his Pilgrimage,' 1613, and 'Purchas his Pilgrim,' 1619. [xlvii. 45]

PURDON, EDWARD (1729–1767), bookseller's hack ; of Trinity College, Dublin ; remembered by Goldsmith's epitaph on him for the Wednesday Club. [xlvii. 46]

PURDY, JOHN (1773–1843), hydrographer ; became hydrographer to the London firm, Laurie & Whittle, 1812 ; published a number of important works, most of which were edited and improved after his death by Alexander George Findlay [q. v.] [xlvii. 46]

PUREFOY, WILLIAM (1580 ?–1659), regicide ; entered parliament in 1627–8 (M.P., Coventry), and sat in the Long parliament (M.P., Warwick) ; held a command in the parliamentary army, and (1648) was a member of the court which tried Charles I., signing the death-warrant ; commanded the forces in Warwickshire, 1659, during Booth's insurrection. [xlvii. 47]

PURFOY, ROBERT (*d.* 1557). [See WARTON.]

PURNELL, ROBERT (*d.* 1666), baptist elder and author ; was a chief founder of the first baptist church at Bristol, 1653. [xlvii. 47]

PURNELL, THOMAS (1834–1889), author ; of Trinity College, Dublin ; was well known in literary society in London ; edited Lamb's 'Correspondence and Works,' 1871. [xlvii. 48]

PURSGLOVE, ROBERT, otherwise SILVESTER (1500 ?–1579), bishop suffragan of Hull ; educated at St. Paul's School, London, and Corpus Christi College, Oxford ; was the last prior of the Augustinian priory, Guisborough ; consecrated bishop of Hull, 1538, and installed archdeacon of Nottingham, 1550 ; deprived of his offices for refusing the oath of supremacy, 1559. [xlvii. 48]

PURTON, WILLIAM (1784–1825), stenographer ; invented a system of shorthand, long known as Richardson's or Counsell's system. [xlvii. 49]

PURVER, ANTHONY (1702–1777), translator of the bible ; became a quaker before the age of thirty ; his 'New and Literal Translation,' known as the 'Quakers' Bible,' published by John Fothergill [q. v.], 1764. [xlvii. 49]

PURVES, JAMES (1734–1795), Scottish sectary ; joined (1755) the 'Fellowship Societies' founded by James Fraser (1639–1699) [q. v.] ; became pastor of a society at Edinburgh, 1776 ; published theological works of a high Arian character. [xlvii. 50]

PURVEY, JOHN (1353 ?–1428 ?), reviser of the Wycliffite translation of the bible ; was intimately associated with Wycliffe at Lutterworth, where he commenced to render Wycliffe's verbatim translation of the Vulgate into vernacular idiom, completing his work at Bristol, c. 1388 ; imprisoned for heresy, 1390 ; recanted, 1401 ; imprisoned by Archbishop Chicheley, 1421. [xlvii. 51]

PUSELEY, DANIEL (1814–1882), author ; published, under the pseudonym of 'Frank Foster,' numerous works, including 'The Rise and Progress of Australia, Tasmania, and New Zealand,' 1857. [xlvii. 53]

PUSEY, EDWARD BOUVERIE (1800–1882), regius professor of Hebrew at Oxford and canon of Christ Church ; was educated at Eton and Christ Church, Oxford ; M.A., 1825 ; elected, 1822, a fellow of Oriel College, Oxford, where he was brought into contact and intimacy with his brother-fellows, Keble and Newman ; on the advice of Charles Lloyd (1784–1829) [q. v.] studied oriental languages and biblical criticism at Göttingen, Berlin, and Bonn, 1825–7 ; appointed regius professor of Hebrew, Oxford, 1828 ; with his assistant lectured nine times a week, and (1832) joined with his brother Philip and Edward Ellerton [q. v.] in founding the Pusey and Ellerton scholarships ; became alarmed by the spread of rationalism in the church of England, and came to the conclusion that it could only be checked by the conviction in the minds of her defenders of her divine institution ; began to work with Newman and Keble on 'Tracts for the Times,' 1833, and was mainly instrumental in bringing about their alteration from stirring appeals to solid doctrinal treatises ; produced 'Tracts' on baptism, 1835, and 'Tracts' on the holy eucharist, 1836 ; when called upon to make some form of declaration which would clearly show his loyalty to the English church (1839), published his 'Letter to the Bishop of Oxford,' in which he distinguished between Anglican and Roman doctrine, and also separated himself from 'ultra protestant' interpretations of the Thirty-nine Articles ; identified himself with Newman when the heads of houses condemned Newman's explanation of the articles in 'Tract No. XC.,' 1841, and from that time became the leader of the Oxford movement ; suspended from the office of university preacher on a charge of heresy, 1843 ; resumed his preaching in 1846, and reiterated the teaching for which he believed he had been condemned ; commenced the establishment of Anglican sisterhoods, 1845 ; was unceasing in his efforts to hinder secession to the Roman church among those who sympathised with his views ; on the occasion of Archdeacon Denison's trial for heresy (1856) published his learned 'Doctrine of the Real Presence' in support of the high Anglican view ; engaged in later life in conflict with the latitudinarian tendency in Oxford and elsewhere ; opposed the reform of the university in 1854, on the ground that it tended to substitute intellectual for moral and religious training, and in 1862 charged Benjamin Jowett [q. v.], regius professor of Greek, before the vice-chancellor's court, with teaching opinions which were not in accordance with the doctrine of the church of England ; desisted from his opposition to the increased endowment of the Greek chair, the court having decided not to hear the case, 1863 ; made efforts to bring about the union of the English and Roman churches from 1865, but saw them annihilated by the decisions of the Vatican council in 1870 ; entertained further projects of union with the Wesleyans and the Eastern church, which proved equally ineffectual ; died at Ascot Priory, Berkshire. He consistently maintained that the true doctrines of the church of England were contained in the writings of the fathers and of Anglican divines of the seventeenth century, and that their significance had afterwards been obscured. 'Pusey House' at Oxford, an institution founded to carry on his work, inherited his library.   [xlvii. 53]

PUSEY, PHILIP (1799–1855), agriculturist ; elder brother of Edward Bouverie Pusey [q. v.] ; of Eton and Christ Church, Oxford ; inherited the family estate, 1828 ; M.P., Chippenham, 1830, Cashel, 1831, Berkshire, 1835–52 ; at first a conservative and protectionist, but after 1847 a free-trader ; espoused the cause of the agricultural tenant, 1847, and endeavoured to procure him compensation for unexhausted improvements ; many of his views embodied in the Agricultural Holdings Bill (passed, 1875) ; took a prominent part in the formation of the Royal Agricultural Society of England (1840), and (1851) was chairman of the agricultural implement department of the Great Exhibition ; published articles and pamphlets on agriculture.   [xlvii. 61]

PUTTA (d. 688), first bishop of Hereford ; consecrated by Theodore, bishop of Rochester, 669 ; was subsequently sheltered by Sexulf, bishop of the Mercians, and resided in the district of the Hecanas (afterwards Herefordshire), whence he is reckoned first bishop of Hereford.   [xlvii. 64]

PUTTENHAM, GEORGE (d. 1590), author ; was the son of Robert Puttenham, a country gentleman ; author of a manuscript prose 'Apologie' for Queen Elizabeth's treatment of Mary Queen of Scots. To him has also been assigned ' The Arte of English Poesie,' which was more probably by his elder brother, Richard Puttenham [q. v.].   [xlvii. 64]

PUTTENHAM, RICHARD (1520?–1601?), reputed author of 'The Arte of English Poesie'; elder brother of George Puttenham [q. v.] ; convicted of rape, 1561 ; was pardoned, but remained on the continent till 1570 ; afterwards resided in England. Edmund Bolton [q. v.], in his 'Hypercritica,' asserted that the 'Arte of Poesie' was the work of 'one of the queen's gentlemen pensioners named Puttenham,' and internal evidence tends to show that the work, which is of an elaborate character, was by one of the sons of Robert Puttenham. The author was a man who had travelled extensively, and he also wrote a series of poems, entitled 'Partheniades,' which are still preserved in the Cotton. MSS.   [xlvii. 64]

PYCROFT, JAMES (1813–1895), author ; younger brother of Sir Thomas Pycroft [q. v.] ; B.A. Trinity College, Oxford, 1836 ; student, Lincoln's Inn, 1836 ; well known as a cricketer ; member of the Lansdown Club ; wrote largely, especially on cricket, and published ' Oxford Memoirs,' 1886.   [xlvii. 67]

PYCROFT, SIR THOMAS (1807–1892), Madras civil servant ; of Trinity College, Oxford ; hon. M.A., 1829 ; entered East India Company's service, 1829 ; became revenue secretary to government, 1850 ; K.C.S.I., 1866 ; retired, 1867. He was the first appointed to the Indian civil service by competitive examination.   [xlvii. 67]

PYE, CHARLES (1777–1864), engraver ; pupil of James Heath (1757–1834) [q. v.] ; chiefly employed on small book illustrations.   [xlvii. 71]

PYE, HENRY JAMES (1745–1813), poetaster and poet-laureate : a descendant of Sir Robert Pye [q. v.] : of Magdalen College, Oxford ; created M.A., 1766, and D.C.L., 1772 ; was a country gentleman of Berkshire ; published 'Poems on various Subjects,' 1787, and translated the ' Poetics ' of Aristotle, 1788 ; became poet-laureate, 1790, and wrote irreproachably patriotic and ludicrously tame official poetry ; published 'Alfred,' an epic poem, 1801 ; was the constant butt of contemporary ridicule.   [xlvii. 68]

PYE, JOHN (fl. 1758–1774), engraver ; pupil of Thomas Major [q. v.] ; engraved in the line manner some admirable landscape plates.   [xlvii. 70]

PYE, JOHN (1782–1874), landscape engraver ; younger brother of Charles Pye [q. v.] ; paid assistant of James Heath (1757–1834) [q. v.] ; the favourite engraver of J. M. W. Turner, after whom he engraved a number of plates, in which for the first time the effects of light and atmosphere were adequately rendered ; received many honours from foreign countries, but was on bad terms with the Royal Academy on account of the refusal of that body to admit engravers to full privileges.   [xlvii. 70]

PYE, SIR ROBERT (d. 1701), parliamentarian ; nephew of Sir Walter Pye [q. v.] ; a colonel of horse under Essex and Fairfax ; M.P., Berkshire, 1654 and 1658 ; took little part in politics after the Restoration ; joined William of Orange on his march to London, 1688.   [xlvii. 71]

PYE, THOMAS (1560–1610), divine ; of Balliol and Merton Colleges, Oxford ; D.D., 1588 ; chaplain of Merton College, Oxford, 1581–6 ; canon of Chichester, 1586–1610 ; published miscellaneous works.   [xlvii. 72]

PYE, SIR THOMAS (1713?–1785), admiral ; grandson of Sir Robert Pye [q. v.] ; entered the navy, 1727 ; promoted captain, 1744 ; rear-admiral, 1758 ; vice-admiral, 1762 ; knighted, 1773 ; admiral, 1773. He was a man of slender ability, thrust into office by the Bathurst interest.   [xlvii. 73]

PYE, SIR WALTER (1571–1635), lawyer ; of St. John's College, Oxford ; barrister, Middle Temple ; was a favourite of Buckingham, who procured his nomination as attorney of the court of wards and liveries, 1621 ; knighted, 1630.   [xlvii. 71]

PYGG, OLIVER (fl. 1565–1591). [See PIGG.]

PYKE, JOHN (fl. 1322 ?). [See PIKE.]

PYLE, THOMAS (1674–1756), divine and author ; M.A. Caius College, Cambridge, 1699 ; a strong whig ; took part in the Bangorian controversy and gained Hoadly's friendship ; prebendary of Salisbury, 1726, but considered too heterodox for further preferment, his opinions being almost openly unitarian.   [xlvii. 74]

PYM, JOHN (1584–1643), parliamentary statesman ; eldest son of Alexander Pym of Brymore, near Bridgwater, Somerset ; educated at Broadgates Hall (Pembroke College), Oxford, and (1602) entered as a student at the Middle Temple ; M.P., Calne, 1614, 1621, and 1624 ; first became a leading speaker after the summer of 1621 ; M.P., Tavistock, 1625, 1626, and 1628 ; one of the managers of Buckingham's impeachment, May 1626 ; supported the Petition of Right, 1628, and took part in the final attack on Buckingham ; opposed the imposition of tonnage and poundage, 1629, but took no part in the disturbance which marked the end of the session, and was not therefore among those subsequently imprisoned by Charles I ; M.P., Tavistock, in the Short parliament, 1640 ; spoke at length in the Short parliament on the grievances of the nation, and resisted the grant of supplies ; drew up a petition after the dissolution and Charles I's ill-success against the Scots, requiring a parliament and demanding the trial of the advisers of Charles I's late measures ; M.P., Tavistock, in the Long parliament, 1640 ; assumed the lead in the attack on government, and (11 Nov. 1640) was empowered to carry up an immediate impeachment of Strafford ; moved the impeachment of Laud, 16 Dec. 1640 ; his influence regarded with peculiar apprehension by the royal party ; was offered the post of chancellor of the exchequer by Charles I's queen, who hoped to win him over to the royalist side ; refused the offer ; declared himself desirous of reforming rather than abolishing episcopacy and the Book of Common Prayer, 1641 ; opposed the abandonment of the impeachment of Strafford in favour of an attainder, but dreading armed intervention decided Strafford's fate by revealing to parliament his knowledge of a design to bring the army up to Westminster ; supported the Root and Branch Bill, 1641, abandoning his former preference for a modified episcopacy ; after the outbreak of the Ulster insurrection took a leading part in preparing the Grand Remonstrance, 1641 ; credited with the intention of impeaching Queen Henrietta Maria by Charles I, who thereupon directed his impeachment with four others, Hampden, Holles, Hesilrige, and Strode (the five members), and on 4 Jan. 1642 came to the Commons with an armed force to arrest them, only to find that they had fled ; escorted back to Westminster in triumph with the other four members by the citizens of London, 11 Jan. 1642 ; member of the committee of safety, July 1642; led parliament in its seizure, on the outbreak of war, of the power of taxation, and (March 1643) proposed an excise, a form of impost hitherto unknown in England; persuaded parliament to take the covenant as the price of the Scottish alliance, 1643; buried at Westminster Abbey, whence his body was ejected after the Restoration.   [xlvii. 75]

PYM, Sir SAMUEL (1778–1855), admiral; brother of Sir William Pym [q. v.]; entered the navy, 1788; commander, 1804; lost a small squadron off Mauritius and became a prisoner of war, 1810, but was acquitted by court-martial; rear-admiral, 1837; K.C.B., 1839; vice-admiral, 1847; admiral, 1852.   [xlvii. 83]

PYM, Sir WILLIAM (1772–1861), military surgeon; of Edinburgh University; served as a medical officer in the West Indies between 1794 and 1796, obtaining great knowledge of yellow fever; became inspector-general of army hospitals, 1816; K.C.H.; first to describe accurately the character of yellow fever in his 'Observations upon Bulam Fever,' 1815.   [xlvii. 84]

PYNCEBECK, WALTER (*fl.* 1327–1333), monk; an inmate of Bury St. Edmunds, where he controlled the monastic vestiary in 1333.   [xlvii. 85]

PYNCHON, WILLIAM (1590–1662), colonist and religious writer; probably educated at Cambridge; emigrated to Massachusetts, 1632, and (1636) founded Springfield; published in English a work controverting the Calvinist view of the atonement, 1650, and was driven to abandon the colony in consequence and return to England.   [xlvii. 85]

PYNE, JAMES BAKER (1800–1870), landscape-painter; exhibited almost entirely with the Society of British Artists; much influenced by Turner's later style.   [xlvii. 85]

PYNE, VALENTINE (1603–1677), master-gunner of England; served in the royal navy, in Charles I's army, and under Prince Rupert; master-gunner, 1666.   [xlvii. 86]

PYNE, WILLIAM HENRY, known as EPHRAIM HARDCASTLE (1769–1843), painter and author; first exhibited at the Royal Academy, 1790; began in 1803 to publish 'Microcosm, or a Picturesque Delineation of the Arts, Agriculture, and Manufactures of Great Britain,' consisting of groups of small figures, cleverly drawn and coloured by hand, and followed it up by several similar works; abandoned art for literature in later life, writing collections of anecdotes and reminiscences under the pseudonym of Ephraim Hardcastle.   [xlvii. 86]

PYNNAR, NICHOLAS (*fl.* 1604–1624), surveyor; came to Ireland (*c.* 1600) as a captain of foot; appointed a surveyor in Ulster, 1618; his report printed in 1757 in Harris's 'Hibernica.'   [xlvii. 87]

PYNSON, RICHARD (*d.* 1530), printer in London; a Norman by birth; succeeded William de Machlinia [q. v.], *c.* 1490, as the chief printer of law books in London; appointed king's printer on the accession of Henry VIII; introduced Roman type into England, 1509. [xlvii. 87]

PYPER, WILLIAM (1797–1861), Scots professor of humanity; of Marischal College, Aberdeen; professor of humanity, St. Andrews, 1844–61; LL.D. Aberdeen.   [xlvii. 88]

PYUS, THOMAS (1560–1610). [See PYE.]

Q

QUÆLLY, MALACHIAS (*d.* 1645), archbishop of Tuam; educated at Paris (D.D.); consecrated archbishop, 1631; raised a body of fighting men on the rebellion, but in 1645 was surprised and slain by Sir Charles Coote.   [xlvii. 88]

QUAIN, Sir JOHN RICHARD (1816–1876), judge; half-brother of Jones Quain [q. v.]; of Göttingen and University College, London (fellow, 1843); LL.B. London, 1839; barrister, Middle Temple, 1851; Q.C., 1866; appointed a judge of the queen's bench, 1871; knighted, 1872.   [xlvii. 89]

QUAIN, JONES (1796–1865), anatomist; M.D. Trinity College, Dublin, 1833; began to teach anatomy in London, 1825; professor of general anatomy at University College, London, 1831, resigning, 1835; his 'Elements of Descriptive and Practical Anatomy' (1828) frequently edited and translated.   [xlvii. 89]

QUAIN, RICHARD (1800–1887), surgeon; brother of Jones Quain [q. v.]; professor of descriptive anatomy at the University of London, 1832, holding office till 1850; F.R.S., 1844; president of the Royal College of Surgeons, 1868; published anatomical works.   [xlvii. 90]

QUAIN, Sir RICHARD, first baronet (1816–1898), physician; M.D. London, 1842; fellow of University College, London, 1843; physician at Brompton Hospital, 1855, and consulting physician, 1875; F.R.C.P., 1851, vice-president, 1889; crown nominee on general medical council, 1863, and president, 1891; member and (1874) chairman of pharmacopœia committee; F.R.S., 1871; physician extraordinary to Queen Victoria, 1890; created baronet of United Kingdom, 1891; edited 'Dictionary of Medicine,' 1882.   [Suppl. iii. 288]

QUARE, DANIEL (1648–1724), clock-maker; practised in Exchange Alley and other parts of London; subjected to some persecution as a quaker; invented repeating watches; made a fine clock for William III, which only required winding once a year, and improved the construction of barometers; master of the Clockmakers' Company, 1708.   [xlvii. 91]

QUARITCH, BERNARD (1819–1899), bookseller; born in Prussian Saxony; employed by Henry George Bohn [q. v.] in London, 1842–4 and 1846–7; opened business independently as bookseller near Leicester Square,

London, 1847; removed to 15 Piccadilly, 1860, and remained there for rest of his life; attended, personally or by deputy, every important book-auction in Europe and America; published from time to time catalogues of his stock, the last of which was 'General Catalogue of Old Books and Manuscripts,' 1887–8, index, 1892, 7 vols. Special catalogues were compiled for him by Mr. Michael Kerney, his literary adviser.   [Suppl. iii. 289]

QUARLES, CHARLES (*d.* 1727), musician; Mus. Bac. Cambridge, 1678; organist at Trinity College, Cambridge, and from 1722 at York Minster.   [xlvii. 92]

QUARLES, FRANCIS (1592–1644), poet; B.A. Christ's College, Cambridge, 1608; studied at Lincoln's Inn; became cup-bearer to the Princess Elizabeth in 1613 on her marriage to the elector palatine; returned to London before 1620; published, 1620, his 'Feast of Wormes,' a paraphrase of Jonah, which was followed by many similar efforts; became private secretary to Archbishop Ussher before 1629; published 'Argalus and Parthenia,' a poetic romance, 1629; retired before 1633 to Essex, where he assured his fame by publishing his 'Emblems' in 1635, the work being quaintly illustrated by William Marshall (*fl.* 1630–1650) [q. v.]; appointed chronologer to the city of London, 1639, and from that time mainly devoted himself to composing prose manuals of piety; wrote in defence of Charles I, in consequence of which his manuscripts were destroyed by parliamentary soldiers. His books were constantly reprinted for more than a century after his death. A complete collection of his 'Works' was edited by Grosart in 1874 for the 'Chertsey Worthies Library.'   [xlvii. 92]

QUARLES, JOHN (1624–1665), poet; son of Francis Quarles [q. v.]; of Exeter College, Oxford; bore arms for Charles I at Oxford and banished; published, in Flanders, 'Fons Lachrymarum,' and, after his return, other works; died of the plague of 1665.   [xlvii. 96]

QUEENSBERRY, DUKES OF. [See DOUGLAS, WILLIAM, first DUKE, 1637–1695; DOUGLAS, JAMES, second DUKE, 1662–1711; DOUGLAS, CHARLES, third DUKE, 1698–1778; DOUGLAS, WILLIAM, fourth DUKE, 1724–1810; SCOTT, Sir HENRY, fifth DUKE, 1746–1812; SCOTT, WALTER FRANCIS, seventh DUKE, 1806–1884.]

QUEENSBERRY, DUCHESS OF (*d.* 1777). [See DOUGLAS, CATHERINE.]

QUEENSBERRY, MARQUISES OF. [See DOUGLAS, WILLIAM, first MARQUIS, 1637–1695; DOUGLAS, SIR JOHN SHOLTO, eighth MARQUIS, 1844–1900.]

QUEENSBERRY, EARLS OF. [See DOUGLAS, SIR WILLIAM, first EARL, *d.* 1640; DOUGLAS, JAMES, second EARL, *d.* 1671; DOUGLAS, WILLIAM, third EARL, 1637–1695.]

QUEKETT, EDWIN JOHN (1808–1847), microscopist; brother of William Quekett [q. v.]; was appointed lecturer on botany at London Hospital, 1835; F.L.S., 1836; genus *Quekettia* named after him. In his house the Royal Microscopical Society originated in 1839. [xlvii. 98]

QUEKETT, JOHN THOMAS (1815–1861), histologist; brother of William Quekett [q. v.]; appointed assistant-conservator of the Hunterian Museum, 1843; made a valuable collection of microscopic preparations, which were purchased by the Royal College of Surgeons, 1846; constituted professor of histology, 1852, and conservator of the Hunterian Museum, 1856; published scientific works. [xlvii. 97]

QUEKETT, WILLIAM (1802–1888), divine; B.A. St. John's College, Cambridge, 1825; distinguished for his social work while a curate in London. He was the subject of Dickens's articles, 'What a London curate can do if he tries,' in 'Household Words' (16 Nov. 1850), and 'Emigration' (*ib.* 24 Jan. 1852). [xlvii. 98]

QUEMERFORD, NICHOLAS (1544?–1599). [See COMBERFORD.]

QUEROUAILLE, LOUISE RENÉE DE, DUCHESS OF PORTSMOUTH AND AUBIGNY (1649–1734). [See KEROUALLE.]

QUESNE, CHARLES LE (1811–1856). [See LE QUESNE.]

QUESNEL or **QUESUEL**, PETER (*d.* 1299?), Franciscan; doctor of the canon law; warden of the Franciscan College at Norwich; wrote 'Directorium Juris in Foro Conscientiæ et Juridiciali,' of which several manuscripts are extant. [xlvii. 98]

QUICK, HENRY (1792–1857), the Cornish poet; wrote rugged verse on local and national events of note. [xlvii. 99]

QUICK, JOHN (1636–1706), nonconformist divine; B.A. Exeter College, Oxford, 1657; ordained presbyter, 1659; ejected from Brixton for nonconformity, 1662, and was afterwards several times imprisoned; published religious treatises. [xlvii. 99]

QUICK, JOHN (1748–1831), actor; joined a theatrical company in his fourteenth year; went to Covent Garden, London, 1767; played at first mainly clowns, rustics, and comic servants; the original Tony Lumpkin, 1773; essayed Richard III to the laughter of the audience, 1790; retired from Covent Garden, London, 1797, and henceforth only appeared intermittently. [xlvii. 100]

QUICK, ROBERT HEBERT (1831–1891), schoolmaster and educational writer; B.A. Trinity College, Cambridge, 1854; assistant-master of Harrow, 1870–4; appointed by the university to lecture at Cambridge on the history of education, 1881; published 'Essays on Educational Reformers,' 1868. [xlvii. 103]

QUILLINAN, DOROTHY (1804–1847), authoress; daughter of William Wordsworth the poet; married to Edward Quillinan [q. v.], 1841; published a 'Journal' of a visit to Spain and Portugal, 1847. [xlvii. 104]

QUILLINAN, EDWARD (1791–1851), poet; entered a cavalry regiment, and in 1814 began seriously to publish verse; settled at Ambleside, near Wordsworth, 1821; most successful in his translation of five books of Camoens's 'Lusiad' (published, 1853, by John Adamson (1787–1855) [q. v.]). [xlvii. 103]

QUIN, EDWARD (*d.* 1823), journalist; founded, in 1803, 'The Traveller,' which was merged (1823) in the 'Globe.' [xlvii. 105]

QUIN, EDWARD (1794–1828), cartographer; son of Edward Quin (*d.* 1823) [q. v.]; published 'An Historical Atlas' (1840), with a 'Universal History from the Creation.' [xlvii. 105]

QUIN, SIR EDWIN RICHARD WINDHAM WYNDHAM-, third EARL OF DUNRAVEN and MOUNT-EARL in the peerage of Ireland, and first BARON KENRY of the United Kingdom (1812–1871), B.A. Trinity College, Dublin, 1833; sat in the Commons in the conservative interest (M.P., Glamorganshire) from 1837–51; succeeded his father as an Irish earl, 1850, and (1866) was created a baron of the United Kingdom; F.R.S., 1834; F.S.A., 1836; a zealous archæologist, writing an architectural history. [xlvii. 105]

QUIN, FREDERIC HERVEY FOSTER (1799–1878), the first homœopathic physician in England; M.D. Edinburgh, 1820; went to Rome, 1820, as physician to the Duchess of Devonshire and (1821) commenced practice at Naples; converted to homœopathy, 1826, and returned to England as physician to Prince Leopold of Saxe-Coburg; began public practice in London, 1832, and was denounced as a quack; founded the British Homœopathic Society, 1844, and the London Homœopathic Hospital, 1850. [xlvii. 106]

QUIN, JAMES (1621–1659), vocalist; son of Walter Quin [q. v.]; of Westminster School and Christ Church, Oxford; M.A., 1646; was ejected from Christ Church, Oxford, as a loyalist, but so charmed Cromwell with his bass voice that he restored him; died insane. [xlvii. 112]

QUIN, JAMES (1693–1766), actor; took to the stage in Dublin and appeared at Drury Lane, London, in 1714 or 1715; first came into note, 1716, as Bajazet in 'Tamerlane'; acted at Lincoln's Inn Fields, London, where he took leading parts in tragedy, 1717–32; subsequently appeared at Covent Garden, London, and, 1734, returned to Drury Lane, London; reappeared at Covent Garden, 1742, and remained there till 1751; rival of Garrick at Covent Garden, 1746 and 1747; lived, after his retirement (1751) in friendship with Garrick. Walpole admired him more than Garrick, but Davies declares that he was unfitted for vigorous parts in tragedy. [xlvii. 107]

QUIN, MICHAEL JOSEPH (1796–1843), traveller and political writer; barrister, Lincoln's Inn; travelled much on the continent, and published a number of books of travel. [xlvii. 111]

QUIN, WALTER (1575?–1634?), poet and preceptor of Charles I; studied at Edinburgh University; was taken into the service of James VI as tutor to his sons, and migrated to England in 1603; published several poems and a life of Lord Bernard Stuart (1619). [xlvii. 111]

QUINCEY, THOMAS DE (1785–1859). [See DE QUINCEY.]

QUINCY, JOHN (*d.* 1722), medical writer; practised medicine as an apothecary and physician in London; M.D. Edinburgh for his 'Medicina Statica Britannica,' 1712; published a number of medical treatises. [xlvii. 112]

QUINCY, ROGER DE, second EARL OF WINCHESTER (1195?–1265), son of Saer de Quincy, first earl of Winchester [q. v.]; succeeded to the title, 1235; married Helen, daughter of Alan, lord of Galloway; became constable of Scotland in right of his wife; took part in the disputes between Henry III and his barons, and on several occasions acted on behalf of the barons. [xlvii. 115]

QUINCY, QUENCY, or QUENCI, SAER, SAHER, or SEER DE, first EARL OF WINCHESTER (*d.* 1219), while a comparatively poor knight married the daughter of Robert III, earl of Leicester, c. 1170, and (1204) succeeded in his wife's right to half the lands of Robert IV, earl of Leicester; created Earl of Winchester, 1207; took part in the barons' struggle against King John, who particularly disliked him during the last few years of his reign on account of his former intimacy with him; his lands confiscated by King John, on which he invited Louis, the dauphin of France, to take the crown; taken prisoner at the battle of Lincoln, 1217; died a crusader at Acre, immediately after his arrival. [xlvii. 116]

QUINTON, JAMES WALLACE (1834–1891), chief commissioner of Assam; B.A. Trinity College, Dublin, 1853; entered the Bengal civil service; served chiefly in the North-West Provinces and Oudh till 1883; became chief commissioner of Assam, 1889; treacherously assassinated at Manipur while on a political mission. [xlvii. 116]

QUIVIL or **QUIVEL**, PETER DE (*d.* 1291), bishop of Exeter; consecrated, 1280; a liberal benefactor to Exeter Cathedral and its clergy. His most memorable work was the reconstruction of the two transept towers of Bishop Warelwast's Norman church. [xlvii. 117]

R

RABAN, EDWARD (d. 1658), printer in Aberdeen : a native of England ; started as a printer in Edinburgh, 1620, after serving as a soldier in the Netherlands ; settled at Aberdeen, where, between 1622 and 1649, he issued, besides academic productions, some interesting Scottish books. [xlvii. 118]

RABY, third BARON (1672–1739). [See WENTWORTH, THOMAS, third EARL OF STRAFFORD.]

RACK, EDMUND (1735 ?–1787), miscellaneous writer ; settled at Bath, 1775 ; established the Bath and West of England Agricultural Society, 1779 ; published religious, agricultural, and other treatises. [xlvii. 118]

RACKETT, THOMAS (1757–1841), antiquary ; M.A. University College, Oxford, 1780 ; rector of Spetisbury in Dorset for more than sixty years. [xlvii. 119]

RADCLIFFE. [See also RATCLIFFE.]

RADCLIFFE, ALEXANDER (fl. 1669–1696), verse-writer ; admitted at Gray's Inn, 1669 ; became a captain in the army, 1696 ; published three ribald poems between 1673 and 1682. [xlvii. 119]

RADCLIFFE, ANN (1764–1823), novelist ; only daughter of William Ward ; married William Radcliffe, a law-student, at the age of twenty-three ; her first novel published, 1789 ; produced 'A Sicilian Romance,' 1790, and 'The Romance of the Forest,' 1791 ; published 'The Mysteries of Udolpho,' 1794, and 'The Italian,' a romance of the inquisition, usually regarded as her best work, 1797 ; wrote nothing subsequently : lived in retirement. She was the founder of a school of romance in which terror and curiosity are aroused by events apparently supernatural, but afterwards naturally explained. [xlvii. 120]

RADCLIFFE or RADCLYFFE, CHARLES, titular EARL OF DERWENTWATER (1693–1746), Jacobite ; brother of Sir James Radcliffe, third earl of Derwentwater [q. v.] ; took part in the rising of 1715, and escaped from Newgate after capture ; assumed the title, 1731 ; became secretary to Prince Charles Edward, and in 1745 was captured off Dogger Bank ; condemned to death and beheaded. [xlvii. 127]

RADCLIFFE, CHARLES BLAND (1822–1889), physician ; M.D. London, 1851 ; became physician at Westminster Hospital in 1857 ; F.R.C.P., 1858 ; Gulstonian lecturer, 1860 ; Croonian lecturer, 1873 ; censor, 1875–6 ; one of the earliest investigators in this country of the electrical physiology of muscle and nerve. [xlvii. 121]

RADCLIFFE or RADCLYFFE, CHARLES EDWARD (1774–1827), lieutenant-colonel ; served in the Peninsular war, 1809–14 ; fought at Waterloo, 1815 ; brevet lieutenant-colonel, 1815. [xlvii. 122]

RADCLIFFE or RADCLYFFE, CHARLOTTE MARIA, COUNTESS OF NEWBURGH (d. 1755), grand-daughter of Sir James Livingstone, first Earl of Newburgh [q. v.] ; succeeded her father Charles Livingstone, second earl of Newburgh, as countess, suo jure, 1694 ; married successively to Thomas Clifford (d. 1718) and to Charles Radcliffe, afterwards titular earl of Derwentwater [q. v.], who after unsuccessfully urging his suit, induced her to marry him by entering her room through the chimney, 1724. [xlvii. 127]

RADCLIFFE, EGREMONT (d. 1578), rebel ; son of Sir Henry Radcliffe, second earl of Sussex [q. v.] ; took part in the rebellion of 1569, and was imprisoned in the Tower of London between 1575 and 1578 ; went to Flanders, 1578, and was beheaded for plotting to poison Don John of Austria. [xlvii. 123]

RADCLIFFE, SIR GEORGE (1593–1657), politician ; B.A. University College, Oxford, 1612 ; barrister, Gray's Inn, 1618, bencher, 1632 ; M.P., 1628 ; a friend of Wentworth, whose private affairs he managed, and with whom he went to Ireland, landing six months before him, 1633 ; Wentworth's chief adviser in all legal and financial matters ; was hindered from bearing witness on Strafford's behalf on his impeachment, but contrived to aid him in preparing his defence ; joined Charles I at Oxford, 1643, and on the surrender of that city refused to take the Duke of York out of England without Charles I's order, though bidden to do so by Queen Henrietta Maria, and handed him over to the Earl of Northumberland ; joined the Duke of York and became his adviser, 1649. [xlvii. 123]

RADCLIFFE, SIR HENRY, second EARL OF SUSSEX (1506 ?–1557), eldest son of Sir Robert Radcliffe, first earl of Sussex [q. v.] : K.B., 1533 ; declared for Queen Mary, 1553, and was made captain-general and a privy councillor. [xlvii. 136]

RADCLIFFE, SIR HENRY, fourth EARL OF SUSSEX (1530 ?–1593), son of Sir Henry Radcliffe, second earl of Sussex [q. v.] ; M.P., Malden, 1555 ; served in Ireland between 1556 and 1565 ; M.P., Carlingford (Irish parliament), 1559 ; M.P., Hampshire, 1571 ; succeeded his brother as earl, 1583 ; K.G., 1589. [xlvii. 143]

RADCLIFFE or RADCLYFFE, SIR JAMES, baronet, third EARL OF DERWENTWATER (1689–1716), was brought up at St. Germain as a companion to James Edward ; returned to England, 1710, but aided the rebellion of 1715, and joined Thomas Forster at Green-rig in October ; taken prisoner at Preston, attainted, and beheaded. On account of his youth and popular manner his death excited general compassion. [xlvii. 126]

RADCLIFFE or RATCLIFFE, JOHN, first BARON FITZWALTER (1452 ?–1496), became a baron in 1485 ; took part in Perkin Warbeck's conspiracy ; attainted, 1495, and beheaded next year. [xlvii. 128]

RADCLIFFE, JOHN (1650–1714), physician ; B.A. University College, Oxford, 1669 ; fellow of Lincoln College, Oxford, 1669–77 ; M.A., 1672 ; he began to practise as a physician at Oxford ; removed to London, where he made twenty guineas a day, 1684 ; became physician to the Princess Anne, 1686 ; offended Anne by styling her distemper nothing but the vapours, and was succeeded by William Gibbons [q. v.], c. 1695 ; annoyed many great people by his extraordinary candour, and declined to visit Queen Anne on her deathbed ; made a number of remarkable cures. The Radcliffe Infirmary and Observatory, Oxford, were built, and Bartholomew's Hospital, London, enlarged from funds bequeathed by him. [xlvii. 129]

RADCLIFFE, JOHN (1690–1729), physician ; M.A. St. John's College, Oxford, 1714 ; M.D., 1721 ; F.R.C.P., 1724 ; physician to St. Bartholomew's Hospital, London. [xlvii. 132]

RADCLIFFE, JOHN NETTEN (1826–1884), epidemiologist ; brother of Charles Bland Radcliffe [q. v.] ; was attached to the headquarters of Omar Pasha as surgeon during the Crimean war. He became an expert on oriental diseases and all questions pertaining to the public health ; made public health inspector, 1869. [xlvii. 132]

RADCLIFFE, NICHOLAS (fl. 1368–1396), opponent of Wycliffe ; a monk of St. Albans ; doctor of theology, Gloucester Hall, Oxford ; was a prominent literary antagonist of Wycliffe, who stigmatised him and the Carmelite, Peter Stokes [q. v.], as the black and white dogs. [xlvii. 133]

RADCLIFFE, RALPH (1519 ?–1559), schoolmaster and playwright ; educated at Brasenose College, Oxford, and (probably) Jesus College, Cambridge ; M.A. Cambridge, 1539 ; opened a school at Hitchin ; wrote several miracle plays for his pupils to act. [xlvii. 133]

RADCLIFFE or RATCLIFFE, SIR RICHARD (d. 1485), adviser of Richard III ; knighted by Edward IV at Tewkesbury ; executed Earl Rivers and others of the queen-dowager's party at Pontefract, 1483 ; loaded with honours and grants by Richard III ; K.G., 1484 ; killed at Bosworth. [xlvii. 134]

RADCLIFFE or RATCLIFFE, SIR ROBERT, first EARL OF SUSSEX, first VISCOUNT FITZWALTER, and second BARON FITZWALTER (1483–1542), son of John Radcliffe, first baron Fitzwalter [q. v.] ; obtained the reversal of his father's attainder in 1506 ; became a prominent courtier under Henry VIII ; K.G., 1524 ; created viscount, 1525 ; privy councillor, 1526 ; created earl, 1529 ; appointed great chamberlain of England, 1540. [xlvii. 135]

RADCLIFFE, ROBERT, fifth EARL OF SUSSEX (1569?–1629), only son of Sir Henry Radcliffe, fourth earl of Sussex [q. v.]; knighted at Cadiz, 1596; acted as earl marshal in 1597 and 1601, and sat in the commission to try Essex in 1601; a patron of men of letters. [xlvi. 144]

RADCLIFFE, SIR THOMAS, third EARL OF SUSSEX (1526?–1583), eldest son of Sir Henry Radcliffe, second earl of Sussex [q. v.]; educated at Cambridge; member of Gray's Inn, 1561; held a command at Pinkie Cleugh, 1547; knight of the shire for Norfolk, 1553; rendered Queen Mary great service in suppressing Wyatt's rebellion; assisted in the marriage negotiations with Philip II, and in 1556 was appointed lord-deputy of Ireland; was a vigorous administrator, carrying his arms through a large part of the country; returned to England on the news of Queen Mary's death, but was reappointed, July 1559, and reintroduced the spiritual supremacy of the crown and the English liturgy; involved (1560–3) in a struggle with Shane O'Neill in Tyrone; failed to subdue O'Neill, and early in 1564 was permitted to resign his office, leaving behind him a reputation for statesmanship which grew with succeeding years; employed to negotiate Queen Elizabeth's marriage with the Archduke Maximilian, 1567, and (1569) was created lord president of the north; dealt successfully with the rebellion of 1569, showing more leniency than Queen Elizabeth approved, and (1570) pursued the rebels into Scotland; supported the project of a French match for Queen Elizabeth both in 1571 and 1578, and thus came into conflict with Leicester. [xlvi. 136]

RADCLIFFE, WILLIAM (1760–1841), improver of cotton machinery; began business at Mellor as a spinner and weaver, 1789; removed to Stockport, 1801; brought out (1804) the 'dressing-machine' invented by his employé, Thomas Johnson; reaped little pecuniary benefit from this and other services rendered to the trade; died in poverty. [xlvi. 145]

RADCLYFFE. [See also RADCLIFFE and RATCLIFFE.]

RADCLYFFE, EDWARD (1809–1863), engraver; son of William Radclyffe (1783–1855) [q. v.]; worked for the 'Art Journal,' and engraved charts for the admiralty. [xlvi. 147]

RADCLYFFE, WILLIAM (1813–1846), portrait-painter; son of William Radclyffe (1783–1855) [q. v.]; practised in London and Birmingham. [xlvi. 147]

RADCLYFFE, WILLIAM (1783–1855), line-engraver; practised in Birmingham, where he formed a school of engravers of great ability. [xlvi. 146]

RADFORD, JOHN (1561–1630), jesuit; educated at Douai; ordained priest, 1587; missioner in England, 1589–1630. [xlvi. 147]

RADFORD, THOMAS (1793–1881), obstetrician; studied at Guy's and St. Thomas's Hospitals, London; elected surgeon to the Manchester and Salford Lying-in Hospital, 1818; M.D. Heidelberg, 1839; F.R.C.S., 1852; author of many papers on midwifery. [xlvi. 147]

RADLEY, WILLIAM DE (d. 1250). [See RALEIGH.]

RADNOR, EARLS OF. [See ROBARTES, SIR JOHN, first EARL, 1606–1685; BOUVERIE, WILLIAM PLEYDELL-, third EARL of the second creation, 1779–1869.]

RADSTOCK, BARONS. [See WALDEGRAVE, WILLIAM, first BARON, 1753–1825; WALDEGRAVE, GEORGE GRANVILLE, second BARON, 1786–1857.]

RADULPH. [See RALPH, RANDOLPH, and RANULF.]

RAE. [See also RAY.]

RAE, ALEXANDER (1782–1820), actor; appeared at Bath as Hamlet, 1806, and at the Haymarket, London, as Octavian, 1806; first appeared at Drury Lane, London, 1812, remaining there till 1820; undertook (1820) the management of the Royalty Theatre, London, which speedily ruined him. [xlvi. 148]

RAE, SIR DAVID, first baronet, LORD ESKGROVE (1724?–1804), lord-justice clerk; studied law at Edinburgh University; became a lord of session, 1782, a lord of justiciary, 1785, and lord-justice clerk, 1799; one of those who tried Thomas Fyshe Palmer [q. v.] and other Scots charged with sedition; created baronet, 1804; was a judge of ability, though with many absurdities of demeanour. [xlvi. 150]

RAE, JAMES (1716–1791), surgeon; established the teaching of clinical surgery at Edinburgh on a firm and broad platform by his lectures at the Royal Infirmary. [xlvi. 150]

RAE, JOHN (1813–1893), Arctic explorer; qualified as a surgeon at Edinburgh, 1833; a surgeon in the employ of the Hudson's Bay Company; joined the first land expedition in search of Sir John Franklin, 1847, and in 1851 he commanded another search party which examined Woilaston Land; obtained decisive intelligence of Franklin's fate from the natives on the west coast of Boothia, and obtained the government reward of 10,000l., 1854; F.R.S., 1880; hon. LL.D. Edinburgh. [xlvi. 151]

RAE, PETER (1671–1748), mechanic and historian; originally a clockmaker; minister of Kirkconnel, 1732–1748; published a 'History of the Rebellion of 1715,' 1718. [xlvi. 153]

RAE, SIR WILLIAM, third baronet (1769–1842), lord advocate; son of Sir David Rae, lord Eskgrove [q. v.]; studied at Edinburgh University; appointed lord advocate, 1819; M.P., Anstruther burghs, 1819–26, Harwich, 1827, Buteshire, 1830 and 1833–42, Portarlington, 1831–2; intimate friend of Sir Walter Scott. [xlvi. 153]

RAE, SIR WILLIAM (1786–1873), naval surgeon; M.D. Edinburgh; L.R.C.P., 1839; F.R.C.S., 1843; knighted, 1858; attained the rank of inspector-general of hospitals and fleets. [xlvi. 155]

RAEBURN, SIR HENRY (1756–1823), portrait-painter; sometimes called the 'Scottish Reynolds'; son of an Edinburgh manufacturer; began to paint water-colour miniatures of his friends at the age of sixteen; married, 1778, Ann Leslie, a widow of fortune, and, on the advice of Reynolds, resolved to study his art in Rome; returned to Edinburgh, 1787, and was for thirty years a fashionable portrait-painter, during which he painted every contemporary of note except Burns; R.A., 1815; knighted, 1822. His works are to be found chiefly in the private houses of Scotland, but the two Edinburgh galleries own many fine examples. [xlvi. 155]

RAFFALD, ELIZABETH (1733–1781), cook and author; daughter of Joshua Whitaker; employed in various families as housekeeper; married John Raffald, head-gardener at Arley, 1763; compiled the first Manchester directory, 1772. [xlvi. 159]

RAFFLES, THOMAS (1788–1863), independent minister; was minister of George Yard Chapel, Hammersmith, 1809–11, and of Newington Chapel, Liverpool, 1811–62; one of the chief founders and organisers of the Lancashire Independent College. [xlvi. 160]

RAFFLES, SIR THOMAS STAMFORD (1781–1826), colonial governor; entered the East India Company's service and landed in Penang, 1805; assisted in the reduction of Java, and was appointed lieutenant-governor, 1811; continued to hold office until the restoration of Java to the Dutch in 1815, and introduced a new system of land tenure and other changes; acquired immense scientific, historical, and philological knowledge in regard to the East India islands, which he embodied in his 'History of Java' (1817); knighted, 1817; from 1818 resided chiefly in Bencoolen, of which he had been appointed governor by Lord Minto; persuaded the company to acquire the island of Singapore, 1819; returned to England, but lost all his papers, besides his immense zoological and botanical collections, owing to the vessel in which they were embarked catching fire, 1824; lived in retirement for the rest of his life near Barnet, occupying himself with the foundation of the Zoological Society, of which he was the first president. [xlvi. 161]

RAFTOR, CATHERINE (1711–1785). [See CLIVE, CATHERINE.]

RAGG, THOMAS (1808–1881), divine and poet; son of George Ragg, a prominent radical; became a bookseller's assistant, 1834; began to publish poetry, and (1839) turned newspaper editor; ordained, 1858, and (1865) appointed perpetual curate of Lawley; published poems and works dealing with the relation of science to theology. [xlvi. 165]

RAGLAN, first BARON (1788–1855). [See SOMERSET, LORD FITZROY JAMES HENRY.]

RAHERE (*d.* 1144), founder of St. Bartholomew's Hospital, London; prebendary of St. Paul's, London; began to build St. Bartholomew's Hospital on its present site in 1123, was its first master till 1137, and obtained a royal charter for it, 1133. [xlvii. 167]

RAIKES, CHARLES (1812–1885), writer on India; commissioner of Lahore; C.S.I., 1866. [xlvii. 167]

RAIKES, HENRY (1782–1854), divine; brother of Thomas Raikes [q. v.]; of Eton and St. John's College, Cambridge; M.A., 1807; chancellor of the diocese of Chester, 1830–54; zealously promoted archæological research in the county; published sermons. [xlvii. 167]

RAIKES, HENRY CECIL (1838–1891), politician; grandson of Henry Raikes [q. v.]; B.A. Trinity College, Cambridge, 1860; barrister, Middle Temple, 1863; entered parliament as a conservative, 1868–80 (M.P., Chester); chairman of committees, 1874–80; M.P., Preston, 1882, Cambridge University, 1882; postmaster-general, 1886–91. [xlvii. 167]

RAIKES, ROBERT (1735–1811), promoter of Sunday schools; a printer at Gloucester; opened his first school in 1780; was not strictly the originator of the idea of teaching children on Sunday, but spread the knowledge of a plan for cheap schools, which was adapted to the wants of the day, and was really the origin of the modern system. [xlvii. 168]

RAIKES, THOMAS (1777–1848), dandy and diarist; nephew of Robert Raikes [q. v.]; educated at Eton; was a London merchant and a governor of the Bank of England; a well-known figure in west-end clubs and an associate of George Brummell. His diary was published in 1356 and 1857. [xlvii. 170]

RAILTON, WILLIAM (*d.* 1877), architect; designed the Nelson memorial in Trafalgar Square, London, in 1839. [xlvii. 171]

RAIMBACH, ABRAHAM (1776–1843), line-engraver; executed, between 1814 and 1825, six large engravings of the pictures of Sir David Wilkie; wrote 'Memoirs and Recollections' (privately printed, 1843). [xlvii. 171]

RAINBOROW, **RAINBOROWE**, or **RAINS-BOROUGH**, THOMAS (*d.* 1648), soldier; son of William Rainborow [q. v.]; served in the parliamentary fleet and army and (1645) received command of a regiment; M.P., Droitwich, 1646; sided with the army in opposing disbandment, 1647; led the republican section among the officers, and opposed further negotiations with Charles I; proceeded to sea as vice-admiral, 1648; occasioned a mutiny by his imperious demeanour, and in May 1648 returned to the army; while besieging Pontefract was surprised by a party of cavaliers, and mortally wounded while resisting capture. [xlvii. 172]

RAINBOROW, WILLIAM (*d.* 1642), naval commander; was a master in the navy in 1626; successfully commanded a punitive expedition to Sallee, 1637. [xlvii. 173]

RAINBOWE, EDWARD (1608–1684), bishop of Carlisle; of Westminster School, Corpus Christi College, Oxford, and Magdalene College, Cambridge; M.A. Cambridge, 1630; D.D., 1646; elected fellow of Magdalene College, Cambridge, 1633; master, 1642; expelled from his mastership by parliament, 1650, but restored, 1660; dean of Peterborough, 1661–4; bishop of Carlisle, 1664–1684; famous as a preacher. [xlvii. 174]

RAINE, JAMES (1791–1858), antiquary and topographer; formed an acquaintance with Surtees, 1812, and became an enthusiastic antiquary and topographer; librarian to the dean and chapter of Durham, 1816–58; rector of Meldon, 1822–58; M.A. Lambeth, 1825; became literary executor to Surtees, and edited the fourth volume of his 'History of Durham,' 1840; published the two volumes of his own 'History of North Durham,' 1830 and 1852; hon. D.C.L. Durham, 1857. [xlvii. 175]

RAINE, MATTHEW (1760–1811), schoolmaster and divine; fellow of Trinity College, Cambridge, 1784; M.A., 1785; D.D., 1799; head-master of Charterhouse School, 1791–1811; F.R.S., 1803; Parr and Porson were his intimate friends. [xlvii. 176]

RAINES, FRANCIS ROBERT (1805–1878), antiquary; perpetual curate of St. James, Milnrow, 1832–78; F.S.A., 1843; helped to found the Chetham Society, 1843,

and contributed some of the most valuable of its works; M.A. Lambeth, 1845. [xlvii. 177]

RAINEY, GEORGE (1801–1884), anatomist; taught anatomy privately in London between 1827 and 1837; M.R.C.S., 1827; became demonstrator at St. Thomas's Hospital, 1846, and was one of the ablest instructors in London; published scientific works. [xlvii. 178]

RAINFORTH, ELIZABETH (1814–1877), vocalist; first sung in public, 1836; subsequently performed at St. James's Theatre, London, the English Opera House, London, Covent Garden, London, and Drury Lane, London. Her voice was soprano. [xlvii. 179]

RAINIER, PETER (1741?–1808), admiral; entered the navy, 1756; attained post rank, 1778; commander-in-chief in the East Indies, 1793–1804, capturing Trincomalee, Amboyna, and Banda Neira; admiral, 1805. [xlvii. 179]

RAINOLDS. [See also REYNOLDS.]

RAINOLDS or **REYNOLDS**, JOHN (1549–1607), president of Corpus Christi College, Oxford; brother of William Rainolds [q. v.]; was a fellow of Corpus Christi College, Oxford (1566–86), where he became famous as Greek reader for his lectures on Aristotle; B.A., 1568; dean of Lincoln, 1593–8; president of Corpus Christi College, Oxford, 1598–1607; took a prominent part in the Hampton Court conference and in the translation of the Prophets for the Authorised Version. [xlvii. 180]

RAINOLDS, WILLIAM (1544?–1594), Roman catholic divine; of Winchester School and New College, Oxford; fellow of New College, Oxford, 1560–72; M.A., 1567; received into the Roman church, 1575; became professor of divinity and Hebrew at the English College at Rheims, and assisted Gregory Martin [q. v.] in preparing his version of the New Testament; published controversial works. [xlvii. 182]

RAINSBOROUGH. [See RAINBOROW.]

RAINSFORD, CHARLES (1728–1809), general; entered the army, 1744, and saw much active service; M.P., Maldon, 1773, Beeralston, 1787, and Newport, 1790; F.R.S., 1779; general, 1795. He left forty volumes of manuscript memoranda, now in the British Museum. [xlvii. 183]

RAINSFORD, MARCUS (*fl.* 1794–1805), author; held a commission in the army, and published accounts of St. Domingo and Hayti, which he had visited. [xlvii. 184]

RAINSFORD, SIR RICHARD (1605–1680), judge; of Exeter College, Oxford; barrister, Lincoln's Inn, 1632 (treasurer, 1660); M.P. for Northampton in Convention parliament of 1660 and Charles II's first parliament; knighted, *c.* 1661; raised to the exchequer bench, 1663; transferred to the king's bench, 1669; removed to make room for Scroggs, 1678. [xlvii. 184]

RAINTON, SIR NICHOLAS (1569–1646), lord mayor of London; member of the Haberdashers' Company; became lord mayor, 1632; president of St. Bartholomew's Hospital, London, 1634–46; imprisoned by Star Chamber (1640) for refusing to furnish a list of citizens able to advance money to Charles I, but released five days later. [xlvii. 185]

RAINY, HARRY (1792–1876), physician; studied at Glasgow and Edinburgh; M.D. Glasgow, 1833; acquired a large practice in Glasgow; professor of forensic medicine at Glasgow University, 1841–62; hon. LL.D. Glasgow University, 1873. [xlvii. 185]

RAITHBY, JOHN (1766–1826), lawyer; barrister, Lincoln's Inn; published anonymously, 'The Study and Practice of the Law considered,' 1798. [xlvii. 186]

RALEGH, SIR CAREW (1550?–1625?), naval commander; brother of Sir Walter Ralegh [q. v.]; M.P., Wiltshire, 1586, Ludgershall, 1589, and Downton, 1604 and 1621; knighted, 1601. [xlvii. 187]

RALEGH, CAREW (1605–1666), politician; only surviving son of Sir Walter Ralegh [q. v.]; of Wadham College, Oxford; was restored in blood, 1628; M.P., Haslemere, 1648–53 and 1659; nominated governor of Jersey, 1660. [xlvii. 205]

RALEGH, SIR WALTER (1552?–1618), military and naval commander and author; son of Walter Ralegh, a Devonshire gentleman; born at Hayes Barton in South

Devon; educated at Oriel College, Oxford; served in France in the Huguenot army at Jarnac and Moncontour, 1569; undertook a 'voyage of discovery' with his half-brother, Sir Humphrey Gilbert, 1578, and (June 1580) sailed to Ireland as captain of a company; put to death the Spanish and Italian garrison of the Fort del Oro at Smerwick in accordance with the lord deputy's order, 1580; was sent to England with despatches, 1581, and at once caught Queen Elizabeth's fancy; remained at court for several years, the recipient of Queen Elizabeth's bounties to an extent which gave much occasion for scandal; obtained numerous grants, and (1584) was knighted; obtained a patent to take possession of un-known lands in America in Queen Elizabeth's name, 1584, and on the return of a preliminary expedition the sea-board of the continent from Florida to Newfoundland was christened Virginia (first settlement made by Sir Richard Grenville (1541?-1591) [q. v.], 1585, abandoned, 1586; after several unsuccessful expeditions, in 1603 the patent lapsed to the crown); never visited Virginia himself, though the traditional story that potatoes and tobacco were intro-duced into England in consequence of these attempts at colonisation is probably correct; placed on a commission to draw up a plan of defence against invasion from Spain, 1588; found his influence somewhat lessened by a quarrel with the new favourite, Essex, 1588, and (1592) was com-mitted to the Tower by Queen Elizabeth, who discovered that he had carried on an intrigue with Eliza-beth Throgmorton; released, but subsequently marrying Elizabeth Throgmorton was forbidden the court; settled at Sherborne and took an active part in parliamentary proceedings; interested himself in the Spanish legend of the fabulous wealth of Manoa, and (1595) undertook an expedition in search of the city; failed to find Manoa, but brought back specimens of goldbearing quartz; took a brilliant part in the expedition against Cadiz, 1596, and (1597) equally distinguished himself in the Azores; deprived of most of his offices on the accession of James I, whose mind had been set against him; was sent to the Tower of London on the charge of conspiring against James I, 1603; found guilty, November 1603; reprieved, December 1603; had apartments in the upper storey of the Bloody Tower, where he lived with his wife and son until 1616, when his friends succeeded in persuading James I to permit him to undertake another expedition to the Orinoco in search of gold, the expenses of the adventure being defrayed by himself and his wife and the gentlemen adventurers who gathered round him; had strict orders not to engage in hostilities with the Spaniards; his fleet scattered by foul winds and storms; on arriving at the Isle de Salut remained behind with the ships, being too feeble from the effects of fever to proceed, and placed the expedition up the river under the command of Laurence Kemys [q. v.], who failed after burning the Spanish settlement of San Tomás; could not induce his men to make another effort, and returned to England, 1618; his punishment demanded by the Spanish minister on the news of the destruction of San Tomás; arrested at Ashburton and lodged in the Tower of London, after an attempt to escape to France; executed in Old Palace Yard, Westminster, in pursuance of his former sentence, 29 Oct. 1618. His remains were buried in St. Margaret's, West-minster. Much of his poetry is lost. About thirty short pieces survive, the principal of which is a fragment called 'Cynthia, the Lady of the Sea.' In prose he published 'A Report of the Truth of the Fight about the Isles of Azores' (1591), 'The Discovery of the Empyre of Guiana' (1596), and his 'History of the World' (1614), which he carried down to B.C. 130. He wrote many essays on political subjects, some of which were published after his death. [xlvii. 186]

RALEGH or **RALEIGH**, WALTER (1586-1646), divine; son of Sir Carew Ralegh [q. v.]; of Winchester College and Magdalen Hall, Oxford; M.A., 1608; created D.D., 1636; held a number of minor preferments, and as a staunch royalist suffered grievously during the civil war; appointed dean of Wells, 1641; made a prisoner, roughly treated, and mortally wounded in a scuffle at Wells. [xlvii. 206]

RALEIGH, ALEXANDER (1817-1880), nonconfor-mist divine; congregational pastor at Greenock, 1845-1847, Rotherham, 1850-5, Glasgow, 1855-8; Canonbury, London, 1858-75, and Kensington, 1875-80; made D.D. Glasgow, 1865. He had a wide reputation as a preacher. [xlvii. 207]

RALEIGH, WILLIAM DE (d. 1250), successively bishop of Norwich and Winchester; appointed one of the justices of the bench and justices itinerant, 1228; consecrated bishop of Norwich in 1239, and translated to Winchester in 1244; had been elected to the see of Winchester in 1238, but his nomination being rejected by Henry III, only obtained admission when supported by an interdict. [xlvii. 208]

RALFE, JAMES (fl. 1820-1829), writer on naval history; author of 'The Naval Biography of Great Britain' (1828) and other works. [xlvii. 208]

RALFS, JOHN (1807-1890), botanist; practised for a time as a surgeon, but in 1837 settled at Penzance, aban-doned his profession, and devoted himself to botany; pre-sident of the Penzance Natural History and Antiquarian Society, 1883-4; published 'British Phænogamous Plants and Ferns,' 1839, and 'The British Desmideæ,' 1848. [xlvii. 209]

RALPH. [See also RANDULF.]

RALPH THE TIMID, EARL OF HEREFORD (d. 1057), Norman noble; came to England (1041) with Edward the Confessor, whose sister, Godgifu, was his mother; became Earl of Worcester in 1042; supported Edward against Godwin in 1051, receiving Swegen's earldom of Hereford-shire; defeated by Ælfgar [q. v.] and his Welsh allies in 1055. [xlvii. 210]

RALPH OF WADER, EARL OF NORFOLK (fl. 1070). [See GUADER, RALPH.]

RALPH OF TOESNY (d. 1102), Norman baron; here-ditary standard-bearer of Normandy; fought at Hast-ings, 1066, and was rewarded by large grants of land; supported William Rufus against his brother Robert. [xlvii. 210]

RALPH OF MORTEMER (d. 1104?). [See MORTIMER.]

RALPH D'ESCURES, sometimes called RALPH DE TURBINE (d. 1122), archbishop of Canterbury; became a monk of Séez, 1079, and abbot, 1089; fled to England from the violence of Robert of Bellême, 1100, and (1108) was consecrated bishop of Rochester; became administrator of the diocese of Canterbury on Anselm's death in 1109, and (1114) was chosen archbishop; refused to consecrate Thurstan [q. v.], archbishop-elect of York, unless he pro-fessed obedience to Canterbury, 1114; soon afterwards pro-ceeded to Rome to represent to Pope Pascal II the ancient privileges of the kingdom, but could not prevent the eventual consecration of Thurstan in 1119 by Pope Calix-tus at Rheims; the controversy still undecided at his death, in spite of Thurstan's having obtained possession of his see; convinced Henry I that the matter concerned the unity of the kingdom, propounding the maxim, 'One primate, one king.' [xlvii. 211]

RALPH, RADULF, RANULF, or RANDULF (d. 1123), chancellor; was chancellor from 1107-8 till his death; his administration was described as unjust and oppressive. [xlvii. 215]

RALPH, called LUFFA (d. 1123), bishop of Chichester; consecrated, 1091; supported Anselm against Rufus, and greatly raised the dignity of his see. [xlvii. 215]

RALPH (d. 1144?), bishop of Orkney; consecrated before 1114 by the archbishop of York, but ignored by the people of the islands, who regarded the primate of Trondhjem as their head; never went into residence, though his cause was espoused by the papacy; friend of Thurstan [q. v.] [xlvii. 216]

RALPH GOBION or GUBIUN (d. 1151), abbot of St. Albans; elected abbot, 1146; remarkable for his love of learning and his large collection of books. [xlvii. 218]

RALPH (d. 1160?), theological writer; was almoner of Westminster and prior of Hurley; one or two of his writings are extant. [xlvii. 217]

RALPH (d. 1174), bishop of Bethlehem and chancellor of the Latin kingdom of Jerusalem; stated by William of Tyre to have been an Englishman; first appears in a charter of 1146 as chancellor under Baldwin III; no-minated archbishop of Tyre, 1147, but his appointment invalidated, 1150, by Eugenius; elected bishop of Beth-lehem, 1156. [xlvii. 217]

RALPH OF ST. ALBANS or **RALPH** OF DUNSTABLE (*fl.* 1180 ?), learned writer; was probably a monk of St. Albans and a native of Dunstable; turned into verse prose lives of St. Alban and St. Amphibalus. [xlvii. 218]

RALPH NIGER (*fl.* 1170). [See NIGER.]

RALPH DE DICETO (*d.* 1202 ?). [See DICETO.]

RALPH OF COGGESHALL (*fl.* 1207). [See COGGESHALL.]

RALPH or **RANDULPH** OF EVESHAM (*d.* 1229), abbot of Evesham; elected abbot, 1214. [xlvii. 218]

RALPH OF BRISTOL (*d.* 1232), bishop of Kildare; consecrated, 1223; wrote a life of St. Laurence O'Toole, archbishop of Dublin. [xlvii. 218]

RALPH OF MAIDSTONE (*d.* 1246), bishop of Hereford; taught in the schools of Oxford and Paris; consecrated bishop, 1234, but resigned, 1239, in order to enter the Franciscan order. [xlvii. 219]

RALPH BOCKING (*d.* 1270). [See BOCKING.]

RALPH OF SHREWSBURY (*d.* 1363), bishop of Bath and Wells; chancellor of Oxford University, 1328; consecrated, 1329; active in reforming abuses, especially in the religious houses of his diocese. [xlvii. 219]

RALPH, GEORGE KEITH (*fl.* 1778-1796), portrait-painter; exhibited at the Royal Academy, 1778-96. [xlvii. 220]

RALPH, JAMES (1705 ?-1762), miscellaneous writer; born in Pennsylvania; accompanied Franklin to England, 1724; attacked Pope in a coarse satire, 1728, and in 1744 and 1746 published a 'History of England' (1688-1727) in two volumes; became subsequently a journalist, and showed sufficient ability to induce the Pelham ministry to purchase his pen. The 'Histoire du Prince Titi' (1736), a eulogy of Prince Frederick, has been incorrectly attributed to him. [xlvii. 221]

RALSTON, RALESTON, or **RAULSTON**, JOHN (*d.* 1452), bishop of Dunkeld; LL.D. 1440; appointed secretary to James II of Scotland, 1444; keeper of the privy seal, 1447-9; bishop of Dunkeld, 1447-52; became high treasurer, 1449. [xlvii. 224]

RALSTON, WILLIAM RALSTON SHEDDEN- (1828-1889), Russian scholar; son of W. P. Ralston Shedden; B.A. Trinity College, Cambridge, 1850; called to the bar; assumed the additional name of Ralston (*c.* 1852), after his father had unsuccessfully claimed the Ralston estates in Ayrshire; assistant in the printed book department at the British Museum (1853-75), where he acquired a knowledge of Russian and edited several Russian translations. [xlvii. 224]

RAM, JAMES (1793-1870), conveyancer and legal author; M.A. Pembroke College, Cambridge, 1823; barrister, Inner Temple, 1823; published legal treatises. [xlvii. 225]

RAM, ROBERT (*fl.* 1643-1655), divine; son of Thomas Ram [q. v.]; graduated at Trinity College, Dublin; was minister of Spalding; supported the cause of parliament in his speeches and writings. [xlvii. 226]

RAM, THOMAS (1564-1634), bishop of Ferns and Leighlin; educated at Eton; fellow of King's College, Cambridge; accompanied Essex to Ireland as chaplain, 1599; consecrated bishop, 1605. [xlvii. 226]

RAMADGE, FRANCIS HOPKINS (1793-1867), medical writer; M.A. and M.B. Trinity College, Dublin, 1819 (incorporated M.B. St. Alban Hall, Oxford, 1821); M.D. Oxford, 1821; F.R.C.P., 1822; censor, 1825; senior physician at the Central Infirmary and Dispensary, London. [xlvii. 227]

RAMAGE, CRAUFURD TAIT (1803-1878), miscellaneous writer; M.A. Edinburgh, 1825; was for fifteen years tutor in the family of Thomas Spring-Rice, first baron Monteagle [q. v.]; became rector of Wallace Hall Academy, 1842; published four anthologies, entitled 'Beautiful Thoughts,' besides other writings. [xlvii. 227]

RAMBERG, JOHANN HEINRICH (1763-1840), historical and portrait painter; born in Hanover; came to England, 1781, and returned to Hanover, 1792, when he was appointed electoral court painter. [xlvii. 228]

RAMESAY, WILLIAM (*fl.* 1645 - 1676). [See RAMSAY.]

RAMKINS, ALEXANDER (1672-1719 ?), adherent of James II; studied at Aberdeen University; fought in Scotland and Ireland at the time of the revolution, and afterwards served in the French army. [xlvii. 228]

RAMSAY, SIR ALEXANDER (*d.* 1342), of Dalhousie, Scottish patriot; held a command in the engagement of Boroughmuir, 1335, and relieved Dunbar, 1338; captured Roxburgh Castle from the English, 1342, but incurred the enmity of William Douglas of Liddesdale, who seized him and left him to perish of hunger in the castle of the Hermitage. [xlvii. 229]

RAMSAY, SIR ALEXANDER (*d.* 1402), of Dalhousie, Scottish noble; killed at Homildon Hill. [xlvii. 230]

RAMSAY, SIR ALEXANDER (*fl.* 1424-1451), Scottish noble; probably grandson of Sir Alexander Ramsay (*d.* 1402) [q. v.]; routed an English force at Piperden, 1435. [xlvii. 230]

RAMSAY, ALLAN (1686-1758), Scottish poet; an Edinburgh wig-maker by trade; became laureate of the Jacobite 'Easy Club,' 1715, and (*c.* 1717) abandoned wig-making for bookselling; published his collected poems, 1721, the 'Tea-table Miscellany,' 1724-7, and (1725) his pastoral drama, 'The Gentle Shepherd,' which achieved instant success; ceased to write after 1730, and in 1755 retired from business; edited a number of ancient Scottish poems, and freely tampered with the text. [xlvii. 230]

RAMSAY, ALLAN (1713-1784), painter; eldest child of Allan Ramsay (1686-1758) [q. v.]; studied in London and on the continent; found employment in Edinburgh as a portrait-painter for some years, but (*c.* 1756) migrated to London, when Walpole considered that he excelled Reynolds as a painter of women; became portrait-painter to George III, 1767. He was one of the Johnsonian group, and was distinguished for knowledge of the world and social charm. [xlvii. 233]

RAMSAY, ANDREW (1574-1659), Scottish divine and Latin poet; educated at St. Andrews; studied theology in France and became professor at Saumur; returned to Scotland, *c.* 1606, and became a minister in Edinburgh, 1614, professor of divinity, 1620, and rector of the college, posts which he resigned in 1626; refused to read Laud's prayer book, and for this was silenced by the privy council, 1637; became a leading covenanter for a time, but (1649) was deposed for refusing to preach against the 'engagement'; restored, 1655; published sacred poems in Latin. [xlvii. 234]

RAMSAY, SIR ANDREW, first baronet, LORD ABBOTSHALL (1620 ?-1688), lord provost of Edinburgh; eldest son of Andrew Ramsay [q. v.]; lord provost, 1654-7 and 1662-73; knighted, 1655 and 1660; created baronet, 1669; named privy councillor and admitted lord of session, 1671; became very unpopular, and was obliged to resign his offices, 1673. [xlvii. 235]

RAMSAY, SIR ANDREW CROMBIE (1814-1891), geologist; devoted himself to the study of geology from an early age, and (1841) obtained employment on the geological survey; was appointed professor of geology at University College, London, 1847, but still preserved his connection with the survey, of which he became senior director for England and Wales, 1862, and director-general, 1871; president of the Geological Society, 1862-4; F.R.S. 1862 (royal medallist, 1880); retired from the geological survey and was knighted, 1881; underrated palæontology and petrology, and devoted most of his attention to district stratigraphy. [xlvii. 236]

RAMSAY, ANDREW MICHAEL (1686-1743), tutor to Prince Charles Edward; son of an Ayrshire baker; educated at Edinburgh University; became a Roman catholic in 1710 under the influence of Fénélon, and in 1724 became tutor to Prince James Edward's two sons; came to England, 1728, and was made F.R.S. and LL.D. St. Mary Hall, Oxford; author of a number of works, the most notable being his 'Voyages de Cyrus' (1727), in imitation of 'Télémaque,' and 'Philosophical Principles of Natural and Revealed Religion explained and unfolded in a Geometrical Order,' published, 1749. [xlvii. 238]

RAMSAY, CHARLES ALOYSIUS (*fl.* 1677-1683), writer on stenography; resided in Germany and France; became known as the publisher of a system of shorthand in Latin. [xlvii. 239]

RAMSAY, DAVID (*d.* 1642), courtier; brother of Sir James Ramsay [q. v.]; groom of the bedchamber to Prince Henry; imprisoned in the Tower of London, in consequence of a quarrel with Lord Reay, 1631.
[xlvii. 240]

RAMSAY, DAVID (*d.* 1653 ?), clockmaker to James I and Charles I; appointed clockmaker extraordinary to James I, 1613, and (1618) chief clockmaker; was also a student of the occult sciences and an inventor.
[xlvii. 239]

RAMSAY, EDWARD BANNERMAN (1793–1872), dean of Edinburgh; B.A. St. John's College, Cambridge, 1816; ordained, 1816; went to Edinburgh, 1824; dean of Edinburgh, 1841–72, becoming generally known in Scotland as Dean Ramsay; published (1858) his 'Reminiscences of Scottish Life and Character,' by which he is most widely known. [xlvii. 241]

RAMSAY, FOX MAULE, eleventh EARL OF DALHOUSIE and second BARON PANMURE (1801–1874). [See MAULE, FOX.]

RAMSAY, SIR GEORGE, ninth baronet (1800–1871), philosophical writer; of Harrow and Trinity College, Cambridge; B.A., 1823; M.B., 1826; contributed voluminously to philosophical topics, but made no addition of importance to philosophic inquiry. [xlvii. 242]

RAMSAY, GEORGE, twelfth EARL OF DALHOUSIE and first BARON RAMSAY (1806–1880), entered the navy, 1820; C.B., 1856; succeeded his cousin, Fox Maule Ramsay, eleventh earl of Dalhousie [q. v.], 1874; created Baron Ramsay of the United Kingdom, 1875; admiral, 1875.
[xlvii. 242]

RAMSAY, SIR JAMES (1589 ?–1638), soldier; nearly related to Sir John Ramsay, earl of Holderness [q. v.]; accompanied James VI to England on his accession, and afterwards fought under Gustavus Adolphus; mortally wounded while defending Hanover against the imperialists.
[xlvii. 243]

RAMSAY, JAMES (1624 ?–1696), bishop of Ross; laureated at Glasgow University, 1647; ordained minister of Kirkintilloch, 1653; was transferred to Linlithgow, 1655; rector of Glasgow University, 1665–71; bishop of Dunblane, 1673; translated to Ross, 1684; expelled from office on the abolition of episcopacy; died in great poverty. [xlvii. 244]

RAMSAY, JAMES (1733–1789), divine and philanthropist; studied at King's College, Aberdeen; served as a surgeon in the navy in earlier life, but afterwards took holy orders; settled in the West Indies and interested himself in the negroes; came into collision with the planters; accepted a naval chaplaincy, 1778; presented to a living in Kent, 1781; endeavoured to stimulate a movement in England in favour of the abolition of slavery; bore the brunt of the struggle almost unaided for some time, but latterly was supported by Wilberforce and others. [xlvii. 246]

RAMSAY, JAMES (1786–1854), portrait-painter; began to exhibit at the Royal Academy, 1803; continued to paint until 1849. [xlvii. 247]

RAMSAY, SIR JAMES ANDREW BROUN, tenth EARL and first MARQUIS OF DALHOUSIE (1812–1860), governor-general of India; educated at Harrow and Christ Church, Oxford; B.A., 1833; conservative M.P., Haddingtonshire, 1837; succeeded his father as tenth earl, and entered the House of Lords as second Baron Dalhousie, 1838; became president of the board of trade, 1845, and (1847) governor-general of India; during the second Sikh war established himself at Firozpur, near the scene of operations, and on its conclusion he was created a marquis; declared the Panjáb a British province, 1849, placing it under a board, of which he made Sir Henry Montgomery Lawrence [q. v.] president; issued his famous minute, by which he determined the character of Indian railways, 1853, resolving, in introducing the railway system into India, to avail himself of private enterprise, while providing a system of direct but not vexatious control by government; introduced the electric telegraph and took measures for the suppression of suttee in native states, the suppression of dacoity, the alteration of the postal system, and the removal of imposts which shackled trade; undertook the second Burmese war, 1852, which ended in the annexation of Lower Burma; his policy of annexation much criticised, particularly with reference to his refusal to permit the rulers of various native states to carry on the succession by the expedient of adopting an heir; refused to recognise the adopted heir of the rájá of Sattára, and subsequently annexed Nagpur and Jhánsi; annexed Oudh (one of his latest acts), in accordance with order of the court of directors, on account of maladministration; returned to England, 1856, after protesting against the rashness of reducing the European garrison in order to reinforce the Crimean army; received with great honour on his arrival, but on the outbreak of the mutiny in 1857 was vigorously assailed on account of his policy of annexation and his confidence in the native army, though such charges were not supported by those cognisant of the actual facts of the case. [xlvii. 247]

RAMSAY, SIR JOHN (*d.* 1513), lord of Bothwell; was one of the favourites of James III; escaped the vengeance of the nobles at Lauder Bridge in 1482 on account of his youth; was several times ambassador to the English court, but after the death of James III was forfeited by parliament, 1488, and took refuge with Henry VII; returned to Scotland, 1496, but continued to act in the English interest. [xlvii. 256]

RAMSAY, JOHN (1496 ?–1551), divine; B.A. New Inn Hall, Oxford, 1514; B.D., 1522; successively prior of St. Mary's College, Oxford, and Merton Abbey, Surrey; adopted reformation principles and resigned his priory; wrote two treatises. [xlvii. 257]

RAMSAY, SIR JOHN, BARON OF EAST BARNS, VISCOUNT HADDINGTON and EARL OF HOLDERNESS (1580 ?–1626), favourite of James VI; assisted James VI in the Gowrie conspiracy by killing the Earl of Gowrie and his brother, 1600, for which he was created a baron; accompanied James VI to England, and in 1606 was made a viscount, and in 1621 an earl. [xlvii. 257]

RAMSAY, JOHN (1802–1879), poet; originally a carpet-weaver; travelled through Scotland for fifteen years selling his poems, which were energetic and picturesque. [xlvii. 258]

RAMSAY, SIR JOHN WILLIAM, thirteenth EARL OF DALHOUSIE (1847–1887), son of George Ramsay, twelfth earl of Dalhousie [q. v.]; entered the navy, 1861, but retired, 1879, and devoted himself to study and politics; matriculated at Balliol College, Oxford, 1875; liberal M.P. for Liverpool, 1880; succeeded as earl, 1880; K.T., 1881; became secretary for Scotland, 1886. [xlvii. 243]

RAMSAY or **RAMSEY**, LAURENCE (*fl.* 1550–1588), versifier; attacked the Roman catholics in verse.
[xlvii. 259]

RAMSAY or **RAMSEY**, ROBERT (*fl.* 1609–1639), musician; Mus. Bac. Cambridge, 1616; organist of Trinity College, Cambridge. Several of his compositions have been preserved. [xlvii. 259]

RAMSAY, ROBERT (1842–1882), Australian politician; took his seat in the legislative assembly of Victoria as member for East Bourke, 1870, and (1872) joined the Francis ministry, becoming postmaster-general in 1874; became minister of public instruction, 1875; resigned, 1877, but (March 1880) joined Service's ministry, resigning, June 1880. [xlvii. 260]

RAMSAY or **RAMSEY**, THOMAS (*fl.* 1631–1653), Roman catholic agent; son of a Scottish physician; M.A. Glasgow and Edinburgh; became a Roman catholic abroad, and was sent to England on a mission in 1653, and took the name of Thomas Horsley; arrested soon after his arrival. [xlvii. 260]

RAMSAY, THOMAS KENNEDY (1826–1886), Canadian judge and jurist; emigrated from Scotland in 1847; was admitted to the bar, 1852; Q.C., 1867; became (1873) a puisne judge of the queen's bench in Canada.
[xlvii. 261]

RAMSAY, WILLIAM, of Colluthie, EARL OF FIFE (*fl.* 1356–1360), married Isabel, countess of Fife, 1356, and was invested with the earldom; fought on the French side at Poitiers, 1356. [xlvii. 261]

RAMSAY, WILLIAM, second BARON RAMSAY OF DALHOUSIE and first EARL OF DALHOUSIE (*d.* 1674), succeeded his father as baron. 1629; created earl, 1633; colonel in the covenanting army; aided Argyll against Montrose; supported Charles II in 1651, and was fined by Cromwell, 1654. [xlvii. 262]

RAMSAY or **RAMESEY**, WILLIAM (*fl.* 1645–1676), physician and astrologer; son of David Ramsay (*d.* 1653 ?) [q. v.]; studied at St. Andrews, Edinburgh; M.D. Montpellier, 1652; physician in ordinary to Charles II; M.D. Cambridge by royal mandate, 1668; published medical and astrological works. [xlvii. 262]

RAMSAY, WILLIAM (1806–1865), classical scholar; brother of Sir George Ramsay [q. v.]; M.A. Trinity College, Cambridge, 1836; professor of humanity, Glasgow, 1831–65; published 'An Elementary Manual of Roman Antiquities,' 1859, and editions of Latin classics. [xlvii. 263]

RAMSAY, WILLIAM NORMAN (1782–1815), major in the royal horse artillery; entered the army, 1798; served in Egypt and Spain with the horse artillery; distinguished himself at Fuentes d'Onoro, 1811; brevetmajor, 1813; killed at Waterloo. [xlvii. 263]

RAMSBOTHAM, FRANCIS HENRY (1801–1868), medical writer; M.D. Edinburgh, 1822; F.R.C.P. London, 1844; obstetric physician at the London Hospital; eminent as a lecturer and specialist in obstetrics. [xlvii. 265]

RAMSDEN, JESSE (1735–1800), optician and mechanician; set up as an engraver in 1762, and afterwards took out patents for important improvements in astronomical instruments; was renowned as an instrumentmaker throughout Europe, and had an enormous business, but refused to raise his prices, and left but a small fortune. [xlvii. 265]

RAMSEY. [See RAMSAY.]

RAMSEY, WILLIAM OF (*fl.* 1219). [See WILLIAM.]

RANBY, JOHN (1703–1773), sergeant-surgeon; F.R.S., 1724; became surgeon in ordinary to the king's household, 1738, sergeant-surgeon to George II, 1740, and principal sergeant-surgeon, 1743; induced government to found a corporation of surgeons distinct from that of the barbers, 1745, and became the first master; chief work 'The Method of Treating Gunshot Wounds,' 1744. Fielding introduced him into 'Tom Jones.' [xlvii. 267]

RANBY, JOHN (1743–1820), pamphleteer; natural son of John Ranby [q. v.]; was a tory pamphleteer of some ability. [xlvii. 268]

RAND, ISAAC (*d.* 1743), botanist; was appointed, 1724, *præfectus horti* of Chelsea garden; published botanical treatises; F.R.S., 1739. [xlvii. 268]

RANDALL, JOHN (1570–1622), puritan divine; of St. Mary Hall and Trinity College, Oxford; B.A., 1585; fellow of Lincoln College, Oxford, 1587; M.A., 1589; rector of St. Andrew Hubbard, London, 1599–1622, where he made a reputation as a preacher. [xlvii. 269]

RANDALL, JOHN (*fl.* 1764), schoolmaster and agriculturist; M.A. Christ's College, Cambridge, 1727; carried on a private school at York; published 'The Semi-Virgilian Husbandry.' [xlvii. 269]

RANDALL, JOHN (1715–1799), organist; Mus. Doc. Cambridge, 1756; organist to King's College Chapel, Cambridge, 1745–99; professor of music at Cambridge, 1755–99. [xlvii. 270]

RANDALL, JOHN (1755–1802), shipbuilder; built navy vessels at Rotherhithe for the East India Company and for government; died from the effects of a fever brought on by mortification at a strike of his workmen. [xlvii. 270]

RANDALL, THOMAS (1605–1635). [See RANDOLPH.]

RANDALL, WILLIAM (*fl.* 1584–1603), musician; was epistler at the Chapel Royal, London, 1584; one or two of his compositions survive. [xlvii. 271]

RANDOLPH, BERNARD (1643–1690 ?), writer on Greece; brother of Edward Randolph (1640 ?–1700 ?) [q. v.]; was long engaged in commerce in the Levant, and wrote accounts of the Morea and the Greek Archipelago. [xlvii. 272]

RANDOLPH, CHARLES (1809–1878), marine engineer; educated at Glasgow University; started business in Glasgow, 1834. His firm developed into the Fairfield Shipbuilding Company. [xlvii. 271]

RANDOLPH, EDWARD (*d.* 1566), soldier; probably brother of Thomas Randolph (1523–1590) [q. v.]; em-

ployed in Scotland in Queen Elizabeth's reign and (1563) was made marshal of Havre; became, lieutenant-general of ordnance on his return; killed in battle at Knockfergus. [xlvii. 271]

RANDOLPH, EDWARD (1640 ?–1700 ?), colonial official; prepared a report on Massachusetts in 1676 for the lords of trade and plantation and (1678) was appointed collector and surveyor of customs for New England; subsequently held other offices and was imprisoned, 1689, during the rebellion against Sir Edmund Andros [q. v.] [xlvii. 272]

RANDOLPH, FRANCIS (1752–1831), divine; of Eton and King's College, Cambridge; fellow of King's College, Cambridge, 1775; M.A., 1780; D.D. Dublin, 1806; held several minor preferments; had some reputation as a theologian, and contributed to the Socinian controversy. [xlvii. 273]

RANDOLPH, JOHN, third EARL OF MORAY (*d.* 1346), son of Sir Thomas Randolph, first earl of Moray [q. v.], succeeded his brother Thomas, second earl of Moray, 1332; completely defeated Edward Baliol at Annan, 1332; fought at Halidon Hill, 1333; chosen (*c.* 1334) joint regent of Scotland; completed the liberation of the country by compelling the Earl of Atholl to surrender; was captured by the English, 1335, and remained in captivity till 1341; defeated Baliol at Irvine, 1342; killed at the battle of Neville's Cross. [xlvii. 273]

RANDOLPH, JOHN (1749–1813), successively bishop of Oxford, Bangor, and London; son of Thomas Randolph (1701–1783) [q. v.]; of Westminster School and Christ Church, Oxford; M.A., 1774; D.D. by diploma, 1783; professor of poetry at Oxford, 1776–83; regius professor of Greek, 1782–3; professor of moral philosophy, 1782–6, and regius professor of divinity, 1783–99; consecrated bishop of Oxford, 1799, translated to Bangor, 1807, and to London, 1809. [xlvii. 274]

RANDOLPH, SIR THOMAS, first EARL OF MORAY (*d.* 1332), companion of Robert Bruce and regent of Scotland; joined Bruce after the murder of Red Comyn in 1306, and was taken prisoner at Methven, 1306; deserted Bruce in order to save his own life, and joined in the hunt for him in Carrick; was captured by Douglas, 1308, and made his submission to Bruce; became the most trusted friend and adviser of the Scottish king, and was created Earl of Moray; performed many remarkable feats of arms, including the capture of Edinburgh Castle by escalade in 1314; commanded a division at Bannockburn, 1314; took part in Edward Bruce's Irish expedition, 1315; concluded an offensive and defensive alliance with France, 1326, and on the death of Bruce in 1329 became regent. [xlvii. 275]

RANDOLPH, THOMAS (1523–1590), ambassador; B.A. Christ Church, Oxford, 1545; B.C.L., 1548; principal of Broadgates Hall (Pembroke College), Oxford, 1549–53; retired to France on Queen Mary's accession, but returned, 1559, and was employed by Queen Elizabeth in various diplomatic missions in Scotland; recalled to England, 1566, and appointed postmaster-general, but (1568) was sent on a mission to Russia and obtained special privileges for English merchants; despatched on special missions to France, 1573 and 1576, and afterwards returned to Scotland in order to assist Morton; Morton's fate hastened by his intervention; successfully concluded a treaty with James VI, 1586. [xlvii. 278]

RANDOLPH, THOMAS (1605–1635), poet and dramatist; showed literary leanings as a child; of Westminster School and Trinity College, Cambridge; fellow of Trinity College, Cambridge, 1629; M.A., 1632; made the acquaintance of Ben Jonson and, after becoming famous in Cambridge as a writer of English and Latin verse, went to London in 1632. His plays (including 'Amyntas,' an adaptation from Guarini and Tasso, and 'The Muses' Looking-Glasse') and poems were edited by Mr. W. C. Hazlitt, 1875. [xlvii. 280]

RANDOLPH, THOMAS (1701–1783), president of Corpus Christi College, Oxford; M.A. and D.D. Corpus Christi College, Oxford; fellow of Corpus Christi College, Oxford, 1723; attracted the attention of the bishop of Oxford, John Potter (1674–1747) [q. v.], who, after he became primate, bestowed several preferments on him; became noted as an orthodox theologian, and in 1748 was elected president of Corpus Christi College, Oxford; vicechancellor of Oxford University, 1756. His works were numerous. [xlvii. 282]

RANDOLPH, WILLIAM (1650–1711), colonist; half-brother of Thomas Randolph (1605–1635) [q. v.]; emigrated to Virginia in 1674, where he founded William and Mary College, and attempted to civilise the Indians; member of council, Virginia.　　　　[xlvii. 283]

RANDS, HENRY (d. 1551). [See HOLBEACH, HENRY.]

RANDS, WILLIAM BRIGHTY (1823–1882), 'the laureate of the nursery'; wrote under the pseudonyms of Henry Holbeach and Matthew Browne; after a struggle with poverty became a reporter in the House of Commons; wrote much prose and verse for various periodicals, and was especially esteemed for his poems and fairy tales for children; composed hymns. His best work was his 'Lilliput Lectures,' 1871.　　　　[xlvii. 283]

RANDULF, called LE MESCHIN, EARL OF CHESTER (d. 1129 ?), nephew of Hugh 'of Avranches,' earl of Chester [q. v.]; led the van at Tinchebrai (1106), and succeeded his cousin Richard, earl of Chester, in 1120 in his earldom.　　　　[xlvii. 284]

RANDULF, called DE GERNONS, EARL OF CHESTER (d. 1153), only son of Randulf 'le Meschin,' earl of Chester [q. v.]; succeeded his father shortly before 1130, and after the accession of King Stephen took an important part in English politics; seized (1140) Lincoln Castle, where he was besieged by Stephen, but with the help of his father-in-law, Robert, earl of Gloucester [q. v.], completely defeated Stephen beneath the walls, 1141; came to terms with Stephen, 1142, but in 1144 again took up arms; again made peace, 1146, but was treacherously thrown into prison and compelled to surrender his castles to obtain his freedom; persuaded Henry, Matilda's son, to return to England, 1149, but was won over by the extensive grants King Stephen made him; won over to the side of Duke Henry by the promise of even larger grants, but died before the end of the year, poisoned, it was believed, by William Peverell [q. v.]　　　　[xlvii. 286]

RANELAGH, third VISCOUNT and first EARL OF (1636 ?–1712). [See JONES, RICHARD.]

RANEW, NATHANIEL (1602 ?–1678), ejected minister; M.A. Emmanuel College, Cambridge, 1624 (incorporated at Oxford, 1627); became minister of St. Andrew Hubbard, London, and (1647) was transferred by parliamentary order to Felsted in Essex, where he became a prominent divine; ejected, 1662; settled in Billericay; published 'Solitude improved by Divine Meditation,' 1670.　　　　[xlvii. 288]

RANKEILLOR, LORD (1639–1706). [See HOPE, ARCHIBALD.]

RANKEN, ALEXANDER (1755–1827), author; graduated at Edinburgh; minister of Cambusnethan, 1781–5, and of St. David, Glasgow, 1785–1827; D.D. Glasgow, 1801; moderator of the general assembly, 1811; published an inaccurate 'History of France' (9 vols. 1802–22).　　　　[xlvii. 289]

RANKEN, GEORGE (1828–1856), major, royal engineers; served in Canada, 1850–5, and received the thanks of the legislature for saving the library of the Literary and Historical Society, when the parliament buildings at Quebec were destroyed by fire in 1854; volunteered for the Crimea, 1855, and distinguished himself in the assault on the Redan (September 1855); accidentally killed at Sebastopol. His journals in 'Canada and the Crimea' were published by his brother (1862).　　　　[xlvii. 289]

RANKIN, THOMAS (1738–18¼0), methodist divine; after hearing Whitefield preach at Leith, resolved to become a preacher; became an intimate friend of John Wesley and (1773) was sent to America to reform methodism there; incurred the dislike of the American methodists on account of his mission, and (1777) returned to England; engaged in active labour in England till his retirement in 1783.　　　　[xlvii. 290]

RANKINE, WILLIAM JOHN MACQUORN (1820–1872), civil engineer; studied at Edinburgh University, 1836–8; was a pupil of (Sir) John Benjamin MacNeill [q. v.]; after his apprenticeship returned to Edinburgh and made important contributions to the science of railway locomotion; commenced (c. 1848) the series of researches on molecular physics which occupied him at intervals during the rest of his life, and which constitute his chief claim to distinction in the domain of pure

science; made professor of civil engineering and mechanics at Glasgow, 1855, and about 1858 became president of the Scottish Institution of Engineers.　　　　[xlvii. 290]

RANKINS, WILLIAM (fl. 1587–1601), author; made a vicious attack on the stage in 1587 in his 'Mirrour of Monsters,' but afterwards wrote plays, none of which are extant; author of 'Seaven Satyres' (1598) and probably of 'The English Ape' (1588).　　　　[xlvii. 292]

RANKLEY, ALFRED (1819–1872), painter; exhibited at the Royal Academy, 1841–71.　　　　[xlvii. 292]

RANNULF FLAMBARD (d. 1128). [See FLAMBARD.]

RANSFORD, EDWIN (1805–1876), vocalist and actor; began to play leading characters at the Surrey Theatre, 1831, and afterwards appeared at most of the London theatres, retiring, 1838; produced, from 1845, a series of popular musical entertainments, in which he was chief performer, and composed songs and glees.　　　　[xlvii. 293]

RANSOME, JAMES (1782–1849), agricultural implement maker; elder son of Robert Ransome [q. v.]; continued his father's business, and with his brother, Robert, gained many medals and prizes from the Royal Agricultural Society.　　　　[xlvii. 294]

RANSOME, JAMES ALLEN (1806–1875), agricultural implement maker; eldest son of James Ransome [q. v.]; became a partner in his father's business and (1843) published a history of 'The Implements of Agriculture.'　　　　[xlvii. 294]

RANSOME, ROBERT (1753–1830), agricultural implement maker; commenced business at Norwich, but removed to Ipswich, 1789; took out several patents, including a most important one in 1803 for an improved ploughshare.　　　　[xlvii. 293]

RANSON, THOMAS FRAZER (1784–1828), line-engraver; learned his art at Newcastle-upon-Tyne. His plates include a good portrait of George IV after E. Scott.　　　　[xlvii. 295]

RANULF. [See RALPH and RANDULF.]

RANULF FLAMBARD (d. 1128). [See FLAMBARD.]

RANULF DE GLANVILLE (d. 1190). [See GLANVILLE.]

RANULF DE BLUNDEVILL, EARL OF CHESTER (d. 1232). [See BLUNDEVILL.]

RANULPH BRITO or LE BRETON (d. 1246). [See BRITO.]

RANYARD, ARTHUR COWPER (1845–1894), astronomer; son of Mrs. Ellen Henrietta Ranyard [q. v.]; M.A. Pembroke College, Cambridge, 1868; barrister, Lincoln's Inn, 1871; secretary to the Royal Astronomical Society, 1874–80; between 1871 and 1879 was occupied in compiling for the society a systematised account of all solar eclipses down to 1878; became editor of 'Knowledge,' 1888, and published in it important investigations on nebulæ.　　　　[xlvii. 295]

RANYARD, ELLEN HENRIETTA (1810–1879), founder of the female bible mission; née White; married Benjamin Ranyard, 1839; published 'The Book and its Story,' 1852, and, from 1856, edited 'The Book and its Mission,' a periodical (renamed 'The Missing Link Magazine,' 1865).　　　　[xlvii. 296]

RAPER, HENRY (1767–1845), admiral; entered the navy, 1780; was signal lieutenant to Howe on 1 June 1794; saw much service, mainly in the West Indies, on the Lisbon station, and in the Baltic; admiral, 1841.　　　　[xlvii. 296]

RAPER, HENRY (1799–1859), writer on navigation; eldest son of Henry Raper (1767–1845) [q. v.]; was a lieutenant in the navy, and after retiring (1825) devoted himself to nautical science; published the 'Practice of Navigation,' 1840.　　　　[xlvii. 297]

RAPIN, PAUL DE (1661–1725), historian; generally styled RAPIN-THOYRAS; born at Castres; took refuge in England, 1686, soon after the revocation of the edict of Nantes; afterwards enlisted in Holland, and returned to England with the troops of William of Orange; fought in Ireland and (1693) became tutor to the Duke of Portland's eldest son; subsequently sojourned in various continental towns in poor circumstances, and died at Wesel. His 'History of England,' in French, appeared in 1723 and

1725, and was carried down to the accession of William and Mary. It was translated into English, and continued by various writers, remaining the standard history of England until the publication of Hume's.   [xlvii. 297]

RASBOTHAM, DORNING (1730–1791), author; made collections for the history of Lancashire which were utilised by Edward Baines [q. v.], and wrote 'Codrus, a Tragedy,' 1774.   [xlvii. 300]

RASHLEIGH, PHILIP (1729–1811), antiquary; of New College, Oxford; M.P., Towey, 1765–1802; known latterly as the 'father of the House of Commons'; F.S.A. and F.R.S., 1788; had great knowledge of Cornish mineralogy, and made a valuable collection of minerals.   [xlvii. 300]

RASPE, RUDOLF ERIC (1737–1794), author of the original 'Baron Munchausen'; born in Hanover; studied at Göttingen and Leipzig; became professor at the Collegium Carolinum in Cassel, 1767, and keeper of the landgrave of Hesse's antique gems and medals, which he purloined, and in 1775 fled to England to escape punishment; took to writing for a livelihood; became storekeeper at a Cornish mine, 1782; published 'Baron Munchausen's Narrative,' 1785, the first edition containing only chapters ii–vi. of the current modern version, the other fifteen chapters being added later by another hand, and a parody of James Bruce's 'Travels' being added as a sequel, 1793; obtained money from Sir John Sinclair of of Ulbster by pretending to discover gold and silver on his estate, 1791, an incident commemorated by Sir Walter Scott in the 'Antiquary'; while still masquerading as a mining expert was carried off by scarlet fever at Muckross.
    [xlvii. 301]

RASTALL, WILLIAM DICKINSON (1756–1822). [See DICKINSON, WILLIAM.]

RASTELL, JOHN (d. 1536), printer and lawyer; entered Lincoln's Inn; had an excellent legal practice; M.P., Dunheved, 1529–36; commenced printing before 1516, but passed most of his time in the country, leaving his workmen to attend to the business; embraced reformed opinions, 1530; attacked the practice of paying tithes, 1536, and was thrown into prison, where he died.
    [xlvii. 303]

RASTELL, JOHN (1532–1577), jesuit; fellow of New College, Oxford, 1549; M.A., 1555; on Queen Elizabeth's accession retired to Louvain; entered the jesuit order, 1568; published controversial works; died at Ingoldstadt.
    [xlvii. 304]

RASTELL, WILLIAM (1508?–1565), judge; elder son of John Rastell (d. 1536) [q. v.]; barrister, Lincoln's Inn, 1539; treasurer, 1555; became a puisne judge of the queen's bench, 1558, retiring, 1563; edited 'The Works of Sir Thomas More,' 1557, and several legal treatises.
    [xlvii. 305]

RASTRICK, JOHN (1650–1727), nonconformist minister; M.A. Trinity College, Cambridge, 1674; became vicar of Kirton, 1674, but resigned his living, 1687, and began to preach as a nonconformist, settling at King's Lynn, 1701.   [xlvii. 305]

RASTRICK, JOHN URPETH (1780–1856), civil engineer; took an important part in introducing railways in England, and effected several improvements in steam engines; M.I.C.E., 1827; was one of the judges appointed by the directors of the Liverpool and Manchester railway who in 1829 decided in favour of George Stephenson's Rocket; F.R.S., 1837.   [xlvii. 306]

RASTRICK, WILLIAM (d. 1752), nonconformist divine; son of John Rastrick [q. v.]; succeeded his father as preacher at King's Lynn.   [xlvii. 306]

RATCLIFFE. [See also RADCLIFFE.]

RATCLIFFE, HENRY (1808–1877), vital statistician; became secretary to the order of Odd Fellows, 1848, and compiled actuarial tables in regard to mortality and sickness, which were of great value to friendly societies; a public valuer under the Friendly Societies Act of 1870.
    [xlvii. 307]

RATCLIFFE, JOHN (d. 1610). [See SICKLEMORE.]

RATCLIFFE, JOHN (d. 1776), book-collector; kept a chandler's shop in Southwark and became an ardent book-collector; his library sold by Christie after his death, the sale lasting nine days.   [xlvii. 307]

RATCLIFFE or **RATLIFFE**, THOMAS (d. 1599), divine; of Peterhouse and Trinity College, Cambridge; B.A., 1578; author of the 'Short Svmme of the whole Catechisme,' 1592.   [xlvii. 308]

RATHBONE, HANNAH MARY (1798–1878), authoress of the 'Diary of Lady Willoughby'; granddaughter of Richard Reynolds (1735–1816) [q. v.]; married her half-cousin, Richard, son of William Rathbone (1757–1809) [q. v.], 1817; brought out the 'Diary' in 1844. Her publisher, Thomas Longman, made it an exact imitation of a seventeenth-century volume, and the 'Diary' itself was an excellent imitation of a contemporary account of the civil war. A second part, carrying the narrative down to the Restoration, appeared in 1847.
    [xlvii. 308]

RATHBONE, JOHN (1750?–1807), artist; practised in Manchester, London, and Preston as a landscape painter, both in oil and water colour.   [xlvii. 309]

RATHBONE, WILLIAM (1757–1809), merchant; was educated as a quaker, and took a prominent part in philanthropic enterprise in Liverpool; disowned by the Friends, 1805, for latitudinarian opinions.   [xlvii. 309]

RATHBONE, WILLIAM (1787–1868), philanthropist; eldest son of William Rathbone (1757–1809) [q. v.]; eminent in Liverpool as an educationist and philanthropist; mayor of Liverpool, 1837.   [xlvii. 310]

RATHBORNE, WILSON (1748–1831), captain in the navy; entered the navy as an 'able seaman,' 1773; lieutenant, 1780; commander, 1795; C.B., 1815. [xlvii. 310]

RATSEY, GAMALIEL (d. 1605), highwayman; son of a well-to-do inhabitant of Market Deeping; took to evil courses when a boy and enlisted for service in Ireland in 1600; took to highway robbery on his return in 1603; his exploits noted for daring and rough humour; hanged at Bedford. He is the hero of several ballads and two pamphlets.   [xlvii. 311]

RATTEE, JAMES (1820–1855), wood-carver; commenced business in Cambridge in 1842, where he was employed by the Camden Society; his masterpiece is the reredos in Ely cathedral.   [xlvii. 312]

RATTRAY, SYLVESTER (fl. 1650–1666), medical writer; practised in Glasgow; author of two treatises.
    [xlvii. 312]

RATTRAY, THOMAS (1684–1743), Scottish nonjuring bishop; consecrated, 1727, nonjuring bishop of Brechin, and in the same year assisted to draw up the canons of the Scottish church; was not recognised by a section of the Scottish nonjuring bishops, because the Old Pretender had not assented to his election, and in consequence of some other points of difference; became bishop of Dunkeld, terms having been made in 1731; chosen primus in 1739, when a new dissension arose which remained unhealed until his death; his chief work was 'The Ancient Liturgy of the Church of Jerusalem,' posthumous, 1744.   [xlvii. 312]

RAULSTON, JOHN (d. 1452). [See RALSTON.]

RAUZZINI, MATTEO (1754–1791), singer; brother of Venanzio Rauzzini [q. v.]; born at Rome; came to England with his brother; professor of singing at Dublin.
    [xlvii. 315]

RAUZZINI, VENANZIO (1747–1810), tenor singer; musical composer and teacher; born at Rome; first appeared in England, 1774; devoted himself to teaching, 1777; several of his operas were produced in London.
    [xlvii. 314]

RAVELRIG, LORD (1650?–1710). [See MAITLAND, SIR JOHN, fifth EARL OF LAUDERDALE.]

RAVEN, JOHN SAMUEL (1829–1877), landscape-painter; frequently exhibited at the Royal Academy and British Institution.   [xlvii. 315]

RAVENET, SIMON FRANÇOIS (1721?–1774), engraver; born in Paris; came to London, c. 1750, and founded an important school of line-engraving.
    [xlvii. 315]

RAVENSCROFT, EDWARD (fl. 1671–1697), dramatist; member of the Middle Temple, 1671; Charles II and court pleased by his first play, 'Mamamouchi' (taken from 'Le Bourgeois Gentilhomme'), 1671; regarded by Dibdin as a mere plagiarist; ceased to write in 1697.
    [xlvii. 316]

RAVENSCROFT, THOMAS (1592 ?–1635 ?), musician; published 'Pammelia,' the earliest collection of rounds, catches, and canons printed in England, 1609, and as a supplementary collection, 'Deuteromelia'; published his most famous work, 'The Whole Book of Psalms,' 1621. [xlvii. 318]

RAVENSER, RICHARD DE (d. 1386), clerk in chancery and archdeacon of Lincoln; made keeper of the hanaper, 1357, and archdeacon of Lincoln, 1368; had temporary charge of the great seal, 1377 and 1386. [xlvii. 318]

RAVENSWORTH, second BARON and first EARL OF (1797–1878). [See LIDDELL, SIR HENRY THOMAS, seventh baronet.]

RAVIS, RAVIUS, or **RAUE**, CHRISTIAN (1613–1677), orientalist and theologian; born at Berlin; M.A. Wittenberg, 1636; came to England, 1638, but (1639) proceeded to the Levant in search of manuscripts; became a fellow of Magdalen College, Oxford, 1648; left England to become professor of oriental languages at Upsala, 1650; professor at Frankfort-on-the-Oder, 1672–7. [xlvii. 319]

RAVIS, THOMAS (1560 ?–1609), successively bishop of Gloucester and London; M.A. Christ Church, Oxford, 1582; D.D., 1595; vice-chancellor, 1596 and 1597; dean of Christ Church, Oxford, 1596–1605; consecrated bishop of Gloucester, 1605, and translated to London, 1607. He assisted in translating the New Testament from 1604. [xlvii. 319]

RAWDON, CHRISTOPHER (1780–1858), unitarian benefactor; a mill-owner at Underbank; founded the Rawdon fund for augmenting the stipends of unitarian ministers. [xlvii. 320]

RAWDON, SIR GEORGE, first baronet (1604–1684), soldier; in the service of the first and second Viscounts Conway; sat in the Irish parliament of 1639 as M.P. for Belfast; fought under Monck in the Irish rebellion, and continued to serve in Ulster till 1649; M.P., Carlingford (Irish parliament), 1660; actively promoted the Restoration after the Protector's death; created baronet, 1665. [xlvii. 320]

RAWDON, MARMADUKE (1610–1669), traveller and antiquary; resided in the Canary islands, 1631–56; made extensive manuscript collections, and left an autobiography, edited for the Camden Society, 1863. [xlvii. 322]

RAWDON-HASTINGS, FRANCIS, first MARQUIS OF HASTINGS and second EARL OF MOIRA (1754–1826). [See HASTINGS.]

RAWES, HENRY AUGUSTUS (1826–1885), Roman catholic divine; M.A. Trinity College, Cambridge, 1852; became a Roman catholic, 1856; created D.D. by Pius IX, 1875; well known in London as a preacher and writer. [xlvii. 322]

RAWLE, FRANCIS (1660–1727), colonist; suffered persecution as a quaker, and (1686) emigrated to Pennsylvania, where he filled a number of important offices. [xlvii. 323]

RAWLE, RICHARD (1812–1889), divine; fellow of Trinity College, Cambridge, 1836; M.A., 1838; bishop of Trinidad, 1872–88. [xlvii. 323]

RAWLE, SAMUEL (1771–1860), topographical engraver and draughtsman; engraved for the 'Gentleman's Magazine' and other publications. [xlvii. 324]

RAWLET, JOHN (1642–1686), divine, of Pembroke Hall, Cambridge; well known as a preacher in the north of England; published religious treatises. [xlvii. 324]

RAWLEY, WILLIAM (1588 ?–1667), the 'learned chaplain' of Francis Bacon; B.A., fellow, and tutor of Corpus Christi College, Cambridge, 1610; became Bacon's chaplain and amanuensis, 1618; D.D., 1621; edited Bacon's works and wrote his life. [xlvii. 324]

RAWLIN, RICHARD (1687–1757), independent minister; went to London, 1730, and became pastor at Fetter Lane. [xlvii. 325]

RAWLINS, RICHARD (d. 1536), bishop of St. David's; elected fellow of Merton College, Oxford, 1480, and warden, 1508, but deprived, 1521; D.D., 1495; consecrated bishop, 1523. [xlvii. 325]

RAWLINS, THOMAS (1620 ?–1670), medallist and playwright; worked under Nicholas Briot [q. v.] at the mint; published (1640) 'The Rebellion,' a successful tragedy; nominated chief engraver of the mint, 1647, and actually installed at the Restoration. [xlvii. 326]

RAWLINSON, CHRISTOPHER (1677–1733), antiquary; of Queen's College, Oxford; with Edward Thwaites [q. v.] published Alfred's Saxon version of Boethius, 1698. [xlvii. 327]

RAWLINSON, SIR CHRISTOPHER (1806–1888), Indian judge; of the Charterhouse and Trinity College, Cambridge; M.A., 1831; barrister, Middle Temple, 1831; knighted, 1847; appointed chief-justice of Madras, 1849, retiring, 1859. [xlvii. 327]

RAWLINSON, SIR HENRY CRESWICKE, first baronet (1810–1895), Assyriologist; entered the East India Company's military service, acquired a good knowledge of Persian and the Indian vernaculars, and (1833–9) served in Persia; became political agent at Kandahar, 1840; distinguished himself in the Afghan war of 1842; became political agent in Turkish Arabia, 1843, and (1844) consul at Bagdad; deciphered the celebrated cuneiform inscription of Darius Hystaspes at Behistun, 1846; returned to England, 1855; K.C.B., 1856; M.P., Reigate, 1858–9, Frome, 1865–8; became a member of the India council, 1868; created baronet, 1891; president of the Royal Asiatic Society, 1878–81, and of the Royal Geographical Society, 1871–2 and 1874–5, contributing many valuable papers to both societies. [xlvii. 328]

RAWLINSON, JOHN (1576–1631), principal of St. Edmund Hall, Oxford; of Merchant Taylor's School, London, and St. John's College, Oxford; fellow, 1602; D.D., 1608; principal of St. Edmund Hall, Oxford, 1610–31; chaplain in ordinary to James I; published sermons. [xlvii. 331]

RAWLINSON, RICHARD (1690–1755), topographer and nonjuring bishop; son of Sir Thomas Rawlinson (1647–1708) [q. v.]; of Eton and St. John's College, Oxford; M.A., 1713; F.R.S., 1714; was ordained a nonjuring priest, 1716, and devoted himself to antiquarian pursuits and foreign travel; created D.C.L. Oxford in his absence, 1719; consecrated bishop, 1728; left his valuable manuscripts to the Bodleian Library, among them collections for a continuation of Wood's 'Athenæ'; wrote or edited numerous topographical works. [xlvii. 331]

RAWLINSON, SIR ROBERT (1810–1898), civil engineer; entered employ of Jesse Hartley [q. v.], 1831, and of Robert Stephenson [q. v.], 1836; chief engineer under Bridgewater trust, 1843–7; inspector under Public Health Act, 1848; chief engineering inspector to local government board, 1848–88; head of sanitary commission sent by government to seat of war in Crimea, 1855; knighted, 1883; K.C.B., 1888; M.I.C.E., 1848, and president, 1894; published technical works and reports. [Suppl. iii. 292]

RAWLINSON, SIR THOMAS (1647–1708), lord mayor of London; knighted, 1686; master of the Vintners' Company, 1687 and 1696; chosen lord mayor, 1705. [xlvii. 333]

RAWLINSON, THOMAS (1681–1725), bibliophile; eldest son of Sir Thomas Rawlinson (1647–1708) [q. v.]; of Eton and St. John's College, Oxford; barrister, Middle Temple, 1705; travelled in England and the Low Countries, making collections of books, manuscripts, and pictures; hired London house (1716) for the reception of his library, from which he supplied valuable material for many scholars, including Thomas Hearne. His manuscripts are in the Bodleian Library. Addison satirised him as 'Tom Folio' (Tatler, No. 158). [xlvii. 334]

RAWLINSON, SIR THOMAS (d. 1769), lord mayor of London; grandson of Sir Thomas Rawlinson (1647–1708) [q. v.]; master of the Grocers' Company; elected lord mayor, 1753; knighted, 1760. [xlvii. 334]

RAWLINSON, SIR WILLIAM (1640–1703), serjeant-at-law; barrister, Gray's Inn, 1667; practised as a chancery lawyer; serjeant-at-law, 1686; a commissioner of the great seal, 1689–93; knighted, 1689. [xlvii. 335]

RAWSON, GEORGE (1807–1889), hymn-writer; practised as a solicitor at Leeds; wrote many hymns, including 'By Christ redeemed.' [xlvii. 336]

RAWSON, JOHN, VISCOUNT CLONTARFF (1470?–1547), joined the knights of St. John, 1497, and (1511) became prior of Kilmainham and head of the order in Ireland; made treasurer of Ireland, 1517; on the dissolution of the order of the knights of St. John by Henry VIII was created viscount, 1541.   [xlvii. 336]

RAWSON, SIR WILLIAM (1783–1827), oculist; son of Henry Adams; M.R.C.S., 1807; established himself in London, 1810, and (1814) was made surgeon and oculist extraordinary to George, the prince regent; knighted, 1814; took his wife's name, Rawson, 1825; published three treatises on the eye.   [xlvii. 337]

RAY, BENJAMIN (1704–1760), antiquary; numismatist; M.A. St. John's College, Cambridge, 1730; perpetual curate of Cowbit and Surfleet; secretary of the well-known 'Gentlemen's Society' at Spalding, 1735, and afterwards vice-president.   [xlvii. 338]

RAY, JAMES (*fl.* 1745–1746), chronicler of the '45'; was with the Duke of Cumberland army at Culloden; published 'A Complete History of the Rebellion,' 1746.   [xlvii. 338]

RAY, JOHN (1627–1705), naturalist; spelt his name Wray until 1670; at first of Catharine Hall, Cambridge; fellow of Trinity College, Cambridge, 1649–62; M.A., 1651; junior dean, 1658; commenced his botanical tours, 1658, and with Francis Willughby [q. v.] agreed to attempt a systematic description of the whole organic world, himself undertaking the plants, 1662; published (1670) 'Catalogus Plantarum Angliæ,' which was recast (1690) as 'Synopsis Methodica Stirpium Britannicarum'; on the death of Willughby (1672) took up his friend's unfinished zoological labours; published (1682) his 'Methodus Plantarum Nova,' in which he first showed the true nature of buds, and employed the division of flowering plants into dicotyledons and monocotyledons; produced (1686) the first volume of his general 'Historia Plantarum,' which was followed by a second volume in 1688, and by a third in 1704; devoted his attention to insects from 1690, and at his death left a completed classification and a less complete 'history' of the group, in which he practically adopted the modern division of insects into the Metabola and Ametabola. His herbarium was placed in the botanical section of the British Museum in 1862; his library was sold by auction in 1707. His varied labours have justly caused him to be regarded as the father of natural history in this country, and as a botanist he has won the highest commendation from his greatest successors.   [xlvii. 339]

RAY, MARTHA (*d.* 1779), mistress of the Earl of Sandwich; daughter of a London staymaker; possessed a fine voice, and was a favourite pupil of Guardini. She became the mistress of Sandwich about the age of eighteen, and influenced naval appointments made by him; was shot dead while leaving Covent Garden Theatre by James Hackman [q. v.]   [xxiii. 422]

RAY, THOMAS MATTHEW (1801–1881), secretary of the Loyal National Repeal Association; a *protégé* of Daniel O'Connell [q. v.]; became secretary of the association in 1840; possessed great powers of organisation.   [xlvii. 345]

RAYMAN, JACOB (*fl.* 1641–1648), violin-maker; possibly a Tyrolese by birth; regarded as the founder of violin-making in England. He lived in Southwark.   [xlvii. 345]

RAYMOND LE GROS (*d.* 1182). [See FITZGERALD, RAYMOND.]

RAYMOND, SIR ROBERT, first BARON RAYMOND (1673–1733), lord chief-justice; only son of Sir Thomas Raymond [q. v.]; barrister, Gray's Inn, 1697; solicitor-general, 1710–14; knighted, 1710; attorney-general, 1720–4; conservative M.P. for Bishop's Castle, 1710–13, Yarmouth (Isle of Wight), 1715–17 (unseated on petition), Ludlow, 1719–22, Helston, 1722–4; appointed a puisne judge in the king's bench, 1724; nominated lord chief-justice, 1725; created baron, 1731.   [xlvii. 345]

RAYMOND, SIR THOMAS (1627–1683), judge; barrister, Gray's Inn, 1650; serjeant-at-law, 1677; became a judge on the exchequer bench, 1679; knighted, 1679; transferred to the common pleas, 1680; advanced to the king's bench, 1680.   [xlvii. 346]

RAYNALDE, THOMAS (*fl.* 1540–1551), physician; translated Eucharius Roesslin's 'De Partu Hominis,' 1545. He is probably distinct from Thomas Reynold [q. v.]   [xlvii. 347]

RAYNER, LIONEL BENJAMIN (1788?–1855), actor; appeared at Drury Lane, London, 1822, after acting in the country, and (1831) opened Rayner's New Subscription Theatre, where the Strand Theatre, London, now stands; retired from the stage almost ruined by the venture; a good serio-comic actor.   [xlvii. 347]

RAYNER, SAMUEL (*fl.* 1841–1872), water-colour painter; painted interiors of abbeys, churches, and mansions in the style of George Cattermole [q. v.]   [xlvii. 349]

RAYNOLD. [See RAINOLDS, RAYNALDE, REYNOLD, and REYNOLDS.]

REA, JOHN (*d.* 1681), nursery gardener; lived at Kinlet in Worcestershire; published 'Flora, or a Complete Florilege,' 1665.   [xlvii. 349]

REACH, ANGUS BETHUNE (1821–1856), journalist; studied at Edinburgh University; became parliamentary reporter to the 'Morning Chronicle,' and wrote largely for other periodicals; published novels, and (1849) joined the staff of 'Punch.'   [xlvii. 349]

READ. [See also REATE, REDE, REEDE, and REID.]

READ, CATHERINE (*d.* 1778), portrait-painter; for some years a fashionable artist in London, exhibiting portraits of several of the royal family.   [xlvii. 350]

READ, CHARLES ANDERSON (1841–1878), miscellaneous writer; failed in business and took to literature as a profession; published 'The Cabinet of Irish Literature' (4 vols. 1876–8) and other works.   [xlvii. 350]

READ, DAVID CHARLES (1790–1851), painter and etcher; began work as an etcher at Salisbury, 1826, and produced numerous plates, 1826–44; devoted himself to painting in oils after 1846.   [xlvii. 351]

READ, JOHN (*fl.* 1587–1588), surgeon; practised in Gloucester, and from 1588 in London; published a treatise on wounds, 1588.   [xlvii. 351]

READ, NICHOLAS (*d.* 1787), sculptor; pupil of Louis François Roubiliac [q. v.], whose extravagant style he imitated.   [xlvii. 352]

READ, RICHARD (1745?–1790?), engraver in stipple and mezzotint.   [xlvii. 352]

READ, SAMUEL (1815?–1883), water-colour painter; began to exhibit, 1857; his early sketches chiefly architectural; tried landscape-painting at a later period, but attained little success.   [xlvii. 352]

READ or **READE**, THOMAS (1606–1669), royalist; nephew of Sir Francis Windebank [q. v.]; was appointed Latin secretary to the crown for life, 1620; fellow of New College, Oxford, 1626; D.C.L., 1638; on the outbreak of the civil war enlisted at Oxford as a royalist; went abroad, 1648, and soon afterwards was ordained a Roman catholic priest at Douay; returned at the Restoration, and lived in London.   [xlvii. 353]

READ, SIR WILLIAM (*d.* 1715), empiric; originally a tailor; became an itinerant quack; knighted (1705) for curing seamen and soldiers of blindness gratis; became oculist to Queen Anne, *c.* 1705, and acquired great wealth.   [xlvii. 354]

READ, WILLIAM (1795?–1866), Irish verse-writer; published two volumes of Irish verse, 1818 and 1821.   [xlvii. 354]

READE. [See also READ, REDE, REEDE, and REID.]

READE, CHARLES (1814–1884), novelist and dramatist; grandson of John Scott (1747–1819) [q. v.]; elected fellow of Magdalen College, Oxford, 1835, while retaining his fellowship and college rooms till his death, spent much of his time in London; M.A., 1838; Vinerian fellow, 1842; barrister, Lincoln's Inn, 1843; started as an author with dramas, of which the first appeared at the Olympic, London, in 1851, and the most successful, 'Masks and Faces,' at the Haymarket, London, in 1852; turned his 'Masks and Faces' into a novel under the title of 'Peg Woffington,' 1852, which attained immense popularity; brought out 'It is never too late to mend,' 1856, the first instance of his employment of fiction to expose social abuses ; published his great historical novel, 'The Cloister and the Hearth,' 1861, and (1863) 'Hard Cash' ; published (1867) 'Griffith Gaunt,' which was strangely denounced as demoralising ; in collaboration with Dion Boucicault [q. v.] wrote his novel 'Foul Play,' 1869 ; produced the autobiographical 'Terrible Temptation,' which scandalised the American reviewers, 1871 ; never recovered from the blow caused by the death of his friend Laura Seymour, the actress, 1879 ; gave much of his time and money towards helping the poor. At his best he was an admirable storyteller, but he had an unfortunate weakness for exaggerated effects.   [xlvii. 354]

READE, EDWARD ANDERDON (1807–1886), Anglo-Indian official ; brother of Charles Reade [q. v.]; entered the East India Company's service, 1823 ; senior civilian at Agra on the outbreak of the mutiny with John Russell Colvin [q. v.], and after Colvin's death took temporary command ; earned the gratitude of the loyal after the mutiny by interposing to shield them from an indiscriminate spirit of vengeance, and received many tokens of their affection ; retired 1860, and was made C.B.   [xlvii. 358]

READE, JOHN EDMUND (1800–1870), poetaster and novelist ; chiefly remarkable for his talent for plagiarism, Byron serving as his chief model. In his longest poem, 'Italy,' he reproduced the dying gladiator.   [xlvii. 360]

READE, JOSEPH BANCROFT (1801–1870), chemist, microscopist, and photographic discoverer ; of Trinity and Caius Colleges, Cambridge ; M.A., 1828 ; was successively rector of Stone (1839–59), Ellesborough (1859–63), and Bishopsbourne (1863–70) ; F.R.S., 1838 ; discovered (1839) a method of separating heat-rays from those of light, and effected improvements in photography ; invented 'Reade's kettledrum' (1861), a hemispherical condenser for the microscope.   [xlvii. 360]

READE, ROBERT (d. 1415), successively bishop of Waterford and Lismore, Carlisle, and Chichester ; probably appointed to Waterford and Lismore, 1394 ; translated to Carlisle, 1396, and again to Chichester, 1397.   [xlvii. 361]

READE, WILLIAM WINWOOD (1838–1875), traveller, novelist, and controversialist ; nephew of Charles Reade [q. v.]; of Magdalen Hall, Oxford ; between 1862 and 1866 travelled extensively in Western Africa ; a special correspondent in the Ashanti war, 1873; published novels, and wrote against Roman catholicism and other forms of religion.   [xlvii. 361]

READER, WILLIAM (fl. 1680), portrait-painter ; chiefly known by his portrait of John Blow [q. v.]   [xlvii. 362]

READER, WILLIAM (1782–1852), topographer; was in early life a printer at Coventry, but died in poverty in London ; wrote on Coventry topography. [xlvii. 363]

READING, BURNET (fl. 1776–1822), engraver and draughtsman ; practised in London, and illustrated Granger's 'History of England' (1820 and 1822) and other works.   [xlvii. 363]

READING, JOHN (1588–1667), prebendary of Canterbury ; of Magdalen Hall and St. Mary Hall, Oxford ; M.A., 1610 ; chaplain to Charles I ; prebendary of Canterbury, 1643 ; his livings sequestered and himself imprisoned by the parliamentarians, but restored to his prebend after the Restoration ; published doctrinal works of Calvinistic character.   [xlvii. 363]

READING, JOHN (d. 1692), musician and author of 'Dulce Domum'; was organist of Winchester Cathedral (1675–81), of Winchester College, 1681–92 ; composed the Winchester College song, 'Dulce Domum.'   [xlvii. 365]

READING, JOHN (1677–1764), organist ; became organist at Lincoln Cathedral, 1702, and ultimately master of the choristers ; organist in London after 1707; published two elaborate books of songs and anthems, and composed the tune, 'Adeste Fideles' (well known as 'O come, all ye faithful ').   [xlvii. 365]

READING, ROBERT DE (d. 1325), historian; a monk of Westminster ; author of the portion of the 'Flores Historiarum ' from 1307 to 1325.   [xlvii. 365]

READING, WILLIAM (1674–1744), library keeper at Sion College, London Wall, London ; B.A. University College, Oxford, 1697 ; M.A. St. Mary Hall, Oxford, 1703 ; appointed library keeper of Sion College, London, 1708 ; published an excellent Greek and Latin edition of the early ecclesiastical historians, 1720.   [xlvii. 366]

READY, WILLIAM JAMES DURANT (1823–1873), marine-painter ; exhibited at the Royal Academy, 1867 ; painted chiefly scenes on the south coast of England.   [xlvii. 366]

REAGH, FLORENCE MacCARTHY (1562?–1640?). [See MacCarthy Reagh.]

REAY, BARONS. [See Mackay, Sir Donald, first Baron, 1591–1649 ; Mackay, Sir John, second Baron, fl. 1649–1654.]

REAY, STEPHEN (1782–1861), orientalist ; M.A. St. Alban Hall, Oxford, 1823 : B.D. 1841 ; vice-principal of St. Alban Hall : sub-librarian of the Bodleian Library, 1828–61 ; Laudian professor of Arabic, 1840–61.   [xlvii. 367]

REBECCA, BIAGIO (1735–1808), painter ; born in Italy ; painted portraits and historical subjects of little merit, but was skilled in decorative painting ; A.R.A., 1771.   [xlvii. 367]

RECORDE, ROBERT (1510?–1558), mathematician ; B.A. and perhaps M.A. Oxford ; fellow of All Souls College, Oxford, 1531 ; taught mathematics and other subjects both at Cambridge and Oxford ; died in prison in Southwark, probably in debt ; he was the first writer in English on arithmetic, geometry, and astronomy, and introduced algebra into England ; publishing ' The Grounde of Artes ' (1540), ' The Pathway to Knowledge,' on geometry (1551), ' The Castle of Knowledge,' on astronomy (1551), ' The Whetstone of Witte,' on algebra (1557), and other works, some of which are lost. He discovered the method of extracting the square root of multinomial algebraic expressions, and was the first to use the sign =.   [xlvii. 367]

REDDIE, JAMES (1773–1852), legal author ; studied at Edinburgh University and Glasgow College ; a Scottish advocate and town clerk of Glasgow, 1804–52. He published four legal works.   [xlvii. 369]

REDDING, CYRUS (1785–1870), journalist ; worked as a journalist in London, Paris, and the West of England ; from 1841 devoted himself more exclusively to bookmaking ; published numerous works, including a ' History and Description of Modern Wines,' 1833.   [xlvii. 370]

REDDISH, SAMUEL (1735–1785), actor ; made a reputation in Dublin and appeared at Drury Lane, London, 1767, where he remained during ten seasons ; acted at Covent Garden, London, 1778, but lost his reason, 1779 ; died a lunatic at York asylum.   [xlvii. 371]

REDE. [See also Read, Reade, Reede, and Reid.]

REDE, LEMAN THOMAS [TERTIUS] (1799–1832), miscellaneous writer ; took to the stage and taught elocution ; published a 'Memoir of George Canning' (1827) and other works.   [xlvii. 373]

REDE, Sir RICHARD (1511–1579), master of requests ; of Winchester College and New College, Oxford ; fellow of New College, Oxford, 1528 ; D.C.L., 1540 ; knighted, 1546 ; became lord chancellor of Ireland, 1546, and (1548) master of requests in England. [xlvii. 374]

REDE, Sir ROBERT (d. 1519), chief-justice of the common pleas ; made justice of the king's bench, 1495 ; knighted, 1495 ; made chief-justice of the common pleas, 1506 ; he founded three public lectureships at Cambridge, the endowment being reorganised in 1858, when it was directed that one lecture should be delivered annually by a man of eminence in science or literature.   [xlvii. 373]

REDE or **READE**, WILLIAM (d. 1385), bishop of Chichester ; of Exeter and Merton Colleges, Oxford ; fellow of Merton College, Oxford ; consecrated bishop at Avignon, 1368 ; a trier of petitions in various parliaments, 1369–80 ; built the library at Merton College, Oxford, and bequeathed it many manuscripts ; enjoyed a high reputation as a mathematician and astrologer.   [xlvii. 374]

REDE, WILLIAM LEMAN (1802–1847), dramatist; was brother of Leman Thomas [Tertius] Rede [q. v.], the two being known as 'the inseparables'; wrote farces and extravaganzas. [xlvii. 376]

REDERECH (*fl.* 573–590). [See RHYDDERCH HAEL.]

REDESDALE, EARL OF (1805–1886). [See MITFORD, JOHN THOMAS FREEMAN-.]

REDESDALE, BARONS. [See MITFORD, JOHN FREE-MAN-, first BARON, 1748–1830; MITFORD, JOHN THOMAS FREEMAN-, second BARON, 1805–1886.]

REDESDALE, ROBIN OF (*fl.* 1469). [See ROBIN.]

REDFERN, JAMES FRANK (1838–1876), sculptor; began to exhibit at the Royal Academy in 1859, and executed many works for Gothic church decoration. [xlvii. 376]

REDFORD, GEORGE (1785–1860), nonconformist divine; M.A. Glasgow, 1811; hon. LL.D. Glasgow, 1834; founded the 'Congregational Magazine'; independent minister at Uxbridge, 1812–26, and Worcester, 1826–56. [xlvii. 377]

REDFORD, SIR HENRY (d. 1404 ?), speaker of the House of Commons; represented Lincolnshire in parliament, 1400–1, 1402, and 1404; privy councillor, 1401; elected speaker, 1402. [xlvii. 377]

REDFORD, JOHN (*fl.* 1535), musician, poet, and dramatist; said to have been organist and almoner at St. Paul's, London; composed instrumental works of great importance in musical history, twenty-three of which are in the famous manuscript written by Thomas Mulliner [q. v.] Similar organ pieces are in the Additional MSS. at the British Museum. [xlvii. 378]

REDGRAVE, RICHARD (1804–1888), subject and landscape painter; brother of Samuel Redgrave [q. v.]; a student of the Royal Academy; R.A., 1851; became inspector-general for art in the government school of design in 1857, and also surveyor of the crown pictures. [xlvii. 379]

REDGRAVE, SAMUEL (1802–1876), writer on art; successively private secretary to several English statesmen, including Lord John Russell; published his valuable 'Dictionary of Artists of the English School,' 1874, and was also the author of several other useful works on art. [xlvii. 380]

REDHOUSE, SIR JAMES WILLIAM (1811–1892), oriental scholar; educated at Christ's Hospital, London; employed at Constantinople under the Turkish government and afterwards in the Turkish navy; secretary, Royal Asiatic Society, 1861–4; K.C.M.G., 1888; leading authority on the Osmanli-Turkish language, publishing several treatises and dictionaries in connection with it. [xlvii. 381]

REDINGTON, SIR THOMAS NICHOLAS (1815–1862), Irish administrator; educated at Oscott College and Christ's College, Cambridge; liberal M.P. for Dundalk, 1837–46; appointed under-secretary of state for Ireland, 1846; K.C.B., 1849. [xlvii. 381]

REDMAN, JOHN (1499–1551), master of Trinity College, Cambridge; of Corpus Christi College, Oxford, and St. John's College, Cambridge; M.A. Cambridge, 1530; D.D., 1537; became a fellow of St. John's College, Cambridge, 1530, Lady Margaret professor, 1538–44 and 1549; first master of Trinity College, Cambridge, 1546–51. [xlvii. 382]

REDMAN, SIR RICHARD (d. 1426), speaker of the House of Commons; M.P. for Yorkshire between 1405 and 1421; elected speaker, 1415. [xlvii. 383]

REDMAN, RICHARD (d. 1505), successively bishop of St. Asaph, Exeter, and Ely; probably great-grandson of Sir Richard Redman [q. v.]; perhaps educated at Cambridge; was abbot of Shap; consecrated bishop of St. Asaph, 1471, translated to Exeter, 1496, and to Ely, 1501. He restored the cathedral of St. Asaph. [xlvii. 383]

REDMAN, ROBERT (d. 1540), printer; started business in London, c. 1525; known chiefly as printer of law books. [xlvii. 383]

REDMAN, WILLIAM (d. 1602), bishop of Norwich; fellow of Trinity College, Cambridge; M.A., 1566; D.D., c. 1578; consecrated bishop, 1595; described by Chamberlain as 'one of the wisest of his coat.' [xlvii. 384]

REDMOND, THOMAS (1745 ?–1785), miniature-painter; practised at Bath; exhibited at the Royal Academy and elsewhere. [xlvii. 384]

REDPATH, PETER (1821–1894), Canadian merchant and philanthropist; a leading citizen of Montreal; made munificent donations to the McGill College and University, including a chair of natural philosophy (1871) and the Redpath Museum and Library. [xlvii. 384]

REDVERS, FAMILY OF, so named from the vill of Réviers in the Bessin, held lands in Devonshire and other parts of England after the Conquest. Among its members were Baldwin of Moeles (d. 1100 ?) [q. v.], brother of Richard de Clare (d. 1090 ?) [q. v.], and Baldwin of Redvers, first earl of Devon [q. v.] The earldom became extinct in 1262 and the family in 1293. [xlvii. 385]

REDWALD or **RÆDWALD** (d. 627 ?), king of the East-Angles; reigned during the supremacy of Ethelbert (552 ?–616) [q. v.], king of Kent, under whose influence he accepted Christianity; subsequently worshipped Christ and his old gods at the same time, threw off the control of Ethelbert, and became fourth Bretwalda; defeated Ethelfrid [q. v.] on the bank of the Idle, 617, and placed Edwin [q. v.] on the throne of Northumbria. [xlvii. 386]

REECE, RICHARD (1775–1831), physician; M.R.C.S., 1796; obtained a considerable practice in London, and published a number of medical treatises. [xlvii. 387]

REECE, ROBERT (1838–1891), dramatist; born in Barbados; M.A. Balliol College, Oxford, 1864; student at the Inner Temple, 1860; began to write in 1865, and produced a number of comic pieces and librettos. [xlvii. 387]

REED. [See also READ, READE, REDE, REEDE, and REID.]

REED, ALFRED GERMAN (1847–1895), actor; son of Thomas German Reed [q. v.], into partnership with Richard Corney Grain [q. v.] on his parents' retirement, for the purpose of continuing the 'Entertainment,' and directed the dramatic part of the performances. [xlvii. 396]

REED, ANDREW (1787–1862), philanthropist and independent minister; pastor of the New Road Chapel, London, 1811–31, and of Wycliffe Chapel, London, 1831–1861; commenced the formation of the London Orphan Asylum, 1813, of the Infant Orphan Asylum, 1827, of the Reedham Orphan Asylum, 1841, and of the Hospital for Incurables, 1855; author of several well-known hymns. [xlvii. 388]

REED, SIR CHARLES (1819–1881), chairman of the London school board; son of Andrew Reed [q. v.]; was the founder of the type-founding firm, Sir Charles Reed & Sons, Limited; interested himself in education from early life, and devoted his public life to the affairs of the London school board, of which he was chairman, 1870–81; knighted, 1874; M.P., St. Ives, 1880. He was also an antiquary of some note. [xlvii. 389]

REED, CHARLES EDWARD BAINES (1845–1884), secretary of the British and Foreign Bible Society; eldest son of Sir Charles Reed [q. v.]; of the City of London School and Trinity College, Cambridge; B.A., 1868; one of the secretaries of the Bible Society, 1874–84. [xlvii. 390]

REED, ISAAC (1742–1807), editor of Shakespeare; had a good practice as a conveyancer, but devoted himself as much as possible to literature and archaeology; collected a valuable library at Staple Inn, and (1781) furnished Johnson with notes for his 'Lives of the Poets'; published 'Biographia Dramatica' [see BAKER, DAVID ERSKINE], 1782 and 1785, re-edited Johnson and Steevens's edition of Shakespeare; produced (1803) an elaborate edition of Shakespeare, known as the 'first variorum' [see STEEVENS, GEORGE]. [xlvii. 391]

REED, JOSEPH (1723–1787), dramatist; by trade a ropemaker; produced several plays, which were acted at the London theatres with indifferent success, including a comic opera adapted from Fielding's 'Tom Jones'; as a pungent controversialist was to the front with an attack on Smollett, 1759, and a defence of Garrick, 1772. [xlvii. 392]

REED, JOSEPH CHARLES (1822–1877), landscape-painter; exhibited chiefly at the gallery of the New Water-colour Society. [xlvii. 393]

REED, PRISCILLA (1818–1895), actress; *née* Horton; went on the stage at the age of ten and acted at Covent Garden, the Haymarket, and other London theatres, in tragedy; married Thomas German Reed [q. v.], 1844; possessed a fine contralto voice; was engaged in later life in the 'German Reed's Entertainment.' [xlvii. 395]

REED, TALBOT BAINES (1852–1893), writer of boys' books; son of Sir Charles Reed [q. v.]; published a useful 'History of Old English Letter-foundries,' 1887, but is better known for his tales of school-life and other books for boys. [xlvii. 390]

REED, SIR THOMAS (1796–1883), general; entered the army, 1813; commanded a brigade at Ferozeshah, 1845, was in command of the forces in the Punjab on the outbreak of the mutiny, 1857; general, 1868; G.C.B., 1875. [xlvii. 393]

REED, THOMAS GERMAN (1817–1888), musician; first appeared at the Bath concerts at the age of ten; became musical director at the Haymarket, London, 1838, and with his wife, Priscilla Reed [q. v.], commenced Mr. and Mrs. German Reed's 'Entertainment,' in order to provide dramatic amusement for persons reluctant to visit theatres, 1855. The entertainments began at St. Martin's Hall, 1855, and were removed to 14 Regent Street, 1856, and to St. George's Hall, 1874. They were subsequently carried on by the son, Alfred German Reed [q. v.] [xlvii. 394]

REEDE, JOHN DE, BARON REEDE (1593–1683), of Dutch parentage; acquired title and lands of Renswoude, 1623, and was elected to the States-General of Holland; came to England as joint-ambassador extraordinary, in the attempt to reconcile Charles I and the parliament, 1644, on which occasion he was created a baron by Charles I; failed in consequence of the resentment felt by the Commons at the interposition of the ambassadors, and shortly returned to Holland, where he was afterwards president of the States-General. [xlvii. 396]

REES. [See also RHYS and RICE.]

REES, ABRAHAM (1743–1825), cyclopædist; was resident tutor at the independent academy at Hoxton, 1762–85; tutor in Hebrew and mathematics at Hackney College, 1786–96, and pastor to the Old Jewry congregation, London, 1783–1825; re-edited the 'Cyclopædia' of Ephraim Chambers [q. v.], 1778, 1781–6, and 1788–91; engaged between 1802 and 1820 on 'The New Cyclopædia,' which appeared in forty-five volumes. [xlvii. 397]

REES, DAVID (1801–1869), independent minister and editor; minister at Capel Als, Llanelly; edited the 'Diwygiwr' ('Reformer'), a monthly political journal, 1835–65. [xlvii. 398]

REES, GEORGE (1776–1846), medical writer; M.D. Glasgow, 1801; practised in London; L.R.C.P., 1808; medical superintendent of the Cornwall lunatic asylum, Bodmin; published medical treatises. [xlvii. 398]

REES, GEORGE OWEN (1813–1889), physician; M.D. Glasgow, 1836; physician at Guy's Hospital, London, 1856–73; Gulstonian lecturer, 1845, Croonian lecturer, 1856–8, Harveian orator, 1869, and senior censor, Royal College of Physicians, 1863–4; was constantly associated with Alfred Swaine Taylor [q. v.] in important criminal investigations; one of the first to turn his attention to the chemistry of the urine. [xlvii. 399]

REES, HENRY (1798–1869), Calvinistic methodist leader; superintendent of the Liverpool churches, 1836–1869; as a preacher had hardly a rival in the denomination. [xlvii. 400]

REES, JOSIAH (1744–1804), Welsh presbyterian minister; minister of Gellionen, 1766–1804; and made important contributions to Welsh literature, including several hymns. [xlvii. 400]

REES, OWEN (1770–1837), publisher; son of Josiah Rees [q. v.]; was a partner of Thomas Norton Longman [q. v.], and an intimate friend of the poet Moore. [xlvii. 402]

REES, RICE (1804–1839), Welsh historical scholar, fellow of Jesus College, Oxford, 1828; M.A., 1828; professor at St. David's, Lampeter; published an 'Essay on the Welsh Saints,' 1836. [xlvii. 401]

REES, THOMAS (1777–1864), unitarian minister and historical writer, brother of Owen Rees [q. v.]; hon. LL.D. Glasgow, 1819; minister in Stamford Street, Blackfriars, London, 1823–31; had great knowledge of the history of anti-trinitarian opinion. [xlvii. 401]

REES, THOMAS (1815–1885), independent minister; held several charges in Wales, and wrote on Welsh nonconformist history. [xlvii. 402]

REES, WILLIAM (1802–1883), Welsh minister and author; brother of Henry Rees [q. v.]; held ministerial office in Liverpool for thirty-two years (1843–75); exerted a powerful influence on the politics, poetry, and literature of Wales; possessed great literary versatility, appearing in prose as a biographer, novelist, journalist, divine, and even dramatist, and writing lyric, epic, and occasional verse. [xlvii. 403]

REES, WILLIAM JENKINS (1772–1855), Welsh antiquary; M.A. Wadham College, Oxford, 1797; prebendary of Brecon, 1820–55, and one of the editors of the Welsh MSS. Society. [xlvii. 404]

REEVE, CLARA (1729–1807), novelist; first attempted authorship, 1772, and (1777) produced her most famous work, 'The Champion of Virtue,' entitled in the second and all subsequent editions 'The Old English Baron.' [xlvii. 404]

REEVE, EDMUND (1585?–1647), judge; of Caius College, Cambridge; became member of Gray's Inn, 1607; reader, 1632; justice of common pleas, 1639; adhered to parliament on the outbreak of war. [xlvii. 405]

REEVE, EDMUND (*d.* 1660), divine; was ejected from his vicarage of Hayes-cum-Norwood by the parliamentary 'triers'; wrote on behalf of the high church party. [xlvii. 405]

REEVE, HENRY (1780–1814), physician; helped to found (1805) the 'Edinburgh Medical and Surgical Journal'; subsequently practised at Norwich. [xlvii. 406]

REEVE, HENRY (1813–1895), man of letters; son of Henry Reeve [q. v.]; joined the staff of the 'Times,' 1840, and guided its foreign policy for fifteen years; editor of the 'Edinburgh Review,' 1855–95; edited the 'Greville Memoirs,' 1865; hon. D.C.L. Oxford, 1869; C.B., 1871; vice-president, Society of Antiquaries, 1879–1882; had many friends among men of letters in all parts of Europe. [xlvii. 406]

REEVE, JOHN (1608–1658), sectary; originally a puritan; became a universalist; presented himself and his cousin, Lodowicke Muggleton [q. v.], as the 'two witnesses' of Revelation, 1652; formulated the 'six foundations' of the Muggletonian theology, but had a distinct following known as Reevites. [xlvii. 408]

REEVE, JOHN (1799–1838), actor; began as an amateur, while still a banker's clerk, but in 1819 appeared at Drury Lane, London, as a mimic, and afterwards appeared successfully in comedy and farce at several London theatres; was addicted to excessive drinking and constantly failed to learn his parts, but was so great a favourite with the public that managers were compelled to engage him. [xlvii. 409]

REEVE, JOSEPH (1733–1820), biblical scholar and Latin poet; became a jesuit, 1770; chaplain to Lord Clifford, 1767–1820; published, among other works, a 'History of the Bible,' 1780. [xlvii. 411]

REEVE, LOVELL AUGUSTUS (1814–1865), conchologist; set up a natural-history shop in King William Street, Strand, London; F.L.S., 1846; F.G.S., 1853; published many works, including 'Conchologia Iconica,' 1843–78 (completed by George Brettingham Sowerby, 1812–1884 [q. v.]). [xlvii. 412]

REEVE, RICHARD (1642–1693), Benedictine monk; B.A. Trinity College, Oxford, 1665; joined Roman catholic church, 1667; M.A. Magdalen College, Oxford, 1668; was master of Magdalen School, Oxford, 1670–3; went in 1674 to Douay, where he became a monk; returned to England, 1688; published Latin treatises. [xlvii. 413]

REEVE, THOMAS (1594–1672), royalist divine; M.A. Caius College, Cambridge, 1617; D.D., 1660; incumbent of Waltham Abbey, Essex; published devotional works. [xlvii. 413]

REEVE, SIR THOMAS (d. 1737), judge; barrister, Middle Temple, 1713, bencher, 1720, reader, 1722; K.C., 1718; became judge of the common pleas, 1733; knighted, 1733; became chief-justice of the common pleas in 1736. [xlvii. 414]

REEVE, WILLIAM (1757–1815), actor and musical composer; became an organist, but accepted the post of composer to Astley's (1783); appeared at the Royalty, London, 1787; a successful composer of dramatic music in later life. [xlvii. 414]

REEVES, CHARLES (1815–1866), architect; became architect to the county courts in England and Wales, 1847, and designed sixty-four new courts in various parts of the country. [xlvii. 415]

REEVES, JOHN (1752?–1829), king's printer; of Eton and Merton College, Oxford; B.A., 1775; fellow of Queen's College, Oxford, 1778; M.A., 1778; barrister, Middle Temple, 1779, bencher, 1824; a commissioner of bankruptcy, 1780; appointed king's printer, 1800; author of a 'History of English Law' (5 vols. 1783–1829) and other works. [xlvii. 415]

REEVES, JOHN (1774–1856), naturalist; educated at Christ's Hospital, London; was an inspector of tea in China in the service of the East India Company (1812–31), and devoted his leisure to the study of the natural products of the country, of which he transmitted many specimens to England; F.R.S. and F.L.S., 1817. [xlvii. 416]

REEVES, JOHN SIMS (1818–1900), tenor vocalist; assumed name of Sims, c. 1847; studied pianoforte under Johann Baptist Cramer [q. v.], singing under Tom Cooke and J. W. Hobbs; first appeared publicly as vocalist, 1839, at Newcastle; sang at Grecian Theatre, City Road, London, 1842, and joined Macready's Drury Lane Company; studied under Bordogni in Paris and Alberto Mazzucato in Milan; appeared with success at Drury Lane, London, 1847; made first appearances in oratorio at Worcester and Norwich, 1848, and thenceforward ranked as the premier English tenor; professor of singing at Guildhall School of Music; published 'Life and Recollections,' 1888, and 'My Jubilee,' 1899. [Suppl. iii. 293]

REEVES, WILLIAM (1667–1726), divine; fellow of King's College, Cambridge, and M.A., 1692; became chaplain to Queen Anne; published the 'Apologies of Justin Martyr, Tertullian, and Minucius Felix,' a translation, 1716. [xlvii. 416]

REEVES, WILLIAM (1815–1892), Irish antiquary and bishop of Down, Connor, and Dromore; Berkeley medallist, and (1837) M.B. (B.A., 1835) Trinity College, Dublin; consecrated bishop, 1886; published 'Acts of Archbishop Colton,' 1850, and his most famous work, 'The Life of St. Columba,' 1857. [xlvii. 416]

REGAN, MORICE (fl. 1171), Irish interpreter; was in the service of Diarmaid MacMurchada [q. v.] as interpreter and herald; wrote an account of the English invasion. [xlvii. 418]

REGENBALD (fl. 1062–1066), chancellor of Edward the Confessor; witnessed several charters as 'cancellarius'; appears in 'Domesday' as holding land in several counties. [xlvii. 419]

REGIMORTER or **REGEMORTER**, ASSUERUS (1614–1650), physician; practised in London; M.D. Leyden, 1636 (incorporated at Oxford, 1636); F.R.C.P., 1643, Gulstonian lecturer, 1645, and censor, 1649; part-author of the famous 'Tractatus de Rachitide,' 1650. [xlvii. 419]

REGINALD, called GODFREYSON (d. 944?), king of the Danes; brother of Olaf (d. 941) [q. v.]; was ruling in Northumbria in 943 conjointly with Olaf (d. 981) [q. v.], and accepted Christianity. [xlvii. 419]

REGINALD or **RAINALD** (d. 1097), abbot of Abingdon; a chaplain of William of Normandy, who gave him the abbacy of Abingdon in 1085. The convent was deprived of much of its property by William Rufus. [xlvii. 420]

REGINALD OF CANTERBURY (fl. 1112), Latin poet; native of 'Fagia,' perhaps Tiffauges, in the north of Poitou; became a monk of St. Augustine's, Canterbury. His longest poem is the life of St. Malchus, a Syrian hermit. His poems are among the Cotton MSS. and in the Bodleian Library. [xlvii. 420]

REGINALD (fl. 1125), reputed chancellor of England; was, according to Leland, chancellor to Henry I. [xlvii. 423]

REGINALD OF COLDINGHAM or OF DURHAM (fl. 1162–1173), hagiologist; a monk of Durham; wrote the life of Godric [q. v.], of St. Cuthbert [q. v.], of Oswald (605?–642) [q. v.], and of St. Ebba [q. v.] The first two have been edited for the Surtees Society. [xlvii. 421]

REGINALD, EARL OF CORNWALL (d. 1175), natural son of Henry I; made Cornwall a basis of operations against King Stephen, and was created earl by the Empress Matilda in 1141; remained attached to Henry II until his death. [xlvii. 422]

REGINALD FITZJOCELIN (1140?–1191). [See FITZJOCELIN.]

REGINALD (d. 1200), abbot of Walden; became prior in 1164 and abbot in 1190, on the elevation of the priory into an abbey; erroneously reckoned among the chancellors of England. [xlvii. 423]

REGONDI, GIULIO (1822–1872), guitarist and concertina-player; born at Geneva; arrived in England, 1831, and afterwards developed the capabilities of the concertina. [xlvii. 423]

REGULUS or **RULE** (fl. 8th cent.?), saint; was the legendary founder of the see of St. Andrews, and is a leading character in the story of the journeyings of the relics of St. Andrew. [xlvii. 424]

REID. [See also READ, READE, REDE, and REEDE.]

REID or **RHEAD**, ALEXANDER (1586?–1641), anatomist and surgeon; educated at Aberdeen University (M.A. after 1600); afterwards studied surgery in France; practised in North Wales, acquired fame as a surgeon, and (1632) was appointed lecturer on anatomy at Barber-Surgeons' Hall; published a number of medical works, but made no original additions of importance to the theory of medicine. [xlvii. 424]

REID, ALEXANDER (1747–1823), painter; had a studio at Dumfries at the end of the eighteenth century, and is chiefly remembered in connection with a miniature of Robert Burns, which he painted in 1796. Its identity is uncertain, but a miniature in the Scottish National Portrait Gallery is most probably the authentic portrait. [xlvii. 425]

REID, ALEXANDER (1802–1860), schoolmaster; M.A. Edinburgh; was proprietor and head-master of the Edinburgh Institution, 1850–8; published 'A Dictionary of English Language,' 1844 (18th edit. 1864). [xlvii. 426]

REID, ANDREW (d. 1767?), compiler; published several works on literary and scientific subjects between 1728 and 1767. [xlvii. 426]

REID, DAVID BOSWELL (1805–1863), inventor; son of Peter Reid [q. v.]; obtained medical diploma at Edinburgh, 1830; taught chemistry privately at Edinburgh (1833–47) and published a work on 'Ventilation,' 1844, the principles laid down in it being adopted in the new houses of parliament; died at Washington. [xlvii. 427]

REID, GEORGE WILLIAM (1819–1887), keeper of the department of prints and drawings in the British Museum; appointed an attendant in the department, 1842, assistant, 1865, and keeper, 1866; retired, 1883. His catalogues, both departmental and non-official, are of considerable value. [xlvii. 427]

REID, HUGO (1809–1872), educational writer; son of Peter Reid [q. v.]; went to the United States, 1858; for some years principal of Dalhousie College, Halifax, Nova Scotia; wrote a number of school text-books on scientific subjects. [xlvii. 428]

REID, JAMES SEATON (1798–1851), church historian; M.A. Glasgow, 1816; entered the Irish presbyterian ministry; hon. D.D. Glasgow, 1833; published a 'History of the Presbyterian Church in Ireland,' of which the first volume appeared in 1833. [xlvii. 429]

REID, JOHN (1721–1807), general; entered the army, 1745; became general (1798) after considerable active service; a proficient flute player and a musical composer. He bequeathed 50,000l. to found a chair of music at Edinburgh University. The bequest took effect in 1839. [xlvii. 430]

REID, JOHN (1776–1822), physician; M.D. Edinburgh, 1798; practised in London, and wrote on 'Insanity' (1816) and 'Hypochondriasis' (1821).
[xlvii. 431]

REID, JOHN (1808–1841 ?), compiler of 'Bibliotheca Scoto-Celtica'; nephew of William M'Gavin [q. v.], a Glasgow bookseller. He published his 'Bibliotheca' in 1832, and also wrote biographies and a book on Turkey, 1840; died at Hongkong, whither he had gone to edit an English journal and prepare a Chinese dictionary.
[xlvii. 431]

REID, JOHN (1809–1849), anatomist; took his diploma at Edinburgh, 1840; Chandos professor of anatomy at St. Andrews, 1841–9; published a collection of papers entitled 'Physiological, Anatomical, and Pathological Researches,' 1848.
[xlvii. 432]

REID, MAYNE, originally THOMAS MAYNE REID (1818–1883), novelist; passed an adventurous life in the United States between 1840 and 1849, and served in the Mexican war, 1847; published 'The Rifle Rangers,' 1850, and from that time until his death continued to write romances and tales of adventure, which attained great popularity among boys.
[xlvii. 432]

REID, PETER (1777–1838), educational reformer; studied medicine at Edinburgh University; succeeded in effecting important changes in the methods of teaching at Edinburgh University; was also known as a medical writer.
[xlvii. 427]

REID, RICHARD TUOHILL (d. 1883), jurist; called to the Irish bar, 1853; was Perry professor of jurisprudence in Elphinstone College, Bombay, for over a quarter of a century; edited from 1864 the 'Reports of the High Court.'
[xlvii. 433]

REID, ROBERT (d. 1558), bishop of Orkney; M.A. St. Andrews, 1515; became abbot of Kinloss, 1526, and frequently acted as secretary to James V of Scotland, who employed him on several diplomatic missions to England and France; appointed bishop of Orkney, 1541; after James V's death supported Cardinal Beaton; took part in arranging (1558) Mary Stuart's marriage with the Dauphin; died on the way home. Knox accuses him of being a miser, but without justice.
[xlvii. 433]

REID, ROBERT (1776–1856), architect; designed St. Salvator's College, St. Andrews, 1820.
[xlvii. 435]

REID, ROBERT (1773–1865), topographer and antiquary; educated at Glasgow University; a Glasgow merchant; published 'Glasgow Past and Present,' 1851–6, and 'Glasgow and its Environs,' 1864, both of which works were reprinted in 1884 with additions.
[xlvii. 435]

REID, READ, or RHÆDUS, THOMAS (d. 1624), Latin secretary to James I; brother of Alexander Reid (1586 ?–1641) [q. v.]; M.A. Aberdeen, 1600; taught humanity at Rostock for several years as a 'docent'; became Latin secretary to James I, 1618. By his will he bequeathed his library to Aberdeen town and college, with an endowment, thus founding the first reference library in Scotland.
[xlvii. 435]

REID, THOMAS (1710–1796), philosopher; graduated at Marischal College, Aberdeen, 1726; became librarian of Marischal College, Aberdeen, in 1733; minister of New Machar in 1737, and professor of philosophy at Marischal College, Aberdeen, in 1751; hon. D.D. Marischal College, Aberdeen, 1762; published his 'Inquiry into the Human Mind,' 1764, an answer to Hume, and was appointed (1764) professor of moral philosophy at Glasgow, where he remained till his death; published his essay on the 'Intellectual Powers,' 1785, and that on the 'Active Powers,' 1788. He is the leading representative of the school of common sense, by which phrase he meant not vulgar opinion, but the beliefs common to rational beings as such. His most important doctrine was that belief in an external world is intuitive or immediate.
[xlvii. 436]

REID, THOMAS (1791–1825), naval surgeon; laboured earnestly to improve the condition of prisoners in England, as well as of transported convicts; published two books of travels.
[xlvii. 440]

REID, THOMAS MAYNE (1818–1883). [See REID, MAYNE.]

REID, WILLIAM (1764–1831), minor poet; of Glasgow; wrote humorous verse in Scottish dialect.
[xlvii. 440]

REID, SIR WILLIAM (1791–1858), major-general and colonial governor; entered the royal engineers, 1809, and served in the Peninsular war, 1810–14, and so in the expedition against New Orleans, 1815, and in the expedition against Algiers, 1816; while in the West Indies (1831–4) materially developed the circular theory of hurricanes, publishing (1838) 'An Attempt to develop the Law of Storms'; served in the British legion in Spain, commanding a brigade, 1835–6; F.R.S., 1839; appointed (1839) governor of the Bermudas, when he was so active in improving the condition of the people that he is still remembered as 'the good governor'; transferred to Barbados as governor-in-chief of the Windward islands, 1846, but resigned, 1848; K.C.B., 1851; became governor of Malta, 1851–8; major-general, 1856; author of important works on military subjects.
[xlvii. 440]

REIDFURD, LORD (1645 ?–1711). [See FOULIS, JAMES.]

REIDIE, LORD (d. 1683). [See NEVOY, SIR DAVID.]

REILLY, or more properly **REILY**, HUGH (d. 1695 ?), political writer; master in chancery and clerk of the council in Ireland in James II's reign; accompanied James II into exile; published 'Ireland's Case briefly stated,' 1695 (frequently reprinted under various titles).
[xlviii. 1]

REILLY, THOMAS DEVIN (1824–1854), Irish revolutionary writer; of Trinity College, Dublin; joined the staff of the 'Nation,' 1845, and attached himself to John Mitchel [q. v.]; fled to New York to avoid prosecution, 1848, and afterwards edited the 'Washington Union.'
[xlviii. 1]

REILLY, WILLIAM EDWARD MOYSES (1827–1886), major-general; educated at Christ's Hospital, London; entered the artillery, 1845; served in the Crimea; C.B., 1855; accompanied the French army of the Loire during the Franco-Prussian war; inspector-general of artillery, with rank of major-general, 1885.
[xlviii. 2]

REIMES, PHILIP DE (1246 ?–1296). [See PHILIP.]

REINAGLE, ALEXANDER ROBERT (1799–1877), musician; son of Joseph Reinagle [q. v.]; organist of St. Peter-in-the-East, Oxford, 1823–53; composed the hymn-tune 'St. Peter.'
[xlviii. 4]

REINAGLE, GEORGE PHILIP (1802–1835), marine-painter; son of Ramsay Richard Reinagle [q. v.]; first exhibited at the Royal Academy, 1822; painted incidents of naval engagements, including Navarino, which he witnessed.
[xlviii. 3]

REINAGLE, JOSEPH (1762–1836), music composer; principal 'cello in the Salomon concerts under Haydn; composed for the violin, violoncello, and pianoforte.
[xlviii. 3]

REINAGLE, PHILIP (1749–1833), animal and landscape painter; abandoned portraits for animal-painting, c. 1785; began to exhibit landscapes, 1787; R.A., 1812.
[xlviii. 4]

REINAGLE, RAMSAY RICHARD (1775–1862), portrait, landscape, and animal painter; son of Philip Reinagle [q. v.]; R.A., 1823; compelled to resign in consequence of an attempt to exhibit another artist's picture as his own, 1848.
[xlviii. 4]

REINBALD (fl. 1062–1066). [See REGENBALD.]

REINHOLD, CHARLES FREDERICK (1737–1815), bass singer; son of Thomas Reinhold [q. v.]; originally a chorister at the Chapel Royal, London; began, in 1759, a long career as singer at Marylebone Gardens, London.
[xlviii. 5]

REINHOLD, THOMAS (1690 ?–1751), singer; born in Dresden; followed Handel to London, where he created principal parts in many of Handel's operas and oratorios.
[xlviii. 5]

REISEN, CHARLES CHRISTIAN (1680–1725), gem-engraver; of Norwegian parentage; was examined as an expert at Atterbury's trial, as to the impression of a seal, and had considerable note as an engraver.
[xlviii. 5]

RELHAN, ANTHONY (1715–1776), physician; B.A. Trinity College, Dublin, 1735; studied medicine at Leyden; M.D. Dublin, 1743; practised at Brighton; published a history of Brighton, 1761.
[xlviii. 6]

RELHAN, RICHARD (1754–1823), botanist and editor of Tacitus; son of Anthony Relhan [q. v.]; M.A., 1779, and fellow, 1781, of King's College, Cambridge; F.R.S.; F.L.S., 1788; published 'Flora Cantabrigiensis,' 1785, and edited Tacitus' 'Germania' and 'Agricola,' 1809, and 'Historia,' 1819; genus *Relhania* named after him.   [xlviii. 6]

RELLY, JAMES (1722?–1778), universalist; one of Whitefield's preachers, but (c. 1761) definitely adopted universalism; published religious works.   [xlviii. 7]

RELPH, JOSEPH (1712–1743), Cumberland poet; perpetual curate of Sebergham; his works published (1747) as 'A Miscellany of Poems.'   [xlviii. 8]

REMIGIUS (d. 1092), bishop of Lincoln; contributed, while almoner of Fécamp, a ship and twenty knights to William the Conqueror's force for the invasion of England; consecrated bishop of Dorchester (1067), a see which he transferred to Lincoln, in consequence of the decree of the council of Windsor (1072).   [xlviii. 8]

REMPSTON or **RAMSTON**, Sir THOMAS (d. 1406), constable of the Tower of London; M.P. Nottinghamshire, 1381, 1382, 1393, and 1395; joined Henry, earl of Derby, in France, 1399, and on his accession to the throne as Henry IV had the custody of Richard II as constable of the Tower of London; K.G., 1400; drowned in the Thames.   [xlviii. 9]

REMPSTON or **RAMPSTON**, Sir THOMAS (d. 1458), soldier; son of Sir Thomas Rempston (d. 1406) [q. v.]; M.P. Nottinghamshire, 1413 and 1416; took part in the French wars of Henry V and Henry VI; K.G.   [xlviii. 10]

REMSDYKE, JOHN (fl. 1767–1778). [See Van Rymsdyc, Jan.]

RENAUD, Mrs. (d. 1831). [See Powell, Mrs.]

RENDEL, JAMES MEADOWS (1799–1856), engineer; was employed as a surveyor under Telford, and (c. 1822) set up a business at Plymouth; member of the council of the Royal Society; was specially famous as a constructor of harbours, canals, and docks. Among his works are the Torquay breakwater (1836), the Birkenhead docks, and Portland harbour (1847).   [xlviii. 10]

RENDER, WILLIAM (fl. 1790–1801), grammarian and translator; a native of Germany; studied at Giessen; came to London, c. 1790; translated works by Kotzebue and Goethe, besides publishing several educational manuals.   [xlviii. 12]

RENDLE, JOHN (1758–1815), divine; B.A. Sidney Sussex College, Cambridge, 1781, and fellow; published 'The History of Tiberius' (1814), in which he maintained that Tiberius was a Christian convert.   [xlviii. 12]

RENDLE, WILLIAM (1811–1893), antiquary; practised in Southwark as a physician for nearly fifty years; F.R.C.S., 1873; wrote several valuable treatises on the history of Southwark.   [xlviii. 13]

RENEHAN, LAURENCE (1797–1857), president of Maynooth College; professor of scripture (1827–34), vice-president (1834–45), and president (1845–57) of Maynooth College; made a large collection of Irish ecclesiastical records, which he bequeathed to the college.   [xlviii. 13]

RENNELL, JAMES (1742–1830), geographer; entered the navy, 1756, and the East India Company's service, 1763; appointed surveyor-general of Bengal, 1764, and was employed on the survey of the province—the first prepared—from 1764 to 1777; published his 'Bengal Atlas,' 1779, and other valuable works relating to the geography of Western Asia, Africa, and the Atlantic.   [xlviii. 14]

RENNELL, THOMAS (1787–1824), divine; only son of Thomas Rennell (1754–1840) [q.v.]; of Eton and King's College, Cambridge; M.A., 1813; B.D., 1822; became vicar of Kensington, 1816; published miscellaneous treatises.   [xlviii. 15]

RENNELL, THOMAS (1754–1840), dean of Winchester; educated at Eton; fellow of King's College, Cambridge; M.A. *per literas regias*, 1779; D.D., 1794; master of the Temple, 1797–1827; dean of Winchester, 1805–40; had a high reputation as a scholar and divine.   [xlviii. 16]

RENNIE, GEORGE (1749–1828), agriculturist; wrote on agriculture and kindred subjects.   [xlviii. 17]

RENNIE, GEORGE (1802–1860), sculptor and politician; son of George Rennie (1749–1828) [q. v.]; exhibited statues and busts at the Royal Academy, 1828–37; liberal M.P. for Ipswich, 1841, retiring, 1847; governor of the Falkland islands, whose condition he greatly improved, 1847–55.   [xlviii. 17]

RENNIE, GEORGE (1791–1866), civil engineer; eldest son of John Rennie [q. v.]; educated at St. Paul's School, London, and Edinburgh University; entered into partnership with his brother, Sir John Rennie [q. v.], 1821, and had considerable business as a railway engineer, besides superintending the mechanical business of the firm.   [xlviii. 18]

RENNIE, JAMES (1787–1867), naturalist; M.A. Glasgow, 1815; professor of natural history at King's College, London, 1830–4; emigrated to Australia, 1840; published and edited works on natural history.   [xlviii. 18]

RENNIE, JOHN (1761–1821), civil engineer; younger brother of George Rennie (1749–1828) [q.v.]; studied at Edinburgh University; entered James Watt's employ, 1784; began business on his own account, c. 1791; F.R.S., 1798; had a great reputation as a constructor of canals, docks, harbours, and bridges. Waterloo bridge (1810–17), London bridge, and Southwark bridge (1815–19), were designed by him, as well as the Plymouth breakwater.   [xlviii. 19]

RENNIE, Sir JOHN (1794–1874), civil engineer; son of John Rennie [q.v.]; carried on his father's business after his death, completing London bridge (opened, 1831) and Plymouth breakwater; knighted, 1831; retired, c. 1862.   [xlviii. 20]

RENNIGER or **RHANGER**, MICHAEL (1530–1609), divine; B.A. Cambridge; B.A. Magdalen College, Oxford, 1546; M.A., 1549; D.D., 1573; distinguished as a preacher during Edward VI's reign; retired to the continent on the accession of Queen Mary, but returned on her death and became one of Queen Elizabeth's chaplains; archdeacon of Winchester, 1575; published political treatises.   [xlviii. 21]

RENNY, GEORGE ALEXANDER (1825–1887), major-general, royal artillery; entered the Bengal horse artillery, 1844; behaved with extraordinary gallantry at the siege of Delhi, 1857, and received the Victoria Cross; retired from active service, 1878.   [xlviii. 22]

RENOUARD, GEORGE CECIL (1780–1867), scholar; of St. Paul's School and Charterhouse, London; fellow of Trinity College, Cambridge, 1804; B.A., 1802; M.A. *per literas regias*, 1805; B.D., 1811; afterwards passed some years as a chaplain in the Levant; lord almoner's professor of Arabic at Cambridge, 1815–21; rector of Swanscombe, 1818–67; R.A.S., 1824. His contributions to classical and oriental study were numerous and important.   [xlviii. 22]

RENOUF, Sir PETER LE PAGE (1822–1897), egyptologist, oriental scholar, and theologian; born in Guernsey; educated at Pembroke College, Oxford; came in contact with the tractarians and entered the Roman church, 1842; professor of ancient history and afterwards of eastern languages at Roman catholic university of Ireland, 1855–54; studied egyptology, and published in 'Atlantis,' 1863, a defence of the science against attacks of Sir George Cornewall Lewis [q. v.]; attacked doctrine of papal infallibility in an essay, 1868, which was placed on the 'Index'; advocated foundation of Roman catholic college at Oxford, 1864; government inspector of schools, 1866; keeper of Egyptian and Assyrian antiquities in British Museum, 1885–91; president (1887) of Society of Biblical Archæology, to whose publications he contributed; knighted, 1896.   [Suppl. iii. 294]

RENWICK, JAMES (1662–1688), Scottish covenanter; threw in his lot with the Cameronians in 1681, after a liberal education at Edinburgh University (M.A., 1681); publicly proclaimed the Lanark declaration, 1682, and proceeded to study at Groningen; was ordained and (1683) entered on his Scottish ministry; became famous as a field preacher and (1685) refused to join Argyle's insurrection because it was not based on the covenant; captured (1688) and executed in the Grassmarket on 17 Feb. after refusing to petition for a reprieve; celebrated as the last of the martyrs of the covenant.   [xlviii. 23]

RENWICK, WILLIAM (1740 ?–1814), naval surgeon and author; captured by John Paul Jones [q. v.] in the Scarbrough in 1779, and wrote a description of the engagement in heroic verse; published a number of pamphlets and poems.   [xlviii. 25]

RENZY or **RENTSI**, SIR MATTHEW DE (1577–1634), Irish writer; a native of Cologne; was an officer of the customs in Ireland. None of his writings (which are said to have included an Irish grammar and dictionary) are extant.   [xlviii. 26]

REPINGTON or **REPYNGDON**, PHILIP (d. 1424), bishop of Lincoln and cardinal; educated at Broadgates Hall, Oxford; was the most prominent supporter of Wycliffe at Oxford; was excommunicated, 1382, but after a few months abjured his heresies and was restored; made chaplain to Henry IV, 1400; consecrated bishop of Lincoln, 1405; created a cardinal, 1408; resigned his bishopric, 1419.   [xlviii. 26]

REPPES, WILLIAM (d. 1550). [See RUGG.]

REPTON, GEORGE STANLEY (d. 1858), architect; son of Humphry Repton [q. v.]; assisted his father to design the Brighton Pavilion; made a runaway match with Lady Elizabeth Scott, eldest daughter of Lord Eldon, 1817.   [xlviii. 30]

REPTON, HUMPHRY (1752–1818), landscape-gardener; lost his fortune and became a professional landscape gardener, being employed by the chief noblemen of the day; published a number of treatises, including ' An Inquiry into the Changes of Taste in Landscape Gardening,' 1806.   [xlviii. 28]

REPTON, JOHN ADEY (1775–1860), architect; assisted his father by preparing architectural designs as adjuncts to landscape gardening; contributed to ' Archæologia.'   [xlviii. 29]

RERESBY, SIR JOHN, baronet (1634–1689), author of 'Travels and Memoirs'; travelled on the continent during the Commonwealth, and in 1675 entered parliament (M.P., Aldborough) as a supporter of the court. His 'Memoirs' appeared in 1734, and his 'Travels and Memoirs' were published together in 1813.   [xlviii. 30]

RESBURY, NATHANIEL (1643–1711), divine; M.A. Emmanuel College, Cambridge, 1672 (incorporated at Oxford, 1673; D.D. Merton College, Oxford, 1692); became chaplain in ordinary to William and Mary, 1691; published theological treatises.   [xlviii. 32]

REUTER, ADAM (fl. 1608–1626), author; a native of Kottbus in Silesia; resided many years at Oxford, having become a member of Exeter College, and wrote against the papacy.   [xlviii. 32]

REVANS, SAMUEL (1808–1888), colonist; proceeded to New Zealand, 1840; published the 'New Zealand Gazette,' the first newspaper in that colony.   [xlviii. 33]

REVELEY, WILLEY (d. 1799), architect; edited vol. iii. of Stuart's 'Antiquities of Athens,' 1794.   [xlviii. 33]

REVELL or **RIVELL**, SIR RICHARD (d. 1222), knight and landowner; sheriff of Devonshire and Cornwall in Richard I's reign.   [xlviii. 34]

REVETT, NICHOLAS (1720–1804), architect and draughtsman; became acquainted with James Stuart (1713–1788) [q. v.] at Rome, and was associated with him in preparing and publishing the first volume of the 'Antiquities of Athens' (1762); subsequently prepared the 'Antiquities of Ionia' (1769–97) for the Society of Dilettanti.   [xlviii. 34]

REYNARDSON, SIR ABRAHAM (1590–1661), lord mayor of London; became master of the Merchant Taylors' Company, 1640; lord mayor, 1648–9; deposed and heavily fined (1649) for manifesting royalist sympathies; was knighted at the Restoration, but declined the mayoralty on account of ill-health.   [xlviii. 35]

REYNELL, CAREW (1636–1690), economic writer; a Hampshire country gentleman; of Wadham College, Oxford; student, Middle Temple, 1654; author of 'The True English Interest,' 1674, a work accepting the mercantile theory without question.   [xlviii. 36]

REYNELL, CAREW (1698–1745), successively bishop of Down and Connor and of Derry; fellow of New College, Oxford, 1711; M.A., 1719; D.D., 1730; consecrated bishop of Down and Connor, 1739; translated to Derry, 1743.   [xlviii. 37]

REYNELL, EDWARD (1612–1663), divine; of Exeter College, Oxford, and the Middle Temple; rector of West Ogwell; published several pieces in prose and verse; committed suicide.   [xlviii. 37]

REYNER, CLEMENT (1589–1651), abbot of Lambspring or Lansperg in Germany; born in Yorkshire; became a Benedictine, 1610, and first abbot of Lansperg, 1643; died at Hildesheim. He edited 'Apostolatus Benedictinorum in Anglia,' the history of the Benedictine Order in England.   [xlviii. 38]

REYNER, EDWARD (1600–1668), ejected minister; M.A. St. John's College, Cambridge, 1624; rector of St. Peter at Arches, Lincoln, 1627, ejected, 1662; published religious treatises.   [xlviii. 38]

REYNER, WILLIAM (fl. 1615–1619), translator; published Latin versions of Roman catholic controversial treatises.   [xlviii. 38]

REYNES, JOHN (fl. 1527–1544), stationer and bookbinder in London.   [xlviii. 39]

REYNOLD, THOMAS (fl. 1541–1555), London printer; frequently confused with Thomas Raynalde [q. v.], whose first book he printed.   [xlvii. 347]

REYNOLDS, SIR BARRINGTON (1786–1861), admiral; son of Robert Carthew Reynolds (1748 ?–1811) [q. v.]; entered the navy, 1795; saw much active service; admiral, 1860; G.C.B., 1861.   [xlviii. 39]

REYNOLDS, CHRISTOPHER AUGUSTINE (1834–1893), first Roman catholic archbishop of South Australia; went to Australia, 1855, as a Roman catholic priest and (1873) was consecrated bishop of Adelaide; nominated archbishop by Pope Leo XIII, 1887.   [xlviii. 40]

REYNOLDS, EDWARD (1599–1676), bishop of Norwich; fellow of Merton College, Oxford, 1619; M.A., 1624, and D.D., 1648 (also incorporated at Cambridge); warden of Merton College, Oxford, 1660–1; consecrated bishop, 1661; a moderate Anglican; published sermons and short religious works.   [xlviii. 40]

REYNOLDS, EDWARD (1629–1698), archdeacon of Norfolk; son of Edward Reynolds (1599–1676) [q. v.]; of Merton and Magdalen Colleges, Oxford; B.A., 1649; made fellow of Magdalen College, Oxford, by the parliamentary visitors; D.D., 1676; archdeacon of Norfolk, 1661–98.   [xlviii. 41]

REYNOLDS, FRANCES (1729–1807), painter; sister of Sir Joshua Reynolds [q. v.]; a friend of Dr. Johnson, whose portrait she painted.   [xlviii. 67]

REYNOLDS, FREDERIC (1764–1841), dramatist; of Westminster School and the Middle Temple; began writing for the stage, 1785, and composed nearly one hundred tragedies and comedies, many of which were printed.   [xlviii. 41]

REYNOLDS, FREDERIC MANSEL (d. 1850), author; eldest son of Frederic Reynolds [q. v.]; edited 'The Keepsake' and published (1833) ' Miserrimus: a Tale,' founded on the inscription in Worcester Cathedral on the gravestone of Thomas Morris (1660–1748) [q. v.]   [xlviii. 42]

REYNOLDS, GEORGE NUGENT (1770 ?–1802), Irish poet; a gentleman of Leitrim; author of 'Kathleen O'More' (1800) and other popular lyrics. In 1830 Campbell's 'Exile of Erin' was claimed for him by his relatives.   [xlviii. 42]

REYNOLDS, GEORGE WILLIAM MACARTHUR (1814–1879), author and politician; became editor of the 'London Journal,' 1846; started 'Reynolds's Miscellany,' 1846, and 'Reynolds's Weekly Newspaper,' 1850; appeared as a chartist leader, 1848, retaining his connection with the movement till 1856; was an advocate of extreme measures and a supporter of James [Bronterre] O'Brien [q. v.]; wrote a number of novels of a sensational character.   [xlviii. 43]

REYNOLDS, HENRY (fl. 1627–1632), poet and critic; friend of Drayton and the author of a translation of Tasso's 'Aminta' (1628) and of an essay on the nature of poetry, 1632.   xlviii. 45]

REYNOLDS, HENRY REVELL (1745–1811), physician; of Lincoln College, Oxford, Trinity College, Cambridge, and Edinburgh; M.D. Cambridge, 1773; settled in London, 1772; registrar, 1781–3, Gulstonian lecturer, 1775, and Harveian orator, 1776, of the Royal College of Physicians; became physician-in-ordinary to George III, 1806. [xlviii. 45]

REYNOLDS, HENRY ROBERT (1825–1896), congregational divine; grandson of Henry Revell Reynolds [q. v.]; educated at Coward College, London; B.A. London, 1848; fellow of University College, London, 1848; ordained pastor of congregational church at Halstead, Essex, 1846; minister of East Parade Chapel, Leeds, 1849; president, 1860–94, of Cheshunt College; co-editor of 'British Quarterly Review,' 1866–74; editor of 'Evangelical Magazine,' 1877–82; published theological works. [Suppl. iii. 295]

REYNOLDS, JAMES (1686–1739), judge; nephew of Sir John Reynolds [q. v.]; M.A., 1705, and fellow of St. John's College, Cambridge; barrister, Lincoln's Inn, 1712; M.P., Bury St. Edmunds, 1717; appointed puisne judge in the king's bench, 1725, and lord chief-baron of the exchequer, 1730; retired, 1738. [xlviii. 45]

REYNOLDS, SIR JAMES (1684–1747), judge; barrister, Lincoln's Inn, 1710; appointed baron of the court of exchequer, 1740; knighted, 1745. [xlviii. 46]

REYNOLDS, JAMES (1805–1866), orientalist; B.A. St. Catharine's College, Cambridge, 1826; perpetual curate of St. Mary's Chapel, Great Ilford, 1837; secretary to the Oriental Translation Fund of the Royal Asiatic Society; published translations from the Persian and Arabic. [xlviii. 46]

REYNOLDS, JOHN (1549–1607). [See RAINOLDS.]

REYNOLDS or **REINOLDS,** JOHN (1584–1614), epigrammatist; fellow of New College, Oxford, 1602; B.C.L., 1607; published 'Epigrammata,' 1611. [xlviii. 47]

REYNOLDS, JOHN (fl. 1621–1650), author; a merchant of Exeter; published several translations from the French and Dutch, besides some original verse. [xlviii. 47]

REYNOLDS, SIR JOHN (1625–1657), soldier; probably a member of the Middle Temple; joined the parliamentary army, and (1648) commanded a regiment of horse; took part in the Irish campaigns; M.P., Galway and Mayo, 1654, Waterford and Tipperary, 1656; knighted, 1655; commanded the English force which co-operated with the French in Flanders, 1657; perished at sea when returning to England. [xlviii. 47]

REYNOLDS, JOHN (1667–1727), dissenting minister; of Pembroke College, Oxford; ordained to Oldbury Chapel, 1699, and afterwards to the presbyterian congregation at Shrewsbury; published several religious treatises. [xlviii. 49]

REYNOLDS, JOHN (1713 ?–1788), admiral; entered the navy as a 'volunteer per order,' 1728; lieutenant, 1736; governor of Georgia, 1754–9; admiral, 1787. [xlviii. 50]

REYNOLDS, JOHN HAMILTON (1796–1852), poet; educated at St. Paul's School, London; published two volumes of verse in 1814; friend and correspondent of Keats from 1816; entered a solicitor's office, 1818, but continued to write both prose and verse; clerk to the county court in the Isle of Wight; best remembered for his 'Romance of Youth' and some sonnets. [xlviii. 50]

REYNOLDS, SIR JOHN RUSSELL, first baronet (1828–1896), physician; grandson of Henry Revell Reynolds [q. v.]; M.D. London, 1852; F.R.S., 1869; became physician-in-ordinary to the queen's household, 1878; president, Royal College of Physicians, 1893–5; created baronet, 1895; wrote on nervous diseases and edited the 'System of Medicine,' 1866–79. [xlviii. 52]

REYNOLDS, JOHN STUCKEY (1791–1874), founder of the Home and Colonial Training College in Gray's Inn Road, London; was a clerk in the treasury office; erected several infant schools in various parts of London, and founded the training college in 1836 to train teachers in Pestalozzian methods. [xlviii. 53]

REYNOLDS, SIR JOSHUA (1723–1792), portrait-painter; born at Plympton-Earl's in Devonshire; son of

the Rev. Samuel Reynolds, master of the Plympton-Earl's grammar school; showed an early talent for portraiture, and was apprenticed to Thomas Hudson (1701–1779) [q. v.]; between 1743 and 1749 painted portraits at London and Plymouth; taken by Commodore Keppel to the Mediterranean, 1749; spent three years in study in Italy, and returned to London, where he soon put all rivals at a distance, and in 1759 had 156 sitters; his art between 1753 and 1760 represented in the National Gallery by the Lord Ligonier on horseback and the portrait of Anne, countess of Albemarle; made an income of about 6,000l. a year, which he spent largely in buying pictures; was by 1760 intimately acquainted with Garrick, Goldsmith, and Johnson; removed, 1760, from Great Newport Street to Leicester Fields, where he lived till his death; mainly identified, as regards his profession of portrait-painter, with the whig party, to which his early patrons had belonged; founded the Literary Club, 1764, to give, as he said, Dr. Johnson unlimited opportunities of talking; selected as president of the Royal Academy on its foundation in 1768; knighted, 1769; immediately took the most active part in organising the Academy and its schools; subsequently devoted more of his time to pictures of the imagination, the number of his sitters having decreased; hon. D.C.L. Oxford, 1773; selected mayor of Plymouth, 1773; compelled to cease painting by the partial failure of his eyesight, 1790; buried in the crypt of St. Paul's Cathedral. He was the greatest portrait-painter that England has produced, and is ranked by Ruskin as one of the seven supreme colourists. His literary works consist mainly of his 'Discourses,' which probably received some polish from Johnson, Burke, Malone, and others, before they were published, but were essentially his own both in style and thought. [xlviii. 53]

REYNOLDS, RICHARD (d. 1535), martyr; studied at Christ's College, Cambridge; B.D., 1513; one of the foremost scholars of the day; executed for refusing to accept the royal supremacy over the church. [xlviii. 67]

REYNOLDS or **RAINOLDE,** RICHARD (d. 1606), divine and chronicler; of St. John's College, Cambridge; M.A. Trinity College, Cambridge, 1553; held several ecclesiastical preferments in Essex; published a work in rhetoric, 1563, and another on the Roman emperors, 1571. [xlviii. 68]

REYNOLDS, RICHARD (1674–1743), successively bishop of Bangor and Lincoln; LL.B. Trinity Hall, Cambridge, 1695; LL.D. Sidney Sussex College, Cambridge, 1701; was bishop of Bangor, 1721–3; bishop of Lincoln, 1723–43. [xlviii. 69]

REYNOLDS, RICHARD (1735–1816), quaker-philanthropist; was the proprietor of large ironworks in Staffordshire; retired from business, 1789, and was distinguished by his munificent charitable gifts. [xlviii. 69]

REYNOLDS, SIR ROBERT (fl. 1640–1660), lawyer; brother of Sir John Reynolds [q. v.]; M.P., Hindon, Long parliament; took the parliamentary side in the civil war; refused to act as a commissioner on Charles I's trial; became solicitor-general, 1650; disappeared from public life in 1653, but returned on Cromwell's death and (1660) became attorney-general; promoted the Restoration and was knighted by Charles II, 1660. [xlviii. 71]

REYNOLDS, ROBERT CARTHEW (d. 1804), lieutenant in the navy; son of Robert Carthew Reynolds (1748 ?–1811), [q. v.]; died from wounds received at Martinique after showing great gallantry. [xlviii. 72]

REYNOLDS, ROBERT CARTHEW (1748 ?–1811), rear-admiral; entered the navy, 1759; saw much service during the French wars; rear-admiral, 1808; perished in a storm on the coast of Jutland. [xlviii. 71]

REYNOLDS, SAMUEL HARVEY (1831–1897), divine and journalist; educated at Radley and Exeter College, Oxford; fellow of Brasenose College, Oxford, 1856; M.A., 1857; entered Lincoln's Inn, 1858; ordained priest, 1865; successively Latin lecturer, tutor, and bursar at Brasenose College, Oxford; held college living of East Ham, 1871–93; leader-writer on staff of 'The Times,' 1873–96; edited Homer's 'Iliad,' 1870, and other classics, and published original essays on various subjects. [Suppl. iii. 296]

REYNOLDS, SAMUEL WILLIAM (1773–1835), mezzotint engraver and landscape-painter; engraved many fine works which created much enthusiasm among French artists; successfully employed etching to strengthen the mezzotint. [xlviii. 72]

REYNOLDS, SAMUEL WILLIAM (1794–1872), portrait-painter; son of Samuel William Reynolds (1773–1835) [q. v.]; exhibited at the Royal Academy. [xlviii. 73]

REYNOLDS, THOMAS (*fl.* 1541–1555). [See REYNOLD.]

REYNOLDS, THOMAS (1667 ?–1727), presbyterian minister; pastor to a congregation in Great Eastcheap, London, 1695–1727; opposed the growth of arian tendencies among the English presbyterians. [xlviii. 74]

REYNOLDS, THOMAS (1752–1829), antiquary; M.A. Lincoln College, Oxford, 1777; rector of Little Bowden, 1776–1829; his principal work, 'Iter Britanniarum,' 1799 (an edition of the British portion of Antoninus's 'Itinerary'). [xlviii. 75]

REYNOLDS, THOMAS (1771–1836), informer; became a United Irishman, 1797, but turned informer in 1798, while financially embarrassed, and betrayed the provincial committee to the police; retired to Paris, 1822. [xlviii. 75]

REYNOLDS, WALTER (*d.* 1327), archbishop of Canterbury; employed, like other secular-minded clerks in Edward I's rougher business; became a favourite of Edward II, who made him bishop of Worcester, 1307, and lord chancellor, 1310; became archbishop of Canterbury by a papal bull, in spite of the previous election of Thomas de Cobham [q. v.] by the Canterbury monks, 1313; supported Edward II in political disputes, and several times attempted mediation: succeeded in introducing a considerable measure of ecclesiastical reform; made his peace with Queen Isabella on the overthrow of Edward II; crowned Edward III at Westminster, and became a member of his council, but had little influence on affairs. [xlviii. 77]

REYNOLDS, WILLIAM (1544 ?–1594). [See RAINOLDS.]

REYNOLDS, WILLIAM (1625–1698), dissenting minister; M.A. Emmanuel College, Cambridge, 1648 (incorporated at Oxford, 1649); became joint-minister at Nottingham with John Whitlock [q. v.], 1651, both being ejected, 1662, and several times imprisoned, but returning to Nottingham in 1687. [xlviii. 80]

REYNOLDS, WILLIAM (1758–1803), inventor; eldest son of Richard Reynolds (1735–1816) [q. v.]; was associated with his father in the management of the works and collieries of Ketley; obtained a patent (1799) for preparing iron for conversion into steel by the use of manganese. [xlviii. 70]

RHAM, WILLIAM LEWIS (1778–1843), agriculturist; born at Utrecht; M.A. Trinity College, Cambridge, 1810; prebendary of Salisbury, 1806; appointed vicar of Winkfield, 1808; opened a school of industry at Winkfield, 1835; member of the Royal Agricultural Society, and a great authority on agricultural methods; contributed to the 'Library of Useful Knowledge' a manual on 'Flemish Industry.' [xlviii. 81]

RHEAD, ALEXANDER (1586 ?–1641). [See REID.]

RHEES, MORGAN JOHN (1760–1804), divine; baptist minister at Peny-garn, Monmouthshire; was a strong republican, and (1794) emigrated to Pennsylvania, where he became a noted preacher. [xlviii. 82]

RHESE. [See RHYS and RICE.]

RHIND, ALEXANDER HENRY (1833–1863), antiquary; studied at Edinburgh University; early devoted himself to the study of Scottish antiquities; compelled, from 1853, to travel in consequence of weak health; published (1862) 'Thebes, its Tombs and their Tenants,' the result of a sojourn in Egypt, besides less important treatises. [xlviii. 82]

RHIWALLON AP CYNFYN (*d.* 1069), Welsh prince; received North Wales in 1163 as a tributary of Edward the Confessor; fell in battle. [xlviii. 83]

RHODES, EBENEZER (1762–1839), topographer; a master-cutler; published 'Peak Scenery,' 1818–24, which remains a standard work on Derbyshire. [xlviii. 83]

RHODES, HUGH (*fl.* 1550–1555), author of the 'Book of Nurture' (1550 ?); published also 'The Chyld-Byshop' (1555), a fulsome panegyric on Queen Mary. [xlviii. 84]

RHODES, JOHN N. (1809–1842), painter; exhibited rustic scenes and groups of cattle at the Royal Academy and elsewhere, 1839–42. [xlviii. 84]

RHODES, RICHARD (*d.* 1668), poet and dramatist; student, Christ Church, Oxford; B.A., 1662; author of 'Flora's Vagaries' (published, 1670), a comedy. [xlviii. 84]

RHODES, RICHARD (1765–1838), engraver; produced chiefly small line-engravings for illustrated books, in the style of James Heath (1757–1834) [q. v.] [xlviii. 84]

RHODES, WILLIAM BARNES (1772–1826), dramatic writer; chief teller in the Bank of England, 1823–6; author of the long-popular burlesque 'Bombastes Furioso' (1813), which had been produced at the Haymarket, London, in 1810. [xlviii. 85]

RHODRI MAWR, i.e. THE GREAT (*d.* 877), Welsh king; son of Merfyn Frych [q. v.], on whose death, in 844, he became ruler of North Wales; chiefly occupied in withstanding the incursions of the Danes; fell in battle against the English. [xlviii. 85]

RHODRI AB OWAIN (*d.* 1195), Welsh prince; son of Owain Gwynedd [q. v.]; drove his elder brother, David, out of Anglesey in 1175, and ruled there till 1191, when he was dispossessed by his nephews. [xlviii. 85]

RHUN AP MAELGWN (*fl.* 547), British king; succeeded his father, Maelgwn Gwynedd [q. v.], as ruler of North Wales, 547. Legend connected him with King Arthur, and he appears in the Triads as one of the three 'blessed rulers' of Britain. [xlviii. 86]

RHYDDERCH HAEL, i.e. THE LIBERAL, or HEN, i.e. THE AGED (*fl.* 580), British king; reigned in Alclud or Dumbarton, but is almost unnoticed in early records. It is, however, generally believed that he was the victor in the battle of Arderydd, 573. [xlviii. 86]

RHYDDERCH, RODERICK, or ROGERS, JOHN (*d.* 1735), printer; settled in Shrewsbury, 1708; printed a number of books connected with Wales, 1708–28. [xlviii. 87]

RHYGYFARCH, wrongly called Rhyddmarch, and in Latin, Ricemarchus (1056–1099), clerk of St. David's; eldest son of Sulien [q. v.]; author of the oldest extant life of St. David, preserved among the Cotton. MSS., and printed in Rees's 'Cambro-British Saints.' [xlviii. 87]

RHYS AB OWAIN (*d.* 1078), Welsh prince; became sole ruler of South Wales, 1076, but was dispossessed, 1078, by Trahaearn ap Caradog. [xlviii. 88]

RHYS AP TEWDWR (*d.* 1093), Welsh king; became king of South Wales on the death of his cousin, Rhys ab Owain [q. v.], in 1078, but was much harassed by the princes of North Wales, whom he decisively defeated in 1081; killed in battle against the Norman settlers in Brecknock. [xlviii. 88]

RHYS AP GRUFFYDD (1132 ?–1197), prince of South Wales; son of Gruffydd ab Rhys (*d.* 1137) [q. v.]; became sole ruler of the Welsh in Dyfed, Ceredigion, and Ystrad Tywi, 1155; engaged in a long struggle with Henry II, whom, however, he supported during the rebellion of 1173–4; eventually acknowledged Henry II's supremacy, but on the accession of Richard I resumed his independence. [xlviii. 89]

RHYS GOCH AP RHICERT (*fl.* 1300), Welsh poet; lived in Glamorgan. His poems first became known through their publication in the Iolo MSS. [xlviii. 91]

RHYS GOCH ERYRI, i.e. of Snowdon (1310 ?–1400 ?), Welsh poet; lived near Bedd Gelert. Seven of his poems have been printed, but a large number remain unprinted in the British Museum among the Cymrodorion MSS. [xlviii. 91]

RHYS (or RICE) AP THOMAS (1449–1525), supporter of Henry VII; formed a fighting force of several thousand men in South Wales, with whom he joined the Earl of Richmond (afterwards Henry VII) after his landing in 1485; knighted, 1485; received numerous honours and preferments from Henry VII. [xlviii. 91]

RHYS, IOAN DAFYDD, or JOHN DAVID (1534–1609), Welsh grammarian; studied at Christ Church, Oxford, and in several Italian universities; published (1592) a Welsh grammar, still extant.   [xlviii. 92]

RHYS, MORGAN (1710?–1779), Welsh hymn-writer; a Calvinistic methodist preacher of the Cilycwm circuit; published a collection of twenty-two hymns in 1760, a second collection in 1767, and a third in 1770–1.
          [xlviii. 92]
RHYSBRACH, JOHN MICHAEL (1693?–1770). [See RYSBRACK.]

RIALL, SIR PHINEAS (1775–1850), general; entered the army, 1794; served in the West Indies and Canada; appointed governor of Grenada, 1816; knighted, 1833; general, 1841.   [xlviii. 93]

RICARDO, DAVID (1772–1823), economist; the son of a Dutch jew, who made a fortune on the London stock exchange early in life; through the perusal of the ' Wealth of Nations' became interested in the scientific treatment of economic questions; had become a leading authority upon the subject by 1817, and, in accordance with the wishes of his friends for a more systematic exposition of his theories, published his well-known ' Principles of Political Economy and Taxation,' 1817, in which he elaborated his theory of rent, exhibited the relation between rent, profit, and wages, and traced the incidence of taxation; retired from business, 1814, and settled in Gloucestershire; M.P., Portarlington, 1819–23; though an independent thinker, generally supported the radical party; soon became accepted in the house as an authority on financial matters. He was the principal founder of the classical school of political economy.
          [xlviii. 93]
RICARDO, JOHN LEWIS (1812–1862), free-trader; nephew of David Ricardo [q. v.]; M.P., Stoke-upon-Trent, 1841–62; supported the repeal of the corn laws and navigation laws.   [xlviii. 97]

RICART, ROBERT (*fl.* 1466–1508), town clerk of Bristol; compiled the ' Mayor's Register,' a record of the ancient usages of the city, which was edited for the Camden Society in 1872.   [xlviii. 97]

RICAUT, SIR PAUL (1628–1700). [See RYCAUT.]

RICCALTOUN, ROBERT (1691–1769), Scottish divine; educated at Edinburgh University; minister of Hopekirk, 1725–69; befriended and encouraged James Thomson, author of the 'Seasons'; published an ode on ' Winter,' in Savage's 'Miscellany,' 1726; engaged in the 'Marrow controversy.'   [xlviii. 97]

RICCIO or **RIZZIO**, DAVID (1533?–1566), secretary to Mary Queen of Scots; son of a musician at Pancalieri, near Turin; began life in the service of the archbishop of Turin; accompanied the ambassador of the Duke of Savoy to Scotland, 1561, and (1564) became French secretary to Mary Queen of Scots, his appointment marking a change in her policy, which now became independent both of the Guises and the Scottish lords; arranged the marriage with Darnley, and practically superseded Maitland of Lethington as secretary of state; with his new position of authority assumed a haughty demeanour; exasperated the Scottish nobles by his assumption of superiority, and in particular annoyed Darnley, Mary's husband, who found himself excluded from political power; was suspected by Darnley of being the queen's lover; was at length seized in the queen's presence by an armed band, including Darnley and Morton, and despatched in an antechamber.   [xlviii. 98]

RICE AP **THOMAS** (1449–1525). [See RHYS.]

RICE, EDMUND IGNATIUS (1762–1844), founder of the Roman catholic institute known as the ' Irish Christian Brothers'; was owner of a provision merchant's business at Waterford; began (*c.* 1802) to educate the children of Waterford gratuitously, and with the other directors took religious vows and became known as the ' Christian Brothers,' 1808 (the order was sanctioned by Pius VII, 1820); elected superior-general, 1822. The schools eventually spread over the greater part of Ireland; and in 1896 numbered three hundred, with an average daily attendance of thirty thousand pupils. [xlviii. 100]

RICE, GEORGE (1724–1779), politician; of Christ Church, Oxford; M.P., Carmarthenshire, 1754–79; supported Lord North; treasurer of the king's chamber, 1770; privy councillor, 1770.   [xlviii. 102]

RICE, JAMES (1843–1882), novelist; of Queens' College, Cambridge; chiefly known for his literary partnership with (Sir) Walter Besant, which commenced in 1872 with ' Ready Money Mortiboy' and continued till the close of his life; published, with (Sir) Walter Besant, 'The Golden Butterfly,' 1876, and 'The Seamy Side,' 1881, among other works; published independently a history of the British turf, 1879.   [xlviii. 102]

RICE, SIR JOHN AP (*d.* 1573?). [See PRICE.]

RICE or **PRICE**, RICHARD (*fl.* 1535–1579), author; brother of Ellis Price [q. v.]; abbot of Conway, 1536; published two theological treatises.   [xlviii. 103]

RICE, SIR STEPHEN (1637–1715), chief-baron of the exchequer in Ireland; appointed a baron by James II, 1686, and chief baron, 1687; took a large share in re-modelling the Irish corporations; on the overthrow of James II escaped reprisals under the articles of Limerick.
          [xlviii. 103]
RICE, THOMAS SPRING, first BARON MONTEAGLE (1790–1866). [See SPRING-RICE.]

RICEMARCHUS (1056–1099). [See RHYGYFARCH.]

RICH, BARNABE (1540?–1617), author and soldier; fought in Queen Mary's war with France (1557–8) and in the Low Countries, rising to the rank of captain; began to write in 1574, and for nearly fifty years devoted his leisure to the production of romances in the style of Lyly's ' Euphues,' pamphlets, and reminiscences; found a patron in Sir Christopher Hatton [q. v.], and (1584) held a military command in Ireland; his admirers in his own day numerous, but chiefly drawn from the less cultivated classes. His extant printed works are twenty-four in number, and several others exist in manuscript. From the second story (' Apolonius and Silla') in ' Riche his Farewell to Militarie profession' (1581) Shakespeare drew the plot of ' Twelfth Night.'   [xlviii. 105]

RICH, CHRISTOPHER (*d.* 1714), theatrical manager; originally an attorney; purchased a share in the management of the Theatre Royal (afterwards Drury Lane), London, 1688; controlled (1706–7) the three London playhouses (Drury Lane, Dorset Garden, and Haymarket), but alienated all who came in contact with him by his avarice and oppression of the actors; Drury Lane closed in consequence of his arbitrary measures by the lord chamberlain, 1709, until the orders for the redress of the actor's grievances had been complied with; soon afterwards lost his hold on the theatre and began to erect a new one in Lincoln's Inn Fields, London, but died before its completion.   [xlviii. 108]

RICH, CLAUDIUS JAMES (1787–1820), traveller; born at Dijon; passed his childhood at Bristol; acquired a great mastery of eastern languages; in 1803 entered the East India Company's service, and afterwards travelled in Asia Minor, Egypt, and Syria; East India Company's resident at Baghdad; died of cholera at Shiraz. His oriental collections were purchased by the trustees of the British Museum.   [xlviii. 110]

RICH, EDMUND (1170?–1240). [See EDMUND.]

RICH, SIR HENRY, first BARON KENSINGTON and first EARL OF HOLLAND (1590–1649), son of Robert Rich, first earl of Warwick, by his wife Penelope Rich [q. v.]; of Emmanuel College, Cambridge; knighted, 1610; M.P., Leicester, 1610 and 1614; enabled by natural qualifications to rise rapidly as a courtier; created Baron Kensington, 1623 and (1624) made Earl of Holland and employed to negotiate the marriage of Charles I and Henrietta Maria; enjoyed Queen Henrietta Maria's favour, and intrigued against Charles I's ministers; became general of the horse, 1639, and took an inglorious part in the Scottish war; joined the parliamentary party, 1642, but (1643) returned to Charles I's side; met an ungracious reception, and at the close of the year was partially reconciled to the parliament; took up arms for Charles I, in consequence of the refusal of the Commons to grant pecuniary compensation for his losses, 1648; captured at St. Neots, July 1648; beheaded, in spite of Fairfax's intercession.   [xlviii. 111]

RICH, JEREMIAH (*d.* 1660?), stenographer; an eminent practitioner of shorthand; pupil of his uncle, William Cartwright, whose system he elaborated in a number of treatises, in some of which he claimed the methods as his own invention. [xlviii. 114]

RICH, JOHN (1682?–1761), pantomimist and theatrical manager; son of Christopher Rich [q. v.]; opened the new theatre at Lincoln's Inn Fields, London, 1714; began to develop the pantomime, 1716, in which genre he himself always played Harlequin; produced a pantomime annually, 1717–60; opened the house at Covent Garden, 1732, where Garrick appeared in 1746. [xlviii. 115]

RICH, MARY, COUNTESS OF WARWICK (1625–1678), daughter of Richard Boyle, first earl of Cork [q. v.]; married (1641) Charles Rich, fourth earl of Warwick; developed a pietistic temperament, which led to her house in Essex becoming the resort of puritan divines; some devotional writings by her published, 1686; her diaries preserved in the British Museum. [xlviii. 118]

RICH, SIR NATHANIEL (1585?–1636), merchant adventurer; member of Gray's Inn, 1610; M.P., Totnes, 1614, East Retford, 1621, Harwich, 1624–5 and 1626–9, Newport (Isle of Wight), 1625; knighted, 1617; took part in forming a company of adventurers for the plantation of Providence and Henrietta, 1630, and (1635) became deputy-governor. [xlviii. 119]

RICH, NATHANIEL (*d.* 1701), soldier; entered the life-guards of Earl of Essex, 1642; became colonel of a regiment of horse in the 'new model'; M.P., Cirencester, 1649; was inclined to the views of the Fifth-monarchy men and (1655) was deprived of his command and imprisoned for opposing Cromwell's government; restored to his command, 1659, but cashiered by Monck for resisting the Restoration, 1660; was arrested during the excitement caused by Venner's plot, 1661, and remained in confinement till 1665. [xlviii. 119]

RICH, PENELOPE, LADY RICH (1562?–1607), daughter of Walter Devereux, first earl of Essex [q. v.]; when a girl of fourteen won the admiration of (Sir) Philip Sidney, whom her father desired that she should marry; married to Robert Rich, third baron Rich (afterwards earl of Warwick), 1581; in consequence of her distaste for the marriage, encouraged the attentions of Sir Philip Sidney, who celebrated her charms and his affection in the series of sonnets afterwards collected under the title 'Astrophel and Stella' (1591); became Lord Mountjoy's mistress after Sidney's death, and from 1601 lived in open adultery, her husband abandoning her, according to her own statement, after the execution of her brother, the second Earl of Essex; divorced by Lord Rich, 1605, on which she married Mountjoy, now become Earl of Devonshire. [xlviii. 120]

RICH, SIR RICHARD, first BARON RICH (1496?–1567), lord chancellor; studied at the Middle Temple (reader, 1529); returned to the reformation parliament for Colchester, 1529; became solicitor-general, 1533; knighted, 1533; afterwards basely procured evidence against Fisher by visiting him in prison and pledging Henry VIII's word that the conversation should be regarded as confidential; perjured himself against Sir Thomas More at More's trial; knight of the shire for Essex and elected speaker, 1536; during 1536 and succeeding years occupied himself largely in the suppression of monasteries; shared Cromwell's unpopularity, but deserted him in his disgrace; took an active part in persecuting the reformers, and, according to Anne Askew's statement, racked her with his own hands; created Baron Rich after the accession of Edward VI; appointed lord-chancellor, 1548; conducted the bill of attainder against Seymour through parliament, 1549, and afterwards joined Warwick in effecting the overthrow of Protector Somerset; employed by Warwick in proceedings against Gardiner and Bonner, as well as in the measures against Mary; resigned the great seal, 1551; after signing the proclamation in favour of Lady Jane Grey, 1553, went down to Essex and declared for Queen Mary, during whose reign he distinguished himself by his severities against the protestants; founded Felstead grammar school, 1564. [xlviii. 123]

RICH, RICHARD (*fl.* 1609–1610), author of 'Newes from Virginia'; sailed for Virginia in 1609 with Captain Christopher Newport [q. v.]; published on his return to England a narrative in verse entitled 'Newes from Virginia' (1610), containing also an account of his shipwreck on the Bermudas. The work probably suggested scenes in Shakespeare's 'Tempest.' [xlviii. 126]

RICH, ROBERT (*fl.* 1185–1240), biographer; younger brother of Edmund (Rich) [q. v.], archbishop of Canterbury, whose lifelong companion he was; present at Edmund's death, 1240; wrote a life of his brother, which seems to be identical with that preserved in Cotton. MS. Faustina B. i. ff. 180–3, in the British Museum, and in Fell MS. 1, vol. iv. in the Bodleian Library. It has been printed in Wallace's 'Life of St. Edmund.' [xlviii. 127]

RICH, SIR ROBERT, second EARL OF WARWICK (1587–1658), eldest son of the first earl of Warwick and Penelope, Lady Rich [q. v.]; educated at Emmanuel College, Cambridge; K.B., 1603; member of the Inner Temple, 1604; M.P., Maldon, 1610 and 1614; succeeded his father in 1619, and occupied himself largely with the colonisation of America and with privateering ventures, which involved him in controversy with the great merchant companies; during the early part of Charles I's reign gradually became estranged from the court; was associated with the foundation of the colonies of New Plymouth, Massachusetts, and Connecticut; refused to subscribe to the forced loan of 1626 and to pay ship-money, and protected the puritan clergy; arrested and his papers searched on the dissolution of the Short parliament, 1640; active in raising forces for parliament on the outbreak of civil war; gained the fleet, July 1642, and (1643) was appointed lord high admiral; nominated head of a commission for the government of the colonies, 1643; assisted in 1644 with the foundation of Rhode Island; generally exerted his authority in behalf of religious freedom; endeavoured unsuccessfully (1648) to regain the fleet, the greater part of which had revolted to Charles I, but was able to organise a new one; after the abolition of the House of Lords was removed by the independents from the post of lord high admiral; took no part in public affairs during the Commonwealth, but received support and encouragement from Cromwell. His grandson, Robert Rich, married the Protector's daughter. [xlviii. 128]

RICH, ROBERT (*d.* 1679), quaker and universalist; a rich merchant and shipowner of London; became a quaker, 1654, and (1655) an adherent of James Nayler [q. v.], whom he loyally assisted during his trial and punishment; renowned for his charity, which was distributed to all creeds without distinction. [xlviii. 133]

RICH, SIR ROBERT, fourth baronet (1685–1768), field-marshal; entered the army, 1700, and served under Marlborough; M.P., Dunwich, 1715–22, Beeralston, 1724, St. Ives, 1727–41; consistently supported Sir Robert Walpole; fought at Dettingen, 1743; general, 1747; field-marshal, 1757. [xlviii. 134]

RICH, SIR ROBERT, fifth baronet (1714–1785), lieutenant-general; son of Sir Robert Rich, fourth baronet [q. v.]; entered the army, 1735; severely wounded at Culloden, 1746; fought at Minorca, 1756; lieutenant-general, 1760; involved in a dispute with government, 1768, which resulted in his dismissal from the service. [xlviii. 135]

RICH-JONES, WILLIAM HENRY (1817–1885). [See JONES.]

RICHARD I, called RICHARD CŒUR-DE-LION (1157–1199), king of England; thirdson of Henry II and Eleanor of Poitou; born at Oxford 8 Sept. 1157; betrothed (1160) to Alice, daughter of Louis VII, a source of many future troubles; acknowledged Duke of Aquitaine, 1170; joined his brothers in rebelling against their father, Henry II, 1173–4, but was forced to submit, and afterwards occupied himself in reducing the local magnates of Aquitaine; completely established the ducal authority, but on becoming (1183) heir to the English throne on the death of his elder brother Henry, was called upon by his father to give up Aquitaine to his brother John; compromised the matter by a nominal surrender to Eleanor in 1185; suspecting that his father intended to disinherit him, allied himself with the French king, Philip Augustus, against his father, 1188; succeeded to the English throne, 1189; immediately began his preparations for the third crusade, having already (1187) taken the cross; added to his inherited wealth, which was insufficient, by the sale of

crown domains and rights; joined Philip Augustus at
Messina, 1190, when he compelled Tancred, the Sicilian
king, to pay him forty thousand ounces of gold; arrived at
Cyprus, 1191, and, the pseudo-emperor, Isaac Comnenus,
having refused to recompense some pilgrims he had
plundered, proceeded to conquer the island and to add its
treasures to his hoard; reached Acre, June 1191, which surrendered on 12 July; advanced on Ascalon, August 1191,
Philip having already returned to France; defeated
Saladin near Arsuf, and towards the end of December
1191 was at Beit-Nuba, only twelve miles off Jerusalem,
but judged it too late in the year to attempt the siege;
retired to Ascalon, which he fortified; again reached
Beit-Nuba, only again to retire, June 1192, and in July
relieved Jaffa and defeated Saladin under its walls;
accepted, since troubles in England rendered his return
imperative, a three years' truce, by which the crusaders
were allowed to visit Jerusalem; set sail for England in
October of the same year; while attempting to travel
through Germany in disguise was arrested near Vienna
and imprisoned at Durrenstein; handed over by the Duke
of Austria to the Emperor Henry VI, and was compelled
to pay a ransom of a hundred and fifty thousand marks,
besides doing homage for England; set free, March 1194,
his arrival in England at once frustrating the attempt of
his brother John to usurp his authority; intended to
return to the East, but found himself unable to depart
owing to the alliance of John and Philip Augustus; left
England for the last time, May 1194, landed in Normandy,
and, after completely defeating Philip, restored the ducal
authority in Aquitaine; made peace (1196) with Philip,
who, fearing attack, had again (1195) invaded Normandy;
defeated Philip near Gisors, 1198, war having again
broken out; mortally wounded by an arrow while besieging
the castle of Chaluz in order to seize a newly found
treasure; his body buried at Fontevrault, and his heart
at Rouen. He married Berengaria of Navarre [q. v.]

[xlviii. 136]

RICHARD II (1367–1400), 'of Bordeaux'; king of
England; younger son of Edward, Prince of Wales [q. v.];
born at Bordeaux, 6 Jan. 1367; created Prince of
Wales, 1376; succeeded Edward III, June 1377, but the
actual control of government was at first seized by parliament and afterwards passed to Lancaster; met at
Smithfield the peasant insurgents who, led by Wat Tyler
[q. v.], had risen in revolt (1381) against the attempt to
levy a tax of a shilling a head on every person over
fifteen, and after the death of their leader succeeded in
pacifying them; granted them charters of freedom, but
when the revolt was at an end revoked these concessions;
proclaimed a general pardon, December 1381, after the
execution of the leaders; married, January 1382, Anne,
sister of Wenceslaus, king of Bohemia; on the attainment of his majority found parliament (1382) reluctant
to surrender the strict control which it had exercised
over the crown during the minority; appointed Michael
de la Pole (1330 ?–1389) [q. v.] chancellor without reference
to parliament, 1383; showed signs of a disposition to
oppose Lancaster; accepted Lancaster's explanation when
the old charges of treason against him were revived, 1384;
created his uncles, Edmund and Thomas, dukes of York
and Gloucester, in the hope of playing them off against
Lancaster; got rid of Lancaster by allowing him to
go on his long-delayed expedition to Spain, by which,
however, the leadership of the magnates was left to
Gloucester, a more dangerous person; provoked the
nobles by his determination to rule through the upstart
Pole, now earl of Suffolk, as chancellor, and Robert de
Vere, created duke of Ireland; compelled by Gloucester
(1386) to agree to a commission of eleven magnates, with
extensive powers for the reform of the household and
realm, but (August 1387) obtained an opinion from the
judges that the commission was unlawful; his power
overthrown by the magnates, headed by Gloucester,
December 1387; his adherents proscribed and executed
by the 'merciless' parliament; regained the ascendency
(May 1389), dismissed the counsellors imposed on him, and
replaced them by others of his own choice; subsequently
pursued a policy of conciliation, but lost popularity after
Queen Anne's death (1394) by his marriage (November
1396) with Isabella, daughter of Charles VI of France;
the feeling against him fanned by Gloucester; resolved
on a *coup d'état*, perhaps fearing a repetition of the
proceedings of 1386; got the three leaders, Gloucester,
Arundel, and Warwick, into his power, July 1397;
summoned parliament, September 1397, and had these

three lords condemned to death as traitors, the upshot
being that Arundel was beheaded and Gloucester died
in custody at Calais under suspicious circumstances,
while Warwick alone obtained pardon; at Shrewsbury
had the acts of the 'merciless' parliament annulled
and restitution ordered to the heirs of its victims; was
again involved in difficulties by the action of Henry of
Lancaster, duke of Hereford, in accusing the Duke of
Norfolk of treasonable designs, with reference to which it
was arranged that they should settle their quarrel by
single combat; forbade the combat on the day appointed
for the battle, and sentenced Hereford to ten years'
banishment and Norfolk to perpetual exile; from this
time exercised the royal authority with great arbitrariness,
exacting heavy fines and contributions from his subjects;
deprived the exiled Hereford of his succession on the
death of the Duke of Lancaster in February 1399; went
over to Ireland, April 1399, to avenge the death of the
Earl of March; heard that in his absence the Duke of
Hereford had landed in Yorkshire, and hurried back to
Milford to meet him; found himself unable to raise a
sufficient force, and after wandering about in North
Wales surrendered to Hereford, August 1399; resigned
the crown, September 1399, and was imprisoned finally at
Pontefract; a rising in his favour set on foot, January
1400; died at Pontefract, probably by a violent death,
14 Feb. 1400. The belief that he had escaped from captivity,
and was still alive in Scotland, was widely prevalent even
so late as 1417, but has little probability.   [xlviii. 145]

RICHARD III (1452–1485), king of England;
eleventh child of Richard, third duke of York [q. v.];
born at Fotheringay Castle on 2 Oct. 1452; created Duke
of Gloucester, June 1461; accompanied Edward IV in his
flight to Holland, September 1470, and (1471) commanded
the vanguard at Barnet and Tewkesbury; reported,
perhaps truly, to have butchered young Edward, prince of
Wales, after Tewkesbury, and murdered Henry VI in the
Tower of London a fortnight later; rewarded by Edward IV with large grants of land, including the possessions of the Earl of Oxford; quarrelled with his brother
Clarence on his marriage to Anne, the younger daughter
of the Earl of Warwick, Clarence, who had married
the elder, desiring to retain the whole of Warwick's
estates; was not, however, directly responsible for the
death of Clarence in 1478, though there was a suspicion
that he had helped indirectly to bring it about; commanded a Scottish expedition (1482) which captured
Berwick and advanced as far as Edinburgh; left by
Edward IV (died 9 April 1483) in charge of his family
and kingdom during the minority of his successor;
resolved, in conjunction with Hastings, to overthrow the
party of the Woodvilles, the relatives of the queen-
mother; seized Edward V's maternal uncles, Rivers and
Grey, at Stony-Stratford, and took Edward V under his
own protection; was recognised by the council as protector on his arrival in London, but in the meantime
became an object of apprehension, after the complete overthrow of the Woodville party, to Hastings and some of
the council, who consequently desired to get Edward V out
of his power; had Hastings and several others seized in
the council itself (13 June), and Hastings immediately
executed, a step which was followed twelve days later by
the execution of Rivers and Grey; employed Archbishop
Bourchier to persuade the queen-mother, who was in
sanctuary at Westminster, to deliver up the Duke of York,
and sent the Duke of York to keep his brother company
in the Tower of London; was offered the crown in an
incomplete parliament, shortly after Dr. Shaw, preaching
at St. Paul's Cross, London, 22 June, had declared Edward IV and his children illegitimate; began his reign,
26 June 1483; by his usurpation alienated many of the
nobility who had supported him as protector; even
Buckingham, his chief adherent, becoming disaffected;
cabals against him set on foot over all the southern
counties, public feeling being further scandalised by the
news of the death of the princes in the Tower of London;
a rebellion against him headed by Buckingham, who,
however, was captured and executed in November 1483;
defeated and slain at Bosworth, chiefly through the
treachery of the Stanleys, by Henry, earl of Richmond, to
whom had descended the Lancastrian claim to the throne,
and who had invaded England in vindication of it; buried
at Grey Friars, London. His nickname Crouchback had
its rise in a real, though probably slight, bodily deformity.

[xlviii. 158]

RICHARD, EARL OF CORNWALL and KING OF THE
ROMANS (1209–1272), second son of King John ; chosen
leader of an expedition fitted out in 1225 to win back the
Aquitanian heritage of the English kings ; succeeded
in recovering Gascony before the close of the year, and
(1227) having concluded a truce with Louis IX returned
to England ; brought into connection with the growing
baronial opposition by a violent quarrel with Henry III,
concerning the possession of a manor, the connection
being strengthened by his marriage (1231) with
Isabella, daughter of William Marshal, first earl of
Pembroke [q. v.] ; took the cross, 1236, but his departure delayed by domestic troubles ; headed the opposition
to the foreigners brought over to England by Henry III's
marriage, and for a short time was a popular hero, but
in 1239 he became reconciled to Henry III ; left England
for Palestine, June 1240, and in October 1240 landed at
Acre ; after fortifying Ascalon and concluding a treaty
with the sultan of Krak, returned to England, 1242 ;
after the death of Isabella in 1240 married Sanchia,
daughter of the Count of Provence and sister of the
queens of England and France, 1243 ; bound closely to
the court by this second marriage, and henceforth was
the political ally of his brother ; by his change of
policy left room for the rise of Simon de Montfort ; was
appointed joint-regent of England with Queen Eleanor
during Henry III's absence in Gascony, 1253, and, May 1254,
became sole regent ; assisted Henry III in his financial
difficulties, and posed as a neutral in the quarrels between
the barons and the foreign favourites ; received the
offer of the German crown, and early in 1257 was elected
king of the Romans by four of the seven electors, though
in April the remaining three chose Alfonso X of Castile ;
was crowned at Aachen, May 1257, and succeeded in
establishing his authority generally in the Rhine
countries ; was not acknowledged by the rest of Germany, and when his money came to an end was generally
deserted ; returned to England to raise fresh supplies,
1259 ; again crossed to Germany, 1260, but, October 1260, was
back in England, and never again succeeded in establishing himself permanently in Germany ; espoused his
brother's side in the barons' war, and was taken prisoner
at the battle of Lewes, 1264, but after the battle of
Evesham, 1265, was unconditionally released ; despite
his hard treatment counselled moderation, and (1268) paid
his last visit to Germany ; his eldest son, Henry, was
murdered by the younger De Montfort ; attacked (1271)
by paralysis, of which he eventually died. [xlviii. 165]

RICHARD, EARL OF CAMBRIDGE (d. 1415), second
son of Edmund de Langley, first duke of York [q. v.] ;
created Earl of Cambridge, 1414 ; married Anne, daughter
of Roger (VI) de Mortimer and through this connection
was led to become centre of a plot to place his wife's
brother, Edmund, earl of March, on the throne, a scheme
which was revealed by Mortimer, who had not been a
conspirator, to Henry V, when that king was starting for
France in July 1415 ; attainted and executed ; the attainder was reversed in 1461. [xlviii. 175]

RICHARD, third DUKE OF YORK (1411–1460), only
son of Richard, earl of Cambridge [q. v.] ; was paternal
grandson of Edmund, fifth son of Edward III, and
maternal great-great-grandson of Lionel, Edward III's
third son ; succeeded his uncle, Edward Plantagenet
[q. v.], as third duke of York, 1415, and (1425) inherited
the possessions of his uncle, Edmund (IV) de Mortimer,
fifth earl of March [q. v.] ; after serving for a year in
France, 1436–7, married (1438) Cicely, daughter of Ralph
Neville, first earl of Westmorland [q. v.] ; a second time
(1440) appointed Henry VI's lieutenant in France, where
he remained till the close of 1445 ; appointed the king's
lieutenant in Ireland, a convenient place of banishment,
1447 ; being discontented with the government, landed at
Beaumaris, August 1450, and, in spite of armed attempts
to hinder him, forced his way into Henry VI's presence at
the head of four thousand men, and was promised by
Henry VI a place in the new council to be appointed ;
for the next two years was involved in a contest with
Somerset, which terminated in March 1452 in an ineffectual attempt to have him removed from the king's counsels ; after a year's retirement was recalled to the
king's council during Henry's first fit of imbecility,
October 1453, Somerset being sent to the Tower of London ;
in spite of the claims of Henry VI's queen was elected protector by the lords, March 1454 ; his protectorate revoked
in consequence of the king's recovery, February 1455,

Somerset being released in March. An immediate reversal
of policy following, he was with his friends driven from
power ; took up arms in company with Salisbury and
Warwick, and on 22 May 1455 defeated the royal forces at
the battle of St. Albans, in which Henry VI was wounded
and Somerset slain ; again proclaimed protector, November 1455, in consequence of Henry VI's illness ; was
discharged of his office by Henry VI in parliament,
February 1456, but remained a councillor ; consistently
opposed by Queen Margaret and the young Duke of
Somerset, in consequence of which the old feuds revived
late in 1458 ; compelled to seek refuge in Wales, October
1459, and (November 1459) was attainted ; crossed to
Ireland at the end of 1459 ; returned to England on
Warwick and Salisbury's victory at Northampton, 1460 ;
went to Westminster and openly claimed the crown,
September 1460 ; obtained promise of succession to the
crown, October 1460, and made protector, November
1460 ; besieged in Wakefield Castle, December 1460,
having gone north to quell the rising instigated there
by Queen Margaret ; attacked the enemy and fell fighting, 30 Dec. His head was placed on the walls of York.
[xlviii. 176]

RICHARD, DUKE OF YORK (1472–1483), second son
of Edward IV ; created Duke of York, 1474 ; married to
Anne, daughter of John Mowbray, fourth duke of Nor-
folk, 1478 ; given up, by the persuasion of Cardinal
Bourchier, by his mother, who, on the overthrow of the
Woodville party in 1483, had sought sanctuary with him at
Westminster, and placed with his brother in the Tower of
London ; murdered there with his brother by Richard III's
orders two months after his brother's deposition in June.
[xlviii. 185]

RICHARD FITZSCROB (fl. 1052–1060), Norman
baron ; settled in Herefordshire in the time of Edward
the Confessor ; was not expelled by Godwin in 1052, but
died before the time of Domesday. He is said to have
erected Richard's Castle in Herefordshire, the first regular
castle in England. [xlviii. 185]

RICHARD DE CAPELLA (d. 1127), bishop of Hereford ;
' custos sigilli regis' in 1119 ; consecrated bishop, 1121.
[xlviii. 186]

RICHARD DE BELMEIS (d. 1128). [See BELMEIS.]

RICHARD (d. 1139), first abbot of Fountains ; established the new community of Fountains in 1132 on the
Cistercian model, and was chosen abbot. [xlviii. 186]

RICHARD called FASTOLF (d. 1143), second abbot of
Fountains ; an original member of the convent ; succeeded the first abbot Richard (d. 1139) [q. v.]
[xlviii. 188]

RICHARD OF HEXHAM (fl. 1138–1154), chronicler
and prior of Hexham ; elected prior, 1141 ; wrote an
account of the early history of Hexham, known as the
' Brevis Annotatio,' and printed in Raine's ' Priory of
Hexham ' (Surtees Soc.) ; also complied ' De gestis regis
Stephani et de bello Standardii ' (1135–9), preserved in
C.C.C. Cambr. MS. (193, f. 3), and translated by Stevenson
in ' Church Historians.' [xlviii. 187]

RICHARD DE BELMEIS (d. 1162). [See BELMEIS.]

RICHARD (d. 1170), sixth abbot of Fountains ; a
native of York ; appointed abbot by St. Bernard ; raised
his convent to a high pitch of excellence by his strict
discipline. [xlviii. 188]

RICHARD OF ST. VICTOR (d. 1173 ?), theologian ; a
native of Scotland ; became a canon in the abbey of St.
Victor, Paris. His writings resemble those of his master,
Hugh of St. Victor, in their abuse of allegory and verbal
antithesis. His philosophy is characterised by mysticism.
A large number of his works are printed in Migne's
' Patrologia ' (vol. cxcvi.) ; others ascribed to him remain
in manuscript. [xlviii. 188]

RICHARD STRONGBOW, second EARL OF PEMBROKE
AND STRIGUL (d. 1176). [See CLARE, RICHARD DE.]

RICHARD (d. 1177 ?), bishop of St. Andrews ; elected
to the bishopric, 1163 ; consecrated, 1165 ; succeeded in
preventing the sacrifice of the independence of the Scottish church at the treaty of Falaise in 1174, and afterwards resisted the pretensions of the see of York at
Northampton in 1176. The independence of the Scottish
church was assured by Clement III in 1188.
[xlviii. 190]

RICHARD (*fl.* 1180–1183), called the 'Premonstratensian'; abbot of an unknown English præmonstratensian house; wrote a 'Life of St. Ursula,' still extant, and possibly some other extant theological treatises.
[xlviii. 197]

RICHARD (*d.* 1184), archbishop of Canterbury; was appointed prior of St. Martin's, Dover, 1157; elected archbishop by the English bishops, 1173, in spite of the wish of the monks of the chapter, who desired Odo (*d.* 1200) [q. v.]; consecrated, 1174, in spite of the opposition of the younger Henry (Henry II's son) at Anagni, by Alexander III; diligent in promoting the material prosperity of his see, but failed to satisfy the requirements of the extreme clerical party.   [xlviii. 191]

RICHARD OF ILCHESTER (*d.* 1188), bishop of Winchester; archdeacon of Poitiers (1162–73) and a baron of the exchequer; elected bishop of Winchester, 1173, continuing to fulfil his judicial functions, and frequently serving Henry II in a diplomatic capacity. [xlviii. 194]

RICHARD OF DEVIZES (*fl.* 1189–1192), chronicler; a monk of St. Swithun's, Winchester; wrote a chronicle of the deeds of Richard I from his accession to October 1192, which was edited by Howlett for the Rolls Series in 1886. To him is also generally ascribed 'Annales de Wintonia,' printed in Luard's 'Annales Monastici.'
[xlviii. 197]

RICHARD OF ELY (*d.* 1194 ?), historian; a monk of Ely; wrote an account of Ely, not extant, but quoted by Thomas of Ely.   [xlviii. 198]

RICHARD OF ELY (*d.* 1198). [See FITZNEALE, RICHARD.]

RICHARD ANGLICUS (*fl.* 1196–1226), lawyer; an Englishman by birth; taught at Bologna, where in 1226 he was archdeacon and rector of the law school; author of the famous 'Ordo Judiciarius.'   [xlvi. 103]

RICHARD DE TEMPLO (*fl.* 1190–122°), reputed author of the 'Itinerarium Regis Ricardi'; may be identical with a chaplain of the templars and a dependant of the Earl of Leicester of that name. The 'Itinerarium,' which is the chief authority for the third crusade, is, however, probably a free translation from a long French poem, by Ambrose, a priest-clerk, who accompanied Richard I on the third crusade. In this case Richard de Templo was only the translator, though he appears to have made independent additions.   [xlviii. 198]

RICHARD OF WETHERSHED (*d.* 1231). [See GRANT, RICHARD.]

RICHARD OF CORNWALL (*fl.* 1237), prebendary of Lincoln; must be distinguished from the Franciscan Richard of Cornwall (*fl.* 1238–1259) [q. v.] [xlviii. 200]

RICHARD DE MORINS (*d.* 1242). [See MORINS.]

RICHARD OF WENDOVER (*d.* 1252), physician; physician to Gregory IX, and afterwards canon of St. Paul's, London; most probably identical with the famous physician, Richard Anglicus, or the Englishman, the author of 'Practica sive Medicamenta Ricardi.' A number of his treatises are preserved in manuscript, chiefly in the libraries of Oxford and Cambridge.   [xlviii. 201]

RICHARD ANGLICUS (*d.* 1252). [See RICHARD OF WENDOVER.]

RICHARD DE WYCHE (1197 ?–1253), bishop of Chichester; studied at Oxford, where he became M.A. and chancellor; made by Edmund Rich chancellor of Canterbury; elected bishop of Chichester in spite of the opposition of Henry III, 1244; rigidly maintained ecclesiastical discipline, and made various regulations for the improvement of the ritual of his church; was canonised in 1262.
[xlviii. 202]

RICHARD OF CORNWALL (*fl.* 1238–1259), called also Richard Rufus, Ruys, Rosso, or Rowse; B.D. Oxford; a Franciscan teacher; lectured at Paris and Oxford. His commentary on Bonaventure's third book of sentences is preserved in manuscript at Assisi.   [xlviii. 200]

RICHARD DE GRAVESEND (*d.* 1279). [See GRAVESEND.]

RICHARD DE SWINFIELD (*d.* 1317). [See SWINFIELD.]

RICHARD DE ABYNDON, ABENDON, or ABINGDON (*d.* 1327 ?), judge; appointed chamberlain of North Wales, 1284; prebendary of Dublin, 1285; appointed a baron of the exchequer, 1299; prebendary of Lichfield, 1304.   [xlviii. 204]

RICHARD OF WALLINGFORD (1292 ?–1336), abbot of St. Albans; according to Leland, fellow of Merton College, Oxford; B.D. Oxford; elected abbot, 1327; his rule hampered by his leprosy; appointed a coadjutor, 1333; renowned for sanctity, and the most skilful man of his time in the liberal sciences and mechanical arts. Several of his treatises are extant in manuscript.
[xlviii. 205]

RICHARD DE BURY (1281–1345). [See BURY.]

RICHARD WETHERSET (*fl.* 1350). [See WETHERSET.]

RICHARD (*d.* 1360). [See FITZRALPH, RICHARD.]

RICHARD OF MAIDSTONE (*d.* 1396). [See MAIDSTONE.]

RICHARD OF CIRENCESTER (*d.* 1401 ?). [See CIRENCESTER.]

RICHARD, EDWARD (1714–1777), Welsh poet; founded a free grammar school at his native village, Ystrad Meurig, which became one of the most famous in Wales, towards the close of the eighteenth century; author of some of the best specimens of pastoral poetry in the Welsh language. A collection of his writings appeared in 1811.   [xlviii. 207]

RICHARD, HENRY (1812–1888), politician; a native of Wales; congregational pastor in the Old Kent Road, London, 1835–50, when he relinquished the ministry; often called the apostle of peace from his making the advocacy of arbitration as a method for settling international disputes, the chief work of his life; became secretary of the Peace Society, 1848, and took part in a series of international peace congresses, which continued until the outbreak of the Crimean war; liberal M.P. for the Merthyr boroughs, 1868–88; carried a motion in the House of Commons in favour of international arbitration, 1873, and presided at some of the sittings of the peace congress at Paris. 1878; became a member of the royal commission on education, 1886; author of various pamphlets.   [xlviii. 208]

RICHARDS, ALFRED BATE (1820–1876), dramatist, journalist, and a chief promoter of the volunteer movement of 1859; B.A. Exeter College, Oxford, 1841; barrister, Lincoln's Inn, 1845; published poems and tragedies, the first being 'Crœsus, King of Lydia,' 1845; first editor of the 'Daily Telegraph,' 1855; on the commencement of the volunteer movement raised (1859) the 3rd City of London rifle corps, of which he remained colonel till 1869.   [xlviii. 210]

RICHARDS, DAVID (1751–1827), Welsh poet; best known as 'Dafydd Ionawr'; for some years a school teacher; abandoned teaching in order to devote himself to writing religious poetry, 1792; took charge of the free school at Dolgelly, 1800–7, but devoted his closing years entirely to writing Welsh religious verse. A collected edition of his poems appeared in 1851.   [xlviii. 211]

RICHARDS, EVAN (1770–1832). [See PRICHARD.]

RICHARDS, GEORGE (1767–1837), poet and divine; of Trinity College, Oxford; fellow of Oriel College, Oxford, 1790–6; M.A., 1791; D.D., 1820; vicar of St. Martin's-in-the-Fields, London, 1824–37; published verse.   [xlviii. 212]

RICHARDS, HENRY BRINLEY (1819–1885), pianist and composer; gained a high position as a pianist in London, and wrote a large number of piano pieces, part-songs, songs, and choruses, including 'God bless the Prince of Wales' (1862), the Welsh national anthem.
[xlviii. 212]

RICHARDS, JACOB (1660 ?–1701), colonel and military engineer; studied the art of sieges in Hungary and the Morea, 1685–6; accompanied Kirke's expedition to Ireland, 1689; appointed chief engineer in Ireland, 1690; served under William III, Marlborough, and Ginkell; transferred to Flanders, 1692; appointed third engineer of the kingdom, 1698. His diaries are preserved in the Stowe MSS. at the British Museum.   [xlviii. 213]

RICHARDS, JAMES BRINSLEY (1846–1892), journalist; spent several years in France as secretary to Drouyn de Lhuys and the Duc Decazes; became 'Times' correspondent at Vienna, 1885, and was transferred to Berlin, 1892. [xlviii. 214]

RICHARDS, JOHN (1669–1709), major-general; brother of Jacob Richards [q. v.]; served with the Venetians against the Turks, in the Polish army, and in the Portuguese service during the war of the Spanish succession; governor of Alicant, 1707–9; killed by an explosion during the siege of Alicant. [xlviii. 214]

RICHARDS, JOHN INIGO (d. 1810), landscape-painter and scene-painter; first exhibited with the Society of Artists, 1763; became (1768) one of the foundation members of the Royal Academy, where he exhibited landscapes and figure-subjects for forty years; became principal scene-painter of Covent Garden, 1777; secretary to the Royal Academy, 1788. [xlviii. 215]

RICHARDS, MICHAEL (1673–1721), brigadier-general; master-surveyor or surveyor-general of the ordnance; brother of Jacob Richards [q. v.]; served in Ireland (1691) and Flanders (1692–6), and under Marlborough (1704–6); was appointed Galway's chief engineer in Spain, 1707, and served in many of the great engagements of the war of the Spanish succession; promoted brigadier-general, 1711; appointed chief-engineer of Great Britain, 1711. [xlviii. 216]

RICHARDS, NATHANIEL (d. 1652), dramatist; LL.B. Caius College, Cambridge, 1634; for some time master of St. Alban's school, London; published 'The Celestiall Pvblican,' 1630, and 'The Tragedy of Messallina,' 1640. [xlviii. 217]

RICHARDS, SIR RICHARD (1752–1823), judge; of Jesus College, Oxford; B.A. Wadham College, Oxford, 1774; fellow of Queen's College, Oxford, 1776 (M.A., 1777); barrister, Inner Temple, 1780; appointed baron of the exchequer, 1814; knighted, 1814; appointed lord chief-baron, 1817. [xlviii. 218]

RICHARDS, THOMAS (d. 1564?), translator; B.D. Oxford, 1515, Cambridge, 1517; elected prior of Totnes, 1528; is said to have translated the 'Consolatio Philosophiæ' of Boethius. [xlviii. 219]

RICHARDS, THOMAS (1710?–1790), Welsh lexicographer; compiled 'Antiquæ Linguæ Britannicæ Thesaurus,' 1753, a Welsh-English dictionary (4th edit. 1838). [xlviii. 219]

RICHARDS, WILLIAM (1643–1705), author; M.A. Trinity College, Oxford, 1666; fellow, 1666–75; rector of Helmdon, 1675–89; published 'Wallography' (1682), a small satirical work on Wales, and 'The English Orator,' 1680. [xlviii. 219]

RICHARDS, WILLIAM (1749–1818), historian of King's Lynn; baptist pastor at Lynn, 1778–1818; published 'The History of Lynn,' 1812, and other works. [xlviii. 219]

RICHARDS, WILLIAM UPTON (1811–1873), divine; M.A. Exeter College, Oxford, 1839; vicar of All Saints', Marylebone, 1849–73; published religious treatises. [xlviii. 221]

RICHARDS, SIR BENJAMIN WARD (1828–1896), physician; studied at Glasgow, and was licentiate of Faculty of Physicians and Surgeons, 1850, M.A. and M.D. St. Andrews, 1854, and hon. LL.D., 1877; M.R.C.S. London, 1856; F.R.C.S., 1865; F.R.S., 1867; physician to Royal Infirmary for Diseases of Chest, City Road, 1856, and to London Temperance Hospital, 1892; president of Medical Society of London, 1868; F.S.A., 1877; knighted, 1893; published scientific and miscellaneous writings; originated and edited 'Journal of Public Health and Sanitary Review' (1855). [Suppl. iii. 297]

RICHARDSON, CAROLINE (1777–1853), poetess; wife of George Richardson; published a volume of 'Poems' in 1829, a novel, and several tales and essays. [xlviii. 223]

RICHARDSON, CHARLES (1775–1865), lexicographer; kept a well-known school on Clapham Common till 1827; chief work, a 'New English Dictionary,' 1835–7. [xlviii. 221]

RICHARDSON, CHARLES JAMES (1806–1871), architect; master of the architectural class in the school of design at Somerset House, 1845–52; formed a valuable collection of drawings by English artists, now at South Kensington Museum, and published several architectural treatises. [xlviii. 222]

RICHARDSON, CHARLOTTE CAROLINE (1775–1850?), poetess; born of poor parents named Smith; married, in 1802, a shoemaker named Richardson, who died in 1804, leaving his wife destitute; published (1806), by subscription, a volume of verse, which was followed by other poems. [xlviii. 222]

RICHARDSON, CHRISTOPHER (1618–1698), nonconformist divine; M.A. Trinity College, Cambridge; obtained rectory of Kirkheaton, 1646; ejected, 1662; removed, in 1687, to Liverpool, where he became the founder of nonconformity. [xlviii. 223]

RICHARDSON, DAVID LESTER (1801–1865), poet and miscellaneous writer; became a major in the Bengal service; edited several newspapers at Calcutta, and published prose and verse. [xlviii. 223]

RICHARDSON, EDWARD (1812–1869), sculptor; began to exhibit at the Royal Academy, 1836; refused admission to the Society of Antiquaries for his restoration of the effigies of the knights templars in the Temple Church in 1842; restored other ancient monuments and statues. [xlviii. 224]

RICHARDSON, FRANCES MARY (1785–1861). [See CURRER.]

RICHARDSON, GABRIEL (d. 1642), author; M.A. Brasenose College, Oxford, 1608; B.D., 1619; fellow of Brasenose College, Oxford, 1607–35; rector of Heythrop, 1635–42; published a treatise 'Of the State of Europe,' 1627. [xlviii. 224]

RICHARDSON, GEORGE (1736?–1817?), architect; was in full professional practice in London towards the end of the eighteenth century; in his old age fell into poverty and was relieved by Nollekens; published works on decorative art and architecture. [xlviii. 225]

RICHARDSON, GEORGE (1773–1862), quaker; began preaching at twenty, and for forty years visited all parts of the British isles on religious tours; published tracts and pamphlets. [xlviii. 225]

RICHARDSON, GEORGE FLEMING (1796?–1848), geologist; employed at the British Museum (1838–48) for ten years; F.G.S., 1839; published useful geological handbooks, besides essays in general literature; committed suicide. [xlviii. 226]

RICHARDSON, JAMES (1806–1851), African traveller; attached himself to the English Anti-Slavery Society, and (1845) penetrated through Algiers and Tripoli to Ghadames and Ghat; proceeded by the same route in search of Lake Tchad, 1850; died of fever at Ungouratona within fifteen days of the lake. He wrote three large books of travels, two of which were published posthumously, besides several pamphlets. [xlviii. 226]

RICHARDSON, JOHN (d. 1625), biblical scholar; B.A. Clare Hall, Cambridge, 1581; fellow of Emmanuel College, Cambridge; M.A., 1585; D.D., 1597; appointed regius professor of divinity at Cambridge, 1607; master of Peterhouse, Cambridge, 1609–15; translated the portion from the Chronicles to Ecclesiastes inclusive in the authorised version of the bible; master of Trinity College, Cambridge, 1615–25. [xlviii. 227]

RICHARDSON, JOHN (1580–1654), bishop of Ardagh; M.A. Trinity College, Dublin; fellow, 1600; consecrated bishop, 1633; fled to England on the outbreak of the rebellion in 1641; his commentary on the Old Testament published posthumously, 1655. [xlviii. 228]

RICHARDSON, JOHN (1647–1725?), nonjuror; fellow of Emmanuel College, Cambridge, 1674–85; ejected (1690) from the rectory of North Luffenham, to which he had been appointed, 1685; published an able 'Vindication of the Canon of the New Testament against Toland,' 1700. [xlviii. 251]

RICHARDSON, JOHN (1664–1747), Irish divine; B.A. Trinity College, Dublin, 1688; appointed rector of Annagh, 1693; author of theological works in English and Irish. [xlviii. 228]

RICHARDSON, JOHN (1667–1753), quaker; travelled through England preaching, as well as in Ireland and America; his journal published, 1757. [xlviii. 229]

RICHARDSON, JOHN (*fl.* 1777–1798), writer on brewing; published 'The Principles of Brewing,' 1798, being the first writer to treat the subject scientifically. [xlviii. 229]

RICHARDSON, JOHN (1741–1811 ?), orientalist; M.A. by diploma, Wadham College, Oxford, 1780; member of the Middle Temple, 1781; published, besides other works, a 'Dictionary of Persian, Arabic, and English' (1777), which, however, was little else than an abridgment of Meninski's 'Oriental Thesaurus.' It was finally reconstructed by Dr. Steingass, after several revisions, in 1892. [xlviii. 229]

RICHARDSON, JOHN (1767 ?–1837), itinerant showman; began life in the workhouse at Great Marlow, and made his first experiment as a showman at Bartholomew Fair in 1796. Many actors, who afterwards rose to distinction, appeared in his show, including Edmund Kean. His favourite haunts were Bartholomew Fair and Greenwich. [xlviii. 230]

RICHARDSON, Sir JOHN (1771–1841), judge; of Harrow and University College, Oxford; M.A., 1795; barrister, Lincoln's Inn, 1803; puisne judge of the court of common pleas, 1818–24; knighted, 1819; compelled by ill-health to pass his later life at Malta. [xlviii. 231]

RICHARDSON, JOHN (1797–1863), journalist; born in Ontario; served in the British legion in Spain; became 'Times' correspondent in Canada, 1858; afterwards removed to the United States, and continued to write for the press till his death. [xlviii. 232]

RICHARDSON, JOHN (1780–1864), solicitor; friend of Cockburn, Jeffrey, Thomas Campbell, and Sir Walter Scott; practised in Westminster as a parliamentary solicitor. [xlviii. 231]

RICHARDSON, Sir JOHN (1787–1865), Arctic explorer and naturalist; studied medicine, and (1807) was gazetted assistant-surgeon in the royal navy; M.D. Edinburgh, 1816; appointed surgeon and naturalist to Franklin's polar expedition, 1819, which, after passing the winter on the Saskatchewan, succeeded in reaching Fort Providence in 1821; F.R.S., 1825; accompanied Franklin in his second expedition to the mouth of the Mackenzie, 1825; separated from Franklin, 1826, and explored the coast to the Coppermine River and the Great Slave Lake; appointed physician to the Royal Hospital at Haslar, 1838; became inspector of hospitals, 1840; knighted, 1846; conducted a search expedition for Franklin, 1847; returned, 1849; C.B., 1850; published his 'Journal,' 1851; LL.D. Dublin, 1857; published works on ichthyology and polar exploration. [xlviii. 233]

RICHARDSON, JOHN (1817–1886), Cumberland poet; originally a mason; became a schoolmaster, and wrote voluminously in the Cumberland vernacular; had a great local reputation. [xlviii. 235]

RICHARDSON, Sir JOHN LARKINS CHEESE (1810–1878), speaker of the legislative council of New Zealand; entered the Bengal artillery, 1828; major, 1854; settled in Otago, New Zealand, 1856; became postmaster-general in the Weld ministry, 1864; elected speaker of the legislative council, 1868; knighted, 1874; died at Dunedin. [xlviii. 236]

RICHARDSON, JONATHAN, the elder (1665–1745), portrait-painter and author; succeeded Kneller and Dahl in the patronage of the public as a portrait-painter; executed portraits of Pope, Prior, Steele, and many others, and also obtained some distinction by his treatises on painting; his 'Theory of Painting' (1715) for many years a standard work; published also poems and literary criticisms. [xlviii. 236]

RICHARDSON, JONATHAN, the younger (1694–1771), portrait-painter; only son of Jonathan Richardson the elder [q. v.]; followed his father's profession, but is best known for his association with his father's literary productions. [xlviii. 238]

RICHARDSON, JOSEPH (1755–1803), author; of St. John's College, Cambridge; barrister, Middle Temple; devoted himself to journalism, becoming one of the proprietors of the whig journal, the 'Morning Post'; M.P., Newport, Cornwall, 1796–1803; author of poems, dramatic pieces, and satires. [xlviii. 238]

RICHARDSON, JOSEPH (1814–1862), flautist; became professor of the flute at the Royal Academy of Music, 1837; became principal flautist in Queen Victoria's band. [xlviii. 239]

RICHARDSON, MOSES AARON (1793–1871), antiquary; brother of Thomas Miles Richardson [q. v.]; published a number of works on the antiquities of the northern English counties; subsequently emigrated to Melbourne (1850), where he died. [xlviii. 239]

RICHARDSON, RICHARD (1663–1741), botanist and antiquary; of University College, Oxford; student at Gray's Inn, 1681; practised as a physician at North Bierley; engaged in botanical researches, and formed a valuable library of botanical and historical works, which passed to his descendant, Frances Mary Richardson Currer [q. v.] [xlviii. 240]

RICHARDSON, ROBERT (*fl.* 1530–1543), divine; a canon of Cambuskenneth; converted to protestantism, and employed by Henry VIII in 1543 to preach in Scotland. [xlviii. 242]

RICHARDSON, ROBERT (d. 1578), lord high treasurer of Scotland; M.A. St. Andrews, 1533; was appointed prior of St. Mary's, Isle of Trail, 1559, and lord high treasurer, 1561; adhered to the party of the lords after the fall of Mary Queen of Scots and (1571) vacated the office of treasurer. [xlviii. 241]

RICHARDSON, ROBERT (1732–1781), divine; only son of William Richardson (1698–1775) [q. v.]; prebendary of Lincoln Cathedral and chaplain in ordinary to the king. [xlviii. 252]

RICHARDSON, ROBERT (1779–1847), physician and traveller; studied at Glasgow and Edinburgh universities; M.D. Edinburgh, 1807; travelling physician to Charles John Gardiner, second viscount Mountjoy; joined Somerset Lowry Corry, second earl of Belmore, and a party in a tour through Europe, Egypt, and Palestine, 1816; claims to have been the first Christian traveller admitted to Solomon's mosque; published 'Travels,' 1822. [xlviii. 242]

RICHARDSON, SAMUEL (*fl.* 1643–1658), controversialist; probably a soldier and army preacher in the early part of the civil wars; published a number of treatises on political and religious subjects characterised by boldness of thought. [xlviii. 242]

RICHARDSON, SAMUEL (1689–1761), novelist; born in Derbyshire; was apprenticed to a stationer, and started in business as a printer, first in Fleet Street, London, and then in Salisbury Court, London, where he lived for the rest of his life; published his first novel, 'Pamela,' 1740, which was soon translated into French and Dutch; still more successful with 'Clarissa Harlowe' (1740), which won him a European fame; his 'Sir Charles Grandison' (1753), though it never held so high a position as 'Clarissa,' received with equal enthusiasm. His novels represented the didacticism of his time, and owe their power mainly to their earnestness, minute realism, and sentimentalism. Among their admirers were Diderot, Rousseau, and, later, Macaulay. [xlviii. 243]

RICHARDSON, SAMUEL (d. 1805), stenographer; a 'particular baptist' pastor in Chester; author of 'A New System of Shorthand' (1800), which, necessitating the use of specially ruled paper, never had much vogue. [xlviii. 247]

RICHARDSON, Sir THOMAS (1569–1635), judge; barrister, Lincoln's Inn, 1595; Lent reader, 1614; serjeant-at-law, 1614; speaker of the House of Commons in 1621 (M.P., St. Albans); knighted, 1621; became chief-justice of common pleas, 1626; refused (1628) to allow Felton to be racked to induce confession, a step which marks an epoch in the history of criminal jurisprudence; became chief-justice of the king's bench, 1631, and came into conflict with Laud for suppressing 'wakes' or Sunday revels. [xlviii. 247]

RICHARDSON, THOMAS (1771–1853), quaker and financier; one of the original partners of the firm Overend, Gurney & Co. [see GURNEY, SAMUEL], and a great benefactor to the Society of Friends. [xlviii. 248]

RICHARDSON, THOMAS (1816–1867), industrial chemist; invented (1840) a process for purifying 'hard' lead, and (1844) began the manufacture of superphosphates at Blaydon; lecturer on chemistry, Durham University, and M.A., 1856; F.R.S., 1866; published chemical treatises. [xlviii. 249]

RICHARDSON, THOMAS MILES (1784 - 1848), landscape-painter ; began to contribute to the Royal Academy, 1818 ; member of the New Water-colour Society. [xlviii. 250]

RICHARDSON, VAUGHAN (1670 ?–1729), organist and composer ; organist of Winchester Cathedral, 1693–1729 ; composed services, songs, and anthems. [xlviii. 250]

RICHARDSON, WILLIAM (1698–1775), antiquary : nephew of John Richardson (1647–1725 ?) [q. v.] ; M.A. Emmanuel College, Cambridge, 1723 ; D.D., 1735 ; prebendary of Lincoln Cathedral, 1724–60 ; F.S.A., 1735 ; master of Emmanuel College, Cambridge, 1736–75 ; vice-chancellor of Cambridge University, 1737 and 1769 ; one of George II and George III's chaplains, 1746–68 ; precentor, Lincoln Cathedral, 1760–75 ; edited Godwin's ' De Præsulibus Angliæ Commentarii,' 1743. [xlviii. 251]

RICHARDSON, WILLIAM (1743–1814), professor of humanity at Glasgow University ; M.A. Glasgow ; appointed professor, 1772 ; published miscellaneous works, including essays on Shakespeare's characters and ' Poems and Plays,' 1805. [xlviii. 252]

RICHARDSON, WILLIAM (1740–1820), writer on geology and agriculture ; M.A. Trinity College, Dublin ; fellow, 1766 ; D.D., 1778 ; afterwards rector of Moy ; published pamphlets on geological and agricultural subjects. [xlviii. 253]

RICHEY, ALEXANDER GEORGE (1830–1883), Irish historian ; B.A. Trinity College, Dublin, 1853 ; LL.D., 1873 ; called to the Irish bar, 1855 ; Q.C., 1871 ; deputy regius professor of feudal and English law at Trinity College, Dublin ; author of ' Lectures on the History of Ireland ' (1869–70) and other works. [xlviii. 253]

RICHMOND, DUKES OF. [See FITZROY, SIR HENRY, first DUKE, 1519–1536 ; STUART, LUDOVICK, first DUKE of the second creation, 1574–1624 ; STUART, SIR JAMES, first DUKE of the third creation, 1612–1655 ; STUART, SIR CHARLES, third DUKE, 1640–1672 ; LENNOX, SIR CHARLES, first DUKE of the fourth creation, 1672–1723 ; LENNOX, SIR CHARLES, second DUKE, 1701–1750 ; LENNOX, CHARLES, third DUKE, 1735–1806 ; LENNOX, CHARLES, fourth DUKE, 1764–1819 ; LENNOX, SIR CHARLES GORDON-, fifth DUKE, 1791–1860.]

RICHMOND, DUCHESSES OF. [See FITZROY, MARY, d. 1557 ; STUART, FRANCES TERESA, 1648–1702.]

RICHMOND, EARLS OF. [See PETER OF SAVOY, d. 1268 ; TUDOR, EDMUND, 1430 ?–1456.]

RICHMOND, COUNTESS OF (1443–1509). [See BEAUFORT, MARGARET.]

RICHMOND, ALEXANDER BAILEY (fl. 1809–1834), reputed government spy ; by trade a weaver ; when at Pollockshaws led an agitation for an increase of wages, 1812 ; entered into relations with government after being outlawed for his share in the strike, and in 1817 betrayed the Glasgow reform committee, the members of which were arrested ; invariably denied his actual guilt, but in a libel action in 1834 against Tait's ' Edinburgh Magazine,' brought by him in consequence of his being termed a contemptible informer, was nonsuited. [xlviii. 254]

RICHMOND, GEORGE (1809–1896), portrait-painter ; son of Thomas Richmond [q. v.] ; was inspired in early life by William Blake [q. v.] ; began to exhibit at the Royal Academy, c. 1825 ; turned his attention to portrait-painting, 1831 ; achieved a world-wide fame by his portrait in water-colour of William Wilberforce ; paid a two years' visit to Italy, 1837, resuming his labours in 1839, and continuing them for over forty years ; began to paint in oil after 1846 ; gave up regular work, 1881, but still painted occasionally and occupied himself with sculpture. Among his sitters were Earl Granville, Keble, Hallam, Macaulay, Faraday. [xlviii. 255]

RICHMOND, LEGH (1772–1827), evangelical divine ; M.A. Trinity College, Cambridge, 1799 ; while a curate in the Isle of Wight wrote three famous tales of village life, of which the earliest and most popular was ' The Dairyman's Daughter ' (1809) ; became rector of Turvey, 1805 ; edited ' Fathers of the English Church,' 1807–12. [xlviii. 258]

RICHMOND, THOMAS (1771–1837), miniature-painter ; a pupil of his mother's cousin, George Engleheart [q. v.] ; was employed by the royal family. [xlviii. 259]

RICHSON, CHARLES (1806–1874), educational reformer ; M.A. St. Catharine's Hall, Cambridge, 1845 ; became a canon of Manchester Cathedral, 1854 ; for thirty years was one of the most prominent public men in Manchester ; secretary of the Church Education Society, 1843, assisting to establish the Manchester commercial schools. Many of his views were embodied in Forster's Education Act of 1870. [xlviii. 259]

RICHTER, CHRISTIAN (1682 ?–1732), miniature-painter ; born at Stockholm ; came to England, c. 1702 ; imitated the style of his fellow-countryman and patron, Michael Dahl [q. v.] [xlviii. 260]

RICHTER, HENRY JAMES (1772–1857), painter ; began to exhibit at the Royal Academy, 1788 ; painted mainly figures of a domestic nature of scenes from Shakespeare, ' Don Quixote,' and the like. [xlviii. 260]

RICHWORD, WILLIAM (d. 1637) [See RUSHWORTH.]

RICKARDS, SIR GEORGE KETTILBY (1812–1889), political economist ; of Westminster School and Eton College, and Balliol, Trinity, and Queen's Colleges, Oxford ; M.A., 1836 ; fellow of Queen's College, 1836–43 ; barrister, Inner Temple, 1837 (bencher, 1873) ; counsel to the speaker of the House of Commons, 1851–82 ; Drummond professor of political economy at Oxford, 1851–7 ; K.C.B., 1882. [xlviii. 261]

RICKARDS, SAMUEL (1796–1865), divine ; fellow of Oriel College, Oxford, 1819–22 ; M.A., 1820 ; rector of Stowlangtoft, 1832–65 ; published devotional works. [xlviii. 261]

RICKETTS, SIR HENRY (1802–1886), Indian civil servant ; entered the Bengal civil service, 1821 ; commissioner of Cuttack, 1836–9 ; commissioner of Chittagong, 1841–8 ; a member of the board of revenue, 1849–56 ; and a member of the governor-general's council, 1858–60 ; retired in consequence of ill-health, 1860 ; K.C.S.I., 1866. [xlviii. 262]

RICKHILL, SIR WILLIAM (fl. 1378–1407), judge ; nominated a justice of the common pleas, 1389 ; sent (1397) to Calais to obtain the confession of the Duke of Gloucester, which was afterwards read in parliament. [xlviii. 263]

RICKINGHALE, JOHN (d. 1429), bishop of Chichester ; D.D. Cambridge ; master of Gonville Hall (now Gonville and Caius College), Cambridge, 1416–26 ; consecrated bishop, 1426. [xlviii. 264]

RICKMAN, JOHN (1771–1840), statistician ; of Magdalen College, Oxford ; B.A. Lincoln College, Oxford, 1792 ; became secretary to Charles Abbot (Baron Colchester) [q. v.] and prepared the first census act (1800) ; became second clerk assistant at the House of Commons, 1814, and (1820) clerk assistant ; prepared annual abstracts of the poor-law returns, 1816–36 ; friend of Lamb and Southey. He devised the methods to be employed in the census, and prepared the reports published in 1801, 1811, 1821, and 1831, besides making elaborate calculations as to the population of preceding periods. [xlviii. 264]

RICKMAN, THOMAS ' CLIO ' (1761–1834), bookseller and reformer ; was known as 'Clio' in his youth for his precocious poetical and historical taste, and wrote much under that sobriquet ; settled in London as a bookseller, 1783 ; was an early friend of Paine, and got into trouble for selling Paine's works ; wrote a number of radical works, besides contributing to the ' Black Dwarf ' and other weekly journals. [xlviii. 266]

RICKMAN, THOMAS (1776–1841), architect ; began to practise in Liverpool, c. 1815 ; published a series of lectures on English styles of architecture, 1817, which became well known, and reached a seventh edition in 1881 ; built the ' New ' court of St. John's College, Cambridge, 1826 ; published architectural treatises. [xlviii. 267]

RICRAFT, JOSIAH (fl. 1645–1679), author ; a merchant of London and a writer of much repute among the presbyterians ; renounced his principles at the Restoration ; a Middlesex magistrate in 1679. [xlviii. 268]

RIDDELL, HENRY SCOTT (1798–1870), minor poet, originally a Selkirkshire shepherd; studied at St. Andrews; was minister of Caerlanrig (1833–41), Teviothead; confined in an asylum on account of insanity, 1841–4; on his release returned to Teviothead; author of 'The Crook and Plaid,' 'Scotland Yet,' and other popular songs; his 'Poetical Works' brought out, 1871.			[xlviii. 269]

RIDDELL, JAMES (d. 1674), Scottish merchant and manufacturer; an Edinburgh merchant; became commissary-general to the Scottish forces, 1645, and made the acquaintance of Cromwell and Monck.			[xlviii. 269]

RIDDELL, JAMES (1823–1866), classical scholar; M.A. and (1844) fellow of Balliol College, Oxford; senior proctor, 1862; prepared editions of the 'Odyssey' for the Oxford series, and of the 'Apology' of Plato for Benjamin Jowett [q. v.], the master of Balliol.			[xlviii. 270]

RIDDELL, JOHN (1785–1862), peerage lawyer; made a study of Scottish peerage law, and published treatises on genealogical questions.			[xlviii. 271]

RIDDELL, ROBERT (d. 1794), antiquary and patron of Burns; entered the army and (1780) attained the rank of captain, but passed much of his life in antiquarian pursuits on his estate at Friars Carse; F.S.A.; hon. LL.D. Edinburgh, 1794; remembered chiefly as the friend of Robert Burns, Friars Carse being within a mile of Burns's farm of Ellisloun; composed airs for several of the poet's songs.			[xlviii. 271]

RIDDELL, SIR THOMAS (d. 1652), royalist; M.P. for Newcastle in the Short parliament, 1640; knighted; held Tynemouth Castle against the parliamentarians, 1644–5; died in exile at Antwerp.			[xlviii. 272]

RIDDLE, EDWARD (1788–1854), mathematician and astronomer; mathematical master at the Royal Naval Hospital, Greenwich, 1821–51; F.R.A.S. and member of the council, 1825–51; published a 'Treatise on Navigation and Nautical Astronomy,' 1824 (8th edit. 1864); re-edited Hutton's 'Mathematical Recreations' (1840, 1854), and published some sixteen papers on astronomical subjects.			[xlviii. 273]

RIDDLE, JOSEPH ESMOND (1804–1859), scholar and divine; M.A. St. Edmund Hall, Oxford, 1831; incumbent of St. Philips, Leckhampton, 1840–59; joint-editor of a Latin dictionary with John T. White and of an 'English-Latin Dictionary' with Thomas Kerchever Arnold [q. v.]; wrote largely on religious and miscellaneous topics.			[xlviii. 274]

RIDEL, GEOFFREY (d. 1120), judge; drowned in the 'White Ship' disaster of 1120, when he is referred to by Henry of Huntingdon as 'justiciarum totius Angliæ.'			[xlviii. 274]

RIDEL, GEOFFREY (d. 1189), bishop of Ely; probably great-nephew of Geoffrey Ridel (d. 1120) [q. v.]; became archdeacon of Canterbury, 1163; a prominent opponent of Thomas Becket; a baron of exchequer, 1165; excommunicated by Becket, 1169, but released before 1173, when he was chosen bishop of Ely; shared with the bishops of Winchester and Norwich the office of chief justiciar, 1179–80. He built the western transept of Ely Cathedral, of which the southern half still remains.			[xlviii. 275]

RIDER. [See also RYDER.]

RIDER or **RYDER**, JOHN (1562–1632), lexicographer and bishop of Killaloe; M.A. Jesus College, Oxford, 1583; rector of Winwick, 1597–1615; bishop of Killaloe, 1613–1632; published (1589) 'Bibliotheca Scholastica,' an elaborate English-Latin and Latin-English dictionary, which was recast and reissued in 1617, 1626, 1633, and 1640.			[xlviii. 277]

RIDER, WILLIAM (1723–1785), miscellaneous writer; of St. Mary Hall and Jesus College, Oxford; B.A.; 1745; chaplain and surmaster (1763–83) at St. Paul's School, London; published several miscellaneous compilations.			[xlviii. 278]

RIDEVALL or **RIDEVANS**, JOHN DE (fl. 1330), Franciscan; was divinity reader of his order at Oxford. Works by him are extant in manuscript at Oxford, Cambridge, Worcester, and Venice.			[xlviii. 278]

RIDGE, JOHN (1590?–1637?), puritan divine; B.A. St. John's College, Oxford, 1612; admitted vicar of Antrim (1619), where in 1626 he established the Antrim meeting, the model of numerous English county assemblies

of independents, both during the Commonwealth and after the Toleration Act of 1689; silenced by Henry Leslie [q. v.], 1636, on which he retired to Scotland.			[xlviii. 279]

RIDGEWAY, SIR THOMAS, first baronet, first BARON RIDGEWAY, and first EARL OF LONDONDERRY (1565?–1631), of Exeter College, Oxford; student, Inner Temple, 1583; high sheriff of Devonshire, 1600; M.P., Devonshire, 1604–6; became treasurer in Ireland, 1606, and took an important part in preparing for the Ulster settlement by surveying the escheated counties and other labours, himself receiving, as an undertaker, two thousand acres in Tyrone; purchased a baronetcy, 1611; created Baron Ridgeway, 1616; nominated Earl of Londonderry, 1623.			[xlviii. 279]

RIDGEWAY, WILLIAM (d. 1817), law reporter; B.A. Trinity College, Dublin, 1787; LL.D., 1795; called to the Irish bar; acted as crown counsel in several state trials; published reports of proceedings in cases brought before the Irish courts.			[xlviii. 281]

RIDGLEY, THOMAS (1667?–1734), independent theologian; became assistant to Thomas Gouge (1665?–1700) [q. v.] in Thames Street, London, 1695, and succeeded him, 1700; elected divinity tutor (1712) to the Fund Academy, Moorfields, London; upheld orthodox opinions against prevalent tendencies to Arianism and Arminianism, being himself a Sabellian; D.D. by diploma, Aberdeen; published theological works.			[xlviii. 282]

RIDLEY, GLOCESTER or GLOSTER (1702–1774), miscellaneous writer; of Winchester College and Trinity and New Colleges, Oxford; B.C.L., 1729; D.D. by diploma, 1767; fellow of New College, Oxford, 1724–34; prebendary of Salisbury Cathedral, 1766–74; published sermons, poems, critical treatises, and biographies.			[xlviii. 282]

RIDLEY, HUMPHREY (1653–1708), physician; of Merton College, Oxford; M.D. Leyden, 1679; incorporated M.D. Cambridge, 1688; F.R.C.P., 1692; Gulstonian lecturer, 1694; published (1695) an important work on 'The Anatomy of the Brain,' which established his reputation as an anatomist, and 'Observationes,' 1703.			[xlviii. 283]

RIDLEY, JAMES (1736–1765), author; eldest son of Glocester Ridley [q. v.]; of Winchester School and University College, Oxford; B.A. New College, Oxford, 1760; fellow of New College, Oxford, 1755–62; incumbent of Romford, 1762–5; chiefly remembered as the author of 'Tales of the Genii' (1764), which professed to be a translation, but were in reality entirely his own, though skilfully modelled on the 'Arabian Nights.' The work went through many editions (the latest appearing in 1861), and was translated into French (1766) and German (1765–6).			[xlviii. 284]

RIDLEY, LANCELOT (d. 1576), divine; first cousin of Nicholas Ridley [q. v.]; M.A., 1527, and D.D., 1540–1, Clare Hall, Cambridge; was a vigorous protestant under Edward VI, and was deprived of his rectory of Willingham under Queen Mary; afterwards (1560–76) rector of Stretham; published three expositions on various books of the New Testament.			[xlviii. 285]

RIDLEY, MARK (1560–1624), physician; son of Lancelot Ridley [q. v.]; M.A. Clare Hall, Cambridge, 1584; went to Russia and became chief physician to the czar, Boris Gudonoff; settled in London on the czar's death, 1598; censor of the Royal College of Physicians, 1607, 1609–13, 1615, and 1618; published a treatise on the magnet, 1613.			[xlviii. 285]

RIDLEY, NICHOLAS (1500?–1555), successively bishop of Rochester and London; of an ancient border family; elected a fellow of Pembroke Hall, Cambridge, c. 1524; M.A., 1526; afterwards studied at the Sorbonne and Louvain; became one of Cranmer's chaplains, 1537, and began, though gradually, to reject many Roman doctrines; D.D. Cambridge, 1540; became master of Pembroke Hall, Cambridge, 1540, and king's chaplain; canon of Canterbury, 1541; canon of Westminster, 1545; nominated bishop of Rochester, 1547, and (1548) was one of the visitors of Cambridge University, when he pronounced in favour of reformed opinions; installed Bonner's successor in the bishopric of London, 1550, where he exerted himself to propagate reformed opinions and to improve the condition of the poor; on Edward's death denounced Queens Mary and Elizabeth as illegitimate at St. Paul's Cross, London, but on perceiving that Lady Jane Grey's cause was lost, flung himself on Queen Mary's mercy; sent to the Tower of London (June 1553), excepted from the amnesty, and deprived of his bishopric; after Wyatt's rebellion was sent to Oxford with Latimer and Cranmer, and declared a heretic after a debate in the divinity school (April 1554); condemned on the capital charge of heresy, September 1555, and burnt alive, 16 Oct. 1555. He published hardly anything in his lifetime, but several theological treatises appeared posthumously. In 1841 the 'Works of Nicholas Ridley' were edited for the Parker Society by Henry Christmas. [xlviii. 286]

RIDLEY, SIR THOMAS (1550?-1629), chancellor of Winchester; of Eton and King's College, Cambridge; M.A., 1574; D.D., 1583; incorporated D.C.L. at Oxford, 1598; fellow of King's College, Cambridge; became headmaster of Eton, 1580; became, before 1599, a master in chancery, chancellor of Winchester, and vicar-general to Archbishop George Abbot [q. v.]; M.P., Wye, 1586-7; Lymington, 1601; knighted, 1619; published 'A View of the Civile and Ecclesiastical Law,' 1607. [xlviii. 290]

RIDLEY, WILLIAM HENRY (1816-1882), religious writer; student of Christ Church, Oxford, 1836-41; M.A., 1840; rector of Hambledon, 1840-82; published theological works. [xlviii. 290]

RIDOLFI or **RIDOLFO**, ROBERTO DI (1531-1612), conspirator; born at Florence; belonged to the great Florentine family of Ridolfi di Piazza; was brought up as a banker; entered into mercantile relations with London merchants, and after Queen Mary's accession settled in London, where in Queen Elizabeth's reign Sir William Cecil and others employed him in financial business; intrigued with the French and Spanish ambassadors; privy to the Northern rebellion, 1569, but though arrested on suspicion, was not proved guilty; engaged (1570) in a fresh conspiracy, in which Norfolk was implicated, to overthrow Queen Elizabeth's government with the aid of a Spanish army; his agent, Charles Baillie [q. v.], arrested at Dover, April 1571, while he himself was absent at Brussels, and his English confederates shortly afterwards arrested; retired to Italy and settled finally at Florence; admitted to the Florentine senate, 1600. [xlviii. 290]

RIDPATH, GEORGE (d. 1726), whig journalist; studied at Edinburgh; imprisoned at Edinburgh (1681) for burning Pope Innocent XI in effigy, and banished the country; went to London and adopted literature as a profession; wrote under the name of Will Laick, attacked the Scottish bishops, and defended the English presbyterians; was, before the union, loud on Scotland's commercial wrongs, and for some years conducted the 'Flying Post or Postman,' a whig journal; committed to Newgate for libelling government in the 'Observer,' 1712; fled, after conviction, to Holland, whence he upheld the Hanoverian succession; returned to England and received some minor offices under George I, but (c. 1723) fell under suspicion of bigamy, and avoided his old friends. [xlviii. 292]

RIDPATH or **REDPATH**, GEORGE (1717?-1772), historian of the Scottish border; minister of Stitchell, 1742-72; left in manuscript 'The Border History of England and Scotland' (published, 1776). [xlviii. 295]

RIDPATH, PHILIP (1721-1788), Scottish minister; brother of George Ridpath (1717?-1772) [q. v.]; edited his brother's 'Border History,' and (1785) published an edition of Boethius's 'Consolation of Philosophy.' [xlviii. 295]

RIEL, LOUIS (1844-1885), Canadian insurgent leader; became secretary in 1869 of an association to resist the incorporation of the North-West Territories in the Canadian Dominion in the half-breed interest; became (December 1869) president of a provisional government at Fort Garry, which was suppressed by the Red River Expedition in September 1870, after which he fled to the United States; became president of a second provisional government, 1885, and began active warfare; captured and executed. [xlviii. 295]

RIEVAULX, ETHELRED OF (1109?-1166). [See ETHELRED.]

RIGAUD, JOHN FRANCIS (1742-1810), painter; born at Turin; studied painting in Italy; came to London, 1771; R.A., 1784. As an historical painter he had little merit, but ranks high as a portrait-painter. [xlviii. 296]

RIGAUD, STEPHEN FRANCIS DUTILH (1777-1861), painter; only son of John Francis Rigaud [q. v.]; engaged chiefly in historical painting, and assisted his father in decorative work. [xlviii. 297]

RIGAUD, STEPHEN JORDAN (1816-1859), bishop of Antigua; eldest son of Stephen Peter Rigaud [q. v.]; fellow of Exeter College, Oxford, 1838-41; M.A., 1842; D.D., 1854; consecrated bishop of Antigua, 1858; published various works, and edited his father's 'Correspondence of Scientific Men,' 1841. [xlviii. 298]

RIGAUD, STEPHEN PETER (1774-1839), mathematical historian and astronomer; fellow of Exeter College, Oxford, 1794-1810; M.A., 1799; F.R.S., 1805; Savilian professor of geometry, 1810-27; Savilian professor of astronomy, 1827-39; remarkable as an astronomer for accurate knowledge of the literature and history of the subject. He wrote several important works, including an 'Historical Essay on the First Publication of Newton's "Principia,"' 1838; edited others, and published a number of important papers in various scientific periodicals. [xlviii. 298]

RIGBY, ALEXANDER (1594-1650), parliamentary colonel and baron of the exchequer; student of Gray's Inn, 1610; sat in the Short parliament as M.P., Wigan, 1640; nominated one of the deputy-lieutenants of Lancashire, 1642; became a colonel in the parliamentary forces; appointed a baron of the exchequer, 1649, and (1650) a commissioner of the high court of justice. [xlviii. 299]

RIGBY, EDWARD (1747-1821), physician; published a work on uterine hæmorrhage in 1776, which was translated into French and German; visited France, 1789, his 'Letters from France' forming a useful supplement to Arthur Young's observations; practised in Norwich; mayor of Norwich, 1805. [xlviii. 301]

RIGBY, EDWARD (1804-1860), obstetrician; son of Edward Rigby (1747-1821) [q. v.]; M.D. Edinburgh, 1825; studied midwifery at Berlin and Heidelberg and became physician at the Lying-in Hospital at Lambeth; F.L.S.; F.R.C.P., 1843; regarded as the first obstetric physician in London after Sir Charles Locock [q. v.] retired from practice. [xlviii. 301]

RIGBY, ELIZABETH, afterwards LADY EASTLAKE (1809-1893). [See EASTLAKE.]

RIGBY, JOSEPH (d. 1671), parliamentarian; brother of Alexander Rigby [q. v.]; educated at Eton; rose to be lieutenant-colonel in the parliamentary army, 1650; published 'The Drunkard's Prospective,' 1656, directed against alcoholic drink. [xlviii. 302]

RIGBY, RICHARD (1722-1788), politician; entered parliament as M.P., Castle Rising, 1745, and attached himself to Frederick, prince of Wales; M.P., Sudbury, 1747, Tavistock, 1754-84; afterwards transferred his allegiance to the Duke of Bedford, whose secretary he became in 1758, when Bedford was made lord-lieutenant of Ireland; appointed master of the rolls for Ireland, 1759, vice-treasurer for Ireland, 1765, and paymaster of the forces, 1768; took a prominent part in opposing Wilkes, 1769, and (1778) objected to a public funeral to Chatham; succeeded as paymaster by Burke, 1784; died, leaving 'near half a million of public money.' [xlviii. 302]

RIGG or **RIGGE**, AMBROSE (1635?-1705), quaker; became a quaker, c. 1653, and, in spite of continued persecution, preached persistently in the southern counties till 1662, when he was arrested and kept in gaol for seven years; published religious works. [xlviii. 304]

RIGGE, ROBERT (d. 1410). [See RYGGE.]

RIGHTWISE or **RITWYSE**, JOHN (d. 1532?), grammarian; of Eton and King's College, Cambridge; B.A., 1513; became surmaster of St. Paul's School, London, 1517, and high master, 1522; removed for neglect, 1531; chiefly remembered as a composer of plays and interludes. [xlviii. 305]

RILEY, CHARLES REUBEN (1752?-1798). [See RYLEY.]

RILEY, HENRY THOMAS (1816-1878), translator and antiquary; educated at Charterhouse School, London, and Trinity and Clare Colleges, Cambridge; M.A. Clare College, 1859; incorporated at Exeter College, Oxford, 1870; barrister, Inner Temple, 1847, but made a living in earlier life by hack-writing; edited several 'Chronicles and Memorials' for the master of the rolls, and (1869) became an additional inspector of the newly created Historical Manuscripts Commission. [xlviii. 306]

RILEY or **RYLEY**, JOHN (1646–1691), portrait-painter; pupil of Gerard Soest [q. v.]; painted portraits of Charles II and James II and his queen; appointed court-painter to William and Mary. [xlviii. 307]

RIMBAULT, EDWARD FRANCIS (1816–1876), musical author and antiquary; was a founder of the Musical Antiquarian Society, of which he became secretary, and for which he edited a number of works; also edited the Motet Society's publications from 1841; F.S.A., 1842. He was organist of various London churches. [xlviii. 307]

RIMMER, ALFRED (1829–1893), artist and author; engaged in trade in Canada, 1858–70, subsequently settling in Chester; published a number of illustrated works on English topography. [xlviii. 308]

RIMMINGTON, SAMUEL (1755 ?–1826), lieutenant-general, royal artillery; entered the army, 1771; fought in the war of American independence; colonel, 1808; lieutenant-general, 1821. [xlviii. 308]

RIMSTON or **REMINGTON**, WILLIAM (*fl.* 1372), theological writer; doctor of theology at Oxford; chancellor of Oxford University, 1372. [xlviii. 308]

RING, JOHN (1752–1821), surgeon; educated at Winchester College; began to practise in London, 1774; became a friend of Edward Jenner [q. v.], 1799, and rendered most important services to the cause of vaccination; published numerous tracts on vaccination. [xlviii. 309]

RINGROSE, BASIL (*d.* 1686), buccaneer and author; was with the buccaneers at Darien in 1680; he returned to England, 1682; his journal published as a second volume of the 'History of the Buccaneers,' 1685; sailed (1684) for the South Seas in the Cygnet, whose captain joined the buccaneers; slain by the Spaniards in Mexico. [xlviii. 310]

RINGSTEAD, THOMAS DE (*d.* 1366), bishop of Bangor; doctor of theology at Cambridge; subsequently became a Dominican, and (1357) was papally provided to the see of Bangor; said to be the author of a work on the Proverbs of Solomon, of which three copies are extant at Oxford. [xlviii. 310]

RINTOUL, ROBERT STEPHEN (1787–1858), journalist; set up as a printer at Dundee, 1809; edited (1811–1825) the 'Dundee Advertiser,' a paper which became one of the chief liberal journals in Scotland; went to London, 1826, and (1828) founded the 'Spectator,' which he sold in 1858. The 'Spectator' took a prominent part in the discussion of all questions of social and political reform. [xlviii. 311]

RINUCCINI, GIOVANNI BATTISTA (1592–1653), archbishop of Fermo, and papal nuncio in Ireland; born in Rome; son of a Florentine patrician; became archbishop of Fermo, 1625; appointed papal nuncio in Ireland, 1645; interfered in the negotiations between the royalists and the Roman catholic confederates, on his arrival in Ireland, by proposing conditions which it was out of the power of Charles I to grant; consequently quarrelled with the Irish catholic royalists, and as soon as a treaty was concluded with Ormonde (March 1646) set to work to annul it, with the support of Owen Roe O'Neill [q. v.], the consequence being that Ormonde's peace was rejected by a great part of Ireland; severely reprimanded from Rome for exceeding his instructions; persisted, and finally drove Ormonde to come to terms with the English parliament; rendered extremely unpopular by the victories of Inchiquin, who had declared for parliament; warned by the confederates (January 1649) to 'intermeddle not in any of the affairs of this kingdom'; left Ireland, February 1649, and returned to Rome, where he received an honourable reception; died at Fermo of apoplexy. Though his political conduct in Ireland was unwise, his ecclesiastical duties were well performed, and in his distribution of Irish church patronage he took great care to make good appointments. [xlviii. 312]

RIOLLAY, FRANCIS (1748–1797), physician; born in Brittany; educated at Trinity College, Dublin (B.A.); incorporated at Oxford, 1777; M.A. Oxford, 1780; M.D., 1784; practised in London; Gulstonian lecturer, 1787, Harveian orator, 1787, and Croonian lecturer, 1788–90. [xlviii. 315]

RIOS, JOSEPH DE MENDOZA Y (1762–1816). [See MENDOZA.]

RIOU, EDWARD (1758 ?–1801), captain in the navy; captain, 1791; led the detached squadron against the defences of Copenhagen, where he was killed by a cannon-shot. [xlviii. 315]

RIPARIIS, DE. [See REDVERS.]

RIPLEY, GEORGE (*d.* 1490 ?), alchemist; an Augustinian and a canon of Bridlington; was undoubtedly the most widely studied of the late alchemists; compiled, 1471, 'The Compound of Alchemie,' and, 1476, 'Medulla Alchimiæ.' [xlviii. 316]

RIPLEY, THOMAS (*d.* 1758), architect; originally a carpenter; owed his advancement in life to Sir Robert Walpole's patronage; built Wolterton House, 1724–30, and the Admiralty, Whitehall, 1724–6. [xlviii. 317]

RIPON, first EARL OF (1782–1859). [See ROBINSON, FREDERICK JOHN.]

RIPPINGILLE, EDWARD VILLIERS (1798 ?–1859), painter and writer on art; began to exhibit at the Royal Academy, 1813; chiefly painted pictures of English country life; contributed to 'Bentley's Magazine' and the 'Art Journal.' [xlviii. 318]

RIPPON, JOHN (1751–1836), baptist divine; pastor in Carter Lane and New Park Street, London (1773–1836); edited 'Baptist Annual Register,' 1790–1802; compiled a well-known 'Selection of Hymns,' 1827. [xlviii. 318]

RIPPON, THOMAS (1761–1835), chief cashier of the Bank of England; brother of John Rippon [q. v.]; succeeded Abraham Newland [q. v.] as cashier. [xlviii. 318]

RISDON, TRISTRAM (1580 ?–1640), topographer; author of a 'Chorographical Description or Survey of Devon,' first printed by Edmund Curll [q. v.] in a garbled edition in 1714. An excellent edition appeared in 1811. [xlviii. 319]

RISHANGER, WILLIAM (1250 ?–1312 ?), monk of St. Albans and chronicler; became a Benedictine of St. Albans Abbey, 1271; author of 'Narratio de Bellis apud Lewes et Evesham' (edited for the Camden Society, 1840), and of a chronicle of 'Gesta Edwardi Primi.' Riley also assigns to him a longer chronicle of English history edited by him for the Rolls Series in 1865. [xlviii. 319]

RISHTON, EDWARD (1550–1586), Roman catholic divine; B.A. Brasenose College, Oxford, 1572; studied at Douay; condemned to death for officiating in England and banished, 1581; died of the plague near Ste.-Ménehould. Several of his works are extant. [xlviii. 321]

RISHTON, NICHOLAS (*d.* 1413), diplomatist; educated at New College, Oxford; held several minor ecclesiastical preferments, and was employed in negotiations with the French, 1403–5; an English representative at the council of Pisa. [xlviii. 321]

RISING, JOHN (1756–1815), portrait and subject painter; regularly exhibited at the Royal Academy, 1785–1815. [xlviii. 322]

RISLEY, THOMAS (1630–1716), nonconformist divine; fellow of Pembroke College, Oxford, 1654–62; M.A., 1655; built a chapel at Culcheth after the passing of the Toleration Act in 1689, and ministered there till his death. [xlviii. 322]

RITCHIE, ALEXANDER HANDYSIDE (1804–1870), sculptor; studied at Rome under Thorwaldsen, and from 1838 practised successfully at Edinburgh. [xlviii. 323]

RITCHIE, JOHN (1809–1850), sculptor; younger brother of Alexander Handyside Ritchie [q. v.]; worked for a time with his brother. His fine group, 'The Deluge,' was suggested by a dream. [xlviii. 323]

RITCHIE, JOHN (1778–1870), journalist; one of the founders of the 'Scotsman' (1817); became sole proprietor shortly after 1831. [xlviii. 325]

RITCHIE, JOSEPH (1788 ?–1819), African traveller; a surgeon by profession; commissioned by government to undertake the exploration of the Nigritian Soudan by way of Tripoli and Fezzan, *c.* 1818; died at Murzuk. [xlviii. 323]

RITCHIE, LEITCH (1800 ?–1865), novelist; was employed as a clerk in Glasgow, but (*c.* 1820) adopted literature as a profession; published novels and other works, and during the latter part of his life edited 'Chambers's Journal.' [xlviii. 324]

RITCHIE, WILLIAM (1781-1831), journalist; younger brother of John Ritchie (1778-1870) [q. v.]; joined Charles Maclaren [q. v.] and others in 1817 in founding the 'Scotsman,' of which he and Maclaren were joint-editors until his death. [xlviii. 325]

RITCHIE, WILLIAM (1790-1837), physicist; professor of natural philosophy at London University, 1832-1837. [xlviii. 326]

RITCHIE, Sir WILLIAM JOHNSTONE (1813-1892), chief-justice of Canada; born at Annapolis, Nova Scotia; educated at Pictou College, Nova Scotia; member for St. John's in the Nova Scotia assembly, 1846-51; became puisne judge of New Brunswick, 1855; chief-justice of New Brunswick, 1865; puisne judge of the Dominion supreme court, 1875, and chief-justice of Canada, 1879; knighted, 1881. [xlviii. 326]

RITSCHEL, GEORGE (1616-1683), divine; born in Bohemia; came to England, 1641; left England on the outbreak of the civil war, returning, 1644; rector of Hexham, 1656?-1683; published one religious and one metaphysical work in Latin. [xlviii. 327]

RITSON, ISAAC (1761-1789), translator; schoolmaster at Penrith; published a translation of the 'Hymn to Venus,' 1788. [xlviii. 331]

RITSON, JONATHAN (1776?-1846), wood-carver; completed the work of Grinling Gibbons at Arundel and Petworth. [xlviii. 331]

RITSON, JOSEPH (1752-1803), antiquary; settled in London, 1775, as a conveyancing clerk, and (1780) began business on his own account; high bailiff of the liberty of the Savoy, 1784-1803; zealously studied English literature and history; attacked Warton's 'History of English Poetry,' 1782, and Johnson and Steevens's edition of Shakespeare, 1783; attacked also Steevens's editorial successors, Isaac Reed and Malone; detected the Ireland forgeries, 1795; was one of the earliest collectors of local verse, and (1783) published a 'Select Collection of English Songs,' in which he attacked Percy's 'Reliques,' and in subsequent works on the same subject threw doubt on the existence of the manuscript whence Percy claimed to have derived his ballads; demonstrated that many of John Pinkerton's 'Select Scottish Ballads' were forgeries, 1784; visited Paris, 1791, and from that time showed a close sympathy with the French revolution; produced (1802) his useful 'Bibliographia Poetica'; became insane, 1803, shortly before his death. [xlviii. 327]

RITTER, HENRY (1816-1853), artist; born at Montreal; practised at Düsseldorf, chiefly affecting sea-pieces. [xlviii. 331]

RITWYSE, JOHN (d. 1532?). [See RIGHTWISE.]

RIVAROL, LOUISA HENRIETTA, MADAME DE (1749?-1821), translator; only child of Mather Flint; born at Remiremont; married the so-called Comte de Rivarol, the future satirist of the revolution, c. 1780; obtained a divorce (1794) from her husband, who had deserted her; translated several English works into French. [xlviii. 331]

RIVAULX or **RIVALLIS,** PETER DE (d. 1258?), favourite of Henry III; said to have been a son or nephew of Peter des Roches (d. 1238) [q. v.]; made treasurer, 1232, but (1234) deprived of his offices in consequence of the opposition to the Poitevin favourites; restored to favour, 1236; again treasurer, 1257. [xlviii. 332]

RIVERS, EARLS OF. [See WOODVILLE, RICHARD, first EARL, d. 1469; WOODVILLE, ANTHONY, second EARL, 1442?-1483; SAVAGE, RICHARD, fourth EARL of the second creation, 1660?-1712.]

RIVERS, first BARON (1722?-1803). [See PITT, GEORGE, first BARON.]

RIVERS, ANTONY, alias THOMAS BLEWETT (fl. 1601-1606), jesuit; was secretary to Henry Garnett [q. v.] In 1692 Shirley's tragedy, 'The Traytor,' was reissued, with a dedication unwarrantably attributing it to Rivers, [xlviii. 333]

RIVERS, AUGUSTUS HENRY LANE FOX PITT- (1827-1900). [See PITT-RIVERS.]

RIVERS, THOMAS (1798-1877), nurseryman; especially noted for his collection of roses at his nurseries at Sawbridgeworth and for his development of the culture of small fruit trees. [xlviii. 333]

RIVERS, WILLIAM (1788-1856), lieutenant in the navy; entered the Victory, 1795; lost a leg at Trafalgar, 1805; adjutant of Greenwich Hospital, 1826-56. [xlviii. 333]

RIVERSTON, titular BARON OF (d. 1715). [See NUGENT, THOMAS.]

RIVETT or **REVETT,** JOHN (1624-1674), brazier; concealed and (1660) handed over to Charles II the brazen statue of Charles I (made by Hubert Le Sueur [q. v.]), which the parliament, on Charles I's execution, sold him as old metal and ordered to be destroyed. [xxxiii. 129]

RIVIERE, HENRY PARSONS (1811-1888), water-colour painter; brother of William Riviere [q. v.]; began to exhibit in 1832; went to Rome, 1865, and remained there till near the end of his life, exhibiting in England views of Rome and the neighbourhood. [xlviii. 334]

RIVIERE, ROBERT (1808-1882), bookbinder; brother of William Riviere [q. v.]; commenced business in 1829 in Bath, and removed, in 1840, to London, where his excellent taste and workmanship made him famous.
[xlviii. 334]

RIVIERE, WILLIAM (1806-1876), historical painter; began to exhibit at the Royal Academy, 1826.
[xlviii. 335]

RIVINGTON, CHARLES (1688-1742), publisher; took over the premises and trade of Richard Chiswell (1639-1711) [q. v.] in 1711, and soon became the leading theological publisher. [xlviii. 335]

RIVINGTON, CHARLES (1754-1831), publisher; son of John Rivington (1720-1792) [q. v.]; carried on his father's business, at first with his brother Francis Rivington [q. v.], and after his death alone. [xlviii. 337]

RIVINGTON, FRANCIS (1745-1822), publisher; eldest son of John Rivington (1720-1792) [q. v.]; carried on his father's business with his brother Charles Rivington (1754-1831) [q. v.] [xlviii. 337]

RIVINGTON, FRANCIS (1805-1885), publisher; son of Charles Rivington (1754-1831) [q. v.]; succeeded to his father's business, 1831; retired, 1859; published 'Tracts for the Times' and other tractarian writings.
[xlviii. 336]

RIVINGTON, JAMES (1724-1803), publisher; son of Charles Rivington (1688-1742) [q. v.]; emigrated to New England in 1760, where he started 'Rivington's New York Gazette' (1777). [xlviii. 336]

RIVINGTON, JOHN (1720-1792), publisher; son of Charles Rivington (1688-1742) [q. v.]; succeeded to his father's business, and in 1760 became publisher to the Society for Promoting Christian Knowledge. [xlviii. 336]

RIVINGTON, JOHN (1779-1841), publisher; eldest son of Francis Rivington (1745-1822) [q. v.]; admitted into the firm in 1810. [xlviii. 337]

RIZZIO, DAVID (1533?-1566). [See RICCIO.]

ROACH, JOHN (fl. 1794-1796), bookseller and compiler; kept a shop in Drury Lane, London, where he sold odd volumes and indelicate prints. [xlviii. 337]

ROACH, RICHARD (1662-1730), divine; of Merchant Taylors' School, London, and St. John's College, Oxford; M.A., 1688; B.D., 1695; rector of St. Augustine's, Hackney, 1690-1730; a follower of Mrs. Jane Lead [q. v.]; published mystical treatises. [xlviii. 338]

ROACH-SMITH, CHARLES (1807-1890). [See SMITH.]

ROB DONN (1714-1778). [See MACKAY, ROBERT.]

ROB ROY (1671-1734). [See MACGREGOR, ROBERT.]

ROB ROY (pseudonym). [See MACGREGOR, JOHN, 1825-1892.]

ROBARTES or **ROBERTES,** FOULK (1580?-1650), divine; M.A. Christ's College, Cambridge, 1602; B.D. Trinity College, Cambridge, 1609; incorporated B.D. Oxford, 1621; installed a prebendary of Norwich Cathedral, 1616, but during the civil war died in poverty.
[xlviii. 338]

ROBARTES, FRANCIS (1650 ?–1718), politician and musician ; son of Sir John Robartes, first earl of Radnor [q. v.] ; sat in parliament from 1673 till his death ; known as a musical composer and as a writer on the theory of sound. [xlviii. 338]

ROBARTES, SIR JOHN, first EARL OF RADNOR, second BARON ROBARTES, and second baronet (1606–1685), of Exeter College, Oxford ; succeeded his father as second baron Robartes, 1634 ; voted with the popular party during the Long parliament ; he became a colonel in Essex's army, and in 1644 held the rank of field-marshal ; was a strong presbyterian, and after Charles I's execution took no further share in public affairs ; made at the Restoration lord-deputy of Ireland, an office which he exchanged for that of lord privy seal ; closely associated with Clarendon's opponents from 1663 ; appointed lord-lieutenant of Ireland, 1669 ; recalled, 1670 ; created Earl of Radnor, 1679 ; appointed lord president of the council, 1679. [xlviii. 339]

ROBBERDS, JOHN GOOCH (1789–1854), unitarian minister ; pastor of Cross Street, Manchester, 1811–54 ; published sermons, tracts, and lectures. [xlviii. 341]

ROBE, JAMES (1688–1753), Scottish presbyterian divine ; studied at Glasgow University ; minister of Kilsyth, 1713–53 ; published religious works. [xlviii. 341]

ROBE, SIR WILLIAM (1765–1820), colonel, royal artillery ; entered the army, 1781 ; served in Holland, 1793–4 and 1799, at Copenhagen, 1807, and in the Spanish peninsula, 1808–12 ; K.C.B., 1815 ; K.H. ; regimental colonel, 1815. [xlviii. 342]

ROBE, WILLIAM LIVINGSTONE (1791–1815), lieutenant, royal artillery ; eldest son of Sir William Robe [q. v.] ; served in the peninsula, 1808–14 ; lieutenant, 1808 ; fell at Waterloo. [xlviii. 343]

ROBERDEAU, JOHN PETER (1754–1815), dramatist ; settled at Chichester, 1796 ; wrote many plays of indifferent merit, chiefly for the provincial theatres. [xlviii. 343]

ROBERT I (1274–1329). [See BRUCE, ROBERT DE, VIII.]

ROBERT II (1316–1390), THE STEWARD, king of Scotland ; son of Walter III, steward of Scotland, by Marjory, daughter of Robert the Bruce ; declared heir presumptive, 1318 ; succeeded to his father's office and estates, 1326 ; led the second division of the Scottish army at Halidon Hill, 1333 ; with Moray was chosen regent, 1334 ; lost his authority in consequence of Edward III's successes, 1335, but in 1338 again became regent, and in 1341 regained Edinburgh from the English ; vacated the regency, David II having returned from France ; resumed his authority as king, May 1341 ; resumed the regency when David II was captured at Neville's Cross, 1346 ; his hopes of the crown impaired by David II's recognition of Edward III as his successor, 1363 ; imprisoned with his three sons by David II as a measure of security ; released, 1370, and peacefully succeeded to the throne on David II's death, 1371 ; took no personal share in the war with England, which was renewed in 1378 and continued intermittently till his death ; his second son Robert, duke of Albany, named guardian of the kingdom, 1389 ; died at Dundonald. [xlviii. 344]

ROBERT III (1340 ? – 1406), king of Scotland ; originally known as John, earl of Carrick ; eldest son of Robert II [q. v.] ; changed his name on succeeding to the throne in 1390 ; created Earl of Atholl, 1367, and Earl of Carrick, 1368 ; disabled from bodily exertion by an accident which took place before his father's death ; never personally governed, all the power of administration being in the hands of his younger brother, Robert Stewart, first duke of Albany [q. v.] ; his heir, the Duke of Rothesay, created lieutenant of the kingdom, 1399, arrested by Albany, 1402, the order being in his father's name, and perhaps put to death in prison, on which Albany resumed the regency ; died at Rothesay. [xlviii. 347]

ROBERT, DUKE OF NORMANDY (1054 ? – 1134), eldest son of William I [q. v.] ; received the investiture of Maine, 1069, but was unable to prevail on his father to give him actual possession of the county ; rebelled, 1077, and (1079) accidentally wounded his father at Gerberoi ; subsequently made his submission and was recognised as heir of Normandy, which he inherited on

William I's death in 1087 ; having emptied his treasury, sold the Cotentin to his brother Henry, 1088 ; his duchy of Normandy invaded by his brother, William II, 1089 ; came to an agreement with William II, 1091, and with him drove Henry out of the Cotentin ; shared his possessions ; took the cross and pledged his duchy to William II for five years for the sum of ten thousand marks, 1096 ; set out in October, and after joining the other crusaders reached Constantinople early in the summer of 1097 ; distinguished himself by his valour at Dorylæum, and in the march to Antioch led the advanced guard ; by his prowess enabled the crusaders to defeat Corbogha in a great battle under the walls of Antioch, June 1098 ; refused the sovereignty of Jerusalem, and in the autumn left Palestine ; did not, however, reach Normandy till September 1100, and thus lost his opportunity of the English succession on the death of William II, but was freed by that event from the necessity of redeeming Normandy from pledge ; urged by Rannulf Flambard [q. v.], invaded England, July 1101, but made a treaty with Henry I ; ceded the county of Evreux to Henry I, 1104 ; his duchy of Normandy invaded by Henry I, who was indignant at his misgovernment of it, 1105 ; defeated by Henry I and taken prisoner at the battle of Tinchebrai, 1106 ; passed the rest of his life in confinement in England ; was probably well treated, the statement that he was blinded after being detected in plotting treason being unsupported by adequate authority. [xlviii. 349]

ROBERT, EARL OF GLOUCESTER (d. 1147), a natural son of Henry I, who bestowed on him the hand of Mabel, daughter of Robert Fitzhamon (d. 1107) [q. v.], and the whole of her father's heritage in Normandy, Wales, and England ; created Earl of Gloucester, c. 1122 ; on Henry I's death (1135) submitted to Stephen ; quarrelled with Stephen, 1137, who soon afterwards confiscated his English and Welsh estates, and (1139) landed in England in company with Matilda ; captured Stephen under the walls of Lincoln, 1141, but before the close of the year was himself made prisoner at Stockbridge and exchanged for Stephen ; defeated Stephen at Wilton, 1143, but spent the rest of his life in desperate efforts to hold his ground, in spite of the rapid disintegration of the Angevin party ; died at Bristol. [xlviii. 356]

ROBERT OF JUMIÈGES (fl. 1037–1052), archbishop of Canterbury ; became abbot of Jumièges, 1037 ; accompanied Edward the Confessor to England, 1043 ; was consecrated bishop of London, 1044, and became the head of the Norman opposition to Godwin ; appointed archbishop of Canterbury, 1051 ; by inflaming Edward's resentment against Godwin, succeeded in driving the earl into exile, September 1051 ; fled to Normandy on Godwin's return in 1052 ; outlawed by the witan and deposed ; went to Rome and procured the support of the pope, who ordered his reinstatement, but in spite of that could not regain possession of his see ; died at Jumièges. [xlviii. 358]

ROBERT THE STALLER (fl. 1066), otherwise known as Robert FitzWimarc ; 'staller' in the court of Edward the Confessor ; supported William the Norman, 1066. [xlviii. 359]

ROBERT D'OILGI, D'OILLY, or D'OYLY I (d. 1090 ?), Norman baron ; came to England with William I, and obtained large grants of land in the midland counties. Some of his buildings at Oxford are still extant, including the tower of St. Michael's Church and the keep of Oxford Castle. [xlviii. 359]

ROBERT OF MORTAIN, COUNT OF MORTAIN (d. 1091 ?). [See MORTAIN.]

ROBERT LOSINGA (d. 1095). [See LOSINGA.]

ROBERT (d. 1103), crusader and martyr ; an Englishman of good family ; followed Edgar Atheling to Palestine on crusade ; taken prisoner at Ramlah and, refusing to deny Christ, was put to death. [xlviii. 361]

ROBERT FITZHAMON (d. 1107). [See FITZHAMON.]

ROBERT OF BELLÊME, EARL OF SHREWSBURY (fl. 1098). [See BELLÊME.]

ROBERT DE BEAUMONT, COUNT OF MEULAN (d. 1118). [See BEAUMONT.]

ROBERT BLOET (d. 1123). [See BLOET.]

ROBERT (d. 1139), first abbot of Newminster ; entered the Benedictine abbey at Whitby, but afterwards joined the Cistercian order, and in 1132 assisted to found the abbey of Fountains; became first abbot of Newminster, 1137. [xlviii. 361]

ROBERT D'OILGI II (*fl.* 1130–1142), baron; elder son of Robert d'Oilgi I (*d.* 1090?), was 'constabularius regis Henrici primi'; assisted the Empress Matilda against King Stephen. [xlviii. 360]

ROBERT THE ENGLISHMAN, ROBERT DE KETENE, or ROBERT DE RETINES (*fl.* 1141–1143), first translator of the Koran; travelled widely and learned Arabic in Asia; was living in Spain, near the Ebro, 1141–3, and subsequently became archdeacon of Pampeluna; translated the Koran into Latin for Peter the Venerable, abbot of Cluny, between 1141 and 1143. His translation was first printed at Basle in 1543. Many other works ascribed to him. [xlviii. 362]

ROBERT PULLEN (*d.* 1147?). [See PULLEN.]

ROBERT DE BETHUNE (*d.* 1148), bishop of Hereford; a native of Bethune in Artois; entered the house of the Augustinian canons at Llanthony, where he became prior; consecrated bishop of Hereford, 1131; followed the political guidance of Henry of Winchester during the troubles of Stephen's reign; died while attending the council of Rheims. [xlviii. 364]

ROBERT OF 'SALESBY' (*fl.* 1132–1148), chancellor of Sicily; was one of the many Englishmen who found employment under the Norman kings of Sicily; was chancellor as early as 1132, and attested charters of King Roger at least as late as 1148. [xlviii. 365]

ROBERT (*d.* 1159), bishop of St. Andrews; probably consecrated in 1125; the priory of St. Andrews founded during his rule by David I. [xlviii. 366]

ROBERT OF MELUN (*d.* 1167), bishop of Hereford; an Englishman by birth; went to France, *c.* 1120, and taught philosophy at Paris and Melun; recalled to England by Thomas Becket and elected bishop of Hereford, 1163; supported Henry II in his controversy with Becket, though with moderation; enjoyed great renown as a theologian and teacher. In philosophy he was a realist, but stopped short of anything like heterodoxy. His great work was 'Summa Theologiæ.' [xlviii. 366]

ROBERT OF SHREWSBURY (*d.* 1167), hagiologist; became abbot of Shrewsbury before 1160, and wrote an extant 'Life of St. Wenefred.' [xlviii. 368]

ROBERT, EARL OF LEICESTER (1104–1168). [See BEAUMONT, ROBERT DE.]

ROBERT FITZHARDING (*d.* 1170). [See FITZHARDING.]

ROBERT OF BRIDLINGTON or ROBERT THE SCRIBE (*fl.* 1160–1170), theologian; became prior of Bridlington, *c.* 1160. He owed his name of 'Scribe' to his many writings, chiefly commentaries on portions of the bible. [xlviii. 368]

ROBERT OF CRICKLADE, also called CANUTUS (*fl.* 1157–1170), historical writer; chancellor of the university of Oxford, 1159; was also prior of St. Frideswide; wrote a life of Thomas Becket. [xlviii. 368]

ROBERT (*d.* 1178), abbot of Glastonbury; wrote lives of two of the bishops of Winchester, printed in Wharton's 'Anglia Sacra.' [xlviii. 369]

ROBERT FITZSTEPHEN (*d.* 1183?). [See FITZSTEPHEN.]

ROBERT DE MONTE (1110?–1186), chronicler; born at Torigni-sur-Vire; was abbot of Mont St. Michel, 1154–1186; continued the work of William of Jumièges and the chronicle of Sigebert of Gemblours. [xlviii. 369]

ROBERT FOLIOT (*d.* 1186). [See FOLIOT.]

ROBERT DE STUTEVILLE (*d.* 1186). [See STUTEVILLE.]

ROBERT, EARL OF LEICESTER (*d.* 1190). [See BEAUMONT, ROBERT DE.]

ROBERT DE BEAUFEU (*fl.* 1190). [See BEAUFEU.]

ROBERT DE TURNHAM (*d.* 1211). [See TURNHAM.]

ROBERT DE VIEUXPONT or VIPONT (*d.* 1228). [See VIEUXPONT.]

ROBERT (*d.* 1235?), saint; lived at Knaresborough as a hermit; often confused with Robert (*d.* 1139) [q. v.], first abbot of Newminster; canonised before 1252. [xlviii. 361]

ROBERT RICH (*fl.* 1185–1240). [See RICH.]

ROBERT DE LEXINTON (*d.* 1250). [See LEXINTON.]

ROBERT DE THWENG, THWING, or TWENG (1205?–1268?). [See THWENG.]

ROBERT ANGLICUS (*fl.* 1272), author; wrote a commentary on John de Sacrobosco's treatise 'De Sphæra.' [xlviii. 372]

ROBERT OF SWAFFHAM (*d.* 1273?), historian of the abbey of Peterborough; continued the history of the abbey commenced by Hugh (*fl.* 1107?–1155?) [q. v.] [xlviii. 370]

ROBERT DE STICHIL (*d.* 1274). [See STICHIL.]

ROBERT THORPE (*fl.* 1290). [See THORPE.]

ROBERT OF GLOUCESTER (*fl.* 1260–1300), historian; known only from the English metrical chronicle of the history of England to 1270, which bears his name; may have been an inhabitant of Gloucester. [xlviii. 370]

ROBERT OF LEICESTER (*fl.* 1320). [See LEICESTER.]

ROBERT THE ENGLISHMAN, also called ROBERTUS PERSCRUTATOR (*fl.* 1326), author; wrote several extant treatises on medicine and alchemy. [xlviii. 371]

ROBERT MANNYNG or DE BRUNNE (*fl.* 1288–1338). [See MANNYNG.]

ROBERT OF AVESBURY (*fl.* 1356), historian; compiled a history of the 'Mirabilia Gesta' of Edward III down to 1356, printed in the Rolls Series, 1889. [xlviii. 372]

ROBERT DE THORPE, SIR (*d.* 1372). [See THORPE.]

ROBERT DE STRETTON (*d.* 1385). [See STRETTON.]

ROBERT WIKEFORD (*d.* 1390). [See WIKEFORD.]

ROBERT OF WOODSTOCK (*d.* 1428). [See HEETE, ROBERT.]

ROBERTON, JAMES, LORD BEDLAY (1590?–1664), Scottish judge; M.A. Glasgow, 1609; appointed professor of philosophy and humanity, Glasgow, 1618; appointed judge in the admiralty court, 1626; retired during Cromwell's supremacy; made an ordinary lord of session, 1661. [xlviii. 372]

ROBERTON, JOHN (1797–1876), surgeon; appointed surgeon to the Manchester Lying-in Hospital, 1827; helped much to extend the fame of the Manchester school of obstetrics. [xlviii. 373]

ROBERTS, SIR ABRAHAM (1784–1873), general; entered the army, 1803; served in India and Afghanistan with distinction for over fifty years; G.C.B., 1873. He was the father of Field-Marshal Earl Roberts, K.G. [xlviii. 374]

ROBERTS, ARTHUR (1801–1886), author; eldest son of William Roberts (1767–1849) [q. v.]; published his father's biography. [xlviii. 397]

ROBERTS, BARRÉ CHARLES (1789–1810), antiquary; B.A. Christ Church, Oxford, 1808; made a fine collection of English coins, now in possession of the trustees of the British Museum. [xlviii. 374]

ROBERTS, BARTHOLOMEW (1682?–1722), pirate; was captured by pirates in 1718, and joined their company; killed in 1722 off Cape Lopez while in action with a man-of-war. [xlviii. 375]

ROBERTS, DAVID (1757–1819), lieutenant-colonel; entered the army, 1794; served in the Spanish peninsula, 1808–13; brevet lieutenant-colonel, 1813; author of 'The Military Adventures of Johnny Newcome,' 1815. [xlviii. 375]

ROBERTS, DAVID (1796–1864), painter; began to practise his art as scene-painter to a travelling company; began to exhibit at the Royal Academy, 1826; travelled extensively, and painted landscapes of all parts of Europe, as well as of Syria and the Holy Land. [xlviii. 376]

ROBERTS, EMMA (1794?–1840), author; resided for some years in India with her married sister, and published several works on that country, including 'Scenes and Characteristics of Hindostan,' 1835. [xlviii. 377]

ROBERTS, FRANCIS (1609–1675), puritan; M.A. Trinity College, Oxford, 1632; joined the presbyterian party at the outbreak of the civil war, and was instituted to Wrington; conformed at the Restoration, and was left undisturbed; created D.D. Dublin, when chaplain to Essex, lord-lieutenant of Ireland; left several theological treatises. [xlviii. 377]

ROBERTS, GEORGE (*fl.* 1721–1726), mariner; reputed author of 'The Four Years' Voyages of Capt. George Roberts' (1726), which is sometimes assigned to Defoe. [xlviii. 378]

ROBERTS, GEORGE (*d.* 1860), antiquary; mayor of Lyme Regis, 1848–9 and 1854–5; published, besides other works, the 'Life, Progresses, and Rebellion of James, Duke of Monmouth,' 1844. [xlviii. 378]

ROBERTS, GEORGE EDWARD (1831–1865), geologist; author of 'The Rocks of Worcestershire,' 1860, and other geological treatises. [xlviii. 379]

ROBERTS, GRIFFITH (*fl.* 1567–1585), Welsh grammarian; M.D. Siena; published a Welsh treatise on grammar at Milan in 1567, which was reprinted in 1857. [xlviii. 379]

ROBERTS or **ROBARTS**, HENRY (*fl.* 1585–1616), author; author of a number of works of extreme rarity, mainly panegyrics and romances; attached to the court of James I. [xlviii. 379]

ROBERTS, HENRY (*d.* 1876), architect; interested himself in the housing of the poor of London, and also of Belgium and Italy. [xlviii. 380]

ROBERTS, SIR HENRY GEE (1800–1860), majorgeneral; entered the East India Company's service, 1818; took a distinguished part in the Sikh wars and in the Indian mutiny; major-general, 1854; K.C.B., 1859. [xlviii. 380]

ROBERTS, JAMES (*fl.* 1564–1606), printer; printed editions of several of Shakespeare's plays, including 'The Marchaunt of Venyce' (1600), 'A Midsummer Night's Dream' (1600), and 'Hamlet' (1604). [xlviii. 382]

ROBERTS, JAMES (*fl.* 1766–1809), portrait-painter. [xlviii. 382]

ROBERTS, JOHN (1576–1610), Benedictine monk; educated at St. John's College, Oxford; ordained priest at Valladolid, 1602; came to England as a missioner; was arrested in England and executed. [xlviii. 383]

ROBERTS, JOHN (1623?–1684), quaker and humorist; joined the parliamentary army, and (1655) became a quaker; suffered persecution, but was befriended by Nicholson, bishop of Gloucester. [xlviii. 383]

ROBERTS, JOHN (1712?–1772), politician; was private secretary to Henry Pelham, and was rewarded for his services with a series of sinecures; M.P., Harwich, 1761–72. [xlviii. 384]

ROBERTS, JOHN (1749–1817). [See SION LLEYN.]

ROBERTS, JOHN (1767–1834), Welsh divine; became co-pastor of Llanbrynmair independent church, 1796, and sole pastor, 1798. A theological work by him, 'Dybenion Marwolaeth Crist' (1814), provoked a tedious controversy. [xlviii. 385]

ROBERTS, JOHN (1822–1877), Welsh musician; better known as IEUAN GWYLLT; published (1859) his tune-book, 'Llyfr Tonau,' which at once became popular; composed twenty-one or more tunes, of which some half-dozen are still in popular use; contributed miscellaneous articles to the 'Traethodydd,' the Welsh quarterly. [xlviii. 386]

ROBERTS, JOHN (1804–1884), Welsh writer and independent minister, better known as 'J. R.'; son of John Roberts (1767–1834) [q. v.]; held pastorates in Wales and London, and edited 'Y Cronicl,' 1857–84. [xlviii. 387]

ROBERTS, JOHN CHRISTOPHER (1739–1810), politician; son of John Roberts (1712?–1772) [q. v.]; was made secretary of the province of Quebec, 1768, and afterwards commissary-general. [xlviii. 385]

ROBERTS, JOSEPH (1795–1849), missionary; sent to Ceylon by the Wesleyan Missionary Society, 1819; published a translation of extracts from the Tamil work 'Sakaa Thevan Saasteram,' 1831. [xlviii. 387]

ROBERTS, LEWES or LEWIS (1596–1640), merchant and economic writer; a director of the East India Company; wrote several works on English trade with foreign countries. [xlviii. 388]

ROBERTS, MARY (1788–1864), author; educated as a quaker; published works on subjects connected with natural history, including 'Annals of My Village,' 1831. [xlviii. 388]

ROBERTS, MICHAEL (1817–1882), mathematician; B.A. Trinity College, Dublin, 1838; fellow, 1843; professor of mathematics at Trinity College, Dublin, 1862–79; discovered many properties of geodesic lines and lines of curvature on the ellipsoid. [xlviii. 389]

ROBERTS, PETER (1760?–1819), divine and antiquary; M.A. Dublin; held successively several livings; chief works, 'Sketch of the Early History of the Cymry,' 1803, and 'Cambrian Popular Antiquities,' 1815. [xlviii. 389]

ROBERTS, RICHARD (1789–1864), inventor; settled in Manchester; patented the self-acting mule, 1825, and invented the radial arm for winding in, 1832; subsequently made several important inventions in connection with railways and steamships. [xlviii. 390]

ROBERTS, RICHARD (1810–1883), author; also known as GRUFFYDD RHISIART; son of John Roberts (1767–1834) [q. v.]; wrote a good deal of prose and verse for 'Y Cronicl' and other magazines. [xlviii. 393]

ROBERTS, SAMUEL (1763–1848), author and pamphleteer; known as the 'Pauper's Advocate'; a Sheffield silversmith by trade and author of an immense number of books and pamphlets on political and social subjects; friend of James Montgomery the poet. [xlviii. 391]

ROBERTS, SAMUEL (1800–1885), social and political reformer; eldest son of John Roberts (1767–1834) [q. v.]; pastor of Llanbrynmair, 1834–57; became a leader of public opinion among Welsh nonconformists; founded (1843) 'Y Cronicl,' a cheap monthly journal, which attained great influence in Wales; went to Tennessee, 1857, where he established a Welsh settlement, which was unsuccessful; returned to Wales, 1867. [xlviii. 391]

ROBERTS, THOMAS (1749?–1794?), artist; chiefly devoted himself to parklike landscape, and imitated Dutch foliage pencilling; exhibited, from 1773, with the Society of Artists in the Strand, London. [xlviii. 393]

ROBERTS, THOMAS SAUTELLE (1760?–1826), artist; brother of Thomas Roberts [q. v.]; exhibited landscapes at the Royal Academy, 1789–1811. [xlviii. 393]

ROBERTS, SIR WILLIAM, first baronet (1605–1662), parliamentarian; entered at Gray's Inn, 1622; knighted, 1624; sided with parliament on the outbreak of the civil war; became a member of the council of state, 1653; sat in Cromwell's House of Peers, 1657; created baronet, 1661. [xlviii. 394]

ROBERTS, WILLIAM (1585–1665), bishop of Bangor; fellow of Queens' College, Cambridge; consecrated, 1637; suffered much during the civil war through adhering to Charles I. [xlviii. 394]

ROBERTS, WILLIAM (1767–1849), barrister and author; educated at Eton and St. Paul's School, London; M.A. Corpus Christi College, Oxford, 1791; barrister, Middle Temple, 1806; edited the 'British Review,' 1811–1822, and had a literary quarrel with Byron; published 'Memoirs of Hannah More,' 1834. [xlviii. 395]

ROBERTS, SIR WILLIAM (1830–1899), physician; educated at University College, London; B.A. London, 1851; M.B., 1853; M.D., 1854; M.R.C.S. England, 1853; physician to Manchester Royal Infirmary, 1855–83; lecturer on anatomy and physiology at Royal [Pine Street] School of Medicine, Manchester; lecturer on pathology, 1859, and on principles and practice of medicine, 1863, at Owens College; first joint-professor of medicine at the Victoria University, 1873–6; F.R.C.P., 1865; F.R.S., 1877; knighted, 1885; fellow (1892) of London University, which he represented on the General Medical Council, 1896–9; published medical treatises. [Suppl. iii. 298]

ROBERTS, WILLIAM HAYWARD (*d.* 1791), poet and biblical critic; M.A. King's College, Cambridge, 1760; created D.D. Cambridge, 1773; became a fellow of Eton College, 1771, and provost, 1781; principal work 'Judah Restored' (1774), a poem in blank verse. [xlviii. 397]

ROBERTS, WILLIAM PROWTING (1806–1871), solicitor and trades-union advocate; educated at Charterhouse School; practised as a solicitor at Bath, and became associated with the leading chartists; concerned in nearly all the law affairs of the trades-unions from 1843. [xlviii. 398]

ROBERTSON, LORD (1794–1855). [See ROBERTSON, PATRICK.]

ROBERTSON, ABRAHAM (1751–1826), astronomer and mathematician; M.A. Christ Church, Oxford, 1782; F.R.S., 1795; Savilian professor of geometry, 1797–1810, of astronomy, 1810–26; chief work 'Sectionum Conicarum Libri VII,' 1792. [xlviii. 398]

ROBERTSON, ALEXANDER, thirteenth BARON OF STRUAN (1670?–1749), educated at St. Andrews; succeeded his father as baron of Struan and chief of the clan Robertson, 1688; joined Dundee and was attainted, and escaped to France; obtained a remission, 1703, and joined Mar, 1715; was taken at Sheriffmuir, but escaped to France; obtained a remission, 1731, and took no active part in the rising of 1745. [xlviii. 399]

ROBERTSON, ANDREW (1777–1845), miniature-painter; brother of Archibald Robertson (1765–1835) [q. v.]; studied at Marischal College, Aberdeen; started practice as a miniature-painter at Aberdeen; came to London, 1801, and became a leading miniature-painter. [xlviii. 401]

ROBERTSON, ARCHIBALD (1765–1835), miniature-painter; educated at Aberdeen; came to London, 1786, and thence removed to New York, where he painted Washington and other leading Americans, and became a prominent citizen. [xlviii. 401]

ROBERTSON, ARCHIBALD (d. 1847), major-general; entered the East India Company's service, 1800; major-general, 1837; elected a director, 1840. [xlviii. 402]

ROBERTSON, ARCHIBALD (1789–1864), medical writer; M.D. Edinburgh, 1817; settled at Northampton, 1818, after serving as assistant-surgeon in the navy; physician to the Northampton infirmary, 1820–53; F.R.S., 1836. [xlviii. 402]

ROBERTSON, BARTHOLOMEW (fl. 1617–1620), divine; published devotional works. [xlviii. 403]

ROBERTSON, DAVID (1795–1854), bookseller; carried on business at the Trongate, Glasgow, from 1823; gradually added publishing to his original trade. [xlviii. 403]

ROBERTSON, DONALD (fl. 1636–1660), tutor of Struan; the son of the tenth Baron of Struan; became head of the clan during the minority of his nephew, Alexander; joined Montrose, 1645; rewarded with a pension at the Restoration. [xlviii. 403]

ROBERTSON, EBEN WILLIAM (1815–1874), historical writer; B.A. Worcester College, Oxford, 1837; barrister, Lincoln's Inn, 1845; was high sheriff and deputy-lieutenant of Leicestershire; published (1862) 'Scotland and her Early Kings,' and 'Historical Essays,' 1872. [xlviii. 404]

ROBERTSON, FREDERICK WILLIAM (1816–1853), divine; educated at Edinburgh University and Brasenose College, Oxford; M.A., 1844; ordained, 1840; became incumbent of Trinity Chapel, Brighton, 1847; gradually acquired great influence among all ecclesiastical parties throughout England, while belonging exclusively to none; his 'Literary Remains,' which include 'Two Lectures on the Influence of Poetry on the Working Classes,' 1852, and a translation of Lessing's 'Education of the Human Race,' published, 1876; his 'Life and Letters' published by the Rev. Stopford A. Brooke, 1865. [xlviii. 404]

ROBERTSON, GEORGE (1748?–1788), landscape-painter; studied in London and Rome; exhibited at the Incorporated Society of Artists' exhibitions. [xlviii. 407]

ROBERTSON, GEORGE (1750?–1832), topographical writer; published several works, including a 'Topographical Description of Ayrshire,' 1820, and 'Rural Recollections,' 1829. [xlviii. 407]

ROBERTSON, GEORGE CROOM (1842–1892), philosopher; educated at Marischal College, Aberdeen; M.A., 1861; elected professor of mental philosophy and logic in University College, London, 1866; became editor of 'Mind,'

1876; published a monograph upon Hobbes in Blackwood's 'Philosophical Classics,' 1886. In philosophy his affinities were chiefly with the school represented by the Mills and Bain. [xlviii. 408]

ROBERTSON, JAMES (1720?–1788), governor of New York; entered the army as a private; obtained a commission, 1740; made governor of New York, 1779; lieutenant-general, 1782. [xlviii. 409]

ROBERTSON, JAMES (1714–1795), orientalist; studied under Schultens at Leyden and graduated there; was professor of Hebrew at Edinburgh University, 1751–1795; published 'Grammatica Linguæ Hebrææ,' 1758. [xlviii. 409]

ROBERTSON, JAMES (d. 1820), Benedictine monk; entered the monastery of the Scottish Benedictines at Ratisbon at an early age, and was afterwards a priest in Galloway; employed by Canning on a secret political mission in Denmark, 1808; returned (1815) to Ratisbon, where he interested himself in the education of the deaf and dumb. [xlviii. 410]

ROBERTSON, JAMES (1783–1858). [See WALKER, JAMES ROBERTSON-.]

ROBERTSON, JAMES (1803–1860), divine; M.A. Aberdeen, 1820; became minister of Ellon, 1832, and (1843) professor of divinity and church history in Edinburgh University; moderator of the general assembly, 1856. [xlviii. 410]

ROBERTSON, JAMES BURTON (1800–1877), historian; translated Schlegel's 'Philosophy of History,' 1835, and Möhler's 'Symbolism,' 1843; became professor of geography and modern history in the Roman catholic university of Dublin, 1855. [xlviii. 411]

ROBERTSON, JAMES CRAIGIE (1813–1882), canon of Canterbury; M.A. Trinity College, Cambridge, 1838; ordained, 1836; canon of Canterbury, 1859; published his 'Church History' between 1850 and 1873, and issued a revised edition, 1874–5; published also 'Becket: a Biography,' 1859, and other works. [xlviii. 412]

ROBERTSON, JOHN (1712–1776), mathematician; mathematical master at Christ's Hospital, London, 1748–1755; first master of the Royal Naval Academy at Portsmouth, 1755–66, and clerk and librarian to the Royal Society, 1768–76. [xlviii. 413]

ROBERTSON, JOHN (1767–1810), minor poet; a native of Paisley; wrote several lyrics; committed suicide near Portsmouth. [xlviii. 413]

ROBERTSON, SIR JOHN (1816–1891), Australian statesman; emigrated to New South Wales in early childhood, and in 1835 became a squatter; returned to the New South Wales legislative assembly in the liberal interest, 1856, subsequently holding other seats, and (1858) joined the Cowper ministry; formed (1860) his first ministry, which went out of office, 1863; again premier, 1860–70, 1875–March 1877, August–December 1877, and 1885; opposed the federation movement, and advocated free trade. [xlviii. 413]

ROBERTSON, JOHN PARISH (1792–1843), merchant and author; a Scottish merchant; devoted himself to opening South America to British trade; published several works on Paraguay and La Plata. [xlviii. 415]

ROBERTSON, JOSEPH (1726–1802), divine; B.A. Queen's College, Oxford, 1749; became vicar of Horncastle, 1779; had considerable reputation as a literary critic, writing in the 'Critical Review' and the 'Gentleman's Magazine.' [xlviii. 415]

ROBERTSON, JOSEPH (1810–1866), Scottish historian and record scholar; studied at Marischal College, Aberdeen; intimate friend of John Hill Burton [q. v.]; assisted (1839) to found the Spalding Club; appointed historical curator of the records in the Edinburgh Register House, 1853; edited 'Concilia Ecclesiæ Scoticanæ' for the Bannatyne Club, 1866. [xlviii. 416]

ROBERTSON, JOSEPH CLINTON (1788–1852), joint compiler of the 'Percy Anecdotes'; was by trade a patent agent in Fleet Street, London; published with Thomas Byerley [q. v.] 'The Percy Anecdotes' (1821–3) in twenty volumes. [xlviii. 417]

ROBERTSON, PATRICK, LORD ROBERTSON (1794–1855), Scottish judge; called to the Scottish bar, 1815;

was appointed a lord of session, 1843; lord rector of Marischal College and university of Aberdeen, and made LL.D., 1848; named by Scott 'Peter o' the Painch' from the rotundity of his figure; published indifferent verse. [xlviii. 417]

ROBERTSON, ROBERT (1742–1829), physician; served in the navy as surgeon's mate and surgeon (1761–1791); created M.D. Aberdeen, 1779; physician to Greenwich Hospital, 1793; F.R.S., 1804; published medical observations. [xlviii. 418]

ROBERTSON or **ROBINSON**, THOMAS (*fl.* 1520–1561), dean of Durham; of Queen's and Magdalen Colleges, Oxford; M.A., 1525; became master of Magdalen College School, 1526, and treasurer of Salisbury Cathedral, 1540; dean of Durham, 1557, deprived, 1559; assisted in compiling Lily's 'Latin Grammar.' [xlviii. 418]

ROBERTSON, THOMAS (*d.* 1799), divine; minister of Dalmeny, 1775–99; hon. D.D. Edinburgh, 1792; published a 'History of Mary Queen of Scots,' 1793, and other works. [xlviii. 419]

ROBERTSON, THOMAS CAMPBELL (1789–1863), Indian civil servant; entered the Bengal civil service, 1805; became a member of the supreme council, 1838, and lieutenant-governor of the North-west Provinces, 1840; retired, 1843. [xlviii. 419]

ROBERTSON, THOMAS WILLIAM (1829–1871), actor and dramatist; appeared at Wisbech, 1834, as Rob Roy's son; came to London, 1848; produced his first piece, 'A Night's Adventures,' at the Olympic, 1851; married Elizabeth Burton, 1856, and acted with her in various parts of Ireland and England; retired from the stage and wrote and translated plays for Lacy, and finally produced 'David Garrick,' which was well received at the Haymarket in 1864; subsequently produced 'Society' (1865) and 'Ours' (1866), which established his reputation, and in 1867 reached his high-water mark in 'Caste'; continued to write plays in rapid succession till his death. [xlviii. 420]

ROBERTSON, WILLIAM (*d.* 1686?), lexicographer; graduated at Edinburgh; was appointed university teacher of Hebrew at Cambridge, 1680; published numerous treatises on the Hebrew language. [xlviii. 423]

ROBERTSON, WILLIAM (1705–1783), theological writer; M.A. Glasgow, 1724; distinguished himself in 1725 by successfully resisting the usurpation by the principal of the students' right to elect the rector of Glasgow University; was ordained deacon, 1728, and subsequently received several Irish preferments; he adopted heterodox opinions, *c.* 1760, and resigned his benefices, 1764; removed to London, 1767; made D.D. Glasgow, 1768; afterwards removed to Wolverhampton, where he finally became a unitarian. He had considerable reputation as a pamphleteer. [xlviii. 423]

ROBERTSON, WILLIAM (1721–1793), historian; educated at Edinburgh University; presented to the parish of Gladsmuir, 1743, and transferred to Lady Yester's Chapel at Edinburgh, 1756; commenced, 1753, his 'History of Scotland,' which was published in 1759, and met with enormous success; appointed principal of Edinburgh University, 1762; elected moderator of the general assembly, and made historiographer for Scotland, 1763; published his 'History of Charles V,' 1769, which rendered his fame European, his 'Introduction,' an estimate of the 'dark ages,' being one of the first successful attempts in England at historical generalisation on the basis of large accumulations of fact; published a fascinating 'History of America,' 1777, in which the part relating to the English colonies was hindered from completion by the outbreak of the American war; spent his later years in retirement, but retained his post as principal of Edinburgh University till 1792. The best collective edition of his works was published at Oxford in eight volumes, 1825. [xlviii. 425]

ROBERTSON, WILLIAM (1740–1803), deputy-keeper of the records of Scotland; studied at King's College, Aberdeen; became secretary to the Earl of Findlater and Seafield, 1766; appointed deputy-keeper of the records, 1773; besides publishing several important manuscripts, commenced to issue 'The Records of the Parliament of Scotland,' of which one volume appeared before his death. [xlviii. 430]

ROBERTSON, WILLIAM BRUCE (1820–1886), divine; studied at Glasgow and Halle; minister of the secession church at Irvine, 1843–78; famous as a preacher, and author of a well-known translation of 'Dies Iræ.' [xlviii. 431]

ROBERTSON, SIR WILLIAM TINDAL (1825–1889), physician; matriculated at London University; M.D. Edinburgh, 1853; practised at Nottingham, and for nearly twenty years acted as physician to the Nottingham general hospital; F.R.C.P., 1874; M.P., Brighton, 1886; knighted, 1888. [xlviii. 432]

ROBERTSON, MRS. WYBROW (1847–1884). [See LITTON, MARIE.]

ROBETHON, JOHN (*d.* 1722), secretary to George I; a Huguenot refugee; came to England, *c.* 1689, and was employed by William III; on William's death entered the service of George William, duke of Zell, and in 1705 that of George Lewis, afterwards George I, in which latter capacity he dealt with the correspondence of George with the English whigs; accompanied George I to England, 1715, and was used by Sunderland to alienate George I from Walpole; his influence diminished on Walpole's return to power. [xlviii. 432]

ROBIN HOOD. [See HOOD, ROBIN.]

ROBIN OF REDESDALE (*fl.* 1469), rebel captain; led a rising in Yorkshire against Edward IV, instigated by Warwick and Clarence, 1469. He was doubtless either Sir William Conyers (*d.* 1495) of Marske, or his brother, Sir John Conyers of Hornby, who afterwards made his peace with Edward IV and was a favourite of Henry VII. [xlviii. 433]

ROBIN DDU O FON (1744?–1785). [See HUGHES, ROBERT.]

ROBIN DDU O'R GLYN (1769?–1835). [See DAVIES, ROBERT.]

ROBIN AB GWILYM DDU (1767–1850). [See WILLIAMS, ROBERT.]

ROBINS, BENJAMIN (1707–1751), mathematician and military engineer; became distinguished in early life as a mathematician and afterwards as a pamphleteer; F.R.S., 1727; Copley medallist, 1747; published (1742) his best-known work, 'New Principles of Gunnery,' which was translated into German by Euler; went to India as engineer-general to repair the forts of the East India Company, 1749; died in Madras. His 'Mathematical Tracts' (2 vols.) were published in 1761 by James Wilson. [xlviii. 434]

ROBINS, GEORGE HENRY (1778–1847), auctioneer; began to exercise his trade at the age of nineteen, and was in much request for fifty years through his ready wit and power of repartee; his most notable sale, that of Horace Walpole's collections at Strawberry Hill, 1842. [xlviii. 436]

ROBINS, JOHN (1500?–1558), astrologer; elected fellow of All Souls College, Oxford, 1520; made a canon of Christ Church, Oxford, 1532; M.A.; B.D., 1531; canon of Windsor, 1543; chaplain successively to Henry VIII and Queen Mary; left several astrological tracts in manuscript. [xlviii. 437]

ROBINS, JOHN (*fl.* 1650–1652), ranter; a small farmer, sold his land and came to London, where he was known as 'the ranters' god,' and claimed power to raise the dead; thrown into Clerkenwell prison, 1651; set at liberty in 1652 on recantation. [xlviii. 437]

ROBINS, SANDERSON (1801–1862), divine; M.A. Exeter College, Oxford, 1825; held several benefices in the south of England; a broad churchman; published pamphlets on education, advocating in his 'Letter to . . . Lord John Russell,' 1851, state education on the lines subsequently carried out in the act of 1870. [xlviii. 438]

ROBINSON, ANASTASIA, afterwards COUNTESS OF PETERBOROUGH (*d.* 1755), singer; studied under Dr. Croft and Sandoni; performed on operatic stage, 1714–1724; married Lord Peterborough secretly, *c.* 1722, and publicly at Bristol, 1735; conducted a musical academy at Parson's Green. [xlix. 1]

ROBINSON, ANTHONY (1762–1827), unitarian; pastor of baptist church, Worship Street, London; sugar refiner in London, 1796; published historical and other writings. [xlix. 3]

ROBINSON, BENJAMIN (1666–1724), presbyterian divine ; minister at Findern, 1688, Hungerford, 1693, and Little St. Helen, Bishopsgate Street, London, 1700 ; lecturer at Salters' Hall, 1705 ; published writings on doctrine of Trinity. [xlix. 3]

ROBINSON, BRYAN (1680–1754), physician ; M.D. Trinity College, Dublin, 1711 ; professor of physic, 1745 ; fellow, 1712, and president, 1718, 1727, and 1739, of King and Queen's College of Physicians ; practised in Dublin ; published mathematical and medical works. [xlix. 4]

ROBINSON, Sir BRYAN (1808 – 1887), colonial judge ; educated at Trinity College, Dublin ; called to bar in Nova Scotia, 1831 ; master of chancery, 1834 ; Q.C. and member of executive council, 1843 ; puisne judge, 1858–78 ; knighted, 1877 ; died in England. [xlix. 5]

ROBINSON, Sir CHRISTOPHER (1766 – 1833), admiralty lawyer ; M.A. Magdalen College, Oxford, 1789 ; D.C.L., 1796 ; entered College of Advocates, 1796 ; knighted and appointed king's advocate, 1809 ; tory M.P. for Callington, 1818–20 ; chancellor of diocese of London, and judge of consistory court, 1821 ; judge of high court of admiralty, 1828 ; privy councillor, 1828 ; published legal writings. [xlix. 5]

ROBINSON, CLEMENT (fl. 1566–1584), song-writer ; edited and probably contributed to ' A Boke of very pleasaunte Sonettes,' 1566 (not extant : reprinted, 1584, with title, ' A Handefull of pleasant Delites '). [xlix. 6]

ROBINSON, DANIEL GEORGE (1826–1877), colonel, royal engineers ; studied at Addiscombe ; first lieutenant, Bengal engineers, 1847 ; appointed to Indian survey, 1850 ; lieutenant-colonel, 1862 ; director-general of Indian telegraphs, 1865 ; colonel, 1874 ; died at sea. [xlix. 6]

ROBINSON, FREDERICK JOHN, Viscount Gode-rich, afterwards first Earl of Ripon (1782–1859), son of Thomas Robinson, second baron Grantham [q. v.] ; educated at Harrow and St. John's College, Cambridge ; M.A., 1802 ; entered Lincoln's Inn, 1802 ; tory M.P. for Carlow borough, 1806, and Ripon, 1807 ; under-secretary for colonies, 1809 ; lord of admiralty, 1810 ; privy councillor, 1812 ; joint paymaster-general of forces, 1813–17 ; introduced bill (which was passed) prohibiting importation of corn until average price of wheat in England should be 80s. per quarter, 1815 ; chancellor of exchequer, 1823–7 ; obtained grant towards erection of building at British Museum to receive Royal Library, 1823 ; introduced extensive fiscal reforms ; created Viscount Goderich, 1827 ; secretary for war, commissioner for Indian affairs, and leader of House of Lords, 1827 ; prime minister after Canning's death, August 1827 ; resigned, 1828 ; secretary for war and colonies, 1830 ; resigned and accepted post of lord privy seal, 1833 ; created Earl of Ripon, 1833 ; resigned office, 1834 ; president of the board of trade, 1841 ; president of the board of control for Indian affairs, 1843–6 ; D.C.L. Oxford, 1839 ; F.R.S., 1828. [xlix. 7]

ROBINSON, Sir FREDERICK PHILIPSE (1763–1852), general ; born near New York ; ensign in loyal American regiment in war of independence, 1777 ; lieutenant, 38th foot, 1780 ; major, 127th foot, 1794 ; colonel, 1810 ; commanded brigade in Spain, 1812–14, and in Canada, 1814–16 ; major-general, 1814 ; commanded troops in Windward and Leeward islands, 1816–21 ; governor of Tobago ; colonel, 59th regiment, 1827, and of 39th, 1840 ; G.C.B., 1838 ; general, 1841. [xlix. 11]

ROBINSON, GEORGE (1737 – 1801), bookseller ; worked before 1764 with Rivington the publisher. [xlix. 12]

ROBINSON, HASTINGS (1792–1866), divine ; of Rugby and St. John's College, Cambridge ; M.A., 1818 ; D.D., 1836 ; fellow and assistant-tutor, 1816–27 ; held living of Great Warley, 1827 ; honorary canon of Rochester, 1862 ; F.S.A., 1824 ; edited classical and other works. [xlix. 13]

ROBINSON, HENRY (1553 ?–1616), bishop of Carlisle ; M.A. Queen's College, Oxford, 1575 ; fellow, 1575 ; D.D., 1590 ; principal of St. Edmund Hall, Oxford, 1576–1581 ; provost of Queen's College, Oxford, 1581–98 ; bishop of Carlisle, 1598–1616 ; commissioner for ecclesiastical causes, 1599 ; entered Gray's Inn, 1601 ; took part in Hampton Court conference, 1603. [xlix. 13]

ROBINSON, HENRY (1605 ?–1664 ?), merchant and economical writer ; of St. John's College, Oxford ; freeman of Mercers' Company, 1626 ; comptroller for sale of royal lands, 1653 ; published works on economical questions, and in his controversial writings opposed William Prynne. [xlix. 14]

ROBINSON, HENRY CRABB (1775–1867), diarist ; articled as attorney at Colchester ; entered solicitor's office in London, 1796 ; travelled in Germany and Bohemia, and met Goethe and Schiller, 1800–2 ; studied at Jena University, 1802–5 ; ' Times ' correspondent at Altona ; foreign editor of ' Times ' ; special ' Times ' correspondent in Peninsula, 1808–9 ; barrister, Middle Temple, 1813 ; leader of the Norfolk circuit ; retired, 1828 ; he was a founder of the Athenæum Club and of University College, London, and was acquainted with many notable persons of his day ; F.S.A., 1829 ; his ' Diary ' and ' Letters ' published posthumously. [xlix. 15]

ROBINSON, HERCULES (1789 – 1864), admiral ; brother of Sir Bryan Robinson [q. v.] ; entered navy, 1800 ; lieutenant, 1807 ; served in Baltic and Atlantic ; post captain, 1814 ; commander-in-chief regulating fishery on Labrador coast, 1820 ; retired, 1846 ; vice-admiral, 1856 ; admiral, 1862. [xlix. 17]

ROBINSON, Sir HERCULES GEORGE ROBERT, first Baron Rosmead (1824–1897), colonial governor ; son of Hercules Robinson [q. v.] ; educated at Sandhurst ; first lieutenant, 87th regiment, 1844 ; retired, 1846 ; president of Montserrat, West Indies, 1854 ; lieutenant-governor of St. Christopher, 1855 ; governor of Hongkong, 1859–65, Ceylon, 1865–72, and New South Wales, 1872–9 ; negotiated cession of Fiji islands, 1874 ; governor of New Zealand, 1879–80 ; governor of Cape Colony and high commissioner of South Africa, 1880–9 ; negotiated terms of peace with the Boers, 1881 ; came to England to assist in settling revised convention, 1884 ; obtained despatch of Sir Charles Warren's expedition, which resulted in annexation of Bechuanaland to British dominions, 1885, concluded treaty with Lobengula, largely due to energy of Cecil Rhodes, 1888 ; created baronet, 1891 ; returned to South Africa as governor, 1895 ; negotiated (1896) at Pretoria for release of men who, without Robinson's sanction or knowledge, had raided (1895), under Dr. Jameson, the frontier of the South African republic ; raised to English peerage, 1896 ; retired from governorship, 1897 ; knighted, 1859 ; G.C.M.G., 1875 ; privy councillor, 1882. [Suppl. iii. 300]

ROBINSON, HUGH (1584 ?–1655), divine ; of Winchester and New College, Oxford ; M.A., 1611 ; D.D., 1627 ; chief master of Winchester School, 1613–27 ; canon of Lincoln, 1625 ; archdeacon of Gloucester, 1634 ; lost canonry and archdeaconry during civil war ; took covenant and accepted from parliament living of Hinton ; published educational works. [xlix. 17]

ROBINSON, JOHN (d. 1598), divine ; B.A. and fellow, Pembroke Hall, Cambridge, 1554 ; M.A., 1557 ; incorporated at Oxford, 1563 ; president of St. John's College, Oxford, 1564–72 ; B.D., 1567 ; D.D. Cambridge, 1583 ; archdeacon of Lincoln, 1586 ; canon of Gloucester, 1594. [xlix. 18]

ROBINSON, JOHN (1576 ?–1625), pastor of the pilgrim fathers ; probably studied at Cambridge ; held a cure at Norwich, and is said to have held and been suspended from a benefice in Norfolk ; emigrated to Amsterdam and joined separatists, 1608 ; removed, with a section of the community, to Leyden, and was ordained pastor, William Brewster [q. v.] being a ruling elder, 1609 ; entered Leyden University, 1615 ; signed, with Brewster, ' seven articles ' presented to privy council detailing scheme for emigration to America, 1617 ; perhaps wrote address alleged to have been delivered on departure of pilgrims in charge of Brewster, 1620 ; died at Leyden ; published controversial works. [xlix. 18]

ROBINSON, JOHN (1617–1681), royalist ; of Christ Church, Oxford ; entered Gray's Inn, 1637 ; lieutenant-colonel of royalist forces, 1643 ; deprived of estates by parliament ; fled to Isle of Man and France ; returned on Restoration ; M.P., Beaumaris, 1661–79 ; vice-admiral of North Wales, 1666–81. [xlix. 22]

ROBINSON, JOHN (1650–1723), bishop of London ; M.A. Brasenose College, Oxford, 1684 ; fellow of Oriel

College, 1675–86 ; D.D. Lambeth, 1696, and Oxford, 1710 ; chaplain (c. 1680) to English embassy at Swedish court, where he remained more than twenty-five years, and during absence of Philip Warwick, the envoy, filled successively posts of resident and envoy extraordinary ; held benefice of Lastingham, 1697–1709 ; accompanied Charles XII to Narva, 1700 ; interpreter to Marlborough during negotiations with Sweden, 1707 ; returned to England, and was appointed dean of Windsor and of Wolverhampton and registrar of knights of Garter, 1709 ; bishop of Bristol, 1710 ; governor of London Charter-house and dean of Chapel Royal, London ; lord privy seal, 1711 ; appointed first English plenipotentiary at peace conference at Utrecht, 1712, and was first to sign treaty, 1713 ; bishop of London, 1714–23 ; privy councillor, 1714 ; published sermons and an 'Account of Sueden' (1695). [xlix. 23]

ROBINSON, JOHN (1715–1745), portrait-painter. [xlix. 26]

ROBINSON, JOHN (1682–1762), organist of Westminster Abbey, 1727 till death. [xlix. 26]

ROBINSON, JOHN (1727–1802), politician ; articled to Richard Wordsworth, attorney, grandfather of the poet ; practised as attorney in St. Lawrence, Appleby ; entered Gray's Inn, 1759 ; tory M.P. for Westmoreland, 1764–74 ; secretary of treasury, 1770–82 ; M.P., Harwich, 1774–1802 ; D.C.L. Oxford, 1773 ; surveyor-general of woods and forests, 1787 ; mentioned in 'Rolliad,' 'Probationary Odes,' and Junius's letters. [xlix. 26]

ROBINSON, JOHN, D.D. (1774–1840), divine ; master of Ravenstonedale grammar school, 1795–1818 ; held livings in Westmoreland, 1818–40 ; published scholastic and other works. [xlix. 28]

ROBINSON, SIR JOHN BEVERLEY, first baronet (1791–1863), chief-justice of Upper Canada ; born at Berthier, Quebec ; entered attorney's office ; volunteer in militia in American war ; clerk of house of assembly for Upper Canada, 1814 ; called to bar, c. 1815 ; solicitor-general, 1815 ; attorney-general, 1818 ; member of assembly ; speaker of legislative council, 1828–40 ; chief-justice of Upper Canada, 1829 ; C.B., 1850 ; created baronet, 1854 ; D.C.L. Oxford, 1855. [xlix. 28]

ROBINSON, JOHN HENRY (1796–1871), line-engraver ; practised as portrait-engraver and book-illustrator ; with eight other engravers petitioned House of Commons for investigation into state of the art of engraving in this country, 1836 ; A.R.A., 1856 ; R.A., 1867. [xlix. 29]

ROBINSON, MRS. MARTHA WALKER (1822–1888), married the Rev. John Robinson, 1861 ; compiled, under maiden name (Freer) works on French history. [xlix. 30]

ROBINSON, MARY (1758–1800), known as 'Perdita' ; actress, author, and mistress of George, prince of Wales (afterwards George IV) ; née Darby ; born at Bristol and educated there and at Chelsea (where she afterwards kept a school with her mother) and Marylebone ; became acquainted with Thomas Hull [q. v.] and David Garrick ; secretly married Thomas Robinson, 1774 ; imprisoned for debt in King's Bench prison ; through Garrick's influence appeared successfully as Juliet at Drury Lane, London, 1776 ; played Lady Anne in 'Richard III,' 1777, and other Shakespearean parts ; attracted (1778) attention of Prince of Wales and became his mistress ; deserted by prince ; received pension from Fox ; devoted herself to literature ; produced several poems, plays, and stories, and is said to have taken part under various signatures in the Della Cruscan literature. Her portrait was painted by Reynolds, Romney, Hoppner, Gainsborough, and others. [xlix. 30]

ROBINSON, MARY (fl. 1802), called 'Mary of Buttermere' ; a noted Cumberland beauty ; was married, under false pretences, by the impostor John Hatfield [q. v.], 1802, and on account of the imposition practised upon her became the subject of numerous verses, dramas, and tales. [xxv. 153]

ROBINSON, MATTHEW (1628–1694), divine and physician ; M.A. St. John's College, Cambridge, 1652 ; fellow, 1650 ; held living of Burneston, 1651–82 ; licensed as physician ; published 'Annotations on New Testament,' 1690. [xlix. 33]

ROBINSON, NICHOLAS (d. 1585), divine ; M.A. Queens' College, Cambridge, 1551 ; fellow ; D.D., 1566 ; bursar, 1551–3 ; dean, 1578 ; university proctor, 1552 ;

vice-president, 1561 ; subscribed Roman catholic articles, 1555 ; ordained, 1557 ; archdeacon of Merioneth, 1562 ; bishop of Bangor, 1566–85 ; supported protestant cause ; took considerable interest in Welsh history and made translations from Welsh. [xlix. 34]

ROBINSON, NICHOLAS (1697 ?–1775), physician ; native of Wales ; M.D. Rheims, 1718 ; practised in London ; L.R.C.P., 1727 ; published medical works. [xlix. 36]

ROBINSON, PETER FREDERICK (1776–1858), architect ; F.S.A., 1826 ; one of first vice-presidents of Institute of British Architects, 1835–9 ; published architectural works. [xlix. 36]

ROBINSON, RALPH (fl. 1551), translator ; M.A. Corpus Christi College, Oxford, 1544 ; fellow, 1542 ; liveryman of Goldsmiths' Company ; clerk in service of Cecil (afterwards Lord Burghley) ; published translation of More's 'Utopia,' 1551. [xlix. 37]

ROBINSON, RALPH (1614–1655), puritan divine ; M.A. St. Catharine Hall, Cambridge, 1642 ; presbyterian minister of St. Mary Woolnoth, Lombard Street, London, c. 1642 ; imprisoned on charge of complicity in conspiracy of Christopher Love [q. v.] ; pardoned. [xlix. 37]

ROBINSON, RICHARD (fl. 1574), servant in household of Earl of Shrewsbury. Published poetical writings. [xlix. 38]

ROBINSON, RICHARD (fl. 1576–1600), author and compiler ; sometimes erroneously identified with preceding ; freeman of Leathersellers' Company ; co-operated with Thomas Churchyard [q. v.] in translating Meteren's 'Historiæ Belgicæ' (1602), and published other works. [xlix. 37]

ROBINSON, RICHARD, first BARON ROKEBY in Irish peerage (1709–1794), divine ; of Westminster and Christ Church, Oxford ; M.A., 1733 ; B.D. and D.D., 1748 ; prebendary of York, 1738 ; chaplain to Duke of Dorset ; lord-lieutenant of Ireland, 1751 ; bishop of Killala, 1752, of Leighlin and Ferns, 1759, and Kildare, 1761 ; dean of Christ Church, Dublin, 1761 ; archbishop of Armagh, 1765 ; vice-chancellor of Dublin University ; created Baron Rokeby of Armagh, 1777 ; first prelate of order of St. Patrick ; a lord justice for Ireland, 1787 ; did much to beautify the town and cathedral of Armagh. [xlix. 39]

ROBINSON, ROBERT (1735–1790), baptist minister and hymn-writer ; joined Calvinists, 1755 ; assistant-minister at Norwich Tabernacle, c. 1758 ; seceded and formed independent church in St. Paul's parish, Norwich ; pastor of Stone Yard Baptist Chapel, Cambridge, 1761 ; published religious controversial and other works ; wrote eleven hymns issued by Whitefield, 1757. [xlix. 40]

ROBINSON, ROBERT (1727 ?–1791), dissenting minister ; educated at Plaisterers' Hall, London ; minister at Old Chapel, Dukinfield, 1752–5, and at Dob Lane chapel, near Manchester, 1755–77 ; published several discourses. [xlix. 43]

ROBINSON, SIR ROBERT SPENCER (1809–1889), admiral ; entered navy, 1821 ; commander, 1838 ; held command in Channel fleet, 1850–2, and in Baltic, 1855 ; controller of navy, 1861–71 ; lord of admiralty, 1868–71 ; vice-admiral, 1866 ; civil K.C.B., 1868 ; admiral, 1871. [xlix. 43]

ROBINSON, SAMUEL (1794–1884), Persian scholar ; educated at Manchester New College (then at York) ; in business as cotton manufacturer successively at Manchester and Dukinfield ; retired, 1860 ; president of Manchester New College, 1867–71 ; published translations from the German and Persian. [xlix. 44]

ROBINSON, SIR SEPTIMUS (1710–1765), brother of Richard Robinson, baron Rokeby [q. v.] ; of Christ Church, Oxford ; served with French army, and subsequently with English in Flanders ; lieutenant-colonel, 1754 ; knighted, 1760. [xlix. 40]

ROBINSON, SIR TANCRED (d. 1748), physician and naturalist ; M.B. St. John's College, Cambridge, 1679 ; F.R.S., 1684 ; M.D. Cambridge, 1685 ; F.R.C.P., 1687, and censor, 1693 and 1717 ; physician-in-ordinary to George I, by whom he was knighted ; contributed to 'Philosophical Transactions,' and wrote on natural history. [xlix. 45]

ROBINSON, THOMAS (fl. 1520–1561). [See ROBERTSON.]

ROBINSON, THOMAS (*fl.* 1588–1603), lutenist and composer ; born in England ; practised profession at court of Denmark ; published a book of musical instruction, 1603. [xlix. 46]

ROBINSON, THOMAS (*fl.* 1622), pamphleteer ; probably studied at Cambridge ; went to sea ; entered English nunnery at Lisbon as secretary and mass-priest ; published in London an account of the immoral practices of the inmates, 1622. [xlix. 46]

ROBINSON, THOMAS (*d.* 1719), author ; rector of Ousby, 1672–1719 ; published works on natural history. [xlix. 46]

ROBINSON, THOMAS (*d.* 1747), entered Lincoln's Inn, 1730 ; published 'Common Law of Kent,' 1741. [xlix. 47]

ROBINSON, THOMAS, first BARON GRANTHAM (1695–1770), diplomatist ; of Westminster and Trinity College, Cambridge ; minor fellow, 1719 ; secretary to English embassy at Paris, 1723 ; M.P. for Thirsk, 1727–34 ; one of the three English representatives at congress of Soissons, 1728–9 ; ambassador at Vienna, 1730–48 ; represented England in negotiations with Maria Theresa and Frederick the Great, 1740–8 ; joint-plenipotentiary of England in peace negotiations at Aix-la-Chapelle, 1748 ; returned to England, 1748 ; one of lords commissioners of trade ; M.P., Christchurch, 1748–61 ; privy councillor, 1750 ; secretary of state for southern department and leader of House of Commons, 1754–5 ; raised to peerage, 1761 ; joint postmaster-general, 1765–6. [xlix. 47]

ROBINSON, SIR THOMAS, first baronet (1700 ?–1777), called 'Long Sir Thomas,' colonial governor ; brother of Richard Robinson, baron Rokeby [q. v.] ; studied architecture in Greece and Italy ; M.P., Morpeth, 1727 ; married Elizabeth, daughter of Charles Howard, third earl of Carlisle, and widow of Nicholas, lord Lechmere, 1728 ; created baronet, 1731 ; resided at Rokeby in the North Riding, Yorkshire ; commissioner of excise, 1735–42 ; governor of Barbados, 1742–7 ; acquired shares in Ranelagh Gardens, London, and became director of entertainments ; practically made the Rokeby of which Scott wrote, but was compelled to dispose of it in 1769. [xlix. 49]

ROBINSON, THOMAS, second BARON GRANTHAM (1738–1786), eldest son of Thomas Robinson, first baron Grantham [q. v.] ; of Westminster and Christ's College, Cambridge ; M.A. 1757 ; M.P., Christchurch, 1761 ; secretary of British embassy to intended congress at Augsburg, 1761 ; commissioner of trade and plantations, 1766, and first commissioner, 1780–2 ; vice-chamberlain of household and privy councillor, 1770 ; ambassador at Madrid, 1771–9 ; foreign secretary, 1782–3. [xlix. 51]

ROBINSON, THOMAS (1749–1813), divine ; M.A. and fellow, Trinity College, Cambridge, 1775 ; vicar of St. Mary's, Leicester, 1778 ; published religious works. [xlix. 52]

ROBINSON, THOMAS (1790–1873), divine ; educated at Rugby and Trinity College, Cambridge ; M.A., 1816 ; M.A. Oxford, 1839 ; D.D., 1844 ; ordained priest, 1816 ; chaplain to Reginald Heber [q. v.], bishop of Calcutta, 1825 ; lord almoner's professor of Arabic, Cambridge, 1837–54 ; master of the Temple, 1845–69 ; rector of Therfield, 1853–60 ; canon of Rochester, 1854 ; published Persian translation of Old Testament and other works. [xlix. 53]

ROBINSON, THOMAS ROMNEY (1792–1882), astronomer ; B.A. Trinity College, Dublin, 1810 ; fellow, 1814 ; deputy-professor of natural philosophy, Trinity College, Dublin ; in charge of Armagh Observatory, 1823 ; rector of Carrickmacross, 1824–82 ; prebendary of St. Patrick's, Dublin, 1872 ; member of nautical almanac committee, 1830 ; invented cup-anemometer, completed, 1846 ; F.R.A.S., 1830 ; F.R.S., 1856, and royal medallist, 1862 ; president, Royal Irish Academy, 1851–6 ; D.D., LL.D. (Dublin and Cambridge) ; D.C.L. (Oxford) ; wrote on astronomical, physical, and other subjects. [xlix. 53]

ROBINSON, WILLIAM (*d.* 1768), architect and surveyor ; published two technical architectural treatises. [xlix. 55]

ROBINSON, WILLIAM (1720 ?–1775), architect ; clerk of works to Greenwich Hospital, 1746 ; assisted Walpole in executing the plans for Strawberry Hill, 1750–75 ; secretary to board of works. [xlix. 55]

ROBINSON, WILLIAM (1726 ?–1803), friend of Thomas Gray the poet ; educated at Westminster and St. John's College, Cambridge ; fellow, 1752 ; M.A., 1754 ; held various livings. [xlix. 55]

ROBINSON, WILLIAM (1799–1839), portrait-painter ; pupil of Sir Thomas Lawrence [q. v.] [xlix. 56]

ROBINSON, WILLIAM (1777–1848). topographer and solicitor ; barrister, Middle Temple, 1827 ; F.S.A., 1819 ; LL.D. Aberdeen, 1822 ; published legal writings and topographical works relating to London districts. [xlix. 56]

ROBINSON, WILLIAM (*d.* 1870), reporter in the admiralty court ; son of Sir Christopher Robinson [q. v.] ; D.C.L. Balliol College, Oxford, 1829 ; entered College of Advocates, 1830 ; published reports. [xlix. 6]

ROBINSON, SIR WILLIAM CLEAVER FRANCIS (1834–1897), colonial governor ; brother of (Sir) Hercules Robinson, afterwards first baron Rosmead [q. v.] ; held various administrative positions and was governor of Prince Edward Island (whose political union with Canada he assisted to bring about), 1870–3, Western Australia, 1874–7, 1880–3, and 1890–5, Straits Settlements, 1877–80, and South Australia, 1883–9, and acting governor of Victoria, 1889 ; G.C.M.G., 1887 ; published musical compositions. [Suppl. iii. 303]

ROBINSON-MONTAGU, HENRY, sixth BARON ROKEBY in Irish peerage (1798–1883), general ; colonel, 1846 ; commanded division in Crimea ; general, 1869 ; succeeded to peerage, 1847 ; G.C.B., 1875. [xlix. 57]

ROBINSON-MORRIS, MATTHEW, second BARON ROKEBY in Irish peerage (1713–1800), son of Matthew Robinson ; LL.B. Trinity Hall, Cambridge, 1734 ; fellow ; M.P. for Canterbury, 1747 and 1754 ; assumed name of Morris ; succeeded his cousin, Richard Robinson [q. v.], in title, 1794 ; published political pamphlets. [xlix. 56]

ROBINSON-MORRIS, MORRIS (*d.* 1829), nephew of preceding, whom he succeeded as third Baron Rokeby ; published a political pamphlet. [xlix. 57]

ROBISON, JOHN (1739–1805), scientific writer ; M.A. Glasgow, 1756 ; appointed by board of longitude to make trial voyage to Jamaica in charge of John Harrison's chronometer, 1762 ; returned to Glasgow and became acquainted with James Watt ; lecturer on chemistry, Glasgow, 1766 ; anticipated Mayer in discovery that law of force is approximately in inverse square, 1769 ; held with rank of colonel, mathematical chair attached to sea cadet corps, St. Petersburg, 1772 ; professor of natural philosophy, Edinburgh, 1773 ; first general secretary, Royal Society of Edinburgh, 1783 ; published scientific works and contributed to 'Encyclopædia Britannica.' [xlix. 57]

ROBISON, SIR JOHN (1778–1843), inventor ; son of John Robison [q. v.] ; educated at Edinburgh ; entered service of nizam of Hyderabad as contractor for the establishment and maintenance of military service ; left India, 1815 ; one of the founders of Scottish Society of Arts, 1821, secretary, 1822–4, and president, 1841–2 ; knighted, 1838 ; invented many ingenious contrivances, and wrote extensively on scientific subjects. [xlix. 58]

ROBOTHOM, JOHN (*fl.* 1654), divine ; minister of Rumbold's Wyke, *c.* 1648–51 ; preacher at Dover, 1654 ; subsequently minister of Upminster, whence he was ejected, 1660 ; published religious works. [xlix. 59]

ROBSART, AMY (1532 ?–1560). [See DUDLEY, AMYE, LADY.]

ROBSON, CHARLES (1598–1638), divine ; M.A. Queen's College, Oxford, 1619 ; B.D., 1629 ; fellow, 1620–31 ; chaplain at Aleppo, 1624–30 ; vicar of Holme-Cultram, 1632–8 ; published account of journey to Aleppo (1628). [xlix. 60]

ROBSON, EDWARD (1763–1813), author ; nephew of Stephen Robson [q. v.] ; associate of Linnean Society, 1789 ; published botanical writings. [xlix. 62]

ROBSON, GEORGE FENNELL (1788–1833), water-colour painter ; exhibited at Royal Academy from 1807 ; president of Oil and Water-colour Society (now Royal Society of Painters in Water-colours), 1819–20. [xlix. 61]

ROBSON, JAMES (1733–1806), bookseller; entered (*c.* 1749) shop of J. Brindley, New Bond Street, London, whom he succeeded, 1759; high sheriff of Westminster, 1797; member of the Booksellers' Dining Club at the Shakspeare Tavern.   [xlix. 61]

ROBSON, STEPHEN (1741–1779), botanist; linen manufacturer and grocer at Darlington; published botanical works.   [xlix. 62]

ROBSON, THOMAS FREDERICK (1822?–1864), actor; his real name THOMAS ROBSON BROWNHILL; worked as copperplate engraver; joined acting profession and was engaged under Rouse at Grecian Saloon, London, *c.* 1845; in Dublin, 1850–3, playing Bottom in 1851; joined Olympic company, London, 1853; showed remarkable power in burlesque and farce, and in some serious parts; undertook with Emden management of Olympic, 1857. His most successful parts were in the 'Yellow Dwarf' (Planché, 1854), Medea in Brough's 'Medea' (1856), and Sampson Burr in the 'Porter's Knot' (1858). [xlix. 63]

ROBSON, WILLIAM (1785–1863), schoolmaster; published historical and other works and translations from French.   [xlix. 64]

ROBY, JOHN (1793–1850), organist; organist at independent chapel, Rochdale; managing partner in banking firm at Rochdale, 1819; retired, 1847; published poetical and other writings, including 'Traditions of Lancashire,' 1829 and 1831.   [xlix. 65]

ROBY, WILLIAM (1766–1830), congregational divine; brother of John Roby [q. v.]; classical master at Bretherton grammar school, Lancashire; minister in Manchester, 1795–1830; published religious writings.
     [xlix. 65]

ROCHARD, SIMON JACQUES (1788–1872), miniature-painter; born in Paris; patronised by Napoleon I and by court at Brussels; came to London, *c.* 1815; exhibited at Royal Academy, 1816–45; retired (1846) to Brussels, where he died.   [xlix. 66]

ROCHARD, FRANÇOIS THÉODORE (*d.* 1858), portrait-painter; brother of Simon Jacques Rochard [q. v.]; exhibited at Royal Academy, 1820–55.   [xlix. 66]

ROCHE, SIR BOYLE, baronet (1743–1807), politician; entered army; served in American war; obtained office in Irish revenue department, *c.* 1775; M.P. (Irish parliament) for Tralee, and subsequently for Gowran, 1777–83, Portarlington, 1783–90, Tralee, 1790–7, and Old Leighlin, 1798 till the union; created baronet, 1782; chamberlain to vice-regal court; rendered government great services in connection with volunteer convention of 1783; celebrated as a perpetrator of 'bulls.'   [xlix. 66]

ROCHE, DAVID, VISCOUNT FERMOY (1573?–1635), succeeded to title, 1600; loyal during the rebellion of Hugh O'Neill, second earl of Tyrone [q. v.]; rewarded by James I.
     [xlix. 68]

ROCHE, EUGENIUS (1786–1829), journalist; born in Paris; came to London, *c.* 1804; engaged in several unsuccessful journalistic enterprises; editor of the 'Day,' 1810, later of 'National Register,' and (*c.* 1813) of the 'Morning Post.'   [xlix. 68]

ROCHE, JAMES (1770–1853), the 'Roscoe of Cork'; born at Cork; wine merchant at Bordeaux; left France, 1797; established (1800) bank at Cork, which suspended payment, 1819; commercial and parliamentary agent for counties Cork, Youghal, and Limerick, 1819–26; local director at Cork of National Bank of Ireland, 1832–53; contributed to magazines under initials essays on literary topics which evinced much literary taste.   [xlix. 69]

ROCHE, MAURICE, VISCOUNT FERMOY (1595?–1660?), rebel son of David Roche, viscount Fermoy [q. v.]; imprisoned in Dublin for papistical inclinations, 1624; outlawed for share in rebellion, 1643; excepted from pardon, 1652, his estates being sequestrated. [xlix. 68]

ROCHE, MICHAEL DE LA (*fl.* 1710–1731), French protestant refugee; engaged in literary work in London; conducted periodical 'Memoirs of Literature,' 1710–14 and 1717; edited (1717–19) 'Bibliothèque Angloise' (a periodical written in French and published at Amsterdam), and subsequently other periodicals.   [xlix. 69]

ROCHE, PHILIP (*d.* 1798), Irish rebel; Roman catholic priest at Poulpearsay, co. Wexford; joined rebels before battle of Tubberneering, 4 June 1798; elected com-

mander of rebels at Slyeeve-Keelter, near New Ross; captured after battle of Vinegar Hill, and hanged.
     [xlix. 70]

ROCHE, MRS. REGINA MARIA (1764?–1845), novelist; born in Ireland of parents named Dalton; published (1793–1834) sixteen novels, including 'Children of the Abbey,' 1798.   [xlix. 71]

ROCHE, ROBERT (1576–1629), poetaster; B.A. Magdalen Hall, Oxford, 1599; vicar of Hilton, 1617–29; published didactic doggerel verse.   [xlix. 71]

ROCHEAD, JOHN THOMAS (1814–1878), architect; practised in Glasgow, 1841–70.   [xlix. 71]

ROCHES, PETER DES (*d.* 1238). [See PETER.]

ROCHESTER, EARLS OF. [See WILMOT, HENRY, first EARL, 1612?–1658; WILMOT, JOHN, second EARL, 1647–1680; HYDE, LAURENCE, first EARL of the Hyde family, 1641–1711.]

ROCHESTER, COUNTESS OF (*d.* 1725). [See HYDE, JANE.]

ROCHESTER, VISCOUNT (*d.* 1645). [See CARR, ROBERT, afterwards EARL OF SOMERSET.]

ROCHESTER, SIR ROBERT (1494?–1557), comptroller of the household to Queen Mary; attached to Princess Mary's household, of which he managed the finances, 1547, and was appointed comptroller, 1551; imprisoned for refusing to carry the council's orders to Mary forbidding mass in her household, 1551–2; K.B. and comptroller of the royal household. 1553; knight of the shire for Essex, 1553–5; chancellor of duchy of Lancaster, 1554; on royal commission for treaty regarding Queen Mary's marriage with Philip II of Spain.   [xlix. 72]

ROCHESTER, SOLOMON DE (*d.* 1294), judge; took orders; justice in eyre for Middlesex, 1274, Worcestershire, 1275, and subsequently for Essex and other counties; dismissed and fined for maladministration of justice and corruption, 1289; prebendary of St. Paul's Cathedral; probably died by poison.   [xlix. 73]

ROCHFORD, EARLS OF. [See ZUYLESTEIN, WILLIAM HENRY, first EARL, 1645–1709; ZUYLESTEIN, WILLIAM NASSAU DE, second EARL, 1681–1710; ZUYLESTEIN, FREDERICK NASSAU DE, third EARL, 1682–1738; ZUYLESTEIN, WILLIAM HENRY, fourth EARL, 1717–1781.]

ROCHFORD, VISCOUNT (*d.* 1536). [See BOLEYN, GEORGE.]

ROCHFORD, SIR JOHN DE (*fl.* 1390–1410), mediæval writer; knighted before 1386; accompanied Henry IV to Wales, 1405; wrote 'Notabilia extracta . . . de viginti uno libris Flavii Josephi' (finished, 1406).   [xlix. 74]

ROCHFORT, ROBERT (1652–1727), Irish judge; recorder of Londonderry, 1680; joint-commissioner for great seal, 1690; attorney-general of Ireland, M.P., co. Westmeath, and speaker of the Irish House of Commons, 1695; chief baron of exchequer, 1707–14; friend of Swift.
     [xlix. 74]

ROCHFORT, SIMON (*d.* 1224), first English bishop of Meath, 1194; one of judges in suit for possession of body of Hugh de Lacy (*d.* 1186) [q. v.]   [xlix. 75]

ROCK, DANIEL (1799–1871), ecclesiologist; educated at St. Edmund's College, near Ware, and at English College, Rome; ordained priest, 1824; D.D.; engaged on 'London mission,' 1825–7; priest of Roman catholic congregation of Buckland, 1840–54; one of first canons of Southwark Cathedral, 1852; published religious and archæological works.   [xlix. 75]

ROCKINGHAM, second MARQUIS OF (1730–1782). [See WATSON-WENTWORTH, CHARLES.]

ROCKINGHAM, first BARON (1584–1653). [See WATSON, SIR LEWIS.]

ROCKRAY, EDMUND (*d.* 1597), puritan divine; M.A. Queens' College, Cambridge, 1564; B.D., 1570; fellow, *c.* 1560; canon of Rochester, 1577; suspended for nonconformity, 1584–8.   [xlix. 76]

ROCKSTRO, WILLIAM SMITH (1823–1895), musician; pupil of Mendelssohn, Hauptman, and Plaidy; studied at Leipzig, 1845–6; pianist, teacher, and composer in London; devoted his attention to musical archæology and ecclesiastical music; teacher of counterpoint and plain-song in Royal College of Music, 1891 ; published 'General History of Music,' 1886. Among his best compositions is the madrigal 'O too cruel fair' (1883) in the manner of Palestrina. [xlix. 76]

RODD, EDWARD HEARLE (1810–1880), ornithologist ; qualified as solicitor, 1832 ; practised in partnership, 1833–78, at Penzance ; published works on ornithology. [xlix. 77]

RODD, HORATIO (*fl.* 1859), brother of Thomas Rodd the younger [q. v.], with whom he was in partnership ; subsequently picture-dealer and printseller in London ; published miscellaneous writings. [xlix. 78]

RODD, THOMAS, the elder (1763–1822), bookseller ; educated at Charterhouse School, London, and in France ; opened bookseller's shop in London, retiring 1821 ; published poetical and other writings. [xlix. 78]

RODD, THOMAS, the younger (1796–1849), bookseller ; son of Thomas Rodd the elder [q. v.], whom he assisted ; carried on the business from 1821 ; published miscellaneous writings. [xlix. 78]

RODDAM, ROBERT (1719–1808), admiral ; entered navy, 1735 ; lieutenant, 1741 ; commander, 1746 ; postcaptain, 1747 ; served successively in North Sea, at New York, and in the West Indies, where he was captured by French, 1757 ; exchanged, 1759 ; rear-admiral of white, 1778 ; commander-in-chief at Nore ; admiral of the blue, 1793 ; senior admiral of the red. [xlix. 79]

RODEN, EARLS OF. [See JOCELYN, ROBERT, first EARL, 1731–1797 ; JOCELYN, ROBERT, third EARL, 1788–1870.]

RODEN, WILLIAM THOMAS (1817–1892), engraver and portrait-painter. [xlix. 79]

RODERIC THE GREAT (*d.* 877). [See RHODRI MAWR.]

RODERIC O'CONNOR (1116 ?–1198). [See O'CONNOR.]

RODERICK, RICHARD (*d.* 1756), critic and versifier ; M.A. Queens' College, Cambridge, 1736 ; F.R.S., 1750 ; F.S.A., 1752 ; coadjutor of Thomas Edwards (1699–1757) [q. v.] in 'Canons of Criticism.' [xlix. 80]

RODES, FRANCIS (1530 ?–1588), judge ; educated at St. John's College, Cambridge ; barrister, Gray's Inn, 1552 ; raised to degree of coif, 1578 ; justice of common pleas, 1585 ; took part in trial of Mary Queen of Scots, 1586. [xlix. 80]

RODGER, ALEXANDER (1784–1846), minor poet ; son of a farmer at Mid-Calder, Midlothian ; worked successively as silversmith at Edinburgh and handloom weaver at Glasgow ; joined staff of 'Spirit of the Union,' a seditious weekly paper at Glasgow ; imprisoned as suspected person : on staff of 'Glasgow Chronicle,' *c.* 1832, and subsequently of the 'Reformer's Gazette' ; published poetical writings. [xlix. 80]

RODINGTON, JOHN (*d.* 1348), Franciscan of convent of Stamford ; D.D. Oxford ; provincial minister of order in England ; left manuscripts. [xlix. 81]

RODNEY, GEORGE BRYDGES, first BARON RODNEY (1719–1792), admiral ; educated at Harrow ; entered navy as volunteer per order, 1732 ; captain, 1742 ; in North Sea, 1744 ; took part in defeat of French under L'Etenduère, 1747 ; governor of Newfoundland, 1748–52 ; rear-admiral, 1759 ; bombarded and blockaded Havre, 1759 and 1760 ; commander-in-chief on Leeward Islands station, 1761 ; reduced Martinique and took possession of St. Lucia, Grenada, and St. Vincent, 1762 ; baronet, 1764 ; governor of Greenwich Hospital, 1765–70 ; M.P., 1751 ; M.P., Northampton, 1768 ; held command at Jamaica, 1771–4 ; rear-admiral, 1771 ; being in pecuniary difficulties owing to his pay being in arrears, lived at Paris, 1775–8 ; admiral, 1778 ; defeated Spanish off Cape St. Vincent, and was nominated extra K.B., 1780 ; proceeded to West Indies and took command of fleet on Leeward Islands station ; fought indecisive battle off Martinique with French under Guichen ; seized St. Eustatius, 1781 ; resigned command, owing to ill-health, to Sir Samuel (afterwards Viscount) Hood [q. v.], 1781 ; rejoined Hood, 1782 ; defeated French under De Grasse off Dominica, received thanks of parliament, and was raised to peerage as Baron Rodney of Stoke-Rodney. His portrait was painted by Reynolds and Gainsborough. [xlix. 81]

RODNEY, JOHN (1765–1847), chief secretary to government of Ceylon ; son of George Brydges Rodney, first baron Rodney [q. v.] ; studied at Royal Academy, Portsmouth ; served under his father at St. Vincent and in other engagements ; lieutenant, commander, and captain, 1780 ; lost his leg owing to an accident, 1795, and was superseded ; chief secretary to government of Ceylon, 1803–32. [xlix. 86]

RODWELL, GEORGE HERBERT BUONAPARTE (1800–1852), author and musician ; pupil of Vincent Novello [q. v.] and Sir Henry Bishop [q. v.] ; professor of harmony and composition at Royal Academy of Music, 1828 ; proprietor of Adelphi Theatre, London, 1825 ; director of music at Covent Garden Theatre, London, 1836 ; composed dramatic pieces and songs, and published works on music, and other writings. [xlix. 87]

RODWELL, JOHN MEDOWS (1808–1900), orientalist ; M.A. Gonville and Caius College, Cambridge, 1833 ; honorary fellow, 1886 ; rector of St. Peter's, Saffron Hill, London, 1836–43 ; held rectory of St. Ethelburga's, Bishopsgate, London, 1843 till death, but retired from residential duty, *c.* 1878 ; translated the Koran into English, 1861. [Suppl. iii. 303]

ROE, GEORGE HAMILTON (1795–1873), physician ; M.D. Edinburgh, 1821 ; L.R.C.P. London, 1823 ; M.A. and M.D. (1827) Trinity College, Dublin ; incorporated M.D. Oxford, 1828 ; F.R.C.P., 1836 ; physician to Westminster Hospital, 1825–54 ; Harveian orator, Royal College of Surgeons, 1856, and conciliarius, 1864, 1865, and 1866. [xlix. 88]

ROE, JOHN SEPTIMUS (1797–1878), explorer ; educated at Christ's Hospital, London ; midshipman, 1813 ; accompanied Captain F. P. King in expeditions to northwest coast of Australia, 1818 and 1821 ; served in Burmese war, 1825–7 ; surveyor-general of Western Australia, 1828– *c.* 1870 ; member of executive and legislative council of the colony ; F.L.S., 1828. [xlix. 88]

ROE, RICHARD (*d.* 1853), author ; probably B.A. Dublin, 1789 ; took holy orders ; published 'New System of Shorthand,' poetical and other works. [xlix. 89]

ROE, SIR THOMAS (1581 ?–1644), ambassador ; commoner of Magdalen College, Oxford, 1593 ; esquire of the body to Queen Elizabeth during last years of reign ; knighted, 1605 ; sent by Henry, prince of Wales, on voyage of discovery in search of gold to West Indies and South America, 1610–11, and twice subsequently ; served in Netherlands, 1613 ; M.P., Tamworth, 1614 ; carried out successful mission as lord ambassador to court of Jehângîr, Mogul emperor of Hindustan, with object of arranging commercial treaty, 1615–18, and laid foundation of greatness of British India ; visited Persia on homeward journey ; as ambassador to Ottoman Porte, 1621–8, secured privileges of English merchants and improved relations between England and Algiers ; succeeded in attaching Bethlen Gabor, prince of Transylvania, to the protestant alliance ; mediated successfully between kings of Sweden and Poland, 1629–30 ; chancellor of order of Garter, 1637 ; ambassador in negotiations with imperial, French, and Swedish plenipotentiaries for settlement of terms of general peace, 1638–42 ; privy councillor and M.P. for Oxford university, 1640 ; ambassador extraordinary at Vienna, 1642–3 ; left diplomatic memoirs and correspondence (part published). [xlix. 89]

ROEBUCK, JOHN (1718–1794), inventor ; studied chemistry and medicine at Edinburgh ; M.D. Leyden, 1742 ; established a chemical laboratory at Birmingham ; invented improved methods of refining precious metals and several improvements in processes for production of chemicals, including manufacture of sulphuric acid ; established manufactory of sulphuric acid at Prestonpans, 1749 ; formed company for manufacture of iron on river Carron, Stirlingshire, *c.* 1760, the Carron manufactory subsequently becoming famous for production of ordnance (hence name carronade), and in 1762 patented a process of iron manufacture involving the use of pit coal ; lost large sums of money owing to lack of success with coal-mines and salt-works leased at Borrowstounness, Linlithgowshire, where he was afterwards employed by his creditors as manager ; member of Royal Societies of London and Edinburgh ; friend and patron of James Watt. [xlix. 93]

ROEBUCK, JOHN ARTHUR (1801–1879), politician ; grandson of John Roebuck [q. v.] ; born at Madras ;

educated in Canada; barrister, Inner Temple, 1831; joined northern circuit; Q.C. and bencher of his inn, 1843; agent in England for house of assembly of Lower Canada, 1835; M.P., Bath, 1832–7 and 1841–7; published weekly pamphlets supporting his political views as an 'independent member'; an original member of Reform Club, 1836–64; M.P., Sheffield, 1849–68 and 1874–9; moved, 1855, for committee of inquiry into conduct of Crimean war, with result that Aberdeen's government resigned and Palmerston, who succeeded as premier, appointed Sebastopol committee, with Roebuck as chairman; chairman of Administrative Reform Association, 1856; a supporter of Lord Beaconsfield's policy, 1877–9; privy councillor, 1878; published political works. [xlix. 95]

ROEBUCK, THOMAS (1781–1819), orientalist; cadet in East India Company's service, 1801; captain, 1815; published works in or relating to Hindustani and Persian. [xlix. 97]

ROESTRATEN, PIETER VAN (1627–1700), painter; born at Haarlem, Holland; worked successfully in England as painter of portraits and still life. [xlix. 98]

ROETTIERS, JAMES (1663–1698), medallist; son of John Roettiers [q. v.], whom he assisted at the mint; assistant-engraver, 1690–7. [xlix. 98]

ROETTIERS, JAMES (1698–1772), medallist; son of James Roettiers (1663–1698) [q. v.]; engraver-general of Low Countries, 1733–72. [xlix. 98]

ROETTIERS, JAMES (1707–1784), medallist and goldsmith; son of Norbert Roettiers [q. v.]; 'engraver of mint' to Pretender, 1727. [xlix. 101]

ROETTIERS, ROETTIER, or ROTIER, JOHN (1631–1703), medallist; perhaps born at Antwerp; engraver at mint, 1661; appointed one of chief engravers, 1662; assisted at different periods by Joseph, James, and Norbert, his sons; produced medals commemorating Restoration and official coronation medals for James II and William and Mary; removed from office owing to theft by labourers of dies for coins, 1697. [xlix. 98]

ROETTIERS, NORBERT (1665 ?–1727), medallist; son of John Roettiers [q. v.]; official assistant-engraver at mint, 1690; attached himself to Stuarts at St. Germain, c. 1695; appointed engraver to mint by James Edward, the Old Pretender, for whom he made English and Scottish coins inscribed James III and James VIII; engraver-general of French mint, 1703. [xlix. 100]

ROGER DE BRETEUIL, EARL OF HEREFORD (fl. 1071–1075). [See FITZWILLIAM, ROGER.]

ROGER DE MONTGOMERY, EARL OF SHREWSBURY AND ARUNDEL (d. 1093 ?), son of Roger the Great, who was cousin of William the Conqueror, Ralph de Mortimer [q. v.], and William FitzOsbern [q. v.]; trusted supporter of Duke William; fought at Domfront, 1048; contributed sixty ships for English invasion, which he accompanied; returned to Normandy, 1067, and was left as guardian of the duchy jointly with Matilda; obtained earldom of Shrewsbury, 1071; founded Shrewsbury Abbey, 1083–7; secretly supported Robert against William Rufus, but fought with William Rufus at Rochester, 1088; became monk at Shrewsbury; built many castles on the Welsh borders; benefactor to the monks. [xlix. 101]

ROGER THE POITEVIN (fl. 1088–1102), earl of Lancaster; son of Roger de Montgomery [q. v.]; fought against William Rufus at Rochester, 1088, but was afterwards taken into favour; joined his brother, Robert of Bellême, against Henry I, 1102; expelled from England. [xlix. 102]

ROGER BIGOD (d. 1107), founder of the house of Bigod in England after the Conquest; endowed by 1079 with the forfeited estates of Ralph de Guader, earl of Norfolk [see GUADER, RALPH]; appears in Domesday as holding six lordships in Essex and 117 in Suffolk; received from Henry I gift of Framlingham, which became principal stronghold of himself and descendants. [v. 22]

ROGER INFANS (fl. 1124), chronologer; wrote, c. 1124, on method of computing the calendar. [xlix. 106]

ROGER OF SALISBURY (d. 1139), called ROGER THE GREAT; originally a priest near Caen; entered service of Henry I as steward; chancellor, 1101; appointed bishop of Salisbury, 1102, but not consecrated till 1107; justiciar; took Stephen's side, 1135, and contributed largely to his

success; continued as justiciar, and exercised great influence over government of kingdom, and consequently excited enmity of barons of his party; summoned by Stephen to Oxford and arrested, 1139; his castles surrendered and his power curtailed. He renewed and adorned the cathedral of Salisbury and built several castles, including Devizes. The administrative system of secular government was remodelled under his direction. [xlix. 103]

ROGER PAUPER (fl. 1139), chancellor; son of Roger of Salisbury [q. v.]; chancellor to King Stephen till 1139. [xlix. 106]

ROGER OF FORD (fl. 1170), called also Roger Gustun, Gustum, and Roger of Cîteaux; Cistercian monk of Ford, Devonshire; wrote 'Account of Revelations of St. Elizabeth of Schonau' and other works. [xlix. 106]

ROGER OF HEREFORD (fl. 1178), writer on mathematics and judicial astrology; probably educated at Cambridge. [xlix. 107]

ROGER (d. 1179), divine; son of Robert, earl of Gloucester (d. 1147) [q. v.]; cousin of Henry II, who appointed him bishop of Worcester, 1163; one of bishops charged to convey to Pope Alexander III Henry II's appeal against Archbishop Thomas Becket; denounced for supporting Thomas, whom he followed into exile; contrived to regain in some measure Henry II's favour, while continuing his friendship with Thomas; sent, after murder of Thomas, to intercede in Henry II's behalf with the legate, Archbishop William of Sens, and afterwards with Pope Alexander III, 1171; died at Tours. [xlix. 107]

ROGER OF PONT L'ÉVÊQUE (d. 1181), archbishop of York; 'Neustrian' scholar, brought up in court of Theobald [q. v.], archbishop of Canterbury; one of King Stephen's chaplains; sent by King Stephen on mission to Rome, 1152; archbishop of York, 1154; present at council of Tours, 1163; joined Henry II in contest with Thomas Becket, archbishop of Canterbury; papal legate in England, 1164; performed coronation ceremony for Henry II's son, 1170, in spite of Becket's protests and express orders of Pope Alexander III; was probably ultimately responsible for murder of Becket; obtained decision in Lateran council, 1179, that no profession of obedience was due from York to Canterbury; legate for Scotland, 1180; excommunicated William the Lion for contumacy, 1181; buried at York. [xlix. 109]

ROGER OF HOVEDEN or HOWDEN (d. 1201 ?). [See HOVEDEN.]

ROGER (d. 1202), bishop of St. Andrews; son of Robert de Beaumont, third earl of Leicester (d. 1190) [q. v.]; high chancellor of Scotland, 1178–89; elected bishop of St. Andrews, 1189, and consecrated, 1198; perhaps abbot of Melrose. [xlix. 111]

ROGER OF CROYLAND (d. 1214 ?), prior of Preston, c. 1213; revised (1213) a life of Becket made by an Evesham monk. [xlix. 112]

ROGER DE WENDOVER (d. 1236). [See WENDOVER.]

ROGER DE WESHAM or WESEHAM (d. 1257). [See WESHAM.]

ROGER DE THURKILBI (d. 1260). [See THURKILBI.]

ROGER DE LEYBOURNE (d. 1271). [See LEYBOURNE.]

ROGER OF WALTHAM (d. 1336), clerk in service of Antony Bek (d. 1310) [q. v.], bishop of Durham; prebendary of St. Paul's, London, 1316; keeper of Edward II's wardrobe, 1322–3; wrote philosophical and other works. [xlix. 112]

ROGER OF CHESTER (fl. 1339). [See CHESTER.]

ROGER OF ST. ALBANS (fl. 1450), Carmelite friar in London; wrote genealogical table showing descent of Henry VI from Adam. [xlix. 113]

ROGERS, BENJAMIN (1614–1698), musician; chorister of St. George's Chapel, Windsor; organist of Christchurch Cathedral, Dublin, 1639–41; driven away by Irish rebellion, 1641; lay clerk of St. George's Chapel, Windsor, 1660; organist to Eton College, 1662; informator choristarum, Magdalen College, Oxford, 1665–85; Mus. Doc. Oxford, 1669; composed several services and other church music, besides glees and songs. [xlix. 113]

ROGERS, CHARLES (1711–1784), art collector; in custom house, 1731; clerk of certificates, 1747; F.S.A., 1752; F.R.S., 1757. Collected works of art, including pictures, prints, and illuminated manuscripts, which, on his death, passed to William Cotton (d. 1791), and were ultimately bequeathed to the Plymouth Proprietary Library; published collection of engraved facsimile drawings, and other works. [xlix. 114]

ROGERS, CHARLES (1825–1890), Scottish author; educated at St. Andrews, and was licensed by the presbytery; chaplain of garrison at Stirling, 1855–63; founded and edited shortlived 'Stirling Gazette'; resigned chaplaincy and devoted himself to literary work in England, 1863; founded, besides several societies for distribution of tracts, the Grampian Club, 1868, for issue of Scottish antiquarian works, and claimed to be founder of Royal Historical Society (1868), of which he was secretary and historiographer till 1880; D.D. St. Andrews, 1881; wrote and edited miscellaneous works. [xlix. 115]

ROGERS, DANIEL (1538?–1591), diplomatist; son of John Rogers (1500?–1555) [q. v.]; born at Wittenberg; came to England, 1548; naturalised, 1552; studied at Wittenberg and Oxford (B.A., 1561); secretary of fellowship of English merchants at Antwerp, 1575; engaged in diplomatic business in Low Countries, 1576–8; went on mission to Duke of Saxony, 1580, but was arrested on imperial territory and imprisoned till c. 1584; clerk of privy council, 1587. [xlix. 116]

ROGERS, DANIEL (1573–1652), divine; M.A. Christ's College, Cambridge, 1599; fellow, 1600–8; strongly advocated puritanism; successively minister of Haversham, and lecturer at Wethersfield; suspended by Laud, 1629; published religious works from the Calvinistic standpoint. [xlix. 117]

ROGERS, SIR EDWARD (1498?–1567?), esquire of body to Henry VIII; M.P., Somerset, 1553, 1558, 1559, and 1563–7; knighted, 1549; abroad during Queen Mary's reign; vice-chamberlain, captain of guard, and privy councillor, 1558; comptroller of household, 1560–5. [xlix. 118]

ROGERS, EZEKIEL (1584?–1661), divine; son of Richard Rogers (1550?–1618) [q. v.]; M.A. Christ's College, Cambridge, 1604; private chaplain; held living of Rowley; suspended for puritanism; emigrated to New England, 1638; pastor of township of Rowley, established by fellow colonists. [xlix. 119]

ROGERS, FRANCIS JAMES NEWMAN (1791–1851), legal writer; educated at Eton and Oriel College, Oxford; M.A., 1815; barrister, Lincoln's Inn, 1816, and Inner Temple, 1820; K.C., 1837; deputy judge-advocate-general, 1842; published legal works. [xlix. 119]

ROGERS, FREDERIC, BARON BLACHFORD (1811–1889), educated at Eton and Oriel College, Oxford, where he was intimate with Froude and John Henry Newman; Craven scholar, 1829; M.A., 1835; B.C.L., 1838; fellow of Oriel College, Oxford, 1833; barrister, Lincoln's Inn, 1831; Vinerian scholar, 1834, and fellow, 1840; in sympathy with and (1845) contributor to the tractarian movement; one of founders of 'Guardian' newspaper, 1846; registrar of joint-stock companies, 1844; commissioner of lands and emigration; permanent under-secretary of state for colonies, 1860–71; G.C.M.G., 1883; privy councillor, 1871; raised to peerage, 1871. [xlix. 119]

ROGERS, GEORGE (1618–1697), physician; M.A. Lincoln College, Oxford, 1641; M.B., 1642; M.D. Padua, where he became English consul; incorporated M.D. Oxford, 1648; practised in London from c. 1654; F.R.C.P., 1664, and president, 1688. [xlix. 120]

ROGERS, HENRY (1585?–1658), divine; M.A. Jesus College, Oxford, 1608; D.D., 1637; prebendary of Hereford, 1616; deprived by parliamentarians, 1645; published theological works. [xlix. 121]

ROGERS, HENRY (1806?–1877), 'Edinburgh' reviewer and Christian apologist; apprenticed as surgeon; entered congregationalist ministry, 1829; lecturer on rhetoric and logic, Highbury College, 1832; professor of English language and literature, University College, London, 1836, and of English, mathematics, and mental philosophy, Spring Hill College, Birmingham, 1839; began connection with 'Edinburgh Review,' 1839. Contributed to the 'Encyclopædia Britannica' and published works, including 'The Eclipse of Faith,' 1852, a piece of clever dialectics, which achieved high popularity. [xlix. 121]

ROGERS, ISAAC (1754–1839), watchmaker; apprenticed in London; freeman of Clockmakers' Company, 1776; master, 1824; member of Levant Company; designed two regulators. [xlix. 122]

ROGERS, JAMES EDWIN THOROLD (1823–1890), political economist; of King's College, London, and Magdalen Hall, Oxford; M.A., 1849; curate of St. Paul's, Oxford; abandoned clerical profession; first Tooke professor of statistics and economic science, King's College, London, 1859–90; Drummond professor of political economy, Oxford, 1862–7; became intimate with Cobden, whose views he adopted; instrumental in obtaining Clerical Disabilities Relief Act, of which he was first to avail himself, 1870; engaged in political agitation; M.P., Southwark, 1880–5, Bermondsey, 1885-6; lecturer in political economy, Worcester College, Oxford, 1883; re-elected Drummond professor, 1888; published works on economics and economic history, including 'History of Agriculture and Prices' (6 vols.), 1866–87. [xlix. 123]

ROGERS, JOHN (1500?–1555), martyr; B.A. Pembroke Hall, Cambridge, 1526; rector of Holy Trinity, London, 1532–4; chaplain to English merchant adventurers at Antwerp, 1534; became intimate with Tindal, was converted to protestantism, and took charge of protestant congregation at Wittenberg, c. 1537; supplied with prefatory matter and marginal notes and prepared for publication Tindal's version of the bible, 1536, published at Antwerp, 1537, known as 'Matthew's Bible,' the dedication being signed with pseudonym, 'Thomas Matthew'; rector of St. Margaret Moyses, London, and vicar of St. Sepulchre, London, 1550; prebendary of St. Paul's, London, 1551; divinity lecturer at St. Paul's, London; temporarily suspended for declining to conform to ordinances respecting vestments; deprived of emoluments of his benefices for preaching against popery, 1553; imprisoned in Newgate, 1554; sentenced to death as heretic, 1555; burnt at Smithfield, the first victim of the Marian persecution. [xlix. 126]

ROGERS, JOHN (1540?–1603?), diplomatist; son of John Rogers (1500?–1555) [q. v.]; born at Wittenberg; came to England, 1548; M.A. St. John's College, Cambridge, 1567; fellow; LL.D., 1574; joined College of Advocates, 1574; M.P., Wareham, 1585, 1586, and 1589; chancellor of Wells Cathedral, 1596–1603; employed on several diplomatic missions abroad. [xlix. 129]

ROGERS, JOHN (1572?–1636), puritan divine; educated at Cambridge; vicar of Dedham, 1605–36, his lecture being suppressed, on ground of his nonconformity, 1629–31. [xlix. 129]

ROGERS, JOHN (1627–1665?), Fifth-monarchy man; son of Nehemiah Rogers [q. v.]; joined advanced puritans, and was turned out of doors by his father; servitor at King's College, Cambridge; received presbyterian ordination, 1647; minister of Purleigh; went to London and joined independents; lecturer at St. Thomas Apostle's, London; sent by parliament to Dublin as preacher, 1650; returned to England, 1652; joined Fifth-monarchy men; denounced as a conspirator, 1654, and imprisoned; released, 1657; sent to Tower of London on charges of conspiracy, 1658; proceeded to Ireland; became chaplain in Fairfax's regiment, and subsequently took refuge in Holland; studied medicine at Leyden and Utrecht; M.D. Utrecht; returned to England, 1662; admitted M.D. Oxford, 1664; published controversial works. [xlix. 130]

ROGERS, JOHN (1610–1680), nonconformist divine; M.A. Wadham College, Oxford, 1635; vicar of Croglin, 1661; ejected, 1662. [xlix. 130]

ROGERS, JOHN (1630–1684), divine; son of Nathaniel Rogers [q. v.], with whom he emigrated to New England, 1636; graduated in theology and medicine at Harvard University; president of Harvard, 1682. [xlix. 135]

ROGERS, JOHN (1679–1729), divine; M.A. Corpus Christi College, Oxford, 1700; took orders; fellow, 1706; D.D., 1719; vicar of Buckland, 1704; rector of Wrington, 1716; chaplain in ordinary to George II, then prince of Wales, 1726; vicar of St. Giles, Cripplegate, London, 1728; published sermons and controversial works. [xlix. 133]

ROGERS, JOHN (1740 ?–1814), Irish seceding divine; minister at Cahans, co. Monaghan, 1767; opposed relaxation of penal laws against Roman catholics, 1782; professor of divinity for Irish burgher synod, 1796; clerk of synod, 1779–1814; published religious writings. [xlix. 133]

ROGERS, JOHN (1778–1856), divine; of Eton and Trinity College, Oxford; M.A., 1810; rector of Mawnan, 1807–38; canon-residentiary of Exeter, 1820; supervised Hebrew bible, published by Society for Promoting Conversion of Jews, 1812; published religious works. [xlix. 134]

ROGERS, JOSEPH (1821–1889), medical practitioner; brother of James Edwin Thorold Rogers [q. v.]; medical officer to Strand workhouse, London, 1856–68, and of Westminster infirmary, 1872; founder and president of Poor Law Medical Officers' Association. [xlix. 125]

ROGERS, JOSIAS (1755–1795), navy captain; entered navy, 1771; commander, 1780; wounded and captured in engagement off Cape May, 1782; exchanged; captain, 1787; flag-captain to Sir John Jervis (afterwards Earl of St. Vincent), 1790; joined fleet in West Indies, 1793, and died of yellow fever. [xlix. 134]

ROGERS, NATHANIEL (1598–1655), divine; M.A. Emmanuel College, Cambridge, 1621; curate at Bocking; adopted puritan views; rector of Assington; sailed for New England, 1636; pastor of Ipswich, Massachusetts, 1638; member of synod. [xlix. 135]

ROGERS, NEHEMIAH (1593–1660), divine; brother of Timothy Rogers (1589–1650?) [q. v.]; of Merchant Taylors' School, London, and Emmanuel College, Cambridge; M.A., 1618; fellow of Jesus College, Cambridge; prebendary of Ely, 1636; rector of St. Botolph's, Bishopsgate, London, 1642; sequestered of rectory and prebend, 1643; pastor at St. Osyth, near Colchester; held living of Doddinghurst, near Brentwood, c. 1657; published treatises on the parables. [xlix. 136]

ROGERS, PHILIP HUTCHINGS (1786 ?–1853), painter; educated under John Bidlake [q. v.], Plymouth; exhibited at Royal Academy, 1808–51. [xlix. 137]

ROGERS, RICHARD (1532 ?–1597), divine; M.A. Christ's College, Cambridge, 1552; B.D., 1562; M.A. Oxford, 1560; archdeacon of St. Asaph, c. 1559; prebendary of St. Paul's, London, 1566; suffragan bishop of Dover, 1568; dean of Canterbury, 1584–97; master of Eastgate Hospital, Canterbury, 1595. [xlix. 137]

ROGERS, RICHARD (1550 ?–1618), puritan divine; M.A. Christ's College, Cambridge, 1574; lecturer at Wethersfield, c. 1577; temporarily suspended for petitioning against Whitgift's three articles, 1583; joined Cartwright's presbyterian movement, signed Book of Discipline, and in consequence frequently suffered persecution; published religious works. [xlix. 138]

ROGERS, ROBERT (1727–1800), colonel; born at Dunbarton, New Hampshire; commanded 'Rogers's Rangers' in war with French in North America, 1755–60; visited England, where he came to attract George III's notice by publishing his journals; governor of Mackinaw, Michigan, 1765; after various misfortunes became colonel in the British army in America and raised 'queen's rangers'; published topographical and historical memoirs and other works; died in England. [xlix. 138]

ROGERS, SAMUEL (1763–1855), poet; entered bank in which his father was partner, in Cornhill, London; began contributing to 'Gentleman's Magazine,' 1781; published, 1792, 'Pleasures of Memory,' which achieved popularity; on death of his father, 1793, he became possessed of comfortable means and grew intimate with most eminent men of his day; visited Paris, where he cultivated tastes as an art connoisseur; attained high position among men of letters, many of whom were indebted to his influence or personal generosity; printed privately, 1808, and published, 1810, a fragmentary epic on 'Columbus,' and other poems in following years, including 'Human Life' (1819) and 'Jacqueline,' which was printed in the same volume with Byron's 'Lara' (1814); was offered but declined the laureateship, 1850. [xlix. 139]

ROGERS, THOMAS (d. 1616), protestant divine; M.A. Christ Church, Oxford, 1576; rector of Horningsheath, 1581–1616; opposed Dr. Bound in sabbatarian controversy; chaplain to Bancroft, whom he aided in literary

work; published two works on the English creed, and other writings. [xlix. 142]

ROGERS, THOMAS (1660–1694), divine; of Trinity College and Hart Hall, Oxford; M.A., 1682; rector of Slapton, near Towcester, 1690; published miscellaneous writings. [xlix. 143]

ROGERS, THOMAS (1760–1832), divine; B.A. Magdalene College, Cambridge, 1783; head-master, Wakefield grammar school, 1795–1814; chaplain of West Riding house of correction, 1817; published lectures. [xlix. 144]

ROGERS, TIMOTHY (1589–1650 ?), puritan divine; preacher at Steeple, 1621; vicar of All Saints', Sudbury, 1636; published writings. [xlix. 144]

ROGERS, TIMOTHY (1658–1728), nonconformist minister; educated at Glasgow University; assistant to John Shower [q. v.] in London, 1690–1707; published sermons and other writings. [xlix. 144]

ROGERS, WILLIAM (*fl.* 1580–1610), engraver; probably studied copper-plate engraving in school of Wierix family, Antwerp, and is first Englishman who is known to have practised the art. Among plates by him are some rare portraits of Queen Elizabeth. [xlix. 145]

ROGERS, WILLIAM (1819–1896), educational reformer; educated at Eton and Balliol College, Oxford; M.A., 1844; studied theology at Durham; perpetual curate, 1845, of St. Thomas's, Charterhouse, London, where he did much to ameliorate social condition of his parishioners by means of education; member of royal commission on popular education, 1858; chaplain in ordinary to Queen Victoria, 1857; prebendary of St. Paul's, London, 1862; rector of St. Botolph's, Bishopsgate, London, 1863. He founded numerous schools, and was active in reconstructing Alleyn's charity at Dulwich, 1871. [xlix. 145]

ROGERS, WILLIAM GIBBS (1792–1875), woodcarver; studied style of Grinling Gibbons [q. v.], and gained considerable reputation; employed on carvings in Kensington Palace and Pavilion, Brighton. [xlix. 146]

ROGERS, WOODES (d. 1732), commander-in-chief of two private men-of-war fitted out by Bristol merchants to cruise against Spaniards in South Sea, 1708; reached Juan Fernandez, 1709, and found Alexander Selkirk [q. v.]; proceeded to coast of Peru, sacked Guayaquil, and after several engagements returned to England, 1711; published journal of the voyage, 1712; rented Bahama islands from lords proprietors and obtained commission as governor, 1717; arrived at Nassau, 1718, and, after facing serious opposition from pirates, returned, 1721; appointed (1728) captain-general and governor-in-chief of Bahama islands, where he died. [xlix. 147]

ROGERSON, JOHN BOLTON (1809–1859), poet; worked in mercantile firm and afterwards with solicitor in Manchester; kept bookshop, 1834–41; contributed to newspapers, and subsequently engaged in journalistic and other enterprises; published poems. [xlix. 148]

ROGET, PETER MARK (1779–1869), physician and savant; studied medicine at Edinburgh (M.D., 1798) and in London; physician to infirmary at Manchester, 1805; L.R.C.P., 1809; physician to Northern Dispensary, which he projected, 1810; physician to Spanish embassy, 1820, and to Milbank penitentiary, 1823; commissioned by government to inquire into water supply of metropolis, 1827–8; first Fullerian professor of physiology, Royal Institution, 1833–6; F.R.S., 1815, after reading of paper on a new sliding rule which he contrived; secretary to Royal Society and editor of the 'Proceedings,' 1827–49; F.R.C.P., 1831, Gulstonian lecturer, 1831, and censor, 1834 and 1835; took active part (1837) in establishment of University of London; published 'Thesaurus of English Words and Phrases,' 1852. [xlix. 149]

ROKEBY, BARONS. [See ROBINSON, RICHARD, first BARON, 1709–1794; ROBINSON-MORRIS, MATTHEW, second BARON, 1713–1800; ROBINSON-MONTAGU, HENRY, sixth BARON, 1798–1883.]

ROKEBY, JOHN (d. 1573 ?) canonist; D.C.L. St. Nicholas's Hostel, Cambridge, 1533; member of Doctors' Commons, 1537; counsel for Henry VIII in his divorce; held prebends in York and Southwell. [xlix. 151]

ROKEBY, RALPH (*d.* 1575), secretary of council of north ; educated at Queens' College, Cambridge ; member of Lincoln's Inn. [xlix. 152]

ROKEBY, RALPH (1527 ?-1596), master of requests ; educated at Cambridge ; barrister, Lincoln's Inn ; chief-justice of Connaught, 1570 ; bencher of Lincoln's Inn, 1572 ; master of requests, 1576 ; master of St. Catherine's Hospital, London, 1580. [xlix. 152]

ROKEBY, SIR THOMAS DE (*d.* 1356), justiciar of Ireland ; knighted by :Edward III, 1327 ; commanded royal escort in Scotland, 1336 ; governor of Stirling Castle, 1336–42, and Edinburgh Castle, 1338–42 ; sheriff of Yorkshire, 1337 and 1343 ; justiciar of Ireland, 1349–55, and 1356. [xlix. 152]

ROKEBY, THOMAS DE (*d.* 1418), soldier ; M.P., Yorkshire, 1406, and sheriff, 1408 and 1412 ; defeated Percy, earl of Northumberland, at Bramham Moor, 1408. [xlix. 153]

ROKEBY, SIR THOMAS (1631 ?-1699), judge ; B.A. Catharine Hall, Cambridge, 1650 ; fellow, 1650–1 ; barrister, Gray's Inn, 1657 ; ancient, 1676 ; serjeant-at-law and puisne judge in common pleas, 1689 ; knighted, 1689 ; removed to king's bench, 1695. [xlix. 153]

ROKEBY, WILLIAM (*d.* 1521), archbishop of Dublin ; doctor of canon law, Oxford ; fellow of King's Hall, Cambridge ; held stall of St. Andrew's at Beverley, 1503 ; bishop of Meath and privy councillor, Ireland, 1507 ; archbishop of Dublin, 1512–21 ; lord chancellor of Ireland, 1512. [xlix. 154]

ROKESLEY, GREGORY DE (*d.* 1291), goldsmith and wool merchant ; alderman of Dowgate ward, London ; sheriff, 1264 and 1270 ; mayor of London, 1274–81 and 1285 ; king's chamberlain, 1276 ; master of exchange throughout England, or chief director of royal mint, 1278 ; one of representatives of London at parliament held at Shrewsbury to conduct trial of David of Wales, 1283 ; dismissed for answering summons to royal commission without robes of office, 1285. [xlix. 155]

ROKEWODE, AMBROSE (1578 ?-1606). [See ROOKWOOD.]

ROKEWODE, JOHN GAGE (1786–1842), antiquary ; educated at jesuit college, Stonyhurst ; barrister, Lincoln's Inn, 1818 ; F.S.A., 1818 ; F.R.S. ; director of Society of Antiquaries, 1829 till death ; published topographical works relating to Suffolk. [xlix. 156]

ROLFE, JOHN (1585–1622), colonist ; sailed from England, 1609, and, having been wrecked on Bermudas, reached Virginia, 1610, and there introduced regular cultivation of tobacco, 1612 ; married, 1613, Pocahontas (1595–1617), the newly converted daughter of Powhattan, overking of Indian tribes from Atlantic coast to 'falls of the rivers' ; came, 1616, to England with his wife, who died, 1617 ; returned to Virginia, where he died. Pocahontas was introduced into Ben Jonson's 'Staple of News ' (1625). [xlix. 157]

ROLFE, ROBERT MONSEY, BARON CRANWORTH (1790–1868), lawyer ; of Winchester and Trinity College, Cambridge ; M.A., 1815 ; fellow of Downing College ; barrister, Lincoln's Inn, 1816 ; appointed K.C. and called within bar, 1832 ; bencher of Lincoln's Inn, 1832–9 ; serjeant-at-law, 1839 ; M.P., Penryn and Falmouth, 1832 ; solicitor-general, 1834, in Melbourne's first administration, and in 1835, when he was knighted ; baron of exchequer ; took seat on bench, 1839 ; commissioner of great seal, 1850 ; vice-chancellor and privy councillor, 1850 ; created Baron Cranworth of Cranworth, Norfolk, 1850 ; one of the first lords justices on creation of court of appeal in chancery, 1851 ; lord chancellor, 1852 ; presided over royal commission for consolidation of statutes, 1854 ; a governor of the Charterhouse, London, 1855 ; resigned office on Lord Derby's accession to power, 1858 ; brought forward 'Cranworth's Act' for shortening of conveyances, 1860 ; reappointed lord chancellor on Lord Westbury's retirement, 1865 ; resigned, 1866. [xlix. 158]

ROLLAND, JOHN (*fl.* 1560), Scottish poet ; presbyter of diocese of Glasgow ; notary at Dalkeith, 1555 ; wrote 'Court of Venus ' (*c.* 1560) and ' The Seven Sages ' (1560), two poems, published probably posthumously. [xlix. 161]

ROLLE, HENRY (1589 ?-1656), judge ; of Exeter College, Oxford ; barrister, Inner Temple, 1618, bencher, 1633, reader, 1637 and 1638 ; recorder of Dorchester, 1636 ; serjeant-at-law, 1640 ; M.P., Callington, Cornwall, 1614–1624 ; joined parliamentarians during civil war ; judge of king's bench, 1645 ; chief-justice of king's bench, 1648 ; lord chief-justice of upper bench, and member of council of state, 1649 ; commissioner of exchequer, 1654 ; resigned, 1655. Left legal reports and abridgments, which were published posthumously. [xlix. 162]

ROLLE, JOHN (1598–1648), merchant and politician ; brother of Henry Rolle [q. v.] ; engaged in Turkey trade in London ; M.P., Callington, Cornwall, 1626 and 1628, and Truro in Short and Long parliaments ; his goods seized on refusal to pay tonnage and poundage, 1628 ; compensation made to him, 1644. [xlix. 163]

ROLLE, JOHN, BARON ROLLE OF STEVENSTONE (1750–1842), M.P., Devonshire, 1780, 1784, and 1790 ; staunch adherent of Pitt ; hero of the ' Rolliad,' ; received title of Baron Rolle of Stevenstone, 1796. [xlix. 163]

ROLLE, RICHARD DE HAMPOLE (1290 ?-1349), hermit and author ; educated at Oxford ; took up abode as hermit in a wood at Thornton, his native place in Yorkshire, subsequently establishing himself successively at Dalton, near Rotherham, and Hampole, near Doncaster, where he died, his grave being said to possess miraculous healing powers. He translated portions of bible into English, and occasionally wrote in the Northumbrian dialect. His works include two Latin ethical treatises, ' De Emendatione Vitæ,' and ' De Incendio Amoris,' translated by Richard Misyn in 1434 and 1435 respectively, an English poem, 'The Pricke of Conscience ' (printed by Richard Morris for Philological Society, 1863), and an English paraphrase of Psalms and Canticles (Clarendon press, 1884). [xlix. 164]

ROLLE or **ROLLS**, SAMUEL (*fl.* 1657–1678), divine ; of Trinity College, Cambridge ; held benefice of Dunton ; ejected, 1662 ; doctor of physic, Cambridge, 1675 ; chaplain in ordinary to Charles II, 1678 ; published religious works. [xlix. 167]

ROLLESTON, GEORGE (1829–1881), physician ; M.A. Pembroke College, Oxford, 1853 ; Sheppard fellow, 1851–62 ; studied medicine at St. Bartholomew's Hospital, London ; M.D., 1857 ; F.R.C.P., 1859 ; physician to British civil hospital at Smyrna, 1855–7 ; assistant-physician, Hospital for Sick Children, Great Ormond Street, London, 1857 ; physician to Radcliffe Infirmary, Oxford, and Lee's reader in anatomy at Christ Church, Oxford ; Linacre professor of anatomy and physiology, 1860–81 ; sided with Huxley in dispute with Owen in reference to Darwinian theory ; published ' Forms of Animal Life,' 1870 ; F.R.S., 1862 ; fellow of Merton College, Oxford, 1872 ; Harveian orator, Royal College of Surgeons, 1873 ; published papers and addresses. [xlix. 167]

ROLLO, ANDREW, fifth BARON ROLLO (1700–1765), soldier ; distinguished himself at Dettingen, 1743 ; lieutenant-colonel, 1756 ; served in Louisburg expedition, and conquest of Canada, 1758–60 ; colonel and brigadier-general in America, 1760 ; in West Indies, 1761–2. [xlix. 169]

ROLLO, JOHN (*d.* 1809), surgeon ; studied medicine at Edinburgh ; surgeon in artillery, 1776 ; served in West Indies ; returned to Woolwich as surgeon-general, *c.* 1781 ; M.D. ; published surgical works. [xlix. 169]

ROLLO, sometimes called **ROLLOCK**, SIR WILLIAM (*d.* 1645), royalist ; captain in General King's lifeguards ; major in Montrose's army, 1644 ; captured by Argyll, but released, it is said, on promise to assassinate Montrose, to whom, however, he disclosed the scheme ; taken prisoner at Philiphaugh and executed. [xlix. 170]

ROLLOCK, HERCULES (*fl.* 1577–1619), schoolmaster ; brother of Robert Rollock [q. v.] ; graduated at St. Andrews ; master of high school, Edinburgh, 1584 ; wrote Latin verses. [xlix. 170]

ROLLOCK, PETER (*d.* 1626 ?), Scottish divine and lawyer ; passed advocate before 1573 ; titular bishop of Dunkeld, 1585 ; extraordinary lord of council, 1587 ; ordinary lord of session, 1598–1610 ; accompanied James VI of Scotland to England, 1603, and was naturalised ; resigned bishopric, 1605; displaced from privy council and bench, 1610, but was restored to seat in privy council, 1616, and reappointed extraordinary lord of session, 1619. [xlix. 170]

ROLLOCK or **ROLLOK**, ROBERT (1555?–1599), divine; brother of Hercules Rollock [q. v.]; M.A. St. Salvator's College, St. Andrews; professor; examiner of arts, and director of faculty of arts, 1580; first principal of newly founded college, afterwards Edinburgh University, 1583 till death; professor of theology, 1587; one of three ministers chosen to remonstrate with James VI for his 'hard dealing with the kirk,' 1596, but subsequently supported James VI's policy; minister of Upper Tolbooth and of Magdalen Church, afterwards Greyfriars, Edinburgh, 1598; published theological writings. [xlix. 171]

ROLPH, JOHN (1793–1870), Canadian politician; born at Thornbury, Gloucestershire; studied medicine in London; barrister, Inner Temple; went to Canada, 1820; called to bar, 1821; member of assembly for Middlesex, Upper Canada, 1825; member of executive council, 1836; joined William Lyon Mackenzie [q. v.] in plot against existing government, 1837, and on its failure fled to Russia; returned to Canada on declaration of amnesty, 1843; member of assembly for Norfolk, 1845; retired from political life, 1857. [xlix. 173]

ROLT, Sir JOHN (1804–1871), judge; born at Calcutta; apprenticed as woollendraper in London; clerk in Doctors' Commons, 1827; barrister, Inner Temple, 1837; Q.C.,1846; M.P., Western Gloucestershire, 1857–67; appointed attorney-general and knighted, 1866; lord justice of appeal and privy councillor, 1867. [xlix. 173]

ROLT, RICHARD (1725?–1770), author; held post in excise, but lost it through joining Jacobites, 1745; went to Dublin and subsequently gained living in London by miscellaneous authorship; composed many cantatas and other pieces for Vauxhall, Drury Lane, and other London theatres; engaged with Christopher Smart [q. v.] to write monthly miscellany, 'The Universal Visitor'; published miscellaneous works, including 'A Dictionary of Trade and Commerce,' for which Dr. Johnson wrote the preface, 1756. [xlix. 174]

ROMAINE, WILLIAM (1714–1795), divine; M.A. Christ Church, Oxford, 1737; chaplain to Sir Daniel Lambert during year of office as lord-mayor of London, 1741; lecturer in united parishes of St. George's, Botolph Lane, London, and St. Botolph's, Billingsgate, London, 1748; lecturer at St. Dunstan's-in-the-West, London, 1749; additional preacher at St. George's, Hanover Square, London, 1750; professor of astronomy at Gresham College, London; became supporter of Whitefield, 1755, and consequently was compelled to resign lectureship at St. George's; chaplain to Lady Huntingdon; held curacies in London and (1766–95) the living of St. Anne's, Blackfriars; published religious treatises and pamphlets. [xlix. 175]

ROMAINE, WILLIAM GOVETT (1815–1893), lawyer; M.A. Trinity College, Cambridge, 1859; barrister, Inner Temple, 1839; deputy judge-advocate of army in east, 1854; C.B. and second secretary to admiralty, 1857; judge-advocate-general in India, 1869–73; member, 1876, and, later, president of Egyptian Conseil du Trésor; comptroller-general in Egypt. [xlix. 177]

ROMANES, GEORGE JOHN (1848–1894), man of science; was born at Kingston, Canada West, 1848, but came with his parents to England at an early age; B.A. Gonville and Caius College, Cambridge, 1870; honorary fellow, 1892; Burney prizeman, 1873; formed friendship with Darwin; studied physiology at University College, London, 1874–6; engaged in researches on medusæ and echinoderms; F.R.S., 1879; made investigations respecting mental faculties of animals in relation to those of man, 1881–3; held professorship at Edinburgh, 1886–90; Fullerian professor of physiology at Royal Institution, 1888–91; expounded in paper contributed to Linnean Society, 1886, theory of physiological isolation, dealing with the possible evolution of a distinct species from an isolated group of an original species; zoological secretary of Linnean Society; incorporated M.A. Oxford; founded Romanes lecture at Oxford, 1891; hon. LL.D. Aberdeen, 1882. His publications include 'Candid Examination of Theism,' 1878, 'Animal Intelligence,' 1881, 'Mental Evolution in Animals,' 1883, 'Mental Evolution in Man,' 1888, and 'Darwin and after Darwin,' 1892. [xlix. 177]

ROMANS, BERNARD (1720?–1784?), engineer; born in Holland; educated in England; employed by British government as civil engineer in North America; government botanist in East Florida, 1760–71; joined provincials on outbreak of revolution; constructed fortifications of Fort Constitution, 1775; captain of Pennsylvania artillery, 1776; captured by British, 1779, and subsequently practised as engineer in England; disappeared mysteriously on voyage to New York, 1784; published works on natural history of Florida, history of Netherlands, and other subjects. [xlix. 180]

ROMANUS (*fl.* 624), bishop of Rochester, 624; probably came to Britain as missionary with Augustine. [xlix. 181]

ROMANUS or **LE ROMEYN**, JOHN, the elder (*d.* 1255), ecclesiastic; canon of York before 1218; archdeacon of Richmond, 1241 till *c.* 1247; treasurer of York, 1247. [xlix. 181]

ROMANUS or **LE ROMEYN**, JOHN, the younger (*d.* 1296), divine; son of John Romanus the elder [q. v.]; educated at Oxford; prebendary of Lincoln, 1258; chancellor of Lincoln, 1275; professor of theology at Paris; prebendary of York, 1279; archbishop of York, 1285; summoned to render military service against Scotland, 1291; engaged in dispute with Antony Bek I [q. v.] concerning relations of see of Durham to that of York. [xlix. 181]

ROMER, EMMA, afterwards Mrs. ALMOND (1814–1868), vocalist; first appeared at Covent Garden, London, 1830; at English Opera House (Lyceum), London, and later again at Covent Garden, where she gained great reputation, 1835; married George Almond, 1835; took chief parts in opera at Drury Lane, London, 1837; undertook management of Surrey Theatre, London, 1852. [xlix. 183]

ROMER, ISABELLA FRANCES (*d.* 1852), miscellaneous writer. [xlix. 184]

ROMER, JOHN LAMBERTUS (1680–1754?), engineer; son of Wolfgang William Romer [q. v.]; served in artillery train in Flanders and Spain; ensign, 1708; lieutenant, 1713; engineer at Sheerness, 1715; engineer in charge of northern district and Scotland, 1720; captain, 1739; director of engineers, 1742. [xlix. 185]

ROMER, WOLFGANG WILLIAM (1640–1713), military engineer; born at the Hague; entered service of Prince of Orange, whom he accompanied to England, having gained rank of colonel; engineer in Ireland, 1690–1692; took part in campaigns of 1690 and 1691; chief engineer to ordnance train of Mediterranean expedition, 1693; reported on defences of Guernsey, 1694; as chief engineer, accompanied Lord Bellamont to New York, 1697; fortified Boston harbour, 1701–3; engaged in fortifying Portsmouth, 1708. [xlix. 184]

ROMILLY, HUGH HASTINGS (1856–1892), explorer; of Winchester, Repton, and Christ Church, Oxford; entered mercantile firm in Liverpool; held government appointments in Fiji islands; deputy-commissioner for Western Pacific, 1881; acted as administrator of New Guinea, 1885–6; C.M.G., 1886; deputy-commissioner and consul of New Hebrides and Solomon islands, 1887–90; published topographical works. [xlix. 186]

ROMILLY, JOHN, first BARON ROMILLY (1802–1874), lawyer; son of Sir Samuel Romilly [q. v.]; M.A. Trinity College, Cambridge, 1826; barrister, Gray's Inn, 1827; bencher; liberal M.P., Bridport, 1832–5 and 1846, and Devonport, 1847–52; Q.C., 1843; solicitor-general, 1848; attorney-general, 1850; privy councillor, 1851; master of rolls, 1851–73; created Baron Romilly of Barry, Gloucestershire, 1865. [xlix. 186]

ROMILLY, JOSEPH (1791–1864), divine; fellow, Trinity College, Cambridge, 1815; M.A., 1816; took holy orders; opposed catholic emancipation, 1829; registrary of the university, 1832–61; arranged and catalogued all university papers. [xlix. 187]

ROMILLY, Sir SAMUEL (1757–1818), law reformer; embraced Rousseau's doctrines at an early age; barrister, Gray's Inn, 1783, treasurer, 1803; made acquaintance of Dumont, the Genevese preacher; exposed several anomalies of criminal law in anonymous 'Observations on "Thoughts on Executive Justice" [by Martin Madan],' 1786; published, 1790, translation of letters by Dumont on events of 1789; K.C., 1800; chancellor of county palatine of Durham, 1805–15 ; solicitor-general to administration of 'All the Talents' ; knighted, 1806 ; M.P., Queenborough, 1806–7, Horsham, 1807 (unseated on petition), Wareham, 1808–12, Arundel, 1812, and Westminster, 1818 ; effected great reforms in code of criminal punishment: favoured the emancipation of Roman catholics and abolition of slavery ; published 'Observations on Criminal Law of England,' 1810, and other works ; committed suicide on death of his wife. His memoirs appeared posthumously. [xlix. 188]

ROMNEY, EARL OF (1641–1704). [See SIDNEY, HENRY.]

ROMNEY, GEORGE (1734–1802), painter ; second son of a builder and cabinet-maker of Dalton-in-Furness ; apprenticed, 1755, to Edward Steele (d. 1760 ?) [q. v.], a portrait-painter then at Kendal ; married Mary Abbott, 1756 ; started independently as portrait-painter at Kendal ; came to London, leaving his wife, from whom he remained separated, 1762 ; perhaps gained prize from Society of Arts for picture 'Death of General Wolfe,' 1763 ; studied in Paris, 1764 ; gained second premium, fifty guineas, from Society of Arts for 'Death of King Edmund,' 1765 ; visited Italy, 1772 ; made acquaintance of William Hayley [q. v.], whose friend he remained till death ; copied various works, including Raphael's 'Transfiguration,' then the altar-piece of San Pietro in Montorio ; settled at 32 Cavendish Square, London ; patronised by Duke of Richmond, Georgiana, duchess of Devonshire, and other fashionable sitters ; professional rival of Reynolds, who showed him marked hostility ; between 1782 and 1785 he produced many portraits and sketches of Emma Hart, afterwards Lady Hamilton [q. v.] ; visited Paris, 1790, being accompanied by Hayley, and being welcomed by Madame de Genlis and other persons of distinction ; contributed three works to Boydell's 'Shakespeare Gallery,' 1791, a project which he warmly supported. His portrait (1782) is in the National Portrait Gallery. [xlix. 191]

ROMNEY, JOHN (1758–1832), son of George Romney [q. v.] ; M.A. and fellow, St. John's College, Cambridge, 1785 ; B.D., 1792 ; non-resident rector of Southery, 1788–1799 ; rector of Thurgarton and Cockley Clay, 1804 ; published memoir of his father, the painter, 1830. [xlix. 199]

ROMNEY, JOHN (1786–1863), engraver. [xlix. 200]

ROMNEY, PETER (1743–1777), painter ; brother of George Romney [q. v.], to whom he was apprenticed at Kendal ; made various efforts to establish connection as portrait-painter, but was unsuccessful in consequence of his irregular habits. [xlix. 200]

ROMNEY, SIR WILLIAM (d. 1611), governor of Merchant Adventurers' Company ; incorporator and one of first directors of East India Company ; governor, 1606 ; alderman of London, 1602, sheriff, 1603 ; knighted, 1603 ; actively promoted expeditions to discover North-west Passage, 1601 and 1610. [xlix. 200]

RONALDS, EDMUND (1819–1889), chemist ; nephew of Sir Francis Ronalds [q. v.] ; studied on continent ; Ph.D. Giessen ; lecturer in chemistry at St. Mary's and Middlesex Hospitals ; professor of chemistry, Queen's College, Galway, 1849–56 ; director of Bonnington chemical works, 1856–78 ; published writings. [xlix. 201]

RONALDS, SIR FRANCIS (1788–1873), electrician and meteorologist ; studied practical electricity under Jean André de Luc ; made experiments (1816) which resulted in invention of a telegraphic instrument based on principle of synchronously revolving discs ; published an account of the invention, 1823 ; invented and patented a perspective tracing instrument, 1825 ; honorary director and superintendent, Meteorological Observatory, Kew, 1843–52 ; F.R.S., 1844 ; devised system of automatic registration for meteorological instruments by means of photography, 1844–5 ; subsequently lived chiefly on continent ; knighted, 1871 ; left valuable library of electrical works containing some manuscripts by himself. [xlix. 201]

RONAYNE, JOSEPH PHILIP (1822–1876), engineer ; entered office of Sir John Benjamin McNeill [q. v.], civil engineer, of London and Glasgow ; subsequently engaged in many railway and hydraulic enterprises in British islands and in California ; M.I.C.E., 1856 ; M.P., Cork, 1872–6. [xlix. 204]

ROOKE, SIR GEORGE (1650–1709), admiral ; nephew of Lawrence Rooke [q. v.] ; lieutenant, 1672 ; captain, 1673 ; supported revolution of 1688 ; rear-admiral of red, 1690 ; took part in battle of Beachy Head ; vice-admiral of blue, 1692 ; fought with distinction in battle of Barfleur ; appointed to convoy outward-bound Mediterranean trade consisting of English and Dutch ships, 1693 ; retreated before French fleet off Cape St. Vincent, losing many merchant ships ; admiral of blue and lord commissioner of admiralty, 1694 ; admiral of white, 1695 ; commander-in-chief of Mediterranean fleet, 1695–6 ; commander in Channel, 1696 and 1697 ; M.P., Portsmouth, 1698 ; commanded fleet in Sound to support Charles XII of Sweden against Danes, 1700 ; commander-in-chief of Cadiz expedition of English and Dutch ships, 1702 ; failed in this expedition, but defeated and destroyed French and Spanish fleet at Vigo ; returned to England : privy councillor ; commander-in-chief of grand fleet, 1703 ; captured Gibraltar ; engaged French fleet in battle off Gibraltar, which, though indecisive, resulted in retreat of French ; returned to England, and owing to party prejudice was superseded in command. [xlix. 204]

ROOKE, SIR GILES (1743–1808), judge ; educated at Harrow and St. John's College, Oxford ; M.A., 1766 ; fellow of Merton College, Oxford, 1766–85 ; barrister, Lincoln's Inn, 1766 ; king's serjeant, 1793 ; knighted and appointed to puisne judgeship of common pleas, 1793. [xlix. 208]

ROOKE, JOHN (1780–1856), writer on political economy and geology ; originally a farmer ; studied political economy and became zealous advocate of free trade. [xlix. 208]

ROOKE, LAWRENCE (1622–1662), astronomer ; of Eton and King's College, Cambridge ; fellow, 1643 ; M.A., 1647 ; fellow commoner, Wadham College, Oxford, 1650 ; professor of astronomy, 1652–7, and of geometry, 1657–62, Gresham College, London ; assisted in formation of Royal Society ; published astronomical works, and left similar writings which appeared posthumously. [xlix. 209]

ROOKE, WILLIAM MICHAEL (1794–1847), musician ; born at Dublin, where he worked with his father, a tradesman ; deputy-leader at Dublin Theatre Royal, 1817 ; went to London ; perhaps director at English opera, Drury Lane, London, 1821 ; produced his most successful opera, 'Amilie,' at Covent Garden, London, 1837. [xlix. 210]

ROOKER, EDWARD (1712?–1774), engraver in London ; became celebrated for architectural plates ; exhibited, 1760–8, at Incorporated Society of Artists, of which he was an original member. [xlix. 210]

ROOKER, MICHAEL, called MICHAEL ANGELO ROOKER (1743–1801), engraver and painter ; son of Edward Rooker [q. v.], under whom and Paul Sandby [q. v.] he studied ; A.R.A., 1770 ; contributed plates to Kearsley's 'Copper-Plate Magazine' (1775–7) and other publications ; scene-painter at Haymarket Theatre, London ; exhibited water-colour landscapes at Royal Academy. [xlix. 211]

ROOKWOOD or **ROKEWODE**, AMBROSE (1578?–1606), conspirator ; educated in Flanders, whither his family, who were Roman catholics, had fled from persecution ; succeeded to his father's estates at Stanningfield, 1600 ; indicted for recusancy, 1605 ; joined Robert Catesby in 'gunpowder plot' ; arrested at Holbeach, and executed at Old Palace Yard, Westminster, with Winter, Keyes, and Fawkes. [xlix. 211]

ROOKWOOD, AMBROSE (1664–1696), Jacobite ; brigadier under James II ; executed at Tyburn. [xlix. 212]

ROOM, HENRY (1802–1850), portrait-painter ; exhibited at Royal Academy from 1826. [xlix. 212]

ROOME, EDWARD (d. 1729), song-writer ; brought up as lawyer ; solicitor to treasury, 1728 ; aroused by his writings enmity of Pope, who satirised him in 'Dunciad' ; wrote some songs in 'Jovial Crew' produced at Drury Lane, London, 1731. [xlix. 212]

ROOS. [See ROS.]

ROOTH, DAVID (1573–1650). [See ROTHE or ROTH.]

ROPER, ABEL (1665–1726), tory journalist ; apprenticed as publisher in London, and subsequently set up business independently ; said to have been first printer of 'Lilliburlero' ; imprisoned on charge of aiding

revolutionary conspirators by his publications, 1696;
started, 1695, ' Post Boy,' tory newspaper, with which he
was connected till c. 1714.   [xlix. 213]

ROPER, MARGARET (1505–1544), daughter of Sir
Thomas More [q. v.]; married William Roper [q. v.],
c. 1525; according to Stapleton, privately purchased the
head of her dead father a month after it had been exposed on London bridge, and preserved it in spices till
her death; buried in Chelsea church. An ancient leaden
box discovered in the Roper vault at St. Dunstan's
church, Canterbury, where her husband was buried, was
opened in June 1824, and contained a head which was
assumed to be More's.   [xxxviii. 439]

ROPER, ROPER STOTE DONNISON (1771–1823?),
legal writer; barrister, Gray's Inn, 1799; his works include ' Treatise upon Law of Legacies,' 1799. [xlix. 214]

ROPER, SAMUEL (d. 1658), antiquary; aided Dugdale in his history of Warwickshire; probably served as
colonel in parliamentary army.   [xlix. 215]

ROPER, WILLIAM (1496–1578), biographer of Sir
Thomas More [q. v.]; held jointly with his father, and
afterwards alone, till 1577, clerkship of pleas of court of
king's bench; married, 1525, Margaret [see ROPER, MAR-
GARET], daughter of Sir Thomas More, whose biography
he subsequently compiled (published, Paris, 1626); M.P.,
Bramber, 1529, Rochester, 1545 and 1554, Winchelsea,
1553, Canterbury, 1555 and 1558; summoned before privy
council for sympathy with Roman catholics, 1568, but
discharged on bond for his good behaviour. [xlix. 215]

RORY or **RURY OGE** (d. 1578). [See O'MORE, RORY.]

RORY O'MORE (fl. 1620–1652). [See O'MORE, RORY.]

ROS or **ROOS** OF HAMLAKE, BARON (d. 1543). [See
MANNERS, THOMAS, afterwards first EARL OF RUTLAND.]

ROS or **ROSSE**, JOHN DE (d. 1332), bishop of
Carlisle; prebendary of Hereford; archdeacon of Salop
before 1308 till 1318; papal chaplain and auditor, c. 1317;
canon of Wells and Salisbury, c. 1318; bishop of Carlisle,
1325–32.   [xlix. 216]

ROS, JOHN DE, BARON ROS (d. 1338), admiral;
second son of William de Ros [q. v.]; in Edward II's
household, c. 1322; joined Queen Isabella, 1326; seneschal
of Edward III's household; joint-admiral of fleets in
Thames and northwards, 1337.   [xlix. 220]

ROS, ROBERT DE (d. 1227), surnamed FURFAN,
baron; bailiff and castellan of Bonneville-sur-Touques,
Lower Normandy, 1195; sent with others by King John
to arrange meeting with William the Lion, c. 1199; received grant of lands in Northumberland, including Wark,
where he built a castle, 1200; assumed temporarily the
monastic habit, 1212; joined barons against King John,
c. 1215; excommunicated by Innocent IV, 1216; one of
last barons who continued resistance; submitted to
Henry III; witnessed third issue of Great Charter, 1225;
again took monastic habit, c. 1227; married Isabella,
daughter of William the Lion.   [xlix. 216]

ROS, ROBERT DE, BARON ROS OF WARK (d. 1274),
son of Robert de Ros (d. 1227) [q. v.]; justice itinerant,
1234; marshal of household to Henry III; one of
guardians of Alexander III's queen, Margaret, daughter
of Henry III, 1252; deprived of lands for cruelty to Margaret, c. 1255; joined barons in civil war, c. 1263.
     [xlix. 218]

ROS, WILLIAM DE, second BARON ROS (d. 1317),
born before 1260; son of Robert de Ros, first baron Ros
of Helmsley or Hamlake (d. 1285), nephew of Robert de
Ros (d. 1274) [q. v.]; accompanied Edward I to Wales,
1277; one of claimants to Scottish crown, 1291, but withdrew claim; served in Gascony, 1297; joint-defender of
Northumberland against Scots, 1307.   [xlix. 219]

ROSA, CARL AUGUST NICHOLAS (1843–1889),
musician; born at Hamburg, his surname being Rose;
studied at Leipzig and Paris; formed Carl Rosa Opera
Company in London, 1875, when he changed his name to
Rosa; subsequently played successfully at many theatres.
     [xlix. 220]

ROSA, THOMAS (1575?–1618). [See ROSS, THOMAS.]

ROSAMOND THE FAIR (d. 1176?). [See CLIFFORD,
ROSAMOND.]

ROSCARROCK, NICHOLAS (1549?–1634?), poetical
writer; B.A. (? Exeter College), Oxford, 1568; entered
Inner Temple, 1572; imprisoned in Tower of London as
Roman catholic, 1580–6, and in Fleet, London, 1594; lived
at Haworth Castle from 1607; contributed verses to
Tottell's edition of John Bossewell's ' Workes of Armorie '
(1572) and other publications.   [xlix. 220]

ROSCOE, HENRY (1800–1836), biographer; son of
William Roscoe [q. v.]; articled as solicitor in Liverpool,
1817; barrister, Inner Temple, 1826; his works include
life of William Roscoe (1833).   [xlix. 221]

ROSCOE, THOMAS (1791–1871), author and translator; son of William Roscoe [q. v.]; published miscellaneous writings.   [xlix. 222]

ROSCOE, WILLIAM (1753–1831), historian; assisted
his father in market-gardening; articled as attorney at
Liverpool; admitted attorney of court of king's bench,
1774; retired from profession and devoted himself to
literary studies; engaged as partner and manager in
banking business in Liverpool, 1799; studied botany;
F.L.S., 1805; whig M.P. for Liverpool, 1806–7; lost
money owing to run on and subsequent suspension of
payment by his bank, 1816; promoter and first president
of Liverpool Royal Institution, 1817; was declared bankrupt, 1820, and provided for by benevolence of friends.
His works include ' Life of Lorenzo de' Medici,' 1795,
' Life and Pontificate of Leo the Tenth,' 1805; an edition
of Pope's works and several volumes of verse, including
' The Butterfly's Ball and the Grasshopper's Feast,' 1807
(now a children's classic). He formed collection of books
and prints, part of which went, after his pecuniary
disaster, to the Liverpool Athenæum.   [xlix. 222]

ROSCOE, WILLIAM CALDWELL (1823–1859), poet
and essayist; son of William Stanley Roscoe [q. v.];
educated at University College, London; graduated,
London, 1843; called to bar, 1850; works include two
tragedies.   [xlix. 225]

ROSCOE, WILLIAM STANLEY (1782–1843), minor
poet; son of William Roscoe [q. v.]; educated at Peterhouse, Cambridge; partner in his father's bank.
     [xlix. 225]

ROSCOMMON, EARL OF (1633?–1685). [See DILLON,
WENTWORTH, fourth EARL.]

ROSE or **ROSS**, ALEXANDER (1647?–1720). [See
ROSS.]

ROSE, CALEB BURRELL (1790–1872), geologist;
apprenticed as surgeon; studied medicine at Guy's and
St. Thomas's Hospitals, London; F.R.C.S., 1846; published
writings on Norfolk geology.   [xlix. 226]

ROSE, GEORGE (1744–1818), statesman; educated at
Westminster School; entered navy; served principally in
West Indies; left navy, 1762; clerk in record office of exchequer; secretary to board of taxes, 1777; secretary to
treasury during Shelburne's ministry, 1782–3, and during
Pitt's ministry, 1784–1801; M.P., Launceston, 1784;
appointed for life master of pleas in court of exchequer;
M.P., Lymington, 1788, and Christchurch, 1790–1818;
privy councillor, 1802; vice-president of board of trade
and joint-paymaster-general during Pitt's second administration, 1804–6; vice-president of board of trade and
treasurer of navy, 1807–12; deputy-warden of New Forest,
1808; subsequently again treasurer of navy; wrote
chiefly on financial subjects.   [xlix. 226]

ROSE, SIR GEORGE (1782–1873), judge; of humble
parentage; educated at Westminster and Peterhouse and
Trinity College, Cambridge; M.A., 1835; barrister, Inner
Temple, 1809; K.C. and bencher of his inn, 1827; reader,
1834, and treasurer, 1835; appointed judge of court of re-
view and knighted, 1831; master in chancery, 1840–58;
F.R.S., 1834; F.G.S.; first chairman of Law Life Insurance
Society, 1844; published legal writings.   [xlix. 230]

ROSE, GEORGE (1817–1882), dramatist, novelist, and
humorous entertainer; clerk in custom house; entered
Magdalen Hall, Oxford, 1841; M.A., 1848; held curacies
at Camberwell and Christ Church, Hoxton; assistant-
reader at Temple; joined Roman catholic church, 1855;
adopted literary career and produced several successful
dramatic pieces; contributed, under pseudonym 'Arthur
Sketchley,' to ' Routledge's Annual,' 1866, and subse-

quently to 'Fun,' monologues of Mrs. Brown, which were published in book form; afterwards toured round the world as public entertainer. [xlix. 230]

ROSE, SIR GEORGE HENRY (1771–1855), diplomatist; son of George Rose (1744–1818) [q. v.]; M.A. St. John's College, Cambridge, 1795; held diplomatic appointment at the Hague, 1792, and Berlin, 1793–4; M.P., Southampton, 1794–1813; deputy paymaster-general of land forces, 1805; British minister at Munich, 1813, and Berlin, 1815; M.P., Christchurch, 1818–44; privy councillor, 1818; published religious pamphlets and other writings. [xlix. 231]

ROSE, HENRY JOHN (1800–1873), theologian; educated at St. Peter's and St. John's Colleges, Cambridge; M.A., 1824; B.D., 1831; fellow of St. John's College, Cambridge, 1824–36; B.D. Oxford, 1851; minister of St. Edward's, Cambridge, 1832–3; Hulsean lecturer, 1833; rector of Houghton Conquest, 1837–73; archdeacon of Bedford, 1866–73; published religious works, and assisted his brother, Hugh James Rose (1795–1838) [q. v.], in many publications; one of revisers of authorised Old Testament. [xlix. 232]

ROSE, HUGH HENRY, BARON STRATHNAIRN (1801–1885), field-marshal; born and educated at Berlin; ensign, 1820; major, 1826; lieutenant-colonel, 1839; selected, 1840, for special service in Syria, against Mehemet Ali's Egyptian army; deputy adjutant-general to Omar Pasha; colonel (local rank) and commander of British detachments in Syria; consul-general for Syria, 1841; secretary of embassy at Constantinople and brevet-colonel, 1851; chargé d'affaires in place of Sir Stratford Canning, 1852; appointed, on declaration of war against Russia by England and France, queen's commissioner at headquarters of French commander-in-chief, with local rank of brigadier-general; served at Alma and Inkerman; major-general, 1854; K.C.B., 1855; commander of legion of honour; volunteered for service in India, 1857; took Ráthgarh and Garhákóta, relieved Ságar, and captured important pass of Máltún, 1858; defeated Tántia Topi; took Kúnch and Kálpi; won victory at Morár; retook Gwáliár; resigned command to Napier and took command at Bombay of Puná division; G.C.B. and colonel, lieutenant-general and commander-in-chief of Bombay army, and, later, commander-in-chief in India, with local rank of general, 1860; K.C.S.I., 1861; G.C.S.I., 1866; returned to England, 1865; D.C.L. Oxford, 1865; commander of forces in Ireland, 1865–70; created Baron Strathnairn of Strathnairn and Jánsi, 1866; president of army transport committee; general, 1867; colonel, royal horse guards, 1869; hon. LL.D. Dublin, 1870; field-marshal, 1877. [xlix. 233]

ROSE, HUGH JAMES (1795–1838), theologian; brother of Henry John Rose [q. v.]; B.A. Trinity College, Cambridge, 1817; frequently select preacher at Cambridge between 1825 and 1834; prebendary of Chichester, 1827–1833; perpetual curate of St. Thomas's, Southwark, 1835–1838; founded 'British Magazine . . of Ecclesiastical Information,' 1832; professor of divinity at Durham, 1833–4; principal of King's College, London, 1836; left England for his health; died at Fiesole. He engaged in many literary undertakings, including 'Encyclopædia Metropolitana,' which he edited from 1836. Rose's 'New Biographical Dictionary' (12 vols., 1840–8), projected by him, was edited by others after his death. [xlix. 240]

ROSE, HUGH JAMES (1840–1878), military chaplain; son of Henry John Rose [q. v.]; M.A. Oriel College, Oxford, 1867; held several posts as military chaplain; 'Times' correspondent in Spain; published works on Spain. [xlix. 233]

ROSE, JOHN (?) AUGUSTUS or AUGUSTE (1757–1841), usher to the French national convention in 1793; perhaps born in Scotland; said to have served in American war; usher to French national assembly, c. 1790; was entrusted with duty of arresting two brothers Robespierre and their comrades, 1794, and had to escape after executing his mission, but returned later; attached to French chamber of peers, 1814. [xlix. 242]

ROSE, SIR JOHN (1820–1888), Canadian statesman; born in Aberdeenshire; educated at King's College, Aberdeen; went to Canada, 1836; called to bar of Lower Canada, 1842; Q.C., 1848; member for Montreal, 1857; solicitor-general for Lower Canada, 1857; minister of public works, 1858–61; represented protestant interests at London conference on Canadian federation, 1867; privy councillor and first minister of finance for Dominion; resigned office and settled in England, c. 1868; G.C.M.G., 1878; privy councillor, 1886; receiver-general for duchy of Lancaster, 1883. [xlix. 242]

ROSE, SAMUEL (1767–1804), friend of Cowper; son of William Rose [q. v.]; educated at Glasgow; barrister, Lincoln's Inn, 1796; counsel to Duke of Kent; assisted Cowper after 1787; edited legal and other works. [xlix. 243]

ROSE, WILLIAM (1719–1786), translator; educated at Marischal College, Aberdeen; conducted school at Kew, and, from 1758, at Chiswick; published translations from Sallust (1757). [xlix. 243]

ROSE, WILLIAM STEWART (1775–1843), poet; son of George Rose (1744–1818) [q. v.]; educated at Eton; M.P., Christchurch, 1796, Chiltern Hundreds, 1800; reading clerk of House of Lords and clerk of private committees, 1800–24; formed friendship with Scott, 1803; travelled on continent, 1814–18. His publications include a rhymed translation from the 'Amadis' of Herberay des Essarts (1803) and a metrical version of Ariosto (1823–31). [xlix. 244]

ROSEBERY, EARLS OF. [See PRIMROSE, ARCHIBALD, first EARL, 1661–1723; PRIMROSE, ARCHIBALD JOHN, fourth EARL, 1783–1868.]

ROSEINGRAVE, DANIEL (1655?–1727), musician; organist at Winchester Cathedral, 1681–92, Salisbury Cathedral, 1692–1700, and St. Patrick's and Christchurch Cathedrals, Dublin, from 1698; wrote vocal music. [xlix. 245]

ROSEINGRAVE, RALPH (1695–1747), organist; son of Daniel Roseingrave [q. v.]; succeeded his father at Dublin, 1727. [xlix. 246]

ROSEINGRAVE, THOMAS (1690?–1755?), musician; brother of Ralph Roseingrave [q. v.]; studied harpsichord under Domenico Scarlatti in Italy; organist of St. George's, Hanover Square, London, 1725–37; for some time a successful teacher. His compositions include sonatas, fugues, and three anthems. [xlix. 246]

ROSEN, FRIEDRICH AUGUST (1805–1837), Sanskrit scholar; born in Hanover; studied at Leipzig, Berlin, and Paris; professor of oriental languages at University College, London, 1828–30, of Sanskrit, 1836; prepared text and Latin translation of the 'Rigveda' (vol. i. published, 1838). [xlix. 247]

ROSENBERG, GEORGE FREDERIC (1825–1869), painter; associate of 'Old Water-colour' Society, 1847. [xlix. 247]

ROSENHAGEN, PHILIP (1737?–1798), divine; of St. Paul's School, London, and St. John's College, Cambridge; M.A., 1763; Platt fellow, 1761–71; rector of Mountnessing; military chaplain; retired to continent owing to gambling excesses, c. 1770–80; rector of Little Easton, 1781; archdeacon of Colombo, where he died; wrote in Wilkes's cause and claimed authorship of 'Junius' in hopes of getting pension to cease writing. [xlix. 248]

ROSEWELL, SAMUEL (1679–1722), divine; son of Thomas Rosewell [q. v.]; ordained, 1705; lecturer at Founders' Hall, Lothbury, London, 1713–19. [xlix. 249]

ROSEWELL, THOMAS (1630–1692), nonconformist minister; B.A. Pembroke College, Oxford, 1651; rector of Roade, 1653, and of Sutton-Mandeville, 1657; ejected, 1662; chaplain to Lady Hungerford, 1663–71, and to Philip Wharton, fourth baron Wharton [q. v.], 1674; presbyterian minister at Rotherhithe, 1674; arrested on false charge of treasonable preaching, 1684; found guilty by Judge Jeffreys, but discharged on bail; published pamphlets. [xlix. 249]

ROSIER, JAMES (1575–1635), voyager; sailed with Bartholomew Gosnold [q. v.] to New England, 1602, and with George Weymouth [q. v.], 1605. Published account of latter voyage. [xlix. 251]

ROSMEAD, BARON (1824–1897). [See ROBINSON, SIR HERCULES GEORGE ROBERT.]

ROSS, DUKE OF (1476?–1504). [See STEWART, JAMES.]

ROSS, EARLS OF. [See MACDONALD, DONALD, ninth EARL, *d.* 1420 ? ; MACDONALD, ALEXANDER, tenth EARL, *d.* 1449 ; MACDONALD, JOHN, eleventh EARL, *d.* 1498 ?]

ROSS, MOTHER (1667–1739). [See DAVIES, CHRISTIAN.]

ROSS, ALEXANDER (1591–1654), divine ; educated at King's College, Aberdeen ; schoolmaster at Southampton, 1616 ; chaplain, *c.* 1622, to Charles I, who presented him to vicarage of Carisbrooke ; published, in Latin and English, poetical and other works. He is mentioned in Hudibras, pt. i. canto ii. [xlix. 251]

ROSS or **ROSE**, ALEXANDER (1647 ?–1720), Scottish divine ; M.A. King's College, Aberdeen, 1667 ; minister at Old Church, Perth, 1672–83 ; professor of divinity at Glasgow, 1683 ; D.D. and principal of St. Mary's College, St. Andrews ; bishop of Moray, 1687 ; bishop of Edinburgh, 1688 ; refused allegiance to William and Mary ; deprived by act abolishing episcopacy, 1689 ; pursued policy of consecrating bishops without jurisdiction. [xlix. 252]

ROSS, ALEXANDER (1699–1784), Scottish poet ; M.A. Marischal College, Aberdeen, 1718 ; schoolmaster, 1732–84, at Lochlee, Angus, where he was also session clerk, precentor, and notary public ; published volume of verse containing 'The Fortunate Shepherdess,' 1768, and left poetical manuscripts. [xlix. 254]

ROSS, ALEXANDER (1742–1827), general ; ensign, 1760 ; captain, 1775 ; served in American war ; aide-de-camp, 1780, to Cornwallis, whose intimate friend he became ; major, 1780 ; served in India ; colonel, 1793 ; surveyor-general of ordnance, 1795 ; general, 1812 ; governor of Fort George. [xlix. 255]

ROSS, ALEXANDER (1783–1856), fur trader ; born in Nairnshire ; emigrated to Canada, 1805 ; accompanied Pacific Fur Company's expedition to Oregon, 1810–12 ; joined (1813) North-West Company, to whom Astoria (founded, 1811) had been made over by Pacific Company, and received command of Oakinacken ; commanded fort of Nez Percés, 1818 ; joined Hudson Bay Company, 1821 ; settled in Red River settlement, and subsequently took prominent part in its organisation ; published topographical works. [xlix. 256]

ROSS, ANDREW (1773–1812), colonel ; ensign, 1789 ; captain of an independent company of foot, 1792 ; served in Ireland ; major, 1794 ; aide-de-camp to Sir Hew Whitefoord Dalrymple [q. v.], 1795–7 ; lieutenant-colonel, 1800 ; at Gibraltar, 1802 ; active in suppressing mutiny ; colonel and aide-de-camp to George III, 1809. [xlix. 257]

ROSS, ARTHUR (*d.* 1704), Scottish divine ; educated at St. Andrews ; minister of Kinernie ; signed declaration of synod of Aberdeen in favour of establishing episcopacy, 1660 ; bishop of Argyll, 1675, and of Galloway, 1679 ; archbishop of Glasgow, 1679, and of St. Andrews, 1684 ; favoured toleration of Roman catholics, 1686 ; refused allegiance to William III ; deprived of see by act abolishing episcopacy, 1689 ; published sermons. [xlix. 257]

ROSS, DAVID (1728–1790), actor ; educated at Westminster ; played in Dublin, 1749 ; engaged by Garrick at Drury Lane, London, 1751–6, and achieved considerable popularity, his parts including Buckingham ('Henry VIII'), Banquo, and Edgar ('Lear') ; at Covent Garden, London, 1757–67, playing Othello, Hamlet, and other Shakespearean characters ; patentee and manager of a theatre in Edinburgh, 1767 ; reappeared at Covent Garden, London, 1770 ; last appeared, 1778. [xlix. 259]

ROSS, GEORGE (1814–1863), legal writer ; grandson of Sir John Lockhart Ross [q. v.] ; called to Scottish bar, 1835 ; professor of Scots law, Edinburgh University, 1861. [xlix. 260]

ROSS, SIR HEW DALRYMPLE (1779–1868), field-marshal ; cadet at Woolwich, 1793 ; sub-lieutenant, royal artillery, 1795 ; captain-lieutenant and adjutant at Woolwich, 1803 ; captain, 1806 ; commanded 'Chestnut' troop in Peninsula, 1809–14 ; brevet-major, 1811 ; in Waterloo campaign, 1814–15 ; lieutenant-colonel, 1825 ; commanded royal artillery in northern district under Sir John Byng (afterwards Lord Strafford) [q. v.], 1828 ; held delegated command in four northern counties of the district ; colonel, 1837 ; deputy adjutant-general of artillery at headquarters, 1840–54 ; lieutenant-general of ordnance, 1854 ; prepared

artillery for Crimea ; general, 1854 ; on commander-in-chief's staff as adjutant-general of artillery, 1855–8 ; G.C.B., 1855 ; field-marshal and lieutenant-governor of Chelsea Hospital, 1868. [xlix. 261]

ROSS, HORATIO (1801–1886), sportsman ; joined light dragoons, 1819 ; retired with rank of captain, 1826 ; M.P., Aberdeen boroughs, 1831, and Montrose, 1832–4 ; captain of Scottish team in match for Elcho Shield, 1862, and took part in the match five times ; published, 1880, introduction to Macrae's 'Deerstalking.' [xlix. 264]

ROSS, JAMES (1835–1871), chief-justice of Manitoba ; son of Alexander Ross (1783–1856) [q. v.] ; educated at Toronto University ; took part in administration of Manitoba (Red River Settlement) ; chief-justice, 1870. [xlix. 256]

ROSS, JAMES (1837–1892), physician ; M.D. Aberdeen, 1864 ; practised at Newchurch, Rossendale ; removed, 1876, to Manchester, where he became pathologist to the infirmary, assistant-physician, 1878, and physician, 1888 ; F.R.C.P., 1882 ; professor of medicine, Owens College, Manchester, 1887 ; published 'Treatise on Diseases of Nervous System,' 1881. [xlix. 265]

ROSS, SIR JAMES CLARK (1800–1862), rear-admiral ; entered navy, 1812 ; lieutenant, 1822 ; accompanied Sir William Edward Parry [q. v.] in voyages in 1819–20, 1821–3, 1824–5, and 1827 ; commander, 1827 ; accompanied Felix Booth expedition, 1829–33, and discovered magnetic pole, 1831 ; post-captain, 1834 ; employed on magnetic survey of United Kingdom, 1838 ; commanded expedition for geographical discovery in Antarctic, 1839–43 ; published account of voyage, 1847 ; gold medallist, geographical societies, London and Paris, 1842 ; knighted, 1843 ; hon. D.C.L. Oxford, 1844 ; held command in expedition to relieve Franklin, 1848–9 ; rear-admiral ; F.R.S., 1828. [xlix. 265]

ROSS, JOHN (1411 ?–1491). [See ROUS.]

ROSS or **ROSSE**, JOHN (1719–1792), bishop of Exeter ; M.A. St. John's College, Cambridge, 1744 ; incorporated at Oxford, 1744 ; D.D. Cambridge, 1756 ; fellow of St. John's College, Cambridge, 1744–70 ; preacher at the Rolls, and king's chaplain, 1757 ; held benefice of Frome, 1760–1792 ; canon of Durham, 1769–78 ; bishop of Exeter, 1778 ; F.R.S., 1758 ; edited Cicero's 'Letters,' 1749. [xlix. 266]

ROSS, JOHN (1763–1837), musician ; organist of St. Paul's Episcopal Church, Aberdeen, 1783–1836 ; composed pianoforte and vocal pieces. [xlix. 267]

ROSS, SIR JOHN (1777–1856), Arctic navigator ; brother of Andrew Ross [q. v.] ; entered service of East India Company, 1794 ; lieutenant in navy, 1805 ; commander, 1812 ; in Baltic and North Sea, 1812–17 ; went in search of North-West Passage, 1818 and 1829–33, when Boothia peninsula, King William Land, and Gulf of Boothia were surveyed ; post-captain, 1818 ; K.C.B., 1834 ; published accounts of voyages, 1819 and 1835 ; gold medallist, geographical societies of London and Paris, 1834 ; consul at Stockholm, 1839–46 ; went on unsuccessful private expedition in search of Franklin, 1850 ; rear-admiral ; published works on nautical subjects. [xlix. 267]

ROSS, JOHN (1800 ?–1865 ?). [See DIX.]

ROSS, SIR JOHN LOCKHART (1721–1790), vice-admiral ; son of Sir James Lockhart ; entered navy, 1735 ; commander, 1755 ; post-captain, 1756 ; in Channel, 1756–7 ; in North Sea, Channel, and Quiberon Bay, 1758–60 ; assumed name of Ross on succeeding to Ross estate of Balnagowan, 1760 ; M.P., Lanark boroughs, 1761 ; rear-admiral, 1779 ; served in Channel, North Sea, and Mediterranean, 1779–82 ; vice-admiral, 1787. [xlix. 269]

ROSS, JOHN MERRY (1833–1883), Scottish writer ; LL.D. Glasgow, 1874 ; sub-editor of Chambers's 'Encyclopædia,' 1859 ; a work by him on 'Scottish History and Literature' appeared posthumously (1884). [xlix. 271]

ROSS, JOHN WILSON (1818–1887), author ; born at Belmont, St. Vincent ; educated at King's College, London ; secretary to vendue-master of Berbice, British Guiana ; subsequently engaged in literary work in London ; published 'Tacitus and Bracciolini : the Annals forged in Fifteenth century,' 1878, and other works in prose and verse. [xlix. 271]

ROSS, PATRICK (1740 ?–1804), practitioner-engineer and ensign in corps of engineers, 1758 ; lieutenant, 1760 ;

engineer extraordinary and captain-lieutenant, 1763 ; lieutenant-colonel and chief engineer at Madras, 1770 ; member of governor's council ; chief engineer in campaigns against Tanjore, 1771–5 ; reconstructed defences of Fort George ; accompanied Commodore Johnstone's abortive expedition against Dutch settlements at Cape of Good Hope, 1781 ; accompanied Major-General Stuart's army against Tipú, sultan of Maisur, 1783 ; colonel in company's service, 1783 ; joined army under Cornwallis acting against Tipú, 1791–2 ; at siege of Seringapatam, 1792 ; in England, 1793–5 ; brevet colonel in India, 1794, and in army, 1796 ; major-general, 1797 ; superintended at Madras engineering operations in campaigns of 1798 and 1799 ; returned to England ; retired, 1803 ; M.P., Horsham, 1802–4. [xlix. 272]

ROSS, ROBERT (1766–1814), soldier ; educated at Trinity College, Dublin ; ensign, 1789 ; captain and major, 1795 ; as major in 20th foot served in Holland under Duke of York, 1799 ; brevet lieutenant-colonel, 1801 ; in Italy, 1806 ; greatly assisted in defeat of French at Maida ; lieutenant-colonel of 20th, 1808 ; with Sir John Moore in Coruña campaign, 1808 ; at Walcheren, 1809 ; brevet colonel and aide-de-camp to George III, 1810 ; again in Peninsula, 1812 ; commanded expeditionary force, in co-operation with Admiral Sir A. Cochrane, sent against coasts of United States, 1814 ; won battle of Bladensburg and took Washington, 24 Aug. 1814 ; died from wound received at Baltimore. A monument to him is in St. Paul's Cathedral ; the name Ross of Bladensburg was given to his widow and descendants. [xlix. 274]

ROSS, SIR ROBERT DALRYMPLE (1828–1887), Australian statesman ; born at St. Vincent ; educated in England ; clerk in commissariat department in Crimea, 1855 ; senior commissariat officer at Cape Coast Castle, 1856–9 ; deputy assistant-commissary-general, 1858 ; served in China, 1860, in South Australia, 1862, New Zealand, 1864–5 ; returned to England, 1869 ; commissary-general, 1870 ; retired to South Australia, 1871 ; member of assembly, 1875, speaker, 1881 ; knighted, 1886. [xlix. 277]

ROSS, THOMAS (1575 ?–1618), Scottish divine ; M.A. Edinburgh, 1595 ; minister at Cargill, Perthshire, 1606 ; went to Oxford, c. 1615, and being in destitution and perhaps crazed, affixed, 1618, a libellous Latin thesis on door of St. Mary's church ; tried and executed at Edinburgh. [xlix. 278]

ROSS, THOMAS (d. 1675), translator ; B.A. Christ's College, Cambridge, 1642 ; adhered to Charles II in exile ; keeper of Charles II's library, 1661 ; M.A. Oxford, 1663 ; secretary to Henry Coventry (1619–1686) [q. v.] on embassy to Swedish court, 1663 ; published a translation from Silius Italicus, and other writings. [xlix. 278]

ROSS, WILLIAM, twelfth BARON ROSS of Hawkhead (1656 ?–1738), took part in opposition to covenanters, c. 1679 ; major under Graham of Claverhouse, 1683 ; made member of Scottish privy council, 1686, but dismissed by James II ; supported claims of William and Mary at the revolution ; temporarily imprisoned on charge of connection with Montgomery plot, 1690 ; appointed, after Queen Anne's accession, lord high commissioner to church of Scotland ; commissioner for the union. [xlix. 279]

ROSS, WILLIAM (1762–1790), Gaelic poet ; schoolmaster at Gairloch ; two volumes of his poems were published posthumously. [xlix. 280]

ROSS, SIR WILLIAM CHARLES (1794–1860), miniature-painter ; studied at Royal Academy, 1808 ; assistant to Andrew Robertson [q. v.], c. 1814 ; patronised by English and other royal families ; R.A., 1842 ; obtained extra premium in Westminster Hall competition, 1843. His miniatures include portraits of Queen Victoria, Duchess of Kent, Prince Albert, and Queen Adelaide. [xlix. 280]

ROSSE, EARLS OF. [See PARSONS, SIR LAWRENCE, second EARL, 1758–1841 ; PARSONS, WILLIAM, third EARL, 1800–1867.]

ROSSE, JOHN DE (d. 1332). [See ROS.]

ROSSETER, PHILIP (1575 ?–1623), lutenist ; one of James I's musicians, c. 1604 ; joint-patentee of company of 'Children of the Revels to the Queen,' 1610 ; published books of music and instruction for lute and other instruments. [xlix. 282]

ROSSETTI, CHRISTINA GEORGINA (1830–1894), poetess ; sister of Dante Gabriel Rossetti [q. v.] ; born in London ; her first productions were printed privately, 1842 and 1847 ; contributed to the 'Germ' under pseudonym 'Ellen Alleyne,' 1850 ; published 'Goblin Market' (her best work), 1862, 'Commonplace' (stories), 1870, 'Sing Song' (nursery rhymes), 1872, and subsequently composed mainly devotional literature ; for many years an invalid. [xlix. 282]

ROSSETTI, DANTE GABRIEL (1828–1882), painter and poet ; son of Gabriele Rossetti, who came to England, 1824, and was professor of Italian, King's College, London, 1831 ; educated at King's College, London, where he studied drawing under John Sell Cotman [q. v.] ; adopted art as profession, 1842 ; studied at Royal Academy, 1846 ; began, 1845, translations from Dante and contemporaries, published in 1861 ; wrote 'Blessed Damozel,' 'The Portrait,' 'Retro me Sathanas,' and 'The Choice,' c. 1847 ; studied painting under Ford Madox Brown, 1848 ; met Woolner, Holman Hunt, and Millais, and founded pre-Raphaelite school of painting ; exhibited 'Girlhood of Mary Virgin,' 1849 ; lived at 14 Chatham Place, Blackfriars Bridge, London, from 1852 ; gained patronage of Ruskin, who had defended pre-Raphaelites in 'The Times' ; made acquaintance of Sir Edward Burne-Jones, Mr. Swinburne, and William Morris ; between 1850 and 1860 painted most of his best works, including the illustrations to the 'Vita Nuova' ; married, 1860, Elizabeth Eleanor Siddal (d. 1862) ; removed to Tudor House, Cheyne Walk, where he lived with his brother (W. M. Rossetti), Mr. Swinburne, and Mr. George Meredith ; painted 'Beata Beatrix,' 'Monna Vanna,' and other famous pictures, chiefly single figures ; published 'Poems,' 1870 ; suffered from neuralgia and consequent insomnia, and became enslaved to habit of taking chloral ; his last great picture, 'Dante's Dream,' painted 1869–71 ; published 'Ballads and Sonnets,' 1881. His portrait by his own hand is in the National Portrait Gallery. [xlix. 284]

ROSSETTI, LUCY MADOX (1843–1894), painter ; daughter of Ford Madox Brown, under whom she studied ; married W. M. Rossetti, 1874. [xlix. 289]

ROSSETTI, MARIA FRANCESCA (1827–1876), author of 'A Shadow of Dante,' 1871 ; sister of Dante Gabriel Rossetti [q. v.] ; published religious works ; entered Anglican sisterhood at All Saints' Home, Margaret Street, London, 1874. [xlix. 283]

ROSSI, JOHN CHARLES FELIX (1762–1839), sculptor ; studied, 1781, at Royal Academy, where he gained a travelling studentship and went to Rome, 1785–1788 ; R.A., 1802 ; sculptor to prince-regent and William IV ; executed many monuments in St. Paul's Cathedral. [xlix. 290]

ROSSLYN, EARLS OF. [See WEDDERBURN, ALEXANDER, first EARL, 1733–1805 ; ERSKINE, SIR JAMES ST. CLAIR, second EARL, 1762–1837.]

ROST, REINHOLD (1822–1896), orientalist ; born at Eisenburg, Saxen-Altenburg ; Ph.D. Jena, 1847 ; oriental lecturer at St. Augustine's Missionary College, Canterbury, 1851–96 ; secretary to Royal Asiatic Society, 1863 ; librarian at India office, 1869 ; hon. LL.D. Edinburgh, 1877 ; companion of Indian Empire, 1888 ; was familiar with over twenty oriental languages, and published and edited oriental works. [xlix. 290]

ROSWORME or ROSWORM, JOHN (fl. 1630–1660), military engineer ; born in Germany ; served as military engineer on continent and in Ireland ; settled, 1642, in Manchester, which town he contracted to defend against James Stanley, lord Strange (afterwards seventh earl of Derby) [q. v.] ; withstood siege and secured Manchester for parliamentarians ; lieutenant-colonel of Ashton's foot regiment, 1643 ; directed siege of Liverpool, taken 1644 ; engineer-general of all garrisons and forts in England, 1651 ; colonel, 1655 ; published account of his services in Manchester, 1649. [xlix. 291]

ROTELANDE, HUE DE, or RUTLAND, HUGH OF (fl. 1185), Anglo-Norman poet ; connected with English district on Welsh border ; wrote two Anglo-Norman romances in verse, 'Ipomedon' and 'Prothesilaus.' [xlix. 293]

ROTHE, BERNARD (1695–1768). [See ROUTH.]

ROTHE or ROTH, DAVID (1573–1650), Roman catholic divine ; born at Kilkenny ; graduated B.D. at Douay ; returned to Ireland, c. 1609 ; vicar-general of

Armagh ; deputy to Peter Lombard, primate of Ireland ; bishop of Ossory, 1618 ; vice-primate ; senior bishop of Ireland ; obtained deanery of Kilkenny, 1641 ; regulated catholic confederacy, 1642 ; attempted to escape from Cromwell when marching on Kilkenny, but was captured and died soon after ; published treatises, and left unfinished manuscript history of diocese of Ossory.
[xlix. 293]

ROTHE, MICHAEL (1661–1741), Jacobite ; lieutenant James II's royal Irish footguards, under Duke of Ormonde, 1686 ; continued allegiance to James II, and was promoted captain at the revolution ; served in campaign of 1689–91, and fought at battle of Boyne, 1690 ; joined French service, 1691 ; served in Flanders, 1693, and Germany, 1694 ; with Moselle army, 1695 ; colonel, 1701 ; served in Germany, 1701, in Vosges, 1703, and at Blenheim, 1704 ; brevet-brigadier, 1706 ; with Rhine army, 1706–9 and 1713 ; at Malplaquet, 1709 ; brevet major-general, 1710 ; in Flanders, 1710–12 ; obtained command of his regiment, which became known by his name, 1718 ; in Spain, 1719–20 ; lieutenant-general of armies of George I, 1720 ; died at Paris. [xlix. 296]

ROTHE, ROBERT (1550–1622), antiquary ; cousin of David Rothe [q. v.] ; Dublin barrister ; M.P., co. Kilkenny, 1585 ; recorder of Kilkenny, 1609 ; bencher of King's Inns, Dublin, and treasurer, 1620 ; left manuscript 'Register of Pedigree of late Thomas, Earl of Ormond and Ossory' (1616), and 'Register of Antiquities of Kilkenny.'
[xlix. 297]

ROTHERAM, CALEB (1694–1752), minister of dissenting congregation at Kendal, 1716 ; conducted dissenting academy at Kendal, 1733–51 ; M.A. and D.D. Edinburgh, 1743 ; published a religious dissertation.
[xlix. 298]

ROTHERAM, EDWARD (1753 ?–1830), navy captain ; brother of John Rotheram (1750 ?–1804) [q. v.] ; seaman in navy, 1777 ; acting lieutenant, 1780–3, in West Indies ; lieutenant, 1783 ; in action of 1 June 1794 ; commander, 1794 ; captain, 1800 ; at Trafalgar, 1805 ; in Channel, 1805–8 ; C.B., 1815 ; captain of Greenwich Hospital, 1828. [xlix. 298]

ROTHERAM, JOHN (1725–1789), theologian ; B.A. Queen's College, Oxford, 1749 ; assistant at Codrington College, Barbados ; returned to England, 1757 ; Percy fellow, University College, Oxford, 1760–7 ; preacher at Chapel Royal, Whitehall ; published religious works.
[xlix. 299]

ROTHERAM, JOHN (1750 ?–1804), natural philosopher ; born at Newcastle ; studied under Linnæus and Bergmann at university of Upsala, Sweden, where he graduated ; assistant-professor of chemistry, Edinburgh, 1793 ; professor of natural philosophy, St. Andrews, 1795–1804 ; published works on natural philosophy.
[xlix. 300]

ROTHERHAM, SIR JOHN (1630–1696 ?), judge ; fellow of Lincoln College, Oxford, 1648 ; M.A., 1652 ; incorporated at Cambridge, 1653 ; barrister, Gray's Inn, 1655 ; ancient, 1671, treasurer, 1686 ; one of counsel for defence of Richard Baxter [q. v.], 1685 ; serjeant-at-law and baron of exchequer, 1687 ; knighted, 1687. [xlix. 300]

ROTHERHAM, THOMAS (1423–1500), archbishop of York ; known as THOMAS SCOT ; educated at King's College, Cambridge (perhaps also at Eton and Oxford) ; D.D. Oxford and Cambridge, 1463 ; prebendary of Lincoln, 1462, and of Salisbury, 1465 ; keeper of privy seal to Edward IV, 1467 ; bishop of Rochester, 1468–71 ; provost of college of Beverley, c. 1468–72 ; ambassador to Louis XI of France, 1468 ; joint-ambassador to Charles of Burgundy, 1471 ; bishop of Lincoln, 1471–80 ; chancellor, 1474 ; accompanied Edward on French expedition, 1475 ; archbishop of York, 1480–1500 ; deprived of chancellorship and temporarily imprisoned for adherence to Queen Elizabeth Woodville on Edward IV's death, 1483 ; several times chancellor of Cambridge University ; benefactor of Oxford, and particularly of Lincoln College ; master of Pembroke Hall, Oxford, 1480. [xlix. 301]

ROTHERY, HENRY CADOGAN (1817–1888), lawyer ; son of William Rothery [q. v.] ; M.A. St. John's College, Cambridge, 1845 ; entered Doctors' Commons ; from 1842 was employed in ecclesiastical and admiralty courts ; register of privy council in ecclesiastical and maritime causes, c. 1853 ; wreck commissioner, 1876 ; published legal works. [xlix. 303]

ROTHERY, WILLIAM (1775–1864), lawyer ; chief of office of king's proctor in Doctors' Commons ; admiralty referee on slave trade matters, 1821–60.
[xlix. 303]

ROTHES, DUKE OF (1630–1681). [See LESLIE, JOHN.]

ROTHES, EARLS OF. [See LESLIE, GEORGE, fourth EARL, d. 1558 ; LESLIE, ANDREW, fifth EARL, d. 1611 ; LESLIE, JOHN, sixth EARL, 1600–1641 ; LESLIE, JOHN, seventh EARL and first DUKE, 1630–1681 ; LESLIE, JOHN, eighth EARL, 1679–1722 ; LESLIE, JOHN, ninth EARL, 1698 ?–1767.]

ROTHES, MASTER OF (d. 1554). [See LESLIE, NORMAN.]

ROTHESAY, DUKE OF (1378 ?–1402). [See STEWART, DAVID.]

ROTHSCHILD, SIR ANTHONY DE (1810–1876), second son of Nathan Meyer Rothschild [q. v.] ; in business under his brother Lionel Nathan de Rothschild [q. v.] ; created baronet, 1847 ; Austrian consul-general, 1858 ; presiding warden of great synagogue, London, 1855–75 ; first president of newly instituted united synagogue in London, 1870. [xlix. 309]

ROTHSCHILD, FERDINAND JAMES DE (1839–1898), virtuoso ; great grandson of Meyer Amschel Rothschild ; born in Paris ; settled in England, 1860 ; resided at Waddesdon, Buckinghamshire, where he collected works of art, left by his will to the British Museum ; liberal-unionist M.P., Aylesbury division, 1885–98.
[Suppl. iii. 304]

ROTHSCHILD, LIONEL NATHAN DE (1808–1879), banker ; eldest son of Nathan Meyer Rothschild [q. v.] ; educated at Göttingen ; succeeded, 1836, to chief management of Rothschild banking-house in England ; assumed, 1838, dignity of Austrian baron conferred on his father ; negotiated loans for Irish famine, 1847, Crimean expenses, 1856, and Turkey, 1858, and engaged in many other national financial transactions ; elected whig M.P. for city of London, 1847, but not allowed to sit, owing to refusal as a Jew of the necessary oath ; repeatedly re-elected, and finally allowed to sit, 1858 ; re-elected, 1859, 1865, and 1869 ; interested himself in many philanthropic movements ; for some time president of the great synagogue, London ; he is the original of Sidonia in Disraeli's 'Coningsby.' [xlix. 304]

ROTHSCHILD, MEYER AMSCHEL DE (1818–1874), sportsman and collector of art treasures ; fourth son of Nathan Meyer Rothschild [q. v.] ; known as 'Baron Meyer' ; lived at Mentmore ; liberal M.P. for Hythe, 1859–74. His daughter Hannah (d. 1890) married, 1878, Archibald Philip Primrose, fifth and present earl of Rosebery. [xlix. 309]

ROTHSCHILD, NATHAN MEYER (1777–1836), financier and merchant ; born at Frankfort-on-Maine, where his father conducted business as banker, money-changer, and dealer in curiosities ; attracted notice of William IX, landgrave of Hesse Cassel (known after 1803 as Elector William I), who appointed him court agent, 1801, and supported him in his career as loan contractor to European governments ; established a branch of the business in London in 1805, while his brothers, James and Solomon, settled respectively in Paris and Vienna ; came to England first in 1797, and was naturalised, 1804 ; opened business house at New Court, St. Swithin's Lane, London ; engaged by government in payment of foreign subsidies ; acted as agent for English government in Peninsular war ; undertook loans for many European countries ; made baron of Austrian empire, 1822, but never assumed title ; consul-general of Austria in England, 1822.
[xlix. 306]

ROTHWELL, EDWARD (d. 1731), dissenting minister ; ordained minister of Poulton-in-the-Fylde, 1693, and subsequently held other charges ; published theological treatises. [xlix. 309]

ROTHWELL, RICHARD (1800–1868), painter ; assistant to Sir Thomas Lawrence in London ; exhibited at Royal Academy from 1830. [xlix. 310]

ROTIER. [See ROETTIERS.]

ROUBILIAC or ROUBILLAC, LOUIS FRANÇOIS (1695–1762), sculptor ; born at Lyons ; probably settled permanently in England after 1730; gained patronage of Horace Walpole's brother Edward; assistant to Cheere at his stoneyard at Hyde Park Corner, London, and later to Jonathan Tyers [q. v.]; executed statue of Handel erected at Vauxhall, London, 1738; opened business independently, and executed monuments and busts of many celebrated persons. Many of his works, including the well-known Nightingale monument, are at Westminster; his full-length of Shakespeare, executed for Garrick, 1758, is in the British Museum. [xlix. 310]

ROUCLIFFE, SIR BRIAN (d. 1494), judge; third baron of exchequer, 1458; frequently counsel to Sir William Plumpton [q. v.]; second baron, 1483. [xlix. 312]

ROUGH. [See also Row.]

ROUGH, JOHN (d. 1557), Scottish protestant minister; educated at St. Leonard's College, St. Andrews; entered monastery at Stirling, but left it to become chaplain to Regent Arran, 1543; prohibited from preaching; chaplain to garrison at St. Andrews; went to England, 1547, and entered service of Lord-protector Somerset; minister of secret society of protestants in London, 1557; arrested and burned at Smithfield. [xlix. 313]

ROUGH, WILLIAM (d. 1838), lawyer and poet; of Westminster and Trinity College, Cambridge; M.A., 1799; barrister, Inner Temple, 1801; serjeant-at-law, 1808; president of court of justice for united colony of Demerara and Essequibo, 1816–21; puisne judge in Ceylon, 1830–6; chief-justice of supreme court, 1836–8; knighted, 1837; published dramatic and other poetical works; died in Ceylon. [xlix. 313]

ROUMARE, WILLIAM DE, EARL OF LINCOLN (fl. 1140), supported Henry I in rebellion of Hugh de Gournay, 1118–19; rebelled against Henry I in Normandy, but was reconciled, 1128; one of justiciars entrusted with the duchy of Normandy, 1137; created Earl of Lincoln, 1138, but was probably subsequently deprived of earldom. [xlix. 314]

ROUPELL, GEORGE LEITH (1797–1854), physician; educated at Greenwich and Gonville and Caius College, Cambridge; M.D., 1825; F.R.C.P., 1826; censor, 1829, 1837, and 1838; Croonian lecturer, 1832 and 1833; physician to St. Bartholomew's Hospital, London, 1834; published medical works. [xlix. 315]

ROUS, FRANCIS (1579–1659), puritan; B.A. Broadgates Hall (afterwards Pembroke College), Oxford, 1597; graduated at Leyden, 1599; entered Middle Temple, 1601, but retired to Landrake, where he produced several theological works; M.P., Truro, 1626, in Short and Long parliaments, 1640, and also in 1654, Tregony, 1628–9; Devonshire, 1653, and Cornwall, 1656; took covenant, 1643; provost of Eton College, 1644; member of Derby house committee, 1648; joined independents, 1649; speaker of Little parliament, and member of Protector's council of state, 1653; published writings. [xlix. 316]

ROUS, HENRY JOHN (1795–1877), admiral and sportsman; educated at Westminster; entered navy, 1808; post-captain, 1823; retired from active service, 1835, and devoted himself to horseracing; steward of Jockey Club; became public handicapper, c. 1855; conservative M.P. for Westminster, 1841; lord of admiralty, 1846; admiral of blue, 1863, and of white, 1864. [xlix. 317]

ROUS or **ROSS**, JOHN (1411?–1491), antiquary of Warwick; educated at Oxford; chaplain, c. 1445 till death, of chapel at Guy's Cliffe, near Warwick, built by Richard Beauchamp, earl of Warwick [q. v.], in 1423; wrote historical works, disfigured by party leanings, including accounts of earls of Warwick, and 'Historia Regum Angliæ,' of which manuscripts are extant. [xlix. 318]

ROUS, JOHN (1584–1644), diarist; M.A. Emmanuel College, Cambridge, 1607; presented to living of Stanton-Downham, 1623; kept, from 1625–41, a diary, edited for Camden Society, 1856. [xlix. 320]

ROUS, JOHN (fl. 1656–1695), quaker; born in Barbados; went to Rhode Island, America, 1657, to preach and proselytise, and after suffering much persecution came to England, 1659; settled in London as West India merchant; joint-author of pamphlets. [xlix. 320]

ROUSBY, CLARA MARION JESSIE (1852?–1879), actress; daughter of Dr. Dowse, inspector-general of hospitals; married Wybert Rousby, a Jersey actor and manager, 1868; first appeared in London, 1869, at Queen's Theatre, Long Acre, where she remained till 1871; subsequently played at Princess's, Olympic, and Drury Lane; her characters include Rosalind and Cordelia. [xlix. 321]

ROUSE or **RUSSE**, JOHN (1574–1652), librarian; B.A. Balliol College, Oxford, 1599; fellow of Oriel College, 1600; M.A., 1604; chief librarian of Bodleian Library, 1620; formed friendship with Milton, who wrote a mock-heroic ode to him, 1647. [xlix. 322]

ROUSSEAU, JACQUES (1626–1694), painter; born in Paris; studied under the Dutch painter, Herman van Swanevelt; member of French Academy; went to Switzerland and Holland, and, later, came to England on revocation of edict of Nantes; assisted in decorating Montagu House (afterwards British Museum); employed by William III at Hampton Court. [xlix. 322]

ROUSSEAU, SAMUEL (1763–1820), printer and orientalist; apprenticed to John Nichols the printer; taught himself several classical, oriental, and modern languages; opened printing office in London, where he produced many oriental books. [xlix. 323]

ROUSSEL, THEODORE (1614–1689). [See RUSSEL.]

ROUTH, BERNARD (1695–1768), Irish jesuit; entered Society of Jesus, 1716; professed of four vows, 1734; professor in Irish College, Poitiers; on editorial staff of 'Journal de Trévoux,' Paris, 1739–43; confessor of Princess Charlotte de Lorraine at Mons, 1764; published poetical and critical works. [xlix. 323]

ROUTH, MRS. MARTHA (1743–1817), quakeress; née Winter; principal of Friends' boarding-school at Nottingham; 'acknowledged minister,' 1773; married Richard Routh of Manchester, 1776; made missionary tours in British islands and America; left journal (part published, 1822). [xlix. 324]

ROUTH, MARTIN JOSEPH (1755–1854), divine; fellow, Magdalen College, Oxford, 1775; M.A., 1776; senior proctor, 1784; D.D. and president of Magdalen College, Oxford, 1791 till death; instituted rector and vicar of Tilehurst, and received priest's orders, 1810; edited 'Reliquiæ Sacræ,' a collection of writings of ecclesiastical authors of second and third centuries, and other works. [xlix. 324]

ROUTH, SIR RANDOLPH ISHAM (1785?–1858), commissary-general in the army; educated at Eton; entered commissariat department of army; saw much foreign service, and was senior commissariat officer at Waterloo, 1815; knighted, 1841; K.C.B., 1848; published work on commissariat service. [xlix. 326]

ROUTLEDGE, GEORGE (1812–1888), publisher; apprenticed to bookseller at Carlisle; opened bookseller's business in London, 1836; started as publisher at 36 Soho Square, 1843; established branch in New York, 1854; retired from business, 1887. His publications include the 'Railway Library,' ultimately numbering 1,060 volumes, at one shilling each, 'Routledge's Universal Library,' edited by Henry Morley, and 'Shakespeare,' edited by Howard Staunton, illustrated by Sir John Gilbert. [xlix. 326]

ROW. [See also ROUGH.]

ROW, JOHN (1525?–1580), Scottish reformer; M.A. St. Leonard's College, St. Andrews; practised as advocate in St. Andrews' consistorial court; represented John Hamilton, archbishop of St. Andrews, at papal court, 1550; licentiate of laws, university of Rome, 1556; LL.D. Padua; returned to Scotland as papal nuncio to examine causes of spread of heretical opinions, 1558–9; converted to protestantism; minister and vicar of Kennoway, 1560; minister of Middle Church, Perth; on commissions which drew up first and second 'Books of Discipline.' [xlix. 327]

ROW, JOHN (1568–1646), Scottish ecclesiastical historian; son of John Row (1525?–1580) [q. v.]; M.A. Edinburgh, 1590; ordained minister of Carnock, Dunfermline, 1592; prominent member of the anti-episcopal party. Wrote and circulated in manuscript 'Historie of Kirk of Scotland, 1558–1637' (printed, 1842). [xlix. 329]

ROW, JOHN (1598?–1672?), divine; son of John Row (1568–1646) [q. v.]; M.A. St. Leonard's College, St. Andrews, 1617; master of grammar school, Kirkcaldy, 1619; rector of grammar school, Perth, 1632–41; minister of St. Nicholas Church, Aberdeen, 1641; teacher of Hebrew at Marischal College, Aberdeen; strongly advocated subscription to covenant; appointed to revise new metrical version of Psalms 90 to 120, 1647; appointed by Cromwell's parliament principal of King's College, Aberdeen, 1652; deposed, 1661; published Hebrew grammar and lexicon, and wrote continuation (1637–9) to his father's history of the kirk. [xlix. 330]

ROW, THOMAS (1786–1864), baptist minister; published hymns and religious writings. [xlix. 331]

ROW, WILLIAM (1563–1634), Scottish presbyterian divine; son of John Row (1525?–1580) [q. v.]; graduated at Perth, 1587; minister of Forgandenny; protested against restoration of episcopacy, 1602–6; imprisoned, 1607–14, for opposing appointment of permanent moderator. [xlix. 331]

ROWAN, ARCHIBALD HAMILTON (1751–1834), United Irishman; son of Gawin Hamilton; adopted name of Rowan on inheriting property from his grandfather, c. 1767; educated at Queens' College, Cambridge; served as lieutenant-colonel in Portugal, 1777; lived in Paris, 1781–4; removed to Ireland, 1784; brought himself into notice, c. 1788, by publication of 'Investigation of Sufferings of Mary Neal,' whose seduction by a person of high station had been allowed to pass unpunished; original member of Northern Whig Club, Belfast, 1790; joined Society of United Irishmen, 1791; arrested on unfounded charge of distributing a seditious pamphlet, 1792; received bail, but on being brought to trial was found guilty, though defended by Curran, and imprisoned at Dublin, 1794; escaped to France and subsequently proceeded to America; obtained pardon, and returned to England, 1803; resided at Killyleagh Castle, Ireland; warmly supported catholic emancipation. [xlix. 332]

ROWAN, ARTHUR BLENNERHASSETT (1800–1861), divine; M.A. Trinity College, Dublin, 1827; D.D., 1854; rector of Kilgobbin, Clonfert, 1854; archdeacon of Ardfert, 1856; published antiquarian and other works. [xlix. 335]

ROWAN, SIR CHARLES (1782?–1852), chief commissioner of police; ensign in 52nd foot, 1797; captain, 1803; served in Sicily, 1806-7, Sweden, 1808, and Peninsular and Waterloo campaigns; major, 52nd regiment, 1811; brevet lieutenant-colonel, 1812; first chief commissioner of police, 1829; K.C.B., 1848. [xlix. 335]

ROWAN, FREDERICA MACLEAN (1814–1882), author; niece of Sir Charles Rowan [q. v.]; born in West Indies and lived successively in Copenhagen, Weimar, Paris, and London; secretary to Sir Francis Henry Goldsmid [q. v.]; published 'History of French Revolution,' 1844, and translations from French, Swedish, and German, including 'Stunden der Andacht' (attributed to Zschokke). [xlix. 336]

ROWAN, GAWIN WILLIAM ROWAN HAMILTON (1783–1834), son of Archibald Hamilton Rowan [q. v.]; entered navy, 1801; lieutenant, 1809; post-captain, 1812; on South American station, c. 1824; retired owing to ill-health. [xlix. 334]

ROWAN, SIR WILLIAM (1789–1879), field-marshal; brother of Sir Charles Rowan [q. v.]; ensign in 52nd foot, 1803; lieutenant, 1804; in Sicily, 1806-7, Sweden, 1808, and Peninsula, France, and Waterloo campaigns; lieutenant-colonel, 1819; civil and military secretary in Canada, 1823–9, and commanded forces there, 1849–55; general, 1862; field-marshal, 1877; G.C.B., 1856. [xlix. 336]

ROWBOTHAM, THOMAS CHARLES LEESON (1823–1875), painter; born in Dublin; member of New Society (now Royal Institute) of Painters in Watercolours, 1851; professor of drawing at Royal Naval School; published volumes of views in British islands. [xlix. 337]

ROWE. [See also Row.]

ROWE, BENONI (1658–1706), nonconformist minister; brother of Thomas Rowe (1657–1705) [q. v.]; pastor in Fetter Lane, London, 1699. [xlix. 348]

ROWE, MRS. ELIZABETH (1674–1737), author; née Singer; married Thomas Rowe (1687–1715) [q. v.], 1710;

published, 1696, poems by 'Philomela'; enthusiastically praised by Klopstock, Wieland, and Dr. Johnson. Her writings, the most popular of which were compositions in epistolary form, include 'Friendship in Death' (1728) and 'Letters Moral and Entertaining' (1729–33); her 'Miscellaneous Works' published, 1739. [xlix. 338]

ROWE, GEORGE ROBERT (1792–1861), physician; M.C.S. London, 1812; served as surgeon in Peninsular war; M.R.C.P., 1840; practised at Chigwell, and, later, in London; published medical works. [xlix. 339]

ROWE, HARRY (1726–1800), showman; born of poor parents; trumpeter in Duke of Kingston's light horse; fought at Culloden, 1746; gained living as puppet showman; patronised by John Croft [q. v.], who caused to be printed, and probably furnished annotations for, 'Macbeth, with notes by Harry Rowe,' 1797; published also a musical farce. [xlix. 339]

ROWE, JOHN (1626–1677), nonconformist divine; B.A. Emmanuel College, Cambridge, 1646; incorporated B.A. Oxford, and M.A., 1648; fellow of Corpus Christi College, Oxford, 1649; preacher at Westminster Abbey, 1654; deprived at Restoration; published religious works. [xlix. 340]

ROWE, JOHN (1764–1832), unitarian minister; joint-pastor, 1787, and sole pastor, 1789, at High Street Chapel, Shrewsbury; joint-pastor at Lewin's Mead Chapel, Bristol, 1798; founded Western Unitarian Society. [xlix. 341]

ROWE, NICHOLAS (1674–1718), poet and dramatist; educated at Westminster School; barrister, Middle Temple; abandoned legal profession for that of playwright, and made the acquaintance of Pope and Addison; produced at Lincoln's Inn Fields, London, his tragedies, 'The Ambitious Stepmother,' 1700, 'Tamerlane,' 1702, and 'Fair Penitent' (adapted from Massinger's 'Fatal Dowry'), 1703; his 'Ulysses' was staged in 1706, his 'Royal Convert' at the Haymarket, London, in 1707, and 'Jane Shore' and 'Lady Jane Grey' in 1714 and 1715 respectively, at Drury Lane, London; produced an unsuccessful comedy, 'The Biter,' at Lincoln's Inn Fields, London, 1704; published, 1709, an edition of Shakespeare's plays, with biographical preface and emendations of the text of the fourth folio, which his edition followed; divided and numbered acts and scenes on rational principles, and modernised grammar, spelling, and punctuation; under-secretary to Duke of Queensberry, 1709-11; poet laureate, 1715; land surveyor of customs of port of London, 1715; clerk of council of George, Prince of Wales; clerk of presentations to Thomas Parker, first earl of Macclesfield [q. v.], 1718; buried in Westminster Abbey. His portrait was twice painted by Kneller. His poetical works include a famous translation of Lucan (1718). His collected works appeared, 1727. [xlix. 341]

ROWE or **ROE**, OWEN (1593?–1661), regicide; worked as haberdasher in London; took part in foundation of colonies of Massachusetts and the Bermudas; captain of green regiment of London trained bands, 1642; colonel, 1646; member of court which tried Charles I, and signed death-warrant; deputy-governor of the Bermudas, 1655; acted with Monck's opponents, 1659; convicted as regicide, 1660; died in prison in Tower of London. [xlix. 345]

ROWE, RICHARD (1828–1879), journalist successively in Edinburgh (on 'Scotsman') and in London; published stories for children under pseudonyms Charles Camden and Edward Howe. [xlix. 346]

ROWE, SAMUEL (1793–1853), topographer; apprenticed to bookseller at Kingsbridge; started business at Plymouth, 1813; entered Jesus College, Cambridge, c. 1822; M.A., 1833; took holy orders; vicar of Crediton, 1835; chief work, 'Perambulation of . . . Dartmoor' (1848). [xlix. 346]

ROWE, SIR SAMUEL (1835–1888), colonial governor and surgeon; qualified as medical practitioner, 1856; appointed on army medical staff, 1862, and afterwards acted as colonial surgeon at Lagos; returned on leave, 1864; graduated in medicine and surgery, Aberdeen, 1865; magistrate and clerk of council at Lagos, 1869; staff-surgeon in army, 1870; surgeon-major, 1873; served in Ashanti war, 1873; brigade-surgeon, 1876; governor successively of Gambia, Sierra Leone, 1876-7, West Africa settlements, 1877 and 1884, and Gold Coast and Lagos, 1881; K.C.M.G., 1880; LL.D. Aberdeen, 1886. [xlix. 347]

ROWE, THOMAS (1657–1705), independent divine and philosophical teacher; pastor successively of independent church in Holborn and Basinghall Street, London; lecturer at Pinners' Hall, London, 1699. [xlix. 347]

ROWE, THOMAS (1687–1715), author; son of Benoni Rowe [q. v.]; husband of Elizabeth Rowe [q. v.]; educated at Charterhouse and Leyden; wrote lives of classical heroes overlooked by Plutarch (published posthumously, 1728). [xlix. 338]

ROWELL, GEORGE AUGUSTUS (1804–1892), meteorologist; originally followed trade of cabinet-maker; studied astronomy; published letters and papers on meteorological subjects; assistant in Ashmolean Museum, and, 1860, in Oxford University Museum. [xlix. 348]

ROWLAND. [See also ROWLANDS.]

ROWLAND, DANIEL (1778–1859), antiquary; educated at Shrewsbury; barrister in London; settled in London, 1846; F.S.A.; printed privately account of Nevill family. [xlix. 349]

ROWLAND, DAVID (*fl.* 1569–1586), author; educated at St. Mary's Hall, Oxford; travelled as private tutor, and subsequently taught Greek and Latin; published translation from Mendoza's 'Lazarillo de Tormes,' 1576. [xlix. 349]

ROWLAND, JOHN (1606–1660), divine; M.A. Corpus Christi College, Oxford, 1626; rector of Foot's Cray, Kent 1634; chaplain in Sir Jacob Astley's royalist regiment; probably took refuge in Netherlands; published at Antwerp two attacks on Milton, 1651 and 1652. [xlix. 349]

ROWLANDS, DANIEL (1713–1790), Welsh methodist; ordained deacon, 1733; priest, 1735; with Howel Harris [q. v.] founded Welsh Calvinistic methodism; deputy-moderator, 1743, and subsequently chairman of methodist 'association' for control of societies; quarrelled with Harris, 1746, and finally separated from him, 1751; suspended by Bishop Squire from exercise of clerical functions, 1763; preached at 'new church,' Llangeitho; published religious works in Welsh and English. [xlix. 350]

ROWLANDS, HENRY (1551–1616), Welsh divine; M.A. St. Mary Hall, Oxford, 1577; D.D., 1605; prebendary of Bangor, 1584–94; dean, 1593, and bishop, 1598, of Bangor. [xlix. 351]

ROWLANDS, HENRY (1655–1723), Welsh divine; held living of Llanidan, 1696; published work on antiquities of Anglesey. [xlix. 351]

ROWLANDS *alias* VERSTEGEN, RICHARD (*fl.* 1565–1620), antiquary; educated at Christ Church, Oxford; set up printing business in Antwerp and assumed his grandfather's name of Verstegen; removed, c. 1587, to Paris, where he published a work against Queen Elizabeth's treatment of Roman catholics in England, and was imprisoned. His works include 'Antiquities concerning the English Nation,' 1605. [xlix. 352]

ROWLANDS, SAMUEL (1570?–1630?), writer of tracts in prose and verse between 1598 and 1628; his works, all of which are bibliographical rarities, include 'The Betraying of Christ,' 1598; 'Greenes Ghost,' 1602, 'Hell's Broke Loose,' 1605, 'Democritus, or Doctor Merryman his Medicines against Melancholy Humors,' 1607, 'Humors Looking Glasse,' 1608, and 'Martin Mark-all' (an account of the habits and language of thieves), 1610, and 'The Melancholie Knight,' 1615. [xlix. 353]

ROWLANDS, WILLIAM (1802–1865), known as GWILYM LLEYN, Welsh bibliographer; weaver in Carnarvonshire; joined Wesleyans, c. 1820; acted as lay-preacher, and (1831–64) served many chapels in Cardiff circuit; settled at Oswestry, 1864; published religious works, and a bibliographical record of books printed in and relating to Wales from 1546 to 1800. [xlix. 356]

ROWLANDSON, MARY (*fl.* 1682), colonist; daughter of John White of New England; married Joseph Rowlandson, first minister of Lancaster, Massachusetts; captured by Indians, 1675; published account of captivity. [xlix. 357]

ROWLANDSON, THOMAS (1756–1827), artist and caricaturist; studied at Royal Academy and in Paris;

exhibited at Royal Academy from 1775; settled in London as portrait-painter, 1777; journeyed frequently on continent; developed tendency to caricature, c. 1781, and rapidly won celebrity; executed for Ackermann's monthly 'Poetical Magazine,' 1809, plates for which William Combe [q. v.] supplied verses, republished (1812) in volume-form as 'Tour of Dr. Syntax'; second and third 'Tours' followed in 1820 and 1821; produced several series of humorous plates. [xlix. 357]

ROWLEY, SIR CHARLES, baronet (1770–1845), admiral; son of Sir Joshua Rowley [q. v.]; entered navy, 1785; lieutenant, 1789; flag-captain to Sir Charles Cotton, 1800; at Walcheren, 1809, Cadiz, 1810, in Adriatic, 1811; created baronet, 1836; G.C.B., 1840; admiral, 1841; commander-in-chief at Portsmouth, 1842–5. [xlix. 359]

ROWLEY, JOHN (1768?–1824), major-general; educated at Royal Military Academy, Woolwich; second lieutenant, royal artillery, 1786; transferred to engineers, 1787; first lieutenant, 1792; adjutant of engineers at Woolwich, 1795–9; chief engineer's aide-de-camp at board of ordnance, 1799; deputy-inspector-general of fortifications, 1811; major-general, 1821. [xlix. 359]

ROWLEY, SIR JOSHUA, baronet (1730?–1790), vice-admiral; son of Sir William Rowley [q. v.]; lieutenant, 1747; captain; commanded reinforcement to Byron in West Indies, 1779; rear-admiral of blue, 1779; commanded Jamaica station, 1782–3; created baronet, 1786; vice-admiral of white, 1787. [xlix. 360]

ROWLEY, SIR JOSIAS, baronet (1765–1842), vice-admiral; grandson of Sir William Rowley [q. v.]; midshipman, 1780; lieutenant, 1783; commander, 1794; post-captain, 1795; served in East Indies, 1799–1802; fought at Finisterre, 1805, and Buenos Ayres and Monte Video; took part in capture of Bourbon, 1810; created baronet, 1813; rear-admiral, 1814; K.C.B., 1815; vice-admiral, 1825; commander-in-chief in Mediterranean, 1833–7; G.C.M.G., 1834; G.C.B., 1840. [xlix. 361]

ROWLEY, SAMUEL (*d.* 1633?), dramatist; attached, before 1598, to service of Philip Henslowe, theatrical manager, probably as reviser of manuscript plays; produced independently or in collaboration several plays on biblical history and other subjects, none of which is extant, excepting 'When you see me you know me, or Chronicle Historie of Henrie VIII,' 1605; with William Bird was paid 4l. by Henslowe for making addition to Marlowe's 'Faustus,' 1602; 'The Noble Sovldier,' 1634, has been attributed to him. [xlix. 362]

ROWLEY, THOMAS (pseudonym). [See CHATTERTON, THOMAS, 1752–1770.]

ROWLEY, WILLIAM (1585?–1642?), dramatist; actor in Queen Anne's company before 1610; met Thomas Middleton, 1614, in collaboration with whom his best work was done; played under Henslowe's management at the 'Hope'; retired from acting profession, c. 1627. He wrote, unassisted, 'A new Wonder,' 1632, 'All's lost by Lust, 1633, 'A Match at Midnight,' 1633, and 'A Shoomaker a Gentleman,' 1638. He collaborated in 'A Fair Quarrel,' 1617, 'The Changeling,' performed, 1621, and others with Middleton, 'The Birth of Merlin,' printed, 1662, perhaps with Shakespeare, 'Fortune by Land and Sea,' printed, 1655, with Heywood 'The Thracian Wonder,' printed, 1661, with Webster, and other pieces with Ford, Massinger, and Dekker. [xlix. 363]

ROWLEY, SIR WILLIAM (1690?–1768), admiral; entered navy, 1704; lieutenant, 1708; captain, 1716; in Mediterranean, 1741; rear-admiral of white, 1743; at Toulon, 1744; admiral of the fleet, 1744; admiral of blue, 1747, and of white, 1748; rear-admiral of Great Britain, 1747; lord of admiralty, 1751; K.B., 1753; admiral of fleet and commander-in-chief, 1762. [xlix. 365]

ROWLEY, WILLIAM (1742–1806), surgeon; studied at St. Thomas's Hospital, London; in army, 1760–5; began practice in London as 'man-midwife,' 1766; M.D. St. Andrews, 1774; L.R.C.P., 1784; M.B., 1788, St. Alban Hall, Oxford; published medical works. [xlix. 366]

ROWNING, JOHN (1701?–1771), divine; M.A. Magdalene College, Cambridge, 1728; fellow; rector of Anderby; published 'System of Natural Philosophy,' 1735, and other works. [xlix. 367]

ROWNTREE, JOSEPH (1801–1859), quaker; grocer in York; member of Merchants' Company; interested in educational schemes of Society of Friends; mayor of York, 1858; published pamphlets. [xlix. 367]

ROWSE, RICHARD (*fl.* 1238–1259). [See RICHARD OF CORNWALL.]

ROWSON, SUSANNA (1762–1824), *née* Haswell; born at Portsmouth, but went to America at early age; returned to England, 1778; married William Rowson, 1786; published novels which achieved considerable success, the most popular being 'Charlotte Temple' (1790), but her husband becoming bankrupt, went on the stage; appeared at Edinburgh, 1792–3; toured in America, 1793–1797; opened school, 1797, at Boston, where she died. [xlix. 367]

ROWTHALL, THOMAS (*d.* 1523). [See RUTHALL.]

ROXBURGH, DUKES OF. [See KER, JOHN, first DUKE, *d.* 1741; KER, JOHN, third DUKE, 1740–1804; KER, JAMES INNES-, fifth DUKE, 1738–1823.]

ROXBURGH, EARL OF (1570?–1650). [See KER, ROBERT.]

ROXBURGH, WILLIAM (1751–1815), botanist; educated at Edinburgh University; qualified as surgeon, and served on one of East India Company's ships; M.D. 1776; surgeon on Madras establishment, 1780; appointed by the company botanist in Carnatic; superintendent of Calcutta Botanic Garden, 1793; R.A.S.; F.L.S.; fellow of Royal Society of Arts; published works relating to Indian botany; left botanical manuscripts. [xlix. 368]

ROXBY, ROBERT (1809?–1866), actor; son of William Roxby Beverley; appeared at St. James's Theatre, London, 1839; managed Theatre Royal, Manchester, 1843; at Lyceum, London, 1847–55; played subsequently at Drury Lane, London (of which he was during eleven years stage-manager) and Princess's, London. [xlix. 370]

ROY, JOHN (1700–1752). [See STEWART, JOHN.]

ROY, WILLIAM (*fl.* 1527–31), friar; educated at Cambridge; friar observant in Franciscan cloister at Greenwich; acted as Tyndale's amanuensis at Cologne and Worms in translating New Testament, 1525–6; published religious works; probably burned in Portugal, *c.* 1531. [xlix. 370]

ROY, WILLIAM (1726–1790), colonel in engineers; assistant to Lieutenant-colonel Watson, deputy quartermaster-general under Duke of Cumberland, 1746; aided Watson in making military map of Scotland; commissioned as practitioner-engineer, 1755; employed in reconnaissance of coasts of Kent and Sussex threatened by French invasion, 1755; took part in expedition against Rochefort, 1757; sub-engineer, lieutenant, and captain in corps of engineers, 1759; major and deputy quartermaster-general of South Britain, 1761; surveyor-general of coasts and engineer for military surveys for Great Britain, 1765; F.R.S., 1767; F.S.A.; major-general, 1781; director and lieutenant-colonel of royal engineers, and colonel in engineers, 1783; colonel of 30th foot, 1786; Copley medallist for work in connection with determining relative positions of observatories of Paris and Greenwich, 1785. Left in manuscript 'Military Antiquities of Romans in Britain'; published archæological and scientific writings. [xlix. 371]

ROYDON, SIR MARMADUKE (1583–1646), merchant and royalist; apprenticed to Bordeaux merchant in London and became his factor in France; freeman of Clothworkers' Company; one of first 'planters' in Barbados; fought for Charles I in civil war; knighted, 1643; governor of Faringdon, 1645. [xlix. 373]

ROYDON, MATTHEW (*fl.* 1580–1622), poet; M.A. Oxford, 1580; intimate with Sidney, Marlowe, Spenser, Lodge, and Chapman. His most celebrated poem is his 'Elegie, or Friends passion for his Astrophill' (on Sidney's death), printed in Spenser's 'Colin Clout,' 1595, and in all later editions of Spenser's works. [xlix. 374]

ROYLE, JOHN FORBES (1799–1858), surgeon and naturalist; educated at Military Academy at Addiscombe; surgeon in East India Company's service; joined medical staff of Bengal army, 1819; superintendent of garden at Saharunpore, 1823; made valuable collection of economic plants; returned to England, 1831; professor of materia medica, King's College, London; F.R.S., 1837; F.L.S.,

1833; fellow and secretary of Geological and Royal Horticultural societies; one of founders of Philosophical Club, 1847; works include 'Illustrations of Botany and Natural History of Himalayan Mountains' (1839). [xlix. 375]

ROYSTON, RICHARD (1599–1686), bookseller to Charles I, Charles II, and James II; confined in Fleet prison for printing books against parliament, 1645; published 'Εἰκὼν Βασιλική,' 1648; received from Charles II monopoly of printing Charles I's works, 1660; master of Stationers' Company, 1673 and 1674. [xlix. 376]

RUADHAN (*d.* 585?), Irish saint; son of Fergus; studied in St. Finnian's school at Clonard, co. Meath; founded religious community of Lothra, co. Tipperary; entered into dispute concerning a fugitive, whom he protected, with Diarmait, king of Ireland, on whose residence, Tara, he laid the curse that it should be uninhabited after Diarmait's time. His day is 15 April. [xlix. 376]

RUD, THOMAS (1668–1733), divine; M.A. Trinity College, Cambridge, 1691; head-master at Newcastle grammar school and master of St. Mary's Hospital, Newcastle, 1699–1710; rector of Washington, 1729; prebendary of Ripon collegiate church, 1728; published several works and left manuscript catalogue of manuscripts at Durham Cathedral. [xlix. 377]

RUDBORNE or **RODEBURNE**, THOMAS (*d.* 1442), bishop of St. David's; bursar, Merton College, Oxford, 1399–1400; dean of Tamworth, 1413; warden of Merton College, Oxford, 1416; chaplain to Henry V in Normandy, 1417; prebendary of Sarum, 1419; chancellor of Oxford University, 1420; bishop of St. David's, 1433. [xlix. 377]

RUDBORNE, THOMAS (*fl.* 1460), monk of St. Swithun's, Winchester; wrote historical works, including 'Historia Major,' 1454, and 'Annales Breves Ecclesiæ Wintoniensis a Bruto ad Henricum VI regem,' 1440. [xlix. 378]

RUDD, ANTHONY (1549?–1615), bishop of St. David's; M.A. and major fellow, Trinity College, Cambridge, 1570; D.D., 1583; dean of Gloucester, 1584–94; bishop of St. David's, 1594–1615; summoned to Hampton Court conference; published sermons. [xlix. 378]

RUDD, SAYER (*d.* 1757), divine; minister at Turners' Hall, Philpot Lane, London, 1725–33; studied midwifery at Paris; M.D. Leyden; practised in London; disowned by Calvinistic baptists owing to alleged unitarianism, 1735; conformed to established church, 1738, and held livings in Kent; kept school at Deal; published religious and other works. [xlix. 379]

RUDD, THOMAS (1584?–1656), captain and military engineer; served in Low Countries; chief military engineer for Wales, 1627; superintended defence and harbour works at Portsmouth and Dover, 1639–42; chief engineer to royalists during civil war; published mathematical and other works. [xlix. 380]

RUDDER, SAMUEL (*d.* 1801), printer at Cirencester; published topographical works relating to Gloucestershire. [xlix. 380]

RUDDIMAN, THOMAS (1674–1757), philologist; educated at King's College, Aberdeen; M.A., 1694; employed in Advocates' Library, Edinburgh, 1700; assistant-librarian, 1702; started as book auctioneer, 1707; prepared for press editions of several well-known books, including George Buchanan's works (1715); opened printing business, 1715; acquired, 1729, 'Caledonian Mercury' (which he had printed since 1724), the organ of Prince Charles Edward in 1745; joint-printer to Edinburgh University, 1728; chief librarian, 1730–52, to Advocates' Library, of which, with assistance of Walter Goodall (1706?–1766) [q. v.], he began to issue a catalogue; joined controversy with the Rev. George Logan [q. v.] on subject of hereditary succession to throne, 1747–50; assisted Ames in 'Typographical Antiquities,' 1749; published 'Rudiments of Latin Tongue,' 1714. [xlix. 381]

RUDGE, EDWARD (1763–1846), botanist and antiquary; educated at Queen's College, Oxford; studied and published work on botany of Guiana, 1805–7; F.S.A.; member of Linnean Society, 1802; F.R.S., 1805; conducted excavations at Evesham Abbey. [xlix. 383]

RUDGE, EDWARD JOHN (1792–1861), antiquary; son of Edward Rudge [q. v.]; M.A. Caius College, Cambridge; barrister; F.S.A. [xlix. 384]

RUDGE, THOMAS (1754–1825), divine; M.A. Worcester College, Oxford, 1783; B.D., 1784; archdeacon of Gloucester, 1814; chancellor of diocese of Hereford, 1817; published historical works relating to Gloucestershire. [xlix. 384]

RUDHALL, ABRAHAM, the younger (1680–1735), bell-founder; son of Abraham Rudhall the elder [q. v.], with whom he worked; the business carried on after his death by his son and grandson. [xlix. 384]

RUDHALL, ABRAHAM, the elder (1657–1736), bell-founder; cast, with his son, bells for St. Bride's, Fleet Street (1710 and 1718), St. Dunstan's-in-the-East, London, and St. Sepulchre's, London. [xlix. 384]

RUDING, ROGERS (1751–1820), numismatist; M.A. and fellow, Merton College, Oxford, 1775; B.D., 1782; held living of Malden, 1793; F.S.A.; published 'Annals of Coinage of Britain,' 1817–19. [xlix. 385]

RUDYERD, SIR BENJAMIN (1572–1658), politician and poet; educated at Winchester College and St. John's College, Oxford; barrister, Inner Temple, 1600; intimate friend of Ben Jonson and William Herbert, earl of Pembroke; knighted and appointed surveyor for life of court of wards, 1618; M.P. for Portsmouth, 1620, 1624, 1625, Old Sarum, 1626, Downton, 1628, Wilton, 1640 (twice); supported Buckingham and the government from 1623, but (c. 1628) assumed part of mediator between Charles I and parliament, and (1642) vigorously attacked Charles I's evil counsellors; took the two covenants. He interested himself in colonial enterprise, and was one of incorporators of Providence Company, 1630. His works were published posthumously. [xlix. 385]

RUE. [See DE LA RUE.]

RUFF, WILLIAM (1801–1856), educated for law; sporting reporter for 'Bell's Life,' 1821–53; published annual 'Guide to Turf,' 1842–54. [xlix. 389]

RUFFHEAD, OWEN (1723–1769), miscellaneous writer; barrister, Middle Temple, 1747; started 'Con-Test' periodical in support of government, 1757. He published an edition of 'Statutes at Large from Magna Charta to 1763,' 1762–5, 'Life of Pope' (digested from Bishop Warburton's materials at his request), 1769, and other works. [xlix. 389]

RUFUS (d. 1128). [See BELMEIS or BEAUMEIS, RICHARD DE.]

RUFUS, GEOFFREY (d. 1140), chancellor to Henry I, c. 1124; bishop of Durham, 1133; supported Stephen. [xlix. 390]

RUFUS, RICHARD (fl. 1238–1259). [See RICHARD OF CORNWALL.]

RUGG or **REPPES**, WILLIAM (d. 1550), divine; D.D. Caius College, Cambridge, 1513; prior of cell of Yarmouth, 1520; sub-prior of Norwich, 1526; abbot of St. Bennet's, Hulme, 1530; favoured Henry VIII's divorce from Catherine of Arragon; bishop of Norwich, 1536; concerned in compilation of 'Bishops' Book'; resigned bishopric through financial embarrassments, 1549. [xlix. 390]

RUGGE, ROBERT (d. 1410). [See RYGGE.]

RUGGE, THOMAS (d. 1672 ?). kept manuscript diary entitled 'Mercurius Politicus Redivivus,' 1659–72, now in British Museum. [xlix. 391]

RUGGLE, GEORGE (1575–1622), author of 'Ignoramus'; M.A. Trinity College, Cambridge, 1597; fellow of Clare Hall, 1598–1620; one of two taxors of university, 1604; M.A. Oxford, 1605; wrote Latin comedy, 'Ignoramus,' ridiculing pettifogging lawyers on occasion of dispute (1611–12) as to precedence between mayor of Cambridge and vice-chancellor of the university; the play twice performed before James I in 1615, and aroused considerable resentment among lawyers. 'Ignoramus' was printed in 1630; English translations by Robert Codrington [q. v.] and Edward Ravenscroft [q. v.] were issued in 1662 and 1678 respectively. [xlix. 392]

RUGGLES, THOMAS (1737 ?–1813), writer on poor-law. [xlix. 393]

RUGLEN, EARL OF (1724–1810). [See DOUGLAS, WILLIAM, third EARL OF MARCH and fourth DUKE OF QUEENSBERRY.]

RULE, SAINT (fl. 8th cent. ?) [See REGULUS.]

RULE, GILBERT (1629 ?–1701), nonconformist divine; educated at Glasgow University; sub-principal, King's College, Aberdeen, 1651; perpetual curate at Alnwick, 1656; ejected, 1662; M.D. Leyden, 1665; practised at Berwick; preached at meeting-house at Linton Bridge, 1679; imprisoned on Bass Rock for lecturing at St. Giles's Church, Edinburgh, 1680; discharged and banished from kingdom; colleague of Daniel Williams [q. v.] at Dublin, 1682–7; became minister at Greyfriars Church, Edinburgh, 1688; principal of Edinburgh University, 1690; published religious works. [xlix. 393]

RULE, WILLIAM HARRIS (1802–1890), divine; after trying to make living as portrait-painter, and village schoolmaster at Newington, Kent, he was ordained Wesleyan preacher, 1826; resident missionary at Malta, 1826–7; missionary in St. Vincent, 1827–31; Wesleyan pastor at Gibraltar, 1832; returned home, 1842, and was engaged in ministerial duty in England, 1842–68; joint-editor at Wesleyan conference office, 1851–7; minister to Wesleyan soldiers at Aldershot, 1857–65; published 'History of Inquisition' (1874) and other works. [xlix. 394]

RUMBOLD, SIR ARTHUR CARLOS HENRY, fifth baronet (1820–1869), colonial administrator; grandson of Sir George Berriman Rumbold [q. v.]; ensign, 1837; served in Crimea, 1855; colonel in the imperial Ottoman army; administrator of St. Christopher and Aquilla, 1867. [xlix. 396]

RUMBOLD, SIR GEORGE BERRIMAN, second baronet (1764–1807), diplomatist; born at Calcutta; son of Sir Thomas Rumbold [q. v.]; succeeded to baronetcy, 1791; ambassador to Hanse Towns, and minister residentiary of Great Britain at Hamburg, 1803; arrested by order of Fouché on charge of conspiring against French; conveyed to Paris and thence to England, 1804; replaced at Hamburg, 1806. [xlix. 395]

RUMBOLD, HENRY (1617–1690), diplomatist; resided chiefly in Spain as wine-merchant during civil war; consul at Cadiz and Puerto Sta Maria, 1660–3; returned to England, 1663; held as sinecures consulates of Malaga, San Lucar, and Seville. [xlix. 399]

RUMBOLD, RICHARD (1622 ?–1685), conspirator; soldier in parliamentary army, c. 1641; served at Dunbar and Worcester; lieutenant in Colonel Packer's horse, 1659; carried on trade of maltster at Rye House, Hertfordshire; indicted of high treason for complicity in Rye House plot, 1683; fled to Holland; colonel of horse regiment in Argyll's expedition to Scotland, 1685; captured and executed. [xlix. 396]

RUMBOLD, SIR THOMAS, first baronet (1736–1791), Indian administrator; writer in East India Company's service, 1752; joined company's military service, and served under Lawrence and Clive; captain, 1757; aide-de-camp to Clive at Plassey; chief of Patna, c. 1763; member of Bengal council, 1766–9; M.P., New Shoreham, 1770; governor of Madras, 1777; created baronet, 1779; readjusted system of payment of rents from Northern sircars, and the nabob of Arcot; reduced Pondicherry and Mahé, and occupied the Guntur sircar; made preparations to resist invasion of Carnatic by Haidar Ali, and resigned on account of ill-health, 1780; dismissed from service of company by court of directors, who held him responsible for invasion of Carnatic; on parliamentary inquiry being instituted he was defended by George Hardinge [q. v.] and acquitted; M.P., Yarmouth, Isle of Wight, 1781, and Weymouth, 1784–90. [xlix. 397]

RUMBOLD, WILLIAM (1613–1667), cavalier; brother of Henry Rumbold [q. v.]; attended Charles I until after the battle of Naseby, when he retired to Spain; returned, 1649, and acted as Charles II's financial agent and secretary to secret royalist council; imprisoned about two years by Cromwell; engaged in Sir George Booth's plot; surveyor-general of customs, 1663. [xlix. 399]

RUMFORD, COUNT VON (1753–1814). [See THOMPSON, SIR BENJAMIN.]

RUMOLD, in Irish RUTHMAEL (d. 775 ?), divine; consecrated bishop, and laboured in Ireland in eighth century; travelled on continent, and finally founded a settlement at Mechlin. His festival is given variously as 1 or 3 July. [xlix. 400]

RUMSEY, WALTER (1584–1660), Welsh judge; of Gloucester Hall, Oxford; barrister, Gray's Inn, 1608 (ancient, 1622, bencher, 1631, Lent reader, 1633, dean of chapel, 1640); judge of great sessions for counties of Brecknock, Glamorgan, and Radnor, 1631 (removed by parliament, 1647); nominated knight of Royal Oak, 1660. [xlix. 401]

RUNCIMAN, ALEXANDER (1736-1785), painter; studied with his brother, John Runciman [q. v.], in Italy, where he met Henry Fuseli [q. v.]; settled in Edinburgh; drawing-master at Scottish academy; painted two celebrated ceilings at Penicuik for Sir James Clerk. [xlix. 401]

RUNCIMAN, JAMES (1852-1891), journalist; board school teacher; contributed to 'Teacher,' 'Schoolmaster,' and 'Vanity Fair'; sub-editor of 'Vanity Fair,' 1874, and of 'London,' c. 1880; B.Sc. London, 1876. Published miscellaneous writings, of which the best are descriptions of fisher life on North Sea. [xlix. 402]

RUNCIMAN, JOHN (1744-1768), painter; brother of Alexander Runciman [q. v.] [xlix. 402]

RUNDALL, MARY ANN (d. 1839), educational writer; kept ladies' school at Bath. Published 'Symbolic Illustrations of English History,' 1815. [xlix. 403]

RUNDELL, MRS. MARIA ELIZA (1745-1828), writer on cookery; née Ketelby; married Thomas Rundell; published 'New System of Domestic Cookery,' 1808, and other works. [xlix. 403]

RUNDLE, ELIZABETH (1828-1896). [See CHARLES, MRS. ELIZABETH.]

RUNDLE, THOMAS (1688 ?-1743), bishop of Derry; D.C.L. Exeter College, Oxford, 1723; member of Whiston's 'Society for Promoting Primitive Christianity'; was prebendary of Salisbury, 1716; archdeacon of Wilts, 1720; treasurer of Sarum, 1721; received stall at Durham, 1722; master of Sherburn Hospital, 1728; bishop of Derry, 1735-43; published sermons; his 'Letters' appeared 1789. [xlix. 403]

RUNNINGTON, CHARLES (1751-1821), legal writer; barrister, Inner Temple, 1778; serjeant-at-law, 1787; chief commissioner in insolvency, 1815-19. [xlix. 405]

RUPERT, PRINCE, COUNT PALATINE OF RHINE and DUKE OF BAVARIA, afterwards DUKE OF CUMBERLAND and EARL OF HOLDERNESS (1619-1682), third son of Elizabeth, queen of Bohemia, and Frederick V, elector palatine; born at Prague; served as volunteer under Prince of Orange in invasion of Brabant, 1635; came to England, and was created M.A. Oxford, 1636; at siege of Breda, 1637; captured during invasion of Westphalia, 1638; released, 1641; in England, 1642; appointed by Charles I general of the horse; gained, at Worcester, 1642, first victory of the war; commanded right wing of Charles I's horse at Edgehill, 1642; took Cirencester; unsuccessfully attempted Bristol, March 1643; took Birmingham, April 1643; gained victory at Chalgrove Field, June 1643; forced capitulation of Bristol, July 1643; at Newbury, September 1643; created Earl of Holderness and Duke of Cumberland, January 1644; relieved Newark, March 1644; defeated parliamentarians at Stockport, May 1644; captured Liverpool, June 1644; failed to relieve York, and was defeated with Newcastle at Marston Moor, June 1644; appointed general, 1644; suppressed rising in Wales, February 1645; relieved Chester; took Leicester, May 1645; distinguished himself at Naseby, where royalists were defeated, June 1645; occupied Bristol; urged Charles I to make peace, July 1645; surrendered Bristol to Fairfax (September), and was deprived of commissions (October); in siege of Oxford, and on its capitulation ordered (January 1646) to leave England; went to St. Germain, July 1646; appointed mareschal-de-camp, with command of English troops in French service; accompanied Prince Charles to Holland, 1648; commanded fleet sent to assist Ormonde in Ireland, 1649; relieved Scilly isles; blockaded by Blake at mouth of Tagus, 1650; escaped to Mediterranean, made piratical cruise, and reached Barbados, 1652; returned to France, 1653; in Germany, 1654-60; returned to England, 1660; privy councillor, and commissioner for government of Tangier, 1662; one of the patentees of Royal African Company, 1663; admiral of white under Duke of York at Solebay, 1665; shared command with Monck against Dutch, 1666; held command at Woolwich, 1667; constable of Windsor Castle, 1668; received charter for Hudson Bay Company, 1670; vice-admiral of England on outbreak of second Dutch war, 1672; general on sea and land, and, later, admiral of fleet, 1673; fought unsuccessful battles off Schoneveldt and Texel; first lord of the admiralty, 1673-1679. Buried in Henry VII's Chapel, Westminster; his portrait painted by Lely. [xlix. 405]

RUPIBUS, PETER DE (d. 1238). [See PETER DES ROCHES.]

RUSH, ANTHONY (1537-1577), divine; M.A. Magdalen College, Oxford, 1558; master of Canterbury grammar school, 1561; canon of Windsor and D.D. Cambridge, 1565; chaplain to Queen Elizabeth and canon of Canterbury, 1568; dean of Chichester, 1570-7. [xlix. 417]

RUSH, JAMES BLOMFIELD (d. 1849), murderer; a tenant farmer on the estate of Isaac Jermy (1789-1848), [q. v.], who sympathised with the claimants to Jermy's estate and shot him and his son. [xlix. 341]

RUSHOOK, THOMAS (fl. 1388), bishop; provincial of Dominican order in England, 1373-82; temporarily deposed, 1378-9; confessor to Richard II, 1379; bishop of Llandaff, 1383, and of Chichester, 1385; supported Richard II; found guilty of treason, 1388; banished to Ireland; bishop of Kilmore, c. 1388. [xlix. 417]

RUSHOUT, SIR JOHN, fourth baronet (1684-1775); politician; M.P. for Malmesbury, 1713 and 1715, and Evesham, 1722-68; lord-commissioner of treasury, 1742; treasurer of navy, 1743; privy councillor, 1744; father of House of Commons when he retired in 1768. [xlix. 418]

RUSHTON, EDWARD (1550-1586). [See RISHTON.]

RUSHTON, EDWARD (1756-1814), poet; apprenticed to firm of West India shippers at Liverpool; lost his sight while serving as mate in slaving expedition to Guinea coast; published poem condemning American war, 1782; kept tavern at Liverpool; edited 'Liverpool Herald'; published poems and political writings. His sight was restored, 1807. [xlix. 419]

RUSHTON, EDWARD (1796-1851); son of Edward Rushton (1756-1814) [q. v.]; printer and stationer; called to bar; stipendiary magistrate at Liverpool, 1839. [xlix. 419]

RUSHWORTH, JOHN (1612 ?-1690), historian; M.A. Queen's College, Oxford, 1649; barrister, Lincoln's Inn, 1647; clerk-assistant to House of Commons, 1640; secretary to general and council of war on organisation of new model army; accompanied Fairfax in campaigns of 1645, 1646, and 1648; secretary to Cromwell, 1650; member of committee for reformation of law, 1652; M.P., Berwick, 1657, 1659, 1660, 1679, and 1681; secretary to council of state, 1660; secretary to lord keeper, 1667; spent last six years of life in king's bench prison. He wrote 'Historical Collections' (to year 1648), which was issued between 1659 and 1701 (8 vols.) [xlix. 419]

RUSHWORTH, JOHN (1669-1736), surgeon; practised at Northampton; discovered efficacy of cinchona bark for gangrene, 1721; with Sir Samuel Garth [q. v.] suggested foundation of local infirmaries and dispensaries; published surgical works. [xlix. 422]

RUSHWORTH or **RICHWORTH**, WILLIAM (d. 1637), Roman catholic divine; born in Lincolnshire; educated at English College, Douay; general prefect, 1618; joined catholic English mission. Left in manuscript religious writings. [xlix. 423]

RUSKIN, JOHN (1819-1900), author, artist, and social reformer; son of John James Ruskin (1785-1864), who entered partnership as wine merchant in London, 1809; brought up on strict puritanical principles; educated by Dr. Andrews, father of Coventry Patmore's first wife, and under the Rev. Thomas Dale (1797-1870) [q. v.] at Camberwell; studied at King's College, London; learned drawing under Copley Fielding and J. D. Harding; entered Christ Church, Oxford, 1836; won Newdigate prize, 1839; contributed verse to 'Friendship's Offering,' and other miscellanies; travelled for his health, 1840-1; B.A., 1842; M.A., 1843; his first published writings were articles in Loudon's 'Magazine of Natural History,' 1834; made acquaintance of Turner, 1840; paid first visit to Venice, 1841; published, 1843, first volume of 'Modern Painters, by a Graduate of Oxford' (his name first appeared on title-page in edition of 1851); second volume published 1846, the authorship being by that time an open secret; the third and fourth volumes appeared 1856, the fifth, 1860; married, 1848, Euphemia Chalmers Gray, daughter of George Gray, a lawyer of Perth; made acquaintance of Millais,

1851; delivered at Edinburgh, 1853, lectures on 'Architecture and Painting,' published, 1854; his marriage annulled on his wife's suit, which he did not defend, 1855; published, 1849, 'Seven Lamps of Architecture,' which had considerable influence in encouraging the Gothic revival of the time, and 'Stones of Venice,' 3 vols. 1851–3; warmly defended the pre-Raphaelites in letters to 'The Times,' and in pamphlets, 1851; published annually, 1855–9, 'Notes on the Royal Academy'; arranged Turner drawings at National Gallery; took charge of drawing classes at Working Men's College, Great Ormond Street, London, 1854–8; published 'Elements of Drawing,' 1856, and 'Elements of Perspective,' 1859; honorary student of Christ Church, Oxford, 1858; devoted himself to economic studies, and published 'Unto this Last' (some of the papers being first contributed to 'Cornhill Magazine'), 1860, 'Munera Pulveris' (contributed in part to 'Fraser's Magazine'), 1862, 'Gold,' 1863, 'Time and Tide,' 1867, and various letters and pamphlets, 1868, advocating a system of national education, the organisation of labour, and other social measures; honorary LL.D. Cambridge, 1867; between 1855 and 1870 he delivered in all parts of the country lectures, some of which were published in 'Sesame and Lilies,' 1865, 'The Crown of Wild Olive,' 1866, and 'The Ethics of the Dust,' 1866; removed, 1871, to Brantwood, Coniston Lake, where he remained till death; established 'Fors Clavigera,' a monthly letter 'to the workmen and labourers of Great Britain,' and founded, 1871, the guild of St. George on principles that 'food can only be got out of the ground and happiness out of honesty,' and that 'the highest wisdom and the highest treasure need not be costly or exclusive'; engaged in several industrial experiments, including the revival of the hand-made linen industry in Langdale, and the establishment of a cloth industry at Laxey, Isle of Man; inspired and was first president of 'The Art for Schools Association'; first Slade professor of art at Oxford, 1870–9; again filled the post, 1883–4, and published eight volumes of lectures; founded a drawing school at Oxford and endowed a drawing-master; honorary fellow of Corpus Christi College, Oxford, 1871; suffered at times from brain fever after 1878; published at intervals during 1885–9 'Præterita,' an autobiography which was never completed; died from influenza, 20 Jan. 1900, and was buried at Coniston. A bibliography of his writings by Thomas J. Wise and James P. Smart was issued, 1893. Many of the illustrations to his works were executed from his own drawings. He inherited from his father a large fortune, all of which was dispersed, chiefly in charitable and philanthropic objects, before his death.

[Suppl. iii. 305]

RUSSEL. [See also RUSSELL.]

RUSSEL, ALEXANDER (1814–1876), journalist; apprenticed to printer in Edinburgh; contributed to 'Tait's Magazine'; edited 'Berwick Advertiser,' 1839, 'Fife Herald' (Cupar), 1842, and a journal at Kilmarnock, c. 1844; editor, c. 1848 till death, of 'Scotsman'; exerted himself to further objects of Anti-Cornlaw League, part of his plans being opposition to all interference of ministers of religion in politics. [xlix. 423]

RUSSEL, ANTONY (1663 ?–1743), portrait-painter; son of Theodore Russel [q. v.]; friend of George Vertue [q. v.] [xlix. 425]

RUSSEL, GEORGE (1728–1767), poet; born in Minorca; B.A. St. Mary Hall, Oxford, 1750; rector of Schull, co. Cork, 1753–67. Works published, 1769.

[xlix. 424]

RUSSEL, JOHN (1740 ?–1817), Scottish divine; licensed preacher, 1768; minister at Kilmarnock, 1774; held second charge of Stirling, 1800–17; satirised by Robert Burns. [xlix. 424]

RUSSEL, ROUSSEEL, or RUSSELL, THEODORE (1614–1689), portrait-painter; born in London of Dutch parents; assistant to Vandyck, many of whose portraits he copied. [xlix. 425]

RUSSEL, WILLIAM (d. 1702), baptist minister; B.A. Cambridge; created M.D., 1688; pastor of baptist congregation at High Hall, West Smithfield, London, before 1670; probably practised as physician from c. 1680; published controversial pamphlets. [xlix. 425]

RUSSELL. [See also RUSSEL.]

RUSSELL, ALEXANDER (1715 ?–1768), physician; educated at Edinburgh; physician to English factory at Aleppo, 1740–53; published 'Natural History of Aleppo,' 1756; F.R.S., 1756; L.R.C.P. and M.D. Glasgow, 1760; physician to St. Thomas's Hospital, 1760. [xlix. 426]

RUSSELL, ARTHUR TOZER (1806–1874), divine; of Merchant Taylors' School, Manchester College, York, and St. John's College, Cambridge; LL.B., 1830; after holding other livings, became rector of Southwick, 1874; published hymns and other writings. [xlix. 427]

RUSSELL, SIR CHARLES, third baronet (1826–1883), lieutenant-colonel; educated at Eton; ensign, 1843; captain in grenadiers, 1853; served in Crimea; deputy assistant quartermaster-general; V.C., 1857; lieutenant-colonel, 1858; conservative M.P. for Berkshire, 1865–8, and Westminster, 1874–82. [xlix. 428]

RUSSELL, CHARLES, first BARON RUSSELL OF KILLOWEN (1832–1900), lord chief-justice of England; nephew of Charles William Russell [q. v.]; admitted solicitor, 1854; practised in county courts of Down and Antrim; studied at Trinity College, Dublin; barrister, Lincoln's Inn, 1859; joined northern circuit; Q.C., 1872; independent liberal M.P. for Dundalk, 1880–5, South Hackney, 1885, 1886, 1892; attorney-general, 1886 and 1892; vigorously advocated home rule; leading counsel for Parnell in Parnell Commission, 1888–9; with Sir R. Webster represented Great Britain in Behring Sea arbitration, 1893, and was made G.C.M.G.; made lord of appeal and raised to peerage for life, 1894; appointed later in same year, on death of Sir John Duke Coleridge, baron Coleridge [q. v.], lord chief-justice; presided at trial of Jameson raiders, 1896; one of arbitrators at Paris, 1899, to determine boundaries of British Guiana and Venezuela under treaty of 1897; introduced secret commissions bill in House of Lords, 1900; published writings on legal and educational questions. [Suppl. iii. 327]

RUSSELL, CHARLES WILLIAM (1812–1880), president of Maynooth College; educated at Maynooth College; Dunboyne student, 1832; professor of humanity, 1835; apostolic vicar of Ceylon, 1842; professor of ecclesiastical history, Maynooth, 1845, and president, 1857; took part in tractarian movement; published antiquarian and other writings. [xlix. 428]

RUSSELL, SIR DAVID (1809–1884), general; cornet, 1828; captain, 1833; brevet colonel, 1854; served in Indian mutiny; general, 1877; K.C.B., 1871.

[xlix. 429]

RUSSELL, EDWARD, EARL OF ORFORD (1653–1727), admiral; lieutenant, 1671; captain, 1672; joined service of Prince of Orange, c. 1683; M.P., Launceston, 1689, Portsmouth, 1690, Cambridgeshire, 1695; treasurer of navy, 1689, and admiral of blue under Torrington, whom he succeeded, 1690; with Dutch defeated French off Cape Barfleur, 1692; dismissed from command for not completing destruction of French fleet, 1693; reinstated, 1693; first lord of admiralty, 1694–9, 1709–10, and 1714–17; served in Mediterranean, 1694–5; created Baron of Shingey, Viscount Barfleur, and Earl of Orford, 1697; one of lords justices, 1697, 1698, and 1714; commissioner for union, 1706. [xlix. 429]

RUSSELL, LORD EDWARD (1805–1887), admiral; son of John Russell, sixth duke of Bedford [q. v.]; lieutenant, 1826; captain, 1833; M.P., Tavistock, 1841–7; naval aide-de-camp to Queen Victoria, 1846–50; served at Sebastopol, 1854; C.B., 1855; admiral, 1867. [xlix. 431]

RUSSELL, LADY ELIZABETH (1528–1609). [See HOBY, ELIZABETH, LADY.]

RUSSELL, FRANCIS, second EARL OF BEDFORD (1527 ?–1585), son of John Russell, first earl of Bedford [q. v.]; of King's Hall, Cambridge; K.B., 1547; M.P., Buckinghamshire, 1547–52; witnessed deed by which Edward VI settled the crown on Lady Jane Grey, 1553; imprisoned, 1553–5; escaped to continent; returned, 1558; privy councillor, 1558; took active part in religious settlement; warden of east marches, governor of Berwick, and K.G., 1564; commissioner to treat as to Mary Queen of Scots' marriage, 1564; lord president of Wales and lieutenant of Garter, 1576; chief-justice and justice in eyre of royal forests south of Trent, 1584. [xlix. 431]

RUSSELL, FRANCIS, fourth EARL OF BEDFORD (1593–1641), son of Sir William Russell, first baron Russell of Thornhaugh [q. v.]; knighted, 1607; succeeded his cousin Edward, third earl of Bedford, 1627 ; M.P., Lyme Regis, 1610-11 ; built square of Covent Garden, c. 1631 ; headed association which undertook draining of fens ; prominent in opposition to Charles I, 1640 ; privy councillor, 1641 ; endeavoured to mediate between Charles I and parliament. [xlix. 433]

RUSSELL, FRANCIS, fifth DUKE OF BEDFORD (1765-1802), son of Francis Russell, marquis of Tavistock ; succeeded his grandfather, John Russell, fourth duke of Bedford [q. v.], 1771 ; of Westminster School and Trinity College, Cambridge ; attached himself to the party of Fox ; one of the friends of George, prince of Wales ; built Russell and Tavistock Squares, London, c. 1800 ; member of original board of agriculture, 1793 ; first president of Smithfield Club, 1798. [xlix. 435]

RUSSELL, FRANCIS CHARLES HASTINGS, ninth DUKE OF BEDFORD (1819-1891), son of Lord George William Russell [q. v.] ; served in Scots fusilier guards, 1835-45 ; M.P., Bedfordshire, 1847-72 ; succeeded his cousin William Russell, eighth duke of Bedford, 1872 ; president of Royal Agricultural Society, 1879 ; K.G., 1880 ; committed suicide. [xlix. 437]

RUSSELL, LORD GEORGE WILLIAM (1790-1846), major-general ; son of John Russell, sixth duke of Bedford [q. v.] ; educated at Westminster and Woodnesborough ; cornet and lieutenant, 1806 ; aide-de-camp to Sir G. Ludlow at Copenhagen, 1807 ; served in Peninsula, 1809 and 1810-12 ; aide-de-camp to Wellington, 1812 ; major, 1813 ; M.P., Bedford ; aide-de-camp to Wellington while ambassador at Paris, 1817 ; major-general, 1841 ; held several diplomatic appointments, and was ambassador at Berlin, 1835-41 ; G.C.B. (civil), 1838. [xlix. 437]

RUSSELL, SIR HENRY (1751-1836), judge ; of Charterhouse School and Queens' College, Cambridge ; M.A., 1775 ; commissioner in bankruptcy, 1775 ; barrister, Lincoln's Inn, 1783 ; appointed puisne judge in supreme court of judicature, Bengal, and knighted, 1797 ; chief-justice of supreme court, 1807-13 ; created baronet, 1812 ; privy councillor, 1816. [xlix. 438]

RUSSELL, HENRY (1812-1900), vocalist and song-composer ; appeared at Surrey Theatre, London, 1828 ; chorus-master at Her Majesty's Theatre, London ; went to Canada and America, where, and from 1841 in England, he made a great reputation by his rendering of songs of a domestic character ; composed numerous settings to songs, some of which were expressly written for him by Dr. Charles Mackay [q. v.] His most popular song was 'Cheer, boys, cheer.' [Suppl. iii. 332]

RUSSELL, JAMES (1754-1836), surgeon ; F.R.C.S. Edinburgh, 1777, president, 1797 ; surgeon to Royal Infirmary, Edinburgh ; first professor of clinical surgery, Edinburgh University, 1803-34 ; original fellow, and subsequently vice-president, Royal Society, Edinburgh ; collected pictures ; published surgical works. [xlix. 439]

RUSSELL, JAMES (1786-1851), surgeon ; studied at Guy's Hospital, London ; L.R.C.P., 1808 ; honorary surgeon to Birmingham Dispensary, 1815-25 ; sanitary inspector at Birmingham ; one of founders of Birmingham Medical Benevolent Society ; wrote on scientific and medical subjects ; F.R.C.S., 1843. [xlix. 440]

RUSSELL, JAMES (1790-1861), barrister ; graduated at Glasgow ; barrister, Inner Temple, 1822 ; reporter in courts of lord chancellor and master of rolls till 1834 ; Q.C., 1841 ; leader of Vice-chancellor Knight-Bruce's court ; lost eyesight through overwork ; edited 'Annual Register' ; published 'Reports.' [xlix. 441]

RUSSELL, JOHN (fl. 1450), mediæval writer ; in service of Humphrey, duke of Gloucester ; wrote 'Book of Nurture' (ed. Dr. Furnivall, Roxburghe Club, 1867, and E.E.T.S., 1868). [xlix. 441]

RUSSELL, SIR JOHN (fl. 1440-1470), speaker of House of Commons ; M.P., 1423 ; speaker, 1423, 1432, and 1450. [xlix. 441]

RUSSELL, JOHN (d. 1494), bishop of Lincoln ; educated at Winchester College and New College, Oxford ; fellow, 1449-62 ; LL.B. and LL.D., 1459 ; moderator in canon law school, 1461 ; archdeacon of Berkshire, 1466 ; keeper of privy seal, 1474-83 ; negotiated marriage between Edward IV's daughter Cicely and James, son of king of Scotland, 1474 ; prebendary of St. Paul's Cathedral, 1474 ; bishop of Rochester, 1476-80, and of Lincoln, 1480-94 ;

chancellor of England, 1483 ; employed by Henry VII in negotiations with king of Scots and with Brittany, 1486 ; chancellor of Oxford University, 1483-94 ; wrote 'Propositio Clarissimi Oratoris, Magistri Johannis Russell' (printed with Caxton's type, probably at Bruges), a speech delivered on embassy to invest Charles the Bold with Garter, 1470, and legal and religious treatises. [xlix. 442]

RUSSELL, JOHN, first EARL OF BEDFORD (1486 ?-1555), gentleman of privy chamber, 1506 ; captain in expedition to France, 1513 ; knighted, c. 1513 ; at tournament at Paris, 1514 ; at Field of Cloth of Gold, 1520 ; accompanied expedition of Thomas Howard, earl of Surrey (afterwards third Duke of Norfolk) [q. v.], to France, 1522 ; knight-marshal of household, 1523 ; went on secret mission to obtain alliance of Duke of Bourbon, 1523, and after many adventures returned, 1525 ; ambassador to Pope Clement, 1527 ; bailiff of Burley in New Forest, 1528 ; took active part in suppressing Pilgrimage of Grace, 1536 ; comptroller of king's household, 1537 ; privy councillor, 1538 ; created Baron Russell of Chenies and elected K.G., 1539 ; high steward of duchy of Cornwall ; lord high-admiral of England, 1540-2 ; high steward of Oxford University, 1542 ; lord privy seal, 1542, 1547, and 1553 ; took part in suppression of Western rebellion, 1549 ; created Earl of Bedford, 1550 ; signed Edward VI's letters patent limiting crown to Lady Jane Grey, but subsequently joined Queen Mary's party ; joint-ambassador to Philip of Spain to conclude marriage treaty, 1554. [xlix. 444]

RUSSELL, JOHN, fourth DUKE OF BEDFORD (1710-1771), second son of Wriothesley Russell, second duke of Bedford ; succeeded his brother, third duke of Bedford, 1732 ; joined opposition to Sir Robert Walpole ; privy councillor ; first lord of admiralty in Pelham's administration ; lord justice of Great Britain, 1745, 1748, and 1750 ; colonel of foot regiment, which he raised for George II, 1745 ; secretary for southern department on Chesterfield's resignation of seals, 1748 ; K.G., 1749 ; resigned seals, 1751 ; started, with Beckford, anti-ministerial paper, 'The Protestor,' edited by James Ralph [q. v.], 1753 ; lord-lieutenant of Ireland in Duke of Devonshire's administration, 1756-7 ; lord high constable at George III's coronation, 1760 ; accepted privy seal, 1760 ; ambassador for treaty of peace with France, 1762-3 ; president of council, 1763-7 ; supported Grafton's government, but took no office, 1767. His portrait, painted by Gainsborough, 1764, was copied by Reynolds. [xlix. 447]

RUSSELL, JOHN (1745-1806), portrait-painter ; apprenticed to Francis Cotes [q. v.] ; practised art in London, and produced many portraits, chiefly in coloured crayons ; exhibited at Royal Academy from 1769, and obtained gold medal, 1770, for figure of 'Aquarius' ; R.A., 1788 ; executed portraits of George III's queen and George, prince of Wales, 1789-90, and other members of royal family, and was styled painter to George III, Prince of Wales, and Duke of York. His portraits include 'Mother's Holiday' (Mrs. Jeans and her sons), 1796, Philip Stanhope, son of Lord Chesterfield, Bartolozzi, Cowper, Mrs. Jordan, Mrs. Siddons, Sheridan, and Robert Merry (Della Crusca) ; published 'Elements of Painting with Crayons,' 1772. [xlix. 452]

RUSSELL, JOHN, sixth DUKE OF BEDFORD (1766-1839), grandson of John Russell, fourth duke of Bedford [q. v.] ; member of Society of Friends of the People ; M.P., Tavistock, 1788-1802 ; succeeded to the dukedom on the death of his brother, Francis Russell, fifth duke of Bedford [q. v.], 1802 ; privy councillor, 1806, and lord-lieutenant of Ireland, 1806-7 ; K.G., 1830 ; rebuilt Covent Garden market, London, 1830 ; interested himself in agriculture, art, and natural history. [xlix. 454]

RUSSELL, JOHN (1787-1863), divine ; educated at Charterhouse School ; M.A. Christ Church, Oxford, 1809 ; head-master of Charterhouse, London, 1811-32 ; prebendary and, later, canon-residentiary of Canterbury ; president of Sion College, London, 1845 and 1846 ; rector of St. Botolph's, Bishopsgate, London, 1832-63 ; published 'History of Sion College' and other works. [xlix. 454]

RUSSELL, JOHN, VISCOUNT AMBERLEY (1842-1876), son of Lord John Russell, first earl Russell [q. v.] ; of Harrow, Edinburgh, and Trinity College, Cambridge ; liberal M.P., Nottingham, 1866-8. [xlix. 454]

RUSSELL, LORD JOHN, first EARL RUSSELL (1792-1878), statesman ; third son of John Russell, sixth duke of Bedford [q. v.] ; educated at Westminster and Edinburgh

University ; travelled on continent ; whig M.P., Tavistock, 1813 ; opposed suspension of Habeas Corpus Act, 1817 ; re-elected for Tavistock, 1818 ; delivered, 1819, first of his speeches on parliamentary reform, which he strenuously advocated till 1832 ; M.P., Huntingdonshire, 1820 ; returned for Irish borough of Bandon, 1826–30 ; moved successfully repeal of Test and Corporation Acts, 1828 ; paymaster-general of forces (without seat in cabinet) and M.P., Tavistock, 1831 ; moved unsuccessfully Government Reform Bill in House of Commons, 1831 ; member for South Devon, 1831 ; member of cabinet ; introduced Reform Bill second time, 24 June, and third time, 12 Dec., and it was passed, 1832 ; advocated Irish church reform, 1833 ; recognised as leader of whigs in House of Commons in Melbourne's administration, 1834 ; M.P., Stroud, home secretary and leader of House of Commons in Melbourne's administration, 1835 ; diminished number of offences liable to capital punishment, 1837 ; colonial secretary under Melbourne, 1839 ; led opposition to Peel's administration, 1841 ; supported repeal of corn laws by Peel, 1845 ; first lord of treasury and premier, 1846 ; member for city of London, 1847 ; introduced measures for alleviating condition of Ireland ; passed bill for removing Jewish disabilities, 1848 ; resigned, 1851, but returned to office ; demanded Palmerston's resignation on ground of exceeding his authority in recognising government formed by Napoleon after *coup d'état* of 2 Dec. 1851 ; resigned, 1852 ; foreign secretary in Aberdeen's ministry, 1852, resigned, 1853, and remained in cabinet without office ; suggested and carried into effect separation of war and colonial departments, 1854 ; president of council, 1854 ; . retired, 1855 ; refused office under Palmerston and became plenipotentiary at Vienna congress, but subsequently (February) accepted secretaryship of colonies ; resigned, July 1855 ; supported Palmerston during Indian mutiny ; opposed Disraeli's Reform Bill, 1859 ; again returned for city of London, 1859 ; foreign secretary under Palmerston ; advocated ' Italy for the Italians ' ; accompanied Queen Victoria on visit to Germany, 1860 ; created Earl Russell of Kingston Russell and Viscount Amberley of Amberley and Ardsalla, 1861 ; maintained neutrality between belligerents in American civil war ; K.G., 1862 ; prime minister on death of Palmerston, 1865 ; resigned, 1866, when his official life terminated ; published ' Memoirs of Affairs of Europe,' 1824, ' Essay on English Constitution,' 1821, ' Letters of Fourth Duke of Bedford,' 1842–6, and other works ; president of the Royal Historical Society, 1872–8. [xlix. 454]

RUSSELL, JOHN (1795–1883), ' the sporting parson ' ; educated at Plympton, Tiverton, and Exeter College, Oxford ; B.A., 1818 ; ordained priest, 1820 ; curate, 1820, at George Nympton, and, 1826, at Iddesleigh, where he kept pack of foxhounds ; received perpetual curacy of Swymbridge, 1831 ; rector, 1880 till death, of Black Torrington, where he started a pack of harriers ; did much to further agricultural improvement. [xlix. 464]

RUSSELL, JOHN FULLER (1814–1884), divine ; son of Thomas Russell (1781 ?–1846) [q. v.] ; LL.B. Peterhouse, Cambridge, 1839 ; held perpetual curacy of St. James, Enfield, 1851–4 ; rector of Greenhithe, 1856 ; member of council of Society of Antiquaries ; published theological and other works. [xlix. 465]

RUSSELL, JOHN SCOTT (1808–1882), naval architect ; graduated at Glasgow ; received large gold medal of Edinburgh Royal Society for paper on laws governing resistance of water to motion of floating bodies, 1837 ; discovered wave of translation and developed wave-line system of construction of ships ; manager of shipbuilding works at Greenock ; F.R.S. and M.I.C.E., 1847 ; secretary of Society of Arts, 1845–50 ; royal commissioner for Great Exhibition (1851) ; advocated ironclad man-of-war ; shipbuilder on Thames ; constructed Great Eastern steamship ; published works on shipbuilding. [xlix. 465]

RUSSELL, JOSEPH (1760–1846), writer on agriculture. [xlix. 466]

RUSSELL, LUCY, COUNTESS OF BEDFORD (d. 1627), patroness of poets ; daughter of John Harington, first baron Harington of Exton [q. v.] ; married Edward Russell, third earl of Bedford, 1594 ; repeatedly mentioned by the chief men of letters of the day, including Ben Jonson, Donne, Daniel, Drayton, and Chapman. [xlix. 467]

RUSSELL, MICHAEL (1781–1848), bishop of Glasgow and Galloway ; M.A. Glasgow, 1806 ; LL.D., 1820 ; deacon,

1808 ; minister of St. James's Chapel, Leith, 1809 ; dean of diocese of Edinburgh, 1831 ; bishop of Glasgow and Galloway, 1837 ; D.C.L. Oxford, 1842 ; published historical, topographical, and other writings. [xlix. 467]

RUSSELL, ODO WILLIAM LEOPOLD, first BARON AMPTHILL (1829–1884), son of Lord George William Russell [q. v.] ; attaché at embassy at Vienna, 1849 ; at foreign office, 1850–2 ; engaged in diplomatic service at Paris and Vienna ; at Constantinople, 1854 ; at Washington under Lord Napier, 1857 ; secretary (resident in Rome, 1858–70) of legation at Florence, 1858, and at Naples, 1860 ; assistant under-secretary at foreign office, 1870 ; on special mission to headquarters of German army at Versailles, 1870–1 ; ambassador at Berlin, 1871 ; privy councillor, 1872 ; G.C.B., 1874 ; G.C.M.G., 1879 ; raised to peerage, 1881. [xlix. 468]

RUSSELL, PATRICK (1629–1692), archbishop of Dublin, 1683 ; did much to restore discipline of church after accession of James II, 1685 ; imprisoned on flight of James II ; died in prison. [xlix. 469]

RUSSELL, PATRICK (1727–1805), physician and naturalist ; half-brother of Alexander Russell [q. v.] ; M.D. Edinburgh ; physician to English factory at Aleppo, 1753 ; settled in London, 1772 ; F.R.S., 1777 ; botanist to East India Company in Carnatic, 1785–9 ; published ' Treatise on Plague ' (1791) and other writings. [xlix. 469]

RUSSELL, RACHEL, LADY RUSSELL (1636–1723), second daughter of Thomas Wriothesley, fourth earl of Southampton [q. v.] ; married as her second husband William Russell, lord Russell [q. v.], 1669 ; acted as her husband's ' writer ' during his trial, and made strenuous efforts to save his life ; was subsequently intimate with Queen Mary and Princess Anne ; corresponded with Tillotson ; her letters transcribed from the manuscript in Woburn Abbey, first published, 1773. [xlix. 480]

RUSSELL, RICHARD (d. 1771), M.D. Rheims, 1738 ; extra L.R.C.P. London, 1742 ; F.R.S., 1752 ; published medical works. [xlix. 470]

RUSSELL, SAMUEL THOMAS (1769 ?–1845), actor ; played juvenile parts under Charles Dibdin [q. v.], 1782 ; appeared as Charles Surface in ' School for Scandal,' Drury Lane, London, 1795 ; took Richmond Theatre, 1796 ; at Drury Lane, 1797 ; stage-manager at the Surrey, London, under Robert William Elliston [q. v.], 1812, and later at Olympic, London ; at Haymarket, London, 1814–18 ; stage-manager at Drury Lane, 1819–21 ; managed Brighton Theatre ; stage-manager at Haymarket, 1837–8, and again at Drury Lane, 1839 ; played Jerry Sneak (his greatest part) to Dowton's Major Sturgeon at Her Majesty's, London, 1840. Among his best characters were the Copper Captain (' Rule a Wife and have a Wife '), Paul Pry, Rover, and Young Rapid. [xlix. 471]

RUSSELL, THEODORE (1614–1689). [See RUSSEL.]

RUSSELL, THOMAS (1762–1788), poet ; of Winchester College and New College, Oxford ; B.A., 1784 ; ordained priest, 1786 ; died of phthisis. His ' Sonnets and Miscellaneous Poems ' appeared, 1789. His sonnets entitle him to an important place among those who revived the sonnet in England. [xlix. 472]

RUSSELL, THOMAS (1767–1803), United Irishman ; accompanied 52nd regiment to India as volunteer, 1782 ; received commission ; held commission in 64th regiment in Ireland ; made acquaintance of Theobald Wolfe Tone [q. v.], 1789 ; sold commission, 1791 ; engaged actively in work of United Irish Society ; librarian of Belfast library, 1794 ; arrested with other United Irishmen, 1796, and confined in Newgate, Dublin, till 1798, when he was banished to Fort George, Scotland ; liberated, 1802 ; went to Paris, where he met Robert Emmet [q. v.] and entered into his plans ; proceeded to Ireland in hope of raising Ulster, 1803 ; arrested, found guilty of high treason, and executed at Downpatrick. [xlix. 473]

RUSSELL or CLOUTT, THOMAS (1781 ?–1846), independent divine ; adopted name of Russell, c. 1820 ; published, under name Cloutt, hymns and sermons, and edited works of John Owen (1616–1683) [q. v.]. [xlix. 475]

RUSSELL, THOMAS MACNAMARA (1740 ?–1824), admiral ; entered merchant service, and later (c. 1766) navy, and served as seaman, midshipman, and master's mate, and was lieutenant, 1776 ; captain, 1781 ; on West Indian station, 1789–92 and 1796–9 ; at reduction of St. Lucia and Trinidad ; in Downs, 1803 ; commander-in-chief of North Sea squadron, 1807 ; took possession of Heligoland, 1807 ; admiral, 1812. [xlix. 475]

RUSSELL, SIR WILLIAM, first BARON RUSSELL OF THORNHAUGH (1558 ?–1613), son of Francis Russell, second earl of Bedford [q. v.] ; of Magdalen College, Oxford ; commanded company against Fiagh O'Byrne [q. v.] in Ireland, 1581 ; knighted, 1581 ; lieutenant-general of cavalry under Leicester in expedition to Netherlands, 1585 ; governor of Flushing, 1587–8 ; supported Leicester in his quarrel with the estates ; M.A. Oxford, 1594 ; lord-deputy of Ireland, 1594–7 ; relieved Enniskillen, which was besieged by Sir Hugh Maguire [q. v.] and O'Donnell ; engaged, in co-operation with Sir John Norris, in extended operations against Tyrone, O'Donnell, the Burkes, Fiagh MacHugh, and Maguire ; captured Fiagh O'Byrne, 1597 ; returned to England, 1597 ; commander of forces in west, 1599 ; raised to peerage by James I, 1603. [xlix. 476]

RUSSELL, SIR WILLIAM, first baronet (d. 1654), treasurer of the navy ; free brother of East India Company, 1609 ; director, 1615 ; director of company of Merchants of London, 1612 ; bought treasurership of navy, 1618, and held office till c. 1627 ; reappointed, 1630 ; created baronet, 1630. [xlix. 479]

RUSSELL, WILLIAM, LORD RUSSELL (1639–1683), 'the patriot' ; son of William Russell, fifth earl (afterwards first duke) of Bedford [q. v.] ; educated at Cambridge ; M.P. for Tavistock, 1660–78 ; married, 1669, Rachel Wriothesley (1636–1723), widow of Francis, lord Vaughan, and second daughter of Thomas Wriothesley, fourth earl of Southampton [q. v.] ; supported politics of country party, attacked Buckingham, 1674, and Danby, 1675 ; succeeded to courtesy title of Lord Russell, 1678 ; proposed address for removal of Duke of York from Charles II's presence and councils, 1678 ; M.P., Bedfordshire, 1679 ; privy councillor ; attacked Lauderdale in council, and withdrew from council, 1680 ; backed with Cavendish bill of indictment of Duke of York as popish recusant, 1680 ; seconded introduction of Exclusion Bill in Oxford parliament, 1681 ; in communication with Prince of Orange ; sent to Tower of London on charge of complicity in Rye House plot, 1683 ; pleaded 'not guilty,' but was convicted of high treason and executed at Lincoln's Inn Fields, London. His attainder was reversed on accession of William and Mary, and his father was created duke in 1694. His portrait painted by Lely. [xlix. 480]

RUSSELL, WILLIAM (1634 – 1696 ?), chemist in ordinary to Charles II ; published 'Physical Treatise,' 1684. [xlix. 426]

RUSSELL, WILLIAM, first DUKE OF BEDFORD (1613–1700), son of Francis, fourth earl of Bedford [q. v.] ; educated at Magdalen College, Oxford ; K.B., 1626 ; M.P. for Tavistock in Long parliament ; general of horse in parliamentary army, 1642 ; besieged Sherborne Castle ; fought at Edgehill, 1642 ; abandoned parliamentary cause and was pardoned by Charles I, 1643 ; fought at Newbury, but returned to parliamentarians, 1643 ; continued work begun by his father of draining fens, 1649 ; governor of Plymouth, 1671 ; joint-commissioner for execution of office of earl marshal, 1673 ; privy councillor, 1689 ; created Duke of Bedford and Marquis of Tavistock, 1694, and Baron Howland of Streatham, 1695. His portrait painted by Kneller and Vandyck. [xlix. 485]

RUSSELL, WILLIAM (1741–1793), historian ; apprenticed to bookseller and printer at Edinburgh, 1756 ; obtained patronage of Lord Elibank ; adopted literary profession in London, 1767 ; hon. LL.D. St. Andrews, 1792 ; published 'History of America' (1779) and 'History of Modern Europe' (1779–84), and other works. [xlix. 487]

RUSSELL, WILLIAM (1777–1813), musician ; organist to Great Queen Street Chapel, London, 1793–8, of St. Anne's, Limehouse, London, 1798–1801, and of Foundling Hospital, London, 1801 ; Mus. Bac. Oxford, 1808 ; composed sacred music, songs, and theatrical pieces ; wrote settings for Smart's 'Ode on St. Cecilia's Day' (1800) and 'Redemption of Israel.' [xlix. 488]

RUSSELL, WILLIAM (1740–1818), merchant and reformer ; engaged in export trade from Birmingham to Russia, Spain, and United States ; advocated political measures of reform, including repeal of Test and Corpora-

tion Acts ; retired, c. 1792 ; travelled in America and Europe. [xlix. 488]

RUSSELL, SIR WILLIAM (1773–1839), M.D. Edinburgh ; practised in Calcutta ; returned to London before 1832 ; created baronet, 1832. [xlix. 489]

RUSSELL, WILLIAM (1780–1870), son of John Russell (1745–1806), exhibited portraits at Royal Academy, 1805–9. [xlix. 453]

RUSSELL, SIR WILLIAM, second baronet (1822–1892), son of Sir William Russell (1773–1839) [q. v.] ; cornet, 7th hussars, 1841 ; major, 1857 ; aide-de-camp to Lord Clarendon, when lord-lieutenant of Ireland, 1850–52 ; M.P., Dover, 1857–9 ; served in Indian mutiny ; C.B., 1859 ; liberal M.P. for Norwich, 1860–74 ; lieutenant-general, 1881. [xlix. 489]

RUSSELL, WILLIAM ARMSTRONG (1821–1879), divine ; educated at Trinity College, Dublin ; missionary at Ningpo, China ; first missionary bishop of North China, 1872 ; published work on Chinese language, and translated portions of scriptures and common prayer into Chinese. [xlix. 489]

RUSSELL, SIR WILLIAM OLDNALL (1785–1833), judge ; son of Samuel Oldnall ; adopted name Russell, 1816 ; M.A. Christchurch, Oxford, 1807 ; barrister, Lincoln's Inn, 1809 ; serjeant-at-law, 1827 ; knight and chief-justice of Bengal, 1832 ; published 'Treatise on Crimes,' 1819, and other legal works. [xlix. 490]

RUSSEN, DAVID (fl. 1705), author ; published, 1703, 'Iter Lunare, or a Voyage to the Moon,' an account and criticism of Cyrano de Bergerac's 'Selenarchia.' [l. 1]

RUST, CYPRIAN THOMAS (1808–1895), divine ; baptist minister at Colchester, 1838 ; joined church of England ; LL.B. Queen's College, Cambridge, 1856 ; rector of Westerfield, 1875–90 ; published works relating to Hebrew scriptures and other writings. [l. 2]

RUST, GEORGE (d. 1670), bishop of Dromore ; M.A. St. Catharine's Hall, Cambridge, 1650 ; fellow of Christ's College, 1649–59 ; dean of Connor, 1661 ; bishop of Dromore, 1667–70 ; published theological treatises. [l. 1]

RUSTAT, TOBIAS (1606 ?–1694), university benefactor ; apprenticed to barber-surgeon in London ; entered service of William Feilding, earl of Denbigh [q. v.], and later that of George Villiers, second duke of Buckingham ; servant of Prince of Wales (Charles II) ; escaped to continent with Buckingham, 1648 ; yeoman of robes to Charles II, 1650–85 ; M.A. per literas regias, Cambridge, 1674 ; his portrait painted by Lely ; benefactor of Jesus and other Cambridge colleges. [l. 2]

RUTHALL or **ROWTHALL**, THOMAS (d. 1523), bishop of Durham ; educated at Oxford ; incorporated D.D. Cambridge, 1500 ; secretary to Henry VII, subsequently to Henry VIII ; prebendary and dean of Lincoln, 1505 ; privy councillor ; bishop of Durham, 1509 ; keeper of privy seal, 1516. [l. 3]

RUTHERFORD, ANDREW, first EARL OF TEVIOT (d. 1664), educated at Edinburgh ; entered French service and attained rank of lieutenant-general ; created Baron Rutherford, 1661, and Earl of Teviot, 1663 ; governor, 1663, of Tangier, where he was killed in sally against Moors. [l. 4]

RUTHERFORD, DANIEL (1749–1819), physician and botanist ; son of John Rutherford (1695–1779) [q. v.] ; M.A. Edinburgh ; obtained M.D., 1772, with dissertation establishing distinction between carbonic acid gas and nitrogen ; professor of botany and keeper of Royal Botanic Garden, Edinburgh, 1786 ; physician in ordinary to royal infirmary, 1791 ; F.L.S., 1796 ; published botanical and medical writings. [l. 5]

RUTHERFORD, JOHN (d. 1577), Scottish divine ; studied at Bordeaux and Paris ; professor of humanity at St. Mary's College, 1560, principal of St. Salvator's College, St. Andrews ; ordained minister of Cults, 1563 ; published 'De Arte Disserendi,' 1577. [l. 6]

RUTHERFORD, JOHN (1695–1779), physician ; educated at Edinburgh ; apprenticed as surgeon ; M.D. Rheims, 1719 ; professor of practice of medicine, 1726–65, at Edinburgh, where he began clinical teaching of medicine. His daughter, Anne, married Sir Walter Scott's father. [l. 6]

RUTHERFORD, SAMUEL (1600–1661), Scottish divine; graduated at Edinburgh, 1621, and was regent of humanity, 1623–6; pastor of Anwoth, Galloway, 1627; published treatise against Arminianism, and was suspended for nonconformity by high commission at Edinburgh, 1636; ordered to reside, during Charles I's pleasure, at Aberdeen; member of Glasgow assembly, 1638; professor of divinity, St. Mary's College, St. Andrews; one of commissioners of church of Scotland to Westminster Assembly, 1643; principal of St. Mary's College, St. Andrews; rector of university of St. Andrews, 1651; took part in opposing the 'engagement' and overturning government; joined those who condemned the treaty with Charles II as sinful; deprived of offices at Restoration. [l. 7]

RUTHERFORD, WILLIAM (1798?–1871), mathematician; mathematical master at Royal Military Academy, Woolwich, 1838–64; honorary secretary, Royal Astronomical Society, 1845 and 1846; published mathematical writings. [l. 9]

RUTHERFORD, WILLIAM (1839–1899), physiologist; M.D. Edinburgh, 1863; studied on continent; professor of physiology at King's College, London, 1869, and at Edinburgh, 1874–99; Fullerian professor of physiology at Royal Institution, London, 1871; his works include 'Text Book of Physiology,' 1880. [Suppl. iii. 333]

RUTHERFORTH, THOMAS (1712–1771), divine; M.A. St. John's College, Cambridge, 1733; regius professor of divinity and D.D., 1745; F.R.S., 1743; chaplain to Frederick, prince of Wales, and, later, to the princess dowager; archdeacon of Essex, 1752; published treatises on natural science and other subjects. [l. 10]

RUTHERFURD, ANDREW, LORD RUTHERFURD (1791–1854), Scottish judge; educated at Edinburgh; passed advocate, 1812; solicitor-general for Scotland, 1837; lord advocate and M.P. for Leith Burghs, 1839; resigned office, 1841, on Peel's accession to power; took active part in parliamentary proceedings relating to Scotland; chosen lord rector of Glasgow University, 1844; supported abolition of corn laws, 1845; reappointed lord advocate, 1846; member of commission on marriage laws, 1847; moved successfully for bill to amend law of entail in Scotland, 1848; appointed ordinary lord of session and privy councillor, and took seat on bench as Lord Rutherfurd, 1851. [l. 11]

RUTHVEN, ALEXANDER (1580?–1600), master of Ruthven; third son of William Ruthven, fourth baron Ruthven and first earl of Gowrie [q. v.]; educated at Perth and Edinburgh University; became gentleman of bedchamber to James VI, and was a favourite of the queen; said to have been engaged, 1600, in plot to capture James VI, whom he decoyed to the house of his brother John Ruthven, third earl of Gowrie [q. v.], near Perth; killed there by Sir John Ramsay. The account is given by King James himself, and there are several theories as to its truth. [l. 13]

RUTHVEN, EDWARD SOUTHWELL (1772–1836), Irish politician; son of Edward Trotter; assumed name of Ruthven, 1800; educated at Wadham College, Oxford; whig M.P., Downpatrick, 1806–7, 1830, and 1831, and Dublin, 1832; supported Reform Bill, 1831; again returned for Dublin, 1835, but unseated on petition. [l. 15]

RUTHVEN, JOHN, third EARL OF GOWRIE (1578?–1600), son of William Ruthven, fourth baron Ruthven and first earl of Gowrie [q. v.]; succeeded his brother in earldom, 1588; M.A. Edinburgh, 1593; provost of Perth, 1592; supported extreme protestant party; studied at Padua, and was elected rector of the university; attended convention of estates and headed opposition to James VI, who proposed to maintain by taxation an army to ensure his succession to English throne; said to have been in communication with Sir Robert Logan [q. v.] respecting plot to convey James VI to Logan's stronghold of Fast Castle; was at his house at Perth in 1600 when his brother Alexander Ruthven [q. v.] arrived with James VI, and after his brother's alleged assault on James VI was killed by James VI's attendants while attempting to avenge his brother's death. It is doubtful whether Gowrie and his brother wished to make away with James VI, or obtain from him a settlement of his debts, or whether James VI, who owed Gowrie large sums of money, invented the story to hide a plot, on his own part, of assassination. The family estates were forfeited, and the name and honours decreed by parliament to be extinct. [l. 15]

RUTHVEN, PATRICK, third BARON RUTHVEN (1520?–1566), eldest son of William Ruthven, second baron Ruthven [q. v.]; educated at St. Andrews University; commanded forces of Perth against Lord Gray, 1544; delivered up Perth to English, 1548; commanded footmen in army sent to France, 1552; succeeded his father, 1552; annually elected provost of Perth, 1553–66; joined Argyll in enforcing the Reformation in Scotland, 1559; took part in capture of Perth from French; supported suspension of Mary of Guise, queen dowager, from office of regent, 1559; on commission for treaty of Berwick, 1560; privy councillor of Mary Queen of Scots, 1563, but continued to support protestantism; advocated the Darnley marriage, and took Mary's part in subsequent rebellion of Moray, 1565; assisted in murder of Rizzio, 1566, and subsequently fled to England, where he wrote description of the murder, known as the 'Relation.' [l. 20]

RUTHVEN, PATRICK, EARL OF FORTH AND BRENTFORD (1573?–1651), captain of regiment of Scots in Sweden, 1612; colonel, c. 1618; fought with distinction at Dirschau, and was knighted by Gustavus Adolphus, 1627; commander of Swedish garrison of Ulm, 1632; received earldom of Kirchberg; major-general, 1632; at capture of Landsberg; lieutenant-general to Banier in Thuringia; muster-master-general of forces in Scotland, 1638; created Baron Ruthven of Ettrick, 1639; commander of Berwick Castle; surrendered Berwick to covenanters after severe attack, 1640; created Earl of Forth, 1642; fought at Edgehill, 1642, and appointed general-in-chief of Charles I's army; wounded in unsuccessful attempt to raise siege of Reading, 1643; created Earl of Brentford, 1644; declared traitor by Scottish parliament, 1644; obtained surrender of Essex's army at Lostwithiel, 1644; superseded by Prince Rupert, 1644; chamberlain to Charles, prince of Wales, whom he accompanied to Jersey and France, 1646; with Charles II in Scotland, 1650. [l. 22]

RUTHVEN, WILLIAM, second BARON RUTHVEN (d. 1552), grandson of first Lord Ruthven; custodian and constable of king's hospital, near Speygate, Perth, 1528; extraordinary lord of session, 1533; privy councillor, 1542; chosen one of guardians of Mary Queen of Scots, 1543; keeper of privy seal, 1546. [l. 24]

RUTHVEN, WILLIAM, fourth BARON RUTHVEN and first EARL OF GOWRIE (1541?–1584), second son of Patrick Ruthven, third baron Ruthven [q. v.]; joined conspiracy against Rizzio, 1566, and subsequently accompanied his father to England; denounced as rebel, 1566, but pardoned; appointed with Lord Lindsay to have charge of Mary Queen of Scots during her imprisonment at Lochleven; assisted in obtaining her demission of government to her son, 1567; took part in several engagements against her supporters; lord high treasurer for life, 1571; commissioner for pacification of Perth, 1573; one of Morton's representatives at convention at Stirling, 1578; lord of the articles under Morton; extraordinary lord of session, 1578; created Earl of Gowrie, 1581; entered conspiracy known as 'Raid of Ruthven,' by which James VI was induced to go to Gowrie's seat at Ruthven, and was practically placed under custody of the conspirators, 1582; member of new privy council, 1583; pardoned for share in Ruthven raid; joined with Angus, Mar, and others plot to capture Stirling Castle, 1584; arrested, convicted of high treason, and beheaded at Stirling. [l. 25]

RUTLAND, DUKES OF. [See MANNERS, JOHN, first DUKE, 1638–1711; MANNERS, CHARLES, fourth DUKE, 1754–1787; MANNERS, CHARLES CECIL JOHN, sixth DUKE, 1815–1888.]

RUTLAND, EARLS OF. [See MANNERS, THOMAS, first EARL, d. 1543; MANNERS, HENRY, second EARL, d. 1563; MANNERS, EDWARD, third EARL, 1549–1587; MANNERS, ROGER, fifth EARL, 1576–1612; MANNERS, FRANCIS, sixth EARL, 1578–1632; MANNERS, JOHN, eighth EARL, 1604–1679.]

RUTLAND, HUGH OF (fl. 1185). [See ROTELANDE, HUE DE.]

RUTLEDGE, JAMES or JOHN JAMES (1743–1794), miscellaneous writer; born probably at Dunkirk; served in Berwick's Franco-Irish cavalry regiment, and subsequently lived by his pen; prominent at Paris during revolution; a leading member of Cordeliers' Club till 1791; published works in French. [l. 29]

RUTT, JOHN TOWILL (1760–1841), politician ; educated at St. Paul's School, London ; entered his father's business of wholesale merchant in drugs in London ; joined Society for Constitutional Information, 1780 ; active member of 'Society of Friends of the People' ; aided in founding, and contributed regularly to, 'Monthly Repository,' acting occasionally as editor ; published miscellaneous works. [l. 30]

RUTTER, JOHN (1796–1851), quaker ; settled as bookseller and printer at Shaftesbury, c. 1818 ; gave up business and studied law, c. 1830 ; published topographical works. [l. 30]

RUTTER, JOSEPH (fl. 1635), poet ; tutor to two sons of Edward Sackville, fourth earl of Dorset [q. v.] ; published 'The Shepheard's Holy Day' (1635) and other poetical works. [l. 31]

RUTTY, JOHN (1698–1775), physician ; M.D. Leyden, 1723 ; practised in Dublin, 1724–75 ; quaker ; kept 'a spiritual diary and soliloquies,' 1753–74 ; published works on medical subjects, a 'History of the Quakers in Ireland, 1653–1751' (1751), and a 'Natural History of County of Dublin' (1772). [l. 31]

RUTTY, WILLIAM (1687–1730), physician ; M.D. Christ's College, Cambridge, 1719 ; F.R.C.P., 1720 ; osteology lecturer at Barber-Surgeons' Hall, 1721, viscera lecturer, 1724, and muscular lecturer, 1728 ; Gulstonian lecturer, 1722 ; F.R.S., 1720. [l. 32]

RUVIGNY, second MARQUIS DE (1648–1720). [See MASSUE DE RUVIGNY, HENRI DE.]

RYALL, HENRY THOMAS (1811–1867), engraver ; pupil of Samuel William Reynolds (1773–1835) [q. v.] ; engraved plates for Lodge's ' Portraits,' and other works ; appointed honorary engraver to Queen Victoria for engraving Leslie's 'Christening of Princess Royal' ; executed plates after Landseer, and occasionally exhibited paintings in oils. [l. 32]

RYAN, DANIEL FREDERICK (1762 ?–1798), Irish loyalist ; educated at Trinity College, Dublin ; army surgeon in 103rd regiment, under Sir Ralph Abercromby [q. v.] ; editor of 'Dublin Journal,' 1784 ; captain of St. Sepulchre's yeomanry corps ; died from wounds received while assisting Henry Charles Sirr [q. v.] and Swan in arresting Lord Edward Fitzgerald [q. v.] [l. 33]

RYAN, EDWARD (d. 1819), divine ; M.A. Trinity College, Dublin, 1773 ; LL.B., 1779 ; D.D., 1789 ; prebendary of St. Patrick's, Dublin, 1790–1819 ; published theological works. [l. 34]

RYAN, SIR EDWARD (1793–1875), judge ; B.A. Trinity College, Cambridge, 1814 ; barrister, Lincoln's Inn, 1817 ; appointed puisne judge of supreme court of Calcutta and knighted, 1826 ; chief-justice of presidency of Bengal, 1833 ; returned to England, 1843 ; privy councillor, 1843 ; civil service commissioner, 1855 ; first commissioner, 1862 ; F.G.S., 1846 ; F.R.S., 1860 ; published legal works. [l. 34]

RYAN, LACY (1694 ?–1760), actor ; educated at St. Paul's School, London ; entered solicitor's office ; adopted theatrical profession ; played various Shakespearean characters in London at Drury Lane, Lincoln's Inn Fields, and Covent Garden, including Hamlet, Iago, and Edgar (in ' King Lear ') at Lincoln's Inn Fields. [l. 35]

RYAN, MICHAEL (fl. 1800), medical writer ; M.D· Edinburgh, 1784 ; F.R.C.S. Ireland ; practised at Kilkenny, and later at Edinburgh ; probably M.R.C.S. London ; published medical works. [l. 37]

RYAN, MICHAEL (1800–1841), physician and author; M.R.C.S. and M.R.C.P. London ; physician to Metropolitan Free Hospital ; edited ' London Medical and Surgical Journal,' 1832–8 ; published medical and surgical works. [l. 36]

RYAN, MICHAEL DESMOND (1816–1868), journalist; son of Michael Ryan (fl. 1800) [q. v.] ; studied medicine at Edinburgh ; sub-editor of ' Musical World,' 1846–68 ; connected, as musical critic, with several journals ; published songs and other writings. [l. 37]

RYAN, RICHARD (1796–1849), bookseller ; published plays, songs, and other writings, including ' Biographia Hibernica,' 1819–21. [l. 37]

RYAN, VINCENT WILLIAM (1816–1888), divine ; M.A. Magdalen Hall, Oxford, 1848 ; D.D., 1853 ; principal of Church of England Metropolitan Training Institution, Highbury, 1850 ; bishop of Mauritius, 1854 ; returned home, 1867 ; archdeacon of Craven, 1875 ; went on special mission to Mauritius, 1872 ; published religious and other writings. [l. 38]

RYCAUT or **RICAUT**, SIR PAUL (1628–1700), traveller and author ; B.A. Trinity College, Cambridge, 1650 ; secretary in Turkish embassy of Heneage Finch, second earl of Winchilsea [q. v.], 1661 ; consul of Levant Company at Smyrna, 1667 ; published ' Present State of Ottoman Empire,' 1668, and ' History of Turkish Empire, 1623–77,' 1679 ; knighted and sworn privy councillor and judge of admiralty in Ireland, 1685 ; appointed resident in Hamburg and the Hanse Towns, 1689 ; recalled, 1700 ; F.R.S., 1666 ; translated from the Spanish ; his portrait painted by Lely. [l. 38]

RYDER. [See also RIDER.]

RYDER, SIR ALFRED PHILLIPPS (1820–1888), admiral of the fleet ; entered navy, 1833 ; lieutenant, 1841 ; captain, 1848 ; in Channel, 1853–7 ; in Russian war; controller of coastguard, 1863–6 ; vice-admiral, 1872 ; commander-in-chief in China, 1874–7 ; admiral, 1877 ; commander-in-chief at Portsmouth, 1879–82 ; K.C.B., 1884 ; admiral of fleet, 1885. [l. 40]

RYDER, SIR DUDLEY (1691–1756), judge ; studied at Edinburgh and Leyden ; barrister, Middle Temple, 1725 ; entered Lincoln's Inn, 1726, bencher, 1733, treasurer, 1734, and master of library, 1735 ; M.P., St. Germans, 1733, and Tiverton, 1734 ; solicitor-general, 1733 ; attorney-general, 1737 ; knighted, 1740 ; prosecuted for crown captured rebels of 1745 ; lord chief-justice of king's bench, 1754 ; privy councillor. He was created Baron Ryder of Harrowby, but died before ceremony of kissing hands. [l. 40]

RYDER, DUDLEY, first EARL OF HARROWBY and VISCOUNT SANDON, and second BARON HARROWBY (1762–1847), son of Nathaniel Ryder, first baron Harrowby [q. v.] ; M.A. St. John's College, Cambridge, 1782 ; M.P., Tiverton, 1784 ; under-secretary for foreign affairs, 1789 ; privy councillor, 1790 ; paymaster of forces and vice-president of board of trade, 1791 ; treasurer of navy, 1800–1; succeeded his father, 1803 ; foreign secretary under Pitt, 1804, but resigned owing to ill-health ; chancellor of duchy of Lancaster, with seat in cabinet, 1805 ; went on peace mission to Berlin, Vienna, and St. Petersburg, 1805 ; president of board of control, 1809 ; created Earl of Harrowby and Viscount Sandon, 1809 ; president of council, 1812–27 ; chairman of lords' committee on currency, 1819 ; retired from office on death of Canning ; supported parliamentary reform ; D.C.L. Oxford, 1814 ; LL.D. Cambridge, 1833. [l. 42]

RYDER, DUDLEY, second EARL OF HARROWBY (1798–1882), son of Dudley Ryder, first earl of Harrowby [q. v.] ; M.A. Christ Church, Oxford, 1832 ; D.C.L., 1848 ; M.P., Tiverton, 1819, 1820, 1826, and 1830 ; lord of admiralty, 1827–8 ; secretary to India board, 1830–1 ; M.P., Liverpool, 1831, 1832, 1835, 1837, and 1841–7 ; supported Reform Bill ; commissioner for inquiry into army punishments, 1835 ; followed Peel in adoption of free-trade principles, 1845 ; ecclesiastical commissioner, 1847 ; succeeded his father, 1847 ; chancellor of duchy of Lancaster and privy councillor, 1855 ; lord privy seal, 1855–7 ; resigned from ill-health, 1857 ; admitted to order of Garter, 1859 ; first standing committee of cabinet established at his instance ; moved rejection of Gladstone's Irish Church Bill, 1869 ; chairman of Maynooth commission ; member of the first Oxford University and other commissions ; F.R.S., 1853. [l. 44]

RYDER, DUDLEY FRANCIS STUART, third EARL OF HARROWBY (1831–1900), second son of Dudley Ryder, second earl of Harrowby [q. v.] ; of Harrow and Christ Church, Oxford ; M.A., 1878 ; M.P. for Lichfield, as supporter of Palmerston, 1856–9, and for Liverpool, 1868–1882 ; succeeded to peerage, 1882 ; member of first London school board ; privy councillor, 1874 ; vice-president of committee of council on education, 1874 ; president of board of trade, 1878–80 ; lord privy seal, 1885–6. He was largely responsible for Education Act, 1876. [Suppl. iii. 334]

RYDER, HENRY (1777–1836), successively bishop of Gloucester and of Lichfield and Coventry ; son of Nathaniel Ryder, first baron Harrowby ; M.A. St. John's College, Cambridge, 1798 ; D.D., 1813 ; rector of Lutterworth, 1801, and vicar of Claybrook, 1805; canon of Windsor, 1808; 'lecturer of St. George's'; dean of Wells, 1812; bishop of Gloucester, 1815; established Gloucester Diocesan Society, 1816; translated to see of Lichfield, 1824; organised Church Building Association in his diocese; published religious writings.   [l. 45]

RYDER, JOHN (1697?-1775), archbishop of Tuam; M.A. Queens' College, Cambridge, 1719; D.D., 1741; vicar of Nuneaton, 1721; bishop of Killaloe, 1742; translated to see of Down and Connor, 1743; archbishop of Tuam, and bishop of Ardagh, 1752.   [l. 47]

RYDER, JOHN (1814-1885), actor; appeared with Macready at Drury Lane, London, as Duke Frederick ('As you like it'), 1842; accompanied Macready to America, 1843 and 1848; played Claudius to Macready's Hamlet at Princess's Theatre, London, 1845, and other Shakespearean parts at various theatres. Hubert (in 'King John') was one of his best characters.   [l. 47]

RYDER, NATHANIEL, first BARON HARROWBY (1735-1803), son of Sir Dudley Ryder [q. v.]; M.A. Clare Hall, Cambridge, 1756; M.P., Tiverton, 1756-76; created Baron Harrowby, 1776.   [l. 42]

RYDER, RICHARD (1766-1832), home secretary; son of Nathaniel Ryder, first baron Harrowby [q. v.]; of Harrow and St. John's College, Cambridge; M.A., 1787; barrister, Lincoln's Inn, 1791, bencher, 1812, and treasurer, 1819; M.P., Tiverton, 1795-1830; second justice of great sessions for Carmarthenshire, Cardiganshire, and Pembrokeshire, 1804; lord commissioner of treasury, privy councillor, and judge advocate-general, 1807; home secretary, 1809-12.   [l. 48]

RYDER, THOMAS (1735-1790), actor; trained as printer; appeared at Smock Alley Theatre, Dublin, under Thomas Sheridan (1719-1788) [q. v.], as Captain Plume ('Farquhar's 'Recruiting Officer'), 1757; toured in Ireland, c. 1765-70, and subsequently opened at Smock Alley Theatre, which he managed, 1772-82, with decreasing success; appeared, 1787, as Falstaff ('Henry IV') at Covent Garden; excelled in low comedy; published two plays.   [l. 49]

RYDER, THOMAS (1746-1810), engraver; pupil of James Basire (1730-1802) [q. v.]; studied at Royal Academy; best known by works in stipple.   [l. 50]

RYDER or RITHER, SIR WILLIAM (1544?-1611), lord mayor of London; apprenticed as haberdasher; introduced into England stockings knitted of woollen yarn; member of Haberdashers' Company; alderman and (1591) sheriff of London; lord mayor, 1600; knighted for loyalty to Queen Elizabeth during Essex's rebellion, 1601; 'collector-general' of James I's 'customs inwards,' 1603; appointed collector for life of toll, tonnage, and poundage in London, 1606; president of Bridewell and Bethlehem hospitals, 1600-5.   [l. 50]

RYE, EDWARD CALDWELL (1832-1885), entomologist; educated at King's College School, London; edited 'Zoological Record,' and was co-editor of 'Entomologist's Monthly Magazine'; librarian of Royal Geographical Society.   [l. 52]

RYERSON, EGERTON (1803-1882), divine; born in Canada; worked on his father's farm; joined methodist church, 1821; assistant-teacher in London district grammar school, Ontario; admitted methodist minister on Niagara circuit, c. 1824; edited 'Christian Guardian,' 1829; delegate to Wesleyan conference in England, 1833; one of originators of Victoria College, Coburg, Ontario (first president, 1841); superintendent of schools in Upper Canada, 1844-76; severed his connection with Wesleyan methodists, 1854; LL.D. Middletown University, 1842; D.D. Victoria College, 1866; wrote historical, autobiographical, and other works.   [l. 52]

RYERSON, WILLIAM (1791-1882), soldier and Irvingite minister; brother of Egerton Ryerson [q. v.]; born near Fredericton, New Brunswick; took part in war of 1812-14, as lieutenant in the 18th Norfolk regiment of Canadian militia; entered methodist ministry, 1819; delegate to conference in England, 1831; converted to the views of Edward Irving; returned to Canada and established the catholic apostolic church there, acting as its head till 1872.   [l. 53]

RYGGE, RIGGE, or RUGGE, ROBERT (d. 1410), divine; fellow of Exeter College, Oxford, 1362-72, and

later of Merton College, Oxford, and was bursar, 1374-5; D.D. c. 1380; chancellor of the university, 1381-8 and 1391; chancellor of Exeter Cathedral, and vicar-general for bishop of Exeter, 1400; bishop's proctor in convocation, 1404. At Oxford he at first persistently favoured the Wycliffites, but was finally compelled to abandon them.   [l. 53]

RYLAND, HERMAN WITSIUS (1760-1838), Canadian statesman; son of John Collett Ryland [q. v.]; master and deputy paymaster-general under Burgoyne and Cornwallis in America, 1781-2; civil secretary to governors-in-chief of British North America, 1793-1813; exerted great influence on administration of affairs in Lower Canada.   [l. 54]

RYLAND, JOHN (1717?-1798), friend of Dr. Johnson; West India merchant on Tower Hill, London; member of the London King's Head, Ivy Lane (1749-53), and Essex Head clubs.   [l. 55]

RYLAND, JOHN (1753-1825), baptist minister; son of John Collett Ryland [q. v.]; entered ministry, 1771; assisted his father at Northampton till 1786, when he received sole charge of congregation; minister of Broadmead chapel and president of baptist college, Bristol, 1793-1825; secretary, 1815-25, of Baptist Missionary Society, of which he was a founder; published religious writings, including hymns.   [l. 55]

RYLAND, JOHN COLLETT (1723-1792), divine; baptist pastor at Warwick, where he kept a school, 1750; minister and schoolmaster at Northampton, 1759-86; removed school to Enfield, 1786; published educational, religious, and other works.   [l. 56]

RYLAND, JONATHAN EDWARDS (1798-1866), man of letters; son of John Ryland (1753-1825) [q. v.]; educated at Edinburgh University; mathematical and classical tutor at Mill Hill College, and, later, teacher at Bradford College; published translations and other writings.   [l. 57]

RYLAND, WILLIAM WYNNE (1732-1783), engraver; apprenticed to Simon François Ravenet [q. v.]; studied in France and Italy; engraver to George III; member of Society of Arts, 1765; exhibited portraits at Royal Academy; opened print-shops in Cornhill, London, and, later, in Strand, London; hanged for forging and uttering bills of exchange. He executed plates in the 'chalk' or dotted manner.   [l. 58]

RYLANDS, JOHN (1801-1888), merchant; established with his brothers and (1819) with his father, as weaver of cotton goods at St. Helens and afterwards at Wigan; became sole proprietor, 1847; converted business into limited company, 1873; spent large sums in printing religious works for free distribution in England, France, and Italy. The John Rylands Library (opened 1900) erected as a memorial at Manchester by his widow.   [l. 59]

RYLANDS, PETER (1820-1887), politician; engaged in manufacture of sailcloth at Warrington; member of Anti-Cornlaw League; M.P., Warrington, 1868-74, and Burnley, 1876-87; published writings on religious topics.   [l. 60]

RYLE, JOHN CHARLES (1816-1900), bishop of Liverpool; of Eton and Christ Church, Oxford; B.A., 1838; M.A., 1871; D.D., 1880; took holy orders, 1841-2; rector of St. Thomas, Winchester, 1843, and of Helmingham, Suffolk, 1844; vicar of Stradbroke, 1861; honorary canon of Norwich, 1872; dean of Salisbury, 1880; first bishop of Liverpool, 1880-1900. He belonged to the Evangelical school; published religious writings.
            [Suppl. iii. 334]

RYLEY. [See also RILEY.]

RYLEY or RILEY, CHARLES REUBEN (1752?-1798), painter; exhibited at Royal Academy.   [l. 60]

RYLEY, JOHN (1747-1815), mathematician; employed as husbandman and cloth manufacturer in Yorkshire; studied mathematics and became master at Drighlington grammar school, 1774; opened a school at Pudsey, 1775; master at Beeston, 1776; head-master of Bluecoat school, Leeds, 1789-1815; published mathematical writings.   [l. 61]

RYLEY, SIR PHILIP (d. 1733), surveyor of royal woods and forests; son of William Ryley the younger [q. v.]; serjeant-at-arms, attending lord treasurer of

England before 1702 and after 1706 ; agent of exchequer : commissioner of excise, 1698 ; surveyor of royal woods and forests ; knighted, 1728.			[l. 64]

RYLEY, SAMUEL WILLIAM (1759-1837), actor and author ; son of Samuel Romney, a grocer in London ; apprenticed to woollen manufacturer in Yorkshire ; joined on sharing terms theatrical company at Newcastle, 1783 ; met with misfortune and became strolling actor : subsequently played Sir Peter Teazle at Drury Lane, London, 1809 ; assumed name Ryley, c. 1797 ; annual benefits held for him at Liverpool towards the end of his life ; wrote plays, songs, and memoirs.			[l. 61]

RYLEY, WILLIAM, the elder (d. 1667), herald and archivist ; studied at Middle Temple ; clerk of records in Tower, c. 1620 ; Bluemantle pursuivant of arms, 1633 ; Lancaster herald, 1641 ; supported parliamentarians, but was more than once suspected of treachery ; keeper of records, 1644 ; Norroy king-of-arms, 1646 ; Clarenceux king-of-arms, 1659 ; proclaimed Charles II, 1660, but was reduced to rank of Lancaster herald on Restoration ; buried in east cloister, Westminster Abbey ; associated with his son William Ryley the younger [q. v.] in publication of ' Placita Parliamentaria. Or pleadings in Parliament,' 1661.			[l. 63]

RYLEY, WILLIAM, the younger (d. 1675), archivist ; son of William Ryley the elder [q. v.] ; barrister, Inner Temple, 1665 ; employed under his father in record office.			[l. 64]

RYMER, JAMES (fl. 1775-1822), surgeon ; studied medicine and anatomy at Edinburgh ; surgeon's mate in navy, 1770 ; surgeon, 1775 ; served in Mediterranean, West Indies, and North America ; left navy, c. 1782 ; F.R.C.S. London, 1815 ; published medical works. [l. 65]

RYMER, THOMAS (1641-1713), author and archæologist ; educated at Sidney Sussex College, Cambridge ; barrister, Gray's Inn, 1673 ; published 'Tragedies of the Last Age consider'd,' 1678, and A Short View of Tragedy,' containing an attack on 'Othello,' 1692 ; historiographer to William III, 1692 ; appointed by government, 1693, to edit a collection of public conventions of Great Britain with other powers, the work appearing as ' Fœdera,' 20 vols. 1704-35, vols. xvi-xx. being edited by Robert Sanderson, the latest document included dated 1654 ; new editions brought out, 1737-45 (at the Hague) and 1816-30 (incomplete, undertaken by Record Commission). He also published poems and a play in rhymed verse entitled 'Edgar, or the English Monarch.'			[l. 65]

RYSBRACK, JOHN MICHAEL (JOANNES MICHIEL) (1693 ?-1770), sculptor ; born on continent ; studied in

Antwerp ; came to England, 1720. Many of his works are in Westminster Abbey.			[l. 68]

RYTHER, AUGUSTINE (fl. 1576-1590), engraver ; associated with Christopher Saxton [q. v.] in engraving maps of English counties, published, 1576-9, and with Jodocus Hondius [q. v.] and others in charts for 'The Mariner's Mirrour,' 1588 ; translated from Ubaldini and engraved plates for ' Discourse concerninge Spanishe Fleet,' 1588.			[l. 69]

RYTHER, JOHN (1634 ?-1681), nonconformist divine ; educated at Sidney Sussex College, Cambridge ; vicar of Frodingham, whence he was ejected : vicar of Ferriby ; ejected, 1662 ; published religious works.			[l. 70]

RYTHER, JOHN (d. 1704), nonconformist divine ; son of John Ryther (1634 ?-1681) [q. v.] ; chaplain on merchant ships trading to Indies ; minister at Nottingham, 1689 ; left manuscript journals.			[l. 70]

RYVES, BRUNO (1596-1677), divine ; B.A. New College, Oxford, 1616 ; M.A. Magdalen College, 1619 ; D.D., 1639 ; entered Gray's Inn, 1634 ; vicar of Stanwell ; deprived by parliament, 1642 ; chaplain to Charles I, c. 1640 ; appointed dean of Chichester, 1646 ; installed dean, 1660, and made master of Chichester Hospital ; chaplain in ordinary to Charles II ; dean of Windsor, 1660 ; scribe of order of Garter, 1661 ; rector of Haseley, and Acton ; published 'Mercurius Rusticus,' royalist periodical (nineteen numbers from August 1642).			[l. 70]

RYVES, ELIZABETH (1750-1797), author ; wrote plays (never acted), one novel, and several volumes of poems.			[l. 71]

RYVES, GEORGE FREDERICK (1758-1826), rearadmiral ; educated at Harrow ; entered navy, 1774 ; lieutenant, 1779 ; commander, 1795 ; captain, 1798 ; on coast of Egypt, 1801 ; in Mediterranean under Nelson, 1803-4 ; in Baltic, 1810 ; rear-admiral, 1825.			[l. 72]

RYVES, Mrs. LAVINIA JANETTA HORTON DE SERRES (1797-1871). [See SERRES.]

RYVES, SIR THOMAS (1583 ?-1652), civilian ; of Winchester and New College, Oxford ; fellow, 1598 ; D.C.L., 1610 ; advocate of Doctors' Commons, 1611 ; judge of faculties in prerogative court of Ireland, 1617 ; resigned office ; returned to England ; practised in admiralty court ; king's advocate, 1623 ; master of requests extraordinary, 1626 ; judge of the admiralty of Dover, 1636, and subsequently of Cinque ports ; fought for Charles I ; knighted, 1644 ; published writings on law and naval history.			[l. 72]

S

SABERET or **SABA** (d. 616 ?). [See SEBERT.]

SABIE, FRANCIS (fl. 1587-1596), poetaster ; schoolmaster at Lichfield in 1587 ; published three volumes of verse, 'The Fisher-man's Tale' (2 parts) and 'Pan's Pipe' (1595) and 'Adam's Complaint' (1596).			[l. 74]

SABINE, SIR EDWARD (1788-1883), general ; second lieutenant, royal artillery, 1803 ; second captain, 1813 ; served in Niagara frontier campaign, 1814 ; returned home, 1816 ; F.R.S., 1818 ; astronomer to Arctic expeditions in search of north-west passage under John Ross (1777-1856) [q. v.], 1818, and William Edward Parry [q. v.], 1819-20 ; Copley medallist, Royal Society, 1821 ; made voyages to conduct experiments in magnetic inclination, 1821 and 1823 ; joint-commissioner with Sir John Herschel to act with French commission in determining difference of longitude between Paris and Greenwich, 1825 ; first captain, 1827 ; one of secretaries of Royal Society, 1829 ; appointed one of three scientific advisers of admiralty, 1828 ; assisted in magnetic survey of British islands, 1834-6 ; brevet-major, 1837 ; member of committee to consider establishment of magnetic stations throughout British empire, 1836-9, and subsequently superintendent of the system of observations and editor of ' Observations' ; general secretary of British Association, 1839-59 (except-ing 1852) ; began contributing to Philosophical Trans-actions' a survey of distribution of magnetism over the

globe, 1840 ; foreign secretary to Royal Society, 1845, treasurer, 1850, and president, 1861-71 ; colonel, 1851 ; major-general, 1856 ; repeated magnetic survey of British isles, 1861 ; lieutenant-general, 1865 ; civil K.C.B., 1869 ; general, 1870 ; D.C.L. Oxford and LL.D. Cambridge, 1855 ; member of Linnean, Royal Astronomical, and other learned societies.			[l. 74]

SABINE, JOSEPH (1662 ?-1739), general ; appointed captain in Ingoldsby's foot, 1689 ; brevet-colonel in Herbert's regiment, 1703 ; served in Low Countries and in war of Spanish succession ; M.P., Berwick-on-Tweed, 1727 ; general, 1730, and governor of Gibraltar, where he died.			[l. 78]

SABINE, JOSEPH (1770-1837), writer on horticulture : brother of Sir Edward Sabine [q. v.] ; practised as barrister till 1808 ; inspector-general of assessed taxes, 1808-35 ; F.R.S., 1779 ; original F.L.S., 1798 ; honorary secretary of Horticultural Society, 1810-30, contributing extensively to its 'Transactions' ; subsequently treasurer and vice-president of Zoological Society.			[l. 79]

SABRAN, LEWIS (1652-1732), jesuit ; born at Paris ; educated at English jesuit college, St. Omer ; professed of four vows, 1688 ; royal chaplain at St. James's Palace, London, 1685 ; escaped to France at revolution ; principal of episcopal seminary at Liège, 1699-1708 ; provincial of

English province, 1708; rector of college at St. Omer, 1712; spiritual father at English College, Rome, 1715; published theological works. [l. 79]

SACHEVERELL, HENRY (1674?–1724), political preacher; of Magdalen College, Oxford; M.A., 1695; fellow, 1701–13; pro-proctor, 1703; D.D., 1708; bursar, 1709; incorporated at Cambridge, 1714; advocated in sermons and pamphlets high church and tory cause; chaplain of St. Saviour's, Southwark, 1705; preached sermons at Derby and at St. Paul's, London, 1709, favouring non-resistance, and condemning toleration and occasional conformity (both sermons printed, 1709, and declared by House of Commons to be seditious libels); impeached (his counsel including Simon Harcourt (1661?–1727) [q. v.]); found guilty and suspended from preaching for three years, much popular feeling being excited in his favour; presented to living of Selattyn, 1710, and to living of St. Andrew's, Holborn, London, 1713; died from effects of accident. [l. 80]

SACHEVERELL, WILLIAM (1638–1691), politician; entered Gray's Inn, 1667; M.P., Derbyshire, 1670 and 1679; opposed court policy; moved successfully that popish recusants be deprived of military office, 1673; on committee to prepare Test Bill, 1673; urged necessity of return to policy of triple alliance, 1677; took prominent part in parliamentary investigation of Oates's pretended popish plot, and for some time presided over committee of secrecy; supported motion for removal of James, duke of York, from royal presence and counsels, and supported Exclusion Bill, 1679; served on committee which drew up articles of Danby's impeachment, 1678; member for Heytesbury in Convention parliament; lord of admiralty in William III's first administration till December 1689; M.P., Nottinghamshire, 1691. [l. 83]

SACKVILLE, CHARLES, sixth EARL OF DORSET and first EARL OF MIDDLESEX (1638–1706), poet; son of Richard Sackville, fifth earl of Dorset, and Frances, daughter of Lionel Cranfield, first earl of Middlesex; M.P., East Grinstead, 1660; led life of dissipation with Sir Charles Sedley [q. v.] and others; volunteered in fleet fitted out against Dutch, 1665, and took part in battle of 3 June; created Baron Cranfield and Earl of Middlesex, 1675; withdrew from court during James II's reign; lord chamberlain of household, 1689–97; received Garter, 1691; thrice acted as regent during William III's absence. His poems appeared with Sedley's in 1701, his best being the song 'To all you ladies now on land,' 1665. Dryden dedicated several poems to him. [l. 86]

SACKVILLE, CHARLES, second DUKE OF DORSET (1711–1769), son of Lionel Cranfield Sackville, first duke of Dorset [q. v.]; of Westminster School and Christ Church, Oxford; M.A., 1730; intimate friend of Frederick, prince of Wales; M.P., East Grinstead, 1734–41 and 1761–5, Sussex, 1742–7, and Old Sarum, 1747–54; high steward of honour at Otford, 1741; lord of treasury, 1743–7; master of horse to Frederick, prince of Wales, 1747; privy councillor, 1766. [l. 88]

SACKVILLE, SIR EDWARD, fourth EARL OF DORSET (1591–1652), son of Robert Sackville, second earl of Dorset [q. v.]; succeeded his brother Richard (1590–1624), 1624; educated at Christ Church, Oxford, and perhaps at Cambridge; M.P., Sussex, 1614 and 1621–2, being one of leaders of popular party; K.B., 1616; held subordinate command at battle of Prague, 1620; ambassador to Louis XIII, 1621; governor of Bermuda Islands Company, 1623; commissioner for planting Virginia, 1631 and 1634; K.G., 1625; privy councillor, 1626; lord chamberlain to Queen Henrietta Maria, 1628; lord commissioner of admiralty, 1628; assisted in draining parts of Lincolnshire, 1631; commissioner of regency, 1640 and 1641; supported Charles I in civil war; present at Edgehill, 1642; commissioner of Charles I's treasury, 1643; lord chamberlain of household, 1644–6; keeper of privy seal and president of council, 1644. [l. 89]

SACKVILLE, GEORGE, first VISCOUNT SACKVILLE (1716–1785). [See GERMAIN.]

SACKVILLE, JOHN FREDERICK, third DUKE OF DORSET (1745–1799), grandson of Lionel Cranfield Sackville, first duke of Dorset [q. v.]; educated at Westminster; M.P., Kent, 1768; succeeded his uncle Charles

Sackville, second duke of Dorset [q. v.], 1769; privy councillor, 1782; ambassador extraordinary to France, 1783–9; K.G., 1788; patron of cricket; lord steward of royal household, 1789–99. [l. 92]

SACKVILLE, LIONEL CRANFIELD, first DUKE OF DORSET (1688–1765), son of Charles Sackville, sixth earl of Dorset [q. v.]; educated at Westminster; succeeded to earldom, 1706; constable of Dover Castle and lord warden of Cinque ports, 1708–13, 1714–17, 1728; envoy extraordinary to notify George I of Queen Anne's death, 1714; groom of stole, first lord of bedchamber, privy councillor, and K.G., 1714; created Duke of Dorset, 1720; lord-lieutenant of Ireland, 1730–7 and 1750–5; lord president of council, 1745; master of horse, 1755–7; constituted constable of Dover Castle and lord warden of Cinque ports for life, 1757; D.C.L. Oxford, 1730; frequently acted as one of lords justices of Great Britain. His portrait was painted by Kneller. [l. 92]

SACKVILLE, SIR RICHARD (d. 1566), first cousin of Anne Boleyn; educated at Cambridge; barrister, Gray's Inn; Lent reader, 1529; M.P., Arundel, 1529; treasurer of army; chancellor of court of augmentations, 1548; knighted, 1549; privy councillor, 1554; M.P., Portsmouth, 1554, Kent, 1558, and Sussex, 1563–6; received charge of Margaret, countess of Lennox, 1561. It was owing to his encouragement that Roger Ascham [q. v.] wrote his 'Scholemaster.' [l. 95]

SACKVILLE, RICHARD, fifth EARL OF DORSET (1622–1677), son of Sir Edward Sackville, fourth earl of Dorset; M.P., East Grinstead, 1640–3; imprisoned by parliament, 1642; lord sewer at coronation of Charles II, 1661; member of Inner Temple, 1661; F.R.S., 1665; contributed to 'Jonsonus Virbius' (1638). [l. 91]

SACKVILLE, ROBERT, second EARL OF DORSET (1561–1609), son of Thomas Sackville, first earl of Dorset [q. v.]; educated by Roger Ascham [q. v.]; M.A. Hart Hall, Oxford, 1579; entered Inner Temple, 1580; M.P., Sussex, 1585, 1593, 1598, 1601, and 1604–8, and Lewes, 1588; engaged in trading ventures; endowed Sackville College for the poor, East Grinstead. [l. 96]

SACKVILLE, THOMAS, first EARL OF DORSET and BARON BUCKHURST (1536–1608), son of Sir Richard Sackville [q. v.]; perhaps educated at Hart Hall, Oxford, and St. John's College, Cambridge; barrister, Inner Temple; planned, began, and wrote 'Induction' for 'Myrrovre for Magistrates' (1559–63), completed by William Baldwin [q. v.] and George Ferrers [q. v.]; collaborated (he probably wrote only last two acts) with Thomas Norton (1532–1584) [q. v.] in 'Tragedy of Gorboduc,' the first English tragedy in blank verse, acted in Inner Temple hall, 1561; grand master of order of freemasons, 1561–7; M.P., Westmoreland, 1558, East Grinstead, 1559, Aylesbury, 1563; knighted and raised to peerage, 1567; M.A. Cambridge, 1571; privy councillor; commissioner at state trials; announced to Mary Queen of Scots sentence of death, 1586; sent (1587) to survey position of affairs in Low Countries after Leicester's return (1586); commissioner for ecclesiastical causes, 1588; K.G., 1589; ambassador to Low Countries, 1589; one of commissioners who signed treaty with France, 1591; renewed treaty with united provinces, 1598; lord treasurer, 1599 till death; lord high steward, presiding at Essex's trial, 1601; created Earl of Dorset, 1604; commissioner for peace with Spain, 1604; chancellor of Oxford University, 1591; incorporated M.A. Oxford, 1592. His poetical works were collected, 1859. [l. 96]

SACROBOSCO, CHRISTOPHER (1562–1616). [See HOLYWOOD.]

SACRO BOSCO, JOHANNES DE (fl. 1230). [See HOLYWOOD or HALIFAX, JOHN.]

SADDINGTON, JOHN (1634?–1679), early Muggletonian; wrote religious works, printed posthumously. [l. 100]

SADDLER, JOHN (1813–1892), line-engraver; pupil of George Cooke (1781–1834) [q. v.]; exhibited at Society of British Artists and Royal Academy between 1862 and 1883. [l. 101]

SADINGTON, SIR ROBERT DE (d. c. 1350), judge; appears as advocate between 1329 and 1336; J.P., Leicestershire and Rutland, 1332; chief baron of exchequer, 1334, and also treasurer, 1340; chancellor, 1343–1345; reappointed chief baron, 1345. [l. 101]

SADLEIR, FRANC (1774–1851), scholar; M.A. and fellow, Trinity College, Dublin, 1805; B.D. and D.D., 1813; Donnelan lecturer, 1816, 1817, and 1823; Erasmus Smith professor of mathematics, 1824–36; regius professor of Greek, 1833–8; provost of Trinity College, Dublin, 1837–51; published sermons. [l. 102]

SADLEIR, JOHN (1814–1856), Irish politician and swindler; educated at Clongowes College; solicitor in Dublin; a director of Tipperary joint-stock bank; chairman of London and County Joint-Stock Bank, 1848; M.P., Carlow, 1847, and Sligo, 1853; junior lord of treasury, 1853; committed suicide on the failure of the Tipperary bank (then managed by his brother James), which his fraudulent practices had helped to bring about. Mr. Merdle in Dickens's 'Little Dorrit' is drawn from him. [l. 102]

SADLER, ANTHONY (*fl.* 1640), clergyman; M.A. Exeter College, Oxford, 1624; M.D., 1633; perhaps rector of West Thurrock, 1628. [l. 104]

SADLER, ANTHONY (*fl.* 1630–1680), divine; B.A. St. Edmund Hall, Oxford, 1632; presented to living of Mitcham, *c.* 1660; accused of disorderly practices; appointed to Berwick St. James; threatened with suspension for debauchery, 1681; published works of a political character. [l. 103]

SADLER, JOHN (*d.* 1595 ?), divine; M.A. Corpus Christi College, Cambridge, 1540; original fellow of Trinity College, 1546; rector of Sudborough, 1568; published translation from Flavius Vegetius Renatus. [l. 104]

SADLER, JOHN (1615–1674), master of Magdalene College, Cambridge; M.A. Emmanuel College, Cambridge, 1638; studied at Lincoln's Inn; master in ordinary in court of chancery 1644; master of requests; town-clerk of London, 1649; master of Magdalene College, Cambridge, 1650–60; M.P., Cambridge, 1653, and Great Yarmouth, 1658; first commissioner under great seal, 1659; lost all offices after Restoration; published historical and other works. [l. 104]

SADLER, MICHAEL FERREBEE (1819–1895), theologian; son of Michael Thomas Sadler [q. v.]; B.A. St. John's College, Cambridge, 1847; prebendary of Wells; rector of Honiton, 1864–95; published theological works. [l. 105]

SADLER, MICHAEL THOMAS (1780–1835), social reformer; while still young assisted methodist movement; engaged in business as importer of Irish linens at Leeds, 1800; took, as tory, enthusiastic interest in politics; opposed catholic emancipation, 1813; published 'Ireland: its Evils and their Remedies,' 1828; issued, 1830, 'Law of Population,' expounding theory that 'prolificness of human beings . . . varies inversely as their number,' which was attacked by Macaulay in 'Edinburgh Review'; tory M.P., Newark, 1829 and 1830, and Aldborough, Yorkshire, 1831–2; moved unsuccessfully for establishment of poor-law for Ireland, and moved resolution for bettering condition of agricultural poor in England, 1831; chosen parliamentary leader of the cause of radical working men; introduced bill for regulating labour of young people in mills and factories, 1831, and subsequently acted as chairman of committee to which it was referred; F.R.S., 1832; published pamphlets and speeches. [l. 105]

SADLER, **SADLEIR**, or **SADLEYER**, Sir RALPH (1507–1587), diplomatist; in service of Thomas Cromwell, afterwards earl of Essex; gentleman of Henry VIII's privy chamber, *c.* 1536; sent to Scotland to advise King James to adopt an ecclesiastical policy antagonistic to Rome; one of Henry VIII's principal secretaries of state, *c.* 1537; knighted, 1542; sent to reside in Edinburgh on death of James V with view of preventing revival of influence of Cardinal Beaton; treasurer of navy in Earl of Hertford's raid on Scotland; one of council of twelve to assist executors in government of kingdom and guardianship of Edward VI, 1547; accompanied Hertford to Scotland as high treasurer of army; knight-banneret after battle of Pinkie, 1547; became agent of Cecil, 1558; had principal share in arranging treaty of peace and alliance between England and Scotland, 1560; chancellor of duchy of Lancaster, 1568; one of commissioners to treat with Scottish commissioners concerning Mary Queen of Scots, 1568; paymaster-general in Sussex's expedition to quell

rebellion on behalf of Duke of Norfolk and Mary Queen of Scots; guardian of Mary Queen of Scots, 1580–1; envoy to James VI, 1587. [l. 109]

SADLER, THOMAS, in religion VINCENT FAUSTUS (1604–1681), Benedictine; entered order of St. Benedict and made profession at Dieulouard, 1622; cathedral prior of Chester and definitor of the province, 1661; published religious works. [l. 111]

SADLER, THOMAS (*fl.* 1670–1700), painter; son of John Sadler (1615–1674) [q. v.]; pupil of Lely; drew portrait of John Bunyan, 1685. [l. 105]

SADLER, THOMAS (1822–1891), divine; educated at University College, London, and at Bonn; Ph.D. Erlangen, 1844; unitarian minister at Rosslyn Hill Chapel, Hampstead, 1846–91; published religious works; edited Crabb Robinson's 'Diaries,' 1869. [l. 112]

SADLER, WINDHAM WILLIAM (1796 – 1824), aëronaut; educated as engineer; gave up service of first Liverpool Gas Company to become professional aëronaut; crossed St. George's Channel from Dublin to Holyhead, 1817; died of injuries from balloon accident. [l. 112]

SADLINGTON, MARK (*d.* 1647); divine; B.A. Christ's College, Cambridge, 1581; fellow of Peterhouse College, Cambridge; M.A., 1584; lecturer, 1588; master of St. Olave's grammar school, Southwark, 1591–4; vicar of Sunbury, 1603–47; some historical writings have been attributed to him. [l. 113]

SAEBBI (*d.* 695 ?). [See SEBBI.]

SÆLRÆD (*d.* 746). [See SELRED.]

SÆWULF (*fl.* 1102), traveller and pilgrim to Syria; left manuscript account of journey from Monopoli to Palestine and back to Dardanelles. [l. 113]

SAFFERY, Mrs. MARIA GRACE (1772 – 1858), poet; *née* Andrews; married, 1799, John Saffery, baptist minister at Salisbury, where she conducted a girls' school; published sacred and other poems. [l. 114]

SAFFOLD, THOMAS (*d.* 1691), empiric; licensed by bishop of London to practise as a physician, 1674; practised in London; died under his own treatment. [l. 114]

SAFRED (*d.* 1204). [See SEFFRID.]

SAGE, JOHN (1652 – 1711), Scottish nonjuring divine; M.A. St. Salvator's College, St. Andrews, 1669; minister of east quarter in Glasgow, 1685; clerk of presbytery and synod; driven from Glasgow to Edinburgh by Cameronian outbreak; banished from Edinburgh for officiating as nonjuror, 1693; privately consecrated at Edinburgh as bishop without diocese or jurisdiction, 1705; published works relating to religious questions. [l. 115]

SAHAM, WILLIAM DE (*d.* 1304 ?), judge of king's bench under Edward I till 1289; constantly employed in judicial *itinera*. [l. 116]

SAINBEL or **SAINT BEL**, CHARLES VIAL DE (1753–1793), veterinary surgeon; born at Lyons; studied under Claude Bourgelat; assistant-surgeon and public demonstrator at veterinary college at Lyons, 1773; distinguished himself during epizootic among horses in France, 1774; assistant-professor, Royal Veterinary College, Paris; veterinary surgeon and physician at Lyons; equerry to Louis XVI and chief of *manège* at academy at Lyons; came to England, 1788; Veterinary College of London instituted with Sainbel as professor, 1791; wrote works on veterinary surgery (some published posthumously). [l. 116]

SAINSBURY, WILLIAM NOEL (1825 – 1895), historical writer; assistant-keeper of records, 1887–91; published historical works and calendars of state papers. [l. 117]

ST. ALBANS, DUKE OF (1670–1726). [See BEAUCLERK, CHARLES.]

ST. ALBANS, DUCHESS OF (1777 ?–1837). [See MELLON, HARRIOT.]

ST. ALBANS, EARL OF (*d.* 1684). [See JERMYN, HENRY.]

ST. ALBANS, VISCOUNT (1561–1626). [See BACON, FRANCIS.]

ST. ALBANS, ALEXANDER OF (1157–1217). [See NECKAM.]

ST. ALBANS, ROGER OF (*fl.* 1450). [See ROGER.]

ST. ALBANS, WILLIAM OF (*fl.* 1178). [See WILLIAM.]

ST. AMAND, ALMARIC DE (*fl.* 1240), crusader; godfather to future Edward I, 1239; .went on crusade, 1240. [l. 118]

ST. AMAND, ALMARIC DE, third BARON DE ST. AMAND (1314?–1382), descendant of Almaric de St. Amand (*fl.* 1240) [q. v.]; served in Scotland, 1338 and 1355, and in France, 1342, 1345 and 1346, 1358 and 1368; justiciar of Ireland, 1357–9. [l. 118]

ST. AMAND, JAMES (1687–1754), antiquary; educated probably at Westminster and at Lincoln College, Oxford; left to Bodleian Library collection of books, coins, prints, and manuscripts, including notes used by Warton in his Theocritus, 1770. [l. 118]

ST. ANDRÉ, NATHANAEL (1680–1776), anatomist; born in Switzerland; came early to England; local surgeon to Westminster Hospital; anatomist to George I's household, 1723; lost court favour owing to belief in fraud practised by Mary Toft [q. v.] and marriage (1730) with Lady Elizabeth Capel, wife of Samuel Molyneux [q. v.], immediately on her husband's death, which he was erroneously suspected of hastening. His portrait is in Hogarth's engraving, 'Cunicularii,' 1726. [l. 119]

ST. AUBYN, CATHERINE, afterwards MRS. MOLESWORTH (*d.* 1836), amateur artist; sister of Sir John St. Aubyn (1758–1839) [q. v.]; her etchings were privately printed. [l. 120]

ST. AUBYN, SIR JOHN, third baronet (1696–1744), politician; M.A. Exeter College, Oxford, 1721; M.P. Cornwall, 1722–44; joined opposition to Walpole; friend of Dr. William Borlase [q. v.] and Pope. [l. 120]

ST. AUBYN, SIR JOHN, fifth baronet (1758–1839), educated at Westminster; sheriff of Cornwall, 1781; M.P. Truro, 1784, Penryn, 1784–90, and Helston, 1807–12; F.L.S.; F.S.A., 1783; F.R.S., 1797; collected fossils and minerals; his portrait painted by Reynolds. [l. 121]

SAINT-CARILEF or **SAINT-CALAIS**, WILLIAM OF (*d.* 1096). [See CARILEF.]

ST. CLAIR. [See SINCLAIR.]

SAINTE-MÈRE-EGLISE (*d.* 1224). [See WILLIAM.]

SAINT-ÉVREMOND, CHARLES DE MARGUETEL DE SAINT DENIS DE (1613?–1703), soldier and poet; born perhaps at Saint-Denis-le-Guast, Normandy; studied at Jesuit Collège de Clermont, Paris, Caen University and Collège d'Harcourt, Paris; ensign in French army; captain, 1637; adopted views of Gassendi; lieutenant in Duc D'Enghien's guards, 1642; fought at Rocroi (1643), Friedburg (1644), and Nordlingen (1645); served in Flanders, 1646, and in Catalonia, 1647; cashiered, 1648; 'maréchal de camp' in French king's armies during civil war, 1652; served in Spanish war in Flanders, 1654–9; accompanied embassy to England to congratulate Charles II on accession, 1661; had accompanied Mazarin, 1659, to conclude peace of Pyrenees, and wrote an attack on Mazarin and his policy, which being discovered on Mazarin's death (1661), compelled him to leave France; came to England, where he was intimate with Grammont and other courtiers; in Low Countries, 1664–70; again in England, 1670–1703; attached himself to service of Duchess of Mazarin, 1675; buried in Westminster Abbey. He wrote occasional poems, some plays, and various essays, dialogues, dissertations, and reflections; a pirated selection in English appeared 1700, and an authentic edition, 1705. [l. 122]

ST. FAITH'S, BENEDICT OF (*fl.* 1400), Carmelite of St. Faith's, near Norwich. [l. 125]

ST. FAITH'S, JOHN OF (*d.* 1359), theological writer; educated at Carmelite house of St. Faith's, near Norwich; studied at Oxford; governor of Carmelites of Burham Norton; wrote theological works, a work on Aristotle's 'De Cœlo et Mundo,' a concordance to Thomas Aquinas and a 'Tabula Juris.' [l. 124]

ST. FAITH'S, PETER OF (*d.* 1452), prior of Carmelite house of St. Faith's, near Norwich; master in theology, Cambridge; doctor of Sorbonne, Paris; wrote theological works. [l. 125]

ST. FAITH'S, ROBERT OF (*d.* 1386), theologian; Carmelite of St. Faith's, near Norwich; papal nuncio to Spain and England; died in Spain. [l. 125]

ST. FAITH'S WILLIAM OF (*d.* 1372), theologian; Carmelite of St. Faith's, near Norwich; D.D. Cambridge. [l. 125]

SAINT-GEORGE, SIR HENRY, the elder (1581–1644), Garter king-of-arms; son of Sir Richard Saint-George [q. v.]; Richmond herald, 1616; knighted by Gustavus Adolphus, 1627; Norroy king-of-arms, 1635; M.D. Oxford, 1643; Garter king-of-arms, 1644; left heraldic manuscripts. [l. 125]

SAINT-GEORGE, SIR HENRY, the younger (1625–1715), Garter king-of-arms; son of Sir Henry Saint-George the elder; Garter king-of-arms, 1703. [l. 125]

ST. GEORGE, SIR JOHN (1812–1891), general; first lieutenant, royal artillery, 1829; lieutenant-colonel, 1854; instructor in practical artillery, Woolwich, 1844–6; commanded siege-train in Crimea, 1855; C.B., 1856; commanded artillery in Malta; colonel, 1857; director of ordnance, 1863–8; major-general, 1865; British delegate at St. Petersburg conference, 1868; general, 1877; G.C.B., 1889; colonel-commandant, R.A., 1872. [l. 125]

SAINT-GEORGE, SIR RICHARD (*d.* 1635), herald; Norroy king-of-arms, 1603; knighted, 1616; Clarenceux king-of-arms, 1623; commissioned with Sir John Borough, Norroy king-of-arms, to institute visitations in any part of England, several of which were printed; left genealogical manuscripts. [l. 126]

SAINT-GEORGE, SIR THOMAS (1615–1703), Garter king-of-arms; son of Sir Henry Saint-George the elder; Garter king-of-arms, 1686. [l. 126]

SAINT-GERMAN, CHRISTOPHER (1460?–1540), legal writer and controversialist; educated at Oxford, perhaps at Exeter College; barrister, Inner Temple; published religious controversial treatises and 'Doctor and Student,' a legal handbook, in Latin, 1523. Translations in English appeared, 1530 and 1531. [l. 127]

ST. GERMANS, third EARL OF (1798–1877). [See ELIOT, EDWARD GRANVILLE.]

ST. GILES, JOHN OF (*fl.* 1230). [See JOHN.]

ST. HELENS, BARON (1753–1839). [See FITZ HERBERT, ALLEYNE.]

ST. JOHN, BAYLE (1822–1859), author; son of James Augustus St. John [q. v.]; studied with view to artistic profession; assisted his father in 'History of Customs of Greece'; travelled in Egypt, 1846 and 1851; lived in Paris, 1848–51; contributed to 'Chambers's Journal' and 'Household Words'; correspondent at Paris of 'Daily Telegraph.' His publications include works of travel and fiction and various treatises. [l. 128]

ST. JOHN, CHARLES GEORGE WILLIAM (1809–1856), sportsman and naturalist; clerk in treasury, 1828, but soon retired on private means and devoted himself to sport, chiefly in Scotland; published 'Short Sketches of Wild Sports and Natural History of Highlands,' 1846, and other works. [l. 128]

SAINT-JOHN, HENRY, first VISCOUNT BOLINGBROKE (1678–1751), statesman; son of Sir Henry St. John and Lady Mary, second daughter of Robert Rich, second earl of Warwick [q. v.]; educated at Eton and, perhaps, Christ Church, Oxford; M.P. for family borough of Wootton-Bassett, 1701; supported Harley and tory party; appointed to prepare and bring in bill for security of protestant succession, 1701; received doctor's degree, Oxford, 1702; secretary at war, 1704–8; secretary of state, 1710; member for Berkshire, 1710; responsible for expedition to Canada, 1710; created Viscount Bolingbroke and Baron St. John of Lydiard Tregoze, 1712; went to Paris to make final arrangements for peace, 1712; again took charge of peace negotiations, treaty of Utrecht being signed, 1713; privately negotiated with Pretender; dismissed from office on accession of George I; founded 'Brothers Club,' to direct patronage of literature and rival 'Whig Kit-Cat Club,' 1711; a motion for his impeachment carried, bill of attainder passed, and his name erased from roll of peers, 1714; fled to France; secretary of state to James the Pretender, who gave him patent for an earldom; drew up the Old Pretender's declaration for invasion, promising security for church of England, the assurance being eventually removed from the document by the Old Pretender's priests, 1715 ; dismissed from the Old Pretender's service, 1716 ; occupied himself with philosophical studies in France ; pardoned, 1723 ; returned to London and joined Walpole's party ; enabled, by act passed 1725, to inherit and acquire real estate, though still excluded from House of Lords ; became estranged from Walpole owing to his opposition to this act ; settled at Dawley, near Uxbridge, and became object of Pope's reverence ; attacked the Walpoles and the government's foreign policy in papers contributed to 'Craftsman,' and in other writings, from 1726 ; wrote, c. 1730, philosophical fragments partly versified by Pope in 'Essay on Man' ; contributed to 'Craftsman' 'Dissertation on Parties,' 1733 ; gave up the contest with Walpole, 1735, and retired to Chanteloup in Touraine , wrote essays upon history in form of letters to friends, and upon political subjects (including 'Patriot King,' 1738), but after 1739 ceased to influence politics. He left his works, published and unpublished, to David Mallet [q. v.] A 'Collection of Political Tracts ' by him appeared, 1748, and Mallet published the collected works, 5 vols. 1754. His greatest powers lay in the art of oratory ; his policy was a kind of democratic toryism, anticipating Disraeli's attacks upon the 'Venetian aristocracy.' [l. 129]

ST. JOHN, HORACE STEBBING ROSCOE (1832-1888), journalist : son of James Augustus St. John [q. v.] ; for many years political leader-writer on 'Daily Telegraph ' ; became bankrupt, 1862 ; published historical and other works. [l. 144]

ST. JOHN, JAMES AUGUSTUS (1801-1875), author and traveller : assistant-editor under James Silk Buckingham [q. v.] of 'Oriental Herald,' 1824 ; with David Lester Richardson [q. v.] started 'Weekly Review,' 1827 ; resided on continent and subsequently travelled, mostly on foot, in Egypt and Nubia ; political leader-writer to 'Daily Telegraph.' His works include accounts of his travels and a 'Life of Sir Walter Raleigh,' 1868. [l. 145]

SAINT-JOHN, JOHN DE (d. 1302), governor of Porchester Castle ; extensive landowner ; took part in Edward I's invasions of Wales, 1277 and 1282 ; attended Edward I in Aquitaine, 1286–9 ; on mission to Nicholas IV respecting crusade, 1291 ; Edward I's lieutenant in Gascony, 1293 ; returned (1294) on Philip the Fair gaining possession of Gascon strongholds ; seneschal and chief counsellor to Edward's son John of Brittany when lieutenant in Aquitaine, 1294 ; made (1295) extensive conquests in Garonne valley which, excepting Bayonne, were soon won back by Philip's brother, Charles of Valois ; defeated and captured by French near Bellegarde, 1297 ; released after treaty of L'Aumône, 1299 ; warden of Galloway, Dumfries, and adjacent marches, 1301. [l. 145]

ST. JOHN, JOHN (1746-1793), author ; nephew of first Viscount Bolingbroke ; educated at Trinity College, Oxford : barrister, Middle Temple, 1770 ; M.P., Newport, Isle of Wight, 1773–4 and 1780–4, and Eye, 1774–80 ; surveyor-general of land revenues of crown, 1775-84 ; published 'Mary Queen of Scots,' a tragedy produced at Drury Lane, London, by Mrs. Siddons and Kemble, 1789, and other works. [l. 148]

ST. JOHN, OLIVER, first VISCOUNT GRANDISON and BARON TREGOZ (1559-1630), lord-deputy of Ireland ; B.A. Trinity College, Oxford, 1578 ; entered Lincoln's Inn, 1580 ; killed George Best [q. v.] in duel and fled to continent, 1584 ; promoted captain ; commanded Essex's horse at siege of Rouen, 1591 ; returned to England, 1592 ; M.P. Cirencester, 1593 ; fought at battle of Nieuport, 1600, accompanied Mountjoy to Ireland, 1601 ; knighted, 1601 M.P., Portsmouth, 1604–7 ; master of ordnance in Ireland, 1605–14 ; Irish privy councillor, 1605 ; commissioner for plantation of Ulster, 1608 ; M.P., Roscommon (Irish parliament), 1613 ; lord-deputy of Ireland, 1616–22 ; English privy councillor, 1622 ; created Viscount Grandison of Limerick in Irish peerage, 1623 ; lord high treasurer of Ireland, 1625 ; made Baron Tregoz of Highworth in English peerage, 1626 ; on council of war, 1624. [l. 148]

ST. JOHN, OLIVER (1603-1642), son of Oliver St. John, fourth baron St. John of Bletsho and first earl of Bolingbroke [q. v.] ; M.P., Bedfordshire, 1624, 1625, 1626, and 1629 ; K.B., 1625 ; known by courtesy title of Lord St. John ; raised regiment for parliament on outbreak of war ; held Hereford, 1642 ; died from wounds received at Edgehill. [l. 151]

ST. JOHN, OLIVER, fourth BARON ST. JOHN OF BLETSHO and first EARL OF BOLINGBROKE (1580 ?-1646), M.P., Bedfordshire, 1601 and 1604 ; K.B., 1610 ; succeeded his father, 1618 ; created Earl of Bolingbroke, 1624 ; joined parliamentarians, 1642 ; named by parliament lord-lieutenant of Bedfordshire, took covenant, and was lay member of Westminster Assembly, 1643 ; one of commissioners for custody of great seal, 1643. [l. 150]

ST. JOHN, OLIVER (1598 ?-1673), chief-justice ; educated at Queens' College, Cambridge ; barrister, Lincoln's Inn, 1626 ; connected with company for plantation of Providence island ; counsel for Lord Saye and John Hampden in their resistance to payment of ship-money, 1637 ; M.P., Totnes, in Short and Long parliaments, 1640 ; opened attack on ship-money, 1640 ; solicitor-general, 1641–3 ; promoted bill for Strafford's attainder ; drew up Root and Branch and Militia Bills ; enabled by ordinance to perform duties of the attorney-general, who had joined Charles I, 1644 ; took solemn league and covenant ; one of commissioners to treat for peace at Uxbridge, 1645 ; sided with army against parliament, 1647 ; chief-justice of common pleas, 1648 ; refused to act as commissioner for trial of Charles I ; with Walter Strickland selected by parliament to negotiate alliance (the negotiations failed) between United Provinces and England, 1651 ; chancellor of Cambridge University 1651 ; commissioner of treasury, 1654 ; devoted himself exclusively to judicial duties ; member of council of state, 1659 and 1660 ; published his 'Case' to counteract rumours as to his share in Charles I's execution and his relations with the Cromwells, and escaped punishment other than perpetual incapacitation from office, 1660 ; left England, 1662. He was related to Cromwell by marriage. [l. 151]

ST. JOHN, SIR OLIVER BEAUCHAMP COVENTRY (1837-1891), lieutenant-colonel ; educated at East India Company's College, Addiscombe ; first lieutenant, Bengal engineers, 1858 ; went to India, 1859 ; took charge of fifth telegraph division (in Persia) in Lieutenant-colonel Stewart's expedition to establish telegraphic communication from India to Bosphorus, 1863–7 ; director of field telegraph and army signalling department of Abyssinian field force, 1867 ; captain, 1869 ; principal of Mayo College, Ajmir, 1875 ; major, 1876 ; chief political officer attached to Kandahar field force, 1878 ; C.S.I., 1879 ; political agent for Southern Afghanistan, 1880 ; fought at the Halmand and Maiwand, and was at Kandahar during investment ; officiating agent to governor-general for Baluchistan, 1881 ; K.C.S.I., 1882 ; lieutenant-colonel, 1886 ; resident and chief commissioner at Maisur and Kurg, 1889 ; published works on natural history and other subjects ; died at Quetta. [l. 157]

ST. JOHN, PERCY BOLINGBROKE (1821-1889), journalist : son of James Augustus St. John [q. v.], whom he accompanied on his travels ; edited 'Mirror of Literature,' 1846, and 'London Herald,' 1861 ; works include translations of Gustave Aimard's Indian tales. [l. 158]

ST. LAWRENCE, SIR CHRISTOPHER, twentieth or more properly eighth BARON HOWTH (d. 1589), called 'Blind Earl' ; sat in first Irish parliament of Queen Elizabeth's reign ; rendered assistance against Shane O'Neill ; knighted at Drogheda, 1569 ; joined agitation of Pale against cess and was imprisoned, 1578, but released with reprimand ; opposed Sir John Perrot [q. v.] in attempt to induce parliament to consent to composition for cess, 1586 ; perhaps contributed to 'Book of Howth.' [l. 159]

ST. LAWRENCE, SIR CHRISTOPHER, twenty-second or tenth BARON HOWTH (1568 ?-1619), son of Sir Nicholas St. Lawrence, twenty-first baron Howth [q. v.] ; served under Essex in Leinster. 1599, and under Lord-deputy Mountjoy, 1600–5, against O'Neill, O'Donnell, and Tyrone ; in service of Archduke, 1606–7 ; imprisoned on charge of complicity in conspiracy against Irish government, but released, 1608 ; charged (1609) with manslaughter of a servant of Sir Roger Jones, who had offended him, and forbidden to leave Ireland ; pardoned, 1611 ; sat in parliament, 1612. [l. 160]

ST. LAWRENCE, NICHOLAS, sixteenth or fourth BARON HOWTH (d. 1526), son of Robert St. Lawrence, fifteenth baron Howth [q. v.] ; Lancastrian ; attended Dublin parliaments, 1490 and 1493 ; served with Lord Kildare in repelling invasion of Pale, 1504 ; lord chancellor of Ireland, 1509-13. [l. 162]

ST. LAWRENCE, SIR NICHOLAS, twenty-first or ninth BARON HOWTH (1550 ?-1607), son of Sir Christopher St. Lawrence, twentieth baron Howth (d. 1589) [q. v.]; knighted, 1588; served with Sir William Russell, first baron Russell (1558 ?-1613) [q. v.] against Fiagh O'Byrne [q. v.], 1595. [l. 160]

ST. LAWRENCE, ROBERT, fifteenth or third BARON HOWTH (d. 1483), grandson of Christopher St. Lawrence, thirteenth lord Howth, created peer by writ, c. 1429; succeeded his father, c. 1463; chancellor of green wax of exchequer, 1467; lord chancellor of Ireland, 1483. [l. 163]

ST. LEGER, SIR ANTHONY (1496 ?-1559), lord-deputy of Ireland; studied at Cambridge and Gray's Inn; agent of Thomas Cromwell in suppressing abbeys; member of jury of Kent which found against Anne Boleyn, 1536; gentleman of Henry VIII's privy chamber, 1538; knighted, 1539; escorted Anne of Cleves to England, 1539; lord-deputy of Ireland, 1540; subdued the Kavanaghs, O'Mores, O'Conors, O'Tooles, Desmond, MacGillapatrick of Ossory, MacWilliam of Connaught, O'Donnell, and finally O'Neill; passed act giving Henry VIII and heirs title of King of Ireland, 1541; K.G.; confirmed as deputy by Edward VI, 1547; returned to England, 1548, but was reconstituted lord-deputy, 1550; recalled for alleged papistical practices, 1551; acquitted by privy council, 1552, and reappointed, 1553; recalled on being charged by Sir William Fitzwilliam (1526-1599) [q. v.] with falsifying accounts, 1556; died while proceedings were in progress. [l. 163]

ST. LEGER, FRANCIS BARRY BOYLE (1799-1829), novelist; educated at Rugby; in Indian civil service, 1816-21; edited 'Album,' from 1822; published poems and novels. [l. 167]

ST. LEGER, SIR WARHAM (1525 ?-1597), soldier; son of Sir Anthony St. Leger [q. v.]; probably served in Somerset's invasion of Scotland, 1547; prisoner in Scotland till 1550; Irish privy councillor; knighted, 1565; appointed president of Munster, 1566, Queen Elizabeth refusing to confirm appointment; in England, 1569-79; provost-marshal of Munster, 1579-89; assistant to court of high commission in Ireland, 1583. [l. 167]

ST. LEGER, SIR WARHAM (d. 1600), soldier; nephew of Sir Warham St. Leger (1525 ?-1597) [q. v.]; served in Ireland from c. 1574; Irish privy councillor, c. 1589; knighted and made governor of Leix, 1597; killed in combat with Hugh Maguire [q. v.] [l. 168]

ST. LEGER, SIR WILLIAM (d. 1642), president of Munster; son of Sir Warham St. Leger (d. 1600) [q. v.]; served in army in Holland, c. 1608-16; knighted, 1618; commanded company of foot in Ireland, 1624; lord president of Munster, 1627-42; privy councillor, 1627; freeman of Cork, 1628; M.P., co. Cork, 1634 and 1639; took part in organising army raised by Wentworth for invasion of Great Britain, 1640-1; engaged till death in campaigns against rebels in great Irish rebellion. [l. 168]

SAINT LEGER or **SALINGER**, WILLIAM (1600-1665), jesuit; born at Kilkenny; entered Society of Jesus at Tournai, 1621; professed of four vows, 1635; rector of Kilkenny College, 1650; published life of Archbishop Walsh, 1665. [l. 171]

ST. LEONARDS, BARON (1781-1875). [See SUGDEN, EDWARD BURTENSHAW.]

ST. LIFARD, GILBERT OF (d. 1305). [See GILBERT.]

ST. LIZ, SIMON DE, EARL OF NORTHAMPTON (d. 1109). [See SENLIS.]

ST. LO, EDWARD (1682 ?-1729), rear-admiral; entered navy, 1695; captain, 1703; served in West Indies, North Sea, Channel, and Baltic; at blockade of Porto Bello, 1727-8; rear-admiral, 1729. [l. 171]

ST. LO, GEORGE (d. 1718), naval commander; lieutenant, 1678; captain, 1682; wounded and captured by French at Brest, 1690; commissioner of prizes, 1692; extra commissioner of navy, 1693; resident commissioner at Plymouth, 1695, and Chatham, 1703; commander-in-chief in Medway and at Nore, 1712-14. [l. 172]

ST. MAUR. [See SEYMOUR.]

ST. MOLYNS, LORD OF (d. 1554). [See KAVANAGH, CAHIR MAC ART.]

SAINTON, PROSPER PHILIPPE CATHERINE (1813-1890), violinist; born at Toulouse; professor of violin at Toulouse conservatoire, 1840-5, and at Royal Academy of Music, London, 1845-90. [l. 172]

SAINTON-DOLBY, CHARLOTTE HELEN (1821-1885), contralto singer; wife of Prosper Philippe Catherine Sainton [q. v.]; married, 1860; studied at Royal Academy of Music; first sang at Leipzig, 1841, under Mendelssohn, who wrote subsequently contralto music in 'Elijah' to suit her voice; opened vocal academy in London, 1872; published musical compositions. [l. 173]

ST. PAUL, JOHN DE (1295 ?-1362), archbishop of Dublin; clerk in chancery before 1318; joint-guardian of great seal, 1334; prebendary of Chichester, 1336; master of rolls, 1337; imprisoned for malversation, 1340; archdeacon of Cornwall and prebendary of York, 1346; archbishop of Dublin, 1349-62; chancellor of Ireland, 1350-4 and 1354-6; privy councillor, 1358. [l. 173]

ST. QUINTIN, SIR WILLIAM, second baronet (1660 ?-1723), politician; M.P. for Kingston-upon-Hull, 1695-1723; joint vice-treasurer, receiver-general, and paymaster of Ireland, 1720-3. [l. 174]

ST. VICTOR, RICHARD OF (d. 1173 ?). [See RICHARD.]

ST. VINCENT, EARL OF (1735-1823). [See JERVIS, JOHN.]

SAKER, EDWARD (1831-1883), actor; educated as architect; joined Edinburgh theatrical company, 1857; managed Edinburgh Royal Theatre, 1862-5, and Alexandra, Liverpool, 1867-83; produced many Shakespearean plays. [l. 175]

SAKER, HORATIO (fl. 1850), actor; brother of Edward Saker [q. v.]; played low comedy parts at Edinburgh, 1850-2, and subsequently at Princess's, London. [l. 175]

SALA, GEORGE AUGUSTUS HENRY (1828-1896), journalist; educated in Paris; studied drawing in London; worked successively as clerk, scene-painter at Princess's and Lyceum theatres, London, and as book illustrator; editor of 'Chat,' 1848; wrote regularly for 'Household Words,' 1851-6; sent by Dickens to Russia at close of Crimean war to write descriptive articles for 'Household Words,' 1856; contributed to 'All the Year Round' from 1858; formed friendship with Edmund Yates [q. v.]; contributed (1859) 'Twice Round the Clock' to Vizetelly's 'Welcome Guest,' which for a short time he edited; contributed 'Echoes of the Week' to 'Illustrated London News,' 1860-86, and contributed to 'Sunday Times' and several provincial papers, 1886-94; founded (1860) and edited 'Temple Bar,' 1860-6; joined staff of 'Daily Telegraph,' 1857, and subsequently excited ridicule by his 'turgid' style; special correspondent of 'Telegraph' in American civil war, 1863, and afterwards in various countries. Published novels and other works; much of his journalistic writing reappeared in book form. [l. 175]

SALABERRY, CHARLES MICHEL DE (1778-1829), Canadian soldier; lieutenant; served eleven years in West Indies under Robert Prescott [q. v.]; major and aide-de-camp to Major-general Rottenberg in Canada, 1811; lieutenant-colonel, 1812; defeated Americans at Chateauguay, 1812; C.B.; member of legislative chamber, 1818. [l. 178]

SALCOT, JOHN (d. 1557). [See CAPON, JOHN.]

SALE, FLORENTIA, LADY (1790 ?-1853), née Wynch; married Sir Robert Henry Sale [q. v.], 1809; was in Kabul, 1842; shared the horrors of the British retreat, and was taken captive, but with her party was rescued by Sir Richmond Shakespeare; died at Cape Town. Her 'Journal' was published in 1843. [l. 188]

SALE, GEORGE (1697 ?-1736), orientalist; entered Inner Temple, 1720; practised as solicitor; one of correctors of Arabic New Testament issued by S.P.C.K., 1726; published (1734) translation of the Koran, which remains the best version in any language; contributed oriental biographies to 'General Dictionary,' 1734, and assisted in 'Universal History'; one of the founders of Society for Encouragement of Learning. His oriental manuscripts are in the Bodleian Library. [l. 179]

SALE, GEORGE CHARLES (1796-1869), organist; son of John Sale [q. v.] [l. 181]

SALE, JOHN (1758–1827), vocalist and composer; chorister of Windsor and Eton, 1767–75, and lay vicar, 1777–96; gentleman of Chapel Royal, London, 1788; vicar-choral of St. Paul's, London, 1795, and almoner and master of choristers, 1800–12; lay vicar of Westminster Abbey, 1796–1800; published glees. [l. 181]

SALE, JOHN BERNARD (1779–1856), organist; son of John Sale [q. v.]; lay vicar of Westminster, 1800 and 1806; organist of St. Margaret's, Westminster, 1809, and at Chapel Royal, London, 1838; teacher of singing to Princess (afterwards Queen) Victoria, 1826. [l. 181]

SALE, SIR ROBERT HENRY (1782–1845), colonel; ensign, 1795; lieutenant, 1797; served against Tipu Sultan, 1798–9, Dhundia Wagh, 1799–1800, and Paichi Raja, 1800–1; captain, 1806; served against the dewan of Travancore, 1809; in expedition against Mauritius, 1810; major, 1813; commanded regiment in Burmese war, 1824; fought at Kamandin and Kamarut; commanded column in advance from Rangoon, 1824; reduced province of Bassein, 1825; lieutenant-colonel, 1825; distinguished himself in operations at Prome, 1825–1826; C.B., 1826; brevet-colonel, 1838; commanded advanced brigade in first Afghan campaign, 1838–40; entered Kandahar, April 1839; arrived at Kabul, July 1839, and commanded storming column; K.C.B., 1839; second in command under Sir Willoughby Cotton in Afghanistan, 1839; gained victories at Charikar, Jalgah, Babu-Kush-Ghar, and in Kohistan valley, 1840; on rising of hillmen, 1841, advanced to clear passes to Jalalabad; occupied Khurd Kabul and Tezin, and after engagements at Pari-dara and Kotal-i-Jagdalak reached Gandamak, 30 Oct. 1841, and (though ordered, 10 Nov., to return to Kabul) Jalalabad, 12 Nov.; defended Jalalabad until 7 April 1842, when he defeated Akbar Khan, who fled towards Kabul; G.C.B.; defeated enemy at Jagdalak pass, 8 Sept., and encamped at Kabul, 15 Sept.; returned to India, October; thanked by parliament and promoted colonel, 1843; quartermaster-general in East Indies, 1844; served in Sikh war; died from effects of wounds received at battle of Mudki. [l. 181]

SALE-BARKER, LUCY ELIZABETH DRUMMOND DAVIES (1841–1892), author; married John Sale-Barker, her second husband, 1865; published books for the young. [l. 189]

SALESBURY. [See SALISBURY.]

'**SALESBY**,' ROBERT OF (*fl.* 1132–1148). [See ROBERT.]

SALGADO, JAMES (*fl.* 1680), Spanish refugee; converted from Romanism to protestantism; came to England, *c.* 1677; studied at Oxford; published religious works. [l. 189]

SALISBURY, EARLS OF. [See LONGESPÉE, WILLIAM DE, first EARL of the Longespée family, *d.* 1226; LONGESPÉE, WILLIAM DE, second EARL, 1212?–1250; MONTACUTE, WILLIAM DE, first EARL of the Montacute family, 1301–1344; MONTACUTE, WILLIAM DE, second EARL, 1328–1397; MONTACUTE, JOHN DE, third EARL, 1350?–1400; MONTACUTE, THOMAS DE, fourth EARL, 1388–1428; NEVILLE, RICHARD, first EARL of the Neville family, 1400–1460; NEVILLE, RICHARD, second EARL, 1428–1471; CECIL, ROBERT, first EARL of the Cecil family, 1563?–1612; CECIL, JAMES, third EARL, *d.* 1683; CECIL, JAMES, fourth EARL, *d.* 1693.]

SALISBURY, COUNTESS OF (1473–1541). [See POLE, MARGARET.]

SALISBURY, ENOCH ROBERT GIBBON (1819–1890), barrister; called to bar, Inner Temple, 1852; went North Wales circuit; M.P. for Chester, 1857; collected and published works on books relating to Wales. [l. 190]

SALISBURY or **SALESBURY**, HENRY (1561–1637?), Welsh grammarian; M.A. St. Alban Hall, Oxford, 1588; physician at Denbigh; published Welsh grammar, 1593, and left unfinished manuscript of Welsh-Latin dictionary. [l. 190]

SALISBURY, JOHN DE (*d.* 1180). [See JOHN.]

SALISBURY, JOHN (1500?–1573), bishop of Sodor and Man; M.A. Cambridge, 1523; B.D., 1534; Benedictine of Bury St. Edmunds; graduated in laws, Oxford, 1530; prior of St. Faith's, Horsham; abbot of St. Mary's, Titchfield; suffragan bishop of Thetford, 1536; archdeacon of Anglesey, 1537; lost preferments, 1554, but was subsequently restored; chancellor of Lincoln, 1554; bishop of Sodor and Man, 1571–3. [l. 191]

SALISBURY, JOHN (1575–1625), Welsh jesuit; joined jesuits, 1605; professed father, 1618; missioner in North Wales; founded and became superior of college of St. Francis Xavier, 1622; published translations into Welsh. [l. 192]

SALISBURY, JOHN (*fl.* 1627), member of English College at Rome; published a Latin poem. [l. 192]

SALISBURY, JOHN (*fl.* 1695), first printer and editor of 'Flying Post,' 1695; probably grandson of Thomas Salisbury (1567?–1620?) [q. v.] [l. 195]

SALISBURY, RICHARD ANTHONY (1761–1829), botanist; son of Richard Markham, cloth-merchant of Leeds; educated at Edinburgh University; assumed name Salisbury under conditions of a bequest, 1785; wrote on botanical subjects, appropriating much of other men's work; honorary secretary, Horticultural Society, London, 1809–10. Left incomplete materials for 'Genera Plantarum,' published by John Edward Gray, 1866. [l. 192]

SALISBURY, ROGER OF (*d.* 1139). [See ROGER.]

SALISBURY or **SALESBURY**, THOMAS (1555?–1586), conspirator; entered Gray's Inn, 1573; in service of Earl of Leicester; joined secret society for protecting jesuit missionaries in England, *c.* 1580; arrested for complicity in Babington's conspiracy, 1586; admitted undertaking to stir up sedition in favour of Mary Queen of Scots, but denied intention of murdering Queen Elizabeth; executed. [l. 194]

SALISBURY or **SALBERYE**, THOMAS (1567?–1620?), printer and Welsh poet; apprenticed, 1581; freeman of Stationers' Company, 1588; printed Psalms in Welsh metres, 1603, and other works of protestant character. [l. 195]

SALISBURY, SALESBURY, or **SALUSBURY**, SIR THOMAS, second baronet (*d.* 1643), poet; educated at Jesus College, Oxford; entered Inner Temple, 1631; succeeded to baronetcy, 1631; M.P., Denbighshire, 1640–3; fought for Charles I in civil war; D.C.L. Oxford, 1642; published 'History of Joseph,' a poem, 1636. [l. 195]

SALISBURY or **SALESBURY**, WILLIAM (1520?–1600?), lexicographer; born in Denbighshire; educated at Oxford; studied law at Thavies Inn and Lincoln's Inn; converted to protestantism before 1550; edited and published, *c.* 1546, collection of Welsh proverbs compiled by Gruffydd Hiraethog [q. v.], probably earliest extant book printed in Welsh; issued 'Dictionary in Englyshe and Welshe,' 1547; probably translated 'Latenye [Litany] in Welshe,' printed by Walley, 1563; entrusted by bishops of Welsh sees and of Hereford with translation of bible into Welsh, 1563; translated New Testament, with assistance of Thomas Huett, precentor of St. David's, and Bishop Richard Davies (*d.* 1581) [q. v.] (printed, 1567, by Henry Denham); assisted Davies in translating various works into English; devoted himself after *c.* 1576 to scientific and antiquarian pursuits; published a Welsh book on rhetoric, 1595, and left several manuscripts. [l. 196]

SALISBURY or **SALESBURY**, WILLIAM (1580?–1659?), royalist; of Oriel College, Oxford; knight of shire for Merioneth, 1620–2; raised Welsh foot regiment for Charles I, and received commission of colonel, 1642; governor of Denbigh Castle, 1643; surrendered to General Mytton after long siege, 1646; fined and pardoned by parliament, 1648. [l. 200]

SALISBURY, WILLIAM (*d.* 1823), botanist; nurseryman at Brompton, and (1799) at Cadogan Place, Sloane Street, London, where he held botanical classes; published botanical works. [l. 201]

SALKELD, JOHN (1576–1660), Roman catholic renegade; perhaps educated at Queen's College, Oxford; studied under jesuits at Coimbra and Cordova; joined English mission; converted to protestantism; received living of Wellington, 1613; rector of Church Taunton, 1635; deprived as royalist, 1646; published religious works. [l. 201]

SALKELD, WILLIAM (1671–1715), legal writer; educated at St. Edmund Hall, Oxford; barrister, Middle Temple, 1698; chief-justice of sessions for counties of Carmarthen, Cardigan, and Pembroke, 1713; serjeant-at-law, 1715; published legal writings. [l. 202]

SALL, ANDREW (1612–1682), Irish jesuit; born at Cashel; educated at St. Omer; rector of Irish College, Salamanca, 1652–5; professed of four vows, c. 1657; provincial superior of Irish jesuits, c. 1662; announced conversion to church of England, 1674; D.D. Trinity College, Dublin; published at Oxford religious apology for himself, 1676; D.D. Oxford, 1676; prebendary of St. Patrick's, Dublin, 1675; chancellor of Cashel, 1676; domestic chaplain to Charles II; lived at Oxford, 1675–80, and at Dublin, 1680–2; left unfinished an edition of William Bedell's [q. v.] translation of Old Testament into Irish; published religious and philosophical writings. [l. 202]

SALMON, ELIZA (1787–1849), vocalist; *née* Munday; first appeared in oratorio at Covent Garden, 1803; married James Salmon, 1806; sang at Three Choirs Festivals, 1812–24; lost her voice, 1825; died in poverty. [l. 204]

SALMON, JOHN (d. 1325), bishop of Norwich; prior of Ely before 1291; bishop of Norwich, 1299–1325; negotiated Edward II's marriage, 1307; went on mission to Pope Clement IV to obtain absolution for Piers Gaveston, 1309; elected ordainer, 1310; chancellor, 1319–23. [l. 205]

SALMON, JOHN DREW (1802?–1859), manager of Wenham Lake Ice Company; F.L.S., 1852; published and left in manuscript writings on ornithology and botany. [l. 206]

SALMON, NATHANAEL (1675–1742), historian and antiquary; son of Thomas Salmon (1648–1706) [q. v.]; LL.B. Corpus Christi College, Cambridge, 1695; ordained; curate at Westmill; resigned charge, c. 1714, and practised medicine; published antiquarian and historical works. [l. 206]

SALMON, ROBERT (1763–1821), inventor; clerk of works under Henry Holland (1746?–1806) [q. v.]; architect and mechanist to Francis Russell, fifth duke of Bedford [q. v.], at Woburn Abbey, 1794–1821; invented first haymaking machine, 1814; silver medallist, Society of Arts. [l. 206]

SALMON, THOMAS (1648–1706), divine; M.A. Trinity College, Oxford, 1670; studied music; published 'Essay to the Advancement of Musick,' advocating octave system proposed by William Bathe [q. v.], 1672; held various livings; published also historical treatises. [l. 207]

SALMON, THOMAS (1679–1767), historical and geographical writer; son of Thomas Salmon (1648–1706) [q. v.]; travelled many years abroad; accompanied Anson on voyage round the world, 1739–40; published historical and geographical works, including 'Modern History, or Present State of all Nations,' 1739. [l. 208]

SALMON, WILLIAM (1644–1713), empiric; travelled in various countries as mountebank, and subsequently practised medicine in London; published works on medicine, astrology, drawing, surgery, and other subjects, though he was perhaps only the amanuensis of another person. [l. 209]

SALMON, WILLIAM (*fl.* 1745), carpenter and builder at Colchester; published works on building. [l. 210]

SALOMON, JOHANN PETER (1745–1815), musician; born at Bonn; court musician to elector of Bonn, c. 1757; toured as violinist, 1765; concertmeister to Prince Henry of Prussia; led orchestra at Covent Garden, London, 1781; gave concerts with Mozart and Haydn at Hanover Square rooms, London, 1791–2; took part in establishing Philharmonic Society, 1813; composed operas. [l. 210]

SALOMONS, SIR DAVID, first baronet (1797–1873), lord mayor of London; engaged in commerce in London; a founder of London and Westminster Bank, 1832; liveryman of Coopers' Company; elected alderman for Aldgate ward, 1835, and for Portsoken ward, 1844, but being Jew was not admitted; elected and admitted alderman of Cordwainer ward, 1847; member of Middle Temple, 1849; liberal M.P. for Greenwich, 1851; fined for voting without having been sworn in statutory way; again member for Greenwich, 1859–73; lord mayor, 1855; created baronet, 1869; published works on finance and other subjects. [l. 211]

SALT, HENRY (1780–1827), traveller; sent by government on mission to king of Abyssinia, 1809–11; British consul-general in Egypt, 1815–27; discovered the famous Abu Simbel inscriptions, 1817; collected Egyptian antiquities, some of which he sold to the trustees of the British Museum and others to the French government; F.R.S.; F.L.S.; published illustrations and account of his travels, and other works. [l. 212]

SALT, SAMUEL (d. 1792), politician; entered Middle Temple, 1741, and Inner Temple, 1745; called to bar, 1753; bencher at Inner Temple, 1782, reader, 1787; treasurer, 1788; M.P., Liskeard, 1768–84, and for Aldeburgh, 1784–1790; friend and benefactor of Charles Lamb, whose father was his clerk for nearly forty years. [l. 213]

SALT, SIR TITUS (1803–1876), manufacturer; partner with his father in woolstapling business at Bradford, 1824; introduced Donskoi wool for worsted manufacture; discovered method of manufacturing alpaca, c. 1836; mayor of Bradford, 1848; founded (1851) works which eventually grew into town of Saltaire; president of Bradford chamber of commerce, 1856; liberal M.P., Bradford, 1859–61; created baronet, 1869. [l. 214]

SALT, WILLIAM (1805–1863), Staffordshire antiquary; partner in firm of Stevenson Salt & Sons, bankers of Lombard Street, London; F.S.A.; member of Royal Society of Literature; made archæological collections relating to Staffordshire, purchased (1872) for the county, and located at Stafford. [l. 215]

SALTER, JAMES (*fl.* 1665), author of 'Caliope's Cabinet opened,' 1665. [l. 216]

SALTER, JAMES (1650–1718?), divine; educated at Magdalen College, Oxford; held livings in Cornwall and Devon; published Greek grammar and a sacred poem. [l. 216]

SALTER, JAMES (*fl.* 1723), proprietor of 'Don Saltero's Coffee-house,' Chelsea, where he made a large collection of curiosities (sold by auction, 1799). [l. 216]

SALTER, JAMES (d. 1767), clergyman; son of James Salter (1650–1718?) [q. v.]; B.A. New Inn Hall, Oxford; vicar of St. Mary Church, 1718–67. [l. 216]

SALTER, JOHN WILLIAM (1820–1869), geologist; apprenticed to James de Carle Sowerby [q. v.], 1835; engaged in illustrating works on natural history; assisted Adam Sedgwick [q. v.], 1842–6; assistant to Edward Forbes [q. v.] in geological survey, 1846; F.G.S., 1846; palæontologist to the survey, 1854–63; wrote extensively on palæontology and geology. [l. 217]

SALTER, SAMUEL (d. 1756?), divine; D.D. Corpus Christi College, Cambridge, 1728; prebendary of Norwich, 1728; archdeacon of Norfolk, 1734; member of Dr. Johnson's circle of friends. [l. 217]

SALTER, SAMUEL (d. 1778), master of the London Charterhouse; son of Samuel Salter (d. 1756?) [q. v.]; of Charterhouse School, London, and Corpus Christi College, Cambridge; M.A., 1737; fellow, 1735–8; prebendary of Gloucester, 1738, of Norwich, 1744; D.D. Lambeth, 1751; preacher at Charterhouse from 1754, and ma ter, 1761–78; published religious and other writings. [l. 217]

SALTER, THOMAS (*fl.* 1580), author of 'A Mirrhor mete for all Mothers,' 1579, and other works of puritan tendency. [l. 218]

SALTER, THOMAS FREDERICK (*fl.* 1814–1826), author; published 'The Angler's Guide,' for fishing in London district, 1814. [l. 219]

SALTER, WILLIAM (1804–1875), painter; resided in Italy, 1827–33; finished picture, 'The Waterloo Banquet at Apsley House,' 1841; member of Society of British Artists, 1846, and, later, vice-president. [l. 219]

SALTHOUSE, THOMAS (1630–1691), quaker; converted to quakerism by George Fox at Swarthmoor, 1652; frequently fined and imprisoned for preaching; published religious works. [l. 219]

SALTMARSH, JOHN (d. 1647), mystical writer; M.A. Magdalene College, Cambridge; advocated episcopacy, but subsequently adopted Calvinistic views; joined controversy, 1643–4, with Thomas Fuller (1608–1661) [q. v.]; rector of Brasted, 1645; army chaplain under Sir Thomas Fairfax (afterwards third Baron Fairfax) [q. v.], 1646; published controversial and other religious writings. [l. 220]

SALTONSTALL, CHARLES (*fl.* 1642), writer on navigation; brother of Wye Saltonstall [q. v.]; sea-captain; published 'Navigator,' 1642. [l. 222]

P p

SALTONSTALL, SIR RICHARD (1521 ?–1601), lord mayor of London ; master of Skinners' Company, 1589, 1593, 1595, and 1599 ; M.P., city of London, 1586 ; sheriff, 1588 ; lord mayor, 1597–8 ; knighted, 1598 ; governor of Merchant Adventurers' Company ; interested in East India Company. [l. 223]

SALTONSTALL, RICHARD (1586–1658), colonist ; nephew of Sir Richard Saltonstall (1521 ?–1601) [q. v.] ; justice of West Riding, Yorkshire ; knighted, 1618 ; member and assistant, Massachusetts Bay Company, 1629 ; in Massachusetts, 1630–1. [l. 223]

SALTONSTALL, WYE (*fl.* 1630–1640), translator ; grandson of Sir Richard Saltonstall (1521 ?–1601) [q. v.] ; educated at Queen's College, Oxford, and, perhaps, at Gray's Inn ; published or left in manuscript verse translations from Ovid and other works. [l. 224]

SALTOUN, sixteenth BARON (1785–1853). [See FRASER, ALEXANDER GEORGE.]

SALTREY, HENRY OF (*fl.* 1150). [See HENRY.]

SALTWOOD, ROBERT (*fl.* 1540), monk of St. Augustine's, Canterbury ; wrote ' Comparyson betwene iiij byrdes,' a poem in seven-line stanzas, printed *c.* 1550. [l. 225]

SALUSBURY. [See SALISBURY.]

SALVEYN, SIR GERARD (*d.* 1320), judge ; employed on mission to France, 1303 ; justice of trailbaston in Yorkshire, 1304 ; knight of shire for Yorkshire, 1304 and 1307, and sheriff, 1311–14 ; escheator north of Trent, *c.* 1307–9 ; imprisoned for oppression, 1314–15 ; supported Thomas of Lancaster, 1318, but was pardoned. [l. 225]

SALVIN, ANTHONY (1799–1881), architect ; pupil of John Nash [q. v.] ; practised in London ; executed restorations at Tower of London, Windsor, and other castles and country seats ; F.R.I.B.A., 1836, vice-president, 1839, and gold medallist, 1863 ; F.S.A., 1824–81 ; exhibited at Royal Academy, 1823–36. [l. 225]

SALVIN, OSBERT (1835–1898), naturalist ; son of Anthony Salvin [q. v.] ; of Westminster School and Trinity Hall, Cambridge ; M.A., 1860 ; honorary fellow, 1897 ; travelled in Central America and other parts of the world collecting natural-history specimens ; Strickland curator of ornithology at Cambridge, 1874–82 ; F.Z.S., 1860 ; F.L.S., 1864 ; F.R.S., 1873 ; edited, conjointly with Mr. F. D. Godman, ' Biologia Centrali-Americana,' and published scientific writings. [Suppl. iii. 335]

SALWEY, HUMPHREY (1575 ?–1652), parliamentarian ; educated at Brasenose College, Oxford, and Inner Temple ; took side of parliament in civil war ; appointed but refused to serve as judge at Charles I's trial, 1649. [l. 226]

SALWEY, RICHARD (1615–1685), parliamentarian ; grocer in London ; M.P., Appleby, 1645 ; member of commissions on Irish matters, 1646 and 1650 ; English ambassador at Constantinople, 1654 ; member of committee of safety and of council of state, May 1659 ; commissioner for navy, 1659 ; imprisoned on suspicion of complicity in Farnley Wood plot, 1663–4. [l. 226]

SAMBLE, RICHARD (1644–1680), quaker minister and travelling preacher ; published religious works. [l. 228]

SAMELSON, ADOLPH (1817–1888), ophthalmic surgeon ; born at Berlin ; M.D. Berlin, 1840 ; practised at Zehdenick, Brandenburg, and subsequently took up diseases of eye at Berlin ; compelled, through political opinions, to leave country, and began practice at Manchester, 1857 ; published surgical and other writings. [l. 228]

SAMMES, AYLETT (1636 ?–1679 ?), antiquary ; M.A. Christ's College, Cambridge, *c.* 1659 ; incorporated at Oxford, 1677 ; entered Inner Temple, 1657 ; published ' Britannia Antiqua Illustrata,' 1676. [l. 229]

SAMPSON. [See also SAMSON.]

SAMPSON, HENRY (1629 ?–1700), nonconformist minister and physician ; son of William Sampson (1590 ?–1636 ?) [q. v.] ; B.A. and fellow, Pembroke Hall, Cambridge, 1650 ; M.A., 1653 ; rector of Framlingham, 1650 ; deprived, 1660 ; M.D. Leyden, 1668 ; practised in London ; honorary F.R.C.P., 1680 ; published archæological and religious works. [l. 229]

SAMPSON, HENRY (1841–1891), journalist ; entered printing office, *c.* 1853 ; engaged in sporting journalism ; editor of ' Fun,' 1874–8 ; as part proprietor and editor, with pseudonym ' Pendragon,' started ' Referee,' 1877. [l. 230]

SAMPSON, RICHARD (*d.* 1554), bishop of Coventry and Lichfield ; of Clement Hostel and Trinity Hall, Cambridge ; D.C.L., 1513 ; chaplain to Wolsey ; advocate, 1515 ; dean of St. Stephen's, Westminster, and of Chapel Royal, London, and Henry VIII's chaplain, 1516 ; archdeacon of Cornwall, 1517 ; prebendary of Newbold, 1519 ; resident ambassador to Spain, 1522–5 ; dean of Windsor, 1523–36 ; prebendary of St. Paul's, London, 1526–34, of Lincoln, 1527 ; archdeacon of Suffolk, 1529 ; supported Henry VIII's divorce ; prebendary and dean of Lichfield, 1533 ; treasurer of Salisbury, 1534 ; bishop of Chichester, 1536–43, of Coventry and Lichfield, 1543–54 ; lord-president of Wales ; published theological treatises. [l. 230]

SAMPSON, THOMAS (1517 ?–1589), puritan divine ; of Pembroke Hall, Cambridge ; entered Inner Temple, 1547 ; converted to protestantism ; rector of All Hallows, Bread Street, London, 1551 ; dean of Chichester, 1552 ; fled to continent, 1556, and returned on Queen Elizabeth's accession ; canon of Durham, 1560 ; dean of Christ Church, Oxford, 1561, deprived and placed temporarily in confinement, 1565 ; prebendary and penitentiary of St. Paul's, London, 1570 ; master of Wigston's hospital, Leicester, 1567–89 ; published religious works ; concerned in translation of Geneva Bible, published, 1560. [l. 232]

SAMPSON, WILLIAM (1590 ?–1636 ?), dramatist ; of humble birth ; joined (1612) with Gervase Markham in writing tragedy on story of Herod (published, 1622) ; subsequently produced independently ' The Vow Breaker,' printed 1636, and, perhaps, ' The Widow's Prize,' licensed for publication, 1653. [l. 233]

SAMPSON, WILLIAM (1764–1836), United Irishman and jurist ; educated at Trinity College, Dublin, and Lincoln's Inn ; called to Irish bar ; wrote against Irish government in ' Northern Star ' at Belfast ; joined United Irishmen ; took lead in movement for arming against French, 1797 ; contributed to the ' Press,' the Dublin organ of United Irishmen ; imprisoned on suspicion of holding French commission, 1798 ; arrested on suspicion of writing pamphlet by Edward Cooke (1755–1820) [q. v.] against union, 1799 ; banished to France, and subsequently to America ; practised at American bar ; published ' Memoirs ' and legal and other writings ; died at New York. [l. 234]

SAMS, JOSEPH (1784–1860), orientalist ; successively schoolmaster and bookseller at Darlington ; travelled in Europe and the East in search of antiquities, which he collected and catalogued. [l. 236]

SAMSON (*fl.* 550), British saint ; educated at monastic school at Llantwit Major ; ordained by Dubricius (Dyfrig) [q. v.] ; abbot of a monastery, possibly on Caldy island ; established community on banks of Severn ; abbot of monastery of Germanus ; consecrated bishop ; built monastery of Dol in Brittany, where he died. [l. 237]

SAMSON (*d.* 1112), bishop of Worcester ; born at Douvres, near Caen ; brother of Thomas of Bayeux (*d.* 1100) [q. v.] ; studied at Liège and Angers ; clerk in William I's chapel ; canon and treasurer of church of Bayeux, 1082 ; consecrated bishop of Worcester and admitted to priest's orders, 1096 ; buried in Worcester Cathedral. [l. 238]

SAMSON (1135–1211), abbot of St. Edmund's ; born at Tottington ; M.A. Paris ; made monastic profession, 1166 ; mitred abbot of St. Edmund's, 1182 ; appointed by Pope Lucius III judge delegate in ecclesiastical causes, 1182 ; exempted, with his successors, from metropolitan jurisdiction, 1188 ; fought at siege of Windsor, 1193 ; visited Richard I, when captive, in Germany ; justice errant ; one of papal commissioners for settling quarrel between Archbishop Hubert and Canterbury monks, 1200 ; wrote theological treatises. His rule was successful, morally and financially, and he added extensively to the abbey buildings. The abbot Samson of Carlyle's ' Past and Present ' is rather a rhetorical construction than a historical personage. [l. 238]

SAMUDA, JOSEPH D'AGUILAR (1813–1885), engineer ; entered partnership, 1832, with his brother Jacob (*d.* 1844) ; engaged chiefly in building marine engines, 1832–42, and in laying down railway lines on atmospheric principle, 1842–8; began construction of iron steamships for war and merchant navies, 1843; original treasurer and member of council of Institution of Naval Architects, 1860; M.I.C.E., 1862; liberal M.P for Tavistock, 1865–1868, and for Tower Hamlets, 1868–80; wrote on engineering subjects. [l. 240]

SAMUEL, EDWARD (1674–1748), Welsh divine; of Oriel College, Oxford; held successively rectories in Merionethshire and Denbighshire; translated religious books into Welsh; published Welsh works in verse and prose. [l. 241]

SAMUEL, GEORGE (d. 1823?), landscape-painter; exhibited at Royal Academy, 1786–1823. [l. 241]

SAMUEL, RICHARD (fl. 1770–1786), portrait-painter; exhibited at Royal Academy, 1772–9. [l. 242]

SAMUEL, WILLIAM (fl. 1551–1569), divine; in service of Duke of Somerset; published religious and poetical works. [l. 242]

SAMWAYS or **SAMWAIES**, PETER (1615–1693), royalist divine; of Westminster School and Trinity College, Cambridge; M.A., 1641; D.D., 1660; vicar of Cheshunt; expelled by parliamentarians; obtained preferment at Restoration; prebendary of York, 1668; published religious works. [l. 242]

SAMWELL, DAVID (d. 1799), surgeon; accompanied Captain Cook on third voyage of discovery, as surgeon's first mate; subsequently lived in London. [l. 243]

SANCHO, IGNATIUS (1729–1780), negro writer; born at sea; brought to England at early age; butler to second Duchess of Montagu, 1749–51, and subsequently served George Montagu, fourth duke of Manchester [q. v.]; formed acquaintance with Sterne, 1766; grocer in Charles Street, Westminster, 1773, where he spent latest years in writing letters in Sterne's manner. His 'Letters' were published, 1782. [l. 243]

SANCROFT, WILLIAM (1617–1693), archbishop of Canterbury; M.A. Emmanuel College, Cambridge, 1641; D.D., 1662; fellow and tutor, 1642; bursar, 1644; published attack on Calvinism, 1658; studied at Padua; returned home, 1660; chaplain to Bishop Cosin; employed in Savoy conference; Charles II's chaplain, 1661; prebendary of Durham, 1662; master (1662–4) of Emmanuel College, Cambridge, where he founded new chapel; dean of York, and, later, of St. Paul's, London; greatly assisted in work connected with rebuilding St. Paul's Cathedral, 1666; archdeacon of Canterbury, 1668–70; archbishop of Canterbury, 1678; crowned James II, 1685; refused to serve in high commission court established by James II; refused to read James II's declaration of liberty of conscience, and signed, with six bishops, petition to James II, 1688; imprisoned in Tower of London; tried on charge of seditious libel and acquitted; signed declaration calling on William of Orange to assist in procuring peace and a 'free parliament,' 1688, but was in favour of appointing him merely *custos regni*, not king; suspended, 1689, and deprived, 1690; published treatises and prepared for the press Laud's 'Memorials.' [l. 244]

SANCTOFIDENSIS, JOHANNES (d. 1359). [See ST. FAITH'S, JOHN OF.]

SANCTO FRANCISCO, ANGELUS À (1601–1678). [See ANGELUS.]

SANCTO FRANCISCO, BERNARD À (1628–1709). [See EYSTON, BERNARD.]

SANCTO GERMANO, JOHANNES DE (fl. 1170). [See JOHN.]

SANDALE, JOHN DE (d. 1319), bishop of Winchester; one of Edward I's clerks, 1294; controller of receipts in Gascony, 1297; treasurer, 1299, and subsequently chancellor, St. Patrick's, Dublin; chamberlain of Scotland, c. 1303–1307; chancellor of exchequer, 1307–8; lieutenant for treasurer, 1308–10; treasurer, 1310–11, 1312, and 1318; held various prebends; archdeacon of Richmond, 1309; chancellor, 1314–18; bishop of Winchester, 1316–19. [l. 250]

SANDARS, THOMAS COLLETT (1825–1894), editor of Justinian; B.A. Balliol College, Oxford, 1848; fellow of Oriel College, Oxford, 1849; M.A., 1851; called to bar, 1851; edited Justinian's 'Institutes,' 1853. [l. 251]

SANDBY, PAUL (1725–1809), watercolour-painter and engraver; held appointment in military drawing department at Tower of London, 1741; assisted Colonel David Watson in survey of highlands; draughtsman to survey till 1751; illustrated several volumes, and burlesqued many of Hogarth's works; exhibited at Society of Artists, 1760–8, and was director, 1765; chief drawing-master, Royal Military Academy, Woolwich, 1768–97; original R.A., 1768, and exhibited between 1769 and 1809; introduced into England 'aquatint' process of engraving; pioneer of topographical art in England. [l. 251]

SANDBY, THOMAS (1721–1798), draughtsman and architect; kept with his brother, Paul Sandby [q. v.], an academy at Nottingham; private secretary and draughtsman to William Augustus, duke of Cumberland, 1743, and accompanied him in Flanders and Scotland, 1743–8; deputy-ranger of Windsor Great Park, 1746–98; formed Virginia Water, and made alterations in Windsor Park; original R.A., 1768; first professor of architecture to Academy, 1770; built Freemasons' Hall, Queen Street, Lincoln's Inn Fields, London, 1776; joint architect with James Adam [q. v.] of his majesty's works, 1777; master-carpenter of his majesty's works in England, 1780. [l. 254]

SANDEMAN, ROBERT (1718–1771), Scottish sectary; educated at Edinburgh; came under influence of John Glas [q. v.], whose views he adopted; linen manufacturer at Perth, 1736–44; elder in Glassite community, 1744; exercised ministry successively in Perth, Dundee. Edinburgh, and London (1760); went to New England, 1764, and founded church at Portsmouth, new Hampshire, 1765; published letters and other writings. [l. 255]

SANDEMAN, SIR ROBERT GROVES (1835–1892), major; educated at St. Andrews; appointed to 33rd Bengal infantry, 1856; served with Probyn's horse in mutiny; magistrate of Dera Ghází Khán, 1866; conducted negotiations which led to treaty with khan of Khalat, 1876; C.S.I., 1877; agent to governor-general in Baluchistán, 1877–92; major; K.C.S.I., 1879; aided Sir Frederick (afterwards Lord) Roberts in transport service to Quetta and Kandahar, 1880. [l. 256]

SANDERS. [See also SAUNDERS.]

SANDERS, *alias* BAINES, FRANCIS (1648–1710), jesuit; born in Worcestershire; studied at St. Omer, and English College, Rome; joined jesuits, 1674; professed of four vows, 1684; confessor to exiled James II at St. Germain; published religious works. [l. 257]

SANDERS, FRANCIS WILLIAMS (1769–1831), conveyancer; barrister, Lincoln's Inn, 1802; practised as conveyancer; published legal writings. [l. 258]

SANDERS, GEORGE (1774–1846), portrait-painter; apprenticed as coach-painter at Edinburgh; from 1807 worked as miniaturist in London and subsequently as portrait-painter. [l. 258]

SANDERS or **SAUNDERS**, JOHN (1750–1825), painter; studied at Royal Academy; exhibited portraits and other pictures from 1771; practised successively at Norwich and Bath. [l. 258]

SANDERS or **SANDER**, NICHOLAS (1530?–1581), controversialist and historian; fellow, New College, Oxford, 1548; B.C.L., 1551; lectured on canon law; D.D. Rome; ordained priest; in attendance successively on cardinal legate Stanislaus Hosius, and Commendone; at Louvain, 1565–72; regius professor of theology, Louvain; joined controversy provoked by Bishop Jewel's challenge; published his great work, 'De Visibili Monarchia Ecclesiae,' 1571; in Madrid working for dethronement of Queen Elizabeth in favour of Roman catholic sovereign, 1573; sent as papal nuncio to Ireland to excite rebellion, 1579; secured adherence of Desmond; after many times narrowly escaping capture died of dysentery; left historical and other manuscripts, printed posthumously. [l. 259]

SANDERS, ROBERT (1727–1783), compiler; became hack-writer in London, c. 1760; compiled 'Newgate Calendar,' 1764, 'Complete English Traveller, or Survey of England and Wales,' 1771, and other works. [l. 262]

SANDERS, WILLIAM (1799–1875), geologist; corn merchant at Bristol; F.G.S., 1839; F.R.S., 1864; made careful survey of geology of Bristol district. [l. 262]

SANDERS, WILLIAM RUTHERFORD (1828–1881), physician: educated at High School, Edinburgh, and at Montpell'er; B.-ès.-L., 1844; M.D. Edinburgh, 1849; studied medicine in Paris and Heidelberg; pathologist to Royal Infirmary, Edinburgh; conservator of museum of Royal College of Surgeons, Edinburgh, 1853; physician to Royal Infirmary, 1861; professor of pathology, Edinburgh, 1869–81; afflicted with right hemiplegia and aphasia, 1880; published medical writings. [l. 263]

SANDERSON, JAMES (1769?-1841?), musician; led orchestra at Astley's Theatre, London, 1788; composer and musical director at Royal Circus, London, 1793; published musical compositions; composed the accepted tune of 'Comin' thro' the Rye.' [l. 264]

SANDERSON, JOHN (d. 1602), Roman catholic divine; M.A. Trinity College, Cambridge, 1561; logic reader, 1562: expelled from university for suspicious doctrine; went to Douay; ordained priest; D.D. Douay; divinity professor in English College, Rheims, 1580; produced religious and other writings. [l. 264]

SANDERSON, ROBERT (1587–1663), bishop of Lincoln; B.A. and fellow, Lincoln College, Oxford, 1606; M.A., 1608; D.D., 1636; reader in logic, 1608; prebendary of Southwell, 1619, and of Lincoln, 1629; rector of Boothby Pagnell, 1619 (sequestered, 1643); regius professor of divinity at Oxford, 1642; ejected by parliamentary visitors, 1648, but reinstated, 1660; bishop of Lincoln, 1660–3; moderator at conference with presbyterians at the Savoy, London, 1661; published philosophical and religious works; author of the second preface, 'It hath been the wisdom,' &c., to the Book of Common Prayer. [l. 265]

SANDERSON, ROBERT (1660–1741), historian; educated at St. John's College, Cambridge; clerk in Rolls Chapel, London; contributed largely to compilation of Rymer's 'Fœdera,' and published vols. xvi–xx. (1715–1735) after Rymer's death: one of founders of revived Society of Antiquaries, 1717; usher of high court of chancery, 1726; left manuscript history of reign of Henry V. [l. 266]

SANDERSON, THOMAS (1759–1829), poet; schoolmaster at Greystoke, near Penrith, 1778; lived in seclusion at Sebergham; schoolmaster successively at Blackhall and Beaumont; published 'Original Poems,' 1800, and other works. His 'Life and Remains' appeared, 1829. [l. 267]

SANDERSON, SIR WILLIAM (1586?-1676), historian; secretary to Henry Rich, earl of Holland [q. v.], when chancellor of Cambridge University; took side of royalists; gentleman of privy chamber to Charles II: knighted; his works include a history of Mary Queen of Scots and her son James, 1656, and a history of Charles I, 1658, which involved him in a controversy with Peter Heylyn [q. v.] [l. 268]

SANDFORD. [See also SANFORD.]

SANDFORD, DANIEL (1766–1830), bishop of Edinburgh; M.A. Christ Church, Oxford, 1791; D.D., 1802; opened episcopal chapel in Edinburgh, 1792; bishop of Edinburgh, 1806–30; published religious writings. [l. 268]

SANDFORD, SIR DANIEL KEYTE (1798–1838), professor of Greek at Edinburgh; son of Daniel Sandford [q. v.]; M.A. Christ Church, Oxford, 1825; D.C.L., 1833; professor of Greek, Glasgow University, 1821; knighted, 1830; M.P., Paisley, 1834–5; author of translations from the Greek and educational Greek works; joint-editor of 'Popular Encyclopædia.' [l. 269]

SANDFORD, FRANCIS (1630–1694), herald; B.A. Trinity College, Dublin; rougedragon pursuivant, College of Arms, 1661; Lancaster herald, 1676–89; confined for debt in Newgate prison, London, where he died; chief work, 'Genealogical History of Kings of England,' 1677. [l. 270]

SANDFORD, FRANCIS RICHARD JOHN, first BARON SANDFORD (1824–1893), son of Sir Daniel Keyte Sandford [q. v.]; M.A. Balliol College, Oxford, 1858; in education office, 1848–68 and 1870–84; assistant undersecretary in colonial office, 1868–70; knighted, 1862; K.C.B., 1879; privy councillor, 1885; created Baron Sandford, 1891. [l. 271]

SANDFORD, FULK DE (d. 1271), also called FULK DE BASSET, archbishop of Dublin; nephew of Sir Philip Basset [q. v.]; archdeacon of Middlesex, 1244; prebendary, treasurer, and chancellor of St. Paul's, London; appointed, 1256, archbishop of Dublin by Pope Alexander IV, who quashed election of Ralph de Norwich [q. v.] approved by Henry III; accepted by Henry III; temporarily deputy-justice of Ireland, 1265; buried in St. Patrick's Cathedral, Dublin. [l. 271]

SANDFORD, SIR HERBERT BRUCE (1826–1892), colonel; son of Sir Daniel Keyte Sandford [q. v.]; served in Bombay artillery in Indian mutiny; colonel, 1865; K.C.M.G., 1877. [l. 270]

SANDFORD or SANFORD, JAMES (fl. 1567), author; perhaps tutor to William Herbert, third earl of Pembroke [q. v.]; published translations, including tales from Plutarch, and a version from a French translation of Epictetus. [l. 272]

SANDFORD, SAUNFORD, or SAMPFORD, JOHN DE (d. 1294), archbishop of Dublin; perhaps brother of Fulk de Sandford [q. v.]: escheator of Ireland, 1271 and 1272; justice in eyre in Ulster, 1281; prebendary of Dublin; treasurer of Ferns, c. 1269; dean of St. Patrick's, Dublin, 1275; chosen archbishop of Dublin, 1284; confirmed in appointment by Pope Honorius IV, 1285; temporarily keeper of Ireland, 1288–90 on sudden death of Viceroy Stephen de Fulburne; one of ambassadors to negotiate alliance with Adolph of Nassau, 1294. [l. 273]

SANDFORD or SANFORD, JOHN (1565?-1629), poet and grammarian; M.A. Balliol College, Oxford, 1595; corrector to press at Oxford, 1592; chaplain of Magdalen College, Oxford, 1593–1616; domestic chaplain to Archbishop Abbot, c. 1614: held rectories in Kent; published Latin verse, and grammars of French, Latin, Italian, and Spanish. [l. 275]

SANDFORD, JOHN (1801–1873), divine; son of Daniel Sandford [q. v.]; of Glasgow University and Balliol College, Oxford; M.A., 1841; B.D., 1845; honorary canon of Worcester, 1844; archdeacon of Coventry, 1851; examining chaplain to Bishop of Worcester, 1853–60; Bampton lecturer at Oxford, 1861; active member of lower house of convocation; published religious works. [l. 275]

SANDFORD, SAMUEL (fl. 1661–1699), actor; joined D'Avenant's company at Lincoln's Inn Fields, London; original Worm in Cowley's 'Cutter of Coleman Street,' 1661; migrated with the company under Lady D'Avenant to Dorset Garden, London, c. 1671; at Theatre Royal, London, 1682; under Betterton at Lincoln's Inn Fields, London, 1695; acted in plays by Dryden, Sedley, and Otway; most popular in 'disagreeable characters.' [l. 276]

SANDHURST, BARON (1819–1876). [See MANSFIELD, SIR WILLIAM ROSE.]

SANDILANDS, JAMES, first BARON TORPHICHEN (d. 1579), preceptor of Torphichen and head of knights hospitallers of Scotland, and M.P., 1543; privy councillor, 1546; signed act approving of 'Book of Discipline,' 1561; resigned possessions of order of St. John for temporal lordship of Torphichen, 1563. [l. 278]

SANDILANDS, JAMES, seventh BARON TORPHICHEN (d. 1753), served as lieutenant-colonel, 7th dragoons under Marlborough, and against rebels of 1715. [l. 279]

SANDSBURY or SANSBURY, JOHN (1576–1610), of Merchant Taylors' School and St. John's College, Oxford; M.A., 1601; B.D., 1608; vicar of St. Giles's, Oxford, 1607; published Latin verse. [l. 279]

SANDWICH, EARLS OF. [See MONTAGU, EDWARD, first EARL, 1625–1672; MONTAGU, JOHN, fourth EARL, 1718–1792.]

SANDWICH, HENRY DE (d. 1273), bishop of London; probably brother of Ralph de Sandwich [q. v.]; prebendary of St. Paul's, London; bishop of London, 1262; sympathised with baronial party, but frequently acted as mediator during barons' war; suspended by papal legate, Ottobon, 1266; for refusing to publish papal sentence of excommunication against Simon de Montfort and his abettors; restored, 1272. [l. 277]

SANDWICH, RALPH DE (d. 1308?), judge; probably brother of Henry de Sandwich [q. v.]; knight; keeper of royal wardrobe; joined barons, 1264; entrusted by Simon de Montfort with great seal, 1265; custodian of Arundel Castle, 1277; constable of Tower of London, 1285-8, and 1290 till death, and warden of the city of London, 1285-1286, 1287-8, and 1290-5; on commission of judges that condemned William Wallace [q. v.], 1305. [l. 280]

SANDWITH, HUMPHRY (1822-1881), army physician; qualified by London University and College of Surgeons; house surgeon to Hull Infirmary, 1847; travelled in Mesopotamia; correspondent of 'The Times,' 1853; staff surgeon in Beatson's corps of Bashi-Bazouks, 1854; inspector-general of hospitals and head of medical staff under Colonel (afterwards Sir William Fenwick) Williams [q. v.] in Armenia, 1855; at defence of Kars; in London, 1856; published narrative of adventures, 1856; C.B.; D.C.L. Oxford; colonial secretary in Mauritius, 1857-9; in Servia, 1872-7, where he advocated cause of Servian refugees; published works of political tendency. [l. 281]

SANDYS, CHARLES (1786-1859), antiquary; admitted solicitor, 1808; practised at Canterbury till 1857; F.S.A., 1846; published and left in manuscript antiquarian works. [l. 283]

SANDYS, EDWIN (1516?-1588), archbishop of York; M.A. St. John's College, Cambridge, 1541; D.D., 1549; proctor, 1542; master of Catharine Hall, Cambridge, 1549 (deprived, 1553); canon of Peterborough, 1549; prebendary of Carlisle, 1552; vice-chancellor of Cambridge University, 1553; supported Lady Jane Grey's cause; imprisoned in Tower of London and Marshalsea; was released and made escape to continent; returned to England, 1559; bishop of Worcester, 1559-70; signed the articles of 1562; one of translators of 'Bishops' Bible,' 1565; bishop of London, 1570-6; joined ecclesiastical commission, 1571; took part in translating bible of 1572; archbishop of York, 1576-88; published sermons and other works. [l. 283]

SANDYS, Sir EDWIN (1561-1629), statesman: son of Edwin Sandys [q. v.]; of Merchant Taylors' School, London, and Corpus Christi College, Oxford; M.A., 1583; B.C.L., 1589; fellow, 1580; prebendary of York, 1582-1602; entered Middle Temple, 1589; M.P., Andover, 1586, and Plympton, 1589 and 1593; travelled abroad with Cranmer, 1593; wrote 'Europæ Speculum,' 1599 (piratically published as 'Relation of State of Religion,' 1605); returned to England, 1599; knighted, 1603; M.P., Stockbridge, 1604, assuming leading position in House of Commons; on committee to consider 'great contract,' 1610; on committee to consider impositions, 1613, when he enunciated principle that there were certain reciprocal conditions of the constitution which neither king nor people might violate with impunity; dismissed by council; free brother of East India Company, 1618; served on company's committee, 1619-23 and 1625-9; member of Somers Islands Company, 1615; member of council for Virginia, 1607; joint-manager of Virginia Company, 1617, and treasurer, 1619-20; organised government of the colony, 1619, and inaugurated an era of prosperity; being suspected of designing to establish republican and puritan state in America, he was accused of malversation of funds and transmission of false news, and temporarily imprisoned in Tower of London, 1621, Virginia Company's charter being annulled and government of colony assumed by crown, 1624; M.P., Sandwich, 1621, Kent, 1624, and Penryn, 1625 and 1626. [l. 286]

SANDYS, GEORGE (1578-1644), poet; son of Edwin Sandys [q. v.]; educated at St. Mary Hall, Oxford; went abroad, 1610, and travelled in Italy, Turkey, Egypt, and Palestine; published 'Relation of a Journey,' 1615; treasurer of Virginia Company, 1621; accompanied Sir Francis Wyatt to Virginia, 1621, and was nominated member of council when crown assumed government, 1624; reappointed, 1626 and 1628; gentleman of privy chamber to Charles I; published a translation of Ovid's 'Metamorphoses,' 1621-6, 'Paraphrase upon the Psalmes' in verse, 1636 (music by Henry Lawes [q. v.] being added in an edition in 1638), 'Christ's Passion, a Tragedy,' a translation in heroic verse from Latin of Grotius, 1640, and 'Paraphrase of Song of Solomon,' in verse, 1641; agent in London to Virginia Company, 1638; petitioned unsuccessfully for re-establishment of company's old privileges of government, 1642. [l. 290]

SANDYS, SAMUEL, first BARON SANDYS OF OMBERSLEY (1695?-1770), educated at New College, Oxford;

M.P., Worcester. 1718-43; several times unsuccessfully introduced Pensions Bill; opposed Excise Bill; moved, unsuccessfully, address for removal of Walpole, 1741; privy councillor, 1742; chancellor of exchequer, 1742-3; member of committee of inquiry into Lord Orford's conduct, 1742; created Baron Sandys, 1743; treasurer of the chamber, 1747-55; speaker of House of Lords, 1756; warden and chief justice in eyre of king's (George II and George III) forests south of Trent, 1756 and 1759-61; first lord of trade and plantations, 1761-3. [l. 293]

SANDYS, WILLIAM, BARON SANDYS OF 'THE VYNE' (d. 1540), knight of the body to Henry VIII, 1509; constable of Southampton, 1510; treasurer of Calais, 1517-26; K.G., 1518; took leading part in festivities at Field of Cloth of Gold; created Baron Sandys of 'The Vyne,' 1523; took part with Fox in founding Guild of Holy Ghost at Basingstoke, 1524; lord chamberlain and captain of Guisnes, 1526. [l. 295]

SANDYS, WILLIAM (1792-1874), antiquary; educated at Westminster; solicitor in London, 1814-73; F.S.A.; collaborated with Forster in 'History of the Violin,' 1864, and published antiquarian works relating chiefly to music and songs. [l. 296]

SANFORD. [See also SANDFORD.]

SANFORD, JOHN LANGTON (1824-1877), historical writer; educated at University College, London; barrister, Lincoln's Inn, 1855; joint-editor of 'Inquirer,' 1852-5; published historical writings. [l. 296]

SANFORD or **SANDFORD**, JOSEPH (d. 1774), scholar and book-collector; M.A. Exeter College, Oxford, 1715; B.D., 1726; fellow of Balliol College, Oxford, 1715 till death; rector of Duloe, 1722, and also of Huntspill, 1739-1774. [l. 296]

SANGAR, GABRIEL (d. 1678), ejected minister; M.A. Magdalen Hall, Oxford, 1632; rector of Steeple Ashton, 1660; ejected, 1662; published religious works. [l. 297]

SANGER, JOHN (1816-1889), circus proprietor; began with his brother George conjuring exhibition at Birmingham, 1845; started a circus entertainment at Lynn; leased Agricultural Hall, Islington, and (1871) Astley's Amphitheatre, London; subsequently dissolved partnership, each brother continuing independently. [l. 297]

SANGSTER, SAMUEL (1804?-1872), line-engraver; pupil of William Finden [q. v.] [l. 298]

SANLEGER. [See SAINT LEGER.]

SANQUHAR, sixth BARON (d. 1612). [See CRICHTON, ROBERT.]

SANSETUN, BENEDICT OF (d. 1226), bishop of Rochester; precentor of St. Paul's, London, 1203; head justice for four home counties, 1212; consecrated bishop of Rochester, 1215. [l. 298]

SANSUM, ROBERT (d. 1665), rear-admiral; commanded vessel attending on army in Scotland, 1652; in North Sea from 1655; rear-admiral of white, 1664; killed in battle off Lowestoft. [l. 298]

SANTLOW, HESTER (fl. 1720-1778), actress; married Barton Booth [q. v.], 1719; originally a dancer who had lived under protection of Duke of Marlborough. [v. 375]

SANTRY, BARON (1603-1672). [See BARRY, JAMES.]

SAPHIR, ADOLPH (1831-1891), theologian; born at Pesth; converted to Christianity by Jewish mission of church of Scotland, 1843; studied for ministry at Edinburgh, Berlin, Glasgow (M.A., 1854), and Aberdeen; licensed and appointed missionary to Jews, 1854; at Hamburg, 1854-6; hon. D.D. Edinburgh, 1878; at Belgrave presbyterian church, 1880-8; published religious works. [l. 298]

SAPIENS, BERNARD (fl. 865). [See BERNARD.]

SARAVIA, HADRIAN À (1531-1613), divine; born at Hesdin in Artois; took part in drawing up Walloon confession of faith; removed to Channel islands, 1560; professor of divinity at Leyden, 1582, and pastor of French reformed church; rector of Tattenhill, 1588; held various prebends; one of translators of new version of scriptures, 1607; rector of Great Chart, 1610-13; published religious treatises. [l. 299]

SARGANT, WILLIAM LUCAS (1809–1889), educational reformer and political economist; educated at Trinity College, Cambridge; entered his father's business of maker of military arms at Birmingham; published works on education and political economy. [l. 301]

SARGENT, JOHN (1780–1833), divine; of Eton and King's College, Cambridge; M.A., 1807; held various rectories; published biographical writings. [l. 301]

SARGENT, JOHN GRANT (1813–1883), quaker; made acquaintance of the American quaker John Wilbur (1774–1856), and founded the Fritchley Friends, 1870; published religious works. [l. 302]

SARGENT, JOHN NEPTUNE (1826–1893), lieutenant-general; lieutenant in 95th foot, 1846; served in Hongkong, 1847–50; captain, 1853; in Turkey, 1854; fought at Alma, Inkermann, and Redan, 1855; brevet-major, 1855; on committee of three officers to examine equipment of armies in Crimea, 1855; second lieutenant-colonel, first battalion, 1859; British commandant at Taku forts, 1860; C.B., 1862; colonel, 1864; appointed to brigade depot at Milford Haven, 1873, and at Oxford, 1874; major-general, 1877; commander of troops in China and Straits Settlements, 1882; lieutenant-general, 1884; colonel, first battalion Inniskilling Fusiliers, 1891. [l. 303]

SARIS, JOHN (d. 1646), merchant and sea-captain; one of factors for East India Company at Bantam, 1605–9; again at Bantam, 1611, when he sailed to Japan, 1612, and obtained emperor's commission authorising the company's agents to reside and trade in Japan; returned to England, 1614. [l. 304]

SARJEAUNT, JOHN (1622–1707). [See SERGEANT.]

SARMENTO, JACOB DE CASTRO (1692–1762), physician; born in Portugal; M.D. Coimbra, 1717; came to England as rabbi of Jews of Portugal resident in London; L.R.C.P., 1725; M.D., Aberdeen, 1739; F.R.S., 1730; published medical works. [l. 305]

SARSFIELD, PATRICK, titular EARL OF LUCAN (d. 1693), born at Lucan; educated at a French military college; lieutenant-colonel of Dover's horse, 1685; colonel, 1686; received from James II command of Irish troops in England; followed the king to France and accompanied him to Ireland, 1689; privy councillor and colonel of horse, 1689; brigadier; took Sligo and assisted in defence of Galway and in securing of Connaught; major-general; fought at Boyne, 1690; assisted in defence of Limerick; governor of Galway and Connaught; received patent as Earl of Lucan, 1691; commanded reserve at Aughrim, 12 July 1691, and after treaty of Limerick, 24 Sept., sailed to France, joining French service with many of his troops; received from the exiled James second troop of lifeguards; commanded Irish soldiers intended for invasion of England, 1692; maréchal-de-camp; fought at Steenkirk, 1692; mortally wounded at Landen, 1692. [l. 305]

SARTORIS, MRS. ADELAIDE (1814?–1879). [See KEMBLE, ADELAIDE.]

SARTORIUS, FRANCIS (1734–1804), painter; son and pupil of John Sartorius (1700?–1780?) [q. v.]; painted sporting subjects; exhibited at Royal Academy. [l. 310]

SARTORIUS, SIR GEORGE ROSE (1790–1885), admiral of the fleet; entered navy, 1801; lieutenant, 1808; captain, 1814; in Bay of Biscay, 1814–15, when Napoleon II surrendered; engaged by Dom Pedro to command Portuguese regency fleet against Dom Miguel, 1831–3; knighted, 1841; admiral, 1861; K.C.B., 1865; vice-admiral of United Kingdom, 1869; admiral of fleet, 1869; G.C.B., 1880. [l. 308]

SARTORIUS, JOHN (1700?–1780?), animal-painter; exhibited chiefly at Free Society of Artists. [l. 309]

SARTORIUS, JOHN F. (1775?–1831?), painter of sporting subjects; son of John N. Sartorius [q. v.]; exhibited at Royal Academy, 1802–27. [l. 310]

SARTORIUS, JOHN N. (1755?–1828?), painter of sporting subjects; son of Francis Sartorius [q. v.]; exhibited at Royal Academy, 1781–1824. [l. 310]

SASS, HENRY (1788–1844), painter; exhibited at Royal Academy from 1807; travelled in Italy, 1815–17, and published account of journey, 1818; opened drawing

school at Charlotte Street, Bloomsbury, London, which he conducted till 1842. [l. 310]

SASS or **SASSE**, RICHARD (1774–1849), landscape-painter; half-brother of Henry Sass [q. v.]; exhibited at Royal Academy, 1791–1813; teacher in drawing to Princess Charlotte. [l. 311]

SASSOON, SIR ALBERT ABDULLAH DAVID, first baronet (1818–1896), merchant; born at Bagdad, whence his father, David Sassoon (1792–1864), who was a merchant there, removed to Bushire, and later to Bombay; educated in India; head of firm at Bombay, 1864; constructed Sassoon dock at Colaba, Bombay, 1872–5; C.S.I., 1867; member of Bombay legislative council, 1868–72; K.B., 1872; settled in England; created baronet, 1890; spent large sums in philanthropic works in India and England. [l. 311]

SATCHWELL, BENJAMIN (1732–1809), founder of the Leamington Spa Charity; shoemaker at Leamington Priors; discovered saline springs, 1784, and was chiefly instrumental in promoting prosperity of the modern town of Leamington; instituted, 1806, Leamington Spa Charity. [l. 312]

SAUL, ARTHUR (d. 1585), divine; M.A. Magdalen College, Oxford, 1549; fellow, c. 1546–1553; expelled by Bishop Gardiner, 1553; at Strasburg during Queen Mary's reign; canon of Salisbury, 1559, and of Gloucester, 1565. [l. 313]

SAUL, ARTHUR (fl. 1614), writer on chess; probably son of Arthur Saul (d. 1585) [q. v.]; author of treatise on use of arquebus; published book on chess, 1614. [l. 313]

SAULL, WILLIAM DEVONSHIRE (1784–1855), geologist; F.G.S., 1831; F.S.A., 1841; F.R.A.S.; published writings relating to geology. [l. 313]

SAULT, RICHARD (d. 1702), mathematician and editor; kept a mathematical school near Royal Exchange, London, 1694; joint-editor with Dunton, the publisher, of 'Athenian Gazette,' 1691; removed, c. 1700, to Cambridge, where he died; published mathematical and other works. [l. 313]

SAUMAREZ, JAMES, BARON DE SAUMAREZ (1757–1836), admiral; born at St. Peter Port; lieutenant, 1776; in Victory, the Channel flagship, 1778–81; in action at Dogger Bank, 1781; in West Indies, 1782; made important capture of French ship off Cherbourg, and was knighted, 1793; employed in blockade of Brest, 1795–6; at battle of St. Vincent, 1797, and Nile, 1798; made rear-admiral and baronet, 1801; with Brest fleet, 1801; made unsuccessful attack on French off Algeciras, but soon after defeated French and Spanish, and was made K.B., 1801; commanded Guernsey station, 1803–7; vice-admiral and second in command of fleet off Brest, 1807; commanded squadron in Baltic, 1808–13; admiral, 1814; rear-admiral of United Kingdom, 1819, and vice-admiral, 1821; commander-in-chief at Plymouth, 1824–7; raised to peerage, 1831; general of marines, 1832. [l. 314]

SAUMAREZ, PHILIP (1710–1747), navy captain; entered navy, 1726; lieutenant, 1737; captain, 1743; captured French ship in Soundings, 1746; with Anson at Cape Finisterre, 1747, and later with Hawke in action of 14 Oct., when he was killed. [l. 317]

SAUMAREZ, RICHARD (1764–1835), surgeon; brother of James, baron de Saumarez [q. v.]; studied medicine at London Hospital; surgeon at Magdalen Hospital, Streatham, 1788–1805; practised in London till 1818; published physiological and other works. [l. 318]

SAUMAREZ, THOMAS (d. 1766), navy captain; brother of Philip Saumarez [q. v.]; captain, 1748; captured French ship Belliqueux in Bristol channel, 1758, and commanded her in West Indies, 1761. [l. 318]

SAUMAREZ, SIR THOMAS (1760–1845), general; brother of James, baron de Saumarez [q. v.]; served in North America during revolutionary war; president and commander-in-chief of New Brunswick, 1813; general, 1838. [l. 317]

SAUNDERS, SIR CHARLES (1713?–1775), admiral; entered navy, 1727; lieutenant, 1734; with George (afterwards Baron) Anson [q. v.] 1739; commander and captain, 1741; on home station, 1745; assisted in defeat by Hawke of French under M. de l'Etenduère,

14 Oct. 1747; M.P., Plymouth, 1750, Heydon, 1754–75;
commodore and commander-in-chief on Newfoundland
station, 1752; comptroller of navy, 1755; commander-
in-chief of fleet for the St. Lawrence, 1759; returned to
England after surrender of Quebec; commander-in-chief
in Mediterranean, 1760; K.B., 1761; lord of admiralty,
1765, and first lord, 1766; admiral, 1770. [l. 319]

SAUNDERS, SIR EDMUND (d. 1683), judge; born
of poor parents; gained living by irregular employment
in Clement's Inn; barrister, Middle Temple, 1664; began,
1666, his 'Reports' in king's bench, which, extending to
1672, were first published, 1686; appeared as counsel for
Strafford, 1680, and against Anthony Ashley Cooper,
1681; bencher of Middle Temple, 1682; lord chief-justice
of king's bench, 1682; made serjeant-at-law and knighted,
1683. [l. 321]

SAUNDERS, SIR EDWARD (d. 1576), judge; educated at Cambridge; entered Middle Temple; Lent reader,
1533; autumn reader, 1539; king's serjeant, 1547; recorder of Coventry; M.P., Coventry, 1541, Lostwithiel,
1547, and Saltash, 1553; justice of common pleas, 1553;
justice of common pleas in county palatine of Lancaster,
1554; knighted, 1555; chief-justice of queen's bench,
1555; degraded to position of chief-baron of exchequer,
1559. [l. 322]

SAUNDERS, ERASMUS (1670–1724), divine; M.A.
Jesus College, Oxford, 1696; D.D., 1712; prebendary of
St. David's, 1709; published religious works. [l. 323]

SAUNDERS, SIR GEORGE (1671?–1734), rear-admiral; served some years in merchant service; entered
navy, 1689; lieutenant, 1694; commander and captain,
1702; on Irish station, 1702–10; in Channel, 1710–15;
in Baltic, 1717, and Mediterranean, 1718–20, under Byng;
knighted, 1720; commissioner of victualling office, 1721–
1727; extra commissioner of navy, 1727–9; comptroller
of treasurer's account, 1729–34; M.P., Queenborough,
1728; rear-admiral, 1732. [l. 324]

SAUNDERS, GEORGE (1762–1839), architect; surveyor for Middlesex; designed extensions of British
Museum, 1804; F.S.A., 1808; F.R.S.; published papers
on architectural subjects. [l. 324]

SAUNDERS, HENRY (1728–1785), schoolmaster;
B.A. Oriel College, Oxford, 1750; curate of Wednesbury
and (c. 1756) of Shenstone; usher at King Edward's School,
Birmingham; master of Halesowen school, 1771, and
curate of Oldbury; wrote history of Shenstone, published,
1794. [l. 325]

SAUNDERS, JOHN (1810–1895), author; edited William Howitt's 'Living Political Reformers'; formed connection with Charles Knight (1791–1873) [q. v.], for
whom he wrote much of 'Old England' and 'London';
contributed to 'Penny Magazine' articles on Chaucer,
which formed basis of introduction to 'Canterbury Tales,'
1846; founded 'People's Journal,' 1846; his blank-verse
tragedy, 'Love's Martyrdom,' produced by Buckstone,
at Haymarket, London, 1855; published poems and several
novels. [l. 325]

SAUNDERS, JOHN CUNNINGHAM (1773–1810),
ophthalmic surgeon; apprenticed as surgeon, 1790–5;
studied at St. Thomas's and Guy's hospitals, London;
demonstrator in anatomy at St. Thomas's, 1797, holding
the post, with a short interval, till death; took prominent
part in founding Royal London Ophthalmic Hospital;
published works on the eye and ear. [l. 326]

SAUNDERS, KATHERINE (afterwards MRS.
COOPER) (1841–1894), novelist; daughter of John Saunders [q. v.]; married the Rev. Richard Cooper, 1876; published works of fiction, 1873–93. [l. 326]

SAUNDERS, LAURENCE (d. 1555), martyr; educated
at Eton and King's College, Cambridge; M.A., 1554;
B.D.; prebendary of York, 1552; rector of All Hallows,
Bread Street, London, 1553; apprehended by Bonner,
1554, condemned for heresy, and burned at Coventry.
[l. 327]

SAUNDERS, MARGARET (fl. 1702–1744), actress;
played Flareit in Cibber's 'Love's Last Shift' at Haymarket, London, and was the original Wishwell in Cibber's
'Double Gallant,' 1707; at Drury Lane, London, 1708–9,
again at Haymarket, London, 1709–10, and from 1711–21
at Drury Lane; after retirement (1721) was a friend and
confidential attendant of Mrs. Oldfield. [l. 327]

SAUNDERS or SANDERS, RICHARD (1613–1687?),
astrologer; practised astrology and cheiromancy from
c. 1647; published astrological and similar works.
[l. 328]

SAUNDERS, RICHARD HUCK- (1720–1785), physician; studied at St. Thomas's Hospital, London; surgeon in Lord Sempill's regiment, 1745–8; M.D. Marischal
College, Aberdeen, 1749; surgeon to 33rd regiment, 1750;
in Malta, 1750–3; served in America, 1755–62; settled in
London; F.R.C.P., 1784; physician to Middlesex Hospital,
1766–8, and to St. Thomas's, London, 1768–77. [l. 329]

SAUNDERS, THOMAS WILLIAM (1814–1890),
police magistrate; barrister, Middle Temple, 1837; metropolitan police magistrate at Thames police-court, London,
1878–90; published, independently or in collaboration,
numerous legal works and compilations. [l. 329]

SAUNDERS, WILLIAM (1743–1817), physician;
M.D. Edinburgh, 1765; practised in London; physician to
Guy's Hospital, London, 1770–1802; F.R.C.P., 1790, and
censor, 1791, 1798, 1805, and 1813; Gulstonian lecturer,
1792; Harveian orator, 1796; F.R.S., 1793; physician to
George, prince regent, 1807; first president of Royal
Medical and Chirurgical Society, 1805; published medical
works. [l. 330]

SAUNDERS, WILLIAM (1823–1895), journalist and
politician; opened quarries near Box tunnel, c. 1844;
started 'Plymouth Western Morning News,' 1860, and
'Eastern Morning News' (Hull), 1864; started (1863)
Central Press news-agency, which became Central News
Agency, 1870; liberal M.P. for East Hull, 1885, and Walworth, 1892; published political writings. [l. 331]

SAUNDERS, WILLIAM WILSON (1809–1879), entomologist; educated at East India Company's academy,
Addiscombe; obtained commission in engineers; in India,
1830–1; resigned commission and became underwriter at
Lloyd's; F.L.S., 1833, and treasurer, 1861–73; president
of Entomological Society, 1841–2 and 1856–7; F.R.S.,
1853; F.Z.S., 1861; president, Royal Horticultural
Society; published writings on entomology and botany.
[l. 331]

SAUNDERSON, MRS. (d. 1711), actress; member of
the Lincoln's Inn company; married Thomas Betterton
[q. v.] the actor; pensioned after her husband's death by
Queen Anne; her Lady Macbeth much admired by Colley
Cibber [q. v.] [iv. 436]

SAUNDERSON or SANDERSON, NICHOLAS
(1682–1739), mathematician; lost his eyes through small-
pox in infancy; mathematical teacher at Cambridge,
1707; made M.A. by special patent from Queen Anne,
1711, and was elected professor of mathematics; LL.D.,
1728; F.R.S., 1719; member of Spitalfields Mathematical
Society (fl. 1717–1845). His 'Algebra' (1740) and other
mathematical writings printed posthumously. [l. 332]

SAUNFORD. [See SANDFORD.]

SAURIN, WILLIAM (1757?–1839), politician; B.A.
Trinity College, Dublin, 1777; entered Lincoln's Inn;
called to Irish bar, 1780; opposed the union, 1798;
M.P., Blessington, 1799, continuing his opposition to the
union; attorney-general for Ireland, 1807–22; promoted
an anti-catholic agitation, and was accordingly removed
by Wellesley, 1822; resumed practice at Chancery bar,
1822; active promoter of formation of Brunswick Club,
1828; retired from practice, 1831. [l. 333]

SAUTRE, WILLIAM (d. 1401). [See SAWTREY.]

SAVAGE, SIR ARNOLD (d. 1375), politician; served
in France, 1345; warden of coasts of Kent, 1355; mayor
of Bordeaux, 1359–63. [l. 335]

SAVAGE, SIR ARNOLD (d. 1410), speaker of the
House of Commons; son of Sir Arnold Savage (d. 1375)
[q. v.]; served with John of Gaunt in Spain, 1386; constable of Queenborough, 1392–6; knight of shire for
Kent, 1390; speaker of House of Commons, 1401 and
1404; formulated petitions that redress of grievances
should precede supply; member of council of Henry,
prince of Wales; again represented Kent, 1402; member
of great council, 1404–6. [l. 335]

SAVAGE, HENRY (1604?–1672), divine; M.A. Balliol College, Oxford, 1630; fellow, 1628; B.D., 1637;

master of Balliol, 1651–72; D.D., 1651; chaplain in ordinary to Charles II, 1660; canon of Gloucester, 1665; published theological works and an historical volume relating to Balliol College (1668). [l. 336]

SAVAGE, JAMES (1767–1845), antiquary; in business with his brother, William Savage (1770–1843) [q. v.], as printer and bookseller at Howden, 1790; went to London, 1803; assistant-librarian to London Institution, 1806; subsequently edited 'Dorset County Chronicle'; published antiquarian works relating to Somerset, Dorset, and Yorkshire. [l. 337]

SAVAGE, JAMES (1779–1852), architect; studied at Royal Academy; exhibited between 1799 and 1832; designed Ormond Bridge (1805) and Richmond Bridge (1808) over Liffey, Dublin; architect to Society of Middle Temple, 1830; F.R.I.B.A.; published 'Observations on Styles in Architecture,' 1836. [l. 338]

SAVAGE, Sir JOHN (d. 1492), politician and soldier; brother of Thomas Savage (d. 1507) [q. v.]; K.B., 1465; mayor of Chester, 1484 and 1485; fought for Henry of Richmond at Bosworth, and on Richmond's accession as Henry VII received large grants of land; K.G., 1488; killed at siege of Boulogne. [l. 338]

SAVAGE, JOHN (d. 1586), Roman catholic conspirator; served with Duke of Parma in Low Countries; joined conspiracy of John Ballard [q. v.] and Babington for murder of Queen Elizabeth and release of Mary Queen of Scots, 1586; one of six nominated to assassinate Queen Elizabeth; arrested and hanged. [l. 339]

SAVAGE, JOHN (fl. 1690–1700), engraver and printseller in London; executed portraits of several eminent persons of his day, including 'the Antipapists.' [l. 339]

SAVAGE, JOHN (1673–1747), divine; of Westminster School and Emmanuel College, Cambridge; M.A., 1698; B.D. and D.D. Christ Church, Oxford, 1707; held livings of Bigrave, 1701–8, and Clothall, 1708–47; published historical and other works, besides translations from French, Spanish, and Latin. [l. 340]

SAVAGE, JOHN (1828–1888), Irish poet; studied at art schools of Royal Dublin Society; joined revolutionary clubs in Dublin; proprietor of 'Irish Tribune'; took part in rising in south; fled to New York, 1848; literary editor of 'Irish Citizen,' New York, 1854; editor, 1857, and, later, proprietor of 'The States,' Washington; Fenian agent in Paris, 1868; published poetical and historical works. [l. 341]

SAVAGE, Sir JOHN BOSCAWEN (1760–1843), major-general; ensign, 1762; lieutenant of marines, 1777; captain, 1793; in actions off L'Orient, St. Vincent, and at Nile; at Copenhagen, 1801; lieutenant-colonel of marines, 1815; K.C.H., 1833; K.C.B., 1839; major-general, 1837. [l. 341]

SAVAGE, MARMION W. (1803–1872), novelist; B.A. Trinity College, Dublin, 1824; held position under Irish government in Dublin; editor of 'Examiner,' London; published novels. [l. 342]

SAVAGE, RICHARD, fourth EARL RIVERS (1660?–1712), general; M.P., Wigan, 1681; lieutenant in fourth troop of horse-guards, 1686; joined William of Orange on his landing; member for Liverpool in Convention parliament; fought in attack on Cork, 1690; accompanied William III to Flanders, 1691 and 1692; received command of third troop of horse-guards, 1692; major-general, 1693; succeeded to earldom, 1694; lieutenant-general in Flanders, 1702; commanded force which was intended to proceed to France, but which subsequently proceeded to Lisbon, 1706–7; returned home, 1708; general of horse, 1708; constable of Tower of London, 1709; plenipotentiary to elector of Hanover, 1710; master of ordnance and colonel of blues, 1711; intimate with Swift and with Harley's circle; member of the Saturday Club. [l. 342]

SAVAGE, RICHARD (d. 1743), poet; probably of humble birth, but claimed to be illegitimate son of Richard Savage, fourth earl Rivers [q. v.], by Anne, daughter of Sir Richard Mason, and wife of Charles Gerard, second earl of Macclesfield [q. v.], who treated him with marked hostility; turned to literature for livelihood; gained friendship of Wilks the comedian, and of Steele, by his comedy, 'Love in a Veil,' acted at Drury Lane, London, 1718; played at Drury Lane, London, title-rôle in his tragedy, 'Sir Thomas Overbury,' 1723; the story of his birth published by Aaron Hill in the 'Plain Dealer,'

1724; condemned to death for killing a gentleman in a tavern, 1727, but pardoned, 1728; published works in verse (including 'The Bastard,' 1728) and prose relating to story of his birth, but agreed to abstain from further attacks on receipt of pension from Lord Tyrconnel, Mrs. Brett's nephew; published, 1729, 'The Wanderer,' which he considered his masterpiece; applied, unsuccessfully, for post of poet laureate, 1730, but obtained pension from Queen Caroline on condition of celebrating her birthday annually with an ode, and assumed title of 'volunteer laureate'; made acquaintance of Dr. Johnson, c. 1737; subsequently lived in great poverty, and died at Bristol. A complete edition of his works was published, 1775. [l. 345]

SAVAGE, Sir ROLAND (d. 1519), lord of Lecale, co. Down; seneschal of Ulster, 1482; deprived of estates as rebel, c. 1515. [l. 348]

SAVAGE, SAMUEL MORTON (1721–1791), divine; appointed by trustees of William Coward (d. 1738) [q. v.] assistant-tutor in natural science and classics at Fund Academy, London, 1744; pastor (1757–87) to independent congregation at Duke's Place, St. Mary Axe, London; held divinity chair at the academy (then removed to Hoxton Square), London, 1762–85; published sermons. [l. 349]

SAVAGE, THOMAS (d. 1507), archbishop of York; brother of Sir John Savage (d. 1492) [q. v.]; LL.D. Cambridge; chaplain to Henry VII, 1485; concluded treaty of Medina del Campo, 1488; represented England at Boulogne conference, 1490; bishop of Rochester, 1492–6, and London, 1496–1501; archbishop of York, 1501–7. [l. 350]

SAVAGE, THOMAS (fl. 1620), colonist; went to Virginia with Captain Christopher Newport, 1608; Indian interpreter to Virginia Company. [l. 350]

SAVAGE, THOMAS (1608–1682), major; apprenticed to Merchant Taylors, London, 1621; went with Sir Harry Vane to Massachusetts, 1635; freeman of Boston, 1636; founded, with William Coddington [q. v.], settlement of Rhode island, 1638; captain of artillery company, Boston, 1651; represented Boston at general court, 1654; several times speaker of assembly; commanded state forces against Philip, chief of the Narragansets, 1675. [l. 350]

SAVAGE, WILLIAM (d. 1736), divine; M.A. Emmanuel College, Cambridge, 1693; D.D., 1717; master of Emmanuel College, Cambridge, 1719–36; vice-chancellor of Cambridge, 1724; incumbent of St. Anne's, Blackfriars, London, 1720. [l. 340]

SAVAGE, WILLIAM (1770–1843), printer and bookseller; in business at Howden, 1790–7; brother of James Savage (1767–1845) [q. v.]; printer to Royal Institution, London, c. 1799; began business as printer in London, 1803; published 'Dictionary of Art of Printing,' 1840–1. [l. 351]

SAVARIC (d. 1205), divine; treasurer of Sarum, 1180; with Richard I on crusade; elected bishop of Bath in his absence, and consecrated at Rome, 1192; engaged in negotiations with the emperor Henry VI for Richard I's release, 1193, and present at conclusion of treaty at Worms; appointed by the emperor Henry VI chancellor of Burgundy, 1194; obtained from Pope Celestine III privilege declaring Glastonbury united to Bath, with equal rights as cathedral church, 1195; on appeal of monks of Glastonbury procured second privilege from Pope Celestine III, 1196, and obtained possession of abbey of Glastonbury, 1197, but was deprived by Richard I, 1198; obtained King John's consent again to take possession, 1199, the union of the churches being confirmed by Pope Innocent III, 1200; granted charter to city of Wells, 1201. [l. 351]

SAVERY, THOMAS (1650?–1715), military engineer; patented invention for rowing vessels by means of paddle-wheels, 1696, and machine for raising water, embodying practical application of steam-power, 1698; captain of engineers, 1702; surveyor to waterworks at Hampton Court, 1714; published accounts of his inventions. [l. 354]

SAVILE, BOURCHIER WREY (1817–1888), divine; of Westminster and Emmanuel College, Cambridge; M.A., 1842; rector of Dunchideock-with-Shillingford St. George, 1872–88; discredited the belief in the Jewish origin of the English people, 1880; published theological works. [l. 355]

SAVILE, Sir GEORGE, MARQUIS OF HALIFAX (1633–1695), son of Sir William Savile of Thornhill (d. 1644), royalist governor successively of Sheffield and York, and

Anne, daughter of Thomas Coventry, first baron Coventry [q. v.], who subsequently remarried Sir Thomas Chicheley [q. v.]; M.P. for Pontefract in Convention, 1660; captain of Prince Rupert's horse, 1667; created Baron Savile of Eland and Viscount Halifax, 1668; commissioner of trade, 1669; privy councillor, 1672; sent on mission to Louis XIV, 1672; opposed Test Acts; created Earl of Halifax, 1679; opposed bill for exclusion of James from succession, 1679; opposed also execution of Stafford, 1679; in communication with William of Orange; elevated to rank of marquis, 1682; lord privy seal, 1682–5; circulated in manuscript his pamphlet, 'Character of a Trimmer' (printed, with title inscribed 'By the Honourable Sir W[illiam] C[oventry],' 1688), in which he urged Charles II to free himself from the influence of his brother in hope of obtaining succession of Monmouth, president of council, 1685; opposed repeal of Test and Habeas Corpus Acts; was dismissed from council, 1685; framed petition to James II demanding summoning of free parliament, and dismissal of Roman catholics from office, 1688; sent by James II, with Godolphin and Nottingham, to try and arrange compromise with William of Orange; presided over council of lords which provided for safety of London; chairman of meeting of peers who requested William of Orange to undertake provisional government and summon Convention; chosen regular speaker of peers on meeting of Convention, 1689; requested Prince and Princess of Orange to accept crown; lord privy seal, 1689–90; struck off council as persistent absentee, 1692. His pamphlets were collected, 1700. [l. 356]

SAVILE, Sir GEORGE, eighth baronet (1726–1784), politician; served as captain against rebels, 1745; M.A. and LL.D. Queens' College, Cambridge, 1749; M.P., Yorkshire, 1759–83; successfully introduced Nullum Tempus Bill, 1768; made several unsuccessful efforts from 1771 to bring in a bill to secure rights of electors; supported, in a remarkable speech, clerical petition for relief from subscription to Thirty-nine Articles, 1772; supported resistance of the American colonies, 1775; successfully brought in bill for relief of Roman catholics from certain obsolete penalties and disabilities, 1778, and in consequence was subjected to attacks of Gordon rioters, 1780; presented petition for economical reforms, 1779; unsuccessfully introduced bill to secure protestant religion from popish encroachments; moved, unsuccessfully, for select committee of inquiry on occasion of North's loan; resigned seat from ill-health, 1783; F.R.S.; vice-president of Society of Arts. Some of his letters on political subjects were printed posthumously. [l. 364]

SAVILE, Sir HENRY (1549–1622), scholar; matriculated at Brasenose College, Oxford, 1561; fellow of Merton College, 1565; M.A., 1570; lectured in mathematics; for brief period resident for Queen Elizabeth in Low Countries; tutor in Greek to Queen Elizabeth; warden of Merton College, Oxford, 1585–1622; translated 'Histories of Tacitus,' 1591; secretary of Latin tongue to Queen Elizabeth; held *in commendam* deanery of Carlisle, 1595; provost of Eton (retaining wardenship of Merton College), 1596; knighted, 1604; one of scholars commissioned to prepare authorised translation of bible; published edition of St. Chrysostom, 1610–13, printed by the king's printer; published edition of Xenophon's 'Cyropædia,' 1613; assisted Bodley in founding his library; founded Savile professorships of geometry and astronomy at Oxford; left manuscripts, now in Bodleian Library. [l. 367]

SAVILE, Sir HENRY, first baronet (1579–1632), son of Sir John Savile (1545–1607) [q. v.]; studied at Merton College, Oxford, and Middle Temple; knighted, 1603; created baronet, 1611; M.P., Aldborough, 1604–11 and 1614; vice-president of council of north before 1627. [l. 372]

SAVILE, HENRY (1642–1687), diplomatist; gentleman of bedchamber to Duke of York, 1665; took part in fights with Dutch off North Foreland, 1666, and in Burlington Bay (of which he wrote an account), 1672; envoy extraordinary to Louis XIV; groom of chamber to Charles II; M.P., Newark, 1677; envoy in Paris, 1679–82; vice-chamberlain, 1680; commissioner of admiralty, 1682–1684; re-appointed vice-chamberlain by James II, holding office till 1687. His correspondence was published, 1858. [l. 370]

SAVILE, JEREMIAH (*fl.* 1651), musician; taught music in London during Commonwealth; composed part-song 'The Waits,' first published, 1667. [l. 371]

SAVILE, Sir JOHN (1545–1607), judge; brother of Sir Henry Savile (1549–1622) [q. v.]; educated at Brasenose College, Oxford, and Middle Temple; autumn reader, 1586; M.P., Newton, Lancashire, 1572; serjeant-at-law, 1594; baron of exchequer, 1598; knighted, 1603; chief-justice of county palatine of Lancaster, 1604; original member of Society of Antiquaries, 1572. [l. 371]

SAVILE, JOHN, first BARON SAVILE OF PONTEFRACT (1556–1630), politician; M.P., Lincolnshire, 1586; sheriff of Lincolnshire, 1600; knight of shire for York, 1597, 1614, 1624, and 1626; *custos rotulorum* of West Riding of Yorkshire; ejected from office, 1615, but reappointed, 1626; privy councillor; comptroller of household, 1627–1630; created Baron Savile, 1627. [l. 372]

SAVILE, JOHN, first BARON SAVILE OF RUFFORD (1818–1896), diplomatist; clerk in librarian's department at foreign office, 1841; attaché at Berlin, 1842; transferred to St. Petersburg, 1849; secretary of legation at Washington, 1854; at Madrid, 1858; secretary to embassy at Constantinople, and later at St. Petersburg, 1860; envoy to king of Saxony, 1866; transferred to Brussels, *c.* 1869; British minister in Rome and privy councillor, 1883; retired from service, 1888, and was raised to peerage; G.C.B., 1885; collected pictures and antiquities. [l. 373]

SAVILE, THOMAS (*d.* 1593), antiquary; brother of Sir Henry Savile (1549–1622) [q. v.]; M.A. Merton College, Oxford, 1585; fellow, 1580; proctor, 1592; wrote letters on British antiquities, printed posthumously. [l. 370]

SAVILE, THOMAS, first VISCOUNT SAVILE OF CASTLEBAR in Irish peerage, second BARON SAVILE OF PONTEFRACT, and first EARL OF SUSSEX in English peerage (1590?–1658?), son of John Savile, first baron Savile of Pontefract [q. v.]; member of Inner Temple, 1610; knighted, 1617; M.P., Yorkshire, 1624; joint-steward and warden of forest of Gualtres and gentleman of privy chamber to Charles I, 1626; elected member for York, 1628, but unseated on petition; created Viscount Savile, 1628; promised assistance to Scottish invading army, and sent letter signed by himself and with forged signatures of Bedford, Essex, Brooke, Warwick, Scrope, and Mandeville (forgery condoned on plea that he acted on patriotic grounds); privy councillor, 1641; lord president of council of north and lord-lieutenant of Yorkshire; commissioner of regency, 1641; treasurer of household, 1641; prevented presentation of anti-royalist petition by people of Yorkshire, 1642, and was declared incapable of sitting in parliament; vindicated his conduct to parliament, and was promised protection; imprisoned in Newark Castle by royalist general, Newcastle; defended himself to Charles I and was pardoned, 1643; created Earl of Sussex, 1644; was impeached of treason to Charles I, 1645, and succeeded in joining parliamentarians; took covenant, 1646; died in retirement. [l. 374]

SAVILE, WILLIAM, second MARQUIS OF HALIFAX (1665–1700), son of George Savile, first marquis of Halifax [q. v.], by Dorothy, daughter of Henry Spencer, first earl of Sunderland; M.A. Christ Church, Oxford, 1681; M.P., Newark, 1689–95. [l. 362]

SAVIOLO, VINCENTIO (*fl.* 1595), writer on fencing; born at Padua; entered service of Earl of Essex; published, 1595, 'Practise,' a work on fencing with which Shakespeare was familiar. [l. 377]

SAVONA, LAURENCE WILLIAM OF (*fl.* 1485), Franciscan of London; D.D. Cambridge; published 'Margarita Eloquentiæ,' 1480. [l. 377]

SAVORY, Sir WILLIAM SCOVELL, first baronet (1826–1895), surgeon; studied at St. Bartholomew's Hospital, London; M.R.C.S., 1847; M.B. London, 1848; lecturer on general anatomy and surgery, St. Bartholomew's, 1859; surgeon, 1867–91; governor of the hospital 1891; lecturer on surgery, 1869–89; F.R.C.S., 1852, member of council, 1877, and president, 1885–9; Hunterian professor of comparative anatomy and physiology, 1859–61; Bradshaw lecturer, 1884; opposed Lister's antiseptic method of surgery, 1879; surgeon extraordinary to Queen Victoria, 1887; created baronet, 1890; F.R.S., 1858; published surgical works. [l. 378]

SAVOY, BONIFACE OF (*d.* 1270). [See BONIFACE.]

SAVOY, PETER OF, EARL OF RICHMOND (*d.* 1268). [See PETER.]

SAWBRIDGE, JOHN (1732?–1795), lord mayor of London; M.P., Hythe, 1768; helped to form society known as Supporters of Bill of Rights; sheriff of London and alderman of ward of Langbourn, 1768; lord mayor of London, 1775; M.P., London, 1774, 1780, 1784, and 1790. [l. 379]

SAWREY, SOLOMON (1765–1825), surgeon; member of Corporation of Surgeons, 1796; demonstrator to Andrew Marshal, M.D. (1742–1813), under whom he had studied; published surgical works. [l. 380]

SAWTREY or **SAWTRE**, JAMES (*fl.* 1541), protestant writer; published 'Defence of Marriage of Preistes,' 1541. [l. 380]

SAWTREY, WILLIAM (*d.* 1401), lollard; charged with heresies before Bishop Henry le Despenser [q. v.], 1399; probably implicated in rising of Earls of Kent and Huntingdon, 1400; attached to St. Osyth's, London, 1401; condemned by Archbishop Thomas Arundel [q. v.] on various charges of heresy, and burnt at Smithfield, being first victim of statute 'De Hæretico Comburendo.' [l. 380]

SAWYER, EDMUND (*d.* 1759), master of chancery; member of Inner Temple and (1718) of Lincoln's Inn; master in Chancery, 1738; compiled 'Memorials' collected from papers of Sir R. Winwood, 1725. [l. 381]

SAWYER, HERBERT (1731?–1798), admiral; entered navy, 1747; lieutenant, 1756; captain, 1759; served on coast of France; in West Indies, 1778–9; at relief of Gibraltar, 1781; commodore and commander-in-chief at Halifax; admiral, 1795. [l. 381]

SAWYER, Sir ROBERT (1633–1692), lawyer; 'chamber fellow' with Samuel Pepys at Magdalene College, Cambridge; first Craven scholar, 1649; Dennis fellow, 1654; M.A. and incorporated at Oxford, 1655; barrister, Inner Temple, and treasurer, 1683–8; M.P., Chipping Wycombe, 1673; knighted, 1677; speaker, April-May, 1678; assisted in drafting Exclusion Bill; attorney-general, 1681; represented crown on second occasion on which the case against city of London charter was argued, 1682; conducted Rye House plot prosecutions, 1683–4; appeared against Algernon Sidney, 1683, and against Titus Oates, 1685; obtained conviction of Sir Thomas Armstrong [q. v.], 1684; senior counsel for the seven bishops, 1688; member for Cambridge University in Convention parliament, 1689; attacked for his conduct in case of Sir Thomas Armstrong and expelled from house, 1690, but was again returned for Cambridge later in year. [l. 381]

SAXBY, HENRY LINCKMYER (1836–1873), physician; studied at Edinburgh; M.D. St. Andrews, 1862; practised at Unst, 1863–71; published writings on ornithology. [l. 384]

SAXE-COBURG-GOTHA, DUKE OF (1844–1900). [See ALFRED ERNEST ALBERT.]

SAXON, JAMES (*d.* 1817?), portrait-painter; exhibited at Royal Academy between 1795 and 1817; practised in St. Petersburg after 1810; painted portrait of Sir Walter Scott, 1805. [l. 384]

SAXONY, DUCHESS OF (1156–1189). [See MATILDA.]

SAXTON, Sir CHARLES (1732–1808), navy captain; entered navy, 1745; lieutenant; in East Indies, *c.* 1753–1760; captain, 1762; in West Indies, 1780; in action off Chesapeake, 1781; in Jamaica, 1782–3; commissioner of navy at Portsmouth, 1789; created baronet, 1794. [l. 384]

SAXTON, CHRISTOPHER (*fl.* 1570–1596), topographical draughtsman; educated at Cambridge; surveyed and drew maps of every county in England and Wales, published, 1579. [l. 385]

SAXULF or **SEXUULFUS** (*d.* 691?), Mercian divine; probably builder and first abbot of monastery of Medeshamstede (Peterborough); bishop of Mercia, *c.* 675 till 679, when Mercian diocese was divided into five dioceses, of which he perhaps took mid-Anglia. [l. 385]

SAY, FREDERICK RICHARD (*fl.* 1826–1858), portrait-painter; son of William Say (1768–1834) [q. v.]; exhibited at Royal Academy, 1826–54. [l. 389]

SAY, GEOFFREY DE, BARON DE SAY (1305?–1359), second baron by writ; served against Scots, 1327; attended tournament at Dunstable, 1333; captain and admiral of the fleet from Thames westward, 1336; in Flanders, 1338; constable of Rochester Castle, 1356. [l. 386]

SAY, SIR JOHN (*d.* 1478), politician; M.P., Cambridge, 1447 and 1449; speaker of House of Commons, 1449; indicted of treason after Cade's rebellion, 1450, but acquitted; M.P., Herefordshire, 1453, 1455, 1463, and 1467; speaker, 1463–5 and 1467–8; K.B., 1465. [l. 387]

SAY, SAMUEL (1676–1743), dissenting minister; co-pastor with Samuel Baxter at Ipswich, 1725; pastor of congregation at Long Ditch (Princes Street), Westminster, 1734–43; poetical and other writings by him were published posthumously. [l. 388]

SAY, WILLIAM (1604–1665?), regicide; B.A. University College, Oxford, 1623; entered Middle Temple, 1631; bencher, 1654; supported parliamentarians; M.P. for Camelford in Long parliament, 1647; signed Charles I's death-warrant; member of committee of safety, 1659; was exempted from act of indemnity, 1660, and fled to continent. [l. 389]

SAY, WILLIAM (1768–1834), mezzotint engraver; pupil of James Ward (1769–1859) [q. v.]; executed some engravings for Turner's 'Liber Studiorum'; engraver to Duke of Gloucester, 1807. [l. 389]

SAYE and **SELE**, first VISCOUNT (1582–1662). [See FIENNES, WILLIAM.]

SAYE or **SAY** and **SELE**, BARON (*d.* 1450). [See FIENNES, JAMES.]

SAYER, AUGUSTIN (1790–1861), physician; B.A., 1811, and M.A., 1813 (university unknown); M.D. Leyden, 1815; F.R.C.P., 1843; president, Royal Medical and Chirurgical Society, 1840; physician to Duke of Kent; physician to Lock Hospital and Asylum; published works relating to sanitary reform. [l. 390]

SAYER or **SEARE**, ROBERT, in religion GREGORY (1560–1602), Benedictine; B.A. Peterhouse, Cambridge, 1581; studied at college of Douay (then temporarily at Rheims) and at English College, Rome; Benedictine monk, 1588, at Monte Cassino, where he became professor of moral philosophy; at monastery of St. George, Venice, 1595–1602; published theological works. [l. 390]

SAYERS, FRANK (1763–1817), poet; studied surgery under John Hunter in London and medicine and science at Edinburgh; M.D. Hardervyck; abandoned medicine for literature; lived at Norwich; works include 'Dramatic Sketches of Northern Mythology,' 1790. [l. 391]

SAYERS or **SAYER**, JAMES (1748–1823), caricaturist; articled as attorney at Yarmouth; worked from *c.* 1780 as political caricaturist in London, supporting Pitt against Fox; appointed marshal of court of exchequer when Pitt succeeded to office. [l. 392]

SAYERS, TOM (1826–1865), pugilist; bricklayer at Brighton, and (1848) in London; began pugilistic career, 1849, when he beat Crouch at Greenhithe; beaten by Nat Langham, 1853; won champion's belt, 1857; his last fight was with the American John C. Heenan (the Benicia Boy), at Farnborough, 1860, the result being declared a draw. [l. 392]

SAYLE, WILLIAM (*d.* 1671), colonist; councillor in the Bermudas, 1630; governor, 1641–2 and 1643; reappointed with two colleagues, 1644; again governor, 1658–1662; governor of Charlestown, the nucleus of South Carolina, 1670. [l. 393]

SAYWELL, WILLIAM (1643–1701), divine; fellow, St. John's College, Cambridge, 1666; M.A., 1667; incorporated at Oxford, 1669; D.D.; prebendary of Ely and master of Jesus College, Cambridge, 1679–1701; chancellor of diocese of Chichester, 1672–1701; archdeacon of Ely, 1681–1701; published Latin verse and controversial treatises. [l. 394]

SCALBY, **SCALLEBY**, or **SCHALBY**, JOHN DE (*d.* 1333), registrar and canon of Lincoln Cathedral. [l. 394]

SCALES, BARON (1442?–1483). [See WOODVILLE or WYDEVILLE, ANTHONY, second EARL RIVERS.]

SCALES, THOMAS DE, seventh BARON SCALES (1399?-1460), served under John of Lancaster, duke of Bedford [q. v.], in French wars, 1422; K.G., 1425; captain of St. James de Beuvron; sent to Brittany by Bedford to aid John V against Alençon, 1431; seneschal of Normandy, c. 1434; took part in capture of Meaux and in defeat of Richemont before Avranches, 1439; raised force against Jack Cade and commanded in fight on London Bridge, 1450; took side of Lancastrians; assisted in defence of Tower of London, 1460, and was murdered while going to seek sanctuary at Westminster. [l. 395]

SCAMBLER, EDMUND (1510?-1594), bishop of Norwich; educated at Peterhouse, Queens', and Jesus colleges, Cambridge; B.A., 1542; D.D., 1564; incorporated at Oxford, 1584; chaplain to Archbishop Parker, 1558; prebendary of York and canon of Westminster, 1560; bishop of Peterborough, 1561-84, and of Norwich, 1584-94; assisted in translation of 'Bishops' Bible'; published religious writings. [l. 396]

SCANDRETT, SCANDRET, or **SCANDERET,** STEPHEN (1631?-1706), puritan divine; M.A. Wadham College, Oxford, 1659; incorporated at Cambridge, 1659, and became 'conduct' of Trinity College, Cambridge; expelled from office, 1660; received presbyterian ordination; published theological writings. [l. 396]

SCARBOROUGH, EARL OF (d. 1721). [See LUMLEY, RICHARD.]

SCARBURGH, SIR CHARLES (1616-1694), physician; of St. Paul's School, London, and Caius College, Cambridge; M.A. and fellow, 1640; ejected during great rebellion; M.D. Merton College, Oxford, 1646; incorporated M.D. Cambridge, 1660; F.R.C.P. London, 1650; censor, 1655, 1664, and 1665; Lumleian lecturer, 1656; anatomical reader to Barber Surgeons' Company, 1649; original F.R.S.; physician to Charles II, 1660, and subsequently to James II, Queen Mary, and Prince George of Denmark; knighted, 1669; published a work on dissection, and left mathematical manuscripts. [l. 397]

SCARDEBURG, ROBERT DE (fl. 1341), chief-justice of common pleas in Ireland, 1331-4; judge of king's bench in England, 1334-9 and 1341-4, and of common pleas, 1339-41. [l. 398]

SCARGILL, WILLIAM PITT (1787-1836), divine; minister of Churchgate Street Chapel, Bury St. Edmunds, 1812-32; joined established church, 1832, and made precarious living as author; published tales and other writings. [l. 398]

SCARISBRICK, EDWARD (1639-1709). [See NEVILLE, EDWARD.]

SCARLE, JOHN DE (d. 1403?), divine; clerk in chancery, 1378 and 1397; prebendary of Aberguylly, 1379; keeper of rolls, 1394-7; chancellor, 1399-1401; archdeacon of Lincoln, 1401. [l. 399]

SCARLETT, JAMES, first BARON ABINGER (1769-1844), born in Jamaica; entered Inner Temple, 1785; B.A. Trinity College, Cambridge, 1789; barrister, Inner Temple, 1791; K.C. and bencher, 1816; M.A., 1794; whig M.P. for Peterborough, 1819, 1820-2, and 1823-30; on committee to inquire into laws relating to capital punishment in felonies; knighted and appointed attorney-general in Canning's ministry, 1827-8, and in Wellington's, 1829-30; successfully brought in bill for improving administration of justice, 1830; M.P., Malton, 1830; opposed Reform Bill, 1831; tory M.P. for Cockermouth, 1831, and for Norwich, 1832; privy councillor, serjeant-at-law, and chief baron of exchequer, 1834; created Baron Abinger of Abinger in Surrey and of city of Norwich and LL.D. Cambridge, 1835. Several of his speeches were published. [l. 399]

SCARLETT, SIR JAMES YORKE (1799-1871), general; son of James Scarlett, first baron Abinger [q. v.]; of Eton and Trinity College, Cambridge; cornet, 1818; major, 5th dragoon guards, 1830; conservative M.P. for Guildford, 1836-41; commanded his regiment, 1840-54; appointed to command of heavy brigade in Turkey, 1854; went to Sebastopol, September 1854; led charge of heavy brigade at Balaclava, 25 Oct. 1854; major-general; K.C.B., 1855; proceeded to England, 1855, but was appointed to command entire British cavalry in Crimea and returned; at conclusion of war

commanded cavalry in Aldershot district; transferred to Portsmouth; adjutant-general, 1860; commander of Aldershot camp, 1865-70; G.C.B., 1869. [l. 402]

SCARLETT, NATHANIEL (1753-1802), bookseller; educated at Merchant Taylors' School, London; successively shipwright, accountant, and bookseller in Strand, London; produced, with assistance, translation of New Testament, published, 1798. [l. 404]

SCARLETT, PETER CAMPBELL (1804-1881), diplomatist; son of James Scarlett, first baron Abinger [q. v.]; of Eton and Trinity College, Cambridge; attaché at Constantinople, 1825, and at Paris, 1828; C.B. and secretary of legation at Florence, 1854; envoy extraordinary at Rio Janeiro, 1855; minister at Florence, 1858-60; envoy extraordinary at Athens, 1862, and in Mexico, 1864-7. [l. 404]

SCARLETT, ROBERT (1499?-1594), known as 'Old Scarlett'; sexton at Peterborough Cathedral before 1535 till 1594; a portrait of him is in the cathedral. [l. 405]

SCARTH, ALICE MARY ELIZABETH (1848-1889), author; daughter of Harry Mengden Scarth [q. v.] [l. 406]

SCARTH, HARRY MENGDEN (1814-1890), antiquary; M.A. Christ's College, Cambridge, 1841; incorporated at Oxford, 1842; held livings in Somerset; prebendary of Wells, 1848; rural dean of Portishead, c. 1880; published antiquarian writings. [l. 405]

SCATCHERD, NORRISSON CAVENDISH (1780-1853), antiquary; barrister, Gray's Inn, 1806; F.S.A., 1851; published antiquarian writings. [l. 406]

SCATTERGOOD, ANTONY (1611-1687), divine; B.A. Trinity College, Cambridge, 1633; chaplain at Trinity College, Cambridge, 1637-40; rector of Winwick, 1641-1687; canon of Lincoln, 1641; chaplain and librarian to bishop of Lincoln; D.D. Cambridge, 1663; prebendary of Lichfield, 1664-82; D.D. Oxford, 1669; published biblical criticism, and added many references to a folio bible printed at Cambridge, 1678. [l. 406]

SCATTERGOOD, SAMUEL (1646-1696), divine; son of Antony Scattergood [q. v.]; B.A. Trinity College, Cambridge, 1665; M.A. and fellow, and incorporated at Oxford, 1669; vicar of St. Mary's, Lichfield, 1678-81, of Ware, and, later, of Blockley, 1681; prebendary of Lichfield, 1682, and of Lincoln, 1683; his sermons were published posthumously. [l. 407]

SCHALBY, JOHN DE (d. 1333). [See SCALBY.]

SCHALCH, ANDREW (1692-1776), master-founder; born at Schaffhausen; employed in cannon foundry at Douay; came to England; master-founder of the Warren (afterwards the Arsenal), Woolwich, 1716-76. [l. 407]

SCHANCK, JOHN (1740-1823), admiral; entered navy as seaman, 1758; lieutenant, 1776; in charge of naval establishment at St. John, Canada; attached to Burgoyne's army, 1777; captain, 1783; successfully submitted to admiralty scheme for boat with sliding keel; superintendent of coast defence; vice-admiral, 1810; admiral, 1821. [l. 408]

SCHARF, GEORGE (1788-1860), draughtsman and lithographer; born at Mainburg, Bavaria; studied at Munich; joined English army, 1814, and was at Waterloo; went to London, 1816, and practised as lithographer and painter; exhibited at Royal Academy from 1817. [l. 409]

SCHARF, SIR GEORGE (1820-1895), writer on art; son of George Scharf [q. v.]; educated at University College School, London; studied at Royal Academy; accompanied Sir Charles Fellows to Asia Minor, 1840; draughtsman to government expedition to Asia Minor, c. 1843; devoted himself to illustration of books, including Dr. Smith's classical dictionaries; assisted Charles Kean in scenery and costumes in his Shakespearean revivals, 1851-1857; art lecturer at Queen's College, Harley Street, London; art secretary to Manchester exhibition, 1857; first secretary of National Portrait Gallery, 1857; received title of director, 1882; F.S.A., 1852; C.B., 1885; retired and was made K.C.B., 1895; wrote extensively on subject of portraiture. [l. 410]

SCHARPE, GEORGE (d. 1638), physician; born in Scotland; studied medicine at Montpellier, where he graduated, 1607, and was professor of medicine, 1619; vice-chancellor of the faculty, 1632; professor of medicine at Bologna, 1634; published medical writings.   [l. 411]

SCHAUB, SIR LUKE (d. 1758), diplomatist; in charge of English embassy at Vienna, 1715; attached to English mission at Copenhagen, 1716; private secretary to James, afterwards first earl Stanhope, 1717; English agent at Madrid, 1718; knighted, 1720; English ambassador at Paris, 1721-4; intimate with George II.   [l. 412]

SCHAW, WILLIAM (1550-1602), architect; 'master of works' in household of James VI, whom he accompanied in Denmark, 1589-90; did much to develop free-masonry in Scotland; executed repairs at many Scottish castles.   [l. 413]

SCHAW, WILLIAM (1714?-1757), physician; M.D. Edinburgh, 1735, and Cambridge, 1753; F.R.C.P. London, 1754; published medical writings.   [l. 414]

SCHEEMAKERS, PETER (1691-1770), sculptor; born at Antwerp; with Laurent Delvaux [q. v.] worked for Francis Bird [q. v.] in London; in Rome, 1728-35; practised in London from 1735-69. Many of his works are in Westminster Abbey.   [l. 414]

SCHEEMAKERS, THOMAS (1740-1808), sculptor; son of Peter Scheemakers [q. v.]; exhibited at Royal Academy between 1765 and 1804.   [l. 414]

SCHETKY, JOHN ALEXANDER (1785-1824), amateur painter in water-colours; served in Portugal as assistant-surgeon in 3rd dragoon guards; surgeon on Portuguese staff, 1812; member of Associated Painters in Water-colours; deputy-inspector of hospitals on west coast of Africa, 1823.   [l 414]

SCHETKY, JOHN CHRISTIAN (1778-1874), marine painter; brother of John Alexander Schetky [q. v.]; educated at high school, Edinburgh; studied drawing under Alexander Nasmyth [q. v.]; exhibited at Royal Academy between 1805 and 1872; junior professor of civil drawing at Royal Military College, Great Marlow, 1808-1811; professor of drawing in Royal Naval College, Portsmouth, 1811-36, and at military college, Addiscombe, 1836-55; marine painter in ordinary to George IV and William IV and, from 1844, to Queen Victoria.   [l. 415]

SCHEUTZER, JOHN GASPAR (1702-1729), physician; born in Switzerland; graduated at Zürich, 1722; came to England; F.R.S., 1724; L.R.C.P., 1725; created M.D. Cambridge, 1728; published work on smallpox.   [l. 416]

SCHEVEZ or **SCHIVES**, WILLIAM (d. 1497), archbishop of St. Andrews; studied at Louvain; master of hospital of St. Mary of Brechin; archdeacon of St. Andrews, 1459; 'coadjutor of St. Andrews,' 1477; archbishop of St. Andrews, 1478; frequently employed on political missions; joined conspiracy of nobles against James III, and retained power under new king.   [l. 417]

SCHIAVONETTI, LUIGI (1765-1810), line-engraver; born at Bassano, Italy; came to England, 1790; was assisted by Bartolozzi, and subsequently practised independently.   [l. 417]

SCHIAVONETTI, NICCOLÒ (1771-1813), engraver; brother of Luigi Schiavonetti [q. v.], whom he assisted.   [l. 417]

SCHIMMELPENNINCK, MRS. MARY ANNE (1778-1856), author; daughter of Samuel Galton and his wife Lucy Barclay (d. 1817); married Lambert Schimmelpenninck of Bristol, 1806; published miscellaneous works, including (1822) a sketch of the modern history of the Moravians, which sect she had joined, 1818.   [l. 417]

SCHIPTON, JOHN OF (d. 1257). [See JOHN.]

SCHMIDT, BERNARD (1630?-1708). [See SMITH.]

SCHMITZ, LEONHARD (1807-1890), scholar; born at Eupen, near Aix-la-Chapelle; studied at Bonn; Ph.D., 1841; assisted in founding (c. 1843) 'Classical Museum' quarterly, which he conducted till 1849; published translation of Niebuhr's 'Lectures on History of Rome,' 1844; rector of high school, Edinburgh, 1845-66; tutor to Albert Edward, prince of Wales, 1859, and Duke of Edinburgh, 1862-3; principal of London International College, Isleworth 1866-74; LL.D. Aberdeen, 1849, and Edinburgh, 1886; translated learned works from English into German and from German into English.   [l. 418]

SCHNEBBELIE, JACOB (1760-1792), topographical draughtsman; confectioner successively at Canterbury and Hammersmith; became drawing-master; draughtsman to Society of Antiquaries; produced many topographical drawings.   [l. 420]

SCHNEBBELIE, ROBERT BREMMEL (d. 1849?), topographical artist; son of Jacob Schnebbelie; exhibited at Royal Academy, 1803-21.   [l. 420]

SCHOLEFIELD, JAMES (1789-1853), classical scholar; of Christ's Hospital, London, and Trinity College, Cambridge; fellow, 1815-27; M.A., 1816; perpetual curate of St. Michael's, Cambridge, 1823; regius professor of Greek, 1825-53; published collected works of Peter Paul Dobree [q. v.], 1831-5; canon of Ely, 1849; published religious and classical works, including an edition of Porson's 'Four Tragedies of Euripides,' 1826; commemorated by the Scholefield theological prize founded at Cambridge, 1856.   [l. 420]

SCHOLEFIELD, JOSHUA (1744-1844), banker and merchant at Birmingham; radical M.P. for Birmingham, 1832, 1835, 1837, and 1841.   [l. 421]

SCHOLEFIELD, WILLIAM (1809-1867), politician; son of Joshua Scholefield [q. v.]; first mayor of Birmingham, 1838; radical M.P. for Birmingham, 1847, 1852, and 1857-67.   [l. 421]

SCHOLES, JAMES CHRISTOPHER (1852-1890), antiquary; author of a 'History of Bolton,' issued 1892.   [l. 422]

SCHOMBERG, SIR ALEXANDER (1720-1804), navy captain; son of Meyer Löw Schomberg [q. v.]; entered navy, 1743; captain, 1757; served at Louisbourg, and (1759) at capture of Quebec; took part in reduction of Belle-isle, 1761; served off Brest and in Bay of Biscay, 1761-3; commander of Dorset yacht attached to lord-lieutenant of Ireland, 1771-1804; knighted, 1777.   [l. 422]

SCHOMBERG, ALEXANDER CROWCHER (1756-1792), author; son of Raphael Schomberg [q. v.]; of Winchester College and Magdalen College, Oxford; M.A., 1781; probationer fellow, 1782; senior dean of arts, 1791; published poetical writings and treatises on jurisprudence.   [l. 423]

SCHOMBERG, ALEXANDER WILMOT (1774-1850), admiral; son of Sir Alexander Schomberg [q. v.]; lieutenant, 1793; captain, 1801; rear-admiral, 1830; admiral, 1849; published work on shipbuilding.   [l. 423]

SCHOMBERG, CHARLES, second DUKE OF SCHOMBERG (1645-1693), son of Frederick Herman, first duke of Schomberg [q. v.], with whom he served as lieutenant-colonel in Roussillon, 1674; served under Créqui in war against Holland; joined service of elector of Brandenburg, and was major-general of infantry and governor of Magdeburg; attended his father in England, 1688; succeeded his father (by limitation), 1690; lieutenant-general in Savoy, 1691; conducted expedition into Dauphiné, 1692; died of wounds received at Marsaglia.   [l. 431]

SCHOMBERG, SIR CHARLES MARSH (1779-1835), commodore; lieutenant, 1795; flag-lieutenant to George Keith Elphinstone, viscount Keith [q. v.], in Egyptian campaign, 1800-1; commander, 1802; captain, 1803; at Malta, 1803-7; senior officer at Mauritius, 1810-13; C.B., 1815, in Mediterranean, 1820-4; commodore and commander-in-chief at Cape of Good Hope, 1828-32; nominated K.C.H. and knighted, 1832; lieutenant-governor of Dominica.   [l. 424]

SCHOMBERG or **SCHÖNBERG**, FREDERICK HERMAN, DUKE OF SCHOMBERG (1615-1690), born at Heidelberg; his mother, Anne, daughter of Edward Sutton, ninth lord Dudley; studied at Sedan, Paris, and Leyden; volunteer in army of Frederick Henry, prince of Orange, 1633; served with Swedish army in Germany under Bernhard of Weimar, 1634; under Rantzau in Franche-Comté, 1636, and in Holstein and East Friesland, 1637; lieutenant in service of Frederick Henry, 1639; at capture of Gennep, 1641; served under Prince de Tarente in Holland, 1645; first gentleman of chamber to William II of Orange; captain in Scottish guards in French army, with rank of maréchal-de-camp, 1652-4; raised infantry regiment in Germany, and was lieutenant-general, 1655; governor of St. Guislain, 1655; surrendered to Spaniards, 1657; captured and became governor of Bourbourg, 1657;

at battle of the Dunes, 1658; governor of Winoxbergen, 1658; maréchal-de-camp in Portuguese service and general of forces in province of Alemtejo, 1660; in England, 1660, and created by Charles II baron of Tetford; served against Don John, 1660-8; defeated Don John at Almeixal or Estremos, 1663, and received chief command and title of Count of Mertola; defeated Don John at Montes Claros, and later Prince of Parma and Marquis of Caracena on the Cebora, 1665; went to Rochelle after peace between Spain and Portugal, 1668, and resided at Coubert in France, 1668-71; came to England, 1673, and entered services as commander under Prince Rupert; returned to Coubert, 1673, and commanded army between Sambre and Meuse; received rank of duc; commander-in-chief of forces in Roussillon, 1674-6; defeated by Spanish at Ceret; took Bellegarde, 1675; marshal, 1675; appointed to army in Flanders under Duke of Orleans, 1676, and commanded attack on Condé; at capture of Valenciennes and Cambray, 1677; commanded army on Meuse, 1677-8; occupied duchy of Cleves, 1679; commanded under Louis XIV in Flanders on renewal of war with Spain, 1684, and took part in capture of Luxembourg; allowed to retire to Portugal after revocation of edict of Nantes, 1685; entered service of elector of Brandenburg, and became general-in chief of armies, 1687; accompanied William of Orange to England, 1688; received order of Garter, and was made master-general of ordnance; created Baron of Teyes, Earl of Brentford, Marquis of Harwich, and Duke of Schomberg, 1689; commander-in-chief of forces in Ireland; conducted campaign in Ireland, 1689-90, and was killed at battle of Boyne; buried in St. Patrick's Cathedral, Dublin. [l. 424]

SCHOMBERG, ISAAC (1714-1780), physician; son of Meyer Löw Schomberg [q. v.]; born at Schweinberg; educated at Merchant Taylors' School, London; practised medicine in London; studied medicine at Trinity College, Cambridge, and graduated M.D., 1749; summoned by president and censors of College of Physicians, 1747, to present himself for examination as licentiate, but declined, on which his practice was interdicted till 1765, when he was admitted licentiate; fellow, 1771; censor, 1773 and 1778; attended Garrick in his last illness. [l. 432]

SCHOMBERG, ISAAC (1753-1813), navy captain; entered navy, 1770; lieutenant, 1777; first lieutenant under Prince William [see WILLIAM IV] in West Indies, 1786; superseded, 1787; under Cornwallis in East Indies, 1789-90; captain, 1790; at battle of 1 June 1794; commissioner and deputy-comptroller of navy, 1808-13; published 'Naval Chronology,' 1802. [l. 433]

SCHOMBERG, MEINHARD, DUKE OF LEINSTER and third DUKE OF SCHOMBERG (1641-1719), son of Frederick Herman, duke of Schomberg [q. v.]; lieutenant-colonel with his father in Portugal, 1660-8; naturalised French subject, 1668; brigadier and maréchal-de-camp in wars against Holland; served against Turks in Hungary, 1686; general of cavalry and colonel of dragoons in service of Elector Frederick William; came to England, 1689; fought as general of horse at the Boyne and Limerick, 1690; created Baron of Tarragh, Earl of Bangor, and Duke of Leinster, 1692; lieutenant-general of British forces; succeeded his brother Charles Schomberg [q. v.] as Duke of Schomberg, 1693; privy councillor, 1695; K.G., 1703; commander of English auxiliary forces in war of Spanish succession, 1703-4; buried in Westminster Abbey. [l. 434]

SCHOMBERG, MEYER LÖW (1690-1761), physician; born at Fetzburg, Germany; M.D. Giessen, 1710; came to England, c. 1720; L.R.C.P. London, 1722; F.R.S., 1726; practised in London. [l. 435]

SCHOMBERG, RAPHAEL or RALPH (1714-1792), physician and miscellaneous writer; son of Meyer Löw Schomberg [q. v]; born at Schweinberg; educated at Merchant Taylors' School, London; studied medicine abroad; M.D. Aberdeen; practised successively at Yarmouth, Bath, and Reading; F.S.A., 1752; published miscellaneous writings. [l. 436]

SCHOMBURGK, RICHARD (1811-1890), botanist; brother of Sir Robert Hermann Schomburgk [q.v.]; born at Freiburg; educated at Berlin and Potsdam; botanist to British Guiana boundary expedition, 1840-2; director of botanic gardens, Adelaide, 1866-90. [l. 438]

SCHOMBURGK, SIR ROBERT HERMANN (1804-1865), traveller; born at Freiburg; educated in Germany; surveyed littoral of Anegada, one of Virgin islands, 1831; explored British Guiana under direction of Royal Geographical Society, 1831-5, and was awarded gold medal, 1840; government commissioner for surveying and making boundaries of British Guiana, 1841-3, establishing 'Schomburgk line'; knighted, 1844; British consul at San Domingo, 1848, and at Bangkok, 1857-64; Ph.D. Königsberg; M.D. Jena; published descriptions of British Guiana and Barbados. [l. 437]

SCHONAU, ANIAN DE (d. 1293), bishop of St. Asaph; probably born in Netherlands; prior of Dominican house at Rhuddlan; bishop of St. Asaph, 1268; said to have been confessor to Edward I and to have accompanied him on crusade; arrested and detained by Edward I in England, c. 1283, perhaps for failure to excommunicate Welsh disturbers of peace. [l. 438]

SCHORLEMMER, CARL (1834-1892), chemist; born at Darmstadt; studied chemistry at Heidelberg and Giessen; assistant in Manchester College laboratory, 1861; lecturer, 1873; professor of organic chemistry, 1874; established hypothesis that normal paraffins form a single, not a double, series; F.R.S., 1871; honorary LL.D. Glasgow, 1888; began publication, with Roscoe, of 'Systematic Treatise on Chemistry' (in English and German, first vol. 1877); published other chemical works and translations in German and English, and left unfinished a German manuscript history of chemistry. [l. 439]

SCHREIBER, LADY CHARLOTTE ELIZABETH (1812-1895), Welsh scholar; daughter of Albemarle Bertie, ninth earl of Lindsey; married, 1833, Sir Josiah John Guest (1785-1852) [q. v.], whose ironworks at Dowlais she managed after his death; married, 1855, Charles Schreiber, M.D. (d. 1884); collected old china, fans, and playing-cards, and presented many specimens to the South Kensington and British museums; published 'Mabinogion' from old Welsh manuscripts with translations (1838-49), and works relating to her collections. [l. 440]

SCHROEDER, HENRY (1774-1853), topographer and engraver; practised under name William Butterworth; published topographical and other works, and was one of compilers of 'Pigott's General Directory.' [l. 441]

SCHULENBURG, COUNTESS EHRENGARD MELUSINA VON DER, DUCHESS OF KENDAL (1667-1743), born at Emden, Saxony; maid of honour to Duchess (from 1692, Electress) Sophia at Hanover; gained favour of Sophia's son, Prince George (afterwards George I), and was one of his mistresses from 1698; came to England, c. 1714; created Baroness of Dundalk, Countess and Marchioness of Dungannon, and Duchess of Munster in Irish peerage, 1716, and Baroness of Glastonbury, Countess of Feversham and Duchess of Kendal, 1719; created by Charles VI princess of the empire under title of Princess of Eberstein, 1723; exercised considerable influence in politics; accompanied George I to Germany, 1727, and after his death lived in retirement at Kendal House, Isleworth. [l. 441]

SCHWANFELDER, CHARLES HENRY (1773-1837), painter; trained as painter of clock-faces, tea-trays, and snuff-boxes, at Leeds; subsequently practised as landscape-painter and animal-painter; exhibited at Royal Academy, 1809-1826. [l. 443]

SCHWARTZ or **SWARTZ**, CHRISTIAN FRIEDRICH (1726-1798), Indian missionary; born at Sonnenburg, Prussia; educated at university of Halle, where he assisted Schultz in new edition of Tamil bible; ordained at Copenhagen, 1749; went with Schultz and others to Danish mission at Tranquebar, 1750; received charge of district south of the Caveri; at Trichinopoly, 1762; chaplain to Major Preston's troops, 1764, at siege of Madura, where Christ's Church was dedicated, 1766; chaplain to troops at Trichinopoly, 1768-78; took up residence at Tanjore, 1778; went on secret mission to Hyder Ali; instituted system of government schools; appointed government interpreter; died at Tanjore. [l. 443]

SCHWARTZ, MARTIN (d. 1487), captain of German mercenaries sent by Margaret, dowager duchess of Burgundy, to aid Lambert Simnel, 1487; killed in battle at Stoke, near Newark. [l. 446]

SCHWEICKHARDT, HEINRICH WILHELM (1746–1797), landscape-painter; born in Brandenburg; came to London, c. 1786; exhibited at Royal Academy, 1788–96. [l. 446]

SCLATER, EDWARD (1623–1699 ?), divine; educated at Merchant Taylors' School, London, and St. John's College, Oxford; M.A., 1648; refused covenant and was ejected from St. John's by parliamentary visitors, 1648; perpetual curate of St. Mary's, Putney, 1663; turned Roman catholic on accession of James II, but again joined church of England, 1688; published works vindicating his changes of opinion. [l. 446]

SCLATER, WILLIAM (1575–1626), divine; of Eton and King's College, Cambridge; fellow, 1596; M.A., 1599; rector of Pitminster, 1604–19; received living of Limpsham, 1619, but returned to Pitminster, where he died; published religious works. [l. 447]

SCLATER, WILLIAM (1609–1661), divine; son of William Sclater (1575–1626) [q. v.]; educated at Eton and King's College, Cambridge; fellow, 1629–33; M.A.; priest, c. 1630; prebendary of Exeter and rector of St. Stephen's, Exeter, 1641; driven from livings, 1644; D.D., 1651; conformed and was rector of St. Peter-le-Poer, Broad Street, London, 1650–61; published religious works. [l. 448]

SCLATER, WILLIAM (1638–1717 ?), nonjuring divine; son of William Sclater (1609–1661) [q. v.]; of Merchant Taylors' School, London, and Pembroke College, Oxford; vicar of Bramford Speke, 1663; refused oath of allegiance after revolution and was ejected; published controversial writings. [l. 448]

SCLATER-BOOTH, GEORGE, first BARON BASING (1826–1894), of Winchester College and Balliol College, Oxford; B.A., 1847; barrister, Inner Temple, 1851; conservative M.P. for North Hampshire, 1857; financial secretary to treasury, 1868; president of local government board, 1874–80; chairman of grand committees in house, 1880; raised to peerage, 1887; privy councillor; LL.D.; F.R.S. [l. 449]

SCOBELL, HENRY (d. 1660), clerk of the parliament: appointed for life, 1648; joint-licenser of newspapers and political pamphlets, 1649; assistant-secretary to council of state, 1653; published works on parliamentary procedure. [l. 449]

SCOFFIN, WILLIAM (1655 ?–1732), nonconformist minister at Sleaford; published religious and other works. [li. 1]

SCOGAN or **SCOGGIN,** HENRY (1361 ?–1407), poet; disciple of Chaucer; tutor to four sons of Henry IV; succeeded his brother John as lord of Haviles, 1391; some of his poems have been accepted as Chaucer's. [li. 1]

SCOGAN, JOHN (fl. 1480), fool at court of Edward IV; perhaps M.A. Oriel College, Oxford, and fool at Edward IV's court, whence he was temporarily banished to France. It is not improbable that his biography, which is supplied in his 'Jests,' said to have been compiled by Andrew Boorde [q. v.], is apocryphal and that Scogan is a fictitious hero. [li. 2]

SCOLES, JOSEPH JOHN (1798–1863), architect; studied abroad with Joseph Bonomi the younger [q. v.]; practised in London; F.R.I.B.A., 1835; published topographical and archæological works. [li. 3]

SCOLOKER, ANTHONY (fl. 1548), printer and translator; established printing press in London, 1547, and at Ipswich, 1548; translated works into English from German, Dutch, and French. [li. 4]

SCOLOKER, ANTHONY (fl. 1604), author of 'Daiphantus, or the Passions of Loue,' which contains references to Shakespeare. 1604. [li. 4]

SCORBURGH, SIR ROBERT DE (d. 1340), baron of the exchequer; baron of exchequer and knight, 1332; chief baron of exchequer at Dublin, 1334; justice of king's bench in Dublin, 1337. [li. 5]

SCORESBY, WILLIAM (1760–1829), arctic navigator; apprenticed on vessel trading to Baltic, 1780; employed in Greenland whale fishery, 1785–90; captain, 1790; retired, 1823. In 1806 he reached the latitude of 81° 30' longitude, long the highest reached by any ship. [li. 5]

SCORESBY, WILLIAM (1789–1857), son of William Scoresby (1760–1829) [q. v.]; served under his father between 1800 and 1806; studied at Edinburgh University; volunteered for service with fleet at Copenhagen, 1807; served as captain in Greenland fishery, made several scientific observations, and occupied himself with arctic problems; F.R.S. Edinburgh, 1819; entered Queens' College, Cambridge, 1823; F.R.S., 1824; chaplain of mariners' church, Liverpool, 1827; incumbent of Bedford Chapel, Exeter, 1832; B.D., 1834; D.D., 1839; vicar of Bradford, 1839–47; made a voyage to Australia to carry out magnetic observations, 1856; published scientific works relating chiefly to the Arctic seas. [li. 6]

SCORESBY-JACKSON, ROBERT EDMUND (1835–1867). [See JACKSON.]

SCORY, JOHN (d. 1585), bishop successively of Rochester, Chichester, and Hereford; Dominican friar at Cambridge, c. 1530; B.D., 1539; chaplain to Cranmer, 1541; examining chaplain to Ridley, c. 1550; bishop of Rochester, 1551; translated to Chichester, 1552; deprived on Queen Mary's accession, but recanted and officiated in London diocese; retired to Emden, Friesland; returned, 1558; bishop of Hereford, 1559–85; published religious works. [li. 8]

SCOT. [See also SCOTT.]

SCOT, DAVID (1770 ?–1834), divine; educated at Edinburgh; licensed preacher, 1795; M.D., 1812; studied oriental languages; held living of Corstorphine, 1814–33; professor of Hebrew, St. Mary's College, St. Andrews, 1833; published miscellaneous works. [li. 9]

SCOTLAND, HENRY OF (1114 ?–1152). [See HENRY.]

SCOTSTARVET, SIR JOHN OF (1585–1670). [See SCOTT, SIR JOHN.]

SCOTT. [See also SCOT.]

SCOTT, ALEXANDER (1525 ?–1584 ?), poet; probably lived in or near Edinburgh; wrote short poems preserved only in Bannatyne manuscript, compiled, 1568. [li. 10]

SCOTT, ALEXANDER JOHN (1768–1840), naval chaplain; of Charterhouse School and St. John's College, Cambridge; B.A., 1791; chaplain with Captain Sir John Collins, 1793, and of Sir Hyde Parker's flagship, 1795; accompanied Parker to West Indies, and held living in Jamaica; joined Parker at Copenhagen and was secretary to conference on shore; accompanied Nelson to Mediterranean (1803) as private secretary and interpreter, and was chaplain of the Victory; attended Nelson at his death; D.D. Cambridge; presented to crown living of Catterick, and appointed chaplain to George, prince regent, 1816. [li. 10]

SCOTT, ALEXANDER JOHN (1805–1866), divine; M.A. Glasgow, 1827; assistant in London to Edward Irving [q. v.], 1828; received invitation to pastorate of Scottish church at Woolwich, 1830, but refused subscription to Westminster confession of faith and was deprived of license, 1831; minister of congregation at Woolwich till 1846; professor of English language and literature, University College, London, 1848; first principal of the Owens College, Manchester, 1851–7; took part in starting Manchester Working Men's College. [li. 12]

SCOTT, ANDREW (1757–1839), Scottish poet; son of a labourer; enlisted and served in American war of independence, and was subsequently a farm labourer at Bowden; published several volumes of poems. [li. 13]

SCOTT, BENJAMIN (1788–1830), divine; youngest son of Thomas Scott (1747–1821) [q. v.]; M.A. Queens' College, Cambridge, 1813; vicar of Bidford and of Priors Salford, 1828; wrote sermons, published, 1831. [li. 75]

SCOTT, BENJAMIN (1814–1892), chamberlain of London; junior clerk in office of chamberlain of London; chief clerk, 1841; chamberlain of London, 1853 and 1858 till shortly before death, his financial knowledge being of great value to the corporation; social reformer and author of miscellaneous works. [li. 14]

SCOTT, CAROLINE LUCY, LADY SCOTT (1784–1857), novelist; daughter of Archibald, first baron Douglas (1748–1827); married Admiral Sir George Scott, 1810; published novels and other works. [li. 14]

SCOTT or **SCOT**, CUTHBERT (*d.* 1564), bishop of Chester; fellow, Christ's College, Cambridge, 1537; M.A., 1538, D.D., 1547; prebendary of York: master of Christ's College, Cambridge, 1553–6; D.D. Oxford, and prebendary of St. Paul's, London, 1554; vice-chancellor of Cambridge, 1554 and 1556; bishop of Chester, 1556; opposed ecclesiastical changes under Queen Elizabeth, was fined and imprisoned in Fleet, 1559–63; retired to Louvain, where he died. [li. 15]

SCOTT, DANIEL (1694–1759), theological writer; educated at Merchant Taylors' School, London, and studied for ministry at Gloucester and Leyden; LL.D. Leyden, 1719; joined Mennonite communion at Utrecht; probably exercised ministry at Colchester and in London; published theological works and an appendix to Stephanus's 'Thesaurus.' [li. 15]

SCOTT, DAVID (1806–1849), painter; son of Robert Scott (1777–1841) [q. v.]; worked as an engraver, but took to painting, and was one of founders of Edinburgh Life Academy Association, 1827; exhibited at Scottish Academy from 1828, and at Royal Academy, 1840 and 1845; in Italy, 1832. Among his best works are illustrations to the 'Ancient Mariner' and Professor Nichol's 'Architecture of the Heavens.' [li. 16]

SCOTT, ELIZABETH (1708 ?–1776), sister of Thomas Scott (1705–1775) [q. v.]; wrote, before 1750, many hymns, which subsequently were published in various collections. [li. 73]

SCOTT or **SCOT**, GEORGE (*d.* 1685), author; son of Sir John Scott or Scot [q. v.]; published, 1685, 'Model of Government of East New Jersey, America,' for which he received a grant of land from the proprietors of East New Jersey; died on outward voyage. [li. 18]

SCOTT, SIR GEORGE GILBERT (1811–1878), architect; grandson of Thomas Scott (1747–1821) [q. v.]; in office of Henry Roberts, a pupil of Sir Robert Smirke [q. v.], 1832–4; practised independently and in partnership with W. B. Moffat, 1834–45, and erected many buildings of the workhouse class; won open competition for church of St. Nicholas at Hamburg, 1844; appointed restoring architect to Ely Cathedral, 1847, and subsequently to cathedrals of Hereford, Lichfield, Salisbury, and Ripon, and executed restorations at many other cathedrals; architect to dean and chapter of Westminster Abbey, 1849; R.A., 1861; appointed architect for India office, 1858, and was compelled to abandon his original Gothic design for one in the Italian manner; subsequently commissioned to complete the block of buildings by the erection of the home and colonial offices; carried out Albert Memorial, 1864; designed St. Pancras station and hotel, London, 1865, and at about the same time buildings of Glasgow University; president of Royal Institute of British Architects, 1873–6; professor of architecture at Royal Academy from 1868; knighted, 1872; buried in Westminster Abbey. His excessive energy in restoration and renovation led to the establishment, in the last year of his life, of the Society for Protection of Ancient Buildings. He published works and pamphlets on architectural subjects. [li. 19]

SCOTT, GEORGE LEWIS (1708–1780), mathematician; barrister, Middle Temple; F.S.A., 1736; F.R.S., 1737; sub-preceptor to Prince George (afterwards George III), 1750; commissioner of excise, 1758–80; pupil of De Moivre and a celebrated mathematician. [li. 23]

SCOTT or **SCOT**, GREGORY (*d.* 1576), divine; of Eton and King's College, Cambridge; M.A., 1557; prebendary of Carlisle, 1564; chancellor of Carlisle, 1569, and vicar-general, 1570. [li. 23]

SCOTT, HARRIET ANNE, LADY SCOTT (1819–1894), *née* Shank; married Sir James Sibbald David Scott [q. v.], 1844; published novels. [li. 24]

SCOTT, HELENUS (1760–1821), physician; on medical staff of East India Company at Bombay, and subsequently at Bath; M.D. in practice, Aberdeen, 1797; L.R.C.P., 1815; wrote paper on use of nitromuriatic acid in medicine. [li. 24]

SCOTT, HENRY, first EARL OF DELORAINE (1676–1730), son of James Scott, duke of Monmouth [q. v.]; created Earl of Deloraine, 1706; chosen one of Scottish representative peers, 1715, 1722, and 1727; received order of Bath, 1725, and was gentleman of bedchamber to George I. [li. 24]

SCOTT, HENRY, third DUKE OF BUCCLEUCH and fifth DUKE OF QUEENSBERRY (1746–1812), son of Francis Scott, earl of Dalkeith; succeeded his grandfather as Duke of Buccleuch, 1751; educated at Eton; travelled abroad with Dr. Adam Smith [q. v.], author of the 'Wealth of Nations,' as tutor; first president of the Royal Society of Edinburgh, 1783; K.T., 1767; K.G., 1794; succeeded William Douglas, fourth duke of Queensberry [q. v.], as fifth duke, 1810; friend of Sir Walter Scott. [li. 25]

SCOTT, HENRY YOUNG DARRACOTT (1822–1883), major-general, royal engineers; educated at Military Academy, Woolwich; first lieutenant, royal engineers, 1843; senior instructor in field works at Woolwich, 1851; first captain and instructor in surveying at Brompton, Chatham, 1855; perfected the Scott selenitic lime; lieutenant-colonel, 1863; constructed Albert Hall, Kensington, 1866; C.B., 1871; retired as honorary major-general, 1871; F.R.S., 1875; for many years secretary to the Great Exhibition commissioners; wrote on engineering subjects. [li. 26]

SCOTT, HEW (1791–1872), divine; M.A. Aberdeen; preferred to charge of West Anstruther, 1839; D.D. St. Andrews; published 'Fasti Ecclesiæ Scoticanæ,' 1866–71. [li. 27]

SCOTT, SIR JAMES (*fl.* 1579–1606), politician; grandson of Sir William Scott or Scot, lord Balwearie (*d.* 1532) [q v.]; knighted, 1590; assisted Bothwell in attempt to seize James VI of Scotland at Falkland Palace, 1592; imprisoned at Edinburgh for complicity with Bothwell, Angus, Erroll, and Huntly, in plot against James VI, 1594; fined, but obtained remission. [li. 27]

SCOTT, JAMES (known as FITZROY and as CROFTS), DUKE OF MONMOUTH AND BUCCLEUCH (1649–1685), natural son of Charles II, by Lucy, daughter of Richard Walters of Haverfordwest; born at the Hague; entrusted on his mother's death to the care of Lord Crofts, as whose kinsman he passed; instructed in protestant religion; acknowledged by Charles II as his son, 1663, and made Baron Tyndale, Earl of Doncaster, Duke of Monmouth, and K.G.; married Anne Scott, countess of Buccleuch, and took surname of Scott, 1663; captain of Charles II's lifeguard of horse, 1668; privy councillor, 1670; captain-general of Charles II's forces, 1670; served against Dutch, 1672 and 1673; chancellor of Cambridge University, 1674; served against the French at Ostend and Mons, 1678; identified himself with protestant movement in England; quelled insurrection which ensued in Scotland on murder of Archbishop Sharp, 1679; deprived of commission as general, in consequence of reaction in favour of Duke of York, and banished, 1679; retired to Holland, but returned immediately and was deprived of all offices; deprived of chancellorship of Cambridge, 1682; made progress through west of England, and was arrested at Taunton, but released on bail; joined Russell, Essex, and Sidney in plot to murder Charles II and Duke of York; in conjunction with Essex, Howard, Russell, Hampden, and Sidney arranged for risings in England and Scotland; was promised pardon, having revealed to Charles II all he knew of the conspiracy after its discovery, but was banished from the court; retired to Zealand, 1684; treated with marked respect by Prince of Orange, who, however, dismissed him on death of Charles II; arranged with Argyll and Ferguson expedition to England; landed at Lyme Regis, 11 June 1685, and claimed as 'head and captain-general of protestant forces of the kingdom' a 'legitimate and legal' right to the crown; was proclaimed king at Taunton, 20 June; defeated by Feversham and Churchill at Sedgemoor, 5 July; escaped, but was captured; executed in the Tower of London, 15 July. Portraits of him by Lely and W. Wissing are in the National Portrait Gallery. [li. 28]

SCOTT, JAMES (1733–1814), political writer; of St. Catharine Hall and Trinity College, Cambridge; M.A., 1760; D.D., 1775; fellow of Trinity College, Cambridge, 1758; lecturer at St. John's, Leeds, 1758–69; curate at Edmonton, 1760–1; published political and religious writings in verse and prose. [li. 37]

SCOTT, SIR JAMES (1790 ?–1872), admiral; entered navy, 1803; lieutenant, 1809; flag-captain to Sir George Cockburn (1772–1853) [q. v.] in West Indies, 1834–6, and to Rear-admiral Ross in Pacific, 1837–40; on China station, 1840–1; K.C.B., 1862; admiral, 1865. [li. 37]

SCOTT, JAMES ROBERT HOPE- (1812–1873). [See HOPE-SCOTT.]

SCOTT, SIR JAMES SIBBALD DAVID, second baronet (1814–1885), antiquary; B.A. Christ Church. Oxford, 1835; succeeded to baronetcy, 1851; F.S.A.; published 'The British Army: its Origin, Progress, and Equipment,' 1868–80. [li. 38]

SCOTT, SIR JOHN (d. 1485), of Scot's Hall; son of Sir William Scott (d. 1350) [q. v.]; sheriff of Kent, 1460; knight and comptroller of Edward IV's household, 1461; engaged in diplomatic missions; M.P., Kent, 1467; lieutenant of Dover Castle, warden of Cinque ports, and marshal of Calais, 1470. [li. 106]

SCOTT or **SCOT**, JOHN (fl. 1530), printer in London; perhaps apprenticed to Wynkyn de Worde; printed books between 1521 and 1537. [li. 38]

SCOTT, JOHN (1484?–1533), son of Sir William Scott (1459–1524) [q. v.]; knighted for distinguished service in Low Countries, 1511; sheriff of Kent, 1527. [li. 106]

SCOTT or **SCOT**, JOHN (fl. 1552–1571), printer in Edinburgh and St. Andrews; his first dated book published in 1552, his last in 1571. [li. 39]

SCOTT, SIR JOHN (1570–1616), son of Sir Thomas Scott (1535–1594) [q. v.]; served in Low Countries, and was knighted, 1588; M.P., Kent, 1604–11, Maidstone, 1614; member of council of Virginia, 1607; councillor of Virginia Company of London, 1609. [li. 107]

SCOTT or **SCOT**, SIR JOHN (1585–1670), Scottish lawyer; succeeded to family office of director of chancery, 1606; educated at St. Leonard's College, St. Andrews; barrister, 1606; knighted and made privy councillor, 1617; ordinary lord of session, 1632; accepted covenant; served on war committee during war with England, 1648 and 1649; lost office of judge and director of chancery during Commonwealth, and retired to Scotstarvet, where he attracted round him as a liberal patron the learned Scotsmen of the time. He established a professorship of Latin at St. Andrews. His first wife (of three) was Anne, sister of William Drummond [q. v.] of Hawthornden. [li. 39]

SCOTT, JOHN (1639–1695), divine; B.D. and D.D. New Inn Hall, Oxford, 1685; held rectories in London; canon of St. Paul's, London, 1685–95; published religious works. [li. 41]

SCOTT, JOHN (fl. 1654–1696), adventurer; arrested by Dutch for treasonable practice with English on Long island, New Netherlands, 1654; president of provisional government formed by English settlers on Long island, 1663; joined Titus Oates in accusing Pepys and Sir Anthony Deane of betraying admiralty secrets to French, 1677. [li. 41]

SCOTT, JOHN (1730–1783), quaker poet; contributed to 'Gentleman's Magazine' from 1753; acquaintance of Dr. Johnson; works include 'Poetical Works' (1782) and 'Critical Essays' (posthumously, 1785). [li. 42]

SCOTT, JOHN, EARL OF CLONMELL (1739–1798), Irish judge; studied at Trinity College, Dublin, and at Middle Temple; called to Irish bar, 1765; M.P., Mullingar, 1769; K.C., 1770; solicitor-general, 1774; attorney-general and privy councillor, 1777; dismissed from office for denying right of Great Britain to bind Ireland by acts of parliament, 1782; chief-justice of king's bench in Ireland, 1784; created Viscount Clonmell, 1789, and earl, 1793; won considerable unpopularity by tyrannical treatment of the defendant John Magee (d. 1809) [q. v.], 1789. [li. 43]

SCOTT, afterwards **SCOTT-WARING**, JOHN (1747–1819), agent of Warren Hastings; brother of Jonathan Scott [q. v.]; entered service of East India Company, c. 1766, and became major in Bengal division of forces; commanded battalion of sepoys at Chanar, 1780; sent (1781) as political agent to England by Warren Hastings, whose affairs he conducted with great industry and small judgment, and whose impeachment was probably due to his injudicious zeal in his behalf; M.P., West Looe, 1784–90, Stockbridge, 1790; assumed name of Waring, 1798; published political writings. [li. 46]

SCOTT, JOHN (1783–1821), journalist; educated at Marischal College. Aberdeen; employed in war office, London; editor, 1813–c. 1816, of 'Drakard's Newspaper,' afterwards (1814) 'The Champion'; travelled on continent, and published volumes relating to his tours; first editor (1820–1) of 'London Magazine,' to which Lamb and other illustrious writers contributed; died from wounds received in a duel with Jonathan Christie, a friend of Lockhart. whom Scott had attacked in the magazine. [li. 47]

SCOTT, JOHN (1774–1827), engraver; studied drawing and engraving, and was employed by Robert Pollard [q. v.]; executed portraits of racehorses for 'Sporting Magazine.' [li. 48]

SCOTT, JOHN (1777–1834), divine; son of Thomas Scott (1747–1821) [q. v.]; M.A. Magdalene College, Cambridge, 1803; held successively several preferments in Yorkshire; published a 'Life' of his father. [li. 75]

SCOTT, JOHN, first EARL OF ELDON (1751–1838), fellow, University College, Oxford, 1767; M.A., 1773; high steward of the university and D.C.L., 1801; barrister, Middle Temple, 1776, bencher, 1783, and treasurer, 1797; pupil of Matthew Duane [q. v.]; K.C., 1783; M.P., Weobley, 1783–96, Boroughbridge, 1796; chancellor of county palatine of Durham, 1787; knighted and appointed solicitor-general, 1788; defended government scheme for providing for regency by means of a bill passed by fictitious commission under great seal; attorney-general, 1793; serjeant-at-law, privy councillor, member of board of trade, and lord chief-justice of common pleas, 1799; created Baron Eldon of Eldon, 1799; lord chancellor, 1801; surrendered seals after Pitt's death, 1806; acted as adviser of Caroline, princess of Wales, 1806; resumed great seal in Portland administration, 1807; pursued vigorous policy for subjugation of Napoleon I; transferred his counsels from Princess Caroline to her husband, Prince of Wales, afterwards George IV; received titles of Viscount Encombe and Earl of Eldon, 1821; succeeded on woolsack by Lord Lyndhurst, 1827; actively opposed parliamentary Reform Bill. His decrees were seldom appealed from and hardly ever reversed. He was F.R.S., F.S.A., a governor of the Charterhouse, London, and a trustee of the British Museum. [li. 49]

SCOTT, JOHN (1798–1846), surgeon; educated at Charterhouse, London; apprenticed to Sir William Blizard [q. v.]; L.S.A., 1819; M.R.C.S., 1820; surgeon to Ophthalmic Hospital, Moorfields, 1826; surgeon to London Hospital, 1831–45; introduced passive treatment of diseased joints; published surgical works. [li. 56]

SCOTT, JOHN (1794–1871), horse-trainer; rode as light-weight jockey for several owners; trainer to Mr. Houldsworth of Rockhill, 1815, and to Hon. E. Petre at Mansfield, c. 1822; purchased training stables at Whitewall House, Malton, 1825, and resided there till death. [li. 57]

SCOTT, JONATHAN (1754–1829), orientalist; brother of John Scott, afterwards Scott-Waring [q. v.]; served in 29th native infantry in Carnatic and was captain, 1778; Persian secretary to Warren Hastings; returned to England, c. 1785; published translations of several oriental works, and translated and revised Galland's French version of the 'Arabian Nights,' 1811; professor of oriental languages at Royal Military College, 1802–5, and at East India College, Haileybury; honorary D.C.L. Oxford, 1805. [li. 58]

SCOTT, JOSEPH NICOLL (1703?–1769), dissenting minister; assisted his father in dissenting ministry at Hitchin, c. 1725–38; adopted Arian views and became lecturer at French church, St. Mary-the-Less; studied medicine at Edinburgh; M.D., 1744; practised in Norwich; published theological writings. [li. 59]

SCOTT or **SCOT**, MICHAEL (1175?–1234?), scholar; of Scottish birth; studied at Oxford and on continent, writing an 'Abbreviatio Avicennæ' at Toledo; attached to court of Emperor Frederick II, to whom he was probably official astrologer, and at whose request many of his works were written; possibly held benefices in Italy; sent by Frederick, c. 1230, on mission to universities of Europe to communicate to them versions of Aristotle made by Michael and others; probably died in Italy. Several legends of his demon horse and demon ship have given a theme for literary treatment to many great writers from Dante ('Inferno,' c. xx.) to Sir Walter Scott ('Lay of Last Minstrel'). His works, which have been printed, include: 'Liber Physiognomiæ,' 1477; a translation of Aristotle's 'De Animalibus,' published perhaps separately, 1493, and with Aristotle's works at Venice, 1496; and 'Quæstio Curiosa de Natura Solis et Lunæ,' printed in 'Theatrum Chemicum,' vol. v., Strasburg, 1622. Works on astronomy and alchemy, besides various translations, still remain in manuscript. [li. 59]

SCOTT, MICHAEL (1789–1835), author; educated at Glasgow; went to Jamaica, 1806, and entered, 1810, at Kingstown, business involving frequent journeys by sea and road, which supplied him with materials for 'Tom Cringle's Log,' published in 'Blackwood's Magazine,' 1829–33 (printed anonymously in book form at Paris, 1836). [li. 62]

SCOTT or **SCOT**, PATRICK (*fl.* 1620), author; in service of James I, 1618; probably occasionally tutor to Prince Charles; published 'The Tillage of Light,' an alchemical work, 1623, and moral writings. [li. 63]

SCOTT or **SCOT**, REGINALD or REYNOLD (1538 ?– 1599), author; educated at Hart Hall, Oxford; M.P., New Romney, 1588–9; published 'Perfect Platform of a Hop-garden,' 1574 (the first practical treatise on hop culture in England), and 'The Discouerie of Witchcraft,' 1584, a work which was written with the aim of preventing persecution of poor, aged, and simple persons who were popularly believed to be witches. Shakespeare drew from the latter work hints for his picture of the witches in Macbeth. [li. 63]

SCOTT, ROBERT (1777–1841), articled as engraver at Edinburgh, where he subsequently practised independently; executed plates for several publications, including the 'Scots Magazine.' [li. 65]

SCOTT, ROBERT (1811–1887), divine; B.A. Christ Church, Oxford, 1833; fellow of Balliol College, Oxford, and tutor, 1835; prebendary of Exeter, 1845–66; master of Balliol College, 1854–70; Dean Ireland's professor of exegesis, 1861–70; dean of Rochester, 1870–87; collaborated with Dr. H. G. Liddell in the Greek-English lexicon published 1843. [li. 65]

SCOTT, ROBERT BISSET (1774–1841), military writer; lieutenant in Tower Hamlets militia, 1807; started weekly paper, 'The Military Register,' 1814; served against Dom Miguel in Portugal, 1830; published 'Military Law of England,' 1810, and other writings. [li. 66]

SCOTT, ROBERT EDEN (1770–1811), philosopher; M.A. University and King's College, Aberdeen, 1785; co-professor of natural philosophy and, later, professor of Greek, mathematics, and moral philosophy, Aberdeen; published philosophical works. [li. 66]

SCOTT, SAMUEL (1710 ?–1772), marine painter; contributed, with William Hogarth [q. v.], illustrations to 'Five Days' Peregrination' in Isle of Sheppey, written (1732) by Ebenezer Forrest [q. v.] and published, 1782. [li. 66]

SCOTT, SAMUEL (1719–1788), brother of John Scott (1730–1783) [q. v.]; quaker minister at Hertford. His diary was published, 1809. [li. 42]

SCOTT, SARAH (*d.* 1795), novelist; daughter of Matthew Robinson; sister of Mrs. Elizabeth Montagu [q. v.]; married, *c.* 1751, George Lewis Scott [q. v.] from whom she separated, living with Lady Barbara Montagu, sister of George Montagu Dunk, second earl of Halifax [q. v.]; published novels and historical works, including 'Life of Theodore Agrippa d'Aubigné' (1772). [li. 67]

SCOTT or **SCOT**, THOMAS (1423–1500). [See ROTHERHAM.]

SCOTT or **SCOT**, THOMAS, LORD PETGORMO (1480 ?– 1539), judge; son of Sir William Scott, Lord Balwearie [q. v.]; appointed ordinary judge, 1532; justice clerk, 1535. [li. 67]

SCOTT, SIR THOMAS (1535–1594), grandson of Sir John Scott (1484 ?–1533) [q. v.]; knighted, 1571; high sheriff of Kent, 1576, and knight of shire in parliaments of 1571 and 1586; chief of Kentish force to oppose Spanish Armada. [li. 107]

SCOTT or **SCOT**, THOMAS (*fl.* 1605), poet; perhaps identical with Thomas Scott (1580 ?–1626) [q. v.]; published 'Four Paradoxes,' 1602, and 'Philomythie or Philomythologie,' 1610, a satire, of which a 'Second Part' appeared in 1616. [li. 70]

SCOTT, THOMAS (1580 ?–1626), political writer; B.D. and chaplain to James I in 1616; incorporated B.D. Peterhouse, Cambridge, 1620; rector of St. Saviour's, Norwich; published, 1620, 'Vox Populi,' a tract directed against the Spanish marriage, containing a fictitious account of Count Gondomar's reception by the council of state on his return to Madrid in 1618; this was widely received as genuine history, and was suppressed by royal authority; preacher to English garrison at Utrecht, 1623; assassinated; wrote against the Roman catholics and Spain. [li. 68]

SCOTT or **SCOT**, THOMAS (*d.* 1660), regicide; educated at Westminster School and at Cambridge; M.P., Aylesbury, 1645; joined army and signed covenant, 1647; signed Charles I's death-warrant, 1649; appointed to manage home and foreign intelligence for the state 1649; M.P. for Wycombe in Protector's first parliament, and was excluded from house for refusing to acknowledge Protector; M.P., Aylesbury, 1656, and was again excluded till 1658; M.P., Wycombe (in Richard Cromwell's parliament); member of council of state, 1659; received charge of intelligence department, 1660, and, later, was secretary of state; supported Monck; fled to Flanders, but surrendered to Charles II's resident at Brussels; brought to England and executed. [li. 70]

SCOTT, THOMAS (1705–1775), divine; brother of Joseph Nicoll Scott [q. v.]; colleague to Samuel Baxter at St. Nicholas Street Chapel, Ipswich, 1734, and sole pastor, 1740 till 1761, when he received a colleague; minister at Hapton, 1774; published hymns and other poetical writings. [li. 72]

SCOTT, THOMAS (1747–1821), divine; apprenticed as surgeon and apothecary at Alford, but was dismissed for misconduct; employed as a grazier; studied privately; joint-chaplain at Lock Hospital, London, 1785, and sole chaplain, 1802; produced, 1788–92, in weekly parts, a commentary on the bible, the publication of which involved him in pecuniary difficulties until 1813; rector of Aston Sandford, 1801–21; published religious writings, five volumes of 'Theological Works' appearing, 1805–8. [li. 73]

SCOTT, THOMAS (1780–1835), divine; son of Thomas Scott (1747–1821) [q. v.]; M.A. Queens' College, Cambridge, 1808; rector of Wappenham, 1833; published religious writings. [li. 75]

SCOTT, THOMAS (1745–1842), general; ensign, 1761; lieutenant, 1765; captain, 1777; in Netherlands under Sir Ralph Abercromby, 1793; lieutenant-colonel, 1794; took part in campaign against Tipu Sultan, 1799; brevet colonel, 1801; deputy inspector-general of recruiting service in North Britain, 1803; lieutenant-general, 1813; general, 1830. [li. 75]

SCOTT, THOMAS (1808–1878), freethinker; educated in France as Roman catholic; page at court of Charles X; issued, between 1862 and 1877, many tracts and works by various hands advocating free thought. [li. 76]

SCOTT, SIR WALTER (1490 ?–1552), Scottish chieftain; succeeded his father, Sir Walter Scott of Buccleuch, 1504; knighted, 1513; fought at Flodden, 1513; joined party of John Stewart, duke of Albany [q. v.], 1515, and maintained opposition to Queen Margaret and her government; defeated by Angus near Melrose, 1526; took refuge in France, 1526–8; joined party opposing marriage of infant Queen Mary of Scotland to an English prince, 1542; fought at Ancrum, 1545, and Pinkie, 1547; killed by partisans of house of Ker of Cessford, with whom he had an old feud. [li. 76]

SCOTT, WALTER, first BARON SCOTT OF BUCCLEUCH (1565–1611), son of Sir Walter Scott of Buccleuch (*d.* 1574); summoned before privy council with other border chiefs to answer for good rule on borders, 1587; knighted, 1590; keeper of Liddesdale, 1591; gave oath to concur in pursuit of Bothwell, but his fidelity being doubted was banished, 1591; returned, 1592; member of commission for pursuit of Bothwell, 1594; opposed Mar, 1595; delivered William Armstrong of Kinmont (*fl.* 1596) [q. v.] from Carlisle Castle, 1596; tried by joint English and Scottish commission and sent abroad, 1597; commanded regiment of borderers under Maurice, prince of Orange, against Spaniards in Netherlands, 1604; created Baron Scott of Buccleuch, 1606. [li. 77]

SCOTT, WALTER (1550 ?–1629 ?), of Harden, freebooter; assisted Francis Stewart, fifth earl of Bothwell [q. v.] in his plundering exploits; joined Sir Walter Scott, first Baron Scott of Buccleuch [q. v.], in rescue of William Armstrong of Kinmont (*fl.* 1596) [q. v.], 1596. [li. 79]

SCOTT, WALTER, EARL OF TARRAS (1644-1693), grandson of Walter Scott (1550 ?-1629 ?) [q. v.] ; married Lady Mary Scott, countess of Buccleuch, 1659, and received dignity for life of Earl of Tarras, 1660 ; condemned for complicity in plots for exclusion of Duke of York from throne, 1685, but was pardoned. [li. 79]

SCOTT, WALTER, of Satchells (1614 ?-1694 ?), captain and genealogist ; served under Walter Scott, first earl of Buccleuch, in Holland, 1629 ; author of metrical history of family of Scot, 1688, which he dictated, being ignorant of writing. [li. 80]

SCOTT, SIR WALTER (1771-1832), novelist and poet ; born in College Wynd, Edinburgh ; son of Walter Scott (1729-1799), a writer to the signet ; educated at the high school and university, Edinburgh, and was apprenticed to his father, 1786, as writer to the signet ; called to bar, 1792 ; formed close friendship with William Erskine (afterwards Lord Kinneder) [q. v.] ; made numerous excursions, collecting ballads and exploring the country ; began study of German, 1792 ; became quartermaster of a body of volunteer cavalry raised in 1797 ; met Charlotte Mary Carpenter, whom he married, 1797 ; settled in Edinburgh ; published a translation of Bürger's 'Lenore' and other ballads, which met with some success, 1799 ; appointed sheriff-depute of Selkirkshire, 1799 ; published 'Border Minstrelsy,' 3 vols., 1802-3, and 'Lay of Last Minstrel,' 1805 ; took up residence at Ashestiel on the Tweed, near Selkirk, 1804 ; obtained one of clerkships of court of session, 1806 ; became secretly a partner in Ballantyne's printing business, 1805, and arranged that his books should be printed by Ballantyne ; secretary to parliamentary commission on Scottish jurisprudence, 1807 ; published 'Marmion,' 1808, and edition of Dryden with 'Life,' 1808 ; assisted in scheme for starting 'Quarterly Review,' 1808-9 ; supplied half capital for new publishing firm of John Ballantyne & Co., 1809 ; published 'Lady of the Lake,' 1810 ; purchased Abbotsford on the Tweed, 1812 ; published 'Rokeby,' 1812, and 'Triermain,' 1813 ; on dissolution of Ballantyne's publishing firm (1813), made John Ballantyne his agent for managing the printing business, which involved him in considerable financial difficulties ; issued edition of Swift, 19 vols., 1814 ; published 'Lord of the Isles,' 1815, and 'Harold the Dauntless' (his last poem of any length), 1817 ; published anonymously the novels 'Waverley,' 1814, 'Guy Mannering,' 1815, 'The Antiquary,' 1815, 'The Black Dwarf' and 'Old Mortality' (together as the first series of 'Tales of my Landlord'), 1816, 'Rob Roy,' 1817, 'Heart of Midlothian,' 1818 (second series of 'Tales of my Landlord'), 'Bride of Lammermoor' and 'Legend of Montrose' (third series of 'Tales of my Landlord'), 1819, 'Ivanhoe,' 1820, really 1819, 'Monastery,' 1820, 'Abbot,' 1820, 'Kenilworth,' 1821, 'Pirate,' 1821, 'Fortunes of Nigel,' 1822, 'Peveril of the Peak,' 1823, 'Quentin Durward,' 1823, 'St. Ronan's Well,' 1823, 'Red Gauntlet,' 1824, 'Tales of the Crusaders,' 'The Betrothed,' and 'The Talisman,' 1825, 'Woodstock,' 1826, 'Chronicles of the Canongate : Two Drovers ; Highland Widow ; Surgeon's Daughter,' 1827, 'Tales of a Grandfather' (first series, 1828, second series, 1829, third series, 1830, fourth series, 1830), 'Chronicles of the Canongate (second series), St. Valentine's Day, or Fair Maid of Perth,' 1828, 'Anne of Geierstein,' 1829, 'Tales of my Landlord (fourth series), Count Robert of Paris,' 'Castle Dangerous,' 1832 ; created baronet, 1820 ; president of Royal Society of Scotland, 1820 ; member of Roxburghe Club, 1823 ; founded Bannatyne Club, 1823 ; ruined (1826) by the stoppage of payment by Hurst, Robinson & Co., which involved the fall of Constable and Ballantyne (Scott's publisher), whom he had again taken into partnership in 1822, the catastrophe being probably in a large measure due to his extravagance ; thenceforth worked heroically to meet his creditors till his death, when the balance of debt was paid off with sums realised on the security of copyrights. He attacked, 1826, the proposal of government to suppress circulation of small bank-notes, in 'Thoughts on proposed change of Currency,' three letters by 'Malachi Malagrowther' to 'Edinburgh Weekly Journal' ; published 'Life of Napoleon,' 1827 ; published collected edition of 'Waverley Novels,' with notes, 1829-33 ; died at Abbotsford after suffering from apoplexy and paralysis, and having travelled on the continent for his health. A monument to him was inaugurated in Edinburgh, 1846. His life by John Gibson Lockhart [q. v.], husband of Scott's daughter,

Charlotte Sophia, was published in 1837. He is now lineally represented by the family of his granddaughter, the Hon. Mrs. Mary Monica Maxwell Scott. [li. 80]

SCOTT, WALTER FRANCIS, fifth DUKE OF BUCCLEUCH and seventh DUKE OF QUEENSBERRY (1806-1884), grandson of Henry Scott, third duke of Buccleuch [q. v.], succeeded to title, 1819 ; M.A. St. John's College, Cambridge, 1827 ; lord privy seal, 1842-6 ; lord president of council, 1846 ; hon. D.C.L. Oxford, 1834 ; built the pier and breakwater at Granton, 1835-42 ; hon. LL.D. Cambridge, 1842, and Edinburgh, 1874 ; chancellor of Glasgow University, 1877. [li. 25]

SCOTT, SIR WILLIAM (d. 1350), judge ; serjeant-at-law, 1335 ; knight and justice of common pleas, 1337 ; probably built Scot's Hall at Orlestone. [li. 105]

SCOTT, SIR WILLIAM (1459-1524), of Brabourne : K.B., privy councillor, and comptroller of Henry VII's household, 1489 ; lieutenant of Dover Castle, warden of Cinque ports, and marshal of Calais, 1491 ; sheriff of Kent, 1491, 1501, and 1516. [li. 106]

SCOTT or SCOT, SIR WILLIAM, LORD BALWEARIE (d. 1532), Scottish judge : accompanied James IV on expedition into England, 1513 ; chosen commissioner to parliament and appointed one of lords of articles for the barons, 1524 ; styled justice, 1524 ; nominated first justice on temporal side on institution of college of justice, 1532. [li. 107]

SCOTT, SIR WILLIAM, LORD CLERKINGTON (d. 1656), lord of session ; knighted, 1641 ; clerk of session : ordinary lord of session, 1649 ; M.P., Haddingtonshire, 1645. [li. 108]

SCOTT, SIR WILLIAM (1674 ?-1725), of Thirlestane ; member of Faculty of Advocates, 1702 ; contributed to Dr. Archibald Pitcairne's 'Selecta Poemata,' published, 1726. [li. 108]

SCOTT, WILLIAM, BARON STOWELL (1745-1836), maritime and international lawyer ; scholar of Corpus Christi College, Oxford, 1761 ; fellow and tutor of University College, Oxford, 1765 ; M.A., 1767 ; B.C.L., 1772 ; Camden reader in ancient history, 1773-85 ; intimate with Dr. Johnson ; D.C.L. and member of Faculty of Advocates at Doctors' Commons, 1779 ; barrister, Middle Temple, 1780 ; advocate-general for office of lord high admiral, 1782 ; appointed registrar of court of faculties, 1783 ; judge of consistory court of London, 1788-1820 ; knighted, 1788 ; George III's advocate-general, 1788 ; vicar-general for province of Canterbury, 1788 ; commissary of city and diocese of Canterbury ; chancellor of diocese of London : master of faculties, 1790 ; bencher of his inn, 1794, and treasurer, 1807 ; privy councillor, 1798 ; judge of high court of admiralty, 1798-1828 ; M.P., Downton, 1784, but unseated on petition ; regained and held seat, 1790 ; M.P., Oxford University, 1801-21, in the main opposing reform ; created Baron Stowell of Stowell Park, 1821. On many maritime points his judgments are still the only law. [li. 108]

SCOTT, WILLIAM (1797-1848), jockey ; brother of John Scott (1794-1871) [q. v.], with whom he was from 1825 in partnership at the Whitewall training stables ; obtained between 1825 and 1847 many successes as jockey ; bred Sir Tatton Sykes, his own horse, 1843. [li. 112]

SCOTT, WILLIAM (1813-1872), divine : of Merchant Taylors' School, London, and Queen's College, Oxford ; M.A., 1839 ; vicar of St. Olave's, Jewry, London, with St. Martin Pomeroy, London, 1860 ; active member of high church party ; co-editor, and for some time sole editor, of 'Christian Remembrancer,' 1841-68 ; one of founders of, and constant contributor to, 'Saturday Review' ; president of Sion College, 1858 ; edited Laurence's 'Lay Baptism invalid,' 1841, and published religious writings. [li. 112]

SCOTT, WILLIAM BELL (1811-1890), poet and painter ; son of Robert Scott (1777-1841) [q. v.] ; studied drawing at Trustees' Academy, Edinburgh, and in London ; exhibited at Royal Academy, 1842-69 ; master in government schools of design, Newcastle-on-Tyne, 1843-64 ; artist employed in decoration and examiner in art schools, South Kensington, 1864-85 ; published five volumes of verse, the best of which is of a mystical and metaphysical character, and works relating to art ; he edited a series of English poets. [li. 113]

SCOTTOW, JOSHUA (1618–1693), colonist; went to Massachusetts, c. 1634; member of 'old church,' at Boston, 1639; a shipowner and merchant; published pamphlets on colonial affairs.   [li. 114]

SCOTUS, DUNS (1265?–1308?). [See DUNS, JOANNES SCOTUS.]

SCOTUS or **ERIGENA**, JOHN (*fl.* 850), philosopher; of Irish origin; employed as teacher at court of King Charles the Bald, afterwards emperor, c. 847; produced, 851, at instance of Hincmar, archbishop of Rheims, 'De Prædestinatione'; probably engaged in controversy touching the Holy Communion which agitated the Frankish domain, c. 840–50; made, probably before 859, by command of Charles the Bald, translations of the books 'De Cælesti Ierarchia,' 'de Ecclesiastica Ierarchia,' 'de Divinis Nominibus,' 'de Mystica Theologia,' and 'Epistolæ,' falsely ascribed to Dionysius the Areopagite; perhaps identical with one John who went to England with Grimbald on a request from Alfred for teachers from Gaul, and was established at Malmesbury. All his known works, which include a series of commentaries on Dionysius the Areopagite, and translations, were collected by H. J. Floss in Migne's 'Patrologia Latina,' cxxii. (1853); two other works claiming his authorship have since come to light. The leading principle of his philosophy is that of the unity of nature, proceeding from (1) God, the first and only real being; through (2) the creative ideas to (3) the sensible universe, which ultimately is resolved into (4) its first Cause.   [li. 115]

SCOTUS, MACARIUS (*d.* 1153). [See MACARIUS.]

SCOTUS, MARIANUS (1028–1082?). [See MARIANUS.]

SCOUGAL, HENRY (1650–1678), Scottish divine; son of Patrick Scougal [q. v.]; M.A. King's College, Aberdeen, 1668; professor; precentor in cathedral of Aberdeen, 1672–3; professor of divinity at King's College, Aberdeen, 1673–8; chief work, with preface by Gilbert Burnet, 'Life of God in the Soul of Man' (anonymous, 1677), which has become a religious classic.   [li. 120]

SCOUGAL or **SCOUGALL**, JOHN (1645?–1730?), portrait-painter; lived at Advocates' Close, Edinburgh, where he fitted up a picture gallery.   [li. 121]

SCOUGAL or **SCOUGALL**, PATRICK (1607?–1682), bishop of Aberdeen; graduated at Edinburgh, 1624; presented to parish of Leuchars, 1644; assisted Charles II in Scotland, 1650; received living of Salton, 1658; bishop of Aberdeen, 1664–82; maintained firm opposition to Test Act, 1681.   [li. 121]

SCOULER, JOHN (1804–1871), naturalist; M.D. Glasgow, 1827; LL.D., 1850; made voyage under Hudson's Bay Company, as surgeon and naturalist, to Columbia river, 1824–5; practised medicine at Glasgow; professor of geology in Andersonian University, 1829, and of mineralogy, and subsequently geology, zoology, and botany, to Royal Dublin Society, 1834; F.L.S., 1829; published papers on natural history, and was joint-founder of 'Glasgow Medical Journal.'   [li. 122]

SCOVELL, SIR GEORGE (1774–1861), general; cornet and adjutant, 1798; went with 57th foot to Peninsula, 1808, and served in quartermaster-general's department throughout the war; lieutenant-colonel, 1812; commanded staff corps of cavalry, 1813, and in Waterloo campaign, when he was assistant quartermaster-general; colonel, 1825; general, 1854; lieutenant-governor of military college, Sandhurst, 1829–37, and governor, 1837–56; G.C.B., 1860.   [li. 123]

SCRATCHLEY, SIR PETER HENRY (1835–1885), major-general; born in Paris; studied at Royal Military Academy, Woolwich; lieutenant, royal engineers, 1854; in Crimea, 1855–6; adjutant of royal engineers at Cawnpore, 1857; accompanied Brigadier-general Walpole to Itawa, Manipuri, and Fathgarh, 1857–8; at siege of Lucknow, 1858; adjutant of engineers under Sir Hope Grant, and commander of engineers under Wetherall in Oudh campaigns, 1858–9; superintended defence works at Melbourne, 1860–3, and was colonial engineer and military storekeeper; returned to England, 1863; assistant-inspector of works for manufacturing departments of army, 1864, and subsequently inspector of works; lieutenant-colonel, 1877; accompanied Sir William Jervois to Australia to advise on defences of Australian colonies,

1877; vice-president of commission to report on military defences of New South Wales, 1881; major-general, 1882; returned to England, 1883; high commissioner for south-east New Guinea, 1884; K.C.M.G., 1885.   [li. 123]

SCRIBA or **THE SCRIBE**, ROBERT (*fl.* 1160–1170). [See ROBERT OF BRIDLINGTON.]

SCRIMGEOUR, SIR JAMES (1550?–1612). [See SCRYMGEOUR.]

SCRIMGER, HENRY (1506–1572). [See SCRYMGEOUR.]

SCRIVEN, EDWARD (1775–1841), engraver; pupil of Robert Thew [q. v.]; executed portraits and other plates, various publications, including 'British Gallery of Portraits,' 1809–17.   [li. 125]

SCRIVENER, FREDERICK HENRY AMBROSE (1813–1891), divine; M.A. Trinity College, Cambridge, 1838; head-master of Falmouth school, 1846–56; rector of St. Gerrans, Cornwall, 1862; prebendary of Exeter, 1874; vicar of Hendon, 1876; LL.D. St. Andrews, 1872; D.C.L. Oxford, 1876; assisted in revised version of New Testament, 1870–82; published works relating to text of New Testament.   [li. 126]

SCRIVENER, MATTHEW (*fl.* 1660), divine; of Catharine Hall, Cambridge; vicar of Haslingfield; published religious works.   [li. 126]

SCROGGS, SIR WILLIAM (1623?–1683), lawyer; M.A. Pembroke College, Oxford, 1643; barrister, Gray's Inn, 1653; knighted after Restoration; elected bencher of Gray's Inn, 1669; king's serjeant, 1669; justice of common pleas, 1676; lord chief-justice of England, 1678; presided at trials of several victims of Titus Oates's plot, and though he displayed brutal zeal for the protestant cause on many occasions, he was fruitlessly charged by Oates and Bedloe before the privy council with depreciating their evidence and setting at liberty 'persons accused upon oath before him of high treason'; subsequently impeached before the House of Commons and removed from office, 1681.   [li. 127]

SCROGGS, SIR WILLIAM (1652?–1695), lawyer; son of Sir William Scroggs (1623?–1683) [q. v.]; B.A. Magdalen College, Oxford, 1673; barrister, Gray's Inn, 1676, bencher, 1681, and treasurer, 1687–8; appointed K.C. and knighted, 1681.   [li. 131]

SCROOP, LAURENCE (1577–1643). [See ANDERTON.]

SCROPE or **SCROOPE**, ADRIAN (1601–1660), regicide; of Hart Hall, Oxford; entered Middle Temple, 1619; major in Colonel Richard Graves's regiment of horse, 1646, and succeeded to command, 1647; at siege of Colchester, 1648; defeated and captured Earl of Holland at St. Neots; signed Charles I's death-warrant; governor of Bristol, 1649–55; member of council for government of Scotland, 1655; surrendered on Charles II's proclamation, 1660, and though House of Commons voted that he should have benefit of act of indemnity, was excepted from pardon by the Lords; executed at Charing Cross, London.   [li. 132]

SCROPE or **SCROOPE**, SIR ADRIAN (*d.* 1667), soldier; sometimes confused with his distant kinsman Adrian Scrope (1601–1660) [q. v.]; served in Charles I's army during civil war; K.B., 1660.   [li. 133]

SCROPE or **SCROOP**, SIR CARR, first baronet (1649–1680), son of Sir Adrian Scrope (*d.* 1667) [q. v.]; M.A. Wadham College, Oxford, 1667; created baronet, 1667; went to London, became one of companions of Charles II, and was well known as a versifier and man of fashion.   [li. 133]

SCROPE, SIR GEOFFREY LE (*d.* 1340), judge; brother of Sir Henry le Scrope (*d.* 1336) [q. v.]; king's serjeant, 1316; accompanied Edward II in campaign against barons. 1321–2; judge of common pleas, 1323; chief-justice of king's bench, 1324; removed from office after Edward II's deposition, but pardoned and reinstated, 1328; resigned office, 1338; Edward III's secretary, 1339; at siege of Tournay, 1340; died at Ghent.   [li. 134]

SCROPE, GEORGE JULIUS POULETT (1797–1876), geologist and political economist; brother of Charles Edward Poulett Thomson, baron Sydenham [q. v.]; of Harrow, Pembroke College, Oxford, and St. John's College, Cambridge; B.A., 1821; travelled in Italy, Sicily, and Germany, and studied volcanic districts; married daughter of William Scrope (1772–1852) [q. v.] and assumed her name,

1821; joint-secretary of Geological Society, 1825; published important geological works; M.P., Stroud, 1833–68; published volumes and pamphlets advocating free trade and various social reforms, especially that of the poor law; Wollaston medallist, Geological Society, 1867. [li. 135]

SCROPE, SIR HENRY LE (d. 1336), judge; brother of Sir Geoffrey le Scrope [q. v.]; was an advocate in 1307; justice of common pleas, 1308; attached himself to Edward II; chief-justice of king's bench, 1317–23; justice of forests north of Trent, c. 1323; second justice of common pleas, 1327; chief-baron of exchequer, 1330–6. [li. 137]

SCROPE, HENRY LE, first BARON SCROPE OF MASHAM (1315–1391), son of Sir Geoffrey le Scrope [q. v.]; fought at Halidon Hill, 1333, and Sluys, 1340; served with Edward III in Brittany, 1342, in Flanders, 1345, in Picardy, 1355, and at Paris, 1360; at siege of Calais, 1347; warden of Calais and Guisnes, 1361–70; joint-warden of west march towards Scotland, 1370; steward of household, 1371. [li. 138]

SCROPE, HENRY LE, third BARON SCROPE OF MASHAM (1376 ?–1415), grandson of Henry le Scrope, first baron Scrope of Masham [q. v.]; succeeded his father, 1406; went on mission to France with Henry Beaufort, 1409; treasurer and K.G., 1410; superseded on Henry V's accession, but entrusted with several delicate foreign negotiations; executed, and his estates forfeited for complicity in plot discovered at Southampton to dethrone Henry V. [li. 139]

SCROPE, HENRY LE, ninth BARON SCROPE OF BOLTON (1534–1592), marshal of army sent by Queen Elizabeth to assist Scottish protestants at Leith, 1560; governor of Carlisle and warden of west marches, 1562–92; took charge of Mary Stuart at Bolton, 1568; suppressed rising of Earls of Northumberland and Westmoreland in favour of Mary Stuart, 1569; member of council of north, 1574; K.G., 1584. [li. 140]

SCROPE, JOHN LE, fifth BARON SCROPE OF BOLTON (1435–1498), supported Yorkists; fought with Warwick at Northampton, received Garter from Edward IV; went on mission with Earl Rivers to Rome, 1474; constable of Exeter Castle; governor of the fleet; assisted in raising siege of Norham Castle, 1497. [li. 141]

SCROPE, JOHN (1662 ?–1752), judge; entered service of Duke of Monmouth; barrister, Middle Temple, 1692; baron of the court of exchequer in Scotland, 1708–1724; commissioner of great seal, 1710; M.P., Ripon, 1722, Bristol, 1727, Lyme Regis, 1734–52; secretary to treasury, 1724–52; recorder of Bristol; a staunch supporter of Walpole. [li. 141]

SCROPE, RICHARD LE, first BARON SCROPE OF BOLTON (1327 ?–1403), lawyer; son of Sir Henry le Scrope (d. 1336) [q.v.]; knighted at Neville's Cross; served with John of Gaunt at Najara, 1367, and in many subsequent expeditions till 1385; treasurer, 1371–5; joint-warden of west marches against Scotland, 1375; steward of household to Richard II; chancellor, 1378–80 and 1381–2; sided with Richard II's opponents in crisis of 1386–9, but was pardoned by him, 1397. [li. 142]

SCROPE, RICHARD LE (1350 ?–1405), archbishop of York; son of Henry le Scrope, first baron Scrope of Masham [q.v.]; probably graduated in law at Cambridge; LLD., 1386; presented to rectory of Ainderby Steeple, near Northallerton, 1367; chancellor of Cambridge University, 1378; dean of Chichester, c. 1383; elected bishop of Chichester, 1385, but Thomas Rushook [q. v.] substituted for him by Richard II; notary of the curia and bishop of Coventry and Lichfield, 1386; archbishop of York, 1398; supported revolution of 1399; resisted spoliation of the church proposed by 'unlearned parliament,' 1404, and took up arms at York in concert with Northumberland and Bardolf, who raised standard of rebellion beyond the Tyne; induced by treachery to surrender to Westmoreland at Shipton Moor; condemned and executed at York; popularly known in the north as Saint Richard Scrope. [li. 144]

SCROPE, THOMAS (d. 1491), divine; also called BRADLEY from his birthplace; Carmelite at Norwich; became anchorite before 1426; sent as papal legate to Rhodes; consecrated at Rome by Nicholas V bishop of Dromore, Ireland, 1450; vicar-general of bishop of Norwich, 1450, and was suffragan till 1477; held livings in Norfolk; wrote religious and historical works. [li. 147]

SCROPE, WILLIAM LE, EARL OF WILTSHIRE (1351 ?–1399), son of Richard le Scrope, first baron Scrope of Bolton [q. v.]; served with John of Gaunt at Harfleur, 1369, in Guienne, 1373 and 1378, and with Charles, duke of Durazzo, at Venice, 1379; seneschal of Gascony, 1383–1392; captain of Cherbourg, 1386–9, and of Brest, 1389; vice-chamberlain of Richard II's household, 1393; bought Isle of Man, 1393; K.G. and constable of Beaumaris and of Dublin Castle, 1394; chamberlain of household and of Ireland, 1395; assisted Richard II, 1397, against his antagonists of 1388, and received earldom of Wiltshire; ambassador to Scotland and captain of Calais Castle, 1398; treasurer of England, 1398; left by Richard II to assist regent (Duke of York) during his absence in Ireland, 1399; arrested by Henry IV at Bristol and executed. [li. 148]

SCROPE, WILLIAM (1772–1852), artist and sportsman; exhibited views at Royal Academy and British Institution; F.L.S.; published works on deerstalking and salmon-fishing. [li. 150]

SCRYMGEOUR or **SCRIMGER**, HENRY (1506–1572), professor of civil law at Geneva; studied philosophy at St. Andrews, proceeded to university of Paris, and subsequently read civil law at Bruges; secretary to Bernard Bocnetel, bishop of Rennes; abandoned Roman catholicism for protestantism; professor of philosophy, and (1565) of civil law at Geneva; member of council of forty, 1570; companion of Calvin, Beza, George Buchanan, and other leading reformers; left in manuscript valuable notes on works of several classical authors. [li. 150]

SCRYMGEOUR, SIR JAMES (1550 ?–1612), of Dudhope, constable of Dundee; succeeded to hereditary offices of standard-bearer and constable of Dundee, 1576; favourite of James VI; banished from three kingdoms for joining with the Gowrie party, 1582, but fled to England, and in 1586 was again James VI's favourite; provost of Dundee, 1588; M.P., Dundee, 1600 and 1605, Forfarshire, 1605 and 1607. [li. 151]

SCRYMGEOUR, JAMES, second VISCOUNT DUDHOPE (d. 1644), royalist; son of John Scrymgeour, first viscount Dudhope [q. v.]; killed at Marston Moor. [li. 152]

SCRYMGEOUR, JOHN, first VISCOUNT DUDHOPE (d. 1643), M.P., Forfarshire, 1612, 1617, and 1621, Argyllshire, 1628–33; created Viscount Dudhope, 1641. [li. 152]

SCRYMGEOUR, JOHN, third VISCOUNT DUDHOPE and first EARL OF DUNDEE (d. 1668), royalist leader; son of James Scrymgeour, second viscount Dudhope [q.v.]; served at Preston and Worcester, 1651, and in north with Middleton, 1654; made privy councillor and created Earl of Dundee, 1660. [li. 152]

SCUDAMORE, SIR CHARLES (1779–1849), physician; studied at Guy's and St. Thomas's hospitals, London; M.D. Glasgow, 1814; admitted L.R.C.P., 1814; practised in London; physician to Prince Leopold of Saxe-Gotha, 1820; attended Duke of Northumberland at Dublin when lord-lieutenant, 1829, and was knighted; published medical works. [li. 152]

SCUDAMORE, FRANK IVES (1823–1884), postoffice reformer and writer; educated at Christ's Hospital, London; entered post office, 1841; chief examiner of united departments of receiver-general and accountant-general, 1852; receiver and accountant-general, 1856; instrumental in elaborating scheme for government savings bank, founded 1861; chief agent for government in negotiations for acquiring telegraphs, 1865–70; assistant-secretary, 1863, and subsequently second secretary of post office; C.B., 1871; resigned, 1875; engaged by Ottoman government to organise Turkish international post office. [li. 153]

SCUDAMORE, JOHN, first VISCOUNT SCUDAMORE (1601–1671), son of Sir James Scudamore, whose 'warlike deeds' are celebrated in the 'Faërie Queene' (book iv.); M.A. Magdalen College, Oxford, 1642; captain of horse in Herefordshire; created baronet, 1620; M.P., Herefordshire, 1620 and 1624, Hereford, 1625 and 1628; member of council of the marches, 1623; created Baron Dromore and Viscount Scudamore of Sligo, 1628; ambassador at Paris,

1635-6; joint-ambassador, 1636-9; high steward of Hereford city and cathedral, 1639; surrendered to Waller at Hereford, 1643; kept in confinement till 1647; devoted later years to study and to relieving impoverished divines. [li. 154]

SCUDAMORE, WILLIAM EDWARD (1813-1881), divine; fellow of St. John's College, Cambridge, 1837; M.A., 1838; rector of Ditchingham, 1839-81; his opinions fashioned in some degree by the Oxford movement; published devotional works, including 'Steps to the Altar,' 1846, and 'Incense for the Altar,' 1874. [li. 157]

SCUDDER, HENRY (d. 1659?), divine; of Christ's College, Cambridge; presented to living of Collingbourne-Ducis, 1633; member of committee for scriptures, 1648; published religious works, including 'The Christian's Daily Walke in Holy Securitie and Peace' (6th edit. 1635). [li. 158]

SCULLY, DENYS (1773-1830), Irish political writer; of Trinity College, Dublin; called to Irish bar, 1796; one of the leading catholic agitators; published political writings. [li. 159]

SCULLY, VINCENT (1810-1871), Irish political writer; son of Denys Scully [q. v.]; of Trinity College, Dublin, and Trinity College, Cambridge; called to Irish bar, 1833; Q.C., 1840; M.P., Cork, 1852-7 and 1859-65; published political pamphlets. [li. 159]

SEAFIELD, EARLS OF. [See OGILVY, JAMES, first EARL, 1664-1730; OGILVY, JAMES, third EARL, 1714?-1770.]

SEAFORD, BARONS. [See ELLIS, CHARLES ROSE, first BARON, 1771-1845; ELLIS, CHARLES AUGUSTUS, second BARON, 1799-1868.]

SEAFORTH, EARLS OF. [See MACKENZIE, KENNETH, fourth EARL, d. 1701; MACKENZIE, WILLIAM, fifth EARL, d. 1740.]

SEAFORTH and **MACKENZIE,** BARON (1754-1814). [See HUMBERSTON, FRANCIS MACKENZIE.]

SEAGAR, JOHN (d. 1656), M.A. St. Mary Hall, Oxford, 1620; received living of Broadclyst, 1631. [li. 197]

SEAGER, CHARLES (1808-1878), orientalist; M.A. Worcester College, Oxford, 1839; pupil of Dr. Pusey, under whom he lectured in Hebrew; took orders in established church; tractarian; seceded to Rome, 1843; first professor of Hebrew and comparative philology at catholic university college, Kensington; member of council of Society of Biblical Archæology; works include a translation of Professor Simonis's 'Smaller Hebrew and Chaldee Lexicon,' 1832. [li. 159]

SEAGER, EDWARD (1812-1883), lieutenant-general; cornet, 1841; major, 1858; in Crimea, 1854-5; in Central India, 1858-9; lieutenant-colonel, 1864; quartermaster-general in Dublin district, 1870; inspector of yeomanry cavalry at York, 1873-8; lieutenant-general, 1881; C.B., 1877. [li. 160]

SEAGER, FRANCIS (fl. 1549-1563). [See SEGAR.]

SEAGRAVE, ROBERT (1693-1760?), divine; M.A. Clare Hall, Cambridge, 1718; joined Oxford methodist movement; preacher at Lorimers' Hall, Cripplegate, London, 1739; published works in defence of Whitefield, besides hymns and other religious writings. [li. 161]

SEALLY, JOHN (1747?-1795), miscellaneous writer; perhaps identical with 'John Sealy'; B.A. Hertford College, Oxford, 1764; established school in Bridgwater Square, Westminster, 1767; vicar of East Meon with Froxfield and Steep, Hampshire, 1790; F.R.S., 1791; M.A.; LL.D.; published miscellaneous writings. [li. 161]

SEAMAN, LAZARUS (d. 1675), puritan divine; M.A. Emmanuel College, Cambridge, 1631; rector of Allhallows, Bread Street, London, 1642-62; member of Westminster Assembly of Divines, 1643; master of Peterhouse Cambridge, 1644-60; signed 'Vindication' by Cornelius Burges [q. v.], protesting against Charles I's trial, 1649; D.D., 1649; vice-chancellor, 1653, and visitor, 1654, of his university; published religious writings. [li. 162]

SEAMAN, WILLIAM (1606-1680), orientalist; M.A. Balliol College, Oxford, 1626; rector of Upton-Scudamore,

1628-80; entered service of Sir Peter Wyche (d. 1643) [q. v.], English ambassador at Constantinople; published first translation of New Testament into Turkish, 1666, a Turkish grammar, 1670, and other works. [li. 163]

SEAMUS DALL (fl. 1712). [See MACCUAIRT, JAMES.]

SEARCHFIELD, ROWLAND (1565?-1622), bishop of Bristol; of Merchant Taylors' School and St. John's College, Oxford; M.A., 1590; D.D., 1608; vicar of Charlbury, 1606; bishop of Bristol, 1619-22. [li. 164]

SEARLE, THOMAS (1777-1849), rear-admiral; entered navy, 1789; commander, 1799; served on north coast of France, 1804-6; in Mediterranean, 1806-9 and 1811-12; C.B., 1815; in Channel, 1818-21; captain of Victory guardship at Portsmouth, 1836-9 rear-admiral, 1846. [li. 164]

SEATON. [See also SETON.]

SEATON, BARON (1778-1863). [See COLBORNE, SIR JOHN.]

SEATON, EDWARD CATOR (1815-1880), physician; M.D. Edinburgh, 1837; surgeon to North Aylesford Union, Rochester; began practice in London, 1841; took part in founding Western Medical Society; original member of Epidemiological Society, for a committee of which he drew up report on small-pox and vaccination, presented to parliament, and resulting in Compulsory Vaccination Act, 1853; inspector under general board of health, 1858; F.R.C.P., 1872; medical officer to local government board, 1876; published 'Handbook of Vaccination' (1868) and other works. [li. 165]

SEATON, JOHN THOMAS (fl. 1761-1806), portrait-painter; member of Incorporated Society of Artists. [li. 166]

SEATON, THOMAS (1684-1741), divine; fellow and M.A. Clare Hall, Cambridge, 1708; vicar of Ravenstone, 1721-41; founded, by legacy, Seatonian prize for sacred poetry at Cambridge; published hymns and other religious writings. [li. 166]

SEATON, SIR THOMAS (1806-1876), major-general; cadet in East India Company's service, 1822; ensign in native infantry of Bengal army, 1823; captain, 1834; joined regiment at Kabul, 1839; took part in defence of Jalalabad, 1841-2; C.B. and major (local rank), 1842; regimental major, 1852; lieutenant-colonel in army, 1854; his regiment in mutiny, 1857; lieutenant-colonel, 1st European fusiliers, 1857; held Fatehgarh and defeated Oudh mutineers at Bunhagong, 1858; K.C.B., 1858; retired as major-general, 1859; published 'From Cadet to Colonel,' an autobiography, 1866. [li. 167]

SEAWARD, JOHN (1786-1858), civil engineer; began life as surveyor and architect; superintended construction of Gordon's, Dowson's, and other Thames docks; made drawings for new London bridge, 1823; established Canal Ironworks, Millwall, 1824; M.I.C.E., 1826; invented tubular boilers used in the navy. [li. 168]

SEAWARD, SAMUEL (1800-1842), engineer; brother of John Seaward [q. v.], with whom he worked from c. 1826, and brought out direct acting naval engines, 1836; F.R.S.; with his brother invented and improved many engineering contrivances. [li. 168]

SEAXBURGH (d. 673). [See SEXBURGHA.]

SEBBI, SAEBBI, or **SEBBA** (d. 695?), became king of East-Saxons, c. 665, reigning conjointly with his nephew, Sigheri [q. v.], under overlordship of king of Mercia; resigned crown and took monastic habit, c. 695, dying soon afterwards; buried in St. Paul's Church, London. [li. 169]

SEBERT. [See also SIGEBERT.]

SEBERT, SABERET, or **SABA** (d. 616?), first Christian king of East-Saxons; received Mellitus [q. v.] as teacher and bishop; perhaps buried in Westminster Abbey. [li. 169]

SEBRIGHT, SIR JOHN SAUNDERS, seventh baronet (1767-1846), politician and agriculturist; served in army on staff of Lord Amherst; M.P., Herefordshire, 1807 till end of first reformed parliament; practically an advanced whig, though disclaiming connection with any party; seconded Russell's motion for leave to bring in first Reform Bill, 1831; published works on animals. [li. 170]

SECKER, THOMAS (1693–1768), archbishop of Canterbury; educated with view to dissenting ministry under Samuel Jones (1680 ?–1719) [q. v.]; studied medicine in London and Paris, 1716–20; M.D. Leyden, 1721; graduated at Exeter College, Oxford; prebendary of Durham, 1727; chaplain to George II, 1732; D.C.L., 1733; bishop of Bristol, 1734, and of Oxford, 1737; dean of St. Paul's, London, 1750; archbishop of Canterbury, 1758; deprecated the progress of methodism, but did not persecute its adherents; published sermons, charges, and other works, including ' Lectures on the Church Catechism ' (posthumously, 1769). [li. 170]

SECKER, WILLIAM (d. 1681 ?), divine; preached at Tewkesbury and afterwards at All Hallows, London Wall; published sermons. [li. 173]

SECKFORD or **SACKFORD**, THOMAS (1515 ?–1588), lawyer; barrister, Gray's Inn, 1540; Lent reader, 1555; surveyor of court of wards and liveries; steward of court of Marshalsea; on commission for causes ecclesiastical, 1570; M.P., Ipswich, 1572. [li. 173]

SECURIS, JOHN (fl. 1566), medical writer; born in England; studied in Paris and afterwards at Oxford; probably licensed to practise physic by bishop of Salisbury, where he lived; published medical and other works. [li. 174]

SECURIS or **HATCHETT**, MICHAEL (fl. 1545), doctor at Salisbury; left medical manuscripts. [li. 174]

SEDDING, EDMUND (1836–1868), architect and musician; architect successively in Bristol, London, and Penzance; published carols and other musical compositions. [li. 175]

SEDDING, JOHN DANDO (1838–1891), architect; brother of Edmund Sedding [q. v.]; entered office of George Edmund Street [q. v.], 1858; endeavoured to form a school of carvers and modellers from nature; F.R.I.B.A., 1874; diocesan architect for Bath and Wells; works by him published posthumously. [li. 175]

SEDDON, FELIX JOHN VAUGHAN (1798–1865), orientalist; registrar of Rangpur, Bengal, 1820; professor of oriental languages, King's College, London, 1833; preceptor to nawab Nizam; assisted in translating bible into some Indian language. [li. 176]

SEDDON, JOHN (1644–1700), master of Sir John Johnson's writing school, Priest's Court, Foster Lane, Cheapside, London; published calligraphic works. [li. 176]

SEDDON, JOHN (1719–1769), unitarian divine; educated at Glasgow University; assistant to Joseph Mottershead [q. v.] at Cross Street, Manchester; religious writings by him published posthumously. [li. 176]

SEDDON, JOHN (1725–1770), dissenting minister; educated at Glasgow University; minister of Cairo Street Chapel, Warrington; secretary and librarian of Warrington academy, the scheme for promotion of which he had actively assisted, 1757; rector and professor of belles lettres, 1767; entered into controversy with John Taylor (1694–1761) [q. v.] respecting forms of prayer; editor and joint-author of 'A Form of Prayer and a New Collection of Psalms,' 1763. [li. 177]

SEDDON, THOMAS (1753–1796), divine; of Hart Hall, Oxford; curate of chapelry of Stretford, near Manchester, 1777–96; incumbent of Lydgate, Saddleworth, 1789; published sermons and other works. [li. 178]

SEDDON, THOMAS (1821–1856), landscape-painter; studied ornamental art in Paris; furniture designer in London; took part in establishing school of drawing and modelling, Camden Town, London, 1850; exhibited at Royal Academy from 1852. [li. 178]

SEDGWICK, ADAM (1785–1873), geologist; B.A. Trinity College, Cambridge, 1808; fellow, 1810; Woodwardian professor of geology at Cambridge, 1818; president of Geological Society, 1831; Wollaston medallist, 1851; F R.S., 1830, and Copley medallist, 1863; president of British Association, 1833, and of geological section, 1837, 1845, 1853, and 1860; honorary D.C.L. Oxford, 1860; honorary LL.D. Cambridge, 1866; member of royal commission of inquiry into condition of Cambridge University, 1850–2; made secretary to Prince Albert when elected chancellor of Cambridge University, 1847; prebendary of

Norwich, 1834; published in scientific magazines papers dealing with geological and other subjects; did much to augment the geological collection of his university. [li. 179]

SEDGWICK, AMY (afterwards MRS. PARKES, MRS. PEMBERTON, and MRS. GOOSTRY) (1830–1897), actress; appeared at Haymarket, London, 1857, and was original Hester Grazebrook in Taylor's 'Unequal Match'; managed Haymarket, 1866; appeared last in London at Haymarket, 1877; subsequently instructed pupils and gave dramatic recitals. [Suppl. iii. 336]

SEDGWICK, DANIEL (1814–1879), hymnologist; shoemaker in London; started as dealer in second-hand books, 1837; published reprints of hymn-writers of seventeenth and eighteenth centuries and catalogues of rare religious poetry; recognised as foremost living hymnologist. [li. 182]

SEDGWICK, JAMES (1775–1851), author; of Pembroke College, Oxford; barrister, Middle Temple, 1801; commissioner of excise at Edinburgh, 1809, and chairman of excise board, 1811; examiner of droits of admiralty accounts, 1815; chairman of board of stamps, 1817–26; published works on legal and political subjects. [li. 182]

SEDGWICK, JOHN (1601 ?–1643), puritan divine; M.A. Magdalen Hall, Oxford, 1625; B.D., 1633 (incorporated at Cambridge, 1638); rector of St. Alphege, London, 1641; chaplain to Earl of Stamford's regiment. [li. 184]

SEDGWICK, OBADIAH (1600 ?–1658), puritan divine; brother of John Sedgwick [q. v.]; M.A. Magdalen Hall, Oxford, 1623; B.D., 1630; chaplain to Sir Horace Vere, baron Vere of Tilbury [q. v.], whom he accompanied to Low Countries; chaplain to regiment of foot raised by Denzil Holles [q. v.], 1642; member of Westminster Assembly, 1643; rector of St. Andrew's, Holborn, London, 1645–6, and of St. Paul's, Covent Garden, London, 1646–56; published religious works. [li. 183]

SEDGWICK, ROBERT (d. 1656), governor of Jamaica; brother of William Sedgwick [q. v.]; perhaps went to New England, 1635; freeman of Massachusetts, 1637; captain of Charlestown trained band; one of founders of 'Military Company of Massachusetts,' 1638; major-general of Massachusetts forces, 1652; served against French in Acadia, which he added to British dominions, 1654; one of civil commissioners for government of Jamaica, 1655. [Suppl. iii. 337]

SEDGWICK, THOMAS (fl. 1550–1565), Roman catholic divine; fellow successively of Peterhouse and Trinity College, Cambridge; D.D.; rector of Erwarton, 1552; Lady Margaret professor of divinity, Cambridge, 1554–6; incorporated D.D. Oxford, 1554; regius professor of divinity, 1557; vicar of Gainsford and rector of Stanhope, 1558. [li. 184]

SEDGWICK, WILLIAM (1610 ?–1669 ?), puritan divine and mystic; M.A. Pembroke College, Oxford, 1631; incorporated M.A. Cambridge, 1635; chaplain to foot regiment raised by Sir William Constable [q. v.], 1642; chief preacher in Ely, 1644–60; conformed and was rector of Mattishall Burgh, 1663; published religious works. [li. 185]

SEDLEY, CATHARINE, COUNTESS OF DORCHESTER (1657–1717), only child of Sir Charles Sedley [q. v.]; mistress of Duke of York (afterwards James II), by whom she had several children; created Baroness of Darlington and Countess of Dorchester, 1686; married Sir David Colyear, second baronet, 1696; celebrated as a wit. [li. 185]

SEDLEY, SIR CHARLES (1639 ?–1701), wit and dramatic author; of Wadham College, Oxford; entered parliament after the Restoration as one of members (barons) for New Romney; achieved notoriety as a fashionable profligate; wrote two tragedies and three comedies, besides prose pieces and poems (collected in 'A New Miscellany' and in a 'Collection of Poems,' 1701). [li. 187]

SEDULIUS (d. 828), biblical commentator; probably of Irish birth; son of Feradach, abbot of Kildare; wrote Latin commentaries on St. Paul's Epistles and Gospel of St. Matthew. [li. 187]

SEEBOHM, HENRY (1832–1895), quaker ornithologist; settled as manufacturer of steel at Sheffield; travelled abroad for purposes of ornithological study;

joined British Ornithologists' Union and Zoological Society, 1873; F.R.G.S., 1878, and secretary, 1890–5; F.L.S., 1879; published ornithological works. [li. 189]

SEED, JEREMIAH (1700–1747), divine; M.A. Queen's College, Oxford, 1725; fellow, 1732; rector of Knight's Enham, 1741–7; published religious writings. [li. 189]

SEELEY, SIR JOHN ROBERT (1834–1895), historian and essayist; son of Robert Benton Seeley [q. v.]; of City of London School and Christ's College, Cambridge; B.A., 1857; obtained senior chancellor's medal; fellow and classical lecturer; chief classical assistant at City of London School, 1859; professor of Latin at University College, London, 1863; published, 1865, 'Ecce Homo,' a work which attracted immediate attention and provoked a storm of controversy; professor of modern history at Cambridge, 1869–95; fellow of Gonville and Caius College, Cambridge, 1882; K.C.M.G., 1894; died of cancer. In his lectures he adopted, though he did not formulate, the view that 'history is past politics, and politics present history.' His publications include 'The Life and Times of Stein,' 1878, 'The Expansion of England,' 'The Growth of British Policy,' 1895, and 'Lectures on Political Science,' 1895. [li. 190]

SEELEY, LEONARD BENTON (1831–1893), author; son of Robert Benton Seeley [q. v.]; educated at City of London School and Trinity College, Cambridge; fellow, 1854; M.A., 1855; barrister, Lincoln's Inn, 1855; published 'Horace Walpole and his Works,' 1884, and other volumes. [li. 193]

SEELEY, ROBERT BENTON (1798–1886), publisher and author; served with his father, Leonard Benton Seeley, in bookselling and publishing business in Fleet Street, London, and, with partners, controlled publishing branch, 1826–57; connected with many religious and philanthropic movements. His publications were mainly confined to books expounding evangelical opinions. His original works include 'Essays on the Church,' 1834, and 'The Greatest of the Plantagenets, Edward I,' 1860. [li. 193]

SEEMAN or **ZEEMAN**, ENOCH (1694–1744), portrait-painter; born at Danzig, Germany; practised in London. [li. 194]

SEEMANN, BERTHOLD CARL (1825–1871), botanist and traveller; born at Hanover; graduated at Göttingen; studied botany at Kew, 1844–6; naturalist to H.M.S. Herald in voyages on west coast of America and in the Arctic seas, 1847–51; published 'Narrative of the Voyage,' 1853, and was made Ph.D. Göttingen; joint-editor of German journal of botany, 'Bonplandia,' 1853–62; commissioned with Colonel Smythe, R.A., to report on Fiji islands, 1860; began publication of 'Journal of Botany,' 1863; subsequently introduced to Venezuela and Nicaragua; F.L.S., 1852; vice-president, Anthropological Society; F.R.G.S.; published numerous scientific treatises; died at Javali. [li. 194]

SEFFRID, **SEFRID**, **SEINFRID**, or **SAFRED II** (d. 1204), bishop of Chichester; successively archdeacon, dean (1178), and bishop (1180) of Chichester; restored a large part of his cathedral church after the fire of 1187; sided with monks of Christ Church, Canterbury, in quarrel with Archbishop Baldwin. [li. 195]

SEGAR or **SEAGER**, FRANCIS (fl. 1549–1563), translator and poet; probably freeman of Stationers' Company, 1557. His works include 'Certayne Psalmes ... drawen into Englishe metre,' 1553, and a poem on Richard Plantagenet in the 'Myrrour for Magistrates,' 1563. [li. 196]

SEGAR, SIMON (fl. 1656–1712), author of 'Honores Anglicani'; great-grandson of Sir William Segar [q. v.]; member of Gray's Inn, 1656; library keeper, 1674; published 'Honores Anglicani,' 1712. [li. 198]

SEGAR, SIR WILLIAM (d. 1633), herald; Portcullis pursuivant, 1585; Somerset herald, 1589; Norroy king-of-arms, 1593; appointed, 1603, Garter king-of-arms in succession to Sir William Dethick [q. v.], who was, however, reinstated; returned to the office, 1607; knighted, 1616; works include 'Baronagium Genealogicum: or the Pedigrees of the English Peers' (published, 1764–84). [li. 197]

SEGRAVE, GILBERT DE (d. 1254), judge; son of Stephen de Segrave (d. 1241) [q. v.]; justice of forests south of Trent, 1242; accompanied Henry III in Gascony, 1254; was captured by citizens of Pons and died in prison. [li. 198]

SEGRAVE, GILBERT DE (d. 1313?), doctor of theology and canon law, Oxford; prebendary of Lincoln, 1297; sacristan of chapel of St. Sepulchre, York, till 1304. [li. 199]

SEGRAVE, GILBERT DE (d. 1316), bishop of London; son of Nicholas de Segrave, first baron Segrave [q. v.]; subdeacon; prebendary of Lincoln, 1302, and probably later of St. Paul's, London; precentor of St. Paul's, 1310; bishop of London, 1313–16. [li. 199]

SEGRAVE, SIR HUGH (d. 1385?), knight and keeper of castle of Brustwick and forests of Kingswood and Filwood, Gloucestershire; member of Richard II's council, 1377; steward of Richard II's household, 1380; received custody of great seal, 1381; treasurer of England, 1381, till death. [li. 199]

SEGRAVE, JOHN DE (1256?–1325), baron; son of Nicholas de Segrave, first baron Segrave [q. v.]; served against Llywelyn of Wales, 1277 and 1282; constantly employed in Scottish wars from 1291; attached himself to Roger Bigod, fifth earl of Norfolk [q. v.], 1297; signed barons' letter to Pope Boniface VIII, 1301; warden of Scotland, 1302–6; at siege of Stirling, 1304; appointed justice and captain in Scotland south of Forth on final departure of Edward I; escorted Wallace to London, 1305; head of commission for Wallace's trial; justice of forests beyond Trent, c. 1307–10; warden of Scotland, 1309; joined barons against Gaveston, 1310; keeper of forests this side of Trent, 1312; fought at Bannockburn, 1314; member of continual council, 1318; joint-captain of troops going to Gascony under Edmund of Woodstock, earl of Kent [q. v.], 1324; died in Aquitaine. [li. 200]

SEGRAVE, NICHOLAS DE, first BARON SEGRAVE (1238?–1295), son of Gilbert de Segrave (d. 1254) [q. v.]; attached himself to Simon de Montfort, 1258; shared in excommunication brought against rebel party, 1263; defended Northampton against Henry III, and, on its capture, escaped to London; at Lewes, 1264, and Evesham, 1265, when he was captured and suffered confiscation; escaped to isle of Ely and was excommunicated; subsequently submitted to Prince Edward, on which his lands were restored; took part in Welsh campaigns, 1277 and 1282; one of the judges of suit as to Scottish succession. [li. 202]

SEGRAVE, NICHOLAS DE, LORD OF STOWE (d. 1322), son of Nicholas de Segrave, first baron Segrave [q. v.]; fought at Falkirk, 1298, and at siege of Carlaverock, 1300; took part in Scottish campaigns of 1303 and 1304; imprisoned in Tower of London for proceeding to France in midst of Scottish campaign; pardoned and restored to favour; adhered to Edward II and supported Piers Gaveston; governor of Northampton and marshal of England, 1309; engaged in Scotland, 1310; attached himself to Thomas, earl of Lancaster (1277?–1322) [q. v.], c. 1316, and served under him against Scots, 1318. [li. 204]

SEGRAVE or **SEDGRAVE**, STEPHEN DE (d. 1241), took orders, but abandoned clerical profession; constable of Tower of London, 1203; prominent as a judge and justice itinerant, from 1217; custodian of Sauvey Castle, Leicestershire, 1220; one of justiciaries on Henry III's departure for Brittany, 1230; chief justiciar, 1232; supported system of administration by foreigners; deprived of office on reconciliation of Henry III with lords, 1234; restored to favour, 1236; justice of Chester; entered Augustinian abbey of St. Mary des Prés. [li. 205]

SEGRAVE, STEPHEN DE (d. 1333), archbishop of Armagh; studied at Cambridge; chancellor of Cambridge University, 1303–6; doctor of canon law; clerk in royal household; rector of Stowe, 1300–18; dean of Glasgow and canon of Dunkeld, c. 1309; canon of Lincoln, c. 1318, and of St. Paul's, London, c. 1319; archbishop of Armagh, 1323. [li. 206]

SEGUARDE, JOHN (fl. 1414), rhetorician and poet; master of grammar school, Norwich; left poetical and other manuscripts. [li. 207]

SEGUIER, JOHN (1785–1856), artist; partner with his brother as picture-restorer; studied at Royal Academy. [li. 208]

SEGUIER, WILLIAM (1771–1843), artist; brother of John Seguier [q. v.]; pupil of George Morland [q. v.]; practised as topographical and portrait painter; art expert; conservator of royal picture galleries under George IV, William IV, and Queen Victoria; first keeper of National Gallery; superintendent of British Institution. [li. 207]

SEGUIN, ANN CHILDE (1814–1888), singer; wife of Arthur Edward Shelden Seguin [q. v.]; married c. 1831; subprofessor at Royal Academy of Music; subsequently taught music in New York. [li. 209]

SEGUIN, ARTHUR EDWARD SHELDEN (1809–1852), bass singer; educated at Royal Academy of Music; engaged at various London theatres till 1838; went (1838) to America, where he founded 'Seguin Troup' operatic company. [li. 208]

SEIRIOL (fl. 530), Welsh saint; founded monastery of Penmon, Anglesey; cousin of Maelgwn Gwynedd [q. v.]. A legend about him and his friend St. Cybi [q. v.] was embodied, though not quite correctly, by Matthew Arnold in a sonnet. [li. 209]

SELBORNE, EARL OF (1812–1895). [See PALMER, ROUNDELL.]

SELBY, CHARLES (1802?–1863), actor and dramatist; member of company at Strand Theatre, London, 1832; with Macready at Drury Lane, London, 1841–2, subsequently playing principally character parts at various London theatres; his last appearance at Drury Lane, 1863; wrote many plays of the lightest description; published 'Maximums and Speciments of William Muggins,' 1841. [li. 209]

SELBY, PRIDEAUX JOHN (1788–1867), naturalist; of University College, Oxford; high sheriff for Northumberland, 1823; published 'Illustrations of British Ornithology,' 1825–34; founded with Sir William Jardine [q. v.] and Dr. G. Johnston, 'Magazine of Zoology and Botany,' 1837, and was joint-editor; F.L.S.; honorary M.A. Durham, 1839; published 'British Forest Trees,' 1842. On his death some of his natural-history collections were presented to Cambridge University. [li. 210]

SELBY, WALFORD DAKIN (1845–1889), antiquary; junior clerk in Record Office, 1867, and ultimately superintendent of the search-room; joint-founder, 1883, and director-in-chief and honorary treasurer, 1883–9, of Pipe Roll Society; published antiquarian writings and compilations. [li. 211]

SELDEN, JOHN (1584–1654), jurist; educated at Chichester under Hugh Barker [q. v.] and at Hart Hall, Oxford; entered Clifford Inn, 1602, and Inner Temple, 1604; barrister, Inner Temple, 1612; bencher, 1633; steward to Henry Grey, ninth earl of Kent [q. v.]; published, 1617, 'History of Tythes,' many passages in which, and in the preface, gave offence to the clergy; his 'History of Tythes' suppressed by public authority; took active part in preparation of the protestation of the Commons, 1621, and was temporarily placed in private custody; returned to parliament as burgess for Lancaster, 1623; M.P., Great Bedwin, 1626; took prominent part (1626) in impeachment of Buckingham; counsel for Sir Edmund Hampden, who had been committed to prison for refusing to lend money to Charles I on his sole demand, and disputed legality of detention on warrant which did not specify the offences, 1627; M.P., Ludgershall, 1628; chairman of committee to consider precedents as to imprisonment without cause assigned; supported (1629) petition of printers and booksellers against Laud's interference with their trade, and took active part in discussion on tonnage and poundage; imprisoned in consequence of his action in the house; liberated, 1631; M.P. for Oxford University in Long parliament; opposed crown on question of ship-money; on committees to draw up articles of impeachment of Laud, 1641, and to examine Charles I's violation of privileges of parliament, 1642; sat in Assembly of Divines at Westminster, 1643; received office of clerk and keeper of records of the Tower of London, 1643; member of committee to manage the admiralty, 1645; member of committee to hear appeals from parliamentary visitors to Oxford University, 1647; after 1649 took no further part in public affairs and abstained from expressing any opinion. He won fame as an orientalist by his treatise 'De Diis Syris,' 1617, and subsequently made a valuable collection of oriental manuscripts,

most of which passed at his death into the Bodleian Library. His work in this direction consisted chiefly in the exposition of rabbinical law. His 'Table Talk,' containing reports of his utterances from time to time during the last twenty years of his life, composed by his secretary, Richard Milward [q. v.], appeared in 1689. His works include 'Titles of Honour,' 1614, an edition of Eadmer [q. v.], 1623, 'Marmora Arundelliana,' 1624, 'De Successionibus,' 1631, 'Mare Clausum,' 1635, 'De Jure Naturali,' 1640, 'Judicature in Parliament,' 1640, 'Privileges of Baronage,' 1642, 'Fleta,' 1647, and 'On the Nativity of Christ,' 1661. His works were collected by Dr. David Wilkins, 1726. [li. 212]

SELKIRK, fifth EARL OF (1771–1820). [See DOUGLAS, THOMAS.]

SELKIRK, ALEXANDER (1676–1721), prototype of 'Robinson Crusoe'; son of John Selcraig, shoemaker, of Largo; ran away to sea, 1695, and returned home, 1701; joined privateering expedition of Captain William Dampier [q. v.] to South Seas, 1703; sailing master on Cinque ports under Thomas Stradling, with whom he quarrelled, 1704; put ashore on uninhabited island of Juan Fernandez; rescued, 1709, by Captain Woodes Rogers [q. v.] in a new expedition of Dampier, who obtained for him command of the Increase; sailing master of a new prize, 1710; arrived in England, 1711; retired to Largo and, later, lived in London; subsequently resumed his life as sailor. Defoe, who published 'Robinson Crusoe,' 1719, probably did not know Selkirk personally. [li. 224]

SELLAR, ALEXANDER CRAIG (1835–1890), barrister; son of Patrick Sellar [q. v.]; M.A. Balliol College, Oxford, 1865; called to Scottish bar, 1862; legal secretary to the lord-advocate, 1870–4; liberal M.P. for Haddington Burghs, 1882–5, and for Partick division of Lanarkshire, 1885; liberal whip, 1885–8. [li. 226]

SELLAR, PATRICK (1780–1851), factor to George Granville Leveson-Gower, first duke of Sutherland [q. v.] till 1818. [li. 225]

SELLAR, WILLIAM YOUNG (1825–1890), professor of Latin in Edinburgh University; son of Patrick Sellar [q. v.]; educated at Glasgow and Balliol College, Oxford; M.A., 1850; fellow of Oriel College, Oxford, 1848; assistant-professor of Latin at Glasgow, 1851–3, and of Greek at St. Andrews, 1853–9; professor of Greek at St. Andrews, 1859–63, and of Latin at Edinburgh, 1863–90; published works on classical authors. [li. 226]

SELLER, ABEDNEGO (1646?–1705), nonjuring divine; educated at Lincoln College, Oxford; vicar of Charles at Plymouth, 1686; deprived, 1690; published religious works. [li. 226]

SELLER, JOHN (fl. 1700), hydrographer to Charles II; published maps, also 'The English Pilot' and 'The Sea Atlas,' 1671. [li. 227]

SELLON, BAKER JOHN (1762–1835), lawyer; of Merchant Taylors' School, London, and St. John's College, Oxford; B.C.L., 1785; barrister, Inner Temple, 1792; police magistrate at Union Hall, 1814, and at Hatton Garden, London, 1819–34; published legal works. [li. 228]

SELLON, PRISCILLA LYDIA (1821–1876), founder of Society of Sisters of Mercy of the Holy Trinity, Devonport, branches of which were afterwards established in many centres of population; her enterprise was attacked or defended in numerous pamphlets. Dr. Pusey took a warm interest in her scheme. [li. 228]

SELLYNG, RICHARD (fl. 1450), author of a poem, 'Evidens to Beware and Gode Counsayle' (Harl. MS. 7333, f. 36 a). [li. 229]

SELRED or **SÆLRÆD** (d. 746), king of East-Saxons, succeeded. c. 709, Offa (fl. 709) [q. v.] [li. 229]

SELVACH (d. 729), king of Scottish Dalriada; probably son of Fearchair Fada (the Long) [q. v.]; king of Scottish Dalriada before 697; defeated Britons at Minverce, 717; slew his brother Ainbhealach in battle at Finglen, 719; defeated by Duncan MacBecc in sea-fight at Ardannisby, 719; became priest, 723; defeated by Eochadh, and lost sovereignty, 727. [li. 229]

SELWYN, SIR CHARLES JASPER (1813–1869), lawyer; son of William Selwyn (1775–1855) [q. v.]; of Eton and Trinity College, Cambridge; fellow; M.A., 1839;

LL.D., 1862; barrister, Lincoln's Inn, 1840; bencher, 1856; Q.C., 1856; M.P., Cambridge University, 1859-68; appointed solicitor-general and knighted, 1867; lord-justice of appeal and privy councillor, 1868.   [li. 230]

SELWYN, GEORGE AUGUSTUS (1719-1791), wit and politician; of Eton and Hart Hall, Oxford; rusticated, 1745; clerk of the irons and surveyor of meltings of the mint (sinecures); M.P. for family borough of Ludgershall, 1747, and for Gloucester, 1754-80; received sinecure of registrar of court of chancery in Barbados, paymaster of the works (till 1782), and surveyor-general of works (1783); elected to White's, 1744, and was member of the Jockey Club in 1767.   [li. 231]

SELWYN, GEORGE AUGUSTUS (1809-1878), bishop of Lichfield; son of William Selwyn (1775-1855) [q. v.]; of Eton and St. John's College, Cambridge; M.A., 1834; fellow and D.D. *per literas regias*, 1842; curate at Windsor; bishop of New Zealand, 1841; greatly influenced the development of the colonial church; attended first Pan-Anglican synod in England, 1867; bishop of Lichfield, 1868; published sermons and other religious writings. Selwyn College, Cambridge, was erected by public subscription in his memory, and incorporated, 1882. [li. 232]

SELWYN, JOHN RICHARDSON (1844-1898), bishop of Melanesia; son of George Augustus Selwyn (1809-1878) [q. v.]; born at Waimaté, New Zealand; of Eton and Trinity College, Cambridge; M.A., 1870; vicar of St. George's, Wolverhampton; joined Melanesian mission, and reached Norfolk island, 1873; bishop of Melanesia, 1877; returned to England owing to ill-health, 1890; master of Selwyn College, Cambridge, c. 1890 till death; published 'Pastoral Work in the Colonies,' 1897. [Suppl. iii. 338]

SELWYN, WILLIAM (1775-1855), lawyer; of Eton and St. John's and Trinity Colleges, Cambridge; M.A., 1800; barrister, Lincoln's Inn, 1807; treasurer, 1840; recorder of Portsmouth, 1819-29; K.C., 1827; published legal writings.   [li. 233]

SELWYN, WILLIAM (1806-1875), divine; son of William Selwyn (1775-1855) [q. v.]; of Eton and St. John's College, Cambridge; fellow, 1829; M.A., 1831; D.D., 1864; held various livings from 1831; canon residentiary of Ely, 1833-75; Lady Margaret professor, 1855; member of cathedrals commission, 1852; published religious works.   [li. 233]

SEMPILL. [See also SEMPLE.]

SEMPILL, FRANCIS (1616?-1682), Scottish ballad-writer; probably educated for the law; sheriff-depute of Renfrewshire, 1677; widely known as a poet and wit; wrote occasional pieces on social and political subjects.   [li. 234]

SEMPILL, HEW, eleventh LORD SEMPILL (d. 1746), colonel; ensign, 1719; served in Spain and Flanders; major, 26th (Cameronians), 1718; colonel of Black Watch, 1741; served in Flanders, 1743; colonel of 25th foot, 1745; acted as brigadier-general at Culloden, 1746.   [li. 235]

SEMPILL or **SEMPLE**, HUGH, HUGO SEMPILIUS (1596-1654), mathematician; born at Craigevar, Scotland; aggregated to Society of Jesus at Toledo, 1615; rector of Scottish College, Madrid; published mathematical works.   [li. 235]

SEMPILL, SIR JAMES (1566-1625), of Beltrees; educated with young King James VI and at St. Andrews; agent to James VI in London, 1599; knighted, 1600; went on embassy to France, 1601; published controversial works; assisted James VI in preparing for press his 'Basilicon Doron,' 1599.   [li. 235]

SEMPILL or **SEMPLE**, ROBERT, third LORD SEMPILL (d. 1572), governor and constable of castle of Douglas, 1533; succeeded his father, 1548; supported queen-regent, Mary of Guise, against lords of congregation; signed band in support of Mary Queen of Scots and Darnley, 1561, but after murder of Darnley joined opposition to Mary; fought at Carberry Hill, 1567; joint-lieutenant of the western parts, 1568; prisoner of the Hamiltons, 1570.   [li. 237]

SEMPILL, ROBERT (1530?-1595), Scottish ballad-writer; spent early life in Paris; fled at massacre of St. Bartholomew, 1572; probably with Morton's army during siege of Edinburgh. In his ballads he appears as a staunch supporter of the reformers.   [li. 238]

SEMPILL, ROBERT (1595?-1665?), Scottish poet; son of Sir James Sempill [q. v.]; educated at Glasgow University; wrote, c. 1640, 'Life and Death of Habbie Simson,' included in Watson's 'Choice Collection,' 1706-9. [li. 236]

SEMPILL or **SEMPLE**, WILLIAM (1546-1633), soldier of fortune; attached as a boy to court of Mary Queen of Scots; joined Scottish regiment under Colonel William Stewart, in service of Prince of Orange; commanded company, 1582, in garrison of Liere, which he betrayed to Duke of Parma; employed in political missions by Philip II of Spain; arrested and imprisoned in Edinburgh, 1588; escaped to Low Countries; lived at Spanish court as 'gentleman of the mouth' to King Philip III; designed and endowed at Madrid missionary college for Scottish Roman catholics, 1623.   [li. 239]

SEMPLE. [See also SEMPILL.]

SEMPLE, DAVID (1808-1878), antiquary; practised as conveyancer in Paisley; F.S.A., Scotland; published works dealing mainly with local history.   [li. 240]

SEMPLE, GEORGE (1700?-1782?), Irish architect; designed and erected steeple of St. Patrick's Cathedral, Dublin, 1749, and Essex Bridge across the Liffey, 1752-4.   [li. 240]

SEMPLE (*alias* SEMPLE-LISLE), JAMES GEORGE (*fl.* 1799), adventurer; born at Irvine; served in America and was prisoner, 1776-7; spent some time on continent, perhaps in service of Frederick the Great and Prince Potemkin; was convicted of fraud in England and repaired to Paris; transported from England for fraud, 1795, and after returning was confined in Tothill Fields prison, London.   [li. 241]

SEMPLE, ROBERT (1766-1816), traveller and governor under the Hudson's Bay Company; born of British parents at Boston; became associated with London firms; chief agent of Hudson's Bay Company's factories and territories, 1815; published accounts of his journeys; killed in quarrel with caravan of North-West Company.   [li. 241]

SEMPRINGHAM, GILBERT OF (1083?-1189). [See GILBERT.]

SENAN (488?-544?), saint; descended from Conaire I, king of Ireland; studied for religious life under Cassidan; perhaps visited Rome and Tours; settled on Great island, Cork Harbour; bishop of Iniscathaigh, at mouth of Shannon. His day in the calendar is 8 March.   [li. 242]

SENATUS, called BRAVONIUS (d. 1207), divine; successively precentor, librarian, and, till 1196, prior of Worcester; wrote concordance of the gospels.   [li. 243]

SENCHAN (*fl.* 649), Irish bard; became chief bard of Connaught during reign of Guaire (649-62); his only extant work, beginning 'Rofich fergus fichit catha co cunnigi' in the 'Book of Leinster.'   [li. 243]

SENEX, JOHN (d. 1740), cartographer and engraver; bookseller in Salisbury Court, Fleet Street, London, 1719; F.R.S., 1728.   [li. 244]

SENGHAM, WILLIAM (*fl.* 1260), Austin friar; sent from Rome to teach in England; wrote religious works.   [li. 244]

SENHOUSE, SIR HUMPHREY FLEMING (1781-1841), navy captain; entered navy, 1797; lieutenant, 1802; served under Sir Israel Pellew [q. v.] in Mediterranean, West Indies, and at Trafalgar, 1804-6; held a command on Spanish main and in Leeward islands, 1806-8; at Martinique, 1809; post captain, 1814; lay captain to Sir Henry Hotham [q. v.], 1815 and 1831-4; K.C.H., 1832; knighted, 1834; served in China, 1839-41; nominated C.B. after death.   [li. 244]

SENHOUSE, RICHARD (d. 1626), bishop of Carlisle; M.A. St. John's College, Cambridge, 1598 (incorporated at Oxford, 1600); D.D., 1622; fellow, 1598; dean of Gloucester, 1621; bishop of Carlisle, 1624.   [li. 245]

SENHOUSE or **SEVER**, WILLIAM (d. 1505), bishop of Durham; entered Benedictine order; educated at Oxford; subdeacon of St. Mary's Abbey, York, 1468-1502; abbot, 1485; bishop of Carlisle, 1495, and of Durham, 1502.   [li. 245]

SENIOR, NASSAU WILLIAM (1790–1864), economist; of Eton and Magdalen College, Oxford; M.A., 1815; probationary fellow, 1812; Vinerian scholar, 1813; barrister, Lincoln's Inn, 1819; member of political economy club, 1823; professor of political economy at Oxford, 1825–30, and 1847–52; he was appointed member of poor-law commission, 1833, and wrote its report, 1834; master in chancery, 1836–55; contributed important political articles to 'Edinburgh Review' after 1840; Cossa places him first among English economists between Ricardo and J. S. Mill. His publications include 'An Outline of Science of Political Economy,' 1836, and 'Biographical Sketches,' 1863. [li. 245]

SENLIS or **ST. LIZ**, SIMON DE, EARL OF NORTHAMPTON AND HUNTINGDON (d. 1109), fought with Rufus in Normandy, 1098; went on crusade after 1100. Built Northampton Castle and founded priory of St. Andrew, Northampton. [li. 248]

SENLIS, SIMON II DE, EARL OF NORTHAMPTON (d. 1153), son of Simon de Senlis or St. Liz, earl of Northampton and Huntingdon [q. v.]; fought for Stephen at Lincoln, 1141, and subsequently remained faithful to Matilda; received earldom of Huntingdon, 1152. [li. 248]

SEPPINGS, SIR ROBERT (1767–1840), naval architect; apprenticed as working shipwright in Plymouth dockyard, 1782, and became master shipwright assistant; invented machinery called 'Seppings blocks' for suspending vessels in dock, 1800; Copley medallist, 1803; master shipwright at Chatham, 1804; invented system of diagonally bracing and trussing frame timbers of ships; surveyor of navy, 1813–32; F.R.S., 1814; knighted, 1819; D.C.L. Oxford, 1836. His improved methods of shipbuilding are now universally adopted. [li. 249]

SÉQUARD, CHARLES EDWARD BROWN- (1817–1894). [See BROWN-SÉQUARD.]

SERES, WILLIAM (d. 1579?), printer; in partnership with John Day (1522–1584) [q. v.] till c. 1550, and with Anthony Scoloker (fl. 1548) [q. v.]; received patent to be sole printer of primers (i.e. forms of private prayer) and psalters, 1554; imprisoned and deprived of patent during Queen Mary's reign, but released by Queen Elizabeth, who restored it; member of old Stationers' Company and master of new company, 1570, 1571, and 1575–6–7. [li. 251]

SERGEANT. [See also SARGENT.]

SERGEANT, JOHN (1622–1707), Roman catholic controversialist; B.A. St. John's College, Cambridge, 1643; secretary to Thomas Morton, bishop of Durham; converted to Roman catholic church; ordained priest at English College, Lisbon; joined English mission, 1652; published a 'Literary Life' of himself, 1700, and many controversial works, which elicited replies from Hammond, Bramhall, Casaubon, Stillingfleet, Tillotson, Gataker, and others. [li. 251]

SERGISON, CHARLES (1654–1732), commissioner of navy; dockyard clerk, 1671; clerk to clerk of the acts, 1675; clerk of the acts, 1689–1719; collected manuscripts relating to navy. [li. 254]

SERLE, AMBROSE (1742–1812), Calvinistic writer; entered navy, and was captain, 1795; under-secretary for colonies, 1772; clerk of reports, 1776; accompanied British army in America, 1776–8; commissioner of transport service and prisoners of war, 1795, 1803, and 1809; published Calvinistic writings. [li. 254]

SERLO (fl. 960?), Benedictine of St. Augustine's, Canterbury; wrote 'Monachorum Libidines.' [li. 255]

SERLO OF BAYEUX (1036?–1104), monkish writer; perhaps monk of Mount St. Michael and chaplain to William (afterwards the Conqueror); received abbey of Gloucester, 1072; perhaps wrote 'Super Oratione Dominica.' [li. 255]

SERLO (d. 1147), fourth dean of Salisbury; first abbot of Cirencester, 1117. [li. 255]

SERLO, called GRAMMATICUS (1109–1207?), monkish writer; became monk of Fountains Abbey, 1138; at monastery of Kirkstall, near Leeds, 1147 till death; wrote poetical and other works. [li. 254]

SERMON, WILLIAM (1629?–1679), physician; practised at Bristol during plague, 1666 till 1669;

attended George Monck, duke of Albemarle [q. v.], for dropsy, and claimed to have cured him, 1669; M.D. Cambridge, 1670; physician in ordinary to Charles II; published medical writings. [li. 255]

SERRES, DOMINIC (1722–1793), marine-painter; born at Auch, Gascony; served as sailor and as master of trading vessel to the Havannah; was captured by British frigate and brought to England, c. 1758; original member of Royal Academy, 1768, and librarian, 1792; marine-painter to George III. [li. 256]

SERRES, JOHN THOMAS (1759–1825), marine-painter; son of Dominic Serres [q. v.]; drawing-master at Chelsea; exhibited at Royal Academy from 1780; marine-painter to George III, 1793; marine draughtsman to admiralty, 1793; married, 1791, Olivia Wilmot, by whose intrigues and extravagance he was ruined; died in rules of King's Bench. [li. 256]

SERRES, LAVINIA JANETTA HORTON DE (1797–1871), daughter of Mrs. Olivia Serres [q. v.]; married Anthony Ryves, a portrait-painter, 1822, and was divorced, 1841; called herself Princess Lavinia of Cumberland and Duchess of Lancaster, and published writings relating to her claim to the title. [li. 258]

SERRES, MRS. OLIVIA (1772–1834), painter and writer; daughter of a house-painter of Warwick named Wilmot; married John Thomas Serres [q. v.], 1791, and was separated from him, 1804; exhibited at Royal Academy, 1794–1808; landscape-painter to George, prince of Wales, 1806; claimed to be natural daughter of Henry Frederick, duke of Cumberland and Strathearn [q. v.], brother of George III, 1817; asserted herself to be legitimate daughter of Duke of Cumberland, and assumed title of Princess Olive of Cumberland, 1820; arrested for debt, 1821; published poetical and other writings; died within rules of King's Bench. [li. 257]

SERVICE, JAMES (1823–1899), politician and pioneer colonist of Melbourne; born in Ayrshire; emigrated to Melbourne and founded commercial firm of John Service & Co., 1853; member for Melbourne in legislative assembly, 1857; minister for lands, 1859–60; passed Torrens act for facilitating transfer of real property, 1860; member for Maldon and treasurer, 1874; member for Castlemaine, 1883; premier of Victoria, 1883–5; brought about Sydney conference, 1882; carried bill for creation of federal council of Australasia, 1884; member of legislative council for Melbourne province. [Suppl. iii. 339]

SERVICE, JOHN (1833–1884), Scottish divine; educated at Glasgow University; edited 'Dumbarton Herald,' 1857; minister at St. John's presbyterian church, at Hobart Town, Tasmania, 1866–70, and at Inch, near Stranraer, Scotland, c. 1871; D.D. Glasgow, 1877; minister at Hyndland, Glasgow, 1878–84; published religious and other writings. [li. 259]

SETCHEL, SARAH (1803–1894), water-colour painter; exhibited at Royal Academy from 1831; member of New Society of Painters in Water-colours, 1841. [li. 259]

SETON, SIR ALEXANDER (fl. 1311–1340), keeper of Berwick (appointed, 1327); surrendered Berwick to English after long siege, 1333. [li. 260]

SETON, SIR ALEXANDER, first EARL OF HUNTLY (d. 1470), received baronies of Gordon, and assumed style of Lord Gordon and Huntly, 1408; accompanied Margaret of Scotland to France on marriage with dauphin Louis, 1436; created Earl of Huntly, 1449; lieutenant-general of the kingdom, 1452; defeated Crawford near Brechin; held command at siege of Roxburgh Castle, 1460. [li. 260]

SETON, ALEXANDER (d. 1542), Scottish friar and reformer; educated at St. Andrews; opposed action of the bishops, c. 1535, and was compelled to retire to England; recanted, 1541; chaplain to Charles Brandon, duke of Suffolk. [li. 261]

SETON, SIR ALEXANDER, first EARL OF DUNFERMLINE (1555?–1622), son of George Seton, fifth baron Seton [q. v.]; studied at jesuit college, Rome; received priory of Pluscardine, 1565; perhaps took holy orders; studied law in France; passed advocate in Scotland; privy councillor, 1585; lord president of court of session, 1593; chief of the Octavians, 1596; became nominally a protestant, but sympathised with Roman catholics; lord of parliament, privy councillor, and guardian of James VI's son Charles (afterwards Charles I), 1598; vice-chancellor and commissioner for union with England, 1604; chancellor, 1604–8; created Earl of Dunfermline, 1606; member of English privy council, 1609; custodian of palace and park of Holyrood, and one of new Octavians, 1611; James I's commissioner at parliament of Edinburgh, 1612.

                                        [li. 261]

SETON, ALEXANDER, sixth EARL OF EGLINTON (1588–1661). [See MONTGOMERIE.]

SETON, ALEXANDER, VISCOUNT KINGSTON (1621 ?–1691), son of George Seton, third earl of Winton [q. v.]; educated in France; declined to subscribe covenant, and was excommunicated, 1644; in attendance on Prince Charles in France; created Viscount Kingston after Charles II's coronation at Scone, 1651. [li. 264]

SETON, SIR ALEXANDER, LORD PITMEDDEN (1639 ?–1719), judge; admitted advocate of Scottish bar, 1661; knighted, 1664; ordinary lord of session, 1677; M.P., Aberdeenshire; lord of justiciary, 1682; created baronet of Nova Scotia, 1684; opposed James II on question of repeal of test and penal law, and was removed from office, 1686. [li. 264]

SETON, ALEXANDER (1814–1852), lieutenant-colonel; second lieutenant, 21st fusiliers, 1832; captain, 1842; exchanged into 75th; assistant quartermaster-general in Ireland, 1849–50; lieutenant-colonel, 1851; perished in wreck during voyage to Cape of Good Hope. [li. 265]

SETON, CHARLES, second EARL OF DUNFERMLINE (d. 1673), son of Sir Alexander Seton, first earl of Dunfermline [q. v.]; one of leaders of Scottish covenanting army which opposed Charles I, 1639; frequently sent on missions to Charles I; privy councillor in England, 1640; Charles I's commissioner to general assembly of kirk of Scotland, 1642; appointed to treat with Charles I after his surrender at Newcastle, 1646; supported 'engagement,' 1648; retired to France; accompanied Charles II in Scotland; privy councillor, 1660; extraordinary lord of session and lord of the articles, 1667; lord privy seal, 1671.

                                        [li. 265]

SETON, SIR CHRISTOPHER (1278 ?–1306); in service of Edward I of England, 1303–6; married Lady Christina Bruce, sister of Robert Bruce [q. v.], and supported Bruce's claims to Scottish crown; captured by English at London, and hanged as traitor. [li. 266]

SETON, GEORGE, first BARON SETON (d. 1478), friend of Robert Bruce [q. v.]; accompanied Lord-chancellor Crichton on embassy to France and Burgundy, 1448; created peer of parliament, 1448; ambassador to England, 1472 and 1473. [li. 267]

SETON, GEORGE, fourth BARON SETON (d. 1549), great-grandson of George Seton, first baron Seton [q. v.]; studied at St. Andrews and in Paris; member of parliamentary committee *pro judicibus*, 1526; extraordinary lord of session, 1533; entrusted (1543) with the custody of Cardinal Beaton, whom he permitted to return to St. Andrews; took field against Hertford, 1544. [li. 267]

SETON, GEORGE, fifth BARON SETON (1530 ?–1585), son of George Seton, fourth baron Seton [q. v.]; lord provost of Edinburgh, 1557 and 1559; on triumph of protestant party went to Paris, 1560, but returned, and was master of Queen Mary's household, 1561; devoted supporter of Queen Mary after marriage with Darnley and Bothwell, assisting her in escape from Loch Leven, 1568; captured at Langside; sent with the Lady Northumberland on embassy to Duke of Alva, c. 1571, and obtained money from Flanders, 1572; made peace with Morton's government after fall of Edinburgh; opposed reinstatement of Morton in power, 1578; intercepted Queen Elizabeth's ambassador, Bowes, and was denounced as rebel, 1578; signed bond to serve James VI of Scotland, 1579; sat on assize for Morton's trial, 1581. [li. 268]

SETON, GEORGE, third EARL OF WINTON (1584–1650), succeeded to earldom, 1607; supported 'engagement' for Charles I's rescue, 1648. [li. 270]

SETON, GEORGE, fifth EARL OF WINTON (d. 1749), succeeded to earldom, 1704; joined rising of 1715; taken prisoner at Preston; sentenced to death, but escaped; died at Rome. [li. 270]

SETON, JOHN (1498 ?–1567), Roman catholic divine; fellow of St. John's College, Cambridge; M.A., 1532;

D.D., 1544; chaplain to Bishop Fisher; chaplain to Gardiner, bishop of Winchester, c. 1554; canon of Winchester, 1553; prebendary of York, 1554; incorporated D.D. Oxford, 1554; persecuted for his religion; died at Rome. His philosophical treatise, 'Dialectica,' appeared, 1572.

                                        [li. 271]

SETON, SIR JOHN, LORD BARNS (d. 1594), Scottish judge; son of George Seton, fifth baron Seton [q. v.]; master of stable to James VI of Scotland before 1581; privy councillor, 1587; extraordinary lord of session, 1588. [li. 272]

SETON or **SETONE,** THOMAS DE (*fl.* 1344–1357), chief-justice of the king's bench; king's serjeant, 1345; judge, probably in king's bench, c. 1354; judge of common pleas, 1355; temporarily chief-justice of king's bench 1357. [li. 272]

SETON, SIR WILLIAM, second baronet of Pitmedden (d. 1744), son of Sir Alexander Seton, lord Pitmedden [q. v.]; M.P., Aberdeen, in Scottish parliament, 1702–6; commissioner for union. [li. 265]

SETTLE, ELKANAH (1648–1724), city poet; of Trinity College, Oxford; produced 'Cambyses, King of Persia: a Tragedy,' which was acted at Lincoln's Inn, 1666, and was first of a series of bombastic dramas which endangered at court Dryden's popularity as a dramatist: Dryden, in consequence, vented his resentment in second part of 'Absalom and Achitophel,' 1682; published 'Absalom Senior, or Achitophel Transpros'd,' 1682, and 'Reflections on several of Mr. Dryden's Plays,' 1687; wrote against Roman catholics; recanted, 1683, and published 'A Narrative of the Popish Plot,' exposing Oates's perjuries; appointed city poet, 1691; found employment soon after the revolution as writer of drolls for Bartholomew Fair; died in the Charterhouse. [li. 272]

SETTLE, THOMAS (*fl.* 1575–1593), divine; of Queens' College, Cambridge; minister at Boxted; imprisoned in Gatehouse for nonconformity, 1586–92 and 1593; joined Brownists, 1592. [li. 275]

SEVENOKE, SIR WILLIAM (1378 ?–1433 ?), lord mayor of London; apprenticed as ironmonger in London; joint-master of Grocers' Company, 1406; warden of London Bridge, 1404; sheriff, 1412; alderman of Tower ward, 1414; lord mayor of London, 1418; M.P., London, 1417. [li. 276]

SEVER, HENRY (d. 1471), divine; of Merton College, Oxford; senior proctor, 1427; D.D.; chaplain and almoner to Henry VI; first provost of Eton College, 1440–2; chancellor of Oxford University, 1442; prebendary, 1445, and chancellor, 1449, of St. Paul's Cathedral, London; warden of Merton College, Oxford, 1456. [li. 276]

SEVER, WILLIAM (d. 1505). [See SENHOUSE.]

SEVERN, ANN MARY (1832–1866). [See NEWTON.]

SEVERN, JOSEPH (1793–1879), painter; apprenticed as engraver; studied at Royal Academy schools; joined Keats circle, c. 1816; gold medallist, Royal Academy, 1818; accompanied Keats to Italy, 1820, and attended him at his death, 1821; obtained travelling pension from Royal Academy, 1821; practised at Rome; married Elizabeth, daughter of Archibald Montgomerie, lord Montgomerie, 1828; in England, 1841–60; British consul at Rome, 1860–72; died at Rome. [li. 277]

SEWALL DE BOVILL (d. 1257), archbishop of York; prebendary of York, c. 1237, dean, 1240, archbishop, 1256 (elected, 1255); suspended and excommunicated for disputing Pope Alexander IV's right to appoint to vacant deanery, 1257. [li. 279]

SEWALL, SAMUEL (1652–1730), colonist and judge; emigrated to Newbury, Massachusetts, in childhood; M.A. Harvard, 1674; member of court of assistants for Massachusetts, 1684; chief-justice, 1718–28. His diary, 1674–1729, has been published. [li. 279]

SEWARD, ANNA (1747–1809), authoress, known as the 'Swan of Lichfield'; daughter of Thomas Seward [q. v.]; lived at Lichfield, 1754–1809; first met, c. 1776, Boswell, whom she afterwards supplied with particulars concerning Johnson; subsequently made acquaintance of Mr. and Mrs. Piozzi [q. v.], and frequently met Dr. Darwin, Thomas Day, Richard Lovell Edgeworth, Dr. Parr, Howard, the prison reformer, and Dr. Johnson; visited by Scott at Lichfield, 1807; bequeathed to Scott her literary works and remains, and to Archibald Constable, the

Edinburgh publisher, her letters; her posthumous compositions edited and poetical works published by Scott, with a memoir, 1810. Six volumes of letters appeared in 1811. Her earliest poems appeared in the 'Batheaston Miscellany,' edited by Anna, lady Miller [q. v.]
[li. 280]

SEWARD, THOMAS (1708–1790), divine; educated at Westminster School and St. John's College, Cambridge; M.A., 1734; prebendary of Lichfield; prebendary of Salisbury, 1755; resided at Lichfield, where he frequently entertained Dr. Johnson; published religious and poetical writings; edited, with Sympson, the 'Works' of Beaumont and Fletcher, 1750.   [li. 282]

SEWARD, WILLIAM (1747–1799), man of letters; of Harrow, Charterhouse, and Oriel College, Oxford; travelled on continent; acquired love of literature and the fine arts; made acquaintance of the Thrales and Dr. Johnson, with whom he became intimate; member of Eumelean Club and Johnson's Essex Club; F.R.S. and F.S.A., 1779; contributed to newspapers and magazines, and published 'Anecdotes of some Distinguished Persons,' 1795–7, and 'Biographia,' 1799.   [li. 282]

SEWARD, WILLIAM WENMAN (*fl.* 1800), writer on Irish politics and topography.   [li. 283]

SEWEL, WILLIAM (1654–1720), quaker historian; born of English parents at Amsterdam; apprenticed as weaver; journalist in Amsterdam. His publications include 'History of the Rise, Increase, and Progress of the Christian People called Quakers' (in Dutch, 1717, and in English, 1722), and a 'Dictionary of English-Dutch,' 1691.
[li. 283]

SEWELL, ANNA (1820–1878), author; daughter of Mary Sewell [q. v.]; published 'Black Beauty,' the 'autobiography' of a horse, 1877.   [li. 288]

SEWELL, GEORGE (*d.* 1726), controversialist and hack writer; of Eton and Peterhouse, Cambridge; B.A., 1709; studied medicine at Leyden; M.D. Edinburgh, 1725; practised medicine in London and later in Hampstead, but subsequently became a bookseller's hack, publishing numerous poems, translations, and political and other pamphlets; wrote at first in tory interest, but afterwards attached himself to cause of Sir Robert Walpole. His works include 'Tragedy of Sir Walter Raleigh,' 1719 (produced at Lincoln's Inn Fields, 1719) and 'Poems on Several Occasions,' 1719.   [li. 285]

SEWELL, HENRY (1807–1879), first premier of New Zealand; brother of Richard Clarke Sewell [q. v.]; solicitor; secretary and deputy-chairman of Canterbury Association for Colonisation of New Zealand, 1850; sent to New Zealand to wind up affairs of the association, 1852; began practice as solicitor at Lyttleton, 1853; member for Christchurch of House of Representatives 1854–61; first premier, 1856; colonial treasurer and commissioner of customs, 1856–9; attorney-general, 1861–2; member of legislative council for Wellington, 1861; minister of justice, 1864–5 and 1869–72; returned to England, 1876.   [li. 286]

SEWELL, JONATHAN (1766–1839), chief-justice of Lower Canada; born at Cambridge, Massachusetts; educated at Bristol grammar school; called to bar of Lower Canada, 1789; solicitor-general, 1793; attorney-general and advocate-general, 1795; member of House of Assembly, *c.* 1795; chief-justice of Quebec, speaker of legislative council, and president of executive council, 1808; introduced into procedure of courts rules of practice which roused strong opposition; honorary LL.D. Harvard; published miscellaneous writings.   [li. 286]

SEWELL, MARY (1797–1884), author; daughter of John Wright, a quaker; governess at school in Essex; married Isaac Sewell, 1819; joined church of England, 1835; interested in philanthropic movements; published verses and stories with object of inculcating moral virtues; her poems collected as 'Stories in Verse,' 1861, and as 'Poems and Ballads,' 1886.   [li. 287]

SEWELL, RICHARD CLARKE (1803–1864), legal writer; of Winchester and Magdalen College, Oxford; M.A., 1829; fellow, 1837–56; senior dean of arts, 1838; D.C.L., 1840; prælector of natural philosophy, 1843; barrister, Middle Temple, 1830; practised in Australian criminal law courts; reader in law to Melbourne University, 1857; published legal works.   [li. 288]

SEWELL, SIR THOMAS (*d.* 1784), master of the rolls; barrister, Middle Temple, 1734; K.C. and bencher of his inn, 1754; practised in chancery courts; M.P., Harwich, 1758–61, Winchelsea, 1761–8; master of rolls, 1764–84; knight and privy councillor, 1764.   [li. 288]

SEWELL, WILLIAM (1780–1853), veterinarian; obtained diploma, 1799; assistant to Edward Coleman (1764 ?–1839), second principal of Veterinary College, London; made supposed discovery of channel pervading the 'medulla spinalis,' 1803; rediscovered neurotomy, 1818; president of Veterinary Medical Society, 1835–6; principal of Veterinary College, 1839; president of Royal College of Veterinary Surgeons, 1852. [Suppl. iii. 340]

SEWELL, WILLIAM (1804–1874), divine; brother of Richard Clarke Sewell [q. v.]; of Winchester and Merton College, Oxford, where he was postmaster, 1822–1827; M.A., 1829; D.D., 1857; Petrean fellow of Exeter College, 1827; tutor of Merton College, Oxford, 1831–53; sub-rector and divinity reader, 1835; dean, 1839; White's professor of moral philosophy, 1836–41; left tractarianism, seeing its Romanising tendencies; assisted in founding St. Columba's College, Rathfarnham, near Dublin, 1842, and St. Peter's College, Radley, near Oxford, 1847; lived at Deutz to avoid his creditors, 1862–70; published miscellaneous works.   [li. 290]

SEXBURGA, **SEAXBURG**, or **SEXBURH** (*d.* 673), wife of Cenwalh [q. v.], king of West-Saxons, whom she succeeded on his death.   [li. 291]

SEXBURGA, SAINT (*d.* 699 ?), queen of Kent and second abbess of Ely; daughter of Anna (*d.* 654), king of East-Angles; married, *c.* 640, Earconbert, king of Kent; founded monastery for nuns in Isle of Sheppey, and became abbess; second abbess of Ely, *c.* 679–*c.* 699. Her day is 6 July.   [li. 291]

SEXBY, EDWARD (*d.* 1658), author of 'Killing no Murder'; entered Cromwell's regiment of horse, *c.* 1643; took leading part in movement against disbanding army, 1647; captain, and governor of Portland, 1649; raised foot regiment, 1650, and became colonel; took part in siege of Tantallon Castle, 1651; deprived of commission, 1651; on political mission in France, 1652–3; took part in schemes for joint rising of royalists and levellers, 1655; negotiated in Flanders with Count Fuensaldanha, governor of Spanish Netherlands, and Don John of Austria, for invasion of England and assassination of Cromwell, 1656; came to England, 1657, and was arrested; published 'Killing no Murder,' an apology for tyrannicide, 1657; died in Tower of London.   [li. 292]

SEXRED or **SEXRÆD** (*d.* 626), king of the East-Saxons; son of Sebert (*d.* 616 ?) [q. v.]; succeeded his father as king of East-Saxons, 616, and reigned conjointly with two brothers; opposed introduction of Christianity; killed in fight with West-Saxons.   [li. 293]

SEXTEN, RICHARD (*d.* 1568). [See ARGENTINE, RICHARD.]

SEYER, SAMUEL (1757–1831), divine; M.A. Corpus Christi College, Oxford, 1780; master of Royal Fort school, 1790; rector of Filton, 1824; published works relating to history of Bristol.   [li. 294]

SEYFFARTH, MRS. LOUISA (1798–1843). [See SHARPE.]

SEYMOUR, MRS. (*fl.* 1717–1723), actress; at Drury Lane, London, 1717–18, and at Lincoln's Inn Fields, London, from 1718; played various Shakespearean characters; married, 1723, the actor Anthony Boheme (*d. c.* 1730). Among her best characters were the Queen ('Don Carlos') and Belvidera.   [li. 294]

SEYMOUR, AARON CROSSLEY HOBART (1789–1870), hymn-writer; brother of Michael Hobart Seymour [q. v.]; member of religious group formed by Selina Hastings, countess of Huntingdon [q. v.], whose biography he published, 1839. His 'Vital Christianity' (1810) contains his hymns and other religious writings. [li. 295]

SEYMOUR, ALGERNON, seventh DUKE OF SOMERSET (1684–1750), son of Charles Seymour, sixth duke of Somerset [q. v.]; joined army under Marlborough at Brussels, 1708; colonel, 1740; general of horse and governor of Minorca, 1737–42.   [li. 299]

SEYMOUR, LADY CATHERINE, COUNTESS OF HERTFORD (1538 ?–1568), daughter of Henry Grey, duke of Suffolk [q. v.], and sister of Lady Jane Grey [see DUDLEY,

LADY JANE]; married, 1553, Henry Herbert, afterwards second earl of Pembroke [q. v.]; divorced after Lady Jane Grey's execution; secretly married Edward Seymour, earl of Hertford [q. v.], 1560, and was consequently imprisoned in Tower of London, 1561, under act of 1536, which made it treason for person of royal blood to marry without sovereign's consent; her second marriage declared invalid by a commission with Parker at its head, 1562; died, still a prisoner, at Cockfield Hall. [li. 296]

SEYMOUR, CHARLES, sixth DUKE OF SOMERSET (1662–1748), son of Charles Seymour, second baron Seymour of Trowbridge (d. 1665); succeeded his brother Francis as duke of Somerset, 1678; educated at Trinity College, Cambridge; married Elizabeth Percy, daughter and heiress of Josceline, eleventh and last earl of Northumberland, and Countess of Ogle, 1682; gentleman of bedchamber, 1683; K.G., 1684; colonel of Queen's dragoons (now 3rd hussars), 1685; lost offices for refusing to introduce at St. James's the papal nuncio d'Adda, 1687; took up arms for Prince of Orange, 1688; chancellor of Cambridge University, 1689, and was incorporated D.C.L. Oxford, 1702; speaker of Lords, 1690; joint-regent, 1701; master of horse, 1702; commissioner for union with Scotland, 1706; enjoyed with his wife the confidence of Queen Anne; supported Marlborough, 1708; lost his place in council, 1711; reinstated as master of horse by George I, but was dismissed, 1716, and lived thenceforth in retirement on his estates; member of the Kit-Cat Club. [li. 297]

SEYMOUR, EDWARD, first EARL OF HERTFORD and DUKE OF SOMERSET (1506 ?–1552), the Protector; son of Sir John Seymour (1476 ?–1536), and brother of Jane Seymour, third wife of Henry VIII; perhaps educated successively at Oxford and Cambridge; accompanied Duke of Suffolk to Calais, 1523, and was knighted; esquire of Henry VIII's household, 1524; master of horse to Duke of Richmond, 1525; accompanied Wolsey on embassy to French king, 1527; esquire of body to Henry VIII, 1530; accompanied Henry VIII to Boulogne to meet Francis I, 1532; gentleman of privy chamber, 1536; created Viscount Beauchamp of Hache, Somerset, 1536; governor and captain of Jersey and chancellor of North Wales, 1536; privy councillor, 1537; created Earl of Hertford, 1537; sent to provide for defences of Calais and Guisnes, 1539; met Anne of Cleves at Calais and returned with her to London, 1539; K.G., 1541; warden of Scottish marches, 1542; lord high admiral, 1542; lord great chamberlain, 1543; lieutenant-general in the north, 1544; took Blackness Castle and pillaged Edinburgh, 1544; lieutenant of kingdom during Henry VIII's absence in France, 1544, but later was with Henry VIII at capture of Boulogne; sent with Gardiner to treat with Emperor Charles at Brussels, 1544; took command at Boulogne, 1545, and defeated French under Marshal De Biez; lieutenant-general in the north, 1545; lieutenant and captain-general of Boulogne and the Boulonnois, 1546; lieutenant-general of the army in France, 1546; took active part in Surrey's trial, 1547; arranged with Paget to conceal fact of Henry VIII's death (28 Jan. 1547), and having brought Edward VI to London, had the death announced; given title of Protector, 31 Jan.; appointed high steward of England for Edward VI's coronation, treasurer of exchequer, and earl marshal; created Duke of Somerset, 16 Feb.; obtained patent as governor and Protector, with power to act with or without advice of the council, 12 March, 1547; chancellor of Cambridge University, 1547; introduced radical religious reforms, an act of uniformity being passed, 1549; sought to win over the Scots, but in consequence of their resistance, which was encouraged by France, made expedition to Scotland and won decisive victory at Musselburgh, 1547; he lost much of his popularity owing to attainder of his brother, Thomas Seymour, baron Seymour of Sudeley [q. v.], 1549, and his religious innovations and other measures, which produced rebellions in various parts of the country; an indictment of his rule drawn up by Warwick, on which he was sent to the Tower of London, and in January 1550 deposed from protectorate; set at liberty and pardoned, February 1550; readmitted to privy council (April) and made gentleman of king's chamber (May); lord-lieutenant of Buckinghamshire and Berkshire, 1551; arrested, October 1551, on charge of conspiring with Arundel Paget and Sir Thomas Palmer (d. 1553) [q. v.] (who revealed the plot) to raise the country and murder Warwick; condemned for felony and beheaded on Tower Hill, though

the plot rests on no satisfactory evidence; buried in St. Peter's Chapel in the Tower of London. His portrait was painted by Holbein. He did much to give practical effect to the protestant revolution, and his actions give evidence of lofty aims. He built Somerset House in the Strand. He married (1) Catherine (d. before 1540), daughter of Sir William Fillol, and (2) Anne (1497–1587), daughter of Sir Edward Stanhope. [li. 299]

SEYMOUR, EDWARD, BARON BEAUCHAMP (1561–1612), son of Edward Seymour, earl of Hertford (1539 ?–1621) [q. v.]; educated at Magdalen College, Oxford; implicated with Sir John Smith (d. 1600 ?) [q. v.] in treasonable proceedings in Essex, 1596. Many unsuccessful attempts were made to establish his legitimacy, and had it been established he would have been, through his mother Catherine Seymour [q. v.], heir to the throne on Queen Elizabeth's death. [li. 311]

SEYMOUR, EDWARD, EARL OF HERTFORD (1539 ?–1621), son of Edward Seymour, earl of Hertford and duke of Somerset [q. v.], by second wife; educated with Prince Edward and knighted at his coronation, 1547; became de jure Duke of Somerset, 1552, but his title and estates forfeited in the same year through the malice of his father's enemies; created Baron Beauchamp and Earl of Hertford, 1559; secretly married Lady Catherine Grey [see SEYMOUR, CATHERINE], 1560, and was imprisoned in Tower of London on marriage becoming known, 1561; in custody till 1571; created M.A. Cambridge, 1571; member of Gray's Inn, 1572; lord-lieutenant of Somerset and Wiltshire, 1602 and 1608; ambassador extraordinary at Brussels, 1605; high steward of revenues to Queen Anne, 1612–19. [li. 310]

SEYMOUR, SIR EDWARD, fourth baronet (1633–1708), speaker of the House of Commons; M.P., Gloucester, 1661; brought in impeachment of Earl of Clarendon, 1667; treasurer of navy; speaker of House of Commons, and privy councillor, 1673; M.P., Devonshire, 1679, and again elected speaker, but rejected by Charles II; co-operated with Halifax and opposed Exclusion Bill; M.P., Exeter, 1685, maintaining opposition to catholic party; succeeded to baronetcy, 1685; joined William of Orange at Exeter, 1688, but opposed offer of crown to him, 1689; later, however, took the oath to the new sovereigns, 1689; lord of treasury, 1692; member of cabinet, 1692–4; M.P., Totnes, 1694, and again for Exeter, 1698; comptroller of Queen Anne's household, and ranger of Windsor Forest, 1702; dismissed from council, 1704. [li. 312]

SEYMOUR, EDWARD ADOLPHUS, eleventh DUKE OF SOMERSET (1775–1855), of Eton and Christ Church, Oxford; M.A., 1794; honorary D.C.L., 1810; succeeded to dukedom, 1793; F.R.S., 1797; F.S.A., 1816; F.L.S., 1820, and president, 1834–7; president of Royal Institution and, 1801–38, of Royal Literary Fund; K.G., 1837; published mathematical treatises. [li. 315]

SEYMOUR, EDWARD ADOLPHUS SEYMOUR, twelfth DUKE OF SOMERSET (1804–1885), son of Edward Adolphus Seymour, eleventh duke of Somerset [q. v.]; of Eton and Christ Church, Oxford; married Jane Georgiana, granddaughter of Richard Brinsley Sheridan [q. v.]; M.P., Okehampton, 1830, Totnes, 1834–55; lord of treasury, 1835; secretary to board of control, 1839; under-secretary for home department, 1841; anti-protectionist; first commissioner of works, with seat in cabinet, 1851–2; succeeded to dukedom, 1855; first lord of admiralty, 1859–66; K.G., 1862; created Earl St. Maur of Berry Pomeroy, 1863. [li. 315]

SEYMOUR, EDWARD JAMES (1796–1866), physician; M.A. Jesus College, Cambridge, 1819; M.D., 1826; studied medicine in London, Edinburgh, and Paris; F.R.C.P., 1823, Gulstonian lecturer, 1829, censor, 1830, Croonian lecturer, 1831, and consiliarius, 1836; physician to St. George's Hospital, London, 1828–47; physician to H.R.H. the Duke of Sussex; metropolitan commissioner in lunacy, 1831–9; F.R.S., 1841; published medical works. [li. 316]

SEYMOUR, FRANCIS, first BARON SEYMOUR OF TROWBRIDGE (1590 ?–1664), son of Edward Seymour, lord Beauchamp [q. v.]; knighted, 1613; M.P. for Wiltshire, 1620 and 1625, and was sheriff of Wiltshire, 1626; M.P. for both Wiltshire and Marlborough, 1628; supported Wentworth's Habeas Corpus Bill; M.P. for Wiltshire in Short parliament, 1640, and in Long parliament; created Baron Seymour of Trowbridge, 1641; joined Charles I at

York, 1642 ; chancellor of duchy of Lancaster, 1645, and was reappointed at Restoration ; at Oxford when it surrendered, 1645, and admitted to composition. His house at Marlborough was used as an inn till 1842, when it became Marlborough College. [li. 317]

SEYMOUR, FRANCIS (INGRAM), second MARQUIS OF HERTFORD (1743-1822), son of Francis Seymour-Conway, first marquis of Hertford [q. v.] ; of Eton and Christ Church, Oxford ; M.A., 1762 ; M.P., Lisburne (Irish House of Commons), 1761-8 ; privy councillor for Ireland, 1765 ; chief secretary to the lord-lieutenant, 1765-6 ; constable of Dublin Castle, 1766 ; member for Lostwithiel in English House of Commons, 1766-8, and for Oxford, 1768-1794 ; lord of treasury, 1774-80 ; cofferer of household, 1780 ; privy councillor for Great Britain, 1780 ; opposed repeal of American tea duty, 1774 ; advocated political union of Great Britain and Ireland with independence of Irish parliament ; took title of Earl of Yarmouth, 1793 ; ambassador extraordinary to Berlin and Vienna, 1793-4 ; succeeded as Marquis of Hertford, 1794 ; master of horse, 1804-6 ; K.G., 1807 ; lord-chamberlain of household, 1812-1821 ; vice-admiral of Suffolk, 1822. [li. 318]

SEYMOUR, SIR FRANCIS (1813-1890), general ; ensign, 1834 ; lieutenant, 1837 ; accompanied Prince Albert of Saxe-Coburg during travels in Italy, 1839, and was groom in waiting to him after marriage to Queen Victoria, 1840, and to queen, 1861 ; captain, 1840 ; obtained company in Scots fusiliers, 1850 ; served in Crimea, 1854 ; C.B., 1857 ; major-general, 1864 ; created baronet, 1869 ; commanded troops in Malta, 1872-4 ; K.C.B., 1875 ; general, 1877. [li. 319]

SEYMOUR, FREDERICK BEAUCHAMP PAGET, first BARON ALCESTER (1821-1895), admiral ; educated at Eton ; entered navy, 1834 ; commander, 1847 ; took Meteor floating battery to Crimea and back to Portsmouth, 1855-6 ; ! commanded naval brigade in New Zealand during Maori war, 1860-1 ; C.B., 1861 ; rear-admiral, 1870 ; lord of admiralty, 1872-4 and 1883-5 ; commanded Channel fleet, 1874-7 ; vice-admiral, 1876 ; commander-in-chief in Mediterranean, 1880-3 ; G.C.B., 1881 ; commanded bombardment of Alexandria, 1882, and was raised to peerage. [li. 320]

SEYMOUR, SIR GEORGE FRANCIS (1787-1870), admiral ; son of Lord Hugh Seymour [q. v.] ; entered navy, 1797 ; lieutenant, 1804 ; served in West Indies, and was wounded at St. Domingo, 1806 ; captain, 1806 ; with Lord Gambier's fleet off Basque roads, 1809 ; in West Indies, 1813-14 ; C.B., 1815 ; serjeant-at-arms to House of Lords, 1818-41 ; naval aide-de-camp to William IV, 1830 ; master of robes, 1830-7 ; K.C.H., 1831 ; G.C.H., 1834 ; rear-admiral, 1841 ; lord of admiralty, 1841-4 ; commander-in-chief in Pacific, 1844-8 ; vice-admiral, 1850 ; admiral, 1857 ; G.C.B., 1860 ; admiral of fleet, 1866. [li. 321]

SEYMOUR, GEORGE HAMILTON (1797-1880), diplomatist ; of Eton and Merton College, Oxford ; M.A., 1823 ; private secretary to Lord Castlereagh, 1822 ; minister resident at Florence, 1830 ; envoy extraordinary to Belgian court, 1836, Lisbon, 1846, St. Petersburg, 1851-4, and Austria, 1855 ; privy councillor, 1855 ; G.C.H., 1836 ; G.C.B., 1847. [li. 321]

SEYMOUR, HENRY (1612-1686), page of honour to Charles I ; attached to Charles II during civil war, and employed as his agent in England from 1651 ; prisoner in England, 1654-7 ; M.P., East Looe, 1660-81 ; groom of bedchamber, comptroller of customs, and clerk of the hanaper. [li. 322]

SEYMOUR, HENRY (1729-1805), politician ; groom of bedchamber ; M.P., Totnes, 1763, Huntingdon, 1768-74, and Evesham, 1774-80 ; married, 1775, and settled at Prunay, near Versailles, 1778 ; became lover of Madame Du Barry, from whom he received many letters, and was separated from his wife ; in England, 1792-1805. [li. 323]

SEYMOUR, LORD HENRY (1805-1859), one of the founders of the Jockey Club at Paris, 1833 ; son of Francis Charles Seymour, third marquis of Hertford ; born in Paris, and lived there throughout his life. [li. 323]

SEYMOUR, LORD HUGH (1759-1801), vice-admiral ; son of Francis Seymour-Conway, first marquis of Hertford [q. v.] ; entered navy, 1770 ; captain, 1779 ; at relief of Gibraltar, 1782 ; became intimate with George, prince of Wales ; lord of admiralty, 1795-8 ; vice-admiral, 1799 ; commander-in-chief in Jamaica, 1799-1801. [li. 323]

SEYMOUR, JAMES (1702-1752), painter of hunting subjects and portraits of racehorses. [li. 324]

SEYMOUR, JANE (1509 ?-1537). [See JANE.]

SEYMOUR, SIR MICHAEL, first baronet (1768-1834), admiral ; entered navy, 1780 ; lieutenant, 1790 ; commander, 1795 ; in Channel, 1796-1800 ; captain, 1800 ; attached to Channel fleet, 1806 ; captured after stubborn fight the French frigate Thétis, off Isle Groix, 1808, and French frigate Niémen, off Ushant, 1809 ; created baronet, 1809 ; in Channel, 1812-14 ; K.C.B., 1815 ; appointed to royal yacht, Prince Regent, 1819, and to George IV's yacht, Royal George, 1825 ; commissioner at Portsmouth, 1829-1832 ; rear-admiral and commander-in-chief in South America, 1832-4. [li. 324]

SEYMOUR, SIR MICHAEL (1802-1887), admiral ; son of Sir Michael Seymour, first baronet [q. v.] ; entered navy, 1813 ; studied at Royal Naval College, Portsmouth ; lieutenant, 1822 ; captain, 1826 ; on South American station, 1827-9 and 1833-5 ; wrecked on coast of Chili, 1835 ; flag-captain to Sir Francis William Austen [q. v.] on North American and West Indies station, 1845-8 ; superintendent of Sheerness dockyard, 1850, and at Devonport, 1851 ; captain of fleet in Baltic, 1854 ; rear-admiral, 1854 ; commander of China station, 1856 ; captured Canton, 1857 ; forced passage of Pei-ho, 1858 ; G.C.B., 1859 ; M.P. for Devonport, 1859-63 ; admiral, 1864 ; commander-in-chief at Portsmouth, 1866 ; vice-admiral of United Kingdom, 1875. [li. 326]

SEYMOUR, MICHAEL HOBART (1800-1874), divine ; M.A. Trinity College, Dublin, 1832 ; admitted ad eundem, Oxford, 1836, and comitatis causa, 1865 ; ordained priest, 1824 ; secretary to Irish Protestant Association ; held lectureships in London, 1834-44 ; wrote against Roman catholics. [li. 327]

SEYMOUR, ROBERT, pseudonymous editor of Stow's 'Survey of London.' [See MOTTLEY, JOHN, 1692-1750.]

SEYMOUR, ROBERT (1800 ?-1836), book illustrator ; apprenticed as pattern-drawer ; practised as artist and, subsequently, as book illustrator ; began copper engraving, 1827, and, later, worked chiefly for reproduction by lithography ; from 1831-6 he executed woodcuts for 'Figaro in London' ; executed illustrations for Hervey's 'Book of Christmas,' 1835 ; produced the plates for the first part (1836) of 'Pickwick Papers,' Dickens being employed originally to write for the illustrations ; committed suicide. His lithographed works include 'Humorous Sketches,' 1833-6. [li. 328]

SEYMOUR, THOMAS, BARON SEYMOUR OF SUDELEY (1508 ?-1549), brother of Edward Seymour, first duke of Somerset [q. v.] : in service of Sir Francis Bryan [q. v.], 1530 ; knighted, 1537 ; accompanied Sir Anthony Browne (d. 1548) [q. v.] on embassy to French court, 1538 ; on mission to Ferdinand, king of Hungary, 1540-2 ; joint-ambassador to regent of Netherlands, 1543 ; marshal of English army in Netherlands under Sir John Wallop [q. v.], 1543 ; appointed master of ordnance for life, 1544 ; served in France, 1544 ; admiral of fleet, 1544, serving against French, 1544-5 ; commissioner to arrange terms with France, 1546 ; privy councillor, 1547 ; created Baron Seymour, K.G., and lord high admiral, 1547 ; secretly married the queen-dowager, Catherine Parr, 1547 ; endeavoured to turn Edward VI against the Protector and formed project for marrying Edward VI to Lady Jane Grey ; lieutenant-general of the south during the Protector's invasion of Scotland, 1547 ; engaged in privateering enterprises ; pressed his suit for hand of Princess Elizabeth, Catherine Parr having died 5 Sept. 1548, and was arrested and imprisoned in Tower, 1549 ; found guilty of treason and executed. [li. 330]

SEYMOUR, WILLIAM, first MARQUIS and second EARL OF HERTFORD and second DUKE OF SOMERSET (1588-1660), son of Edward Seymour, earl of Hertford (1539 ?-1621) [q. v.] ; privately married to Arabella Stuart [see ARABELLA], 1610, and was confined in Tower of London ; escaped, and on Arabella's death went to Paris ; made his peace with James VI and returned to England, 1616 ; K.B., 1616 ; married again ; took courtesy title of Lord Beauchamp, 1618, and was called to House of Lords as Baron Beauchamp, 1621 ; succeeded his grandfather as Earl of

Hertford, 1621 ; privy councillor, 1640 ; created Marquis of Hertford, 1640 ; governor to Charles, prince of Wales, 1641 ; commissioner of array for western counties, 1642 ; took Hereford, 1642 ; reduced Cirencester (February) ; defeated Sir William Waller [q. v.] at Lansdown (5 July) and took Bristol (26 July), 1643 ; in charge of Oxford, 1645, and on its surrender (1646) compounded for his estates on the terms of the articles ; attended Charles I during confinement ; received Garter and barony of Seymour and dukedom of Somerset, 1660. 　　[li. 333]

SEYMOUR, WILLIAM DIGBY (1822 - 1895) lawyer ; B.A. Trinity College, Dublin, 1844 ; LL.D. 1872 ; barrister, Middle Temple, 1846 ; M.P., Sunderland, 1852 ; recorder of Newcastle, 1854 ; engaged in commercial transactions, became financially involved, and was censured by benchers of Middle Temple, 1859 ; M.P., Southampton, 1859 ; Q.C. in county palatine of Lancaster, 1860, and for England, 1861 ; judge of county court circuit No. 1, 1889-95 ; published political and other works. 　　[li. 335]

SEYMOUR-CONWAY, FRANCIS, first MARQUIS OF HERTFORD (1719-1794). [See CONWAY.]

SEYMOUR-CONWAY, FRANCIS CHARLES, third MARQUIS OF HERTFORD (1777-1842), son of Francis (Ingram) Seymour, second marquis of Hertford [q. v.] ; B.A. St. Mary Hall, Oxford, 1796 ; M.P., Oxford, Lisburne, and Camelford, 1819-22 ; K.G., 1822 ; vice-chamberlain to George, prince regent ; original of Marquis of Steyne in 'Vanity Fair.' 　　[li. 319]

SHAA. [See SHAW.]

SHACKLETON, ABRAHAM (1697-1771), schoolmaster ; successively teacher in school at Skipton and private tutor at Duckett's Grove, co. Carlow, Ireland ; opened boarding-school at Ballytore, co. Kildare, 1726, and was head-master till 1756 ; Edmund Burke was one of his pupils. 　　[li. 336]

SHACKLETON, JOHN (d. 1767), portrait-painter ; court painter, 1749 ; painted portraits of George II, Queen Caroline, and other members of royal family, from 1730. 　　[li. 337]

SHACKLETON, RICHARD (1728-1792), son of Abraham Shackleton [q. v.] ; educated at his father's school with Burke, whose lifelong friend he became, and at Trinity College, Dublin ; head-master of school at Ballytore, 1756-79. Letters from Burke to him are printed in 'Leadbeater Papers.' 　　[li. 336]

SHACKLOCK, RICHARD (fl. 1575), Roman catholic divine ; M.A. and fellow, Trinity College, Cambridge, 1559 ; published translation of Cardinal Hosius's 'De Heresibus,' and other writings. 　　[li. 337]

SHADRACH, AZARIAH (1774-1844), Welsh evangelical writer ; entered independent ministry and preached, 1798, in North Wales, where he subsequently held various charges ; published Welsh works. 　　[li. 337]

SHADWELL, CHARLES (fl. 1710-1720), dramatist ; son of Thomas Shadwell [q. v.] ; his plays published, 1720. 　　[li. 343]

SHADWELL, SIR CHARLES FREDERICK ALEXANDER (1814-1886), rear-admiral ; son of Sir Lancelot Shadwell [q. v.] ; studied at Royal Naval College, Portsmouth ; entered navy, 1829 ; commander, 1846 ; served in Burmah war, 1852 ; captain and C.B., 1853 ; on China station, 1856-60 ; at capture of Canton, 1857 and in attack on Taku forts, 1859 ; F.R.S., 1861 ; rear-admiral, 1869 ; commander-in-chief in China, 1871-5 ; K.C.B., 1873 ; president of Royal Naval College, Greenwich, 1878-81 ; published writings on naval astronomy. 　　[li. 338]

SHADWELL, SIR JOHN (1671-1747), physician ; son of Thomas Shadwell [q. v.] ; M.A. All Souls College, Oxford, 1693 ; M.D., 1700 ; F.R.S., 1701 ; physician extraordinary to Queen Anne, 1709, and physician in ordinary, 1712, continuing in the post under George I and George II ; F.R.C.P., 1712 ; knighted, 1715. [li. 338]

SHADWELL, SIR LANCELOT (1779-1850), lawyer ; educated at Eton and St. John's College, Cambridge ; fellow, 1801 ; M.A., 1803 ; honorary LL.D., 1842 ; barrister, Lincoln's Inn, 1803, bencher, 1822, and treasurer, 1833 ; practised in court of chancery ; K.C., 1821 ; M.P., Ripon, 1826 ; last vice-chancellor of England,

1827 till death ; privy councillor and knight, 1827 ; joint-commissioner of great seal, 1835-6 and 1850. 　　[li. 339]

SHADWELL, LAWRENCE (1823-1887), general ; son of Sir Lancelot Shadwell [q. v.] ; educated at Eton ; ensign, 1841 ; served in China, Punjab, and the Crimea ; military assistant at war office, 1866-71 ; C.B., 1869 ; general, 1881. 　　[li. 340]

SHADWELL, THOMAS (1642 ?-1692), dramatist and poet ; educated at Caius College, Cambridge, and entered Middle Temple ; produced the 'Sullen Lovers,' based on Molière's 'Les Fâcheux,' at Lincoln's Inn Fields, London, 1668 ; produced dramatic pieces, including an opera, the 'Enchanted Island ' (from Shakespeare's 'Tempest'), 1673, 'Timon of Athens,' 1678, the 'Squire of Alsatia,' 1688, and the 'Scowrers,' 1691 ; was at open feud with Dryden from 1682, the two poets repeatedly attacking one another in satires, among which were Dryden's 'Medal' and 'MacFlecknoe,' and Shadwell's 'The Medal of John Bayes,' 1682, and a translation of the 'Tenth Satire of Juvenal,' 1687 ; superseded Dryden as poet-laureate and historiographer royal at the revolution. 　　[li. 340]

SHAFTESBURY, EARLS OF. [See COOPER, ANTHONY ASHLEY, first EARL, 1621-1683 ; COOPER, ANTHONY ASHLEY, third EARL, 1671-1713 ; COOPER, ANTHONY ASHLEY, seventh EARL, 1801-1885.]

SHAIRP, JOHN CAMPBELL (1819-1885), professor of poetry at Oxford ; educated at Glasgow University and Balliol College, Oxford ; won Newdigate prize, 1842 ; assistant-master at Rugby, 1846 ; assistant-professor of Greek at Glasgow, 1856, and of Latin at St. Andrews, 1857 ; professor of Latin at St. Andrews, 1861-72 ; principal of United College, St. Andrews, 1868 ; professor of poetry at Oxford, 1877-87 ; LL.D. Edinburgh, 1884. His works include 'Kilmahoe, and other Poems,' 1864 ; 'Studies in Poetry and Philosophy,' 1868, 'Culture and Religion,' 1870, 'Burns ' ('English Men of Letters' series), 1879, and 'Aspects of Poetry,' 1881. 　　[li. 343]

SHAKERLEY, JEREMY (fl. 1651), astronomer ; made second observation of transit of Mercury at Surat ; 1651 ; published astronomical and mathematical works. 　　[li. 345]

SHAKESPEAR, JOHN (1774-1858), orientalist ; studied Arabic under Richardson and James Golius in London ; oriental professor at Royal Military College, Marlow, 1805 ; professor of Hindustani at East India Company's college, Addiscombe, 1809-29 ; published Hindustani dictionary and grammar. 　　[li. 345]

SHAKESPEAR, SIR RICHMOND CAMPBELL (1812-1861), soldier and administrator ; cousin of William Makepeace Thackeray [q. v.] ; educated at Charterhouse ; studied at East India Company's college, Addiscombe ; second lieutenant, Bengal artillery, 1828 ; political assistant to Major Elliott D'Arcy Todd [q. v.] in mission to Herat, 1839 ; sent to khan of Khiva to negotiate for surrender of Russian prisoners, 1840, and conducted prisoners to Russia ; knighted, 1841 ; military secretary to Sir George Pollock [q. v.] at Peshawar and in march to Kabul, 1842 ; deputy-commissioner of Sagar, 1843 ; served at Maharajpur, 1843 ; in political charge of Gwalior, 1844-8 and 1849-51 ; captain, 1846 ; served with distinction at Chillianwalla and Gujerat, in second Sikh war, 1849 ; political agent at Jodpur, 1851 ; resident of Baroda, 1857, and political commissioner of district, 1858, with command of northern division of Bombay army and rank of br:gadier-general ; lieutenant-colonel, 1858 ; agent to governor-general for central India, 1859 ; C.B., civil division, 1860. 　　[li. 346]

SHAKESPEARE, WILLIAM (1564-1616), dramatist and poet, eldest son and third child of John Shakespeare and Mary, daughter of Robert Arden, a well-to-do farmer of Wilmcote, was born at Stratford-on-Avon, 22 or 23 April 1564. His father was a trader in agricultural produce at Stratford, chamberlain of the borough (1561-1564), auditor of the borough accounts, alderman (1565), and bailiff (1568), but was eventually involved in debt, and deprived of his alderman's gown, 1586. The poet entered the free grammar school at Stratford, c. 1571, when Walter Roche was master ; studied the Latin language and literature ; left school, c. 1577, and joined his father, who seems at this period to have been a butcher. He married (1582) Anne, doubtless daughter of Richard Hathaway of Shottery, who bore him a daughter, Susanna, 1583, within six months of the marriage. Shakespeare was probably forced into marrying by his wife's friends, who were anxious to protect her reputation. Leaving Stratford, 1585, to avoid prosecution for poaching at Charlecote, the property of Sir Thomas Lucy (afterwards caricatured as Justice Shallow), he spent some time, perhaps as a schoolmaster, in a neighbouring village, and arrived in London in 1586. He soon engaged in some subordinate capacity at one of the two theatres (The Theatre or The Curtain) then existing in London, and before long became a member of the Earl of Leicester's company of actors, a company which passed under the patronage successively of Ferdinando Stanley, lord Strange, afterwards Earl of Derby (in 1588), Henry Carey, first lord Hunsdon, lord chamberlain (in 1594), his son, George Carey, second lord Hunsdon, and lord chamberlain (in 1597); it became the king's company of players in 1603. He acted with this company at the Rose (opened 1592), The Curtain, the Globe (opened, 1599), and after c. 1610 the Blackfriars Theatre; possibly made tours through the English country towns; appeared in many of his own plays, and took part in the original performances of Jonson's 'Every Man in his Humour' (1598) and 'Sejanus' (1603). As a dramatist he gained his earliest experience by revising or rewriting plays purchased by the manager of his theatre. 'Love's Labour's Lost,' the first of his dramatic productions, written c. 1591, revised probably for a performance at court, 1597, was published, 1598. There were produced about the same time 'The Two Gentlemen of Verona' (the story of which is the same as that of 'The Shepardess Felismena' in George de Montemayor's pastoral romance 'Diana') and the 'Comedy of Errors' (perhaps founded on a play, 'The Historie of Error,' acted, 1576), both of which were first printed in the folio of 1623. His first tragedy, 'Romeo and Juliet' (based on an Italian romance frequently translated into English), written in 1591, was first printed anonymously and surreptitiously in quarto, 1597 (authentic second quarto, 1599). The three parts of his 'Henry VI' were acted in 1592; the first part was first published in 1623, the second part anonymously in 1594 as 'The first part of the contention betwixt the two famous houses of Yorke and Lancaster,' and the third part, in 1595, as 'The True Tragedie of Richard, Duke of Yorke, and the death of good King Henry the Sixt,' but both the second and third parts underwent revision by himself before they were included in the 1623 folio. The original draft of the three parts of his 'Henry VI' was possibly by Greene and Peele, Shakespeare joining Marlowe in a revision which resulted in 'The Contention' and the 'True Tragedie,' and being again aided by Marlowe in the final revision. After 'Henry VI,' Shakespeare composed 'Richard III' and 'Richard II,' both of which were published anonymously in 1597; his 'Titus Andronicus,' much of which was perhaps written by Kyd, was published in quarto in 1594 (only one copy extant, new edit. 1600); his comedy 'The Merchant of Venice' (probably acted in 1594, printed, 1600) was based on material in Giovanni Fiorentino's collection of Italian novels 'Il Pecorone' and the 'Gesta Romanorum,' besides earlier plays. In 1594 he adapted 'King John' (printed, 1623) from 'The Troublesome Raigne of King John' (1591). He is also credited on somewhat slender grounds with portions of 'Arden of Feversham' (1592) and 'Edward III' (1596).

Meanwhile Shakespeare published the love poems 'Venus and Adonis' and 'Lucrece' respectively in 1593 and 1594, each with a dedication to Henry Wriothesley, earl of Southampton, with whom, in the latter year, he was doubtless on terms of intimate friendship. Summoned with the most famous actors of the day to perform at court, Christmas 1594, he was thenceforth shown special favour by Queen Elizabeth. His 'Sonnets,' which were printed 1609, were probably written between 1591 and 1594; their intensity of feeling has led readers to assume that they have an autobiographical significance. Most of them trace the course of the writer's affection for a young patron of rank and beauty, and may be addressed to Shakespeare's only known patron, Southampton; but the emotion is probably for the most part of dramatic temper, and is a masterly imaginative rendering of that spirit of adulation which poets of the day habitually paid their patrons. The publisher Thomas Thorpe issued the 'Sonnets' in 1609 with a dedication to 'Mr. W. H., the onlie begetter' of these ensuing sonnets (who was doubtless some friend of Thorpe, through whose good offices the manuscript had reached his hands, 'begetter' being used

in the sense of 'getter' or 'procurer'): the theory that Mr. W. H. was Shakespeare's patron, and that the initials are those of William Herbert, third earl of Pembroke [q. v.], is inadmissible. Shakespeare probably wrote 'A Midsummer Night's Dream' (printed, 1600) at the end of 1595, and produced about the same time 'All's well that ends well,' the plot of which was drawn from Painter's 'Palace of Pleasure' (No. xxxviii.) (first printed in the folio of 1623). His play, 'The Taming of the Shrew,' c. 1596 (also first printed in the folio), mainly a revision of an old play, owed something to the 'Supposes' of George Gascoigne [q. v.]. Shakespeare returned to Stratford, c. 1596, and there relieved his family from financial embarrassments, which had steadily increased since his departure. He purchased New Place, the largest house in the town, 1597, but he does not appear to have settled permanently there till 1611, by which year he had by further purchases built up an estate at Stratford. He wrote, c. 1597, 'Henry IV,' parts i. and ii., from Holinshed's 'Chronicles,' and from a popular piece, 'The Famous Victories of Henry V'; both parts of 'Henry IV' were printed,—in 1598 and 1600 respectively. He probably wrote 'The Merry Wives of Windsor' by command of Queen Elizabeth (printed in an imperfect form in 1602, the first complete version being that of the 1623 folio), the plot of the play being probably suggested by an Italian novel. His 'Henry V' was performed early in 1599 (an imperfect draft printed, 1600, the perfected play supplied in the first folio). In 1599 he also produced his three most perfect essays in comedy—'Much Ado about Nothing,' 'As you like it,' and 'Twelfth Night' (the first of these published in 1600, the remaining two not printed until they appeared in the folio); the story of Hero and Claudio in 'Much Ado' was drawn from an Italian source; 'As you like it' was a dramatic adaptation of Lodge's romance 'Rosalynde, Euphues Golden Legacie' (1590), and the story of 'Twelfth Night' was taken from the 'Historie of Apolonius and Silla' in 'Riche his Farewell to Militarie Profession' (1581), an English rendering of a tale in Cinthio's 'Hecatommithi.' Meanwhile his name was applied by unprincipled publishers to such writings of obscure men as 'The Tragedie of Locrine,' 1595, 'The Puritaine, or the Widdow of Watling-streete,' 1607, 'The True Chronicle Historie of Thomas, Lord Cromwell,' 1613, 'The Life of Oldcastle,' 1600, 'The London Prodigall,' 1605, 'The Yorkshire Tragedy,' 1608, and an old play on the subject of King John, 1611. Only two sonnets and three poems from 'Love's Labour's Lost' appeared in 'The Passionate Pilgrim, by W. Shakespeare,' 1599, the bulk of the volume being by Richard Barnfield and others. Shakespeare's name was also appended to 'a poetical essaie on the Turtle and the Phœnix,' which was published in Robert Chester's 'Love's Martyr,' a collection of poems by Marston, Chapman, Jonson, and others, 1601.

Shakespeare's 'Julius Cæsar,' taken from North's translation of 'Plutarch's Lives,' was produced in 1601 (first printed version extant in the 1623 folio), and 'Hamlet,' the story of which was accessible in Belleforest's 'Histoires Tragiques,' was played in the following year. He wrote 'Troilus and Cressida' (the story of which was based upon Chaucer's 'Troilus and Cresseide') probably in 1603 (two quarto editions, 1609); his 'Othello' and 'Measure for Measure,' the stories of which were drawn from Cinthio, were acted in 1604 (neither printed in Shakespeare's lifetime); the plot of his 'Macbeth' (finished, 1606) was drawn from Holinshed's 'Chronicle of Scottish History,' and was doubtless designed as a tribute to the nationality of the king, James I; his 'King Lear,' also mainly founded on Holinshed, was produced 1606 (two slightly differing versions printed in 1608, and a third included in the folio of 1623). 'Timon of Athens' and 'Pericles' quickly followed (the latter was first printed in a mangled form in 1608, and was included in Shakespeare's collected works for the first time, 1664): both were written in collaboration with another dramatist, perhaps George Wilkins [q. v.]; possibly in 'Timon' some additional assistance was given by William Rowley. Shakespeare derived the story of 'Timon' partly from Painter's 'Palace of Pleasure' and partly from Plutarch's 'Marc Antony,' and that of 'Pericles' from the 'Apollonius of Tyre' in John Gower's 'Confessio Amantis.' In both 'Antony and Cleopatra' and 'Coriolanus,' Shakespeare closely followed North's 'Plutarch': they were probably written in 1608 (first printed in 1623). In 'Cymbeline' (acted in 1610 or 1611) Shakespeare combined a fragment of British history freely adapted from Holinshed with the story of Ginevra in Boccaccio's 'Decameron.' He based 'A Winter's Tale ' (played in 1611) on Greene's romance ' Pandosto,' 1588 (afterwards called 'Dorastus and Fawnia '). His play, ' The Tempest,' probably written in 1611, was in all likelihood the latest drama that he completed, hints for portions of the story being derived from Sylvester Jourdain or Jourdan [q. v.] and one speech from Montaigne's essays (1603). He abandoned dramatic composition, c. 1611, but there can be little doubt that he left with the manager of his company unfinished drafts of more than one play, which John Fletcher (1579–1625) [q. v.] and others completed. These included ' The History of Cardenio, by Fletcher and Shakespeare ' (licensed for publication, 1653, but not issued from the press, and probably identical with the lost play 'Cardano,' which was acted in 1613), ' The Two Noble Kinsmen,' and ' Henry VIII.' The ' Two Noble Kinsmen ' embodied Chaucer's ' Knight's Tale of Palamon and Arcite,' and was printed in 1634. ' Henry VIII' perhaps contains some work from the pen of Massinger, as well as Fletcher ; it was acted in 1613, and included in the folio of 1623.

Shakespeare spent the concluding years of his life (1611–16) mainly at Stratford, but paid frequent visits to London till 1614, and continued his relations with actors and poets till the end. He purchased a house in Blackfriars, 1613 ; took a prominent part in social and civic affairs at Stratford, having become a joint-owner of the tithes of Old Stratford, Welcombe, and Bishopton, and in 1614, having indemnified himself against personal loss, joined in an unsuccessful attempt to enclose the Stratford common fields. He drafted his will, January 1616, and completed it in March. He died 23 April (O.S., i.e. 3 May), after entertaining Ben Jonson and Drayton at New Place, and was buried on 25 April (O.S.) in Stratford Church, where before 1623 a monument, with a bust by a London sculptor, Gerard Johnson, was erected. His wife died in 1623, and Elizabeth (d. 1670), daughter of Susannah, his eldest daughter, and of John Hall [q. v.], was his last surviving descendant. Her second husband was John Barnard, who was knighted in 1661. By Lady Barnard's will New Place was sold in 1675.

Two portraits of Shakespeare may be regarded as fully authenticated, the bust in Stratford Church, and the frontispiece to the folio of 1623, engraved by Martin Droeshout [q. v.]. The ' Droeshout' or ' Flower ' portrait, now at Stratford, has been claimed as the original picture, whence the engraving was made ; the ' Ely House' portrait, also at Stratford, is probably of early date, and other portraits, less fully authenticated, exist. The Garrick Club possesses a bust believed to be of seventeenth-century workmanship. A mask, said to have been taken from Shakespeare's face after death, is in private hands at Darmstadt. A monument designed by William Kent (1684–1748) [q. v.], with a statue by Peter Scheemakers [q. v.], was erected in Poets' Corner, Westminster Abbey, in 1741. The birthplace at Stratford was acquired by the public and converted into a museum in 1846. The site of New Place and Anne Hathaway's cottage were similarly purchased in 1861 and 1892 respectively. A memorial at Stratford, consisting of a theatre, picture gallery, and library, was opened in 1879.

Shakespeare's plays were first collected in 1623, when a folio edition was published containing all the plays excepting ' Pericles.' A second folio edition appeared in 1632, a third in 1663, with a reissue, including ' Pericles ' and six spurious plays, in 1664, and a fourth, with the same additions, in 1685. Collected editions of the works have since been edited by Nicholas Rowe (1709–10), Alexander Pope (1725), Lewis Theobald (1733), Sir Thomas Hanmer (1744), Bishop Warburton (1747), Dr. Johnson (1765), Edward Capell (1768), Edmund Malone (1790), Johnson and Steevens, ' Variorum ' (1773), William Harness (1825), Samuel Weller Singer (1826), Thomas Campbell (1838), Charles Knight (1838–43), Bryan Waller Procter (1839–43), John Payne Collier (1841–4), Samuel Phelps (1851–4), J. O. Halliwell (1853–61), Nikolaus Delius (Elberfeld, 1854–61), Alexander Dyce (1857), Richard Grant White (Boston, 1857–65), Howard Staunton (1858–60), W. G. Clark, J. Glover, and Dr. Aldis Wright (' Cambridge,' 1863–9), and Rev. H. N. Hudson (Harvard, 1881). [li. 348]

SHALDERS, GEORGE (1825 ?–1873), landscapepainter ; exhibited at Royal Academy from 1848. [li. 397]

SHANK, JOHN (1740–1823). [See SCHANCK.]

SHANKS, JOHN (d. 1636), actor ; in companies successively of Lord Pembroke, Queen Elizabeth, Charles Howard, earl of Nottingham, and Prince Henry ; joined king's company, c. 1619, and remained in it during the early years of Charles I's reign ; his name in the list of principal players in the 1623 Shakespeare folio ; held shares in Blackfriars and Globe theatres. [li. 397]

SHANNON, EARL OF (1682–1764). [See BOYLE, HENRY.]

SHARDELOWE or **SCHERDELOW**, SIR JOHN DE (d. 1344 ?), advocate ; judge of court of common pleas, 1332–42 ; knighted, 1332 ; trier of petitions in parliament of 1343. [li. 398]

SHARESHULL, WILLIAM DE (fl. 1360), advocate ; king's serjeant in 1331 ; K.B. and member of Edward III's council of advisers, 1332 ; judge of king's bench, 1333, but was removed to common pleas, 1333 ; chief-baron of exchequer, 1344–5 ; returned to common pleas, 1345 ; chief-justice of king's bench, 1350–7. [li. 399]

SHARINGTON or **SHERINGTON**, SIR WILLIAM (1495 ?–1553), vice-treasurer of the mint at Bristol ; in service of Sir Francis Bryan [q. v.] ; page of king's robes ; vice-treasurer of mint at Bristol, 1546 ; K.B., 1547 ; perpetrated extensive frauds at mint and sought protection of Thomas Seymour, baron Seymour of Sudeley [q. v.], in whose plots he assisted ; arrested and attainted, but received pardon ; sheriff of Wiltshire, 1552. [li. 399]

SHARMAN-CRAWFORD, WILLIAM (1781–1861). [See CRAWFORD.]

SHARP. [See also SHARPE.]

SHARP, ABRAHAM (1651–1742), mathematician ; apprenticed to merchant, but abandoned business and studied mathematics ; employed by John Flamsteed [q. v.] in Greenwich observatory, 1676–90 ; taught mathematics in London from 1690 ; celebrated for skill in graduating instruments ; published ' Geometry Improved,' 1717. [li. 400]

SHARP, SIR CUTHBERT (1781–1849), antiquary ; educated under Dr. Burney at Greenwich ; served as cavalry officer in Ireland during rebellion, c. 1799 ; visited Paris, 1803, and was for some years detained as prisoner of war ; collector of customs successively at Sunderland and Newcastle-on-Tyne ; published antiquarian works, including ' History of Hartlepool' (1816). [li. 401]

SHARP, GRANVILLE (1735–1813), philanthropist ; son of Thomas Sharp (1693–1758) [q. v.] ; apprenticed as linendraper in London ; studied Greek and Hebrew ; member of Fishmongers' Company, 1757, entered ordnance department, 1758, and was clerk in ordinary, 1764–76 ; became involved in the struggle for liberation of slaves in England, and engaged in various actions at law which resulted (1775) in the formulation of the principle ' that as soon as any slave sets foot upon English territory he becomes free ' ; advocated cause of American colonies, and joined crusade against the press-gang ; prominent in founding a society for abolition of slavery, 1787, British and Foreign Bible Society, 1804, and Society for Conversion of Jews, 1808. His works include many pamphlets on the movements in which he was interested, besides religious, historical, and other treatises. [li. 401]

SHARP, ISAAC (1806–1897), missionary ; educated at a Friends' school in Essex ; began to preach, 1832, was ' recorded ' minister, 1843, and subsequently preached in many parts of the world. [Suppl. iii. 341]

SHARP, JACK (d. 1431), lollard rebel ; weaver at Abingdon ; when bailiff (1431) headed a movement of lollards of the southern midlands ; arrested and executed at Abingdon or Oxford. [li. 404]

SHARP, JAMES (1613–1679), archbishop of St. Andrews ; M.A. King's College, Aberdeen, 1637 ; professor of philosophy, St. Andrews University ; presented to church of Crail, 1649 ; adhered, on the division of the kirk, to the resolutioners in opposition to the protesters, and came to be regarded as head of the party ; seized by Cromwell's forces, 1651, and imprisoned in Tower of London till 1652 ; assisted Monck in his schemes for the Restoration, 1659, and was sent to Charles II at Breda, 1660 ; for some time acted ostensibly as the representative of the resolutioners and

Q q

presbyterianism, but really in the interest of episcopacy; Charles II's chaplain in Scotland; professor of divinity, St. Mary's College, St. Andrews, 1661; was consecrated archbishop of St. Andrews, 1661, and immediately put in force severe measures for the annihilation of covenanting principles; murdered by covenanters on Magus Muir; portrait painted by Lely. [li. 404]

SHARP, JOHN (1572?–1648?), Scottish divine; M.A. St. Andrews, 1592; minister of Kilmany, Fife, 1601; he was clerk to assembly which met at Aberdeen in opposition to commands of James VI, 1605, and was banished, 1606; professor of theology in college of Die, in Dauphiné, France, 1608–30; professor of divinity at Edinburgh, 1630 till death; published theological works. [li. 407]

SHARP, JOHN (1645–1714), archbishop of York; B.A. Christ's College, Cambridge, 1663; M.A., 1667; incorporated at Oxford, 1669; domestic chaplain to Sir Heneage Finch [q. v.], 1667–76; prebendary of Norwich and incumbent of St. Bartholomew's, Exchange, London, 1675; rector of St. Giles-in-the-Fields, London, 1675; D.D. Cambridge, 1679; dean of Norwich, 1681; chaplain in ordinary to James II, 1686; suspended for preaching sermons held to reflect on James II, 1686–7; refused to read declaration of indulgence, 1688; dean of Canterbury and commissioner for reform of liturgy and the ecclesiastical courts, 1689; archbishop of York, 1691; privy councillor, 1702; commissioner for Scottish union; published sermons, and left in manuscript 'Observations on Coinage of England,' and an account of the archbishopric of York. A collected edition of his works appeared, 1754. [li. 408]

SHARP or SHARPE, LEONEL (1559–1631), divine; educated at Eton and King's College, Cambridge; M.A., 1584; D.D., 1603; chaplain to Earl of Essex at Tilbury camp, 1588, accompanying him to Cadiz, 1589, and Portugal, 1596; royal chaplain, c. 1601; archdeacon of Berkshire and rector of North Moreton, 1605; chaplain to Henry, prince of Wales; imprisoned in Tower of London, 1614–15, on suspicion of endeavouring to stir up strife between English and Scottish factions at court; D.D. Oxford, 1618; published religious writings. [li. 411]

SHARP, MICHAEL WILLIAM (d. 1840), painter; exhibited at Royal Academy from 1801; his works chiefly portraits and domestic scenes. [li. 412]

SHARP, PATRICK (d. 1615), Scottish theologian; master of Glasgow grammar school, 1574; principal of Glasgow University, 1585; appointed with others by general assembly to organise church in opposition to government, 1596; supported James I at Hampton Court in debate on questions at issue with kirk, 1606; constant moderator to Glasgow presbytery in absence of bishop, 1606; took part in Falkland conference, 1609; appointed to Scottish court of high commission, 1610. [li. 412]

SHARP, RICHARD (1759–1835), known as 'Conversation Sharp'; born in Newfoundland; partner in commercial firms in London; whig M.P. for Castle Rising, 1806–12, Portarlington, Ireland, 1816 and 1818–19, and Ilchester, 1826–7; took a keen interest in politics and literature, and his friends at various periods numbered the most eminent men of the day; an original member of the society for reform of parliament known as 'Friends of the People,' 1791, and of the Literary Society, 1806; F.S.A., 1787; F.R.S., 1806; published 'Letters and Essays in Prose and Verse,' 1834. [li. 413]

SHARP, SAMUEL (1700?–1778), surgeon; apprenticed to William Cheselden [q. v.], 1724; studied in France; freeman of Barber-Surgeons' Company, 1731; obtained diploma, 1732; surgeon to Guy's Hospital, London, 1733–57; F.R.S. and member of Paris Royal Society, 1749; travelled in Italy, 1765, and issued 'Letters from Italy,' 1766; published surgical treatises which form the link connecting the old methods of surgery as represented by Cheselden with the new as represented by William Hunter. [li. 414]

SHARP, SAMUEL (1814–1882), geologist; assisted in conducting 'Stamford Mercury' newspaper; F.S.A.; F.G.S., 1862; published 'Rudiments of Geology,' 1875, and writings on local antiquities of Stamford. [li. 415]

SHARP, THOMAS (1693–1758), divine; son of John Sharp (1645–1714) [q. v.]; M.A. Trinity College, Cambridge, 1716; fellow; D.D.; prebendary of Southwark

and (1719) of York; rector of Rothbury and archdeacon of Northumberland, 1723; prebendary of Durham, 1732; official to dean and chapter of Durham, 1755; published theological and biographical works. [li. 416]

SHARP, THOMAS (1770–1841), antiquary; hatter at Coventry, 1784–1804; studied local antiquities and made extensive topographical and other antiquarian collections. His works include 'A Dissertation on the Pageants, or Dramatic Mysteries, anciently performed at Coventry,' 1825, and 'Ancient Mysteries and Moralities,' edited from Digby MSS., 1835. [li. 416]

SHARP, WILLIAM (1749–1824), engraver; apprenticed to Barak Longmate [q. v.]; carried on business successively in Bartholomew Lane, London, Vauxhall, London, and Chiswick; executed plates after Guido, West, Trumbull, and Reynolds; friend of Thomas Paine and Horne Tooke, and member of Society for Constitutional Information. [li. 417]

SHARP, WILLIAM (1805–1896), surgeon and physician; educated at Westminster; articled as surgeon, 1821; studied in London; L.S.A., 1826; M.R.C.S., 1827; practised till 1843 at Bradford, where he was surgeon to the infirmary, 1829; F.R.S., 1840; 'reader in natural philosophy,' 1849–50, at Rugby school, where his energy had led to establishment of science teaching; adopted methods of homœopathists, and engaged extensively in medical investigations; received degree of M.D. from archbishop of Canterbury, 1856; published medical works. [li. 418]

SHARPE. [See also SHARP.]

SHARPE, BARTHOLOMEW (fl. 1679–1682), buccaneer; perhaps one of party of English and French buccaneers who sacked Porto Bello, 1679; cruised with English party in Bay of Panama and on coast of Peru; headed company in island of Quibo, 1680, and on expedition to Juan Fernandez, where he was temporarily deposed from command; cruised in West Indies, 1681; returned to England, 1682; arrested and tried for piracy, but acquitted. [li. 419]

SHARPE, CHARLES KIRKPATRICK (1781?–1851), antiquary and artist; M.A. Christ Church, Oxford, 1806; resided at Edinburgh, living mainly as a literary recluse; made acquaintance of Scott, 1802, and became his lifelong friend; made extensive antiquarian collections. His works include an edition of Kirkton's 'Secret and True History of the Church of Scotland,' 1817, and 'Portraits of an Amateur' (a volume of etchings), 1833. [li. 420]

SHARPE, CHARLOTTE (d. 1849), portrait-painter; exhibited from 1817; sister of Louisa Sharpe [q. v.] [li. 425]

SHARPE, DANIEL (1806–1856), geologist; brother of Samuel Sharpe [q. v.], with whom he was partner in Portuguese mercantile business; resided in Portugal, 1835–1838; wrote important papers on geology of Portugal and various districts in Great Britain and on the continent; F.R.S., 1850; F.L.S.; F.Z.S; treasurer of Geological Society, 1853, and president, 1856. [li. 421]

SHARPE, EDMUND (1809–1877), architect; M.A. St. John's College, Cambridge, 1836; studied architecture in France and Germany; pupil of John Rickman [q. v.]; practised at Lancaster, 1836–51; abandoned architecture for engineering, and engaged in railway construction, 1851; F.R.I.B.A., 1848; published architectural works. [li. 422]

SHARPE, ELIZA (1796–1874), artist; sister of Louisa Sharpe [q. v.]; member, 1829–72, of 'Old' Water-colour Society. [li. 425]

SHARPE, GREGORY (1713–1771), divine; of Westminster School and Trinity College, Cambridge; LL.D., 1747; incorporated at Oxford, 1751; took orders in English church; vicar of All Saints', Birling, 1743–56; prebendary of Salisbury, 1757–71; chaplain to Frederick, prince of Wales, and to George III; master of Temple, 1763–71; F.R.S., 1754; published theological and classical writings. [li. 423]

SHARPE, JAMES (1577?–1630), Roman catholic divine; born in Yorkshire; ordained priest at St. Alban's College, Valladolid, 1604; entered Society of Jesus, 1608; professor of Hebrew at Louvain; professed of four vows, 1622; worked on English mission; published and left in manuscript religious writings. [li. 424.

SHARPE, LEWIS (*fl.* 1640), author of the 'Noble Stranger,' a comedy, 1640. [li. 424]

SHARPE, LOUISA, afterwards MRS. SEYFFARTH (1798–1843), water-colour painter; exhibited miniature portraits at Royal Academy, 1817–29; member of 'Old' Water-colour Society, 1829; married Professor Woldemar Seyffarth of Dresden, 1834. [li. 424]

SHARPE, MARY ANNE (*d.* 1867), artist; sister of Louisa Sharpe [q. v.]; exhibited portraits and domestic subjects at Royal Academy and Society of British Artists. [li. 425]

SHARPE, ROGER (*fl.* 1610), author; published, 1610, 'More Fooles yet,' a collection of epigrams. [li. 424]

SHARPE, SAMUEL (1799–1881), Egyptologist; brother of Daniel Sharpe [q. v.]; entered banking firm of Samuel and Henry Rogers (his uncles), 1814 (partner, 1821–61); F.G.S., *c.* 1827; published works on Egyptian history and hieroglyphics; began a revision of authorised version of New Testament, 1840, and was one of scholars representing unitarians in connection with arrangements for revised version of 1870; wrote a Hebrew history and grammar; president of British and Foreign Unitarian Association, 1869–70, and of Manchester College (now at Oxford), 1876–8; liberal benefactor of University College, London. [li. 425]

SHARPEIGH, ALEXANDER (*fl.* 1607–1613), merchant and sea-captain; factor of Levant Company at Constantinople; captain in service of East India Company and general of fourth voyage to East Indies, 1608; reached Agra, 1609; agent for company at Bantam, 1613. [li. 427]

SHARPEY, WILLIAM (1802–1880), physiologist; studied medicine and surgery at Edinburgh, London, and Paris; M.D. Edinburgh, 1823; practised at Arbroath, 1824–6; joint-lecturer on systematic anatomy at Edinburgh from 1832; professor of anatomy and physiology, University College, London, 1836–74; F.R.S., 1839, member of council, 1844, and secretary, 1853–72; member of general medical council, 1861–76; hon. LL.D. Edinburgh, 1859; examiner in anatomy, London University from 1840; published physiological writings. [li. 427]

SHARPHAM, EDWARD (*fl.* 1607), author; member of Middle Temple, 1594; published two plays, 'The Fleire' and 'Cupid's Whirligig,' 1607. [li. 429]

SHARPLES or **SHARPLESS**, JAMES (1750 ?–1811), portrait-painter; exhibited at Royal Academy, 1779–85; went to America, *c.* 1796. A portrait by him of George Washington is in the National Portrait Gallery. [li. 429]

SHARPLES, JAMES (1825–1893), painter; worked as an ironfounder at Bury; studied drawing, and painted portraits and other pictures. [li. 430]

SHARPLES, ROLINDA (*d.* 1838), artist; daughter of James Sharples (1750 ?–1811) [q. v.]; honorary member of Society of British Artists. [li. 430]

SHARROCK, ROBERT (1630–1684), divine; educated at Winchester College and New College, Oxford; fellow, 1649; D.C.L., 1661; prebendary of Winchester, 1665; held livings in Hampshire; archdeacon of Winchester, 1684; published botanical, philosophical, and other works. [li. 430]

SHAW, ALEXANDER (1804–1890), surgeon; brother of Sir Charles Shaw [q. v.]; M.A. Glasgow, 1822; studied at Middlesex Hospital, London, and was surgeon, 1842–1872, and consulting surgeon, 1872; L.S.A., 1827; F.R.C.S., 1843; held various offices in Royal Medical and Chirurgical Society; published works chiefly relating to discoveries of Sir Charles Bell [q. v.], his brother-in-law. [li. 431]

SHAW, SIR CHARLES (1795–1871), brigadier-general; brother of Alexander Shaw [q. v.]; educated at St. Andrews and Edinburgh; ensign, 1813; in Waterloo campaign, 1813–15; on half-pay, 1818; captain and commander of Leith volunteer sharpshooters; engaged in wine-business at Leith; captain of light infantry marines in liberating army of Portugal, 1831; major, 1832; colonel, 1833; came to England, 1835, but returned to serve against Carlists in Spain; took San Sebastian, 1836; brigadier-general; resigned and returned home, 1836; chief commissioner of police at Manchester, 1839–42; died at Homburg-von-der-Hohe. [li. 432]

SHAW, CUTHBERT (1739–1771), poet; son of a shoemaker in Yorkshire; successively usher in schools and actor; published poems, including 'The Race. By Mercurius Spur,' 1766. a satire on living poets. [li. 433]

SHAW, DUNCAN (1725–1795), Scottish divine; M.A. King's College, Aberdeen, 1747; licensed preacher, 1752; minister at Rafford, 1753–83, and at Aberdeen, 1783–95; D.D. Marischal College, Aberdeen, 1774; published religious writings. [li. 434]

SHAW or **SHAA**, SIR EDMUND (*d.* 1487 ?), lord mayor of London; member and master of Goldsmiths' Company; sheriff of London, 1474; alderman of Cheap ward, 1485; lord mayor, 1482; intimate with Edward IV; privy councillor of Richard III; endowed a school at Stockport. [li. 434]

SHAW, SIR FREDERICK, second baronet (1799–1876), Irish politician; of Trinity College, Dublin, and Brasenose College, Oxford; B.A. Oxford, 1819; recorder of Dundalk, 1826, and of Dublin, 1828–76; tory M.P. for Dublin, 1830 and 1831, and for Dublin University, 1832–1848; Irish privy councillor, 1834; succeeded his elder brother in baronetcy, 1869. [li. 435]

SHAW, GEORGE (1751–1813), naturalist; M.A. Magdalen Hall, Oxford, 1772; ordained deacon, 1774, but abandoned church as profession; studied medicine at Edinburgh and Oxford; M.B. and M.D. Oxford, 1787; botanical lecturer at Oxford; joint-founder and vice-president of Linnean Society, 1788; F.R.S., 1789; assistant-keeper, 1791, and keeper, 1807 till death, of natural-history section of British Museum; published works relating to natural history. [li. 436]

SHAW, HENRY (1800–1873), antiquary and draughtsman; assisted John Britton (1771–1857) [q. v.] in 'Cathedral Antiquities of England'; works include 'Details of Gothic Architecture,' 1823, 'Handbook of Art of Illumination,' 1866; F.S.A., 1833; largely employed in illuminating publications and addresses. [li. 436]

SHAW, SIR JAMES (1764–1843), chamberlain of London; born in Scotland; member of London firm of commercial house of George and Samuel Douglass; alderman of Portsoken ward, 1798; sheriff of London and Middlesex, 1803; lord mayor of London, 1805; independent tory M.P., city of London, 1806–18; created baronet, 1809; chamberlain of London, 1831–43. [li. 437]

SHAW, JOHN (1559–1625), divine; B.A. Queen's College, Oxford, 1584; vicar of Woking, 1588; deprived for nonconformity, 1596; published poetical writings. [li. 438]

SHAW or **SHAWE**, JOHN (1608–1672), puritan divine; educated at Christ's College, Cambridge; M.A., 1630; chaplain to Philip Herbert, earl of Montgomery and fourth earl of Pembroke [q. v.]; vicar of Rotherham, 1639; accompanied Pembroke to Berwick; chaplain to Henry Rich, earl of Holland [q. v.], 1641; fled from Rotherham after outbreak of civil war, 1643; rector of Lymm, 1643; scribe to assembly of ministers at York, 1644; rector of Scrayingham; lecturer at Hull, where he was master of the Charter House, 1651; chaplain of parliamentary commissioners to Charles I at Newcastle, 1646; royal chaplain, 1660; inhibited from preaching at his church at Hull, 1661, but retained mastership till 1662, when he resigned; published religious writings. [li. 438]

SHAW, JOHN (1614–1689), divine; B.A. Brasenose College, Oxford, 1632; vicar of Alnham, *c.* 1636; rector of Whalton, 1645, and subsequently of Bolton in Craven; lecturer at Newcastle, 1662; published religious writings. [li. 438]

SHAW, JOHN (1789–1815), corporal, 2nd life guards; enlisted as private, 1807, and attracted notice by his skill as a boxer and swordsman; entered prize ring, 1812, and won a fight at Coombe-Warren; defeated Edward Painter [q. v.], 1815; accompanied his regiment at Waterloo, where he died after displaying extraordinary feats of valour. [Suppl. iii. 341]

SHAW, JOHN (1792–1827), surgeon; brother of Sir Charles Shaw [q. v.]; pupil of (Sir) Charles Bell [q. v.], who became his brother-in-law; lecturer at Great Windmill Street school, London; surgeon to Middlesex Hospital, London, 1825; published works on anatomy and surgery. [li. 440]

SHAW, JOHN (1776–1832), architect; articled to George Gwilt the elder [q. v.]; began practice, 1798; F.L.S.; F.R.S.; F.S.A.; F.R.I.B.A.; architect to Christ's Hospital, London. [li. 440]

SHAW, JOHN (1803–1870), architect; son of John Shaw (1776–1832) [q. v.]; succeeded as architect to Christ's Hospital, London; built Wellington College, Sandhurst, 1855–9. [li. 441]

SHAW, JOSEPH (1671–1733), legal writer; educated at Trinity College, Oxford; entered Middle Temple, 1695; published legal writings and letters to his patron, Anthony Ashley Cooper, third earl of Shaftesbury [q. v.] [li. 441]

SHAW, LACHLAN (1692–1777), Scottish divine; M.A. King's College, Aberdeen, 1711; studied theology at Edinburgh; held collegiate charge at Elgin, 1734–74; published antiquarian and historical works, including 'History of Moray,' 1775. [li. 441]

SHAW, MARY (1814–1876), contralto singer; daughter of John Postans; studied at Royal Academy of Music and under Sir George Smart; first appeared in public, 1834, and subsequently took part regularly in many important concerts in England and on continent till *c.* 1843; married, 1835, Alfred Shaw, who became insane, *c.* 1843. [li. 441]

SHAW, PATRICK (1796–1872), lawyer; brother of Sir Charles Shaw [q. v.]; called to Scottish bar, 1819; sheriff of chancery, 1848–69; published reports and other legal writings. [li. 442]

SHAW, PETER (1694–1763), physician; practised successively in Scarborough and London; M.D.; F.R.C.P., 1754; physician extraordinary to George II, and M.D. Cambridge, 1752; physician in ordinary to George II, 1754, and to George III, 1760; published original medical works, besides editions of the works of Bacon and Boyle, and several translations and adaptations. [li. 442]

SHAW or **SHAA**, RALPH or JOHN (*d.* 1484), prebendary of London, 1477; brother of Sir Edmund Shaw [q. v.]; supported Richard III. [li. 435]

SHAW, ROBERT BARKLEY (1839–1879), traveller; educated at Marlborough and Trinity College, Cambridge; settled as tea-planter at Kangra in the Himalayas, 1859; first Englishman to reach Yarkund, 1868, and Kashgar, 1869; published account of travels, 1871; accompanied Sir Douglas Forsyth on official mission to Yarkund, 1870; received patron's gold medal from Royal Geographical Society, 1872; British joint-commissioner in Ladak; resident at Mandalay, 1878–9; died at Mandalay; his works include treatises on oriental languages [li. 443]

SHAW, SAMUEL (1635–1696), nonconformist divine; B.A. St. John's College, Cambridge, 1650; rector of Long Whatton, 1658; removed from living, 1661; master of grammar school at Ashby-de-la-Zouche, 1668–96; published religious works, comedies, and other writings. [li. 444]

SHAW, STEBBING (1762–1802), topographer; of Repton and Queens' College, Cambridge; fellow, 1786; M.A., 1787; B.D., 1796; tutor to (Sir) Francis Burdett [q. v.]; travelled with Sir Egerton Brydges in Derbyshire and Leicestershire, and printed results of observations in the 'Topographer,' 1789–91, edited by Brydges and himself; rector of Hartshorn, 1799; F.S.A., 1795; published 'History and Antiquities of Staffordshire,' 1798–1801. [li. 445]

SHAW, THOMAS (1694–1751), African traveller; M.A. Queen's College, Oxford, 1720; chaplain to English factory at Algiers, 1720; returned to England, 1733; elected, in his absence, fellow of Queen's College, 1727; D.D., 1734; vicar of Godshill, 1734; F.R.S., 1734; principal of Edmund Hall, Oxford, 1740; regius professor of Greek, 1741; vicar of Bramley, 1742–51; published 'Travels, or Observations relating to Barbary and the Levant,' 1738. [li. 446]

SHAW, THOMAS BUDGE (1813–1862), author; educated under Samuel Butler (1774–1839) [q. v.] at Shrewsbury, and at Trinity College, Cambridge; B.A., 1836; M.A., 1851; settled at St. Petersburg, 1841; professor of English literature at Imperial Alexander Lyceum, St. Petersburg, 1842; lector of English literature at St.

Petersburg University, *c.* 1851; tutor and professor of English to grand dukes of Russia, 1853–62; chief work, 'Outlines of English Literature,' 1848. [li. 447]

SHAW, WILLIAM (1550–1602). [See Schaw.]

SHAW, WILLIAM (1749–1831), Gaelic scholar; M.A. King's College, Glasgow, 1772; private tutor in London; became member of Dr. Johnson's literary circle; entered ministry of church of Scotland and was presented to parish of Ardelach, 1779; resigned charge, 1780; travelled in Scotland and Ireland, and published 'Galic and English Dictionary,' 1780; published writings denying the authenticity of Macpherson's 'Ossian'; published 'Memoirs of . . . Dr. Johnson,' 1785; joined English church and was rector of Chelvey, 1795; B.D. Emmanuel College, Cambridge, 1800. [li. 448]

SHAW, WILLIAM (1797–1853), agriculturist; educated at Wadham College, Oxford; barrister, Inner Temple, 1833; helped to found Royal Agricultural Society, 1838 (first secretary, 1838–9, member of council, 1839); started and conducted, with Cuthbert William Johnson [q. v.], the 'Farmers' Almanack and Calendar,' 1838; published, 1849, with Henry Corbet, digest of evidence given before committee of House of Commons, presided over by Philip Pusey [q. v.], 1848; died in pecuniary embarrassment in Australia. [li. 448]

SHAW, WILLIAM (1823–1895), Irish politician; educated at Trinity College, Dublin; studied for congregational ministry at Highbury, London; minister of independent church in Cork, 1846–50; adopted mercantile career, 1850; liberal M.P. for Bandon, 1868–74, and for co. Cork, 1874–85; supported home rule and was chairman of Irish party, 1879–80; member of Bessborough commission, 1880; seceded from Irish party, 1881, but gave general support to William Ewart Gladstone [q. v.]; declared bankrupt, 1886. [li. 449]

SHAW-KENNEDY, SIR JAMES (1788–1865). [See Kennedy.]

SHAW-LEFEVRE, CHARLES, VISCOUNT EVERSLEY (1794–1888), M.A. Trinity College, Cambridge, 1819; barrister, Lincoln's Inn, 1819; M.P., Downton, 1830, for Hampshire, 1831, and for northern division of Hampshire, 1832–57; chairman of select committee on procedure, 1838; speaker of House of Commons, 1839–57, setting himself to reform procedure; created Viscount Eversley, 1857; ecclesiastical commissioner, 1859; G.C.B., 1885. [li. 450]

SHAW-LEFEVRE, SIR JOHN GEORGE (1797–1879), public official; brother of Sir James Shaw-Kennedy [q. v.]; of Eton and Trinity College, Cambridge; senior wrangler, 1818; fellow, 1819; barrister, Inner Temple, 1825; bencher, 1850; practised as conveyancer; appointed to settle divisions of counties for purposes of Reform Act, 1832; under-secretary to Edward Smith Stanley (afterwards thirteenth earl of Derby) [q. v.] at colonial office, 1833; on commission which founded colony of Australia, 1834; commissioner for carrying into effect new Poor-law Amendment Act, 1834; vice-chancellor of London University, 1842–62; joint-assistant secretary to board of trade, 1841; on ecclesiastical commission, 1847; deputy-clerk of the parliaments, 1848, and clerk, 1855–1875; served on inquiry into Indian civil service, 1851; civil service commissioner, 1855; F.R.S., 1820; K.C.B., 1857; D.C.L. Oxford, 1858. [li. 451]

SHAWE. [See Shaw.]

SHAXTON, NICHOLAS (1485?–1556), divine; B.A. Cambridge, 1506; fellow of Gonville Hall, Cambridge; M.A., 1510; president of Physick's Hostel, which was attached to Gonville Hall 1512–13; university preacher, 1520; B.D., 1521; member of committee of divines who discussed question of Henry VIII's marriage with Catherine of Arragon; favoured Henry VIII's views; treasurer of Salisbury Cathedral, 1533; almoner to Anne Boleyn; canon of Westminster, 1534; bishop of Salisbury, 1535, when he acknowledged Henry VIII as supreme head of church; resigned bishopric on passing of the six articles, 1539, and was committed to custody of bishop Clerk; pardoned, 1540, but prohibited from preaching; held parochial charge at Hadleigh, whence he was summoned and arraigned for heresy, 1546; was condemned to be burned, but recanted; master of St. Giles's Hospital, Norwich, 1546–7; suffragan to Thomas Thirlby [q. v.], bishop of Ely, during Queen Mary's reign. [ii. 452]

SHEA, DAVID (1777–1836), translator; educated at Dublin University; clerk in mercantile establishment at Malta; assistant-professor in oriental department of East India Company's College, Haileybury; member of committee of Oriental Translation Fund; published translations from oriental works. [li. 454]

SHEAFFE, SIR ROGER HALE (1763–1851), general; born in Boston, America; ensign, 1778; lieutenant-colonel, 49th foot, 1798; served in Holland, 1799, Baltic, 1801, and Canada, 1802–11 and 1812–13; major-general, 1811; commanded British at recapture of Queenstown, 1812; defended York (now Toronto), 1813; baronet of Great Britain, 1813; colonel, 36th foot, 1829; general, 1838. [li. 455]

SHEARES, HENRY (1753–1798), United Irishman; brother of John Sheares [q. v.]; educated at Trinity College, Dublin; held commission in 51st regiment, but resigned; called to bar, 1789; visited France with his brother, by whom he was governed in political actions; executed before Newgate prison. [li. 457]

SHEARES, JOHN (1766–1798) United Irishman; brother of Henry Sheares [q. v.]; B.A. Trinity College, Dublin, 1787; called to Irish bar, 1788; visited France and became imbued with political principles of the revolution; barrister in Dublin; joined United Irishmen; contributed to anti-government newspaper, the 'Press'; arrested with his brother for complicity in rising of 1798; found guilty of high treason and executed. [li. 455]

SHEARMAN or **SHERMAN**, WILLIAM (1767–1861), physician; M.D. Edinburgh, 1807; physician to Charing Cross Hospital, London; president of Medical Society of London, 1824; published medical works. [li. 1]

SHEBBEARE, JOHN (1709–1788), political writer; practised as a surgeon in Exeter and Bristol; imprisoned for reflections on legislature in novel 'Marriage,' 1754; fined, imprisoned, and pilloried for political libel in 'Sixth Letter to the People of England,' 1758; after release, having attacked Wilkes and advocated peace with France, received pension from Grenville, 1762; defended American policy of George III against Burke and Price; his name coupled by whigs with that of Johnson as pensioner; attacked Smollett and Scotch critics; published as 'History of the Sumatrans,' 1763, a satire on whig policy and panegyric of George III; author of a work on Jersey, 1771, and medical treatises. [lii. 1]

SHEDDEN-RALSTON, WILLIAM RALSTON (1828–1889). [See RALSTON.]

SHEE, GEORGE DARELL (1843–1894), recorder of Hythe; LL.B. Trinity Hall, Cambridge, 1866; barrister, Middle Temple, 1867; recorder of Hythe, 1883. [lii. 7]

SHEE, SIR MARTIN ARCHER (1769–1850), portrait-painter and president of the Royal Academy; educated in Dublin; R.A., 1800; a founder of British Institution, 1807; president of the Royal Academy, 1830–50; defended Academy from attacks in press and parliament; introduced written discourses to students; published poems, two works, and a play. [lii. 4]

SHEE, SIR WILLIAM (1804–1868), judge; called from Lincoln's Inn, 1828; serjeant-at-law, 1840; queen's serjeant, 1857; as M.P., Kilkenny county, 1852–7, took charge of Sharman Crawford's Tenants' Right Bill, and Napier's Tenants' Improvement Compensation Bill; defended William Palmer (1824–1856) [q. v.] and appeared for plaintiff in Roupell case; justice of queen's bench, 1863–8; knighted, 1864; first Roman catholic judge since the revolution; his 'Papers, Letters, and Speeches' privately printed,' 1862–3. [lii. 5]

SHEEHAN, JOHN (1812–1882), journalist and author; member of the Comet Club, Dublin; imprisoned for libel as sub-editor of the 'Comet,' 1833; represented the 'Constitutional' in Paris and Madrid, 1836–7; proprietor and editor of the 'Independent,' 1852; contributed to 'Bentley Ballads'; the original of Thackeray's Captain Shandon. [lii. 7]

SHEEHY, NICHOLAS (1728–1766), Irish priest; executed on charge of complicity in murder of the informer Bridge. [lii. 8]

SHEEPSHANKS, ANNE (1789–1876), founder of exhibition and other endowments at Cambridge Universities; sister of Richard Sheepshanks [q. v.] [lii. 10]

SHEEPSHANKS, JOHN (1787–1863), art amateur; presented to the nation his collection of works by British artists, 1857. [lii. 8]

SHEEPSHANKS, RICHARD (1794–1855), astronomer; brother of John Sheepshanks [q. v.]; fellow of Trinity College, Cambridge, 1817 (tenth wrangler, 1816); M.A., 1819; secretary of Royal Astronomical Society from 1829; F.R.S., 1830; scientific adviser of Edward Troughton [q. v.] in south equatoreal case; carried on controversies with Charles Babbage [q. v.] and others; member of commissions on weights and measures, 1838 and 1843; his reconstructed standard of length adopted, 1855; determined longitudes of Antwerp and Brussels, 1838, of Valentia, Kingstown, and Liverpool, 1844; devised method of driving an equatoreal by clockwork. [lii. 9]

SHEERES, SIR HENRY (d. 1710), military engineer and friend of Pepys; employed at Tangier, 1669–84; served against Monmouth, 1685; knighted and named surveyor of ordnance by James II; twice imprisoned on suspicion of Jacobitism under William III; trustee of Irish grants, 1700; published 'Essay on Certainty and Causes of the Earth's Motion' (1698) and other works. [lii. 10]

SHEFFIELD, first EARL OF (1735–1821). [See HOLROYD, JOHN BAKER.]

SHEFFIELD, EDMUND, first BARON SHEFFIELD (1521–1549), author of lost sonnets; grandson of Sir Robert Sheffield [q. v.]; created a peer, 1547; his death in Ket's rebellion commemorated in epitaph by Barnabe Googe [q. v.] [lii. 16]

SHEFFIELD, SIR EDMUND, first EARL OF MULGRAVE (1564?–1646), grandson of Edmund Sheffield, first baron Sheffield [q. v.]; succeeded as third Baron Sheffield, 1568; served under Leicester in the Netherlands; knighted and granted manor of Mulgrave for services against Spanish armada; K.G., 1593; governor of Brill, 1599; president of the north and lord-lieutenant of Yorkshire, 1603–19; member of councils of Virginia and New England companies; created Earl of Mulgrave, 1626; joined opposition. [lii. 11]

SHEFFIELD, EDMUND, second EARL OF MULGRAVE (1611?–1658), vice-admiral of Yorkshire and member of Cromwell's council; grandson of Sir Edmund Sheffield, first earl of Musgrave [q. v.] [lii. 12]

SHEFFIELD, GEORGE (1839–1892), landscape-painter; member of Manchester Academy; celebrated for drawings in sepia and black and white. [lii. 12]

SHEFFIELD, JOHN (fl. 1643–1647), divine; M.A. Peterhouse, Cambridge; rector of St. Swithin, London, 1643–60. [lii. 16]

SHEFFIELD, JOHN, third EARL OF MULGRAVE, afterwards first DUKE OF BUCKINGHAM AND NORMANBY (1648–1721), patron of Dryden and friend of Pope; son of Edmund Sheffield, second earl of Mulgrave [q. v.]; served against the Dutch under Charles II; commanded expedition for relief of Tangier, 1680; banished from court for courting Princess Anne, 1682; privy councillor and lord chamberlain, 1685; member of high commission court, 1686; lord-lieutenant of East Riding, 1687; submitted to William III, but joined opposition; received pension and was created Marquis of Normanby, 1694, but was dismissed from privy council, 1696; restored by Anne and appointed lord privy seal, 1702; created duke of Normanby, 1703; compelled to resign his appointment, 1705; commissioner for Scottish union, 1706; corresponded with Electress Sophia and advocated her invitation to England; lord president of the council, 1710–14; a lord justice, 1714; buried in Westminster Abbey. He published 'Essay on Poetry' and (probably) 'Essay on Satire,' 'Account of the Revolution,' and poetical works, including a recast of 'Julius Cæsar' into two plays. The fourth edition of his collected works was published in 1753. [lii. 13]

SHEFFIELD, JOHN (1654?–1726), nonconformist divine and friend of Locke; presbyterian pastor in St. Thomas Street, Southwark, 1697. [lii. 15]

SHEFFIELD, SIR ROBERT (d. 1518), speaker of House of Commons; knighted after battle of Stoke, 1487; recorder of London; speaker, 1510 and 1512. [lii. 16]

SHEIL, Sir JUSTIN (1803–1871), general and diplomatist; ambassador in Persia, 1844–54; major-general, 1859; served in Bengal army in India and Persia; secretary to British legation at Teheran, 1836–44; K.C.B., 1855. [lii. 16]

SHEIL, RICHARD LALOR (1791–1851), politician and dramatist; brother of Sir Justin Sheil; educated at Stonyhurst and Trinity College, Dublin; B.A., 1811; his play 'Adelaide, or the Emigrants,' produced at Dublin, 1814; barrister, Lincoln's Inn, 1814; his 'Apostate' played at Covent Garden, 1817, 'Bellamira,' 1818, and 'Evadne,' 1819; collaborated with Banim in 'Damon and Pythias'; protested against O'Connell's refusal of concessions to protestant supporters of catholic emancipation, but afterwards joined him in agitation; his indictment for libel not proceeded with by Canning, 1827; urged opposition to government candidate in Clare, 1828; addressed hostile protestant meeting on Penenden Heath; admitted to inner bar, 1830; returned for Lord Anglesey's borough of Milborne Port, 1830; sat for Louth county, 1831–2; elected as repealer for Tipperary county, 1833; acquitted by parliamentary committee on charge of political double dealing; spoke effectively on foreign questions; opposed Irish Municipal Corporation Bill, 1836, but helped to bring about Lichfield House compact and accepted office, 1837; vice-president of board of trade, 1838–41; sat for Dungarvan from 1841; counsel for John O'Connell [q. v.], 1843; master of the mint, 1846–50; died soon after appointment as minister at Florence. His 'Sketches Legal and Political' (originally contributed to 'New Monthly') were published posthumously. [lii. 17]

SHIELDS or **SHIELDS**, ALEXANDER (1660?–1700), covenanter; M.A. Edinburgh, 1675; when preacher to Scottish presbyterians in London arrested for refusing oath of allegiance, 1685; made modified submission in Scotland, but subsequently retracted; escaped disguised from Bass Rock, 1686; joined James Renwick [q. v.]; preached at field meetings; took part in renewing of covenant at Borland Hill, 1689; received into fellowship after submission to general assembly, 1690; appointed chaplain to Cameronian regiment, 1691, to second charge at St. Andrews, 1697; went to Darien settlement, 1699; died of fever in Jamaica; published 'A Hind let Loose' (1687, printed in Holland), vindicating historically Renwick's position, 'Life and Death of James Renwick' (posthumous), and other covenanting treatises. [lii. 21]

SHEILS, ROBERT (d. 1750). [See SHIELS.]

SHELBURNE, second EARL OF (1737–1805). [See PETTY. WILLIAM, first MARQUIS OF LANSDOWNE.]

SHELDON, EDWARD (1599–1687), translator from the French. [lii. 23]

SHELDON, GILBERT (1598–1677), archbishop of Canterbury; M.A. Trinity College, Oxford, 1620; B.A. 1617; incorporated at Cambridge, 1619; fellow of All Souls College, Oxford, 1622; D.D., 1634; chaplain to lord keeper Coventry; vicar of Hackney, 1633; rector of Newington, 1639; warden of All Souls College, Oxford 1626–48, restored to the wardenship, 1659; friend of Hyde and Falkland; took part in negotiations at Uxbridge, 1644, and attended Charles I at Oxford, Newmarket, and in Isle of Wight; imprisoned at Oxford, 1648; became bishop of London, dean of the chapel royal, London, and master of the Savoy, London, 1660, the Savoy conference being held at his lodgings; virtually primate during Juxon's old age; archbishop of Canterbury, 1663–1677; prominent adviser of Charles II; severe against dissenters, but frequently protected them; remained at Lambeth during the plague; active and liberal promoter of rebuilding of St. Paul's Cathedral, London; greatly interested in church beyond the seas; as chancellor of Oxford built the Sheldonian Theatre (1669) at his own expense, and encouraged Anthony à Wood. [lii. 24]

SHELDON, JOHN (1752–1808), anatomist; after lecturing under William Hunter (1718–1783) [q. v.] at Great Windmill Street, London, carried on private anatomical school in Great Queen Street, London, 1777–88; professor of anatomy to Royal Academy, 1782; F.R.S., 1784; surgeon to Westminster Hospital, 1786, to Devon and Exeter Hospital, 1797; made voyage to Greenland to test method of catching whales; reputed first Englishman to make balloon ascent; published 'History of the Absorbent

System,' 1784, 'Essay on Fracture of the Patella,' &c. (1789). [lii. 26]

SHELDON, NATHANIEL (1705–1780). [See ELLIOT.]

SHELDON, RALPH (1623–1684), antiquary and patron of learning; nephew of Edward Sheldon [q. v.]; left in manuscript 'Catalogue of Nobility of England since Norman Conquest.' [lii. 23]

SHELDON, RICHARD (d. 1642?), divine; imprisoned as jesuit, 1610; became royal chaplain, and published anti-catholic works. [lii. 27]

SHELDRAKE, TIMOTHY (fl. 1759), author of 'Botanicum Medicinale' (1759) and meteorological treatises; M.D. [lii. 27]

SHELFORD, LEONARD (1795–1864), legal writer; barrister, Middle Temple, 1827; works include 'Real Property Statutes,' 1834, 'Law of Railways,' 1845, and 'Law of Joint Stock Companies,' 1863. [lii. 28]

SHELLEY, GEORGE (1666?–1736?), writing-master at Christ's Hospital, London (1714–36), and author of calligraphical works. [lii. 28]

SHELLEY, MARY WOLLSTONECRAFT (1797–1851), second wife of Percy Bysshe Shelley [q. v.]; daughter of William Godwin the elder [q. v.] and Mary Wollstonecraft Godwin [q. v.]; brought up by her stepmother with the Clairmonts; went to the continent with Shelley, July 1814, and married him, December 1816; saw much of Byron, Trelawny, and the Leigh Hunts; left Genoa for England, 1823; contributed to annuals and Lardner's 'Cabinet Cyclopædia'; travelled on the continent, 1840–3; settled annuity on Hunt; published 'Frankenstein,' 1818, 'The Last Man,' 1826, the autobiographical 'Lodore' (1835), and other works; edited Shelley's works, 1839–40. [lii. 29]

SHELLEY, PERCY BYSSHE (1792–1822), poet; born at Field Place, Warnham; educated at Sion House, Brentford, and Eton, where he was unhappy, but consoled himself with scientific researches; while at school published his romance 'Zastrozzi'; issued 'St. Irvyne, or the Rosicrucian,' and 'Original Poetry by Victor and Cazire,' 1810; while at University College, Oxford, composed with Thomas Jefferson Hogg [q. v.] 'Posthumous Fragments of Margaret Nicholson'; sent down after circulation of 'Necessity of Atheism,' 1811; in London made acquaintance of Harriet Westbrook; married her at Edinburgh, 1811; whilst at Keswick was received by Southey, and opened correspondence with Godwin; addressed meetings and wrote pamphlets in Ireland, 1812; from Lynmouth addressed remonstrance to Lord Ellenborough for condemning publisher of Paine's 'Age of Reason'; suffered supposed attempt at assassination at Tanyrallt, North Wales, 1813; his 'Queen Mab' privately printed the same year, unknown till piratically published, 1821; his 'Refutation of Deism' issued anonymously, 1815; left England with Mary Godwin; returned within six weeks; received income from his father and made settlement on Harriet Shelley; his 'Alastor,' written while living near Windsor, published, 1816; fled to continent to avoid Godwin's demands for money; travelled with Byron in Switzerland, and composed 'Mont Blanc'; refused custody of elder children by decision of Eldon; while living at Great Marlow gave money to Leigh Hunt and made acquaintance of Peacock and Keats; issued political pamphlets and published 'Revolt of Islam,' 1818; left England for Italy; translated Plato's 'Symposium' and finished 'Rosalind and Helen' at Lucca; visited Byron at Venice; went to Naples and Rome; published 'The Cenci' at Leghorn, 1819, and 'Prometheus Unbound' at London, 1820; produced 'Ode to the West Wind' while at Florence, 1819; removed to Pisa at end of 1819; produced there many of his best lyrics; his 'Epipsychidion' and 'Adonais' (1821) inspired by Emilia Viviani and death of Keats; visited Byron at Ravenna; produced 'Hellas' and translation from Goethe and Calderon, 1822; removed to Lerici; visited the Hunts at Pisa; sailed from Leghorn for Spezzia with Edward Elliker Williams [q. v.] and was lost in a storm; his body, when recovered, cremated in presence of Byron, Trelawny, and Hunt, and the ashes buried in protestant cemetery, Rome. His 'Posthumous Poems' (including 'Julian and Maddalo,' 'The Witch of Atlas,' and 'Epistle to Maria Gisborne') were printed, 1824, but immediately withdrawn and followed by many pirated editions, no perfect collection being issued till that of Mrs. Shelley. 'Relics of Shelley' were edited by Dr. Garnett, 1862, and a virtually complete collection of Shelley's writings, by Mr. Buxton Forman, 1876–80. Only two genuine portraits are extant ; there are monuments at Christchurch, Hampshire, and University College, Oxford. [lii. 31]

SHELLEY, SIR RICHARD (1513 ?–1589 ?), last grand prior of Knights of St. John in England ; son of Sir William Shelley [q. v.] ; claimed to be the first Englishman to visit Constantinople since its capture by the Turks ; sent on many diplomatic missions by Henry VIII, Edward VI, and Mary ; made turcopolier, 1557 ; received pension from Philip II of Spain and employed by him till his appointment as grand prior, 1566 ; lived at Venice from 1569, rendering some services to the English government. [lii. 40]

SHELLEY, SAMUEL (1750–1808), miniature-painter ; exhibited at Royal Academy, 1774–1804 ; afterwards treasurer of Old Water-colour Society. [lii. 41]

SHELLEY or **DE CONCHES**, WILLIAM (d. 1155 ?). [See WILLIAM.]

SHELLEY, SIR WILLIAM (1480 ?–1549 ?), judge ; judge of sheriff's court, 1517 ; recorder of London, 1520 ; judge of common pleas, 1527 ; twice summoned to parliament ; employed in many important state trials ; his youngest brother the Shelley of 'Shelley's case.' [lii. 41]

SHELTON, JOHN (d. 1845), colonel ; served in the Peninsula and in Walcheren with 9th foot, losing his right arm at San Sebastian ; with 44th in first Burmese war ; commanded regiment in India, 1827–40 ; commanded brigade in Afghanistan, 1841 ; joined William George Keith Elphinstone [q. v.] at Cabul after murder of Sir Alexander Burnes [q. v.] ; defeated by Afghans in a sortie ; did good service in retreat to Jellalabad ; hostage in enemy's hands after evacuation, 1842 ; honourably acquitted by court-martial, 1843 ; died from effects of horse accident. [lii. 42]

SHELTON, SHELDON, or **SHILTON**, SIR RICHARD (d. 1647), solicitor-general ; employed by Duke of Buckingham ; solicitor-general, 1625–34 ; M.P., Bridgnorth, 1626 and 1628 ; treasurer of Inner Temple, 1628 ; ecclesiastical commissioner, 1633. [lii. 43]

SHELTON, THOMAS (fl. 1612–1620), first translator of 'Don Quixote' into English ; employed by Theophilus Howard, second earl of Suffolk [q. v.] ; his version of part i. (based on reprint by Roger Velpius, 1607) issued, 1612 ; translation of part ii. issued with 2nd edition of part i., 1620, probably also his work ; his translation reprinted in 'Tudor Translations,' 1896. [lii. 44]

SHELTON, THOMAS (1601–1650 ?), stenographer ; published 'Tachygraphy,' 1638, and 'Zeiglographia' (a new system), 1649 ; the Psalms in his system of shorthand issued, 1660. [lii. 45]

SHELVOCKE, GEORGE (fl. 1690–1728), privateer ; served some time in the navy ; given by London merchants command of privateer Speedwell under orders of Clipperton in the Success, 1719 ; designedly separated from his consort for two years and conducted independent cruise ; under ambiguous colours extorted ransom from Portuguese ship on coast of Brazil ; caused a black albatross to be shot in rounding Cape Horn, the incident being suggested by Wordsworth to Coleridge, 1797 ; sacked Payta ; wrecked on Juan Fernandez ; built new ship and captured the Jesu Maria : after short reunion with the Success left her in Jesu Maria : captured the Santa Familia and La Concepcion, 1721 : sailed in former for China ; sold her there and divided the treasure : acquitted on technical grounds when charged with piracy, but fled the country : published, 1726, account of his voyage, mentioning gold of California and guano of Peru : his account partially discredited by that of Betagh, 1728. [lii. 46]

SHENSTONE, WILLIAM (1714–1763), poet ; contemporary of Dr. Johnson at Pembroke College, Oxford ; studied poetry there with Richard Graves the younger [q. v.] and Richard Jago [q. v.], and privately printed some occasional verse ; published anonymously 'The Judgment of Hercules,' 1741, and 'The Schoolmistress,' 1742 ; his 'Pastoral Ballad' (1755) and other poems (1758) issued by Dodsley ; devoted much care to laying out the

Leasowes estate ; consulted by Percy when compiling 'Reliques of English Poetry' ; his writings published collectively by Dodsley, 1764–9 ; his 'Schoolmistress' praised by Dr. Johnson and Goldsmith, and his elegies by Burns. [lii. 48]

SHENTON, HENRY CHAWNER (1825–1846), sculptor ; son of Henry Chawner Shenton (1803–1866) [q. v.]. [lii. 50]

SHENTON, HENRY CHAWNER (1803–1866), line-engraver ; best known by his plates after Charles Landseer's 'Tired Huntsman,' R. Crosse's 'Cœur de Lion,' and J. R. Dicksee's 'Labour of Love.' [lii. 50]

SHENTON, WILLIAM KERNOT (1836–1877), sculptor ; brother of Henry Chawner Shenton (1825–1846) [q. v.] [lii. 50]

SHEPARD. [See also SHEPHEARD, SHEPHERD, SHEPPARD.]

SHEPARD, THOMAS (1604–1649), puritan divine ; M.A. Emmanuel College, Cambridge, 1627 ; interdicted from preaching in dioceses of London and York ; settled in New England, 1635, becoming pastor of Newtown, afterwards Cambridge, Massachusetts ; a chief founder of Harvard College ; his 'Sincere Convert' (1641) and 'Sound Beleever' (1645) translated into American-Indian ; published 'The clear Sun-Shine of the Gospel breaking forth upon the Indians,' 1648 (reprinted, 1834 and 1865) ; his work, 'My Birth and Life,' first printed, 1832 ; collective edition issued, 1853 (Boston). [lii. 50]

SHEPARD, THOMAS (1635–1677), pastor of Charlestown, 1659 ; son of Thomas Shepard (1604–1649) [q. v.] [lii. 51]

SHEPESHEVED, WILLIAM DE (fl. 1320 ?), Cistercian and chronicler. [lii. 51]

SHEPHEARD, GEORGE (1770 ?–1842), water-colour painter and engraver. [lii. 52]

SHEPHEARD, GEORGE WALWYN (1804–1852), water-colour painter ; son of George Shepheard [q. v.] [lii. 52]

SHEPHERD, ANTONY (1721–1796), Plumian professor of astronomy at Cambridge ; fellow of Christ's College, Cambridge, 1747–83 ; M.A., 1747 ; D.D., 1766 ; Plumian professor, 1760 ; F.R.S., 1763 ; master of mechanics to George III, 1768 ; canon of Windsor, 1777 ; friend of Captain Cook. [lii. 52]

SHEPHERD, GEORGE (fl. 1800–1830), water-colour painter ; in much repute as topographical artist. [lii. 52]

SHEPHERD, GEORGE SIDNEY (d. 1858), water-colour painter ; son of George Shepherd [q. v.] [lii. 53]

SHEPHERD, JOHN (fl. 1554), musical composer ; organist and choirmaster of Magdalen College, Oxford, and fellow, 1549–51 ; Mus. Doc. Oxon., 1554 ; probably afterwards attached to Chapel Royal, London ; composed four masses (unpublished) and many anthems ; credited with 'O Lord, the Maker of all things,' in Durham seventeenth-century choir-books ; classed by Morley among famous English masters. [lii. 53]

SHEPHERD, JOHN (1759–1805), author of 'Critical and Practical Elucidation of Book of Common Prayer' (1797–8) ; M.A. Queen's College, Oxford, 1787 ; curate of Paddington, 1785–99. [lii. 54]

SHEPHERD, LUKE (fl. 1548), satirical poet ; twice imprisoned for his 'John Bon and the Mast Person,' 1548 (reprinted 1807 and 1852). [lii. 54]

SHEPHERD, RICHARD (1732 ?–1809), divine and author ; M.A. Corpus Christi College, Oxford, 1757 ; D.D., 1788 ; chaplain to Thomas Thurlow [q. v.] ; archdeacon of Bedford, 1783 ; Bampton lecturer, 1788 ; rector of Wetherden and Helmingham, 1792–1809 ; published poems, theological treatises, and devotional works. [lii. 55]

SHEPHERD, RICHARD HERNE (1842–1895), bibliographer ; edited various English classics, including Lamb's 'Poetry for Children' ; printed Coleridge's 'Osorio,' 1873, and unauthorised issues of early poems by Tennyson, 1875, Mrs. Browning, 1878, and Thackeray, 1887 ; published also 'Waltoniana' (1878), and bibliographies of Ruskin (1879), Dickens (1880), Thackeray (1881), Carlyle (1881), Mr. Swinburne (1887), and Tennyson (1896). [lii. 55]

SHEPHERD, SIR SAMUEL (1760–1840), lawyer ; barrister, Inner Temple, 1781 ; king's serjeant, 1796 ;

solicitor-general, 1813 ; knighted, 1814 ; attorney-general, 1817 ; lord chief-baron of the Scottish exchequer, 1819–30 ; privy councillor, 1819 ; his career hindered by deafness ; friend of Scott and Lyndhurst.   [lii. 56]

SHEPHERD, THOMAS HOSMER (*fl.* 1825–1840), painter of buildings and streets in London and other cities.   [lii. 53]

SHEPHERD, WILLIAM (1768–1847), unitarian minister of Gateacre, Liverpool ; radical and author ; friend of William Roscoe [q. v.] ; took charge of Gilbert Wakefield's children when he was in prison, and adopted daughter of Jeremiah Joyce [q. v.] ; published ' Life of Poggio Bracciolini ' (1802) and other works ; collaborated with Joyce and Lant Carpenter in ' Systematic Education ' (1815).   [lii. 57]

SHEPPARD, ELIZABETH SARA (1830 – 1862), novelist ; published 'Charles Auchester (1853), in which Mendelssohn appears as Seraphael, 'Counterparts, or the Cross of Love ' (1854), and other works ; a protégée of Disraeli.   [lii. 58]

SHEPPARD, SIR FLEETWOOD (1634–1698), courtier and poet ; M.A. Christ Church, Oxford, 1657 ; protégé of Charles Sackville, earl of Dorset [q. v.] ; steward of Nell Gwyn and tutor to her son, Charles Beauclerk [q. v.] ; first patron of Prior ; knighted by William III, and named usher of the black rod, 1694 ; published 'The Calendar Reformed ' (1687), and other fugitive pieces.   [lii. 58]

SHEPPARD, JOHN (1702–1724), criminal (' Jack Sheppard ') ; son of a carpenter ; brought up in Bishops-gate workhouse ; arrested as runaway apprentice, 1723 ; incited to theft by ' Edgeworth Bess ' and Poll Maggott ; effected escapes from St. Giles's Roundhouse and New Prison ; offended Jonathan Wild [q. v.], who secured his capture ; condemned to death at Old Bailey, but escaped from condemned hold ; again arrested near Finchley Common ; subsequently escaped up the chimney of the ' Castle,' Newgate ; finally taken when in liquor, and hanged at Tyburn before huge concourse ; subject of many eighteenth-century plays and ballads, and of novel by Ainsworth.   [lii. 60]

SHEPPARD, JOHN (1785–1879), author of ' Thoughts preparative or persuasive to Private Devotion ' (1823) and other works.   [lii. 62]

SHEPPARD or **SHEPHERD**, NICHOLAS (*d.* 1587), master of St. John's College, Cambridge, 1553 ; M.A., 1558 ; vice-master of Trinity College, Cambridge, 1564–8 ; master of St. John's College, 1569–74 ; archdeacon of Northampton, 1571.   [lii. 62]

SHEPPARD, ROBERT (*fl.* 1730–1740), engraver.   [lii. 62]

SHEPPARD, SAMUEL (*fl.* 1646), amanuensis of Ben Jonson and royalist writer.   [lii. 63]

SHEPPARD, WILLIAM (*fl.* 1650–1660), portrait-painter ; protégé of Thomas Killigrew the elder [q. v.]   [lii. 63]

SHEPPARD, WILLIAM (*d.* 1675 ?), legal writer ; serjeant-at-law, 1656 ; clerk of the upper bench and puisne judge of the County Palatine during Commonwealth ; published numerous legal treatises, including ' Grand Abridgement of Common and Statute Law,' 1675, ' The Precedent of Precedents,' 1655, ' Law of Common Assurances,' 1650.   [lii. 63]

SHEPPEY, JOHN DE (*d.* 1360), bishop of Rochester ; D.D. Oxford ; prior of Rochester, 1333–53 ; envoy to Spain, 1345 ; bishop of Rochester, 1353–60 ; treasurer of England, 1356–8 ; a famous preacher.   [lii. 64]

SHEPREVE or **SHEPERY**, JOHN (1509 ?–1542), hebraist ; M.A. Corpus Christi College, Oxford, 1533 ; Greek reader at Corpus Christi College, Oxford ; Hebrew professor at Oxford, *c.* 1538 ; author of 'Summa et Synopsis Novi Testamenti ' in verse (published, 1560), &c. ; eulogised by Leland.   [lii. 64]

SHEPREVE or **SHEPERY**, WILLIAM (1540–1598), Roman catholic divine and writer (Scepreus) ; nephew of John Shepreve [q. v.] ; B.A. Corpus Christi College, Oxford, 1560 ; retired to Rome in reign of Queen Elizabeth (D.D. Rome) and died there.   [lii. 65]

SHEPSTONE, SIR THEOPHILUS (1817–1893), South African statesman ; Kaffir interpreter at Capetown,

1835 ; British resident among Fingo and other tribes, 1839 ; agent for natives in Natal, 1845, secretary for native affairs, 1856 ; arranged succession of Cetewayo, 1872 ; conferred with colonial secretary in England, 1874 and 1876, and created K.C.M.G. ; annexed Transvaal, 1877, and administered it till 1879 ; administrator of Zululand, 1884.   [lii. 65]

SHERARD, JAMES (1666–1738), botanist and apothecary ; received hon. M.D. from Oxford (1731) and fellowship of College of Physicians (1732) after carrying out (1728) his brother's scheme of an Oxford botanical endowment ; his garden at Eltham noted for rare plants.   [lii. 66]

SHERARD, WILLIAM (1659–1728), botanist ; brother of James Sherard [q. v.] ; of Merchant Taylors' School and St. John's College, Oxford (D.C.L., 1683) ; studied at Paris under Tournefort and at Leyden with Paul Hermann ; made botanical excursion to Geneva, Rome, and Naples ; while consul for Turkish company at Smyrna (1702–16) made botanical and antiquarian journeys in Asia Minor ; F.R.S., 1718 ; brought John James Dillenius [q. v.] to England ; founded chair of botany at Oxford ; published catalogue of plants introduced at Paris by Tournefort, and Introduction to Hermann's ' Paradisus Batavus ' (1689) ; assisted Ray and other botanists ; plant named after him in Linnean classification.   [lii. 67]

SHERATON, THOMAS (1751–1806), furniture maker and designer ; published 'Cabinet-maker and Uphol-sterer's Drawing Book,' 1791 (3rd edit. 1802), and 'Cabinet Dictionary,' 1803, also devotional works ; advocated severe style, and adhered to it except in his later designs.   [lii. 68]

SHERBORNE or **SHIRBURN**, ROBERT (1440 ?–1536), bishop of Chichester ; fellow of New College, Oxford, 1474 ; master of St. Cross Hospital, Winchester ; archdeacon of Buckinghamshire, Huntingdonshire, and Taunton, 1496 ; envoy to the papal court, 1496, 1502, and 1504, and to Scotland, 1503 ; dean of St. Paul's, London, 1499 ; forged papal bull appointing himself to see of St. David's, 1505 ; bishop of Chichester, 1508–36 ; acquiesced reluctantly in Reformation ; founded prebends at Chichester and grammar school at Rolleston.   [lii. 69]

SHERBROOKE, VISCOUNT (1811–1892). [See LOWE, ROBERT.]

SHERBROOKE, SIR JOHN COAPE (1764–1830), general ; as lieutenant-colonel of the 33rd foot served in the Netherlands, 1794, and the Mysore war, 1799, commanding right column at storming of Seringapatam ; held commands in Sicily, 1805–8 ; Wellesley's second in command in Peninsular campaign of 1809 ; K.B. after Talavera ; returned to England in bad health ; lieutenant-governor of Nova Scotia during second American war ; governor-general of Canada, 1816–18 ; G.C.B., 1815.   [lii. 70]

SHERBURNE, SIR EDWARD (1618–1702), clerk of the ordnance and translator ; royalist commissary-general of artillery at Edgehill, 1642 ; friend of Shirley and Thomas Stanley [q. v.] ; travelled with Sir John Coventry, 1654–9 ; chief author of ' Rules and Orders ' long in use in ordnance office ; knighted, 1682 ; published ' Poems and Translations,' 1651, renderings in verse of Seneca's tragedies (1701), and the ' Sphere ' of Manilius (1675). [lii. 72]

SHERER, MOYLE (1789–1869), author of books of travel ; served with 34th in the Peninsula till captured at pass of Maya, 1813 ; returned from India by overland route and issued 'Scenes and Impressions in Egypt and Italy,' 1824 ; published also 'Sketches of India,' 1821, ' Recollections of the Peninsula,' 1823, ' Story of a Life ' (1825), novels, and a life of Wellington (in Lardner).   [lii. 73]

SHERFIELD, HENRY (*d.* 1634), puritan ; a governor of Lincoln's Inn from 1622 ; M.P., Southampton, 1614–24, Salisbury, 1624–9 ; attacked Buckingham and Richard Neile [q. v.] ; fined by Star-chamber for destroying painted church window at Winterbourne Earls.   [lii. 74]

SHERIDAN, MRS. CAROLINE HENRIETTA (1779–1851), novelist ; daughter of Colonel Callander, afterwards Sir James Campbell (1745–1832) [q. v.] ; married Thomas, son of Richard Brinsley Sheridan, 1805, and became mother of ' the three beauties'; on her husband's death resided at Hampton Court ; published 'Carwell, or Crime and Sorrow' (1830), and two other novels.   [lii. 74]

SHERIDAN, CHARLES FRANCIS (1750–1806), author and politician; brother of Richard Brinsley Sheridan [q. v.]; Irish secretary-at-war, 1782–9; member of Irish parliament, Belturbet, 1776, Rathcormack, 1783–1800; received pensions for himself and wife; published 'History of late Revolution in Sweden' (1778) and political pamphlets. [lii. 75]

SHERIDAN, Mrs. ELIZABETH ANN (1754–1792), vocalist; first wife of Richard Brinsley Sheridan [q. v.]; as Miss Linley celebrated for her singing in oratorios and for her beauty and virtue; sat to Reynolds for St. Cecilia and the Virgin; assisted her husband in management of Drury Lane, London; canvassed for Fox, 1790; died of consumption. [lii. 76]

SHERIDAN, Mrs. FRANCES (1724–1766), author; married Thomas Sheridan (1719–1788) [q. v.], 1747; published 'Memoirs of Miss Sidney Bidulph,' 1761, 1767, and 'History of Nourjahad' (posthumous, 1767); her comedy 'The Discovery' produced successfully by Garrick at Drury Lane, London, 1763; died at Blois. [lii. 77]

SHERIDAN, HELEN SELINA, afterwards COUNTESS OF DUFFERIN and COUNTESS OF GIFFORD (1807–1867), song-writer; eldest of 'the three beauties,' daughters of Tom Sheridan [q. v.]; married Commander Blackwood, 1825, and became mother of first Marquis of Dufferin; admired by Benjamin Disraeli [q. v.]; married, on his death-bed, George Hay, earl of Gifford, 1862; her comedy 'Finesse' played by Buckstone and Wigan at Haymarket, London, 1863; some of her songs published, 1894. [lii. 77]

SHERIDAN, RICHARD BRINSLEY (1751–1816), dramatist and parliamentary orator; son of Thomas Sheridan (1719–1788) [q. v.]; educated at Harrow, 1762–8; collaborated with Nathaniel Brassey Halhed [q. v.] in an edition of Aristænetus, 1771; contributed verses to 'Bath Chronicle'; escorted Miss Linley from Bath to France, 1772, and fought two duels with Major Mathews, her persecutor; married her, 1773; his comedy 'The Rivals,' produced at Covent Garden, London, January 1775, at first a failure; his 'St. Patrick's Day' and 'The Duenna' played the same year, the latter running seventy-five nights; acquired Garrick's share in Drury Lane, London, and became manager, 1776; produced 'The Rivals' there, 1777, also 'A Trip to Scarborough' and 'The School for Scandal' (8 May); his famous farce 'The Critic' first given, 1779, and 'Pizarro,' 1799; his new theatre opened, 1794, but destroyed by fire, 1809, motion being made to adjourn House of Commons in respect for his loss; elected to the Literary Club, 1777; returned for Stafford as supporter of Fox, 1780; declined gift of money offered by American congress for speeches against the war; undersecretary for foreign affairs in Rockingham ministry, 1782; secretary to the treasury in coalition ministry, 1783; confidential adviser to George, prince of Wales; made great speech of nearly six hours in moving adoption of the Oude charge against Warren Hastings, 1787, and in replying to defence on that charge, 1794; his speech as manager of impeachment (June 1788) the topic of the day; spoke twelve times for reform of Scottish royal burghs, 1787–94; replied to Mornington's speech against French republic, 1794; thanked by Dundas for patriotic speech, 1797; opposed Irish union, 1799; upheld liberty of press in spite of constant calumnies; treasurer of the navy in ministry of 'all the Talents,' 1806–7; M.P., Westminster, 1806–7, Ilchester, 1807–12; arrested for debt, 1813; suffered from brain disease in last years; receiver of the duchy of Cornwall in his last years, but had no pension; did not die 'a neglected pauper'; received a grand public funeral. There are several portraits of him by Reynolds. [lii. 78]

SHERIDAN, THOMAS, the elder (fl. 1661–1688), Jacobite and author; fellow of Trinity College, Dublin, 1667 (B.A. 1664); F.R.S., 1679; imprisoned in connection with 'Popish plot,' 1680; chief secretary for Ireland, 1687; private secretary to James II in exile; his 'Discourse on Rise and Power of Parliaments' (1677) reprinted as 'Revelations in Irish History,' 1870. [lii. 85]

SHERIDAN, THOMAS (1687–1738), Dublin schoolmaster and friend of Swift; nephew of William Sheridan [q. v.]; M.A. Trinity College, Dublin, 1714; D.D., 1726; constant companion of Swift when in Ireland, but finally alienated him by convicting him of avarice; published translations of Persius, Juvenal, and the 'Philoctetes.' [lii. 86]

SHERIDAN, THOMAS, the younger (d. 1746), tutor to Prince Charles Edward; son of Thomas Sheridan (fl. 1661–1688) [q. v.]; accompanied Prince Charles Edward to Scotland, 1745, and was knighted by him. [lii. 86]

SHERIDAN, THOMAS (1719–1788), actor, lecturer on elocution, and author; son of Thomas Sheridan (1687–1738) [q. v.]; of Westminster School and Trinity College, Dublin; played Richard III at Dublin, 1743; several years manager of Theatre Royal, Dublin; married Frances Chamberlaine after Kelly riots; played at Covent Garden, London, 1754–6, and Drury Lane, London, 1763; lectured in English towns; procured Dr. Johnson and himself pensions; gave readings in London with Henderson; published 'General Dictionary of the English Language' (1780), works on education, lectures, and an edition of Swift's works, 1784. [lii. 87]

SHERIDAN, TOM (1775–1817), colonial treasurer at Cape of Good Hope; son of Richard Brinsley Sheridan [q. v.] [lii. 85]

SHERIDAN, WILLIAM (1636–1711), bishop of Kilmore; brother of Thomas Sheridan (fl. 1661–1688) [q. v.], secretary to James II; dean of Down, 1669; D.D. of Dublin, 1682; bishop of Kilmore, 1682–93; chaplain to Ormonde; a nonjuror. [lii. 88]

SHERIFF, LAURENCE (d. 1567), founder of Rugby school; a native of Rugby; became a London grocer (second warden of Grocers' Company, 1566); connected with household of Princess Elizabeth, and granted arms by her when queen; left bequests and endowments of a school at Rugby, which was founded immediately after his death. [lii. 89]

SHERINGHAM, ROBERT (1602–1678), linguist; fellow of Caius College, Cambridge; M.A. 1626 (incorporated at Oxford, 1628); ejected from fellowship for royalism, 1644, but restored, 1660; taught Hebrew and Arabic in Holland; published Latin translation of 'Joma. Codex Talmudicus' with commentary, 1648, and 'De Anglorum Gentis Origine Disceptatio,' 1670. [lii. 89]

SHERINGTON or SHERRINGTON, SIR WILLIAM (1495?–1553). [See SHARINGTON.]

SHERLEY. [See also SHIRLEY.]

SHERLEY or SHIRLEY, THOMAS (1638–1678), physician; grandson of Sir Thomas Shirley (1564–1630?) [q. v.]; physician in ordinary to Charles II; imprisoned by Commons for appealing to House of Lords against a member whom they had declared exempt from lawsuits during session, 1675. [lii. 90]

SHERLOCK, MARTIN (d. 1797), traveller; of Trinity College, Dublin; chaplain to Frederick Augustus Hervey, fourth earl of Bristol [q. v.] and bishop of Derry; travelled extensively in central Europe and Italy; saw Frederick the Great at Potsdam, 1779, and Voltaire at Ferney; vicar of Castlecomer and Kilglass, 1782; archdeacon of Killala, 1788; published 'Lettres d'un Voyageur Anglois,' 1779, 'Nouvelles Lettres,' 1780, 'Letters on several Subjects,' 1781, and 'Consiglio ad un Giovane Poeta,' 1779. [lii. 90]

SHERLOCK, PAUL (1595–1646), superior of Irish College, Salamanca; author of three books of commentaries on the Song of Solomon (1634, 1637, 1640), and other works. [lii. 91]

SHERLOCK, RICHARD (1612–1689), divine; uncle of bishop Thomas Wilson (1663–1755) [q. v.]; M.A. Trinity College, Dublin, 1633; captured by Fairfax at Nantwich, 1644; chaplain to royalist governor of Oxford; afterwards to Sir R. Bindloss at Berwick and the eighth Earl of Derby at Lathom; employed by Derby in Isle of Man; rector of Winwick, 1660–89; published 'Mercurius Christianus: the Practical Christian,' 1673, a treatise against quakerism, 1654, and other works. [lii. 92]

SHERLOCK, THOMAS (1678–1761), bishop of London; son of William Sherlock (1641?–1707) [q. v.]; at Eton with Walpole, Townshend, and Pelham; fellow of St. Catharine's Hall, Cambridge, 1698; M.A., 1701, and master of St. Catharine's Hall, Cambridge, 1714–19; as master of the Temple, 1704–53, obtained reputation as a preacher; when vice-chancellor at Cambridge arranged university archives and defended rights of university against Bentley; dean of Chichester, 1715; took part in

Bangorian controversy, and fell into disgrace; bishop of Bangor, 1728-34, of Salisbury, 1734-48, of London, 1748-1761; declined see of York, 1743, and the primacy, 1747; supported Walpole in House of Lords; as bishop of London issued popular pastorals and cultivated good relations with dissenters; left library to Cambridge University; published 'Tryal of the Witnesses of the Resurrection of Jesus,' 1729, a treatise on prophecy against deists, 1725, and other controversial works. [lii. 93]

SHERLOCK, WILLIAM (1641 ?-1707), dean of St. Paul's; of Eton and Peterhouse, Cambridge; M.A., 1663; rector of St. George's, Botolph Lane, London, 1669; lecturer at St. Dunstan's-in-the-West; prebendary of St. Paul's, London, 1681; master of the Temple, 1685-1704; upheld duty of passive obedience, but refused to read declaration for liberty of conscience, 1687; opposed succession of William and Mary, but took the oaths, 1690; dean of St. Paul's, London, 1691-1707; his 'Practical Discourse concerning Death' (1689) translated into French and Welsh; issued numerous controversial treatises, including 'The Knowledge of Jesus Christ,' 1674 (against John Owen (1616-1683) [q. v.]), 'Case of Resistance,' 1684, 'Preservative against Popery,' 1688, 'Vindication of Doctrine of the Trinity,' 1690, and 'Present State of the Socinian Controversy,' 1698. [lii. 95]

SHERLOCK, WILLIAM (*fl.* 1759-1806), portrait-painter and engraver; director of Incorporated Society of Artists, 1774. [lii. 97]

SHERLOCK, WILLIAM P. (*fl.* 1800-1820), water-colour painter and etcher. [lii. 97]

SHERMAN, EDWARD (1776 - 1866), coach-proprietor and carrier. [lii. 97]

SHERMAN, JAMES (1796-1862), dissenting divine; minister of Lady Huntingdon's chapel, Bristol, Castle Street, Reading (1821-36), Surrey Chapel, Blackfriars, London (1836-54), and Blackheath; powerful preacher and popular author of devotional treatises. [lii. 97]

SHERMAN, JOHN (*d.* 1671), historian of Jesus College, Cambridge; educated at Queens' College, Cambridge; 'president' of Jesus College, Cambridge, 1662-71; D.D. by royal mandate, 1665; archdeacon of Salisbury, 1670-1; his Latin history of the college printed by Halliwell, 1840. [lii. 98]

SHERRING, MATTHEW ATMORE (1826-1880), missionary at Benares and Mirzapore; LL.D. University College, London, 1849; M.A. London, 1850; published 'Indian Church during Great Rebellion,' 1859, 'Hindoo Tribes and Castes,' 1872-81, 'History of Protestant Missions in India,' 1875, and other works. [lii. 98]

SHERRY, JOHN (*d.* 1551), archdeacon of Lewes, 1541. [lii. 99]

SHERRY or **SHIRRYE**, RICHARD (*fl.* 1550), author; head-master of Magdalen College School, Oxford, 1534-40; chief work, 'A Treatise of the Figures of Grammer and Rhetorike,' 1555. [lii. 99]

SHERWEN, JOHN (1749 - 1826), physician and archæologist; M.D. Aberdeen, 1798; practised at Enfield and Bath; published part of a work maintaining the genuineness of the 'Rowley' poems (1809) and medical treatises. [lii. 99]

SHERWIN, CHARLES (*fl.* 1780), engraver; brother and assistant of John Keyse Sherwin [q. v.] [lii. 100]

SHERWIN, JOHN KEYSE (1751 ?-1790), engraver and draughtsman; studied under Bartolozzi and at the Academy; exhibited chalk drawings, 1774-84; published original plates, including 'The Finding of Moses,' 1789, and portraits of Mrs. Siddons and Mrs. Hartley, 1782; also engravings after Reynolds ('The Fortune Teller,' &c.), Guido, and other masters; engraver to George III, 1785. [lii. 100]

SHERWIN, RALPH (1550-1581), jesuit; of Exeter College, Oxford (M.A. 1574), and the English College, Rome; twice racked in the Tower of London and executed at Tyburn with Edmund Campion [q. v.] [lii. 101]

SHERWIN, RALPH (1799-1830), actor; played at Drury Lane, London, 1823-6. [lii. 101]

SHERWIN, WILLIAM (1607 - 1687 ?), divine; minister of Wallington, 1645-60; author of theological works. [lii. 102]

SHERWIN, WILLIAM (*fl.* 1670-1710), line-engraver and one of the earliest workers in mezzotint; son of William Sherwin (1607-1687 ?) [q. v.] [lii. 102]

SHERWOOD. [See also SHIRWOOD.]

SHERWOOD, MRS. MARY MARTHA (1775-1851), authoress; daughter of George Butt [q. v.]; at school with Mary Russell Mitford [q. v.] and Letitia Elizabeth Landon [q. v.]; her 'Susan Gray' (1802) very successful; married Captain Henry Sherwood, 1803; while in India devoted much attention to soldiers' orphans, and wrote 'Little Henry and his Bearer,' the 'Indian Pilgrim,' and other works; published numerous stories and tracts, including 'History of the Fairchild Family' (pts. i. 1818, ii. 1842, iii. 1847). [lii. 102]

SHERWOOD, ROBERT (*fl.* 1632), lexicographer; B.A. Corpus Christi College, Cambridge, 1626; wrote, 1622, a French-English dictionary to be appended to the new edition of the English-French dictionary of Randle Cotgrave [q. v.] [lii. 104]

SHERWOOD, WILLIAM (*d.* 1482), bishop of Meath; bishop, 1460-82; deputy-viceroy, 1475-7; chancellor of Ireland, 1475-81. [lii. 104]

SHEWEN, WILLIAM (1631 ?-1695), quaker; published 'The True Christian's Faith and Experience' (1675), and other works. [lii. 104]

SHIELD, WILLIAM (1748-1829), musical composer; principal viola for eighteen years at the Italian opera, London, and composer at Covent Garden, London, 1778-1797; a founder of the Glee Club, 1793; master of musicians in ordinary, 1817; composed 'The Wolf,' 'The Arethusa,' and other songs, besides music to thirty dramatic pieces; published treatises on musical theory, and collections of ballads, glees, string music, &c. [lii. 104]

SHIELDS, ALEXANDER (1660 ?-1700). [See SHEILDS.]

SHIELS, **SHIELLS**, or **SHIELDS**, ROBERT (*d.* 1753), compiler; employed as amanuensis on Dr. Johnson's 'Dictionary'; a chief contributor to the 'Lives of the Poets of Great Britain and Ireland to the time of Dean Swift,' 1753; published 'Musidorus,' 1748, and other poems. [lii. 105]

SHILLETO, ARTHUR RICHARD (1848-1894), scholar; son of Richard Shilleto [q. v.]; of Harrow and Trinity College, Cambridge; M.A. 1875; master of Ulverston school, 1879-82; published translations of Pausanias, Plutarch's 'Morals,' and Josephus; annotated Burton's 'Anatomy of Melancholy.' [lii. 106]

SHILLETO, RICHARD (1809-1876), classical scholar; of Shrewsbury and Trinity College, Cambridge (second classic, 1831); M.A., 1835; thirty years leading Cambridge coach; fellow of Peterhouse, Cambridge, 1867; edited Demosthenes's 'De Falsa Legatione' (1844), and Thucydides, bk. i. and part of ii.; published 'Thucydides or Grote,' 1851; contributed to 'Notes and Queries' under the anagram Charles Thiriold; composed skits in Latin, Greek, and English. [lii. 106]

SHILLIBEER, GEORGE (1797-1866), pioneer of omnibuses in London; built omnibuses in Paris, 1825; introduced omnibuses from Paris into London, 1829; ruined by railway competition; patented funeral coach. [lii. 107]

SHILLING, ANDREW (*d.* 1621), commander in East India Company; one of chief masters of the navy, 1603; took part in expedition to India, 1617, and conveyed home Sir Thomas Roe [q. v.]; mortally wounded in victory of his squadron over Portuguese on Persian coast. [lii. 107]

SHILLITOE, THOMAS (1754-1836), quaker; having realised a competence as shoemaker, turned itinerant preacher; visited chief countries of Europe and had interviews with several sovereigns; in America, 1826-9; president of British and Foreign Temperance Society, 1833; his 'Journal' printed, 1839. [lii. 108]

SHIPLEY, SIR CHARLES (1755-1815), general; ensign, 1771; suspended from the army for a year for employing private negroes on government works in Antigua, 1792; captured by French off Barbados, 1794; commanding royal engineer under Abercromby in Trinidad and Porto Rico, 1797; took part in capture of various

West Indian islands, 1799, of St. Lucia, 1803, and of Surinam, 1804 ; accompanied expedition against Danish West Indies, 1807 : knighted, 1808 : took leading part in capture of Martinique, 1809, and Guadeloupe, 1810, and recapture of latter, 1815 ; died governor of Grenada, 1813–1815.   [lii. 109]

SHIPLEY, CONWAY (1782–1808), captain in the navy ; son of William Davies Shipley [q. v.] ; killed in Sir Charles Cotton's [q. v.] Tagus expedition.   [lii. 114]

SHIPLEY, GEORGIANA (d. 1806), artist : cousin of Georgiana Cavendish, duchess of Devonshire [q. v.], by whom she was introduced to Francis Hare-Naylor [q. v.] ; married Hare-Naylor ; friend of Clotilda Tambroni, the female professor of Greek at Bologna : returned to England with her husband and devoted herself to painting ; died at Lausanne.   [xxiv. 374]

SHIPLEY, JONATHAN (1714–1788), bishop of St. Asaph and friend of Franklin ; of St. John's College and Christ Church, Oxford ; M.A., 1738 ; rector of Silchester and Sherborne St. John, 1743 ; chaplain-general in Fontenoy campaign, 1745 ; canon of Christ Church, Oxford, 1748 ; dean of Winchester and rector of Chilbolton, 1760 ; bishop of Llandaff, 1769 ; bishop of St. Asaph, 1769–88 ; vigorous opponent of American policy of George III and advocate of repeal of laws against protestant dissenters and of parliamentary reform ; intimate with Burke and Reynolds.   [lii. 110]

SHIPLEY, WILLIAM (1714–1803), originator of the Society of Arts ; brother of Jonathan Shipley [q. v.] ; established 'Shipley's Academy,' Strand, London ; registrar of Society of Arts till 1760 ; founded Kentish Society for Promotion of Useful Knowledge ; his portrait painted by Cosway (a former pupil).   [lii. 112]

SHIPLEY, WILLIAM DAVIES (1745–1826), dean of St. Asaph ; son of Jonathan Shipley [q. v.] ; educated at Westminster School, Winchester College, and Christ Church, Oxford ; M.A., 1771 ; vicar of Wrexham and Llanarmon yn Ial and chancellor of St. Asaph ; dean of St. Asaph, 1774–1826 ; his prosecution for seditious libel, 1783–5, in connection with Sir William Jones's 'Principles of Government' led to establishment of rights of juries in libel actions ; father-in-law of Reginald Heber [q. v.] and of Dr. Pelham Warren [q. v.]   [lii. 113]

SHIPMAN, THOMAS (1632–1680), author of 'Carolina, or Loyal Poems' (1683) : of St. John's College, Cambridge ; friend of Abraham Cowley [q. v.] and Thomas Flatman [q. v.]   [lii. 114]

SHIPP, JOHN (1784–1834), soldier and author ; enlisted in 22nd foot, 1797 ; received commission in 65th for bravery in Mahratta campaign, 1804–5 ; sold out to pay debts, 1808 ; enlisted in 24th dragoons and again won his commission ; sentenced to dismissal for reflections on superior officers, 1823, but received pension from East India Company on selling out, 1825 ; died master of Liverpool workhouse ; published Memoirs of his military career (1829 ; last ed. 1890), 'Flogging and its Substitutes' (1831), and other works.   [lii. 115]

SHIPPARD, ALEXANDER (1771–1841), rear-admiral ; cut out vessels off the Texel, 1797 ; landed Georges Cadoudal, 1803, and Pichegru, 1804 ; received promotion and sword of honour for gallant action off Boulogne, 1804 ; attained post rank, 1806 ; rear-admiral, 1838 ; died in Malta.   [lii. 116]

SHIPPARD, WILLIAM (1764–1856), captain in the navy ; brother of Alexander Shippard [q. v.] : present at battles of St. Vincent, 1797, and Copenhagen, 1801.   [lii. 116]

SHIPPEN, ROBERT (1675–1745), principal of Brasenose College, Oxford ; B.A. Merton College, Oxford, 1696 ; fellow of Brasenose College ; M.A., 1699 ; Gresham professor of music, 1705–10 ; principal of Brasenose, 1710–45 ; vice-chancellor of Oxford University, 1718–22 ; rector of Whitechapel, 1716.   [lii. 118]

SHIPPEN, WILLIAM (1673–1743), parliamentary Jacobite : brother of Robert Shippen [q. v.] : of Westminster School and Trinity College, Cambridge ; B.A., 1694 ; M.P., Bramber, 1707–13, Newton, 1714–43 ; published satires on whigs, 1708 ; commissioner to investigate charges against Marlborough, 1711 ; opposed offer of reward for apprehension of James Edward, the Old Pretender, 1714, impeachment of Harley, and Septennial Bill,

1716 ; sent to the Tower of London for words reflecting on George I, 1718 ; moved reduction of civil list, 1727 ; opposed excise scheme, 1733, but refused to concur in motion for removal of Walpole, 1741.   [lii. 117]

SHIPTON, MOTHER, reputed prophetess ; first mentioned in tract of 1641 (probably compiled in York) as prophesying death of Cardinal Wolsey and others, the tract being widely circulated and much imitated (reprinted, 1869) ; a so-called account of her, 'Life and Death of Mother Shipton,' brought out by Richard Head [q. v.], 1667 (reprinted, 1871) ; biographical details supplied in 'Wonderful History' (1686) additions (including predictions of steam-engine and telegraph) made to Head's 'Life' of her by Charles Hindley, 1862. There are spurious memorial stones, one in the museum of the Yorkshire Philosophical Society at York, the other, 'Old Mother Shipton's tomb,' at Williton, Somerset.   [lii. 119]

SHIPTON, JOHN (1680–1748), surgeon ; consulted in case of Queen Caroline (1737).   [lii. 120]

SHIPTON, WILLIAM (fl. 1659), author of 'Dia : a poem,' 1659.   [lii. 120]

SHIRBURN, ROBERT (1440?–1536). [See SHERBORNE.]

SHIRLEY or **SHERLEY**, SIR ANTHONY (1565–1635 ?), adventurer ; B.A. Hart Hall, Oxford, 1581 ; fellow of All Souls College, Oxford, 1581 ; served in Netherlands, 1586, and under Essex in Normandy, 1591 ; imprisoned for accepting knighthood from Henry of Navarre, 1593 ; commanded expedition against Portuguese settlement of San Thomé, 1596 ; took Santiago (Cape Verde islands), landed in Dominica and Margarita (Venezuela), explored Jamaica, and returned home by Newfoundland ; accompanied Essex's 'Island Voyage,' 1597 ; left Venice, 1599, with instructions from Essex to proceed to Persia on political and commercial mission ; received from Shah Abbas the rank of mirza and grants of religious and trade privileges ; returned to Europe as his envoy ; badly received by the tsar Boris, but entertained by Emperor Rudolph II and the Pope Clement VIII ; disavowed by English government and imprisoned by Venetians, 1603 ; undertook mission to Morocco for Rudolph II, 1605–6, and was created count of the empire ; led unsuccessful expedition for king of Spain against Turkish possessions in the Levant, 1609, but received pension ; lived in poverty at Madrid till his death ; published narrative of his travels in Persia, 1613.   [lii. 121]

SHIRLEY, EVELYN PHILIP (1812–1882), archæologist ; of Eton and Magdalen College, Oxford ; M.A., 1837 ; M.P., Monaghan, 1841–7, South Warwickshire, 1853–65 ; the Mr. Ardenne of 'Lothair' ; trustee of National Portrait Gallery and Rugby School ; hon. LL.D. Dublin, 1881 ; author of 'Stemmata Shirleiana,' 1841, and 'The Sherley Brothers,' 1848 ; published 'The Noble and Gentle Men of England' (1859), 'History of County of Monaghan' (1879), and other works.   [lii. 124]

SHIRLEY, HENRY (d. 1627), author of 'The Martyr'd Souldier' (1638) ; son of Sir Thomas Shirley (1564–1630 ?) [q. v.] ; his murder referred to in Prynne's 'Histriomastix.'   [lii. 125]

SHIRLEY, SIR HORATIO (1805–1879), general ; cousin of Evelyn Philip Shirley [q. v.] ; entered the army, 1825 ; commanded 88th foot in Crimea ; C.B., 1856 ; K.C.B., 1869 ; general, 1877.   [lii. 125]

SHIRLEY, JAMES (1596–1666), dramatic poet ; educated at Merchant Taylors' School, London ; migrated from St. John's College, Oxford, and graduated at St. Catharine's, Cambridge, c. 1618 ; printed poem 'Eccho' ('Narcissus'), 1618 ; master of St. Albans grammar school, 1623–5, but soon became Roman catholic ; his first play (printed as 'Schoole of Complement,' 1631), licensed, 1626 ; patronised by Queen Henrietta Maria, and associated with Massinger, Ford, and other dramatists and poets ; attacked Prynne in 'A Bird in a Cage' (licensed as 'The Beauties'), 1633 ; supplied text of Inns of Court masque, 'Triumph of Peace,' 1634 ; produced, while in Ireland (1636–40), four plays, of which 'The Royal Master' was acted before the lord-deputy at Dublin Castle : continued to produce plays till their interdiction by parliament, 1642 ; accompanied his patron, Newcastle, in the campaigns of 1642–4 ; under protection of Thomas Stanley (1625–1678) [q. v.] published 'Poems,' 1646, and wrote commendatory prefaces to unprinted plays of Beaumont and Fletcher; published educational treatises; died from miseries caused by Great Fire. His chief plays were 'The Traitor' (1631; printed, 1635) and 'The Cardinal' (licensed, 1641, printed, 1652), tragedies; 'Hyde Park' (licensed, 1632, printed, 1637), 'The Gamester' (licensed, 1633, acted 1634, adapted by Garrick and others), 'The Coronation' (licensed 1635, printed 1640 — sometimes ascribed to Fletcher), 'The Lady of Pleasure' (1635), 'The Sisters' (licensed, 1642, printed, 1653), comedies; and 'The Contention of Ajax and Ulysses' (1659), dramatic entertainment (containing the famous dirge, 'The glories of our mortal state,' which is said to have terrified Oliver Cromwell). He was disparaged by Dryden ('MacFlecknoe'), but his reputation was revived by Richard Farmer [q. v.] and Charles Lamb; works edited by Alexander Dyce, 1833.   [lii. 126]

SHIRLEY, JOHN (1366?-1456), transcriber of Chaucer and Lydgate; epitaph in St. Bartholomew-the-Less, London, preserved by Stow.   [lii. 133]

SHIRLEY, JOHN (*fl.* 1678), medical writer.   [lii. 134]

SHIRLEY, JOHN (1648-1679), author of 'Life of Sir Walter Raleigh'; M.A. Trinity College, Oxford, 1671.   [lii. 134]

SHIRLEY, JOHN (*fl.* 1680-1702), author of 'Triumph of Wit' (1688) and other works; perhaps son of James Shirley [q. v.]   [lii. 134]

SHIRLEY, LAURENCE, fourth EARL FERRERS (1720-1760), murderer; hanged at Tyburn after trial by peers; his wife (afterwards Lady Frederick Campbell) accidentally burned to death, 1807.   [lii. 134]

SHIRLEY or **SHERLEY**, ROBERT, called SIR ROBERT or COUNT SHIRLEY (1581?-1628), envoy in service of shah of Persia; accompanied his brother, Sir Anthony Shirley [q. v.], to Persia, but remained behind when he left; married a noble Circassian; left Persia to negotiate alliance against Turkey with European princes, 1608; entertained by Sigismund III of Poland and created count palatine by Emperor Rudolph II; well received by Pope Paul V; after visiting Spain came to England, 1611, but was opposed by Levant merchants; stayed a year with Emperor Jehangir at Surat on return journey; after narrowly escaping being poisoned, left Persia on second mission, 1615; stayed in Spain, 1617-22; visited Gregory XV at Rome; received by James I, 1624, and assigned a residence, but was dismissed on arrival of another envoy, 1627; died in disgrace soon after return to Persia; his portrait painted by Vandyck.   [lii. 136]

SHIRLEY, SIR ROBERT (1629-1656), royalist; fellow-commoner of Corpus Christi College, Cambridge; succeeded as fourth baronet of Eatington, 1646; several times imprisoned for royalist plots, and died in the Tower of London; left money for distressed royalists.   [lii. 137]

SHIRLEY, SIR THOMAS (1542-1612), of Wiston; M.P., Sussex and Steyning; knighted, 1573; sheriff of Sussex and Surrey, 1578; as treasurer-at-war to English army in the Netherlands involved himself in debts to the crown; freedom from arrest claimed for him under privilege of parliament, 1604; said to have suggested creation of baronets.   [lii. 138]

SHIRLEY, SIR THOMAS (1564-1630?), adventurer; son of Sir Thomas Shirley (1542-1612) [q. v.]; of Hart Hall, Oxford; served in the Netherlands and in Ireland; knighted, 1589; imprisoned by Queen Elizabeth for secret marriage, 1591; M.P., Hastings, 1601, and Steyning; captured by Turks while privateering in the Levant, 1603; imprisoned in the Tower of London for interference with Levant Company, 1607; sold Wiston.   [lii. 138]

SHIRLEY, SIR THOMAS (1769-1800), general; son of William Shirley (1694-1771) [q. v.]; governor of Leeward islands, 1781; created baronet, 1786.   [lii. 143]

SHIRLEY, WALTER (1725-1786), hymn-writer; brother of Laurence Shirley, fourth earl Ferrers [q. v.]; B.A. New College, Oxford, 1746; rector of Loughrea, Galway; active methodist preacher and sometime chaplain to Countess of Huntingdon (his cousin); took part with Calvinists against Wesley; author of well-known hymns.   [lii. 139]

SHIRLEY, WALTER AUGUSTUS (1797-1847), bishop of Sodor and Man; grandson of Walter Shirley [q. v.]; fellow of New College, Oxford, 1818; chaplain at Rome, 1826-7; incumbent of Shirley, Wiston, and Brailsford; archdeacon of Derby, 1840; bishop of Sodor and Man, 1847; a moderate evangelical.   [lii. 140]

SHIRLEY, WALTER WADDINGTON (1828-1866), regius professor of ecclesiastical history at Oxford; son of Walter Augustus Shirley [q. v.]; educated under Arnold at Rugby; fellow and tutor of Wadham College, Oxford, 1852; regius professor, 1863-6; edited 'Fasciculi Zizaniorum,' 1858, and 'Letters illustrative of Reign of Henry III,' 1862; took up independent theological position.   [lii. 141]

SHIRLEY, WASHINGTON, fifth EARL FERRERS (1722-1778), vice-admiral; elected F.R.S., 1761, for observations on transit of Venus.   [lii. 135]

SHIRLEY, WILLIAM (1694-1771), colonial governor; emigrated to Boston, 1731; governor of Massachusetts, 1741-56, of the Bahamas, 1759-70; directed capture of Louisburg, 1745; instigated expulsion of French from Canada, and held command in North America after Braddock's death; published vindication of his military conduct, 1758; died at Roxbury, Massachusetts.   [lii. 142]

SHIRLEY, WILLIAM (*fl.* 1739-1780), dramatist and Portugal merchant; his 'Edward the Black Prince' played by Garrick and Barry at Drury Lane, London, 1750; produced also other tragedies and burlesques; attacked Garrick in 'Brief Remarks on original and present state of the Drama,' 1758.   [lii. 143]

SHIRREFF, EMILY ANNE ELIZA (1814-1897), pioneer of women's education; collaborated with her sister (afterwards Mrs. Maria Grey) in 'Letters from Spain and Barbary,' and other works; published 'Intellectual Education and its influence on Character and Happiness of Women,' 1858; mistress of Girton College, 1870; co-founder of National Union for improving Education of Women,' 1871; assisted in foundation of Froebel Society, 1875; published works on Kindergarten system, Froebel, etc.   [lii. 144]

SHIRREFF, JOHN (1759-1818), agricultural writer; published surveys of the West Riding of Yorkshire and of Orkney and Shetland; won premium from board of agriculture for his 'Best Mode of cropping old Pasture Grounds,' 1801.   [lii. 145]

SHIRREFS, ANDREW (1762-1807?), Scottish poet; M.A. Marischal College, Aberdeen, 1783; edited 'Caledonian Magazine'; went to London, 1798; his 'Jamie and Bess' (pastoral comedy) acted at Aberdeen, 1787, and Edinburgh, 1796; published dialect poems, 1790.   [lii. 145]

SHIRRYE, RICHARD (*fl.* 1550). [See SHERRY.]

SHIRWOOD. [See also SHERWOOD.]

SHIRWOOD, JOHN (*d.* 1494), bishop of Durham; M.A. University College, Oxford, 1450; brought Greek authors from Italy; Edward IV's advocate at Rome; chancellor of Exeter, 1460; archdeacon of Richmond, 1465; prebendary of York, 1471; partisan of Richard III; bishop of Durham, 1485-94; went from Burgundy to Rome, where he died; his Greek library discovered by Bishop Tunstall; author of 'Liber de Ludo Arithmomachia' (1482).   [lii. 146]

SHIRWOOD, ROBERT (*fl.* 1520), hebraist and Greek scholar; studied at Oxford; published exegetical work on Ecclesiastes (1523).   [lii. 146]

SHIRWOOD, WILLIAM (*fl.* 1260), schoolman; treasurer of Lincoln; eulogised by Roger Bacon.   [lii. 146]

SHOBERL, FREDERIC (1775-1853), author; edited 'New Monthly Magazine,' Ackermann's 'Repository of Arts' (1809-28), and other publications; published histories of Oxford and Cambridge, 'Narrative of Events in and near Leipzig, 1813-14,' and other works, and translations of French and German authors.   [lii. 147]

SHORE, JANE (*d.* 1527?), mistress of Edward IV; daughter of a Cheapside mercer and wife of Lombard Street goldsmith; exercised great influence over Edward IV by her beauty and wit; afterwards mistress of Thomas Grey, first marquis of Dorset [q. v.]; accused by Richard III of sorcery, imprisoned and made to do penance, 1483; died in poverty; two portraits of her at Eton, which she is said to have saved from destruction.   [lii. 147]

SHORE, JOHN, first BARON TEIGNMOUTH (1751–1834), governor-general of India; went to India as writer, 1768; member of revenue council at Calcutta, 1775–80, and afterwards of the committee of revenue; returned to England with Warren Hastings [q. v.], 1785; as member of supreme council of Bengal, 1787–9, drew up minute which forms basis of Bengal zámindari system, and initiated several of Cornwallis's reforms; gave evidence in favour of Hastings, 1797; created baronet, 1792; governor-general of India, 1793–8; pursued passive policy, but settled Oude succession; created an Irish peer, 1798. After returning to England he became P.C. and member of the board of control, and thrice gave evidence before House of Commons on Indian affairs; identified himself with the Clapham sect, and was first president of British and Foreign Bible Society; published 'Memoirs of Sir William Jones' (1804), and other works. [lii. 149]

SHORE, LOUISA CATHERINE (1824–1895), poet; youngest daughter of Thomas Shore [q. v.]; collaborated with her sister Arabella in 'War Lyrics' (1855), 'Elegies and Memorials' (1890), and other volumes; published also 'Hannibal, a Poem' (1861). [lii. 151]

SHORE, MARGARET EMILY (1819–1839), author; sister of Louisa Catherine Shore [q. v.] [lii. 151]

SHORE, THOMAS (1793–1863), author of 'The Churchman and the Freethinker' (1863); nephew of John Shore, first baron Teignmouth; taught Earl Canning and the second Earl Granville. [lii. 151]

SHOREDITCH or **SHORDYCH**, SIR JOHN DE (d. 1345), diplomatist; chief clerk of the common bench under Edward II; second baron of the exchequer, 1336; employed in negotiations with France by Edward II and Edward III, with Austria, 1335, and the Pope Clement VI, 1343; murdered by his servants. [lii. 152]

SHORT, AUGUSTUS (1802–1883), first bishop of Adelaide; of Westminster and Christ Church, Oxford (censor, 1833); M.A., 1826; incumbent of Ravensthorpe, 1835; Bampton lecturer, 1846; bishop of Adelaide, 1847–1881. [lii. 152]

SHORT, CHARLES WILLIAM (1799–1857), author of military treatises; brother of Augustus Short [q. v.] [lii. 153]

SHORT, JAMES (1710–1768), optician; graduated at Edinburgh; mathematical tutor to duke of Cumberland; F.R.S., 1737; the first to give to specula a true parabolic figure; made Gregorian for king of Spain, 1752; observed transits of Mercury, 1753, and Venus, 1761, and deduced authoritative solar parallax; determined difference of longitude between Greenwich and Paris. [lii. 153]

SHORT, THOMAS (1635–1685), physician; B.A. St. John's College, Cambridge, 1653; created M.D. by royal mandate, 1668; F.R.C.P., 1675; joined Roman catholics, but was saved from the consequences of an order of the House of Lords for the ejection of Roman catholics by the fact that by design no quorum was present at the meeting held for the carrying out of the order. [lii. 154]

SHORT, THOMAS (1690?–1772), medical writer; practised at Sheffield; published 'General Chronological History of the Air,' 1749, 'New Observations on the Bills of Mortality,' 1750, 'Treatise on Cold Mineral Waters,' 1766, and other works. [lii. 154]

SHORT, THOMAS VOWLER (1790–1872), bishop of St. Asaph; educated at Westminster; censor of Christ Church, Oxford, 1816–29; M.A., 1815; D.D., 1837; friend of Keble and Pusey; rector of St. George's, Bloomsbury, 1834; deputy-clerk of the closet, 1837; bishop of Sodor and Man, 1841–6, of St. Asaph, 1846–70; published 'Sketch of History of Church of England,' 1832. [lii. 155]

SHORTALL, SEBASTIAN (d. 1639), titular abbot of Bective and Latin poet. [lii. 155]

SHORTLAND, EDWARD (1812–1893), writer on New Zealand, son of Thomas George Shortland [q. v.]; M.A. Pembroke College, Cambridge, 1839; protector of aborigines in New Zealand, 1842; published 'Southern Districts of New Zealand,' 1851, 'Maori Religion and Mythology,' 1882. [lii. 155]

SHORTLAND, JOHN (1769–1810), captain in the navy; wrecked on Norfolk island with John Hunter (1738–1821) [q. v.]; transport agent for Egyptian expe-

dition, 1801; mortally wounded during engagement with French in West Indies [lii. 156]

SHORTLAND, PETER FREDERICK (1815–1888), vice-admiral; son of Thomas George Shortland [q. v.]; seventh wrangler at Cambridge, 1842; surveyed coast of Nova Scotia and took soundings from Aden to Bombay; published, among other works, 'Sounding Voyage of H.M.S. Hydra,' 1868, 'Nautical Surveying' (posthumous). [lii. 156]

SHORTLAND, THOMAS GEORGE (1771–1827), captain in the navy; promoted for cutting out the Aventurier in bay of Corréjou, 1798; flag-captain to Sir Thomas Louis [q. v.] in Dardanelles, 1807; commanded Valiant in Walcheren expedition, 1809; died resident commissioner of Jamaica. [lii. 157]

SHORTLAND, WILLOUGHBY (1804–1869), colonial administrator; son of Thomas George Shortland [q. v.]; colonial secretary in New Zealand, 1840–3, and acting governor, 1842–3; president of Nevis, 1845; governor of Tobago, 1854–6. [lii. 157]

SHORTON, ROBERT (d. 1535), archdeacon of Bath; M.A. Jesus College, Cambridge, 1503; fellow of Pembroke Hall, Cambridge, 1505; B.D., 1509; hon. D.D. Oxford, 1525; dean of the chapel to Wolsey; first master of St. John's College, Cambridge, 1511–16; master of Pembroke Hall, Cambridge, 1518–34; almoner to Queen Catherine of Arragon, whom he supported in convocation; master of her college at Stoke-by-Clare, 1529; archdeacon of Bath, 1535; benefactor to Cambridge colleges. [lii. 158]

SHOVELL, SIR CLOWDISLEY (1650–1707), admiral of the fleet; probably with Sir John Narbrough [q. v.] in South Sea voyage and at Solebay; commanded boats at burning of ships in Tripoli harbour, 1676; cruised in Mediterranean against Barbary pirates, 1677–86; commanded Edgar at Bantry Bay and was knighted, 1689; rear-admiral in command of squadron in Irish sea, 1690; co-operated in capture of Duncannon Castle; broke French line at battle of Barfleur, 1692; joint-admiral of the fleet after Russell's supersession; second in command in expedition against Camaret Bay, St. Malo, and Dunkirk, 1695; commanded Channel fleet, 1696–7, 1699, 1701, 1703; M.P. for Rochester, 1698–1707; comptroller of victualling, 1699–1704; took part with Rooke in capture of Gibraltar, 1704, and action off Malaga, 1704; admiral and commander-in-chief of the fleet, 1705; co-operated with Peterborough at Barcelona, 1705, and with Duke of Savoy at Toulon, 1707, destroying French Mediterranean fleet; perished in wreck on Bishop and Clerk rocks, Scilly islands; his monument in Westminster Abbey and portraits in National Portrait Gallery and at Greenwich. [lii. 159]

SHOWER, SIR BARTHOLOMEW (1658–1701), lawyer; barrister, Middle Temple, 1680 (treasurer, 1699); prominent as pamphleteer for court party, 1683; deputy-recorder of London, 1685; knighted, 1687; recorder, 1688 (February–November); counsel for crown against seven bishops; defended Sir John Fenwick [q. v.], 1696, and other Jacobites; acted for 'Old' East India Company, 1698; published squib against Dean Sherlock, 1696; the Vagellius of Garth's 'Dispensary.' [lii. 161]

SHOWER, JOHN (1657–1715), nonconformist divine; brother of Sir Bartholomew Shower [q. v.]; assistant to Vincent Alsop [q. v.], 1679–83; resident in Holland, 1684–6, and lecturer at English presbyterian church, Rotterdam, 1687–91; pastor at Curriers' Hall, London Wall, Jewin Street, London, and Old Jewry, London, 1691–1715; published devotional works. [lii. 162]

SHRAPNEL, HENRY (1761–1842), inventor of the Shrapnel shell; served with royal artillery in Flanders and was wounded at Dunkirk, 1793; first assistant-inspector, 1804; retired from active service as major-general, 1825; lieutenant-general, 1837; his shell recommended for adoption, 1803, and successfully used at Surinam, 1804; highly commended by Wellington in the Peninsula, by Sir G. Wood at Waterloo, and by subsequent commanders in the field; the inventor inadequately pensioned, 1814, and promised baronetcy by William IV, 1837; other improvements in artillery due to him. [lii. 163]

SHREWSBURY, DUKE OF (1660–1718). [See TALBOT, CHARLES.]

SHREWSBURY, EARLS OF. [See ROGER DE MONT-GOMERY, d. 1093 ?; HUGH OF MONTGOMERY, d. 1098; BELLÉME, ROBERT OF, fl. 1098; TALBOT, JOHN, first EARL, 1388 ?-1453 ; TALBOT, JOHN, second EARL, 1413 ?-1460 ; TALBOT, GEORGE, fourth EARL, 1468-1538 ; TALBOT, FRANCIS, fifth EARL, 1500-1560 ; TALBOT, GEORGE, sixth EARL, 1528 ?-1590 ; TALBOT, GILBERT, seventh EARL, 1553-1616.]

SHREWSBURY, COUNTESS OF (1518-1608). [See TALBOT, ELIZABETH.]

SHREWSBURY, RALPH OF (d. 1363). [See RALPH.]

SHREWSBURY, ROBERT OF (d. 1167). [See ROBERT.]

SHRUBSOLE, WILLIAM (1729-1797), author of 'Christian Memoirs' (1776) ; preached at Sheerness, 1763-1793. [lii. 165]

SHRUBSOLE, WILLIAM (1760-1806), organist at Spa Fields Chapel, London ; friend of Edward Perronet [q. v.], and composer of the tune ' Miles Lane.' [lii. 166]

SHRUBSOLE, WILLIAM (1759-1829), secretary to London Missionary Society and hymn-writer ; son of William Shrubsole (1729-1797) [q. v.] [lii. 165]

SHUCKARD, WILLIAM EDWARD (1802-1868), entomologist ; nephew of William Bernard Cooke [q. v.] ; librarian to Royal Society, 1835-43 ; edited ' Lloyd's List,' 1844-61 ; published ' Elements of British Entomology,' 1839, ' British Coleoptera,' 1840, ' British Bees,' 1866 ; edited and translated German works. [lii. 166]

SHUCKBURGH, SIR RICHARD (1596-1656), royalist ; B.A. Lincoln College, Oxford, 1615 ; M.P. for Warwickshire in Long parliament ; knighted at Edgehill, 1642 ; defended Shuckburgh against parliament ; imprisoned in Kenilworth Castle. [lii. 166]

SHUCKBURGH-EVELYN, SIR GEORGE AUGUSTUS WILLIAM, sixth baronet (1751-1804), mathematician ; descendant of Sir Richard Shuckburgh [q. v.] ; of Rugby and Balliol College, Oxford ; B.A. 1772 ; M.P., Warwickshire, 1780-1804 ; F.R.S., 1774 ; F.S.A., 1777 ; assumed additional name, 1793 ; published ' Observations made in Savoy to ascertain Height of Mountains by the Barometer,' 1777 ; made investigations concerning measures of length, capacity, and weight. [lii. 167]

SHUCKFORD, SAMUEL (d. 1754), author of ' Sacred and Profane History of the World' (1728) ; M.A. Caius College, Cambridge, 1720 ; Lambeth D.D. ; prebendary of Canterbury, 1738. [lii. 168]

SHULDHAM, MOLYNEUX, BARON (1717 ?-1798), admiral ; present at attack on Carthagena, 1741 ; captured by French off Martinique, 1756 ; took part in reduction of Guadeloupe, 1759 ; commander on Newfoundland station, 1772-5, on coast of North America, 1775-6 ; created an Irish peer, 1776 ; admiral of the white, 1793. [lii. 168]

SHUTE or **SHUTTE**, CHRISTOPHER (d. 1626), author of 'Testimonie of a True Faith ' (1577) ; M.A. Pembroke College, Cambridge, 1568 ; B.D., 1580 ; vicar of Giggleswick, 1576-1626. [lii. 169]

SHUTE, JOHN (fl. 1550-1570), architect, limner, and author of 'The First and Chief Groundes of Architecture ' (1563). [lii. 170]

SHUTE, JOHN (fl. 1562-1573), translator of Italian and French works. [lii. 170]

SHUTE (afterwards **SHUTE-BARRINGTON**), JOHN, first VISCOUNT BARRINGTON (1678-1734). [See BARRINGTON.]

SHUTE, JOSIAS or JOSIAH (1588-1643), archdeacon of Colchester ; M.A. Trinity College, Cambridge, 1609 ; rector of St. Mary Woolnoth, Lombard Street, London, 1611-43 ; son of Christopher Shute [q. v.] ; chaplain to East India Company, 1632 ; archdeacon of Colchester, 1642. [lii. 170]

SHUTE, ROBERT (d. 1590), judge ; barrister, Gray's Inn, 1552 ; recorder of Cambridge, 1558, and M.P., 1572 ; treasurer of Gray's Inn, 1576 ; second baron of the exchequer, 1579 ; judge of queen's bench, 1586-90. [lii. 171]

SHUTE, ROBERT (d. 1621), recorder ; son of Robert Shute (d. 1590) [q. v.] ; clerk of common pleas, 1616 ; recorder of London, 1621. [lii. 171]

SHUTE, SAMUEL (1662-1742), governor of Massachusetts ; son-in-law of Joseph Caryl [q. v.] and pupil of Charles Morton (1627-1698) [q. v.] ; served under Marlborough, attaining rank of lieutenant-colonel ; governor of Massachusetts, 1716-27 ; left America, 1723, having had constant differences with colonial assembly. [lii. 171]

SHUTE-BARRINGTON, WILLIAM WILDMAN, second VISCOUNT (1717-1793). [See BARRINGTON.]

SHUTER, EDWARD (1728 ?-1776), comedian ; of low extraction ; played Cibber's 'Schoolboy' at Covent Garden and Drury Lane, London, 1745 ; acted in London under Garrick at Covent Garden, 1746, Foote at Haymarket, and Garrick and Lacy at Drury Lane, 1747 ; original Sir Gregory Gazette in Foote's ' Knights,' 1749 ; took minor comic parts at Drury Lane, 1749-53, distinguishing himself as Master Stephen ('Every Man in his Humour ') and Scrub (' Beaux' Stratagem ') ; his parts at Covent Garden included Falstaff, Mercutio, Bayes, Sir John Brute, Polonius ; the original Croaker (' Goodnatured Man '), 1768, Hardcastle, 1773, Sir Anthony Absolute, 1775 ; a follower of Whitefield, but a wit, drunkard, and gambler. [lii. 172]

SHUTTLEWOOD, JOHN (1632-1689), conductor of nonconformist academy at Sulby ; minister of Ravenstone and Hugglescote, 1654-62 ; preached at conventicles, and was frequently fined and imprisoned for nonconformity. [lii. 174]

SHUTTLEWORTH, SIR JAMES PHILLIPS KAY-(1804-1877). [See KAY-SHUTTLEWORTH.]

SHUTTLEWORTH, OBADIAH (1675-1734), organist of the Temple and St. Michael's, Cornhill, London, 1724-1734, and violinist. [lii. 175]

SHUTTLEWORTH, PHILIP NICHOLAS (1782-1842), bishop of Chichester ; educated at Winchester and New College, Oxford ; M.A., 1811 ; D.D., 1822 ; warden of New College, Oxford, 1822-40, and bishop of Chichester, 1840-2 ; wrote against the tractarians, and published 'Paraphrastic Translation of Apostolic Epistles' (1829). [lii. 175]

SHUTTLEWORTH, ROBERT JAMES (1810-1874), botanist and conchologist ; educated at Geneva ; also studied medicine at Edinburgh ; lived in Switzerland from 1834, but died at Hyères ; assisted scientific travellers ; intimate with Meissner and Jean de Charpentier ; published ' Nouvelles Observations sur la Matière coloriante de la neige rouge,' 1840, ' Notitiæ Malacologicæ,' 1856 (part ii. German, 1878) ; honorary Ph.D. of Basle ; his collection of shells at Berne, and herbarium in British Museum. [lii. 176]

SIBBALD, JAMES (1590 ?-1650 ?), Scottish royalist divine ; B.D. Marischal College, Aberdeen, 1630 ; D.D. Marischal College and King's College, Aberdeen, 1637 ; admitted to first charge in St. Nicholas' Church, 1626 ; one of the six harmonising divines (1637) who questioned lawfulness of the covenant, 1638 ; joined Charles I at Berwick, 1639, but soon returned ; silenced and deposed for refusing to take the covenant and for Arminianism, 1640 ; went to Ireland, and died of the plague at Dublin. [lii. 177]

SIBBALD, JAMES (1745-1803), Edinburgh bookseller and author of 'Chronicle of Scottish Poetry' (1802) ; carried on large circulating library ; conducted ' Edinburgh Magazine,' 1785-92, and befriended Burns ; lived in Soho, London, 1794-7 ; published 'The Vocal Magazine,' 1797, and 'Record of the Public Ministry of Jesus Christ,' 1798. [lii. 178]

SIBBALD, SIR ROBERT (1641-1722), president of Edinburgh Royal College of Physicians ; M.D. Leyden, 1661 ; M.D. Angers, 1662, studying also in Paris and London ; with Dr. Andrew Balfour instituted Botanical Garden at Edinburgh, 1667 ; physician to Charles II and geographer of Scotland, 1682 ; president of Edinburgh Royal College of Physicians, 1684 ; first professor of medicine at Edinburgh University, 1685 ; temporarily converted to Romanism and obliged to leave Edinburgh for London ; published ' History, Ancient and Modern, of Sheriffdoms of Fife and Kinross,' 1710, ' Scotia Illustrata,' 1684, and many geographical and antiquarian works ; his ' Remains ' (with autobiography) printed, 1837. [lii. 179]

SIBBALD, WILLIAM (d. 1650), adherent of Montrose; M.A. Aberdeen, 1639; accompanied his secret journey to Scotland, 1644; deserted during highland campaign, but soon rejoined; fled to Holland after Philiphaugh; tortured and beheaded at Edinburgh after his return. [lii. 182]

SIBBES, **SIBBS**, or **SIBS**, RICHARD (1577–1635), puritan divine; scholar and fellow of St. John's College, Cambridge; M.A., 1602; deprived of taxatorship and lectureship at Holy Trinity, Cambridge, by high commission, 1615; preacher at Gray's Inn, 1617–35; master of St. Catharine's Hall, Cambridge, 1626–35; twice offered provostship of Trinity College, Dublin; published many devotional works, including 'The Saint's Cordials,' 1629, and 'The Bruised Reede and Smoaking Flax,' 1630; collected editions issued, 1809, 1812, and 1862-3 (ed. Dr. Grosart). [lii. 182]

SIBERCH, JOHN (fl. 1521–1522), first Cambridge printer; came probably from Cologne and was known to Erasmus; Bullock's 'Oratio' to Wolsey (1521) his first impression. [lii. 184]

SIBLEY, GEORGE (1824–1891), civil engineer; educated at University College, London; employed in India, 1851–75; chief engineer of N.W. Provinces, 1859, of the East India railway, 1868; designed brick arch bridges over the Adjai and More; completed Allahabad Jumna bridge; constructed works at Delhi; founded engineering scholarships at Calcutta. [lii. 184]

SIBLEY, SEPTIMUS (1831–1893), physician and author of 'History of Cholera Epidemic in 1854'; brother of George Sibley [q. v.] [lii. 185]

SIBLY, EBENEZER (d. 1800), astrologer and medical writer. [lii. 185]

SIBLY, MANOAH (1757–1840), Swedenborgian; brother of Ebenezer Sibly; principal of chancery office, Bank of England, 1815–40; published 'Defence of the New Church' (1815) and translations of works by Placidus de Titis. [lii. 185]

SIBORNE or **SIBORN**, WILLIAM (1797–1849), author of 'History of the War in France and Belgium in 1815' (1844); served with 9th foot in army of occupation in France, 1815–17; assistant military secretary to successive commanders of the forces in Ireland, 1826–43; secretary of military asylum, Chelsea, 1844–9; published topographical treatises; constructed model of field of Waterloo, 1830–8 (at United Service Institution); his 'Waterloo Letters' edited by his son, 1891. [lii. 185]

SIBSON, FRANCIS (1814–1876), physician; friend and pupil of Thomas Hodgkin [q. v.] at Guy's; surgeon to Nottingham General Hospital, 1835–48, and intimate of Charles Waterton [q. v.]; M.D. of London. 1848; F.R.C.P., 1853; F.R.S., 1849; first physician to St. Mary's Hospital, London; Gulstonian, Croonian, and Lumleian lecturer; active member of senate of London University; died at Geneva; published important paper on changes of the internal organs, 1844, elaborated in 'Medical Anatomy' (1855–69); 'Collected Works' edited by Dr. William Miller Ord, 1881. [lii. 186]

SIBSON, THOMAS (1817–1844), artist and friend of William Bell Scott [q. v.]; brother of Francis Sibson [q. v.]; died at Malta. [lii. 187]

SIBTHORP, CHARLES DE LAET WALDO (1783–1855), politician and colonel of South Lincoln militia; nephew of John Sibthorp [q. v.]; served with 4th dragoon guards in the Peninsula; represented Lincoln, 1826–55 (except 1833–4); opposed catholic emancipation, parliamentary reform, and free trade; originated Chandos clause in Reform Bill; obtained reduction of grant to Prince Albert; an able but eccentric speaker. [lii. 188]

SIBTHORP, SIR CHRISTOPHER (d. 1632), justice of king's bench in Ireland, 1607-32, and controversialist. [lii. 188]

SIBTHORP, JOHN (1758–1796), botanist; M.A. Lincoln College, Oxford, 1780; as Radcliffe travelling fellow of University College, Oxford, studied at Edinburgh and Montpellier; succeeded his father (Humphrey) as Sherardian professor of botany, Oxford, but returned to the continent; examined illustrated codex of Dioscorides at Vienna; with Ferdinand Bauer visited Crete, the Ægæan isles, Athens, Smyrna, and Constantinople, 1786; studied fauna and flora of Cyprus, and returned to Greece, 1787;

published 'Flora Oxoniensis,' 1794; revisited Greece and the Troad and stayed in the Ionian islands, 1794-5; contracted chill at Nicopolis; F.R.S., 1789; endowed chair of rural economy at Oxford; his 'Flora Græca' and 'Floræ Græcæ Prodromus' edited by Dr. James Edward Smith [q. v.] and Dr. John Lindley. [lii. 189]

SIBTHORP, RICHARD WALDO (1792–1879), divine; brother of Charles Sibthorp [q. v.]; M.A. Magdalen College, Oxford, 1816; fellow, 1818; vicar of Tattersall, 1819; minister of Percy Chapel, St. Pancras, London, 1825-9; incumbent of St. James's, Ryde, 1830–41; was received into Roman church by Cardinal Wiseman, 1841, and took priest's orders, but reverted, 1843; established St. Anne's bede-house at Lincoln; readmitted to Anglican functions, 1857, but again Romanised, 1865, and preached at St. Barnabas pro-cathedral, Nottingham; published devotional and apologetical works. [lii. 190]

SIBTHORP or **SYBTHORPE**, ROBERT (d. 1662), royalist divine; fellow of Trinity College, Cambridge, 1618; M.A., 1619 (incorporated at Oxford, 1619); D.D. Cambridge, c. 1626; vicar of St. Sepulchre, Northampton, 1619–29; asserted doctrine of passive obedience in assize sermon, 1627; included in pardon granted to Roger Manwaring [q. v.] and made chaplain to Charles I; rector of Burton Latimer, 1629; as commissary of Peterborough zealous repressor of puritanism; joined Charles I at Oxford, 1643; his livings sequestrated, 1647, but restored at Restoration; confused by Anthony à Wood with Robert Sibthorp, bishop of Limerick. [lii. 191]

SICKLEMORE or **RATCLIFFE**, JOHN (d. 1610), governor of Virginia; one of the founders of Jamestown; made governor of Virginia after deposition of Edward Maria Wingfield [q. v.], 1607; quarrelled with John Smith (1580 ?–1631) [q. v.]; returned to England, 1608, but went back next year and arrested Smith; murdered by Indians. [lii. 192]

SIDDALL or **SYDDALL**, HENRY (d. 1572), divine; B.A. Cardinal College (Christ Church), Oxford, 1532; B.Can.L., 1535: D.D., 1552; ejected from Cardinal College, Oxford, by Henry VIII, 1532, but subsequently employed by him; canon of Christ Church, Oxford, 1547; a zealous protestant under Edward VI, Romanist under Mary I, and Anglican again in Queen Elizabeth's reign; witnessed Cranmer's fifth recantation. [lii. 193]

SIDDONS, MRS. HARRIET (1783–1844), actress; daughter of Charles Murray [q. v.] and wife of Henry Siddons [q. v.]; appeared at Covent Garden, London, 1798–1805, playing leading Shakespearean parts; at Drury Lane, London, 1805–9, playing Juliet with Elliston; afterwards assisted her husband at Edinburgh. [lii. 194]

SIDDONS, HENRY (1774–1815), actor; son of Sarah Siddons [q. v.]; educated at Charterhouse for the church; played at Covent Garden, London, 1801-5, and Drury Lane, London, 1805-9; as manager of Edinburgh Theatre, 1809–15, received encouragement from Sir Walter Scott [q. v.], and produced creditable plays. [lii. 194]

SIDDONS, MRS. SARAH (1755–1831), actress; daughter of Roger Kemble [q. v.]; acted when very young in company with William Siddons; married him, 1773, after attempts by her parents at separation; while playing with her husband at Cheltenham attracted attention as Belvidera, 1774; engaged by Garrick at Drury Lane, London, 1775–6, opening with Portia and ending with Lady Anne ('Richard III'), but failed decidedly; gained brilliant success at Manchester under Tate Wilkinson, 1776–7, in Euphrasia ('Grecian Daughter'), and other characters; appeared, 1777–81, at Bath and Bristol under Palmer, in great variety of parts, including most of those which became celebrated; re-engaged at Drury Lane, London, 1782; triumphed completely as Isabella (Garrick's version of 'Fatal Marriage'), Euphrasia, Belvidera, and Zara ('Mourning Bride'); visited Liverpool, Dublin, and Cork; played first Shakespearean characters (Isabella and Constance) in London, 1783; appeared at Edinburgh, 1784; first gave Lady Macbeth in London, 1785, and Volumnia ('Coriolanus'), 1788; retired temporarily, 1789–91; played the Queen in 'Richard II,' 1791, in 'Hamlet,' 1796, Mrs. Haller ('The Stranger'), 1798, Elvira ('Pizarro'), 1799, the last being the only capital part among those she 'created'; played Hermione in 'Winter's Tale,' 1801-2; acted at Covent Garden, London, 1806–12, giving her farewell performance in Lady Macbeth; she subsequently made incidental appearances for her children and the

Theatrical Fund ; gave private readings at Windsor Castle and to guests in Upper Baker Street, London ; much annoyed in last years by her sister, Mrs. Curtis ('Anne of Swansea ') ; buried in Paddington churchyard; her statue by Chantrey in Westminster Abbey. She won praise from Christopher North, Hazlitt, Byron, Haydon, Erskine, and Leigh Hunt, and converted Horace Walpole, but inspired more admiration than affection. A picture of her by Reynolds as the 'Tragic Muse' is at Dulwich. She executed busts of herself and brother John Philip Kemble [q. v.] [lii. 195]

SIDENHAM, CUTHBERT (1622-1654). [See SYDENHAM.]

SIDGWICK, HENRY (1838-1900), philosopher; educated at Rugby and Trinity College, Cambridge; thirty-third wrangler, senior classic, and first chancellor's medallist, 1859 ; fellow and assistant-tutor of Trinity College, Cambridge, 1859 ; lecturer in moral philosophy, 1869 ; advocated abolition of religious tests; resigned fellowship, 1869, on conscientious grounds; appointed to 'prælectorship on moral and political philosophy' at Trinity College, Cambridge, 1875 ; Knightsbridge professor, 1883-1900 ; honorary fellow of his college, 1881, and again ordinary fellow, 1885 ; subscribed to, and energetically supported, scheme for providing a system of lectures for girls at Cambridge, which was carried out by opening of Newnham Hall, 1876 ; married, 1876, Eleanor Mildred, sister of Right Hon. A. J. Balfour (Mrs. Sidgwick became vice-president of North Hall (added to Newnham, 1880) and president of Newnham on death of Anne Jemima Clough [q. v.], 1892) ; Sidgwick successfully advocated admission of women to university and examinations, 1881 ; member of general board of studies of Cambridge University, 1882-99 ; on council of senate, 1890-8 ; president of Society for Psychical Research, 1882-5 and 1888-93. He published 'Ethics of Conformity and Subscription,' 1871, 'Methods of Ethics,' 1874, 'Principles of Political Economy,' 1883, 'Scope and Method of Economic Science,' 1885, 'Outlines of History of Ethics,' 1886, and 'Elements of Politics,' 1891. As a philosopher he was greatly influenced by the teaching of John Stuart Mill [q. v.] [Suppl. iii. 342]

SIDLEY. [See also SEDLEY.]

SIDLEY, SAMUEL (1829-1896), portrait and subject painter. [lii. 202]

SIDMOUTH, VISCOUNT (1757-1844). [See ADDINGTON, HENRY.]

SIDNEY or **SYDNEY**, ALGERNON (1622-1683), republican ; accompanied his father, Robert Sidney, second earl of Leicester [q. v.], to Denmark and Paris ; served under his brother, Lord Lisle, against the Irish rebels, 1642 ; took up arms against Charles I, and was wounded at Marston Moor, 1644 ; governor of Colchester, 1645 ; M.P., Cardiff, 1646 ; lieutenant general of horse in Ireland, 1647 ; appointed governor of Dublin, but immediately superseded ; governor of Dover, 1648-50 ; nominated commissioner for trial of Charles I, but opposed constitution and proceedings of high court as invalid, as well as the subsequent 'engagement' approving them ; member of council of state, 1653 ; held aloof from the protectorate after dissolution of the Rump ; again member of council of state, 1659 ; chief of four commissioners who mediated between Sweden and Denmark at Elsinore, 1659-60. Refusing to give pledges to Charles II, he remained abroad ; at Rome, 1660-3 ; his attempts to obtain foreign military employment frustrated by English influence: his life attempted at Augsburg ; went to Holland, 1665 ; afterwards lived in France ; negotiated with Louis XIV, with the view of raising a revolt in England, 1666 ; came to England on private business, 1677, and remained ; unable to obtain a seat in parliament, but exercised much influence ; vindicated himself in interview with Charles II from charge of complicity in nonconformist plot ; intimate with republicans, but quarrelled with Shaftesbury ; received money from French ambassador and co-operated with him on foreign questions, but ridiculed his pretensions to direct opposition ; said to have drafted answer to Charles II's reasons for dissolving Oxford parliament ; discussed question of insurrection with whig leaders, January 1683 ; sent to Tower of London after discovery of Rye House plot (June) ; tried before Jeffreys on three overt charges of treason (November) ; defended himself ably, but convicted ; drew up petitions setting forth illegality of his trial and for commutation of sentence ; executed on

Tower Hill (December) ; his body buried at Penshurst ; his vindication allowed to be published by government ; his 'Discourses concerning Government' (answer to Filmer) first printed, 1698, an edition containing letters and report of trial being issued, 1763, further revised and added to, 1773. [lii. 202]

SIDNEY, LADY DOROTHY, afterwards COUNTESS OF SUNDERLAND (1617-1684), 'Sacharissa.' [See SPENCER.]

SIDNEY, SIR HENRY (1529-1586), thrice lord-deputy of Ireland and president of Wales ; son of Sir William Sidney [q. v.] ; one of the four gentlemen of the privy chamber of Edward VI ; knighted, 1550 ; undertook mission to France, 1552 ; accompanied Bedford to Spain, 1554 ; went to Ireland as vice-treasurer, 1556 ; took part in Sussex's expedition into Ulster, and acted as lord justice during his absences, 1558 ; president of Wales, 1559-86 ; sent on missions to France and Scotland, 1562 ; K.G., 1564 ; appointed lord deputy of Ireland, 1565 ; during his first period of government restored Calvagh O'Donnell [q. v.], garrisoned Derry, and crushed Shane O'Neill [q. v.] ; decided in favour of Ormonde and deposed Desmond, replacing him in the government of Munster by his brother, and rebuilt Dublin Castle ; his Munster policy reversed after his return ; regained favour by the help of Sir William Cecil [q. v.], and returned to Ireland, 1568 ; reduced the rebellious Butlers, 1569, carried an act for the erection of schools under English masters, 1570, encouraged settlers from the Low Countries at Swords, and 'shired' county Longford, but resigned from vexation at insufficient support from Queen Elizabeth, 1571 ; spent four years at court and in Wales ; a third time lord-deputy, 1575 ; pacified Ulster, made a tour of inspection in Munster, annexed Thomond as County Clare to Connaught, and divided that province into four shires ; crushed the revolt of Clanricarde's sons in Galway and the opposition of the gentry of the Pale to the cess ; defeated Rory Oge O'More [q. v.] ; settled dispute between Desmond and Drury ; recalled, 1578, owing to discontent at his expenditure ; visited Lord Grey de Wilton (now deputy) at Wilton, 1580 ; again talked of for Ireland, 1582 ; died prematurely old at Ludlow ; buried at Penshurst. [lii. 210]

SIDNEY or **SYDNEY**, HENRY, EARL OF ROMNEY (1641-1704), partisan of William of Orange ; brother of Algernon Sidney [q. v.] ; groom of the bedchamber to James, duke of York, and master of horse to the duchess, 1665 ; envoy to France, 1672 ; master of the robes, 1677 ; M.P. for Bramber, 1679 ; as envoy to the Hague, 1679-81, gained confidence of William of Orange ; general of British regiments in Dutch service, 1681-5 ; took secret invitation to William, and through intrigue with his wife communicated with Sunderland, 1688 ; accompanied William to England and Ireland ; privy councillor and Viscount Sydney, 1689 ; secretary of state, 1690-1 ; lord-lieutenant of Ireland, 1692 ; master-general of ordnance, 1693 ; created an earl, 1694 ; a lord justice, 1697 ; groom of the stole, 1700-2 ; the handsomest man of his time ; his portrait painted by Lely. [lii. 217]

SIDNEY, MARY, COUNTESS OF PEMBROKE (1555 ?-1621). [See HERBERT, MARY.]

SIDNEY, SIR PHILIP (1554-1586), soldier, statesman, and poet ; son of Sir Henry Sidney [q. v.] ; educated at Shrewsbury and Christ Church, Oxford ; intimate with Sir Fulke Greville (afterwards Lord Brooke) [q. v.] and Camden, and favoured by Sir William Cecil (Burghley) ; well received at French court, 1572, but left it for Lorraine and Germany after the St. Bartholomew's massacre ; at Frankfort came under influence of Languet, whom he accompanied to Vienna, 1573 ; visited Venice (meeting Tintoretto and Paolo Veronese), Genoa, and Padua, 1573-4 ; accompanied Languet to Poland, and again resided in Austria, 1575 ; took part in festivities at Kenilworth, 1576 ; became acquainted with Walter Devereux, first earl of Essex [q. v.], and his daughter Penelope ('Stella') ; travelled with his father in Ireland, 1576 ; entrusted with diplomatic missions to the elector palatine and the Emperor Rudolf II, 1577 ; made a great impression on William (the Silent) of Orange ; presented to Queen Elizabeth a masterly defence of Sir Henry Sidney's Irish policy ; attended her at Audley End, and was eulogised in Harvey's 'Gratulationes,' 1578 ; saw much of Spenser at Leicester House, and received dedication of his 'Shepherd's Calendar' ; became member of the Areopagus, 1579 (a club formed chiefly for the purpose of naturalising the classical metres in English verse), and began to compose verses; incurred disfavour of Queen Elizabeth by refusing to apologise to the Earl of Oxford and by submitting treatise condemning proposed marriage with Anjou, 1580; M.P. for Kent, 1581, in which year he took part in tournament at Whitehall; knighted and named master of the horse, 1583; married Frances, daughter of Walsingham, but continued to address sonnets to 'Stella'; had frequent discussions with Giordano Bruno at Greville's house; joint master of ordnance, 1585; showed strong interest in the colonisation of America, and received dedications of Hakluyt's 'Voyages'; undertook abortive mission to France, 1584; advocated in parliament legislation against jesuits, and urged on Queen Elizabeth aggressive policy towards Spain; made secret attempt to join Drake's expedition, 1585; recalled to court, but made governor of Flushing; appealed to Burghley and Walsingham for more vigorous measures; with Prince Maurice surprised Axel, 1586; joined as volunteer attack on Spanish convoy for relief of Zutphen; wounded in thigh, and died at Arnhem after twenty-six days; his public funeral in St. Paul's Cathedral, London, delayed by financial difficulties; among the two hundred poetic memorials evoked by his death are Spenser's 'Astrophel' (including contributions by Countess of Pembroke and Ralegh), a sonnet by James VI, an elegy by Breton, and eclogue by Drayton. Numerous portraits and miniatures are at Penshurst and elsewhere. None of his works appeared in his lifetime. The 'Arcadia,' written for the amusement of the Countess of Pembroke (his sister), a medley of prose romance and pastoral eclogues, was first published, 1590; the 3rd edition (1598) contained 'Apologie for Poetrie,' 'Astrophel and Stella,' and other poems. It enjoyed undisputed vogue for a century, afforded hints to Shakespeare and Spenser, was much imitated, continued, and epitomised, supplied plots to several plays, and was translated into French (1624) and German (1629), but adversely criticised by Walpole and Hazlitt. 'Astrophel and Stella' (sonnets in Shakespearean form) appeared (at first unauthorised), 1591, with revisions and additions, in 'Arcadia,' 1598; reprinted in Arber's 'English Garner,' and edited by A. W. Pollard, 1891. The 'Apologie for Poetrie' (answer to Gosson's 'Schoole of Abuse') was first printed, 1595; edited by Lord Thurlow (1810), Professor Arber (1868), and E. S. Shuckburgh (1891). Sidney's version of the Psalms was published in 1823, and in Ruskin's 'Bibliotheca Pastorum' (1877); his collective poetical works were edited by Dr. Grosart, 1873. [lii. 219]

SIDNEY, PHILIP, third EARL OF LEICESTER (1619–1698), parliamentarian; brother of Algernon Sidney [q. v.]; styled Lord Lisle, 1626–77; commanded cuirassiers in second Scottish war; M.P. for Yarmouth (I. of W.) in Short and Long parliaments; as lieutenant-general of horse in Ireland supported parliamentary commissioners against Ormonde, 1642–3; lord-lieutenant, 1646–7; declined to act as commissioner for trial of Charles I, but was member of several of the republican councils of state, and of the two protectorate councils; pardoned at Restoration. [lii. 234]

SIDNEY, ROBERT, VISCOUNT LISLE and first EARL OF LEICESTER of a new creation (1563–1626), soldier; second son of Sir Henry Sidney [q. v.]; M.P., Glamorganshire, 1585 and 1592, Kent, 1597; accompanied his brother, Sir Philip [q. v.], to Flushing, and was with him at Zutphen and Arnhem; sent on mission to Scotland, 1588; returned to Netherlands as governor of Flushing and commander of a troop of horse; wounded at siege of Steenwyck, 1592; undertook special mission to Henri IV, 1593; distinguished at battle of Turnhout, 1598; chief channel of communication between the court and Essex during the disturbances due to Essex's rebellion of 1601; created Baron Sidney by James I, 1603, Viscount Lisle, 1605, and Earl of Leicester, 1618; member of Virginia, East India, and N.-W. Passage companies; created K.G. after arranging for surrender of Flushing, 1616; ecclesiastical commissioner, 1620; member of council of war, 1621; wrote words for Dowland's songs; his life at Penshurst described in poem by Ben Jonson. [lii. 236]

SIDNEY, ROBERT, second EARL OF LEICESTER (1595–1677), father of Algernon Sidney and of 'Sacharissa'; son of Robert Sidney, viscount Lisle and first earl of Leicester [q. v.]; of Christ Church, Oxford; K.B., 1610; admitted to Gray's Inn, 1618; styled Lord Lisle, 1618–26; served in Netherlands, 1614–16; sat in parliament successively for Wilton, Kent, and Monmouthshire;

married Dorothy Percy, 1616; employed on embassies to Denmark and Holstein, 1632, and to France, 1636–41; P.C., 1639; appointed lord-lieutenant of Ireland, 1641, but never assumed the office; with Charles I at Oxford, 1643–4, but distrusted on account of his moderation or irresolution; retired to Penshurst, where he entertained the royal children, 1649–50; passively accepted Commonwealth, but concurred in Restoration. [lii. 237]

SIDNEY, SAMUEL (1813–1883), author of 'Book of the Horse' (1873); son of Abraham Solomon, but assumed name of Sidney; edited 'Sidney's Emigrant's Journal,' 1848–50; assistant-commissioner for exhibition, 1850–1; as secretary of Agricultural Hall organised first horse show, 1864; published works on railways and agricultural subjects. [lii. 239]

SIDNEY, SIR WILLIAM (1482?–1554), soldier; accompanied Thomas, lord Darcy [q. v.] to Spain, 1511; captain of the 'Great Bark' at Brest and commander of English right at Flodden, 1513; undertook mission to France, 1515; attended Henry VIII at Field of Cloth of Gold; accompanied Suffolk's French expedition, 1523; tutor and steward to Prince Edward, 1538; granted Penshurst, 1552. [lii. 210]

SIEMENS, SIR WILLIAM (1823–1883), metallurgist and electrician; born at Lenthe, Hanover, and educated at Magdeburg and Göttingen; sold an electrical invention in England, 1843; introduced 'chronometric governor' and 'anastatic printing,' 1844; patented regenerative steam engine and condenser, 1847; first great success, water-meter of 1851; regenerative furnace of brothers Siemens applied to melting and reheating of steel, 1857, and afterwards to glass-making and other industrial processes; works carried on at Landore, 1869–88. Siemens was naturalised, 1859; specially elected to Institute of Civil Engineers, 1860; F.R.S., 1862; won medals at London, 1862, Paris, 1867; became London agent of electrical firm of Siemens & Halske; established works at Charlton, 1866; laid Atlantic cable and designed cable-ship Faraday, 1874; announced principle of the dynamo simultaneously with Sir Charles Wheatstone [q. v.] and Cromwell Fleetwood Varley [q. v.], 1867; invented electric furnace, 1879, bathometer, and electric thermometer; applied electric power to Portrush railway, 1883; took out 113 patents; president of British Association, 1882; of Society of Telegraph Engineers (twice), Mechanical Engineers, 1872, Iron and Steel Institute, 1877; hon. D.C.L. of Oxford and LL.D. of Dublin and Glasgow; received Howard prize, 1883, Bessemer medal, 1875, and many foreign orders; knighted, 1883; memorial window erected to him in Westminster Abbey and electrical laboratory at King's College; collected works edited by E. F. Bamber, 1889. [lii. 240]

SIEVIER, ROBERT WILLIAM (1794–1865), stipple-engraver and sculptor; exhibited at Royal Academy, 1822–1844; F.R.S., 1840; executed busts of Albert, prince consort, and king of Prussia, and statue of Jenner in Gloucester Cathedral. [lii. 244]

SIGEBERT or SEBERT (d. 616?). [See SEBERT.]

SIGEBERT or SEBERT, 'the Little' (fl. 626), king of the East-Saxons; son of Sebert or Saberet (d. 616?) [q. v.] [lii. 244]

SIGEBERT (d. 637?), king of the East-Angles; became king, c. 631; baptised when exile in Gaul; aided Saint Felix [q. v.] and Saint Fursa [q. v.] to Christianise his kingdom and establish boys' school; resigned crown and received tonsure, but headed East-Anglians against Penda [q. v.], by whom he was defeated and slain. [lii. 244]

SIGEBERT or SEBERT, 'the Good' (fl. 653), king of the East-Saxons; succeeded Sigebert the Little; baptised under influence of Oswy [q. v.] at At-Wall; slain by kinsmen after rebuke by St. Cedd [q. v.], possibly because he bore it patiently. [lii. 245]

SIGEBERT (d. 756?), king of the West-Saxons; succeeded Cuthred [q. v.]; deposed, but allowed to retain Hampshire; slain at Privets-flood after putting to death Cumbran the ealdorman. [lii. 245]

SIGERED or SIGERÆD (fl. 762), king of Kent. [lii. 246]

SIGERED or SIGERÆD (fl. 799), king of the East-Saxons. [lii. 246]

SIGERIC or SIRIC (d. 994), archbishop of Canterbury; abbot of St. Augustine's, 980; bishop of Ramsbury, 985; archbishop of Canterbury, 990–4, going to Rome for archiepiscopal pall; said to have ejected secular monks from Christ Church, Canterbury. [lii. 246]

SIGFRID or SIGFRITH (d. 689), joint-abbot of St. Peter's, Wearmouth, 686–9. [lii. 246]

SIGHARD (fl. 695), king of the East-Saxons and under-king of Kent. [lii. 247]

SIGHERI or SIGHERE (fl. 665), king of the East-Saxons; son of Sigebert the Little [q. v.]; reigned conjointly with his uncle Sebbi [q. v.] and his cousin Sighard [q. v.]; husband of St. Osyth [q. v.] [lii. 247]

SIGILLO, NICHOLAS DE (fl. 1170), judge; perhaps identical with Nicholas 'capellanus regis,' sheriff of Essex and Hertfordshire (1164–9), dean of Tilbury (1169), and archdeacon of Coventry (1179). [lii. 248]

SIHTRIC, SIGTRYGGR, or SIDROC (d. 871), 'the Old'; heathen earl at battle of Ashdown, 871, where he fell with Sihtric, Sigtryggr, or Sidroc 'the Young' [q. v.] [lii. 248]

SIHTRIC, SIGTRYGGR, or SIDROC (d. 871), 'the Young'; heathen earl at Ashdown, 871, where he fell. [lii. 248]

SIGHTRIC or SIGTRYGGR (d. 927), king of the Black Gall and White Gall; brought fleet to Dublin, 888; won battle near Wexford, 916, and plundered Leinster; defeated king Niall (870 ?–919) [q. v.], 919; ruled 'Danes' and Northumbrians, 925–7; married Æthelstan's sister. [lii. 248]

SIHTRIC or SIGTRYGGR (fl. 962), Northman, surnamed Cam. [lii. 249]

SIHTRIC or SIGTRYGGR (d. 1042), king of Dublin; son of Olaf Sitricson [q. v.]; surnamed Silki-skegg; defeated by Brian [q. v.], 1000, whose daughter he married; plundered Kells, 1019; defeated on land by Leinstermen, 1020, and at sea by king Niall (d. 1062) [q. v.] of Ulster, 1022; made pilgrimage to Rome, 1028; won victory at Boyne mouth, 1032; passed over sea, 1035; patron of poet Gunnlaug Snakestongue; traditional founder of Christ Church, Dublin. [lii. 249]

SIKES, SIR CHARLES WILLIAM (1818–1889), projector of post-office savings banks (scheme first broached in an anonymous letter to the 'Leeds Mercury,' 1850); knighted, 1881. [lii. 249]

SILLERY, CHARLES DOYNE (1807–1837), poet; published 'Vallery, or the Citadel of the Lake,' 1829, and three other volumes of verse. [lii. 250]

SILLETT, JAMES (1764–1840), painter; exhibited at Academy, 1796–1837; president of Norwich Society of Artists, 1815; published 'Grammar of Flower Painting,' 1826. [lii. 250]

SILVER, GEORGE (fl. 1599), author of 'Paradoxes of Defence,' maintaining superiority of short sword over Italian rapier. [lii. 250]

SILVESTER. [See also SYLVESTER.]

SILVESTER DE EVERDON (d. 1254). [See EVERDON.]

SILVESTER, SIR PHILIP CARTERET, second baronet (1777–1828), captain in the navy; son of Philip Carteret [q. v.]; assumed name of Silvester, 1822; captured Dutch vessel with military stores, 1805; distinguished as volunteer in Walcheren expedition, 1809; captured detachments of Boulogne flotilla in sight of Napoleon, 1811; C.B., 1815; succeeded maternal uncle in baronetcy. [lii. 251]

SILVESTER, ROBERT (1500 ?–1579). [See PURSGLOVE.]

SILVESTER, TIPPING (1700–1768), divine; M.A. Pembroke College, Oxford, 1724; fellow; vicar of Shabbington, 1737–68; published 'Poems and Translations' (1733), and unimportant theological treatises. [lii. 252]

SIMCOCKS, MANNERS, or GROSVENOR, JOHN (1609–1695), jesuit; died at the court of St. Germain. [lii. 252]

SIMCOE, HENRY ADDINGTON (1800–1868), theologian; son of John Graves Simcoe [q. v.]; M.A. Wadham College, Oxford, 1825; curate, afterwards vicar, of Egloskerry; author and printer of theological works. [lii. 252]

SIMCOE, JOHN GRAVES (1752–1806), first governor of Upper Canada: of Eton and Merton College, Oxford; commanded queen's rangers in American war; first governor of Upper Canada, 1792–4; governor of San Domingo, 1794–7; named commander-in-chief in India, 1806, but died before assuming office. [lii. 253]

SIME, JAMES (1843–1895), author and journalist; M.A. Edinburgh, 1867; studied in Germany; published 'History of Germany,' 1874, and lives of Lessing (1877), Schiller (1882), and Goethe (1888), with other works [lii. 253]

SIMEON or SYMEON OF DURHAM (fl. 1130), precentor of Durham and compiler of 'Historia Ecclesiæ Dunelmensis' (first printed, 1732) and 'Historia Regum Anglorum et Dacorum'; his complete works edited by Thomas Arnold (Rolls Series, 1882, 1885). [lii. 254]

SIMEON STOCK, SAINT (1165 ?–1265), general of Carmelite friars; bachelor in theology, Oxford; vicar-general in the west, 1215; general of the order, 1245; obtained revision of Carmelite rule, 1248; propagator of the 'scapular'; died at Bordeaux. [lii. 255]

SIMEON OF WARWICK (d. 1296), abbot of St. Mary's, York, 1258, and Benedictine historian. [lii. 255]

SIMEON, CHARLES (1759–1836), divine: educated at Eton and Cambridge; fellow of King's College, Cambridge, 1782 (B.A., 1783), vice-provost, 1790–2; as incumbent of Holy Trinity, Cambridge, 1783–1836, became influential evangelical leader; one of the founders of Church Missionary Society; founded trust for acquiring church patronage; his 'Horæ Homileticæ' collected, 1819–20; complete works issued, 1840. [lii. 255]

SIMEON, SIR JOHN, first baronet (1756–1824), master in chancery; brother of Charles Simeon [q. v.]; of Merton College, Oxford; barrister, Lincoln's Inn, 1779; recorder of Reading, 1779–1807; master in chancery, 1795–1824; M.P., Reading, 1797–1802 and 1806–18; head of commission to administer estates of George III; created a baronet, 1815. [lii. 257]

SIMEON or SIMONS, JOSEPH, verè EMMANUEL LOBB (1594–1671), provincial of English jesuits (1667–1671) and dramatist: reconciled James, duke of York, to the Roman catholic church, 1669; his tragedies acted in Italy and Spain. [lii. 257]

SIMEONIS, SYMON (fl. 1322), Irish Franciscan and traveller in Egypt and Palestine; his 'Itineraria' printed at Cambridge, 1778. [lii. 258]

SIMMONS, BARTHOLOMEW (1804–1850), Irish poet; author of 'Napoleon's Last Look.' [lii. 258]

SIMMONS, SAMUEL (1777 ?–1819), actor: appeared at Covent Garden, London, 1785: played there (1796–1819) secondary parts, including Mordecai ('Love à la Mode'), Matthew Fainwou'd ('Raising the Wind'), Alibi ('Sleep Walker'), and Moses in 'School for Scandal.' [lii. 258]

SIMMONS, SAMUEL FOART (1750–1813), physician: M.D. Leyden, 1776; F.R.S., 1779: physician to St. Luke's Hospital, London, 1781–1811; attended George III when insane, 1803 and 1811; edited 'London Medical Journal'; published medical works and 'Life and Writings of William Hunter' (1783). [lii. 259]

SIMMONS, WILLIAM HENRY (1811–1882), mezzotint engraver; engraved plates after Faed, Landseer, Holman Hunt, Millais, and other artists. [lii. 260]

SIMMS, FREDERIC WALTER (1803–1865), engineer: received Telford medal, 1842; reported on railways for India, 1845–50; published works on engineering, including 'Practical Tunnelling' (1844). [lii. 261]

SIMMS, WILLIAM (1793–1860), mathematical-instrument maker; brother of Frederic Walter Simms [q. v.]; partner of Edward Troughton [q. v.]; F.R.S., 1852. [lii. 261]

SIMNEL, LAMBERT (fl. 1487–1525), personator of Edward, earl of Warwick (1475–1499) [q. v.]; born, c. 1475, of humble parentage; educated by Richard Simon, a priest; taken by him to Ireland and declared to be

Clarence's son, 1486; recognised by Margaret of Burgundy; crowned at Dublin as Edward VI, 1487; defeated and captured at Stoke-on-Trent, but pardoned.
[lii. 261]

SIMON DE SENLIS, EARL OF NORTHAMPTON and HUNTINGDON (*d.* 1109). [See SENLIS.]

SIMON DU FRESNE, FRAXINETUS, or ASH (*fl.* 1200), poet; canon of Hereford, and friend of Giraldus Cambrensis [q. v.] [lii. 263]

SIMON OF TOURNAY (*fl.* 1184-1200). [See TOURNAY.]

SIMON DE WELLS (*d.* 1207), bishop of Chichester; archdeacon of Wells, 1199, 'archiepiscopi vicecancellarius'; bishop of Chichester, 1204-7; died in France.
[lii. 263]

SIMON OF MONTFORT, EARL OF LEICESTER (1208 ?-1265). [See MONTFORT.]

SIMON DE WAUTON (*d.* 1266). [See WAUTON.]

SIMON OF FAVERSHAM (*fl.* 1305), philosophical writer; prebendary of Hereford; chancellor of Oxford; archdeacon of Canterbury, 1305. [lii. 263]

SIMON TUNSTED (*d.* 1369). [See TUNSTED.]

SIMON SUDBURY (*d.* 1381). [See SUDBURY.]

SIMON THE ANCHORITE (*fl.* 1512-1529), author of 'The Fruyte of Redemcyon' (Wynkyn de Worde, 1514); lived in Allhallows, London Wall, London. [lii. 264]

SIMON THE LITTLE (1530 ?-1606). [See SIMWNT.]

SIMON, ABRAHAM (1622 ?-1692 ?), medallist; brother of Thomas Simon [q. v.]; employed by Queen Christina of Sweden; came to England, *c.* 1642; cast models of eminent contemporaries, including Charles II and Henry Cromwell; wax portrait of himself in British Museum. [lii. 264]

SIMON, JOHN (1675 ?-1751), engraver; Huguenot refugee. [lii. 265]

SIMON, SIR JOHN (1818-1897), serjeant-at-law; LL.B. of London, 1841; barrister, Middle Temple, 1842 (second Jewish barrister admitted); defended Simon Bernard, 1858; serjeant-at-law, 1864; liberal M.P. for Dewsbury, 1868-88; knighted, 1886; a founder of Anglo-Jewish Association. [lii. 265]

SIMON, THOMAS (1623 ?-1665), medallist and seal-engraver; joint chief graver to the royal mint, 1645; sole chief graver, 1649-60; engraved dies for Cromwell's projected coinages of 1656 and 1658, his portrait for the Dunbar medal, and the great seals of 1648, 1651, and 1661; died of the plague. [lii. 265]

SIMONS, JOSEPH (1594-1671). [See SIMEON.]

SIMPSON. [See also SIMSON.]

SIMPSON or **SYMPSON**, CHRISTOPHER (1605 ?-1669), violist and writer on music; served as royalist in Great Rebellion; published 'The Division Violist' (1659), 'Principles of Practical Musick' (1665), and other works.
[lii. 267]

SIMPSON, DAVID (1745-1799), divine; M.A. St. John's College, Cambridge, 1772; deprived of curacy at Macclesfield for methodistical preaching; incumbent of Christ Church, Macclesfield, 1779-99; published 'Plea for Religion and the Sacred Writings,' 1797, 'Apology for Doctrine of the Trinity,' 1798, and other works.
[lii. 268]

SIMPSON or **SIMSON**, EDWARD (1578-1651), author of 'Chronicon Historiam Catholicam complectens' (1652); fellow of Trinity College, Cambridge, 1601-28; M.A., 1603; D.D., 1618; rector of Eastling, 1618, and Pluckley.
[lii. 269]

SIMPSON, ELSPETH (1738-1791). [See BUCHAN.]

SIMPSON, SIR GEORGE (1792-1860), administrator of Hudson's Bay Company's territory; traversed North American continent, 1828; organised north-western expedition of 1837; knighted, 1841; made 'overland' journey round the world, 1841-2, and published an account, 1847; assisted arctic expeditions; Falls on Peace River and a cape named after him. [lii. 269]

SIMPSON, JAMES (1781-1853), advocate, author and friend of Scott; published 'Visit to Flanders and the Field of Waterloo,' 1815, 'Paris after Waterloo,' 1853, and works on education. [lii. 270]

SIMPSON, SIR JAMES (1792-1868), general; served with grenadier guards in Peninsula, 1812-13; wounded at Quatre Bras; commanded 29th foot at Mauritius; second in command to Sir Charles James Napier [q. v.] in Kacchi expedition, 1845; chief of the staff in Crimea, 1854, and successor to Lord Raglan in the command; G.C.B. and general after capture of Sebastopol; resigned, November 1855. [lii. 270]

SIMPSON, SIR JAMES YOUNG, first baronet (1811-1870), physician; son of a baker; M.D. Edinburgh, 1832; professor of midwifery, 1839; introduced use of chloroform, 1847; awarded Monthyon prize of Académie des Sciences, 1856; created a baronet and D.C.L. of Oxford, 1866; made important contributions to science of obstetrics; anticipated discovery of Röntgen rays; received public funeral at Edinburgh; Maternity Hospital founded to his memory; bust erected to him in Westminster Abbey; published ' Obstetric Memoirs and Contributions' (1855-6); his 'Anæsthesia,' 1871, 'Clinical Lectures on Diseases of Women,' 1872, and 'Archæological Essays,' 1873, issued posthumously. [lii. 272]

SIMPSON, MRS. JANE CROSS (1811-1886), hymn-writer; sister of Henry Glassford Bell [q. v.]; married J. Bell Simpson, 1837; her best hymns in 'Lyra Britannica' (1867), Martineau's hymns, and 'Scottish Evangelical Hymnal,' 1878; published also poems and tales, often under pseudonym 'Gertrude.' [lii. 273]

SIMPSON, JOHN (1746-1812), author of 'Essays on the Language of Scripture,' 1806; educated at Warrington Academy and Glasgow University; sometime Unitarian minister of High Pavement Chapel, Nottingham.
[lii. 274]

SIMPSON, JOHN (1782-1847), portrait-painter.
[lii. 274]

SIMPSON, JOHN PALGRAVE (1807-1887), dramatist and novelist; M.A. Corpus Christi College, Cambridge, 1832; described his continental experiences in 'Letters from the Danube,' 1847, and 'Pictures from Revolutionary Paris,' 1849; published four novels and numerous plays, including 'A Scrap of Paper' (produced, 1861), and 'Lady Dedlock's Secret' (produced, 1864). [lii. 274]

SIMPSON, NATHANIEL (1599-1642), author of 'Arithmeticæ Compendium,' 1622; fellow of Trinity College, Oxford (M.A., 1623). [lii. 275]

SIMPSON, RICHARD (1820-1876), Roman catholic writer and Shakespearean scholar; B.A. Oriel College, Oxford, 1843; vicar of Mitcham, 1844-5; edited the 'Rambler' and (1862-4) 'Home and Foreign Review'; assisted William Ewart Gladstone [q. v.] with 'Vaticanism'; published 'Life of Edmund Campion,' 1867, 'Introduction to Philosophy of Shakespeare's Sonnets,' 1868, 'The School of Shakespeare,' 1872, 'Sonnets of Shakespeare Selected,' 1878. [lii. 276]

SIMPSON, ROBERT (1795-1867), united presbyterian minister of Sanquhar; published works on the covenanters and 'History of Sanquhar,' 1853. [lii. 276]

SIMPSON, SIDRACH (1600 ?-1655), independent minister; of Emmanuel College, Cambridge; joined independent church at Rotterdam, 1638; afterwards pastor of a rival church; resumed lectureship at St. Margaret's, Fish Street, London, 1641; member of Westminster Assembly and one of the five authors of the 'Apologeticall Narration' (1643); master of Pembroke Hall, Cambridge and rector of St. Mary Abchurch, London, 1650; rector St Bartholomew, Exchange, London 1653; one of the 'triers,' 1654; imprisoned for preaching against Cromwell; published controversial treatises. [lii. 277]

SIMPSON, THOMAS (*fl.* 1620), court musician to Count of Schaumburg; published collections of music at Frankfort, 1611, and Hamburg (posthumous), 1621.
[lii. 278]

SIMPSON, THOMAS (1710-1761), mathematician; 'the oracle of Nuneaton, Bosworth, and the environs': professor of mathematics at Royal Academy, Woolwich, 1743; F.R.S., 1745; edited 'Ladies' Diary,' 1754-60; published 'New Treatise on Fluxions,' 1737, revised as 'Doctrine and Application of Fluxions,' 1750, and other mathematical treatises. [lii. 279]

S.MPSON, THOMAS (1808-1840), arctic explorer; nephew of Sir George Simpson [q. v.]; M.A. King's College, Aberdeen, 1829; second in command of the Hudson's Bay Company's expedit.on under Peter Warren Dease, which explored the north-western coast of North America, 1836–9 ; killed by gunshot wound ; his 'Narrative of Discoveries on North Coast of America' published, 1843. [lii. 279]

SIMPSON or **SYMPSON**, WILLIAM (1627 ?–1671), quaker ; appeared in sackcloth in various towns, and practised other acts of religious fanaticism ; accompanied John Burneyeat [q. v.] to Barbados and died there. [lii. 280]

SIMPSON, WILLIAM (1823–1899), artist and war correspondent ; entered architect's office in Glasgow, 1835 ; apprenticed as lithographer ; employed by Day & Son, lithographers, in London, 1851 ; accompanied British army in Crimea for purpose of making drawings for 'Illustrations of the War in the East,' published by Colnaghi & Son, 1855–6 ; commissioned by Day & Son to make sketches in India, 1858 ; joined staff of 'Illustrated London News,' 1866, and subsequently acted as war-artist in Abyssinia, 1868, Franco-Prussian war, 1870, and Afghanistan, 1878–9, and made numerous journeys as artist and correspondent ; associate of Institute of Painters in Water-colours, 1874, and full member, 1879 ; original member, 1883, of Institute of Painters in Oil Colours (now Society of Oil Painters) ; F.R.G.S. ; hon. A.R.I.B.A. ; member of Royal Asiatic Society ; founded with Samuel Birch (1813–1885) [q. v.] Society of Biblical Archæology ; published works illustrated by himself. [Suppl. iii. 345]

SIMS, JAMES (1741–1820), president of Medical Society of London ; M.D. Leyden, 1764 ; published 'Observations on Epidemic Disorders,' 1773, and other medical works of wide circulation. [lii. 281]

SIMS, JOHN (1749–1831), botanist and physician ; M.D. Edinburgh, 1774 ; physician to Princess Charlotte ; F.R.S. and an original F.L.S. ; edited Curtis's 'Botanical Magazine,' 1801–28 ; joint-editor of 'Annals of Botany,' 1805–6. [lii. 281]

SIMSON. [See also SIMPSON.]

SIMSON, ALEXANDER (1570 ? – 1639), divine ; laureated at Glasgow University, 1590 ; son of Andrew Simson (d. 1590 ?) [q. v.] ; minister of Merton, 1597–1632 ; imprisoned for sermon at Edinburgh, 1621. [lii. 282]

SIMSON, ANDREW (d. 1590 ?), Scottish divine ; studied at St. Andrews ; author of 'Rudimenta Grammatices' ; master of Perth grammar school, 1550–60 minister and grammar-school master of Dunbar, 1564 ; minister of Dalkeith, 1582 ; devised formula of modified subscription to Act of Uniformity. [lii. 282]

SIMSON, ANDREW (1638–1712), author of 'Large Description of Galloway' (printed, 1823) ; M.A. Edinburgh, 1661 ; episcopalian minister at Kirkinner, and afterwards of Douglas ; finally printer and author in Edinburgh. [lii. 283]

SIMSON, ARCHIBALD (1564 ? – 1628), Scottish divine ; brother of Alexander Simson [q. v.] ; M.A. St. Andrews, 1585 ; succeeded his father as minister of Dalkeith ; adhered to general assembly against James I, 1605 ; as secretary of the meeting which drew up protest of 1617 deprived and imprisoned, but restored on submission ; author of theological works and 'Life of Patrick Simson.' [lii. 283]

SIMSON, JOHN (1668 ?–1740), Scottish theologian ; M.A. Edinburgh, 1692 ; minister of Troqueer, 1705–8 ; professor of divinity at Glasgow, 1708–29 ; censured by general assembly for unorthodoxy, 1717 ; attacked for heterodox teaching on the incarnation, 1726, and despite explanations and withdrawals suspended from all ecclesiastical functions, 1729 ; his 'Case' printed, 1715, and 'Continuations,' 1727–9. [lii. 284]

SIMSON, PATRICK (1556–1618), divine ; son of Andrew Simson (d. 1590 ?) [q. v.] ; graduated at St. Mary's College, St. Andrews, 1574 ; minister of Spott, 1577, Cramond, 1580, and Stirling, 1590–1618 ; opposed introduction of episcopacy, and drew up protest of 1606, but had much influence with James VI, and was generally respected : Greek and Hebrew scholar ; author of 'History of the Church,' published, 1624. [lii. 286]

SIMSON, ROBERT (1687–1768), mathematician ; nephew of John Simson [q. v.] ; M.A. Glasgow, 1711 ; professor of mathematics, 1712–61 ; published 'Elements

of Euclid,' 1756, 'Sectionum Conicarum Libri V,' 1735, a restoration of the 'Loci Plani' of Apollonius, 1749, and other works, some of them posthumous. [lii. 287]

SIMSON, THOMAS (1696–1764), first professor of medicine at St. Andrews (1722–64) ; brother of Robert Simson [q. v.] ; published medical works. [lii. 288]

SIMSON, WILLIAM (d. 1620 ?), Scottish divine ; son of Andrew Simson (d. 1590 ?) [q. v.] ; minister of Dumbarton, 1601 ; author of treatise on Hebrew accents, 1617. [lii. 283]

SIMSON, WILLIAM (1800–1847), historical and landscape painter ; exhibited at Royal Academy (from 1830), British Institution, and Scottish Academy. [lii. 288]

SIMWNT FYCHAN, i.e. SIMON THE LITTLE (1530 ?–1606), Welsh bard ; of Tybrith ; 'pencerdd' at Caerwys, 1568 ; probable author of 'Pum Llyfr Cerddwriaeth.' [lii. 289]

SINCLAIR, ANDREW (d. 1861), botanist and surgeon ; collected plants in Mexico and Central America, 1837–8, and afterwards in Australia and New Zealand ; colonial secretary in New Zealand, 1844–56 ; drowned in crossing the Rangitata river, New Zealand. [lii. 289]

SINCLAIR, CATHERINE (1800–1864), novelist ; daughter of Sir John Sinclair by his second wife ; published 'Holiday House' and other children's books. 'Scotland and the Scotch' (1840), and many novels. [lii. 290]

SINCLAIR, GEORGE, fourth EARL OF CAITHNESS (d. 1582), peer of parliament, 1542 ; imprisoned and fined for neglecting to attend the regent's courts, 1555 ; joined invitation of catholic nobles to Mary Stuart ; opposed ratification of 'Confession of Faith,' 1560 ; hereditary justiciar in Caithness, 1566 ; implicated in Darnley's murder, but presided at trial of Bothwell ; signed letter of rebel lords to Queen Elizabeth, 1570 ; accused of instigating crimes in the north. [lii. 290]

SINCLAIR, GEORGE, fifth EARL OF CAITHNESS (1566 ?–1643), succeeded his grandfather ; engaged in feud with Sutherland ; committed outrage on servants of Earl of Orkney ; put down rebellion of Orkney's son, and received a pension, 1615 ; obliged to resign it and sheriffdom of Caithness to obtain pardon for outrages on Lord Forbes ; driven to Shetland by commission of fire and sword, 1623, but soon allowed to return and meet his creditors. [lii. 292]

SINCLAIR or **SINCLAR**, GEORGE (d. 1696), author of 'Satans Invisible World discovered ' (1685) ; professor of philosophy at Glasgow, 1654–66 ; obliged to resign for non-compliance with episcopacy, but reappointed after the revolution ; professor of mathematics, 1691–6 ; associated with the inventor in using the diving-bell, 1655 ; one of the first to utilise the barometer ('baroscope') in Scotland ; his 'Hydrostaticks' (1672) attacked by James Gregory (1638–1675) [q. v.] of St. Andrews ; superintended laying of Edinburgh water-pipes, 1673–4 ; published works on mathematics, natural philosophy, and astronomy. [lii. 293]

SINCLAIR, GEORGE (1786–1834), author of 'Hortus Gramineus Woburnensis' (1816), describing experiments with grasses made when gardener to the Duke of Bedford, under the superintendence of Sir Humphry Davy [q. v.] ; edited botanical works. [lii. 294]

SINCLAIR, SIR GEORGE (1790–1868), politician and author ; brother of Catherine Sinclair [q. v.] ; friend of Byron at Harrow ; printed (1826) 'Narrative' of interview with Napoleon I at Göttingen ; as M.P. for Caithness (1811–41) advocated catholic emancipation and emancipation of slaves ; joined party of Stanley and Graham, and succeeded Sir John Sinclair [q. v.] in baronetcy, 1835 ; chairman of Sir Francis Burdett's election committee, 1837 ; joined free church of Scotland ; published works on Scottish church question, a pamphlet on the fall of Charles X, and other writings. [lii. 295]

SINCLAIR, SIR HENRY (d. 1330 ?), warrior ; son of Sir William Sinclair (fl. 1266–1303) [q. v.] ; captured by Edward I at Dunbar, 1296 ; provost, 1299 ; sheriff of Lanark, 1305 ; fought for Bruce at Bannockburn ; received pension, 1328. [lii. 308]

SINCLAIR, Sir HENRY, EARL or PRINCE OF ORKNEY (*d.* 1400 ?), son of Sir William Sinclair (*d.* 1330) [q. v.]; earldom awarded to him by Hacon VI of Norway, 1379; conquered Faroe isles (Frislanda), 1391; wrested Shetland from Malise Sperra; made voyage across Atlantic with Antonio Zeno and explored Greenland. [lii. 296]

SINCLAIR, HENRY, second EARL OF ORKNEY (*d.* 1418), admiral of Scotland; captured at Homildon Hill, 1402; taken with James I on voyage to France, 1406. [lii. 296]

SINCLAIR, HENRY (1508-1565), president of the court of session and bishop of Ross; brother of Oliver Sinclair [q. v.]; studied at St. Leonard's College, St. Andrews; lord of session, 1537; abbot of Kilwinning, 1541; negotiator of treaty with Flanders, 1548; dean of Glasgow, 1550; in France, 1550-4; commissioner for treaties of Carlisle, 1556, and Upsettlington, 1559; lord president of the court of session, 1558; bishop of Ross; member of Mary Stuart's privy council, 1561; denounced by Knox, but maintained neutral religious attitude; wrote additions to Boece's 'History of Scotland'; died at Paris. [lii. 297]

SINCLAIR, JAMES (*d.* 1762), general; brother of John Sinclair (1683-1750) [q. v.]; colonel of royal Scots regiment, 1737; lieutenant-general commanding forces in Flanders, 1745; commanded abortive expedition against Port L'Orient, 1746; M.P., Dysart, 1722, 1727, and 1747, Sutherland, 1736 and 1741, and Fife county, 1754 and 1761; ambassador at Vienna and Turin; general, 1761; died governor of Cork. [lii. 298]

SINCLAIR, JAMES, fourteenth EARL OF CAITHNESS (1821-1881), inventor of a steam carriage, gravitating compass, and tape-loom; a lord in waiting, 1856-8 and 1859-66; representative peer, 1858-66; created British peer (Baron Barrogill), 1866; published 'Lectures on Popular and Scientific Subjects,' 1877. [lii. 298]

SINCLAIR, JOHN (*d.* 1566), bishop of Brechin; brother of Henry Sinclair (1508-1565) [q. v.], bishop of Ross; lord of session, 1540; dean of Restalrig; married Mary Queen of Scots to Darnley, 1565; bishop of Brechin, 1565-6; denounced by Knox; probable author of Sinclair's 'Practicks.' [lii. 299]

SINCLAIR, JOHN, seventh BARON SINCLAIR (1610-1676), covenanter; member of general assembly of 1638, and of committee of estates, 1641, 1643, 1645; joined Charles II, 1650; captured at Worcester and imprisoned till Restoration; privy councillor of Scotland, 1661. [lii. 299]

SINCLAIR, JOHN (1683-1750), master of Sinclair; Jacobite; while serving with Marlborough in Flanders sentenced to death for shooting Captain Shaw, 1708; fled to Prussia till pardoned, 1727; captured Hanoverian stores at Burntisland, but not distinguished at Sheriffmuir, 1715; pardoned, 1726; his 'Memoirs of the Rebellion' printed, 1858. [lii. 300]

SINCLAIR, Sir JOHN, first baronet (1754-1835), president of the board of agriculture; educated at Edinburgh, Glasgow, and Oxford universities (Trinity College); barrister, Lincoln's Inn, 1782; M.P., Caithness, 1780, Lostwithiel, 1784-1811; created baronet, 1786; formed 'armed neutrality' party; president of the board of agriculture, 1793-8 and 1806-13; carried Enclosure Bill in Commons, 1796; suggested issue of exchequer bills; wrote pamphlets against Pitt ministry, 1798; privy councillor, 1810; took part in the currency controversy; commissioner of excise, 1811. As an agriculturist he initiated sheep-shearings, introduced improved methods of tillage, and new breeds of live stock in northern Scotland, and obtained establishment of the board of agriculture, 1793. He carried out a 'Statistical Account of Scotland' (1791-9), and a system of county reports for Great Britain; superintended publication of Macpherson's Ossianic transcripts (1807), and published 'History of the Public Revenue' (1784), and treatises on northern agriculture. [lii. 301]

SINCLAIR, JOHN (1791-1857), tenor singer; appeared in opera at Covent Garden, London, 1810-17; studied at Paris, Milan, and Naples, and sang in Italy, 1822-3, creating the part of Idreno in 'Semiramide'; reappeared at Covent Garden, London, 1823, and afterwards at the Adelphi, Drury Lane, London, and in America; composed Scottish songs. [lii. 305]

SINCLAIR, JOHN (1797-1875), divine; of Edinburgh University; M.A. Pembroke College, Oxford, 1822; secretary of the National Society, 1839, vicar of Kensington, 1843, and archdeacon of Middlesex, 1844; published 'Life and Times of Sir John Sinclair' (1837), his father. [lii. 305]

SINCLAIR, OLIVER (*fl.* 1537-1560), Scottish general at Solway Moss; favourite of James V; opposed protestant and English influence; captured at Solway Moss, 1542; released on parole and conditionally on furthering English interests. [lii. 306]

SINCLAIR, Sir ROBERT, BARON STEVENSON (1640 ?-1713), Scottish judge; one of Argyll's counsel, 1661; dean of faculty, 1670; lord of session and sheriff of Haddington, 1689; privy councillor and baron of exchequer, 1690, but never took his seat, and resigned, 1693. [lii. 307]

SINCLAIR, Sir WILLIAM, or WILLIAM DE SAINT CLAIR (*fl.* 1266-1303), Scottish baron; of Roslin; guardian of Alexander, prince of Scotland; one of the envoys to negotiate French marriage for him; sheriff of Dumfries and justiciar of Galloway; partisan of Baliol; taken by English at Dunbar, 1294; escaped from Gloucester Castle, 1303. [lii. 307]

SINCLAIR or **SAINT CLAIR**, Sir WILLIAM (*d.* 1330), of Roslin; son of Sir Henry Sinclair (*d.* 1330 ?) [q. v.]; accompanied Sir James Douglas (1286 ?-1330) [q. v.] to take the heart of Bruce to Palestine; slain with him by Saracens in Andalusia. [lii. 308]

SINCLAIR, WILLIAM (*d.* 1337), bishop of Dunkeld; son of Sir William Sinclair (*fl.* 1266-1303) [q. v.]; bishop of Dunkeld, 1312; known as the 'king's bishop,' after his repulse of English at Donibristle, 1317; crowned Edward Baliol, 1332. [lii. 308]

SINCLAIR, Sir WILLIAM, third EARL OF ORKNEY and first EARL OF CAITHNESS (1404 ?-1480), chancellor of Scotland; son of Henry Sinclair, second earl of Orkney [q. v.]; hostage for James I, 1421; acknowledged Norwegian jurisdiction on investiture with earldom, 1434; as high admiral of Scotland conveyed Princess Margaret to France, 1436; summoned to Norway, 1446; there probably received diploma setting forth pedigree; began foundation of Roslin, 1446; assisted in repelling English invasion, 1448; created Lord Sinclair, 1449, and Earl of Caithness, 1455; chancellor of Scotland, 1454-6; active against the Douglases; one of the regents and ambassador to England, 1461; resigned Orkney to Scottish crown, 1471, receiving lands in Fife and a pension in exchange; envoy to England, 1472-3. [lii. 309]

SINCLAIR, WILLIAM (1804-1878), divine; brother of John Sinclair (1797-1875) [q. v.]; served in Madras cavalry; afterwards graduated at Oxford (M.A. St. Mary Hall, 1837), and was president of the Union; incumbent of St. George's, Leeds, 1837-57; rector of Pulborough, 1857-78; published 'The Dying Soldier,' 1838, and 'Sepoy Mutinies,' 1857. [lii. 310]

SINDERCOMBE or **SINDERCOME**, MILES (*d.* 1657), conspirator; when quartermaster in regiment of (Sir) John Reynolds (*d.* 1657) [q. v.] joined mutiny of levellers, 1649; a chief agent in Robert Overton's plot against Monck, 1655; sentenced to death for attempt to assassinate Cromwell, but committed suicide in the Tower of London. [lii. 311]

SINGER, ELIZABETH (1674-1737). [See ROWE, MRS. ELIZABETH.]

SINGER, GEORGE JOHN (1786-1817), electrician; invented gold-leaf electrometer; published 'Elements of Electricity and Electro-chemistry,' 1814. [lii. 311]

SINGER, JOHN (*fl.* 1594-1602), actor and dramatist; reputed author of 'Quips upon Questions,' 1600 (reprinted, 1875). [lii. 312]

SINGER, JOSEPH HENDERSON (1786-1866), bishop of Meath; fellow of Trinity College, Dublin, 1810 (M.A., 1811, and D.D., 1825); regius professor of divinity, 1850; archdeacon of Raphoe, 1851; bishop of Meath, 1852-66. [lii. 312]

SINGER, SAMUEL WELLER (1783-1858), author; brother of George John Singer [q. v.]; sometime bookseller in St. James's Street; friend of Francis Douce [q.v.]; issued 'The Book printed at Oxford in MCCCCLXVIII' (Rufinus on the Apostles' Creed), 1812; edited for Chiswick Press reprints of rare English sixteenth-century works; compiled 'Researches into History of Playing Cards,' 1816; printed Spence's 'Anecdotes,' 1820; edited 'Correspondence of Henry Hyde, Earl of Clarendon,' 1828; published also an edition of Shakespeare, 1826; attacked genuineness of Collier's corrections, 1853, and Madden's 'Glossary of Havelock the Dane,' 1829; librarian to Royal Institution, 1827-35.   [lii. 313]

SINGLETON, HENRY (1766-1839), painter; exhibited many years at the Royal Academy; painted group of academicians, 1793; his portrait of Lord Howe in National Portrait Gallery; executed also portraits of Boswell and Lord Nelson.   [lii. 314]

SINGLETON, ROBERT or JOHN (d. 1544), Roman catholic divine; educated at Oxford; executed at Tyburn for treason.   [lii. 315]

SINGLETON, ROBERT CORBET (1810-1881), joint-editor of 'Anglican Hymn-Book,' 1871; M.A. Trinity College, Dublin, 1833; warden of St. Columba's College, Rathfarnham, 1843; of Radley, 1847-51; translated Virgil, 1855; composed and translated hymns. [lii. 315]

SINGLETON, THOMAS (1783-1842), archdeacon of Northumberland: of Eton and Corpus Christi College, Oxford; M.A., 1826; archdeacon of Northumberland and rector of Howick, 1826; letters on ecclesiastical commission addressed to him by Sydney Smith [q. v.] [lii. 315]

SINNICH, JOHN (d. 1666), theologian; professor of theology at Louvain, 1648-66; founder of bursaries for Irish students.   [lii. 316]

SION or **JOHN**, LLYWELYN (1520 ?-1616). [See LLYWELYN OF LLANGEWYDD.]

SION TREREDYN (fl. 1651). [See EDWARDS, JOHN.]

SION Y POTIAU (1700 ?-1776). [See EDWARDS, JOHN.]

SION LLEYN, or JOHN ROBERTS (1749-1817), Welsh poet; of Pwllheli.   [lii. 316]

SION GLANYGORS (1767-1821). [See JONES, JOHN.]

SIRR, HENRY CHARLES (1764-1841), chief of Dublin police ('town-major'); served in the army, 1778-1790, town-major of Dublin, 1796-1826; arrested Peter Finnerty [q. v.], 1797; wounded Lord Edward Fitzgerald, 1798; mulcted in damages for false imprisonment, 1802; arrested Robert Emmet [q. v.], 1803.   [lii. 317]

SIRR, HENRY CHARLES (1807-1872), author of 'China and the Chinese' (1849) and 'Ceylon and the Cingalese' (1850); second son of Henry Charles Sirr (1764-1841) [q. v.]   [lii. 317]

SIRR, JOSEPH D'ARCY (1794-1868), author of lives of Archbishops Trench (1845) and Ussher; brother of Henry Charles Sirr (1807-1872) [q. v.]   [lii. 317]

SITRIC. [See SIHTRIC.]

SIWARD (d. 1048), coadjutor archbishop of Canterbury; succeeded Æthelwine [q. v.] as abbot of Abingdon; bishop of Upsala as coadjutor to Eadsige [q. v.], 1042-8.   [lii. 318]

SIWARD, EARL OF NORTHUMBERLAND (d. 1055), called the STRONG (Digera); probably came to England with Canute and received earldom of Deira on division of Northumbria; ravaged Worcestershire for Hardecanute [q. v.], 1041; became earl of all Northumbria after slaying his wife's uncle; held also earldom of Huntingdon; upheld Edward the Confessor [q. v.] against Godwin, 1051; invaded Scotland, defeated Macbeth [q. v.], and established Malcolm III as king of Cumbria, 1054.   [lii. 318]

SIWARD (d. 1075), bishop of Rochester; abbot of Chertsey; bishop, 1058-75.   [lii. 319]

SKAE, DAVID (1814-1873), physician-superintendent of Royal Edinburgh Asylum, Morningside, 1846-73; hon. M.D. St. Andrews, 1842; Morrisonian lecturer on insanity, 1873; made new classification of the insane. [lii. 320]

SKEFFINGTON, CLOTWORTHY, seventh VISCOUNT and second EARL OF MASSEREENE (1742-1805), of Corpus Christi College, Cambridge; imprisoned for debt at Fort l'Evêque and La Force, 1770-89.   [lii. 320]

SKEFFINGTON, SIR JOHN, second VISCOUNT MASSEREENE (d. 1695), supporter of William of Orange; succeeded as fifth baronet, 1647; M.P., co. Antrim, 1661; became viscount on death of his father-in-law, 1665; custos

of Londonderry county, 1666; commissioner of revenue 1673; assisted citizens of Derry and Enniskilleners, and was proscribed by Tyrconnel, 1689; active in Irish parliament, 1692.   [lii. 321]

SKEFFINGTON, JOHN SKEFFINGTON FOSTER, tenth VISCOUNT MASSEREENE (1812-1863), minor poet; of Eton and Christ Church, Oxford; K.P., 1851.
    [lii. 321]

SKEFFINGTON, SIR LUMLEY ST. GEORGE (1771-1850), fop and playwright; succeeded as second baronet of Skeffington Hall, Leicestershire: admitted into Carlton House circle; invented Skeffington brown; caricatured by Gillray, and satirised by Byron and Moore; produced at Covent Garden, London, 'The Word of Honour,' 1802, at Drury Lane, London, 'The High Road to Marriage,' 1803, and 'The Sleeping Beauty,' 1805; lived many years within rules of King's Bench.   [lii. 322]

SKEFFINGTON, SIR WILLIAM, called 'The Gunner' (d. 1535), lord-deputy of Ireland; sheriff of Warwickshire and Leicestershire, 1509; master of the ordnance; lord-deputy of Ireland, 1529-32 and 1534-5, being recalled from Ireland by influence of Kildare, 1532, but again appointed after his fall, 1534; put down rebellion of Lord Thomas Fitzgerald of Offaly, capturing Maynooth with heavy artillery; stormed Dungarvan; his son the inventor of 'Skeffington's daughter.'   [lii. 323]

SKELATER, JOHN FORBES- (1733-1808). [See FORBES.]

SKELTON, BEVIL (fl. 1661-1692), diplomatist; groom of the bedchamber and lieutenant-colonel, 1672; envoy at Vienna and Venice; as envoy in Holland warned James II of William of Orange's designs, and attempted to prevent the sailing of Argyll's and Monmouth's expeditions; at Versailles supported French attempt to hinder William's invasion; imprisoned on recall, but soon appointed lieutenant of the Tower of London; employed by James II in exile, and became Romanist.   [lii. 325]

SKELTON, JOHN (1460 ?-1529), poet; native of Norfolk; educated both at Oxford and Cambridge (M.A., 1484); created 'poet-laureate' by both universities, and perhaps by the crown; composed poem on death of Edward IV, 1483, and elegies on Henry Percy, fourth earl of Northumberland, 1489, and Henry VII, 1509; translated 'Pelerinage de la Vie Humaine' for Countess of Richmond; tutor to Prince Henry (Henry VIII), and enjoyed court favour despite his outspokenness; was admitted to orders, 1498, and became parson of Diss; wrote poems against Christopher Garneys or Garnysshe [q. v.] by order of Henry VIII; patronised by the Countess of Surrey (mother of the poet) and Wo sey; attacked Wolsey in 'Colyn Cloute,' 'Speake Parrot,' and other poems, and is said to have been imprisoned by him; died in sanctuary at Westminster. Of his works, 'The Bowge of Court' was printed by Wynkyn de Worde, 'Garlande of Laurell' (enumerating his productions) by Rycharde Faukes (1523), 'Phylyp Sparowe' (praised by Coleridge) by Rychard Kele, and others, 'Colyn Cloute' (which gave suggestions to Spenser) by Thomas Godfrey, Kele, and others. He probably invented his favourite metre. His 'Balade of the Scotyshe Kynge' (on Flodden) is one of the earliest extant ballads. Imperfect collected editions appeared, 1520, 1560, 1570; first complete edition, 1568; works edited by Dyce, 1843. Anecdotes of him appeared in the popular 'Merie Tales' (1566) and similar collections.   [lii. 327]

SKELTON, SIR JOHN (1831-1897), author who adopted pseudonym 'Shirley'; studied at Edinburgh University; admitted advocate, 1854; secretary to Scottish board of supervision (public health), 1868, chairman, 1892; vice-president of Scottish local government board, 1894-7; hon. LL.D. of Edinburgh, 1878; K.C.B., 1897; friend of James Anthony Froude, Dante Rossetti, and Sir Noel Paton; contributed to 'Fraser' and 'Blackwood'; works include 'Maitland of Lethington and the Scotland of Mary Stuart,' 1887-8, and other works defending Mary Queen of Scots, 'Benjamin Disraeli,' 1868, official works on public health, 'Essays of Shirley,' 1882, and 'Table Talk of Shirley,' 1895-6   [lii. 332]

SKELTON, JOSEPH (fl. 1820-1850), topographical and antiquarian engraver; brother of William Skelton [q. v.]   [lii. 335]

SKELTON, PHILIP (1707-1787). Irish divine and author; scholar of Trinity College, Dublin, 1726; B.A.,

1728 ; curate to Dr. Samuel Madden [q. v.] and afterwards at Monaghan ; came to London to publish his ' Ophiomaches, or Deism Revealed,' 1748 : incumbent of Templecarn on Lough Derg, 1750–9, of Devenish, 1759–66, of Fintona, 1766, devoting himself to his poor parishioners : issued ironical ' Vindication ' of Bishop Hoadly and ' Proposal for the Revival of Christianity,' 1736 ; published also ' Discourses Controversial and Practical on various Subjects,' 1754 ; gave profits of sale of collected works (1770) to Magdalen charity. [lii. 333]

SKELTON, WILLIAM (1763–1848), line-engraver ; best known by plates after Beechey. [lii. 335]

SKENE, FELICIA MARY FRANCES (1821–1899), novelist ; daughter of James Skene [q. v.]; born at Aix in Provence ; organised band of nurses under Sir Henry Wentworth Acland [q. v.] during outbreak of cholera at Oxford, 1854. Her publications include memoirs of her cousin, Alexander Penrose Forbes [q. v.], a volume of poems, and several novels. [Suppl. iii. 347]

SKENE, GILBERT (1522 ?–1599). [See SKEYNE.]

SKENE, SIR JAMES (d. 1633), president of the court of session ; son of Sir John Skene [q. v.]; lord of session, 1612 ; president, 1626–33 ; created Nova Scotia baronet, 1630. [lii. 337]

SKENE, JAMES (1775–1864), friend of Sir Walter Scott ; admitted to Scottish bar, 1797 ; served with Edinburgh light horse ; studied in Germany ; member of Royal Society of Edinburgh ; secretary to board of trustees and manufactures ; lived in Greece, 1838–44 ; executed ' Series of Sketches of existing Localities alluded to in Waverley Novels,' 1829 ; edited Spalding's ' History of the Troubles,' 1828 ; his manuscript memoranda utilised by Lockhart. [lii. 335]

SKENE, SIR JOHN, LORD CURRIEHILL (1543 ?–1617), clerk-register and lord of session : regent in St. Mary's College, St. Andrews, 1564–5 ; visited Scandinavia and Paris ; advocate, 1575 ; granted pension by Morton for preparing digest of laws ; accompanied James VI to Denmark ; as joint king's advocate zealous in witch prosecution : ambassador to Holland, 1591 ; lord clerk-register and lord of session, with title of Lord Curriehill, 1594–1611 ; prepared revision of Scottish laws, 1597 : one of the Octavians, 1596–7 ; his work on the laws of Scotland previous to James I (' Regiam Majestatem ') printed at public expense, 1609. [lii. 336]

SKENE, JOHN (d. 1644), reputed compiler of ' Ancient Scottish Melodies' (printed, 1838) ; brother of Sir James Skene [q. v.] [lii. 338]

SKENE, WILLIAM FORBES (1809–1892), author of ' Celtic Scotland' (1876–80), second son of James Skene [q. v.]; clerk of the bills in court of session : historiographer of Scotland, 1881 ; D.C.L. of Oxford, 1879 : published ' The Highlanders of Scotland,' 1837, ' The Four Ancient Books of Wales,' 1868 ; contributed important introduction to ' Collection of Gaelic Poetry' (1862) ; edited ' Chronicles of the Picts and Scots' (1867) and Fordun (1871) ; effected union of St. Vincent's church with episcopal church of Scotland. [lii. 338]

SKERNING or **SKERVINGE**, ROGER DE (d. 1278), bishop of Norwich : prior of Benedictines, 1257 : bishop of Norwich, 1266–78 : laid Norwich under interdict after burning of the cathedral, 1272. [lii. 340]

SKETCHLEY, ARTHUR (1817–1882) (pseudonym). [See ROSE, GEORGE.]

SKEVINGTON. [See also SKEFFINGTON.]

SKEVINGTON or **PACE**, THOMAS (d. 1533), bishop of Bangor : abbot of Beaulieu : abbot of Waverley : bishop of Bangor, 1509–33 ; built tower and nave of his cathedral. [lii. 340]

SKEWES, JOHN (d. 1544). [See SKUISH.]

SKEY, FREDERIC CARPENTER (1798–1872), surgeon : pupil of Abernethy : taught surgery in Aldersgate Street school of medicine, London : assistant-surgeon, 1827, lecturer on anatomy, 1843–65, and surgeon, 1854–64, at St. Bartholomew's Hospital, London ; F.R.S., 1837 ; professor of human anatomy to College of Surgeons, 1852, president, 1863 ; president of Medical and Chirurgical Society, 1859 ;

C.B. for services as chairman of committee on contagious diseases : published ' Operative Surgery,' 1851, and ' Hysteria,' 1867. [lii. 340]

SKEYNE, GILBERT (1522 ?–1599), physician ; M.A. and M.D. King's College, Aberdeen ; professor of medicine at King's College, Aberdeen, 1556 ; doctor of medicine to James VI, 1581 ; his ' Breve Descriptioun of the Pest,' 1568 (reprinted, 1860), the earliest Scottish medical work. [lii. 341]

SKINNER. [See also SKYNNER.]

SKINNER, JAMES (1778–1841), commander of Skinner's horse : served in the Mahratta army ; joined English, 1803, and distinguished himself against Holkar, the Pindarees, and (1825) at the storming of Bhurtpore ; created C.B., 1828, and received grants of land from Indian government ; built St. James's Church, Delhi, in fulfilment of a vow ; died at Hansi. [lii. 342]

SKINNER, JAMES (1818–1881), theological writer, hymn-writer, and friend of Pusey : son of John Skinner [q. v.], dean of Dunkeld ; B.A., 1836, and M.A., 1840, Marischal College, Aberdeen, and fellow ; foundation scholar (1833) and fellow of Durham University ; senior curate of St. Barnabas, Pimlico, London, 1851–5 ; organised E.C.U., 1859 ; incumbent of Newland, 1861–77 ; published ' Daily Service Hymnal,' 1864, ' Synopsis of Moral and Ascetical Theology,' posthumously, 1882, and other works. [lii. 343]

SKINNER, JOHN (1721–1807), song-writer : episcopalian minister of Longside, Aberdeenshire, 1742 ; imprisoned for preaching, 1753 ; corresponded with Burns, who secured his best songs for Johnson's ' Musical Museum ' ; wrote ' Tullochgorum,' ' Ewie wi' the Crookit Horn,' and other favourites ; published also ' Ecclesiastical History of Scotland ' (1788) ; his ' Songs and Poems ' edited by H. G. Reid, 1859. [lii. 343]

SKINNER, JOHN (1744–1816), bishop of Aberdeen ; son of John Skinner (1721–1807) [q. v.]; studied at Marischal College, Aberdeen ; episcopalian minister in Aberdeenshire : coadjutor to Bishop Kilgour, 1782 ; bishop of Aberdeen, 1786–1816 (primus, 1788) : obtained removal of penal restrictions on Scottish episcopal church (1792) and effected union with it of Scottish Anglican congregations (1804) : published theological treatises and ' Theological Works,' with life of his father. [lii. 344]

SKINNER, JOHN (1772–1839), antiquary : M.A. Trinity College, Oxford, 1797 ; incumbent of Camerton, 1800–39 : bequeathed to British Museum ninety-eight manuscript volumes of travels and researches with watercolour drawings ; committed suicide. [lii. 346]

SKINNER, JOHN (1769–1841), dean of Dunkeld ; studied at Marischal College, Aberdeen ; published ' Annals of Scottish Episcopacy, 1788–1816' (1818) ; son of John Skinner (1744–1816) [q. v.] [lii. 346]

SKINNER, JOHN EDWIN HILARY (1829–1894), special correspondent of ' Daily News' ; LL.D. London, 1861 : barrister, Lincoln's Inn, 1861 : reported for the ' Daily News' Danish war, Austro-Prussian campaign, and Franco-German war ; advocated independence of Canada and cession of Crete to Greece ; assistant-commissioner in Cyprus, 1881 : died in Algeria. [lii. 346]

SKINNER, MATTHEW (1689–1749), serjeant-at-law : great-grandson of Robert Skinner [q. v.] ; of Westminster School and Christ Church, Oxford : called from Lincoln's Inn, 1716 : recorder of Oxford, 1721, and M.P., 1734–8 ; chief-justice of Chester, 1738–49 ; appeared for crown against rebels, 1746 : published his father's (Robert Skinner's) ' Reports,' 1728. [lii. 347]

SKINNER, ROBERT (1591–1670), successively bishop of Bristol, Oxford, and Worcester : fellow of Trinity College, Oxford, 1613 ; M.A., 1614 ; D.D. by diploma. 1636 ; rector of Pitsford and chaplain in ordinary, 1628, of Launton, 1631 ; bishop of Bristol, 1636–41, of Oxford, 1641–63, and of Worcester, 1663–70 ; committed to the Tower of London for protest, 1641 : sequestered during Commonwealth, but licensed to preach, and conferred orders. [lii. 347]

SKINNER, STEPHEN (1623–1667), Lincoln physician and author of ' Etymologicon Linguæ Anglicanæ' (printed, 1671) : M.A. Christ Church, Oxford, 1646 ; M.D. of Heidelberg, 1654 ; lived much on the continent. [lii. 348]

SKINNER or **SKYNNER**, THOMAS (1629 ?–1679), Colchester physician and historical writer; of St. John's College, Cambridge; M.D. St. John's College, Oxford, 1672; continued Bates's 'Elenchi Motuum Nuperorum' (part iii, 1676) and compiled 'Life of General Monk' (printed, 1723). [lii. 348]

SKINNER, THOMAS (1800 ?–1843), soldier and author; commanded 31st foot in Afghanistan, 1842–3, and was made C.B. and brevet lieutenant-colonel, 1842; published 'Excursions in India' (1832) and 'Adventures during a Journey Overland to India' (1836). [lii. 349]

SKINNER, THOMAS (1804–1877), engineer; grandson of William Skinner (1700–1780) [q. v.]; commissioner of public works and auditor-general in Ceylon; his 'Fifty Years in Ceylon' published, 1891. [lii. 349]

SKINNER, WILLIAM (1700–1780), chief engineer of Great Britain; employed at Gibraltar, 1724–46, including first siege (1727), and became chief engineer, 1741; as chief engineer of North Britain constructed Fort George or Arderseer (completed, 1759); reported on Irish fortifications, 1756; chief engineer of Great Britain, 1757–80; criticised adversely Tyrawley's works at Gibraltar, 1758, and made subsequent reports; lieutenant-general, 1770; his drawings in British Museum and at Chatham. [lii. 350]

SKINNER, WILLIAM (1778–1857), bishop of Aberdeen; son of John Skinner (1744–1816) [q.v.]; of Marischal College, Aberdeen, and Wadham College, Oxford; M.A. and D.D. Oxford, 1819; assisted his father at Aberdeen; bishop of Aberdeen, 1816–57; elected primus, 1841; excommunicated Sir William Dunbar for not following Scottish ritual, 1843. [lii. 351]

SKIP, JOHN (d. 1552), bishop of Hereford; of Gonville Hall, Cambridge (scholar, 1513, fellow, 1516, M.A., 1518, D.D., 1535, master, 1536–40); president of Physick Hostel, 1519–21; chaplain and almoner of Queen Anne Boleyn; canon of Westminster, 1535; archdeacon of Suffolk, 1536, of Dorset, 1539; bishop of Hereford, 1539–1552; protested against first prayer book of Edward VI. [lii. 352]

SKIPPE or **SKIPP**, JOHN (1742 ?–1796 ?) amateur artist; of Merton College, Oxford. [lii. 353]

SKIPPON, PHILIP (d. 1660), soldier; served under Sir Horace Vere in the Palatinate and Netherlands, being wounded at Breda, 1625 and 1637; admitted to artillery company, 1639; named commander of city trained bands and of parliamentary guard, 1642; served under Essex as 'sergeant-major-general' at siege of Reading, relief of Gloucester, in Cornwall, and at first and second battles of Newbury, 1642–4; as sergeant-major-general under Fairfax severely wounded at Naseby; directed siege of Oxford, 1645; escorted convoy to Scots. 1646; appointed marshal-general of expedition to Ireland, 1647; as M.P. for Barnstaple presented letter of 'agitators' to parliament; attempted to mediate between army and parliament; commander of London militia, 1648; member of first, second, third, and fifth republican councils of state and of both Cromwellian councils; major-general of London district; M.P., Lyme, 1654 and 1656; member of Cromwell's House of Lords, 1657; reappointed to London command by restored parliament; published three devotional works for soldiers. [lii. 353]

SKIPWITH, SIR WILLIAM DE (fl. 1380), judge; said to have been first reader at Gray's Inn; king's serjeant, 1354; judge of common pleas, 1359; chief-baron, 1362–5; removed for misconduct, but appointed chief-justice of king's bench in Ireland, 1370, and restored to English judgeship, 1376; frequently employed as trier of parliamentary petitions and other judicial work under Richard II; supported lords appellant. [lii. 356]

SKIRLAW, WALTER (d. 1406), bishop successively of Lichfield, Bath. and Durham; graduated M.A. and LL.D. at Oxford; archdeacon of East Riding of Yorkshire; canon of Beverley; dean of St. Martin's-le-Grand, London; went on diplomatic mission to Italy, 1381–3; keeper of the privy seal, 1384; provided to see of Lichfield, 1385, but translated to Bath and Wells before enthronement; bishop of Durham, 1388–1406; employed in negotiations with France, Flanders, and Scotland under Richard II; chief plenipotentiary of Henry IV in France; built chapel at Swine, tower and chapter-house at Howden, bridges

over Tees and Wear; contributed largely to works at Durham and York; endowed fellowships at University College, Oxford. [lii. 357]

SKIRVING, ADAM (1719–1803), Jacobite song-writer. [lii. 358]

SKIRVING, ARCHIBALD (1749–1819), Scottish portrait-painter; son of Adam Skirving [q. v.]; best known by crayon of Burns. [lii. 359]

SKOGAN, JOHN (fl. 1480). [See SCOGAN.]

SKOT. [See SCOTT.]

SKRINE, HENRY (1755–1803), author of 'Three Tours in North of England and in Scotland' (1795) and other books of travel. [lii. 359]

SKUISH or **SKEWES**, JOHN (d. 1544), author of 'Brevyat of a Cronacle made by Mathewe Paris' (MS.); of Lincoln's Inn; employed by Wolsey; owned property in Cornwall. [lii. 359]

SKYNNER, SIR JOHN (1724 ?–1805), chief-baron of the exchequer; of Westminster School and Christ Church, Oxford; B.C.L., 1751; barrister, Lincoln's Inn, 1748; K.C. and attorney-general of duchy of Lancaster, 1771; M.P., Woodstock, 1771–7; second judge on Chester circuit, 1772; recorder of Oxford, 1776; chief-baron, 1777–86; privy councillor, 1787. [lii. 360]

SKYNNER, LANCELOT (1766 ?–1799), captain in the navy; commanded the Beaulieu at reduction of St. Lucia, 1796; lost in Lutine while convoying treasure from Yarmouth to the Texel. [lii. 361]

SLACK, HENRY JAMES (1818–1896), author and journalist; proprietor and editor of 'Atlas,' 1852; edited 'Intellectual Observer' and 'Student' from 1862; president of Sunday League; secretary and president (1878) of Microscopical Society; published 'Marvels of Pond Life,' 1861, and 'Ministry of the Beautiful,' 1850; joint-editor of 'Memorial edition' of works of William Johnson Fox [q. v.] [lii. 361]

SLADE, SIR ADOLPHUS (1804–1877), vice-admiral and traveller; son of Sir John Slade [q. v.]; present at Navarino, 1827; head of Turkish navy as Mushaver Pasha, 1839–66; K.C.B., 1858; vice-admiral, 1873; published 'Records of Travel in Turkey, Greece, &c.,' 1833, 'Turkey, Greece, and Malta,' 1837, 'Travels in Germany and Russia,' 1840, and 'Turkey and the Crimean War,' 1867. [lii. 362]

SLADE, FELIX (1790–1868), founder of professorships of fine art at Oxford, Cambridge, and London; bequeathed to British Museum valuable collections of glass, engravings, and other articles of vertu. [lii. 362]

SLADE, JAMES (1783–1860), divine and author; fellow of Emmanuel College, Cambridge (ninth wrangler, 1804); examining chaplain to George Henry Law [q. v.]; king's preacher for county of Lancaster; prebendary of Chester, 1816; vicar of Bolton-le-Moors, 1817–56; advocate of church reform; published 'Annotations on the Epistles,' 1816, and devotional and educational works. [lii. 363]

SLADE, SIR JOHN, first baronet (1762–1859), general; commanded hussar brigade under Sir John Moore, 1808, and brigade of dragoons in Peninsula, 1809–13; beaten by Lallemand at Llera, 1812; created baronet, 1831; general, 1837. [lii. 364]

SLADE, MATTHEW (1569–1628 ?), divine and friend of Casaubon; B.A. St. Alban Hall, Oxford, 1589; elder of Brownist Church at Amsterdam, and rector of the Academy; published work against Conrad Vorstius, 1612–1614. [lii. 365]

SLADE, MATTHEW (1628–1689), author of 'Dissertatio epistolica de Generatione Animalium contra Harveium' (1666); grandson of Matthew Slade (1569–1628 ?) [q. v.] [lii. 365]

SLADE, WILLIAM (fl. 1380), philosopher; monk of Buckfastleigh. [lii. 365]

SLADEN, SIR CHARLES (1816–1884), Australian statesman; of Ripple Park, Kent; educated at Shrewsbury School and Trinity Hall, Cambridge; B.A., 1837; LL.D., 1867; settled at Geelong, Victoria, 1842; treasurer and member of legislative council, 1854; member of House of Assembly and treasurer in first ministry of responsible government, 1857; led conservative party in legislative council, 1864-8; premier in minority, 1868; opposed Graham Berry's administration, 1876-80; K.C.M.G., 1875. [lii. 365]

SLADEN, SIR EDWARD BOSC (1827-1890), Indian officer; served in second Burmese war, 1852-3, and operations against Yun-za-lin rebels, 1856-7; with Madras fusiliers in mutiny; as agent to chief commissioner at Mandalay, saved Europeans in disturbances of 1866, and negotiated commercial treaty, 1867; undertook political mission to Chinese frontier, 1868; commissioner of Arakan, 1876-85; knighted, 1886. [lii. 366]

SLANE, PHILIP OF (d. 1326), bishop of Cork; bishop, 1321; author of abridgment of 'Topographia Hiberniæ.' [lii. 367]

SLANEY, ROBERT AGLIONBY (1792-1862), advocate of rural and economic reform; studied at Trinity College, Cambridge; barrister, Lincoln's Inn, 1817; M.P., Shrewsbury, 1826-35, 1837-41, and 1847-62; chairman of committees on education (1838) and health of town poor (1840); commissioner on health of towns, 1843-6; high sheriff of Shropshire, 1854; died from effects of accident at International Exhibition. [lii. 367]

SLANNING, SIR NICHOLAS (1606-1643), royalist; knighted, 1632; served in first Scottish war; M.P. for Plympton in Short parliament and Penrhyn in Long parliament; voted against Strafford's attainder; distinguished as general of ordnance in army of Sir Ralph Hopton [q. v.]; mortally wounded at storming of Bristol. [lii. 368]

SLARE or **SLEAR**, FREDERICK (1647?-1727), physician and chemist; showed experiments on spermatozoa before Royal Society, 1679, and was elected fellow, 1680; M.D. Oxford, 1680; member of council of Royal Society and of College of Physicians; showed experiments on phosphorus; published 'Experiments . . . upon Oriental and Bezoar-Stones,' 1715, disproving miraculous virtues of animal calculi, and 'Account of the Pyrmont Waters,' 1717; defended inoculation. [lii. 369]

SLATE, RICHARD (1787-1867), independent minister at Stand and Preston; published 'Select Nonconformists' Remains' (1814), 'Brief History of Lancashire Congregational Union' (1840). [lii. 370]

SLATER. [See also SCLATER.]

SLATER, SAMUEL (d. 1704), nonconformist; M.A. Emmanuel College, Cambridge, 1658; ejected from Suffolk benefices, 1662; succeeded Stephen Charnock [q. v.] as minister in Crosby Square, London, 1680; published 'Poems,' 1679. [lii. 370]

SLATTERY, MICHAEL (1785-1857), Roman catholic archbishop of Cashel; M.A. Trinity College, Dublin; professor of philosophy at Carlow College, 1809-15; president of Maynooth, 1833; archbishop of Cashel, 1834-1857; opposed Peel's educational proposals of 1845. [lii. 371]

SLATYER or **SLATER**, WILLIAM (1587-1647), divine; M.A. and fellow of Brasenose College, Oxford, 1611; D.D., 1623; treasurer of St. David's Cathedral, 1616; rector of Romney and Otterden; reprimanded by high commission in connection with 'Psalmes or Songs of Zion,' 1630; published also elegies on Anne of Denmark, and 'History of Great Britain in Latin and English Verse,' 1621, and the Psalms with tunes, 1643. [lii. 371]

SLAUGHTER, EDWARD (1655-1729), hebraist; rector of English (jesuit) College, Liège; published Hebrew grammar, 1699. [lii. 372]

SLAUGHTER, STEPHEN (d. 1765), portrait-painter and keeper of the royal collection of pictures. [lii. 372]

SLEATH, JOHN (1767-1847), high master of St. Paul's School, London; of Rugby, and Lincoln and Wadham colleges, Oxford; M.A., 1793; D.D., 1814; assistant-master at Rugby, 1787; high master of St. Paul's School, London, 1814-37; F.S.A., 1815; F.R.S., 1820; chaplain in ordinary, 1825; sub-dean of Chapel Royal, London, 1833. [lii. 372]

SLEEMAN, SIR WILLIAM HENRY (1788-1856), Indian official and major-general; served in Nepal war, 1814-16; superintended suppression of Thuggi and dacoity, 1835-41; political resident in Gwalior, 1843-9; resident at Lucknow, 1849-54; died on homeward

voyage; published 'Rambles and Recollections of an Indian Official,' 1844, a vocabulary of Thug language and other works. [lii. 373]

SLEIGH, WILLIAM CAMPBELL (1818-1887), serjeant-at-law; of St. Mary Hall, Oxford; barrister, Middle Temple, 1846; held first brief for Arthur Orton [q. v.] in civil action, 1871; leading counsel to Bank; practised at Melbourne bar, 1877-86. [lii. 374]

SLEZER, JOHN (d. 1714), designer of 'Theatrum Scotiæ' (1693; ed. Dr. Jamieson, 1874); came to Scotland from Holland, 1669; patronised by Charles II and Duke of York; entrusted with superintendence of ordnance; sent to Holland for guns and gunners, 1680; captain of Artillery Company, 1690; tax levied for continuation of his 'Theatrum.' [lii. 374]

SLINGSBY, GUILFORD (1610-1643), secretary to Strafford and vice-admiral of Munster; mortally wounded at Guisborough; brother of Sir Robert Slingsby [q. v.] [lii. 378]

SLINGSBY, SIR HENRY (1602-1658), royalist; created Nova Scotia baronet, 1638; served under Lord Holland against Scots, 1639; as M.P. for Knaresborough voted against Strafford's attainder, but supported proposal to deprive bishops of peerage; served under Newcastle, 1643-4; joined Charles I at Oxford, and accompanied him after Naseby; at surrender of Newark, 1646; refused oaths to Commonwealth; executed on Tower Hill for tampering with officers of Hull garrison while imprisoned there; his 'Diary' (1638-48) published by Sir Walter Scott (abbreviated), 1806; edited with additions by Rev. D. Parsons, 1836. [lii. 375]

SLINGSBY, MARY, LADY SLINGSBY (d. 1694), actress; appeared as Mrs. Lee at Dorset Garden, London, 1672-81, playing Queen Margaret in Crowne's adaptation of Henry VI, and leading parts in contemporary pieces; married (probably) Sir Charles Slingsby, second baronet (nephew of Sir Robert); as Lady Slingsby at Theatre Royal and Dorset Garden, 1682-5. [lii. 377]

SLINGSBY, SIR ROBERT (1611-1661), comptroller of the navy; cousin of Sir Henry Slingsby [q. v.]; commanded squadron in Channel, 1640-2; imprisoned as royalist, 1642; undertook mission to Paris and Amsterdam, 1644; created a baronet at Restoration; comptroller of the navy, 1660-1; his 'Discourse upon the Past and Present State of His Majesty's Navy' printed, 1801 and 1896. [lii. 378]

SLOANE, SIR HANS, first baronet (1660-1753), physician; studied at Paris and Montpellier; M.D. Orange, 1683; F.R.S., 1685; lived in house of Thomas Sydenham [q. v.]; physician to governor of Jamaica, 1687-9; as secretary of Royal Society, 1693-1712, revived 'Transactions'; president, 1727-41; foreign member of Academy of Sciences at Paris, St. Petersburg, and Madrid; president of Royal College of Physicians, 1719-35; attended Queen Anne; created baronet, 1716; first physician to George II, 1727, to Christ's Hospital, 1694-1730; purchased manor of Chelsea, 1712, and founded Botanic Garden, 1721; published catalogue (Latin) of Jamaica plants (1696), and 'Voyage to Islands of Madera, Barbadoes, Nieves, St. Christopher's and Jamaica' (1707, 1725); monument to him in Chelsea churchyard; his collections purchased by the nation and placed in Montague House, 1754 (afterwards the British Museum). [lii. 379]

SLOPER, EDWARD HUGH LINDSAY (1826-1887), pianoforte teacher and composer. [lii. 380]

SMALBROKE, RICHARD (1672-1749), bishop successively of St. Davids and of Lichfield and Coventry; demy and fellow (1698) of Magdalen College, Oxford; M.A., 1695; D.D., 1708; chaplain to Archbishop Tenison and rector of Hadleigh, 1709; canon of Hereford, 1710; last treasurer of Llandaff, 1712; rector of Withington, 1716; bishop of St. Davids, 1726-31, of Lichfield and Coventry 1731-49; published controversial treatises against William Whiston [q. v.] and Thomas Woolson [q. v.] [lii. 380]

SMALL, JOHN (1726-1796), major-general and lieutenant-governor of Guernsey; served under Amherst in Canada, 1757-9; raised highlanders in Nova Scotia, 1775; commanded battalion of engineers against Americans, 1775-82; lieutenant-governor of Guernsey, 1793; major-general, 1794. [lii. 382]

SMALL, JOHN (1828–1886), librarian of Edinburgh University and Edinburgh College of Physicians ; M.A. Edinburgh, 1847 ; hon. LL.D., 1886 ; president of Library Association, 1880 ; edited 'English Metrical Homilies,' 1862, works of Gavin Douglas, 1874, Sir David Lyndesay's 'Monarchie,' 1865–6, Dunbar's Poems, 1884–92, Laing's 'Remains of Early Scottish Poetry,' 1884–92 ; also published biographical and historical works.   [lii. 382]

SMALLE, PETER (*fl.* 1596–1615), author of 'Mans May or a Moneths minde' (1615) : B.C.L. St. John's College, Oxford, 1602 ; rector of Pinnock, 1604.   [lii. 382]

SMALLWOOD, CHARLES (1812–1872), professor of meteorology at Montreal ; professor, 1858–72.   [lii. 383]

SMALRIDGE, GEORGE (1663–1719), bishop of Bristol and dean of Christ Church, Oxford . educated at Lichfield, and afterwards at Westminster School, at expense of Elias Ashmole [q. v.] ; as tutor of Christ Church, Oxford, issued 'Auctio Davisiana,' 1689 ; M.A., 1689 ; D.D., 1701; prebendary of Lichfield, 1693 ; one of the writers against Bentley's 'Dissertation on the Phalaris Letters,' his share being an attempt to prove that the dissertation was not written by Bentley, 1698 ; deputy to regius professor of divinity at Oxford, 1700–7 ; chaplain to Queen Anne, 1710 ; canon of Christ Church, Oxford. 1711 ; dean of Carlisle, 1711–13 ; dean of Christ Church, 1713 ; bishop of Bristol, 1714–19 ; refused to sign declaration against James Edward, the Old Pretender, and was dismissed from lord almonership ; the 'Favonius' of the 'Tatler'; his sermons praised by Dr. Johnson.   [lii. 383]

SMALWOODE, JOHN (*d.* 1520). [See WINCHCOMBE.]

SMART, BENJAMIN HUMPHREY (1786 ?–1872), writer on elocution and metaphysics.   [lii. 385]

SMART, CHRISTOPHER (1722–1771), poet ; educated at Durham school and Cambridge ; B.A., 1742 ; fellow of Pembroke College, Cambridge, 1745 ; won the Seaton'an prize, 1750–3 and 1755 ; contributed to 'The Student'; introduced by Burney to John Newbery [q. v.], for whom he conducted 'The Midwife, or Old Woman's Magazine,' 1751–3, and other periodicals ; his 'Poems on Several Occasions,' including 'The Hop Garden,' issued by Newbery, 1752 ; published the 'Hilliad' against 'Sir' John Hill (1716 ?–1775) [q. v.], 1753 ; prose version of Horace, 1756 ; co-editor of 'Universal Visiter,' 1756–9 ; benefit performance given for him by Garrick, 1759 ; twice immured in a madhouse ; his 'Song to David' first issued, 17 3 ; visited by Dr. Johnson ; produced libretto 'Hannah,' 1764, metrical versions of Phædrus and of the Psalms, 1765 ; lived in last years and died within rules of King's Bench ; collected poems (omitting 'Song of David'), issued, 1791.   [lii. 386]

SMART, SIR GEORGE THOMAS (1776–1867), musician and orchestral conductor ; chorister in Chapel Royal, London ; sang at first Handel commemoration, Westminster (1784), and conducted the last (1834) ; knighted in Dublin, 1811 ; original member of Philharmonic Society ; produced in England Beethoven's 'Mount of Olives,' 1814, Mendelssohn's 'St. Paul,' 1836 ; joint-organist of Chapel Royal, London, 1822 ; as musical director at Covent Garden, London, produced Weber's 'Oberon' ; conducted music at funeral of George IV and coronations of William IV and Queen Victoria ; composed church music and glees ; edited Gibbons's first set of madrigals and Handel's Dettingen 'Te Deum.'   [lii. 389]

SMART, HENRY (1778–1823), violinist ; brother of Sir George Thomas Smart [q. v.]   [lii. 390]

SMART, HENRY HAWLEY (1833–1893), novelist ; served in 1st regiment foot in Crimea and Indian mutiny ; with 17th in Canada, 1858–64 ; published (1869–93) numerous novels excelling in racing, hunting, and military incidents.   [lii. 391]

SMART, HENRY THOMAS (1813–1879), organist and composer ; son of Henry Smart [q. v.] ; designed many organs ; composed organ music, anthems, part-songs, a cantata ; granted civil list pension.   [lii. 390]

SMART, JOHN (1741–1811), miniature-painter ; friend of Cosway ; exhibited with Society of Artists, 1762–83 (vice-president, 1783) ; practised in India, 1784–97 ; afterwards exhibited at Royal Academy.   [lii. 391]

SMART, PETER (1569–1652 ?), puritan divine : of Westminster School and Broadgates Hall, Oxford : M.A., 1595 ; master of Durham school, 1598 ; chaplain to Bishop William James (1542–1617) [q. v.] : master of St. Edmund's Hospital, Gateshead ; prebendary of Durham : deprived, fined, and imprisoned four years for sermon (1628) against ritual in the cathedral ; restored by Long parliament ; took the covenant, 1643 ; gave evidence at Laud's trial ; obtained sequestered livings ; published puritan tracts.   [lii. 392]

SMEATON, JOHN (1724–1792), civil engineer ; as a boy made models of fire engines and lathes : educated at Leeds grammar school : elected F.R.S., 1753 ; awarded gold medal for 'Experimental Enquiry concerning the Natural Powers of Wind and Water to Turn Mills,' 1759 ; studied canal and harbour systems of Holland, 1754 ; constructed third Eddystone lighthouse, 1756–9 ; built arched bridges at Perth, Banff, and Coldstream ; made Forth and Clyde canal : founded Smeatonian Club, 1771 ; published account of Eddystone Lighthouse, 1792.   [lii. 393]

SMEDLEY, EDWARD (1788–1836), author : of Westminster School and Trinity College, Cambridge ; M.A., 1812 ; fellow of Sidney Sussex College, Cambridge, 1812 ; Seatonian prizeman, 1813, 1814, 1827, 1828 ; preacher at St. James's, Tottenham Court Road : prebendary of Lincoln, 1829 ; edited 'Encyclopædia Metropolitana' ; published 'Religio Clerici,' 1821, 'Sketches from Venetian History,' 1831–2, 'History of Reformed Religion in France,' 1832–4, 'History of France,' 1836, and prize poems. His poems collected, 1837.   [lii. 395]

SMEDLEY, FRANCIS EDWARD (1818–1864), novelist ; cripple from childhood ; his 'Frank Fairlegh' (1850) originally contributed anonymously to Sharpe's 'London Magazine' : published also 'Lewis Arundel' (1852) from same magazine, which he edited for two years : edited three numbers of 'George Cruikshank's Magazine' ; published 'Harry Coverdale's Courtship,' and with Edmund Yates 'Mirth and Metre,' 1855.   [lii. 396]

SMEDLEY, JONATHAN (*fl.* 1689–1729), dean of Clogher ; M.A. Trinity College, Dublin, 1698 : dean of Killala, 1718–24, of Clogher, 1724–7 : published whig pamphlets and verses : wrote pasquinades against Swift and Pope, to which they replied ; left Ireland for Madras, 1729.   [lii. 397]

SMEE, ALFRED (1818–1877), surgeon and metallurgist : of St. Paul's School and King's College, London ; appointed surgeon to Bank of England, 1841, to Aldersgate Street Dispensary, London, 1842, and to Central London Ophthalmic Institution ; awarded Isis medal of Society of Arts for his battery ; F.R.S., 1841 ; initiated educat'onal lectures of London Institution ; invented 'gum and chalk' splints ; published 'Elements of Electro-Metallurgy,' 1840, 'Elements of Electro-Biology,' 1849, 'My Garden ; its Plan and Culture,' 1872, and medical works.   [lii. 398]

SMEETON, GEORGE (*fl.* 1800–1828), printer and compiler : issued 'Reprints of Rare and Curious Tracts relating to English History,' 1820, 'Biographica Cur'osa,' 1822, 'Doings in London,' 1828.   [lii. 399]

SMELLIE, WILLIAM (1697–1763), man-midwife : friend of Dr. William Cullen [q. v.] and of Smollett : came to London from Lanark, 1739, and acquired large practice ; taught midwifery and published obstetrical treatises ; hon. M.D. Glasgow, 1745.   [lii. 399]

SMELLIE, WILLIAM (1740–1795), Edinburgh printer, naturalist, and antiquary : printed and contributed to first edition of 'Encyclopædia Britannica,' 1771 ; secretary of Newtonian Club, 1778, and of Scottish Antiquaries' Society, 1793 (original member and keeper of natural history museum) : noticed in Burns's 'Crochallan Fencibles' ; published an account of Scottish Antiquarian Society (1782–4), 'The Philosophy of Natural History' (1790–9), posthumous lives of Lord Kames, Hume, Adam Smith, and J. Gregory, M.D., and an edition of Buffon.   [lii. 400]

SMELT, LEONARD (1719 ?–1800), captain in royal engineers and sub-governor to George, prince of Wales and Prince Frederick ; saw service as engineer at Dettingen, Fontenoy, and in Scotland : reported on defences of Newfoundland, 1751 ; had charge of northern military district of England, 1757 ; deputy-governor to royal princes, 1771–1781 ; deputy-ranger of Richmond Park ; favourite of George III and of literary society.   [lii. 401]

SMETHAM, JAMES (1821–1889), painter and essayist; befriended by Rossetti, Ruskin, and others. but unsuccessful as painter; produced etchings and drawings illustrative of his own conceptions; 'Literary Works' (containing memoir of Reynolds and study of Blake), issued 1893; his 'Letters' appeared 1891. [lii. 403]

SMETHURST, JOHN (1793–1859), unitarian minister of Moreton Hampstead; undertook mission to Ulster, 1821. [lii. 404]

SMETON, THOMAS (1536–1583), principal of Glasgow University; educated at Perth and St. Salvator's College, St. Andrews; friend of Andrew Melville at Paris; visited Rome and Geneva; in Paris on St. Bartholomew's Day, 1572; minister of Paisley Abbey and dean of faculty at Glasgow, 1577; moderator of general assembly, 1579 and 1583; principal of Glasgow University, 1580–3: published reply to the work of Archibald Hamilton (d. 1593) [q. v.], 'De Confusione apud Scotos' with life of Knox. [lii. 404]

SMIBERT or **SMYBERT**, JOHN (1684–1751), portrait-painter; worked in Italy, 1717–20; accompanied Bishop (then dean) Berkeley to America, 1728, and painted a group of the expedition; settled at Boston, U.S.A., and painted many portraits there. [lii. 405]

SMIBERT, THOMAS (1810–1854), author; edited and contributed to 'Chambers's Journal,' 1837–42; his 'Condé's Wife' acted at Edinburgh, 1842; published 'Clans of the Highlands' (1850), and lyrical poems (1851). [lii. 405]

SMIRKE, SIR EDWARD (1795–1875), lawyer and antiquary; third son of Robert Smirke [q. v.]; of St. John's College, Cambridge, and Middle Temple; M.A. 1820; recorder of Southampton, 1846–55; attorney-general to Albert Edward, prince of Wales, 1852; vice-warden of the stannaries of Cornwall and Devon, 1853–70; knighted, 1870; president of Royal Institution of Cornwall, 1861–3 and 1865–7; edited law reports and wrote on history of tin mines and procedure in stannaries court. [lii. 406]

SMIRKE, RICHARD (1778–1815), antiquarian draughtsman; brother of Sir Edward Smirke [q. v.] [lii. 407]

SMIRKE, ROBERT (1752–1845), painter; exhibited with Society of Artists and at the Academy, 1786–1813; R.A., 1793; painted for Boydell's 'Shakespeare Gallery' and Bowyer's 'History of England,' and designed many illustrations. [lii. 406]

SMIRKE, SIR ROBERT (1781–1867), architect; second son of Robert Smirke [q. v.]; studied in Italy, Greece, and Sicily, and published 'Specimens of Continental Architecture,' 1806; gained first prize for 'navy memorial,' 1817; designed British Museum and post-office (St. Martin's-le-Grand, London); rebuilt Covent Garden, London, 1809; erected library and dining hall, Inner Temple; restored York minster; R.A., 1811; treasurer, 1820–50; knighted, 1832. [lii. 407]

SMIRKE, SYDNEY (1798–1877), architect; brother of Sir Robert Smirke [q. v.]; completed restoration of Temple Church, London, 1841; built British Museum reading-room, 1854–7; twice restored Savoy Chapel, London; completed Burlington House exhibition galleries, London, 1870; R.A., 1859; professor of architecture, 1861–5; treasurer, 1871; founded Architects' Benevolent Society, 1852; published architectural works. [lii. 408]

SMITH. [See also SMYTH and SMYTHE.]

SMITH, AARON (d. 1697?), solicitor to the treasury; a whig plotter at the time of the Popish plot; arrested at the time of the Rye House plot, and not released till March 1688; appointed solicitor to treasury and public prosecutor, 1689; detected a more or less imaginary conspiracy in Lancashire, 1694; dismissed for malversation, 1696. [liii. 1]

SMITH, AARON (fl. 1823), seaman; charged with piracy in the West Indies, 1823, but his piratical acts shown to have been committed upon compulsion; published (1824) a 'Narrative' of his sufferings, and subsequently brought a charge of libel against a man who styled him a pirate, obtaining 10l. damages. [liii. 2]

SMITH, ADAM (1723–1790), political economist; studied at Glasgow University and as a Snell exhibitioner at Balliol College, Oxford; perhaps B.A., 1744; after some literary lectures at Kirkcaldy, was elected (1751) to chair of logic at Glasgow, and next year transferred to chair of moral philosophy, lecturing on theology, ethics, jurisprudence. and political institutions: appointed vice-rector, 1762: frequently visited Edinburgh and became intimate with Hume; published his 'Theory of the Moral Sentiments,' 1759; his lectures the means of his attaining a foreign tutorship to the Duke of Buccleuch; saw Hume, Turgot, and others in Paris, and Voltaire at Geneva; returned to London, 1766, and settled, 1767, in Kirkcaldy on a pension from the Duke of Buccleuch; acquired from the 'physiocrats' the perception that a 'scheme of distribution' was necessary, having previously worked out his theory upon the division of labour, money, prices, and differences of wages, and published (1776) his great book, 'The Wealth of Nations,' which originated the study of political economy as a separate science; his book recognised as a po itical as well as economic authority, being studied, among others, by Pitt; edited the autobiography of Hume, with an account of his last illness, 1777; elected lord rector of Glasgow University, 1787; member of Dr. Johnson's Club. [liii. 3]

SMITH, ALBERT RICHARD (1816–1860), author and lecturer; educated at Merchant Taylors' School, London; studied at Middlesex Hospital, began writing for 'Punch,' and (1842) sent 'The Adventures of Mr. Ledbury' to Bentley's; brought out 'Christopher Tadpole,' 1848; wrote a number of extravaganzas, and was well known for his entertainments at the Egyptian Hall—the 'Overland Mail,' 'Mont Blanc,' 1852, and 'China.' [liii. 10]

SMITH, ALEXANDER (fl. 1714–1726), biographer of highwaymen; called Captain Smith; wrote 'Lives of Highwaymen,' 1714, lives of celebrated beauties, 1715, and lives of 'Bayliffs,' Jonathan Wild, and others. [liii. 12]

SMITH, ALEXANDER (1684–1766), Roman catholic prelate; consecrated bishop of Mosinopolis in partibus infidelium, 1735; succeeded to the vicariate of the lowland district of Scotland, 1746. [liii. 13]

SMITH, ALEXANDER (1760?–1829). [See ADAMS, JOHN.]

SMITH, ALEXANDER (1830–1867), Scottish poet; a lace pattern designer in Glasgow; patronised by Gilfillan and George Henry Lewes; published in 1853 'Life Drama' and other poems, which made a sensation; satirised by Aytoun in 'Firmilian': published sonnets on the Crimean war with his friend Dobell, 1855, and 'Dreamthorp' (essays), 1863. [liii. 13]

SMITH, SIR ANDREW (1797–1872), director-general, army medical department; served at the Cape and in Natal, 1821–37; wrote on zoology of South Africa; director-general of the army and ordnance medical departments, 1853–8; blamed for his administration of medical department in the Crimea; K.C.B., 1859. [liii. 15]

SMITH, ANKER (1759–1819), engraver; became a famous engraver of small plates in line; A.R.A., 1797. [liii. 15]

SMITH, AQUILLA (1806–1890), Irish antiquary; studied at Trinity College, Dublin; M.D. honoris causa, Dublin, 1839; king's professor of materia medica and pharmacy in the school of physic, Dublin, 1864–81; collector of coins; wrote on archæological, numismatic, and medical subjects. [liii. 16]

SMITH, ARCHIBALD (1813–1872), mathematician; of Glasgow and Trinity College, Cambridge; senior wrangler, 1836; M.A., 1839; barrister, Lincoln's Inn, 1841; F.R.S., 1856; rewarded by government, 1872; wrote on the deviation of the compass. [liii. 16]

SMITH, ARTHUR W. W. (1825–1861), entertainer; managed entertainments for his brother Albert Richard Smith [q. v.], and also for Charles Dickens [q. v.] [liii. 16]

SMITH, AUGUSTUS JOHN (1804–1872), lessee of the Scilly isles; B.A. Christ Church, Oxford, 1826; obtained lease of islands under the crown, 1834, for ninety-nine years; largely rebuilt and reorganised industries at Scilly; M.P., Truro, 1857–65. [liii. 17]

SMITH, BARBARA LEIGH (1827–1891). [See BODICHON.]

SMITH, BENJAMIN (d. 1833), engraver; practised in the stipple manner of his master Bartolozzi. [liii. 18]

SMITH, BENJAMIN (1783–1860), politician; son of William Smith (1756–1835) [q. v.]; supported corn law repeal as M.P. for Norwich, 1838 and 1841–7   [liii. 150]

SMITH (formerly **SCHMIDT**), BERNARD (1630 ?–1708), called Father Smith; organ-builder; came from Halle in Charles II's time; built organ for Westminster Abbey and for Sheldonian Theatre at Oxford and Durham Cathedral; built also organ for St. Paul's, London, 1697, and for Trinity College, Cambridge.   [liii. 18]

SMITH, CHARLES (1715 ?–1762), Irish county historian; wrote histories of Down (1744), Waterford (1746), Cork (1750), and Kerry (1756), which were praised by Macaulay.   [liii. 20]

SMITH, CHARLES (1713–1777), writer on the corn trade; earned praise of Adam Smith by his treatise on the import and export laws.   [liii. 20]

SMITH, CHARLES (1749 ?–1824), painter; native of the Orkneys; painted in India, 1783 : published a 'Trip to Bengal' (musical entertainment), 1802.   [liii. 21]

SMITH, CHARLES (1786–1856), singer; chorister of Chapel Royal, London, 1796; became organist at the Welbeck Chapel and (1816) at Liverpool; wrote songs and operettas.   [liii. 21]

SMITH, SIR CHARLES FELIX (1786–1858), lieutenant-general; served as engineer in Spain, with distinction at Gibraltar, December 1811; served at Vittoria and in Wellington's army of occupation, 1815–18; in West Indies, 1823–37; as commanding engineer at Gibraltar, 1838–42, gaining K.C.B. for gallantry at St. Jean d'Acre; lieutenant-general, 1851, and colonel-commandant, royal engineers, 1856.   [liii. 21]

SMITH, CHARLES HAMILTON (1776–1859), soldier and writer on natural history; of Flemish origin; served in English army, 1797–1820; wrote military part of Coxe's 'Marlborough,' and many military and natural-history books.   [liii. 24]

SMITH, CHARLES HARRIOT (1792–1864), architect; became an authority on building-stone and ornamental stone-carving, and published 'Lithology,' 1842.   [liii. 25]

SMITH, CHARLES JOHN (1803–1838), engraver; executed plates for Stothard and John Gough Nichols [q. v.], 1829; F.S.A., 1837.   [liii. 26]

SMITH, CHARLES ROACH (1807–1890), antiquary; a great collector of, and authority on, Roman and British antiquities; sold a collection in 1856 to British Museum for 2,000l.; wrote largely for 'Archæologia' and 'Numismatic Chronicle' and edited 'Antiquarian Notes' for 'Gentleman's Magazine,' besides helping to found British Archæological Association in 1843, and publishing useful 'Collectanea.'   [liii. 26]

SMITH, CHARLOTTE (1749–1806), poetess and novelist; daughter of Nicholas Turner; married Richard Smith, a merchant, 1765, who became bankrupt; produced some successful novels, 'Emmeline,' 1788, 'Celestina,' 1792, 'Desmond,' 1792, 'The Old Manor House,' 1793, and 'Conversations introducing Poetry,' 1804.   [liii. 27]

SMITH, COLVIN (1795–1875), portrait-painter; studied at London and Rome; settled at Edinburgh, 1826; painted Scott, Jeffrey, and Macintosh, and exhibited at the Royal Scottish Academy.   [liii. 29]

SMITH, EDMUND (1672–1710), poet; son of Edmund Neale; adopted name of Smith from his guardian; of Westminster School and Christ Church, Oxford; M.A., 1696; expelled from Christ Church for lampooning Dr. Aldrich, 1705; adapted 'Phædra and Hippolitus' from Racine, 1707; wrote elegy on John Philips, 1708.   [liii. 30]

SMITH or **SMYTH**, EDWARD (1665–1720), bishop of Down and Connor; M.A. and fellow, 1684; D.D., 1696, and later vice-chancellor of Dublin University; chaplain to William III; consecrated bishop, 1699.   [liii. 31]

SMITH, EDWARD (1818 ?–1874), physician and medical writer; M.D. London, 1843; LL.B., 1848; F.R.C.S., 1851; studied physiological chemistry; made F.R.S., 1860; lecturer, Charing Cross Hospital, London, 1853; published medical works.   [liii. 31]

SMITH, ELIZABETH (1776–1806), oriental scholar; born near Durham; learned Hebrew and Syriac, 1796–9;

her 'Vocabulary, Hebrew, Arabic, and Persian,' printed, 1814.   [liii. 32]

SMITH, ERASMUS (1611–1691), educational benefactor; Turkey merchant; army contractor, 1650; obtained large grants of land in Tipperary, 1652; founded grammar schools and lectureships in Ireland.   [liii. 33]

SMITH, FRANCIS (*fl.* 1770), painter; born in Italy; exhibited oriental views at the Royal Academy, 1770–3.   [liii. 34]

SMITH, SIR FRANCIS PETTIT (1808–1874), inventor of screw-propeller for steamships; constructed a model quite independently of other experimenters in 1836; by his experiments on the Archimedes steamer in 1839 led the admiralty to construct the Rattler in 1841–3 with Smith's four-bladed screw; knighted, 1871.   [liii. 34]

SMITH, FREDERICK WILLIAM (*d.* 1835), sculptor; son of Anker Smith [q. v.]; modelled some fine groups, 1818–28.   [liii. 16]

SMITH, GABRIEL (*d.* 1783), engraver; engraved after Watteau, Boucher, and French school, 1765–80.   [liii. 36]

SMITH, GEORGE (1693–1756), nonjuring divine; of Durham; son of John Smith (1659–1715) [q. v.]; studied at Queen's College, Oxford, and Inner Temple; was a student of early English history and antiquities; completed his father's 'Bede,' 1722, and edited other learned works; consecrated nonjuring bishop, 1728.   [liii. 36]

SMITH, GEORGE (1713–1776), landscape-painter; studied under his brother William (1707–1764) [q. v.]; exhibited landscapes, 1760–70; patronised by Duke of Richmond.   [liii. 37]

SMITH, GEORGE (1797 ?–1850), captain in navy; invented a new method of sighting guns, and wrote professionally.   [liii. 38]

SMITH, GEORGE (1800–1868), historian and theologian; a Cornwall notability and keen antiquary; R.A.S. and F.S.A.; issued numerous religious and archæological volumes, including 'The Cassiterides,' 1863.   [liii. 38]

SMITH, GEORGE (1815–1871), bishop of Victoria; M.A. Magdalen Hall, Oxford, 1843; missionary to China; consecrated bishop of Victoria in Hongkong, 1847; wrote on consular cities of China and on Japan.   [liii. 39]

SMITH, GEORGE (1840–1876), Assyriologist; devoted his leisure as a bank-note engraver to studying Assyrian inscriptions at British Museum; encouraged by Rawlinson and Birch; deciphered the Chaldæan account of the deluge from Layard's tablets, 1872; made three great excavating expeditions to the site of Nineveh at the expense of the 'Daily Telegraph' and British Museum authorities, whose collection he vastly enriched; died near Aleppo, leaving valuable Assyriological works.   [liii. 39]

SMITH, GEORGE (1831–1895), philanthropist; started life as a brickmaker; educated himself; strenuously advocated the cause of women and children employed in brickworks, on canal boats, and in caravans; his agitation highly successful; wrote several books, and in 1885 received a grant from royal bounty.   [liii. 41]

SMITH, GEORGE (1824–1901), publisher, and founder and proprietor of the 'Dictionary of National Biography'; joined in 1838 the firm of Smith & Elder, publishers and East India agents, of 65 Cornhill, London, which his father had founded in partnership with Alexander Elder in 1816, soon after coming in youth to London from his native town of Elgin. In 1843 Smith took charge of some of the firm's publishing operations, and on his father's death in 1846 became sole head of the firm. Under his control the business quickly grew in both the India agency and publishing directions. The chief authors whose works he published in his early career were John Ruskin, Charlotte Brontë, whose 'Jane Eyre' he issued in 1848, and W. M. Thackeray, whose 'Esmond' he brought out in 1851. In 1853 he took a partner, H. S. King, and, after weathering the storm of the Indian Mutiny, started in 1859 'The Cornhill Magazine,' with Thackeray as editor, and numerous leading authors and artists as contributors. In 1865 Smith founded the 'Pall Mall Gazette,' a London evening newspaper of independent character and literary quality, which remained his property till 1880. In 1868 he dissolved partnership with King, leaving him to carry on the India agency branch of the old firm's business, and himself taking over the publishing branch, which he thenceforth conducted at 15 Waterloo Place, London, and soon extended in many ways, among others by the publication of medical books. His chief authors now included Robert Browning, Matthew Arnold, (Sir) Leslie Stephen, and Miss Thackeray (Mrs. Ritchie), all of whom were intimate personal friends. Meanwhile he engaged with great success in many mercantile ventures, including the purchase, with two others, in 1873, of the Apollinaris mineral water. In 1882 he gave proof of his public spirit by setting on foot the 'Dictionary of National Biography,' which was completed under the successive editors Sir Leslie Stephen and Mr Sidney Lee in sixty-three volumes (1885-1900), with three supplementary volumes (1901). Smith's portrait was painted by Mr. G. F. Watts, R.A., 1876, and posthumously by the Hon. John Collier, 1901. A tablet to his memory was placed by his friends in the crypt of St. Paul's Cathedral, 1902.   [Suppl. i. p. xi.]

SMITH, GEORGE CHARLES (1782-1863), 'boatswain Smith'; pressed into navy; served at Copenhagen, 1801; left navy, 1803; became a baptist pastor and devoted himself to open-air preaching to sailors and watermen; founded the first sailors' home, in 1828, in Wellclose Square, London, performing other missionary work both as a preacher and a pamphleteer.   [liii. 42]

SMITH, GERARD EDWARD (1804-1881), botanist and divine; of Merchant Taylors' School, London, and St. John's College, Oxford; B.A., 1829; produced a catalogue of rare phanerogamous plants, 1829; wrote on the flora of Derbyshire, and was the first to recognise several British plants.   [liii. 43]

SMITH, SIR HARRY GEORGE WAKELYN, first baronet (1787-1860), victor of Aliwal; served in South America, 1807, at Coruña, Fuentes d'Onoro, Ciudad Rodrigo, and Badajos, also in battles of 1812-14, and at Bladensburg and Waterloo; took a leading part in subduing the Kaffirs, 1836; went out to India as adjutant-general under Gough, 1842; served in Gwalior and Sikh campaigns, leading the charge against the Sikhs at Aliwal, 28 Jan. 1846, and commanding first division of infantry at Sobraon, 1846; made baronet and major-general, and in 1847 governor of the Cape; routed (1848) at Boom Plaatz the Boers under Pretorius, who resented extension of British territory, many of them subsequently crossing the Vaal and founding the Transvaal state; resisted the landing of convicts at the Cape, 1849; put down another Kaffir rebellion, 1850; his connection with South Africa, whence he returned in 1852, commemorated by the names of the towns of Harrismith, Ladysmith, Whittlesey his native town, and Aliwal.   [liii. 43]

SMITH, HENRY (1550?-1591), puritan divine; of Queens' College, Cambridge, and Lincoln College, Oxford; B.A. Oxford, 1579; became a great preacher at St. Clement Danes, where he was lecturer from 1587; known as 'silver-tongued Smith'; dedicated his collected sermons to Lord Burghley, who defended him when attacked by the bishop of London for his puritan inclinations.   [liii. 48]

SMITH, HENRY (1620-1668?), regicide; B.A. St. Mary Hall, Oxford, 1640; student of Lincoln's Inn, 1640; M.P., Leicestershire, 1640; signed Charles I's death-warrant, 1649; attainted, 1660, but respited; probably died in prison.   [liii. 49]

SMITH, HENRY JOHN STEPHEN (1826-1883), mathematician; son of a Dublin barrister; went to Rugby and won the Balliol scholarship (classical), 1844; fellow of Balliol College, Oxford, 1849; M.A., 1855; mathematical tutor at Balliol, though equally brilliant in classics; elected Savilian professor of geometry, 1860; F.R.S. and F.R.A.S., 1861; the greatest disciple of Gauss; elucidated the theory of numbers, his mathematical papers being collected in 1894.   [liii. 50]

SMITH, HORATIO ('Horace') (1779-1849), poet and author; brother of James Smith (1775-1839) [q. v.]; gained an introduction to the literary world through Richard Cumberland the dramatist, and fame in 1812 as joint-author with his brother James of 'Rejected Addresses,' his best parodies being those of Byron and Scott; subsequently wrote novels, including 'Brambletye House,' 1826 (imitation of Sir Walter Scott); published many other works: the 'Tin Trumpet' (a medley), 1836; aided Campbell on the 'New Monthly'; his 'Poetical Works' collected, 1846.   [liii. 53]

SMITH, HUGH (1736?-1789), medical writer; M.D. Leyden, 1755; compiled 'The Family Physician,' 1760.   [liii. 55]

SMITH, HUGH (d. 1790), medical writer; M.D. Edinburgh, 1755; L.R.C.P., 1762; wrote on 'Blood-letting,' 1761.   [liii. 55]

SMITH, HUMPHREY (d. 1663), quaker; joined the quakers, 1654; died in Winchester gaol, leaving 'Visions' and other tracts.   [liii. 55]

SMITH, JAMES (1605-1667), divine and poet; of Christ Church and Lincoln College, Oxford; D.D., 1661; chaplain to Earl of Holland; became archdeacon of Barnstaple and rector of Exminster, 1664; wrote verse, and, together with his correspondent, Sir John Mennes, was strongly represented in 'Wits' Recreations,' 1640, 'Musarum Deliciæ,' 1655, and 'Wit Restored,' 1658, a series of rather free anthologies.   [liii. 56]

SMITH, JAMES (1645-1711), Roman catholic prelate; D.D. Douay, 1680; elected president of Douay College, 1682; was one of four catholic vicars apostolic, 1687, bishop of 'Calliopolis,' 1688, and was spoken of for a cardinalate in 1700.   [liii. 57]

SMITH, JAMES (1775-1839), author and humorist; elder brother of Horatio Smith [q. v.]; succeeded his father as solicitor to board of ordnance, 1812; produced with his brother 'Rejected Addresses,' 1812, and 'Horace in London,' 1813; also wrote clever nonsense for Charles Mathews.   [liii. 57]

SMITH, JAMES (1789-1850), agricultural engineer; invented a reaping-machine, 1811; devised a system of deep ploughing and thorough draining for his farm at Deanston; wrote upon the 'subsoil plough,' 1831.   [liii. 58]

SMITH, JAMES, 'Smith of Jordanhill' (1782-1867), geologist and man of letters; merchant by profession; studied glacial questions; wrote on the 'Newer Pliocene,' 1862, and on the 'Voyage and Shipwreck of St. Paul,' 1848; an authority on ancient shipbuilding and navigation.   [liii. 59]

SMITH, JAMES (1805-1872), merchant; wrote largely, 1863-70, upon the 'Quadrature of the Circle,' a problem which he imagined he had solved.   [liii. 60]

SMITH, SIR JAMES EDWARD (1759-1828), botanist; studied at Edinburgh, and in 1784 purchased Linnean collections; founded Linnean Society, 1788; knighted, 1814; produced numerous botanical works of high value, including 'English Botany' (illustrated by Sowerby), 1790-1814, in 36 vols., and 'Introduction to Botany' and 'English Flora,' 1824-8.   [liii. 61]

SMITH, JAMES ELIMALET, 'Shepherd Smith' (1801-1857), divine and essayist; studied at Glasgow University; influenced by John Wroe, the Southcottian prophet, and by Robert Owen, for whom he lectured; started (1834) his own organ, 'The Shepherd'; became essayist to the new 'Family Herald,' 1843; published 'Divine Drama of History and Civilisation,' 1854.   [liii. 64]

SMITH, JAMES HICKS (1822-1881), barrister-at-law; son of Jeremiah Smith (1771-1854) [q. v.]; compiled 'Reminiscences' and antiquities of Manchester. [liii. 66]

SMITH or SMYTH, SIR JEREMIAH (d. 1675), admiral; adhered to Cromwell, 1653; fought in Dutch war, 1665, against Tromp.   [liii. 65]

SMITH, JEREMIAH (d. 1723), divine; wrote on 'Trinity' during Salters' Hall debates, 1719.   [liii. 65]

SMITH, JEREMIAH (1771-1854), master of Manchester grammar school; M.A. Hertford College, Oxford, 1797; D.D., 1811.   [liii. 65]

SMITH, JEREMIAH FINCH (1815-1895), prebendary of Lichfield; son of Jeremiah Smith (1771-1854) [q. v.]; edited 'Manchester School Register,' 1874.   [liii. 66]

SMITH or SMYTHE, SIR JOHN (1534?-1607), diplomatist and military writer; first cousin of Edward VI, through his mother; entered Queen Elizabeth's service, 1574; knighted, 1576; criticised Leicester's force at Tilbury, and wrote commending use of archery; was slighted by Queen Elizabeth; reported to Burghley for treasonable talk, and confined, 1596-8.   [liii. 66]

SMITH or SMYTH, JOHN (*d.* 1612), the Se-baptist; Fellow of Christ's College, Cambridge, and (1579) M.A.; wrote tracts in defence of baptist principles, and was known among English at Amsterdam as Se-baptist (self-baptiser); his religious views and tracts incoherent and distracted. [liii. 68]

SMITH, JOHN (1563-1616), divine; M.A. St. John's College, Oxford, 1585; B.D., 1591; fellow of his college; lecturer at St. Paul's Cathedral, 1592; wrote controversial tracts. [liii. 70]

SMITH, JOHN (1580-1631), soldier and colonist; of Willoughby; travelled in South-eastern Europe, 1601-5; set out with Virginia colonists in December 1606; said to have been rescued when taken prisoner by the Indians by the Indian princess Pocahontas [see ROLFE, JOHN], 1607; became head of colony, 1608, and explored coasts of Chesapeake; visited New England, 1614; later produced maps and pamphlets in London on behalf of American colonisation; buried in St. Sepulchre's, London. [liii. 70]

SMITH or SMYTH, JOHN (1567-1640), genealogist; steward of Berkeley family at Netley; wrote valuable lives of the first twenty-one lords of Berkeley, first edited, 1821. [liii. 73]

SMITH, SIR JOHN (1616-1644), royalist; fought in the Netherlands; joined royalist party in civil war; knighted on the field at Edgehill for saving the royal standard; killed at Cheriton. [liii. 73]

SMITH, JOHN (1618-1652), Cambridge Platonist; M.A. Emmanuel College, Cambridge, 1644; lectured at Queens' College, Cambridge; his select discourses published, 1660. [liii. 74]

SMITH, JOHN (*fl.* 1633-1670), writer on trade; privately sent to visit the Shetlands and report on their industries, 1633; wrote on British fisheries, husbandry and trade. [liii. 75]

SMITH, JOHN (1630-1679), physician; M.A. Brasenose College, Oxford, 1653; M.D., 1652; F.R.C.P.; published in 1366 a curious book on old age. [liii. 75]

SMITH, JOHN (*fl.* 1673-1680),'philomath'; wrote on clocks, 1675, oil-painting, 1676, the weather-glass, 1688, and hydropathy ('The Curiosities of Common Water,' 1722). [liii. 75]

SMITH, JOHN (1659-1715), divine; grandson of Matthew Smith (1589-1640) [q. v.]; educated at St. John's College, Cambridge; M.A., 1681; D.D., 1696; became treasurer of Durham, but spent much time at Cambridge studying for an edition of Bede (completed by his son, George Smith (1693-1756) [q. v.], in 1722). [liii. 76]

SMITH or SMYTH, JOHN (1662-1717), dramatist; M.A. Magdalen College, Oxford, 1686; usher at Magdalen College school, 1689-1717; published a comedy (1691) and burlesques. [liii. 76]

SMITH, JOHN (1655-1723), politician; of St. John's College, Oxford, and the Middle Temple; sat in parliament from 1678; M.P., Ludgershall, 1678-9, 1680-1, and 1688-9, Beeralston, 1681-5, Andover, 1695-1713, East Looe, 1715-23; as a stout whig, acting as whip for the party; elected speaker, 1705, for three years; chancellor of the exchequer, 1708-10; friend of Godolphin. [liii. 77]

SMITH, JOHN (1657-1726), judge; of Lincoln College, Oxford; barrister, Gray's Inn, 1684; became a baron of exchequer, 1702, and lord chief-baron of exchequer, 1708. [liii. 77]

SMITH, JOHN (1652?-1742), mezzotint engraver; engraver after Kneller, Lely, Dahl, and many classical painters; sold prints in Covent Garden, London. [liii. 78]

SMITH, JOHN (*fl.* 1747), author of 'Chronicon-Rusticum-Commerciale'; LL.B. Trinity Hall, Cambridge, 1725; settled in Lincolnshire; published 'Chronicon Rusticum-Commerciale, or Memoirs of Wool,' a standard work, 1747. [liii. 78]

SMITH, JOHN (1717-1764), painter; brother of George Smith (1713-1776) [q. v.]; executed landscapes, sometimes on same canvas with his brother. [liii. 37]

SMITH, JOHN (1747-1807), antiquary and Gaelic scholar; hon. D.D. Edinburgh, 1787; published 'Gaelic Antiquities,' 1780, 'Life of St. Columba' (translated from Cummin and Adamnan), 1798, and other works. [liii. 79]

SMITH, JOHN (1790-1824), missionary; went out to evangelise negroes of Demerara in 1817, and was arrested for refusing to take up arms against insurgent slaves, and died in prison. [liii. 79]

SMITH, JOHN (1749-1831), water-colour painter; known as ' Warwick Smith '; patronised by the Earl of Warwick; joined Water-colour Society, 1805; executed views in Italy and the Lakes. [liii. 80]

SMITH, SIR JOHN (1754-1837), general; served under Sir William Howe and Sir Henry Clinton in America, 1777-81; captured at Yorktown, 1781, but soon released; commanded artillery at St. Vincent and Trinidad, 1797, and under Duke of York in Dutch expedition, 1799; G.C.H., 1831; became colonel of horse artillery, 1833; general, 1837. [liii. 80]

SMITH, JOHN (1797-1861), musician; became vicar-choral of St. Patrick's, Dublin, 1819, and wrote cathedral music. [liii. 81]

SMITH, JOHN ABEL (1801-1871), banker and politician; M.A. Christ's College, Cambridge, 1827; M.P., Midhurst, 1830, Chichester, 1831-59, and 1863-8; took an active part in first Reform Bill. [liii. 82]

SMITH, JOHN CHALONER (1827-1895), author of ' British Mezzotinto Portraits '; B.A. Trinity College, Dublin, 1848; engineer of Irish railways, 1857-94; produced a notable catalogue of mezzotints with biographical notes, in four parts, 1878-84. [liii. 82]

SMITH, JOHN CHRISTOPHER (1712-1795), musician; born at Anspach; a pupil of Handel, for whom he acted as amanuensis; appointed first organist of Foundling Hospital, 1750; carried on Handel's oratorios until 1774; presented Handel's scores and harpsichord to George III. [liii. 82]

SMITH, JOHN GORDON (1792-1833), professor of medical jurisprudence; graduated in medicine at Edinburgh, 1810; wrote on forensic medicine, and lectured on it as professor at London University, but had no pupils; resigned and died in a debtor's prison. [liii. 83]

SMITH, SIR JOHN MARK FREDERICK (1790-1874), general; served under Sir John Stewart in South Italy, 1809; commanding royal engineer of London district, 1830; knighted, 1831; inspector-general of railways, 1840; M.P., Chatham, 1857-68; colonel commandant, royal engineers, 1860; general, 1863; translated Marmont's 'Present State of the Turkish Empire,' 1839. [liii. 84]

SMITH, JOHN ORRIN (1799-1843), wood-engraver; became a very delicate wood-engraver; illustrated Curmer's 'Paul et Virginie,' 1835, Wordsworth's 'Greece,' 1840, and other works. [liii. 85]

SMITH, JOHN PRINCE (1774?-1822), law reporter; barrister, Gray's Inn, 1801; edited the 'Law Journal' and king's bench reports, 1807. [liii. 85]

SMITH, JOHN PRINCE (1809-1874), political economist; advocated free trade principles in Germany as a journalist; wrote several German works, and translated Hager's 'Political Economy,' 1844. [liii. 86]

SMITH, JOHN PYE (1774-1851), nonconformist divine; son of a Sheffield bookseller; theological tutor at Homerton College, 1806-51; published 'Scripture Testimony to the Messiah,' 1818-21, and 'Relation between the Holy Scriptures and some parts of Geological Science,' 1839. [liii. 86]

SMITH, JOHN RAPHAEL (1752-1812), portrait-painter and engraver; began life as a linendraper at Derby; made famous by his engravings after Reynolds, Romney, Gainsborough, and others; turned from miniature painting and engraving to crayon portrait drawing. [liii. 87]

SMITH, JOHN RUSSELL (1810-1894), bookseller; sold topographical and philological books in Old Compton Street, Soho, London; began publishing in Soho Square, London, 1842, retiring, 1884, when his 'Library of Old Authors' (a series of reprints) was sold to William Reeves for 1,000*l*. [liii. 88]

SMITH, JOHN SIDNEY (1804-1871), legal writer; M.A. Trinity Hall, Cambridge, 1850; barrister, Middle Temple, 1845; published a useful 'Treatise on the Practice of the Court of Chancery,' 1834-5. [liii. 88]

SMITH, JOHN STAFFORD (1750–1836), composer and musical antiquary ; became organist of Chapel Royal, London, 1802 ; published his 'Musica Antiqua,' 1812, besides anthems and glees. [liii. 89]

SMITH, JOHN THOMAS (1766–1833), topographical draughtsman and antiquary ; entered the studio of Nollekens, 1778 ; compiled antiquities of London, 1791–1800 ; appointed keeper of prints and drawings at British Museum, 1816 ; published 'Nollekens and his Times,' 1828, and 'Book for a Rainy Day,' posthumous, 1845. [liii. 89]

SMITH, JOHN THOMAS (1805–1882), colonel, royal engineers ; appointed superintending engineer at Madras, 1839 ; built a lighthouse and reorganised the Madras mint ; lieutenant-colonel. 1854 ; was made mint-master at Calcutta, 1855, greatly improving the machinery ; honorary colonel, 1854 ; wrote on currency, exchange, and professional subjects. [liii. 90]

SMITH, JOHN WILLIAM (1809–1845), legal writer ; of Westminster School and Trinity College, Dublin ; special pleader at Inner Temple ; published 'Compendium of Mercantile Law,' 1834, and 'Leading Cases' (10th ed. 1896), and other works, showing great legal acumen and learning. [liii. 92]

SMITH, JOSEPH (1670–1756), provost of Queen's College, Oxford ; B.A. Queen's College, Oxford, 1694 ; M.A. by diploma, 1697 ; fellow, 1698 ; made chaplain to Caroline, princess of Wales, 1715 ; provost of Queen's College, Oxford, 1730–56 ; obtained several donations and legacies for the college ; wrote works against deists and nonjurors. [liii. 92]

SMITH, JOSEPH (1682–1770), British consul at Venice ; known as a collector of objects of vertu ; prepared, 1729, an exact reproduction of the 1527 edition of Boccaccio's 'Decamerone' ; British consul at Venice, 1740–60 ; his books and art treasures sold to George III, 1765. Most of his books are now in the King's Library at the British Museum. [liii. 93]

SMITH, JOSEPH (1733 ?–1790), soldier ; served as ensign under Clive in Carnatic, 1752 ; captain, 1754 ; accompanied expedition under Lieutenant-colonel Heron to Madura, 1755 ; temporarily commanded garrison at Trichinopoli, 1757 ; assisted in reduction of Kárikál, 1760 ; major, 1760 ; colonel, 1766 ; commanded forces intended to co-operate with Nizám Ali against Haidar Ali, 1776, and when Haidar joined the Nizám worsted the combined armies and concluded treaty with the Nizám, 1768 ; major-general ; took Tanjore, 1773. [Suppl. iii. 348]

SMITH, JOSHUA TOULMIN (1816–1869), publicist and constitutional lawyer ; articled to a Birmingham solicitor ; lectured in America ; returned to England, 1842 ; barrister, Lincoln's Inn, 1849 ; devoted much time to sanitary and municipal reform, writing on 'Local Self Government' and on 'The Parish' ; established the 'Parliamentary Remembrancer,' 1857 ; wrote on 'English Gilds' and in defence of the Hungarian movement and on geological and antiquarian subjects. [liii. 94]

SMITH, JOSIAH WILLIAM (1816–1887), legal writer ; LL.B. Trinity Hall, Cambridge, 1841 ; barrister, Lincoln's Inn, 1841 ; bencher, 1861 ; Q.C., 1861 ; issued 'Manual of Equity,' 1845, of 'Real and Personal Property,' 1855, and of 'Common Law,' 1864. [liii. 95]

SMITH, SIR LIONEL, baronet (1778–1842), lieutenant-general ; served in West Indies and was made governor of Windward and Leeward islands, 1833, but was unpopular as a favourer of slaves ; created baronet, 1837 ; governor of Mauritius, 1840–2 ; G.C.B., 1841. [liii. 96]

SMITH, MATTHEW (1589–1640), royalist ; barrister, Inner Temple ; member of the council of the north, 1639 ; left in manuscript two dramatic pieces and annotations on Littleton's 'Tenures.' [liii. 76]

SMITH, MATTHEW (*fl.* 1695), informer ; trafficked in Jacobite secrets and charged Shrewsbury and Vernon with complicity and Jacobite designs of 1695 ; wrote tracts and extorted blackmail, but was effectually silenced in 1700. [liii. 97]

SMITH, MICHAEL WILLIAM (1809–1891), general ; served as colonel of dragoons during Indian mutiny ; mainly in pursuit of Tantia Topi ; C.B., 1859 ; general, 1877 ; wrote on 'Cavalry Outpost Drill' and 'Skirmishing,' 1867. [liii. 98]

SMITH, MILES (*d.* 1624), bishop of Gloucester ; of Corpus Christi and Brasenose Colleges, Oxford ; M.A., 1576 ; D.D., 1594 ; became a distinguished oriental scholar and one of translators of authorised version ; consecrated bishop, 1612 ; was opposed to ceremonies and allowed Gloucester Cathedral to fall into decay, but was overruled by his dean, Laud. [liii. 98]

SMITH, MILES (1618–1671), secretary of Archbishop Sheldon, 1660 ; B.A. Magdalen College, Oxford, 1638 ; B.C.L., 1646 ; produced a metrical version of the Psalms, 1668. [liii. 99]

SMITH, SIR MONTAGU EDWARD (1809–1891), judge ; barrister, Gray's Inn, 1835 ; bencher, Middle Temple, 1853 ; M.P., Truro, 1859 ; made a justice of common pleas by Lord Westbury, 1865 ; knighted, 1865. [liii. 99]

SMITH, PERCY GUILLEMARD LLEWELLIN (1838–1893), general ; lieutenant, royal engineers, 1855 ; constructed defences at Portland, Portsmouth, Malta ; wrote notes on building construction (1875–9) ; retired with the honorary rank of major-general, 1887. [liii. 91]

SMITH, PHILIP (1817–1885), writer on ancient history ; brother of Sir William Smith [q. v.] ; B.A. London, 1840 ; master of Mill Hill school ; published 'Student's' histories, 1862–78. [liii. 100]

SMITH, PLEASANCE, LADY (1773–1877), centenarian ; of Lowestoft ; married, 1796, Sir James Edward Smith [q. v.] ; was painted by Opie ; published a memoir of her husband, 1832 ; retained her faculties until the last, numbering among her friends Sarah Austin, Whewell, and Stanley, and receiving a message from Queen Victoria, 1873. [liii. 100]

SMITH, RICHARD (1500–1563), Roman catholic divine ; fellow of Merton College, Oxford, 1527 ; M.A., 1530 ; D.D., 1536 ; retracted his views under Edward VI, but was restored as regius professor of divinity at Oxford by Queen Mary ; combated Cranmer in argument ; fled to Douay, 1559 ; became chancellor of university there, 1562 ; wrote many controversial works. [liii. 101]

SMITH, RICHARD (1566–1655), bishop of Chalcedon ; studied under Bellarmine at Rome ; chosen vicar-apostolic for England and Scotland, 1625 ; resided at Turvey and at the French embassy, where his sermons drew large congregations, in spite of a proclamation for his arrest ; being suspended by Pope Urban VIII for his arbitrary treatment of the regulars, found refuge at the English Austin nunnery in Paris, and died there ; wrote controversial works in English and in Latin. [liii. 102]

SMITH or **SMYTH**, RICHARD (1590–1675), bookcollector ; formed a valuable library in Little Moorfields, London, catalogued and sold in 1682 for 1,414*l.* ; best known as the compiler of the 'Obituary of Richard Smyth (1627–74),' extant in Sloane MS. 886 British Museum, printed, 1849. [liii. 103]

SMITH, RICHARD BAIRD (1818–1861), chief engineer at the siege of Delhi ; fought at Aliwal and Sobraon, 1846, and at Chilianwala (1849), and Gujrat, during second Sikh war ; during furlough wrote an elaborate report on 'Italian Irrigation,' 1852 ; appointed superintendent of canals in North-West Provinces, 1854 ; proceeded from Rurki, which he had successfully defended, to Delhi in June 1857, and forced on the bombardment and assault in September in spite of a painful wound and reluctance of Sir Archdale Wilson [q. v.] to take responsibility ; promoted colonel, 1859, and mint master at Calcutta ; made a survey of the great famine of 1861 ; left several works on irrigation. [liii. 104]

SMITH, RICHARD JOHN (1786–1855), actor ; known as O Smith ; seen as a boy as Ariel at Bath ; after adventures as a sailor on the Gaboon river, and as a strolling player in the provinces, was engaged by Elliston at the Surrey, London, 1810 ; played 'Obi' in melodrama and 'The Bottle Imp' at the Lyceum, London ; was eminent in assassins, sorcerers, moss-troopers, and infernal parts, mostly at Drury Lane, London, or the Adelphi, London ; formed large dramatic collections now in British Museum. [liii. 107]

SMITH, ROBERT (*fl.* 1689–1729), schoolmaster ; educated at Marischal College, Aberdeen ; became schoolmaster at Glamis and published verses. [liii. 109]

SMITH, ROBERT (1689-1768), mathematician and founder of Smith's prizes at Cambridge; M.A. Trinity College, Cambridge, 1715; LL.D., 1723; D.D. *per literas regias*, 1739; became senior fellow of Trinity College, Cambridge, Plumian professor of astronomy, and master of Trinity College, Cambridge, 1742; left large sums for university and college purposes, besides pictures and sculptures; wrote on 'Optics,' 1738, and 'Harmonics,' 1749. [liii. 109]

SMITH, ROBERT, first BARON CARRINGTON (1752-1838), son of a banker; M.P., Nottingham, 1779-97; attached himself to Pitt and was rewarded by a peerage, 1796. [liii. 111]

SMITH, ROBERT ANGUS (1817-1884), chemist; was educated at his native Glasgow and under Liebig in Germany; Ph.D. Giessen, 1841; settled as consulting chemist in Manchester, 1844; studied organic impurities of the air; became inspector of alkali works, 1863; wrote on 'Disinfectants,' 1869, 'Air and Rain,' 1872; did valuable work as pioneer 'chemist of sanitary science.' [liii. 112]

SMITH, ROBERT ARCHIBALD (1780-1829), musical composer; became musical conductor at Paisley, and in 1823 at Edinburgh, where he also gave lessons; wrote sacred music and melodies for songs by Tannahill and others. [liii. 114]

SMITH, ROBERT HENRY SODEN (1822-1890), keeper of the art library, South Kensington; obtained his keepership in 1868 and organised library, compiling several catalogues. [liii. 115]

SMITH, SIR ROBERT MURDOCH (1835-1900), major-general, archæologist, and diplomatist; educated at Glasgow; obtained commission in royal engineers, 1855; commanded party of sappers which accompanied archæological expedition under (Sir) Charles Thomas Newton [q. v.] to Asia Minor, and discovered real site of mausoleum at Halicarnassus, 1856-9; explored cities of the Cyrenaica in North Africa, 1860-1; employed on Persian section of line of telegraph from England to India, 1863; director of Persian telegraph at Teheran, 1865-85; director of Science and Art Museum, Edinburgh, 1885; director-in-chief of Indo-European telegraph department, 1887; retired from army as major-general, 1887; went on special mission to Persia to adjust differences arising from occupation of Jashk by British-Indian troops, 1887; K.C.M.G., 1888; published archæological and other writings. [Suppl. iii. 349]

SMITH, ROBERT PAYNE (1819-1895). [See PAYNE SMITH.]

SMITH, ROBERT PERCY, BOBUS SMITH (1770-1845), advocate-general of Bengal; elder brother of Sydney Smith [q. v.]; of Eton and King's College, Cambridge; M.A., 1797; barrister, Lincoln's Inn; appointed advocate-general, 1803; returned home rich in 1810; M.P., Grantham, 1812, Lincoln, 1820-6; renowned for his wit and his Latin verses. [liii. 116]

SMITH (afterwards VERNON), ROBERT VERNON BARON LYVEDEN (1800-1873), son of Robert Percy Smith [q. v.]; studied at Eton and Christ Church, Oxford; B.A., 1822; student, Inner Temple, 1822; M.P., Tralee, 1829 and 1830, Northampton, 1831-59; junior lord of treasury under Melbourne; president of board of control under Palmerston, 1855-8; raised to peerage, 1859. [liii. 116]

SMITH, SAMUEL (1587-1620), writer on logic; M.A. Magdalen College, Oxford, 1612; M.B., 1620; wrote a manual of his subject, Oxford, 1613. [liii. 117]

SMITH, SAMUEL (1584-1662?), ejected divine; of St. Mary Hall, Oxford; perpetual curate of Cound and Cressage, 1648; ejected at the Restoration; wrote sermons and edifying tracts in numbers, 1618-58. [liii. 117]

SMITH, SIR SIDNEY (1764-1840). [See SMITH, SIR WILLIAM SIDNEY.]

SMITH, STEPHEN (1623-1678), quaker and foreign merchant; travelled with George Fox and wrote pious tracts. [liii. 118]

SMITH, STEPHEN CATTERSON (1806-1872), portrait-painter; settled at Dublin; was very successful at portraits, first in black chalk, afterwards after Lawrence's manner; president of Royal Hibernian Academy, 1859-1864. [liii. 118]

SMITH, SYDNEY (1771-1845), canon of St. Paul's; educated at Winchester College and New College, Oxford; fellow of New College, Oxford, 1791; took orders, 1794; became tutor to Michael Hicks Beach, residing at Edinburgh, where he was intimate with Jeffrey, Brougham, and Horner; projected, and with the first two of these started the 'Edinburgh Review,' 1802; proceeded to London, though his resources were slender, 1803; lectured on moral philosophy at Royal Institution to large audiences, 1804-6, and shone among whigs at Holland House; published the 'Plymley Letters' in defence of catholic emancipation, 1807; settled at his living of Foston, near York, 1808; was given a prebend at Bristol, 1828, and made a canon-residentiary of St. Paul's, London, 1831; followed Paley in theology; a reformer, but opposed the ballot; published sermons and other writings, taking a purely secular view of the religious establishment; known, liked, and honoured, for his manliness, honesty, and exuberant drollery and wit. [liii. 119]

SMITH, THEOPHILUS AHIJAH (1809-1879), philanthropist; son of George Charles Smith [q. v.]; aided his father at Sailors' Society and became secretary of the Protestant Association. [liii. 43]

SMITH, THEYRE TOWNSEND (1798-1852), divine; originally a presbyterian; studied at Glasgow University and Queens' College, Cambridge; M.A., 1830; became Hulsean lecturer, 1839, and vicar of Wymondham, 1848; published lectures and sermons. [liii. 123]

SMITH, SIR THOMAS (1513-1577), statesman, scholar, and author; became fellow of Queens' College, Cambridge, 1530; M.A., 1533; public orator at Cambridge, 1538; went to Paris and Padua (D.C.L. Padua), and endeavoured to reform Greek pronunciation at Cambridge; became regius professor of civil law and vice-chancellor, 1544; appointed secretary of state, 1548; knighted, 1548; went on several missions abroad; lived in retirement during Queen Mary's reign, and resigned his post as provost of Eton; sent ambassador to France by Queen Elizabeth, 1562, returning to England, 1566; readmitted to privy council, 1571, and reappointed secretary of state, 1572. Six years after his death was published (in English) his important work on the Tudor constitution, 'De Republica Anglorum.' [liii. 124]

SMITH, SIR THOMAS (1556?-1609), master of requests; M.A. Christ Church, Oxford, 1578; became Latin secretary, and was knighted in 1603. [liii. 127]

SMITH or SMYTHE, SIR THOMAS (1558?-1625), merchant; son of a London haberdasher; acquired wealth by trade; elected first governor of East India Company, October 1600; acquitted of the charge of complicity in Essex's rebellion; knighted, 1603; re-elected governor, 1603, and made treasurer of Virginia Company, 1620; amassed a fortune and endowed a free school and charities at Tonbridge. [liii. 128]

SMITH, THOMAS (*fl.* 1600-1627), soldier; published 'The Art of Gunnery,' 1600 (with additions, 1627). [liii. 129]

SMITH, THOMAS (1615-1702), bishop of Carlisle; M.A. Queen's College, Oxford, 1639; chaplain to Charles II; became dean, 1672, and, 1684, bishop of Carlisle; endowed Carlisle grammar school. [liii. 130]

SMITH, THOMAS (d. 1708), captain in the navy and renegade; did good service by gaining intelligence of French fleet off Brest, 1693; obtained a small command, but was neglected and eventually dismissed for irregularities in 1703; joined a French privateer, 1707, captured the English ship Nightingale, and in her was taken and subsequently executed. [liii. 130]

SMITH, THOMAS (1638-1710), nonjuring divine and scholar; became a fellow of Magdalen College, Oxford, 1667; M.A., 1663; D.D., 1683; went for three years to Constantinople as chaplain, 1668; was ejected from Magdalen as an anti-papist in 1688, but refused to subscribe oaths to William and Mary; became librarian of the Cottonian Library; wrote learned works on the Turks, 1672, on the Seven Churches and on the Greek church; left valuable books and manuscripts to his friend Thomas Hearne [q. v.]. [liii. 131]

SMITH, THOMAS (d. 1762), admiral; obtained popularity by compelling a French corvette to salute British flag near Plymouth, 1728; became commander-in-chief in the Downs, 1755, and next year presided at court-martial of Admiral Byng [q. v.]; admiral of the blue, 1757. [liii. 133]

SMITH, THOMAS (*d.* 1767), known as 'Smith of Derby'; landscape-painter; painted picturesque views of Derbyshire, Cumberland, and Yorkshire. [liii. 134]

SMITH, THOMAS ASSHETON (1776–1858), sportsman; of Eton and Christ Church, Oxford; M.P.,;Andover, 1821–31, Carnarvonshire, 1832–41; a great cricketer; became master of Quorn hounds, 1806–16, of a Hampshire pack at Penton, 1826, and afterwards at Tedworth; greatly improved his Carnarvonshire estates, and introduced novelties in yacht construction. [liii. 134]

SMITH, THOMAS BARRY CUSACK- (1795–1866), judge; son of Sir William Cusac Smith [q. v.]; B.A. Trinity College, Dublin, 1813; became attorney-general for Ireland, 1842; prosecuted O'Connell; M.P. for Ripon; became master of the rolls. [liii. 156]

SMITH, THOMAS SOUTHWOOD (1788–1861), sanitary reformer; became unitarian minister at Edinburgh and at the same time studied medicine, graduating M.D., 1816; helped to found 'The Westminster Review,' 1824, The Useful Knowledge Society, and 'The Penny Cyclopædia,' Health of Towns Association, and similar bodies; wrote valuable works on epidæmics and sanitary improvements; Bentham left his body by will to Smith for dissection in 1832. [liii. 135]

SMITH, WALTER (*fl.* 1525), author of an account (verse) of a roguish adventuress, 'The Widow Edyth, Twelue Merry Gestys,' 1525. [liii. 137]

SMITH, WENTWORTH (*fl.* 1601–1623), dramatist; wrote, in partnership with others, numerous plays for the Admiral's Company at the Rose Theatre, London; also wrote 'The Hector of Germanie' (published, 1615) and one or two other plays printed as by W. Smith. [liii. 137]

SMITH or **SMYTH**, WILLIAM (1460 ?–1514), bishop of Lincoln and co-founder of Brasenose College, Oxford; educated in a noble family; became a member of Henry VII's council, 1486; bishop of Coventry and Lichfield, 1493; chancellor of Oxford University, 1495; translated to Lincoln, 1496; became lord president of Wales, 1501; with Richard Sutton in 1512 founded Brasenose College, Oxford, the first statutes of which he drew up. He had made other charitable bequests, but is said to have peopled Lincoln Cathedral with William Smiths, probably his kinsmen. [liii. 138]

SMITH, WILLIAM (*fl.* 1596), poet; a disciple of Spenser; published (1596) a collection of sonnets called 'Chloris.' One of these, a description of the world, had appeared in 'The Phœnix-nest,' 1595, signed 'W. S., gentleman.' [liii. 141]

SMITH, WILLIAM (1550 ?–1618), herald; educated at Oxford University; created Rouge Dragon, 1597; wrote on the county palatine of Chester, 1585 (work printed, 1656), besides many genealogical works. [liii. 142]

SMITH, WILLIAM (*fl.* 1660), author; wrote, in defence of the quakers, 'The Wisdom of the Earthly Wise confounded,' 1679. [liii. 143]

SMITH, WILLIAM (*d.* 1673), quaker; joined quakers, 1658; frequently imprisoned, many times in Nottingham gaol, where he wrote voluminous tracts. [liii. 143]

SMITH, WILLIAM (*d.* 1696), actor; joined the Duke of York's company under Sir William D'Avenant; created many parts in plays by Dryden, Etherege, Otway, and Lee; played successively at Dorset Garden, London, Theatre Royal, London, and Little Lincoln's Inn Fields, London; quitted the stage, 1685–95, owing to a cabal of Mohawks against him; was persuaded by Betterton and Congreve to reappear, and was cordially welcomed as Scandal in 'Love for Love.' [liii. 144]

SMITH, WILLIAM (*fl.* 1726), surveyor to Royal African Company; issued a survey of Guinea, 1726. [liii. 146]

SMITH, WILLIAM (1651 ?–1735), antiquary; fellow of University College, Oxford, 1675; M.A., 1675; published 'Annals' of his college, 1728. [liii. 145]

SMITH, WILLIAM (1707–1764), painter; brother of George Smith (1713–1776) [q. v.] of Chichester; practised portraiture in London and Gloucester. [liii. 37]

SMITH, WILLIAM (1711–1787), translator from the Greek; M.A. New College, Oxford, 1737; D.D., 1758; became dean of Chester, 1758; published translations of Longinus, Thucydides, and Xenophon, all now superseded. [liii. 146]

SMITH, WILLIAM (1730 ?–1819), actor; known as 'Gentleman Smith'; of Eton and St. John's College, Cambridge, whence he was rusticated; obtained an engagement at Covent Garden, London, through Spranger Barry; after playing there twenty-one years appeared at Drury Lane, London, under Garrick as Richard III in 1774, his last'part being Charles Surface on the same stage in 1788; gained notoriety by marrying the sister of a peer; unsurpassed as Charles Surface. [liii. 147]

SMITH, WILLIAM (1756–1835), politician; son of a London merchant; M.P., Sudbury, 1784–90, Camelford, 1791, Sudbury, 1796–1802, Norwich, 1802, 1807, 1812, 1818, 1820, and 1826–30; became a follower of Fox, a defender of Priestley, and a great abolitionist and emancipator; opposed the war with France; attacked Southey as a renegade; friend of Samuel Rogers, Wilberforce, Sir James Stephen, Opie, and Cotman. [liii. 149]

SMITH, WILLIAM (1769–1839), geologist and engineer; obtained as a canal surveyor a great insight into stratigraphy, and projected a great map of English strata; became known as an authority on drainage and irrigation, obtaining an extensive practice as an engineer; his map published, 1815, obtaining by it wide fame as a geologist; gave lectures from 1824–8, when he became land-steward of the Hackness estate; obtained the Wollaston medal, 1831, and a pension from the government; his fossils bought by the British Museum; the real founder of stratigraphical geology. [liii. 151]

SMITH, WILLIAM (1808–1876), printseller; sold the Sheepshanks (Dutch and Flemish portions) and other collections of engravings to British Museum, and took part in managing the Art Union of London and in establishing the National Portrait Gallery; F.S.A., 1852. [liii. 153]

SMITH, SIR WILLIAM (1813–1893), lexicographer; educated at University College, London, and Gray's Inn; contributed to 'Penny Cyclopædia'; edited classical texts, and wrote a large portion of Smith's 'Dictionary of Greek and Roman Antiquities' (1842); brought out subsequently dictionaries of Greek and Roman biography, of the bible, of Christian antiquities and Christian biography; became adviser to John Murray, initiating the 'Principia' series and the 'Student's manuals'; knighted, 1892; annotated Gibbon; editor of the 'Quarterly Review,' 1867–93. [liii. 153]

SMITH, WILLIAM (1816–1896), actuary and translator of Fichte; was apprenticed to a bookseller, but became in 1847 manager of the Law Life Assurance Association; was known in Edinburgh as a strong liberal; made a mark in letters by translating the works of Fichte for John Chapman's 'Catholic Series.' [liii. 154]

SMITH, SIR WILLIAM CUSAC, second baronet (1766–1836), Irish judge; of Eton and Christ Church, Oxford; B.A., 1788; a friend of Burke; was made K.C. and entered parliament (Donegal), 1795; solicitor-general, 1800; baron of exchequer, 1801; unsuccessfully attacked for showing political bias by O'Connell; wrote verses and pamphlets in defence of union. [liii. 155]

SMITH, WILLIAM HENRY (1808–1872), philosopher and poet; educated at Glasgow; knew Maurice, Sterling, Mill; wrote largely for 'Blackwood'; is known by two philosophical dialogues, 'Thorndale' and 'Gravenhurst, 1857 and 1861, and by the memoir prefixed to 'Gravenhurst' in 1875 by Smith's widow. [liii. 156]

SMITH, WILLIAM HENRY (1825–1891), statesman; entered his father's news agency business in Strand, 1841 (junior partner, 1846); developed profits enormously by securing railway bookstall monopoly, and developing a circulating library; M.P. for Westminster from 1868; member of first London school board, 1871; joined Disraeli's cabinet as first lord of admiralty, 1877; became first lord of treasury and leader of the House of Commons under Lord Salisbury as premier in 1886. His widow was created Viscountess Hambleden, 1891. [liii. 157]

SMITH, WILLIAM ROBERTSON (1846–1894), theologian and Semitic scholar; educated at Aberdeen, Edinburgh (New College), and Bonn; was also much influenced by Ritschl at Göttingen; became (1870) professor of Old Testament exegesis at the Free Church College,

Aberdeen, and a member of the Old Testament revision committee, 1875 ; dismissed from his Aberdeen chair in 1881 for the advanced character of his biblical articles in the 'Encyclopædia Britannica' (9th ed.), of which work he became co-editor with Spencer Baynes in 1881 ; professor of Arabic at Cambridge from 1883.   [liii. 160]

SMITH, Sir WILLIAM SIDNEY, known as Sir SIDNEY SMITH (1764–1840), admiral ; entered navy, 1777 ; fought at St. Vincent, 1780, at Dominica, 1782 ; studied French at Caen, 1785–7 ; sent home with despatches after evacuation of Toulon, 1793 ; captured off Havre in 1796 while conducting a cutting-out expedition from the Diamond frigate and imprisoned two years in the Temple, Paris ; upon his escape, 1798, was put in command of the Tigre in Levant ; undertook defence of Saint Jean d'Acre, May 1799, and finally after heroic efforts repulsed the French ; served subsequently mainly in Mediterranean and Lisbon ; theatrical and fond of self-laudation, but brave and energetic ; admiral, 1821 ; G.C.B., 1838 ; died at Paris and was buried in the Père Lachaise.   [liii. 162]

SMITH, WILLIAM TYLER (1815–1873), obstetrician ; M.B. London, 1840 ; M.D., 1848 ; became physician at St. Mary's Hospital ; wrote for 'Lancet,' and expanded his papers into 'Manual of Obstetrics,' 1858 ; helped to found Obstetrical Society of London, and tried to promote Seaford into a popular watering-place.   [liii. 167]

SMITH, WILLOUGHBY (1828–1891), telegraphic engineer ; entered Gutta Percha Company's service and had charge of cable-laying and electrical department, introducing many improvements ; assisted in laying Dover and Calais cables, 1849–51 ; wrote on the 'Progress of Submarine Telegraphy,' 1891.   [liii. 168]

SMITH-NEILL, JAMES GEORGE (1810–1857). [See NEILL.]

SMITHSON, HARRIET CONSTANCE (afterwards MADAME BERLIOZ) (1800–1854), actress ; born at Ennis ; first seen at the Crow Street Theatre, Dublin, in 1815, when she played Lady Teazle ; was engaged by Elliston at Birmingham, and appeared at Drury Lane, London, on 20 Jan. 1818 as Letitia Hardy ; seen to great advantage in the provinces in such parts as Desdemona ; played at Boulogne and Calais, 1824, and in 1828 accompanied Macready to Paris ; reappeared there at the Théâtre Italien and Odéon in 1832, playing Jane Shore, Juliet, and Ophelia, and created a furore of some months' duration at Paris, where her Irish accent was unperceived. Hector Berlioz, the composer, became enamoured of 'la belle Smidson,' and in October 1833 married her at the British embassy, Paris. She was separated from her husband in 1840, but was supported by him until her death.   [liii. 168]

SMITHSON, Sir HUGH, afterwards PERCY, first DUKE OF NORTHUMBERLAND, of the third creation (1715–1786). [See PERCY.]

SMITHSON, JAMES, known in early life as JAMES LEWIS or LOUIS MACIE (1765–1829), founder of Smithsonian Institution at Washington ; illegitimate son of Hugh Smithson Percy, duke of Northumberland [q. v.] ; born in France but matriculated from Pembroke College, Oxford, as James Louis Macie in 1782 ; was already distinguished as a student of mineralogy and chemistry by 1786 ; F.R.S., 1786 ; contributed valuable analyses to the 'Philosophical Transactions' (1802–17), and eighteen articles to Thomson's 'Annals of Philosophy' (1819–25) ; spent much time abroad in Berlin, Rome, Florence, Geneva, and, latterly, Paris, among his correspondents being Davy, Gilbert, Banks, Thomson, Black, Arago, Biot, and Klaproth ; died and was buried at Genoa. His politics appear to have been republican, and by his will he left over 100,000l. to the United States of America to found at Washington, as the Smithsonian Institution, an establishment for the increase and diffusion of knowledge. The institution was inaugurated in 1846, and the handsome buildings now comprise a national museum (mainly zoological and ethnological) and an astrophysical observatory. His own scientific papers nearly all perished in a fire at the institution in 1865.   [liii. 171]

SMITZ, CASPAR (d. 1707 ?), painter ; of Flemish origin ; exhibited fruit and flower pieces, also small portraits, and penitent Magdalenes, mainly in London and Dublin.   [liii. 173]

SMOLLETT, Sir JAMES (1648–1731), provost of Dumbarton ; an active supporter of the revolution ; knighted by William III, 1698, and made judge of commissary court, Edinburgh ; commissioner of the union, 1707 ; M.P., Dumbarton ; settled at Bonhill.   [liii. 174]

SMOLLETT, TOBIAS GEORGE (1721–1771), novelist ; grandson of Sir James Smollett [q. v.] ; born at Dalquhurn, Cardross ; educated at Glasgow University ; proceeded to London with a play to make his fortune, 1739 ; sailed as surgeon on the Cumberland in Ogle's West India squadron, 1741–3 ; settled as surgeon in Downing Street ; published 'Roderick Random,' a novel of eccentric and picaresque order, inspired by 'Gil Blas,' 1748 ; published 'Peregrine Pickle,' 1751, 'Ferdinand Count Fathom,' 1753, 'Sir Launcelot Greaves,' 1762, and 'Humphrey Clinker,' 1771 ; settled at Chelsea, 1753, and undertook vast labours as a compiler, founding 'The Critical Review,' 1756, and bringing out a large 'History of England' in 1757 ; imprisoned for libel, 1759 ; edited the unsuccessful 'Briton,' 1762 ; went abroad, 1763, and published ably written 'Travels,' 1766, and a coarse and ruthless satire on public affairs in England from 1754 to 1769 entitled 'Adventures of an Atom,' 1769 ; revisited Scotland and Bath in 1766 ; left England, 1769, and died at Monte Nero, near Leghorn, on 17 Sept. 1771. As a novelist he had a vigorous originality and power of characterisation which often degenerated into caricature ; few imaginative writers have had more numerous imitators.   [liii. 174]

SMYTH. [See also SMITH and SMYTHE.]

SMYTH, CHARLES PIAZZI (1819–1900), astronomer ; son of William Henry Smyth [q. v.] ; born at Naples ; assistant in Royal Observatory, Cape of Good Hope, 1835 ; astronomer-royal for Scotland, 1845–1888 ; made experiments at Teneriffe on telescopic vision, 1856 ; elected F.R.S., 1857, but resigned, 1874, on the society denying him the reading of a paper on his interpretation of the design of the 'Great Pyramid' ; member of Royal Astronomical Society, 1846 ; hon. LL.D. Edinburgh ; published 'Our Inheritance in the Great Pyramid,' 1864, 'Teneriffe, an Astronomical Experiment,' 1858, and numerous other writings.   [Suppl. iii. 350]

SMYTH, EDWARD (1749–1812), sculptor ; son of a Meath stonecutter ; worked under Simon Vierpyl and Henry Darley, and was employed by James Gandon to execute sculpture for the Dublin custom house (1760–70), for the Irish parliament house, the town courts, the castle chapel, O'Connell Bridge, and other buildings.
          [liii. 184]

SMYTH, JAMES CARMICHAEL (1741–1821), medical writer ; born in Fifeshire ; M.D. Edinburgh, 1764 ; travelled abroad ; appointed physician to the Middlesex Hospital, 1768 ; voted 5,000l. by parliament (1802) for experiments with nitrous acid gas for prevention of contagion in cases of fever ; wrote several treatises on this subject, 1780 and 1805, establishing his claim to priority as a discoverer ; added his mother's name Smyth to his own surname Carmichael ; was one of George III's physicians ; F.R.S., 1779.   [liii. 184]

SMYTH, Sir JAMES CARMICHAEL, first baronet (1779–1838), governor of British Guiana ; eldest son of James Carmichael Smyth [q. v.] ; entered the royal artillery from Woolwich, 1794 ; transferred to royal engineers, 1795 ; after service against the Dutch in South Africa (1796) was promoted and (1805) joined Sir David Baird's expedition to the Cape of Good Hope as commanding royal engineer ; was absent from the battle of Blaauwberg, but greatly assisted Baird after the surrender of Capetown, and repaired the defences of Table Bay ; was with Sir John Moore at Coruña ; served in the expedition to Holland, 1814 ; responsible for the assault of Bergenop-Zoom on 8 March ; subsequently strengthened Antwerp and other fortresses against the French ; served on Wellington's staff at Quatre Bras and Waterloo, entered Paris with him, and commanded royal engineers at Cambray until December 1815 ; created baronet, 1821 ; made governor of the Bahamas, 1829, and of British Guiana, 1833, where he carried through with firmness the emancipation of slaves ; died at George Town, Demerara.
          [liii. 185]

SMYTH, JOHN (1775 ?–1834 ?), sculptor ; son of Edward Smyth [q. v.] ; executed statues for public buildings in Dublin.   [liii. 184]

SMYTH, SIR JOHN ROWLAND (*d.* 1873), lieutenant-general; educated at Trinity College, Dublin; entered 16th lancers, 1821; served in Canada and in the Gwalior (1843) and Sutlej (1846) campaigns; badly wounded at Aliwal leading a charge with his regiment against the Sikh cavalry; colonel of 6th dragoon guards, 1868; lieutenant-general, 1870. [liii. 187]

SMYTH, JOHN TALFOURD (1819?–1851), a self-taught, but finished engraver; worked upon plates for the 'Art Journal' after Wilkie, Mulready, and others at Edinburgh. [liii. 187]

SMYTH, SIR LEICESTER (1829–1891), general; educated at Eton; entered the rifle brigade, 1845; served in the Kaffir war, fighting at Berea, 1852; was aide-de-camp to Lord Raglan. fought at Alma and Inkerman. and brought home despatches on the fall of Sebastopol; assistant military secretary in the Ionian islands, 1856–1861; commanded at the Cape, 1880–5; acted as high commissioner for South Africa, 1882–3; K.C.M.G., 1884; general, 1885; K.C.B., 1886; appointed governor of Gibraltar, 1890. [liii. 188]

SMYTH, PATRICK JAMES (1826–1885), Irish politician; joined the Repeal Association, 1844, siding with the 'Young Ireland' party; after the failure of the insurrection of 1848 escaped to America disguised as a drover; wrote for Irish journals in America; visited Tasmania and planned the escape of John Mitchel [q. v.]; returned to Ireland, 1856, and for a short time owned 'The Irishman'; M.P., Westmeath, 1871–80, Tipperary, 1880–2; lost popularity in Ireland through his hostility to Parnell and the Land League. [liii. 188]

SMYTH, RICHARD (1826–1878), Irish politician; studied at Bonn and Glasgow (M.A., 1850); became (1870) Dill professor of theology, Magee College, Londonderry, and moderator of the presbyterian church; supported Gladstone's Irish policy as M.P. for Londonderry, 1874–8. [liii. 189]

SMYTH, ROBERT BROUGH (1830–1889), mining surveyor; worked in Derwent ironworks, migrated to Victoria, 1852, and became secretary and inspector of mines (1870) and director of geological survey; went subsequently to India and helped to promote a disastrous boom in gold-mines there; wrote handbooks for prospectors and handbooks to gold-fields, and a work on aborigines of Victoria, 1878. [liii. 189]

SMYTH, SIR WARINGTON WILKINSON (1817–1890), mineralogist; born at Naples; son of William Henry Smyth [q. v.]; M.A. Trinity College, Cambridge, 1844; studied geology in Germany on Worts foundation, and was appointed mining geologist to the geological survey, 1844; appointed (1851) lecturer on mining in the school of mines, and inspector of crown minerals, 1857; appointed mineral surveyor to the duchy of Cornwall, of which he had an unrivalled geological knowledge, 1852; knighted, 1887; wrote, besides a treatise on coal-mining (1866), a pleasant record of 'A Year with the Turks' (1854), describing his own travels of ten years back. [liii. 190]

SMYTH, WILLIAM (1765–1849), professor of modern history at Cambridge; son of a Liverpool banker; eighth wrangler, Peterhouse, Cambridge, 1787; M.A., 1790; his father's bank having failed, went as tutor to Richard Brinsley Sheridan's elder son Thomas, and had frequent skirmishes with the great wit while attempting to obtain arrears of salary; was tutor of Peterhouse, 1806; made regius professor of modern history, 1807. His lectures on modern history (2 vols. 1840) were revised by Professor Adam Sedgwick; his lectures on the French revolution were published, 1840. He was very popular in society, talked well, gave concerts, and wrote verses, publishing 'English Lyrics' in 1797. [liii. 191]

SMYTH, WILLIAM HENRY (1788–1865), admiral and scientific writer; served in East India Company's ship Cornwallis, 1804; was transferred in it to the navy, 1805; saw active service in the East; after service off Spain made commander, 1815, and appointed to survey coasts of Sicily and adjacent shores of Italy and Africa, his results appearing in a 'Memoir of the Resources, Inhabitants, and Hydrography of Sicily and its Islands' and 'A Sketch of Sardinia,' 1828; promoted post-captain and retired from active service. Devoting himself to the life of a savant, he became vice-president of the Royal Society,

a founder of the Royal Geographical Society (1830), a director of the Society of Antiquaries, contributing numerous papers to learned publications, writing also on 'The Cycle of Celestial Objects' (1844), for which he gained the Astronomical Society's medal, 'The Mediterranean' (1854), and 'The Sailor's Word-book' (1867), and translating treatises by Arago. [liii. 192]

SMYTHE. [See also SMITH and SMYTH.]

SMYTHE, DAVID, LORD METHVEN (1746–1806), Scottish judge; raised to Scots bench as Lord Methven, 1793, and was commissioner of justiciary, 1796–1804. [liii. 193]

SMYTHE, EMILY ANNE, VISCOUNTESS STRANGFORD (*d.* 1887), daughter of Sir Francis Beaufort (1774–1857) [q. v.]; married Percy Ellen Frederick William Smythe, eighth viscount Strangford of Ireland [q. v.], 1862; as a descendant of the Beauforts of the crusades was given by the patriarch of Jerusalem the order of the Holy Sepulchre; organised a fund for the relief of the Bulgarian peasants, 1876; went to the seat of war in Turkey, 1877, in order to superintend a hospital she had established for Turkish soldiers; died at sea. She published 'Egyptian Sepulchres and Syrian Shrines,' 1861, and a work on the eastern shores of the Adriatic. [liii. 198]

SMYTHE, GEORGE AUGUSTUS FREDERICK PERCY SYDNEY, seventh VISCOUNT STRANGFORD and second BARON PENSHURST (1818–1857), born at Stockholm, where his father was minister; went to Eton and St. John's College, Cambridge, where he wrote promising verse; M.A. *jure natalium*, 1840; M.P., Canterbury, 1841; became one of Disraeli's Young England party, and was the type of the hero in 'Coningsby,' 1844; became foreign under-secretary in Peel's second ministry, followed Peel in 1846, broke with Disraeli's party, and 'committed political suicide' by his abstention from debate; fought with Colonel Frederick Romilly the last duel in England, 1852; from 1847 wrote much and brilliantly in the press (especially 'Morning Chronicle') and in the reviews. [liii. 193]

SMYTHE, JAMES MOORE (1702–1734), playwright; third son of Arthur Moore [q. v.]; a well-known fop of the Queen Anne period; wrote for Drury Lane Theatre, London, a dull comedy, 'The Rival Modes' (January 1727), which brought him 400*l.* (for his creditors) and the lasting resentment of Pope (see 'Dunciad' and second 'Moral Essay'). [liii. 195]

SMYTHE, PERCY CLINTON SYDNEY, sixth VISCOUNT STRANGFORD and first BARON PENSHURST (1780–1855), diplomatist; entered the service from Trinity College, Dublin (B.A., 1800), and became secretary of legation at Lisbon, 1802; published 'Poems from the Portuguese of Camoëns,' a smooth version (often reissued), 1803; while at Lisbon counselled prince regent of Portugal to sail for Brazil (November 1807), and later, at Canning's desire, drew up a report, which was much contested, of Portuguese situation; became ambassador at Stockholm, 1817, at Constantinople, 1820; and at St. Petersburg for a few months only, 1824; friend of Moore, Croker, and Rogers; devoted his leisure latterly to literature, and edited 'Household Expenses of Princess Elizabeth' for Camden Society. [liii. 195]

SMYTHE, PERCY ELLEN FREDERICK WILLIAM, eighth VISCOUNT STRANGFORD and third BARON PENSHURST (1826–1869), philologist; youngest son of Percy Clinton Sydney Smythe, sixth viscount Strangford [q. v.]; went from Merton College, Oxford, as student attaché at Constantinople, and became oriental secretary there, 1857–1858; mastered Persian, Greek, Turkish, Arabic, Hindustani, and other eastern tongues; wrote brilliantly on topics of the near East, mainly for 'Pall Mall Gazette,' and contributed chapters to 'Eastern Shores of the Adriatic' (1863), written by his wife, Emily Anne, viscountess Strangford [q. v.] [liii. 197]

SMYTHE, SIR SIDNEY STAFFORD (1705–1778), judge; B.A. St. John's College, Cambridge, 1724; called from Inner Temple, 1724; became K.C. and a bencher, and M.P. for East Grinstead, 1747; knighted, 1750; lord chief baron, 1772; resigned, 1777. [liii. 198]

SMYTHE, WILLIAM JAMES (1816–1887), general; entered Woolwich from Antrim, 1830; obtained commission in royal artillery, 1833; served in Kaffir war, 1835, St. Helena, Nova Scotia, and on royal commission upon military education abroad, 1856; went to Fiji to report upon cession to England, 1859; made meteorological observations, and supervised his wife Sarah Maria Smythe's 'Ten Months in Fiji Islands' (1864); after four years in India settled in Ireland; colonel, R.A., 1880, retired general, 1881; left 3,000*l.* to the Royal Irish Academy. [liii. 199]

SMYTHIES, CHARLES ALAN (1844–1894), bishop of Zanzibar; born in London; educated at Felsted, Trinity College, Cambridge (B.A., 1866), and Cuddesdon; became vicar of Roath, near Cardiff, 1880; sailed for Zanzibar as second bishop of universities mission in Central Africa, in succession to Bishop Edward Steere, 1884; worked with the greatest energy at organising the mission and training native teachers, travelling thousands of miles on foot; raised 11,000*l.* in England for a suffragan bishop for Nyasa district, 1890; succumbed to malarial fever, May 1894, and was buried at sea between Zanzibar and Aden. [liii. 201]

SNAGGE, THOMAS (1536–1592), speaker of House of Commons; barrister, Gray's Inn, 1554; at Gray's Inn, 1563, 'double reader,' 1574; M.P., Bedfordshire, 1571; attorney-general for Ireland, 1577–80; serjeant-at-law and treasurer of his inn, 1580, being at the time M.P. for Bedford; was chosen speaker, holding the office for two sessions, 1588. [liii. 202]

SNAPE, ANDREW (1675–1742), provost of King's College, Cambridge; educated at Eton and King's College, Cambridge; M.A., 1697; D.D., 1705; master of Eton, 1711; gave offence at court by his attacks on Benjamin Hoadly (1676–1761) [q. v.], and was removed from the list of royal chaplains; chosen provost of King's College, Cambridge, 1719. [liii. 203]

SNAPE, EDMUND (*fl.* 1576–1608), puritan; went to Jersey and framed a Calvinistic discipline for Huguenot ministers there; M.A. Merton College, Oxford, 1584; summoned with Cartwright before high commission for attempting to introduce presbyterian usages into England, and was imprisoned for a short while, 1590. [liii. 203]

SNATT, WILLIAM (1645–1721), nonjuring divine; graduated from Magdalen College, Oxford (B.A., 1664); vicar of Seaford, 1679; associated with Jeremy Collier in giving absolution to Parkyns and Friend, conspirators against William III in 1696; found guilty of serious misdemeanour, but treated leniently. [liii. 204]

SNELL, HANNAH (1723–1792), female soldier; stated in a chap-book history of her adventures, issued in 1750, to have enlisted in 1745, to have served in the fleet, and to have received a pension for wounds received at Pondicherry. The facts were much embellished, but there was probably a kernel of truth as in the cases of Phœbe Hessel, Christian Davies, and Mary Anne Talbot. Hannah, who was thrice married, died in Bedlam. [liii. 205]

SNELL, JOHN (1629–1679), founder of Snell exhibitions at Balliol College, Oxford; studied at Glasgow University; fought on the royalist side at Worcester; secretary to Monmouth; left estates in trust for the further education of Glasgow scholars at Oxford. In 1693 chancery decided that Snell exhibitions should go to Balliol College. [liii. 206]

SNELLING, THOMAS (1712–1773), numismatist; sold book and coins, on which he wrote several treatises published, 1757–76, at 163 Fleet Street, London; chief works, three 'Views,' respectively of silver, gold, and copper coins of England, 1762, 1763, 1766. [liii. 207]

SNETZLER, JOHN or JOHANN (1710?–1774?), organ-builder; native of Passau; settled in England and built fine organs at Lynn (1754), Halifax (1766), and St. Martin's, Leicester (1774). [liii. 207]

SNOW, JOHN (1813–1858), anæsthetist; M.D. London, 1844; discovered that cholera was communicated by contaminated water, and introduced scientific use of ether (first adopted in America) into English surgery practice, 1846–7; published 'Chloroform and other Anæsthetics,' 1858. [liii. 207]

SNOW, WILLIAM PARKER (1817–1895), mariner, explorer, and writer; born at Poole; after a wild life in the Australian bush and in West Africa became a literary amanuensis in London, transcribing for Macaulay the first two volumes of the 'History'; served on a Franklin search vessel, 1850, and subsequently on a missionary ship off Patagonia; wrote for New York booksellers between 1858 and 1864; wrote also on Arctic subjects and on (1857) 'Tierra del Fuego.' [liii. 208]

SNOWDEN, JOHN (1558–1626). [See CECIL.]

SOAMES, HENRY (1785–1860), ecclesiastical historian; son of a shoemaker; passed from St. Paul's School, London, to Wadham College, Oxford (M.A., 1810); became Bampton lecturer and chancellor of St. Paul's, London, 1842; edited Mosheim, 1841 (4th ed. by Stubbs, 1863), and wrote 'History of Reformation,' 1826–8, 'Anglo-Saxon Church,' 1835, and 'Elizabethan Religious History,' 1839. [liii. 209]

SOANE, GEORGE (1790–1860), miscellaneous author; son of Sir John Soane [q. v.]; B.A. Pembroke College, Cambridge, 1811; writer of numerous novels, plays, and translations. [liii. 211]

SOANE, SIR JOHN (1753–1837), founder of Soane Museum; son of a mason named Swan; taken into George Dance's office; gained Royal Academy silver medal for an architectural drawing, and went to Rome in 1777 as travelling student; after a wealthy marriage became, in 1788, architect of the Bank of England, rebuilding the whole structure and gaining a great reputation for the work; R.A., 1802; succeeded Dance as professor of architecture at the Academy, 1806, and began to collect the museum of paintings (including Hogarth's 'Rake's Progress' and 'Election'), sculpture, drawings, and gems in a house in Lincoln's Inn Fields, which in 1833 he presented with its contents to the nation; knighted, 1831. In philanthropic endeavour Soane was munificent, but he is said to have declined a baronetcy in order to spite his son George Soane [q. v.] [liii. 211]

SOEST, GERARD (*d.* 1681), portrait-painter; native of Soest, near Utrecht; came to London in 1656 and obtained many commissions; painted Colonel Blood and Bishop Cartwright, and might have rivalled Lely but for his uncouth demeanour. [liii. 211]

SOLANDER, DANIEL CHARLES (1736–1782), botanist; native of Norrland, in Sweden; noticed by Linnæus at Upsala, and recommended by him to naturalists in England, where he arrived in 1760; familiarised English botanists with Linnean system, and was made assistant-librarian to catalogue natural-history collections at British Museum, employing a deputy there from 1768, when he accompanied (Sir) Joseph Banks on Cook's voyage in Endeavour; went with Banks to Iceland, 1772, and became his secretary and librarian in Soho Square, London, until in 1773 he was made keeper of natural history department, British Museum. [liii. 212]

SOLANUS, MOSES or MOÏSE DU SOUL (*d.* 1735?), Greek scholar; a refugee from Saumur; came from Amsterdam to England; was encouraged by Bentley; projected an elaborate 'Lucian' and published a fine edition of Plutarch's 'Lives' (5 vols. London, 1729). [liii. 213]

SOLE, WILLIAM (1741–1802), botanist; educated at King's School, Ely; went as surgeon to Bath to be near his relative, Christopher Anstey [q. v.] the poet; studied grasses, and issued (1798) his chief botanical work, 'Menthæ Britannicæ.' [liii. 213]

SOLLY, EDWARD (1819–1886), chemist and antiquary; studied chemistry at Berlin; lectured at Royal Institution, 1841; published 'Rural Chemistry,' 1843; professor of chemistry at Addiscombe, 1845–9; had a large antiquarian library; wrote much in 'Notes and Queries' and edited 'Titles of Honour' (1879) for Index Society. [liii. 214]

SOLLY, SAMUEL (1805–1871), surgeon; son of Isaac Solly, a Baltic merchant; apprenticed to Benjamin Travers [q. v.] of St. Thomas's Hospital, London, and became surgeon and lecturer there (1853). He was F.R.S. (1836) and president of Royal Medical and Chirurgical Society, 1867–8. A good clinical teacher and operator, he wrote 'Surgical Experiences,' 1865, and professional treatises. [liii. 214]

SOLLY, THOMAS (1816–1875), philosophical writer; after studying at Caius College, Cambridge, and Inner Temple (barrister, 1841), became lecturer on English language and literature at Berlin University, 1843; published a 'Syllabus of Logic,' 1839, 'A Coronal of English Verse,' 1864, and other works, and contributed to Cohn's 'Shakespeare in Germany.' [liii. 215]

SOLME or **SOLEMAN**, THOMAS (*d.* 1541). [See SOULEMONT.]

SOLME, THOMAS (*fl.* 1540–1553). [See SOME.]

SOLMS, HEINRICH MAASTRICHT, COUNT OF SOLMS-BRAUNFELS (1636–1693), general in the Dutch service; entered Dutch army, *c.* 1670, rose to be general, 1680, sailed with Prince of Orange, October 1688, and led Dutch guards into Westminster; he was distinguished at the Boyne, but much censured for not supporting English brigade under Mackay at Steinkirk; died from a cannon-shot wound at Neerwinden. [liii. 215]

SOLOMON, ABRAHAM (1823–1862), painter; learned his art in Sass's school, Bloomsbury, London; exhibited game and costume canvases regularly at Royal Academy, 1841–62. He was a good colourist, and showed marked advance in some of his later pictures, especially 'Waiting for the Verdict,' 1857. [liii. 216]

SOLUS, SAINT (*d.* 790 ?), an English monk who settled in Suabia under Charles the Great. [liii. 217]

SOME, ROBERT (1542–1609), master of Peterhouse, Cambridge; fellow of Queens' College, Cambridge, 1562; M.A., 1565; D.D., 1580; appointed master of Peterhouse, Cambridge, 1589, and was vice-chancellor four times; steered a middle course between high Anglicans and puritans; wrote a 'Treatise of the Sacraments' (1582), and tried to interpose as moderator in Mar-Prelate controversy (1588). [liii. 217]

SOME or **SOLME**, THOMAS (*fl.* 1540–1553), protestant divine; an unwilling monk, took up advanced protestant views; an active preacher under Edward VI; fled abroad on Mary's accession; his treatise, the 'Lord's Flail,' burned by Bonner, 1546. [liii. 218]

SOMER, HENRY (*fl.* 1407–1413), chancellor of the exchequer; friend of Hoccleve and possibly of Chaucer; made baron of exchequer, 1407, chancellor, 1413. [liii. 218]

SOMER, SEMUR, SOMERARIUS, JOHN (*fl.* 1380), Minorite astronomer; of Oxford; wrote a calendar, dated 1380, with astronomical tables. [liii. 218]

SOMER, PAUL VAN (1576–1621). [See VAN SOMER.]

SOMERCOTE, SWINERCOTE, or SOMERTON, LAWRENCE (*fl.* 1254), canonist; canon of Chichester, 1247; wrote on 'Canonical Election of Bishops,' 1254. [liii. 219]

SOMERCOTE or **UMMARCOTE**, ROBERT (*d.* 1241), cardinal; of English birth; favoured by Langton, entered papal curia and was made cardinal by Gregory IX, 1238. [liii. 219]

SOMERLED, LORD OF THE ISLES (*d.* 1164). [See SUMERLED.]

SOMERS, EDMUND SIGISMUND (1759 ?–1824), physician; studied at Dublin and Edinburgh; M.D. Edinburgh, 1783; served in Jamaica and in Peninsula under Wellington. [liii. 219]

SOMERS or **SUMMERS**, SIR GEORGE (1554–1610), discoverer of Bermudas; served on buccaneering voyage under Sir Amyas de Preston [q. v.]; took part in Islands' Voyage, 1597; knighted, 1603; commanded a fleet conveying settlers for Virginia, as one of founders of South Virginia Company, 1609; wrecked on Bermudas or Summer islands; took possession of islands for king of England in July, 1609; died there; his shipwreck and sojourn in Bermudas commemorated by Silvester Jourdain [q. v.], whence Shakespeare derived some details of 'The Tempest.' [liii. 220]

SOMERS or **SOMMERS**, JOHN, BARON SOMERS (1651–1716), lord chancellor of England; son of John Somers, a Worcestershire attorney; educated at Worcester Cathedral school and Trinity College, Oxford; called to the bar from Middle Temple, 1676; counsel for seven bishops, June 1688; M.P., Worcester, 1689; asserted virtual abdication of James II, and presided over the drafting of the Declaration of Rights; made solicitor-general and knighted, 1689; became lord-keeper, 1693, member of the Kit-Cat Club and friend and patron of Addison, Congreve, Steele, Vertue, Tindal, Rymer, and, for a time, Swift, who dedicated to him the 'Tale of a Tub,' 1704; with Montagu, Locke, and Newton planned in 1695 the reform of the currency; lord high chancellor of England, 1697; created Baron Somers of Evesham,

1697; possessed great influence, second only to that of Sunderland, with William III, and was one of the council of regency during William III's absence in Holland; on William III's return in 1698 shared his unpopularity as the abettor of a policy necessitating a large standing army, and after repeated attacks by the country party he had to surrender the great seal, 1700; a demand raised in 1700 for his impeachment on account of his share in the secret partition treaties of 1698-9; was acquitted, and would have been restored to power but for William III's death, upon which he joined the whig party, exercising great influence, especially in settling terms of union with Scotland, 1707; sworn president of the council, 1708; fell with the junto in the autumn of 1710. Somers was a great lawyer, but his influence and capacity as a statesman have perhaps been unduly magnified by Macaulay and others. His four political tracts of 1681 are models of lucid presentation. [liii. 221]

SOMERS, ROBERT (1822–1891), journalist; edited 'Scottish Herald,' 1844, and after its amalgamation with the 'Witness' managed that paper under Hugh Miller [q. v.]; from 1849 to 1859 edited 'North British Daily Mail'; wrote for 'Encyclopædia Britannica.' [liii. 229]

SOMERSAM, RICHARD (*d.* 1531). [See BAYFIELD, RICHARD.]

SOMERSET, DUKES OF. [See BEAUFORT, JOHN, first DUKE, 1403–1444; BEAUFORT, EDMUND, second DUKE, *d.* 1455; BEAUFORT, HENRY, third DUKE, 1436–1464; SEYMOUR, EDWARD, first DUKE of the Seymour family, 1506 ?–1552; SEYMOUR, WILLIAM, second DUKE, 1588–1660; SEYMOUR, CHARLES, sixth DUKE, 1662–1748; SEYMOUR, ALGERNON, seventh DUKE, 1684–1750; SEYMOUR, EDWARD ADOLPHUS, eleventh DUKE, 1775–1855; SEYMOUR, EDWARD ADOLPHUS, twelfth DUKE, 1804–1885.]

SOMERSET, EARLS OF. [See MOHUN, WILLIAM DE, *fl.* 1141; BEAUFORT, JOHN, first EARL, 1373 ?–1410; CARR, ROBERT, *d.* 1645.]

SOMERSET, CHARLES, EARL OF WORCESTER (1460 ?–1526), bastard son of Henry Beaufort, third duke of Somerset; fought at Bosworth, and was employed by Henry VII on important embassies, 1490–1505; chamberlain as Lord Herbert of Raglan, 1505; negotiated with Louis XII, Maximilian, and Charles V, 1515–18; created Earl of Worcester, 1514. [liii. 230]

SOMERSET, EDWARD, fourth EARL OF WORCESTER (1553–1628), great-grandson of Charles Somerset, earl of Worcester [q. v.]; succeeded Essex as Queen Elizabeth's master of the horse, 1601; examined conspirators of 1605; became lord privy seal, 1616, and was great chamberlain at Charles I's coronation. [liii. 231]

SOMERSET, EDWARD, sixth EARL and second MARQUIS of WORCESTER and titular EARL OF GLAMORGAN (1601–1667), as Lord Herbert served for Charles I in South Wales and garrisoned Raglan Castle; defeated by Waller at Highnam, March 1643; created Earl of Glamorgan, 1644, and selected by Charles I to distribute honours and raise troops in Ireland; possibly exceeded his commission (which Charles I eventually disavowed, 1646) by throwing himself into the arms of Rinuccini and the ultramontane party in Ireland; his appointment as lord-lieutenant requested of Charles I by the papal nuncio, but the Anglo-Irish preferred Ormonde; went to Paris, 1648; compelled by his narrow means to return to England, 1652; imprisoned for two years, but released in October 1654, and later given a pension of 3*l.* a week; recovered the bulk of his estates at the Restoration, and gave his time to mechanical experiments; published (1663) his 'Century of Inventions,' written in 1655, in which he suggested a calculating machine (No. 84) and an hydraulic machine (No. 68) 'for driving up water by fire.' This was a very ingenious adumbration of a steam pumping-engine, but there is no evidence of any practical attempt by Worcester to give effect to such an idea. [liii. 232]

SOMERSET, LORD EDWARD (1776–1842). [See SOMERSET, LORD ROBERT EDWARD HENRY.]

SOMERSET, LORD FITZROY JAMES HENRY, first BARON RAGLAN (1788–1855), youngest son of fifth Duke of Beaufort; served at Roliça and Vimeiro as

Wellesley's aide-de-camp; fought at Busaco, Fuentes d'Onoro and Badajoz; wounded when close to Wellington at Waterloo; secretary at Horse Guards, 1827 – 52, when he succeeded Wellington as commander of the forces and was made Baron Raglan; selected to command British troops for Crimea, 1854; accepted position at Sebastopol; won battle of Alma, 20 Sept. 1854; blamed Lucan for blunder and loss of light brigade at Balaclava, 25 Oct. 1854; showed judgment and almost rash bravery at Inkerman on 5 Nov., and was thanked by Queen Victoria; made the scapegoat of mismanagement during the terrible winter of 1854–5; suffered intensely owing to the failure of the mistimed attack on the Malakhoff and Redan, 18 June 1855, and died ten days later 'the victim of England's unreadiness for war.'   [liii. 237]

SOMERSET, LORD GRANVILLE CHARLES HENRY (1792 – 1848), chancellor of duchy of Lancaster; second son of Henry Charles Somerset, sixth Duke of Beaufort; M.A. Christ Church, Oxford, 1817; M.P., Monmouthshire, 1828–48; supported Liverpool and subsequently Peel; chancellor of duchy, 1841–6.   [liii. 245]

SOMERSET, HENRY, first DUKE OF BEAUFORT (1629–1700), son of Edward Somerset, second Marquis of Worcester; renounced catholicism and was friendly with Cromwell, on whose death, however, he demanded a full and free parliament; sat in Convention, November 1659; favoured Restoration; succeeded as third marquis of Worcester in 1667; president of council of Wales, 1672; K.G., 1672; opposed exclusion, and was made Duke of Beaufort, 1682; opposed both Monmouth and Prince of Orange, but was reconciled to William III; maintained great state in retirement at Badminton.   [liii. 242]

SOMERSET, HENRY, second DUKE OF BEAUFORT (1684–1714), grandson of Henry Somerset, first duke of Beaufort; pillar of the tory party, and a member of Swift's 'Brothers' Club; K.G., 1712.   [liii. 244]

SOMERSET, HENRY, seventh DUKE OF BEAUFORT (1792–1853), aide-de-camp to the Duke of Wellington in the Peninsula, 1812–14; M.P., Monmouth, 1813–32; M.P., West Gloucestershire, 1835; K.G., 1842. A typical tory and sportsman, he figured in the 'Badminton Hunt' and in Nimrod's sporting sketches.   [liii. 244]

SOMERSET or **SOMERSETH**, JOHN (d. 1455 ?), physician to Henry VI; studied at Paris; M.D.; attended Henry VI constantly as doctor and astrologer; chancellor of exchequer, 1441–6, and executor of Humphrey of Gloucester.   [liii. 245]

SOMERSET, POULETT GEORGE HENRY (1822–1875), aide-de-camp to Lord Raglan; nearly killed at Inkerman; subsequently M.P. for Middlesex. [liii. 242]

SOMERSET, LORD ROBERT EDWARD HENRY (1776–1842), general; known as Lord Edward Somerset; served in Holland and throughout Peninsular campaign, 1809–14; led cavalry brigade under Uxbridge at Waterloo, was thanked by parliament, and appointed to command first brigade of cavalry in the army of occupation in France; general, 1841.   [liii. 246]

SOMERSET, WILLIAM, third EARL OF WORCESTER (1526–1589), served at coronations of Edward VI and Queens Mary and Elizabeth; took part in trials of Protector Somerset, Norfolk, and Mary Queen of Scots; went to Paris on an embassy, 1573; raised land force against Armada, 1588.   [liii. 247]

SOMERVILLE, ALEXANDER (1811–1885), social reformer; son of a Lothian carpenter; after serving in army wrote on economic subjects, especially corn-law reform; collected facts for Cobden; wrote for 'Manchester Examiner' and other journals; published 'Autobiography of a Working Man,' 1848, and other books.   [liii. 248]

SOMERVILLE, ALEXANDER NEIL (1813–1889), Scots divine; a pioneer of Scots free church, 1844; journeyed on missions in India, 1874, Spain, Africa, and elsewhere, making many converts.   [liii. 249]

SOMERVILLE, ANDREW (1808–1834), painter; R.S.A.; exhibited at Edinburgh, 1830–4.   [liii. 249]

SOMERVILLE, HUGH, fifth BARON SOMERVILLE (1483 ?–1549), joined James V at Stirling in 1528; taken prisoner at Solway Moss, 1542; took a pension

from Henry VIII, and joined 'English party' among Scots.   [liii. 250]

SOMERVILLE, JAMES, sixth BARON SOMERVILLE (d. 1569), son of Hugh Somerville, fifth baron Somerville [q. v.]; employed by Mary of Guise in negotiating with Châtelherault; fought at Langside, 1568.   [liii. 251]

SOMERVILLE, JAMES (1632–1690), family historian; fought in covenanting army under General Leslie, and was at rout of Dunbar, September 1650; joined Scots royalists, but took little further part in affairs; his 'Memorie of the Somervilles' (1679) edited by Sir Walter Scott in 1815.   [liii. 251]

SOMERVILLE or **SOMERVILE**, JOHN (1560–1583), traitor; of Roman catholic faith; formed design to shoot Queen Elizabeth, was sentenced to death, December 1583, and found strangled in the Tower of London. [liii. 252]

SOMERVILLE, JOHN SOUTHEY, fifteenth BARON SOMERVILLE (1765–1819), succeeded his uncle to title and estates, 1796; representative Scots peer; ousted Sinclair from presidency of board of agriculture, 1798; aided George III in introducing merino sheep; invented a plough; published agricultural works.   [liii. 253]

SOMERVILLE, MARY (1780 – 1872), scientific writer; daughter of Sir William George Fairfax [q. v.]; read Newton's 'Principia' in Latin; married, as a second husband, in 1812, William Somerville (1771–1860) [q. v.], and moved in a brilliant intellectual circle; wrote on spectrum and on Laplace; her best work, 'The Connection of the Physical Sciences,' 1834, which illustrates in its able summary the width of her scientific acquirements.   [liii. 254]

SOMERVILLE, THOMAS (1741–1830), historian; after education at Edinburgh, visited London in 1769, and associated with Hume, Robertson, Franklin, and other eminent men; appointed minister at Jedburgh, 1772; wrote useful histories of Restoration and fall of Stuarts, 1792, and of Queen Anne, 1798, and an interesting autobiography, first published, 1861.   [liii. 255]

SOMERVILLE, WILLIAM (1675–1742), poet; of an ancient Gloucestershire family; educated at Winchester College and New College, Oxford; fellow of New College, Oxford; student at the Middle Temple, 1696; led a country and sporting life, devoting leisure to letters; his poem of four books in blank verse, 'The Chase,' published first in 1735; his hawking poem, 'Field Sports,' a kind of supplement, published, 1742.   [liii. 256]

SOMERVILLE, WILLIAM (1771–1860), physician; eldest son of Thomas Somerville [q. v.]; surgeon at Capetown, 1795; travelled among Kaffirs, the journey being described in an appendix to Barrow's 'Cochin China,' 1806; hospital inspector in Canada; married in 1812 Mary Somerville [q. v.]; F.R.S., 1817; became physician to Chelsea Hospital, London, 1819.   [liii. 258]

SOMERVILLE, SIR WILLIAM MEREDYTH, BARON ATHLUMNEY in the peerage of Ireland, and BARON MEREDYTH in the peerage of the United Kingdom (1802–1873), represented Drogheda in liberal interest, 1837–52; became chief secretary for Ireland, 1847–52; raised to peerage, 1863; supported William Ewart Gladstone's land bill, 1870, and Irish church bill.   [liii. 258]

SOMMERS, WILLIAM (d. 1560), Henry VIII's fool; amused Henry VIII by his jokes on Wolsey; was painted with Henry VIII, and was not without influence at court; left court in 1547. Nash and other writers introduced him as a chorus, or one of the *dramatis personæ*, into their plays.   [liii. 259]

SOMNER, WILLIAM (1598–1669), Anglo-Saxon scholar; registrary of Canterbury diocese for a while under Laud; a zealous antiquary and loyalist; wrote on Canterbury and Kent, but is best known for his version of 'Anglo-Saxon Laws,' 1568, and his 'Dictionarium Saxonico-Latino-Anglicum,' 1659.   [liii. 260]

SONDES, SIR GEORGE, EARL OF FEVERSHAM (1600–1677), royalist; K.B., 1626; suffered in estate and was in prison, 1645–50, but suffered more in mind by fratricidal act of his younger son, Freeman, who was hanged for killing his brother George, 1655; for his unwavering loyalty was made an earl in 1676, but died without issue.   [liii. 261]

SONMANS, WILLIAM (d. 1708). [See SUNMAN.]

SOONE or **ZOONE**, WILLIAM (*fl.* 1540–1575), professor of law at Louvain and cartographer; published maps at Cologne, based mainly on Ortelius, 1572. [liii. 262]

SOOWTHERN, JOHN (*fl.* 1584). [See SOUTHERN.]

SOPWITH, THOMAS (1803–1879), mining engineer; studied stratigraphical geology, and directed attention of British Association and Royal Society to bearing of railway cuttings upon subject; F.R.S., 1845; wrote valuable technical works. [liii. 263]

SOROCOLD, THOMAS (1561–1617), divine; M.A. Brasenose College, Oxford, 1585; rector of St. Mildred's, Poultry, London, 1590–1617; published 'Supplications of Saints,' 1608. [liii. 264]

SOTHEBY, CHARLES (*d.* 1854), rear-admiral; son of William Sotheby [q. v.]; took part in the battle of the Nile, 1798, and in the operations in Egypt, 1801, and against the Turks, 1807. [liii. 268]

SOTHEBY, SAMUEL (1771–1842), auctioneer and antiquary; nephew of John Sotheby, who founded Covent Garden sale-room, London, for books and prints, 1744; moved business to Strand, 1817; issued many important catalogues. [liii. 264]

SOTHEBY, SAMUEL LEIGH (1805–1861), auctioneer and antiquary; son of Samuel Sotheby [q. v.]; took his accountant Wilkinson into partnership as salesman, 1843, and devoted himself to cataloguing; wrote on early printing and 'Block Books,' 1858, and Milton's autograph, 1861. [liii. 265]

SOTHEBY, WILLIAM (1757–1833), author; served in dragoons, 1774–80; studied classics zealously; mixed in first-rate literary circles; prominent in Dilettante Society from 1792; issued 'Poems,' 1790; made a highly eulogised version of Virgil's 'Georgics' (1800), also original verses which fell flat; produced unacted tragedies; devoted himself latterly to a verse translation of Homer, 1830–4; maintained affectionate terms with Sir Walter Scott, and wrote of his death. [liii. 265]

SOTHEL, SETH (*d.* 1697), colonial governor; after adventures among Algerine pirates was (1683–91) governor of the Carolines. [liii. 268]

SOTHEREY, SIMON (*fl.* 1396). [See SOUTHREY.]

SOTHERN, EDWARD ASKEW (1826–1881), actor; son of a Liverpool merchant; played Claude Melnotte at St. Heliers, 1849; played subsequently in provinces and America with slender encouragement; first appeared in New York as Lord Dundreary, a brainless peer, in 'Our American Cousin,' 1858, not a striking part until worked up by Sothern; introduced the part at the Haymarket, London, 1861, and carried the part, though nearly a failure at first, through 496 nights, the caricature, which grew into a series of monologues, eventually becoming the talk of London; his next best part, David Garrick, 1864; revisited America, 1875–8; celebrated as a wag and practical joker; ambitious of shining as a tragedian, though his real vein was eccentric comedy. [liii. 268]

SOTHERN, LYTTON EDWARD (1856–1887), actor; son of Edward Askew Sothern [q. v.]; acted in London, Philadelphia, and Australia. [liii. 271]

SOTHERON-ESTCOURT, THOMAS HENRY SUTTON (1801–1876). [See ESTCOURT.]

SOTHERTON, JOHN (1562–1631?), judge; of a Suffolk family; M.A. Christ Church, Oxford, 1586; barrister, Inner Temple, 1597; bencher, 1610; cursitor baron of exchequer, 1610. [liii. 271]

SOULEMONT, SOLEMAN, or **SOLME**, THOMAS (*d.* 1541), French secretary of Henry VIII; native of Jersey; entered Henry VIII's and then Cromwell's service; clerk of parliaments, 1540; a 'learned antiquary.' [liii. 271]

SOULIS, SIR JOHN DE (*d.* 1321?), Scots soldier; supported claim of Balliol, by whom he was appointed co-guardian of Scots realm with John Comyn; negotiated with France and papacy; banished, 1304; lived in France till death. [liii. 272]

SOUTH, SIR JAMES (1785–1867), astronomer; observed in London with Sir John Frederick William Herschel [q. v.] and in Paris with Laplace, 1825; president in 1829, as one of founders of Astronomical Society; knighted, 1830; failed with a great telescope he projected at Campden Hill; published pamphlets. [liii. 272]

SOUTH, JOHN FLINT (1797–1882), surgeon; half-brother of Sir James South [q. v.]; lectured at St. Thomas's Hospital, London; developed historical side of his subject, and wrote 'Memorials of the Craft of Surgery' (edited by D'Arcy Power, 1882). [liii. 274]

SOUTH, ROBERT (1634–1716), divine; student of Christ Church, Oxford, 1651–5; M.A., 1657; travelled abroad; public orator, Oxford, 1660–7; rector of Islip, 1678; made in his 'Animadversions' of 1690 a crushing attack on William Sherlock, whom he accused in 1695 of Tritheism; was offered, but declined, see of Rochester in 1713; though a court preacher, was homely, pithy, and often very humorous in the pulpit; his sermons frequently reissued and collected. [liii. 275]

SOUTHAMPTON, DUKE OF (1662–1730). [See FITZROY, CHARLES.]

SOUTHAMPTON, EARLS OF. [See FITZWILLIAM, WILLIAM, *d.* 1542; WRIOTHESLEY, THOMAS, first EARL 1505–1550; WRIOTHESLEY, HENRY, second EARL, 1545–1581; WRIOTHESLEY, HENRY, third EARL, 1573–1624; WRIOTHESLEY, THOMAS, fourth EARL, 1607–1667.]

SOUTHAMPTON, BARON (1737–1797). [See FITZROY, CHARLES.]

SOUTHCOTE, JOHN (1511–1585), judge; serjeant-at-law, 1559; raised to queen's bench, 1563; sat as assessor at trial of Norfolk, 1572. [liii. 277]

SOUTHCOTT, JOANNA (1750–1814), fanatic; a Devonshire farmer's daughter; in domestic service for many years; began in 1792 to write doggerel prophecies, and broke with her methodist connections; began to attract notice and make converts in 1801, when she set forth her claims in a pamphlet; interpreted strange dreams, and in 1802 declared that she was about to bring into the world a spiritual man, Shiloh; died of brain disease: a self-convinced impostor. [liii. 277]

SOUTHERN, HENRY (1799–1853), founder of 'Retrospective Review'; M.A. Trinity College, Cambridge, 1822; founded the 'Retrospective Review,' 1820, and edited it till 1826; joined diplomatic service, and died minister at Rio de Janeiro. [liii. 279]

SOUTHERN or **SOOWTHERN**, JOHN (*fl.* 1584), poetaster; published in 1584 a now very rare volume of somewhat clumsy sonnets, based on those of Ronsard, and addressed to his Mistresse Diana. [liii. 280]

SOUTHERNE, THOMAS (1660–1746), dramatist; born at Oxmantown and educated at Trinity College, Dublin; M.A., 1696; entered Middle Temple, 1678, and four years later produced 'The Loyal Brother,' manifesting writer's strong tory sympathies; after 1688, having to fall back on drama for a livelihood, attached himself to Dryden, and produced 'The Fatal Marriage,' 1694, and 'Oroonoko,' 1696. Though his later plays were inferior, the two plays mentioned held the stage nearly a hundred years. [liii. 280]

SOUTHESK, EARL OF (1575–1658). [See CARNEGIE, SIR DAVID.]

SOUTHEY, MRS. CAROLINE ANNE (1786–1854), poetess; daughter of Captain Charles Bowles; began to write in 1816; encouraged by Robert Southey to publish 'The Widow's Tale,' 1822, and similar metrical narratives; corresponded regularly with Southey, and married him in 1839, his health being then greatly on the wane. [liii. 282]

SOUTHEY, HENRY HERBERT (1783–1865), physician; M.D. Edinburgh, 1806; younger brother of Robert Southey [q. v.]; F.R.C.P., 1823; became physician to George IV, 1823, and to Queen Adelaide; F.R.S., 1825; commissioner in lunacy, 1836; Harveian orator, 1847; published 'Observations on Pulmonary Consumption,' 1814. [liii. 283]

SOUTHEY, ROBERT (1774–1843), poet and man of letters; expelled from Westminster School for a precocious protest against flogging; proceeded in 1792 to Balliol College, Oxford, where he pursued his private studies without interference, and began 'Joan of Arc,' an epic; visited there by Coleridge; converted by him to unitarianism and pantisocracy; married Edith Fricker (*d.* 1837) and visited Spain, 1795, Portugal, 1800; there finished 'Thalaba' and planned 'History of Portugal'; published 'Thalaba,' 1801, 'Madoc,' 1805; 'Curse of Kehama,' his chief epic, published, 1810; settled at Keswick and set to work compiling and translating from Spanish; began in 1808 thirty years' work as a regular contributor to the 'Quarterly' at 100*l*. an article; his admirable short 'Life of Nelson' expanded from an article, 1813; accepted in 1813 the laureateship, which had been offered to Scott; his 'Vision of Judgment' (parodied by Byron), published, 1821; his 'Life of Wesley,' 1820, his well-filled commonplace-books, 'Omniana' and 'The Doctor,' 1812 and 1837, and his standard 'Life' and edition of Cowper, 1833–7; remained friendly with Wordsworth, and in 1839 contracted a second marriage with Caroline Bowles; enjoyed from 1835 a pension of 300*l*., granted by Peel.   [liii. 284]

SOUTHGATE, HENRY (1818–1888), anthologist; a London print-auctioneer; compiled useful treasuries of quotation, notably 'Many Thoughts of Many Minds,' 1857, and 'Noble Thoughts in Noble Language,' 1871. [liii. 290]

SOUTHGATE, RICHARD (1729–1795), numismatist; B.A. St. John's College, Cambridge, 1749; a London curate, then rector of Warsop, and assistant-librarian, British Museum, from 1784; formed a great collection of ancient coins and medals ('Museum Southgatianum') and aided Pinkerton in his 'Essay on Medals,' 1784.
[liii. 291]

SOUTHREY or **SOTHEREY**, SIMON (*fl.* 1397–1401), Benedictine monk; D.D. Oxford; prior of St. Albans, 1397–*c*. 1401; wrote treatises against Wycliffites.
[liii. 291]

SOUTH-SAXONS, kings of. [See ÆLLA ,*d*. 514?; OSMUND, *fl.* 758.]

SOUTHWELL, EDWARD (1671–1730), statesman; son of Sir Robert Southwell (1635–1702) [q. v.]; of Merton College, Oxford; clerk to the council, 1699; vice-admiral of Munster, 1699; secretary of state for Ireland, 1702; joint-commissioner of the privy seal, 1701 and 1716; M.P., Rye, 1707–11, Tregony, 1711 and 1713, Preston, later in 1713; M.P., Kinsale (Irish parliament), till 1730; clerk to the crown and prothonotary of the king's bench, 1715; secretary of state, 1720.   [liii. 302]

SOUTHWELL, *verè* BACON, NATHANAEL (1598–1676), jesuit; on mission in England, 1622–8; returned to English College, Rome; completed 'Bibliotheca Scriptorum Societatis Jesu,' 1676.   [liii. 292]

SOUTHWELL, SIR RICHARD (1504–1564), courtier and official; of a Suffolk house; a tool of the court and Cromwell against monasteries, 1535–9; knighted, 1542; was a privy councillor under Edward VI; master of ordnance, 1554–60.   [liii. 292]

SOUTHWELL, SIR ROBERT (*d.* 1559), master of the rolls; younger brother of Sir Richard Southwell [q .v.]; knighted, 1537; profited greatly by suppression of monasteries, and was made master of rolls, 1542.   [liii. 293]

SOUTHWELL, ROBERT (1561?–1595), jesuit and poet; educated at Douay and Rome; took Roman orders and came on English mission, 1586, with Henry Garnett [q. v.]; became in 1589 domestic chaplain to Countess of Arundel; wrote religious tracts; captured when going to celebrate mass in 1592; subsequently tortured and executed. He left 'St. Peter's Complaint, with other poems,' 1595, 'Mæoniæ,' 1595, and 'A Foure-fould Meditation,' containing devotional poetry of a very high order, notably the 'Burning Babe,' admired by Ben Jonson.   [liii. 294]

SOUTHWELL, ROBERT (1607–1677), vice-admiral of Munster; collector of the port of Kinsale, 1631–54; sovereign of Kinsale, 1657; vice-admiral of Munster, 1670.
[liii. 300]

SOUTHWELL, SIR ROBERT (1635–1702), diplomatist; son of Robert Southwell (1607–1677) [q. v.]; B.A. Queen's College, Oxford, 1655; entered Lincoln's Inn, 1654; knighted, 1665; succeeded to his father's office in Munster, 1677; hon. D.C.L. Oxford, 1677; English envoy in Portugal, 1665–8, and after other diplomatic work became principal secretary of state for Ireland, 1690; P.R.S., 1690–5.   [liii. 299]

SOUTHWELL, *verè* BACON, THOMAS (1592–1637), jesuit; educated at Rome; theological professor at Liège, 1627–35; wrote some controversial tracts in Latin.
[liii. 303]

SOUTHWELL, THOMAS, first BARON SOUTHWELL (1667–1720), rose to importance in Ireland under William

III; fostered linen industry and protestant immigration; ennobled in 1717.   [liii. 303]

SOUTHWELL, WILLIAM (1669–1719), colonel of 6th foot; brother of Thomas Southwell, first baron Southwell [q. v.]; fought in Flanders and Spain with much gallantry, 1694–1708. especially at Barcelona, 1705; colonel, 1706; M.P., Baltimore (Irish House of Commons), 1715–19.   [liii. 304]

SOWERBY, GEORGE BRETTINGHAM, the elder (1788–1854), conchologist and artist; F.L.S., 1811; assisted his father and elder brother, and issued independently catalogues of shells and molluscs.   [liii. 304]

SOWERBY, GEORGE BRETTINGHAM, the younger (1812–1884), conchologist and artist; eldest son of George Brettingham Sowerby the elder [q. v.]; F.L.S., 1844; produced 'Conchological Illustrations,' 1841, and a number of handbooks on shells.   [liii. 305]

SOWERBY, HENRY (1825–1891), mining expert; brother of George Brettingham Sowerby the younger [q. v.]; assistant-librarian to the Linnean Society, 1843–1852; wrote on 'Popular Mineralogy,' 1850; went to Australia, 1854.   [liii. 305]

SOWERBY, JAMES (1757–1822), naturalist and artist; abandoned study of flower-painting for that of botany; his great work on 'English Botany' issued, 1790–1814; published also 'English Fungi,' 1797–1815, and compilations on mineralogy, conchology, and the like.
[liii. 305]

SOWERBY, JAMES DE CARLE (1787–1871), naturalist and artist; eldest son of James Sowerby [q. v.]; F.L.S., 1823; secretary of Royal Botanic Society and Gardens, 1838; executed botanical and also mineralogical and conchological plates, and aided his father and brother in many compilations.   [liii. 307]

SOWERBY, JOHN EDWARD (1825–1870), botanical draughtsman; illustrated botanical works, and brought out an 'Illustrated Key' to British wildflowers, 1865.
[liii. 308]

SOYER, ALEXIS BENOÎT (1809–1858), cook; the 'Mirobolant' of Thackeray's 'Pendennis'; left Paris in 1830, served Duke of Cambridge, and became chef at Reform Club, 1837; proceeded in 1855 to Scutari, reorganised victualling of the hospitals, and introduced a cooking wagon; wrote several cookery books, including a 'History of Food in all Ages,' 1853.   [liii. 308]

SOYER, ELIZABETH EMMA (1813–1842), painter; wife of Alexis Benoit Soyer [q. v.]; a pupil of F. Simoneau; excelled in depicting street arabs, exhibiting with success, 1823–42.   [liii. 309]

SPALDING, JOHN (*fl.* 1650), Scottish historian; of Aberdeen; wrote the valuable annalistic 'History of the Troubles and Memorable Transactions in Scotland,' 1624–1645 (first published, 1792); the 'Spalding Club' named after him.   [liii. 310]

SPALDING, SAMUEL (1807–1843), writer on moral philosophy; M.A. London, 1840; wrote an essay (based on Mackintosh) on 'The Philosophy of Christian Morals,' issued, 1843.   [liii. 310]

SPALDING, WILLIAM (1809–1859), author; M.A. Marischal College, Aberdeen, 1827; published a valuable book on 'Italy,' 1841, also a 'History of English Literature,' 1853, and contributed to 'Edinburgh Review,' especially on Shakespearean subjects.   [liii. 310]

SPARK, THOMAS (1655–1692), classical scholar; M.A. Christ Church, Oxford, 1679; D.D., 1691; chaplain to Judge Jeffreys; dedicated an edition of Zosimus to Busby, 1679; annotated Lactantius, 1684.   [liii. 311]

SPARKE, EDWARD (*d.* 1692), divine; M.A. Clare Hall, Cambridge, 1633; B.D., 1640 (incorporated at Oxford, 1653); chaplain to Charles II. His devotional work, 'Scintillula Altaris,' 1652, reached many editions.
[liii. 311]

SPARKE or **SPARKES**, JOSEPH (1683–1740), antiquary; B.A. St. John's College, Cambridge, 1704; edited, in two folio volumes, 'Historiæ Anglicanæ Scriptores varii,' 1723.   [liii. 312]

SPARKE, THOMAS (1548–1616), divine; fellow of Magdalen College, Oxford, 1569; M.A., 1574; D.D., 1581; a conforming puritan of note and prebendary of Lincoln and rector of Bletchley, attended Hampton Court conference, 1603 ; was influenced by James I and wrote a 'Brotherly Persuasion to Unity and Uniformity,' 1607 ; wrote other controversial treatises. [liii. 312]

SPARKE, WILLIAM (1587-1641), chaplain to Buckingham ; fellow of Magdalen College, Oxford ; M.A., 1609 ; B.D., 1629 ; wrote religious tracts. [liii. 313]

SPARROW, ANTHONY (1612-1685), royalist divine ; fellow of Queens' College, Cambridge, 1633 ; became bishop of Exeter, 1667, of Norwich, 1676 ; wrote a valuable 'Rationale upon the Book of Common Prayer,' 1657 (re-edited by Newman, 1839). [liii. 313]

SPARROW, JOHN (1615-1665 ?), mystic ; of the Inner Temple; a student of Jacob Boehme, issued 'prophetical passages,' and a mystical commentary on Genesis, 1654. [liii. 314]

SPEARMAN, ROBERT (1703-1761), eccentric theologian ; pupil of John Hutchinson (1674-1737) [q. v.]; published 'An Enquiry after Philosophy and Theology,' 1755. [liii. 314]

SPEARS, ROBERT (1825-1899), unitarian preacher and journalist ; master of new connexion methodists' school at Scotswood-on-Tyne, 1846 ; joined unitarians, 1849 ; minister at Sunderland, 1852-8 ; originated 'Christian Freeman' magazine, 1856 ; established 'Christian Life' weekly paper, 1876 ; founded unitarian chapel at Highgate, London, 1886, co-secretary, 1867, and general secretary, 1869-76, of British and Foreign Unitarian Association ; published biographical and theological works. [Suppl. iii. 351]

SPEDDING, JAMES (1808-1881), editor of Bacon's 'Works'; educated at Bury St. Edmunds and Trinity College, Cambridge ; junior optime, 1831 ; held a temporary post in colonial office, but in 1841 devoted himself to study of Bacon; contributed to the 'Gentleman's Magazine' (August 1850) a discussion on Shakespeare and Fletcher's respective shares in 'Henry VIII' (reprinted by the New Shakespere Society), 1874 ; published Bacon's 'Life and Letters,' 7 vols. 1861-74, as a supplement to Bacon's 'Works' in 7 vols., 1857-9 (the 'Life' abridged, 1878) ; remained through life the close friend of the Tennysons, Sir Henry Taylor, and Edward FitzGerald. Several essays by him were published after his death, which was due to an accident. [liii. 315]

SPEECHLY, WILLIAM (*fl.* 1776-1820), agriculturist; gardener to William Henry Cavendish Bentinck, third duke of Portland [q. v.] ; published a manual of 'Rural Economy,' 1820, and essays. [liii. 316]

SPEED, ADOLPHUS (*fl.* 1652), agricultural writer; commenced his 'Adam out of Eden,' 1626 (published, 1659) ; wrote also a 'Cornucopia,' 1652 ; lifelong ally of Samuel Hartlib. [liii. 317]

SPEED, JOHN (1552 ?-1629), historian and cartographer ; brought up as a tailor by his father ; settled in Moorfields, London, and obtained a post in custom-house, 1598 ; made various maps of English counties, and was encouraged by Camden, Cotton, and others, whose 'Society of Antiquaries' he joined, to write his carefully digested 'History of Great Britaine,' 1611 ; wrote also 'A Cloude of Witnesses' confirming 'God's Holie Word,' 1616. [liii. 318]

SPEED, JOHN (1595-1640), scholar: son of John Speed (1552 ?-1629) [q. v.] ; M.A. St. John's College, Oxford, 1620 ; M.D., 1628 ; wrote tracts and 'Stonehenge,' a pastoral, 1635. [liii. 319]

SPEED, JOHN (1628-1711), author ; son of John Speed (1595-1640) [q. v.] ; fellow of St. John's College, Oxford, 1647 ; M.A., 1660 ; M.D., 1666 ; wrote 'Batt upon Batt,' a poem, and formed manuscript collections relating to Southampton, of which he was mayor in 1681 and 1694. [liii. 319]

SPEED, SAMUEL (*d.* 1681), stationer and bookseller of Fleet Street, London ; wrote in doggerel 'Fragmenta Carceris,' 1674, and 'Prison Pietie.' [liii. 320]

SPEED, SAMUEL (1631-1682), divine ; eldest son of John Speed (1595-1640) [q. v.] ; of Westminster School and Christ Church, Oxford ; student; M.A., 1660 ; was presented to vicarage of Godalming after Restoration, with other benefices; published (1678) a version of the 'Romæ Antiquæ Descriptio' of Valerius Maximus. [liii. 320]

SPEGHT, THOMAS (*fl.* 1598), editor of Chaucer and schoolmaster ; M.A. Peterhouse, Cambridge, 1573 ; possibly head-master of Ely Cathedral school, 1572 ; edited, 1598, 'The Workes of our Antient and learned English Poet, Geffrey Chaucer.' A new edition was called for in 1602, in which he availed himself of the criticism and aid of a former Chaucer editor's son, Francis Thynne. [liii. 320]

SPEKE, GEORGE (*d.* 1690), royalist ; suffered heavily during civil war ; M.P., Somerset, 1679 ; joined Green Ribbon Club, and was punished by fine for abetting Monmouth supporters in 1685. [liii. 322]

SPEKE, HUGH (1656-1724 ?), political agitator ; son of George Speke [q. v.] ; of St. John's College, Oxford, and Lincoln's Inn ; reflected on the Duke of York in a pamphlet on the murder of Essex, 1683 ; sent to prison by Jeffreys for three years on a charge of sedition, 1683 ; on the news of the Prince of Orange's landing in 1688 offered his services to James II, but betrayed him to the Prince of Orange ; in a 'Secret History of the Revolution' (1715) claimed that he had forged the printed 'declaration' which set the mob upon the catholics ; failed miserably in his attempts to extort bribes for these 'services.' [liii. 322]

SPEKE, JOHN HANNING (1827-1864), African explorer and discoverer of the source of the Nile ; served in Punjab under the first Viscount Gough, but left India, 1854, to explore Somaliland under (Sir) Richard Burton; set out in 1856 under Burton to investigate Lake Nyassa, and discovered Lakes Tanganyika and Victoria Nyanza, the latter independently of Burton ; his theory that V. Nyanza was the 'source reservoir' of the Nile subsequently confirmed by himself and Grant in the summer of 1862 ; his 'Journal of the Discovery of the Nile,' published, 1863 ; gave information to (Sir) Samuel White Baker [q. v.] which enabled him to discover the third lake, Albert Nyanza ; was, with Grant, the first European to cross equatorial Africa. [liii. 324]

SPELMAN, CLEMENT (1598-1679), cursitor baron of exchequer ; of Queens' College, Cambridge ; barrister, Gray's Inn, 1624 ; wrote in support of his father, Sir Henry Spelman's [q. v.] views of sacrilege ; bencher of Gray's Inn, 1660 ; cursitor baron of the exchequer, 1663-78. [liii. 327]

SPELMAN or **YALLOP**, EDWARD (*d.* 1767), author and translator ; published well-known versions of Xenophon's 'Anabasis,' 1742, and of fragments of Polybius, 1743, and Dionysius Halicarnassus, 1758. [liii. 328]

SPELMAN, SIR HENRY (1564 ?-1641), historian and antiquary ; studied at Trinity College, Cambridge (B.A., 1583), and Lincoln's Inn ; M.P., Castle Rising, 1597 ; commissioner on unsettled Irish lands, 1617 ; settled in London for study, 1612, and (1613) printed his 'De non temerandis Ecclesiis,' material for his much more elaborate work, the 'History of Sacrilege' (published, 1698) ; his 'Glossary' of obsolete Latin and old English terms published, 2 vols., 1626, 1664 ; subsequently published compilations on 'Councils of the Church,' the 'Tenures by Knight Service'; founded a short-lived Anglo-Saxon readership at Cambridge, 1635. [liii. 328]

SPELMAN, SIR JOHN (1495 ?-1544), judge of king's bench ; reader of Gray's Inn, 1514 and 1519 ; a discreet courtier ; appointed a judge of king's bench, 1533, and special commissioner at trials of More, Fisher, and Anne Boleyn. [liii. 333]

SPELMAN, SIR JOHN (1594-1643), royalist and author ; son of Sir Henry Spelman [q. v.] ; educated at Cambridge, Gray's Inn, and Paris, and in Italy ; gained Charles I's favour early in civil war ; knighted, 1641 ; brought out some learned pamphlets, and compiled a 'Life of King Alfred' (published, 1678). [liii. 333]

SPENCE, BENJAMIN EDWARD (1822-1866), sculptor ; studied under R. J. Wyatt and John Gibson ; exhibited at Royal Academy five times, 1849-66. [liii. 334]

SPENCE, ELIZABETH ISABELLA (1768-1832), author ; wrote novels and home-travel sketches, 1799-1823. [liii. 334]

SPENCE, GEORGE (1787-1850), jurist ; M.A. Glasgow, 1805 ; M.P. successively for Reading and Ripon, 1826-32 ; a pioneer of chancery reform ; improved legal education ; published a standard work on chancery jurisdiction, 1846-9. [liii. 335]

SPENCE, JAMES (1812–1882), surgeon; studied at Edinburgh; taught anatomy and surgery there, 1834–1882; appointed professor of surgery, 1864; a great operating surgeon of the older school.   [liii. 335]

SPENCE, JOSEPH (1699–1768), anecdotist and friend of Pope; of Winchester School and Magdalen Hall and New College, Oxford; fellow of New College, Oxford, 1720; M.A., 1727; succeeded Thomas Warton (1688 ?–1745) [q. v.] as professor of poetry at Oxford, 1728; accompanied young men of rank on foreign tours, and in 1742 was given as a sinecure the regius professorship of modern history at Oxford; published 'Polymetis' (a treatise on classical mythology), 1747; took notes of the conversation of Pope and his circle. His admirable literary anecdotes were used by Dr. Johnson and others, but not published until 1820, when two editions appeared simultaneously, the best by Samuel Weller Singer [q. v.]   [liii. 336]

SPENCE, THOMAS (1750–1814), bookseller and author of the Spencean scheme of land nationalisation; submitted his plan of corporate land tenure, upon semi-socialistic principles, to a local philosophical society in 1775; expelled from the society for hawking his pamphlets; was consistently persecuted for his views and his pamphlets on the rights of man, the millennium, the natural state of man, phonetic spelling, and other schemes. His views found many supporters, but were directly challenged by Malthus.   [liii. 338]

SPENCE, WILLIAM (1783–1860), entomologist: collaborated with William Kirby [q. v.] in the celebrated 'Introduction to Entomology,' 1815–26; wrote also some economic treatises; president, 1847, of the Entomological Society, which he had helped to found in 1833.
                    [liii. 340]

SPENCER. [See also DESPENSER and SPENSER.]

SPENCER, AUBREY GEORGE (1795–1872), first bishop of Newfoundland; of Magdalen Hall, Oxford; after work in the Bermudas was appointed bishop of Newfoundland, 1839; laid first stone of the cathedral of St. John's, Newfoundland; translated to Jamaica, 1843.
                    [liii. 340]

SPENCER, Sir AUGUSTUS ALMERIC (1807–1893), general; grandson of George Spencer, fourth duke of Marlborough [q. v.]; commanded 44th regiment at Alma and Inkerman; wounded during the siege of Sebastopol, June 1855; C.B.; obtained the Crimea medal; commanded in 1860 a division of Madras army as major-general; commander-in-chief of Bombay army, 1869; general, 1875.   [liii. 341]

SPENCER, Sir BRENT (1760–1828), general; served with distinction in the West Indies, 1779–82, 1790–4, and again as brigadier-general in 1797 against Toussaint l'Ouverture; commanded 40th regiment in the Duke of York's expedition to the Helder, 1799; commanded at Aboukir Bay and Alexandria under Moore and Abercromby, 1801; returned to England and became an equerry of George III; served at Copenhagen and Cadiz, and was second in command to Wellesley at Roliça and Vimiera; K.B., 1809; returned to Peninsula, 1810, and commanded a division at Busaco and at Fuentes d'Onoro; superseded by Graham, 1811; general, 1825. His pessimistic letters home had shaken Wellington's faith in his capacity.   [liii. 341]

SPENCER, 'BUCK' (1743–1803). [See WOODHAM, MRS.]

SPENCER, CHARLES, third EARL OF SUNDERLAND (1674–1722), statesman and bibliophile; second son of Robert Spencer, second earl of Sunderland [q. v.]; early contracted a taste for rare books, and began to develop a library at Althorp; entered parliament for Tiverton in 1695 as a zealous whig, affecting the airs of a republican; married Anne Churchill, 1700, thus gaining the support of Marlborough, whose approximation to the orthodox whig party the alliance served to further; went out as an envoy extraordinary to Vienna, 1705; through his father-in-law's influence was named secretary of state for the southern department, appointing Addison as his under-secretary, 1706; especially hated by Harley and the high church tories, who persuaded Queen Anne to dismiss him, 1710; his impeachment desired by the extreme section of the tories, who came into power in the autumn of 1710;

during last years of Queen Anne was in constant communication with Hanover; his zeal very displeasing to the heads of the whig party; on Queen Anne's death was excluded from the lords justices and sent to Ireland as viceroy; became lord privy seal, 1715, but had no real influence; fomented opposition to Townshend and Walpole with considerable success, ousting them from office in 1717, and himself becoming first lord of the treasury, March 1718; on account of the threatening attitude of Walpole and the general feeling that he was largely responsible for the South Sea fiasco, was forced to resign early in 1721 in favour of his rival; still retained influence with George I, though this did not prevent his coquetting with the tories. As a politician he was singularly unattractive, cross-grained, and tactless, but in the main honest and zealous for liberty.   [liii. 343]

SPENCER, CHARLES, third DUKE OF MARLBOROUGH and fifth EARL OF SUNDERLAND (1706–1758), third son of Charles Spencer, third earl of Sunderland [q. v.]; grandson of the great Duke of Marlborough; succeeded in turn to both titles, 1729 and 1733; opposed the court down to 1738 in order to curry favour with the old duchess; accepted a colonelcy of the 38th foot and a place in the bedchamber, 1738; commanded a brigade at Dettingen, 1743, and the abortive expedition against St. Malo in 1758; despatched with an English contingent to join Prince Ferdinand in Westphalia, 1758; died suddenly at Munster.
                    [liii. 349]

SPENCER, LORD CHARLES (1740–1820), politician; sat for Oxfordshire as moderate whig, 1761–84 and 1796–1801; admiralty lord, 1779; vice-treasurer of Ireland, 1782; postmaster-general, 1801–6; master of the mint, 1801–6.   [liii. 352]

SPENCER, DOROTHY, COUNTESS OF SUNDERLAND (1617–1684), Waller's 'Sacharissa'; courted at Penshurst from c. 1634 till 1639 by Waller, whose attachment seems to have been mainly literary; married, 1639, Henry, lord Spencer (created Earl of Sunderland shortly before his death from a wound received at Newbury, 1643); retired to Althorp after her husband's death, and assisted many distressed clergy and royalists; married (Sir) Robert Smythe, 1652; spent much time at Halifax's seat of Rufford, and often met her old admirer Waller, whose attentions have made her name and beauty famous.
                    [liii. 352]

SPENCER, GEORGE, fourth DUKE OF MARLBOROUGH (1739–1817), son of Charles Spencer, third duke of Marlborough [q. v.]; captain of the 20th foot, 1756; left the army, 1758; obtained office in the Grenville ministry as lord privy seal, 1763–5; hon. D.C.L. Oxford, 1763; K.G., 1768; took little part in political affairs after his early years.   [liii. 354]

SPENCER, GEORGE, fifth DUKE OF MARLBOROUGH (1766–1840), of Eton and Christ Church, Oxford; M.A., 1786; D.C.L., 1792; M.P., Oxfordshire, 1790–6, Tregony, 1802–4; a lord of the treasury, 1804–6; spent enormous sums on his gardens and library of early printed books at White Knights, near Reading, giving 2,260l. for Valderfen's edition of the 'Decameron' at the Duke of Roxburghe's sale, 1812.   [liii. 354]

SPENCER, GEORGE JOHN, second EARL SPENCER (1758–1834), M.A. Trinity College, Cambridge, 1778; M.P., Northampton, 1780, Surrey, 1782; succeeded his father, John Spencer, first earl Spencer, in the upper house in 1783; deserted the extreme whig faction as a follower of Burke; made first lord of the admiralty by Pitt, 1794; improved the naval administration, and helped to achieve great victories, such as St. Vincent and Camperdown, by his organising skill; the mutinies of Spithead and the Nore put down under his rule; singled out Nelson and sent him to win the battle of the Nile; K.G., 1799; resigned office with Pitt, 1801; home secretary, 1806–7; while in retirement helped to form the Roxburghe Club, 1812, and rehabilitated the Althorp Library, as described by Thomas Frognall Dibdin [q. v.] in his 'Bibliotheca Spenceriana.' The collection went in 1892 to form the nucleus of the Rylands Library at Manchester.   [liii. 355]

SPENCER, GEORGE TREVOR (1799–1866), bishop of Madras; B.A. University College, Oxford, 1822; consecrated, 1837; created D.D., 1847; remained in India for twelve years, publishing journals of his southern visitations; appointed chancellor of St. Paul's Cathedral, 1860.
                    [liii. 356]

SPENCER, GERVASE (d. 1763), miniature-painter; began by copying a portrait of one of the family in which he was servant; produced artistic miniatures in ivory and enamel. [liii. 357]

SPENCER, HENRY LE (d. 1406). [See DESPENSER, HENRY LE.]

SPENCER, HENRY, first EARL OF SUNDERLAND (1620-1643), created M.A. Magdalen College, Oxford, 1636; fought for Charles I and was killed by Falkland's side at Newbury, 20 Sept. 1642; married in 1639 Lady Dorothy Sidney [see SPENCER, DOROTHY], and had issue Robert, second earl of Sunderland [q. v.]. [liii. 368]

SPENCER, LORD HENRY JOHN (1770-1795), second son of George Spencer, fourth duke of Marlborough [q. v.]; educated at Eton and Oxford; showed great promise as envoy at the Hague, Stockholm, and Berlin, 1790-5. [liii. 355]

SPENCER, SIR JOHN (d. 1610), lord mayor of London; a Levant merchant; visited by Queen Elizabeth at Canonbury, London, 1581; kept his mayoralty, 1594-5, at Crosby Place, London; knighted, 1595; a noted hunter down of papists. [liii. 357]

SPENCER, JOHN (1559-1614). [See SPENSER.]

SPENCER, JOHN (1601-1671), controversialist; entered Society of Jesus, 1626; professor at Liège and missioner at Antwerp; became superior of Worcester district, 1658; wrote several controversial works against John Lenthall, bishops Gunning, Pearson, and others. [liii. 358]

SPENCER, JOHN (1630-1693), master of Corpus Christi College, Cambridge; became fellow there, c. 1655; master of the college, 1667-93; M.A., 1652; D.D., 1665; was an erudite hebraist, and in his 'Dissertatio de Urim et Thummim,' 1669, and 'De Legibus Hebræorum,' laid the foundations of the science of comparative religion, tracing the connection between the rites of the Hebrew religion and those practised by kindred Semitic races. [liii. 359]

SPENCER, JOHN CHARLES, VISCOUNT ALTHORP and third EARL SPENCER (1782-1845), eldest son of George John Spencer, second earl Spencer [q. v.]; left in childhood to the care of servants; went to Harrow, 1790; became devotedly attached to field-sports; M.A. Trinity College, Cambridge, 1802; his debts and clumsy manners a source of embarrassment to his parents, who tried in vain to interest him in foreign art and manners; became M.P. for Okehampton, 1804, and supported Pitt; M.P., St. Albans, 1806, Northamptonshire, 1806-34; rarely spoke in parliament, devoting himself to the Pytchley hunt, prize fights, and races; drawn into active politics by his admiration for Fox; joined the advanced whig party, voting with Whitbread, Mackintosh, Romilly, and Brougham; from 1815 to 1820 studied economic history and working-class grievances, supporting Huskisson and even Joseph Hume; became in 1830 leader of the whig opposition in the Commons, and on Wellington's resignation in December chancellor of the exchequer and leader in the lower house under Earl Grey; behaved with signal industry and honesty of purpose; returned to office with an increased whig majority, 1831, and showed his zeal for the Reform Bill by the vigour with which he rallied his followers on its rejection by the lords in October; resigned again in May 1832, but had to return to office in a few days, and saw the Reform Bill pass the lords on 4 June 1832; depressed by the intrigues of O'Connell, 1833-4; lost influence at the time of the rise of Peel; he retained office reluctantly till his succession to the earldom, 1834; withdrew with satisfaction to country pursuits, emerging only in 1841 to pronounce in favour of the repeal of the corn laws. Almost devoid of political ambition, he stepped at one stroke to the leadership of the House of Commons, and won absolute trust from friends and opponents alike by his truthfulness and integrity. Macaulay said of him that he had 'the temper of Lord North with the principles of Romilly.' [liii. 360]

SPENCER, ROBERT, first BARON SPENCER OF WORMLEIGHTON (d. 1627), the descendant of a knightly family which had derived great wealth from sheep-breeding; reputed the richest man in England; created baron by James I, 1603; active as an opponent of Bacon at the latter's trial; an adherent of Southampton, and a subscriber to the Virginia Company. [liii. 367]

SPENCER, ROBERT, second EARL OF SUNDERLAND (1640-1702), only son of Henry Spencer, first earl of Sunderland, by his wife, Dorothy ('Sacharissa') [see SPENCER, DOROTHY]; born at Paris; succeeded to the title, 1643; studied in Southern Europe and at Christ Church, Oxford, showing much precocity; married, in 1665, a rich heiress, Anne Digby; after paying assiduous court to Charles II's mistresses, obtained political employment on embassies to Madrid and to Paris, 1671-2; early in 1679, upon payment of 6,000l., succeeded Williamson as secretary of state for the northern department; during the next eighteen months was in the inner cabinet, and exercised much influence; dismissed for his intrigues with the demagogues and exclusionists (February 1681), on which he recanted, made abject submission to James, duke of York, and regained his place in 1683, striving especially to oust Halifax and Rochester from favour; as a strenuous supporter of the royal prerogative, no less than as a subtle contriver of expedients, commended himself to James II on his accession in 1685, and showed his skill by the way in which he avoided being compromised by Monmouth; his unscrupulous intrigues against his chief rival with James II, Rochester, consummated by his throwing in his lot with the victorious catholic party, and by his gaining the complete confidence of James II's queen; supported the repeal of the Test Act, the recall of the three British regiments from Holland, and the committal of the seven bishops; renounced protestantism, 1687, but was disturbed by the internal feuds of the catholic party, and was all the time making overtures to the Prince of Orange; was sceptical of the success of an invasion, but flattered himself that he might act as mediator between king and parliament; advised remedial measures when too late; fled in female disguise to Rotterdam early in November 1688; reverted to protestantism, and from Rotterdam sent William of Orange (William III) numerous explanations and suggestions, which convinced William that his skill as a wirepuller was indispensable; advised William III to confide in a united whig ministry in preference to a composite body of whigs and tories, and by his own diplomatic skill made the scheme a success; endeavoured to obtain ostensible position and power, and (1697) was made lord chamberlain and one of the lords justices; his appointment strongly resented, even the whig junto, though they owed him much, shrinking from his defence; hastily resigned office, but retained his great wealth and much of his influence until his death. He has generally been considered, and probably with justice, as the craftiest, most rapacious, and most unscrupulous of all the politicians of his age. [liii. 368]

SPENCER, SIR ROBERT CAVENDISH (1791-1830), captain in the navy; served against New Orleans in 1813, and commanded the Naiad against Algiers, 1824; employed on the coast of Greece during the war of independence; K.C.H. and knighted, 1828; reputed a pattern commander; died off Alexandria. [liii. 377]

SPENCER, THOMAS (1791-1811), independent divine; trained at the Hoxton College (entering the pulpit at seventeen); obtained great repute as a preacher in London, at Brighton, and, in 1811, at Liverpool; his 'Sermons' printed posthumously, 1829. [liii. 378]

SPENCER, THOMAS (1796-1853), writer on social subjects; ninth wrangler, St. John's College, Cambridge, 1820; came under Charles Simeon's influence at Cambridge, 1816-20; fellow of St. John's College, Cambridge, 1823; became a zealous social reformer in his curacy of Hinton Charterhouse, 1826-47; a keen opponent of slavery, the corn laws, intemperance, and pauperism; published pamphlets. [liii. 378]

SPENCER, WILLIAM GEORGE (1790-1866), mathematician; elder brother of Thomas Spencer (1796-1853) [q. v.]; taught private pupils in mathematics with much originality and success; published 'Inventional Geometry,' 1860, a work of which the soundness of both principle and method is widely recognised; invented a system of lucid shorthand. Both works have been edited by his son, Mr. Herbert Spencer. [liii. 379]

SPENCER, WILLIAM ROBERT (1769-1834), poet and wit; educated at Harrow and Christ Church, Oxford; mixed freely in the society of Sheridan, Fox, Sydney Smith, and Horner; translated from the German of Bürger; attracted Byron by his society verse, and Christopher North by his ballads ; died after a life of extravagance in poverty and obscurity at Paris. [liii. 380]

SPENDER, LILY, known as MRS. JOHN KENT SPENDER (1835–1895), novelist ; *née* Headland ; wrote for ' London Quarterly ' and other reviews, and produced over twenty novels, 1869–95. [liii. 380]

SPENS, SIR JAMES (*fl.* 1598-1630), Scots adventurer and diplomatist ; attempted, unsuccessfully, to settle the island of Lewis, 1598 ; entered service of Charles IX of Sweden ; knighted ; envoy from James I to Gustavus Adolphus, 1612 ; served as intermediary between Gustavus and England, 1623–7 and 1629–30. [liii. 381]

SPENS, SIR JOHN (1520 ?–1573), of Condie ; queen's advocate ; educated at St. Salvator's College, St. Andrews ; was made a judge in 1560, holding at the same time the office of queen's advocate ; showed sympathy with Knox, but adhered to Mary Stuart's party, and prosecuted officially both the murderer of Riccio and that of Darnley ; remained in office until his death. [liii. 382]

SPENS, THOMAS DE (1415 ?–1480), bishop of Aberdeen ; went on embassies to Henry VI of England, 1446, and to Charles VII of France, 1449 ; became bishop of Aberdeen, 1449 ; keeper of the privy seal, 1458 ; went on missions to Edward IV and to Charles the Bold ; gave information to Edward IV of a conspiracy against him formed at Bruges ; was captured by English war-ships as he was escorting the Duke of Albany to Scotland, 1464, but well treated by Edward IV and sent back to Scotland ; helped to secure the meeting between Edward IV and Louis XI at Pecquigny, and to maintain the peace between James III and Edward IV ; again keeper of the Scots privy seal, 1468–71 ; treated at Alnwick for a permanent peace with the English, 1471, the treaty being eventually signed in 1473 ; negotiated the betrothal of Prince James [IV] with Cecilia, youngest daughter of Edward IV, 1474 ; rebuilt the bishop's palace, and was a munificent benefactor of St. Machar's Cathedral, Aberdeen. [liii. 382]

SPENSER. [See DESPENSER and SPENCER.]

SPENSER, EDMUND (1552 ?–1599), poet ; elder son of John Spenser, described as a ' gentleman ' and a journeyman in the art of clothmaking ; born probably, *c.* 1552, in East Smithfield, London, whither his father had migrated from the Burnley district of Lancashire ; his hereditary connection with this district confirmed by the dialect employed in the ' Shepheard's Calendar ' and other early pieces ; educated at Merchant Taylors' School ; matriculated sizar from Pembroke Hall, Cambridge, May, 1569 ; at Cambridge ; studied Latin, Greek, French, and Italian assiduously, making influential friends ; M.A., 1576 ; while still at Cambridge, contributed fourteen sonnet ' Visions ' from Du Bellay to an edifying ' Theatre for Worldlings,' 1568 ; obtained in 1578, through his college friend, Gabriel Harvey, a place in Leicester's household ; became, through Leicester, acquainted with Sir Philip Sidney ; with Sidney, Dyer, and Drant formed a literary club styled the Areopagus ; while under Leicester's roof and in love with a fair ' Rosalind ' (probably a yeoman's daughter), made experiments, at the instance of Harvey and Edward Kirke, in classical measures ; published (with archaic glossary suggested partly by Kirke) the ' Shepheard's Calendar ' (twelve eclogues), 1579, and began the ' Faerie Queene ' ; his ' Shepheard's Calendar ' enthusiastically received ; was appointed secretary to Arthur Grey, fourteenth lord Grey de Wilton [q. v.], then going to Ireland as lord deputy, 1580 ; was well rewarded for his work in Ireland, which remained his home until within a month of his death ; left the neighbourhood of Dublin for Kilcolman Castle upon an estate he had acquired near Cork, 1588 ; occupied himself with literary work, writing his elegy on ' Astrophel ' (Sidney) in 1586, and preparing for the press his ' Faerie Queene,' three books of which were entrusted to the printer on the poet's visit to London, November 1589 ; reluctantly returned to Kilcolman, 1591, and penned ' Colin Clouts come home again ' (printed, 1595), by the reputation of the ' Faerie Queene ' led the publisher Ponsonby to collect his minor verse and *juvenilia*, in part rewritten, as ' Complaints, containing sundrie small poems of the worlds vanitie,' 1590 ; married (1594) Elizabeth Boyle, whom he had wooed in his ' Amoretti,' and celebrated the marriage in his splendid ' Epithalamion ' (the two printed together, 1595) ; published the second instalment of three books of

the ' Faerie Queene ' and ' Foure Hymnes,' 1596, being in London for the purpose at Essex House, where he wrote his ' Prothalamion,' and also his well-informed, though one-sided, prose ' View of the Present State of Ireland ' ; returned to Kilcolman, depressed both in mind and health, 1597 ; his castle of Kilcolman burned, October 1598, in a sudden insurrection of the natives, chiefly O'Neills, under the ' sugan ' Earl of Desmond, on which, with his wife and four children, he was compelled to flee for refuge to Cork ; sent over to England early in December 1598 with a despatch from the president of Munster to the government in London ; died in distress, if not actual poverty, at a lodging in King Street, Westminster, a month later ; buried near his favourite Chaucer in Westminster Abbey. Four portraits of him are extant. His main achievement, the moral and allegorical, but pre-eminently pictorial, ' Faerie Queene,' was the only great poem that had been written in England since Chaucer died. As a scholar ranking near Milton and Gray, as a metrist and inventor of the Spenserian stanza, and as ' the poet's poet,' his high position and influence in our poetic literature cannot be overestimated. [liii. 384]

SPENSER, JOHN (1559–1614), president of Corpus Christi College, Oxford ; M.A. Corpus Christi College, Oxford, 1581 ; elected president, 1607, having been previously fellow and Greek reader at the college ; took part in the authorised version of 1611, being upon the New Testament committee ; was at great pains in bringing out in complete form the work of his friend Richard Hooker [q. v.], 1604. [liii. 398]

SPERLING, JOHN (1793–1877), lieutenant, royal engineers ; served in Holland under Sir James Carmichael Smyth [q. v.], 1813–14 ; prepared defence against Napoleon's invasion of 1815, was at Waterloo, and Paris, 1816 ; retired from service in 1824, and wrote a diary of his active service, published, 1872. [liii. 399]

SPICER, HENRY (1743 ?–1804), miniature portrait-painter ; exhibited, 1765–1804 ; painter in enamel to George, prince of Wales. [liii. 400]

SPIERS, ALEXANDER (1807–1869), lexicographer ; doctor of philosophy, Leipzig ; English teacher at Paris ; produced, after fourteen years' work, his ' General English and French Dictionary ' 1846, which won him a cross of the Legion of Honour. [liii. 401]

SPIGURNEL, HENRY (1263 ?–1328), judge ; was summoned to parliaments of Edward I and Edward II, and made a justice of oyer and terminer, 1300 ; sent on a mission to papal court, 1311 ; interpreted the ordinances, 1312 ; retired, 1327. [liii. 401]

SPILLAN, DANIEL (*d.* 1854), scholar and medical writer ; educated at Trinity College, Dublin ; M.A. and M.B., 1826 ; unsuccessful in practice ; wrote manuals of therapeutics, clinics, chemistry and medicine, and translated from Sophocles, Tacitus, and Livy ; died in St. Pancras workhouse, London. [liii. 402]

SPILLER, JAMES (1692–1730), comedian ; son of ' the ' Gloucester carrier ; learned painting, but drifted as a player to Drury Lane, London ; played with Pinkethman at Greenwich, 1710, and three years later settled under John Rich at Lincoln's Inn Fields, London, playing such parts as Iachimo, Pistol, Pandarus, Dr. Caius, Marplot, Sir Politick Would-be, and Brainworm ; frequently confined in the Marshalsea for debt, an inn near Clare Market, London, which he frequented becoming noted as the " Spiller's Head.' [liii. 402]

SPILSBURY, JOHN (1730 ?–1795 ?), engraver ; drawing-master at Harrow ; executed heads, and fifty engravings from gems, 1785. [liii. 404]

SPILSBURY, JONATHAN (*fl.* 1760–1790), engraver ; practised mainly in mezzo-portraits, but engraved some subject-pieces after Rembrandt, Rubens, and Murillo. [liii. 404]

SPILSBURY, MARIA (*d.* 1820 ?), rural painter ; daughter of Jonathan Spilsbury [q. v.] ; exhibited domestic and rural pieces, 1792–1813, and a few etchings. [liii. 404]

SPINCKES, NATHANIEL (1653–1727), nonjuror ; Rustat scholar of Jesus College, Oxford ; M.A., 1677 ; became chaplain to first Duke of Lauderdale, 1681, and a close friend of his fellow-chaplain, George Hickes [q. v.], deprived of preferments, 1690, upon declining to take oath of allegiance to William and Mary; became a leader among nonjurors, and was consecrated a bishop among them by Hickes, 1713; friend of the pious Robert Nelson; published sermons and devotions. [liii. 405]

SPITTLEHOUSE, JOHN (*fl.* 1653), pamphleteer; fought against Charles I from 1644; remained until battle of Worcester with the Roundhead army, of which he wrote several vindications. [liii. 406]

SPODE, JOSIAH (1754-1827), potter; of Stoke-upon-Trent; improved the old willow pattern, jasper, cream, and black ware; opened a large London warehouse; commenced making porcelain with improved (bone) paste in 1800; made potter to George III, 1806; the most successful china manufacturer of his time. [liii. 406]

SPOFFORTH, REGINALD (1770-1827), glee composer; composed about seventy lively glees for 'Nobleman's Catch Club' and other clubs, besides stage music; a good pianist. [liii. 407]

SPOONER, CHARLES (*d.* 1767), mezzotint engraver; a skilful copyist; engraved many good portraits in Dublin, 1749-56, and afterwards in London. [liii. 407]

SPOONER, CHARLES (1806-1871), veterinary surgeon; passed the Royal Veterinary College, 1829, and was appointed veterinary surgeon to the Zoological Society; was appointed demonstrator of anatomy at the Royal Veterinary College, 1839, and principal and chief professor, 1853, and by 1858 was president of the incorporated Royal College of Veterinary Surgeons. [liii. 407]

SPOONER, WILLIAM CHARLES (1809?-1885), veterinary surgeon; son of a Blandford innkeeper; practised at Southampton; studied chemical manures; was a great judge of horses, and wrote two treatises on veterinary matters, but was chiefly known for his standard work on 'Sheep,' 1844. [liii. 408]

SPORLEY or SPORTE, RICHARD (*d.* 1490?), historian; monk of Westminster, *c.* 1430; wrote a collection of annals, 1043-1483. [liii. 409]

SPOTTISWOOD or SPOTSWOOD, ALEXANDER (1676-1740), colonial governor; fought at Blenheim in Bath's regiment; made governor of Virginia, 1710; a successful administrator, but superseded in 1722, though he remained in colony; major-general, 1740. [liii. 409]

SPOTTISWOOD, JAMES (1567-1645), bishop of Clogher; graduated at Glasgow University, 1583; accompanied James VI to Denmark, 1589; persuaded by Whitgift to take orders in Anglican church, and (1621) was made bishop of Clogher; fled to England, 1641; died and was buried at Westminster. [liii. 410]

SPOTTISWOOD, SPOTISWOOD, or SPOTSWOOD, JOHN (1510-1585), Scots reformer; studied at Glasgow (M.A., 1536), but proceeded to London and was admitted to orders by Cranmer, *c.* 1540; became intimate with Knox; sat on committee for 'First Book of Discipline'; was ecclesiastical superintendent of Lothian, and officiated at coronation of James VI. [liii. 411]

SPOTTISWOOD, SPOTTISWOODE, SPOTISWOOD, or SPOTSWOOD, JOHN (1565-1639), archbishop of St. Andrews and Scots historian; studied at Glasgow under James and Andrew Melville, 1580-1; M.A., 1581; accompanied Duke of Lennox to France and James I to London, 1603; made by James I archbishop of Glasgow in place of Beaton, and a member of the Scots privy council, since he found him a thorough erastian and a pliant instrument in subjugating the kirk; became archbishop of St. Andrews, 1615; secured the passing of the Five Articles of Perth in 1618, and retained the favour of Charles I; tried, however, to prevent the introduction of the liturgy in 1637, and to modify the policy of Charles I; had to take refuge at Newcastle, and was deposed by the assembly; proceeded to London, and died there; buried in Westminster Abbey. [liii. 412]

SPOTTISWOOD, SPOTTISWOODE, or SPOTIS-WOOD, JOHN (1666-1728), Scots advocate and legal author; studied at Edinburgh University; became professor of law there, 1703; edited his grandfather, Sir Robert Spottiswood's, 'Practicks of the Laws of Scotland,' 1706, and other legal works. [liii. 415]

SPOTTISWOOD, SIR ROBERT (1596-1646), Scottish judge; studied at Glasgow (M.A., 1613), at Exeter College, Oxford, and in France; promoted to Scots bench, 1622;

president of the court of session, 1633; assailed by covenanters in 1638 and had to take to flight; joined Charles in Scotland; taken prisoner with Montrose at Philiphaugh, 1645, and executed. His 'Practicks of the Law of Scotland' published by his grandson, John Spottiswood [q. v.], 1706. [liii. 416]

SPOTTISWOODE, ARTHUR COLE (1808-1874), major-general; served with distinction at Bhartpur and at Benares during mutiny; colonel, 1858; retired with rank of major-general, 1861. [liii. 417]

SPOTTISWOODE, WILLIAM (1825-1883), mathematician and physicist; son of a partner in Eyre & Spottiswoode's; obtained a scholarship at Balliol College, Oxford, and a university mathematical scholarship; B.A., 1845; worked on curves and surfaces and the polarisation of light, and was a successful lecturer and writer on polarisation and electrical discharge; president of the Royal Society, 1878-83. [liii. 418]

SPRAGGE, SIR EDWARD (*d.* 1673), admiral; born in Ireland; knighted, 1665; took part in the great battle of June 1666 under Prince Rupert, and commanded at Sheerness in 1667, when the Dutch forced the Medway; destroyed the Algerine fleet in Bugia Bay, 1671, and took a brilliant part in battle of Solebay, 1672; admiral of the blue, 1672; served in three actions during 1673, in the third of which, against Cornelis Tromp, on 11 Aug., he was drowned. [liii. 418]

SPRAT, THOMAS (1635-1713), bishop of Rochester and dean of Westminster; studied at Wadham College, Oxford; M.A., 1657; D.D., 1669 (incorporated at Cambridge, 1671); one of the scientific circle from which sprang the Royal Society; his poem on the death of Cromwell published, with others, by Dryden and Waller, 1659; published a stinging reply to Sorbière's remarks on England, 1664, and a history of the Royal Society, of which he was (1663) one of the first fellows, 1667; published (1668) an account of Cowley, for whose monument he wrote the inscription; supposed to have taken some part in Buckingham's 'Rehearsal'; noted as a preacher, and in 1680 made canon of Windsor; promoted dean of Westminster, 1683, bishop of Rochester, 1684; given by James II a seat on the new ecclesiastical commission, 1686; read the Declaration of Indulgence to empty benches in Westminster Abbey, 1688; subsequently assisted at the coronation of William and Mary; drew up an admirable narrative of Robert Young's plot, of which he was a victim, being arrested, 1692; directed Wren's repairs at Westminster Abbey, and gave facilities for Dryden's burial; buried in Westminster Abbey; celebrated in literature for the excellent prose style of his sermons. [liii. 419]

SPRATT, JAMES (1771-1853), naval commander; fought with great bravery at Trafalgar, 1805; was forced to invalid by wounds, and was given command of a prison ship at Plymouth, 1815; retired, 1817, having during his service saved nine men from drowning. [liii. 424]

SPRATT, THOMAS ABEL BRIMAGE (1811-1888), vice-admiral, hydrographer, and author; eldest son of James Spratt [q. v.]; commanded vessels doing surveying work in the Mediterranean; laid down positions for ships during Crimean war; promoted captain, 1855; C.B., 1855; F.R.S., 1856; retired, 1870; published log-books of his Mediterranean surveys, 1847-65. [liii. 424]

SPRENGER, ALOYS (1813-1893), orientalist; native of Tyrol; studied at Vienna and Paris; naturalised in England, 1838; appointed principal of Mohammedan college, Delhi, 1848; while at Delhi, Lucknow, and Calcutta translated important Hindustani, Arabic, and Persian texts, including the 'Gulistan' of Saadi, 1851, and began an elaborate 'Life of Mohammad'; left India, 1857, and settled at Heidelberg. [liii. 425]

SPRIGG, JOSHUA (1618-1684), divine; of New Inn Hall, Oxford; M.A. Edinburgh, 1639; a retainer of Sir Thomas Fairfax; made fellow and bursar of All Souls College, Oxford, by the parliamentarians, 1649; opposed the execution of Charles I, and retired from Oxford at the Restoration; published a judicious compilation called 'Anglia Rediviva,' 1647, upon the successes of Fairfax's army. [liii. 426]

SPRIGG, WILLIAM (*fl.* 1657), pamphleteer; brother of Joshua Sprigg [q. v.]; fellow of Lincoln College,

Oxford, from 1652 till the Restoration ; M.A., 1655 ; published philosophical essays and ' A modest Plea for an Equal Commonwealth,' 1657.   [liii. 427]

SPRING, TOM (1795–1851). [See WINTER, THOMAS.]

SPRING-RICE, THOMAS, first BARON MONTEAGLE OF BRANDON in Kerry (1790–1866), B.A. Trinity College, Cambridge, 1811 ; represented Limerick in the whig interest from 1820 ; suggested Irish reforms to Canning's government ; secretary to treasury in Grey's administration, 1830–4 ; chancellor of exchequer in Melbourne's second administration, 1835–9 ; introduced the penny-postage scheme, 1839, but having lost popularity, especially with the radicals, was not adopted for the speakership, as he had hoped ; retired and was made a peer, 1839.
       [liii. 427]

SPRINT, JOHN (d. 1590), treasurer of Salisbury Cathedral ; of Corpus Christi College, Oxford ; D.D. Christ Church, Oxford, 1574 ; dean of Bristol, 1571 ; treasurer of Salisbury Cathedral, 1584.   [liii. 429]

SPRINT, JOHN (d. 1623), theologian ; student of Christ Church, Oxford, 1592 ; M.A., 1599 ; appointed vicar of Thornbury, 1610, and after conforming reluctantly to the Anglican ritual published several treatises in defence of it, 1607–13.   [liii. 429]

SPROTT, GEORGE (d. 1608), conspirator ; convicted of having forged three letters purporting to be from Robert Logan to John Ruthven, third earl of Gowrie [q. v.], concerning the murder of James VI ; found guilty of complicity in the conspiracy and executed.   [liii. 430]

SPROTT or **SPOTT**, THOMAS (fl. 1270 ?), historian and monk of St. Augustine's, Canterbury ; wrote a history of that foundation, a fragment of which is now among the Cottonian MSS., British Museum.
       [liii. 430]

SPRUCE, RICHARD (1817–1893), botanist and traveller ; began working upon mosses when a master at St. Peter's School, York ; went to the Pyrenees, and (1849) to South America with Hooker and Bentham ; discovered many new plants in the Amazon region, where he met Wallace ; collected cinchona plants for India, and returned home in 1864, much enfeebled in health, to work out his results, in aid of which, having had severe losses, he received a small government grant.
       [liii. 431]

SPRY, HENRY HARPUR (1804–1842), writer on India ; surgeon on Bengal staff ; F.R.S., 1841 ; published ' Modern India,' 1837.   [liii. 432]

SPRY, SIR RICHARD (1715–1775), rear-admiral ; captured by the Spaniards while in command of the Comet bomb, 1744 ; served under Boscawen at Pondicherry ; at Louisbourg, 1758 ; commanded (1772) a squadron in the Channel ; knighted, 1773.   [liii. 432]

SPURGEON, CHARLES HADDON (1834–1892), preacher ; born at Kelvedon, Essex ; became usher in a school at Newmarket, 1849 ; left independents and became a zealous baptist in 1850 ; became pastor of the baptist congregation at Waterbeach, 1852 ; came to London, 1854, and became so popular a preacher that Exeter Hall could not hold his hearers ; the Metropolitan Tabernacle, to hold 6,000 persons, having been opened in 1861, he ministered there till his death ; was a convinced Calvinist, adhering staunchly to that system of theology, though his resentment at what he called the down-grade development of modern biblical criticism led to his withdrawing from the Baptist Union in 1887 ; his pulpit, as well as his private utterances, marked by a rich vein of humour ; his sermons, which were far famed, were published at the rate of one a week ; author of ' John Ploughman's Talks,' 1869, ' John Ploughman's Pictures,' 1880, and other works ; edited the ' Treasury of David,' 1870–85.
       [liii. 433]

SPURGIN, JOHN (1797–1866), medical writer ; proceeded from Caius College, Cambridge, to Edinburgh, but returned and became M.D., 1825 ; F.R.C.P., 1826 ; censor, 1829 ; Harveian orator, 1851 ; published medical lectures, 1853–60 ; physician to the Foundling Hospital, London, 1835–66 ; projected an edition of Swedenborg's philosophical works.   [liii. 435]

SPURSTOWE, WILLIAM (1605 ?– 1666), puritan divine ; M.A. Emmanuel College, Cambridge, 1630 ;

fellow of Catharine Hall, Cambridge ; put into the mastership of Catharine Hall by the puritans, 1645 ; objected to the execution of Charles I, but lost his mastership at the Restoration ; one of the five divines who wrote, in 1641, as ' Smectymnuus.'   [liii. 435]

SPYNIE, BARONS. [See LINDSAY, ALEXANDER, first BARON, d. 1607 ; LINDSAY, ALEXANDER, second BARON, d. 1646 ; LINDSAY, GEORGE, third BARON, d. 1671.]

SQUIRE, EDWARD (d. 1598), alleged conspirator ; employed in Queen Elizabeth's stables ; became mixed up with the jesuits, and was charged with an attempt to assassinate Queen Elizabeth by poisoning her saddle, and executed on slight grounds.   [liii. 436]

SQUIRE, JOHN (1780–1812), brevet lieutenant-colonel, royal engineers ; served under Abercromby in Holland and Egypt ; travelled through Syria and Greece ; was employed on lines of Torres Vedras, 1810, and in bridging the Guadiana ; suffered in health after Badajoz, and died at Truxillo.   [liii. 437]

SQUIRE, SAMUEL (1713 - 1766), bishop of St. Davids ; fellow of St. John's College, Cambridge, 1735 ; M.A., 1737 ; curried favour with Newcastle and Chesterfield, obtained a deanery at Bristol, 1760, and the see of St. Davids, 1761 ; published historical essays, and fostered Anglo-Saxon studies in Cambridge.   [liii. 439]

SQUIRE, WILLIAM (d. 1677), controversialist ; B.A. Trinity Hall, Cambridge, 1650 ; M.A., Brasenose College, Oxford, 1653 ; chaplain of All Souls College and fellow of University College, Oxford ; wrote two tracts on the ' Unreasonableness ' of Romanists shortly before his death.   [liii. 440]

STACK, EDWARD (d. 1833), general ; of Irish birth ; entered French army, but quitted it for Irish brigade ; narrowly escaped being shot as a spy by Napoleon I ; general in the British army, 1830.   [liii. 441]

STACK, RICHARD (d. 1812), author ; M.A. Trinity College, Dublin, 1779 ; fellow, 1779 ; D.D., 1786 ; vice-president of Royal Irish Academy, contributing to ' Transactions ' and writing lectures.   [liii. 441]

STACKHOUSE, JOHN (1742–1819), botanist ; fellow of Exeter College, Oxford, 1761–4 ; studied seaweeds and was an early F.L.S. ; published the ' Nereis Britannica ' (on sea-wracks), 1795, and other standard botanical memoirs.   [liii. 441]

STACKHOUSE, THOMAS (1677–1752), theologian ; of Durham and St. John's College, Cambridge ; was a poor curate at Shepperton, at Amsterdam, and at Finchley ; obtained vicarage of Benham Valence, 1733 ; latterly worked for booksellers at Chelsea ; produced a ' History of the Bible,' 1737, and many short histories and abridgments.
       [liii. 442]

STACKHOUSE, THOMAS (d. 1784), writer ; younger son of Thomas Stackhouse (1677–1752) [q. v.] ; compiled several school-books, 1762–81.   [liii. 443]

STACKHOUSE, THOMAS (1756–1836), antiquary and theologian ; nephew of Thomas Stackhouse (d. 1784) [q. v.] ; wrote on the ' Ancient Barrows,' 1806, and ' Remains of Ancient Pagan Britain,' 1833 ; wrote also school-books and obituaries of quakers, having joined that denomination.   [liii. 443]

STAFFORD, MARQUIS OF (1721–1803). [See LEVESON-GOWER, GRANVILLE.]

STAFFORD, VISCOUNT (1614–1680). [See HOWARD, WILLIAM.]

STAFFORD, ANTHONY (1587–1645 ?), devotional writer ; of Oriel College and Inner Temple ; created M.A., 1623 ; published ' The Female Glory ' (a panegyric of the Blessed Virgin), 1635.   [liii. 444]

STAFFORD, EDMUND DE (1344–1419), bishop of Exeter ; dean of York, 1385 ; keeper of the privy seal, 1389 ; consecrated bishop of Exeter, 1395 ; lord chancellor from 1396 till the abdication of Richard II in 1399 ; assented to the deposition of Richard II ; again lord chancellor, 1403 ; was regarded as the second founder of Stapeldon Hall, Oxford, the name of which was changed to Exeter College in his day.   [liii. 445]

STAFFORD, EDWARD, third DUKE OF BUCKING-HAM (1478–1521), eldest son of Henry Stafford, second duke of Buckingham [q. v.]; sworn privy councillor, 1509; attended court functions; was at Gravelines with Henry VIII, 1520; condemned and executed, charges of disloyalty to Henry VIII having been trumped up against him in 1521. [liii. 446]

STAFFORD, SIR EDWARD (1552?–1605), diplomatist; carried on negotiations for a union between Queen Elizabeth and Henry, duke of Anjou, 1579; knighted, 1583; ambassador at Paris, 1583–90. [liii. 447]

STAFFORD, HENRY, second DUKE OF BUCKINGHAM (1454?–1483), grandson of Humphrey Stafford, first duke [q. v.]; pronounced sentence as high steward on Clarence, 1478; joined Richard of Gloucester (afterwards Richard III), 1483, and acted as great chamberlain at his coronation; raised a force against Richard III three months later; his army rendered useless by the floods of the river Wye and Severn, and himself captured and executed at Salisbury. [liii. 448]

STAFFORD, HENRY, first BARON STAFFORD (1501–1563), courtier; K.B., 1532; M.P., Stafford, 1547; supported successively Henry VIII, Protector Somerset, Queen Mary, and Queen Elizabeth. [liii. 450]

STAFFORD, HUGH DE, second EARL OF STAFFORD (1342?–1386), second son of Ralph de Stafford, first earl of Stafford [q. v.]; went with John of Gaunt to France, 1373; K.G., 1375; officiated at coronation of Richard II, 1377, and was member of his council; having lost his eldest son by treachery, went on pilgrimage to Jerusalem, and died at Rhodes. [liii. 458]

STAFFORD, HUMPHREY, first DUKE OF BUCKINGHAM (1402–1460), accompanied Henry VI abroad, 1430; captain of Calais, 1442; created Duke of Buckingham, 1444, and warden of Cinque ports, 1450; opposed the Duke of York; subsequently tried to reconcile Queen Margaret with the Yorkists, but was killed at the battle of Northampton. [liii. 451]

STAFFORD, HUMPHREY, EARL OF DEVON (1439–1469), fought for and was knighted by Edward IV at Towton, 1461; won numerous honours, was made a privy councillor, and Earl of Devon, 1469; sent to oppose Robin of Redesdale, 1469, but quarrelled with William Herbert, first earl of Pembroke [q. v.], and retired with all his troops, on which Edward IV ordered his execution. [liii. 453]

STAFFORD, JOHN (d. 1452), archbishop of Canterbury; D.C.L. of Oxford before 1413; appointed archdeacon of Salisbury, 1419, and keeper of the privy seal, 1421; joined party of Henry Beaufort; consecrated bishop of Bath and Wells, 1425; first to have the title of 'lord chancellor,' 1432; archbishop of Canterbury, 1443–52. [liii. 454]

STAFFORD, JOHN (1728–1800), independent divine; a wool-comber by trade; became minister of New Broad Street chapel, London, 1758; published Calvinistic treatises. [liii. 455]

STAFFORD, RALPH DE, first EARL OF STAFFORD (1299–1372), served Edward III in Flanders, 1338–40; led reinforcements to Britanny, 1342; taken prisoner at Vannes and exchanged; seneschal of Aquitaine, 1345; fought at Crecy and at siege of Calais; defeated French near Agen, 1352; fought in Scotland and (1356) at Poitiers; assisted at treaty of Bretigny, 1360; died at Tonbridge. [liii. 456]

STAFFORD, SIR RICHARD, styled 'of Clifton' (fl. 1337–1369), seneschal of Gascony; brother of Ralph de Stafford, first earl of Stafford [q. v.] [liii. 457]

STAFFORD, RICHARD (1663–1703), Jacobite pamphleteer; of Magdalen Hall, Oxford, and the Middle Temple; distributed rabid Jacobite tracts; showed signs of lunacy, and was sent to Bedlam, 1691. [liii. 459]

STAFFORD, RICHARD ANTHONY (1801–1854), surgeon; attracted notice of Abernethy at St. Bartholomew's Hospital, London; studied in Paris; wrote on spine and urethra. [liii. 459]

STAFFORD, THOMAS (1531?–1557), rebel; travelled in Italy and Poland; opposed Queen Mary's Spanish marriage, and, claiming royal descent on both sides, sailed from Dieppe, by connivance of Henri II, with two ships, and made a landing at Scarborough, April 1557, but was taken and hanged. [liii. 460]

STAFFORD, SIR THOMAS (fl. 1633), reputed author of 'Pacata Hibernia'; knighted by Chichester in Ireland, 1611; inherited the manuscripts of George Carew, earl of Totnes [q. v.], and from them compiled his impartial history of the Irish wars ('Pacata Hibernia'), 1633. [liii. 461]

STAFFORD, WILLIAM (1554–1612), alleged author of 'Compendious Examination of certain ordinary Complaints'; of Winchester College and New College, Oxford; fellow of New College, Oxford, 1573; implicated obscurely in a plot of 1586. The book attributed to him, upon social distress under Edward VI, was probably in reality by John Hales (d. 1571) [q. v.] [liii. 462]

STAFFORD, WILLIAM (1593–1684), pamphleteer; created M.A. Christ Church, Oxford, 1618; wrote on war from parliamentarian standpoint, 1644–6. [liii. 463]

STAGG, JOHN (1770–1823), Cumberland poet; lost eyesight in his youth; described Cumberland peasantry in his poems, 1804, and his 'Cumberland Minstrel,' 1821. [liii. 463]

STAGGINS, NICHOLAS (1650?–1700), musician; master of his majesty's music, 1675; Mus.Doc. Cambridge, 1682; composed birthday music and songs. [liii. 464]

STAINER, SIR RICHARD (d. 1662). [See STAYNER.]

STAINES, SIR THOMAS (1776–1830), captain in the navy; served in the Victory under Hood, 1795, and under Jervis, 1796; captured by Spaniards, 1798; served on Foudroyant under Nelson, and afterwards at siege of Toulon; promoted captain, 1806; had great success in South of Spain and Naples; knighted, 1809, and appointed to Britain frigate; accidentally struck on Pitcairn's island, 1813, and sent account of its colony to England. [liii. 464]

STAINTON, HENRY TIBBATS (1822–1892), entomologist; began studying smaller lepidoptera, 1840; published numerous books on British insects, especially the tineidæ; founded magazines; president of the Entomological Society, 1881–2; secretary of Ray Society, 1861–72; F.R.S., 1867. [liii. 466]

STAIR, EARLS OF. [See DALRYMPLE, SIR JOHN, first EARL, 1648–1707; DALRYMPLE, JOHN, second EARL, 1673–1747; DALRYMPLE, JOHN, fifth EARL, 1720–1789; DALRYMPLE, JOHN, sixth EARL, 1749–1821; DALRYMPLE, SIR JOHN HAMILTON MACGILL, eighth EARL, 1771–1853.]

STAIR, first VISCOUNT (1619–1695). [See DALRYMPLE, SIR JAMES.]

STAIRS, WILLIAM GRANT (1863–1892), captain and traveller; born at Halifax, Nova Scotia; gazetted lieutenant, royal engineers, 1885; sailed on Emin relief expedition, 1886; journeyed with Stanley through central forest of Africa, and explored the Mountain of the Moon, 1888; took command of Belgian expedition to south of Congo Free State, 1891; died on way back from Katanga. [liii. 467]

STALEY or **STAYLEY**, WILLIAM (d. 1678), victim of the popish plot; a catholic goldsmith and banker; charged with treason by the informer Carstairs; tried by Chief-justice Scroggs, and hanged at Tyburn. [liii. 468]

STALHAM, JOHN (d. 1681), puritan divine; said to have been educated at Oxford; vicar of Terling, 1632; a strong puritan and congregationalist; wrote much against quakers; ejected, 1662. [liii. 469]

STAMFORD, EARLS OF. [See GREY, HENRY, first EARL, 1599?–1673; GREY, THOMAS, second EARL, 1654–1720.]

STAMFORD, SIR WILLIAM (1509–1558). [See STANFORD.]

STAMPE, WILLIAM (1611–1653?), divine; M.A. Pembroke College, Oxford, 1633 (incorporated at Cambridge, 1640); D.D., 1643; fellow of Pembroke College, Oxford; vicar of Stepney, 1641; sequestered by Westminster Assembly as a loyalist; chaplain to Elizabeth, queen of Bohemia; died at the Hague. [liii. 469]

STANBRIDGE, JOHN (1463–1510), grammarian; fellow of New College, Oxford, 1481, and M.A.; became rector of Winwick and prebendary of Lincoln, 1509;

wrote 'Vocabula,' 'Vulgaria,' 'Accidentia,' and other glossaries and grammars printed by Wynkyn de Worde.
[liv. 470]

STANBURY, STANBERY, or STANBRIDGE, JOHN (d. 1474), bishop of Hereford ; D.D. Exeter College, Oxford ; confessor to Henry VI, and first provost of Eton ; bishop of Hereford, 1453–74. [liii. 471]

STANDISH, ARTHUR (fl. 1611), writer on agriculture ; published the 'Commons' Complaint,' 1611, advocating systematic planting. [liii. 471]

STANDISH, FRANK HALL (1799–1840), connoisseur and author ; wrote on Voltaire, on northern capitals of Europe, and on Seville, where he lived ; bequeathed his fine collection of pictures and manuscripts to King Louis-Philippe of France. [liii. 472]

STANDISH, HENRY (d. 1535), bishop of St. Asaph : D.D. ; preached at Henry VIII's court ; maintained that the clergy were liable to punishment in secular courts, but by Henry VIII's favour escaped punishment by convocation ; opposed Colet and Erasmus, and was very hostile to heresy ; bishop of St. Asaph, 1518–35 ; consecrated Cranmer, 1533. [liii. 472]

STANDISH, JOHN (1507 ?–1570), archdeacon of Colchester ; of Brasenose and Corpus Christi colleges, Oxford ; M.A., 1531 ; D.D., 1541 ; chaplain to Edward VI ; conformed subsequently both under Queen Mary and Queen Elizabeth ; wrote several tracts. [liii. 473]

STANDISH, MYLES (1584–1656), colonist ; of Lancashire ; a descendant of the Duxbury branch of the family ; served under the Veres in the Netherlands before 1603 ; embarked on Mayflower from Leyden, 1620, and settled at New Plymouth ; chosen military captain of the colony, 1621 ; awed the Indians by his rapid and well-concerted measures, and ensured the success of the Plymouth colony ; died at Duxbury, New England ; his estate still in the possession of descendants on the north side of the bay. His daring exploits against the Indians are celebrated in poems by Longfellow and Lowell.
[liii. 474]

STANFIELD, CLARKSON (1793–1867), marine and landscape painter ; son of James Field Stanfield [q. v.] ; entered the merchant service, 1808, and was pressed into the navy, 1812, but left the sea, 1818 ; became scene-painter finally at Drury Lane, London, and painted a drop-scene for Dickens ; R.A., 1835 ; painted 'The Battle of Trafalgar,' 1836 ; settled at Hampstead, 1847 ; styled the English Vandevelde ; famous for his cloud-forms.
[liii. 476]

STANFIELD, GEORGE CLARKSON (1828–1878), painter ; son of Clarkson Stanfield [q. v.] ; exhibited, 1844–1876. [liii. 478]

STANFIELD, JAMES FIELD (d. 1824), actor and author ; wrote 'Observations on a Guinea Voyage,' 1788, and 'The Guinea Voyage,' 1789, against the slave traffic, of which he had had some experience ; had the direction of a theatrical company in the north of England.
[liii. 478]

STANFORD, CHARLES (1823–1886), divine ; minister at Devizes ; became president of the London Baptist Association, 1882 ; published Philip Doddridge, D.D., 1880, and other memorial lives. [liii. 478]

STANFORD, STAMFORD, or STAUNFORD, SIR WILLIAM (1509–1558), judge ; of Oxford and Gray's Inn; barrister, 1536 ; M.P., Stafford, 1541, 1545–7 ; Newcastle-under-Lyme, 1547–52 ; appointed justice of common pleas, 1555 ; knighted, 1555 ; chief work, 'Les Plees del Coron,' 1560. [liii. 479]

STANGER, CHRISTOPHER (1759–1834), physician ; studied at Edinburgh and abroad ; M.D. Edinburgh, 1783; Gresham professor of medicine, 1790 ; became physician to Foundling Hospital, London, 1792 ; unsuccessfully contested admission to the fellowship of the Royal College of Physicians ; published medical tracts. [liii. 479]

STANHOPE, LADY, and COUNTESS OF CHESTERFIELD (d. 1667). [See KIRKHOVEN or KERCKHOVEN, CATHERINE.]

STANHOPE, CHARLES (1673–1760), of Elvaston, brother of William Stanhope, first earl of Harrington [q. v.] ; M.P., Milborne Port, 1717–22, Aldborough, 1722–1734, and Harwich, 1734–41 ; under-secretary for southern department, 1714–17 ; as secretary to the treasury

(1720–1), charged with illegitimate dealing in South Sea stock, but acquitted ; treasurer of the chamber, 1722.
[liv. 40]

STANHOPE, CHARLES, third EARL STANHOPE (1753–1816), politician and man of science ; grandson of James Stanhope, first earl Stanhope [q. v.] ; educated at Eton and Geneva ; styled Lord Mahon till succession to peerage, 1786 ; F.R.S., 1772 ; married Lady Hester, sister of the second William Pitt, 1774 ; constructed two calculating machines, c. 1777 ; harangued Gordon rioters, 1780 ; elected for Chipping Wycombe by Shelburne's influence, 1780 ; advocated cessation of American war and parliamentary reform, 1781 ; opposed coalition of Fox and North ; attacked Pitt's proposals for sinking fund, 1786 ; became permanently estranged from Pitt on French revolution question ; chairman of 'Revolution Society,' 1788 ; patented steam-vessels, 1790 and 1807 (approved by admiralty, 1795–6) ; letters by him against false assignats and on treatment of negroes printed at Paris, 1791-2 ; published answer to Burke's speech on the revolution, 1790 ; moved to acknowledge French republic, 1794 ; introduced motions against interferences in French affairs, 1794 and 1795 ; on defeat withdrew from parliament till 1800 ; frequently caricatured by Gillray, 1791–1808 ; his London house fired by rioters, 1794 ; 'Moral Epistle' addressed to him by Landor, 1795 ; issued pamphlet against Irish union, 1799 ; proposed peace with Napoleon, 1800 ; his process of stereotyping acquired by Clarendon Press, Oxford, 1805, also his iron hand-press and logotypes ; carried Gold Coin and Banknote Bill, 1811, also motions for committees to revise statutes and unify weights and measures, 1816 ; disinherited all his children ; invented a microscopic lens and projected a canal from Holsworthy to Bristol Channel ; published 'Principles of Science of Tuning Instruments with Fixed Tones,' 1806, and 'Principles of Electricity,' 1779. [liv. 1]

STANHOPE, CHARLES, third EARL OF HARRINGTON (1753–1829), general ; M.P., Thetford, 1774–6, Westminster, 1776–9 ; ensign, 1769 ; served in America, 1776 ; aide-de-camp to Burgoyne at Saratoga, news of which he carried home, 1777 ; captain, 3rd foot-guards, 1778 ; succeeded to peerage, 1779 ; raised and commanded regiment in Jamaica, 1780–1 ; colonel of 1st life-guards and gold stick, 1792 ; privy councillor, 1798 ; commander-in-chief in Ireland, 1805–12 ; governor of Windsor, 1812 ; special envoy to Vienna, 1805, Berlin, 1806 ; bearer of great standard at coronation of George IV ; introduced new sword, 1792. [liv. 5]

STANHOPE, CHARLES, fourth EARL OF HARRINGTON (1780–1851), styled Lord Petersham till 1829; colonel, 1814 ; a lord of the bedchamber, 1812 and 1820–1829 ; designed Petersham overcoat and Petersham snuff-mixture. [liv. 6]

STANHOPE, SIR EDWARD (1546 ?–1608), chancellor of the diocese of London ; son of Sir Michael Stanhope [q. v.] ; scholar and fellow of Trinity College, Cambridge (M.A., 1566, LL.D., 1575) ; incorporated M.A. at Oxford, 1566 ; prebendary of York, 1572–91 ; advocate at Doctors' Commons, 1576 ; master in chancery, 1577 ; vicar-general of Canterbury, c. 1583 ; M.P., Marlborough, 1584–5 and 1586–7 ; member of ecclesiastical commission, 1587 ; chancellor of London diocese, 1591–1608 ; served on Whitgift's London commission, 1594, piracy inquiry, 1601, and Ralegh's trial, 1603 ; knighted, 1603 ; benefactor of Trinity College, Cambridge, Hull, and other places ; began 'Lodge Book' at Trinity College, Cambridge.
[liv. 7]

STANHOPE, EDWARD (1840–1893), statesman ; second son of Philip Henry Stanhope, fifth earl Stanhope [q. v.] ; of Harrow and Christ Church, Oxford ; fellow of All Souls College, Oxford, 1863 ; barrister, Inner Temple, 1865 ; M.P., Mid-Lincolnshire, 1874, Horncastle division, 1885 ; as parliamentary secretary to board of trade largely responsible for Merchant Shipping Act, 1876 ; under-secretary for India, 1878–80 ; vice-president of committee of council on education with seat in cabinet, 1885 ; president of board of trade, 1885 ; as colonial secretary, 1886, issued invitations for colonial conference of 1888 ; as secretary for war (1887–92) completed Cardwell system, reorganised manufacturing departments, established army service corps, passed Imperial Defence Act (1888), revised conditions of promotion and retirement of officers (1889), adopted magazine rifle, and appointed committee to inquire into terms of service (1891).
[liv. 8]

STANHOPE, GEORGE (1660–1728), dean of Canterbury; elected from Eton to King's College, Cambridge; M.A., 1685; D.D., 1697; chaplain to William and Mary; Boyle lecturer, 1701; vicar of Deptford and chaplain to Queen Anne, 1702; dean of Canterbury, 1704–28; Tuesday lecturer at St. Lawrence Jewry, London, 1704–8; prolocutor of lower house of convocation, 1713, and twice afterwards; broke up meeting, 1718, to prevent reading of Tenison's 'protestation' in favour of Hoadly; lost royal chaplaincy, probably in consequence of his action; famous preacher; published translations, including 'Epictetus,' 1694, Charron's 'Books on Wisdom,' 1697, Marcus Aurelius, 1697, and the 'Imitatio Christi' ('The Christian's Pattern,' 1698, ed. Henry Morley, 1886); his 'Paraphrase and Comment on the Epistles and Gospels' (1705, 1706, and 1708) a favourite eighteenth-century book. [liv. 10]

STANHOPE, LADY HESTER LUCY (1776–1839), eccentric; eldest daughter of Charles Stanhope (afterwards) third earl Stanhope [q. v.]; housekeeper and trusted confidant of her uncle, William Pitt, 1803–6; retired to Wales after death of favourite brother and Sir John Moore at Coruña, 1808; finally left England for the Levant, 1810; made pilgrimage to Jerusalem; crossed the desert, and camped with Bedouins amid ruins of Palmyra, 1813; settled on Mount Lebanon, 1814, building walled group of houses; intrigued against British consuls and incited Druses against Ibrahim Pasha; protected Europeans after Navarino, 1827; adopted Eastern habits, and practised judicial astrology; visited at Djouni by Lamartine, Kinglake, and others; her conversations recorded by the physician Charles Lewis Meryon [q. v.]; heavily involved in debt; after appropriation of pension to creditors wrote letters to Palmerston and Queen Victoria; died deserted and plundered. [liv. 12]

STANHOPE, JAMES, first EARL STANHOPE (1673–1721), grandson of Philip Stanhope, first earl of Chesterfield [q. v.]; educated at Eton and Trinity College, Oxford; volunteer in Flanders, 1694–5; received commission in 1st footguards; colonel, 1702; M.P., Newport, 1701, Cockermouth, 1702–13; Spanish secretary to Ormonde at Cadiz, 1702; served under Marlborough, 1703, and in Portugal, 1703–4, and became brigadier; gave valuable assistance to Peterborough at Barcelona, 1705; British minister in Spain, 1706; urged on Archduke Charles aggressive measures; unjustly blamed by Peterborough for the reverse at Almanza, 1707; appointed commander of British forces in Spain, 1708; took Port Mahon, 1708; received overtures from Orleans; as manager of Sacheverell's impeachment made able speech, 1710; won cavalry action at Almenara, and victory for allies at Saragossa, 1710; surprised by Vendôme and obliged to capitulate at Brihuega; detained prisoner nearly two years; declined Bolingbroke's offer to present him to Louis XIV; a leader of whig opposition; M.P., Wendover, 1713, Newport, 1715; took leading part in securing Hanoverian succession; secretary of state for southern department and privy councillor, 1714; carried impeachment of Ormonde; had chief direction of measures for suppression of Jacobite rising, 1715; active in passing of Septennial Act, but especially in foreign affairs; while with George I at Hanover arranged with Dubois alliance with France and the Dutch, 1716; unjustly charged with treachery to colleagues by Townshend and Walpole; head of the treasury and chancellor of the exchequer, 1717; returned to secretaryship, 1718; created Viscount Stanhope of Mahon, 1717, Earl Stanhope, 1718; negotiated quadruple alliance against Spain, and compelled her to accede to it, 1719; saved Sweden from coalition against her by despatching fleet to the Baltic, 1719; obtained repeal of Schism Act and assisted Sunderland in pressing on Peerage Bill (rejected in Commons), 1718–19; died after vehement speech on South Sea question; monument to him by Rysbrack in Westminster Abbey. [liv. 14]

STANHOPE, JOHN, first BARON STANHOPE OF HARRINGTON (1545?–1621), third son of Sir Michael Stanhope [q. v.]; member of council of the north; treasurer of the chamber, 1596–1616; knighted, 1596; M.P., Preston, 1597, Northamptonshire, 1601, Newtown, 1604; a commissioner for union, 1603, and a peer, 1605; member of council of Virginia Company, 1609; signed warrant for torture of Edmond Peacham [q. v.], 1615. [liv. 19]

STANHOPE, LEICESTER FITZGERALD CHARLES, fifth EARL OF HARRINGTON (1784–1862), third son of Charles Stanhope, third earl of Harrington [q. v.];

entered army, 1799; deputy quartermaster-general in India, 1817; C.B. for services in Mahratta war, 1818; colonel, 1837; defended Indian policy of Marquis of Hastings; went to Greece as agent of English committee, 1823; met Byron in Cefalonia and Mavrocordato at Missolonghi, where he established a Greek newspaper, formed an artillery corps, and prevented Greek fleet from dispersing; favoured Western Greeks and establishment of a republic; recalled owing to complaints of Turkish government, 1824; brought home Byron's remains and gave information to Moore; received Greek order of the Redeemer, 1838; published 'Greece in 1823 and 1824,' 1824; contributed to W. Parry's 'Last Days of Lord Byron' (Paris edition); succeeded to earldom, 1851. [liv. 20]

STANHOPE, SIR MICHAEL (d. 1552), partisan of Protector Somerset; received from Henry VIII grants of monastic property in Nottinghamshire; lieutenant of Kingston-upon-Hull, 1542; M.P., Nottinghamshire. 1545–7; employed in connection with Scottish wars; knighted and made deputy of Somerset (brother-in-law) in governorship of Edward VI, c. 1547; keeper of Windsor park and governor of Hull, 1547; sent to Tower of London on Somerset's fall, 1549; reappointed at Hull, 1550; beheaded for conspiring against Northumberland. [liv. 21]

STANHOPE, PHILIP, first EARL OF CHESTERFIELD (1584–1656), royalist; created Baron Stanhope of Shelford, 1616, Earl of Chesterfield, 1628; raised regiment of dragoons for Charles I, 1642; obliged to surrender at Lichfield. [liv. 22]

STANHOPE, PHILIP, second EARL OF CHESTERFIELD (1633–1713), grandson of Philip Stanhope, first earl of Chesterfield [q. v.]; said to have declined Cromwell's offer of military command and his daughter's hand; sent to the Tower of London for duelling, 1658, and again on suspicion of plotting with royalists, 1659; killed a man in a duel, but was pardoned by Charles II, 1660; chamberlain to Catherine of Braganza, 1662–5; colonel of foot regiment, 1667–8, of Holland regiment. 1682–4; privy councillor, 1681; refused to act as regent for James II after the revolution, but declined office from William III; refused to abjure the Pretender at coronation of Anne; friend of Charles Cotton and patron of Dryden; his letters and autobiographical fragment printed, 1835. [liv. 23]

STANHOPE, PHILIP, fifth EARL OF CHESTERFIELD (1755–1815), cousin and godson of Philip Dormer Stanhope, fourth earl of Chesterfield [q. v.], who directed his education; pupil of Dr. William Dodd [q. v.], who was hanged for forging his name to a bond; enjoyed favour of George III; privy councillor, 1784, and (nominal) ambassador to Spain, 1784–7; master of the mint, 1789–90, joint postmaster-general, 1790, master of the horse, 1798–1804; K.G., 1805; replaced old mansion of Bretby by modern residence. [liv. 36]

STANHOPE, PHILIP DORMER, fourth EARL OF CHESTERFIELD (1694–1773), statesman, wit, and letter-writer; grandson of Philip Stanhope, second earl of Chesterfield [q. v.]; studied for a year at Trinity Hall, Cambridge; by influence of kinsman, James (afterwards Earl) Stanhope [q. v.], named gentleman of bedchamber to Prince of Wales (afterwards George II), and was elected as whig M.P. for St. Germans, 1715, though a minor; formed intimacy with Pope; cultivated acquaintance of Henrietta Howard, mistress of Prince George, and incurred enmity of his wife Caroline; M.P., Lostwithiel, 1722–5; captain of gentlemen-pensioners, 1723–5; rejected Walpole's offer of the order of the Bath, and quarrelled with him, 1725; succeeded to peerage, 1726; privy councillor, 1727; accepted the Hague embassy, 1728; formed intimacy with Mlle. du Bouchet, mother (1732) of his natural son; negotiated marriage of Prince of Orange with Anne, princess royal of England; K.G. and lord steward, 1730; temporarily reconciled with Walpole; signed treaty with Spain and Holland guaranteeing Pragmatic Sanction, 1731; retired from embassy, 1732; dismissed from lord stewardship for opposition to Excise Bill, 1733; attacked ministry in 'Fog's Journal,' 1734; offended George II by marrying Petronilla Melusina von der Schulenburg (Countess of Walsingham), daughter of the Duchess of Kendal, 1733; threatened lawsuit against the crown to recover legacy bequeathed by George I to his wife's mother, and received 20,000l. to stay proceedings; made witty speech, 1737 (published, 1749) against bill for licensing theatres; visited Voltaire at Brussels (1741) and frequented society of men of letters in Paris ; contributed to fall of Walpole, but continued in opposition ; denounced in parliament proposal to hire Hanoverian troops, and attacked new ministers in the press in letters signed ' Geffery Broadbottom,' 1743 ; acknowledged leader of opposition in House of Lords ; received legacy from Dowager duchess of Marlborough in reward for political conduct, 1744, but entered Pelham ministry on retirement of Carteret, 1744 ; as envoy to the Hague induced Holland to take part in Austrian succession war, 1745 ; as viceroy in Ireland, 1745-6, kept the country quiet by his tolerant policy, and encouraged national industries ; as secretary for the northern department, 1746-8, thwarted in his pacific policy by his colleague Newcastle ; declined dukedom ; ' Apology for a late Resignation,' 1748, inspired or partially written by him ; introduced bill for reform of the calendar, 1751 ; in last speech denounced subsidy treaties with Prussia and Hesse-Cassel, 1755 ; on invitation of the court overcame Newcastle's objections to take office with Pitt, 1757 ; built (1749) Chesterfield House, South Audley Street, London, and formed picture galleries there and at Blackheath ; wrote much in the ' World,' and corresponded with Voltaire and other French friends ; elected to Académie des Inscriptions, 1755 ; patronised men of letters ; the prospectus of Dr. Johnson's ' Dictionary ' addressed to him, 1747 ; eulogised Johnson's ' Dictionary ' in the ' World,' 1754 ; bore no malice for Dr. Johnson's letter (1755), rebuking him for neglect, and disclaimed responsibility for alleged refusal to receive him ; maintained from 1737 an almost daily correspondence with his natural son, procuring his entrance into parliament and diplomatic employment as envoy to the diet (1763) and minister at Hamburg (1756-64) and Dresden (1764-8) ; addressed similar letters (236 extant) to his godson and heir-presumptive, 1761-70 ; his posthumous reputation injured by hostility of leading contemporaries ; caricatured as Sir John Chester in ' Barnaby Rudge' ; his political insight proved by prophecy (1753) of French revolution ; his immorality much exaggerated, and his worldliness tempered by real affection ; political tracts and contributions to periodicals (' Common Sense,' 1737-9, ' The World,' 1753-6) only publications authorised in his lifetime ; his ' Letters ' to his natural son published by widow (Mrs. Eugenia Stanhope) of the latter, 1774, ' Supplement,' 1787, French version, 1775, German, 1774-6 ; ' Miscellaneous Works ' (including ' Memoirs of his Life ') prepared by Maty, and supplementary letters, with ' Characters of Eminent Personages,' 1777 ; ' Miscellaneous Works ' collected, 1779 ; his ' Letters ' relative to the education of his godson published, 1817. Collective editions of letters and literary works edited by Lord Mahon, 1845-53, and John Bradshaw, 1892 ; extracts from other unpublished letters in Ernst's ' Life of Chesterfield ' (1893). [liv. 24]

STANHOPE, PHILIP HENRY, fifth EARL STANHOPE (1805-1875), historian ; grandson of Charles Stanhope, third earl Stanhope [q. v.] ; styled Viscount Mahon, 1816-55 ; B.A. Christ Church, Oxford, 1827, hon. D.C.L., 1834 ; conservative M.P., Wootton Bassett, 1830-2, Hertford, 1835-52 ; under-secretary for foreign affairs, 1834-5 ; president, Society of Arts, 1846-75 ; procured passing of bill amending copyright law, 1842 ; secretary to board of control (India), 1845-6 ; supported corn law repeal, 1846 ; one of Peel's literary executors ; examiner at Oxford, 1855, and founder of prize for historical essay ; obtained parliamentary grant for formation of National Portrait Gallery, and became chairman of trustees, 1857 (opened at Great George Street, Westminster, 1859, since thrice removed) ; lord rector, Aberdeen, 1858 ; effected removal of three state services from prayer-book, 1859 ; created LL.D. Cambridge, 1864 ; Historical Manuscripts Commission largely due to him, 1869 ; proposed parliamentary grant for excavation of Troy ; foreign associate of Institut de France, 1872 ; chairman of copyright commission, 1875 ; his ' History of the War of Succession in Spain, 1702-14,' 1832, based largely on papers of first Earl Stanhope ; published ' History of England from Peace of Utrecht to Peace of Versailles, 1713-83,' 1836-63, ' Life of the Right Hon. William Pitt, with Extracts from his unpublished Correspondence,' etc., 1861-2 (last ed., 1879), ' History of England, comprising the Reign of Queen Anne until the Peace of Utrecht,' 1870, and other works, including ' Life of Belisarius,' 1829, ' Spain under Charles II,' 1840, ' Essai sur la Vie du Grand Condé,' 1842 (in English, 1845), ' Memoirs of Sir Robert Peel,' 1856-7, collections of essays, and ' Notes of Conversations with Wellington,' 1888 ; edited ' Letters

of Philip Dormer, Earl of Chesterfield ' (1845, 1853), ' Secret Correspondence connected with Mr. Pitt's return to office in 1804 ' (1852), and other works. [liv. 37]

STANHOPE, WILLIAM, first EARL OF HARRINGTON (1690 ?-1756), diplomatist and statesman ; served in Spain ; colonel of dragoons and M.P. for Derby, 1715 ; special envoy at Madrid, 1717-18, at Turin, 1718 ; as volunteer with French army concerted attack on Spanish ships at St. Andero ; British ambassador in Spain, 1719-1727 ; obtained from Ripperda revelation of articles of secret treaty of Vienna, 1726 ; engaged in fruitless negotiations for cession of Gibraltar ; his correspondence with Marquis de la Paz published, 1726-7 ; vice-chamberlain and privy councillor, 1727 ; plenipotentiary at Aix-la-Chapelle and Soissons, 1728-30 ; procured treaty of Seville (England, France, and Spain), 1729 ; created Baron Harrington, 1730 ; secretary of state for northern department, May 1730-41 ; supported George II's Hanoverian policy against the Walpoles ; propounded plan for ultimatum to France, but was obliged to carry out peace policy of Walpole in preliminaries of 1735 ; negotiated treaty for neutrality of Hanover without knowledge of Walpole, 1741 ; president of the council, 1741 ; created Earl of Harrington, 1742 ; a lord justice, 1743 ; succeeded Carteret as secretary of state, 1744 ; resigned, 1746, after George II's vain attempt to detach him from the Pelhams ; returned with Pelhams, but exchanged (October) seals for lord-lieutenancy of Ireland ; his vice-royalty (1746-51) marked by beginning of Irish parliamentary opposition. [liv. 40]

STANHOPE, WILLIAM, second EARL OF HARRINGTON (1719-1779), known as ' Peter Shambles' ; son of William Stanhope, first earl of Harrington [q. v.] ; distinguished at Fontenoy ; general, 1770 ; M.P. (Viscount Petersham), Bury St. Edmunds, 1747-56 ; his wife a beauty and friend of Horace Walpole. [liv. 44]

STANIHURST, RICHARD (1547-1618). [See STANYHURST.]

STANLEY, MRS. (1796 ?-1861). [See FLEMING.]

STANLEY, ARTHUR PENRHYN (1815-1881), dean of Westminster ; son of Edward Stanley (1779-1849) [q. v.] ; at Rugby under Arnold ; scholar of Balliol College, Oxford ; Ireland scholar and Newdegate prizeman, 1837 ; as fellow of University College, Oxford, gained prizes for Latin, English, and Ellerton essays, 1839, 1840 ; helped to promote petition for relief of clergy from subscription to damnatory clauses of Athanasian creed ; published ' Life of Dr. Arnold,' 1844 ; opposed degradation of William George Ward [q. v.] and agitation against Dr. Hampden ; resigned fellowship, 1850 ; secretary of Oxford University commission, 1850-2 ; canon of Canterbury, 1851 ; travelled in Egypt and Palestine, 1852-3 ; published ' Memorials of Canterbury,' 1854, ' Commentary on Epistles to the Corinthians,' 1855, ' Sinai and Palestine,' 1856 ; Oxford professor of ecclesiastical history, 1856 (installed canon of Christ Church, 1858) ; examining chaplain to (Archbishop) Tait ; published ' Lectures on History of the Eastern Church,' 1861, ' Lectures on History of the Jewish Church,' 1863, 1865, 1876 ; supported Jowett's right to salary as Greek professor and cause of Bishop Colenso ; defended ' Essays and Reviews ' in ' Edinburgh Review,' 1861 ; accompanied Albert Edward, prince of Wales on eastern tour, 1862 ; dean of Westminster, 1864-81 ; his views embodied in ' Essays, chiefly on Questions of Church and State, from 1850 to 1870,' 1870 ; endeavoured to attract men of all shades of religious opinion to the abbey ; issued ' Memorials of Westminster Abbey,' 1868 ; conducted Anglican ceremony at marriage of Duke of Edinburgh and Grand Duchess Marie at St. Petersburg, 1874. [liv. 44]

STANLEY, CHARLOTTE, COUNTESS OF DERBY (1599-1664), daughter of Claude de la Trémoille, duc de Thouars ; married to James Stanley, lord Strange, afterwards seventh Earl of Derby [q. v.], 1626 ; held Lathom House against parliamentarians, February to May, 1644 ; afterwards retired to Isle of Man ; alleged to have persecuted William Christian [q. v.] for surrendering the island, 1651. [liv. 48]

STANLEY, EDWARD, first BARON MONTEAGLE (1460 ?-1523), fifth son of Thomas Stanley, first earl of Derby [q. v.] ; sheriff of Lancashire, 1485 ; distinguished himself at Flodden, 1513, and in French war ; K.G., 1514 ; created Baron Monteagle, 1514 ; at Field of Cloth of Gold, 1520 ; commenced religious foundation at Hornby. [liv. 49]

STANLEY, EDWARD, third EARL OF DERBY (1508–1572); signed petition to Pope Clement VII for Henry VIII's divorce, 1530 ; present at interview between Henry VIII and Francis I, 1532 ; K.B., 1533 ; prominent in suppressing northern rebellions, 1536 and 1537 ; K.G., 1547 ; privy councillor, 1551, under special conditions ; assessor at trial of Somerset, 1551 ; lord-lieutenant of Lancashire, 1552 ; regular member of privy council, 1553 ; special commissioner for trial of Lady Jane Grey ; helped to try protestants ; retained as privy councillor by Queen Elizabeth ; lord-lieutenant of Cheshire and Lancashire, 1569 ; gave warning of insurrection of 1569, but regarded with suspicion by government. [liv. 50]

STANLEY, EDWARD (1779–1849), bishop of Norwich ; uncle of Edward John Stanley, second baron Stanley of Alderley [q. v.] ; sixteenth wrangler from St. John's College, Cambridge, 1802 ; incumbent of Alderley, 1805–37 ; keenly interested in education ; published 'Familiar History of Birds,' 1836 ; lectured on geology ; advocated church reform, 1831 ; chairman of board of guardians, 1834 ; bishop of Norwich, 1837–49 ; enforced Plurality and Non-residence Act ; appointed rural deans ; instituted annual confirmations ; supported whig measures in House of Lords ; advocate of admission of nonconformists to National schools, of ragged schools, and of temperance. [liv. 52]

STANLEY, EDWARD (1793–1862), surgeon ; trained at St. Bartholomew's Hospital, London ; M.R.C.S., 1814 ; Jacksonian prizeman, 1815 ; lecturer on anatomy, St. Bartholomew's, 1826–48, surgeon, 1838–61 ; F.R.S., 1830 ; life member of council, Royal College of Surgeons, 1832, professor of human anatomy and physiology, 1835, Hunterian orator, 1839, president, 1848, 1857 ; surgeon extraordinary to Queen Victoria, 1858 ; president of Royal Medical and Chirurgical Society ; published important treatises on diseases of the bones, 1849. [liv. 53]

STANLEY, EDWARD GEORGE GEOFFREY SMITH, fourteenth EARL OF DERBY (1799–1869), statesman ; son of Edward Smith Stanley, thirteenth earl of Derby [q. v.] ; of Eton and Christ Church, Oxford (hon. D.C.L., 1852) ; won chancellor's Latin verse prize, 1819 ; whig M.P., Stockbridge, 1822–6, Preston, 1826–30, Windsor, 1831–2, North Lancashire, 1832–44 ; under-secretary for the colonies under Canning and Goderich ; as Irish secretary (1830–3) under Earl Grey attacked by O'Connell, whom he challenged ; prosecuted O'Connell for breach of Association Act, 1831 ; moderate supporter of parliamentary reform, pressing for concessions within the cabinet ; after defeat of ministers on Lyndhurst's amendment (May 1832) supported full reform scheme ; introduced Reform Bill for Ireland, 1832 ; instituted Irish board of works ; introduced Irish Education Act, 1831 ; passed measures making tithe composition in Ireland compulsory, 1832 ; carried Peace Preservation Act and Irish Church Temporalities Act, 1833, though opposed by Althorp in the cabinet ; as colonial secretary carried act for abolition of slavery, 1833 ; resigned, 1834, being opposed to appropriation of Irish church revenues for secular purposes ; his independent party named by O'Connell the 'Derby Dilly'; joined conservative opposition, 1835 ; compelled whig government to modify Irish disendowment proposals ; colonial secretary under Peel, 1841–4 ; called up to House of Lords as Lord Stanley of Bickerstaffe, 1844 ; resigned on Peel's declaration in favour of immediate free trade ; declined to form protectionist ministry, 1846, but reluctantly accepted leadership of anti-freetraders ; made brilliant speeches in parliament on foreign affairs, 1848–51 ; attempted to form conservative ministry, 1851 ; succeeded to earldom, 1851 ; formed protectionist ministry (February 1852), but failed to secure majority at general election (July), and resigned (December) after defeat on the budget ; on Aberdeen's defeat (1855) again tried to form ministry ; attacked foreign policy of Palmerston ministry, 1855–8 ; during his second premiership (1858–9) settled the Orsini dispute with France, the Cagliari question with Naples, and difficulties with America concerning the right of search ; introduced bill for equalisation of town and country franchise, but was beaten on clause disfranchising forty-shilling freeholders ; dissolved parliament ; resigned on carrying of Hartington's vote of want of confidence ; created extra K.G. ; came to understanding with Palmerston ; prevented English intervention in German-Danish war, 1864 ; during third administration (1866–8) concerted with Disraeli

parliamentary Reform Bill of 1867 ; resigned, February 1868 ; called ' the Rupert of debate ' by Lord Lytton in the ' New Timon ' ; success of movement for relief of cotton famine largely due to him ; devoted to classical scholarship and sport ; chancellor of Oxford University, 1852 ; Derby scholarship founded to commemorate him, 1870 ; published miscellaneous works, including a version of the ' Iliad ' (issued privately, 1862, published, 1864). [liv. 54]

STANLEY, EDWARD HENRY, fifteenth EARL OF DERBY (1826–1893), statesman ; eldest son of Edward George Geoffrey Smith Stanley, fourteenth earl of Derby [q. v.]; of Rugby and Trinity College, Cambridge ; M.A., 1848, hon. LL.D., 1862 (D.C.L. Oxford, 1853) ; one of ' the Apostles ' ; travelled in North America and West Indies, 1848, Jamaica and Ecuador, 1849–50, Bengal, 1852 ; M.P., King's Lynn, 1848–69 ; under-secretary for foreign affairs, 1852 ; declined Palmerston's offer of colonial secretaryship, 1855 ; joined opposition to Crimean war ; member of commission on army purchase ; colonial secretary, and (after passing of India bill) Indian secretary in second Derby ministry (1858–9) ; in cabinet supported disfranchising clauses of Reform Bill ; member of Cambridge University commission ; president Indian army and patent laws commissions ; offered crown of Greece, 1863 ; made able speech seconding Grosvenor's amendment to Reform Bill of 1866 ; suggested as head of a ministry, 1866 ; foreign secretary under Derby and Disraeli, 1866–8 ; mediated between France and Prussia, postponing war by his ' collective guarantee ' of Luxemburg, 1867 ; declined interference in Crete and Italy ; in Alabama case admitted principle of arbitration ; supported Reform Bill ; led opposition to Irish disestablishment half-heartedly, 1869 ; succeeded as earl, 1869 ; as foreign secretary (1874–8) in Disraeli's second ministry accepted with hesitation purchase of Suez Canal shares and Austrian proposals for reforms in Turkey, demanded punishment of perpetrators of Bulgarian atrocities, and initiated Constantinople conference on Turkish reform (1876) ; resigned on Disraeli's ordering of British fleet to the Dardanelles, 1878 (January) ; resumed office on countermanding of order, but again resigned on calling out of the reserves (March) ; opposed acquisition of Cyprus and first Afghan war, 1879 ; left conservatives, 1880 ; as colonial secretary under Gladstone, 1882 (December)–1885, resisted further annexation of tropical colonies, concluded convention of 1884 with the Boers, and discouraged Australian federation ; K.G., 1884 ; joined liberal unionists, and led them in House of Lords, 1886–91 ; presided over labour commission, 1892 ; chancellor of London University, 1891–1893 ; lord rector of Glasgow University, 1868–71, Edinburgh University, 1875–80. [liv. 61]

STANLEY, EDWARD JOHN, second BARON STANLEY OF ALDERLEY and first BARON EDDISBURY OF WINNINGTON (1802–1869), statesman ; B.A. Christ Church, Oxford, 1825 ; whig M.P., Hindon, 1831, North Cheshire, 1832–41 and 1847–8 ; under-secretary for home department, 1834, foreign department, 1846–52 ; paymaster-general, 1841 ; privy councillor and liberal whip ; created Baron Eddisbury, 1848 ; succeeded to Stanley barony, 1850 ; president of board of trade, 1855–8 ; postmaster-general, 1860–6. [liv. 64]

STANLEY, EDWARD SMITH, thirteenth EARL OF DERBY (1775–1851) ; M.A. Trinity College, Cambridge, 1795 ; whig M.P., Preston, 1796–1812, Lancashire, 1812–32 ; summoned as Baron Stanley of Bickerstaffe, 1832 ; succeeded to earldom, 1834 ; K.G., 1839 ; president of Linnean Society, 1828–33 ; president of Zoological Society ; formed private menagerie at Knowsley ; 'Stanley Crane' named after him ; his museum given to Liverpool. [liv. 66]

STANLEY, FERDINANDO, fifth EARL OF DERBY (1559 ?–1594), son of Henry Stanley, fourth earl of Derby [q. v.] ; M.A. St. John's College, Oxford, 1589 ; as mayor of Liverpool raised troop of horse, 1588 ; summoned as Baron Strange, 1589 ; succeeded to earldom and sovereignty of Man, 1593 ; panegyrised by Spenser, as ' Amyntas,' Nash, and Chapman. [liv. 67]

STANLEY, HANS (1720 ?–1780), politician ; M.P., St. Albans, 1743–7, Southampton, 1754–80 ; a lord of the admiralty, 1757–65 ; employed by Pitt as chargé d'affaires to conduct negotiations at Paris, 1761 ; failed ; privy councillor, 1762 ; governor of Isle of Wight, 1764 ; cofferer of the household, 1766–74, and from 1776 ; Sloane trustee ; left works in manuscript ; intimate with Helvetius ; committed suicide at Althorp. [liv. 68]

STANLEY, HENRIETTA MARIA, LADY STANLEY OF ALDERLEY (1807–1895), married Edward John Stanley, second baron Stanley of Alderley [q. v.], 1826; rendered useful service to whig party; friend of Carlyle, Frederick Denison Maurice, and Jowett; promoter of women's education. [liv. 65]

STANLEY, HENRY, fourth EARL OF DERBY (1531–1593), son of Edward Stanley, third earl of Derby [q. v.]; styled Lord Strange till succession, 1572; hostage in France, 1550; gentleman of the privy chamber to Edward VI, 1547, to Philip of Spain, 1554; alleged himself to have been employed by Somerset to exercise influence and watch over Edward VI; married, 1555, Margaret Clifford, granddaughter of Mary Tudor, sister of Henry VIII; summoned as Baron Strange, 1559; commissioner for ecclesiastical causes; member of council of the north; K.G., 1574; privy councillor, 1585; commissioner at trial of Mary Queen of Scots, 1586, to treat with Spain, 1588; lord high steward, 1589. [liv. 70]

STANLEY, JAMES (1465?–1515), bishop of Ely; son of Thomas Stanley, first earl of Derby [q. v.]; M.A. Oxford, D.Can.L., 1506; warden of collegiate church of Manchester, 1485; dean of St. Martin-le-Grand, London, 1485; archdeacon of Richmond, 1500; prebendary of Salisbury, 1505; bishop of Ely by papal bull, 1506–15; took part in foundation of St. John's and Christ's colleges, Cambridge; compiled statutes for Jesus College, Cambridge; denounced by protestants for loose morals. [liv. 70]

STANLEY, JAMES, seventh EARL OF DERBY (1607–1651), 'the Martyr Earl'; M.P. (Lord Strange), Liverpool, 1625; K.B., 1626; summoned as Baron Strange, 1628; lord-lieutenant of North Wales; encouraged minor authors and actors; attended Charles I at York, 1639–40; said to have mustered sixty thousand Lancashire and Cheshire royalists; attempted to recover Manchester for Charles I, 1642; seized magazines; impeached and outlawed by parliament; succeeded to earldom, 1642; twice defeated near Warrington; took Preston, 1643; repulsed Brereton at Warrington, but was defeated at Whalley, 1643; with Rupert in the north, 1644, leading the assault at Bolton; after Marston Moor, 1644, withdrew to Man, rejecting terms, for six years; landed in Lancashire, 1651, and saw Charles II, but failed to gain over presbyterians; routed at Wigan by Robert Lilburne [q. v.]; after Worcester (3 Sept. 1651) conducted Charles II to Boscobel; captured, condemned as traitor by court-martial, and executed; his 'Discourse concerning Government of Isle of Man' printed in Peck's 'Desiderata Curiosa,' 1732. [liv. 71]

STANLEY, SIR JOHN (1350?–1414), founder of house of Stanley; acquired Knowsley and Lathom by marriage with Isabel Latham, c. 1385; deputy for De Vere in Ireland, 1386, lieutenant, 1389–91; held posts on Welsh and Scottish borders; regranted Irish office by Henry IV, 1399; superseded, 1401; steward of Prince Henry's household from 1403; K.G., 1405; granted the Isle of Man, 1405; died Henry V's lieutenant in Ireland. [liv. 75]

STANLEY, JOHN (1714–1786), musician; accidentally blinded in childhood; organist of All Hallows, Bread Street, London, at eleven; organist of St. Andrew's, Holborn, 1726–86, and Inner Temple, 1734–86; Mus.Bac. Oxford, 1730; played organ concertos at Vauxhall; led subscription concerts with violin; invented apparatus for teaching music to the blind; his oratorio 'Jephthah' performed, 1757; carried on Covent Garden Lent oratorios with John Christopher Smith [q. v.], 1760–74, and afterwards with Thomas Linley the elder [q. v.]; composed 'Zimri,' 1760, 'Arcadia' (dramatic pastoral), 1762, 'Fall of Egypt,' 1774; led George III's band, 1782; set Warton's birthday ode, 1786; published twelve cantatas, organ voluntaries, and concertos. [liv. 74]

STANLEY, MONTAGUE (1809–1844), actor and landscape-painter; played at York under name of Manby, 1824, at Edinburgh in his own name, 1826–38, visiting Dublin, 1830, London, 1832–3; left the stage, 1838; A.R.S.A., 1839. [liv. 75]

STANLEY, THOMAS (1406?–1459), first BARON STANLEY; son of Sir John Stanley [q. v.]; lieutenant-governor of Ireland, 1431–7; M.P., Lancashire, 1446–55; comptroller of the household, c. 1447; lord chamberlain and privy councillor, c. 1455; K.G.; created peer, 1456. [liv. 76]

STANLEY, THOMAS, first EARL OF DERBY (1435?–1504), succeeded his father, Thomas Stanley, as second Baron Stanley, 1459; married Eleanor Neville before 1460; with Henry VI at Northampton (1460), but made chief-justice of Chester and Flint by Edward IV, 1461; again Lancastrian on restoration of Henry VI, 1470; privy councillor and lord steward after Warwick's defeat, 1471; held commands in France, 1475, and Scotland, 1482; married, c. 1482, Margaret Beaufort, countess of Richmond; imprisoned for support of Edward V, 1483, but continued in offices by Richard III, and named K.G. and constable of England; took up neutral position at Bosworth (1485), but crowned the victor; created by Henry VII Earl of Derby, 1485, and continued in all his offices. [liv. 75]

STANLEY, THOMAS (d. 1570), bishop of Sodor and Man; second son of Edward Stanley, first baron Monteagle [q. v.]; appointed bishop, 1530, deprived, 1545, restored, 1556; his metrical chronicle of Stanleys of Lathom in Halliwell's 'Palatine Anthology' (1850). [liv. 50]

STANLEY, THOMAS (1625–1678), classical scholar; descendant of Edward Stanley, third earl of Derby [q. v.]; M.A. Pembroke Hall, Cambridge, 1641; travelled; financially assisted Sir Edward Sherburne [q. v.], John Hall (1627–1656) [q. v.], and James Shirley [q. v.]; intimate with William Hammond [q. v.], and with Lovelace (his cousin); published poems and translations, 1647–51, including versions of Tasso, Petrarch, and Lope de Vega, and of Greek and late Latin poets; his Latin and Greek translations edited by Brydges, 1814–15; his version of Anacreon reprinted, 1893; published also 'History of Philosophy' (4 vols.), 1655, 1656, 1660, 1662 (mainly biographical), long a standard work; his edition of Æschylus (1663) republished, 1745, revised by Richard Porson [q. v.] 1795 and 1806, and by Samuel Butler (1774–1839) [q. v.], 1809–16, criticised by Charles James Blomfield [q. v.]; his manuscript notes on classical authors in Cambridge University Library; at the time of the Bentley-Boyle controversy Bentley was accused of using without acknowledgment his comments on Callimachus. [liv. 78]

STANLEY, VENETIA (1600–1633). [See DIGBY, VENETIA, LADY.]

STANLEY, SIR WILLIAM (d. 1495), lord chamberlain to Henry VII; brother of Thomas Stanley, first earl of Derby [q. v.]; made chamberlain of Chester by Edward IV, 1461; rewarded further after Hexham and Towton; made justiciar of North Wales and granted estates in Derbyshire by Richard III; was denounced as traitor by his nephew, Lord Strange, and outlawed; joined Richmond at end of battle of Bosworth, deciding the day by bringing three thousand men into action; K.G. and lord chamberlain, 1485; beheaded as accomplice of Warbeck. [liv. 81]

STANLEY, SIR WILLIAM (1548–1630), adventurer; of Hooton; volunteer under Alva, 1567–70; served Queen Elizabeth in Ireland, 1570–85; knighted, 1579; took part in hunting down of Desmond and Fitzgerald of Imokelly and reduction of Munster, 1583; sheriff of Cork and temporary governor of Munster, 1584; wounded in expedition against Ulstermen, 1584–5; raised men in Ireland for service in Netherlands, but meditated treachery, 1585–6; distinguished at Zutphen, 1586; English governor of Deventer, betraying it to Spanish, 1587; pensioned by Spain; advised invasion of England from Ireland; returned to Netherlands to act with Armada, 1588; with Spanish in France, 1596–7, in Netherlands, 1598–1603; negotiated with English government for pardon; Spanish governor of Mechlin; died at Ghent. [liv. 82]

STANLEY, WILLIAM (1647–1731), dean of St. Asaph; B.A. St. John's College, Cambridge, 1666; fellow of Corpus Christi College, Cambridge, 1669; master, 1693–8; M.A., 1670; created D.D. 1694; chaplain to Princess of Orange, 1685; clerk of the closet and canon of St. Paul's, London, 1689; archdeacon of London, 1692; dean of St. Asaph, 1706–31; the Stentor of the 'Tatler'; defrayed cost of act relieving relicts of Welsh clergy from mortuary fees; works include 'Faith and Practice of a Church of England-Man,' 1688. [liv. 84]

STANNARD, ALFRED (1806–1889), landscape-painter; brother of Joseph Stannard [q. v.] [liv. 85]

STANNARD, JOSEPH (1797–1830), painter; exhibited with Norwich Society, 1811–16, at Royal Academy and British Institution, 1820–9. [liv. 85]

STANNUS, Sir EPHRAIM GERRISH (1784-1850), major-general; ensign, Bombay army, 1800; promoted major for services in Pindari war, 1818; private secretary to Mountstuart Elphinstone; lieutenant-colonel, 9th native infantry, 1822; C.B., 1823; first British resident in Persian Gulf, 1823-6; lieutenant-governor of East India College, Addiscombe, 1834-50; knighted, 1837; major-general, 1838. [liv. 86]

STANSFELD, Sir JAMES (1820-1898), politician; educated at University College, London; B.A., 1840; LL.B., 1844, barrister, Middle Temple, 1849; intimate with Mazzini; liberal M.P. for Halifax, 1859-95; advocated cause of Italian unity; junior lord of admiralty, 1863; charged with being in correspondence with conspirators against NapoleonIII,and though his explanationwasregarded byPalmerston as satisfactory resigned office, 1864; under-secretary of state for India, 1866; third lord of treasury, 1868; privy councillor, 1869; financial secretary to treasury, 1869; president of poor law board,1871; president of local government board, 1871-4, and April-July, 1886; G.C.B., 1895. [Suppl. iii. 352]

STANWIX, JOHN (1690?-1766), lieutenant-general; entered army, 1706; lieutenant-colonel, 1745; M.P., Carlisle, 1746, Appleby, 1761; governor of Carlisle, 1752; of Isle of Wight, 1763; colonel-commandant of royal Americans (king's royal rifle corps), 1756; in Pennsylvania, 1757-60; built Fort Stanwix, 1758; lieutenant-general, 1761; lost in Irish Channel. [liv. 86]

STANWIX, RICHARD (1608-1656), divine; M.A. Queen's College, Oxford, 1632; fellow; B.D., 1639; incorporated at Cambridge, 1640; chaplain to lord keepers Coventry and Finch; published a devotional work, 1652. [liv. 87]

STANYAN, ABRAHAM (1669?-1732), diplomatist; student, Middle Temple, 1690; while envoy (1705-9) to Swiss cantons co-operated with Dutch envoy in obtaining for king of Prussia succession to Neufchatel; undertook secret mission to Piedmont, 1710; negotiated with emperor Charles VI and Duke of Savoy, 1712; M.P., Buckingham, 1715; envoy extraordinary to the emperor Charles VI, 1716-17; ambassador extraordinary at Constantinople, 1719-20; clerk in privy seal office; member of Kit-Cat Club, but friend of Pope; published 'Account of Switzerland,' 1714. [liv. 87]

STANYAN, TEMPLE (d. 1752), author of 'Grecian History,' 1739 (translated by Diderot, 1743); brother of Abraham Stanyan [q. v.]; of Westminster School and Christ Church, Oxford; under-secretary of state, 1715-19; clerk to privy council, 1719. [liv. 88]

STANYHURST, JAMES (d. 1573), speaker of the Irish House of Commons; speaker, 1557, 1560, 1568; recorder of Dublin; secured passing of statute of uniformity, 1560; proposed system of national education, 1570; friend of Edmund Campion [q. v.] and Sir Henry Sidney [q. v.] [liv. 89]

STANYHURST, RICHARD (1547-1618), translator of Virgil; son of James Stanyhurst [q. v.]; B.A. University College, Oxford, 1568; student at Furnivall's Inn and Lincoln's Inn; published Latin commentaries on Porphyry, 1570; contributed 'Description of Ireland' and 'History of Ireland' to Holinshed's 'Chronicles,' 1577; became a Romanist abroad, c. 1580; his grotesque translation into English heroics of the first four books of the 'Æneid,' with some original poems and epitaphs, printed at Leyden, 1582 (reprinted by Arber, 1880), and London, 1583; praised as a disciple by Gabriel Harvey [q. v.], but ridiculed by Nash and Bishop Hall; issued at Antwerp 'De rebus in Hibernia gestis,' 1584, and a Latin life of St. Patrick, 1587; plotted with Roman catholic exiles in Flanders; advised Spanish court, 1590-5; named chaplain to governor of the Netherlands, c. 1602; wrote devotional works; corresponded with Archbishop Ussher (his nephew) and replied (1615) to his attack on the pope; died at Brussels. [liv. 86]

STANYHURST, WILLIAM (1602-1663), jesuit and religious writer; son of Richard Stanyhurst [q. v.] [liv. 91]

STAPELDON, WALTER DE (1261-1326), bishop of Exeter; professor of canon law, Oxford; chaplain to Pope Clement V; precentor of Exeter; bishop of Exeter, 1307-1326; accumulated material, and contributed largely to rebuilding of cathedral; undertook missions to France, 1306, 1313, and 1319; joined lords ordainers, 1310; with his brother founded Stapeldon Hall (afterwards Exeter College), Oxford, 1314; appointed to hold parliament in Edward II's absence, 1314; lord high treasurer, 1320; tried to mediate between Edward II and Thomas of Lancaster, 1321; forced to flee from Gascony as a favourite of Edward II, 1325; murdered by mob while in charge of London. [liv. 92]

STAPLES or **STAPLE**, EDWARD (1490?-1560?), bishop of Meath; educated at Oxford and Cambridge; M.A., 1514, D.D., 1526; canon of Cardinal College (Christ Church), Oxford, 1525; chaplain to Henry VIII; master of St. Bartholomew's Hospital, 1528; bishop of Meath by provision, 1530; compelled to flee to England by Kildare's rebellion, 1534; with George Browne (d. 1556) [q. v.] introduced Irish reformation; deprived by Queen Mary on account of his marriage. [liv. 93]

STAPLETON, AUGUSTUS GRANVILLE (1800-1880), author of 'Political Life of George Canning, 1822-1827,' 1831, and 'George Canning and his Time,' 1859; B.A. St. John's College, Cambridge, 1823; Canning's private secretary; commissioner of customs, 1827; contributed political reminiscences to 'Macmillan's Magazine'; published political pamphlets. [liv. 94]

STAPLETON, BRIAN DE (1321?-1394), of Wighill, knight; brother of Miles de Stapleton (d. 1364) [q. v.]; sent to help the Black Prince in Aquitaine, 1369; served under William de Montacute, second earl of Salisbury [q. v.]; captain and warden of Calais, 1380, of Guisnes Castle, 1381-3; K.G., 1382; gave evidence in Scrope-Grosvenor case; hero of several legends. [liv. 95]

STAPLETON, GREGORY (1748-1802), Roman catholic prelate; procurator of English College, Douay, 1773-85; president of English College, St. Omer, 1787; imprisoned by revolutionists at Dourlens; president of St. Edmund's College, Hertfordshire, 1795-1800; bishop of Hierocæsarea and vicar-apostolic of Midlands, 1800-2; died at St. Omer. [liv. 95]

STAPLETON, MILES DE (d. 1314), baron; connected by marriage with elder line of Bruces; served Edward I in Scotland and Gascony; director of household of Edward, prince of Wales; steward of Edward II's household, 1307-8; adherent of Thomas of Lancaster; thrice summoned to parliament, 1313; his chapel of St. Nicholas in North Moreton Church still standing; slain at Bannockburn. [liv. 96]

STAPLETON, MILES DE (d. 1364), of Bedale and Ingham; grandson of Miles de Stapleton (d. 1314) [q. v.]; in early life called 'of Cotherstone'; distinguished in French wars; an original K.G.; envoy of Edward III to Philip of Navarre, 1358; negotiated at Bretigny, 1360; rewarded with annuity, 1361; supported John de Montfort in Brittany; died probably of wounds received at Auray; parts of his church at Ingham existing. [liv. 97]

STAPLETON, Sir MILES, first baronet (1628-1707), nephew of Sir Robert Stapleton [q. v.]; created baronet, 1662; charged with complicity in plot of Sir Thomas Gascoigne [q. v.], 1680; acquitted, 1681. [liv. 101]

STAPLETON or **STAPILTON**, Sir PHILIP (1603-1647), parliamentarian; fellow-commoner, Queens' College, Cambridge, 1617; knighted, 1630; M.P., Boroughbridge, in Long parliament; with Hampden attended Charles I in Scotland, 1641; parliamentary commissioner in Yorkshire, 1642; commander of Essex's bodyguard and colonel of horse, 1642; did good service at Edgehill, 1642, Chalgrove Field, 1643, and first battle of Newbury, 1643; sent by Essex to represent state of western army to parliament, 1643; member of committee of safety, 1642, of committee of both kingdoms, 1644; opposed self-denying ordinance and planned accusation of Cromwell; impeached with the eleven members by the army, 1647; escaped to Calais, and died there. [liv. 98]

STAPLETON or **STAPYLTON**, Sir ROBERT (d. 1669), dramatist and translator; Benedictine of Douay, 1625; became protestant; knighted, 1642; accompanied Charles I to Oxford after Edgehill; created D.C.L., 1642; gentleman usher to privy chamber, 1660; published four plays (three acted), some verses, and translations, including 'Pliny's Panegyricke,' 1644, and Musæus, 1645. [liv. 100]

STAPLETON, THEOBALD (*fl.* 1636), Irish priest; author of 'Catechismus seu Doctrina Christiana Latino-Hibernica' (1639, Brussels), first Irish book in Roman type. [liv. 101]

STAPLETON, THOMAS (1535-1598), Roman catholic controversialist; of Winchester College and New College, Oxford (fellow, 1553); B.A., 1556; prebendary of Chichester, 1558, deprived for Romanism, 1563; D.D. and public professor of divinity, Douay, 1571; canon of St. Amatus, Douay; professor of holy scripture and canon of Louvain, 1590; dean of Hilverenbeeck; named prothonotary apostolic, 1597, but never went to Rome. His works (collected, 1620) include controversial treatises against Jewel and other protestants, a translation of Bede's 'History of the Church of England,' 1565, 'Tres Thomæ' (St. Thomas, Becket, and More), 1588, and a metrical autobiography in Latin. [liv. 101]

STAPLETON, THOMAS (1805-1849), antiquary; vice-president Society of Antiquaries, 1846; F.R.S.; published, 'Magni Rotuli Scaccarii Normanniæ sub Regibus Angliæ,' 1841-4; edited works for Camden Society. [liv. 104]

STAPLEY, ANTHONY (1590-1655), regicide; M.P., New Shoreham, 1624-5, Lewes, 1628, Sussex, 1640, 1653-4; colonel and governor of Chichester, 1642-5; signed death-warrant of Charles I; member of council of state, 1649-1653; vice-admiral of Sussex, 1650; member of interim council and of supreme assembly, 1653. [liv. 104]

STAPLEY, SIR JOHN, first baronet (1628-1701), second son of Anthony Stapley [q. v.]; M.P., Sussex, 1654, 1656, Lewes, 1661; plotted with John Hewit or Hewett (1614-1658) [q. v.] and others to restore Charles II, 1657-8; created baronet, 1660. [liv. 105]

STARK, ADAM (1784-1867), antiquary; published histories of Gainsborough (1817), the bishopric of Lincoln (1852), and printing (1855). [liv. 106]

STARK, JAMES (1794-1859), landscape-painter; elected to Norwich Society of Artists, 1812; exhibited in London, 1814-18, and after 1830; student at Royal Academy, 1817; awarded premium by British Institution, 1818; his 'Scenery of Rivers of Norfolk' completed, 1834; his works exhibited at Norwich, 1887. [liv. 106]

STARK, WILLIAM (1740-1770), physician; studied at Glasgow and Edinburgh; under John Hunter (1728-1793) [q. v.] at St. George's Hospital, London; M.D. Leyden, 1766; made experiments on diet, dying from effects; his 'Works' edited, 1788. [liv. 107]

STARKE, MARIANA (1762?-1838), pioneer of guide-books ('Travels in Europe,' &c.); published also plays and other works; died at Milan. [liv. 107]

STARKEY, GEOFFREY (*fl.* 1440). [See GEOFFREY THE GRAMMARIAN.]

STARKEY, GEORGE (*d.* 1665), empiric; born in the Bermudas; M.A. Harvard, 1646; claimed medical degree; practised in English settlements in America, and met the mysterious 'Eirenæus Philalethes' [q. v.]; proceeded to England between 1646 and 1650; sold quack medicines, 1650-66; published medical tracts, a royalist pamphlet, 'Liquor Alchahest,' 1675, and prefaces to 'The Marrow of Alchemy by Eirenæus Philoponus Philalethes,' 1654; often confused with last named [see EIRENÆUS PHILALETHES]; died after dissecting plague patient. [liv. 107]

STARKEY, SIR HUMPHREY (*d.* 1486), chief-baron of the exchequer; of the Inner Temple; counsel for John Paston [q. v.], 1464, 1466; serjeant-at-law, 1478; chief-baron, 1483-6; knighted; judge of common pleas under Richard III and Henry VII. [liv. 108]

STARKEY, RALPH (*d.* 1628), transcriber and collector of state papers and manuscripts; confidential papers of William Davison (1541?-1608) [q. v.] seized by government in his house, 1619; his papers now in the Harleian collection, British Museum. [liv. 109]

STARKEY, THOMAS (1499?-1538), author of 'Exhortation to Christian Unity' (or 'Treatise against Papal Supremacy') and 'Dialogue between Pole and Lupset' (ed. J. M. Cowper, 1871); M.A. Magdalen College, Oxford, 1521, fellow, 1522-4; incumbent of Great Mongeham, 1530; LL.D. while with Reginald Pole in Italy; chaplain to Henry VIII and Countess of Salisbury,

1534; suggested (1533) reference to a general council of the divorce question; master of college of Corpus Christi, London, 1536; his letters edited by S. J. Herrtage, 1878. [liv. 109]

STARKIE, THOMAS (1782-1849), legal writer; senior wrangler and first Smith's prizeman, 1803; M.A. St. John's College, Cambridge, 1806; barrister, Lincoln's Inn, 1810; K.C. at Lancaster; Q.C.; member of commission on amendment of the law; Downing professor of law, Cambridge, 1823-49; judge of Clerkenwell county court, 1847-9; wrote on the 'law of evidence,' 1824. [liv. 110]

STARLEY, JAMES (1831-1881), machinist; brought out 'European' sewing machine, 1857; patented 'Ariel' and other improved bicycles; brought out 'Coventry' tricycle, 1876; his masterpiece the 'Salvo' quadricycle. [liv. 111]

STATHAM, NICHOLAS (*d.* 1472), author of 'Epitome Annalium Librorum temp. Henrici Sexti' (Pynson [1495?]); reader, Lincoln's Inn, 1471. [liv. 112]

STAUNFORD, SIR WILLIAM (1509-1558). [See STANFORD.]

STAUNTON, EDMUND (1600-1671), president of Corpus Christi College, Oxford; scholar of Corpus Christi College, Oxford, 1615, fellow, 1617; M.A., 1623, D.D., 1634; incumbent of Bushey, and of Kingston-on-Thames; member of Westminster Assembly of Divines, and preacher in the abbey, 1643; president of Corpus Christi College, Oxford, 1648; ejected, 1660; preached in conventicles, 1662-71; Salters' Hall built for him; published puritan tracts. [liv. 112]

STAUNTON, FRANCIS FRENCH (1779?-1825), lieutenant-colonel; ensign, Bombay army, 1798; lieutenant-colonel, 1823; served in Mysore war, and (1801) Egypt; repulsed peshwa's army at Korigaum, 1817; C.B.; died at sea. [liv. 113]

STAUNTON, SIR GEORGE LEONARD (1737-1801), diplomatist; M.D. Montpellier, 1758; friend of Dr. Johnson, 1759-62, and of Burke later; practised in West Indies, 1762-70; in Grenada, 1772-9; sometime attorney-general; active in defence of Grenada, 1779; while secretary to Lord Macartney at Madras undertook mission to Warren Hastings, 1782, and negotiated treaty with Tippu Sultan, 1784; pensioned by East India Company and created Irish baronet, 1785; F.R.S., 1787; hon. D.C.L. Oxford, 1790; secretary to Macartney's embassy to China, 1792; published an account, 1797; buried in Westminster Abbey. [liv. 113]

STAUNTON, SIR GEORGE THOMAS (1781-1859), writer on China; son of Sir George Leonard Staunton [q. v.]; accompanied Macartney's Chinese embassy, 1792; at Canton, 1798 to 1817; interpreter, 1808; chief of factory, 1816-17; introduced vaccination into China, 1805; member of abortive embassy to Pekin, 1816; M.P., St. Michael's, 1818-26, Heytesbury, 1830-1, Portsmouth, 1838-52; co-founder of Royal Asiatic Society, 1823; F.R.S., 1803; hon. D.C.L. Oxford, 1818; works include 'Fundamental Laws,' 1810 (first Chinese book Englished), and biographical memoirs. [liv. 114]

STAUNTON, HERVEY DE (*d.* 1327), judge; held livings in Norfolk; went to Rome, 1300; justice itinerant in Cornwall, 1302, Durham, 1303; judge of common pleas, 1306; chancellor of the exchequer, 1316-23 and 1324-6; chief-justice of king's bench, 1323-4, of common pleas, 1326-7; adherent of Edward II; his foundation of Michael House, Cambridge, absorbed in Trinity College. [liv. 115]

STAUNTON, HOWARD (1810-1874), chess-player and editor of Shakespeare; reputed son of fifth Earl of Carlisle; defeated chess champion of Europe (St. Amant), 1843, Horwitz and Harrwitz, 1846; beaten in international tournament, 1851, and by Baron von Heydebrand, 1852; edited 'Chess-Player's Chronicle,' 1840-54; published 'Chess-Player's Handbook,' 1847; his 'Chess: Theory and Practice,' edited by R. B. Wormald, 1876; issued his edition of Shakespeare, 1857-60 (reissued, 1864); 'Great Schools of England,' 1865; wrote articles on 'Unsuspected Corruptions of Shakespeare's Text' for 'Athenæum,' 1872-4. [liv. 116]

STAVELEY, SIR CHARLES WILLIAM DUNBAR (1817-1896), general; son of William Staveley (1784-1854) [q. v.]; educated at Scottish military academy; entered army, 1835; aide-de-camp to governor of Mauritius, 1840–1843, to governor-general, British North America, 1846–7; assistant military secretary, Hongkong, 1848–51; aide-de camp to Duke of Cambridge at Alma and Balaclava, 1854; C.B. for services with Eyre's brigade, 1855; led brigade in Peking expedition, 1860; defeated Taepings and recommended Gordon for command of Chinese forces, 1862; major-general, 1867; led first division in Abyssinian campaign, 1867–8; commander-in-chief at Bombay, 1874–1878; general, 1877; G.C.B., 1884. [liv. 117]

STAVELEY, THOMAS (1626–1684), author of 'The Romish Horseleech,' 1674, and posthumous historical works; barrister, Inner Temple, 1654; steward of Leicester court of records, 1672; his Leicester collections printed by Nichols. [liv. 118]

STAVELEY, WILLIAM (1784–1854), lieutenant-general; served with Caithness legion, 1798–1804; entered staff corps, 1804; on quartermaster-general's staff throughout Peninsular war; guided stormers at Ciudad Rodrigo; on headquarters staff at Waterloo, 1815; sent to communicate with Blucher; brevet lieutenant-colonel and C.B., 1815; wounded at Paris while directing carrying out of convention; acting governor of Mauritius, 1842; major-general, 1846; held command at Hongkong, 1847–50, Bombay, 1851–2; commander-in-chief at Madras, 1853–4. [liv. 119]

STAWELL or **STOWELL**, SIR JOHN (1599–1662), royalist; gentleman-commoner, Queen's College, Oxford, 1616; M.P., Somerset, 1625, in Long parliament, and 1661–2; K.B., 1625; sheriff of Somerset, 1628; raised five regiments for Charles I; governor of Taunton; M.A. and M.D. Oxford, 1643; advocated association of western counties under Prince Charles, 1645; captured at Exeter, 1646; imprisoned, 1646–60, and fined; his son created Baron Stawell, 1683. [liv. 120]

STAWELL, SIR WILLIAM FOSTER (1815–1889), first chief-justice of Victoria; B.A. Dublin, 1837, LL.D., 1874; Irish barrister, 1839; admitted to Melbourne bar, 1842; advocated separation of Port Phillip from New South Wales; first attorney-general of Victoria, 1851–5, drafting early laws and preparing Constitution Act, 1854–1855; member for Melbourne and attorney-general, 1855–1857; chief-justice, 1857–86; knighted, 1858; lieutenant-governor, 1887–9; K.C.M.G., 1886; died at Naples. [liv. 121]

STAYLEY, GEORGE (1727–1779?), actor and playwright; played in Dublin, 1752–66, and at the Canongate Music Hall, Edinburgh, 1766; a riot caused by his not being re-engaged at Edinburgh, 1767; published 'Life and Opinions of an Actor,' 1762. [liv. 121]

STAYLEY, WILLIAM (d. 1678). [See STALEY.]

STAYNER, SIR RICHARD (d. 1662), admiral; commanded the Foresight in actions off Portland (February), and the Gabbard (June), and in battle of 29–31 July, 1653; captured great part of Spanish West Indian treasure fleet off Cadiz, 1656; knighted for services in Blake's destruction of Spanish ships at Santa Cruz, 1657; rear-admiral of the fleet which brought Charles II to England, 1660; again knighted; died at Lisbon, vice-admiral of Mediterranean fleet. [liv. 122]

STEARNE. [See STERN and STERNE.]

STEBBING, HENRY (1687–1763), divine; M.A. St. Catharine Hall, Cambridge, 1712, D.D., 1730, fellow, 1710–1713; incorporated at Oxford, 1738; preacher at Gray's Inn, 1731; chaplain to George II, 1732; chancellor of Sarum, 1739; rector of Redenhall, 1748–63; attacked Warburton's 'Divine Legation'; wrote against Benjamin Hoadly and George Whitefield [q. v.] [liv. 123]

STEBBING, HENRY (1716–1787), son of Henry Stebbing (1687–1763) [q. v.]; fellow of St. Catharine Hall, Cambridge; preacher at Gray's Inn, 1750–87. [liv. 124]

STEBBING, HENRY (1799–1883), divine and author; M.A. St. John's College, Cambridge, 1827; D.D., 1839; incorporated at Oxford, 1857; F.R.S., 1845; acting editor of the 'Athenæum' almost from its beginning, 1828; chaplain to University College Hospital, 1834–79; rector of St. Mary Somerset, London, 1857, with parishes added to it, 1866 and 1879; published a continuation to 1837 of Hume and Smollett's 'History,' 'Lives of the Italian poets' (1831; reissued, 1832, 1860), and other works. [liv. 124]

STEDMAN, CHARLES (1753–1812), author of 'History of the Origin, Progress, and Termination of the American war,' 1794; born at Philadelphia and educated at William and Mary College, Virginia; commissary with Sir William Howe's troops during American war; twice wounded and twice captured; received post in English stamp office, 1797. [liv. 125]

STEDMAN, JOHN ANDREW (1778–1833), general in the Dutch army; served against French, 1794, against English, 1799 and 1839; general of brigade in French army at Dresden and Bautzen, 1813; commanded Dutch reserves at Waterloo. [liv. 126]

STEDMAN, JOHN GABRIEL (1744–1797), soldier and author; born in Holland; served in Scots brigade in Dutch army, 1760–72 and 1777–83; volunteer in expedition against revolted negroes in Surinam, 1772–7; major in British army (Scots brigade), 1793, lieutenant-colonel, 1796; published narrative of the Surinam expedition (with plates by Bartolozzi and Blake), 1796 (2nd ed., 1806). [liv. 126]

STEDMAN, ROWLAND (1630?–1673), nonconformist divine; scholar of Balliol College, Oxford, 1649; M.A., 1656; rector of Hanwell, 1657, of Wokingham, 1660; ejected, 1662; published devotional works. [liv. 128]

STEEL, SIR SCUDAMORE WINDE (1789–1865), lieutenant-general; lieutenant, Madras army, 1806; served in Mahratta war, 1817–18, and first Burmese war, 1826; military secretary at Madras, 1832–45; planned and executed reduction of Coorg, 1834; C.B., 1838; commanded Madras division in second Burmese war, 1852–3; K.C.B., 1853; lieutenant-general, 1861. [liv. 128]

STEELE, ANNE (1717–1778), hymn-writer; published as Theodosia 'Poems on Subjects chiefly devotional,' 1760 (reissued, 1780); complete works issued by Daniel Sedgwick [q. v.], 1863. [liv. 128]

STEELE, CHRISTOPHER (fl. 1756), portrait-painter; known as 'Count Steele'; friend of Romney. [liv. 129]

STEELE, JOSHUA (1700–1791), author of 'Essay towards establishing the Melody and Measure of Speech ... by certain Symbols,' 1775 ('Prosodia Rationalis,' 1779); member of Society of Arts, 1756; lived on estates in Barbados from 1780; established Bridgetown Society of Arts, 1781; made his negroes copyholders, 1789. [liv. 129]

STEELE or **STEEL**, RICHARD (1629–1692), nonconformist divine; sizar, St. John's College, Cambridge, 1642; incorporated M.A. at Oxford, 1656; rector of Hanmer, 1650–62; ordainer of Philip Henry [q. v.], 1657, and Matthew Henry [q. v.], 1687; resigned living, 1662; author of 'The Tradesman's Calling,' 1684 ('Religious Tradesman'). [liv. 129]

STEELE, SIR RICHARD (1672–1729), author and politician; born at Dublin a few weeks before Addison, his schoolfellow at Charterhouse, London; postmaster, Merton College, Oxford, 1691–4; cadet in life-guards, 1694; dedicated mourning verses on Queen Mary to John, baron Cutts [q. v.]; became his secretary, 1696–7; received commission; published 'The Christian Hero,' 1701; his comedy, 'The Funeral,' acted at Drury Lane, London, 1701 (published same year), noticed by William III; captain of foot, 1702; his 'Lying Lover' given at Drury Lane, London, 1703 (published, 1704), and 'The Tender Husband,' partly by Addison, 1703 (printed); gentleman waiter to Prince George of Denmark, 1706; named gazetteer by Harley, 1707; married secretly Miss Mary Scurlock (second wife), 1707; his letters to her presented to British Museum, 1787; began the 'Tatler,' April 1709; carried it on with help of Addison till January 1711, writing himself as 'Isaac Bickerstaff' 188 numbers out of 271; commissioner of stamps, 1710; lost gazetteership for satirising Harley, 1710; with Addison carried on the 'Spectator,' 1711–12, writing 236 papers and sketching the Spectator Club (No. 2); carried on the 'Guardian' as non-political till attacked by the tory 'Examiner,' 1713; resigned office and pension and was elected M.P. for Stockbridge, 1713; attacked government on demolition of Dunkirk question; conducted the whig 'Englishman,' October 1713–February 1714; issued 'The Crisis' in favour of Hanoverian succession, January 1714, answered by Swift's 'Public Spirit of the Whigs'; expelled House of Commons for seditious libel (March); published 'Poetical Miscellanies,' 1714, and further political pamphlets; on accession of George I named J.P., deputy-lieutenant for Middlesex, surveyor of Hampton Court stables, and supervisor of Drury Lane Theatre, London; issued 'The Ladies' Library' and 'Mr. Steele's Apology,' 1714: M.P., Boroughbridge, 1715, Wendover, 1722; knighted, 1715; established the 'Censorium' in Villiers Street, London, 1715; commissioner for Scottish forfeited estates, 1716; his denunciation in the 'Plebeian' (1718) of Sunderland's Peerage Bill answered by Addison in the 'Old Whig,' causing quarrel and withdrawal of Drury Lane patent, 1720 (restored, 1721); issued 'The Theatre' and pamphlets against South Sea mania, 1720; published second edition of Addison's 'Drummer,' with reply to Tickell's charges, 1721; his last comedy, 'The Conscious Lovers,' produced at Drury Lane, London, 1722. [liv. 130]

STEELE, THOMAS (1788–1848), O'Connell's 'head pacificator'; B.A. Dublin, 1810; M.A. Cambridge, 1820; raised money for and joined rising against Ferdinand VII of Spain, 1823–4; though protestant, O'Connell's chief supporter in Clare election, 1828; at second election fought duel with William Smith O'Brien [q. v.]; tried with O'Connell, 1843; supported him against Young Irelanders; attempted suicide after his death; wrote on Shannon navigation, and published (1824) 'Notes of the War in Spain.' [liv. 137]

STEELE, SIR THOMAS MONTAGUE (1820–1890), general; ensign, 1838; aide-de-camp to governor of Madras, 1842–8; military secretary in Crimea, 1854–5; brevet colonel and C.B., 1854; general, 1877; commander-in-chief in Ireland, 1880–5; G.C.B., 1887. [liv. 138]

STEELE, WILLIAM (d. 1680), lord chancellor of Ireland; of Cains College, Cambridge; barrister, Gray's Inn, 1637; commissioner for martial law, 1644; recorder of London, 1649; M.P., London, 1654; disabled by illness from taking part in trial of Charles I; prosecuted royalists, 1649; member of committee to reform the law, 1652; serjeant-at-law, 1654; chief-baron of the exchequer, 1655; lord chancellor of Ireland, 1656; proclaimed Richard, but quarrelled with Henry Cromwell; commissioner to govern Ireland for Long parliament, 1659; went to Holland, 1660, but returned unmolested. [liv. 138]

STEELL, GOURLAY (1819–1894), animal-painter; studied under Sir William Allan [q. v.] and Robert Scott Lauder [q. v.]; first exhibited at Scottish Academy, 1832; R.S.A., 1859; animal-painter to Queen Victoria for Scotland, 1872; curator of Scottish National Gallery, 1882. [liv. 139]

STEELL, SIR JOHN (1804–1891), sculptor; brother of Gourlay Steell [q. v.]; studied at Trustees' Academy, Edinburgh, and in Rome; modelled 'Alexander taming Bucephalus,' 1833; executed statue of Queen Victoria for Royal Institution, of Scott, Wellington, and others at Edinburgh, Lord Dalhousie (Calcutta), Burns (New York); knighted on inauguration of Scottish memorial to Prince Albert, 1876; modelled numerous busts; R.S.A., 1829; sculptor to Queen Victoria for Scotland, 1838; introduced artistic bronze casting into Scotland. [liv. 140]

STEERE, EDWARD (1828–1882), missionary bishop; B.A. London, 1847, LL.D., 1850; barrister, Inner Temple, 1850; rector of Little Steeping, 1859–73; accompanied Bishop William George Tozer to the Shiré, East Africa, 1862; had temporary charge of Zanzibar mission, 1866–8; addressed church congress on slave trade, 1871; bishop of Central Africa, 1874–82; penetrated into Nyassa district, 1875–6, and founded Masai station; preached in England, 1877; D.D. Oxford, 1877; opened Zanzibar Cathedral, 1879; visited England, 1882; published books on English brotherhoods (1856), persecutions of the church (1859), the Central African mission, and East African dialects, 'Handbook of Swahili' (1870), and 'Swahili Tales' (1871); died at Zanzibar. [liv. 141]

STEEVENS. [See also STEPHENS and STEVENS.]

STEEVENS, CHARLES (1705–1761), rear-admiral; lieutenant, 1729; commanded fireship at attack on Carthagena, 1741; assisted in capture of Magnanime, 1748; took reinforcements to East Indies, 1757; second in command under Pocock in actions in April and August, 1758, and 10 Sept. 1759; wounded and promoted rear-admiral; co-operated with Coote in capture of Pondicherry, 1761. [liv. 143]

STEEVENS, GEORGE (1736–1800), commentator on Shakespeare; of Eton and King's College, Cambridge; issued reprints of twenty quarto editions of Shakespeare's plays, 1766; at Dr. Johnson's suggestion published another fully annotated edition, 1773, reissued, 1778; attacked by Joseph Ritson [q. v.] and others; contributed to Reed's 'Biographia Dramatica' (1782); assisted Dr. Johnson in 'Lives of the Poets'; contributed anecdotes to Hawkins's edition of Dr. Johnson's works, 1787; member of 'The Club,' 1774, and Essex Head Club, 1783; F.S.A. and F.R.S., 1767; constantly quarrelled with literary associates; attacked the Rowley poems and the supporters of their genuineness; satirised literary crazes; forged letter of George Peele describing meeting with Shakespeare; issued his edition of Shakespeare (without poems) to displace Malone's, 1793; called by Gifford 'the Puck of Commentators'; assailed the Irelands, writing inscription for Gillray's caricature, 1795–7; joint-editor with Bishop Percy of Surrey's poems, 1795; left Hogarth prints to William Windham, and Shakespeares to Earl Spencer and Isaac Reed [q. v.]; his unpublished notes embodied by Reed in new Shakespeare, 1803 ('first variorum'); his librarys old, 1800; his second folio Shakespeare bought for George III, now in British Museum. [liv. 144]

STEEVENS, GEORGE WARRINGTON (1869–1900), journalist; educated at City of London school; B.A. Oxford and London, 1892; fellow of Pembroke College, Oxford, 1893; edited 'Cambridge Observer,' 1893; on staff of 'Pall Mall Gazette,' 1893–5; joined staff of 'Daily Mail,' 1896; special correspondent successively in United States, Greece, Germany, Egypt and Soudan, India, Rennes (for trial of Captain Alfred Dreyfus), and South Africa; died of enteric fever at Ladysmith during the siege. His publications include 'Monologues of the Dead,' 1895, and several volumes of articles reprinted from the 'Daily Mail.' [Suppl. iii. 354]

STEEVENS, RICHARD (1653–1710), chief founder of Steevens's hospital, Dublin; B.A. Dublin, 1675, M.D., 1687; took deacon's orders; president, Irish College of Physicians, 1710. [liv. 148]

STENHOUSE, JOHN (1809–1880), chemist; studied chemistry at Glasgow and Giessen; LL.D. Aberdeen, 1850; chemical lecturer at St. Bartholomew's Hospital, London, 1851–7; assayer to the mint, 1865–70; F.R.S., 1848; a founder of Chemical Society; invented charcoal air-filters and respirators; took out many patents; discovered betorcinol; published chemical papers. [liv. 149]

STENHOUSE, WILLIAM (1773?–1827), Scottish antiquary; edited Johnson's 'Musical Museum' (reprinted, 1839). [liv. 149]

STENNETT, JOSEPH (1663–1713), seventh-day baptist; Sunday lecturer, Paul's Alley, Barbican, London; eight of his hymns still in use; works collected, 1732, but some not included. [liv. 150]

STENNETT, JOSEPH (1692–1758), baptist minister; son of Joseph Stennett (1663–1713) [q. v.]; D.D. [liv. 150]

STENNETT, SAMUEL (1728–1795), baptist minister; minister at Little Wild Street, London, 1758–95; son of Joseph Stennett (1692–1758) [q. v.]; D.D. Aberdeen, 1763; works collected, 1824. [liv. 150]

STEPHANOFF, FRANCIS PHILIP (1790?–1860), historical and genre painter; exhibited at Royal Academy and British Institution, 1807–45, with 'Old' Water-colour Society, 1815–20; gained prize at Westminster Hall competition, 1843. [liv. 150]

STEPHANOFF, JAMES (1788?–1874), watercolour-painter; brother of Francis Philip Stephanoff [q. v.]; associate 'Old' Water-colour Society, 1819; historical painter in water-colours to William IV, 1830; a founder of Sketching Society. [liv. 151]

STEPHEN (1097?–1154), king of England; son of Stephen Henry, count of Blois, and Adela [q. v.], daughter of William I; brought up by Henry I; knighted and granted lands in England and county of Mortain; acquired Alençon, 1118; constantly with Henry I after death of his son William; swore first of lay barons to acknowledge Empress Matilda [q. v.] as heir to England and Normandy, 1126, also her son, 1133; claimed English crown, 1135; chosen king by London; crowned at Westminster, 1135; issued charter; acknowledged in Normandy; recognised by Pope Innocent II, despite Matilda's appeal, 1136; bought off David I of Scotland; issued second charter, 1136, promising to surrender lands afforested by Henry I; crushed barons at Norwich, Bampton, and Exeter; made truce with Geoffrey of Anjou, 1137; drove back Scots, 1138; alienated barons by favouring foreigners and extravagance; took Shrewsbury, 1138; took Leeds Castle (Kent) and made treaty with Scotland, but failed before Ludlow, 1139; arrested Bishop Roger of Salisbury [q. v.] and his son and nephew; crushed revolt of Isle of Ely and took Bungay Castle, 1140; defeated and captured, after gallant fight, at Lincoln by Robert, earl of Gloucester [q. v.], 1141; imprisoned at Bristol and deposed by church council, but soon released in exchange for Gloucester, and again crowned, 1141; first English king who allowed tournaments; took Oxford and blockaded Matilda in the castle, 1142; routed near Wilton, 1143; failed elsewhere, but was successful against Gloucester in the west, 1144; defeated barons in Norfolk and Essex, 1145; regained Bedford, built Crowmarsh, and compelled Randulf of Chester to surrender Lincoln, 1146; reduced earls of Chester and Pembroke, 1149; failed before Worcester Castle, 1150-1; at feud with the papacy, 1147-1151, causing interdict, 1148; failed to obtain papal sanction for coronation of his son Eustace, 1152; made truce with Henry of Anjou at Crowmarsh, 1153; concluded treaty of Wallingford, 1153, obtaining crown for life, but giving up succession; lost his only surviving son, 1154; buried in Feversham Abbey (his foundation).   [liv. 151]

STEPHEN, usually known as STEPHEN OF WHITBY (d. 1112), abbot of St. Mary's, York; prior of Whitby; removed house to Lastingham, finally to York; visited by William II; his account of the foundation in Dugdale's ' Monasticon.'   [liv. 156]

STEPHEN, SAINT (d. 1134). [See HARDING.]

STEPHEN DE TOURS or DE MARZAI (d. 1193), seneschal of Anjou; royal chamberlain; when seneschal of Anjou fired Le Mans to defend it from the French king, Philip Augustus; imprisoned by Richard I on his accession, but subsequently continued in authority; his death foretold by a wizard. He has been wrongly identified with Stephen de Turnham [q. v.]   [lvii. 370]

STEPHEN DE TURNHAM (d. 1215). [See TURNHAM.]

STEPHEN DE LEXINTON (fl. 1250). [See LEXINTON.]

STEPHEN OF EXETER (fl. 1265), supposed author of ' Annales Domus Montis Fernandi' (Armagh MS.)   [liv. 157]

STEPHEN DE GRAVESEND (d. 1338). [See GRAVESEND.]

STEPHEN LANGTON (d. 1228). [See LANGTON.]

STEPHEN, SIR ALFRED (1802-1894), chief-justice of New South Wales; nephew of James Stephen (1758-1832) [q. v.]; born in St. Christopher's; barrister, Lincoln's Inn, 1823; as solicitor-general (1825-32) and attorney-general (1833-7) organised courts and passed numerous statutes in Van Diemen's Land; chief-justice, New South Wales, 1844-73; lieutenant-governor, 1875-91; president of first legislative council, 1856-7; knighted, 1846; C.B., 1862; G.C.M.G., 1884; privy councillor, 1893; president of colonial commission for revising statute law, 1870; obtained consolidation of criminal law, 1883; carried divorce law, 1890; died at Sydney; his ' Jottings from Memory' privately printed, 1889.   [liv. 157]

STEPHEN, EDWARD (1822-1885), Welsh musician ('Tanymarian'); independent minister; self-taught musician; composed 'Ystorm Tiberias,' first Welsh oratorio, 1851-2 (revised score, 1887); edited Welsh independent hymnals, 1860, 1868, 1879.   [liv. 158]

STEPHEN, SIR GEORGE (1794-1879), lawyer and author; fourth son of James Stephen (1758-1832) [q. v.]; solicitor; formed plan for 'Agency Committee' of Anti-Slavery Society; solicitor under act for relieving imprisoned pauper debtors; knighted, 1837; barrister, Gray's Inn, 1849; emigrated to Melbourne, 1855; published 'Adventures of a Gentleman in Search of a Horse,' by Caveat Emptor, 1835, 'Adventures of an Attorney in Search of Practice,' 1839, 'Anti-Slavery Recollections,' 1854, and other works; died at Melbourne.   [liv. 159]

STEPHEN, HENRY JOHN (1787-1864), legal writer; brother of Sir George Stephen [q. v.]; of St. John's

College, Cambridge; barrister, 1815; serjeant-at law and common law commissioner, 1828; said to have declined judgeship from unwillingness to pronounce capital sentences; bankruptcy commissioner, 1842-54; published treatise on principles of pleading, 1824, 'Summary of the Criminal Law,' 1834, and 'New Commentaries on the Laws of England,' 1841-5 (10th edit. 1895).   [liv. 160]

STEPHEN, JAMES (1758-1832), master in chancery; barrister, 1782; practised in St. Christopher's, 1783-94, afterwards in English prize appeal court of privy council; sent information on slave-trade to the abolitionist Wilberforce; brother-in-law and active supporter of Wilberforce; issued 'War in Disguise' against evasions of British regulations by neutral traders, 1805; M.P., Tralee, 1808-12, East Grinstead, 1812-15; resigned seat on refusal of government to support registration of slaves; master in chancery, 1811-31; adherent of 'Clapham Sect'; chief work, 'Slavery in the British West India Colonies delineated' (vol. i. 1824, vol. ii. 1830).   [liv. 161]

STEPHEN, SIR JAMES (1789-1859), colonial under-secretary; son of James Stephen (1758-1832) [q. v.]; LL.B. Trinity Hall, Cambridge, 1812; barrister, Lincoln's Inn, 1811; permanent counsel to colonial office and board of trade, 1825; under-secretary for colonies, 1836-47; called 'Mr Over-secretary Stephen' from his influence; prepared bill abolishing slave-trade, 1833; much concerned in establishment of responsible government in Canada; K.C.B. and privy councillor on resigning undersecretaryship, 1847; professor of modern history, Cambridge, 1849-59, at East India College, Haileybury, 1855-7; published 'Essays in Ecclesiastical Biography,' 1849, and 'Lectures on the History of France,' 1852.   [liv. 163]

STEPHEN, SIR JAMES FITZJAMES, first baronet (1829-1894), judge; son of Sir James Stephen [q. v.]; of Eton, King's College, London, and Trinity College, Cambridge; B.A., 1851; a friend of Sir Henry Sumner Maine [q. v.]; barrister, Inner Temple, 1854; began to write for 'Saturday Review,' 1855; secretary to education commission, 1858-61; counsel for Rowland Williams [q. v.] in 'Essays and Reviews' case, 1861; intimate with Froude and Carlyle; contributed to 'Fraser' and the 'Cornhill,' 1860-3; chief writer on 'Pall Mall Gazette,' 1865-9; acted for Jamaica committee against Governor Eyre, 1867; Q.C., 1868; legal member of council in India, 1869-72, being chiefly responsible for Evidence Act (1872), member of Metaphysical Society; occupied in attempted codification of English law, 1873-4 and 1876-8; professor of common law at Inns of Court, 1875; member of legal commissions, 1876-8; defended Lytton's Indian policy, 1877-8; judge of high court, 1879-91; chairman of ordnance commission, 1886; created baronet on retirement from bench, 1891; K.C.S.I., 1877; hon. D.C.L. Oxford, 1878; LL.D. Edinburgh, 1884; chief works, 'General View of the Criminal Law of England' (1863, 1890), 'History of the Criminal Law,' 1883, and 'Story of Nuncomar and Sir Elijah Impey,' 1885.   [liv. 164]

STEPHEN, JAMES KENNETH (1859-1892), author of 'Lapsus Calami,' and other verses (collected, 1896); son of Sir James Fitzjames Stephen [q. v.]; of Eton and King's College, Cambridge; Whewell scholar, 1881; fellow, 1885; president of Cambridge Union, 1882, and an 'apostle'; tutor to Duke of Clarence, 1883; issued 'The Reflector,' 1888.   [liv. 167]

STEPHENS. [See also STEEVENS and STEVENS.]

STEPHENS, ALEXANDER (1757-1821), biographical writer; educated at Aberdeen; lived in Jamaica; barrister, Middle Temple; conducted 'The Templar'; edited early volumes of 'Annual Biography and Obituary'; chief work, 'Memoirs of John Horne Tooke,' 1813.   [liv. 168]

STEPHENS, CATHERINE, COUNTESS OF ESSEX (1794-1882), vocalist and actress; sang under direction of Gesualdo Lanza [q. v.], 1807-12; appeared successfully at Covent Garden, London, in 'Artaxerxes,' 1813, remaining there till 1822; principal soprano at concert of ancient music, 1814; played Ophelia and Desdemona, 1814, Imogen, 1815; created Susanna in 'Marriage of Figaro,' 1819, and various parts in adaptations of Scott 1816-20; with Elliston at Drury Lane, London, 1823-7; again at Covent Garden, London, 1828; unsurpassed for her rendering of ballads; coupled by Hazlitt with Kean as dramatic artist, and highly praised by Leigh Hunt; retired, 1835; married fifth Earl of Essex 1838.   [liv. 168]

STEPHENS, CHARLES EDWARD (1821–1892), musician; nephew of Catherine Stephens [q. v.]; organist at London churches; treasurer of Philharmonic Society, 1880. His compositions include a symphony in G minor (Philharmonic, 1891). [liv. 170]

STEPHENS, EDWARD (*d.* 1706), pamphleteer; practised at common law bar, but afterwards took orders; called 'Abbat Stephens' for theological learning; son-in-law of Sir Matthew Hale [q. v.] and editor of his 'Contemplations' (1676); published political tracts, 1689–90; attacked Romanists, quakers, and erastians; his 'Liturgy of the Ancients' (1696) reprinted, 1848. [liv. 170]

STEPHENS, EDWARD BOWRING (1815–1882), sculptor; student, Royal Academy, 1836; exhibited there, 1838–9 and 1842–82, receiving gold medal for 'Battle of Centaurs and Lapithæ,' 1843; in Rome, 1839–1841; A.R.A., 1864; had two groups at exhibition of 1851. [liv. 171]

STEPHENS, GEORGE (1800–1851), dramatist; his tragedy 'Martinuzzi' played by Phelps at English Opera House, London, 1841; published tragedies, romances, and 'Dramas for the Stage,' 1846. [liv. 172]

STEPHENS, GEORGE (1813–1895), runic archæologist; of University College, London; at Stockholm, 1834–51; issued text-books and translations for Swedish students; assisted in foundation of Society for Publication of Ancient Swedish Texts, 1843; translated the Anglo-Saxon poem 'The Phœnix,' 1844; catalogued English and French manuscripts in royal library, 1847; lector in English at Copenhagen University, 1851, in Anglo-Saxon, 1852, professor of English and Anglo-Saxon, 1855–93; Ph.D. Upsala, 1877; knight of Scandinavian orders; F.S.A.; furnished quotations for 'New English Dictionary'; chief work, 'The Old Northern Runic Monuments of Scandinavia and England now first collected and deciphered' (vols. i. 1866, ii. 1868, iii. 1884; abridged, 1884), valuable for materials, but severely criticised for defective philology. [liv. 173]

STEPHENS, HENRY (1795–1874), author of 'The Book of the Farm,' 1842–4 (often reprinted); of Edinburgh University; studied agriculture in Berwickshire, 1815–18, and on the continent, 1818–19; introduced improvements on farm at Balmadies, Forfarshire, 1820–30; at Bonnington, near Edinburgh, produced agricultural works alone and in collaboration; edited agricultural periodicals. [liv. 174]

STEPHENS, JAMES FRANCIS (1792–1852), entomologist; educated at Christ's Hospital, London; in admiralty, 1807–45; wrote on birds in Shaw's 'General Zoology,' 1815–25; assisted in arranging insects at British Museum from 1818, publishing 'Catalogue of British Lepidoptera,' 1850–2; F.L.S., 1815, F.Z.S., 1826; chief work, 'Illustrations of British Entomology,' 1827–37 (suppl. 1846). [liv. 175]

STEPHENS, JANE (1813?–1896), actress; gained first success at Olympic, London, as Mrs. Willoughby in 'Ticket of Leave,' 1863; Nurse in 'Romeo and Juliet,' 1867; subsequently played old women's parts; last appearance at the Shaftesbury, London, 1889. [liv. 176]

STEPHENS, JEREMIAH (1591–1665), coadjutor of Sir Henry Spelman [q. v.] in first volume of his 'Concilia' (1639); M.A. Brasenose College, Oxford, 1615; B.D., 1628; chaplain of All Souls College, Oxford; rector of Quinton, 1622, Wootton, 1626; prebendary of Lincoln, 1639, of Sarum, 1660; deprived, 1644; reinstated, 1660; edited St. Gregory 'de Cura Pastorali,' 1629, and works by Cyprian and Spelman. [liv. 176]

STEPHENS, JOHN (*fl.* 1615), author of 'Satyrical Essayes, Characters, and others,' 1615 (partly reprinted by Halliwell-Phillipps, 1857); of Lincoln's Inn. [liv. 177]

STEPHENS, JOSEPH RAYNER (1805–1879), agitator; brother of George Stephens (1813–1895) [q. v.]; methodist missioner at Stockholm, 1826–9; chaplain to British ambassador and friend of Montalembert; Wesleyan minister in England, 1829–34; joined chartists, 1838; arrested for attending unlawful meeting at Hyde, 1838; sentenced to find sureties for five years, 1839; preached and conducted papers at Ashton-under-Lyne, 1840–51, at Stalybridge, 1852–75. [liv. 178]

STEPHENS, NATHANIEL (1606?–1678), nonconformist divine; M.A. Magdalen Hall, Oxford, 1628; took the covenant, 1642; rector of Fenny Drayton, 1659–62; held discussions with George Fox (1624–1691) [q. v.], Gerard Winstanley [q. v.], and anabaptists; published work on the Apocalypse, 1656, and controversial tracts. [liv. 179]

STEPHENS, SIR PHILIP, first baronet (1725–1809), secretary of the admiralty, 1763–95; secretary to George Anson, baron Anson [q. v.]; F.R.S., 1771; M.P., Sandwich, 1768–1806; created baronet, 1795; granted special pension, 1806. [liv. 179]

STEPHENS, ROBERT (1665–1732), historiographer royal; barrister, Middle Temple, 1689; F.S.A., 1717; chief solicitor of the customs; historiographer royal, 1726–32; collected and published, with introduction, letters of Francis Bacon in reign of James I, 1702; his 'Letters and Remains of Lord Chancellor Bacon,' 1734, edited by his widow; his catalogue of letters and papers connected with Bacon in British Museum. [liv. 180]

STEPHENS or STEVENS, THOMAS (1549?–1619), jesuit missionary and author; educated at Winchester; entered Society of Jesus at St. Andrew's College, Rome; went as missionary to East Indies, 1579, and laboured at Portuguese settlement at Goa till death; spiritual coadjutor, 1588; published works on the Canarese language and other writings. [Suppl. iii. 355]

STEPHENS, THOMAS (1821–1875), Welsh scholar; chemist at Merthyr Tydfil; high constable, 1858; won prizes at eisteddfodau, 1840–58; his prize essay of 1848 (Abergavenny) published as 'The Literature of the Kymry,' 1849 (German translation, 1861); disproved Welsh claim to discovery of America, 1858, the essay 'Madoc' being published, 1893; established mediæval origin of the Triads; his work on 'The Gododin of Aneurin Gwawdrydd' edited for Cymmrodorion Society, 1888. [liv. 180]

STEPHENS, WILLIAM (1647?–1718), whig divine; M.A. St. Edmund Hall, Oxford, 1671 (incorporated at Cambridge), B.D., 1678; rector of Sutton, and archdeacon, 1690; preached strong whig sermon before House of Commons, 1700 (reprinted, 1752); wrongly sentenced for libel, 1706; published 'Account of the Growth of Deism in England,' 1696. [liv. 181]

STEPHENS, WILLIAM (1671–1753), president of Georgia; of Winchester and King's College, Cambridge; M.A., 1688; M.P., Newport (Isle of Wight), 1702–22; colonel of militia; met James Edward Oglethorpe [q. v.] in South Carolina, 1736; settled in Georgia, 1737; president of Georgia, 1743–50; published 'Journal of the Proceedings in Georgia, beginning October 20, 1737,' 1742 (rare). [liv. 182]

STEPHENSON, GEORGE (1781–1848), inventor and founder of railways; son of a fireman at Wylam, near Newcastle; employed in father's colliery; engine-man at Willington Ballast Hill, 1802; removed to Killingworth, 1804, and Montrose, 1807; returned to Killingworth, 1808, becoming engine-wright to the colliery, 1812; designed safety lamps, 1815, simultaneously with Sir Humphry Davy [q. v.]; presented with testimonial and 1,000*l.*, 1818; his first locomotive tried successfully, 1814; his engine with steam blast patented, 1815; railroad laid down under his direction for Hetton colliery, 1819–23; engineer of Stockton and Darlington railway (opened 1825); made survey for proposed Manchester and Liverpool line, 1824 (opened, 1830); appointed engineer, 1826; won prize for engine with 'The Rocket,' having tubular boiler, 1829; chief engineer to line connecting Birmingham with Manchester and Liverpool, begun 1833, lines between northern towns, 1836, Derby-Leeds railway, 1837; increased speed to twenty-nine miles an hour by application of Gurney's steam-jet; vice-president, mechanical science section, British Association, 1838; tried to check railway mania of 1844; overcame supporters of atmospheric railways, 1845; first president, Institution of Mechanical Engineers, 1847; visited Belgium and Spain; knighted by Leopold I, 1835; refused British honours; memorial hall opened at Chesterfield, where he died, 1879. [liv. 183]

STEPHENSON, HENRY PALFREY (1826–1890), gas engineer; student at engineering college, Putney; founded Putney Club; M.I.C.E., 1864. [liv. 187]

STEPHENSON, JAMES (1808–1886), engraver ; practised in Manchester, 1838–47, engraving members' card for Anti-Cornlaw League and portraits of Lancashire celebrities ; exhibited at Royal Academy from 1856. [liv. 187]

STEPHENSON, ROBERT (1803–1859), civil engineer ; son of George Stephenson [q. v.] ; apprenticed at sixteen to viewer of Killingworth colliery ; studied at Edinburgh University, 1822 ; employed in Newcastle locomotive factory, 1823 ; superintended mines in Columbia, 1824–7 ; took important part in constructing 'The Rocket' and devising improvements, 1827–33 ; constructed London and Birmingham line, 1833–8 ; built high-level bridge, Newcastle, and Victoria bridge, Berwick, Menai tubular girder bridge (opened, 1850), Victoria bridge, Montreal (1859) ; awarded gold medal at French exhibition, 1855 ; conservative M.P., Whitby, 1847–59 ; president, Institution of Civil Engineers, 1856–7 ; F.R.S., 1849 ; D.C.L. Oxford, 1857 ; received Belgian and Norwegian orders ; buried in Westminster Abbey. [liv. 188]

STEPHENSON, SAMUEL MARTIN (1742–1833), Irish presbyterian divine and physician ; ordained minister of Grey Abbey, co. Down, though declining subscription to Westminster confession, 1774 (resigned, 1785) ; studied medicine at Dublin and Edinburgh ; M.D. Edinburgh, 1776 ; physician in Belfast, 1785 ; fever specialist and co-founder of dispensary, 1792, and fever hospital, 1797 ; his name replaced on ministerial roll by Ulster synod, 1818 ; published theological and Irish topographical works. [liv. 189]

STEPHENSON, THOMAS (1552–1624), jesuit ; tried for high treason and imprisoned in Tower of London, 1584–5 ; novice at Brünn, 1585, spiritual coadjutor, 1597 ; Hebrew and Greek professor at Prague and Olmütz ; secretary to Robert Parsons (1546–1610) [q. v.] at Rome ; again English missioner, 1605–20 ; published religious works ; died at Watten. [liv. 190]

STEPNEY, CATHERINE, LADY (d. 1845), novelist ; née Pollok ; married Sir Thomas Stepney, baronet, 1813 ; her first book published, 1806, last, 1841. [liv. 190]

STEPNEY, GEORGE (1663–1707), diplomatist and poet ; friend at Westminster of Charles Montagu (afterwards Earl of Halifax) [q. v.] ; major fellow, Trinity College, Cambridge, 1687 ; M.A., 1689 ; envoy to Brandenburg, 1692, 1698, to the emperor, 1693, Saxony, 1695, to German princes and Frankfort congress, 1696–7 ; commissioner of trade, 1697–1707 ; envoy to Vienna, 1702–6, to the Hague, 1706 ; buried in Westminster Abbey. He contributed to Dryden's 'Miscellany Poems' and translation of Juvenal · a political tract by him (1701) in Somers collection. [liv. 190]

STERLING. [See also STIRLING.]

STERLING, SIR ANTHONY CONINGHAM (1805–1871), author of 'Story of the Highland Brigade in the Crimea' (published, 1895, founded on 'Letters ... by a Staff Officer,' 1857) ; brother of John Sterling [q. v.] ; ensign, 1826 ; brigade-major and assistant-adjutant-general to highland division in Crimea, 1854–5 ; colonel, 1857 ; military secretary to Colin Campbell in India, 1858–9 ; accused by him of suppressing Colonel Pakenham's name in recommendations for K.C.B. ; K.C.B., 1860. [liv. 192]

STERLING, EDWARD (1773–1847), journalist ; of Trinity College, Dublin, and Irish bar ; volunteer during Irish rebellion, 1798 ; issued pamphlet 'Military Reform,' 1811 ; correspondent of 'The Times,' 1811–15, member of staff, 1815–40. [liv. 193]

STERLING, JAMES (fl. 1718–1755), playwright ; M.A. Trinity College, Dublin, 1733 ; his 'Parricide' (1736) acted at Goodman's Fields, London, 1735 ; published 'Poetical Works,' 1734 ; migrated to Maryland, c. 1740, as preacher. [liv. 192]

STERLING, JOHN (1806–1844), author ; son of Edward Sterling [q. v.] ; of Trinity College, then of Trinity Hall, Cambridge, 1824–7 ; an 'apostle' and speaker at the union ; through his tutor, Julius Charles Hare [q. v.], came to know Coleridge and Wordsworth ; friend of Frederick Denison Maurice [q. v.] and Richard Chenevix Trench [q. v.] ; with Maurice conducted the 'Athenæum,' July to December 1828 ; meditated accompanying volunteer expedition against Ferdinand VII of Spain, but stayed behind to marry, 1830 ; manager of sugar estate in St.

Vincent, 1831–2 ; studied philosophy in Germany, 1833 ; curate of J. C. Hare at Hurstmonceaux, 1834–5 ; became acquainted with Carlyle, 1835 ; contributed to 'Blackwood's Magazine,' 1837–8, and 'London and Westminster Review' ; Sterling Club (founded, 1838) called after him ; in Rome, 1838–9 ; introduced to Caroline Fox's circle, 1839 ; reviewed Tennyson's 'Poems' in 'Quarterly,' September 1842 ; his 'Essays and Tales' edited by Julius Charles Hare [q. v.], 1848 ; rendered famous by Carlyle's biography, 1851. [liv. 192]

STERN, HENRY AARON (1820–1885), missionary to Jews ; born in Hesse-Cassel, and educated at Frankfort ; entered Hebrew college of London Jews' Society, 1842 ; missionary to Jews and Moslems in Asia Minor and Persia, 1844–53 ; ordained deacon (at Jerusalem), 1844, priest (in London), 1849 ; missionary at Constantinople, 1853–6 ; after other missionary journeys went to Abyssinia, 1859 ; imprisoned and tortured by King Theodore, 1863–7 ; liberated, 1868 ; D.D. Canterbury, 1881 ; works include two books on Abyssinia (1862 and 1868). [liv. 195]

STERNE or **STEARNE,** JOHN (1624–1669), founder of Irish College of Physicians ; related to (Archbishop) James Ussher [q. v.] ; scholar, Trinity College, Dublin, 1641, fellow, 1643 ; studied medicine at Sidney Sussex College, Cambridge, 1643–9, and at Oxford ; first Hebrew lecturer at Dublin University, 1656 ; M.D., 1658 ; LL.D., professor of law and senior fellow, 1660 ; professor of medicine, 1662 ; physician in Dublin ; Trinity Hall, Dublin, constituted as College of Physicians, with him as president, 1660, and incorporated, 1667 ; his works chiefly theological. [liv. 197]

STERNE or **STEARNE,** JOHN (1660–1745), bishop of Clogher ; son of John Sterne or Stearne (1624–1669) [q. v.] ; M.A. Trinity College, Dublin, 1681, D.D., 1705 ; dean of St. Patrick's, Dublin, 1702–12 ; intimate with Swift, who obtained for him see of Dromore, 1713 ; translated to Clogher, 1717 ; vice-chancellor, Dublin University, 1721 ; gave money to erect printing-house, 1726 ; founded exhibitions at Trinity College, Dublin ; bequeathed also books and valuable manuscripts ; his 'Tractatus de Visitatione Infirmorum' (1697) translated as 'The Curate's Manual,' 1840. [liv. 198]

STERNE, LAURENCE (1713–1768), humorist and sentimentalist ; great-grandson of Richard Sterne [q. v.] ; born at Clonmel ; the son of a subaltern in the army ; after some years' wandering spent eight years at school in Halifax ; left penniless ; sent to Cambridge by a cousin (Richard) ; sizar, Jesus College, 1733, exhibitioner, 1734 ; matriculated, 1735 ; intimate with John Hall-Stevenson [q. v.] ; M.A., 1740 ; curate of Buckden ; became vicar of Sutton-in-the-Forest, 1738, and prebendary of York, 1741, also obtaining a sinecure office ; married Miss Lumley, 1741 ; first used epithet 'sentimental' in letter, 1740 ; obtained, by wife's influence, Stillington, parish adjoining Sutton, 1743, being also chaplain to fourth Earl of Aboyne ; interested in local private enclosure acts, 1756, 1766 ; dabbled in painting and music ; joined in orgies of 'Demoniacks' at Hall-Stevenson's house ; showed affection for his only child ; troubled by his mother's demands for money ; said to have let her die of starvation ; published, 1750, assize sermon, inserted in 'Tristram Shandy' ; satirised Yorkshire lawyer as 'Trim' in sketch first published, 1769, as 'A Political Romance addressed to —— Esq. of York' (rare), afterwards reprinted as 'History of a Warm Watch Coat' ; unfaithful to his wife, who became insane, 1758 ; began 'Tristram Shandy,' 1759 ; carried on flirtation with Mademoiselle Fourmantelle ; vols. i. and ii. of his 'Tristram Shandy' printed at York by publisher of sermons, 1760 ; taken by Croft to London, where he was well received in society ; second edition of his 'Tristram' and 'Sermons of Mr. Yorick' issued by Dodsley, 1760, the latter being commended by Gray ; his 'Tristram Shandy' unpopular in Yorkshire on account of its recognisable portraits of local characters, such as Dr. John Burton (1710–1771) [q. v.] ('Slop') ; denounced by Dr. Johnson, Richardson, Horace Walpole, Goldsmith, and others, on moral and literary grounds ; ineffectual attempts made by Warburton to restrain his obscenity ; many pamphlets issued against him, 1760–1 ; received perpetual curacy of Coxwold, 1760 ; called house at Coxwold (which now has tablet) Shandy Hall ; visited London to superintend publication of vols. iii. and iv. of 'Tristram,' 1761 ; preached at Foundling Hospital, London ; vols. v. and vi. of 'Tristram' dedicated to Lord Spencer, issued for him by Becket

December 1761 ; went abroad for his health, January 1762 ;
well received in Paris salons ; entertained by Fox at St.
Germain ; joined by wife and daughter ; lived at Toulouse,
and, till February 1764, in the south of France ; left wife
and daughter behind at Montauban, by their wish ; spent
April–May 1764 in Paris, seeing much of Wilkes and
preaching at English ambassador's chapel ; published
books vii. and viii. of 'Tristram,' 1765 ; painted by Gainsborough at Bath, 1765 ; began seven months' tour described in 'Sentimental Journey,' October 1765 ; went by
Paris, Lyons, and Savoy to Italy ; well received at Rome,
where he met Smollett ('Smelfungus'); in Naples, February 1766 ; in Yorkshire again, June 1766 ; issued book ix.
of 'Tristram Shandy,' with dedication to Chatham, containing sentence supposed to have suggested Burns's
lines about the 'guinea stamp,' 1767 ; also published
vols. iii. and iv. of 'Sermons,' Voltaire being among the
subscribers ; during visit to London, December 1766 to
May 1767, met, at house of Sir William James [q. v.],
Mrs. Eliza Draper [q. v.] ; kept journal addressed to her
('The Bramine's Journal'; manuscript in British Museum), April to August 1767, after her departure for
India ; after two months' visit from wife and daughter
at Coxwold, arranged permanent separation ; parted
reluctantly with daughter ; his 'Sentimental Journey'
issued, 1768 ; died of pleurisy in Old Bond Street lodgings,
London ; buried in St. George's cemetery, Bayswater Road,
London ; body said to have been 'resurrected' and sold
to Charles Collignon [q. v.], the skeleton being long preserved at Cambridge ; inscription on stone at St. George's
erected by 'two brother masons' inaccurate ; left no will,
and died insolvent ; wife and daughter relieved through
subscriptions collected by Hall-Stevenson and Mrs. Draper,
and by publication (1769) of three more volumes of
sermons ; publication of his letters to Mrs. Draper
threatened by widow in default of blackmail ; his letters
published by his daughter (Madame Medalle), 1775 ; publication of 'Letters of Yorick to Eliza' (1766–7) authorised
by Mrs. Draper, 1775. The 'Letters from Eliza to Yorick,'
1775, and 'Letters supposed to have been written by
Yorick and Eliza,' 1779, are forgeries.

Among fraudulent imitations of his writings were John
Carr's third volume of 'Tristram Shandy,' 1760, J. Hall-
Stevenson's continuation of the 'Sentimental Journey,'
1769, and Richard Griffith's 'Posthumous Works of a late
celebrated Genius,' 1770 (included in first collected edition).
His works contain many literary thefts, and the general
scheme of 'Tristram' closely resembles that of John
Dunstan's 'A Voyage round the World . . . the rare
adventures of Don Kainophilus' (1720 ?). But his style
is original, and his characters are of the first class. First
collective edition of 'Tristram Shandy' published, 1767,
last, 1779 ; 'Sermons of Mr. Yorick,' first reissued collectively, 1775, last, 1787 ; 'Sentimental Journey' reissued
with plates, 1792 ; first collective edition of complete
works (without letters) published, 1779 (Dublin) ; best
early edition (with letters and Hogarth's plates) published,
1780 ; Dr. J. P. Browne's (containing much newly recovered correspondence), 1873. 'The 'Sentimental Journey' has been often translated.   [liv. 199]

STERNE, RICHARD (1596 ?–1683), archbishop of
York ; scholar, Trinity College, Cambridge, 1614. M.A.,
1618, B.D., 1625 (Oxford, 1627) ; fellow, Benet (Corpus
Christi) College, 1620 ; master of Jesus College, Cambridge, 1634 (deprived, 1644) ; chaplain to Laud, c. 1633 ;
rector of Yelverton and Harleton, 1634–44 ; D.D., 1635 ;
arrested for royalism at Cambridge and imprisoned, 1642–
1645 ; allowed to attend Laud in Tower of London, 1645 ;
bishop of Carlisle, 1660–4 ; said to have been a reviser
of prayer-book, 1662 ; archbishop of York, 1664–83 ;
founded scholarships at Jesus and Corpus Christi Colleges,
Cambridge ; assisted Brian Walton [q. v.] with Polyglott,
and published 'Summa Logicæ,' 1685 ; 'Whole Duty of
Man,' ascribed to him among others, probably by Richard
Allestree [q. v.]   [liv. 221]

STERNHOLD, THOMAS (d. 1549), joint versifier of
the Psalms with John Hopkins (d. 1570) [q. v.] ; according to Wood, of Christ Church, Oxford ; groom of the
robes to Henry VIII, 1538, receiving legacy from him ;
probably M.P., Plymouth, 1545–7 ; nineteen psalms by
himself only (in metre of 'Chevy Chase') contained in
first edition of Psalms (undated, dedicated to Edward VI) ; seven added in second edition (1549), and
three in edition of 1561 ; forty in complete collections.
                                               [liv. 223]

STERRY, NATHANIEL (d. 1698), dean of Bocking ;
fellow of Merton College, Oxford, 1649 ; B.A. Cambridge,
1648 ; B.D. Oxford, 1675 ; dean of Bocking, 1674–98.
                                               [liv. 225]

STERRY, PETER (d. 1672), Cromwell's chaplain ;
brother of Nathaniel Sterry [q. v.] ; fellow of Emmanuel
College, Cambridge, 1636 ; M.A., 1637 ; member of Westminster Assembly ; Cambridge platonist ; preacher to
council of state, 1649 ; after Restoration held conventicle ;
satirised in 'Hudibras' ; chief work, 'Discourse of the
Freedom of the Will' (posthumous), 1675.   [liv. 224]

STEUART. [See also STEWARD, STEWART, and
STUART.]

STEUART, SIR HENRY SETON, first baronet (1759–
1836), of Allanton ; agriculturist ; claimed for his family
ancestry of the Stewarts of Lennox, Darnley, and Castlemilk, 1799 ; served in the army, 1778–87 ; advocated canal
from Lancashire coalfields to Edinburgh, 1801 ; edited
Sallust, 1806 ; LL.D. (Edinburgh) and F.R.S.E. ; his
system of transplantation adopted by Sir Walter Scott
at Abbotsford ; his 'Planter's Guide,' 1828 (reissued, 1848),
reviewed by Sir Walter Scott and 'Christopher North' ;
created baronet, 1814.   [liv. 225]

STEUART or STEWART, SIR JAMES (1635–1715),
lord-advocate ; barrister, 1661 ; outlawed as contriver of
Argyll's rebellion, 1685 ; pardoned by William of Orange ;
as lord-advocate of Scotland, 1692–1709, introduced legal
reforms.   [liv. 227]

STEUART, SIR JAMES, the elder (afterwards
DENHAM) (1712–1780). [See DENHAM.]

STEUART (formerly DENHAM), SIR JAMES, the
younger (1744–1839). [See DENHAM.]

STEUART-SETON, REGINALD MACDONALD
(1778–1838), sheriff of Stirlingshire and friend of Scott ;
originally Macdonald of Staffa ; son-in-law of Sir Henry
Seton Steuart [q. v.]   [liv. 227]

STEVENS, ALFRED (1818–1875), artist ; son of a
house-painter ; enabled to study art in Italy, 1833–42, by
private liberality ; employed by Thorwaldsen at Rome,
1841–2 ; teacher in school of design, London, 1845–7 ;
employed by Hoole & Co. of Sheffield ; gained first prize
for designs in metal-work at exhibition of 1851 ; executed
Wellington monument at St. Paul's Cathedral (unfinished) ;
designed vases and lions at British Museum.   [liv. 227]

STEVENS, FRANCIS (1781–1823), landscape-painter ;
exhibited at Royal Academy, 1804–5, 1819, and 1822 ;
member of Water-colour Society, 1809.   [liv. 229]

STEVENS, GEORGE ALEXANDER (1710–1784),
author of 'A Lecture upon Heads' ; wrote 'The History
of Tom Fool' (1760), and various other pieces ; his
lectures first given in the Haymarket, London, 1764, and
afterwards in the country and in America ; his 'Lecture
on Heads' published spuriously, 1770 ; sold to Charles Lee
Lewes [q. v.], 1774 (first authentic edition, 1785) ; published 'Songs, Comic and Satyrical' (cuts by Bewick),
1772 ; sole dramatic success, 'The Trip to Portsmouth'
(acted, 1773).   [liv. 229]

STEVENS or STEPHENS, JOHN (d. 1726), translator and antiquary ; said to have served in James II's
army in Ireland ; described in his books as 'Captain' ;
translated Bæda's 'Ecclesiastical History,' and Portuguese, Spanish (including Quevedo's 'Pablo de Segovia'),
and French works ; published also translation and
abridgment of Dugdale's 'Monasticon,' 1718 (continuation, 1722).   [liv. 231]

STEVENS, RICHARD JOHN SAMUEL (1757–1837),
musician ; friend of Samuel Birch (1757–1841) [q. v.] ;
organist at Temple Church, London, 1786, at Charterhouse, London, 1796–1837 ; Gresham professor of music,
1801–37 ; edited collection of sacred music, 1802 ; composed
glees, sonatas, and songs.   [liv. 232]

STEVENS, WILLIAM (1732–1807), biographer and
editor of William Jones of Nayland [q. v.], 1801 ; published posthumous sermons of his cousin, bishop George
Horne [q. v.] ; his 'Essay' (1799) against relaxation
of subscription to Thirty-nine Articles thrice reissued ;
joined William Jones in founding 'Society for the Reformation of Principles' ; 'Nobody's Friends' (club)
founded in his honour, c. 1800, originating from pseudonym used by him in pamphlet ; treasurer, Queen Anne's
Bounty.   [liv. 233]

STEVENS, WILLIAM BAGSHAW (1756–1800), poet; demy of Magdalen College, Oxford, 1772–94, fellow, 1794–5; M.A., 1779, D.D., 1797; head-master of Repton, 1779–1800; chaplain to Sir Francis Burdett [q. v.]; incumbent of Seckington and Kingsbury, 1799; published poems, 1775, 1782; contributed to 'Gentleman's Magazine' as M.C.S. [liv. 233]

STEVENSON. [See also STEPHENSON.]

STEVENSON, LORD (1640?–1713). [See SINCLAIR, SIR ROBERT.]

STEVENSON, ALAN (1807–1865), civil engineer; son of Robert Stevenson [q. v.]; M.A. and Fellowes prizeman, Edinburgh University, 1826; M.I.C.E., 1830; F.R.S.E., 1838; hon. LL.D. Glasgow, 1840; engineer to Scottish lighthouse commissioners from 1843; designed ten lighthouses, including Skerryvore lighthouse tower (finished, 1843), introducing prismatic rings; his 'Account of the Skerryvore Lighthouse' (1848) expanded into 'Rudimentary Treatise' on lighthouses, 1850. [liv. 234]

STEVENSON, DAVID (1815–1886), civil engineeer; son of Robert Stevenson [q. v.]; educated at Edinburgh; managing partner of Stevenson engineering firm; reported on and executed works for improvement of rivers in northern England and Scotland; M.I.C.E., 1844, member of the council, 1877–83; vice-president, Royal Society of Edinburgh, 1873–7; engineer to northern lighthouse board, 1853; constructed numerous beacons and lighthouses; devised 'aseismatic arrangement' for those in Japan; introduced use of paraffin in lighthouses, 1870; president, Royal Scottish Society of Arts, 1869; works include 'Application of Marine Surveying and Hydrometry to Practice of Civil Engineering,' 1842, and 'Life of Robert Stevenson,' 1878. [liv. 235]

STEVENSON, GEORGE (1799–1856), Australian journalist and agriculturist; in Canada, Central America, and West Indies, 1820–30; edited the 'Globe' (London), 1835–6; private secretary to first governor of South Australia and first clerk of legislative council, 1836–8; established 'South Australian Gazette,' 1836; conducted 'South Australian Register,' 1840–2, 'South Australian Gazette,' 1845–51; made agricultural experiments, and established vineyards; in Victoria diggings, 1851–3; assisted Lord Dalling in book on France, 1834; died coroner of Adelaide. [liv. 236]

STEVENSON, GEORGE JOHN (1818–1888), hymnologist and author; head-master of Lambeth Green parochial school, London, 1848–55; edited 'Wesleyan Times,' 1861–7, and 'Union Review,' 1882; published 'Methodist Hymn Book and its Associations,' 1869 (enlarged, 1883), and religious biographies. [liv. 237]

STEVENSON, JOHN (1778–1846?), ophthalmic surgeon; studied at St. Thomas's and Guy's hospitals, London; M.R.C.S., 1807; founded Royal Infirmary for Cataract, Little Portland Street, London, 1830; oculist and aurist to William IV and Leopold I, king of the Belgians; published medical works. [liv. 237]

STEVENSON, SIR JOHN ANDREW (1760?–1833), musical composer; chorister and afterwards vicar-choral at St. Patrick's and Christ Church, Dublin; created Mus.Doc. Dublin, 1791; knighted, 1803; best known by symphonies and accompaniments to Moore's Irish melodies. [liv. 238]

STEVENSON, JOHN HALL-, originally JOHN HALL (1718–1785), friend of Laurence Sterne [q. v.]; met Sterne at Jesus College, Cambridge; assumed wife's surname, c. 1738; inherited Skelton Castle ('Crazy Castle'), Yorkshire, from maternal aunt; formed 'club of demoniacks' and entertained Sterne there; acquainted with Wilkes and Horace Walpole, and claimed friendship of Rousseau; the Eugenius of Sterne's works; imitated 'Tristram Shandy' and wrote continuation of 'Sentimental Journey,' 1769; published pamphlets in verse; his chief work, 'Crazy Tales,' 1762, reprinted privately, 1894; works collected, 1795. [liv. 238]

STEVENSON, JOSEPH (1806–1895), historian and archivist; educated at Durham School and Glasgow University; entered manuscript department, British Museum, 1831; sub-commissioner of public records, 1834–9; librarian

and keeper of Durham records, 1841; hon. M.A. Durham; incumbent of Leighton Buzzard, 1849–62; suggestor of Rolls series, 1856; became Roman catholic, 1863, priest, 1872; professed of three vows as jesuit, 1885; received civil list pension, 1872; examined for government and transcribed from Vatican archives; hon. LL.D. St. Andrews, 1885; edited works for Rolls series, various archæological clubs and societies, and collection of 'Church Historians of England'; calendared Elizabethan state papers (foreign i.-vii.); published books on Wyclif (1885), 'Marie Stuart' (1886), and other historical works. [liv. 240]

STEVENSON, MATTHEW (*fl.* 1654–1685), minor poet; works include 'The Tvvelve Moneths,' 1661, and 'Florus Britannicus,' 1662. [liv. 242]

STEVENSON, ROBERT (1772–1850), civil engineer; studied at Andersonian Institute, Glasgow, and at Edinburgh; engineer to Scottish lighthouse board; designed and constructed twenty lighthouses, inventing intermittent and flashing lights; began Bell Rock tower lighthouse, 1807 (finished in five years), on novel design, and with specially invented implements; his bust placed in it; designed many bridges, including Hutchison bridge; suggested modern rails; invented hydrophore; designed eastern road approaches to Edinburgh; M.I.C.E., 1828; F.R.S.E.; wrote 'Account of the Bell Rock Lighthouse,' 1824, technical articles, and scientific papers. [liv. 243]

STEVENSON, ROBERT ALAN MOWBRAY (1847–1900), painter and art critic; son of Alan Stevenson [q. v.]; cousin of Robert Louis Stevenson [q. v.]; M.A. Sidney Sussex College, Cambridge, 1882; studied art in Edinburgh, Antwerp, and Paris; professor of fine arts at University College, Liverpool, 1880–93; art critic to the 'Pall Mall Gazette,' 1893 till death. His publications include 'Peter Paul Rubens,' 1898, 'The Art of Velasquez,' 1895, and 'Velasquez,' 1899. [Suppl. iii. 356]

STEVENSON, ROBERT LOUIS (1850–1894), author and traveller; son of Thomas Stevenson [q. v.]; born in Edinburgh; entered student at Edinburgh University, 1867; pupil of Fleeming Jenkin [q. v.]; silver medallist, Edinburgh Society of Arts, for paper on lighthouse improvements, 1871; abandoned engineering for law; was admitted advocate, 1875, but never practised; composed essay on 'Pentland Rising of 1666' in sixteenth year (printed, 1866); contributed to 'Edinburgh University Magazine,' 1871, to 'Portfolio,' 1873; went on canoe tour in France and Belgium, 1876 (described in the 'Inland Voyage,' 1878); in Paris and Cevennes country, 1878; contributed to 'Cornhill,' 'Temple Bar,' and 'London,' 1876–1878; travelled to California by emigrant ship and train, 1879; though very ill wrote stories and essays; married Mrs. Osbourne, 1880; returned home with her, 1880, after stay at Calistoga (described in 'Silverado Squatters,' 1883); unsuccessful candidate for Edinburgh chair of history and constitutional law, 1881; lived in Scotland, but wintered in Switzerland and France, 1880–3; settled at Bournemouth, 1884; collaborated with Mr. W. E. Henley in 'Beau Austin,' 'Robert Macaire,' and 'Admiral Guinea' (plays); established position as author with 'Strange Case of Dr. Jekyll and Mr. Hyde,' 1886, and 'Kidnapped,' 1886; went to America, 1887; set out on South Sea voyage, June 1888; stayed at Honolulu, visiting leper settlement at Molokai, 1889; first lived in Samoa, 1889–90, where he bought 'Vailima' property; settled there, November 1890; wrote vindication of Father Damien at Sydney, 1890; in Samoa temporarily recovered health; corresponded with men of letters in England; obtained removal of white officials from Samoa, and wrote 'A Footnote to History,' 1893; died suddenly from rupture of a blood-vessel of the brain, and was buried in spot selected by himself on Mount Vaea. His works include 'Travels with a Donkey in the Cevennes,' 1879, 'Virginibus Puerisque,' 1881, 'Treasure Island,' and 'New Arabian Nights,' 1882, 'Prince Otto' and 'Child's Garden of Verses,' 1885, 'Underwoods' and 'Memories and Portraits,' 1887, the 'Master of Ballantrae,' 1889, 'Across the Plains,' 1892, 'Catriona,' 1893, 'The Wrecker,' 1892, and 'The Ebb-Tide,' with Lloyd Osbourne, 1894, and the posthumous 'Vailima Letters,' 1895, 'Weir of Hermiston' (fragment: his best work), 1897, and 'St. Ives' (unfinished), 1897. The collected Edinburgh edition (1894–6, 1896–8) also contains reprints from periodicals, and an unprinted fragment of family history. [liv. 245]

STEVENSON, SETH WILLIAM (1784–1853), antiquary; son of William Stevenson (1741–1821) [q. v.]; proprietor and editor of 'Norfolk Chronicle'; mayor of Norwich, 1832; F.S.A., 1827; his 'Dictionary of Roman Coins' (completed by Frederic William Madden) published, 1889. [liv. 254]

STEVENSON, THOMAS (1818–1887), engineer and meteorologist; son of Robert Stevenson [q. v.]; educated at Edinburgh; joint-engineer to board of northern lighthouses, 1853–85; continued experiments of Alan Stevenson [q. v.] in lighthouse illumination; invented and perfected 'azimuthal condensing system'; president, Royal Society of Edinburgh, 1885; president, Royal Scottish Society of Arts, 1859–60; M.I.C.E., 1864; honorary secretary, Scottish Meteorological Society, 1871; designed (1864) Stevenson screen for thermometers, and made other original contributions to meteorology; wrote on lighthouse illumination and harbour construction. [liv. 255]

STEVENSON, WILLIAM (1719?–1783), physician; M.D. Edinburgh; served in army; practised at Coleraine, Wells (Somerset), Bath, and Newark; Jacobite; opposed bleedings and prevalent use of drugs; published medical works. [liv. 256]

STEVENSON, WILLIAM (1741–1821), proprietor of 'Norfolk Chronicle' and publisher; edited Campbell's 'Lives of British Admirals.' [liv. 254]

STEVENSON, WILLIAM (1772–1829), keeper of treasury records; nonconformist minister, classical tutor, Manchester Academy; farmer; editor of 'Scots Magazine,' c. 1797; keeper of the records in the treasury, 1806–29; published agricultural and other works, compiled 'Annual Register,' and contributed to 'Edinburgh Review' and other periodicals. [liv. 256]

STEVENSON, W. B. (fl. 1803–1825), author of 'A Historical and Descriptive Narrative of twenty years' residence in South America' (1825); imprisoned by Spanish at Concepcion, Callao, and Lima; joined revolutionists at Quito; governor of the Esmeraldas, 1810; secretary to Lord Cochrane, 1818. [liv. 257]

STEVENSON, WILLIAM FLEMING (1832–1886), Irish presbyterian divine; M.A. Glasgow, 1851; hon. D.D. Edinburgh, 1881; studied also in Germany; town missionary in Belfast, 1857; minister of Rathgar, Dublin, 1860–86; convener of Irish General Assembly's foreign missions, 1873; made missionary tour round the world, 1877; professor of evangelistic theology, New College, Edinburgh, 1879–80; moderator of general assembly, 1881; chaplain to viceroy of Ireland, 1886; published 'Praying and Working,' 1862. [liv. 258]

STEWARD. [See also STEUART, STEWART, and STUART.]

STEWARD or **STEWART**, RICHARD (1593?–1651), dean designate of St. Paul's Cathedral and Westminster; of Westminster and Magdalen Hall, Oxford; M.A., 1615, D.C.L., 1624; fellow of All Souls College, Oxford, 1613; canon of Salisbury; clerk of the closet to Charles I, 1633; dean of Chichester, 1635; provost of Eton, 1639–43; dean of the Chapel Royal, 1643; dean designate of St. Paul's, London, 1641, of Westminster, 1645; deprived by parliament; defended episcopacy at Uxbridge conference, 1645; ecclesiastical adviser to Charles II; published theological works; died in Paris. [liv. 258]

STEWARD, ROBERT THE (1316–1390). [See ROBERT II.]

STEWARD, STYWARD, or **WELLS**, ROBERT (d. 1557), first dean of Ely; M.A. Cambridge, 1520; prior of Ely, 1522; maintained validity of Henry VIII's marriage with Catherine of Arragon, 1529, but afterwards carried out royal policy; surrendered Ely monastery, 1559, receiving pensions; dean of Ely, 1541–57; continued 'Historia Eliensis' from 1486 to 1554. [liv. 260]

STEWARD, SIR SIMEON (d. 1629?), poet; related to Robert Steward [q. v.]; of Trinity Hall, Cambridge; knighted, 1603; M.P., Shaftesbury, 1614, Aldeburgh, 1627; his 'Fairy King' (1635) reprinted, 1656, and later by Bliss, 1813, and Mr. A. E. Waite, 1888 ('Elfin Music'). [liv. 261]

STEWARD, THOMAS (1669?–1753), presbyterian divine; minister at Debenham, 1689–1706, Cook Street, Dublin, 1706–24, Bury St. Edmunds, 1724–53; hon. D.D.

Aberdeen, 1733; correspondent of Francis Hutcheson (1694–1746) [q. v.] and Philip Doddridge [q. v.] [liv. 261]

STEWARDSON, THOMAS (1781–1859), portrait-painter; exhibited at Royal Academy, 1804–29; among his sitters Canning, Lord Liverpool, and Grote. [liv. 262]

STEWART. [See also STEUART, STEWARD, and STUART.]

STEWART, ALEXANDER, EARL OF BUCHAN and LORD OF BADENOCH (1343?–1405?), 'the Wolf of Badenoch'; son of Robert II of Scotland by Elizabeth Mure; granted Badenoch, 1371; king's lieutenant north of Forth, 1372; became Earl of Buchan and acquired Ross by marriage, c. 1382; censured for deserting wife by bishops of Moray and Ross, 1389; in revenge burnt Forres and Elgin, 1390; his tomb in church of Dunkeld. [liv. 262]

STEWART, ALEXANDER. EARL OF MAR (1375?–1435), natural son of Alexander Stewart, the 'Wolf of Badenoch' [q. v.]; having previously instigated the murder of her husband, besieged at Kildrummy Isabel (d. 1408), countess of Mar, and heiress of the Douglas estates, 1404; compelled her to make him his heir and to marry him; ambassador to England, 1406–7; helped to restore John of Burgundy at Liège, 1408; defeated Lord of the Isles at Harlaw, 1411; conservator of truce with England and warden of the marches, 1424; though adherent of Albany not disgraced by James I. [liv. 263]

STEWART, ALEXANDER, DUKE OF ALBANY and EARL OF MARCH (1454?–1485), second son of James II of Scotland [q. v.]; earl of March and lord of Annandale, 1455; duke of Albany before 1458; captured by English ship on way to Guelderland, but released, 1454; high admiral of Scotland and warden of the marches; lieutenant of Scotland, 1472; fortified Dunbar against royal forces and was imprisoned at Edinburgh, 1479; escaped to Paris; well received by Louis XI; married (second wife) Anne de la Tour d'Auvergne, 1480; concluded with Edward IV treaty of Fotheringay, 1482, agreeing to rule Scotland as his vassal; returned to Scotland with English army, but agreed to be faithful to James III if restored to his estates, 1482; made truce with English, surrendering Berwick; created earl of Mar and Gairloch, and reconciled to James III; attempted to seize James III's person, 1482; made new treaty with Edward IV, 1483, agreeing to help in conquest of France; after death of Edward IV indicted and outlawed, 1483; fled to England; with Douglas made raid on Lochmaben; accidentally killed in France. [liv. 264]

STEWART, ALEXANDER (1493?–1513), archbishop of St. Andrews; natural son of James IV; appointed archbishop in boyhood; visited the Netherlands and France, c. 1506; studied under Erasmus at Padua, 1508; praised in Erasmus's 'Adagia'; lord chancellor of Scotland, c. 1510; co-founder of college of St. Leonard's, St. Andrews, 1512; killed at Flodden. [liv. 267]

STEWART, ALEXANDER, fifth EARL OF MORAY (d. 1701), Scottish statesman; justice-general, 1674; a lord of the treasury, 1678; extraordinary lord of session, 1680; secretary of state, 1680–8; active in repressing covenanters; high commissioner to Scottish parliament, 1686; K.T., 1687; deprived at revolution. [liv. 268]

STEWART, ALEXANDER, fifth LORD BLANTYRE (d. 1704), raised regiment for William III, and received pension; seceder from convention, 1702; took seat in Scottish parliament, 1703. [liv. 268]

STEWART, ALEXANDER (d. 1795), of Invernahyle, Jacobite; 'out' with Stewarts of Appin, 1715 and 1745; distinguished at Prestonpans, 1745; wounded at Culloden, 1746; pardoned under act of indemnity; introduced Sir Walter Scott to the highlands, 1787. [liv. 269]

STEWART, ALEXANDER PATRICK (1813–1883), physician; M.D. Glasgow, 1838; physician, Middlesex Hospital, 1855–66; F.R.C.P., 1855; active member of British Medical Association; his paper differentiating typhus from typhoid fever (Parisian Medical Society, 1840) reprinted, 1884. [liv. 269]

STEWART, ANDREW, first BARON AVANDALE or AVONDALE (d. 1488), chancellor of Scotland; grandson of Murdac Stewart, second duke of Albany [q. v.]; knighted, and probably educated in England; member of general council at Stirling, 1440; in household of James II; created Baron Avondale, c. 1457; chancellor of Scotland, 1460-82; obtained cession of Orkney and Shetland from Denmark; besieged Albany's castle at Dunbar, 1479; deserted James III at Lauder, 1482; helped to effect agreement between him and Albany, 1482; ambassador to France, 1484. [liv. 270]

STEWART, ANDREW, second BARON OCHILTREE (*fl.* 1548-1598), a lord of the congregation, 1559; signed bond for expulsion of French from Scotland, and subscribed book of discipline, 1560; accompanied Knox to Holyrood, 1563; joined Moray's rising against Darnley's marriage, 1565, and the conspiracy against Riccio; wounded by Herries at Langside, 1568; member of Morton's privy council, 1578; attempted mediation between Huntly and Moray (second earl), 1592; after Huntly's treachery tried to attack him in the highlands, but had to retire to England, 1594; pardoned by James VI, 1595, on agreeing to abandon Bothwell; lieutenant on the borders, 1598. [liv. 271]

STEWART, ANDREW (*d.* 1671), Irish divine; minister of Donaghadee, c. 1615; granted government salary, 1654; helped to draw up 'Act of Bangor,' 1654; ejected, 1661; imprisoned on suspicion of complicity in Blood's plot, 1663; part of his 'Short Account' of the Irish church printed by Dr. W. D. Killen, 1866. [liv. 272]

STEWART, ANTHONY (1773-1846), miniature-painter; executed earliest miniatures of Queen Victoria; exhibited at Royal Academy. [liv. 273]

STEWART or **STUART**, LADY ARABELLA (1575-1615). [See ARABELLA.]

STEWART or **STUART**, ARCHIBALD JAMES EDWARD (1748-1827). [See DOUGLAS, ARCHIBALD JAMES EDWARD, first BARON DOUGLAS OF DOUGLAS.]

STEWART, BALFOUR (1828-1887), physicist and meteorologist; assistant to Professor Forbes at Edinburgh, 1856; director of Kew Observatory, 1859-71; F.R.S., 1862; secretary to government meteorological committee, 1867-9; professor of natural philosophy, Owens College, Manchester, 1870-87; a founder of Society for Psychical Research (president, 1885-7); president of Physical Society and of Manchester Literary and Philosophical society, 1887; Rumford medallist, 1868, for researches on radiant heat, which helped to lay foundation of spectrum analysis; demonstrated applicability of law of radiation to polarised rays of light, 1860; suggested variations in a primary electric current in the sun as cause of auroræ, magnetic storms, and earth currents, 1860; investigated sun-spots; made calculations as to periodic irregularities in terrestrial and solar phenomena; published anonymously with Professor Peter Guthrie Tait 'The Unseen Universe,' 1875 (authorship avowed, 1876), with sequel, 1878. Other works include text-books on physics and work on sun-spots (with Warren de la Rue [q. v.] and Benjamin Loewy), 1865-8. [liv. 273]

STEWART, BERNARD or BERAULT, third SEIGNEUR D'AUBIGNY (1447?-1508). [See STUART.]

STEWART, LORD BERNARD, titular EARL OF LICHFIELD (1623?-1645). [See STUART.]

STEWART, CHARLES, sixth DUKE OF LENNOX and third DUKE OF RICHMOND (1640-1672). [See STUART.]

STEWART, CHARLES (1775-1812), lieutenant-colonel; lieutenant, 71st highlanders, 1791; wounded at Seringapatam, 1792; lieutenant-colonel, 50th foot, 1805; commanded first battalion in Walcheren, 1809, and in the Peninsula, 1811-12; died at Coria. [liv. 276]

STEWART, CHARLES (1764-1837), orientalist; served in Bengal army, 1781-1808; assistant-professor of Persian, Fort William College, Calcutta, 1800-6; professor of Arabic, Persian, and Hindustani at Haileybury, 1807-27; edited and translated oriental works. [liv. 276]

STEWART or **STUART**, CHARLES EDWARD (1720-1788), the Young Pretender. [See CHARLES EDWARD LOUIS PHILIP CASIMIR.]

STEWART, CHARLES JAMES (1775-1837), bishop of Quebec; brother of Sir William Stewart (1774-1827 [q. v.]; B.A. Corpus Christi College, Oxford, 1795;

fellow of All Souls College, Oxford, 1795; D.D., 1816; rector of Overton-Longueville and Botolph Bridge, 1799-1807; S.P.G. missionary at Saint Armand, Misisquoi Bay, Canada, 1807-17, Hatley, 1817-19; bishop of Quebec, 1826-37; died in London. [liv. 277]

STEWART (afterwards **VANE**), CHARLES WILLIAM, third MARQUIS OF LONDONDERRY (1778-1854), half-brother of Robert Stewart, lord Castlereagh [q. v.] (second marquis); entered army, 1794; on Lord Moira's staff in Netherlands, 1794-5; with Austrians on Rhine and Upper Danube, 1795-6; slightly injured by wound; lieutenant-colonel, 5th dragoons, 1797, 18th light dragoons, 1799; under-secretary in Ireland, 1803-7; Irish M.P., Thomastown, 1798-1800; M.P. co. Derry, 1800-14; under-secretary for war, 1807-9; commanded hussar brigade under Sir John Moore, 1808; adjutant-general to Wellington, 1809-12; major-general, 1810; distinguished at Talavera and Fuentes d'Onoro; groom of the bedchamber, 1812; K.B., 1813; British minister to Prussia, 1813; signed treaty with Prussia and Russia at Dresden; severely wounded at Kulm, 1813; induced Bernadotte to take active part for allies; created privy councillor, and Baron Stewart, 1814; ambassador at Vienna during congress, 1814; envoy at Troppau, 1820, Laybach, 1821, Verona, 1822; lord of the bedchamber, 1820-7; succeeded Castlereagh as marquis, 1822; took surname of Vane on second marriage, 1819; appointed to St. Petersburg embassy, 1835, but withdrew owing to parliamentary opposition; travelled in eastern and southern Europe; fought duel with Grattan's son, 1839; general, 1837; K.G., 1852; pall-bearer at Wellington's funeral; published narratives of Peninsular campaigns, 1828, of campaigns of 1813-14, 1830, travels, and 'Memoir and Correspondence of Viscount Castlereagh,' 1848-53. [liv. 278]

STEWART, DAVID, DUKE OF ROTHESAY (1378?-1402), son of Robert III of Scotland; Earl of Carrick on father's accession; pacified northern Scotland, c. 1396; lieutenant of the kingdom and Duke of Rothesay, 1399; married Elizabeth Douglas, 1399; defeated March and his English allies at Cockburnspath; seized by Albany (his uncle) and imprisoned at Falkland, 1402; said to have been starved to death. [liv. 281]

STEWART, DAVID (1772-1829), major-general; of Garth; joined 42nd highlanders, 1787; fought in Flanders, 1794, West Indies, 1795-7; captured on way to Minorca, 1798; severely wounded at Alexandria, 1801; wounded at Maida, 1806; lieutenant-colonel, West India rangers, 1808; at capture of Guadaloupe, 1810; C.B., 1815; major-general, 1825; published 'Sketches . . . of the Highlanders of Scotland'; with Details of the Military Service of Highland Regiments,' 1822; died governor of St. Lucia. [liv. 282]

STEWART, SIR DONALD MARTIN, first baronet (1824-1900), field-marshal; entered East India Company's service as ensign, 9th Bengal native infantry, 1840; major (Bengal staff corps), 1866; general, 1881; field-marshal, 1894; served with distinction in Indian mutiny, 1857-8; brigadier-general in Abyssinian expedition, 1867-1868; C.B., 1868; reorganised convict settlement in Andaman islands, 1869; commander of Lahore division, 1876; commanded Quetta army in Afghan war, 1878-80; K.C.B., 1879; made celebrated march to Kabul, 1880; G.C.B. and created baronet, 1880; commander-in-chief in India, 1880-5; member of council of India, 1885, till death; G.C.S.I., 1885; governor of Chelsea Hospital, 1895. [Suppl. iii. 357]

STEWART, DUGALD (1753-1828), philosopher; son of Matthew Stewart (1717-1785) [q. v.]; educated at Edinburgh High School, and at Edinburgh and Glasgow universities; friend of Thomas Reid (1710-1796) [q. v.] and (Sir) Archibald Alison; associated with his father in Edinburgh mathematical professorship, 1775; lectured for Adam Ferguson [q. v.], 1778-9; Edinburgh professor of moral philosophy, 1785; gave up lecturing, 1809, but retained chair till after death (1820) of his coadjutor, Thomas Brown (1778-1820) [q. v.]; met Burns at Catrine, 1786; visited France in summers of 1788 and 1789; gave offence by sympathy with revolution; supported Sir John Leslie (1766-1832) [q. v], 1805; received sinecure from whigs, 1806; accompanied Lords Lauderdale and Henry Petty to Paris, 1806; monument erected to him upon Calton Hill, Edinburgh; Palmerston, Russell, and Lansdowne (Lord Henry Petty) among his pupils, and Scott among friends; while approximating to empirical school disavowed its developments and retained 'intuitionism'; unable to study Kant. His works, collected by Sir William Hamilton, 1854–60 (11 vols.), include 'Elements of the Philosophy of the Human Mind' (vols. i., 1792, ii., 1814, iii., 1827), 'Outlines of Moral Philosophy,' 1793, 'Lectures on Political Economy' (delivered, 1800), and 'Account of Life and Writings of Thomas Reid,' 1802. [liv. 282]

STEWART, ESMÉ, sixth SEIGNEUR D'AUBIGNY and first DUKE OF LENNOX (1542 ?–1583). [See STUART.]

STEWART or STUART, FRANCIS, fifth EARL OF BOTHWELL (d. 1624). [See HEPBURN.]

STEWART, FRANCES TERESA, DUCHESS OF RICHMOND AND LENNOX (1647–1702). [See STUART.]

STEWART, HELEN D'ARCY CRANSTOUN (1765–1838). [See CRANSTOUN, HELEN D'ARCY.]

STEWART, HENRY, first BARON METHVEN (1495 ?–1551 ?); supported Margaret, Queen-dowager of Scotland, in proclaiming James V, 1524; became James V's treasurer and chancellor, and Queen Margaret's favourite; married her after her divorce from Angus, 1528; imprisoned by Angus; created Baron Methven and master of the artillery by James V, 1528. [liv. 286]

STEWART or STUART, HENRY, LORD DARNLEY (1545–1567), son of Matthew Stewart, fourth or twelfth earl of Lennox [q. v.] and Lady Margaret Douglas [q. v.]; skilful penman and lutenist and expert at physical exercises, but mentally and morally weak; sent by his mother to France with a view to marriage with Mary Stuart, 1560; with his mother confined in London by Queen Elizabeth, 1561, but released and received into favour, 1562; allowed to go to Scotland at Mary Stuart's request, 1565; created Duke of Albany and married to Mary Stuart, 1565, the marriage being without real affection on either side; opposed by Moray; was refused the crown matrimonial and ousted from political influence by David Riccio [q. v.]; his jealousy of Riccio used by the nobles to make him join their conspiracy, 1566; promised to establish protestantism in return for crown matrimonial and right of succession; after death of Riccio betrayed nobles to Mary Stuart and helped her to escape to Dunbar, 1566; temporary reconciliation with Mary Stuart dissolved by discovery of his plot; refused to attend baptism of James VI; only prevented by illness from leaving Scotland; induced by Mary Stuart to leave Glasgow for Edinburgh; murdered at Kirk o' Field. [liv. 287]

STEWART, HENRY, DUKE OF GLOUCESTER (1639–1660). [See HENRY.]

STEWART or STUART, HENRY BENEDICT MARIA CLEMENT (1725–1807), styled by Jacobites Henry IX. [See HENRY.]

STEWART, SIR HERBERT (1843–1885), major-general; ensign 1863; aide-de-camp to commander of Allahabad division, 1868–70; deputy-assistant quartermaster-general, Bengal, 1872–3, for conduct in cholera outbreak, 1870; entered staff college and Inner Temple, 1877; brigade-major of cavalry during Zulu war, 1879; military secretary to Wolseley and brevet lieutenant-colonel, 1880; as chief staff officer to Sir George Pomeroy Colley [q. v.] captured at Majuba, 1881; assistant adjutant-general of cavalry in Egypt, 1882; secured Cairo after Tel-el-Kebir; C.B., brevet-colonel, and aide-de-camp to Queen Victoria; K.C.B. for services in Suakim campaign, 1884; assistant adjutant and quartermaster-general, south-eastern district, 1884; in Lord Wolseley's Gordon relief expedition, 1884–5, commanded desert column to proceed to Metemmeh; repelled Arab attack at Abu Klea, but three days later was mortally wounded; promoted major-general before death; monuments at St. Paul's, London, and Winchester. [liv. 291]

STEWART, SIR HOUSTON (1791–1875), admiral of the fleet; entered navy, 1805; in Walcheren expedition, 1809; Keith's signal-lieutenant in the Channel, 1812–13; flag-captain on Jamaica station, 1817–18; at reduction of Acre, 1840; C.B., 1840; controller-general of the coastguard, 1846–50; a lord of the admiralty, 1850–2; rear-admiral, 1851; commanded at reduction of Kinburn, Black Sea, 1855; commander-in-chief on North American station, 1856–60, at Devonport, 1860–3; G.C.B., 1865; admiral of the fleet, 1872. [liv. 293]

STEWART, JAMES (d. 1309), high steward of Scotland, 1283–1309; a guardian of Scotland under Queen Margaret, 1286; partisan of Bruce; made treaty with France, 1295, but came to terms with Edward I, 1297; sent to negotiate with Wallace before battle of Stirling, 1297; joined him afterwards; envoy to France, 1302; again submitted to English, 1305, but recognised Bruce, 1309. [liv. 294]

STEWART, JAMES, DUKE OF ROSS (1476 ?–1504), son of James III of Scotland; created duke, 1488; archbishop of St. Andrews, 1498; seen by Ariosto at Rome and eulogised in 'Orlando Furioso'; chancellor of Scotland, 1502. [liv. 295]

STEWART, JAMES, EARL OF MORAY (1499 ?–1544), natural son of James IV; granted earldom of Moray, 1501; accused (1517) Lord Home of slaying James IV after Flodden; a guardian of James V and lieutenant-general of French forces in Scotland, 1523; suppressed insurrection of the isles, 1531; warden of east and middle marches, 1532–6; commissioner for marriage of James V and Marie de Bourbon, 1535–6; specially hostile to England; partisan of Beaton; member of council of state, 1543; served against Hertford, 1544. [liv. 295]

STEWART, LORD JAMES, EARL OF MAR, and afterwards of MORAY (1531 ?–1570), natural son of James V; half-brother of Mary Queen of Scots; granted Tantallon, 1536, priory of St. Andrews, 1538; studied at St. Andrews, 1541–4; accompanied Mary Stuart to France, 1548; repelled English raid on Fife, 1549; visited France, 1550, 1552; legitimated, 1551; attended Knox's teaching at laird of Dun's, 1555; signed invitation to him to return, 1557; fell ill after witnessing marriage of Mary Stuart to dauphin, 1557; at first supported regency of Mary of Guise; on discovery of her bad faith headed lords of the congregation, 1559; with Argyll drove French from Perth and attacked Scone; disavowed designs on the crown; procured suspension of the regent and negotiated with Queen Elizabeth for help against the French; concluded treaty at Berwick providing for expulsion of French, but safeguarding of Mary Stuart's sovereign rights, 1560; reoccupied Edinburgh by English help, and concluded treaty confirming that of Berwick, 1560; deputed, 1561, by Scottish estates to sound Mary Stuart after death of Francis II, 1560; strongly dissuaded her from attempting to Romanise Scotland; won confidence of Queen Elizabeth by disclosing his conduct, but deprecated English attempts to prevent or intercept Mary Stuart's return to Scotland; opposed proposal to debar Mary Stuart in Scotland from the mass; privy councillor, 1561; privately granted earldom of Moray, but assumed title Earl of Mar, 1562; virtually home secretary; by expedition against Liddesdale prevented Bothwell's establishment in southern Scotland; formally created Earl of Moray after personal expedition of Mary Stuart against Huntly (holder of title), 1562; on Queen Elizabeth's refusal to recognise Mary as her successor, supported projected Spanish alliance of Mary, 1563; opposed the Darnley match; thenceforth estranged from Mary; attempted capture of Mary and Darnley before marriage, 1565; backed by Knox and Lennox's enemies, but not by bulk of protestants; deceived by Queen Elizabeth; publicly disavowed and insulted by Queen Elizabeth, but granted asylum in England and privately received, 1565; after failure to procure Riccio's intercession joined plot against him; supported charge of infidelity against Mary and promised to acknowledge Darnley; returned after Riccio's assassination, 1566; affected to favour Bothwell's pretensions and was nominally reconciled to Mary; tacitly sanctioned murder of Darnley, though probably not cognisant of Bothwell's plan; left Scotland for France immediately afterwards, 1567; returned on Mary Stuart's abdication at Lochleven; accepted the regency at her personal request, 1567, making great show of reluctance; promoted declaration of her privity to the Darnley murder; secured punishment of subordinates, but took no steps against principal in the crime; took rapid measures to defeat Mary after escape from Lochleven; secured his position as regent by formal sanction of Queen Elizabeth, though pretending approval of the Norfolk marriage scheme; voted against divorce from Bothwell, but after discovery of Norfolk's intrigues excused his apparent approval of them and made revelations; caused Maitland of Lethington to be accused of Darnley's murder, and imprisoned, 1569; captured and imprisoned Northumberland; proposed to Queen Elizabeth imprisonment of Mary Stuart in Scotland, 1569; assassinated at Linlithgow by James Hamilton (*fl.* 1566–1580) [q. v.] of Bothwellhaugh; buried at St. Giles's, Edinburgh; called 'the good regent.' [liv. 297]

STEWART or **STUART**, JAMES, second EARL OF MORAY (*d.* 1592), 'the bonny earl'; assumed title in right of his wife, daughter of the regent Moray, 1580; commissioner under acts against Spanish Armada, 1588, and the jesuits, 1590; assisted laird of Grant against Huntly, 1590; induced to come south on promise of pardon; warrant granted to Huntly against him by James VI, who was said to be jealous of his favour with his queen; slain by Huntly's men at Donibristle, his mother's house having been burned; his corpse long unburied; popular indignation expressed in traditional ballad. [liv. 307]

STEWART, JAMES, of Bothwellmuir, EARL OF ARRAN (*d.* 1596), second son of Andrew Stewart, second baron Ochiltree [q. v.]; served states of Holland against Spanish; gentleman of king's chamber, 1580; on Lennox's behalf accused Morton of Darnley's murder, 1580; privy councillor, 1581; recognised as head of the Hamiltons and granted earldom of Arran, being cousin of James Hamilton, third earl [q. v.], now insane; forbidden the court for insolence to Lennox, but temporarily reconciled with him; caused raid of Ruthven (1581) by 'intrusion' of Robert Montgomerie (*d.* 1609) [q. v.] into Glasgow bishopric; after James VI's escape from protestant lords obtained great influence over him, 1583; given custody of Stirling and Edinburgh castles and made chancellor, 1584; entered into relations with England; procured forfeitures of enemies' lands and order for 'kirk to acknowledge royal supremacy; provost of Edinburgh; his influence with Queen Elizabeth undermined by Patrick, master (afterwards sixth baron) Gray [q. v.], 1585; imprisoned, outlawed, and (1586) banished; returned as Captain James Stewart; failed to regain influence; murdered by nephew of Morton. [liv. 308]

STEWART, JAMES, fourth DUKE OF LENNOX and first DUKE OF RICHMOND (1612–1655). [See STUART.]

STEWART, JAMES (1791–1863), line-engraver; articled with Burnet to Robert Scott (1777–1841) [q. v.]; original member of Scottish Academy, 1826; emigrated to Cape Colony, 1833; died there. [liv. 311]

STEWART or **STUART**, JAMES FRANCIS EDWARD (1688–1766), the Old Pretender. [See JAMES FRANCIS EDWARD STUART.]

STEWART, JOHN, EARL OF BUCHAN (1381?–1424), soldier; son of Robert Stewart, first duke of Albany [q. v.], by second wife; created Earl of Buchan, 1406; chamberlain of Scotland, 1407–24; succeeded as Earl of Ross, 1415; led force to France to serve against English, 1419; after victory of Beaugé, 1421, created constable of France; took Norman fortresses; with his father-in-law, the fourth Earl of Douglas, brought reinforcements from Scotland, 1424; defeated and slain at Verneuil; buried at Tours. [liv. 311]

STEWART, SIR JOHN (1365?–1429), of Darnley, first SEIGNEUR OF AUBIGNY. [See STUART.]

STEWART, JOHN, EARL OF MAR (1457?–1479?), youngest son of James II of Scotland; arrested at instance of Cochrane, James III's favourite; said to have been bled to death in Craigmillar Castle. [liv. 312]

STEWART or **STUART**, SIR JOHN, LORD DARNLEY and first (ninth?) EARL OF LENNOX of the Stewart line (*d.* 1495); grandson of Sir John Stuart of Darnley, seigneur d'Aubigny [q. v.]; claimed half of Lennox earldom, 1460; created lord of parliament as Lord Darnley, *c.* 1461; governor of Rothesay, 1465; granted sasin of principal messuage and half lands of Lennox, but guaranteed life-rent to Baron Avondale, 1473; assumed title of earl; instrument in his favour revoked at instance of another claimant, 1476; joined conspiracy of 1482 against James III; made keeper of Dumbarton Castle, 1488, and allowed to sit in parliament as Lennox under usurpation; headed rising in favour of James IV; surprised and defeated at Tallymoss, 1488; submitted; ultimately obtained possession of Lennox earldom. [liv. 312]

STEWART, SIR JOHN, of Balveny, first EARL OF ATHOLL of a new Stewart line (1440?–1512), son of Jane or Johanna [q. v.], queen-dowager of Scotland, by the black knight of Lorne; created Earl of Atholl, *c.* 1457; granted Balveny, 1460; assisted in subjugation of Angus of the Isles, 1480; received new charter of earldom of Atholl, 1482; one of James III's generals, 1488; imprisoned by James IV, but afterwards favoured. [liv. 314]

STEWART, JOHN, third (or eleventh) EARL OF LENNOX (*d.* 1526), succeeded, 1513; joined Arran's party and seized Dumbarton, 1515; helped to blockade Stirling, 1515; at first opponent, afterwards partisan of Albany; joined Angus's party and helped to surprise Edinburgh, 1524; pensioned by Henry VIII; privy councillor, 1525; entered into plot for deliverance of James V from Angus; defeated near Linlithgow; slain in cold blood by Sir James Hamilton (*d.* 1540) [q. v.] of Finnart. [liv. 315]

STEWART, JOHN, DUKE OF ALBANY (1481–1536), regent of Scotland; son of Alexander Stewart, duke of Albany [q. v.]; brought up in France; invited to Scotland as regent and heir after Flodden, 1513, but remained in France till 1515 as Scottish ambassador; tutor and governor of James V and kingdom, 1515; reduced Hume Castle and detached Arran from the league against him, 1515; his dismissal from regency demanded by Henry VIII, 1516; caused Hume to be executed and seized his estates; declared heir to the kingdom and of his father, 1516; went to France, 1517, taking hostages and leaving French garrisons; negotiated treaty of Rouen with France against England, 1517; procured from Leo X confirmation of Scottish privileges, 1518; detained in France by secret agreement with England; his return much desired; during stay in Scotland, 1521–2, reconciled with Margaret, the queen-dowager, whom he helped to obtain divorce from Angus; charged with undue intimacy with her and designs against James V; formally accused by English herald, war with England following, 1522; invaded England with large army, which, however, refused to fight outside Scotland; after extending truce returned to France, 1522; came to Scotland with French troops and money, 1523; lost prestige by fruitless attack on Wark and retreat, 1523; his regency annulled on proclamation of James V, 1524; held command for Francis I of France in Italian campaign, 1525; obtained divorce of Queen Margaret from Angus, 1527; as French envoy at Rome negotiated marriage of Henry, duke of Orleans (Henri II), with Catherine de' Medici, 1533; also concerned in institution of court of session and endowment from Scottish sees, and in negotiations for French marriage of James V. [liv. 317]

STEWART, JOHN, third EARL OF ATHOLL (*d.* 1542), sumptuously entertained James V and French ambassador in Atholl, 1529. [liv. 315]

STEWART, LORD JOHN (1531–1563), prior of Coldingham; natural son of James V; legitimated, 1552; reckoned by Knox among protestants, but chiefly notable as courtier; favoured by Mary Queen of Scots. [liv. 322]

STEWART, JOHN, fourth EARL OF ATHOLL (*d.* 1578), son of John Stewart, third earl of Atholl [q. v.]; supported Mary, queen-dowager; voted against confession of faith, 1559; joined protestant lords against Huntly and supported Arran's marriage scheme; member of Mary Stuart's first council, 1561; associated with Maitland; favoured as catholic; won confidence of Lennox; leader of Roman catholic nobles after Huntly's fall; with Riccio was Mary's chief counsellor after Darnley marriage; helped to suppress Moray's rising; granted Tantallon Castle; not connected with Riccio's or Darnley's murder; procured Maitland's return to court; one of the leaders against Mary Stuart at Carberry Hill; declared to have been witness of opening of casket letters; member of council of regency during Moray's absence; secretly favoured Mary's restoration after her escape from Lochleven; joined league against James VI's party after the regent Moray's assassination; held convention at Atholl to support Mary, 1570; proceeded against as catholic by the kirk, but declared wish for conversion, 1574; joined Argyll against Morton and became chancellor, 1578; reconciled with Morton by English mediation, 1578; died suddenly under suspicion of poison. [liv. 323]

STEWART, SIR JOHN, first EARL OF TRAQUAIR (*d.* 1659), lord high treasurer of Scotland; privy councillor, 1621; created Baron Stewart of Traquair, 1628, Earl of Traquair, 1633; treasurer depute and extraordinary lord of session, 1630; said to have given casting vote against Balmerino at his trial, but afterwards obtained his pardon, 1634 ; treasurer of Scotland, 1636–41 ; assisted Charles I to introduce the liturgy, but advised cautious policy and moderation towards its opponents ; conveyed arms and ammunition to Dalkeith, but had to surrender to covenanters, 1639 ; joined Charles I at York ; king's commissioner to Edinburgh assembly, 1639 ; assented to abolition of episcopacy and signature of the covenant ; distrusted by both parties ; dismissed and condemned to death, 1641 ; sentence remitted at Charles I's instance ; heavily fined, 1644 ; perhaps betrayed Montrose's plans to Leslie, 1645 ; readmitted to parliament, 1646 ; raised cavalry for the 'engagement' ; taken at Preston, 1648 ; prisoner in England till 1654. [liv. 326]

STEWART, JOHN, called ĪOHN ROY (1700–1752), Jacobite ; lieutenant in Scots greys ; resigned commission ; Jacobite agent ; fought in French army at Fontenoy, 1745 ; commanded 'Edinburgh regiment,' 1745–6 ; favourite with Prince Charles Edward ; escaped with him to France ; died there. He was a noted Gaelic poet. [liv. 328]

STEWART, JOHN (1749–1822), 'Walking Stewart'; refractory at Harrow and Charterhouse School ; went to India, 1763 ; resigned East India writership, 1765 ; general under Hyder Ali ; escaped wounded ; prime minister of nabob of Arcot ; travelled in Persia, Ethiopia, and Abyssinia ; came to Europe through Arabian desert, walking through France and Spain towards England, 1783 ; walked from Calais to Vienna, 1784 ; in North America, 1791 ; met Wordsworth, 1792, De Quincey, 1798–9 ; announced lectures in London, 1803 ; his money claims on Arcot settled by East India Company, c. 1813 ; published discursive philosophical works, including 'Travels to discover the Source of Moral Motion,' c. 1789. [liv. 328]

STEWART or STUART, LOUISA, COUNTESS OF ALBANY (1753–1824), wife of the Young Pretender. [See ALBANY.]

STEWART, LUDOVICK, second DUKE OF LENNOX and DUKE OF RICHMOND (1574–1624). [See STUART.]

STEWART or STUART, MARIA CLEMENTINA (1702–1735), wife of the Old Pretender ; daughter of Prince James Sobieski, eldest son of the king of Poland ; married James Francis Edward Stuart, the Old Pretender [q. v.], 1719 ; left her husband and retired to a nunnery, 1724. [xxix. 202]

STEWART or STUART, MARY (1542–1587), queen of Scots. [See MARY.]

STEWART, MATTHEW, second (or tenth) EARL OF LENNOX (d. 1513), succeeded to Lennox and had sheriffdom of Dumbarton ; slain at Flodden, commanding Scots right wing. [liv. 314]

STEWART, MATTHEW, fourth (twelfth) EARL OF LENNOX (1516–1571), regent of Scotland ; keeper of Dumbarton Castle, 1531 ; commanded Scots men-at-arms in Provence, 1536 ; naturalised in France, 1537 ; induced by French party to return to Scotland, 1543 ; put forward as rival to Arran as next heir after the Princess Mary ; seized Mary of Guise, the queen dowager and Princess Mary at Edinburgh, 1543 ; brought them to Stirling ; disappointed of marriage with Mary of Guise ; opened negotiations with Henry VIII for hand of Lady Margaret Douglas [q. v.] ; joined English party, but came to temporary agreement with Arran, 1544 ; went to London and signed treaty agreeing to surrender Dumbarton and Bute and support English overlordship in exchange for hand of Lady Margaret and the governorship of Scotland, 1544 ; received English estates ; naturalised and married ; as English lieutenant for southern Scotland made attempt against west coast, 1544–5 ; assisted Hertford's invasion, 1545 ; outlawed in Scotland, 1545 ; imprisoned by Queen Elizabeth for design to return to Scotland, 1562, his object being to promote marriage of his son (Darnley) with Mary Queen of Scots ; allowed to go, 1564 ; restored to title and lands, 1564 ; lieutenant over western Scotland, 1565 ; privy to plot against Riccio ; warned Mary of Darnley's wish to leave Scotland ; formally accused Bothwell, 1567 ; prevented from appearing against him ; provisional regent after Mary's surrender ; accused Mary at Westminster conference, 1568 ; lieutenant-general and regent of Scotland, 1570 ; fought against Huntly and the Hamiltons ; held parliament at Edinburgh ; surprised at Stirling by Kirkcaldy of Grange ; rescued by Mar, but stabbed by Captain Calder. [liv. 331]

STEWART, MATTHEW (1717–1785), geometrician ; studied at Glasgow and at Edinburgh under Colin Maclaurin [q. v.] ; gained reputation by his 'General Theorems,' 1746 ; minister of Roseneath, 1745–7 ; professor of mathematics at Edinburgh University, 1747–85, the duties being performed by his son, Dugald Stewart [q. v.], after 1772 ; F.R.S., 1764 ; chief work, 'Tracts, Physical and Mathematical,' 1761, applying geometrical demonstration to astronomy. [liv. 336]

STEWART, MURDAC or MURDOCH, second DUKE OF ALBANY (d. 1425), governor of Scotland ; known as Earl of Fife till death of father, Robert Stewart, first duke of Albany [q. v.], 1420 ; justiciary north of Forth, 1392 ; captured at Homildon, 1402 ; prisoner in England till exchanged for Sir Henry Percy, second earl of Northumberland [q. v.], 1415 ; suspected of delaying James I's liberation ; incompetent and corrupt governor, 1420–4 ; arrested and executed. [liv. 337]

STEWART, PATRICK, second EARL OF ORKNEY (d. 1614), son of Robert Stewart, first earl of Orkney [q. v.] ; granted charter of earldom of Orkney and lordship of Zetland, 1600 ; exercised almost independent sovereignty ; charged with tyranny and cruelty ; tried and sentenced to imprisonment and loss of justiciarship, 1611 ; released, but again imprisoned ; refused all terms ; executed for instigating rebellion of his son. [liv. 337]

STEWART, PATRICK (1832–1865), major, royal (17th Bengal) engineers ; lieutenant, Bengal engineers, 1854 ; brevet major, 1858 ; attached to headquarters staff during relief of Lucknow, 1857, and at siege and capture, 1858 ; accompanied Lord Canning to Allahabad, 1858 ; served on commission to inquire into cause of the great mortality from cholera, 1861–2 ; director-general of government Indo-European telegraph at Bombay, 1863 ; laid cable from Gwadar to Fao ; C.B., 1864. [Suppl. iii, 358]

STEWART, ROBERT, first DUKE OF ALBANY (1340 ?– 1420), regent of Scotland ; third son of Robert Stewart, earl of Strathearn (afterwards Robert II) [q. v.] ; hostage in England, 1360 ; Baron of Menteith on marriage, 1361 ; Earl of Fife and Menteith, 1371 ; hereditary governor of Stirling, 1373 ; placed in line of succession ; chamberlain of Scotland, 1382–1407 ; took part in raids into Northumberland and Cumberland, 1385–6 ; led invasion of 1388 ; provisional guardian of Scotland, 1389–99 ; created Duke of Albany, 1398 ; member of Rothesay's council, 1399 ; reinstated as governor after Rothesay's arrest and death, 1402 ; his forces defeated by English, 1402 ; supposed to have acted with Hotspur, 1403 ; regent of Scotland on capture of Prince James and death of Robert III [q. v.], 1406 ; his supposed connivance at imprisonment of James I in England not substantiated ; crushed rebellion of Donald Macdonald, second lord of the Isles [q. v.], who claimed Albany's earldom of Ross, 1411 ; caused erection of Inverness Castle ; demanded release of James I, 1416 ; protected Thomas Warde, the pretended Richard II of England ; made 'foul raid' against Roxburgh, 1417 ; granted charter, 1420 ; buried at Dunfermline. [liv. 339]

STEWART or STUART, ROBERT, SEIGNEUR D'AUBIGNY (1470 ?–1543), brother of Matthew Stewart, second or tenth earl of Lennox [q. v.] ; served with Scots under Seigneur d'Aubigny ; as marshal of France defeated Colonna at Villa Franca, 1515 ; fought at Marignano ; captured at Pavia. [liv. 314]

STEWART, LORD ROBERT, afterwards EARL OF ORKNEY (d. 1592), natural son of James V ; abbot of Holyrood, 1539 ; privy councillor, 1552 ; acted with lords of congregation ; prominent during French attack on Edinburgh, 1559 ; pensioned by his half-sister, Mary Queen of Scots, 1566 ; reported to have warned Darnley of the plot against him ; exchanged temporalities of Holyrood for those of Orkney, 1569 ; a chief conspirator against Morton, 1580 ; created Earl of Orkney, 1581. [liv. 342]

STEWART, SIR ROBERT (d. 1670 ?), Irish royalist ; accompanied James VI to England, 1603 ; in Swedish service, 1611–17 ; granted Irish estates, 1617 ; raised troops in Scotland for Sigismund III of Poland, 1623 ; at battle of Leipzig and taking of Wurzburg, 1629 ; enlisted Irish troops for Sweden, 1637 ; governor of Culmore Castle, 1638, of Londonderry, 1643–4 ; M.P., Londonderry, 1639 ; received royal commission against Irish rebels, 1641 ; defeated Sir Phelim O'Neill [q. v.] at Glenmaquin,

1642; surprised Owen Roe O'Neill [q. v.], 1643; reluctantly took the covenant; captured Sligo Castle, 1645; refused to obey parliamentary governor of Derry; secured and sent to London, 1648; escaped and joined Clanricarde in Ireland, 1649; after royalist defeat retired to Scotland; reappointed to Derry and Culmore at Restoration. [liv. 343]

STEWART, ROBERT, first MARQUIS OF LONDONDERRY (1739–1821); Irish M.P., co. Down, 1769–83; prominent delegate to second Dungannon convention, 1783; Irish privy councillor; created (Irish) Baron Londonderry, 1789, Viscount Castlereagh, 1795, Earl of Londonderry, 1796, marquis, 1816. [liv. 345]

STEWART, ROBERT, second MARQUIS OF LONDONDERRY, better known as VISCOUNT CASTLEREAGH (1769–1822), statesman; son of Robert Stewart, first marquis of Londonderry [q. v.]; studied at St. John's College, Cambridge, 1788, and abroad; M.P., co. Down (Irish parliament), 1790; M.P., Tregony, 1794–6, Oxford, 1796–7; supported enfranchisement of Irish Roman catholics; at first voted with opposition; as keeper of Irish privy seal, 1797–8, was acting chief secretary to viceroy; forestalled United Irish rebellion by arresting leaders; procured English troops to replace Irish militia; chief secretary for Ireland, 1799–1801, being specially selected by Pitt; impressed on ministry necessity for immediate union; solely responsible for its passing through Irish parliament, 1800, though reluctantly employing corruption; threatened resignation on refusal of ministry to recommend all peerages promised; pressed for introduction of Irish Catholic Emancipation Bill; resigned on George III's refusal, 1801; after union represented co. Down, 1800–5 and 1812–20, Boroughbridge, 1806, Plympton-Earl, 1806–1812, Oxford, 1821–2; had unofficial charge of Addington's Irish measures, 1801; prepared plans for Irish tithe commutation, and recommended state payment of Roman catholic priests; at Pitt's request became president of (East India) board of control under Addington, 1802; supported Lord Wellesley against court of directors and the cabinet, and conducted negotiations with Persia; appointed by Pitt to war and colonial office in addition to board of control, 1805; responsible for abortive Elbe expedition, 1805; attacked Grenville's foreign policy, 1806; again war secretary, 1807; made treaty with Prussia, secured Danish fleet, saved Swedish and Portuguese fleets from Napoleon I, 1807; prepared expedition to Portugal, 1808, vainly endeavouring to secure chief command for Sir Arthur Wellesley; sent Wellesley to Portugal, 1809, and supported him throughout; increased army; his Walcheren expedition delayed and ruined by dissension between commanders and fever, 1809; his supersession agreed upon in cabinet under influence of Canning; declined presidency of council; fought duel with Canning, wounding him, 1809; resigned; supported ministerial policy whilst out of office, 1809–12; member of bullion committee; supported continued suspension of cash payments, 1811; refused peerage; foreign secretary, 1812–22; led House of Commons after Perceval's death; rejected Napoleon I's overtures and increased troops in Peninsula, 1812; brought about peace between Russia and Turkey, Sweden and Russia, and concluded treaties with Russia and Sweden, 1812; increased foreign subsidies, 1813; by his exertions as British plenipotentiary on the continent procured treaty of Chaumont, 1814; arranged with Austria at Dijon affairs of Italy; signed preliminaries of peace at Paris with reservations, after Napoleon's abdication, 1814; opposed to Elba settlement; K.G.; senior British plenipotentiary at congress of Vienna, 1814–15; in consequence of determined opposition on Polish question by Russia and Prussia, concluded offensive and defensive treaty with France and Austria, 1815; peace having meanwhile been made with America, effected a compromise, a paper constitution being granted Poland, Luxemburg given to Netherlands and Genoa to Piedmont, and abolition of slave trade after term of years promised by France and Spain; on Napoleon's escape increased foreign subsidies and refused separate peace; after Waterloo restrained allies from retaliations on France; selected St. Helena and settled terms of Napoleon's confinement; restored Java to the Dutch; defeated in Commons on income tax, 1816; in cabinet opposed resumption of cash payments, 1819; with Sidmouth held responsible for the Six Acts, 1819; measures against Queen Caroline imputed to him, 1820; made treaties with Spain (1817) and Belgium (1818) for aboli-

tion of slave trade: a plenipotentiary at Aix-la-Chapelle, 1818; consolidated settlement of 1815 by further treaties; became Marquis of Londonderry, 1821; superintended home office upon Sidmouth's retirement; his mind affected by work and responsibility; committed suicide at country seat; buried in Westminster Abbey. [liv. 346]

STEWART, SIR ROBERT PRESCOTT (1825–1894), musician; organist of Christ Church and Trinity College, Dublin, 1844; vicar-choral and organist of St. Patrick's, 1852; professor of music, Dublin University, 1861; Mus. Doc.,1851; conductor of Dublin Choral and Philharmonic Societies; knighted, 1872; composed glees, church music, and other works. [liv. 358]

STEWART, SIR THOMAS GRAINGER (1837–1900), physician; M.D. Edinburgh, 1858; president while still undergraduate of Royal Medical Society; studied at Berlin, Prague, and Vienna; F.R.S.E., 1866; professor of practice of physic at Edinburgh University, 1876; physician in ordinary to Queen Victoria in Scotland, 1882; knighted, 1894; represented Edinburgh University at Berlin congress on tuberculosis; president, Edinburgh College of Physicians, 1889–91. His works include essays in pure literature and 'A Practical Treatise on Bright's Disease of the Kidneys,' 1869. [Suppl. iii. 360]

STEWART, WALTER (d. 1177), steward of Malcolm IV of Scotland; Robert II was sixth in descent from him. The surname of the royal house of Stuart probably dates from the reign of Malcolm IV, and the person of Walter, since in the prior reign of David I he had been witness to two charters without the designation of Steward. [xlviii. 344]

STEWART, WALTER (1293–1326), high steward of Scotland; son of James Stewart (d. 1309) [q. v.]; shared command of left wing at Bannockburn, 1314; married Marjory Bruce, 1315; first governor of Scotland, 1316; defended Berwick; engaged in attempted surprise of Edward II at Byland Abbey, 1322. [liv. 295]

STEWART, WALTER, EARL OF ATHOLL (d. 1437), second son of Robert II, by second wife; lord of Brechin by marriage, 1378; keeper of Edinburgh Castle; Earl of Caithness, 1402–30; forwarded return of James I, 1424; granted earldom of Strathearn, 1427; joined plot for assassination of James I that his own grandson might succeed; tortured and executed. [liv. 358]

STEWART or **STUART**, WALTER, first LORD BLANTYRE (d. 1617), lord treasurer of Scotland; educated with James VI under Buchanan; prior of Blantyre; keeper of the privy seal, 1582–96; extraordinary lord of session, 1593; an 'octavian,' 1596; treasurer, 1596–9; imprisoned and compelled to resign by James VI, 1599; commissioner for union with England, 1604; created Baron Blantyre, 1606; assessor at trials of George Sprott [q. v.], 1608, and Balmerino, 1609. [liv. 359]

STEWART, SIR WILLIAM (d. 1402), of Jedworth; sheriff of Teviotdale; not identical with Stewart of Castlemilk; progenitor of earls of Galloway; auditor of customs, 1390; 'borow' of Douglas for middle marches, 1398; taken at Homildon Hill; executed by Hotspur as traitor to England. [liv. 360]

STEWART, WILLIAM (1479–1545), bishop of Aberdeen; dean of Glasgow, 1527; lord treasurer of Scotland, 1530–7; bishop of Aberdeen, 1532–45; ambassador to England and France, 1534; built King's College Library, Aberdeen. [liv. 360]

STEWART, WILLIAM (1481?–1550?), Scots chronicler and verse-writer; first licentiate, St. Andrews, 1501; pensioned by James V; poems ascribed to him in Bannatyne and Maitland collections; his metrical version of Hector Boece [q. v.], containing notable additions, printed by William Barclay Turnbull [q. v.], 1858. [liv. 361]

STEWART, SIR WILLIAM (d. 1588), of Monkton; third son of Andrew Stewart, second lord Ochiltree [q. v.]; routed and wounded when commanding Arran's men after raid of Ruthven, 1582; envoy to France, 1587; accused master of Gray, who was convicted; captured John Maxwell, lord Maxwell (1553–1593) [q. v.], and Lochmaben Castle, 1588; killed in brawl at Edinburgh by Francis Stewart, fifth earl of Bothwell [q. v.]. [liv. 361]

STEWART, SIR WILLIAM (*fl.* 1575-1603), of Houston ; favourite of James VI ; colonel in Dutch service, 1580 ; married Flemish wife ; captain of James VI's guard, 1582 ; joint-ambassador to England, 1583 ; James VI's chief instrument in freeing himself from Ruthven raiders, 1583 ; shared influence over him with Arran ; granted Pittenweem priory, 1583 ; frustrated attempts of insurgents on Stirling, 1584 ; induced James VI, Queen Elizabeth, and Mary Stuart to help him in recovering wife's dowry ; overthrown by coup d'état, 1585 ; dismissed ; James VI's secret agent in Denmark and France, 1586 ; convoyed James VI and his queen from Denmark, 1589 ; again privy councillor ; envoy to Germany, 1590 ; sent to Netherlands to negotiate evangelic alliance, 1593 ; knighted and granted Houston, 1593 ; ' gentleman adventurer ' in Lewis, 1598. [liv. 362]

STEWART, SIR WILLIAM, first VISCOUNT MOUNT-JOY (1653-1692), soldier ; succeeded as second baronet, 1662 ; commissioner of claims under (Irish) acts of settlement and explanation, 1675 ; custos of Donegal, 1678 ; created Viscount Mountjoy, 1683 ; master-general of ordnance for life, 1684 ; volunteer at capture of Buda, 1686 ; brigadier in Ireland, 1687 ; sent by Tyrconnel to Londonderry, 1688 ; promised pardon for Ulstermen and protestant garrison : deceived by Tyrconnel and induced to go to Paris, 1689 ; imprisoned there ; attainted and deprived ; exchanged for Richard Hamilton [q. v.], 1692 ; killed in William III's army at Steenkirk. [liv. 364]

STEWART, SIR WILLIAM (1774-1827), lieutenant-general ; brother of Charles James Stewart [q. v.] ; entered army, 1786 ; on staff of Quiberon expedition, 1795 ; commanded 67th foot in San Domingo, 1795-8 ; volunteer with Austro-Russian army at Zurich, 1799 ; lieutenant-colonel of 'riflemen' (afterwards 95th), 1800 ; wounded at Ferrol, 1800 ; commanded marines at Copenhagen, 1801, writing account of the battle ; intimate with Nelson ; published scheme of reform for British army, 1805 ; commanded brigade in Sicily, 1806 ; failed to take Rosetta, 1807 ; led light brigade in Walcheren expedition, 1809 ; lieutenant-general, 1813 ; K.B. for services at Vittoria, 1813 ; wounded in Dona Maria pass ; present at later actions, being prominent at Aire ; G.C.B., 1815 ; M.P., Saltash, 1795, Wigtonshire, 1796-1816 ; thanked personally by speaker, 1814. [liv. 366]

STEWART-MACKENZIE, MARIA ELIZABETH FREDERICA, LADY HOOD (1783-1862), friend of Sir Walter Scott ; accompanied Sir Samuel Hood (1762-1814) [q. v.], her first husband, to East Indies ; succeeded to headship of clan Mackenzie, 1815 ; married James Alexander Stewart of Glasserton, 1817. [liv. 368]

STICHIL, ROBERT DE (d. 1274), bishop of Durham ; monk of Durham ; prior of Finchale ; bishop of Durham, 1260-74 ; attended council of Lyons ; resigned see ; founded hospital at Greatham ; died at L'Arbresle ; buried at Savigny. [liv. 368]

STIGAND (d. 1072), archbishop of Canterbury ; chaplain to Canute and Harold Harefoot ; chief counsellor of Emma [q. v.] ; appointed to see of Elmham, 1038 ; consecrated, 1043 ; deprived but reinstated, 1044 ; bishop of Winchester, 1047 ; employed in negotiations between Edward the Confessor and Earl Godwin [q. v.], 1051-2 ; uncanonically appointed archbishop, 1052 ; excommunicated by five popes ; received pall from Benedict X (afterwards declared uncanonical), 1058 ; probably did not crown Harold ; joined in electing Edgar Atheling [q. v.] after Hastings ; submitted and helped to crown William I, 1066 ; condemned by papal legates for usurpation, receiving pall from schismatic, and plurality, 1070 ; deprived of Canterbury and Winchester ; imprisoned ; buried in the cathedral abbey of St. Swithin, Winchester. [liv. 369]

STILL, JOHN (1543 ?-1608), bishop of Bath and Wells ; M.A. Christ's College, Cambridge, 1565, D.D., 1575 ; fellow, c. 1562 ; Margaret professor of divinity, Cambridge, 1570-1573 ; rector of Hadleigh, 1571 ; chaplain to Archbishop Parker, 1572 ; canon of Westminster, 1573 ; master of St. John's College, Cambridge, 1574-7, of Trinity, 1577-1608 ; twice vice-chancellor ; archdeacon of Sudbury, 1577 ; chosen Cambridge delegate to diet at Schmalkald, 1578 ; prolocutor of Canterbury convocation, 1589 ; bishop of Bath and Wells, 1593-1608 ; benefactor to Bubwith's Hospital, Wells, and Trinity College, Cambridge ; authorship of 'Gammer Gurton's Needle' (second English

comedy ; played at Christ's College ; published, 1575) attributed to him on inconclusive evidence by Isaac Reed [q. v.] [liv. 370]

STILLINGFLEET, BENJAMIN (1702-1771), botanist and author ; grandson of Edward Stillingfleet (1635-1699) [q. v.] ; scholar and B.A. Trinity College, Cambridge, 1723 ; tutor to Ashe-Windham's son William ; explored Mer de Glace, Chamounix, 1741 ; received pension from Windham, having charge later of his son ; obtained a sinecure through his influence with Lord Barrington ; attended assemblies of Mrs. Agmondesham Vesey at Bath, c. 1748, originating term ' blue-stocking ' by his dress ; became acquainted with Linnean system, 1750-5 ; wrote librettos for oratorios ; ' Paradise Lost ' (1760) set by John Christopher Smith [q. v.], performed at Covent Garden, London, 1760 ; first proposed English names for grasses ; genus of euphorbiaceous plants named after him ; chief works, ' Miscellaneous Tracts relating to Natural History, Husbandry, and Physick,' 1759, containing preface which introduced Linnean principles into England, and ' Observations on Grasses.' [liv. 373]

STILLINGFLEET, EDWARD (1635-1699), bishop of Worcester ; fellow of St. John's College, Cambridge, 1653 ; M.A., 1656 ; incorporated at Oxford, 1677 ; D.D., 1668 ; preacher at Rolls Chapel and reader at the Temple ; prebendary of St. Paul's, London, 1667 ; canon of Canterbury, 1669 ; popular London preacher ; chaplain to Charles II ; friend of Sir Matthew Hale [q. v.] ; archdeacon of London, 1677 ; dean of St. Paul's, London, 1678 ; prolocutor of lower house ; bishop of Worcester, 1689-99 ; member of commission to revise prayer-book and consider ' comprehension ' ; frequent speaker in parliament ; adviser of Tenison when primate ; had controversy with Locke on the Trinity, 1696-7 ; reformed procedure of consistory court ; his manuscripts bought by Harley, books by Narcissus Marsh [q. v.] His works (edited by Bentley, 1710) include ' The Irenicum,' 1659 (suggesting compromise with presbyterians), ' Origines Sacræ,' 1662, also a treatise on jurisdiction of bishops in capital cases, and ' Origines Britannicæ,' 1685. [liv. 375]

STILLINGFLEET, EDWARD (1660 ?-1708), Gresham professor of physic ; son of Edward Stillingfleet (1635-1699) [q. v.] ; M.A. St. John's College, Cambridge, 1685, M.D., 1692 ; F.R.S. and Gresham professor of physic, 1698 ; held various rectories. [liv. 373]

STILLINGTON, ROBERT (d. 1491), bishop of Bath and Wells and lord chancellor ; doctor of civil and canon law, Oxford ; principal, Deep Hall, Oxford, 1442 ; canon of Wells, 1445 ; prebendary of York and Southwell ; dean of St. Martin's, London, 1458-85 ; bishop of Bath and Wells, 1466-91 ; Yorkist keeper of privy seal, 1460 ; lord chancellor, 1467-75, with short intervals ; imprisoned by Edward IV, probably for hostility to the Woodvilles ; supported Richard III ; imprisoned, but pardoned by Henry VII ; again imprisoned for share in Simnel's rebellion ; founded college at Nether Acaster. [liv. 378]

STIRLING. [See also STERLING.]

STIRLING, EARL OF (1567 ?-1640). [See ALEXANDER, SIR WILLIAM.]

STIRLING, CHARLES (1760-1833), vice-admiral ; son of Sir Walter Stirling [q. v.] ; captain, 1783, for capture of American privateer Congress, 1781 ; resident commissioner, Jamaica, 1803-4 ; rear-admiral, 1804 ; with Rochefort squadron took part in action off Cape Finisterre, 1805 ; naval commander of South American expedition, 1806 ; commander-in-chief at the Cape, 1807, in Jamaica, 1811-13 ; vice-admiral, 1810 ; removed and placed on half-pay for corruption, 1814. [liv. 384]

STIRLING, JAMES (1692-1770), mathematician (' the Venetian ') ; educated at Glasgow and Oxford Universities ; expelled from Oxford for corresponding with Jacobites, 1715 ; studied ten years at Venice ; discovered secret of Venetian glass-making ; came to London, c. 1725 ; F.R.S., 1726 ; friend of Newton ; manager to Scots Mining Company, Leadhills, 1735 ; made first survey of the Clyde ; chief work, ' Methodus Differentialis, sive Tractatus de Summatione et Interpolatione Serierum Infinitarum,' 1730 (translated, 1749). [liv. 379]

STIRLING, SIR JAMES, first baronet (1740 ?-1805), lord provost of Edinburgh ; secretary to governor of

Jamaica ; town councillor, Edinburgh, 1771, treasurer, 1773–4, provost, 1790, 1794, and 1798 ; created baronet for services in reform riots, 1792. [liv. 380]

STIRLING, Sir JAMES (1791–1865), admiral and first governor of Western Australia ; nephew of Charles Stirling [q. v.], under whom he served at Finisterre, 1805, in South America, 1807, and West Indies, 1811–13 ; formed settlement in Raffles Bay, Torres Strait, 1826 ; governor of Western Australia, 1829–39 ; rear-admiral, 1851 ; commander in China and East Indies, 1854–6 ; admiral, 1862 ; knight of the Redeemer. [liv. 380]

STIRLING, Mrs. MARY ANN (FANNY), afterwards LADY GREGORY (1815–1895), actress ; *née* Kehl ; first appeared as Fanny Clifton at the Coburg, London ; played leading parts at the Pavilion, London, 1832 ; married Edward Stirling or Lambert ; appeared as Mrs. Stirling at the Adelphi, London, under Mrs. Nisbett ; made hit as Sally Snow ; with Macready at Drury Lane, London, 1842 ; Cordelia to Macready's Lear (Princess's, London), 1845 ; her greatest part Peg Woffington in 'Masks and Faces ' at Haymarket, London, 1852 ; played Lady Bountiful ('Beaux' Stratagem ') and Mrs. Hardcastle, 1879, Mrs. Malaprop, 1880 ; Nurse in 'Romeo and Juliet' at Lyceum, London, 1882 and 1884 ; her last part, Martha, in Wills's 'Faust,' 1885 ; partially retired after 1870 ; recited and taught elocution at Royal Academy of Music ; married Sir Charles Hutton Gregory, 1894. [liv. 381]

STIRLING, ROBERT (1790–1878), inventor of heated air engine and constructor of scientific instruments ; minister of Galston, 1824–78 ; hon. D.D. St. Andrews, 1840. [liv. 383]

STIRLING, Sir THOMAS, first baronet (1733–1808), general ; served in Scots brigade of Holland, 1747–57 ; captain, 42nd highlanders, 1757 ; at conquest of Canada and Martinique, 1759, the Havannah, 1762 ; commanded 42nd foot during American war, 1776–80 ; general, 1801 ; created baronet ; succeeded also to Ardoch baronetcy. [liv. 383]

STIRLING, Sir WALTER (1718–1786), captain in the navy ; lieutenant, 1746 ; captain, 1759 ; knighted after Hood's capture of St. Eustatius, 1780 ; commodore at the Nore, 1782. [liv. 384]

STIRLING-MAXWELL, Sir WILLIAM, ninth baronet (1818–1878), historical writer and virtuoso ; B.A. Trinity College, Cambridge, 1839, M.A., 1843 ; visited Spain and the Levant ; contributed to 'Fraser's Magazine' and the 'Examiner' ; succeeded to Keir estates, 1847 ; M.P., Perthshire, 1852–68 and 1874–8 ; member of universities commission, 1859, of Historical Manuscripts Commission (1872–8), and of Scottish education board ; original member of Philobiblon Society, 1854 ; rector of St. Andrews University, 1862, Edinburgh, 1872 ; succeeded to Maxwell baronetcy, assuming additional name, 1865 ; chancellor of Glasgow, hon. D.C.L. Oxford, and K.T., 1876 ; member of London University senate, 1874–8 ; trustee of British Museum and National Gallery ; breeder of shorthorns and Clydesdale horses ; ardent bibliographer and collector of works of art ; pioneer of Spanish art ; died at Venice. His 'Works' (collected, 1891) include 'Annals of the Artists of Spain,' 1848 ('Velazquez' issued separately, 1855), 'The Cloister Life of Charles V,' 1852 (enlarged, 1891), and monographs on the bibliography of proverbs. [liv. 384]

STISTED, Sir HENRY WILLIAM (1817–1875), lieutenant-general ; ensign, 1835 ; served in Afghanistan and Baluchistan ; lieutenant-colonel, 78th foot, 1850 ; commanded brigade in Persian war, 1856–7 ; led Havelock's advance guard at relief of Lucknow, 1857 ; C.B., 1858 ; commanded second brigade at Bareilly, 1858 ; lieutenant-colonel, 93rd, 1859 ; lieutenant-governor of Ontario, 1867 ; K.C.B., 1871. [liv. 387]

STOCK, JOSEPH (1740–1813), Irish bishop ; scholar, Trinity College, Dublin, 1759, B.A., 1761, fellow, 1763 ; head-master of Portera Royal School, 1795 ; bishop of Killala, 1798–1810, of Waterford and Lismore, 1810–13 ; captured by General Humbert, 1798 ; works include account of French invasion of Mayo, 1799, life of George Berkeley (1685–1753) [q. v.], 1776, and translations of Isaiah and Job. [liv. 388]

STOCK, RICHARD (1569 ?–1626), puritan divine ; scholar, St. John's College, Cambridge, 1587 ; M.A., 1594 ; incorporated at Oxford ; rector of Standlake, 1596, of

All Hallows, Bread Street, London, 1611–26 ; published theological works. [liv. 389]

STOCK, St. SIMEON (1165 ?–1265). [See SIMEON.]

STOCKDALE, JOHN (1749 ?–1814), publisher ; porter to John Almon [q. v.] ; after his retirement set up business ; issued Dr. Johnson's 'Works,' 1787 (editing two volumes), and 'Debates in Parliament,' 1784–90 ; prosecuted for libel in connection with Logan's 'Review of the Charges against Warren Hastings,' 1789 ; defended by Erskine and acquitted ; had to pay damages to Joseph Nightingale [q. v.], 1809. [liv. 389]

STOCKDALE, JOHN JOSEPH (1770–1847), publisher and compiler ; son of John Stockdale [q. v.] ; obtained verdicts in action for libel against Messrs. Hansard (parliamentary publishers), 1836 and 1839, who claimed privilege, and obtained it by act of 1840. [liv. 390]

STOCKDALE, PERCIVAL (1736–1811), author ; studied at Aberdeen, 1754 ; sailed in Byng's expedition for relief of Minorca, 1756 ; went to London, c. 1760, and mixed in literary society ; conducted 'Critical Review' and 'Universal Magazine' ; chaplain of Resolution guardship, 1773–6 ; defended Pope's writings against Warton's essay, 1778 ; rector of Hinxworth, 1780, of Lesbury and Long Houghton, 1783 ; M.A. Lambeth, 1784 ; his numerous works include 'The Poet,' 1773, an edition with biography of Thomson's 'Seasons' (1793), translations, criticism, and 'Memoirs,' 1809. [liv. 390]

STOCKER, THOMAS (*fl.* 1569–1592), translator of Calvin's works and books by French authors. [liv. 392]

STOCKS, ARTHUR (1846–1889), painter ; third son of Lumb Stocks [q. v.] ; exhibited at Royal Academy, 1867–89 ; member of Institute of Painters in Water-colours. [liv. 393]

STOCKS, LUMB (1812–1892), line-engraver ; articled to Charles Rolls ; first exhibited at Royal Academy, 1832 ; executed plates for annuals and Finden's 'Gallery of British Art' ; associate engraver, Royal Academy, 1853 ; R.A., 1871. [liv. 392]

STOCKTON, OWEN (1630–1680), puritan divine ; B.A. Christ's College, Cambridge, 1649 ; senior fellow Caius College, Cambridge, 1652–8 ; received presbyterian ordination, 1655 ; town lecturer at Colchester, 1657–61 ; preached afterwards at Colchester, Ipswich, and Hadleigh ; presented in ecclesiastical court as conventicle holder, 1669 ; benefactor of Caius College, Cambridge, and Harvard ; published devotional works. [liv. 393]

STOCKWOOD, JOHN (*d.* 1610), schoolmaster and divine ; B.A. Heidelberg, 1567 (incorporated, Oxford, 1575) ; M.A. Oxford, 1575, Cambridge, 1579 ; minister of Battle, 1571 ; head-master of Tonbridge school, 1578, vicar, 1585–1610 ; celebrated preacher ; protected by Sir Robert Sidney ; published school manuals and translations of devotional works. [liv. 394]

STOCQUELER, JOACHIM HAYWARD (1800–1885), compiler ; edited papers and published 'Fifteen Months' Pilgrimage through Khuzistan and Persia ' (1832), 'Memorials of Affghanistan ' (1843), and other works while in India, 1821–41 ; lectured in London on Indian subjects and Crimean war, 1841–56 ; correspondent in American war ; his 'Autobiography' suppressed in India, c. 1873 ; published military compilations and historical manuals (as J. H. Siddons). [liv. 395]

STODDART, CHARLES (1806–1842), soldier and diplomatist ; entered staff corps, 1823 ; captain on half-pay, 1834 ; secretary to United Service Institution, 1833–1835 ; military secretary to British envoy in Persia, 1835 ; in Persian camp during siege of Herat, 1837–8 ; presented ultimatum to Mahomed Shah which stopped war, 1838 ; envoy to Bokhara to negotiate release of Russian prisoners and treaty with Nasrulla Khan, 1838 ; imprisoned during some months ; released temporarily, 1839 and 1841 ; communicated to Palmerston ameer's wish for English alliance, 1841 ; again imprisoned, and with Arthur Conolly [q. v.] beheaded, 1842. [liv. 396]

STODDART, Sir JOHN (1773–1856), journalist and judge in Malta ; brother-in-law of Hazlitt ; B.A. Christ Church, Oxford, 1794, D.C.L., 1801 ; king's and admiralty advocate, Malta, 1803–7, chief-justice, 1826–40 ; knighted, 1826 ; contributor to 'Times,' 1812–16 ; conducted 'New

Times,' 1817–26 ; called ' Dr. Slop ' ; published ' Remarks on the Local Scenery and Manners of Scotland,' 1801, legal pamphlets and translations. [liv. 397]

STODDART, THOMAS TOD (1810–1880), angler and author ; published ' The Death-wake,' 1831, ' Angler's Companion to the Rivers and Lakes of Scotland,' 1847, and ' Songs of the Seasons,' 1873 (with autobiography, 1881). [liv. 398]

STOGDON, HUBERT (1692–1728), nonconformist divine ; presbyterian minister near Exeter, 1715, at Wookey, 1718–24 ; rebaptised by immersion ; pædobaptist pastor, Trowbridge, 1724–8 ; published theological works, with posthumous ' Poems and Letters.' [liv. 399]

STOKES, DAVID (1591 ?–1669), divine ; of Westminster School and Trinity College, Cambridge ; M.A. and fellow of Peterhouse, Cambridge, 1618 ; fellow of Eton, 1624 ; canon of Windsor and precentor of Chichester, 1628 ; D.D., 1630 ; deprived as royalist of all benefices ; incorporated at Oxford, 1645 ; reinstated, 1660 ; published theological works. [liv. 399]

STOKES, GEORGE THOMAS (1843–1898), Irish ecclesiastical historian ; B.A. Trinity College, Dublin, 1864, M.A., 1871, D.D., 1886 ; ordained, 1866 ; vicar of All Saints, Newtown Park, co. Dublin, 1868–98 ; prebendary and canon of St. Patrick's Cathedral, Dublin, 1893 ; deputyprofessor and (1883) professor of ecclesiastical history at Dublin ; librarian of St. Patrick's Library, Dublin, 1887 ; chief works, ' Ireland and the Celtic Church,' 1886, ' Ireland and the Anglo-Norman Church,' 1888, ' Commentary on the Acts of the Apostles ' (for the ' Expositor's Bible '), 1891. [Suppl. iii. 361]

STOKES, HENRY SEWELL (1808–1895), Cornish poet ; schoolfellow of Dickens at Chatham ; established ' Cornish Guardian,' 1833 ; mayor of Truro, 1856, town clerk, 1859 ; clerk of the peace for Cornwall, 1865–95 ; entertained Tennyson, 1848 ; published verse. [liv. 399]

STOKES, JOHN LORT (1812–1885), admiral ; entered navy, 1826 ; commanded the Beagle during survey of Timor and New Zealand, 1841–3 ; surveyed New Zealand, 1847–51 ; admiral, 1877 ; published (1846) account of Beagle explorations, 1837–43. [liv. 400]

STOKES, MARGARET M'NAIR (1832–1900), Irish archæologist ; daughter of William Stokes [q. v.] ; published, 1861, an illuminated edition of Sir Samuel Ferguson's poem, ' The Cromlech on Howth,' and was subsequently engaged on numerous publications relating to Irish archæology ; edited and contributed drawings to the Earl of Dunraven's ' Notes on Irish Architecture,' 1875–7 ; her work, ' The High Crosses of Ireland ' (partly published, 1898), remained unfinished at her death. She was an honorary member of the Royal Irish Academy and of the Royal Society of Antiquaries of Ireland. [Suppl. iii. 362]

STOKES, PETER (d. 1399), Carmelite of Hitchin ; D.D. of Oxford ; Archbishop Courtenay's agent in proceedings against Wycliffites at Oxford, 1382 ; wrote work defending William Ockham [q. v.] [liv. 401]

STOKES, WHITLEY (1763–1845), regius professor of medicine, Trinity College, Dublin, 1830–43 ; fellow, 1787, M.D., 1793, senior fellow, 1805, natural-history lecturer, 1816 ; suspended for nationalist opinions, 1798–1800. [liv. 401]

STOKES, WILLIAM (1804–1878), physician ; son of Whitley Stokes [q. v.] ; M.D. Edinburgh, 1825, Dublin, 1839 ; physician to Meath Hospital ; with Robert James Graves [q. v.] reformed chemical teaching ; edited ' Dublin Journal of Medical Science ' ; founded Pathological Society, 1838 ; regius professor of medicine from 1845 ; physician to Queen Victoria in Ireland, 1861 ; F.R.S., 1861 ; president, Royal Irish Academy, 1874 ; awarded Prussian order Pour le Mérite, 1876 ; works include treatises on diseases of the chest (1837) and of the heart (1854). [liv. 401]

STOKES, Sir WILLIAM (1839–1900), surgeon ; son of William Stokes (1804–1878) [q. v.] ; B.A. Trinity College, Dublin, 1859, M.B., M.D., and M.Ch., 1863 ; L.R.C.S. Ireland, 1862, and F.R.C.S., 1874 ; studied at Paris, Berlin, Vienna, and Prague ; practised in Dublin ; professor of surgery at Royal College of Surgeons of Ireland, 1872, president, 1886–7 ; knighted, 1886 ; surgeon in ordinary to Queen Victoria in Ireland, 1892 ; consulting

surgeon to British military forces in Natal, 1900 ; published a life of his father in ' Masters of Medicine ' series, 1898 ; died of pleurisy at Pietermaritzburg. [Suppl. iii. 363]

STOKESLEY, JOHN (1475 ?–1539), bishop of London : fellow of Magdalen College, Oxford, c. 1495, vicepresident, 1505 ; principal of Magdalen Hall, Oxford, 1498 ; chaplain and almoner to Henry VIII, 1509 ; dean of Chapel Royal, London, 1524 ; envoy to France, 1529 ; tried to win over Italian universities to Henry VIII's divorce from Catherine, 1530 ; part-author of book in favour of the divorce, 1531 ; bishop of London, 1530–9 ; concurred in anti-papal measures ; joined Cuthbert Tunstall [q. v.] in remonstrance with Pole, 1537 ; condemned John Frith [q. v.] and other protestants ; opposed translation of bible into English ; resisted Cranmer's visitation ; incurred Cromwell's hostility ; accused of infringing statutes by excusing bull of Martin V, 1538 ; produced royal pardon. [liv. 403]

STONE, ALFRED (1840–1878), musician ; organist at Clifton and Bristol churches ; conducted Bristol Orpheus Society, 1876–8 ; organised and trained choir which won prize at first Crystal Palace music meeting, 1872 ; organised first Bristol musical festival, 1873 ; jointeditor of ' Bristol Tune Book,' 1863 ; advocated tonic sol-fa. [liv. 405]

STONE, ANDREW (1703–1773), under-secretary of state ; M.A. Oxford, 1728 ; as private secretary and undersecretary of state (1734) exercised much influence over Newcastle and Henry Pelham (1695 ?–1754) [q. v.] ; M.P., Hastings, 1741–61 ; joint-secretary to lords justices, 1744 ; commissioner of trade, 1749–61 ; accused of toasting the Pretender, but retained confidence of the court ; treasurer to Queen Charlotte, 1761 ; one of the ' king's friends ' ; left important political correspondence. [liv. 405]

STONE, BENJAMIN (fl. 1630–1642), sword-maker ; established on Hounslow Heath, c. 1630, earliest known English sword-factory. [liv. 407]

STONE, EDMUND (d. 1768), mathematician ; son of a gardener ; self-educated ; F.R.S., 1725 ; died in poverty ; chief works, ' New Mathematical Dictionary,' 1725, and ' The Method of Fluxions, both direct and inverse ' (the former translated, latter original), 1730. [liv. 407]

STONE, EDWARD JAMES (1831–1897), astronomer ; fifth wrangler, 1859 ; fellow, Queens' College, Cambridge, 1859–72, hon. fellow, 1875 ; chief assistant, Greenwich Observatory, 1860–70 ; detected ' variation of latitude ' ; gold medallist, Royal Astronomical Society, 1869 ; astronomer-royal at the Cape, 1870–9 ; received Lalande prize, 1881, for his Cape catalogue of 12,441 stars (completed, 1894) ; observed total solar eclipse of 16 April 1874, and transit of Venus, 8 Dec. 1874 ; Radcliffe observer, Oxford, 1879–97 ; organised transit of Venus expeditions, 1882 ; F.R.S. ; P.R.A.S., 1882–4 ; D.Sc. Padua, 1892 ; made spectroscopic observations of solar eclipse at Novaya Zemlya, 1896. [liv. 408]

STONE, FRANCIS (1738 ?–1813), unitarian ; captain of Charterhouse, London ; M.A. University College, Oxford, 1766 ; became Arian while curate to Henry Taylor [q. v.] ; rector of Cold Norton, Essex, 1765–1808 ; published pamphlet, ' Tyro-Theologus,' 1768 ; chairman of petitioning clergy ; deprived, 1808, for sermon at Danbury, 1806, advocating unitarian views ; supported by unitarians, but died a debtor ; published economical and political pamphlets. [liv. 409]

STONE, FRANK (1800–1859), painter ; self-educated ; associated exhibitor, Water-colour Society, 1833, member, 1842–6 ; first exhibited at Royal Academy, 1837, winning rapid popularity ; A.R.A., 1851 ; intimate with Dickens. [liv. 410]

STONE, GEORGE (1708 ?–1764), archbishop of Armagh ; brother of Andrew Stone [q. v.] ; M.A., 1732, D.D., 1740 ; bishop of Ferns and Leighlin, 1740–3, Kildare, 1743–5, Derry, 1745–7 ; dean of Christ Church, Dublin, 1743–5 ; archbishop of Armagh, 1747–64 ; Irish privy councillor and a lord justice, 1747 ; rival of Boyle ; supported claim of crown to surplus revenues, 1749–53 ; excluded from regency, 1756 ; restored, 1758, but thenceforth shared power with Shannon (Boyle) and Ponsonby ; the ' Cardinal Lapidario ' of ' Baratariana.' [liv. 410]

STONE, GILBERT (*d.* 1417 ?), mediæval letter-writer; prebendary of Wells, 1384, Hereford, and St. Paul's, London, 1412–17; some of his letters in Bodley and James collections, Oxford.   [liv. 412]

STONE, HENRY (*d.* 1653), painter ('Old Stone'); eldest son of Nicholas Stone the elder [q. v.]; successful copyist of Vandyck.   [liv. 414]

STONE, JEROME (1727–1756), self-taught linguist and poet; head-master of Dunkeld grammar school; contributor to 'Scots Magazine.'   [liv. 413]

STONE, JOHN (*d.* 1667), mason and statuary; youngest son of Nicholas Stone the elder [q. v.]; royalist; last survivor of family.   [liv. 415]

STONE, JOHN HURFORD (1763–1818), political refugee; intimate with Price, Priestley, and Madame de Genlis; prominent member of Society of Friends of the Revolution; led English celebrations in Paris of French victories in Belgium, 1792; imprisoned there, 1793 and 1794; lived with Helen Maria Williams [q. v.]; engaged in conspiracy against England, 1795; printer in Paris; naturalised, 1817; published French unitarian pamphlet as 'Photinus,' 1800.   [liv. 413]

STONE, NICHOLAS, the elder (1586–1647), mason, statuary, and architect; worked in Amsterdam under Pieter de Keyser; employed by James I; carried out designs of Inigo Jones; designed and executed porch of St. Mary's, Oxford, and gates of Botanic Garden, Oxford; master-mason and architect at Windsor, 1626; best known for his tombs, including those of Bodley at Oxford and Donne at St. Paul's, London; published 'Enchiridion of Fortification,' 1645.   [liv. 414]

STONE, NICHOLAS, the younger (*d.* 1647), mason and statuary; son of Nicholas Stone the elder [q. v.]; worked under Bernini in Italy.   [liv. 415]

STONE, SAMUEL (1602–1663), puritan divine; M.A. Emmanuel College, Cambridge, 1627; accompanied Thomas Hooker [q. v.] as teacher to New England, 1633, settling at Newtown (Cambridge); removed to Hartford, 1636; published 'A Congregational Church, a Catholike Visible Church,' 1652; died at Hartford.   [liv. 415]

STONE, WILLIAM (1603 ?–1661 ?), proprietary governor of Maryland, 1648–54; condemned to death by parliamentary commissioners, 1654, but pardoned; reappointed councillor, 1659.   [liv. 415]

STONEHENGE (editor of the 'Field'). [See WALSH, JOHN HENRY, 1810–1888.]

STONEHEWER or **STONHEWER**, RICHARD (1728 ?–1809), friend of Gray; scholar, Trinity College, Cambridge, 1747; eighth wrangler, 1750; fellow of Peterhouse, 1751; tutor of Augustus Henry, third duke of Grafton [q. v.]; afterwards private secretary; under-secretary, northern department, 1765, southern, 1766; permanent auditor of excise; obtained for Gray Cambridge professorship; inherited from Mason Gray's library, holograph poems, and correspondence.   [liv. 416]

STONFORD, JOHN DE (1290 ?–1372 ?). [See STOWFORD.]

STONHOUSE, SIR JAMES, eleventh baronet (1716–1795), physician and divine; M.A. St. John's College, Oxford, 1739, M.D., 1746; studied medicine at St. Thomas's Hospital, London, and French universities; practised at Northampton, 1743–63, founding the county infirmary; under influence of Philip Doddridge [q. v.] took holy orders, 1749, but continued medical practice; attended James Hervey (1714–1758) [q. v.] in last illness; rector of Little Cheverell, 1764, with Great Cheverell, 1779; lived in Bristol, preaching there and at Bath; Hannah More's 'Shepherd of Salisbury Plain'; succeeded to baronetcy, 1792; published 'Every Man's Assistant and the Sick Man's Friend,' 1788, and popular devotional tracts.   [liv. 417]

STONOR, JOHN DE (*d.* 1354), judge; summoned to parliament as serjeant, 1313; justice of common pleas, 1320; chief baron of the exchequer, 1329; chief-justice of common pleas, 1329–31, 1334–40, 1342–54; imprisoned, 1340.   [liv. 418]

STOPES, LEONARD (1540 ?–1587 ?), seminary priest; original scholar, St. John's College, Oxford, 1555, afterwards fellow; ejected, 1559; imprisoned at Wisbech on return from continent; exiled.   [liv. 419]

STOPES, RICHARD (*fl.* 1521–1544), last abbot of Meaux or Melsa, Yorkshire; B.D. St. Bernard's College, Oxford, 1521.   [liv. 419]

STOPFORD, JAMES (*d.* 1759), Irish bishop; friend of Swift; scholar, Trinity College, Dublin, 1713, fellow, 1717–27, M.A., 1718; vicar of Finglas, 1727; provost of Tuam, 1730; archdeacon of Killaloe, 1736; dean of Kilmacduagh, 1748; bishop of Cloyne, 1753–9.   [liv. 419]

STOPFORD, JOSHUA (1636–1675), divine; foundation clerk, Magdalen College, Oxford, 1656; M.A. and B.D., 1670; morning lecturer, Old Church, Manchester, 1650; encouraged Booth's rising, 1659; prebendary of York, 1660; vicar of Kirkby Stephen and rector of All Saints', York, 1663; vicar, St. Martin's, York, 1667; his 'Pagano-Papismus' (1675) re-edited, 1844.   [liv. 420]

STOPFORD, SIR ROBERT (1768–1847), admiral; entered navy, 1780; present at relief of Gibraltar, 1781, action of 12 April, 1782, at West Indies, and action of 1 June 1794; commanded Phaeton in retreat of Admiral William Cornwallis [q. v.], 1795; with Nelson in chase to West Indies, 1805; received gold medal for conduct in battle of San Domingo, 1806; in Rio and Copenhagen expeditions, 1806–7; rear-admiral, 1808; blockaded Rochefort and destroyed French ships, 1808; commander at the Cape, 1810; took naval command of Java expedition, 1811; admiral, 1825; G.C.B., 1831; G.C.M.G., 1837; commander at Portsmouth, 1827–30, of Mediterranean fleet, 1837–41; conducted operations against Mehemet Ali, 1840; governor of Greenwich, 1841–7.   [liv. 420]

STORACE, ANNA (or ANN) SELINA (1766–1817), vocalist and actress; pupil of Rauzzini and Sacchini; gained first great success at Florence, 1780; sang at La Scala, Milan, 1782; original Susanna in 'Nozze di Figaro,' Vienna, 1784; married John Abraham Fisher [q. v.]; separated from him; appeared in comic operas in London, 1787; original Margaretta ('No Song no Supper'), 1790, Barbara ('Iron Chest'), 1796; sang at Handel festival, 1791; first played Rosina, 1795; formed connection with John Braham [q. v.]; sang with him in Paris, 1797, Italy, Vienna, and Hamburg, 1798–1801, and afterwards at Covent Garden, London, and Drury Lane, London; retired, 1808.   [liv. 421]

STORACE, STEPHEN (1763–1796), musical composer; brother of Anna Storace [q. v.]; studied at Naples; met Mozart at Vienna; engaged by Linley as composer to Drury Lane, London, 1787; gained great success with his operas, 'The Haunted Tower,' 1789, 'The Pirate,' 1792, and 'The Iron Chest,' 1796; also composed string quartet in which Haydn and Mozart played, and good ballads.   [liv. 423]

STORER, ANTHONY MORRIS (1746–1799), collector; friend of fifth Earl of Carlisle at Eton and Cambridge; accompanied him to America, 1778–9; commissioner of trade, 1781; M.P., Carlisle, 1774–80, Morpeth, 1780–4; intimate with Lord North; sent by Fox to Paris as secretary of legation, 1783, afterwards plenipotentiary; conspicuous in society; assisted Edward Harwood (1729–1794) [q. v.] in 'Views of the Classics'; purchased Purley, 1793; F.S.A., 1777; member of Dilettanti Society, 1790; left library and prints to Eton.   [liv. 423]

STORER, HENRY SARGANT (1795–1837), draughtsman and engraver; exhibited drawings at Royal Academy, 1814–36; collaborated with his father, James Sargant Storer [q. v.] in 'Cathedrals of Great Britain,' 1814–19, 'The Portfolio,' 1823–4, and similar works; engraved independently.   [liv. 424]

STORER, JAMES SARGANT (1771–1853), draughtsman and engraver; collaborated with John Greig in 'Antiquarian and Topographical Cabinet,' 1807–11, and other works, and from 1814 with his son.   [liv. 424]

STORER, THOMAS (1571–1604), author of 'Life and Death of Thomas Wolsey, cardinall' (poem), 1599 (reissued, 1826); student of Christ Church, Oxford, 1587; M.A., 1604.   [liv. 424]

STORKS, SIR HENRY KNIGHT (1811–1874), lieutenant-general; ensign, 1828; assistant adjutant-general in Kaffir war, 1846–7; assistant military secretary, Mauritius, 1849–54; had charge of British establishments in Turkey during Crimean war; K.C.B., 1857; high commissioner of Ionian islands, 1859–63; G.C.M.G., 1860; major-general, 1862; G.C.B., 1864; governor of Malta, 1864–5; special commissioner and governor of Jamaica

1865–6; privy councillor, 1866; controller-in-chief of war office, 1867–70; surveyor-general of ordnance, 1870–4; lieutenant-general, 1871; M.P., Ripon, 1871–4; assisted Cardwell in abolition of purchase. [liv. 425]

STORMONT, first VISCOUNT (*d.* 1631). [See MURRAY, DAVID.]

STORY, EDWARD (*d.* 1503), bishop successively of Carlisle (1468) and Chichester (1477); fellow of Pembroke Hall, Cambridge, *c.* 1444; master of Michaelhouse, 1450; chaplain to Queen Elizabeth (Woodville); twice chancellor of Cambridge; procured annexation to Chichester school of canonry and prebend, 1498, and erected cross. [liv. 426]

STORY, GEORGE WALTER (*d.* 1721), author of 'An Impartial History of the War in Ireland,' 1691, with 'Continuation,' 1693; accompanied (as regimental chaplain) Schomberg to Ireland; present at the Boyne, 1690, and siege of Limerick, 1691; dean of Connor, 1694, of Limerick, 1705. [liv. 427]

STORY, JOHN (1510 ?–1571), Roman catholic martyr; B.C.L. Hincksey Hall, Oxford, 1531, civil law lecturer, 1535, D.C.L., 1538; first regius professor, 1544; advocate, Doctors' Commons, 1539; M.P., Hindon, 1547; recanted, but opposed Act of Uniformity; imprisoned, 1548–9, by House of Commons; retired to Louvain; excepted from pardon, 1552; chancellor of London and Oxford and dean of arches, 1553; active persecutor of protestants; queen's proctor for Cranmer's trial, 1555; M.P., East Grinstead, Bramber, Ludgershall, Downton, 1553–9; opposed admission of papal licenses, 1555; took oath renouncing foreign jurisdiction, 1558; imprisoned, 1560; escaped from Marshalsea to Flanders by help of Spanish ambassador, 1563; said to have instigated establishment of Inquisition at Antwerp, 1565; pensioned by Philip II; kidnapped for English government, 1570; convicted of treason and executed at Tyburn; beatified, 1886. [liv. 427]

STORY, ROBERT (1790–1859), minister of Roseneath, 1818–59; educated at Edinburgh; tutor to James Andrew Broun Ramsay, earl of Dalhousie [q. v.]; exposed his parishioner, Mary Campbell, who claimed 'gift of tongues,' 1830; published 'Peace in Believing,' 1829; part-author of 'The Institute' (satirical poem), 1811. [liv. 430]

STORY, ROBERT (1795–1860), Northumbrian poet; son of a peasant at Wark; schoolmaster at Gargrave; received post in audit office for support of conservatism, 1843; 'Poetical Works' issued by Duke of Northumberland, 1857 (selection edited, 1861). [liv. 430]

STORY, THOMAS (1670 ?–1742), quaker; brother of George Warter Story [q. v.]; assisted by William Penn [q. v.] and appointed registrar of Society of Friends, 1695; accompanied Penn to Ireland, 1698; preceded him to Pennsylvania; recorder of Philadelphia, 1701; treasurer of Pennsylvania Land Company; visited West Indies; returned to London, 1714; preached in Oxford, Holland (1715), Ireland, Scotland, and Bath; his 'Journal' (1747) twice abridged, and reprinted, 1846. [liv. 431]

STOTHARD, MRS. ANNA ELIZA (1790–1883). [See BRAY.]

STOTHARD, CHARLES ALFRED (1786–1821), antiquarian draughtsman; son of Thomas Stothard [q. v.]; student, Royal Academy, 1807; prepared ten parts (first issued, 1811) of 'Monumental Effigies of Great Britain'; as historical draughtsman to Society of Antiquaries made drawings of Bayeux tapestry, writing important essay on its date, 1806 (drawings in 'Vetusta Monumenta' 1821, 1823); F.S.A., 1818; killed by fall from ladder at Beerferris. [liv. 432]

STOTHARD, THOMAS (1755–1834), painter and book-illustrator; student, Royal Academy, 1777; first exhibited at Society of Artists, 1777, at Academy, 1778; began book illustrations, 1779; R.A., 1794, librarian, 1812; designed Wellington's shield, 1814; decorated Burghley House and Advocates' Library, Edinburgh; intimate with Flaxman, Beckford of Fonthill, and Samuel Rogers; among his pictures 'Dryads finding Narcissus,' the 'Canterbury Pilgrims setting forth from the Tabard Inn,' and 'The Vintage'; executed masterly illustrations of Fielding, Richardson, Sterne, 'Robinson Crusoe,' Milton, 'Rape of the Lock,' Shakespeare, Spenser, and Rogers;

his 'Callisto' and 'Zephyrus and Flora' engraved by Blake; his Milton designs by Bartolozzi. [liv. 433]

STOTHERD, RICHARD HUGH (1828–1895), director-general of the ordnance survey; entered royal engineers, 1847; first captain, 1860; brigade-major in North America, 1861–5; organised first field telegraph; caused adoption of Morse signalling system; reported on military operations in France, 1871; president of war office torpedo committee, 1873–6; appointed to Irish ordnance survey, 1881; director-general of United Kingdom survey, 1883–6; C.B. for preparing maps under Redistribution Act, 1884; retired as hon. major-general, 1886; published first English book on submarine mining (2nd edit. 1873). [liv. 437]

STOUGHTON, ISRAEL (*d.* 1645 ?), founder of Dorchester, Massachusetts, 1630; commanded Massachusetts army against Pequot Indians, 1637; assistant, 1637–43; died in England lieutenant-colonel in parliamentary army. [liv. 438]

STOUGHTON, JOHN (1807–1897), ecclesiastical historian; educated at Norwich and Highbury College; congregational co-pastor, Windsor, 1833–43, Hornton Street, Kensington, 1843–74; compiled appendix on nonconformist modes of communicating to fourth report of ritual commission, 1870; professor of historical theology, New College, St. John's Wood, London, 1872–84; arranged conference with churchmen, 1876; lectured in Westminster Abbey on missions, 1877; pall-bearer at Dean Stanley's funeral, 1881; hon. D.D. Edinburgh, 1868; elected to Athenæum Club, 1874; chief works, 'Church and State Two Hundred Years Ago,' 1862, 'Ecclesiastical History of England,' 1867–70, with sequels, 1878, 1884, popular works on foreign reformers, 'Introduction to Historical Theology,' 1880, and autobiographical memoirs. [liv. 439]

STOUGHTON, WILLIAM (1630 ?–1701), governor of Massachusetts; son of Israel Stoughton [q. v.]; B.A. Harvard; incorporated, New College, Oxford, 1652, fellow and M.A., 1653; ejected, 1662; returned to America; assistant, Massachusetts, 1671–86; federal commissioner, 1673–7 and 1680–6; lieutenant-governor, 1692–1701; presided at trial of Salem witches, 1692; founded hall at Harvard. [liv. 438]

STOVIN, SIR FREDERICK (1783–1865), general; ensign, 1800; with Moore at Coruña; aide-de-camp to Alexander Mackenzie Fraser [q. v.] in Walcheren expedition, 1809; aide-de-camp to Picton, afterwards assistant adjutant-general to his division in Peninsula, 1811–14; brevet lieutenant-colonel, 1813; deputy adjutant-general in America, being wounded at New Orleans, 1815; lieutenant-colonel, 92nd foot, 1819–21, 90th, 1821–9; K.C.M.G., 1829; major-general, 1841; groom-in-waiting, 1837–60; general, 1859; G.C.B., 1860. [liv. 440]

STOW, DAVID (1793–1864), educational writer and founder of the Glasgow Normal School; educated at Paisley grammar school; employed in business at Glasgow, 1811; was influenced by the ideas, among others, of Samuel Wilderspin [q. v.], and founded, 1824, his first training school at Drygate; advocated strict moral and physical education; the mixing of both sexes in large classes, and banished corporal punishment and prizes; aided by government; established, on disruption of Scottish church, Free Church Normal College; published, among other works, 'Physical and Moral Training,' 1832. [lv. 1]

STOW, JAMES (*fl.* 1790–1820), engraver. [lv. 2]

STOW, JOHN (1525 ?–1605), chronicler and antiquary; followed at first the trade of a tailor; admitted freeman of Merchant Taylors' Company, 1547; occupied himself from 1560 in collecting and transcribing manuscripts, and in producing original historical works; joined Society of Antiquaries founded by Archbishop Parker, and maintained good relations with him throughout; attacked, but unsuccessfully, by a rival chronicler, Richard Grafton [q. v.]; suspected of partiality for the old faith; was charged, 1568, 1569, and 1570, with being in possession of popish and dangerous writings; was examined before the ecclesiastical commission, but escaped without punishment; spent all his fortune on his literary pursuits, and existed for some time upon charitable contributions; letters patent, 1604, granted to him authorising collection of 'kind gratuities.' His effigy, erected by his wife, still exists in church of St. Andrew Undershaft, Leadenhall Street, London. He was the most accurate and businesslike of the historians of his century. His chief productions are 'The Woorkes of Geffrey Chaucer,' 1561 (his further notes on Chaucer being subsequently printed by Thomas Speght [q. v.], 1598, 'Summarie of Englyshe Chronicles,' 1565 (an original historical work), Matthew of Westminster's 'Flores Historiarum,' 1567, Matthew Paris's 'Chronicle,' 1571; Thomas Walsingham's 'Chronicle,' 1574, 'The Chronicles of England,' 1580 (in subsequent editions styled 'The Annales of England '), the second edition of Holinshed's 'Chronicle,' 1585-7, and lastly 'A Survey of London,' 1598 and 1603 (republished by John Mottley [q. v.], 1754; a modernised edition published by Henry Morley [q. v.], 1876). [lv. 3]

STOWE, WILLIAM HENRY (1825-1855), scholar and journalist; B.A. Wadham College, Oxford, 1848; fellow of Oriel College, Oxford, 1852; entered at Lincoln's Inn; on the staff of 'The Times,' 1852; correspondent in the Crimea, 1855; died of fever at Balaclava. [lv. 6]

STOWEL, JOHN (d. 1799), Manx poet and satirist. [lv. 6]

STOWELL, BARON (1745-1836). [See SCOTT, SIR WILLIAM.]

STOWELL, HUGH (1799-1865), divine; cousin of William Hendry Stowell [q. v.]; M.A. St. Edmund Hall, Oxford, 1826; incumbent of Christ Church, Salford, 1831; an effective preacher and leader of the evangelical party; published religious works. [lv. 7]

STOWELL, SIR JOHN (1599-1662). [See STAWELL.]

STOWELL, WILLIAM HENDRY (1800-1858), dissenting divine; cousin of Hugh Stowell [q. v.]; educated at Blackburn Academy; hon. D.D. Glasgow, 1849; president of Cheshunt College, 1850; pioneer of missions to working men; published theological and historical works. [lv. 7]

STOWFORD or STONFORD, JOHN (1290 ?-1372 ?), judge; a judge of the court of common pleas, 1342-72; acted as chief baron of the exchequer in 1345. [lv. 8]

STRACHAN, ARCHIBALD (d. 1652), colonel; served under Cromwell at Preston, 1648; after the execution of Charles I he signed the covenant at Edinburgh, 1649, and in spite of Alexander Leslie, first earl of Leven [q. v.], was given a command; defeated Montrose in Carbisdale, 1650; present at the battle of Musselburgh and Dunbar, 1650; refused to serve under Leslie, and corresponded with Cromwell, whom he subsequently joined again. [lv. 8]

STRACHAN, SIR JOHN, third baronet (d. 1777), captain in the navy; captured the French privateer Télémaque off Alicante, 1757; subsequently served under Sir Edward (Lord) Hawke [q. v.] [lv. 9]

STRACHAN, JOHN (1778-1867), first bishop of Toronto; M.A. Aberdeen, 1797; became a schoolmaster and went to Canada; became bishop of Toronto, 1839; founded Toronto University. [lv. 10]

STRACHAN, SIR RICHARD JOHN, fourth baronet (1760-1828), admiral; nephew of Sir John Strachan [q. v.]; entered the navy, 1772; present at various naval actions, 1772-1802; succeeded to baronetcy, 1777; captured the French frigate Résolue, 1791, and four French battleships which had escaped from Trafalgar in 1805; K.B., 1806; made naval commander of the ill-fated Walcheren expedition, 1809; admiral, 1821. [lv. 10]

STRACHEY, SIR HENRY, first baronet (1736-1810); politician; grandson of John Strachey [q. v.], private secretary to Lord Clive in India, 1764; M.P., Pontefract, 1768, Bishop's Castle, 1774-8 and 1780-1802, East Grinstead, 1802-7; joint under-secretary of state for home department, 1782; master of George III's household, 1794; created baronet, 1801; F.S.A. [Suppl. iii. 364]

STRACHEY, JOHN (1671-1743), geologist; F.R.S., 1719; said to have first suggested theory of stratification in his work, 'Observations on different Strata of Earths and Minerals,' 1727. [Suppl. iii. 364]

STRACHEY, WILLIAM (fl. 1609-1618), colonist and writer on Virginia; sailed for Virginia on the Sea Venture, 1609, with Sir Thomas Gates [q. v.] and Sir George Somers [q. v.]; wrecked on the Bermudas, 1609, and reached James Town, Virginia, 1610; wrote 'The Historie of Travaile into Virginia,' 1612 (printed, 1849). [lv. 12]

STRADLING, SIR EDWARD (1529-1609), scholar and patron of literature; son of Sir Thomas Stradling [q. v.]; studied at Oxford; M.P., Steyning, 1554, and Arundel, 1557-8; knighted, 1575; wrote account of 'The Winning of the Lordship of Glamorgan,' 1572, incorporated by David Powell [q. v.] in his edition of Humphrey Llwyd's 'Historie of Cambria.' [lv. 13]

STRADLING, SIR EDWARD, second baronet (1601-1644), royalist; eldest son of Sir John Stradling [q. v.]; of Brasenose College, Oxford; M.P., Glamorganshire, 1640; engaged in business undertakings; in the civil war leading royalist in Glamorganshire; taken prisoner at Edgehill, 1642. [lv. 15]

STRADLING, GEORGE (1621-1688), royalist; eighth son of Sir John Stradling [q. v.]; M.A. Jesus College, Oxford, 1647; D.D., 1661; served on royalist side during civil war; dean of Chichester, 1672-88. [lv. 16]

STRADLING, SIR HENRY (fl. 1642), royalist captain; fourth son of Sir John Stradling [q. v.]; captain of the Tenth Whelp under John Pennington [q. v.]; knighted, c. 1642; joined Charles I from Carlisle after surrender, 1645; taken prisoner at Rowton Heath; took part in royalist revolts in South Wales, 1647 and 1648. [lv. 14]

STRADLING, SIR JOHN, first baronet (1563-1637), scholar and poet; adopted by his great-uncle, Sir Edward Stradling (1529-1609) [q. v.]; of Brasenose College and Magdalen Hall, Oxford; B.A., 1584; knighted, 1608; created baronet, 1611; M.P., St. Germans, 1625, Old Sarum, 1625, Glamorganshire, 1626; enjoyed a great reputation for learning; published, among other works, 'Divine Poems,' 1625. [lv. 15]

STRADLING, SIR THOMAS (1498 ?-1571), knight; eldest son of Sir Edward Stradling; sheriff of Glamorganshire, 1547-8; M.P., East Grinstead, 1553, Arundel, 1554; imprisoned in the Tower of London, 1561, on suspicion of popish practices. [lv. 16]

STRAFFORD, EARLS OF. [See WENTWORTH, THOMAS, first EARL, 1593-1641; WENTWORTH, THOMAS, third EARL, 1672-1739; BYNG, SIR JOHN, 1772-1860.]

STRAHAN, GEORGE (1744-1824), friend of Dr. Johnson; second son of William Strahan [q. v.]; M.A. University College, Oxford, 1771; D.D., 1807; vicar of St. Mary's, Islington, 1773; prebendary of Rochester, 1805; rector of Kingsdown, 1820; attended Dr. Johnson on his deathbed; afterwards published Dr. Johnson's 'Prayers and Meditations,' 1785. [lv. 18]

STRAHAN, WILLIAM (1715-1785), printer and publisher; left Scotland and became partner with Millar in London, with whom he produced Johnson's 'Dictionary,' and subsequently with Thomas Cadell the elder [q. v.]; publisher to Thomas Somerville, Hume, Adam Smith, Johnson, Gibbon, Robertson, Blackstone, and others; maintained friendly relations with his clients; M.P., Malmesbury, 1774, Wootton-Bassett, 1780-4. [lv. 17]

STRANG, JOHN (1584-1654), principal of Glasgow University; educated at Kilmarnock and St. Andrews University; M.A., 1600; inducted to the parish of Errol on the recommendation of Alexander Henderson (1583 ?-1646) [q. v.], 1614; member of the general assembly held at Perth and the only D.D. who voted against the five articles; principal of Glasgow University, 1626; maintained a middle course during the subsequent dissensions; accused later of heresy, and resigned his office in 1650; published theological works. [lv. 18]

STRANG, JOHN (1795-1863), author of 'Glasgow and its Clubs'; a wine-merchant; his literary and artistic tastes developed by travels in France and Italy; effected many improvements in Glasgow, his native city; author of 'Germany in 1831,' 1836, the article 'Glasgow' in the 'Encyclopædia Britannica' (8th edit.), and 'Glasgow and its Clubs,' 1855. [lv. 20]

STRANGE. [See also L'ESTRANGE.]

STRANGE, ALEXANDER (1818-1876). lieutenant-colonel and man of science; fifth son of Sir Thomas

Andrew Lumisden Strange [q. v.] ; educated at Harrow ; joined Madras light cavalry, 1834 ; did much work on the trigonometrical survey of India; major, 1859; made inspector (1862) of scientific instruments for use in India on his return to England, 1861 ; lieutenant-colonel, 1861 ; F.R.G.S. and F.R.A.S., 1861 ; F.R.S., 1864.   [lv. 20]

STRANGE, SIR JOHN (1696–1754), master of the rolls ; a pupil of the attorney Salkeld ; barrister, Middle Temple, 1718; as counsel defended Lord Macclesfield, 1725 ; solicitor-general in Walpole's administration, 1737 ; elected recorder of London, 1739, and knighted, 1740 ; M.P., Totnes, 1742 ; master of the rolls, 1750 ; author of 'Reports' published 1755.   [lv. 21]

STRANGE, JOHN (1732–1799), diplomatist and author; second son of Sir John Strange [q. v.]; M.A. Clare Hall, Cambridge, 1755 ; edited his father's ' Reports,' 1755 ; F.R.S. and F.S.A., 1766; British resident at Venice, 1773 ; writer of geological and archæological papers.   [lv. 23]

STRANGE, RICHARD (1611–1682), jesuit ; author of 'The Life of S. Thomas Cantilvpe.'   [lv. 24]

STRANGE, SIR ROBERT (1721–1792), engraver ; apprenticed to Richard Cooper the elder [q. v.] ; fought on the Stuart side at Prestonpans, Falkirk, and Culloden ; studied engraving in Paris under Le Bas, 1749, and returned to London, 1750, with a first-rate reputation ; long deprived by his Jacobitism of court favour ; left England for Italy, 1760 ; returned, 1765 ; excluded, as an engraver, on the foundation of the Royal Academy, 1768, though his rival, Bartolozzi, was elected ; left England again, 1775, for Paris ; introduced to George III by Benjamin West [q. v.], president of the Academy, and engraved Vandyck's Queen Henrietta Maria, Charles I on his horse, 1784, and West's 'Apotheosis of the Royal Children,' 1786 ; knighted, 1787. He stands in the first European rank as a pure historical line-engraver, condemning Bartolozzi's 'stippling' and 'dotting.' His engravings from Vandyck, Titian, Raffaelle, together with the portraits of the royal children, were his chief works.   [lv. 24]

STRANGE, ROGER LE (d. 1311), judge ; a descendant of Guy Le Strange, and perhaps of Hoel II, duke of Brittany (1066–1084) ; justice of the forest on this side of Trent, 1283 ; filled various important judicial, military, and administrative posts in reign of Edward I. [lv. 27]

STRANGE, SIR THOMAS ANDREW LUMISDEN (1756–1841), Indian jurist; second son of Sir Robert Strange [q. v.] ; educated at Westminster School and Christ Church, Oxford ; M.A., 1782 ; barrister, Lincoln's Inn, 1785; chief-justice of Nova Scotia, 1789 ; knighted, 1798 ; recorder of Madras, 1798, where he displayed great firmness and ability, reforming administration of justice and suppressing a mutiny ; D.C.L. Oxford, 1818 ; author of ' Elements of Hindu Law,' 1825.   [lv. 27]

STRANGE, THOMAS LUMISDEN (1808–1884), judge and writer; eldest son of Sir Thomas Andrew Lumisden Strange [q. v.] ; educated at Westminster School ; judge of the high court of judicature, Madras, 1862 ; author of a ' Manual of Hindoo Law,' 1856, and of controversial religious works.   [lv. 28]

STRANGEWAYS, SIR JAMES (d. 1516), speaker of the House of Commons ; M.P., Yorkshire, 1449 and 1460 ; a Yorkist and speaker of Edward IV's first parliament, 1461 ; later supported the Tudor cause.   [lv. 29]

STRANGFORD, VISCOUNTS. [See SMYTHE, PERCY CLINTON SYDNEY, sixth VISCOUNT, 1780–1855 ; SMYTHE, GEORGE AUGUSTUS FREDERICK PERCY SYDNEY, seventh VISCOUNT, 1818–1857 ; SMYTHE, PERCY ELLEN FREDERICK WILLIAM, eighth VISCOUNT, 1826–1869.]

STRATFORD, verè LECHMERE, EDMUND (d. 1640 ?), Roman catholic divine ; D.D. Rheims, 1633 ; author of controversial religious works.   [lv. 29]

STRATFORD, EDWARD, second EARL OF ALDBOROUGH (d. 1801), eldest son of first earl ; M.P., Taunton, 1774 (unseated, 1775) ; M.P., Baltinglass (Irish parliament); voted for the union, 1800 ; called the ' Irish Stanhope ' for his ability and eccentricity.   [lv. 30]

STRATFORD, JOHN DE (d. 1348), archbishop of Canterbury ; brother of Robert de Stratford [q. v.] and kinsman of Ralph de Stratford [q. v.], bishop of London ;

born at Stratford-on-Avon ; educated at Merton College, Oxford ; doctor of civil and canon law before 1311 ; parson of Stratford-on-Avon ; archdeacon of Lincoln, 1319 ; dean of the court of arches and bishop of Winchester, 1323, this last appointment being obtained against King Edward II's wishes, and the temporalities of the see withheld till 1324; restored to favour soon afterwards ; commissioner to treat with France, 1324 and 1325 ; advised Edward II to allow Queen Isabella's visit to France; desired to effect a reconciliation, but finally acquiesced in the election of Edward III, January 1327 ; drew up the six articles containing the reasons for deposition of Edward II, and obtained from Edward II his abdication, 1327 ; appointed chancellor, 1330, and for the next ten years was Edward III's principal adviser ; accompanied Edward III abroad, both disguised, 1331 ; sent on various important missions to France ; archbishop of Canterbury, 1333 ; after being three times chancellor, 1330, 1335, and April 1340, resigned the seal finally, June 1340 ; incurred Edward III's displeasure and took sanctuary at Canterbury, 1340 ; summoned by Edward III to attend at court, on which he appealed to the judgment of his peers; on being refused admittance to the painted chamber by Edward III's chamberlain forced his way in ; formally reconciled to Edward III, after a committee of lords had reported that peers could not be tried outside parliament, 1341. Of his writings the most interesting appear to be his letters, of which some are printed in the ' Litteræ Cantuarienses,' vol. ii.   [lv. 30]

STRATFORD, NICHOLAS (1633–1707), bishop of Chester ; M.A. Trinity College, Oxford, 1656 ; fellow, 1657 ; D.D., 1673 ; warden of the parish church, Manchester, 1667; dean of St. Asaph, 1674–89 ; was fiercely attacked on account of his tolerance of dissenters, and withdrew to London, 1684 ; made bishop of Chester at the revolution, 1689.   [lv. 33]

STRATFORD, RALPH DE (d. 1354), bishop of London ; probably son of Robert de Stratford [q. v.], bishop of Chichester; M.A. and B.C.L. Oxford; bishop of London, 1340–54; supported John de Stratford [q. v.] in assertion of his rights, 1341.   [lv. 34]

STRATFORD, ROBERT DE (d. 1362), bishop of Chichester and chancellor; younger brother of John de Stratford [q. v.] ; educated at Oxford; held several ecclesiastical appointments; was keeper of the great seal, 1331, 1334, and chancellor, 1337 and 1340 ; chancellor of the exchequer, 1331–4 ; chancellor of the university of Oxford, 1335 ; appointed bishop of Chichester, 1337.   [lv. 34]

STRATFORD, WILLIAM SAMUEL (1791–1853), lieutenant, royal navy, and astronomer ; lieutenant, 1815 ; first secretary to the Astronomical Society, 1820 ; F.R.S., 1832 ; author of astronomical works.   [lv. 35]

STRATFORD DE REDCLIFFE, first VISCOUNT (1786–1880). [See CANNING, STRATFORD.]

STRATHALLAN, VISCOUNTS OF. [See DRUMMOND, WILLIAM, first VISCOUNT, 1617 ?–1688 ; DRUMMOND, WILLIAM, fourth VISCOUNT, 1690–1746.]

STRATHEARN, DUKE OF (1745–1790). [See HENRY FREDERICK, DUKE OF CUMBERLAND and STRATHEARN.]

STRATHEARN, MALISE, sixth EARL OF (fl. 1281–1315), and son of fifth earl ; one of the guarantors of the marriage treaty of Margaret of Scotland with Eric of Norway, 1281, and a supporter of Baliol ; invaded England, but took oath of fidelity to Edward I, 1296 ; joined Bruce ; subsequently captured and imprisoned by the English ; set free, 1309.   [lv. 35]

STRATHEARN, MALISE, seventh EARL OF (fl. 1320–1345), commanded the third division of the Scots army at Halidon Hill, 1333.   [lv. 37]

STRATHMORE, EARLS OF. [See LYON, PATRICK, first EARL, 1642–1695 ; LYON, JOHN, ninth EARL, 1737–1776.]

STRATHMORE, COUNTESS OF (1749–1800). [See BOWES, MARY ELEANOR.]

STRATHNAIRN, BARON (1801–1885). [See ROSE, HUGH HENRY.]

STRATTON, ADAM DE (fl. 1265–1290), clerk and chamberlain of the exchequer ; clerk of the works at the palace of Westminster, 1262 ; was promoted to be chamberlain of the exchequer, and amassed great riches ; was convicted of frauds and one of the chief delinquents in the state trials, 1290 ; was disgraced, 1290, but continued to be confidentially employed by the crown. [lv. 37]

STRATTON, JOHN PROUDFOOT (1830-1895), surgeon ; M.D. Aberdeen, 1855 ; officiating resident in Mewar, March 1881, in the western states of Rajputana, July 1881, and in Jeypur, 1882 ; retired as brigade-surgeon, 1885. [lv. 38]

STRAUBENZEE, SIR CHARLES THOMAS VAN (1812-1892). [See VAN STRAUBENZEE.]

STRAUSS, GUSTAVE LOUIS MAURICE (1807 ?-1887), miscellaneous writer ; born at Trois Rivières, Lower Canada ; educated at Magdeburg ; doctor of philosophy, Berlin ; was banished both from Germany and France for complicity in revolutionary plots, and subsequently lived in London ; published ' The Old Ledger, a Novel,' 1865, the criticism of which in the ' Athenæum' led to two libel actions against that journal, in the first of which a compromise was made, while in the second a verdict was given in favour of the defendants. Other works include ' Moslem and Frank,' 1854. [lv. 39]

STREAT, WILLIAM (1600 ?-1666), divine ; M.A. Exeter College, Oxford, 1624 ; rector of South Pool ; published a work on seeming contradictions in the bible, 1654. [lv. 40]

STREATER or **STREETER**, JOHN (*fl.* 1650-1670), soldier and pamphleteer ; quartermaster-general in the army of the Commonwealth in Ireland, 1650-3 ; opposed Cromwell's summary treatment of parliament and was imprisoned in consequence, 1653 ; subsequently took the side of Monck against Lambert ; published political pamphlets. [lv. 40]

STREATER, ROBERT (1624-1680), painter ; excelled in architectural and decorative painting ; extolled by Pepys and Evelyn ; made serjeant-painter by Charles II at the Restoration ; painted the roof of the Sheldonian Theatre at Oxford. [lv. 41]

STREATFEILD, THOMAS (1777-1848), topographer, genealogist, and artist ; B.A. Oriel College, Oxford, 1799 ; curate of Tatsfield ; F.S.A., 1812 ; collected a large amount of material, genealogical and biographical, for a history of Kent, now in the British Museum (first printed in 'Hasted's History of Kent, edited by Henry H. Drake,' 1886). [lv. 41]

STREET, GEORGE EDMUND (1824-1881), architect ; of the same family as Sir Thomas Street [q. v.] ; originally followed his father's profession of solicitor ; assistant of Sir George Gilbert Scott [q. v.] ; his first independent work the designing of Biscovey church ; appointed honorary diocesan architect by Samuel Wilberforce [q. v.] ; carried out many important works in Oxfordshire ; travelled in Germany, France, and Spain ; designed the Crimean Memorial Church at Constantinople (begun, 1864), and the new nave of Bristol Cathedral ; R.A., 1871 ; professor of architecture, Royal Academy, 1881 ; chosen architect of the new Law Courts, 1868, in the carrying out of which he was much hampered by injudicious economy ; among much restoration work carried out restorations at York Minster, 1871, and at cathedrals of Salisbury and Carlisle, rehabilitating fratry of Carlisle Cathedral, *c.* 1871 ; excelled in the building of parish churches ; buried in Westminster Abbey ; author of the article on Gothic architecture in the 'Encyclopædia Britannica ' (9th edit.), and of other works. [lv. 42]

STREET, SIR THOMAS (1626-1696), judge ; of Lincoln College, Oxford ; barrister, Inner Temple, 1653, bencher, 1669 ; M.P. for Worcester, 1659-81 ; judge of the exchequer bench and knighted, 1681 ; removed to common pleas, 1684 ; decided against the king's dispensing power in Godden *v.* Hales. [lv. 45]

STREETER, JOHN (*fl.* 1650-1670). [See STREATER.]

STRETES, **STREETES**, or **STREATE**, GUILLIM or WILLIAM (*fl.* 1546-1556), portrait-painter ; described as a Dutchman ; paid by Edward VI a salary of 62*l*.10*s*. Among his pictures may be mentioned especially that of Henry Howard, earl of Surrey [q. v.], now at Arundel Castle ; and several of Edward VI, inaccurately ascribed to Holbein, are supposed to be his. [lv. 46]

STRETTON, ROBERT DE (*d.* 1385), bishop of Coventry and Lichfield ; chaplain to the Black Prince ; bishop, 1359-85. His consecration was refused on account of his illiteracy, but finally at the instance of Edward III Pope Innocent VI yielded. [lv. 47]

STRICKLAND, AGNES (1796-1874), historian ; educated by her father ; commenced authorship with verse ; granted a civil list pension of 100*l*. in 1870. Her chief prose works were 'Historical Tales of Illustrious British Children,' 1833, and 'Tales and Stories from History,' 1836 (both for children), 'Lives of the Queens of England,' 1840-8, her most successful work, but in which her sister Elizabeth collaborated. and ' Letters of Mary Queen of Scots,' 1843, ' Lives of the Queens of Scotland and English Princesses,' 1850-9 (of which Elizabeth again wrote portions) ; and a novel, ' How will it end ? ' 1865. [lv. 48]

STRICKLAND, HUGH EDWIN (1811-1853), naturalist ; grandson of Edmund Cartwright [q. v.], inventor of the power-loom ; educated by Thomas Arnold (1795-1842) [q. v.], and early gave proof of scientific talent ; entered Oriel College, Oxford, 1829, and attended Buckland's lectures on geology ; M.A., 1835 ; accompanied William John Hamilton [q. v.] in a geological tour through Asia Minor, and traversed Greece, Constantinople, Italy, and Switzerland, 1835 ; visited the north of Scotland, 1837 ; drew up (1841) rules for zoological nomenclature, ultimately with some modifications accepted as authoritative ; while examining a railway cutting at Clarborough was killed by a train. Among several important scientific writings were 'Ornithological Synonyms,' 1855, and ' The Dodo,' 1848. [lv. 50]

STRICKLAND, JANE MARGARET (1800-1888), author ; sister of Agnes Strickland [q. v.] ; author of ' Rome,' 1854, and biographer of Agnes Strickland, 1887. [lv. 50]

STRICKLAND, SIR ROGER (1640-1717), admiral ; commanded the Santa Maria in the four days' fight (1-4 June 1666) ; recaptured the Henry from the Dutch in the battle of Solebay, 1672 ; knighted, 1673 ; admiral of the blue, 1687 ; appointed by James II commander of the fleet in the Narrow Seas ; excited a mutiny by causing mass to be publicly said on board, and was superseded, 1688 ; followed the fortunes of James II at the revolution, and died at St. Germain. [lv. 52]

STRICKLAND, SAMUEL (1809-1867), author ; brother of Agnes Strickland [q. v.] ; emigrated to Canada ; author of ' Twenty-seven Years in Canada,' 1853. [lv. 50]

STRICKLAND, THOMAS JOHN FRANCIS, known as ABBÉ STRICKLAND (1679 ?-1740), bishop of Namur and doctor of the Sorbonne ; fourth son of Sir Thomas Strickland of Sizergh ; brought up in France ; graduated at Douay, 1712 ; endeavoured to effect reconciliation between the English catholics and the government, but unsuccessfully ; made bishop of Namur, 1727 ; resided at Rome as agent of the English government, and was employed by the emperor Charles VI in England in connection with a vain attempt to create war with France. [lv. 53]

STRICKLAND, WALTER (*fl.* 1642-1657), politician ; agent of the Long parliament to the United Provinces, with one interruption, 1642-50 ; M.P., Minehead, 1645, East Riding, 1654, Newcastle, 1656 ; accompanied Oliver St. John (1598 ?-1673) [q. v.] to Holland to negotiate alliance, 1651 ; summoned to Cromwell's House of Lords, 1657 ; member of several councils under the Commonwealth. [lv. 54]

STRICKLAND, WILLIAM (*d.* 1419), bishop of Carlisle ; provided to the bishopric by Pope Benedict XIII, 1400, an appointment which Henry IV refused to recognise till he had been elected by the chapter and confirmed by himself ; commissioner for negotiating peace with Scotland, 1401. [lv. 56]

STRICKLAND, SIR WILLIAM, first baronet (1596 ?-1673), politician ; elder brother of Walter Strickland [q. v.]; knighted, 1630 ; created baronet, 1641 ; vigorously supported the parliamentary cause as M.P., Hedon (Long parliament), and Yorkshire, 1654, 1656, and 1659. [lv. 55]

STRIGUL or **STRIGUIL**, EARL OF (*d.* 1176). [See CLARE, RICHARD DE.]

STRODE, SIR GEORGE (1583-1663), author and royalist ; went to London and entered trade ; wounded at Edgehill, 1642 ; lived abroad after the defeat of Charles I :

returned to London at the Restoration; translated work of Cristofero da Fonseca, 'A Discourse of Holy Love,' 1652. [lv. 56]

STRODE, RALPH (*fl.* 1350–1400), schoolman; said by Dempster to have been a Scot, but was more probably born in the west of England; fellow of Merton College, Oxford, where John Wycliffe was his colleague; opposed Wycliffe and evoked a reply from him; dedicatee, with Gower, of Chaucer's 'Troylus and Cryseyde'; mentioned as 'nobilis poeta' in the 'Vetus Catalogus' of Merton College, Oxford. His chief reputation was acquired as a scholastic philosopher and logician. Fragments of his teaching are preserved in his 'Consequentiæ' and 'Obligationes' (printed, 1477 and 1507). [lv. 57]

STRODE, THOMAS (*fl.* 1642–1688), author of mathematical works; of University College, Oxford. [lv. 59]

STRODE, WILLIAM (1599?–1645), politician; B.A. Exeter College, Oxford, 1617, and student of the Inner Temple, 1614; M.P., Beeralston, 1624, 1625, 1626, and 1628; opposed the action of the speaker in refusing to put Eliot's resolutions to the vote, 1629; proceeded against in the Star-chamber; imprisoned till 1640; after 1640 one of the fiercest of Charles I's enemies; when one of the managers on Strafford's impeachment sought to deprive him of counsel; one of the five members impeached by Charles I, 1642; opposed all attempts at reconciliation with Charles I, and showed himself very active against Laud; buried in Westminster Abbey, but disinterred, 1661. [lv. 59]

STRODE, WILLIAM (1602–1645), poet and dramatist; of Westminster School and Christ Church, Oxford; M.A., 1624; B.D., 1631; wrote 'The Floating Island,' a tragi-comedy acted before Charles I and his queen at Oxford, with music by Lawes, 1636; canon of Christ Church, Oxford, 1638; author of poems included in various collections and of some unprinted. [lv. 61]

STRONG, WILLIAM (*d.* 1654), independent divine; B.A. and fellow of Catharine Hall, Cambridge, 1631; member of the Westminster Assembly, 1645, and preacher to the parliament; published theological works. [lv. 62]

STRONGBOW, RICHARD, second EARL OF PEMBROKE and STRIGUL (*d.* 1176). [See CLARE, RICHARD DE.]

STROTHER, EDWARD (1675–1737), medical writer; M.D. Utrecht, 1720; L.R.C.P., 1721. [lv. 62]

STRUTHERS, JOHN (1776–1853), Scottish poet; at first cowherd and shoemaker; abandoned his trade for literary work, 1819; introduced by Joanna Baillie to Sir Walter Scott; librarian of Stirling's public library, Glasgow, 1833–48; author of 'Anticipation,' 1803, 'The Poor Man's Sabbath,' 1804, 'Dychmont,' 1836, and other poems, as well as pamphlets. [lv. 63]

STRUTHERS, SIR JOHN (1823–1899), anatomist; M.D. Edinburgh, 1845; L.R.C.S. and F.R.C.S. Edinburgh; taught anatomy in extramural school, 1847; assistant surgeon to Royal Infirmary, 1854, and later was appointed full surgeon; professor of anatomy at Aberdeen, 1863–1889; chairman of board of directors of Leith Hospital; president of Royal College of Surgeons, Edinburgh, 1895–1897; knighted, 1898; published anatomical writings. [Suppl. iii. 365]

STRUTT, EDWARD, first BARON BELPER (1801–1880), son of William Strutt [q. v.]; M.A. Trinity College, Cambridge, 1826; student at Lincoln's Inn and the Inner Temple; M.P., Derby, 1830–47, Arundel, 1851–2, Nottingham, 1852–6; as a philosophical radical, intimate with Bentham, the Mills, and Macaulay; chancellor of the duchy of Lancaster in Lord Aberdeen's government, 1852–4; created Baron Belper, 1856; F.R.S., 1860; president of University College, London, 1871; authority on free trade, law reform, and education. [lv. 63]

STRUTT, JACOB GEORGE (*fl.* 1820–1850), painter and etcher. [lv. 64]

STRUTT, JEDEDIAH (1726–1797), cotton-spinner and improver of the stocking-frame; in conjunction with Woollatt took out two valuable patents, 1758 and 1759; entered into partnership with Sir Richard Arkwright [q. v.] [lv. 64]

STRUTT, JOSEPH (1749–1802), author, artist, antiquary, and engraver; apprenticed to William Wynne Ryland [q. v.]; author of many works valuable for their research and engravings, including 'Chronicle of England,' 1777–8, 'Biographical Dictionary of Engravers,' 1785–6, 'Dresses and Habits of the English People,' 1796–9, and 'Sports and Pastimes of the People of England,' 1801. An unfinished novel of Strutt's, completed by Scott, suggested to the latter the publication of his own 'Waverley.' [lv. 65]

STRUTT, JOSEPH (1775–1833), author of 'Commentaries' on the scriptures; eldest son of Joseph Strutt (1749–1802) [q. v.] [lv. 66]

STRUTT, JOSEPH (1765–1844), mayor of Derby; third son of Jedediah Strutt [q. v.]; mayor, 1835; gave an 'arboretum' to Derby. [lv. 65]

STRUTT, WILLIAM (1756–1830), inventor; eldest son of Jedediah Strutt [q. v.]; invented the Belper stove, 1806. [lv. 65]

STRUTT, WILLIAM GOODDAY (1762–1848), governor of Quebec; served at the siege of Gibraltar, 1782; brigadier-general at St. Vincent; major-general, 1798; governor of Quebec, 1800–48. [lv. 67]

STRUTT, WILLIAM THOMAS (1777–1850), miniature-painter; son of Joseph Strutt (1749–1802) [q. v.] [lv. 67]

STRYPE, JOHN (1643–1737), ecclesiastical historian and biographer; educated at St. Paul's School and Jesus College and Catharine Hall, Cambridge; M.A., 1669 (incorporated at Oxford, 1671); held among other church preferments the sinecure rectory of West Tarring; formed a magnificent collection of original documents, mostly of the Tudor period, some acquired by questionable means (now in the Harleian and Lansdowne MSS.). His publications include lives of Cranmer (1694), Sir John Cheke (1705), Grindal (1710), Matthew Parker (1711), and Whitgift (1718); his works published by the Clarendon Press in nineteen volumes; many of his letters in Cambridge University Library. [lv. 67]

STRZELECKI, SIR PAUL EDMUND DE (1796–1873), Australian explorer, known as COUNT STRZELECKI; belonged to a noble Polish family; educated partly at the High School, Edinburgh; undertook the scientific exploration of the interior of Australia, 1839; discovered gold in Wellington district, which, however, was kept a secret for twelve years; author of 'Physical Description of New South Wales,' &c., 1845; K.C.M.G., 1869. [lv. 69]

STUART. [See also STEUART, STEWARD, and STEWART.]

STUART, SIR ALEXANDER (1825–1886), premier of New South Wales; educated at Edinburgh; went to New South Wales, 1851; champion of the denominational system in primary education; defeated the Parkes-Robinson ministry, 1882; premier, 1883; passed his land laws, 1884. [lv. 70]

STUART, ANDREW (*d.* 1801), lawyer; tutor to the children of the sixth Duke of Hamilton; conducted the case against the claimant in the Douglas lawsuit, in which the Duke of Hamilton disputed the identity of Archibald James Edward Douglas, first baron Douglas [q. v.]; fought a duel with Thurlow, the opposing counsel; attacked Lord Mansfield for his decision in 'Letters to Lord Mansfield,' 1773; M.P., Lanarkshire, 1774–84, Weymouth and Melcombe Regis, 1790–1801; appointed to the board of trade, 1779. [lv. 71]

STUART or **STEWART**, BERNARD or BÉRAULT, third SEIGNEUR OF AUBIGNY (1447?–1508), commanded French troops which assisted Richmond at Bosworth, 1485; as lieutenant-general of the French army gained victory of Seminara over the king of Naples, 1495, but was defeated at the same place, 1503; employed by Charles VIII on several missions to Scotland, where he died. [lv. 72]

STUART, LORD BERNARD, titular EARL OF LICHFIELD (1623?–1645), sixth son of Esmé Stuart, third duke of Lennox; fought for Charles I at Edgehill, 1642, Cropredy Bridge, and Naseby; killed at Chester; extolled by Clarendon. [lv. 73]

STUART, CHARLES, sixth DUKE OF LENNOX, third DUKE OF RICHMOND, and tenth SEIGNEUR OF AUBIGNY

(1639-1672), grandson of Esmé Stuart, third duke of Lennox ; created Earl of Lichfield, 1645 ; lived principally in France ; returned to England with Charles II ; succeeded his cousin as Duke of Richmond and Lennox, 1660 ; K.G., 1661 ; imprisoned in the Tower of London, 1665 ; married ' La Belle Stuart ' [see STUART or STEWART, FRANCES TERESA].   [lv. 73]

STUART, SIR CHARLES (1753-1801), general ; fourth son of John Stuart, third earl of Bute [q. v.] ; M.P., Bossiney, 1780 ; captured Minorca from the Spaniards, 1798 ; lieutenant-general, 1798 ; K.B., 1799.
[lv. 74]

STUART, SIR CHARLES, BARON STUART DE ROTHESAY (1779-1845), eldest son of Sir Charles Stuart (1753-1801) [q. v.], general ; G.C.B. and privy councillor, 1812 ; minister at the Hague, 1815-16, ambassador to Paris, 1815-30, and St. Petersburg, 1841-5 ; created Baron Stuart de Rothesay, 1828.   [lv. 75]

STUART, CHARLES EDWARD (1799?-1880), brother of John Sobieski Stolberg Stuart [q. v.] ; with his brother claimed to be descended from Prince Charles Edward Stuart, the young Chevalier ; with his brother fought for Napoleon I at Dresden, Leipzig, and Waterloo ; his real name Allan, which in 1829 was changed to Stuart Allan, and in 1841 to Allan Stuart ; his pretension and his brother's, for which there was no foundation, based on the supposed birth of a son to the Countess of Albany, 1773, who had been handed over to a ' Commodore O'Haleran ' ; succeeded, however, in enlisting the sympathies of many leading persons in Scotland ; author, with his brother, of several works, including ' Bridal of Caölchairn, and other Poems,' 1822, ' Costume of the Clans,' 1843, ' Tales of the Century,' 1847, ' Lays of the Deer Forest,' 1848, and ' Poems,' by Charles Edward Stuart, 1869.   [lv. 104]

STUART, DANIEL (1766-1846), journalist ; assisted his brother-in-law, Sir James Mackintosh [q. v.], as secretary to Society of the Friends of the People ; published ' Peace and Reform against War and Commotion,' 1794 ; purchased the ' Morning Post,' 1795, and converted it into organ of moderate toryism, and had as contributors Mackintosh, Coleridge, Southey, Lamb, Wordsworth ; purchased the ' Courier,' 1796, his success in both ventures being very great.   [lv. 75]

STUART, LORD DUDLEY COUTTS (1803-1854), advocate of the independence of Poland ; eighth son of first Marquis of Bute ; M.A. Christ College, Cambridge, 1823 ; liberal M.P. for Arundel, 1830, 1831, 1833, and 1835, Marylebone, 1847-54 ; obtained parliamentary and charitable relief for the Polish victims ; died at Stockholm, whither he had gone in the hope of persuading the king of Sweden to join western Europe in taking measures for the reconstruction of Poland.   [lv. 76]

STUART, ESMÉ, sixth SEIGNEUR OF AUBIGNY and first DUKE OF LENNOX (1542?-1583), grandson of John Stewart, third or eleventh Earl of Lennox [q. v.] ; sent to Scotland as agent of the Guises to overthrow Morton and restore Roman catholicism, 1579 ; pretended to be a convert to protestantism, and obtained the support of the kirk, which led to Morton's execution, 1581 ; created Duke of Lennox, 1581 ; proposed to lead a Spanish army to invade England, 1582 ; suspicion of his fidelity excited by his quarrel with Arran and rumours of the plot ; obliged on James VI's seizure by the protestant nobles to leave Scotland ; had an interview with Queen Elizabeth, 1583, and left for Paris, where he died.   [lv. 77]

STUART or STEWART, FRANCES TERESA, DUCHESS OF RICHMOND and LENNOX (1647-1702), ' La Belle Stuart,' granddaughter of Walter Stewart or Stuart, first Lord Blantyre [q. v.] ; educated in France and imbued with French tastes ; remarkable for her beauty ; maid of honour to Queen Catherine of Braganza ; mistress of Charles II ; had many lovers and aspirants ; eloped from Whitehall with the third Duke of Richmond, 1667, in consequence of which Charles II, suspecting it to be the work of Clarendon, determined to disgrace the chancellor ; returned to court after her marriage. She was probably the original of the figure of Britannia on the copper coinage.   [lv. 80]

STUART, GILBERT (1742-1786), historian and reviewer ; educated at Edinburgh ; published ' Historical Dissertation on the Antiquity of the English Constitution,' 1768 ; writer in the ' Monthly Review,' 1768-73 ; brought out the ' Edinburgh Magazine and Review,' 1773, which came to an end in 1776 owing to his violence and malicious jealousy ; wrote also, among other works, ' A View of Society in Europe,' 1778, and ' The History of Scotland,' 1782, composed in the Johnsonian or ' balancing style ' ; was one of the principal writers in the ' English Review,' 1783 ; attacked Robertson with great violence, imagining himself to have been injured by the historian.
[lv. 82]

STUART, GILBERT (1755-1828), portrait-painter ; born in Narragansett, Rhode Island, U.S.A. ; came to England and worked with Benjamin West, 1775, returning, 1792 ; the painter of Washington.   [lv. 84]

STUART, HENRY, LORD DARNLEY (1545-1567). [See STEWART.]

STUART, HENRY, DUKE OF GLOUCESTER (1639-1660). [See HENRY.]

STUART, HENRY WINDSOR VILLIERS (1827-1895), of Dromana ; politician ; was ordained, 1850, but surrendered his orders, 1873, and was returned to parliament as M.P. for Waterford, 1873-4 and 1880-5 ; accomplished valuable work in Egypt, 1883 ; his reports published in a blue-book ; wrote largely on Egypt.   [lv. 85]

STUART, JAMES, fourth DUKE OF LENNOX and first DUKE OF RICHMOND (1612-1655), son of Esmé, third duke of Lennox : studied at Cambridge ; a staunch supporter of Charles I, but more from loyalty than devotion to his policy ; granted Charles I large sums in the civil war ; created Duke of Richmond, 1641.   [lv. 85]

STUART, JAMES (1713-1788), painter and architect ; known as ' Athenian Stuart ' ; originally employed in painting fans for Lewis Goupy [q. v.] ; visited Rome, 1741, and Greece, 1751, with Nicholas Revett [q. v.], the result of their expedition to Greece being published in ' The Antiquities of Athens,' 1762, which led to the introduction of Greek architecture in London, Lord Anson's house in St. James's Square, built by Stuart, being perhaps the first of that style ; F.R.S. and F.S.A. ; architect and authority on classical art ; member of the Dilettanti Society.
[lv. 86]

STUART, JAMES (d. 1793), major-general ; brother of Andrew Stuart [q. v.] ; saw much active service from 1758 to 1775, in which latter year he entered the employment of East India Company in Madras ; major-general, 1781 ; while attacking Cuddalore, owing to rivalry of the civil powers, was seized by the Madras government and sent home to England.   [lv. 88]

STUART, JAMES (1741-1815), general ; served in the American war of independence ; in campaigns under Sir Eyre Coote, Sir William Medows, and Cornwallis ; commanded expedition against Ceylon, which he secured, 1796 ; took Seringapatam, 1798 ; general, 1812.   [lv. 89]

STUART, JAMES (1764-1842), historian of Armagh ; B.A. Trinity College, Dublin, 1789 ; called to the Irish bar ; author of ' Historical Memoirs of Armagh,' 1819 ; editor of newspapers and poet.   [lv. 89]

STUART, JAMES (1775-1849), writer to the signet ; studied at Edinburgh University ; a keen whig politician, and attacked violently by the ' Beacon ' and by the ' Glasgow Sentinel,' 1821 ; killed in a duel the writer of one of these articles, Sir Alexander Boswell, 1822, and after a trial, which excited much interest, was acquitted ; after a visit to America, 1828, published ' Three Years in North America,' 1833, displaying a strong bias in favour of the Americans ; inspector of factories, 1836.   [lv. 90]

STUART, SIR JAMES, first baronet (1780-1853), chief-justice of Canada ; solicitor-general of Lower Canada, 1801, but resigned and joined the opposition in the House of Assembly, 1809, and procured impeachment of the chief-justices Sewell and Monk ; active in procuring the union of the two provinces ; appointed attorney-general for Lower Canada, 1825 ; impeached, 1831 ; created baronet, 1841 ; chief-justice of Canada, 1841.   [lv. 91]

STUART or STEWART, SIR JOHN, of Darnley, SEIGNEUR OF AUBIGNY (1365?-1429), as one of the commanders of the Scottish force helped to defeat the English at Beaugé, 1421 ; granted the seigneury of Aubigny, 1422.
[lv. 92]

STUART, JOHN (1700?-1779), superintendent of Indian affairs; went to America with General James E. Oglethorpe, 1733, and was in Fort Loudoun during the French war, when it was besieged by the Cherokee Indians; made terms with Oconostota, who, however, treacherously massacred the garrison; general agent and superintendent of Indian affairs for the southern department, 1763; took part with the royalists in the war of independence; died in England.   [lv. 98]

STUART, JOHN, third EARL OF BUTE (1713-1792), succeeded his father as earl, 1723; educated at Eton; married Mary, only daughter of Lady Mary Wortley Montagu [q. v.], thereby acquiring eventually the Wortley estates; elected a representative peer of Scotland, 1737; took no part, however, in politics during his earlier years, but amused himself in Bute with agriculture, botany, and architecture; introduced by an accident, 1747, to Frederick, prince of Wales, at whose court his influence soon became paramount; assisted the Princess of Wales in imbuing Prince George (George III) with Bolingbroke's principles of absolute monarchy; great scandal caused by his intimate relations with the princess; on accession of George III became practically prime minister; made secretary of state, 1761; got rid of Pitt, his policy being to make peace, but notwithstanding was obliged to declare war with Spain, 1762; succeeded Newcastle as first lord of the treasury, whose retirement he effected by proposing withdrawal of the Prussian subsidy, 1762; K.G., 1762; made secret overtures for peace, and induced Henry Fox [q. v.] to accept leadership of the House of Commons, with whose aid and by bribery he carried addresses approving the terms of the preliminary treaty of Fontainebleau; lost popularity by the treaty of Paris, 1763, being even suspected (probably without foundation) of accepting bribes from France; his unpopularity increased by the cider tax, 1763; resigned, 1763; retained, with George Grenville as prime minister, George III's confidence, and intrigued against that minister, but unsuccessfully; finally retired from George III's business, May 1765; voted against the Stamp Act, 1766, and subsequently travelled abroad incognito. His ability for intrigue did not make up for his lack of administrative talent and of parliamentary experience. He was a patron of literature, giving Dr. Johnson a pension of 300*l.* a year, and a student of botany, privately printing 'Botanical Tables.'   [lv. 92]

STUART, SIR JOHN (1759-1815), lieutenant-general; son of John Stuart (1700?-1779) [q. v.]; count of Maida; born in Georgia, North America; educated at Westminster School; took part in the war against the American colonists, and was present at surrender at Yorktown, 1781; served in the unsuccessful campaign against the French, 1793-5; took part in the capture of Minorca, 1799; at the battle of Alexandria (1801) ensured the victory by his action at a critical moment; gained decisive victory over the French general Reynier in Calabria, 1806, and received pension of 1,000*l.* per annum; made K.B. and Count of Maida; took Ischia and Procida and captured Murat's gunboats, 1809, after which he retired to Messina; repulsed attack of the enemy with great loss near Messina, 1810; complained of want of support from Lord Liverpool and resigned; G.C.B., 1815.   [lv. 98]

STUART, JOHN (1743-1821), Gaelic scholar and minister; D.D. Glasgow, 1795; completed (1767) translation of the Old Testament into Gaelic, already begun by his father.   [lv. 101]

" **STUART**, JOHN (1813-1877), Scottish genealogist and advocate; educated at Aberdeen University; as secretary of the 'Spalding Club,' 1839-70, produced, among other valuable works, 'The Sculptured Stones of Scotland,' 1856, 'The Book of Deer,' 1869, and 'A Lost Chapter in the History of Mary Queen of Scots,' 1874.   [lv. 102]

STUART, JOHN FERDINAND SMYTH (1745-1814), American loyalist; adopted the name of Stuart, 1793; studied medicine at Edinburgh; emigrated to America, but on rebellion breaking out served as a loyalist against the colonists; returned to England at the close of the war; present at capture of St. Lucia; author of 'A Tour in the United States,' 1784, and other works   [lv. 102]

STUART, JOHN McDOUALL (1815-1866), explorer; conducted several expeditions into the interior of Australia; received prize of 2,000*l.* destined for the first colonist who crossed the continent, though John McKinlay

[q. v.] had anticipated him; returned to England, 1864. Stuart's Creek was named after him.   [lv. 103]

STUART, JOHN PATRICK CRICHTON-, third MARQUIS OF BUTE (1847-1900), son of John Stuart, second marquis of Bute (*d.* 1848), and great-great-grandson of John Stuart, third earl of Bute [q. v.]; of Harrow and Christ Church, Oxford; abandoned presbyterian church for that of Rome, 1868, an incident which probably suggested the plot of Disraeli's novel 'Lothair' (1870); inherited large estates in Scotland and in neighbourhood of Cardiff; mayor of Cardiff, 1890; president of University College, Cardiff; active member of Scottish universities commission, 1889; rector of St. Andrews, 1892-8; provost of Rothesay, 1896-9; lord-lieutenant of county of Bute, 1892; K.T., 1875. His works include an English translation of the 'Breviary,' 1879, with numerous historical and critical notes, several translations of the orders of service for the greater church festivals, 'The Language of the Natives of Teneriffe,' 1891, and 'The Arms of the Royal and Parliamentary Burghs,' 1897, with Mr. J. R. N. Macphail and Mr. H. W. Lonsdale. He was a munificent benefactor of St. Andrews and Glasgow universities.
[Suppl. iii. 366]

STUART, JOHN SOBIESKI STOLBERG (1795?-1872), brother of Charles Edward Stuart [q. v.]
[lv. 104]

STUART, LUDOVICK, second DUKE OF LENNOX and DUKE OF RICHMOND (1574-1624), eldest son of Esmé Stuart, first duke of Lennox [q. v.], and next in succession to the Scottish throne; president of the council during the absence of James VI, 1588; lord high admiral, 1591; after James VI's accession to the English throne, 1603, made privy councillor and steward of the household; created Duke of Richmond, 1623; buried in Henry VII's chapel at Westminster.   [lv. 107]

STUART (STEWART), MARY (1542-1587), queen of Scots. [See MARY.]

STUART, PETER (*fl.* 1788-1805), proprietor of 'The Oracle' and 'The Star'; brother of Daniel Stuart [q. v.]   [lv. 76]

STUART, ROBERT, SEIGNEUR OF AUBIGNY (1470?-1543). [See STEWART, ROBERT.]

STUART, ROBERT (1812-1848), author of 'Caledonia Romana,' 1845, a treatise on the influence of the Romans in Scotland, and of poetical works.   [lv. 109]

STUART, WILLIAM (1755-1822), archbishop of Armagh; son of John Stuart, third earl of Bute [q. v.]; of Winchester College and St. John's College, Cambridge; fellow and (1774) M.A.; D.D., 1789; bishop of St. Davids, 1793-1800; archbishop of Armagh, 1800-22.   [lv. 109]

STUART-WORTLEY, LADY EMMELINE CHARLOTTE ELIZABETH (1806-1855), poetess and authoress; daughter of fifth Duke of Rutland; wrote accounts of her travels; was the author of many poetical works; edited the 'Keepsake,' 1837 and 1840; died at Beyrout.
[lv. 109]

STUART-WORTLEY, JAMES ARCHIBALD (1805-1881), youngest son of James Archibald Stuart-Wortley-Mackenzie, first baron Wharncliffe [q. v.]; barrister, Inner Temple, 1831; Q.C., 1841; B.A. Christ Church, Oxford, 1826; fellow of Merton College, Oxford; solicitor-general under Lord Palmerston, 1856-7.   [lv. 113]

STUART-WORTLEY, JOHN, second BARON WHARNCLIFFE (1801-1855), eldest son of James Archibald Stuart-Wortley-Mackenzie, first baron Wharncliffe [q. v.]; B.A. Christ Church, Oxford, 1822; M.P., Bossiney, 1823-32, West Riding, 1841-5; secretary to the board of control, 1830; published pamphlets and an economic work.
[lv. 113]

STUART-WORTLEY-MACKENZIE, JAMES ARCHIBALD, first BARON WHARNCLIFFE (1776-1845), statesman; grandson of John Stuart, third earl of Bute [q. v.]; educated at Charterhouse; served in the army, 1790-1801; tory M.P. for Bossiney, 1797-1818, and for Yorkshire subsequently; mover of the resolution which caused the resignation of the Perceval government, 1812; advocated economy, freedom of wool from duties, and spoke against further agricultural protection, and for amendment of the corn laws; in foreign policy was a follower of Canning and supported catholic emancipation and amendment of game laws; created Baron Wharncliffe,

1826 ; opposed reform, but, considering resistance hopeless, endeavoured to effect a compromise, and, when that failed, advised his friends to support the second reading ; lord privy seal in Peel's ministry, 1834, and president of the council, 1841, but opposed Peel on the corn laws. [lv. 110]

STUBBS, GEORGE (1724–1806), animal-painter and anatomist ; son of a currier ; studied anatomy at York under Charles Atkinson ; visited Italy, 1754, and came to London, 1756, with a considerable reputation ; published ' The Anatomy of the Horse,' 1766, an exhaustive study of the structure of the horse ; executed portraits of horses for Lord Grosvenor, Duke of Richmond, and others, and for the 'Turf Review,' besides imaginative or 'heroic' pictures and rustic subjects ; exhibited at the Royal Academy ; began executing pictures in enamel, 1771 ; many of his works engraved by himself. He was probably the first painter who mastered the anatomy of the horse. [lv. 113]

STUBBS, GEORGE TOWNELEY (1756–1815), engraver ; son of George Stubbs [q. v.] [lv. 116]

STUBBS, STUBBES, or **STUBBE,** HENRY, the younger (1632–1676), physician and author ; son of Henry Stubbs or Stubbe the elder [q. v.] ; educated at Westminster School and introduced by Busby to Sir Henry Vane the younger [q. v.], who became his patron ; M.A. Christ Church, Oxford, where he was highly esteemed for his learning, 1656 ; served in the parliamentary army, 1653–5 ; expelled from Christ Church, Oxford, for writing against the clergy and universities, 1659 ; practised physic at Stratford-on-Avon ; imprisoned for writing a pamphlet denouncing James, duke of York's marriage with Mary of Modena ; described by Wood as ' the most noted Latinist and Grecian of his age . . . a singular mathematician ' ; intimately acquainted with Hobbes ; works include ' The Commonwealth of Oceana put in a Ballance and found too light' (an account of Sparta), 1660, and ' An Epistolary Discourse concerning Phlebotomy,' 1671. [lv. 116]

STUBBS, STUBBES, or **STUBBE,** HENRY, the elder (1606 ?–1678), ejected minister ; M.A. Magdalen Hall, Oxford, 1630 ; ejected from living of Dursley, 1662 ; published theological works. [lv. 117]

STUBBS or **STUBBE,** JOHN (1543 ?–1591), puritan zealot ; B.A. Trinity College, Cambridge, 1561 ; published ' The Discoverie of a gaping gulf,' 1579, condemning the proposed marriage between Queen Elizabeth and Henry, duke of Anjou, though writing of the queen in terms of loyalty and affection, for which he and his publisher Page had their right hands struck off ; remained loyal ; M.P., Great Yarmouth, 1589. He wrote for Burghley ' Defence of the English Catholics.' [lv. 118]

STUBBS or **STUBBES,** PHILIP (*fl.* 1583–1591), puritan pamphleteer ; said to have been kinsman of John Stubbs [q. v.] ; studied at Cambridge and Gloucester Hall, Oxford ; author of ' The Anatomie of Abuses,' 1583, which went quickly through several editions, in which he showed himself the exponent of extreme puritanic views, and which drew a rejoinder from Nashe in the ' Anatomie of Absurditie ' ; published ' A Christal Glasse for Christian Women,' 1591, and puritanical ballads and other works. [lv. 119]

STUBBS, PHILIP (1665–1738), archdeacon of St. Albans ; M.A. Wadham College, Oxford, 1689, and fellow, 1691 ; B.D., 1722 ; rector of Woolwich and afterwards of St. Alphege, London Wall, where his reading of the service was highly eulogised by Steele in the ' Spectator ' ; archdeacon of St. Albans, 1715 ; one of the earliest promoters of the S.P.G. ; published sermons. [lv. 120]

STUBBS, THOMAS (*fl.* 1373), chronicler ; perhaps identical with one Thomas de Stoubbes ordained at Durham, 1344 ; D.D. ; author of the latter portion of the ' Chronicle of the Archbishops of York' (published, 1886), the only work of his now extant. [lv. 121]

STUCLEY or **STUKELY,** SIR LEWIS (*d.* 1620), vice-admiral of Devonshire ; appointed keeper of Ralegh, on his return from the Orinoco, in which capacity his supposed unfair conduct made him intensely unpopular ; charged with clipping coin, 1619, but pardoned ; fled to Lundy, where he is said to have died insane. [lv. 122]

STUCLEY or **STUKELY,** THOMAS (1525 ?–1578), adventurer ; said to have been a natural son of Henry VIII ; entered the service of the Duke of Somerset, and on his arrest escaped to France ; sent to England by Henry II of France, 1552, for information required for his projected attempt on Calais ; betrayed his errand to Cecil, but was himself betrayed to the French king and imprisoned in the Tower of London ; escaped abroad, entered the service of the emperor Charles V and the Duke of Savoy, and was present at the victory of St. Quentin, 1557 ; embarked in a privateering expedition, in which Queen Elizabeth provided one of his six ships, 1563, and robbed the ships of all nations alike for two years, till at length the remonstrances of the foreign powers obliged Elizabeth to arrest him, when he was pardoned ; proceeded to Ireland, recommended by Cecil, but his ambitious schemes in that country discountenanced by Elizabeth, who suspected treasonable designs ; had for some time been corresponding with Philip II, and accepted from him a pension ; escaped to Spain, 1570, where he concocted plots against England, also visiting Paris and the papal court ; joined an expedition against Morocco in the interests of the king of Portugal, and was killed at the battle of Alcazar. [lv. 123]

STUDLEY, JOHN (1545 ?–1590 ?), translator ; of Westminster School and Trinity College, Cambridge ; fellow ; M.A., 1570 ; his translation of Seneca's tragedies, though he was a good classical scholar, remarkable for unnecessary additions and tedious paraphrases ; translated Bale's ' Acta Pontificum Romanorum,' 1574. [lv. 126]

STUKELEY. [See also STUCLEY.]

STUKELEY, WILLIAM (1687–1765), antiquary ; M.B. Bennet (Corpus Christi) College, Cambridge, 1708 ; F.R.S. and secretary to the Society of Antiquaries, which he shared in founding, 1718 ; M.D., 1719 ; F.R.C.P., 1720 ; Gulstonian lecturer, 1722 ; made long antiquarian excursions with Roger Gale [q. v.] and others ; incumbent of All Saints', Stamford, 1729–47 ; rector of St. George-the-Martyr, London, from 1747 ; author of medical and of antiquarian works ; published, among other writings, ' Itinerarium Curiosum,' 1724, and 'Stonehenge,' 1740, being specially interested in Druidism, which he considered the 'aboriginal patriarchal religion ' ; friend of Sir Isaac Newton and of Warburton ; published, 1757, as a genuine work of Richard of Cirencester, Charles Bertram's forgery ' De Situ Britanniæ.' To him was primarily due the error of supposing one Oriuna to have been the wife of Carausius [q. v.], he having read Oriuna for Fortuna on a coin. [lv. 127]

STUMP, SAMUEL JOHN (*d.* 1863), painter and miniaturist ; painted portraits of stage celebrities. [lv. 129]

STURCH, WILLIAM (1753 ?–1838), theological writer and ironmonger ; author of 'Apeleutherus' (1799), sonnets and pamphlets. [lv. 129]

STURGE, JOSEPH (1793–1859), quaker and philanthropist ; a zealous abolitionist ; went to the West Indies in order to supply the government with proofs, and on his return published ' The West Indies in 1837 ' ; a high tribute paid to him by Brougham ; assisted the freed negroes in various ways ; joined the chartists ; advocate of international arbitration ; visited many foreign countries to disseminate his views and attend peace congresses ; one of the deputation from the Society of Friends to protest to the tsar against the Crimean war. [lv. 130]

STURGEON, HENRY (1781 ? – 1814), lieutenant-colonel ; distinguished himself at the siege of Ciudad Rodrigo, at Salamanca, and elsewhere ; lieutenant-colonel, 1812 ; designed the great bridge over the Adour, 1814 ; killed soon afterwards ; mentioned in Wellington's despatches. [lv. 131]

STURGEON, WILLIAM (1783–1850), electrician ; was apprenticed to his father's trade of shoemaker, but enlisted, 1802, and remained in the army till 1820 ; studied science ; opened a shoemaker's shop at Woolwich and contributed scientific papers to various publications ; appointed lecturer in science at East India College, Addiscombe, 1824 ; presented to the Society of Arts improved apparatus for electro-magnetic experiments, which included his soft-iron electro-magnet, the parent of the dynamo, of which he was the original discoverer, 1823, also the inventor of the magneto-electrical machine ; described process of amalgamating the zinc plate of a battery with a film of mercury in ' Experimental Researches,' 1830 ; inventor of the electro-magnetic rotary engine, 1832 ; established ' The Annals of Electricity,' the first electrical journal in England, 1836 ; produced his electro-magnetic coil machine, 1837 ; superintendent of the Victoria Gallery of Practical Science at Manchester : itinerant lecturer from 1843 ; granted a pension by Lord John Russell, 1849. His various writings were collected by himself into one volume, 'Scientific Researches,' shortly before his death [lv. 131]

STURGES, OCTAVIUS (1833 - 1894), physician ; M.D. Emmanuel College, Cambridge, 1867 ; F.R.C.P., 1870 ; author of 'The Natural History . . . of Pneumonia,' 1876, and other works. [lv. 135]

STURGION, JOHN (*fl.* 1657), pamphleteer and anabaptist : imprisoned by Cromwell, 1657. [lv. 135]

STURT, CHARLES (1795–1869), Australian explorer ; educated at Harrow ; entered the army, 1813 ; saw active service at the end of the Peninsular campaign ; entered Paris with his regiment, 1815 ; took an active part in Ireland during the 'Whiteboy' riots ; appointed military secretary to Sir Ralph Darling [q. v.], governor of New South Wales, 1827 ; led several hazardous expeditions into the interior of Australia, the largest river system of Australia being surveyed, and South Australia with its extensive water communications being opened up ; assistant-commissioner of lands in South Australia, 1839 ; founder's gold medallist, Royal Geographical Society, 1847 ; colonial secretary, 1849 ; returned to England, 1853 ; published 'Journals,' 1833, and 'Narrative of an Expedition into Central Australia,' 1849. [lv. 136]

STURT, JOHN (1658–1730), engraver ; associated with John Ayres [q. v.] ; produced his Book of Common Prayer with minute lettering, 1717 ; illustrated numerous religious works, and was inventor of 'medleys.' [lv. 138]

STUTEVILLE, ROBERT DE (*d.* 1186), baron and justiciar ; justice itinerant, 1170–1 ; sheriff of Yorkshire, 1170–5 ; took a prominent part in the capture of William the Lyon (1143–1214) [q. v.], 1174. [lv. 139]

STUTEVILLE, WILLIAM DE (*d.* 1203), justice ; son of Robert de Stuteville [q. v.] ; justice itinerant and sheriff ; took part in the struggle between Richard I and Earl John. [lv. 139]

STYLE, WILLIAM (1603–1679), legal author ; of Queen's and Brasenose colleges, Oxford ; barrister, Inner Temple, 1628 ; compiled 'Regestum Practicale,' 1657, and other works. [lv. 140]

STYLEMAN, HENRY L'ESTRANGE (1815–1862). [See LE STRANGE.]

SUCKLING, ALFRED INIGO (1796–1856), author of 'History and Antiquities of Suffolk,' 1846–8, and other works ; LL.B. Pembroke College, Cambridge, 1824. [lv. 140]

SUCKLING, SIR JOHN (1609–1642), poet ; son of Sir John Suckling, secretary of state, 1622, and descendant of an old Norfolk family ; educated at Trinity College, Cambridge ; admitted at Gray's Inn, and inherited large estates on the death of his father, 1627 ; travelled in France and Italy ; knighted on his return, 1630 ; said to have joined Hamilton's force and to have taken part in the defeat of Tilly before Leipzig, 1631 ; returned, 1632 ; threw himself into all the gaieties of the court ; wrote 'The Session of the Poets,' 1637, and his first play 'Aglaura,' 1637, in producing which he spent large sums on the costumes and scenery ; accompanied Charles I to Scotland with a contingent, 1639, and was ridiculed for the gorgeous clothes with which he bedecked his soldiers ; published 'The Discontented Colonel,' 1640, a play in which he reflected on the disloyalty of the Scots ; advised Charles I in a letter of counsel to 'doe something extraordinary' ; set on foot the 'first army plot,' which, however, was betrayed by George, afterwards Lord Goring [q. v.] and escaped abroad ; is said by Aubrey to have committed suicide at Paris. His chief works are included in 'Fragmenta Aurea,' 1646, and consist of poems, plays, letters, and tracts. His plays are chiefly valuable for their few good lyrics. D'Avenant speaks of his sparkling wit, describing him further as the greatest gallant and gamester of his day. He invented the game of cribbage. [lv. 140]

SUCKLING, MAURICE (1725-1778), uncle of Nelson ; comptroller of the navy, 1775–8 ; fought a spirited action against the French, 1757. [lv. 146]

SUDBURY, SIMON OF (*d.* 1381), archbishop of Canterbury ; doctor of laws, Paris ; entered the service of Pope Innocent VI, and was made bishop of London, 1361 ; said to have told a party of Canterbury pilgrims that plenary indulgence was of no avail, an utterance which stirred up anger among the people ; blamed for abuses in his diocese by Edward III, 1371 ; sent as ambassador abroad on several occasions ; archbishop of Canterbury, 1375 ; tried Wycliffe at Lambeth, 1378 ; made chancellor, 1380 ; imprisoned John Ball (*d.* 1381) [q. v.], 1381, who was, however, released by the rioters on the outbreak of the rebellion ; urged Richard II to subdue them, and was especially hateful to the mob ; seized by the rioters and beheaded on the departure of Richard II from the Tower. He began the rebuilding of the nave of Canterbury Cathedral. [lv. 146]

SUDBURY, WILLIAM (*fl.* 1382), theologian, Benedictine monk, and author. [lv. 149]

SUEFRED (*fl.* 695), king of the East-Saxons. [lv. 149]

SUETT, RICHARD (1755–1805), actor ; began life as a choir-boy at Westminster Abbey ; sang at the Ranelagh Gardens, London, 1769, and elsewhere ; acted innumerable parts at Drury Lane, London, where he first appeared, 1780, and at the Haymarket Opera House, London, during the rebuilding of Drury Lane Theatre, 1791–2 ; his parts mainly those of Shakespearean clowns ; much praised by Lamb and Kemble. [lv. 149]

SUFFELD or **SUTHFELD**, WALTER (*d.* 1257), also called WALTER CALTHORP ; bishop of Norwich, 1244–5 ; the 'Norwich taxation,' the basis of later clerical assessments, made under his direction, 1253 ; built the lady-chapel of the cathedral. [lv. 151]

SUFFIELD, third BARON (1781–1835). [See HARBORD, EDWARD.]

SUFFIELD, ROBERT RODOLPH (1821–1891), successively Dominican friar and unitarian minister ; Dominican, 1860 ; published 'The Crown of Jesus,' 1862 ; became a unitarian minister, 1870. [lv. 152]

SUFFOLK, DUKES OF. [See POLE, WILLIAM DE LA, first DUKE, 1396–1450 ; POLE, JOHN DE LA, second DUKE, 1442–1491 ; BRANDON, CHARLES, first DUKE of the Brandon line, *d.* 1545 ; BRANDON, HENRY, second DUKE, 1535–1551 ; BRANDON, CHARLES, third DUKE, 1537 ?–1551 ; GREY, HENRY, *d.* 1554.]

SUFFOLK, DUCHESS OF (1520–1580). [See BERTIE, CATHARINE.]

SUFFOLK, EARLS OF. [See UFFORD, ROBERT DE, first EARL, 1298–1369 ; POLE, MICHAEL DE LA, first EARL of the Pole family, 1330 ?–1389 ; UFFORD, WILLIAM DE, second EARL, 1339 ?–1382 ; POLE, MICHAEL DE LA, second EARL, 1361 ?–1415 ; POLE, MICHAEL DE LA, third EARL, 1394–1415 ; POLE, SIR EDMUND DE LA, 1472 ?–1513 ; HOWARD, THOMAS, first EARL of the Howard family, 1561–1626 ; HOWARD, THEOPHILUS, second EARL, 1584–1640 ; HOWARD JAMES, third EARL, 1619–1688.]

SUFFOLK, COUNTESS OF (1681–1767). [See HOWARD, HENRIETTA.]

SUGDEN, EDWARD BURTENSHAW, BARON ST. LEONARDS (1781–1875), lord chancellor ; called to the bar from Lincoln's Inn after two years of conveyancing, 1807 ; K.C., 1822 ; tory M.P. for Weymouth and Melcombe Regis, 1828–30, St. Mawes, 1831–2, Ripon, 1837 ; solicitor-general, 1829–30 ; disapproved strongly of Brougham being made chancellor : drew attention to his levity in court ; accused him of jobbery, but made friends with him, 1832 ; Irish chancellor, 1834–5 and 1841–6 ; lord chancellor for less than a year owing to the fall of the government, though he continued to take active legal part in the privy council and House of Lords ; almost infallible as an oracle of law ; published 'Practical Treatise of the Law of Vendors and Purchasers,' 1805, 'Practical Treatise of Powers,' 1808, and learned edition of Gilbert's 'Law of Uses and Trusts,' 1808, which early made his reputation, also many other legal papers. As a law reformer he passed some excellent bills through parliament, mostly connected with wills and trusts. [lv. 152]

SUIDBERT (*d.* 713), apostle of the Frisians ; sent by Egbert to work in northern Europe ; consecrated by St. Wilfrid in England, 693. [lv. 155]

SULCARD or **SULGARD** (*fl.* 1075), chronographer and monk of Westminster ; wrote a history of the monastery. [lv. 155]

SULIEN, SULGEN, or **SULGENUS** (1011-1091), bishop of St. Davids, 1073-8, and again, 1080-6 : the centre of much literary activity. [lv. 155]

SULIVAN, Sir BARTHOLOMEW JAMES (1810-1890), admiral and hydrographer ; son of Thomas Ball Sulivan [q. v.] ; lieutenant on the Beagle, 1831-6, during her celebrated voyage ; carried out the survey of the Falkland islands ; returned home, 1846, and paid special attention to the formation of a naval reserve ; K.C.B., 1869 ; admiral, 1877. [lv. 156]

SULIVAN, THOMAS BALL (1780-1857), vice-admiral ; saw much active service, including the capture of Curaçoa, 1807, and the destruction of the America flotilla in the Patuxent, 1814 ; was chief agent of transports during the Peninsular war, 1809 ; advanced to post rank, 1814 ; C.B., 1815. [lv. 157]

SULLIVAN. [See also O'SULLIVAN.]

SULLIVAN, ALEXANDER MARTIN (1830-1884), Irish politician : joined the revolutionary party of the Young Irelanders ; editor of the nationalist paper, ' Nation,' 1856, which advocated constitutional agitation ; opponent of the Fenians, by whom he was marked out for assassination ; imprisoned for article in the ' Weekly News ' on the ' Manchester Martyrs,' 1868 ; one of the inaugurators of the home rule party under Butt, 1870 ; afterwards supported the more active leadership of Parnell, 1877 ; M.P. for several Irish constituencies ; called to the Irish bar, 1876, and to the English bar, 1877 ; author of ' The Story of Ireland,' and other works. [lv. 157]

SULLIVAN, Sir ARTHUR SEYMOUR (1842-1900), composer ; son of Thomas Sullivan (*d.* 1866), who was bandmaster at Royal Military College, Sandhurst, 1845-56, and professor, 1857-66, at Royal Military School of Music, Kneller Hall ; admitted one of children of Chapel Royal, St. James's, London, 1854 ; won Mendelssohn scholarship, 1856 ; studied at Royal Academy of Music, 1857, and at Conservatorium, Leipzig, 1858-61 ; organist and choir-master of St. Michael's Church, Chester Square, London, 1861-72 ; achieved considerable reputation by performance at Crystal Palace, 1862, of his music to Shakespeare's ' Tempest,' first performed at Leipzig, 1860 ; organist at Royal Italian Opera, Covent Garden Theatre, London ; conductor of Civil Service Musical Society, 1865-9 ; professor of composition at Royal Academy of Music, and of ' pianoforte and ballad-singing ' at Crystal Palace School of Art, 1866 : composed, 1866, comic opera, ' Cox and Box,' adapted by Mr. F. C. Burnand from farce by John Maddison Morton [q. v.], and produced at the Adelphi, 1867 ; composed ' Thespis, or the Gods grown old,' libretto by Mr. W. S. Gilbert, at Gaiety Theatre, London, 1871, the first of a series of comic operas produced in collaboration with Mr. Gilbert, the most popular of which were ' Trial by Jury,' 1875, ' H.M.S. Pinafore,' 1878, and ' The Mikado,' 1885 ; wrote ' Marmion ' for Philharmonic Society, 1867 ; organist and choirmaster of St. Peter's Church, Cranley Gardens, Kensington, London, 1867-72 ; composed oratorio, ' The Prodigal Son,' for Worcester musical festival, 1869, ' Overture di Ballo' for Birmingham festival, 1870, cantata, ' On Shore and Sea,' for opening of International Exhibition, 1871, ' Te Deum ' to celebrate recovery of King Edward VII, then prince of Wales, 1871 ; oratorio, ' Light of the World,' for Birmingham festival, 1873 ; conductor of Royal Aquarium orchestra, 1874-6, Leeds musical festival (triennial), 1880-98, and Philharmonic Society, London, 1885-7 ; first principal of National Training School of Music, South Kensington, London, 1876-81 ; produced setting to Longfellow's ' Golden Legend ' at Leeds festival, 1886, and serious opera, ' Ivanhoe,' at Royal English Opera House, London, 1891 ; F.R.A.M. ; buried in St. Paul's Cathedral. [Suppl. iii. 369]

SULLIVAN, BARRY (1821-1891), actor ; of Irish parentage ; began life as a draper's assistant, but by 1837 had appeared as a professional actor, his first part being that of Young Meadows in Bickerstaff's ' Love in a Village,' at Cork ; acted in several parts of Ireland ; appeared at Edinburgh, 1841, and in England, at Liverpool, 1847, in London, at the Haymarket, 1852, in America, 1858, in Australia, 1863 ; undertook several Shakespearean rôles in London, 1866, and became manager of the Holborn Theatre; acted at the opening of the Memorial Theatre at Stratford, 1879, as Benedick ; far more popular in Ireland and in the north of England than in London. [lv. 159]

SULLIVAN, Sir EDWARD, first baronet (1822-1885), lord chancellor of Ireland ; B.A. Trinity College, Dublin, 1845 : called to the Irish bar, 1848 ; as solicitor-general for Ireland dealt with the Fenian conspiracy, 1865 ; M.P., Cork, 1865 ; performed very valuable services in the conduct of the Irish Church Bill in the House of Commons, 1868, and as master of the rolls, 1870, and chancellor, 1883-5, was the mainstay of the English government ; created baronet, 1881. [lv. 161]

SULLIVAN, FRANCIS STOUGHTON (1719-1776), jurist ; of Trinity College, Dublin ; author of ' An Historical Treatise on the Feudal Law,' 1772. [lv. 162]

SULLIVAN, LUKE (*d.* 1771), engraver and miniaturist ; assistant to Hogarth. [lv. 162]

SULLIVAN, OWEN (1700 ?-1784), Irish Jacobite poet and potato-digger. [lv. 162]

SULLIVAN, Sir RICHARD JOSEPH, first baronet (1752-1806), miscellaneous writer ; F.S.A. and F.R.S., 1785 ; M.P., New Romney, 1787-96, Seaford, from 1802 ; created baronet, 1804 : author of ' An Analysis of the Political History of India,' 1779, ' Thoughts on the Early Ages of the Irish Nation . . . and on . . . the Ancient Establishment of the Milesian Families in that Kingdom,' 1789, and other works. [lv. 163]

SULLIVAN, ROBERT (1800-1868), educational writer and inspector of schools ; M.A. Trinity College, Dublin, 1832 ; LL.D., 1850 ; author of several educational works. [lv. 164]

SULLIVAN, TIMOTHY (1710 ?-1800), Irish itinerant poet ; composed panegyrics, satires, and religious poems. [lv. 164]

SULLIVAN, WILLIAM FRANCIS (1756-1830), author of poems and farces ; son of Francis Stoughton Sullivan [q. v.] ; of Trinity College, Dublin. [lv. 162]

SULMO, THOMAS (*fl.* 1540-1553). [See SOME.]

SUMBEL, MARY (*fl.* 1781-1812). [See WELLS, MRS. MARY.]

SUMERLED or **SOMERLED,** LORD OF THE ISLES (*d.* 1164), obtained possession of nearly all Argyll by defeating the Norse pirates ; seized Man, 1158 ; refusing to hold his possessions as a vassal of Malcolm IV, was defeated and slain near Renfrew, 1164. [lv. 164]

SUMMERS, CHARLES (1827-1878), sculptor ; went to Australia as a gold-digger, 1853 ; designed several monuments and statues in Melbourne. [lv. 165]

SUMMERS, Sir GEORGE (1554-1610). [See SOMERS.]

SUMNER, CHARLES RICHARD (1790-1874), bishop of Winchester ; brother of John Bird Sumner [q. v.], archbishop of Canterbury ; educated at Eton and Trinity College, Cambridge ; M.A., 1817 ; through the Conynghams, to whose sons he had been tutor, was introduced to George IV, 1820 ; created a very favourable impression, George IV's subsequent offer to him of a Windsor canonry nearly leading to the retirement of Lord Liverpool's administration, 1821 ; finally obtained several appointments at court, to which other preferments were added soon afterwards ; made bishop of Llandaff and dean of St. Paul's, London, 1826, and bishop of Winchester, 1827 ; voted for the Catholic Relief Bill, 1829, and thereby forfeited George IV's favour ; proved a zealous and capable administrator of his diocese, urging especially the necessity for new churches and for schools for the poor ; edited and translated Milton's ' De Doctrina Christiana,' 1825 ; author of several sermons. [lv. 165]

SUMNER, JOHN BIRD (1780-1862), archbishop of Canterbury ; educated at Eton and King's College, Cambridge ; elected fellow, 1801 ; Browne medallist. 1800, and Hulsean prizeman, 1802 ; M.A., 1807 ; canon of Durham, 1820 ; published several theological works, 1815-29, reflecting evangelical views ; made by Peel bishop of Chester, 1828, and by Lord John Russell archbishop of Canterbury 1848 ; voted for catholic relief and for the Reform

Bill ; repudiated the Bampton Lectures of Hampden, but did not refuse to consecrate him ; supported the institution of Gorham in the baptismal controversy ; opposed the removal of Jewish disabilities.   [lv. 168]

SUMNER, ROBERT CAREY (1729–1771), master of Harrow ; of Eton and King's College, Cambridge ; fellow, 1750 ; M.A., 1755 ; D.D., 1768 ; the friend of Dr. Johnson and master of Dr. Parr and Sir William Jones ; published 'Concio ad Clerum,' 1768.   [lv. 170]

SUNDERLAND, EARLS OF. [See SPENCER, HENRY, first EARL, 1620–1643 ; SPENCER, ROBERT, second EARL, 1640–1702 ; SPENCER, CHARLES, third EARL, 1674–1722.]

SUNDERLIN, BARON (1738–1816). [See MALONE, RICHARD.]

SUNDON, CHARLOTTE CLAYTON, LADY (d. 1742). [See CLAYTON, CHARLOTTE, LADY SUNDON.]

SUNMAN or **SONMANS**, WILLIAM (d. 1708), portrait-painter ; followed Sir Peter Lely into England ; painter of the imaginary portraits of founders in the Bodleian.   [lv. 171]

SURENNE, JOHN THOMAS (1814–1878), organist and professor of music ; compiler of 'The Dance Music of Scotland,' 1841, and other works.   [lv. 172]

SURR, THOMAS SKINNER (1770–1847), novelist; clerk in the Bank of England.   [lv. 172]

SURREY, DUKE OF (1374–1400). [See HOLLAND, THOMAS.]

SURREY, EARLS OF. [See WARENNE, WILLIAM DE, first EARL, d. 1088 ; WARENNE, WILLIAM DE, second EARL, d. 1138 ; WARENNE, WILLIAM DE, third EARL, d. 1148 ; WARENNE, HAMELIN DE, first EARL OF SURREY and WARENNE, d. 1202 ; WARENNE, WILLIAM DE, second EARL OF SURREY and WARENNE, d. 1240 ; WARENNE, JOHN DE, third EARL OF SURREY and WARENNE, 1231 ?–1304 ; WARENNE, JOHN DE, fourth EARL OF SURREY and WARENNE, 1286–1347 ; FITZALAN, RICHARD III, EARL OF ARUNDEL and SURREY, 1346–1397 ; FITZALAN, THOMAS, EARL OF ARUNDEL and SURREY, 1381–1415 ; HOWARD, THOMAS, EARL OF SURREY and second DUKE OF NORFOLK, 1443–1524 ; HOWARD, HENRY, EARL OF SURREY by courtesy, 1517 ?–1547 ; HOWARD, THOMAS, EARL OF SURREY and third DUKE OF NORFOLK, 1473–1554.]

SURTEES, ROBERT (1779–1834), antiquary and topographer ; B.A. Christ Church, Oxford, 1803 ; spent his life in examining remains of antiquity in the county for his work, 'The History of Durham' (published, 1816–40). Scott included a spurious ballad by him, 'The Death of Featherstonehaugh,' in his 'Ministrelsy of the Scottish Border.' The Surtees Society was founded in his name, 1834.   [lv. 173]

SURTEES, ROBERT SMITH (1803–1864), sporting novelist ; started 'New Sporting Magazine,' 1831, in which he published the sketches of Mr. John Jorrocks, the sporting grocer, published later as 'Jorrocks's Jaunts,' 1838 ; J.P. and high sheriff for Durham, 1856 ; among his other works 'Handley Cross,' 1845, 'Ask Mamma,' 1858, and 'Mr. Facey Romford's Hounds,' published 1865 ; wrote also 'The Horseman's Manual,' 1831.   [lv. 174]

SUSSEX, DUKE OF (1773–1843). [See AUGUSTUS FREDERICK.]

SUSSEX, EARLS OF. [See RADCLIFFE, ROBERT, first EARL, 1483–1542 ; RADCLIFFE, HENRY, second EARL, 1506 ?–1557 ; RADCLIFFE, THOMAS, third EARL, 1526 ?–1583 ; RADCLIFFE, HENRY, fourth EARL, 1530 ?–1593 ; RADCLIFFE, ROBERT, fifth EARL, 1569 ?–1629 ; SAVILE, THOMAS, 1590 ?–1658 ?]

SUTCLIFFE, MATTHEW (1550 ?–1629), dean of Exeter ; major fellow of Trinity College, Cambridge, 1574 ; M.A., 1574 ; LL.D., 1581 ; dean of Exeter, 1588 ; established a college in Chelsea, 1609, 'where learned divines should study and unite in maintenance of all controversies against the papists' (FULLER) ; scheme strongly supported by James I, but a complete failure ; assisted John Smith (1580–1631) [q. v.], and was member of the council for New England, 1620 ; fell into disgrace at court, 1621, on account of his opposition to the Spanish marriage ; published a large number of controversial works directed against the Roman catholics.   [lv. 175]

SUTCLIFFE, THOMAS (1790 ?–1849), adventurer ; entered the navy, and during the blockade of Corfu was taken prisoner, but escaped, 1806 ; severely wounded at Waterloo ; fought for the Columbians against the Spaniards, 1817 ; filled various military and administrative positions in the republic of Chili ; published works mainly on Chili and Peru.   [lv. 177]

SUTHERLAND, DUKES OF. [See LEVESON-GOWER, GEORGE GRANVILLE, first DUKE, 1758–1833 ; LEVESON-GOWER, GEORGE GRANVILLE WILLIAM SUTHERLAND, third DUKE, 1828–1892.]

SUTHERLAND, DUCHESS OF (1806–1868). [See LEVESON-GOWER, HARRIET ELIZABETH GEORGIANA.]

SUTHERLAND, EARLS OF. [See GORDON, JOHN, tenth or eleventh EARL, 1526 ?–1567 ; GORDON, ALEXANDER, eleventh or twelfth EARL, 1552–1594 ; GORDON, JOHN, thirteenth or fourteenth EARL, 1609–1663 ; GORDON, JOHN, fifteenth or sixteenth EARL, 1660 ?–1733.]

SUTHERLAND, JOHN (1808–1891), promoter of sanitary science ; educated at the high school, Edinburgh ; M.D. Edinburgh, 1831 ; inspector under the first board of health, 1848 ; despatched by Palmerston to investigate the sanitary condition of the troops in the Crimea ; carried out great sanitary reforms in the army.   [lv. 178]

SUTHERLAND, ROBERT, sixth EARL OF (d. 1442), present at the battle of Homildon, 1402 ; hostage for James I in England, 1427.   [lv. 179]

SUTHERLAND, WILLIAM, second EARL OF (d. 1325), took part on the side of Bruce at Bannockburn, 1314.   [lv. 179]

SUTHERLAND, WILLIAM, fourth EARL OF (d. 1370), hostage in England for David II, 1353.   [lv. 179]

SUTHERLAND, WILLIAM, fifth EARL OF (d. 1398 ?), according to Froissart, present at the battle of Berwick, 1384.   [lv. 179]

SUTHFIELD, WALTER DE (d. 1257). [See SUFFELD.]

SUTTON. [See also MANNERS-SUTTON.]

SUTTON, SIR CHARLES (1775–1828), colonel ; served with Sir John Moore, and later distinguished himself as colonel of a Portuguese regiment in Peninsular campaign ; K.C.B., 1815.   [lv. 179]

SUTTON, CHRISTOPHER (1565 ?–1629), divine ; of Hart Hall and Lincoln College, Oxford ; M.A. Lincoln College, Oxford, 1589 ; D.D., 1608 ; canon of Westminster, 1605, and of Lincoln, 1618 ; author of devotional works.   [lv. 180]

SUTTON, JOHN DE, sixth BARON DUDLEY (1401 ?–1487). [See DUDLEY, JOHN.]

SUTTON, OLIVER (d. 1299), bishop of Lincoln ; related to the Lexington family ; bishop of Lincoln, 1280–1299 ; involved himself in disputes with the university of Oxford ; joined Archbishop Winchelsey in resisting Edward I's taxation, 1296.   [lv. 180]

SUTTON, SIR RICHARD (d. 1524), co-founder of Brasenose College, Oxford, with William Smith (1460 ?–1514) [q. v.], bishop of Lincoln ; member of the Inner Temple ; appears to have early amassed wealth ; in the privy council, 1498 ; endowed his foundation with several properties, 1519 ; knighted before 1524 ; the first lay founder of a college.   [lv. 181]

SUTTON, SIR RICHARD, second baronet (1798–1855), sportsman ; he was one of the most wealthy men in the country, and devoted himself to sport ; master of the Burton hunt in Lincolnshire, 1822 ; led the Quorn hunt, 1848–55 ; bore the sole cost of the Quorn hunt for some years.   [lv. 182]

SUTTON, ROBERT, first BARON LEXINGTON (1594–1668), M.P., Nottinghamshire, 1625 and 1640 ; served throughout the war on Charles I's side in the garrison at Newark till its surrender, 1646 ; his property sequestered ; obtained some compensation at the Restoration. [lv. 183]

SUTTON, ROBERT, second BARON LEXINGTON (1661–1723), son of Robert Sutton, first baron Lexington [q. v.] ; entered the army, but appears to have resigned his commission as a protest against the illegal conduct of James II, 1686 ; lord of the bedchamber to William III ; sent on various missions abroad ; one of the plenipotentiaries chosen to conclude the peace of Ryswick, 1697 ; conducted negotiations in Spain at the treaty of Utrecht, 1712, for which he was severely censured by Walpole's committee. [lv. 184]

SUTTON, THOMAS (1532–1611), founder of the Charterhouse, London ; is said to have been educated at Eton ; student of Lincoln's Inn ; perhaps related to the Dudley, *alias* Sutton family, earls of Warwick and Leicester ; served in the army at Berwick and elsewhere ; surveyor of the ordnance in the northern parts, 1570 ; obtained leases of land rich in coal in Durham, and made an enormous fortune, which was further increased by his marriage with Elizabeth, widow of John Dudley ; settled in London, 1580 ; gave liberally to public and charitable subscriptions ; purchased the Charterhouse, 1611, where he established a hospital of eighty inmates and a school of forty boys, for which he had already conveyed his estates in Essex ; buried in the chapel there, 1614. He was estimated the richest commoner in England, his estates being reckoned at 5,000*l.* a year and his personalty at 60,410*l.* [lv. 185]

SUTTON, THOMAS (1585–1623), divine ; M.A. Queen's College, Oxford, 1609 ; D.D., 1620 ; fellow, 1611 ; founded and endowed a free school at Bampton, Westmoreland, 1623 ; published some celebrated sermons. [lv. 187]

SUTTON, THOMAS (1767 ?–1835), medical writer ; M.D. Leyden, 1787 ; L.R.C.P., 1790 ; first modern English physician to advocate bleeding ; established the true character of delirium tremens in 'Tracts,' 1813. [lv. 188]

SWADLIN, THOMAS (1600–1670), royalist divine ; B.A. St. John's College, Oxford, 1619 ; created D.D., 1646 ; as curate of St. Botolph, Aldgate, London, obtained celebrity as a preacher ; imprisoned by the parliamentary party, 1642, and his living sequestered ; reinstated at the Restoration, when he obtained other preferments ; D.D. ; author of religious and royalist works. [lv. 188]

SWAFFHAM, ROBERT OF (*d.* 1273 ?). [See ROBERT.]

SWAIN, CHARLES (1801–1874), poet ; began life as clerk in a dye-house, and subsequently carried on the business of an engraver ; published several volumes of poetry, including 'The Mind and other Poems,' 1832. His songs, which include 'I cannot mind my wheel, mother,' and 'Somebody's waiting for somebody,' were many of them set to music and became very popular. [lv. 189]

SWAIN, JOSEPH (1761–1796), hymn-writer and preacher ; author of several volumes of hymns, including 'Walworth Hymns,' 1792. [lv. 190]

SWAINE, FRANCIS (*d.* 1782), marine-painter and one of the earliest English artists whose sea-views possess any merit. [lv. 190]

SWAINE, JOHN (1775–1860), draughtsman and engraver ; but known by his facsimile copies of old prints. [lv. 190]

SWAINE, JOHN BARAK (1815 ?–1838), etcher and artist ; son of John Swaine [q. v.] [lv. 190]

SWAINSON, CHARLES ANTHONY (1820–1887), theologian ; sixth wrangler, Trinity College, Cambridge, 1841 ; fellow of Christ's College, Cambridge, 1841 ; held several clerical posts and became prebendary of Chichester, 1856 ; Norrisian professor of divinity, 1864, and Lady Margaret's reader, 1879 ; master of Christ's College, Cambridge, 1881 ; vice-chancellor, 1885 ; author of theological works, including 'The Greek Liturgies,' 1884, chiefly dealing with the creeds ; follower of Hooker. [lv. 191]

SWAINSON, WILLIAM (1789–1855), naturalist ; obtained a post in the commissariat and went to Malta, 1807, and Sicily, making large collections which he brought to England, 1815 ; made another collection of birds in Brazil, 1816 ; published works, including 'Zoological Illustrations,' 1820–3 ; eleven volumes in Lardner's 'Cabinet Cyclopædia,' and three volumes in Sir William Jardine's 'Naturalist's Library.' He adopted a quinary system based on the circular system of William Sharp Macleay [q. v.] ; emigrated to New Zealand, 1837, and died there. [lv. 192]

SWAINSON, WILLIAM (1809–1883), first attorney-general of New Zealand ; barrister, Inner Temple, 1838 ; attorney-general, 1841, and first speaker of the legislative

council, 1854, New Zealand ; opposed the war with the Maoris, 1862 ; a member of Sir George Grey's ministry, 1879 ; author of works on New Zealand. [lv. 193]

SWALE, SIR RICHARD (1545 ?–1608), civilian ; fellow of Jesus College, Cambridge, 1571 ; M.A., 1572 ; fellow of Caius College, Cambridge, 1576 ; accused by the other fellows of popery, but nevertheless was appointed president, 1582 ; made master in chancery by Sir Christopher Hatton, 1587 ; M.P., Higham Ferrers, 1589 ; prebendary of York, 1589 ; knighted, 1603. [lv. 194]

SWAN, JOSEPH (1791–1874), anatomist ; surgeon to the Lincoln County Hospital, 1814–27 ; never attained any practice, but did much for the science of anatomy, excelling especially as a dissectionist ; F.R.C.S., 1843 ; published 'A Demonstration of the Nerves of the Human Body,' 1830, and other medical works. [lv. 195]

SWAN, WILLIAM (1818–1894), professor of natural philosophy at St. Andrews ; hon. LL.D. Edinburgh, 1869, St. Andrews, 1886 ; professor, 1859–80 ; author of various scientific papers. [lv. 196]

SWANBOROUGH, MRS. ARTHUR (1840 ?–1893). [See BUFTON, ELEANOR.]

SWANLEY, RICHARD (*d.* 1650), naval commander ; performed valuable naval services for the parliament ; reduced the Isle of Wight, 1642, and prevented the Irish reinforcements from landing in Wales. [lv. 196]

SWANSEA, BARON (1821–1894). [See VIVIAN, SIR HENRY HUSSEY.]

SWANWICK, ANNA (1813–1899), authoress ; born at Liverpool ; studied German and Greek at Berlin ; member of councils of Queen's and Bedford colleges, London, and was president of Queen's College ; assisted in founding Girton College, Cambridge ; hon. LL.D. Aberdeen. Her publications include translations from German and Greek dramatists ; her version of Goethe's 'Faust,' 1850–78, in blank verse, is one of the best in existence. [Suppl. iii. 374]

SWEET, ROBERT (1783–1835), horticulturist ; began life as a gardener at Ham Green, near Bristol ; F.L.S., 1812 ; occupied himself latterly in the production of botanical and gardening works ; genus *Sweetia* named after him. [lv. 197]

SWEETMAN, JOHN (1752–1826), United Irishman and Dublin brewer ; identified himself with the movement for removing catholic disabilities ; member of the revolutionary organisation of United Irishmen at Leinster, and arrested, 1798 ; exiled, 1802–20. [lv. 197]

SWEETMAN, MILO (*d.* 1380), archbishop of Armagh ; consecrated, 1360 ; became involved in the dispute concerning the primacy with the archbishop of Dublin ; present at the parliament which passed the statute of Kilkenny, 1367 ; successfully resisted the writs ordering Irish representatives to go to the parliament at Westminster, 1374. [lv. 198]

SWEREFORD, ALEXANDER DE (1176 ?–1246), baron of the exchequer and reputed compiler of the 'Red Book of the Exchequer' ; canon of St. Paul's, London, and treasurer, 1232 ; sent on several important missions by Henry III to Wales and abroad ; appointed baron of the exchequer, 1234 ; famous also as the collector of historical precedents and state papers. [lv. 199]

SWETE or **TRIPE,** JOHN (1752 ?–1821), antiquary ; M.A. University College, Oxford, 1777 ; prebendary of Exeter, 1781 ; contributed to works published or edited by Polwhele. [lv. 200]

SWETNAM, JOSEPH (*fl.* 1617), called the woman-hater ; author of 'The Araignment of lewd, idle, froward and unconstant Women,' 1615, which provoked several rejoinders. [lv. 200]

SWETNAM, SWEETNAM, or **SWEETMAN,** JOSEPH (1577–1622), jesuit and religious author. [lv. 201]

SWEYN or **SVEIN** (*d.* 1014), king of England and Denmark ; son of Harold Blaatand, king of Denmark ; baptised according to the conditions of peace dictated by the Emperor Otho, 965 ; appears to have cast aside Christianity and made war against his father, who was killed in a battle with him, 986, on which he became king ; soon, however, driven from Denmark by Eric the Victorious, he became a sea-rover, invading England with Olaf, 994, when an unsuccessful assault on London was made ; remained for some time ravaging the country, but after further adventures was restored to his kingdom, c. 1000 ; invaded England, 1003, in consequence of the massacre of the Danes on St. Brice's day, 1002, in which his sister Gunhild and her family are said to have perished ; stormed Exeter and ravaged Wiltshire ; burnt and plundered Norwich, 1004 ; again arrived, with Canute, his son, in the Humber, 1013, ravaged the land, and made a complete conquest of the country ; accepted as 'full king,' 1013 ; died soon afterwards, according to the legend, pierced by the spear of St. Edmund, whom he had derided.   [lv. 201]

SWEYN or SWEGEN (d. 1052), eldest son of Earl Godwin [q. v.] ; earl of Oxfordshire, Berkshire, Gloucestershire, Herefordshire, and Somerset ; took the side of his father in his quarrel with Edward the Confessor ; was outlawed several times and made a pilgrimage barefoot to Jerusalem for the murder of his cousin Beorn, 1052.
[lv. 203]

SWIFT, DEANE (1707-1783), author ; cousin of Jonathan Swift [q. v.] ; B.A. St. Mary Hall, Oxford, 1736 ; published 'An Essay upon the Life, Writings, and Character of Dr. Jonathan Swift,' 1755.   [lv. 228]

SWIFT, JONATHAN (1667-1745), dean of St. Patrick's, Dublin, and satirist ; cousin of Dryden and son of Jonathan Swift by Abigail (Erick) of Leicester ; born at Dublin after his father's death ; grandson of Thomas Swift, the well-known royalist vicar of Goodrich, who was descended from a Yorkshire family, a member of which, 'Cavaliero' Swifte, was created Baron Carlingford, 1627 ; educated at Kilkenny grammar school, where Congreve was a schoolfellow, and at Trinity College, Dublin, 1682 ; neglected his studies, showed an impatience of restraint, was publicly censured for offences against discipline, and only obtained his degree by the 'special grace' ; attributed his recklessness himself to the neglect of his family, for whom he felt little regard ; joined his mother at Leicester on the troubles which followed the expulsion of James II ; admitted into the household of Sir William Temple, who had known his uncle Godwin, c. 1692, where he acted as his secretary ; introduced to William III and sent by Temple to him, to convince him of the necessity for triennial parliaments, 1693 ; wrote pindarics, one being printed in the 'Athenian Mercury,' 1692, which, according to Dr. Johnson, provoked Dryden's remark, 'Cousin Swift, you will never be a poet' ; chafed at his position of dependence, and was indignant at Temple's delay in procuring him preferment ; left Temple's service, returned to Ireland, was ordained, 1694, and was given the small prebend of Kilroot ; returned to Temple at Moor Park, 1696 ; read deeply, mostly classics and history, and edited Temple's correspondence ; wrote (1697) 'The Battle of the Books,' which was published in 1704, together with 'The Tale of a Tub,' his famous and powerful satire of theological shams and pedantry ; met 'Stella,' Esther Johnson [q. v.], who was an inmate of Temple's family at the time ; went again to Ireland on the death of Temple, 1699 ; given a prebend in St. Patrick's, Dublin, and Laracor, with other livings ; made frequent visits to Dublin and London ; D.D. Dublin, 1701 ; wrote his 'Discourse on the Dissensions in Athens and Rome' with reference to the impeachment of the whig lords, 1701 ; in his visit to London, 1705 and 1707, became acquainted with Addison, Steele, Congreve, and Halifax ; entrusted (1707) with a mission to obtain the grant of Queen Anne's bounty for Ireland ; wrote some pamphlets on religious or church subjects ; published 'Letter on the Sacramental Test,' 1708, an attack on the Irish presbyterians, which, though anonymous, injured him with the whigs ; in disgust at the whig alliance with dissent, ultimately went over to the tories on his next visit to England, 1710 ; attacked the whig ministers in pamphlets, in the 'Examiner,' November 1710 to June 1711, and wrote the 'Conduct of the Allies,' 1711 ; became dean of St. Patrick's, 1713 ; had already commenced the 'Journal to Stella,' had become intimate with the tory ministers, and had used his influence in helping young and impoverished authors, including Pope and Steele ; returned to England, 1713, to reconcile Bolingbroke and Harley, but in vain ; wrote more pamphlets, notably 'The Public Spirit of the Whigs considered,' 1714, in reply to Steele's 'Crisis,' but at length gave up all for lost and retired to the country ; left for Ireland, 1715, after the fall of the ministry and the death of Queen Anne ; his marriage to Stella, an incident

which still remains unproven, and also his final rupture with 'Vanessa' (Miss Vanhomrigh, whose acquaintance he had made in London), supposed to have taken place about this time ; his rupture with Vanessa the cause of her death, before which she entrusted to her executors his poem 'Cadenus and Vanessa,' which relates the story of their love affair ; though always contemptuous of the Irish, was led, by his personal antipathies to the whigs, to acquire a sense of their unfair dealings with Ireland ; successfully prevented the introduction of 'Wood's Halfpence' into Ireland by his famous 'Drapier Letters,' 1724 ; came to England, 1726, visited Pope and Gay, and dined with Walpole, for whose behoof he afterwards wrote a letter complaining of the treatment of Ireland, which had, however, no effect on the minister ; broke with Walpole in consequence ; was introduced to Queen Caroline, but gained nothing by it ; published 'Gulliver's Travels,' 1726 ; made his last visit to England, 1727, when the death of George I created for a moment hopes of dislodging Walpole ; wrote some of his most famous tracts and some of his most characteristic poems during these last years in Ireland ; kept up his correspondence with Bolingbroke, Pope, Gay, and Arbuthnot, and though remaining aloof from Dublin society, maintained good relations with Lord Carteret, the lord-lieutenant ; attracted to himself a small circle of friends, and was adored by the people ; set up a monument to Schomberg in the cathedral at his own expense, spent a third of his income on charities, and saved up another third to found a charitable institution at his death, St. Patrick's Hospital (opened, 1757) ; symptoms of the illness from which he appears to have suffered all his life very marked, c. 1738 ; buried by the side of Stella, in St. Patrick's, Dublin, his own famous inscription, 'ubi sæva indignatio ulterius cor lacerare nequit,' being inscribed on his tomb. Dr. Johnson, Macaulay, and Thackeray, among many other writers, were alienated by his ferocity, which was, however, the result of noble qualities soured by hard experience. His indignation at oppression and unfairness was genuine. His political writings are founded on common sense pure and simple, and he had no party bias. His works, with the exception of the letter upon the correction of the language, 1712, were all anonymous, and for only one, 'Gulliver's Travels,' did he receive any payment (200l.). A large number of publications appear to have been attributed to him by different editors without sufficient authority.   [lv. 204]

SWIFT, ROBERT (1534 ?-1599), chancellor of Durham ; of the same family as Jonathan Swift [q. v.] ; B.A. St. John's College, Cambridge, 1553 ; fellow ; chancellor of Durham, 1561.   [lv. 227]

SWIFT, THEOPHILUS (1746-1815), Irish writer ; son of Deane Swift [q. v.] ; B.A. St. Mary Hall, Oxford, 1767 ; barrister, Middle Temple, 1774 ; sentenced to twelve months' imprisonment for libelling the fellows of Trinity College, Dublin, 1794.   [lv. 228]

SWINBURNE, HENRY (1560 ?-1623), ecclesiastical lawyer ; matriculated at Hart Hall, Oxford ; B.C.L. Broadgates Hall, Oxford ; author of 'A Briefe Treatise of Testaments and last Willes,' 1590, and 'A Treatise of Spousals,' published, 1686 (the first works written in England on their respective subjects).   [lv. 228]

SWINBURNE, HENRY (1743-1803), traveller ; son of Sir John Swinburne of Capheaton ; educated in France ; visited Italy ; visited Spain with his wife, 1774-6 ; the two Sicilies, Vienna, Frankfort, and Brussels, 1777-9, Italy and Vienna, 1780 ; with his wife formed acquaintances with the chief literati, and received many compliments from the different Roman catholic sovereigns ; again in Paris, 1786-8 ; his eldest son made by Marie-Antoinette one of her pages ; sent on a mission to Paris by the government for the exchange of prisoners, 1796 ; went out as vendue-master to Trinidad, 1801, where he died. He was author of 'Travels through Spain,' 1779, 'Travels in the Two Sicilies,' 1783 and 1785. His letters, under the title of 'The Courts of Europe,' badly edited, were published, 1841.   [lv. 229]

SWINDEN, HENRY (1716-1772), antiquary : author of the 'History . . . of Great Yarmouth,' 1772. [lv. 231]

SWINDEN, TOBIAS (d. 1719), divine ; M.A. Jesus College, Cambridge, 1682 ; published 'An Enquiry into the Nature and Place of Hell,' 1714.   [lv. 231]

SWINERCOTE, LAWRENCE (fl. 1254). [See SOMERCOTE.]

SWINESHEAD, RICHARD (*fl.* 1350), mathematician ; fellow of Merton College, Oxford ; Cistercian monk at Swineshead in Lincolnshire ; author of mathematical and philosophical works. [lv. 231]

SWINEY, GEORGE (1786 ?–1844), founder of the Swiney prize and lectureship ; M.D. Edinburgh, 1816. [lv. 232]

SWINEY, GEORGE (1786–1868), general ; cousin of George Swiney (1786 ?–1844) [q. v.] [lv. 232]

SWINEY, OWEN MAC (*d.* 1754). [See SWINNY.]

SWINFEN, JOHN (1612–1694). [See SWYNFEN.]

SWINFEN, SAMUEL (1679–1734). [See SWYNFEN.]

SWINFIELD or **SWYNFIELD**, RICHARD DE (*d.* 1317), bishop of Hereford ; entered the service of Thomas de Cantelupe, chancellor and partisan of the baronial party, and was given by him several preferments ; accompanied him to Normandy when exiled, and again in his journey to Italy, 1282 ; bishop of Hereford, 1282–1317 ; resisted the extortions of Edward I. He was a bountiful patron of scholars, and a portion of the cathedral was probably built by him. [lv. 232]

SWINFORD, CATHERINE, DUCHESS OF LANCASTER (1350 ?–1403). [See SWYNFORD.]

SWINNERTON, THOMAS (*d.* 1554), protestant divine ; M.A. Cambridge, under the assumed name of John Roberts, 1519 ; author of ' A mustre of scismatyke Bysshoppes of Rome,' 1534. [lv. 234]

SWINNOCK, GEORGE (1627–1673), nonconformist divine ; B.A. Jesus College, Cambridge, 1648 ; fellow of Balliol College, Oxford, 1649 ; M.A. 1650 ; held various incumbencies ; published religious works. [lv. 235]

SWINNY, OWEN MAC (*d.* 1754), playwright. He was manager of the Queen's Theatre, Haymarket, London, 1706, 1710, and 1711 ; after some successes became bankrupt and took refuge abroad, returning 1735. [lv. 235]

SWINSHED, RICHARD (*fl.* 1350). [See SWINESHEAD.]

SWINTON, ALEXANDER, LORD MERSINGTON (1625 ?–1700), Scottish judge ; fought for Charles II and was taken prisoner at Worcester ; advocate, 1671 ; relinquished his profession rather than take the test, 1681 ; restored, 1686 ; made judge, 1688 ; joined the supporters of William III in Scotland at the Revolution. [lv. 236]

SWINTON, ARCHIBALD CAMPBELL (1812–1890), author and politician ; elder brother of James Rannie Swinton [q. v.] ; professor of civil law at Edinburgh, 1852–72. [lv. 237]

SWINTON, JAMES RANNIE (1816–1888), portrait-painter ; worked at the studio of Sir John Watson-Gordon [q. v.] ; at the schools of the Academy, and visited Italy and Spain ; painted the fashionable beauties of the day. [lv. 236]

SWINTON, SIR JOHN (*d.* 1402), Scottish soldier ; killed at Homildon Hill. [lv. 237]

SWINTON, JOHN (1621 ?–1679), Scottish politician ; elder brother of Alexander Swinton [q. v.] ; M.P. for the Merse, 1649 ; joined Cromwell after Dunbar, and was excommunicated by the Scottish kirk and his estates forfeited, 1651 ; under Cromwell's administration of Scotland was appointed commissioner, member of the council of state, and M.P. ; was arrested and imprisoned at the Restoration ; turned quaker, 1657 ; published quaker pamphlets. [lv. 237]

SWINTON, JOHN (1703–1777), historian and antiquary ; F.R.S., 1728 ; fellow of Wadham College, Oxford, 1729 (M.A., 1726) ; B.D., 1759 ; published dissertations and other works, including ' Inscriptiones Citieæ,' 1750. [lv. 239]

SWINTON, JOHN, LORD SWINTON (*d.* 1799), Scottish judge and legal writer ; sat on the bench, 1782–1799 ; a lord of justiciary, 1788–99. [lv. 239]

SWINY, OWEN MAC (*d.* 1754). [See SWINNY.]

SWITHUN, SAINT (*d.* 862), bishop of Winchester ; probably a secular clerk ; an adviser in state matters of Egbert [q. v.], and educator of his son, Ethelwulf [q. v.], who on his accession appointed him bishop of Winchester,

852 ; one of the chief counsellors of this king in ecclesiastical matters. His body was buried, by his own wish, outside the north wall of Winchester minster, but moved inside the cathedral, 971, when innumerable miracles followed, and he was canonised in popular tradition. The shrine was destroyed by Henry VIII. [lv. 239]

SWITZER, STEPHEN (1682 ?–1745), agricultural writer, was well educated, and became a gardener under George London and Henry Wise [q. v.] ; eventually became seedsman in Westminster Hall ; edited a monthly periodical, ' The Practical Husbandman and Planter,' in which he warmly repelled attacks on Virgil's agriculture as represented in the 'Georgics' ; author of several books on gardening. [lv. 241]

SWYNFEN or **SWINFEN**, JOHN (1612–1694), politician ; M.P. for Stafford in the Long parliament, 1640, on the side of the parliament ; excluded by Pride's Purge, 1648 ; restored by Monck ; prominent at the Restoration as an opponent of the court party. [lv. 242]

SWYNFEN or **SWINFEN**, SAMUEL (1679–1734), physician ; grandson of John Swynfen [q. v.] ; M.A. Pembroke College, Oxford, 1703 ; M.D., 1712 ; godfather to Dr. Johnson. [lv. 243]

SWYNFORD, CATHERINE, DUCHESS OF LANCASTER (1350 ?–1403), mistress and third wife of John of Gaunt [q. v.] ; mother of the Beauforts and ancestress of Henry VII ; daughter of Sir Payne Roelt, who came to England with Queen Philippa, her first husband being Sir Hugh Swynford, who belonged to the retinue of John of Gaunt, and who died, 1372 ; became John of Gaunt's mistress and had charge of his children ; married to John of Gaunt on the death of his second wife, 1396. Their issue were legitimised by parliament, 1397, but in 1407 the words ' excepta dignitate regali ' were interpolated. [lv. 243]

SWYNFORD, SIR THOMAS (1368 ?–1433), only legitimate child of Catherine Swynford [q. v.] by her first husband ; supporter of Henry IV's claims, and supposed murderer of Richard II. [lv. 244]

SYBTHORPE, ROBERT (*d.* 1662). [See SIBTHORP.]

SYDDALL, HENRY (*d.* 1572). [See SIDDALL.]

SYDENHAM, BARON (1799–1841). [See THOMSON, CHARLES EDWARD POULETT.]

SYDENHAM or **SIDENHAM**, CUTHBERT (1622–1654), theologian and presbyterian divine ; lecturer at St. John's and St. Nicholas's churches, Newcastle ; author of religious and puritanical works. [lv. 244]

SYDENHAM, FLOYER (1710–1787), translator of Plato ; M.A. Wadham College, Oxford, 1734 ; fellow, 1734 ; barrister, Lincoln's Inn, 1735 ; published, besides his translation (1759–80), 'An Essay on the Divine Names according to the Platonic Philosophy,' 1784. [lv. 245]

SYDENHAM, HUMPHREY (1591–1650 ?), royalist divine ; B.A. Exeter College, Oxford, 1611 ; fellow and M.A. Wadham College, Oxford, 1613 ; prebendary of Wells, 1642 ; received other preferments, from all of which he was ejected by the parliamentary commissioners ; published sermons. [lv. 245]

SYDENHAM, JOHN (1807–1846), antiquary and editor ; author of ' The History of the Town and County of Poole,' 1839. [lv. 246]

SYDENHAM, THOMAS (1624–1689), physician ; entered Magdalen Hall, Oxford, 1642 ; together with his brothers took part in the civil war on the side of the parliament, 1642–5 ; returned to Oxford, 1646, and was advised by Thomas Coxe [q. v.] to apply himself to medicine ; fellow of All Souls College, Oxford, 1648 ; created M.B. by command of the Earl of Pembroke, 1648 ; M.A. later ; received a new commission as captain of cavalry, 1651, and took part in much sharp fighting ; studied medicine at Montpellier, 1659 ; L.R.C.P., 1663 ; gradually made his way in the profession and became one of the most famous of the English physicians, his reputation being especially great on the continent ; author of several Latin medical works. His chief contributions to medicine were his observations on epidemic diseases, his first clear discrimination of certain diseases, his cooling method of treating the smallpox, and his introduction of the use of bark in agues ; these and his method of studying diseases made an epoch in medical science. [lv. 246]

SYDENHAM, WILLIAM (1615–1661), Cromwellian soldier; eldest brother of Thomas Sydenham [q. v.]; fought for the parliament and defeated the royalists in various skirmishes in Dorset; member of the various parliaments of the Commonwealth; avowed conservative principles, and defended 'the liberties of Englishmen'; made by Cromwell councillor and commissioner of the treasury, 1654; took the side of the army against the parliament; after the death of the Protector was expelled from the Long parliament, 1660; perpetually incapacitated from holding office by act of indemnity. [lv. 253]

SYDNEY. [See also SIDNEY.]

SYDNEY, first VISCOUNT (1733–1800). [See TOWNSHEND, THOMAS.]

SYDSERFF, THOMAS (1581–1663), bishop of Galloway; M.A. Edinburgh, 1602; took an active part in the introduction of the English prayer-book, 1633; made bishop of Galloway by Laud, 1635; attacked by the mob and deposed, 1638; appointed bishop of Orkney at the Restoration. [lv. 255]

SYKES, ARTHUR ASHLEY (1684?–1756), latitudinarian divine; educated at St. Paul's School, London, and Corpus Christi College, Cambridge; M.A., 1708; D.D. 1726; held numerous church preferments; a voluminous controversial writer of the school of Hoadly. [lv. 255]

SYKES, GODFREY (1825–1866), decorative artist; decorated the new buildings of the South Kensington Museum. [lv. 256]

SYKES, SIR MARK MASTERMAN, third baronet (1771–1823), book-collector; of Brasenose College, Oxford; M.P., York, 1807–20; his library especially rich in first editions of the classics, specimens of fifteenth-century printing, and Elizabethan poetry, besides manuscripts. [lv. 256]

SYKES, SIR TATTON, fourth baronet (1772–1863), patron of the turf; younger brother of Sir Mark Masterman Sykes [q. v.]; educated at Westminster School and Brasenose College, Oxford; an expert boxer and renowned breeder of sheep and horses, owner of racehorses, rider and master of foxhounds for more than forty years. [lv. 257]

SYKES, WILLIAM HENRY (1790–1872), naturalist and soldier; entered the service of the East India Company, 1803, and saw a good deal of active service; being appointed statistical reporter to the Bombay government, 1824, drew up valuable reports; chairman of the board of directors, 1856; liberal M.P., Aberdeen, 1857–72; F.R.S., 1834, and author. [lv. 258]

SYLVESTER. [See also SILVESTER.]

SYLVESTER, JAMES JOSEPH (1814–1897), mathematician; was educated at a Jewish school in London, at the Royal Institution, Liverpool, and St. John's College, Cambridge; second wrangler, 1837; graduated B.A. Cambridge (after the passing of the Tests Act), 1872; professor of natural philosophy at University College, London, 1837–41; professor of mathematics in the university of Virginia, 1841–5, and at Woolwich, 1855–70; president of the London Mathematical Society, 1866; professor of mathematics at the Johns Hopkin University at Baltimore, 1877–83; Savilian professor of geometry at Oxford, 1883–97; shared with Cayley the work of founding invariant algebra, and enriched the science of number with a body of doctrine on partitions. His writings are collected in four volumes. [lv. 258]

SYLVESTER, JOSUAH (1563–1618), poet; translator of Du Bartas; educated at the school of Hadrian à Saravia [q. v.] at Southampton, where he acquired a sound knowledge of French, and subsequently entered a trading firm; is supposed to have been for some time steward to the Essex family; made groom of his chamber by Prince Henry, c. 1606; became secretary to the merchant adventurers, 1613, and had to reside at Middelburg. Meanwhile he had accomplished a considerable amount of literary work, chiefly translations of the scriptural epics of the Gascon Huguenot, Guillaume de Saluste, seigneur du Bartas, in the rhymed decasyllabic couplet. He had a full sympathy with his original, and his work was much admired by contemporaries, and doubtless influenced Milton indirectly, but after the Restoration was considered pedantic, and ceased to be read. The translation of Du Bartas's 'Canticle' appeared, 1590, of 'La Semaine,' 1592,

and the first collective edition, 1606; author of several other works, mainly religious, but including accounts of Henry of Navarre and St. Louis. [lv. 260]

SYLVESTER, MATTHEW (1636?–1708), nonconformist divine; of St. John's College, Cambridge; vicar of Great Gonerby, 1659, which he resigned in consequence of the Uniformity Act, 1662; Baxter his assistant as pastor of Rutland House; published 'Reliquiæ Baxterianæ,' badly edited and very faulty, 1696; author of sermons and prefaces. [lv. 264]

SYME, EBENEZER (1826–1860), colonial journalist; emigrated to Victoria, 1852, and bought the 'Melbourne Age,' which, as leading liberal organ, had a marked influence on colonial politics. [lv. 265]

SYME, JAMES (1799–1870), surgeon; educated at the high school and university, Edinburgh; after filling many surgical posts and studying in Paris and Germany, started a private surgical hospital, 1829, at Edinburgh, where he inaugurated his system of clinical instruction; appointed crown professor of clinical surgery in Edinburgh University, 1833; recognised as the greatest living authority in surgery; author of several surgical works; his plan of leaving wounds open till all oozing of blood had ceased, adopted by, and often attributed to, Liston. [lv. 266]

SYME, JOHN (1755–1831), friend of Burns; lawyer, ensign, distributor of stamps, 1791; one of Burns's executors. [lv. 267]

SYME, JOHN (1795–1861), portrait-painter; nephew of Patrick Syme [q. v.]; pupil of Sir Henry Raeburn [q. v.] [lv. 267]

SYME, PATRICK (1774–1845), flower-painter and author. [lv. 268]

SYMEON. [See SIMEON.]

SYMES, MICHAEL (1753?–1809), soldier and diplomatist; sent on missions to Burmah, of which he wrote an account; served with Sir John Moore, 1808. [lv. 268]

SYMINGTON, ANDREW (1785–1853), Scottish divine; M.A. Glasgow, 1803; professor of theology in the reformed presbyterian church, 1820; published theological works. [lv. 268]

SYMINGTON, WILLIAM (1763–1831), engineer; took out a patent for an improved form of steam-engine, 1787, and devised the first steam-boat for practical use, the Charlotte Dundas, 1802; his plans not supported; lost by death his patron the Duke of Bridgewater; died in poverty in London. [lv. 269]

SYMINGTON, WILLIAM (1795–1862), divine; younger brother of Andrew Symington [q. v.]; D.D. Edinburgh, 1808; a successful preacher and author; succeeded his brother as professor of theology in the reformed presbyterian church, 1853. [lv. 270]

SYMMONS, CHARLES (1749–1826), man of letters; educated at Westminster School and Glasgow and Cambridge universities; a staunch whig; aroused some hostility by a whig sermon at Cambridge, 1793; rector of Narberth and Lampeter; author of poetical works, a life of Milton, 1806, and of Shakespeare, 1826, and 'The Æneis of Virgil translated,' 1817. [lv. 270]

SYMMONS, JOHN (1781–1842), son of Charles Symmons [q. v.]; translator of the 'Agamemnon' of Æschylus, 1824; of Westminster School and Christ Church, Oxford; M.A., 1806; barrister, Lincoln's Inn, 1807. [lv. 271]

SYMON SIMEONIS (fl. 1322). [See SIMEONIS.]

SYMONDS, JOHN (1730–1807), professor of modern history at Cambridge; B.A. St. John's College, Cambridge, 1752; fellow of Peterhouse, Cambridge, 1753; M.A., 1754; professor, 1771; wrote works urging the revision of the New Testament. [lv. 271]

SYMONDS, JOHN ADDINGTON (1807–1871), physician; educated at Magdalen College school and at Edinburgh; held several posts on the staff of the Bristol Hospital; F.R.C.P., 1857; author of several volumes of essays and lectures, and of papers contributed to medical periodicals. [lv. 272]

SYMONDS, JOHN ADDINGTON (1840–1893), author; son of John Addington Symonds (1807–1871) [q. v.]; educated at Harrow and Balliol College, Oxford, where he gained a first class in classics, the Newdigate prize, a fellowship at Magdalen, 1862, and the English essay prize, subject 'The Renaissance,' 1863; was obliged to reside abroad on account of his health, and finally settled at Davos Platz; brought out 'History of the Italian Renaissance,' 1875–86, a series of picturesque sketches rather than a continuous work, and his prose translation of the 'Autobiography of Benvenuto Cellini,' 1887; published books of poems, including 'Many Moods,' 1878, and 'Animi Figura,' 1882. Among his other prose works were 'Sketches in Italy and Greece,' 1874, 'Introduction to the Study of Dante,' 1872, and 'Walt Whitman,' 1893. He excelled as a translator, his translation of the sonnets of Michael Angelo and Campanella, 1878, being especially famous. [lv. 272]

SYMONDS, RICHARD (1609–1660 ?), Welsh puritan; B.A. Exeter College, Oxford, 1627; taught at Shrewsbury, 1635, where Baxter was his pupil; fled to London on the outbreak of the civil war, and preached in the city; returned to Wales as 'approver of preachers,' 1650. [lv. 275]

SYMONDS, RICHARD (1617–1692 ?), royalist and antiquary; imprisoned as a delinquent at the commencement of the civil war; escaped, joined the royalist army, and took part in the battles of the next two years, including the engagements at Dewsbury and Naseby; he petitioned to be allowed to compound for his delinquency, 1646, and travelled abroad; compiled several note-books, including four published by the Camden Society, as the 'Diary of the Marches of the Royal Army,' 1859. Other works of his contain anecdotes of Cromwell, memoranda of his travels abroad, and genealogical and archæological collections. [lv. 276]

SYMONDS, SIR THOMAS MATTHEW CHARLES (1813–1894), admiral of the fleet; son of Sir William Symonds [q. v.]; tactician and naval reformer; served in the Crimea; admiral of the fleet, 1879; G.C.B., 1880. [lv. 277]

SYMONDS, WILLIAM (1556–1616 ?), divine; M.A. Magdalen College, 1581, and became master of Magdalen school, 1553; created D.D. 1613; held many church preferments, and at one time resided in Virginia; published theological works. [lv. 278]

SYMONDS, SIR WILLIAM (1782–1856), rear-admiral; present at Lord Bridport's action, 1795, and saw a good deal of service; as surveyor of the navy, 1832–47, introduced some important changes in ship construction, notably the elliptical sterns; C.B., 1848; rear-admiral, 1854. [lv. 278]

SYMONDS, WILLIAM SAMUEL (1818–1887), geologist and author; educated at Cheltenham and Christ's College, Cambridge; B.A., 1842; rector of Pendock, 1845; published scientific articles in various periodicals, two novels, which went through several editions, and other works. [lv. 279]

SYMONS, BENJAMIN PARSONS (1785–1878), warden of Wadham College, Oxford, and leader of the evangelical party; M.A., Wadham College, Oxford, 1810; fellow, 1812; D.D., 1831; warden, 1831–71; vice-chancellor of Oxford University, 1844–8. [lv. 280]

SYMONS, GEORGE JAMES (1838–1900), meteorologist; studied at school of mines, Jermyn Street, London; member of Royal Meteorological Society, c. 1855, secretary, 1878–9 and 1882–99, and president, 1880 and 1900; meteorological reporter to registrar-general, 1857 till death; issued, from 1860, thirty-nine annual volumes of statistics of rainfall observations; F.R.S., 1878; began, 1863, issue of a monthly rain circular, which developed, 1866, into 'Monthly Meteorological Magazine,' still in course of publication; published several works on meteorological subjects. [Suppl. iii. 374]

SYMONS, JELINGER COOKSON (1809–1860), miscellaneous writer; B.A. Corpus Christi College, Cambridge, 1832; appointed commissioner to carry out several inquiries by the government; barrister, Middle Temple, 1843; editor of the 'Law Magazine' and inspector of schools, 1848; published miscellaneous works. [lv. 280]

SYMONS, SIR WILLIAM PENN (1843–1899), major-general; ensign, 1863; captain, 1878; served in Kaffraria, 1878, and in Zulu war, 1879; major, 1881; served on staff in expedition to Burma, 1885; commanded Burma column in Chin-Lushai expedition, 1889; C.B., 1890; brigadier-general in command of district in Punjab, 1895; K.C.B., 1898; commander of troops in Natal, May 1899; temporary lieutenant-general of fourth division of South Africa field force, October 1899; major-general; died of wounds received at storming of Talana hill, near Dundee. [Suppl. iii. 375]

SYMPSON, CHRISTOPHER (1605 ?–1669). [See SIMPSON.]

SYMPSON, WILLIAM (1627 ?–1671). [See SIMPSON.]

SYMSON or **SYMPSON**, PATRICK (1556–1618). [See SIMSON.]

SYNDERCOMB, MILES (d. 1657). [See SINDERCOMBE.]

SYNGE, CHARLES (1789–1854), lieutenant-colonel; served in the Peninsular campaign and distinguished himself at Salamanca; lieutenant-colonel, 1821. [lv. 281]

SYNGE, EDWARD (d. 1678), Irish bishop; brother of George Synge [q. v.]; of Trinity College, Dublin; bishop of Limerick, 1661; translated to Cork, Cloyne, and Ross, 1663. [lv. 282]

SYNGE, EDWARD (1659–1741), archbishop of Tuam; son of Edward Synge (d. 1678) [q. v.]; educated at Christ Church, Oxford; B.A., 1677; M.A. Trinity College, Dublin; vicar of Christ Church, Cork; appointed bishop of Raphoe, 1714, and archbishop of Tuam, 1716; resigned a fourth part of his tithes for the improvement of livings in his diocese; became privy councillor, 1716, and one of the keepers of the great seal in 1717–18; opposed the Toleration Bill, 1719; published religious tracts and sermons. [lv. 281]

SYNGE, GEORGE (1594–1653), bishop of Cloyne; brother of Edward Synge (d. 1678) [q. v.]; bishop of Cork, Cloyne, and Ross; M.A. Balliol College, Oxford, 1616; consecrated bishop, 1638–53; was nominated to the archbishopric of Tuam, 1647, but failed to obtain possession on account of the war. [lv. 281]

SYNGE, WILLIAM WEBB FOLLETT (1826–1891), diplomatist and author; attached to the British legation at Washington, 1853; appointed secretary to Sir William Gore Ouseley's mission to Central America, 1856; commissioner for the Sandwich islands, 1861; commissary judge in Cuba, 1865; contributed to 'Punch,' the 'Standard,' and the 'Saturday Review,' and was the author of some other works. [lv. 283]

SYNTAX, DOCTOR. [See COMBE, WILLIAM, 1741–1823.]

SYRACUSE (SYRACUSANUS), RICHARD OF (d. 1195). [See PALMER.]

T

TAAFFE, DENIS (1743?-1813), Irish political writer; brought up a Roman catholic priest, but became a protestant, and subsequently a catholic again; joined the United Irishmen and fought during the rebellion in Wexford; chief work, a 'History of Ireland,' 1809-11; published also pamphlets. [lv. 284]

TAAFFE, FRANCIS, fourth VISCOUNT TAAFFE and third EARL OF CARLINGFORD (1639-1704), Austrian field-marshal; second son of Theobald Taaffe, second viscount Taaffe [q. v.]; entered the service of Charles, duke of Lorraine, and saw much active service on the continent, assisting to relieve Vienna, 1683; found favour with William III, who received him, 1699, and on Leopold, duke of Lorraine's reinstatement in his dominions, 1697, was made governor of Nancy. [lv. 284]

TAAFFE, JOHN (fl. 1685-1708), informer; alias THOMAS O'MULLEN and FATHER VINCENT; after the revolution turned protestant, and was employed by the government in collecting evidence against the Jacobites. [lv. 285]

TAAFFE, NICHOLAS, sixth VISCOUNT TAAFFE (1677-1769), lieutenant-general in the Austrian army; served in the war of the Polish succession, 1734-5, and against the Turks, 1737-9, and was present, at the age of eighty, at the battle of Kolin, 1757; ancestor of the late president of the Austrian ministry. [lv. 286]

TAAFFE, THEOBALD, second VISCOUNT TAAFFE and first EARL OF CARLINGFORD (d. 1677), grandson of Sir William Taaffe [q. v.]; commanded the forces of the catholic confederation in Connaught, 1644, and Munster, 1647; defeated by Lord Inchiquin, 1647; employed in negotiations between Queen Henrietta Maria and the Duke of Lorraine; created Earl of Carlingford at the Restoration. [lv. 287]

TAAFFE, SIR WILLIAM (d. 1627), sheriff of Sligo; sheriff, 1588; distinguished himself on the landing of the Spaniards at Kinsale, 1601, and in expeditions against the Irish; knighted, 1605. [lv. 288]

TABLEY, BARONS DE. [See LEICESTER, SIR JOHN FLEMING, 1762-1827; WARREN, JOHN BYRNE LEICESTER, 1835-1895.]

TABOR or **TALBOR**, SIR ROBERT (1642?-1681), physician; perfected the cure of ague by quinine; cured Charles II and the dauphin; published 'Πυρετολογία,' 1672; knighted, 1678. [lv. 288]

TACHÉ, ALEXANDRE ANTONIN (1823-1894), Roman catholic archbishop; educated at Quebec and Montreal; went as a missionary to the Indians on the great lakes, and showed much energy in founding missions; the most influential person in the North-West Territories; published works on Canada. [lv. 289]

TACHÉ, SIR ETIENNE PASCAL (1795-1865), premier of Canada; uncle of Alexandre Antonin Taché [q. v.]; a physician; speaker of the legislative assembly and premier, 1856; knighted, 1858. [lv. 290]

TACHÉ, JEAN CHARLES (1820-1893), physician and author; elder brother of Alexandre Antonin Taché [q. v.] [lv. 289]

TAGART, EDWARD (1804-1858), unitarian divine; minister of Little Portland Street Chapel, London, 1833; F.L.S., F.G.S., and F.S.A.; visited the unitarians in Transylvania, 1858; published 'Locke's Writings and Philosophy,' 1855, denying Hume's scepticism to have been its outcome. [lv. 290]

TAGLIONI, MARIE (1809-1884), the 'most prominent danseuse of the century'; made her début in Vienna, 1822, appearing in Paris, 1827, and in London, 1829, her great parts there being in 'La Sylphide,' in 'La Gitana,' in the 'Pas de Quatre,' 1845, and in 'Pas des Déesses,' 1846; died in straitened circumstances at Marseilles. [lv. 291]

TAILOR. [See also TAYLER and TAYLOR.]

TAILOR, ROBERT (fl. 1614), dramatist; author of 'The Hog hath lost his Pearle,' 1614, a play valuable as a storehouse of dramatic allusions; a work entitled 'Sacred Hymns,' 1615, also attributed to him. [lv. 292]

TAIRCELL (d. 696). [See DAIRCELL.]

TAIT, ARCHIBALD CAMPBELL (1811-1882), archbishop of Canterbury; born at Edinburgh, his family being originally Aberdeenshire yeomen; brought up as a presbyterian and educated at Edinburgh High School, Glasgow University, and Balliol College, Oxford, where he was scholar; took a first-class in classics, 1833; fellow, 1834, and one of the most influential tutors in the university; took charge of the parish of Baldon, 1836; visited Germany, 1839; his conduct during the Oxford movement characterised by broadness of view and tolerance; one of those who condemned 'Tract XC.,' 1841, and signed the counter-memorial in favour of Dr. Renn Dickson Hampden [q. v.], 1847; succeeded Arnold as head-master of Rugby, 1842; appointed dean of Carlisle, 1849; made bishop of London, 1856; showed great firmness and at the same time broad-mindedness in his treatment of the church controversies of the day connected with ritualism and the freedom of opinion of the clergy, especially in the 'Essays and Reviews' case, 1860, and in the Colenso case, 1862; withdrew the licence of Poole, curate of St. Barnabas, Pimlico, on account of his practice of confession, 1858; showed himself a vigorous evangeliser, and preached in omnibus yards, Covent Garden market, London, and elsewhere; began the building of new churches; founded the Diocesan Home Mission, 1857, and the Bishop of London's Fund, 1866; supported the Divorce Bill, 1857, with modifications to suit the conscientious views of the clergy, and also the relaxation in the forms of subscription demanded from the clergy, 1865; obtained the opening of Westminster Abbey for the evening services, and worked hard during the cholera epidemic, 1866; became archbishop of Canterbury, 1869; at first opposed the Irish Church Bill, but subsequently recognised the inevitable, the eventual settlement being largely owing to his patience and good sense; showed sympathy with the Old Catholic movement abroad, declared against the use of the Athanasian Creed in the public services, and was instrumental in passing the Public Worship Regulation Act, 1874, though the final bill was not the measure which he had intended or desired; supported the Burial Act, 1880. No archbishop probably since the Reformation had so much weight in parliament or in the country generally. [lv. 292]

TAIT, JAMES HALDANE (1771-1845), rear-admiral; saw much active service; commanded the Jane in the North Sea, 1799, and captured fifty-six French and Dutch vessels; rear-admiral, 1841. [lv. 299]

TAIT, ROBERT LAWSON (1845-1899), surgeon; L.R.C.P. and L.R.C.S. Edinburgh, 1866; began practice in Birmingham, 1870; F.R.C.S. Edinburgh, 1870, and England, 1871; surgeon to Hospital for Diseases of Women, 1871-93; gained Hastings gold medal of British Medical Association, 1873; performed operations for removal of an ovary for suppurative disease and extirpation of the uterine appendages to arrest growth of a bleeding myoma, 1872; one of founders of British Gynæcological Society; professor of gynæcology at Queen's College, Birmingham, 1887; professor of anatomy at Royal Society of Artists and Birmingham School of Design; published 'Diseases of Women,' 1877, and other works. [Suppl. iii. 352]

TAIT, WILLIAM (1793-1864), publisher of 'Tait's Edinburgh Magazine,' 1832-64, a literary and radical magazine, to which Mill, Cobden, and Bright contributed. [lv. 300]

TALBOT, CATHERINE (1721-1770), author; niece of Charles Talbot [q. v.], lord chancellor; with her mother lived with Thomas Secker [q. v.], archbishop of Canterbury; educated by Secker; became well-known in society. Among her works published after her death are 'Reflections on the Seven Days of the Week,' 1770, 'Essays,' 1772, and her 'Letters,' 1809. [lv. 300]

TALBOT, CHARLES, twelfth EARL and only DUKE OF SHREWSBURY (1660-1718), son of the eleventh earl; became a protestant, 1679, probably owing to the influence of Tillotson; was given places and employments by Charles II and James II, but nevertheless was one of the foremost in bringing about the revolution; took 12,000l. to Holland for the support of William III, 1688, and landed with him in England; made secretary of state, 1689, but resigned, 1690, on the refusal of the tory parliament to pass the Abjuration Bill; resumed office after much hesitation, 1694, his inconsistent conduct being, it is said, the result of communications with James II; became K.G., Duke of Shrewsbury, and head of the administration, 1694, and during William III's absence, 1695 and 1696, was one of the lords justices, and carried on a regular correspondence with William III; charges of complicity in Jacobite intrigues brought against him, 1696; withdrew from public affairs and finally resigned, 1700, though William III readily accepted his explanations; left England and went to Rome, whence he wrote his celebrated letter to Somers, Had I a son, I would sooner bind him a cobbler than a courtier, and a hangman than a statesman'; refused all invitations to serve the state till 1710, when he was instrumental in bringing about the fall of the whigs and became lord chamberlain; appointed ambassador to France, 1712; seems to have disapproved of the Utrecht negotiations and was recalled; made lord-lieutenant of Ireland, 1713; at the great crisis on the death of Queen Anne, 1714, acted a courageous part as treasurer and lord justice, it being chiefly owing to his conduct that the Hanoverian succession was assured; became lord chamberlain to the new king, but was not included in the cabinet council. He was a man of great personal attractions, and was called by Swift 'the favourite of the nation.'   [lv. 301]

TALBOT, CHARLES, BARON TALBOT OF HENSOL (1685-1737), lord chancellor; eldest son of William Talbot [q. v.], bishop of Durham; of Eton and Oriel College, Oxford; B.A., 1704; fellow of All Souls College, Oxford, 1704; admitted at the Inner Temple, 1707, and at Lincoln's Inn, 1719; M.P., Tregony, 1720, Durham, 1722-7 and 1727-34; LL.B. Lambeth, 1714; solicitor-general, 1726, and lord-chancellor, 1733; created D.C.L., 1735.   [lv. 307]

TALBOT, SIR CHARLES CHETWYND, second EARL TALBOT OF HENSOL (1777-1849), eldest son of the first Earl Talbot; created M.A. Christ Church, Oxford, 1797; lord-lieutenant of Ireland, 1817-22; K.C., 1821; supported the extinction of the duties on corn, and made K.G., 1844.   [lv. 308]

TALBOT, EDWARD (1555-1595). [See KELLEY.]

TALBOT, ELIZABETH, COUNTESS OF SHREWSBURY (1518-1608), known as 'Bess of Hardwick'; daughter and co-heiress of John Hardwick of Hardwick, Derbyshire; married successively Robert Barlow of Barlow, near Dronfield, Sir William Cavendish, 1549, who purchased the estate of Chatsworth, Sir William St. Loe, and George Talbot, sixth earl of Shrewsbury [q. v.]; inherited their whole estates from all her four husbands, her income being estimated at 60,000l. a year; Mary Queen of Scots entrusted to the care of her and her husband, the sixth earl, 1569, at Tutbury; married her daughter to Charles Stuart, and was imprisoned for a short time in the Tower of London in consequence (Arabella Stuart being the issue of this marriage). She built, besides Chatsworth (not the present building), Hardwick Hall, and many other houses.   [lv. 309]

TALBOT, FRANCIS, fifth EARL OF SHREWSBURY (1500-1560), second son of George Talbot, fourth earl of Shrewsbury [q. v.]; accompanied Henry VIII to Calais, 1522, and assisted his father in suppressing the Pilgrimage of Grace, 1536-7; made president of the council of the north; took part in the proceedings against Seymour and Somerset; acquiesced in Northumberland's rule, but welcomed the accession of Queen Mary.   [lv. 311]

TALBOT, GEORGE, fourth EARL OF SHREWSBURY and EARL OF WATERFORD (1468-1538), son of John Talbot, third earl of Shrewsbury; K.G., 1488; appointed to several offices of state by Henry VIII; ambassador to Pope Julius II, 1511, and to Ferdinand of Arragon, 1512, to conclude alliance against France; commanded division in France, 1513; present at the Field of the Cloth of Gold, 1520; suppressed the northern rebellion, 1536; received grants of monastery lands   [lv. 313]

TALBOT, GEORGE, sixth EARL OF SHREWSBURY (1528?-1590), elder son of Francis Talbot, fifth earl of Shrewsbury [q. v.]; took part in Somerset's invasion of Scotland; married 'Bess of Hardwick' [see TALBOT, ELIZABETH], 1568, and was chosen by Queen Elizabeth keeper of Mary Queen of Scots, who remained his ward at Tutbury, Chatsworth, Sheffield Castle, and other of his

country places, 1569-84; much trusted by Queen Elizabeth.   [lv. 314]

TALBOT, GILBERT DE, first BARON TALBOT (1277?-1346), took part in Edward I's expedition into Scotland, 1293; took up arms against the Despensers and was captured at Boroughbridge, 1322; justice of South Wales.   [lv. 316]

TALBOT, GILBERT, seventh EARL OF SHREWSBURY (1553-1616), second son of George Talbot, sixth earl of Shrewsbury [q. v.]; married Mary Cavendish, daughter of 'Bess of Hardwick' [see TALBOT, ELIZABETH], who had married his father; joined in 'Bess of Hardwick's' intrigues against his father; on his father's death quarrelled with various members of the family and his tenantry; arrested by order of Queen Elizabeth, 1595, but sent to invest Henri IV with the Garter, 1596. [lv. 317]

TALBOT, JAMES, first BARON TALBOT DE MALAHIDE in the peerage of the United Kingdom, 1856 (1805-1883), son of James Talbot, third baron in the Irish peerage; M.A. Trinity College, Cambridge, 1830; lord-in-waiting, 1863-6; president, Archæological Society, 1863-1883, and Royal Irish Academy; F.R.S. and F.S.A., 1858.   [lv. 318]

TALBOT, JOHN, first EARL OF SHREWSBURY (1388?-1453), second son of Richard Talbot, fourth Baron Talbot; summoned to parliament in right of his wife as Lord Furnivall or Lord Talbot of Hallamshire, 1409-21; deputy-constable of Montgomery Castle; assisted in capture of Harlech Castle, 1409; imprisoned by Henry V on suspicion of lollard tendencies, 1413, but soon released and made lieutenant of Ireland, 1414; present at the sieges of Melun, 1420, and Meaux, 1421; fought at Verneuil, and won the Garter, 1424; surprised and reduced a number of Irish chiefs, 1424; accompanied Bedford to France, 1427, and after much fighting was made governor of Anjou and Maine and of Falaise; present at the siege of Orleans, 1429; taken prisoner at battle near Patay, remaining captive till 1431; performed many brilliant services in France, including the reconquest of the pays de Caux, the capture of Ivry, and the capture of Harfleur; made constable of France and Earl of Salop, 1422; sent again to govern Ireland, 1455, and created Earl of Waterford; sent to assist Somerset in Normandy, 1448; on the capitulation of Rouen remained as a hostage for the surrender of Harfleur; finally despatched on an expedition to Aquitaine; took Bordeaux and the whole Bordelais, but was defeated and slain at Castillon. He owed his reputation mainly to his dash and daring. [lv. 319]

TALBOT, JOHN, second EARL OF SHREWSBURY (1413?-1460), son of John Talbot, first earl of Shrewsbury [q. v.]; served in France, 1434 and 1442; chancellor of Ireland, 1446; treasurer of England, 1456; chief butler, 1458; killed fighting on Henry VI's side at Northampton.   [lv. 323]

TALBOT, SIR JOHN (1769?-1851), admiral; entered the navy on the Boreas, with Nelson as captain, 1784; saw much service; captured the Ville de Milan and her prize, the Cleopatra, 1805, and as captain of the Victorious took the French 74-gun ship Rivoli after a severe engagement, 1812; admiral, 1841; G.C.B., 1842.   [lv. 324]

TALBOT, MARY ANNE (1778-1808), the 'British Amazon'; served as a drummer-boy in Flanders, 1792, and as cabin-boy in the Le Sage, and afterwards in the Brunswick, when she was wounded in the great battle of 1 June 1794; after subsequent adventures became a servant and received a small pension. Her history was embodied by her employer, Robert S. Kirby, in his 'Wonderful Museum,' second volume, 1804.   [lv. 325]

TALBOT, MONTAGUE (1774-1831), actor and manager of Belfast, Newry, and Londonderry theatres, 1809-21; acted first in Ireland, where he had some success, then in Wales, London, and Liverpool, under the name of Montague; acted at Drury Lane, London, under his own name, 1799 and 1800, and also in Dublin, where he became a great favourite, and greatly preferred to Charles Mathews, who was received with cries of 'Talbot.' His acting is not generally criticised favourably, and he failed to maintain his position on the London stage. His best characters were Lothario, Edgar in Lear, and old men such as Wolsey.   [lv. 326]

TALBOT, PETER (1620-1680), titular archbishop of Dublin and jesuit; second son of Sir William Talbot [q. v.];

engaged in various plots to gain assistance for Charles II, travelling about between Ireland and the continent, but apparently trusted by no party; came to England at the Restoration; consecrated archbishop of Dublin at Ghent, 1669; engaged in a dispute about precedency with the primate, Oliver Plunket [q. v.]; received a pension of 200*l.* from Charles II, and lived at Poole Hall in Cheshire unmolested; was arrested for supposed complicity in the popish plot, 1678, and died in Newgate prison, Dublin.
[lv. 327]

TALBOT, RICHARD DE, second BARON TALBOT (1302?–1356), eldest son of Gilbert de Talbot, first baron Talbot [q. v.]; like his father, sided with the Lancastrian nobles against Edward II, and was captured with him at Boroughbridge, 1322; joined Edward III and Isabella on their landing in England, 1326; supported Baliol in Scotland, 1332, but on Baliol being driven out was taken prisoner; present at the siege of Tournay, 1340, and at that of Morlaix, 1342; served apparently in the Crécy campaign and at Calais, 1346.
[lv. 329]

TALBOT, RICHARD (*d.* 1449), archbishop of Dublin and lord chancellor of Ireland; younger brother of John Talbot, first earl of Shrewsbury [q. v.]; archbishop, 1417; chancellor of Ireland, 1423; acted frequently as deputy during absence of the viceroys in Ireland; summoned to England charged with abetting rebellion, 1429; opposed the government of the Earl of Ormonde, and both ordered to appear in England to answer for their conduct, 1442 and 1443.
[lv. 330]

TALBOT, RICHARD, EARL and titular DUKE OF TYRCONNEL (1630–1691), youngest son of Sir William Talbot [q. v.]; taken prisoner at the rout of Preston's army, 1647; was wounded at the siege of Drogheda, but escaped abroad; returning to England, was arrested by Cromwell on suspicion of plotting his murder, 1655, but also accused by Clarendon of being in the Protector's pay; gentleman of the Duke of York's bedchamber at the Restoration; imprisoned for challenging Ormonde, 1661; fought in the naval action at Lowestoft, 1665; engaged in various love affairs; as spokesman of the Irish Roman catholics opposed Ormonde in Ireland, and was again imprisoned, 1670; arrested for supposed complicity in the 'popish plot,' 1678; given command of the army in Ireland, Ormonde being recalled, and on accession of James II made Earl of Tyrconnel, with chief power in Ireland, and with the object of repealing Act of Settlement, bringing back Roman catholic domination, and making James II independent in England by means of an Irish army; protestant forces disbanded and oath of supremacy dispensed with; made viceroy, 1687; despatched three thousand men to King James's assistance in England; met James II at Kinsale; instigator of all James II's violent proceedings, including the attainder of 2,455 protestant landowners; made duke; commanded at the battle of the Boyne, 1690; advised James's retreat to France, and was left with full powers in Ireland; accused of treachery by the Irish party; left for France after the raising of the siege of Limerick, where he gained the full confidence of James and Louis XIV; returned with money and arms as lord-lieutenant, 1691, and commander-in-chief; died of apoplexy shortly after the battle of Aughrim.
[lv. 331]

TALBOT, ROBERT (1505?–1558), antiquary; scholar at Winchester College; fellow of New College, Oxford, 1521; M.A., 1529; got into trouble as a reformer; friend of Leland and praised by Camden and Lambarde; his only published work, 'Annotationes in eam partem Antonini itinerarii quæ ad Britanniam pertinet.' [lv. 336]

TALBOT, THOMAS (*fl.* 1580), antiquary; clerk of the records in the Tower of London before 1580; compiler of many unpublished collections in the Harleian, Cottonian, and Lansdowne MSS. [lv. 337]

TALBOT, THOMAS (1771–1853), colonist; younger brother of Sir John Talbot (1769?–1851) [q. v.]; ensign, 1783; attached to the staff of John Graves Simcoe [q. v.]; founded twenty-eight townships on the north of Lake Erie. [lv. 337]

TALBOT, SIR WILLIAM, first baronet (*d.* 1633), Irish politician; 'legal oracle of the catholic party in the Irish House of Commons'; one of the deputies sent to James I on their behalf; imprisoned in the Tower of London, 1613; created baronet and given grants of land, 1622. [lv. 338]

TALBOT, WILLIAM (1659?–1730), bishop of Durham; M.A. Oriel College, Oxford, 1680; dean of Worcester, 1691; bishop of Oxford, 1699; supported the condemnation of Sacheverell, 1710; bishop of Durham, 1721; author of sermons. [lv. 339]

TALBOT, WILLIAM HENRY FOX (1800–1877), pioneer of photography; educated at Harrow; scholar of Trinity College, Cambridge; Porson prizeman, 1820; twelfth wrangler and second chancellor's medallist, 1821; M.A., 1825; invented 'photogenic drawing,' 1839, which, improved by the 'talbotype' method, subsequently patented by him, was the foundation of the photography of the present day; discovered method of taking instantaneous photographs, 1851, and of photographic engraving, 1852; author of mathematical works, of 'The Pencil of Nature,' the first book illustrated without aid from the artist, 1844–6, and of other books; F.R.A.S., 1822; F.R.S., 1831; M.P., Chippenham, 1833–4. [lv. 339]

TALBOYS, DAVID ALPHONSO (1790?–1840), bookseller at Oxford; translator of Heeren's 'Researches,' 1832. [lv. 341]

TALBOYS, GILBERT, LORD TALBOYS (*d.* 1530), keeper of Harbottle Castle, 1509; served in French war, 1513; became insane, 1517. [lv. 342]

TALBOYS or **TAILBOYS**, SIR WILLIAM, styled EARL OF KYME (*d.* 1464), fined 3,000*l.* for assaulting Suffolk, 1449; adherent of the Lancastrian cause; fought at St. Albans, 1461, Hedgeley Moor, 1464, and Hexham, 1464; captured soon after the battle of Hexham and beheaded. [lv. 341]

TALFOURD, FRANCIS (1828–1862), dramatist; eldest son of Sir Thomas Noon Talfourd [q. v.]; educated at Eton and Christ Church, Oxford; barrister, Middle Temple, 1852; writer of popular burlesques.
[lv. 342]

TALFOURD, SIR THOMAS NOON (1795–1854), judge and author; educated at Mill Hill dissenting school, and at Reading under Richard Valpy [q. v.]; read law with Joseph Chitty the elder [q. v.]; published 'Poems on various Subjects,' 1811; contributed to the 'Pamphleteer,' the 'New Monthly Magazine,' and the 'Retrospective Review,' especially articles of dramatic criticism, and made acquaintance of Lamb, Wordsworth, and Coleridge; joined the Oxford circuit and became 'Times' reporter; made serjeant, 1833, and justice of the common pleas, 1849; M.P., Reading, 1835, 1837, and 1841; introduced the Custody of Infants Bill and Copyright Bill; best known for his tragedy 'Ion,' 1835, a drama conceived in the Greek spirit. Amongst his other publications may be noticed his 'Letters' (1837) and 'Memorials' (1848) of Lamb, and his articles on Lord Eldon and Lord Stowell in the 'Quarterly Review,' December 1844. [lv. 343]

TALHAIARN (1810–1869). [See JONES, JOHN.]

TALIESIN (*fl.* 550), British bard; perhaps a mythic personage; first mentioned in the 'Saxon Genealogies' appended to the 'Historia Britonum,' *c.* 690. A mass of poetry, probably of later date, has been ascribed to him, and legends told concerning him, printed as 'Hanes Taliesin' in the 'Cambrian Quarterly Magazine' for 1833. The village of Taliesin in Cardiganshire has sprung up near the supposed site of his grave. The 'Book of Taliesin,' fourteenth century, is a collection of poems by different authors and of different dates. [lv. 346]

TALLENTS, FRANCIS (1619–1708), ejected divine; fellow of Magdalene College, Cambridge; received presbyterian ordination, 1648; curate of St. Mary's, Shrewsbury, 1653; ejected, 1662; after Monmouth's rebellion confined in Chester Castle, 1685; presented purse of gold to James II in recognition of the indulgence, 1686; author of sermons and controversial religious works. [lv. 347]

TALLIS, THOMAS (1510?–1585), musician; organist at Waltham Abbey, 1540; granted half the lease of the manor of Minster in Thanet by Queen Mary, 1557; with William Byrd [q. v.] was given, by Queen Elizabeth, a monopoly of music-printing for twenty-one years, 1576; buried in Greenwich parish church, since pulled down. During life some five of his anthems were published in Day's 'Certayne Notes,' 1560, and he composed eight tunes for Archbishop Parker's 'Psalter,' 1567, and a ninth, intended for 'Veni Creator Spiritus.' Others were published in Barnard's 'Selected Church Musick,' 1641,

Lowe's 'Short Directions for Cathedral Service,' 1661, Bryce's 'Cathedral Music,' 1760 and 1763, and in other collections, but many of his works remain in manuscript. He excelled in his sacred vocal compositions; he was one of the first to compose settings of the Anglican ' service.' He represents the reaction from the excessive complications usual in his day, his litany is ' one of the finest pieces of ancient church music extant,' and the responses and some of his hymn-tunes, including 'Glory to Thee, my God, this Night,' are in general use, while his seven-voiced ' Miserere' is a ' masterpiece of speculative art' (RITTER).   [lv. 348]

TALMAN, JOHN (d. 1726), amateur artist; son of William Talman [q. v.]; first director of the Society of Antiquaries, 1718.   [lv. 351]

TALMAN, WILLIAM (fl. 1670–1700), architect of Chatsworth and other houses, and of the alterations to Hampton Court Palace.   [lv. 351]

TALMASH, THOMAS (1651?–1694). [See TOLLE-MACHE.]

TALSARN (1796–1857). [See JONES, JOHN.]

TANCRED, CHRISTOPHER (1689–1754), benefactor and horsedealer; published 'Essay for a general Regulation of the Law,' 1727, in which he elaborated reforms a century in advance of his age; left his property to found twelve Tancred studentships at Cambridge and Lincoln's Inn, and for the maintenance of twelve persons in a hospital.   [lv. 352]

TANDY, JAMES NAPPER (1740–1803), United Irishman; born in Dublin; began life as a small tradesman; attacked municipal corruption and became very popular in the city; declared warmly for the American colonies, 1775; became an enthusiastic volunteer, and continued in violent opposition to the government of Ireland; instrumental in returning Grattan for Dublin, 1790; a leader of the protestant section and upholder of the French revolution; arrested for challenging the attorney-general, 1792; liberated on prorogation of parliament, and instituted unsuccessful proceedings against the Earl of Westmorland, the lord-lieutenant, for false imprisonment; on rejection of the catholic petition commenced further agitation; raised two battalions in Dublin, but the movement failing through the energy of the government, fled to America; visited Paris, 1798, and was given command by the Directory of the Anacreon corvette, with a body of soldiers, with whom he landed in Donegal; issued an absurd proclamation, and took to drinking habits; escaped to Bergen, and travelling to Hamburg was there arrested; taken to Ireland and convicted, but not executed, since doubts arose as to the legality of his arrest; finally liberated through representations made by Bonaparte at the treaty of Amiens; reached Bordeaux, 1802; well known as the hero of ' The Wearing of the Green.'   [lv. 353]

TANFIELD, SIR LAWRENCE (d. 1625), judge; M.P. for Woodstock, 1584, Oxfordshire, 1604; admitted to the Inner Temple, 1569; knighted and made judge, 1606; chief-baron of the exchequer, 1625; well reputed of by his contemporaries, but in some quarters accused of corruption, fraud, and oppression.   [lv. 357]

TANKERVILLE, EARLS OF. [See GREY, JOHN, d. 1421; GREY, FORDE, d. 1701.]

TANNAHILL, ROBERT (1774–1810), Scottish songwriter; educated in Paisley; brought up as a silk-weaver; visited by James Hogg (1770–1835) [q. v.], 1810; drowned himself at Paisley. His poems were published, 1807, the most complete edition being that of David Semple [q. v.], 1873. Among his songs which entitle him to rank with the greatest of Scottish song-writers are ' Braes o' Gleniffer' and ' Jessie the Flower o' Dunblane.'   [lv. 357]

TANNER, JOHN SIGISMUND (d. 1775), medallist and engraver at the royal mint.   [lv. 358]

TANNER, THOMAS (1630–1682), historian; B.A. Pembroke Hall, Cambridge, 1650; fellow of New College, Oxford, 1651; M.A. Edinburgh and Oxford, 1652; ejected, 1660; author of 'The Entrance of Mazzarini,' 1657, and other works.   [lv. 359]

TANNER, THOMAS (1674–1735), bishop of St. Asaph and antiquary: educated at Queen's College, Oxford; M.A., 1696; D.D., 1710; fellow of All Souls College, Oxford, 1696; chancellor of Norwich diocese, 1701; canon of

Ely, 1713, of Christ Church, Oxford, 1724; bishop of St. Asaph, 1732–5; author of two well-known works, 'Notitia Monastica,' 1695, and 'Bibliotheca Britannico-Hibernica,' published, 1748, an account of all authors flourishing within the three kingdoms at the beginning of the seventeenth century, which long remained the highest authority; supplied the addition to the history of Wiltshire in Gibson's edition of Camden's 'Britannia'; his collections on the county presented by his son to the Bodleian Library; one of the literary executors of Wood, publishing, with some modifications, his continuation of his 'Athenæ Oxonienses,' 1721.   [lv. 359]

TANNER, THOMAS HAWKES (1824–1871), physician; M.D. St. Andrews, 1847; member of the Royal College of Physicians, 1850; gynæcologist and consulting practitioner; published medical works.   [lv. 362]

TANNOCK, JAMES (1784–1863), shoemaker; house-painter and subsequently portrait-painter.   [lv. 362]

TANS'UR, WILLIAM (1699?–1783), psalmodist.
                                                     [lv. 363]

TANSWELL, JOHN (1800–1864), archæologist; author of ' The History and Antiquities of Lambeth,' 1858.   [lv. 363]

TANY, THOMAS (fl. 1649–1655), fanatic and goldsmith; claimed to be 'a Jew of the tribe of Reuben,' 1649; proclaimed the rebuilding of the Temple, 1650, and himself as 'high priest,' Earl of Essex, heir to the throne, and king of France; imprisoned in Newgate for blasphemy, 1651; assaulted men at the parliament-house, 1654, and finally disappeared; author of pantheistic tracts, illiterate, but with occasional beauties. [lv. 363]

TANYMARIAN (1822–1885). [See STEPHEN, EDWARD.]

TAPP, JOHN (fl. 1596–1615), writer on navigation; author of ' The Arte of Navigation,' translated from the Spanish by Richard Eden [q. v.] and now ' corrected . . . by J. T.,' 1596.   [lv. 364]

TARA, VISCOUNT (1585–1655). [See PRESTON, THOMAS.]

TARBAT, VISCOUNT (1630–1714). [See MACKENZIE, GEORGE.]

TARLETON, SIR BANASTRE, baronet (1754–1833), general; educated at Liverpool and Oxford; became cornet in George III's dragoon guards, 1775, and accompanied Cornwallis to America; took part in the attack under Clinton on Charleston, and in the capture of New York and other places, also in the seizure of General Lee and in the operations of January 1777 under Cornwallis; present (1777) at the battle of Brandywine and capture of Germantown and Philadelphia; took part in Clinton's march to New York; distinguished himself in the capture of Charleston, 1780; defeated Burford at Waxhaws and gained honourable mention in despatches at Cornwallis's victory (1780) at Camden, and elsewhere; defeated Sumpter at Blackstock Hill, but suffered a reverse at Cowpens; defeated Lafayette and Wayne near Jamestown, 1781, held Gloucester, and on capitulation of that place with Yorktown, returned to England, 1782; M.P., Liverpool, 1790–1806 and 1807–12; held several home military appointments; published 'History of the Campaigns of 1780 and 1781,' 1781; general, 1812; created baronet, 1815; G.C.B., 1820.   [lv. 364]

TARLTON, RICHARD (d. 1588), actor; of humble origin and imperfect education; introduced to Queen Elizabeth through the Earl of Leicester, whose servant his ' happy unhappy answers' had attracted; instituted one of Queen Elizabeth's twelve players, 1583; attained an immense popularity by his comic acting, improvisations of doggerel verse—'Tarletonizing'—and jigs; led a dissipated life and died in poverty; probably to be identified with Spenser's 'Pleasant Willy' and Shakespeare's Yorick; reputed author of several songs, which were, however, probably wrongly ascribed to him. Many fictitious anecdotes connected with him were published, notably ' Tarlton's Jests,' 1592?–1611?, in three parts.
                                                     [lv. 369]

TARRAS, EARL OF (1644–1693). [See SCOTT, WALTER.]

TARRING, JOHN (1806–1875), architect; 'the Gilbert Scott of the dissenters.'   [lv. 371]

TARVER, EDWARD JOHN (1841–1891), architect; son of John Charles Tarver [q. v.]   [lv. 372]

TARVER, JOHN CHARLES (1790-1851), educational writer; born at Dieppe, and together with his parents thrown into prison on the outbreak of the war with England, 1793; educated in France; published 'Royal Phraseological English-French and French-English Dictionary,' 1845; tutor to Prince George, duke of Cambridge, 1818; French master at Eton, 1826; author also of 'L'Inferno, en français,' 1824, and other French educational works. [lv. 371]

TASCHEREAU, ELZEAR ALEXANDRE (1820-1898), Canadian cardinal; educated at the Quebec seminary; ministered to Irish emigrants stricken with typhus on Grosse island, 1847; superior of the Quebec seminary and rector of Laval University, 1842; archbishop of Quebec, 1871-98; first Canadian cardinal, 1886. [lv. 372]

TASKER, WILLIAM (1740-1800), poet and antiquary; B.A. Exeter College, Oxford, 1762; rector of Iddesleigh; 'a well-known physiognomist' and Greek scholar; his interview with Dr. Johnson, 1779, one of the most life-like passages in Boswell; author of· Ode to the Warlike Genius of Great Britain,'_ 1778, 'An Ode to Curiosity' (2nd edit. 1779), translations, and other works. [lv. 373]

TASSIE, JAMES (1735-1799), modeller; began life as a stonemason; invented, together with Quin, the 'white enamel composition' used for his medallion portraits and reproduction of gems; produced a large number of reproductions of gems enumerated by Rudolf Eric Raspe [q. v.] in his 'Descriptive Catalogue,' 1791. [lv. 374]

TASSIE, WILLIAM (1777-1860), modeller; nephew of James Tassie [q. v.], to whose business he succeeded, the collection of impressions amounting finally to twenty thousand specimens; his portrait medallions inferior to his uncle's. [lv. 375]

TASWELL-LANGMEAD, THOMAS PITT (1840-1882). [See LANGMEAD.]

TATE, ALEXANDER NORMAN (1837-1892), analytical chemist; devoted himself especially to the study of American petroleum, and wrote 'Petroleum and its Products,' 1863; practised in Liverpool and elsewhere; specialist in the analysis of oils and fats; founded the Liverpool operatives' science classes, 1871. [lv. 375]

TATE, CHRISTOPHER (1811-1841), sculptor. [lv. 376]

TATE, FRANCIS (1560-1616), antiquary; of Magdalen College, Oxford; barrister, Middle Temple, 1587; original member and secretary of the Society of Antiquaries; M.P., Northampton, 1601, Shrewsbury, 1604-11; justice itinerant in Wales; J.P., Glamorganshire, Brecknockshire, and Radnorshire; his antiquarian collections afterwards used by Camden and others. [lv. 376]

TATE, GEORGE (1745-1821), admiral in the Russian navy; said to have distinguished himself in engagements against the Turks and Swedes; wounded at the capture of Ismail, 1790. [lv. 377]

TATE, GEORGE (1805-1871), topographer and naturalist; brother of Thomas Tate [q. v.]; began life as a linendraper; postmaster, 1848; active in all public movements in the town; published 'History of Alnwick,' 1865-9, besides works on archæology and natural history. [lv. 377]

TATE, SIR HENRY, first baronet (1819-1899), public benefactor; entered firm of sugar refiners at Liverpool; patented invention for cutting up sugar-loaves, 1872; came to London, 1880, and rapidly made large fortune from 'Tate's cube sugar'; formed at Park Hill, Streatham, a valuable collection of works by contemporary masters, which he offered to the nation on condition that the government should find a site for a gallery which he would build; the building erected on ground occupied by Millbank Prison (demolished, 1893), and opened, 1897, as National Gallery of British Art (known as the 'Tate Gallery'); created baronet, 1898. [Suppl. iii. 378]

TATE, JAMES (1771-1843), schoolmaster and author; educated at Richmond School and at Sidney Sussex College, Cambridge; M.A., 1797; fellow, 1795; master of Richmond grammar school, 1796-1833; an admirable classical scholar and successful schoolmaster; chief work, 'Horatius Restitutus,' 1832. [lv. 378]

TATE, NAHUM (1652-1715), poetaster and dramatist; B.A. Trinity College, Dublin, 1672; published a volume of poems, 1677, and brought out several plays, his alteration of 'King Lear,' in which Cordelia survives and marries Edgar, holding the stage till about 1840; wrote, with Dryden's assistance, the second part of 'Absalom and Achitophel,' 1682; appointed poet laureate, 1692, and historiographer-royal, 1702; published, with Nicholas Brady [q. v.], the well-known 'New Version of the Psalms' in metre, 1696; the Christmas hymn, 'While shepherds watched,' attributed to him; wrote mainly as editor or translator; his chief original poem being 'Panacea—a Poem on Tea,' 1700. In the 'Dunciad' his work is labelled as 'Tate's poor page.' [lv. 379]

TATE, THOMAS (1807-1888), mathematician; brother of George Tate (1805-1871) [q. v.]; mathematical and scientific master at Battersea, 1840-9, and Kneller colleges, 1849-56; F.R.A.S., 1851; inventor of the 'Tate' double-piston air-pump; published mathematical works and a 'Philosophy of Education,' 1854. [lv. 380]

TATE, WILLIAM (1750?-1806), portrait-painter. [lv. 381]

TATE, ZOUCH (1606-1650), parliamentarian; nephew of Francis Tate [q. v.]; cf Trinity College, Oxford; mover of the self-denying ordinance, 1644. [lv. 377]

TATHAM, CHARLES HEATHCOTE (1772-1842), architect; worked under Henry Holland (1746?-1806) [q. v.], and designed the decorations for Drury Lane Theatre, London; visited Italy, 1794; published 'Ancient Ornamental Architecture at Rome and in Italy,' 1799, and collected a fine assemblage of antique fragments, now in Sir John Soane's collection; exhibited at the Royal Academy, and carried out architectural and decorative work in various houses in the severe classical style; fell into pecuniary difficulties, 1834; made warden of Holy Trinity Hospital, Greenwich. [lv. 381]

TATHAM, EDWARD (1749-1834), controversialist; of Queen's College, Oxford; M.A., 1776; fellow of Lincoln College, Oxford, 1781, appointed rector, 1792-1834; D.D., 1787; preached a famous sermon, c. 1802, on the disputed verse in St. John's first epistle (v. 7); opposed the new examinations; published 'The Chart and Scale of Truth by which to find the Cause of Error' (his Bampton lectures, 1790), a famous series of discourses embodying a new system of logic, much praised by Burke, and other political and miscellaneous works and pamphlets. [lv. 382]

TATHAM, JOHN (*fl.* 1632-1664), dramatist and city poet; writer of the city pageants, 1657-64, and author of several plays—'Love crowns the End,' 1640, 'The Distracted State,' 1651, aimed against sectaries and the Scots, 'The Scots Figgaries,' 1652, and 'The Rump,' 1660, which had considerable influence in preparing the political transition of several pageants, and of at least two volumes of verse, 'Fancies Theater,' 1640, and 'Ostella,' 1650. [lv. 384]

TATHAM, WILLIAM (1752-1819), soldier and engineer; went to America, 1769, and became a clerk in a merchant's office; took part in the revolutionary war; fought at the siege of Yorktown, 1781, and was employed in various official capacities; author of several works; committed suicide. [lv. 385]

TATTAM, HENRY (1789-1868), Coptic scholar; incumbent of Stanford Rivers, 1849; hon. LL.D. Trinity College, Dublin, 1845; D.D. Göttingen, and doctor of philosophy, Leyden; archdeacon of Bedford, 1845; F.R.S., 1835; works include 'A Compendious Grammar of the Egyptian Language,' 1830, 'The Ancient Coptic Version of the Book of Job,' 1846. [lv. 386]

TATTERSALL, GEORGE (1817-1849), 'Wildrake,' artist; grandson of Richard Tattersall [q. v.]; published 'The Lakes of England,' 1836, with beautiful outline drawings; 'Sporting Architecture,' 1841; 'Cracks of the Day,' 1841, and with Henry Alken [q. v.] illustrated Nimrod's 'Hunting Reminiscences,' 1843, the engravings in the two latter works being greatly prized. He also contributed illustrations of great merit to other works. [lv. 388]

TATTERSALL, RICHARD (1724-1795), founder of 'Tattersall's'; second son of Edmund Tattersall of Ridge and Hurstwood; became stud-groom to Evelyn Pierrepont, second Duke of Kingston [q. v.]; set up as a horse-auctioneer at Hyde Park Corner, 1766, where his honesty and businesslike precision brought him the highest patronage; fitted up his 'subscription rooms' and entertained the Prince of Wales (George IV), Charles Fox, Windham, and others, at his seat, Highflyer Hall, near Ely. [lv. 387]

TATTERSALL, WILLIAM DE CHAIR (1752–1829), editor of psalmodies; educated at Westminster School and Christ Church, Oxford; M.A., 1777; rector of Westbourne; published 'A Version or Paraphrase of the Psalms by J. Merrick, adapted to the Purposes of Devotion,' 1789, and the 'Improved Psalmody,' 1794.
[lv. 388]

TATWIN, TATUINI, or TADWINUS (d. 734), archbishop of Canterbury, 731; a Mercian and priest of a monastery called Briudun or Bredon, in Worcestershire; he bore a high character for religion, prudence, and sacred learning. Forty enigmas written in Latin hexameters are attributed to him, and other poems. [lv. 389]

TAUBMAN, MATTHEW (d. 1690 ?), city poet; author of 'An Heroic Poem to his Royal Highness the Duke of York,' 1682, 'Loyal Poems and Satyrs,' 1685, and various pieces celebrating the inauguration of the lord mayors.
[lv. 390]

TAUBMAN, NATHANAEL (d. 1720 ?), chaplain at Leghorn and author; son of Matthew Taubman [q. v.]
[lv. 390]

TAUNTON, first BARON (1798–1869). [See LABOUCHERE, HENRY.]

TAUNTON, JOHN (1769–1821), surgeon; became a pupil of Henry Cline [q. v.] at St. Thomas's Hospital, London; demonstrator of anatomy at Guy's Hospital, London, and surgeon to the city dispensary, 1801; founded the City of London Truss Society, 1807. [lv. 390]

TAUNTON, SIR WILLIAM ELIAS (1773–1835), justice of the king's bench, 1830; educated at Westminster and Christ Church, Oxford; chancellor's prizeman for the English essay, 1793; M.A., 1796; barrister, Lincoln's Inn, 1799; published legal works. [lv. 391]

TAUTPHŒUS, BARONESS VON, originally JEMIMA MONTGOMERY (1807–1893), novelist of foreign manners; author of 'The Initials,' 1850, and other novels of merit.
[lv. 391]

TAVERNER, JOHN (fl. 1530), musician; presumably identical with the 'Taverner of Boston,' who was made by Wolsey master of the choristers at Cardinal College (Christ Church), c. 1525; composed masses, motets, and songs, but, as far as is known, no instrumental music, almost all remaining in manuscript; last of the pre-Reformation composers. [lv. 392]

TAVERNER, JOHN (1584–1638), professor of music at Gresham College; grandson of Richard Taverner [q. v.]; M.A. Trinity College, Cambridge, 1605 (incorporated at Oxford, 1606); professor, 1610–38. [lv. 395]

TAVERNER, RICHARD (1505 ?–1575), religious reformer and author; often confused with John Taverner (fl. 1530) [q. v.]; educated at Cardinal's College, Oxford, and at Cambridge; M.A.; patronised by Wolsey, and, on his fall, by Cromwell, for whom he wrote works supporting the Reformation, including his English version of the bible, 1539, which was a revised edition of Matthew's, and a commentary on the epistles and gospels, 1540; clerk of the privy seal, 1536, which he retained till the accession of Queen Mary; sent to the Tower of London, 1541, on the fall of Cromwell, but released, and was granted by Henry VIII various estates; M.P., Liverpool, 1545; licensed to preach, 1552; under Queen Elizabeth J.P. and high sheriff of Oxfordshire; author of several religious works and translations from Erasmus. [lv. 393]

TAVERNER, ROGER (d. 1582), economic writer; brother of Richard Taverner [q. v.]; educated at Cambridge; wrote on the scarcity of provisions; became surveyor-general of woods, c. 1540; M.P., Launceston, 1554. [lv. 394]

TAVERNER, WILLIAM (d. 1731), dramatist; procurator-general of the court of arches at Canterbury; author of 'The Artful Husband' (produced, 1717), and of other plays of little merit. [lv. 396]

TAVERNER, WILLIAM (1703–1772), procurator-general and artist; son of William Taverner (d. 1731) [q. v.] [lv. 396]

TAXSTER or TAYSTER, JOHN DE (d. 1265 ?), chronicler; Benedictine monk of Bury St. Edmunds; writer of a chronicle beginning with the creation of the world, and terminating in the year 1265, of which the latter portion from towards the middle of the thirteenth century is by far the most valuable; a strong partisan of Simon de Montfort. [lv. 396]

TAYLER. [See also TAILOR and TAYLOR.]

TAYLER, CHARLES BENJAMIN (1797–1875), writer for the young; M.A. Trinity College, Cambridge, 1822; incumbent of St. Peter's, Chester, 1836; author of religious manuals for the young. [lv. 397]

TAYLER, FREDERICK (1802–1889), landscape-painter; educated at Eton and Harrow; studied at the Academy and elsewhere, at Paris under Vernet, and in Italy; president of the 'Old Water-colour' Society, 1858–1871; excelled as painter of 'elegant' sporting and pastoral scenes in water-colour. [lv. 398]

TAYLER, JOHN JAMES (1797–1869), unitarian divine; educated at Manchester College, York; B.A. Glasgow, 1818; minister at Mosley Street Chapel, Manchester; visited Germany, 1835, became professor of ecclesiastical history at Manchester New College, 1840, professor of theology, 1852, and principal, 1853; published religious and other works. [lv. 399]

TAYLER, JOSEPH NEEDHAM (1785–1864), rear-admiral; entered the navy on the Royal George, 1796, and witnessed the mutiny at Spithead, 1797; wounded at the siege of St. Sebastian; C.B., 1815; rear-admiral, 1846.
[lv. 400]

TAYLER, WILLIAM (1808–1892), Indian civilian; younger brother of Frederick Tayler [q. v.]; educated at the Charterhouse, London; appointed assistant-commissioner of Cuttack, 1830; during the mutiny he committed grave mistakes; suspended, 1859; published works dealing with his case and on India. [lv. 400]

TAYLOR. [See also TAILOR and TAYLER.]

TAYLOR, ABRAHAM (fl. 1727–1740), independent tutor; minister at Deptford, 1728; preacher and divinity tutor; D.D.; published religious and controversial works.
[lv. 402]

TAYLOR, ALFRED SWAINE (1806–1880), medical jurist; student of Guy's and St. Thomas's hospitals, London; travelled and studied abroad; professor of medical jurisprudence at Guy's Hospital, 1831–77, and lecturer on chemistry, 1832–70; authority as a witness in poisoning trials; invented valuable improvements in Talbot's photographic processes, including the use of hyposulphate of lime as a 'fixer'; editor of the 'London Medical Gazette,' 1844–51; F.R.C.P., 1853; F.R.S., 1845; published, among other books, 'A Manual of Medical Jurisprudence,' 1844, 'The Principles and Practice of Medical Jurisprudence,' 1865, and 'Poisons in Relation to Medical Jurisprudence and Medicine,' 1848, standard works throughout the world. [lv. 402]

TAYLOR, MRS. ANN, originally ANN MARTIN (1757–1830), authoress; married Isaac Taylor (1759–1829) [q. v.]
[lv. 416]

TAYLOR, ANN (1782–1866). [See GILBERT, MRS. ANN.]

TAYLOR, BROOK (1685–1731), mathematician; LL.D. St. John's College, Cambridge, 1714; corresponded with John Keill [q. v.] and sent a solution of the problem involved in Kepler's second law of planetary motion to John Machin, 1712; F.R.S., 1712, and first secretary, 1714; published solution of the problem of the centre of oscillation, 1714 (obtained in 1708); published his 'Methodus Incrementorum Directa et Inversa,' 1715 (the first treatise dealing with the calculus of finite differences), containing 'Taylor's Theorem,' and other original solutions and formulas; 'Linear Perspective,' 1715, 'New Principles of Linear Perspective,' 1719, and other works.
[lv. 404]

TAYLOR, SIR BROOK (1776–1846), ambassador; brother of Sir Herbert Taylor [q. v.]; G.C.H., 1822.
[lv. 413]

TAYLOR, CHARLES (1756–1823), scholar and engraver; son of Isaac Taylor (1730–1807) [q. v.]; articled to his father and studied under Bartolozzi; editor of revised Calmet's 'Dictionary of the Bible'; published 'Picturesque Beauties of Shakespeare,' 1783, and other works. [lv. 405]

TAYLOR, CHRISTOPHER (*d.* 1686), quaker schoolmaster; brother of Thomas Taylor (1618–1682) [q. v.]; B.A. Magdalen College, Oxford, 1636; became puritan minister; converted by George Fox, 1652; started a school at Waltham Abbey, 1670; followed William Penn to Pennsylvania, 1682; published religious works. [lv. 467]

TAYLOR, DAN (1738–1816), founder of the new connexion of general baptists; son of a miner in Yorkshire; joined the Wesleyans, 1759, but withdrew, 1762; baptised in the river Idle, 1763, and ordained baptist pastor at Wadsworth; did not leave the old 'general assembly' till 1803, though the formation of a 'new connexion' was resolved upon under his auspices at Lincoln on the spread of anti-trinitarian views in the general assembly, 1769; author of religious works. [lv. 405]

TAYLOR, EDGAR (1793–1839), solicitor, legal writer, translator, and biographer; dissenter; grandson of John Taylor (1694–1761) [q. v.]; author of 'German Popular Stories,' translated from the Grimms, 1824–6, 'The New Testament . . . revised' (posthumous), 1840, and other works. [lv. 407]

TAYLOR, EDWARD (1784–1863), Gresham professor of music; son of John Taylor (1750–1826) [q. v.]; ironmonger at Norwich; promoter of the first triennial Norwich musical festival, 1824, and vocalist; friend of Spohr, whose works he translated and introduced at Norwich; Gresham professor, 1837–63; author of songs, words of songs, adaptations, and other works. [lv. 407]

TAYLOR, EMILY (1795–1872), authoress; sister of Edgar Taylor [q. v.] [lv. 407]

TAYLOR, GEORGE LEDWELL (1788–1873), architect; travelled abroad and discovered the famous Theban lion at Chaeronea, 1818; surveyor of buildings to the naval department, 1824; laid out Westbourne Terrace, London, and neighbouring squares, 1843–8; wrote 'The Stones of Etruria and Marbles of Antient Rome,' 1859, and other works. [lv. 408]

TAYLOR, HARRIETTE DEBORAH (1807–1874). [See LACY.]

TAYLOR, HELEN (1818–1885), writer of religious works for children; granddaughter of Isaac Taylor (1759–1829) [q. v.] [lv. 417]

TAYLOR, HENRY (1711–1785), theological writer; educated at Hackney and at Queens' College, Cambridge; fellow, 1733; M.A., 1735; rector of Wheatfield and other livings; espoused the Apollinarian heresy in 'The Apology of Ben Mordecai,' 1771–7. [lv. 409]

TAYLOR, SIR HENRY (1800–1886), author of 'Philip van Artevelde'; held a small official appointment in London, 1817–20; returned home, 1820, and wrote poetry and articles on Moore and Lord John Russell accepted by the 'Quarterly Review'; wrote also for the 'London Magazine'; given an appointment in the colonial office, 1824; became acquainted with Southey, Wordsworth, Mill, and Sir James Stephen [q. v.]; finished his tragedy, 'Isaac Comnenus,' 1828, a failure; published 'Philip van Artevelde,' 1834, which was a great success (though failing on the stage in 1847), and 'The Statesman,' an ironical exposition of the arts of succeeding, 1836; supported the policy of 'melioration' and not abolition of the slave laws, advised the suppression of the West Indian assemblies, and approved of Governor Eyre's action, 1865. 'Philip van Artevelde' (modelled upon the Elizabethan drama) has great interest as a psychological study. [lv. 410]

TAYLOR, SIR HERBERT (1775–1839), lieutenant-general; a good linguist; employed by Lord Grenville as his secretary and in the foreign office; saw active service in the Duke of York's campaign in the Netherlands, and made lieutenant in the 2nd dragoon guards; served on foreign missions; secretary to the Duke of York, 1794, to George III, 1805, to Queen Charlotte and to William IV; commissioner by the regency act of George III's estate; lieutenant-general, 1825; adjutant-general of the forces, 1828; defended George III and George IV in 'Remarks,' &c., 1838; G.C.B., 1834. [lv. 413]

TAYLOR, ISAAC (1730–1807), engraver; made his way to London, *c.* 1752; executed plates for the 'Gentleman's Magazine,' and concentrated his attention on book illustration, including those for Owen's 'Dictionary,' Chambers's 'Cyclopædia,' and Richardson's 'Sir Charles Grandison,' 1778; excelled also as a portrait-painter; fellow and secretary of the Society of Artists. [lv. 414]

TAYLOR, ISAAC (1759–1829), engraver and writer for the young; son of Isaac Taylor (1730–1807) [q. v.]; brought up in the studio of his father; engraved plates for Boydell's bible and 'Shakespeare'; published 'Specimens of Gothic Ornaments selected from the Parish Church of Lavenham,' 1796, and produced other successful engravings; nonconformist pastor of Ongar, where he published a series of children's manuals. [lv. 415]

TAYLOR, ISAAC (1787–1865), artist, author, and inventor; son of Isaac Taylor of Ongar (1759–1829) [q. v.]; began life as an engraver; his work much admired by Rossetti and Gilchrist; early turned his attention to literature, and wrote a large number of works, including 'The Elements of Thought,' 1823, 'The Natural History of Enthusiasm,' 1830, by which he is best known, 'Fanaticism,' 1833, 'Spiritual Despotism,' 1835, 'Ancient Christianity and the Doctrines of the Oxford Tracts,' 1839–40, and 'The Restoration of Belief,' 1855; regarded by some as the greatest lay theologian since Coleridge; his attention especially drawn to the problems presented by the corruptions of the Christian church; perfected an ingenious machine for engraving upon copper. [lv. 417]

TAYLOR, JAMES (1745–1797), china-painter and magazine-illustrator; brother of Isaac Taylor (1730–1807) [q. v.] [lv. 415]

TAYLOR, JAMES (1753–1825), engineer; educated at Edinburgh University; became tutor to the sons of Patrick Miller [q. v.], and suggested to him the employment of William Symington's steam-engine in his boats. [lv. 419]

TAYLOR, JAMES (1788–1863), bimetallist and author; brother of John Taylor (1781–1864) [q. v.] [lv. 447]

TAYLOR, JAMES (1813–1892), divine and M.A. St. Andrews, 1843; minister at St. Andrews and Glasgow; secretary to the Scottish board of education, 1872, advocate of popularly elected educational authorities, clear and accurate historian; author of 'The Pictorial History of Scotland,' 1852–9, and other works. [lv. 420]

TAYLOR, JANE (1783–1824), writer for the young; daughter of Isaac Taylor (1759–1829) [q. v.]; together with her sister Ann published 'Original Poems for Infant Minds,' 1804, which attained an immense popularity, and 'Rhymes for the Nursery,' 1806, which included her poem 'Twinkle, twinkle, little Star'; published, with her sister, 'Hymns for Infant Minds,' 1810, and other works; published, among other books, 'Display, a Tale for Young People,' 1815, and 'Contributions of Q.Q.,' 1824; admired by Browning and Sir Walter Scott. [lv. 420]

TAYLOR, JEFFERYS (1792–1853), writer for children; youngest son of Isaac Taylor (1759–1829) [q. v.]; invented a ruling-machine for engravers; author of humorous and fanciful children's books. [lv. 422]

TAYLOR, JEREMY (1613–1667), bishop of Down and Connor, and administrator of Dromore; descendant of Rowland Taylor [q. v.], the martyr; Perse scholar at Gonville and Caius College, Cambridge, 1628; fellow, 1633; M.A., 1634; attracted Laud's attention by his preaching in London; sent by Laud to Oxford; made fellow of All Souls College, Oxford, 1635; M.A. University College, Oxford, 1635; chaplain to Laud and to Charles I; of high repute as a casuistical preacher; rector of Uppingham, 1638; preached his 'gunpowder treason' sermon in St. Mary's, Oxford, 1638, upholding the penal legislation of Queen Elizabeth; made rector of Overstone, 1643; taken prisoner in the royalist defeat before Cardigan Castle, 1645; retired to Golden Grove, Carmarthenshire, where some of his best work, including the 'Liberty of Prophesying,' 1646, the 'Holy Living,' 1650, and the 'Holy Dying,' 1651, was composed; received from Charles I, shortly before his execution, his watch and some jewels; preached in London occasionally; prisoner at Chepstow, 1655; accepted lectureship at Portmore, near

Lisburn, 1658 ; dedicated his 'Ductor Dubitantium,' 1660, to Charles II ; made bishop (1661) of Down and Connor, where he was involved in disputes with the independent clergy ; appointed also 'administrator' of Dromore diocese, where he built the present cathedral (consecrated, 1661) ; dedicated to Ormonde his treatise on 'Confirmation,' 1663 ; published his 'Dissuasive from Popery,' 1664 ; pleaded for an English bishopric, 1664. His 'Liberty of Prophesying' is a practical rather than theoretical treatise on tolerance, while the 'Holy Living' and 'Holy Dying,' with the 'Worthy Communicant,' 1660, may be said to offer 'a complete summary of the duties, and specimen of the devotions, of a Christian' (HEBER). His literary genius is best seen in his sermons. He was also a writer of verse described as 'Eloquence, not Poetry.' Among his other works may be mentioned 'A Discourse of Auxiliary Beauty,' 1656, and 'A Discourse of Friendship,' 1657. [lv. 422]

TAYLOR, JOHN (d. 1534), master of the rolls ; of humble origin ; doctor of civil and canon law of some foreign university (incorporated at Cambridge, 1520, Oxford, 1522) ; prebendary of Lichfield, 1509, and of Westminster, 1518 ; sent on various missions abroad ; accompanied Henry VIII in his campaign in France, 1513, and to the Field of the Cloth of Gold, 1520 ; ambassador to France, 1526 and 1531 ; master of the rolls, 1527. [lv. 429]

TAYLOR, JOHN (1503 ?-1554), bishop of Lincoln ; probably a relative of John Taylor (d. 1534) [q. v.] ; M.A. Queens' College, Cambridge, 1527 ; fellow, c. 1524 ; master of St. John's College, Cambridge, 1538, which post he was obliged to resign owing to dissensions, 1547 ; dean of Lincoln, 1544–52 ; was imprisoned for reformed opinions, 1546, but soon retracted ; under Edward VI supported the marriage of priests, and was one of the commissioners appointed to draw up the first Prayer-book, 1548 ; bishop of Lincoln, 1552 ; deprived, 1554. [lv. 430]

TAYLOR, JOHN (d. 1555). [See CARDMAKER.]

TAYLOR, JOHN (1580–1653), the 'water-poet' ; born of humble parentage at Gloucester ; sent to Gloucester grammar school, but being 'mired' in his Latin accidence, was apprenticed to a London waterman ; pressed into the navy, and was present at the siege of Cadiz, 1596 ; retiring, became a Thames waterman and collector of the lieutenant of the Tower's perquisite of wine ; discharged before 1622 ; increased his diminishing earnings by rhyming, and had a great talent for expressing himself in rollicking prose and verse ; ridiculed in his 'Sculler,' 1612, Thomas Coryate [q. v.], who appealed to 'superior powers' to defend him ; obtained the patronage of Ben Jonson and other men of genius, and diverted both court and city ; arranged the water pageant at the marriage of the Princess Elizabeth, 1613, and composed the triumphs at the pageants of the lord mayors ; visited the continent, 1616 ; went on foot from London to Braemar, 1618 ; started from London to Queenborough in a brown-paper boat and narrowly escaped drowning ; visited the queen of Bohemia at Prague, 1620, and accomplished other journeys, each one resulting in a booklet with an odd title ; on the outbreak of plague retired to Oxford, 1625, and was lodged in Oriel College ; again visited Oxford, 1642 ; at surrender of Oxford, 1645 ; returned to London and took the Crown public-house (now the Ship) in Hanover Court, Long Acre ; published a collective edition of his works, 'All the Workes of Iohn Taylor, the Water Poet,' 1630 (with other pieces were reprinted by the Spenser Society, 1868–9). As literature his books do not rank high, but they are of great value to the historian and antiquary. [lv. 431]

TAYLOR, JOHN (1600 ?-1655), diplomatist ; student at the Inner Temple, 1619 ; employed at foreign embassies ; sent to Vienna to accomplish the restitution of the Palatinate to the elector, exceeded his instructions, and was recalled and committed to the Tower of London ; subsequently agent for Charles II at foreign courts. [lv. 438]

TAYLOR, JOHN (1694–1761), dissenting divine and hebraist ; ordained by dissenting ministers, 1716 ; went to Norwich, 1733 ; founded the Octagon chapel there, 1754 ; D.D. Glasgow ; divinity tutor in Warrington academy, 1757 ; author of several important works, including 'The Scripture Doctrine of Original Sin,' 1740 (against Calvinistic views), and 'A Paraphrase . . . on the Epistle to

the Romans,' 1745, 'The Hebrew Concordance adapted to the English Bible,' 1754–7 (the first serious attempt to fix the primitive meaning of Hebrew roots), and 'The Scripture Account of Prayer,' 1761. [lv. 439]

TAYLOR, JOHN (1704–1766), classical scholar ; sizar at St. John's College, Cambridge, 1721 ; M.A., 1728 ; fellow, 1729 ; patronised by Carteret ; chancellor of Lincoln, 1744 ; canon of St. Paul's, London, 1757 ; F.R.S. and F.R.A.S. ; published excellent editions of Lysias, 1739, 'Demosthenes contra Leptinem,' 1741, and other works. [lv. 440]

TAYLOR, JOHN (1703–1772), itinerant oculist ; commonly known as the 'Chevalier' ; studied at St. Thomas's Hospital, London ; practised at Norwich and journeyed through England, France, and Holland ; M.D. Basle, 1733, Liège and Cologne, 1734 ; possessed much skill as an operator, but advertised like a charlatan ; was the subject of many satires ; author of treatises on the eye and a bombastic autobiography. [lv. 441]

TAYLOR, JOHN (1724–1787), oculist ; son of John Taylor (1703–1772) [q. v.] ; published a scurrilous 'Life' of his father, 1761. [lv. 442]

TAYLOR, JOHN (1711–1788), friend of Dr. Johnson ; educated with Dr. Johnson at Lichfield grammar school ; of Christ Church, Oxford ; rector of Market Bosworth, 1740 ; chaplain to the Duke of Devonshire, 1737 ; prebendary of Westminster, 1746 ; often visited by Dr. Johnson at his residence at Ashbourne ; supplied information to Boswell for the 'Life' ; author of sermons believed to be largely Johnson's composition. [lv. 442]

TAYLOR, JOHN (1745 ?-1806), landscape-painter. [lv. 446]

TAYLOR, JOHN (d. 1808), writer on India ; officer in the Bombay army. [lv. 443]

TAYLOR, JOHN (1743–1818), baptist minister ; younger brother of Dan Taylor [q. v.] [lv. 406]

TAYLOR, JOHN (d. 1821), translator from the Sanskrit ; M.D. Edinburgh, 1804. [lv. 444]

TAYLOR, JOHN (1750–1826), hymn-writer and founder of the literary family of the Taylors of Norwich ; grandson of John Taylor (1694–1761) [q. v.] ; prominent member of the Octagon chapel, Norwich ; author of songs, including 'The Trumpet of Liberty,' 1791, verses and hymns. [lv. 444]

TAYLOR, JOHN (1757–1832), miscellaneous writer ; son of John Taylor (1724–1787) [q. v.] ; oculist to George III ; dramatic critic of the 'Morning Post,' and later editor ; proprietor of the 'True Briton,' and of the 'Sun' ; author of 'Monsieur Tonson' (a dramatic poem, rehearsed at Drury Lane, London, 1821), and other works. [lv. 445]

TAYLOR, JOHN (1739–1838), portrait-painter. [lv. 446]

TAYLOR, SIR JOHN (1771–1843), lieutenant-general ; commanded a battalion of the Connaught rangers ; in the Peninsular war ; severely wounded at Orthes ; K.C.B., 1834 ; lieutenant-general, 1837. [lv. 446]

TAYLOR, JOHN (1779–1863), mining engineer ; son of John Taylor (1750–1826) [q. v.] [lv. 457]

TAYLOR, JOHN (1781–1864), publisher ; proprietor of the 'London Magazine' and editor (1821–4) ; author of 'The Identity of Junius . . . established,' 1816, which first publicly identified Junius with Sir Philip Francis [q. v.], and of books on the currency. [lv. 446]

TAYLOR, JOHN (1829–1893), author ; elected librarian of the Bristol Library Society, 1863 ; writer on the history and antiquities of Bristol and the west. [lv. 447]

TAYLOR, JOHN EDWARD (1791–1844), founder of the 'Manchester Guardian' ; educated at his father's classical school at Manchester ; became partner in a cotton manufactory ; one of the founders of the Junior Literary and Philosophical Society ; contributed powerful liberal articles to the 'Manchester Gazette' ; indicted for libel of John Greenwood, 1819, but calling evidence of truth acquitted by the jury ; signed the 'Declaration and Protest' on the occasion of the 'Peterloo Massacre,' 1819, and published 'Notes and Explanations . . . relative to the Internal State of the Country,' 1819 ; founded the 'Manchester Guardian,' 1821. [lv. 448]

TAYLOR, JOHN ELLOR (1837–1895), popular science writer; editor of the 'Norwich People's Journal' and scientific lecturer; author of 'Half-hours at the Seaside,' 1872, and other popular scientific works; editor of 'Hardwicke's Science Gossip,' 1872–93.　　[lv. 450]

TAYLOR, JOHN SYDNEY (1795–1841), journalist; B.A. Trinity College, Dublin, 1814; barrister, Middle Temple, 1824; contributor to 'Morning Chronicle'; editor of the 'Morning Herald'; author of works on punishment of crime.　　[lv. 450]

TAYLOR, JOSEPH (1586?–1653?), actor; acted at the Globe and Blackfriars theatres, London; one of the king's players; one of the twenty-six 'principal actors in all these plays' mentioned in the list prefixed to the folio 'Shakespeare' of 1623, two of his parts being Hamlet and Othello; acted in Jonson's and in Beaumont and Fletcher's plays.　　[lv. 451]

TAYLOR, MEADOWS [PHILIP MEADOWS TAYLOR] (1808–1876), Indian officer and novelist; great grandson of John Taylor (1694–1761) [q. v.]; entered the house of a Bombay merchant, and subsequently the nizam's service in a military, and then civil, capacity; 'Times' correspondent, 1840–53; carried out pacification of the state of Shorapore, 1841, and on the outbreak of the mutiny kept the district of Booldana in North Berar quiet; author of 'Confessions of a Thug,' 1839, a very successful book, and of five other brilliant novels delineating epochs of Indian history, also of 'Story of My Life' (edited by his daughter, 1877).　　[lv. 452]

TAYLOR, MICHAEL ANGELO (1757–1834), politician; son of Sir Robert Taylor [q. v.]; B.A. Corpus Christi College, Oxford, 1778; M.A. St. John's College, Oxford, 1781; called to the bar at Lincoln's Inn, 1774; M.P., Poole, 1784–90, Heytesbury, 1790–1, Aldborough, 1796–1800, Durham, 1800–2, Rye, 1806–7, Ilchester, 1807–12, Poole, 1812–18, Durham, 1818–31, Sudbury, 1832–4; called Father of the House; began as a tory and supporter of Pitt, but gradually became whig, voting for dismissal of the tory ministers, 1797; one of the managers at impeachment of Warren Hastings; drew attention to chancery delays and defective condition of the London streets, the Metropolitan Paving Act, 1817, being still called by his name; privy councillor, 1831.　　[lv. 453]

TAYLOR, MICHAEL WAISTELL (1824–1892), antiquary and physician; M.D. Edinburgh, 1843; discovered the contamination of milk by scarlet fever; made several local archæological discoveries; published 'Old Manorial Halls of Cumberland and Westmoreland,' 1892. [lv. 455]

TAYLOR, PETER or PATRICK (1756–1788), decorative artist; painted one of the few authentic portraits of Burns.　　[lv. 455]

TAYLOR, PETER ALFRED (1819–1891), radical politician; silk mercer; friend of Mazzini and chairman of the Society of Friends of Italy; M.P., Leicester, 1862–1884; represented the Manchester school.　　[lv. 455]

TAYLOR, PHILIP (1786–1870), civil engineer; son of John Taylor (1750–1826) [q. v.]; began life as a surgeon and chemist; invented wooden pill-boxes; took out a patent for lighting buildings by oil-gas, 1824, and for other inventions; founded engineering and other works in France.　　[lv. 456]

TAYLOR, POLICARPUS (d. 1780), rear-admiral; took part in the engagement off Havana, 1748; rear-admiral 'in the fleet,' 1762.　　[lv. 457]

TAYLOR, REYNELL GEORGE (1822–1886), general of the Indian army; the 'Bayard of the Punjab'; fought in the Gwalior campaign and first Sikh war, when he was wounded, 1845; worked at Lahore and in the Punjab under the Lawrences, 1847; ruler of Peshawur; captured the fort of Lukkee in the second Sikh war, 1849; given the Star of India, 1866; general, 1880.　　[lv. 457]

TAYLOR, RICHARD (1781–1858), printer and naturalist; son of John Taylor (1750–1826) [q. v.]; partner with his father in a printing business in London; fellow of various scientific societies and F.S.A.; editor of scientific publications.　　[lv. 458]

TAYLOR, RICHARD COWLING (1789–1851), antiquary; engaged on the ordnance survey and in reporting on mining properties at home and in America; published archæological and geological works.　　[lv. 459]

TAYLOR, ROBERT (1710–1762), physician; M.D. Trinity College, Cambridge, 1737; obtained a large practice in London; F.R.C.P., 1749; Harveian orator, 1755; P.R.S., 1752, and physician to George II; published medical works.　　[lv. 459]

TAYLOR, SIR ROBERT (1714–1788), architect; among other productions sculptured the monuments to Cornwall and Guest at Westminster Abbey, 1743–6; built many country houses, Stone Buildings, Lincoln's Inn, 1756, and additions to the Bank of England and other London edifices; knighted when sheriff of London, 1782–1783; left the bulk of his property for the teaching of modern languages at Oxford.　　[lv. 460]

TAYLOR, ROBERT (1784–1844), deïstical writer; M.R.C.S., 1807; later studied for the church at St. John's College, Cambridge; B.A., 1813; curate of Midhurst and Eastbourne, 1813; became a sceptic, 1818, and resigned, but recanted; failing to get preferment again, lectured publicly in London, attacking the church; sentenced to a year's imprisonment for blasphemy, 1828; became acquainted with Richard Carlile [q. v.], with whom he set out on a lecturing tour; convicted again of blasphemy, 1831, and imprisoned for two years; married an elderly lady of property, 1833, and escaped to France to avoid an action for breach of promise to another lady; became a surgeon; ignorant of philology; published writings on Christianity, expounding it as a scheme of solar myths. 　　[lv. 461]

TAYLOR, ROWLAND (d. 1555), martyr; converted to protestantism by William Turner (d. 1568) [q. v.]; LL.D. Cambridge, 1534; domestic chaplain to Cranmer, 1540; incumbent of Hadleigh, 1544; arrested and examined before Gardiner, 1554, and burnt on Aldham Common, near Hadleigh, 1555; represented by Foxe as the beau-ideal of a parish priest and a man of ability and learning. [lv. 463]

TAYLOR, SAMUEL (fl. 1786–1816), stenographer; published 'An Essay intended to establish . . . an universal System of Stenography,' 1786, Pitman's system being an adaptation of it.　　[lv. 464]

TAYLOR, SILAS (1624–1678). [See DOMVILLE.]

TAYLOR, SIMON (d. 1772), botanical painter; painted Lord Bute's rare plants.　　[lv. 465]

TAYLOR, SUSANNAH (1755–1823), well-known for her literary predilections; née Cook; married John Taylor (1750–1826) [q. v.], in 1777.　　[lv. 444]

TAYLOR, THOMAS (1576–1633), puritan divine; B.D. Christ's College, Cambridge, 1628; D.D. Oxford, 1630; preached before Queen Elizabeth at St. Paul's Cross, London; called 'a brazen wall against popery,' but denounced Bancroft's severe treatment of the puritans; minister of St. Mary Aldermanbury, London, 1625; published religious works.　　[lv. 465]

TAYLOR, THOMAS (1618–1682), quaker; educated at Oxford; incumbent of a living in Westmoreland; followed George Fox, and imprisoned for many years; author of religious addresses.　　[lv. 466]

TAYLOR, THOMAS (1738–1816), Wesleyan minister; joined the methodists, 1748; itinerant minister, 1761–1816, relating his experiences in his 'Autobiography'; president of the conference, 1796 and 1809; writer of religious books.　　[lv. 467]

TAYLOR, THOMAS (1758–1835), Platonist; received an irregular education; obtained a clerkship in Lubbock's bank; devoted himself to the translation and exposition of Plato, Aristotle, and the Neo-Platonists and Pythagoreans; defective in critical scholarship, never doubting the historic personality of Orpheus and the authenticity of the 'Hymns'; esteemed the mystical neo-Pythagorean mathematics the true science; visited Oxford, 1802, where he was heartily welcomed; author of translations of the Orphic Hymns, Plato, Aristotle, Proclus, Porphyry, Apuleius, Pausanias, and other ancient writers; published also dissertations and miscellanies, including an attack on the mathematician Wallis's arithmetic of infinites.　　[lv. 468]

TAYLOR, THOMAS (d. 1848), botanist; B.A. Trinity College, Dublin, 1807; M.D.; published 'Muscologia Britannica,' 1818, with Sir William Jackson Hooker [q. v.]; contributed to the 'Flora Antarctica.'　　[lv. 470]

TAYLOR, THOMAS EDWARD (1811-1883), politician; captain in the guards and colonel of militia; M.P. in Dublin, 1841-83; conservative whip; chancellor of the duchy of Lancaster, 1868 and 1874. [lv. 471]

TAYLOR, THOMAS GLANVILLE (1804-1848), astronomer; entered the Royal Observatory, Greenwich, 1820; director of Madras Observatory, 1830; F.R.A.S., 1844; published the 'Madras General Catalogue' of stars, 1844. [lv. 471]

TAYLOR, TOM (1817-1880), dramatist and editor of 'Punch'; distinguished himself at Glasgow University and Trinity College, Cambridge; fellow, 1842; M.A., 1843; professor of English literature at London University, 1845; barrister, Inner Temple, 1846; secretary to the board of health, 1854; wrote for the 'Morning Chronicle,' 'Daily News,' 'Punch,' 'Times,' and 'Graphic'; editor of 'Punch,' 1874-80; author of numerous works, including biography of Haydon, 1853, 'Leicester Square,' 1874, and successful plays, including 'To Parents and Guardians,' 1845, and 'Our American Cousin,' 1858, and three historical dramas. [lv. 472]

TAYLOR, WILLIAM (d. 1423), heretic; M.A. Oxford and priest; burnt at Smithfield. [lv. 474]

TAYLOR, WILLIAM (1765-1836), man of letters; travelled abroad, and was introduced to Goethe; became an enthusiast for German literature and the French revolution; attended the debates in the national assembly at Paris, 1790; translated Bürger's 'Lenore' into English ballad metre, 1790, Lessing's 'Nathan' and Goethe's 'Iphigenia'; wrote numerous articles in the 'Monthly Review,' 'Critical Review,' 'Athenæum,' and other periodicals; abounding in new ideas, and extending the English literary outlook; became intimate with Southey, 1798; contributed to the 'Annual Anthology,' 1799-1800; published 'Tales of Yore,' 1810; 'English Synonyms Described,' 1813, and his *magnum opus*, the 'Historic Survey of German Poetry,' 1828-30. [lv. 474]

TAYLOR, WILLIAM BENJAMIN SARSFIELD (1781-1850), painter of landscapes and military subjects; elder brother of John Sydney Taylor [q. v.] [lv. 477]

TAYLOR, WILLIAM COOKE (1800-1849), miscellaneous writer; B.A. Trinity College, Dublin, 1825; edited several of Pinnock's catechisms; settled in London, 1829; contributed to the 'Athenæum,' and produced a vast number of books, mostly historical and educational, and translations; LL.D. Dublin, 1835; ardent advocate for national education and free trade; leading and original member of the British Association; statistical writer for the Irish government, 1847; contributor to the 'Evening Post' in support of the executive, and writer of party pamphlets. [lv. 478]

TAYLOR, WITTEWRONGE (1719?-1760), captain in the navy; took part in the action off Havana, 1748, and the blockade of Brest, 1758-9, with Sir Edward (afterwards Lord) Hawke [q. v.]; shipwrecked off Bolt Head in the Ramillies. [lv. 479]

TAYLOR, ZACHARY (1653-1705), the 'Lancashire Levite'; M.A. Jesus College, Cambridge, 1678; rector of Croxton, 1695; published 'Submission and Obedience to the present Government,' 1690, and other tracts exposing the foibles of dissenters. [lv. 480]

TEACH or **THATCH**, EDWARD (d. 1718), pirate; known as Blackbeard; said to have been a native of Bristol and employed as a privateer in the West Indies in the war of the Spanish succession: after the peace plundered all impartially: became a terror in the West Indies and off Carolina and Virginia; was wrecked in Topsail Inlet, North Carolina, and surrendered at Bathtown; his conduct connived at by Governor Eden, in consequence of which he continued his acts of piracy, but was finally killed; though brutal and treacherous, became the ideal pirate of romance. [lvi. 1]

TEDDEMAN, SIR THOMAS (d. 1668?), vice-admiral; rear-admiral in the action off Lowestoft, 1665; knighted, 1665; present at the attack on Bergen and capture of Dutch ships, 1665; vice-admiral in the fight, 1-4 June 1665; vice-admiral of the white, 1666. [lvi. 2]

TEELING, BARTHOLOMEW (1774-1798), United Irishman; visited France to bring about invasion of Ireland, 1796; served under the name of Biron with Hoche;

landed with the French army at Killala, 1798; was captured and executed. [lvi. 3]

TEELING, CHARLES HAMILTON (1778-1850), Irish journalist; brother of Bartholomew Teeling [q. v.], and United Irishman; author of 'Personal Narrative of the Rebellion of 1798,' 1828; edited various journals.
[lvi. 3]

TEESDALE, SIR CHRISTOPHER CHARLES (1833-1893), major-general, R.A.; aide-de-camp to William Fenwick Williams [q. v.] when British commissioner with the Turkish army in war with Russia; performed valuable and brilliant services in defence of Kars, 1854-5, and at battle of Kars, when he was wounded; became prisoner of war at the capitulation to the Russians; liberated, made C.B., and officer of the Legion of Honour, 1856; V.C., 1857; equerry to the Prince of Wales (now Edward VII), 1858, and aide-de-camp to Queen Victoria, 1877; major-general, 1887; K.C.M.G., 1887. [lvi. 3]

TEGAI (1805-1864). [See HUGHES, HUGH.]

TEGG, THOMAS (1776-1845), bookseller; after some adventures went to London, 1796; opened a shop at 111 Cheapside, 1805, and made a great reputation by his cheap reprints and abridgments; sold fifty thousand copies of 'The Whole Life of Nelson' after Trafalgar, and realised large sums by Hone's 'Everyday Book and Table Book,' 1824; published handbooks and other works.
[lvi. 6]

TEGG, WILLIAM (1816-1895), publisher and bookseller, son of Thomas Tegg [q. v.]; publisher of school and juvenile books, of reprints of standard works and books for export; author of various compilations.
[lvi. 7]

TEGID (1792-1852). [See JONES, JOHN.]

TEIGNMOUTH, first BARON (1751-1834). [See SHORE, JOHN.]

TEILO (fl. 550), British saint; born near Tenby of noble parentage; said with Paulinus and David (d. 601?) [q. v.] to have been consecrated bishop at Jerusalem; became bishop of Llandaff on his return and chief of the churches of 'dextralis Britannia,' other accounts making him successor to David. [lvi. 7]

TELFAIR, CHARLES (1777?-1833), naturalist; practised as a surgeon in Mauritius; established the botanical gardens at Mauritius and Réunion; died at Port Louis. [lvi. 8]

TELFER, JAMES (1800-1862), minor poet; shepherd and country schoolmaster; published 'Border Ballads and Miscellaneous Poems,' 1824, and prose writings.
[lvi. 8]

TELFORD, THOMAS (1757-1834), engineer; son of a Dumfriesshire shepherd; worked as a mason; became early interested in literature; published poetry in Ruddiman's 'Edinburgh Magazine,' 1779, and 'Eskdale,' 1784, which was praised by Southey; worked at Edinburgh as a mason, 1780; went to London, 1782; became surveyor of public works for Shropshire; engineer of the Ellesmere canal, 1793, in which capacity he built the remarkable aqueducts over the Ceiriog valley at Chirk, 1796-1801, and Dee, 1795-1805; inspected the harbours of Scotland, and drew up exhaustive reports; constructed the Caledonian canal, the most conspicuous of his achievements, but not the most useful, and which proved a financial failure, and opened up the northern counties of Scotland by 920 miles of new roads and 120 new bridges, advancing country 'at least a century'; carried out improvements of Scottish harbours, including those of Wick, Aberdeen, Peterhead, Banff, Leith, and Dundee; constructed canals and roads in England, and the Gotha canal between the Baltic and North Sea, 1808-10; first president and one of the founders of the Institute of Civil Engineers, 1818; erected the Menai Bridge (begun, 1819) on the suspension principle (scarcely tried before in England); built bridges at Tewkesbury, 1826, Gloucester, 1828, and Glasgow and on the Clyde, 1833, opened 1835; drew up plans for improvement of Dover harbour, 1834; buried in Westminster Abbey. Throughout he was animated by great public spirit; a man of generous and social disposition and of literary inclinations, the intimate friend of Campbell and Southey; wrote autobiography, published, 1838, as well as contributions to the 'Edinburgh Encyclopædia' and to other works. [lvi. 9]

TELYNOG (1840-1865). [See EVANS, THOMAS.]

T t

TEMPEST, PIERCE (1653–1717), printseller ; brother of Sir John Tempest, first baronet ; best known by his 'Cryes of the City of London,' 1711. [lvi. 14]

TEMPLE, EARL (1711–1779). [See GRENVILLE, RICHARD TEMPLE.]

TEMPLE, DOROTHY (1627–1695), wife of Sir William Temple (1628–1699) [q. v.] ; daughter of Sir Peter Osborne (1584–1653) [q. v.] ; married Sir William Temple, 1655 ; helped her husband in many of his schemes, and was a friend of Queen Mary II ; her letters to Temple, which attracted Macaulay, published, 1888. [lvi. 50]

TEMPLE, HENRY, first VISCOUNT PALMERSTON (1673 ?–1757), son of Sir John Temple (1632–1704) [q. v.]; joint-chief-remembrancer of the Irish court of exchequer, 1680 ; created Viscount Palmerston of Palmerston, co. Dublin, 1723 ; M.P., East Grinstead, 1727–34, Bossiney, 1734–41, and Weobly, 1741–7 ; supporter of Walpole ; improved houses at East Sheen and Broadlands ; quarrelled with Swift, 1726. [lvi. 15]

TEMPLE, HENRY, second VISCOUNT PALMERSTON (1739–1802), grandson of Henry Temple, first viscount [q. v.] ; M.P., East Looe, 1762–8, Southampton, 1768–74, Hastings, 1774–80, and 1780–4, Boroughbridge, 1784–90, Newport (Isle of Wight), 1790–6, and Winchester, 1796–1802 ; lord of the admiralty, 1766, and of the treasury, 1777 ; was fond of travel and social life, the assemblies at Hanover Square, London, being famous ; acquainted with Gibbon, Wilkie, and Reynolds ; member of 'The Club,' 1784 ; D.C.L. Oxford, 1773 ; writer of verses and of the 'Diary in France during July and August, 1791' (published, 1885). [lvi. 15]

TEMPLE, HENRY JOHN, third VISCOUNT PALMERSTON (1784–1865), statesman ; elder son of Henry Temple, second viscount Palmerston [q. v.]; born at Broadlands, near Romsey, Hampshire ; educated at Harrow, Edinburgh, and St. John's College, Cambridge ; M.A. *jure natalium*, Cambridge, 1806 ; succeeded to the peerage, 1802 ; tory M.P. for Newport, Isle of Wight, 1807 ; lord of the admiralty in the Portland ministry, when he made his first speech (vindicating diplomatic secrecy), 1808; refused seat in the cabinet offered by Perceval, but accepted secretaryship-at-war, 1809 ; retained secretaryship through successive administrations till 1828, showing energy in carrying out reforms and maintaining his rights ; wounded by a would-be assassin, 1818 ; elected M.P. for Cambridge University, 1811–31, when he was rejected through his support of parliamentary reform : for Bletchingley, 1831, South Hampshire, 1832, and Tiverton, 1835–65 ; offered by Canning chancellorship of the exchequer, but excluded from that office by George IV, 1827 ; remained, however, a Canningite all his life ; continued in Goderich's and in Wellington's ministries, but left with the Canningites, 1828 ; made his first great speech on foreign affairs, attacking the government's policy towards Portugal and Greece, 1829, and supported catholic emancipation ; became foreign secretary in Lord Grey's administration, 1830, which office, except during Peel's administration for four months, he held during eleven years ; effected the independence of Belgium in spite of great difficulties, and prevented acceptance of the Belgian throne by the Duc de Nemours, 1830–1 ; obtained the Volo to Arta frontier for Greece, 1832 ; G.C.B., 1832 ; supported Isabella in Spain and Donna Maria in Portugal against the pretenders, Don Carlos and Dom Miguel, by his quadruple alliance, 1834, and sent troops to Spain ; supported Turkey, in whose regeneration he believed, against the encroachments of Russia, but failed to prevent the treaty of Unkiar Skelesi between Russia and Turkey, 1833, and was obliged by French patronage of Mohammed Ali to make a treaty with Russia, Austria, and Prussia to defend Turkish territory against the Egyptians, 1840 ; opposed by the cabinet and court, threatened his resignation ; baffled Mohammed Ali and concluded a convention closing the Bosphorus and Dardanelles to ships of all nations, 1841 ; declared war against China, annexed Hongkong, and obtained opening of five ports, 1840–1 ; effected slave trade convention, 1841 ; showed great prescience and firmness throughout, and raised English prestige abroad ; 'had created Belgium, saved Portugal and Spain from absolutism, rescued Turkey from Russia, and the highway to India from France,' and had maintained peace ; attacked in opposition, 1841–6, the 'imbecility' and 'sacrifices' of the government; became foreign secretary again in Lord John Russell's administra-

tion, 1846 ; preserved Swiss independence from Austrian and French interference ; refused further support of England to the Orleanist dynasty, owing to the Spanish marriages, 1846 ; sent a fleet to re-establish the queen of Portugal, 1846 ; maintained attitude of neutrality through the revolution period, desiring the establishment of a stable government in France and Italian independence ; through a dictatorial letter to Spain caused the English minister's dismissal from Madrid, 1848 ; allowed Woolwich to furnish arms to the Sicilian insurgents ; procured better terms for Sardinia by his intercession, 1849 ; expressed England's 'disgust' at Austrian severities, and supported Turkey, at the risk of war, in her refusal to give up to Russia and Austria Polish and Hungarian refugees, 1849 ; compelled Greece to accept his terms in the Pacifico affair and blockaded the Piræus, 1850, on which occasion he made his famous ' civis Romanus ' speech, and defeated the foreign and English conspiracies to overthrow him ; brought upon himself by his independent action as foreign minister Queen Victoria's memorandum of 12 Aug. 1850, and having expressed his approval of Napoleon's *coup d'état*, 1851, was dismissed by Lord John Russell ; the government itself defeated on an amendment moved by him shortly afterwards ; refused to join, but supported Lord Derby's government ; on its fall became home secretary in Lord Aberdeen's ministry, 1852 ; resigned on the question of reform, but returned to office, 1853 ; advocated in vain vigorous action in resisting Russia ; on the outbreak of war proposed the Crimean campaign ; the conduct of the war refused him by Aberdeen, on which Russell resigned, and the ministry fell, 1855 ; became prime minister at a time of immense difficulty and danger ; compelled by France and Austria to agree to the treaty of Paris (1856), by which, however, the integrity of Turkey was guaranteed ; K.G., 1856 ; opposed French projects for partition of Turkish territories in Africa; opposed the construction of the Suez Canal ; defeated on the China war question, but returned to power again with increased majority at general election, 1857 ; underrated at first seriousness of Indian mutiny, but took prompt measures for relief of English garrisons ; was defeated on the Conspiracy to Murder Bill, 1858, and resigned, but again became prime minister, 1859 ; supported advance of Italy towards independence ; strengthened the national defences ; warden of the Cinque ports, 1861 ; lord rector of Glasgow University, 1863 ; hon. D.C.L. Oxford, 1862, and LL.D. Cambridge, 1864 ; maintained neutrality during the American civil war, but on seizure of passengers on a British steamer sent guards to Canada, while the escape of the Alabama from Birkenhead was caused by the hesitation of the law officers ; attempted in vain to protect the Poles, 1863, and Denmark from Austria and Prussia ; buried in Westminster Abbey. [lvi. 16]

TEMPLE, JAMES (*fl.* 1640–1668), regicide ; served in the parliamentary army ; commissioner for the sequestration of delinquents' estates, 1643 ; M.P. for Bramber in the Long parliament, 1645 ; governor of Tilbury fort, 1649 ; one of Charles I's judges, signing the death-warrant, 1649 ; was excepted from the act of oblivion, 1660 ; arrested and tried, but adducing evidence of services to the royalists escaped execution. [lvi. 33]

TEMPLE, SIR JOHN (1600–1677), master of the rolls in Ireland : son of Sir William Temple (1555–1627) [q. v.] ; educated at Trinity College, Dublin ; entered the personal service of Charles I ; knighted, 1628 ; master of the rolls in Ireland, 1640, suspended, 1643, reappointed, 1655, and confirmed at the Restoration ; assisted the government on outbreak of the rebellion, 1641, but took the parliamentary side in civil war, and was imprisoned and suspended, 1643 ; M.P. for co. Meath, 1642, 1646 ; published his 'Irish Rebellion,' inflaming popular indignation against the Irish, 1646 ; joint-administrator of the great seal of Ireland, 1647, but voting for compromise with Charles I was excluded from the house ; served on various commissions ; received grants of land ; made privy councillor at the Restoration. [lvi. 34]

TEMPLE, SIR JOHN (1632–1704), speaker of the Irish parliament ; son of Sir John Temple (1600–1677) [q. v.] ; solicitor-general of Ireland, 1660 ; knighted, 1661 ; M.P., Carlow, and speaker of the Irish parliament, 1661 ; attorney-general, 1690. [lvi. 35]

TEMPLE, SIR PETER, second baronet of Stowe (1592–1653), parliamentarian ; M.P., Buckingham ; knighted, 1641. [lvi. 37]

TEMPLE, PETER (1600–1663), regicide ; of Temple Hall ; member of the county association for defence, 1642 ; captain of horse ; accused of cowardice at Leicester, 1645 ; signed Charles I's death-warrant, 1649 ; excepted from the act of oblivion at the Restoration, and imprisoned in the Tower of London till his death, his estate being confiscated. [lvi. 36]

TEMPLE, Sir RICHARD, third baronet (1634–1697), politician ; son of Sir Peter Temple, second baronet of Stowe ; M.P., Warwickshire, 1654, Buckingham, 1659 and 1660–97 (except in the parliament of 1679) ; a secret royalist ; K.B., 1661 ; senior commissioner of customs, 1671 ; prominent member of the country party ; zealous against those accused in the Popish plot, and for the exclusion bill ; dismissed by James II ; later supporter of William III in the Commons ; author of works on taxation and the coinage. [lvi. 37]

TEMPLE, Sir RICHARD, Viscount Cobham and fourth baronet of Stowe (1669 ?–1749), general ; eldest son of Sir Richard Temple (1634–1697) [q. v.] ; succeeded his father, 1697 ; M.P., Buckinghamshire, 1704 and 1705, Buckingham, 1708 and 1710 ; served as colonel in Marlborough's campaigns, especially distinguishing himself at Lille, 1708 ; made baron, 1714, and Viscount Cobham, 1718, by George I ; captured Vigo, 1719 ; opposed Walpole's scheme of excise, and in consequence was dismissed from his regiment ; joined the faction known as the 'boy patriots' ; on Walpole's fall joined Wilmington and the Pelhams ; created field-marshal and appointed colonel of horse guards, 1742 ; resigned his commission as a protest against the Hanoverian policy ; rebuilt Stowe and laid out the famous gardens ; patron of literati and celebrated by Pope and Congreve ; member of the Kit-Cat Club. [lvi. 38]

TEMPLE, Sir THOMAS (1614–1674), governor of Acadia ; grandson of Sir Richard Temple, first baronet of Stowe ; appointed governor of Acadia by Oliver Cromwell ; resisted French claims in Acadia till its cession (1667) to the French ; created baronet of Nova Scotia, 1662. [lvi. 40]

TEMPLE, Sir WILLIAM (1555–1627), fourth provost of Trinity College, Dublin ; belonged to the Stowe family ; educated at Eton and King's College, Cambridge ; fellow, 1578 ; M.A. 1581 (incorporated at Oxford, 1581) ; champion of the Ramist system of logic ; published several tracts attacking the followers of Aristotle, and an annotated edition of Ramus's 'Dialectics,' 1584 (dedicated to Sir Philip Sidney) ; became master of Lincoln grammar school and Sir Philip Sidney's secretary, 1585 ; with Sidney at his death in 1586 ; became secretary to the Earl of Essex ; M.P., Tamworth, 1597 ; his fortunes prejudiced by Essex's fall ; made provost of Trinity College, Dublin, 1609, where he carried out many useful reforms ; master in chancery at Dublin, 1610 ; M.P. in the Irish parliament for Dublin University, 1613 ; knighted, 1622. [lvi. 40]

TEMPLE, Sir WILLIAM (1628–1699), statesman and author ; son of Sir John Temple (1600–1677) [q. v.] ; of Emmanuel College, Cambridge ; travelled abroad and studied foreign languages ; met Dorothy Osborne [q. v.], whom in 1655 he married ; resided in Ireland and became Irish M.P. ; settled at Sheen, 1663 ; sent on a mission to the prince-bishop of Munster, 1665, which proved entirely unsuccessful ; subsequently made envoy at Brussels and baronet, 1666 ; visited the Hague, cultivated relations with John de Witt, and effected the triple alliance between England, Holland, and Sweden, aiming at the protection of Spain from French ambition, 1668 ; appointed ambassador at the Hague, but his useful political plans entirely frustrated by Charles II's secret understanding with Louis XIV ; ordered to return privately to England, 1670 ; being received coldly withdrew to Sheen ; wrote his 'Essay upon the Present State . . . of Ireland,' 1668, condemning the 'late settlement,' but recommending despotic severity ; published 'Essay upon the Original and Nature of Government,' 1671 (anticipating Filmer's patriarchal theory), 'Observations upon . . . the Netherlands,' 1672, and his majestic 'Letter to the Countess of Essex' ; went again to the Hague, 1674, where he brought about marriage between William of Orange and Mary ; offered secretaryship of state, 1677 ; took part in the conference at Nimeguen, but disapproved of the treaty, 1679 ; was offered secretaryship again, and again refused it ; privy council revived under his sponsorship, 1679,

but inner committee soon formed, with himself as member, though his toleration and opposition to Charles II's arbitrary government soon caused his exclusion from the king's counsels and retirement to his 'nectarines' at Sheen ; struck off list of privy councillors, 1681 ; purchased Moor Park ; took no part in the revolution, but presented himself at Windsor after James II's second flight ; refused the secretaryship ; received Swift in his house as secretary and was aided by him in editing his 'Memoirs' ; visited frequently and consulted by William III ; published his two volumes of Essays ('Miscellanea'), 1680 and 1692, including that on 'Ancient and Modern Learning,' a literary and not a critical essay ; uncritically considered the 'Epistles of Phalaris' to be genuine, and began, but did not publish, a reply to Bentley ; published 'An Introduction to the History of England,' 1695, and 'Poems by Sir W. T.' (privately printed) ; buried in Westminster Abbey. As author his prose marks development in refinement, rhythmical finish, and emancipation from long parentheses and superfluous quotations. His writings are now, however, chiefly valuable for the picture they afford of the cultured gentleman of the period. [lvi. 42]

TEMPLE, WILLIAM JOHNSTONE or JOHNSON (1739–1796), essayist ; friend of Gray and Boswell ; educated with Boswell at Edinburgh University ; scholar of Trinity Hall, Cambridge, 1759 ; law student with Boswell in London, 1762 ; returned to Cambridge ; LL.B. Cambridge, 1765 ; became acquainted with Gray and with Dr. Johnson, 1766 ; rector of Mamhead ; wrote a character of Gray, subsequently incorporated by Dr. Johnson in 'Lives of the Poets' ; vicar of Gluvias, 1776 ; published 'An Essay on the Clergy,' 1774, and other works. He was grandfather of Dr. Frederick Temple, archbishop of Canterbury. [lvi. 51]

TEMPLEMAN, PETER (1711–1769), physician ; educated at the Charterhouse School, Trinity College, Cambridge, and Leyden ; M.D. Leyden, 1737 ; keeper of reading room at British Museum, 1758 ; corresponding member of foreign societies and author. [lvi. 53]

TEMPLETON, JOHN (1766–1825), Irish naturalist ; associate of the Linnean Society ; added *Rosa hibernica* and *Orobanche rubra* to the list of Irish flora ; contributed important articles to Smith's 'English Botany,' 'Flora Britannica,' and works on every branch of natural history, his collection of mosses and lichens being very extensive. [lvi. 54]

TEMPLETON, JOHN (1802–1886), tenor vocalist ; took the part of Don Ottavio in 'Don Giovanni' ; sang with Malibran, 1833–6. [lvi. 55]

TEMPLO, RICHARD DE (*fl.* 1190–1229). [See RICHARD.]

TENCH, WATKIN (1759 ?–1833), soldier and author ; served in America as lieutenant of marines and was taken prisoner, 1778 ; accompanied Arthur Phillip [q. v.] to Australia, 1787, and published 'A Narrative of the Expedition to Botany Bay,' 1789, and 'A Complete Account of . . . Port Jackson,' 1793 ; taken prisoner on board the Alexandra by the French, 1794 ; published 'Letters written in France,' 1796 ; major-general, 1811. [lvi. 55]

TENISON, EDWARD (1673–1735), bishop of Ossory ; cousin of Thomas Tenison [q. v.] ; educated at St. Paul's School ; B.A. Corpus Christi College, Cambridge, 1694 ; LL.B. Lambeth, 1697 ; D.D. Lambeth, 1731 ; prebendary of Canterbury, 1709 ; bishop of Ossory, 1731–5 ; edited two books of Columella, 1732, and published sermons. [lvi. 56]

TENISON, RICHARD (1640 ?–1705), bishop of Meath ; kinsman of Thomas Tenison [q. v.] ; educated at Trinity College, Dublin ; M.A. ; created D.D. Trinity College, Dublin, 1682 ; chaplain to the Earl of Essex, lord lieutenant ; appointed bishop of Killala, 1682 ; fled to England at the revolution ; bishop of Clogher, 1691 ; translated to Meath, 1697. [lvi. 56]

TENISON, THOMAS (1636–1715), archbishop of Canterbury ; educated at Norwich free school ; scholar of Corpus Christi College, Cambridge, 1653 ; fellow, 1659 ; M.A. 1660 (incorporated at Oxford, 1664) ; D.D., 1680 ; as vicar of St. Andrew-the-Great, Cambridge, gained credit by his ministrations during the plague ; published 'The Creed of Mr. Hobbes examined,' 1670, and in 1678, 'Baconiana' and 'A Discourse of Idolatry' ; after other church preferments, became rector of St. Martin-in-the-fields, London, 1680; published 'An Argument for Union,' 1683; ministered to Monmouth before execution, 1685; won fame by his controversy with the jesuits and published several pamphlets; attacked Louis XIV; joined the seven bishops in their celebrated declaration, 1688; active in philanthropic works; established a school and the first public library in London in his parish, 1695; preached the funeral sermon on Nell Gwynne; made archdeacon of London by William III, 1689; prominent for his 'moderation towards dissenters'; bishop of Lincoln, 1691–4; archbishop of Canterbury, 1694; revived jurisdiction of the archbishop's court and deprived bishop Thomas Watson (1637–1717) [q. v.] of his see for simony; voted for attainder of Sir John Fenwick, 1696; lost favour in Queen Anne's reign; urged the electress Sophia to come to England; took active measures to secure accession of George I; one of the founders of the S.P.G.   [lvi. 57]

TENNANT, CHARLES (1768–1838), manufacturing chemist; studied bleaching processes at Wellmeadow; took out patent for a bleaching liquor, proved, however, in Tennant v. Slater to have been employed before; established chemical works at St. Rollox, near Glasgow, 1800.   [lvi. 60]

TENNANT, SIR JAMES (1789–1854), brigadier-general; educated at Marlow military school; took part in capture of Cape Town, 1806, and in that of Kalinjar, 1812; in successful operations on the Ramgarh ridge, 1814–15; employed in the Pindari and Maratha war, 1817–1819; present at the taking of Bhartpur, 1825; member of special committee of artillery officers, 1836, and as such performed valuable services; lieutenant-colonel, 1837; commanded fort artillery in the Gwalior campaign, 1843; commandant of artillery at Cawnpore, 1844; commanded artillery at battle of Chilianwala and Gujerat; mentioned in despatches, received thanks of parliament and made C.B., 1849; K.C.B., 1852; died at Mian Mir.   [lvi. 61]

TENNANT, JAMES (1808–1881), mineralogist; purchased mineral business in London; teacher of geological mineralogy and of geology at King's College and Woolwich; superintended the recutting of the Koh-i-nor; F.G.S., 1838; published works dealing with gems and fossils.   [lvi. 62]

TENNANT, SMITHSON (1761–1815), chemist; educated at Edinburgh, Christ's College, and Emmanuel College, Cambridge; M.D. Cambridge, 1796; F.R.S., 1785; Copley medallist, Royal Society, 1804; professor of chemistry at Cambridge, 1813; supplied the analytical proof of the composition of fixed air, proved the diamond to consist of carbon, and in 1804 discovered osmium and iridium.   [lvi. 63]

TENNANT, WILLIAM (1784–1848), linguist and poet; studied at St. Andrews University; learned Hebrew, Arabic, Syriac, and Persian; parish schoolmaster; professor of Hebrew and oriental languages, St. Mary's College, St. Andrews, 1834–48; among other works published poems, 'The Anster Concert,' 1811, and 'Anster Fair,' 1812, the latter immediately making him famous; author also of historical and biblical dramas, and of a 'Syriac and Chaldee Grammar,' 1840.   [lvi. 64]

TENNENT, HAMILTON TOVEY- (1782–1866). [See TOVEY-TENNENT.]

TENNENT, SIR JAMES EMERSON, first baronet (1804–1869), traveller, politician, and author; educated at Trinity College, Dublin; visited Greece and other countries, 1824; called to the bar at Lincoln's Inn, 1831; M.P., Belfast, 1832; supporter of Earl Grey till 1834, and later of Peel; promoter of the Copyright of Designs Bill; secretary to the India board, 1841–3; knighted, 1845; filled various official posts at home and at Ceylon; hon. LL.D., 1861; created baronet, 1867; F.R.S., 1862; author of several works, including 'Ceylon,' 1859.   [lvi. 65]

TENNYSON, ALFRED, first BARON TENNYSON (1809–1892), poet; fourth son of George Tennyson, rector of Somersby; born at Somersby; educated chiefly by his father; published with his brother Charles 'Poems by two Brothers,' 1827; matriculated at Trinity College, Cambridge, 1828; became acquainted, among others, with Arthur Hallam; studied seriously and won chancellor's medal for English verse with 'Timbuctoo,' 1829; published 'Poems, chiefly Lyrical,' 1830; travelled with Hallam in the Pyrenees and on the Rhine, 1832; pub-

lished (1832) 'Poems,' including some of his noblest pieces (unfavourably reviewed); wrote (1833) sections of 'In Memoriam' and 'The Two Voices,' both being the expression of his grief for Hallam, who had died in 1833; became engaged to Emily Sellwood, though not married till 1850; resided successively with his family after leaving Somersby, 1837, in Epping Forest, and at Tunbridge Wells and Boxley; introduced to Gladstone, 1837; published 'Poems,' 1842, which went through many editions and was attacked by Lord Lytton; lost money in Allen's 'wood-carving by machinery,' and given by Peel pension of 200l.; published the 'Princess,' 1847, and 'In Memoriam,' 1850, the latter being welcomed with greater appreciation by the public than by the critics and theologians of the time; poet laureate on the death of Wordsworth, 1850; travelled in Italy with his wife, 1851; resided at Twickenham; wrote the 'Ode' on the death of Wellington, and the 'Charge of the Light Brigade,' 1854; took up his residence at Farringford, Isle of Wight, 1853; published 'Maud,' 1855, the poem being universally disliked at the time; published 'Idylls of the King' in 1859, from which date his fame and popularity continued till his death, his treatment of the Arthurian legends at once taking hold of the popular imagination; travelled in England and abroad, 1860–2; published 'Enoch Arden,' 1864, the volume including 'The Northern Farmer: Old Style,' one of his most popular pieces; published the 'Holy Grail' and other poems, 1869; began building Aldworth, his second residence, near Haslemere, 1868; published 'Gareth and Lynette,' 1872, 'Queen Mary,' 1875, and 'Harold,' 1876, literary dramas; 'The Falcon' and 'The Cup,' 1884; reprinted 'The Lover's Tale,' 1879; visited Venice, Bavaria, and Tyrol, 1880; published 'Ballads and Poems,' 1880; produced 'The Promise of May,' 1882, and 'Becket,' 1884; made a peer, 1884; published 'Tiresias and other Poems,' 1885, 'Locksley Hall, sixty years after,' 1886; wrote 'Vastness,' 1887; produced 'Demeter and other Poems,' 1889, including 'Merlin and the Gleam' and 'Crossing the Bar'; brought out 'Robin Hood,' 1891, and 'Lines on the Death of the Duke of Clarence,' 1892; buried in Westminster Abbey. A 'life' of him was published by his son, 1897.   [lvi. 66]

TENNYSON, CHARLES (1808–1879). [See TURNER, CHARLES TENNYSON.]

TENNYSON, FREDERICK (1807–1898), poet; elder brother of Alfred Tennyson [q. v.]; educated at Eton; distinguished himself at Trinity College, Cambridge; B.A., 1832; contributed to the 'Poems by Two Brothers,' and published 'Days and Hours,' 1854, 'The Isles of Greece,' 1890, and other volumes of verse.   [lvi. 75]

TENTERDEN, titular EARL OF (d. 1695). [See HALES, SIR EDWARD.]

TENTERDEN, BARONS. [See ABBOTT, CHARLES, first BARON, 1762–1832; ABBOTT, CHARLES STUART AUBREY, third BARON, 1834–1882.]

TEONGE, HENRY (1621–1690), chaplain in the navy and diarist; his 'Diary of Henry Teonge, 1675–1679,' being published, 1825.   [lvi. 76]

TERILL, ANTHONY (1621–1676). [See BONVILLE, ANTHONY.]

TERNAN or **TERRENAN** (d. 431?), archbishop of the Picts; 'a disciple of the blessed Palladius' [q. v.]; died and was buried at Banchory on the Dee; also identified with Torannan, abbot of Bangor.   [lvi. 77]

TERNAN, FRANCES ELEANOR (1803?–1873). [See JARMAN.]

TERNE, CHRISTOPHER (1620–1673), physician; M.D. Leyden (incorporated first at Cambridge and then at Oxford); F.R.C.P., 1655; lecturer and author; F.R.S.   [lvi. 77]

TERRICK, RICHARD (1710–1777), bishop of Peterborough and of London; M.A., 1733; D.D., 1747, Clare College, Cambridge; fellow, 1731; preacher at the Rolls Chapel, 1736–57; chaplain to the speaker and canon of Windsor and St. Paul's; chaplain to George II; vicar of Twickenham, 1749; bishop of Peterborough, 1757; attaching himself to Bute became bishop of London and privy councillor, 1764; prosecuted mass-houses, 1765. [lvi. 78]

TERRIEN DE LA COUPERIE, ALBERT ÉTIENNE JEAN BAPTISTE (d. 1894), orientalist; born in Normandy; descendant of the Cornish Terrien family; studied oriental languages at Hongkong; published 'Du Langage,' 1867; demonstrated affinity between Chinese characters and early Akkadian hieroglyphics; R.A.S., 1879; professor of comparative philosophy at University College, London, 1884; published 'The Oldest Book of the Chinese,' 1892, and several other works, mostly dealing with Chinese.   [lvi. 79]

TERRISS, WILLIAM (1847–1897), actor; his true name WILLIAM CHARLES JAMES LEWIN; educated at Christ's Hospital, London; joined the merchant service, but ran away; after other adventures appeared first as actor at Prince of Wales's Theatre, Birmingham, 1867; played numerous parts, including many original ones, in various London theatres, including that of Squire Thornhill in Wills's 'Olivia,' 1878, at the Court Theatre, Château-Renaud in the 'Corsican Brothers' at the Lyceum, 1880, and Shakespearean characters; accompanied Irving to America, 1883, and Miss Millward, 1889; assassinated while entering the Adelphi Theatre, London.   [lvi. 80]

TERROT, CHARLES (1758–1839), general, royal artillery; as lieutenant took part in repulse of the Americans at Three Rivers, Canada, 1776, and in capture of Ticonderoga, 1777; employed on Canadian defences, 1780–4; took part in the campaign against the French in Madras, 1792–3, and in the Duke of York's campaign in the Netherlands, 1798; thanked for his services at Walcheren, 1809; major-general, 1811; general, 1837.   [lvi. 81]

TERROT, CHARLES HUGHES (1790–1872), bishop of Edinburgh; descendant of French exiled protestants; B.A. and fellow of Trinity College, Cambridge, 1812; Seatonian prizeman, 1816; pastor of St. Peter's, Edinburgh, 1817; bishop, 1841–62; published sermons and charges.   [lvi. 83]

TERRY, DANIEL (1780?–1829), actor and playwright; played first at Bath Heartwell in the 'Prize,' and subsequently joined the companies of the elder Macready and Stephen Kemble [q. v.]; acted also in Liverpool and Edinburgh; appeared first in London at the Haymarket, 1812; played there and at Covent Garden numerous parts, including Shakespeare and Sheridan characters, and many original rôles, his acting of Frederick William of Prussia in Abbott's 'Youthful Days of Frederick the Great,' 1817, raising his reputation to its highest point; played subsequently at Drury Lane; became, with Frederick Henry Yates [q. v.], manager of the Adelphi, 1825, but lost his powers through financial worry; intimate with Sir Walter Scott [q. v.], whose manner and speech he imitated, and with whom he corresponded, advising him on many literary questions and on the building of Abbotsford; his acting highly esteemed by Scott; expressed well the workings of powerful or agonised minds, and in comedy excelled in old men.   [lvi. 83]

TERRY, EDWARD (1590–1660), writer of travels; M.A. Christ Church, Oxford, 1614; went to India as chaplain in the East India Company's fleet, 1616, and in a mission to Mandoa, 1617; published 'A Voyage to East India,' 1655, and other works.   [lvi. 86]

TERRY or **TIRREYE**, JOHN (1555?–1625), divine; of Winchester College and New College, Oxford; fellow of New College, Oxford, 1576; M.A., 1582; anti-Roman catholic writer.   [lvi. 87]

TESDALE, **TEASDALE**, or **TISDALE**, THOMAS (1547–1610), 'co-founder of Pembroke College, Oxford'; maltster. The feoffees under his will acquiesced in the project of a new college, and the existing foundation of Broadgates Hall 'was erected by the name of Pembroke College,' 1624.   [lvi. 87]

TESIMOND, *alias* GREENWAY, OSWALD (1563–1635), jesuit; *alias* PHILIP BEAUMONT; educated at Rome and joined jesuits, 1584; came to England and was charged with complicity in the 'Gunpowder plot'; was arrested, but escaped abroad and died at Naples; his 'autobiography' printed in Morris's 'Troubles of our Catholic Forefathers.'   [lvi. 87]

TEVIOT, EARL OF (d. 1664). [See RUTHERFORD, ANDREW.]

TEVIOT, VISCOUNT (1652?–1711). [See LIVINGSTONE, SIR THOMAS.]

TEWKESBURY, JOHN (d. 1369). [See TUNSTED, SIMON.]

THACKERAY, FRANCIS (1793–1842), author of 'A History of William Pitt, Earl of Chatham,' 1827, and other works; curate; M.A. Pembroke College, Cambridge, 1817; uncle of William Makepeace Thackeray [q. v.]   [lvi. 88]

THACKERAY, FREDERICK RENNELL (1775–1860), general; brother of George Thackeray [q. v.] and cousin of William Makepeace Thackeray [q. v.]; served as lieutenant, R.E., at Gibraltar and in the East Indies, and at the capture of Surinam, 1799, and Swedish, Dutch, and Danish islands, 1801, by Trigge; commanded engineers at successful attack on Castle of Scylla, 1809; mentioned in despatches for services in taking of Santa Maura, Ionian islands, and promoted major, 1810; took part with the Anglo-Sicilian army in Peninsular campaign; present at battle of Castalla, and at investment of Tarragona, 1813; colonel, R.E., 1825; C.B., 1831; general, 1854.   [lvi. 88]

THACKERAY, GEORGE (1777–1850), provost of King's College, Cambridge; brother of Frederick Rennell Thackeray [q. v.]; of Eton and King's College, Cambridge; fellow of King's College, 1800; M.A., 1805; D.D. by royal mandate, 1814; provost of King's College, 1814–1850; book-collector and chaplain to George III and his successors.   [lvi. 90]

THACKERAY, WILLIAM MAKEPEACE (1811–1863), novelist; born at Calcutta; only child of Richmond Thackeray, collector in India; descended from a Yorkshire yeoman family; sent to England, 1817; educated at Chiswick, at the Charterhouse, London, 1822–8, under John Russell (1787–1863) [q. v.], and at Trinity College, Cambridge, 1829–30, where he studied little, but wrote numerous verses; travelled abroad and visited Goethe at Weimar; entered the Middle Temple, 1831, but soon abandoned the legal profession; purchased 'The National Standard and Journal of Literature, Science, Music, Theatricals, and the Fine Arts,' 1833, which was unsuccessful; had meanwhile spent his fortune and settled at Paris to study drawing; engaged in various literary experiments; published 'Flore et Zéphyr' (satirical drawings), 1836, and became Paris correspondent of the 'Constitutional,' which failed; married Isabella Shawe, 1836; returned to England, 1837; wrote for 'The Times,' for 'Fraser's Magazine,' to which he contributed the 'Yellowplush Correspondence,' and for other journals; separated from his wife on account of her insanity; published the 'Paris Sketch-book,' 1840, 'Comic Tales and Sketches,' 1841, the 'History of Samuel Titmarsh and the Great Hoggarty Diamond,' 1841, the 'Irish Sketchbook,' 1843 (the result of a tour in Ireland in 1842), 'Cornhill to Cairo,' 1846, and the 'Luck of Barry Lyndon,' 1846, none of these, however, being successful; contributed to 'Punch,' 1842–54, both with pen and pencil, and gained celebrity by the 'Snob Papers,' which first appeared in 'Punch'; published a 'Christmas-book' yearly, 1846–50; published 'Vanity Fair,' 1847–8, which completely established his reputation; and 'Pendennis,' 1848–50, the latter embodying experience of his early life, though the characters in it cannot be identified with their originals; elected to the Athenæum Club, 1851; lectured on the 'English Humorists,' 1851; published 'Esmond,' 1852; lectured in America, 1852–3; wrote 'The Newcomes,' 1853; visited Switzerland and Rome; produced 'The Rose and the Ring,' 1854; lectured on 'The Four Georges' in America, 1855, and afterwards in England, 1856; contested Oxford city unsuccessfully as a liberal, 1857; published 'The Virginians,' 1857–9; quarrelled with Edmund Yates [q. v.] on account of the latter's personalities, which led to withdrawal of Yates from the Garrick Club, and also to a coolness with Dickens; reconciled with Dickens shortly before his death, although the two great novelists never felt much mutual attraction; became editor of the 'Cornhill,' 1860–2, to which he contributed 'Lovel the Widower,' 1860, 'The Adventures of Philip,' 1861–2, 'Denis Duval,' and the 'Roundabout Papers,' which had great success, though his tenderheartedness and unbusinesslike habits prevented his being a good editor. The first collective edition of his works appeared in 22 vols., 1867–9.   [lvi. 90]

THACKWELL, SIR JOSEPH (1781–1859), lieutenant-general; served with 15th light dragoons in retreat to Coruña; present at battles of Vittoria, the Pyrenees,

Orthes, and Toulouse ; recommended for a brevet majority ; lost his left arm at Waterloo ; commanded his regiment, 1820-32 ; present at capture of Ghazni ; commanded cavalry in the Gwalior campaign, 1843, being mentioned in despatches after battle of Maharajpur, 1844, and at Sobraon in first Sikh war, 1846 ; commanded cavalry at Chilianwala ; received thanks of parliament and made G.C.B., 1849 ; lieutenant-general, 1854.
[lvi. 106]

THACKWELL, OSBERT DABITÔT (1837-1858), lieutenant ; son of Sir Joseph Thackwell [q. v.] ; lieutenant, 1856 ; killed at Lucknow. [lvi. 107]

THANE, JOHN (1748-1818), printseller and engraver ; editor of ' British Autography,' &c., 1793.
[lvi. 107]

THANET, ninth EARL OF (1767-1825). [See TUFTON, SACKVILLE.]

THAUN, PHILIP DE (*fl.* 1120). [See PHILIP.]

THAYRE, THOMAS (*fl.* 1603-1625), medical writer ; published a ' Treatise of the Pestilence,' 1603.
[lvi. 107]

THEAKSTON, JOSEPH (1772 - 1842), sculptor ; carved draperies and accessories of Chantrey's statues ; ablest ornamental carver of his time. [lvi. 108]

THEED, WILLIAM (1764-1817), painter of classical subjects ; designer for Messrs. Wedgwood and others ; R.A., 1813. [lvi. 108]

THEED, WILLIAM (1804-1891), sculptor ; son of William Theed (1764-1817) [q. v.] ; studied at the Royal Academy and in Italy under Thorvaldsen and others ; executed many well-known statues, busts, and groups, including 'Africa' for the Albert Memorial. [lvi. 108]

THEINRED (*fl.* 1371), musical theorist ; Benedictine monk; wrote ' De legitimis ordinibus Pentacordorum et Tetracordorum,' 1371. [lvi. 109]

THELLUSSON, PETER (1737-1797), merchant ; of Huguenot family ; born in Paris ; came to London and was naturalised, 1762 ; famous for his eccentric will, which left a large fortune to accumulate for several generations ; his will held valid by Lord Loughborough, 1799, but act passed, 1800, prohibiting such accumulations for the future. [lvi. 109]

THELWALL, ALGERNON SYDNEY (1795-1863), son of John Thelwall [q. v.] ; clergyman ; M.A. Trinity College, Cambridge, 1826 ; published religious works.
[lvi. 113]

THELWALL, SIR EUBULE (1562-1630), principal and benefactor of Jesus College, Oxford ; B.A. Trinity College, Cambridge, 1577 ; M.A. Oxford, 1580 ; barrister, Gray's Inn, 1595, treasurer, 1625 ; master in chancery, 1617 ; knighted, 1619 ; principal of Jesus College, Oxford, 1621-30 ; M.P., Denbighshire, 1624-5, 1626, and 1628-9.
[lvi. 110]

THELWALL, JOHN (1764 - 1834), reformer and lecturer on elocution ; began life in his father's business as mercer, then became tailor and attorney's clerk ; gave up his legal work through scruples ; maintained himself by his pen ; published ' Poems upon various Subjects,' 1787 ; editor of the ' Biographical and Imperial Magazine ' ; carried away by French revolutionary doctrines ; made an eloquent speech at Coachmakers' Hall, 1790 ; supported Horne Tooke [q. v.] at Westminster, and joined the Society of the Friends of the People ; obtained great notoriety by his sallies ; arrested, 1794, and sent to the Tower of London with Horne Tooke, but acquitted ; published ' Poems written in the Tower and Newgate,' 1795 ; left London, but denounced the government in ' Lectures upon Roman History ' ; abandoned politics and became lecturer on elocution ; established institution in London for the cure of defects in speech, 1809 ; published ' Treatment of Cases of Defective Utterance,' 1814 ; advocated reform in his journal, ' The Champion,' 1818, which proved a failure ; published works dealing with elocution and political questions. [lvi. 110]

THEOBALD or TEDBALDUS (*d.* 1161), archbishop of Canterbury ; came of a Norman knightly family settled near Thierceville ; monk of Bec ; abbot, 1137 ; archbishop of Canterbury, 1138 ; after some hesitation joined the Empress Maud against King Stephen, but returned to his allegiance to Stephen on the king's release, 1141, and crowned him at Canterbury ; attached to his household rising men of legal and political talent,

including Thomas (Becket) [q. v.] ; introduced study of civil law into England, and brought over Vacarius of Mantua [q. v.], the famous jurist ; involved in disputes with Henry, bishop of Winchester, who as legate till the death of Pope Innocent II, 1143, caused a division of authority ; engaged in disputes with St. Augustine's and Christ Church convent, Canterbury ; went to Rome, 1143, and being supported by Bernard of Clairvaux obtained satisfaction from the new pope, Eugenius III, and was made legate by 1150 ; was refused by Stephen permission to attend the pope's council at Rheims, 1148, but managed to cross the Channel secretly in a boat ; on his return was exiled and his revenues seized ; forced to go back to France ; published an interdict of the pope which was little observed ; returned to England, became reconciled to King Stephen, and received submission of the monks at St. Augustine's ; refused to crown Stephen's son, Eustace, king, 1152, and was imprisoned, but escaped to Flanders ; recalled by Stephen under threat of an interdict ; brought about reconciliation between Stephen and Henry, duke of Normandy, 1153, and on death of Stephen maintained order in the kingdom till Henry's arrival, 1154 ; recommended Archdeacon Thomas Becket to Henry II as chancellor to secure continuity in his ecclesiastical policy, his hopes, however, being disappointed ; wished him to be his successor ; buried in Canterbury Cathedral. During his primacy he successfully resisted the efforts of the monasteries to rid themselves of episcopal control. He supported Stephen as the king recognised by the pope, but opposed him whenever he resisted the will of the church, the church becoming under him more powerful and more dependent on the pope. He may be said to have been the founder of canonical jurisprudence in England. [lvi. 113]

THEOBALD, LEWIS (1688-1744), editor of Shakespeare ; became an attorney, but soon abandoned the law for literature ; published an ode on the union, 1707, and translations of Plato, Æschylus, Sophocles, Aristophanes, and Homer, poems, essays, biographies, and dramatic works ; accused of scandalous plagiarism in respect of his ' Perfidious Brother,' 1715 ; published 'Shakespeare restored, or a Specimen of the many Errors as well committed as unamended by Mr. Pope in his late Edition of this Poet,' 1726, exposing Pope's incapacity as a critic ; made the hero of the ' Dunciad,' and ridiculed in the ' Miscellanies,' 1727-8, at the same time that his best corrections were incorporated in Pope's second edition of Shakespeare ; defended himself in ' The Author,' 1729 ; produced the ' Double Falsehood,' a tragedy, 1727, as a work of Shakespeare's, though probably from his own pen ; edited the posthumous works of Wycherley, and contributed notes to Cook's ' Hesiod,' 1728 ; failed in his candidature for the poet laureateship, 1730 ; contributed valuable emendations on Æschylus, Athenæus, and other Greek writers, to ' Miscellaneous Observations on Authors, Ancient and Modern,' by Zachary Pearce [q. v.], 1731 ; published an edition of Shakespeare, 1734, which raised him to the front rank of Shakespearean commentators ; pursued by poverty ; wrote various tragedies and operas, and was engaged on an edition of Beaumont and Fletcher at the time of his death. [lvi. 118]

THEODORE (602 ?-690), archbishop of Canterbury ; native of Tarsus in Cilicia ; studied at Athens ; well versed in literature, and Greek and Latin, and called the ' philosopher ' ; while a monk at Rome was consecrated by Pope Vitalian archbishop of Canterbury, 668 ; arrived at Canterbury, 669 ; made a tour throughout the island ; imposed the Roman order and was the first archbishop to whom the whole English church agreed in submitting ; together with Hadrian, now made abbot of St. Augustine's, founded a school of learning at Canterbury ; held a synod at Hertford, 673, which was the first time that the English church acted as one body ; subdivided many of the dioceses, before conterminous with the kingdoms, and created many new bishoprics ; separated the diocese of Wilfrid (the country north of the Humber) into four (afterwards five) dioceses, and appointed bishops to them, Wilfrid being left the see of York, on which Wilfrid, having appealed to Rome, was authorised by Pope Agatho to expel the new bishops and appoint his own ; made peace between Egfrid of Northumbria and Ethelred of Mercia, 679 ; divided Mercia into five dioceses ; held a synod at Hatfield, 680, to declare orthodoxy of the English church ; reconciled to Wilfrid, 686 ; a great organiser, the effects of his work existing to the present day ; gave the church unity and order, his autocratic spirit, however, leading him into unfair treatment of Wilfrid ; never regarded by the monks as a saint ; scholar, and author, at least in part, of the ' Penitential,' of considerable ecclesiastical and historical interest. [lvi. 122]

THEODORE ÉTIENNE, BARON DE NEUHOFF (*d.* 1756), adventurer and king of Corsica ; married an Irish lady named Sarsfield, a member of the suite of Queen Elizabeth Farnese of Spain ; absconded from Spain, 1720 ; visited England and Holland, subsequently residing at Florence in the imperial service, until he went to Corsica ; was proclaimed king of Corsica, 1736, but lost his throne ; failed to regain it by English aid and came to England an exile ; was imprisoned for debt in the Fleet, but obtained his discharge under the Insolvent Act. [xx. 232]

THERRY, JOHN JOSEPH (1791-1864), patriarch of the Roman catholic church in New South Wales ; born at Cork ; one of the priests sent out by the English government to New South Wales, 1819 ; laid the foundation-stone of St. Joseph's chapel (now part of Sydney Roman catholic cathedral), 1829. [lvi. 126]

THERRY, SIR ROGER (1800-1874), judge in New South Wales ; called to the Irish bar, 1824, to the English bar, 1827 ; went to New South Wales, 1829 ; attacked on account of his Roman catholic leanings ; attorney-general, 1841 ; puisne judge of the supreme court and primary judge in equity, New South Wales, 1846 ; wrote ' Reminiscences,' 1863, and edited George Canning's speeches. [lvi. 126]

THESIGER, ALFRED HENRY (1838-1880), lord justice of appeal ; son of Frederick Thesiger, first baron Chelmsford [q. v.] ; M.A. Christ Church, Oxford, 1862 ; barrister, Inner Temple, 1862 ; Q.C., 1873 ; lord justice of appeal and privy councillor, 1877-80. [lvi. 127]

THESIGER, SIR FREDERICK (*d.* 1805), naval officer ; uncle of Frederick Thesiger, first Baron Chelmsford [q. v.] ; aide-de-camp to Rodney, 1782 ; served in the Russian navy and distinguished himself in the war between Russia and Sweden ; left on death of the Empress Catherine, 1797 ; aide-de-camp to Nelson at the battle of Copenhagen, and took flag of truce to the crown prince through the enemy's fire, his knowledge of the Baltic proving of great value in subsequent operations ; promoted post-captain and knighted. [lvi. 127]

THESIGER, FREDERICK, first BARON CHELMSFORD (1794-1878), lord chancellor ; entered the navy and present at seizure of Danish fleet at Copenhagen, 1807 ; joined his father, collector of customs at St. Vincent, 1811 ; returned to England and was called to the bar from Gray's Inn, 1818 ; leader in the home circuit ; K.C., 1834 ; conservative M.P. successively for Woodstock, 1840, Abingdon, 1844, and Stamford, 1852 ; hon. D.C.L. Oxford, 1842 ; F.R.S., 1845 ; solicitor-general, 1844 ; attorney-general, 1845 till the fall of Peel's administration, 1846, and again in Lord Derby's, 1852 ; made Baron Chelmsford and lord chancellor, 1858-9 and 1866-8. [lvi. 128]

THEW, ROBERT (1758-1802), engraver ; son of an innkeeper ; executed many excellent engravings, including plates for John Boydell's [q. v.] Shakespeare. [lvi. 129]

THEYER, JOHN (1597-1673), antiquary ; educated at Magdalen College, Oxford ; created M.A., 1643 ; practised law in London ; served in Charles I's army ; presented to Charles I his ' Aerio Mastix,' 1643 ; a portion of his collection of manuscripts is now in the British Museum. [lvi. 130]

THICKNESSE, formerly FORD, ANN (1737-1824), authoress and musician ; a favourite in society on account of her beauty and talent, her Sunday concerts being famous ; sang, ' accompanying herself on the musical glasses,' in public, in spite of her father's violent measures to prevent her ; married Philip Thicknesse [q. v.], 1762, after whose death she was arrested in France, 1792 ; published ' Instructions for playing on the Musical Glasses,' 1761, and ' The School for Fashion,' a novel, 1800. [lvi. 130]

THICKNESSE, GEORGE (1714-1790), schoolmaster ; brother of Philip Thicknesse [q. v.] ; chaplain of St. Paul's School, London, 1737, and high master, 1748-69. [lvi. 131]

THICKNESSE, PHILIP (1719-1792), lieutenant-governor of Landguard Fort ; began life as apothecary, but went out to Georgia with Oglethorpe, 1735 ; served as

lieutenant in Jamaica against runaway negroes ; became captain of marines, 1741 ; purchased lieutenant-governorship of Landguard Fort, 1766 ; imprisoned and fined for libelling Colonel Francis Vernon, 1762 ; patronised Gainsborough ; wrote letters in the ' Crisis ' signed ' Junius,' 1775, denouncing a decision against him in the House of Lords ; travelled abroad and died near Boulogne ; author, among other works, of ' Junius Discovered,' 1789, in which he discovered Junius in Horne Tooke. [lvi. 132]

THIERRY, CHARLES PHILIP HIPPOLYTUS, BARON DE (1793-1864), colonist ; a French refugee ; of Magdalen Hall, Oxford, and Queens' College, Cambridge ; attempted unsuccessfully to form an empire in New Zealand ; became a colonist ; died at Auckland. [lvi. 134]

THIMELBY, RICHARD (1614-1680). [See ASHBY.]

THIRLBY, STYAN (1686 ?-1753), critic and theologian ; of Jesus College, Cambridge ; B.A., 1704 ; fellow, 1712 ; published ' The University of Cambridge Vindicated,' 1710 (against Bentley), and several books on divinity, including his splendid edition of ' Justini Philosophi et Martyris Apologiæ duæ, et Dialogus cum Tryphone Judæo,' 1722, ' railed against classical studies and Bentley ' ; contributed notes to Theobald's ' Shakespeare.' [lvi. 134]

THIRLBY or **THIRLEBY,** THOMAS (1506 ?-1570), only bishop of Westminster and successively bishop of Norwich and Ely ; educated at Trinity Hall, Cambridge ; fellow ; doctor of civil law, 1528 ; doctor of canon law, 1530 ; patronised by Cranmer and commended by him to Henry VIII ; archdeacon of Ely and member of convocation which recognised Henry VIII's ecclesiastical supremacy, 1534 ; dean of the Chapel Royal, London ; member of the council of the north, 1536 ; ambassador to Francis I, 1538 ; as prolocutor of Canterbury convocation signed decree annulling Henry VIII's marriage with Anne of Cleves, 1540 ; commissioner to deliberate on religious doctrines ; made bishop of Westminster, 1540 ; privy councillor ; ambassador to the Emperor Charles V in Spain, 1542 and 1545 ; declared in parliament his objections to the abolishment of the ' elevation ' and ' the adoration,' 1549, and voted against Act of Uniformity ; bishop of Norwich, 1550 ; served on various commissions and embassies ; at heart a Roman catholic ; translated by Queen Mary from Norwich to Ely, 1554 ; presided at the trial of Bishop Hooper and others ; ambassador to the pope, 1555 ; assisted at the degradation of Cranmer, 1556 ; commissioner to treat for the restoration of Calais, 1558 ; refused to take oath of supremacy to Queen Elizabeth, and deposed, 1559, and continuing to preach against the Reformation was imprisoned, 1560. [lvi. 135]

THIRLESTANE, BARON MAITLAND OF (1545 ?-1595). [See MAITLAND, SIR JOHN.]

THIRLWALL, CONNOP (1797-1875), historian and bishop of St. David's ; son of Thomas Thirlwall [q. v.] ; educated at the Charterhouse, London, and Trinity College, Cambridge, where he greatly distinguished himself ; Bell and Craven scholar, 1815 ; fellow and B.A., 1818 ; travelled abroad ; barrister, Lincoln's Inn, 1825 ; published his work on Schleiermacher's ' Critical Essay on the Gospel of St. Luke,' 1825 ; returned to Cambridge ; took orders, 1827 ; became tutor and lecturer ; published with Hare, translation of the first volume of Niebuhr's ' Rome,' 1828, and essays ; wrote ' Letter on the Admission of Dissenters to Academical Degrees,' 1834, deprecating inclusion of religious teaching in the instruction at Cambridge, and was obliged to resign college appointments ; given living of Kirby Underdale by Brougham ; completed his ' History of Greece,' 1835-44 ; made bishop of St. David's by Melbourne, 1840 ; showed great energy, learning to preach in Welsh, visiting every part of his large diocese, and building numerous churches ; supported abolition of Jewish disabilities, 1848, and disestablishment of the Irish church, 1869 ; buried in Westminster Abbey in the same grave with Grote. [lvi. 138]

THIRLWALL, THOMAS (*d.* 1827), rector of Bower's Gifford, and author. [lvi. 138]

THIRNING, WILLIAM (*d.* 1413), chief-justice of the common pleas ; chief-justice, 1396-1413 ; the proceedings of 1388 relating to the judges reversed owing to his opinion, 1398 ; obtained from Richard II his abdication. [lvi. 141]

THISTLEWOOD, ARTHUR (1770-1820), Cato Street conspirator ; said to have been illegitimate son of William

Thistlewood, a Lincolnshire farmer; developed revolutionary sympathies by reading Paine's works and by visits to America and Paris; ensign in the militia, 1798; after death of his wife drifted to London from Lincoln and joined the Spencean Society; organised mutiny at Spa Fields, 1816, to inaugurate a revolution which proved a failure; arrested, but acquitted, 1817; imprisoned for sending a challenge to Lord Sidmouth, 1818; on his release, 1819, became one of a secret directory of thirteen pledged to violent measures; planned assassination of the cabinet ministers when dining at Lord Harrowby's house in Grosvenor Square, London, 1820, Edwards, however, one of the conspirators, reporting everything to the government, and most of the party being apprehended in a loft in Cato Street, London; escaped after killing a policeman, but captured the day after; was convicted of high treason and hanged. [lvi. 142]

THOM, ALEXANDER (1801–1879), founder of 'Thom's Almanac'; son of Walter Thom [q. v.]; founded 'Thom's Almanac,' 1844, and published 'A Collection of Tracts and Treatises' concerning Ireland, 1860. [lvi. 145]

THOM, JAMES (*fl.* 1815), subject-painter. [lvi. 146]

THOM, JAMES (1802–1850), sculptor; self-taught artist; began life as an apprentice to builders; sculptured figures of Tam o' Shanter and Souter Johnnie, which were secured for the Burns monument, Ayr; attracted great notice in London, and executed other groups; went to America, executed replicas, a statue of Burns, and ornamental work; died at New York. [lvi. 145]

THOM, JOHN HAMILTON (1808–1894), unitarian divine; became a unitarian after reading works of Channing; minister at Renshaw Street Chapel, Liverpool, 1831–54 and 1857–66; editor of the 'Christian Teacher,' 1838; contributed to the Liverpool unitarian controversy, 1839; author of 'Life of Blanco White,' 1845, and of several important works, including 'Laws of Life after the Mind of Christ,' 1883 and 1886. [lvi. 146]

THOM, JOHN NICHOLS (1799–1838). [See TOM.]

THOM, WALTER (1770–1824), miscellaneous writer; editor of the 'Dublin Journal.' [lvi. 145]

THOM, WILLIAM (1798?–1848), Scottish poet; a weaver; contributed 'The Blind Boy's Pranks,' part i., to the 'Aberdeen Herald,' 1841, which attracted much notice; published 'Rhymes and Recollections,' 1844; settled in London, where he found supporters and admirers; died in poverty at Dundee. [lvi. 147]

THOMAS, EARL OF LANCASTER, LEICESTER, DERBY, LINCOLN, and SALISBURY (1277?–1322), eldest son of Edmund, earl of Lancaster [see LANCASTER], brother of Edward I; at Edward II's accession made steward of England; became the enemy of Gaveston, who defeated him in arms; attended the parliament of 1310, and obliged Edward II to consent to the appointment of the twenty-eight 'ordainers,' of whom he was one, and to the supersession of his authority; banished Gaveston, who, however, returned, 1312; brought about the death of Gaveston after his surrender to the Earl of Pembroke at Scarborough under guarantee of safe conduct; was pardoned by Edward II, but refused to be reconciled with Hugh le Despenser, 1313, or to accompany Edward II to Scotland; after Bannockburn obtained complete control of Edward II; engaged in a private war with the Earl of Warenne; accompanied Edward II to the siege of Berwick, 1318, but soon quitted him, and was accused of having taken bribes from the enemy; obliged Edward II to consent to banishment of the Despensers, 1321, but after the capture of Leeds Castle showed hesitation in assisting his friends in the south, 1322, and meeting the royal forces; taken at Boroughbridge and beheaded. Though afterwards made into a saint and martyr through popular idealisation and Edward II's misgovernment, he showed no patriotism or prudence. [lvi. 148]

THOMAS, OF BROTHERTON, EARL OF NORFOLK, and MARSHAL OF ENGLAND (1300–1338), eldest child of Edward I by his second wife, Margaret, sister of Philip the Fair; created Earl of Norfolk, 1312, and marshal of England, 1316; acted as warden of England during Edward II's absence in Scotland, 1319; adhered to Edward II in the struggle against Thomas of Lancaster, 1321, but was one of the first to join Queen Isabella on her landing, 1326; received grants of estates of the Despensers

and others, and married his son to Mortimer's daughter; becoming discontented joined the conference of the magnates in St. Paul's, London, 1329, and welcomed Edward III's attainment of power. [lvi. 152]

THOMAS OF WOODSTOCK, EARL OF BUCKINGHAM and DUKE OF GLOUCESTER (1355–1397), seventh and youngest son of Edward III and Philippa of Hainault; styled Earl of Essex in right of his wife Eleanor, daughter of Bohun, earl of Hereford; constable of England, 1376; Earl of Buckingham and knighted, 1377; averted landing of French and Spaniards at Dover, 1380, and captured eight Spanish ships off Brest; led expedition to the assistance of the Duke of Brittany, which came to nothing, since the duke made peace with Charles VI; mortified by John of Gaunt's conduct towards him, Richard II's attempts at arbitrary government drawing them together later; dispersed insurgents in Essex, 1381; associated with Gaunt in expeditions and negotiations; supported him when accused of treason; created Duke of Gloucester, 1385; placed himself at the head of the opposition to Richard II; one of the judges who condemned Suffolk, 1386; threatened Richard II with the fate of Edward II; with other lords routed De Vere at Radcotbridge, 1388; chiefly responsible for the vindictiveness of the Merciless parliament; held the reins of power till 1389, when Richard II resumed the government; obtained money and lands for himself, and chief-justiceship of Chester; arrested by Richard II after further provocation at Pleshey, 1397; was taken to Calais and announced as dead in September, but interviewed by Sir William Rickhill [q. v.], 8 Sept., when he handed to him a written confession; announced again as dead, 24 Sept., probably murdered, Halle and Serle being executed for the deed subsequently by Henry IV. He composed, c. 1390, 'L'Ordonnance d'Angleterre pour le Camp à l'outrance, ou gaige de bataille.' [lvi. 153]

THOMAS, DUKE OF CLARENCE (1388?–1421), second son of Henry IV by Mary de Bohun; lieutenant of Ireland, 1401; commanded the fleet which burnt vessels at Sluys and ravaged the coast of Normandy, 1405; captain of Guines, 1407; arrested Earl of Kildare in Ireland and made raid into Leinster, 1408; returned to England, quarrelled with the Beauforts, and on their fall, 1412, supplanted Henry, prince of Wales in the government; made Duke of Clarence, 1412; commanded an expedition to France; served at the siege of Harfleur, 1415; received the Emperor Sigismund at Dartford, 1416; took part in the great expedition, 1417, which ended in Henry V's triumphal entry into Paris, 1420; appointed lieutenant of France at Henry V's departure, 1421, and, impatient to win a victory like Agincourt, attacked the French with his cavalry only at Beaugé and was defeated and slain; buried at Canterbury. [lvi. 158]

THOMAS OF BAYEUX (*d.* 1100), archbishop of York; a native of Bayeux; son of Osbert, a priest, and brother of Samson (*d.* 1112) [q. v.], bishop of Worcester; educated by Odo [q. v.], bishop of Bayeux; studied in France, Germany, and Spain; accompanied Odo to England, and was made one of the Conqueror's chaplains; appointed archbishop of York, 1070; refused profession of obedience to Lanfranc, archbishop of Canterbury, but was obliged by William I to yield, and the question being decided by a council of bishops at Windsor, 1072, in favour of Canterbury, was blamed by Pope Alexander II, according to a York historian, for yielding; failed also in claim to estates held by the bishop of Worcester; present at council of London, 1075, when place of the archbishop of York was decided to be on the right of the archbishop of Canterbury; claimed Lincoln for his province, 1092; at the consecration of Anselm successfully objected to Canterbury being styled 'the metropolitan church of all Britain,' 1093; noted for his learning and skill in music; engaged in disputes without personal bitterness; rebuilt or restored his cathedral; introduced the system which became general in secular chapters, and carried out many reforms; wrote the epitaph in elegiac verse placed on the tomb of the Conqueror. [lvi. 160]

THOMAS (*d.* 1114), archbishop of York; son of Samson (*d.* 1112) [q. v.], bishop of Worcester; brought up by his uncle, Thomas of Bayeux [q. v.]; provost of Beverley, 1092; one of William II's chaplains; made archbishop of York, 1108, when the dispute commenced with Anselm concerning the profession of obedience; made profession after Anselm's death by command of Henry I, but not in consequence of any legal decision, 1109, and received his pall from the legate Ulric ; was buried in York Minster. [lvi. 163]

THOMAS, known as THOMAS À BECKET (1118 ?-1170), archbishop of Canterbury ; son of Gilbert Becket, of a Norman family of knights ; portreeve of London ; educated at Merton Priory, London, and Paris ; became a 'notary' ; entered the service of Archbishop Theobald [q. v.] ; accompanied Theobald to Rome, 1143 ; driven away by the jealousy of Roger of Pont l'Evêque [q. v.] ; studied canon law at Bologna and Auxerre ; accompanied Theobald to the council of Rheims, 1148 ; prevented the coronation of King Stephen's son Eustace, 1152 ; archdeacon of Canterbury, 1154 ; chancellor, 1155, in which capacity he co-operated with Henry II in his policy, an extraordinary intimacy growing up between them ; ambassador to France to propose marriage between Henry II's eldest son and Louis VII's daughter, when his magnificence made a great impression ; supported Henry II's expedition against Toulouse, 1159, when the church was disproportionately taxed, and in which he performed great military services ; became unwillingly archbishop of Canterbury, 1162, and refused to remain chancellor ; at a council at Woodstock successfully opposed Henry II on a point of taxation (the first case of such opposition in English history), 1163 ; endeavoured to reclaim alienated property of his see, even from the crown ; prohibited marriage of Henry II's brother, William of Anjou, to the Countess of Warenne ; opposed royal jurisdiction over criminous clerks ; on Henry II's calling upon the bishops at Westminster to confirm 'his grandfather's customs,' refused ; afterwards on a supposed order from Pope Alexander III, submitted at Clarendon, 1164, but refused to seal the Constitutions of Clarendon, then drawn up ; summoned to Northampton to account for various sums of money, on which occasion he appeared at the council, holding his cross, appealed to Pope Alexander III, and being refused a safe-conduct, fled secretly to Louis VII of France ; obtained condemnation of the constitutions from Pope Alexander III ; resided at Pontigny Abbey and at Sens, while Henry confiscated the property of his see and banished his friends, to which he replied with threats of excommunication, 1166, a personal interview at Montmirail subsequently failing to effect a reconciliation, and the quarrel being embittered by the coronation of the young Prince Henry by Roger of York and other bishops, in spite of Pope Alexander III's and the primate's prohibition, 1170 ; suspended Archbishop Roger and all the bishops who had taken part in the ceremony ; returned, however, to England, Henry II having promised amends for this violation of his rights, but was met by a demand for the absolution of all the suspended bishops, which he refused ; set out for Winchester, but was ordered to return to Canterbury ; excommunicated those in possession of his estates ; was murdered by Hugh de Morville (d. 1204) [q. v.], William de Tracy [q. v.] Reginald Fitzurse [q. v.], Richard le Breton, and others in Canterbury Cathedral, 29 Dec., his shrine becoming the most famous in Christendom and Henry II doing public penance at his tomb, 1174 ; many hospitals and churches named in his honour. The shrine was broken up, 1538, and St. Thomas was ordered to be styled ' Bishop Becket,' and all images of him to be destroyed. [lvi. 165]

THOMAS, known as THOMAS BROWN (fl. 1170), officer of the exchequer ; served under the Norman kings of Sicily, and later in the English exchequer. [lvi. 173]

THOMAS, called of BEVERLEY (fl. 1174), hagiographer ; wrote ' life' of St. Margaret of Jerusalem, his sister. [lvi. 173]

THOMAS OF ELY (fl. 1175), historian and monk of Ely ; author of a history of Ely and other works. [lvi. 173]

THOMAS (fl. 1200 ?) romance-writer ; produced versions of the romances of ' King Horn' and ' Tristan' in French ; generally identified with ' Thomas von Britanie.' [lvi. 174]

THOMAS DE MARLEBERGE (d. 1236). [See MARLEBERGE.]

THOMAS WALLENSIS or OF WALES (d. 1255). [See WALLENSIS or GUALENSIS.]

THOMAS DE HIBERNIA (d. 1270). [See HIBERNIA.]

THOMAS DE WYKES (fl. 1258-1293). [See WYKES.]

THOMAS OF ERCELDOUNE or **THOMAS** THE RHYMER (fl. 1220 ?-1297 ?). [See ERCELDOUNE.]

THOMAS OF CORBRIDGE (d. 1304). [See CORBRIDGE.]

THOMAS THE ENGLISHMAN (d. 1310). [See JORZ or JOYCE, THOMAS.]

THOMAS HIBERNICUS or DE HIBERNIA (fl. 1306-1316), known also as PALMERANUS or PALMERSTON, theological writer ; wrote ' Tabula originalium sive Manipulus Florum,' 1306, and other works. [lvi. 174]

THOMAS DE LA MORE (fl. 1327-1351). [See MORE.]

THOMAS OF HATFIELD (d. 1381). [See HATFIELD.]

THOMAS OF ASHBORNE (fl. 1382), theological controversialist ; master in theology, Oxford. [lvi. 175]

THOMAS ASHEBURNE (fl. 1384), poet : scholar of Corpus Christi College, Oxford, and Carmelite of Northampton ; wrote an English theological poem, formerly in the Cottonian MSS., which has been burnt. [lvi. 175]

THOMAS DE NEWENHAM (fl. 1393). [See NEWENHAM.]

THOMAS OF NEWMARKET (fl. 1410 ?), arithmetician ; M.A. Cambridge ; wrote a ' Commentum in Computum Ecclesiasticum Dionysi' (Exigui), and other works. [lvi. 175]

THOMAS NETTER or WALDEN (d. 1430). [See NETTER.]

THOMAS THE BASTARD (d. 1471). [See FAUCONBERG, THOMAS.]

THOMAS AB IEUAN AP RHYS (d. 1617 ?), Welsh bard and farmer ; writer of ballads. [lvi. 175]

THOMAS OF ST. GREGORY (1564-1644). [See HILL, THOMAS.]

THOMAS, ARTHUR GORING (1850-1892), musical composer ; studied at Paris and at the Royal Academy ; composed ' The Light of the Harem,' ' Esmeralda,' and other operas, besides cantatas, songs, and other music. [lvi. 176]

THOMAS, DAVID (1760 ?-1822), known as ' Dafydd Ddu Eryri,' Welsh poet and schoolmaster ; published poems on ' The Life of Man,' 1789, ' Liberty,' 1790, and ' Truth,' 1791 ; published ' Corph y Gainc' (collection of Welsh poems, some original), 1810. [lvi. 176]

THOMAS, DAVID (1813-1894), divine : minister of the congregational church at Chesham, and (1844-77) of the independent church at Stockwell ; published ' The Augustine Hymn-book,' 1866, containing original hymns of his own, ' The Homilist' (commenced in 1852), and other works, chiefly religious ; originated the university of Wales at Aberystwyth, 1872 ; started ' The Dial ' newspaper, 1860, and the ' Cambrian Daily Leader,' 1861. [lvi. 177]

THOMAS, EDWARD (1813-1886), Indian antiquary ; son of Honoratus Leigh Thomas [q. v.] ; went to India as ' writer' in service of East India Company, 1832 ; Indian judge ; published ' Chronicles of the Pathan Kings of Delhi,' 1847, Prinsep's ' Essays on Indian Antiquities,' ' Useful Tables,' 1858, and other noteworthy works in which he broke new ground. [lvi. 178]

THOMAS, ELIZABETH (1677-1731), poetaster ; known as ' Corinna,' a name given to her by Dryden, with whom she corresponded ; sold letters of Pope to Curll for publication, 1726 ; probably subsisted by blackmailing ; concocted a fictitious account of Dryden's death, 1727 ; died in poverty ; author of ' Poems on several Occasions,' 1722, ' Codrus, or the Dunciad Dissected,' 1729, and other works. [lvi. 178]

THOMAS, ERNEST CHESTER (1 50-1892), bibliographer ; B.A. Trinity College, Oxford, 1875 ; barrister, Gray's Inn, 1881 ; edited the ' Philobiblon of Richard de Bury,' 1888 ; translated Lange's ' Geschichte des Materialismus,' 1880-1. [lvi. 179]

THOMAS, FRANCIS SHEPPARD (1794 ?-1857), archivist ; secretary at the Public Record Office ; author of ' Handbook to Public Records,' 1853, and other works. [lvi. 180]

THOMAS, FREDERICK JENNINGS (1786–1855), rear-admiral; present in action of 22 July 1805, and present at Trafalgar on the Spartiate; defended Cadiz against the French, 1809–11; rear-admiral, 1846. [lvi. 180]

THOMAS, GEORGE (1756 ?–1802), adventurer in India and Irishman; sailor in the navy, but deserting became commander of the begum of Sirdhana's army, 1787, and of Appa Rao's forces; governor of Meerut, 1792; asserted his independence, and became master of extensive Sikh territories, 1797–9, but was driven out with French assistance, 1802; famous for his military genius and recklessness. [lvi. 181]

THOMAS, GEORGE HOUSMAN (1824 – 1868), painter; illustrated a New York paper, 1846, and contributed to the 'Illustrated London News' from Rome, 1849; painted pictures for Queen Victoria. [lvi. 182]

THOMAS, HONORATUS LEIGH (1769–1846), surgeon; worked under John Hunter; surgeon in the army and navy; fellow of the Royal College of Surgeons on its foundation, 1843; F.R.S. 1806; Hunterian orator, 1827; published medical works. [lvi. 182]

THOMAS, JOHN (1691–1766), successively bishop of Lincoln and Salisbury; son of a drayman; of Merchant Taylors' School and Catharine Hall, Cambridge; M.A., 1717, and D.D., 1728 (incorporated at Oxford, 1728); favourite of George II on account of his knowledge of German; bishop of Lincoln, 1744, and of Salisbury, 1761–6. [lvi. 183]

THOMAS, JOHN (1696–1781), successively bishop of Peterborough, Salisbury, and Winchester, 1761; educated at Charterhouse, London, and Christ Church, Oxford; M.A., 1719; D.D., 1731; fellow of All Souls College, Oxford, 1720; chaplain to George II, 1742; bishop of Peterborough, 1747–57, of Salisbury, 1757–61, of Winchester, 1761–81; preceptor to George, prince of Wales, 1752. [lvi. 183]

THOMAS, JOHN (1712–1793), bishop of Rochester; of Queen's College, Oxford; D.C.L., 1742; rector of Bletchingley, 1738; chaplain to George II and George III; dean of Westminster and of the order of the Bath, 1768; bishop of Rochester, 1774–93; author of sermons. [lvi. 184]

THOMAS, JOHN (1813–1862), sculptor and architectural draughtsman; employed by Sir Charles Barry [q. v.] on the decorations of the Houses of Parliament; executed also several groups, figures, and vases. [lvi. 184]

THOMAS, JOHN (1795–1871), musical composer; Welsh song-writer and schoolmaster; published 'Y Caniedydd Cymreig,' the 'Cambrian Minstrel,' 1845, and poems. [lvi. 185]

THOMAS, JOHN (1821–1892), independent minister; brother of Owen Thomas [q. v.]; pastor of the Tabernacle, Liverpool, 1854; journalist, lecturer, and political speaker; visited the United States, 1865 and 1876; published miscellaneous works. [lvi. 186]

THOMAS, JOHN EVAN (1809–1873), sculptor. [lvi. 186]

THOMAS, JOHN FRYER (1797–1877), secretary to the Madras government; chief secretary to the government of Madras, 1845; member of the governor's council, 1850; writer of very able minutes; authority on native education; supporter of the missionaries. [lvi. 186]

THOMAS, JOHN WESLEY (1798–1872), translator of Dante; Wesleyan minister; published translation of the 'Inferno,' 1859; 'Purgatorio,' 1862, and 'Paradiso,' 1866. [lvi. 187]

THOMAS, JOSHUA (d. 1759 ?), clergyman; vicar of Kerry, 1758; translated into Welsh Scott's 'Christian Life,' 1752. [lvi. 188]

THOMAS, JOSHUA (1719–1797), Welsh writer; published an important history of the baptists in Wales, 1778. [lvi. 187]

THOMAS, LEWIS (fl. 1587–1619), preacher; B.A. Brasenose College, Oxford, 1587; author of two volumes of sermons. [lvi. 188]

THOMAS, MATTHEW EVAN (1788 ?–1830), architect. [lvi. 188]

THOMAS, SIR NOAH (1720–1792), physician; M.A., 1746, and M.D., 1753, St. John's College, Cambridge;

F.R.S., 1757; F.R.C.P., 1757; Gulstonian lecturer, 1759; censor, 1761, 1766, 1767, and 1781; physician in ordinary to George III, 1775; knighted, 1775. [lvi. 188]

THOMAS, OWEN (1812–1891), Calvinistic methodist minister; pastor at Newtown, Montgomeryshire, at Jewin Crescent, London, and Liverpool, and moderator of the general assembly; celebrated preacher and author of several works. [lvi. 189]

THOMAS, RICHARD (1777–1857), admiral; entered the navy, 1790; was present at the reduction of Tobago, Martinique, and St. Lucia, 1792, and commanded a boat in the attack on Fort Royal; present at the battle of Cape St. Vincent, 1797; commander-in-chief in the Pacific, 1841–4; admiral, 1854. [lvi. 189]

THOMAS, SAMUEL (1627–1693), nonjuror; son of William Thomas (1593–1667) [q. v.], rector of Ubley; fellow of St. John's College, Oxford, 1651, but deprived, 1660; M.A., 1651 (incorporated at Cambridge, 1653); prebendary of Wells, 1681, but refusing to take oaths at accession of William and Mary was deprived, 1691; author of controversial religious writings. [lvi. 190]

THOMAS, SIDNEY GILCHRIST (1850–1885), metallurgist and inventor; educated at Dulwich College; became schoolmaster and was clerk at police-courts; studied metallurgy, and experimented; discovered method for eliminating phosphorus from pig-iron in the Bessemer converter, 1875, enabling phosphoric ores to be used; secured a large fortune by his patents; paid a triumphal visit to America, 1881; travelled abroad in search of health; died at Paris. [lvi. 190]

THOMAS, THOMAS (1553–1588), printer and lexicographer; of Eton and King's College, Cambridge; fellow, 1574; M.A., 1579; first printer to Cambridge University, 1582; issued Ramus's 'Dialectics' by (Sir) William Temple [q. v.], 1584; his press seized by the Stationers' Company, but his rights upheld by Lord Burghley, chancellor; author of a Latin dictionary, 1587 (14th ed. 1644). [lvi. 192]

THOMAS, VAUGHAN (1775 – 1858), antiquary; fellow of Corpus Christi College, Oxford; M.A., 1800; B.D., 1809; vicar of Stoneleigh and other livings; author of 'The Italian Biography of Sir Robert Dudley, Knight,' 1861, and of other works. [lvi. 193]

THOMAS, WILLIAM (d. 1554), Italian scholar and clerk of the council to Edward VI; a Welshman and probably educated at Oxford; lived abroad, chiefly in Italy; wrote there a defence of Henry VIII, 1552; wrote 'Principal Rvles of the Jtalian Grammer, with a Dictionarie' (printed, 1550), the first published in England; returned to England, 1549; published 'The Historie of Italie,' 1549; published 'Of the Vanitee of this World,' 1549; made clerk of the privy council, 1550; given a prebend in St. Paul's, London, and other rewards; member of the embassy sent to France, 1551; became political instructor to Edward VI and drew up discourses for his use; dedicated to him his translation of Barbaro's voyages to the east, 1551; lost all his preferments at accession of Queen Mary; took active part in Wyatt's conspiracy, 1553–4; arrested; attempted suicide; racked and accused of conspiring Mary's death, and executed. [lvi. 193]

THOMAS, WILLIAM (1593–1667), ejected minister; M.A. Brasenose College, Oxford, 1615; rector of Ubley, 1616; an earnest puritan; refused to read 'The Book of Sports,' 1633; was suspended, but restored; took the 'covenant,' 1643; carried on a controversy with Thomas Speed, and wrote 'Rayling Rebuked' and other pamphlets; declined to conform to Act of Uniformity, and was ejected, 1662; author of several works, mostly theological. [lvi. 196]

THOMAS, WILLIAM (1613–1689), bishop of St. David's and Worcester successively; educated at Carmarthen grammar school and St. John's College, Oxford; fellow of Jesus College, Oxford; M.A., 1635; vicar of Laugharne; ejected, 1644, restored, 1660; created D.D. Oxford, 1660; rector of Lampeter Velfrey, and chaplain to the Duke of York, 1601, whom he attended in his engagements with the Dutch; dean of Worcester, 1665; rector of Hampton Lovett, 1670; bishop of St. David's, 1677, where he identified himself thoroughly as a Welshman with the interests of his diocese; bishop of Worcester, 1683; known for his hospitality and charities;

entertained James II; refused to distribute among his clergy the declaration of indulgence, 1688, and also to take oath of allegiance to William III, being suspended in consequence, 1689; author of pamphlets and sermons. [lvi. 197]

THOMAS, WILLIAM (1670–1738), antiquary; grandson of William Thomas (1613–1689) [q. v.], bishop of Worcester; educated at Westminster School and Trinity College, Cambridge; M.A., 1695; D.D., 1729; rector of St. Nicholas, Worcester, 1723; edited Dugdale's 'Antiquities of Warwickshire,' 1730; author of antiquarian works. [lvi. 199]

THOMAS, WILLIAM (*fl.* 1780–1791), architect. [lvi. 199]

THOMAS, WILLIAM (ISLWYN) (1832–1878), Welsh poet and methodist minister of Mynyddislwyn; published 'Barddoniaeth [poetry] gan Islwyn,' 1854, 'Caniadau [Songs of] Islwyn,' 1867, and other volumes of verse and sermons; acknowledged as the finest Welsh poet of the century. [lvi. 200]

THOMAS, WILLIAM LUSON (1830–1900), founder of the 'Graphic' and 'Daily Graphic'; brother of George Housman Thomas [q. v.], with whom he worked as woodengraver in Paris; assistant to William James Linton [q. v.]; opened independently an engraving establishment; associate, 1864, and full member, 1875, of Institute of Painters in Water-colours; worked as engraver for 'Illustrated London News'; founded the 'Graphic' weekly newspaper, 1869; had much to do with introduction of photographic method of reproduction; founded 'Daily Graphic,' the first daily illustrated paper, 1890. [Suppl. iii. 379]

THOMASON, SIR EDWARD (1769–1849), manufacturer and inventor; took out numerous patents; completed series of sixty medals on bibl. subjects, 1830, presented to the European sovereigns; knighted, 1832. [lvi. 200]

THOMASON, GEORGE (*d.* 1666), collector of Commonwealth and civil war publications, and bookseller; published a trade catalogue, 1647; a collector of oriental works bought from him for Cambridge, 1648; implicated in the royalist plot, 1651; collected nearly 23,000 articles and transcripts of nearly one hundred manuscripts, 1641–1662, arranged chronologically in 1983 volumes (presented by George III to the British Museum, 1762). [lvi. 201]

THOMASON, JAMES (1804–1853), lieutenant-governor; registrar and judge in the Bengal civil service; secretary to government, 1830; magistrate and collector of Azamgarh, 1832; held other official posts; lieutenant-governor of the North-Western Provinces, 1843–53; appointed governor of Madras on the day of his death. [lvi. 202]

THOMASSON, THOMAS (1808–1876), manufacturer and political economist; cotton-spinner; chief promoter of anti-cornlaw agitation, which he aided greatly by subscriptions. [lvi. 203]

THOMLINSON or TOMLINSON, MATTHEW (1617–1681), soldier; colonel of horse in the new model army; one of the officers presenting the remonstrance to parliament, 1647; took charge of Charles I, 1648, till execution, but refused to be his judge; followed Cromwell to Scotland, 1650; member of the council of state on expulsion of the Long parliament; employed in Ireland; knighted, but suspected of disaffection by Henry Cromwell, 1657; impeached by the parliamentary party, 1660; escaped punishment at the Restoration. [lvi. 204]

THOMLINSON, ROBERT (1668–1748), benefactor of Newcastle-on-Tyne; of Queen's College and St. Edmund Hall, Oxford; M.A., 1692 (incorporated at Cambridge, 1719); D.D. King's College, Cambridge, 1719; vice-principal, St. Edmund Hall, Oxford, 1692; rector of Whickham, 1712, and prebendary of St. Paul's, London, 1719; founded public library at Newcastle-on-Tyne, and other institutions. [lvi. 205]

THOMOND, third MARQUIS OF (1769–1855). [See O'BRIEN, JAMES.]

THOMOND, EARLS OF. [See O'BRIEN, MURROUGH, first earl, *d.* 1551; O'BRIEN, CONOR, third earl, 1534?–1581; O'BRIEN, DONOUGH, fourth earl, *d.* 1624; O'BRIEN, BARNABAS, sixth earl, *d.* 1657.]

THOMPSON. [See also THOMSON, TOMPSON, and TOMSON.]

THOMPSON, SIR BENJAMIN, COUNT VON RUMFORD (1753–1814), born at North Woburn, Massachusetts; attended lectures at Harvard University; became a schoolmaster and then major in a provincial regiment; imprisoned for lukewarmness in the cause of liberty, 1775; subsequently sailed for England; given employment at the colonial office; occupied himself with scientific experiments and wrote paper on the cohesion of bodies; F.R.S., 1779; under-secretary for the colonies, 1780; returned to America as lieutenant-colonel of George III's American dragoons; was (1784–1795) in the service of the elector of Bavaria, where he carried out important reforms, and a monument was erected to him in the 'English Garden,' which he laid out, at Munich; made Count von Rumford and knighted, 1784; introduced improvements in Dublin hospitals and workhouses, 1796; inaugurated in London many social reforms, and made mechanical inventions with a view to ameliorating domestic life; the first to determine that 'heat is a mode of motion'; credited also with other discoveries and practical suggestions on cooking and fuel; gave 1,000*l.* to the Royal Society for the purchase of medals, 1796, and to the American Academy; under his will a professorship at Harvard University was established; founded the Royal Institution, London, 1799; published essays; died at Auteuil. [lvi. 205]

THOMPSON, BENJAMIN (1776?–1816), dramatist; translated Kotzebue's dramas; author of two original plays and other works. [lvi. 208]

THOMPSON, CHARLES, baronet (1740?–1799), vice-admiral; entered the navy, 1755; commanded the Alcide in the action off the Chesapeake, 1781, and in that of 12 April, 1782; took part in the capture of Martinique and Guadeloupe, 1793; vice-admiral, 1795; commanded the Britannia and second in command at battle of Cape St. Vincent, 1797; made a baronet, but having censured the execution of mutineers was removed by Lord St. Vincent, 1797. [lvi. 209]

THOMPSON, CHARLES (1791–1843), engraver; brother of John Thompson (1785–1866) [q. v.] [lvi. 217]

THOMPSON, CHARLES THURSTON (1816–1868), engraver and photographer; son of John Thompson (1785–1866) [q. v.] [lvi. 217]

THOMPSON, EDWARD (1738?–1786), commodore and author; educated at Harrow; entered the navy after some sea-service, 1755, and took part in blockade of Brest and battle of Quiberon Bay, 1759; wrote the 'Meretriciad' (1755?), and other 'Meretricious Miscellanies,' plays, and 'A Sailor's Letters,' 1767; promoted captain, 1772; took part in the relief of Gibraltar by Rodney; employed in settling Demerara and Essequibo, 1781; court-martialled for loss of Guiana colonies, 1782, but honourably acquitted; edited Andrew Marvell's works; wrote poems and sea-songs. [lvi. 209]

THOMPSON, GEORGE (1804–1878), anti-slavery advocate; delivered lectures; went to America and organised the movement there, 1834; denounced by President Jackson and was obliged to escape to England, 1835; supported parliamentary reform and Anti-Cornlaw League; an admirable speaker. [lvi. 211]

THOMPSON, GILBERT (1728–1803), physician in the city; quaker; M.D. Edinburgh, 1753; published three works. [lvi. 211]

THOMPSON, SIR HARRY STEPHEN MEYSEY, first baronet (1809–1874), agriculturist; graduated at Trinity College, Cambridge, in mathematical honours; studied entomology under Charles Darwin and agriculture abroad and in different parts of England; one of the founders of the Royal Agricultural Society, 1838; carried out important though incomplete experiments; discovered the value of covered fold yards; a successful chairman of the North-Eastern Railway Company; liberal M.P. for Whitby, 1859–65; deputy-lieutenant of Yorkshire; created baronet, 1874; contributed papers on agricultural topics to 'Tait's Magazine,' 1840, and to 'Journal of the Royal Agricultural Society.' [lvi. 211]

THOMPSON, HENRY (1797–1878), miscellaneous writer; M.A. St. John's College, Cambridge, 1825; vicar of Chard, 1853; author of religious works, editions of the Latin classics, and other books. [lvi. 213]

THOMPSON, HENRY LANGHORNE (1829–1856), soldier; educated at Eton; lieutenant, Bengal native infantry ; fought and was wounded in second Burmese war, 1852–3 ; distinguished himself at Kars, 1855 ; honorary C.B., 1856.   [lvi. 213]

THOMPSON, JACOB (1806–1879), landscape-painter ; was apprenticed to a house-painter, but became student at the Royal Academy, 1829 ; exhibited pictures of high-land country scenes, portraits, and classical and scriptural subjects.   [lvi. 214]

THOMPSON, JAMES (1817–1877), journalist and local historian ; contributed to his father's paper, ' The Leicester Chronicle ' ; published ' A History of Leicester, from the time of the Romans to the end of the Seventeenth Century,' 1849, ' A History of Leicester in the Eighteenth Century,' 1871, ' An Essay on English Municipal History,' 1867, and other works ; F.R.H.S.   [lvi. 214]

THOMPSON, THOMSON, or **TOMSON,** JOHN (*fl.* 1382), Carmelite ; B.D. Oxford ; member of the council which pronounced judgment on Wycliffe's doctrines, 1382 ; his works not known to be extant.   [lvi. 215]

THOMPSON, Sir JOHN, first BARON HAVERSHAM (1647–1710), nephew of George Thomson (*fl.* 1643–1668) [q. v.] ; made baronet, 1673 ; M.P., Gatton, 1685–96 ; one of the earliest supporters of William III ; created Baron Haversham, 1696 ; lord of the admiralty, 1699, but re-signed, 1701, and joined the tories.   [lvi. 215]

THOMPSON, JOHN (1776–1864), admiral ; entered the navy, 1787 ; present in the action off Toulon, 1795 ; wrecked in the Tagus, 1796, when he was thanked for his services in saving life ; distinguished himself in several expeditions ; admiral, 1860.   [lvi. 216]

THOMPSON, JOHN (1785–1866), wood-engraver ; executed numerous book illustrations, the design for Mulready's envelope, 1852, and Britannia, still on Bank of England notes, 1839 ; his work much appreciated abroad, and his cuts in Fairfax's 'Tasso' and Puckle's 'Club' especially famous.   [lvi. 217]

THOMPSON, Sir JOHN SPARROW DAVID (1844–1894), premier of Canada ; born at Halifax, Nova Scotia ; began life as a lawyer and reporter in the assembly there ; Q.C., 1879 ; premier of Nova Scotia, 1881, and judge of the supreme court of Nova Scotia, 1882 ; became minister of justice for Canada, 1885 ; K.C.M.G., 1888 ; premier of Canada, 1892 ; arbitrator on the Behring Sea fisheries question at Paris, 1893 ; died suddenly at Windsor after being sworn privy councillor.   [lvi. 217]

THOMPSON, JOHN VAUGHAN (1779–1847), zoologist ; present (as assistant surgeon) at taking of Demerara and Berbice, 1803 ; published zoological discoveries, and on return to England, 1809, was made F.L.S., 1810 ; investigated extinct birds during visit to Madagascar and Mauritius, 1812–16 ; district medical inspector at Cork, 1816, where he made his important discoveries on the feather-star, polyzoa, barnacles, and crustacea ; went to Sydney as officer of health in charge of convict medical department, 1835 ; died at Sydney.   [lvi. 218]

THOMPSON, Sir MATTHEW WILLIAM, baronet (1820–1891), railway director ; M.A. Trinity College, Cambridge, 1846 ; barrister, Inner Temple, 1847 ; became manager of his uncle's brewery at Bradford, 1857, and mayor, 1862 ; chairman of the Midland Railway Company, 1865, and of the Forth Bridge Company ; baronet, 1890 ; M.P., Bradford, 1867.   [lvi. 220]

THOMPSON, PISHEY (1784–1862), historian of Boston ; published ' The History and Antiquities of Boston,' 1856.   [lvi. 220]

THOMPSON, SAMUEL (1766–1837), founder of the ' Freethinking Christians ' ; began life as a watchmaker and wine merchant ; turned seriously to religion and became a preacher ; seceded with others from the universalists, 1798, and founded the sect named ' The Church of God ' or ' Freethinking Christians,' 1799 ; protested against religious marriage ; conducted services at meeting houses in Jewin Crescent, London, and High Holborn, London, and, after another schism at Clerkenwell expelled, 1834, but elected elder of another ' church of God ' ; author of religious books and articles.   [lvi. 221]

THOMPSON, THEOPHILUS (1807–1860), physician ; studied at St. Bartholomew's Hospital, London, and Edinburgh (M.D., 1830), and at Paris ; physician to Marlborough Street Consumption Hospital, London, 1847 ; introduced cod-liver oil and other useful medicines ; F.R.S., 1846 ; published medical works.   [lvi. 222]

THOMPSON, THOMAS (1708 ?–1773), missionary and apologist for the African slave trade ; M.A. Christ's College, Cambridge, 1735 ; fellow, 1738 ; vicar of Eleham, 1761 ; published ' The African Trade for Negro Slaves consistent with . . . Humanity,' 1772.   [lvi. 222]

THOMPSON, THOMAS (1817–1878). [See THOMSON.]

THOMPSON, Sir THOMAS BOULDEN, first baronet (1766 ?–1828), vice-admiral ; nephew of Edward Thompson [q. v.] ; served under Nelson at Teneriffe, 1797 ; was wounded at Santa Cruz ; as captain of the Leander had great share in the victory of the Nile, but returning home was captured by the French ; complimented at court-martial on his gallant defence ; lost a leg at the battle of Copenhagen, 1801 ; created baronet, 1806 ; M.P., Rochester, 1807–18 ; vice-admiral, 1814 ; G.C.B., 1822.   [lvi. 223]

THOMPSON, THOMAS PERRONET (1783–1869), general and politician ; B.A. Queens' College, Cambridge, as seventh wrangler ; entered the navy as midshipman, 1803 ; fellow of Queens' College, Cambridge, 1804 ; entered the army, 1806 ; captured by the Spaniards at Buenos Ayres, 1807 ; governor of Sierra Leone, 1808 ; took part in the Peninsular war, and subsequently in several Indian expeditions, in one of which, at Soor, he was defeated by Arabs, 1820 ; on return home, 1822, published several articles, mostly on economic and political subjects, including the popular 'Catechism on the Corn Laws,' 1827 ; F.R.S., 1828 ; published 'Geometry without Axioms,' 1830 ; editor of the 'Westminster Review,' 1829 ; M.P. for Hull as a philosophic radical,' 1835–7, Bradford, 1847–52 and 1857–9 ; produced numerous articles on free trade ; published ' Exercises, Political and others,' 1842, ' Catechism on the Currency,' 1848, and other works.   [lvi. 224]

THOMPSON or **THOMSON**, Sir WILLIAM (1678–1739), judge ; barrister, Middle Temple, 1698 ; M.P., Orford, 1708–10, Ipswich, 1713 (unseated, 1714), and 1715–1729 ; recorder of London and knighted, 1715 ; solicitor-general, 1717, but dismissed, 1720 ; baron of the exchequer, 1729.   [lvi. 226]

THOMPSON, WILLIAM (1712 ?–1766 ?), poet ; M.A. Queen's College, Oxford, 1739 ; fellow rector of Hampton Poyle ; author of 'Sickness,' 1745, and other poems ; imitated Spenser.   [lvi. 227]

THOMPSON, WILLIAM (1730 ?–1800), portrait-painter and author.   [lvi. 227]

THOMPSON, WILLIAM (1785 ?–1833), political economist ; born in co. Cork, where he became an extensive landowner ; made acquaintance of Bentham, and supported Robert Owen's system of co-operation ; published 'Inquiry into Principles of Distribution of Wealth,' 1824, expounding principles of scientific socialism on theory of the injustice of unearned income and private property ; published also an ' Appeal ' for sexual equality and other writings ; bequeathed his property to trustees for promulgating principles of Robert Owen, but his will was disputed by his heirs-at-law, who ultimately obtained judgment in their favour.   [Suppl. iii. 380]

THOMPSON, WILLIAM (1805–1852), naturalist ; began life as a linendraper ; travelled abroad and published valuable papers ; author of the 'Natural History of Ireland,' published, 1849–56.   [lvi. 227]

THOMPSON, WILLIAM (1811–1889), pugilist ; known as ' Bendigo ' ; defeated Benjamin Caunt [q. v.], 1835, Leechman, Langan, Looney, Deaf Burke, and Tom Paddock, 1850 ; was beaten by Caunt, 1838, and again defeated him, 1845 ; the Australian city Bendigo said to be called after him ; became a dissenting minister.   [lvi. 228]

THOMPSON, WILLIAM HEPWORTH (1810–1886), master of Trinity College, Cambridge ; educated at Trinity, where his tutor was George Peacock (1791–1858) [q. v.] ; B.A., 1832, with high classical and mathematical honours ; obtained second chancellor's medal for classics ; fellow, 1834, and tutor, 1844 ; M.A., 1835 ; regius professor of Greek, 1853–66 ; canon of Ely, 1853, his lectures and scholarship being highly appreciated ; published splendid editions, with learned notes and masterly introductions, of Plato's 'Phædrus,' 1868, and 'Gorgias,' 1871, an important dissertation on the 'Sophist,' 1857, and several other works; master of Trinity College, Cambridge, 1866–1886; vice-chancellor, 1867–8. [lvi. 228]

THOMS, WILLIAM JOHN (1803–1885), antiquary; clerk in the secretary's office at Chelsea Hospital; helped by Francis Douce [q. v.], published 'Early Prose Romances,' 1827–8, and 'Lays and Legends' (2 vols.), 1834; edited 'The Original,' 1832; F.S.A., 1838; secretary of the Camden Society, 1838–73; published 'The Book of the Court,' 1838, and other antiquarian works, and an edition of 'Reynard the Fox,' 1844; appointed clerk of the House of Lords, 1845; published 'Gammer Gurton's Famous Histories,' 1846, and 'Gammer Gurton's Pleasant Stories,' 1846; started 'Notes and Queries,' 1849; appointed deputy-librarian of the House of Lords, 1863, and published many other works of interest. [lvi. 230]

THOMSON. [See also THOMPSON, TOMPSON, and TOMSON.]

THOMSON, ALEXANDER (1763–1803), poet; author of 'Whist,' 1791, and other poems. [lvi. 232]

THOMSON, ALEXANDER (1817–1875), architect; known as 'Greek Thomson'; partner with John Baird of Glasgow, where he designed numerous buildings in the Greek style. [lvi. 232]

THOMSON, ALLEN (1809–1884), biologist; son of John Thomson (1765–1846) [q. v.]; educated at Edinburgh and Paris; visited the schools and museums of Germany, Holland, and Italy, M.D. Edinburgh, 1830; lectured on physiology and on microscopic anatomy; professor of physiology at Edinburgh, 1842–8, and of anatomy at Glasgow, 1848–77; F.R.S., 1848; president of the British Association, 1876; hon. LL.D. Edinburgh, 1871, Glasgow, 1877; hon. D.C.L. Oxford, 1832; the first of the great biologists of the century; anatomist rather than physiologist. [lvi. 233]

THOMSON, ANDREW MITCHELL (1779–1831), Scottish divine; of Edinburgh University; minister of St. George's, Edinburgh, 1814; leader of the evangelical party in the Scottish church and reformer; attacked the British and Foreign Bible Society for binding up the Apocrypha with the Bible, 1827; published religious works. [lvi. 234]

THOMSON, ANTHONY TODD (1778–1849), physician; M.D. Edinburgh, 1799; practised in London, 1800; a founder of the Chelsea Dispensary, 1812, and one of the editors of 'The Medical Repository'; appointed professor of materia medica and therapeutics at London University, 1828, and professor of medical jurisprudence, 1832; F.R.C.P., 1842; carried out valuable and original researches into the composition of alkaloids and iodides, and extended botanical knowledge; author of 'The Conspectus Pharmacopœiæ,' 1810, and other medical works. [lvi. 235]

THOMSON, CHARLES EDWARD POULETT, BARON SYDENHAM (1799–1841), governor-general of Canada; brother of George Julius Poulett Scrope [q. v.]; after spending some years abroad in his father's commercial business, became M.P. for Dover, 1826; M.P., Manchester, frequently from 1832; vice-president of the board of trade, 1830, president, 1834; carried out many reforms and measures; made governor-general of Canada, 1839, when he accomplished union of the different provinces; created Baron Sydenham, 1840. [lvi. 236]

THOMSON, SIR CHARLES WYVILLE (1830–1882), naturalist; educated at Edinburgh University; filled many professional appointments, including that of professor of natural history at Edinburgh from 1870; organised sounding expeditions to the north of Scotland, 1868, and Mediterranean, 1870, and another through various parts of the world, 1872–6, and published accounts of these expeditions in 'The Depths of the Sea,' 1873, and 'The Voyage of the Challenger,' 1877; F.R.S., 1869, and recipient of many academical and foreign distinctions; knighted, 1876. [lvi. 237]

THOMSON, DAVID (*d.* 1815), musician; brother of George Thomson (1757–1851). [lvi. 242]

THOMSON, DAVID (1817–1880), professor of natural philosophy at Aberdeen, 1845; was educated abroad, at Glasgow University, and at Trinity College, Cambridge; M.A. Cambridge, 1845; professor, King's College, Aberdeen, 1845–60, Aberdeen (the reconstituted university), 1860–80; a famous teacher; wrote 'Acoustics' in the 'Encyclopædia Britannica,' ninth edition. [lvi. 238]

THOMSON, SIR EDWARD DEAS (1800–1879), Australian official and politician; made clerk of the council, New South Wales, 1827; colonial secretary and member of executive and legislative councils, 1837; as leader of the house showed great capacity in dealing with several important questions; proposed motion for Australian federation, 1857; K.C.M.G., 1874. [lvi. 239]

THOMSON, GEORGE (*fl.* 1643–1668), parliamentarian; served with Sir William Waller [q. v.] in his western campaign, 1644; M.P., Southwark, 1645–53 and 1659–60, and commissioner of customs, 1652, and later of army and navy; dismissed, 1653; became Fifth-monarchy man; intrigued against the Restoration. [lvi. 240]

THOMSON, GEORGE (*fl.* 1648–1679), medical writer; served under Prince Maurice in the civil war; M.D. Leyden, 1648; published 'Loimologia,' 1665 (on the plague), 'Galeno-pale,' 1665, 'Aἱματίασις,' 1670 (against bloodletting), and other works, which excited violent controversies. [lvi. 240]

THOMSON, GEORGE (1782 ?–1838), tutor in Sir Walter Scott's household, *c.* 1811–20, and supposed original of 'Dominie Sampson'; an expert fencer and bold rider, notwithstanding the loss of a leg, but very eccentric; became tutor to sons of Mrs. Dennistoun of Colgrain, 1820. [lvi. 241]

THOMSON, GEORGE (1757–1851), collector of Scottish music; clerk to the Board of Trustees for the Encouragement of Scottish Manufactures; published collections of Scottish, Welsh, and Irish airs, for which Haydn, Beethoven, and others provided accompaniments, and Burns, Scott, Byron, and other poets new words. [lvi. 242]

THOMSON, GEORGE (1799–1886), lieutenant-colonel, Bengal engineers; joined Bengal sappers, 1818; assisted in capture of Arakan, 1825, and was mentioned in despatches; appointed executive engineer, 1825; chief engineer of the army invading Afghanistan, 1838; bridged the Indus at Rohri in eleven days; rendered valuable services in march to Candahar and Kabul under Sir John Keane [q. v.]; successfully stormed Ghazni, 1839; received thanks of the government and made brevet-major and C.B., 1839; retired from the service, 1841, in consequence of a dispute; lieutenant-colonel, 1854. [lvi. 242]

THOMSON, HENRY (1773–1843), painter; R.A., 1802; painted mythological and domestic subjects and portraits, and designed illustrations for Sharpe's 'Poets' and other works; keeper of the Royal Academy, 1825, resigning from illness after two years. [lvi. 244]

THOMSON, HENRY WILLIAM (BYERLEY) (1822–1867), jurist; son of Anthony Todd Thomson [q. v.]; of University College, London, and Jesus College, Cambridge (B.A., 1846); barrister, Inner Temple, 1849; puisne judge of the supreme court of Colombo; published 'Institutes of the Laws of Ceylon,' 1866, and other works. [lvi. 245]

THOMSON, JAMES (1700–1748), poet; born at Ednam; son of a Scottish minister; educated at Southdean parish school, Jedburgh, and Edinburgh University; studied the English poets and wrote verse in the 'Edinburgh Miscellany,' 1720; went to London, 1725, and became tutor to Thomas Hamilton (afterwards seventh Earl of Haddington) at Barnet; introduced to Arbuthnot, Gay, Pope, and others; published 'Winter,' 1726, 'Summer,' 1727, 'Spring,' 1728, 'Autumn,' 1730 (the last first appearing in 'The Seasons,' 1730), and minor poems; produced 'Sophonisba' at Drury Lane, London, 1730; became tutor to Charles Richard Talbot and travelled abroad; given by Talbot's father, the chancellor, secretaryship of briefs, 1733, which, however, he lost, 1737; resided at Richmond; published 'Liberty,' 1734–6, and 'Agamemnon,' a play, 1738; through Lyttelton obtained pension from Frederick, prince of Wales, 1738; wrote 'Rule Britannia,' appearing first in 'The Masque of Alfred,' 1740; spent several years in revising 'The Seasons'; made surveyor-general of the Leeward islands by Lyttelton, 1744; produced 'Tancred and Sigismunda,' 1752, patronised by Pitt and Lyttelton, and in which Garrick played Tancred; produced 'The Castle of Indolence : an allegorical Poem,'

1748 ; buried in Richmond Church ; his 'Coriolanus' produced, 1749, and his 'Works' by Lyttelton, 1750, in which many alterations were made in the text. 'The Seasons' first challenged the artificiality of English poetry, and inaugurated a new era by their sentiment for nature. The poems were translated into many languages, and made a great impression in France. [lvi. 246]

THOMSON, JAMES (1786–1849), mathematician; M.A. Glasgow, 1812 ; appointed professor of mathematics at the Academical Institution, Belfast, 1815 ; hon. LL.D. Glasgow, 1829 ; professor of mathematics, Glasgow University, 1832–49 ; author of mathematical school-books. [lvi. 254]

THOMSON, JAMES (1788–1850), engraver ; engraved mainly portraits. [lvi. 255]

THOMSON, JAMES (1768–1855), co-editor of the 'Encyclopædia Britannica,' third edition, with George Gleig [q. v.] ; hon. D.D. St. Andrews, 1842 ; wrote several articles, including those on 'Scripture,' 'Septuagint,' and 'Superstition,' in the 'Encyclopædia Britannica' ; minister of Eccles, 1805–47. [lvi. 255]

THOMSON, JAMES (1834–1882), poet and pessimist ; became army schoolmaster and made friends with Charles Bradlaugh [q.v.] ; discharged for breach of discipline, 1862 ; wrote for the 'National Reformer,' and took active part in propaganda of free thought ; lived a sad and isolated life in London, aggravated by poverty, dipsomania, and depression ; chief works, 'The City of Dreadful Night' (contributed to the 'National Reformer,' 1874, first published, 1880), and 'Vane's Story, Weddah and Om-el-Bonain, and other Poems,' 1881. [lvi. 256]

THOMSON, JAMES (1800–1883), architect ; designed Cumberland Terrace and Place, Regent's Park, and other buildings in London and the provinces. [lvi. 257]

THOMSON, JAMES (1822–1892), professor of engineering ; son of James Thomson (1786–1849) [q. v.] and brother of Lord Kelvin ; professor of civil engineering in Queen's College, Belfast, 1857–73, and at Glasgow, 1873–1889 ; invented the 'Vortex Water-wheel,' 1850, and other appliances ; contributed numerous scientific papers to the 'Proceedings' of the Royal Society and other publications ; hon. LL.D. Glasgow, 1870, and Dublin, 1878 ; F.R.S., 1877. [lvi. 257]

THOMSON, JAMES BRUCE (1810–1873), pioneer of criminology ; educated at Glasgow University ; surgeon to Perth prison, 1858 ; published papers in the 'Journal of Mental Science' ; first medical writer to investigate relations of crime to disease. [lvi. 258]

THOMSON, JOHN (1778–1840), landscape-painter ; succeeded his father as minister of Dailly, 1799, and was given living of Duddingston, 1805 ; became the greatest Scottish landscape-painter of the time. [lvi. 259]

THOMSON, JOHN (1805–1841), musical writer ; son of Andrew Mitchell Thomson [q. v.] ; Reid professor of musical theory at Edinburgh, 1839–41 ; composer of operas and other works. [lvi. 260]

THOMSON, JOHN (1765–1846), physician and surgeon ; studied at Glasgow and Edinburgh ; became house surgeon at the Royal Infirmary, Edinburgh, 1791 ; president of the Medical Society, 1791 ; professor of surgery at the College of Surgeons, Edinburgh, 1805 ; and of military surgery at Edinburgh University, 1806 ; M.D. Aberdeen, 1808 ; lectured on various subjects ; visited European medical schools ; professor of general pathology, Edinburgh, 1832–41 ; reputed the most learned physician in Scotland ; author of 'The Elements of Chemistry and Natural History,' 1798, and some medical works. [lvi. 260]

THOMSON, JOHN COCKBURN (1834–1860), Sanskrit scholar ; brother of Henry William Thomson [q. v.] ; of Trinity College and St. Mary Hall, Oxford ; B.A. St. Mary Hall, 1857 ; published a translation of 'The Bhagavad-Gita,' 1855, and other works. [lvi. 245]

THOMSON, JOSEPH (1858–1894), African explorer ; showed early great interest in and talent for geology, and contributed papers on formations in his father's quarry at Gatelawbridge ; medallist for geology and natural history at Edinburgh, 1877 ; geologist to expedition of Alexander Keith Johnston the younger [q. v.] to Central Africa, 1878–80, becoming leader on death of Johnston, 1879 ; led expedition for opening up of route between the east coast and northern shore of Victoria Nyanza, 1882–3, traversing country of the dreaded Masai, visiting the lake, and reaching Rabai ; presented with gold medal of Royal Geographical Society, 1885 ; led expedition for the National African Company to Sekoto, and made valuable treaties, 1885 ; explored the Atlas mountains in Morocco, 1888 ; led another expedition for the South African Company, 1890–1, his explorations beginning at Quilimane and ending at Kwa Chepo, in which his health was permanently injured ; made most extensive additions to the geological map of Africa and valuable contributions to zoology and botany ; author of 'To the Central African Lakes and Back,' 1881, 'Through Masai Land,' 1885, 'Travels in the Atlas and Southern Morocco,' 1889, and other works, besides numerous contributions to periodicals. [lvi. 262]

THOMSON, KATHARINE (1797–1862), miscellaneous writer ; *née* Byerley ; married Anthony Todd Thomson [q. v.], 1820 ; published works of anecdotal biography and historical novels. [lvi. 265]

THOMSON, RICHARD (*d.* 1613), biblical scholar and divine ; called 'Dutch Thomson' ; M.A., 1591 (fellow, 1587), Clare Hall, Cambridge ; incorporated at Oxford, 1596 ; one of the translators of the Old Testament ; published religious and controversial works. [lvi. 266]

THOMSON, RICHARD (1794–1865), antiquary ; seed-merchant ; joint-librarian of the London Institution, 1834, the catalogue being largely his work ; arranged antiquities found in the Royal Exchange excavations ; published 'Account of Processions and Ceremonies observed in the Coronation of the Kings and Queens of England,' 1820, and other works. [lvi. 267]

THOMSON, ROBERT DUNDAS (1810–1864), medical officer of health and author ; son of James Thomson (1768–1855) [q. v.] ; studied at Glasgow and Giessen under Liebig ; M.D. Glasgow, 1831 ; turned his attention to investigation of constituents of food ; assisted his uncle, Thomas Thomson (1773–1852) [q. v.] at Glasgow ; chemical lecturer, St. Thomas's Hospital, London, 1852 ; medical officer of health for Marylebone, London, 1856, and authority on sanitation ; F.R.S., 1854 ; F.R.C.P., 1864 ; author of works relating to medical and other science. [lvi. 268]

THOMSON, ROBERT WILLIAM (1822–1873), engineer ; was sent to America to be a merchant, but returning took up engineering ; encouraged by Faraday and employed by Robert Stephenson ; took out a patent for indiarubber tyres, 1845, and one for a 'fountain pen,' 1849, and others connected with motive power ; devised new machinery for manufacturing sugar in Java, 1852 ; the first portable steam-crane, hydraulic docks, 1860, and his traction engine, 1867. [lvi. 268]

THOMSON, THOMAS (1768–1852), jurist and legal antiquary ; brother of John Thomson (1778–1840) [q. v.] ; M.A. Glasgow, 1789 ; admitted advocate, 1793 ; one of Sir Walter Scott's closest friends ; contributed three articles to the 'Edinburgh Review' and occasionally acted as editor ; deputy clerk-register of Scotland, 1806 ; removed, 1839, on account of his carelessness in expenditure ; succeeded Scott as president of the Bannatyne Club, 1832 ; rendered the public records accessible, and published several works with that object, involving immense labour. [lvi. 269]

THOMSON, THOMAS (1773–1852), chemist ; M.D. Edinburgh, 1799 ; contributed articles to the 'Encyclopædia Britannica,' and published his 'System of Chemistry,' 1802 ; opened chemical laboratory for instruction, said to be first in England ; invented Allan's 'Saccharometer' ; F.R.S., 1811 ; visited Sweden, 1812, and published account of his travels ; lecturer in chemistry, 1817, and regius professor at Glasgow University ; supported Dalton's atomic theory ; published 'An Attempt to establish the First Principles of Chemistry by Experiment,' 1825, and other scientific works. [lvi. 271]

THOMSON, THOMAS (1817–1878), naturalist ; son of Thomas Thomson (1773–1852) [q. v.] ; showed early remarkable scientific ability ; M.D. Glasgow, 1839 ; appointed curator of the Asiatic Society's museum at Calcutta, 1840, but sent to Afghanistan and was taken prisoner at Ghuznee, 1842, escaping however by bribing his captor ; served through the Sutlej campaign ; held several botanical appointments at Calcutta ; F.R.S., 1855 ; published 'Flora Indica,' 1855, and other works. [lvi. 272]

THOMSON, THOMAS NAPIER (1798–1869), historian and biographer ; of Glasgow University ; minister to the Scottish church at Maitland, New South Wales, 1831 ; returned to England, 1835 ; contributed to the 'Pictorial History of England,' 1838, and other works ; edited Chambers's 'Biographical Dictionary of Eminent Scotsmen,' published, 1869-71. [lvi. 273]

THOMSON, WILLIAM (1746–1817), miscellaneous writer ; was educated at St. Andrews and Edinburgh Universities ; became librarian to the eighth Earl of Kinnoull [q. v.], and minister, but was obliged by the complaints of his parishioners to resign ; settled in London, 1778, and did much literary work on various subjects. [lvi. 274]

THOMSON, WILLIAM (1802–1852), physician ; son of John Thomson (1765–1846) [q. v.], and half-brother of Allen Thomson [q. v.] ; M.D. Marischal College, Aberdeen, 1831 ; filled several posts as physician and lecturer at Edinburgh and Glasgow ; published medical works. [lvi. 275]

THOMSON, WILLIAM (1819–1890), archbishop of York ; educated at Shrewsbury ; scholar and fellow (1840) of Queen's College, Oxford ; M.A., 1844 ; published 'Outlines of the Laws of Thought,' 1842, which brought him early reputation ; was ordained, but returned to Queen's College as tutor ; Bampton lecturer, 1853 ; a zealous supporter of university reform ; provost of Queen's College, Oxford, 1855 ; preacher at Lincoln's Inn, 1858 ; chaplain to Queen Victoria, 1859 ; severed himself from the writers of 'Essays and Reviews,' and replied by 'Aids to Faith,' 1861 ; contributed 'Introduction to the Synoptical Gospels' to the 'Speaker's Commentary' ; appointed bishop of Gloucester and Bristol, 1861, and archbishop of York, 1862 ; showed a keen interest in social, economic, and political questions ; gained especially the confidence of working men, and greatly strengthened position of the northern church ; in the reconstitution of the ecclesiastical court of appeal supported the judicial rights of the bishops ; introduced Dilapidations Act, 1871 ; joined Archbishop Tait in bill for regulation of public worship, 1874 ; conducted his own case in the matter of Tristram's election, 1887, and successfully challenged the court's jurisdiction ; proceeded against Voysey for heresy, 1869, but always supported toleration. [lvi. 276]

THORBURN, GRANT (1773–1863), original of Galt's 'Lawrie Todd,' and author ; nail-maker at Dalkeith ; emigrated to New York, 1794, where, after several vicissitudes, he became a successful seed-merchant ; published 'Forty Years' Residence in America ; or the Doctrine of a particular Providence exemplified in the Life of Grant Thorburn,' 1834, and other works. [lvi. 279]

THORBURN, ROBERT (1818–1885), miniature-painter ; patronised by fashionable society ; painted miniatures of Queen Victoria ; A.R.A., 1848. [lvi. 280]

THORESBY, JOHN (d. 1373), archbishop of York and chancellor ; entered the service of William de Melton [q. v.] ; sent on several missions to Rome ; became notary in chancery and king's clerk ; obtained numerous ecclesiastical preferments ; appointed master of the rolls, 1341 ; temporary keeper of the great seal, 1343 ; keeper of the privy seal, 1345 ; commissioner to treat with France, 1346 ; attended Edward III at Calais, and made bishop of St. David's, 1347, and of Worcester, 1349 ; chancellor, 1349–56 ; appointed archbishop of York, 1351 ; guardian of the kingdom, 1355 ; commissioner to treat with the Scots, 1357 ; settled dispute between Canterbury and York, the arrangement being that each primate should be allowed to bear his cross erect in the other's province ; built the lady-chapel in the minster and commenced the choir. [lvi. 280]

THORESBY, RALPH (1658–1725), antiquary and topographer ; belonged to the same family as John Thoresby [q. v.], the archbishop ; educated at Leeds, and brought up to trade, but turned his attention to antiquarian research ; indicted under the Conventicle Act, 1683 ; F.R.S., 1697 ; imprisoned for debt, 1698 ; conformed to the church of England, 1699 ; published the 'Ducatus Leodiensis,' 1715, and 'Vicaria Leodiensis,' 1724 ; collected

a celebrated 'museum of rarities' ; the first Yorkshire antiquary to publish important work, his 'Ducatus,' though not scholarly nor accurate, being a useful compilation. His diary was published, 1830. [lvi. 282]

THORIE or **THORIUS**, JOHN (fl. 1586–1593), translator from the Spanish ; B.A. Christ Church, Oxford, 1586 ; wrote five sonnets in the 'Pierce's Supererogation' (1593) of his friend Gabriel Harvey [q. v.] [lvi. 284]

THORIUS, RAPHAEL (d. 1625), physician ; studied at Oxford and Leyden (M.D.) ; practised in London ; wrote 'Hymnus Tabaci,' 1610, 'Hyems,' 1625, and other poems. [lvi. 284]

THORKILL. [See THURKILL.]

THORN, SIR NATHANIEL (d. 1857), lieutenant-general ; took part with the buffs in Peninsular campaign ; was wounded and highly distinguished himself ; brevet-major, 1814 ; K.H., 1832 ; colonel of the buffs, 1854, and lieutenant-general, 1854 ; K.C.B., 1857. [lvi. 285]

THORN, WILLIAM (fl. 1397). [See THORNE.]

THORN, SIR WILLIAM (1781–1843), soldier and military historian ; joined the 29th light dragoons, 1799 ; served in the Maratha war, 1803–6, especially distinguishing himself at battle of Laswari, where he was wounded ; took part in the capture of Mauritius, 1810, and in conquest of Java, 1811 ; thanked in orders for his services ; promoted brevet-major and deputy quarter-master general of the forces in Java ; took part in the capture of Palembang, 1812 ; wrote two books of military memoirs. [lvi. 285]

THORNBOROUGH, JOHN (1551–1641), bishop of Worcester ; M.A. Magdalen College, Oxford, 1575, B.D., 1582 ; chaplain to Earl of Pembroke and Queen Elizabeth ; received many preferments ; dean of York, 1589 ; bishop of Limerick, 1593–1603, of Bristol, 1603–17, of Worcester, 1617–41 ; showed himself zealous against recusants and in raising forced loans ; author of writings supporting the union with Scotland and of other works. [lvi. 286]

THORNBROUGH, SIR EDWARD (1754–1834), admiral ; went to sea with his father, 1761 ; wounded on the North American station, 1775 ; wrecked while commanding the Blonde, near Seal island, 1782 ; joined the Latona, 1792, and was publicly commended for detaining French squadron, 1793 ; assisted the Bellerophon in the battle, 1 June 1794 ; took part in Quiberon expedition, 1795, and in capture of French squadron off Tory island, 1798 ; held various commands ; admiral, 1813 ; G.C.B., 1825 ; vice-admiral of the United Kingdom, 1833 ; had few rivals as a practical seaman. [lvi. 287]

THORNBURY, GEORGE WALTER (1828–1876), miscellaneous writer ; contributed articles to Farley's 'Bristol Journal,' and published poems at the age of seventeen ; joined staff of the 'Athenæum,' and was associated with Dickens in 'Household Words' and 'All the Year Round' ; contributed articles on art and miscellaneous papers to the magazines ; wrote 'Life of J. M. W. Turner,' under Ruskin's observation, 1861, novels, and other works. [lvi. 289]

THORNDIKE, HERBERT (1598–1672), Anglican divine ; M.A. Trinity College, Cambridge, 1620, major fellow, 1620 ; studied theology, oriental languages, and rabbinical literature ; made prebendary of Lincoln, 1636 ; Hebrew lecturer at Trinity College, Cambridge, 1640, and senior bursar ; published 'Of the Government of Churches' and 'Of Religious Assemblies,' 1641 ; deprived of his living during the civil war and of his work at Cambridge ; contributed the Syriac portion to Walton's 'Polyglott' and wrote his 'Epilogue,' 1659, advocating return to the primitive catholic church, and other treatises ; prebendary of Westminster, 1661 ; took part in the Savoy conference, 1661, and in the revision of the prayer-book. [lvi. 290]

THORNE, JAMES (1795–1872), Bible Christian ; preached through various parts of Devonshire and Kent with remarkable success ; noted for his earnest eloquence and ready wit ; editor of the 'Bible Christian Magazine,' 1828–66. [lvi. 292]

THORNE, JAMES (1815–1881), antiquary ; contributed articles on antiquarian and topographical subjects to various periodicals, including 'Rambles by Rivers' in 'The Land we live in' ; published 'Handbook to the Environs of London,' 1876. [lvi. 293]

THORNE, JOHN (d. 1573), musical composer and poet; probably connected with York Minster, where he is buried; skilled also in logic.   [lvi. 293]

THORNE, Sir RICHARD THORNE- (1841-1899), physician; studied at St. Bartholomew's Hospital, London; M.R.C.S., 1863; L.R.C.P., 1865; M.B. London, 1866; physician to Hospital for Diseases of the Chest, City Road, London, 1868; inspector in medical department of privy council, 1871; principal medical officer to local government board, 1892; F.R.C.P., 1875; his Milroy lectures on diphtheria published, 1891; permanent lecturer on public health at St. Bartholomew's, London, 1891; F.R.S., 1890; crown nominee on general medical council, 1895; K.C.B., 1897.   [Suppl. iii. 382]

THORNE, ROBERT (d. 1527), merchant and geographical writer; perhaps a commissioner for the office of admiral of England in Bristol, 1510; carried on business at Seville; wrote to Henry VIII, 1527, exhorting him to take in hand expeditions to the Indies by the north-east, and sending a map; fourteen hundred ducats contributed by his firm to Sebastian Cabot's voyage, 1526. [lvi. 294]

THORNE, WILLIAM (fl. 1397), historian; monk of St. Augustine's, Canterbury; visited Rome, 1387, and wrote detailed account of the corruption there; wrote a history of monks of St. Augustine's (printed by Twysden in 'Decem Scriptores,' 1652).   [lvi. 295]

THORNE, WILLIAM (1568 ?-1630), orientalist and Hebrew scholar; fellow of New College, Oxford, 1587; M.A., 1593; D.D., 1602; regius professor of Hebrew, 1598-1604; appointed dean of Chichester, 1601.   [lvi. 295]

THORNHILL, Sir JAMES (1675-1734), painter; studied under Thomas Highmore [q. v.]; travelled abroad; employed by Queen Anne on important works at Hampton Court, Greenwich, and Windsor; designed paintings for the dome of St. Paul's, London; decorated Greenwich Hospital and many country houses; copied Raphael's cartoons at Hampton Court; painted portraits of Sir Isaac Newton, Steele, Bentley, and others; founded an unsuccessful academy; became sergeant-painter to George I, and was knighted, 1720; repurchased the old family seat at Thornhill, in Dorset; M.P., Melcombe Regis, 1722-34.   [lvi. 295]

THORNHILL, WILLIAM (fl. 1737-1755), surgeon; nephew of Sir James Thornhill [q. v.]; surgeon to the Bristol Infirmary, 1737-55; one of the earliest English surgeons to practise suprapubic lithotomy.   [lvi. 297]

THORNTON, BONNELL (1724-1768), miscellaneous writer and wit; scholar of Westminster and contemporary of William Cowper; M.A., 1750, and M.B., 1754, Christ Church, Oxford; contributed to periodicals; one of the 'Nonsense Club,' which opened the 'Exhibition by the Society of Sign-painters' in ridicule of the Society of Arts, 1754; published, with Colman, 'The Connoisseur,' 1754; became, with Colman, proprietor of 'St. James's Chronicle'; published a burlesque 'Ode on St. Cæcilia's Day,' 1763, and 'Battle of the Wigs: an additional Canto to Dr. Garth's . . . Dispensary,' 1767; his translation of a few of the comedies of Plautus much praised by Southey; diverted Dr. Johnson by his witty sallies.   [lvi. 297]

THORNTON, Sir EDWARD (1766-1852), diplomatist; brother of Thomas Thornton (d. 1814) [q. v.]; educated at Christ's Hospital, London; third wrangler, 1789, and M.A. and fellow, Pembroke College, Cambridge, 1798; filled various diplomatic posts; negotiated treaties of alliance with Sweden and Russia, 1811; minister of Portugal, 1817; G.C.B., 1822.   [lvi. 299]

THORNTON, EDWARD (1799-1875), author of a 'History of the British Empire in India,' 1841-5, and other works on India; in the East India House, 1814-57, and head of the maritime department from 1847.
                [lvi. 300]

THORNTON, EDWARD PARRY (1811-1893), Indian civilian; grandson of Samuel Thornton [q. v.]; commissioner at Rawul Pindi, 1849; distinguished himself by arresting Nadir Khan, 1852, on which occasion he was wounded, and in the mutiny by suppressing revolt of the Hazarah tribes, 1857; judicial commissioner for the Punjaub and C.B., 1860; published a work on the Thugs, 1837.   [lvi. 299]

THORNTON, GILBERT DE (d. 1295), judge; king's advocate; sent to Ireland on Edward I's service, 1284;

chief-justice of the king's bench, 1290; summoned to parliament, 1295; compiled compendium of Henry de Bracton's work.   [lvi. 300]

THORNTON, HENRY (1760-1815), philanthropist and economist; son of John Thornton (1720-1790) [q. v.]; banker; M.P., Southwark, 1782-1815; independent politician; voted for reform and catholic emancipation; a high authority on finance; supported Pitt's measures; member of the bullion committee, 1811; governor of the Bank of England; published 'Enquiry into the Nature and Effects of the Paper Credit of Great Britain,' 1802; influential member of the 'Clapham Sect'; connected with Wilberforce, who resided with him; organised the Sierra Leone colony; first treasurer of the Society for Missions (afterwards the Church Missionary Society) and of the British and Foreign Bible Society; spent immense sums on charity; author of family prayers and some other works.
                [lvi. 301]

THORNTON, JOHN (1720-1790), supporter of the first generation of 'Evangelicals'; spent large sums in circulating bibles and purchasing advowsons; assisted John Newton and Cowper.   [lvi. 301]

THORNTON, JOHN (1783-1861), commissioner of inland revenue and author; son of Samuel Thornton [q. v.]
                [lvi. 307]

THORNTON, ROBERT (fl. 1440), transcriber of the 'Thornton Romances.'   [lvi. 303]

THORNTON, ROBERT JOHN (1768 ?-1837), botanical and medical writer; son of Bonnell Thornton [q. v.]; M.B. Trinity College, Cambridge, 1793; studied at Guy's Hospital, London; travelled abroad and began to practise in London, 1797; wrote 'New Illustration of the Sexual System of Linnæus,' a great work, 1797-1807, and other botanical works, including 'The British Flora,' 1812, for which he organised an unsuccessful lottery, and numerous medical and other works.   [lvi. 304]

THORNTON, SAMUEL (1755-1838), director of the Bank of England, 1780-1833; son of John Thornton (1720-1790) [q. v.], and brother of Henry Thornton [q. v.]; tory M.P. for Kingston-upon-Hull, 1784-1806, Surrey, 1807-12 and 1813-18; spoke on commercial questions, and defended interests of the Bank of England; governor of Greenwich and president of Guy's Hospital, London.   [lvi. 306]

THORNTON, THOMAS (d. 1814), writer on Turkey; brother of Sir Edward Thornton [q. v.]; was engaged in trade and visited Constantinople; published 'The Present State of Turkey,' 1807.   [lvi. 307]

THORNTON, THOMAS (1757-1823), sportsman; revived falconry and made a sporting tour in the highlands, 1786, publishing an account, 1804; visited France and saw Napoleon, 1802; published 'A Sporting Tour in France,' 1806; died at Paris.   [lvi. 307]

THORNTON, THOMAS (1786-1866), journalist; employed in the custom-house; published works concerning East Indian trade; joined staff of 'The Times,' 1825; wrote 'Notes of Cases in the Ecclesiastical and Maritime Courts,' 1850, reports of parliamentary debates, and other works.   [lvi. 308]

THORNTON, Sir WILLIAM (1779 ?-1840), lieutenant-general; joined the 89th foot, 1796; aide-de-camp to Sir James Henry Craig [q. v.] at Naples and Messina, 1805-6; went to Canada as his military secretary, 1807; commanded the 85th at siege of St. Sebastian and subsequent operations, and was promoted brevet-colonel; commanded a brigade and defeated the Americans at Bladensburg, but being severely wounded became prisoner of war, 1814; distinguished himself and was wounded in attack on New Orleans; K.C.B., 1836; lieutenant-general, 1838; colonel of the 85th, 1839; committed suicide.
                [lvi. 309]

THORNTON, WILLIAM THOMAS (1813-1880), author; son of Thomas Thornton (d. 1814) [q. v.]; secretary for public works to the India office, 1858; C.B., 1873; able adherent and intimate friend of Mill; author of 'Over-population and its Remedy,' 1845 (advocating subdivision of land and deprecating state interference), 'A Plea for Peasant Proprietors,' 1848, 'On Labour,' 1869, and other works.   [lvi. 310]

THORNYCROFT, MARY (1814-1895), sculptor; daughter of John Francis [q.v.], sculptor; married Thomas Thornycroft [q. v.], 1840.   [lvi. 311]

THORNYCROFT, THOMAS (1815–1885), sculptor; studied under John Francis (1780-1861) [q. v.]; executed the group of Commerce on the Albert Memorial, and other statues. [lvi. 312]

THOROLD, ANTHONY WILSON (1825–1895), bishop of Winchester; M.A., 1850, D.D., by diploma, Queen's College, Oxford, 1877; incumbent successively of St. Giles-in-the-Fields, Curzon Chapel, and St. Pancras, London; bishop of Rochester, 1877-90, of Winchester, 1890-5; author of devotional works. [lvi. 312]

THOROLD, THOMAS (1600-1664.) [See CARWELL.]

THOROTON, ROBERT (1623-1678), antiquary; J.P. at the Restoration; enforced stringently the conventicle laws; published 'Antiquities of Nottinghamshire,' 1677. [lvi. 313]

THOROTON, THOMAS (1723-1784), politician; political agent of the Duke of Rutland and M.P., Boroughbridge, 1757, Newark, 1761; corresponded with John Manners, marquis of Granby [q. v.]; secretary to the board of ordnance, 1763. [lvi. 314]

THORP, CHARLES (1783-1862), first warden of Durham University; son of Robert Thorp [q. v.], archdeacon of Durham; M.A.,1806, and D.D., 1835, University College, Oxford; fellow, 1803; rector of Ryton; supporter of savings banks; archdeacon of Durham, 1831; first appointed warden of Durham University, 1833. [lvi. 314]

THORP, ROBERT (1736-1812), archdeacon of Durham; senior wrangler, Peterhouse, Cambridge, 1758; M.A., 1761; author of 'Excerpta quædam e Newtoni Principiis,' 1765, and other works. [lvi. 314]

THORPE, BENJAMIN (1782-1870), Anglo-Saxon scholar; studied at Copenhagen under Rask, and published Rask's 'Anglo-Saxon Grammar' in English, 1830; edited and translated 'Cædmon's Metrical Paraphrase of . . . the Scriptures,' 1832; published 'Ancient Laws and Institutes of England,' 1840; an edition of 'Florence of Worcester,'1848-9, 'Anglo-Saxon Poems of Beowulf,'1855, 'The Anglo-Saxon Chronicle' for the Rolls Series, 1861, 'Diplomatarium Anglicum Ævi Saxonici,' 1865, and other works; granted a pension of 160l., 1835, raised later to 200l. [lvi. 315]

THORPE, FRANCIS (1595-1665), judge; B.A. St. John's College, Cambridge, 1613; barrister, 1621, and bencher of Gray's Inn, 1632; recorder of Beverley, 1623, of Hull, 1639; made public speech at reception of Charles I there, 1639; witness at Strafford's trial, 1641; colonel in the parliamentary army and 'recruiter' to the Long parliament; judge for the northern circuit, 1649; delivered a 'charge' at York justifying Charles I's execution; judge for the western circuit, 1652; M.P., Beverley, 1654-5, and the West Riding, 1656-8; refused to try the northern insurgents, 1655; was excluded from parliament, 1656; pardoned at the Restoration. [lvi. 316]

THORPE or **THORP**, JOHN DE, BARON THORPE (d. 1324), judge; summoned among the magnates to join expedition to Gascony, 1293; knight of the shire for Norfolk, 1305; attended Edward II's first parliament; received special summons as baron, 1309; justice itinerant and sheriff of Norfolk. [lvi. 318]

THORPE, JOHN (fl. 1570-1610), architect and surveyor; built probably, or had a share in building, Kirby Hall, Northamptonshire, Longford Castle, Wiltshire, and Holland House, Kensington (first design), Rushton Hall, Northamptonshire, and Audley End, Essex; others ascribed to him without sufficient authority; left a 'folio of plans,' mostly drawings from finished buildings; wrongly confused with John of Padua [see PADUA, JOHN OF.] [lvi. 318]

THORPE, JOHN (1682-1750), antiquary; M.A., 1704; M.D., 1710, University College, Oxford; F.R.S., 1705; assisted Sir Hans Sloane [q. v.] in 'Philosophical Transactions'; practised at Rochester and studied antiquities and history of Kent; his collections, 'Registrum Roffense,' published by his son, 1769. [lvi. 320]

THORPE, JOHN (1715-1792), antiquary; son of John Thorpe (1682-1750) [q. v.]; M.A. University College, Oxford, 1738; published 'Custumale Roffense,' 1788. [lvi. 321]

THORPE, ROBERT DE (fl. 1290), judge; justice of the common pleas, 1289. [lvi. 321]

THORPE or **THORP**, ROBERT DE (1294?-1330?), justice itinerant; son of John de Thorpe, baron Thorpe [q. v.] [lvi. 318]

THORPE or **THORP**, SIR ROBERT DE (d. 1372), chancellor; educated at Cambridge; king's serjeant, 1345; second master of Pembroke Hall, Cambridge, 1347-1364; chief-justice of the common pleas, 1356; chancellor, 1371. [lvi. 321]

THORPE, THOMAS (d. 1461), speaker of the House of Commons; M.P., Northamptonshire, 1449; remembrancer and baron of the exchequer, but dismissed by John Tiptoft, earl of Worcester [q. v.], 1452; chosen speaker in the Lancastrian parliament, 1452-3, and privy councillor, 1453; imprisoned, 1453, when Fortescue (while suggesting his release) refused to determine the privileges of parliament; liberated, 1455; baron of the exchequer, 1458; drew up Yorkist attainders in parliament of Coventry, 1459; taken prisoner, 1460, and beheaded by the mob at Haringay. [lvi. 322]

THORPE, THOMAS (1570?-1635?), publisher of Shakespeare's 'Sonnets'; stationer's assistant; there existing then no author's copyright, procured and published Marlowe's translation of the 'First Book of Lucan,' 1600, several plays by Chapman and Ben Jonson, and 'Shakespeare's Sonnets,' 1609, obtained for him probably by W[illiam] H[all]; brought out also other works, including the writings of John Healey [q. v.], prefaced by him with obsequious and fantastic addresses to Healey's patrons. [lvi. 323]

THORPE or **THORP**, SIR WILLIAM DE (fl. 1346-1352), chief-justice of the king's bench, 1346; sentenced to imprisonment and forfeiture for bribery, 1350; second baron of the exchequer, 1352. [lvi. 324]

THORPE, WILLIAM (d. 1407?), Wycliffite; educated at Oxford; tried for heresy by Thomas Arundel [q. v.]; said to have been burnt at Saltwood; author of 'The Examination of William Thorpe' and 'A Short Testament to his Faith.' [lvi. 325]

THRALE, MRS. (1741-1821). [See PIOZZI, HESTER LYNCH.]

THRELKELD, CALEB (1676-1728), botanist; M.A. Glasgow, 1698; M.D. Edinburgh, 1713; lived at Dublin; published 'Synopsis Stirpium Hibernicarum,' 1727. [lvi. 325]

THRING, EDWARD (1821-1887), schoolmaster; educated at Ilminster, Eton, and King's College, Cambridge; Porson prizeman, 1844. and fellow; appointed head-master of Uppingham, 1853; advanced the school to a foremost position; wrote several books on English grammar, to which he attached great importance, making it serve as a basis for what he called 'sentence anatomy,' and wrote on education, including 'The Theory and Practice of Teaching,' 1883, and 'Miscellaneous Addresses,' 1887, characterised by a deep sense of the moral purpose in education; founder of the Headmasters' Conference, 1869; established the first public school mission to the London poor; author of sermons, poems, and other works. [lvi. 325]

THROCKMORTON, FRANCIS (1554-1584), conspirator; nephew of Sir Nicholas Throckmorton [q. v.]; matriculated at Hart Hall, Oxford, 1572; student of the Inner Temple; a zealous catholic; engaged in plots abroad against the English government; arrested in England while organising communications between Mary Queen of Scots and Mendoza and Thomas Morgan (1543-1606?) [q. v.] in Paris, incriminating documents being found at his house, 1583; confessed under torture to furthering Guise's designs upon England; executed at Tyburn. [lvi. 327]

THROCKMORTON, JOB (1545-1601), puritan controversialist; first cousin of Francis Throckmorton [q. v.]; B.A. Oxford; M.P., East Retford, 1572-83, Warwick, 1586-7; assisted John Penry [q. v.] in his campaign against the bishops, 1588, part of the Mar-prelate tracts being secretly printed at his house; indicted for association with religious malcontents, 1590, but acquitted; defended himself from the charge of complicity, and published 'Defence of Throckmorton,' 1594. [lvi. 329]

THROCKMORTON or **THROGMORTON**, SIR JOHN (d. 1445), under-treasurer of England; ancestor of Sir Nicholas Throckmorton [q. v.]; knight of the shire for

Worcestershire, 1414, 1420, 1422, and 1432 ; J.P. ; served the Earl of Warwick in various capacities ; chamberlain of the exchequer and under-treasurer of England, 1440. [lvi. 330]

THROCKMORTON, MICHAEL (*d.* 1558), secretary of Cardinal Pole at Rome ; uncle of Sir Nicholas Throckmorton [q. v.] [lvi. 331]

THROCKMORTON, SIR NICHOLAS (1515-1571), diplomatist : joined household of Catherine Parr, his relative, 1543 ; became a sturdy protestant ; M.P., Malden, 1545, sitting in the House of Commons almost continuously till 1567 ; much liked by Edward VI ; accompanied Somerset to Scotland, 1547 ; knighted ; appointed knight of the privy chamber ; present at the siege of Boulogne, 1549-50 ; signed document giving the crown to Lady Jane Grey, 1553, but appears to have performed useful services for the Princess Mary on Edward VI's death ; sent to the Tower of London on charge of complicity in Wyatt's rebellion, 1554, but acquitted ; on accession of Queen Elizabeth was appointed chief butler, chamberlain of the exchequer, and ambassador to France, 1560, to protest against the assumption of the arms of England ; entered there into friendly relations with Mary Stuart ; reconciled Elizabeth to Mary Stuart's settlement in Scotland ; urged Elizabeth to ally herself with the foreign protestants ; remonstrated with her on proposed marriage with Leicester, 1560 ; captured by the catholics at the battle of Dreux, 1562 ; negotiated the treaty of Troyes, 1564 ; sent to Scotland to prevent Mary Stuart's marriage with Darnley, 1565 ; created M.A. Oxford, 1566 ; was sent again to Mary Stuart, now imprisoned in Lochleven Castle, 1567, but only gained Elizabeth's reproaches ; imprisoned on suspicion of sympathy with the rebellion of the northern catholics, 1569. [lvi. 330]

THROGMORTON. [See THROCKMORTON.]

THROSBY, JOHN (1740-1803), antiquary ; parish clerk of St. Martin's, Leicester ; chief works, ' The Memoirs of the Town and County of Leicester,' 1777, and 'The History . . . of Leicester,' 1791. [lvi. 334]

THRUPP, DOROTHEA ANN (1779-1847), author ; half-sister of Frederick Thrupp [q. v.] [lvi. 336]

THRUPP, FREDERICK (1812-1895), sculptor ; studied at Sass's and the Royal Academy, and visited Italy ; executed a large number of sculptures, including 'The Prodigal Returned,' 1832 (his first exhibit at the Academy), ' Mother and Children,' 1837, ' Arethusa,' 1843, and ' Boys with a Basket of Fruit,' 1844 ; the statue of Sir Thomas Buxton, 1846, and of Wordsworth in Westminster Abbey by him ; carved subjects from the 'Pilgrim's Progress ' and George Herbert's poems ; engraved also designs for illustrations to 'Paradise Lost' and other works. [lvi. 335]

THRUPP, JOHN (1817-1870), historical writer ; nephew of Frederick Thrupp [q. v.]; published ' Historical Law-Tracts,' 1843, and the ' Anglo-Saxon Home,' 1862. [lvi. 336]

THRUPP, JOSEPH FRANCIS (1827-1867), divine ; nephew of Frederick Thrupp [q. v.] ; M.A. Trinity College, Cambridge, 1852 ; fellow ; contributed to the 'Speaker's Commentary ' and to Smith's ' Dictionary of the Bible.' [lvi. 337]

THURCYTEL (*d.* 975), abbot of Crowland ; kinsman probably of Archbishop Oswald of York and friend of St. Dunstan ; restored and endowed the abbey, and obtained charter from King Edgar, still extant. [lvi. 337]

THURKILBI, ROGER DE (*d.* 1260), judge ; itinerant justice in various parts of England ; sat also at Westminster ; described in ' Flores Historiarum' as second to none ; his decisions among the few mentioned in thirteenth-century treatises. [lvi. 337]

THURKILL, THORKILL, or TURGESIUS (*d.* 845), Danish king of North Ireland ; perhaps identical with Ragnar Lodbrok, the half-mythical king of Denmark and Norway ; conquered the north of Ireland and Dublin, 832 ; taken prisoner by Malachy [see MAELSECHLAINN I], and drowned. [lvi. 339]

THURKILL or THORKILL, THE EARL (*fl.* 1012-1023), Danish invader ; commanded Danish fleet, 1009, and led raids in southern and eastern counties of England ; present at murder of Ælfheah [q. v.], 1012 ; en-

tered Ethelred's service, became probably a Christian, and fought against Sweyn ; supported Cnut and took part in battle of Assandun, 1015 ; made Earl of East-Anglia, 1017 ; banished by Cnut, 1021, but made his viceroy in Denmark, 1023. [lvi. 340]

THURLAND, SIR EDWARD (1606-1683), judge ; barrister, Inner Temple, 1634 ; member for Reigate in the Short, Convention, and Restoration parliaments ; recorder of Reigate and Guildford, 1661 ; solicitor to James, duke of York, and knighted, 1665 ; baron of the exchequer, 1673 ; friend of Evelyn and Jeremy Taylor. [lvi. 340]

THURLOE, JOHN (1616-1668), secretary of state ; studied law at Lincoln's Inn and entered the service of Oliver St. John (1598 ?-1673) [q. v.]; filled several posts, and was made secretary to the council of state, 1652 ; took important part in raising Cromwell to the Protectorate ; M.P., Ely, 1654 and 1656, Cambridge University, 1659 ; given charge of intelligence and postal departments, and made member of the council ; acted with great vigilance and success ; spokesman of the government in parliament ; one of those with whom Cromwell was wont to ' lay aside his greatness,' but had little influence on his policy ; desired Cromwell to accept the crown ; was opposed to the military faction ; governor of the Charterhouse, 1657 ; chancellor of Glasgow University, 1658 ; supported government of Richard Cromwell ; accused of arbitrary government by the republican and royal opposition ; relieved of his functions on restoration of Long parliament, 1659, but reappointed secretary of state on readmission of secluded members, 1660 ; accused of high treason at the Restoration, but liberated. His vast correspondence is the chief authority for the history of the Protectorate ; seven volumes were published in 1742. [lvi. 341]

THURLOW, EDWARD, first BARON THURLOW (1731-1806), lord chancellor ; educated at Seckars school, Scarning, and King's school, Canterbury ; Perse scholar at Gonville and Caius College, Cambridge, but removed for misconduct ; barrister, Middle Temple, 1754, treasurer, 1770 ; distinguished himself by his discomfiture of Fletcher Norton [q. v.] in Robinson *v.* Lord Winchilsea, 1758 ; argued for the defendant in Tonson *v.* Collins [see TONSON, JACOB], 1761 ; K.C., 1762 ; M.P., Tamworth, 1765, and recorder, 1769 ; retained for the appellants to the lords in Douglas *v.* Hamilton, when the decision of the court of session was reversed, 1769, and fought a duel with the Duke of Hamilton's agent, Andrew Stuart [q. v.]; appointed solicitor-general, 1770, and attorney-general, 1771 ; overthrew Lord Mansfield's doctrine of perpetual copyright in Donaldson *v.* Becket, 1774, but opposed legislative settlement ; established his fame as constitutionalist ; inflexibly maintained right of England to exert her full might in dispute with American colonies ; made chancellor and Baron Thurlow, 1778 ; established his ascendency over the peers ; refused to listen to Lord Shelburne's representations on the misgovernment of Ireland, 1779 ; acted as king's chancellor ; remained in power during the Rockingham and Shelburne ministries, 1782-3, but was obliged to resign by Fox, 1783 ; resumed office under Pitt ; presided at Warren Hastings's trial, 1788 ; intrigued with George, prince of Wales, against Pitt and was obliged to resign, 1792 ; courted George, prince of Wales, and defended the interests of the slave-trader. His political principles were merely a high view of royal prerogative and an aversion to change. [lvi. 344]

THURLOW, afterwards HOVELL-THURLOW, EDWARD, second BARON THURLOW (1781-1829), minor poet ; son of Thomas Thurlow [q. v.], bishop of Durham ; M.A. Magdalen College, Oxford, 1801 ; clerk of the hanaper ; author of ' Poems,' 1813, and other volumes of verse, including 'Angelica' (an attempt to continue Shakespeare's ' Tempest '), 1822. [lvi. 349]

THURLOW, THOMAS (1737-1791), bishop of Durham ; brother of Edward Thurlow, first Baron Thurlow [q. v.]; fellow of Magdalen College, Oxford, 1759 ; M.A., 1761 ; D.D., 1772 ; dean of St. Paul's, London, 1782-7 ; bishop of Durham, 1787-91. [lvi. 350]

THURMOND, MRS. (*fl.* 1715-1737), actress ; *née* Lewis ; married John Thurmond the younger, dancer in Dublin ; played the original Cosmelia in the ' Doting Lovers,' 1715, and other parts, at Lincoln's Inn Fields, London ; at Drury Lane, London, 1718-32 ; played Desdemona, Lady Macduff, Lady Wronghead in the ' Provoked

Husband' and numerous other parts, some original; acted, 1732, at Goodman's Fields, London, Almira in the 'Mourning Bride,' and again, 1734–7, at Drury Lane, London, Marcia in 'Cato,' Queen in 'Henry VIII' and Richard III,' Lucy Lockit in the 'Beggar's Opera,' Zara in the 'Mourning Bride,' and Queen in Dryden's 'Spanish Friar.' [lvi. 350]

THURNAM, JOHN (1810–1873), craniologist; quaker; F.R.C.P., 1859; M.D. Aberdeen, 1846; medical superintendent at asylum, Devizes; published 'Observations . . . on the Statistics of Insanity,' 1843, and 'Two Principal Forms of Ancient British and Gaulish Skulls,' 1865, and other works. [lvi. 351]

THURSBY, JOHN DE (d. 1373). [See THORESBY.]

THURSTAN or **TURSTIN** (d. 1140), archbishop of York; native of Bayeux; prebendary of St. Paul's, London; clerk and favourite of William Rufus; secretary of Henry I; elected archbishop of York, 1114, but his consecration withheld by Ralph, archbishop of Canterbury, on account of his refusal to profess obedience; supported by successive popes in opposition to Henry I; visited Louis VI, 1118; visited Pope Calixtus in France, 1119, and, contrary to his promise, was consecrated by him, and bull issued freeing church of York from the profession; was forbidden by Henry I to return to England; rendered useful services in negotiations between England and France, and was reinvested with archbishopric by Henry I, 1120; returned to England, 1121; refused to acknowledge the new archbishop of Canterbury, William of Corbeil (d. 1126) [q. v.], as primate of all England, 1123, both archbishops visiting Rome, 1123 and 1125, when, though the dispute was not settled, a legatine commission was granted to Archbishop William; failed in obliging John, bishop of Glasgow, to acknowledge the authority of York; forbidden to bear his cross erect or to place the crown on the king's head at Westminster, 1126; consecrated Robert (d. 1159) [q. v.] as bishop of St. Andrews without any profession of obedience, 1128; gave land for founding of Fountains Abbey, 1132; on David of Scotland preparing to invade England, 1137, persuaded him to accept truce; on the invasion, 1138, animated the lords to resist the enemy, and gathered forces at York which beat the Scots at the battle of the Standard; exhorted by St. Bernard not to resign his see; entered the Cluniac order, and died at Pontefract priory. He was largely concerned in the growth of monasticism in the north; three tracts are attributed to him. [lvi. 352]

THURSTON, JOHN (1774–1822), draughtsman; worked under James Heath (1757–1834) [q. v.]; designer of highly successful book illustrations, including those to Thomson's 'Seasons,' 1805, and Shakespeare's works, 1814. [lvi. 357]

THURSTON, SIR JOHN BATES (1836–1897), colonial governor; after several adventures, including shipwreck at Samoa, became consul for Fiji, 1869; obtained remarkable influence, and was made colonial secretary of the new colony, 1874; lieutenant-governor, 1886; governor of the Western Pacific, 1887; K.C.M.G., 1887; F.L.S. and F.R.G.S. [lvi. 357]

THURTELL, JOHN (1794–1824), murderer; son of the mayor of Norwich; failed as a bombasin manufacturer and took to prize-fighting and gambling; lost money, amongst others, to William Weare, whom he murdered on the St. Albans road, 1823; was convicted, his accomplices turning king's evidence, in spite of a powerful speech in his own defence, and hanged. [lvi. 358]

THURVAY, SIMON (fl. 1184–1200). [See TOURNAY, SIMON OF.]

THWAITES, EDWARD (1667–1711), Anglo-Saxon scholar; M.A. Queen's College, Oxford, 1697; ordained and elected fellow and 'Anglo-Saxon preceptor,' 1698; edited 'Dionysii Orbis Descriptio,' 1697; published 'Heptateuchus,' 'Liber Job et Evangelium Nicodemi Anglo-Saxonice,' 1698, 'Notæ in Anglo-Saxonum nummos,' 1708, and other works; appointed regius professor of Greek, 1708, and Whyte's professor of moral philosophy, 1708; received grant of money from Queen Anne. [lvi. 360]

THWAITES, GEORGE HENRY KENDRICK (1811–1882), botanist and entomologist; studied cryptogams and made important observations on diatoms; contributed to the 'Gardeners' Chronicle'; made superintendent of botanical gardens, Peradeniya, Ceylon, 1849, where he did valuable work on flowering plants; applied botany to tropical agriculture; published 'Enumeratio Plantarum Zeylaniæ,' 1859–64; F.R.S., 1865; C.M.G., 1878. [lvi. 361]

THWAYT, WILLIAM OF (d. 1154). [See FITZ-HERBERT, WILLIAM.]

THWENG, MARMADUKE, first BARON THWENG (d. 1322), grandson of Robert de Thweng [q. v.]; prominent in the Scots wars; summoned to parliament as baron, 1307. [lvi. 362]

THWENG, THWING, or **TWENG,** ROBERT DE (1205 ?–1268 ?), opponent of Henry III's foreign ecclesiastics, one of whom had been intruded into his living of Kirkleatham; organised riots, 1232; justified his conduct before Henry III and obtained satisfaction on a visit to Pope Gregory IX, 1239; joined Richard of Cornwall's crusade, 1240. [lvi. 362]

THYER, ROBERT (1709–1781), Chetham librarian, 1732, and editor of Butler's 'Remains,' 1759; praised by Dr. Johnson; B.A. Brasenose College, Oxford, 1730. [lvi. 363]

THYNNE, FRANCIS (1545 ?–1608), or 'Botevile,' Lancaster herald; son of William Thynne [q. v.]; member of Lincoln's Inn, 1561; admitted attorney; imprisoned for debt, 1573–6; employed with others in revising and continuing Holinshed's 'Chronicle'; criticised Speght's 'Chaucer' in letter entitled 'Animadversions,' 1599; assisted him in a second edition; created Lancaster herald, 1602; left numerous works in manuscript, some of which have been printed, including 'The Perfect Ambassadovr.' [lvi. 363]

THYNNE, SIR JOHN (d. 1580), builder of Longleat; introduced at court by his uncle William Thynne [q. v.]; became steward to Somerset; accompanied him in his Scottish expedition, 1547; wounded at Pinkie, 1547; knighted and allowed to quarter the Scots lion on his arms, 1547; imprisoned on the fall of Somerset, 1551–2; continued a zealous protestant through Mary's reign; controller of Princess Elizabeth's household; M.P., Wiltshire, 1559, Great Bedwin, 1562–3, and Heytesbury, 1572, and J.P.; built Longleat House, probably from his own plans, 1567–79; entertained Queen Elizabeth, 1575. [lvi. 365]

THYNNE, JOHN ALEXANDER, fourth MARQUIS OF BATH (1831–1896), great-grandson of Thomas Thynne, first marquis of Bath [q. v.]; of Eton and Christ Church, Oxford; lord-lieutenant of Wiltshire, 1889; ambassador at Lisbon, 1858, and at Vienna, 1867. [lvi. 366]

THYNNE, THOMAS, OF LONGLEAT (1648–1682), 'Tom of Ten Thousand'; of Eton and Christ Church, Oxford; succeeded to Longleat on death of his uncle, Sir James Thynne, 1670; M.P., Wiltshire, 1670–82; attached himself first to James, duke of York, but afterwards to Monmouth; the Issachar of 'Absalom and Achitophel'; presented petition to Charles II for the punishment of popish plotters, 1680; one of the grand jury of Middlesex who ignored bill against Shaftesbury, 1681; removed from command of Wiltshire militia for his hostility to the court, 1681; married Elizabeth, heiress of the Percy estates [see PERCY, LADY ELIZABETH], 1681, and was murdered by Königsmark, one of her suitors. [lvi. 367]

THYNNE, SIR THOMAS, first VISCOUNT WEYMOUTH (1640–1714), matriculated from Christ Church, Oxford, 1657; envoy to Sweden, 1666; M.P., Oxford University, 1674–8, Tamworth, 1678–82; second baronet on death of his father, Sir Henry Thynne, 1681; owner of Longleat on murder of his cousin Thomas Thynne (1648–1682) [q. v.], and created Baron Thynne and Viscount Weymouth, 1682; one of the four lords dispatched to invite William of Orange to England, 1688; voted for a regency; opposed William III's government; privy councillor in Queen Anne's reign; custos rotulorum of Wiltshire. [lvi. 368]

THYNNE, THOMAS, third VISCOUNT WEYMOUTH and first MARQUIS OF BATH (1734–1796), statesman; travelled on the continent and fell into dissipated courses; joined the Bedford party and was made viceroy of Ireland, 1765, never going there, however; secretary for northern department in Grafton's ministry, 1768; neglected duties of his office, but made powerful speeches in parliament; gained George III's favour by his vigour in suppressing the Wilkes riots; transferred to the southern department, on Shelburne's resignation; suddenly left office when war became imminent with Spain, concerning dispute as to the Falkland islands, 1770 ; was reappointed, 1775, and represented government in the Lords ; showed hesitation and want of foresight in foreign affairs ; declared motion for withdrawing troops from America an infringement of the prerogative ; was proposed for the treasury by the king and made K.G., 1778 ; took northern department in addition to his own office, 1779, and resigned both the same year ; received no office from Pitt, 1783 ; hon. LL.D. Cambridge, 1769 ; master of Trinity House, 1770 ; governor of the Charterhouse, London, 1778 ; created Marquis of Bath, 1789.   [lvi. 369]

THYNNE, WILLIAM (*d.* 1546), editor of Chaucer's works ; '*alias* Botevile' ; clerk of the kitchen and of the green cloth to Henry VIII, and recipient of numerous grants and appointments ; enthusiastic student of Chaucer and first editor of his works, 1532, with dedication to Henry VIII, written by Sir Brian Tuke [q. v.]   [lvi. 373]

TIBETOT. [See TIPTOFT.]

TICHBORNE, CHIDIOCK (1558 ?–1586), conspirator ; an ardent papist ; joined the Babington conspirators, 1586, in plot to assassinate Queen Elizabeth ; being arrested, pleaded guilty, and was executed.   [lvi. 374]

TICHBORNE, SIR HENRY (1581 ?–1667), governor of Drogheda ; captain of a regiment of foot in Ireland ; made governor of Lifford ; knighted, 1623 ; appointed commissioner of plantations in Londonderry, receiving himself large grants, 1623 ; on outbreak of rebellion, 1641, was made governor of Drogheda and defended the town heroically against the insurgents for four months ; on its relief by Ormonde captured with him Dundalk by storm, 1642 ; sworn lord-justice, 1642 ; returned to England and was taken prisoner by the parliament, bearing back instructions to Ormonde for a peace with the catholics, 1645 ; being liberated on exchange became again governor of Drogheda ; fought gallantly at Dungan Hill, 1647 ; obtained grant of Beaulieu, co. Louth.   [lvi. 375]

TICHBORNE, SIR HENRY, BARON FERRARD (1663–1731), grandson of Sir Henry Tichborne (1581 ?–1667) [q. v.] ; created Baron Ferrard of Beaulieu, 1715.
    [lvi. 376]

TICHBORNE, ROBERT (*d.* 1682), regicide ; a linen-draper and captain in the London trained bands, 1643 ; lieutenant of the Tower of London, 1647 ; extreme republican and independent ; signed Charles I's death-warrant ; commissioner to settle government of Scotland, 1651 ; sat for London in the Little parliament and in Cromwell's House of Lords ; knighted, 1655, and made lord mayor of London, 1656 ; one of the 'conservators of liberty' set up by the army, 1659 ; sentenced to death at the Restoration, and imprisoned for life ; author of religious works.   [lvi. 377]

TICKELL, MRS. MARY (1756 ?–1787). [See LINLEY, MARY.]

TICKELL, RICHARD (1751–1793), pamphleteer and dramatist ; grandson of Thomas Tickell [q. v.] ; barrister, Middle Temple ; obtained a pension by writing for the government, and commissionership in the stamp office, 1781 ; produced 'The Camp' at Drury Lane, London, 1778, 'Anticipation' ; a satirical forecast of parliamentary proceedings, 1778, and other works ; connected through his wife with Sheridan, he transferred his pen to Fox's party ; elected member of Brooks's Club, 1785 ; killed himself by jumping from a window.   [lvi. 378]

TICKELL, THOMAS (1686–1740), poet ; M.A. Queen's College, Oxford, 1709 ; fellow, 1710 ; published 'Oxford,' a poem, 1707 ; professor of poetry at Oxford, 1711 ; produced a poem much praised by Pope and Addison 'On the Prospect of Peace,' 1712 ; contributed verse to the 'Guardian,' 'Spectator,' and other publications ; employed by Addison when secretary to the lord-lieutenant of Ireland, 1714 ; published translation of the first book of the 'Iliad' at the same time as Pope, which occasioned the quarrel between Pope and Addison, 1715 ; made under-secretary by Addison, now secretary of state, 1717 ; edited Addison's 'Works,' publishing in the first volume his celebrated elegy on the death of Addison, 1721 ; published 'Kensington Gardens,' 1722 ; made secretary to the lords justices in Ireland, 1724, when friendly intercourse passed between him and Swift.   [lvi. 380]

TIDCOMB or **TIDCOMBE,** JOHN (1642–1713), lieutenant-general ; servitor at Oriel College, Oxford, 1661 ; commanded an Irish regiment and served in Portugal ; lieutenant-general, 1708 ; member of the 'Kit-Cat Club.'
    [lvi. 382]

TIDD, WILLIAM (1760–1847), legal writer ; barrister, Inner Temple, 1813 ; author of 'Practice of the Court of King's Bench,' 1790 and 1794, and other legal works.
    [lvi. 382]

TIDEY, ALFRED (1808–1892), miniature-painter ; executed miniatures for Queen Victoria ; exhibited at the Royal Academy.   [lvi. 383]

TIDEY, HENRY (1814–1872), water-colour painter ; brother of Alfred Tidey [q. v.] ; painter of portraits and later of historical and poetical subjects ; member of the Society of Painters in Water-colours.   [lvi. 383]

TIDFERTH or **TIDFRITH** (*d.* 823 ?), ninth bishop of Dunwich ; succeeded, *c.* 798 ; made profession of obedience to Ethelheard, archbishop of Canterbury ; attended council at Clovesho, 803.   [lvi. 383]

TIDY, CHARLES MEYMOTT (1843–1892), sanitary chemist ; M.B. Aberdeen, 1866 ; professor of chemistry at the London Hospital, 1876 ; reader of medical jurisprudence to the Inns of Court ; public analyst and deputy medical officer of health for London ; invented new method of analysing water, 1879, and published numerous works on sanitary and chemical science and legal medicine.   [lvi. 384]

TIERNAN or **TIGHEARNAN,** O'ROURKE (*d.* 1172). [See O'ROURKE.]

TIERNEY, GEORGE (1761–1830), statesman ; was educated at Eton and Peterhouse, Cambridge ; LL.B., 1784 ; barrister ; M.P., Colchester, 1788, Southwark, 1796 ; opposed Pitt ; continued his attendance in the house on withdrawal of Fox and his party, 1798, and deeply offended them ; fought duel with Pitt, who had accused him of obstruction ; attacked Pitt's finance, but became treasurer of the navy in Addington's ministry, 1802 ; made president of the board of control, 1806 ; returned to opposition on retirement of Grenville, and led the party, 1817–21 ; joined Canning as master of the mint, and quitted office finally with Goderich, 1828.   [lvi. 385]

TIERNEY, MARK ALOYSIUS (1795–1862), Roman catholic historian ; ordained priest, 1818 ; became chaplain to twelfth Duke of Norfolk, 1824 ; F.S.A., 1833 ; F.R.S., 1841 ; opposed Cardinal Wiseman and papal domination ; edited Dodd's 'Church History of England,' 1839–43.   [lvi. 386]

TIERNEY, SIR MATTHEW JOHN, first baronet (1776–1845), physician ; supporter of vaccination ; M.D. Glasgow, 1802 ; practised at Brighton ; appointed physician to George IV and William IV ; created baronet, 1818.   [lvi. 387]

TIFFIN, WILLIAM (1695 ?–1759), stenographer ; B.A. Caius College, Cambridge, 1716 ; chaplain of Wigston's Hospital, Leicester ; author of 'A New Help and Improvement of the Art of Swift-Writing,' 1751.
    [lvi. 388]

TIGHE, MRS. MARY (1772–1810), poet ; *née* Blachford ; married her cousin, Henry Tighe, 1793 ; published 'Psyche,' 1805.   [lvi. 388]

TIGHEARNACH (*d.* 1088). [See O'BRAEIN.]

TILBURY, GERVASE OF (*fl.* 1211). [See GERVASE.]

TILLEMANS, PETER (1684–1734), painter and draughtsman ; painted country seats and sporting subjects, and made drawings for Bridge's 'History of Northamptonshire.'   [lvi. 389]

TILLESLEY, RICHARD (1582–1621), archdeacon of Rochester ; M.A., 1607, and D.D., 1617, St. John's College, Oxford ; archdeacon of Rochester, 1614, prebendary, 1615 ; published 'Animadversions upon Mr. Selden's "History of Tithes,"' 1619.   [lvi. 389]

TILLEY, SIR SAMUEL LEONARD (1818–1896), Canadian statesman ; born at Gagetown, New Brunswick ; became leader of the liberals in the New Brunswick legislature and carried the union, 1866 ; C.B., 1867 ; held office in the Macdonald ministries, 1868–73 and 1878–1885 ; lieutenant-governor of New Brunswick, 1873–8 and 1885–93 ; as minister of finance formulated the 'national policy' ; K.C.M.G., 1879.   [lvi. 390]

TILLINGHAST, JOHN (1604–1655), Fifth-monarchy man; B.A. Caius College, Cambridge, 1625; rector of Streat, 1637, but became an independent; held the rectory of Trunch, Norfolk; remonstrated with Cromwell, 1655; published religious works. [lvi. 391]

TILLOCH, ALEXANDER (1759–1825), inventor (1784) of stereotyping; son of John Tulloch; changed his name to Tilloch after 1787; editor of the 'Star,' 1789–1821; established the 'Philosophical Magazine,' 1797; joined the Sandemanians and wrote on scriptural prophecy. [lvi. 391]

TILLOTSON, JOHN (1630–1694), archbishop of Canterbury; born at Old Haugh End, Halifax; descendant of the Tilstons of Cheshire and son of a prosperous and dissenting cloth-worker; B.A. Clare Hall, Cambridge, 1650; fellow, 1651; M.A., 1654; D.D., 1666; became chaplain to Sir Edmond Prideaux [q. v.] and tutor to his son, 1656 or 1657; deprived of his fellowship, 1661; ordained without subscription by Thomas Sydserf [q. v.], probably c. 1661; auditor on nonconforming side at Savoy conference; rector of Kedington, 1663, but resigned, 1664; preacher at Lincoln's Inn and lecturer at St. Lawrence Jewry, London; his pulpit ceasing to be a puritan stronghold, and his innovation in style, introducing clearness greater brevity, and addresses to reason and feeling, being very welcome; preached on 'The Wisdom of being Religious,' 1664, against atheism, and published his 'Rule of Faith,' 1666, against the Roman catholics; chaplain to Charles II; dean of Canterbury, 1670, and canon of St. Paul's, London, 1675; drafted a bill with Baxter for comprehending the nonconformists; created much stir by his sermon at Whitehall denying right to make proselytes from 'the establish'd religion,' 1680; made dean of St. Paul's, London, and exercised archiepiscopal jurisdiction on suspension of Sancroft, 1689; appointed archbishop of Canterbury, 1691; published four lectures on the Socinian controversy, delivered in 1679–80, as answer to doubts of his orthodoxy; buried in St. Lawrence Jewry, London. He was perhaps the only primate who took first rank in his day as a preacher. [lvi. 392]

TILLY, WILLIAM, OF SELLING (d. 1494). [See CELLING, WILLIAM.]

TILNEY, CHARLES (1561–1586), cousin of Edmund Tilney [q. v.]; took part in Babington's conspiracy and suffered death. [lvi. 399]

TILNEY, EDMUND (d. 1610), master of the revels in the royal household, 1579–c. 1609; controlled the court entertainments and licensed plays for the public; wrote 'A Briefe and Pleasant Discourse of Duties in Mariage,' 1568. [lvi. 399]

TILNEY, JOHN (fl. 1430), Carmelite friar; doctor of theology at Cambridge; wrote several treatises. [lvi. 399]

TILSLEY, JOHN (1614–1684), puritan divine; M.A. Edinburgh, 1637; present at the taking of Preston, 1643; made vicar of Deane, Lancashire, 1643; one of the ordaining ministers; petitioned parliament to set up presbyterianism in Lancashire, and was one of the principal and most intolerant members; ejected, 1662, and silenced for nonconformity, 1678. [lvi. 400]

TILSON, HENRY (1659–1695), portrait-painter; studied under Lely; committed suicide. [lvi. 400]

TILT, JOHN EDWARD (1815–1893), physician; M.D. Paris, 1839; original fellow of the Obstetrical Society and president, 1874–5; published works on diseases of women. [lvi. 401]

TIMBERLAKE, HENRY (d. 1626), traveller; visited Jerusalem, 1602; member of the Company of Merchant Adventurers, formed 1612; wrote a 'True and Strange Discourse of the Trauailes of two English Pilgrimes,' 1603. [lvi. 401]

TIMBERLAKE, HENRY (fl. 1765), born in Virginia; engaged in subduing the Cherokee Indians; brought three chiefs to England to see George III, 1762; published 'Memoirs,' 1765. [lvi. 401]

TIMBRELL, HENRY (1806–1849), sculptor; gold medallist and travelling student of the Royal Academy; executed groups and busts. [lvi. 402]

TIMBRELL, JAMES C. (1810–1850), painter; brother of Henry Timbrell [q. v.] [lvi. 402]

TIMBS, JOHN (1801–1875), author; apprenticed to a printer and druggist at Dorking; editor of the 'Mirror of Literature,' 1827–38, and of other periodicals, and sub-editor of the 'Illustrated London News,' 1842–58; F.S.A., 1854; published anecdotic works. [lvi. 402]

TIMPERLEY, CHARLES H. (1794–1846?), writer on typography; enlisted in the 33rd foot; wounded at Waterloo; became a printer; published 'Songs of the Press,' 1833, 'The Printer's Manual,' 1838, and 'A Dictionary of Printers and Printing,' 1839. [lvi. 403]

TINDAL, MATTHEW (1657–1733), deist; B.A., 1676, and D.C.L. Exeter College, Oxford, 1685; fellow at All Souls College, Oxford, 1678; turned catholic during James II's reign; advocate at Doctors' Commons; gave opinion that pirates could be tried notwithstanding commission from James II, 1693; published 'The Rights of the Christian Church asserted,' 1706, which excited many replies, and was burnt with Sacheverell's sermon, 1710, by order of the House of Commons; attacked Walpole for resigning, 1717; published 'Christianity as Old as the Creation,' 1730, expounding rationalistic opinions; author of several other works or pamphlets. [lvi. 403]

TINDAL, NICHOLAS (1688–1774), historical writer; nephew of Matthew Tindal [q. v.]; M.A. Exeter College, Oxford, 1713; rector of Hatford, 1716; vicar of Great Waltham, 1721; was appointed master of the Royal Free School at Chelmsford, 1731, and chaplain to Greenwich Hospital, 1738; published a translation and continuation of Rapin's 'History of England,' 1725–45, and an abridgment of Spence's 'Polymetis,' 1764, and some other works. [lvi. 405]

TINDAL, SIR NICHOLAS CONYNGHAM (1776–1846), chief-justice of the common pleas; great-grandson of Nicholas Tindal [q. v.]; M.A. Trinity College, Cambridge, 1802; fellow, 1801; chancellor's gold medallist; hon. D.C.L. Oxford, 1814; successfully claimed in Ashford v. Thornton right of wager of battle for his client; counsel for Queen Caroline; M.P. Wigtown Burghs, 1824, Harwich, 1826; solicitor-general and knighted, 1826; chief-justice of the common pleas, 1829. [lvi. 406]

TINDAL, WILLIAM (d. 1526). [See TYNDALE.]

TINDAL, WILLIAM (1756–1804), antiquary; grandson of Nicholas Tindal [q. v.]; fellow of Trinity College, Oxford, 1778; M.A., 1778; chaplain of the Tower of London; published a history of Evesham, 1794, and other works; committed suicide. [lvi. 407]

TINMOUTH, JOHN DE (fl. 1366), historian; vicar of Tynemouth and Benedictine monk at St. Albans; author of 'Historia Aurea a Creatione ad Tempus Edwardi III,' and other works. [lvi. 408]

TINNEY, JOHN (d. 1761), engraver. [lvi. 408]

TIPPER, JOHN (d. 1713), almanac-maker; commenced the 'Ladies' Diary' (almanac and serial collection of mathematical papers), 1704, editing it himself till 1713; founded 'Great Britain's Diary,' 1710. [lvi. 408]

TIPPING, WILLIAM (1598–1649), author; B.A. Queen's College, Oxford, 1617; joined the parliament and took the covenant; took living of Shabbington; published 'A Discourse of Eternity,' 1633, and other works. [lvi. 408]

TIPTOFT or **TIBETOT,** JOHN, BARON TIPTOFT (1375?–1443); descended from Robert de Tiptoft [q. v.]; began life in service of Earl of Derby; was rewarded by various grants; M.P., Huntingdonshire, 1403–4, 1404, and 1405–6; elected speaker, 1406, his tenure of office being marked by important advances in the power of the Commons and by persecution of the lollards; held many appointments at court and abroad; received forfeited lands of Owen Glendower; treasurer of England, 1408; made seneschal of Aquitaine by Henry V, 1415; negotiated alliances with foreign princes; appointed treasurer of Normandy, 1417; negotiated the peace, 1419; member of the privy council during Henry VI's minority; summoned to parliament as Baron Tiptoft, 1426; steward of the household, 1428–32; commanded troops in France, 1429 and 1436. [lvi. 409]

TIPTOFT or **TIBETOT,** JOHN, EARL OF WORCESTER (1427?–1470), son of John, baron Tiptoft [q. v.]; educated at Balliol College, Oxford; created Earl of Worcester, 1449; a Yorkist; appointed treasurer of the exchequer, 1452; joint-commissioner to keep guard by sea

1454 ; deputy of Ireland, 1457 ; chief-justice of North Wales, 1461, on Edward IV's accession ; held various high offices ; failed to prevent escape of Queen Margaret, 1463 ; as deputy of Ireland executed the Earl of Desmond and two of his infant sons, 1467, and, as constable of England, 1462–7 and 1470, was guilty of great cruelties, including the execution of John, earl of Oxford, 1462, Sir Ralph Grey, and Lancastrians, 1464, and twenty of Clarence's party, taken at sea, who were hanged and impaled, 1470 ; called 'the butcher of England' ; on flight of Edward IV was taken and executed. He was eulogised by Caxton and famous for his scholarship, having studied Latin at Padua, heard John Argyropoulos lecture on Greek at Florence, and translated Cicero's 'De Amicitia' and 'The Declaration of Nobleness,' by Buonaccorso.
[lvi. 411]

TIPTOFT, ROBERT DE, sometimes styled BARON TIBETOT or TIPTOFT (d. 1298), governor of various castles ; accompanied Edward I to the Holy Land ; suppressed revolt of Rhys ab Mereduc, 1287–8 ; served in France and in Scotland. [lvi. 414]

TIRECHAN (fl. 7th cent.), bishop and saint ; wrote 'Collections' relating to St. Patrick. [lvi. 414]

TIREL or **TYRRELL**, WALTER (fl. 1100), reputed slayer of William Rufus ; son and successor of Walter Tirel, lord of Poix in Picardy ; was generally believed to have shot the arrow that killed William Rufus, but denied having done so. [lvi. 414]

TIRWHIT, SIR ROBERT (d. 1428). [See TYRWHITT.]

TISDAL, PHILIP (1703–1777), Irish politician ; B.A. Dublin, 1722 ; entered the Middle Temple, 1728 ; called to the Irish bar, 1733 ; M.A. Dublin University, 1739–76 Armagh, 1776 ; succeeded his father as registrar of the court of chancery, 1742 ; judge of the prerogative court, 1745 ; solicitor-general, 1751 ; attorney-general, 1760 ; principal secretary of state and manager of the House of Commons, 1763 ; died in Belgium. [lvi. 415]

TISDAL or **TISDALL**, WILLIAM (1669–1735), controversialist and acquaintance of Swift ; fellow of Trinity College, Dublin, 1696 ; D.D., 1707 ; lost Swift's friendship by his courtship of 'Stella,' 1704 ; vicar of Belfast, 1712 ; wrote against the dissenters. [lvi. 416]

TISDALE, **TYSDALL**, or **TYSDALE**, JOHN (fl. 1550–1563), printer and stationer ; original member of the Company of Stationers. [lvi. 416]

TITCOMB, JONATHAN HOLT (1819–1887), bishop of Rangoon ; of St. Peter's College, Cambridge ; M.A., 1845 ; D.D. honoris causa, 1877 ; perpetual curate of St. Andrew-the-Less, Cambridge, 1845–59 ; vicar of St. Stephen's, South Lambeth, 1861, and lectured in London ; rural dean of Clapham and honorary canon of Winchester ; first bishop of Rangoon, 1877–82 ; bishop for Northern and Central Europe, 1884–6 ; published 'Personal Recollections of Burma,' 1880, and religious works.
[lvi. 417]

TITE, SIR WILLIAM (1798 – 1873), architect ; assisted David Laing (1774–1856) [q. v.] ; built the Royal Exchange, London, 1844, numerous railway stations, and London edifices ; president of the Architectural Society ; M.P., Bath, 1855–73 ; opposed Scott's Gothic government offices ; largely concerned in construction of the Thames embankment ; knighted, 1869 ; C.B., 1870 ; F.R.S., 1835 ; F.S.A., 1839. [lvi. 418]

TITIENS (correctly **TIETJENS**), TERESA CAROLINE JOHANNA (1831–1877), operatic singer ; of Hungarian birth ; a soprano of great sweetness and power, her best parts including Lucrezia, Semiramide, and Lenora ; singer of sacred music. [lvi. 419]

TITLEY, WALTER (1700–1768), envoy extraordinary at Copenhagen ; of Westminster and Trinity College, Cambridge ; M.A., 1726 ; wrote Latin verses and 'imitated' Horace. [lvi. 419]

TITUS, SILIUS (1623 ?–1704), politician ; of Christ Church, Oxford, and the Middle Temple ; took part in the siege of Donnington Castle on the parliament side, 1644 ; one of Charles I's household, Isle of Wight, 1647 ; became royalist and devised plans for Charles I's escape ; entered service of Charles II ; but after the battle of Worcester applied to Cromwell for leave to return to England ; correspondent of Clarendon ; intermediary between the

royalists and levellers, and intimate with Edward Sexby [q. v.] ; made keeper of Deal Castle at the Restoration ; became one of the leaders of the House of Commons during the excitement of the popish plot and Extension Bill ; very zealous against Lord Stafford ; a humorous and vigorous speaker ; saw through James II's favour to the dissenters, but became privy councillor, 1688 ; transferred his allegiance to William III ; M.P., Ludlow, 1690–5.
[lvi. 420]

TOBIAS (d. 726), ninth bishop of Rochester ; consecrated, c. 696 ; pupil of Theodore and Hadrian.
[lvi. 422]

TOBIN, GEORGE (1768–1838), rear-admiral ; brother of John Tobin [q. v.] ; was present at the action in West Indies, 12 April 1782 ; captured the Cyane, 1805 ; co-operated with the army in France and Spain, 1813–14 ; C.B., 1815 ; rear-admiral, 1837. [lvi. 422]

TOBIN, JOHN (1770–1804), dramatist ; brother of George Tobin [q. v.], solicitor ; author of the 'Honey Moon,' 1805, the 'Curfew,' 1807, the 'School for Authors,' 1808, and other plays, all posthumous. [lvi. 422]

TOCLIVE, RICHARD (d. 1188). [See RICHARD OF ILCHESTER.]

TOD, JAMES (1782–1835), colonel and Indian diplomatist ; obtained East Indian cadetship and went to Bengal, 1799 ; lieutenant, Bengal infantry, 1800 ; surveyed and collected topographical information ; organised intelligence department at Rowtah during operations against the Pindharis, 1817 ; appointed political agent in western Rajput states, 1818 ; resigned, 1822 ; lieutenant-colonel, 1826 ; published 'Annals and Antiquities of Rajasthan,' 1829–32, and 'Travels in Western India,' posthumous, 1839. [lvi. 424]

TODD, ALPHEUS (1821–1884), librarian of the parliament of Canada ; published 'The Practice and Privileges of the two Houses of Parliament,' 1840, and 'On Parliamentary Government in England,' 1867–9, and other works ; librarian of the parliament of the Dominion, 1867–84 ; minister of the 'Catholic Apostolic Church.'
[lvi. 425]

TODD, ELLIOTT D'ARCY (1808–1845), British resident at Herat ; lieutenant in the Bengal artillery, 1823 ; took part in second siege of Bhartpur, 1825 ; studied Persian and became instructor in artillery to the Persian army, 1834 ; military secretary to Sir Henry Lindesay Bethune [q. v.] at Tabriz, 1836 ; accompanied John McNeill [q. v.] to Herat, 1838, and took despatches thence to Simla by Kandahar and Peshawar ; military secretary to Sir William Hay Macnaghten [q. v.] when envoy to the amir of Afghanistan, and made treaty with Shah Kamran at Herat ; political agent at Herat, 1841, when, having proofs of Kamran's bad faith, he withdrew to Candahar ; angrily dismissed by Lord Auckland, the governor-general ; rejoined his regiment ; promoted captain and killed at Firozshah. [lvi. 426]

TODD, HENRY JOHN (1763–1845), editor of Milton and author ; chorister at Magdalen College, Oxford ; tutor and lecturer at Hertford College, Oxford ; M.A., 1786 ; held various livings ; librarian at Lambeth Palace, and royal chaplain ; rector of Settrington, 1820, prebendary of York, 1830, and archdeacon, 1832 ; published the 'Poetical Works of Milton,' 1801, and edition of Spenser, 1805, and of 'Johnson's Dictionary,' 1818, and numerous original works, including a life of Cranmer, 1831.
[lvi. 428]

TODD, HUGH (1658 ?–1728), author ; B.A. Queen's College, Oxford, 1677 ; fellow of University College, 1678 ; M.A., 1679, and D.D., 1692 ; prebendary of Carlisle, 1685 ; rector of Arthuret and vicar of Penrith St. Andrew ; quarrelled with his bishop, William Nicolson [q. v.], and was excommunicated, but continued to officiate ; published poems and miscellaneous works, including translations from Plutarch and Nepos. [lvi. 430]

TODD, JAMES HENTHORN (1805–1869), Irish scholar and regius professor of Hebrew at Dublin ; brother of Robert Bentley Todd [q. v.] ; B.A. Dublin, 1825 ; fellow, 1831, and tutor ; D.D., 1840 ; contributed to various publications ; Donnellan lecturer, 1838–9 ; published his lectures as 'Discourses on the Prophecies,' 1840 ; treasurer, 1837, and precentor, 1864, of St. Patrick's, Dublin ; regius professor of Hebrew at Dublin, 1849, and librarian, 1852 ; classified the manuscripts, added many books, and compiled a catalogue ; founded the Archæological Society, 1840, acted as secretary and contributed to its publications; published 'St. Patrick, Apostle of Ireland,' 1864 and other important works; consulted by statesmen and theologians. [lvi. 430]

TODD, ROBERT BENTLEY (1809-1860), physician; brother of James Henthorn Todd [q. v.]; B.A. Trinity College, Dublin, 1829; lectured in London on anatomy; D.M. Oxford, 1836; professor of physiology at King's College, London, 1836-53; Gulstonian, 1839, and Lumleian lecturer, 1849; F.R.S., 1838; examiner for London University, 1839-40; instrumental in founding King's College Hospital, London, 1840, and St. John's House Institution for nurses; F.R.C.S., 1844; established large private practice; revolutionised treatment of fevers; contributed many works to medical science, including 'The Cyclopædia of Anatomy and Physiology,' which he edited, 1835-59. [lvi. 432]

TODHUNTER, ISAAC (1820-1884), mathematician; attended evening classes at University College; M.A. London; scholar and gold medallist; senior wrangler and Smith's prizeman, Cambridge, 1848, and fellow of St. John's College, Cambridge, 1849; published mathematical treatises, mostly elementary; F.R.S., 1862; an accomplished linguist. [lvi. 434]

TOFT or **TOFTS**, MARY (1701?-1763), 'the rabbit-breeder'; said to have given birth to rabbits (the fraud occasioning a torrent of pamphlets and squibs); confessed afterwards to the imposture. [lvi. 435]

TOFTE, ROBERT (d. 1620), poet and translator; travelled in France and Italy; published 'Laura,' 1597, and 'Alba,' 1598, reference being made in the latter to 'Love's Labour's Lost,' also 'The Fruits of Jealousie,' 1615; translated from the Italian, including Ariosto's 'Tales and Satires,' and from the French. [lvi. 436]

TOFTS, KATHERINE, afterwards SMITH (1680?-1758?), vocalist; sang at Drury Lane concerts; rival of Francesca Margherita de l'Épine [q. v.]; took part in 'Arsinoë,' 1705, 'Camilla,' 'Love's Triumph,' and other operas; a soprano greatly extolled by contemporaries; after her retirement from the stage, 1709, said to have lost her reason. [lvi. 437]

TOFTS, MARY (1701?-1763). [See TOFT.]

TOLAND, JOHN (1670-1722), deist; studied at the college, Glasgow, at Leyden, and Oxford; M.A. Edinburgh, 1690; published 'Christianity not Mysterious,' 1696, the first act of warfare between the deists and the orthodox; returned to Ireland, 1697; coupled with Locke as a Socinian, and denounced from the pulpit, his book ordered to be burnt by the House of Commons, and himself arrested; retreated to England; edited Milton's prose works, 1698, and other authors; wrote pamphlets defending the Act of Succession, and formed one of the mission to the Electress Sophia, 1701; on his return wrote 'Vindicius Liberius,' and recanted his former opinions; assisted by Shaftesbury; visited the courts of Hanover and Berlin and published an account, 1705; was admitted to Sophie Charlotte's philosophical conversations, and wrote letters to her ('Serena'); wrote pamphlets in defence of Harley and Marlborough; travelled abroad again; resided in Holland; returned to England, 1710, and wrote pamphlets against Sacheverell and Jacobitism, and the 'Art of Restoring,' 1714, accusing Oxford of intending to play the rôle of Monck; returned to speculations in 'Nazarenus,' 1718, 'Tetradymus,' 1720, and 'Pantheisticon,' 1720; author of several other works. [lvi. 438]

TOLER, JOHN, first EARL OF NORBURY (1745-1831), chief-justice of the common pleas in Ireland; M.A. Dublin, 1766; called to the Irish bar, 1770; M.P., Tralee, 1776, Philipstown, 1783, Gorey, 1790; K.C., 1781; opposed Flood's bill for reform, 1783; solicitor-general, 1789; opposed Grattan's motion reprobating sale of places and peerages, 1790; gave consistent support to Earl of Westmoreland, 1790-3, and Lord Camden, his indifference to propriety and broad humour giving him success over his opponents; moved rejection of catholic relief bill, 1795; attorney-general, 1798; showed cruelty in prosecution of the rebels; made chief-justice of the common pleas and Baron Norbury, 1800; showed gross partiality, buffoonery, and scanty legal knowledge on the bench; famous for his bons mots; had great influence in the government as a supporter of protestant ascendency; retired and was created earl, 1827. [lvi. 442]

TOLFREY, WILLIAM (1778?-1817), orientalist; served in Mysore war and Mahratta campaigns, 1803-4; distinguished himself at Assaye; assistant-commissioner of revenue in Ceylon, 1813; translated New Testament into Pali. [lvi. 444]

TOLLEMACHE, TALMASH, or TALMACH, THOMAS (1651?-1694), lieutenant-general; served in Flanders and Tangier in Coldstream guards; appointed colonel of fusiliers, 1685, but resigned on discovering James II's political designs; served again in Holland and landed with William of Orange at Torbay; made governor of Portsmouth and colonel of Coldstream guards, 1689; M.P., Malmesbury, 1689, Chippenham, 1691; served under Marlborough in Netherlands; distinguished himself at Aghrim and siege of Limerick, 1691; promoted lieutenant-general on dismissal of Marlborough, 1692; saved English foot at Steinkirk, 1692, and Neerwinden, 1693; commanded the disastrous expedition against Brest, 1694, the failure perhaps being occasioned by treacherous communications from England; was wounded, and died at Plymouth. [lvi. 444]

TOLLER, SIR SAMUEL (d. 1821), advocate-general of Madras; barrister, Lincoln's Inn; advocate-general at Madras, 1812; knighted; published legal works; died in India. [lvi. 447]

TOLLET, ELIZABETH (1694-1754), poetess. [lvi. 448]

TOLLET, GEORGE (1725-1779), Shakespearean critic; nephew of Elizabeth Tollet [q. v.]; barrister, Lincoln's Inn, 1745; contributed notes to Johnson and Steevens's edition of Shakespeare. [lvi. 448]

TOM or **THOM**, JOHN NICHOLS (1799-1838), impostor and madman; son of an innkeeper and farmer; clerk and subsequently hop-dealer at Truro; joined Spencean Society; was regarded by his family as insane and disappeared; reappeared at Canterbury, styling himself Sir William Percy Honeywood Courtenay, earl of Devon, knight of Malta, and king of Jerusalem; nominated M.P. for Canterbury, 1832; convicted of perjury, 1833, but placed in an asylum; on release lived at farmhouse between Canterbury and Faversham; declared himself the Messiah, showed stigmata and attracted disciples; shot a constable while serving warrant upon him for enticing away a farmer's labourers, and a lieutenant sent to apprehend him with soldiers; killed with eight rioters in Blean Wood. [lvii. 1]

TOMBES, JOHN (1603?-1676), baptist divine; M.A. Magdalen Hall, Oxford, 1624; lecturer at St. Martin Carfax, 1624-30; vicar of Leominster, where his preaching was very popular; held several other livings; being a presbyterian declined to baptise infants; appealed to the Westminster Assembly on this subject and published tracts; master of the Temple, 1645-7; had interview with Cromwell, 1646; organised baptist church; engaged in public debate with Baxter, 1650, and others; author of tracts against pædobaptists, quakers, and papists. [lvii. 2]

TOMBS, SIR HENRY (1824-1874), major-general; lieutenant, Bengal artillery, 1841; mentioned in despatches for Gwalior campaign, 1844; distinguished himself in both Sikh wars, being present at battles of Mudki, 1845, Firozshah, 1845, Aliwal, 1846, Ramnagar, 1848, Chilianwala, 1849, and Guzerat, 1849; recommended for brevet majority; during the mutiny distinguished himself in defeat of the rebels at Ghazi and Badli-ke-Serai, and throughout siege of Delhi; made V.C. and C.B.; commanded his troop at Lucknow, 1858, and in subsequent operations in Rohilkhand; promoted brevet-colonel and eulogised by Lord Panmure, 1858; brigadier-general commanding artillery at Gwalior, 1863; commanded force which recaptured Dewangiri, 1864; K.C.B., 1868; commanded Allahabad division, 1871. [lvii. 4]

TOMES, SIR JOHN (1815-1895), dental surgeon; invented dental forceps and studied histology of bone and teeth; delivered lectures at Middlesex Hospital which marked new era in dentistry; administered ether for dental operations, 1847; contributed important papers to 'Philosophical Transactions,' 1849-56; induced Royal College of Surgeons to grant licence in dental surgery, 1858; one of the chief founders of the Odontological Society, 1856, and Dental Hospital, 1858; secured passing of Dentists Act, 1878; F.R.C.S., 1883; knighted, 1886; published works on dentistry. [lvii. 6]

TOMKINS, CHARLES (*fl.* 1779), topographical and antiquarian draughtsman and aquatint engraver; brother of Peltro William Tomkins [q. v.] [lvii. 9]

TOMKINS, GILES (*d.* 1668?), musician; brother of John Tomkins (1586–1638) [q. v.], whom he succeeded as organist at King's College, Cambridge; choirmaster at Salisbury Cathedral; household musician to Charles I, 1630. [lvii. 11]

TOMKINS, JOHN (1586–1638), musician; brother of Thomas Tomkins (*d.* 1656) [q. v.]; organist of King's College, Cambridge, 1606; Mus.Bac. Cambridge, 1608; organist of St. Paul's, London, *c.* 1619; epistler and gospeller, Chapel Royal, London; composed anthems; the Thomalin of three of Phineas Fletcher's eclogues. [lvii. 10]

TOMKINS, JOHN (1663?–1706), quaker annalist; published 'Piety Promoted, in a Collection of Dying Sayings of . . . Quakers,' 1701, and other works. [lvii. 7]

TOMKINS, MARTIN (*d.* 1755?), Arian divine; studied at Utrecht and Leyden; dissenting minister at Stoke Newington, 1707, but resigned, 1718, on account of Arian sympathies; chief work, 'A Sober Appeal to a Turk or an Indian concerning the plain Sense of Scripture relating to the Trinity,' 1723. [lvii. 8]

TOMKINS, NATHANAEL (*d.* 1681), prebendary of Worcester, 1629; son of Thomas Tomkins (*d.* 1656) [q. v.]; B.D. Balliol College, Oxford, 1629. [lvii. 10]

TOMKINS, PELTRO WILLIAM (1759–1840), engraver and draughtsman; pupil of Francesco Bartolozzi [q. v.]; produced many fine plates and illustrations for Sharpe's 'British Poets' and other works; projected 'The British Gallery of Art' and 'The Gallery of the Marquess of Stafford' (both appearing, 1818); drawing-master in George III's reign to the princesses. [lvii. 8]

TOMKINS, THOMAS (*fl.* 1604–1615). [See TOMKIS.]

TOMKINS, THOMAS (*d.* 1656), musician; brother of John Tomkins (1586–1638) [q. v.]; studied under William Byrd [q. v.]; Mus.Bac. Oxon., 1607; organist of Worcester Cathedral and (1621) of the Chapel Royal, London; composed 'Songs' and (published, 1668) 'Musica Deo Sacra,' besides pieces remaining in manuscript. [lvii. 9]

TOMKINS, THOMAS (1637?–1675), divine; son of John Tomkins (1586–1638) [q. v.]; M.A. Balliol College, Oxford, 1658; fellow of All Souls College, Oxford, 1657; D.D. Cambridge, 1673; published 'The Rebel's Plea,' 1660, criticising Baxter's constitutional theories, and other works; rector of St. Mary Aldermary, London, 1665; chaplain to Gilbert Sheldon [q. v.] and assistant licenser of books; rector of Great Chart, 1667, of Lambeth, 1669; chancellor and prebendary of Exeter. [lvii. 11]

TOMKINS, THOMAS (1743–1816), calligrapher; kept a writing-school in Foster Lane, London; produced ornamental titles to books and other work, attaining the highest eminence in his art; published 'The Beauties of Writing,' 1777, and other works. [lvii. 12]

TOMKINSON, THOMAS (1631–1710?), Muggletonian; tenant-farmer; visited Lodowicke Muggleton [q. v.], 1662; fined and excommunicated for recusancy, 1674; ablest of the Muggletonian writers; published 'The Muggletonians Principles Prevailing,' 1695, and other works. [lvii. 13]

TOMKIS or **TOMKYS**, THOMAS (*fl.* 1604–1615), dramatist; fellow of Trinity College, Cambridge, 1604; M.A., 1604; wrote 'Albumazar' (comedy), 1615, on visit of James I to Cambridge, for the revival of which Dryden composed a prologue, 1668; author probably also of 'Lingua' (comedy), 1607; both his comedies founded on Italian models. [lvii. 13]

TOMLINE, SIR GEORGE PRETYMAN (1750–1827), tutor of the younger Pitt and bishop of Winchester; belonged to an old Suffolk family; of Pembroke Hall, Cambridge; senior wrangler and Smith's prizeman, 1772; fellow and tutor, 1773; M.A., 1775; university moderator, 1781; Pitt's tutor, 1774, and his private secretary, 1783–7, and given a Westminster prebend and other preferment; F.R.S., 1785; assisted Pitt in finance; became bishop of Lincoln and dean of St. Paul's, London, 1787; exercised ecclesiastical patronage and gave political advice; published 'Elements of Christian Theology,' 1818; opposed to Pitt's relationship with Addington; suggested Pitt's

guarantee to George III concerning catholic emancipation; arranged payment of Pitt's debts; took name of Tomline on large estate being left to him, 1803; was refused archbishopric by George III, 1804; attended Pitt on his deathbed and left literary executor; published 'A Refutation of Calvinism,' 1811; bishop of Winchester, 1820–7; published his memoir of Pitt, 1793; established claim to Nova Scotia baronetcy, 1823. [lvii. 14]

TOMLINS, ELIZABETH SOPHIA (1763–1828), authoress; sister of Sir Thomas Edlyne Tomlins [q. v.] [lvii. 18]

TOMLINS, FREDERICK GUEST (1804–1867), journalist and publisher; contributed to 'Weekly Times,' 'Morning Advertiser,' and other journals; founder of the Shakespeare Society, 1840; wrote mainly on the drama. [lvii. 18]

TOMLINS, SIR THOMAS EDLYNE (1762–1841), legal writer; of Queen's College, Oxford; barrister, Inner Temple, 1783; editor of 'St. James's Chronicle'; counsel to chief secretary for Ireland and (parliamentary) to Irish chancellor of the exchequer, 1801; knighted, 1814; assistant-counsel to treasury, 1818; chief work, 'A Familiar Explanation of the Law of Wills and Codicils,' 1785. [lvii. 17]

TOMLINS, THOMAS EDLYNE (1804–1872), legal writer; nephew of Sir Thomas Edlyne Tomlins [q. v.] [lvii. 18]

TOMLINSON, CHARLES (1808–1897), scientific writer; of Wadham College, Oxford; kept a day-school with his brother at Salisbury; attended science lectures at University College, London; contributed papers to magazines; published 'The Student's Manual of Natural Philosophy,' 1838; lecturer on experimental science, King's College School, London; made important discoveries concerning surface tension of liquids; F.C.S., 1867; F.R.S., 1872; Dante lecturer, University College, London, 1878–80; author of miscellaneous works. [lvii. 18]

TOMLINSON, MATTHEW (1617–1681). [See THOMLINSON.]

TOMLINSON, NICHOLAS (1765–1847), vice-admiral; severely injured in explosion on the Duke of Athol, 1783; present at fifth action between Suffren and Sir Edward Hughes [q. v.]; performed 'dashing exploits' on French coast, 1794; captured the Revanche and other vessels; fitted out a privateer, 1797; vice-admiral, 1841. [lvii. 19]

TOMLINSON, RICHARD (1827–1871). [See MONT-GOMERY, WALTER.]

TOMOS GLYN COTHI (1766–1833). [See EVANS, THOMAS.]

TOMPION, THOMAS (1639–1713), 'father of English watchmaking'; freeman of the Clockmakers' Company, 1671; made clocks for Royal Observatory, 1676; under direction of Robert Hooke [q. v.] made one of the first English watches with balance spring, 1675; patented the cylinder escapement with Houghton and Barlow, 1695; made barometers and sundials for William III, and clock in Pump-room, Bath, 1709, still in working order; 'left English watches and clocks the finest in the world.' [lvii. 20]

TOMPSON, RICHARD (*d.* 1693?), printseller. [lvii. 21]

TOMS, PETER (*d.* 1777), painter and herald; painted drapery for Sir Joshua Reynolds and others; Portcullis pursuivant, 1746; original R.A., 1768. [lvii. 22]

TOMSON, LAURENCE (1539–1608), politician, author, and transcriber; demy and fellow of Magdalen College, Oxford; M.A., 1564; accompanied Sir Thomas Hoby [q. v.] to France, 1566; M.P., Weymouth and Melcombe Regis, 1575–87, Downton, 1588–9; travelled extensively and knew many languages; employed by Walsingham; author of theological and commercial works. [lvii. 22]

TOMSON, RICHARD (*fl.* 1588), mariner; traded in the Mediterranean; sailed to Algiers to ransom those captured in his ship Jesus, 1583; corresponded with Walsingham and Robert Cecil; fought against the Armada, 1588. [lvii. 22]

TONE, THEOBALD WOLFE (1763–1798), United Irishman; son of Peter Tone, Dublin coachmaker; entered Trinity College, Dublin, 1781; nearly expelled; eloped with Matilda Witherington and neglected his studies; B.A., 1785; entered Middle Temple as student, 1787, and was joined by a younger brother; forwarded to Pitt scheme for a military colony in the South Sea islands, which was left unnoticed ; called to Irish bar, 1789 ; soon turned his attention to politics ; published 'A Review of the Conduct of Administration,' 1790, and 'Hibernicus,' arraigning the government and asserting Irish independence ; became an ardent republican : published 'An Argument on behalf of the Catholics of Ireland,' 1791, to promote union of dissenters with catholics against government ; joined Belfast volunteers ; founded with Russell and Tandy club of United Irishmen in Dublin ; became assistant-secretary to the Catholic Committee, 1792 ; took active part in agitation and in great catholic convention in Tailors' Hall ; accompanied delegation to present petition to George III ; suspension of agitation contrary to his hopes, 1793 ; was voted 1,500*l.* and gold medal ; compromised himself with William Jackson (1737 ?–1795) [q. v.], the French spy, 1794, and was allowed by government to sail for America, 1795 ; went to Paris, 1796, to promote French expedition against Ireland ; made chef-de-brigade and adjutant-general by Hoche ; took part in Hoche's expedition, which never effected a landing, and in another under Dutch auspices, which never started, 1797 ; finally accompanied small expedition under Hardy in the Hoche, which struck to Borlase off Lough Swilly ; was tried by court-martial, condemned to death, and being refused a soldier's execution committed suicide ; wrote 'Journals.'   [lvii. 23]

TONE, WILLIAM THEOBALD WOLFE (1791–1828), soldier ; son of Theobald Wolfe Tone [q. v.] ; educated by the French republic ; entered the French army and fought in Germany, 1813 ; author, and editor of his father's writings.   [lvii. 29]

TONG, WILLIAM (1662–1727), presbyterian divine ; minister at Chester, Knutsford, Coventry, and at Salters' Hall Court, Cannon Street, London ; maintained orthodoxy on the Trinity in conferences, 1718–19 ; successful preacher ; Williams and Barnes trustee, and distributor of the *regium donum* ; published 'A Defence of Mathew Henry, with a History of Nonconformity,' 1693, and other works.   [lvii. 29]

TONGE or **TONGUE,** ISRAEL or EZEREL [EZREEL] (1621–1680), divine and ally of Titus Oates ; B.A. University College, Oxford, 1643 ; left Oxford to avoid bearing arms for Charles I ; returned and was made fellow, 1648 ; rector of Pluckley, 1649 ; D.D., 1656 ; fellow of Durham College, 1656–9 ; chaplain at Dunkirk, 1660–1 ; after other moves and changes became rector of St. Michael's, Wood Street, London, St. Mary Stayning, London, and Aston, Herefordshire ; made acquaintance with Titus Oates, 1676, and became his willing dupe ; worked up Oates's inventions into narrative of the 'Popish plot,' 1678 ; communicated with Danby and had interviews with Charles II ; prevailed on Sir Edmund Berry Godfrey [q. v.] to take down Oates's depositions, and inaugurated the reign of terror ; withdrew, however, from association with Oates, but gave evidence in the House of Commons, 1679 ; wrote numerous diatribes against the jesuits.   [lvii. 30]

TONKIN, THOMAS (1678–1742), Cornish historian ; of Queen's College, Oxford, and Lincoln's Inn ; lived on his Cornish estates ; collected topographical and genealogical information, and projected a history of Cornwall.   [lvii. 33]

TONNA, CHARLOTTE ELIZABETH (1790–1846), miscellaneous writer ; *née* Browne ; married Captain Phelan, and secondly, Lewis Hippolytus Joseph Tonna [q. v.] ; edited protestant magazines ; wrote anti-catholic tracts and Orange songs, including 'The Maiden City' and 'No Surrender,' and many other works.   [lvii. 34]

TONNA, LEWIS HIPPOLYTUS JOSEPH (1812–1857), author ; naval schoolmaster, and later secretary to Royal United Service Institution ; published ultra-protestant works.   [lvii. 35]

TONNEYS, TONEYS, or **TONEY,** JOHN (*d.* 1510 ?), grammarian ; D.D. Cambridge, 1502 ; provincial of Austin-friars ; wrote 'Rudimenta Grammatices,' and other works.   [lvii. 35]

TONSON, JACOB (1656 ?–1736), publisher ; set up business at the Judge's Head, Chancery Lane, London, 1677 ; purchased copyright of 'Paradise Lost' ; was much associated with Dryden ; published many of his plays and other pieces, the 'Miscellany,' his translation of Virgil, 1697, and 'The Fables,' 1699 ; moved to Gray's

Inn Gate ; secretary of the Kit-Cat Club ; met Addison in Holland, 1703, and published his 'Remarks on several Parts of Italy,' 1705 ; published Dryden's 'Alexander's Feast,' 1707, verses by Pope in sixth 'Miscellany,' 1709, and Rowe's 'Shakespeare,' 1709 ; moved to the Shakespeare's Head, 1710, where Swift met Addison and Steele ; joint-publisher with Buckley of the 'Spectator' from 1712 ; published Addison's 'Cato,' 1713 ; printed Steele's 'Ladies' Library,' 1714 ; made printer of parliamentary votes ; bought Addison's 'The Drummer,' 1715 ; published Tickell's 'Iliad,' 1715 ; made large fortune by South Sea stock and Law's Mississippi scheme ; became stationer to public offices, 1720 ; published, besides those named, several celebrated works, including Steele's 'Conscious Lovers' and Pope's 'Shakespeare,' 1725.   [lvii. 35]

TONSON, JACOB (*d.* 1767), publisher ; great-nephew of Jacob Tonson (1656 ?–1736) [q. v.] ; paid Warburton 500*l.* for editing Shakespeare, 1747 ; eulogised by Dr. Johnson.   [lvii. 38]

TONSON, RICHARD (*d.* 1772), M.P., Wallingford, 1747, New Windsor, 1768 ; brother of Jacob Tonson (*d.* 1767) [q. v.]   [lvii. 38]

TONSTALL, CUTHBERT (1474–1559). [See TUNSTALL.]

TOOKE. [See also TUKE.]

TOOKE, ANDREW (1673–1732), master of the London Charterhouse ; educated at Charterhouse ; scholar of Clare Hall, Cambridge ; M.A., 1697 ; usher at Charterhouse, 1695 ; Gresham professor of geometry, 1704–29 ; F.R.S., 1704 ; master, 1728–32 ; published mainly translations.   [lvii. 39]

TOOKE, GEORGE (1595–1675), soldier and writer ; took part in unsuccessful expedition under Sir Edward Cecil, viscount Wimbledon [q. v.] against Cadiz, 1625, and wrote an account, 'The History of Cales Passion,' 1652 (in prose and verse) ; resided on his estate of Popes, Hertfordshire ; intimate with Selden and Hales ; author also of 'The Legend of Britamart,' 1646, and other works.   [lvii. 39]

TOOKE, JOHN HORNE (1736–1812), politician and philologist ; son of a poulterer named Horne ; lost sight of one eye fighting with a schoolfellow ; senior optime and B.A. St. John's College, Cambridge, 1758 ; entered Inner Temple ; incumbent of chapel of ease, Brentford, 1760, but being unsuited to clerical duties travelled abroad as tutor to son of John Elwes [q. v.] ; returning, wrote 'The Petition of an Englishman,' violently defending Wilkes, 1765 ; travelled abroad again as tutor ; abandoned clerical dress ; made acquaintance with Wilkes and Sterne and visited Voltaire ; supported Wilkes at the Middlesex election, 1768 ; accused George Onslow (1731–1792) [q. v.] of selling an office and was fined 400*l.* by Lord Mansfield (verdict set aside on appeal) ; organised 'Society for supporting the Bill of Rights' ; supposed author or part author of addresses to George III, 1770 ; quarrelled with Wilkes, and seceding formed the Constitutional Society, 1771 ; resigned his living, 1773 ; was summoned before the House of Commons on account of violent attack on the speaker, Norton, but escaped punishment, 1774 ; fined and imprisoned for publishing resolution to raise a subscription for American colonists, 1778 ; refused admission to the bar ; inherited some fortune from his father and lived in London, giving famous suppers and engaging in political discussions ; added name of his friend, William Tooke, to his own, 1782 ; published ''Επεα πτερόεντα, or the Diversions of Purley,' 1786 and 1798, which established his reputation as a philologist ; joined 'Society for Constitutional Information,' 1780 ; supported reform and Pitt against Fox, 1788 ; published 'Two Pair of Portraits,' contrasting the Pitts and the Foxes ; contested Westminster against Fox, 1790 ; tried for high treason, 1794, but acquitted ; hostile to the whig aristocracy ; contested Westminster again unsuccessfully, 1796 ; returned for Old Sarum, 1801, but act was passed declaring clergymen ineligible for seats in House of Commons ; received much society at his house at Wimbledon, including Thurlow, Erskine, Bentham, Coleridge, Paine, Godwin, and others ; the shrewdest of the Wilkes agitators, and an old-fashioned radical, who appealed to Magna Charta, but ridiculed the 'rights of man.' His philology, with reference to which subject he emphasised the necessity of studying Gothic and Anglo-Saxon, was intended to subserve a nominalism of the type of Hobbes.   [lvii. 40]

TOOKE, THOMAS (1774–1858), economist; son of William Tooke (1744–1820) [q. v.]; follower of Ricardo, Horner, and Huskisson, and supporter of report of bullion committee, 1810; published 'Thoughts and Details on the High and Low Prices of the last Thirty Years,' 1823, and other pamphlets combating view that fall of prices was result of return to cash payments; published the 'History of Prices,' 1838–57; opposed the 'currency theory' and the act of 1844; published 'Enquiry into the Currency Principle,' 1844; free-trader and part-founder of the Political Economy Club, 1821; F.R.S., 1821; correspondant de l'Institut de France.   [lvii. 47]

TOOKE, WILLIAM (1744–1820), historian of Russia; chaplain of the English church at Cronstadt, 1771, and at St. Petersburg, 1774; published, among other works, 'A History of Russia from Rurik to . . . Catherine II,' 1800, and other books on Russia; edited the 'New and General Biographical Dictionary,' 1798.   [lvii. 49]

TOOKE, WILLIAM (1777–1863), president of the Society of Arts; son of William Tooke (1744–1820) [q. v.]; solicitor; took prominent part in formation of St. Katharine's Docks, 1825, and in foundation of the London University, 1823, and Royal Society of Literature; F.R.S., 1818; president of the Society of Arts, 1862; M.P., Truro, 1832–7; compiled a work on the 'Monarchy of France,' 1855.   [lvii. 50]

TOOKER or **TUCKER**, WILLIAM (1558?–1621), divine; educated at Winchester College; fellow of New College, Oxford, 1577; M.A., 1583; D.D., 1594; archdeacon of Barnstaple; chaplain to Queen Elizabeth; rector of Kilkhampton, West Dean, and Clovelly; dean of Lichfield, 1605; published 'Charisma sive Donum Sanationis,' 1597, vindicating royal power of curing king's evil, and other works.   [lvii. 51]

TOOTEL, HUGH (1672–1743). [See DODD, CHARLES.]

TOPCLIFFE, RICHARD (1532–1604), persecutor of Roman catholics; M.P. for Beverley, 1572, and Old Sarum, 1586; hunted out popish recusants and jesuits; 'topcliffizare,' used in court language for hunting a recusant, derived from his name; racked prisoners in his own house; cruelly treated Robert Southwell (1561?–1595) [q. v.], and was imprisoned; included in commission against the jesuits, 1593; imprisoned again, 1594–5; engaged in torturing gipsies and others, 1596–71; obtained the Fitzherberts' house at Padley.   [lvii. 52]

TOPHAM, EDWARD (1751–1820), journalist and play-writer; educated at Eton and Trinity College, Cambridge; travelled abroad and in Scotland; published 'Letters from Edinburgh,' 1776; entered life-guards; wrote tory 'Address to Edmund Burke on Affairs in America,' 1777; associated with Horne Tooke, Wilkes, and Sheridan; wrote several popular epilogues; produced 'Deaf Indeed,' 1780, 'The Fool,' 1786, and other plays; started 'The World,' daily paper, 1787, to which he contributed 'The Schools' and 'Life of the late John Elwes'; tried for libelling the third Earl of Cowper, but eventually acquitted, 1791; satirised by Gillray and other caricaturists.   [lvii. 53]

TOPHAM, FRANCIS WILLIAM (1808–1877), water-colour painter; began life as an engraver; exhibited water-colours at the Royal Academy, 1832, and elsewhere, chiefly scenes of Irish and Welsh peasant life; one of Dickens's 'splendid strollers,' 1850; painted Spanish subjects after a visit to Spain, 1854–9, and Italian scenes, 1864; died at Cordova.   [lvii. 55]

TOPHAM, JOHN (1746–1803), antiquary; of Lincoln's Inn; deputy-keeper of state papers, 1781, and commissioner in bankruptcy, 1783; bencher of Gray's Inn, 1787; treasurer of Society of Antiquaries, 1787; librarian to archbishop of Canterbury; edited 'Rotuli Parliamentorum' (1278–1503), 1767–77, Fortescue's and Glanville's works, and published various papers.   [lvii. 56]

TOPHAM, THOMAS (1710?–1749), 'the strong man'; son of a carpenter; innkeeper; performed various feats of strength in London, Ireland, and the provinces; stabbed his wife and killed himself.   [lvii. 56]

TOPLADY, AUGUSTUS MONTAGUE (1740–1778), divine; educated at Westminster and Trinity College, Dublin; B.A., 1760; incumbent of Broad Hembury, 1768; published 'Rock of Ages' in the 'Gospel Magazine,' 1775; published 'The Historic Proof of the Doctrinal Calvinism

of the Church of England,' 1774, and 'The Scheme of Christian and Philosophical Necessity asserted,' 1775, and engaged in violent controversy with Wesley.   [lvii. 57]

TOPLEY, WILLIAM (1841–1894), geologist; assisted in survey of the Weald, 1862, and prepared memoir, 1875; contributed various papers to 'Quarterly Journal of the Geological Society'; surveyed formations in north of England and Sussex; worked at the survey office, London, from 1880; secretary of various societies; F.R.S., 1888.   [lvii. 59]

TOPSELL, EDWARD (d. 1638?), divine and author; of Christ's College, Cambridge; rector of East Hoathly, 1596; perpetual curate of St. Botolph, Aldersgate, London, 1604; held several other preferments; published 'The Historie of Foure-footed Beastes,' 1607, and 'The Historie of Serpents,' 1608, and religious works.   [lvii. 59]

TORKINGTON, SIR RICHARD (fl. 1518), English priest and pilgrim; rector of Mulberton, 1511; travelled to the Holy Land and back through Italy, 1517–8, and wrote an account, published, 1883.   [lvii. 60]

TORPHICHEN, BARONS. [See SANDILANDS, JAMES, d. 1753; SANDILANDS, JAMES, seventh BARON, d. 1753.]

TORPORLEY, NATHANIEL (1564–1632), mathematician; B.A. Christ Church, Oxford, 1584; M.A. Brasenose College, Oxford, 1591; rector of Salwarpe and of Liddington; patronised by ninth Earl of Northumberland; secretary to François Viète of Fontenay, mathematician; published 'Diclides Cœlometricæ,' 1602.   [lvii. 61]

TORR, WILLIAM (1808–1874), agriculturist; farmed at Riby, North Lincolnshire; raised famous breeds of Leicester sheep, thorough-bred ponies, and shorthorn cattle; elected to council of Royal Agricultural Society, 1857; judge of live-stock in England and abroad.   [lvii. 61]

TORRE, JAMES (1649–1699), antiquary and genealogist; belonged to old Lincolnshire family; B.A. Magdalene College, Cambridge, 1669; studied at the Inner Temple; published 'Antiquities Ecclesiastical of the City of York,' 1691, and compiled 'English Nobility and Gentry.'   [lvii. 62]

TORRENS, SIR ARTHUR WELLESLEY (1809–1855), major-general; son of Sir Henry Torrens [q. v.]; page of honour to Prince Regent; lieutenant, grenadier guards, 1825; fought against rebels in Canada, 1838; commanded 23rd royal Welsh fusiliers in Barbados; commanded infantry brigade at Alma and Balaclava; distinguished himself and was wounded at Inkerman, 1854; received thanks of parliament; promoted major-general and K.C.B., 1854; died at Paris.   [lvii. 63]

TORRENS, SIR HENRY (1779–1828), major-general; entered the army, 1793; took part with 63rd foot in expedition under Abercromby against St. Lucia and St. Vincent, 1796, and in campaigns in Portugal, 1798, and Netherlands, 1799, being wounded at Egmont-op-Zee; commanded Surrey rangers in Nova Scotia, 1800–1, and 68th foot during Maratha war; took part in disastrous attack on Buenos Ayres, 1807; accompanied Wellesley as military secretary to Portugal, 1808, and was present at battles of Roliça and Vimeiro; received Portuguese decorations; military secretary to commander-in-chief, 1809; aide-de-camp to Prince Regent, 1812; major-general, 1814; K.C.B., 1815; adjutant-general of the forces, 1820; revised infantry regulations. [lvii. 65]

TORRENS, HENRY WHITELOCK (1806–1852), Indian civil servant; son of Sir Henry Torrens [q. v.]; educated at Charterhouse and Christ Church, Oxford; B.A., 1828; clerk in foreign office; obtained writership in Indian civil service; assistant to collector of Meerut, 1829; secretary to board of customs at Calcutta, 1840; agent to governor-general of Murshidabad, 1847; published one volume of an excellent translation of the 'Arabian Nights,' 1838, and other works.   [Suppl. iii. 383]

TORRENS, ROBERT (1780–1864), political economist; cousin of Sir Henry Torrens [q. v.]; as captain in royal marines defended Isle of Anholt against the Dutch, 1811; colonel of Spanish legion in Peninsular war; colonel, 1837; published 'An Essay on the External Corn Trade,' 1815, and 'An Essay on the Reduction of Wealth,' 1821; one of the first economists to attribute production of wealth to land, labour, and capital; influenced Peel and Ricardo; M.P., Ashburton, 1831–5; advocated colonisation of South Australia, and published book on the subject, 1835; editor of the 'Traveller' and 'Globe'; F.R.S., 1818. [lvii. 66]

TORRENS, Sir ROBERT RICHARD (1814–1884), son of Robert Torrens [q. v.]; first premier of South Australia; of Trinity College, Dublin; emigrated to South Australia, 1840; premier and colonial treasurer, 1857; author of 'Torrens Act' to substitute title by public registration for the old conveyancing system, 1858; returned to England; M.P., Cambridge, 1868; G.C.M.G., 1884; wrote pamphlets dealing with Torrens Act. [lvii. 68]

TORRENS, WILLIAM TORRENS McCULLAGH (1813–1894), politician and author; B.A., 1833, and LL.D. Dublin, 1842; called to Irish bar, 1836, and English, 1855; assistant-commissioner on Irish poor-relief commission, 1835; joined Anti-Cornlaw League, and published 'The Industrial History of Free Nations,' 1846; M.P., Dundalk, 1847–52, Yarmouth, 1857, Finsbury, 1865–85; independent liberal; supported legislation for amelioration of condition of the poor; published 'Memoirs of Viscount Melbourne,' 1878, 'History of Cabinets,' 1894, and other works. [lvii. 68]

TORRIGIANO, PIETRO (1472–1522), sculptor and draughtsman; born at Florence; one of the artists protected by Lorenzo de' Medici; broke Michelangelo's nose in a quarrel and was banished; became soldier in papal army and fought at Garigliano, 1503; returned to Florence and became one of the best sculptors there; came to England and executed Henry VII's tomb in Westminster Abbey and that of the Countess of Richmond, also the altar at the head of Henry VII's tomb, destroyed in 1641; later settled at Seville and executed works there, including a Madonna and Child for the Duke of Arcas, and which, disappointed with the payment received, he dashed to pieces; was sentenced to death for sacrilege and imprisoned; said to have starved himself to death in prison; Benvenuto Cellini refused to accompany him to England because of his injury to Michelangelo. [lvii. 69]

TORRINGTON, EARL OF (1647–1716). [See HERBERT, ARTHUR.]

TORRINGTON, VISCOUNT (1663–1733). [See BYNG, GEORGE.]

TORRY, PATRICK (1763 – 1852), bishop of St. Andrews, Dunkeld, and Dunblane; ordained priest of Scottish episcopal church, 1783; assistant, 1789, and sole pastor, 1791–1837, of congregation at Peterhead; bishop of Dunkeld, 1808 till death; received style of bishop of united dioceses of St. Andrews, Dunkeld, and Dunblane, 1844; published, 1850, 'Prayer-book,' which claimed to be embodiment of usages of the episcopal church of Scotland, and occasioned much opposition, led by Charles Wordsworth [q. v.]; his 'Prayer-book' was censured by Scottish episcopal synod and suppressed. [Suppl. iii. 384]

TORSHELL or **TORSHEL,** SAMUEL (1604–1650), puritan divine; rector of Bunbury, Cheshire; tutor to Charles I's two younger children; preacher at Cripplegate; author of religious works. [lvii. 71]

TOSTIG, TOSTI, or **TOSTINUS** (d. 1066), earl of the Northumbrians; son of Earl Godwin [q. v.], whose banishment he shared in Flanders, 1051; married Judith, daughter of Count Baldwin IV of Flanders; returned to England, 1052; made Earl of Northumbria, Northamptonshire, and Huntingdonshire by King Edward, 1055; ruled with severity; sent Malcolm III of Scotland help against Macbeth; benefactor to church at Durham; went to Rome, 1061, and pleaded cause of Aldred [q. v.]; joined Harold in invading Wales, 1063; treacherously murdered two thegns and Gospatric, a noble, 1064; was declared an outlaw by the thegns, Morcar [q. v.] being chosen as earl instead, 1065, and his deposition confirmed by Edward, who, it is said, was persuaded by Harold; was forced to go into exile, and retired to Flanders; on death of Edward, 1066, ravaged Isle of Wight, the east coast, and Lindesey, but being driven off retired to Malcolm in Scotland; joined Harold Hardrada and accompanied invaders to York, where they defeated Edwin and Morcar; was vanquished at Stamford Bridge by Harold and killed. [lvii. 71]

TOTINGTON or **TOTTINGTON,** SAMSON DE (1135–1211). [See SAMSON.]

TOTNES, EARL OF (1555–1629). [See CAREW, GEORGE.]

TOTO, ANTHONY (fl. 1518–1543), painter; native of Florence, and pupil of Ghirlandajo; brought to England by Pietro Torrigiano [q. v.]; executed work for Henry VIII; naturalised, 1538; appointed serjeant-painter, 1543. [lvii. 74]

TOTTEL, RICHARD (d. 1594), publisher; carried on business at The Hand and Star within Temple Bar, 1553–94; held several patents for printing and publishing; member of the Stationers' Company on its foundation, 1557; master, 1578 and 1584; published mostly law-books, but also More's 'Dialogue of Comfort,' 1553, Lydgate's 'Fall of Princes,' 1554, Surrey's 'Æneid,' 1557, Tottel's 'Miscellany,' 1557, and other works. [lvii. 74]

TOTTENHAM, CHARLES (1685–1758), Irish politician; Irish M.P. for New Ross; rode sixty miles in the night to parliament, and gave casting vote against handing over Irish surplus to England, 1731; sheriff of co. Wexford, 1737. [lvii. 75]

TOUCHET, GEORGE (d. 1689?), Benedictine monk; brother of James Touchet, third earl of Castlehaven [q. v.]; chaplain to Catherine of Braganza, but banished, 1675, and excluded by parliament from succession to title; published 'Historical Collections,' 1674. [lvii. 76]

TOUCHET, JAMES, seventh BARON AUDLEY (1465?–1497), descended from Adam de Audley, temp. Henry I; K.B., 1475; succeeded as baron, 1491; accompanied Henry VII in French expedition, 1492; led rebellion, 1497; defeated at Blackheath, captured, and beheaded. [lvii. 76]

TOUCHET, JAMES, BARON AUDLEY of Hely or Heleigh, third EARL OF CASTLEHAVEN (1617?–1684), eldest son of second earl; instrumental in bringing his father to justice for unnatural offences, 1631; created Baron Audley of Hely, 1633, forfeited by his father for felony; travelled to Rome; joined Charles I at Berwick, 1639; offered his services to government on outbreak of Irish rebellion, 1641, but his offer declined, he being a Roman catholic; hesitated to join Ormonde at battle of Kilrush, 1642, and was imprisoned on charge of high treason; escaped and joined army of confederate catholics, and performed brilliant and useful services; promoted cessation in Ireland; present at siege and rendition of Duncannon, 1645, but failed to take Youghal; joined Ormonde on refusal of O'Neill and nuncio to accept peace made with the confederates, 1646, and advised making terms with parliament rather than the council; fought under Prince Rupert at Landrecies; attended Charles I's queen and the prince of Wales at St. Germain; returned with Ormonde to Ireland, 1648; appointed general of the horse to reduce fortresses holding out for O'Neill, 1649; shared Ormonde's defeat at Rathmines, 1649; threw fifteen hundred men into Wexford and forced Ireton to raise siege of Duncannon; appointed commander of Leinster forces; captured Athy, 1650, but failed to relieve Tecroghan; on departure of Ormonde became commander-in-chief of Munster and Clare, but failed to prevent progress of Cromwell's forces or capitulation of Limerick, 1651; left for France; served under Condé at fight in Faubourg St.-Antoine; taken prisoner by Turenne at Comercy; commanded an Irish regiment in Spanish service and took part in various sieges, and 1658] in battle of the Dunes; returned to England at Restoration; served in several naval actions against the Dutch, 1665–7, and landed two thousand four hundred recruits at Ostend; present at battle of Senef, 1674; commanded Spanish foot, 1676; served at Maastricht and Charleroi, and was present at battle before Mons, 1678; published 'Memoirs,' 1680. [lvii. 77]

TOULMIN, CAMILLA DUFOUR, afterwards MRS. NEWTON CROSLAND (1812–1895), miscellaneous writer; contributed to periodicals; published novels, translations, 'Landmarks of a Literary Life,' 1893, and other works. [lvii. 81]

TOULMIN, JOSHUA (1740–1815), dissenting historian and biographer; presbyterian minister of Colyton, 1761, and Taunton, 1765; excited hostility by his Socinian views and liberal politics; a founder of the Western Unitarian Society, 1792; minister of the New Meeting,

Birmingham, 1803 ; author of numerous works, including ' Memoirs . . . of Faustus Socinus,' 1777, ' Life . . . of John Biddle ' [q. v.], 1789, and edition of Neal's ' History of the Puritans,' 1793-7.   [lvii. 82]

TOULMIN SMITH, JOSHUA (1816-1869). [See SMITH.]

TOUNSON. [See TOWNSON.]

TOUP, JONATHAN (or JOANNES) (1713-1785), philologer and classical editor ; educated at Exeter College, Oxford ; M.A., 1756 ; curate successively of Philleigh, 1736, and of Buryan, 1738 ; rector of St. Martin's-by-Looe, 1750-85 ; published ' Emendations in Suidam,' 1760-6, followed by an ' Epistola Critica ' to Warburton, 1767, and ' Curæ novissimæ . . . in Suidam,' 1775 ; contributed notes to Warton's ' Theocritus,' 1770, and published further emendations in ' Curæ Posteriores,' 1772 ; produced a famous edition of ' Longinus,' containing numerous emendations, 1778 ; contributed notes to Sammet's ' Epistolæ ' of Æschines, 1771, and Shaw's ' Apollonius Rhodius,' 1779, and other works ; friend and correspondent of Warburton and Hurd ; prebendary of Exeter, 1774, and vicar of St. Merryn, 1776.   [lvii. 83]

TOURAINE, DUKES OF. [See DOUGLAS, ARCHIBALD, first DUKE, 1369 ?-1424 ; DOUGLAS, ARCHIBALD, second DUKE, 1391 ?-1439 ; DOUGLAS, WILLIAM, third DUKE, 1423 ?-1440.]

TOURNAY, SIMON OF (*fl.* 1180-1200), schoolman : supposed to have been native of Cornwall : established himself at Paris by 1180, and was regent of arts : follower of Aristotle, and hence accused of heresy : three volumes of his lectures extant at Oxford in the Balliol and Merton MSS.   [lvii. 86]

TOURNEUR, TURNOUR, or **TURNER,** CYRIL (1575 ?-1626), dramatist : published ' The Revenger's Tragædie,' 1607, a work of great tragic intensity : author of ' The Atheists Tragedie,' 1611, and other plays and works, including panegyric of Sir Francis Vere : was employed in the Netherlands, and served as Sir Edward Cecil's secretary in the unsuccessful Cadiz expedition, 1625 : was disembarked among the sick in Ireland, and died there. His ' Plays and Poems ' were edited by John Churton Collins, 1878.   [lvii. 87]

TOURS, BERTHOLD (1838-1897), musician and musical editor ; organist ; chief editor of Novello, Ewer & Co., and composer of services and songs.   [lvii. 89]

TOURS, STEPHEN DE (*d.* 1193). [See STEPHEN.]

TOVEY, DE BLOSSIERS (1692-1745), author of ' Anglia Judaica ' : B.A. Queen's College, Oxford, 1712 ; fellow of Merton College, Oxford, and M.A., 1715 ; barrister, Inner Temple, 1717 ; D.C.L. Oxford, 1721 ; vicar of Embleton : principal of New Inn Hall, Oxford, 1732-45 ; published ' Anglia Judaica,' 1738.   [lvii. 89]

TOVEY-TENNENT, HAMILTON (1782-1866), soldier ; lieutenant, Bombay service, 1798 ; fought against the Mahrattas ; wounded at Bhurtpore, 1805 ; secretary to Mountstuart Elphinstone ; governor of Bombay ; lieutenant-colonel, 1824.   [lvii. 90]

TOWERS, JOHN (*d.* 1649), bishop of Peterborough ; fellow of Queens' College, Cambridge, 1608 ; M.A., 1606 ; D.D. *per literas regias*, Oxford, 1624 ; held numerous preferments ; dean of Peterborough, 1630 ; prebendary of Westminster, 1634 ; bishop of Peterborough, 1639 ; supporter of the royal prerogative ; follower of Laud ; signed the bishops' protest, 1641, and was imprisoned by the parliament.   [lvii. 90]

TOWERS, JOHN (1747 ?-1804), independent preacher ; brother of Joseph Towers [q. v.] ; wrote against Martin Madan [q. v.]   [lvii. 92]

TOWERS, JOSEPH (1737-1799), biographer ; edited the ' British Biography,' 1766-72 ; hon. LL.D. Edinburgh, 1779 ; joint-editor of ' Biographia Britannica,' 1778-93 ; dissenting minister at Highgate and elsewhere, and published a history of Frederick III of Prussia, 1788.   [lvii. 91]

TOWERS, JOSEPH LOMAS (1767 ?-1831), unitarian minister and author ; son of Joseph Towers [q. v.]   [lvii. 91]

TOWERS, WILLIAM (1617 ?-1666), divine ; son of John Towers (*d.* 1649) [q. v.] ; M.A. Christ Church, Oxford, 1641 ; B.D., 1646 ; prebendary of Peterborough, 1641.   [lvii. 91]

TOWERSON, GABRIEL (*d.* 1623), captain and agent for East India Company ; made several voyages to India, and commanded the Hector ; visited Batavia and Amboyna, 1622 ; tortured and killed with others by the Dutch at Amboyna.   [lvii. 92]

TOWERSON, GABRIEL (1635 ?-1697), divine and theological writer ; M.A. Queen's College, Oxford, 1657 ; fellow of All Souls College, Oxford, 1660 ; rector of Welwyn and St. Andrew Undershaft ; D.D. Lambeth, 1678 ; author of theological works and verses.   [lvii. 93]

TOWERSON, WILLIAM (*fl.* 1555-1577), merchant and navigator ; made three voyages to the Guinea coast, 1555, 1556, and 1557.   [lvii. 93]

TOWGOOD, MATTHEW (*fl.* 1710-1746), minister ; cousin of Michaijah Towgood [q. v.]   [lvii. 95]

TOWGOOD, MICHAIJAH (1700-1792), dissenting minister ; pastor successively at Moreton Hampstead, Crediton, and Exeter ; of high Arian principles ; published the ' Dissenting Gentleman's Letters,' 1746-8, and other works.   [lvii. 94]

TOWGOOD, RICHARD (1595 ?-1683), dean of Bristol ; M.A. Oriel College, Oxford, 1618 ; B.D., 1633 ; master of the grammar school, College Green, Bristol ; vicar of All Saints, 1619, and St. Nicholas, Bristol, 1626 ; chaplain to Charles I ; sequestered, 1645 ; imprisoned and sentenced to death ; later rector of Tortworth, and at Restoration returned to St. Nicholas ; prebendary of Bristol, 1660, and dean, 1667 ; chaplain to Charles II and vicar of Weare.   [lvii. 95]

TOWNE, CHARLES (*d.* 1850 ?), artist ; exhibited at Royal Academy and Liverpool Academy ; painted landscapes and animals.   [lvii. 95]

TOWNE, FRANCIS (1740-1816), landscape-painter.   [lvii. 96]

TOWNE, JOHN (1711 ?-1791), controversialist ; M.A. Clare Hall, Cambridge, 1736 ; vicar of Thorpe-Ernald, 1740 ; archdeacon of Stowe, 1785 ; prebendary of Lincoln ; rector of Little Paunton ; author of controversial works.   [lvii. 96]

TOWNE, JOSEPH (1808-1879), modeller ; gained Society of Arts' gold medal for models of the brain in wax, 1827 ; constructed over a thousand models of anatomical preparations at Guy's Hospital, London, and lectured there on organs of the senses ; sculptured also busts and statues.   [lvii. 96]

TOWNELEY or **TOWNLEY**, CHARLES (1737-1805), collector of classical antiquities ; succeeded to his father's estate of Townley, 1742 ; educated at Douay College ; visited Italy and made collections mostly of marbles and terra-cotta reliefs, which he placed at 7 Park Street, Westminster ; collection purchased after his death by the British Museum.   [lvii. 97]

TOWNELEY, CHRISTOPHER (1604-1674), antiquary ; called ' The Transcriber ' ; attorney ; transcribed public records for projected history of Lancashire.   [lvii. 98]

TOWNELEY, FRANCIS (1709-1746), Jacobite ; entered service of French king and distinguished himself at siege of Phillipsburg ; made colonel by Louis XV to raise forces in England for Prince Charles Edward ; joined Prince Charles Edward at Manchester, 1745, and accompanied him to Derby and back to Carlisle ; captured there on surrender of town to Duke of Cumberland, and executed.   [lvii. 99]

TOWNELEY, JOHN (1697-1782), translator of ' Hudibras ' into French ; brother of Francis Towneley [q. v.] ; entered Gray's Inn, 1715 ; distinguished himself at siege of Phillipsburg ; assisted Prince Charles Edward in Scotland, 1745 ; returned to Paris ; translated ' Hudibras ' into French verse, 1757.   [lvii. 100]

TOWNLEY, SIR CHARLES (1713-1774), Garter king-of-arms ; York herald in College of Arms, 1735 ; knighted at George III's coronation, 1761 ; Garter principal king-of-arms, 1773.   [lvii. 101]

TOWNLEY, JAMES (1714–1778), author of 'High Life below Stairs'; brother of Sir Charles Townley [q. v.]; of Merchant Taylors' School and St. John's College, Oxford; M.A. 1738; third undermaster at Merchant Taylors', London, 1748–53; grammar-master at Christ's Hospital, 1753; head-master at Merchant Taylors', 1760; revived dramatic performances at Merchant Taylors'; produced 'High Life below Stairs' at Drury Lane, London, 1759, and other farces; held living of St. Benet's, Gracechurch Street, London, Hendon, and other preferments. [lvii. 101]

TOWNLEY, JAMES (1774–1833), Wesleyan divine; minister, 1796; D.D. Princeton, 1822; secretary of Wesleyan Missionary Society; president of Wesleyan Conference, 1829; published religious works. [lvii. 102]

TOWNSEND. [See also TOWNSHEND.]

TOWNSEND, AURELIAN (*fl.* 1601–1643), poet; steward to Robert Cecil; friend of Ben Jonson and Herbert; accompanied Herbert on a tour abroad, 1608; enjoyed high literary reputation at court of Charles I; became composer of court masques, 1631, and wrote 'Albion's Triumph' and 'Tempe Restored,' 1632; granted freedom from arrest for debt, 1643; lyrics by him in various miscellanies. [lvii. 103]

TOWNSEND, GEORGE (1788–1857), author; M.A. Trinity College, Cambridge, 1816; curate successively of Littleport, Hackney, and Farnborough; professor at Sandhurst, 1816; published 'Œdipus Romanus,' in reply to Drummond's 'Œdipus Judaicus,' 1811, 'The Old Testament arranged in Historical and Chronological order,' 1821, and 'The New Testament arranged in Historical and Chronological order,' 1826; prebendary of Durham, 1825–57; held livings in Durham diocese; went to Rome to convert Pope Pius IX, 1850. [lvii. 104]

TOWNSEND, GEORGE HENRY (*d.* 1869), compiler; nephew of George Townsend [q. v.]; author of 'Russell's History of Modern Europe epitomised,' 1857, and other works; edited 'Men of the Time,' 1868; committed suicide. [lvii. 105]

TOWNSEND, ISAAC (*d.* 1765), admiral; commanded various ships and in the Shrewsbury took part in the reduction of Cartagena, 1741; admiral of the blue, 1747; as governor of Greenwich Hospital had custody of Admiral John Byng [q. v.]; senior admiral, 1762. [lvii. 105]

TOWNSEND, JOHN (1757–1826), founder of the London Deaf and Dumb Asylum; independent minister at Kingston and Bermondsey; founded at Bermondsey deaf and dumb asylum, 1792; assisted in establishing the London Missionary Society, 1794; published religious works. [lvii. 106]

TOWNSEND, JOSEPH (1739–1816), geologist; M.A. Clare College, Cambridge, 1765, and fellow; studied medicine at Edinburgh; travelled; became chaplain to Duke of Atholl and rector of Pewsey; author of 'The Physician's Vade Mecum,' 1781, 'The Character of Moses established,' 1812–15, and other works. [lvii. 106]

TOWNSEND or **TOWNESEND**, RICHARD (1618?–1692), parliamentary colonel; assisted in defence of Lyme Regis, 1644, and in siege of Pendennis Castle, 1646; took part in Inchiquin's victory over Taaffe, near Mallow, Ireland, 1647; deserted parliamentary cause with Inchiquin, but returned; went back to Ireland and engaged in plots to get possession of Youghal for Cromwell, 1649; M.P., Baltimore (Irish parliament), 1661; high sheriff of Cork, 1671; organised protestant defence there, 1685; besieged and compelled to surrender to the Irish in his mansion at Castletownshend, 1690. [lvii. 107]

TOWNSEND, RICHARD (1821–1884), mathematician; M.A. Trinity College, Dublin, 1852; fellow, 1845, tutor, 1847; F.R.S., 1866; appointed professor of natural philosophy at Dublin, 1870; published 'Chapters on the Modern Geometry of the Point, Line, and Circle,' between 1863 and 1865. [lvii. 108]

TOWNSEND, WILLIAM CHARLES (1803–1850), historical and legal writer; M.A. Queen's College, Oxford, 1827; barrister, Lincoln's Inn, 1828; recorder of Macclesfield, 1833; Q.C., 1850; works include 'The History . . . of the House of Commons,' 1843–4. [lvii. 108]

TOWNSHEND. [See also TOWNSEND.]

TOWNSHEND, CHARLES, second VISCOUNT TOWNSHEND (1674–1738), statesman; son of Sir Horatio, first viscount Townshend [q. v.]; succeeded to peerage, 1687; educated at Eton and King's College, Cambridge; travelled abroad; though brought up a tory seceded to the whig junto; supported religious liberty against Occasional Conformity Bill; a negotiator of treaty of union, 1706; privy councillor, 1707; plenipotentiary to Netherlands, 1709; negotiated with France a treaty with the States-General guaranteeing Hanoverian succession, and conventions guaranteeing the empire, 1710; recalled, 1711, on change of administration, and for having exceeded his instructions in negotiating barrier treaty; voted enemy of his country, 1712; in opposition countenanced agitation for repeal of union; was made secretary for northern department on accession of George I; procured paymaster-generalship for Walpole; married Walpole's sister, 1713; concerned in proceedings against negotiators of Treaty of Utrecht, and showed promptitude and severity in insurrection of 1715; approved of Septennial Act; co-operated with Stanhope in making definite barrier treaty, 1715, and alliance with the emperor, 1716, but was accused of obstructing French alliance, and of design to place George, prince of Wales on the throne; lost power by not accompanying George I to Hanover, 1716, and by not conciliating his favourites; dismissed and made lord-lieutenant of Ireland, 1717, but again dismissed on not giving government full support; made president of council in Stanhope's administration, 1720, and on his death again secretary for northern department, 1721; his integrity untouched by the South Sea disclosures, and his patience and acumen shown in investigation of Layer and Atterbury plots; supported prerogative; obtained Bolingbroke's partial restitution; thwarted Carteret's schemes by allying himself with the Duchess of Kendal, 1723; K.G., 1724; became dissatisfied with Austria and the quadruple alliance, and effected treaty of Hanover with France and Russia, 1725; forced emperor to separate from Spain, 1727; misled by spurious version of Austro-Spanish treaty, made subsidiary treaty with Duke of Brunswick-Wolfenbüttel; brought over the Hanoverian League to the side of Spain, and agreed to treaty of Seville, 1729, which paved the way for alliance between Spain and France and jeopardised peace of Europe; on king of Prussia declaring for the emperor, desired war, but was successfully opposed by Walpole and Queen Caroline; resigned, 1730; devoted himself at Rainham to agriculture. [lvii. 109]

TOWNSHEND, CHARLES, third VISCOUNT TOWNSHEND [q. v.]; son of Charles, second Viscount Townshend [q. v.]; lord of the bedchamber; lord-lieutenant of Norfolk, 1730–8; M.P., Great Yarmouth, 1722–3. [lvii. 116]

TOWNSHEND, CHARLES (1725–1767), chancellor of the exchequer; second son of Charles, third viscount Townshend [q. v.]; educated with Wilkes and Dowdeswell at Leyden; M.P. for Yarmouth, 1747–61; elected for Harwich, 1761; opposed Hardwicke's Marriage Bill, 1753; lord of the admiralty, 1754; resigned, 1755, and attacked Newcastle for employing German mercenaries; privy councillor, 1757; secretary-at-war, 1761; resigned, 1762, but became president of board of trade, 1763; refused to join Grenville's administration and went into opposition; made a great speech against legality of general warrants, and wrote pamphlet, 1764; became paymaster on dismissal of Fox, 1765, and retained office through Rockingham's administration; chancellor of exchequer in Chatham's ministry, 1766; opposed Chatham's India policy, and 'pledged himself to find a revenue in America,' 1767; made his famous 'champagne speech,' 1767; suspended legislative functions of New York assembly, 1767; established commissioners of customs in America and port duties, but did not live to see results. His eloquence was by some of the best judges placed above that of Burke, but his political career was spoilt by instability and lack of principle. [lvii. 117]

TOWNSHEND, CHARLES, first BARON BAYNING (1728–1810), son of William Townshend [q. v.]; of Eton and Clare Hall, Cambridge; M.A., 1749; M.P., Yarmouth, 1761–84; lord of the admiralty, 1765; held other offices, and created Baron Bayning of Foxley, 1797. [lvii. 120]

TOWNSHEND, CHARLES FOX (1795–1817), nephew of George, second marquis Townshend [q. v.]; founder of the Eton Society commonly called 'Pop,' 1811; M.A., St. John's College, Cambridge, 1816. [lvii. 120]

TOWNSHEND, CHAUNCEY HARE (1798-1868), poet; M.A. Trinity Hall, Cambridge, 1824; chancellor's medallist for poem 'Jerusalem,' 1817; took holy orders; published 'Poems,' 1821, and other works. [lvii. 121]

TOWNSHEND, GEORGE (1715-1769), admiral; son of Charles Townshend, second viscount Townshend [q. v.]; served in and commanded various ships; present at action off Toulon, 1744; commanded squadron in co-operation with insurgent Corsicans; drew off on seeing supposed French ships, and his conduct (1747) severely re-primanded; admiral, 1765. [lvii. 121]

TOWNSHEND, GEORGE, fourth VISCOUNT and first MARQUIS TOWNSHEND (1724-1807), son of Charles Towns-hend, third viscount Townshend [q. v.]; M.A. St. John's College, Cambridge, 1749; captain, 7th dragoons; joined Duke of Cumberland's army abroad; fought at Culloden, 1746, and Laufeld, 1747; was appointed aide-de-camp; lieutenant-colonel, 1st foot guards, 1748, but retired owing to difference with Duke of Cumberland, 1750; supposed to have inspired pamphlet severely criticising the duke's military capacity; brought in Militia Bill, 1757; created enemies by his caricatures; on retirement of Cumberland made colonel and aide-de-camp to George II; brigadier-general under Wolfe in Quebec expedition, 1759; com-manded left wing on heights of Abraham, and on Wolfe's death took chief command, 13 Sept. 1759; accused of ingratitude towards Wolfe, and his conduct severely criticised in 'A Letter to an Hon. Brigadier-General,' 1760; privy councillor, 1761; lieutenant-general of the ordnance, 1763; became fourth Viscount Townshend, 1764, and lord-lieutenant of Ireland, 1767; resided there and endeavoured to break down the government by 'undertakers'; promised restriction of pension list, *habeas corpus*, and other boons, but met with great opposition, 1768; granted new peerages, places, and pensions; ob-tained prorogation of parliament, 1769; obtained majority by flagrant corruption and lowered his office; took to dissipated habits; recalled, 1772; reappointed master-general of the ordnance; created marquis, 1786; lord-lieutenant of Norfolk, 1792; field-marshal, 1796.
[lvii. 123]

TOWNSHEND, GEORGE, second MARQUIS TOWNS-HEND, EARL OF LEICESTER, and BARON DE FERRARS of Chartley (1755-1811), son of George Townshend, first marquis Townshend [q. v.]; captain of dragoons, 1773; created Earl of Leicester, 1784; master of the mint, 1790-1794; joint postmaster-general, 1794-9; lord steward of the household, 1799-1802; president of the Society of Antiquaries, 1784; F.R.S.; British Museum trustee.
[lvii. 126]

TOWNSHEND, GEORGE FERRARS, third MAR-QUIS TOWNSHEND (1778-1855), son of George Townshend, second marquis Townshend [q. v.]; disinherited.
[lvii. 127]

TOWNSHEND, HAYWARD (*fl.* 1601), author of 'Historical Collections' (relating to the last four parlia-ments of Queen Elizabeth), published, 1680; B.A. St. Mary Hall, Oxford, 1595; barrister, Lincoln's Inn, 1601; M.P., Bishop's Castle, 1597 and 1601. [lvii. 127]

TOWNSHEND, SIR HORATIO, first VISCOUNT TOWNSHEND (1630?-1687), son of Sir Roger Townshend, first baronet; created M.A. Cambridge, 1645; M.P., Nor-folk, 1659; member of council of state, 1659; active in procuring restoration of Charles II; one of the deputies sent to the Hague, 1660; created Baron Townshend, 1661; signed address for dissolution of parliament, 1675; created viscount, 1682. [lvii. 128]

TOWNSHEND, HORATIO (1750-1837), Irish writer; M.A. Trinity College, Dublin, 1776; incumbent of Ross-carbery, co. Cork; published 'Statistical Survey of the County of Cork,' 1810, and other works. [lvii. 128]

TOWNSHEND, SIR JOHN (1564-1603), soldier; son of Sir Roger Townshend (1543?-1590) [q. v.] [lvii. 130]

TOWNSHEND, JOHN (1789-1845), colonel; as cap-tain of 14th light dragoons served throughout Peninsular war; brevet-major, 1819; served in America and India; aide-de-camp to Queen Victoria and colonel, 1841; suc-ceeded to Castle Townshend estates, 1827. [lvii. 129]

TOWNSHEND, SIR ROGER (*d.* 1493), judge and founder of the Townshend family; governor of Lincoln's Inn, 1461, 1463, 1465, and 1466; M.P., Bramber, 1467, Calne, 1472; legal adviser to the Pastons, from whom he

bought land; king's serjeant, 1483; justice of the com-mon pleas, *c.* 1484; knighted, 1486; served on various commissions. [lvii. 129]

TOWNSHEND, SIR ROGER (1543?-1590), courtier; of East Rainham; of Trinity College, Cambridge; held court offices under Queen Elizabeth; served against Armada and was knighted at sea. [lvii. 130]

TOWNSHEND, ROGER (1708-1760), cavalry officer; son of Charles Townshend, second viscount Townshend [q. v.]; M.P., Great Yarmouth, 1737-8-47, Eye, 1747-8; aide-de-camp to George II at Dettingen, 1743.
[lvii. 116]

TOWNSHEND, THOMAS (1701-1780), teller of the exchequer; son of Charles Townshend, second viscount Townshend [q. v.]; M.A. King's College, Cambridge, 1727; M.P., Winchelsea, 1722-7, Cambridge University, 1727-74; teller of the exchequer, 1727-80. [lvii. 116]

TOWNSHEND, THOMAS, first VISCOUNT SYDNEY (1733-1800), statesman; son of Thomas Townshend (1701-1780) [q. v.]; M.A. Clare College, Cambridge, 1753; M.P. for Whitchurch, Hampshire, 1754-83; clerk of the board of green cloth, 1760; dismissed, 1762; spoke against American mutiny bill, 1765; lord of the treasury under Rockingham; joint-paymaster of the forces in Pitt-Grafton ministry, 1767, but resigned, 1768; remained in opposition and attacked North and the 'king's friends'; war secretary in Rockingham's administration, 1782; home secretary in Shelburne's; created Baron Sydney, 1783; home secretary again under Pitt, 1783; Sydney in Australia named after him; disagreed with Pitt's India bill and slave regulation bill; resigned, 1789, and was created viscount, with 2,500*l.* a year. [lvii. 131]

TOWNSHEND, WILLIAM (1702?-1738), son of Charles Townshend, second viscount Townshend [q. v.]; M.P., Great Yarmouth, 1723-38. [lvii. 116]

TOWNSON, **TOUNSON**, or **TOULSON**, ROBERT (1575-1621), bishop of Salisbury; M.A. Queens' College, Cambridge, 1595, fellow, 1597; D.D. Oxford, 1613; held livings of Wellingborough and Old; royal chaplain and dean of Westminster, 1617; attended Ralegh to the scaffold; bishop of Salisbury, 1620-1. [lvii. 133]

TOWNSON, ROBERT (*fl.* 1795-1798), traveller and mineralogist; M.D. Göttingen, 1795; chief work 'The Philosophy of Mineralogy,' 1798. [lvii. 133]

TOWNSON, THOMAS (1715-1792), divine; matricu-lated from Christ Church, Oxford, 1733; fellow of Mag-dalen College, Oxford, 1737, M.A., 1739, D.D., 1779; held living of Blithefield, and other preferments; archdeacon of Richmond, 1781; published theological works.
[lvii. 133]

TOWRY, GEORGE HENRY (1767-1809), captain in the navy; served in various ships; captured the Minerve, 1795; commanded Diadem at Cape St. Vincent, 1797.
[lvii. 134]

TOWSON, JOHN THOMAS (1804-1881), scientific writer; watchmaker; invented means of photographing on glass and sensitive photographic papers; discovered the quickest route across the Atlantic to be by sailing the great circle; appointed scientific examiner of masters at Liverpool, 1850, and examiner in compasses; published 'Practical Information on the Deviation of the Com-pass,' and other works. [lvii. 135]

TOY, HUMPHREY (1540?-1577), printer; son of Robert Toy [q. v.]; warden of the Stationers' Company, 1571-3; printed 'Grafton's Chronicle,' 1569, and other works. [lvii. 136]

TOY, JOHN (1611-1663), author; M.A. Pembroke College, Oxford, 1634; head-master of King's school, Worcester, *c.* 1643-63; vicar of Stoke Prior, 1641-63; published 'Worcesters Elegie and Eulogie,' 1638, and 'Quisquiliæ Poeticæ,' 1662. [lvii. 136]

TOY, ROBERT (*d.* 1556), printer; benefactor of the Stationers' Company. [lvii. 136]

TOYNBEE, ARNOLD (1852-1883), social philosopher and economist; son of Joseph Toynbee [q. v.]; originally of Pembroke College, Oxford; B.A. Balliol College, Ox-ford, 1878, and tutor; disciple of Thomas Hill Green [q. v.]; studied economics; gave lectures on industrial problems to working-men audiences in London and else-where (published in 'Industrial Revolution'), 1884;

intimate with Jowett, Green, and Nettleship; though a socialist, opposed Henry George's theories; his 'Industrial Revolution' published, 1884. Toynbee Hall in Whitechapel, London, was established in his memory. [lvii. 136]

TOYNBEE, JOSEPH (1815–1866), aural surgeon; assisted Sir Richard Owen at Royal College of Surgeons; F.R.S., 1842; F.R.C.S., 1843; surgeon to St. James's and St. George's Dispensary, London; aural surgeon and lecturer at St. Mary's Hospital, London, 1852; placed aural surgery on firm basis; chief work, 'The Diseases of the Ear,' &c., 1860. [lvii. 138]

TOZER, AARON (1788–1854), captain in the navy; entered navy, 1801; wounded at capture of French frigate Didon, 1805; served at reduction of Madeira, in West Indies, in Walcheren expedition, and in Mediterranean; severely wounded at attack on Cassis, 1813; post-captain, 1830. [lvii. 139]

TOZER, HENRY (1602–1650), puritan royalist; M.A. Exeter College, Oxford, 1626; B.D., 1636; bursar and subrector; imprisoned and expelled from his lectureship, 1648; lecturer at Carfax, Oxford; vicar of Yarnton; published religious works. [lvii. 140]

TRACY, RICHARD (d. 1569), protestant reformer; son of William Tracy (d. 1530) [q. v.]; B.A. Oxford, 1515; M.P., Wootton Bassett, 1529; wrote protestant treatises; employed in visiting monasteries in Gloucestershire; J.P., Gloucestershire, 1537; lost favour at Cromwell's fall and his books ordered to be burnt, 1546; published work on the sacraments, 1548; imprisoned, 1551–2; prosecuted in Mary's reign; high sheriff for Gloucestershire, 1560–1. [lvii. 140]

TRACY, ROBERT (1655–1735), judge; younger son of Robert Tracy, second Viscount Tracy; Irish judge, 1699; baron of the exchequer in England, 1700; removed to common pleas, 1702; tried Jacobites at Carlisle, 1716. [lvii. 142]

TRACY, WILLIAM DE (d. 1173), murderer of Thomas (Becket) [q. v.]; had been Thomas's 'man' when chancellor; assisted in his murder at Canterbury Cathedral, 1170; surrendered himself to Pope Alexander III; set out for the holy land, but died at Cosenza, Sicily, from a horrible disease. He granted the manor of Doccombe to the chapter of Canterbury in expiation of his crime. [lvii. 142]

TRACY, WILLIAM (d. 1530), justice of the peace in the reigns of Henry VII and Henry VIII; adopted Luther's views and expressed his belief in the doctrine of justification by faith in a will which was pronounced heretical by convocation (1532), and became a sort of sacred text to the reformers. [lvii. 140]

TRADESCANT, JOHN (d. 1637 ?), traveller, naturalist, and gardener; employed by Robert Cecil, earl of Salisbury, Lord Wotton, and Duke of Buckingham; author (almost certainly) of 'A voiag of ambasad,' 1618, describing voyage under Sir Dudley Digges [q. v.] to Archangel, and containing the earliest account extant of Russian plants; joined expedition of Sir Samuel Argall [q. v.] against Algerine pirates, 1620, and brought back, among other things, the 'Algier apricot'; appears to have entered Charles I's service; established at South Lambeth his physic garden, the first in England. [lvii. 143]

TRADESCANT, JOHN (1608–1662), traveller and gardener; son of John Tradescant (1637 ?) [q. v.]; gathered 'flowers, plants, shells, etc.,' in Virginia for collection at Lambeth, 1637; succeeded his father as gardener to Charles I and his queen; published 'Museum Tradescantianum,' 1656; bestowed collection, which became famous, on Elias Ashmole [q. v.], 1659, who presented it to the university of Oxford, 1683. Among the trees and shrubs introduced by him and his father were the lilac, acacia, and occidental plane. [lvii. 145]

TRAHAEARN AB **CARADOG** (d. 1081), Welsh prince; ruler of greater part of North Wales; vanquished by Gruffydd ab Cynan and Rhys ab Tewdwr, and slain at Mynydd Carn, South Cardiganshire. [lvii. 147]

TRAHERNE, JOHN MONTGOMERY (1788–1860), antiquary; M.A. Oriel College, Oxford, 1813; took orders, 1812; F.R.S., 1823; F.S.A., 1838; chancellor of Llandaff, 1844; authority on Glamorganshire genealogies and archaeology; edited 'The Stradling Correspondence,' 1840, and published other works. [lvii. 148]

TRAHERON, BARTHOLOMEW (1510 ?–1558 ?), protestant writer; brought up by Richard Tracy [q. v.]; friar minorite; B.A. Cambridge, 1533; relinquished his habit; travelled abroad and joined Bullinger at Zurich, 1537; entered Cromwell's service, 1539, and escaped from court at his fall; joined Calvin at Geneva, 1546, and adopted Calvinism; M.P., 1548; strove unsuccessfully for unambiguous 'reformation of the Lord's Supper'; disputed with Hooper on predestination; made keeper of Edward VI's library, 1549, and tutor to Duke of Suffolk, 1550; contributed to 'Epigrammata Varia,' 1551; dean of Chichester, though not in orders, 1552; resigned, 1552, and made canon of Windsor; went abroad on Mary's accession; lectured at Frankfort and Wesel, and published controversial and other writings. [lvii. 148]

TRAIL, ROBERT (1642–1716), presbyterian divine; distinguished himself at Edinburgh University; excepted from act of indemnity as a 'Pentland rebel,' 1667; joined his father and other exiles in Holland; minister at Cranbrook, 1670; subsequently minister in London; published 'A Vindication of the Protestant Doctrine . . . from the unjust charge of Antinomianism,' 1692, and sermons. [lvii. 150]

TRAIL, WALTER (d. 1401), bishop of St. Andrews; graduated with distinction at Paris; doctor of civil and canon law; held church appointments in Scotland; referendarius at papal court; bishop of St. Andrews, 1385–1401; crowned Robert III, 1390, and exercised great influence in Scotland; ambassador to France, 1391. [lvii. 151]

TRAILL, HENRY DUFF (1842–1900), author and journalist; of Merchant Taylors' School and St. John's College, Oxford; B.A., 1865; B.C.L., 1868; D.C.L., 1873; barrister, Inner Temple, 1869; on staff of 'Pall Mall Gazette,' 1873–80, and 'St. James's Gazette,' 1880–2; contributed to 'Saturday Review'; chief political leader-writer on 'Daily Telegraph,' 1882–97; editor of the 'Observer,' 1889–91; first editor of 'Literature,' 1897 till death; works include 'Life of Sir John Franklin,' 1896, 'Number Twenty,' 1892, 'The New Fiction,' 1897 (collections of essays), and 'The New Lucian' (a series of 'Dialogues of the Dead'), 1884. [Suppl. iii. 385]

TRAILL, THOMAS STEWART (1781–1862), professor of medical jurisprudence; M.D. Edinburgh, 1802; appointed professor of medical jurisprudence, Edinburgh University, 1832; editor of eighth edition of 'Encyclopædia Britannica'; published scientific and medical works. [lvii. 151]

TRAIN, JOSEPH (1779–1852), Scottish antiquary and correspondent of Sir Walter Scott; labourer's son; served in militia, 1799–1802; obtained through his colonel post as excise officer; published 'Poetical Reveries,' 1806, and 'Strains of the Mountain Muse,' 1814, which attracted Sir Walter Scott's attention; corresponded with, and collected valuable materials for, Scott; supplied also information for Lockhart's 'Life of Burns' and Chalmers's 'Caledonia'; published 'Account of the Isle of Man,' 1845, and 'The Buchanites,' 1846. [lvii. 151]

TRANT, 'SIR' NICHOLAS (1769–1839), brigadier-general in the Portuguese army; served with the 84th foot and Irish brigade; took part in expeditions to Minorca (1798) and Egypt; military agent in Portugal, 1808; accompanied Wellesley with Portuguese corps and present at Roliça and Vimeiro; commanded Portuguese force and joined advance to the Douro; made governor of Oporto; captain in staff corps, 1809; gained successes over Masséna during retreat to Torres Vedras, including capture of five thousand prisoners, 1810; knight-commander of the Tower and Sword, 1811; brevet-major, 1815. [lvii. 153]

TRAPP, JOHN (1601–1669), divine; M.A. Christ Church, Oxford, 1624; head-master of Stratford-upon-Avon school, 1622; vicar of Weston-on-Avon, 1636; sided with the parliament, and rector of Welford, 1646–60; published commentaries on the bible, characterised by quaint humour and profound scholarship, and other works; a distinguished preacher. [lvii. 155]

TRAPP, JOSEPH (1679–1747), poet and pamphleteer; grandson of John Trapp [q. v.]; fellow of Wadham College, Oxford, c. 1703; M.A., 1702 (incorporated at Cambridge, 1714); contributed poems to Oxford collections; published translations and 'Abramule,' a play, 1704;

first professor of poetry at Oxford, 1708-18 ; published his lectures as 'Prælectiones Poeticæ,' 1711, 1715, and 1736 ; assisted Sacheverell at his trial, 1709, and wrote high church tory tracts ; chaplain to Sir Constantine Phipps, Irish lord-chancellor, 1711, and to Bolingbroke, 1712 ; wrote 'Peace, a Poem,' 1713 ; held several London lectureships and livings ; published sermons, 1739 ; engaged in controversy with dissenters and wrote against Roman catholics ; D.D. Oxford, 1728 ; president of Sion College ; published translation of the 'Æneis' in blank verse, 1718-35, and other works. [lvii. 155]

TRAQUAIR, first EARL OF (d. 1659). [See STEWART, SIR JOHN.]

TRAVERS, BENJAMIN (1783-1858), surgeon ; studied under Sir Astley Paston Cooper [q. v.] ; demonstrator of anatomy at Guy's Hospital, London, and surgeon to East India Company, 1809 ; surgeon to London Eye Infirmary, 1810 ; F.R.S., 1813 ; surgeon to St. Thomas's Hospital, London, 1815, and lecturer ; Hunterian orator, 1838 ; P.R.S., 1847 and 1856 ; surgeon to Queen Victoria ; raised science of eye-surgery ; published medical works. [lvii. 158]

TRAVERS, SIR EATON STANNARD (1782-1858), rear-admiral ; served off Holland, in West Indies, on Spanish Main, off French coast, and Mediterranean ; took part in Walcheren expedition ; said to have engaged over a hundred times with the enemy ; repeatedly recommended and thanked for good conduct ; K.H., 1834 ; rear-admiral, 1855. [lvii. 159]

TRAVERS, JAMES (1820-1884), general ; lieutenant, Bengal infantry ; served in Afghan war, 1841-2, and mentioned in despatches for services at battles of Sikandarabad, Babawalli, and also at Sobraon, 1846 ; brevet-major, 1846 ; commanded forces at Indur in mutiny, 1857, charged guns of mutineers, defended residency, and obtained V.C ; commanded Mirat division, 1869 ; C.B., 1873 ; general, 1877 ; published 'The Evacuation of Indore,' 1876. [lvii. 160]

TRAVERS, JOHN (d. 1620), brother of Walter Travers [q. v.] ; rector of Farringdon ; B.A. and fellow, Magdalen College, Oxford, 1569. [lvii. 164]

TRAVERS, JOHN (1703 ?-1758), musician ; organist of the Chapel Royal, London, 1737-58 ; composed chiefly church music. [lvii. 161]

TRAVERS, REBECCA (1609-1688), quakeress ; née Booth ; married William Travers, tobacconist ; friend of James Nayler [q. v.] ; heckled incumbent of St. John the Evangelist's, London ; fearless and powerful preacher ; visited prisons and the sick ; published religious works. [lvii. 161]

TRAVERS, WALTER (1548 ?-1635), puritan divine ; a senior fellow of Trinity College, Cambridge, 1569 ; M.A. Christ's College, Cambridge, 1569 ; visited Geneva, and formed friendship with Beza ; published 'Ecclesiasticæ Disciplinæ . . . explicatio,' 1574 (translated by Thomas Cartwright (1535-1603) [q. v.]) ; D.D. Oxford, 1576, but declined to subscribe ; ordained by Cartwright and others at Antwerp ; subsequently chaplain to Burghley and tutor to Robert Cecil ; lecturer at the Temple, 1581, and during Hooker's mastership, confuting in the afternoon what Hooker preached in the morning ; provost of Trinity College, Dublin, 1595-8. [lvii. 162]

TRAVIS, GEORGE (1741-1797), archdeacon of Chester ; M.A. St. John's College, Cambridge, 1768 ; chancellor's medallist, 1765 ; vicar of Eastham, 1766 ; rector of Handley, 1787 ; prebendary of Chester, 1783, archdeacon, 1786 ; his 'Letters to Edward Gibbon' in defence of the genuineness of 1 John v. 7, 1784, answered by Porson in 'the most acute and accurate piece of criticism which has appeared since the days of Bentley' (GIBBON). [lvii. 164]

TREBY, SIR GEORGE (1644 ?-1700), judge ; barrister, Middle Temple, 1671 ; bencher, 1681 ; M.P., Plympton, 1677 till the end of Charles II's reign ; chairman of committee for investigating 'Popish plot' ; succeeded Jeffreys as recorder of London, 1680 ; knighted, 1681 ; defended Sir Patience Ward [q. v.] and Sandys in East India case, and corporation rights in quo warranto proceedings ; dismissed in consequence, 1683 ; one of the counsel for the seven bishops, 1688 ; was restored to recordership 1688, and headed procession of city magnates to meet William

of Orange ; solicitor-general, 1689 ; attorney-general, 1689 ; piloted Bill of Rights through House of Commons ; chief-justice of the common pleas, 1692. [lvii. 165]

TREDENHAM, JOHN (1668 - 1710), politician ; student of the Inner Temple and Christ Church, Oxford ; M.P., St. Mawes, 1690-1705 and 1707-10 ; refused to sign voluntary association of loyalty to William III, 1696 ; arrested on suspicion ; incurred odium through associating with Poussin, the French agent, 1701. [lvii. 166]

TREDGOLD, THOMAS (1788-1829), engineer ; carpenter and architect's clerk ; self-educated ; published 'Elementary Principles of Carpentry,' 1820, the first serious attempt in England to determine data of resistance, and other works, including 'The Steam Engine,' 1827. [lvii. 167]

TREDWAY, LETICE MARY (1593-1677), English abbess in Paris ; took the veil at Augustinian convent, Douay, 1615 ; founded, with Thomas Carre [q. v.], convent for English girls at Paris, 1634. [lvii. 168]

TREE, ANN MARIA (1801-1862). [See BRADSHAW.]

TREE, ELLEN (1805-1880). [See KEAN, MRS. ELLEN.]

TREGELLAS, WALTER HAWKEN (1831-1894), miscellaneous writer ; draughtsman in the war office ; published 'Cornish Worthies,' 1884, and other works ; contributed to periodicals, also articles on Cornishmen to the 'Dictionary of National Biography.' [lvii. 169]

TREGELLES, EDWIN OCTAVIUS (1806-1886), civil engineer and quaker minister ; engineer of Southampton and Salisbury railway, 1835 ; preached and visited West Indies, Northern Europe, and the Hebrides. [lvii. 169]

TREGELLES, SAMUEL PRIDEAUX (1813-1875), biblical scholar ; nephew of Edwin Octavius Tregelles [q. v.] ; employed at ironworks, Neath Abbey ; studied Greek, Hebrew, Chaldee, and Welsh ; took pupils at Falmouth, 1835 ; successively quaker, Plymouth brother, and presbyterian ; superintended, publication of concordances in London, 1837 ; published 'The Book of Revelation,' edited from ancient authorities,' 1844 ; deciphered and collected numerous manuscripts at home and abroad for his new Greek text of the New Testament ; published 'Account of the Printed Text,' 1854, and the text, 1857-1872 ; LL.D. St. Andrews ; received pension of 200l. from civil list. [lvii. 170]

TREGIAN, FRANCIS (1548-1608), Roman catholic exile ; attended Elizabeth's court to assist persecuted catholics ; imprisoned for twenty-eight years, and his property confiscated for harbouring Cuthbert Mayne [q. v.], popish priest, 1577 ; retired to Spain. [lvii. 171]

TREGONWELL, SIR JOHN (d. 1565), civilian ; D.C.L. Oxford, 1522 ; principal of Vine Hall, Oxford ; commissary-general in court of admiralty, 1535 ; agent of Henry VIII in various capacities, especially in dissolution of the monasteries ; master in chancery, 1539 ; chancellor of Wells Cathedral, 1541-3 ; commissioner of the great seal, 1550 : knighted, 1553, and favoured by Queen Mary ; M.P., Scarborough, 1553. [lvii. 172]

TREGOZ, BARON (1559-1630). [See ST. JOHN, OLIVER.]

TREGURY or TREVOR, MICHAEL (d. 1471), archbishop of Dublin ; M.A. and D.D. Oxford ; fellow of Exeter College, Oxford, 1422-7 ; first rector of Caen University, 1440 ; chaplain to Henry VI and his queen ; dean of St. Michael's, Penkridge, 1445 ; archbishop of Dublin, 1449-71. [lvii. 173]

TRELAWNY, CHARLES (1654-1731), major-general ; brother of Sir Jonathan Trelawny [q. v.] ; served with Monmouth in Holland, 1673, and with Turenne on the Rhine, 1674 ; deserted to William of Orange, 1688 ; fought at battle of the Boyne, 1690 ; governor of Dublin ; took part in siege of Cork and was promoted major-general, 1690 ; resigned his regiment, 1692 ; governor of Plymouth, 1696. [lvii. 174]

TRELAWNY, EDWARD (1699-1754), governor of Jamaica ; son of Sir Jonathan Trelawny [q. v.] ; of Westminster School and Christ Church, Oxford ; M.P. for West Looe, 1724-33, East and West Looe, 1734-5 ; governor of Jamaica, 1738-52 ; settled the Maroons and proved very efficient administrator ; took part in expedition against Cartagena, 1742, against San Domingo, 1748. [lvii. 174]

TRELAWNY, EDWARD JOHN (1792–1881), author and adventurer ; entered navy, 1805 ; deserted at Bombay and made his way to Eastern Archipelago ; returned to England and visited Switzerland ; met Shelley and Byron in Italy, 1821 ; present at Leghorn when Shelley and Williams were drowned ; prepared Shelley's tomb at Rome ; took part in Greek struggle for independence, 1823, and married, as his second wife, Tersitza, sister of the insurgent chief Odysseus ; wrote letters on Byron's death and fall of Missolonghi ; published his classical ' Adventures of a younger Son,' 1831 ; visited America ; swam across the river at Niagara between the rapid and the falls and performed other exploits ; idolised by London society ; published ' Records of Shelley, Byron, and the Author,' 1858 ; lived to be the distinguished survivor of the Byronic age ; brilliant but inaccurate conversationalist ; sat for the old seaman in Millais's ' North-West Passage ' ; buried by Shelley's side at Rome ; distinguished as an author for his graphic and living descriptions, but also for a tendency to romance. [lvii. 175]

TRELAWNY, Sir JOHN (*fl.* 1422), knight ; claimed descent from family settled at Trelawne, Cornwall, before the Conquest ; M.P. for Cornwall ; fought at Agincourt, 1415. [lvii. 178]

TRELAWNY, Sir JONATHAN, third baronet (1650–1721), bishop successively of Bristol, Exeter, and Winchester ; son of second baronet and descended from Sir John Trelawny [q. v.] ; of Westminster and Christ Church, Oxford ; M.A., 1675 ; given livings of St. Ive and Southill ; one of the builders of Wren's Tom tower at Christ Church, Oxford, 1681–2 ; showed great activity on Monmouth's landing, and signed militia commissions ; bishop of Bristol, 1685–9 ; showed intense loyalty to the crown, but refused to sign address in favour of declaration of indulgence, 1687 ; assisted French protestant ministers ; attended James II with the bishops' petition, and was imprisoned with them in the Tower of London, tried for seditious libel and acquitted ; enthusiastically supported by the Cornishmen ; took oaths to William and Mary ; bishop of Exeter, 1689–1707 ; established his right as visitor at Exeter College, Oxford ; took the side of Anne and the Churchills against William III, 1691 ; supported Atterbury in revival of convocation ; bishop of Winchester, 1707–21. [lvii. 179]

TRELAWNY, Sir WILLIAM, sixth baronet (*d.* 1772), cousin of Edward Trelawny [q. v.] ; M.P., West Looe, 1756–67 ; died at Spanish Town. [lvii. 175]

TREMAMONDO. [See ANGELO, DOMENICO.]

TREMAYNE, EDMUND (*d.* 1582), clerk of the privy council ; entered service of Edward Courtenay, earl of Devonshire, 1553 ; employed by Cecil in Ireland to send information, 1569 ; clerk of the privy council, 1571 ; published ' Causes why Ireland is not Reformed,' 1571, and ' Matters wherewith the Queen of Scots may be Charged,' 1572 ; M.P., Plymouth, 1572 ; succeeded to family estate of Collacombe, 1572. [lvii. 184]

TREMAYNE or **TREMAINE**, Sir JOHN (*d.* 1694), lawyer ; counsel for the crown and in several important cases ; appointed king's serjeant and knighted, 1689 ; M.P., Tregony, 1690 ; his ' Placita Coronæ ' published, 1723. [lvii. 185]

TREMAYNE, RICHARD (*d.* 1584), younger brother of Edmund Tremayne [q. v.] ; M.A. and fellow of Exeter College, Oxford, 1553 ; fled to Germany at Mary's accession, 1553 ; made archdeacon of Chichester by Elizabeth, 1559 ; treasurer of Exeter Cathedral. [lvii. 185]

TREMELLIUS, JOHN IMMANUEL (1510–1580), hebraist ; son of a Jew of Ferrara ; studied at Padua ; converted by Cardinal Pole ; afterwards became protestant ; fled successively from Lucca and Strasburg ; resided with Cranmer at Lambeth, 1547 ; made ' king's reader of Hebrew ' at Cambridge, 1549 ; prebendary of Carlisle, 1552 ; on accession of Mary left England ; tutor to children of Duke of Deux-Ponts, 1555, imprisoned by him for Calvinism ; professor of Old Testament studies at Heidelberg, 1561 ; visited England, 1565 ; expelled from Heidelberg, 1576, by the new Lutheran elector ; taught Hebrew at Sedan College, and died there ; published translation of the bible from Hebrew and Syriac into Latin, 1569–79, and other works. [lvii. 186]

TREMENHEERE, HUGH SEYMOUR (1804–1893), publicist and author ; son of Walter Tremenheere [q. v.] ; fellow of New College, Oxford, 1824–56 ; M.A., 1832 ; barrister, Inner Temple, 1834 ; revising barrister, 1837 ; served on various commissions and wrote reports ; inspector of schools, 1840 ; assistant poor-law commissioner, 1842 ; C.B., 1871 ; works include ' A Manual of the Principles of Government,' 1882. [lvii. 187]

TREMENHEERE, WALTER (1761–1855), colonel of marines ; present at actions of the Doggerbank, 1781, and Brest, 1805, and at capture of Martinique and Gaudeloupe, 1794–5 ; K.H., 1832. [lvii. 187]

TRENCH, FRANCIS CHENEVIX (1805–1886), divine and author ; son of Melesina Trench [q. v.] ; M.A. Oriel College, Oxford, 1859 ; rector of Islip ; published miscellaneous works. [lvii. 188]

TRENCH, FREDERICK CHENEVIX (1837–1894), major-general ; son of Richard Chenevix Trench [q. v.] ; served at siege of Delhi and Lucknow, and with Hodson's horse ; C.M.G., 1887 ; published military works. [lvii. 194]

TRENCH, Sir FREDERICK WILLIAM (1775–1859), general ; 1st foot guards ; served in Sicily, 1807, and in Walcheren expedition, 1809 ; assistant, 1811, and deputy quartermaster-general, 1813 ; aide-de-camp to George IV, 1825 ; conservative M.P., St. Michael, 1807–12, Dundalk, 1812–18, Cambridge, 1819–32, Scarborough, 1835–47 ; planned Thames Embankment ; K.C.H., 1832 ; general, 1854. [lvii. 189]

TRENCH, MELESINA (1768–1827), author ; *née* Chenevix ; married, first, Colonel Richard St. George, 1786, who died 1788 ; travelled in Germany 1797 and 1800 ; met Nelson and Lady Hamilton ; married Richard Trench, 1803 ; petitioned Napoleon for her husband's release, 1806 ; wrote ' Remains ' (journal and correspondence) and poems. [lvii. 189]

TRENCH, POWER LE POER (1770–1839), archbishop of Tuam ; brother of Richard le Poer Trench, second earl of Clancarty [q. v.] ; B.A. Dublin, 1791 ; held benefices of Creagh and Rawdenstown ; captain of yeomanry, 1798 ; successively bishop of Waterford, 1802–1810, Elphin, 1810–19, and archbishop of Tuam, 1819–39 ; promoted the ' second reformation ' in Ireland ; president of the Irish Society. [lvii. 191]

TRENCH, RICHARD CHENEVIX (1807–1886), archbishop of Dublin ; son of Melesina Trench [q. v.] ; of Harrow and Trinity College, Cambridge ; M.A., 1833 ; studied Spanish literature, and became acquainted with Maurice, Tennyson, and others ; travelled abroad and took part in expedition of Torrijos to Spain, 1830 ; special preacher at Cambridge, 1843 ; Hulsean lecturer, 1845 and 1846 ; rector of Itchenstoke, 1844 ; professor of divinity at King's College, London, 1846–58 ; dean of Westminster, 1856, where he instituted evening nave services ; archbishop of Dublin, 1863 ; opposed Irish church disestablishment ; and, after passing of the act, kept Irish church united ; author of works dealing with history and literature, poetry, divinity, and philology, including ' The Study of Words ' in 1851, ' Notes on the Parables of our Lord,' 1841, and ' Notes on the Miracles of our Lord,' 1846 ; displays great excellence in his sonnets and lyrics ; as philologist popularised scientific study of language ; suggested Oxford English dictionary. [lvii. 191]

TRENCH, RICHARD LE POER, second EARL of CLANCARTY and first VISCOUNT CLANCARTY (1767–1837), diplomatist ; son of first earl ; Irish barrister ; M.P., Newton Limavady, 1796, and co. Galway, 1798 till the union ; first opposed, but afterwards supported, the union ; M.P., co. Galway (British parliament), as supporter of Pitt ; representative peer, 1808 ; president of board of trade, 1813 ; joint postmaster-general, 1814 ; ambassador to William of the Netherlands, 1813 ; plenipotentiary at congress of Vienna, 1814 ; sent to adjust disputes between Bavaria and Baden, 1815 ; ambassador again to the Netherlands, 1816–22 ; created Baron Trench, 1815, and Viscount Clancarty in the peerage of United Kingdom, 1823 ; Marquis of Hunsdon in Netherlands, 1818 ; opposed catholic emancipation, 1829. [lvii. 194]

TRENCH, WILLIAM STEUART (1808–1872), Irish land agent and author ; nephew of first Lord Ashtown ; educated at Trinity College, Dublin ; Royal Agricultural

Society's gold medallist ; agent to the Shirley and other estates ; published 'Realities of Irish Life,' 1868, 'Ierne,' 1871, and tales. [lvii. 196]

TRENCHARD, Sir JOHN (1640–1695), secretary of state ; studied at New College, Oxford, and Middle Temple ; M.P., Taunton, 1679, 1681, Dorchester, 1688, Thetford, in the Convention parliament, Poole, 1690 ; promoted Oates's designs ; took prominent part in exclusion debates and shared in plots ; arrested, but acquitted ; on Monmouth's landing, 1685, escaped to the continent ; pardoned by James II, 1687 ; remonstrated with James II, 1688 ; knighted, 1689 ; serjeant to William and Mary and chief-justice of Chester, 1689 ; secretary for northern department, 1692. [lvii. 196]

TRENCHARD, JOHN (1662–1723), political writer ; educated at Trinity College, Dublin, and called to the bar ; commissioner of forfeited estates in Ireland ; wrote pamphlets against 'standing armies' and 'superstition,' and, with Thomas Gordon (d. 1750) [q. v.], 'The Independent Whig' and 'Cato's Letters.' [lvii. 198]

TRENGROUSE, HENRY (1772–1854), inventor of the 'Rocket' life-saving apparatus, 1808 (adopted, 1818). [lvii. 199]

TRESHAM, FRANCIS (1567?–1605), betrayer of the 'Gunpowder plot' ; son of Sir Thomas Tresham (1543?–1605) [q. v.]; took part in Essex's rebellion, 1601, and was imprisoned ; implicated in mission to the king of Spain ; obtained copy of Blackwell's book on equivocation ; was initiated into Gunpowder plot, but revealed it to his relative Lord Monteagle ; was arrested and confessed knowledge, but died before trial. [lvii. 200]

TRESHAM, HENRY (1749?–1814), historical painter ; exhibited at Dublin ; accompanied John Campbell Cawdor to Italy and studied there ; exhibited at Royal Academy, 1789–1806 ; R.A., 1799 ; collector of pictures and decorative objects ; published verse. [lvii. 202]

TRESHAM, Sir THOMAS (d. 1471), speaker of the House of Commons ; son of William Tresham (d. 1450) [q. v.]; brought up in Henry VI's household ; M.P., Buckinghamshire, 1447, Huntingdonshire, 1449, Northamptonshire, 1459 ; controller of the household ; fought with Lancastrians at St. Albans, 1455 ; speaker of the parliament at Coventry, 1459 ; knighted by Henry VI's son after battle of St. Albans, 1461 ; taken prisoner at Towton and attainted, but pardoned ; imprisoned, but released at restoration of Henry VI, 1470 ; proclaimed traitor on Edward IV's return, 1471 ; fought at Tewkesbury ; promised pardon, but beheaded. [lvii. 203]

TRESHAM, Sir THOMAS (d. 1559), grand prior of order of St. John in England ; grandson of Sir Thomas Tresham (d. 1471) [q. v.]; sheriff of Northamptonshire, 1524–6 and 1539–40 ; knighted before 1530 ; M.P., Northamptonshire, 1542 ; proclaimed Queen Mary at Northampton, 1553 ; grand prior, 1557 ; sat in House of Lords. [lvii. 204]

TRESHAM, Sir THOMAS (1543?–1605), popish recusant ; son of Sir Thomas Tresham (d. 1559) [q. v.]; knighted, 1577 ; imprisoned seven years for harbouring Campion, 1581. [lvii. 204]

TRESHAM, WILLIAM (d. 1450), speaker of the House of Commons ; lawyer ; M.P., Northamptonshire, 1423–50 ; speaker, 1439, 1442, 1447, and 1449 ; Yorkist ; active in Suffolk's impeachment ; murdered by Lancastrians. [lvii. 205]

TRESHAM, WILLIAM (d. 1569), divine ; M.A., 1520, and D.D., 1532, Oxford, and registrar, 1524–9 ; canon of Christ Church, Oxford, 1532 ; vice-chancellor, 1532–47, 1556, and 1558 ; held livings of Towcester and Bugbrooke ; disputed with Peter Martyr concerning eucharist, 1549 ; imprisoned for catholic opinions, 1551 ; favoured by Queen Mary and given preferment ; disputed with Cranmer, Latimer, and Ridley, 1554–5 ; refused oath of supremacy to Queen Elizabeth, and was deprived of all preferments except Towcester. [lvii. 206]

TRESILIAN, Sir ROBERT (d. 1388), chief-justice of the king's bench ; fellow of Exeter College, Oxford, c. 1354 ; Cornwall, 1368 ; J.P., 1377, and steward of Cornwall ; king's serjeant and justice of the king's bench at beginning of reign of Richard II's reign ; chief-justice, 1381 ; tried John Ball (d. 1381) [q. v.] and his followers ; refused to encroach on lord mayor's jurisdiction in case

of John de Northampton [q. v.], 1384 ; one of Richard's advisers in declaring commission of 1386 unlawful, 1387 ; hanged at Tyburn for treason. [lvii. 206]

TREVELYAN, Sir CHARLES EDWARD (1807–1886), governor of Madras ; writer in Bengal civil service, 1826 ; assistant to Sir Charles Metcalfe, commissioner at Delhi, 1827 ; deputy-secretary to government at Calcutta, 1831 ; married Hannah Moore, Macaulay's sister, 1834 ; wrote 'On the Education of the People of India,' 1838 ; assistant-secretary to the treasury, London, 1840–59 ; administered Irish relief works, 1845–7 ; K.C.B., 1848 ; introduced new system of admission into civil service, 1853 ; became governor of Madras, 1859 ; recalled for publicly opposing financial policy of Calcutta, 1860 ; returned to India as finance minister, 1862, and carried out great reforms ; published 'The Application of the Roman Alphabet to all the Oriental Languages,' 1834, and other works. [lvii. 208]

TREVELYAN, RALEIGH (1781–1865), miscellaneous writer ; M.A. St. John's College, Cambridge, 1807 ; barrister, Lincoln's Inn, 1810 ; succeeded to Netherwitton estates, 1818 ; author of poems and other works. [lvii. 209]

TREVELYAN, Sir WALTER CALVERLEY, sixth baronet (1797–1879), naturalist ; M.A. University College, Oxford, 1822 ; studied science at Edinburgh ; published scientific articles and edited the 'Trevelyan Papers,' with Sir Charles Edward Trevelyan [q. v.]; F.G.S. [lvii. 210]

TREVENEN, JAMES (1760–1790), lieutenant, R.N., and captain in Russian navy ; served with James Cook (1728–1799) [q. v.] on the Resolution, 1776, and James King (1750–1784) [q. v.] on the Discovery, 1779 ; took part (on the Resistance) in capture of the Coquette, 1783 ; entered Russian service, 1787, and served against Sweden ; fatally wounded in action at Viborg Bay, 1790. [lvii. 210]

TREVERIS, PETER (fl. 1527), printer, mostly of grammatical tracts, also of 'Polychronicon,' 1527. [lvii. 212]

TREVET, Sir THOMAS (d. 1283), justice itinerant for Dorset and the neighbouring counties, 1268–71 ; tried the rioters who burnt Norwich Cathedral, 1272. [lvii. 234]

TREVISA, JOHN DE (1326–1412), author ; fellow of Exeter (1362–9) and of Queen's (1369–79) colleges, Oxford ; expelled, 1379 ; chaplain and vicar of Berkeley ; translated for fourth Baron Berkeley Higden's 'Polychronicon,' 1387, and other Latin works. [lvii. 212]

TREVITHICK, RICHARD (1771–1833), 'father of the locomotive engine' ; famous for quickness at figures and herculean strength ; engineer at Ding Dong Mine, near Penzance, 1797, introduced several improvements, including double-acting water-pressure engine, 1800, thus perfecting the vacuum engine ; after preliminary experiments completed first steam carriage to carry passengers, at Redruth, 1801 ; devised improved locomotive, the first tried on a railway, at Pen-y-darran, 1804, and another for a steam circus, 1808 ; erected the first 'Cornish engine,' 1812, and started application of steam to agricultural processes ; despatched nine engines to Peru mines, 1814, which proved very successful ; went to Peru, 1816 ; made and lost many fortunes till war of independence, when machinery was wrecked ; prospected in Costa Rica, 1826–1827 ; met Robert Stephenson [q. v.] at Carthagena ; arrived penniless at Falmouth, and his petition to government was disregarded ; visited Holland, 1829 ; projected other schemes, including improvements in propulsion of steamboats ; was buried at expense of workmen at Hall's factory in Dartford churchyard ; as inventor, 'one of the greatest that ever lived.' [lvii. 213]

TREVOR, ARTHUR HILL-, third VISCOUNT DUNGANNON of the second creation in the peerage of Ireland (1798–1862), son of second viscount ; M.A. Christ Church, Oxford, 1825 ; M.P., New Romney, 1830, Durham, 1831, 1855 ; vigorous opponent of parliamentary municipal reform ; supported property qualification of members, revival of convocation, national education connected with the church, and control of beer-shops ; elected representative peer, 1855 ; opposed in the Lords Divorce and Deceased Wife's Sister Bills ; published political pamphlets and a history of William III, 1835–6. [lvii. 217]

TREVOR, GEORGE (1809–1888), divine ; clerk at the India House, 1825 ; attended political meetings with

Benjamin D'Israeli; M.A. Magdalen Hall, Oxford, 1847; chaplain at Madras, 1836; deputy of S.P.G. for York; canon of York and chaplain of Sheffield church; instrumental in reviving convocation of York; held living of Burton Pidsea, and later of Beeford; high churchman and published 'The Catholic Doctrine of the Holy Eucharist,' 1869, and several other works; well known as author and orator; D.D. Durham. [lvii. 218]

TREVOR or TREVAUR, JOHN (*d*..1410), bishop of St. Asaph; precentor of Bath and Wells, 1386; bishop, 1394; was employed by, but deserted, Richard II, and was made chamberlain of Chester, Flint, and North Wales immediately by Henry IV; supported unlimited royal prerogative; was sent to Spain and accompanied army into Scotland, 1400; fought at Shrewsbury, 1403, but joined Glendower, 1404; fled to Scotland, 1405, and subsequently went on mission to France. [lvii. 220]

TREVOR, SIR JOHN (1626–1672), secretary of state; son of Sir John Trevor (*d*. 1673) [q. v.]; M.P., Flintshire, 1646 and 1654, Arundel in Convention parliament, and Great Bedwin in Long parliament of the Restoration; member of trade committee, 1656, and commissioner for forests, 1657; admitted to Monck's council, 1660; took part in Paris in negotiations with Louis XIV, Holland, and Spain, 1668; knighted and appointed secretary of state, 1668. [lvii. 221]

TREVOR, SIR JOHN (*d*. 1673), parliamentarian; of Trevalyn, Denbighshire; knighted, 1619; M.P., Denbighshire, 1620, Flintshire, 1624 and 1625, and Great Bedwin, 1628, and Grampound in the Long parliament; member of council of state, 1651, and of various committees; favoured Restoration. [lvii. 221]

TREVOR, SIR JOHN (1637–1717), judge and speaker of the House of Commons; barrister, 1661, treasurer, 1674, and reader, 1675, of the Inner Temple; knighted, 1671; M.P., Castle Rising, 1673, Beeralston, 1678–9 and 1679–81, Denbighshire, 1681, Denbigh, 1685, Beeralston, 1689, Yarmouth (Isle of Wight), 1689–90; chairman of various committees and courted protestant interest; speaker, 1685 and 1690–5; master of the rolls, 1685, and proved successful judge; remained faithful to James II and was displaced, 1688, but reinstated, 1693; deprived of speakership for taking bribes, 1695; constable of Flint Castle, 1705; *custos rotulorum* of Flint. [lvii. 222]

TREVOR, JOHN HAMPDEN-, third VISCOUNT HAMPDEN (1749–1824), diplomatist; son of Robert Hampden-Trevor, first viscount Hampden and fourth Baron Trevor [q. v.]; M.A. Christ Church, Oxford, 1773; minister at Munich, 1780, Turin, 1783–98. [lvii. 223]

TREVOR, MARCUS, first VISCOUNT DUNGANNON of the first creation and BARON TREVOR of Rose Trevor in peerage of Ireland (1618–1670); 'commander' in co. Down, 1641; came to England, 1643, and fought at Marston Moor, 1644; served in Cornwall under Hopton, 1645–6; fought for the parliament against Irish rebels, 1647, but joined Ormonde, 1649, and helped to defend Drogheda; wounded at fight near Wexford; changed sides again, 1650; made ranger at Ulster, 1660, and created Baron Trevor and Viscount Dungannon, 1662. [lvii. 224]

TREVOR, MICHAEL (*d*. 1471). [See TREGURY.]

TREVOR, RICHARD (1707–1771), bishop of St. David's and of Durham; son of Thomas, baron Trevor of Bromham [q. v.]; D.C.L. Queen's College, Oxford, 1731; fellow of All Souls College, Oxford, 1727; bishop of St. David's, 1744, and of Durham, 1752. [lvii. 225]

TREVOR, ROBERT HAMPDEN-, first VISCOUNT HAMPDEN and fourth BARON TREVOR (1706–1783), son of Thomas Trevor, first baron Trevor of Bromham [q. v.]; B.A. Queen's College, Oxford, 1725; fellow of All Souls College, Oxford, 1725; secretary to legation, 1734, and minister at the Hague, 1739–46; corresponded with Horatio Walpole; made commissioner of revenue in Ireland, 1750; F.R.S., 1764; author of Latin poems. [lvii. 226]

TREVOR, SIR SACKVILL (*fl*. 1604), naval commander; brother of Sir Thomas Trevor [q. v.]; captured four Spanish vessels off coast of Spain, 1602; knighted, 1604. [lvii. 227]

TREVOR, SIR THOMAS (1586–1656), judge; brother of Sir Sackvill Trevor [q. v.]; barrister, Inner Temple,

1603; reader, 1620; knighted, 1619; exchequer judge, 1625; delivered judgment for government against Hampden in ship-money case, 1638; impeached, 1641, and fined 6,000*l*.; on outbreak of civil war refused to follow Charles I to Oxford, but abandoned public life on Charles I's execution. [lvii. 228]

TREVOR, THOMAS, BARON TREVOR of Bromham (1658–1730), judge; son of Sir John Trevor (1626–1672) [q. v.]; barrister, Inner Temple, 1680; solicitor-general, 1692; M.P., Plympton, 1692–8, Lewes, 1701; attorney-general, 1695; opposed Sir John Fenwick's attainder, 1696; chief-justice of the common pleas, 1701; commissioner to arrange union with Scotland, 1706; created Baron Trevor, 1712; removed at accession of George I; lord privy seal, 1726–30; president of the council, 1730. [lvii. 228]

TRICHRUG, IAGO (1779–1844). [See HUGHES, JAMES.]

TRIGGE, FRANCIS (1547 ?–1606), divine and economic writer; M.A. University College, Oxford, 1572; rector of Welbourn; wrote treatises condemning the commercial morality of the time, enclosure of commons, and conversion of arable land into pastures. [lvii. 230]

TRIMEN, HENRY (1843–1896), botanist; M.B. London, 1865; became assistant in botanical department at British Museum, 1861; published with Dyer the 'Flora of Middlesex,' 1869; editor of the 'Journal of Botany,' 1871; published with Bentley 'Medicinal Plants,' 1875–1880; director of botanical gardens at Peradeniya, Ceylon, 1879; F.R.S., 1888; published 'A Handbook to the Flora of Ceylon,' 1893. [lvii. 230]

TRIMLESTON, third BARON (1470–1538). [See BARNEWALL, JOHN.]

TRIMMER, JOSHUA (1795–1857), geologist; grandson of Mrs. Sarah Trimmer [q. v.]; employed on geological survey; wrote 'Practical Geology and Mineralogy,' 1841, and several papers; made important advances in classification of superficial deposits. [lvii. 231]

TRIMMER, MRS. SARAH (1741–1810), author; daughter of John Joshua Kirby [q. v.]; made favourable impression on Dr. Johnson; married James Trimmer of Brentford, 1762; published 'Easy Introduction to the Knowledge of Nature,' 1782, and 'Sacred History,' 1782–1784; started Sunday schools at Brentford, 1786; had interview with Queen Charlotte, 1786; published 'The Œconomy of Charity,' 1786, and other works, including the 'Story of the Robins' and 'Fabulous Histories,' 1786. [lvii. 231]

TRIMNELL, CHARLES (1630 ?–1702), rector of Abbots Ripton. [lvii. 233]

TRIMNELL, CHARLES (1663–1723), successively bishop of Norwich and Winchester; M.A. New College, Oxford, 1688 (incorporated, Cambridge, 1695); D.D. Oxford, 1699; preacher at Rolls Chapel, 1688; chaplain to Earl of Sunderland; prebendary of Norwich, 1691; held successively various livings; archdeacon of Norfolk, 1698; wrote pamphlets upholding rights of crown as against convocation, 1701–2; bishop of Norwich, 1708–21; clerk of the closet to George I; bishop of Winchester, 1721–3. [lvii. 233]

TRIPE, JOHN (1752 ?–1821). [See SWETE, JOHN.]

TRIPP, HENRY (*d*. 1612), author and translator; M.A. Pembroke Hall, Cambridge, 1571; rector of St. Faith's, London; author of 'Brief Aunswer to Maister Pownd's Six Reasons,' 1581, and translations from the Latin. [lvii. 234]

TRIVET or TREVET, NICHOLAS (1258 ?–1328), historian; son of Sir Thomas Trevet [q. v.]; taught at Oxford; works include theological and philological writings, and 'Annales sex Regum Angliæ' (1136–1307), last edited, 1845. [lvii. 234]

TRIVET, SIR THOMAS (*d*. 1388), soldier; served in Poitou, 1375, in Aquitaine, in Spain, 1378–9, Brittany, 1379–1381, where he greatly distinguished himself, and Flanders, 1383; besieged at Bourbourg; convicted on his return of having taken bribes from the French to surrender, and was imprisoned; supported Richard II and was imprisoned at Dover, 1388. [lvii. 236]

TROKELOWE, THROKLOW, or THORLOW, JOHN DE (*fl.* 1330), chronicler and monk of St. Albans; wrote 'Annales' of reign of Edward II (edited by Thomas Hearne, 1729), a work once attributed to Rishanger.
[lvii. 237]

TROLLOPE, SIR ANDREW (*d.* 1461), soldier; served in the French wars, 1449–50; sergeant-porter at Calais; concerned in conspiracy of Alençon, 1454; returned to England with Warwick, 1459, but became Lancastrian; commanded at Wakefield, 1460, and St. Albans, 1461; knighted; killed at Towton. [lvii. 238]

TROLLOPE, ANTHONY (1815–1882), novelist and post-office official; son of Thomas Anthony Trollope [q. v.]; was educated as a town-boy at Harrow; obtained clerkship in post-office, 1834; post-office surveyor in Ireland, 1841; published his first novel, 'The Macdermots of Ballycloran,' 1847, and other failures; became inspector of postal deliveries in south-west rural districts of Ireland, and obtained thus immense stock of information; gained success with 'The Warden,' 1855, followed, among others, by 'Barchester Towers,' 1857, 'The Three Clerks,' 1858, 'Framley Parsonage,' 1861, 'Orley Farm,' 1862, 'The Small House at Allington,' 1864, 'Can you forgive her?' 1864, and 'The Last Chronicle of Barset,' 1867; despatched on missions abroad to Egypt, 1858, and West Indies, and also visited America, 1862, Australia, and New Zealand, 1871–2, South Africa, 1878; published 'The West Indies and the Spanish Main,' 1859, 'North America,' 1862, and other works; given charge of eastern postal district in England, 1859, but being disappointed of promotion retired, 1866; claimed invention of pillar-box; published series of political novels, starting with 'Phineas Finn,' 1869, also 'He knew he was Right,' 1869, 'The way we live now,' 1875, 'Nina Balatka,' 1867, and 'Linda Tressel,' 1868, in Blackwood; besides a large number of other works, including his autobiography, 1875–6. [lvii. 238]

TROLLOPE, ARTHUR WILLIAM (1768–1827), head-master of Christ's Hospital, London; educated there and at Pembroke College, Cambridge, where he distinguished himself; M.A., 1794; D.D., 1815; head-master of Christ's Hospital, 1799–1826; held several livings. [lvii. 242]

TROLLOPE, EDWARD (1817–1893), bishop of Nottingham and antiquary; M.A. St. Mary Hall, Oxford, 1859; rector of Leasingham; prebendary of Lincoln, 1860; archdeacon of Stow, 1867; bishop suffragan of Nottingham, and D.D., 1877; instrumental in establishing see of Southwell, 1884; supervised church restorations; wrote antiquarian books, including a 'Manual of Sepulchral Memorials,' 1858. [lvii. 243]

TROLLOPE, FRANCES (1780–1863), novelist; formerly Milton; married Thomas Anthony Trollope [q. v.], 1809; after visiting America, 1827–30, wrote 'Domestic Manners of the Americans,' 1832, and also produced books on Belgium, Paris, and Vienna; published, among many other novels, 'The Vicar of Wrexhill,' 1837, and 'The Widow Barnaby,' 1838; highly incensed Americans by her description of American society; settled at Florence, 1855; died at Florence. [lvii. 243]

TROLLOPE, GEORGE BARNE (*d.* 1850), rear-admiral; C.B., 1815; half-brother of Sir Henry Trollope [q. v.]; rear-admiral, 1849. [lvii. 248]

TROLLOPE, SIR HENRY (1756–1839), admiral; entered navy, 1771; served in North America; said to have assisted in battles of Lexington and Bunker's Hill; supported attempt of army to join Burgoyne, 1777; commanded the Kite, 1778–81, in the Downs; captured prizes and defended merchant ships; captured the Hebe, 1782; as captain of the Glatton drove into port squadron of Helvoetsluys, and ensured safety of merchantmen, 1796; performed valuable services in the mutiny, 1797; took part in battle of Camperdown and was knighted, 1797; was refused pension, 1805; admiral, 1812; G.C.B., 1831; committed suicide. [lvii. 246]

TROLLOPE, THEODOSIA (1825–1865), author; *née* Garrow; wrote on 'Social Aspects of the Italian Revolution' in the 'Athenæum,' and contributed to other periodicals; married Thomas Adolphus Trollope [q. v.], 1848; created a salon at Florence. [lvii. 248]

TROLLOPE, THOMAS ADOLPHUS (1810–1892), author; eldest son of Thomas Anthony Trollope [q. v.];

accompanied his father to America, 1828; B.A. Magdalen Hall, Oxford, 1835; embarked on literary profession under his mother's auspices; contributed to Dickens's 'Household Words'; settled at Florence, 1843, where his house became the meeting-place for many English and foreign authors; supported Italian revolutionary movement; published a large number of works, including books on Tuscan subjects, reminiscences, and several novels; given order of St. Maurice and St. Lazarus by Victor Emmanuel, 1862; correspondent of 'Daily News' at Florence and of 'Standard,' 1873, at Rome; returned to England, 1890. [lvii. 249]

TROLLOPE, THOMAS ANTHONY (1774–1835), barrister; cousin of Sir Henry Trollope [q. v.]; Winchester scholar; B.C.L. New College, Oxford, 1801; barrister, Middle Temple, 1804; ruined himself by scheme for selling fancy goods at Cincinnati. [lvii. 244]

TROLLOPE, WILLIAM (1798–1863), author; son of Arthur William Trollope [q. v.]; M.A. Pembroke College, Cambridge, 1824; incumbent of St. Mary's, Green Ponds, Tasmania; published exegetical works on the New Testament. [lvii. 242]

TROSSE, GEORGE (1631–1713), nonconformist divine; educated for trade in France and Portugal; took to dissipated habits; was placed with a physician at Glastonbury, and finally went to Pembroke College, Oxford, 1658; became dissenting minister at Exeter; was imprisoned for conventicle preaching, 1685; published religious works and autobiography. [lvii. 250]

TROTTER, CATHARINE (1679–1749). [See COCKBURN.]

TROTTER, COUTTS (1837–1887), vice-master of Trinity College, Cambridge; nephew of Henry Dundas Trotter [q. v.]; M.A. Trinity College, Cambridge, 1862; fellow, 1861; studied in Germany; lecturer in physical science, 1869–84; vice-master, 1885; performed valuable services in carrying out statutes of 1882. [lvii. 252]

TROTTER, HENRY DUNDAS (1802–1859), rear-admiral; served in East and West Indies; commanded Curlew on West African coast and captured pirates, 1833; commanded expedition to the Niger, 1841, to make treaties; commodore at Cape of Good Hope on outbreak of Crimean war; rear-admiral, 1857. [lvii. 252]

TROTTER, JOHN (1757–1833), army contractor; uncle of Henry Dundas Trotter [q. v.]; established Soho Bazaar, 1815. [lvii. 253]

TROTTER, JOHN BERNARD (1775–1818), author; brother of Edward Southwell Ruthven [q. v.]; B.A. Trinity College, Dublin, 1795; student at the Temple; secretary to Fox; Irish barrister, 1802; published political tracts and other works; died in great destitution. [lvii. 254]

TROTTER, THOMAS (1760–1832), physician to the fleet and author; M.D. Edinburgh, 1788; surgeon's mate in Channel Fleet, 1779, at battle of the Doggerbank, 1781; promoted surgeon, 1782; served on a slaver; as physician to Channel fleet (1794–5) was present at battle of 1 June, 1794; published medical works and verses. [lvii. 254]

TROUBRIDGE, SIR EDWARD THOMAS (*d.* 1852), rear-admiral; son of Sir Thomas Troubridge [q. v.]; entered navy, 1797; present at battle of Copenhagen, 1801; served on the Victory, 1803; assisted in destroying Dutch ships, 1806; lord of the admiralty, 1835; C.B., 1838; rear-admiral, 1841. [lvii. 255]

TROUBRIDGE, SIR THOMAS, first baronet (1758?–1807), rear-admiral; entered navy, 1773; served in East Indies and on various ships; present at battles off Sadras and Trincomalee, 1782, and Hughes's actions, 1782–3; captured on the Castor, 1794; present at action off the Hyères, 1795, on the Culloden, and at battle of St. Vincent, 1797, where he led the line and was warmly praised for his gallant conduct; failed in attack on Santa Cruz, and at battle of the Nile struck on a shoal; received, however, gold medal; assisted Nelson at Naples and Malta; created baronet, 1799; lord of the admiralty, 1801; rear-admiral, 1804; lost in the Blenheim proceeding from Madras to the Cape. [lvii. 256]

TROUBRIDGE, SIR THOMAS ST. VINCENT HOPE COCHRANE (1815–1867), colonel; son of Sir Edward Thomas Troubridge [q. v.]; served at Gibraltar and the West Indies, and in Canada and the Crimea; fought at Alma, 1854, and lost right leg and left foot at Inkerman ; C.B. ; aide-de-camp to Queen Victoria ; brevet-colonel ; received Legion of Honour ; deputy adjutant-general, 1857. [lvii. 258]

TROUGHTON, EDWARD (1753–1835), scientific instrument maker ; joined his brother in London as mechanician, and later carried on business by himself ; original member R.A.S. and F.R.S., 1810; invented new mode of graduating arcs of circles, 1778 ; contrived mural circles and erected them at Greenwich, 1812, and other places, and also telescopes ; made the ' beam-compass ' and ' hydrostatic balance ' ; contributed to the ' Edinburgh Cyclopædia.' [lvii. 259]

TROUGHTON, JOHN (1637 ?–1681), nonconformist divine; became blind from small-pox ; fellow of St. John's College, Oxford, and B.A., 1659; nonconformist minister and religious author. [lvii. 260]

TROUGHTON, WILLIAM (1614 ?–1677 ?), nonconformist divine; of Queen's College, Oxford ; chaplain to Robert Hammond [q. v.], 1647 ; obtained preferment ; independent preacher ; published religious works.
[lvii. 260]

TROY, JOHN THOMAS (1739–1823), Roman catholic archbishop of Dublin ; joined Dominican order at Rome, 1756; rector of St. Clements at Rome ; bishop of Ossory, 1776 ; archbishop of Dublin, 1784 ; condemned Whiteboys ; instrumental in founding Maynooth College. [lvii. 261]

TRUBBEVILLE or **TRUBLEVILLE,** HENRY DE (*d.* 1239). [See TURBERVILLE.]

TRÜBNER, NICHOLAS (NIKOLAUS) (1817–1884), publisher ; born at Heidelberg ; became clerk at Longman's ; entered into partnership with Delf, and afterwards with David Nutt ; developed American trade and visited United States ; competent orientalist and critic ; published, among other works, ' Bibliographical Guide to American Literature,' 1855, ' Trübner's American and Oriental Record,' ' Trübner's Oriental Series,' and ' British and Foreign Philosophical Library.' [lvii. 262]

TRUBSHAW, JAMES (1777–1853), engineer ; employed at Buckingham Palace and elsewhere ; gained local reputation at Stone ; constructed Grosvenor Bridge (single-arched) at Chester, 1833, declared by Thomas Telford [q. v.] impracticable, and Exeter Bridge, Derby.
[lvii. 263]

TRUMAN, JOSEPH (1631–1671), ejected minister and metaphysician ; M.A. Clare College, Cambridge, 1654; rector of Cromwell; near Nottingham ; ejected, 1662; frequently indicted for nonconformity ; published ' The Great Propitiation,' 1669, dealing with the doctrine of justification by faith and contending for the all-sufficiency of the Mosaic law ; published also ' A Discourse of Natural and Moral Impotency,' 1671. [lvii. 263]

TRUMBULL, CHARLES (1646–1724), chaplain to Sancroft: brother of Sir William Trumbull [q. v.] ; B.A. Christ Church, Oxford, 1667 ; D.C.L. All Souls College, Oxford, 1677. [lvii. 267]

TRUMBULL, WILLIAM (*d.* 1635), diplomatist ; resident in the Netherlands, 1609–25 ; recalled on rupture with Spain ; M.P., Downton, 1626 ; clerk of privy council, 1626 ; granted Easthampstead Park, 1628, and appointed muster-master-general. [lvii. 264]

TRUMBULL, SIR WILLIAM (1639–1716), secretary of state ; grandson of William Trumbull [q. v.] ; entered St. John's College, Oxford, 1655 ; fellow of All Souls College, Oxford, 1657 ; D.C.L., 1667 ; student at Middle Temple, 1657 ; practised in ecclesiastical and admiralty courts ; chancellor of Rochester diocese and clerk of the signet, 1682 ; with Pepys accompanied Lord Dartmouth as judge-advocate to Tangier, 1683 ; knighted, 1684 ; envoy to France, 1685 ; assisted English protestants there and was recalled ; M.P., East Looe, 1685–7 ; ambassador to Turkey, 1686–91 ; governor of Hudson's Bay and Turkey companies ; lord of the treasury, 1694 ; secretary of state, privy councillor, and secretary to lords justices, 1695 ; M.P., Oxford University, 1695–8 ; was acquainted with Dryden and Pope, and is eulogised in their works.
[lvii. 265]

TRURO, BARON (1782–1855). [See WILDE, THOMAS.]

TRUSLER, JOHN (1735–1820), eccentric divine, literary compiler, and medical empiric ; B.A. Emmanuel

College, Cambridge, 1757 ; translated Italian burlettas ; held several curacies, chaplaincy to the Poultry-Compter, and city lectureship ; studied medicine ; brought out series of sermons for use of clergymen ; established book-selling business ; works include ' Hogarth Moralized,' 1768, ' The Habitable World,' 1788–97, and part i. of an autobiography. [lvii. 268]

TRUSSELL, JOHN (*fl.* 1636–1642), historical writer ; mayor of Winchester ; published ' A Continuation of the . . . History of England,' 1636, and the 'Touchstone of Tradition,' 1642; contributed to 'Annalia Dubrensia,' 1636. [lvii. 269]

TRUSSELL, THOMAS (*fl.* 1610–1625), of Billesley ; soldier and author ; brother of John Trussell [q. v.]
[lvii. 269]

TRUSSELL or **TRUSSEL,** WILLIAM (BARON TRUSSELL) (*fl.* 1327), adherent of Thomas of Lancaster ; fought at Boroughbridge, 1322, and fled to France on Lancaster's fall ; returned with Isabella, 1326 ; tried and sentenced elder Despenser to be hanged ; as procurator of parliament renounced allegiance to Edward II at Berkeley, 1327 ; had for a time commission of oyer and terminer ; was sent on various foreign missions to Rome, Spain and Portugal, France and Flanders ; granted lordship of Bergues, 1331.
[lvii. 270]

TRYE, CHARLES BRANDON (1757–1811), surgeon ; studied under John Hunter (1728–1793) [q. v.] ; house surgeon to Westminster Hospital and assisted John Sheldon [q. v.] ; subsequently surgeon to Gloucester infirmary ; established lying-in charity at Gloucester ; F.R.S., 1807 ; published medical works. [lvii. 271]

TRYON, SIR GEORGE (1832–1893), vice-admiral ; entered the navy, 1848 ; served in the Crimea, in royal yacht, 1858 ; commander of the Warrior, Channel fleet, 1861, first British sea-going ironclad ; director of transports in Annesley Bay for Abyssinian expedition, 1867 ; private secretary to Mr. Goschen, 1871 ; commanded the Raleigh, 1874–7 ; on committee for revision of signal-book, 1877 ; commanded Monarch in Mediterranean, 1878, and performed valuable services off coast of Tunis, 1881 ; secretary of the admiralty, 1882–4 ; rear-admiral, 1884 ; commanded on Australian station and formulated colonial defence ; K.C.B., 1887 ; superintendent of reserves, 1888, and commanded fleet in summer manœuvres ; vice-admiral, 1889 ; commanded on Mediterranean station, 1891 ; was lost in the Victoria in collision with the Camperdown, caused by his error, off Tripoli. [lvii. 272]

TRYON, THOMAS (1634–1703), 'Pythagorean' ; as a boy was employed in spinning and shepherding ; trudged to London and apprenticed himself to a hatter ; read works of Behmen and became a Pythagorean, refusing to eat all meat and fish ; visited Barbados and traded in ' beavers ' ; wrote several works of mystical philosophy and dietetics, including ' Health's Grand Preservative,' 1682 ; forms a link between the Behmenists and early quakers. [lvii. 274]

TRYON, WILLIAM (1725–1788), governor of New York ; of same family as Sir George Tryon [q. v.] ; lieutenant-colonel, 1st foot guards ; became governor of North Carolina, 1765, of New York, 1771 ; on outbreak of rebellion remained on board ship ; re-entered New York with Howe, 1776 ; commanded Surrey regiment, made successful expedition into Connecticut, and issued letters of marque ; lieutenant-general, 1782. [lvii. 276]

TUATHAL (*d.* 544), king of Ireland ; called Maelgarbh, Roughcrown ; succeeded his cousin Muircheartach Mor [q. v.], 533 ; defeated the Cianachta. [lvii. 277]

TUCHET. [See TOUCHET.]

TUCKER, ABRAHAM (1705–1774), philosopher ; gentleman commoner of Merton College, Oxford, 1721, where he studied philosophy, mathematics, French and Italian, and music ; bought Betchworth Castle, near Dorking, 1727, and studied agriculture ; wrote ' The Light of Nature Pursued,' published, 1768–78, and other works of discursive philosophising, eulogised by Paley.
[lvii. 277]

TUCKER, BENJAMIN (1762–1829), secretary of the admiralty ; at first purser in the navy ; secretary to Lord St. Vincent, and assisted him in his attack on prevalent abuses ; surveyor-general of the duchy of Cornwall, 1808.
[lvii. 279]

TUCKER, CHARLOTTE MARIA (1821–1893), known as A.L.O.E. (A Lady of England); writer for children; daughter of Henry St. George Tucker [q. v.]; wrote mainly tales of allegorical form; went to India as Zenana missionary, 1875; died at Amritsar. [lvii. 279]

TUCKER, HENRY ST. GEORGE (1771–1851), Indian financier; obtained writership in East India Company's service, 1792, at Calcutta; captain of cavalry corps; military secretary to Lord Wellesley, 1799; accountant-general, 1801–4, and again in 1805, when he incurred unpopularity by advocating retrenchments; underwent imprisonment for attempted rape, 1806; filled various posts, and became secretary in colonial and financial department, 1812; left India, 1815; elected director of East India Company, 1826, chairman, 1834 and 1847; published two tragedies and works on Indian finance. [lvii. 280]

TUCKER, JOSIAH (1712–1799), economist and divine; M.A. St. John's College, Oxford, 1739; D.D., 1755; minor canon of Bristol and domestic chaplain to Bishop Butler; appointed prebendary of Bristol, 1756, and dean of Gloucester, 1758; wrote tract against 'going to war for the sake of trade,' 1763, which originated correspondence with and a translation by Turgot; defended clerical subscription to the thirty-nine articles; maintained desirability of separation from the colonies, and addressed 'Cui Bono?' arguing the war with America a mistake for all concerned to Necker, 1781; anticipated some of Adam Smith's arguments against monopolies; author of economic, political, and religious works. [lvii. 282]

TUCKER, THOMAS TUDOR (1775–1852), rear-admiral; brother of Henry St. George Tucker [q. v.]; entered navy, 1793, and assisted at reduction of Cape of Good Hope, battle of St. Domingo, 1806, reduction of Guadeloupe, 1810, and capture of American frigate Essex near Valparaiso, when he was severely wounded, 1814; C.B., 1840; rear-admiral, 1846. [lvii. 284]

TUCKER, WILLIAM (1558?–1621). [See TOOKER.]

TUCKER, WILLIAM (1589?–1640?), colonist; appears to have sailed for Virginia, 1610, in the Mary and James; leading colonist at Kiccowtan. [lvii. 285]

TUCKEY, JAMES KINGSTON (1776–1816), commander R.N. and explorer; entered navy, 1793; served at reduction of Trincomalee, 1795, and of Amboyna, where he was wounded; shared in capture of the Forte, 1799; went out on the Calcutta, 1802, to establish colony at Port Phillip, and published account, 1804; captured by the French on return home and detained prisoner till 1814; commander, 1814; wrote 'Maritime Geography and Statistics,' 1815; commanded expedition to the Congo, 1816, and died of exhaustion; left a 'Narrative.' [lvii. 285]

TUCKNEY, ANTHONY (1599–1670), puritan divine; M.A. Emmanuel College, Cambridge, 1620, fellow and tutor; D.D., 1649; town preacher, 1629, and vicar, 1633, of Boston; prepared doctrinal formularies in the Westminster Assembly, 1643; received rectory of St. Michael-le-Querne, Cheapside, London; master of Emmanuel College, Cambridge, 1645–53; vice-chancellor, 1648 and 1653; corresponded with Whichcote on his rationalistic tendencies, 1651; master of St. John's College, Cambridge, 1653–61; a 'trier,' 1654; regius professor of divinity, 1656; removed, 1661; arrested for nonconformist preaching, 1665; published sermons. [lvii. 286]

TUDOR, EDMUND, EARL OF RICHMOND (EDMUND OF HADHAM) (1430?–1456), eldest son of Owen Tudor [q. v.]; knighted by Henry VI, 1449; created Earl of Richmond, 1453, and declared legitimate; great forester of Braydon Forest, 1453, and privy councillor. [lvii. 288]

TUDOR, JASPER, EARL OF PEMBROKE and DUKE OF BEDFORD (JASPER OF HATFIELD) (1431?–1495), second son of Owen Tudor [q. v.]; knighted, 1449; created Earl of Pembroke, 1453; fought on Henry VI's side at battle of St. Albans, 1455; employed in Wales, 1457; K.G., 1459; took Denbigh, 1460; defeated by Edward IV at Mortimer's Cross, 1461; took part in invasion of the north, 1462; retired to Scotland and was attainted; landed in North Wales, 1468, but was finally defeated; landed with Warwick, 1470; fled with his nephew Henry (afterwards Henry VII) after battle of Tewkesbury to Wales, thence to Brittany and to Paris, 1483; accompanied Henry to Milford Haven and to Bosworth, 1485; created Duke of Bedford, 1485; held various

high offices; earl-marshal, 1492; active in suppressing Lovel and Stafford, and Simnel insurrections; commander in France, 1492. [lvii. 288]

TUDOR, MARGARET (1443–1509). [See BEAUFORT, MARGARET.]

TUDOR, MARGARET (1489–1541). [See MARGARET.]

TUDOR, OWEN (d. 1461), grandfather of Henry VII; belonged to old Welsh family; became clerk of the wardrobe to Catherine of Valois [q. v.], widow of Henry V, to whom he was perhaps legally married; was twice confined in Newgate and escaped; pleaded his cause before the council, 1437; given annuity by Henry VI; captured at battle of Mortimer's Cross, 1461, and beheaded. [lvii. 290]

TUDWAY, THOMAS (d. 1726), musician; choir-boy in Chapel Royal, London, after Restoration, and tenor in choir of St. George's, Windsor, 1664; organist of King's College, Cambridge, 1670, Pembroke College, Cambridge, and University Church; professor of music at Cambridge, 1705; Mus.Doc., 1705; composer and organist to Queen Anne; degraded from degrees and appointments for punning on the Duke of Somerset's restricted bestowal of patronage among the members of the university, 1706, but reinstated on public retractation, 1707; compiled for Lord Oxford collection of church music; composed church music, songs, and catches. [lvii. 291]

TUER, ANDREW WHITE (1838–1900), publisher and writer on Bartolozzi; entered partnership with Mr. Field (d. 1891) as stationer and printer in London, 1862; founded, 1877, and edited 'Paper and Printing Trades Journal'; began, 1877, publishing business, which was turned into a limited company as the Leadenhall Press, 1892; collected works of art of all kinds; F.S.A., 1890; published 'Bartolozzi and his Works,' 1882, 'London Cries,' 1883, and works relating to literature and children's books of George III's reign. [Suppl. iii. 387]

TUFNELL, HENRY (1805–1854), politician; B.A. Christ Church, Oxford, 1829; student at Lincoln's Inn, 1827; private secretary to Sir Robert John Wilmot-Horton, and afterwards to Lord Minto; treasury lord, 1840; whig M.P., Devonport, 1840–54; secretary to the treasury, 1846. [lvii. 293]

TUFNELL, THOMAS JOLLIFFE (1819–1885), surgeon; assistant-surgeon to 44th regiment at Calcutta, 1841, and later to 3rd dragoon guards in Ireland; F.R.C.S. of Ireland, 1845, and president, 1874–5; surgeon to Dublin military prison and several hospitals; regius professor of military surgery, Dublin, 1851–60; accompanied Scottish regiment to Crimea, 1854; published surgical works. [lvii. 293]

TUFTON, SACKVILLE, ninth EARL OF THANET (1767–1825), nephew of John Frederick Sackville, third Duke of Dorset [q. v.]; travelled abroad; created riot in court at trial of Arthur O'Connor [q. v.] at Maidstone, 1798, and was imprisoned and fined. [lvii. 294]

TUKE, SIR BRIAN (d. 1545), secretary to Henry VIII; king's bailiff of Sandwich, 1508; clerk of the signet, 1509; clerk of the council at Calais, 1510; J.P. for Kent, 1512; knight of the king's body, 1516; 'governor of the king's ports,' 1517; secretary to Wolsey, and later French secretary to Henry VIII, 1522; treasurer of the household, 1528; patron of learning; celebrated by Leland and often painted by Holbein. [lvii. 295]

TUKE, DANIEL HACK (1827–1895), physician; son of Samuel Tuke [q. v.]; after some hesitation applied himself to study of mental disease; distinguished himself at St. Bartholomew's Hospital, London; M.D. Heidelberg, 1853; wrote essay 'On the Progressive Changes in the Moral Management of the Insane,' 1854, which gained a prize, and, with Bucknill, 'A Manual of Psychological Medicine,' 1858; visited foreign asylums; became consulting physician in London, 1875, examiner, and lecturer; LL.D. Glasgow, 1883; published other medical works. [lvii. 296]

TUKE, HENRY (1755–1814), quaker writer; son of William Tuke [q. v.]; engaged in business at York; quaker minister; chief work, 'The Principles of Religion as professed by . . . the Quakers,' 1805. [lvii. 297]

TUKE, JAMES HACK (1819–1896), philanthropist and quaker; son of Samuel Tuke [q. v.]; employed in his father's business at York, 1835, but became partner in a bank, 1852, removing to Hitchin, Hertfordshire; studied social questions, wrote papers on education, and devoted himself to public objects; visited America, 1845 and 1880; distributed money in Paris after the siege, 1871, and in Ireland, 1846–7; published 'Irish Distress and its Remedies,' 1880, and set on foot large scheme of emigration to America, assisted by the government; recommended bills for establishing light railways, 1889, and Congested Districts Board, 1891, of which he was an active member; elected member of Athenæum and Reform Clubs, 1884; instrumental in establishing 'Emigrants' Information Office,' 1886; published several pamphlets and letters relating to Ireland, and other works.   [lvii. 297]

TUKE, SIR SAMUEL, first baronet (d. 1674), royalist and playwright; admitted, Gray's Inn, 1635; entered royal army, commanded at Lincoln, and fought at Marston Moor, 1644; served under Goring in the west, 1645; defended Colchester, 1648; resided abroad during Protectorate, and attended Duke of Gloucester; turned Roman catholic; at Restoration was sent on missions to French court; created baronet, 1664; original F.R.S.; his tragi-comedy, 'The Adventures of Five Hours,' 1663, much lauded by Pepys.   [lvii. 299]

TUKE, SAMUEL (1784–1857), philanthropist and quaker; eldest son of Henry Tuke [q. v.]; entered his father's business at York; collected evidence on insanity and wrote papers, including 'Description of the Retreat,' 1813, founded by his father and grandfather, constituting earliest account of humane treatment of insane; interested himself in education, various good works and public objects; published works on prominent quakers.
     [lvii. 301]

TUKE, THOMAS (d. 1657), royalist divine; M.A. Christ's College, Cambridge, 1603; minister at St. Giles's-in-the-Fields, London, 1616; vicar of St. Olave's, Jewry, London, 1617; sequestered and imprisoned 1643; published religious works.   [lvii. 302]

TUKE, WILLIAM (1732–1822), founder of the York Retreat, erected, 1796, for humane treatment of insane, first establishment of the kind in England; tea and coffee merchant in York, and quaker.   [lvii. 303]

TULK, CHARLES AUGUSTUS (1786–1849), Swedenborgian; of Westminster School and Trinity College, Cambridge; assisted in founding 'society' for publishing Swedenborg's works, 1810, and was connected with the 'Hawkstone Meeting'; studied physical science and social questions; magistrate; M.P., Sudbury, 1820–6, Poole, 1835–7; author of Swedenborgian works.   [lvii. 303]

TULL, JETHRO (1674–1741), agricultural writer; matriculated, St. John's College, Oxford; barrister, Gray's Inn, 1699, bencher, 1724; farmed at Howberry, near Wallingford, where he invented his drill, c. 1701; removed to 'Prosperous' farm, near Hungerford, Berkshire, c. 1709; travelled abroad, 1711–14; introduced system of pulverising ground; published 'The Horse-hoing Husbandry,' 1733, and other agricultural treatises; was much attacked and accused of plagiarism. Voltaire followed his method at Ferney.   [lvii. 304]

TULLIBARDINE, MARQUIS OF (d. 1746). [See MURRAY, WILLIAM.]

TULLOCH, SIR ALEXANDER MURRAY (1803–1864), major-general; educated for the law at Edinburgh; joined 45th regiment in Burmah, 1826; exposed scandals connected with the soldiers' food, health, pay in bad coinage, and pension frauds; colonel, 1854; investigated with Sir John McNeill [q. v.] commissariat in Crimea, 1854, when report severely blamed general officers for improper distribution, and aroused controversy between Tulloch and Kinglake; published 'The Crimean Commission and the Chelsea Board,' 1857; K.C.B., 1857; major-general, 1859.   [lvii. 306]

TULLOCH, JOHN (1823–1886), principal of St. Andrews; distinguished himself at St. Andrews University; assistant-minister at Dundee, 1844–5; travelled abroad; contributed to periodicals, 1848–53; appointed principal and professor of theology at St. Mary's College, St. Andrews, 1854; delivered lectures at Edinburgh on reformation leaders, 1859, and was appointed chaplain to Queen Victoria; chief clerk, 1875, of general assembly, and moderator, 1878; visited America, 1874, and lectured; opposed church disestablishment; conducted services in Westminster Abbey, 1878; LL.D. Glasgow, 1879, and Edin-

burgh, 1884; edited 'Fraser's Magazine,' 1879; dean of the Chapel Royal, London, 1882; lectured on church defence, 1882, 'Literary and Intellectual Revival of Scotland in the Eighteenth Century,' 1883, and 'Movements of Religious Thought in the Nineteenth Century,' 1884–5; a broad-minded theologian, but champion of orthodoxy; founder of Scottish liberal church party; published 'Rational Theology and Christian Philosophy in England in the Seventeenth Century,' 1872, and other important works; contributed to 'Encyclopædia Britannica' (9th edit.)
     [lvii. 307]

TULLY or **TULLIE**, GEORGE (1652 ?–1695), controversial writer; possibly nephew of Thomas Tully [q. v.]; fellow, Queen's College, Oxford, 1679; M.A., 1678.
     [lvii. 310]

TULLY, THOMAS (1620–1676), divine; fellow of Queen's College, Oxford, 1643; M.A., 1642; appointed principal of St. Edmund Hall, Oxford, 1658; rector of Grittleton, 1658; royal chaplain, 1660; D.D., 1660; dean of Ripon, 1673; strict Calvinist; published controversial works.   [lvii. 310]

TUNSTALL or **TONSTALL**, CUTHBERT (1474–1559), master of the rolls and bishop successively of London and Durham; studied at Oxford and Cambridge; LL.D. Padua; became learned in Greek, Hebrew, mathematics, and civil law; extolled by Erasmus; friend of More and leaders of the renascence; rector of Harrow-on-the-Hill, 1511; prebendary of Lincoln, 1514; archdeacon of Chester, 1515; ambassador to Prince of Castile at Brussels, 1515–16; master of the rolls, 1516; prebendary of York, 1519; sent ambassador to Charles V, 1519 and 1525; dean and prebendary of Salisbury, 1521; bishop of London, 1522–30; keeper of the privy seal, 1523; visited his diocese, 1526, and prohibited Tyndall's 'New Testament'; accompanied Wolsey to France, 1527, and negotiated treaty of Cambray; bishop of Durham, 1530; during ecclesiastical revolution remained faithful to Roman catholic dogma, but obeyed passively civil power; president of council of the north, 1537; envoy to Scotland and France; took part (1541) in drawing up 'Institution of a Christian Man,' passing of Six Articles Act, 1539, and publication of the 'Great Bible'; executor to Henry VIII's will, 1547; voted against Uniformity Act, 1549, but carried out its provisions when law; accused of inciting rebellion, 1550, and confined to his house in London, and wrote 'De Veritate Corporis et Sanguinis . . . in Eucharistia'; deprived, 1553; was restored on Queen Mary's succession, but refrained from persecution of the protestants; refused oath of supremacy and again deprived by Queen Elizabeth, 1559; author of works, mostly religious.   [lvii. 310]

TUNSTALL, JAMES (1708–1762), divine and classical scholar; M.A. St. John's College, Cambridge, 1731; fellow and tutor; D.D., 1744; public orator, 1741–6; obtained several livings, including Minster and Great Chart, 1747; chaplain to Archbishop Potter, 1743; treasurer and canon of St. David's, 1746; vicar of Rochdale, 1757; carried on controversy with Middleton, questioning genuineness of Cicero's letters to Brutus; published miscellaneous works.   [lvii. 315]

TUNSTALL, MARMADUKE (1743–1790), naturalist; of Wycliffe Hall, Yorkshire; educated at Douay; published 'Ornithologia Britannica,' 1771; F.R.S., 1771.
     [lvii. 316]

TUNSTALL or **HELMES**, THOMAS (d. 1616), Roman catholic martyr; studied at Douay; missioner in England; executed at Norwich.   [lvii. 316]

TUNSTED, SIMON (d. 1369), Minorite friar and miscellaneous writer; joined Greyfriars at Norwich; distinguished for learning and piety; doctor of theology, master of Minorites at Oxford, 1351, and minister provincial, 1360; author of commentary on Aristotle's 'Meteora,' additions to Richard of Wallingford's 'Albion,' and perhaps of valuable treatise 'Quatuor Principalia Musicæ.'   [lvii. 317]

TUPPER, MARTIN FARQUHAR (1810–1889), author of 'Proverbial Philosophy'; belonged to old Huguenot family; M.A. Christ Church, Oxford, 1835, and barrister, Lincoln's Inn, 1835; published 'Proverbial Philosophy,' poem, 1838, which had a world-wide success (his name, however, in due time becoming a synonym for the commonplace), and numerous other works, including his naive 'Autobiography,' 1886 ; urged necessity for national defence ; ingenious inventor ; F.R.S., 1845 ; D.C.L. Oxford, 1847. [lvii. 318]

TURBE, WILLIAM DE (1095 ?-1174). [See WILLIAM.]

TURBERVILLE, DAUBENEY (1612-1696), physician ; M.A. Oriel College, Oxford, 1640 ; M.D., 1660 ; royalist soldier ; eye specialist. [lvii. 320]

TURBERVILLE or **TURBERVILE**, EDWARD (1648 ?-1681), informer ; Roman catholic ; entered household of Lady Molyneux ; served in French army, and studied at Douay ; pretended, at Lord Stafford's trial, that he had been importuned by him to kill Charles II, but later gave evidence against Stephen College and Shaftesbury, 1681. [lvii. 320]

TURBERVILLE or **TURBERVILE**, GEORGE (1540 ?-1610 ?), poet ; great-nephew of James Turberville [q. v.] ; scholar of Winchester and (1561) fellow of New College, Oxford ; admired at the Inns of Court for excellence in poetry ; secretary to Thomas Randolph, ambassador to Russia, 1568 ; published 'Epitaphs, Epigrams, Songs, and Sonets,' 1567 ; ' Poems describing . . . Russia,' 1568, ' The Booke of Faulconrie,' 1575 ; ' Tragical Tales,' 1587 (from the Italian) ; translated Ovid's 'Heroycall Epistles,' 1567, ' Mantuan,' 1567, and ' Mancinus,' 1568 ; commended by Harington and Puttenham ; familiarised employment of Italian models ; pioneer in use of blank verse. [lvii. 321]

TURBERVILLE, **TRUBBEVILLE**, or **TRUBLE-VILLE**, HENRY DE (d. 1239), seneschal of Gascony ; famous soldier ; adhered to King John ; took part in victory over French fleet in Dover Straits, 1217 ; seneschal of Gascony, 1226-31 and 1234-8 (with short break, 1237) ; distinguished himself in Welsh war, 1233, and took Carmarthen ; sent to aid the Emperor Frederick II against the Lombards, 1238. [lvii. 323]

TURBERVILLE, HENRY (d. 1678), Roman catholic controversialist ; private chaplain ; published 'An Abridgment of Christian Doctrine,' 1649, and 'A Manual of Controversies,' 1654. [lvii. 324]

TURBERVILLE or **TURBERVYLE**, JAMES (d. 1570 ?), bishop of Exeter ; fellow of New College, Oxford ; M.A.,1520 ; graduated D.D. abroad (incorporated, 1532) ; bishop of Exeter, 1555 ; refused oath of supremacy and deprived, 1559. [lvii. 325]

TURBINE, RALPH DE (d. 1122). [See RALPH D'ESCURES.]

TURFORD, HUGH (d. 1713), quaker writer ; schoolmaster at Bristol ; published 'Grounds of a Holy Life,' 1702. [lvii. 325]

TURGEON, PIERRE FLAVIEN (1787-1867), Roman catholic archbishop of Quebec ; director of Quebec seminary, 1821 ; coadjutor, 1834 ; archbishop, 1850 ; supported English policy ; organised province and founded Laval University, 1852. [lvii. 326]

TURGES or **TURGESIUS** (d. 845). [See THURKILL.]

TURGOT (d. 1115), bishop of St. Andrews ; belonged to good Saxon family ; was imprisoned at Norman Conquest, but escaped and was welcomed by king of Norway ; shipwrecked on English coast ; studied under Aldwin at Jarrow ; became monk and subsequently prior of Durham, 1087, and archdeacon ; assisted in founding new cathedral, 1093, and in translation there of remains of St. Cuthbert, 1104 ; bishop of St. Andrews, 1109 ; probably author of ' Life of St. Margaret, Queen of Scotland,' and her spiritual adviser. [lvii. 326]

TURLE, HENRY FREDERIC (1835-1883), editor of ' Notes and Queries ' ; son of James Turle [q. v.] ; sub sequently assistant to William John Thoms [q. v.], editor of 'Notes and Queries,' 1870 ; editor, 1878. [lvii. 327]

TURLE, JAMES (1802-1882), organist and composer ; chorister at Wells, 1810-13 ; organist successively of Christ Church, Surrey, and St. James's, Bermondsey ; first connected with Westminster Abbey, 1817 ; organist, 1831-82 ; composer mostly of church music. [lvii. 328]

TURMEAU, JOHN (1777-1846), miniature-painter ; exhibited at Royal Academy, 1794-1836. [lvii. 329]

TURMEAU, JOHN CASPAR (1809-1834), architect ; son of John Turmeau [q. v.] [lvii. 329]

TURNBULL, GEORGE (1562 ?-1633), Scots jesuit ; professor and controversial writer. [lvii. 329]

TURNBULL, JOHN (fl. 1800-1813), traveller ; made voyage to Pacific islands and published ' A Voyage round the World,' 1804. [lvii. 329]

TURNBULL, WILLIAM (d. 1454), bishop of Glasgow, 1447 ; founder of Glasgow University, 1451. [lvii. 330]

TURNBULL, WILLIAM (1729 ?-1796), physician ; published medical works. [lvii. 330]

TURNBULL, WILLIAM BARCLAY DAVID DONALD (1811-1863), architect and antiquary ; admitted advocate, 1832 ; founded Abbotsford book-printing club, and edited several works for the society at Edinburgh ; became Roman catholic, 1843 ; barrister, Lincoln's Inn, 1856 ; edited for Rolls Series ' The Buik of the Cronicles of Scotland . . . by William Stewart,' 1858 ; assistant under record commission, 1859, compiling calendars of state papers ; obliged to give up employment owing to suspicions aroused by his religion, 1861 ; edited large number of old authors, translated from the French, and published genealogical works. [lvii. 330]

TURNER, MRS. ANNE (1576-1615), murderess ; wife of George Turner [q. v.] ; intimate with, and perhaps daughter of the astrologer, Simon Forman [q. v.] ; abetted Countess of Essex in poisoning Sir Thomas Overbury (1581-1613) [q. v.], 1613 ; was hanged at Tyburn. [lvii. 337]

TURNER, CHARLES (1774-1857), engraver ; engraved plates for Joseph Mallord William Turner's ' Liber Studiorum ' ; engraver to George III, 1812 ; exhibited at Royal Academy, 1810-57. [lvii. 331]

TURNER, CHARLES TENNYSON (1808-1879), poet ; elder brother of Alfred Tennyson, first Baron Tennyson [q. v.], with whom he published ' Poems by Two Brothers,' 1827 ; B.A. Trinity College, Cambridge, 1832 ; vicar of Grasby ; changed his name to Turner on succeeding to a great-uncle's property, 1830 ; published sonnets, 1830, 1864, 1868, and 1873.. [lvii. 332]

TURNER, CYRIL (1575 ?-1626). [See TOURNEUR.]

TURNER, DANIEL (1667-1741), physician ; member of the Barber-Surgeons' Company ; L.R.C.P., 1711 ; published medical works. [lvii. 332]

TURNER, DANIEL (1710-1798), hymn-writer ; schoolmaster at Hemel Hempstead, and baptist minister successively at Reading and Abingdon ; published hymns, sermons, and other works. [lvii. 333]

TURNER, DAWSON (1775-1858), botanist and antiquary ; entered Pembroke College, Cambridge ; joined the Yarmouth bank, 1796 ; published ' The Botanist's Guide through England and Wales,' 1805, ' Natural History of Fuci,' 1808-19, and other works. [lvii. 334]

TURNER, DAWSON WILLIAM (1815-1885), philanthropist and educational writer ; son of Dawson Turner [q. v.] ; demy of Magdalen College, Oxford ; M.A., 1840 ; D.C.L., 1862. [lvii. 335]

TURNER, EDWARD (1798-1837), chemist ; M.D. Edinburgh, 1819 ; studied chemistry and mineralogy abroad ; professor of chemistry, University College, London, 1828-37 ; F.R.S., c. 1831 ; published 'Elements of Chemistry,' 1827. [lvii. 335]

TURNER, FRANCIS (1638 ?-1700), bishop of Ely ; son of Thomas Turner (1591-1672) [q. v.] ; scholar of Winchester ; probationary fellow of New College, Oxford, 1655 ; M.A., 1663 ; D.D., 1669 ; master of St. John's College, Cambridge, 1670-9 ; vice-chancellor, 1678 ; bishop of Rochester, 1683, of Ely, 1684 ; joined in the bishops' petition, 1688, but refused oath of allegiance to William and Mary, and was deprived, 1690 ; corresponded with the exiled James II and was frequently arrested. [lvii. 336]

TURNER, GEORGE (d. 1610), physician ; M.A. St. John's College, Cambridge, 1576 ; M.D. abroad ; F.R.C.P., 1588, censor, 1591, 1592, 1597, 1606, and 1607, and treasurer, 1609-10. [lvii. 337]

TURNER, SIR GEORGE JAMES (1798-1867), lord justice of appeal in chancery ; brother of William Turner (1792-1867) [q. v.] ; M.A., 1822, and fellow, Pembroke

College, Cambridge; barrister, Lincoln's Inn, 1821; Q.C., 1840; M.P., Coventry, 1847-51; carried ' Turner's Act' to simplify chancery proceedings; vice-chancellor, privy councillor, and knighted, 1851; member of commission for reform of chancery practice, 1852; lord justice of appeal in chancery, 1853; hon. D.C.L. Oxford, 1853. [lvii. 338]

TURNER, JAMES (*d.* 1664), parliamentary colonel; executed for burglary. [lvii. 340]

TURNER, SIR JAMES (1615-1686?), soldier and author; M.A. Edinburgh, 1631; enlisted in service of Gustavus Adolphus under Sir James Lumsden [q. v.], and served in Germany, 1632-4; joined Scottish army in England and Ireland and Scotland; took part in invasion of England, 1645; adjutant-general, 1647; joined Hamilton's expedition into England, 1648; returned to Scotland, 1650, and accompanied Charles II to battle of Worcester, 1651; joined Charles II in Paris; employed on royalist missions; knighted at Restoration; commanded forces in south-west Scotland to crush opposition of covenanters, 1666; captured by the rebels; escaped, but was deprived of his commissions, 1668; granted pension by James II; published 'Pallas Armata' (military essays), 1683, and memoirs; probably original of Dugald Dalgetty. [lvii. 338]

TURNER, JOSEPH MALLORD (or MALLAD) WILLIAM (1775-1851), landscape-painter; son of a London barber; sold drawings at a very early age; entered Academy schools, 1789, and was admitted to Reynolds's studio; exhibited first drawing, view of Lambeth Palace at Royal Academy, 1790; contributed drawings to Walker's 'Copper-plate Magazine' and Harrison's 'Pocket Magazine,' and made sketching tours; paid visits to Thomas Monro (1759-1833) [q. v.], called by Ruskin Turner's true master; executed drawings in neutral tint; made tour in the north, which resulted in great development, and exhibited at the Royal Academy, 1798, 'Morning on the Coniston Fells, Cumberland,' and other pictures; exhibited Welsh subjects and his first naval battle-piece, 'The Battle of the Nile,' 1799; entered his 'first style,' 1800-20, in which he imitated various old masters, his work including Alpine scenes, 1803, after a tour abroad; 'Shipwreck,' 1805, 'Sun rising through Vapour,' 1807, 'Crossing the Brook,' 'Dido building Carthage,' 1815, also 'Liber Studiorum,' 1807-19; R.A., 1802; professor of perspective, 1808; visited Devonshire, the north, Scotland, the continent, and Italy; from 1820 to 1835 ceased to imitate, and aimed at ideal compositions; executed drawings for 'Rivers of England' and 'Harbours of England,' 1824; painted the 'Bay of Baiæ,' 1823, 'Dido directing the Equipment of the Fleet,' 1828, and 'Ulysses deriding Polyphemus,' sometimes regarded as his masterpiece, 1829; executed illustrations for Rogers's 'Italy,' 1830, and several other publications; visited south of France, Italy, Rome, 1828, and Venice, *c.* 1832; painted series of splendid pictures of Venice, and the famous 'Fighting Téméraire,' 1839; entered his 'third period,' 1835-45; travelled in France and Italy, 1836; exhibited 'The Slave Ship,' 1840; some of his later works severely criticised and ridiculed; his reputation greatly increased by publication of Ruskin's 'Modern Painters,' 1843; during next five years produced characteristic and inimitable works, including pictures from sketches in Switzerland, such as 'The Splugen,' Venetian subjects, such as 'The Approach to Venice,' 1843, together with 'Snowstorm,' 1842, and 'Rain, Steam, and Speed,' 1844, and attempts to represent vague thoughts in colour language, such as 'War—the Exile'; completed his 'third' period, 1845, his later pictures including 'Whalers,' a new class of subject; buried in St. Paul's Cathedral. [lvii. 341]

TURNER, MATTHEW (*d.* 1788?), chemist and freethinker; furnished chemical appliances to Josiah Wedgwood; published an answer to Dr. Priestley's 'Letters to a Philosophical Unbeliever,' 1782. [lvii. 350]

TURNER, PETER (1542-1614), physician; son of William Turner (*d.* 1568) [q. v.]; M.A. Cambridge; M.D. Heidelberg, 1571 (incorporated at Oxford and Cambridge); physician at St. Bartholomew's Hospital, London; M.P. for Bridport; puritan. [lvii. 351]

TURNER, PETER (1586-1652), mathematician; son of Peter Turner (1542-1614) [q. v.]; B.A. Christ Church, Oxford, 1605; fellow of Merton College, Oxford, 1607, M.A., 1612; Gresham professor of geometry, 1620-31;

Savilian professor, 1631-48; directed by Laud, assisted in revision of the university statutes, 1634; enlisted for Charles I under Sir John Byron, first baron Byron [q. v.], 1641, and was captured and imprisoned; ejected, 1648. [lvii. 351]

TURNER, RICHARD (*d.* 1565?), protestant divine; M.A. Magdalen College, Oxford, 1529; fellow, 1529; D.D., 1552; curate to Ralph Morice [q. v.]; chaplain to Cranmer; obtained various preferments; indicted for non-compliance with Six Articles Act, 1543; prebendary of Windsor and vicar of Dartford; fled to Basle at Queen Mary's accession; restored, 1559. [lvii. 351]

TURNER, RICHARD (1753-1788), author; son of Richard Turner (1724?-1791) [q. v.]; writer of standard school text-books. [lvii. 352]

TURNER, RICHARD (1724?-1791), divine and author; vicar of Elmley Castle and rector of Little Comberton, 1754; hon. LL.D. Glasgow, 1785; wrote educational works. [lvii. 352]

TURNER, ROBERT (*d.* 1599), Roman catholic divine; professor at Douay, Rome, Eichstadt, and Ingolstadt; rector of Ingolstadt University and D.D.; canon of Breslau and Latin secretary to Archduke Ferdinand; author of Latin sermons. [lvii. 353]

TURNER, ROBERT (*fl.* 1640-1664), astrologer and botanist; B.A. Christ's College, Cambridge, 1640; published 'Μικρόκοσμος,' 1654, 'Βοτανολογία,' 1664, with other astrological works and translations. [lvii. 354]

TURNER, SAMUEL (*d.* 1647?), royalist; son of Peter Turner (1542-1614) [q. v]; M.A. St. Alban Hall, Oxford, 1604; M.D. Padua; M.P., Shaftesbury, 1626, and in the Long parliament; also in Charles I's Oxford parliament; attacked Buckingham in House of Commons, 1626; voted against Strafford's attainder, 1641; defeated parliamentarians at Henley, 1643. [lvii. 354]

TURNER, SAMUEL (1749?-1802), Asiatic traveller; captain, East India service; led expedition to Thibet, 1783-4, and wrote an account, 1800; present at siege of Seringapatam, 1794; F.R.S., 1801. [lvii. 354]

TURNER, SAMUEL (1765-1810), Irish informer; B.A., 1784, and LL.D. Dublin, 1787; barrister and United Irishman; fled abroad, 1797, but returned, 1803; enjoyed friendship of O'Connell, but had betrayed the cause. [lvii. 355]

TURNER, SHARON (1768-1847), historian; attorney; studied Icelandic and Anglo-Saxon literature, and published his chief work, 'History of England from the earliest period to the Norman Conquest,' 1799-1805, a complete revelation; F.S.A.; received civil list pension. [lvii. 356]

TURNER, SYDNEY (1814-1879), dean of Ripon; son of Sharon Turner [q. v.]; B.A. Trinity College, Cambridge, 1836, and of Reformatory School at Red Hill; inspector of reformatories; dean of Ripon, 1875-6. [lvii. 357]

TURNER, THOMAS (1591-1672), dean of Canterbury; M.A. St. John's College, Oxford, 1618; fellow; created D.D., 1633; received numerous preferments; chaplain successively to Laud and Charles I; dean of Rochester, 1642, of Canterbury, 1644; attended Charles I devotedly; subsequently was deprived and imprisoned; reinstated at Restoration. [lvii. 357]

TURNER, THOMAS (1645-1714), president of Corpus Christi College, Oxford; son of Thomas Turner (1591-1672) [q. v.]; scholar and fellow of Corpus; M.A., 1669; D.D., 1683; archdeacon of Essex and canon of St. Paul's, London; president of Corpus Christi College, Oxford, 1688-1714; erected the fellows' buildings, 1712. [lvii. 358]

TURNER, THOMAS (1749-1809), potter; son of Richard Turner (1724?-1791) [q. v.]; excellent chemist and designer; succeeded to 'The Salopian China Warehouse' pottery works; introduced 'willow pattern.' [lvii. 359]

TURNER, THOMAS (1793-1873), surgeon; studied at Guy's and St. Thomas's hospitals, London, and at Paris; house-surgeon at Manchester Infirmary, 1817-20; instrumental in establishing Manchester schools of medicine and surgery; surgeon to Deaf and Dumb Institution, 1825, and to Royal Infirmary, Manchester, 1830; professor of philosophy at Manchester Royal Institution, 1843; F.R.C.S., 1843; published medical works. [lvii. 360]

TURNER, THOMAS HUDSON (1815–1852), antiquary; held post at record office in the Tower of London; edited 'Manners and Household Expenses of England in the Thirteenth and Fifteenth Centuries,' 1841, and published other works. [lvii. 361]

TURNER, SIR TOMKYNS HILGROVE (1766?–1843), general; ensign, 1782; served in Holland, 1793–4; brevet-colonel, serving in Egyptian campaign, 1801; fought at Aboukir Bay and Alexandria; brought to England the Rosetta stone; received foreign decorations; assistant and quartermaster-general, 1803; brigadier-general to staff in South America, 1807; colonel of 19th foot, 1811; hon. D.C.L. Oxford, knighted, and appointed lieutenant-governor of Jersey, 1814–16, of Bermuda, 1825–1831; general, 1830; G.C.H. and groom of the bedchamber; published archæological works. [lvii. 361]

TURNER, WILLIAM (d. 1568), dean of Wells; physician and botanist; M.A. Pembroke Hall, Cambridge, 1533; fellow and (1538) senior treasurer; intimate with Ridley and Latimer; published at Cambridge several works, including 'Libellus de re Herbaria,' 1538; left Cambridge, 1540; travelled abroad, studied botany, and became intimate with Gesner and others; returned to England at accession of Edward VI; became chaplain and physician to Duke of Somerset; M.P. and prebendary of York; dean of Wells, 1550; deprived, 1553; lived abroad during Mary's reign; reinstated, 1560; opposed all ceremonial; suspended for nonconformity, 1564; wrote botanical works, including his 'Herbal,' which marks start of scientific botany in England; his religious controversial works forbidden to be read in England in English; said to have introduced lucern into England. [lvii. 363]

TURNER, WILLIAM (1653–1701), divine; M.A. St. Edmund Hall, Oxford, 1675; incumbent of Walberton and Binstead; chief work, 'Compleat History of the most Remarkable Providences ... in this Present Age,' 1697 [lvii. 366]

TURNER, WILLIAM (1651–1740), musician; chorister at Christ Church, Oxford, and Chapel Royal, London, one of the authors of the 'Club Anthem'; sang in choirs of Lincoln Cathedral, St. Paul's, London, and Westminster; gentleman of the Chapel Royal, London, 1669; Mus.Doc. Cambridge, 1696; composed secular and sacred music, including various anthems. [lvii. 366]

TURNER, WILLIAM primus (1714–1794), dissenting divine; minister at Wakefield and elsewhere; contributed to Priestley's 'Theological Repository' and 'Harmony of the Evangelists.' [lvii. 367]

TURNER, WILLIAM, tertius (1788–1853), dissenting minister; son of William Turner (1761–1859) [q. v.]; M.A. Glasgow, 1806; mathematical and philosophical tutor, Manchester College; chief work, 'Lives of Eminent Unitarians,' 1840–3. [lvii. 368]

TURNER, WILLIAM, secundus (1761–1859), dissenting divine; son of William Turner (1714–1794) [q. v.]; minister at Newcastle; published several works. [lvii. 367]

TURNER, WILLIAM (1789–1862), 'Turner of Oxford'; artist; taught at Oxford; painted pictures of English scenery. [lvii. 368]

TURNER, WILLIAM (1792–1867), diplomatist and author; brother of Sir George James Turner [q. v.]; entered foreign office; attached to embassy at Constantinople; published 'Journals of a Tour in the Levant,' 1820; envoy to Columbia, 1829–38. [lvii. 368]

TURNERELLI, EDWARD TRACY (1813–1896), artist; son of Peter Turnerelli [q. v.]; sketched Russian monuments for the czar, 1836–54; projector of 'people's tribute' to Lord Beaconsfield, 1878; published miscellaneous works. [lvii. 370]

TURNERELLI, PETER (1774–1839), sculptor; grandson of Italian refugee; gained medal at Royal Academy; instructor to princesses, 1797–1801; executed busts, including those of Wellington, Blücher, George III, O'Connell, Princess Charlotte, and Prince Leopold, and memorials, including that of Burns at Dumfries; represented sitters in ordinary costume. [lvii. 369]

TURNHAM, ROBERT DE (d. 1211), baron; brother of Stephen de Turnham [q. v.]; took part in third cru-

sade; justiciar of Cyprus, 1191; commanded Richard I's forces in Anjou, 1197; John's seneschal in Poitou and Gascony, 1201–5. [lvii. 370]

TURNHAM, STEPHEN DE (d. 1215), justice; brother of Robert de Turnham [q. v.]; went on third crusade; escorted Berengaria to Rome, 1193; justice itinerant in Richard I's and John's reigns. [lvii. 370]

TURNOR, SIR CHRISTOPHER (1607–1675), judge; M.A. Emmanuel College, Cambridge, 1633; barrister, Middle Temple, 1633; bencher, 1654; joint receiver-general of South Wales, 1639–62; baron of exchequer and knighted at Restoration; served on several important commissions. [lvii. 371]

TURNOR, EDMUND (1755?–1829), antiquary; descended from Sir Edmund Turnor, brother of Sir Christopher Turnor [q. v.]; M.A. Trinity College, Cambridge, 1781; F.S.A., 1778; F.R.S., 1786; M.P., Midhurst, 1802–6; published 'Chronological Tables ... of the County of Lincoln,' 1779, and other works. [lvii. 372]

TURNOR, SIR EDWARD (1617–1676), judge; entered Queen's College, Oxford, 1632; barrister, Middle Temple, 1640; treasurer, 1662; M.P., Essex; K.C., 1660; knighted, 1660; speaker of the House of Commons, 1661; solicitor-general; lord chief-baron of exchequer, 1670. [lvii. 373]

TURNOR, SIR EDWARD (1643–1721), gentleman of the privy chamber; M.P., Oxford; son of Sir Edward Turnor (1617–1676) [q. v.] [lvii. 373]

TURNOUR, CYRIL (1575?–1626). [See TOURNEUR.]

TURNOUR, GEORGE (1799–1843), orientalist; entered Ceylon civil service, 1818; identified King Piyadassi with Asóka; edited the 'Mahávamsa,' 1836. [lvii. 374]

TUROLD (fl. 1075–1100), romance-writer; supposed author of the 'Chanson de Roland.' [lvii. 374]

TURPIN, RICHARD (1706–1739), robber; son of an innkeeper at Hempstead, Essex; joined gang of robbers; entered into partnership with the highwayman Tom King on the Cambridge road, 1735, whom he shot by accident; escaped to Yorkshire; arrested for horse-stealing and hanged at York, the romances connected with his name being legendary. [lvii. 375]

TURQUET DE **MAYERNE**, SIR THEODORE (1573–1655). [See MAYERNE.]

TURSTIN (d. 1140). [See THURSTAN.]

TURSWELL, THOMAS (1548–1585), canon of St. Paul's, London; M.A. King's College, Cambridge, 1574; canon of St. Paul's, London, 1580; possible author of 'A View of certain Wonderfull Effects of late Dayes,' 1578. [lvii. 376]

TURTON, JOHN (1735–1806), physician; M.A. Queen's College, Oxford, 1759; M.D. University College, Oxford, 1767; obtained Radcliffe travelling fellowship, 1761; F.R.S., 1763; F.R.C.P., 1768; physician to George III and royal family. [lvii. 376]

TURTON, THOMAS (1780–1864), bishop of Ely; senior wrangler, Catharine Hall, Cambridge, 1805; fellow, 1806; tutor, 1807; M.A., 1808; B.D., 1816; Lucasian professor of mathematics, 1822; regius professor of divinity, 1827; dean of Peterborough, 1830, of Westminster, 1842; bishop of Ely, 1845; vigorous controversial writer; composed church music. [lvii. 377]

TURTON, WILLIAM (1762–1835), conchologist; M.A. and M.B. Oriel College, Oxford, 1791; practised at Swansea; F.L.S., 1809; chief work, 'A Conchological Dictionary of the British Islands,' 1819. [lvii. 377]

TUSSAUD, MARIE, MADAME TUSSAUD (1760–1850), founder of the wax-work exhibition; née Gresholtz; born at Berne; assisted her uncle Curtius in his 'Cabinet de Cire' in the Palais Royal, Paris; taught Madame Elisabeth; modelled heads of victims of the Terror; married Tussaud; separated from him, 1800, and, migrating to England, transferred museum to Lyceum, Strand, London, 1802, later to Blackheath, and finally settled at Baker Street, London. [lvii. 378]

TUSSER, THOMAS (1524?–1580), agricultural writer and poet; chorister at St. Paul's, London; went to Eton, King's College, and Trinity Hall, Cambridge;

joined the court as musician to William Paget, first baron Paget [q. v.] ; farmed at Cattiwade, Suffolk, and introduced culture of barley; died prisoner for debt in London; published 'Hundreth Good Pointes of Husbandrie,' 1557 (amplified in editions, 1570, 1573), verse of quaint and pointed expression, many proverbs being traceable back to this work. [lvii. 379]

TUTCHIN, JOHN (1661 ?-1707), whig pamphleteer ; published 'Poems,' 1685 ; took part in Monmouth's rebellion, 1685, and was sentenced to seven years' imprisonment by Jeffreys, who was bribed afterwards to recommend pardon ; clerk in victualling office, c. 1692, but dismissed ; published 'The Foreigners : a Poem,' 1700, attacking William III and the Dutch, and provoking Defoe's 'The True-born Englishman' ; was arrested ; established 'The Observator,' 1702, whig organ, and attacked the tories ; published 'A Dialogue between a Dissenter and the "Observator,"' 1703, defending Defoe; was prosecuted by attorney-general, 1703 ; tried subsequently for attack on naval administration, but escaped on technical grounds ; an ally of Defoe, though frequently quarrelling with him. [lvii. 381]

TUTHILL, Sir GEORGE LEMAN (1772-1835), physician ; M.A., 1809, and M.D., 1816, Caius College, Cambridge ; kept prisoner in France for several years ; F.R.S., 1810 ; F.R.C.P., 1817 ; Gulstonian lecturer, 1818 ; censor, 1819 and 1830 ; knighted, 1820 ; physician to Westminster and other hospitals ; active promoter of 'Pharmacopœia Londiniensis,' 1824. [lvii. 384]

TUTTIETT, LAWRENCE (1825-1897), hymn-writer ; canon of St. Ninian's Cathedral, Perth, 1877 ; published 'Hymns for Churchmen,' 1861. [lvii. 384]

TWEDDELL, JOHN (1769-1799), classical scholar ; M.A. Trinity College, Cambridge, 1793, where he distinguished himself ; fellow, 1792 ; published 'Prolusiones Juveniles,' 1792; travelled abroad, 1795, and died at Athens. His valuable journals and pictures disappeared. [lvii. 384]

TWEDDELL, RALPH HART (1843-1895), engineer and inventor of hydraulic riveter ; patented portable hydraulic apparatus, 1865, and stationary hydraulic riveting machine, 1866 ; designed portable riveting machine, 1871. [lvii. 385]

TWEEDDALE, MARQUISES OF. [See HAY, JOHN, second EARL and first MARQUIS, 1626-1697 ; HAY, JOHN, second MARQUIS, 1645-1713 ; HAY, JOHN, fourth MARQUIS, d. 1762 ; HAY, GEORGE, eighth MARQUIS, 1787-1876 ; and HAY, ARTHUR, ninth MARQUIS, 1824-1878.]

TWEEDIE, ALEXANDER (1794-1884), physician ; M.D. Edinburgh, 1815 ; house-surgeon to Edinburgh Royal Infirmary ; F.R.C.P., 1838 ; Lumleian lecturer, 1858-9 ; physician to London Fever Hospital, 1824 ; F.R.S., 1838 ; published medical works. [lvii. 386]

TWEEDIE, WILLIAM MENZIES (1826-1878), portrait-painter ; exhibited at Royal Academy. [lvii. 387]

TWELLS, LEONARD (d. 1742), divine ; B.A. Jesus College, Cambridge, 1704 ; M.A. Oxford, by diploma, 1733 ; created D.D. Oxford, 1740 ; prebendary of St. Paul's, London ; published controversial and religious works. [lvii. 387]

TWENG, ROBERT DE (1205 ?-1268 ?). [See THWENG.]

TWINE. [See TWYNE.]

TWINING, ELIZABETH (1805-1889), philanthropist and botanist ; daughter of Richard Twining (1772-1857) [q. v.] [lvii. 388]

TWINING, RICHARD (1749-1824), director of East India Company and tea-merchant ; wrote journals and letters. [lvii. 387]

TWINING, RICHARD (1772-1857), tea-merchant ; F.R.S. ; son of Richard Twining (1749-1824) [q. v.] [lvii. 388]

TWINING, THOMAS (1735-1804), translator of Aristotle's 'Poetics' ; half-brother of Richard Twining (1749-1824) [q. v.] ; scholar and fellow, Sidney Sussex College, Cambridge ; M.A., 1763 ; rector of St. Mary's, Colchester, 1788-1804 ; published translation of the 'Poetics,' 1789 ; left interesting correspondence ; musician and linguist. [lvii. 389]

TWINING, THOMAS (1776-1861), resident successively at Santipore and Behar ; son of Richard Twining (1749-1824) [q. v.] [lvii. 388]

TWINING, THOMAS (1806-1895), authority on technical education ; son of Thomas Twining (1776-1861) [q. v.] [lvii. 388]

TWINING, WILLIAM (1790-1835), army surgeon ; F.R.C.S. ; hospital assistant throughout Peninsular war and present at Waterloo ; senior assistant at Calcutta hospital ; author of 'Clinical Illustrations of . . . Diseases of Bengal,' 1832, and other writings. [lvii. 389]

TWINING, WILLIAM (1813-1848), physician and author; of Rugby and Balliol College, Oxford; son of Richard Twining (1772-1857) [q. v.] [lvii. 388]

TWISDEN. [See TWYSDEN.]

TWISLETON, EDWARD TURNER BOYD (1809-1874), politician ; fellow of Balliol College, Oxford, 1830-1838 ; M.A., 1834 ; barrister, Inner Temple, 1835 ; served on numerous commissions, 1839-70 ; published, 'The Tongue not Essential to Speech,' 1873. [lvii. 390]

TWISS, FRANCIS (1760-1827), compiler ; brother of Richard Twiss [q. v.] ; married Fanny Kemble, sister of Mrs. Siddons, and kept with her girls' school at Bath ; published index to Shakespeare, 1805. [lvii. 390]

TWISS, HORACE (1787-1849), wit and politician ; son of Francis Twiss [q. v.]; barrister, Inner Temple, 1811, treasurer, 1838 ; contributed squibs to the papers ; K.C., 1827 ; M.P., Wootton Bassett, 1820-30, Newport (Isle of Wight), 1830-1 ; judge-advocate of the fleet, 1825 ; under-secretary of war and colonies, 1828-30 ; vehemently opposed reform ; wrote for 'The Times' ; vice-chancellor of duchy of Lancaster, 1844 ; published a life of Lord Eldon, 1844. [lvii. 391]

TWISS, RICHARD (1747-1821), miscellaneous writer ; brother of Francis Twiss [q. v.] ; published 'Travels through Portugal and Spain,' 1775, and other works ; F.R.S., 1774. [lvii. 392]

TWISS, Sir TRAVERS (1809-1897), civilian ; M.A., 1832, and D.C.L., 1841, University College, Oxford ; bursar and tutor and public examiner ; barrister, Lincoln's Inn, 1840, bencher, 1858 ; Drummond professor of political economy, 1842-7 ; professor of international law, King's College, London, 1852-5 ; regius professor of civil law, Oxford, 1855-70 ; Q.C., 1858 ; chancellor of London diocese, 1858 ; admiralty advocate-general, 1862 ; knighted, 1867 ; took important part in congress at Berlin, 1884-5 ; chief work, 'The Law of Nations considered as Independent Political Communities,' 1861-3. [lvii. 393]

TWISS, WILLIAM (1745-1827), general, colonel-commandant, royal engineers ; employed at Gibraltar and Portsmouth ; aide-de-camp to William Phillips [q. v.], taking part in operations against the French, 1776 ; superintended construction of fleet for Lake Champlain which defeated French ; as commanding engineer took part in capture of Ticonderoga, 1777 ; taken prisoner at Saratoga, but exchanged ; employed in various parts of Canada and at Portsmouth and elsewhere ; commanding engineer of southern district, and of Duke of York's army in Holland, 1799 ; colonel-commandant, R.E., 1809, lieutenant-general, 1812 ; author of several useful military inventions. [lvii. 396]

TWISSE, WILLIAM (1578 ?-1646), puritan divine ; nephew of Thomas Bilson [q. v.] ; M.A. New College, Oxford, 1604 ; D.D., 1614 ; probationer fellow, 1596 ; chaplain to Elizabeth, queen of Bohemia, at Heidelberg, 1613, but recalled and made rector of Newington Longueville ; vicar of Newbury, 1620 ; protested against the 'Declaration of Sports' ; prolocutor of Westminster Assembly, 1643, but opposed alienation of church property ; published controversial works. [lvii. 397]

TWM SHON CATTI (1530-1620 ?). [See JONES, THOMAS.]

TWYFORD, JOSIAH (1640-1729), potter ; worked with John Philip Elers [q. v.] and learnt his secrets ; set up manufactory of stone wares at Shelton. [lvii. 399]

TWYFORD, Sir NICHOLAS (d. 1390), lord mayor of London ; warden of Goldsmiths' Company ; goldsmith to Edward III, 1360 ; sheriff, 1378 ; belonged to John of

Gaunt's party; rival of Sir Nicholas Brembre [q. v.]; present with Sir William Walworth [q. v.] at Wat Tyler's death, 1381, and was knighted; lord mayor, 1388. [lvii. 400]

TWYNE, BRIAN (1579?–1644), Oxford antiquary; son of Thomas Twyne [q. v.]; fellow, Corpus Christi College, Oxford, 1605; M.A., 1603; B.D., 1610; vicar of Rye, 1614; published 'Antiquitatis Academiæ Oxoniensis Apologia,' 1608, and 'Account of the Musterings of the University of Oxford' (printed, 1733); made valuable collections on early history and antiquities of Oxford; one of the editors of Laud's university statutes. [lvii. 401]

TWYNE, JOHN (1501?–1581), schoolmaster and author; B.C.L. Oxford, 1525; master of grammar school, Canterbury; M.P., Canterbury, 1553 and 1554; mayor, 1554; often in trouble with the authorities; wrote ' De Rebus Albionicis' (published, 1590), 'Communia Loca,' and other works. [lvii. 402]

TWYNE, LAWRENCE (*fl.* 1576), translator; son of John Twyne [q. v.]; B.C.L. All Souls College, Oxford, 1564; fellow; published 'Patterne of Painefull Aduentures,' 1576. [lvii. 403]

TWYNE, THOMAS (1543–1613), physician; son of John Twyne [q. v.]; fellow of Corpus Christi College, Oxford, 1564; M.A., 1568; M.D. Oxford, 1593; M.D. Cambridge; practised at Lewes; author of several works, including the completion (Bks. xi., xii., and xiii.) of Thomas Phaer's translation of the ' Æneid.' [lvii. 403]

TWYSDEN, JOHN (1607–1688), physician; brother of Sir Roger Twysden [q. v.]; educated at University College, Oxford; barrister, Inner Temple, 1634; M.D. Angers, 1646; F.R.C.P., 1664; chief work, 'Medicina veterum Vindicata,' 1666. [lvii. 404]

TWYSDEN, SIR ROGER, second baronet (1597–1672), historical antiquary; brother of Sir Thomas Twysden [q. v.]; educated at St. Paul's School and Emmanuel College, Cambridge; occupied himself in improving his property at Roydon Hall, and in study; refused to pay ship-money; M.P. for Kent in Short parliament, but alienated from parliament by cause of subsequent proceedings; signed petition from Kent, 1642, and was summoned before the House as delinquent; released on bail, but imprisoned again on publication of the 'Instructions,' 1642; being discovered endeavouring to escape abroad, was imprisoned and his estates sequestrated, 1643; returned to Kent, 1650, and engaged in literary pursuits; at Restoration became deputy-lieutenant, but remained unreconciled to the court and government; published ' The Commoners Liberty,' 1648, 'Historiæ Anglicanæ Scriptores Decem,' 1652, a work which entitles him to rank among the pioneers in English mediæval history, and 'An Historical Vindication of the Church of England,' 1657; left an unfinished treatise and manuscripts. [lvii. 404]

TWYSDEN or **TWISDEN**, SIR THOMAS (1602–1683), judge; brother of Sir Roger Twysden [q. v.]; of Emmanuel College, Cambridge; barrister, Inner Temple, 1626; bencher, 1646; though staunch royalist became serjeant-at-law under Commonwealth, and defended Cony, 1655, for which he was imprisoned; confirmed in status at Restoration, made judge in king's bench, and knighted; created baronet, 1666; son of the judge of the regicides. [lvii. 409]

TYE, CHRISTOPHER (1497?–1572), musician; chorister at King's College, Cambridge; master of the choir boys at Ely, 1543; Mus.Doc. Cambridge, 1545; obtained living of Doddington, Newton-cum-Capella, and Wilbraham Parva; published ' Actes of the Apostles,' 1553, with music, excellent compositions as part-songs, some of which, with alterations, have become well-known hymntunes, such as 'Winchester,' sung to 'While shepherds watched'; composer of anthems and other music, mostly sacred. [lvii. 410]

TYERMAN, DANIEL (1773–1828), missionary; congregational minister at Newport, Isle of Wight, and elsewhere; visited southern stations of London Missionary Society, and died at Antananarivo; author of religious works and journals. [lvii. 413]

TYERS, JONATHAN (*d.* 1767), proprietor of Vauxhall Gardens; opened them, 1732; instituted concerts and enjoyed patronage of Frederick, prince of Wales, and fashionable society. [lvii. 414]

TYERS, THOMAS (1726–1787), author; son of Jonathan Tyers [q. v.]; M.A. Exeter College, Oxford, 1745; barrister, Inner Temple, 1757; joint-manager with his brother of Vauxhall Gardens, 1767; favourite with Dr. Johnson, and described in the 'Idler' as 'Tom Restless'; published 'Political Conferences,' 1780, and biographical essays. [lvii. 414]

TYLDEN, SIR JOHN MAXWELL (1787–1866), lieutenant-colonel; brother of William Burton Tylden [q. v.]; served in Monte Video, 1807, and Java expeditions, 1811; in Peninsular war, 1813, and in America, 1814; knighted, 1812; J.P. and D.L. [lvii. 415]

TYLDEN, RICHARD (1819–1855), captain, R.E.; son of William Burton Tylden [q. v.]; commanded district at the Cape and defeated Kaffirs; promoted brevetcolonel; fought at Alma and was present at his father's death, 1854; distinguished himself at Sebastopol; promoted brevet lieutenant-colonel; was twice severely wounded; made aide-de-camp to Queen Victoria, colonel, and C.B., 1855; died at Malta. [lvii. 417]

TYLDEN, THOMAS (1624–1688). [See GODDEN, THOMAS.]

TYLDEN, WILLIAM BURTON (1790–1854), colonel, R.E.; brigadier-general; brother of Sir John Maxwell Tylden [q. v.]; as lieutenant, R.E., employed at Gibraltar, Malta, and Messina, 1808–12; was commanding R.E. at capture of Santa Maria, 1814, and of Genoa; mentioned in despatches, and promoted brevet-major; served in Netherlands and France, 1815, and elsewhere; took part in battle of the Alma, 1854; died of cholera. [lvii. 416]

TYLDESLEY, SIR THOMAS (1596–1651), royalist general; of Morleys Hall, Astley; served in German wars; commanded regiments raised by himself at Edgehill, 1642; stormed Burton-upon-Trent; made knight and brigadier; governor of Lichfield, 1645; surrendered at Appleby, 1648; landed with Derby in Lancashire; defeated and slain at Wigan Lane. [lvii. 417]

TYLER, SIR CHARLES (1760–1835), admiral; entered navy, 1771; served on various stations; served under Nelson, 1795–1802; severely wounded at Trafalgar, 1805, and granted pension; received surrender of Russian fleet at Lisbon, 1808; commander-in-chief at the Cape, 1812–15; admiral, 1825; G.C.B., 1833. [lvii. 418]

TYLER, SIR GEORGE (1792–1862), vice-admiral; son of Sir Charles Tyler [q. v.]; lieutenant-governor of St. Vincent, 1833–40; vice-admiral, 1857. [lvii. 419]

TYLER, JAMES ENDELL (1789–1851), divine; fellow, 1812, and tutor, 1818–26, of Oriel College, Oxford; M.A., 1813; incumbent of St. Giles-in-the-Fields, London, 1826; canon of St. Paul's, London, 1845; published religious works. [lvii. 419]

TYLER, TEGHELER, or **HELIER**, WALTER or WAT (*d.* 1381), rebel; to be distinguished from John Tyler who killed collector of poll-tax; leader in the rebellion, 13 and 14 June 1381; presented demands to Richard II at Smithfield on 15th, and was killed by Lordmayor Walworth and (according to Froissart) Ralph Standish. [lvii. 420]

TYLER, WILLIAM (*d.* 1801), sculptor and architect; director of Society of Artists; original R.A., 1768. [lvii. 421]

TYLOR, ALFRED (1824–1884), geologist; quaker and brassfounder; published 'On Changes of Sea Level,' 1853, and other works. [lvii. 422]

TYMME, THOMAS (*d.* 1620), translator and author; rector of St. Antholin, Budge Row, London, and of Hasketon; translated De la Ramée's history of French civil wars, 1574, and published translations and 'A Siluer Watchbell' (19th edit. 1659), a popular book of devotion. [lvii. 422]

TYMMS, SAMUEL (1808–1871), antiquary; bookseller at Lowestoft; studied antiquities, especially those at Bury St. Edmunds; F.S.A., 1853, and local secretary; chief work, 'Bury Wills and Inventories,' 1850. [lvii. 423]

TYNDALE, WILLIAM (*d.* 1536), translator of the bible; M.A. Magdalen Hall, Oxford, 1515; subsequently studied at Cambridge; before 1522 preached in Gloucestershire and introduced the new learning; involved in disputes with the clergy; translated Erasmus's 'Enchiridion

Militis Christiani'; was summoned before William of Malvern and rebuked for his proceedings; determined to translate New Testament into vernacular: removed to London, 1523; left for Hamburg to accomplish his translation, 1524, and visited Luther at Wittenberg; commenced printing at Cologne, 1525, but was stopped by injunction from Cologne senate; completed work at Worms in different form, and introduced copies into England, which were denounced, contrary to Wolsey's advice, by the bishops, 1526, and copies destroyed; was himself ordered to be seized at Worms by Wolsey; escaped to protection of Philip the Magnanimous, landgrave of Hesse, at Marburg; became Zwinglian; published 'Parable of the Wicked Mammon,' 1528 (denounced by More), and 'The Obediece of a Christen man,' 1528, laying down supreme authority of scripture in the church and of king in state; approved by Henry VIII; went to Hamburg, and subsequently to Antwerp; wrote 'The Practyse of prelates,' 1530, denouncing Roman hierarchy, Wolsey's administration and divorce proceedings, and lost Henry VIII's favour; engaged in bitter controversy with More, and wrote 'An answere unto Sir Thomas Mores dialoge,' 1531; his surrender demanded by Henry VIII from the emperor, 1531, which being refused, instructions were issued for kidnapping him; left Antwerp, but returned, 1533, and occupied himself in revising translation of the Bible; betrayed by Henry Phillips to imperial officers, who arrested him for heresy; imprisoned at Vilvorde, 1535, and strangled and burned at the stake there, in spite of Cromwell's intercession. He was one of the most remarkable of the Reformation leaders; his original writings show sound scholarship, but his translation of the bible—consisting of New Testament, 1525, Pentateuch, c. 1530, and Jonah, 1531—the accuracy of which has been endorsed by translators of authorised version, is his surest title to fame. [lvii. 424]

TYNDALL, JOHN (1820–1893), natural philosopher; born at Leighlin Bridge, co. Carlow; employed on surveys and as railway engineer; teacher of mathematics and surveying at Queenwood College, Hampshire, with Frankland; studied with him at Marburg under Bunsen, 1848–1850; Ph.D. Marburg, 1850; published, with Knoblauch, investigation 'On the Magneto-optic Properties of Crystals,' 1850; went to Berlin and published other papers on same subject, afterwards collected in 'Diamagnetism,' 1870; returned to Queenwood, 1851; F.R.S., 1852; formed friendship with Huxley; lectured at Royal Institution and became professor of natural philosophy there, 1853, and colleague of Faraday, whom he succeeded as superintendent, 1867–87; made important investigations in Penrhyn slate-quarries, and subsequently in the Alps, with Huxley, upsetting the plastic theory; embodied their investigations in 'The Glaciers of the Alps,' 1860; made first ascent of the Weisshorn, 1861; conducted his important researches on 'Radiant Heat in its relation to Gases and Vapours,' 1859–71; removed all vagueness regarding the once widely received doctrines of spontaneous generation, his memoirs being collected in 'Contributions to Molecular Physics,' 1872, and 'Floating Matter of the Air,' 1881; Rumford medallist, 1869; M.D. Tübingen; succeeded Faraday as scientific adviser to Trinity House and Board of Trade, 1866, and undertook investigations embodied in 'On Sound,' 1867, and others on light: resigned, 1883; gave lectures in America, 1872–3, and published their substance in 'Light,' 1873, also 'Heat considered as a Mode of Motion,' 1863, and other works. As writer Tyndall did much in popularising science, his works being translated into most European and some Eastern languages and widely read throughout the world. [lvii. 431]

TYRAWLEY, BARONS. [See O'HARA, SIR CHARLES, first BARON, 1640 ?–1724; O'HARA, JAMES, second BARON, 1690–1773.]

TYRCONNEL, EARL and titular DUKE OF. [See TALBOT, RICHARD, 1630–1691.]

TYRIE, JAMES (1543–1597), jesuit theologian; studied at St. Andrews University; was carried abroad by Edmund Hay [q. v.]; became jesuit at Rome, 1563; professor and subsequently rector of Clermont College; wrote a 'Refutation' in answer to John Knox, 1573, and disputed publicly with Andrew Melville at Paris, 1574; concerned in affair of the Spanish Blanks, 1593.
[lvii. 436]

TYRONE, EARLS OF. [See O'NEILL, CON BACACH, first EARL, 1484 ?–1559?; O'NEILL, HUGH, 1540 ?–1616,

and O'NEILL, SHANE, second EARLS, 1530 ?–1567; POWER, RICHARD, first EARL of the Power family, 1630–1690.]

TYRRELL, ANTHONY (1552–1610?), renegade priest and spy; descendant of Sir John Tyrrell [q. v.]; born abroad; graduated B.A. abroad; frequently arrested and rearrested in England, and concerned in the 'devil hunting' at Denham, 1585; communicated with Burghley from his prison and made disclosures concerning Babington conspirators and other plotters; became spy, and after escaping abroad again and showing much vacillation, pronounced recantation at St. Paul's Cross and obtained livings of Southminster and Dengie; fell into disreputable company, tried to escape abroad and was imprisoned; wrote his 'Confession,' 1602, and was liberated; died a Roman catholic in Belgium. [lvii. 437]

TYRRELL, FREDERICK (1793–1843), surgeon; surgeon at St. Thomas's Hospital, London, 1822, and lecturer on anatomy; assistant-surgeon to London Eye Infirmary, 1820; Arris and Gale lecturer; published 'Diseases of the Eyes,' 1840. [lvii. 439]

TYRRELL or TYRELL, SIR JAMES (d. 1502), supposed murderer of the princes in the Tower of London; grandson of Sir John Tyrrell [q. v.]; strong Yorkist; knighted after battle of Tewkesbury, 1471; M.P., Cornwall, 1477; fought under Richard III in Scotland, and was made knight-banneret, 1482; master of the horse to Richard III; according to 'Historie of Kyng Rycharde the Thirde,' instrumental in murder of the princes; became steward of duchy of Cornwall and chamberlain of exchequer; given posts in Wales by Henry VII and general pardons; lieutenant of castle of Guisnes, 1486; was concerned in Suffolk's flight, 1501, and beheaded, having confessed to murder of the princes. [lvii. 440]

TYRRELL, JAMES (1642–1718), historical writer; M.A. Queen's College, Oxford, 1663; barrister, Inner Temple, 1666; J.P. and deputy-lieutenant for Buckinghamshire, but deprived by James II for refusing to support 'declaration of indulgence,' 1687; intimate friend of Locke; chief work, 'Patriarcha non Monarcha,' 1681, advocating limited monarchy, in reply to Filmer's 'Patriarcha.' [lvii. 441]

TYRRELL, SIR JOHN (d. 1437), speaker of the House of Commons; M.P. for Essex, 1411 and 1413; present at Agincourt, 1415; sheriff, 1423; speaker, 1427, 1431, 1437; treasurer to Henry VI. [lvii. 442]

TYRRELL, SIR THOMAS (1594–1672), judge; belonged to family of Sir John Tyrrell [q. v.]; barrister, Inner Temple, 1621, bencher, 1659; deputy-lieutenant for Buckinghamshire, 1642; served under Bedford and Essex, and fought at Lostwithiel, 1644; M.P., Aylesbury, 1659–1660; joint-commissioner of great seal and serjeant-at-law; at Restoration knighted and justice of common pleas; served on various commissions. [lvii. 443]

TYRRELL, WALTER (fl. 1100). [See TIREL.]

TYRWHITT, JOHN (1601–1671). [See SPENCER.]

TYRWHITT, RICHARD ST. JOHN (1827–1895), writer on art; M.A. Christ Church, Oxford, 1852; student and tutor; vicar of St. Mary Magdalen, Oxford, 1858–72; exhibited at Royal Academy and elsewhere; author of 'A Handbook of Pictorial Art,' 1866, and other works.
[lvii. 444]

TYRWHITT or TIRWHIT, SIR ROBERT (d. 1428), judge; advocate in Richard II's reign; member of council of duchy of Lancaster; serjeant on Henry IV's accession, 1399; judge of king's bench and knighted, 1408.
[lvii. 445]

TYRWHITT, ROBERT (1735–1817), unitarian; brother of Thomas Tyrwhitt [q. v.]; fellow of Jesus College, Cambridge, 1759; resigned, 1779; a founder of London 'Unitarian Society,' 1791, but withdrew; contributed to 'Commentaries and Essays.' [lvii. 445]

TYRWHITT, THOMAS (1730–1786), classical commentator; educated at Eton and Queen's College, Oxford; fellow of Merton, 1755; M.A., 1756; published works while undergraduate; barrister, Middle Temple, 1755; deputy-secretary at war, 1756; clerk of the House of Commons, 1762–8; edited 'Proceedings . . . of the House of Commons, 1620–1,' 1766, and Elsinge's 'Manner of holding Parliaments,' 1768; credited with knowledge of 'almost every European tongue,' and master of English and classical literature; published anonymously 'Observations . . . upon . . . Shakespeare,' 1766, ' Canterbury Tales of Chaucer,' 1775, 'Poems supposed to have been written . . . by Thomas Rowley' (chief work exposing the Rowley forgeries), 1777 and 1778, and editions and emendations of classical authors, including ' Aristotelis de Poetica Liber, Græce et Latine,' posthumous, 1794, and ' De Lapidibus,' 1781, boldly assigning the latter work (Λιθικά), to the era of Constantius ; F.R.S., 1771, and trustee of the British Museum, 1784. [lvii. 446]

TYSDALE, JOHN (*fl.* 1550-1563). [See TISDALE.]

TYSILIO (*fl.* 600), British saint; founded Meifod Church, Montgomeryshire; reputed by tradition, but without foundation, poet and historian. [lvii. 448]

TYSON, EDWARD (1650-1708), physician; M.A. Magdalen Hall, Oxford, 1673; M.D. Cambridge; F.R.C.P., 1683 ; censor, 1694 ; physician to Bridewell and Bethlehem hospitals ; lectured on anatomy to Barber Surgeons ; published first in England monographs on particular animals ; declared the pigmies, cynocephali, satyrs, and sphinges of the ancients to have been merely apes in ' Orang Outang,' 1699. [lvii. 448]

TYSON, MICHAEL (1740-1780), antiquary and artist ; fellow of Corpus Christi College, Cambridge, 1767 ; bursar, 1774 ; M.A., 1767 ; made tour in north and Scotland with Richard Gough [q. v.], 1766 ; contributed to Mason's life of Gray ; F.S.A. and F.R.S. ; rector of Lambourne, 1778 ; Whitehall preacher, 1776 ; executed engravings, etchings, and miniatures, and contributed to ' Philosophical Transactions' and other publications. [lvii. 449]

TYSON, RICHARD (1680-1750), physician; son of Edward Tyson [q. v.]; M.D. Pembroke Hall, Cambridge, 1715 ; president, Royal College of Physicians, 1746-50 ; Harveian orator, 1725. [lvii. 450]

TYSON, RICHARD (1730-1784), physician; greatnephew of Edward Tyson [q. v.]; M.A. Oriel College, Oxford, 1753 ; M.D., 1760; censor, Royal College of Physicians, 1763, 1768, 1773, and 1776. [lvii. 450]

TYTLER, ALEXANDER FRASER, LORD WOODHOUSELEE (1747-1813), historian ; son of William Tytler [q. v.]; studied at Edinburgh University ; Scottish barrister, 1770 ; published 'The Decisions of the Court of Session,' 1778 ; became professor of universal history at Edinburgh University, and published ' Elements of General History,' 1801, and other historical works ; judge-advocate of Scotland, 1790; published ' Essay on the Principles of Translation,' 1791, ' Memoirs . . . of . . . Lord Kames,' 1807, and numerous miscellaneous works ; judge of session as Lord Woodhouselee, 1802 ; lord of justiciary, 1811. [lvii. 450]

TYTLER, HENRY WILLIAM (1752-1808), physician and translator : brother of James Tytler [q. v.]; translated Callimachus, 1793. [lvii. 452]

TYTLER, JAMES (1747 ?-1805), 'Balloon Tytler,' miscellaneous writer ; unsuccessful surgeon and apothecary at Edinburgh and Leith ; printed several works in debtors' refuge at Holyrood with press constructed by himself; edited and wrote large portions of second and third editions of ' Encyclopædia Britannica'; first in Great Britain to ' navigate the air,' 1784 ; published ' The Observer,' weekly paper, 1786, and verses and historical works ; published ' A Pamphlet on the Excise ' and ' The Historical Register,' 1792, and fled to America to escape arrest, where he died. [lvii. 452]

TYTLER, PATRICK FRASER (1791-1849), Scottish historian ; son of Alexander Fraser Tytler, lord Woodhouselee [q. v.]; studied at Edinburgh University ; wrote ' Essay on the History of the Moors during their Government in Spain ' ; became Scottish barrister, 1813 ; visited Paris ; made acquaintance with Archibald Alison [q. v.], Sir Walter Scott, and others ; king's counsel in exchequer, 1816 ; published ' The Life of the Admirable Crichton,' 1819 ; took part with Scott in forming Bannatyne Club, 1822 ; published ' History of Scotland,' 1828-43, ' England under the Reign of Edward VI and Mary,' 1839, and several other works, including ' Scotland,' in seventh edition of ' Encyclopædia Britannica,' 1839. [lvii. 453]

TYTLER, WILLIAM (1711-1792), Scottish historian ; educated at Edinburgh University ; writer to the signet ; joined the Select Society ; apologist of the Scottish queen in ' The Inquiry . . . into the Evidence against Mary Queen of Scots,' 1759 ; published ' The Poetical Remains of James I,' 1783 ; discovered James I's ' Kingis Quair.' [lvii. 455]

U

UBALDINI, PETRUCCIO (1524 ?-1600 ?), illuminator and scholar ; native of Tuscany ; came to England, 1545 ; employed by Henry VIII in Italy ; employed by Edward VI ; accompanied the English forces into Scotland, 1549 ; wrote a description of England, 1551 ; resided in Venice, c. 1552-62 ; resided in England, c. 1562-86 ; published, 1581, ' Vita di Carlo Magno,' the first Italian book printed in England ; went to the Low Countries, 1586 ; wrote narrative of the Spanish Armada, 1588 ; published lives of illustrious English and Scottish ladies, 1591 ; published accounts of Rome, Naples, and Tuscany, 1594 and 1597 ; published ' Rime,' 1596 ; works illuminated by him in British Museum Library. [lviii. 1]

UCHTRED. [See UHTRED.]

UCHTRYD (the Welsh form of UHTRED) (*d.* 1148), bishop ; a Welshman ; archdeacon of Llandaff, c. 1126 ; elected bishop of Llandaff, 1134, and consecrated, 1140 ; traditional uncle of Geoffrey of Monmouth [q. v.] [lviii. 3]

UDALL. [See also UVEDALE.]

UDALL, EPHRAIM (*d.* 1647), royalist divine ; son of John Udall [q. v.]; M.A. Emmanuel College, Cambridge, 1614 ; incumbent of Teddington, 1615 ; rector of St. Augustine's, Watling Street, London, 1634 ; a puritan, but ejected by parliament for defending episcopacy, 1643 ; published theological tracts. [lviii. 3]

UDALL or **UVEDALE**, JOHN (1560 ?-1592), puritan ; entered Cambridge University, 1578 ; M.A. Trinity College, Cambridge, 1584 ; friend and fellow-student of John Penry [q. v.]; incumbent of Kingston-on-Thames before 1584 ; published sermons, 1584-6 ; prosecuted for hostility to episcopacy, 1586 ; conferred with Penry, 1587 ; published anonymously, through Robert Waldegrave's [q. v.] press, ' The State of the Church,' and ' A Demonstration ' against the bishops, 1588 ; deprived of his benefice, July 1588 ; preacher at Newcastle-on-Tyne, December 1588 ; imprisoned on suspicion of complicity in Penry's Mar-Prelate tracts, January 1590 ; sentenced to death, 1591 ; pardoned, June 1592, but died soon after. His commentary on the Lamentations of Jeremiah and Hebrew grammar and dictionary appeared posthumously, 1593. [lviii. 4]

UDALL or **UVEDALE**, NICHOLAS (1505-1556), dramatist and scholar ; a native of Hampshire ; scholar of Winchester College, 1517 ; scholar of Corpus Christi College, Oxford, 1520 ; fellow, 1524 ; suspected of Lutheranism, 1526 ; M.A., 1534 ; published selections from Terence, with English version, 1533 ; head-master of Eton, 1534 ; a flogging master ; dismissed for misconduct, 1541 ; perhaps had his 'Ralph Roister Doister ' (printed, 1566), the earliest known English comedy, acted by Eton boys before 1541 ; vicar of Braintree, 1537-44 ; published an English version of part of Erasmus's 'Apophthegms,' 1542, and took part in the English version of Erasmus's ' Paraphrase of the New Testament,' published, 1548 ; employed by Edward VI to reply to the Devonshire catholics, 1549 ; translated Peter Martyr's [see VERMIGLI] discourse on the Lord's Supper, 1550, and Thomas Gemini's [q. v.] ' Anatomia,' 1552 ; prebendary of Windsor, 1551 ; rector of Calborne, Isle of Wight, 1553 ; received into favour by Queen Mary and Stephen Gardiner ; play-writer to Queen Mary, 1554 ; head-master of Westminster School, 1554-6. [lviii. 6]

UFFORD, JOHN DE (*d.* 1349). [See OFFORD.]

UFFORD, SIR RALPH DE (*d.* 1346), lord justice of Ireland, 1344. [lviii. 10]

UFFORD, ROBERT DE (*d.* 1298), younger son of a Suffolk landowner, John de Peyton; took his surname from his lordship of Ufford, Suffolk: attended Edward I on his crusade; lord justice of Ireland, 1276–81; built Roscommon Castle. [lviii. 10]

UFFORD, ROBERT DE, first EARL OF SUFFOLK of his house (1298–1369), succeeded to his estates, 1316; came of age, 1318; knighted; attended Edward III to Amiens, 1329; granted Orford castle and lands in Norfolk, 1330; joined movement against Mortimer, 1330; rewarded by lands and offices; summoned as a baron, 1332; a chief counsellor of Edward III; served against the Scots, 1335–7; created Earl of Suffolk, 1337; envoy to France, 1337, 1338; in attendance on Edward III in Brabant, 1339; taken prisoner near Lille, and ransomed, 1340; K.G.; served in Brittany, 1342; envoy to Pope Clement VI at Avignon, 1343; admiral of the northern fleet, 1344–7; accompanied Edward III to France, 1346; fought at Crecy, 1346; a commissioner to treat with the French, 1348–50; fought Spanish off Winchelsea, 1350; accompanied Black Prince to Aquitaine, 1355; led raids into French territory, 1355–6; distinguished himself at Poitiers, 1356; employed on embassies up to 1362; removed Leiston Abbey to a new site, 1363. [lviii. 9]

UFFORD, WILLIAM DE, second EARL OF SUFFOLK of his house (1339?–1382), second son of Robert de Ufford, earl of Suffolk [q. v.]; summoned as a baron, 1364; succeeded to earldom, 1369; served in France, 1370; accompanied John of Gaunt through France, 1373; K.G., 1375; opposed John of Gaunt in the Good parliament, 1376; employed under Richard II in Norfolk and Suffolk, 1377; served in France and Brittany, 1377–8, and in Scotland, 1380; sought by the revolted Norfolk peasants to be their leader, June 1381; employed in suppressing the rising, June–August, 1381; took a leading part against John of Gaunt, October 1381. The title died with him, and the estates lapsed to the crown. [lviii. 13]

UGHTRED, SIR ANTHONY (*d.* 1534), soldier; marshal of Tournay, 1514; captain of Berwick, 1523–8; governor of Jersey. [lviii. 16]

UGHTRED, SIR THOMAS, styled BARON UGHTRED (1291?–1365), succeeded to his estates in Yorkshire, 1309; served at the siege of Berwick, 1319; M.P., Yorkshire, 1320, 1330, and 1332; supported Edward II against Thomas of Lancaster [q. v.], 1322; knighted, 1324; accompanied Edward Baliol in his invasion of Scotland, 1332; made baron of Innerwick by Baliol; covered Baliol's retreat, 1334; governor of Perth, 1338, but surrendered, 1339; served in France, 1340, 1347, 1360; said to have been summoned as a peer, 1343–64, but was probably only knight of the shire for Yorkshire, 1344 and 1352. [lviii. 15]

UHTRED or **UCHTRED** (*d.* 1016), Earl of Northumbria; helped Bishop Ealdhun to fix his see at Durham, 995; married Ecgfrida, Ealdhun's daughter; defeated an invasion of the Scots under Malcolm II, 1006: received his father's earldom from Ethelred II; married Ethelred's daughter Ælfgifu; submitted to King Sweyn, 1013; resisted Canute, 1015–16; slain by Canute's order. [lviii. 16]

UHTRED, **UTRED**, or **OWTRED** (1315?–1396), Benedictine theologian; called also JOHN UTRED, and (from his birthplace, Boldon, North Durham) UHTRED BOLEDUNUS or BOLTON; entered the Benedictine order, 1332; sent to London, 1337, to Oxford, 1340, to Stamford, 1344, and again to Oxford before 1347: said to be B.D., 1354, and D.D., 1357; attacked the friars; prior of Finchale Abbey, 1367, and afterwards; sub-prior of Durham, 1368 and 1381; envoy to Pope Gregory XI, 1373; attended the great council at Westminster, 1374; in Oxford, 1383; published monastic and religious treatises. [lviii. 17]

ULECOT, PHILIP DE (*d.* 1220), judge; constable of Chinon, 1205; ransomed from the French, 1207; one of King John's evil counsellors; sheriff of Northumberland; employed by King John to hold the north for him; continued in office by Henry III; a justice itinerant in the north, 1219. [lviii. 18]

ULFCYTEL or **ULFKETEL** (*d.* 1016), earl of the East-Angles; made peace with King Sweyn, 1004; fought against the Danes at Thetford; defeated by them near Ipswich, 1010; fell in battle at Assandun. [lviii. 18]

ULLATHORNE, WILLIAM BERNARD (1806–1889), Roman catholic prelate; son of a Yorkshire grocer; went to sea, 1821; entered as 'Bernard' the Benedictine order, 1825; ordained priest, 1831; stationed at Sydney, Australia, 1833–6, 1838–40; wrote and agitated against the transportation system, 1836–8; D.D., 1837; stationed at Coventry, 1841; consecrated bishop *in partibus*, with charge of west England, 1846; transferred to central England district, 1848; bishop of Birmingham, 1850–88; attended the Vatican council, 1870; titular archbishop of Cabasa, 1888; published theological tracts and occasional pamphlets. [lviii. 19]

ULLERSTON, RICHARD (*d.* 1423), theological writer; fellow of Queen's College, Oxford, 1391–1403; senior bursar, 1396–7; D.D., 1394; prebendary of Salisbury, 1403; rector of Beeford, 1407; chancellor of Oxford University, 1408. [lviii. 21]

ULSTER, EARLS OF. [See COURCI, JOHN DE, *d.* 1219?; LACY, HUGH DE, *d.* 1242?; BURGH, WALTER DE, called EARL OF ULSTER, *d.* 1271; BURGH, RICHARD DE, second EARL of the Burgh family, 1259?–1326; BURGH, WILLIAM DE, third EARL, 1312–1332; LIONEL OF ANTWERP, 1338–1368; MORTIMER, ROGER (VI) DE, 1374–1398; MORTIMER, EDMUND (IV) DE, 1391–1425.]

ULTAN (*d.* 656), of Ardbrecain; Irish saint; tribal bishop of central Meath; commemorated on 4 Sept. [lviii. 21]

UMFRAVILLE, GILBERT DE, EARL OF ANGUS (1244?–1307), son of Matilda, heiress of the Celtic earls of Angus, and of Gilbert de Umfraville (*d.* 1245); of a Norman stock (originally from Amfreville, département Eure) long settled at Redesdale, Northumberland; ward of Simon de Montfort, and compelled to side with him in the barons' wars; fought against the barons, 1264; styled Earl of Angus, *c.* 1267; summoned to the English parliament (generally as 'Gilbert de Umfraville'), and to the Scottish parliament; accepted Edward I as arbiter of Scotland, 1291; accepted John Baliol as king of Scotland, 1292; served in Gascony, 1294; fought for Edward I against Baliol and Wallace, 1296–8. [lviii. 21]

UMFRAVILLE, GILBERT DE (1310–1381), son of Robert de Umfraville, earl of Angus [q. v.]; summoned to the English parliament as Earl of Angus; joined Edward Baliol in his attempt on Scotland, 1332–4; fought at Neville's Cross, 1346; entailed Redesdale on his half-brother, 1378. [lviii. 23]

UMFRAVILLE, GILBERT DE (1390–1421), popularly styled 'Earl of Kyme'; son of Sir Thomas de Umfraville (1362–1391), eldest son of Sir Thomas de Umfraville [q. v.]; inherited, 1391, Harbottle and Redesdale, and Kyme in Kesteven; a royal ward in charge successively of his uncle, Robert de Umfraville (*d.* 1436) [q. v.], of Hotspur, and, 1403, of George Dunbar, earl of March; came of age and was knighted, 1410; went to help Philip of Burgundy, 1411; served at Calais, 1412; fought in Henry V's French wars, 1415–19; granted Amfreville and other Norman estates; envoy to the French court, 1419; accompanied Henry V to Paris, 1420; marshal of France, 1421; killed in battle at Baugé. [lviii. 24]

UMFRAVILLE, ROBERT DE, EARL OF ANGUS (1277–1325), son of Gilbert de Umfraville, earl of Angus [q. v.]; succeeded, 1307; fought for Edward II against the Scots and the barons; taken prisoner at Bannockburn, 1314, and deprived of his Scottish title and estates; married the heiress of Kyme, Lincolnshire. [lviii. 23]

UMFRAVILLE, ROBERT DE (*d.* 1436), younger son of Sir Thomas de Umfraville [q. v.]; constantly engaged in border warfare with the Scots; nicknamed 'Robin Mendmarket'; sheriff of Northumberland; inherited Redesdale and Kyme from his nephew, Gilbert de Umfraville (1390–1421) [q. v.]; last of the male line of the Umfravilles of Redesdale. [lviii. 25]

UMFRAVILLE, SIR THOMAS DE (*d.* 1386), half-brother of Gilbert de Umfraville (1310–1381) [q. v.], from whom he inherited Redesdale and Kyme. [lviii. 23]

UMMARCOTE, ROBERT (d. 1241). [See SOMERCOTE.]

UMPHELBY, FANNY (1788–1852), author of 'The Child's Guide to Knowledge,' 1825. [lviii. 26]

UNDERDOWN, THOMAS (fl. 1566–1587), poet and translator; published 'The excellent Historye of Theseus and Ariadne,' 1566, Heliodorus's 'Æthiopian Historie,' 1569, and Ovid 'against Ibis,' with an appendix of legends, 1569. [lviii. 26]

UNDERHILL, CAVE (1634–1710?), actor; son of a London clothworker; entered Merchant Taylors' School, 1645; a leading member of the Duke of York's company, 1661, of the joint company, 1682; a principal player of comic parts, 1661–1702; appeared occasionally, 1704–10. [lviii. 27]

UNDERHILL, EDWARD (fl. 1539–1562), the 'hot gospeller'; occurs as gentleman pensioner, 1539–62; served in Hainault, 1543, and France, 1544; a forward protestant in Edward VI's reign; served at Boulogne, 1549; imprisoned for a lampoon on Queen Mary, 1553. [lviii. 29]

UNDERHILL, JOHN (1545?–1592), bishop of Oxford; at Winchester School, 1556; fellow of New College, Oxford, 1561–76; M.A., 1568; chaplain to Dudley, earl of Leicester; rector of Lincoln College, Oxford, by Leicester's influence, 1577–90; D.D., 1581; after other benefices, rector of Witney, 1587; bishop of Oxford, 1589–92. [lviii. 30]

UNDERHILL, JOHN (d. 1672), colonist; of a Warwickshire family; served in the Netherlands, and, 1625, against Cadiz; taken as military instructor to New England, 1630; joint-leader against the Pequot Indians, 1637; governor of Dover colony, Piscataqua; served the Dutch against the Indians in New Netherlands, 1643, and resided in other colonies. [lviii. 31]

UNDERWOOD, MICHAEL (1736–1820), man-midwife; studied in London and Paris; practised in London as a surgeon, and, from 1784, as man-midwife; published surgical treatises. [lviii. 31]

UNTON or **UMPTON**, SIR HENRY (1557?–1596), diplomatist and soldier; M.A. Oriel College, Oxford, 1590; entered Middle Temple, 1575; travelled in France and Italy; M.P., New Woodstock, 1584–5; served in the Low Countries, 1585–6; knighted, 1586; envoy to Henry IV of France, 1591–2; M.P., Berkshire, 1593; envoy to France, 1595; died at La Fère; part of his official despatches published. [lviii. 32]

UNWIN, MARY (1724–1796), the friend of Cowper; née Cawthorne; married Morley Unwin, 1744; resided in Huntingdon, 1748; took William Cowper, the poet, as a boarder, October 1765; widowed, July 1767; took Cowper with her to Olney, September 1767, and to Weston, 1786; a marriage with Cowper projected in 1772 stopped by his insanity. [lviii. 34]

UNWIN, WILLIAM CAWTHORNE (1745?–1786), correspondent of Cowper; eldest son of Mary Unwin [q. v.]; M.A. Christ's College, Cambridge, 1767; rector of Stock, 1769. [lviii. 35]

UNWONA (d. 800?), sixth bishop of Leicester; succeeded, c. 781; reputed a Welshman and a scholar. [lviii. 35]

UPCOTT, WILLIAM (1779–1845), antiquary and autograph collector; natural son of Ozias Humphry [q. v.], who bequeathed him his correspondence, engravings, etc.; assistant-librarian of the London Institution, 1806–34; his collections sold by auction, 1846; published a catalogue of his papers, 1836, and a bibliography of English topography, 1818; edited antiquarian works. [lviii. 36]

UPHAM, EDWARD (1776–1834), orientalist; bookseller in Exeter; mayor of Exeter, 1809; chief works, 'The History and Doctrine of Buddhism,' 1829, 'History of the Ottoman Empire from its Establishment till the year 1828,' 1829, and a translation of the sacred and historical books of Ceylon, 1833. [lviii. 37]

UPINGTON, SIR THOMAS (1845–1898), South African statesman; M.A. Trinity College, Dublin, 1868; an Irish barrister, 1867; settled in Cape Colony, 1874; attorney-general there, 1878–81, 1886–90, 1896–8; premier, 1884–6; K.C.M.G., 1887; judge of the supreme court, 1892–6. [lviii. 38]

UPPER OSSORY, LORD OF (1535?–1581). [See FITZPATRICK, SIR BARNABY.]

UPTON, ARTHUR (1623–1706), Irish presbyterian; a royalist; refused the 'Engagement'; sat in the Irish parliament successively for Carrickfergus and co. Antrim, 1661–1701; raised a foot regiment for William III; attainted by James II's Irish parliament, 1689. [lviii. 38]

UPTON, JAMES (1670–1749), schoolmaster; educated at Eton; fellow of King's College, Cambridge; M.A., 1701; assistant-master at Eton; taught school at Ilminster, 1724–30; master of Taunton grammar school, 1730–49; beneficed in Somerset, 1711–49; edited classical texts, including Theodore Gulston's Latin version of 'Poetics of Aristotle' (1623), 1696. [lviii. 39]

UPTON, JOHN (1707–1760), editor of Spenser; younger son of James Upton [q. v.]; fellow of Exeter College, Oxford, 1728–36; M.A., 1732; beneficed in Somerset and Gloucestershire; edited Spenser's 'Faerie Queen,' 1758. [lviii. 39]

UPTON, NICHOLAS (1400?–1457), writer on heraldry; at Winchester School, 1408; fellow of New College, Oxford, 1415; B.C.L.; a soldier in France; present at the siege of Orleans, 1428; perhaps B.Can.L. Oxford, 1438; held cathedral preferment at Wells, 1431, St. Paul's, London, 1443, and Salisbury, 1446; rector successively of Chedsey, Stapylford, and Farleigh; solicited at Rome the canonisation of Bishop Osmund (d. 1099) [q. v.], 1452–3; compiled a large treatise 'de officio militari' (printed, 1654). [lviii. 39]

UPTON, SIR NICHOLAS (d. 1551), knight of St. John of Malta; killed by sunstroke while defending Malta against the Turks. [lviii. 40]

URCHARD, SIR THOMAS (1611–1660). [See URQUHART.]

URE, ANDREW (1778–1857), chemist and scientific writer; educated at Edinburgh and Glasgow Universities: M.D. Glasgow, 1801; professor of chemistry in Anderson's College, Glasgow, 1804–30; director of Glasgow Observatory, 1809; inaugurated popular scientific lectures; F.R.S., 1822; analytical chemist in London, 1830–57; published 'Dictionary of Chemistry,' 1821, 'Dictionary of Arts, Manufactures, and Mines,' 1853, and other works. [lviii. 40]

URE, DAVID (d. 1798), geologist; a Glasgow weaver; M.A. Glasgow, 1776; assistant-minister at East Kilbride; minister of Uphall, 1796–8; published geological tracts, 1793–7. [lviii. 41]

URI, JOANNES (1726–1796), orientalist; born at Körös, Hungary; studied at Leyden; edited a Hebrew etymology and the 'Burda' (Arabic poem), 1761; resided in Oxford, 1766–96; compiled a defective 'Catalogue of Bodleian Oriental MSS.,' 1787; edited Persian, Turkish, and Hebrew pieces. [lviii. 42]

URIEN (fl. 570), British prince; historically 'Urbgen,' prince of part of North Britain; slain in battle with the Northumbrian Angles (appendix to NENNIUS, c. 690); mythologically he appears in 'Malory' as King Vryens of the land of Goire (Gower, according to Glamorganshire antiquaries). [lviii. 42]

URQUHART, DAVID (1805–1877), diplomatist; educated in France, Geneva, and Spain, 1817–21; at Oxford, 1822; travelled in the East; served in Greek navy, 1827–8; surveyed Greek frontier, 1830; attached to Sir Stratford Canning's Constantinople mission, 1831–2; sent to Constantinople to report on British trade, 1834; secretary of embassy at Constantinople, 1836; recalled, 1837, for hostility to Russia; M.P., Stafford, 1847–52; a bitter opponent of Palmerston; wrote and agitated in favour of Turkish autonomy; withdrew, in ill heath, to Montreux, Switzerland, 1864; published notes of travel and political and diplomatical papers; died at Naples. [lviii. 43]

URQUHART, THOMAS (fl. 1650?), violin-maker; of London. [lviii. 45]

URQUHART or **URCHARD**, SIR THOMAS (1611–1660), of Cromarty; author and translator; eldest son of Sir Thomas Urquhart; of King's College, Aberdeen; travelled in France, Spain, and Italy; fought at Turriff against the Covenanters, 1639; withdrew to London, May 1639; knighted, 1641; published 'Epigrams,' 1641; returned to Scotland to arrange his affairs, 1642; went abroad, 1642-5 ; published ' Trissotetras,' a trigonometrical work, 1645 ; resided in Cromarty Tower, 1645-50 ; joined the Inverness rising to proclaim Charles II, 1649 ; followed Charles II to Worcester, where many of his manuscripts were destroyed by the parliamentarians, 1651 ; prisoner in the Tower of London and at Windsor, 1651-2 ; published the Urquhart genealogy (Παντοχρονοχανον), 1652, and an invective ('Εκσκυβάλαυρον) against Scottish presbyterians, 1652 ; visited Scotland on parole, 1652-3 ; published scheme for a universal language in his 'Logopandecteision,' 1653, and part of his translation of Rabelais, 1653 ; died abroad. A further portion of Rabelais was printed, 1693 ; his miscellaneous works were collected, 1774 and 1834. [lviii. 46]

URRY or **HURRY**, Sir JOHN (d. 1650), professional soldier ; of Pitfichie, Aberdeenshire ; served abroad ; lieutenant-colonel in Scotland ; solicited to join, but subsequently revealed the plot known as the ' Incident,' October 1641 ; officer in the English parliamentary army at Edgehill and Brentford, 1642 ; went over to Charles I, 1643 ; fought at Chalgrove, 1643, and was knighted ; fought at Marston Moor, 1644 ; surrendered to the parliament, but was soon released on parole, 1644 ; attached himself to the Scottish army ; sent, with William Baillie, against Montrose, March 1645 ; routed at Auldearn, May 1645 ; went back to the royalists ; accompanied Hamilton's army to Preston, 1648 ; escaped to the continent ; major-general in Montrose's descent, January 1650 ; taken prisoner at Carbisdale ; beheaded at Edinburgh.
[lviii. 50]

URRY, JOHN (1666-1715), editor of Chaucer ; student of Christ Church, Oxford ; B.A., 1686 ; a nonjuror, 1689 ; undertook to edit Chaucer, 1711 ; tampered with the text ; his edition completed by others and published, 1721. [lviii. 52]

URSE D'ABETOT (fl. 1086), sheriff of Worcestershire ; occurs in ' Domesday ' as a great landowner in Gloucester, Worcester, Hereford, and Warwick ; oppressed Worcester, Pershore, and Evesham monasteries ; reputed founder of Malvern priory ; helped to crush the Earl of Hereford's revolt, 1074. The estates passed, through a daughter, to the Beauchamp family. [lviii. 52]

URSULA, SAINT (d. 238, or 283, or 451), patroness of virgins ; described as only daughter of Deonotus, a British prince ; sailed with ten virgin companions and eleven thousand virgin attendants to Cologne ; visited Rome ; massacred at Cologne on her return, with her company, by the Huns. The legend occurs in the eighth century, was developed in the twelfth century, and popularised by Geoffrey of Monmouth. The Ursuline nuns, named after her, were founded in 1537. Many attempts have been made to get rid of the difficulties involved in the number eleven thousand, culminating in Rettberg's conjecture that XI.M.V. (meaning ' eleven martyred virgins') was misread ' eleven thousand virgins.' [lviii. 53]

URSWICK, CHRISTOPHER (1448-1522), diplomatist and churchman ; educated at Cambridge ; LL.D. ; confessor to Lady Margaret Beaufort, and to Henry VII ; negotiated the marriage treaty between Henry (then Earl of Richmond) and Elizabeth of York, 1484 ; accompanied Henry to England, 1485 ; master of King's Hall, Cambridge, 1485-8 ; envoy to Pope Innocent VIII, 1486, to Castile, 1488, to France, 1489 and 1492, to Scotland, 1492 and 1493, to the king of the Romans, 1496 ; dean of York, 1488-94 ; dean of Windsor, 1495-1522 ; rector of Hackney, London, 1502-22 ; held much cathedral and parochial preferment ; friend of Erasmus. [lviii. 55]

URSWICK, SIR THOMAS (d. 1479), judge ; Yorkist ; recorder of London, 1455 ; M.P., London, 1461 and 1467 ; admitted Edward IV to London, 1471 ; knighted, 1471 ; chief-baron of the exchequer, 1472. [lviii. 56]

URWICK, THOMAS (1727-1807), independent divine ; of Glasgow University ; pastor in Worcester, 1754-75, Narborough, 1775-9, and Clapham, 1779-1807 ; published sermons. [lviii. 57]

URWICK, WILLIAM (1791-1868), congregational divine ; pastor at Sligo, 1816-26, and in Dublin, 1826-68 ; D.D. Connecticut, 1832 ; professor in the Dublin Theological Institute, 1832 ; published biographies of congregational worthies, autobiographical notes, hymns, and controversial pamphlets. [lviii. 57]

USCYTEL or **USKETILLUS** (d. 971). [See OSKYTEL.]

USHER. [See also USSHER.]

USHER, JAMES (1720-1772), schoolmaster ; educated at Trinity College, Dublin ; embraced Romanism ; failed as a farmer, and as a linendraper in Dublin ; kept a school for Roman catholic youth at Kensington, 1767-72 ; published philosophical essays, 1764-71. [lviii. 58]

USHER, RICHARD (1785-1843), clown ; son of a travelling showman ; appeared as a clown at Liverpool, 1807 ; chief clown at Astley's Amphitheatre, London, 1809 ; writer and inventor of several stock pantomimes.
[lviii. 59]

USK, ADAM OF (fl. 1400). [See ADAM.]

USK, THOMAS (d. 1388), author of ' The Testament of Love,' formerly ascribed to Chaucer ; native of London ; private secretary to John de Northampton [q. v.], the Wycliffite lord mayor of London, 1381-3 ; prisoner in Newgate, 1384 ; procured his pardon by turning informer against his patron ; under-sheriff of London, by Richard II's mandate, October 1387 ; proceeded against by the ' Merciless ' parliament, February 1388 ; executed. ' The Testament of Love ' is an allegorical prose work, written by Usk in prison to enlist sympathy (printed as Chaucer's, 1532 ; the Chaucerian attribution disproved, 1866).
[lviii. 60]

USSHER, AMBROSE (1582 ?-1629), scholar ; M.A. and fellow of Trinity College, Dublin, 1601 ; his manuscript compilations, biblical, Hebrew, Arabic, and mathematical, in Trinity College Library. [lviii. 62]

USSHER, HENRY (1550 ?-1613), archbishop of Armagh ; native of Dublin ; educated at Cambridge (B.A., 1570), Paris, and Oxford (M.A., 1572) ; treasurer of Christ Church, Dublin, 1573 ; archdeacon of Dublin, 1580 ; sent to London to oppose a proposed university in Dublin, 1584 ; sent to London to solicit the foundation of Trinity College, Dublin, 1591 ; obtained the charter, 1592 ; archbishop of Armagh, 1595-1613. [lviii. 62]

USSHER, HENRY (d. 1790), astronomer ; fellow of Trinity College, Dublin, 1764 ; D.D., 1779 ; professor of astronomy, 1783 ; F.R.S., 1785 ; started Dunsink observatory, Dublin ; published astronomical papers.
[lviii. 63]

USSHER, JAMES (1581-1656), archbishop of Armagh ; son of a Dublin lawyer ; scholar of Trinity College, Dublin, 1594, at its foundation ; fellow, 1599-1605 ; M.A., 1601 ; lay preacher at Christ Church, Dublin ; sent to England to buy books for Trinity College Library, 1602 ; chancellor of St. Patrick's, Dublin, and rector of Finglas, 1605 ; professor of divinity, Dublin, 1607-21 ; rector of Assey, 1611-26 ; published his first work, ' De . . . Ecclesiarum . . . Successione,' 1613 ; D.D., 1614 ; drafted the Irish convocation articles, 1615 ; vice-chancellor of Trinity College, Dublin, 1617 ; rector of Trim, 1620 ; bishop of Meath, 1621 ; resided in England, studying, 1623-6 ; archbishop of Armagh, 1625 ; incorporated D.D. at Oxford, 1626 ; defended the catholic penal laws, 1626-1627 ; corresponded with Laud, 1628-40 ; discountenanced Bishop William Bedell's idea of reviving the Irish language in the service, 1629 ; accepted, at Strafford's command, the English Thirty-nine Articles, but rejected the 1604 Anglican canons in favour of new Irish canons, 1634 ; drafted a scheme of modified episcopacy acceptable to the puritans (printed without his leave, 1641) ; pleaded with Charles I not to sacrifice Strafford ; bishop of Carlisle in commendam, February 1642 to autumn 1643 ; voted a pension by parliament, September 1643 (first payment made, December 1647) ; objected to the Westminster Assembly, 1643 ; preacher at Lincoln's Inn, 1647 ; offered a pension by Richelieu, c. 1649 ; buried in Westminster Abbey ; his library bought by the state, 1656, and placed in Trinity College, Dublin, 1661 ; his chronology still the standard adopted in editions of the English bible ; learned in patristic literature and ancient Irish history ; collected works published, 1847-64.
[lviii. 64]

USSHER, ROBERT (1592-1642), Irish bishop ; son of Henry Ussher (1550 ?-1613) [q. v.] ; fellow of Trinity College, Dublin, 1611 ; B.D., 1621 ; elected provost of Trinity College, Dublin, 1627, but election annulled ; rector of Lurgan, 1629 ; provost of Trinity College, Dublin, 1630-4 ; bishop of Kildare, 1635-42. [lviii. 63]

USSHER, Sir THOMAS (1779–1848), rear-admiral; son of Henry Ussher (d. 1790) [q. v.]; entered navy, 1791; lieutenant, 1797; commander, 1806; captain, 1808; conveyed Napoleon from Fréjus to Elba, 1814; knighted, 1831; rear-admiral, 1846.   [lviii. 72]

UTENHOVE, JOHN (d. 1565), reformer; native of Ghent; left Flanders for religion's sake, 1544; resident in England, 1548–53, co-operating with John Laski [q. v.] in organising churches for protestant refugees; planted a colony of Flemish weavers at Glastonbury; again in England, 1558; 'first elder' of the Dutch church, London; published a Latin narrative of his church, some psalms in Dutch verse, and other writings.   [lviii. 73]

UTHER PENDRAGON, father of King Arthur; hero of romance, according to which he was brother of Aurelius Ambrosianus, who claimed descent from Constantine the Tyrant, and headed a war against the Saxons.   [ii. 126]

UTRED (1315?–1396). [See UHTRED.]

UTTERSON, EDWARD VERNON (1776?–1856), literary antiquary; educated at Eton; LL.B. Trinity Hall, Cambridge, 1801; barrister, Lincoln's Inn, 1802; one of the six clerks in chancery, 1815–42; edited reprints of scarce English books, 1812–39; issued similar reprints from his private 'Beldornie press,' Ryde, 1840–3.
                    [lviii. 73]

UVEDALE. [See also UDALL.]

UVEDALE or WOODHALL, JOHN (d. 1549?), contractor and official; carrier for the royal household, 1488; commissariat officer at Flodden, 1513; clerk of the pells, 1516; speculated in crown leases of mines; secretary to Henry Fitzroy, duke of Richmond [q. v.], 1525–8; secretary to Anne Boleyn, 1533–5; secretary to the council in the north, 1536–9, 1545; treasurer of the garrisons in the north, 1542 till death.   [lviii. 74]

UVEDALE or UVEDALL, RICHARD (d. 1556), conspirator; governor of Yarmouth Castle, Isle of Wight; a protestant; privy to Sir Henry Dudley's anti-Spanish

plot, January 1556; sent to the Tower of London, March 1556; turned informer; executed.   [lviii. 75]

UVEDALE, ROBERT (1642–1722), schoolmaster and horticulturist; educated at Westminster School; fellow of Trinity College, Cambridge, 1664; M.A., 1666; LL.D., 1682; master of the grammar school and proprietor of a boarding school at Enfield, 1664; non-resident rector of Orpington, 1696; cultivated exotic plants in hot-houses; his herbarium in the Sloane collection.   [lviii. 76]

UVEDALE, THOMAS (fl. 1712), translator of Philip de Comines's memoirs, 1712.   [lviii. 77]

UVEDALE, Sir WILLIAM (1455–1524), soldier and courtier; of Wickham, Hampshire, and Titsey, Surrey; sheriff of Hampshire, 1480, 1487, and 1493; governor of Porchester, 1483; attainted by Richard III, 1484, but pardoned; esquire of the body of Henry VII, c. 1486; K.B., 1489; employed on public service in Wales, 1512; a commissioner of musters for Hampshire, 1522.
                    [lviii. 77]

UVEDALE, Sir WILLIAM (d. 1542), of More Crichel; comptroller of Poole port, 1515; customer of wools, London, 1522–35; knighted, 1533.   [lviii. 78]

UWINS, DAVID (1780?–1837), medical writer; studied in London hospitals: M.D. Edinburgh, 1803; practised at Aylesbury; physician to various London dispensaries, and, 1828, to Peckham lunatic asylum; became a homœopathist; works include a 'Treatise on Nervous and Mental Disorders,' 1830.   [lviii. 78]

UWINS, THOMAS (1782–1857), painter in oil and water colours; art student in London; apprenticed to an engraver, 1797; professional miniature portrait-painter from 1798; exhibited at the Royal Academy, 1799–1808, and from 1830; illustrated books from 1808; visited France to paint vintage scenes, 1817, and Scotland to illustrate Sir Walter Scott's works, 1820–2, and Italy, 1824–31; R.A., 1838; keeper of the National Gallery, 1847–55.   [lviii. 79]

UXBRIDGE, EARLS OF. [See PAGET, HENRY, first EARL, d. 1743; PAGET, HENRY, second EARL, 1719–1769; PAGET, HENRY WILLIAM, first MARQUIS OF ANGLESEY, 1768–1854.]

V

VACARIUS (1115?–1200?), civilian; probably of Bologna; called to England, c. 1143, in the interest of Archbishop Theobald [q. v.]; lectured on Justinian at Oxford, 1149; abridged Justinian, as a text-book for Oxford students; silenced by King Stephen, c. 1152; long in the service of Roger of Pont l'Evêque [q. v.]; prebendary of Southwell, 1167   [lviii. 80]

VACHER, CHARLES (1818–1883), painter in water-colours; art student in London; travelled in Italy, France, Germany, Algeria, Egypt; exhibited in London, 1838–81.
                    [lviii. 81]

VALENCE, AYMER DE (d. 1260). [See AYMER.]

VALENCE, AYMER DE, EARL OF PEMBROKE (d. 1324). [See AYMER.]

VALENCE, WILLIAM DE, titular EARL OF PEMBROKE (d. 1296). [See WILLIAM.]

VALENTIA, VISCOUNT (1585–1660). [See ANNESLEY, SIR FRANCIS.]

VALENTINE, BENJAMIN (d. 1652?), parliamentarian; M.P., St. Germans, 1629; joined in forcing Speaker Finch to allow Sir John Eliot [q. v.] to read his resolutions against Charles I, 2 March 1629; imprisoned, 1629–30; condemned and fined, February 1630; prisoner, with considerable liberty, in the Gatehouse, London, 1630, but rigorously confined, 1630–40; M.P., St. Germans, in the Long parliament; voted compensation by parliament before 1648.   [lviii. 81]

VALLANCEY, CHARLES (1721–1812), antiquary; son of a French protestant; officer of engineers; engineer in ordinary in Ireland, 1762; general, 1803; F.R.S., 1784; ignorant of Irish; published worthless tracts on Irish philology and history, 1772–1802.   [lviii. 82]

VALLANS, WILLIAM (fl. 1578–1590), poet; a Hertfordshire salter; published, in unrhymed hexameters, 'A Tale of Two Swannes,' descriptive of places in Hertfordshire, 1590.   [lviii. 83]

VALOGNES or VALONIIS, PHILIP DE (d. 1215), baron of Panmure; grandson of one of William the Conqueror's officers; migrated to Scotland before 1165; an intimate friend of William the Lion, and hostage for him, 1174 and 1209; granted Panmure and Benvie; high chamberlain of Scotland, 1180–1215.   [lviii. 83]

VALPY, ABRAHAM JOHN (1787–1854), editor and printer; second son of Richard Valpy [q. v.]; educated at Reading grammar school and Pembroke College, Oxford (M.A. and fellow, 1811); published excerpts from Cicero, 1804, and Latin verses, 1809; publisher and part-editor of numerous classical texts and journals, London, 1807–37; reprinted the Delphin classics, 1819–30.
                    [lviii. 84]

VALPY, EDWARD (1764–1832), classical scholar; B.D. Trinity College, Cambridge, 1810; assistant-master at Reading; high master of Norwich school, 1810; beneficed in Norfolk, 1819–32; edited an annotated Greek testament and school books.   [lviii. 85]

VALPY, FRANCIS EDWARD JACKSON (1797–1882), schoolmaster; son of Richard Valpy [q. v.]; educated at Reading school; M.A. Trinity College, Cambridge, 1824; head-master of Reading school, 1830, but proved a failure; master of Burton-on-Trent school; rector of Garveston, 1854; published classical schoolbooks.   [lviii. 86]

VALPY, RICHARD (1754–1836), schoolmaster; native of Jersey; educated partly in Normandy and partly at Guildford school; published verse, 1772; scholar of Pembroke College, Oxford, 1773; B.A., 1776; D.D., 1792;

assistant-master at Bury St. Edmunds, 1777 ; very successful head-master of Reading school, 1781-1830 ; non-resident rector of Stradishall, 1787 ; published classical and other school-books, 1809-16. [lviii. 85]

VANAKEN, JOSEPH (1699 ?-1749). [See VAN HAECKEN.]

VANBRUGH, CHARLES (d. 1745), son of Sir John Vanbrugh [q. v.] ; educated at Lausanne ; ensign in the Coldstream guards, 1739 ; mortally wounded at Fontenoy. [lviii. 93]

VANBRUGH or **VANBURGH**, SIR JOHN (1664-1726), dramatist, architect, and herald ; son of a London tradesman ; of Flemish descent ; studied in France, 1683-1685, forming architectural tastes ; entered the army, 1686 ; prisoner in France, 1690-2, latterly in the Bastille ; captain, 1696 ; comptroller of the board of works, 1702-12, and again, 1715 ; brought out 'The Relapse,' 1696, with immense success, 'Æsop,' 1697 (adapted from the French of Edmond Boursault), and 'The Provok'd Wife,' 1697 ; severely censured in Jeremy Collier's [q. v.] 'Short View,' 1698, and issued the same year a feeble 'Vindication'; brought out, 1700, a prose version of Beaumont and Fletcher's 'Pilgrim,' and 'The False Friend,' 1702 (adapted from Le Sage) ; also 'Squire Trelooby,' 1704 (adapted, jointly with Congreve and Walsh, from Molière) ; brought out 'The Country House,' 1705 (adapted from the French of Carton Dancourt), 'The Confederacy,' one of the most licentious pieces of the comic drama after the Restoration, 1705 (also from Dancourt), and 'The Mistake,' 1705 (adapted, jointly with Betterton, from Molière) ; his 'Journey to London,' completed by Colley Cibber and brought out, 1728 ; manager of Haymarket Theatre, London, 1705-7 ; designed Castle Howard, 1701 (completed, 1714), his own Haymarket Theatre, London, 1705, and Blenheim Palace, Woodstock, 1705 (completed by Sarah, duchess of Marlborough, from Vanbrugh's designs, but without his help, 1724) ; 'restored' Kimbolton Castle, 1707, and designed the Clarendon Building, Broad Street, Oxford, 1711, jointly with Nicholas Hawksmoor [q. v.] ; worked on country seats in a ponderous style of architecture ; 'Carlisle' herald, to qualify for office, 1703, Clarenceux king-at-arms, 1704-26 ; knighted, 1714 ; acted as Garter, 1715-18, the claim of John Anstis the younger [q. v.] being allowed in 1718 ; disliked in the College of Arms, owing to his ridicule of its formalities. His correspondence is partly published in 'Gentleman's Magazine,' 1736-9, and 'Athenæum,' 1890). His collected dramatic works appeared, 1730. [lviii. 86]

VANCE, ALFRED GLENVILLE (1838 ?-1888), actor and pantomimist ; 'the great Vance,' real name ALFRED PECK STEVENS ; originally a solicitor's clerk in London ; acted in the north of England ; made his mark in London music-halls ; died while performing at Sun Music Hall, Knightsbridge. [lviii. 94]

VAN CEULEN, CORNELIUS JANSSEN (1593-1664 ?). [See JANSSEN.]

VANCOUVER, CHARLES (fl. 1785-1813), agriculturist ; an American ; published a compendium of science, 1785 ; invited English settlers to Kentucky, 1788 ; reported on English farming for the board of agriculture (Cambridgeshire, 1794 ; Essex, 1795) ; described the drainage of the fens, 1794 (published, 1801) ; returned to Kentucky, c. 1798 ; again in England, 1806 ; reported on Devonshire, 1808, and Hampshire, 1813. [lviii. 95]

VANCOUVER, GEORGE (1758-1798), explorer ; sailed on James Cook's (1728-1779) [q. v.] second voyage, 1772, as seaman ; seaman (afterwards midshipman) on Cook's third voyage ; returned, 1780 ; served as lieutenant in the West Indies, 1781-3, 1786-9 ; commander, 1790 ; captain, 1794 ; sailed on a voyage of discovery round the Cape of Good Hope, 1791 ; surveyed the south-west of Australia and of New Zealand ; surveyed the Pacific coast of North America, sailing round 'Vancouver' island, 1792-4 ; returned by Cape Horn, 1795 ; his 'Voyage' published posthumously, 1798. [lviii. 96]

VANDELEUR, SIR JOHN ORMSBY (1763-1849), general ; infantry officer, 1781-92 ; exchanged into the dragoons, 1792 ; served in Flanders, 1794-5, and at the Cape of Good Hope, 1796 ; lieutenant-colonel, 1798 ; served with distinction in India, 1803-5 ; major-general, 1811 ; in the Peninsular war commanded an infantry brigade, 1811, an infantry division, 1812-13, a cavalry brigade,

1813 ; commanded the fourth cavalry brigade at Waterloo; K.C.B., 1815 ; general, 1838. [lviii. 97]

VANDENHOFF, CHARLOTTE ELIZABETH (1818-1860), actress ; daughter of John M. Vandenhoff [q. v.] ; first appeared in London, 1836 ; brought out a comedy, 1852 ; married Thomas Swinbourne, an actor, 1856. [lviii. 99]

VANDENHOFF, JOHN M. (1790-1861), actor ; of Dutch descent ; born at Salisbury ; educated at Stonyhurst ; acted in the west of England, 1808-13, at Liverpool, 1814-20, in London, 1820-39, and occasionally at Edinburgh, 1822-57 ; visited America, 1837 ; acted chiefly in the country, 1839-58. [lviii. 98]

VANDEPUT, GEORGE (d. 1800), admiral ; illegitimate son of Sir George Vandeput, baronet (d. 1784) ; lieutenant, 1759 ; in command of ships, 1764-93 ; rear-admiral, 1793 ; admiral, 1799 ; died at sea. [lviii. 99]

VANDERBANK, JOHN (1694 ?- 1739), portrait-painter ; son of Peter Vanderbank [q. v.] ; born in England ; illustrated 'Don Quixote,' 1738 ; painted Sir Isaac Newton. [lviii. 100]

VANDERBANK or **VANDREBANC**, PETER (1649-1697), engraver, chiefly of portraits ; born in Paris ; came to England, 1674. [lviii. 100]

VAN DER DOORT [DORT], ABRAHAM (d. 1640), medallist ; native of Holland ; in the service of Henry, prince of Wales, 1612 ; designer of coinage, 1625 ; keeper of Charles I's collections, 1628-40 ; compiled a catalogue of the collections, 1638 ; committed suicide. [lviii. 101]

VAN DER EYDEN, JEREMIAH (d. 1695), portrait-painter ; native of Brussels ; assistant to Sir Peter Lely. [lviii. 101]

VAN DER GUCHT, BENJAMIN (d. 1794), painter; son of Gerard Van der Gucht [q. v.] ; art-student in London ; painted theatrical portraits ; a noted picture-dealer; accidentally drowned. [lviii. 102]

VAN DER GUCHT, GERARD (1696-1776), engraver; son of Michael Van der Gucht [q. v.] ; born in London ; book-illustrator and picture-dealer. [lviii. 102]

VAN DER GUCHT, JAN (1697-1728 ?), engraver; son of Michael Van der Gucht [q. v.] [lviii. 102]

VAN DER GUCHT, MICHAEL (1660-1725), engraver ; born in Antwerp ; came to London, 1690 ; book-illustrator ; instructor of George Vertue [q. v.] [lviii. 101]

VANDERLINT, JACOB (d. 1740), author of 'Money Answers all Things' (1734), an economic treatise ; a London timber-merchant. [lviii. 102]

VAN DER MYN or **VAN DER MIJN**, HERMAN (1684-1741), portrait-painter ; born in Amsterdam ; resided in London, 1718-36 and 1741. [lviii. 102]

VAN DER VAART, JAN (1647-1721), painter and mezzotint-engraver ; born in Haarlem ; came to London, 1674 ; a noted painter of landscapes, portraits, and still-life ; one of the earliest mezzotint-engravers ; from 1713 specialised as a restorer of pictures. [lviii. 103]

VAN DE VELDE, WILLEM, the elder (1610-1693), marine-painter ; born in Leyden ; originally a sailor-boy ; came to England, 1675. [lviii. 103]

VAN DE VELDE, WILLEM, the younger (1633-1707), painter ; son of Willem Van de Velde the elder [q. v.] ; came to England, c. 1675 ; produced copies in oil of his father's sketches. [lviii. 103]

VAN DIEST, ADRIAEN (1656-1704), landscape-painter ; son of Willem Van Diest, a Dutch marine-painter ; came to England, c. 1673. [lviii. 104]

VAN DYCK, SIR ANTHONY (ANTHONIS, ANTOON) (1599-1641), painter and etcher ; a younger son of an Antwerp silk-mercer ; pupil of the painter Hendrik Van Balen, 1609 ; opened a studio in Antwerp, 1615, painting portraits, and heads for Christ and his apostles ; freeman of St. Luke's Guild, Antwerp, 1619 ; intimate friend and assistant of Rubens, 1619-20 ; invited to England by Thomas Howard, second earl of Arundel [q. v.] or his countess, 1620 ; employed by James I, November 1620-February 1621 ; travelled in Italy, 1621-5 ; visited Aix ; resided in Antwerp, painting and etching, c. 1626-c. 1632 ; brought to England by Charles I ; had his studio in Blackfriars, London, 1632; knighted, 1632; pensioned, 1633; visited Antwerp, 1634–5; painting portraits in England, 1635–40; a libertine; forced by Charles I to marry Mary Ruthven, 1640; went to Antwerp, 1640, and to Paris, 1641; returned to London, 1641. His method of work was to make a first sketch and take notes for the guidance of the assistants who executed the portrait, after which he added the finishing touches. [lviii. 104]

VANDYKE, PETER (*fl.* 1767), painter; native of Holland; assistant to Sir Joshua Reynolds; exhibited in London, 1762–7; settled in Bristol; painted portraits of Coleridge and Southey. [lviii. 111]

VANE, ANNE (1705–1736), the subject of Dr. Johnson's line, 'Yet Vane could tell what ills from beauty spring'; daughter of Gilbert Vane, baron Barnard; maid of honour to Queen Caroline; mistress of Frederick, prince of Wales. [lviii. 112]

VANE, FRANCES ANNE, VISCOUNTESS VANE (1713–1788), nicknamed 'Lady Fanny'; *née* Hawes; married, 1732, Lord William Douglas (*d.* 1734); married, 1735, William, second viscount Vane; became infamous for gambling and profligacy; contributed chapter eighty-one to Smollett's 'Peregrine Pickle'; a confirmed invalid from 1768. [lviii. 112]

VANE, SIR HENRY, the elder (1589–1655), secretary of state; originally styled Henry Fane, of Hadlow; entered Brasenose College, Oxford, 1604; entered at Gray's Inn, 1606; knighted, 1611; purchased carver's place at court, 1612, share in the subpœna office in chancery, 1613, and cofferership to Prince Charles, 1617; cofferer, 1625, comptroller, 1629, and treasurer, 1639–41, of the household; M.P., Lostwithiel, 1614, Carlisle, 1621, 1624–6, and Retford, 1628–9; sent to solicit help for the Palatinate to Holland, 1629–30, and to the king of Sweden, 1631, but was unsuccessful; sold Hadlow; accumulated wealth by court practices, and bought lands in Kent and Yorkshire, and Raby and Barnard Castles in Durham; privy councillor, 1630; constantly employed on administrative commissions, 1630–40; opposed the war with Scotland, 1639; personally aggrieved by Strafford, 1640; secretary of state, by the Marquis of Hamilton's influence, 1640–1; M.P., Wilton, and spokesman for Charles I in the Short parliament, May 1640; employed in negotiations with the Scots, 1640; M.P., Wilton, in the Long parliament, 1640–1653; approved of the impeachment of Strafford; gave evidence, March 1641, implying that in May 1640 Strafford had advised Charles I to bring the Irish army into England; a commissioner of the treasury, 1641; accompanied Charles I to Scotland, August 1641; dismissed from all his places, November 1641; joined the parliamentary leaders; parliamentary lord-lieutenant of Durham, but powerless there, 1642; served on the committee of both kingdoms from 1644; compensated by parliament for damage to his Durham estates by the royal troops; M.P., Kent, 1654. [lviii. 113]

VANE, SIR HENRY, the younger (1613–1662), statesman; eldest son of Sir Henry Vane the elder [q. v.]; educated at Westminster School, at Oxford, 1629, and abroad; adopted decided puritan views, 1628; attached to the embassy at Vienna, 1631; returned to England, 1632; resolved to go to New England for freedom of conscience; resided in Boston, 1635–7; governor of Massachusetts, 1636–7; entangled in the doctrinal controversies of the colonists; returned to England, 1637; treasurer of the navy, 1639–41; M.P., Hull, in the Short parliament, April 1640; knighted, 1640; married, and received Raby Castle from his father, July 1640; showed Pym his father's memorandum of Strafford's advice (5 May 1640) to Charles I, September 1640; M.P., Hull, in the Long parliament, November 1640; Strafford's fate sealed by his copy of the memorandum, April 1641; advocated abolition of episcopacy, May 1641; dismissed by Charles I from his treasurership of the navy, December 1641; a leader of the war party in parliament; parliamentary treasurer of the navy, 1642–50; conducted negotiations with Scots at Edinburgh, 1643; virtual leader of the House of Commons, 1643–6; rejected Charles I's overtures to dissociate him from the parliament, 1644; a commissioner at the treaty of Uxbridge, 1645; urged the reorganisation of the army; offended the presbyterians by insisting on toleration; rejected fresh overtures to Charles I, 1646; a commissioner to treat with the army leaders at Wycombe, 1647; distrusted both by the presby-

terians and the levellers; a commissioner to treat with Charles I at Newport, 1648; took no part in Charles I's trial; member of the parliamentary council of state, 1649; a leading man in all affairs of the Commonwealth, home, colonial, military, and naval, 1649–53; a close friend of Cromwell, 1650–3; sent to Scotland to settle Scottish affairs, 1651; came into collision with Cromwell, from wishing to perpetuate the Long parliament, 1653; retired to Belleau, 1653; imprisoned for a pamphlet against Cromwell's arbitrary government, 1656; M.P., Whitchurch, in Richard Cromwell's parliament, February 1659; effected the abolition of the protectorate; in the restored Long parliament was commissioner of the navy and virtual foreign minister, May 1659; laboured to reconcile the army and the parliament; became distrusted by all parties; expelled from the Long parliament, January 1660; put in custody, February; partially excluded from indemnity by the 'Convention' parliament, June 1660; prisoner in the Tower of London, and in the Scilly islands; his death demanded by the Cavalier parliament, July 1661; condemned and executed on Tower Hill; a religious enthusiast; published several treatises of mystical divinity; published also speeches. [lviii. 116]

VANE, SIR RALPH (*d.* 1552). [See FANE.]

VANE, THOMAS (*fl.* 1652), Romanist convert; D.D. Christ's College, Cambridge; rector of Crayford; embraced Romanism; settled in Paris as a physician; published Romanist tracts, 1646–52. [lviii. 129]

VANE, WILLIAM HARRY, first DUKE OF CLEVELAND of the second creation and third EARL OF DARLINGTON (1766–1842); styled Viscount Barnard; of Christ Church, Oxford; M.P., Totnes, 1788–90, Winchelsea, 1790–1792; a whig; succeeded as Earl of Darlington, 1792; created marquis, 1827, and duke, 1833, of Cleveland; fox-hunter and patron of the turf. [lviii. 130]

VANE-STEWART, CHARLES WILLIAM, third MARQUIS OF LONDONDERRY (1778–1854). [See STEWART.]

VAN HAECKEN (**VAN AKEN**), JOSEPH (1699?–1749), painter; born in Antwerp; came to England, *c.* 1719; practised as portrait-painter; assistant to various portrait-painters. [lviii. 131]

VANHOMRIGH, ESTHER (1690–1723), 'Vanessa'; friend of Dean Swift; of Dutch descent; the intimacy between her and Swift recorded in Swift's poem 'Cadenus and Vanessa' (written in 1713, published in 1726, after Vanessa's death, by her executors); conceived a hopeless passion for Swift; wrote a letter to Stella [see JOHNSON, ESTHER], or, according to another account, to Swift himself, asking if he was married to Stella, 1723; died of shock occasioned by Swift's anger at her action. [lv. 215]

VAN HUYSUM, JACOB (JAMES) (1687?–1746), flower-painter; born in Amsterdam; came to England, *c.* 1721. [lviii. 131]

VANKOUGHNET, PHILIP MICHAEL SCOTT (1822–1869), Canadian statesman; born at Cornwall, Ontario; served in the militia, 1837; barrister, 1843; minister of agriculture, 1856; chief commissioner of crown lands, 1858; chancellor of Upper Canada, 1862–9. [lviii. 131]

VAN LAUN, HENRI (1820–1896), author; born in Holland; educated in France; settled in England, 1848; teacher of French; examiner in French for various government departments; published a French grammar, 1863, a 'History of French Literature,' 1876, and a history of the French revolution, 1878; translated Taine's 'English Literature,' 1871, Molière, 1875, La Bruyère, 1885, and 'Gil Blas,' 1886. [lviii. 132]

VAN LEEMPUT, REMIGIUS (1609?–1675), painter; often called M. Remy; born in Antwerp; came to England before 1640; copied portraits by Lely and Van Dyck. [lviii. 132]

VAN LEMENS, BALTHASAR (1637–1704), painter; born in Antwerp; made sketches for London engravers. [lviii. 133]

VAN MILDERT, WILLIAM (1765–1836), the last bishop of Durham with palatine dignity; of Dutch extraction; son of a London distiller; at Merchant Taylors' School, 1779–84; B.A. Queen's College, Oxford, 1787; M.A., 1790; rector of Bradden, 1795, and of St. Mary-le-Bow, London, 1796–1820; Boyle lecturer, 1802–4; vicar of Farningham, 1807–13; preacher at Lincoln's Inn,

1812–19; Bampton lecturer, 1813; D.D., 1813; regius professor of divinity, Oxford, 1813–19; bishop of Llandaff, 1819–26; dean of St. Paul's, London, 1820–6; bishop of Durham, 1826–36; joined in founding Durham University, 1832; published sermons, charges, and theological tracts. [lviii. 133]

VANNES, PETER (*d.* 1563), diplomatist; born in Lucca; assistant to Andrea Ammonio [q. v.], Henry VIII's secretary, 1513; secretary to Wolsey, 1514; Latin secretary to Henry VIII and Edward VI; incorporated B.D. Cambridge, 1523; visited Rome, 1526; accompanied Wolsey to France, 1527; resident in Rome, vainly soliciting Henry VIII's divorce, 1529; held various prebends from 1529; envoy to Rome, 1533; archdeacon of Worcester, 1534; dean of Salisbury, 1540–7 and 1553–63; rector of Tredington, 1542; English ambassador at Venice, 1550–6. [lviii. 134]

VAN NOST, JOHN (*d.* 1780), sculptor; of Dublin. [lviii. 136]

VAN RYMSDYK, ANDREW (*d.* 1780), engraver; son of Jan Van Rymsdyk [q. v.] [lviii. 136]

VAN RYMSDYK, JAN (*fl.* 1767–1778), painter and engraver; native of Holland; portrait-painter; began mezzotint-engraving, 1767; settled at Bristol. [lviii. 136]

VANS, SIR PATRICK, LORD BARNBARROCH (*d.* 1597), Scottish judge; rector of Wigton; inherited Barnbarroch, Wigtownshire, 1568; lord of session as Lord Barnbarroch, 1576; privy councillor, 1587; ambassador to Denmark, 1587; accompanied James VI to Denmark, 1589; possibly the 'Sir Patrick Spens' of the old ballad. [lviii. 136]

VANSITTART, GEORGE HENRY (1768–1824), general; studied at Strasbourg and Brunswick; lieutenant, 1787; captain, 1790; lieutenant-colonel, 1794; served at Toulon, 1793, at the Cape, 1795, and in the West Indies, 1803; major-general, 1803; general, 1821. [lviii. 137]

VANSITTART, HENRY (1732–1770), governor of Bengal; of Dutch extraction; younger son of a London merchant; a profligate youth; writer in the East India Company's service at Fort St. Davids, 1746; made friendship there with Clive; visited England, 1751; sent to negotiate with the French East India Company, 1754–5; member of the council, 1757; took part in the defence of Madras, 1759; temporary governor of Fort St. George, 1759–60; his governorship of Bengal (1760–4) marked by the deposition of Mir Jafar, subadar of Bengal, and the appointment of Mir Kásim, 1760, by friction with the military officers of the company, 1761, by vain efforts to check the corruption of the company's administration, and by war with Mir Jafar, 1763; returned to England, 1764; coldly received by the company and by Clive; published a 'Narrative' of his governorship, 1766; M.P., Reading, 1768; director of the East India Company, 1769; touched at the Cape, 1769, when on his way to India to report on the administration of Bengal; his ship never heard of afterwards. [lviii. 137]

VANSITTART, HENRY (1777–1843), vice-admiral; put on ship's books, 1788; on service almost uninterruptedly, 1791–1814; lieutenant, 1795; captain, 1801; rear-admiral, 1830; vice-admiral, 1841. [lviii. 140]

VANSITTART, NICHOLAS, first BARON BEXLEY (1766–1851), chancellor of the exchequer; a younger son of Henry Vansittart (1732–1770) [q. v.]; M.A. Christ Church, Oxford, 1791; hon. D.C.L., 1814; barrister, Lincoln's Inn, 1791; wrote pamphlets in favour of Pitt's administration, 1793–6; M.P., 1796–1823, latterly for Harwich; supported Addington's administration; envoy to Denmark, 1801; secretary of the treasury, 1801–4 and 1806–7; chief secretary for Ireland, 1805; chancellor of the exchequer, 1812–23; urged the union of the English and Irish exchequers, 1817; chancellor of the duchy of Lancaster, 1823–8; created Baron Bexley, 1823, and pensioned. [lviii. 140]

VANSITTART, ROBERT (1728–1789), jurist; educated at Winchester School; fellow of All Souls College, Oxford; D.C.L., 1757; barrister, Inner Temple, 1753; recorder of Maidenhead, 1763, of Windsor, 1770; regius professor of civil law, Oxford, 1767–89; F.S.A., 1767. [lviii. 144]

VAN SOMER, PAUL (1576–1621), portrait-painter; born in Antwerp; had a studio at Amsterdam, 1604; came to England, *c.* 1606; the favourite painter of James I's court. [lviii. 145]

VAN SOMER, PAUL (*d.* 1694), mezzotint-engraver; came from Amsterdam to London, 1674. [lviii. 145]

VAN SON, JAN FRANS (FRANCIS), erroneously written VAN ZOON (1658–1718 ?), painter of still-life; son of an Antwerp flower-painter; settled in London. [lviii. 145]

VAN STRAUBENZEE, SIR CHARLES THOMAS (1812–1892), general; of Dutch extraction; born in Malta; ensign, 1828; major, 1843; served in Ceylon, 1829–33, and in India, 1833–7 and 1842–5; lieutenant-colonel, 1851; in command at the Piræus, 1854–5; brigadier-general, May 1855; commanded brigade in the Crimea, 1855–6; commanded British contingent in Chinese war, 1857–60; K.C.B., 1858; major-general, 1859; held command in India, 1862–5; governor of Malta, 1872–8; general, 1875; retired, 1881. [lviii. 146]

VAN VOERST, ROBERT (1596–1636), engraver; native of Holland; pupil of Crispin de Passe the elder; came to England, 1628; engraved portraits, partly after Van Dyck. [lviii. 147]

VARDY, JOHN (*d.* 1765), architect; clerk of works in London at the Horse Guards, 1751, and at Kensington Palace and Chelsea Hospital. [lviii. 148]

VARLEY, CORNELIUS (1781–1873), water-colour painter and inventor; sketched early in life; maker of philosophical instruments; invented improvements in lens-making; went back to art, 1800; exhibited at the Royal Academy, 1803 and 1821–59; exhibited at the Water-colour Society, 1805–21; experimented in electricity. [lviii. 148]

VARLEY, CROMWELL FLEETWOOD (1828–1883), electrical engineer; son of Cornelius Varley [q. v.]; employé of the International Telegraph Company, 1846–1868; introduced improvements in telegraphic apparatus, 1854–70; consulted as expert about laying the second Atlantic cable, *c.* 1860; F.R.S., 1871; published papers on electricity and telegraphy. [lviii. 149]

VARLEY, JOHN (1778–1842), landscape-painter; worked for portrait-painters, 1792; sketched on the Thames and about London; became an art-teacher in London, latterly very successful, and boarding his pupils; sketched in Wales and the north and west of England, 1798–1803; exhibited at the Royal Academy, 1798–1803, and at the Water-colour Society, 1805–42; published treatises on art, 1815–18; a close friend of William Blake, 1819–27; believed in astrology; in constant difficulties through generosity to others. [lviii. 150]

VARLEY, WILLIAM FLEETWOOD (1785–1856), artist; exhibited at the Royal Academy, 1804–18; art-teacher. [lviii. 153]

VARLO or **VARLEY**, CHARLES (1725 ?–1796 ?), agriculturist; native of Yorkshire; visited Ireland, 1746, and introduced flax-growing; farmed land in Leitrim, 1748; mobbed in Dublin, 1760, for exporting Irish cattle; invented a winnowing-machine, 1772; being hoaxed by forged deeds went to America, 1784, to claim the governorship of New Jersey; returned, *c.* 1786; published treatises on agriculture, 1770–96. [lviii. 153]

VASCUS, JOHN (1490 ?–1538 ?). [See VAUS.]

VASHON, JAMES (1742–1827), admiral; served continuously in the navy, 1755–1808; lieutenant, 1774; commander, 1779; rear-admiral, 1804; admiral, 1814. [lviii. 154]

VASSALL, JOHN (*d.* 1625), colonial pioneer; protestant refugee from Normandy; apparently a ship-master in 1577; commanded a ship against the Armada, 1588; member of the London Virginia Company, 1609. [lviii. 155]

VASSALL, SAMUEL (1586–1667), parliamentarian; a younger son of John Vassall [q. v.]; merchant in London, trading with America, Guinea, &c.; an original member of the Massachusetts Company, 1628; refused to pay Charles I's demand of tonnage and poundage, 1628 and 1630; imprisoned on that account, 1628–36, and his goods retained; M.P., London, in the Short and the

Long parliaments, 1640; solicited parliament for compensation for losses in resisting tonnage and poundage, 1641–60; advanced money to pay the parliament troops in Ireland, 1646, and had difficulty in obtaining repayment, 1647; visited Carolina, 1663 ; probably died abroad.
[lviii. 156]

VASSALL, SPENCER THOMAS (1764 – 1807), soldier ; served at Gibraltar, 1782, and in Flanders ; lieutenant-colonel, 1801; served at the Cape, 1806 ; mortally wounded at Monte Video. [lviii. 156]

VASSALL, WILLIAM (1592–1655), colonist ; a younger son of John Vassall [q. v.]; visited Massachusetts, 1630 ; settled at Plymouth, Massachusetts, 1635–46 ; resided in Barbados, 1650–5. [lviii. 156]

VAUGHAN, BENJAMIN (1751–1835), politician ; educated at nonconformist seminaries, Cambridge, and Edinburgh ; unitarian ; merchant in London ; supporter of Lord Shelburne : sympathised with the American insurgents, the Irish conspirators, and the French revolutionists ; visited Paris, 1790 ; M.P., Calne, 1792 ; fled to avoid persecution for treason to France, 1794 ; imprisoned by the Carmelites, but, owing to the goodwill of Robespierre, only for a short time : advised Robespierre to surround France with a fringe of free and allied states, 1794 ; emigrated to America, 1798 : published political tracts, 1789–96. [lviii. 158]

VAUGHAN, CHARLES JOHN (1816–1897), dean of Llandaff ; of Rugby and Trinity College, Cambridge; senior classic, 1838 ; fellow, 1839 ; M.A., 1841 ; D.D., 1845 ; vicar of St. Martin's, Leicester, 1841–4 ; head-master of Harrow, 1844–59; vicar of Doncaster, 1860–9 ; for love of the church privately trained ordination candidates in ministerial work, 1861–97; master of the Temple, 1869–1894 ; dean of Llandaff, 1879–97; published scripture commentaries and devotional works, 1859–90.
[lviii. 159]

VAUGHAN, SIR CHARLES RICHARD (1774–1849), diplomatist ; of Rugby and Merton College, Oxford ; M.A., 1798 ; fellow of All Souls College, Oxford, 1798 ; M.B., 1800 ; travelled on the continent, 1801–3, in Western and Central Asia, 1804–6, in Spain, 1808 ; secretary of embassy in Spain, 1810–19, in Paris, 1820–2 ; ambassador to Switzerland, 1823–4, to the United States, 1825–35; knighted, 1833 ; afterwards travelled on the continent. [lviii. 161]

VAUGHAN, EDWARD (d. 1522), bishop of St. David's ; LL.D. Cambridge ; vicar of St. Matthew's, Friday Street, London, 1487 ; vicar of Islington ; prebendary, 1493–1509, and treasurer, 1503–9, of St. Paul's, London ; bishop, by papal provision, of St. David's, 1509 ; built much at St. David's. [lviii. 161]

VAUGHAN or VYCHAN, SIR GRIFFITH (d. 1447), soldier ; son of Griffith ap Ieuan, who rebelled with Glendower (1403) ; styled Sir Griffith 'Vaughan,' i.e. the ' younger,' 1406 ; inherited lands in Montgomeryshire : fought at Agincourt, 1415 ; captured Sir John Oldcastle in Montgomeryshire, 1417; outlawed and beheaded.
[lviii. 162]

VAUGHAN, SIR HENRY, the elder (1587 ?–1659 ?), royalist : acquired Derwydd, Carmarthenshire, by marriage ; M.P., Carmarthen, 1621–9, and Carmarthenshire, in the Short parliament, 1640, and in the Long parliament, November 1640, till expelled, February 1644 ; knighted, 1643 ; royalist major-general in Pembrokeshire, 1643, but driven out by Rowland Laugharne [q. v.], 1644 ; fined as a delinquent, 1644 and 1645 ; taken prisoner at Naseby, 1645 ; in prison in London, 1645–c. 1659.
[lviii. 163]

VAUGHAN, SIR HENRY, the younger (1613–1676), royalist ; son of Sir Henry Vaughan the elder [q. v.] ; taken prisoner at Tenby, 1648; knighted, 1661 : M.P., Carmarthenshire, 1668–76. [lviii. 164]

VAUGHAN, HENRY, 'SILURIST' (1622–1695), poet ; entered Jesus College, Oxford, 1638 ; studied law in London ; medical practitioner in Brecknock, 1645, and in Newton-by-Usk, 1650–95 ; published ' Poems,' 1646, ' Silex Scintillans ' (sacred poems), first part, 1650, second part, containing the magnificent 'They are all gone into the world of light,' 1655, ' Olor Iscanus,' poems and prose translations, 1651 ; ' The Mount of Olives,' 1652, and ' Flores Solitudinis,' 1654, the last two being English versions of Latin devotional tracts,

'Hermetical Physick' (from the Latin), 1655 ; ' Thalia Rediviva ' (poems), 1678 ; Wordsworth's ' Ode on the Intimations of Immortality ' suggested by his ' Retreat ' ; his collected works published, 1871. He was called ' Silurist ' from the fact that the county of his birth, Brecknockshire, was anciently inhabited by the Silures.
[lviii. 164]

VAUGHAN, HENRY (1766–1844). [See HALFORD, SIR HENRY.]

VAUGHAN, HENRY (1809–1899), collector of works of art, and especially the pictures of Turner, Stothard, Flaxman, and Constable ; F.S.A., 1879 ; one of founders of Burlington Fine Arts Club. By his will his collections were distributed among various public institutions.
[Suppl. iii. 388]

VAUGHAN, HENRY HALFORD (1811–1885), historian ; son of Sir John Vaughan (1769–1839) [q. v.] : of Rugby and Christ Church, Oxford ; fellow of Oriel, 1835–1842 ; barrister, Lincoln's Inn, 1840 ; regius professor of modern history, Oxford, 1848–58 ; published historical lectures, notes on Shakespeare, and versions of Welsh proverbs. [lviii. 166]

VAUGHAN, JOHN, first EARL OF CARBERY (1572 ?–1634), of Jesus College, Oxford ; entered the Middle Temple, 1596 ; inherited Golden Grove, Carmarthenshire, 1598; served in Ireland, 1599 ; M.P., Carmarthenshire, 1601 and 1620–2 ; comptroller of the household to Prince Charles ; accompanied Charles to Madrid, 1623 ; created, in the Irish peerage, Baron Vaughan, 1621, and Earl of Carbery, 1628. [lviii. 171]

VAUGHAN, SIR JOHN (1603–1674), judge ; of Christ Church, Oxford ; barrister, Inner Temple, 1630 ; friend of John Selden ; M.P., Cardigan, 1628, April 1640, and in the Long parliament, 1640 till expelled, 1645 ; consulted by Charles I at Newport, 1648 ; imprisoned ; M.P., Cardiganshire, 1661–8 ; a leader of the country party ; active in the impeachment of Clarendon, 1667 ; knighted, 1668 ; chief-justice of the common pleas, 1668. [lviii. 167]

VAUGHAN, JOHN, third and last EARL OF CARBERY (1640–1713), second son of Richard Vaughan, second earl of Carbery [q. v.] ; of Christ Church, Oxford ; entered the Inner Temple, 1658 ; knighted, 1661 ; M.P., Carmarthen, 1661–79, Carmarthenshire, 1679–81 and 1685–7 ; styled, by courtesy, Lord Vaughan from 1667 ; governor of Jamaica, 1674–8 ; succeeded as earl, 1686. [lviii. 173]

VAUGHAN, SIR JOHN (1748 ?–1795), lieutenant-general ; captain of dragoons, 1755 ; served in Germany ; major, 1759 ; served in America as lieutenant-colonel, 1760–7, and as major-general, 1776–9 ; M.P., Berwick, 1774–95 ; M.P. in the Irish parliament, 1776–83 ; governor of Berwick, 1779–95 ; served in the West Indies, 1780–2 ; accused of peculation at the taking of St. Eustatius; lieutenant-general, 1782 ; K.B., 1792 ; commander of the Leeward islands ; died at Martinique. [lviii. 168]

VAUGHAN, SIR JOHN (1769–1839), judge ; of Rugby and Queen's College, Oxford ; hon. D.C.L., 1813 ; barrister, Lincoln's Inn, 1791 ; recorder of Leicester, 1798 ; serjeant-at-law, 1799 ; king's serjeant, 1816 ; baron of the exchequer, 1827–34 ; knighted, 1828 ; justice of the common pleas, 1834–9. [lviii. 169]

VAUGHAN, RICE (fl. 1638–1672), legal writer ; entered Gray's Inn, 1638 ; author of ' Plea for the Common Laws,' 1651, ' Practica Walliæ,' a guide to the Welsh courts, 1672, and a posthumous ' Discourse of Coin,' 1675.
[lviii. 170]

VAUGHAN, RICHARD (1550 ?–1607), bishop of London ; M.A. St. John's College, Cambridge, 1577 ; D.D., 1589 ; chaplain to his relative, John Aylmer, bishop of London, who made him rector of Chipping Ongar, 1578, of Little Canfield, 1580, of Great Dunmow, 1592, of Moreton, 1592, and of Stanford Rivers, 1594 ; prebendary of St. Paul's, London, 1583, of Wells, 1593 ; archdeacon of Middlesex, 1588 ; bishop of Bangor, 1595–7 ; archdeacon of Anglesey, 1596; bishop of Chester, 1597–1604 ; bishop of London, 1604–7. [lviii. 170]

VAUGHAN, RICHARD, second EARL OF CARBERY (1600 ?–1686), eldest son of John Vaughan, first earl of Carbery [q. v.] ; styled ' Lord Vaughan ' ; travelled, c. 1622 ; knighted, 1626 ; M.P., Carmarthenshire, 1624–9 ; succeeded to earldom, 1634 ; created Baron Vaughan (English peerage), 1643 ; royalist commander in Pembrokeshire, 1643, but driven out by Rowland Laugharne [q. v.], 1644 ; fined as delinquent, 1644 and 1645 ; pardoned by parliament, 1647 ; afterwards remained neutral ; gave asylum to Jeremy Taylor [q. v.] ; lord president of the marches, 1660–72 ; befriended Samuel Butler [q. v.], the author of ' Hudibras.' [lviii. 171]

VAUGHAN, ROBERT (1592–1667), Welsh antiquary : of Oriel College, Oxford ; published ' British Antiquities Revived,' 1662 ; his valuable Welsh MSS. (the ' Hengwrt MSS.') now at Peniarth, Merionethshire. [lviii. 174]

VAUGHAN, ROBERT (1795–1868), congregational divine ; pastor at Worcester, 1819–25 ; pastor in Kensington, 1825–43 ; professor of history, University College, London, 1834–43 ; D.D. Glasgow, 1836 ; president of the Lancashire Independent College, Manchester, 1843–57 ; afterwards pastor at Uxbridge and Torquay ; editor of the ' British Quarterly,' 1845–65 ; published histories of the Stuart and Commonwealth periods, monographs on Wycliffe, and other works. [lviii. 175]

VAUGHAN, ROBERT ALFRED (1823–1857), congregational divine ; eldest son of Robert Vaughan (1795–1868) [q. v.] ; B.A. London, 1842 ; student at the Lancashire Independent College, Manchester, 1843–6, and at Halle, 1846–7 ; minister at Bath, 1848–50, and Birmingham, 1850–5 ; published verses, 1844 ; contributed to the ' British Quarterly ' from 1845 ; published ' Hours with the Mystics,' 1856. [lviii. 176]

VAUGHAN, ROGER WILLIAM BEDE (1834–1883), Roman catholic prelate : educated at Downside College, Bath, and at Rome ; entered the Benedictine order, 1854 ; ordained priest, 1859 ; professor at Belmont, near Hereford, 1861, and principal, 1862–73 ; coadjutor to the archbishop of Sydney, 1873 ; archbishop of Sydney, 1877 ; published a life of Aquinas, 1872, and sermons, 1865–82. [lviii. 177]

VAUGHAN, ROWLAND (*fl.* 1629–1658), Welsh author : studied at Oxford ; inherited Caer Gai, Merionethshire, 1629 ; a royalist captain ; his house burnt and his estate forfeited, 1645 ; imprisoned, 1650 ; recovered his estate, 1660 ; published Welsh versions of devotional books, 1630–1658 ; wrote Welsh verse. [lviii. 178]

VAUGHAN, STEPHEN (*d.* 1549), diplomatist ; a London merchant (governor of the Merchant Adventurers' Company, 1534), frequently visiting Antwerp ; in the service of Thomas Cromwell, 1524 ; molested as a protestant, 1529 and 1532 ; agent at Antwerp for Henry VIII, 1530–46 ; employed on a mission to France, 1532, and to Germany, 1533 ; clerk in chancery, 1534 ; spy on Queen Catherine at Kimbolton, 1536 ; an official of the mint, 1537–49 ; envoy to Milan, 1538, to Flanders, 1541 ; granted church lands, 1544 ; M.P., Lancaster, 1547. [lviii. 179]

VAUGHAN, Sir THOMAS (*d.* 1483), soldier ; a Yorkist partisan ; attainted, 1459 ; personal servant of Edward IV, 1461 ; chamberlain to Edward, prince of Wales, 1471 ; knighted, 1475 ; executed at Pontefract by Richard III. [lviii. 180]

VAUGHAN, THOMAS (1622–1666), alchemist and poet ; twin brother of Henry Vaughan, ' Silurist ' [q. v.] ; of Jesus College, Oxford ; B.A. and fellow, 1642 ; rector of St. Bridget's, Brecknockshire, 1640 ; withdrew to Oxford, 1642 ; had a controversy with Henry More (1614–1687) [q. v.], 1650–1 ; disciple of Cornelius Agrippa ; published alchemical works under the pseudonym ' Eugenius Philalethes,' 1650–7 ; wrote Latin and English verse. [lviii. 181]

VAUGHAN, THOMAS (*fl.* 1772–1820), dramatist ; solicitor in Westminster ; brought out two farces, 1776, ' Fashionable Follies,' a novel, 1782, and a comedy, 1784. [lviii. 182]

VAUGHAN, THOMAS (1782–1843), vocalist ; chorister of Norwich ; choirman in the Chapel Royal, London, 1799, at Westminster, and, 1803, St. Paul's, London ; leading tenor soloist from 1811. [lviii. 183]

VAUGHAN, WILLIAM (1577–1641), poet and colonial pioneer ; M.A. Jesus College, Oxford, 1597 ; travelled in France and Italy ; LL.D. Vienna (incorporated at Oxford, 1605) ; acquired Torcoed by marriage ; published ' The Spirit of Detraction,' 1611, to clear himself of slanders ; bought an interest in Newfoundland, 1616, and sent out settlers, 1617–18 ; visited his colony, 1622 ; published ' The Golden Fleece,' 1626, (allegory in praise of his colony), and ' The Newlanders Cure,' 1630, an account of its diseases ;

published also ' The Golden Grove,' a critique of contemporary manners, 1600, ' Directions for Health,' 1600, Latin poems, and devotional tracts. [lviii. 183]

VAUGHAN, Sir WILLIAM (*d.* 1649), royalist : served in Ireland, 1643, in Cheshire, 1644 ; governor of Shrawardine Castle, 1644 ; joined Charles I at Newport, 1645 ; fought at Naseby, 1645 ; in attendance on Charles I in Wales, autumn of 1645 ; cavalry commandant in Wales : defeated at Denbigh, November 1645 ; fell back on Worcester, 1646 ; joined Lord Astley, 1646 ; crushed at Stow-on-the-Wold, 1646 ; escaped to Holland ; major-general in Ireland, 1648 ; killed in battle at Rathmines. [lviii. 185]

VAUGHAN, WILLIAM (*d.* 1719), a Londoner ; emigrated to Portsmouth, New England, 1667. [lviii. 185]

VAUGHAN, WILLIAM (1716 ?–1780 ?), Jacobite soldier ; a Herefordshire catholic : joined Prince Charles Edward at Preston, 1745 ; lieutenant-colonel ; escaped after Culloden to France, 1746 ; accompanied Prince Charles to Madrid, 1747 ; entered the Spanish service ; major-general, 1777 ; went to Buenos Ayres, 1778. [lviii. 187]

VAUGHAN, WILLIAM (1752–1850), merchant and author ; a director of the Royal Exchange Assurance Corporation, London, 1783–1829 ; advocated canal extension, 1791 ; published pamphlets urging extension of London docks, 1793–7. [lviii. 187]

VAUS or **VASCUS**, JOHN (1490 ?–1538 ?), Scottish grammarian ; native of Aberdeen : studied at Paris ; Latin professor, Aberdeen, 1516, till death ; published a Latin grammar, 1522 (valuable to the students of early Scots dialect). [lviii. 188]

VAUTOR, THOMAS (*fl.* 1619), musician ; servant of Buckingham's father ; Mus.Bac. Oxford, 1616 ; dedicated ' Madrigals ' to Buckingham, 1619. [lviii. 188]

VAUTROLLIER, THOMAS (*d.* 1587 ?), printer ; Huguenot refugee ; freeman of the Stationers' Company, 1564 ; owned press in Blackfriars, 1570 ; fined for printing unlicensed books, 1578–9 ; left his press in his wife's charge and started bookselling in Edinburgh, 1580 ; returned to London, but left to avoid prosecution ; printed six works (including James VI's poetical ' Essayes ') at Edinburgh, 1584, and two works in 1585 ; returned to London ; his impression of John Knox's ' History of the Reformation' suppressed ; translated a French tractate on ' Apostasi,' 1587. [lviii. 189]

VAUX, ANNE (*fl.* 1605–1635), recusant ; third daughter of William Vaux, third baron Vaux [q. v.] ; under the name of Mrs. Perkins harboured the jesuit Henry Garnett ; her house frequented by the gunpowder plotters at Wandsworth, 1604, and at Enfield, 1605 ; imprisoned at Hindlip, when Garnett was arrested there, 1606 ; her school, near Derby, for Roman catholic youth closed by the privy council, 1635. [lviii. 190]

VAUX, EDWARD, fourth BARON VAUX OF HARROWDEN (1591–1661), succeeded to the barony, 1595 ; lived chiefly on the continent. [lviii. 196]

VAUX, LAURENCE (1519–1585), Roman catholic divine ; B.D. Corpus Christi College, Oxford, 1556 ; fellow of Manchester collegiate church, and warden, 1558 ; withdrew with the college vestments and plate to Ireland, 1559 ; visited England, 1561 ; withdrew to Louvain before 1564 ; visited Rome, 1566 ; brought to England papal decree forbidding attendance at Anglican services, 1566 ; published his ' Catechism ' at Louvain, 1567 ; became an Augustinian canon, 1572 ; sent on the English mission, 1580 ; prisoner in London, 1580–5. [lviii. 191]

VAUX, Sir NICHOLAS, first BARON VAUX of HARROWDEN (*d.* 1523), courtier and soldier ; son of Sir William Vaux [q. v.] ; page to Margaret, countess of Richmond ; restored to his estates by Henry VII's first parliament, 1485 ; fought against Lambert Simnel at Stoke, 1487 ; knighted ; enclosed much common-land in Buckinghamshire and Northamptonshire, 1490–1509 ; governor of Guisnes, near Calais, 1502–23 ; married Anne Green, a great territorial heiress, 1507 ; entertained Henry VIII at Harrowden, 1511 ; served in France, 1513–14 ; a member of the embassy to France, 1518 ; prosecuted for enclosing common-land, 1519 ; in attendance on Henry VIII in France, 1520 ; created Baron Vaux of Harrowden, 1523. [lviii. 192]

VAUX, THOMAS, second BARON VAUX OF HARROW-DEN (1510–1556), poet; son of Sir Nicholas Vaux, first baron Vaux [q. v.]; educated at Cambridge; succeeded to barony, 1523; attended Wolsey to France, 1527, and Henry VIII, 1532; resigned captaincy of Jersey, 1536; verses by him appeared posthumously in Tottel's 'Miscellany,' 1557, and 'The Paradyse of daynty deuises,' 1576. [lviii. 194]

VAUX, SIR WILLIAM (*d.* 1471), Lancastrian leader; of Harrowden, Northamptonshire; attainted and his estates confiscated by Edward IV's first parliament, 1461; killed in battle at Tewkesbury. [lviii. 192]

VAUX, WILLIAM, third BARON VAUX OF HARROW-DEN (1542 ?–1595), son of Thomas Vaux, second baron Vaux [q. v.]; succeeded to barony, 1556; harboured Edmund Campion [q. v.], 1580; imprisoned and fined, 1581. [lviii. 196]

VAUX, WILLIAM SANDYS WRIGHT (1818–1885), antiquary; entered Westminster School, 1831; M.A. Balliol College, Oxford, 1842; entered British Museum service, 1841, and was keeper of coins and medals, 1861–1870; catalogued Bodleian coins, 1871–6; published works on Greek, Egyptian, and Assyrian art and history. [lviii. 196]

VAVASOUR, JOHN (*d.* 1506 ?), judge; serjeant-at-law, 1478; king's serjeant, 1483; recorder of York, 1486; justice of common pleas, 1490. [lviii. 197]

VEAL or **VEALE**. [See also VEEL.]

VEAL, GEORGE (*fl.* 1774–1818). [See COLLIER, JOEL.]

VEDDER, DAVID (1790–1854), Scottish poet; native of Orkney; captain of a whaler, 1812; excise officer, 1820–52; published poems, 1828–42; edited 'Reynard the Fox,' 1852. [lviii. 197]

VEEL or **VEAL**, EDWARD (1632 ?–1708), nonconformist tutor; M.A. Christ Church, Oxford, 1654; presbyterian minister of Dunboyne, 1655; fellow of Trinity College, Dublin; B.D., 1661; left Ireland, 1662; had a church in Wapping, 1668, and a school in Stepney; published sermons. [lviii. 198]

VEEL, **VEALE**, or **VEIL**, ROBERT (1648–1674 ?), poetaster; of St. Edmund Hall, Oxford; lived in London; published 'New Court Songs,' 1672. [lviii. 198]

VEEL, THOMAS (1591 ?–1663), royalist; governor of Berkeley Castle, 1644; fined for delinquency; fought at Worcester, 1651; took part in the Gloucestershire rising, 1659, and had his estates confiscated; given a post at the Exchange, 1662. [lviii. 198]

VEITCH. [See also VETCH.]

VEITCH, JAMES, LORD ELIOCK (1712–1793), Scottish judge; Scottish advocate, 1738; visited Germany and began a correspondence with Frederick the Great, 1739; sheriff-depute of Peebles, 1747; M.P., Dumfriesshire, 1755–1760; a lord of session, 1761. [lviii. 199]

VEITCH, JOHN (1829–1894), man of letters; educated at Peebles, Edinburgh University, and Free Church college; influenced by Sir William Hamilton (1788–1856) [q. v.]; assistant to Hamilton when logic professor, Edinburgh, 1856–60; logic professor at St. Andrews, 1860, and at Glasgow, 1864–94; hon. LL.D. Edinburgh, 1872; published memoirs of Dugald Stewart, 1857, and Sir William Hamilton, 1869; poems, 1875–89; philosophical works, 1885–95, including 'Dualism and Monism,' 1895, and critiques of Scottish border poetry, 1887–93. [lviii. 199]

VEITCH, WILLIAM (1640–1722), covenanter; M.A. Glasgow, 1659; licensed to preach, 1664; outlawed, 1667; lived in England as 'Mr. Johnson,' latterly as pastor in Northumberland (1671–9); prisoner on the Bass, 1679; aided the Earl of Argyll's escape, 1681; fled to Holland, 1683; tried to raise Northumberland against James II, 1685; pastor at Beverley; subsequently held charges in Scotland; published sermons and controversial tracts. [lviii. 200]

VEITCH, WILLIAM (1794–1885), classical scholar; educated at Jedburgh and Edinburgh University; licentiate of the Scottish church; private tutor in Edinburgh from 1843; hon. LL.D. Edinburgh, 1866; published 'Greek Verbs, Irregular and Defective,' 1848; edited classical texts. [lviii. 201]

VELEY, MARGARET (1843–1887), novelist and poet; began to publish, 1870; issued 'For Percival,' her best novel, 1878. [lviii. 201]

VELLEY, THOMAS (1748 ?–1806), botanist; D.C.L. Oxford, 1787; studied the algæ; wrote on marine plants. [lviii. 202]

VENABLES, EDMUND (1819–1895), antiquary and divine; of Merchant Taylors' School; M.A. Cambridge, 1845; curate at Hurstmonceux, 1844–53; removed to Bonchurch, 1853; precentor of Lincoln, 1867–95; published guide-books to the Isle of Wight and Lincoln City; contributed to encyclopædias and biblical and biographical dictionaries. [lviii. 202]

VENABLES, EDWARD FREDERICK (1818–1858), a hero of the Indian mutiny; inherited a Shropshire estate, 1856; indigo-planter near Azimghur; rescued the Europeans there, July 1857; led the cavalry in the victory at Mandori, September 1857; mortally wounded in action. [lviii. 203]

VENABLES, GEORGE STOVIN (1810–1888), journalist; educated at the Charterhouse, London; fellow and tutor of Jesus College, Cambridge; M.A., 1835; barrister, Inner Temple, 1836; retired from practice, 1882; contributed to the 'Saturday Review,' 1855, and to 'The Times,' 1857–88; friend of Alfred Tennyson. [lviii. 204]

VENABLES, ROBERT (1612 ?–1687), soldier; lieutenant-colonel in the parliamentary army; wounded at Chester, 1645; governor of Liverpool, 1648; served with success in Ireland, 1649–54; sent, with Admiral Penn, against the Spanish West Indies, 1654; routed at Hispaniola, 1655; successful at Jamaica, 1655; sent to the Tower of London, September 1655; cashiered, October 1655; governor of Chester, 1660; remained a nonconformist; bought Wincham; published a treatise on angling, 1662. [lviii. 205]

VENDIGAID, CADWALADR (*d.* 664 ?). [See CADWALADR.]

VENDRAMINI, FRANCESCO (*fl.* 1805), engraver; settled at St. Petersburg, *c.* 1805. [lviii. 207]

VENDRAMINI, GIOVANNI (1769–1839), line and stipple engraver; an Italian; came to England, 1788; pupil of Bartolozzi; visited Russia, 1805–7. [lviii. 206]

VENN, HENRY (1725–1797), evangelical divine; son of Richard Venn [q. v.]; M.A. Jesus College, Cambridge, 1749; fellow of Queens' College, Cambridge, 1749–57; curate of Clapham, 1754; vicar of Huddersfield, 1759; rector of Yelling, 1771–97; published sermons and devotional works. [lviii. 207]

VENN, HENRY (1796–1873), divine; son of John Venn (1759–1813) [q. v.]; fellow of Queens' College, Cambridge, 1819–29; B.D., 1828; vicar of Drypool, 1827; incumbent of St. John's, Holloway, London, 1834–46; honorary secretary of the Church Missionary Society, 1841–73; published sermons, pamphlets, and memoirs. [lviii. 208]

VENN, JOHN (1586–1650), regicide; warden of the Merchant Taylors' Company, 1641; traded in wool with the west of England and Ireland; a member of the Massachusetts Company, 1629–44; captain in the artillery company, 1636; M.P., London, in the Long parliament, 1640; colonel of foot in the parliamentary army, 1642; governor of Windsor, 1642–5; in command at Northampton, 1646; afterwards resided at Hammersmith and attended parliament; signed Charles I's death warrant. [lviii. 209]

VENN, JOHN (1647–1687), master of Balliol College, Oxford, 1678–87; vice-chancellor of Oxford University, 1686–7. [lviii. 210]

VENN, JOHN (1759–1813), divine; son of Henry Venn (1725–1797) [q. v.]; M.A. Cambridge, 1784; rector of Clapham, 1792–1813; a founder of the Church Missionary Society, 1797, and member of the 'Clapham sect.' [lviii. 208]

VENN, RICHARD (1691–1740), divine; educated at Blundell's school, Tiverton, and Sidney Sussex College, Cambridge; M.A., 1716; rector of St. Antholin's, London, 1725–40; published sermons. [lviii. 210]

VENNAR or **VENNARD**, RICHARD (*d.* 1615 ?), author; of Balliol College, Oxford; travelled; entered Lincoln's Inn, 1581; visited Scotland and flattered

James VI, 1600; imprisoned on his return; published 'Right Way to Heauen,' 1601, flattering Queen Elizabeth; cheated many people by taking entrance money for a masque, which, though promised, was never performed, 'Englands Ioy' at the Swan, 1602; published an 'Apology' for his conduct, 1614; died in a debtor's prison. [lviii. 210]

VENNER, THOMAS (d. 1661), plotter; a cooper; resident in Massachusetts, 1638; Fifth-monarchy preacher in London; planned a rising, 1657; prisoner in the Tower of London, 1657-9; headed a rising to set up the Fifth monarchy, 1661; executed. [lviii. 212]

VENNER, TOBIAS (1577-1660), medical writer; M.A. Oxford, 1603; M.D., 1613; practised, from 1603, at Petherton, and, in the season, at Bath; published 'The Bathes of Bathe,' 1620, 'Via recta ad vitam longam,' 1620, and a polemic against tobacco, 1621. [lviii. 212]

VENNING, JOHN (1776-1858), philanthropist; a London merchant; resident in St. Petersburg, 1793; settled in Norfolk, 1830; advocated prison reform.
[lviii. 213]

VENNING, RALPH (1621?-1674), nonconformist divine; M.A. Emmanuel College, Cambridge, 1650; lecturer in Southwark; ejected, 1663; preacher at Pewterers' Hall, London, 1663-74; published sermons and tracts.
[lviii. 213]

VENNING, WALTER (1781-1821), philanthropist; a London merchant; resided at St. Petersburg, 1799-1807; advocated prison reform, 1815-21; died at St. Petersburg.
[lviii. 214]

VENNOR, HENRY GEORGE (1840-1884), Canadian meteorologist; born and educated at Montreal; attached to the Canadian geological survey, 1865-81; published the 'Vennor Almanac,' 1877, and a 'Monthly Bulletin,' 1882, forecasting the weather; wrote on Canadian ornithology. [lviii. 214]

VENTRIS, SIR PEYTON (1645-1691), judge; barrister, Middle Temple, 1661; M.P., Ipswich, 1689; justice of the common pleas, and knighted, 1689; his 'Reports,' from 1645 to 1691, published, 1696. [lviii. 215]

VERBRUGGEN, JOHN (fl. 1688-1707?), a favourite actor on the London stage; nicknamed Alexander, 1688-1694. [lviii. 216]

VERBRUGGEN, MRS. SUSANNA (1667?-1703), actress; daughter of Percival, a London actor; married, July 1686, William Mountfort [q. v.]; married secondly, c. 1693, John Verbruggen [q. v.]; the leading London actress in comedy from her first appearance in 1681.
[lviii. 215]

VERDON or VERDUN, BERTRAM DE (d. 1192), judge; sheriff of Warwickshire and Leicestershire, 1168-1183; a justiciary, 1175-8; a justice itinerant, 1175-9; founded Croxden Abbey, 1176; seneschal of Ireland, 1184-1186; accompanied Richard I to Palestine, 1190-1; died at Joppa. [lviii. 217]

VERDON, THEOBALD DE, the elder (1248?-1309), baron; son and heir of John de Verdon; visited Ireland, 1275, 1285, 1295-9; personally attended the parliament at Lincoln, 1301. [lviii. 218]

VERDON, THEOBALD DE, the younger (d. 1316), baron; son and heir of Theobald de Verdon the elder [q. v.]; substitute for his father in the Scottish campaign, 1298; knighted, 1298; summoned to parliament, 1299; succeeded to the estates, 1309; lieutenant of Ireland, 1313.
[lviii. 219]

VERE, FAMILY OF, derived from Ver, near Bayeux; founded in England by Aubrey ('Albericus') de Vere, who received from the Conqueror the great estates of thegn Wulfwine in Essex and neighbouring counties. The chief seat of the Veres was at Castle Hedingham, Essex, where their great stone keep still stands. Their burial-place was Earl's Colne priory, founded by them. The badge was a blue boar ('verres'), and the motto Vero nil verius. The house became extinct in 1703, in Aubrey de Vere, twentieth earl [q. v.] [lviii. 219]

VERE, AUBREY DE (d. 1141), great chamberlain; successor of 'Albericus' de Vere 'senior'; joint-sheriff of London, 1125; joint-sheriff of eleven counties, 1130; appointed hereditary great chamberlain, 1133; adherent of King Stephen; killed in a riot in London. [lviii. 220]

VERE, AUBREY DE, first EARL OF OXFORD (d. 1194), son of Aubrey de Vere (d. 1141) [q. v.]; count of Guines in right of his wife, 1139?-1145; adopted the cause of Empress Maud; created earl by her, 1142, with the choice of his own title; confirmed by Henry II as earl of Oxford, 1156. [lviii. 221]

VERE, AUBREY DE, tenth EARL OF OXFORD (1340?-1400), second son of John de Vere, seventh earl of Oxford [q. v.]; steward of Havering forest, 1360, and of Hadley Castle, &c., 1378; accompanied the Black Prince to Aquitaine, 1367; steward of Wallingford honour, &c., 1375-82; an envoy to France, 1376 and 1383; chamberlain of the household, 1381; fought in Scotland, 1385; removed from court by the Merciless parliament, 1388; was created Earl of Oxford, 1393, and received the entailed estates, but not the lord chamberlainship; became tenth earl by succession on the reversal of the attainder of his nephew, Robert de Vere, ninth earl [q. v.], 1397; attainder replaced, 1399. [lviii. 221]

VERE, AUBREY DE, twentieth EARL OF OXFORD (1626-1703), son and heir of Robert de Vere, nineteenth earl; succeeded, 1632; brought up in Friesland; officer in the Dutch service till 1648; his estates sequestrated by parliament, 1651; imprisoned as a royalist, 1654 and 1659; an envoy to recall Charles II, 1660; lord-lieutenant of Essex and colonel of 'the Oxford blues' regiment, 1661; privy councillor, 1669; pensioned, 1670; opposed James II's arbitrary measures, 1688; joined the Prince of Orange, 1688; lieutenant-general, 1689; fought at the Boyne; a whig lord. [lviii. 222]

VERE, SIR AUBREY DE (1788-1846). [See DE VERE.]

VERE, SIR CHARLES BROKE (1779-1843), major-general; named Charles Broke; took the name Vere, 1822; ensign, 1796; major, 1808; lieutenant-colonel, 1812; quartermaster-general, 1815; served in Holland, 1799, at Buenos Ayres, 1807, throughout the Peninsular war, 1809-14, and at Waterloo; K.C.B., 1815; tory M.P. for East Suffolk, 1835-43; major-general, 1837. [lviii. 225]

VERE, EDWARD DE, seventeenth EARL OF OXFORD (1550-1604), poet; only son of John de Vere, sixteenth earl of Oxford [q. v.]; styled Lord Bulbeck; of Queens' and St. John's Colleges, Cambridge, from 1558; succeeded to the earldom, 1562; a royal ward in Cecil's (Burghley's) household; a prominent figure at Elizabeth's court, 1564-82; married, 1571, Anne Cecil (Burghley's daughter, who died 1588); angry at the prosecution of the Duke of Norfolk, 1572; withdrew to Flanders, but was brought back, 1574; travelled in Italy, 1575-6; patron of a company of players; quarrelled with Sir Philip Sidney, 1579; in disgrace at court on account of his violent temper, 1582-3; sat as judge of Mary Queen of Scots, 1586; served against the Armada, 1588; alienated his estates; officiated as lord great chamberlain, 1603; verses by him printed in miscellanies, 1576-1600; collected edition, 1872.
[lviii. 225]

VERE, SIR FRANCIS (1560-1609) soldier; brought up by Sir William Browne; visited Poland, 1580; accompanied Leicester's expedition to Holland, 1585; served in Lord Willoughby de Eresby's horse from 1586; captain, 1586; distinguished himself in the defence of Sluys, June-August, 1587, and of Bergen-op-Zoom, 1588; knighted; visited England, 1588; second in command of the English contingent in Holland, 1589; acting commander from August 1589; relieved Rheinberg, 1589; took part in a brilliant series of sieges and surprises, from that of Breda, 1589, to that of Groningen, 1594; in the regular pay of the Dutch states from 1593; served with the Cadiz expedition, 1596, and the Azores expedition, 1597; returned to Holland, 1597; took part in the victory at Turnhout, 1597; negotiated agreement between Dutch states and Queen Elizabeth, 1598; appointed governor of Brill in the autumn of 1598; returned to Holland, 1599; took part in the victories at Bommel, 1599, and Nieuport, 1600; successfully defended Ostend, 1601-2; dangerously wounded at Grave, 1602; retired from the Dutch service, 1604; paid a final visit to Holland, 1605-6; governor of Portsmouth, 1606; his 'Commentaries,' an account of his services, published, 1657; a benefactor of the Bodleian Library, Oxford. [lviii. 229]

VERE, HENRY DE, eighteenth EARL OF OXFORD (1593-1625), son of Edward de Vere, seventeenth earl of

Oxford [q. v.] ; succeeded, 1604 ; entered the Inner Temple, 1604 ; hon. M.A. Oxford, 1605 ; K.B., 1610 ; travelled, chiefly in Italy, 1613–18 ; admitted hereditary great chamberlain, 1619 ; served in the Palatinate, 1620 ; prisoner in the Tower of London, 1621 and 1622–3, through offence given to Buckingham ; went to serve in Holland, 1624 ; died at the Hague. [lviii. 234]

VERE, SIR HORACE, BARON VERE OF TILBURY (1565–1635), soldier ; served under his brother, Sir Francis Vere [q. v.], in Holland, 1590–4, and at Cadiz, 1596 ; knighted, 1596 ; distinguished himself at Nieuport, 1600, and Ostend, 1602 ; took over from Sir Francis Vere command of English in Holland, 1604 ; distinguished himself at the recovery of Sluys, 1604, and in the defeat of Mulheim, 1605 ; returned to England ; governor of Brill, 1609–16 ; served at Juliers, 1610 ; governor of Utrecht, 1618 ; sailed from England in command of the English troops for the Palatinate, 1620 ; garrisoned the Palatinate, winter, 1620 ; forced to capitulate at Mannheim, 1622 ; returned to England, 1623 ; master-general of the ordnance ; repulsed by Spinola at Breda, 1625 ; returned to England ; created Baron Vere, 1625 ; served at the sieges of Bois-le-Duc, 1629, and Maastricht, 1632. [lviii. 235]

VERE, JOHN DE, seventh EARL OF OXFORD (1313–1360), succeeded his uncle, April 1331 ; served in Scotland, 1333, 1335, and 1343, in Flanders, 1339, in Brittany, 1342, 1345, at Crecy, 1346, and at Poitiers, 1356 ; died in the Burgundy campaign. [lviii. 239]

VERE, JOHN DE, twelfth EARL OF OXFORD (1408 ?–1462), succeeded his father, 1417 ; married the heiress of the barony of Plaiz before 1429 ; served in France, 1436 and 1441 ; executed on charge of planning a Lancastrian rising. [lviii. 240]

VERE, JOHN DE, thirteenth EARL OF OXFORD (1443–1513), son of John de Vere, twelfth earl [q. v.] ; succeeded, 1462 ; obtained the reversal of the attainder [see AUBREY DE VERE, tenth EARL], 1464 ; imprisoned as a suspected Lancastrian, 1468 ; helped to restore Henry VI, 1470 ; escaped to France from Hammes field, 1471 ; seized St. Michael's Mount, 1473 ; prisoner in Hammes Castle, near Calais, 1474–84 ; attainted, 1475 ; joined Richmond (Henry VII) in Paris, 1484 ; accompanied him to England ; fought at Bosworth, 1485 ; obtained reversal of his attainder and the hereditary chamberlainship ; constable of the Tower of London, 1485, with many other places ; fought at Stoke, 1487, and in Picardy, 1492 ; joined in suppressing the Cornish insurgents, 1497 ; entertained Henry VII at Castle Hedingham, 1498. [lviii. 240]

VERE, JOHN DE, fifteenth EARL OF OXFORD (1490 ?–1540), courtier of Henry VIII ; knighted, 1513 ; succeeded his uncle, 1514 ; the first protestant Earl of Oxford. [lviii. 242]

VERE, JOHN DE, sixteenth EARL OF OXFORD (1512 ?–1562), son of John de Vere, fifteenth earl of Oxford [q. v.] ; succeeded, 1562 ; served in France, 1544 ; declared for Queen Mary, 1553 ; entertained Queen Elizabeth at Castle Hedingham, 1561. [lviii. 242]

VERE, ROBERT DE, third EARL OF OXFORD (1170 ?–1221), second son of Aubrey de Vere, first earl of Oxford [q. v.] ; married, c. 1208, the heiress of the Buckinghamshire Bolebecs ; succeeded his brother, 1214 ; one of the twenty-five executors of Magna Charta. [lviii. 243]

VERE, ROBERT DE, ninth EARL OF OXFORD and DUKE OF IRELAND (1362–1392), succeeded his father, 1371 ; married Philippa de Couci, 1378 ; became a bosom friend of Richard II, 1381 ; granted lands and stewardships, 1382–5 ; accompanied Richard II to Scotland, 1385 ; created Marquis of Dublin, 1385, with regal powers in Ireland, and Duke of Dublin, 1386 ; exercised these powers through a deputy, Sir John Stanley, 1385–8 ; attended Richard II during his summer progress, 1387 ; divorced his wife, 1387 (divorce annulled, 1389) ; charged by the lords appellant with treason, 1387 ; escaped to Chester, raised troops, and marched on London ; deserted by his troops at Witney ; escaped in disguise to London, and withdrew to the Netherlands, and thence to Paris ; attainted, 1388 ; settled at Louvain, c. 1389 ; killed in a boar-hunt ; solemnly re-buried at Earl's Colne by Richard II, 1395. [lviii. 243]

VEREKER, CHARLES, second VISCOUNT GORT (1768–1842), entered the navy, 1782 ; M.P., Limerick,

1790–1817 ; lieutenant-colonel of the Limerick militia ; checked the French under Humbert at Sligo, 1798 ; opposed the union, 1799 ; succeeded his uncle in the peerage, 1817 ; Irish representative peer, 1820. [lviii. 247]

VERELST, HARMEN (1643 ? – 1700 ?), painter ; went to London, 1683. [lviii. 249]

VERELST, HARRY (d. 1785), governor of Bengal ; went to Bengal, 1750 ; imprisoned by Suraj ud Dowlah, 1758 ; in charge of Chittagong, 1761–5 ; governor of Bengal, 1767–9, carrying out Clive's policy ; returned to England, 1770 ; ruined by litigation raised by corrupt Bengal influences ; published a narrative of ' English Government in Bengal,' 1772 ; died at Bologne. [lviii. 248]

VERELST, SIMON (1644–1721 ?), flower and portrait painter ; native of the Hague ; came to London, 1669, and was for a time highly popular. [lviii. 249]

VERELST, WILLEM (fl. 1740), portrait-painter in London. [lviii. 250]

VERGIL, POLYDORE (1470 ?–1555 ?), historian : born at Urbino ; studied at Bologna and Padua ; secretary to the Duke of Urbino ; published ' Proverbiorum Libellus,' Venice, 1498, anticipating Erasmus's ' Adagia' ; published ' De Inventoribus Rerum,' Venice, 1499 (enlarged, 1521) ; resided in England as sub-collector of Peter's pence, 1502–15 ; non-resident rector of Church Langton, 1503 ; prebendary of Hereford, 1507–55, of Lincoln, 1507, and of St. Paul's Cathedral, London, 1513–55 ; archdeacon of Wells, 1508–54 ; asked by Henry VII to write the history of England, 1505 ; naturalised, 1510 ; visited Rome, 1514 ; imprisoned, at Wolsey's instance, 1515 ; visited Rome, 1516 ; returned to England, 1517 ; edited Gildas, 1525 ; published his ' Anglicæ Historiæ Libri xxvi.,' Basle, 1534 (brought down to 1509, continued to 1538 in the 1555 edition), of special value for Henry VII's reign ; returned to Italy, 1551 ; published other treatises and translations. [lviii. 250]

VERMIGLI, PIETRO MARTIRE (1500–1562), reformer ; known as PETER MARTYR ; born in Florence ; Augustinian monk at Fiesole, 1516, and Padua, 1519 ; D.D. Padua ; learnt Greek and Hebrew ; sent to different towns as Lent or Advent preacher from 1527 ; head of the convent at Spoleto, 1530, and Naples, 1533 ; read Bucer and Zuingli ; removed to Lucca, 1541 ; fled from Italy as a suspected heretic, 1542 ; divinity-professor at Strasburg, 1542–7 ; married an ex-nun there ; brought to London by Cranmer, 1547 ; incorporated D.D. and appointed divinity professor at Oxford, 1548 ; canon of Christ Church, Oxford, 1551 ; one of the commissioners to revise the ecclesiastical code, 1551 (this code was published, 1571) ; his wife buried in Christ Church Cathedral, 1553 (exhumed, 1557. reinterred, 1558) ; left England, 1553 ; divinity professor at Strasburg, 1554 ; Hebrew professor at Zürich, 1556 ; corresponded with English protestants ; attended the conference at Poissy, 1561 ; published theological treatises and commentaries from 1543 ; died at Zürich. [lviii. 253]

VERMUYDEN, SIR CORNELIUS (1595 ?–1683 ?), engineer ; native of Holland ; repaired the Thames embankments in Essex, 1621 ; encountered much opposition in his drainage of part of the fens, 1622, and of Axholme, 1626 ; granted portions of the reclaimed lands, 1625–9 ; knighted, 1629 ; engineer of the ' Bedford level' to drain the 'Great Fens,' 1629–37, 1649–56 ; sent by Cromwell to solicit a close alliance with Holland, 1653 ; projected the drainage of Sedgemoor, 1656. [lviii. 256]

VERNEUIL, JOHN (1583 ? – 1647), sub-librarian (1618 till death) of the Bodleian Library ; born in Bordeaux ; M.A. Montauban ; came to Oxford, 1608 ; incorporated as M.A. 1625 ; catalogued sermons ; published translations. [lviii. 259]

VERNEY, SIR EDMUND (1590 – 1642), soldier ; studied at St. Alban Hall, Oxford ; travelled in Holland and France ; knighted, 1611 ; visited Madrid ; servant of Prince Charles, 1613 ; followed Charles to Madrid, 1623 ; M.P., Buckingham, 1624, Aylesbury, 1628, Chipping Wycombe in the Short and Long parliaments, 1640 ; opposed Charles I's arbitrary measures ; lent Charles I much money ; knight-marshal of the palace and keeper of

Marshalsea prison, 1626; attended Charles I to Scotland, 1639; appointed standard-bearer, 1642; slain at Edgehill. [lviii. 260]

VERNEY, SIR EDMUND (1616 – 1649), royalist soldier; son of Sir Edmund Verney (1590-1642) [q. v.]; at Winchester, 1634, and Magdalen Hall, Oxford, 1636; served in Scotland, 1639, in Flanders and Scotland, 1640, in Ireland, 1642; knighted, 1644; defended Chester, 1644-1646; withdrew to Paris before 1648; returned to Ireland with Ormonde, 1649; slain at Drogheda. [lviii. 261]

VERNEY, SIR FRANCIS (1584-1615), pirate; of Trinity College, Oxford, 1600; knighted, 1604; sold his estate; deserted his wife and went abroad, 1608; joined the pirates of Algiers; died at Messina. [lviii. 262]

VERNEY, SIR HARRY, second baronet (1801-1894), son of Sir Harry Calvert [q. v.]; succeeded to his father's baronetcy, 1826; assumed the name Verney on succeeding in 1827 to the Claydon estate in Buckinghamshire; educated at Harrow and Sandhurst; military attaché at Stuttgart, 1818-20; travelled in South America, 1827-9; studied in Cambridge, 1831-3; liberal M.P. for Buckingham, 1832-35. [lviii. 263]

VERNEY, JOHN (1699-1741), judge; of New College, Oxford, 1714; hon. D.C.L., 1737; barrister, Middle Temple, 1721; M.P., Downton, 1722-34; chief-justice of Chester, 1734; master of the rolls, 1738. [lviii. 267]

VERNEY, SIR RALPH, first baronet (1613-1696), politician; eldest son of Sir Edmund Verney (1590-1642) [q. v.]; educated at Magdalen Hall, Oxford; M.P., Aylesbury, in the Short and Long parliaments, 1640; opposed to Laud; knighted, 1641; took notes of proceedings in the Long parliament (published, 1845); refused the covenant and went abroad, 1643; his estates confiscated, 1646, but restored, 1650; returned to England, 1653; imprisoned, 1655; created baronet, 1661; M.P., Buckingham, 1680, 1685, 1689. [lviii. 264]

VERNEY, RALPH, second EARL VERNEY and third VISCOUNT FERMANAGH in the peerage of Ireland (1712?-1791), whig politician; succeeded his father, 1752; M.P., Wendover, 1753, and Buckinghamshire, 1768-91; patron of Edmund Burke; squandered his estate. [lviii. 265]

VERNEY, RICHARD, third BARON WILLOUGHBY DE BROKE (1621-1711), of Belton; sheriff of Rutland, 1682; knighted, 1685; M.P., Warwickshire, 1685, 1690; established his claim to the barony, 1695. [lviii. 266]

VERNON, FAMILY OF, named from Vernon, département Eure, Normandy. Richard de Vernon came to England with William I, and settled at Shipbrook, Cheshire. William de Vernon, tempore Henry III, acquired Haddon Hall, Derbyshire, by marriage with the heiress of the Avenels. Dorothy Vernon (d. 1584), daughter and heiress of Sir George Vernon (d. 1567), the last male representative of the family's main branch, eloped with Sir John Manners, by whom she was ancestress of the Dukes of Rutland, and thus Haddon Hall passed into their possession. [lviii. 279]

VERNON, AUGUSTUS HENRY, sixth BARON VERNON (1829-1883), eldest son of George John Warren Vernon, fifth baron Vernon [q. v.]; born at Rome; captain in the guards, retired, 1851; succeeded, 1866. [lviii. 276]

VERNON, EDWARD (1684-1757), admiral; second son of James Vernon [q. v.]; entered the navy, 1700; engaged in active service, 1701-7, chiefly in the Mediterranean, 1707-12, chiefly in the West Indies, 1715-17, 1719-1721, and 1726-8, chiefly in the Baltic, and 1739-42, in the West Indies; lieutenant, 1702; captain, 1706; admiral, 1745; M.P., Penryn, 1722; advocated war with Spain, 1731; took the defenceless Porto Bello, 1739, but, in conjunction with Brigadier-general Wentworth, failed miserably at Cartagena, in 1741, at Santiago in Cuba, and Panama; first to issue rum diluted with water ('grog'), 1740; bought Nacton; M.P., Ipswich; given command in North Sea, 1745; attacked the admiralty in anonymous pamphlets, 1745-6; cashiered, 1746. [lviii. 267]

VERNON, SIR EDWARD (1723-1794), admiral; educated at Portsmouth Royal Academy, 1735-9; on active service, chiefly in the Mediterranean, 1739-62; lieutenant, 1743; captain, 1753; employed on harbour duty, 1763-76; knighted, 1773; commander-in-chief in the East Indies, 1776-81; rear-admiral, 1779; admiral, 1794. [lviii. 272]

VERNON, EDWARD VENABLES (1757 - 1847). See HARCOURT, EDWARD.]

VERNON, FRANCIS (1637?-1677), traveller; educated at Westminster School, 1649, and Christ Church, Oxford, 1654; M.A., 1660; travelled; secretary to the embassy to Sweden, 1668, and at Paris, 1669-71; travelled through Dalmatia and Greece to Persia; murdered near Ispahan. [lviii. 273]

VERNON, SIR GEORGE (1578?-1639), judge; barrister, Inner Temple, 1604; baron of the exchequer and knighted, 1627; justice of the common pleas, 1631; member of the ecclesiastical commission court, 1632; pronounced ship-money legal, 1637. [lviii. 274]

VERNON, GEORGE (1637-1720), divine; M.A. Brasenose College, Oxford, 1660; chaplain of All Souls College, Oxford; rector of Sarsden, 1663; rector of Bourton-on-the-Water, Gloucestershire; wrote against John Owen the independent, 1670, and Sir Thomas Overbury the younger, 1677; published 'Life of Peter Heylin,' 1681. [lviii. 274]

VERNON, GEORGE JOHN WARREN, fifth BARON VERNON (1803-1866), of Sudbury, Derbyshire; styled George John Venables Vernon; M.P., Derbyshire, 1831-5; succeeded to barony, 1837; lived mostly in Florence; published Dante texts and commentaries, including 'L'Inferno di Dante Alighieri disposto in ordine grammaticale,' 1858-1865. [lviii. 275]

VERNON, JAMES (1646-1727), secretary of state; M.A. Christ Church, Oxford, 1669; incorporated M.A. Cambridge, 1676; political agent in Holland, 1672; attached to the Paris embassy, 1673; secretary to the Duke of Monmouth, 1674-8; edited the official 'London Gazette,' 1678-89; M.P., Cambridge University, 1678-9; assistant in the secretary of state's office, 1689, 1692, 1694; a commissioner of prizes, 1693-1705; M.P., Penryn, 1695-8, Westminster, 1698-1702, Penryn, 1705-10; traced out Sir John Fenwick's plot, 1696; principal secretary of state, 1698-1702; teller of the exchequer, 1702-10. [lviii. 277]

VERNON, JOSEPH (1738?-1782), actor and singer; sang soprano at Drury Lane, London, 1751; singer of tenor parts and actor of comedy at Drury Lane, 1754; married at the Savoy Chapel, London, 1754; withdrew to Dublin, to escape the odium incurred by his marriage being annulled; a favourite at Drury Lane, 1762-81; composed songs; compiled a song-book, 1782. [lviii. 278]

VERNON or PEMBRUGE, SIR RICHARD DE (d. 1451), of Haddon, Derbyshire; acquired the Pembruge estates by marriage; M.P., Derbyshire, 1422 and 1426; speaker of the House of Commons, 1426. [lviii. 279]

VERNON, RICHARD (1726-1800), 'father of the turf'; some time captain in the guards; M.P. successively for Tavistock, Bedford, Okehampton, and Newcastle-under-Lyme, 1754-90; a founder of the Jockey Club; began training horses at Newmarket, c. 1753. [lviii. 280]

VERNON, ROBERT (1774-1849), art patron; contractor for army horses, c. 1799; bought pictures, mostly by British artists, from 1820; presented 157 of them to the nation, 1847. [lviii. 281]

VERNON, ROBERT, BARON LYVEDEN (1800-1873). [See SMITH, ROBERT VERNON.]

VERNON, THOMAS (1654-1721), law reporter; of Hanbury Hall, Worcestershire; barrister, Middle Temple, 1679; practised in chancery; whig M.P., Worcester, 1715-1721; compiled reports of chancery decisions (1681-1718), published in 1726-8. [lviii. 282]

VERNON, THOMAS (1824?-1872), line-engraver. [lviii. 283]

VÉRON, JOHN (d. 1563), protestant controversialist; born near Sens; studied at Orleans, 1534; came to England, 1536; studied at Cambridge; rector of St. Alphage, Cripplegate, London, 1552-4; imprisoned for seditious preaching, 1553-8; prebendary of St. Paul's, London, 1559-63; rector of St. Martin's, Ludgate, London, and vicar of St. Sepulchre, London, 1560-3; published controversial tracts and translations, 1548-62; a Latin-English dictionary by him brought out, 1575. [lviii. 283]

VERRIO, ANTONIO (1639?-1707), decorative painter; born near Otranto; history-painter in France; employed by Charles II and James II to decorate Windsor Castle, &c., and by William III and Anne to decorate Hampton

Court; decorated many English noblemen's seats; satirised by Pope for the 'sprawling' appearance of the figures in his decorative painting. [lviii. 284]

VERSTEGEN, RICHARD (*fl.* 1565-1620). [See ROWLANDS, RICHARD.]

VERTUE, GEORGE (1684-1756), engraver and antiquary; worked for Michael Van der Gucht [q. v.]; set up for himself, 1709; a prolific engraver of portraits; travelled about England, engraving objects of antiquarian interest; official engraver to the Society of Antiquaries, 1717-56; designed the Oxford almanacs, 1723-51; collected materials for the history of art in England. [lviii. 285]

VERULAM, BARON (1561 - 1626). [See BACON, FRANCIS.]

VESCI, BARONS. [See CLIFFORD, HENRY DE, first BARON, 1455 ?-1523; CLIFFORD, HENRY DE, second BARON, 1493-1542; CLIFFORD, HENRY DE, third BARON, *d.* 1570.]

VESCY or **VESCI,** EUSTACE DE (1170 ?-1216), baron; served with Richard I in Palestine, 1195; envoy from King John to William the Lion of Scotland, 1199; served in Ireland, 1210; fled to Scotland to escape a charge of treason, 1212; married an illegitimate daughter of William the Lion; recalled by King John, 1213; one of the barons who forced John to sign Magna Charta, and one of the twenty-five executors of it; excommunicated, 1216; killed at Barnard Castle. [lviii. 286]

VESCY, JOHN DE (*d.* 1289), baron; of Alnwick; succeeded his father, 1253; supported Simon de Montfort; summoned to parliament, 1265; wounded at Evesham, 1265; in rebellion, 1267, but subdued by Prince Edward; accompanied Prince Edward to Palestine, 1270; served in Wales, 1277 and 1282; envoy to Aragon, 1282, and Holland, 1285. [lviii. 287]

VESCY, WILLIAM DE (1249 ?-1297), baron; held Gloucester for the barons, 1265; served in Wales, 1277 and 1282; succeeded his brother, John de Vesey [q. v.], in the estates, 1289; advanced a claim to the Scottish crown, 1290; inherited Kildare from his mother, Agnes Marshall, 1290; lord justice of Ireland, 1290-4; sent on a mission to Gascony, 1295; surrendered Kildare Castle to Edward I, 1297. [lviii. 288]

VESCY, WILLIAM DE (*d.* 1314), styled 'of Kildare'; bastard son of William de Vescy (1249 ?-1297) [q. v.]; given the De Vesci estates in Yorkshire by his father, 1297; served in Scotland, 1300; sold Alnwick to the Percies, 1309; summoned to parliament, 1313 and 1314; killed at Bannockburn. [lviii. 289]

VESEY, BARON (1783-1843). [See FITZGERALD, WILLIAM VESEY.]

VESEY, ELIZABETH (1715 ?-1791), leader of literary society; daughter of Sir Thomas Vesey [q. v.]; married William Handcock, and secondly, before 1746, Agmondesham Vesey, friend of Edmund Burke and member of Dr. Johnson's club; had a literary 'salon' in London, 1770-84; became imbecile, 1789. [lviii. 289]

VESEY, JOHN (1638-1716), archbishop of Tuam; educated at Westminster School; M.A. Trinity College, Dublin, 1667; D.D., 1672; beneficed in Cloyne diocese, 1661; archdeacon of Armagh, 1662-3: dean of Cork, 1667; bishop of Limerick, 1673; archbishop of Tuam, 1678; warden of Galway; withdrew to London, 1689; returned to Ireland, 1692; published sermons. [lviii. 290]

VESEY, SIR THOMAS, first baronet (1668 ?-1730), Irish bishop; son of John Vesey [q. v.]; entered Christ Church, Oxford, from Eton, 1689; fellow of Oriel College, Oxford, 1695; M.A., 1697; married a Surrey heiress; created baronet, 1698; bishop of Killaloe, 1713, of Ossory, 1714. [lviii. 291]

VESTRIS, MADAME (1797-1856). [See MATHEWS, LUCIA ELIZABETH.]

VETCH, JAMES (1789-1869), engineer; educated at the military academies at Great Marlow and, 1805, Woolwich; served in the royal engineers, 1808-24; captain, 1813; mining engineer in Mexico, 1824-9, 1832-5; F.R.S., 1830; resided in England after 1835, working on railways, drainage schemes, and harbours; projected a ship-canal at Suez, 1839-43, opposed by Palmerston; published antiquarian and engineering treatises. [lviii. 292]

VETCH, SAMUEL (1668-1732), colonist; son of William Veitch (1640-1722) [q. v.]; educated at Utrecht; officer in the Dutch army; accompanied the Prince of Orange to England, 1688; officer in the Cameronian regiment at Dunkeld, 1689, Steinkirk, 1692, and Landen, 1693; captain in William Paterson's Darien colony, 1698; settled in Albany, New York, 1699; employed to negotiate with the Indians, 1700 and 1702, and with the Canadian French, 1705; visited London to urge the conquest of Canada, 1708 and 1709; colonel of the colonial troops at the conquest of Nova Scotia, 1710; governor of Nova Scotia, 1710-13, 1715-17; came to England to solicit his arrears of pay, 1719; neglected; died in a debtor's prison. [lviii. 293]

VEYSEY or **VOYSEY,** JOHN, *alias* HARMAN (1465 ?-1554), bishop of Exeter; son and heir of William Harman (*d.* 1470) of Moor Hall, Sutton-Coldfield; took the name of Veysey or Voysey, *c.* 1488; fellow of Magdalen College, Oxford, 1486-7; LL.D., 1494; chaplain to Elizabeth, consort of Henry VII, 1489; rector of Clifton-Reynes, 1496-9; held chancellorship of Lichfield, 1498-1502; archdeacon of Chester, 1499-1515; canon of Exeter, 1503-9; vicar of St. Michael's, Coventry, 1507-20; dean of Exeter, 1509-19; canon of St. Stephen's, Westminster, 1514-18; dean of Windsor, 1515-19; dean of Wolverhampton, 1516-21; bishop of Exeter, 1519-51 and 1553-4; attended Henry VIII to France, 1520; president of the court of the marches of Wales, 1526; lived at Moor Hall, administering his diocese by deputy; forced by Edward VI's courtiers to alienate to them much property of the see; removed, 1551, but was restored by Queen Mary; benefactor of Sutton-Coldfield. [lviii. 296]

VIAL DE **SAINBEL,** CHARLES (1753-1793). [See SAINBEL.]

VICARS, HEDLEY SHAFTO JOHNSTONE (1826-1855), soldier; born in the Mauritius; entered the army, 1843; captain, 1854; from 1851 worked for the moral and religious welfare of the troops; killed in the trenches at Sebastopol. [lviii. 298]

VICARS, JOHN (1580 ?-1652), poetaster; usher at Christ's Hospital, London; presbyterian; published doggerel verses, 1617-41; wrote against episcopacy and against the independents, 1641-8; printed a narrative of the civil war, 'Jehovah Jireh' (1641-3) in 1644, continued in 'Gods Arke,' 1646; mentioned in 'Hudibras.' [lviii. 298]

VICARS, THOMAS (*fl.* 1607-1641), divine; fellow of Queen's College, Oxford, 1616; M.A., 1615; B.D., 1622; vicar of Cowfold and Cuckfield, Somerset; published devotional works. [lviii. 299]

VICARY, THOMAS (*d.* 1561), surgeon; his name spelt also Vicars, Vikers; surgeon to Henry VIII, 1528, and sergeant-surgeon, 1536-61; several times master of the Barber-Surgeons Company, London, from 1530; granted church lands, 1542; governor of St. Bartholomew's Hospital, 1548, and resident director, 1554-61. An anatomical treatise, wrongly attributed to him, appeared, 1577. [lviii. 300]

VICCARS, JOHN (1604-1660), biblical scholar; B.A. Christ's College, Cambridge, 1622; M.A. Lincoln College, Oxford, 1625; rector of South Fambridge, 1640, and of Battlesden; ejected, 1646; went abroad; published, 1639, a commentary on the Psalms, drawn from ten languages. [lviii. 301]

VICKERS, ALFRED (1786-1868), landscape-painter; exhibited in London, 1813-59. [lviii. 301]

VICKERS, ALFRED GOMERSAL (1810-1837), marine-painter; son of Alfred Vickers [q. v.] [lviii. 301]

VICKRIS, RICHARD (*d.* 1700), quaker; son of a Bristol merchant; visited France; prosecuted for recusancy, 1680; wrote pamphlets in defence of quakerism. [lviii. 301]

VICTOR, BENJAMIN (*d.* 1778), theatrical manager; originally a London barber; tradesman in Norwich, 1722; linendraper in London; deputy-manager of a Dublin theatre, 1746-59; treasurer of Drury Lane, London, 1760-78; poet-laureate of Ireland, 1755; published pamphlets and wretched verse, 1722-76, memoirs of Barton Booth, 1733, and a history (covering 1710 to 1771) of the stage in London and Dublin, 1761-71. [lviii. 302]

VICTOR, FERDINAND FRANZ EUGEN GUSTAF ADOLF CONSTANTIN FRIEDRICH OF HOHENLOHE-LANGENBURG, PRINCE, for many years known as COUNT GLEICHEN (1833-1891), admiral and sculptor; third and youngest son of Prince Ernest of Hohenlohe-Langenburg, and of Princess Féodore, daughter of Ernest Charles, reigning prince of Leiningen, by Princess Victoria of Saxe-Coburg-Saalfeld, afterwards Duchess of Kent; his mother was thus half-sister to Queen Victoria; midshipman in British navy, 1848; flag-lieutenant to Sir Harry Keppel in China, 1856; retired on half-pay owing to ill-health, 1866; K.C.B. and governor and constable of Windsor Castle, 1867; married, 1861, Laura Williamina, daughter of Admiral Sir George Francis Seymour [q. v.], and assumed title of Count Gleichen; devoted himself successfully to sculpture; G.C.B. and admiral, 1887.

[Suppl. iii. 388]

VICTORIA, QUEEN OF THE UNITED KINGDOM OF GREAT BRITAIN AND IRELAND, and EMPRESS OF INDIA (1819-1901), granddaughter of George III, and only child of George III's fourth son, Edward Augustus, duke of Kent (d. 1820), by Mary Louisa Victoria, fourth daughter and youngest child of Francis Frederick Antony (1750-1806), reigning duke of Saxe-Coburg-Saalfeld (afterwards Gotha), and widow of Ernest Charles, reigning prince of Leiningen (d. 1814), was born at Kensington Palace, 24 May 1819. She was baptised, 24 June, Alexandrina Victoria, the first name being after Alexander I, czar of Russia, who was one of her sponsors. She lived from 1820 with the Duchess of Kent at Kensington Palace. Her early education was undertaken by Fräulein Louise Lehzen (created Hanoverian baroness, 1827), and, from 1827, by the Rev. George Davys, and many tutors and mistresses who worked under his supervision. Music and art were favourite studies. In 1830 the Duchess of Northumberland was appointed her governess. From 1832 onwards the Duchess of Kent and the princess made extended tours in England. She was confirmed at Chapel Royal, St. James's, 1835, celebrated her coming of age, 24 May 1837, and on 20 June 1837 succeeded to the throne, on the death of her uncle, William IV. The queen met her first privy council on the day of the king's death, and she was formally proclaimed on the following day. On her accession the union between England and Hanover, which had existed since 1714, was dissolved. She was instructed in the duties of her station by Lord Melbourne, the prime minister and leader of the whig party, who also undertook the duties of private secretary for all public business. Melbourne thus became the queen's constant companion. In private matters the Baroness Lehzen continued to fill till 1842 the secretarial office for private business, which she had filled before the queen's accession. Baron Stockmar, who had been sent by King Leopold to direct the princess's political education as soon as she reached her majority, was also in attendance on her. On 13 July she took up her official residence in Buckingham Palace. On 20 Nov. she opened her first parliament, reading her own speech, as was her custom until her widowhood, whenever she attended in person. Parliament granted her an annuity of 385,000l. She had in addition the revenues of the duchies of Lancaster and Cornwall (about 27,500l. annually); the duchy of Cornwall, which passed to the Prince of Wales at his birth in 1841, ultimately produced more than 66,000l., while the yearly income from the duchy of Lancaster rose to more than 60,000l. In 1839 the queen discharged the debts of her father, the late Duke of Kent. The coronation took place on 28 June, 1838. In the early months of 1839 the queen was subjected to much unfavourable comment owing to her passive attitude towards Lady Flora Hastings [q. v.], daughter of the Marquis of Hastings, who was lady-in-waiting to the Duchess of Kent at Buckingham Palace, and was improperly suspected by some of the queen's attendants of immoral conduct. In the same year, 1839, Melbourne's whig ministry resigned and the queen commissioned Sir Robert Peel, the leader of the conservative opposition in the lower house, to form a government. Peel, in consultation with his friends, decided that the ladies holding the higher posts in the queen's household must be displaced if the conservative ministers were to receive adequate support from the crown. The queen, misunderstanding Peel's intentions, refused to accept his proposals. He accordingly declined to proceed to the formation of a government, and the whigs returned to office. In October 1839 the queen's first cousins, Prince Albert of Saxe-Coburg Gotha, and his elder brother Ernest, who had

already stayed at Kensington in 1836, visited Windsor, and on 15 Oct. the queen offered Prince Albert marriage. The marriage took place on 10 Feb. 1840. Prince Albert received a grant from parliament of 30,000l. annually, and the queen gave him, by royal warrant, precedence next after herself. The first attempt on the queen's life was made, 10 June, 1840, by Edward Oxford, a potboy, who was found to be insane. The queen's first child, Victoria Adelaide Mary Louisa, was born on 21 Nov. 1840. In 1841 the queen came for the first time into conflict with Palmerston, the foreign minister, whose Eastern policy seemed likely to bring about a war between England and France. In June 1841 parliament was dissolved and the ensuing election produced a tory majority. Melbourne resigned and Peel was called upon to form a ministry. On 9 Nov. 1841, the queen's second child, Albert Edward, prince of Wales (now Edward VII), was born. In June 1842 the queen made her first railway journey, travelling from Slough to Paddington. On 30 May and 3 July second and third attempts on her life were made by John Francis and John William Bean. In the autumn of this year the queen paid her first visit to Scotland, journeying by sea from Woolwich to Granton. Princess Alice was born on 25 April 1843. In September the queen visited Louis-Philippe at Château d'Eu, near Tréport. This was the first occasion on which the queen had trodden foreign soil, and the first occasion on which an English sovereign had visited a French sovereign since Henry VIII appeared on the Field of the Cloth of Gold at the invitation of Francis I in 1520. Prince Alfred was born 6 Aug. 1844. Louis-Philippe returned the queen's visit in October 1844, this being the first time that a French monarch voluntarily landed on English shores. The queen opened the new Royal Exchange, London, 28 Oct. 1844. In the autumn of 1845 she visited Germany for the first time, and stayed at Rosenau, Prince Albert's birthplace. In 1845 the state of agricultural distress which prevailed throughout the United Kingdom forced Peel to advocate the repeal of the corn laws, a step which he and his party were pledged to oppose. The queen firmly supported him, but Peel deemed it just that the opposite party, which had lately championed the reform, should carry it out. He accordingly resigned, and the queen sent for Lord John Russell. Russell, however, was unable to face difficulties chiefly arising from the distrust in which Palmerston was held by the queen and many members of his own party. Peel resumed power, and on 26 June 1846 the corn-law bill passed its third reading in the Lords, but on the same night the government was defeated on the second reading of a coercion bill for Ireland, and Peel's resignation followed. Lord John Russell formed a new ministry, and the queen, with much misgiving, agreed to Palmerston's return to the foreign office. In the meantime the Princess Helena was born, 25 May 1846.

In 1844 the queen had purchased the estate of Osborne, in the Isle of Wight; the foundations of her palace there were laid in 1845, and the whole was completed, 1851. In 1848 the queen leased Balmoral House, and purchased it in 1852, when Balmoral Castle was begun; it was finished in 1854. Here a part of every spring and autumn was spent during the rest of the queen's life. In June 1849 the queen made her first visit to Ireland, going by sea from Cowes to the Cove of Cork, on which she bestowed the name of Queenstown. Subsequently she stayed four days in Dublin. Her third son, Arthur, was born on 1 May 1850.

Meanwhile the breach between the foreign minister, Palmerston, and the crown had been growing wider, and in 1850 the queen was compelled to state definitely her demands in regard to his future conduct. She required, firstly, that he should inform her distinctly of his proposed course of action in any given case, and, secondly, that he should not arbitrarily modify or alter any measure which had once received her sanction. Palmerston affected pained surprise; but his method of procedure underwent no permanent change. In February 1851 the government was outvoted on a question of electoral reform, and Lord John Russell resigned. The conservative leader, Lord Stanley, afterwards Lord Derby, declined to form a government, and Russell was recalled. In this year the queen threw herself with great spirit into the arrangements connected with the Great Exhibition. The removal of Palmerston from the ministry followed at the end of this year, and was a source of relief to the queen. On 2 Dec. Prince Louis Napoleon, by a coup d'état, made himself absolute head of the French government. The queen and Lord John viewed with detestation Napoleon's accession to power and the means of its accomplishment. Palmerston, however, expressed his approbation to the French ambassador Walewski, without communicating either with the queen or with his colleagues. Lord John, who proposed that for the present England should extend to Napoleon the coldest neutrality, summarily demanded Palmerston's resignation. The seals of the foreign office were accordingly transferred to the queen's friend, Lord Granville. Early in 1852 a militia bill occasioned the defeat and consequent resignation of the ministry. Lord Derby formed a conservative government, with Disraeli as chancellor of the exchequer and leader of the House of Commons. A general election in July left the conservatives in the minority. The Duke of Wellington died on 14 Sept. In December Disraeli's budget was rejected by a small majority, and Lord Derby resigned. A coalition ministry of conservatives and liberals was formed by the queen's wish by Lord Aberdeen, the foreign and home offices being taken respectively by Clarendon and Palmerston.

An alliance between England and France became inevitable late in 1853, owing to the position of affairs in eastern Europe. In the autumn Russia pushed her claims to protect the Greek Christians of the Turkish empire with such violence as to extort from Turkey a declaration of war. British popular opinion demanded the immediate intervention of England in behalf of Turkey. Napoleon offered to join his army with that of England, and the king of Sardinia promised to follow his example. But other foreign sovereigns endeavoured privately to influence the queen in favour of peace. Her attitude to all her continental correspondents was irreproachable, but the rumour spread that she and her husband were employing their foreign intimacies against the country's interest; and as the winter of 1853–4 progressed without any signs of decisive action on the part of the English government, popular indignation burst in its fullest fury on the head of Prince Albert. The tide of abuse was temporarily checked when, 27 Feb. 1854, the queen announced in the House of Lords the breakdown of negotiations with Russia. War was formally declared next day, and France and Sardinia renewed their promises of alliance. The queen evinced great personal interest in the progress of the Crimean war, and initiated or supported all manner of voluntary measures for the comfort of the troops. In January 1855 the government was defeated on a hostile motion for inquiry into the management of the war, and the queen reluctantly bade Palmerston form an administration ; subsequently, however, she gave him her full confidence, and when the treaty of peace was signed, 30 March 1856, she acknowledged that the successful issue of the war was mainly due to him. In April 1855 the Emperor Napoleon visited the queen at Windsor, and was dissuaded from his intention of taking command in person of the French troops in the Crimea. In May the queen distributed with her own hands war medals to the returned soldiers, a function that had not previously been performed by sovereigns. In August the queen and Prince Albert visited the emperor at Paris ; this was the first occasion on which an English sovereign had entered the French capital since the infant Henry VI went to be crowned in 1422. In June 1856 the queen instituted the Victoria Cross for acts of conspicuous valour in war, and herself decorated the first recipients on 26 June 1857. On 25 June 1857 the queen conferred on Prince Albert the title of prince consort. During this year (1857) the progress of the Indian mutiny caused the queen acute distress. In February Palmerston resigned on the defeat of a bill making conspiracy to murder, hitherto a misdemeanor, a felony ; this had been introduced in consequence of a plot hatched in England to destroy the emperor and empress of the French by an explosive bomb which was thrown in the Opera House in Paris. Lord Derby formed a new ministry. In August the queen visited Napoleon at Cherbourg, and afterwards made an extended tour in Germany. On 25 Jan. 1858 her eldest daughter, the princess royal, married Prince Frederick, afterwards Crown Prince of Prussia. While the Indian mutiny was in course of suppression the East India Company was abolished, its territories and powers transferred to the crown, and the administration placed in the hands of the secretary of state, who was assisted by a council of fifteen, The scheme for the actual reorganisation of the Indian government, in which the queen was deeply interested, received the royal assent, 2 Aug. 1858.

The queen's tranquillity of mind was at this time greatly disturbed by the part Napoleon was playing in European politics. He had threatened to join the king of Sardinia in an endeavour to expel Austria from Lombardy and Venetia. The prospect of war between France and Austria gave the queen peculiar anxiety owing to Austria's proximity to Prussia, with whose reigning house her daughter had recently become allied by marriage. Austria took the initiative by declaring war on Sardinia, and Napoleon immediately entered the field in behalf of Sardinia. The queen was successful in dissuading Prussia from interference. The prompt triumph of French arms brought hostilities to a close, but the queen's fears of the sequel were increased by a change of ministry, which brought Palmerston into power as premier, and Russell as foreign secretary. Palmerston and Russell agreed in a resolve to serve the interests of Italy at the expense of Austria. The queen, however, contrived to persuade her ministers to adopt a policy of strict neutrality. In May 1859 a volunteer force was called into existence, and in July 1860 the queen personally inaugurated the National Rifle Association as a complement to the volunteer movement ; in the same year she instituted the queen's prize (250l.), which was thenceforth awarded annually. In September 1860 the queen and prince consort made a second journey to Coburg to visit Stockmar, who had lived there in retirement since 1857. On 4 Feb. 1861 the queen opened parliament in person ; this was the last occasion in which she delivered with her own voice the speech from the throne. On 16 March the queen's mother died at Frogmore after a brief illness. In the later months of this year the health of the prince consort gradually failed. Early in December he persuaded the British ministers to adopt a conciliatory attitude towards the United States respecting the Trent affair, and on 14 Dec. he died.

The sense of desolation which the queen experienced on her husband's death never wholly left her. She long remained in retirement, and never ceased to wear mourning for him. In the two years that followed her bereavement she lived in complete seclusion, but engaged assiduously in official work. General the Hon. Charles Grey, a younger son of the second Earl Grey, who had been since 1846 private secretary to the prince consort, was appointed to the same post in the queen's service, and continued in this capacity until his death in 1870. His place was then taken by General Sir Henry Ponsonby, who died in 1895, and was succeeded by Colonel Sir Arthur Bigge, who survived the queen. On 1 July 1862 the queen attended, in deep mourning, the marriage of Princess Alice to Prince Louis of Hesse. At the close of this year it was proposed to confer the crown of Greece upon her second son, Prince Alfred. The offer caused her much perplexity. The crown was finally given to George, son of Prince Christian of Schleswig-Holstein-Sonderburg-Glucksburg (who became king of Denmark on 15 Nov. 1863) ; he was brother of the affianced bride of the Prince of Wales. The marriage of the Prince of Wales took place, 10 March 1863. The queen visited Germany in the autumn, and while at Coburg had an interview with the Emperor Francis Joseph of Austria, who was returning from Frankfurt, where a conference of German sovereigns had been held to consider a form of confederation of the German states, which seemed likely to exclude Prussia. The queen endeavoured to influence the emperor of Austria in behalf of Prussia. Towards the close of 1863 the queen gave close attention to the struggle brought about by the conflicting claims of Germany and Denmark to the duchies of Schleswig-Holstein. Her sympathies were with Germany, while those of her ministers and people were with the Danes. In February 1864 hostilities broke out between Austria and Prussia on the one hand and Denmark on the other. The Danes were promptly defeated. The queen succeeded in enforcing on her government a policy of strict neutrality. In June the German allies occupied the disputed duchies.

Meanwhile a feeling had been growing throughout the country that the queen's prolonged seclusion was contrary to the nation's interest. She replied guardedly to the popular outcry in a letter to 'The Times' newspaper (1864), stating her desire to meet the wishes of her subjects so far as her health, strength, and spirits might allow. The queen was acutely distressed at the deaths of Palmerston on 18 Oct. 1865, and of King Leopold on 10 Dec. Palmerston's place as prime minister was taken by Lord John Russell. On 10 Feb. 1866 the queen opened parliament in person. Later in the year the disputes between Prussia and Austria in regard to the final allotment of the conquered duchies of Schleswig-Holstein culminated in a desperate conflict between the two powers. The struggle hopelessly divided the queen's family in Germany. The queen bade Lord Russell take every step to prevent war. In June war was declared, and the queen's perplexity was increased by the defeat and subsequent resignation of Russell's government on the question of reform of the franchise. Russell retired from public life; he died 4 June 1878. In July the conservative leader, Lord Derby, formed a new ministry, with Disraeli as chancellor of the exchequer and leader of the House of Commons. Prussia's triumph in the war was quickly assured; Hanover was converted into a Prussian province, and by the victory at Sadowa, near Königgrätz (3 July 1866), Prussia was finally placed at the head of the whole of north Germany, and Austria was compelled to retire from the German confederation.

With the object of perpetuating her husband's memory, the queen published in 1867 a minute account of the early years of the prince consort, which had been prepared under her direction by her private secretary, General Grey. In 1870 she entrusted the continuation of this biography to (Sir) Theodore Martin; this work appeared in five volumes, 1874–80. The queen's 'Leaves from a Journal of our Life in the Highlands, 1848–61,' appeared privately in 1867, and publicly in 1868. A second part, 'More Leaves,' followed in 1883, covering the years 1862–82.

In February 1867 the queen opened parliament in person. In May of the same year she laid the foundation of the Royal Albert Hall, which was erected in her husband's memory. In this year she encouraged the government to settle the question of franchise, and Disraeli's reform bill passed through parliament. In July 1867 the queen received visits from the khedive of Egypt and the sultan of Turkey. In February 1868 Disraeli became prime minister in succession to Lord Derby. In April Gladstone brought forward his first and main resolution in favour of the disestablishment of the Irish church. The government resisted him and was defeated, and Disraeli tendered his resignation. On 5 May Disraeli announced in parliament that the queen had decided, on her own responsibility, to reject his resignation, and to dissolve parliament as soon as the arrangements for appeal to the electors, newly enfranchised under the reform bill, were complete. Disraeli's action in giving the queen the choice of two alternatives excited hostile comment. In August she paid her first visit to Switzerland, travelling incognito under the name of the Countess of Kent. In a general election at the close of this year Disraeli's government was defeated. In December Gladstone became prime minister. The first measure which he introduced was the bill for the disestablishment of the Irish church, and despite her disapproval of it the queen recognised that its adoption was inevitable. Accordingly she exerted, through Archbishop Tait, her influence against the opposition of the House of Lords, and the bill was passed (June 1869).

In 1870 the queen watched with close attention the struggle between France and Germany, and when, in 1870, Napoleon declared war, she regarded his action as wholly unjustified. On his overthrow, however, she welcomed the Empress Eugénie to England, and when the emperor joined the empress at Chislehurst, 1871, the queen extended to him a sympathy which continued until his death, 9 Jan. 1873. In 1870 Cardwell, the secretary for war, instituted a scheme for the reorganisation of the army, and on 28 June, with some reluctance, the queen signed an order in council deposing the commander-in-chief from his place of sole and immediate dependence on the crown. Later in the year her ministers caused her prerogative to be exercised in order to circumvent the opposition of the House of Lords to a bill passed in the House of Commons for the abolition of military promotion by purchase. She opened parliament in person, February 1871. On 21 March Princess Louise was married to the Marquis of Lorne, eldest son of the Duke of Argyll ; this was the first time in English history that the sovereign sanctioned the union of a princess with one who was not a member of a reigning house since Mary, sister of Henry VIII, married, in 1515, Charles Brandon, duke of Suffolk. During this period much antiroyalist feeling was fostered in certain classes of the community in England. In March 1872 Sir Charles W. Dilke, M.P. for Chelsea, introduced into parliament a motion which aimed at a complete reform of the civil list. The proposal was rejected by a large majority, but the feeling which inspired it remained alive in the country until the queen conspicuously modified her habits of seclusion. In March 1873 Gladstone resigned on the defeat of his Irish university bill, but on Disraeli's refusal to take his place he returned to office.

In January 1874 the queen's second son, Prince Alfred, married at St. Petersburg the Grand Duchess Marie Alexandrovna, Czar Alexander II's only daughter. The match was of little political importance. In the same month parliament was dissolved and a conservative government came into power, with Disraeli as prime minister. With Disraeli the queen was in complete sympathy, and it was in conformity with his views in regard to British intervention in foreign politics that she exerted her influence in 1875 to avert the hostilities which again threatened between France and Germany. In 1875 the Prince of Wales, as representative of the queen, made a state tour through India, and in May 1876 the designation of Empress of India was conferred on her by the Royal Titles Bill. In February 1876, and again in February 1877, the queen opened parliament in person. In 1876–8 the queen gave much attention to the position of affairs in eastern Europe. The subject races of the Turkish empire in the Balkans had threatened the Porte with revolt in 1875, and there was the likelihood that Russia, to serve her own ends, might come to the rescue of the insurgents. Beaconsfield adopted Palmerston's policy of 1854, and declared that British interests required the maintenance of the sultan's authority inviolate. Gladstone, who had in 1876 announced his retirement from public life, emerged from his seclusion to oppose the bestowal on Turkey of any English support. The queen used, without success, her private influence to dissuade Russia from interference, and on Russia's declaration of war with Turkey, April 1877, she firmly supported Beaconsfield in a diplomatic struggle which brought Russia to the brink of hostilities with England. The question was settled by the congress of Berlin, June 1878, when Beaconsfield, who acted as English envoy, obtained, in his own phrase, ' peace with honour.'

In April 1879 the queen paid her first visit to Italy, staying at Baveno on Lago Maggiore. The queen again opened parliament in person in February 1880, and in March, after the dissolution, she visited Germany. The ensuing election brought the liberals into power, and the queen reluctantly commissioned Gladstone to form a government. She was seriously perturbed by plans for the further reorganisation of the army. She was unremitting in her admonitions to the government to take vigorous steps in Afghanistan, 1880, and in the Transvaal, 1880–1, and the policy of peace which followed the defeat of General Colley at Majuba Hill, 28 Feb. 1881, conflicted with her views. On 19 April 1881 Beaconsfield died, and the queen treated his loss as a personal bereavement. During the war in Egypt occasioned by Arabi Pasha's rebellion (1882) the queen continued to urge her ministers to energetic action. After the pacification of Egypt she devised a new decoration of the royal red cross for nurses who had rendered efficient service in war. The queen's life was for the fifth time threatened by assassination at Windsor on 2 March 1882, when Roderick Maclean, a lunatic, fired a pistol at her, fortunately without effect. On 4 Dec. 1882 the queen inaugurated the new law courts in the Strand. In 1883–4 Egypt, which was now practically administered by England, became the centre of renewed anxieties. In 1883 the inhabitants of the Soudan revolted. The English ministry decided to abandon the territory, but undertook to relieve several Egyptian garrisons remaining in the Soudan in positions of great peril. General Gordon was despatched to Khartoum, the capital of the disturbed district, with a view to negotiation with the rebels. He was besieged in Khartoum by the mahdi's forces. The queen repeatedly warned the government of the necessity for sending him relief, and in the autumn of 1884 a British army was sent out under Lord Wolseley, but Gordon was killed before a rescue could be effected. The queen reproached her ministers with the death of Gordon, which she regarded as a public disaster. Throughout 1885 she maintained her interest in the operations in the Soudan. The queen lent her support to the Franchise Bill, which, after some opposition from the lords, was passed concurrently with the Redistribution of Seats Bill before the end of the year (1884). She spent the spring of 1885 at Aix-les-Bains, and on her return journey visited

Darmstadt and made the acquaintance of Prince Henry of Battenberg, who on 23 July married the queen's youngest daughter, Princess Beatrice. In June the government was defeated on its budget proposals, and Gladstone resigned. Lord Salisbury at once took office as prime minister, but the general election which followed the dissolution in November left the conservatives in a minority, and in January 1886 Salisbury's government was outvoted. Five days previously the queen had opened parliament in person, as it proved, for the last time. Gladstone resumed power, and at once committed his party to the policy of home rule for Ireland. The queen disliked the proposal, and Gladstone's Home Rule Bill was decisively rejected by the House of Commons (7 June). At Gladstone's instance parliament was dissolved; he resigned without meeting the new parliament, where his party was small, and Lord Salisbury for the second time formed a government. In this year (1886) the queen manifested great interest in the Colonial and India exhibition at South Kensington organised by the Prince of Wales (afterwards King Edward VII). On 21 June 1887 and the following days she took part in the public ceremonies in celebration of her jubilee, and on 6 July she laid the foundation-stone of the Imperial Institute, which was erected by public subscription to commemorate the fifty years of her reign.

In March 1888 the queen for the first time visited Florence, and afterwards proceeded to Charlottenburg, the palace of the dying Emperor Frederick. In March 1889 she stayed at Biarritz, and thence visited the queen-regent of Spain at San Sebastian. This was the first occasion on which an English sovereign had visited that country, though Charles I and Charles II went thither as princes. In July the approaching majority of the Prince of Wales's eldest son and the approaching marriage of his eldest daughter compelled the queen to appeal to parliament on the question of suitable provision for the third generation of her family. Precedent justified public provision for all children of the sovereign's sons, and the queen agreed to forego any demand in behalf of her daughters' children. The matter was settled, with Gladstone's assistance, by a grant to the Prince of Wales of 36,000l. annually for his children's support. Gladstone's intervention was always remembered by the queen with gratitude. In August 1889 she welcomed her grandson, the German emperor, William II, on his first visit to England since his accession to the throne. The emperor caused the queen to be gazetted honorary colonel of his first regiment of horse guards, on which she bestowed the title of Queen of England's Own. In 1892 a general election returned a majority of home rulers, and Gladstone filled the post of prime minister for the fourth time. In September 1893 his Home Rule Bill, which had passed through the House of Commons, was rejected by the House of Lords. In March 1894 the queen accepted Gladstone's resignation and chose Lord Rosebery to succeed him. In this year the government made further changes in the war office, which strictly limited to five years the tenure of the post of commander-in-chief, and thus finally disposed of the queen's cherished fiction that the head of the army was her permanent personal deputy. The ministry fell in June, and Lord Salisbury resumed office as premier and foreign secretary, with Mr. Chamberlain as colonial secretary. In the spring of 1895 the queen was at Cannes, in 1896 and 1897 at Nice, and in 1898 and 1899 at Cimiez. On 22 June 1897 she took part in a state procession through London to celebrate her 'diamond Jubilee,' the completion of the sixtieth year of her rule. During the closing years of her reign the queen gave close attention to the numerous expeditions in which her armies were engaged, and she was gratified when the rebellion in the Soudan was finally crushed at the battle of Omdurman, 2 Sept. 1898. On the outbreak of the Boer war in 1899, when she was convinced that the peace which she was always anxious to preserve could not be maintained, she exerted her utmost energy to urge her ministers to conduct hostilities with all possible promptitude and effect. To encourage her soldiers she went, in the spring of 1900, for the fourth time to Ireland, whence the armies in the field had been largely recruited. She held her last drawing-room in Buckingham Palace, 4 May. She gave her assent to the Australian commonwealth bill, 27 Aug. In October a general election was deemed necessary by the government, and on the return of a conservative majority Lord Salisbury remained prime minister, but resigned the foreign secretaryship to Lord Lansdowne, formerly minister of war.

Throughout the summer the queen experienced acute distress at the accounts of suffering which reached her from South Africa, and her personal sympathy with her troops was intensified by the death of her grandson, Prince Christian Victor of Schleswig-Holstein, from enteric fever contracted in active service. In the autumn of 1900 the queen showed signs of general physical decay, and on 22 Jan. 1901 she died. Her body was conveyed with military honours from Osborne through London to Windsor, and was placed (4 Feb.) in the mausoleum at Frogmore, which had been completed in 1868, and already contained the remains of her husband. On the day following her death her eldest son was proclaimed King Edward VII.

Among the most notable portraits of the queen are paintings or drawings by Sir William Beechey, R.A., 1821; Sir George Hayter, 1833 and 1838; Sir David Wilkie, 1839; Sir Edwin Landseer, 1839 and 1866; F. Winterhalter, 1845 and other years; Baron H. von Angeli, 1875 (of which a copy by Lady Abercromby is in the National Portrait Gallery, London), 1885, and 1897; and M. Benjamin Constant, 1900. Sculptured presentations include a bust by Behnes, 1827; a plaster bust by Sir Edgar Boehm (in National Portrait Gallery); a statue at Winchester by Mr. Alfred Gilbert, R.A.; and a statue at Manchester by Mr. Onslow Ford, R.A. A national memorial in sculpture to be designed by Mr. Thomas Brock, R.A., with an architectural setting by Mr. Aston Webb, A.R.A., is to be placed in the Mall opposite Buckingham Palace. [Suppl. iii. 389]

VIDAL, ROBERT STUDLEY (1770–1841), antiquary; a Devonshire squire; barrister, Middle Temple; benefactor of St. John's College, Cambridge. [lviii. 303]

VIDLER, WILLIAM (1758–1816), universalist; independent preacher, 1777; baptist minister, 1780; adopted universalist views, 1792; became a unitarian, 1802; minister of a chapel, Battle, 1780–96, and in London, 1794–1815; a bookseller, 1796–1806; joint-editor of a theological magazine, 1797–1805. [lviii. 303]

VIEUXPONT or **VIPONT** (DE VETERI PONTE), ROBERT DE (d. 1228), baron of Westmorland; one of King John's evil counsellors; gaoler of Arthur of Brittany at Rouen, 1203; granted barony of Appleby or Westmorland, and lordships in Yorkshire and Normandy, 1203; sheriff of various English counties, 1207–13; in attendance on John in Ireland, 1210; fought in Wales, 1212; supported John against the barons; joint-custodian for John of Yorkshire castles, 1216; surrendered the castles he held, 1223; justice itinerant, 1219 and 1226. [lviii. 304]

VIGANI, JOHN FRANCIS (1650?–1712), chemist; born at Verona; travelled in Spain, France, Holland; published 'Medulla Chymiæ,' Danzig, 1682; taught chemistry at Cambridge from 1683; professor of chemistry, 1703–12. [lviii. 305]

VIGER, DENIS BENJAMIN (1774–1861), Canadian statesman; educated at Montreal; a barrister; member of the Montreal legislature, 1808–38; came to England to state the French Canadian case, 1828–30; imprisoned for seditious newspaper articles, 1838–40; member of the Canadian legislature, 1841–55; in the ministry, 1843–6; LL.D., 1855; published pamphlets. [lviii. 306]

VIGER, JACQUES (1787–1858), Canadian antiquary; educated at Montreal; served in the militia, 1812–15; lieutenant-colonel; mayor of Montreal, 1833; collected materials for the history of Canada. [lviii. 307]

VÍGFÚSSON, GÚDBRANDR (1828–1889), Icelandic scholar; born and educated in Iceland; went to Copenhagen, 1849; worked in the Arna-Magnæan Scandinavian library; published 'Timatàl,' a chronology of Icelandic literature, 1855; edited sagas and folk-lore, 1858–87; came to Oxford, 1866; edited Richard Cleasby's Icelandic dictionary, 1873; joint-editor of the 'Corpus Poeticum Boreale,' 1883; lecturer on Icelandic, Oxford University, 1884; published philological papers. [lviii. 307]

VIGHARD (d. 664). [See WIGHARD.]

VIGNE, GODFREY THOMAS (1801–1863), traveller; barrister, Lincoln's Inn, 1824; published narratives of his travels in the United States, 1831, Central Asia, 1832–9, Mexico and Central America, 1852. [lviii. 309]

VIGNOLES, CHARLES BLACKER (1793–1875), engineer ; articled to a solicitor, 1807 ; entered Sandhurst, 1810 ; served in the army, 1813–16 ; lieutenant, 1815 ; engaged on the South Carolina survey, 1816–23 ; a leading railway engineer, 1825–65 ; professor of civil engineering, University College, London, 1841 ; F.R.S., 1855 ; published geographical and astronomical notes.
[lviii. 309]

VIGORS, NICHOLAS AYLWARD (1785 – 1840), zoologist ; of Trinity College, Oxford ; ensign in the Peninsula, 1809–11 ; M.A. Oxford, 1818 ; D.C.L., 1832 ; F.R.S., 1826 ; F.S.A.; landowner in co. Carlow, 1828 ; Irish M.P., Carlow, 1832, co. Carlow, 1837–40 ; published papers on birds, 1825–39.
[lviii. 310]

VILLETTES, WILLIAM ANNE (1754–1808), lieutenant-general ; educated at Bath and St. Andrews University ; entered the army, 1775 ; lieutenant-colonel, 1791 ; lieutenant-general, 1805 ; served at Toulon, 1791, in Corsica, 1794–5, and in Portugal, 1796 ; governor of Malta, 1801–7 ; governor of Jamaica, 1807 ; died there.
[lviii. 311]

VILLIERS (afterwards PALMER), BARBARA, COUNTESS OF CASTLEMAINE and DUCHESS OF CLEVELAND (1641–1709), daughter of William Villiers, second viscount Grandison (d. 1643) ; a London beauty, 1656 ; married Roger Palmer (d. 1705) [q. v.], 1659 ; mistress of Charles II, 1660 ; Countess of Castlemaine by her husband's elevation to the Irish peerage, 1661 ; forced as lady of the bedchamber on Queen Catherine, 1662 ; assigned rooms in Whitehall ; procured the dismissal of Sir Edward Nicholas [q. v.], secretary of state, 1662 ; her miscellaneous amours notorious, 1662 ; embraced Romanism, 1663 ; accompanied the court to Oxford, 1665 ; instrumental in securing Clarendon's dismissal, 1667 ; trafficked in the sale of court places and offices ; pensioned, 1669 ; created Duchess of Cleveland, 1670 ; supplanted in Charles II's graces by Louise Renée de Kéroualle [q. v.], 1674 ; resided in Paris, 1677–84 ; obtained the dismissal of Ralph Montagu, ambassador at Paris, 1678 ; married Robert Feilding [q. v.], 1705 (marriage annulled, 1707) ; resided latterly at Chiswick. Of her children Charles II acknowledged the paternity of (1) Anne (afterwards Countess of Sussex), born 1661 ; (2) Charles (duke of Southampton), born 1662 : (3) Henry (duke of Grafton), born 1663 ; (4) Charlotte (afterwards countess of Lichfield), born 1664 ; (5) George (duke of Northumberland), born 1665. Barbara, born 1672, was popularly assigned to John Churchill ; and a boy, born 1686, to Cardonnell Goodman, an actor.
[lviii. 312]

VILLIERS, CHARLES PELHAM (1802–1898), statesman ; educated at Haileybury and St. John's College, Cambridge (B.A., 1824) ; adopted Jeremy Bentham's political views, 1825 ; barrister, Lincoln's Inn, 1827 ; assistant poor-law commissioner, 1832 ; official of the court of chancery, 1833–52 ; M.P., Wolverhampton, 1835–1898 ; declared for free-trade, 1836 ; moved a resolution against the corn-law, 1838, repeating it year by year till its abolition in 1846 ; sat on the parliamentary committee on the import duties on corn, 1840 ; judge-advocate general, 1852–8 ; privy councillor, 1853 ; president of the poor-law board, 1859–66 ; in receipt of an ex-minister's pension, 1866 till death ; his statue erected in Wolverhampton, 1879 ; opposed home rule for Ireland ; last speech in parliament, 1885.
[lviii. 318]

VILLIERS, CHRISTOPHER, first EARL OF ANGLESEY (1593 ?–1630), younger brother of George Villiers, first duke of Buckingham [q. v.] ; gentleman of the bedchamber to James I, 1617 ; master of the robes : enriched by a pension, by traffic in places, by illegal monopolies, and patents ; created Baron Villiers of Daventry and Earl of Anglesey, 1623.
[lviii. 323]

VILLIERS, SIR EDWARD (1585 ?–1626), president of Munster ; eldest half-brother of George Villiers, first duke of Buckingham [q. v.] ; knighted, 1616 ; master of the mint, 1617–22 and 1624–5 ; comptroller of the court of wards, 1618 ; M.P., Westminster, 1620–5 ; envoy to the elector palatine, 1620 and 1621 ; president of Munster, 1625 ; enriched by monopolies and patents.
[lviii. 324]

VILLIERS, EDWARD, first EARL OF JERSEY (1656–1711), brother of Elizabeth Villiers [q. v.] ; master of the horse to Queen Mary II, 1689 ; knight marshal of the household, 1689 ; created Viscount Villiers of Dartford,

1691 ; envoy to Holland, 1695, 1697, and to Paris, 1698–9 ; created Earl of Jersey, 1697 ; a lord justice of Ireland, 1697–9 ; secretary of state, 1700–1 ; lord chamberlain, 1700–4.
[lviii. 325]

VILLIERS, ELIZABETH, COUNTESS OF ORKNEY (1657 ?–1733), styled ' Mrs. Villiers,' accompanied Princess Mary to Holland as maid of honour, 1677 ; became mistress of the Prince of Orange ; came to England with Mary, 1689 ; granted portion of James II's Irish estates, 1689 (grant annulled, 1699) ; poisoned William III's mind against Marlborough ; cast off by William, 1694 ; married, 1695, to Lord George Hamilton [q. v.], who was, 1696, created Earl of Orkney.
[lviii. 326]

VILLIERS, FRANÇOIS HUET (1772 ?–1813), portrait-painter and etcher ; born in Paris ; son of a French painter, Jean-Baptiste Huet ; exhibited at Paris, 1799–1801 ; settled in London and exhibited there, 1803–13.
[lviii. 327]

VILLIERS, SIR GEORGE (d. 1606), knight, of Brooksby ; sheriff of Leicestershire, 1591 ; married (second wife) Mary Beaumont (created in 1618 Countess of Buckingham, d. 1630).
[lviii. 324]

VILLIERS, GEORGE, first DUKE OF BUCKINGHAM (1592–1628), court favourite ; a younger son, by his second marriage, of Sir George Villiers [q. v.] ; trained for a page's place ; visited France, 1610–13 ; introduced to James I, 1614 ; appointed cupbearer, 1614 ; gentleman of the bedchamber, 1615 ; knighted and pensioned ; master of the horse, 1616 ; K.G., 1616 ; created Viscount Villiers, 1616, and given an estate ; created Earl of Buckingham, 1617, and Marquis of Buckingham, 1618 ; married a Romanist, Lady Katherine Manners, 1620 ; obtained the dismissal of his court rivals, the Howard family, 1618 ; undertook the administration, acting himself as lord high admiral, 1619 ; advised an expedition to the Palatinate, February 1620, but intrigued with Gondomar, the Spanish ambassador, to defeat it, 1620 and 1621 ; parliament checked in its censure of the monopolies in which his brothers had speculated, by his disowning his brothers, 1621, sheltering himself behind James I's name, and dissolving parliament ; shrank from supporting Bacon, 1621 ; dissuaded by Laud from professing Romanism, 1622 ; forced James I and Prince Charles to the Madrid journey, 1623 ; arrived with Charles at Madrid ; quarrelled with the Spanish court, and left Madrid, August 1623 ; had been created Duke of Buckingham, 1623, in his absence ; failing to force the council into war with Spain, 1624, had parliament called and the Spanish negotiations broken off ; became warden of the Cinque ports, 1624 ; originally urged on the match with Henrietta Maria, 1624–5 ; took offence, 1625, on Richelieu's refusal of his terms, and grossly insulted King Louis ; the expedition under Count Mansfeld sent by him to the Palatinate a few months before (January 1625) a failure ; supplies refused by parliament if he was to have the sole conduct of the war, July, on which it was dissolved, August 1625 ; the squadron lent by him to Richelieu used contrary to his hopes by the French minister against Rochelle, 1625 ; irritated the French by setting on foot search for contraband of war ; the Cadiz expedition under his favourite, Sir Edward Cecil, a failure, October 1625 ; promised large subsidies to Denmark and Holland, 1625, and planned the relief of Rochelle, 1626 ; the parliament of February 1626 dissolved, June 1626, to prevent it carrying out his impeachment ; his overtures to Spain for peace rejected, February 1627 ; sent Pennington to make war on French shipping in March 1627 ; personally sailed to relieve Rochelle, June, but failed shamefully, July–October 1627, and was infatuated enough to reject French proposals for peace, December 1627 ; urged Charles I to raise a standing army, partly of German mercenaries, January 1628 ; action against him prevented by the prorogation of the parliament which had voted supplies on Charles I's acceptance of the Petition of Right, June 1628 ; urged on a new Rochelle expedition, and was assassinated by John Felton (1595 ?–1628) [q. v.], 23 Aug., at Portsmouth.
[lviii. 327]

VILLIERS, GEORGE, second DUKE OF BUCKINGHAM (1628–1687), son of George Villiers, first duke of Buckingham [q. v.] ; succeeded, August 1628 ; brought up with Charles I's children ; studied at Trinity College, Cambridge ; M.A., 1642 ; joined Charles I in Oxford, winter, 1642 ; served under Rupert, 1643 ; travelled in Italy ;

X X

received back his sequestered estates, on the plea of youth, 1647; joined the Surrey insurgents, was routed at St. Neots, and fled to Holland, 1648; his estates definitely confiscated, 1651; admitted privy councillor, 1650; urged conciliation of the presbyterians; accompanied Charles II to Scotland, 1650, and to Worcester, 1651; escaped to Holland, 1651; tried to make peace with parliament, 1652 and 1653; was in disgrace with the queen-mother, 1652, with Charles II, 1654, and Clarendon, 1656; returned to England, 1657; married Fairfax's daughter, 1657; prisoner in the Tower of London, 1658–9; recovered estates at the Restoration; gentleman of the bedchamber, 1660–7; lord-lieutenant of the West Riding, 1661–7; privy councillor, 1662–7; intrigued against Clarendon, 1663–7; served at sea against the Dutch, 1665; influential member of the 'Cabal' administration, 1667–9; advocated alliance with France and toleration at home; seduced the Countess of Shrewsbury and mortally wounded the earl in a duel, January 1668, but was pardoned, February; master of the horse, by purchase, July 1668; at feud with York and with Ormonde; displaced by Arlington in Charles II's confidence and kept ignorant of the private negotiations with Louis, April 1669, and the secret treaty of Dover, May 1670; envoy to Paris, July 1670, to the Prince of Orange, and to Paris, June 1672; lieutenant-general, May 1673; quarrelled openly with Arlington, 1673, whom Charles supported; being attacked by the Lords for the Shrewsbury scandal, and by the Commons for the French treaty, January 1674, was dismissed from his offices; joined the country party; opposed the non-resistance oath, and moved a bill to relieve protestant dissenters, 1675; prisoner in the Tower of London, 1677; intrigued against Charles II getting supplies, 1678–9, and laboured to have a whig parliament; disapproved of the Exclusion Bill, 1680–1; the Zimri of Dryden's 'Absalom and Achitophel,' 1681; restored to court favour, 1683; published pamphlets in favour of toleration, 1685; lived in retirement in Yorkshire, 1686. He had dabbled in chemistry, and spent much in building and laying out gardens. He wrote verses, satires, and some pieces for the stage, particularly 'The Rehearsal,' brought out 1671, ridiculing contemporary dramatists. His 'Miscellaneous Works' were first collected, 1704–5. [lviii. 337]

VILLIERS, GEORGE BUSSY, fourth EARL OF JERSEY and seventh VISCOUNT GRANDISON (1735–1805), styled 'Viscount Grandison' by courtesy; M.P., Tamworth, 1756–65, Aldborough, 1765–8, Dover, 1768–9; vice-chamberlain of the household, 1765; succeeded to the earldom, 1769; held various offices at court from 1769. [lviii. 346]

VILLIERS, GEORGE CHILD-, fifth EARL OF JERSEY and eighth VISCOUNT GRANDISON (1773–1859), son of George Bussy Villiers, fourth earl of Jersey [q. v.]; styled by courtesy 'Viscount Grandison'; educated at Harrow; M.A. St. John's College, Cambridge, 1794; married, 1804, the prospective heiress of the banker Robert Child, and assumed, 1819, Child as an additional name; succeeded to earldom, 1805 · held court offices.
[lviii. 346]

VILLIERS, GEORGE WILLIAM FREDERICK, fourth EARL OF CLARENDON and fourth BARON HYDE (1800–1870), entered the diplomatic service; attaché at St. Petersburg, 1820; a commissioner of customs, 1823; negotiated a commercial treaty with France, 1831; ambassador at Madrid, 1833–9; succeeded his uncle in the peerage, 1838; lord privy seal, 1839–41; president of the board of trade, 1846; lord-lieutenant of Ireland, 1847–52; foreign minister, 1853–8, and so responsible for the Crimean war and the terms of the treaty of Paris (1856); chancellor of the duchy of Lancaster, 1864; foreign minister, 1865–6 and 1868–70, and so responsible (1869) for the terms of the Alabama settlement. [lviii. 347]

VILLIERS, HENRY MONTAGU (1813–1861), bishop of Durham; student of Christ Church, Oxford, 1830–8; M.A., 1837; D.D., 1856; vicar of Kenilworth, 1837; rector of St. George's, Bloomsbury, London, 1841–56; canon of St. Paul's, London, 1847–56; bishop of Carlisle, 1856; translated to Durham, 1860; published sermons and charges. [lviii. 350]

VILLIERS, JOHN, VISCOUNT PURBECK (1591 ?–1657), elder brother of George Villiers, first duke of Buckingham [q. v.]; knighted, 1616; groom of the bedchamber to Prince Charles, 1616; created Viscount Purbeck, 1619; became insane, 1620; deserted (1621) by his wife,

who had a son by Sir Robert Howard, 1624 [see DANVERS, ROBERT, called VISCOUNT PURBECK]; married again. [lviii. 351]

VILLIERS, JOHN (1677 ?–1723), styling himself 'Viscount Purbeck' and, after 1687, 'third earl of Buckingham'; married, c. 1700; unsuccessfully claimed the earldom, 1709 and 1720. [lviii. 351]

VILLIERS, JOHN CHARLES, third EARL OF CLARENDON (1757–1838), second son of Thomas Villiers, first earl of Clarendon [q. v.]; M.A. St. John's College, Cambridge, 1776; LL.D., 1833; barrister, Lincoln's Inn, 1779; M.P., Old Sarum, 1784–90, Dartmouth, 1790–1802, Wick burghs, 1802–5, Queenborough, 1807–12 and 1820–4; privy councillor, 1787; comptroller of the household, 1787; warden of forests north of Trent, 1790; colonel of yeomanry, 1794; ambassador to Portugal, 1808–10; succeeded his brother in the peerage, 1824. [lviii. 352]

VILLIERS, ROBERT, called VISCOUNT PURBECK, 1621 ?–1674. [See DANVERS, ROBERT]

VILLIERS, THOMAS, first EARL OF CLARENDON (1709–1786), second son of William Villiers, second earl of Jersey [q. v.]; educated at Cambridge: envoy to Warsaw, 1737, to Dresden, 1740, to Vienna, 1742, and to Warsaw, 1744; arranged peace between Frederick the Great and Augustus of Saxony, 1745; ambassador at Berlin, 1746–8; M.P., Tamworth, 1747–56; created Baron Hyde of Hindon, June 1756; privy councillor, 1763; held minor ministerial offices; created Earl of Clarendon, 1776; created a count in Prussia, 1782. [lviii. 352]

VILLIERS, THOMAS HYDE (1801–1832), politician; M.A. St. John's College, Cambridge, 1825; in the colonial office, 1822–5; agent for Berbice and Newfoundland; disciple of John Stuart Mill [q. v.]; M.P., Hedon, 1826–30, Wootton Bassett, 1830, and Bletchingley, 1831; travelled in Ireland, 1828. [lviii. 353]

VILLIERS, WILLIAM, second EARL OF JERSEY (1682 ?–1721), son of Edward Villiers, first earl of Jersey [q. v.]; M.A. Queens' College, Cambridge, 1700; M.P., Kent, 1705–8. [lviii. 326]

VILLIERS STUART, HENRY WINDSOR (1827–1895). [See STUART.]

VILLULA, JOHN DE (d. 1122). [See JOHN.]

VILVAIN, ROBERT (1575 ?–1663), physician; born and educated in Exeter; fellow of Exeter College, Oxford, 1599–1611; M.A., 1600; M.D., 1611; practitioner in Exeter, 1612–63; published English and Latin trifles; benefactor of Exeter College, Oxford, and of Exeter Cathedral library. [lviii. 354]

VINCE, SAMUEL (1749–1821), mathematician and astronomer; a Suffolk bricklayer; usher at Harleston, Norfolk; senior wrangler, 1775; fellow of Sidney Sussex College, Cambridge; M.A., 1778; beneficed in Norfolk, 1784; F.R.S., 1786; astronomy professor, Cambridge, 1796; archdeacon of Bedford, 1809; published mathematical and astronomical works. [lviii. 355]

VINCENT, AUGUSTINE (1584 ?–1626), herald; studied the records in the Tower of London; Rouge Rose pursuivant, 1616; acted as deputy for Camden, 1618; Rouge Croix pursuivant, 1621; Windsor herald, 1624; wrote against Ralph Brooke, 1621. [lviii. 356]

VINCENT, GEORGE (1796–1836 ?), landscape-painter; born and educated in Norwich; pupil of John Crome [q. v.]; exhibited, chiefly Norfolk views, at Norwich, 1811–31, and in London, 1814–31; resided in London from 1818; published etchings, 1821–7. [lviii. 357]

VINCENT, HENRY (1813–1878), political agitator; printer's apprentice at Hull, 1825; came to London, c. 1835; abandoned his trade; chartist agitator, 1838; his conviction at the Monmouth assizes, August 1839, the occasion of the great Newport miners' riot, November 1839; imprisoned again, 1840–1; journalist, lay-preacher, and lecturer on social questions from 1841; unsuccessful parliamentary candidate, 1841–52; lectured in the United States, 1866, 1867, 1869, and 1875. [lviii. 358]

VINCENT, JOHN (1591–1646), puritan; of New College, Oxford, 1609; beneficed in Cornwall, but ejected for nonconformity; intruded rector of Sedgefield, 1643.
[lviii. 360]

VINCENT, JOHN PAINTER (1776–1852), surgeon; trained in London; assistant-surgeon, 1807, and surgeon, 1816–47, to St. Bartholomew's Hospital, London; P.R.C.S., 1832 and 1840.   [lviii. 359]

VINCENT, NATHANIEL (1639?–1697), nonconformist divine; third son of John Vincent [q. v.]; chorister of Corpus Christi College, Oxford, 1648; M.A., Christ Church, Oxford, 1657; chaplain of Corpus Christi College, Oxford; nominated fellow of Durham College, 1657; intruded rector of Langley Marish, 1650; ejected, 1662 nonconformist preacher in Southwark, 1666; imprisoned, 1670; prosecuted again, 1682 and 1686; published devotional works and sermons.   [lviii. 360]

VINCENT, PHILIP (*fl.* 1638), author of a narrative of the conflict of the New England colonists with the Pequot Indians, and of a description of the desolation of Germany, both published in 1638; appears to have visited Guiana, New England (*c.* 1632), and South Germany (*c.* 1636).   [lviii. 361]

VINCENT, RICHARD BUDD (1770?–1831), served in the navy, 1781–1816; lieutenant, 1790; captain, 1805; saved a convoy by sacrificing his unseaworthy sloop-of-war, 1805; C.B., 1815.   [lviii. 362]

VINCENT, THOMAS (1634–1678), nonconformist divine; second son of John Vincent [q. v.]; M.A. Christ Church, Oxford, 1654; intruded rector of St. Mary Magdalene, Milk Street, London, 1656; ejected, 1662; preacher and schoolmaster at Hoxton; published an account of the great plague, 1667, and sermons.   [lviii. 363]

VINCENT, WILLIAM (1739–1815), dean of Westminster; at Westminster School, 1747–57; M.A. Trinity College, Cambridge, 1764; D.D., 1776; usher at Westminster, 1761, second master, 1771, and head-master, 1788–1802; beneficed in London, 1778–1807; sub-almoner, 1784; canon, 1801, and dean of Westminster, 1802–15; rector of Islip, Oxfordshire, 1807–15; superintended restoration works in Westminster Abbey from 1807; some of his Latin verses translated by Cowper; published pamphlets, sermons, and, 1797–1813, treatises on ancient geography.   [lviii. 363]

VINER, CHARLES (1678–1756), jurist; of Hart Hall, Oxford, 1695; published 'Abridgment of Law and Equity,' 23 vols., 1742–53 (the index by Robert Kelham [q. v.], produced, 1758); founder of the Vinerian common law professorship, scholarships, and fellowships at Oxford.   [lviii. 365]

VINER, SIR ROBERT, first baronet (1631–1688), lord mayor of London; apprentice and then partner with his uncle, Sir Thomas Viner [q. v.], goldsmith and banker of London; alderman of London, 1666; sheriff, 1666; lord mayor, 1674; knighted, 1665; created baronet, 1666; erected the equestrian statue of Charles II in Stocks Market, London, May 1672 (taken down, 1736); did a large business for government; ruined by the dishonest closing of the exchequer, 1672; bankrupt; his bankruptcy finally settled by act of parliament, 1699.   [lviii. 366]

VINER, SIR THOMAS, baronet (1588–1665), lord mayor of London; came to London, 1600; brought up by Samuel Moore, goldsmith; alderman of London, 1646–1660, sheriff, 1648, lord mayor, 1653; knighted, 1654; created baronet, 1661; did much government banking business from James I's to Charles II's time; benefactor of the Goldsmiths' Company.   [lviii. 368]

VINER, WILLIAM LITTON (1790–1867), composer of church music; organist at Bath, 1820, and at Penzance, 1835; emigrated, 1859; died in Massachusetts.   [lviii. 369]

VINES, RICHARD (1585–1651), colonist; born in Devonshire; studied medicine; explored Maine, 1609; agent for Sir Ferdinando Gorges [q. v.] in Massachusetts, 1615–40; acting-governor of Massachusetts, 1643–5; planter in Barbados, *c.* 1646–51.   [lviii. 369]

VINES, RICHARD (1600?–1656), puritan divine; M.A. Magdalene College, Cambridge, 1627; schoolmaster at Hinckley, 1624–*c.* 1642; non-resident rector of Weddington, 1628, and of Caldecote, 1630; preacher at Nuneaton; an active member of the Westminster Assembly from June 1643; intruded rector of St. Clement Danes, London, 1643–5; intruded master of Pembroke Hall,

Cambridge, 1644–50; refused the 'engagement,' 1649; minister of St. Lawrence Jewry, London, 1650–6; published sermons.   [lviii. 369]

VINING, FREDERICK (1790?–1871), comedian; first appeared on the provincial stage, 1806, and in London, 1813.   [lviii. 371]

VINING, GEORGE J. (1824–1875), actor; son of James Vining [q. v.]; educated in France; a London bank-clerk; first appeared in London (Marylebone Theatre), 1847.   [lviii. 371]

VINING, JAMES (1795–1870), actor; appeared on the London stage, 1828–60.   [lviii. 371]

VINSAUF, GEOFFREY DE (*fl.* 1200), poet; called also 'Anglicus'; styled 'de Vino Salvo,' from a treatise on vine-culture, formerly attributed to him; compiled a once popular art of poetry, 'Poetria Novella'; adherent of Richard I; visited Italy and was favoured by Pope Innocent III.   [lviii. 372]

VINT, WILLIAM (1768–1834), congregational divine; minister at Idle, near Leeds, 1790–1834; divinity tutor of a nonconformist seminary at Idle (known from 1826 as Airedale Independent College), 1800–34; published sermons and theological pieces at a private press at Idle, 1824–34.   [lviii. 373]

VIOLET, PIERRE (1749–1819), miniature-painter and etcher; in Paris, 1789; exhibited in London, 1790–1819, miniatures and fancy subjects; published etchings, 1810, and a treatise on miniature-painting before 1788.   [lviii. 373]

VIOLET, THOMAS (*fl.* 1634–1662), goldsmith and alderman of London; imprisoned for exporting gold and silver, 1634; turned informer against other merchants, 1635; imprisoned as a royalist, 1642, 1644–8; informer against exporters of silver, 1652–3; published pamphlets against the exportation of coin.   [lviii. 374]

VIOLETTI, EVA MARIA (1724–1822), wife of Garrick; reputed daughter of Veigel, a Viennese citizen; came to London, 1746; dancer at the Haymarket; guest of the Earl and Countess of Burlington, who, on her marriage (1749) to Garrick, settled 6,000*l.* on her.   [xxi. 19]

VIRGILIUS, SAINT (*d.* 785). [See FERGIL.]

VIRTUE, GEORGE (1793?–1868), London publisher; brought out books illustrated by fine copper and steel engravings; proprietor of the 'Art Journal.'   [lviii. 374]

VIRTUE, JAMES SPRENT (1829–1892), art publisher; son of George Virtue [q. v.]; manager of the New York branch, 1848–55; manager of the London publishing house, 1855; proprietor of the 'Art Journal,' 1855–92.   [lviii. 374]

VITALIS, ORDERICUS (1075–1143?). [See ORDERICUS.]

VITELL or **VITELLS**, CHRISTOPHER (*fl.* 1555–1579), familist; originally a joiner of Delft; came to England before 1555; prisoner for Arianism in London, *c.* 1558; apostle of the 'family of love' in Cambridgeshire and Essex; issued translations of familist tracts, 1574.   [lviii. 375]

VITELLI, CORNELIO (*fl.* 1489), earliest teacher of Greek at Oxford; born in the Romagna; lectured on Greek in New College, Oxford, 1475–89, in Paris, 1489, and in Exeter College, Oxford, 1491; published classical commentaries.   [lviii. 376]

VIVARES, FRANÇOIS (1709–1780), landscape-engraver; a Frenchman; came to London, 1727; engraved from landscape-painters for John Boydell; kept a print-shop, 1750–80.   [lviii. 376]

VIVARES, THOMAS (*fl.* 1770–1790), engraver; son and assistant of François Vivares [q. v.]   [lviii. 376]

VIVES, JOHANNES LUDOVICUS (1492–1540), scholar; born at Valentia in Spain; went to Paris, 1509; resided chiefly at Bruges, 1512–23; published his first book, Paris, 1514; lectured on Latin authors at Louvain, 1520, 1521–2; wrote a commentary on Augustine's 'De Civitate Dei,' 1521–2; introduced to Henry VIII and his Spanish consort at Bruges, 1521; invited by Henry VIII to England, 1523; D.C.L. Oxford; in residence at Corpus Christi College, Oxford, 1523; fellow of Corpus Christi

College, Oxford; went to Bruges; again visited England, 1527; offended Henry VIII by supporting Queen Catherine, and the queen by withdrawing his advocacy after imprisonment, 1528; withdrew to Bruges; published his chief philosophical treatises, including those on education, 1529–31; died at Bruges; a voluminous writer in theology, philology, philosophy, law, and history; collected works first published, 1555; a fuller edition, 1782–1790. [lviii. 377]

VIVIAN, SIR CHARLES CRESPIGNY, second BARON VIVIAN (1808–1886), son of Sir Richard Hussey Vivian, first baron Vivian [q. v.]; served in the army, 1825–34; major, 1834; M.P., Bodmin, 1835–42; succeeded to barony, 1842; lord-lieutenant of Cornwall, 1856–77. [lviii. 380]

VIVIAN, SIR HENRY HUSSEY, first BARON SWANSEA (1821–1894), educated at Eton, Cambridge, and abroad; copper merchant in Liverpool, 1842; patented metallurgical processes, 1843–69; director of smelting works at Swansea, 1845–94; took an active part in public affairs in South Wales; liberal M.P., Truro, 1852–7, Glamorganshire, 1857–85, Swansea, 1885, 1886, and 1892–3; created baronet, 1852; Baron Swansea, 1893. [lviii. 379]

VIVIAN, SIR HUSSEY CRESPIGNY, third BARON VIVIAN (1834–1893), diplomatist; eldest son of Sir Charles Crespigny Vivian, second baron Vivian [q. v.]; clerk in foreign office, 1851–72; agent at Alexandria, 1873, 1876–9, at Bucharest, 1874–6; ambassador at European courts, 1879–93; British plenipotentiary to the slave-trade conference at Brussels, 1889, and G.C.M.G. [lviii. 380]

VIVIAN, SIR RICHARD HUSSEY, first BARON VIVIAN (1775–1842), lieutenant-general; entered the army, 1793; captain, 1794; lieutenant-colonel, 1804; lieutenant-general, 1827; served in Flanders, 1794–5, Holland, 1799, Spain, 1808–9, 1813–14, at Waterloo and in France, 1815–1818; commander of the forces in Ireland, 1831; master-general of the ordnance, 1835; K.C.B., 1815; M.P., Truro, 1820–5, Windsor, 1826–31, East Cornwall, 1837–41; created baronet, 1828; privy councillor, 1835; created Baron Vivian, 1841; died at Baden-Baden. [lviii. 380]

VIVIAN, SIR ROBERT JOHN HUSSEY (1802–1887) general; natural son of Sir Richard Hussey Vivian [q. v.]; lieutenant in the East India Company's service, 1819; captain, 1825; major-general, 1854; general, 1870; served in the Burmese war, 1824–6; served, with frequent furloughs, in India, 1827–54; commanded Turkish contingent in Crimea, 1855–6; K.C.B., 1857; retired, 1877. [lviii. 383]

VIZETELLY, FRANK (1830–1883 ?), artist; first worked for the 'Pictorial Times'; editor of 'Le Monde Illustré,' Paris, 1857–9; war correspondent of the 'Illustrated London News,' 1859 till death; perished with Hicks Pasha in the Sudan. [lviii. 386]

VIZETELLY, HENRY (1820–1894), artist and publisher; of Italian extraction; son of a London publisher; wood-engraver; started the 'Pictorial Times,' 1843, and the 'Illustrated News,' 1855; correspondent of the 'Illustrated London News' at Paris, 1865–72, and Berlin, 1872; wrote much and translated much, 1867–90; publisher in London, 1879, issuing translations of French fiction; fined for issuing an English version of Zola's 'La Terre,' 1888; imprisoned for repeating his offence, 1889; published an autobiography, 1893. [lviii. 384]

VOELCKER, JOHN CHRISTOPHER AUGUSTUS (1822–1884), agricultural chemist; pharmacist at Frankfort-on-Main; studied chemistry at Göttingen, 1844–6; Ph.D.; went to Edinburgh, 1847; chemistry professor at Cirencester Agricultural College, 1849–63; consulting agricultural chemist, 1855–84; resided in London from 1863; F.R.S., 1870; contributed to scientific journals. [lviii. 386]

VOGEL, SIR JULIUS (1835–1899), premier of New Zealand; educated at University College School, London, and Royal School of Mines; emigrated to Victoria goldfields; settled in Dunedin, New Zealand, 1861; started 'Otago Daily Times'; member of Otago provincial council, 1862; head of provincial executive, 1866–9; member of New Zealand House of Representatives, 1863; colonial treasurer, 1869, in cabinet of Sir William Fox [q. v.], and later head of post office and of departments of customs and telegraphs; premier; adopted policy of borrowing money in London for development of natural resources of the island, and when, 1876, he resigned premiership and came to England as agent-general, left New Zealand prosperous; knighted, 1875; resigned agent-generalship and returned to colonial parliament as member for Christ Church, 1884; treasurer under radical chief, Sir Robert Stout, 1884–7; leader of opposition, 1887; published 'Great Britain and her Colonies,' 1865, and other works; died in England. [Suppl. iii. 500]

VOKES, FREDERICK MORTIMER (1846–1888), actor in burlesque and dancer; went on the stage, 1854; appeared jointly with his sisters as 'The Vokes Children,' 1861, and afterwards as 'the Vokes family'; met with great success in London, the provinces, France, and America. [lviii. 387]

VOKES, JESSIE CATHERINE BIDDULPH (1851–1884), actress and dancer. [lviii. 388]

VOKES, ROSINA (1858–1894), actress in burlesque; married Cecil Clay, 1870; toured in the United States, 1885–93. [lviii. 388]

VOKES, VICTORIA (1853–1894), actress and singer. [lviii. 387]

VOKINS, JOAN (d. 1690), quakeress; née Bunce; married Richard Vokins of West Challow; preached in America and the West Indies, 1680–1, and in Ireland, 1686; her writings published, 1691. [lviii. 388]

VOLENTIUS, THOMAS (1582–1660 ?). [See WILLIS.]

VOLUSENE, FLORENCE (1504 ?–1547 ?), scholar, whose surname was possibly 'Wolson' or 'Wolsey'; born in Elginshire; educated at Aberdeen; resided in Paris, 1528–35, first as tutor to Wolsey's son (Thomas Wynter), then as political agent for Thomas Cromwell; lecturer on Latin authors at Carpentras, near Avignon, 1536–46; died at Vienne, Dauphiné; published, at Lyons, 'Commentatio quædam,' (devotional tract) and 'De Animi Tranquillitate' (philosophical dialogue), 1543; wrote Latin verses. [lviii. 389]

VON HOLST, THEODOR (1810–1844), historical painter; of Livonian extraction; born and trained in London; exhibited in London, 1827–44. [lviii. 391]

VORTIGERN (fl. 450), philologically 'supreme lord'; historically, according to Gildas, supplemented by Bede, the prince of south-east Britain, who called in the Saxons to repel the northern tribes; traditionally, according to Nennius and Geoffrey of Monmouth, the traitor who, for love of the beautiful Saxon, Rowena, ruined the British cause; conjectured by some modern writers to have been leader of a native, at feud with a Roman, party among the Britons. [lviii. 391]

VOS or **VOSSIUS**, GERARD JOHN (1577–1649), scholar; born near Heidelberg; professor at Leyden, 1622; invited to England and made canon of Canterbury, 1629; history professor at Amsterdam, 1633; author of a 'Historia Pelagiana.' [lviii. 392]

VOSSIUS, ISAAC (1618–1689), scholar; son of Gerard John Vos [q. v.]; born at Leyden; edited the 'Periplus' of Scylax, 1639; visited Italy, 1642; edited seven epistles of St. Ignatius, 1646; royal librarian at Stockholm, 1649–52; supported the Septuagint against the received chronology, 1659–61; wrote against Cartesianism, 1662–3; edited Pliny's 'Natural History,' 1669; invited to England by Dr. John Pearson, 1670; hon. D.C.L. Oxford, 1670; canon of Windsor, 1673–89; published 'De Poematum cantu,' a treatise on prosody, 1673, and 'De . . . Oraculis,' 1679; edited Catullus, 1684, and Juvenal, 1685; published 'Observationes' on classical topics, 1685; worked also on Lucretius, Anacreon, Hesychius of Alexandria, and Arrian. His library of manuscripts went to Leyden, 1710; his correspondence is largely in the Bodleian. [lviii. 392]

VOWELL, JOHN (1526 ?–1601). [See HOOKER, JOHN.]

VOYSEY, alias HARMAN, JOHN (1465 ?–1554). [See VEYSEY.]

VULLIAMY, BENJAMIN LEWIS (1780–1854), clockmaker, of London; published treatises on clock-work, 1828–48. [lviii. 396]

VULLIAMY, GEORGE JOHN (1817–1886), architect; second son of Benjamin Lewis Vulliamy [q. v.]; pupil of Sir Charles Barry [q. v.], 1836–41; settled in London, 1843; architect to the metropolitan board of works, 1861–1886. [lviii. 396]

VULLIAMY, LEWIS (1791–1871), architect; pupil of Sir Robert Smirke [q. v.]; settled in London, 1822; designed many churches and mansions. [lviii. 397]

VYCHAN (*fl.* 1230-1240). [See EDNYVED.]

VYCHAN, HOWEL (*d.* 825). [See HOWEL.]

VYCHAN, SIMWNT (1530 ?-1606). [See SIMWNT.]

VYNER. [See VINER.]

VYSE, RICHARD (1746-1825), general; entered the army, 1763; colonel of dragoons, 1781; served in Flanders, 1794; M.P., Beverley, 1806; general, 1812.   [lviii. 398]

VYSE, RICHARD WILLIAM HOWARD (1784-1853), major-general; son of Richard Vyse [q. v.]; assumed Howard as additional name, 1812, on succeeding

to Northamptonshire estates; entered the army, 1800; captain, 1802; major-general, 1846; M.P., Beverley, 1807-1812, Honiton, 1812-18; hon. D.C.L. Oxford, 1810; high sheriff for Buckinghamshire, 1824; explored the Pyramids, 1835-7.   [lviii. 398]

VYVYAN, SIR RICHARD RAWLINSON, eighth baronet (1800-1879), of Trelowarren; of Harrow and Christ Church, Oxford; succeeded to title and estates, 1820; tory M.P., Cornwall, 1825, 1826, 1830, Okehampton, 1831, Bristol, 1832 and 1835, Helston, 1841-57; high sheriff for Cornwall, 1840; published philosophical treatises, 1825-45.   [lviii. 399]

W

WAAD or **WADE**, ARMAGIL (*d.* 1568), styled ' the English Columbus'; native of Yorkshire; B.A. Magdalen College, Oxford, 1532; sailed to Cape Breton and Newfoundland, 1536; clerk of the council at Calais, 1540; chief clerk to the privy council, 1552-3; M.P., Wycombe, 1547-53; granted Milton Grange, Oxfordshire, 1554; envoy to Holstein, 1559; employed on the public service, 1562 and 1566.   [lviii. 400]

WAAD, SIR WILLIAM (1546-1623), diplomatist; a younger son of Armagil Waad [q. v.]; succeeded to the estate, 1568; entered Gray's Inn, 1571; travelled; collected news for Burghley in Paris, 1576, in Italy, 1578-9, at Strasburg, 1580, and in Paris, 1580; ambassador to Portugal, 1580; returned to England, 1581; clerk of the privy council, 1583-1613; employed on foreign missions, 1583-5; seized Mary Stuart's papers, 1586; envoy to France, 1587; M.P., Thetford, 1588, Preston, 1601, West Looe, 1605; tracked out Roderigo Lopez's plot, 1594, and other catholic schemes; knighted, 1603; investigated the Main and By plots, 1603, and Gunpowder plot, 1605; lieutenant of the Tower, 1605-13; a member of the Virginia Company, 1609.   [lviii. 401]

WACE (*fl.* 1170), chronicler; born in Jersey; educated at Caen; wrote many narrative poems in French (remains printed, 1836-79); began, at Henry II's instance, ' Roman de Rou' (a history of the ruling Norman house to 1107), 1160; prebendary of Bayeux, 1169. [lviii. 404]

WADD, WILLIAM (1776-1829), surgeon; educated at Merchant Taylors' School and St. Bartholomew's Hospital, London; practised surgery in London; published surgical treatises, 1809-24, and professional chit-chat, 1824-7; accidentally killed at Killarney.   [lviii. 405]

WADDELL, PETER HATELY (1817-1891), Scottish divine; educated at Glasgow; free church minister at Girvan, 1844-61; independent minister in Glasgow, 1862-1888; American D.D.; edited Burns, 1867-9, and the Waverley novels, 1882-5; turned the Psalms, 1871, and Isaiah, 1879, into ' Scottis.'   [lviii. 405]

WADDILOVE, ROBERT DARLEY (1736-1828), dean of Ripon; originally Robert Darley; added Waddilove on succession to property; of Westminster and Clare Hall, Cambridge; M.A., 1762; non-resident incumbent in Yorkshire; embassy chaplain at Madrid, 1771-9; examined manuscripts and pictures in Spain; prebendary of Ripon, 1780, of York, 1782; archdeacon of East Riding, 1786; dean of Ripon, 1791-1828; LL.D. Lambeth. [lviii. 406]

WADDING, LUKE (1588-1657), Franciscan; native of Waterford; educated in Portugal; became a Franciscan, 1607; president of the Irish College, Salamanca, 1617; chaplain to the Spanish embassy at Rome, 1618-57; founder and first rector of St. Isidore's College (for Irish students), Rome, 1625-40; instigated Irish rebellion of 1641; published history of Franciscans and theological tractates.   [lviii. 407]

WADDING, PETER (1581 ?-1644), jesuit; native of Waterford; educated at Douay; M.A., D.D., and LL.D.; became a jesuit, 1601; theology professor successively at Louvain, Antwerp, Prague, Gratz; published theological works.   [lviii. 408]

WADDINGTON, CHARLES (1796-1858), military engineer; educated at Addiscombe; second lieutenant, Bom-

bay engineers, 1813; captain, 1825; major-general, 1854; served in India, 1814-47, 1854-8, and at Aden, 1847-54.   [lviii. 408]

WADDINGTON, EDWARD (1670 ?-1731), bishop of Chichester; educated at Eton; fellow of King's College, Cambridge; M.A., 1695, D.D., 1710; rector of Wexham, 1702, of All Hallows the Great, London, 1712; fellow of Eton, 1720; bishop of Chichester, 1724-31; published sermons.   [lviii. 409]

WADDINGTON, GEORGE (1793-1869), traveller and church historian; at the Charterhouse, London, 1808-11; fellow of Trinity College, Cambridge, 1817; M.A., 1818; D.D., 1840; travelled in Ethiopia, 1821, and Greece, 1823-4; published a church history, 1833, and an account of the reformation in Germany, 1841; vicar of Masham, 1833-40; dean of Durham, 1840-69.   [lviii. 410]

WADDINGTON, JOHN (1810-1880), congregational divine; studied at Airedale College; pastor at Stockport, 1833, and in Southwark, 1846; D.D.; published memoirs of congregationalists, histories of congregationalism, and sermons.   [lviii. 410]

WADDINGTON, SAMUEL FERRAND (*fl.* 1790-1812), politician; educated in Germany; hop merchant near Tonbridge; opposed war with the French republic, 1795; answered Edmund Burke, 1796; published pamphlets on the hop trade and on political questions.   [lviii. 411]

WADE or **WAAD**, ARMAGIL (*d.* 1568). [See WAAD.]

WADE, SIR CLAUDE MARTINE (1794-1861), colonel; served in India, 1809-44; captain, 1825; lieutenant-colonel and knighted, 1839; employed in negotiations with Ranjit Singh, 1823-44; forced the Khaibar Pass and entered Kabul, 1839; political agent at Indore, 1840-4.   [lviii. 411]

WADE, GEORGE (1673-1748), field-marshal; an Irishman; ensign, 1690; lieutenant-colonel, 1703; served in Flanders, 1692 and 1702-3, in Spain, 1704-10; distinguished himself in the battles of Almanza, 1707, and Saragossa, 1710, and at the taking of Minorca, 1708; major-general, 1714; M.P., Hindon, 1715; stationed at Bath to overawe the western Jacobites, 1715; served in the Vigo expedition, 1719; M.P., Bath, 1722-48; sent to the highlands, 1724, where he made military roads, 1726-1733; lieutenant-general, 1727; field-marshal, 1743; commanded in Flanders, 1744-5; commander-in-chief in England, 1745; sent against Prince Charles Edward; superseded for failing to stop his march.   [lviii. 413]

WADE, JOHN (1788-1875), author; leader-writer in the ' Spectator,' 1828-58; published ' The Black Book,' an exposure of sinecures, 1820-3, a British history, 1839, a gazetteer of the world, 1853, and popular treatises on social questions; granted a civil-list pension, 1862.   [lviii. 416]

WADE, JOSEPH AUGUSTINE (1796 ?-1845), composer; native of Dublin; opera-conductor in London; among other works brought out an oratorio, 1824, and an opera, 1826; died insane.   [lviii. 417]

WADE, NATHANIEL (*d.* 1718), conspirator; entered the Middle Temple, 1681; privy to the Rye House plot, 1683; escaped to Holland; served as major in Monmouth's invasion, June 1685; taken prisoner, October

1685; turned king's evidence; pardoned, 1686; town-clerk of Bristol, by James II's appointment, 1687.
[lviii. 418]

WADE, THOMAS (1805–1875), poet; resided in London; published poems, showing Shelley's influence, 'Tasso,' 1825, and 'Mundi et cordis . . . Carmina,' 1835; brought out 'Woman's Love' (otherwise 'Duke Andrea'), a romantic drama, 1828, 'The Phrenologists' (farce), 1830, and 'The Jew of Arragon' (tragedy), 1830; published verse pamphlets, 1837–9; edited 'Bell's Weekly Messenger'; withdrew to Jersey and edited there 'The British Press'; died at Jersey.
[lviii. 418]

WADE, SIR THOMAS FRANCIS (1818–1895), diplomatist; brought up at Mauritius, 1823–7, and the Cape, 1829–32; at Harrow, 1832–7, and Trinity College, Cambridge, 1837–8; entered the army, 1838; lieutenant, 1841; studied Chinese during the voyage to Hongkong, 1841–2; interpreter at Hong-Kong, 1843–51; vice-consul at Shanghai, 1852; Chinese secretary at Hong-Kong, 1855; attached to Lord Elgin's Chinese missions, 1857 and 1860; member of the Pekin legation, 1861–71, and ambassador there, 1871–83; K.C.B., 1875; Chinese professor, Cambridge, 1888; bequeathed his Chinese books to Cambridge University; published papers on China and the Chinese language, 1849–81.
[lviii. 420]

WADE, WALTER [d. 1825), Irish botanist; M.D., practising in Dublin, 1790; lectured on botany; made botanical tours in Ireland; published papers on Irish flora, 1794–1804, synopses of his lectures, and other botanical papers.
[lviii. 421]

WADE or **WAAD**, SIR WILLIAM (1546–1623). [See WAAD.]

WADER, RALPH, EARL OF NORFOLK (fl. 1070). [See GUADER.]

WADESON, ANTHONY (fl. 1600), playwright; author probably of 'Look about you,' a comedy, 1600; wrote also a sequel, 1601, 'The . . . humorous Earle of Gloster, with his conquest of Portugall,' now lost.
[lviii. 422]

WADESON, RICHARD (1826–1885), colonel; private soldier, 1843; serjeant-major, 1854; lieutenant, 1857; V.C.; captain, 1864; brevet-colonel, 1880; distinguished himself, especially in the Delhi campaign, 1857; lieutenant-governor of Chelsea Hospital, 1885. [lviii. 422]

WADHAM, JOHN (d. 1411), justice of the common pleas, 1388–97.
[lviii. 423]

WADHAM, NICHOLAS (1532–1609), founder of Wadham College, Oxford; married Dorothy Petre (1534–1618), 1555; lived retiredly at Merefield; built an alms-house at Ilton, 1606; his plans for a college at Oxford carried on by his widow, 1610, and Wadham College completed, July 1613.
[lviii. 423]

WADMORE, JAMES (1782–1853), collector of objects of vertu; a land-surveyor.
[lviii. 424]

WADSWORTH, JAMES, the elder (1572?–1623), jesuit; B.D. Emmanuel College, Cambridge, 1600; beneficed in Suffolk, 1598–1604; embassy chaplain at Madrid, 1605; official of the inquisition, Seville; English tutor to the infanta Maria, 1623.
[lviii. 424]

WADSWORTH, JAMES, the younger (1604–1656?), Spanish scholar; son of James Wadsworth the elder [q. v.]; taken to Spain, 1610; educated at Seville, Madrid, and, 1618–22, St. Omer; prisoner in Algiers, 1623; named 'captain' in the Spanish service; a government spy in England, 1625, and in Brussels and Paris, 1626; prisoner at Calais, 1627; published his 'English-Spanish Pilgrim,' 1629 (enlarged, 1630); a common informer against Romanists from 1630; published translations from the Spanish.
[lviii. 425]

WADSWORTH, THOMAS (1630–1676), nonconformist divine; fellow of Christ's College, Cambridge, 1652–4; M.A., 1654; intruded rector of St. Mary's, Newington, 1653–60; 'lecturer' in London, 1660–2; published sermons.
[lviii. 426]

WAFER, LIONEL (1660?–1705?), buccaneer; ship's surgeon, 1677–9, in a voyage to Java; surgeon at Port Royal, Jamaica, 1680; surgeon on board an English pirate in the Pacific; lamed while crossing the Isthmus of Darien, 1681, and resided for some months among the

Darien Indians; picked up by William Dampier [q. v.], with whom he subsequently cruised in the West Indies; went a buccaneering voyage with Edward Davis (fl. 1683–1702) [q. v.], 1683; settled in Virginia; returned to England, 1691; published his narrative, 1699; urged the colonisation of Darien, 1704.
[lviii. 427]

WAGER, SIR CHARLES (1666–1743), admiral; served in the navy, 1690–9, 1701–6, chiefly in the Mediterranean; in command at Jamaica, 1707–9; enriched by prize-money, defeating a Spanish treasure-fleet, 1708; at Cartagena; rear-admiral, 1707; knighted, 1709; employed at the admiralty office, 1715–33; blockaded Cadiz, 1727–8; admiral, 1731; first lord of the admiralty, 1733–1742.
[lviii. 428]

WAGER, LEWIS (fl. 1566), author of an interlude (1566), 'Repentaunce of Marie Magdalene'; rector of St. James's, Garlickhithe, 1560.
[lviii. 431]

WAGER, WILLIAM (fl. 1566), author of two interludes, 'The longer thou livest, the more foole thou art' and 'The cruell Debtter' (1566); other pieces attributed to him.
[lviii. 430]

WAGHORN, MARTIN (d. 1787), navy captain; served in the navy, 1762–4 and 1778–85; captain of the Royal George when she sank, 29 Aug. 1782; acquitted by a competent court-martial.
[lviii. 431]

WAGHORN, THOMAS (1800–1850), pioneer of the overland route (from Cairo to Suez) to India; served in the navy, 1812–17; pilot in the Bengal service, 1819–24; commanded a sloop in the Burmese war, 1824–5; advocated the overland route, 1827; established its feasibility, 1829; organised the transport service for it, before 1841; lieutenant, R.N., 1842; published pamphlets, 1831–46.
[lviii. 431]

WAGSTAFFE, JOHN (1633–1677), author of 'Witchcraft Debated' (1669), questioning the possibility of witchcraft; educated at St. Paul's School, London; M.A. Oriel College, Oxford, 1656.
[lviii. 432]

WAGSTAFFE, SIR JOSEPH (fl. 1642), royalist; major in the French service; lieutenant-colonel in the parliamentary army, 1642; changed sides, 1643; royalist major-general; knighted, 1644; headed the Wiltshire rising, 1655; petitioned for reward, 1662.
[lviii. 433]

WAGSTAFFE, THOMAS, the elder (1645–1712), nonjuror; educated at Charterhouse, London, and New Inn Hall, Oxford; M.A., 1667; incumbent of Martinsthorpe, 1669; chancellor of Lichfield, 1684; rector of St. Gabriel Fenchurch, London, 1684; ejected as a nonjuror, 1691; physician; consecrated nonjuring bishop of Ipswich, 1694; published pamphlets.
[lviii. 433]

WAGSTAFFE, THOMAS, the younger (1692–1770), nonjuror; second son of Thomas Wagstaffe the elder [q. v.]; ordained nonjuring priest, 1719; keeper of the nonjurors' church registers: Anglican chaplain to the Chevalier St. George and Prince Charles Edward at Rome, before 1738; collated manuscripts at the Vatican; published pamphlets.
[lviii. 435]

WAGSTAFFE, WILLIAM (1685–1725), physician; M.A. Lincoln College, Oxford, 1707; M.D., 1714; physician to St. Bartholomew's Hospital, 1720; his 'Miscellaneous Works' published, 1725.
[lviii. 436]

WAINEWRIGHT, THOMAS GRIFFITHS (1794–1852), poisoner and art critic; art-student in London, 1814; wrote art critiques for the 'London Magazine,' 1820–3; exhibited at the Royal Academy, 1821–5; forged an order on the Bank of England, 1826; poisoned several relatives to secure money, 1828–30; imprisoned at Paris; transported for the 1826 forgery, 1837; died, a convict, in Tasmania.
[lviii. 437]

WAINFLEET, WILLIAM OF (1395?–1486). [See WAYNFLETE.]

WAIT, DANIEL GUILFORD (1789–1850), hebraist; educated at University College, Oxford, and St. John's College, Cambridge; LL.D. Cambridge, 1824; rector of Blagdon, 1819; published sermons and works of textual criticism, 1811–48; issued 'Jewish . . . Antiquities,' 1823.
[lviii. 438]

WAITE or **WAYTE**, THOMAS (fl. 1634–1668), regicide; colonel in the parliamentary army, 1643; governor of Burley House, 1644–5; M.P., Rutland, 1646–

1653; suppressed the Peterborough rising, 1648; gave evidence against the Duke of Hamilton; one of Charles I's judges; imprisoned from 1660. [lviii. 439]

WAITHMAN, ROBERT (1764-1833), politician; made a competence as a London linendraper; agitated against war with the French republic, 1794; alderman of London, 1818, sheriff, 1820, lord mayor, 1823, and M.P., London, 1818-20, 1826-33; published pamphlets.
[lviii. 440]

WAKE, HEREWARD THE (*fl.* 1070). [See HEREWARD.]

WAKE, SIR ISAAC (1580?-1632), diplomatist; entered Christ Church, Oxford, 1593; fellow of Merton College, Oxford, 1598; M.A., 1603; public orator, 1604; welcomed James I to Oxford, 1605 (the event described in his 'Rex Platonicus,' 1607); secretary of embassy at Venice, c. 1610, and Turin, c. 1614; ambassador, with occasional absences on missions, at Turin, 1615-30; knighted, 1619; M.P., Oxford University, 1624; ambassador at Paris, 1631; published Latin speeches, &c.; died at Paris. [lviii. 441]

WAKE, THOMAS (1297-1349), baron; succeeded his father, 1300; his chief estates in Lincolnshire; a royal ward; married Blanche, daughter of Henry of Lancaster [q. v.]; given possession of his estates, 1317; joined the rising against Edward II and the Despensers, 1326; constable of the Tower of London, 1326; joined the rising against Isabella and Mortimer, 1328; fined and deprived of his offices, 1329; restored to his lands and offices, 1331; governor of the Channel islands; imprisoned, 1340.
[lviii. 442]

WAKE, WILLIAM (1657-1737), archbishop of Canterbury; M.A. Christ Church, Oxford, 1679; D.D., 1689; chaplain to the embassy at Paris, 1682-5; preacher at Gray's Inn, 1688-96; canon of Christ Church, Oxford, 1689-1702; dean of Exeter, 1703; rector of St. James's, Westminster, 1693-1706; bishop of Lincoln, 1705; translated to Canterbury, 1716; negotiated for union with the French Jansenists, 1717-20; published theological treatises; bequeathed his library to Christ Church, Oxford.
[lviii. 445]

WAKEFELD, ROBERT (d. 1537), orientalist; studied at Cambridge before 1514, and abroad; Hebrew professor at Louvain, 1519, Tübingen, 1520-3; taught Hebrew at Cambridge, 1524, and Oxford, 1530; wrote in favour of Henry VIII's divorce, 1528; canon of Christ Church, Oxford, 1532; his treatises the first in England (1524) to employ Hebrew and Arabic type. [lviii. 446]

WAKEFIELD, THOMAS (d. 1575), hebraist; M.A. Cambridge; first regius professor of Hebrew, Cambridge, 1540; taught, 1540-9 and 1553-69; probably rejected protestantism. [lviii. 448]

WAKEFIELD, ARTHUR (1799-1843), colonist; son of Edward Wakefield [q. v.]; captain in the navy; founded Nelson, New Zealand, 1841; killed in battle with the Maoris. [lviii. 457]

WAKEFIELD, DANIEL (1776-1846), writer on political economy, son of Priscilla Wakefield [q. v.]; barrister, Lincoln's Inn, 1802; equity draughtsman.
[lviii. 448]

WAKEFIELD, EDWARD (1774-1854), author of 'Ireland : statistical and political,' 1812; son of Priscilla Wakefield [q. v.]; farmer at Romford; land-agent in London. [lviii. 448]

WAKEFIELD, EDWARD GIBBON (1796-1862), colonial statesman; son of Edward Wakefield [q. v.]; employed at the embassy at Turin, 1814-16; eloped with a ward of court, 1816; attached to the embassy at Paris, 1820-6; abducted an heiress, 1826; imprisoned, 1826-9, and his marriage cancelled by parliament; urged reforms in the administration of the Australian colonies, 1829-49; procured the discontinuance of free grants of land in New South Wales, 1831; secured formation of South Australian Association, 1834 (colony founded, 1836); London agent of the New Zealand Land Company, 1839-46; emigrated to Wellington, New Zealand, 1853; published political pamphlets. [lviii. 449]

WAKEFIELD, EDWARD JERNINGHAM (1820-1879), colonist; son of Edward Gibbon Wakefield [q. v.]; visited Canada, 1838, and New Zealand, 1839-44; published notes of his New Zealand experiences, 1845; settled in New Zealand, 1853; published a narrative of the Canterbury settlement, 1868. [lviii. 452]

WAKEFIELD, FELIX (1807-1875), engineer; son of Edward Wakefield [q. v.]; superintendent of public works, Tasmania, before 1847; visited New Zealand, 1851-4; lieutenant-colonel and constructor of the Balaclava to Sebastopol railway, 1855; returned to New Zealand, 1863. [lviii. 457]

WAKEFIELD, GILBERT (1756-1801), scholar and controversial writer; second wrangler, Jesus College, Cambridge, 1776; fellow, 1776-9; curate at Stockport and Liverpool; adopted unitarian views; classical tutor at Warrington unitarian college, 1779-83; private tutor at Nottingham, and afterwards at Hackney; published 'Silva critica,' 1789; maintained the inutility of Greek accents; edited the 'Georgics,' 1788, some Greek plays, and Horace, 1794, and Lucretius, 1796-9; conceived a violent hatred of Pitt and of Porson, assailing Porson's 'Hecuba' (1797) in a 'Diatribe Extemporalis'; imprisoned for a seditious pamphlet, 1799-1801; published also theological tractates; edited some English authors. [lviii. 452]

WAKEFIELD, PETER OF (d. 1213), hermit; known also as PETER OF PONTEFRACT; predicted, 1212, that before Ascension day, 1213, King John's crown would pass to another; prediction fulfilled in John's submission to the pope; put to death by John at Wareham.
[lviii. 455]

WAKEFIELD, MRS. PRISCILLA (1751-1832), author and philanthropist; a quakeress; married, 1771, Edward Wakefield (1750-1826), a London merchant; resided at Tottenham, where she instituted a lying-in charity, 1791, and a savings bank, 1798; published educational works for children. [lviii. 455]

WAKEFIELD, WILLIAM HAYWARD (1803-1848), colonist; son of Edward Wakefield [q. v.]; imprisoned, 1826-9, for abetting an abduction by his brother, Edward Gibbon Wakefield [q. v.]; entered the Portuguese army, 1829; colonel in the Spanish army; went to New Zealand as agent for the New Zealand Land Company, 1840; his large purchases of Maori lands annulled by the colonial government, 1840-1; founded Wellington, 1840, and settled there. [lviii. 456]

WAKEMAN, SIR GEORGE (*fl.* 1668-1685), physician; a Roman catholic; studied at St. Omer and Pavia, and probably at Paris; imprisoned as a royalist, c. 1659; created baronet, 1661; appointed physician to Queen Catherine, 1670; accused by Titus Oates of planning to poison Charles II, 1678; acquitted, 1679; went abroad; returned to London before 1685. [lix. 1]

WAKEMAN, *alias* WICHE, JOHN (d. 1549), first bishop of Gloucester; known as John Wiche; a Benedictine; possibly B.D. Oxford, 1511; possibly of Evesham Abbey, 1513; prior and, 1534, abbot of Tewkesbury; surrendered Tewkesbury to Henry VIII, 1539; took the name Wakeman; bishop of Gloucester, 1541-9. [lix. 2]

WAKERING, JOHN (d. 1425), bishop of Norwich; incumbent of St. Benet Sherehog, London, 1389-96; clerk in chancery, 1395; chancellor of the county of Lancaster, 1399; master of the rolls, 1405-15; archdeacon of Canterbury, 1409; keeper of the privy seal, 1415; consecrated bishop of Norwich, 1416; joint-envoy to the council of Constance, 1416-18; persecuted the lollards; much employed in state affairs, 1422-5. [lix. 3]

WAKLEY, THOMAS (1795-1862), medical reformer; studied surgery in London, 1815-17; practised surgery in London from 1818; seriously injured and his house burned, probably by the Thistlewood gang, 1820; became acquainted with William Cobbett [q. v.]; founded the 'Lancet,' 1823, to report medical lectures and hospital cases and to expose nepotism in hospital appointments; M.P., Finsbury, 1835-52; recognised authority in medical matters; coroner of West Middlesex, 1839-62; exposed the adulteration of food stuffs, 1851-60; died at Madeira.
[lix. 4]

WALBRAN, JOHN RICHARD (1817-1869), Yorkshire antiquary; wine merchant in Ripon; mayor of Ripon, 1856; superintended the excavations at Fountains Abbey; published Yorkshire guide-books and local histories, 1841-64. [lix. 8]

WALBURGA or **WALPURGA** (*d.* 779 ?), of English birth; sister of Willibald [q. v.]; abbess of Heidenheim, *c.* 761. [lix. 9]

WALCHER (*d.* 1080), bishop of Durham; native of Lorraine; secular priest; connected with Liège; consecrated bishop of Durham, 1071; replaced secular priests by monks in his great churches; benefactor of Jarrow and Wearmouth monasteries; administered Waltham Abbey; acted as Earl of Northumberland, 1074; won popular hatred, owing to the tyranny of his favourite officers; murdered in a tumult. [lix. 9]

WALCOT, HUMPHREY (1586–1650), royalist; high sheriff of Shropshire, 1631. [lix. 10]

WALCOT, SIR THOMAS (1629–1685), judge; son of Humphrey Walcot [q. v.]; barrister, Middle Temple, 1653; practised in the court of the marches of Wales; recorder of Bewdley, 1671–85; a justice in North Wales, 1676, and chief-justice there, 1681; M.P., Ludlow, 1679–1681; knighted, 1681; justice of the king's bench, 1683. [lix. 10]

WALCOTT, MACKENZIE EDWARD CHARLES (1821–1880), ecclesiologist; at Winchester School, 1837–40; M.A. Exeter College, Oxford, 1847; B.D., 1866; curate in and near London, 1845–53; minister of Berkeley chapel, Mayfair, London, 1867–70; precentor of Chichester, 1863–1880; wrote much on churches and cathedrals, 1847–79. [lix. 11]

WALDBY, ROBERT (*d.* 1398), archbishop of York; a Yorkshireman; Austin friar; accompanied the Black Prince to Gascony, 1355; D.D. Toulouse; envoy to Spain, 1383; bishop of Aire, Gascony, 1387; archbishop of Dublin, 1390–6; chancellor of Ireland, 1392–3; bishop of Chichester, February 1396; archbishop of York, 1397–8. [lix. 12]

WALDEGRAVE, SIR EDWARD (1517 ?–1561), politician; inherited Borley, Essex, 1543; granted church lands, 1548; in the service of Princess Mary; imprisoned for suffering mass in her household, 1551–2; M.P., Wiltshire, 1553, Somerset, 1554, Essex, 1558; privy councillor and master of the great wardrobe, 1553; knighted, 1553; granted crown lands, 1553, 1557; chancellor of the duchy of Lancaster, 1557–8; recusant prisoner in the Tower of London, 1558–61. [lix. 13]

WALDEGRAVE, FRANCES ELIZABETH ANNE, COUNTESS WALDEGRAVE (1821–1879), daughter of John Braham [q. v.]; married firstly, 1839; married secondly, 1840, George Edward, seventh earl Waldegrave (*d.* 1846); inherited his estates, 1846; married thirdly, 1847, George Granville Harcourt (*d.* 1861), of Nuneham; became a leader in London society, establishing a salon, which was much frequented by the chiefs of the liberal party; restored Strawberry Hill; married fourthly, 1863, Chichester Fortescue, afterwards Baron Carlingford [q. v.] [lix. 14]

WALDEGRAVE, GEORGE GRANVILLE, second BARON RADSTOCK (1786–1857), eldest son of William Waldegrave, first baron Radstock [q. v.]; served in the navy, 1798–1815; captain, 1807; C.B., 1815; rear-admiral, 1841; vice-admiral, 1851. [lix. 15]

WALDEGRAVE, HENRY, first BARON WALDEGRAVE (*d.* 1689), of Chewton, Somerset; fourth baronet; a Roman catholic; married Henrietta, natural daughter of James II, 1684; created Baron Waldegrave, 1686; comptroller of the household, 1687; withdrew to Paris, 1688. [lix. 16]

WALDEGRAVE, JAMES, first EARL WALDEGRAVE (1685–1741), succeeded his father, Henry Waldegrave, first baron Waldegrave [q. v.], 1689; educated in France; embraced protestantism, 1719; a lord of the bedchamber, 1723; envoy to Paris, 1725; ambassador at Vienna, 1727–1730, and Paris, 1730–40; created Earl Waldegrave, 1729; K.G., 1738; his correspondence (1728–39) in the British Museum. [lix. 16]

WALDEGRAVE, JAMES, second EARL WALDEGRAVE (1715–1763), educated at Eton; succeeded his father, James Waldegrave, first earl Waldegrave [q. v.]; lord of the bedchamber, 1743; chief confidant of George II, 1743–60; governor of the Prince of Wales (afterwards George III), 1752–6; premier, 8–12 June 1757; K.G., 1757; his 'memoirs' published, 1821. [lix. 16]

WALDEGRAVE, JOHN, third EARL WALDEGRAVE (*d.* 1784), second son of James Waldegrave, first earl Waldegrave [q. v.]; distinguished himself at St. Malo,

1758, and Minden, 1759; succeeded to the earldom, April 1763; lieutenant-general, 1772. [lix. 19]

WALDEGRAVE or **WALGRAVE**, SIR RICHARD (*d.* 1402), of Smallbridge; M.P., Suffolk, in most parliaments from 1376 to 1390; speaker of the House of Commons, 1381–2. [lix. 20]

WALDEGRAVE, ROBERT (1554 ?–1604), puritan printer; printer's apprentice in London, 1568; free of the Stationers' Company, 1576; issued his first publication, 1578; his press destroyed for issuing John Udall's [q. v.] treatise against episcopacy, 1588; imprisoned, autumn, 1588; printed at East Molesey John Penry's [q. v.] first Marprelate tract, 1588; moved his press to Fawsley, 1588, and to Coventry, 1589; visited La Rochelle, 1590; published many books at Edinburgh, 1590–1603; king's printer in Scotland, 1591; returned to London, 1603. [lix. 20]

WALDEGRAVE, SAMUEL (1817–1869), bishop of Carlisle; second son of the eighth Earl Waldegrave; a double-first at Oxford, 1839; fellow of All Souls College, Oxford, 1839–45; M.A., 1842; D.D. by diploma, 1860; rector of Barford St. Martin, 1844; Bampton lecturer, 1854; canon of Salisbury, 1857; bishop of Carlisle, 1860–9; published sermons and charges. [lix. 22]

WALDEGRAVE, SIR WILLIAM (*fl.* 1689), physician; M.D. Padua, 1659; a Roman catholic; physician to Mary Beatrice, queen of James II. [lix. 22]

WALDEGRAVE, WILLIAM, first BARON RADSTOCK (1753–1825), admiral; second son of John Waldegrave, third earl Waldegrave [q. v.]; served at sea, 1766–83, 1790, 1793–1802; lieutenant, 1772; captain, 1776; rear-admiral, 1794; third in command at St. Vincent, 1797; created Baron Radstock in the Irish peerage, 1800; admiral, 1802; G.C.B., 1815. [lix. 23]

WALDEN, BARONS HOWARD DE. [See GRIFFIN (formerly WHITWELL), JOHN GRIFFIN, 1719–1797; ELLIS, CHARLES AUGUSTUS, 1799–1868.]

WALDEN, ROGER (*d.* 1406), archbishop of Canterbury; incumbent of St. Helier's, Jersey, 1371; resident chiefly in Jersey till 1386; held benefices also in Yorkshire, 1374, Leicestershire, Westmoreland, 1385, and Essex, 1391; held prebends in Lincoln, Salisbury, Lichfield, Exeter, and St. Paul's, London; treasurer of Calais, 1387–92; rector of St. Andrew's, Holborn, London, 1391; secretary to Richard II; lord high treasurer, 1395–8; dean of York, *c.* 1395; archbishop of Canterbury during Arundel's exile, 1398; prisoner in the Tower of London, 1400; bishop of London, 1405–6. [lix. 24]

WALDEN, THOMAS (*d.* 1430). [See NETTER.]

WALDHERE or **WALDHERI** (*fl.* 705), bishop of London, 693; dead before 716. The grant to Peterborough attested by him and Archbishop Theodore [q. v.] is a forgery. [lix. 26]

WALDIE, CHARLOTTE ANN, afterwards MRS. EATON (1788–1859), visited Brussels, 1815; published a 'Narrative' of her Waterloo experiences, 1817, a description of Rome, 1820, and two novels; married Stephen Eaton, 1822. [lix. 26]

WALDIE, JANE, afterwards MRS. WATTS (1793–1826), landscape-painter; published 'Sketches' of her 1816–17 continental tour; married Captain George Augustus Watts, 1820. [lix. 26]

WALDRIC (*d.* 1112). [See GALDRIC.]

WALDRON, FRANCIS GODOLPHIN (1744–1818), writer and actor; occurs occasionally as acting in London, from 1769; brought out some feeble comedies and adaptations, 1773–1804; published a history of the English stage, 1800; edited collections of scarce tracts and some biographical collections. [lix. 27]

WALDRON, GEORGE (1690–1730 ?), author; educated at Queen's College, Oxford; revenue officer in Man; published speeches and occasional poems, 1716–23; his 'Description of the Isle of Man' published, 1731. [lix. 28]

WALE, SIR CHARLES (1763–1845), general; entered the army, 1779; lieutenant at Gibraltar, 1781–2; lieutenant-colonel, 1798; served in the West Indies, 1810–15; major-general, 1811; K.C.B., 1815; general, 1838. [lix. 28]

WALE, FREDERICK (1822–1858), soldier; served in India, 1840–58; captain, 1852; distinguished himself as a commander of native horse, 1858; killed in action. [lix. 29]

WALE, SAMUEL (*d.* 1786), historical painter; pupil of Francis Hayman [q. v.]; exhibited, 1760–78; professor of perspective to the Royal Academy, 1768, and librarian, 1782–6. [lix. 29]

WALEDEN, HUMPHREY DE (*d.* 1330?), judge; occurs as king's clerk, in charge of estates, from 1290; submitted to Edward I's taxation of the clergy, 1297; baron of the exchequer, 1306–7; acted occasionally as justice, 1309–14; steward of Windsor park and other crown estates, 1320; baron of the exchequer, 1324, till death. [lix. 30]

WALERAND, ROBERT (*d.* 1273), judge; partisan and household officer of Henry III; frequently employed as custodian of manors and castles, 1246–62; sheriff of Gloucestershire, 1246, of Kent, 1261; justiciar, 1251–8; seneschal of Gascony, 1252; in attendance on Henry III in Gascony, 1253–4; envoy to Pope Alexander IV, 1255, to Germany, 1256, to France, 1257 and 1262; justiciar, 1256; warden of the Cinque ports, 1262; declared by the barons one of Henry III's evil counsellors, 1263; fought on Henry III's side, 1264; rewarded by grants of lands, 1265; envoy to the Welsh, 1267; justiciar, 1268–71; one of Prince Edward's trustees, 1270. [lix. 31]

WALES, JAMES (1747–1795), painter; painted portraits and landscapes at Aberdeen; exhibited portraits in London, 1783–91; resided in India, painting portraits of native princes and sketching architectural remains, 1791–5. [lix. 33]

WALES, OWEN OF (*d.* 1378). [See OWEN.]

WALES, WILLIAM (1734?–1798), mathematician; astronomical observer to the Hudson's Bay transit of Venus expedition, 1769, and to James Cook's second, 1772–4, and third, 1776–80, voyages; F.R.S., 1776; mathematical master at Christ's Hospital, London, *c.* 1781–98; published astronomical and statistical papers. [lix. 33]

WALEY, JACOB (1818–1873), legal writer; educated in London; barrister, Lincoln's Inn, 1842; an eminent conveyancer; a leading member of the Jewish community; professor of political economy, University College, London, 1854–66. [lix. 34]

WALEY, SIMON WALEY (1827–1875), amateur musician; stock-exchange broker; a leading member of the London Jews; published music and notes of travel. [lix. 35]

WALEYS or **WALENSIS**. [See also WALLENSIS.]

WALEYS, WALEIS, WALLEIS, or GALEYS, SIR HENRY LE (*d.* 1302?), mayor of London; sheriff of London, 1270; mayor of Bordeaux, 1275; knighted, *c.* 1281; mayor of London, 1273–4, 1281–4, and 1298; while in office was severe against disturbers of the peace and against short-weight bakers and millers; M.P., London, 1283; often abroad on Edward I's business, 1288–97; owned much property in London. [lix. 35]

WALFORD, CORNELIUS (1827–1885), writer on insurance; solicitor's clerk; insurance agent at Witham, 1848; barrister, Middle Temple, 1860; director of various banking and insurance societies in London, 1860–85; published standard works on insurance, 1857–78, and collections concerning famines, fairs, gilds, 1877–84. [lix. 37]

WALFORD, EDWARD (1823–1897), compiler; scholar of Balliol College, Oxford, 1841; M.A., 1847; ordained, 1846; embraced Romanism; journalist in London, 1858–69; edited numerous biographical, genealogical, and topographical works, 1855–94. [lix. 39]

WALFORD, THOMAS (1752–1833), antiquary; major of militia, 1797; F.S.A., 1788; published 'The Scientific Tourist,' containing descriptions of ancient monuments, 1818. [lix. 40]

WALHOUSE, afterwards **LITTLETON**, EDWARD JOHN, first BARON HATHERTON (1791–1863). [See LITTLETON.]

WALKDEN, PETER (1684–1769), presbyterian minister; native of Lancashire; M.A. in Scotland; pastor in Yorkshire, 1709, and Lancashire, 1711–44, and at Stock-

port, 1744–69. His diary for 1725 and 1729–30 has been printed. [lix. 40]

WALKELIN or **WALCHELIN** (*d.* 1098), bishop of Winchester; appointed bishop, 1070, by his kinsman, the Conqueror; unsuccessfully proposed substituting secular canons for monks at Winchester, *c.* 1072; built Winchester new cathedral, 1079–93; destroyed the old Saxon minster, 1093; joint-regent of England during Rufus's absence, 1097–8. [lix. 40]

WALKER, ADAM (1731?–1821), author and inventor; native of Westmoreland; self-taught; mathematical teacher in the north; became a travelling lecturer on physics; settled in London; employed at Eton and Winchester; published tracts on ventilation and notes of his lectures. [lix. 42]

WALKER, ALEXANDER, first baronet (1764–1831), brigadier-general; served in the Bombay army, 1780–99; lieutenant, 1788; captain, 1797; political agent in Baroda, 1800–8; lieutenant-colonel, 1808; returned to England, 1810; brigadier-general and governor of St. Helena, 1822–1830; his collection of oriental manuscripts preserved in the Bodleian. [lix. 42]

WALKER, SIR ANDREW BARCLAY (1824–1893), benefactor of Liverpool; a wealthy brewer; mayor of Liverpool, 1873–4, 1875–7; built Liverpool art gallery and the laboratories of Liverpool University College; knighted, 1877; created baronet, 1886. [lix. 44]

WALKER, ANTHONY (1726–1765), draughtsman and engraver; son of a Yorkshire tailor; pupil of John Tinney [q. v.]; a noted book illustrator. [lix. 44]

WALKER, SIR BALDWIN WAKE, first baronet (1802–1876), admiral; entered navy, 1812; lieutenant, 1820; captain, 1838; in the Turkish navy, latterly as Yavir Pasha, 1838–45; K.C.B., 1841; re-entered the British navy, 1845; surveyor of the navy, 1848–60; created baronet, 1856; rear-admiral, 1858; commander-in-chief at the Cape, 1861–4; admiral, 1870. [lix. 44]

WALKER, SIR CHARLES PYNDAR BEAUCHAMP (1817–1894), general; ensign, 1836; captain, 1846; lieutenant-colonel, 1855; served in the Crimea, 1854, India, 1859, and China, 1860; colonel, 1860; military attaché in Prussia, 1865–77; major-general, 1873; inspector-general of military education, 1878–84; K.C.B., 1881; general, 1884. [lix. 45]

WALKER, CHARLES VINCENT (1812–1882), electrical engineer; published treatises on electricity, 1841–1850; electrician to the South-Eastern Railway, 1845–82; introduced improvements in telegraphy, 1848–9; F.R.S., 1855. [lix. 46]

WALKER, CLEMENT (*d.* 1651), presbyterian leader; a Somerset squire; student of the Middle Temple, 1611; took the parliamentary side, 1642; imprisoned for pamphlets accusing Nathaniel Fiennes of treachery at Bristol, 1643; M.P., Wells, 1645 till expelled by 'Pride's Purge,' 1648; vigorously opposed the independents; wrote against parliamentary misrule, 1647; prisoner in the Tower of London, 1649 till death, on account of his 'History of Independency,' part i., 1648, part ii., 1649, part iii. (posthumously), 1651. [lix. 47]

WALKER, DEANE FRANKLIN (1778–1865), science lecturer; son of Adam Walker [q. v.] [lix. 42]

WALKER, SIR EDWARD (1612–1677), herald; servant of Thomas Howard, earl of Arundel, 1633–9; pursuivant, 1635; Chester herald, 1638; in attendance on Charles I, 1642–5; secretary at war, 1642; a secretary of the privy council, 1644; Norroy king-of-arms, 1644; Garter, 1645; knighted, 1645; in France, 1647–8; secretary to Charles I at Newport, 1648; clerk of the council to Charles II at the Hague, 1649, and at Cologne, 1655; accompanied Charles (II) to Scotland, 1650; returned to Holland, 1650; secretary at war to Charles II, 1656; a clerk of council, 1660; ejected Sir Edward Bysshe [q. v.], the parliamentary Garter king-of-arms, 1660; quarrelled with his fellow heralds; collected narratives of the civil war, 1664; purchased Shakespeare's house at Stratford-on-Avon, 1675; wrote heraldic tracts. [lix. 48]

WALKER, ELIZABETH (1800–1876), engraver and portrait-painter; daughter of Samuel William Reynolds [q. v.]; married, 1829, William Walker (1791–1867) [q. v.]; exhibited at the Royal Academy, 1818–50. [lix. 89]

WALKER, FREDERICK (1840–1875), painter; a Londoner; architect's clerk, 1855; art student, 1857; wood-engraver's apprentice, 1858; a prolific book-illustrator, 1859–65; exhibited in oil and water colours, 1863–1875. [lix. 51]

WALKER, GEORGE (1581 ?–1651), puritan divine; born in Lancashire; M.A. St. John's College, Cambridge, 1611; rector of St. John Evangelist, Watling Street, London, 1614–51; incorporated B.D. at Oxford, 1621; engaged in controversies with Socinians, 1614, and Romanists, 1623–4; censured by Laud, 1635; published a Sabbatarian treatise, 1638; imprisoned for factious preaching, 1638–1641; member of the Westminster Assembly, 1643; published theological tracts. [lix. 53]

WALKER, GEORGE (1618–1690), governor of Londonderry; educated at Glasgow; incumbent of Lissan, co. Derry, 1669, and of Donaghmore, Tyrone, 1674; raised a regiment at Dungannon, 1688; joint-governor of Derry during its famous siege, April–July 1689, the town being relieved by water in July; sent to ask pecuniary relief for Derry in London, August 1689; published a narrative of the siege of Derry, 1689; bishop designate of Derry; honorary D.D. Cambridge and Oxford; at Belfast, March 1690; killed at the battle of the Boyne. [lix. 54]

WALKER, GEORGE (d. 1777), privateer; served in the Dutch navy in the Levant; a mercantile captain; commanded, on the American and French coasts, a privateer ship, 1739–44, and a privateer squadron, 1744–8; mercantile captain in the North Sea trade. [lix. 56]

WALKER, GEORGE (1734 ?–1807), dissenting divine and mathematician; studied mathematics at Edinburgh, 1751, and Glasgow, 1752–4; presbyterian minister at Durham, 1757–62, in Norfolk, 1762–72, and at Nottingham, 1774–98; professor at Manchester College, 1798–1803; an active politician; published sermons and mathematical works. [lix. 58]

WALKER, GEORGE (1772–1847), novelist; a London bookseller and music publisher, 1789–1847; published romances and verses, 1792–1824. [lix. 59]

WALKER, GEORGE (1803–1879), writer on chess; son of George Walker (1772–1847) [q. v.]; a leading chess-player, 1840–7; a London stockbroker, 1847–79; published chess treatises, 1832–50. [lix. 60]

WALKER, GEORGE ALFRED (1807–1884), sanitary reformer; studied medicine in London; qualified as a surgeon, 1831; visited Paris, 1836; medical practitioner in London; agitated against burying in churches and in city churchyards, 1839–51. [lix. 61]

WALKER, SIR GEORGE TOWNSHEND, baronet (1764–1842), general; entered the army, 1782; lieutenant, 1783; captain, 1791; lieutenant-colonel, 1798; major-general, 1811; distinguished himself at Vimiera, 1808; commanded a Portuguese brigade, 1811; severely wounded at Badajoz, 1812; commanded a British brigade, and afterwards a division, 1813; wounded at Orthez, 1814; K.C.B., 1815; G.C.B., 1817; lieutenant-general, 1821; commander-in-chief at Madras, 1826–31; created baronet, 1835; lieutenant-governor of Chelsea Hospital, 1837–42; general, 1838. [lix. 61]

WALKER, GEORGE WASHINGTON (1800–1859), missionary; draper's assistant at Newcastle-on-Tyne; joined the quakers, 1827; went on a missionary tour to Australia and Tasmania, 1831–8, and South Africa, 1838–1840; married and settled as a draper at Hobart Town, 1840; published tracts. [lix. 63]

WALKER, SIR HOVENDEN (d. 1728), rear-admiral; an Irishman; captain in the navy, 1692–9, 1701–11; rear-admiral and knighted, 1711; failed in an attempt on Quebec, 1711; commander-in-chief at Jamaica, 1712; removed from the list of admirals, 1715; went to Carolina, c. 1716; published a journal of his Canada expedition, 1720; resided latterly in Ireland. [lix. 64]

WALKER, JAMES (1748–1808 ?), mezzotint engraver; pupil of Valentine Green [q. v.]; published portraits, 1780–3; went to St. Petersburg as court engraver, 1784; returned to England, 1802. [lix. 66]

WALKER, JAMES (1764–1831), rear-admiral; served in the navy, 1776–83, 1789–95, 1797–1818; lieutenant, 1781; travelled on the continent, 1783–8; commander,

1794; under censure for overstepping orders, 1795–7; captain, 1797; distinguished himself at Camperdown, 1797, and Copenhagen, 1801; C.B., 1815; rear-admiral, 1821. [lix. 67]

WALKER, JAMES (1770 ?–1841), Scottish episcopalian bishop; educated at Marischal College, Aberdeen, and St. John's College, Cambridge (B.A., 1793; D.D., 1826); travelling tutor in Germany, c. 1799; incumbent of St. Peter's Chapel, Edinburgh; bishop of Edinburgh and professor in the Scottish episcopalian theological college, 1830–41; primus, 1837; published sermons. [lix. 68]

WALKER, SIR JAMES (1809–1885), colonial governor; educated at Edinburgh; clerk in the colonial office, 1825; official at Honduras, 1837, in the West Indies, 1839–69, and Bahamas, 1869–71; K.C.M.G., 1869. [lix. 69]

WALKER, JAMES ROBERTSON- (1783–1858), captain R.N.; by birth James Robertson; took the additional name Walker, 1824; served in the navy, 1801–15; lieutenant, 1808; defeated and taken prisoner by the Americans on Lake Champlain, September 1814; commander, 1815; captain, 1851. [lix. 69]

WALKER, JAMES THOMAS (1826–1896), general, royal engineers; son of a Madras civil servant; born at Cannanore, South India; trained at Addiscombe and Chatham; second lieutenant, Bombay engineers, 1844; reached Bombay, 1846; served in the Punjaub campaign, 1848–9; surveyed the northern frontier, 1849–53; frequently employed in expeditions against the hill tribes, 1849–60; lieutenant, 1853; officially connected with the trigonometrical survey of India, 1853–60; field-engineer at Delhi, 1857; captain, 1857; major, 1858; superintendent of the trigonometrical survey, 1861–83; lieutenant-colonel, 1864; visited Russia, 1864; edited the official account of the trigonometrical survey from 1871; surveyor-general of India, 1878–83; major-general, 1878; general, 1884; F.R.S., 1865; hon. LL.D. Cambridge, 1883; wrote on geographical and geodetical subjects. [lix. 70]

WALKER, JOHN (d. 1588), divine; B.A. Cambridge, 1547; D.D., 1569; incumbent of Alderton, before 1562; preacher at Ipswich and, 1564, Norwich; canon of Norwich, 1569, and of St. Paul's, London, 1575–88; archdeacon of Essex, 1571–85; rector of Laindon, 1573; wrote theological tracts. [lix. 72]

WALKER, JOHN (1692 ?–1741), classical scholar; educated at Wakefield School and Trinity College, Cambridge; B.A., 1713; M.A. and fellow, 1717; went to Paris, 1719, as emissary of Bentley, for purpose of collecting various readings for proposed Græco-Latin New Testament projected by Bentley, c. 1716; at Paris, Brussels, and elsewhere he collated numerous manuscripts; many of his collections in Trinity College Library, Cambridge; dean and rector of Bocking, 1725; chancellor of St. David's, 1727; D.D., 1728; archdeacon of Hereford, 1729; rector of St. Mary Aldermary, and incumbent of St. Thomas the Apostle, London, 1730; chaplain to George II. [Suppl. iii. 502]

WALKER, JOHN (1674–1747), ecclesiastical historian; fellow of Exeter College, Oxford, 1695–1700; M.A., 1699; rector of St. Mary Major, Exeter, 1698; hon. D.D. Oxford, 1714; prebendary of Exeter, 1714; published his account of the sufferings of the clergy during the Commonwealth period, 1714; rector of Upton Pyne, 1720–47; his manuscript collections in the Bodleian. [lix. 72]

WALKER, JOHN (fl. 1800), landscape-engraver; son of William Walker (1729–1793) [q. v.] [lix. 44]

WALKER, JOHN (1731–1803), botanist; born and educated in Edinburgh; minister of Glencorse, Midlothian, 1758–62, of Moffat, 1762–83, and of Colinton, 1783; sent to report on the Hebrides, 1764; honorary M.D. Glasgow, and D.D. Edinburgh, 1765; professor of natural history, Edinburgh, 1779–1803; published botanical papers. [lix. 74]

WALKER, JOHN (1732–1807), lexicographer; acted in the provinces and in London; acted in Dublin, 1758–62 and 1767; quitted the stage, 1768; taught school at Kensington, 1769–71; became a travelling lecturer on elocution; embraced Romanism; projected his 'Pronouncing Dictionary,' 1774, published it, 1791; published text-books of elocution and English grammar. [lix. 74]

WALKER, JOHN (1759–1830), man of science; a Cumberland blacksmith; engraver at Dublin, 1779–83; quaker schoolmaster at Dublin, 1783–94; published a text-book of geography, 1788, and a 'Universal Gazetteer,' 1795; studied medicine in London, 1795, and Paris, 1797; M.D. Leyden, 1799; visited Naples and Egypt, 1800–2; public vaccinator in London, 1802–30; published miscellaneous tracts. [lix. 75]

WALKER, JOHN (1770–1831), antiquary; at Winchester School, 1783–8; B.C.L. Brasenose College, Oxford, 1797; fellow of New College, Oxford, 1797; vicar of Hornchurch, 1819–31; published 'Oxoniana,' 1809, 'Letters written by Eminent Persons,' 1813, and other miscellaneous collections; edited the 'Oxford Herald' and the 'Oxford University Calendar,' 1810. [lix. 76]

WALKER, JOHN (1768–1833), founder of the 'Walkerites'; scholar, 1788, and fellow, 1791–1804, of Trinity College, Dublin; B.D., 1800; abandoned Anglicanism and founded an extreme Calvinist sect, styling itself 'The Church of God,' in Dublin, 1804; private tutor in Dublin, 1804–19, and in London from 1819; returned to Dublin, 1833; published classical, mathematical, and controversial works. [lix. 77]

WALKER, JOHN (1781?–1859), druggist in Stockton-on-Tees, 1818; invented a friction match, 1827. [lix. 77]

WALKER, JOSEPH COOPER (1761–1810), Irish antiquary; published papers on Irish history and antiquities, and on the Italian drama. [lix. 78]

WALKER, OBADIAH (1616–1699), Oxford Romanist; a Yorkshireman; fellow of University College, Oxford, 1633, till ejected by the parliamentary visitors, 1648; came under the influence of Abraham Woodhead [q. v.]; M.A., 1638; tutor and bursar of his college; visited Rome, 1648; private tutor in Surrey, 1650; recovered his fellowship, 1660; visited Rome, 1661–5; recovered his tutorship, 1665; a delegate of the Oxford University Press, 1667; elected master of University College, Oxford, June 1676; suspected of Romanism, 1678–80; publicly professed Romanism after James II's accession, January 1686; opened a Romanist chapel in his college, August 1686, and a Romanist press, 1687; left Oxford, November 1688; prisoner in the Tower of London, December 1688–January 1690; ejected from his mastership, February 1689; excepted from the act of pardon, 1690; withdrew to the continent; lived latterly on private charity in London; published educational works and theological treatises. [lix. 78]

WALKER, RICHARD (1679–1764), vice-master of Trinity College, Cambridge; fellow of Trinity College, Cambridge; M.A., 1710; D.D., 1728; curate at Upwell, 1708; junior bursar of Trinity College, Cambridge, 1717, and vice-master, 1734; supported the master, Richard Bentley (1662–1742) [q. v.], throughout his quarrel with the fellows of Trinity College; appointed professor of moral philosophy, Cambridge, 1744; rector of Thorpland, 1745–57, and of Upwell, 1757; founded the University Botanical Garden, Cambridge, 1762. [lix. 81]

WALKER, ROBERT (d. 1658?), portrait-painter; painted portraits of Cromwell and other parliamentary leaders. [lix. 82]

WALKER, ROBERT (1709–1802), styled 'Wonderful Walker' in Cumberland peasantry; native of, schoolmaster of, and finally, 1735 till death, curate of Seathwaite, Borrowdale, Cumberland; commemorated by Wordsworth. [lix. 82]

WALKER, ROBERT FRANCIS (1789–1854), translator; chorister of Magdalen College, Oxford; chaplain of New College, Oxford, 1812; M.A., 1813; curate at Purleigh, 1819–48; translated German evangelical theology, 1835–44. [lix. 83]

WALKER, SAMUEL (1714–1761), evangelical divine; B.A. Exeter College, Oxford, 1736; travelling tutor in France, 1738–40; vicar of Lanlivery, 1740–6; rector of Truro, 1746–61; vicar of Talland, 1746–52; correspondent of John and Charles Wesley; many of his sermons published posthumously. [lix. 84]

WALKER, SAYER (1748–1826), physician; presbyterian minister at Enfield; M.D. Aberdeen, 1791; accoucheur in London from 1792. [lix. 85]

WALKER, SIDNEY (1795–1846). [See WALKER, WILLIAM SIDNEY.]

WALKER, THOMAS (1698–1744), actor and dramatist; found acting in tragedy and comedy in London, 1714–42, especially as Captain Macheath in the 'Beggar's Opera,' 1728; brought out some poor adaptations and other pieces, 1724–30; died in Dublin on tour. [lix. 85]

WALKER, THOMAS (1784–1836), police magistrate and author; son of a Manchester cotton-merchant; M.A. Trinity College, Cambridge, 1811; barrister, Inner Temple, 1812; police magistrate at Lambeth, 1829; published works in favour of poor-law reform. [lix. 86]

WALKER, THOMAS (1822–1898), journalist; bred a carpenter in Oxford; self-taught; reporter in London, 1846; a sub-editor of the 'Daily News,' 1851, and editor, 1858–69; editor of the 'London Gazette,' 1869–89. [lix. 87]

WALKER, THOMAS LARKINS (d. 1860), architect; pupil of Augustus Charles Pugin [q. v.]; designed several churches and mansions, 1838–42; published architectural treatises; died at Hong Kong, 1860. [lix. 88]

WALKER, WILLIAM (1623–1684), schoolmaster; B.A. Trinity College, Cambridge; head-master of Louth and Grantham schools; vicar of Colsterworth; published grammatical text-books, including, 1673, 'A Treatise of English Particles.' [lix. 88]

WALKER, WILLIAM (1729–1793), engraver; a prolific book-illustrator. [lix. 44]

WALKER, WILLIAM (1767?–1816), lecturer on astronomy; eldest son of Adam Walker [q. v.] [lix. 42]

WALKER, WILLIAM (1791–1867), engraver; learnt engraving in Edinburgh; went to London, 1815; engraved portraits and subject-pictures. [lix. 88]

WALKER, WILLIAM SIDNEY (1795–1846), always called SIDNEY WALKER; Shakespearean critic; began writing verses, 1805; at Eton, 1811–15; B.A. Trinity College, Cambridge, 1819; fellow, 1820–9; published verses, 1813–16; edited 'Corpus Poetarum Latinorum,' 1828; dependent on private charity from 1830; his letters and poems published, 1852, and his Shakespeare notes edited by Lettsom as 'Shakespeare's Versification,' 1854, and 'A Critical Examination of the Text of Shakespeare,' 1860. [lix. 89]

WALKER-ARNOTT, GEORGE ARNOTT (179·–1868). [See ARNOTT.]

WALKINGAME, FRANCIS (fl. 1751–1785), writing-master at Kensington; published 'The Tutor's Assistant,' a school arithmetic, 1751. [lix. 90]

WALKINGTON, NICHOLAS DE (fl. 1193?). [See NICHOLAS.]

WALKINGTON, THOMAS (d. 1621), author of 'The Optick Glasse of Humors' (a forerunner of Burton's 'Anatomy of Melancholy'), 1607, and some expository tracts; M.A. St. John's College, Cambridge, 1600; D.D. Cambridge, 1613; fellow, 1602; vicar of Raunds, 1608; rector of Wadingham St. Mary, 1610; vicar of Fulham, 1615. [lix. 91]

WALKINSHAW, CLEMENTINA (1726?–1802), mistress of Prince Charles Edward; daughter of a Romanist Scottish Jacobite exile; bred at Rome; met Charles Edward in Scotland, 1746; joined him, probably in Paris, 1752; travelled with him as his wife under various aliases; believed by the Jacobites to have betrayed Prince Charles Edward's plans to her sister Catherine, a confidante of George III's mother; gave birth to a daughter, Charlotte Stuart (legitimated, 1784, died, 1789), October 1753; separated from Prince Charles Edward in consequence of his ill-usage, 1760; pensioned by his father, James 'III,' and, 1766, by his brother, the Cardinal of York; styled Comtesse d'Albertroff; withdrew to Switzerland, 1792; died at Freiburg. [lix. 91]

WALL, JOHN (1588–1666), divine; educated at Westminster and Christ Church, Oxford; M.A., 1611; D.D., 1623; vicar of St. Aldate's, Oxford, 1617; canon of Christ Church, Oxford, 1632, and of Salisbury, 1644, both till death; benefactor of Oxford city; published sermons. [lix. 93]

WALL, JOHN (1708–1776), physician ; entered Worcester College, Oxford, 1726 ; fellow of Merton College, Oxford, 1735 ; M.D., 1759 ; practised at Worcester, 1736–1776 ; published medical tracts, 1744–75. [lix. 93]

WALL, JOSEPH (1737–1802), governor of Goree (Senegambia) ; an Irishman ; entered Trinity College, Dublin, 1752 ; entered the army, 1760 ; served at Havana, 1762 ; captain, 1763 ; official of the East India Company at Bombay ; secretary at Goree, 1773 ; visited Ireland and London ; lieutenant-governor of Goree, 1779–82 ; fled to France to escape prosecution for murderous cruelty during his governorship, 1784 ; returned to England, 1797 ; at last brought to trial, 1802, and executed. [lix. 94]

WALL, MARTIN (1747–1824), physician ; son of John Wall (1708–1776) [q. v.] ; educated at Winchester ; fellow of New College, Oxford, 1763–78 ; M.D., 1777 ; physician to the Radcliffe infirmary, 1775, and lecturer on chemistry, Oxford, 1781 ; professor of clinical medicine, 1785–1824 ; F.R.C.P., 1787 ; Harveian orator, 1788 ; F.R.S., 1788. [lix. 95]

WALL, RICHARD (1694–1778), Spanish statesman ; an Irishman ; served in the Spanish fleet, 1718 ; captain of dragoons ; secretary to the Spanish embassy at St. Petersburg, 1727 ; served in Italy and the West Indies ; negotiated the peace of Aix-la-Chapelle, 1747–8 ; Spanish ambassador in London, 1748 ; recalled to Madrid, 1752 ; foreign minister ; secretary of state, 1754–64 ; pensioned ; lived latterly at Granada. [lix. 96]

WALL, WILLIAM (1647–1728), divine ; M.A. Queen's College, Oxford, 1670 (incorporated at Cambridge, 1676) ; hon. D.D., 1720 ; appointed vicar of Shoreham, 1674 ; rector of Milton-next-Gravesend, 1708–28 ; published treatises on 'Infant Baptism,' 1705–20, and on biblical criticism. [lix. 97]

WALLACE, EGLANTINE, LADY WALLACE (d. 1803), authoress ; née Maxwell ; married, 1770, Thomas Dunlop Wallace, who styled himself a baronet ; separated from her husband, c. 1783 ; travelled from 1789 ; published verses, three comedies, and other writings ; died at Munich. [lix. 97]

WALLACE, GEORGE (d. 1805 ?), Scottish advocate (1754) ; son of Robert Wallace (1697–1771) [q. v.] ; published verses and Scottish law tracts. [lix. 103]

WALLACE, GRACE, LADY WALLACE (d. 1878), authoress ; née Stein ; married, 1829, Sir Alexander Don (d. 1826), baronet ; married, 1836, Sir James Maxwell Wallace ; translated, from German and Spanish, romances and collections of letters. [lix. 98]

WALLACE, JAMES (d. 1678), covenanter ; inherited Auchans, Ayrshire, 1641 ; lieutenant-colonel in the parliamentary army ; served in Ireland, 1642–5 ; taken prisoner at Kilsyth, 1645 ; governor of Belfast, 1649 ; taken prisoner at Dunbar, 1650 ; joined the Pentland rising, 1666 ; escaped to Holland ; outlawed, 1667 ; died at Rotterdam. [lix. 98]

WALLACE, JAMES (d. 1688), writer on Orkney ; M.A. Aberdeen, 1659 ; minister of Ladykirk, Orkney, c. 1660 ; minister of Kirkwall, 1672 ; his 'Description of Orkney' published, 1693. [lix. 99]

WALLACE, JAMES (fl. 1684–1724), M.D. ; son of James Wallace (d. 1688) [q. v.] ; republished his father's book, 1700 ; F.R.S. ; visited Darien ; published a history of Scotland, 1724. [lix. 100]

WALLACE, SIR JAMES (1731 – 1803), admiral ; served in the navy, 1748–82 and 1790–7, chiefly in the West Indies and on the North American coast ; lieutenant, 1755 ; commander, 1762 ; captain, 1771 ; knighted, 1777 ; rear-admiral, 1794 ; admiral, 1801. [lix. 100]

WALLACE, SIR JOHN ALEXANDER DUNLOP AGNEW (1775 ?–1857), general ; son of Eglantine Wallace, lady Wallace [q. v.] ; ensign, 1787 ; captain, 1796 ; lieutenant-colonel, 1804 ; served in India, 1789–96, Minorca, 1798, Egypt, 1801–2, and with distinction in the Peninsula, 1809–12 ; major-general, 1819 ; K.C.B., 1833 ; general, 1851. [lix. 101]

WALLACE, SIR RICHARD, baronet (1818–1890), connoisseur ; supposed natural son of Maria (Fagnani), marchioness of Hertford ; brought up as Richard Jackson,

chiefly at Paris ; sold his art collections at Paris, 1857 ; inherited Hertford House, London, from his half-brother, 1870 ; equipped ambulances for the French service and helped besieged Paris, 1870–1 ; created baronet, 1871 ; M.P., Lisburn, 1873–85 ; founded the Hertford British hospital in Paris ; died in Paris ; the great Hertford-Wallace collection of pictures was bequeathed to the nation by his widow, 1897. [lix. 102]

WALLACE, ROBERT (1697–1771), writer on population ; entered Edinburgh University, 1711 ; minister of Moffat, 1723–33, of Grey Friars, Edinburgh, 1733–8, and of New North Church, Edinburgh, 1738–71 ; hon. D.D. Edinburgh, 1759 ; published dissertations on social questions, 1753–61 ; believed to have stimulated Malthus by a passage in his 'Various Prospects of Mankind, Nature, and Providence,' 1761. [lix. 103]

WALLACE, ROBERT (1791–1850), unitarian divine ; studied at the unitarian college, York, 1810–15 ; had a private school at Chesterfield, 1815–31 ; theological professor at Manchester College, 1840–6 ; unitarian minister at Bath, 1846 ; contributed to theological journals ; compiled 'Anti-trinitarian Biography,' 1850. [lix. 103]

WALLACE, ROBERT (1773–1855), postal reformer ; inherited Kelly, Ayrshire, 1805 ; agitated for parliamentary reform ; M.P., Greenock, 1831–46 ; advocated penny postage. [lix. 104]

WALLACE, ROBERT (1831–1899), divine and member of parliament ; M.A. St. Andrews University, 1853 ; licensed preacher, 1857 ; held charge of Trinity College Church, Edinburgh, 1860–71, and of Old Greyfriars, 1871 ; D.D. Glasgow, 1869 ; appointed by crown professor of church history, Edinburgh University, 1872 ; supported theological views and ecclesiastical reforms advocated by Dr. Robert Lee (1804–1868) [q. v.], and took prominent part in religious controversy ; left church, 1876, and was editor of the 'Scotsman' newspaper, 1876–80 ; called to bar at Middle Temple, 1883 ; radical M.P. for East Edinburgh, 1886–99. [Suppl. iii. 504]

WALLACE, THOMAS, BARON WALLACE (1768–1844), educated at Eton and Christ Church, Oxford ; M.A., 1790 ; D.C.L., 1793 ; M.P., Grampound, 1790, Penrhyn, 1796, Hindon, 1802, Shaftesbury, 1807, Weymouth, 1812, 1818, 1820, and 1826, and Cockermouth, 1813 ; a commissioner of the admiralty, 1797–1800, and of the India board, 1800–4, 1807–16 ; vice-president of the board of trade, 1818–23 ; master of the mint, 1823–7 ; created Baron Wallace, 1828. [lix. 105]

WALLACE, VINCENT (1813–1865.) [See WALLACE, WILLIAM VINCENT.]

WALLACE, SIR WILLIAM (1272 ?–1305), Scottish patriot and hero of romance ; occurs as WALAYS and WALLENSIS ; second son of Malcolm Wallace, a small landowner at Elderslie, near Paisley ; had an elder brother, Malcolm, a knight, killed after 1299, and a younger brother, John, executed in 1307 ; educated partly at Dundee ; organised the Scottish insurgents in the name of King John [de Baliol] of Scotland in the spring of 1297 ; killed Sir William Hezelrig, the English sheriff of Lanark, 1297 ; became joint-warden of Scotland ; defeated at Irvine, July 1297 ; retired to Selkirk forest, August ; drove the English out of Perth, Stirling, and Lanark shires, 1297 ; besieged Dundee and Stirling castles ; defeated the English army at Stirling bridge, September 1297 ; raised, partly by compulsion, a larger army ; drove out more English garrisons ; ravaged Northumberland, Westmoreland, and Cumberland, 1297 ; protected the monks of Hexham, 1297 ; is found styled, in a charter, knight, and warden of Scotland, March 1298 ; defeated with great slaughter by Edward I at Falkirk, 22 July 1298 ; resigned the wardenship of Scotland ; kept up a guerilla warfare till August 1299 ; withdrew to France after August 1299 ; sought aid for Scotland from Norway and France, and solicited the intervention of Pope Boniface VIII ; imprisoned for a time at Amiens, c. 1300 ; possibly visited Rome ; finally denied help by Pope Boniface VIII, August 1302, and by Philip of France, November 1302 ; conducted a guerilla warfare in Scotland, 1303–5 ; was outlawed by Edward I, 1304 ; taken prisoner by treachery near Glasgow ; brought to London, 22 Aug. 1305, tried in Westminster Hall, 23 Aug., and executed 24 Aug., his quarters gibbeted at Newcastle-on-Tyne, Berwick, Stirling, and Perth. [lix. 106]

WALLACE, WILLIAM (1768-1843), mathematician; bookbinder's apprentice and bookseller's shopman in Edinburgh; mathematical teacher at Perth, 1794, and Great Marlow military school, 1803; professor of mathematics, Edinburgh, 1819-38; LL.D. Edinburgh, 1838; inventor of the eidograph and the chorograph; contributed to mathematical journals. [lix. 115]

WALLACE, WILLIAM (1844-1897), philosopher; educated at St. Andrews and Balliol College, Oxford; M.A., 1871; fellow of Merton College, Oxford, 1867, and tutor, 1868-97; Whyte professor of moral philosophy, Oxford, 1882-97; chief works, 'The Logic of Hegel' (translated from Hegel's 'Encyclopædia of Philosophical Sciences'), 1873, 'Hegel's Philosophy of Mind' (translation), and 'The Life of Arthur Schopenhauer,' 1890.
 [lix. 116]

WALLACE, WILLIAM VINCENT (1813-1865), musical composer; generally called VINCENT WALLACE; organist of Thurles Cathedral, 1829?; professional musician in Dublin, 1829-34; a good violinist; went to Australia, 1835; went on professional tours in Tasmania, New Zealand, India, and South America; brought out two operas in London, 1845 and 1847; visited Germany and North and South America; returned to England, 1853; brought out four operas, 1860-3; died in South France; a voluminous composer. [lix. 116]

WALLACK, HENRY JOHN (1790-1870), actor; first appeared in America, 1821, and in London, 1829; died in New York. [lix. 117]

WALLACK, JAMES WILLIAM (1791?-1864), actor; appeared in pantomime, 1798; acted chiefly in London, 1804-45, with occasional visits to Dublin and the United States; withdrew to the United States, 1845; settled in New York as manager of Wallack's theatre, 1852; excellent in melodrama and light comedy, indifferent in tragedy. [lix. 117]

WALLACK, JOHN JOHNSTONE (1819-1888), actor; known as LESTER WALLACK; son of James William Wallack [q. v.]; born in New York; acted in the provinces and Dublin; met with great success in the United States, 1847 onwards; died in Connecticut; published memoirs. [lix. 119]

WALLENSIS, WALENSIS, or **GALENSIS,** JOHN (*fl.* 1215), canon lawyer; of Welsh origin; probably lecturer at Bologna; wrote legal treatises. [lix. 119]

WALLENSIS or **WALEYS,** JOHN (*fl.* 1283), Franciscan; D.D. Oxford; theological teacher in the Franciscan school in Oxford, and 1260, at Paris; envoy to the insurgent Welsh, 1282; died in Paris; theological writings of his are found in numerous manuscripts and early printed editions. [lix. 119]

WALLENSIS or **GUALENSIS,** THOMAS (*d.* 1255), bishop of St. David's; a Welshman; canon of Lincoln, 1235; D.D. Paris, 1238; archdeacon of Lincoln, 1238; bishop of St. David's, 1247-55; joined in excommunicating all violators of the Great Charter, 1253. [lix. 121]

WALLENSIS, THOMAS (*d.* 1310). [See JORZ.]

WALLENSIS or **WALEYS,** THOMAS (*d.* 1350?), Dominican; probably a Welshman; educated at Oxford and Paris; D.D.; imprisoned at Avignon for asserting the papally condemned doctrine of the saints' immediate vision of God, 1333-4; some theological treatises by him, including a commentary on St. Augustine's 'De Civitate Dei,' are extant in manuscripts. [lix. 121]

WALLER, AUGUSTUS VOLNEY (1816-1870), physiologist; brought up a vegetarian; M.D. Paris, 1840; practitioner in Kensington, 1841-51; F.R.S., 1851; conducted physiological researches at Bonn, 1851-6, and Paris, 1856; professor of physiology, Birmingham, 1858; practitioner at Geneva, 1868; invented the degeneration method of studying the paths of nerve impulses; published important papers on the nervous system; died at Geneva. [lix. 122]

WALLER, EDMUND (1606-1687), poet; inherited Beaconsfield, Buckinghamshire, 1616; educated at Eton and King's College, Cambridge; student of Lincoln's Inn, 1622; M.P. (possibly for Amersham), 1621, Ilchester, 1624, Chipping Wycombe, 1626, Amersham, 1628 and 1640; married Anne Banks (*d.* 1634), a London heiress,

1631; paid poetic court to 'Sacharissa' [see SPENCER, DOROTHY], 1635; his verses circulated in manuscript; M.P., St. Ives, Long parliament, 1640; defended episcopacy, 1641; conducted the impeachment of Sir Francis Crawley [q. v.], 1641; opposed the raising of troops by parliament, 1642; commissioner to treat with Charles I at Oxford, February 1643; leader in a plot ('Waller's plot') to seize London for Charles I, May 1643; informed against his fellow-plotters to save his life; expelled from the House of Commons, July 1643; prisoner in the Tower of London, 1643-4; fined and banished, November 1644; married Mary Bracey (*d.* 1677) and withdrew to Paris; his 'poems' published, 1645; was pardoned, November 1651, by Cromwell's influence, on which he returned to England; a commissioner of trade, 1655; published laudatory verses on Cromwell, 1655, and poems of rejoicing on Cromwell's death, 1658, and Charles II's Restoration, 1660; M.P., Hastings, 1661, sitting in the House of Commons till death; constantly advocated toleration; published 'Divine Poems,' 1685. A 'Second part' of his poems appeared posthumously, 1690.
 [lix. 123]

WALLER, SIR HARDRESS (1604?-1666?), regicide; knighted, 1629; acquired Castletown, Limerick, by marriage, 1630; served as colonel against the Irish rebels, 1641; visited England to ask help for Ireland from parliament and Charles I, 1642; governor of Cork, 1644; commanded a parliamentary regiment in England, April 1645-9; acted as one of Charles I's judges, 1649; major-general in the re-conquest of Ireland, 1650-1; supported Cromwell, 1653; granted lands in county Limerick, 1657; seized Dublin castle, 1659; sent to England, 1659; withdrew to France, c. 1660; stood his trial as a regicide, October 1660; imprisoned, October 1660 till death.
 [lix. 127]

WALLER, HORACE (1833-1896), writer on Africa; visited Central Africa, 1861-2; beneficed in Essex, 1870, and Northamptonshire, 1874-95; wrote against the slave-trade. [lix. 129]

WALLER, JOHN FRANCIS (1810-1894), author; B.A. Trinity College, Dublin, 1831; called to the Irish bar, 1833; contributed verse and prose to the 'Dublin University Magazine'; hon. LL.D. Dublin, 1852; lived latterly in London as a man of letters. [lix. 129]

WALLER, RICHARD (1395?-1462?), soldier and official; fought at Agincourt, 1415; warder of the Duke of Orleans while prisoner, 1415; fought at Verneuil, 1424; sheriff of Surrey and Sussex, 1434, and of Kent, 1438; master of the household to Cardinal Beaufort, 1439; served in France, 1443; an official of Henry VI, 1450-8; employed by Edward IV, 1461. [lix. 130]

WALLER, SIR WILLIAM (1597?-1668), parliamentary general; of Magdalen Hall, Oxford; served in Bohemia, 1620, and the Palatinate, 1621-2; knighted, 1622; married a Devonshire heiress; fined for brawling at court; M.P., Andover, Long parliament, 1640; colonel of parliamentary horse; took Portsmouth and other royalist holds, 1642; hence nicknamed 'William the Conqueror'; commanded an army in the west, 1643, taking Malmesbury and relieving Gloucester (March), defeating the royalists in Monmouth and Wales, taking Hereford (April), fighting Sir Ralph Hopton at Lansdowne (5 July), being defeated at Roundway Down (17 July), falling back to Bristol and returning to London (August); obtained fresh troops in London, November, 1643; defeated Lord Crawford at Alton, December 1643; took Arundel Castle, January, 1644; defeated the royalists at Cheriton, March 1644; advanced on Oxford, May 1644; worsted at Cropredy Bridge, June 1644; shared the command at Newbury, October 1644; sent to relieve Taunton, February 1645, but removed from command by the self-denying ordinance, April 1645; became a presbyterian leader in parliament; regarded by the army as their chief enemy, 1647; began to levy troops to resist the army, June 1647; withdrew to France, August 1647; returned and urged making terms with Charles I, 1648; kept prisoner by the army, 1648-51; arrested on suspicion by Cromwell, 1658; actively plotted for a royalist rising in the spring of 1659; prisoner in the Tower of London, 1659; recovered his place in parliament, February 1660; sat on the council of state and urged Charles II's recall; M.P., Westminster, 1660, in the Convention parliament, but obtained nothing at the Restoration. His autobiographical papers appeared posthumously. [lix. 131]

WALLER, SIR WILLIAM (d. 1699), informer; son of Sir William Waller (1597?-1668) [q. v.]; a Middlesex justice; active against Romanists during 'the popish plot,' 1678-9; removed from the commission of the peace, April, 1680; M.P., Westminster, 1679 and 1681; fled to Holland, 1682; returned to England, November, 1688. [lix. 135]

WALLEYS. [See WALLENSIS.]

WALLICH, GEORGE CHARLES (1815-1899), naturalist; son of Nathaniel Wallich [q. v.]; M.D. Edinburgh, 1836; army surgeon in India, 1838-56; published two works on marine biology, including 'The North Atlantic Sea-bed,' 1862. [lix. 136]

WALLICH, NATHANIEL (1786-1854), botanist; a Dane; M.D. Copenhagen; surgeon at Serampore, India, 1807-13; superintendent of Calcutta botanic gardens, 1815-50; collected plants in India and Burmah; brought great collections to London, 1828; F.R.S., 1829; R.A.S.; published 'Plantæ Asiaticæ Rariores,' 1830-2; went back to India, c. 1833; explored Assam; returned to England, 1847; settled in London. [lix. 135]

WALLINGFORD, VISCOUNT (1547-1632). [See KNOLLYS, WILLIAM, EARL OF BANBURY.]

WALLINGFORD, JOHN OF (d. 1258), compiler or transcriber of a chronicle (A.D. 449-1035); became a monk of St. Albans, 1231. [lix. 136]

WALLINGFORD, RICHARD OF (1292?-1336). [See RICHARD.]

WALLINGFORD, WILLIAM (d. 1488?), abbot of St. Albans; entered St. Albans very young; afterwards studied at Oxford; archdeacon of the abbey before 1451; candidate for the abbotship, 1452; prior, retaining the archdeaconry, 1465; elected abbot, 1476; possibly patron of the printing press at St. Albans, 1480-6; an able administrator; added to the abbey buildings. [lix. 136]

WALLINGTON, NEHEMIAH (1598-1658), puritan; a turner in London; prosecuted for owning prohibited puritan books, 1639; kept notes of private and public matters, 1583 onwards. [lix. 138]

WALLIS, MISS, afterwards MRS. CAMPBELL (fl. 1789-1814), actress; acted in Dublin (c. 1782), in the provinces, in London (1789), in Bath and Bristol (1789-94), in London (1794-7); married, and left the stage, 1797; reappeared, without success, in London, 1813, and in Bath, 1813-14. [lix. 139]

WALLIS, GEORGE (1740-1802), physician; M.D.; practised in York, and 1776 onwards in London; published dramatic pieces, satires, and medical tracts. [lix. 140]

WALLIS, GEORGE (1811-1891), keeper of South Kensington Museum; art teacher in Manchester (1832-7), London (1841-3), and Birmingham (1852-8); keeper of the art collections, South Kensington, 1858-90; on the staff of the London exhibitions of 1851 and 1862, and of the British section of the Paris exhibitions of 1855 and 1867; wrote on artistic and technical instruction. [lix. 140]

WALLIS, HENRY (1805?-1890), book-illustrator; picture-dealer in London. [lix. 148]

WALLIS, JOHN (1616-1703), mathematician; educated at Felsted school, 1630, and Emmanuel College, Cambridge, 1632; M.A., 1640; domestic chaplain to Mary (Tracy), baroness Vere, in London; employed by the parliament to decipher intercepted despatches, 1642-5; inherited a considerable estate, 1643; beneficed in London, 1643; secretary of the Westminster Assembly, 1644; intruded fellow of Queens' College, Cambridge, 1644; settled in London and attended a weekly scientific club; Savilian professor of geometry, Oxford, 1649-1703, and keeper of the archives, 1658-1703; published an English grammar, 1652; D.D. Oxford, 1654; published his famous 'Arithmetica Infinitorum,' 1655, which contained the germs of the differential calculus; exposed Thomas Hobbes's ignorance of mathematics, from 1655; confirmed in his offices, 1660, but remained a strong whig; deciphered intercepted despatches for William III, 1690; opposed the adoption of the Gregorian calendar, 1692; published a collection of his mathematical works, 1693-9, and of his theological tracts, 1691; introduced the principles of analogy and continuity into mathematical science,

and widened the range of the higher algebra; invented the symbol for infinity ∞; edited classical mathematical authors, 1676-88. [lix. 141]

WALLIS, JOHN (1714-1793), county historian; B.A. Queen's College, Oxford, 1737; M.A., 1740; curate at Simonburn, c. 1746-72, and at Billingham, 1776-92; published 'Miscellany in prose and verse,' 1748, and 'Natural History and Antiquities of Northumberland,' 1769. [lix. 145]

WALLIS, JOHN (1789-1866), topographer; a solicitor; M.A. Exeter College, Oxford, 1821; vicar of Bodmin, 1817-66; published maps and directories for Bodmin district and for Cornwall, 1816-48. [lix. 146]

WALLIS, SIR PROVO WILLIAM PARRY (1791-1892), admiral; born at Halifax, Nova Scotia; served at sea, 1804-57; lieutenant, 1808; took part in the Shannon-Chesapeake encounter, 1813; commander, 1813; captain, 1819; rear-admiral, 1851; K.C.B., 1860; admiral of the fleet, 1877. [lix. 146]

WALLIS, RALPH (d. 1669), nonconformist pamphleteer; schoolmaster at Gloucester, 1648; issued coarse pamphlets under the name of 'The Cobler of Gloucester,' or 'Sil Awl,' against the clergy, 1660-8; under arrest, September 1664, and April 1665. [lix. 147]

WALLIS, ROBERT (1794-1878), line-engraver; engraved many of Joseph Mallord William Turner's [q. v.] landscapes. [lix. 148]

WALLIS, SAMUEL (1728-1795), captain in the navy; served at sea, 1743-80; lieutenant, 1748; captain, 1757; sailed round the Horn, through Polynesia, and back by the Cape, 1766-8; a commissioner of the navy, 1782-3 and 1787-95. [lix. 148]

WALLMODEN, AMALIE SOPHIE MARIANNE, COUNTESS OF YARMOUTH (1704-1765), née von Wendt; native of Hanover; married, 1727; had an intrigue with George II at Hanover, 1735; installed in St. James's Palace, 1738; divorced, 1739; created countess, 1740; returned to Hanover, 1760. [lix. 149]

WALLOP, SIR HENRY (1540?-1599), lord justice of Ireland; of Farleigh-Wallop, Hampshire; knighted, 1569; M.P., Southampton, 1572; vice-treasurer of Ireland, 1579-99; served on many commissions; received grants of Irish lands; proposed the plantation of Munster, 1580; joint lord justice, 1582-4; travelled through Limerick and Kerry, 1584; founded the English settlement at Enniscorthy, 1585; quarrelled with Sir John Perrot [q. v.]; resided in England, 1589-95, discharging his vice-treasurership by deputy; entertained Queen Elizabeth at Farleigh-Wallop, 1591; unsuccessful in negotiating with Hugh O'Neill, second earl of Tyrone [q. v.], 1596; his colony at Enniscorthy destroyed by the Irish, 1598; died at Dublin. [lix. 150]

WALLOP, SIR JOHN (d. 1551), soldier and diplomatist; served in the Low Countries, 1511; knighted before 1513; served at sea against the French, 1513-14; envoy to the Netherlands, 1515; fought against the Moors at Tangier, 1516; served in Ireland, 1518-21, and France, 1522-3; high marshal of Calais, 1524; envoy to the Netherlands, Germany, Austria, and Poland, 1526-7; envoy to France, 1528; keeper of Dytton Park, 1529; ambassador in France, 1532-7; inherited Farleigh-Wallop, Hampshire, from his uncle, 1535; granted church lands, 1538; ambassador in France, 1540; recalled on a charge of treason, January 1541, but pardoned, on his abject apology, March 1541; captain of Guisnes, 1541-51; commanded the English contingent in north France, 1543; K.G., 1544; died at Guisnes. [lix. 152]

WALLOP, JOHN, first EARL OF PORTSMOUTH (1690-1762), of Farleigh-Wallop, Hampshire; travelled on the continent, 1708; M.P., Hampshire, 1715-20; a commissioner of the treasury, 1717-20; created Viscount Lymington, 1720; lord-lieutenant of Hampshire, 1733-42; governor of the Isle of Wight, 1734-42 and 1746; created Earl of Portsmouth, 1743. [lix. 155]

WALLOP, RICHARD (1616-1697), judge; of Bugbrooke; B.A. Pembroke College, Oxford, 1635; barrister, Middle Temple, 1646; leading counsel in defence of whigs in the state trials, 1679-86; cursitor baron of the exchequer, 1696. [lix. 156]

WALLOP, ROBERT (1601–1667), regicide; of Far-leigh-Wallop, Hampshire; educated at Hart Hall, Oxford; anti-royalist; M.P., Andover, 1621–2 and 1623–4, Hampshire, 1625 and 1625–6, Andover, 1627–53, Hampshire, 1658–9, Whitchurch, April 1660; an active member of the Long parliament; sat as judge on Charles I's trial, but did not sign the death-warrant; member of councils of state, June 1649 to February 1651, December 1651 to March 1653, May 1659 to April 1660; expelled the House of Commons and excepted from the act of pardon, June 1660; imprisoned in the Tower of London, 1660–7. [lix. 156]

WALMESLEY, CHARLES (1722–1797), Roman catholic prelate and mathematician; native of Lancashire; educated at Douay and Paris; a Sorbonne D.D.; Benedictine monk, 1739; travelled in Italy; published important astronomical and mathematical papers, 1745–61; F.R.S., 1750; titular bishop of Rama, December 1756; resided at Bath, administering the western district, 1757–1797; published a church history, 1771. [lix. 157]

WALMESLEY, SIR THOMAS (1537–1612), judge; native of Lancashire; barrister, Lincoln's Inn, 1567; bencher, 1574; serjeant-at-law, 1580; M.P., Lancashire, 1588–9; justice of the common pleas, 1589–1611; knighted, 1603; voted against the claim of the *post nati*, 1607–8; accumulated great wealth. [lix. 159]

WALMISLEY or **WALMSLEY**, GILBERT (1680–1751), friend of Dr. Johnson; a native of Lichfield; of Trinity College, Oxford; barrister, Inner Temple, 1707; registrar of the ecclesiastical court of Lichfield. [lix. 160]

WALMISLEY, THOMAS ATTWOOD (1814–1856), musician; son of Thomas Forbes Walmisley [q. v.]; pupil of Thomas Attwood (1765–1838) [q. v.]; organist at Croydon, 1831; organist of Trinity and St. John's colleges, Cambridge, 1833–56; professor of music, Cambridge, 1836–56; M.A. Cambridge, 1841; Mus.Doc., 1848; composed church music and madrigals. [lix. 161]

WALMISLEY, THOMAS FORBES (1783–1866), glee composer and organist; chorister of Westminster Abbey; at Westminster School, 1793–8; pupil of Thomas Attwood (1765–1838) [q. v.]; organist in London, 1810–54. [lix. 161]

WALMODEN, AMALIE SOPHIE MARIANNE, COUNTESS OF YARMOUTH (1704–1765). [See WALLMODEN.]

WALMSLEY, GILBERT (1680–1751). [See WALMISLEY.]

WALMSLEY, SIR JOSHUA (1794–1871), politician; schoolmaster in Westmoreland, 1807, and Liverpool, 1811; corn-merchant in Liverpool, 1814; agitated against the duties on corn; mayor of Liverpool, 1838; knighted, 1840; M.P., Bolton, 1849–52, Leicester, 1852–7. [lix. 162]

WALMSLEY, THOMAS (1763–1805), landscape-painter; scene-painter in London and Dublin; exhibited landscapes in London, 1790–6; engravings after his pictures issued, 1792–1810. [lix. 162]

WALPOLE, EDWARD (1560–1637), jesuit; heir of Houghton, Norfolk; entered Peterhouse, Cambridge, 1576; embraced Romanism; disinherited, and took the name Poor; became intimate with John Gerard (1564–1637) [q. v.], 1587; withdrew to Rome, 1590; ordained priest, 1592; joined the jesuits, 1592; went to Tournay, 1592; outlawed, 1597; mission-priest in England under the name of Rich, 1598; pardoned, 1605. [lix. 163]

WALPOLE, GEORGE (1758–1835), soldier; a younger son of Horatio, second baron Walpole of Wolterton; cornet, 1777; lieutenant-colonel of dragoons, 1792; as local major-general reduced the Jamaica insurgents, 1795–6; M.P., Derby, 1797–1806; a supporter of Fox; under-secretary for foreign affairs, 1806–7; M.P., Dungarvan, 1807–20. [lix. 163]

WALPOLE, HENRY (1558–1595), jesuit; educated at Norwich, 1566, and Peterhouse, Cambridge, 1575; student of Gray's Inn, 1578; published a eulogy of Edmund Campion [q. v.], 1581; withdrew to Rheims, 1582, and Rome, 1583; joined the jesuits, 1584; ordained priest, 1588; chaplain in the Spanish army in Flanders, 1589–91; englished Robert Parsons' (1546–1610) [q. v.] 'Responsio ad edictum,' Bruges, 1592; sent to attend Parsons in Spain, 1592; sent to England, 1593; arrested in Yorkshire, 1593; prisoner in the Tower of London, February 1594–March 1595; tried and executed at York. [lix. 164]

WALPOLE, HORATIO or HORACE, first BARON WALPOLE OF WOLTERTON (1678–1757), diplomatist; a younger brother of Sir Robert Walpole, first earl of Orford [q. v.]; educated at Eton; fellow of King's College, Cambridge, 1702; student of Lincoln's Inn, 1700; whig M.P. for Castle Rising, 1702, 1705, 1708, 1710, and 1713, Beeralston, 1715, East Looe, 1718, Great Yarmouth, 1722, 1727, and 1730, Norwich, 1734–56; secretary to various envoys and ministers, 1706–10 and 1715–16; an under-secretary of state, 1714; secretary of the treasury, 1715–17; surveyor of the plantation revenues, 1717, for life; secretary to the lord-lieutenant of Ireland, 1720; secretary to the treasury, 1721; ambassador to the Hague, May 1722, and at Paris, 1723–30, where he gained the confidence of Cardinal Fleury; cofferer of the household, 1730; privy councillor, 1730; ambassador at the Hague, 1733–40; visited the court at Hanover, 1736; advocated a good understanding with Prussia, 1738–40; defended his brother's, Sir Robert's, administration, 1742–3; advocated alliance with Prussia, 1747–8; created Baron Walpole, 1756; published political pamphlets; much satirised by contemporaries for the coarseness of his speech and manners. [lix. 166]

WALPOLE, HORATIO or HORACE, fourth EARL OF ORFORD (1717–1797), author; fourth son of Sir Robert Walpole, first earl of Orford [q. v.]; at Eton, 1727–34, and King's College, Cambridge, 1735–9; given various lucrative offices, 1737–8; travelled in France and Italy with Thomas Gray, the poet, 1739–41; M.P., Callington, 1741–53, Castle Rising, 1754–7, Lynn, 1757–67; settled at Strawberry Hill, Twickenham, which he made into 'a little Gothic castle,' 1747; collected articles of vertu; established there a private press, 1757–89, at which he printed his 'Catalogue of Royal and Noble Authors,' 1758, 'Anecdotes of Painting in England,' 1762–71, 'Catalogue of Engravers in England,' 1763, the 'Gothic romance' of 'The Castle of Otranto,' 1764 (from a fictitious black-letter original), and a description of his house and his collections, 1774 (enlarged edition, 1784), and other works (verse and prose) and editions; visited Paris, 1765, 1767, and 1775; published 'Historic Doubts on Richard III,' 1768, and the 'Mysterious Mother' (tragedy), 1768; neglected the poet, Thomas Chatterton's, appeal for help, 1769; gave an asylum to Catherine Clive [q. v.] before 1785, and to Agnes and Mary Berry [q. v], 1791; succeeded his nephew in the earldom, 1791; his Strawberry Hill collections sold, 1842; his collected 'Works' published, 1798, his autobiographical treatises, 1805, 1859, and his correspondence, 1857–9. [lix. 170]

WALPOLE, MICHAEL (1570–1624?), jesuit; born in Norfolk; attached himself to John Gerard (1564–1637) [q. v.], 1588; joined jesuits, 1593; chaplain in London to Doña Luisa de Carvajal, 1606–10, 1613–14; withdrew to Spain; published theological tracts, 1608–16. [lix. 176]

WALPOLE, RALPH DE (*d.* 1302), bishop of Ely; probably a Walpole of Houghton; D.D., possibly of Cambridge; rector of Somersham; archdeacon of Ely, 1268–88; elected bishop of Norwich, 1288; consecrated, 1289; opposed Edward I's taxation of the clergy, 1297; translated to Ely by Pope Boniface VIII, 1299; made new statutes for the Ely chapter. [lix. 176]

WALPOLE, RICHARD (1564–1607), jesuit; born in Norfolk; scholar of Peterhouse, Cambridge, 1579; withdrew to Rheims, 1584, and Rome, 1585; ordained priest, 1589; attended Robert Parsons in Spain from 1589; rector of the college at Valladolid, 1592; joined the jesuits, *c.* 1593; accused of devising Edward Squire's [q. v.] plot, 1598; died at Valladolid. [lix. 178]

WALPOLE, ROBERT (1650–1700), of Houghton; a leading whig squire; M.P., Castle Rising, 1689, 1695, 1698. [lix. 179]

WALPOLE, SIR ROBERT, first EARL OF ORFORD (1676–1745), statesman; third son of Robert Walpole (1650–1700) [q. v.]; at Eton, 1690–6; scholar of King's College, Cambridge, 1696–8; became heir to the estate, 1698; succeeded to the estate, November 1700; pushed forward by the interest of Sarah, duchess of Marlborough; M.P., Castle Rising, 1701–2, King's Lynn, 1702–12 and 1713–42; at once took an active part in the business of the Commons; from first to last favoured religious toleration; recognised as a leader of the whig party, 1703; one of the council to Prince George of Denmark, lord high admiral, 1705; secretary at war, 1708–10, and treasurer of the navy, 1710–11; leader of the House of Commons; recognised as a great financier, 1711; shared in Marlborough's fall; leader of the opposition against Harley, January 1711; expelled the House of Commons and imprisoned in the Tower of London on a vexatious charge of venality in the navy office, 1712; wrote pamphlets against the tory administration, 1712–13; advocated the Hanoverian succession, April 1714; distrusted by George I through the intrigues of Bothmar and the German court favourites; paymaster of the forces, 1714; privy councillor, 1714; conducted the impeachment of Bolingbroke, Ormonde, Oxford (Harley), and Stafford, 1715; tracked out the arrangements for the 1715 rising, and sternly punished its leaders; prime minister and chancellor of the exchequer, 1715–17; seriously ill, spring 1716; opposed George I's demands for war with Russia and for payment for his German troops, 1716; devised the first general sinking fund, March 1717; driven from office by the intrigues of Stanhope and Sunderland, April 1717; joined the tories in protesting against a standing army, 1717; successfully opposed the proposal to limit the number of peers, 1718; opposed the government's encouragement of the South Sea Company, 1720; made money by prudent speculation in South Sea Stock, and gained the friendship of Caroline, princess of Wales, by directing her speculations, May 1720; began to form a gallery of pictures; rebuilt Houghton (1722–38); called upon to help the government through the South Sea collapse, September 1720; prime minister and chancellor of the exchequer, 1721; encouraged trade by removing duties on imported raw materials and on many exports, 1721; managed the proceedings against Francis Atterbury [q. v.], 1722; vainly tried to carry out the patent of William Wood, [q. v.] for coining half-pence for Ireland, 1722–5; intrigued against by John, baron Carteret [q. v.], and Bothmar, 1723; enforced the unpopular malt-tax on Scotland, 1724–1725; advised the impeachment of the lord chancellor, Sir Thomas Parker, first earl of Macclesfield [q. v.], February 1725; K.B., 1725; K.G., 1726, the first commoner 'Blue-ribbon' since 1660; censured Townshend for precipitancy in forming an alliance with France and Prussia against Spain and Austria, 1725; steadily cultivated friendship with France, 1726, the opposition, led by William Pulteney [q. v.], desiring an Austrian alliance; intrigued against by Bolingbroke and George I's favourites, 1726; seriously ill, 1727; coldly treated by George II on his accession, June 1727, but, by the help of an appeal to George II's love of money, was continued in office, being re-appointed first lord of the treasury and chancellor of the exchequer, 1727; vilely attacked by the tory press as bribed by France to sacrifice English interests, 1730–1; encouraged colonial trade by removing restrictions, 1730–1735; quarrelled definitively with Townshend, 1730; failed, through popular clamour, to carry his excellent excise proposals, 1733; opposed George II and his queen's wish for armed intervention in favour of Austria, 1734; succeeded in bringing about peace by the treaty of Vienna, 1735; lost the favour of dissenters by opposing the repeal of the Test Act, proposed by the opposition whigs, 1736–9; lost favour in Scotland by the repressive measures occasioned by the Porteous riot, 1736; offended Frederick, prince of Wales, by refusing his demand for an increased allowance, 1737; his influence in the House of Commons visibly diminished, 1737; vainly endeavoured to stifle the popular clamour for war with Spain, 1738–9; thwarted by Newcastle and others of his colleagues; twice offered to resign, but was implored by George II to retain office; vainly opposed George II's wish to fight for the pragmatic sanction, spring 1741; motions for his removal defeated in both houses of parliament, February 1741; defeated in the new House of Commons, 28 Jan. 1742; resigned all his offices, and was pensioned and created Earl of Orford, February 1742; proposals to impeach his conduct for supposed ministerial corruption when in office baffled, March–June 1742; retired to Houghton; his advice still pleaded for by George II, 1743; advocated peace, 1744; died in debt. He was the first minister since the Restoration who made a special study of finance and commerce, and laid the foundations of free trade and modern colonial policy. His grandson sold his fine collection of pictures to the Tsarina Catherine II. [lix. 178]

WALPOLE, ROBERT (1781–1856), classical scholar; M.A. Trinity College, Cambridge, 1809; B.D., 1828; travelled in Greece; beneficed in Norfolk, 1809, and London, 1828; a Norfolk landowner; published 'Comicorum

Græcorum Fragmenta,' 1805, notes of eastern travel, 1817–20, and other works. [lix. 207]

WALPOLE, Sir ROBERT (1808–1876), lieutenant-general; ensign, 1825; captain, 1834; lieutenant-colonel, 1847; stationed at Corfu, 1847–56; commanded in India a brigade, November 1857, and a division, February 1858; defeated with heavy loss at Fort Ruiya, April 1858; K.C.B.; stationed at Gibraltar, 1861–4, and at Chatham, 1864–6; major-general, 1862; lieutenant-general, 1871. [lix. 207]

WALPOLE, SPENCER HORATIO (1806–1898), home secretary; educated at Eton and Trinity College, Cambridge; B.A., 1828; honorary LL.D., 1860; barrister, Lincoln's Inn, 1831; Q.C., 1846; practised in the rolls court till 1852; conservative M.P., Midhurst, 1846–56, and Cambridge University, 1856–82; home secretary, 1852, 1858–9, 1866; driven from office by popular clamour at his management of the Hyde Park monster meetings, May 1867; an ecclesiastical commissioner, 1856–8, 1862–6; chairman of the Great Western Railway. [lix. 209]

WALPURGA, Saint (d. 779?). [See WALBURGA.]

WALROND, HUMPHREY (1600?–1670?), deputy-governor of Barbados; inherited Sea, near Ilminster, Somerset, 1621; a lukewarm royalist; taken prisoner at Bridgwater, 1645; compounded for his estate, 1646; sold it and went to Barbados before 1649; raised a royalist force in Barbados; proclaimed Charles II, May 1650; deprived of his command by the new governor, Francis Willoughby, baron Willoughby [q. v.] of Parham, 1650; banished by Sir George Ayscue, March 1652; entered the Spanish service in the West Indies; created Marquess de Vallado, 1653; returned to Barbados before April 1660; deputy-governor there, 1660–3; tried to stir up a mutiny, 1663; threatened with imprisonment in London, 1664; disappeared, probably to the Spanish West Indies. [lix. 211]

WALSH, ANTOINE VINCENT (1702–1763), Jacobite; of Irish extraction; born at St. Malo; served in the French navy; shipowner at Nantes; took Prince Charles Edward to Scotland in his own brig, the Doutelle, 1745; knighted by Prince Charles and created an Irish earl by 'James III'; ennobled by Louis XV, 1755; died in St. Domingo. [lix. 212]

WALSH, EDWARD (1756–1832), physician; a native of Waterford; M.D. Glasgow, 1791; army surgeon in Ireland, 1798, in Holland, 1799, in Canada, throughout the Peninsular war, and at Waterloo; published verses and a 'Narrative of the Expedition to Holland,' 1800. [lix. 213]

WALSH, EDWARD (1805–1850), Irish poet; a hedge-school teacher; collected Irish traditional tales and poetry; national school teacher in co. Waterford, 1837–43; contributed to nationalist journals; published songs and translations of Irish poetry, 1844–7. [lix. 213]

WALSH, JOHN (1725?–1795), secretary to Clive; paymaster of the troops, Madras; private secretary to Robert Clive, first baron Clive [q. v.], 1757–9; returned to lay Clive's plans before Pitt, 1759; F.R.S., 1770; bought Warfield Park, Berkshire, 1771; conducted experiments on the torpedo fish. [lix. 214]

WALSH, JOHN (1835–1881), Irish poet; national school teacher in Waterford and Tipperary counties. [lix. 215]

WALSH, JOHN (1830–1898), archbishop of Toronto; a native of Kilkenny; went to Montreal, 1852; bishop of Sandwich, 1864; removed his see to London, Ontario, 1869; archbishop of Toronto, 1889–98. [lix. 215]

WALSH, Sir JOHN BENN, first BARON ORMATHWAITE (1798–1881), of Warfield Park, Berkshire; educated at Eton and Christ Church, Oxford; high sheriff of Berkshire, 1823, of Radnorshire, 1825; succeeded as second baronet, 1825; tory M.P., Sudbury, 1830–4, 1837–40, and Radnorshire, 1840–68; lord-lieutenant of Radnorshire, 1842–75; created Baron Ormathwaite, 1868; published political pamphlets. [lix. 216]

WALSH, JOHN EDWARD (1816–1869), Irish judge; son of Robert Walsh [q. v.]; B.A. Trinity College, Dublin, 1836; Irish barrister, 1839; published 'Ireland Sixty Years Ago,' 1847; attorney-general for Ireland, 1866; Irish master of the rolls, 1866; died at Paris. [lix. 216]

WALSH, JOHN HENRY (1810–1888), writer on sport under the pseudonym of STONEHENGE; a Londoner;

qualified as a surgeon, 1844; practised in London and Worcester: settled in London, 1852; edited 'The Coursing Calendar' from 1856, and 'The Field' from 1857; conducted experiments on sporting guns, 1858-83; published works on dogs, horses, guns, sports, domestic economy, medicine, cookery. [lix. 217]

WALSH, NICHOLAS (d. 1585), bishop of Ossory; son of Patrick Walsh (d. 1578), bishop of Waterford; studied at Paris, Oxford, and Cambridge; B.A. Cambridge, 1563; M.A., 1567; chancellor of St. Patrick's, Dublin, 1571; joined John Kearney [q. v.] in translating the New Testament into Irish, 1573; bishop of Ossory, 1577; murdered. [lix. 218]

WALSH, PETER (1618?-1688), in Latin VALESIUS; Irish Franciscan; born at Mooretown, co. Kildare; was educated at Louvain, where he joined the Franciscans; divinity lecturer in Kilkenny convent, 1646; encouraged the Irish catholic party to resist the proposals of the nuncio Giovanni Battista Rinuccini [q. v.], and to make peace with Ormonde, 1646-8; preached against Cornelius Mahony [q. v.] in defence of Charles I's title to Ireland, 1647; made guardian of Kilkenny convent by the Irish leaders, 1648-50; chaplain with Castlehaven's army in Munster, 1650-1; withdrew to London, 1652; visited Madrid, 1654, and Holland; lived obscurely in London, 1655-60; published pamphlets on Irish affairs, 1660-2; proposed a 'loyal remonstrance' to be addressed by Irish catholics to Charles II repudiating papal infallibility and promising undivided civil allegiance to the crown, in hope of securing favourable terms for Irish catholics; actively canvassed in favour of this remonstrance among Irish clerics and laity in London, 1661-2, and in Dublin, 1664-5, and again, 1665-1669; but his exertions rendered fruitless by opposition from Rome; settled in London, 1669, living on good terms with the Anglican clergy, and being pensioned by Ormonde; excommunicated by the Franciscan chapter-general at Valladolid, 1670; published controversial letters against the claims of Pope Gregory VII, 1672-84, a reply to Bishop Thomas Barlow's 'Popery,' 1686, and other works. [lix. 218]

WALSH, RICHARD HUSSEY (1825-1862), political economist; B.A. Trinity College, Dublin, 1847; student of Lincoln's Inn, 1848; lecturer on political economy at Dublin, 1850; government official in the Mauritius, 1857-62; chief work, 'An Elementary Treatise on Metallic Currency,' 1853. [lix. 224]

WALSH, ROBERT (1772-1852), miscellaneous writer; B.A. Trinity College, Dublin, 1796; curate of Finglas, co. Dublin, 1806-20; embassy chaplain at Constantinople, 1820 and 1831-5; hon. M.D. Aberdeen and LL.D. Dublin; embassy chaplain at St. Petersburg, and Rio de Janeiro, 1828-31; rector of Kilbride, Wicklow, 1835-9, and of Finglas, 1839-52; published a 'History of the City of Dublin,' 1815, notes of his travels and other works. [lix. 224]

WALSH, WILLIAM (1512?-1577), bishop of Meath; a Cistercian; D.D.; commissioner to eject married clergy in Meath diocese, 1553; appointed bishop of Meath, 1554; employed on government commissions, 1556-9; deposed by Queen Elizabeth, 1560; prisoner in Dublin, 1565-72; withdrew to Alcalá, Spain; died there. [lix. 225]

WALSH, WILLIAM (1663-1708), critic and poet; entered Wadham College, Oxford, 1678, but did not graduate; whig M.P. for Worcestershire, 1698, 1701, 1702, Richmond, Yorkshire, 1705-8; gentleman of the horse to Queen Anne; wrote poems, 1692 (first printed in Tonson's 'Miscellany,' pt. iv. 1716); collaborated with Vanbrugh in an adaptation from Molière, 1704; friend and literary adviser of Alexander Pope, whom he advised to be a 'correct' poet, that being the 'only way left of excellency,' 1706; chief prose work, a 'Dialogue concerning Women, being a Defence of the Sex,' 1691; his collected verses and letters published posthumously. [lix. 226]

WALSHE, WALTER HAYLE (1812-1892), physician; born in Dublin; studied medicine in Paris, 1832-5; M.D. Edinburgh, 1836; practitioner in London, 1838; a noted medical professor in University College, London, 1841-62; published and translated medical treatises. [lix. 227]

WALSINGHAM, PETRONILLA MELUSINA VON DER SCHULENBURG, COUNTESS OF (1693-1778), natural daughter of George I and the Duchess of Kendal, and wife of Philip Dormer Stanhope, fourth earl of Chesterfield; countess of Walsingham in her own right, 1722; formally married Philip Dormer Stanhope, fourth earl of Chesterfield [q. v.], who thereby gave offence to George II, 1733. [liv. 27]

WALSINGHAM, first BARON (1719-1781). [See GREY, WILLIAM DE.]

WALSINGHAM, FAMILY OF. Assumed to have been named from Walsingham, Norfolk. Alan Walsingham was cordwainer of London in 1415. His son, Thomas Walsingham (d. 1456), bought Scadbury, Chislehurst, 1424. Scadbury was sold in 1655 by Sir Thomas Walsingham (d. 1669), in whose grandson, James Walsingham (1646-1728), the main line came to an end. Sir Francis Walsingham [q. v.] belonged to a cadet branch. [lix. 228]

WALSINGHAM, SIR EDMUND (1490?-1550), lieutenant of the Tower of London; of Scadbury, Kent; knighted at Flodden, 1513; attended Henry VIII to France, 1520; lieutenant of the Tower of London, 1525-1547; granted church lands, 1539; M.P., Surrey, 1544. [lix. 228]

WALSINGHAM, EDWARD (fl. 1643-1654), royalist and author; private secretary to George Digby, second earl of Bristol [q. v.], 1643; hon. M.A. Oxford, 1643; resided in Oxford, 1643-5; published elegies on cavaliers, 1644-5; went to Henrietta Maria's court in Paris, 1646; embraced Romanism; envoy to Ormonde in Ireland, 1648; resided in Paris, 1649-54; attempted the conversion of Henry, duke of Gloucester, 1654; published, 1652, 'Arcana Aulica, or Walsingham's Manual,' a piracy from the French of Eustache du Refuge; perhaps entered a convent abroad. [lix. 230]

WALSINGHAM, SIR FRANCIS (1530?-1590), statesman; inherited Foot's Cray, 1534; brought up as a zealous protestant; at King's College, Cambridge, 1548-1550; student of Gray's Inn, 1552; travelled, during Queen Mary's reign, studying foreign politics, 1553-8; M.P., Banbury, 1559, Lyme Regis, 1563-7, and Surrey, 1574-90; collected foreign intelligence for Cecil (Burghley); chief of the secret service in London, 1569; tracked out the conspiracy of Roberto di Rodolfi [q. v.], 1569; envoy to Paris, to ask indulgence for the Huguenots, August 1570; ambassador at Paris, to negotiate a French alliance and Queen Elizabeth's marriage with Anjou, 1570-3; vainly pressed Elizabeth to make war on Spain, 1571-85; protected English protestants during the St. Bartholomew massacre, 1572; secretary of state, 1573-90; employed in foreign affairs, but his advice neglected by Elizabeth; organised at his own expense a secret service to discover the plans of Spain and the jesuits; knighted, 1577; unwilling envoy to the Netherlands with peace proposals, 1578; sold Foot's Cray and settled at Barn Elms, Surrey, 1579; envoy to France to negotiate a new treaty, 1581, and made bold to suggest discontinuing the proposed match between Alençon and Elizabeth; unwilling envoy to Scotland, 1583; encouraged colonial enterprises; secured the conviction of William Parry [q. v.], 1585, of Anthony Babington [q. v.], 1586, and of Mary Queen of Scots, 1586, and her execution, 1587; entertained Elizabeth at Barn Elms, 1585, 1588, 1589; involved in debt through being security for his son-in-law, Sir Philip Sidney, 1586; provided for a theological lecture at Oxford, 1586; chancellor of the duchy of Lancaster, 1587; vainly urged Elizabeth to make preparations for the Armada, 1587, and to supply adequate ammunition to the fleet, 1588. Large numbers of his official papers and correspondence are in the Public Record Office, the British Museum, and the archives at Hatfield. Some have been printed; others calendared. [lix. 231]

WALSINGHAM, FRANCIS (1577-1647), jesuit; assumed the name JOHN FENNELL; educated at St. Paul's School, London; took Anglican orders, 1603; went to Rome, 1606; was ordained priest and joined the jesuits, 1608; visited England, 1609, to distribute his 'Search made into Matters of Religion,' a persuasive to Romanism; mission priest in England, 1616; published 'Reasons for embracing the Catholic Faith,' 1618. [lix. 240]

WALSINGHAM or **WALSINGAM**, JOHN (*d.* 1340 ?), theologian ; a Carmelite friar ; studied at Oxford and Paris ; D.D. ; provincial of the English Carmelites, 1326 ; summoned to the papal court at Avignon, 1328, to dispute against William Ockham [q. v.] ; probably died there. Two treatises are assigned to him by Tritheim. [lix. 241]

WALSINGHAM, THOMAS (*d.* 1422 ?), monk and historian ; our chief authority for Richard II, Henry IV, and Henry V ; precentor and superintendent of the scriptorium of St. Albans Abbey ; compiled 'Chronica Majora,' now lost, *c.* 1380, and 'Chronicon Angliæ' from 1328 to 1388 ; prior of Wymundham, 1394–1409 ; returned to St. Albans, 1409 ; compiled 'Ypodigma Neustriæ,' a record of events in Normandy, finished 1419, and perhaps 'Historia Anglicana' from 1272 to 1422. [lix. 242]

WALSINGHAM, SIR THOMAS (1568–1630), patron of the poets Thomas Watson, Christopher Marlowe, and George Chapman ; inherited Scadbury, 1589 ; entertained Queen Elizabeth there, and was knighted, 1597 ; knight of the shire for Kent, 1614 ; M.P. for Rochester, with an interval, 1597–1626. His wife, Ethelred or Awdrey (Shelton) (*d.* 1631) was a favourite of James I's queen, Anne of Denmark, 1603–19. [lix. 229]

WALTER OF LORRAINE (*d.* 1079), bishop of Hereford ; a native of Lorraine ; chaplain to Edith or Eadgyth (*d.* 1075) [q. v.], the Confessor's queen ; consecrated at Rome, 1061 ; oppressed by William the Conqueror ; attended Lanfranc's councils, 1072 and 1075. [lix. 244]

WALTER OF ESPEC (*d.* 1153). [See ESPEC.]

WALTER OF PALERMO (*fl.* 1170), archbishop of Palermo; an Englishman ; sent by Henry II to be tutor of William II of Sicily ; archdeacon of Cefalù ; dean of Girgenti ; archbishop of Palermo, 1168 ; chancellor of Sicily. [lix. 244]

WALTER DE COUTANCES (*d.* 1207). [See COUTANCES.]

WALTER DE KIRKHAM (*d.* 1260). [See KIRKHAM.]

WALTER DE MERTON (*d.* 1277). [See MERTON.]

WALTER OF COVENTRY (*fl.* 1293 ?). [See COVENTRY.]

WALTER DE HEMINGFORD, HEMINGBURGH, or GISBURN (*fl.* 1300). [See HEMINGFORD.]

WALTER OF EXETER (*fl.* 1301). [See EXETER.]

WALTER OF EVESHAM or WALTER ODINGTON (*fl.* 1320), Benedictine writer ; a monk of Evesham ; compiled a calendar there, beginning 1301 ; made astronomical observations in Oxford, 1316 ; lodged in Merton College, *c.* 1330 ; manuscript tracts by him in Oxford and Cambridge libraries. His valuable 'De Speculatione Musices' has been printed. [lix. 245]

WALTER OF SWINBROKE (*fl.* 1350). [See BAKER, GEOFFREY.]

WALTER, HENRY (1785–1859), divine and antiquary; B.A. St. John's College, Cambridge, 1806 ; fellow, 1806–24 ; M.A., 1809 ; B.D., 1816 ; F.R.S., 1819 ; natural philosophy professor at Haileybury College, 1806–30 ; rector of Haselbury Bryant, 1821–59 ; edited theological works. [lix. 246]

WALTER, HUBERT (*d.* 1205). [See HUBERT.]

WALTER or **FITZWALTER**, JOHN (*d.* 1412 ?), astrologer ; of Oxford and Winchester. [lix. 247]

WALTER, SIR JOHN (1566–1630), judge ; of Brasenose College, Oxford ; created M.A., 1613 ; barrister, Inner Temple, 1590, bencher, 1605, autumn reader, 1607 ; practised in the exchequer and chancery ; Oxford university counsel ; attorney-general and trustee to Prince Charles, 1613 ; knighted, 1619 ; M.P., East Looe, 1620–2 and 1624 ; chief-baron of the exchequer, 1625 ; obsequious to Charles I on taxation questions, but opposed him on the law of treason ; ordered not to act as judge, 1630. [lix. 247]

WALTER, JOHN (1739–1812), founder of 'The Times' ; son of a London coal-merchant ; coal-merchant, 1755–81, and underwriter, 1770–82; bankrupt owing to the loss of shipping during the American war, 1782 ; bought Henry Johnson's 'logotype' patent for printing by founts of whole words, 1782 ; bought printing premises

in Printing House Square. London, 1784 ; opened his 'logographic' press there ; practised 'logographic' printing for several years ; printed books, 'Lloyd's List' from 1785, and, 1787–1805, the custom-house papers ; started his newspaper called 'The Daily Universal Register,' price twopence halfpenny, 1 Jan. 1785, to report fully parliamentary debates and to review home and foreign affairs ; fined for 'libel,' 1786 ; altered title of newspaper to 'The Times or Daily Universal Register,' price threepence, on 1 Jan. 1788, and to 'The Times,' 18 March 1788 ; imprisoned, 1789–91, for reflecting on George III's sons ; retired to Teddington, 1795, giving up the direct management of the paper, but retaining the proprietorship ; prosecuted for libel, 1799. [lix. 248]

WALTER, JOHN (1776–1847), chief proprietor of 'The Times' newspaper ; second son of John Walter (1739–1812) [q. v.] ; educated at Merchant Taylors' School and Trinity College, Oxford ; joint-manager of 'The Times,' *c.* 1797 ; sole manager from 1803 ; sole editor, 1803–10 ; joint-editor with (Sir) John Stoddart [q. v.], 1811–15, with Thomas Barnes (1785–1841) [q. v.], 1815–1841, and with John Thaddeus Delane [q. v.] from 1841 ; offended the government by the independent criticisms which appeared in 'The Times,' 1804–5 ; lost the government advertisements and the printing for the custom-house, and was long persecuted by the government ; introduced the system of sending special correspondents to report on events abroad, 1805 ; was the first to give its special prominence to 'the leading article' ; thanked by the merchants of London for his strenuous opposition to Napoleon, 1814 ; adopted the steam printing-press, November 1814 ; bought Bear Wood, Berkshire ; M.P., Berkshire, 1832–7 ; strongly opposed the new poor-law for England, 1834, and for Ireland, 1837 ; exposed great commercial frauds, 1840 ; M.P., Nottingham, 1841. [lix. 252]

WALTER, JOHN (1818–1894), chief proprietor of 'The Times' newspaper ; eldest son of John Walter (1776–1847) [q.v.] ; educated at Eton and Exeter College, Oxford ; M.A., 1843 ; barrister, Lincoln's Inn, 1847 ; joined his father in the management of 'The Times,' 1840 ; showed friendliness to the Oxford tractarians ; sole manager, 1847 ; resigned the management to Mowbray Morris ; employed as editors John Thaddeus Delane [q. v.], 1847–78, Thomas Chenery [q. v.], 1878–84, and George Earle Buckle from 1884 ; devised and introduced the 'Walter' printing-press, 1869 ; M.P., Nottingham, 1847–1859, and Berkshire, 1859–65 and 1868–85. [lix. 256]

WALTER, LUCY (1630 ?–1658), known also as MRS. BARLOW, and incorrectly as WALTERS and WATERS, mother of James, duke of Monmouth ; daughter of a Welsh royalist ; went to the Hague, 1644 ; mistress of Colonel Robert Sidney, 1644, of Charles II, 1648–50, of Henry Bennet, 1650, and others ; gave birth, 9 April 1649, to a son, James, of whom Charles II was father, and a daughter, Mary, 6 May 1651 ; at Cologne, 1656 ; bribed by Charles II's friends to return to England ; arrested as a spy in London, 1656 ; sent back to Holland, 1656 ; died in Paris. From 1673 to 1680 it was industriously reported that Charles II had legally married her in the presence of John Cosin (afterwards bishop of Durham), and that Sir Gilbert Gerard, Cosin's son-in-law, had the proofs of the marriage in a 'black box.' Charles II issued three declarations denying a marriage, January–June 1678. [lix. 259]

WALTER, RICHARD (1716 ?–1785), chaplain in the navy ; B.A. Sidney Sussex College, Cambridge, 1738 ; fellow ; M.A., 1744 ; chaplain with George Anson during the first part of his voyage, 1740–2 ; chaplain at Portsmouth dockyard, 1745–85 ; published the narrative of Anson's voyage, 1748. [lix. 260]

WALTER, THEOBALD (*d.* 1205 ?). [See BUTLER.]

WALTER, WILLIAM (*fl.* 1520), translator ; 'servant' of Sir Henry Marney (created Baron Marney, 1523) ; published three metrical translations from Latin, 'Guystarde and Sygysmonde,' 1532, and 'The Spectacle of Lovers' and 'Tytus and Gesyppus,' undated. [lix. 261]

WALTERS, EDWARD (1808–1872), architect ; employed in Turkey on government buildings, 1832–7 ; a leading architect in Manchester, 1839–65. [lix. 262]

WALTERS, JOHN (1759–1789), poet ; eldest son of John Walters (1721–1797) [q. v.] ; entered Jesus College, Oxford, 1777 ; M.A., 1784 ; fellow ; sub-librarian of the

Bodleian ; master of Cowbridge, and, 1784, of Ruthin school ; rector of Efenechtyd ; published translations from Welsh poetry, 1772, poems, 1780, and sermons. [lix. 263]

WALTERS, JOHN (1721–1797), Welsh lexicographer ; rector of Llandough and vicar of St. Hilary, Glamorganshire, 1759 ; prebendary of Llandaff ; wrote poems and sermons in Welsh ; published an admirable ' English-Welsh Dictionary,' 1770–94. [lix. 262]

WALTERS, LUCY (1630 ?–1658). [See WALTER.]

WALTHAM, JOHN DE (d. 1395), bishop of Salisbury and treasurer of England ; a secular priest ; a favourite of Richard II ; prebendary of Southwell, Lichfield, 1361, and York, 1370, with other preferments ; master of the rolls, 1381–6, introducing the practice of writs of subpœna ; temporary keeper of the great seal, 1382, 1383 ; archdeacon of Richmond, 1385 ; keeper of the privy seal, 1386 ; bishop of Salisbury, 1388 ; lord high treasurer, 1391–5 ; buried, by Richard II's order, in the royal chapel, Westminster. [lix. 263]

WALTHAM, ROGER OF (d. 1336). [See ROGER.]

WALTHEOF, in Latin WALDEVUS or GUALLEVUS (d. 1076), earl of Northumberland ; son of Siward (d. 1055) [q. v.], earl of Northumbria ; educated for the church ; Earl of Huntingdon and Northampton shires, c. 1065 ; taken to Normandy by the Conqueror, 1067 ; joined the Danish invaders in the massacre of the French garrison of York, 1069 ; pardoned by William I, 1070 ; married Judith, William's niece ; appointed Earl of Northumberland, 1072 ; on friendly terms with Bishop Walcher [q. v.] ; murderously followed up a blood feud, 1073 ; privy to the plot of Ralph Guader [q. v.], earl of Norfolk, 1075 ; confessed his share in it to Lanfranc, and to William in Normandy ; arrested on suspicion of having invited the Danish fleet to the Humber, December 1075 ; imprisoned at Winchester ; executed there ; regarded by the English as a martyr ; miracles reported to be wrought at his tomb in Crowland Abbey. [lix. 265]

WALTHEOF (d. 1159), saint and abbot of Melrose ; second son of Simon de Senlis, earl of Northampton and Huntingdon [q. v.], by Matilda, eldest daughter of Waltheof (d. 1076) [q. v.] ; Augustinian monk at Nostal ; prior of Kirkham ; joined the Cistercians as more ascetic ; monk at Wardon and Rievaulx ; elected abbot of Melrose, 1148 ; venerated as a saint ; miracles wrought at his tomb. [lix. 267]

WALTON. [See also WAUTON.]

WALTON, BRIAN or BRYAN (1600 ?–1661), bishop of Chester and editor of the ' English Polyglot Bible ' ; a Yorkshireman ; of Magdalene College and Peterhouse, Cambridge ; B.A., 1620 ; D.D., 1639 ; curate in Suffolk, 1623 ; incumbent of St. Martin's Orgar, London, 1628–41, and of Sandon, Essex, 1636–41 ; wrote a treatise on London tithes, 1634 (published, 1752) ; king's chaplain ; ejected from his livings for ritualism, 1641 ; imprisoned, 1642 ; withdrew to Oxford and studied oriental languages ; incorporated D.D. at Oxford, 1645 ; fined as a delinquent, 1647 ; returned to London, 1647 ; invited subscriptions for his ' Polyglot,' 1652 ; issued it with the help of many scholars, 1654–7, adding critical prolegomena ; published an introduction to oriental languages, 1655 ; restored to his benefices, 1660 ; consecrated bishop of Chester, 1660. [lix. 268]

WALTON, CHRISTOPHER (1809–1877), theosopher ; came from Lancashire to London, 1830 ; a silk-mercer ; then a jeweller ; a Wesleyan methodist ; published notes on the life of William Law (the same work containing discussions on mysticism, especially as represented by Boehme and Freher), 1854 ; his collection of manuscripts and theosophic collections now in the Dr. Williams Library, London. [lix. 271]

WALTON, ELIJAH (1832–1880), painter of mountain scenery in oil and watercolours ; art student in Birmingham and London ; sketched in Switzerland, Egypt, Syria, Greece, Norway, 1860–70 ; published illustrated books. [lix. 272]

WALTON, SIR GEORGE (1665–1739), admiral ; in active service, 1690–1736 ; lieutenant, 1690 ; commander, 1697 ; ably seconded Rodney in the West Indies, 1702 ; commander-in-chief at Portsmouth, 1712 ; captured a Spanish squadron off Sicily, 1718 ; famous for the laconic

(but fictitious) report, ' the number as per margin ' (ships captured and destroyed in the engagement) ; knighted, 1722 ; rear-admiral, 1723 ; admiral, 1734. [lix. 272]

WALTON, ISAAC (1651–1719), divine ; son of Izaak Walton [q. v.] ; M.A. Christ Church, Oxford, 1676 ; travelled in Italy, 1675 ; prebendary of Salisbury, 1678–1719 ; rector of Poulshot, 1680–1719. [lix. 276]

WALTON, IZAAK (1593–1683), author of ' The Compleat Angler ' ; born in Stafford ; apprentice to a London ironmonger ; in business for himself in London, 1614 ; freeman of the Ironmongers' Company, 1618 ; wrote verses before 1619 ; contributed copies of verses to books by his friends, 1638–61 ; favoured the royalists, 1642 ; married his second wife, 1646 ; lived with Bishop George Morley at Farnham, 1662–78 ; lived at Winchester with his son-in-law, Dr. William Hawkins, canon of Winchester, 1678–83 ; published his biographies of Dr. John Donne, 1640, of Sir Henry Wotton, 1651, of Richard Hooker, 1665, of George Herbert, 1670, and of Bishop Robert Sanderson, 1678 ; ' The Compleat Angler ' first appeared in 1653, and the second edition in 1655. Cotton wrote his dialogue between ' Piscator ' and ' Viator ' in 1676, and it was published as a second part in the ' Compleat Angler,' 5th ed., 1676. [lix. 273]

WALTON, JAMES (1802–1883), manufacturer and inventor ; a Yorkshireman ; cloth-friezer, and afterwards machine-manufacturer, near Halifax ; removed to Lancashire before 1846 ; introduced improvements in cotton-spinning machinery, 1834–40 ; bought Dolforgan Hall, Montgomeryshire, 1870. [lix. 277]

WALTON, JOHN (fl. 1410), poet ; monk of Osney ; wrote a verse translation of Boethius ' De Consolatione Philosophiæ ' (published, 1525). [lix. 278]

WALTON, JOHN (d. 1490 ?), archbishop of Dublin ; probably the same with John Walton, who, as monk of Osney, graduated B.A. at Oxford, 1450 ; abbot of Osney, 1452 ; D.D., 1463 ; consecrated archbishop of Dublin, 1472 ; resigned, 1484. [lix. 278]

WALTON or **WAUTON**, SIR THOMAS (1370 ?–1437?), speaker of the House of Commons in 1425 ; of Great Staughton ; M.P., Huntingdonshire, 1397, 1400, and 1402, Bedfordshire, May 1414, Huntingdonshire, November 1414, 1420, and 1422, Bedfordshire, 1419, 1425, and 1432 ; sheriff of Bedfordshire, 1415–16, 1428–9, 1432–3 ; chamberlain of North Wales, 1422. [lix. 279]

WALTON, VALENTINE (d. 1661 ?), regicide ; of Great Staughton ; married Oliver Cromwell's sister, 1619 ; M.P., Huntingdonshire, in the Long parliament, 1640 ; raised a troop of horse for the service of parliament, 1642 ; taken prisoner at Edgehill, 1642 ; parliamentary colonel of foot, 1643 ; governor of Lynn, 1643 ; sat as judge at Charles I's trial and signed the warrant, 1649 ; member of the parliamentary council of state ; resumed his seat in parliament, 1659 ; commissioner of the navy ; commissioner for the government of the army, October 1659–February 1660 ; secured Portsmouth for the parliament ; commanded a regiment ; excepted from the act of pardon, 1660 ; fled to Germany. [lix. 279]

WALTON, WILLIAM (1784–1857), writer on Spain ; educated in Spain and Portugal ; travelled in Spanish America ; British agent in San Domingo, 1802–9 ; wrote against the government policy in Spain and Portugal, from 1810 ; advocated the naturalisation of the alpaca. [lix. 280]

WALWORTH, COUNT JENISON (1764–1824). [See JENISON, FRANCIS.]

WALWORTH, SIR WILLIAM (d. 1385), lord mayor of London ; probably a native of Durham ; apprenticed to John Lovekyn [q. v.], fishmonger, London ; alderman, 1368 ; sheriff, 1370 ; mayor of London, 1374 ; one of the city deputation to Edward III, 1376 ; lent money to Richard II from 1377 ; an adherent of the Duke of Lancaster, 1378 ; built a chantry chapel for ten chantry priests in St. Michael's, Crooked Lane, c. 1380 ; mayor of London, 1381 ; held London Bridge against Wat Tyler, 13 June, 1381 ; killed Tyler in Richard II's presence, 15 June, 1381, and was knighted for it ; a commissioner to suppress the rising and quiet Kent, 1381–2 ; M.P., London, 1383 ; had a fine collection of books ; a figure of him displayed in the mayoral pageant, 1616, 1799. [lix. 281]

WALWYN, WILLIAM (*fl.* 1649), pamphleteer; silk-man in London; took the parliamentary side; advocated religious toleration; a leader of the 'levellers,' 1647; imprisoned, 1649; published pamphlets defending himself, 1646–51; not identical with the William Walwyn who was appointed canon of St. Paul's, London, in 1660.
[lix. 284]

WANDESFORD, CHRISTOPHER (1592–1640), lord deputy of Ireland; of Clare College, Cambridge, *c.* 1607–1612; student of Gray's Inn, 1612; inherited Kirklington, Yorkshire, 1612; a personal friend of Sir Thomas Wentworth; M.P., Aldborough, 1621 and 1624, Richmond, Yorkshire, 1625 and 1626, Thirsk, 1628; an opponent of Charles I; led the attack on Buckingham, 1628; changed over to the king's side, 1629; accompanied Wentworth to Ireland; Irish privy councillor and master of the rolls, 1633; served as a lord justice during Wentworth's absence, 1636 and 1639; acquired Castlecomer, Kilkenny, 1637; lord-deputy of Ireland, 1640; unsuccessful in handling the Irish parliament, 1640; died in Dublin.
[lix. 285]

WANDESFORD, SIR CHRISTOPHER, second VIS-COUNT CASTLECOMER (*d.* 1719), succeeded to the Irish peerage, 1707; M.P., Morpeth, 1710–13, Ripon, 1715; governor of Kilkenny, 1715; secretary at war, 1718.
[lix. 287]

WANLEY, HUMFREY (1672–1726), antiquary; draper's apprentice at Coventry, 1687–94; read widely; went to Oxford, 1695; assistant in the Bodleian Library, 1696; prepared the index to Edward Bernard's 'Cata-logue of MSS.,' 1697; prepared a catalogue of Anglo-Saxon manuscripts, 1700; assistant-secretary, 1700, and secretary, 1702–8, of the S.P.C.K., London; catalogued the Harleian MSS., 1708; librarian to the first and second earls of Oxford; F.S.A., 1717; his correspondence in the British Museum and the Bodleian. [lix. 287]

WANLEY, NATHANIEL (1634–1680), divine and compiler; M.A. Trinity College, Cambridge, 1657; rector of Beeby; vicar of Trinity Church, Coventry, 1662; pub-lished 'The Wonders of the Little World' (an anecdotal treatise on mankind), 1678, and other works. [lix. 289]

WANOSTROCHT, NICOLAS (1745–1812), teacher of French; a Belgian; came to England before 1780; had a private school at Camberwell, 1795; published a French grammar, 1780, and vocabulary, 1783, and other school-books. [lix. 290]

WANOSTROCHT, NICHOLAS (1804–1876), cricketer; had a private school at Camberwell, 1824–30, and at Blackheath, 1830–58; a leading cricketer, playing under the name of N. FELIX, 1828–51; published 'Felix on the Bat,' 1845. [lix. 290]

WANSEY, HENRY (1752?–1827), antiquary; a clothier of Warminster; F.S.A., 1789; made collections for the history of Warminster hundred; published pam-phlets, 1780–1814. [lix. 291]

WARBECK, PERKIN (1474–1499), Pretender; son of John Osbeck or De Werbecque, controller of Tournay; went to Portugal as page to a Yorkist lady, wife of Sir Edward Brampton; accompanied a Breton, Pregent Meno, to Ireland, 1491; thought by people in Cork to be a son of George, duke of Clarence, or of Richard III; became assured of the support of the Earls of Desmond and Kildare, and gave out that he was Richard, duke of York, son of Edward IV; learnt English; wrote to James IV of Scotland, February 1492; went to France, on Charles VIII's invitation, October 1492; acknowledged by Margaret, dowager-duchess of Burgundy [q. v.], to be her nephew, November 1492; his banishment demanded by Henry VII, July 1493; went to Vienna, November 1493; recognised as Richard IV, king of England, and supplied with money for his expedition by the Emperor Maximilian I, 1494; denounced as an impostor at Mechlin by Garter king-of-arms; his English adherents arrested and executed, 1495; repulsed at Deal, July 1495, and at Waterford; welcomed by James IV at Stirling, November 1495; married Lady Catherine Gordon (*d.* 1537); accom-panied James IV on a raid into Northumberland, pro-claiming himself King Richard IV, September 1496; sailed to Cork, July 1497; landed in Cornwall, proclaim-ing himself King Richard IV; advanced to Exeter; taken prisoner, September 1497; confessed his imposture at

Taunton, October 1497; prisoner in the Tower of London, November 1497–November 1499; hanged, after an at-tempted escape. [lix. 291]

WARBURTON, BARTHOLOMEW ELLIOTT GEORGE, usually known as ELIOT WARBURTON (1810–1852), miscellaneous writer; an Irishman; member of the Cambridge University Dramatic Club, 1830; of Queens' and Trinity Colleges, Cambridge; M.A. Trinity College, Cambridge, 1837; Irish barrister, 1837; pub-lished, 1845, 'The Crescent and the Cross,' an account of his 1843 Eastern tour; published biographies of Prince Rupert and other cavaliers, 1849, historical novels, and other works; perished in a burning steamer. [lix. 294]

WARBURTON, GEORGE DROUGHT (1816–1857), writer on Canada; an Irishman; educated at Wool-wich; served in the artillery, 1833–54; stationed in Canada, 1844–6; major; M.P., Harwich, 1857; published 'Hochelaga' (an account of Canada), 1846, and other works. [lix. 296]

WARBURTON, HENRY (1784?–1858), philosophical radical; educated at Eton and Trinity College, Cam-bridge; M.A., 1812; timber-merchant at Lambeth; F.R.S., 1809; M.P., Bridport, 1826–41, Kendal, 1843–7; advocated the foundation of London University, 1826, medical reform, 1827–34, the repeal of the duties on news-papers and corn, and penny postage. [lix. 296]

WARBURTON, JOHN (1682–1759), herald and anti-quary; exciseman in Yorkshire; F.R.S., 1719–57; F.S.A., 1720; Somerset herald, 1720–59; collected scarce books and manuscripts; sold some of his manuscripts to the Earl of Oxford, July 1720; his cook, Betsy Baker, said to have destroyed unique Elizabethan and Jacobean plays; published maps of several counties, and, 1753, a survey of the Roman wall; his collections sold by auction, 1766.
[lix. 297]

WARBURTON, SIR PETER (1540?–1621), judge; barrister, Lincoln's Inn, 1572; sheriff of Cheshire, 1583; M.P., Chester, 1587–98; serjeant-at-law, 1593; justice of the common pleas, 1600–21; knighted, 1603. [lix. 299]

WARBURTON, PETER (1588–1666), judge; of Hef-ferston Grange, Cheshire; B.A. Brasenose College, Ox-ford, 1606; barrister, Lincoln's Inn, 1612; took the par-liamentary side; justice of Chester, 1647; serjeant-at-law, 1649; justice of the common pleas, 1649; justice of the upper bench, 1655; removed at the Restoration.
[lix. 299]

WARBURTON, PETER EGERTON (1813–1889), Australian explorer; educated in France; served in the army, 1831–53; captain, 1845; major, 1853; in command of the South Australian police, 1853–67, and volunteers, 1869–77; travelled overland from Adelaide to Perth, 1872–4, experiencing much privation; C.M.G., 1875; published a narrative of his 'Journey,' 1875; died at Adelaide. [lix. 300]

WARBURTON, SIR ROBERT (1842–1899), warden of the Kyber; studied at Addiscombe and Woolwich; ob-tained commission in royal regiment of artillery, 1861; went to India, 1862, exchanged to 21st Punjab infantry, 1866, and served in Abyssinian campaign, 1868; political officer of the Kyber, 1879; major, 1881; lieutenant-colonel, 1887; C.S.I., 1890; brevet-colonel, 1893; resigned, 1897; served with Tirah expedition, 1897–9; K.C.I.E., 1898. His reminiscences were published, 1900, under title, 'Eighteen Years in the Kyber.' [Suppl. iii. 504]

WARBURTON, ROWLAND EYLES EGERTON-(1804–1891), poet; of Arley Hall, Cheshire; educated at Eton and Corpus Christi College, Oxford; travelled; high sheriff of Cheshire, 1833; published 'Hunting Songs,' 1846, and other verses, 1855–79. [lix. 301]

WARBURTON, THOMAS ACTON (*d.* 1894), writer of legal and historical books; a barrister; vicar of Iffley, 1853–76, and of St. John's, East Dulwich, 1876–88.
[lix. 295]

WARBURTON, WILLIAM (1698–1779), bishop of Gloucester; articled to a Nottinghamshire attorney, 1714–19; ordained, 1723; published translations from Latin, 1724, and pamphlets on chancery procedure and on prodigies, 1727; vicar of Greaseley, 1727–8; honorary M.A. Cambridge, 1728; rector of Brant Broughton, 1728–57?; non-resident vicar of Frisby, 1730–56; read widely; had a large literary correspondence; published 'The Alliance between Church and State,' 1736, and 'The

Divine Legation of Moses,' part i., 1737, part ii., 1741, the latter (a work famous for its paradoxical view) maintaining the law of Moses to be of divine origin, inasmuch as through its not containing a socially essential doctrine, viz. that of future rewards and punishments, it must have been supported by an 'extraordinary providence'; plunged by the 'Legation' into controversies with his critics, 1738–65; chaplain to Frederick, prince of Wales, 1738; gained Alexander Pope's friendship by publishing a defence of his 'Essay on Man,' 1739; advised Pope to add a fourth book to the 'Dunciad,' and furnished him with notes ridiculing Richard Bentley's 'Milton'; wrote against Viscount Bolingbroke, 1742–55; preacher at Lincoln's Inn, 1746; published an edition of Shakespeare, 1747, which was sharply criticised by Thomas Edwards (1699–1757) [q. v.] and others; began a friendship with Richard Hurd [q. v.], 1749; published 'Julian,' a theological work, 1750; having been left Pope's literary executor in 1744, brought out an edition of Pope's works, 1751, and put up a monument to him in Twickenham church, 1761; prebendary of Gloucester, 1753–5; king's chaplain and D.D. Lambeth, 1754; prebendary of Durham, 1755–79; dean of Bristol, 1757; bishop of Gloucester, 1759–79; published 'The Doctrine of Grace,' an argument against John Wesley's views, 1762; preached against the slave trade, 1766; his 'Collected Works' edited by Hurd, 1788. [lix. 301]

WARD. [See also WARDE.]

WARD, SIR EDWARD (1638-1714), judge; barrister, Inner Temple, 1664; practised in the exchequer court; a whig; one of the counsel for William Russell, lord Russell, 1683; withstood Chief-justice Jeffreys's browbeating, 1684; declined a justiceship of the common pleas, 1689; attorney-general and knighted, 1693; bought Stoke-Doyle, Northamptonshire, 1694; chief-baron of the exchequer, 1695–1714. [lix. 311]

WARD, EDWARD (1667-1731), humorist; born in Oxfordshire; visited the West Indies; kept a tavern in London; published a great number of coarse poems, printed 1691–1734, satirising the whigs and the low-church party, and descriptive of life in London; pilloried for an attack on the government, 1705; issued 'The London Spy,' in parts, 1698–1709, 'Hudibras Redivivus,' 1705–7, and other works of coarse humour. [lix. 312]

WARD, EDWARD MATTHEW (1816-1879), historical painter; trained in London; exhibited a portrait, 1834; visited Paris, Venice, Rome, Munich, 1836–9; exhibited at the Royal Academy, 1840–79, chiefly pictures illustrative of English history in the seventeenth and eighteenth centuries and of the French revolution and the first empire; painted frescoes for the houses of parliament, 1853; R.A., 1855. [lix. 314]

WARD, GEORGE RAPHAEL (1798-1878), engraver; son of James Ward (1769-1859) [q. v.]; engraved chiefly portraits. [lix. 317]

WARD, SIR HENRY GEORGE (1797-1860), colonial governor; of Gilston Park, Hertfordshire; eldest son of Robert Plumer Ward [q. v.]; attaché at Stockholm, 1816, the Hague, 1818, and Madrid, 1819; minister to Mexico, 1823–4 and 1825–7; published 'Mexico in 1825–7'; liberal M.P. for St. Albans, 1832–7, Sheffield, 1837–49; advocated disestablishment of the Irish church; secretary of the admiralty, 1846; G.C.M.G., 1849; governor of the Ionian islands, 1849–55; governor of Ceylon, 1855-60; governor of Madras, June 1860; died at Madras. [lix. 316]

WARD, HUGH (1580?-1635). [See MACANWARD, HUGH BOY.]

WARD, JAMES (1769-1859), engraver and painter; trained in London; exhibited paintings, chiefly of animals, 1790–1855; R.A., 1811. [lix. 317]

WARD, JAMES (1800-1885), pugilist and artist; son of a London butcher; cabin-boy on a collier; a London coal-whipper; a professional prize-fighter, 1821–32; 'British champion,' July 1825 and July 1831; tavern-keeper in Liverpool, 1832–53, and in London from 1853; exhibited oil-paintings of some merit, 1846–60. [lix. 317]

WARD, JAMES CLIFTON (1843-1880), geologist; trained in the Royal School of Mines, 1861; attached to the geological survey in Yorkshire, 1865–9, and in the Lake district, 1869–77; curate at Keswick, 1878; vicar of Rydal, 1880; published geological papers and text-books. [lix. 319]

WARD, JOHN (fl. 1613), composer; published 'English Madrigals,' 1613; composed anthems. [lix. 319]

WARD, JOHN ? (fl. 1601-1615), pirate; known as CAPTAIN WARD; a Feversham fisherman; probably seaman in the West Indies; petty officer in a king's ship at Portsmouth, c. 1601; seized a ship at Portsmouth and sailed on a piratical cruise, 1603; a renegade and pirate at Tunis, 1615, where he built himself a palace; cruised under the Turkish or Tunisian flag, especially against the Venetians and Knights of Malta. [lix. 320]

WARD, JOHN (fl. 1642-1643), poet; a parliamentary trooper, 1642; published, 1642, 'The Taking of Winchester,' lauding the parliamentary army, and 'An Encouragement to Warre' (reissued in 1643 as 'The Christian's Incouragement'), denouncing the cavaliers. [lix. 321]

WARD, JOHN (1679?-1758), biographer; clerk in the navy office; schoolmaster in Moorfields, 1710; professor of rhetoric, Gresham College, London, 1720–58; F.R.S., 1723; F.S.A., 1736; hon. LL.D. Edinburgh, 1751; published treatises on rhetoric, dissertations on classical topics, and 'The Lives of the Professors of Gresham College,' 1740; manuscript antiquarian collections by him in the British Museum library. [lix. 321]

WARD, JOHN (1781-1837), mystic; born near Cork; without education; learned to be a shipwright at Bristol, 1793, and a shoemaker in London, 1797; shipwright at sea, 1801–3; married, 1803; shoemaker, 1803–27; successively a Calvinist, methodist, baptist, a Sandemanian preacher (1813); refused admission to the Southcottians (1814); founded a church of his own, styling himself 'Zion' or 'Shiloh,' 1827; travelled in the north of England preaching, 1829–37; several times imprisoned between 1828 and 1834; published several tracts, treating the biblical narrative as allegory, 1829–37, and left hundreds of others in manuscript. [lix. 322]

WARD, JOHN (1805-1890), diplomatist; inspector of prisons, 1837; secretary to the New Zealand Colonisation Company, 1838; consul-general at Leipzig, 1845, and at Hamburg to the Hanse Towns, 1860–70. [lix. 323]

WARD, JOHN (1825-1896), naval captain and surveyor; served in the navy, 1840–70; lieutenant, 1850; captain, 1873; employed on survey duty on the Scottish coast, 1855–6, and in Chinese waters, 1858–66. [lix. 324]

WARD, JOHN WILLIAM, first EARL OF DUDLEY of Castle Dudley, Staffordshire, and fourth VISCOUNT DUDLEY AND WARD (1781-1833), educated at Oriel and Corpus Christi Colleges, Oxford, and at Edinburgh; M.A. Oxford, 1813; tory M.P., Downton, 1802, Worcestershire, 1803, Petersfield, 1806, Wareham, 1807, Ilchester, 1812, and Bossiney, 1819–23; travelled, 1814–22; succeeded his father as fourth Viscount Dudley and Ward, 1823; foreign secretary, 1827–8; created Earl of Dudley, 1827; placed under restraint, 1832. [lix. 324]

WARD, JOSHUA (1685-1761), quack doctor; nicknamed 'Spot' Ward, from a birth-mark; fraudulently tried to enter parliament for Marlborough, 1717; fled to St. Germain; maintained himself by the sale of his universal remedy, his 'drop and pill,' a dangerous compound of antimony; pardoned, 1733; much patronised in London by admirers, and satirised in the newspapers; amassed a fortune; published some pamphlets. [lix. 326]

WARD, MARTIN THEODORE (1799?-1874), painter of dogs and horses; pupil of Landseer; exhibited, 1820–1850; afterwards lived in retirement at York. [lix. 344]

WARD, MARY (1585-1645), founder of a female order modelled on the rule of the jesuits; niece of John Wright (1568?-1605) [q. v.]; educated in Roman catholic faith; went to St. Omer, 1606, and entered the community of the Colettines, but left the convent, 1607; obtained from archdukes of Brussels land for a convent near Gravelines, and formed a community; returned to St. Omer, 1609, and founded in the Grosse Rue another community which chiefly concerned itself with education of girls; adopted rules of Society of Jesus for her community, adapting them for use of women, 1611; removed to a subordinate community which had been established at Liège, 1617; obtained leave from Pope Gregory XV to establish a house in Rome, 1622 ; suffered persecution and proceeded with community to Munich, 1626 ; obtained support of Emperor Ferdinand and established herself in Vienna, 1627 ; aroused considerable ecclesiastical opposition, and accordingly returned to Munich, 1630 ; received permission from Pope Urban VIII to establish second house in Rome, 1634 ; fled from persecution to London, 1638, and lived with community in Strand till 1642 ; sought refuge in Yorkshire at outbreak of civil war. [Suppl. iii. 506]

WARD, NATHANIEL (1578–1652), puritan divine ; entered Emmanuel College, Cambridge, 1596 ; M.A., 1603 ; studied law ; travelled ; chaplain at Elbing, 1620–4 ; rector of Stondon Massey, 1628 ; deprived by Laud for nonconformity, 1633 ; minister in Massachusetts, 1634–6 ; joint-author of the 1641 New England code of laws ; returned to England, 1646 ; rector of Shenfield, 1648–52 ; published theological tracts. [lix. 328]

WARD, NATHANIEL BAGSHAW (1791–1868), botanist ; visited Jamaica, 1804 ; medical practitioner in London ; an enthusiastic botanist and plant-cultivator ; invented the ‘Wardian’ case for transporting plants, 1829 ; F.R.S., 1852. [lix. 328]

WARD, SIR PATIENCE (1629–1696), lord mayor of London ; a Yorkshireman ; apprenticed to a London merchant taylor, 1646–53 ; master of the Merchant Taylors’ Company, 1671 ; knighted, 1675 ; alderman and sheriff, 1670, and lord mayor, 1680, of London ; expressed strong protestant opinions ; probably directed the additional inscription to the effect that the fire of London (1666) was caused by the papists to be placed on the Monument ; presented the unpalatable city addresses to Charles II, May–July, 1681 ; convicted of perjury in defence of Sir Thomas Pilkington, 1683 ; escaped to Holland ; pardoned, 1688 ; M.P., London, 1689 ; a commissioner of the customs, 1689–96 ; colonel of militia, 1689 and 1691. [lix. 329]

WARD, ROBERT PLUMER (1765–1846), novelist and politician ; called Robert Ward till 1828, when he took the additional name of Plumer ; of Westminster School and Christ Church, Oxford ; travelled ; barrister, Inner Temple, 1790 ; a partisan of Pitt ; wrote on legal and political questions, 1795–1838 ; M.P., Cockermouth, 1802–6, Haslemere, 1807–23 ; under-secretary for foreign affairs, 1805–6 ; a commissioner of the admiralty, 1807–11 ; clerk of the ordnance, 1811–23 ; published three society novels, 1825, 1827, 1841 ; high sheriff of Hertfordshire, 1830 ; kept a political diary from 1809. [lix. 331]

WARD, SAMUEL (1577–1640), of Ipswich ; puritan divine ; scholar of St. John’s College, Cambridge, 1594 ; B.A., 1597 ; an original fellow of Sidney Sussex College, 1599–1604 ; M.A., 1600 ; B.D., 1607 ; puritan ‘lecturer’ at Haverhill, Suffolk, and, 1603–35, at Ipswich ; married, 1604 ; imprisoned for an anti-Spanish engraving, 1621 ; prosecuted for nonconformity, 1622–3 ; suspended for puritanical preaching, 1635 ; withdrew to Holland ; returned to Ipswich before 1638 ; published theological tracts and sermons. [lix. 333]

WARD, SAMUEL (d. 1643), master of Sidney Sussex College, Cambridge ; scholar of Christ’s College, Cambridge ; fellow of Emmanuel College, 1595–9 ; M.A., 1596 ; fellow of Sidney Sussex College, 1599, and master, 1610–1643 ; D.D., 1610 ; king’s chaplain, 1611 ; one of the translators of the Apocrypha ; archdeacon of Taunton, 1615 ; prebendary of Wells, 1615, of York, 1618 ; delegate at the synod of Dort, 1619 ; Lady Margaret professor of divinity, Cambridge, 1623–43 ; a leading puritan and Calvinist ; refused the covenant, 1643 ; published theological treatises. [lix. 335]

WARD, SETH (1617–1689), bishop of Salisbury ; M.A. Sidney Sussex College, Cambridge, 1640 ; fellow, 1640–4 ; lectured on mathematics, 1643 ; instructed by William Oughtred [q. v.] ; wrote against the covenant, 1643 ; ejected from his fellowship, 1644 ; private tutor at Aspenden, 1645–9 ; incorporated M.A. at Oxford. 1649 ; held the Savilian professorship of astronomy, Oxford, 1649–61 ; D.D., 1654 ; advanced a theory of planetary motion on the assumption of a centre of uniform motion ; published ‘Vindiciæ Academiarum,’ against critics of university education, 1654, and critiques of Thomas Hobbes, 1656, being associated with John Wallis (1616–1703) [q. v.] in his controversy with the latter ; nominated precentor of Exeter, 1656 ; elected principal of Jesus College, Oxford,

but ejected by Cromwell, 1657 ; intruded president of Trinity College, Oxford, September 1659 to August 1660 ; beneficed in London, Devon, and Cornwall, 1661–2 ; prebendary, 1660, dean, 1661, and bishop, 1662–7, of Exeter ; translated to Salisbury, 1667 ; severe against dissenters ; chancellor of the Garter, 1671 ; published sermons and theological and mathematical treatises. [lix. 336]

WARD, THOMAS (1652–1708), controversialist ; a Yorkshireman ; embraced Romanism ; soldier of the pope’s guard ; resided in England, 1685–8 ; died in France ; published controversial tracts, 1686–8 ; other pieces by him published posthumously. [lix. 340]

WARD, THOMAS, BARON WARD of the Austrian Empire (1809–1858), a Yorkshire jockey ; went as jockey to Hungary, 1823 ; entered the service of Charles Louis of Bourbon, duke of Lucca, 1827 ; made his master’s peace with Austria, 1843 ; styled baron, and minister of the household to Charles Louis, 1846 ; when his master became Duke of Parma, 1847, was chief minister of Parma, holding that place till 1854 ; created baron of the Austrian empire, 1849 ; envoy to Great Britain, 1849 ; died in Austria. [lix. 340]

WARD or **WARDE, WILLIAM** (1534–1604 ?), physician ; educated at Eton ; fellow of King’s College, Cambridge, 1553–68 ; M.A., 1558 ; M.D., 1567 ; medical lecturer at Cambridge, 1596 ; translated, from French, Alessio of Piedmont’s medical ‘Secrets,’ and other works, 1558–62. [lix. 341]

WARD, WILLIAM (1769–1823), baptist missionary ; printer in Derby, Stafford, and, 1794, Hull ; a local preacher ; superintendent of the baptist missionary press in Bengal, 1799–1818 ; travelled in Great Britain, Germany, and the United States, collecting funds for the baptist college at Serampúr, 1818–21 ; wrote on Indian missions, 1811–21 ; died at Serampúr. [lix. 342]

WARD, WILLIAM (1766–1826), engraver ; trained in London ; engraved, chiefly in mezzotint, portraits and landscapes. [lix. 343]

WARD, WILLIAM (1787–1849), financier ; trained at Antwerp ; merchant in London, 1810 ; director of the Bank of England, 1817 ; a famous cricketer ; bought the lease of Lord’s cricket ground to save it from being sold for building purposes, 1825 ; tory M.P., London, 1826–31. [lix. 344]

WARD, WILLIAM GEORGE (1812–1882), Roman catholic theologian and philosopher ; eldest son of William Ward (1787–1849) [q. v.] ; at Winchester School, 1823–9 ; scholar of Lincoln College, Oxford, 1833 ; fellow of Balliol, 1834–45 ; mathematical lecturer, 1834–41, bursar, 1842 ; M.A., 1837 ; adopted John Henry Newman’s [q. v.] views, c. 1838 ; wrote in defence of Newman’s Tract XC, 1841 ; published ‘The Ideal of a Christian Church,’ a Romanist treatise, 1844, and hence was nicknamed ‘Ideal Ward’ ; removed from his degree for heresy, February 1845 ; inherited estates, 1849 ; moral philosophy lecturer in St. Edmund’s College, Ware, 1851–1858 ; Ph.D., by Pope Pius IX, 1854 ; edited the ‘Dublin Review,’ 1863–78, writing against liberal theology and in favour of papal infallibility ; wrecked Newman’s projected Romanist college at Oxford ; resided latterly in the Isle of Wight ; published controversial treatises, 1852–80. [lix. 344]

WARD, WILLIAM JAMES (1800 ?–1840), mezzotint engraver, chiefly of portraits ; son of William Ward (1766–1826) [q. v.] [lix. 348]

WARD-HUNT, GEORGE (1825–1877). [See HUNT.]

WARDE, SIR EDWARD CHARLES (1810–1884), general ; son of Sir Henry Warde [q. v.] ; served in the artillery, 1828–69 ; commanded the siege-train at Sebastopol ; K.C.B., 1869 ; major-general, 1866 ; general, 1877. [lix. 348]

WARDE, SIR HENRY (1766–1834), general ; ensign, 1783 ; captain, 1790 ; lieutenant-colonel, 1794 ; brigadier-general, 1807 ; commanded a brigade in Spain, 1808–9 ; took part in the capture of the Mauritius, 1810 ; governor of the Mauritius, 1811–13 ; lieutenant-general, 1813 ; K.C.B., 1815 ; governor of Barbados, 1821–7 ; general, 1830 ; G.C.B., 1831. [lix. 348]

WARDE, JAMES PRESCOTT (1792–1840), actor ; real name Prescott, added the name Warde professionally ; appeared at Bath, 1813–18, 1823, in London, 1818–20, 1825–38 ; died in poverty. [lix. 349]

WARDE, LUKE (*fl.* 1587), sea captain; sailed with Sir Martin Frobisher [q. v.], 1576–8, and with Edward Fenton [q. v.], 1582–3; commanded a queen's ship, 1587–1591; fought against the Armada, 1588.   [lix. 350]

WARDEN, WILLIAM (1777–1849), naval surgeon; trained at Montrose and Edinburgh; surgeon in the navy, 1795–1849; M.D. St. Andrews, 1811; M.D. Edinburgh, 1824; in attendance on Napoleon during his voyage and in St. Helena, 1815; censured for publishing, 1816, garbled notes of his conversations with Napoleon.   [lix. 350]

WARDER, JOSEPH (*fl.* 1688–1718), author of 'The True Amazons,' a treatise on bees, 1693; physician at Croydon before 1688.   [lix. 351]

WARDLAW, ELIZABETH, LADY (1677–1727), supposed authoress of the ballad of 'Hardyknute'; *née* Halket; married, 1696, Sir Henry Wardlaw of Pitcruivie; published, as an old ballad, 'Hardyknute,' 1719; reputed authoress of 'Sir Patrick Spens,' and other ballads.   [lix. 352]

WARDLAW, HENRY (*d.* 1440), bishop of St. Andrews; educated at Oxford, and, 1383, Paris; studied civil law at Orleans before 1388; D.Can.L.; nephew of Walter Wardlaw [q. v.]; held canonries of Glasgow, Moray, and Aberdeen, and other preferments; long resided at Avignon; consecrated bishop of St. Andrews, 1403; tutor to James I of Scotland; restored St. Andrews Cathedral; founded the university of St. Andrews, February 1411; crowned James I and his queen, 1424; burned Wycliffites, 1407 and 1432.   [lix. 352]

WARDLAW, RALPH (1779–1853), Scottish congregational divine; entered Glasgow University, 1791; studied for the ministry of the secession (burgher) church, 1795–1800; congregational minister in Glasgow, 1803–1853, and from 1811 divinity professor in the congregational seminary there; honorary D.D. Yale, 1818; published hymns, sermons, and tracts on social and theological questions.   [lix. 353]

WARDLAW, WALTER (*d.* 1390), cardinal; secretary to David II; archdeacon of Glasgow; bishop of Glasgow, 1368–90; cardinal, 1381.   [lix. 354]

WARDLE, GWYLLYM LLOYD (1762 ?–1833), soldier and politician; of Hartsheath; yeomanry officer in Ireland, 1798; titular lieutenant-colonel; M.P., Okehampton, 1807–12; attacked, and by a parliamentary committee procured the retirement of, Frederick, duke of York, commander-in-chief, for granting commissions through his mistress, Mary Anne Clarke [q. v.], 1809; thanked by the city of London; suspected of collusion with Mrs. Clarke, July 1809; went abroad to escape his creditors; died in Florence.   [lix. 355]

WARDROP, JAMES (1782–1869), surgeon; trained in Edinburgh, 1797, London, 1801, and Vienna, 1803; ophthalmic surgeon in Edinburgh, 1804–8, and London, 1808–1869; M.D. St. Andrews, 1834; lectured on surgery from 1826; published surgical treatises.   [lix. 355]

WARE, HUGH (1772 ?–1846), colonel in the French army; a United Irishman; joined the insurgents, 1798; taken prisoner; allowed to go abroad, 1802; served in the French Irish legion, 1803–15; captain, 1804; received the cross of the Legion of Honour, 1812; colonel, 1815; died at Tours.   [lix. 357]

WARE, ISAAC (*d.* 1766), architect; studied in Italy; clerk of works in the government service, 1728–66; also engaged in private practice; published architectural drawings and treatises.   [lix. 358]

WARE, SIR JAMES (1594–1666), Irish historian; M.A. Trinity College, Dublin, 1616; collected Irish manuscripts and studied Irish history and antiquities; knighted, 1629; auditor-general of Ireland, 1632–49 ?, and 1660–6; M.P., Dublin University, 1634–7, 1661; sent on a mission to Charles I at Oxford, 1644; hon. D.C.L. Oxford; prisoner in the Tower, 1644–5; a hostage in England, 1647; banished from Dublin by Michael Jones [q. v.], 1649; resided in London, 1651–60; returned to Dublin, 1660; published important contributions to Irish history and biography, 1626–65.   [lix. 359]

WARE, JAMES (1756–1815), surgeon; trained at Portsmouth, 1770, and London, 1773–6; ophthalmic surgeon in London, 1777–1815; F.R.S., 1802; published professional papers and treatises, 1780–1812.   [lix. 360]

WARE, SAMUEL HIBBERT- (1782–1848). [See HIBBERT.]

WARE, WILLIAM OF (*fl.* 1300 ?). [See WILLIAM.]

WARELWAST, WILLIAM DE (*d.* 1137), bishop of Exeter; a Norman; 'king's clerk'; envoy to the pope from William Rufus, 1095, 1098, and from Henry I, 1103, 1105–6, 1119, and 1120; employed by Rufus to search Anselm's baggage, 1097, and by Henry I to arrange for Anselm's return, 1100–7; consecrated bishop of Exeter, 1107; attended the councils of Troyes, 1107, Rheims, 1119, and Northampton, 1131; became blind; began rebuilding Exeter Cathedral; founded Plympton priory; re-founded Launceston and Bodmin priories.   [lix. 361]

WARENNE, EARL OF (1307 ?–1376). [See FITZALAN, RICHARD II.]

WARENNE, GUNDRADA DE, COUNTESS OF SURREY (*d.* 1085). [See GUNDRADA.]

WARENNE, DE, FAMILY OF, took its name from the castle of Varenne (called later Bellencombre) on the river Varenne, département Seine-Inférieure; founded in England by William Warenne, first earl of Surrey [q. v.]; held at one time great estates in twelve English counties; chief seats at Lewes in Sussex and Conisborough, Yorkshire; in 1148 the family property passed to an heiress, Isabel de Warenne [q. v.]; was continued by her son, William de Warenne (*d.* 1240) [q. v.], taking his mother's name; acquired the earldom of Sussex after 1243 on the extinction of the De Albini family. A cadet branch acquired the De Wirmgay estates, Norfolk, by marriage, and became extinct about 1209; the legitimate main line expired with John de Warenne (1286–1347) [q. v.]

WARENNE, HAMELIN DE, EARL OF WARENNE or SURREY (*d.* 1202), illegitimate son of Geoffrey 'Plantagenet,' count of Anjou (*d.* 1151), and therefore half-brother of Henry II; married Isabella de Warenne [q. v.]; styled De Warenne and Earl of Surrey in right of his wife from 1163; denounced Thomas Becket as a traitor, 1164; remained faithful to Henry II, 1174 and 1189; escorted Princess Joan to Provence, 1176; present at the coronation of Richard I, 1189; opposed Prince John's intrigues, 1191; present at King Richard's second coronation, 1194, and at King John's, 1199; built the great keep at Conisborough; entertained King John at Conisborough, 1201.   [lix. 362]

WARENNE, ISABEL DE (*d.* 1199), only daughter and heiress of William de Warenne, third earl of Surrey (*d.* 1148) [q. v.]; married, before 1153, King Stephen's second son, William (*d.*, without issue, 1159); married, *c.* 1163, Hamelin de Warenne [q. v.]   [lix. 375]

WARENNE, JOHN DE, EARL OF SURREY or EARL WARENNE (1231 ?–1304), son of William de Warenne, earl of Warenne or Surrey (*d.* 1240) [q. v.]; long a royal ward; under the guardianship of Peter of Savoy [q. v.]; married, 1247, Alice de Lusignan, Henry III's half-sister; accompanied Prince Edward to Gascony and Spain, 1254; granted the 'third penny' of Sussex, 1256; took Henry III's side against the barons, 1258–9; acted with Simon de Montfort, 1260–3; returned to Henry III's side, 1263; besieged by Montfort in Rochester Castle, 1264; fought on Henry III's side at Lewes, May 1264; escaped to France; his lands confiscated by the barons, June 1264; joined Prince Edward at Ludlow, 1265; fought at Evesham, 1265; reduced Kent, 1265; pardoned for all his offences against Henry III, 1268; took the cross, 1268, but did not go on crusade; fined for turbulence, 1270; took the oaths to Edward I, 1272; served in Wales, 1277; led the opposition to the 1278 *quo warranto* writs, declaring that he held his lands 'by the sword,' 1279; after the death of his sister Isabella (widow of Hugh de Albini, earl of Sussex, *d.* 1243) in 1282, assumed the title of Earl of Sussex; served in Wales, 1282–3; was granted Bromfield and Yale by Edward I, 1282, and built Dinas Bran Castle on the Dee; sent on a mission to Scotland, 1285; fought in Wales, 1287 and 1294; negotiated with the Scots the treaties of Salisbury, 1289, and Brigham, 1290; custodian of the sea-coast, 1295; raised troops in Wales, and led them to Scotland in Edward I's invasion, 1296; took Dunbar Castle, April 1296; appointed warden of Scotland, August 1296; spent the winter and next spring and summer in the north of England; superseded in August, but re-appointed in September, 1297; routed by Wallace at Stirling Bridge, 11 Sept. 1297; ordered to lead fresh troops into Scotland, December 1297; raised the siege of Roxburgh, January 1298; fought at Falkirk, July 1298; besieged Caerlaverock Castle, July 1300.

[lix. 364]

WARENNE, JOHN DE, EARL OF SURREY AND SUSSEX, or EARL WARENNE (1286–1347); succeeded his grandfather in the estates and peerage, 1304; married to Joan of Bar (*d.* 1361), 1306; summoned to parliament, May 1306; quarrelled with Peter de Gaveston, 1307; reconciled to him, 1309; accompanied Edward II to Scotland, 1310; overran Selkirkshire, 1311; joined the barons' party; took Gaveston prisoner, under terms of protection, at Scarborough, 1312; being incensed at Gaveston's execution, went over to Edward II, August 1312; pardoned for all his offences against Edward II, 1313; refused to follow Edward to Bannockburn, June 1314; excommunicated for open adultery; agreed to pay a yearly allowance to his wife, February 1316; helped Thomas, earl of Lancaster's countess to elope, May 1317; stripped of great portions of his estates by Lancaster, 1317–19; served against the Scots, July 1319; joined Edward II against Lancaster, 1322, and recovered his Welsh lands; sent with troops into Aquitaine, 1325–6; took Edward II's side against Queen Isabella, and recovered his lands, May 1326; made his peace with Queen Isabella; counselled Edward II's abdication, January 1327; attended Edward III's coronation, March 1327; a commissioner to treat with the Scots, 1327; granted fresh estates, 1327–33; given the earldom of Strathern by Edward Baliol, 1333; accompanied Baliol to Scotland, 1333 and 1335; acted as sheriff of Surrey and Sussex, 1339; his estates reverted to the crown, and his earldom went to Richard Fitzalan II, earl of Arundel (1307 ?–1376) [q. v.] [lix. 368]

WARENNE or **WARREN,** WILLIAM DE, first EARL OF SURREY (*d.* 1088), fought as a knight at the battle of Mortemer, 1054; married Gundrada [q. v.] of Flanders; granted Mortemer Castle by Duke William; fought at Hastings, 1066; received great grants of lands and built castles at Lewes in Sussex, Reigate in Surrey, and Castle Acre in Norfolk; granted Conisborough, Yorkshire, 1069; fought against the refugees into Ely, 1071; joint chief justiciar, 1075; helped to suppress the rebellion of the Earls of Hereford and Norfolk; founded the Cluniac priories of St. Pancras, Lewes, 1077, and of Castle Acre; fought in Main, 1085; remained faithful to Rufus, 1088; granted the earldom of Surrey, *c.* 1088; fatally wounded at the siege of Pevensey Castle.

[lix. 372]

WARENNE or **WARREN,** WILLIAM DE, second EARL OF SURREY (*d.* 1138), frequently described as EARL OF WARENNE; elder son of William de Warenne (*d.* 1088) [q. v.]; took part in the defence of Courcy against Duke Robert, 1091; unsuccessful suitor, *c.* 1094, for Matilda, afterwards consort of Henry I; joined Duke Robert when he invaded England, 1101; withdrew to Normandy; pardoned by Henry II, 1103; fought in Normandy, 1106, 1119, 1135; attended Stephen's court at Westminster, 1136. [lix. 374]

WARENNE or **WARREN,** WILLIAM DE, third EARL OF SURREY (*d.* 1148), eldest son of William de Warenne, second earl of Surrey [q. v.]; succeeded his father, 1138; supported King Stephen, 1141–2; fought at Lincoln, 1141; went with the crusaders, 1147; killed near Laodicea. His estates passed to his daughter, Isabel de Warenne [q. v.]

[lix. 375]

WARENNE, WILLIAM DE, EARL OF WARENNE or SURREY (*d.* 1240), son of Hamelin de Warenne [q. v.]; succeeded to the title and estates, 1202; lost the estates in Normandy, 1204; granted Grantham and Stamford by King John, 1205; accompanied John to France, 1206; sided with John against the pope and against the barons; one of John's sureties for the keeping of Magna Charta, June 1215; granted forfeited lands in Norfolk, 1216; warden of the Cinque ports, 1216; supported Louis of France, June 1216 to April 1217; then joined Henry III and obtained grants of land; married, 1225, Matilda, co-heiress of William Marshal, first earl of Pembroke [q. v.]; one of the three regents, 1230; became surety for Hubert de Burgh, 1232; made a member of the king's council, 1237; sent to Oxford to protect the legate Otho, 1238; founded Reigate priory.

[lix. 375]

WARFORD *alias* WARNEFORD and WALFORD, WILLIAM (1560–1608), jesuit; scholar of Trinity College, Oxford, 1576, fellow, 1578, M.A., 1582; went to Rheims, 1582, and Rome, 1583; ordained priest, 1584; visited England, 1591; joined the jesuits, 1594; went to Spain, 1599; published doctrinal tracts under the pseudonym of George Doulye; died at Valladolid.

[lix. 378]

WARHAM, WILLIAM (1450 ?–1532), archbishop of Canterbury; a native of Hampshire; of Winchester College; fellow of New College, Oxford, 1475; LL.D. Oxford before 1488; LL.D. Cambridge, 1500; advocate in the court of arches, 1488; went on legal business to Rome, 1490, and Antwerp, 1491; went on a political mission to Flanders, 1493; precentor of Wells, 1493; master of the rolls, 1494–1502; rector of Barley, 1495–1501, and of Cottenham, 1500–1; archdeacon of Huntingdon, 1496; joint-envoy to Scotland, 1497, to the Duke of Burgundy, 1496–9, and to the Emperor Maximilian, 1499 and 1501–2; consecrated bishop of London, 1502; lord 'keeper,' 1502–1504, and lord 'chancellor,' 1504–15; translated to Canterbury, 1504; chancellor of Oxford University, 1506–32; crowned Henry VIII and Catherine of Aragon, 1509; befriended Erasmus from 1509; had a controversy about jurisdiction with his suffragans, 1512; had trouble with Wolsey through Wolsey's legatine precedence, 1518–23; attended Henry VIII to France, 1520; forced by Henry VIII to collect subsidies and loans in Kent, 1523–5; approached by Wolsey with the suggestion that Henry VIII's marriage with Catherine of Aragon was null, May 1527; afraid to act as counsel for Queen Catherine, 1528; forced by Henry VIII to advise Pope Clement VII to annul the marriage, 1530; proposed by Henry VIII to Pope Clement VII as a competent judge to determine the divorce suit, 1531; protested against the measures taken by parliament since 1529 against the pope's authority, 1532; bequeathed books to Winchester College and to New College and All Souls College, Oxford. [lix. 378]

WARING, EDWARD (1734–1798), mathematician; educated at Shrewsbury School; entered Magdalene College, Cambridge, 1753; senior wrangler, 1757; fellow, 1758–76; Lucasian professor of mathematics, 1760–98; F.R.S., 1763–95; M.D. Cambridge, 1767; published treatises on algebra, 1762–92. [lix. 383]

WARING, JOHN BURLEY (1823–1875), architect; studied architecture and painting in Bristol, 1836, and London, 1840–3; studied art and architecture in frequent continental tours, 1843–69; art commissioner at several exhibitions; a Swedenborgian; fancied himself a prophet; published architectural, archæological, and theological treatises. [lix. 385]

WARING, JOHN SCOTT (1747–1819). [See SCOTT, afterwards SCOTT-WARING, JOHN.]

WARING, ROBERT (1614–1658), author; educated at Westminster School; student of Christ Church, Oxford, 1632–48; M.A., 1637; elected professor of ancient history, 1647; deprived, 1648; visited France; settled in London; published anonymously political pamphlets, 1646, and 'Amoris Effigies' (Latin verse), 1648.

[lix. 386]

WARING, WILLIAM (1610–1679), jesuit; known as FATHER HARCOURT or BARROW; born in Lancashire; educated at St. Omer; joined the jesuits, 1632; missioner in London, 1644–79; arrested, May 1679; executed, June.

[lix. 386]

WARINGTON, ROBERT (1807–1867), chemist; at Merchant Taylors' School, 1818–22; apprentice to a manufacturing chemist, 1822–7; assistant to the chemistry professor, London University, 1828; chemist to a brewery, 1831–9; honorary secretary to the London Chemical Society, 1841–51; chemist to the London Apothecaries' Society, 1842–67; F.R.S., 1864. [lix. 387]

WARKWORTH, JOHN (*d.* 1500), reputed author of manuscript additions to Caxton's 'Brute,' published (1839) as 'Warkworth's Chronicle'; fellow of Merton College, Oxford; resident in Oxford, 1446–57; beneficed in Cambridgeshire, 1458–1500; master of Peterhouse, Cambridge, 1473–1500. [lix. 387]

WARMESTRY, GERVASE (1604–1641), poet; native of Worcester; educated at Westminster School; M.A. Christ Church, Oxford, 1628; student of the Middle

Temple, 1628 ; registrar of Worcester diocese ; published, 1628, ' Virescit vulnere virtus,' a political poem. [lix. 388]

WARMESTRY, THOMAS (1610–1665), dean of Worcester ; M.A. Oxford, 1631 ; D.D., 1642 ; of puritan leanings, but a royalist ; rector of Whitchurch, Warwick, 1635–46 ; withdrew to London, 1646 ; compounded for his estate, 1653 ; lecturer at St. Margaret's, Westminster, 1657 ; master of the Savoy, 1660 ; prebendary of Gloucester, 1660 ; dean of Worcester, 1661, and vicar of Bromsgrove, 1662–5 ; published devotional and controversial tracts. [lix. 389]

WARMINGTON, WILLIAM (*fl.* 1577–1612), Roman catholic divine ; entered Oxford University, 1577 ; withdrew to Douay, before 1579 ; ordained priest, 1580 ; sent to England, 1581 ; banished, 1585 ; chaplain to Cardinal William Allen ; returned to England, 1594 ; imprisoned, 1608 ; released on signing the oath of allegiance, 1612 ; published pamphlets justifying his action ; pensioned by Thomas Bilson [q. v.], bishop of Winchester. [lix. 390]

WARNE, CHARLES (1802–1887), archæologist ; travelled in France ; F.S.A., 1856 ; made collections concerning prehistoric and ancient remains in Dorset ; published accounts of his researches, 1836–72. [lix. 390]

WARNEFORD, SAMUEL WILSON (1763–1855), philanthropist ; a man of great wealth ; M.A. Oxford, 1786 ; married a Berkshire heiress, 1796 ; D.C.L. Oxford, 1810 ; rector of Lydiard Millicent, 1809–55 ; vicar of Bourton-on-the-Hill, 1810–55 ; honorary canon of Gloucester, 1844 ; founder of Warneford lunatic asylum, Oxford ; benefactor of the diocese of Gloucester ; benefactor of Leamington, Birmingham, and other places. [lix. 391]

WARNEFORD, WILLIAM (1560–1608). [See WARFORD.]

WARNER or GARNIER (*fl.* 1106), monk of Westminster ; wrote homilies (now lost). [lix. 392]

WARNER, SIR EDWARD (1511–1565), lieutenant of the Tower ; a decided protestant ; received grants of church lands ; M.P., Grantham, 1545–53 ; gave evidence against Lord Surrey, 1546 ; took part in defending Norwich against Robert Kett [q. v.], 1549 ; lieutenant of the Tower of London, 1552–3 ; favoured Lady Jane Grey ; imprisoned, 1554–5 ; lieutenant of the Tower of London, 1558–65 ; master of St. Katherine's Hospital, London, 1560 ; M.P., Norfolk, 1563 ; sent on a mission to Holland, 1565. [lix. 392]

WARNER, EDWARD (*fl.* 1632–1640), colonist ; son of Sir Thomas Warner [q. v.] ; deputy-governor of St. Kitts, 1629 ; governor of Antigua, 1632 ; his wife and children kidnapped by the Caribs, 1640. [lix. 404]

WARNER, FERDINANDO (1703–1768), miscellaneous writer ; LL.D., 1754 ; vicar of Ronde, Wiltshire, 1730 ; vicar of St. Michael's, Queenhithe, London, 1747 ; rector of Barnes, Surrey, 1758 ; published dogmatical and liturgical tractates, a church history, and, 1763–7, contributions to Irish history. [lix. 393]

WARNER, JOHN (*d.* 1565), physician ; fellow of All Souls College, Oxford, 1520, and warden, 1536–55 and 1559–65 ; M.A., 1525 ; M.D., 1535 ; the first regius professor of medicine, 1546–54 ; archdeacon of Cleveland, 1547–64, and of Ely, 1556–*c.* 1559 ; prebendary of St. Paul's, London, 1547, Winchester, 1550, and Salisbury, 1559 ; rector of Hayes, 1557 ; dean of Winchester, 1559–65. [lix. 393]

WARNER, JOHN (1581–1666), bishop of Rochester ; demy of Magdalen College, Oxford, 1599 ; fellow, 1604–10 ; M.A., 1605 ; D.D., 1616 ; beneficed in London, 1614, and Kent, 1619 ; prebendary of Canterbury, 1616 ; a violent royalist ; dean of Lichfield, 1633–7 ; appointed bishop of Rochester, 1637 ; attended Charles I at York, 1640 ; attended convocation and joined in framing new canons, 1640 ; impeached, August, and imprisoned, December, 1641 ; excluded from the House of Lords, February 1642 ; ejected from his see, 1643 ; published a pamphlet against the sale of church lands, 1646, and one of abhorrence of Charles I's execution, February 1649 ; compounded for his estates, 1649 ; restored to his see, 1660, and to parliament, 1661 ; benefactor of Bromley College, Kent ; founded exhibitions for Scottish episcopalians in Balliol College, Oxford. [lix. 394]

WARNER, JOHN (1628–1692), jesuit ; born in Warwickshire ; ordained priest in Spain ; professor at Douay ; joined jesuits, 1663 ; rector of Liège, 1678 ; provincial of the jesuits, 1679 ; rector of St. Omer, 1683–6 ; confessor to James II in England, 1686–8, and France, 1689 ; published theological tractates, 1661–88 ; died at Paris. [lix. 395]

WARNER, JOHN (1673 ?–1760), horticulturist ; grew vines, fruit-trees, and exotic plants at Rotherhithe, 1720. [lix. 396]

WARNER, JOHN (1736–1800), classical scholar ; son of Ferdinando Warner [q. v.] ; educated at St. Paul's School, London, and Trinity College, Cambridge ; M.A., 1761 ; D.D., 1773 ; rector of Hockliffe, 1771, and, later, of Stourton ; embassy chaplain at Paris, 1790. [lix. 396]

WARNER, JOSEPH (1717–1801), surgeon ; born in Antigua ; pupil of Samuel Sharpe [q. v.], 1741 ; qualified as a surgeon, 1741 ; army surgeon in Scotland, 1745 ; surgeon of Guy's Hospital, London, 1746–80 ; a leading practitioner in London ; F.R.S., 1750 ; published surgical treatises. [lix. 396]

WARNER, MARY AMELIA (1804–1854), actress ; *née* Huddart ; married, 1837, Robert William Warner ; appeared in the provinces, *c.* 1828, in Dublin, 1829, 1831–1836, in London, 1830, 1836–51, and in America, 1851, 1853 ; joint-manager of Sadler's Wells Theatre, London, 1844–6 ; manager of Marylebone Theatre, London, 1846–1848 ; obtained her chief successes as Evadne (' The Bridal ') and Imogen. [lix. 397]

WARNER, PHILIP (*d.* 1689), colonist ; a younger son of Sir Thomas Warner [q. v.] ; commanded a regiment in the reduction of Dutch and French Guiana, 1667, and in Antigua, 1671 ; governor of Antigua, 1672 ; prisoner in London, 1675–6, for a massacre of natives in Dominica ; dismissed the king's service, 1677 ; speaker of the Antigua assembly, 1679. [lix. 404]

WARNER, RICHARD (1713 ?–1775), botanist and scholar ; B.A. Wadham College, Oxford, 1734 ; studied at Lincoln's Inn ; had a botanical garden ; published a flora for Woodford, 1771 ; compiled a glossary (manuscript in British Museum) to Shakespeare ; translated various plays of Plautus into prose, and the 'Captivi' into verse ; benefactor of Wadham College, Oxford. [lix. 398]

WARNER, RICHARD (1763–1857), divine and author ; educated at Christ Church grammar school, Hampshire, and, 1787–9, Oxford ; curate in Hampshire, *c.* 1790 ; curate of St. James's, Bath, 1795–1817 ; rector of Great Chalfield, 1809–57, and of Chelwood, near Bristol, 1827–57 ; fixed the site of the Roman Clausentum at Bitterne Farm, near Southampton ; published notes of tours in the south and west of England and in Wales, also sermons, devotional books, and antiquarian notes. [lix. 399]

WARNER, SAMUEL ALFRED (*d.* 1853), inventor ; offered the admiralty explosive machines (an ' invisible shell ' and ' a long range ') of his invention, 1830 ; believed to be a monomaniac, on inquiry, 1842. [lix. 402]

WARNER, SIR THOMAS (*d.* 1649), West Indian colonist ; born in Suffolk ; captain in James I's guards ; visited Surinam (Dutch Guiana), 1620, and conceived the idea of a West Indian settlement ; founded a colony in St. Kitts, 1624 ; visited England, 1625 ; appointed governor of St. Kitts, Nevis, Barbados, and Montserrat, September 1625 ; commanded a privateer in the English Channel, spring 1626 ; returned to St. Kitts, autumn 1626 ; had trouble with French settlers, 1627–35, and Spanish filibusters, 1629 ; visited England, and was knighted, 1629 ; colonised Nevis, 1628, and Antigua and Montserrat, 1632 ; attempted to colonise St. Lucia, 1639–41 ; visited England, 1636 ; parliamentary governor of the Caribee islands, 1643 ; died at St. Kitts. [lix. 402]

WARNER, THOMAS (1630 ?–1675), nicknamed ' INDIAN WARNER,' because son of Sir Thomas Warner [q. v.] and a Carib woman ; joined the Caribs and fought against the whites, 1645 ; governor of Dominica, 1664–75 ; prisoner to the French, 1666–7 ; was treacherously killed by his brother Philip Warner [q. v.], but, according to another account, fell in fight with the English. [lix. 404]

WARNER, WILLIAM (1558 ?–1609), poet ; studied at Oxford ; attorney in London ; published, 1585, ' Pan his Syrinx,' seven prose tales ; published a translation of the 'Menæchmi' of Plautus, 1595. His chief work is 'Albion's England,' a metrical British history, with mythical and fictitious episodes, extending in the first (1586) edition from Noah to the Norman Conquest; brought down to James I's reign in 1606; complete edition (posthumously), 1612. Meres, in his 'Palladis Tamia' (1598), associated him with Spenser as one of the two chief English heroic poets, and with Spenser, Daniel, Drayton, and Breton, as a lyric poet. Drayton also eulogised him. [lix. 405]

WARRE, SIR WILLIAM (1784–1853), lieutenant-general; ensign, 1803; captain, 1806; aide-de-camp in Portugal, 1808, and in Sir John Moore's expedition, 1808–9; Portuguese major; aide-de-camp to Beresford, 1809–12; lieutenant-colonel, 1813; stationed at the Cape, 1813–21; attached to the quartermaster-general's department, 1823–37; C.B., 1838; knighted, 1839; lieutenant-general, 1851. [lix. 407]

WARREN. [See also WARENNE.]

WARREN, AMBROSE WILLIAM (1781?–1856), line-engraver; son of Charles Warren [q. v.] [lix. 409]

WARREN, ARTHUR (*fl.* 1605), poet; in prison for debt, 1604; published, 1605, in six-line stanzas, 'The Poore Mans Passions' and 'Pouerties Patience,' two poems; probably author of various commendatory verses, signed 'A. W.,' which appeared, 1575–96; not improbably the author of the verses signed 'A. W.,' in Davison's 'Poetical Rhapsodie,' 1602. [lix. 408]

WARREN, CHARLES (1767–1823), line-engraver; engraved on metal for calico-printing; from 1802 a noted book-illustrator. [lix. 409]

WARREN, SIR CHARLES (1798–1866), major-general; ensign, 1814; captain, 1822; stationed in Cape Colony, and travelled in the interior, 1822–5; served in India, 1830–8; major, 1834; served in China, 1841–4; lieutenant-colonel, 1842; served in the Crimea, 1854–6; stationed at Malta, 1856–61; major-general, 1858; K.C.B., 1865. [lix. 409]

WARREN, FREDERICK (1775–1848), vice-admiral; son of Richard Warren (1731–1797) [q. v.]; entered the navy, 1789; lieutenant, 1794; captain, 1801; defeated a Danish gunboat flotilla in the Belt, May 1809; rear-admiral, 1830; commander-in-chief at the Cape, 1831–4; admiral-superintendent at Plymouth, 1837–41; vice-admiral, 1841. [lix. 411]

WARREN, GEORGE JOHN VERNON, fifth BARON VERNON (1803–1866). [See VERNON.]

WARREN, JOHN (1730–1800), bishop of Bangor; scholar of Caius College, Cambridge; M.A., 1754; D.D., 1772; beneficed in Cambridgeshire, 1754–79; prebendary of Ely, 1768; bishop of St. David's, 1779; translated to Bangor, 1783; published sermons. [lix. 412]

WARREN, JOHN (1796–1852), mathematician; brother of Sir Charles Warren [q. v.]; educated at Westminster School; fellow and tutor of Jesus College, Cambridge; B.A., 1818; F.R.S., 1830; beneficed in Cambridgeshire and Huntingdonshire; chancellor of Bangor; published a mathematical treatise and papers, 1828–9. [lix. 411]

WARREN, SIR JOHN BORLASE (1753–1822), admiral; of Stapleford, Nottinghamshire; entered Emmanuel College, Cambridge, 1769; M.A., 1776; had his name on ship's books, 1771–4; M.P., Marlow, 1774; created baronet, 1775; bought Lundy Island; served in the navy, 1777–82 and 1793–1814; captain, 1781; commodore, 1794; defeated French squadrons, April and August 1794; had charge of the naval arrangements for the French royalist attempt in La Vendée, June–October, 1794; destroyed many armed French vessels, 1796; intercepted and defeated the French fleet conveying Hoche to Ireland, October 1798; rear-admiral, 1799; captured a French squadron, 1806; admiral, 1810; G.C.B., 1815. [lix. 412]

WARREN, JOHN BYRNE LEICESTER, third and last BARON DE TABLEY (1835–1895), poet; of Tabley House, Cheshire; brought up in Italy and Germany; educated at Eton and Christ Church, Oxford; M.A., 1860; barrister, Lincoln's Inn, 1860; published small volumes of poetry under the pseudonym of 'George F. Preston,' 1859–62, and of 'William Lancaster,' 1863–8; published

an essay on Greek coins as illustrative of Greek federal history, 1863; published, anonymously, 'Philoctetes,' 1866, and 'Orestes,' 1868, tragedies; resided in London from 1871; published verses in his own name, 1873–6, and a 'Guide-book to Bookplates,' 1880; compiled a flora of Cheshire; succeeded to the peerage, 1887; published his selected poems, 1893–5. [lix. 415]

WARREN, JOHN TAYLOR (1771–1849), physician; pupil of John Hunter (1728–1793) [q. v.]; army-surgeon, 1793–1820; accompanied Sir John Moore's expedition, 1808–9. [lix. 416]

WARREN, JOSEPH (1804–1881), musician; organist in London, 1843; edited music; compiled musical instruction-books; re-edited William Boyce's 'Cathedral Music,' 1849. [lix. 417]

WARREN, LEMUEL (1770–1833), major-general; entered the army, 1787; captain, 1793; lieutenant-colonel, 1804; major-general, 1819; served in Flanders, 1794–6, West Indies, 1796, Holland, 1799, Egypt, 1801, Sicily, 1809, and the Peninsula. [lix. 417]

WARREN, MATTHEW (1642–1706), nonconformist; of St. John's College, Oxford; preacher at Otterford, 1661–2; trained candidates for the nonconformist ministry from 1671; pastor at Taunton, 1687–1706. [lix. 418]

WARREN, PELHAM (1778–1835), physician; son of Richard Warren (1731–1797) [q. v.]; M.B. Trinity College, Cambridge, 1800; M.D., 1805; practitioner in London from 1800; physician of St. George's Hospital, London, 1803–16; F.R.C.P., 1806, censor, 1810, Harveian orator, 1826, elect, 1829; F.R.S., 1813. [lix. 418]

WARREN, SIR PETER (1703–1752), vice-admiral; an Irishman; entered the navy, 1717; lieutenant, 1723; captain, 1727; commodore, 1744; served on the American station, 1735–41; served in the West Indies, 1742–5, making immense prize-money; naval commander at the taking of Louisbourg, 1745; vice-admiral, 1747; M.P., Westminster, 1747–52; monument to him in Westminster Abbey. [lix. 419]

WARREN, SIR RALPH (1486?–1553), lord mayor of London; in business as a mercer, 1508; freeman, 1507, warden, 1521, and master of the Mercers' Company, 1530 and 1542; lent money to the crown; alderman, 1528–53; sheriff, 1528–9, and lord mayor of London, 1536–7 and 1544; sat on several government commissions. [lix. 420]

WARREN, RICHARD (1731–1797), physician; B.A. Jesus College, Cambridge, 1752; fellow, 1752–9; M.D., 1762; practised in London, 1756–97; F.R.C.P., 1763, Gulstonian lecturer, 1764, Harveian orator, 1768, censor, 1764, 1776, 1782, elect, 1784; physician to the Middlesex Hospital, 1756–8, to St. George's Hospital, London, 1760–6; physician to George, prince of Wales, 1787. [lix. 421]

WARREN, SIR RICHARD AUGUSTUS (1705?–1775), Jacobite; an Irishman; in business in Marseilles, 1744; captain in the Franco-Irish regiment, August 1745; aide-de-camp in Scotland to Lord George Murray (1700?–1760) [q. v.], October 1745; colonel, November 1745; sent to ask French help, April 1746; sent back to fetch off Prince Charles, August–October 1746; created baronet, and, 1750, a 'brigadier-general' by 'James III'; aide-de-camp to Marshal Saxe, 1746–8; a naturalised Frenchman, 1764; commandant at Belleisle, 1764–75. [lix. 422]

WARREN, SIR SAMUEL (1769–1839), rear-admiral; served at sea, 1782–1823; lieutenant, 1793; captain, 1802; knighted, 1835; rear-admiral, 1837; K.C.B., 1839. [lix. 423]

WARREN, SAMUEL (1781–1862), divine; sent to sea, 1794; prisoner in France, May 1794–5; Wesleyan preacher in Lancashire; expelled for faction, 1835. His followers, 'the Warrenites,' joined with other seceders to form the 'United Methodist Free Churches,' but he himself took Anglican orders, 1838, and was rector of All Souls, Ancoats, 1840–62. [lix. 423]

WARREN, SAMUEL (1807–1877), novelist; son of Samuel Warren (1781–1862) [q. v.]; studied medicine at Edinburgh, 1826–7; entered Inner Temple, 1828; special pleader, 1831–7; barrister, 1837; bencher, 185.; issued many legal text-books and some political tracts, 1835–56; F.R.S., 1835; Q.C., 1851; hon. D.C.L. Oxford, 1853; recorder of Hull, 1852-74; M.P., Midhurst, 1856-9; a master in lunacy, 1859-77; published his novels, ' Passages from the Diary of a Late Physician,' 1830, 'Ten Thousand a Year,' 1839, 'Now and Then,' 1847; published 'The Lily and the Bee,' 1851, and miscellanies. [lix. 423]

WARREN, THOMAS (1617?-1694), nonconformist divine; M.A. Cambridge; intruded rector of Houghton, 1650; was episcopally ordained, 1660, and retained his rectory, 1661; ejected for nonconformity, 1662; pastor at Romsey, 1672-90. [lix. 426]

WARREN, WILLIAM (*fl.* 1581), author of two poems (1) a dialogue (now lost) between a citizen and a soldier, 1578, and (2) 'The Nurcerie of Names' of Englishwomen, 158!. [lix. 426]

WARRINGTON, EARLS OF. [See BOOTH, HENRY, first EARL, 1652-1694; BOOTH, GEORGE, second EARL, 1675-1758.]

WARRISTON, LORD (1610?-1663). [See JOHNSTON, ARCHIBALD.]

WARTER, JOHN WOOD (1806-1878), divine and antiquary; educated at Shrewsbury School and Christ Church, Oxford; M.A., 1834; B.D., 1841; embassy chaplain at Copenhagen, 1830-3; vicar of West Tarring, 1834-78; married Robert Southey's daughter, 1834; published collections for the history of West Tarring, 1853-1860; collected notes of Shropshire antiquities (partly published posthumously, 1886-91); published sermons and tracts and edited part of Southey's collections. [lix. 427]

WARTON, JOSEPH (1722-1800), critic; elder son of Thomas Warton the elder [q. v.]; educated at Winchester School, 1735, and Oriel College, Oxford, 1740; B.A., 1744; M.A. by diploma, 1759; D.D., 1768; curate at Basingstoke and Chelsea; rector of Winslade, 1748, and of Wickham, Hampshire, 1783-1800, with other benefices; prebendary of St. Paul's, London, 1782, and Westminster, 1788; travelling chaplain with the Duke of Bolton, April to September, 1751; second master of Winchester, 1755, and conspicuously unsuccessful head-master, 1766-93; verses of his printed, 1739; published two volumes of 'Odes,' 1744, 1746, showing unusual feeling for nature; edited and partly translated Virgil, 1753; contributed to Dr. Johnson's 'Adventurer,' 1753-6; published 'Essays' on Pope, 1756 and 1782, severely criticising the 'correct' school, of which Pope was the founder; edited Pope's works, 1797; began an edition of Dryden; friend of Dr. Johnson and his circle. [lix. 428]

WARTON, ROBERT (*d.* 1557), or PUREFOY, bishop of Hereford; Cluniac monk; possibly B.D. Cambridge, 1535; abbot of Bermondsey, which he surrendered to Henry VIII, 1538; bishop of St. Asaph, 1536; lived chiefly at Denbigh; translated to Hereford, 1554. [lix. 431]

WARTON, THOMAS, the elder (1688?-1745), professor of poetry (1718-28) at Oxford; demy, Magdalen College, Oxford, 1706-17; fellow, 1717-24; M.A., 1712; B.D., 1725; circulated Jacobite verses, 1717-18; vicar of Basingstoke and master of Basingstoke school, 1723-45; beneficed also in Surrey and Sussex; his 'Poems' published posthumously, 1748. [lix. 431]

WARTON, THOMAS, the younger (1728-1790), historian of English poetry; son of Thomas Warton the elder [q. v.]; entered Trinity College, Oxford, 1744; M.A., 1750; fellow, 1751-90; tutor; B.D., 1767; friend of Dr. Johnson and his circle; his first verses published, 1745-7; made his mark by a poem in praise of Oxford, 'The Triumph of Isis,' 1749; published an account of antiquities at Winchester, 1750, and a satire, 'Newmarket,' 1751; contributed verses to most Oxford contemporary collections; edited two collections of verses, 'The Union,' 1753, and 'The Oxford Sausage,' 1764; put out 'Observations' on Spenser's 'Faery Queen,' 1754 (enlarged, 1762); professor of poetry, Oxford, 1757-67; edited classical texts, 1758-70; issued a skit on Oxford guide-books, 'A Companion to the Guide,' 1760; published lives of Dr. Ralph Bathurst, 1761, and Sir Thomas Pope, 1772; rector of Kiddington, 1771; issued his 'History of English Poetry' (to the end of the Elizabethan age), 1774-81; attacked the Chatterton forgeries, 1782; published a history of Kiddington, 1783; Camden professor of ancient history, Oxford, 1785-90; poet-

laureate, 1785-90, his official odes being much ridiculed; edited Milton's early poems, 1785; his own collected poems issued, 1791. [lix. 432]

WARWICK, DUKE OF (1425-1445). [See BEAUCHAMP, HENRY DE.]

WARWICK, EARLS OF. [See NEWBURGH, HENRY DE, *d.* 1123; PLESSIS or PLESSETIS, JOHN DE, *d.* 1263; MAUDUIT, WILLIAM, 1220-1268; BEAUCHAMP, GUY DE, *d.* 1315; BEAUCHAMP, THOMAS DE, *d.* 1401; BEAUCHAMP, RICHARD DE, 1382-1439; NEVILLE, RICHARD, 1428-1471, the 'king-maker'; EDWARD, 1475-1499, son of GEORGE PLANTAGENET, duke of Clarence; DUDLEY, JOHN, 1502?-1553, afterwards DUKE OF NORTHUMBERLAND; DUDLEY, AMBROSE, 1528?-1590; DUDLEY, SIR ROBERT, 1573-1649; RICH, ROBERT, 1587-1658.]

WARWICK, COUNTESS OF (1625-1678). [See RICH, MARY.]

WARWICK, GUY OF, in romance. [See GUY.]

WARWICK, SIR PHILIP (1609-1683), politician and historian; his father organist of Westminster Abbey and the Chapel Royal, London; chorister at Westminster; visited France and Geneva; secretary to George, baron Goring, and, 1636, to Lord-treasurer Juxon; student of Gray's Inn, 1638; clerk of the signet, 1638; hon. B.C.L. Oxford, 1638; M.P., Radnor, in the Long parliament, 1640, till expelled, 1644; opposed Strafford's attainder; sat in Charles I's parliament at Oxford; twice sent to urge Newcastle to march south, 1643; negotiated the surrender of Oxford, 1646; secretary to Charles I at Hampton Court, 1647, and Newport, 1648; compounded for his estate, 1649; imprisoned as a suspect, 1655; knighted, 1660; M.P., Westminster, 1661-78; managed the treasury for Thomas Wriothesley, fourth earl of Southampton [q. v.], 1660-7; urged war with France, 1668; opposed toleration of dissenters, 1672; his 'Discourse of Government' appeared, 1694, and his 'Memoires,' 1701. [lix. 437]

WARWICK, PHILIP, the younger (*d.* 1683), ambassador; son of Sir Philip Warwick [q. v.]; envoy to Sweden, 1680. [lix. 439]

WARWICK, SIMEON OF (*d.* 1296). [See SIMEON.]

WASE, CHRISTOPHER, the elder (1625?-1690), scholar; educated at Eton; fellow of King's College, Cambridge, 1648; ejected and went abroad; M.A., 1655; head-master of Dedham school, 1665, of Tonbridge, 1662-1668; esquire bedell of law and supervisor of the University Press, Oxford, 1671-90; published Greek and Latin pieces. [lix. 439]

WASE, CHRISTOPHER, the younger (1662-1711), divine; son of Christopher Wase the elder [q. v.]; M.A. Corpus Christi College, Oxford, 1685; B.D., 1694; vicar of Preston, 1687-90. [lix. 440]

WASEY, WILLIAM (1691-1757), physician; of Caius College, Cambridge; M.A., 1716; M.D., 1723; studied at Leyden, 1716; practitioner in London; physician to Westminster Hospital, London, 1719-33, and St. George's Hospital, London, 1733; F.R.C.P., 1724; censor, 1731, 1736, 1739, and 1748; president, 1750, 1751, 1752, and 1753. [lix. 440]

WASHBOURN, JOHN (1760?-1829), compiler of 'Bibliotheca Gloucestrensis,' a bibliography of civil war tracts concerning Gloucester, 1823-5; a unitarian; printer and bookseller in Gloucester. [lix. 440]

WASHBOURNE, THOMAS (1606-1687), canon of Gloucester; M.A. Balliol College, Oxford, 1628; B.D., 1636; D.D., 1660; rector of Loddington, 1639, and of Dumbleton, 1640; prebendary of Gloucester, 1643, and readmitted, 1660; vicar of St. Mary's, Gloucester, 1660-8; published poems and sermons. [lix. 440]

WASHINGTON, JOHN (1800-1863), rear-admiral; entered the navy, 1812; lieutenant, 1821; travelled much, 1822-53; secretary of the Royal Geographical Society, 1836-41; captain, 1842; engaged on the east coast survey, 1841-7; F.R.S., 1845; assistant-hydrographer, and, 1855-1862, hydrographer; rear-admiral, 1862; died at Havre. [lix. 441]

WASSE, JOSEPH (1672-1738), scholar; entered Queens' College, Cambridge, 1691; M.A. and fellow, 1698; B.D., 1707; rector of Aynhoe, 1711; published classical texts, his critical edition of Sallust (1710) being based on a collation of nearly eighty manuscripts. [lix. 442]

WASTELL, SIMON (*d.* 1632), schoolmaster; B.A. Queen's College, Oxford, 1585; master of Northampton school before 1592; published a metrical version of John Shaw's summary of the bible, 1623. [lix. 442]

WAT TYLER (*d.* 1381). [See TYLER.]

WATERFORD, EARL OF (1468-1538). [See TALBOT, GEORGE.]

WATERHOUSE, SIR EDWARD (1535-1591), chancellor of the exchequer (1586-9) in Ireland; went to Ireland with Sir Henry Sidney [q. v.]; official in Ireland, 1565-91; obtained grants of Irish lands and offices; retired to Woodchurch, 1591. [lix. 442]

WATERHOUSE, EDWARD (*fl.* 1622), author of a pamphlet on Virginia. [lix. 444]

WATERHOUSE, EDWARD (1619-1670), author; F.R.S., *c.* 1663; LL.D. Cambridge, 1668; ordained, 1668; published tracts, chiefly on heraldry, 1653-67. [lix. 444]

WATERHOUSE, GEORGE (*d.* 1602), musician; went from Lincoln Cathedral choir to the Chapel Royal, London, 1588; Mus.Bac. Oxford, 1592; wrote on musical theory; his canons, 1163 in number, on the plain-song 'Miserere' preserved in manuscript in the Cambridge University Library. [lix. 445]

WATERHOUSE, GEORGE ROBERT (1810-1888), naturalist; architect in London; devoted to entomology; curator of the London Zoological Society, 1836-43; entrusted by Darwin with the task of describing the mammals and coleoptera collected in the voyage of the Beagle; keeper of the mineralogical and geological branch, British Museum, 1851-7, of the department of geology, 1857-80; published natural-history papers and treatises. [lix. 446]

WATERLAND, DANIEL (1683-1740), theologian; fellow of Magdalene College, Cambridge, 1704; M.A., 1706; D.D., 1717; beneficed in Norfolk, 1713, London, 1721, and Middlesex, 1730; master of Magdalene College, Cambridge, 1713-40; chancellor of York, 1722; prebendary of Windsor, 1727; archdeacon of Middlesex, 1730; published polemical treatises against Arians and deists, 1719-1737, and a history of the Athanasian creed, 1723; his collected works published, 1823. [lix. 446]

WATERS, SIR JOHN (1774-1842), lieutenant-general; a Welshman; entered the army, 1797; lieutenant, 1799; captain, 1803; intelligence officer in Spain, 1808-14; major, 1809; served at Waterloo, 1815; lieutenant-colonel, 1817; K.C.B., 1832; lieutenant-general, 1841. [lix. 448]

WATERS, LUCY (1630 ?-1658). [See WALTER, LUCY.]

WATERTON, CHARLES (1782-1865), naturalist; a Roman catholic; educated at Stonyhurst, 1796-1800; visited Spain, 1802; resided in British Guiana, 1804-12; inherited Walton Hall, Yorkshire, 1806; travelled in Guiana, 1813, 1816, 1820, 1824, his famous ride on a cayman taking place on his 1820 expedition; visited Rome, 1817 and 1841; visited the United States and the West Indies, 1824; published an account of his 'Wanderings,' 1825; prepared his specimens according to a method of his own, by which internal stuffing was rendered unnecessary; published three series of essays in natural history, 1838, 1844, 1857. [lix. 449]

WATERTON, EDMUND (1830-1887), antiquary; son of Charles Waterton [q. v.]; formed a collection of rings. [lix. 451]

WATERWORTH, WILLIAM (1811-1882), jesuit; educated at Stonyhurst; joined the jesuits, 1829; ordained priest, 1836; served churches in England, 1850 till death; published polemical tractates. [lix. 451]

WATH, MICHAEL (*fl.* 1314-1347), judge; found as an attorney, 1314-21, as rector of Beeford, 1321, as rector of Wath, 1327; clerk of chancery, 1328; prebendary of Southwell, 1330, with other ecclesiastical preferment; master of the rolls, 1334-7; clerk of chancery, 1338-40; a commissioner of the great seal, 1339. [lix. 452]

WATHEN, JAMES (1751 ?-1828), traveller; nicknamed 'Jemmy Sketch'; a Hereford glover; made many pedestrian tours in Great Britain and Ireland from 1787,

and described them in the 'Gentleman's Magazine'; published, 1814, an account of a voyage in 1811 to India and China; visited Byron in Italy, 1816. [lix. 452]

WATKIN, WILLIAM THOMPSON (1836-1888), archæologist; a Liverpool merchant; published 'Roman Lancashire,' 1883, 'Roman Cheshire,' 1886; his manuscript collections in the Chetham Library, Manchester. [lix. 453]

WATKINS, CHARLES (*d.* 1808), legal writer; conveyancer in London, 1799-1808; published 'Principles of Conveyancing,' 1800, and other legal works. [lix. 453]

WATKINS, CHARLES FREDERICK (1793-1873), author; of Christ's College, Cambridge; vicar of Brixworth, 1832-73; published 'Eidespernox,' 1821, and other poems and prose works. [lix. 453]

WATKINS, JOHN (*fl.* 1792-1831), miscellaneous author; a schoolmaster in Devonshire; compiled biographical works, 1800-31, including a 'Universal Biographical and Historical Dictionary,' 1800. [lix. 454]

WATKINS, MORGAN (*fl.* 1653-1670), quaker; of Herefordshire; imprisoned in London, 1660 and 1665; published religious tractates. [lix. 454]

WATSON, ALEXANDER (1815 ?-1865), divine; son of Joseph Watson [q. v.]; M.A. Corpus Christi College, Cambridge, 1840; held various curacies and benefices, 1840-65; edited and published sermons. [lx. 17]

WATSON, ANTHONY (*d.* 1605), bishop of Chichester; fellow of Christ's College, Cambridge, 1572; M.A., 1575; D.D., 1596; rector of Cheam, 1581-1605, and of Storrington, 1592-1605; dean of Bristol, 1590-7; chancellor of Wells, 1592-6; lord almoner, 1595-1605; bishop of Chichester, 1596-1605. [lx. 1]

WATSON, SIR BROOK, first baronet (1735-1807), merchant and official; went to sea before 1749; commissary at the sieges of Beauséjour, 1755, and Louisbourg, 1758; merchant in London, 1759; commissary-general in Canada, 1782-3, Flanders, 1793-5, and in Great Britain from 1798; M.P., London, 1784-93; a director of the Bank of England; alderman, 1786, sheriff, 1786, and lord mayor of London, 1796-7; created baronet, 1803. [lx. 1]

WATSON, CAROLINE (1761 ?-1814), engraver in stipple; daughter of James Watson (1739 ?-1790) [q. v.]. [lx. 10]

WATSON, CHARLES (1714-1757), rear-admiral; entered the navy, 1728; lieutenant, 1735; captain, 1738; commodore on the North American station, 1748; rear-admiral, 1748; commander-in-chief in the East Indies, 1754-7; co-operated with Robert Clive in reducing Gheriah, February 1756, recovering Calcutta, December 1756, reducing Chandernagore, March 1757, and crushing Suráj ud Dowlah, June 1757; his name, by Clive's contrivance, fraudulently attached to a fictitious treaty to deceive Omichund; died in Bengal; monument in Westminster Abbey. [lx. 2]

WATSON, CHRISTOPHER (*d.* 1581), historian and translator; M.A. Cambridge, 1569; probably beneficed in Norfolk; published a translation of Polybius, and a life of Henry V, 1568; published a catechism, 1579; his manuscript notes concerning Durham are in the British Museum. [lx. 3]

WATSON, DAVID (1710-1756), translator; native of Brechin; M.A. St. Andrews; published a text and prose version of Horace, 1741, and a manual of classical mythology, 1752. [lx. 3]

WATSON, DAVID (1713 ?-1761), major-general; royal engineers; lieutenant of foot, 1733; captain, 1745; lieutenant-colonel, 1746; military engineer in Flanders, 1742-5, serving at Dettingen, 1743, and Fontenoy, 1745; military engineer in Scotland, 1745-54, serving at Falkirk, January 1746, and Culloden, April 1746, and superintending the military survey of Scotland, 1747-54; planned defensive works in the south of England, 1755-6; captain, royal engineers, 1757; served against St. Malo, 1758; quartermaster-general in Germany, 1758-61; distinguished himself at Minden, 1759; major-general, 1759. [lx. 4]

WATSON, GEORGE (1723 ?-1773), divine; scholar, 1744, and fellow, 1747-54, of University College, Oxford; M.A., 1746; published theological tracts. [lx. 5]

WATSON, GEORGE (1767-1837), portrait-painter ; pupil of Alexander Nasmyth [q. v.], and, 1785-7, of Sir Joshua Reynolds [q. v.] ; settled as an artist in Edinburgh ; first president of the (Royal) Scottish Academy, 1826-37. [lx. 6]

WATSON, HENRY (1737-1786), engineer colonel ; educated at Woolwich ; ensign, 1755 ; lieutenant, 1757 ; served at Belleisle, 1761, and Havana, 1762 ; captain, 1763 ; field-engineer in Bengal, 1764, and chief engineer, 1765 ; constructed docks at Calcutta ; returned to England ; translated Euler on shipbuilding, 1776 ; again served in India, 1780-6. [lx. 6]

WATSON, HEWETT COTTRELL (1804 - 1881), botanist ; inherited a Derbyshire estate, c. 1826 ; studied phrenology and natural history in Edinburgh, 1828-32 ; settled at Thames Ditton, 1833 ; published phrenological treatises, 1836 ; edited the 'Phrenological Journal,' 1837-1840 ; visited the Azores, 1842 ; edited the 'London Catalogue of British Plants,' 1844-74 ; contributed an article 'On the Theory of Progressive Development ' to the 'Phytologist,' 1845 ; published a classification of British plants according to local distribution, ' Cybele Britannica,' with supplements and a 'Compendium,' 1847-72, and 'Topographical Botany,' 1873-4, with other botanical tracts. [lx. 7]

WATSON, JAMES (d. 1722), Scottish printer ; printer in Edinburgh from 1695 ; imprisoned for a pamphlet on the Darien grievance, 1700 ; published the ' Edinburgh Gazette' from 1700, and the 'Edinburgh Courant' from 1705 ; published ' Comic and Serious Scottish Poems,' 1706-11 ; opened a bookseller's shop, 1709 ; joint king's printer in Scotland, 1711. [lx. 9]

WATSON, JAMES (1739 ?-1790), mezzotint engraver: an Irishman ; trained in London ; engraved portraits after Reynolds ; exhibited engravings, 1762-75. [lx. 10]

WATSON, JAMES (1766 ?-1838), agitator ; probably an apothecary in Bloomsbury ; became, with his son James (d. 1836), a leader of the tavern club, which advocated the communistic views of Thomas Spence [q. v.], c. 1814 ; a leader of the riotous mob, December 1816 ; acquitted of a charge of high treason, June 1817 ; withdrew to America. [lx. 10]

WATSON, JAMES (1799-1874), radical publisher ; warehouseman in Leeds, 1817; became a freethinker, 1819 ; salesman in London for Richard Carlile [q. v.], 1822; imprisoned, 1823 ; compositor and manager of Carlile's business, 1825 ; adopted Robert Owen's co-operative schemes, 1826 ; storekeeper of the Co-operative Association, 1828 ; printer and publisher, 1831, issuing, among other books, cheap reprints of Tom Paine's works ; imprisoned, 1833 and 1834 ; a leading chartist, 1837 ; joined Mazzini's ' International League,' 1847 ; agitated for freedom of the press. [lx. 12]

WATSON, JOHN (d. 1530), friend of Erasmus ; fellow of Peterhouse, Cambridge, 1501-16 ; travelled in Italy ; rector of Elsworth, 1516, and of St. Mary Woolnoth, London, 1523 ; master of Christ's College, Cambridge, 1517-30 ; D.D. Cambridge, 1517 ; prebendary of Southwell, 1523 ; one of the divines selected to answer for Cambridge University Henry VIII's questions about his divorce. [lx. 13]

WATSON, JOHN (1520-1584), bishop of Winchester ; fellow of All Souls College, Oxford, 1540 ; M.A., 1544 ; prebendary of Winchester, 1551 ; rector of Kelshall and of Winchfield, 1554, with other benefices ; chancellor of St. Paul's, 1558 ; archdeacon of Surrey. 1559 ; master of St. Cross, Winchester, 1568 ; dean of Winchester, 1570, and bishop, 1580-4. [lx. 13]

WATSON, JOHN (1725-1783), antiquary ; fellow of Brasenose College, Oxford, 1746 ; M.A., 1748 ; curate at Halifax, 1750-4 ; incumbent of Ripponden, near Halifax, 1754-66 ; F.S.A., 1759 ; rector of Stockport, 1769 ; published ' History and Antiquities of . . . Halifax,' 1775, and 'Memoirs of the . . . Earls of Warren and Surrey,' 1776 ; made large historical collections for Cheshire. [lx. 14]

WATSON, JOHN DAWSON (1832-1892), artist ; trained at Manchester, 1847, and London, 1851 ; exhibited in Manchester, 1851, and in London, 1859-92 ; member of the Society of Painters in Water-colours, 1869 ; a prolific book illustrator ; painted in water-colours. [lx. 15]

WATSON, JOHN FORBES (1827-1892), writer on India ; M.A. and M.D. Aberdeen, 1847 ; army surgeon in Bombay, 1850-3 ; director of the India Museum, London, 1858-80 ; attached to the Indian department of the international exhibitions, 1862, 1868, 1873 ; published works on Indian food-grains, textile manufactures, and plant-names. [lx. 15]

WATSON, JOHN SELBY (1804-1884), author and murderer ; M.A. Trinity College, Dublin, 1844 ; curate in Somerset, 1839-41 ; schoolmaster in Stockwell, London, 1844-70 ; married, 1845 ; condemned to penal servitude for life for murdering his wife, 1871 ; edited classical texts and translations ; compiled biography of Porson, 1861. [lx. 16]

WATSON, JONAS (1663-1741), artillery officer ; served in Ireland and Flanders ; lieutenant-colonel, 1727 ; commanded the artillery at Gibraltar, when besieged, 1727 ; killed at Carthagena. [lx. 19]

WATSON, JOSEPH (1765 ?-1829), author of treatises on deaf and dumb instruction ; pupil of Thomas Braidwood [q. v.] ; master of the Kent Road deaf and dumb asylum, London. [lx. 17]

WATSON, JOSHUA (1771-1855), philanthropist ; a London wine-merchant, 1792-1814 ; a leader of the pre-Tractarian high-church party ; first treasurer of the National Society, 1811-42 ; an active member of most church institutions and associations, and one of the ' Hackney Phalanx' ; hon. D.C.L. Oxford, 1820. [lx. 17]

WATSON, JUSTLY (1710 ?-1757), military engineer ; son of Jonas Watson [q. v.] ; artillery officer at Gibraltar, 1727 ; joined the engineers, 1732 ; served at Carthagena, 1741, and in the futile attempts on Cuba, 1741, and Panama, 1742 ; stationed at Jamaica, 1742-4 ; surveyed Darien and Florida, 1743 ; served in the descent on Brittany, 1746 ; chief engineer in the Medway district, 1748 ; reported on West African stations, 1755-6 ; stationed in Nova Scotia, 1757, and died there ; lieutenant-colonel, royal engineers, 1757. [lx. 19]

WATSON, SIR LEWIS, first BARON ROCKINGHAM (1584-1653), of Rockingham Castle, Northamptonshire ; entered Magdalen College, Oxford, 1599 ; student of the Middle Temple, 1601 ; knighted, 1608 ; a courtier, and a friend of George Villiers, first duke of Buckingham [q. v.] ; M.P., Lincoln, 1614, 1621, 1624 ; created baronet, 1621 ; sheriff of Northamptonshire, 1632-3 ; arrested for allowing parliament troops to occupy Rockingham Castle, 1643 ; joined Charles I at Oxford ; created Baron Rockingham, 1645 ; compounded for his estates, 1647. [lx. 20]

WATSON, MUSGRAVE LEWTHWAITE (1804-1847), sculptor, etcher, and painter in water-colours ; solicitor's apprentice at Carlisle. 1821 ; practised drawing ; art student in London, 1824, and Rome ; opened a studio in London, 1828 ; exhibited at the Royal Academy, 1829-47 ; executed 'The Battle of St. Vincent' bas-relief on the Nelson Monument. [lx. 21]

WATSON, PETER WILLIAM (1761-1830), botanist ; tradesman in Hull ; devoted to natural science ; a landscape-painter ; published, 1824-5, ' Dendrologia Britannica,' an account of foreign trees and shrubs adapted to the climate of Britain. [lx. 22]

WATSON, RICHARD (1612-1685), royalist writer ; a Londoner ; M.A. Caius College, Cambridge, 1636 ; fellow, 1636-44 ; ejected by the parliament ; master of Perse School, Cambridge, 1636-42 ; royalist chaplain in Paris ; restored to his fellowship, 1660 ; D.D. Oxford, 1662 ; rector of Pewsey, 1662 ; prebendary of Salisbury, 1666, with other preferment ; published verses praising Charles I, treatises against presbyterianism and puritanism, and other controversial works, 1649-84. [lx. 22]

WATSON, RICHARD (1737-1816), bishop of Llandaff ; scholar of Trinity College, Cambridge, 1757 ; second wrangler, 1759 ; fellow, 1760 ; M.A. 1762 ; professor of chemistry, 1764 ; F.R.S., 1769 ; D.D. and regius professor of divinity, 1771 ; made a discovery which led to the black-bulb thermometer ; prebendary, 1774, and archdeacon of Ely, 1779-82 ; offended the court by a whig sermon, 1776 ; rector of Northwold, 1779-81; rector of Knaptoft, 1781 ; bishop of Llandaff, 1782 ; inherited an estate, 1786 ; wrote in favour of Pitt's war policy, 1798 ; advocated the union with Ireland, 1799 and Roman catholic emancipation, 1804; published chemical researches, controversial tracts, and sermons and charges; defended Christianity against Edward Gibbon, 1776, and Thomas Paine, 1796; his advice to government (1787) on improvements in gunpowder said to have resulted in a saving of 100,000l. a year. [lx. 24]

WATSON, RICHARD (1781–1833), methodist divine; apprenticed to a joiner at Lincoln, 1795; Wesleyan preacher, 1796–1801; minister of the methodist 'New connexion,' 1803–7; editor of the 'Liverpool Courier,' 1808; Wesleyan minister, 1812–33; London secretary to Wesleyan missions, 1816–27, 1832–3; agitated for abolition of slavery, 1825–32; published a life of John Wesley, papers on Wesleyan missions, theological text-books, and sermons. [lx. 27]

WATSON, ROBERT (fl. 1555), protestant; a civilian; steward to Archbishop Cranmer; imprisoned as a protestant, 1554–5; went abroad on his release; published, 1556, 'Ætiologia,' an account of his trial. [lx. 29]

WATSON, ROBERT (fl. 1581–1605), almanac-maker; of Queens' College and Clare Hall, Cambridge; B.A. Clare Hall, Cambridge, 1585; licensed to practise physic, 1589; settled at Braintree; first known issue of his almanac, 1595, latest, 1605. [lx. 29]

WATSON, ROBERT (1730?–1781), historian; professor of logic, St. Andrews; principal of St. Salvator's College, 1777; minister of St. Leonard's parish, St. Andrews, 1777; published histories of 'Philip II. of Spain,' 1777, and, posthumously (1783), of 'Philip III.' [lx. 29]

WATSON, ROBERT (1746–1838), adventurer; rose to be 'colonel' in Washington's army; M.D.; secretary to Lord George Gordon, 1780; an advocate of revolution; imprisoned as a political suspect, 1796–8; fled to Paris and became English tutor to Napoleon; known as 'Chevalier Watson'; principal of Scots College, Paris, c. 1802–8; teacher of English in Rome, 1816–19; purchased at Rome the 'Stuart papers' from an attorney, who had been confidential agent to Henry, cardinal York (1725–1807) [q. v.], 1817 (papers seized by the Vatican, and finally delivered to the prince regent); obtained in all 3,600l. from the English ministry for his find; committed suicide in London; published life of Lord George Gordon, 1795; edited 'Political Works' of Fletcher of Saltoun, 1798, and, 1821, Chevalier Johnstone's 'Memoirs of . . . 1745.' [lx. 30]

WATSON, RUNDLE BURGES (1809–1860), captain, R.N.; lieutenant, 1829; captain, 1842; commanded a squadron in the Baltic, 1854–5. [lx. 30]

WATSON, SAMUEL (1663–1715), sculptor in wood and stone; employed at Chatsworth, 1693–1707. [lx. 31]

WATSON, THOMAS (1513–1584), bishop of Lincoln; fellow of St. John's College, Cambridge, 1535; M.A., 1537; D.D., 1554; a humanist; wrote a Latin tragedy, 'Absolon (Absalom)'; rector of Wyke Regis, 1545; chaplain to Stephen Gardiner [q. v.], 1545–53; imprisoned, 1547–8 and 1550; a leading Roman catholic preacher in London, 1553–8; master of St. John's College, Cambridge, 1553–4; dean of Durham, 1553–7; one of the disputants against Cranmer at Oxford, 1554; one of Cardinal Pole's commission to visit Cambridge University, 1557; bishop of Lincoln, 1557; deprived of his see, June 1559; kept in custody, 1559–84. [lx. 31]

WATSON, THOMAS (1557?–1592), poet; possibly educated at Oxford; law-student in London; studied Italian and French poetry; circulated in manuscript Latin poems, and Latin versions of some of Petrarch's sonnets; visited Paris, 1581, and formed a friendship with Sir Francis Walsingham [q. v.]; published a Latin version of the 'Antigone' of Sophocles, with an appendix of Latin allegorical poems and experiments in Latin metres, 1581; contributed commendatory verses, Latin and English, to his friends' books; published, 1582, 'Ἑκατομπαθία, or Passionate Centurie of Loue,' eighteen-line English poems (called 'sonnets'), reflecting classical and French and Italian poems, and being in some cases translations; published Latin versions of Tasso's 'Aminta,' 1585, and of 'Raptus Helenæ' from the Greek of Coluthus, 1586; his version of the 'Aminta' rendered into English, without authority, by Abraham Fraunce [q. v.], 1587; published 'The first Sett of Italian Madrigalls Englished,'

1590, and an 'Eglogue' (Latin and English) on Walsingham's death, 1590. His Latin pastoral 'Amyntæ Gaudia,' appeared posthumously in 1592, and 'The Tears of Fancie,' sixty English sonnets, in 1593; a few previously unpublished poems appeared in 'The Phœnix Nest,' 1593, and 'England's Helicon,' 1600. His sonnets were closely studied by Shakespeare and other contemporaries. He was the 'Amyntas' of Spenser's 'Colin Clout's come home again' (1595), and was declared by Francis Meres to be the equal of Petrarch, Theocritus, and Virgil. [lx. 34]

WATSON, THOMAS (d. 1686), puritan divine; educated at Emmanuel College, Cambridge; chaplain to Mary, widow of Horace Vere, baron Tilbury; intruded minister of St. Stephen's, Walbrook, London, 1646; joined in the London ministers' petition against Charles I's execution, 1649; imprisoned as a suspected royalist intriguer, 1651; ejected from St. Stephen's, 1660; preacher in London, 1660–80; published devotional works, 1652–1669. His 'Body of Practical Divinity' appeared posthumously, 1692. [lx. 37]

WATSON, THOMAS (1637–1717), bishop of St. David's; fellow of St. John's College, Cambridge, 1660; M.A., 1662; D.D., 1675; rector of Burrough Green, Cambridgeshire; a strong supporter of James II; bishop of St. David's, 1687; opposed William III's government, 1692–6; involved in a controversy with his registrar, Robert Lucy, 1694; accused of simony, 1695; found guilty and deprived of his see, 1699; vainly tried, 1700–5, to obtain reversal of the sentence, which his friends believed to have been influenced by his Jacobite opinions. [lx. 38]

WATSON, THOMAS (d. 1744), captain in the navy; lieutenant, 1733; lost his ship, the Northumberland, in a badly fought action, 1744; died of wounds. [lx. 40]

WATSON, THOMAS (1743–1781), engraver; engraved portraits, both in stipple and mezzotint; printseller in London. [lx. 41]

WATSON, SIR THOMAS, first baronet (1792–1882); physician; fellow of St. John's College, Cambridge, 1816; studied medicine in London and Edinburgh; M.D. Cambridge, 1825; became a leading physician in London, 1825–70; F.R.C.P., 1826, Gulstonian lecturer, 1827, Lumleian lecturer, 1831, and censor, 1828, 1837, and 1838; physician to Middlesex Hospital, London, 1827–43; professor at University College, London, 1828–31, and at King's College, London, 1831–40; F.R.S., 1859; created baronet, 1866; active member of College of Physicians; published 'Lectures on the . . . Practice of Physic,' 1843. [lx. 41]

WATSON, WALTER (1780–1854), Scottish poet; private in the Scots greys, 1799–1802; afterwards a weaver; published songs and verses, 1808, 1823, 1843; his 'Select Poems' published, 1853. [lx. 42]

WATSON, WILLIAM (1559?–1603), conspirator; visited Oxford, 1569; went to Rheims, 1575; secular priest, 1586; sent on the English mission; imprisoned, 1586, and again, 1587; protested against Anthony Babington's plot, 1587; escaped to Liège, 1588; mission priest in west of England, 1590; imprisoned, 1597 and 1599–1602; opposed the appointment of George Blackwell [q. v.] as archpriest, 1600; strenuously opposed the jesuits, and especially their project of conveying the English crown to the infanta of Spain; author, or part-author, of four books printed at Rheims, 1601, against Robert Parsons and the jesuits, the longest being 'Ten Quodlibeticall Questions concerning Religion and State'; negotiated with Bishop Richard Bancroft about an oath of allegiance which Roman catholics might conscientiously take, 1602; provoked by James I's failure to obtain toleration for Roman catholics, became a leader of the 'Bye' or 'Priests' Plot,' and privy to the 'Main' plot, 1603; informed against by the jesuits; executed at Winchester. [lx. 42]

WATSON, SIR WILLIAM (1715–1787), physician and naturalist; apothecary's apprentice in London, 1730; apothecary, 1738; F.R.S., 1741; honorary M.D., Halle, 1757; physician to Foundling Hospital, London, 1762–87; F.R.C.P., 1784, and censor, 1785 and 1786; knighted, 1786; published botanical papers from 1744, notes of electrical experiments, 1745–63, and some medical papers, 1762–8. [lx. 45]

WATSON, Sir WILLIAM (1744–1825 ?), physician ; M.D. ; F.R.S., 1767 ; knighted, 1796 ; probably son of Sir William Watson (1715–1787) [q. v.] [lx. 47]

WATSON, WILLIAM, LORD WATSON (1827–1899), judge : educated at Glasgow and Edinburgh ; LL.D. Edinburgh, 1876 ; admitted advocate, 1851 ; appeared for defence of Dr. Edward William Pritchard [q. v.] the poisoner, 1865 ; solicitor-general for Scotland, 1874 : dean of Faculty of Advocates, 1875 ; lord advocate and M.P. for Glasgow and Aberdeen universities, 1876 ; privy councillor, 1878 ; appointed ordinary lord of appeal and created life peer, 1880. [Suppl. iii. 508]

WATSON, Sir WILLIAM HENRY (1796–1860), judge ; officer of dragoons in the Peninsula, 1812–14, and at Waterloo, 1815 ; called to bar at Lincoln's Inn, 1832 ; M.P. Kinsale, 1841–7, and Hull, 1854–6 ; baron of the exchequer and knighted, 1856 ; published two legal treatises, 1825–7. [lx. 47]

WATSON-WENTWORTH, CHARLES, second MARQUIS OF ROCKINGHAM (1730–1782), styled Viscount Higham from 1734, and Earl of Malton from 1746 ; of Westminster School and St. John's College, Cambridge ; served as volunteer against the Scottish insurgents, 1746 ; created Earl of Malton in the Irish peerage, 1750 ; succeeded to the marquisate, 1750 ; held decided whig opinions ; lord of the bedchamber, 1751–62 ; lord-lieutenant of North and East Ridings of Yorkshire, 1751 ; vice-admiral of Yorkshire, 1755 ; out of favour and dismissed from his offices, 1762 ; premier of a coalition ministry, July 1765 ; mortified George III by repealing the Stamp Act, opposing grants to the king's brothers, and condemning general warrants ; dismissed from office, July 1766 ; failed to form a whig ministry, 1767 ; a leader of the opposition in the House of Lords, 1768–81 ; supported proposals to grant independence to the American colonies and partial enfranchisement of Roman catholics, 1778 ; prime minister, March 1782. [lx. 48]

WATT, JAMES (1698–1782), merchant ; chief magistrate of Greenock, 1751. [lx. 51]

WATT, JAMES (1736–1819), engineer ; suffered throughout life from weak health ; studied geometry, 1749 ; showed great manual dexterity ; served for a year under a London philosophical-instrument maker : mathematical-instrument maker in the precincts of Glasgow University, 1757 ; while repairing a model of John Newcomen's steam-engine, discovered the cause of its waste of power, 1764 ; devised the separate condenser and the air-pump, to obviate the defect, 1765 ; went into partnership with John Roebuck [q. v.] to construct improved steam-engines, but their experimental engine proved unsatisfactory ; employed in survey work for canals and harbours, c. 1760–74 ; patented his 'Watt' steam-engine, 1769 ; obtained a prolongation of his patent, 1775 ; in partnership with Matthew Boulton [q. v.], at Soho Engineering Works, Birmingham, 1775–1800 ; frequently visited Cornwall to superintend construction of engines to drain mines ; experimented to obtain rotary motion from his reciprocating engine, at first by applying the crank, c. 1780, afterwards by the 'Sun-and-planet' wheel, 1781 ; made use of the expansiveness of steam to obtain the double stroke, 1782, and introduced other mechanical improvements, 1784 ; adopted the centrifugal governor for regulating speed of steam-engines ; patented a fuel-saving furnace, his last patent, 1785 ; engaged in litigation to protect his patents, 1792–1800 ; invented copying-ink, 1780 ; independently discovered the composition of water (his 'dephlogisticated air' = oxygen and 'phlogiston'= hydrogen), 1782–3 ; projected the screw-propeller, 1784 ; retired and devoted himself to mechanical and chemical research ; F.R.S., 1785 ; LL.D. Glasgow, 1806 ; accorded a monument in Westminster Abbey. [lx. 51]

WATT, JAMES (1769–1848), engineer ; son of James Watt (1736–1819) [q. v.] ; resided in Paris, 1789–94 ; partner in Boulton & Watt, engineers, Birmingham, 1794 ; fitted the Caledonia with engines, and steamed to Holland and up the Rhine, this being the first steamship to leave an English port, 1817 ; improved marine engines. [lx. 62]

WATT, JAMES HENRY (1799–1867), line-engraver and book illustrator. [lx. 62]

WATT, ROBERT (1774–1819), bibliographer ; began life as ploughboy ; studied in Glasgow University, 1792–5, and Edinburgh, 1795–7 ; schoolmaster at Symington, Ayrshire, 1797–8 ; completed his medical course at Glasgow, 1798–9 ; practitioner in Paisley, 1799, and in Glasgow, c. 1810–17 ; published medical papers ; M.D. Aberdeen, 1810 ; published 'Catalogue of Medical Books,' 1812 ; physician to Glasgow infirmary, 1814 ; compiled 'Bibliotheca Britannica,' a general catalogue of authors, with index of subjects, which was published posthumously, 1819–24. [lx. 63]

WATTS, ALARIC ALEXANDER (1797–1864), poet ; journalist in London, 1818 ; editor of 'Leeds Intelligencer,' 1822–5 ; editor of 'Manchester Courier,' 1825–6 ; published 'Poetical Sketches,' 1823 ; edited 'Literary Souvenir,' an annual, 1824–38 ; published occasional volumes of verses, partly his own, partly fugitive pieces by other authors, from 1828 ; edited 'United Service Gazette,' 1833–47 ; bankrupt through failure of his numerous newspaper ventures, 1850 ; published 'Lyrics of the Heart,' 1850 ; furnished the letterpress of Turner's 'Liber Fluviorum,' 1853 ; obtained civil list pension, 1854 ; brought out first issue of 'Men of the Time,' 1856. [lx. 65]

WATTS, GILBERT (d. 1657), divine : M.A. Lincoln College, Oxford, 1614 ; fellow, 1621–57 ; D.D., 1642 ; rector of Willingale Doe, 1642–7 ; translated Bacon's 'De Aug mentis Scientiarum,' 1640. [lx. 66]

WATTS, HENRY (1815–1884), chemist ; B.A. London, 1841 ; assistant-professor of chemistry, University College, London, 1846–57 ; translated and expanded Leopold Gmelin's 'Handbuch der Chemie,' eighteen volumes, 1848–72 ; edited the Chemical Society's 'Journal ' from 1849 ; F.R.S., 1866 ; edited Watts's 'Dictionary of Chemistry,' 1868, with supplements, 1872–81. [lx. 66]

WATTS, HUGH (1582 ?–1643), bell-founder of Leicester : cast bells, 1600–43, known as 'Watts's Nazarenes,' from his favourite inscription ; his peal of ten bells for St. Margaret's, Leicester, said to have been the finest in England at the time ; mayor of Leicester at Charles I's visit, 1634. [lx. 67]

WATTS, ISAAC (1674–1748), hymn-writer ; son of a nonconformist schoolmaster ; educated at Stoke Newington nonconformist academy, 1690–4 ; wrote his first hymn, 'Behold the glories of the Lamb,' c. 1695 ; private tutor, 1696–1702 ; nonconformist minister in London, 1702–48 ; hon. D.D. Edinburgh, 1728 ; composed six hundred hymns, including 'Jesus shall reign where'er the sun,' ' Our God, our help in ages past,' and other standard hymns ; published 'Horæ Lyricæ,' religious poems, 1706, ' Hymns,' 1707, ' Divine Songs,' hymns for children, 1715, and a selection of metrical ' Psalms of David,' 1719 ; published doctrinal treatises, of Arian tendency, 1722–46, broaching a theory held also by Henry More [q. v.] ; compiled educational manuals, including ' Logic,' 1725, and ' Scripture History,' 1732 ; accorded a monument in Westminster Abbey ; his 'Collected Works' published, 1810. [lx. 67]

WATTS, MRS. JANE (1793–1826). [See WALDIE, JANE.]

WATTS, Sir JOHN (d. 1616), merchant and shipowner ; served in one of his own ships against the Armada, 1588 ; fitted out privateers ; alderman of London ; governor of the East India Company, 1601 ; knighted, 1603 ; an active member of the Virginia Company. [lx. 70]

WATTS, JOHN (1818–1887), educational and social reformer ; self-taught ; lectured in many towns in favour of Robert Owen's communistic ideas ; settled in Manchester, 1841 ; Ph.D. Giessen, 1844 ; advocated, in Manchester and district, public parks, rate-supported schools, free libraries, co-operation, technical education ; published many pamphlets on educational and economic questions. [lx. 71]

WATTS, RICHARD (1529–1579), founder of Watts's charity (an almshouse and wayfarers' rest) at Rochester ; victualling contractor, 1550 ; deputy-victualler to the navy, 1554 and 1559 ; surveyor of ordnance, Upnor, 1562 ; M.P., Rochester, 1563–7 ; entertained Queen Elizabeth, 1573. [lx. 72]

WATTS, ROBERT (1820-1895), Irish presbyterian divine; educated at Belfast and at Lexington and Princeton, United States; minister in Philadelphia, 1853-63, and in Dublin, 1863-6; professor in the presbyterian college, Belfast, 1866-95; published theological papers, including critiques of Professor Tyndall, 1874, and of Herbert Spencer, 1875. [lx. 73]

WATTS, THOMAS (1811-1869), keeper of printed books at the British Museum: acquired most European and some oriental languages; advocated general reading room for British Museum Library, 1836; employed on the library staff from 1838, selecting foreign literature and classifying acquisitions: superintendent of reading-room, 1857; keeper of printed books, 1866; published bibliographical and philological papers. [lx. 73]

WATTS, WALTER HENRY (1776-1842), journalist and miniature-painter; exhibited miniatures at Royal Academy, 1808-30; member of the Society of Associated Artists in Water-colours, 1808; parliamentary reporter to 'Morning Post,' 1803-13, and to 'Morning Chronicle,' 1813-40; edited 'Annual Biography and Obituary,' 1817-1831. [lx. 74]

WATTS, WILLIAM (1590?-1649), chaplain to Prince Rupert; M.A. Caius College, Cambridge, 1614; travelled on continent; vicar of Barwick, 1624-48; rector of St. Alban, Wood Street, London, 1625-42; army chaplain to Lord Arundel, 1639, and to Prince Rupert, 1642-9; hon. D.D. Oxford, 1639; translated 'Confessions of St. Augustine,' 1631 (edited by Pusey, 1838); edited 'Historia Major' of Matthew Paris, 1640. [lx. 75]

WATTS, WILLIAM (1752-1851), line-engraver: edited 'Copper-plate Magazine' from 1774; published 'Seats of the Nobility and Gentry,' 1779-86; published 'Views' in Scotland, 1791-4, in London and Westminster, 1800, in Turkey, 1801, and in Bath and Bristol, 1819. [lx. 76]

WAUCHOPE, ANDREW GILBERT (1846-1899), major-general; midshipman in navy, 1860; obtained discharge, 1862, and received commission in 42nd regiment, 1865; lieutenant, 1867; in charge of Papho district, Cyprus, 1878-80; C.M.G., 1880; captain, 1878; served in Egypt, 1882; major, 1884; in Soudan, 1884; brevet lieutenant-colonel, 1884; in Nile expedition, 1884-5; colonel, 1888; C.B., 1893; commanded brigade in expedition for reconquest of Soudan, 1898; major-general, 1898; commanded highland brigade in General Lord Methuen's column in Transvaal, 1899, and was killed at Magersfontein. [Suppl. iii. 509]

WAUCHOPE, SIR JOHN (d. 1682), covenanter: of Niddrie Marischal, Midlothian; knighted, 1633; served in Argyll's army, 1645. [lx. 76]

WAUGH, ALEXANDER (1754-1827), Scottish divine; educated at Edinburgh University, 1770, in the secession church seminary, 1774, and at Aberdeen University, 1777; M.A. Aberdeen, 1778; D.D., 1815; minister at Newtown, near Melrose, 1780-2, and of the Wells Street congregational church, London, 1782; went on missionary tours in France, Ireland, and Scotland; published sermons, 1825. [lx. 76]

WAUGH, SIR ANDREW SCOTT (1810-1878), major-general, royal engineers; educated at Addiscombe and Chatham; lieutenant, Bengal engineers, 1827; went to India, 1829; an extremely accurate worker for trigonometrical survey of India, 1832-43; surveyor-general of India, 1843-61; captain, 1844; lieutenant-colonel, 1847; F.R.S., 1858; returned to England, 1861; major-general and knighted, 1861. [lx. 77]

WAUGH, EDWIN (1817-1890), Lancashire poet and miscellaneous writer; called 'the Lancashire Burns'; son of a Rochdale shoemaker: self-taught; a journeyman printer: traveller for a Manchester printing firm; published 'Sketches of Lancashire Life and Localities,' 1855; made his mark by the song, 'Come whoam to the childer an' me,' 1856; published 'Poems and Songs,' 1859, and numerous prose and verse pieces connected with Lancashire; granted a civil list pension, 1881. [lx. 79]

WAUTON. [See also WALTON.]

WAUTON, WATTON, WALTON, or WALTHONE, SIMON DE (d. 1266), bishop of Norwich: 'king's clerk' to King John; incumbent of St. Andrew, Hastings, 1206; a justice itinerant, 1246; rector of Stoke Prior, Herefordshire, 1253; chief-justice of common pleas, 1257; conse-

crated bishop of Norwich, 1258; supported Henry III against the barons. [lx. 81]

WAY, ALBERT (1805-1874), antiquary; son of Lewis Way [q. v.]; M.A. Trinity College, Cambridge, 1834; travelled on continent and in Palestine; fellow of Society of Antiquaries, 1839, and director, 1842-6; edited 'Promptorium Parvulorum' (Camden Soc.), 1843-65. [lx. 81]

WAY, SIR GREGORY HOLMAN BROMLEY (1776-1844), lieutenant-general; ensign, 1797; captain, 1802; served at Malta, 1800, and Buenos Ayres, 1807; major, 1808; taken prisoner at Roliça, 1808; served at Oporto, 1809, Talavera and Busaco, 1810, and Albuera, 1811; lieutenant-colonel of 29th foot, 1811-13; invalided and knighted, 1814; C.B., 1815, and deputy adjutant-general in North Britain, 1815-22; lieutenant-general, 1841. [lx. 82]

WAY, LEWIS (1772-1840), advocate of conversion of the Jews; M.A. Merton College, Oxford, 1796; called to bar, Inner Temple, 1797; took holy orders; founded Marbœuf (English protestant) chapel, Paris. [lx. 81]

WAY or WEY, WILLIAM (1407?-1476). [See WEY.]

WAYLETT, MRS. HARRIET (1798-1851), actress; née Cooke; appeared on the Bath stage, 1816; married Waylett (d. 1840), an actor, 1819; appeared at the Adelphi, London, 1820, in Birmingham, 1823, and in Dublin, 1828; manager of Strand Theatre, London, 1834; long a favourite actress of soubrette parts and a singer in London and the provinces; retired from the stage, 1843; married George Alexander Lee [q. v.], c. 1840. [lx. 83]

WAYNFLETE or WAINFLEET, WILLIAM OF (1395?-1486), bishop of Winchester: lord chancellor of England and founder of Magdalen College, Oxford; son of Richard Patyn, of Wainfleet; probably educated at Winchester College and New College, Oxford; master of St. Mary Magdalen Hospital, Winchester, 1426; fellow of Eton, 1440, and provost, 1443; a great favourite of Henry VI; added to the buildings at Eton; bishop of Winchester, 1447-86; founded in Oxford a hall dedicated to St. Mary Magdalen, 1448; a commissioner to negotiate with Jack Cade, 1450; approved of the ascendency of Richard, duke of York, 1454; lord chancellor, 1456-60; dissolved Magdalen Hall and founded St. Mary Magdalen College, Oxford, 1458; opposed the Yorkists, 1459; submitted to Edward IV, 1461; released Henry VI from the Tower of London, 1471; again submitted to Edward IV, 1471; entertained Edward IV and afterwards Richard III at Oxford, 1483; founded free school at Wainfleet, 1484. [lx. 85]

WAYTE, THOMAS (fl. 1634-1668). [See WAITE.]

WEALE, JOHN (1791-1862), publisher; began business in London, c. 1820; published educational text-books in classics, science, architecture, and engineering. [lx. 89]

WEARG, SIR CLEMENT (1686-1726), solicitor-general; called to bar, Inner Temple, 1711; whig M.P., Helston, 1724; solicitor-general and knighted, 1724; wrote on the law of divorce, 1723-6. [lx. 89]

WEATHERHEAD, GEORGE HUME (1790?-1853), medical writer; M.D. Edinburgh, 1816; L.R.C.P., 1820; published medical treatises and translations, 1819-42. [lx. 90]

WEATHERSHED or WETHERSHED, RICHARD OF (d. 1231). [See GRANT, RICHARD.]

WEAVER, JOHN (d. 1685), politician; M.P., Stamford, 1645-59; a recognised leader of the independents, 1647; refused to sit as one of Charles I's judges, 1649; a commissioner for government of Ireland, 1650-3; member of council of state, 1659-60. [lx. 90]

WEAVER, JOHN (1673-1760), dancing-master, and the original introducer of pantomimes into England; resided in Shrewsbury; brought out in London ballets (called 'pantomimes'), 1702, 1707, 1716-33, occasionally taking part himself in their performance; published treatises on dancing, 1706-28. [lx. 91]

WEAVER, ROBERT (1773-1852), congregational divine and antiquary; pastor at Mansfield,1802-52; published a dissertation on ancient stone monuments in Britain, entitled 'Monumenta Antiqua,' ascribing the remains of pre-Roman times to Phœnician influence, 1840, and theological and controversial works. [lx. 92]

WEAVER, THOMAS (1616–1663), poetaster; M.A. Christ Church, Oxford, 1640; chaplain of Christ Church, Oxford, 1641–8; ejected as a royalist; published 'Songs and Poems of Love and Drollery,' 1654; exciseman at Liverpool, 1660. The ' T. W., Gent.' who published, 1647, 'Plantaganets Tragicall Story,' a chronicle-poem on Richard III, is probably a different person. [lx. 93]

WEAVER, THOMAS (1773–1855), geologist; educated at Fribourg, 1790–4; government geologist in co. Wicklow; mining geologist in Mexico and United States; F.R.S., 1826; published papers on geology of Gloucestershire, Somerset, and Ireland, and on carboniferous rocks of America. [lx. 94]

WEBB. [See also WEBBE.]

WEBB, MRS. (d. 1793), actress; née Child; known successively as Mrs. Day and Mrs. Webb; first acted at Norwich; a popular actress in Edinburgh, 1772–8; a good actress of grotesque parts at Haymarket and Covent Garden Theatres, London, 1778–93. [lx. 94]

WEBB, BENJAMIN (1819–1885), ecclesiologist; educated at St. Paul's School, London, 1828–38; M.A. Trinity College, Cambridge, 1845; secretary of the Cambridge Camden Society, and, 1848–63, of the London Ecclesiological Society; incumbent of Sheen, Staffordshire, 1851–62, and of St. Andrews, Well Street, London, 1862–1885; prebendary of St. Paul's, London, 1881; editor of 'Church Quarterly Review,' 1881–5; translated foreign theological works; published 'Sketches of Continental Ecclesiology,' 1847, and ecclesiological papers. [lx. 95]

WEBB, DANIEL (1719 ?–1798), author; entered New College, Oxford, 1735; published 'Beauties of Painting,' 1760, 'Beauties of Poetry,' 1762, 'Literary Amusements,' 1787, and similar works. [lx. 96]

WEBB, FRANCIS (1735–1815), miscellaneous writer; educated in Daventry nonconformist seminary; pastor at Honiton; baptist minister in St. Paul's Alley, London, 1758–66; deputy-searcher at Gravesend, 1766–77, and at Poole, 1777; secretary to the envoy to Hesse Cassel, 1786, and to Paris, 1801; published pamphlets in the whig interest, 1772 and 1775, verses, 1788–1811, and sermons. [lx. 96]

WEBB, FRANCIS CORNELIUS (1826–1873), physician and medical writer; educated at University College, London, 1843; M.D. Edinburgh, 1850; F.R.C.P., 1873; lectured in London on medical jurisprudence and on natural history; published papers on epidemics and sanitation; edited 'Medical Times and Gazette.' [lx. 97]

WEBB, GEORGE (1581–1642), bishop of Limerick; M.A. Corpus Christi College, Oxford, 1605; vicar of Steeple Aston; rector of SS. Peter and Paul, Bath, 1621; D.D. and chaplain to Prince Charles, 1624; bishop of Limerick, 1634; published theological and educational works. [lx. 98]

WEBB or **WEBBE**, JOHN (1611–1672), architect; educated at Merchant Taylors' School; pupil of Inigo Jones [q. v.]; supervised the building of Greenwich Palace, 1661–6, and of Burlington House, London, 1664–6; designed several country houses; edited Inigo Jones's tract on Stonehenge, 1655, and published 'Vindication of Stonehenge Restored,' 1665. [lx. 98]

WEBB, SIR JOHN (1772–1852), director-general, ordnance medical department; assistant army surgeon, 1794; field inspector, 1801; director-general, 1813; served in Netherlands, 1794, West Indies, 1795–8, Egypt, 1801–6; knighted, 1821; published account of outbreak of plague among forces in Egypt, 1801–3; C.B., 1850. [lx. 99]

WEBB, JOHN (1776–1869), divine and antiquary; educated at St. Paul's School, London; M.A. Wadham College, Oxford, 1802; rector of Tretire; minor canon of Worcester, 1811, and of Gloucester; F.S.A., 1819; wrote words for oratorios. His works include accounts of Herefordshire in the civil war and of Gloucester Abbey. [lx. 100]

WEBB, JOHN RICHMOND (1667 ?–1724), general; cornet of dragoons, 1687; colonel of foot, 1695; tory M.P. for Ludgershall, 1690–1710, 1715, 1722; served in Flanders, 1702–3; brigadier-general at Blenheim, 1706; major-general at Ramillies, 1706, and Oudenarde, 1708; became centre of tory agitation against Marlborough because

the credit of protecting convoy, September 1708, from superior French force was assigned in despatches not to Webb, but to his whig subordinate, William Cadogan (1675–1726) [q. v.]; lieutenant-general and pensioned, 1709; severely wounded at Malplaquet, 1709; governor of Isle of Wight and M.P. for Newport, 1710–15; general, 1712; commander of land forces in Great Britain, 1712–15; dismissed from office on accession of George I. [lx. 100]

WEBB, JONAS (1796–1862), stockbreeder; farmer at Babraham, 1822; a leading exhibitor of Southdown sheep, 1840–62, and of shorthorn cattle, 1838–62. [lx. 103]

WEBB, MATTHEW (1848–1883), known as ' Captain Webb,' the Channel swimmer; apprentice in mercantile marine, 1862, mate, 1866, and captain, 1875; swam from Dover to Calais in twenty-two hours, August 1875; drowned in attempt to swim Niagara rapids. [lx. 104]

WEBB, PHILIP BARKER (1793–1854), botanist; of Harrow and Christ Church, Oxford; entered Lincoln's Inn, 1812; B.A., 1815; studied geology under William Buckland [q. v.]; travelled in Italy, Greece, and the Troad, 1817–18, re-discovering the Scamander and Simois; collected natural-history specimens in Spain, 1826, Portugal and Morocco, 1827, Canary islands, 1828–30, Italy, 1848–50, and west of Ireland, 1851; among his works (French, Italian, and English), dissertations on topography of the Troad, 1820 and 1844, and treatises on natural history of Spain, Portugal, and Morocco, 1838 and 1853, and of Canary islands, 1836–50; his collections kept in the museum at Florence. [lx. 105]

WEBB, PHILIP CARTERET (1700–1770), antiquary and politician; a London attorney; of the Middle Temple and Lincoln's Inn; secretary of bankrupts in court of chancery, c. 1746–66; F.S.A., 1747; F.R.S., 1749; M.P., Haslemere, 1754–68; joint solicitor to treasury, 1756–65; leading official in prosecution of John Wilkes, 1763; published, among other works, pamphlets against the Pretender, 1745, and against Wilkes, 1763, and legal tracts; collected copies of public records, coins, and antique marbles and bronzes. [lx. 107]

WEBB, THOMAS WILLIAM (1807–1885), astronomer; son of John Webb (1776–1869) [q. v.]; M.A. Magdalen Hall, Oxford, 1832; minor canon of Gloucester; incumbent of Hardwick, 1856–85; prebendary of Hereford; an excellent observer, studying particularly lunar phenomena; published popular treatises on astronomy and optics. [lx. 108]

WEBBE. [See also WEBB.]

WEBBE, EDWARD (fl. 1590), master-gunner and adventurer; servant at Moscow to Anthony Jenkinson, 1566–9; enslaved by Crim Tartars at burning of Moscow, 1571; master-gunner at taking of Tunis by Don John of Austria, 1572; gunner in the Turkish service; ransomed, 1588; master-gunner under Henri IV at Ivry, 1590; published his narrative, c. 1590. [lx. 109]

WEBBE, JOSEPH (fl. 1612–1633), grammarian and physician; M.D., perhaps of Padua; published astrological tract at Rome, 1612; translated Cicero's 'Familiar Epistles,' c. 1620; published two tracts advocating colloquial teaching of languages, 1622–3; taught school in the Old Bailey, London, 1623; published tract on Latin prosody, 1626. [lx. 110]

WEBBE, SAMUEL, the elder (1740–1816), composer; bred a cabinet-maker; member, 1771, and secretary, 1794–1812, of Catch Club; librarian of Glee Club, 1787; organist to chapels of Sardinian and Spanish embassies; teacher of church music; composed numerous glees, catches, part-songs, motets, antiphons, and other music. [lx. 110]

WEBBE, SAMUEL, the younger (1770 ?–1843), teacher and composer; son of Samuel Webbe the elder [q. v.]; organist in Liverpool, 1798; music-teacher in London, 1817; organist to chapel of Spanish embassy; again organist in Liverpool; composed glees, madrigals, motets, and anthems, and other church music. [lx. 111]

WEBBE, WILLIAM (fl. 1586–1591), author of 'A Discourse of English Poetrie,' 1586, containing valuable information about contemporary poets; college friend at Cambridge of Edmund Spenser; B.A. St. John's College,

y y

Cambridge, 1573 ; tutor in gentlemen's families in Essex, 1583–91 ; one of the school which protested against rhyme and wished to naturalise classical metres.
[lx. 111]

WEBBER, JOHN (1750 ?–1793), landscape-painter ; of Swiss extraction ; art student at Berne, 1763–6, and Paris, 1766–71 ; decorative painter in London ; exhibited portrait at Royal Academy, 1776 ; draughtsman on Captain James Cook's third voyage, 1776–80 ; published coloured etchings of places visited on that voyage, 1787–92 ; exhibited English, Welsh, Swiss, and North Italian views at Royal Academy, 1784–93 ; R.A., 1791.   [lx. 112]

WEBER, HENRY WILLIAM (1783–1818), editor of plays and romances ; of German extraction ; born at St. Petersburg ; amanuensis in Edinburgh to Sir Walter Scott, 1804 ; became insane, 1813. His publications include reprints of old ballads and romances, 1808–10, slovenly editions of dramas of John Ford, 1811, and Beaumont and Fletcher, 1812, and 'Illustrations of Northern Antiquities from . . . Romances,' 1814.
[lx. 113]

WEBER, OTTO (1832–1888), painter of landscapes and animals ; born in Berlin ; exhibited in Paris, 1864–9 ; settled in London, 1872 ; member of the Institute of Painters in Oil-colours ; exhibited at Royal Academy, 1874–88.   [lx. 113]

WEBSTER, ALEXANDER (1707–1784), Scots writer ; son of James Webster [q. v.] ; minister of Culross, 1733–7, and of Tolbooth Church, Edinburgh, 1737–1784 ; a staunch Hanoverian ; drew up actuarial scheme for church of Scotland, 1742–4 (published, 1748) ; moderator of general assembly, 1753 ; collected census statistics for Scotland, 1755 ; hon. D.D. Edinburgh, 1760 ; dean of Chapel Royal, London, 1771 ; published sermons.
[lx. 114]

WEBSTER, MRS. AUGUSTA (1837–1894), poet ; née (Julia Augusta) Davies ; educated at Cambridge and Paris ; married, 1863 ; published, under pseudonym of Cecil Home, poems, 1860 and 1864, and a novel, 1864 ; member of London school board, 1879–82. Her works include, poems, 'Dramatic Studies,' 1866, 'Portraits,' 1870 (including 'The Castaway,' a poem which won the admiration of Browning), 'A Book of Rhyme,' 1881, also dramatic pieces, 'The Auspicious Day,' 1872, 'Disguises,' 1879, 'In a Day,' 1882, 'The Sentence,' 1887 ; and translations from Greek, 'Prometheus Bound,' 1866, and 'Medea,' 1868, besides essays.   [lx. 115]

WEBSTER, BENJAMIN NOTTINGHAM (1797–1882), actor and dramatist ; played harlequin, and acted small parts at Warwick, c. 1818, and other midland towns and in Ireland ; dancer and actor of minor parts in various London theatres, 1819–20, in Birmingham and north of England, 1821–3, and at Drury Lane, London, 1823–8 ; recognised as a leading comedian from 1829, acting in London at Haymarket, Drury Lane, Covent Garden, and Adelphi theatres, and creating many parts in contemporary comedy ; long manager of Haymarket and Adelphi theatres ; compiled about a hundred comedies and farces, mainly adaptations from French, from 1837 ; retired from stage, 1874 ; last appeared, 1875.   [lx. 116]

WEBSTER, JAMES (1658 ?–1720), Scottish divine ; educated at St. Andrews ; imprisoned as a covenanter ; minister of Liberton, 1688, and of the collegiate church, Edinburgh, 1693–1720.   [lx. 114]

WEBSTER, JOHN (1580 ?–1625 ?), dramatist ; son of a London tailor ; freeman of Merchant Taylors' Company, 1604 ; collaborated with Drayton, Anthony Munday, Middleton, and Thomas Dekker in producing 'Cæsar's Fall' and 'Two Harpes,' and with Chettle, Dekker, Heywood, and Wentworth Smith in producing 'Lady Jane,' and with Chettle, Dekker, and Heywood in producing 'Christmas comes but once a year,' for Philip Henslowe's company, 1602 ; collaborated with Dekker in two comedies, 'Westward Hoe' and 'Northward Hoe,' 1603–4 (published, 1607), and possibly with William Rowley in 'A Cure for a Cuckold' (printed, 1661) ; completed for stage John Marston's 'Malcontent,' 1604 ; with Dekker wrote verses for Stephen Harrison's 'Arches of Triumph,' 1604, describing James I's formal entry into London ; with Heywood and Tourneur published elegies on Prince Henry, 1612 ; brought out a weak tragi-comedy, 'The Devil's Law Case,' before 1619 ; compiled 'Monuments of Honor,' a pageant for the lord mayor's procession, 1624.

His tragedies, founded on Italian *novelle*, and approaching in tragic power nearest of his contemporaries to Shakespeare, are 'The White Divel,' produced, c. 1608, 'Appius and Virginia,' c. 1609, 'Duchess of Malfi,' c. 1616. Lost plays are a tragedy on contemporary French history, entitled 'Guise,' and (written in conjunction with John Ford, c. 1624) 'A late Murder of the Son upon the Mother.' The attribution to him of a share in 'The Thracian Wonder' (printed 1661) and 'The Weakest goes to the Wall' (comedy, printed, 1600) is erroneous. Collected editions of his plays were published, 1830, by Alexander Dyce, and, 1856, by William Hazlitt.   [lx. 120]

WEBSTER, JOHN (1610–1682), puritan writer ; latinised as 'Johannes Hyphastes' ; probably studied at Cambridge ; curate of Kildwick in Craven, 1634 ; master of Clitheroe grammar school, 1643 ; chaplain and surgeon in parliamentary army ; intruded vicar of Mitton, Yorkshire, c. 1649 ; popular preacher and theological disputant in London, 1653 ; practised medicine at Clitheroe, 1657–1682 ; published two devotional works, 'The Saint's Guide,' 1653, and 'The Judgment Set and the Books opened,' 1654 ; adversely criticised university education in 'Academiarum Examen,' 1654 ; ridiculed the credulity of Henry More (1614–1687) [q. v.] and others in 'The Displaying of Supposed Witchcraft,' 1677 ; has been confused with John Webster the dramatist.   [lx. 125]

WEBSTER, THOMAS (1773–1844), geologist ; educated at Aberdeen ; travelled in England and France, making architectural sketches ; architect in London ; published valuable memoirs on upper secondary and tertiary strata of Isle of Wight and south-east of England ; curator of Geological Society's Museum ; professor of geology, University College, London, 1842–4.
[lx. 126]

WEBSTER, THOMAS (1810–1875), barrister ; M.A. Trinity College, Cambridge, 1835 ; called to bar, Lincoln's Inn, 1841 ; F.R.S., 1847 ; a leading authority on patent law ; published works on navigation of the Mersey, 1848–1857.   [lx. 126]

WEBSTER, THOMAS (1800–1886), painter and etcher ; chorister, St. George's Chapel, Windsor ; art-student in London, 1821 ; exhibited, 1823–79, chiefly scenes from school and village life ; R.A., 1846.   [lx. 127]

WEBSTER, WILLIAM (1689–1758), divine ; M.A. Caius College, Cambridge, 1716 ; D.D., 1732 ; curate in London, 1716 ; rector of Depden, 1733 ; vicar of Ware and Thundridge, 1740 ; published, among other works, 'Remarks on the Divine Legation' (of William Warburton [q. v.], Pope's friend), 1739, and 'A Complete History of Arianism from 306 to 1666,' 1735 ; put into the 'Dunciad,' 1742.   [lx. 127]

WECKHERLIN, GEORG RUDOLPH (1584–1653), under-secretary of state ; native of Stuttgart ; studied law at Tübingen ; entered the Würtemberg diplomatic service ; employed on diplomatic missions in Germany, France, and England ; married an English lady, 1616 ; under-secretary of state in England, 1624–41 ; 'secretary for foreign tongues' to the parliament, 1644–9 ; retired in ill-health ; recalled to assist John Milton in Latin secretaryship, March to December 1652 ; wrote verses in English, French, German. His English verses include 'Triumphal Shows . . . at Stutgart,' 1616, and 'Panegyricke to Lord Hay,' 1619. His German verses imitate English and French models.   [lx. 128]

WEDDELL, JAMES (1787–1834), navigator ; merchant seaman ; sent prisoner to Rainbow frigate for mutiny, 1808 ; rated as midshipman for good conduct ; an efficient master on king's ships, 1810–16 ; commanded Leith sealing-ships in Antarctic Ocean, 1819–24 ; discovered islands in Antarctic ; published, 1825, 'Voyage towards the South Pole . . . 1822–4.'   [lx. 129]

WEDDELL, JOHN (1583–1642), sea-captain ; officer in East India Company's service, 1617–26, 1628–33 ; commanded squadron which helped shah of Persia to take Ormuz from Portuguese, 1622 ; joined Dutch in destroying Portuguese squadron in Persian Gulf, 1624 ; censured by the company for illicit private trading, 1626 ; commanded king's ship Rainbow, 1627–8 ; an adherent of Duke of Buckingham, 1628 ; unjustly held responsible by the company for loss of his ship by fire, 1633 ; commanded Sir William Courten's [q. v.] rival trading fleet to India and China, 1636–40 ; died in India.   [lx. 130]

WEDDERBURN, ALEXANDER (1581–1650?), Latin scholar; educated at Aberdeen; completed for press his brother's (David Wedderburn [q. v.]) commentary on Persius, printed 1664. [lx. 135]

WEDDERBURN, SIR ALEXANDER (1610–1676), of Blackness, Forfarshire; town-clerk of Dundee, 1633–75; pensioned by Charles I, 1640, and by Charles II, 1664; knighted, 1640; M.P., Dundee, 1644–51. [lx. 132]

WEDDERBURN, ALEXANDER, first BARON LOUGHBOROUGH and first EARL OF ROSSLYN (1733–1805), lord chancellor: educated at Dalkeith school and, 1746, at Edinburgh University; Scottish advocate, 1754; left Scottish bar after insulting in open court Lord-president Craigie, 1757; called to bar, Inner Temple, 1757; a favourite of the Earl of Bute; M.P., Ayr burghs, 1761–8, Richmond, Yorkshire, 1768–9, Bishop's Castle, 1769–74, and Okehampton, 1774–8; bencher, Lincoln's Inn, 1773; deserted the tories and spoke in favour of John Wilkes, 1769; violently attacked Lord North's administration, 1770; returned to the tories, accepting the solicitor-generalship, 1771; attorney-general, 1778; chief-justice of common pleas, 1780–93; created Baron Loughborough, 1780; lord chancellor, 1793–1801; created Earl of Rosslyn, 1801. [lx. 132]

WEDDERBURN, DAVID (1580–1646), Latin poet; master of Aberdeen grammar school, 1602–40; professor in Marischal College, Aberdeen, 1614–24; official Latin poet of Aberdeen city, 1620–46; compiled a Latin grammar, 1630. His verses include elegies on Prince Henry, 1612, King James, 1625, and Arthur Johnston [q. v.], 1641. [lx. 134]

WEDDERBURN, JAMES (1495?–1553), Scottish poet; educated at St. Andrews, 1514; embraced protestantism; merchant at Dieppe and Rouen; satirised the Romanists in 'Beheading of John Baptist,' a tragedy, and 'Dionysius the Tyrant,' a comedy, acted at Dundee, 1539–40; wrote religious and anti-Romanist ballads to go to popular tunes, issued as broadsheets, *c.* 1540, afterwards (1567) included in 'Ane Compendious Booke of Godly and Spirituall Songs'; fled to France to escape prosecution for heresy, *c.* 1540; died in France. [lx. 136]

WEDDERBURN, JAMES (1585–1639), bishop of Dunblane; educated at St. Andrews; tutor in Isaac Casaubon's family; beneficed in England, 1615–36; helped Laud to compile the Scottish liturgy; divinity professor, St. Andrews, 1617; D.D. St. Andrews before 1623; canon of Ely, 1626; prebendary of Wells, 1631; dean of Chapel Royal, Stirling, 1635; bishop of Dunblane, 1636; deposed by general assembly, 1638. [lx. 137]

WEDDERBURN, JOHN (1500?–1556), Scottish poet; M.A. St. Andrews, 1528; chaplain of St. Matthew's chapel, Dundee, 1532; embraced protestantism, and, like his brother, James Wedderburn (1495?–1553) [q. v.], wrote anti-Romanist ballads; withdrew to Wittemberg, 1540; returned to Dundee and printed his ballads, 1542; fled to England, 1546. [lx. 136]

WEDDERBURN, SIR JOHN (1599–1679), physician; graduated at St. Andrews, 1618; professor of philosophy, St. Andrews, 1620–30; king's physician in Scotland; knighted; in attendance on the prince (Charles II) in Holland; incorporated M.D. Oxford, 1646; bequeathed his library to St. Andrews University. [lx. 138]

WEDDERBURN, SIR JOHN, baronet (1704–1746), Jacobite; succeeded as fifth baronet of Blackness, 1741; taken prisoner at Culloden, 1746; executed. [lx. 138]

WEDDERBURN, SIR PETER (1616?–1679), Scottish judge; styled Lord Gosford; M.A. St. Andrews, 1636; admitted advocate, 1642; a royalist; knighted, 1660; keeper of signet, 1660; clerk to privy council, 1661–8; lord of session, 1668–79; published 'Decisions of Court of Session . . . 1668 till . . . 1677.' [lx. 139]

WEDDERBURN, ROBERT (1510?–1557?), Scottish poet; M.A. St. Leonard's College, St. Andrews, 1530; chaplain of St. Katherine's Chapel, Dundee; vicar of Dundee; wrote anti-Romanist ballads like his brother, James Wedderburn (1495?–1553) [q. v.]; published in 'Ane Compendious Booke of Godly and Spirituall Songs,' 1567; withdrew to Paris under suspicion of protestantism, *c.* 1534; returned to Scotland, 1546. [lx. 137]

WEDDERBURN, WILLIAM (1582?–1660), Scottish divine; master of Aberdeen grammar school, 1617; a regent of Marischal College; minister of Bethelnay, Old Meldrum, 1633, and of Innernochtie, 1651. [lx. 135]

WEDGE, JOHN HELDER (1792–1872), colonial statesman; government surveyor in Tasmania, 1827; explored large part of Tasmania; land speculator at Port Phillip (Victoria), 1835; returned to Tasmania, 1843; member of Tasmanian legislature, 1855–72. [lx. 139]

WEDGWOOD, HENSLEIGH (1803–1891), philologist; educated at Rugby, and St. John's and Christ's colleges, Cambridge; M.A., 1828; police magistrate, Lambeth, 1832–7; registrar of metropolitan carriages, 1837–49; maintained, against Professor Max Müller, that language was the elaborated imitation of natural sounds; published, among other works, 'Dictionary of English Etymology,' 1857, and 'Contested Etymologies,' 1882. [lx. 140]

WEDGWOOD, JOSIAH (1730–1795), potter; working potter at Burslem, Staffordshire, 1739, first as 'thrower' on the wheel, then as 'modeller'; of an inventive disposition and fond of trying experiments; partner in small pot-works near Stoke, 1751, and at Fenton; opened works of his own at Burslem, 1759, supplying the models and mixing the clays for his workmen with help of his cousin, Thomas Wedgwood; greatly improved ordinary wares, Egyptian ware or black basaltes, and variegated or marbled ware, and, *c.* 1769, perfected cream, afterwards called queen's ware; successfully advocated road-improvement and canal-extension in potteries district; appointed queen's potter, 1762; took into partnership his cousin, Thomas Wedgwood, 1766, and Thomas Bentley, 1768; opened new pot-works at Etruria (a village he had built for his workmen), 1769; made use of sulphate of baryta to produce his fine 'jasper' ware, 1773–80; F.R.S., 1783; F.S.A., 1786; published pamphlets. [lx. 140]

WEDGWOOD, THOMAS (1771–1805), the first photographer; a younger son of Josiah Wedgwood [q. v.]; compelled through ill-health to abandon profession of potter; published researches on heat and light, 1791–2; munificent patron of Samuel Taylor Coleridge [q. v.] 1798, and of Sir John Leslie [q. v.]; invented process of obtaining copies of objects by action of light on paper sensitised by nitrate of soda, 1802. [lx. 146]

WEEDALL, HENRY (1788–1859), president of St Mary's College, Oscott; educated at Oscott; classical tutor, professor of theology, 1818, and president, 1828; D.D. by Leo XII, 1829; mission-priest at Leamington; provost of Birmingham; again president of Oscott College, 1853–9; published sermons. [lx. 147]

WEEKES, HENRY (1807–1877), sculptor; pupil of William Behnes [q. v.]; assistant to Sir Francis Legatt Chantrey [q. v.]; exhibited at Royal Academy, 1828; R.A., 1863; eminent as portrait-sculptor; executed Shelley monument at Christ Church, Hampshire. [lx. 148]

WEELKES, THOMAS (*fl.* 1602), musician; organist of Winchester College; Mus.Bac. Oxford, 1602; organist of Chichester Cathedral; published 'Madrigals,' 1597, 1598, 1600, and 'Ayers,' 1608; contributed 'As Vesta was from Latmos Hill descending' to the 'Triumphs of Oriana'; left in manuscript anthems and instrumental pieces. [lx. 148]

WEEMSE, JOHN (1579?–1636). [See WEMYSS.]

WEEVER, JOHN (1576–1632), poet and antiquary; sizar of Queens' College, Cambridge, 1594–8; published 'Epigrammes,' 1599, containing interesting appreciations of Shakespeare, Spenser, Ben Jonson, and other contemporaries; published 'The Mirror of Martyrs,' 1601 (a poem on Sir John Oldcastle, possibly suggested by Shakespeare's Henry IV); published a thumb-book of devotional verse, entitled 'An Agnus Dei,' 1606; travelled in France and Italy; made antiquarian tours in England, and researches in the Cottonian Library; published 'Ancient Funerall Monuments,' 1631, faulty, but valuable through subsequent destruction of originals. [lx. 149]

WEGUELIN, THOMAS MATTHIAS (*d.* 1828), soldier; ensign, Bengal army, 1781; brevet captain, 1796; served against Tipú Saib, 1790–2; stationed in Oudh, 1799; served at sieges of Gwalior, 1803, and Bhartpur, 1804; major, 1808; commissary-general at Mauritius, 1810–12, and in Bengal, 1812–20; lieutenant-colonel, 1814; colonel, 1823. [lx. 150]

WEHNERT, EDWARD HENRY (1813–1868), water-colour painter; educated at Göttingen; art student in Paris; returned to England, 1837; painted historical pictures, including 'The Prisoner of Gisors'; illustrated books. [lx. 151]

WEIR, THOMAS (1600?–1670), reputed sorcerer; served in Ireland, 1641; major in army; a strict covenanter; chief officer ('major') of Edinburgh town guard, 1650; superintended execution of Montrose; became insane; reputed to possess magic staff, which effected his incantations; burned, along with his sister, for sorcery. [lx. 151]

WEIR, WILLIAM (1802–1858), journalist; educated at Ayr Academy and Göttingen; called to the Scottish bar, 1827; edited 'Glasgow Argus'; journalist in London; joined 'Daily News' staff, 1846; editor of 'Daily News,' 1854–8. [lx. 152]

WEISS, WILLOUGHBY HUNTER (1820–1867), vocalist and composer; first sang in public, Liverpool, 1842; first appeared in opera, Dublin, 1842; a good concert singer and excellent in oratorio; composed setting for Longfellow's 'The Village Blacksmith,' 1854, and other songs and ballads. [lx. 152]

WEIST-HILL, THOMAS HENRY (1828–1891), musician; professor of violin, Royal Academy of Music; eminent concert violinist; musical director, Alexandra Palace, 1873; principal, Guildhall School of Music, 1880–1891; composed music for violin and violoncello. [lx. 153]

WELBY, HENRY (d. 1636), eccentric; entered St. John's College, Cambridge, 1558, and Inner Temple, 1562; became recluse in Grub Street, London, in mortification at the dissolute and violent character of his brother John, 1592, spending all his means in charity. His biography, published 1637, styles him 'The Phœnix of these late Times.' [lx. 153]

WELCH or **WELSH**, JOHN (1570?–1622), presbyterian divine; M.A. Edinburgh, 1588; minister at Selkirk, 1590, Kirkcudbright, 1594, and Ayr, 1600; denounced King James VI in violent sermon at Edinburgh, 1596; imprisoned for attending prohibited general assembly at Aberdeen, 1605; banished, 1606; protestant pastor at Nerac and St. Jean d'Angely; expelled from France by Louis XIII, 1621; returned to London, 1621; King James told by his (Welch's) wife that she had rather 'kep' her husband's head in her lap than have him submit to the bishops, 1622. [lx. 154]

WELCH, JOSEPH (d. 1805), compiler of 'Alumni Westmonasterienses' (printed, 1788); bookseller's assistant at Westminster. [lx. 155]

WELCHMAN, EDWARD (1665–1739), theologian; chorister, Magdalen College, Oxford, 1679–82; fellow, Merton College, Oxford, 1684; M.A., 1688; rector of Lapworth, 1690, and of Solihull, 1736–9; prebendary of St. David's, 1727, and Lichfield, 1732; published annotated edition of Thirty-nine Articles, 1713, and doctrinal treatises and texts. [lx. 156]

WELD, CHARLES RICHARD (1813–1869), author of 'History of the Royal Society,' 1848; educated in France and at Trinity College, Dublin; secretary to Statistical Society, London, 1839; called to the bar, Middle Temple, 1844; assistant-secretary and librarian to Royal Society, 1845–61; published notes of travel, 1850–69; partner in London publishing firm, 1862; British commissioner at Paris exhibition, 1867. [lx. 156]

WELD, SIR FREDERICK ALOYSIUS (1823–1891), colonial governor; educated at Stonyhurst College and in Freiburg; emigrated to New Zealand, 1844; explored uninhabited districts, 1851 and 1855; member of legislature, 1853; minister for native affairs, 1860–1; premier, 1864–5, during Maori war; governor of West Australia, 1869, of Tasmania, 1875, of Straits Settlements, 1880–7; made (1883) the arrangements which led to Negri Sembilan becoming a protected state, and established a British agency in Pahang; returned to England, 1887; G.C.M.G., 1885; published pamphlets on New Zealand affairs, 1851–1869. Port Weld, Perak, is named after him. [lx. 157]

WELD, ISAAC (1774–1856), topographical writer; travelled in United States and Canada, 1795–7, publishing his 'Travels,' 1799; published 'Illustrations of the Scenery

of Killarney,' 1807; sailed in small steam-boat from Dunleary to London, 1815; compiled 'Statistical Survey of . . . Roscommon,' 1838. [lx. 158]

WELD, JOSEPH (1777–1863), of Lullworth Castle, Dorset; entertained the exiled Charles X of France, 1830. [lx. 161]

WELD, **WELDE**, or **WELLS**, THOMAS (1590?–1662), puritan divine; graduated at Cambridge, 1613; vicar of Terling, Essex, 1624; ejected for nonconformity, 1631; pastor of First Roxbury, Massachusetts, 1632; joint-author of 'The Bay Psalm Book' (so styled), a metrical version of the Psalms, 1640, which was the first volume printed in the American colonies; agent for Massachusetts in London, 1641–6; wrote against antinomians, 1644; intruded rector of St. Mary's, Gateshead, 1649; wrote against quakers, 1653–4. [lx. 160]

WELD, THOMAS (1773–1837), cardinal; approved his father's gift of Stonyhurst to the jesuits, c. 1789; transferred Lullworth Castle estate to his brother, Joseph Weld [q. v.], c. 1818; ordained priest, 1821; titular bishop of Amycla, 1826; cardinal, 1830; died at Rome. [lx. 161]

WELDON, SIR ANTHONY (d. 1649?), historical writer; of Swanscombe, Kent; clerk of the kitchen to James I, 1604; clerk of the Green Cloth, 1609–17; knighted, 1617; accompanied James I to Scotland, 1617; dismissed from his court place for satirising the Scots, 1617; took the parliament side; joined in suppressing cavalier risings in Kent, 1643 and 1648; his 'Court and Character of James I,' published 1650, and augmented, 1651, by 'Court of King Charles,' provoked much adverse criticism; wrote a 'Description of Scotland,' published, 1659. [lx. 162]

WELDON, ANTHONY (fl. 1648), colonel; son of Sir Anthony Weldon (d. 1649?) [q. v.]; captain at Duncannon; major of horse in Lincolnshire; petitioned parliament against his superiors, 1643 and 1644; entered Spanish service in Flanders, 1645; canvassed in London for recruits for the Venetian service, 1648; arrested, 1650; allowed to go abroad, 1654; published an autobiographical 'Declaration,' 1649. [lx. 162]

WELDON, JOHN (1676–1736), musician; trained at Eton; organist of New College, Oxford, 1694–1702; gentleman of Chapel Royal, London, 1701, organist, 1708, and composer, 1715; organist of St. Bride's, Fleet Street, London, and, 1726, of St. Martin's-in-the-Fields, London; composed sacred and secular music. [lx. 163]

WELDON, MICHAEL (fl. 1644), colonel; agent for Long parliament in Scotland, 1643; colonel of horse in Scots army, 1644; high sheriff of Northumberland, 1644–1645. [lx. 163]

WELDON, RALPH (fl. 1645), colonel; son of Sir Anthony Weldon (d. 1649) [q. v.]; commanded regiment of foot in Sir William Waller's [q. v.] army, 1644; commanded a brigade at the relief of Taunton and the siege of Bristol, 1645; parliamentarian governor of Plymouth, 1645. [lx. 162]

WELDON, RALPH (1674–1713), Benedictine monk; abjured protestantism, 1687; entered St. Edmund's convent, Paris, 1692; compiled 'A Chronicle of the English Benedictine Monks' (1554–1701), published, 1882; died in Paris. [lx. 164]

WELDON, WALTER (1832–1885), chemist; journalist in London, 1854; edited 'Weldon's Register of Facts,' a literary journal, 1860–4; sought means for recovering the manganese peroxide used up in manufacturing chlorine, c. 1866; patented magnesia-manganese process, 1867, lime manganese process (still employed), c. 1868, and magnesia-chlorine process, c. 1870; F.R.S., 1882; conducted researches into atomic volume and weights. [lx. 164]

WELLBELOVED, CHARLES (1769–1858), unitarian divine and archæologist; student at Homerton academy, 1785–7, and at New College, Hackney; assistant-minister, 1792, and minister, 1801–58, of St. Saviourgate Chapel, York; divinity professor in Manchester College, York, 1803–40; published, among other works, annotations on books of Old Testament, printed 1819–62, papers on antiquities of York city, 1804–52, devotional and controversial tracts, and memoirs of nonconformists. [lx. 165]

WELLES. [See also WELLS.]

WELLES, or **WELLE**, ADAM DE, BARON (d. 1311), held estates in Lincolnshire; accompanied Hugh le Despenser to Gascony, 1294; knighted, c. 1296; fought against the Scots, 1298, 1300, 1303–4, 1309–10; constable of Rockingham Castle, 1299; summoned to parliament, 1299–1311. [lx. 167]

WELLES, JOHN, first VISCOUNT WELLES (d. 1499), son of Lionel, sixth baron Welles [q. v.]; a Lancastrian; fled to Brittany, 1483; fought at Bosworth; created Viscount Welles, 1487. [lx. 169]

WELLES, LIONEL, LEO, or LYON DE, sixth BARON WELLES (1405 ?–1461), soldier; a Lancastrian; succeeded his grandfather in estates, 1421; knighted, 1426; accompanied Henry VI to France, 1430; summoned to parliament, 1432–60; served at Calais, 1436, 1451–6; lord-lieutenant of Ireland, 1438–40; fought at St. Albans, 1461; slain at Towton and attainted. [lx. 168]

WELLES, RICHARD, seventh BARON WELLES (1431–1470), son of Lionel, sixth baron Welles [q. v.]; summoned to parliament, 1455–66, as Baron Willoughby de Eresby in right of his wife; fought on the Lancastrian side at St. Albans, 1461; submitted to Edward IV, 1461; attainder reversed, 1468; beheaded because of rebellion of his son Robert; attainted, 1475. [lx. 168]

WELLES, THOMAS (1598–1660), governor of Connecticut; resided at Rothwell, Northamptonshire, 1634; to avoid persecution for puritan leanings, went as secretary with William Fiennes, first viscount Saye and Sele [q. v.], to New England, 1635; co-founder of Hartford, Connecticut, 1637; treasurer of Connecticut, 1639–51, secretary, 1640–8, deputy-governor or governor, 1654–9. [lx. 169]

WELLESLEY, ARTHUR, first DUKE OF WELLINGTON (1769–1852), field-marshal; fourth son of Garrett Wellesley, first earl of Mornington [q. v.]; spelt his name 'Wesley' till 1798; educated at Eton, Brussels, 1784, and Angers Military Academy, 1786; lieutenant of foot, 1787; captain of dragoons, 1792; aide-de-camp in Ireland to lord-lieutenant, 1787–93; M.P., Trim, 1790–5; lieutenant-colonel, 33rd foot, 1793–1806, and colonel, 1806–13; commanded 33rd foot in Netherlands campaign, 1794–5, being in action at Boxtel, 1794, and Geldermalsen, 1795; led (by evident inefficiency of British officers) to regular study, 1795; commanded 33rd foot in India, 1797–1804; given, by his brother, the Earl of Mornington, the new viceroy, command of the troops at Vellore, 1798–9, and command of a division in invasion of Mysore, 1799; governor of Seringapatam and military and civil administrator in Mysore, 1799–1802; in two campaigns crushed the great freebooter, Dhoondiah Waugh, 1799–1800; moved troops from Trincomalee to Bombay in anticipation of the expedition to Egypt, 1801; prevented by illness from sailing as second in command to Egypt; major-general, 1802; commanded a division to reinstate the peshwah, 1803; chief military and civil administrator in the Deccan, 1803–5; advanced from south against Holkar and Scindiah, taking Ahmednuggur, defeating the Mahrattas at Assye, 23 Sept. 1803, and Argaum, 29 Nov., and storming Gawilghur; concluded peace with rajah of Berar, and with Scindiah, 1803; crushed freebooting band at Perinda, February 1804; revisited Seringapatam; K.B., 1804; resigned his appointments, 1805; commanded brigade at Hastings, 1806; M.P., Rye, 1806, Mitchell, 1807, Newport, 1807–1809; chief secretary for Ireland, 1807–9, during period of unrest; sent on the Copenhagen expedition and defeated Danes at Kiöge, 1807; lieutenant-general, 1808; given command of force sent to Peninsula; defeated Delaborde at Roliça, and Junot at Vimeiro; superseded by Sir Harry Burrard [q. v.]; signed armistice negotiated by Sir Hew Whitefoord Dalrymple [q. v.], preliminary to convention of Cintra, 1808; returned to England and was acquitted by court-martial; reassumed command in Portugal, 1809; forced passage of the Duero and drove Soult out of Oporto; induced by Spanish promises of co-operation to advance into Spain; defeated Victor at Talavera; planned lines of Torres Vedras as a last retreat, 1809; created Viscount Wellington, 1809; steadfastly combated the gloomy views of the war held by the ministry and his own officers; detached division in command of Thomas Graham (1748–1843) [q. v.] to defend Cadiz; fell back from Almeida before Masséna's greatly superior force, clearing the country as he retired, 1810; repulsed Masséna at Busaco, and arrested his advance at

Torres Vedras; much troubled by disaffection among his officers and failure of the ministry to send out reinforcements, 1810; followed sharply on Masséna's retreat from Portugal, 1811; invested Badajoz; repulsed Masséna at Fuentes de Oñoro, but was forced to raise siege by conjunction of Marmont and Dorsenne; invested Ciudad Rodrigo, but was forced to raise siege by Marmont and Dorsenne, 1811; stormed Ciudad Rodrigo, 1812; created Earl of Wellington, 1812; captured Badajoz, but with terrible sacrifice of life; defeated Marmont at the Arapiles Hills, near Salamanca; entered Madrid, 12 Aug. 1812; pressed Clausel back to Burgos; repulsed with loss in assault on Burgos; had to retreat precipitately before Soult and Souham; halted at Ciudad Rodrigo, 1812; created Marquis of Wellington, 1812; visited Cadiz and Lisbon, to obtain heartier co-operation; began final advance from Portuguese frontier, 22 May 1813; concentrated at Toro on the Duero; crushed King Joseph at Vitoria, and drove the French across Pyrenees; field-marshal, 1813; suffered severe loss in assault on St. Sebastian; prevented Soult from relieving Pamplona and St. Sebastian by nine days' fighting, known as the battles of the Pyrenees; carried St. Sebastian, but with grievous sacrifice of life; obtained dismissal of O'Donoju, the anti-British war minister of Spain; forced passage of the Nivelle and of the Nive, and repulsed Soult's sallies from Bayonne, 1813; K.G., 1813; forced passage of the Adour and invested Bayonne, 1814; defeated Soult at Orthes, and at Toulouse, but with heavy loss, 10 April 1814; summoned to Paris to confer with allied kings; sent to Madrid in vain effort to reconcile King Ferdinand and the Spanish leaders; returned to England, and created Duke of Wellington, 1814; ambassador at Paris, August, 1814, and to congress at Vienna, February 1815; assumed command of forces at Brussels, April 1815; concerted plan of campaign with Blücher; expected Napoleon to attack his right wing; surprised by furious attack of Ney on his left wing at Quatre Bras, afternoon of 16 June; fell back to Waterloo, 17 June, in consequence of Blücher's defeat at Ligny; gave battle, 18 June 1815, trusting to Blücher's promise to join him; repulsed the fierce French attacks till Blücher came up and completed the rout of the French army; advanced with Blücher on Paris; persuaded Blücher not to make reprisals on the French capital, and the allied sovereigns to resist Prussian claim for cession of French territory; G.C.B., 1815; had headquarters at Cambray, 1816; given Apsley House and Strathfieldsaye by the nation, 1817; attended conference of Aix-la-Chapelle, 1818; master-general of the ordnance, with seat in the cabinet, 1818–1827; governor of Plymouth, 1819–26; held strong opinions in favour of aristocracy and against catholic emancipation; attended the Vienna-Verona congresses, 1820–2, vainly opposing armed intervention in favour of Spanish absolutism; lord-lieutenant of Hampshire, 1820–1852; lord high constable at the coronations, 1821, 1831, 1838; disapproved of recognition of independence of Spain's American colonies, 1824; envoy to the Emperor Nicholas to discuss the Greek difficulty, 1826; disapproved of the proposal to compel Turkey to grant self-government to Greece, 1826; approved of defence of Portugal from filibustering excursions by Dom Miguel's supporters, but refused to allow attacks on Dom Miguel, when he had gained the throne, 1826; constable of Tower of London, 1826–52; commander-in-chief, 1827–8, and again, 1842–52; refused office under Canning, 1827; reluctantly accepted premiership, 1828; carried, by Peel's help, catholic emancipation, against his own opinions, and, in spite of dissensions in the cabinet and factious interference of George IV's brothers, 1829; distressed at the ascendency obtained by Russia over Turkey, 1829–30; recognised Louis-Philippe as king of France, 1830; resigned office rather than accept parliamentary reform, 1830; lord warden of Cinque ports, 1829–52; temporarily unpopular because of his steady opposition to the Reform Bill, 1831–2; chancellor of Oxford University, 1834–52; premier and home secretary, 1834; foreign secretary in Peel's first ministry, 1834; leader of conservative opposition in House of Lords, 1835–41; capital of New Zealand named after him, 1840; cabinet minister, without office, in Peel's second ministry, 1841–6; urged greater attention to military and naval administration, 1843–7; called in to advise cabinet in Chartist troubles, 1848; frequent visitor at International Exhibition, 1851; accorded national monument in St. Paul's, London, executed by Alfred Stevens [q. v.]; Wellington College, for education of officers' sons, founded as a memorial and opened, 1859 ; his 'Despatches' (1799–1832) published, 1834–80, and his speeches in parliament, 1854. [lx. 170]

WELLESLEY or **WESLEY**, GARRETT, first VISCOUNT WELLESLEY of Dangan and first EARL OF MORNINGTON (1735–1781), son of Richard Colley Wellesley, first baron Mornington [q. v.] ; M.A. Trinity College, Dublin, 1757 ; Mus.Doc., 1764 ; M.P., Trim, 1757 ; succeeded as second baron, 1758 ; created Earl of Mornington, 1760 ; composed glees. [lx. 204]

WELLESLEY, GERALD VALERIAN (1809–1882), dean of Windsor ; third son of Henry Wellesley, first baron Cowley [q. v.] ; M.A. Trinity College, Cambridge, 1830 ; rector of Strathfieldsaye, 1836–54 ; domestic chaplain to Queen Victoria, 1849 ; dean of Windsor, 1854–82. [lx. 206]

WELLESLEY, HENRY, first BARON COWLEY (1773–1847), diplomatist ; youngest son of Garrett Wellesley, first earl of Mornington [q. v.] ; served in army ; secretary to legation, Stockholm, 1792 ; M.P., Trim, 1795 ; private secretary to his brother, the Earl of Mornington, in India, 1798–9 ; returned to England to explain the Mysore war and settlement, 1799–1800 ; lieutenant-governor of territory ceded by Oudh, 1801–2 ; M.P., Eye, 1807–9 ; secretary to treasury, 1808–9 ; ambassador to Spain, 1809–22, to Vienna, 1823–31, to Paris, 1841–6 ; knighted, 1812 ; created Baron Cowley, 1828. [lx. 205]

WELLESLEY, HENRY (1791–1866), scholar and antiquary ; illegitimate son of Richard Colley Wellesley, marquis Wellesley [q. v.] ; student of Christ Church, Oxford, 1811–28 ; M.A., 1818 ; D.D., 1847 ; beneficed in Sussex, 1838–66 ; vice-principal of New Inn Hall, Oxford, 1842, and principal, 1847–66 ; a patron of Italian studies ; edited 'Anthologia Polyglotta,' 1849. [lx. 206]

WELLESLEY, HENRY RICHARD CHARLES, first EARL COWLEY (1804–1884), eldest son of Henry Wellesley, first baron Cowley [q. v.] ; attaché at Vienna, 1824 ; succeeded as second baron, 1847 ; ambassador to Switzerland, 1848, to Germanic confederation at Frankfort, 1851, and at Paris, 1852–67 ; employed in negotiations which led to and closed Crimean war, and in procuring 'the declaration of Paris,' 1856, which abolished privateering ; negotiated at Paris peace with Persia, 1857 ; created Earl Cowley, 1857 ; strove to allay jealousies caused by the Orsini outrage, 1858, by the French naval armaments, 1859, and by annexation of Savoy and Nice, 1860 ; negotiated treaty of commerce with France, 1860. [lx. 207]

WELLESLEY or **WESLEY**, RICHARD COLLEY, first BARON MORNINGTON (1690 ?–1758), named Richard Colley ; M.A. Trinity College, Dublin, 1714 ; took name Wesley or Wellesley on succeeding to cousin's estate, 1728 ; M.P., Trim, 1729–46 ; created Baron Mornington in Irish peerage, 1747 ; founded charity school at Trim, 1748. [lx. 210]

WELLESLEY, RICHARD COLLEY, MARQUIS WELLESLEY (1760–1842), governor-general of India ; eldest son of Garrett Wellesley, first earl of Mornington [q. v.] ; educated at Eton ; student of Christ Church, Oxford ; excellent classical scholar ; succeeded to Irish earldom, 1781 ; M.P., Beeralston, 1787, Windsor, 1790, Old Sarum, 1796 ; sympathised with free trade movement, but opposed parliamentary reform ; member of India board, 1793 ; appointed governor-general of India and created Baron Wellesley in British peerage, 1797 ; found, 1798, British rule in India menaced by French in alliance with Tippú Sahib of Mysore and the nizam of Hyderabad ; prevailed on nizam to dismiss French officers, and secured neutrality of Mahrattas ; declared war on Mysore, 1799 ; replaced Mohammedan dynasty in Mysore by former Hindu dynasty in dependence on British, and annexed part of Mysore for the company ; obtained territory from nizam to pay charges of troops for defence of Hyderabad, disbanding nizam's forces, 1799 ; created Marquis Wellesley in Irish peerage, 1799 ; made the rájás of Tanjore and Surat dependent princes, 1799–1800 ; planned college at Fort William to educate newly arrived civilians, 1800, but plans rejected by London board of directors ; annexed Carnatic by treaty with nawáb, 1801 ; persuaded nawáb of Oudh to cede territory to pay charges of British force for defence of Oudh ; sent (Sir) John Malcolm to urge shah of Persia to attack amír of Afghanistan and avert threatened invasion of India ; wisely disregarded orders

to restore French fortresses after peace of Amiens, 1802 ; commander-in-chief in East Indies ; twice asked to be recalled, in disgust at London directors' interference with his patronage, 1802–3 ; persuaded peshwah to cede territory to pay British force for defence of Poona, 1802 ; forced to make war on the Mahratta princes, Sindia and rájá of Berár, 1803, and Holkar, 1804 ; tried to promote observance of Sunday in India and to repress sedition in native press ; recalled, 1805, in panic caused by defeat of William Monson [q. v.], colonel ; much of his Indian policy immediately reversed, but finally, after much loss and at great cost, resumed ; his Oudh policy attacked in House of Commons, 1806, but approved, 1808 ; ambassador to Spain to concert measures for Peninsular war, 1809 ; foreign secretary in Perceval's cabinet, 1809–12 ; asked by prince regent to form coalition ministry, 1812, but baffled ; favoured free-trade movement and catholic emancipation ; willing to accept Napoleon as constitutional sovereign of France, 1814, and again, 1815 ; as lord-lieutenant of Ireland, 1821–8, and 1833–4, put down white-boy insurrection, suppressed secret societies, reorganised police, removed partisan magistrates, and alleviated the 1822 famine ; passively approved of Reform Bill, 1832 ; lord-steward of the household, 1832–3 ; lord chamberlain, 1835 ; withdrew from public life, 1835 ; his India 'Despatches' printed, 1836–7. [lx. 211]

WELLESLEY, WILLIAM POLE TYLNEY LONG-, fourth EARL OF MORNINGTON and second BARON MARYBOROUGH (1788–1857), son of William Wellesley-Pole, third earl of Mornington [q. v.] ; assumed name Tylney-Long on marriage with heiress of Draycot, 1812 ; M.P.,Wiltshire, 1818–20, St. Ives, 1830–1, Essex, 1831–2 ; succeeded to titles, 1845 ; wasted his property. [lx. 224]

WELLESLEY-POLE, WILLIAM, third EARL OF MORNINGTON in Irish peerage, and first BARON MARYBOROUGH of United Kingdom (1763–1845), second son of Garrett Wellesley, first earl of Mornington [q. v.] ; educated at Eton ; naval officer ; took additional name Pole on succeeding to a cousin's estates, 1778 ; Irish M.P., Trim ; M.P., East Looe, 1790–4, Queen's County, 1801–21 ; clerk of the ordnance, 1802 ; secretary to the admiralty, 1807 ; chief secretary for Ireland, 1809–12, opposing catholic emancipation ; master of the mint, with seat in cabinet in Liverpool ministry, 1814–23 ; created Baron Maryborough, 1821 ; postmaster-general, 1834–5 ; succeeded to Irish earldom, 1842. [lx. 223]

WELLINGTON, DUKE OF (1769–1852). [See WELLESLEY, ARTHUR, first DUKE.]

WELLS. [See also WELLES.]

WELLS, CHARLES JEREMIAH (1799 ?–1879), poet ; friend of William Hazlitt, Leigh Hunt, and, for a time, of John Keats ; lost the friendship of Keats by a practical joke he played upon the poet's brother, Tom ; solicitor in London, 1820–30 ; published 'Stories after Nature,' 1822, and a drama, 'Joseph and his Brethren,' 1824 (under pseudonym of 'H. L. Howard'), reissued, 1876 ; withdrew to country, 1830 ; taught English at Quimper, Brittany, 1840 ; published his tale, 'Claribel,' 1845 ; burnt his manuscripts, 1874, in chagrin at want of recognition ; died at Marseilles. [lx. 225]

WELLS, EDWARD (1667–1727), mathematician, geographer, and divine ; educated at Westminster School, 1680 ; student of Christ Church, Oxford, 1686 ; M.A., 1693 ; D.D., 1704 ; rector of Cotesbach, 1702–27, and Bletchley, 1716–27 ; published, among other works, treatises on geography, 1701, and on geography of New Testament, 1708, and of Old Testament, 1711–12, also some classical texts and translations, scriptural commentaries, and treatises in defence of church ceremonies, 1706, and various polemical writings against validity of presbyterian orders, 1707 ; published 'Elementa Arithmeticæ,' 1698, and 'Young Gentleman's Course of Mathematicks,' 1712–14. [lx. 227]

WELLS, HENRY LAKE (1850–1898), lieutenant-colonel, royal engineers ; lieutenant, 1871 ; lieutenant-colonel, 1896 ; served with distinction in Afghan campaign, 1878–9 ; surveyed telegraph routes in Kashmir, 1879–80, and Persia, 1880 ; director of the Persian telegraph, 1891 ; died at Karachi. [lx. 228]

WELLS, HUGH OF (d. 1235). [See HUGH.]

WELLS, JOCELYN DE (d. 1242). [See JOCELIN.]

WELLS, JOHN (*d.* 1388), opponent of Wycliffe; Benedictine monk of Ramsey; D.D. Oxford, *c.* 1377; head of Gloucester College, the Oxford Benedictine seminary, for thirteen years; active in condemning Wycliffe's doctrines at Oxford, and in the Earthquake council at London, 1382; envoy from English Benedictines to Pope Urban VI, 1387; died at Perugia. [lx. 228]

WELLS, JOHN (1623-1676), puritan divine; educated at Merchant Taylors' School; fellow of St. John's College, Oxford, 1643; created M.A., 1648; vicar of St. Olave Jewry, London; ejected, 1662; published devotional tracts. [lx. 229]

WELLS, MRS. MARY, afterwards MRS. SUMBEL (*fl.* 1781-1811), actress; *née* Davies; married Wells, an actor; nicknamed 'Becky Wells,' and 'Cowslip,' from her part in O'Keeffe's 'Agreeable Surprise'; first appeared in Birmingham; a favourite at Haymarket and Drury Lane, London, 1781-6, and at Covent Garden, London, 1785-7; married Joseph Sumbel, a Jew, secretary to Morocco ambassador; published her 'Memoirs,' 1811. [lx. 230]

WELLS, ROBERT (*d.* 1557). [See STEWARD.]

WELLS, SAMUEL (*d.* 1678), nonconformist divine; M.A. Magdalen Hall, Oxford, 1636; minister at Battersea, 1639; chaplain in parliamentary army, 1644; intruded rector of Remenham, Berkshire, 1646-8; vicar of Banbury, 1648; ejected for nonconformity, 1662. [lx. 231]

WELLS, SIMON DE (*d.* 1207). [See SIMON.]

WELLS, SIR THOMAS SPENCER, first baronet (1818-1897), surgeon; studied surgery at Leeds, at Trinity College, Dublin, 1836, St. Thomas's Hospital, London, 1839-1841, and Paris, 1848; naval surgeon at Malta, 1841-1847; F.R.C.S., 1844, and president, 1883; surgeon of Samaritan Free Hospital for Women, London, 1854, and 1856-78; surgeon to Queen Victoria's household, 1863-1896; hon. M.D. Leyden; created baronet, 1883; perfected ovariotomy, performing one thousand ovarian operations, 1858-80; published medical tracts, 1851-60, and papers on ovarian diseases, 1855-85. [lx. 232]

WELLS, WILLIAM (1818-1889), agriculturist; inherited Holme estate, Huntingdonshire, 1826; educated at Harrow and Balliol College, Oxford; M.A., 1842; drained and reclaimed Whittlesea Mere, near Peterborough, 1851-66; M.P., Beverley, 1852-7, Peterborough, 1868-74; active member of Royal Agricultural Society. [lx. 234]

WELLS, WILLIAM CHARLES (1757-1817), physician; born in South Carolina of Scottish parents; educated at Edinburgh University, 1770-1 and 1775-8; M.D., 1780; newspaper publisher in East Florida, 1782-4; settled as physician in London, 1785; L.R.C.P., 1788; physician to Finsbury Dispensary, 1789-99, and St. Thomas's Hospital, London, 1800-17; published medical papers, treatises on eyesight, and, 1814, an 'Essay on Dew,' which conclusively explained that phenomenon; Rumford medallist of the Royal Society; his autobiography published, 1818. [lx. 235]

WELLS, WILLIAM FREDERICK (1762-1836), watercolour-painter; exhibited at Royal Academy views of Welsh scenery, 1795-1804, and at Society of Painters in Watercolours, 1804-13; drawing-master at Addiscombe College, 1809-29, and in London; published etchings after Gainsborough. [lx. 236]

WELLSTED, JAMES RAYMOND (1805-1842), surveyor and traveller; officer of East India Company's surveying ship in Red Sea, 1830-3; examined Socotra island, 1834; travelled in Oman, 1835 and 1837; retired from service in shattered health, 1839; published narratives of his own travels, and 'Travels in Arabia,' 1838. [lx. 236]

WELLWOOD, SIR HENRY MONCREIFF (1750-1827). [See MONCREIFF.]

WELLWOOD, SIR HENRY MONCREIFF (1809-1883). [See MONCREIFF.]

WELLWOOD, JAMES (1652-1727), physician; educated at Glasgow; M.D. Leyden; accompanied William of Orange to England; F.R.C.P., 1690, censor, 1722; works include 'Vindication of the Revolution,' 1689, and a whig survey of 'Transactions in England' (1588-1688). [lx. 237]

WELLWOOD, SIR JAMES, LORD MONCREIFF (1776-1851). [See MONCREIFF.]

WELLWOOD, WILLIAM (*fl.* 1577-1622). [See WELWOOD.]

WELSBY, WILLIAM NEWLAND (1802?-1864), legal writer; M.A. St. John's College, Cambridge, 1827; called to bar, Middle Temple, 1826; recorder of Chester, 1841; junior counsel to treasury; edited revised editions of standard law-books; joint-author of 'Exchequer Reports,' 'Reports of Mercantile Cases,' and 'Lives of Eminent English Judges.' [lx. 237]

WELSCHE, JOHN (1570?-1622). [See WELCH.]

WELSH, DAVID (1793-1845), Scottish divine; educated at Edinburgh; minister of Crossmichael, 1821, and in Glasgow, 1827; hon. D.D. Glasgow, 1831; church history professor, Edinburgh University, 1831-43, and in Free Church College, Edinburgh, 1844-5; published sermons, and edited Thomas Brown's 'Lectures on the Philosophy of the Human Mind,' 1834. [lx. 237]

WELSH, JAMES (1775-1861), general; captain, Madras infantry, 1799; major, 1807; lieutenant-colonel, 1813; major-general, 1837; general, 1854; in active service in India, 1791-1807, 1809-29, 1837-47, fighting in Wellesley's Mahratta campaigns, 1803-4, quelling projected mutiny at Palamkotta, 1805, and heading storming party at Travancore, 1809; published his 'Reminiscences,' 1830. [lx. 238]

WELSH, JOHN (1824-1859), meteorologist; educated at Edinburgh, 1839-42; employed at Makerstoun observatory, 1842-50, and at Kew observatory, 1850-9; F.R.S., 1857; improved self-recording magnetic instruments. [lx. 239]

WELSH, THOMAS (1781-1848), vocalist; chorister, Wells Cathedral; sang in oratorio, Haymarket, London, 1796; successful operatic singer, actor, teacher of singing; brought out two farces and an opera, 'Kamskatka' wrote instrumental and vocal music. [lx. 240]

WELSTED, LEONARD (1688-1747), poet; of Westminster School, 1703-7, and Trinity College, Cambridge; clerk in secretary of state's office, and, 1725-47, in ordnance office; published his first poem 'Apple-Pye,' 1704, and 'Oikographia,' an autobiographical poem, 1725; issued occasional poems, personal, political, and didactic, 1709-41; translated 'Longinus on the Sublime,' 1712; virulently satirised, and was satirised by, Alexander Pope [q. v.] [lx. 240]

WELSTED, ROBERT (1671-1735), physician; demy of Magdalen College, Oxford, 1689-98; M.A., 1694; practised medicine in Bristol and London; L.R.C.P., 1710; F.R.S., 1718; published Latin medical pieces, and, with Richard West, edited Pindar, 1692. [lx. 242]

WELTON, RICHARD (1671?-1726), nonjuring divine; M.A. Caius College, Cambridge, 1695; D.D., 1708; rector of Whitechapel, 1697-1715, where he caused White Kennett's portrait to be put as Judas in altarpiece, 1713; vicar of East Ham, Essex, 1710-15; refused oaths to George I, and opened nonjuring chapel in Whitechapel, London, 1715; consecrated bishop among nonjurors, 1722; minister of Christ Church, Philadelphia, 1724-5, performing episcopal functions; published sermons; died at Lisbon. [lx. 242]

WELWITSCH, FRIEDRICH MARTIN JOSEF (1807-1872), botanist; born in Carinthia; studied at Vienna; M.D. Vienna, 1836; resident in Portugal, 1839-1853, having charge of botanical gardens at Lisbon and Coimbra, and collecting Portuguese plants, fungi, algæ, molluscs, and insects; travelled in Portuguese West Africa, 1853-60, forming extensive herbarium of tropical plants; met David Livingstone, 1854, in interior; resided in London, comparing his specimens with those in British collections, 1863-72; published, in Portuguese, descriptions of plants; his collections are partly at Lisbon, partly in British Museum. [lx. 243]

WELWOOD. [See also WELLWOOD.]

WELWOOD, ALEXANDER MACONOCHIE-, LORD MEADOWBANK (1777-1861). [See MACONOCHIE.]

WELWOOD or **WELWOD** or **VELVOD**, WILLIAM (*fl.* 1577-1622), professor of mathematics and of law at St. Andrews; discovered principle of the siphon, 1577, and described it (as applied to pumping water) in a Latin pamphlet, 1582 ; professor of mathematics, 1578–87, of law, 1587–97 ; expelled by the royal visitors from his chair, 1597 ; ordered to be replaced by James I, 1600, though it is doubtful whether he was ever actually replaced. His legal works include 'Sea-Law of Scotland,' 1590, 'Abridgement of all Sea-Lawes,' 1613, and three Latin treatises, printed in Holland, 1594, instituting comparison between Roman and Jewish law, reviewing procedure in civil and ecclesiastical courts, and discussing methods of repressing popular outbreaks. [lx. 245]

WEMYSS, DAVID, second EARL OF WEMYSS (1610–1679), while Lord Elcho commanded foot regiment in Scottish army, 1640, and was defeated by Montrose at Tippermuir, 1644, and Kilsyth, 1645 ; succeeded to earldom, 1649. [lx. 246]

WEMYSS, DAVID, third EARL OF WEMYSS (1678–1720), succeeded to earldom, 1705 ; took seat in parliament, 1705 ; a commissioner for the union ; vice-admiral of Scotland, 1707. [lx. 246]

WEMYSS, DAVID, LORD ELCHO (1721–1787), Jacobite ; eldest son of James, fourth earl of Wemyss (d. 1756) ; visited Great Britain as Jacobite agent, 1744 ; commanded Prince Charles Edward's life-guards, 1745–6 ; wrote narrative of the rising ; attainted ; excluded from titles and estates ; died at Paris. [lx. 247]

WEMYSS, DAVID DOUGLAS (1760–1839), general ; as David Douglas was ensign, 1777, and captain, 1783, serving in North America and West Indies, 1777–81, 1786–9 ; assumed name of Wemyss, c. 1790 ; became major, 1791, lieutenant-colonel, 1793, major-general, 1802, and general, 1819, serving in Flanders, 1793, Corsica and Italy, 1794–7, Gibraltar, 1797–1802, and Ceylon, 1803–6. [lx. 247]

WEMYSS, JAMES (1610 ?–1667), master-gunner of England ; came to London, 1630 ; studied and experimented in gunnery ; improved leather guns for field service ; lost his scientific instruments by a fire, 1637 ; master-gunner of England, 1638–48 and 1660–6 ; accompanied Charles I's artillery train to Scotland, 1639 and 1640 ; went over to parliamentary army ; colonel and master of ordnance in Sir William Waller's army ; taken prisoner at Cropredy Bridge, 1644 ; well treated by King Charles I ; tested guns for the parliamentary navy, 1646–7 ; returned to Scotland, 1648 ; general of artillery in Scottish army at Dunbar, 1650, and Worcester, 1651 ; prisoner in Windsor Castle, 1651–60. [lx. 248]

WEMYSS or **WEEMES**, JOHN (1579 ?–1636), divine ; M.A. St. Andrews, 1600 ; minister of Hutton, Berwickshire, 1608, and Dunse, 1613 ; took part in the ritual controversy, 1618–20 ; prebendary of Durham, 1634 ; published 'The Christian Synagogue,' an expository treatise, 1623, and works of practical divinity. [lx. 249]

WENDOVER, RICHARD OF (d. 1252). [See RICHARD.]

WENDOVER, ROGER DE (d. 1236), chronicler and monk of St. Albans ; prior of Belvoir, but recalled, c. 1221, for extravagance ; compiled 'Flores Historiarum,' creation to 1235, of which the portion from 1202 is a first-hand authority. [lx. 250]

WENDY, THOMAS (1500 ?–1560), physician to Henry VIII, Edward VI, and Mary I ; fellow of Gonville Hall, Cambridge, 1519 ; M.A., 1522 ; M.D. Ferrara ; served on ecclesiastical commissions, 1548, 1552, and 1559 ; F.R.C.P., 1551 ; elect, 1552 ; M.P. St. Albans, 1554, and Cambridgeshire, 1555 ; benefactor of Gonville and Caius College, Cambridge. [lx. 252]

WENGHAM, HENRY DE (d. 1262). [See WINGHAM.]

WENHAM, JANE (d. 1730), the last woman condemned for witchcraft in England ; lived at Walkern, Hertfordshire ; tried for witchcraft and found guilty by jury, contrary to assize judge's leading (who, in answer to one of the charges brought against her, remarked that there was no law against flying), 1712, and condemned to death, but pardoned ; her case debated in several pamphlets, 1712. [lx. 253]

WENLOCK, JOHN, BARON WENLOCK (d. 1471), fought in France, 1421 ; constable of Vernon, Normandy, 1422 ; M.P., Bedfordshire, 1433–55 ; usher, and, 1450,

chamberlain to Queen Margaret of Anjou ; attended Richard, duke of York's, mission to France, 1442 ; high sheriff of Buckinghamshire, 1444 ; received back (alienated) Wenlock estate, 1448 ; knighted, c. 1448 ; fought on Lancastrian side at St. Albans, 1455 ; went over to Yorkists ; speaker of House of Commons, 1455 ; Yorkist envoy to Burgundy and France, 1458 ; attainted, 1459 ; took refuge in France ; returned, 1460 ; K.G., 1461 ; fought at Ferrybridge and Towton, 1461 ; created Baron Wenlock and appointed chief butler of England, 1461 ; employed by Edward IV on foreign missions ; lieutenant of Calais, 1469 ; returned to Lancastrian side, 1461 ; slain at Tewkesbury. [lx. 253]

WENMAN, AGNES (d. 1617), née Fermor ; wife of Sir Richard Wenman [q. v.] ; a Roman catholic ; patron of John Gerard (1564–1637), the jesuit [q. v.] ; imprisoned on suspicion of complicity in Gunpowder plot, 1605–6 ; left in manuscript a translation of French version of Johannes Zonaras. [lx. 255]

WENMAN, SIR RICHARD, first VISCOUNT WENMAN (1573–1640), of Thame Park, Oxfordshire ; studied at Oxford, 1587 ; knighted for gallantry at Cadiz, 1596 ; M.P., Oxfordshire, 1620 and 1625 ; high sheriff for Oxfordshire, 1627 ; created Viscount Wenman of Tuam, 1628. [lx. 255]

WENMAN, THOMAS, second VISCOUNT WENMAN (1596–1665), eldest son of Sir Richard Wenman, first viscount Wenman [q. v.] ; knighted, 1617 ; M.P., Brackley, 1620–5, Oxfordshire, 1626, Brackley, 1628, and for Oxfordshire in Long parliament, 1640 ; succeeded to Irish barony, 1640 ; supporter of the parliament ; served on commissions to treat with Charles I, 1642–3, 1644, and 1648 ; excluded by army from parliament as too favourable to Charles I, and imprisoned, 1648 ; bought confiscated estates in Ireland, 1651 ; M.P., Oxfordshire, in Convention parliament, 1660. [lx. 255]

WENMAN, THOMAS FRANCIS (1745–1796), regius professor of civil law, Oxford ; student of University College, Oxford ; fellow of All Souls College, Oxford, 1765 ; D.C.L., 1780 ; barrister, Inner Temple, 1770 ; M.P., Westbury, 1774–80 ; keeper of the Oxford University archives, 1781 ; regius professor of civil law, Oxford, 1789–96 ; studied botany ; left in manuscript a history of All Souls College, Oxford. [lx. 256]

WENSLEYDALE, BARON (1782–1868). [See PARKE, SIR JAMES.]

WENTWORTH, CHARLES WATSON-, second MARQUIS OF ROCKINGHAM (1730–1782). [See WATSON-WENTWORTH.]

WENTWORTH, HENRIETTA MARIA, BARONESS WENTWORTH (1657 ?–1686), mistress of Duke of Monmouth ; only child of Sir Thomas Wentworth, fifth baron Wentworth (1613–1665) [q. v.] ; succeeded her grandfather in barony, 1667 ; acted with Monmouth in masque at court, 1674 ; lived with him at Toddington, Bedfordshire, 1680 ; followed him to Holland, 1684 ; dissuaded Monmouth from entering imperialist service against Turks, 1685, and supplied funds for descent on England ; returned to England, 1685. [lx. 257]

WENTWORTH, SIR JOHN (1737–1820), colonial governor ; son of a merchant of Portsmouth, New Hampshire ; M.A. Harvard College, 1758 ; visited London and pleaded for repeal of Stamp Act, 1765 ; hon. D.C.L. Oxford, 1766 ; governor of New Hampshire, 1766–76, becoming more and more unpopular from efforts to carry out his instructions ; his house pillaged, 1775 ; banished, and property confiscated by state congress, 1778 ; resided in London, 1778–83 ; resided in Halifax, Nova Scotia, as surveyor of king's forests, 1783–92, and as governor of Nova Scotia, 1792–1808 ; created baronet, 1795 ; died at Halifax ; his correspondence, 1767–1808, preserved in public records at Halifax. [lx. 258]

WENTWORTH, PAUL (1533–1593), parliamentary leader ; younger brother of Peter Wentworth (1530 ?–1596) [q. v.] ; lessee from crown of Burnham Abbey, Buckinghamshire ; M.P., Buckingham, 1563–7, Liskeard, 1572–83 ; active in petitioning Queen Elizabeth to name her successor, 1566 ; custodian at Burnham Abbey of Thomas Howard, fourth duke of Norfolk (beheaded, 1572) ; angered Queen Elizabeth by proposing the preaching of a sermon before each meeting of House of Commons, 1581. [lx. 260]

WENTWORTH, PETER (1530 ?–1596), parliamentary leader ; of Lillingstone Lovell ; M.P., Barnstaple, 1571–2, Tregony, 1576–83, Northampton, 1586–7 ; attacked Sir Humphrey Gilbert [q. v.] for subserviency to court, 1571 ; advocated right of House of Commons to discuss Thirty-nine Articles and other church questions in spite of Queen Elizabeth's orders, 1571 ; imprisoned in Tower of London, 1576, for bitter speech against crown interference with House of Commons, and, 1587, for again challenging Elizabeth's absolutism in ecclesiastical affairs, and, 1593–6, for petitioning Elizabeth to name her successor, and advocating right to succession of Edward Seymour, lord Beauchamp ; wrote, 1594, 'A Pithie Exhortation' (printed, 1598), urging Elizabeth to name her successor. [lx. 261]

WENTWORTH, SIR PETER (1592–1675), politician ; of Magdalen Hall, Oxford ; of Lillingstone Lovell, Oxfordshire ; K.B., 1625 ; high sheriff of Oxfordshire, 1634 ; M.P., Tamworth, 1641 ; refused to act as judge of Charles I, 1649 ; served in Commonwealth councils of state ; reviled for immorality by Oliver Cromwell at expulsion of the Rump, 1653 ; re-took his seat in parliament, 1659 ; left legacy to John Milton. [lx. 263]

WENTWORTH, THOMAS, first BARON WENTWORTH of Nettlestead (1501–1551), knighted while serving in France, 1523 ; inherited Nettlestead, Suffolk, 1528 ; created baron, 1529 ; embraced protestantism ; advocated Henry VIII's divorce from Catherine, 1530 ; attended Henry VIII to France, 1532 ; served against Norfolk insurgents, 1549 ; helped to overthrow Protector Somerset, 1549 ; privy councillor, 1549–51 ; lord chamberlain, 1550 ; granted crown lands. [lx. 264]

WENTWORTH, THOMAS, second BARON WENTWORTH of Nettlestead (1525–1584), eldest son of Thomas Wentworth, first baron Wentworth [q. v.] ; perhaps of St. John's College, Cambridge ; knighted while serving in Scotland, 1547 ; M.P., Suffolk, 1547–51 ; succeeded to barony, 1551 ; voted for execution of Somerset, 1551 ; made privy councillor by Queen Mary, 1553 ; sat on commission to try Northumberland and his supporters, 1553 ; deputy of Calais, 1553–8 ; failed to obtain necessary support from England ; neglected warnings of imminent French attack, December 1557 ; surrendered Calais, January 1558 ; prisoner of war in France, 1558–9 ; acquitted of charge of treasonable surrender, 1559 ; sat on commission which condemned Norfolk, 1572. [lx. 265]

WENTWORTH, THOMAS (1568 ?–1628), lawyer ; third son of Peter Wentworth (1530 ?–1596) [q. v.] ; called to bar, Lincoln's Inn, 1594, Lent reader, 1612 ; recorder of Oxford city, 1607–23 ; as M.P., Oxford city, 1604–28, steadily opposed the crown ; discommoned by Oxford University, 1611–14 ; imprisoned for speech against illegal imposts, 1614 ; advocated war with Spain, 1624. [lx. 267]

WENTWORTH, SIR THOMAS, first EARL OF STRAFFORD (1593–1641), statesman ; of Wentworth-Woodhouse, Yorkshire ; educated at St. John's College, Cambridge ; entered Inner Temple, 1607 ; knighted, 1611 ; travelled on continent, 1612–13 ; M.P., Yorkshire, 1614 ; succeeded as second baronet, 1614 ; custos rotulorum, Yorkshire, 1615–1625 ; began feud with Sir John Savile, afterwards first Baron Savile of Pontefract [q. v.], 1617 ; as M.P., Yorkshire, 1621, showed firmness and moderation in opposing the crown ; as M.P., Pontefract, 1624, opposed war with Spain and showed hostility to puritanism ; M.P., Yorkshire, 1625, unseated on Savile's petition, but re-elected ; opposed war with Spain, and expressed resentment at dissolution of parliament ; appointed sheriff of Yorkshire, 1625, to exclude him from new parliament ; opposed Charles I's demands for money, and was removed from commission of peace and replaced by his rival Savile in office of custos rotulorum, 1625 ; imprisoned for refusal to pay the forced loan, 1627 ; in the parliament of 1628 led House of Commons, April–May, in endeavour to bring Charles I to some reasonable compromise as regards forced loans, billeting of soldiers, and imprisonment without cause shown ; offended Charles I by safeguarding the supplies voted against sudden appropriation by crown ; passively accepted the Petition of Right, which was substituted for his own proposals in consequence of Charles I's obstinacy, May–June, 1628 ; taken into court favour ; created Baron and Viscount Wentworth, and made president of council of north, 1628 ; privy coun-

cillor, 1629 ; drawn into friendship with Laud through common aversion to puritanism, 1630 ; as president of north, 1631–2, used fine and imprisonment by court of Star-chamber to break down opposition of northern gentry ; appointed lord-deputy of Ireland, 1632 ; entered Dublin, July 1633, and set himself to establish the royal authority by reducing army to strict discipline, suppressing piracy in St. George's Channel, encouraging linen industry, compelling restitution by nobility of embezzled church property, forcing acceptance by clergy of English Thirty-nine Articles ; obtained supplies from Irish parliament, 1634, on promise of remedial measures, which were partly conceded in 1635 ; laid a heavy hand on English officials in Dublin, 1634–5, e.g. on Sir Paul Crosby, privy councillor, Lord Mountnorris, vice-treasurer, and Adam Loftus, first viscount Loftus of Ely [q. v.], lord-chancellor ; offended Henrietta Maria by refusing pensions on Irish establishment to her favourites ; compelled packed juries to declare all Connaught crown property, 1635, intending to bring in English settlers ; advised Charles I against the naval intervention in foreign affairs which he contemplated to provide a colourable excuse for demanding ship-money, the judges having pronounced in favour of the legality of his right to levy it, 1637 ; advocated invasion of Scotland to crush covenanters and enforce adoption of English liturgy, 1638, but vainly urged Charles I to train his troops before attempting invasion, 1639 ; came to London to prosecute his Irish opponents in Star-chamber court, May 1639 ; became informally Charles I's chief adviser, September 1639 ; advised demand of loan from privy councillors and summoning parliament to vote supplies, promising, as a good example, a large loan from himself and a prompt vote of supplies from Irish parliament ; was created Baron Raby and Earl of Strafford, 1640, thereby deeply offending Sir Henry Vane the elder [q. v.], owner of Raby Castle ; created lord-lieutenant of Ireland, 1640 ; offered service of Irish troops against Scotland and to command them in person ; obtained subsidies to amount of 180,000l. from Irish parliament, March 1640 ; attended Short parliament, April 1640 ; advised Charles I personally to invite peers to insist on Commons voting supplies before discussing grievances ; taken into favour by Henrietta Maria ; vainly advised Charles I to be content with part of the subsidies asked ; assented to dissolution of Short parliament ; in committee of privy council, 5 May 1640, urged collection of funds by force and immediate invasion of Scotland, promising, it was reported, help of Irish troops against both Scottish and English rebels ; popularly styled 'Black Tom Tyrant,' from suspicion of this advice ; vainly urged Charles I to immediate and despotic action, July 1640 ; received patent as captain-general in Ireland, with prospect of employment in Scotland and England, August 1640 ; took command of Charles I's force in Yorkshire, and prevailed on Yorkshire to adopt defensive measures against the invading Scots army, September 1640 ; attended Long parliament on Charles I's personal guarantee of his safety ; urged Charles I to send parliamentary leaders to the Tower of London ; impeached by Commons and sent to the Tower of London, 1640 ; trial opened, March 1641 ; procedure by impeachment abandoned because of favourable impression produced on peers by his vigorous defence and in fear of northern army being brought to coerce parliament ; bill of attainder against him passed by Commons, 21 April, passed by Lords, 8 May, in panic caused by discovery of court plot to release him, and introduce into England Irish and Dutch troops ; his attainder assented to by Charles, 10 May, in dread of mob violence ; executed on Tower Hill, 11 May 1641. [lx. 268]

WENTWORTH, SIR THOMAS, fifth BARON WENTWORTH (1613–1665), eldest son of Thomas Wentworth, fourth baron Wentworth of Nettlestead and first earl of Cleveland [q. v.], styled Lord Wentworth by courtesy from 1626 ; at the court of Queen Elizabeth of Bohemia at the Hague, 1631 ; M.P., Bedfordshire, in Short and Long parliaments, 1640 ; called to peers in his father's barony, 1640 ; commanded troop of horse under Wilmot and Goring, 1644–5 ; held chief command in west, but was routed at Torrington, 1646 ; in attendance on Prince Charles (Charles II) in Scilly, Jersey, Paris, 1649, Scotland, 1650, Worcester, 1651, and abroad, 1651–60 ; colonel of the guards, 1656–60. [lx. 283]

WENTWORTH, SIR THOMAS, fourth BARON WENTWORTH of Nettlestead, and first EARL OF CLEVELAND

(1591–1667), succeeded to barony, 1593 ; entered Trinity College, Oxford, 1602 ; custos rotulorum, Bedfordshire, 1619 ; took seat in the Lords, 1621 ; favourite of Buckingham : created Earl of Cleveland, 1626 ; accompanied Buckingham to Rochelle, 1627 ; was with Buckingham when assassinated, 1628 ; incurred heavy debts, 1630–8, ultimately alienating his whole estate ; served against the Scots, 1639–40 ; attended Strafford on scaffold, 1641 ; colonel of horse in Charles I's army, 1642 ; displayed great military activity, 1644 ; prisoner of war, 1644–8 ; in attendance on Charles II in France and Scotland, 1650 ; covered his flight at Worcester, 1651 ; prisoner of war, 1651–6 ; captain of gentlemen pensioners, 1660. [lx. 284]

WENTWORTH, THOMAS, BARON RABY and third EARL OF STRAFFORD (1672–1739), diplomatist ; page to Queen Mary Beatrice, 1688 ; served in cavalry in Scotland, 1689, and in Holland, 1690–7, with distinction ; major in the guards, 1693 ; succeeded to barony of Raby, 1695 ; envoy to Berlin, 1701 ; served in Flanders, 1702 ; lieutenant-general, 1707 ; ambassador at Berlin, 1703–11, and the Hague, 1711–14 ; created Earl of Strafford, 1711 ; one of the negotiators of peace of Utrecht, 1711–13 ; recalled by George I, 1714, and his pension stopped, 1715 ; proceeded against in parliament for share in treaty of Utrecht, 1715–16 (proceedings dropped, 1717) ; privy to proposed Jacobite insurrection, 1725 ; much of his correspondence preserved in British Museum Library. [lx. 286]

WENTWORTH, WILLIAM (1616–1697), colonist ; emigrated from Lincolnshire, 1636, to avoid molestation as puritan ; finally settled at Dover, New Hampshire, 1649 ; saved Heard's garrison from a massacre planned by the Indians, 1689 ; died at Dover, New Hampshire. [lx. 258]

WENTWORTH, WILLIAM CHARLES (1793–1872), 'the Australian patriot' ; chief founder of colonial self-government ; born on Norfolk Island ; son of a government surgeon ; sent to school at Greenwich, 1800 ; deputy provost-marshal, New South Wales, 1811 ; went on exploring journey across Blue Mountains, 1813 ; entered Peterhouse, Cambridge, 1816 ; published 'Statistical Account of the British Settlements in Australasia,' 1819 ; barrister, Middle Temple, 1822 ; returned to Sydney ; co-proprietor and joint-editor of 'The Australian' newspaper, Sydney, from 1824, advocating admission to political power of the ex-convicts ('emancipists') and discouraging voluntary immigrants ('interlopers') ; obtained, by popular clamour, recall of the governor, Sir Ralph Darling [q. v.], 1831 ; chief adviser of his successor, Sir Richard Bourke [q. v.] ; deeply offended the next governor, Sir George Gipps [q. v.], 1840, by underhand attempt to buy large tracts of land in New Zealand ; member for Sydney in the first New South Wales legislature, 1843 (re-elected, 1848 and 1851) ; leader of the 'pastoral,' or squatter party, from 1843 ; advocated continuance of transportation to provide 'assigned' labourers ; carried, 1849, bill for founding Sydney University (opened 1852) ; bitterly opposed lowering of franchise, 1850 ; his proposal for an hereditary Australian peerage scouted by colonial opinion, and his proposal that no change of constitution should be allowed except by a two-thirds majority of both legislative houses rejected by home government, 1853 ; suggested federal parliament for all Australia, 1857 ; accorded statue in Sydney University, 1861 ; returned finally to England, 1862 ; given a public funeral and buried at Sydney. [lx. 289]

WERBURGA or **WERBURH,** SAINT (d. 700 ?), abbess of Ely ; daughter of Wulfhere [q. v.], king of Mercia ; abbess of Sheppey, of Ely, and in Mercian convents ; her remains, in fear of Danish invasion, c. 875, translated to Chester, where cathedral represents church of her shrine ; patroness of women and children ; commemorated on 3 Feb. [lx. 294]

WERDEN or **WORDEN,** SIR JOHN, first baronet (1640–1716), politician ; son of Robert Werden [q. v.] ; called to bar, Middle Temple, 1660 ; employed in diplomatic service, c. 1665–72 ; created baronet, 1672 ; secretary to James, duke of York ; M.P., Reigate, 1673–9, 1685–7 ; a commissioner of customs, 1685–97 and 1702–14. [lx. 295]

WERDEN or **WORDEN,** ROBERT (d. 1690), soldier ; colonel of horse in Charles I's army ; taken prisoner at Chester, 1645 ; admitted to composition for delinquency, 1646 ; suspected of treasonable designs, 1648–52, 1655 ;

barely escaped with life for joining Sir George Booth's rising, 1659 ; accused of treason by royalists, 1660 ; recovered his estates ; lieutenant, 1665, and lieutenant-colonel, 1672, in Duke of York's guards ; M.P., Chester, 1673–9 and 1685 ; comptroller of Duke of York's household, 1679 ; lieutenant-general, 1688 ; treasurer to Mary II, 1689. [lx. 296]

WERFERTH, WEREFRID, or **HEREFERTH** (d. 915), consecrated bishop of Worcester, 873 ; one of King Alfred's scholar-courtiers, 884 ; translated into Saxon Pope Gregory's 'Dialogues' (manuscripts extant at Cambridge, London, and Oxford). [lx. 297]

WESHAM or **WESEHAM,** ROGER DE (d. 1257), bishop of Lichfield ; D.D. ; divinity lecturer in Franciscan convent, Oxford ; prebendary of Lincoln, 1223 ; dean of Lincoln, 1232 ; bishop of Lichfield, 1245–56, devoting himself to care of diocese and cathedral. [lx. 297]

WESLEY, CHARLES (1707–1788), divine and hymn-writer ; youngest son of Samuel Wesley (1662–1735) [q. v.] ; entered Westminster School, 1716 ; student of Christ Church, Oxford, 1726 ; joined with some fellow-students in a strict method of religious observance and study, whence they were nicknamed 'methodists' ; began his private diary, 1729 ; B.A., 1730 ; M.A., 1733 ; ordained, 1735 ; visited Georgia as secretary to James Edward Oglethorpe [q. v.], the governor, 1736 ; believed himself 'converted,' Whitsunday 1738 ; did much evangelistic work in London, 1738–9 ; settled at Bristol as centre, 1739–56, going on evangelising journeys in west of England and Wales, and to Cornwall, Newcastle-on-Tyne, and (1747–8) to Ireland ; in sharp controversy with the 'conference' of 1755, which showed readiness to separate from Anglican church ; removed, in ill-health, to Bath, 1761 ; developed divergent views on doctrine of 'perfection' from his brother, John Wesley, 1762 ; removed to London, 1771 ; continued to preach as much as his health allowed ; disapproved of John Wesley's ordinations of presbyters from 1784 ; composed over six thousand hymns, of which five hundred are still in use ; some sermons and poetical pieces by him published posthumously. [lx. 298]

WESLEY, CHARLES (1757–1834), musician ; eldest son of Charles Wesley (1707–1788) [q. v.] ; studied music in Bristol and London ; published 'Six Concertos,' eight songs, and other music, before 1784 ; organist in various London churches from 1794. [lx. 302]

WESLEY, JOHN (1703–1791), evangelist and leader of methodism ; a younger son of Samuel Wesley (1662–1735) [q. v.] ; foundationer at Charterhouse, London, 1714 ; scholar of Christ Church, Oxford, 1720 ; B.A., 1724 ; ordained deacon, 1725 ; fellow of Lincoln College, Oxford, 1726–51 ; M.A., 1727 ; curate for his father at Wroot, 1727–9 ; tutor in Lincoln College, Oxford, 1729–1735 ; leader of his brother Charles Wesley's (1707–1788) [q. v.] 'methodist' society in Oxford, 1729, from which year methodism is sometimes dated ; published prayers, 1733 ; accepted charge of the Georgia mission, 1735 ; much influenced by German Moravian brethren during his voyage out and during his first months of residence ; founded at Savannah a religious 'society' on the Moravian model, 1736 ; began correspondence with Zinzendorf, founder of the Moravians, 1737 ; his ministry in Georgia embittered by quarrels, partly provoked by his autocratic church methods, 1736–7 ; published his first hymnal, 1737 ; left Georgia to avoid a libel action, founded on his repelling from communion a Mrs. Williamson, who (as Miss Hopkey) had a short time before rejected his offer of marriage ; after his return met, and was much influenced by, Peter Böhler, a Moravian ; became member of the Moravian 'society' at Fetter Lane chapel, London, 1738 ; believed himself 'converted,' 1738 ; visited Zinzendorf at Herrnhut, 1738 ; appointed his first lay preacher, 1738 ; began field preaching, and opened methodist chapel at Bristol, 1739 ; brought into conflict with Joseph Butler [q. v.] on question of convulsive paroxysms, which were claimed to be manifestations of the Holy Ghost, at his Bristol meetings, 1739 ; bought a disused gun-foundry in London and converted it into methodist chapel, 1739 ; founded a 'united society' for weekday meetings, December 1739, from which the inception of methodism is generally dated ; broke off his membership of the Moravian 'society,' 1740 ; renounced Calvinism by publishing his 'free grace' sermon, preached at Bristol, 1740 ; was personally involved in controversy by this sermon, and

brought about secession from methodists of Welsh Calvinistic Methodists (1743) and of Countess of Huntingdon's connexion (1756); preached University sermons at
Oxford, 1741 and 1744; organised his followers in Bristol
and London in 'class meetings,' to which admission was
by 'society tickets' (of membership), 1742, and divided
the country into 'circuits'; held first methodist 'conversation' or conference, London, 1744, and second (which
acknowledged his title to be 'overseer' of methodists),
1745; published handbooks on various subjects, including
physic, from 1743; went on continual evangelistic journeys, visiting Isle of Man, Ireland forty-two times (from
1747), and Scotland constantly (from 1751); became contracted to Grace Murray, a widow, 1748, but assented to
her marriage with John Bennet, 1749; married Mary
Vazeille, a widow, 1751, who had a serious quarrel with
him, 1755, and separated from him, 1776; found his lay-
preachers ready for separation from Anglican church in
the conference of 1755; found that during his absence in
Ireland they had begun to celebrate the eucharist, 1760;
vainly tried to induce the Calvinists to enter a union of
methodists, 1764; had several of his lay preachers ordained by Erasmus, so-called bishop of Arcadia in Crete,
1764; wrote against the anti-taxation agitation in the
American colonies, 1775-8; executed 'deed of declaration' providing for regulation of methodist chapels and
preachers, 1784; ordained presbyters to confer orders and
administer the sacraments, 1784; preached his last sermon, 23 Feb. 1791; published twenty-three collections of
hymns, 1737-86; published his collected prose 'Works,'
1771-4.   [lx. 303]

WESLEY, SAMUEL, the elder (1662-1735), divine
and poet; originally spelt his name Westley; educated
in London for independent ministry, 1678-83; entered
Exeter College, Oxford, 1683; published volume of verse,
'Maggots,' 1685; B.A., 1688; naval chaplain, c. 1689;
rector of South Ormsby, 1690; joint-editor of 'Athenian
Gazette,' 1691-7; rector of Epworth, 1695-1735, and of
Wroot, 1722-35; involved in pecuniary difficulties by
various accidents; his rectory troubled by a noisy 'spirit,'
1716-17; published much verse and prose, including a
panegyric on Marlborough, 1705, and a hostile criticism
of nonconformist academies, 1703; his dissertations on
Job published posthumously, 1735.   [lx. 314]

WESLEY, SAMUEL, the younger (1691-1739), schoolmaster; eldest son of Samuel Wesley the elder [q. v.];
educated at Westminster School, 1704, and Christ Church,
Oxford, 1711; M.A., 1718; took orders; head-usher, Westminster School, 1713-33; master of Blundell's School,
Tiverton, 1733-9; published poems, 1716-36; friend of
Francis Atterbury [q. v.]   [lx. 317]

WESLEY, SAMUEL (1766-1837), musician; son of
Charles Wesley (1707-1788) [q. v.]; chiefly self-taught;
gave subscription concerts in London from 1779; embraced Roman catholicism, 1784; mental balance disturbed by severe accident, 1787; enthusiastic admirer of
John Sebastian Bach's music from 1800; lectured on
music in London from 1811; organist in Camden Town,
London, 1824; a prolific composer.   [lx. 318]

WESLEY, SAMUEL SEBASTIAN (1810-1876), organ-
ist and composer; natural son of Samuel Wesley (1766-1837)
[q. v.]; chorister, Chapel Royal, London, 1819; organist
of various London churches, 1825-32, Hereford Cathedral,
1832-5, Exeter Cathedral, 1835-41, Leeds parish church,
1842-9, Winchester Cathedral, 1849-65, and Gloucester
Cathedral, 1865-76; Mus.Doc. Oxford, 1839; professor
of the organ, Royal Academy of Music, 1850; granted
civil list pension, 1873; published pamphlets against the
cathedral music of his time; in first rank as composer of
English church music.   [lx. 320]

WESSEX, Kings of. [See WEST-SAXONS.]

WESSINGTON, JOHN (d. 1451), prior of Durham;
Benedictine monk; studied at, and was bursar, 1398, of
Durham College, Oxford; chancellor of Durham Cathedral,
1400, and prior, 1416-46; wrote sermons and treatises on
history of monasticism and of universities, still extant in
manuscript.   [lx. 322]

WEST, MRS. (1790-1876), actress; née Cooke; first
appeared at Bath, 1810, at Covent Garden, London, 1812,
and Edinburgh, 1814; married, 1815; acted at Bath,
1815-17; a leading actress, chiefly in tragedy, Drury
Lane, London, 1818-28; played secondary parts at
Covent Garden, 1835; afterwards played in the provinces.
                                                     [lx. 323]

WEST, BENJAMIN (1738-1820), historical painter;
born of quaker parents in Pennsylvania; self-taught;
painted portraits in Philadelphia and New York; studied
and painted portraits in Italy, 1760-3; exhibited numerous
paintings, historical and scriptural, in London from 1764;
member of the Incorporated Society of Artists, 1765;
much employed by George III, 1767-1811; historical
painter to George III, 1772; an original R.A.; exhibited
at first exhibition of Royal Academy, 1769; president
R.A., 1792; engravings from his pictures very popular;
his best-known picture the 'Death of Wolfe' (exhibited,
1771); first to abandon the Greek and Roman and introduce modern costume into historical painting. [lx. 324]

WEST, CHARLES (1816-1898), physician; studied
in St. Bartholomew's Hospital, London, 1833, Bonn, Paris,
Berlin, and, 1839, Dublin; M.D. Berlin, 1837; physician
and accoucheur, London; physician, Infirmary for Children, and, 1852-75, Hospital for Sick Children; lecturer
on midwifery at Middlesex Hospital, 1845, and St. Bartholomew's Hospital, 1848-60; F.R.C.P., 1848, censor,
1870 and 1882, Croonian lecturer, 1871, Harveian orator,
1874; published lectures on 'Diseases of Infancy and
Childhood,' 1848, and 'Diseases of Women,' 1856, and
other professional papers.   [lx. 327]

WEST, SIR CHARLES RICHARD SACKVILLE-,
sixth EARL DE LA WARR, sixth VISCOUNT CANTELUPE,
and twelfth BARON DE LA WARR (1815-1873), a younger
son of George John Sackville West, fifth earl De La Warr
[q. v.]; ensign, 1833; captain, 1842; aide-de-camp to Sir
Hugh Gough [q. v.] in Sikh war, 1845-6; styled Lord
West from 1850; colonel, 1854; served in Crimea, 1854-5;
major-general, 1864; succeeded to earldom, 1869.
                                                     [lx. 328]

WEST, SIR EDWARD (1782-1828), economist; fellow
of University College, Oxford; M.A., 1807; called to the
bar, Inner Temple, 1814; recorder, and, 1823-8, chief-
justice of Bombay; knighted, 1822; published 'Essay on
Application of Capital to Land,' 1815, stating law of
diminishing returns, and anticipating Ricardo's theory
of rent; published observations on 'The Price of Corn,'
1826.   [lx. 329]

WEST, FRANCIS (1586-1633 ?), colonist; accom-
panied Christopher Newport [q. v.] to Virginia, 1609;
member of council, 1609; owned plantations on James
River; commander at Jamestown, 1612; admiral of New
England, 1622; governor of Virginia, 1628-9; died in
Virginia.   [lx. 329]

WEST, FRANCIS (d. 1652), captain in London
trained bands, 1644; lieutenant of Tower, 1645. [lx. 329]

WEST, FRANCIS ROBERT (1749 ?-1809), draughtsman in crayons; son of Robert West [q. v.]; trained in
Paris; master of Dublin School of Design, 1770-1809.
                                                     [lx. 340]

WEST, GEORGE JOHN SACKVILLE, fifth EARL
DE LA WARR (1791-1869), contemporary of Byron at
Harrow; M.A. Brasenose College, Oxford, 1819; lord of
the bedchamber, 1813 and 1820-8; assumed Sackville as
additional name, 1843; lord-chamberlain, 1841 and 1858-
1859.   [lx. 333]

WEST, GILBERT (1703-1756), author; educated at
Eton and Christ Church, Oxford; B.A., 1725; served in
army and secretary of state's office; clerk of privy council,
1752; paymaster of Chelsea Hospital, London, 1754; published 'Observations on the Resurrection,' 1747 (hon.
D.C.L. Oxford, 1748), a metrical version of 'Odes of
Pindar,' and miscellaneous poetry.   [lx. 330]

WEST, JAMES (1704 ?-1772), politician and antiquary; M.A. Balliol College, Oxford, 1726; called to bar,
Inner Temple, 1728, bencher, 1761, reader, 1767, treasurer,
1768; F.R.S., 1726, and president, 1768; F.S.A., 1727;
M.P., St. Albans, 1741-68, Boroughbridge, 1768-72; joint-
secretary to treasury, 1741-62; recorder of Poole, 1746-72;
collected manuscripts, rare books, prints, coins, pictures.
                                                     [lx. 330]

WEST, MRS. JANE (1758-1852), author; began to
write verses, 1771; published verses, plays, didactic
'Letters,' and works of good moral tone, 1780-1827;
befriended by Thomas Percy [q. v.], the bishop, 1800.
                                                     [lx. 331]

WEST, JOHN, first EARL DE LA WARR (1693-1766),
travelled; clerk-extraordinary of privy council, 1712;
M.P., Grampound, 1715; lieutenant-colonel in guards,

1717; succeeded as seventh (or sixteenth) Baron De La Warr, 1723; treasurer of the household, 1731-6; took active part in debates in the Lords, 1732-54; brigadier at Dettingen, 1743; general of horse, 1765; created earl, 1761. [lx. 332]

WEST, JOHN, second EARL DE LA WARR (1729-1777), son of John West, first earl De La Warr [q. v.]; ensign, 1746; major-general, 1761; styled Viscount Cantelupe from 1761; succeeded to earldom, 1766; lieutenant-general, 1770. [lx. 333]

WEST, SIR JOHN (1774-1862), admiral; entered navy, 1788; captain, 1796; rear-admiral, 1819; K.C.B., 1840; admiral of the fleet, 1858; G.C.B., 1860. [lx. 334]

WEST, JOSEPH (fl. 1669-1685), governor of South Carolina; took out an emigrant party, 1669; settled at Ashley River, 1670; temporary governor, 1671; governor and store-keeper, 1674-82 and 1684-5. [lx. 334]

WEST, NICOLAS (1461-1533), bishop of Ely and diplomatist; educated at Eton; fellow of King's College, Cambridge, 1483-98; LL.D., c. 1485; appointed archdeacon of Derby, 1486; non-resident rector of Egglescliffe, 1499-1515, and Witney, 1502-15; appointed dean of Windsor, 1509; bishop of Ely, 1515-33; constantly employed on complimentary and diplomatic missions to Scotland, Germany, France, and Castile, 1502-25; chaplain to Queen Catherine of Arragon and opposed to the divorce proceedings, 1529; added to buildings of St. George's, Windsor, King's College, Cambridge, Putney parish church, and Ely Cathedral. [lx. 335]

WEST, RAPHAEL LAMAR (1769-1850), painter and book-illustrator; son of Benjamin West [q. v.] [lx. 327]

WEST, RICHARD (fl. 1606-1619), poet; published 'News from Bartolomew Fayre,' 1606, and 'The Court of Conscience,' a satire, 1607; added second part, 1619, to Francis Segar's 'School of Vertue.' [lx. 338]

WEST, RICHARD (d. 1726), lawyer and playwright; called to bar, Inner Temple, 1714, bencher, 1718; counsel to board of trade, 1718; M.P., Grampound, 1721, Bodmin, 1722-6; active manager of Lord-chancellor Macclesfield's impeachment, 1725; lord chancellor of Ireland, 1725; published treatises on law of attainder, 1716, and creation of peers, 1719; brought out 'Hecuba, a tragedy,' 1726. [lx. 338]

WEST, RICHARD (1716-1742), poet; school-friend of Thomas Gray at Eton; entered Middle Temple, 1733; studied at Christ Church, Oxford, 1735-8; some of his letters and poems published posthumously. [lx. 339]

WEST, ROBERT (d. 1770), artist; trained at Paris; head-master of Dublin School of Design. [lx. 340]

WEST, ROBERT LUCIUS (d. 1849), painter of portraits and historical subjects; son of Francis Robert West [q. v.]; exhibited at Royal Academy, 1808; head-master of Dublin School of Design, 1809-49; an original member of Royal Hibernian Academy, 1823. [lx. 340]

WEST, TEMPLE (1713-1757), vice-admiral; entered navy, 1727; captain, 1738; cashiered, 1745, for failure (off Toulon, 1744) to come to close action with French squadron, but reinstated through family influence, 1746; rear-admiral, 1755; second in command under Admiral John Byng [q. v.] in failure at Minorca, 1756; vice-admiral of the blue, 1756. [lx. 341]

WEST, SIR THOMAS, eighth BARON WEST and ninth BARON DE LA WARR (1472 ?-1554), soldier and courtier; knighted while serving in France, 1513; attended Henry VIII to France, 1520; carver to Henry VIII, 1521; high sheriff of Surrey and Sussex, 1524; succeeded to baronies, 1526; assented to Henry VIII's divorce from Catherine, 1530; acted with the opposition peers, 1536-46; disliked dissolution of monasteries and the English service-books; prisoner in Tower of London under suspicion of disaffection, 1538; forced to give Halnaker to Henry VIII in exchange for church lands, 1540; supported Warwick against Somerset, 1547; K.G., 1549; accused his nephew, William West, afterwards first (or tenth) baron De La Warr [q. v.], of attempt to poison him, 1549; joint lord-lieutenant of Sussex, 1551; declared for Queen Mary, 1553. [lx. 341]

WEST, THOMAS, third (or twelfth) BARON DE LA WARR (1577-1618), entered Queen's College, Oxford, 1592; created M.A., 1605; travelled in Italy, 1595; M.P.,

Lymington, 1597; served in Netherlands, 1598, and under Essex in Ireland, 1599; knighted, 1599; imprisoned as privy to Essex's rising, 1602; succeeded to barony, 1602; member of Virginia Company, 1609; appointed governor and took out fresh colonists, 1610; returned and published 'Relation,' giving favourable account of colony, 1611; died in Virginia on second visit. [lx. 344]

WEST, THOMAS (1720-1779), topographer; joined jesuits, 1751; mission-priest in Furness and Westmoreland; published 'Antiquities of Furness,' 1774, 'Guide to the Lakes,' 1778, and archæological papers. [lx. 345]

WEST, WILLIAM (fl. 1568-1594), author of 'Symbolæographia' (published, 1590), a practical guide to English law; entered Middle Temple, 1568. [lx. 346]

WEST, WILLIAM, first (or tenth) BARON DE LA WARR (1519 ?-1595), attainted, 1550, on charge of attempting to poison his uncle Thomas West, ninth baron De La Warr [q. v.]; restored in blood, 1563; believed to have been created by patent Baron De La Warr, 1570; summoned, 1572-92. His title to count in reckoning of old barony rests on decision of lords, 1597. [lx. 344]

WEST, WILLIAM (1770-1854), bookseller and antiquary; apprenticed in London, 1784; bookseller in Cork, 1808-30, Birmingham, and London; published, among other works, 'Tavern Anecdotes, and Reminiscences of Signs,' 1825, autobiographical 'Fifty Years' Recollections,' 1830, a history of Warwickshire, 1830, views of buildings in Staffordshire, 1830-1; and historical collections about printing, 1835, and bookselling, 1839. [lx. 346]

WEST, WILLIAM (1796 ?-1888), comedian and musical composer; appeared at Haymarket, London, 1805; acted in provincial and in minor London theatres; lived to be called 'The Father of the Stage'; composed songs and glees. [lx. 324]

WESTALL, RICHARD (1765-1836), historical painter; apprentice to heraldic engraver, London, 1779-1786; exhibited at Royal Academy from 1784; R.A., 1794; painted chiefly in water-colours, but occasionally in oils; painted chiefly historical subjects, but also portraits and rustic subjects; contributed designs to the 'Shakespeare' and 'Milton' of John Boydell [q. v.]; a prolific book-illustrator. [lx. 347]

WESTALL, WILLIAM (1781-1850), topographical painter; taught by his brother Richard Westall [q. v.]; draughtsman to Matthew Flinders's [q. v.] Australian expedition, 1801-5, making sketches in Australia, China, and Bombay; visited Madeira and Jamaica, 1805-6; exhibited water-colour pictures and drawings of foreign scenes, 1808-30, and of English scenery, 1809-40; A.R.A., 1812; much employed in illustration of topographical works, 1818-31. [lx. 348]

WESTBURY, first BARON (1800-1873). [See BETHELL, RICHARD.]

WESTCOTE, BARONS. [See LYTTELTON, WILLIAM HENRY, first BARON, 1724-1808; LYTTELTON, WILLIAM HENRY, third BARON, 1782-1837; LYTTELTON, GEORGE WILLIAM, fourth BARON, 1817-1876.]

WESTCOTE, THOMAS (fl. 1624-1636), topographer; travelled; saw military service; compiled topographical 'View of Devonshire,' c. 1630, and 'Pedigrees of . . . Devonshire Families' (printed, 1845). [lx. 350]

WESTCOTT, GEORGE BLAGDON (1745 ?-1798), captain in the navy; master's mate, 1768; lieutenant, 1777; captain, 1790; killed in battle of St. Vincent; accorded public monument in Westminster Abbey. [lx. 350]

WESTERN, CHARLES CALLIS, BARON WESTERN (1767-1844), politician and agriculturist; of Felix Hall, Essex; educated at Eton and Cambridge; travelled, collecting busts, urns, and other objects of antiquity; M.P., Maldon, 1790-1812, Essex, 1812-32; advocated agricultural interests and parliamentary reform; created Baron Western of Rivenhall, 1833; improved breed of sheep; published pamphlets on prison discipline, 1821-2, and economic questions, 1822-43. [lx. 351]

WESTFALING or WESTPHALING, HERBERT (1532 ?-1602), bishop of Hereford; student of Christ Church, Oxford, 1547; M.A., 1555; canon, 1562; D.D.,

1566; Lady Margaret professor of divinity, 1562–4; vice-chancellor of Oxford, 1576–7; rector of Brightwell Baldwin, Oxfordshire, 1572; bishop of Hereford, 1586; benefactor of Jesus College, Oxford; published 'Treatise of Reformation in Religion,' 1582. [lx. 352]

WESTFIELD, THOMAS (1573–1644), bishop of Bristol; fellow of Jesus College, Cambridge, 1600–3; M.A., 1596; D.D., 1615; rector of South Somercotes, 1600–5, of St. Bartholomew, Smithfield, London, 1605, and of Hornsey, 1615–37; archdeacon of St. Albans, 1631; bishop of Bristol, 1642; attended opening of Westminster Assembly, 1643; his sermons published posthumously, 1646 and 1660. [lx. 353]

WESTGARTH, WILLIAM (1815–1889), Australian colonist and politician; clerk in office of Australian merchant firm, Leith; general merchant, Melbourne, 1840; actively opposed transportation; represented Melbourne in New South Wales legislature, 1850–3; settled in London as director of Westgarth & Co., colonial brokers, 1857; published 'Report on ... Australian Aborigines,' 1846, historical notes of settlement of Port Phillip or Victoria, 1848–57, and personal recollections of colonial affairs, 1888–9. [lx. 354]

WESTMACOTT, SIR RICHARD (1775–1856), sculptor; trained in Rome under Canova, 1793–7; exhibited at Royal Academy, 1797–1839; R.A., 1811; professor of sculpture, Royal Academy, 1827–57; hon. D.C.L. Oxford, 1836; knighted, 1837; up to 1820 worked chiefly on monumental sculptures, busts and statues, after 1820 chiefly on classical and imaginative works; many of his monuments in Westminster Abbey and St. Paul's, London; executed bronze Achilles in Hyde Park, 1822, and pediment of British Museum portico, 1847. [lx. 355]

WESTMACOTT, RICHARD (1799–1872), sculptor; son of Sir Richard Westmacott [q. v.]; studied in Italy, 1820–6; exhibited at Royal Academy, 1827–55; R.A., 1849; up to 1840 produced chiefly imaginative works, afterwards chiefly portraits and monuments; professor of sculpture, Royal Academy, 1857–67. [lx. 356]

WESTMACOTT, THOMAS (d. 1798), architect; exhibited at Royal Academy, 1796–8. [lx. 356]

WESTMEATH, EARLS OF. [See NUGENT, SIR RICHARD, first EARL, 1583–1642; NUGENT, RICHARD, second EARL, d. 1684; NUGENT, THOMAS, fourth EARL, 1656–1752; NUGENT, JOHN, fifth EARL, 1672–1754.]

WESTMINSTER, first DUKE OF (1825–1899). [See GROSVENOR, HUGH LUPUS.]

WESTMINSTER, MARQUISES OF. [See GROSVENOR, ROBERT, first MARQUIS, 1767–1845; GROSVENOR, RICHARD, second MARQUIS, 1795–1869.]

WESTMINSTER, MATTHEW, name of an imaginary author, to whom is assigned, in a fifteenth-century manuscript, the chronicle 'Flores Historiarum,' compiled by various writers at the abbeys of St. Albans and Westminster, first printed, 1567, reprinted in Rolls Series, 1890. [lx. 357]

WESTMORLAND, BARONS OF. [See CLIFFORD, ROGER DE, fifth BARON, 1333–1389; CLIFFORD, THOMAS DE, sixth BARON, d. 1391?; CLIFFORD, HENRY DE CLIFFORD, tenth BARON, 1455?–1523; CLIFFORD, HENRY DE CLIFFORD, eleventh BARON, 1493–1542; CLIFFORD, HENRY DE, twelfth BARON, d. 1570.]

WESTMORLAND, EARLS OF. [See NEVILLE, RALPH, first EARL of first creation, 1364–1425; NEVILLE, RALPH, second earl, d. 1484; NEVILLE, RALPH, fourth EARL, 1499–1550; NEVILLE, HENRY, fifth EARL, 1525?–1563; NEVILLE, CHARLES, sixth EARL, 1543–1601; FANE, MILDMAY, second EARL of second creation, d. 1665; FANE, JOHN, seventh EARL, 1682?–1762; FANE, JOHN, tenth EARL, 1759–1841; FANE, JOHN, eleventh EARL, 1784–1859; FANE, FRANCIS WILLIAM HENRY, twelfth EARL, 1825–1891.]

WESTMORLAND, COUNTESS OF (1793–1879). [See FANE, PRISCILLA ANNE.]

WESTON, EDWARD (1566–1635), Roman catholic controversialist; studied at Lincoln College, Oxford, 1579, Rheims, and Rome, 1585–91; D.D. Monreale; lecturer on casuistry, Rheims, 1592, and on divinity, Douay, 1593–1603; mission-priest in England, c. 1603–12; canon of Bruges; published doctrinal and polemical works, Latin and English, 1602–31. [lx. 358]

WESTON, EDWARD (1703–1770), didactic writer; son of Stephen Weston (1665–1742) [q. v.]; educated at Eton and King's College, Cambridge; M.A., 1727; under-secretary of state, 1730–46 and 1761–4; editor of 'London Gazette,' 1741–70; chief secretary for Ireland, 1746–51; assailed by Junius under the impression that he was the author of 'A Vindication of the Duke of Grafton'; his works, published anonymously, 1740–68, include 'The Country Gentleman's Advice to' 'his Son,' 1755, 'to his Neighbours,' 1756. [lx. 358]

WESTON, ELIZABETH JANE (1582–1612), learned lady; master of several languages; born in London; removed with her parents to Bohemia; addressed Latin letters and verses to princes and scholars, including Lipsius and Scaliger; married the jurist Johann Leon; her poems printed at Frankfort-on-Oder, 1602. [lx. 359]

WESTON, SIR FRANCIS (1511?–1536), courtier; only son of Sir Richard Weston (1466?–1542) [q. v.]; page to Henry VIII, 1526; gentleman of the privy chamber, 1532; K.B., 1533; executed on charge of misconduct with Anne Boleyn. [lx. 360]

WESTON, HUGH (1505?–1558), dean of Westminster; M.A. Lincoln College, Oxford, 1533; rector of Lincoln College, Oxford, 1538–55; D.D., 1540; Margaret professor of divinity, 1540–9; pluralist in rectories; leader of Roman catholic party; dean of Westminster, 1553–6, and of Windsor, 1556–7; appointed to preside over trial of Cranmer and the disputation between Latimer and Richard Smith, 1554. [lx. 361]

WESTON, JEROME, second EARL OF PORTLAND (1605–1663), son of Richard Weston, first earl of Portland [q. v.]; M.P., Gatton, 1628–9; envoy to France, 1628 and 1632–3; styled Lord Weston from 1633; succeeded to earldom, 1635; governor of Isle of Wight, 1633–42 and 1660–3; joint lord-lieutenant of Hampshire, 1641; imprisoned for plot to deliver Portsmouth to Charles I, 1642–3; resided in Oxford, 1643–6; compounded for delinquency, 1646; sat in Convention parliament, 1660. [lx. 362]

WESTON, SIR RICHARD (1466?–1542), courtier; governor of Guernsey, 1509–42; fought against Moors, 1511; knighted, 1514; in constant personal attendance on Henry VIII as knight of the body from 1516; K.B., 1518; granted Sutton manor, Surrey, 1521; treasurer of Calais, 1525; under-treasurer of England, 1528–42. [lx. 363]

WESTON, RICHARD (d. 1572), judge; called to bar, Middle Temple, before 1554, reader, 1554; bought Skreens, Essex, 1554; M.P., Maldon, 1555; solicitor-general, 1557–1559; justice of common pleas, 1559–72. [lx. 364]

WESTON, RICHARD, first EARL OF PORTLAND (1577–1635), statesman; student of Middle Temple; knighted, 1603; M.P., Maldon, 1601–3, Midhurst, 1604, Essex, 1614, Arundel, 1621; M.P., 1624; M.P., Callington, 1625, Bodmin, 1626; sent, by recommendation of Gondomar, to Brussels and Germany on fruitless endeavour to avert invasion of Palatinate, 1620, and to solicit restoration of Elector Palatine, 1622; as chancellor of the exchequer from 1621, showed financial capacity in providing for necessary expenditure, incurred popular hatred as suspected Roman catholic, and was intrigued against by Henrietta Maria for refusing grants to her favourites; opposed war with Spain, 1623, and France, 1626; created Baron Weston of Neyland, 1628; lord high treasurer, 1628–33; escaped impeachment only by dissolution of parliament, 1629; persuaded Charles I to peace, 1630, and to secret treaty, 1634, with Spain; created Earl of Portland, 1633. [lx. 364]

WESTON, SIR RICHARD (1579?–1652), judge; called to bar, Middle Temple, 1607, bencher, 1626; M.P., Lichfield, 1622; baron of exchequer, 1634–45; knighted, 1635; gave opinion favourable to ship-money, 1636; impeached, 1641; disabled from judicial functions, 1645. [lx. 367]

WESTON, SIR RICHARD (1591–1652), agriculturist; of Sutton, Surrey; knighted, 1622; introduced canal-locks, irrigation to increase hay-crops, and rotation of crops; superintended works (completed, 1653) to make Wey navigable to Guildford, 1635–41, 1650–2; sequestrated as royalist; while residing, 1644–9, in Low Countries, wrote 'Discours of Husbandrie used in Brabant and Flanders.' [lx. 367]

WESTON, Sir RICHARD (1620–1681), judge; called to bar, Gray's Inn, 1649, reader, 1676; pleader of repute, c. 1662; king's serjeant and knighted, 1678; baron of exchequer, 1680–1. [lx. 369]

WESTON, RICHARD (1733–1806), agricultural writer; thread-hosier of Leicester; works include 'Tracts on Practical Agriculture and Gardening,' 1769, 'Flora Anglicana,' 1775–80, and 'The Leicester Directory,' 1794. [lx. 369]

WESTON, ROBERT (1515 ?–1573), lord chancellor of Ireland; fellow of All Souls College, Oxford, 1536; principal of Broadgates Hall, Oxford, 1546–9; D.C.L., 1556; M.P., Exeter, 1553, Lichfield, 1559; dean of arches, 1559–1567; lord-chancellor of Ireland, 1567–73; held, though layman, deanery of St. Patrick's, Dublin, 1567–73, and deanery of Wells, 1570–3. [lx. 370]

WESTON, STEPHEN (1665–1742), bishop of Exeter; educated at Eton; fellow of King's College, Cambridge; M.A., 1690; assistant-master, 1690, and second master, 1693–1707, at Eton; fellow of Eton, 1707; D.D. Oxford, 1711; canon of Ely, 1715–17; vicar of Mapledurham, 1716; bishop of Exeter, 1724; compiled school-books for use at Eton; sermons published posthumously. [lx. 371]

WESTON, STEPHEN (1747–1830), antiquary and man of letters; educated at Blundell's School, Tiverton; fellow of Exeter College, Oxford, 1768–84; M.A., 1770; B.D., 1782; travelled as tutor on continent, 1771; visited Paris, 1791–2, and subsequently; rector of Mamhead, 1777–90, and of Little Hempston, Devon, 1784–1823; F.R.S., 1792; F.S.A., 1794; published notes of travel, classical texts and annotations, notes on Shakespeare, scriptural annotations, and translations from Arabic, Chinese, and Persian, 1776–1828; other works include 'Remains of Arabic in Spanish and Portuguese Languages,' 1810, and 'Greek, Latin, and Sanscrit compared,' 1814. [lx. 372]

WESTON, THOMAS (d. 1643 ?), merchant and colonist; made, at Leyden, 1620, offers to provide shipping to take puritans to New England, which he failed to keep; sent trading-ship to Plymouth, New England, which brought back cargo of timber and fur, 1621; sent out futile private expedition to New England, 1622, and followed it; returned to England. [lx. 374]

WESTON, THOMAS (1737–1776), actor; acted at Bartholomew Fair and Haymarket, London, 1759, and at Dublin, 1760–1; an admired comedian, especially in clown parts, at principal London theatres, 1761–75. [lx. 375]

WESTON, Sir WILLIAM (d. 1540), last prior of knights of St. John in England; distinguished himself at siege of Rhodes, 1522; commanded warship ('the first ironclad') at Crete, 1523; envoy to Henry VIII, 1524; prior in England, 1527; died on day of dissolution of the order. [lx. 377]

WESTON, WILLIAM (1550 ?–1615), jesuit; known also as EDMONDS and HUNT; contemporary of Edmund Campion [q. v.] at Oxford; studied at Paris, and, 1572, Douay; joined jesuits, 1575; trained in Rome and Spain; Greek lecturer at Seville, 1582–4; superior of jesuit mission in England, 1584; reconciled Philip Howard, earl of Arundel [q. v.]; wrote 'Book of Miracles,' describing his activity as exorcist; prisoner in the Clink, 1586–8, Wisbech Castle, 1588–98, and the Tower of London, 1598–1603; quarrelled at Wisbech with Christopher Bagshaw [q. v.] and other secular priests, 1594; allowed to withdraw to continent, 1603; official of colleges at Seville, 1605–14, and Valladolid, 1614; died at Valladolid. [lx. 378]

WESTPHAL, Sir GEORGE AUGUSTUS (1785–1875), admiral; on active service, 1798–1834; wounded at Trafalgar; lieutenant, 1806; captain, 1819; knighted, 1824; rear-admiral, 1851; admiral, 1863. [lx. 380]

WESTPHAL, PHILIP (1782–1880), admiral; on active service, 1794–1847; lieutenant, 1801; captain, 1830; rear-admiral, 1855; admiral, 1866. [lx. 380]

WESTPHALING, HERBERT (1532 ?–1602). [See WESTFALING.]

WEST-SAXONS, kings and queens of. [See CERDIC, l. 534; CEAWLIN, d. 593; CEOLRIC, d. 597; CYNEGILS, l. 643; CENWALH, d. 672; SEXBURGA, d. 673; CYNEWULF,

d. 785; CENTWINE, d. 685; CAEDWALLA, 659 ?–689; INE, d. 726; CUTHRED, d. 754; SIGEBERT, d. 756 ?; BEORHTRIC, d. 802; EGBERT, d. 839.]

WESTWOOD, JOHN OBADIAH (1805–1893), entomologist and palæographer; articled to London solicitor, 1821; secretary of Entomological Society, 1834; first Hope professor of zoology, Oxford, 1861–93; M.A. by decree, 1861; fellow of Magdalen College, Oxford, 1880; published entomological text-books, 1838–89, papers in scientific journals from 1827, and additions to new editions of older works; published, among other palæographical works, 'Palæographia Sacra Pictoria,' 1843–5, 'Facsimiles of Miniatures and Ornaments of Anglo-Saxon and Irish Manuscripts,' 1868, and 'Lapidarium Walliæ,' account of early inscribed stones in Wales, 1876–9. [lx. 381]

WESTWOOD, THOMAS (1814 ?–1888), minor poet; son of Thomas Westwood of Enfield; friend of Charles Lamb, who fostered his literary tastes; published, between 1840 and 1886, several volumes of verse characterised by exquisite taste; went to Belgium as director and secretary of the Tournay railway, 1844, and devoted much attention to collection of a library of works on angling, and subsequently published writings on the bibliography of angling, including 'Chronicle of the Compleat Angler,' 1864, and 'Bibliotheca Piscatoria' (in collaboration with Thomas Satchell, d. 1888), 1883. [Suppl. iii. 510]

WETENHALL, EDWARD (1636–1713), bishop of Kilmore and Ardagh; educated at Westminster School; B.A. Trinity College, Cambridge, 1660; M.A. Lincoln College, Oxford, 1661; prebendary of Exeter, 1667; master of blue-coat school, Dublin, 1672; D.D. Trinity College, Dublin; bishop of Cork and Ross, 1679; resided in Ireland throughout troubles, 1688–9; translated to Kilmore, 1699; urged publication of 'books of religion' in Irish language, 1710; published grammars of Greek and Latin, devotional works, and appeals for mutual forbearance in theological controversy, 1666–1710. [lx. 382]

WETHAM, ROBERT (d. 1738). [See WITHAM.]

WETHERALL, Sir EDWARD ROBERT (d. 1869), major-general; son of Sir George Augustus Wetherall [q. v.]; entered army, 1834; served in Canada, 1837; captain, 1845; assistant quartermaster-general in Crimea, 1854–5; chief of staff to Sir Hugh Henry Rose [q. v.] in central India, 1857–8; K.C.S.I., 1867; major-general, 1869. [lx. 385]

WETHERALL, Sir FREDERICK AUGUSTUS (1754–1842), general; entered army, 1775; served in America, 1776; officer of marines in battle off Cape St. Vincent, 1780; captain, 1781; stationed in Gibraltar, 1783–9; served in Canada and West Indies, 1790–1806; lieutenant-colonel, 1795; major-general, 1809; second in command of Java expedition, 1810; stationed in Mysore, 1811–15; G.C.H., 1833; general, 1837; successively aide-de-camp, equerry, and executor to Duke of Kent. [lx. 383]

WETHERALL, Sir GEORGE AUGUSTUS (1788–1868), general; son of Sir Frederick Augustus Wetherall [q. v.]; lieutenant, 1795; captain, 1805; lieutenant-colonel, 1828; served in India, 1811–31, and Canada, 1837; K.C.B., 1856; general, 1863; G.C.B., 1865; governor of Sandhurst College, 1866. [lx. 384]

WETHERELL, Sir CHARLES (1770–1846), politician and lawyer; demy of Magdalen College, Oxford, 1786–91; M.A., 1793; hon. D.C.L., 1834; barrister, Inner Temple, 1794; bencher, 1816; treasurer, 1825; practised in chancery courts and at parliamentary bar; successfully defended James Watson (1766 ?–1838) [q. v.] in high treason case, 1817; tory M.P., Shaftesbury, 1813–18, Oxford, 1820–6, Hastings, 1826, Plympton Earl, 1826–30, Boroughbridge, 1830–2, violently opposing legal, municipal, and parliamentary reform, and Roman catholic emancipation; solicitor-general, 1824; knighted, 1824; attorney-general, 1826 and 1828; recorder of Bristol; the great Bristol riot caused by his unpopularity, 1831. [lx. 385]

WETHERELL, NATHANIEL THOMAS (1800–1875), geologist; surgeon; collected geological specimens in London district; contributed papers to Geological Society. [lx. 387]

WETHERSET, RICHARD (fl. 1350), theological writer; chancellor of Cambridge University, 1350; works still extant in manuscript. [lx. 387]

WETHERSHED, RICHARD OF (*d.* 1231). [See GRANT, RICHARD.]

WETWANG, SIR JOHN (*d.* 1684), captain in the navy; commanded king's ship in wars against Dutch, 1665–74; convoyed Mediterranean merchant fleet, 1676; knighted, 1680; died in India. [lx. 388]

WEWITZER, MISS (*fl.* 1772–1789), actress at Covent Garden, London, and in Dublin; married, after 1808, James Cuffe, baron Tyrawley. [lx. 389]

WEWITZER, RALPH (1748–1825), comedian; acted in principal London theatres, 1773–1812, with great success in parts representing Germans, Frenchmen, Jews, and old men; brought out pantomimes, 1784 and 1788; published a collection of bons mots entitled 'School for Wits,' 1815, autobiographical 'Dramatic Reminiscences,' and notes of stage history. [lx. 388]

WEY or **WAY**, WILLIAM (1407 ?–1476), traveller and author; M.A. and B.D. Oxford; fellow of Exeter College, Oxford, 1430–42; fellow of Eton College, *c.* 1442; wrote sermons, and itineraries (published, 1857) of his pilgrimages to Compostella, 1456, and Palestine, 1457–8 and 1462. [lx. 390]

WEYLAND, JOHN (1774–1854), writer on the poor laws; called to bar, Inner Temple, 1800; M.P., Hindon, 1830–2; published 'A Short Enquiry into . . . Poor Laws,' 1807, 'Letter . . . on State of Religion in India,' 1813, and other papers. [lx. 390]

WEYLAND, THOMAS DE (*fl.* 1272–1290), judge; sub-deacon; justice itinerant in eastern counties from 1272; justice of common pleas, *c.* 1274, and chief-justice, 1278–89; active in judicial duties, but rapacious in increasing his estates; removed from office and his estates confiscated on Edward I's return to England, when the conduct of the judges during Edward I's absence was investigated, 1289; banished, 1290. [lx. 391]

WEYMOUTH, VISCOUNTS. [See THYNNE, SIR THOMAS, first VISCOUNT, 1640–1714; THYNNE, THOMAS, third VISCOUNT, 1734–1796.]

WEYMOUTH or **WAYMOUTH**, GEORGE (*fl.* 1605), voyager; employed by East India Company to seek for north-west passage to India; penetrated Hudson's Strait, but was forced to return by mutiny, 1602: in second voyage, 1605, traded with natives on New England coast and sailed up a river in Maine. [lx. 393]

WHALEY or **WHALLEY**, THOMAS (1766–1800), Irish politician and eccentric; nicknamed 'Buck' and 'Jerusalem' Whaley; lived extravagantly in Paris, 1782, and Dublin; M.P., Newcastle, co. Down, 1785–90, Enniscorthy, 1797–1800; visited Jerusalem on a wager, 1788–9; revisited Paris, 1790; left autobiography in manuscript. [lx. 393]

WHALLEY. [See also WHALEY.]

WHALLEY, EDWARD (*d.* 1675 ?), regicide; woollen-draper; major in Cromwell's horse, 1643, and lieutenant-colonel, 1644; served with distinction in many actions, 1643–9; one of army leaders who resisted disbandment by parliament, 1647; custodian of Charles I at Hampton Court, 1648; sat as judge and signed Charles I's death-warrant, 1649; served under Cromwell at Dunbar, 1650, and Worcester, 1651; major-general in command of mid-land district, 1655; active supporter of protectorate; sat in Oliver Cromwell's two parliaments, and in his House of Lords, 1657; army agent to negotiate with Monck in Scotland, 1659; escaped to New England, 1660; still alive, 1674. [lx. 394]

WHALLEY, GEORGE HAMMOND (1813–1878), politician; called to bar, Gray's Inn, 1835; assistant tithe commissioner, 1836–47; published articles and treatise on tithe question, first edition, 1838; liberal M.P., Peterborough, 1859–78. [lx. 396]

WHALLEY, JOHN (1653–1724), quack; resided in Dublin, 1682–8 and 1689–1724, selling universal medicines, issuing 'Vox Urani' or 'Advice from the Stars,' an astrological almanac, and pretending to necromancy; visited London, 1688–9, to shun resentment of native Irish and Roman catholics; issued 'Whalley's News Letter,' a libellous weekly journal, from 1714; published astrological works. [lx. 397]

WHALLEY, PETER (1722–1791), author and editor; educated at Merchant Taylors' School, 1731–40; fellow of St. John's College, Oxford, 1743; B.A., 1744; B.C.L., 1768; schoolmaster in Northamptonshire and at Christ's Hospital, London, 1760–76; rector of St. Gabriel Fen-church, London, 1766–91, and of Horley, 1768–91; edited John Bridges's (1666–1724) [q. v.] Northamptonshire collections, 1762–91, and Ben Jonson's 'Works,' 1756; wrote 'Enquiry into the Learning of Shakespeare,' 1748; died at Ostend. [lx. 398]

WHALLEY, RICHARD (1499 ?–1583), politician; in personal service of Henry VIII before 1524; employed to visit lesser monasteries, 1536; granted church lands, 1539; joint-steward to Protector Somerset; M.P., Scarborough, 1547; crown receiver for Yorkshire, 1547–52; commissioner for appropriation of parish chantries, 1547; granted crown lands, 1549; imprisoned as adherent of Somerset, 1551; gave evidence against Somerset; released, with loss of much of his property, 1552; again imprisoned; released by Queen Mary, 1553; M.P., East Grinstead, 1554, and Nottinghamshire, 1555; granted lands by Queen Elizabeth, 1561. [lx. 399]

WHALLEY, THOMAS SEDGWICK (1746–1828), poet and traveller; M.A. St. John's College, Cambridge, 1779; hon. D.D. Edinburgh, 1808; non-resident rector of Hag-worthingham, Lincolnshire, 1772–1828; prebendary of Wells, 1777–1826; lived chiefly on continent, 1783–1808 and 1814–18; published verses, 1779–97, and a tragedy, 1781; died at La Flèche; part of his journals and correspondence published, 1863. [lx. 400]

WHARNCLIFFE, BARONS. [See STUART-WORTLEY-MACKENZIE, JAMES ARCHIBALD, first BARON, 1776–1845; STUART-WORTLEY, JOHN, second BARON, 1801–1855.]

WHARTON, ANNE (1632 ?–1685), poetess; *née* Lee; married Thomas Wharton (afterwards first Marquis of Wharton) [q. v.], 1673; wrote metrical paraphrase of 'Lamentations of Jeremiah' and other verse. [lx. 401]

WHARTON, EDWARD ROSS (1844–1896), philologer and genealogist; of Charterhouse, London, and Trinity College, Oxford; Ireland scholar; fellow of Jesus College, Oxford, 1868–90; M.A., 1870; published 'Etyma Græca,' 1882, 'Etyma Latina,' 1890, and translations from classics; his manuscript history of the family of Wharton in Bodleian Library. [lx. 402]

WHARTON, SIR GEORGE, first baronet (1617–1681), astrologer; studied astronomy and mathematics at Oxford, 1633; published almanac under anagram of George Naworth, 1641–4, and under his own name, 1645, 1647–66, adding to issues after 1657 chronological history of England from 1600; raised troop of horse for Charles I, 1642; defeated at Stow-on-the-Wold, 1643; paymaster to Charles I's artillery, 1644; captain of horse, 1645; began pamphlet war with other almanac-makers, 1645; published 'Bellum Hybernicale . . . Astrologically demonstrated,' 1646–7; issued in London weekly sheet 'Mercurius Elenchicus,' ridiculing parliament, 1647; imprisoned, 1649–50; paymaster of ordnance office, 1660–81; published his 'Poems,' 1661; created baronet, 1677; prose works published, 1683. [lx. 402]

WHARTON, GEORGE (1688–1739), physician; M.D. Cambridge, 1719; F.R.C.P., 1720; censor, 1725, 1729, 1732, and 1734; treasurer, 1727–39. [lx. 417]

WHARTON, HENRY (1664–1695), divine and author; scholar of Caius College, Cambridge, 1680–7; M.A., 1687; literary assistant to Dr. William Cave [q. v.], 1686–7; chaplain to William Sancroft [q. v.], the archbishop, 1688–1693; rector of Minster and of Chartham, 1689–95; published, among other works, 'Treatise of Celibacy of Clergy,' 1688, 'Anglia Sacra' (lives of English prelates to 1540), 1691, 'Specimen of Errors' in Burnet's 'History of the Reformation,' 1693, 'History of Dr. Will. Laud,' 1695; his large manuscript collections in Lambeth Library. [lx. 404]

WHARTON, HENRY THORNTON (1846–1895), physician and scholar; brother of Edward Ross Wharton [q. v.]; M.A. Wadham College, Oxford, 1874; published work on Sappho (text, memoir, selected renderings, and translation), 1885. [lx. 402]

WHARTON or **WARTON**, JOHN (*fl.* 1575–1578), puritan writer; censured popularity of Chaucer's poems in preface to Jud Smith's 'A misticall deuise,' 1575; published metrical satire, 'Whartons Dreame,' 1578; other writings lost. [lx. 407]

WHARTON, PHILIP, fourth BARON WHARTON (1613–1696), succeeded his grandfather in barony, 1625 ; entered Exeter College, Oxford, 1626 ; headed Yorkshire opposition to court exactions, 1640 ; commissioner to treat with Scots at Ripon, 1640 ; champion of the popular party in the Lords, Long parliament, 1640 ; parliamentary lord-lieutenant of Lancashire and Buckingham, 1642 ; abandoned soldiering on his regiment being routed at Edgehill, 1642 ; member of committee of both kingdoms ; lay member of Westminster Assembly, 1643 ; adopted independent views ; voted for self-denying ordinance and creation of new-model army ; commissioner to treat with Scots, 1645 ; declined all share in public affairs during Commonwealth and protectorate ; coldly treated at Restoration ; opposed Conventicle Act, 1670, and the proposed non-resistance oath, 1675 ; prisoner in Tower of London for censuring prolonged prorogation of parliament, 1677 ; retired abroad, 1685 ; strenuously supported William of Orange, 1688–9 ; opposed proposed abjuration oath, 1690. [lx. 407]

WHARTON, PHILIP, DUKE OF WHARTON (1698–1731), only son of Thomas Wharton, first marquis of Wharton [q. v.] ; god-son of William III ; styled Viscount Winchendon, 1706–15 ; succeeded to marquisate, 1715 ; visited Pretender at Avignon and Marie Beatrix at St. Germain, 1716 ; took seat in Irish house of lords, 1717 ; created Duke of Wharton, 1718 ; patron of the turf ; president of ' Hell-fire Club ' (royal proclamation for its suppression issued, 1721) ; took seat in House of Lords, 1719 ; vigorously opposed extension of South Sea Company's charter, 1720, and attainder of Francis Atterbury [q. v.], 1723 ; sold his estates and pictures, 1723–30 ; adopted, at Vienna, 1726, cause of ' James III' and was created ' Duke of Northumberland ' ; at Madrid, 1726, urged Spanish descent in favour of Stuarts, and embraced Roman catholicism ; visited Rome, 1726 ; served against Gibraltar, 1727, and received colonelcy of a Spanish regiment ; outlawed, 1729 ; died in Catalonia ; his writings published, 1731–2. [lx. 410]

WHARTON, PHILIP (pseudonym). [See THOMSON, JOHN COCKBURN, 1834–1860.]

WHARTON, THOMAS, first BARON WHARTON (1495 ?–1568), served against Scots, 1522 ; knighted, c. 1527 ; high sheriff of Cumberland, 1529, 1535, and 1539 ; constantly employed in commissions on border affairs from 1531 ; supported Henry VIII against northern insurgents, 1536 ; employed to visit Cumberland monasteries, 1537 ; deputy-warden of west marches, 1537–49 ; captain of Carlisle, 1541 ; M.P., Cumberland, 1542 ; led raids into Scotland, 1542–3, and inflicted on Scots defeat of Solway Moss ; created Baron Wharton by patent, 1544 ; led raids into Scotland, 1547–8 ; incurred blood-feud with Scottish Maxwells by hanging their hostages, 1548 ; disapproved of the changes in religion, 1549 ; commissioner to treat with Scots, 1550 ; voted for execution of Somerset, 1551 ; deputy-warden of the three marches, 1553, and of east and middle marches only, 1553–68. [lx. 413]

WHARTON, THOMAS, second BARON WHARTON (1520–1572), son of Thomas Wharton, first baron Wharton [q. v.] ; served against Scots ; knighted, 1545 ; M.P., Cumberland, 1545–53, Hedon, 1554, Northumberland, 1555, Yorkshire, 1558 ; high sheriff of Cumberland, 1547 ; steward to Princess Mary, 1552 ; granted crown lands, 1553 ; privy councillor, 1553–9 ; imprisoned as recusant, 1561 ; succeeded to barony, 1568. [lx. 416]

WHARTON, THOMAS (1614–1673), physician ; studied at Cambridge, 1638, and Oxford ; M.D. Oxford, 1647 ; F.R.C.P., 1650, censor, 1658, 1661, 1666, 1667, 1668, and 1673 ; physician to St. Thomas's Hospital, 1659–73, residing in London throughout the plague, 1665–6 ; discovered the sub-maxillary (Wharton's) gland ; published, 1656, ' Adenographia,' a description of the glands. [lx. 416]

WHARTON, THOMAS, first MARQUIS OF WHARTON (1648–1715), statesman ; son of Philip Wharton, fourth baron Wharton [q. v.] ; brought up in puritanical fashion ; travelled, 1663–4 ; M.P., Wendover, 1673–9, and Buckinghamshire, 1679–96 ; leading patron of the turf, 1673–1705 ; supported Exclusion Bill, 1679–80 ; opposed settling revenues for life on James II, 1685 ; published ' Lilli Burlero, Bullen-a-la,' 1687, set to a quick step by Purcell ; joined William of Orange at Exeter, 1688 ; voted for declaring throne vacant, 1689 ; comptroller of the household, 1689–1702 ; succeeded to barony, 1696 ; lord-lieu-

tenant of Oxfordshire, 1697, and of Buckinghamshire, 1702 ; entertained William III at Wooburn, 1698 ; dismissed from his posts by Queen Anne, 1702 ; opposed Occasional Conformity Bill, 1703–4 ; involved in controversy with Commons over Aylesbury franchise case, 1703–5 ; spared no cost to return whigs to parliament, 1705–10 ; commissioner for union with Scotland, 1706 ; created Earl of Wharton, 1706 ; as lord-lieutenant of Ireland, 1708–10, took Joseph Addison as his secretary, refused to have Jonathan Swift as chaplain, and settled Palatinate refugees in Ireland ; urged prosecution of Henry Sacheverell, 1710 ; led opposition to tory government, 1710–14, advocating help for distressed Catalans, censuring treaty of Utrecht, and opposing Schism Bill, 1714 ; joined whig leaders in forcibly taking seat at privy council and proclaiming George I, 1714 ; created Marquis of Catherlough in Irish, and Marquis of Wharton in British, peerage, 1715. [lx. 418]

WHATELY, RICHARD (1787–1863), archbishop of Dublin ; fellow of Oriel College, Oxford, 1811–22 ; M.A., 1812 ; tutor ; D.D., 1825 ; published ' Historic Doubts relative to Napoleon Buonaparte,' 1819, ridiculing David Hume's arguments ; edited anti-Calvinistic treatise on predestination, 1821 ; published sermons, 1821–60 ; Bampton lecturer, 1822, on ' Party Feeling in Matters of Religion ' ; rector of Halesworth, Suffolk, 1822–5 ; principal of St. Alban Hall, 1825–31 ; supposed to be author of anti-Erastian ' Letters on Church of England by an Episcopalian,' 1826 ; published ' Logic ' (a treatise restricting the scope of logic to deduction merely), 1826, ' Rhetoric,' 1828, ' Errors of Romanism,' 1830 ; Drummond professor of political economy, 1829–1831, publishing his ' Introductory Lectures' ; archbishop of Dublin, 1831–63 ; presided over commissions to administer ' united national education ' in protestant and Roman catholic schools, 1831–53, and wrote scriptural manuals for that purpose ; founded political economy chair in Trinity College, Dublin, 1832 ; spoke and wrote against transportation, 1832–40 ; presided over commission on condition of Irish poor, 1833–6 ; voted for repeal of religious tests, 1833–53 ; wrote primers of mental, moral, and economic science for use in Irish schools, 1837–59 ; disapproved of Tithe Commutation Act, 1838 ; wrote against ' Ideal of a Christian Church,' 1844, by William George Ward [q. v.] ; voted for Maynooth grant, 1845 ; contributed munificently to Irish famine fund, 1847 ; edited Edward Copleston's [q. v.] ' Remains,' 1854, Bacon's ' Essays,' 1856, and other works ; published ' Lectures on … Scripture Parables,' 1857, and other expository treatises. [lx. 423]

WHATELY, THOMAS (d. 1772), politician and literary student ; M.P., Ludgershall, Wiltshire, 1761–8, Castle Rising, 1768–72 ; secretary to treasury under George Grenville, 1764–5 ; under-secretary of state under Lord North, 1771–2 ; published pamphlets on national finance, 1765–9, and ' Observations on Modern Gardening,' 1770 ; his ' Remarks ' on Shakespeare's characters of Macbeth and Richard III, published, 1785. [lx. 429]

WHATELY, WILLIAM (1583–1639), puritan divine ; B.A. Christ's College, Cambridge, 1601 ; M.A. St. Edmund Hall, Oxford, 1604 ; vicar of Banbury, 1610–1639 ; published devotional tracts, 1606–37 ; provoked much censure by his tract, ' A Bride-Bvsh,' 1619, allowing adultery or desertion to be valid ground of divorce. [lx. 430]

WHATTON, WILLIAM ROBERT (1790 – 1835), surgeon and antiquary ; F.R.C.S., 1810 ; surgeon to Royal Infirmary, Manchester ; F.S.A. ; F.R.S., 1834 ; advocated a university for Manchester, 1829 ; wrote papers on armorial bearings of Manchester and a history of Manchester grammar school and the Chetham Library. [lx. 431]

WHEARE, DEGORY (1573–1647), historian ; M.A. Broadgates Hall, Oxford, 1600 ; fellow of Exeter College, Oxford, 1602–8 ; travelled as tutor ; first Camden professor of history, Oxford, 1622–47 ; principal of Gloucester Hall, Oxford, 1626–47 ; published, among other works, ' De Ratione … Legendi Historias,' 1623. [lx. 432]

WHEATLEY, BENJAMIN ROBERT (1819–1884), bibliographer ; catalogued many public and private libraries, including that of Athenæum Club, 1843 ; indexed many books, including ' Journal of Statistical Society ' ; librarian of Royal Medical and Chirurgical Society, 1855–84. [lx. 433]

WHEATLEY, MRS. CLARA MARIA (*d.* 1838). [See POPE.]

WHEATLEY, FRANCIS (1747–1801), painter of portraits, portrait groups, landscapes, and scenes from daily or peasant life; first exhibited in London, 1765; first exhibited at Royal Academy, 1778; resided in Dublin and exhibited there, 1779–81; exhibited at Royal Academy, 1784–1801; R.A., 1791; copied Greuze's mannerisms. [lx. 434]

WHEATLEY, WILLIAM OF (*fl.* 1315). [See WILLIAM.]

WHEATLY, CHARLES (1686–1742), divine; educated at Merchant Taylors' School, 1699–1705; fellow of St. John's College, Oxford, 1707–13; M.A., 1713; 'lecturer' in various London churches, 1717–25; vicar of Furneaux Pelham, 1726–42; published sermons, doctrinal tracts, and, 1710, a popular commentary on the Book of Common Prayer. [lx. 435]

WHEATSTONE, SIR CHARLES (1802–1875), man of science and inventor; musical-instrument maker in London, 1823; presented to the Royal Society a memoir explaining 'Chladni's Figures,' 1833; professor of experimental physics, King's College, London, 1834; F.R.S., 1836; hon. D.C.L. Oxford, 1862; hon. LL.D. Cambridge, 1864; knighted, 1868; experimented, *c.* 1823, on sound and light; suggested the stereoscope, and, 1835, spectrum analysis; collaborated with (Sir) William Fothergill Cooke [q. v.] in producing and improving electric telegraph instruments; made important improvements in submarine telegraphy, magneto-electrical machines (dynamos), measurement of electrical force, and automatically recording instruments. [lx. 435]

WHEELER. [See also WHELER.]

WHEELER, DANIEL (1771–1840), quaker missionary; apprentice on merchantman, 1783; midshipman, royal navy, 1784; served in army, 1790–6; joined quakers, 1798; accepted as quaker minister, 1816; manager of Russian imperial farms at Ochta, 1818–28, and Shoosharry, 1828–31, occasionally visiting England; made missionary voyage in Polynesia and Australasia, 1833–8, and missionary tour in North America, 1839; died at New York; his 'Letters and Journals' published, 1835–9; 'Memoirs,' by his son, 1842. [lx. 437]

WHEELER, SIR HUGH MASSY (1789–1857), major-general, Indian army; ensign, 1803; lieutenant-colonel, 1835; brigadier, 1845; K.C.B., 1850; major-general, 1854; served with distinction in Afghan war, 1838–9, and Sikh wars, 1845–9; in command at Cawnpore, 1856; failed to appreciate gravity of impending mutiny, 1857, and to make sufficient preparations for defence of European non-combatants; capitulated on terms, after brave defence; murdered in the first massacre. [lx. 438]

WHEELER, JAMES TALBOYS (1824–1897), historian of India; bookseller in Oxford; issued summaries of ancient and scripture history and of Herodotean geography, 1848–55; employed to report on government records at Madras, 1860; assistant-secretary in the foreign department at Calcutta, 1862; secretary at Rangoon, 1870–3; reported on the records in the home and foreign departments at Calcutta from 1876; retired, 1891. His works on Indian history include 'History of Madras (1639–1748),' 1860–2, 'History of India,' 1867–81, and 'Mahratta States (1627 to 1858),' 1878. [lx. 440]

WHEELER, JOHN (*fl.* 1601–1608), secretary of Merchant Adventurers' Company; published 'Treatise of Commerce,' 1601, and 'Lawes . . . of . . . Merchantes Adventurers of . . . England,' 1608. [lx. 441]

WHEELER, MAURICE (1648?–1727), divine; chaplain of Christ Church, Oxford; M.A., 1670; rector of St. Ebbe's, Oxford, 1670–80; master of Gloucester Cathedral School, 1684–1708; prebendary of Lincoln, 1708; beneficed in Northamptonshire, 1680–1727; published 'The Oxford Almanac for 1673.' [lx. 441]

WHEELER, THOMAS (1754–1847), botanist; student at St. Thomas's Hospital, London, 1767; curator of Society of Apothecaries' Garden, Chelsea, 1778–1820; apothecary to Christ's Hospital, London, 1800, and St. Bartholomew's Hospital, London, 1806–30. [lx. 442]

WHEELOCKE, WHEELOCK, WHELOCKE, WHELOCK, or **WHELOC,** ABRAHAM (1593–1653), linguist;

M.A. Trinity College, Cambridge, 1618; fellow of Clare College, Cambridge, 1619–32; minister of St. Sepulchre's, Cambridge, 1622–42; librarian, Cambridge University, 1629–53; professor of Arabic, 1630; studied Persian; his name suggested for Anglo-Saxon professorship, 1638; published Anglo-Saxon version of Bede, 1643, translated 'Chronologia Saxonica,' and began Anglo-Saxon dictionary. [lx. 443]

WHELER. [See also WHEELER.]

WHELER, SIR FRANCIS (1656?–1694), admiral; lieutenant, 1678; captain, 1680; captured Algerine corsairs, 1681; knighted, 1688; blockaded Brest, 1689; commanded ship in actions off Beachy Head, 1690, and Barfleur, 1692; rear-admiral, 1693; failed in attempts on French West Indies and Canada, 1693; convoyed outward-bound Mediterranean merchantmen, 1694; wrecked, with most of his fleet, in hurricane off Malaga. [lx. 444]

WHELER, SIR GEORGE (1650–1723), traveller; M.A. Lincoln College, Oxford, 1683; D.D., 1702; student, Middle Temple, 1671; travelled in France and Italy, 1673–1675, and in Greece and Levant, 1675–6, collecting plants, coins, classical manuscripts, and antique marbles; published his 'Journey into Greece,' 1682; knighted, 1682; canon of Durham, 1684; rector of Houghton-le-Spring, 1709–23. [lx. 445]

WHELER, GRANVILLE (1701–1770), electrician; son of Sir George Wheler [q. v.]; rector of Leake, Nottinghamshire; F.R.S., 1728; experimented in electricity. [lx. 446]

WHELER, ROBERT BELL (1785–1857), antiquary; solicitor of Stratford-on-Avon; published 'History and Antiquities of,' 1806, and 'Guide to,' Stratford-on-Avon, 1814; 'Account of Birthplace of Shakespeare,' 1829; his collections now in Birthplace Museum. [lx. 446]

WHELPDALE, ROGER (*d.* 1423), bishop of Carlisle; fellow, *c.* 1402, and provost, 1404–21, of Queen's College, Oxford; bishop of Carlisle, 1420; bequeathed books to Balliol and Queen's Colleges, Oxford. [lx. 447]

WHETENHALL, EDWARD (1636–1713). [See WETENHALL.]

WHETHAMSTEDE or **BOSTOCK**, JOHN (*d.* 1465), abbot of St. Albans; became monk at St. Albans after 1401; prior of Gloucester College, Oxford, where he afterwards built library and chapel; D.D.; in first abbacy, 1420–40, repaired conventual buildings, and was involved in many lawsuits; attended council at Pavia, 1423; friend of Humphrey, duke of Gloucester [q. v.]; in second abbacy, 1451–65, built the library at St. Albans; wrote 'Granarium de viris illustribus' (partially preserved), turgid official letters, and doggerel Latin verse. [lx. 447]

WHETSTONE, GEORGE (1544?–1587?), author; spent his patrimony in riotous living; served in Low Countries against Spaniards, 1572–4; prefixed commendatory verses to George Gascoigne's 'Flowers,' 1575; published 'Rocke of Regard,' tales in prose and verse drawn from Italian, interspersed with poems addressed to friends, 1576; published 'Remembraunce,' obituary panegyric, on George Gascoigne, 1577, followed by others on Sir Nich. Bacon, 1579, Sir James Dier, and Thomas Radcliffe, earl of Sussex, 1583, Francis, earl of Bedford, 1585, and Sir Philip Sidney, 1587; published in miscellanies, 1577 and 1578; published, 1578, 'Promos and Cassandra,' a play in rhymed verse (never acted), the plot of which closely resembles Shakespeare's 'Measure for Measure'; sailed in Sir Humphrey Gilbert's [q. v.] Newfoundland voyage, 1578–9; visited Italy, 1580; published 'An Heptameron of Ciuill Discourses,'1582 (prose tales adapted from Giraldi Cinthio), 'A Mirour for Magestrates,' with descriptions of low life in London, 1584, and 'The honorable Reputation of a Souldier,' 1585, a collection of military anecdotes; served in Holland, 1585–6, taking part in the action at Zutphen; published 'The English Myrror,' 1586, containing in second part notices of conspiracies against Queen Elizabeth, and 'The Censure of a loyall Subiect,' 1587, a prose dialogue on the Babington conspiracy. [lx. 449]

WHETSTONE, SIR WILLIAM (*d.* 1711), rear-admiral; captain, 1689; rear-admiral in West Indies, 1702–3, and commander-in-chief, 1705–6; knighted, 1705; cashiered for allowing convoy to be captured by M. de Forbin, the privateer, 1707. [lx. 453]

WHEWELL, WILLIAM (1794–1866), master of Trinity College, Cambridge; schoolfellow at Lancaster grammar school of Sir Richard Owen [q. v.], the naturalist; exhibitioner of Trinity College, Cambridge, 1812; second wrangler and second Smith's prizeman, 1816; fellow, 1817; tutor, 1823–38; learned German thoroughly and helped to introduce the analytical methods of continental mathematicians; published treatises on 'Mechanics,' 1819, and 'Dynamics,' 1823; F.R.S., 1820; went summer tours, 1820–1831, resulting in 'Architectural Notes on German Churches,' 1830 (enlarged, 1835); F.G.S., 1827, and president, 1837–8; professor of mineralogy, Cambridge, 1828–1832; wrote in 1830 'Astronomy and General Physics considered with reference to Natural Theology,' the first of the 'Bridgewater Treatises' (published, 1833); published in the Royal Society's 'Transactions' fourteen laborious memoirs on tides, 1833–50; frequently attended British Association meetings, 1832–62; engaged in controversy with Sir William Hamilton as to value of mathematical training, 1836–7; published 'History of the Inductive Sciences,' 1837, and 'Philosophy of the Inductive Sciences,' 1840; Knightbridge professor of moral philosophy, 1838–55, publishing 'Lectures' on that subject. 1841–52; master of Trinity College, Cambridge, 1841–66; vice-chancellor of Cambridge University, 1843 and 1856; secured election of Prince Consort as chancellor of Cambridge University, 1847, and the institution of 'moral sciences' and 'natural sciences' triposes, 1848; published (anonymously) treatise denying probability of 'Plurality of Worlds,' 1853; enlarged buildings of Trinity College, Cambridge; founded professorship and scholarships for international law; published and edited many other works in natural and mathematical science, philosophy, and theology, and sermons. In philosophy he championed the old-fashioned form of 'intuitionism' against John Stuart Mill.   [lx. 454]

WHICHCORD, JOHN (1823–1885), architect; studied at King's College, London, and at the Royal Academy; travelled abroad; practised, 1850–8, in partnership with Arthur Ashpitel [q. v.], and afterwards independently, in London; president, Royal Institute of British Architects, 1879–81; F.S.A., 1848. His works include Grand Hotel, Brighton, St. Stephen's Club (1874), and many commercial houses in London; published antiquarian writings.   [lxi. 1]

WHICHCOTE or WHITCHCOTE, BENJAMIN (1609–1683), provost of King's College, Cambridge: B.A. Emmanuel College, Cambridge, 1630; M.A. and fellow, 1633; D.D., 1649; Sunday afternoon lecturer, Trinity Church, Cambridge, 1636; college tutor from 1634; rector of North Cadbury, 1643; provost of King's College Cambridge, 1644–60; rector of Milton, Cambridgeshire, c. 1649, till death; vice-chancellor of the university, 1650; ejected from provostship at Restoration; complied with Act of Uniformity and received cure of St. Anne's, Blackfriars, London, 1662; vicar of St. Lawrence Jewry, London, 1668; wrote religious works, published posthumously.   [lxi. 1]

WHICHCOTE, GEORGE (1794–1891), general; educated at Rugby; ensign, 52nd foot, 1811; served in Peninsular war and in Waterloo campaign; exchanged into 4th dragoon guards, 1822; major-general, 1857, general, 1871.   [lxi. 4]

WHICHELO, C. JOHN M. (d. 1865), exhibited water-colour paintings at Royal Academy from 1810. [lxi. 4]

WHIDDON, JACOB (d. 1595), sea-captain and servant of Sir Walter Ralegh; served against the Armada and was with Ralegh in his voyage to Guiana, 1595; died on the return journey at Trinidad.   [lxi. 4]

WHIDDON, SIR JOHN (d. 1576), judge; studied at Inner Temple; treasurer, 1538–40; serjeant, 1547; judge of queen's bench, 1553; knighted, 1555.   [lxi. 5]

WHINCOP, THOMAS (d. 1730), compiled a list of dramatic authors and of English dramas, published with 'Scanderbeg, a Tragedy,' 1747, under the nominal editorship of his widow.   [lxi. 5]

WHINYATES, SIR EDWARD CHARLES (1782–1865), general; studied at Woolwich; lieutenant, royal artillery, 1799; second captain, 1805; served with D troop, horse artillery, in Peninsula; captain, 1813; commanded second rocket troop at Waterloo, 1815; regimental lieutenant-colonel, 1830; K.H., 1823, and C.B.,

1831; director-general of artillery, 1852; commandant at Woolwich, 1852–6; general, 1864; K.C.B., 1860. [lxi. 5]

WHINYATES, FRANCIS FRANKLAND (1796–1887), general; brother of Sir Edward Charles Whinyates [q. v.]; entered East India Company's service as lieutenant-fire-worker in Madras artillery, 1813; left India, 1854; general, 1872.   [lxi. 7]

WHINYATES, FREDERICK WILLIAM (1793–1881), major-general; brother of Sir Edward Charles Whinyates [q. v.]; lieutenant, royal engineers, 1812; retired as major-general, 1855.   [lxi. 7]

WHINYATES, GEORGE BARRINGTON (1783–1808), navy captain; brother of Sir Edward Charles Whinyates [q. v.]; served chiefly in Mediterranean.   [lxi. 7]

WHINYATES, THOMAS (1778–1857), rear-admiral; brother of Sir Edward Charles Whinyates [q. v.]; lieutenant, 1799; commander, 1805; post-captain, 1812; served against United States, 1812; rear-admiral, 1846.   [lxi. 6]

WHIPPLE, GEORGE MATHEWS (1842–1893), physicist; educated at King's College, London; B.Sc. London, 1871; entered Kew Observatory, 1858, and became superintendent, 1876; F.R.A.S., 1872; member of the Meteorological Society, 1874; published scientific writings.   [lxi. 7]

WHISH, SIR WILLIAM SAMPSON (1787–1853), lieutenant-general; lieutenant, Bengal artillery, 1804; captain, 1807; major, 1821; lieutenant-colonel, 1826; C.B. (military), brigadier-general, and member of military board, 1838; major-general, 1841; received command of Punjab division at Lahore, 1848; commanded Multan field force, 1848; took part in siege of Mulraj, 1848–9; K.C.B., 1849; commanded Bengal division, 1849; lieutenant-general, 1851.   [lxi. 8]

WHISTLER, DANIEL (1619–1684), physician; B.A. Merton College, Oxford, 1642; M.A., 1644; M.D. Leyden, 1645; incorporated M.D. Oxford, 1647; professor of geometry at Gresham College, London, 1648; Linacre reader at Oxford, 1648; F.R.C.P., 1649, Harveian orator, 1659, registrar, 1674–82, and president, 1683; published 'De Morbo puerili Anglorum,' a treatise on rickets (reprinted, 1684).   [lxi. 9]

WHISTON, JOHN (d. 1780), bookseller; son of William Whiston [q. v.]; opened in Fleet Street, London, a bookseller's shop which was known as a meeting-place for men of letters. He was one of the earliest issuers of regular priced catalogues.   [lxi. 9]

WHISTON, WILLIAM (1667–1752), divine; B.A. Clare Hall, Cambridge, 1690; fellow, 1691; M.A., 1693; ordained deacon, 1693; chaplain to John Moore (1646–1714) [q. v.], bishop of Norwich; studied Newton's works and published, 1696, 'New Theory of the Earth,' which confirmed the narrative in Genesis on Newtonian grounds; vicar of Lowestoft-with-Kissingland, Suffolk, 1698–1703; deputy to Newton in the Lucasian professorship, 1701; succeeded Newton as professor, 1703; Boyle lecturer, 1707; wrote, 1708, an essay on the 'Apostolic Constitutions' which expounded Arian doctrines and occasioned his banishment from the university and (1710) the loss of his professorship; published 'Primitive Christianity Revived,' 1711, on which convocation voted an address for his prosecution; after some delay proceedings against him dropped; started society for promoting primitive Christianity, 1715; lectured in London, Bristol, Bath, and Tunbridge Wells on various subjects, comprising meteors, eclipses, and earthquakes, which he connected more or less with the fulfilment of prophecies; advocated in his last years a number of theories, the most famous of which was that the Tartars were the lost tribes. His portrait, by Mrs. Hoadly, is in the National Portrait Gallery, London. He issued more than fifty publications on religious, mathematical, and other subjects; his most successful work, a translation of Josephus, appeared, 1737, and has since been the established version.   [lxi. 10]

WHITAKER. [See also WHITTAKER.]

WHITAKER, SIR EDWARD (1660–1735), admiral; lieutenant under Matthew (afterwards Baron) Aylmer [q. v.], 1688; captain, 1690; flag-captain to Aylmer, 1694, and to Sir Clowdisley Shovell [q. v.], 1696; aide-de-camp to Sir George Byng [q. v.] at capture of Gibraltar, 1704; promoted rear-admiral of the blue and knighted, 1706; vice-admiral of blue, 1708, and of white, 1709. [lxi. 14]

WHITAKER, EDWARD WILLIAM (1752–1818), divine; B.A. Christ Church, Oxford, 1777; rector of St. Mary-de-Castro with All Saints, Canterbury, 1783–1818; founded Refuge for the Destitute; published religious and historical works. [lxi. 15]

WHITAKER, SIR FREDERICK (1812–1891), premier of New Zealand; qualified as solicitor in England; settled in practice in New Zealand, 1840; unofficial member of legislative council, 1845; member of provincial council formed under new constitution of 1852; member of legislative council, 1853; member of first general assembly of the colony, 1854; attorney-general, 1855, 1856, 1863, 1876, 1877, and 1887–90; premier, 1863–4 and 1882–3; superintendent of Auckland and member for Parnell in house of representatives, 1865–7; member for Waikato, 1876–7; K.C.M.G., 1884. [lxi. 15]

WHITAKER, JEREMIAH (1599–1654), puritan divine; B.A. Sidney Sussex College, Cambridge, 1619; rector of St. Mary Magdalen, Bermondsey, 1644; member of Westminster Assembly of Divines, 1643, and moderator, 1647. [lxi. 16]

WHITAKER, JOHN (1735–1808), historian of Manchester; B.A. Corpus Christi College, Oxford, 1755; M.A., 1759; fellow, 1763; B.D., 1767; ordained, 1760; F.S.A., 1771; rector of Ruan-Lanyhorn, Cornwall, 1777–1808. His works include 'History of Manchester,' 1771–5 (two volumes only published, but transcript of his manuscript continuation preserved at Chetham Library, Manchester), 'Mary Queen of Scots vindicated,' 1787, and other historical, antiquarian, and religious writings. He left in manuscript the 'Private Life of Mary Queen of Scots,' which was used by George Chalmers in his life of that queen, 1818. [lxi. 17]

WHITAKER, JOHN (1776–1847), member of the musical publishing firm of Button, Whitaker & Co.; composed several songs which attained considerable popularity. [lxi. 18]

WHITAKER, JOSEPH (1820–1895), publisher; apprenticed as bookseller in London; began business independently as theological publisher in Pall Mall; removed to 310 Strand, 1855; edited 'Gentleman's Magazine,' 1856–1859; founded 'Bookseller,' monthly journal, 1858; started annual publication of 'Whitaker's Almanac,' 1868; produced, 1874, 'Reference Catalogue of Current Literature' (latest edition, 1898); F.S.A., 1875. [lxi. 18]

WHITAKER, JOSEPH VERNON (1845–1895), editor; son of Joseph Whitaker [q. v.]; connected from 1875 with the 'Bookseller,' of which he became editor. [lxi. 19]

WHITAKER, THOMAS DUNHAM (1759–1821), topographer; LL.B. St. John's College, Cambridge, 1781; perpetual curate of Holme, Lancashire, 1797; LL.D., 1801; vicar of Whalley, 1809, and also of Blackburn, Lancashire, 1818–21; published topographical writings relating to Lancashire and Yorkshire and other works. [lxi. 19]

WHITAKER, TOBIAS (d. 1666), physician in ordinary to the royal household, 1660; published, 1638, 'The Tree of Humane Life,' advocating the use of wine as a universal remedy against disease. [lxi. 20]

WHITAKER, WILLIAM (1548–1595), master of St. John's College, Cambridge; educated at St. Paul's School, London, and Trinity College, Cambridge; B.A., 1568; major fellow and M.A., 1571; B.D. and incorporated at Oxford, 1578; canon of Norwich, 1578; regius professor of divinity, 1580–95; chancellor of St. Paul's, London; master of St. John's College, Cambridge, 1586–95; created D.D., 1587; canon of Canterbury, 1595; published and left in manuscript writings interpreting the teaching of the church of England in its most Calvinistic sense. [lxi. 21]

WHITAKER, WILLIAM (1629–1672), puritan divine; M.A. Queens' College, Cambridge, 1646; held living of St. Mary Magdalen, Bermondsey, London, from 1654; ejected under Act of Uniformity. [lxi. 23]

WHITBOURNE, SIR RICHARD (fl. 1579–1627), writer on Newfoundland, whither he first journeyed, c. 1579; went with commission from court of admiralty to hold courts of vice-admiralty, this being the first attempt to create a formal court of justice in Newfoundland, 1615; assisted Sir William Vaughan [q. v.] in efforts to form Welsh colony in Newfoundland, 1617; published, 1620, 'Discovrse and Discovery of New-fovnd-land,' which advocated reforms in the plantations and administration of the island and gained the favour of James I; knighted, c. 1623; served as lieutenant in navy, 1627. [lxi. 23]

WHITBREAD, SAMUEL (1758–1815), politician; son of Samuel Whitbread (d. 1796), brewer; educated at Eton, Christ Church, Oxford, and St. John's College, Cambridge; B.A., 1784; whig M.P. for Bedford, 1790; attached himself closely to Fox, and became a leading spirit in opposition to Pitt's government; led the attack by his party on Henry Dundas, first viscount Melville [q. v.], who was suspected of abuses in the naval department, 1805, and subsequently moved Melville's impeachment, and unsuccessfully conducted the case in Westminster Hall; introduced, 1807, an elaborate poor-law bill, some clauses of which afterwards passed their second reading as separate bills; adopted, 1807, a peace policy, and occasioned a party split which resulted in a practical disbandment of the opposition, 1809; expressed disapprobation of regency bill, 1811; made the acquaintance of Caroline, princess of Wales, 1812, and constituted himself her champion in the House of Commons; took much interest in rebuilding and reorganisation of Drury Lane Theatre, London, from 1809; died by his own hand. His portrait was painted by Gainsborough. [lxi. 24]

WHITBREAD, THOMAS (1618–1679). [See HARCOURT, THOMAS.]

WHITBY, DANIEL (1638–1726), polemical divine; B.A. Trinity College, Oxford, 1657; M.A., 1660; fellow, 1664; chaplain to Seth Ward [q. v.], bishop of Salisbury, 1668; prebendary of Salisbury, 1668; B.D. and D.D., and precentor of Salisbury, 1672; produced, from 1664, several anti-Romish controversial writings of considerable popularity, which, however, he lost by publication of 'The Protestant Reconciler,' 1682, pleading for concessions to nonconformists. His works include a 'Paraphrase and Commentary on the New Testament,' 1703, and numerous sermons and theological treatises. [lxi. 28]

WHITBY, STEPHEN OF (d. 1112). [See STEPHEN.]

WHITCHURCH or **WHYTCHURCH**, EDWARD (d. 1561), protestant publisher; probably a grocer in London; joined with Richard Grafton [q. v.] in arranging for distribution of printed copies of the bible in English, and published in London 'Thomas Matthews's Bible' (printed at Antwerp), the first complete version of the bible in English; with Grafton published Coverdale's corrected version of the New Testament (printed at Paris), 1538; with Grafton set up a press in London and published 'The Great Bible,' 1539; with Grafton printed first edition of Book of Common Prayer, 1549. [lxi. 30]

WHITE, ADAM (1817–1879), naturalist; engaged in zoological department of British Museum, 1835–63; F.L.S., 1846–55; published numerous writings relating to insects, crustacea, and mammalia. [lxi. 31]

WHITE, ALICE MARY MEADOWS (1839–1884), composer; née Smith; married Frederick Meadows White, 1867; produced, from 1861, numerous musical compositions. [lxi. 31]

WHITE, ANDREW (1579–1656), jesuit missionary; educated at Douay; secular priest, 1605; returned to England; banished from England, 1606; admitted to Society of Jesus at Louvain, 1607; returned as missioner to England, 1609; professed of the four vows, 1619; went to America and founded Maryland mission, 1633; died in England. He left manuscripts relating to Maryland. [lxi. 32]

WHITE, ANTHONY (1782–1849), surgeon; M.B. Emmanuel College, Cambridge, 1804; apprenticed to Sir Anthony Carlisle [q. v.]; M.R.C.S., 1803; Hunterian orator, 1831, and president, 1834 and 1842; surgeon to Westminster Hospital, London, 1823; consulting surgeon, 1846; the first to excise the head of the femur for disease of the hip-joint. [lxi. 32]

WHITE, BLANCO (1775–1841). [See WHITE, JOSEPH BLANCO.]

WHITE, CHARLES (1728–1813), surgeon ; assisted in founding, 1752, and was surgeon at, Manchester Infirmary ; F.R.S. and M.R.C S., 1762 ; joint-founder of Manchester Lying-in Hospital (now St. Mary's Hospital), 1790 ; published surgical and other works. He was widely known for the revolution he effected in the practice of midwifery. [lxi. 33]

WHITE, FRANCIS (1564 ?–1638), bishop of Ely ; brother of John White (1570 ?–1615) [q. v.] ; B.A. Gonville and Caius College, Cambridge, 1583 ; M.A., 1586 ; D.D., 1618 ; dean of Carlisle, 1622–6 ; senior dean of Sion College, London, 1625 ; bishop of Carlisle, 1626, of Norwich, 1629, and of Ely, 1631–8 ; published religious controversial treatises. [lxi. 34]

WHITE, FRANCIS (d. 1711), original proprietor of White's Chocolate House ; opened Chocolate House on east side of St. James's Street, London, 1693 ; removed to west side, 1697. After his death the business was carried on successively by his widow and, 1729, by his assistant, John Arthur. ' White's ' club most probably originated in the coffee-house, c. 1697. [lxi. 35]

WHITE, FRANCIS BUCHANAN WHITE (1842–1894), botanist and entomologist ; M.D. Edinburgh, 1864 ; assisted in founding Perthshire Society of Natural Science, and was president, 1867–72 and 1884–92 ; contributed largely to the society's ' Proceedings ' and ' Transactions,' and conducted its magazine, ' The Scottish Naturalist,' 1871–82. His ' Flora of Perthshire ' was published posthumously, 1898. [lxi. 35]

WHITE, GEORGE (1684 ?–1732), mezzotint engraver ; son of Robert White (1645–1703) [q. v.] ; executed portraits in pencil, crayon, mezzotint, and oils ; first used the etched line to strengthen mezzotint work. [lxi. 73]

WHITE, GILBERT (1720–1793), naturalist ; born at Selborne, Hampshire ; educated under Thomas Warton (1688 ?–1745) [q. v.] at Basingstoke ; B.A. Oriel College, Oxford, 1743 ; fellow, 1744 ; M.A., 1746 ; curate at Swarraton, and, 1751, to Dr. Bristow, vicar of Selborne ; proctor of Oxford University and dean of Oriel College, Oxford, 1752 ; curate of Durley, near Bishop's Waltham ; incumbent of Moreton-Pinkney, 1757 ; resigned curacy of Durley for that of Faringdon, near Selborne, c. 1758 ; held for a short time curacy of West Deane ; in 1751 began to keep a ' Garden Kalendar,' for which, in 1767, he adopted a more elaborate form, ' Naturalist's Journal ' (diaries in the British Museum) ; made, 1767, acquaintance of Thomas Pennant [q. v.], and began with him a correspondence which formed the basis of White's ' Natural History and Antiquities of Selborne ' ; a series of letters, 1769–87, written to Daines Barrington contained in the second part of his ' Natural History ' ; his book issued by his brother Benjamin White (1725–1794), the publisher, of Fleet Street, London, in 1789, and soon highly valued by naturalists ; contributed to the Royal Society's ' Transactions ' two papers on the ' Hirundines,' 1774 and 1775 ; died at his house, The Wakes, Selborne, and was buried in Selborne churchyard. ' A Naturalist's Calendar . . . extracted from the Papers of the late Rev. Gilbert White, M.A.,' appeared, 1795 ; his ' Works on Natural History,' comprising ' Selborne ' and the ' Naturalist's Calendar,' appeared, 1802, and has been frequently reissued, an edition, 1837, with notes by Bell, Daniell, Owen, and Yarrell, long remaining the standard ; it was revised by Mr. Harting, 1875. In 1876 the correspondence between White and Robert Marsham was printed, and in 1877 appeared the classical edition of White's ' Selborne ' by Thomas Bell (1792–1880) [q. v.] [lxi. 36]

WHITE, HENRY (1812–1880), historical writer ; educated at Trinity College, Cambridge ; Ph.D. Heidelberg ; published ' History of France,' 1850, ' Massacre of St. Bartholomew,' 1867, and other works. [lxi. 48]

WHITE, HENRY KIRKE (1785–1806), poet ; son of a butcher of Nottingham ; articled as lawyer at Nottingham ; contributed verses to ' Monthly Preceptor ' ; published, 1803, ' Clifton Grove . . . with other Poems,' which attracted the favourable notice of Southey, who thenceforth interested himself in White's career ; obtained sizarship at St. John's College, Cambridge, where overwork brought about his death. His ' Remains,' including his fragment, ' The Christiad,' a new concluding stanza to Waller's ' Go, lovely Rose,' and ' Melancholy Hours ' (essays), with a ' life ' by Southey, appeared in 1807. [lxi. 48]

WHITE, HUGH (fl. 1107 ?–1155 ?). [See HUGH.]

WHITE, JAMES (d. 1799), author ; B.A. Trinity College, Dublin, 1780 ; published editions of classical authors, three historical novels, and other writings. [lxi. 50]

WHITE, JAMES (1775–1820), author of ' Falstaff's Letters ' ; educated at Christ's Hospital, London, with Charles Lamb [q. v.], whose lifelong friend he became ; clerk in treasurer's office, 1790 ; founded an advertising agency at 33 Fleet Street, London. He frequently impersonated, in the company of his friends, the character of Falstaff, and published, 1796, ' Original Letters, &c., of Sir John Falstaff and his Friends.' [lxi. 50]

WHITE, JAMES (1803–1862), author ; B.A. Pembroke College, Oxford, 1827 ; vicar of Loxley, 1833 ; retired to Bonchurch, Isle of Wight, where he produced a number of Scottish historical tragedies and other historical and miscellaneous writings, including ' The Eighteen Christian Centuries,' 1858. [lxi. 51]

WHITE, JAMES (1840–1885). [See JEZREEL, JAMES JERSHOM.]

WHITE, JEREMIAH (1629–1707), chaplain to Cromwell ; B.A. Trinity College, Cambridge, 1649 ; M.A., 1653 ; domestic chaplain and preacher to council of state ; left religious writings, published posthumously ; wrote account of sufferings of dissenters after Restoration, not known to be extant. [lxi. 51]

WHITE, JOHN (1510 ?–1560), bishop of Winchester ; educated at Winchester and New College, Oxford ; fellow, 1527–34 ; B.A., 1529 ; M.A., 1534 ; D.D., 1555 ; master of Winchester College ; warden, 1541 ; prebendary of Winchester, 1541 ; imprisoned in the Tower of London, 1551, as opponent of the protestants ; prebendary of Lichfield, 1552 ; bishop of Lincoln, 1554 ; presided at Ridley's trial, 1555 ; bishop of Winchester, 1556 ; preached funeral sermon of Queen Mary, 1558, incurred disfavour of Queen Elizabeth, was deprived of bishopric, 1559, and imprisoned in the Tower of London ; released, 1559 ; wrote theological works in verse and prose. [lxi. 52]

WHITE or **WITH**, JOHN (fl. 1585–1590), Virginian pioneer ; sailed with Sir Richard Grenville, 1585, and was one of the first settlers in Virginia ; returned with Drake, 1586 ; conducted band of settlers sent out by Ralegh, and returned, 1587 ; visited Roanoke, 1590 ; made watercolour drawings of Virginian subjects. [lxi. 54]

WHITE, JOHN (1570–1615), divine ; brother of Francis White (1564 ?–1638) [q. v.] ; B.A. Gonville and Caius College, Cambridge, 1590 ; M.A., 1593 ; D.D., 1612 ; rector of Barsham, Suffolk, 1609 ; chaplain in ordinary to James I, c. 1614 ; published, 1608, ' The Way to the True Church,' a treatise against Romanism, which occasioned considerable controversy. [lxi. 55]

WHITE, alias BRADSHAW, JOHN, afterwards AUGUSTINE (1576–1618), Benedictine monk ; educated at jesuit seminaries at St. Omer and Valladolid ; entered monastery of San Benito, Valladolid ; proceeded to Compostella and as novice took name of Augustine, 1599 ; professed, 1600 ; came as missionary to England, 1603 ; vicar-general, 1604 ; chaplain-general at Ostend to English regiment under Thomas Arundell, first baron Arundell of Wardour [q. v.], in service of Archduke Albert, 1605–6 ; succeeded, in spite of opposition from Parsons and other jesuits, in effecting the foundation of Benedictine monastery of St. Gregory at Douay, 1605 ; brought about reunion of all Benedictines in England into one congregation, but the terms of agreement being resented by many of the brethren was removed and deprived of vicarship, 1612 ; founded and presided over house for English monks in Paris. [lxi. 55]

WHITE, JOHN (1590–1645), parliamentarian ; commonly called CENTURY WHITE ; educated at Jesus College, Oxford ; barrister, Middle Temple, 1618, bencher, 1641 ; joined in forming committee known as feoffees for impropriations, which aimed at making a better provision for puritan preaching ministry, 1625 ; but feoffment dissolved by decree of exchequer chamber, 1633 ; M.P. for Southwark, 1640 ; chairman of committee to inquire into immoralities of the clergy ; vigorously opposed the episcopal system ; did much to assist first colonists of Massachusetts. [lxi. 58]

WHITE, JOHN (1575–1648), puritan divine; called the patriarch of Dorchester; of Winchester College and New College, Oxford; fellow of New College, 1595; M.A., 1601; rector of Holy Trinity, Dorchester, 1606; interested himself, *c.* 1624, in sending out a colony of Dorset men to Massachusetts, and subsequently brought about formation of Massachusetts Company; probably author of the 'Planters' Plea,' published anonymously, 1630; took refuge at the Savoy, London, on outbreak of civil war, 1642; rector of Lambeth, 1643; member of Westminster Assembly of Divines; published religious writings. [lxi. 59]

WHITE, JOHN (1826–1891), historian of the Maoris; went to New Zealand, 1832, and ultimately became magistrate of Central Wanganui; published 'Ancient History of the Maori,' 1889; died at Auckland. [lxi. 61]

WHITE, JOHN MEADOWS (1799?–1863), legal writer; brother of Robert Meadows White [q. v.]; practised as parliamentary solicitor in London; became authority on tithe legislation; published legal writings. [lxi. 75]

WHITE, JOHN TAHOURDIN (1809–1893), scholar; M.A. Corpus Christi College, Oxford, 1839; D.D., 1866; assistant-master, Christ's Hospital, London, 1836–69; rector of St. Martin, Ludgate, London, 1868; published numerous scholastic works and critical editions of classical authors; joint-compiler of White and Riddle's 'Latin-English Dictionary,' 1862. [lxi. 61]

WHITE, JOSEPH (1745–1814), orientalist and theologian; of humble parentage; financially assisted by John Moore (1730–1805) [q. v.] (afterwards archbishop of Canterbury); B.A. Wadham College, Oxford, 1769; M.A., 1773; B.D., 1779; D.D., 1787; Laudian professor of Arabic, 1775–1814; edited for delegates of Clarendon press Harklensian version of New Testament, 1778; Bampton lecture, 1784, taking as his subject a comparison between 'Mahometism' and Christianity; in writing the discourses had great assistance from Samuel Badcock [q. v.], who concealed the secret of his share in the work, which, however, was revealed after Badcock's death; prebendary of Gloucester, 1788; published, 1790, an account of his literary obligations to Badcock; regius professor of Hebrew at Oxford, 1804–14; wrote in connection with textual study of bible; edited Abdullatif's description of Egypt, 1800. [lxi. 62]

WHITE, JOSEPH BLANCO (1775–1841), theological writer; born at Seville; studied for ministry; entered Seville University, 1790, and was ordained subdeacon, 1796; priest, 1800; chaplain in Chapel Royal of St. Ferdinand, Seville, 1802; 'religious instructor' at Pestalozzian school at Madrid; gave up belief in Christianity, abandoned priesthood, and came to England, 1810; conducted the 'Español,' a monthly periodical partly circulated in Spain by the English government in defence of the national cause; again embraced Christianity, 1812, and qualified as English clergyman, 1814; studied at Oxford; tutor to Lord Holland's son, 1815–17; contributed, from 1820, to 'New Monthly,' edited by Thomas Campbell; published 'Evidences against Catholicism,' 1825; received degree of M.A. Oxford in recognition of his services to the church, and settled at Oriel College, 1826; became close friend of Whately, and when Whately was appointed archbishop of Dublin, 1831, accompanied him as tutor to his son and that of his friend Senior; adopted unitarian views and resided at Liverpool, 1835 till death. His publications include 'Observations on Heresy and Orthodoxy,' 1835, and translations into Spanish of Paley's 'Evidences,' 'Book of Common Prayer,' and other works. He wrote the sonnet on 'Night and Death' (published in the 'Bijou,' 1828), which Coleridge declared to be 'the finest and most grandly conceived sonnet in our language.' [lxi. 63]

WHITE, MATTHEW (*fl.* 1610–1630), organist at Christ Church, Oxford, 1611; Mus.Doc. Oxford, 1629; has been confused with Robert White (1540?–1574) [q. v.] [lxi. 72]

WHITE, SIR MICHAEL (1791–1868), lieutenant-general; of Westminster School; lieutenant, 24th dragoons, 1805; served in India; lieutenant-colonel, 1839; commanded cavalry in Afghan campaign, 1842; C.B., 1842; in Sikh wars, 1845–6 and 1848–9; aide-de-camp to Queen Victoria, 1845; colonel, 1846; lieutenant-general, 1860; K.C.B., 1862. [lxi. 67]

WHITE, SIR NICHOLAS (*d.* 1593), master of the rolls in Ireland; recorder of Waterford, *c.* 1564; seneschal of Wexford and constable and ruler of Leighlin and Ferns, 1568; privy councillor, 1569; master of the rolls in Ireland, 1572; supported the agitation of the gentry of the Pale against cess by refusing to sign order for their committal, and excited animosity of Sir Henry Sidney, and was temporarily suspended from office on charge of remissness, 1578; served under Sir William Pelham [q. v.] in Munster, 1580; knighted, 1584, by Sir John Perrot, the lord deputy, subservience to whom earned him the ill-will of the English members of the council, through which, when Perrot was charged with high treason, he (White) was sent to England and committed to the Marshalsea; retained office and died in Ireland. [lxi. 68]

WHITE, RICHARD (*d.* 1584), Roman catholic martyr; educated at St. John's College, Cambridge; schoolmaster in East Denbighshire and Flintshire; fell under influence of one of the Douay missioners, and subsequently suffered martyrdom. [lxi. 70]

WHITE, RICHARD (1539–1611), jurist and historian; of Winchester College and New College, Oxford; B.A., 1559; king's professor of civil and canon laws at Douay, and subsequently 'magnificus rector' of the university; created 'comes palatinus'; ordained priest and appointed canon of St. Peter's, Douay. His works include 'Historiarum (Britanniæ) libri (1–11),' 1597–1607. [lxi. 70]

WHITE, *alias* JOHNSON, RICHARD (1604–1687) devotional writer; educated at English College at Douay; adopted name of Johnson, 1623; confessor of English Augustinian canonesses at St. Monica's, Louvain, 1630–50; left devotional treatises in manuscript. [lxi. 71]

WHITE, ROBERT (1540?–1574), musician; Mus. Bac. Cambridge, 1560; master of choristers at Ely Cathedral, *c.* 1561; master of choristers and organist at Westminster Abbey, *c.* 1570; he attained a high reputation as a composer; published nothing himself; some of his compositions printed in collections published after his death. [lxi. 71]

WHITE, ROBERT (1645–1703), draughtsman and engraver; engraved and drew numerous portraits of public and literary characters of his period. [lxi. 73]

WHITE, ROBERT (1802–1874), antiquary; engaged in the counting-house of a plumber and brassfounder at Newcastle, 1825–65; published works and papers relating to border legends and ministrelsy, several volumes of poems, and other writings. [lxi. 73]

WHITE, ROBERT MEADOWS (1798–1865), Anglo-Saxon scholar; B.A. Magdalen College, Oxford, 1819; M.A., 1822; D.D., 1843; ordained deacon, 1821; priest, 1822; fellow, 1824–47; Rawlinson professor, 1834–9; rector of Slimbridge, 1846–65; edited the 'Ormulum,' a harmonised narrative of the gospels in verse (1852). [lxi. 74]

WHITE, SAMUEL (1733–1811). [See WHYTE.]

WHITE, STEPHEN (1575–1647?), Irish jesuit; educated at Irish seminary at Salamanca; joined jesuits, 1595; professor of scholastic theology at Ingoldstadt, 1606–9; rector of college at Cassel; transcribed many valuable manuscripts, one of which, Adamnan's life of St. Columba, was used by Ussher in his work on ecclesiastical antiquities. Several treatises by him were printed posthumously. [lxi. 75]

WHITE, SIR THOMAS (1492–1567), founder of St. John's College, Oxford; was apprenticed to member of Merchant Taylors' Company and, 1523, began business in London; first renter warden of company, 1530; senior warden, 1533; master, *c.* 1535; alderman for Cornhill, 1544; sheriff, 1547; one of promoters of Muscovy Company, 1553; knighted, 1553; lord mayor of London, 1553; obtained royal licence to found St. John's College, Oxford, 1555; purchased, 1559, Gloucester Hall, Oxford, which he opened as a hall for a hundred scholars, 1560; took part in foundation of Merchant Taylors' School; buried in St. John's College chapel. Portraits of him are at St. John's College. [lxi. 76]

WHITE, THOMAS (1550?–1624), founder of Sion College, London; B.A. Magdalen Hall, Oxford, 1570; M.A., 1573; vicar of St. Dunstan-in-the-West, London, 1575; B.D., 1581; D.D., 1585; prebendary of St. Paul's Cathedral, 1588; treasurer of Salisbury, 1590; canon of Christ Church, Oxford, 1591; canon of Windsor, 1593;

founded White's professorship of moral philosophy at Oxford, 1621 ; made provision in his will for foundation of Sion College, London, designed as a guild of the clergy of London and its suburbs, with an almshouse for twenty persons ; published sermons. His portrait is at Sion College. [lxi. 78]

WHITE, THOMAS (1593–1676), philosopher and controversialist, who wrote under pseudonyms of ALBIUS, ANGLUS, and BLACLOE or BLACKLOW ; educated at English Roman catholic college at St. Omer and Douay, and at Valladolid ; B.D. and teacher of classics, philosophy, and theology at Douay ; president of English college at Lisbon ; priest in England ; again at Douay, 1650 ; finally settled in London, where he published works which occasioned much controversy, including ' Institutiones Sacræ,' 1652, and 'Obedience and Government,' 1655, which were censured by the university of Douay, and, with other writings attacking the pope's personal infallibility, by the court of inquisition. Eventually he recanted his opinions. [lxi. 79]

WHITE, THOMAS (1628–1698), bishop of Peterborough ; B.A. St. John's College, Cambridge, 1646 ; created D.D. Oxford, 1683 ; vicar of Newark-on-Trent, 1660 ; rector of All Hallows the Great, London, 1666–79 ; rector of Bottesford, 1679–85 ; chaplain to the Lady, (afterwards Queen) Anne, daughter of James, duke of York, 1683 ; archdeacon of Nottingham, 1683 ; bishop of Peterborough, 1685 ; one of the six bishops who with Sancroft, archbishop of Canterbury, petitioned against James II's second ' Declaration of Indulgence,' 4 May 1688, and with them was tried and acquitted (June) ; refused oaths to William and Mary, 1689 ; deprived of see, 1690. [lxi. 81]

WHITE, THOMAS (1830–1888), Canadian politician ; born in Montreal ; founded and conducted, 1853–60, ' Peterborough Review ' ; founded ' Hamilton Spectator,' 1864 ; member of Dominion House of Commons for Cardwell, 1878–88 ; did much to assist emigrants to Ontario. [lxi. 83]

WHITE, WALTER (1811–1893), miscellaneous writer ; worked as cabinet-maker at Reading till 1834, and in New York, 1834–9 ; 'attendant' in library of Royal Society, 1844 ; assistant-secretary and librarian, 1861–84 ; published accounts of holiday walks, and other writings. [lxi. 83]

WHITE, WILLIAM (_fl._ 1620), left musical compositions in manuscript ; has been confused with Robert White (1540 ?–1574) [q. v.] [lxi. 73]

WHITE, WILLIAM (1604–1678), divine ; M.A. Wadham College, Oxford, 1628 ; master of Magdalen College school, Oxford, 1632 ; ejected by parliamentary commissioners, 1648 ; rector of Pusey, and _c._ 1662, of Appleton ; published works in Latin under name of 'Gulielmus Phalerius.' [lxi. 84]

WHITE, SIR WILLIAM ARTHUR (1824–1891), diplomatist ; educated at Trinity College, Cambridge ; clerk to consul-general at Warsaw, 1857 ; vice-consul, 1861 ; consul at Danzig, 1864 ; British agent and consul-general in Servia, 1875 ; ably assisted Lord Salisbury at conference of Constantinople, 1876 ; envoy extraordinary and minister plenipotentiary at Bucharest, 1879 ; envoy extraordinary, 1885, and special ambassador extraordinary and plenipotentiary, 1886, at Constantinople ; hon. LL.D. Cambridge, 1886 ; G.C.B. and privy councillor, 1888.
[lxi. 84]

WHITEFIELD, GEORGE (1714–1770), leader of Calvinistic methodists ; born at Gloucester and educated at St. Mary de Crypt school and Pembroke College, Oxford ; B.A., 1736 ; joined ' Society of Methodists' ; 1735 ; ordained deacon, 1736 ; engaged in missionary preaching and gained great popularity, 1737 ; made successful missionary journey to Georgia, 1738–9, and was appointed by the Georgia trustees minister of Savannah ; ordained priest at Christ Church, Oxford, 1739 ; returned to Savannah and founded an orphanage, 1740, the maintenance of which for the remainder of his life was an important factor in his work ; left his work as incumbent of Savannah largely in the hand of a lay delegate, and engaged in evangelical preaching in New York, Pennsylvania, Maryland, Virginia, Carolina, and elsewhere, and was suspended from his ministry for ceremonial irregularities by the commissary's court at Charleston ; proceeded to Boston, where his preaching gave new vitality to the Calvinistic position, and his followers and those

of Wesley thenceforth formed rival parties ; returned to London and opened, 1741, Moorfields tabernacle, a temporary shed, which was replaced by a brick building, 1753 ; preached with great success in Scotland, 1741 and 1742 ; presided at first conference of Calvinistic methodists held at Watford, near Caerphilly, 1743 ; in America, 1744–8 ; domestic chaplain to Lady Huntingdon, 1748 ; visited Scotland, where the synods of Glasgow, Lothian, and Perth passed resolutions intended to exclude him from churches, 1748 ; visited Ireland, 1751, and America, 1751–2 ; compiled his hymn-book, 1753 ; again in America, 1754–5 ; opened, 1756, chapel in Tottenham Court Road, London (rebuilt, 1899), and tabernacle at Bristol ; in America, 1763–5 ; opened Lady Huntingdon's chapels at Bath, 1765, and Tunbridge Wells, 1769, and her college at Trevecca, 1768 ; finally embarked for America, 1769 ; settled conversion of orphanage into Bethesda College (destroyed by fire, 1773) ; published sermons and autobiographical and other writings ; died at Newburyport, Massachusetts. His portrait (_c._ 1737) by John Woolaston is in the National Portrait Gallery. [lxi. 84]

WHITEFOORD, CALEB (1734–1810), diplomatist ; natural son of Charles Whitefoord [q. v.] ; educated at Edinburgh University ; in wine-merchant's office in London ; secretary to commission which concluded peace with United States at Paris, 1782 ; F.R.S., 1784 ; F.S.A. ; published political squibs ; mentioned in Goldsmith's ' Retaliation' ; his portrait painted by Reynolds.
[lxi. 92]

WHITEFOORD, CHARLES (_d._ 1753), soldier ; captain in Royal Irish at Minorca, 1738 ; accompanied West India expedition, 1740 ; fought at Carthagena, and was lieutenant-colonel, 5th marines, 1741 ; fought as volunteer against Scottish rebels, 1745, in which capacity his conduct at Prestonpans suggested to Sir Walter Scott incidents in ' Waverley ' ; colonel, 1752. [lxi. 93]

WHITEHALL, ROBERT (1625–1685), poetaster ; of Westminster and Christ Church, Oxford ; B.A., 1647 ; expelled, 1648 ; submitted to parliamentarians and was elected fellow of Merton College, Oxford, 1650 ; M.A., 1652 ; M.B., 1657 ; tutor to John Wilmot, second earl of Rochester [q. v.] ; subwarden of Merton College, Oxford, 1671 ; published chiefly congratulatory odes. [lxi. 94]

WHITEHEAD, CHARLES (1804–1862), poet, novelist, and dramatist ; published, 1831, ' The Solitary,' a poem, which met with warm approval, and, 1834, ' The Autobiography of Jack Ketch,' the success of which obtained for him an invitation to write humorous letterpress to a monthly issue to be illustrated by Robert Seymour (1800 ?–1836) [q. v.] ; pleaded inability, and recommended Charles Dickens, who accordingly wrote ' Pickwick Papers' ; his career wrecked by intemperance ; died in Australia. His most successful play was the ' Cavalier' (blank verse), 1836. [lxi. 95]

WHITEHEAD, DAVID (1492 ?–1571), divine ; probably educated at Oxford ; took holy orders ; fled to continent on Mary's accession, 1553 ; took charge of exile congregation at Frankfort, 1554 ; supported Richard Cox [q. v.] against Knox, and was chosen pastor, 1555 ; resigned, 1556 ; returned to England on Queen Elizabeth's accession, 1558 ; sequestered for refusing to subscribe, 1564. [lxi. 96]

WHITEHEAD, GEORGE (1636 ?–1723), quaker ; became a quaker about 1650 ; started as itinerant preacher, 1654 ; suffered considerable persecution and was frequently imprisoned ; had many audiences with Charles II, James II (who as a result of his interviews issued a declaration for liberty of conscience), William III, George I, and the Prince of Wales (George II), greatly improving by his efforts the legal status of the Friends, and establishing the sect on a sound civil and political basis ; engaged on many occasions in public disputes, and published controversial works dealing with all the principal features of his creed. [lxi. 98]

WHITEHEAD, HUGH (_d._ 1551), first dean of Durham ; last prior of Durham, 1519–40 ; appointed dean of Durham, 1541 ; implicated in the fictitious charges of treason brought against Cuthbert Tunstall [q. v.], bishop of Durham, 1550–1, and imprisoned in the Tower of London ; died in the Tower of London.
[lxi. 96]

WHITEHEAD, JAMES (1812 - 1885), physician ; F.C.S., 1845 ; M.R.C.P., 1859 ; M.D. St. Andrews, 1850 ; practised in Manchester, where he was joint-founder of the Clinical Hospital for Women and Children, as it was afterwards named ; published medical works. [lxi. 101]

WHITEHEAD, JOHN (1630-1696), quaker ; became quaker, c. 1645 ; first preached, 1652 ; served in the army, 1648-53 ; suffered frequent imprisonment in various parts of the country for his religious views ; published controversial writings. [lxi. 102]

WHITEHEAD, JOHN (1740 ?-1804), physician and biographer ; joined the methodists early in life and acted as lay preacher in Bristol ; became a quaker ; studied medicine at Leyden ; M.D. Leyden, 1780 ; physician to London dispensary, 1781 ; L.R.C.P., 1782 ; returned to methodists, 1784, and with Thomas Coke [q. v.] and Henry Moore (1751-1844) [q. v.] was John Wesley's literary executor ; arranged with Coke and Moore to prepare biography of John Wesley, though eventually, disagreements having arisen, the life was issued by Coke and Moore, 1792 ; having retained John Wesley's papers, published an independent ' Life,' 1793-6. [lxi. 103]

WHITEHEAD, JOHN (1860-1899), ornithologist ; made valuable ornithological collections in Borneo and the Philippines ; published 'Exploration of Mount Kina Balu,' 1893. [lxi. 104]

WHITEHEAD, PAUL (1710-1774), satirist : studied law in the Temple ; confined several years in Fleet prison, London, whence he issued political squibs, including ' State Dunces,' 1733 ; published ' Manners,' 1739, and ' Honour,' 1747 ; paid hanger-on of the ' Prince's friends ' ; secretary and steward of the ' monks of Medmenham Abbey ' ; held a subordinate post in the treasury ; spent last years at Twickenham ; was severely criticised by Churchill in his satires (1763-4) ; collected works published, 1777 ; his portrait painted by Gainsborough. [lxi. 104]

WHITEHEAD, WILLIAM (1715 - 1785), poet laureate ; educated at Winchester ; B.A. Clare Hall, Cambridge, 1739 ; fellow, 1742 ; M.A., 1743 ; tutor to George Bussy Villiers, viscount Grandison (afterwards fourth Earl of Jersey) [q. v.] ; produced at Drury Lane, London, tragedies, the ' Roman Father,' 1750, and ' Creusa,' 1754 ; secretary and registrar of the order of the Bath, c. 1755 ; poet laureate, 1757 ; produced the ' School for Lovers ' (comedy) at Drury Lane, 1762 ; subsequently became Garrick's reader of plays. His productions as poet laureate met with much unfriendly comment, to which he replied in ' A Charge to the Poets,' 1762, but his earlier writings are not without merit. His ' Plays and Poems ' were collected, 1774, and a complete edition of his poems appeared, 1788. [lxi. 106]

WHITEHORNE. [See WHITHORNE.]

WHITEHURST, JOHN (1713-1788), horologer ; engaged in business as maker of chronometers and scientific instruments at Derby, 1736-75 ; was appointed stamper of money-weights, and removed to London, 1775 ; F.R.S., 1779 ; published ' An Attempt towards obtaining invariable Measures of Length, Capacity, and Weight from the Mensuration of Time,' 1787, and other scientific writings. [lxi. 108]

WHITELAW, JAMES (1749-1813), statistician and philanthropist ; B.A. Trinity College, Dublin, 1771 ; held successively livings of St. James's and St. Catherine's, Dublin, and afterwards with St. Catherine's that of Castlereagh ; formed Meath charitable loan, 1808, and other philanthropic institutions ; made census of city of Dublin, 1798-1805 ; began with John Warburton ' History of Dublin,' which was completed by Robert Walsh [q. v.], and published, 1818. [lxi. 109]

WHITELOCKE, BULSTRODE (1605-1675), keeper of the great seal ; son of Sir James Whitelocke [q. v.] ; educated at Merchant Taylors' School and St. John's College, Oxford ; called to bar at Middle Temple, 1626, and was treasurer, 1628 ; M.P., Stafford, 1626 ; member for Marlow in Long parliament ; chairman of committee which managed prosecution of Strafford ; parliamentary governor of Henley, 1644 ; repeatedly engaged in overtures for peace ; one of four commissioners of great seal, 1648 ; member of committee appointed to

draw up charge against king and consider method of trial, but declined to take any part in proceedings ; member of council of state of republic ; one of three commissioners of the great seal, 1649 and 1654-5 ; ambassador to Sweden, 1653-4, where he conducted negotiations for treaty of amity : returned as member for Buckinghamshire, Bedford, and city of Oxford, 1654, and Buckinghamshire, 1656 ; one of commissioners of treasury, 1654 ; deprived of office as commissioner of great seal owing to objections to reform in procedure in court of chancery introduced by Protector, 1655 ; member of committee for trade and navigation, 1655 ; chairman of committee appointed to urge Cromwell to accept crown ; again commissioner of great seal, 1659 ; member and afterwards president of new council of state on fall of Richard Cromwell ; member of committee of safety which succeeded council of state, and of committee to draw up scheme for new constitution ; after Restoration escaped punishment and lived in retirement. He wrote ' Memorials of English Affairs ' (1625 to 1660), first published, 1682, ' Journal of the Swedish Embassy ' (1653-4), first published, 1772, and other biographical and miscellaneous works. An anonymous portrait of Whitelocke is in the National Portrait Gallery. [lxi. 110]

WHITELOCKE, EDMUND (1565-1608), courtier ; brother of Sir James Whitelocke [q. v.] ; B.A. Christ's College, Cambridge, 1585 ; travelled on continent, 1587-99, and served during civil wars in France ; arrested as abettor of Essex's rebellion, 1601, but released ; imprisoned on suspicion of complicity in Gunpowder plot, but discharged without trial. [lxi. 116]

WHITELOCKE, SIR JAMES (1570-1632), judge ; educated at Merchant Taylors' School and St. John's College, Oxford ; fellow, 1589 ; B.C.L., 1594 ; barrister, Middle Temple, 1600, bencher, 1619, reader, 1619 ; recorder of Woodstock, 1606 ; M.P., Woodstock, 1610, 1614, and 1622 ; committed to Fleet for opposing commission on naval reform, 1613 ; invested with coif, and appointed chief-justice of court of session of county palatine of Chester, 1620 ; justice of king's bench, 1624 ; declined to certify the legality of forced loans, 1626 ; member of Society of Antiquaries, c. 1600 ; wrote antiquarian papers. [lxi. 117]

WHITELOCKE, JOHN (1757-1833), lieutenant-general ; ensign, 1778 ; major, 1788 ; lieutenant-colonel, 13th foot, in Jamaica, 1791 ; served against French in San Domingo, 1793-4 ; colonel, 6th West India regiment, and brigadier, 1795 ; major-general and brigadier-general in Guernsey, 1798 ; lieutenant-governor of Portsmouth, 1799 ; lieutenant-general, 1805 ; commanded force sent to recover Buenos Ayres, 1807, made disastrous attempt to take town by assault, and was compelled to conclude treaty and evacuate Monte Video ; cashiered by court martial, 1808. [lxi. 119]

WHITER, WALTER (1758-1832), philologist ; M.A. Clare College, Cambridge, 1784 ; fellow, 1782 ; rector of Hardingham, 1797-1832. His works include ' Universal Etymological Dictionary,' 1822-5, and some Shakespearean annotations. [lxi. 121]

WHITESIDE, JAMES (1804-1876), lord chief-justice of Ireland ; B.A. Trinity College, Dublin, 1832 ; called to Irish bar, 1830 ; Q.C., 1842 ; made notable speech in defence of O'Connell in state trials of 1843 ; leading counsel for defence of William Smith O'Brien [q. v.], 1848 ; conservative M.P., Enniskillen, 1851, and Dublin University, 1859-66 ; solicitor-general for Ireland, 1852 ; attorney-general, 1866 ; chief-justice of queen's bench in Ireland, 1866 ; published ' Italy in Nineteenth Century,' 1848, and other works. [lxi. 122]

WHITFELD or **WHITFIELD**, HENRY (d. 1660 ?), divine ; perhaps held living of Ockley, Surrey, from 1616 ; became nonconformist ; sailed for New England, 1639, and founded Guildford, Connecticut ; returned to England, 1650 ; published religious works. [lxi. 123]

WHITFELD, JOHN CLARKE- (1770-1836), organist ; Mus.Bac. Oxford, 1793 ; organist and choir-master at Armagh Cathedral, 1794-7, and choirmaster at St. Patrick's Cathedral and Christ Church, Dublin, 1798 ; organist and choir-master to Trinity and St. John's colleges, Cambridge ; hon. Mus.Doc. Dublin, 1795, Cambridge, 1799, Oxford, 1810 ; professor of music, Cambridge University, 1821-36 ; organist and choir-master of

Hereford Cathedral, 1820–33 ; composed much sacred music, and set numerous poems by Scott, Byron, and Moore. [lxi. 124]

WHITFORD, ADAM (1624–1647), royalist soldier ; son of Walter Whitford (1581 ?–1647) [q. v.] ; B.A. Christ Church, Oxford, 1646 ; killed at siege of Oxford. [lxi. 128]

WHITFORD, DAVID (1626–1674), soldier and scholar ; son of Walter Whitford (1581 ?–1647) [q. v.] ; of Westminster School and Christ Church, Oxford ; M.A., 1661 ; officer in Charles II's army ; taken prisoner at Worcester, 1651 ; studied at Inner Temple, 1658 ; chaplain to Lord George Douglas's regiment of foot, 1666 ; minister to Scottish regiment in France, 1672 ; rector of Middleton Tyas, 1673 ; published ' Musæi, Moschi, et Bionis quæ extant omnia' (Latin and Greek), 1655, and other works. [lxi. 124]

WHITFORD, JOHN (d. 1667), divine ; son of Walter Whitford (1581 ?–1647) [q. v] ; rector of Ashton, Northamptonshire, 1641 ; ejected, 1645 ; reinstated, 1660. [lxi. 128]

WHITFORD or **WHYTFORD**, RICHARD (fl. 1495–1555 ?), ' the wretch of Syon ' ; fellow of Queens' College, Cambridge, c. 1495 ; made acquaintance of Erasmus ; chaplain to Richard Foxe [q. v], bishop of Winchester, c. 1498 ; entered Brigittine house at Isleworth (known as Syon House), c. 1507, and on its dissolution retired to London ; published devotional and theological works, including 'The following of Christ' (1556), a translation of the ' De Imitatione,' founded on Dr. William Atkinson's translation of 1504. [lxi. 125]

WHITFORD, WALTER (1581 ?–1647), bishop of Brechin ; educated at Glasgow University ; licensed preacher by presbytery of Paisley, 1604 ; minister of Kilmarnock, 1608, of Moffat, 1610, and Failford, 1619 ; signed protestation in support of liberties of kirk, 1617, but afterwards joined royal party ; member of court of high commission, 1619 ; D.D. Glasgow, 1620 ; sub-dean of Glasgow, 1628–39 ; bishop of Brechin, 1635 ; supported Charles I's liturgical changes ; was deposed by Glasgow assembly, 1638 ; rector of Walgrave, 1642 ; expelled by parliamentarians, 1646. [lxi. 127]

WHITFORD, WALTER (d. 1686 ?), soldier ; son of Walter Whitford (1581 ?–1647) [q. v.] ; colonel in royalist army during civil war ; retired to Holland ; murdered, 1649, Isaac Dorislaus (1595–1649) [q. v.], English envoy in Holland and one of Charles I's judges ; accompanied Montrose in Scotland, 1650 ; entered Russian service, c. 1664 ; in England, 1666 ; held commission in guards, but was dismissed as papist. [lxi. 129]

WHITGIFT, JOHN (1530 ?–1604), archbishop of Canterbury ; educated at St. Anthony's school, London, and Pembroke Hall, Cambridge ; B.A., 1554 ; M.A., 1557 ; fellow of Peterhouse, 1555 ; rector of Teversham and chaplain to Richard Coxe, bishop of Ely, 1560 ; B.D., 1563 ; Lady Margaret professor of divinity, Cambridge, 1563–7 ; advocated theories of Calvin, but supported Anglican ritual ; university preacher, 1566 ; created D.D., 1567 ; master of Pembroke Hall, Cambridge, 1567, and of Trinity College, Cambridge, 1567–77 ; regius professor of divinity, 1567–9 ; prebendary of Ely and royal chaplain, 1568 ; revised Cambridge university statutes, 1570 ; vice-chancellor, 1570 and 1573 ; dean of Lincoln, 1571 ; prebendary of Lincoln, 1572 ; bishop of Worcester, 1577 ; vice-president of marches of Wales, c. 1577–80 ; archbishop of Canterbury, 1583–1604 ; enjoyed the favour of Elizabeth and rigorously enforced her policy of religious uniformity ; drew up articles aimed at nonconformist ministers, 1583, and obtained augmentation of powers of high commission court ; privy councillor, 1586 ; being violently attacked in tracts published by John Penry [q.v.] and others under pseudonym of ' Martin Mar-Prelate,' 1588–9, proceeded against the offenders with the utmost severity ; drew up Lambeth articles, adopting Calvinist views of predestination and election, 1595 ; active in anticipating attack on queen in Essex's rebellion, 1601 ; celebrated coronation of James I, 1603 ; attended Hampton Court conference, 1604 ; published tracts and sermons. A collected edition of his works appeared, 1851–3. [lxi. 129]

WHITHORNE or **WHITEHORNE**, PETER (fl. 1550–1563), military writer ; served in armies of Emperor Charles V against Moors, c. 1550 ; published translations of Machiavelli's treatise on art of war (1562), and Fabio Cotta's Italian version of the Greek ' Strategicus' by Onosander (1563). [lxi. 137]

WHITHORNE, THOMAS (fl. 1590), musical amateur ; published collections of part-songs of small merit, 1571 and 1590. [lxi. 137]

WHITING, JOHN (1656–1722), quaker ; suffered much persecution, and was imprisoned at Ilchester, where he and other quaker prisoners held meetings ; released, 1686 ; travelled in various parts of England ; published ' Catalogue of Friends' Books' (1708), and other works, chiefly religious. [lxi. 138]

WHITING, RICHARD (d. 1539), last abbot of Glastonbury ; M.A. Cambridge, 1483 ; D.D., 1505 ; monk of Glastonbury ; acolyte, 1498 ; sub-deacon, 1499 ; deacon, 1500 ; priest, 1501 ; abbot, 1525 ; took oath of supremacy, 1534 ; imprisoned in Tower of London probably on charge relating to his views on succession to the throne, 1539 ; executed on Tor Hill, near Glastonbury. He was ' beatified,' 1896. [lxi. 139]

WHITLOCK, MRS. ELIZABETH (1761–1836), actress ; daughter of Roger Kemble [q. v.] ; appeared, with her sister Sarah (Mrs. Siddons [q. v.]), at Drury Lane, London, as Portia, 1783 ; married, 1785, Charles Edward Whitlock, whom she accompanied to America, whither she again went, 1797 ; probably last appeared as Elwina in ' Percy ' at Drury Lane, 1807. [lxi. 140]

WHITLOCK, JOHN (1625–1709), ejected divine ; M.A. Emmanuel College, Cambridge, 1649 ; minister with William Reynolds (1625–1698) [q. v.] at Leighton Buzzard, 1645, and Aylesbury, 1648 ; with Reynolds refused ' Engagement,' 1649, and was deprived ; vicar of St. Mary's, Nottingham, 1651 ; established presbyterian service ; sequestered, 1662 ; returned to Nottingham, 1687 ; published Life of Reynolds (1698) and other works. [lxi. 141]

WHITLOCK, WILLIAM (d. 1584), historian of Lichfield ; educated at Eton and King's College, Cambridge ; M.A., 1545 ; B.D., 1553 ; vicar of Prescot, 1558 ; rector of Greenford Magna, 1560 ; prebendary of Lichfield, 1561 ; continued to 1559 the manuscript chronicle (extending to 1347) of Thomas Chesterfield [q. v.] [lxi. 141]

WHITMORE, SIR GEORGE (d. 1654), lord mayor of London ; master of Haberdashers' Company ; member of Virginia Company, 1609 ; sheriff of London, 1622 ; alderman, 1621–43 ; lord mayor, 1631 ; knighted, 1632 ; twice imprisoned, 1642 and 1643, for refusing to pay taxes levied by parliament. [lxi. 142]

WHITNEY, GEOFFREY (1548 ?–1601 ?), poet ; studied at Magdalene College, Cambridge ; under-bailiff of Great Yarmouth, c. 1580–6 ; entered Leyden University, 1586, and published in that year ' Choice of Emblems' (printed by Plantin), from which Shakespeare gained his knowledge of the foreign emblematists of the sixteenth century. [lxi. 142]

WHITSHED, SIR JAMES HAWKINS, first baronet (1762–1849), admiral of the fleet ; entered navy, 1773 ; lieutenant, 1778 ; commander, 1780 ; with Rodney in West Indies ; captain, 1780 ; on east coast of Scotland, 1784–7 ; studied at Oxford, 1787–90 ; at Cape St. Vincent, 1797 ; rear-admiral, 1799 ; with Channel fleet, 1799–1801 ; organised Irish sea fencibles, 1803 ; vice-admiral, 1804 ; commander-in-chief at Cork, 1807–10, and at Portsmouth, 1821–4 ; admiral, 1810 ; K.C.B., 1815 ; G.C.B., 1830 ; created baronet, 1834 ; admiral of fleet, 1844. [lxi. 143]

WHITSON, JOHN (1557–1629), merchant and adventurer ; in service of a shipowner at Bristol ; took active part in voyages for settlement of North America ; M.P., Bristol, 1605, 1620, 1625, and 1626. [lxi. 144]

WHITTAKER. [See also WHITAKER.]

WHITTAKER, GEORGE BYROM (1793–1847), bookseller and publisher ; entered partnership with Charles Law in London, c. 1814 ; published for Mrs. Trollope, Colley Grattan, George Croly, Miss Mitford, and Sir Walter Scott ; brought out a series of Greek and Latin classics. [lxi. 144]

WHITTAKER, JAMES WILLIAM (1828–1876), painter in water-colours ; member of Society of Painters in Water-colours, 1864. [lxi. 145]

WHITTAKER, JOHN WILLIAM (1790 ?–1854), divine; Beresford fellow and B.A. St. John's College, Cambridge, 1814; M.A., 1817; D.D., 1830; vicar of Blackburn, Lancashire, 1822–54; honorary canon of Manchester, 1852; assisted in forming Royal Astronomical Society; published '. . . Inquiry into Interpretation of Hebrew Scriptures' (1819) and other works. [lxi. 145]

WHITTINGHAM, CHARLES, 'the uncle,' (1767–1840), printer and founder of Chiswick Press; apprenticed as printer and stationer at Coventry; set up press in London, 1789; rapidly extended business and began printing compact editions of standard authors; brought out with John Sharpe 'British Classics' (1803), 'British Theatre,' and 'British Poets' (1805); started, 1809, paper-pulp manufactory at Chiswick, where he established Chiswick Press, 1810; issued Chiswick edition of 'British Poets' (100 vols.), 1822; took into partnership, 1824, his nephew Charles Whittingham (1795–1876) [q. v.], to whom he resigned sole control, 1838. [lxi. 145]

WHITTINGHAM, CHARLES, 'the nephew,' (1795–1876), printer; nephew of Charles Whittingham (1767–1840) [q. v.]; apprenticed to his uncle, 1810; freeman of Stationers' Company, 1817; liveryman, 1848; in partnership with his uncle, 1824–8; started independently in London, 1828; printed many fine volumes for William Pickering [q. v.]; took over, 1840, control of Chiswick Press, which he removed, 1852, to his London premises at 21 Took's Court, Chancery Lane; retired from active work, 1860, when he took as partner John Wilkins (d. 1869). [lxi. 147]

WHITTINGHAM, SIR SAMUEL FORD (1772–1841), lieutenant-general; entered mercantile house at Bristol; travelled in Spain; ensign, 1803; lieutenant, 1st life guards, 1803; sent by Pitt on secret mission to Peninsula, 1804–5; captain, 1805; transferred to command of troop of 13th light dragoons, 1805; served at Buenos Ayres on staff of John Whitelocke [q. v.]; deputy-assistant quartermaster-general to force under Sir Arthur Wellesley, 1808; brigadier-general in Spanish army, 1809; at Talavera, 1809; commanded Spanish force at Barrosa, 1811; inspector-general of division, 1811; at Palma, Majorca, where he established a military training college, 1812; co-operated with Lord William Bentinck in Spain, 1812–13; lieutenant-general in Spanish army, colonel in British army, and aide-de-camp to prince regent, 1814; knight and C.B., 1815; again in Spain after Napoleon I's escape from Elba; governor-general of Dominica, 1819–21; quartermaster-general in India, 1821–1825; major-general, 1825; K.C.B., 1826; returned to England, 1835; lieutenant-general and commander of forces in Windward and Leeward islands, West Indies, 1836–9; commander of Madras army, 1839–41; wrote on military and political subjects; died at Madras. [lxi. 148]

WHITTINGHAM, WILLIAM (1524 ?–1579), dean of Durham; B.A. Brasenose College, Oxford, 1540; fellow of All Souls College, Oxford, 1545; M.A. Christ Church, Oxford, 1548; associated with English protestant exiles at Frankfort, 1554; followed Knox to Geneva, 1555, and was appointed deacon, 1558, and minister, 1559; assisted in translation of Geneva or 'Breeches' Bible (1560), and produced metrical versions of several of the Psalms, and of the Ten Commandments; returned to England, 1560; dean of Durham, 1563; was charged before commission, 1578, on various counts, including invalidity of his ordination, but died before proceedings terminated. [lxi. 150]

WHITTINGTON, RICHARD (d. 1423), mayor of London; son of Sir William Whittington, perhaps of Pauntley, Gloucestershire; mercer in London; member of common council, 1385 and 1387; alderman for Broad Street ward, 1393; sheriff, 1394; mayor, 1397–8, 1406–7, and 1419–20; possibly M.P. for London, 1416; married Alice, daughter of Sir Ivo Fitzwaryn, who possessed landed property in the south-western counties; acquired considerable wealth, advanced loans to Richard II, Henry IV, and Henry V, and was a liberal benefactor of London; left legacies for rebuilding of Newgate prison, foundation of an almshouse, and the collegiation of church of St. Michael de Paternoster-church as Whittington College (suppressed, 1548). The popular 'legend' of Whittington and his cat, the germ of which is probably of very remote origin, is not known to have been narrated before 1605, when a dramatic version and a ballad were licensed for the press. The story of a cat helping its owner to fortune has been traced in many countries both of southern and northern Europe. [lxi. 153]

WHITTINGTON, WHYTYNTON, or **WHITINTON,** ROBERT (fl. 1519), grammarian; B.A. and laureate in grammar, Magdalen College, Oxford, 1513; published five grammatical treatises, 1512–19, and wrote translations from Cicero and Seneca, published between 1534 and 1554. [lxi. 157]

WHITTLE, PETER ARMSTRONG (1789–1866), Lancashire antiquary; bookseller and printer at Preston, 1810–51; published topographical works. [lxi. 158]

WHITTLESEY or **WITTLESEY,** WILLIAM (d. 1374), archbishop of Canterbury; nephew of Simon Islip [q. v.], the archbishop; LL.D. Oxford; archdeacon of Huntingdon; 'custos' of Peterhouse, Cambridge, 1349–1351; prebendary of Lichfield, 1350, and Lincoln, 1356; vicar-general to Islip; bishop of Rochester, 1360–4, of Worcester, 1364–8; archbishop of Canterbury, 1368–74; buried in Canterbury Cathedral. [lxi. 158]

WHITTY, EDWARD MICHAEL (1827–1860), journalist; son of Michael James Whitty [q. v.]; writer of parliamentary summary of 'Times,' 1846–9; on staff of 'Leader,' to which he contributed sarcastic sketches of parliamentary proceedings; edited 'Northern Whig,' 1857–8; emigrated to Australia; died at Melbourne. [lxi. 160]

WHITTY, MICHAEL JAMES (1795–1873), journalist; edited 'London and Dublin Magazine,' 1823–7; edited 'Liverpool Journal,' 1830–6, and became its proprietor, 1848; issued 'Liverpool Daily Post,' the first penny daily paper published in United Kingdom, 1855. [lxi. 160]

WHITWELL, JOHN GRIFFIN, BARON HOWARD DE WALDEN (1719–1797). [See GRIFFIN, JOHN GRIFFIN.]

WHITWORTH, CHARLES, BARON WHITWORTH (1675–1725), diplomatist; educated at Westminster and Trinity College, Cambridge; B.A., 1699; fellow, 1700; represented England at diet of Ratisbon, 1702; envoy extraordinary to Russia, 1704–10; ambassador to Vienna, 1711; British plenipotentiary at congress of Baden, 1714; envoy extraordinary and plenipotentiary at court of Prussia, 1716–17 and 1719, and at the Hague, 1717–19; British plenipotentiary at congress of Cambray, 1722; M.P., Newport, Isle of Wight, 1722; created Baron Whitworth of Galway, 1721; 'Russia in 1710' printed at Strawberry Hill from his memoranda, 1758. [lxi. 161]

WHITWORTH, SIR CHARLES (1714 ?–1778), author; M.P., Minehead, 1747–61, and 1768–74, Bletchingley, 1761–8, East Looe, 1774, Saltash, 1775; chairman of ways and means, 1768 and 1774–8; knighted, 1768; lieutenant-governor of Gravesend and Tilbury fort, 1758–1778; compiled several works of reference. [lxi. 162]

WHITWORTH, CHARLES, EARL WHITWORTH (1752–1825), diplomatist; ensign, 1st regiment of foot-guards, 1772; lieutenant-colonel, 104th regiment, 1783; envoy extraordinary and minister plenipotentiary to Poland, 1785–9, and at St. Petersburg, 1789–1800; K.B., 1793; created Baron Whitworth of Newport Pratt, Ireland, 1800; on special mission to Copenhagen, 1800; privy councillor, 1800; married widowed Duchess of Dorset, 1801; ambassador at Paris, 1802; retired to London on British declaration of war with France, 1803; lord of bedchamber to George III, 1813; lord-lieutenant of Ireland, 1813–17; created Viscount Whitworth of Adbaston, 1813; G.C.B. and Earl Whitworth, 1815; visited Paris, 1819. His portrait, painted by Sir Thomas Lawrence, is at the Louvre, Paris. [lxi. 163]

WHITWORTH, SIR JOSEPH, first baronet (1803–1887), mechanical engineer; worked as mechanic in Manchester and London; discovered method of producing a truly plane surface; set up as toolmaker at Manchester, 1833; constructed measuring machine by which was elaborated his system of standard measures and gauges; F.R.S., 1857; hon. LL.D. Trinity College, Dublin, 1863; hon. D.C.L. Oxford, 1868; made experiments relating to rifles, and produced, 1857, a rifle which was adopted by war office, 1869; produced Whitworth steel for big guns,

1870 ; created baronet, 1869 ; converted works at Manchester, 1874, into limited liability company which united with firm of Armstrong, Elswick, 1897. [lxi. 166]

WHOOD, ISAAC (1689–1752), portrait-painter ; a skilful imitator of the style of Kneller. [lxi. 170]

WHORWOOD, JANE (*fl.* 1648), royalist ; *née* Ryder ; married Brome Whorwood, 1634 ; rendered Charles I numerous services, 1647–8. [lxi. 170]

WHYTE. [See also WHITE.]

WHYTE, SAMUEL (1733–1811), schoolmaster and author ; cousin of Frances Chamberlain, wife of Thomas Sheridan (1719–1788) [q. v.] ; opened, 1758, school in Dublin, where Richard Brinsley Sheridan was one of his pupils ; published poetical, educational, and other writings. [lxi. 171]

WHYTE-MELVILLE, GEORGE JOHN (1821–1878), novelist and poet ; educated at Eton ; captain, Coldstream guards, 1849 ; served in Crimea as major of Turkish irregular cavalry, 1854 ; devoted himself to literature and field-sports ; died from accident while hunting ; published novels relating to military, sporting, and fashionable life. [lxi. 173]

WHYTEHEAD, THOMAS (1815–1843), missionary and poet ; educated at St. John's College, Cambridge ; Hulsean prizeman, 1835 ; senior classical medallist, 1837 ; fellow, 1837–43 ; M.A., 1840 ; incorporated M.A. Oxford, 1841 ; chaplain to George Augustus Selwyn (1809–1878) [q. v.], bishop of New Zealand, 1841–3 ; published poetical writings. [lxi. 172]

WHYTFORD, RICHARD (*fl.* 1495–1555 ?). [See WHITFORD.]

WHYTT, ROBERT (1714–1766), physician ; M.A. St. Andrews, 1730 ; studied medicine in Edinburgh and London and on the continent ; M.D. Rheims, 1736, and St. Andrews, 1737 ; F.R.C.P. Edinburgh, 1738, and president, 1763–6 ; professor of theory of medicine, Edinburgh University, 1747 ; F.R.S., 1752 ; first physician to George III in Scotland, 1761 ; published 'Nervous, Hypochondriac, or Hysteric Diseases' (1764), and other works. [lxi. 174]

WHYTYNTON or **WHITINTON,** ROBERT (*fl.* 1520). [See WHITTINGTON.]

WIBURN or **WYBURN,** PERCEVAL (1533 ?–1606 ?), puritan divine ; fellow of St. John's College, Cambridge, 1552 ; on continent during Mary's reign ; M.A., 1558 ; prebendary of Norwich and of Rochester, 1561 ; canon of Westminster, 1561 ; vicar of St. Sepulchre's, Holborn, London, 1564 ; refused subscription, 1564 ; was sequestered, but retained prebends, and preached in public. [lxi. 175]

WICHE. [See also WYCHE.]

WICHE, JOHN (*d.* 1549). [See WAKEMAN.]

WICHE, JOHN (1718–1794), baptist minister ; studied at baptist academies at Taunton, Kendal, and Findern ; minister at Salisbury, 1743–6, and at Maidstone, 1746–94 ; abandoned Arian for Socinian views, 1760 ; published religious writings. [lxi. 176]

WICKENS, SIR JOHN (1815–1873), judge ; educated at Eton and Balliol College, Oxford ; M.A., 1859 ; barrister, Lincoln's Inn, 1840 ; bencher, 1871 ; equity counsel to treasury ; vice-chancellor of county palatine of Lancaster, 1868 ; raised to bench as vice-chancellor and knighted, 1871. [lxi. 176]

WICKHAM. [See also WYKEHAM.]

WICKHAM, HENRY LEWIS (1789–1864), barrister ; son of William Wickham [q. v.] ; of Westminster and Christ Church, Oxford ; called to bar at Lincoln's Inn, 1817 ; receiver-general of Gibraltar ; chairman of board of stamps and taxes, 1838–48. [lxi. 178]

WICKHAM, WILLIAM (1761–1840), politician ; educated at Harrow and Christ Church, Oxford ; B.A., 1782 ; M.A., 1786 ; D.C.L., 1810 ; called to bar at Lincoln's Inn, 1786 ; employed by Lord Grenville, then foreign secretary, in secret diplomatic service, 1793–4 ; minister to Swiss cantons, 1795–7 ; under-secretary for home department, 1798–1802 ; envoy to Swiss cantons and Russian and Austrian armies, 1799–1802 ; privy councillor, 1802 ; chief secretary for Ireland, 1802–4. [lxi. 177]

WICKLOW, VISCOUNT (*d.* 1786). [See HOWARD, RALPH.]

WICKWANE or **WYCHEHAM,** WILLIAM DE (*d.* 1285), archbishop of York ; canon and chancellor of York in 1262 ; archbishop, 1279–85 ; came into conflict with monks of Durham, 1280 and 1283 ; made a rule that each archbishop of York should leave a certain amount of stock on the estates of the see ; died at Pontigny. [lxi. 178]

WICLIF, JOHN (*d.* 1384). [See WYCLIFFE.]

WIDDICOMB, HENRY (1813–1868), comedian ; son of John Esdaile Widdicomb [q. v.] ; clerk in customhouse ; adopted theatrical profession, 1831 ; played in London and Liverpool ; joint-manager of Sheffield and Wolverhampton theatres, 1845 ; principal comedian at Surrey Theatre, London, 1848–60. His parts included first Gravedigger in 'Hamlet,' and Jacques Strop in the 'Roadside Inn.' [lxi. 179]

WIDDICOMB or **WIDDICUMB,** JOHN ESDAILE (1787–1854), riding-master and conductor of the ring at Astley's Amphitheatre, 1819–53. [lxi. 179]

WIDDOWES, GILES (1588 ?–1645), divine ; M.A. Oxford, 1614 ; fellow of Oriel College, Oxford, 1610–21 ; rector of St. Martin Carfax, Oxford, 1619–45 ; vice-principal of Gloucester Hall, Oxford, 1621 ; engaged in controversy with Prynne, 1630–1. [lxi. 179]

WIDDRINGTON, RALPH (*d.* 1688), regius professor of Greek at Cambridge ; brother of Sir Thomas Widdrington [q. v.] ; B.A. Christ's College, Cambridge, 1635 ; M.A. 1639 ; fellow ; public orator, 1650 ; regius professor of Greek, 1654 ; D.D., 1661 ; Lady Margaret professor of divinity, 1673. [lxi. 180]

WIDDRINGTON, ROGER (1563–1640), Benedictine monk, whose real name was THOMAS PRESTON ; ordained secular priest at Rome ; joined Benedictines of Monte Cassino, 1590 ; sent on English mission, 1602, and subsequently spent much of his life in prison ; set himself up as champion of the condemned oath of allegiance against the pope's deposing power, publishing several works on the subject, and gained favour of James I and Charles I. [lxi. 180]

WIDDRINGTON, SAMUEL EDWARD (*d.* 1856), writer on Spain ; son of Joseph Cook ; entered navy, 1802 ; served in West Indies ; lieutenant, 1809 ; commander, 1824 ; retired, *c.* 1824 ; lived in Spain, 1829–32, and published, 1834, 'Sketches in Spain during 1829–32' ; assumed surname of Widdrington, 1840 ; F.R.S., 1842 ; F.R.G.S. [lxi. 182]

WIDDRINGTON, SIR THOMAS (*d.* 1664), speaker of House of Commons ; probably studied at Oxford ; called to bar at Gray's Inn ; ancient and bencher, 1639 ; reported cases in court of king's bench, 1625–31 ; recorder of Berwick, 1631, and of York, 1638–*c.* 1662 ; knighted, 1639 ; twice M.P. for Berwick, 1640 ; a commissioner of great seal, 1648–9, 1654–5, and 1660 ; serjeant-at-law and king's serjeant, 1648 ; serjeant for Commonwealth, 1650 ; member of council of state, 1651, 1659, and 1660 ; on treasury commission, 1654–9 ; M.P. for York, 1654, and Northumberland, 1656 ; speaker, 1656 ; lord chief-baron of exchequer, 1658–60 ; M.P. for York in Convention parliament ; lost all offices on Restoration, but regained degree of serjeant ; temporal chancellor of bishopric of Durham, 1660 ; M.P., Berwick, 1661 ; wrote history of York, published, 1897. [lxi. 182]

WIDDRINGTON, WILLIAM, first BARON WIDDRINGTON (1610–1651), sheriff of Northumberland, 1637, and M.P. for county, 1640 ; took up arms for Charles I, 1642 ; knighted, 1642 ; fought under William Cavendish, duke of Newcastle [q. v.] ; commanded garrison of Lincoln, 1643 ; created Baron Widdrington of Blankney, 1643 ; accompanied Newcastle to Hamburg, 1644, and later to Paris ; joined Prince Charles in Low Countries, 1648, accompanied him to England, and died of wounds at Wigan. [lxi. 184]

WIDDRINGTON, WILLIAM, fourth BARON WIDDRINGTON (1678–1743), great-grandson of William Widdrington, first baron [q. v.] ; succeeded to title, 1695 ; joined Jacobite rising under Thomas Forster (1675 ?–1738) [q. v.] and Sir James Radcliffe, third earl of Derwentwater [q. v.], 1715 ; attainted of high treason, 1716 ; sentenced to death, but pardoned. [lxi. 185]

WIDVILE. [See WOODVILLE.]

WIFFEN, BENJAMIN BARRON (1794–1867), biographer; brother of Jeremiah Holmes Wiffen [q. v.]; quaker; engaged as ironmonger at Woburn, 1808–38; visited Spain, 1839, to forward abolition of slave-trade; collected writings of early Spanish reformers, volumes of which he issued privately; published biographies of Spanish reformers. [lxi. 186]

WIFFEN, JEREMIAH HOLMES (1792–1836), translator of Tasso; quaker; opened school at Woburn, 1811; published translation, in Spenserian verse, of fourth book of 'Jerusalem Delivered,' 1821, and complete version, 1824; other works include poetical writings and 'Historical Memoirs of House of Russell,' 1833. [lxi. 187]

WIGAN, ALFRED SYDNEY (1814–1878), actor in London, appeared under name of Sydney or Sidney at Lyceum, 1834; played original John Johnson in Dickens's 'Strange Gentleman' at the St. James's, 1836; with Madame Vestris at Covent Garden, 1839; married Leonora Pincott, 1839 or 1841; gained reputation as Alcibiades Blague in Jerrold's 'Gertrude's Cherries, or Waterloo in 1835'; at the Lyceum with the Keeleys, 1844, and later independently; played the hero of 'Monsieur Jacques' with Miss Mary Ann Stirling [q. v.] at the Olympic, 1847; with Kean at the Haymarket, 1848–9, playing clown in 'Twelfth Night' and Bassanio in 'Merchant of Venice'; among his finest impersonations Achille Talma Dufard in the 'First Night,' 1849, and John Mildmay in Tom Taylor's 'Still Waters run Deep,' 1855; retired, 1872; produced original plays. [lxi. 188]

WIGAN, HORACE (1818?–1885), actor and adapter of plays; brother of Alfred Sydney Wigan [q. v.]; acted in Ireland, and first appeared in London, 1854, at the Olympic, where he continued till 1866; manager of the Mirror (Holborn Theatre), London, 1875; among his most successful parts the original Hawkshaw in Taylor's 'Ticket-of-Leave Man,' 1863. He made many translations and adaptations of foreign dramatic pieces. [lxi. 190]

WIGAN, JOHN (1696–1739), physician and author; of Westminster School and Christ Church, Oxford; M.A., 1721; M.D., 1727; principal of New Inn Hall, Oxford, 1726–32; F.R.C.P., 1732; physician to Westminster Hospital, 1733–7, accompanied, 1738, Mr. (afterwards Sir Edward) Trelawny [q. v.] to Jamaica, where he died; published an edition of Aretæus, 1723, and other writings. [lxi. 192]

WIGAN, LEONORA (1805–1884), actress; *née* Pincott; with Madame Vestris at Olympic, London, 1831; married Alfred Sydney Wigan [q. v.], 1839 or 1841; with the Keeleys at Lyceum, London, 1844. Her parts include Mrs. Candour, Mrs. Malaprop, and Mrs. Hector Sternhold ('Still Waters run Deep'). [lxi. 190]

WIGG, LILLY (1749–1828), botanist; trained as shoemaker; kept school at Yarmouth; bank clerk at Yarmouth, 1801–28; made manuscript collections for history of esculent plants; Fucus (Naccaria) Wigghii named after him. [lxi. 192]

WIGGINTON, GILES (*fl.* 1569–1592), divine; B.A. Trinity College, Cambridge, 1569; fellow; M.A., 1572; vicar of Sedbergh, 1579; deprived on account of his Calvinistic views, 1586, but reinstated, 1592; frequently imprisoned; left theological treatises in manuscript. [lxi. 193]

WIGHARD, WIGHEARD, or **VIGHARD** (*d.* 664), Kentish priest; nominated archbishop of York; died at Rome, whither he had gone for consecration. [lxi. 194]

WIGHT, ROBERT (1796–1872), botanist; educated at Edinburgh; M.D., 1818; assistant-surgeon in East India Company's service, stationed at Madras, 1819; in charge of Madras botanical establishment, 1826–8; surgeon, 1831; entered revenue department as superintendent of cotton cultivation; made valuable collections and published works relating to Indian botany. [lxi. 194]

WIGHTMAN, EDWARD (*d.* 1612), fanatic; the last person burned for heresy in England; claimed to be the person mentioned in Messianic prophecies; suffered death at Lichfield on account of his anti-Trinitarian views and claims to be the promised paraclete. [lxi. 195]

WIGHTMAN, JOSEPH (*d.* 1722), major-general; ensign, 1690; lieutenant and captain, 1693; captain and

lieutenant-colonel, 1st foot guards, 1696; served with Sir Matthew Bridge's regiment in Netherlands and Holland; lieutenant-colonel, 1702; in Spanish peninsula, 1704; brigadier-general, 1707; commander-in-chief in Scotland, 1712; commanded centre of royal force at Sheriffmuir, 1715; governor of Kinsale, 1718. [Suppl. iii. 511]

WIGHTMAN, SIR WILLIAM (1784–1863), judge; M.A. Queen's College, Oxford, 1809; honorary fellow, 1859–63; called to bar, Lincoln's Inn, 1821; junior counsel to treasury; appointed judge of queen's bench and knighted, 1841. [lxi. 196]

WIGHTWICK, GEORGE (1802–1872), architect; entered office of Sir John Soane; opened practice at Plymouth, 1829, and executed numerous works in Devonshire and Cornwall; published architectural and dramatic writings. [lxi. 196]

WIGLAF (*d.* 838), king of Mercia; succeeded Ludecan, 825; driven from throne by Egbert (*d.* 839) [q. v.], king of Wessex, *c.* 828, but restored as under-king of Wessex. [lxi. 197]

WIGMORE, BARONS OF. [See MORTIMER, RALPH (I) DE, *d.* 1104?; MORTIMER, HUGH (I) DE, *d.* 1181; MORTIMER, ROGER (II) DE, sixth BARON, 1231?–1282; MORTIMER, ROGER (IV) DE, eighth BARON, 1287?–1330; MORTIMER, ROGER (V) DE, 1327?–1360; MORTIMER, EDMUND (II) DE, 1351–1381; MORTIMER, ROGER (VI) DE, 1374–1398; MORTIMER, EDMUND (IV) DE, 1391–1425.]

WIGMORE, WILLIAM (1599–1665). [See CAMPION, WILLIAM.]

WIGNER, GEORGE WILLIAM (1842–1884), chemist; worked as bank clerk in London, devoting his leisure to chemical studies; set up as analyst in London; founded Society of Public Analysts, 1875, and was president, 1883; F.C.S.; F.I.C.; published scientific writings. [lxi. 197]

WIGRAM, GEORGE VICESIMUS (1805–1879), exegetical writer; brother of Sir James Wigram; educated at Queen's College, Oxford; joined Plymouth brethren; works deal with study of biblical text. [lxi. 199]

WIGRAM, SIR JAMES (1793–1866), vice-chancellor; fellow, Trinity College, Cambridge, 1817; M.A., 1818; called to bar at Lincoln's Inn, 1819; K.C., 1834; tory M.P. for Leominster, 1841; vice-chancellor, 1841; member of judicial committee of privy council, 1842; knighted, 1842; retired from bench, 1850. [lxi. 198]

WIGRAM, JOSEPH COTTON (1798–1867), bishop of Rochester; brother of Sir James Wigram [q. v.]; M.A. Trinity College, Cambridge, 1823; D.D., 1860; archdeacon of Surrey, 1847; bishop of Rochester, 1860–7; published religious and educational works. [lxi. 198]

WIGTOWN, EARLS OF. [See FLEMING, SIR MALCOLM, *d.* 1360?; FLEMING, JOHN, first EARL, *d.* 1619; FLEMING, JOHN, second EARL, *d.* 1650.]

WIHTGAR (*d.* 544), first king of Isle of Wight; nephew of Cerdic [q. v.]; probably came to England, 514; conquered Isle of Wight, 530, and with his brother Stuf received the island from Cerdic and Cynric [q. v.], 534. [lxi. 199]

WIHTRED (*d.* 725), king of Kent, *c.* 600; great-great-grandson of Ethelbert (552?–616) [q. v.]; drew up one of earliest British codes of law. [lxi. 199]

WIKEFORD, ROBERT DE (*d.* 1390), archbishop of Dublin; fellow of Merton College, Oxford; LL.D.; archdeacon of Winchester, *c.* 1368; prebendary of York, 1370; constable of Bordeaux, 1373–5; archbishop of Dublin, 1375; chancellor of Ireland, 1376, 1377, and 1384–5. [lxi. 200]

WIKES, THOMAS (*fl.* 1258–1293). [See WYKES.]

WILBERFORCE, HENRY WILLIAM (1807–1873), Roman catholic journalist; fourth son of William Wilberforce [q. v.]; B.A. Oriel College, Oxford, 1830; M.A. 1833; entered Lincoln's Inn; took holy orders; vicar of East Farleigh, 1843–50; joined Roman catholic church, 1850; secretary to Catholic Defence Association, 1852; proprietor and editor of 'Catholic Standard,' 1854–63; published works on religious questions. [lxi. 200]

WILBERFORCE, ROBERT ISAAC (1802–1857), archdeacon of East Riding; second son of William Wilberforce

[q. v.]; B.A. Oriel College, Oxford, 1824 ; fellow, 1826 ; M.A., 1827 ; sub-dean and tutor, 1828, his colleagues being John Henry Newman [q. v.] and Richard Hurrell Froude [q. v.] ; identified with tractarian or high-church party ; ordained, 1826 ; priest, 1828 ; received livings of East Farleigh, 1832, Burton Agnes, 1840 ; archdeacon of East Riding, 1841 ; became intimate with Henry Edward Manning [q. v.], and followed his example in joining Roman catholic church, 1854 ; entered Academia Ecclesiastica in Rome, 1855, and was in minor orders when he died ; published religious and historical writings.
[lxi. 201]

WILBERFORCE, SAMUEL (1805–1873), successively bishop of Oxford and Winchester ; third son of William Wilberforce [q. v.] ; B.A. Oriel College, Oxford, 1826 ; M.A., 1829 ; D.D., 1845 ; honorary fellow of All Souls College, Oxford, 1871 ; rector of Brighstone or Brixton, Isle of Wight, 1830–40 ; rural dean of northern division of Isle of Wight, 1836 ; archdeacon of Surrey, 1839 ; canon of Winchester, 1840 ; received living of Alverstoke, 1840 ; chaplain to Prince Albert, 1841 ; sub-almoner to Queen Victoria, 1843 ; dean of Westminster, 1845 ; bishop of Oxford, 1845–69 ; introduced reforms and greatly improved the organisation of his diocese ; determined to attempt the revival of the former power of convocation as a synodical body, 1852, and was successful in obtaining the ultimate restoration to the convocations of Canterbury and York of much of their ancient authority ; earned considerable unpopularity by his action in regard to the appointment of Renn Dickson Hampden [q. v.] to see of Hereford, 1847, having, as bishop of Oxford, signed the letters of request to the court of arches for Hampden's trial ; condemned ' Essays and Reviews,' 1860 ; bishop of Winchester, 1869 ; initiated, 1870, and presided over revision of New Testament. He published ' Journals and Letters of Henry Martyn' [q. v.], ' Agathos and other Sunday Stories,' 1840, ' History of the Protestant Episcopal Church in America,' 1844, and other works.
[lxi. 204]

WILBERFORCE, WILLIAM (1759–1833), philanthropist ; educated at St. John's College, Cambridge ; M.P. for Hull, his native town, 1780 ; became intimate with Pitt, George Selwyn, Fox, Sheridan, and their friends ; M.P., Yorkshire, 1784, 1790, 1796, 1802, 1806, and 1807–12 ; travelled on the continent, 1784–5, in company with Isaac Milner [q. v.], under whose influence he adopted strict religious views ; carried through House of Commons, 1786, bill for amending criminal law, which was rejected in House of Lords ; founded ' Proclamation Society ' for suppression of vice, 1787 ; became parliamentary leader of cause of abolition of slavery, 1787 ; proposed motion for abolition, motion for gradual abolition being eventually carried, 1791, the date fixed for abolition being 1 Jan. 1796 ; failed to obtain leave to bring in bill for abolition, 1795, 1797, and 1798, the bill being again defeated, 1799 ; carried bill for abolition through House of Commons, 1804 (bill rejected by Lords, and on its reintroduction, 1805, thrown out on second reading, but was passed and received royal assent, 1807) ; the ' African Institution ' founded to promote the effective application of his bill ; M.P., Bramber, 1812–25 ; supported extension of missionary teaching in India, and was mainly responsible for foundation of bishopric of Calcutta, 1813 ; continued to advocate various measures relating to slavery question ; took part in founding Church Missionary Society, 1798, and Bible Society, 1803 ; expended most of his fortune in philanthropic objects ; published ' View of the . . . Religious System of professed Christians . . . contrasted with Real Christianity,' 1797, and ' Appeal . . . on behalf of the Negro Slaves in the West Indies,' 1823. His life by his sons Robert and Samuel [q. v.] appeared, 1838. Portraits by John Russell, R.A., and Sir Thomas Lawrence are in the National Portrait Gallery.
[lxi. 208]

WILBRORD or WILLIBRORD, SAINT (657 ?–738 ?). [See WILLIBRORD.]

WILBYE, JOHN (fl. 1598–1614), musician ; regarded as the greatest of English madrigal composers ; published sets of madrigals, 1598 and 1608, and contributed to collections, published in 1601 and 1614.
[lxi. 217]

WILCOCKS, JOSEPH (1673–1756), successively bishop of Gloucester and Rochester ; fellow, Magdalen College, Oxford, 1692–1703 ; M.A., 1698 ; D.D., 1709

chaplain to English factory at Lisbon, 1709 ; chaplain in ordinary to George I ; prebendary of Westminster, 1721 ; bishop of Gloucester, 1721–31 ; dean of Westminster and bishop of Rochester, 1731–56.
[lxi. 218]

WILCOCKS, JOSEPH (1724–1791), antiquary ; son of Joseph Wilcocks (1673–1756) [q. v.] ; M.A. Christ Church, Oxford, 1747 ; F.S.A., 1765 ; his ' Roman Conversations' published, 1792.
[lxi. 218]

WILCOX, THOMAS (1549 ?–1608), puritan divine ; educated at Oxford ; minister in Honey Lane, London ; imprisoned in Newgate for share in composition of ' Admonition to Parliament,' 1572–3, and deprived of ministry ; published religious works and translations.
[lxi. 219]

WILD. [See also WILDE.]

WILD, CHARLES (1781–1835), water-colour artist ; articled to Thomas Malton (1748–1804) [q. v.] ; member of Old Water-colour Society, 1812 ; treasurer, 1822, and secretary, 1827 ; published works on English cathedrals.
[lxi. 221]

WILD or WILDE, GEORGE (1610–1665), bishop of Derry ; fellow, St. John's College, Oxford, 1631–48 ; B.C.L., 1635 ; incorporated at Cambridge, 1635 ; preacher to Charles I at Oxford, 1642 ; D.C.L., 1647 ; bishop of Derry, 1661–5.
[lxi. 221]

WILD, JAMES WILLIAM (1814–1892), architect ; son of Charles Wild [q. v.] ; articled to George Basevi [q. v.] ; accompanied Dr. Lepsius to Egypt, 1842, and travelled abroad till 1848 ; decorative architect to Great Exhibition, 1851 ; curator of Soane Museum, 1878–92.
[lxi. 221]

WILD, JONATHAN (1682 ?–1725), informer ; worked as buckle-maker in London ; became head of a large corporation of thieves, and opened offices in London for recovery and restoration of property stolen by his dependents ; gained notoriety as thief-taker : ultimately hanged at Tyburn for receiving reward for restoring stolen property. Fielding's ' History &c.,' is not historically trustworthy.
[lxi. 222]

WILD or WYLDE, ROBERT (1609–1679), puritan divine and poet ; M.A. St. John's College, Cambridge, 1639 ; D.D., 1660 ; received living of Aynhoe, 1646 ; achieved popularity by many poetical broadsides celebrating Restoration and relating to other public events ; ejected under Act of Uniformity, 1662. His publications include ' Iter Boreale,' 1660, celebrating Monck's march from Scotland to London, and satirical poems.
[lxi. 223]

WILDE, SIR ALFRED THOMAS (1819–1878), lieutenant-general ; educated at Winchester ; ensign in East India Company's army, 1838 ; lieutenant, 19th Madras infantry, 1842 ; quartermaster and interpreter to regiment, 1847 ; adjutant, 3rd Punjab infantry, 1850 ; captain, 1856 ; commanded 4th Punjab infantry against Bozdar Baluchis, 1857 ; served in mutiny campaigns, 1857–8 ; brevet lieutenant-colonel and C.B., 1858 ; commanded corps of guides in Ambala, 1862 ; K.C.B. and major-general, 1869 ; member of council of India and lieutenant-general, 1877.
[lxi. 225]

WILDE, JAMES PLAISTED, first BARON PENZANCE (1816–1899), judge ; of Winchester College and Trinity College, Cambridge ; M.A., 1842 ; barrister, Inner Temple, 1839, bencher, 1856 ; counsel to commissioners of customs, 1840 ; Q.C., 1855 ; counsel to duchy of Lancaster, 1859 ; made baron of exchequer, invested with coif, and knighted, 1860 ; transferred to court of probate and divorce, 1863 ; raised to peerage, 1869 ; retired from judicial duties owing to ill-health, 1872, but undertook office of judge under Public Worship Regulation Act, 1874, and became dean of arches court of Canterbury, master of faculties, and official principal of chancery court of York, 1875 ; retired from bench, 1899 ; served on numerous royal commissions.
[Suppl. iii. 511]

WILDE, JANE FRANCISCA, LADY (1826–1896), née Elgee ; married Sir William Robert Wills Wilde [q. v.], 1851 ; contributed, under pseudonym of ' Speranza,' to ' The Nation,' c. 1845–8 ; published poetical writings, also ' Ancient Cures, Charms, and Usages of Ireland,' 1890, and similar works.
[lxi. 231]

WILDE or WYLDE, JOHN (1590–1669), chief-baron of exchequer ; M.A. Balliol College, Oxford, 1610 ; called to bar at Inner Temple, 1612, bencher, 1628 ; serjeant-at-law, 1636 ; M.P., Droitwich, 1620, 1624, 1625, 1626, 1628, 1640, 1659 ; knight of shire for Worcester ; in Long parliament, 1640 ; lay member of Westminster Assembly, 1643 ; commissioner for great seal, 1643 ; recorder of Worcester, 1646 ; judge of assize in Gloucester, Monmouth, and Hereford, 1646, and subsequently in Oxfordshire and Hampshire ; chief-baron of exchequer, 1646–53 and 1660 ; member of council of state, 1649 and 1650 ; superseded in exchequer at Restoration. [lxi. 226]

WILDE, OSCAR O'FLAHERTIE WILLS (1856–1900), wit and dramatist ; son of Sir William Robert Wills Wilde [q. v.] ; educated at Trinity College, Dublin, and at Magdalen College, Oxford ; B.A. Oxford, 1878 ; gained at Oxford reputation as founder of the æsthetic cult, subsequently caricatured in Gilbert and Sullivan's comic opera 'Patience' ; published 'Poems,' 1881 ; lectured in United States on 'Æsthetic Philosophy,' 1882 ; published several works of fiction, including 'Picture of Dorian Gray' (1891) ; produced several plays, including 'Lady Windermere's Fan,' 1892, 'A Woman of no Importance,' 1893, 'Salomé,' 1893 (in French, played in Paris, 1896), and 'The Importance of being Earnest,' 1895 ; brought unsuccessful action for criminal libel against Marquis of Queensberry and was found guilty under Criminal Law Amendment Act and sentenced to two years' imprisonment with hard labour, 1895 ; released, 1897 ; lived at Berneval, and later in Paris, where he died ; published anonymously 'Ballad of Reading Gaol,' 1898. [Suppl. iii. 513]

WILDE, THOMAS, BARON TRURO (1782–1855), lord chancellor ; of St. Paul's School, London ; admitted attorney, 1805 ; called to bar at Inner Temple, 1817 ; distinguished himself in defence of Queen Caroline, 1820 ; serjeant-at-law, 1824 ; king's serjeant, 1827 ; whig M.P. for Newark-on-Trent, 1831–2 and 1835–41, and Worcester, 1841 ; solicitor-general, 1839 ; knighted, 1840 ; attorney-general, 1841 and 1846 ; chief-justice of common pleas, 1846–50 ; privy councillor, 1846 ; lord chancellor, 1850–2 ; created Baron Truro of Bowes, 1850 ; instituted various chancery reforms. [lxi. 228]

WILDE, SIR WILLIAM, first baronet (1611 ?–1679), judge ; barrister, Inner Temple, 1637, bencher, 1652 ; recorder of London, 1659 ; M.P. for city of London in Convention parliament, 1660 ; created baronet, 1660 ; serjeant-at-law and king's serjeant, 1661 ; judge of common pleas, 1668 ; removed to king's bench, 1673 ; removed for condemning three prisoners on perjured testimony of William Bedloe [q. v.], 1679. [lxi. 230]

WILDE, SIR WILLIAM ROBERT WILLS (1815–1876), surgeon and Irish antiquary ; qualified as surgeon at Dublin, 1837 ; studied in London, Berlin, and Vienna ; practised in Dublin from 1841 ; founded and edited 'Dublin Quarterly Journal of Medical Science' ; published works on ophthalmic and aural surgery and topographical writings relating to Ireland ; received Cunningham gold medal from Royal Irish Academy, 1873. [lxi. 230]

WILDERSPIN, SAMUEL (1792 ?–1866), advocate of infant school system ; clerk in merchant's office ; opened infant school at Spitalfields, 1820, and subsequently spent his life in developing system throughout United Kingdom ; published works on education of the young. [lxi. 232]

WILDMAN, SIR JOHN (1621 ?–1693), politician ; educated at Cambridge ; probably served under Fairfax, 1646–7 ; supported dissentient regiments in attack on Cromwell and his officers, 1647, and was imprisoned in Newgate, 1648 ; major in Colonel John Reynolds's regiment of horse in Ireland, 1649 ; speculated in forfeited lands ; imprisoned in Tower of London, 1655–6, for plotting overthrow of Protector ; imprisoned on suspicion of plotting against government, 1661–7 ; associated with Algernon Sidney and others in schemes against Charles II and Duke of York, c. 1681 ; committed to Tower of London for complicity in Rye House plot, 1683, but discharged, 1684 ; became Monmouth's chief agent in England, but refused to join him when he landed and escaped to Holland, 1685 ; returned with William of Orange ; M.P. for Wootton Bassett in Convention parliament, 1689 ; postmaster-general, 1689–91 ; dismissed on suspicion of intriguing with Jacobites ; knighted, 1692 ; published numerous pamphlets. [lxi. 232]

WILFORD or **WILSFORD**, SIR JAMES (1516 ?–1550), defender of Haddington ; provost-marshal of Somerset's army in invasion of Scotland, 1547 ; knighted, 1547 ;

governor of Haddington, 1548 ; defended Haddington for nearly eighteen months against allied French and Scots, 1548–9 ; captured in attack on Dunbar Castle, 1549, but exchanged in same year. [lxi. 236]

WILFORD, JOHN (*fl.* 1723–1742), bookseller ; issued monthly catalogues, 1723–9 ; published the 'Daily Post-Boy,' c. 1735, issued in weekly parts, 1741, 'Memorials and Characters,' a collection of lives of eminent persons compiled by various authors, including John Jones (1700–1770) [q. v.] [lxi. 237]

WILFORD, RALPH (1479 ?–1499). [See WULFORD.]

WILFORD or **WILSFORD**, SIR THOMAS (1530 – 1604 ?), soldier ; brother of Sir James Wilford [q. v.] ; served in Low Countries ; knighted, 1588 ; superintendent of admiralty works in Dover harbour, 1591 ; governor of Camber Castle, 1593 ; colonel of English force invading France, 1596 ; serjeant-major of force to meet expected Spanish invasion, 1599. [lxi. 236]

WILFRID or **WILFRITH**, SAINT (634–709), bishop of York ; became novice at Lindisfarne ; left England with Benedict Biscop [q. v.], and proceeded to Rome, 653 ; returned to England, 658 ; received monastery of Ripon, c. 661 ; ordained priest, c. 663 ; successful as spokesman of Roman against Columbite party at conference at Streanæshalch (Whitby), 664 ; nominated bishop of York by Bishop Agilbert, and consecrated by him at Compiègne ; Ceadda or Chad [q. v.] appointed by Oswy bishop in his place during his absence, c. 665 ; retired to Ripon and discharged episcopal functions in Mercia and Kent ; regained bishopric on deprivation of Ceadda by Archbishop Theodore [q. v.], 669 ; introduced Benedictine rule into monasteries ; journeyed to Rome to appeal against division of his bishopric (which included Bernicia, Deira, and Lindsey) by Ecgfrid, king of Northumbria, and Theodore, who, in his absence, appointed Bosa [q. v.] in his stead at York (part of the former bishopric), 678 ; reached Rome, 679, and obtained decrees restoring him to bishopric ; returned to England, 680, and was imprisoned by Ecgfrid till 681 ; took refuge in Sussex ; taught the South-Saxons to fish ; built monastery at Selsey ; on Ecgfrid's death became reconciled to Theodore, 686, and was restored to the reduced see of York and monastery of Ripon by Aldfrid, the new king of Northumbria ; quarrelled with king, left York, and received from Ethelred of Mercia bishopric of Leicester, 691 ; came into conflict with Archbishop Brihtwald [q. v.], who wished him to resign episcopal functions ; went to Rome, 704, and appealed successfully to Pope John VI, and, being reconciled to Brihtwald, accepted see of Hexham. His day, 12 Oct. [lxi. 238]

WILKES, JOHN (1727–1797), politician ; educated at Leyden ; F.R.S., 1749 ; admitted to Sublime Society of the Beefsteaks, 1754 ; became intimate with John Armstrong (1709–1779) [q. v.], Thomas Brewster [q. v.], John Hall-Stevenson [q. v.], and Thomas Potter [q. v.], and was initiated by Sir Francis Dashwood [q. v.] into fraternity of Medmenham Abbey ; high sheriff of Buckinghamshire, 1754 ; M.P., Aylesbury, 1757, 1761 ; colonel of Bucks militia, 1762 ; attacked Bute in pamphlets ; founded, 1762, with Churchill, 'The North Briton' : was arrested for libel on George III published in No. 45, 1763, but discharged on ground of privilege as member of parliament, and, after much delay, obtained verdict with damages for illegal arrest against Halifax, the secretary of state, 1769 ; expelled from House of Commons and outlawed for printing and publishing libels, including 'North Briton, No. 45,' and 'An Essay on Woman' (to which was attached an obscene paraphrase of the 'Veni Creator'), probably written by Thomas Potter, 1764 ; retired to Paris ; returned, 1768 ; elected M.P. for Middlesex ; surrendered to his outlawry and committed to King's Bench prison ; his outlawry reversed, June 1768 ; again expelled from House of Commons for libel published in 'St. James's Chronicle,' 1769 ; three times re-elected for Middlesex, but elections annulled, his case being supported by Junius and opposed by Dr. Johnson ; sheriff of London and Middlesex, 1771 ; again returned for Middlesex, 1774, when he took seat without opposition and remained member till 1790 ; lord mayor of London, 1774 ; city chamberlain, 1779–97 ; opposed government in struggle with America. Hogarth caricatured him, and a sketch by Earlom is in the National Portrait Gallery. His works include 'Introduction to the History of England from Revolution to Accession of Brunswick Line,' 1768. [lxi. 242]

WILKES, RICHARD (1691–1760), antiquary and physician; M.A. St. John's College, Cambridge, 1717; fellow, 1717–23; Linacre lecturer, 1718, practised physic at Wolverhampton; published medical writings.

[lxi. 250]

WILKES, Sir THOMAS (1545?–1598), diplomatist; B.A. All Souls College, Oxford, 1573; secretary to Dr. Valentine Dale [q. v.], ambassador to France, 1573; went on secret embassy to Count Frederick, palatine of the Rhine, 1575; followed Huguenot army into France, 1575–1576; clerk of privy council, 1576; sent on mission to Philip II, 1577–8, and to Don John of Austria, 1578; sent to report on condition of Netherlands, 1586; English member of council of state of Netherlands, 1586; returned to England, 1587, and was imprisoned in Fleet prison, London, owing to Leicester's malice; again sent to Netherlands, 1590; on embassy to France, 1592; M.P., Southampton, 1588 and 1593; on embassy to archduke at Brussels, 1594; died at Rouen on embassy to French king.

[lxi. 251]

WILKIE, Sir DAVID (1785–1841), painter; educated under John Strachan [q. v.], afterwards bishop of Toronto; studied at Trustees' Academy of Design, Edinburgh, 1799–1804; painted 'Pitlessie Fair,' 1804; came to London, 1805, and studied at Royal Academy and exhibited 'The Village Politicians,' which attracted considerable notice, 1806; exhibited 'The Blind Fiddler,' 1807, 'The Rent Day,' 1808; R.A., 1811; exhibited 'The Village Festival,' 1811, and 'Blind Man's Buff,' 1813; visited Paris with Haydon, 1814; exhibited 'Distraining for Rent,' 1815; visited Netherlands, 1816; painted 'The Waterloo Gazette' for Duke of Wellington, 1817–21; exhibited 'The Parish Beadle,' and 'The Highland Family,' 1823; travelled on continent, 1825, and was in Spain, 1827–8, where a study of Titian, Velasquez, and Murillo powerfully influenced his style; exhibited 'Preaching of Knox before Lords of Congregation,' 1832, 'Columbus,' and 'The First Earring,' 1835, 'Peep o' Day Boy's Cabin,' 1836; appointed painter in ordinary, 1830, retaining office under William IV and Victoria; knighted, 1836. His portrait, by himself, is in the National Portrait Gallery.

[lxi. 253]

WILKIE, WILLIAM (1721–1772), 'the Scottish Homer'; educated at Edinburgh University; licensed by presbytery of Linlithgow, 1745; assistant, 1753, and sole minister, 1756, of Ratho; professor of natural philosophy, St. Andrews, 1759; hon. D.D. St. Andrews, 1766; published 'The Epigoniad' (1757) in heroic couplets based on fourth book of 'Iliad.'

[lxi. 258]

WILKIN, SIMON (1790–1862), editor of 'Works of Sir Thomas Browne,' 1836; F.L.S.; member of Wernerian Society of Edinburgh; printer and publisher at Norwich.

[lxi. 259]

WILKINS, Sir CHARLES (1749?–1836), orientalist; writer in East India Company's service, 1770; superintendent of factories at Maldah; assisted in establishment of printing-press for oriental languages, 1778, and in foundation of Asiatic Society of Bengal; examiner and visitor of Haileybury College, 1805–36; F.R.S., 1788; D.C.L. Oxford, 1805; knighted, 1833; the first European to study Sanskrit inscriptions, and the first Englishman to gain a thorough grasp of the Sanskrit language; published translations from, and works relating to, Sanskrit, including a translation of the 'Bhagavad-gítá,' 1785. [lxi. 259]

WILKINS, DAVID (1685–1745), scholar: of Prussian parentage; studied abroad and at Oxford and Cambridge; D.D. Cambridge, 1717, and lord almoner's professor of Arabic, 1724; domestic chaplain to Archbishop Wake, 1719; prebendary of Canterbury, 1721; archdeacon of Suffolk, 1724; F.S.A., 1720; librarian at Lambeth, 1715–18; published editions of Latin works; chiefly famous for his 'Concilia Magnæ Britanniæ et Hiberniæ' (446–1717), 1737.

[lxi. 260]

WILKINS, GEORGE (*fl.* 1607), dramatist and pamphleteer; associated as playwright with king's company of actors, of which Shakespeare was a member; collaborated with John Day and William Rowley in 'Travaile of Three English Brothers,' 1607, and probably wrote passages in Shakespeare's 'Timon of Athens' and 'Pericles,' 1608. His independent publications include 'Miseries of Inforst Mariage,' 1607, and a novel entitled 'The Painful Adventures of Pericles' (published, 1608, immediately after the surreptitious publication of Shakespeare's 'Pericles').

[lxi. 261]

WILKINS, GEORGE (1785–1865), divine; brother of William Wilkins [q. v.]; M.A. Caius College, Cambridge, 1810; D.D., 1824; vicar of Lexington, 1813, Lowdham, 1815, and St. Mary's, Nottingham, 1817; prebendary of Southwell, 1823; archdeacon of Nottingham, 1832; published 'Body and Soul' (1822), and other works.

[lxi. 263]

WILKINS, HENRY ST. CLAIR (1828–1896), general; son of George Wilkins (1785–1865) [q. v.]; educated at Addiscombe; lieutenant, Bombay engineers, 1847; captain, 1858; colonel, 1868; major-general, 1877; lieutenant-general, 1878; general, 1882; commanded royal engineers in Abyssinian campaign, 1868; employed in public works department of India.

[lxi. 263]

WILKINS, JOHN (1614–1672), bishop of Chester: B.A. Magdalen Hall, Oxford, 1631; M.A., 1634; vicar of Fawsley, 1637; private chaplain to prince palatine, Charles Lewis, nephew of Charles I; adhered to parliamentary side in civil war and took covenant; B.D., 1648; warden of Wadham College, Oxford, 1648–59; D.D., 1649; centre of group of men who formed Royal Society, 1662, and first secretary; master of Trinity College, Cambridge, 1659; incorporated D.D. Cambridge, 1659; deprived of mastership at Restoration; prebendary of York, 1660; vicar of St. Lawrence Jewry, London, 1662; dean of Ripon, 1663; prebendary and precentor of Exeter, 1667; prebendary of St. Paul's Cathedral, 1668; bishop of Chester, 1668; published 'The Discovery of a World in the Moone,' 1638, 'A Discourse tending to prove that 'tis probable our Earth is one of the Planets,' 1640, 'Mathematical Magick,' 1648, and 'An Essay towards a real Character and a Philosophical Language,' 1668 (suggested by the 'Ars Signorum' of George Dalgarno [q. v.]), and other works.

[lxi. 264]

WILKINS, WILLIAM (1778–1839), architect; brother of George Wilkins (1785–1865) [q. v.]; B.A. Caius College, Cambridge, 1800; fellow; designed, 1804, and carried out, 1807–11, portions of Downing College, Cambridge; designed Haileybury College, 1806; executed much work at Cambridge; designed University College, London, 1827–8, St. George's Hospital, London, 1827–8, and National Gallery, London, 1832–8; pointed out the true meaning of *Scamilli impares* (a device for correcting an optical illusion) in Vitruvius, book v.; published architectural works, including a translation of Vitruvius, 1812. [lxi. 267]

WILKINSON, CHARLES SMITH (1843–1891), geologist; born in Northamptonshire; worked on geological survey in Victoria; F.G.S., 1876; F.L.S., 1881.

[lxi. 269]

WILKINSON, HENRY (1610–1675), canon of Christ Church, Oxford; M.A. Magdalen Hall, Oxford, 1629, B.D., 1638; member of Westminster Assembly; rector of St. Dunstan's-in-the-East, 1645; senior fellow of Magdalen and parliamentary visitor, 1646; canon of Christ Church, Oxford, 1648; D.D., 1649; Margaret professor of divinity, 1652–62; after Restoration preached in conventicles.

[lxi. 269]

WILKINSON, HENRY (1616–1690), principal of Magdalen Hall, Oxford; M.A. Magdalen Hall, Oxford, 1638; parliamentary visitor of Oxford, 1647; B.D. and fellow, and vice-president, Magdalen College, Oxford, 1648; principal of Magdalen Hall, Oxford, 1648; ejected, 1662; Whyte's professor of moral philosophy, 1649–54; published sermons and other works.

[lxi. 270]

WILKINSON, JAMES JOHN (*d.* 1845), judge of county palatine of Durham; published legal works.

[lxi. 271]

WILKINSON, JAMES JOHN GARTH (1812–1899), Swedenborgian; son of James John Wilkinson [q. v.]; M.R.C.S., 1834; established himself in London as homœopathic doctor; member of committee of Swedenborg Society; edited Blake's 'Songs of Innocence and of Experience,' 1839; published 'Improvisations from the Spirit' (poems), 1857; devoted literary energies to translation and elucidation of Swedenborg's writings; his philosophic work highly esteemed by Emerson. [lxi. 271]

WILKINSON, JOHN (1728–1808), ironmaster; established first blast-furnace at Bilston, Staffordshire, c. 1748; set up plant for boring cylinders at Bersham, c. 1756; began manufacture of wrought iron at Broseley; patentee for making lead pipe, 1790; executed large government orders for artillery material. [lxi. 272]

WILKINSON, SIR JOHN GARDNER (1797–1875), explorer and Egyptologist; educated at Harrow and Exeter College, Oxford; lived in Egypt and Nubia, 1821–1833; made journeys of exploration; independently arrived at conclusions respecting hieroglyphics identical with those of Champollion; F.R.S., 1833; knighted, 1839; travelled in Montenegro, Herzegovina, Bosnia, and in Italy, studying the Turin papyrus, of which he published a facsimile; works include a standard 'Manners and Customs of Ancient Egyptians,' 1837. [lxi. 274]

WILKINSON, TATE (1739–1803), actor; took lessons from John Rich [q. v.]; engaged by Garrick, 1757, and in London, Dublin, and elsewhere, made considerable reputation, chiefly as a mimic of popular actors and actresses; partner in management, and, later, sole manager of several theatres in Yorkshire; published 'Memoirs' (1790) and other writings. [lxi. 276]

WILKINSON, WILLIAM (d. 1613), theological writer; M.A. Queens' College, Cambridge, 1575; received, though a layman, prebendal stall in York Cathedral, 1588. [lxi. 278]

WILKS, JOHN (d. 1846), swindler; son of John Wilks (1765 ?–1854) [q. v.]; practised as attorney; whig M.P. for Sudbury, 1826–8; Paris correspondent to 'Standard'; engaged in various fraudulent schemes, including a clerical registry office; published biographical writings. [lxi. 278]

WILKS, JOHN (1765 ?–1854), attorney; radical M.P. for Boston, Lincolnshire, 1830–7. [lxi. 278]

WILKS, MARK (1760 ?–1831), lieutenant-colonel, Madras army; received commission, 1782; lieutenant and aide-de-camp to governor of Fort St. George, 1788; military secretary to Colonel James Stuart in war against Tipu Sahib, 1794; captain, 1798; successively military and private secretary to Governor Lord Clive; major, 1804; lieutenant-colonel, 1808; governor of St. Helena, 1813–15; brevet-colonel, 1814; published 'Historical Sketches of South of India,' 1810–14. [lxi. 279]

WILKS, ROBERT (1665 ?–1732), actor; clerk in office of secretary Sir Robert Southwell (1635–1702) [q.v.]; accompanied William III's army to Ireland; appeared, 1691, as Othello at Smock Alley Theatre, Dublin, where he became popular; in London at Drury Lane, 1699–1706 and 1708–9, at Haymarket, 1706–8 and 1709–10, and again at Drury Lane, 1710–32, his name being associated with management of the two theatres successively, from 1709; won his chief triumphs in the comedy of Farquhar; guardian of Farquhar's orphan daughters. His best parts include Macduff, Sir Harry Wildair, and the Prince of Wales ('First Part of King Henry IV'). [lxi. 280]

WILKS, SAMUEL CHARLES (1789–1872), evangelical divine; M.A. St. Edmund Hall, Oxford, 1816; attached himself to 'Clapham Sect,' and edited its organ, the 'Christian Observer,' 1816–50; held living of Nursling, 1847–72; published tracts and essays. [lxi. 283]

WILKS, WILLIAM (fl. 1717–1723), actor; nephew of Robert Wilks [q. v.]; played at Smock Alley Theatre, Dublin, 1714, and afterwards at Drury Lane, London. His parts include Ferdinand ('Tempest'), 1723. [lxi. 283]

WILLAN, ROBERT (1757–1812), physician and dermatologist; M.D. Edinburgh, 1780; practised successively in Darlington and London; physician to Public Dispensary, London, 1783–1803; L.R.C.P., 1785; received Fothergillian medal from Medical Society of London for classification of skin diseases, 1790; published, in parts, 'Description and Treatment of Cutaneous Diseases,' 1798–1808; F.S.A., 1791; F.R.S., 1809. [lxi. 284]

WILLEHAD or **WILHEAD** (d. 789), divine; of Northumbrian birth; worked as missionary in Germany; bishop of Bremen, c. 787. [lxi. 285]

WILLEMENT, THOMAS (1786–1871), heraldic artist to George IV; F.S.A., 1832; artist in stained glass to Queen Victoria; published works on heraldry. [lxi. 285]

WILLES, GEORGE WICKENS (1785–1846), navy captain; lieutenant, 1801; served in Adriatic and Ionian islands; distinguished in fight with Franco-Neapolitan squadron in Naples Bay, and was promoted commander, 1810; captain, 1814. [lxi. 286]

WILLES, SIR JAMES SHAW (1814–1872), judge; B.A. Trinity College, Dublin, 1836; hon. LL.D., 1860; barrister, Inner Temple, 1840; tubman in court of exchequer, 1851; member of commission on common-law procedure, 1850–4, and of Indian (1861) and English and Irish (1862) law commissions; knighted, and appointed judge of common pleas, 1855; privy councillor, 1871. [lxi. 286]

WILLES, SIR JOHN (1685–1761), chief-justice of common pleas; M.A. Trinity College, Oxford, 1707; D.C.L., 1715; fellow of All Souls College, Oxford; barrister, Lincoln's Inn, 1713; K.C., 1719; M.P., Launceston, 1722–6; judge on Chester circuit, 1726; M.P., Weymouth and Melcombe Regis, 1726, West Looe, 1727–37; attorney-general, 1734; knighted, 1734; chief-justice of common pleas, 1737; senior commissioner of great seal, 1756–7. [lxi. 287]

WILLES or **WILLEY**, RICHARD (fl. 1558–1573), poetical writer; of Winchester College and New College, Oxford; fellow, 1566–8; M.A. Oxford, 1574, and Cambridge, 1578; perhaps edited 'History of trauayle in VVest and East Indies,' 1577; contributed to Hakluyt's 'Voyages'; published poetical writings. [lxi. 288]

WILLET, ANDREW (1562–1621), controversial divine; fellow of Christ's College, Cambridge, 1583–8; M.A. and incorporated at Oxford, 1584; D.D., 1601; took holy orders, 1585; prebendary of Ely, 1587; rector of Barley, 1599–1621; chaplain in ordinary and tutor to Prince Henry; imprisoned for one month for opposing Spanish marriage, 1618; produced numerous works of biblical commentary and theology; his chief publication, 'Synopsis Papismi,' designed as a reply to the jesuit Bellarmine's treatise in support of the papal theory. In doctrine he was Calvinistic in tendency, and a strenuous opponent of the papal claims, but was strongly opposed to 'separatists.' [lxi. 288]

WILLET, THOMAS (1605–1674), first mayor of New York; son of Andrew Willet [q. v.]; accompanied second puritan exodus to Leyden and New Plymouth plantations; assistant-governor of Plymouth colony; founded town of Swansey, Rhode Island, 1660; mayor of New York, 1665 and 1667. [lxi. 292]

WILLETT, RALPH (1719–1795), book-collector; studied at Oriel College, Oxford, and Lincoln's Inn; F.S.A., 1763; F.R.S., 1764; formed valuable collections of early printed books, specimens of block-printing, prints, drawings, and pictures. [lxi. 292]

WILLIAM THE CONQUEROR (1027–1087), king of England; natural son of Robert II, duke of Normandy; born at Falaise; succeeded as duke, 1035; suppressed, with assistance of French king, Henry, rising under Guy, grandson of Richard II of Normandy, and established his power in the duchy, 1047; visited England, 1051; married Matilda, daughter of Count of Flanders, 1053; resisted invasion under Henry of France, 1054–5; received homage of Guy, count of Ponthieu, and Geoffrey of Mayenne; again defeated invasion of Henry and Geoffrey of Anjou, 1058; decreed, 1061, at council held at Caen, ringing of evening bell as a signal for all to shut their doors and not go out again, a custom afterwards introduced into England as curfew; obtained person of Harold (1022 ?–1066) [q. v.], then Earl of Wessex, who had been shipwrecked off Ponthieu, and, 1064, exacted an oath to uphold the duke's claim to succeed to English throne, which had been promised him by Edward the Confessor; invaded England on Harold's accession, 1066; landed at Pevensey (28 Sept.), encamped at Hastings, and defeated Harold at a place eight miles distant afterwards called Battle (14 Oct.); ravaged country and received submission of Londoners, and was crowned at Westminster, 1066; visited Normandy, 1067; quelled insurrection under Harold's sons at Exeter, 1068, and invasion under Sweyn of Denmark in north, 1069–70, deposed Stigand and appointed Lanfranc archbishop of Canterbury, 1070, and organised church as department of government separate from civil administration, and asserted the supremacy of his own will in respect of papal authority; reduced isle of Ely and suppressed rebellion under Hereward [q. v.], 1071; invaded Scotland and received homage of Malcolm, 1072; invaded Maine and received submission of city of Le Mans 1073; suppressed conspiracy formed during his absence in Normandy by Ralph Guader, earl of Norfolk [q. v.], and other barons, 1075; besieged Dol, but was defeated by Philip of France; quelled insurrections under his son Robert, duke of Normandy [q. v.], in Normandy, 1080 and 1082 ; ordered survey, results of which were embodied in Domesday book, 1085 ; engaged in dispute as to right to the French Vexin, and invaded the Vexin and took Mantes, where he met with an accident on horseback and died ; buried at Caen. [lxi. 293]

WILLIAM II (*d.* 1100), king of England ; called Rufus from his ruddy complexion ; third son of William the Conqueror [q. v.] and Matilda of Flanders [q. v.] ; probably born between 1056 and 1060 ; fought with his father against his brother Robert, duke of Normandy [q.v.], 1079 ; succeeded to throne, 1087 ; suppressed insurrection under Odo, bishop of Bayeux [q. v.], 1088 ; invaded Normandy,1091, obtained part as his dominion, and co-operated with Robert in recovery of territory which he had lost ; marched against Malcolm III [q. v.] of Scotland and received his homage ; restored Carlisle and colonised northern districts laid waste by Conqueror, 1092 ; invested Anselm with the archbishopric of Canterbury, 1093, but attempted to obtain his deprivation from Pope Urban, 1095, and finally quarrelled with him, 1097 ; earned unpopularity by his rapaciousness and cruelty ; led expedition to Normandy to assist Robert, 1094, but quarrelled with him and returned, 1094 ; received pledge of duchy of Normandy for 10,000 marks, 1096 ; made unsuccessful expeditions against Welsh insurgents, 1096-7 ; demanded from Philip of France cession of the Vexin, crossed with army to France, 1097, but made small progress against French resistance, and returned, 1099 · he had demanded surrender of Maine, 1096, and was engaged in war with Elias, count of Maine, 1098 and 1099 ; ' loathsome to wellnigh all his people ' (English Chronicle) ; shot, perhaps by Walter Tirel [q. v.], and accidentally, while hunting in New Forest ; buried at Winchester, the clergy of Winchester refusing his corpse religious rites. [lxi. 301]

WILLIAM III (1650–1702), king of England, Scotland, and Ireland ; born at the Hague ; posthumous son of William II, prince of Orange, and Mary [q. v.], daughter of Charles I and princess royal of England ; educated at Leyden ; admitted to council of state, 1667 ; visited England, 1670, and received an honorary degree at each of the universities ; appointed captain-general of Dutch forces, 1672 ; and later proclaimed stadholder, captain-and admiral-general at Vere in Zealand and at Dort; conducted war against France, and concluded treaties of alliance with the empire and Spain ; fought indecisive battle with Condé at Senef, 1674, and suffered reverses at Maestricht, 1676, and Montcassel and Charleroi, 1677 ; married, 1677, Mary, daughter of James, duke of York (afterwards James II of England) ; secured integrity of territories in United Provinces by treaty of Nimeguen, 1678 ; went to England, 1681 ; with aid of Waldeck, carried on schemes for European alliance against France, a basis for which was furnished, 1681, by association formed between United Provinces, Sweden, the empire, and Spain for maintenance of existing treaties, but his work undone by a twenty years' truce, 1684, concluded on basis of existing conquests, which left the European position of France stronger than ever ; endeavoured to prevent sailing of Argyll's and Monmouth's expeditions against James II, prepared at Amsterdam, 1685, and showed anxiety for friendly relations with James II until estranged by James's catholic zeal ; accepted invitation to undertake armed expedition to England, 1688, landed at Brixham, south of Torbay, 5 Nov., and arrived at St. James's, 18 Dec. 1688 ; refused, on James II's flight, to accept throne as by right of conquest, but assumed executive, on which he and Princess of Orange were declared king and queen by declaration of right drawn up by committee of Convention parliament, the succession being to Mary's issue, then to Anne and her issue, and finally, in default, to William's issue ; crowned with his wife, 11 April 1689 ; formed ' grand alliance ' with United Provinces and the empire ; went to Ireland, 1690, and defeated James II and Irish-French army at Boyne ; made expedition to Holland, 1691, to support the confederacy ; sanctioned vigorous treatment of Scottish rebels, which culminated in massacre of Glencoe, 1692 ; again in Holland, 1693, and was defeated at Landen by Luxemburg, who, however, was unable through losses to follow up success ; reopened campaign, 1694 ; took Namur, 1695 ; obtained from Louis XIV a promise not to support his enemies by peace of Ryswyk, 1697 ; engaged in negotiations with Louis XIV on the Spanish succession, and signed partition treaties, 1698 and 1700, but on death of Charles II

of Spain, Louis having acted in direct opposition to the terms of the second treaty, William returned to policy of grand alliance and embarked for Holland, 1701 ; assented to Act of Settlement securing ultimate succession of house of Hanover, 1701 ; died from effects of accident while riding at Hampton Court ; buried at Westminster. Portraits by Jan Wyck are in National Portrait Gallery. [lxi. 306]

WILLIAM IV (1765–1837), king of Great Britain and Ireland ; third son of George III and his queen Charlotte Sophia of Mecklenburg-Strelitz ; served as ' able seaman ' under Captain Robert Digby [q. v.] at relief of Gibraltar, 1780 ; midshipman, 1780 ; at St. Vincent ; K.G., 1782 ; stationed at New York, 1782, and in West Indies ; lieutenant, 1785 ; captain of frigate, 1785 ; associated with Nelson in West Indies ; created Earl of Munster and Duke of Clarence and St. Andrews, 1789 ; commanded Valiant, in English waters, 1790 ; rear-admiral, 1790 ; formed, *c.* 1791, connection with Dorothea Jordan [q. v.], which continued till 1811 ; vice-admiral, 1794 ; admiral, 1799 ; admiral of the fleet, 1811 ; married Adelaide, eldest daughter of George, duke of Saxe-Coburg Meiningen, 1818 ; lord high admiral, 1827 ; succeeded George IV as king, 26 June 1830 ; as king, though wanting in reticence and self-command, displayed the instincts of a statesman ; refused to swamp the majority in the House of Lords which (1832) rejected the Reform Bill (originally brought in in 1831) by creating new peers, but owing to a circular letter sent by him to the tory peers, a hundred of them absented themselves from the division, and the bill became law ; buried at Windsor ; portrait painted by Gainsborough and Sir Thomas Lawrence. [lxi. 325]

WILLIAM THE LYON (1143–1214), king of Scotland ; second son of Henry (1114 ?–1152) [q. v.] of Scotland ; succeeded his brother Malcolm IV [q. v.], 1165 ; accompanied Henry II of England to France ; made alliance with Louis VII, 1168 ; allied with king of France and Henry II's three sons against Henry II, 1173 ; invaded Northumberland and was captured near Alnwick ; released by treaty of Falaise, by which Scotland was completely subjected to England, 1174 ; founded monastery of Arbroath for Tyronesian Benedictines from Kelso, 1178 ; engaged in dispute with Pope Alexander III as to see of St. Andrews, and was ultimately successful in establishing Scottish church as independent of English church, and directly subject only to see of Rome ; obtained from Richard Cœur de Lion restoration of independence of Scottish kingdom by treaty of Canterbury, 1189, in consideration of payment of ten thousand merks (100,000*l.* present value) ; married Ermengarde, daughter of the Viscount of Beaumont, and cousin of Henry II, 1186 ; subdued the Moray highlands, and made Caithness and Sutherland subject to Scottish crown ; demanded of King John restitution of northern earldoms of England, 1199, and, after a period of armed inaction, made peaceable treaty, 1212, without recovering earldoms. Of his laws, which had for their object the better enforcement of the criminal law through the king's officers and the gradual substitution of Norman feudal for the older Celtic customs, few fragments remain. [lxi. 331]

WILLIAM (1103–1120), only son of Henry I, king of England, and his first wife, Matilda of Scotland (1080–1118) [q. v.] ; as his father's destined successor, received homage of Norman barons, 1115, and of English witan, 1116 ; married Matilda, daughter of Fulk V, count of Anjou, 1119 ; invested by Louis VI with duchy of Normandy, 1120 ; drowned in wreck of ' White Ship ' off Barfleur. [lxi. 337]

WILLIAM, DUKE OF GLOUCESTER (1689–1700), son of the Princess Anne (afterwards Queen Anne) and Prince George of Denmark ; declared Duke of Gloucester by William III ; made K.G., 1695 ; appointed to the command of William III's Dutch regiment of foot-guards, 1698. [i. 446]

WILLIAM AUGUSTUS, DUKE OF CUMBERLAND (1721–1765), military commander ; third son of George II, then prince of Wales, by Caroline, daughter of John Frederic, margrave of Brandenburg-Anspach ; created Duke of Cumberland, 1726 ; K.G., 1740 ; educated for navy ; served under Sir John Norris (1660 ?–1749) [q.v.], 1740 ; colonel of Coldstream guards, 1770 ; transferred to 1st guards, 1742 ; privy councillor, 1742 ; major-general, 1742 ; served with the army on the Main at Dettingen ; lieutenant-general, 1743 ; honorary commander of allied forces in Netherlands, 1744; captain-general of British land forces at home and in field, 1745; took part in unsuccessful attempt to relieve Tournay, 1745; took command of second army (the first being under Wade) formed to oppose Prince Charles Edward, 1745, and engaged in indecisive action at Clifton; commanded first army, occupied Stirling and defeated rebels at Culloden, 1746; marched to Inverness and subsequently fixed headquarters at Fort Augustus, hunting down rebels with utmost severity; received thanks of parliament for Culloden and income of 25,000l. a year for himself and heirs; colonel, 15th dragoons; chancellor of St. Andrews University, 1746; resumed command in Holland, 1747; defeated with allies by Saxe at Laeffelt (or Val) and fell back on Maestricht; returned to England, 1748; ardently supported horse-racing, and made course and founded meeting at Ascot; chancellor of Dublin University, 1751; appointed one of lords justices on George II's departure for Hanover, 1755; took command of army of observation formed to cover invasion of Hanover, 1757; defeated by French under Marshal d'Estrées at Hastenbeck; signed treaty of Kloster-Zeven and returned to England, was received angrily by George II, and resigned appointments, 1757; captain-general, 1765; buried at Westminster. His portrait by Reynolds, 1758, is in the National Portrait Gallery. [lxi. 337]

WILLIAM HENRY, first DUKE OF GLOUCESTER of the latest creation (1743–1805), third son of Frederick Louis, prince of Wales [q. v.], by Augusta, daughter of Frederick II, duke of Saxe-Gotha; K.G., 1762; created Duke of Gloucester and Edinburgh and Earl of Connaught, 1764; privy councillor, 1764; secretly married Maria, dowager countess of Waldegrave, 1766, the validity of marriage being allowed, 1773; general, 1772; F.R.S., 1780; field-marshal, 1793. [lxi. 348]

WILLIAM FREDERICK, second DUKE OF GLOUCESTER of the latest creation (1776–1834), son of William Henry, first duke [q. v.]; M.A. Trinity College, Cambridge, 1790; LL.D., 1796; chancellor of Cambridge University, 1811; served as colonel of 1st foot-guards in Flanders, 1794; major-general, 1795; F.R.S., 1797; in Helder expedition, 1799; general, 1808; field-marshal, 1816; K.G., 1794; privy councillor, 1806; governor of Portsmouth, 1827; married his first cousin, Mary, fourth daughter of George III, 1816. [lxi. 349]

WILLIAM FITZOSBERN, EARL OF HEREFORD (d. 1071). [See FITZOSBERN.]

WILLIAM MALET OR MALLET (d. 1071). [See MALET.]

WILLIAM (d. 1075), bishop of London: chaplain to Edward the Confessor [q. v.]; bishop of London, 1051. [lxi. 350]

WILLIAM DE ST. CARILEF or ST. CALAIS (d. 1096). [See CARILEF.]

WILLIAM OF CHESTER (fl. 1109), poet; Benedictine monk of Chester; wrote poems on Anselm. [lxi. 350]

WILLIAM GIFFARD (d. 1129). [See GIFFARD.]

WILLIAM (d. 1135 ?), archbishop of Tyre; born in England; prior of Holy Sepulchre at Jerusalem; archbishop of Tyre, 1128. [lxi. 350]

WILLIAM OF CORBEIL (d. 1136). [See CORBEIL.]

WILLIAM DE WARELWAST (d. 1137). [See WARELWAST.]

WILLIAM OF MALMESBURY (d. 1143 ?), historian; born between 1090 and 1096; educated at Malmesbury Abbey, and became librarian; probably resided some time at Glastonbury, later revisions of his 'Gesta Regum Anglorum' containing notices derived from the history and charters of Glastonbury. His works include 'Gesta Regum Anglorum,' finished in 1125 (the earlier books of which made considerable use of the older ballad literature of England), and its sequel 'Historia Novella,' dealing with English history to 1142, 'Gesta Pontificum Anglorum,' finished 1125, and 'De Antiquitate Glastoniensis Ecclesiæ,' written between 1129 and 1139. [lxi. 351]

WILLIAM (1132 ?–1144), 'saint and martyr of Norwich'; apprenticed as skinner at Norwich, 1142; became associated in dealings with Jews; said to have been murdered by Jews, on what motive it is not known, but, according to hearsay evidence, as a victim in compliance with what was believed to be a Jewish rite. The resting-place of his body in Norwich Cathedral became a centre for pilgrims. [lxi. 354]

WILLIAM OF THWAYT (d. 1154). [See FITZHERBERT, WILLIAM.]

WILLIAM OF CONCHES (d. 1154 ?), natural philosopher, born at Conches, Normandy; studied at Chartres; wrote 'De Philosophia,' afterwards changing its title to 'Dragmaticon,' and other works, including a commentary on Boethius's 'De Consolatione Philosophiæ.' [lxi. 355]

WILLIAM DE WYCUMBE (fl. 1160), biographer; prior of second Llanthony Abbey, Gloucester; wrote life of Robert de Betun (d. 1148), bishop of Hereford. [lxi. 356]

WILLIAM OF YPRES (d. 1165 ?), erroneously styled EARL OF KENT; son of Philip, count of Ypres, younger son of Robert I, count of Flanders; claimed Flemish succession on murder of his half-brother Charles, but Louis of France instated William Clito, son of Robert, duke of Normandy [q. v.]; joined league of English nobles against Clito, 1127; captured by Louis and Clito at Ypres and imprisoned; released, Clito being overcome by a new rival, Thierry of Alsace, 1128; took refuge in England, 1133; fought for Stephen in Normandy, and 1141 at Lincoln; joined Stephen's queen; fought at Winchester; rewarded by Stephen with revenues from crown lands in Kent, but received no earldom; founded Cistercian abbey at Boxley, c. 1144–6. [lxi. 356]

WILLIAM DE TRACY (d. 1173). [See TRACY.]

WILLIAM (1095 ?–1174), bishop of Norwich; surname Turbe, Turbo, or de Turbeville; educated in monastic school at Norwich, and became successively schoolmaster, monk, sub-prior, and prior; supported truth of story of murder of William (1132 ?–1144) [q. v.] by Jews; bishop of Norwich, 1146–74; faithful adherent of Becket; pronounced papal sentence of excommunication against Earl Hugh at Norwich, 1166. [lxi. 358]

WILLIAM OF ST. ALBANS (fl. 1178), hagiologist; monk of St. Albans; wrote lives of Amphibalus and Alban, versified by Ralph of St. Albans [q. v.] [lxi. 360]

WILLIAM OF CROWLAND (d. 1179), abbot of Ramsey, 1161, and of Cluny, 1177; has been confounded with William of Ramsey [q. v.] [lxi. 364]

WILLIAM OF PETERBOROUGH (fl. 1188), theological writer; monk of Ramsey; wrote theological works. [lxi. 360]

WILLIAM FITZSTEPHEN (d. 1190 ?) [See FITZSTEPHEN.]

WILLIAM FITZOSBERT (d. 1196). [See FITZOSBERT.]

WILLIAM OF LONGCHAMP (d. 1197). [See LONGCHAMP.]

WILLIAM OF NEWBURGH (1136–1198 ?), historian; educated at Augustinian priory at Newburgh, Yorkshire. His 'Historia Rerum Anglicarum,' written c. 1198, and comprising history from 1066 to 1198, is the finest historical work extant by an Englishman of the twelfth century. [lxi. 360]

WILLIAM DE LEICESTER, or WILLIAM DU MONT (d. 1213), theologian; studied at Oxford and Paris; chancellor of Lincoln, 1192–1200; wrote theological works. [lxi. 363]

WILLIAM MALET or MALLET (fl. 1195–1215). [See MALET.]

WILLIAM OF RAMSEY (fl. 1219), hagiographer and poet; monk of Crowland; wrote life of Waltheof, a poem on St. Guthlac, and other works. [lxi. 364]

WILLIAM THE TROUVÈRE (fl. 1220 ?), poet; translated Latin tales from 'Miracles of the Virgin' into Anglo-Norman verse. [lxi. 364]

WILLIAM OF SAINTE-MÈRE-EGLISE (d. 1224), bishop of London; in service of Henry II, whom he accompanied abroad, 1187; prebendary of York and dean of St. Martin's, London, 1189; prebendary of Lincoln, c. 1192; employed as justiciar and member of exchequer; bishop of London, 1198; went on diplomatic mission to King Otto, King John's nephew, 1204; with bishops of Ely and

Z Z

Worcester pronounced papal interdict, 1208, and in consequence was banished ; engaged as bearer of papal overtures to John, 1208–13 ; restored, 1213 ; resigned bishopric
to legate Pandulf on account of age, 1221. [lxi. 364]

WILLIAM THE CLERK (*fl.* 1208–1226), Anglo-Norman
poet ; author of ' Frégus et Galienne,' a romance belonging to the Arthurian cycle, and four other Norman
French works. [lxi. 367]

WILLIAM DE LONGESPÉE, third EARL OF SALISBURY
(*d.* 1226). [See LONGESPÉE.]

WILLIAM DE FORS or DE FORTIBUS, EARL OF ALBE-
MARLE (*d.* 1242), great-grandson of Count Stephen ;
supported King John against barons until defection of
Londoners ; one of executors of Magna Charta, but subsequently fought for John, returning to barons after capture of Winchester, and again siding with king after
baronial disasters ; constable of Rockingham and Sauvey
castles, 1216 ; refused to surrender castles on demand of
Hubert de Burgh [q. v.], 1220, but was compelled to submit,
having been excommunicated ; rose in revolt at Bytham,
1221, and was again excommunicated ; captured, pardoned,
and ordered into exile in Holy Land ; remained unmolested in England ; joined Falkes de Breauté and others
in rebellion, 1223, but surrendered to Henry III ; member of
Henry III's council ; ambassador to Antwerp, 1227 ; served
in Brittany, 1230 ; set out for Holy Land, 1241, and died at
sea in Mediterranean. [lxi. 367]

WILLIAM OF DROGHEDA (*d.* 1245 ?), canonist ;
lectured on canon law at Oxford ; wrote ' Summa
Aurea,' a treatise on canon law. [lxi. 370]

WILLIAM OF DURHAM (*d.* 1249), archdeacon of
Durham, 1237 ; rector of Wearmouth ; educated at Oxford
and Paris ; left sum of money for support of masters of
arts studying theology, who subsequently formed community that was nucleus of University College.
[lxi. 370]

WILLIAM DE LONGESPÉE, called EARL OF SALIS-
BURY (1212 ?–1250). [See LONGESPÉE.]

WILLIAM OF NOTTINGHAM (*d.* 1251). [See NOT-
TINGHAM.]

WILLIAM OF YORK (*d.* 1256), bishop of Salisbury ;
justice in Kent and Huntingdon, 1227 ; justice itinerant
at Worcester, Lewes, Gloucester, and Launceston, 1235,
Bedford and St. Albans, 1240, and Bermondsey and
Oxford, 1241 ; one of the three custodians of the realm,
1242 ; bishop of Salisbury, 1246 ; one of deputation sent
to Henry III from bishops in parliament asking for
liberty of ecclesiastical elections, 1253. [lxi. 371]

WILLIAM DE FORS or DE FORTIBUS, EARL OF
ALBEMARLE (*d.* 1260), son of William de Fors (*d.* 1242)
[q. v.] ; married Christina, younger daughter of Alan, lord
of Galloway, and succeeded to third of Galloway ; sheriff
of Cumberland and keeper of Carlisle Castle, 1255–60 ;
took prominent share in Mad parliament at Oxford,
1258 ; one of king's standing council of fifteen.
[lxi. 372]

WILLIAM DE WILTON (*d.* 1264). [See WILTON.]

WILLIAM DE WICKWANE or WYCHEHAM (*d.*
1285). [See WICKWANE.]

WILLIAM DE VALENCE, titular EARL OF PEMBROKE
(*d.* 1296), fourth son of Isabella of Angoulême, widow of
King John, by her second husband, Hugh X of Lusignan,
count of La Marche : came to Henry III's court, 1247 ;
married Joan, daughter of Baron Warin de Munchensi by
Joan, daughter and coheiress of William Marshal, first
earl of Pembroke [q. v.] ; assumed title of Earl of
Pembroke ; knighted, 1247 ; joint-ambassador to France,
1249 ; took the cross, 1250 ; one of twelve nominees of
Henry III in reforming committee appointed by Mad parliament, 1258 ; came into conflict with Simon de Montfort
[q. v.] ; ambassador to Louis, 1263 ; with Henry III at
siege of Northampton, 1264 ; fought for Henry III at
Lewes, and escaped to France ; took part in royalist
restoration, 1265 ; went with Edward to Holy Land, 1270,
returned, 1273 ; commander of army in west Wales, 1282
and 1283 ; one of Edward I's council ; Edward I's agent for
districts ceded by treaty of Amiens, 1279 ; one of negotiators of treaty of Salisbury with Scots, 1289 ; died at
Bayonne ; buried at Westminster. [lxi. 373]

WILLIAM OF HOTHUM (*d.* 1298). [See HOTHUM.]

WILLIAM OF WARE or WILLIAM WARRE, GUARO,
or VARRON (*fl.* 1300 ?), philosopher ; Franciscan ; D.D. of
Paris, where he chiefly lived ; wrote philosophical and
theological works. [lxi. 377]

WILLIAM OF WHEATLEY or WHETLEY (*fl.* 1310),
divine and author ; studied at Oxford and Paris ; rector
of Yatesbury ; wrote philosophical and other works.
[lxi. 377]

WILLIAM OF LITTLINGTON (*d.* 1312), theological
writer ; Carmelite of Stamford ; doctor of theology, Oxford ; opposed division of England arranged at council of
Narbonne, and was excommunicated, 1303 ; provincial of
Holy Land and Cyprus. [lxi. 377]

WILLIAM DE SHEPESHEVED (*fl.* 1320 ?). [See
SHEPESHEVED.]

WILLIAM OF EXETER (*fl.* 1330 ?). [See EXETER.]

WILLIAM DE AYREMINNE (*d.* 1336). [See AYRE-
MINNE.]

WILLIAM OF COVENTRY (*fl.* 1360), Carmelite ; wrote
on history of Carmelites and other subjects.
[lxi. 377]

WILLIAM OF BERTON (*fl.* 1376). [See BERTON.]

WILLIAM OF ALNWICK (*d.* 1449). [See ALNWICK.]

WILLIAM OF WORCESTER or WYRCESTER (1415 ?–
1482 ?). [See WORCESTER.]

WILLIAM DE MACHLINIA (*fl.* 1482–1490). [See
MACHLINIA.]

WILLIAMS, ANNA (1706–1783), poetess and friend
of Dr. Johnson ; daughter of Zachariah Williams [q. v.] ;
became intimate with Dr. Johnson, and from 1752 lived
with him whenever he had a house ; lost her sight through
an eye-operation ; published, 1766, ' Miscellanies in Prose
and Verse,' to which Dr. Johnson and Mrs. Thrale contributed. [lxi. 378]

WILLIAMS, CHARLES (1796–1866), congregational
divine ; minister successively at Newark-upon-Trent,
Salisbury, London, and Sibbertoft ; editor to Religious
Tract Society. [lxi. 398]

WILLIAMS, SIR CHARLES HANBURY (1708–1759),
satirical writer and diplomatist ; son of John Hanbury
[q. v.] ; assumed name of Williams, 1729 ; educated at
Eton ; M.P. for Monmouthshire, 1734–47, and Leominster,
1754–9 ; paymaster of marine forces, 1739–42 ; K.B., 1744 ;
envoy to court of Dresden, 1746 ; envoy extraordinary
at Berlin, at Dresden, 1751–3, Vienna, 1753, again at
Dresden, 1754, St. Petersburg, 1755–7 ; died by his own
hand. He published numerous occasional satirical verses
and other writings ; a fairly complete collected edition
appeared, 1822. [lxi. 379]

WILLIAMS, CHARLES JAMES BLASIUS (1805–
1889), physician ; M.D. Edinburgh, 1824 ; studied in Paris
and London ; L.R.C.P.; F.R.S., 1835 ; professor of medicine and physician to University College, London, 1839 ;
F.R.C.P., 1840 ; censor, 1846 and 1847 ; Lumleian lecturer,
1862 ; took part in founding Consumption Hospital,
Brompton, 1841 ; first president of Pathological Society,
1846 ; physician extraordinary to Queen Victoria, 1874 ;
published ' Principles of Medicine' (1843) and other works.
[lxi. 383]

WILLIAMS, SIR CHARLES JAMES WATKIN
(1824–1884), judge ; studied medicine at University College Hospital ; entered St. Mary Hall, Oxford, 1851 ;
called to bar at Middle Temple, 1854 ; tubman of court
of exchequer, 1859 ; Q.C., 1873 ; liberal M.P. for Denbigh
boroughs, 1868–80, and Carnarvonshire, 1880 ; puisne
judge, 1880 ; published legal writings. [lxi. 384]

WILLIAMS, DANIEL (1643 ?–1716), nonconformist
divine and benefactor ; chaplain to Countess of Meath
(*d.* 1685), 1664 ; preached at Drogheda ; joint-minister at
Wood Street, Dublin, 1667–87 ; retired before animosity of
Roman catholics to London, 1687 ; refused to recognise
James II's right of dispensation on declaration of liberty
of conscience ; presbyterian minister at Hand Alley,
Bishopsgate, London, 1687–1716 ; lecturer at Painters' Hall,
London ; published, 1692, ' Gospel Truth,' founded on his
lectures, and giving rise to controversy, which occasioned
his dismissal from lectureship, 1694 ; opposed bill against
occasional conformity, *c.* 1704 ; headed joint address from

the 'three denominations' on accession of Queen Anne and of George I : left large sums to be devoted chiefly to scholastic and religious purposes. His extensive library formed the nucleus of that now housed at University Hall, Gordon Square, London. [lxi. 385]

WILLIAMS, SIR DAVID (1536 ?-1613), judge ; barrister, Middle Temple, 1576 ; recorder of Brecknock, 1587-1604 ; queen's attorney-general in court of great sessions for counties of Carmarthen, Cardigan, Pembroke, Brecknock, and Radnor ; serjeant-at-law, 1593 ; M.P., Brecknock, 1584-5, 1586-7, 1588-9, and 1597-8 ; knighted and appointed fifth puisne justice of king's bench, 1603. [lxi. 389]

WILLIAMS, DAVID (d. 1794), Welsh hymn-writer ; methodist 'exhorter' ; worked as tailor at Llan Fynydd, and subsequently as schoolmaster in various towns ; joined baptists, 1777 ; published several collections of hymns. [lxi. 390]

WILLIAMS, DAVID (1738-1816), founder of Royal Literary Fund ; studied for dissenting ministry at Carmarthen academy ; ordained minister at Frome, 1758 ; removed to Mint meeting, Exeter, 1761 ; minister at Southwood Lane, Highgate, 1769-73 ; set up school at Chelsea, 1773 ; opened, 1776, chapel in Margaret Street, Cavendish Square, London, where he lectured till 1780 ; founded, 1788, by private subscription, Literary Fund, which was incorporated, 1812 ; became Royal Literary Fund, 1842 ; in Paris, 1792-3 ; published numerous lectures, sermons, and treatises on religious, educational, and other questions. [lxi. 390]

WILLIAMS, DAVID (1792-1850), geologist ; M.A. Jesus College, Oxford, 1820 ; vicar of Kingston and rector of Bleadon ; F.G.S., 1828 ; published papers on geological subjects. [lxi. 393]

WILLIAMS, EDWARD (fl. 1650), author of 'Virgo Triumphans, or Virginia truly valued,' published, 1650. [lxi. 394]

WILLIAMS, EDWARD (1750-1813), nonconformist divine ; independent minister, 1775-7, at Denbigh, and 1777-91, Oswestry, where he took charge of dissenting academy, 1782-91 ; theological tutor at Rotherham, 1795-1813 ; published works of moderate Calvinistic tendency. [lxi. 394]

WILLIAMS, EDWARD (1746-1826), Welsh bard, known as 'Iolo Morgannwg' ; worked as stonemason ; opened bookseller's shop at Cowbridge, 1797, and later took to land surveying at Flemingston ; published 'Poems, Lyric and Pastoral,' 1794 ; became champion of the bardic system, the spurious antiquity of which he accepted in good faith ; one of the three editors of 'Myvyrian Archaiology' (1801). [lxi. 394]

WILLIAMS, EDWARD (1762-1833), antiquary ; educated at Repton and Pembroke College, Oxford ; M.A., 1787 ; fellow of All Souls College, Oxford ; perpetual curate at Battlefield and Uffington, 1786-1833 ; rector of Chelsfield, 1817-33 ; left manuscripts on history and antiquities of Shropshire. [lxi. 395]

WILLIAMS, EDWARD ELLERKER (1793-1822), friend of Shelley ; commissioned in East India Company's cavalry in India, c. 1811 ; made Shelley's acquaintance at Pisa, 1821 ; perished with Shelley in yacht Don Juan sailing from Leghorn to Lerici. [lxi. 396]

WILLIAMS, SIR EDWARD VAUGHAN (1797-1875), judge ; son of John Williams (1757-1810) [q. v.] ; of Winchester College, Westminster School, and Trinity College, Cambridge ; M.A., 1824 ; barrister, Lincoln's Inn, 1823 ; puisne judge of court of common pleas, 1846 ; knighted, 1847 ; privy councillor, 1865. [lxi. 396]

WILLIAMS, ELIEZER (1754-1820), historian and genealogist ; son of Peter Williams [q. v.] ; M.A. Jesus College, Oxford, 1781 ; ordained priest, 1778 ; naval chaplain, 1780 ; evening lecturer at All Hallows, Lombard Street, London ; chaplain to Tilbury fort, 1799 ; vicar of Lampeter, where he kept school, 1805-20 ; published poetical, historical, and genealogical writings. [lxi. 397]

WILLIAMS, FREDERICK SMEETON (1829-1886), congregational divine ; son of Charles Williams (1796-1866) [q. v.] ; studied at University and New colleges, London ; tutor at Congregational Institute, 1861-86 ; published 'Our Iron Roads,' 1852, and other works relating to railways. [lxi. 398]

WILLIAMS, GEORGE (1762-1834), physician ; B.A. Corpus Christi College, Oxford, 1781 ; studied at St. Bartholomew's Hospital, London ; M.D. Oxford, 1788 ; physician to Radcliffe Infirmary, Oxford ; regius and Sherardian professor of botany, 1796-1834 ; Radcliffe librarian, 1810. [lxi. 399]

WILLIAMS, GEORGE (1814-1878), divine and topographer ; educated at Eton and King's College, Cambridge; fellow, 1835-70 ; M.A., 1840 ; incorporated at Oxford, 1847 ; B.D. Cambridge, 1849 ; chaplain to Bishop Alexander at Jerusalem, 1841-3 ; warden of St. Columba's College, Rathfarnham, near Dublin, 1850 ; vice-provost of King's College, Cambridge, 1854-7 ; university pro-proctor, 1858 ; honorary canon of Cumbrae College, 1864, and of Winchester Cathedral, 1874 ; vicar of Ringwood, 1869 ; published 'The Holy City' (1845) and other topographical writings. [lxi. 399]

WILLIAMS, GEORGE JAMES (1719-1805), wit, known as 'Gilly Williams'; son of William Peere Williams [q. v.] ; receiver-general of excise, 1774-1801 ; intimate friend of Dick Edgecumbe and of George Selwyn and Horace Walpole, with whom he corresponded. [lxi. 400]

WILLIAMS, GRIFFITH (1589 ?-1672), bishop of Ossory ; M.A. Jesus College, Cambridge, 1609 ; D.D., 1621 ; incorporated M.A. Oxford, 1610 ; lecturer at St. Paul's Cathedral ; rector of St. Bennet Sherehog, London, 1612 ; suspended for high church sympathies, 1616 ; rector of Llanllechid ; rector of Trefdraeth, 1626 ; prebendary of Westminster, 1628-41 ; dean of Bangor, 1634-72 ; royal chaplain, 1636 ; bishop of Ossory, 1641 ; fled to England on outbreak of Irish rebellion, 1641 ; published vigorous invectives against parliamentarians ; suffered many hardships during war ; spent considerable sums in restoring his cathedral after Restoration ; held prebend of Mayne in his diocese with his bishopric ; published sermons and religious treatises. [lxi. 401]

WILLIAMS, GRIFFITH (1769-1838), Welsh bard ; worked in Lord Penrhyn's quarry, 1790 ; published 'Ffrwyth Awen' (1816) and other writings. [lxi. 403]

WILLIAMS, HELEN MARIA (1762-1827), authoress ; published 'Edwin and Eltruda,' a tale in verse, 1782, and adopted literary profession ; resided chiefly in France after 1788 ; adopted with enthusiasm principles of the revolution ; imprisoned as Girondist by Robespierre, narrowly escaping execution ; published writings relating to France, besides poems and other works. [lxi. 404]

WILLIAMS, HENRY (1792-1867), missionary ; midshipman, 1806 ; saw considerable service, and retired as lieutenant, 1815, receiving half-pay till 1827 ; ordained priest, 1822 ; went as missionary to New Zealand, 1823, and laboured at Paihia, subsequently extending work to Hot Lakes district, the Waikato River, the Bay of Plenty, the east coast, and Otaki ; assisted in obtaining signatures of Maori chiefs to treaty of Waitangi establishing British supremacy, 1840 ; came into conflict with (Sir) George Grey, who erroneously attributed to missionaries responsibility for Maori war, c. 1845 ; died at Pakaraka. [lxi. 405]

WILLIAMS, HUGH WILLIAM (1773-1829), landscape-painter ; travelled in Italy and Greece, and published account of travels, illustrated by engravings from his sketches, 1820, earning name of 'Grecian Williams'; original member of Associated Artists in Water Colour, 1808 ; associate of Royal Institution, Edinburgh. [lxi. 407]

WILLIAMS, ISAAC (1802-1865), poet and theologian ; educated at Harrow and Trinity College, Oxford ; M.A., 1831 ; B.D., 1839 ; fellow ; ordained priest, 1831 ; philosophy lecturer, 1832 ; rhetoric lecturer, 1834-40 ; contributed verses to 'British Magazine'; wrote celebrated tract, No. 80, in 'Tracts for the Times,' on 'Reserve in communicating Religious Knowledge ; stood unsuccessfully for professorship of poetry at Oxford, 1842 ; lived at Stinchcombe from 1848 ; his work in 'Lyra Apostolica' (1836) signed 'ζ'; published volumes of poems, chiefly religious, besides religious works in prose. [lxi. 408]

WILLIAMS, JANE (1806-1885), Welsh historian and miscellaneous writer ; known as 'Ysgafell'; lived at Neuadd Felen, and, from 1856, in London ; published 'History of Wales' (to end of Tudor dynasty), 1869, and other works in verse and prose. [lxi. 411]

WILLIAMS, JOHN, BARON WILLIAMS OF THAME (1500 ?–1559), politician ; clerk of the king's jewels, 1530 ; associated with Thomas Cromwell as treasurer of king's jewels, 1536 ; receiver of lands of Woburn Abbey, 1538 ; sheriff of Oxfordshire, 1538 ; knighted, c. 1537 ; sole keeper of king's jewels, c. 1539–44 ; treasurer of court of augmentations, 1544–53 ; M.P., Oxfordshire, 1542 and 1547–54 ; sent with Wingfield to arrest Protector Somerset, 1549 ; supported Queen Mary's cause ; had temporary custody of Princess Elizabeth, 1554, treating her with much consideration ; created Baron Williams of Thame, 1554 ; chamberlain to Philip II ; lord president of Wales, 1559. [lxi. 412]

WILLIAMS, JOHN (1582–1650), archbishop of York ; B.A. St. John's College, Cambridge, 1601 ; fellow, 1603 ; M.A., 1605 ; received living of Honington, Suffolk, 1605 ; prebendary of Hereford, 1612 ; B.D., 1613 ; prebendary and precentor of Lincoln, 1613 ; prebendary of Peterborough, 1616 ; D.D., 1617 ; dean of Salisbury, 1619, of Westminster, 1620 ; lord-keeper and bishop of Lincoln, 1621 ; gained favour of Buckingham and acted as his adviser ; opposed war with Spain ; removed from office of lord-keeper ; adopted mediatory tone in dispute which ensued over 'Petition of Right,' 1628 ; charged in Starchamber with betraying secrets of privy council, 1628, and with subornation of perjury, 1635, and fined and suspended from exercise of function, 1637, and imprisoned in Tower of London, 1637–40 ; chairman of committee to consider innovations concerning religion, 1641 ; archbishop of York, 1641–50 : retired to Conway on outbreak of war, 1642 ; being put forward as leader by his countrymen after disaster of Naseby, 1645, made terms with parliamentary commander, Mytton. He gave money for building library of St. John's College, Cambridge. [lxi. 414]

WILLIAMS, JOHN (1636 ?–1709), bishop of Chichester ; M.A. Magdalen Hall, Oxford, 1658 ; incorporated at Cambridge, 1660 ; D.D. Cambridge, 1690 ; prebendary of St. Paul's, London, 1683 ; chaplain to William and Mary ; prebendary of Canterbury ; bishop of Chichester, 1696 ; published controversial writings. [lxi. 420]

WILLIAMS, JOHN (1727–1798), nonconformist divine ; studied at Cambrian academy, Carmarthen ; minister at Stamford, Lincolnshire, 1752, Wokingham, Berkshire, 1755, and Sydenham, 1767–95 ; published 'Concordance to Greek New Testament,' 1767, and other works. [lxi. 420]

WILLIAMS, JOHN (1757–1810), lawyer ; M.A. Wadham College, Oxford, 1781 ; fellow, 1780–92 ; barrister, Inner Temple, 1784 ; serjeant-at-law, 1794 ; king's serjeant, 1804 ; brought out with Richard Burn [q. v.] tenth and eleventh editions of Sir William Blackstone's 'Commentaries,' 1787 and 1791. [lxi. 421]

WILLIAMS, JOHN (1745–1818), schoolmaster at Cardigan, 1766–70, and at Ystrad-meurig, where his academy gained great reputation from 1770. [lxi. 427]

WILLIAMS, JOHN (1761–1818), satirist and miscellaneous writer, known by pseudonym 'Anthony Pasquin' ; worked as journalist in Dublin, Brighton, Bath, and London ; lost action for libel against Robert Faulder, the bookseller, for libel in Gifford's 'Baviad and Mæviad,' 1797 ; edited New York democratic paper, 'The Federalist' ; published satirical poems and other writings ; died at Brooklyn. [lxi. 422]

WILLIAMS, JOHN (1796–1839), missionary ; apprenticed to a furnishing ironmonger in London ; entered service of London Missionary Society and went to Papetoai in Eimeo, one of Society islands, 1817 ; proceeded to Raiatea, 1818, established mission station and introduced customs of civilisation ; built a ship for himself and made missionary voyages to Hervey, Cook, Austral, Navigators', and Friendly islands ; came to England, and did much to quicken growing interest in missions, 1834 ; visited Samoan islands, Society Group, and New Hebrides, 1839, and was killed and eaten by natives of Erromanga. He translated the New Testament into the Raratongan language. [lxi. 423]

WILLIAMS, JOHN (1753–1841), banker and mine-adventurer ; manager of Wheal Maiden mine, Burncoose, Cornwall ; worked sulphur mines in co. Wicklow ; developed manganese industry at Calstock, East Cornwall,

1806 ; partner in Cornish bank at Truro, 1810 ; contracted, in conjunction with Messrs. Fox of Falmouth, to build breakwater at Plymouth, 1812 ; retired from business, 1828. On 2 or 3 May 1812 he foresaw in a dream the assassination of Perceval—one of the best-authenticated instances of prevision, or second sight. [lxi. 425]

WILLIAMS, SIR JOHN (1777–1846), judge ; M.A. Trinity College, Cambridge, 1801 ; fellow ; barrister, Inner Temple, 1804 ; junior counsel in trial of Queen Caroline, 1820 ; liberal M.P. for Lincoln, 1822–6, and Winchilsea, 1830–2 ; K.C., 1827 ; solicitor-general and attorney-general to Queen Adelaide, 1830 ; baron of exchequer, 1834 ; knighted and transferred to king's bench, 1834. [lxi. 426]

WILLIAMS, JOHN (1792–1858), archdeacon of Cardigan ; son of John Williams (1745–1818) [q. v.] ; B.A. Balliol College, Oxford, 1814 ; M.A., 1838 ; vicar of Lampeter and master of school established by Eliezer Williams [q. v.], 1820 ; rector of newly established academy at Edinburgh, 1824–7 and 1829–47 ; professor of Latin at London University, 1827–8 ; archdeacon of Cardigan, 1833 ; warden of new school at Llandovery, 1847–53 ; F.R.S. Edinburgh ; one of the greatest classical scholars Wales has produced. His publications include ' Gomer ; or a Brief Analysis of the Language and Knowledge of the Ancient Cymry,' incidentally claiming that Welsh, in its earliest forms, contained vocables expressive of philosophical truths, 1854, and ' Homerus,' 1842. [lxi. 427]

WILLIAMS, JOHN (1811–1862), Welsh antiquary ; known as ' Ab Ithel ' ; B.A. Jesus College, Oxford, 1835 ; M.A., 1838 ; rector of Llan ym Mowddwy, 1849–62 ; rector of Llan Enddwyn and perpetual curate of Llan Ddwywe, 1862 ; formed Cambrian Archæological Association, 1846 ; joint-editor, 1846–51, and sole editor, 1851–3, of 'Archæologia Cambrensis' ; established Cambrian Institute, 1851, and started and edited ' Cambrian Journal.' [lxi. 430]

WILLIAMS, SIR JOHN BICKERTON (1792–1855), nonconformist writer articled as attorney ; admitted attorney, 1816 ; practised at Shrewsbury, 1816–41 ; mayor of Shrewsbury, 1836 ; knighted, 1837 ; F.S.A., 1824 ; fellow of American Antiquarian Society, 1838 ; published biographical and other writings relating to nonconformists. [lxi. 431]

WILLIAMS, JOSEPH (fl. 1673–1700), actor ; entered Dorset Garden company, c. 1673 ; with Theatre Royal company, c. 1682–c. 1695 ; with Betterton at Lincoln's Inn Fields, London, 1700. His parts include Henry VI in Crowne's alterations of Shakespeare's ' Henry VI ' and the Bastard in Tate's alteration of ' King Lear,' 1681. [lxi. 432]

WILLIAMS, JOSHUA (1813–1881), legal author ; educated at University College, London ; barrister, Lincoln's Inn, 1838 ; bencher, 1865 ; conveyancing counsel to court of chancery, 1852 ; Q.C., 1865 ; professor of law of real and personal property to Inns of Court, 1875–80 ; published works on law of real and personal property. [lxi. 433]

WILLIAMS, (MARIA) JANE (1795–1873), musician and compiler ; obtained prize at eisteddfodau held at Abergavenny for best collection of unpublished Welsh music, 1837 (published, 1844). [lxi. 411]

WILLIAMS, MONTAGU STEPHEN (1835–1892), barrister ; educated at Eton ; ensign, 1856 ; barrister, Inner Temple, 1862 ; joined Old Bailey sessions and home circuit ; junior prosecuting counsel to treasury, 1879 ; metropolitan stipendiary magistrate, 1886 ; Q.C., 1888 ; wrote and adapted dramatic pieces, and published autobiographical works. [lxi. 433]

WILLIAMS, MORRIS (1809–1874), Welsh poet, known in bardic circles as ' Nicander ' ; apprenticed as carpenter ; educated with assistance of friends ; M.A. Jesus College, Cambridge, 1838 ; rector of Llan Rhuddlad, Anglesey, 1859 ; rural dean of Talebolion, 1872 ; won several prizes at eisteddfodau ; published works in Welsh. [lxi. 434]

WILLIAMS, MOSES (1686–1742), Welsh antiquary ; B.A. University College, Oxford, 1708 ; sub-librarian at Ashmolean Museum ; ordained deacon, 1709 ; priest, 1713 ; vicar of Llan Wenog, 1715–42 ; incorporated M.A. Cambridge ; rector of Chilton Trinity and St. Mary's, Bridgewater, 1732–42 ; published works relating to Welsh philology and antiquities. [lxi. 435]

WILLIAMS, PENRY (1800?–1885), artist; studied at Royal Academy, and exhibited between 1822 and 1869; settled at Rome, 1827; associate of Society of Painters in Water-colours, 1828–33. [lxi. 435]

WILLIAMS, PETER (1722–1796), Welsh biblical commentator; curate and schoolmaster at Eglwys Cummin, 1741; joined Welsh Calvinistic methodists, 1746; itinerant preacher; published in monthly parts annotated edition of bible in Welsh, 1767–70; expelled from methodist connexion, 1791, on ground that some of his annotations savoured of Sabellianism; preached at chapel at Water Street, Carmarthen, 1791–6; assisted in editorship of earliest Welsh magazine, 'Trysorfa Gwybodaeth, neu Eurgrawn Cymraeg,' 1770; published several volumes of hymns, translations in Welsh, and other works. [lxi. 436]

WILLIAMS, PETER (1756?–1837), Welsh divine; M.A. Christ Church, Oxford, 1783; D.D., 1802; archdeacon of Merioneth, 1802–9; canon of Bangor, 1809–18; published sermons and other writings. [lxi. 438]

WILLIAMS, PETER BAYLY (1765–1836), antiquary; son of Peter Williams (1722–1796) [q. v.]; B.A. Christ Church, Oxford, 1790; incumbent of Llanrug-with-Llanberis, Carnarvonshire, 1792–1836; published antiquarian works relating to Wales. [lxi. 438]

WILLIAMS, RICHARD D'ALTON (1822–1862), Irish poet; studied medicine at Dublin; joined 'Young Ireland' movement; contributed poems to 'Nation'; obtained medical diploma, 1849; professor of belles-lettres at Jesuit College, Springhill, Mobile, America, c. 1851-6. His collected poems appeared, 1894. [lxi. 438]

WILLIAMS, ROBERT or ROGER (*fl.* 1680), mezzotint-engraver; practised in London and brought out portraits, 1680–1704. [lxi. 439]

WILLIAMS, ROBERT (1765–1827), rear-admiral; entered navy, 1777; lieutenant, 1783; at Cape St. Vincent, 1796; commander and acting captain, 1796; captain, 1797; rear-admiral, 1823. [lxi. 439]

WILLIAMS, ROBERT (1787?–1845), physician; M.D. Trinity College, Cambridge, 1816; F.R.C.P., 1817; censor, 1831, and elect, 1844; assistant-physician, 1816, and physician, 1817–45, of St. Thomas's Hospital, London; discovered curative power of iodide of potassium in later stages of syphilis; published 'Elements of Medicine,' 1836–1841. [lxi. 440]

WILLIAMS, ROBERT (1767–1850), Welsh bard; known as 'Robert ap Gwilym Ddu'; published 'Gardd Eifion,' poems, 1841. [lxi. 440]

WILLIAMS, ROBERT (1810–1881), Celtic scholar; M.A. Christ Church, Oxford, 1836; vicar of Llangadwaladr, West Denbighshire, 1837–77; perpetual curate of Rhydycroesau, near Oswestry, 1838–79; rector of Culmington, Herefordshire, 1879–81; honorary canon of St. Asaph, 1872–81; discovered at Peniarth the 'Ordinale de Vita Sancti Mereadoci,' a previously unknown Cornish drama; published 'Lexicon Cornu-Britannicum : a Dictionary of Ancient Celtic Language of Cornwall,' 1865, and other works. [lxi. 440]

WILLIAMS, SIR ROGER (1540?–1595), soldier; page in household of Sir William Herbert, first earl of Pembroke [q. v.]; joined volunteers under Thomas Morgan (*d.* 1595) [q. v.], defending Flushing, 1572; lieutenant to (Sir) John Norris (1547?–1597) [q. v.] in Low Countries, 1577–84; held command and served with distinction in army under Leicester serving in Low Countries, 1585; Zutphen, 1586; knighted, 1586; besieged at Sluys, which was taken by Parma, 1587; master of horse in camp at Tilbury to oppose possible landing of Spanish army, 1588; accompanied Willoughby to Dieppe, 1589, and subsequently served in cause of Henry of Navarre; succeeded Essex as commander of English troops in camp before Rouen, 1592; fought with great valour at siege of Rue, 1592; published 'A Brief Discourse of War,' 1590. [lxi. 441]

WILLIAMS, ROGER (1604?–1683), colonist and pioneer of religious liberty; B.A. Pembroke College, Cambridge, 1626; private chaplain; went to America and became minister at Boston, 1631; assistant-minister at Salem, 1631, and later at Plymouth; formally appointed chief teacher at Salem, 1635; maintained 'dangerous' opinions as to civil authority in matters of conscience,

and was banished from Massachusetts, 1635; settled at Manton's Neck, on east bank of Seekonk river; removed to banks of the 'Mooshausic,' where he founded Providence, 1636; founded first baptist church in Providence, 1639, but soon severed connection with baptists; published 'Key into the Language of America,' 1643, soon after returning to England, and obtained charter giving permission to Providence plantations in Narragansetts Bay to rule themselves, 1644; published 'The Bloudy Tenent,' 1644 (expounding doctrine of liberty of conscience), which was burned by the common hangman; returned to America, 1644; again in England, 1651–4, obtaining assurances of independence of his settlement; president of Rhode Island, 1654–7; elected assistant under new governor, Benedict Arnold, of Rhode Island, 1663, 1667, and 1670; captain in militia in repressing rising of Indians, 1675. His works were reprinted by the Narragansett Club, 1866–74. [lxi. 445]

WILLIAMS, ROGER (*fl.* 1680). [See WILLIAMS, ROBERT.]

WILLIAMS, ROWLAND (1817–1870), Anglican divine; educated at Eton and King's College, Cambridge; fellow, 1839; M.A., 1844; B.D., 1851; vice-principal and professor of Hebrew in Theological College of St. David's, Lampeter, 1850–62; select preacher in Cambridge University, 1854; published 'Christianity and Hinduism' (1856), an expansion of the Muir essay prize, which he gained, 1848; D.D., 1857; held living of Broad Chalke, near Salisbury, 1858; prosecuted and suspended for one year by court of arches for heterodoxy displayed in contribution to 'Essays and Reviews,' 1860, but judgment against him reversed, 1864, by judicial committee of privy council; his translation of 'Hebrew Prophets' issued, 1866–71. [lxi. 450]

WILLIAMS, SAMUEL (1788–1853), draughtsman and wood-engraver; apprenticed as printer at Colchester, where he established himself as wood-engraver; settled in London, 1819; executed illustrations for numerous publications. [lxi. 453]

WILLIAMS, TALIESIN (1787–1847), son of Edward Williams (1746–1826) [q. v.]; edited Iolo MSS. left by his father. [lxi. 395]

WILLIAMS, THOMAS (1513?–1566), speaker of House of Commons; entered Inner Temple, 1539; Lent reader, 1558 and 1561; M.P., Bodmin, 1555, Saltash, 1558, Exeter, 1563; speaker, 1563. [lxi. 454]

WILLIAMS, THOMAS (1550?–1620?), Welsh scholar; educated at Oxford; probably took orders; practised as physician; left manuscript Latin-Welsh dictionary. [lxi. 454]

WILLIAMS, THOMAS (1668–1740), Roman catholic prelate; of a Welsh family; was Dominican friar at Bornhem, near Antwerp, 1686; priest, 1692; rector of Dominican College of St. Thomas Aquinas at Louvain, 1697; provincial of English Dominican province; prior of Bornhem, 1724; bishop of Tiberiopolis, 1725; vicar-apostolic of northern district of England, 1727. [lxi. 455]

WILLIAMS, THOMAS (*fl.* 1830), wood-engraver; brother of Samuel Williams [q. v.], whose pupil he was. [lxi. 454]

WILLIAMS, SIR THOMAS (1762?–1841), admiral; entered navy, 1768; lieutenant, 1779; commander, 1783; captain, 1790; rendered distinguished service in co-operation with army in Low Countries, 1794–5; on Irish station, 1795; knighted after success with two French frigates, 1796; rear-admiral, 1809; at Lisbon, 1810; vice-admiral, 1814; admiral, 1830; G.C.B., 1831. [lxi. 455]

WILLIAMS, THOMAS (1760–1844), Welsh hymn-writer; joined Peter Williams (1722–1796) [q. v.] after his expulsion in forming separate methodist church at Aberthaw, c. 1792, and was pastor, 1798–1827; joined independent denomination, 1814. His poetical works appeared 1882. [lxi. 456]

WILLIAMS, THOMAS WALTER (1763–1833), barrister; educated at St. Paul's School, London; published legal writings; edited 'Law Journal,' 1804–6. [lxi. 457]

WILLIAMS, SIR WILLIAM, first baronet (1634–1700), solicitor-general and speaker of House of Commons; educated at Jesus College, Oxford; called to bar at Gray's Inn, 1658, and was treasurer, 1681; recorder of Chester,

1667-84; M.P., Chester, 1675; became recognised champion of privileges of the house against all extensions of royal prerogative; speaker, 1680 and 1681; leading counsel on whig side in cases involving questions of constitutional law; counsel for Algernon Sidney or Sydney [q. v.]; fined, 1686, at Jeffreys's instigation for licensing, as speaker, publication of Dangerfield's libellous ' Narrative' (1680); again recorder of Chester, 1687; knighted and appointed solicitor-general, 1687-9; appeared for James II against the seven bishops, 1688; created baronet, 1688; sat for Beaumaris in Convention parliament, 1689; on committee to draft bill of rights; K.C., 1689; lord-lieutenant for Merionethshire, 1689-90; queen's solicitor-general, 1692; M.P., Beaumaris, 1695. [lxi. 457]

WILLIAMS, WILLIAM (1717-1791), Welsh hymnwriter; ordained deacon, 1740; became closely connected with methodist movement; made evangelical tours in Wales; published many collections of hymns, which had a large share in the dissemination of methodism; a complete edition appeared, 1811. [lxi. 462]

WILLIAMS, WILLIAM (1739-1817), Welsh antiquary; apprenticed as saddler; land surveyor and clerk in Penrhyn estate office; supervisor of Lord Penrhyn's slate quarries, 1782-1803; published antiquarian writings. [lxi. 464]

WILLIAMS, WILLIAM, known as WILLIAMS OF WERN (1781-1840), Welsh preacher; worked as carpenter; preached in connection with independent church at Pen-y-stryd; studied at dissenting academy, Wrexham; ordained, 1808; made preaching tours in Wales; pastor of Welsh Tabernacle, Great Crosshall Street, Liverpool, 1836-1839. [lxi. 464]

WILLIAMS, WILLIAM (1801-1869), Welsh poet; his bardic name Caledfryn; brought up as weaver; studied for congregational ministry at Rotherham; ordained pastor of Llanerchymedd, Anglesey, 1829; pastor at Carnarvon, 1832-48, Welsh Church, Aldersgate Street, London, 1848-50, Llanrwst, 1850-7, and Groeswen, Glamorganshire, 1857-69; won many prizes at eisteddfodau from 1822; published poems and works on Welsh grammar and prosody. [lxi. 465]

WILLIAMS, WILLIAM (1800-1879), first bishop of Waiapu; brother of Henry Williams [q. v.]; B.A. Magdalen Hall, Oxford, 1825; D.C.L., 1851; ordained, 1824; studied medicine; went to New Zealand, 1826; archdeacon of Waiapu, 1843; bishop, 1859. Published 'Dictionary of New Zealand Language' (1844) and other works. [lxi. 407]

WILLIAMS, SIR WILLIAM FENWICK, baronet 'of Kars' (1800-1883), general; educated at Woolwich; second lieutenant, royal artillery, 1825; second captain, 1840; first captain, 1846; brevet major, 1846; brevet lieutenant-colonel, 1848; brevet colonel, 1854; major-general, 1855; colonel-commandant, royal artillery, 1864; lieutenant-general, 1864; general, 1868; British commissioner for settlement of Turko-Persian boundary, 1848; C.B., 1852; British commissioner with Turkish army in Anatolia, 1854; held Kars against Russians and won battle of Kars, 1855, but was compelled to capitulate; K.C.B., 1856; general-commandant of Woolwich garrison, 1856-9; M.P., Calne, 1856-9; governor of Nova Scotia, 1865; governor-general and commander-in-chief of Gibraltar, 1870-6; G.C.B., 1871; constable of Tower of London, 1881. [lxi. 466]

WILLIAMS, WILLIAM HENRY (1771-1841), physician and author; educated at Bristol Infirmary and St. Thomas's and Guy's hospitals, London; surgeon to East Norfolk militia; M.D. Caius College, Cambridge, 1811; in charge of South Military Hospital, near Ipswich, 1810; F.R.C.P., 1817; F.L.S.; published medical writings. [lxi. 467]

WILLIAMS, WILLIAM MATTIEU (1820-1892), scientific writer; apprenticed as instrument maker in Lambeth, London; studied at Edinburgh University; electrical instrument-maker in Hatton Garden, London; headmaster of Williams Secular School, Edinburgh, on the 'Birkbeck' model, 1848; master of science classes in Birmingham and Midland Institute, 1854-63; delivered Cantor lectures, 1876; F.C.S., 1857; F.R.A.S., 1872; published 'The Chemistry of Iron and Steel Making,' 1890; 'Vindication of Phrenology,' posthumous, 1894, and other works. [lxi. 468]

WILLIAMS, WILLIAM PEERE (1664-1736), law reporter; called to bar at Gray's Inn, 1687; one of counsel for defence of the Jacobite George Seton, fifth earl of Winton [q. v.], 1716; M.P. for Bishop's Castle, 1722-7; collaborated with William Melmoth in edition of Vernon's 'Reports,' 1726-8. [lxi. 469]

WILLIAMS, afterwards **WILLIAMS-FREEMAN**, WILLIAM PEERE (1742-1832), admiral of the fleet; grandson of William Peere Williams [q. v.]; joined navy, 1757; lieutenant, 1764; commander, 1768; captain, 1771; at second relief of Gibraltar, 1781; on half-pay, 1782; rear-admiral, 1794; vice-admiral, 1795; admiral, 1801; assumed name of Freeman, 1821; admiral of fleet, 1830. [lxi. 470]

WILLIAMS, ZACHARIAH (1673?-1755), medical practitioner and inventor; practised as physician and surgeon in South Wales; persuaded himself that he had discovered means of ascertaining longitude by magnetism, and went to London to submit scheme to admiralty; pensioner in Charterhouse, London, 1729-48; continued to importune admiralty in vain; invented a machine for extracting the saltness from sea-water; his 'Account of an Attempt to ascertain the Longitude ... by ... the Magnetical Needle,' 1755, edited by Dr. Johnson. [lxi. 471]

WILLIAMSON, SIR ADAM (1736-1798), lieutenant-general; studied at Woolwich; practitioner engineer, 1753; ensign, 1755; served in North America; engineer extraordinary and captain-lieutenant, 1758; served in West Indies, 1761-2; major, 16th foot, 1770; engineer in ordinary, 1770; lieutenant-colonel, 1775; in North America, 1775-6; colonel, 1782; lieutenant-governor and commander-in-chief at Jamaica, 1790-4; established British protectorate in St. Domingo, 1793, and was governor, 1794; K.B., 1794; lieutenant-general, 1797. [lxii. 1]

WILLIAMSON, ALEXANDER (1829-1890), missionary; ordained at Glasgow, 1855; under London Missionary Society in China, 1855-8; agent in China to National Bible Society of Scotland, 1863-90. [lxii. 2]

WILLIAMSON, JOHN (1751-1818), painter; apprenticed as 'ornamental' painter in Birmingham; portrait-painter in Liverpool, 1783-1818; member of Liverpool Academy. [lxii. 8]

WILLIAMSON, JOHN SUTHER (1775?-1836), colonel, royal artillery; studied at Woolwich; lieutenant, royal artillery, 1794; captain, 1803; major, 1814; C.B., 1815; lieutenant-colonel, 1817; served at Cape of Good Hope, Peninsula, and Waterloo; superintendent of Royal Military Repository, Woolwich; colonel, 1825. [lxii. 2]

WILLIAMSON, SIR JOSEPH (1633-1701), statesman and diplomatist; of Westminster School and Queen's College, Oxford; B.A., 1654; fellow and M.A., 1657; held position in office of Sir Edward Nicholas [q. v.], then secretary of state, 1660-1; keeper of Charles II's library at Whitehall and at the paper office, 1661; called to bar at Middle Temple, 1664; editor, 1665, of 'Oxford Gazette,' which became 'London Gazette,' 1666; M.P. for Thetford, 1669, 1679, 1681, and 1685, and Rochester, 1690 and 1701; knighted and appointed clerk of council in ordinary, 1672; joint British plenipotentiary to congress at Cologne, 1673-4; secretary of state, 1674; LL.D. Oxford, and privy councillor, 1674; fell victim to suspicions aroused by 'popish plot' and was removed from office, 1678; master of Clothworkers' Company, 1676; member of Royal Society, 1663, and president, 1677-80; recorder of Thetford, 1682; joint-plenipotentiary at congress of Nimeguen, 1696; signed, as joint-commissioner, the first partition treaty, 1698. [lxii. 2]

WILLIAMSON, PETER (1730-1799), author and publisher; born in Aberdeenshire; kidnapped in Aberdeen and transported to American plantations, c. 1740; returned, after many adventures, 1757, and published account of his life, for which he was convicted of libel by Aberdeen magistrates, 1758, but subsequently (1762) obtained verdict and damages against corporation; set up as bookseller and publisher in Edinburgh; issued 'Scots Spy,' 1776, and 'New Scots Spy,' periodicals, 1777; instituted penny post in Edinburgh. [lxii. 7]

WILLIAMSON, SAMUEL (1792-1840), landscape painter; son of John Williamson (1751-1818) [q. v.]; member of Liverpool Academy. [lxii. 8]

WILLIAMSON, WILLIAM CRAWFORD (1816–1895), naturalist; apprenticed to an apothecary at Scarborough, 1832; studied in Manchester and at University College, London; M.R.C.S. and L.S.A., 1840; surgeon to Chorlton-on-Medlock dispensary, 1841–68; assisted in foundation of Manchester Institute for Diseases of the Ear, 1855, and was surgeon, 1855–70; first professor of natural history, anatomy, and physiology at the Owens College, Manchester, 1851; professor of 'Natural History,' 1872, and of 'Botany,' 1880–92; resigned as emeritus professor, 1892; worked extensively as popular scientific lecturer; appointed F.R.S., 1854, for monographs on histology of teeth, fish scales, and bone; member of Literary and Philosophical Society of Manchester, 1851; received royal medal of Royal Society, 1874; hon. LL.D. Edinburgh, 1883; Wollaston medallist of Geological Society, 1890; entitled to rank by his study of the plants of the coal-measures as one of the founders of palæobotany. [lxii. 9]

WILLIBALD (700 ?–786), bishop and traveller; son of Winna, sister of Saint Boniface [q. v.]; educated at monastery at Waltham; went on pilgrimage to Rome, c. 721, and proceeded to Syria; at Benedictine monastery of Monte Casino, 728–38; bishop of Eichstädt, 741; became leader of German mission; wrote 'Vita seu Hodœporicon Sancti Willibaldi.' [lxii. 12]

WILLIBRORD or **WILBRORD,** SAINT (657 ?–738 ?), archbishop of Utrecht; a Northumbrian; educated by monks of Ripon; studied at monastery of Rathmelsigi, 677–90; ordained, 690; sent by St. Egbert [q. v.] as missionary to the Frisians, 690, and formed alliance with Pippin of Herstal, 'duke of the Franks'; archbishop of the Frisians, c. 695; built church of St. Saviour at Utrecht, which was granted him by Charles Martel, 722; retired to monastery of Echternach, where he died. [lxii. 13]

WILLIS. [See also WILLES.]

WILLIS, BROWNE (1682–1760), antiquary; of Westminster and Christ Church, Oxford; created M.A., 1720; created D.C.L., 1749; entered Inner Temple, 1700; M.P., Buckingham, 1705–8; took part in reviving Society of Antiquaries, 1717; F.S.A., 1718; published works relating to English cathedrals, a 'History of the Counties, Cities, and Boroughs in England and Wales' (1715), and other antiquarian works; left valuable manuscripts of ecclesiastical topography and biography to the Bodleian Library. [lxii. 15]

WILLIS, FRANCIS (1718–1807), physician; M.A. Brasenose College, Oxford, 1741; fellow and vice-principal; took holy orders; M.B. and M.D., 1759; physician to hospital at Lincoln, 1769; attended George III in his first attack of madness, 1788, and became popular at court. [lxii. 17]

WILLIS, SIR GEORGE HARRY SMITH (1823–1900), general; ensign, 1841; captain, 1850; fought with distinction at the battles of the Alma and Inkerman and at Sebastopol; brevet major, 1854, and brevet lieutenant-colonel, 1856; served also in Algeria and Malta; lieutenant-general, 1880; wounded at Tel-el-Kebir, 1882; thanked by parliament and made K.C.B.; general, 1887; G.C.B., 1895. [Suppl. iii. 515]

WILLIS, HENRY BRITTAN (1810–1884), painter; exhibited at Royal Academy, British Institution, and Suffolk Street Gallery, London, 1844–62; member of Old Water-colour Society, 1863. [lxii. 18]

WILLIS, JOHN (d. 1628 ?), stenographer; M.A. Christ's College, Cambridge, 1596; B.D., 1603; rector of St. Mary Bothaw, Dowgate Hill, London, 1601–6, and of Bentley Parva, Essex, 1606; published 'The Art of Stenographie,' 1602, the first practical and rational scheme of modern shorthand founded on a strictly alphabetical basis, and 'Mnemonica; sive Ars Reminiscendi,' 1618. [lxii. 18]

WILLIS, JOHN WALPOLE (1793–1877), justice of king's bench, Upper Canada; barrister, Gray's Inn, 1817; joined northern circuit; puisne judge of king's bench; received from colonial office warrant to organise court of chancery in Upper Canada, but came into conflict with Sir Peregrine Maitland [q. v.], lieutenant-governor, who removed him; held judicial appointments successively in Demerara and New South Wales (1841–2); published legal works. [lxii. 19]

WILLIS, RICHARD (1664–1734), bishop of Gloucester, Salisbury, and Winchester; B.A. Wadham College Oxford, 1688; fellow of All Souls College, Oxford, 1688; D.D. Lambeth, 1695; lecturer at St. Clement's, Strand, London, 1692; chaplain to William III in Holland, 1694–1695; prebendary of Westminster, 1695; a promoter of Society for Promoting Christian Knowledge, 1699; dean of Lincoln, 1701; bishop of Gloucester, 1714–21; lord almoner, 1717; bishop of Salisbury, 1721–3, and of Winchester, 1723–34. [lxii. 20]

WILLIS, ROBERT (1800–1875), professor of mechanism and archæologist; grandson of Francis Willis [q. v.]; B.A. Gonville and Caius College, Cambridge, 1826; Frankland fellow, 1826; foundation fellow, 1829 ordained priest, 1827; F.R.S., 1830; Jacksonian professor of applied mechanics at Cambridge, 1837–75; invented odontograph, 1837; published 'Principles of Mechanism,' 1841; member of commission appointed to inquire into application of iron to railway structures, 1849; lecturer on applied mechanics at school of mines, 1853; published 'Remarks on Architecture of Middle Ages,' 1835, and 'Architectural Nomenclature of Middle Ages,' 1843; invented the cymagraph, 1841; member of Archæological Institute, 1843. His works include 'Architectural History of Conventual Buildings of Monastery of Christ-church, Canterbury,' 1869, and numerous treatises elucidating the mechanical construction of English cathedrals. [lxii. 21]

WILLIS, ROBERT (1799–1878), medical writer; M.D. Edinburgh, 1819; M.R.C.S. England, 1823; L.R.C.P., 1837; librarian of College of Surgeons, 1827–45; published medical works and translations. [lxii. 23]

WILLIS, THOMAS (1582–1660 ?), schoolmaster; M.A. St. John's College, Oxford, 1609; incorporated at Cambridge, 1619; schoolmaster at Isleworth; published two Latin school-books. [lxii. 24]

WILLIS, THOMAS (1621–1675), physician; M.A. Christ Church, Oxford, 1642; M.B., 1646; M.D., 1660; Sedleian professor of natural philosophy, 1660; F.R.S.; F.R.C.P., 1664; practised in London from 1666; the first to distinguish the form of diabetes known as 'diabetes mellitus'; published 'Cerebri Anatome Nervorumque descriptio et usus,' 1664, and other works; buried in Westminster Abbey. [lxii. 25]

WILLIS, THOMAS (d. 1692), divine; son of Thomas Willis (1582–1660 ?) [q. v.]; M.A. St. John's College, Oxford, 1646; minister of Twickenham, Middlesex, 1646; deprived, 1661; conformed and was rector of Dunton, Buckinghamshire, 1663–92; vicar of Kingston-on-Thames, 1671–92; chaplain in ordinary to Charles II; D.D., 1670; published religious writings. [lxii. 24]

WILLIS, TIMOTHY (fl. 1615), writer on alchemy; of Merchant Taylors' School; fellow of St. John's College, Oxford; B.A. Gloucester Hall, Oxford, 1582; envoy to Muscovy; published works on alchemy. [lxii. 26]

WILLISEL, THOMAS (d. 1675 ?), naturalist; served as foot soldier under Cromwell; engaged by Royal Society to collect zoological and botanical specimens in England and Scotland; gardener to John Vaughan, third earl of Carbery, in Jamaica, 1674 till death. [lxii. 26]

WILLISON, GEORGE (1741–1797), portrait-painter; grandson of John Willison [q. v.]; exhibited at Royal Academy, 1767–77. [lxii. 27]

WILLISON, JOHN (1680–1750), Scottish divine; M.A. Glasgow; licensed by presbytery of Stirling, 1701; ordained minister of Brechin, 1703; minister of South Church, Dundee, 1716; took prominent part in endeavour to prevent schism caused by scceders under Ebenezer Erskine [q. v.]; published religious writings. [lxii. 27]

WILLMORE, ARTHUR (1814–1888), line-engraver; brother of James Tibbitts Willmore [q. v.]; exhibited at Royal Academy between 1858 and 1885. [lxii. 29]

WILLMORE, JAMES TIBBITTS (1800–1863), line-engraver; apprenticed to William Radclyffe (1783–1855) [q. v.]; assistant to Charles Heath (1785–1848) [q. v.]; associate engraver of Royal Academy, 1843. [lxii. 28]

WILLMOTT, ROBERT ARIS (1809–1863), author; of Merchant Taylors' and Harrow schools; B.A. Trinity

College, Cambridge, 1841; incumbent of St. Catherine, Bearwood, 1846-62. His publications include collections of extracts in verse and prose from English writers. [lxii. 29]

WILLOBIE, HENRY (1574?-1596?). [See WIL-LOUGHBY.]

WILLOCK or **WILLOCKS**, JOHN (d. 1585), Scottish reformer: educated at Glasgow University; preacher at St. Catherine's Church, London; resigned charge, 1553, and practised as physician at Emden, Friesland; settled in Scotland, 1558; preached regularly in St. John's Church, Ayr; indicted for heresy and outlawed, 1559; substitute for Knox as minister of St. Giles, Edinburgh, 1559; appointed by committee of parliament superintendent of the west, 1560; on commission appointed to draw up first book of discipline, 1560; moderator of general assembly, 1562, 1564, 1565, and 1568; rector of Loughborough, Leicestershire, 1562-85. [lxii. 30]

WILLOUGHBY. [See also WILLUGHBY.]

WILLOUGHBY DE BROKE, third BARON (1621-1711). [See VERNEY, RICHARD.]

WILLOUGHBY DE ERESBY, BARON (1555-1601). [See BERTIE, PEREGRINE.]

WILLOUGHBY, FRANCIS, fifth BARON WIL-LOUGHBY OF PARHAM (1613?-1666), parliamentary lord-lieutenant of district of Lindsey, Lincolnshire; commanded regiment of horse under Essex, 1642; lord-lieutenant and commander-in-chief in Lincolnshire; besieged by royalists at Gainsborough and surrendered, 1643; captured Bolingbroke Castle, 1643; one of leaders of presbyterians in parliament, 1647; one of seven lords impeached on triumph of independents and army, 1647, and was imprisoned, 1647-8; fled to Holland and joined royalists, 1648; made vice-admiral of fleet in Downs, which revolted from parliament, 1648; governor of Barbados, 1650; repudiated right of parliament to control islanders who were not represented, 1651, but was compelled to treat with Sir George Ayscue, who arrived with parliamentary fleet and effected landing; returned to England, 1652; imprisoned for plotting with royalists, 1655 and 1656; governor of Barbados, St. Kitts, Nevis, Montserrat, and Antigua, 1663; lost at sea in expedition to retake St. Kitts, which the French had occupied, 1666. [lxii. 31]

WILLOUGHBY or **WILLOBIE**, HENRY (1574?-1596?), eponymous hero of poem, 'Willobies Avisa'; educated at St. John's College, Oxford; served in army abroad. He may be identical with the hero of 'Willobie his Avisa,' 1594 (perhaps written by Hadrian Dorrell, probably an assumed name), a poem, the chief interest of which lies in its apparent bearings on the biography of Shakespeare, who has been identified with Willobie's alleged friend figuring in the piece as 'W. S.' [lxii. 35]

WILLOUGHBY, SIR HUGH (d. 1554), sea-captain; served in expedition to Scotland, 1544; knighted, 1544; captain of Lowther Castle, 1548-9; captain of Bona Esperanza in fleet under Richard Chancellor [q. v.] dispatched by Sebastian Cabot to search for north-eastern passage to Cathay and India, 1553; arrived, after erratic passage, at Arzina, near Kegor, Norwegian Lapland, and there perished. [lxii. 36]

WILLOUGHBY, SIR NESBIT JOSIAH (1777-1849), rear-admiral; entered navy, 1790; present at occupation of Amboyna and Banda, 1796; commander, 1799; with Nelson at Copenhagen, 1801; dismissed service for insolence to his captain, 1801; volunteered with Sir John Thomas Duckworth [q. v.] in West Indies, 1803; lieutenant, 1803; served with distinction at blockade of Cape Français; in operations against Curaçoa, 1804; commander, 1808; took part in action at St. Paul's, Mauritius, 1809; promoted post-captain, 1810, for service at Jacotel; at seizure of Isle de la Passe, 1810; defeated by French, but honourably acquitted in subsequent court-martial; volunteered for service with Russian army; accompanied Count Steinheil and was captured by French; imprisoned in Château de Bouillon, and later at Peronne, whence he escaped; C.B.,1815; knighted, 1827; K.C.H., 1832; naval aide-de-camp to Queen Victoria, 1841; rear-admiral, 1847. [lxii. 37]

WILLOUGHBY, RICHARD DE (d. 1362), judge; knight of shire for Nottingham, 1324; chief-justice of common pleas in Ireland, c. 1324-7; justice of common pleas, 1328-30 and 1341-57; justice of king's bench, 1330. [lxii. 40]

WILLOUGHBY, SIR ROBERT, first BARON WIL-LOUGHBY DE BROKE (1452-1502), one of leaders in abortive Lancastrian rising of Henry Stafford, second duke of Buckingham [q. v.], 1483; escaped to Brittany; probably returned with Richmond, 1485; receiver of duchy of Cornwall, 1485; knight of king's body, 1485; king's councillor, 1486; sheriff of Devonshire, 1488; joint leader of expedition for defence of Brittany, 1489; envoy from Henry to Anne, duchess of Brittany, and admiral of the fleet, 1490; marshal of the army, 1492; K.G.; served against Perkin Warbeck, 1497. [lxii. 41]

WILLOUGHBY, WILLIAM, sixth BARON WIL-LOUGHBY OF PARHAM (d. 1673), colonial governor; brother of Francis Willoughby, fifth baron Willoughby [q. v.], whom he succeeded as governor of Barbados and Caribbee islands, 1667; regained Antigua and Montserrat, expelled French from Cayenne, and recaptured Surinam from Dutch. [lxii. 34]

WILLS, SIR CHARLES (1666-1741), general; served with Colonel Thomas Erle's foot regiment in Ireland; captain, 19th foot, 1691; served in Flanders; lieutenant-colonel of Viscount Charlemont's foot regiment in Ireland, 1701 and 1704, and Guadeloupe, 1703; quartermaster-general to Peterborough in Spain, 1705; colonel of regiment of marines, 1705; major-general, 1709; at Almenara and Saragossa, 1710; lieutenant-general, 1710; returned to England, 1710; with George Carpenter [q. v.] defeated Jacobites at Preston, 1715; general commanding foot, 1739; M.P., Totnes, 1714-41; privy councillor to George I; K.B., 1725. [lxii. 43]

WILLS, JAMES (1790-1868), poet and man of letters; educated at Trinity College, Dublin; entered Middle Temple, 1821; contributed to Blackwood's and other magazines; vicar of Suirville, co. Kilkenny, 1846; received living of Kilmacow, 1849, and Attanagh, 1860; published 'Lives of Illustrious and Distinguished Irishmen,' 1839-47; Donellan lecturer, Dublin University, 1855-6. Among his poems is 'The Universe,' which was published by and long attributed to Charles Robert Maturin [q. v.] [lxii. 44]

WILLS, JOHN (1741-1806), benefactor of Wadham College, Oxford; B.A. Hertford College, Oxford, 1761; M.A., 1765; fellow, 1765; warden of Wadham College, 1783-1806; D.D., 1783; vice-chancellor, 1792; made bequests to Wadham College. [lxii. 46]

WILLS, RICHARD (fl. 1558-1573). [See WILLES.]

WILLS, THOMAS (1740-1802), evangelical preacher; B.A. Magdalen Hall, Oxford, 1760; ordained priest, 1764; made acquaintance of Countess of Huntingdon at Bath, 1772; frequently preached in her chapel, and became her chaplain, 1778; minister of Spa Fields chapel, 1782-8; officiated in various London chapels till 1800, when he retired to Boskenna, Cornwall; published sermons and other religious writings. [lxii. 46]

WILLS, WILLIAM GORMAN (1828-1891), dramatist; son of James Wills [q. v.]; educated at Trinity College, Dublin; settled in London; contributed several serial stories to magazines, and practised as portrait painter; began writing for stage, and produced 'Man o' Airlie,' given at Princess's, London, 1867, 'Medea in Corinth,' 1872, 'Charles I' (played by Henry Irving), 1872, and a version of 'Faust,' 1885. [lxii. 47]

WILLS, WILLIAM HENRY (1810-1880), miscellaneous writer; member of original literary staff of 'Punch,' 1841; sub-editor of 'Daily News' under Charles Dickens, 1846; edited 'Chambers's Journal' in Edinburgh; private secretary to Dickens, c. 1849; assistant-editor of 'Household Words,' 1849, and 'All the Year Round,' 1859; retired, 1868; republished his contributions to periodicals. [lxii. 49]

WILLS, WILLIAM JOHN (1834-1861), Australian explorer; studied at Guy's and St. Bartholomew's hospitals, London; emigrated to Victoria; entered, as volunteer, office of surveyor of crown lands for Ballarat district, 1855; on staff of Melbourne magnetic and meteorological observatory, 1858; third in command of expedition sent from Victoria to discover route to north across Australia, 1860; with party reached Torowoto and went on to

Cooper's Creek, whence the route was struck for Adelaide, but eventually died of starvation with all his comrades but one. [lxii. 50]

WILLSHIRE, SIR THOMAS, baronet (1789–1862), general; born at Halifax, Nova Scotia; lieutenant, 38th foot, 1795; joined regiment, 1798; captain, 1804; served in Portugal and Walcheren; in Peninsular war, 1812–14, and Netherlands, 1815; brevet lieutenant-colonel, 1814; commandant of British Kaffraria, 1819; added territory between Fish river and Keiskamma to colony; major in India, 1823; lieutenant-colonel, 1827; commander of Bombay division of infantry, 1839; served with distinction in Afghanistan campaign and captured Kelat, 1839; C.B., 1838: K.C.B., 1839; created baronet, 1840; commandant at Chatham, 1841–6; general and G.C.B., 1861. [lxii. 51]

WILLSON. [See also WILSON.]

WILLSON, EDWARD JAMES (1787–1854), antiquary and architect: practised at Lincoln; executed restorations at Lincoln Castle, 1834–45; contributed to 'Architectural Antiquities' (1807–26) and other works by John Britton [q. v.]; wrote letterpress for 'Specimens' and 'Examples' of Gothic architecture, published by Augustus Charles Pugin [q. v.], 1821–31; mayor of Lincoln, 1852. [lxii. 53]

WILLSON, ROBERT WILLIAM (1794–1866), Roman catholic bishop; brother of Edward James Willson [q. v.]; studied at Old Oscott College, 1816; built church of St. John, Nottingham, 1825–8, and buildings of cathedral of St. Barnabas: consecrated first bishop of Hobart Town, Tasmania, 1842; brought about reform in convict system; resigned preferment and was translated to bishopric of Rhodiopolis, *in partibus infidelium*, 1866. [lxii. 54]

WILLUGHBY. [See also WILLOUGHBY.]

WILLUGHBY, FRANCIS (1635–1672), naturalist; B.A. Trinity College, Cambridge, 1656; M.A., 1659; accompanied John Ray on botanical journey through northern midland counties, 1662; original F.R.S., 1663; travelled with Ray in Europe, collecting natural-history specimens; works include 'Ornithologiæ libri tres,' 1676 (in English, 1678), and 'De Historia Piscium,' 1686. [lxii. 54]

WILLUGHBY, PERCIVALL (1596–1685), writer on obstetrics; educated at Rugby, Eton, and Magdalen College, Oxford; B.A., 1621; extra L.R.C.P., 1641; left manuscript works on obstetrics. [lxii. 57]

WILLYAMS, COOPER (1762–1816), topographer and artist; M.A. Emmanuel College, Cambridge, 1789; vicar of Exning, near Newmarket, 1788; rector of St. Peter, West Lynn, 1793; served as naval chaplain in West Indies, at Guadeloupe (1794), at battle of Nile (1798); published works, illustrated with engravings from his own drawings, relating to places and campaigns with which he was connected. [lxii. 57]

WILLYMAT, WILLIAM (d. 1615), author; rector of Ruskington, Lincolnshire, 1585; published 'A Prince's Looking Glasse' (extracts from James I's 'Basilikon Doron'), 1603, 'A Loyal Svbiect's Looking-Glasse,' 1604, and 'Physicke to cure the most Dangerous Disease of Desperation,' 1605. [lxii. 58]

WILLYMOTT, WILLIAM (d. 1737), grammarian; of Eton and King's College, Cambridge; M.A., 1700; LL.D., 1707; fellow; usher at Eton; opened private school at Isleworth; vice-provost of King's College, 1721; rector of Milton, near Cambridge; published school-books. [lxii. 59]

WILMINGTON, EARL OF (1673?–1743). [See COMPTON, SPENCER.]

WILMOT, SIR CHARLES, first VISCOUNT WILMOT OF ATHLONE (1570?–1644?), of Magdalen College, Oxford; served in Irish wars; captain, 1592; sergeant-major of forces in Munster, 1597; colonel, 1598; knighted, 1599; took prominent part in suppressing Irish rebellion, 1600–1602; governor of Cork, 1601, and of Kerry, 1602; joint-commissioner with Sir George Thornton for government of Munster, 1603 and 1606–7; Irish privy councillor, 1607; member for Launceston in English House of Commons, 1614; president of Connaught, 1616; created Viscount Wilmot in Irish peerage, 1621; general and commander-in-chief of forces in Ireland, 1629; accused of alienating crown lands at Athlone. [lxii. 59]

WILMOT, SIR EDWARD, first baronet (1693–1786), baronet; physician; fellow, St. John's College, Cambridge; M.A., 1718; M.D., 1725; F.R.C.P., 1726; Harveian orator, 1735; F.R.S., 1730; physician-general to army, 1740; physician to Frederick, prince of Wales, and physician in ordinary to George II, 1742; created baronet, 1759; physician in ordinary to George III, 1760. [lxii. 61]

WILMOT, HENRY, first EARL OF ROCHESTER (1612?–1658), son of Sir Charles Wilmot, first viscount Wilmot [q. v.]; captain of horse in Dutch service, 1635; commissary-general of horse in Charles I's army in second Scottish war; M.P., Tamworth (Long parliament); expelled from house for share in plot to overawe parliament with army, 1641; joined Charles I in Yorkshire, 1642; at Edgehill, 1642; defeated Sir William Waller (1597?–1668) [q. v.] near Devizes, 1643, and at Cropredy Bridge, 1644; created Baron Wilmot, 1643; succeeded his father as Viscount Wilmot, 1644; deprived of command on suspicion of treating with parliament, 1644; gentleman of bedchamber to Charles II, 1649; accompanied Charles II to Scotland and in wanderings after battle of Worcester; created Earl of Rochester, 1652; in England directing movements of royalist conspirators, 1655; died at Sluys. [lxii. 61]

WILMOT, JAMES (d. 1808), alleged author of the 'Letters of Junius'; uncle of Mrs. Olivia Serres [q. v.], who put forward the claim that he was the author of 'Junius' in 'The Life of the Author of Junius's Letters, the Rev. James Wilmot, D.D.,' 1813, and published another pamphlet on the same subject, pretending to prove her theory from the evidence of handwriting, 1817. [li. 257]

WILMOT, JOHN, second EARL OF ROCHESTER (1647–1680), poet and libertine; son of Henry Wilmot, first earl of Rochester [q. v.]; M.A. Wadham College, Oxford, 1661; volunteer in unsuccessful assault on Dutch ships at Bergen, 1665; became intimate with George Villiers, second duke of Buckingham, Sir Charles Sedley, and Henry Savile, and soon excelled them all in profligacy; gained reputation for amorous lyrics, obscene rhymes, and mordant satires in verse; gentleman of king's bedchamber, 1666; became patron of Elizabeth Barry [q. v.], and temporarily of several poets, including Dryden; frequently dismissed in disgrace from court; several collections of his poetical writings issued posthumously, that of 1731–2 probably being the most complete. [lxii. 63]

WILMOT, SIR JOHN EARDLEY- (1709–1792), chief-justice of common pleas; educated with Dr. Johnson at King Edward's School, Lichfield, at Westminster School, and Trinity Hall, Cambridge; barrister, Inner Temple, 1732; F.S.A., 1745; knighted, invested with coif, and appointed to puisne judgeship in king's bench, 1755; commissioner of great seal, 1756–7; chief-justice of common pleas, 1766–71; privy councillor, 1766; took part in cases arising from Wilkes's libels. [lxii. 67]

WILMOT, JOHN EARDLEY- (1750–1815), politician and author; son of Sir John Eardley Wilmot [q. v.]; of Westminster School and University College, Oxford; B.A., 1769; fellow of All Souls College, Oxford, 1769; barrister, Inner Temple, 1773; master in chancery, 1781–1804; M.P., Tiverton, 1776–84, Coventry, 1784–96; edited his father's 'Notes and Opinions,' 1802, and published a life of his father and other writings. [lxii. 69]

WILMOT, SIR JOHN EARDLEY EARDLEY-, second baronet (1810–1892), barrister and politician; grandson of John Eardley-Wilmot [q. v.]; of Winchester College and Balliol College, Oxford; B.A., 1831; barrister, Lincoln's Inn, 1842; recorder of Warwick, 1852–74; judge of county court of Bristol, 1854–63, and of Marylebone district, London, 1863–71; conservative M.P. for South Warwickshire, 1874–85; published legal writings. [lxii. 70]

WILMOT, LEMUEL ALLEN (1809–1878), governor of New Brunswick; born at Sunbury, New Brunswick; educated at King's College, Fredericton; attorney, 1830; called to bar of New Brunswick, 1832; liberal member for province of York in house of assembly, 1834; Q.C., 1838; premier and attorney-general, 1848; judge of supreme court, 1851; hon. D.C.L. King's College; advocated union and was lieutenant-governor of New Brunswick, 1868–73. [lxii. 70]

WILMOT, ROBERT (*fl.* 1568–1608), dramatist; rector of North Ockendon, 1582, and of Horndon-on-the-Hill,

1585 ; M.A.; published, 1591, 'The Tragedie of Tancred and Gismund,' a play based on Boccaccio, and the oldest English play of which the plot is certainly taken from an Italian novel. [lxii. 71]

WILMOT, ROBERT (d. 1695), commodore; commanded fire-ship in battle off Beachy Head, 1690 ; commanded expedition to West Indies, 1695 ; died of fever on voyage home. [lxii. 72]

WILMOT-HORTON, SIR ROBERT JOHN (1784–1841). [See HORTON.]

WILSON, MRS. (d. 1786), actress ; née Adcock : appeared at York, 1773, Leeds and Glasgow, 1774 ; at Haymarket, London, 1775 and 1781, and Covent Garden, London, 1776 and 1782–6, and in Liverpool, 1776–7 ; met Richard Wilson (fl. 1774–1792) [q. v.], whom she married, c. 1774. Her parts include Filch (' Beggar's Opera '), 1781, and Maria (' Twelfth Night '). [lxii. 73]

WILSON, AARON (1589–1643), divine ; M.A. Queen's College, Oxford, 1615 ; D.D., 1639 ; chaplain to Charles I, archdeacon of Exeter, and vicar of Plymouth, 1634. [lxii. 104]

WILSON, SIR ADAM (1814–1891), Canadian judge ; born at Edinburgh : emigrated to Upper Canada, 1830, and was called to bar, 1839 ; Q.C., 1850 ; member of legislative assembly for North Riding of York, 1859 and 1862 ; solicitor-general, 1862–3 ; puisne judge of court of queen's bench for Upper Canada, and later of common pleas, 1863, but returned to queen's bench, 1868 ; chief-justice of court of common pleas, 1878 ; chief-justice of court of queen's bench of Ontario, 1884. [lxii. 74]

WILSON, ALEXANDER (1714–1786), professor of astronomy at Glasgow University ; M.A. St.Andrews, 1733; worked as assistant to surgeon and apothecary in London, 1737–9 ; set up type-foundry at St. Andrews, 1742 ; removed it to Camlachie, near Glasgow, 1744 ; first professor of practical astronomy at Glasgow, 1760–84; hon. M.D. St. Andrews, 1763 ; original F.R.S. Edinburgh ; made discovery that sun-spots are cavities in luminous matter surrounding sun, 1769. [lxii. 74]

WILSON, ALEXANDER (1766–1813), ornithologist ; worked as weaver at Lochwinnoch and Paisley ; published poems ; emigrated to America, 1794 ; opened schools near Frankland, Pennsylvania, c. 1795, and at Bloomfield, New Jersey ; received appointment in Union school, near Philadelphia, 1802 ; published seven volumes of ' The American Ornithology,' 1808–13, volumes viii. and ix. appearing posthumously. [lxii. 75]

WILSON, ALEXANDER PHILIP (1770 ?–1851 ?). [See PHILIP, ALEXANDER PHILIP WILSON.]

WILSON, ANDREW (1718–1792), philosophical and medical writer ; M.D. Edinburgh, 1749 ; F.R.C.P. Edinburgh, 1764 ; physician to Medical Asylum, London, before 1777 ; published ' Human Nature surveyed by Philosophy and Revelation,' 1758, and other works. [lxii. 76]

WILSON, ANDREW (1780–1848), landscape-painter ; studied under Alexander Nasmyth [q. v.] and in Royal Academy schools, London, and in Italy ; collected pictures by old masters ; teacher of drawing at Military College, Sandhurst ; master of Trustees' Academy, Edinburgh, 1818 ; lived in Rome, Florence, and Genoa, 1826–47. [lxii. 77]

WILSON, ANDREW (1831–1881),traveller and author ; son of John Wilson (1804–1875) [q. v.] ; educated at Edinburgh and Tübingen ; worked as journalist in India and China ; travelled much in southern China ; contributed largely to ' Blackwood's Magazine ' ; published works relating to his travels and Gordon's Chinese campaigns. [lxii. 78]

WILSON, ANTHONY (fl. 1793), known by pseudonym, ' Henry Bromley,' under which he published ' Catalogue of Engraved British Portraits,' 1793. [lxii. 78]

WILSON, SIR ARCHDALE, first baronet (1803–1874), lieutenant-general ; studied at East India Company's College, Addiscombe ; second lieutenant, Bengal artillery, 1819 ; captain, 1834 ; commanded artillery at Lucknow, 1839 ; superintendent of gun-foundry at Kossipur, 1841–5 ; lieutenant-colonel, 1847 ; served in Punjab campaign, 1848, in Jalandar, 1850–2 ; colonel and commandant of artillery at Mirat, 1856 ; served with distinction at opening of mutiny, and was promoted major-general and placed in command of Delhi field force ; captured Delhi and was made K.C.B., 1857 ; created baronet, as Sir Archdale Wilson of Delhi, 1858 ; commanded artillery at siege of Lucknow, 1858 ; G.C.B., 1867 ; lieutenant-general, 1868. [lxii. 79]

WILSON, ARTHUR (1595–1652), historian and dramatist ; clerk in exchequer office ; gentleman-in-waiting to Robert Devereux, third earl of Essex [q. v.], whom he accompanied on Vere's expedition for defence of Palatinate (1620), Holland (1621–3), at Breda (1624), and at Cadiz (1625) ; gentleman commoner of Trinity College, Oxford, 1631 ; entered service of Sir Robert Rich, second earl of Warwick [q. v.], 1633, and accompanied him to Breda, 1637 ; wrote several plays, of which only one, ' The Inconstant Lady,' is extant. His ' History of Great Britain, being Life and Reign of James I,' appeared, 1653. [lxii. 81]

WILSON, BENJAMIN (1721–1788), painter and man of science ; clerk in registry of prerogative court of Doctors' Commons ; clerk to registrar of Charterhouse; studied painting under Thomas Hudson (1701–1779) [q. v.] ; practised as portrait-painter in Dublin, 1748–50, and in London from 1750 ; received Royal Society's gold medal for electrical experiments, 1760 ; gained patronage of Duke of York and became manager of his private theatre in James Street, Westminster ; succeeded Hogarth as serjeant-painter, 1764, and James Worsdale [q. v.] as painter to board of ordnance, 1767 ; published writings relating to electricity. [lxii. 82]

WILSON, BERNARD or BARNARD (1689–1772), divine and author ; of Westminster and Trinity College, Cambridge ; M.A., 1719 ; D.D., 1737 ; vicar of Newark, 1719 ; prebendary of Lincoln, 1727 ; canon of Lichfield, 1730, and of Worcester, 1734 : master of St. Leonard's Hospital, Newark ; member of Gentleman's Society at Spalding ; published English version of part of De Thou's ' Historia sui Temporis,' 1729–30. [lxii. 84]

WILSON, MRS. CAROLINE (1787–1846), author ; née Fry ; began, 1823, publication of monthly periodical, ' Assistant of Education,' from which she compiled ' The Listener,' 1830 ; married, 1831. Her works include hymns and other religious writings. [lxii. 85]

WILSON, CHARLES HEATH (1809–1882), art teacher and author ; son of Andrew Wilson (1780–1848) [q. v.] ; practised as architect in Edinburgh ; A.R.S.A., 1835–58 ; director of Edinburgh school of art ; headmaster of Glasgow school of design, 1849–64 ; settled at Florence, 1869. [lxii. 86]

WILSON, MRS. CORNWALL BARON (1797–1846), author ; her maiden name, MARGARET HARRIES ; conducted periodicals ' La Ninon,' 1833, and ' The Weekly Belle Assemblée,' from 1833 ; published miscellaneous works. [lxii. 87]

WILSON, DANIEL (1778–1858), bishop of Calcutta ; B.A. St. Edmund Hall, Oxford, 1802 ; M.A., 1804 ; D.D., 1832 ; vice-principal, c. 1807 ; evangelical preacher ; minister of St. John's Chapel, Bloomsbury, London, 1812 ; vicar of St. Mary's, Islington, London, 1824 ; fifth bishop of Calcutta, with quasi-metropolitan jurisdiction over sees of Bombay and Madras ; originated and greatly assisted building of new cathedral at Calcutta, 1839–47 ; published ' Evidences of Christianity ' (a réchauffé of Paley), 1828–30, and other religious works. [lxii. 88]

WILSON, SIR DANIEL (1816–1892), archæologist and educational reformer ; educated at Edinburgh ; honorary secretary of Scottish Society of Antiquaries, 1845 ; professor of history and English literature in Toronto University, 1853, and became president, 1881 ; secured a ' national ' system of university education in Canada ; published ' Archæology and Prehistoric Annals of Scotland,' 1851, and other works. [lxii. 89]

WILSON, EDWARD (d. 1694), ' Beau Wilson ' ; became, c. 1693, the talk of London on account of the expensive style in which he lived, the secret of the source of his wealth never being discovered ; killed in a duel by John Law, afterwards the celebrated financier. [lxii. 90]

WILSON, EDWARD (1814–1878), Australian politician ; employed in bank in London ; went to Australia, 1842 ; engaged in journalism at Melbourne and conducted the ' Argus,' 1847–64, vigorously attacking all kinds of abuses ; founded Acclimatisation Society of Victoria, 1861. [lxii. 91]

WILSON, Sir ERASMUS (1809-1884). [See WILSON, Sir WILLIAM JAMES ERASMUS.]

WILSON, FLORENCE (1504?-1547?). [See VOLUSENE.]

WILSON, GEORGE (*fl.* 1607), writer on cock-fighting; vicar of Wretton, Norfolk; published 'The Commendation of Cockes and Cock-fighting,' 1607. [lxii. 91]

WILSON, GEORGE (1818-1859), chemist and religious writer; brother of Sir Daniel Wilson [q. v.]; studied medicine at Edinburgh; qualified by Royal College of Surgeons, Edinburgh; assistant to Thomas Graham (1805-1869) [q. v.] at University College, London, 1838; M.D. Edinburgh, 1839; 'extra-mural' lecturer on chemistry at Edinburgh; owned congregational church belonging to independent section, 1844; director of Scottish Industrial Museum, 1855; regius professor of technology, Edinburgh University, 1855; president of Royal Scottish Society of Arts. His works include 'Life of Henry Cavendish' (1731-1810) [q. v.], 1851, and 'Researches on Colour-Blindness, 1855, and numerous writings on scientific and religious subjects. [lxii. 92]

WILSON, GEORGE (1808-1870), chairman of Anti-Cornlaw League; engaged in corn trade; starch and gum manufacturer; on foundation of Anti-Cornlaw Association, 1839, and later member of executive committee; became chairman on change of title to Anti-Cornlaw League, 1841, and occupied position till repeal of corn laws, 1846; president of National Reform Union, 1864; chairman of Lancashire and Yorkshire Railway Company, 1867; director of Electric Telegraph Company. [lxii. 94]

WILSON, HARRIETTE (1789-1846), woman of fashion; daughter of John James Dubouchet or De Bouchet, a shopkeeper in Mayfair, London; mistress of Lord Craven; resided much in Paris after *c.* 1820; published, 1825, her 'Memoirs' (perhaps written by John Joseph Stockdale [q. v.], the publisher) in revenge on the Duke of Beaufort, who failed to fulfil generous promises which he made to her. [lxii. 95]

WILSON, HARRY BRISTOW (1774-1853), divine and antiquary; of Merchant Taylors' School and Lincoln College, Oxford; M.A., 1799; D.D., 1818; master of Merchant Taylors' School from 1798; received united parishes of St. Mary Aldermary and St. Thomas the Apostle, London, 1816; published 'History of Merchant Taylors' School,' 1812-14, and other works. [lxii. 96]

WILSON, HENRIETTA (*d.* 1863), author; niece of James Wilson (1795-1856) [q. v.]; published 'Chronicles of a Garden,' 1863, and other works. [lxii. 100]

WILSON, HENRY BRISTOW (1803-1888), divine; son of Harry Bristow Wilson [q. v.]; of Merchant Taylors' School and St. John's College, Oxford; M.A., 1829; B.D., 1834; fellow, 1825-50; Rawlinsonian professor of Anglo-Saxon, 1839-44; vicar of Great Staughton, Huntingdonshire, 1850-88; Bampton lecturer, 1851; sentenced to suspension by court of arches, 1862, for essay on 'The National Church' in 'Essays and Reviews' (1861); decision reversed by judicial committee of privy council, 1863. [lxii. 97]

WILSON, HORACE HAYMAN (1786-1860), orientalist; studied at St. Thomas's Hospital, London; became assistant-surgeon (Bengal) to East India Company, 1808; assay-master at Calcutta mint, 1816; secretary to Asiatic Society of Bengal, 1811; professor of Sanskrit at Oxford, 1832; librarian to East India Company, 1836; director of Royal Asiatic Society, London, 1837-60; F.R.S., 1834; published 'Sanskrit-English Dictionary,' 1819, an edition of the 'Meghadūta,' 1813, and a translation of the 'Rig-Veda' (according to the native school of interpretation), and other works. [lxii. 97]

WILSON, Sir JAMES (1780-1847), major-general; ensign, 1798; major, 1811; major-general, 1838; served in Egypt, 1801; exchanged to 48th, 1803; served in Peninsula, 1809-14; at Albuera, Badajoz, Salamanca, Vittoria, and Toulouse; K.C.B., 1815. [lxii. 99]

WILSON, JAMES (1795-1856), zoologist; brother of John Wilson (1785-1854) [q. v.]; educated at Edinburgh; travelled on continent; made excursions in Scotland with Sir Thomas Dick Lauder [q. v.], at request of fisheries board, 1841, 1843, and 1850; published works on natural history of fishes (1838) and birds (1839), and other zoological writings. [lxii. 99]

WILSON, JAMES (1805-1860), politician and political economist; educated at quaker schools; apprenticed as hat manufacturer at Hawick, Roxburghshire; carried on business in London, 1824-44; published 'Influences of the corn-laws,' 1839, 'Fluctuations of Currency, Commerce, and Manufactures,' 1840, and 'The Revenue,' 1841; established 'The Economist,' weekly paper, 1843; M.P., Westbury, Wiltshire, 1847 and 1852, Devonshire, 1857-9; joint-secretary to board of control, 1848; financial secretary to treasury, 1853-8; vice-president of board of trade and paymaster-general, 1859; privy councillor, 1859; financial member of council of India, 1859; established paper currency in India; reformed system of public accounts. [lxii. 100]

WILSON, JAMES ARTHUR (1795-1882), physician; of Westminster School and Christ Church, Oxford; M.A., 1818; M.D., 1823; Radcliffe travelling fellow, 1821; F.R.C.P., 1825; Lumleian lecturer, 1847 and 1848; Harveian orator, 1850; physician to St. George's Hospital, 1829-57; published medical writings. [lxii. 103]

WILSON, JOHN (1595-1674), lutenist; musician to Charles I, 1635; Mus.Doc. Oxford, 1645; appointed choragus on re-establishment of Oxford professorship of music, 1656; chamber musician to Charles II, 1661; gentleman of Chapel Royal, 1662; possibly identical with Shakespeare's Jack Willson (stage direction, folio of 1623), who sang 'Sigh no more, ladies,' and other lyrics; set to music 'Take, oh! take those lips away,' and published airs and glees. [lxii. 103]

WILSON, JOHN (1627?-1696), playwright; son of Aaron Wilson [q. v.]; of Exeter College, Oxford; barrister, Lincoln's Inn, 1649; recorder of Londonderry, *c.* 1681; perhaps secretary to viceroy of Ireland, 1687; works include 'The Cheats: a Comedy,' 1664, 'Andronicus Commenius: a Tragedy,' 1664, 'The Projectors: a Comedy,' 1665, and 'Belphegor: a Tragi-comedy,' 1691. [lxii. 104]

WILSON, JOHN (*d.* 1751), botanist; land-surveyor's assistant; published 'Synopsis of British Plants,' 1744. [lxii. 106]

WILSON, JOHN (1720-1789), author of 'The Clyde'; parish schoolmaster of Lesmahagow, 1746; master of Greenock grammar school, 1767-87; published, 1760, 'A Dramatic Sketch,' which he afterwards elaborated into 'Earl Douglas,' and issued (1764) with 'The Clyde,' a dramatic descriptive poem of considerable merit. [lxii. 106]

WILSON, Sir JOHN (1741-1793), judge; B.A. and senior wrangler, Peterhouse, Cambridge, 1761; M.A. and fellow, 1764; barrister, Middle Temple, 1766; judge of common pleas and knighted, 1786; commissioner of great seal, 1792-3; F.R.S., 1782. [lxii. 107]

WILSON, JOHN (1800-1849), Scottish vocalist; engaged as compositor by the Ballantynes, and helped to set up 'Waverley Novels'; precentor at St. Mary's Church, Edinburgh, 1825-30; engaged in music-teaching and operatic singing, and subsequently gained considerable reputation as exponent of Scottish song; published songs. [lxii. 107]

WILSON, JOHN (1785-1854), author, the 'Christopher North' of 'Blackwood's' and professor of moral philosophy at Edinburgh; educated at Glasgow University and Magdalen College, Oxford; M.A. Oxford, 1810; contributed to Coleridge's 'Friend'; called to bar at Edinburgh, 1815; joined editorial staff of 'Blackwood's Magazine,' 1817, and, with John Gibson Lockhart [q. v.], was its main support; elected on strength of his tory principles professor of moral philosophy at Edinburgh University, 1820; contributed to 'Blackwood,' 1822-35, his 'Noctes Ambrosianæ' (some of the earlier numbers being by other hands), in which he figured as 'Christopher North' and James Hogg as the 'Ettrick Shepherd'; resigned professorship, 1851. His works were collected by Professor Ferrier, 1855-8. [lxii. 107]

WILSON, JOHN (1774-1855), sea-painter; apprenticed as house-painter at Edinburgh; scene-painter at Astley's Theatre, London; exhibited at Royal Academy (from 1807), the British Institution, Society of British Artists, and [Royal] Scottish Academy; hon. member of Scottish Academy, 1827. [lxii. 112]

WILSON, SIR JOHN (1780–1856), general; ensign, 1794; lieutenant, 1795; served in Egypt, 1801; major, 1802; in Peninsula, 1808, and from 1809; governor of province of Minho, 1811; brevet-colonel and knighted, 1814; major-general, 1825; commanded troops in Ceylon, 1830–8; K.C.B., 1837; general, 1854; colonel, 82nd foot, 1836, and 11th foot, 1841. [lxii. 112]

WILSON, JOHN (1804–1875) missionary and orientalist; studied for ministry at Edinburgh University; studied medicine; joined Scottish Missionary Society; went to Bombay, 1829; founded 'Oriental Christian Spectator' periodical, 1830; established native church on presbyterian principles, and with his wife schools for native children, special attention being given to female education; transferred to church of Scotland, 1835, but quitted it at disruption, 1843; R.A.S., 1836; first partially to decipher rock inscriptions of Asoka at Girnar; published 'The Parsi Religion unfolded,' 1843; F.R.S., 1845; president, 1848, of the 'Cave Temple Commission,' publishing writings relating to the commission's work; his knowledge of archaic alphabets (used for secrecy) and local dialects useful to the government in the Indian mutiny; dean of faculty of arts in new Bombay University, 1857; wrote on Indian religion and customs. [lxii. 113]

WILSON, JOHN (1812–1888), agriculturist; educated at University College, London, and in Paris; principal of Royal Agricultural College, Cirencester, 1846–50; professor of agriculture and rural economy, Edinburgh University, 1854–85; secretary to senate, 1868; emeritus professor, 1885, and honorary LL.D., 1886; published writings on agriculture. [lxii. 115]

WILSON, JOHN MACKAY (1804–1835), author; printer in London; editor of 'Berwick Advertiser,' 1832; published 'Tales of the Borders' in weekly numbers, 1834–5, and other writings. [lxii. 116]

WILSON, JOHN MATTHIAS (1813–1881), president of Corpus Christi College, Oxford; M.A. Corpus Christi College, Oxford, 1839; B.D., 1847; fellow, 1843; president, 1872–81; held Whyte's professorship of moral philosophy, 1846–74; collaborated with Dr. Thomas Fowler in 'Principles of Morals,' published, 1886–7. [lxii. 116]

WILSON, SIR JOHN MORILLYON (1783–1868), commandant of Royal Hospital, Chelsea; midshipman, 1798–1803; ensign, 1804; lieutenant, 1805; major, 1814; lieutenant-colonel, 1815; colonel, 1837; served at Walcheren, in Peninsular war, and in United States of America; adjutant of Royal Hospital, Chelsea, 1822, and major-commandant, 1855–8; C.B. and K.H. [lxii. 117]

WILSON, JOSHUA (1795–1874), barrister; son of Thomas Wilson (1764–1843) [q. v.]; barrister, Inner Temple; published 'Historical Inquiry concerning English Presbyterians,' 1835, and other works. [lxii. 144]

WILSON, MARGARET (1667–1685), 'martyr of the Solway'; suffered death by drowning at Bladenoch for refusing to conform to episcopacy; the incident commemorated in a picture by Millais, 1871. [lxii. 118]

WILSON, MARY ANNE (1802–1867), singer; pupil and subsequently wife of Thomas Welsh [q. v.] [lx. 240]

WILSON, MATTHEW (1582–1656). [See KNOTT, EDWARD.]

WILSON, NICHOLAS (d. 1548), Roman catholic divine; B.A. Christ's College, Cambridge, 1509; D.D., 1533; chaplain and confessor to Henry VIII before 1527; archdeacon of Oxford, 1528; presented to Church of St. Thomas the Apostle, London, 1531; master of Michaelhouse, Cambridge, 1533; opposed Henry VIII in question of divorce; imprisoned for refusing oath relative to succession to the crown, 1534; attainted of misprision of treason and deprived of preferments; took oath, 1537, and was pardoned; dean of collegiate church of Wimborne Minster, Dorset, 1537–47; imprisoned in Tower for assisting persons who denied royal supremacy, 1540–1; prebendary of York and of St. Paul's, London, 1542. [lxii. 119]

WILSON, RICHARD (1714–1782), landscape-painter; portrait-painter in London; went, 1749, to Italy, where he gained reputation as landscape-painter; returned to England, 1756; original member, 1768, of Royal Academy, where he exhibited till 1780; librarian to Royal Academy,

1776; experienced extreme poverty, though reputed the best landscape-painter of the day. Among his most celebrated pictures are 'Niobe,' 1760, and 'View of Rome from the Villa Madama,' 1765. [lxii. 120]

WILSON, RICHARD (fl. 1774–1792), actor; married Mrs. Wilson [q. v.], c. 1774; played comic characters in London at Covent Garden and Haymarket. His parts include Malvolio, Falstaff, and Polonius. [lxii. 74]

WILSON, ROBERT, the elder (d. 1600), actor and playwright; original member of Earl of Leicester's company, 1574; member of Queen Elizabeth's company, 1583–1588; joined Lord Strange's company, 1588; gained great reputation as comic actor. His only extant productions (loosely constructed moralities with very little plot), include 'The Three Ladies of London,' 1584, and 'The Pleasant and Stately Morall of the Three Lordes and Three Ladies of London,' 1590. [lxii. 123]

WILSON, ROBERT, the younger (1579–1610), dramatic hack-writer; employed by Henslowe, 1598–1600; probably son of Robert Wilson the elder [q. v.]; collaborated in many productions with Drayton, Dekker, and Munday and with Drayton, Hathaway, and Munday in 'Sir John Oldcastle' (first part only extant, 1600), described on title-page of one edition as work of Shakespeare. [lxii. 124]

WILSON, ROBERT (1803–1882), engineer; invented screw-propeller for vessels, for which he was awarded a silver medal by Scottish Society of Arts, 1832; invented self-acting motion for steam-hammer, patented, 1843, by James Nasmyth (1808–1890) [q. v.], of whose foundry, near Bridgwater, he was manager, 1838; received grant from war department for use of his double-action screw-propeller as applied to fish torpedo, 1880. [lxii. 125]

WILSON, ROBERT ARTHUR (1820?–1875), Irish humorist and poet; born at Falcaragh, co. Donegal; emigrated to America, 1840, and worked as journalist; returned to Ireland, and subsequently became leader-writer to 'Morning News' (Belfast), to which and other papers he contributed satires and humorous lyrics. 'Reliques of Barney Maglone' (his pseudonym), appeared 1894. [lxii. 126]

WILSON, SIR ROBERT THOMAS (1777–1849), general and governor of Gibraltar; son of Benjamin Wilson [q. v.]; of Westminster School and Winchester College; cornet, 1793; one of eight officers commanding dragoons which routed superior French force at Villiers-en-Couché, preventing capture of Emperor Francis II, 1794; received cross of order of Maria Theresa, rank of baron of holy Roman empire, and knighthood, 1801; lieutenant, 1794; purchased troop, 1796; served at the Helder, 1799, in Egypt, 1801; published 'History of British Expedition to Egypt,' 1802; lieutenant-colonel, 19th light dragoons, 1804, and 20th light dragoons, 1805; served in Cape of Good Hope, 1806; accompanied Lord Hutchinson and king of Prussia to Memel, 1807, and served in subsequent campaign; commandant of Lusitanian legion in Portugal, 1808–9; brevet colonel and aide-de-camp to George III, 1810; accompanied Sir Robert Liston [q. v.] to Constantinople with local rank of brigadier-general in British army, 1811; British commissioner at Krasnoi Pakra, near Moscow, 1811; fought at Lützen and Bautzen, 1813; major-general, 1813; fought at Dresden, Kulm, and Kraupen, 1813; British commissioner with Austrian army at Leitmeritz; served at Leipzig; with Austrian army in Italy; at Vincenza, Verona, and Valeggio, 1814; M.P., Southwark, 1818, 1826, and 1830; dismissed from army for action against mob at Queen Caroline's funeral, 1821; reinstated with rank of lieutenant-general, 1830; colonel of 15th hussars, 1835; general, 1841; governor and commander-in-chief of Gibraltar, 1842; published military and autobiographical works. [lxii. 126]

WILSON, ROWLAND (1613–1650), parliamentarian; lieutenant-colonel of orange regiment of London trained bands; joined Earl of Essex after first battle of Newbury, 1643; colonel, 1646; M.P., Calne, 1646; alderman of London, 1648; member of council of state, 1649; sheriff of London, 1649. [lxii. 131]

WILSON, THOMAS (1525?–1581), secretary of state and scholar; of Eton and King's College, Cambridge; M.A., 1549; published 'Rule of Reason,' 1551, and 'Arte of Rhetorique,' 1551 or 1553; on continent, 1555–60; LL.D. Ferrara, 1559, and was incorporated at Oxford,

1566, and Cambridge, 1571 ; advocate in court of arches, 1561 ; master of St. Catherine's Hospital in the Tower of London and master of requests, 1561 ; M.P., Michael Borough, 1563–7 ; went on diplomatic mission to Portugal, 1567 ; participated in Earl of Leicester's secret negotiations with Spanish ambassador ; published ' The Three Orations of Demosthenes,' 1570, the earliest English translation from Demosthenes ; M.P., Lincoln, 1572–81 ; on embassy to Netherlands, 1574–5 and 1576–7 ; privy councillor and secretary of state, 1578 ; lay dean of Durham, 1580. [lxii. 132]

WILSON, THOMAS (1563–1622), divine ; M.A. Queen's College, Oxford, 1586 ; college chaplain, 1585 ; rector of St. George the Martyr, Canterbury, 1586–1622 ; published ' Christian Dictionarie,' 1612, one of first attempts made at a concordance of the bible in English. [lxii. 136]

WILSON, SIR THOMAS (1560 ?–1629), keeper of the records and author ; B.A. St. John's College, Cambridge, 1583 ; M.A. Trinity Hall, 1587 ; travelled abroad ; translated from Spanish, 1596, Gorge de Montemayor's ' Diana,' a romance from which story of Shakespeare's ' Two Gentlemen of Verona ' is partly drawn ; employed as foreign intelligencer ; in Italy, 1601–2 ; consul in Spain, 1604–5 ; entered service of Sir Robert Cecil, 1605 ; keeper of records at Whitehall, 1606–29 ; clerk of imports, 1606–14 ; knighted, 1618 ; employed to obtain admissions from Ralegh sufficient to condemn him, 1618. [lxii. 136]

WILSON, THOMAS (1663–1755), bishop of Sodor and Man ; B.A. Trinity College, Dublin, 1686 ; studied medicine ; curate of Newchurch Kenyon, Lancashire, 1687–92 ; master of almshouse at Lathom, 1693 ; M.A., 1696 ; bishop of Sodor and Man, 1697 ; resided at Bishop's Court, Kirk Michael ; LL.D. Lambeth, 1698 ; built new churches and established parochial libraries ; published ' Principles and Duties of Christianity, in English and Manks,' the first book published in Manx, 1707 ; supervised translation of gospels and acts into Manx ; D.D. Oxford and Cambridge, 1707 ; drew up ' Ecclesiastical Constitutions ' for restoration of discipline in church, 1707 ; came into conflict with the governor, Alexander Horne, and his successors, Floyd and Thomas Horton, on questions of civil and ecclesiastical authority, 1716 ; accepted office of ' artistes ' of the ' reformed tropus ' (one of three) in the Moravian church, 1749. His collected works appeared, 1781. [lxii. 139]

WILSON, THOMAS (1703–1784), divine ; son of Thomas Wilson (1663–1755) [q. v.] ; M.A. Christ Church, Oxford, 1727 ; D.D., 1739 : one of George II's chaplains, 1737 ; rector of St. Stephen's, Walbrook, London, 1737–1784 ; prebendary of Westminster, 1743 ; rector of St. Margaret's, Westminster, 1753–84. [lxii. 142]

WILSON, THOMAS (1747–1813), schoolmaster ; headmaster of Slaidburn grammar school, 1773 ; master of Clitheroe grammar school, Lancashire, 1775 ; B.D. Trinity College, Dublin, 1794 ; rector of Claughton, near Lancaster, 1807 ; published ' Archæological Dictionary,' 1783. [lxii. 142]

WILSON, THOMAS (1764–1843), nonconformist benefactor ; apprenticed to his father as manufacturer of ribbons and gauzes, and entered partnership, 1785 ; retired, 1798 ; treasurer of Hoxton Academy, London, 1794–1843 ; engaged extensively in building and repairing chapels for congregationalists ; one of first directors of London Missionary Society, 1795 ; original member of council of University College, London, 1825. [lxii. 143]

WILSON, THOMAS (1773–1858), Tyneside poet ; worked as miner ; entered counting-house of Losh, Lubbin & Co., Newcastle, 1803, and became partner, 1805 ; a collective edition of his poems appeared, 1843 (reprinted with additions, 1872). [lxii. 144]

WILSON, WALTER (1781–1847), nonconformist biographer ; bookseller in London ; studied at Inner Temple ; published ' History and Antiquities of Dissenting Churches and Meeting Houses in London, Westminster and Southwark, including the Lives of their Ministers,' 1808–14, and ' Life and Times of Daniel Defoe,' 1830 ; left manuscripts on history of dissent. [lxii. 144]

WILSON, WILLIAM (1690–1741), Scottish divine ; educated at Glasgow University ; licensed preacher by presbytery of Dunfermline, 1713 ; ordained minister of new or west church, Perth, 1716 : ejected from Scottish church for protesting against act of assembly, ordaining that right of presentation, when not exercised by patrons, should be exercised by heritors and elders, and not by congregation, 1733 ; formed, with supporters, ' associate presbytery,' 1733 ; published religious writings. [lxii. 145]

WILSON, WILLIAM (1801–1860), poet and publisher ; edited Dundee ' Literary Olio,' 1823 ; in business in Edinburgh ; went to United States, 1832, and engaged in bookselling and publishing at Poughkeepsie, on the Hudson ; contributed poems to English and American periodicals. [lxii. 146]

WILSON, WILLIAM (1799–1871), botanist ; articled as solicitor at Manchester ; became well known as a bryologist ; discovered the cotoneaster on Great Orme's Head, 1821, and added a species of rose, a fern, and many new mosses to British list ; published ' Bryologia Britannica,' 1855. [lxii. 147]

WILSON, WILLIAM (1783 ?–1873), canon of Winchester ; M.A. Queen's College, Oxford, 1808 ; D.D., 1824 ; fellow, 1815–25 ; dean and bursar, 1822 ; headmaster of St. Bees grammar school, 1811–16 ; vicar of Holy Rood, Southampton, 1824–73 ; canon of Winchester, 1832 ; published ' The Bible Student's Guide,' 1850, and other works. [lxii. 147]

WILSON, WILLIAM (1808–1888), Scottish divine ; educated at Edinburgh University ; D.D., 1870 ; licensed by presbytery of Dumfries, 1830 ; ordained minister of Carmyllie, 1837 ; joined free church ; minister at mariners' church, Dundee, 1848–77 ; senior clerk of free church assembly, 1883 ; published religious works. [lxii. 148]

WILSON, SIR WILLIAM JAMES ERASMUS (1809–1884), surgeon ; studied at St. Bartholomew's Hospital, London, and under (Sir) William Lawrence [q. v.] ; M.R.C.S., 1831 ; demonstrator of anatomy to Richard Quain [q. v.] at University College, London, 1831–6 ; F.R.S., 1845 ; F.R.C.S., 1843 ; founded, 1869, and held, 1869–77, chair of dermatology at Royal College of Physicians, and was president, 1881 ; defrayed expenses of transport of ' Cleopatra's Needle ' to London, 1877–8 ; knighted, 1881 ; published ' Treatise on Diseases of the Skin,' 1842, and other works. [lxii. 148]

WILSON, WILLIAM RAE (1772–1849), author ; practised as solicitor before supreme courts of Scotland ; travelled in Egypt, Palestine, and through greater part of Europe, and published interesting records of his experience ; F.S.A. ; hon. LL.D. Glasgow, 1844. [lxii. 150]

WILSON, SIR WILTSHIRE (1762–1842), lieutenant-general ; studied at Woolwich ; second lieutenant, royal artillery, 1779 ; lieutenant, 1782 ; major, 1804 ; colonel, 1814 ; colonel-commandant, royal artillery, 1828 ; lieutenant-general, 1837 ; served in Flanders, 1793 ; took great part in defence of Nieuport against French under Vandamme, 1793 ; in West Indies, 1800–5 ; commanded royal artillery in northern district, England, 1806, Ceylon, 1810–1815, Canada, 1817–20 ; knight commander of Royal Hanoverian Guelphic order, 1838. [lxii. 150]

WILSON-PATTEN, JOHN, first BARON WINMAR-LEIGH (1802–1892), educated at Eton and Magdalen College, Oxford ; conservative M.P. for Lancashire, 1830–1, North Lancashire, 1832–74 ; firmly advocated all measures for benefit of the industrial population ; chancellor of duchy of Lancaster, 1867 ; privy councillor, 1867 ; chief secretary for Ireland under Disraeli, 1868 ; created Baron Winmarleigh, 1874. [lxii. 151]

WILTON, JOSEPH (1722–1803), sculptor ; pupil of Laurent Delvaux [q. v.] ; studied in Paris, Rome, and Florence ; practised in London from 1755 ; sculptor to George III ; original foundation member of Royal Academy, 1769 ; keeper of Royal Academy, 1786–90 ; his best work decorative sculpture to adorn architectural creations of Sir William Chambers [q. v.] [lxii. 152]

WILTON, WILLIAM DE (d. 1264), judge ; justice itinerant, 1248–50, and 1253, 1255, and 1259–61 ; chief-justice, 1261 ; killed on Henry III's side at battle of Lewes. [lxii. 153]

WILTSHIRE, EARLS OF. [See SCROPE, WILLIAM LE, 1351 ?–1399 ; BUTLER, JAMES, 1420–1461 ; BOLEYN, SIR THOMAS, 1477–1539.]

WIMBLEDON, VISCOUNT (1572–1638). [See CECIL SIR EDWARD.]

WIMPERIS, EDMUND MORISON (1835–1900), water-colour painter; trained as wood-engraver and draughtsman under Myles Birket Foster [q. v.]; member of Society of British Artists, 1870–4; vice-president of Institute of Painters in Water-colours, 1895; painted chiefly landscapes. [Suppl. iii. 516]

WINCH, SIR HUMPHREY (1555 ?–1625), judge; barrister, Lincoln's Inn, 1581; bencher, 1596, autumn reader, 1598; M.P., Bedford, 1593–1606; knighted and made serjeant-at-law; chief-baron of exchequer in Ireland, 1606; lord chief-justice of king's bench in Ireland, 1608; justice of common pleas in England, 1611–25; member of council of Wales, 1623; left legal compilations, published posthumously. [lxii. 153]

WINCH, NATHANIEL JOHN (1769 ?–1838), botanist; F.L.S., 1803, and associate, 1821; secretary to Newcastle Infirmary; published works relating to botany of Northumberland, Cumberland, and Durham. [lxii. 154]

WINCHCOMBE, alias SMALWOODE, JOHN (d. 1520), clothier; known as JACK OF NEWBURY; apprenticed as clothier at Newbury, where subsequently he pursued his trade, his wealth inspiring the authors of numerous chapbook stories; according to a legend led 100 or 250 men, equipped at his own expense, in the battle of Flodden Field. [lxii. 154]

WINCHCOMBE, JOHN (1489 ?–1565 ?), clothier and politician; son of John Winchcombe (d. 1520) [q. v.], whose trade he carried on; on commission of peace for Berkshire, 1541; M.P., West Bedwin, 1545, Reading, 1553. [lxii. 155]

WINCHELSEA, ROBERT DE (d. 1313), archbishop of Canterbury; graduated in arts at Paris and became rector of the university before 1267; D.D. Oxford; chancellor of Oxford, 1288; prebendary of Lincoln; archdeacon of Essex and prebendary of St. Paul's, London, c. 1283; elected archbishop of Canterbury, 1293; travelled to Rome and obtained papal confirmation of election, 1294; published papal bull forbidding clergy to pay taxes to the secular authority; outlawed with clergy by Edward I, who required money for French wars, but reconciled with him, 1297, Pope Boniface VIII making an exception in favour of voluntary gifts and sums raised for national defence, and Edward I conceding his long-promised confirmation of the charters; came into conflict with monks of St. Augustine's, Canterbury, and with bishop of Winchester, who were in the main supported by the pope; entrusted by Boniface VIII with delivery of apostolic mandate to Edward I to withdraw from attacking the Scots, 1300; quarrelled with Edward I on account of living of Pagham, which the king had presented to Theobald, brother of his son-in-law, the Count of Bar; deprived Theobald (who was, however, reappointed by papal provision), presented Pagham to Ralph of Malling, and was excommunicated, 1300, by the abbot of St. Michael's in diocese of Verdun, who was sent to England to secure execution of papal provision; submitted and obtained removal of sentence, 1302; induced clergy to reject law proposed by Edward I, 1305, forbidding export of specie from alien priories; suspended from spiritual and temporal functions by Pope Clement V under influence of Bishop Langton, 1306, and was in exile from England till Edward I's death; restored, through intercession of Edward II, 1308; one of lords ordainers, 1310; excommunicated Piers Gaveston and his abettors, and Langton, 1312; buried at Canterbury. [lxii. 155]

WINCHESTER, MARQUISES OF. [See PAULET, WILLIAM, first MARQUIS, 1485 ?–1572; PAULET, WILLIAM, third MARQUIS, 1535 ?–1598; PAULET, JOHN, fifth MARQUIS, 1598–1675.]

WINCHESTER, EARLS OF. [See QUINCY, SAER DE, d. 1219; QUINCY, ROGER DE, second EARL, 1195 ?–1265; DESPENSER, HUGH LE, 1262–1326.]

WINCHESTER, GODFREY OF (d. 1107). [See GODFREY.]

WINCHESTER, GREGORY OF (fl. 1270). [See GREGORY.]

WINCHESTER, JOHN, or JOHN OF (d. 1460?), bishop of Moray; chaplain to James I of Scotland; prebendary of Dunkeld; canon of Glasgow, 1428; provost of Lincluden, 1435; elected bishop of Moray, 1435, received papal confirmation, 1436, and held bishopric twenty-three years. [lxii. 162]

WINCHESTER, WULSTAN OF (fl. 1000). [See WULSTAN.]

WINCHILSEA, EARLS OF. [See FINCH, HENEAGE, second EARL, d. 1689; FINCH, DANIEL, sixth EARL, 1647–1730; FINCH-HATTON, GEORGE WILLIAM, ninth EARL, 1791–1858.]

WINCHILSEA, COUNTESS OF (d. 1720). [See FINCH, ANNE.]

WINDEBANK, SIR FRANCIS (1582–1646), secretary of state; grandson of Sir Richard Windebank, and son of Sir Thomas Windebank (d. 1607); entered Middle Temple, 1602; travelled on continent; served in office of signet, and was clerk of signet, 1624; joint-secretary of state with Sir John Coke [q. v.], 1632; knighted, 1632; engaged by Charles I in various secret negotiations; appointed to discuss with papal agent, Gregorio Panzani, possibility of union between Anglican and Roman churches, 1634; M.P., Oxford University (Short parliament), 1640, Corfe (Long parliament), 1640; fled to Calais, being accused of signing letters in favour of priests and jesuits, 1640, and arrived at Paris, 1641; died at Paris. [lxii. 162]

WINDELE, JOHN (1801–1865), Irish antiquary; lived at Cork; made many antiquarian expeditions in Ireland; published ' Historical and Descriptive Notices of City of Cork and its Vicinity,' 1839, and other writings, and left antiquarian manuscripts. [lxii. 166]

WINDER, HENRY (1693–1752), dissenting divine and chronologist; studied at Whitehaven academy and Dublin; licensed preacher at Dublin; ordained independent minister of Tunley, Lancashire, 1716; minister of Castle Hey congregation, Liverpool, 1718; removed to chapel in Benn's Garden, Red Cross Street, Liverpool, 1727; D.D. Glasgow, 1740; supported non-subscription; published ' Critical and Chronological History of . . . Knowledge, chiefly Religious,' 1745. [lxii. 166]

WINDET, JAMES (d. 1664), physician; M.D. Leyden, 1655; incorporated at Oxford, 1656; M.R.C.P., 1656; practised in London from 1656; published poetical and other writings in Latin. [lxii. 167]

WINDEYER, CHARLES (1780–1855), parliamentary reporter and Australian magistrate; first recognised reporter in House of Lords; emigrated to New South Wales, 1828; police magistrate for Sydney. [lxii. 168]

WINDEYER, RICHARD (1806–1847), Australian reformer and statesman; son of Charles Windeyer [q. v.]; parliamentary reporter for 'The Times'; barrister, Middle Temple, 1834; emigrated to Australia, 1835; member for Durham in first legislative council, 1843; one of popular leaders against bureaucratic government of Sir George Gipps [q. v.]; originated jury and libel acts of New South Wales; advocated introduction of representative institutions and responsible government; devoted much time to scientific farming. [lxii. 168]

WINDEYER, SIR WILLIAM CHARLES (1834–1897), Australian legislator and judge; son of Richard Windeyer [q. v.]; born in Westminster; taken to New South Wales, 1835; M.A. Sydney University, 1859; called to bar, 1857; liberal M.P. for the Lower Hunter, 1859, and West Sydney, 1860–2 and 1866–72; solicitor-general, 1870; first member for Sydney University, 1876; attorney-general, 1877–9; judge of divorce and matrimonial causes court, and deputy-judge of vice-admiralty court, 1879–96; knighted, 1891; honorary LL.D. Cambridge. [lxii. 169]

WINDHAM. [See also WYNDHAM.]

WINDHAM, SIR CHARLES ASH (1810–1870), lieutenant-general; educated at Sandhurst; ensign and lieutenant, Coldstream guards, 1826; captain and lieutenant-colonel, 1846; served in Canada, 1838–42; colonel, 1854; assistant and quartermaster-general of 4th division of army of the east in Crimea, 1854; at Alma, Balaclava, and Inkerman; C.B., 1855; commanded 2nd brigade of 2nd division, 1855; at assault on the Redan; major-general, 1855; commanded 4th division; chief of staff to Sir William John Codrington [q. v.], 1855; liberal M.P. for East Norfolk, 1857; commanded troops at Cawnpore, 1857; defeated central division of Gwalior troops under Tantia Topi, but was unsuccessful in holding Cawnpore; commanded Lahore division, 1857–1861; lieutenant-general, 1863; K.C.B., 1865; commanded forces in Canada, 1867–70. [lxii. 170]

WINDHAM, JOSEPH (1739-1810), antiquary; educated at Eton and Christ's College, Cambridge; travelled on continent; F.S.A., 1775; F.R.S., 1781; member of Society of Dilettanti, 1779; assisted James Stuart (1713-1788) [q. v.] in 'Antiquities of Athens.' [lxii. 172]

WINDHAM, WILLIAM (1717-1761), colonel; officer in one of Queen Maria Theresa's hussar regiments in Hungary; M.P., Aldeburgh, 1754; supported Pitt's scheme for national militia, 1756; published 'Plan of Discipline,' 1760. [lxii. 172]

WINDHAM, WILLIAM (1750-1810), statesman; son of William Windham (1717-1761) [q. v.]; educated at Eton, Glasgow University, and University College, Oxford; M.A., 1782; hon. D.C.L., 1793; friend of Dr. Johnson and Burke; chief secretary to Northington, lord-lieutenant of Ireland, 1783; M.P., Norwich, 1784-1802; one of members charged with impeachment of Warren Hastings; secretary for war, with seat in cabinet under Pitt, 1794-1801; opposed peace of 1802; assisted Cobbett to found 'Political Register'; M.P., St. Mawes, 1802-6, New Romney, 1806, and Higham Ferrers, 1807-1810; held war and colonial office in Lord Grenville's administration, 1806-7; introduced plan for improving condition of military forces, 1806; his diary published, 1866. [lxii. 172]

WINDSOR, ALICE DE (d. 1400). [See PERRERS.]

WINDSOR, formerly **HICKMAN,** THOMAS WINDSOR, seventh BARON WINDSOR OF STANWELL and first EARL OF PLYMOUTH (1627?-1687), nephew of Thomas Windsor, sixth baron (1590-1641); assumed surname of Windsor in lieu of Hickman; served with royalist army, and was perhaps captain, 1642, and lieutenant-colonel, 1645; probably captured at Naseby, 1645, and fined; took seat as seventh Baron Windsor, 1660; governor of Jamaica, 1661-4, but was only in West Indies, July to October, 1662; master of horse to Duke of York, 1676; governor of Portsmouth, 1681, and of Hull, 1682; created Earl of Plymouth, 1684; privy councillor, 1685. [lxii. 175]

WINDSOR, SIR WILLIAM DE, BARON WINDSOR (d. 1384), deputy of Ireland; king's lieutenant in Ireland, 1369; having adopted, to secure order, measures which Edward III would not support, was recalled; viceroy of Ireland, 1373-6; governor of Cherbourg, 1379; took leading part in putting down peasants' revolt, 1381-2; married Alice Perrers [q. v.] [lxii. 177]

WINDUS, JOHN (fl. 1725), author of 'A Journey to Mequinez,' 1725, written from notes gathered as historian of a mission despatched by George I, 1720, under Commodore Charles Stewart, to treat for peace with emperor of Morocco. [lxii. 179]

WINEFRIDE (Welsh, Gwenfrewi), a legendary saint, supposed to have lived in seventh century; reputed abbess of Gwytherin; her life written by Robert of Shrewsbury [q. v.] Holywell, Flintshire, gains its name from the spring which, according to legend, appeared in the place where her head, which was subsequently reunited to her body, was cut off. [lxii. 179]

WINFRID, afterwards called BONIFACE (680-755). [See BONIFACE.]

WING, TYCHO (1696-1750), astrologer; coroner of Rutland, 1727-42; edited, from 1739, 'Olympia Domata,' the almanac founded by his great-great-uncle, Vincent Wing [q. v.]. [lxii. 180]

WING, VINCENT (1619-1668), astronomer; land-surveyor; published 'Astronomia Britannica,' 1652, and other astronomical writings. [lxii. 179]

WINGATE, EDMUND (1596-1656), mathematician and legal writer; B.A. Queen's College, Oxford, 1614; entered Gray's Inn, 1614; teacher of English language to Princess (afterwards Queen) Henrietta Maria in Paris, c. 1624; published 'L'usage de la règle de proportion en arithmétique,' 1624 (in English, 1626), and other mathematical works, including an edition of 'Britton' [see BRETON, JOHN LE], 1640; sided with parliament in civil war; M.P., Bedfordshire, 1655. [lxii. 180]

WINGATE or **WINYET,** NINIAN (1518-1592). [See WINZET.]

WINGFIELD, SIR ANTHONY (1485?-1552), comptroller of the household; nephew of Sir Humphrey Wingfield [q. v.]; served in France, 1513; knighted, 1513; sheriff of Norfolk and Suffolk, 1515-16; served in France, 1523; M.P., Suffolk, 1529-35 and 1547-52, Horsham, 1544; vice-chamberlain, captain of guard, and privy councillor, 1539; K.G., 1541; joined Warwick's conspiracy against Protector Somerset, 1549; arrested Somerset, 1549; comptroller of the household, 1550; joint lord-lieutenant of Suffolk, 1551. [lxii. 181]

WINGFIELD, ANTHONY (1550?-1615?), reader in Greek to Queen Elizabeth; grandson of Sir Anthony Wingfield [q. v.]; B.A. Trinity College, Cambridge, 1574; fellow, 1576; M.A., 1577; accompanied Lord Willoughby de Eresby on his embassy to Denmark, 1582; public orator at Cambridge, 1581-9; proctor, 1582; M.P., Ripon, 1593. [lxii. 182]

WINGFIELD, EDWARD MARIA (fl. 1607), colonist; grandson of Sir Richard Wingfield (1469?-1525) [q. v.]; one of original patentees of Virginia, 1606; went to America, 1607; first president of council in Virginia, 1607, but was deposed; returned to England, 1608; wrote 'Discourse of Virginia,' published, 1856. [lxii. 183]

WINGFIELD, SIR HUMPHREY (d. 1545), speaker of House of Commons; brother of Sir Richard Wingfield (1469?-1525) [q. v.]; educated at Gray's Inn; Lent reader, 1517; high sheriff of Norfolk and Suffolk, 1520; legal member of king's council, 1526; M.P., Great Yarmouth, 1529; speaker, 1533-6; knighted, 1533 or 1537. [lxii. 184]

WINGFIELD, SIR JOHN (d. 1596), soldier; brother of Anthony Wingfield [q. v.]; captain of foot in Leicester's expedition to Holland, 1585; knighted, 1586; governor of Gertruydenberg, 1587, until its delivery to Spaniards, 1589; master of ordnance in Brittany, 1591; campmaster, with colonel's rank, in Essex's expedition, 1596, to Cadiz, where he was killed. [lxii. 185]

WINGFIELD, LEWIS STRANGE (1842-1891), traveller, actor, writer, and painter; youngest son of Richard Wingfield, sixth viscount Powerscourt; educated at Eton and Bonn; played at Haymarket Theatre, London, 1865, and subsequently at various times acted as newspaper correspondent, travelled in many parts of the world, practised as painter, designed theatrical costumes, and engaged in numerous other pursuits; published novels and other writings. [lxii. 186]

WINGFIELD, SIR RICHARD (1469?-1525), soldier and diplomatist; brother of Sir Robert Wingfield [q. v.]; educated at Cambridge; studied at Gray's Inn; knighted; marshal of Calais, 1511; dispatched with Sir Edward Poynings to Netherlands to arrange holy league between Pope Julius II, England, Arragon and Castile, Maximilian, Prince Charles (afterwards Charles V), and Margaret of Savoy, 1512; knight-marshal of Calais, 1513; on missions to Brussels and Antwerp, 1513; joint-deputy of Calais, 1513; on mission to Margaret of Savoy to arrange marriage of Henry VIII's sister Mary with Prince Charles, 1514-15; accompanied embassy to France, 1515; accredited to court of Brussels, 1516; resigned post at Calais, 1519; English ambassador at court of France, 1520; Henry's representative in mediating between Francis and Charles V, 1521-3; received Garter, 1522; chancellor of duchy of Lancaster, 1524; high steward of Cambridge University, 1524; died while on mission to Spain. [lxii. 187]

WINGFIELD, SIR RICHARD, first VISCOUNT POWERSCOURT (d. 1634), deputy vice-treasurer of Ireland, 1580-c. 1586; served under Sir John Norris (1547?-1597) [q. v.], in Netherlands, 1586, and in Brittany, 1591; served in Ireland, 1595; knighted, 1595; colonel in Essex's expedition to Cadiz, 1596; marshal of army in Ireland, 1600; privy councillor, 1600; served in Ulster, 1600, and at siege of Kinsale, 1601; M.P., Downpatrick, 1613; created Viscount Powerscourt, 1619. [lxii. 190]

WINGFIELD, SIR ROBERT (1464?-1539), diplomatist; brother of Sir Humphrey Wingfield [q. v.] and Sir Richard Wingfield (1469?-1525) [q. v.]; on mission from Henry VII to Maximilian, 1507-8; knighted; councillor and knight of the body, c. 1511; joint-ambassador to council convoked by Julius II at the Lateran, 1511-12; at Vienna, 1514-17; censured by Henry VIII for credulous confidence in Maximilian; king's councillor, 1519; ambassador at Charles V's court, 1520; privy councillor and vice-chamberlain; ambassador to Margaret of Savoy at Brussels, 1522–3; lieutenant of Calais Castle, 1523; at Brussels, 1525–6; deputy of Calais, 1526; mayor of Calais, 1534. [lxii. 191]

WINGHAM or **WENGHAM**, HENRY DE (*d.* 1262), bishop of London; one of king's escheators; chamberlain of Gascony; keeper of great seal, 1255–9; chancellor of Exeter, 1257; dean of St. Martin's; one of twelve nominated by Henry III to draw up provisions of Oxford, 1258; bishop of Winchester, 1259, and later of London. [lxii. 193]

WINI (*d.* 675 ?), bishop of London; bishop of western portion of West-Saxons, with see at Winchester, and, later, sole bishop of West-Saxons, *c.* 663; expelled from bishopric, 666, by Cenwalh, king of West-Saxons; bishop of London, 666. [lxii. 194]

WINKWORTH, CATHERINE (1827–1878), author; sister of Susanna Winkworth [q. v.]; educated privately; studied at Dresden, 1845–6; joined committee for higher education of women, 1868, and became secretary, 1870; best known by her translations of German hymns, 1853 and 1858. [lxii. 194]

WINKWORTH, SUSANNA (1820–1884), translator; met Baron Bunsen at Rome and for some time acted as his literary secretary; published life and letters of Niebuhr, 1853, a translation of the 'Theologia Germanica,' 1854, and other works; engaged in philanthropic enterprises at Bristol. [lxii. 195]

WINMARLEIGH, BARON (1802–1892). [See WILSON-PATTEN, JOHN.]

WINNIFFE, THOMAS (1576–1654), bishop of Lincoln; fellow, Exeter College, Oxford, 1595–1609; M.A., 1601; D.D., 1619; incorporated D.D. Cambridge, 1628; chaplain to Prince Charles (afterwards Charles I); dean of Gloucester, 1624; chaplain to Charles I; dean and prebendary of St. Paul's, London, 1631; bishop of Lincoln, 1642. [lxii. 196]

WINNINGTON, SIR FRANCIS (1634–1700), lawyer; of Trinity College, Oxford; barrister, Middle Temple, 1660, bencher, 1672; autumn reader, 1675; treasurer, 1675; K.C. and attorney-general to Duke of York, 1672; knighted, 1672; solicitor-general, 1674–9; M.P., Windsor, 1677; M.P., Worcester, 1679 (twice) and 1681, and Tewkesbury, 1692–8. [lxii. 197]

WINNINGTON, THOMAS (1696–1746), politician; grandson of Sir Francis Winnington [q. v.]; of Westminster School and Christ Church, Oxford; entered Middle Temple, 1714; M.P., Droitwich, 1726–41, Worcester, 1741–6; supported Walpole; lord of admiralty, 1730; treasurer, 1736–41; cofferer of household, 1741–3; paymaster-general of forces, 1743–6; privy councillor, 1741. [lxii. 198]

WINRAM, GEORGE, LORD LIBBERTOUN (*d.* 1650), Scottish judge; admitted advocate, 1620; presented to Charles I petition of assembly after abolition of episcopacy, 1638; one of commissioners for Midlothian in parliaments of 1643 and 1649; represented general assembly at Westminster Assembly of Divines, 1647; lord of session, 1649; one of Scottish parliamentary commissioners chosen to treat with Charles II, 1649, and after conference with Charles in Jersey brought intelligence to Scotland that Charles would receive commissioners at Breda, 1650; took part in conferences at Breda; fought at Dunbar and died of wounds. [lxii. 199]

WINRAM, **WYNRAM**, or **WINRAHAM**, JOHN (1492?–1582), Scottish reformer; B.A. St. Leonard's College, St. Andrews, 1515; entered Augustinian monastery of St. Andrews, and was third prior, 1534, and sub-prior, 1536; adopted tolerant attitude towards George Wishart (1513?–1546) [q. v.] and Knox, and casting in his lot with reformers was superintendent of Fife, 1561–72 and 1574; member of commission to draw up 'Book of Discipline'; prior of Portmoak; present at Perth convention, 1569, and Leith convention, 1572, and was made archbishop of the diocese on authorisation of 'tulchan' bishops; superintendent of Strathearn, 1572–4. [lxii. 200]

WINSLOW, EDWARD (1595–1655), governor of Plymouth colony; born at Droitwich, Worcestershire; joined English church at Leyden; went to New England in Mayflower, 1620; in England as agent for the colony, 1623–4 and 1624; assistant-governor, 1624–47, excepting 1633, 1636, and 1644, when he was governor; in England as agent for Plymouth and Massachusetts, 1635, when he was imprisoned for preaching and celebrating marriages, though a layman; returned to England to answer charges against colonists of religious intolerance and persecution, 1646; held various offices under Commonwealth; died at sea while accompanying naval expedition against Spanish in West Indies; published controversial and other writings. [lxii. 201]

WINSLOW, FORBES BENIGNUS (1810–1874), physician; educated at University College, London, and Middlesex Hospital; M.R.C.S., 1835; M.D. Aberdeen, 1849; published treatises on insanity; opened private lunatic asylum at Hammersmith, 1847; founded, 1848, and conducted, 1848–64, 'Quarterly Journal of Psychological Medicine'; hon. D.C.L. Oxford, 1853. [lxii. 203]

WINSOR, FREDERICK ALBERT (1763–1830), one of pioneers of gas-lighting; born in Brunswick; obtained patent for 'oven' for manufacture of gas, 1804; lighted with gas part of Pall Mall, London, 1806; obtained patents for new gas furnace and purifiers, 1807, 1808, and 1809; assisted Westminster Gas Light and Coke Company to obtain charter, 1810; founded gas-lighting company in Paris, 1815 (liquidated, 1819); died in Paris. [lxii. 204]

WINSOR, FREDERICK ALBERT (1797–1874), barrister; son of Frederick Albert Winsor (1763–1830) [q. v.]; barrister, Middle Temple, 1840; obtained patent for 'production of light,' 1843. [lxii. 205]

WINSTANLEY, GERRARD (*fl.* 1648–1652), 'digger' or 'leveller'; came into notice, 1649, as joint-leader of party of men who began cultivating waste lands at St. George's Hill, Walton-on-Thames, Surrey, asserting right of common people to do so without paying rent; published tracts relating to this and religious questions; universalist, and, according to Dean Comber, real founder of the quaker sect. [lxii. 206]

WINSTANLEY, HAMLET (1698–1756), painter and engraver; studied under Sir Godfrey Kneller [q. v.] in London; employed at Rome by James Stanley, tenth earl of Derby, 1723–5, in copying works of old masters; painted portraits. [lxii. 207]

WINSTANLEY, HENRY (1644–1703), engineer and engraver; nephew of William Winstanley [q. v.]; clerk of works to Charles II at Audley End and Newmarket, 1666; issued engravings of Audley End, 1676; furnished design for Eddystone lighthouse, 1696, and while superintending construction was captured by French privateer, which destroyed the work, 1697; released, 1697; completed building, and lost life in storm which demolished it, 1703. [lxii. 208]

WINSTANLEY, JOHN (1678?–1750), verse-writer; published 'Poems written occasionally,' Dublin, 1742. [lxii. 209]

WINSTANLEY, THOMAS (1749–1823), scholar; M.A. Brasenose College, Oxford, 1774; D.D., 1799; fellow of Hertford College, Oxford; Camden professor of history, 1790; prebendary of St. Paul's, London, 1794–1810; principal of St. Alban Hall, Oxford, 1797; Laudian professor of Arabic, 1814; edited Aristotle's 'Poetics,' 1780. [lxii. 209]

WINSTANLEY, WILLIAM (1628?–1698), compiler; uncle of Henry Winstanley [q. v.]; barber in London; adopted literary profession; probably wrote the almanacs and chapbooks issued from 1662, under pseudonym of 'Poor Robin.' His compilations include 'The Muses Cabinet,' 1655, 'England's Worthies,' 1660, 'Loyall Martyrology,' 1662, 'The Honour of the Merchant Taylors,' 1668, and 'Lives of the most famous English Poets,' 1687. [lxii. 209]

WINSTON, CHARLES (1814–1864), writer on glass-painting; studied at Inner Temple; special pleader; called to bar, 1845; published several works on glass-painting, and conducted chemical experiments which led to improvement in manufacture of coloured glass; claimed to have discovered the secret of the mediæval processes of glass-painting; member of Archæological Institute. [lxii. 211]

WINSTON, THOMAS (1575–1655), physician; M.A. Clare Hall, Cambridge, 1602; fellow till 1617; F.R.C.P., 1615; professor of physic, Gresham College, London, 1615–42 and 1652–5. [lxii. 212]

WINT, PETER DE (1784–1849). [See DE WINT.]

WINTER, SIR EDWARD (1622?–1686), agent at Fort St. George, Madras; went to India, c. 1630; chief of Masulipatam factory, 1655–8; dismissed for private trading; knighted, 1662; agent at Fort St. George, 1662; accused of fraud but succeeded in securing imprisonment of George Foxcroft, the new agent sent to take his place, 1665, and continued direction of affairs till 1668, when he was compelled to submit, Foxcroft being reinstated; finally returned to England, 1672. [lxii. 212]

WINTER, SIR JOHN (1600?–1673?), secretary to Queen Henrietta Maria; grandson of Sir William Winter [q. v.], and son of Sir Edward Winter by Anne, daughter of Edward Somerset, fourth earl of Worcester [q. v.]; knighted, 1624; frequently gave Charles I pecuniary assistance, and received large grants in Forest of Dean; member of council of Fishing Company; secretary to Queen Henrietta Maria, 1638; master of requests to Queen Henrietta Maria; became object of parliamentary oppression owing to his Roman catholic principles; lieutenant-colonel of Welsh force raised by Marquis of Worcester, 1643; conducted guerilla warfare; defeated at Tidenham, 1644; governor of Chepstow, 1645; confined in Tower of London, 1650–3; employed leisure in making experiments in production of coke, for which he obtained monopoly after Restoration; successful colliery manager in Forest of Dean. [lxii. 213]

WINTER or **WINTOUR**, ROBERT (d. 1606), conspirator; brother of Thomas Winter or Wintour [q. v.]; admitted to Gunpowder plot, 1605; arrested at Hagley, Worcestershire, 1606; wrote confession of his share in conspiracy and was executed. [lxii. 219]

WINTER, SAMUEL (1603–1666), provost of Trinity College, Dublin; of King Henry VIII's school, Coventry, and Queens' College, Cambridge; M.A.; joined independent ministry; chaplain to four parliamentary commissions in Ireland; provost of Trinity College, Dublin, 1651–60; D.D., 1654; took lead in forming clerical association in which independents, presbyterians, and episcopalians could meet in amity; divinity lecturer, 1659; removed from provostship at Restoration. [lxii. 216]

WINTER or **WINTOUR**, THOMAS (1572–1606), conspirator; served in Netherlands; secretary to William Parker, fourth lord Monteagle [q. v.]; became intimate friend of Catesby; sent by Monteagle and Catesby on mission to Philip III of Spain, 1602, to propose invasion of England or obtain money for distressed Roman catholics; became party to Catesby's Gunpowder plot, 1604, and brought Fawkes to England; took prominent part in working of the mine under the parliament house; arrested at Holbeche, 8 Nov. 1605, and conveyed to Tower of London; prepared written confession containing account of plot, 1605, and was executed, 1606. [lxii. 217]

WINTER, THOMAS (1795–1851), pugilist; styled 'Tom Spring'; worked as butcher; adopted boxing as profession, 1814; defeated Ned Painter, 1818, but was beaten by him later in same year; defeated Carter, 1819, Tom Oliver [q. v.], 1821, and others; claimed championship of England on retirement of Tom Cribb [q. v.], 1821; defeated Neat of Bristol, and Langan, an Irishman, 1823; retired from ring; kept Castle Tavern, Holborn, 1828–51. [lxii. 219]

WINTER, or correctly **WYNTER**, SIR WILLIAM (d. 1589), admiral; surveyor of navy, 1549–89; master of ordnance of navy, 1557–89; commanded fleet sent to Forth to watch for French squadron, 1559; with the fleet at Conquêt, 1558, and Havre, 1563; knighted, 1573; took part in battle off Gravelines, 1588; supported charges of dishonesty brought against (Sir) John Hawkins or Hawkyns [q. v.], 1588. [lxii. 220]

WINTERBOTHAM, HENRY SELFE PAGE (1837–1873), politician; grandson of William Winterbotham [q. v.]; educated at University College, London; LL.D. London, 1859; barrister, Lincoln's Inn, 1860; advanced liberal M.P. for Stroud, Gloucestershire, 1867; under-secretary of state for home department, 1871. [lxii. 222]

WINTERBOTHAM, WILLIAM (1763–1829), dissenting minister and political prisoner; silversmith in London; joined Calvinistic methodists; became baptist. 1789; assistant at How's Lane Chapel, Plymouth; fined and imprisoned for preaching seditious sermons, 1793–7; published sermons and historical and other works. [lxii. 222]

WINTERBOTTOM, THOMAS MASTERMAN (1765?–1859), physician; M.D. Glasgow, 1792; went on medical mission to Sierra Leone, c. 1796–1803, and embodied his experiences in two works; practised at South Shields. [lxii. 223]

WINTERBOURNE, THOMAS (d. 1478), divine; archdeacon of Canterbury; dean of St. Paul's, London, 1471. [lxii. 224]

WINTERBOURNE, WALTER (1225?–1305), cardinal; D.D.; entered Dominican order, and was provincial in England, 1290; confessor to Edward I, 1298; made cardinal by Pope Benedict IX, 1304; died at Genoa, having gone abroad to take part in election of Pope Clement V; author of works of scholastic theology (lost). [lxii. 223]

WINTERSEL, WINTERSHALL, WINTERSAL, or **WINTERSHULL**, WILLIAM (d. 1679), actor; member of Queen Henrietta Maria's company, c. 1637–42, and that of Thomas Killigrew the elder [q. v.], after Restoration; famous for his performance of Cokes in Jonson's 'Bartholomew Fair.' [lxii. 224]

WINTERTON, RALPH (1600–1636), physician; educated at Eton and King's College, Cambridge; fellow, 1620; M.A., 1624; licensed to practise medicine, 1631; M.D., 1633; appointed regius professor of physic, 1635; published numerous translations, including a Greek metrical version of aphorisms of Hippocrates (with Latin versions by John Heurnius of Utrecht), 1633. [lxii. 225]

WINTERTON, THOMAS (fl. 1391), theological writer; doctor of theology, Oxford; provincial of Augustinian order, 1389 and 1391; wrote against Wycliffe. [lxii. 226]

WINTHROP, JOHN (1588–1649), governor of Massachusetts; educated at Trinity College, Cambridge; lived at Great Stanbridge, Essex, and gained great moral ascendency among his puritan neighbours; attorney of court of wards and liveries, 1626; entered Inner Temple, 1628; went to Massachusetts after decision, 1629, of court of Massachusetts Company to vest government of colony in the colonists, 1630; settled at Charlestown (now northern suburb of Boston) and received from John Endecott [q. v.] authority which he exercised as acting-governor; established headquarters on peninsula of Shawmut, to which name of Boston was given, 1630; elected governor, 1631, 1632, 1637, 1642, and 1646; made councillor for life, 1636; combated relaxation of religious discipline in government of colony; left a manuscript 'Journal' (1630–49) which was published, 1825–6, and forms staple of all subsequent histories of early New England. [lxii. 226]

WINTHROP, JOHN, the younger (1606–1676), governor of Connecticut; son of John Winthrop (1588–1649) [q. v.]; of Trinity College, Dublin; entered Inner Temple; travelled on continent; joined his father in New England, 1631; assistant, 1634, 1635, 1640, 1641, and 1644–9; governor, 1632, of settlement on river Connecticut (afterwards absorbed in colony of Connecticut); one of magistrates of Connecticut, 1651; deputy-governor, 1659; governor, 1660–76; carried loyal address to Charles II in England, 1662; F.R.S., 1662. [lxii. 231]

WINTON, EARLS OF. [See SETON, GEORGE, third EARL, 1584–1650; SETON, GEORGE, fifth EARL, d. 1749; MONTGOMERIE, ARCHIBALD WILLIAM, first EARL in peerage of United Kingdom, 1812–1861.]

WINTON, ANDREW OF (1350?–1420?). [See WYNTOUN.]

WINTOUR. [See also WINTER.]

WINTOUR, JOHN CRAWFORD (1825–1882), landscape-painter; studied at Trustees' Academy, Edinburgh; associate of Royal Scottish Academy, 1859. [lxii. 232]

WINTRINGHAM, CLIFTON (1689–1748), physician; educated at Jesus College, Cambridge; extra L.R.C.P., 1711; practised at York; physician in York county hospital; his medical works collected by his son, 1752. [lxii. 232]

WINTRINGHAM, SIR CLIFTON, baronet (1710–1794), physician; son of Clifton Wintringham [q. v.];

M.D. Trinity College, Cambridge, 1749; entered army medical service; joint-physician to hospital for service of forces of Great Britain, 1756; physician in ordinary to George III, 1762; knighted, 1762; F.R.O.P., 1763; created baronet, 1774; physician-general to forces, 1786; F.R.S., 1792; published medical writings, and (1752) edited his father's works. [lxii. 233]

WINWOOD, SIR RALPH (1563?-1617), diplomatist and secretary of state; fellow, Magdalen College, Oxford, 1582-1601: B.A., 1582; M.A., 1587; B.C.L., 1591; university proctor, 1592; travelled on continent; secretary, 1599, to Sir Henry Neville, whom he succeeded as ambassador to France, 1601-3; English agent to States-General of Holland, 1603-14; councillor of state in assembly of States-General, 1603; visited England and was knighted, 1607; signed, with Sir Richard Spencer, treaty of the States-General with England, 1608; joined with French ambassador, Boississe, in unsuccessful mediation between protestant princes and the emperor Rudolph II, 1609; appointed secretary of state for life, 1614; M.P., Buckingham, 1614; led House of Commons, 1614; supported theory that power of impositions belonged to hereditary, though not to elective, monarchs; joint-secretary with Sir Thomas Lake, 1616; supported and profited by James I's policy of selling peerages; largely responsible for release of Sir Walter Ralegh, 1616, and for permission covertly given him to pillage Spanish possessions in America; a selection from his papers published, 1725. [lxii. 233]

WINZET, WINYET, or **WINGATE,** NINIAN (1518-1592), Scottish controversialist; perhaps educated at Glasgow; ordained priest, 1540; master of grammar school of Linlithgow, 1552, and subsequently provost of collegiate church of St. Michael, Linlithgow; ejected from office for refusing to sign protestant confession of faith, 1561; Queen Elizabeth's chaplain, c. 1562; exiled, 1563; preceptor of arts in Paris University; abbot of Benedictine monastery of St. James at Ratisbon, 1577-1592; published writings against Knox and Buchanan. [lxii. 236]

WIREKER, NIGEL (*fl.* 1190). [See NIGEL.]

WIRLEY, WILLIAM (1565-1618). [See WYRLEY.]

WISDOM, ROBERT (*d.* 1568), archdeacon of Ely; B.D. (university unknown); committed to Lollards' Tower for heresy, 1540; recanted, 1543; continued to preach reformation doctrines; vicar of Settrington; settled at Frankfort on Queen Mary's accession; returned to England, 1559; archdeacon of Ely, 1560; published metrical version of Psalms, and other works. [lxii. 237]

WISE, FRANCIS (1695-1767), archæologist; M.A. Trinity College, Oxford, 1717; fellow, 1719-46; B.D., 1727; under-keeper of Bodleian Library, 1719; keeper of archives at Oxford, 1726; rector of Rotherfield Greys, near Henley-on-Thames, 1745-67; Radcliffe librarian at Oxford, 1748-67; F.S.A., 1749; published archæological works. [lxii. 238]

WISE, HENRY (1653-1738), gardener; deputy-ranger of Hyde Park and superintendent of royal gardens at Hampton Court, Kensington, and elsewhere, c. 1689; was also gardener to Queen Anne, 1702, and to George I, 1714; published 'The Retir'd Gard'ner,' 1706 (translated from the French), with George London, under whom he studied horticulture, and whose sole partner he had been at the Brompton nursery. [lxii. 239]

WISE, JOHN RICHARD DE CAPEL (1831-1890), author and ornithologist; of Lincoln College, Oxford; travelled abroad and in England collecting birds' eggs; published 'Shakspere: his Birthplace and its Neighbourhood,' 1860, illustrated by W. J. Linton, 'The New Forest' (1862), illustrated by Mr. Walter Crane, and other works. [lxii. 240]

WISE, MICHAEL (1646?-1687), musician and composer; one of children of Chapel Royal, London, in 1660; lay-clerk of St. George's, Windsor, 1663; organist and master of choristers of Salisbury Cathedral, 1668; gentleman of Chapel Royal, London, 1676, almoner and master of the boys at St. Paul's Cathedral, 1687; published and left in manuscript religious and other musical compositions which, with those of Blow and Humphrey, constitute a link between the foreign music encouraged by Charles II and the original work of Purcell. [lxii. 241]

WISE, WILLIAM FURLONG (1784-1844), rear-admiral; entered navy, 1797; lieutenant, 1804; captain, 1806; distinguished at bombardment of Algiers, 1816; C.B., 1816; rear-admiral, 1841. [lxii. 242]

WISEMAN, NICHOLAS PATRICK STEPHEN (1802-1865), cardinal-archbishop of Westminster; born in Seville; went to Waterford, 1805; educated at St. Cuthbert's College, Ushaw; received four minor orders and studied at English College, Rome; doctor in divinity, 1824; ordained priest, 1825; assistant to Abbate Molza, who was compiling Syriac grammar; published oriental researches under title 'Horæ Syriacæ,' 1828; professor supernumerary in chairs of Hebrew and Syro-Chaldaic in Roman Archigymnasium of the Sapienza, 1828; vice-rector of English College, Rome, 1827, rector, 1828-40; published lectures on 'Connection between Science and Revealed Religion,' 1836; in England, 1835-6; assisted in founding 'Dublin Review,' Roman catholic quarterly magazine,'1836; coadjutor to vicar-apostolic of central district of England, 1839; bishop of Melipotamus *in partibus*, and president of Oscott College, 1840; greatly influenced development of the Oxford movement; published 'High Church Claims,' 1841; diplomatic envoy from Pius IX to Palmerston, 1848; pro-vicar apostolic of London district, 1848; vicar-apostolic, 1849; archbishop of Westminster and cardinal, with title of St. Prudentiana, 1850; gained wide repute as lecturer on social, artistic, and literary topics. His works include, 'Fabiola, or the Church of the Catacombs,' a story of the third century, 1854, 'Recollections of the last Four Popes,' 1858, and numerous lectures and sermons. He is the bishop in Browning's 'Bishop Blougram's Apology,' though the poem can hardly be accepted as a serious description of his life and aims. [lxii. 243]

WISEMAN, RICHARD (1622?-1676), surgeon; apprenticed in London; served in Dutch navy; joined royalist army of the west, c. 1644; with Prince Charles after rout at Truro, 1645, and became his immediate medical attendant; captured at Worcester, 1651; practised in London from 1652; freeman of Barber-Surgeons' Company; imprisoned for assisting a royalist, 1654; 'surgeon in ordinary for the person,' 1660; principal surgeon and sergeant-surgeon to Charles II, 1672; master of Barber-Surgeons' Company, 1665; published surgical works; the first to raise the surgical profession from its state of subordination to the physicians. [lxii. 246]

WISHART, GEORGE (1513?-1546), Scottish reformer; perhaps graduated in arts at King's College, Aberdeen; said to have been schoolmaster at Montrose, and, being charged with heresy for teaching Greek New Testament, to have fled the country, 1538; probably visited Germany and Switzerland, c. 1540; became member of Corpus Christi College, Cambridge, c. 1543; probably returned to Montrose, 1543; preached at Dundee, Ayr, Kyle, Mauchlin, Perth, Leith, and Haddington, 1545; arrested by Bothwell; confined at Edinburgh and St. Andrews, 1546; tried by convocation of bishops and other clergy; convicted of heresy and burned at St. Andrews, 1546; teacher and intimate friend of John Knox from 1544. [lxii. 248]

WISHART, GEORGE (1599-1671), bishop of Edinburgh; perhaps educated at Edinburgh and St. Salvator's College, St. Andrews; minister at Monifieth, Forfarshire, 1625; held second charge at St. Andrews, 1626; D.D. St. Andrews, c. 1634; fled to England during presbyterian ascendency; lecturer at St. Nicholas, Newcastle, 1640; captured by Leslie on fall of Newcastle, 1644, and imprisoned at Edinburgh, 1644-5; chaplain to Montrose, whom he accompanied in his wanderings on continent; returned to Newcastle, 1660; bishop of Edinburgh, 1662; published Latin account of Montrose's campaigns, 1647. [lxii. 251]

WISHART, SIR JAMES (*d.* 1723), admiral; captain, 1689; with Sir George Rooke [q. v.] at Cadiz and Vigo, 1702, and in channel, 1703-4; promoted rear-admiral and knighted, 1704; admiral of the blue, 1708; lord of admiralty, 1710; M.P., Portsmouth, 1711-15; admiral of white squadron and commander-in-chief in Mediterranean, 1713; superseded in command, 1714. [lxii. 253]

WISHART, SIR JOHN (*d.* 1576), Scottish judge; studied law at Edinburgh; one of those who signed the 'band,' or first covenant, and confederated themselves under name of the congregation for destruction of Roman catholic church in Scotland, 1557 ; member of council of authority which declared Mary of Guise to have forfeited office of regent, 1559 ; commissioner at convention of Berwick, where terms of treaty were arranged with England against France, 1560 ; temporal lord of the articles, 1560 ; member of temporary governing body formed on death of queen regent, 1560 ; knighted, 1562 ; privy councillor and comptroller and collector-general of teinds, 1562 ; opposed Mary Stuart's marriage with Darnley, was denounced as a rebel, and fled to England, 1565 ; pardoned, 1566 ; joined confederacy against Bothwell, 1567 ; extraordinary lord of session, 1567 ; joined party of Duke of Châtelherault [see HAMILTON, JAMES, second EARL OF ARRAN], 1570 ; constable of Edinburgh ; captured by Morton, 1573 ; deprived of judicial office, but reappointed extraordinary lord of session, 1574. 　　　　　　　　[lxii. 253]

WISHART, ROBERT (*d.* 1316), bishop of Glasgow ; archdeacon of St. Andrews ; bishop of Glasgow, 1270 ; one of six guardians of realm on death of Alexander III, 1286 ; supported Edward I, 1290, and swore fealty to him during his progress through Scotland, 1296, but took up cause of Robert Bruce, *c.* 1299 ; was captured by Edward I, 1301 ; was released on again swearing fealty, but soon joined patriots under Wallace ; officiated at coronation of Bruce, 1306 ; captured after battle of Methven ; imprisoned at Porchester Castle ; released after battle of Bannockburn, 1314. 　　　　　　　　[lxii. 255]

WISSING, WILLEM (1656–1687), portrait-painter; born at Amsterdam ; came to England, *c.* 1680 ; worked for Sir Peter Lely [q. v.]; became favourite painter of James II and Mary of Modena. 　　　　　[lxii. 256]

WITCHELL, EDWIN (1823–1887), geologist ; articled as solicitor at Stroud, where he practised from 1847 ; F.G.S., 1861 ; published work on geology of Stroud, 1882. 　　　　　　　　[lxii. 257]

WITHALS or **WHITHALS,** JOHN (*fl.* 1556), lexicographer ; published 'A Short Dictionarie for Yonge Beginners,' an English-Latin vocabulary for children (earliest edition now discoverable dated 1556), which became a standard school-book, and was frequently reissued until 1634. 　　　　　　　[lxii. 257]

WITHAM, GEORGE (1655–1725), Roman catholic prelate ; brother of Robert Witham [q. v.] ; educated at English College, Douay, and Paris (D.D. Sorbonne, 1688) ; vicar-apostolic of midland district of England and bishop of Marcopolis *in partibus infidelium,* 1703 ; translated to northern district, 1715. 　　　　　　　[lxii. 258]

WITHAM, ROBERT (*d.* 1738), biblical scholar ; educated at English College, Douay, where he became professor of philosophy and divinity ; joined English mission ; president of Douay College, 1714 ; D.D. Douay, 1692 ; published biblical commentaries. 　　　　　　　　[lxii. 258]

WITHAM, THOMAS (*d.*1728), chaplain to James II ; brother of Robert Witham [q. v.] ; educated at Douay and Paris ; D.D. Sorbonne, 1692 ; superior of St. Gregory's seminary, Paris, 1699–1717. 　　　　　[lxii. 258]

WITHENS or **WITHINS,** SIR FRANCIS (1634?–1704). [See WYTHENS.]

WITHER or **WITHERS,** GEORGE (1588–1667), poet and pamphleteer ; educated at Magdalen College, Oxford, 1604–6 ; entered Lincoln's Inn, 1615 ; devoted his energies to literature and gained patronage of Princess Elizabeth ; imprisoned in Marshalsea for his satire, 'Abuses stript and whipt,' 1613 ; wrote in Marshalsea 'The Shepherd's Hunting' (published, 1615), a continuation of William Browne's 'Shepherd's Pipe' (1614), to which he had contributed ; privately printed 'Fidelia,' 1615 (published,1617, and with the lyric, 'Shall I wasting in despair,' 1619) ; again in Marshalsea for his poem 'Wither's Motto. Nec habeo, nec careo, nec curo,' 1621 ; published, 1622, 'Faire-Virtve, the Mistresse of Phil'Arete' ; published subsequently pious exercises and political diatribes, of which 'Halelujah' (1641) alone displays evidence of his early power ; became convinced puritan ; published, 1623, 'Hymnes and Songs of the Church,' which by letter patent was ordered to be inserted in every copy of the authorised 'Psalm-book in meeter,' which the Stationers' Company enjoyed the privilege under earlier patents of publishing ; stated his grievances against the booksellers, resulting

partly from the hostility of the Stationers' Company in 'The Schollers Purgatory,' 1624, ten years after which (1634) the patent directing that his 'Hymnes' should be bound with the authorised Psalms was disallowed by the council ; served as captain of horse against Scottish covenanters, 1639 ; raised troop of horse for parliament, 1642 ; captain and commander of Farnham Castle, 1642 ; captured by royalists, but released ; major ; commissioner for sale of the king's goods, 1653 ; clerk in statute office of court of chancery, 1655 ; imprisoned in Newgate, 1660–1663, for opinions expressed in an unpublished manuscript 'Vox Vulgi' (printed, 1880) ; his last publication, 'Fragmenta Poetica' (1666, re-issued as 'Fragmenta Prophetica,' 1669), a series of extracts from earlier works. His reputation as a poet mainly depends on the collection of pieces which he issued in 1622 with the title 'Juvenilia' ; an enlarged edition followed in 1633. 　　　　[lxii. 259]

WITHERING, WILLIAM (1741–1799), physician, botanist, and mineralogist ; M.D. Edinburgh, 1766 ; chief physician to Birmingham General Hospital ; F.R.S., 1784 ; published 'A Botanical Arrangement of all Vegetables naturally growing in Great Britain,' 1776, and other works, including an account (1785) of the foxglove, which he did much to introduce into the pharmacopœia. 　　　　　　　　[lxii. 268]

WITHERINGTON, WILLIAM FREDERICK (1785–1865), landscape-painter ; studied at Royal Academy, where he exhibited, 1811–65 ; R.A., 1840. 　[lxii. 270]

WITHEROW, THOMAS (1824–1890), Irish divine and historian ; educated at Royal Academical Institution, Belfast ; licensed preacher, 1844 ; professor of church history and pastoral theology at Magee presbyterian college, Londonderry, 1865–90 ; moderator of general assembly, 1878 ; published historical and religious works. 　　　　　　　　[lxii. 270]

WITHERS, THOMAS (1769–1843), captain in navy ; educated at Christ's Hospital, London ; with Horatio (afterwards Viscount) Nelson [q. v.] as midshipman, schoolmaster, and master's mate, 1793–6 ; lieutenant after battle of Cape St. Vincent, 1797 ; commander, 1803 ; agent for transports to the Elbe and Weser, 1805 ; principal agent in Mediterranean, 1810–16 ; post-captain, 1809. 　　　　　　　　[lxii. 271]

WITHERSPOON, JOHN (1723–1794), presbyterian divine and statesman ; laureated at Edinburgh University, 1739 ; ordained to parish of Beith, 1744 ; published 'Ecclesiastical Characteristics,' 1753 ; minister at Paisley, 1757 ; fined, 1776, for libel published in 'Sinners Sitting in the Seat of the Scornful,' 1762 ; honorary D.D. St. Andrews, 1769 ; principal of Princeton College, New Jersey, 1768 ; member of convention for framing first constitution for New Jersey, 1776 ; represented New Jersey in general congress by which constitution of United States was framed, 1776 ; supported a signed Declaration of Independence ; member of secret executive committee ; member of board of war, and, 1778, of committee of the finances ; resumed academic duties, 1783 ; hon. LL.D. Yale College, 1785 ; exercised considerable influence on theological development in the United States. His works were collected, New York, 1800–1, and Edinburgh, 1804–5. 　　　　　　　[lxii. 271]

WITHMAN (*d.* 1047 ?), abbot of Ramsey ; called also Leucander and Andrew ; German by birth ; abbot of Ramsey, 1016 ; went on pilgrimage to Jerusalem, *c.* 1020, and on return resigned abbacy ; lived in retirement at Northeye, near Ramsey. 　　　　　　　[lxii. 274]

WITHRINGTON. [See WIDDRINGTON.]

WITTLESEY, WILLIAM (*d.* 1374). [See WHITTLESEY.]

WIVELL, ABRAHAM (1786–1849), portrait-painter ; apprenticed as hairdresser in London, 1799, and opened business independently, 1806 ; subsequently adopted portrait-painting as profession ; superintendent of fire-escapes to Society for Protection of Life from Fire, 1836–1841 ; settled in Birmingham, 1841 ; published 'Inquiry into History, Authenticity, and Characteristics of Shakespeare Portraits,' 1827. 　　　　　　[lxii. 274]

WIX, SAMUEL (1771–1861), divine ; of Charterhouse, London, and Christ College, Cambridge ; M.A.,1799 ; entered Inner Temple, 1783 ; received living of Inworth, 1802 ; hospitaller and vicar of St. Bartholomew's-the-Less,

London, 1808 ; president of Sion College, London ; F.R.S. ; F.S.A. ; published controversial writings, adopting principles of the old high-church party. [lxii. 275]

WODE. [See WOOD.]

WODEHOUSE. [See also WOODHOUSE.]

WODEHOUSE, SIR PHILIP EDMOND (1811–1887), colonial governor ; writer in Ceylon civil service, 1828 ; assistant-judge at Kandy, 1840 ; government agent for western province, Ceylon, 1843 ; superintendent of British Honduras, 1851 ; governor of British Guiana, 1854 ; governor of Cape of Good Hope and high commissioner of South Africa, 1861–70 ; declared Basutos British subjects, 1868 ; opposed principle of responsible government ; governor of Bombay, 1872–7 ; K.C.B., 1862 ; G.C.S.I., 1877. [Suppl. iii. 516]

WODEHOUSE or **WOODHOUSE,** ROBERT DE (d. 1345 ?), treasurer of the exchequer ; presented to church of Ellon, in diocese of Aberdeen, 1298 ; king's clerk ; king's escheator north and south of Trent, 1311–12 ; prebendary of Lincoln, 1314, and of York, 1317 ; custodian of hospital of St. Nicholas, Pontefract ; baron of exchequer, 1318 ; keeper of wardrobe, 1322–8 ; archdeacon of Richmond, 1328 ; second baron of exchequer, 1329 ; prebendary of St. Mary's, Southwell ; chancellor of exchequer, 1330–1. [lxii. 276]

WODELARKE, ROBERT (d. 1479), founder of St. Catharine's College, Cambridge ; original fellow of King's College, Cambridge ; provost of King's, 1452–79 ; founded St. Catharine's Hall (now college), 1473 ; drew up original statutes and obtained charter from Edward IV, 1475 ; chancellor of Cambridge University, 1459 and 1462. [lxii. 277]

WODENOTE, THEOPHILUS (d. 1662), royalist divine ; educated at Eton and King's College, Cambridge ; fellow ; M.A. ; B.D., 1623 ; D.D., 1630 ; incorporated M.A. Oxford, 1619 ; vicar of Linkinhorne, Cornwall, 1619–51 ; sequestered by parliamentarians, 1651 ; restored, 1660 ; published religious writings. [lxii. 277]

WODENOTH, or **WOODNOTH,** ARTHUR (1590 ?–1650 ?), colonial pioneer ; cousin of Nicholas Ferrar [q.v.] ; in business as goldsmith in London ; member of Virginia Company after 1612 ; deputy-governor of Somers Island Company, 1644. [lxii. 278]

WODHULL, MICHAEL (1740–1816), book-collector and translator ; of Winchester College and Brasenose College, Oxford ; high sheriff for Northamptonshire, 1783 ; collected valuable library, the printed books consisting mainly of first editions of the classics and rare specimens of early printing in the fifteenth century. His publications include the first translation into English verse of all the extant writings of Euripides, 1782. [lxii. 278]

WODROW, ROBERT (1679–1734), ecclesiastical historian ; M.A. Glasgow ; university librarian, 1697–1701 ; licensed preacher, 1703 ; ordained minister, 1703, of Eastwood, near Glasgow, where he remained till his death ; assisted Principal Hadow in drawing up act of assembly relating to filling of vacant ministries, 1731, upholding compliance with law of patronage where it remained in force ; works include 'History of Sufferings of Church of Scotland from Restoration to Revolution,' 1828–30. [lxii. 280]

WOFFINGTON, MARGARET (1714 ?–1760), actress ; daughter of a bricklayer in Dublin ; appeared in lilliputian company in Dublin, at age of ten ; engaged by Thomas Elrington (1688–1732) [q.v.] ; played Ophelia successfully at Smock Alley Theatre, Dublin, 1737, and Sir Harry Wildair, 1740 ; engaged by Rich for Covent Garden, London, 1840, and was immediately successful at Drury Lane, London, 1741, her parts including Rosalind ('As you like it') and Cordelia to Garrick's Lear ; played Lady Anne to Garrick's Richard III at Drury Lane, 1742 ; appeared as Ophelia, Mrs. Ford, Lady Townley, and Portia ('Merchant of Venice'), 1743–4, Isabella ('Measure for Measure'), and Viola ('Twelfth Night'), 1744–5 ; reappeared at Covent Garden, and played Portia ('Julius Cæsar') and Queen Katharine ('Henry VIII'), 1749, Desdemona, Lady Macbeth, 1750, Queen ('Hamlet'), 1750–1 ; in Dublin, 1751–4, at Covent Garden, 1754 ; quarrelled with Mrs. Bellamy, and while performing in Mrs. Bellamy's Statira drove her off the stage and stabbed her ; her last performance, Rosalind ('As you like it'),

1757 ; her most popular character probably Sir Harry Wildair. Her amours were numerous, and for some time she lived with Garrick. [lxii. 281]

WOGAN, (SIR) CHARLES (1698 ?–1752 ?), Jacobite soldier of fortune, known as the Chevalier Wogan ; served under Henry Oxburgh [q.v.], whose force surrendered at Preston, 1715 ; escaped from Newgate prison, 1716 ; took service in Dillon's regiment in France ; served with Ormonde on diplomatic mission from James Edward the Old Pretender to Russia, 1718–19, when he gained celebrity by release of Princess Clementina from Innspruck ; colonel in Spanish army, 1723 ; brigadier-general and governor of La Mancha ; with Duke of York at Dunkirk, 1746 ; died at La Mancha. [lxii. 284]

WOGAN, EDWARD (d. 1654), royalist captain ; probably captain in Okey's dragoons in 'new model' ; deserted parliament's service, 1648, and joined Ormonde in Ireland ; governor of Duncannon, which fortress he held against Ireton, 1649 ; captured and imprisoned in Cork, whence he escaped, 1650 ; fought at Worcester, 1651 ; escaped to France ; landed with several companies at Dover, 1653, and joined Middleton's highland force, 1654 ; died from wound received in skirmish. [lxii. 286]

WOGAN, SIR JOHN (d. 1321 ?), chief-justice and governor of Ireland ; justice itinerant for four northern counties, 1292 ; went to Ireland as chief-justice, 1295 ; led troop of English settlers to aid Edward I in Scotland, 1296–8 ; again in Scotland, 1300–2 ; suppressed knights templars in Ireland, 1308 ; recalled, 1308, but reappointed, 1309 ; defeated (1312) by rebels, who afterwards surrendered. [lxii. 287]

WOGAN, NICHOLAS (1700–1770), Jacobite ; brother of (Sir) Charles Wogan [q.v.] ; found guilty of high treason for complicity in rebellion of 1745, but pardoned ; naturalised French subject, 1724 ; with Prince Charles Edward in Scotland, 1745–6 ; made Chevalier de St. Louis, 1754. [lxii. 285]

WOGAN, THOMAS (fl. 1646–1666), regicide ; M.P., Cardigan, 1646 ; served under Thomas Horton (d. 1649) [q.v.] ; signed Charles I's death-warrant, 1649 ; excepted from Act of Oblivion, 1660, and surrendered ; included in saving clause of suspension from execution. [lxii. 288]

WOGAN, WILLIAM (1678–1758), religious writer ; of Westminster School and Trinity College, Cambridge ; secretary to Duke of Ormonde, lord-lieutenant of Ireland, 1710 ; entered army and was stationed at Dublin ; published religious works, including 'Essay on the Proper Lessons of the Church of England,' 1753. [lxii. 288]

WOIDE, CHARLES GODFREY (1725–1790), oriental scholar ; native of Poland ; educated at Frankfort-on-Oder and Leyden ; preacher at Dutch chapel royal, St. James's Palace, London, 1770 ; reader and chaplain of reformed protestant church in Savoy, London ; F.S.A., 1778 ; studied Sahidic language of Upper Egypt ; assistant-librarian at British Museum, 1782 ; F.R.S., 1785 ; D.C.L. Oxford, 1786. His publications include an edition, 1778, with notes, of the 'Lexicon Ægyptiaco-Latinum' which La Croze had drawn up and Christianus Scholtz had revised, and a facsimile edition of the 'Novum Testamentum Græcum' from the 'Codex Alexandrinus.' [lxii. 289]

WOLCOT, JOHN (1738–1819), satirist and poet, under name of Peter Pindar ; studied medicine in London ; M.D. Aberdeen, 1767 ; physician to Sir William Trelawny, governor of Jamaica, 1767–9 ; ordained deacon and priest in England, 1769 ; incumbent of Vere, Jamaica, 1770 ; physician in general to horse and foot in the island, 1770 ; returned to England, 1773 ; medical practitioner at Truro, Helstone, and Exeter ; abandoned medicine for literature, 1778, and removed to London ; published 'Lyric Odes to the Royal Academicians,' 1782, 1783, 1785, and 'Farewell Odes,' 1786 ; issued various satires on George III from 1785, his only efficient opponent being William Gifford (1756–1826) [q.v.], who attacked him severely in the 'Anti-Jacobin.' His last work was an 'Epistle to the Emperor of China,' 1817, on the occasion of Lord Amherst's unfortunate embassy. [lxii. 290]

WOLF. [See also WOLFE, WOLFF, WOOLF, and WOULFE.]

WOLF, JOSEF (1820–1899), animal-painter ; born at Mörz, Rhenish Prussia ; apprenticed as lithographer at Coblenz ; studied at Antwerp Academy ; came to London,

1848; illustrated Robert Gray's 'Genera of Birds,' and assisted Gould in 'Birds of Great Britain'; prepared plates for 'Zoological Sketches,' 1861-7, and 'Life and Habits of Wild Animals,' 1874; first exhibited at Royal Academy, 1849. [lxii. 294]

WOLFE, ARTHUR, first VISCOUNT KILWARDEN (1739-1803), lord chief-justice of Ireland; B.A. Trinity College, Dublin, 1760; called to Irish bar from Middle Temple, 1766; K.C., 1778; member for Coleraine in Irish House of Commons, 1783, Jamestown, 1790, and Dublin, 1798; solicitor-general, 1787; attorney-general and Irish privy councillor, 1789; appointed chief-justice of king's bench and created Baron Kilwarden of Newlands, 1798; created viscount and peer of United Kingdom 1800; murdered by rebels during Emmet insurrection. [lxii. 294]

WOLFE, CHARLES (1791-1823), poet; B.A. Trinity College, Dublin, 1814; curate of Donoughmore, co. Down, 1818-21. His poems include the famous lines on the burial of Sir John Moore, which were first published in the 'Newry Telegraph,' 1817. [lxii. 295]

WOLFE, DAVID (d. 1578?), papal legate in Ireland; born in Limerick; became jesuit, c. 1550, and was rector of college at Modena; apostolic legate in Ireland, 1560; arrested and imprisoned in Dublin Castle, 1566; escaped to Spain, 1572, but soon returned to Ireland, where he probably died. [lxii. 296]

WOLFE, JAMES (1727-1759), major-general; second lieutenant of marines, 1741; ensign, 1742; in Flanders, 1743; acting-adjutant at Dettingen; lieutenant, 1743; served under Wade, 1744; brigade-major, 1745; served with Wade against Prince Charles Edward, 1745, and was with army defeated under Hawley at Falkirk; on staff at Culloden; brigade-major under Sir John Mordaunt (1697-1780) [q. v.] in Netherlands, 1747; major, 20th foot, 1749, and lieutenant-colonel, 1750; in Scotland, 1749-52; studied in Paris, 1752-3; returned to regiment in Scotland, 1753, and was quartered at Exeter, 1754-5, and Canterbury, 1755-6; introduced system of manœuvres which long remained in use; quartermaster-general in Ireland, 1757-8; quartermaster-general of force under Mordaunt sent against Rochefort, 1758; brigadier in force sent against Louisbourg, 1758; took prominent part in siege of Louisbourg; destroyed French fishing settlement in Gulf of St. Lawrence, 1758, and returned to England; colonel, 67th regiment (formerly second battalion of 20th), 1758; appointed to command, with rank of major-general in America, force to be sent up St. Lawrence against Quebec, 1759; arrived at Halifax, 20 April 1759; advanced from Louisbourg in June; was shot during battle on plains of Abraham, whither he had led his men, having scaled heights above Quebec, and died after hearing that his attack was successful, 13 Sept. A monument to him is in Westminster Abbey. [lxii. 296]

WOLFE, JOHN (d. 1601), printer and publisher; son of Reyner Wolfe [q. v.], whose presses he inherited, working independently of Stationers' Company till 1583; liveryman, 1598; took active part in company's proceedings against Robert Waldegrave [q. v.], printer of Martin Mar-Prelate tracts, 1589; worked in St. Paul's Churchyard, London, 1589-92, and in Pope's Head Alley, Lombard Street, London, 1596-1601. [lxii. 305]

WOLFE, REYNER or **REGINALD** (d. 1573), printer and publisher; born at Strasburg; settled in England before 1537, and established himself at sign of the Brazen Serpent in St. Paul's Churchyard, London; removed to Finsbury Fields, London, 1549; first to hold patent as printer to king in Latin, Greek, and Hebrew; original member of Stationers' Company, 1554; master, 1559, 1564, 1567, and 1572; left manuscript collections for 'Universal History or Cosmography.' [lxii. 304]

WOLFE, alias LACEY, **WILLIAM** (1584-1673). [See LACEY.]

WOLFF, JOSEPH (1795-1862), missionary; born of Jewish parents at Weilersbach, near Bamberg; converted to Christianity, 1812; studied at Vienna, Tübingen, and Rome; expelled from Collegio di Propaganda for erroneous opinions; entered monastery of Redemptorists at Val Sainte, Fribourg; came to London and entered church of England; studied oriental languages at Cambridge; travelled as missionary in Egypt and Sinaitic peninsula, 1821-6, and later in Mesopotamia, Persia,

Tiflis, the Crimea, and European Turkey; travelled from Jerusalem through Central Asia to Calcutta, 1828; visited United States, and was ordained priest, 1838; rector of Linthwaite, Yorkshire, 1838; went to Bokhara to ascertain fate of Charles Stoddart [q. v.] and Captain Arthur Conolly [q. v.], 1843-5; vicar of Ile Brewers, Somerset, 1845-62; published journals of travel. [lxii. 306]

WOLLASTON, FRANCIS (1731-1815), author; grandson of William Wollaston [q. v.]; LL.B. Sidney Sussex College, Cambridge, 1754; entered Lincoln's Inn, 1750; rector of Dengie, 1758; rector and vicar of East Dereham, 1761, and of Chislehurst, 1769-1815; F.R.S., 1769; precentor of St. David's, 1777; rector of St. Vedast, Foster Lane, with St. Michael-le-Querne, London, 1779-1815; published astronomical and other writings. [lxii. 307]

WOLLASTON, FRANCIS JOHN HYDE (1762-1823), natural philosopher; brother of William Hyde Wollaston [q. v.]; of Charterhouse, London, and Sidney Sussex College, Cambridge; senior wrangler, 1783; Taylorian lecturer in mathematics, 1783-5; fellow of Trinity Hall, Cambridge, 1785-93; M.A., 1786; B.D., 1795; Jacksonian professor, 1792-1813, lecturing on chemistry and natural philosophy, 1792-6, on chemistry alone from 1796; given stall in St. Paul's Cathedral, London, 1802; archdeacon of Essex, 1813; rector of East Dereham, 1815. [lxii. 308]

WOLLASTON, GEORGE (1738-1826), divine; brother of Francis Wollaston [q. v.]; M.A. Sidney Sussex College, Cambridge, 1761; D.D., 1774; rector of St. Mary Aldermary with St. Thomas the Apostle, London, 1774-90; F.R.S., 1763; edited, with John Jebb (1736-1786) [q. v.], 'Excerpta quædam e Newtoni Principiis,' 1765. [lxii. 308]

WOLLASTON, THOMAS VERNON (1822-1878), entomologist and conchologist; M.A. Jesus College, Cambridge, 1849; F.L.S., 1847; made collections and published works relating to coleoptera (chiefly of Madeira), and other writings. [lxii. 309]

WOLLASTON, WILLIAM (1660-1724), moral philosopher; M.A. Sidney Sussex College, Cambridge, 1681; assistant-master of Birmingham school, 1682; took priest's orders; inherited fortune from a cousin, and settled in London, devoting himself to writing treatises on philological and ecclesiastical questions; upheld the 'intellectual' theory of morality. His publications include 'Religion of Nature Delineated,' 1724 (printed privately, 1722). [lxii. 310]

WOLLASTON, WILLIAM HYDE (1766-1828), physiologist, chemist, and physicist; son of Francis Wollaston [q. v.]; of Charterhouse, London, and Caius College, Cambridge; M.D., 1793; senior fellow, 1787-1828; F.R.S., 1794; practised as physician at Huntingdon, 1789, and Bury St. Edmunds; F.R.C.P., 1795; censor, 1798, elect, 1824; opened practice in London, 1797; retired, 1800, and took to chemical research; Copley medallist, 1802; secretary of Royal Society, 1804-1816; published fifty-six papers on pathology, physiology, chemistry, optics, mineralogy, crystallography, astronomy, electricity, mechanics, and botany. Notable among his discoveries and inventions are a method for producing pure platinum and welding it into vessels (made, c. 1804, and published as the Bakerian lecture, 1828), the camera lucida (patented, 1807), and the principle that 'galvanic' and 'frictional' electricity are of the same nature; commissioner of Royal Society on board of longitude, 1818-28; F.R.S., 1812; left to Geological Society sum of money which formed 'the Wollaston fund,' and to Royal Society a sum to form the 'Donation Fund.' [lxii. 311]

WOLLEY. [See also WOOLLEY.]

WOLLEY, EDWARD (d. 1684), bishop of Clonfert; educated at the King's School, Shrewsbury; M.A. St. John's College, Cambridge, 1629; D.D. Oxford, 1642, and Cambridge, 1664; domestic chaplain to Charles I and to Charles II while in exile; bishop of Clonfert and Kilmacduagh, 1665; published religious writings. [lxii. 316]

WOLLEY, SIR JOHN (d. 1596), Latin secretary to Queen Elizabeth; fellow, Merton College, Oxford, 1553; M.A., 1557; D.C.L., 1566; in Queen Elizabeth's service in 1563; Latin secretary, 1568; lay prebendary of Wells,

1569, and dean of Carlisle, 1577; privy councillor, 1586; one of commissioners appointed to try Mary Queen of Scots; chancellor of order of Garter, 1589; M.P., East Looe, 1571, Weymouth and Melcombe Regis, 1572, Winchester, 1584 and 1586, Dorset, 1588, and Surrey, 1593; member of court of high commission, 1590; knighted, 1592. [lxii. 316]

WOLLEY or **WOOLLEY**, RICHARD (*fl.* 1667–1694), miscellaneous writer; M.A. Queens' College, Cambridge, 1671; curate in London; employed as hack-writer by John Dunton [q. v.], the bookseller; edited monthly 'Compleat Library; or News for the Ingenious,' 1692–4. [lxii. 317]

WOLLSTONECRAFT, MARY (1759–1797). [See GODWIN, MRS. MARY WOLLSTONECRAFT.]

WOLMAN. [See also WOOLMAN.]

WOLMAN or **WOLEMAN**, RICHARD (*d.* 1537), dean of Wells; studied at Corpus Christi College, Cambridge; principal of St. Paul's Inn, Cambridge, 1510; D.C.L., 1512; admitted advocate, 1514; archdeacon of Sudbury, 1522; canon of St. Stephen's, Westminster, 1524; chaplain to Henry VIII, 1526; master of requests and member of Henry VIII's council, 1526; promoter of king's divorce suit; prebendary of St. Paul's, London, 1527; dean of Wells, 1529; prolocutor of convocation, 1529; canon of Windsor, 1533. [lxii. 318]

WOLRICH, **WOOLRICH**, or **WOOLDRIDGE**, HUMPHREY (1633?–1707), quaker; originally baptist; joined quakers soon after their rise; frequently imprisoned on account of his quaker principles; published religious writings. [lxii. 319]

WOLRICH or **WOLRYCHE**, SIR THOMAS, first baronet (1598–1668), royalist; educated at Cambridge; entered Inner Temple, 1615; M.P., Much Wenlock, 1621, 1624, and 1625; raised regiment for Charles I, and was colonel at outbreak of civil war; governor of Bridgnorth; knighted and created baronet, 1641; conformed to parliament, c. 1645. [lxii. 320]

WOLSELEY, SIR CHARLES (1630?–1714), politician; M.P. for Oxfordshire in Little parliament, 1653, and member of both councils of state; member of council established to advise the Protector; M.P. for Staffordshire in Cromwell's parliaments; one of Cromwell's House of Lords, 1657; member of Richard Cromwell's council; member for Stafford in Convention parliament, 1660; pardoned at Restoration; arrested on suspicion of complicity in Monmouth's rebellion, 1685, but released; published pamphlets on ecclesiastical subjects. [lxii. 320]

WOLSELEY, SIR CHARLES, seventh baronet (1769–1846), politician; travelled abroad; joined reform movement in England, c. 1811; one of founders of Hampden Club; succeeded to baronetcy, 1817; elected 'legislatorial attorney' by reformers of Birmingham, 1819; imprisoned, 1820–1, on charge of sedition and conspiracy; on committee of Middlesex electors to promote reform, 1821, entered Roman catholic church, 1837. [lxii. 322]

WOLSELEY, ROBERT (1649–1697), diplomatist; son of Sir Charles Wolseley (1630?–1714); educated at Trinity College, Oxford; entered Gray's Inn, 1667; envoy from William III to elector of Bavaria, 1692. [lxii. 322]

WOLSELEY, WILLIAM (1640?–1697), brigadier-general; brother of Sir Charles Wolseley (1630?–1714) [q. v.]; captain-lieutenant to Marquis of Worcester's footregiment, 1667, and again, 1673; lieutenant-colonel of Sir John Hanmer's regiment (11th foot), 1689; served in Ireland; colonel of Inniskilling horse, 1689; defeated Justin MacCarthy, titular viscount Mountcashel [q. v.] at Newtown-Butler, 1689; took Cavan, 1690; at battle of Boyne, 1690, and Aughrim, 1691; master-general of ordnance in Ireland, 1692; brigadier of all horse, 1693; lord justice in Ireland and privy councillor, 1696. [lxii. 323]

WOLSELEY, WILLIAM (1756–1842), admiral; born in Nova Scotia; went to Ireland, 1764; served in Jamaica and East Indies (1773–7); lieutenant, 1778; commanded company of naval brigade at Negapatam, 1781, and Fort Ostenberg and Trincomalee, 1782; commander, 1782; captured by French in Ganjam Roads, 1783; released at the peace; in Mediterranean, 1786–9 and 1793–4; in Channel fleet, 1799–1801; rear-admiral,

1804; commanded sea fencibles of all Ireland, 1804–5; admiral, 1819. [lxii. 324]

WOLSEY, THOMAS (1475?–1530), cardinal and statesman; son of Robert Wulcy (or Wolsey) of Ipswich, who is said to have been a butcher; fellow of Magdalen College, Oxford, 1497; M.A. and master of school adjoining Magdalen College; junior bursar, 1498–9; senior bursar, 1499–1500; rector of Limington, 1500; domestic chaplain to Henry Deane [q. v.], archbishop of Canterbury, c. 1501; chaplain to Sir Richard Nanfan [q. v.], 1503; Henry VII's chaplain, 1507; appointed by Henry VII dean of Lincoln, 1509; prebendary of Lincoln, 1509; almoner to Henry VIII, 1509; B.D. and D.D. Oxford, 1510; prebendary of Hereford, 1510; canon of Windsor, 1511; registrar of order of Garter, 1511; privy councillor, 1511; directed plan of operations against France, 1512; dean of Hereford, 1512, of York, 1513; dean of St. Stephen's, Westminster, and precentor of London, 1513; accompanied Henry VIII to Calais and in French campaign, 1513; received from Pope Leo X bishopric of Tournay, 1513, but never obtained possession; bishop of Lincoln, 1514; archbishop of York, 1514; created cardinal by Leo X, with title, 'St. Cæcilia trans Tiberim,' 1515; lord chancellor, 1515; concluded with Ferdinand, whose position in Naples had been threatened by the battle of Marignano, league for commerce and defence against invasion, 1515; papal legate *de latere* as associate of Campeggio, who came to England to urge a crusade, 1518; granted by Pope Leo X administration of bishopric of Bath and Wells, of which Cardinal Adrian de Castello [q. v.] was deprived; signed with Henry VIII and French ambassador secret articles for marriage of dauphin to Princess Mary, and for surrender of Tournay to French, and arranged treaty of alliance with France, 1518, and accompanied Henry to Field of Cloth of Gold, 1520, but meanwhile negotiated marriage between Princess Mary and Emperor Charles of Spain (Charles V of Germany), who had pledged himself to marry the French king's daughter, Charlotte; went to Calais as mediator in dispute between France and the emperor, 1521, and at Henry VIII's instance made with Charles a secret defensive and offensive alliance against France; took part in forming new treaty between Henry VIII and Charles, 1522, by which Charles agreed to marry Mary in 1526, and both monarchs agreed to invade France before May 1524; supported king in demand for money for war, which was granted immediately, 1522; resigned Bath and Wells, and received from pope temporalities of Durham, 1524; concluded treaty with France, 1525; converted into a college (Christ Church, by papal bull, dated 1524) the monastery of St. Frideswide, Oxford, 1525; supported Henry VIII in matter of divorce from Catherine of Arragon, 1527; went as Henry VIII's lieutenant to France and concluded treaties with Francis at Amiens, 1527, and endeavoured to obtain from Pope Clement VII a decretal commission to define the law by which the judges were to be guided, and a dispensation for the new marriage, the only result of which endeavour was that the pope sent Cardinal Campeggio, giving Wolsey no control over the business; received see of Winchester, resigning that of Durham, 1529; incurred, owing to delay in divorce proceedings, dislike of Anne Boleyn, who influenced Henry VIII against him, the result being that a bill of indictment was preferred against him in king's bench, 3 Nov. 1529; acknowledged that he had incurred a *præmunire*; received general pardon, 12 Feb. 1530; retired to Cawood, where he was arrested for high treason on false information given by his physician, Augustine, 4 Nov.; died and was buried at Leicester, where he had arrived on journey to London. [lxii. 325]

WOLSTAN. [See WULFSTAN and WULSTAN.]

WOLSTENHOLME, DEAN, the elder (1757–1837), animal painter; exhibited at Royal Academy, 1803–24. [lxii. 343]

WOLSTENHOLME, DEAN, the younger (1798–1883), animal painter and engraver; son of Dean Wolstenholme the elder [q. v.]; exhibited at Royal Academy. [lxii. 344]

WOLSTENHOLME, SIR JOHN (1562–1639), merchant adventurer; one of incorporators of East India Company, 1600; member of council for Virginia Company, 1609; assisted expeditions to find north-west passage; knighted, 1617; commissioner of navy, 1619; member of king's council for Virginia, 1624; commissioner for plantation of Virginia, 1631. [lxii. 344]

WOLSTENHOLME, JOSEPH (1829–1891), mathematician; graduated as third wrangler, St. John's College, Cambridge, 1850; fellow, 1852; fellow of Christ's College, Cambridge, 1852–69; moderator and examiner in mathematical tripos; mathematical professor at Royal Indian Engineering College, Cooper's Hill, 1871–89; published mathematical works. [lxii. 344]

WOLTON, JOHN (1535?–1594). [See WOOLTON.]

WOLVERTON, second BARON (1824–1887). [See GLYN, GEORGE GRENFELL.]

WOMBWELL, GEORGE (1778–1850), founder of Wombwell's menageries; kept cordwainer's shop in Soho, London; exhibited in 1804 two boa-constrictors with such success that he formed a menagerie, which became the finest travelling collection in England. [lxii. 345]

WOMOCK or **WOMACK**, LAURENCE (1612–1686), bishop of St. David's; B.A. Corpus Christi College, Cambridge, 1632; M.A., 1639; prebendary of Hereford, 1660–1674; archdeacon of Suffolk, 1660–84; D.D., 1661; prebendary of Ely, 1663; bishop of St. David's, 1683; published writings advocating the old liturgy, and the decision of the bishops at the Savoy conference.
[lxii. 346]

WONOSTROCHT, NICHOLAS (1804–1876). [See WANOSTROCHT.]

WOOD, ALEXANDER (1725–1807), surgeon; qualified at Edinburgh; F.R.C.S. Edinburgh, 1756; practised at Edinburgh, where his philanthropy and kindness were proverbial. [lxii. 347]

WOOD, ALEXANDER (1817 – 1884), physician; studied at Edinburgh University; M.D., 1839; extra-mural lecturer on medicine, 1841; president, Edinburgh Royal College of Physicians, 1858–61; representative of the college on general medical council, 1858–73; assessor of university court at Edinburgh, 1864; introduced into practice use of hypodermic syringe for administration of drugs. [lxii. 347]

WOOD, SIR ANDREW (d. 1515), sea-captain and merchant at Leith; served on sea and land chiefly against English; conveyed James III across Forth in flight from rebel lords, 1488, but subsequently accepted the revolution; knighted, c. 1495; overseer of public works and vendor of stores for public service; superintended building of Dunbar Castle, 1497; many of the exploits with which his name has been connected are probably fictitious. [lxii. 348]

WOOD, ANTHONY, or, as he latterly called himself, ANTHONY À WOOD (1632–1695), antiquary and historian; educated at New College School, Oxford, 1641–4, Thame School, 1644–6 (founded by John Williams, baron Williams [q. v.]), and Merton College, Oxford; postmaster; B.A., 1652; submitted to parliamentary visitors, 1648; bible clerk, 1650; M.A., 1655; made collections for history of Oxfordshire, and published 'Historia et Antiquitates Univ. Oxon.,' 1674, of which an English version by him, issued by John Gutch [q. v.], is the standard edition, 1791–6; published 'Athenæ Oxonienses,' 1691–2, a biographical dictionary of Oxford writers and bishops, and was expelled from university at instance of Henry Hyde, second earl of Clarendon, for a libel which the work contained on his father, the first earl, 1693. Several antiquarian manuscripts left by him were published posthumously.
[lxii. 349]

WOOD, SIR CHARLES, first VISCOUNT HALIFAX (1800–1885), of Eton and Oriel College, Oxford; M.A., 1824; liberal M.P. for Grimsby, 1826, Wareham, 1831, Halifax, 1832–65; joint-secretary to treasury, 1832; secretary to admiralty, 1835; chancellor of exchequer, 1846; privy councillor, 1846; succeeded his father in baronetcy, 1846; president of board of control, 1852; first lord of admiralty, 1855; G.C.B., 1856; secretary of state for India, 1859–66; M.P. for Ripon, 1865; created Viscount Halifax of Monk Bretton, 1866; lord privy seal, 1870–4.
[lxii. 353]

WOOD, SIR DAVID EDWARD (1812–1894), general; studied at Woolwich; second lieutenant, royal artillery, 1829; captain, 1846; colonel, 1860; major-general, 1867; colonel commandant, royal artillery, 1876; general, 1877; served against Boers, 1843; in Crimea, 1855; C.B. (military), 1857; in Indian mutiny campaigns, 1857–9; K.C.B., 1859; general commandant of Woolwich garrison, 1869–1874; G.C.B., 1877. [lxii. 354]

WOOD, EDMUND BURKE (1820–1882), Canadian judge and politician; born in Ontario; B.A. Overton College, Ohio, 1848; admitted to Canadian bar as attorney, 1853; called to bar of Ontario, 1854; M.P., West Brant, Ontario, 1863–7; member of Ontario house of assembly, 1867, and of Canadian House of Commons, 1867–72; provincial treasurer of Ohio, 1867–71; Q.C., 1872; member of Canadian House of Commons for West Durham, 1873–4; chief-justice of Manitoba, 1874. [lxii. 354]

WOOD, ELLEN (1814–1887), known as MRS. HENRY WOOD; novelist; née Price; married Henry Wood, 1836; lived mainly abroad, 1836–56; contributed short stories to Bentley's 'Miscellany,' and to Colburn's 'New Monthly Magazine,' where appeared 'East Lynne' (1861), which achieved very great success; became proprietor and conductor of the 'Argosy' magazine, for which she wrote the 'Johnny Ludlow' tales. Among her most popular works are 'Mrs. Halliburton's Troubles,' 1862, 'The Channings,' 1862, and its sequel 'Roland Yorke,' 1869, 'The Shadow of Ashlydyat,' 1863, 'Lord Oakburn's Daughters,' 1864, 'Within the Maze,' 1872, and 'Edina,' 1876. [lxii. 355]

WOOD, SIR GEORGE (1743–1824), judge; articled as attorney; barrister, Middle Temple; M.P., Haslemere, Surrey, 1796–1806; knighted and appointed baron of exchequer, 1807–23. [lxii. 357]

WOOD, SIR GEORGE ADAM (1767–1831), major-general, royal artillery; studied at Woolwich; second lieutenant, royal artillery, 1781; captain, 1800; lieutenant-colonel, 1808; major-general, 1825; served in Flanders, 1793–5, West Indies, 1795–7, Mediterranean, 1806–8, Portugal, 1808–9, and Walcheren, 1809; knighted, 1812; in Holland and Flanders, 1813–14; commanded whole of artillery in Waterloo campaign, 1815, and British artillery in army of occupation in France, 1819; governor of Carlisle, 1825. [lxii. 357]

WOOD, MRS. HENRY (1814–1887). [See WOOD, ELLEN.]

WOOD, HERBERT WILLIAM (1837–1879), major, royal engineers; educated at Cheltenham and East India Company's college, Addiscombe; second lieutenant, Madras engineers, 1855; went to India, 1857; lieutenant, 1858; field engineer in Abyssinian campaign, 1868; major, 1873; explored the Amu Darya, and published 'The Shores of Lake Aral,' 1876; F.R.G.S. [lxii. 358]

WOOD, JAMES (1672–1759), nonconformist minister; known as GENERAL WOOD; minister at Atherton Chapel, 1695–1721; raised troop which served under Sir Charles Wills [q. v.] against Jacobites at Preston, 1715; ministered at new meeting-house at Chowbent in Atherton from 1722. [lxii. 358]

WOOD, JAMES (1760–1839), mathematician; educated at St. John's College, Cambridge; senior wrangler and fellow, 1782; M.A., 1785; D.D., 1815; vice-chancellor of Cambridge University, 1816; master of St. John's College, 1815–39; F.R.S.; dean of Ely, 1820; published mathematical treatises. [lxii. 359]

WOOD, SIR JAMES ATHOL (1756–1829), rear-admiral; brother of Sir Mark Wood [q. v.]; entered navy as able seaman, 1774; lieutenant, 1778; served in West Indies, 1794; captured, while conveying prisoners to France, and confined at Paris, 1794–5; exchanged, 1795; commander, 1795; assisted at capture of Trinidad; captain, 1797; went in charge of convoy, 1804, to West Indies, where he was superseded by Sir John Thomas Duckworth, for a court-martial on whom he applied unsuccessfully; again in West Indies, 1807–9; knighted, 1809; attached to Channel fleet, 1810–12; in Mediterranean, 1812–15; C.B., 1815; rear-admiral, 1821.
[lxii. 360]

WOOD or **WODE**, JOHN (fl. 1482), speaker of House of Commons; probably sheriff of Surrey and Sussex, 1476; speaker, 1482. [lxii. 361]

WOOD, JOHN (d. 1570), secretary of the regent (Lord James Stewart [q. v.], afterwards Earl of Moray, 1531?–1570); son of Sir Andrew Wood [q. v.]; M.A. St. Leonard's College, St. Andrews, 1536; vicar of Largo; accompanied Lord James in embassy to Queen Mary in France, 1561; extraordinary lord of session, 1562; denounced as rebel on rebellion of Earl of Moray, 1565; became secretary to Moray on his return to power as regent, and was employed in all his more confidential and political missions; obtained bishopric of Moray, 1569; assassinated. [lxii. 361]

WOOD, JOHN (*fl.* 1596), medical writer; published 'Practicæ Medicinæ Liber,' a treatise on diseases and disorders affecting the head, 1596. [lxii. 362]

WOOD, JOHN (1705 ?-1754), architect; known as WOOD OF BATH; settled at Bath, 1727, and achieved fame as architect of the Palladian school, owing particularly to his success in the composition of streets and groups of houses; published ' Choir Gaure' (Stonehenge), 1747, and other works. His architectural enterprises include Queen's Square, Bath. [lxii. 363]

WOOD, JOHN (*d.* 1782), architect; son of John Wood (1705 ?-1754) [q. v.], with whom he was associated in many works; constructed various baths at Bath. [lxii. 364]

WOOD, JOHN (1801-1870), painter; studied in Sass's school and in Royal Academy, where he exhibited largely. [lxii. 364]

WOOD, JOHN (1811-1871), geographer; entered East India Company's naval service, 1826, and became captain; assistant to commercial mission to Afghanistan under (Sir) Alexander Burnes [q. v.], 1836, and issued reports on geography of Kábul Valley, and discovered source of the Oxus; manager of Oriental Steam Navigation Company, Sindh, 1857; superintendent of Indus steam flotilla, 1861-1871. [lxii. 364]

WOOD, JOHN (1825-1891), surgeon; studied at King's College, London; M.B. London, 1848; M.R.C.S. and L.S.A., 1849; surgeon to King's College Hospital, London; professor of surgery at King's College, London, 1871; joint-lecturer with (Lord) Lister on clinical surgery, 1877, and emeritus professor of clinical surgery, 1889; F.R.C.S., 1854, member of council, 1879–87, vice-president, 1885, Hunterian professor, 1884–5, and Bradshaw lecturer, 1885; F.R.S., 1871; published surgical works. [lxii. 365]

WOOD, JOHN GEORGE (1827-1889), writer on natural history; M.A. Merton College, Oxford, 1851; chaplain to St. Bartholomew's Hospital, London, 1856–62; reader at Christ Church, Newgate Street, London, 1858–63; lectured in Eng'and and America on natural history; delivered Lowell lectures at Boston, 1883-4; F.L.S., 1854-1877. His numerous works, which aimed at popularising natural history, include 'Illustrated Natural History,' 1853, 'Common Objects of the Seashore,' 1857, of the country, 1858, and of the microscope (in conjunction with Tuffen West), 1861, and an edition of White's ' Natural History of Selborne,' 1854. [lxii. 366]

WOOD, JOHN MUIR (1805-1892), editor of the ' Songs of Scotland ' ; educated at Edinburgh; studied music at Paris and Vienna; engaged in literary pursuits in London; joined his half-brother, George, in business of music-sellers in Edinburgh, and afterwards in Glasgow; collected materials for 'Songs of Scotland,' nominally edited, 1819, by George Farquhar Graham [q. v.], and reissued with notes and additions by Wood, 1887. [lxii. 367]

WOOD, SIR JOHN PAGE, second baronet (1796–1866), chaplain to Queen Caroline; son of Sir Matthew Wood [q. v.]; of Winchester College and Trinity College, Cambridge; LL.B., 1821; chaplain and private secretary to Queen Caroline; chaplain to Duke of Sussex; rector of St. Peter's, Cornhill, London, 1824–66. [lxii. 372]

WOOD, JOHN PHILIP (*d.* 1838), Scottish antiquary and biographer; deaf and dumb from infancy; auditor of excise in Scotland. His publications include an edition of the ' Peerage of Scotland ' of Sir Robert Douglas [q. v.], 1813. [lxii. 368]

WOOD, SIR MARK, first baronet (1747–1829), colonel, Bengal engineers; brother of Sir James Athol Wood [q. v.]; went to India, 1770; received commission in Bengal engineers, 1772, and became colonel, 1795; chief engineer in Bengal, 1790; returned to England, 1793; M.P., Milborne Port, Somerset, 1794, Newark, 1796, and Gatton, Surrey, 1802-18; entered George III's service as colonel, 1795; created baronet, 1808; published account of ' War with Tippoo Sultaun,' 1800, and other works. [lxii. 368]

WOOD, MARSHALL (*d.* 1882), sculptor; brother of Shakspere Wood [q. v.]; exhibited at Royal Academy between 1854 and 1875. [lxii. 377]

WOOD, MARY ANN (1802-1864). [See PATON.]

WOOD, MARY ANNE EVERETT (1818-1895). [See GREEN, MRS. MARY ANNE EVERETT.]

WOOD, SIR MATTHEW, first baronet (1768–1843), municipal and political reformer; serge-maker at Tiverton; apprenticed as chemist and druggist, and opened business independently in London; alderman of Cripplegate Without, London, 1807; sheriff of London and Middlesex, 1809; lord mayor, 1815–16 and 1816–17; took leading part in many city improvements; M.P., city of London, 1817–43; friend and counsellor of Queen Caroline; received baronetcy from Queen Victoria at Guildhall, 1837, this being the first title she bestowed. [lxii. 370]

WOOD or **WOODS, ROBERT** (1622 ?-1685), mathematician; of Eton and Merton College, Oxford; M.A., 1649; fellow of Lincoln College, 1650–60; licensed physician, 1656; supported Commonwealth; went to Ireland, 1660; M.D.; chancellor of diocese of Meath; mathematical master at Christ's Hospital, London; accountant-general of Ireland; F.R.S., 1681; published 'A New Al-moon-ac for Ever,' 1680, and 'The Times Mended,' 1681. [lxii. 372]

WOOD, ROBERT (1717 ?-1771), traveller and politician; travelled in France, Italy, Western Europe, and Asia Minor, with John Bouverie and James Dawkins [q. v.]; published ' Ruins of Palmyra,' 1753, and ' Ruins of Balbec,' 1757; member of Society of Dilettanti, 1763; under-secretary of state, 1756–63; M.P., Brackley, 1761-1771; seized, under warrant and orders of Lord Halifax, John Wilkes's papers, 1763, and was fined in subsequent action for trespass; under-secretary to Lord Weymouth, 1768–70. An essay by him on 'The Original Genius of Homer,' embodying his impressions of the Troad and other writings, appeared posthumously. [lxii. 373]

WOOD, SEARLES VALENTINE, the elder (1798-1880), geologist; officer in East India Company's service, 1811–25; became partner in bank at Hasketon, near Woodbridge; retired, 1835; went to London; joined London Clay Club; curator of Geological Society's museum; member of Palæontographical Society; F.G.S., 1839; Wollaston medallist; published valuable writings on the 'Crag Mollusca,' and presented an unrivalled collection of fossils to British Museum of Natural History. [lxii. 375]

WOOD, SEARLES VALENTINE, the younger (1830-1884), geologist; son of Searles Valentine Wood the elder [q. v.]; educated at King's College, London; admitted solicitor, 1851; retired, 1865; assisted his father in geological pursuits; F.G.S., 1864; made special study of drifts of Suffolk and Essex; published scientific papers. [lxii. 376]

WOOD, SHAKSPERE (1827-1886), sculptor; studied at Royal Academy and in Rome, where he lived many years, and died; published works relating to sculpture of Rome. [lxii. 376]

WOOD, THOMAS (1661-1722), lawyer; nephew of Anthony Wood [q. v.]; fellow of New College, Oxford, 1679; D.C.L., 1703; proctor for his uncle in suit instituted against him for libelling first Earl of Clarendon, 1692-3; barrister, Gray's Inn, 1692; rector of Hardwick, Buckinghamshire, 1704–22; published 'Institute of the Laws of England,' 1720, and other works in verse and prose. [lxii. 377]

WOOD, WESTERN (1804-1863), chemist and druggist; in partnership with his father, Sir Matthew Wood [q. v.]; M.P., city of London, 1861-3. [lxii. 372]

WOOD, SIR WILLIAM (1609-1691), toxophilite; for many years marshal of the Finsbury archers; probably knighted by Charles II; first wearer of the decoration known as the ' Catherine of Braganza Shield,' 1676. [lxii. 378]

WOOD, WILLIAM (1671-1730), ironmaster; stated to have owned large copper and iron works in west of England; obtained patent, 1722, of sole privilege of coining halfpence and farthings for circulation in Ireland; aroused opposition in Ireland, strengthened by Swift's tracts, called ' The Drapier's Letters,' 1724, and surrendered patent, 1725; held patent to strike halfpence, pence, and twopences for English colonies in America. 1722-3. [lxii. 378]

WOOD, WILLIAM (1745–1808), botanist and nonconformist divine; minister successively at Debenham, Suffolk, Stamford, Lincolnshire, Ipswich, 1770–2, and Mill Hill Chapel, Leeds, 1773–1808 ; F.L.S., 1791. [lxii. 379]

WOOD, WILLIAM (1774–1857), zoologist and surgeon; educated at St. Bartholomew's Hospital, London; practised in London, 1801–15, and conducted business as bookseller, 1815–40 ; F.L.S., 1798 ; F.R.S., 1812 ; published zoological works. [lxii. 380]

WOOD, WILLIAM PAGE, BARON HATHERLEY (1801–1881), lord chancellor ; second son of Sir Matthew Wood [q. v.]; of Winchester College and Geneva ; collected evidence for Queen Caroline's case, 1820 ; entered Trinity College, Cambridge, 1820 ; fellow, 1824 ; barrister, Lincoln's Inn, 1827 ; Q.C., 1845 ; advanced liberal M.P. for Oxford, 1847 ; chancellor of duchy and vice-chancellor of county palatine of Lancaster, 1849–51 ; member of commission on court of chancery, 1851 ; appointed solicitor-general and knighted, 1851 ; vice-chancellor, 1853 ; on Cambridge University commission ; lord justice of appeal, 1868 ; appointed lord chancellor and created Baron Hatherley of Hatherley, 1868 ; resigned, 1872 ; published religious and ecclesiastical works. [lxii. 380]

WOODALL, JOHN (1556 ?–1643), surgeon ; military surgeon in Lord Willoughby's regiment, 1591 ; member of Barber Surgeons' Company, 1599, warden, 1627, and master, 1633 ; surgeon to St. Bartholomew's Hospital, 1616–43 ; first surgeon-general to East India Company when formed into joint-stock business, 1612 ; interested in Virginia Company ; published surgical works showing some power of observation. [lxii. 382]

WOODARD, NATHANIEL (1811–1891), founder of the Woodard schools ; M.A. Magdalen Hall, Oxford, 1866 ; curate at New Shoreham, where, 1847, he opened a day school ; opened a boarding-school at Shoreham, 1848, and subsequently devoted his whole attention to organisation and development of large educational schemes for middle classes, the Woodard Society being formed, 1848, to carry them out ; instituted educational centres for east, west, north, south, and the midlands ; canon residentiary of Manchester, 1870 ; hon. D.C.L. Oxford, 1870 ; sub-dean of Manchester, 1881. [lxii. 383]

WOODBRIDGE, BENJAMIN (1622–1684), divine; educated at Magdalen Hall, Oxford ; went to New England, 1639 ; first graduate of Harvard College ; B.A., 1642 ; returned to England; M.A. Oxford, 1648 ; rector of Newbury, 1648 ; assistant for ejection of scandalous ministers, 1654 ; chaplain to Charles II, 1660 ; commissioner at Savoy conference, 1661 ; silenced by Act of Uniformity, 1662 ; conformed, 1665, but subsequently remained much in retirement. [lxii. 385]

WOODBRIDGE, JOHN (1613–1696), brother of Benjamin Woodbridge [q. v.]; studied at Oxford ; went to America, 1634 ; first town-clerk at Newbury, New England ; ordained, 1645 ; in England, 1647–63 ; magistrate of Newbury, New England. [lxii. 386]

WOODBURY, WALTER BENTLEY (1834–1885), inventor of Woodbury-type process ; studied engineering ; went to Australian goldfields, 1852 ; migrated to Batavia, Java, and worked at collodion process of photography ; married a Malay lady; returned to England, 1863 ; settled at Birmingham ; invented Woodbury-type process (1866), and subsequently patented many contrivances in connection with photography. [lxii. 386]

WOODCOCK, MARTIN, alias FARINGTON, JOHN (1603–1646), Franciscan martyr ; born in Lancashire; admitted to Franciscan order at Douay, 1631, and was professed, 1632 ; went on English mission, 1643 ; executed, after two years' imprisonment, at Lancaster. [lxii. 387]

WOODCROFT, BENNET (1803–1879), clerk to commissioners of patents ; in business as silk and muslin manufacturer at Manchester and Salford ; took out patents for many valuable inventions, including 'tappets' for looms (1838) ; opened business as consulting engineer and patent agent, in London, 1846 ; professor of machinery, University College, London, 1847–51 ; superintendent of patent specifications, 1852 ; F.R.S., 1859 ; clerk to commissioners of patents, 1864–76 ; published works relating to inventions and inventors. [lxii. 387]

WOODD, BASIL (1760–1831), hymn-writer ; M.A. Trinity College, Oxford, 1785 ; lecturer of St. Peter's, Cornhill, London, 1784–1808 ; preacher at Bentinck Chapel, Marylebone, London, 1785 ; rector of Drayton Beauchamp, 1808 ; exerted himself successfully in establishing schools ; published 'New Metrical Version of the Psalms, with an Appendice of select Psalms and Hymns,' 1821, and other works. [lxii. 388]

WOODDESON, RICHARD, the elder (1704–1774), divine; M.A. Magdalen College, Oxford, 1725 ; master of free school at Kingston, c. 1733–72. [lxii. 389]

WOODDESON, RICHARD, the younger (1745–1822), jurist ; son of Richard Wooddeson the elder [q. v.]; M.A. Magdalen College, Oxford, 1765 ; D.C.L., 1777 ; fellow, 1772–1823 ; barrister, Middle Temple, 1767 ; bencher, 1799 ; deputy Vinerian professor ; Vinerian fellow, 1776 ; Vinerian professor, 1777–93 ; published lectures as 'Systematical View of the Laws of England,' 1792–4, and other legal works. [lxii. 388]

WOODFALL, GEORGE (1767–1844), printer ; son of Henry Sampson Woodfall [q. v.], with whom he was in partnership, 1767–93 ; carried on business independently till 1840, and with his son, 1840–4 ; stock-keeper of Stationers' Company, 1812 and 1836 ; member of court of assistants, 1825, and master, 1833–4 and 1841 ; F.S.A., 1823 ; fellow of Royal Society of Literature, 1824 ; acquired a high reputation as a printer ; best known by his edition of Junius's 'Letters,' 3 vols. 1812. [lxii. 389]

WOODFALL, HENRY SAMPSON (1739 – 1805), printer and journalist ; of St. Paul's School, London ; apprenticed to his father, printer of the 'Public Advertiser,' 1754 ; conducted 'Public Advertiser,' c. 1758–93, and printed letters of Junius, with whom he had no personal acquaintance ; affirmed that Sir Philip Francis [q. v.] did not write the letters ; retired from business, 1793 ; master of Stationers' Company, 1797. [lxii. 390]

WOODFALL, WILLIAM (1746–1803), parliamentary reporter and dramatic critic ; brother of Henry Sampson Woodfall [q. v.]; apprenticed as bookseller ; employed in printing 'Public Advertiser'; actor and journalist ; edited 'London Packet,' 1772–4 ; on staff of 'Morning Chronicle,' 1774–89 ; established, 1789, the 'Diary,' the first journal to give reports of parliamentary proceedings on the morning after they had taken place. [lxii. 392]

WOODFORD, SIR ALEXANDER GEORGE (1782–1870), field-marshal ; brother of Sir John George Woodford [q. v.]; of Winchester College and Bonnycastle's academy, Woolwich ; ensign, 1794 ; captain, 1799 ; colonel, 1814 ; lieutenant-general, 1838 ; colonel, 40th regiment, 1842 ; general, 1854 ; colonel, Scots fusilier guards, 1861 ; field-marshal, 1868 ; at Copenhagen, 1807 ; in Peninsula, 1811–14 ; Waterloo, 1815 ; C.B. (military), 1815 ; K.C.M.G., 1831 ; governor and commander-in-chief of Gibraltar, 1836–43 ; G.C.B., 1852 ; governor of Chelsea Hospital, 1868–70. [lxii. 392]

WOODFORD, JAMES RUSSELL (1820–1885), bishop of Ely ; educated at Merchant Taylors' School and Pembroke College, Cambridge ; M.A., 1845 ; vicar of Kempsford, 1855 ; honorary canon of Christchurch ; vicar of Leeds, 1868 ; D.D. Lambeth, 1869 ; chaplain to Queen Victoria, 1872 ; bishop of Ely, 1873 ; established theological college, Ely ; published sermons and other writings. [lxii. 394]

WOODFORD, SIR JOHN GEORGE (1785–1879), major-general ; brother of Sir Alexander George Woodford [q. v.]; educated at Harrow ; ensign, 1800 ; at Copenhagen, 1807 ; in Peninsula, 1808–14 ; wounded at Coruña ; captain, 1st grenadier guards, 1814 ; at Waterloo, 1815 ; commanded army of occupation in France, 1818 ; colonel, grenadier guards, at Dublin, 1823 ; carried out numerous reforms in military discipline ; K.H.; major-general, 1837 ; K.C.B., 1838. [lxii. 394]

WOODFORD, SAMUEL (1636–1700), divine and poet ; of St. Paul's School, London, and Wadham College, Oxford ; B.A., 1657 ; entered Inner Temple ; elected to Royal Society, 1664 ; canon of Chichester, 1676, and of Winchester, 1680 ; D.D., 1677 ; published poetical paraphrases of the Psalms, 1667, and the Canticles, 1679. [lxii. 396]

WOODFORD or **WYDFORD,** WILLIAM OF (fl. 1381–1390), opponent of Wycliffe ; Franciscan ; D.D.

Oxford, where he met Wycliffe and gradually became hostile to him; wrote work opposing Wycliffe's repudiation of transubstantiation, 1381, and subsequently repeatedly attacked him in writing; regent-master in theology among minorites at Oxford, 1389; vicar of provincial minster, 1390. [lxii. 396]

WOODFORDE, SAMUEL (1763 - 1817), painter; studied at Royal Academy and in Italy; exhibited at Royal Academy, 1784-6 and 1792-1815; R.A., 1807. [lxii. 397]

WOODHALL or WOODALL. [See UVEDALE.]

WOODHAM, MRS. (1743-1803), singer and actress; previously called SPENCER; pupil of Dr. Arne; for many years a favourite on the Dublin stage; burned in fire at Astley's amphitheatre. [lxii. 398]

WOODHAM or GODDAM, ADAM (d. 1358). [See GODDAM.]

WOODGATE, SIR EDWARD ROBERT PREVOST (1845-1900), major-general; educated at Sandhurst; lieutenant, 4th foot, 1869; in Ashanti war, 1873-4; captain, 1878; staff officer of flying column in Zulu campaign, 1879; brigade-major in West Indies, 1880-5; lieutenant-colonel, 1893; C.B., 1896; colonel, 1897; organised West African regiment at Sierra Leone, 1898; major-general in command of eleventh brigade of fifth division under Sir Charles Warren in South Africa, 1899; K.C.M.G., 1900; died from wounds received at Spion Kop. [Suppl. iii. 517]

WOODHEAD, ABRAHAM (1609 - 1678), Roman catholic controversialist; M.A. University College, Oxford, 1631; fellow, 1633; took holy orders; proctor, 1641; firmly opposed puritan efforts of the government; tutor to George Villiers, second duke of Buckingham [q. v.], and his brother, Lord Francis, c. 1648; ejected from fellowship by parliamentary visitors, 1648; re-instated, 1660; resigned, 1678; joined Roman catholic church, but did not enter priesthood; the 'Whole Duty of Man' erroneously attributed to him; published and left in manuscript controversial and other religious works. [lxii. 398]

WOODHOUSE, JAMES (1735-1820), 'the poetical shoemaker'; worked as shoemaker and schoolmaster at Rowley Regis; published 'Poems on sundry Occasions,' 1764, attracting considerable attention; bailiff on estates of Edward Montagu, husband of Mrs. Elizabeth Montagu [q. v.], c. 1766-78; house steward to Mrs. Montagu, c. 1778-85; complete edition of his works, 1896. [lxii. 400]

WOODHOUSE, PETER (fl. 1605), poet; published 'Democritvs his Dreame, or the Contention betweene the Elephant and the Flea,' 1605, in the 'Epistle Dedicatorie' of which there is a reference to 'Justice Shallowe' and 'his cousen Mr. Weathercocke.' [lxii. 401]

WOODHOUSE, ROBERT DE (d. 1345?). [See WODEHOUSE.]

WOODHOUSE, ROBERT (1773-1827), mathematician; senior wrangler and Smith's prizeman, Caius College, Cambridge, 1795; M.A., 1798; fellow, 1798-1823; F.R.S., 1802; first in England to explain and advocate the notation and methods of the calculus; Lucasian professor of mathematics, 1820, and Plumian professor of astronomy and experimental philosophy, 1822; superintendent of Cambridge observatory; published mathematical works. [lxii. 402]

WOODHOUSE, THOMAS (d. 1573), Roman catholic martyr; ordained priest, 1558; imprisoned as priest in Fleet, London, 1561; admitted to Society of Jesus, 1572; executed at Tyburn on charge of high treason. [lxii. 402]

WOODHOUSELEE, LORD (1747-1813). [See TYTLER, ALEXANDER FRASER.]

WOODINGTON, WILLIAM FREDERICK (1806-1893), sculptor and painter; pupil of Robert William Sievier [q. v.]; exhibited at Royal Academy between 1825 and 1882; curator of school of sculpture at Royal Academy; A.R.A., 1876. [lxii. 403]

WOODLARK, ROBERT (d. 1479). [See WODELARKE.]

WOODLEY, GEORGE (1786-1846), poet and divine; served in navy; edited 'Royal Cornwall Gazette,' 1808; missionary of Society for Promoting Christian Knowledge, in islands of St. Martin and St. Agnes, Scilly,

1820-42; perpetual curate of Martindale, 1843-6; published poems, essays, and other writings. [lxii. 403]

WOODMAN, RICHARD (1524?-1557), protestant martyr; 'iron-maker' at Warbleton; imprisoned as protestant, 1554 to 1555, when his detention was declared illegal; itinerant preacher; arrested, 1557; burned at Lewes. [lxii. 404]

WOODMAN, RICHARD (1784-1859), engraver; apprenticed to Robert Mitchell Meadows; exhibited water-colour paintings and miniatures at Royal Academy, 1820-50. [lxii. 405]

WOODNOTH. [See WODENOTE and WODENOTH.]

WOODROFFE, BENJAMIN (1638-1711), divine; of Westminster School and Christ Church, Oxford; M.A., 1662; incorporated at Cambridge, 1664; tutor at Christ Church, Oxford; F.R.S., 1668; chaplain to Duke of York, 1669, and to Charles II, 1674; canon of Christ Church, Oxford, 1672-1711; D.D., 1673; subdean of Christ Church, Oxford, 1674; rector of St. Bartholomew, near Royal Exchange, London, 1676-1711; canon of Lichfield, 1678-1711; principal of Gloucester Hall, Oxford, 1692; founded Greek College at Oxford, 1697 (demolished, 1806); published religious and other writings. [lxii. 405]

WOODROOFFE, MRS. ANNE (1766-1830), author; née Cox; married, 1803; published 'Shades of Character,' 1824, and other works. [lxii. 407]

WOODROW, HENRY (1823-1876), promoter of education in India; of Rugby and Caius College, Cambridge; M.A., 1849; junior fellow, 1846-54; principal of Martinière College, Calcutta, 1848; secretary to council of education, 1854; inspector of schools in Eastern Bengal, 1855-72; director of public instruction in Bengal, 1876; increased native interest in education. [lxii. 407]

WOODS, JAMES (1672-1759). [See WOOD.]

WOODS, JOSEPH (1776-1864), architect and botanist; entered office of Daniel Asher Alexander [q. v.]; formed, and was first president of, London Architectural Society, 1806; edited and issued, 1816, fourth volume of 'Antiquities of Athens,' by James Stuart (1713-1788) [q. v.]; travelled on continent and studied geology and botany; practised in London, 1819-33; retired, 1833; published 'Tourist's Flora,' 1850, a descriptive catalogue of plants and ferns of British islands and various European countries; F.L.S., F.G.S., and F.S.A. [lxii. 409]

WOODS, JULIAN EDMUND TENISON- (1832-1889), geologist and naturalist; became Roman catholic when young, and joined Passionist order; accompanied Bishop Wilson to Tasmania, 1854; ordained deacon and priest, 1856; missionary priest in south-eastern district of South Australia; vicar-general of diocese, 1867; missionary priest in Queensland, 1873; published 'History of Discovery and Exploration of Australia,' 1865, numerous papers on natural history, geology, and palæontology, and other writings. [lxii. 410]

WOODS, ROBERT (1622?-1685). [See WOOD.]

WOODSTOCK, EDMUND OF, EARL OF KENT (1301-1330). [See EDMUND.]

WOODSTOCK, EDWARD OF (1330-1376). [See EDWARD, PRINCE OF WALES.]

WOODSTOCK, ROBERT OF (d. 1428). [See HEETE, ROBERT.]

WOODSTOCK, THOMAS OF, EARL OF BUCKINGHAM and DUKE OF GLOUCESTER (1355-1397). [See THOMAS.]

WOODVILLE or WYDVILLE, ANTHONY, BARON SCALES and second EARL RIVERS (1442?-1483), son of Richard Woodville, first earl Rivers [q. v.], and Jacquetta, widow of John of Lancaster, duke of Bedford [q. v.]; married, c. 1460, Elizabeth (d. 1473), baroness Scales and Neucelles in her own right; fought for Lancastrians at Towton, but transferred allegiance to Edward IV; recognised as Lord Scales; K.G., 1466; lord of Isle of Wight, 1466; fought celebrated tournament with Bastard of Burgundy, 1467, the battle being declared drawn; member of embassy which arranged match between Duke of Burgundy and Edward IV's sister Margaret, 1467; governor of Portsmouth, 1468; succeeded as Earl Rivers, 1469; lieutenant of Calais; accompanied Edward IV in exile, 1470-1; guardian of Edward, prince of Wales, and chief butler of England, 1473 ; governor to Prince Edward, 1473 ; went to Rome, 1475–6 ; invested by Pope Sixtus IV with title of defender and director of papal causes in England ; on Edward IV's death was suspected of treason by Richard, duke of Gloucester, the protector, and executed. He wrote several translations from French, which were issued by Caxton. [lxii. 410]

WOODVILLE or **WYDEVILLE**, ELIZABETH (1437?-1492). [See ELIZABETH.]

WOODVILLE, LIONEL (1446?-1484), bishop of Salisbury ; son of Richard Woodville, first earl Rivers [q. v.] ; D.D. Oxford : dean of Exeter, 1478 ; chancellor of Oxford University, 1479 ; bishop of Salisbury, 1482 ; took part in organising Buckingham's rebellion, and subsequently fled to Henry of Richmond in Brittany, where possibly he died. [lxii. 414]

WOODVILLE or **WYDEVILLE**, RICHARD, first EARL RIVERS (d. 1469), son of Richard Woodville, who was lieutenant of Calais, 1429, and died, c. 1441 ; knighted by Henry VI at Leicester, 1426 ; served in France ; married secretly, c. 1436, Jacquetta of Luxemburg, widow of John of Lancaster, duke of Bedford [q. v.], and was pardoned, 1437 ; served under Somerset and Talbot in attempt to relieve Meaux, 1439 ; accompanied Duke of York to France, 1441 ; knight banneret and captain of Alençon, 1442 ; created Baron Rivers, 1448 ; took part in suppression of Cade's rising, 1450 ; K.G. and privy councillor, 1450 ; appointed seneschal of Aquitaine, 1450 ; lieutenant to Duke of Somerset when captain of Calais, 1451 ; stationed at Sandwich to guard against landing of exiled Earls of Warwick and March, who had taken refuge at Calais, 1459 ; captured and carried to Calais, 1460 ; escaped ; fought at Towton and accompanied Henry VI in flight to Newcastle ; transferred allegiance, 1461, to Edward IV, who married his daughter Elizabeth, 1464 ; treasurer, 1466 ; created Earl Rivers, 1466 ; high constable of England, 1467 ; taken after Edward IV's defeat at Edgecot and executed at Kenilworth. [lxii. 414]

WOODVILLE, WILLIAM (1752–1805), physician and botanist ; M.D. Edinburgh, 1775 ; physician to Middlesex dispensary, London, 1782 ; L.R.C.P., 1784 ; physician to small-pox and inoculation hospitals at St. Pancras, London, 1791 ; F.L.S., 1791 ; though at first hostile, subsequently adopted and advocated theory of vaccination introduced by Edward Jenner (1749–1823) [q. v.], and published reports relating to practice of vaccination. His works include ' Medical Botany,' 1790–4. [lxii. 417]

WOODWARD, BENJAMIN (1815–1861), architect ; articled as civil engineer : associated with Sir Thomas Deane [q. v.] in building Queen's College, Cork, 1846–8 ; in partnership with Deane and his son, (Sir) Thomas Newenham Deane [q. v.], in Dublin, 1853, and built Trinity College new library, Dublin, 1853–7 ; built the Oxford museum under Ruskin's supervision, 1855–8 ; intimate with Rossetti, Morris, Burne-Jones, younger group of pre-Raphaelites. Both at Dublin and Oxford the experiment was made with some success of leaving sculptural details to the taste of individual workmen. [Suppl. iii. 518]

WOODWARD, BERNARD BOLINGBROKE (1816–1869), librarian ; son of Samuel Woodward [q. v.] ; worked at heraldic drawing for Hudson Gurney [q. v.] ; studied at Highbury College, London ; B.A. London, 1841 ; pastor of independent church at Wortwell-with-Harleston, 1843–8 ; librarian in ordinary to Queen Victoria at Windsor Castle, 1860 ; F.S.A., 1857 ; published historical and other works. [lxii. 417]

WOODWARD, GEORGE MOUTARD (1760?-1809), caricaturist ; practised in London, his work being etched chiefly by Rowlandson and Isaac Cruikshank ; published several volumes of caricatures. [lxii. 418]

WOODWARD, HENRY (1714–1777), actor : of Merchant Taylors' School ; joined Lilliputian troupe of Lun under John Rich [q. v.] at Lincoln's Inn Fields, London, 1729 ; at Goodman's Fields, London, 1730–6, and at Lincoln's Inn Fields, 1737 ; at Drury Lane and Covent Garden, London, 1737–47, playing comedy parts, including Feeble (' 2 Henry IV '), Pistol, and Silvius (' As you Like it '), Sir Andrew Aguecheek, Lucio (' Measure for Measure '), Parolles, Guiderius (' Cymbeline ') ; with Sheridan at Smock Alley, Dublin, 1747 ; again at Drury Lane, London,

1748–58, playing Stephano (' Tempest '), Polonius, Falstaff (' 2 Henry IV '), and Mercutio ; produced and doubtless acted in several pantomimes between 1751 and 1756 ; joint-manager with Spranger Barry [q. v.] of Crow Street Theatre, Dublin, 1758–62, and at Cork, 1761 ; reappeared at Covent Garden, 1763, his parts including Careless (Colman's ' Oxonian in Town ') and Justice Shallow, Captain Absolute ; unsurpassed as Mercutio and Bobadil ; last appeared as Stephano, 1777. [lxii. 419]

WOODWARD, HEZEKIAH or EZEKIAS (1590–1675), nonconformist divine ; B.A. Balliol College, Oxford, 1612 ; opened school at Aldermanbury, c. 1619 ; presbyterian controversialist, but subsequently an independent ; vicar of Bray, near Maidenhead, 1649 ; left Bray to escape ejection, 1660, and subsequently preached at Uxbridge ; published ' Inquiries into the Causes of our Miseries, 1644, and a ' Judgment ' on Edwards's ' Anti-Apologie,' 1644. [lxii. 422]

WOODWARD, JOHN (1665–1728), geologist and physician ; pupil of Dr. Peter Barwick [q. v.] ; professor of physic, Gresham College, London, 1692 ; F.R.S., 1693 ; created M.D. by Thomas Tenison [q. v.], 1695 ; M.D. Cambridge, 1695 ; F.C.P., 1703 : Gulstonian lecturer, 1710–1711 ; published ' Essay toward a Natural History of the Earth,' 1695, in which he recognised existence of various strata in the earth's crust, but overlooked the true disposition of fossils in the strata : served on council of Royal Society, but was expelled, 1710, for insulting Sir Hans Sloane [q. v.] [lxii. 423]

WOODWARD, RICHARD (1726–1794), bishop of Cloyne ; B.C.L. Wadham College, Oxford, 1749 ; D.C.L., 1759 ; dean of Clogher, 1764–81 ; chancellor of St. Patrick's, Dublin, 1772–8 ; one of principal founders of House of Industry in Dublin, 1769 ; bishop of Cloyne, 1781–1794 ; published writings relating to condition of Ireland. [lxii. 425]

WOODWARD, SAMUEL (1790–1838), geologist and antiquary ; apprenticed to manufacturer of camlets and bombazines at Norwich ; clerk in Gurney's (now Barclay's) Bank, Norwich, 1820–38 ; studied history and archæology, and formed collection of fossils and antiquities, and published works relating to Norfolk. [lxii. 426]

WOODWARD, SAMUEL PICKWORTH (1821–1865), naturalist ; son of Samuel Woodward [q. v.] ; collected botanical specimens for Dawson Turner [q. v.] ; held post in library of British Museum, 1838 ; sub-curator to Geological Society of London, at Somerset House, 1839 ; member of Botanical Society of London ; professor of geology and natural history at Royal Agricultural College, Cirencester, 1845 ; first-class assistant in department of geology and mineralogy, British Museum, 1848–65 ; F.G.S., 1854 ; associate of Linnean Society, 1841 ; published ' Manual of the Mollusca,' 1851–6, and other works. [lxii. 426]

WOODWARD, THOMAS (1801–1852), animal painter ; exhibited at Royal Academy and British Institution, 1822–52. [lxii. 427]

WOODWARD, THOMAS JENKINSON (1745?-1820), botanist ; educated at Eton and Clare Hall, Cambridge ; LL.B., 1769 ; F.L.S., 1789 ; joint-author with Samuel Goodenough [q. v.] of ' Observations on the British Fuci,' 1797. [lxii. 427]

WOOLER, THOMAS JONATHAN (1786?-1853), journalist and politician ; printer ; started radical periodical ' The Stage '; printer and editor of ' The Reasoner, 1808 ; succeeded Cobbett as editor of ' The Statesman '; issued ' The Black Dwarf,' 1817–24, setting up his articles without manuscript ; imprisoned at Warwick for assisting in electing Sir Charles Wolseley (1769–1846) [q. v.] ' legislatorial attorney ' for Birmingham, 1819 ; published legal and other writings. [lxii. 428]

WOOLF, ARTHUR (1766–1837), mining engineer ; millwright under Joseph Bramah [q. v.] at Pimlico ; master-engineer, 1795 ; resident engineer at Meux's brewery, 1796–1806 ; took out patents for an improved engine boiler, 1803, and for system facilitating use of steam at high pressure, 1804 and 1805 ; partner in steam-engine factory at Lambeth, 1806 ; took out patent for a certain type of compound (' Woolf ') engine, 1810 ; engaged in mining in Cornwall, introducing many improvements,

which, however, were superseded by the high pressure single-cylinder engine of Richard Trevithick [q. v.]
[lxii. 428]

WOOLHOUSE, JOHN THOMAS (1650?-1734), oculist; groom of chamber to James II, and was appointed his oculist; practised in Paris; F.R.S., 1721; published works in French; described performance of iridectomy for restoration of sight in cases of occluded pupil, 1711.
[lxii. 429]

WOOLL, JOHN (1767-1833), schoolmaster; of Winchester and Balliol New College, Oxford; M.A., 1794; D.D., 1807; fellow, 1788-99; headmaster of Midhurst free grammar school, 1799, and of Rugby School, 1807-28; published poetical and other writings. [lxii. 430]

WOOLLETT, WILLIAM (1735-1785), draughtsman and line-engraver; engraved 'Temple of Apollo' after Claude, 1760, and established his reputation as landscape-engraver; engraved West's 'Death of General Wolfe,' 1776, and received title of 'Historical Engraver to His Majesty'; the first English engraver whose works were admired and purchased on the continent. [lxii. 430]

WOOLLEY or **WOLLEY**, MRS. HANNAH, afterwards MRS. CHALLINOR (*fl.* 1670), writer of works on cookery; worked as private governess; married Francis Challinor, after the death of her first husband, Woolley, 1666. Her works appeared between 1661 and 1675. [lxii. 431]

WOOLLEY, JOHN (1816-1866), first principal of Sydney University; educated at University College, London, and Exeter and University colleges, Oxford; M.A., 1839; D.C.L., 1844; fellow of Exeter College, Oxford, 1840-1; took holy orders, 1840; head-master of King Edward VI's grammar school, Hereford, 1842, of Rossall, 1844, of Norwich grammar school, 1849, and principal of Sydney University, 1852; drowned at sea while returning from visit to London; published 'Introduction to Logic,' 1840, and other works. [lxii. 432]

WOOLLEY, JOSEPH (1817-1889), naval architect; brother of John Woolley [q. v.]; B.A. St. John's College, Cambridge, 1840; M.A., 1843; fellow and tutor, 1840-6; incorporated M.A. Oxford, 1856; ordained, 1846; principal of school of naval construction, Portsmouth, 1848-1853; admiralty inspector of schools, 1853, and government inspector of schools, 1858; took part in founding Institution of Naval Architects, 1860; inspector-general and director of studies at Royal School of Naval Architecture, 1864-73; joint-editor of 'Naval Science,' 1874-5; divested himself of orders, 1865. [lxii. 432]

WOOLMAN, JOHN (1720-1772), quaker essayist; born in West Jersey, America; baker; began to preach against slave trade, c. 1743; came to England, 1772. His 'Journal' appeared, 1775, and his 'Works,' 1774. [lxii. 433]

WOOLNER, THOMAS (1825-1892), sculptor and poet; pupil of William Behnes [q. v.]; studied at Royal Academy, 1842; made acquaintance of Rossetti and became one of the original 'pre-Raphaelite Brethren,' 1847; contributed poems to 'The Germ'; met with small success and went to Australian goldfields, his departure inspiring Madox Brown's picture 'The Last of England,' 1852; practised painting in Melbourne and Sydney till he returned to England, 1854; executed bust of Tennyson, 1857; R.A., 1874, and professor of sculpture, 1877-9; executed portrait-sculptures of the most eminent men of his day, his statue of John Stuart Mill, on the Thames Embankment, London, being among the most notable of his works.
[lxii. 434]

WOOLRIDGE, JOHN (*fl.* 1669-1698). [See WOOLRIDGE.]

WOOLRYCH, HUMPHRY WILLIAM (1795-1871), biographer and legal writer; of Eton and St. Edmund Hall, Oxford; barrister, Lincoln's Inn, 1821; *ad eundem* at Inner Temple, 1830; admitted at Gray's Inn, 1847; serjeant-at-law, 1855; published 'Lives of Eminent Serjeants-at-Law,' 1869, and other biographical works, besides legal text-books and tracts. [lxii. 436]

WOOLSTON, THOMAS (1670-1733), enthusiast and freethinker; M.A. Sidney Sussex College, Cambridge, 1692; fellow, 1691; took orders; prælector, 1694; classical lecturer, 1697; B.D., 1699; adopted from Origen idea of interpreting the scriptures as allegory; published religious controversial tracts and was deprived of fellowship; issued further writings, declaring his intention of found-

ing a new sect; fined and imprisoned (1729) for published 'Discourses' on Christ's miracles; remained in King's Bench till his death. [lxii. 437]

WOOLTON or **WOLTON**, JOHN (1535?-1594), bishop of Exeter; B.A. Brasenose College, Oxford, 1555; lived abroad, 1555-8; canon of Exeter, 1565; first warden of collegiate church of Manchester, 1578; bishop of Exeter, 1578; D.D., 1579; held with bishopric place of archpriest at Haccombe, 1581, and rectory of Lezant, 1584; published theological treatises. [lxii. 439]

WOOTTON. [See also WOTTON.]

WOOTTON, JOHN (1668?-1765), animal and landscape painter; studied under John Wyck [q. v.]; first became known as painter of racehorses at Newmarket; painted many landscapes in the style of Claude and Gaspar Poussin. [lxii. 440]

WORBOISE, EMMA JANE, afterwards MRS. GUYTON (1825-1887), author; published 'Alice Cunningham,' 1846, and subsequently issued about fifty volumes, chiefly stories and novels of a religious and domestic character.
[lxii. 440]

WORCESTER, second MARQUIS OF (1601-1667). [See SOMERSET, EDWARD.]

WORCESTER, EARLS OF. [See PERCY, THOMAS, 1344?-1403; TIPTOFT, JOHN, 1427?-1470; SOMERSET, CHARLES, first EARL, 1460?-1526; SOMERSET, WILLIAM, third EARL, 1526-1589; SOMERSET, EDWARD, fourth EARL, 1553-1628.]

WORCESTER or **BOTONER**, WILLIAM (1415-1482?), chronicler and traveller; studied at Great Hart Hall, Oxford; acted as secretary to Sir John Fastolf; on Fastolf's death, 5 Nov. 1459, he disputed his will made shortly before, leaving John Paston residuary legatee, and obtained some land near Norwich and two tenements in Southwark; travelled in England and left detailed accounts of his journeys; he left also 'Annales rerum Anglicarum,' and other manuscripts. [lxii. 441]

WORDE, WYNKYN DE (*d.* 1534?), printer and stationer; his real name Jan van Wynkyn; born at Worth, in Alsace; came to England and was apprenticed to William Caxton, whose business in Westminster he carried on after Caxton's death; removed to Fleet Street, London, 1500; opened shop in St. Paul's churchyard, London, 1509. The number of books issued from his press was very large, the third edition of the 'Golden Legend,' 1493, 'Vitas Patrum' (translated by Caxton), 1495, second edition of 'Mort d'Arthur,' 1498, and third edition of 'Canterbury Tales,' being among the most notable. [lxii. 443]

WORDEN. [See WERDEN.]

WORDSWORTH, CHARLES (1806-1892), bishop of St. Andrews, Dunkeld, and Dunblane; son of Christopher Wordsworth (1774-1846) [q. v.]; of Harrow and Christ Church, Oxford; won chancellor's prizes for Latin verse, 1827, and Latin essay, 1831; B.A., 1830; travelled as tutor on continent; second master of Winchester College, 1835-46; published 'Græcæ Grammaticæ Rudimenta' (accidence, 1839, syntax, 1843); warden of the new episcopalian Trinity college, at Glenalmond, 1846-54; elected bishop of St. Andrews, Dunkeld, and Dunblane, 1852; took part in eucharistic controversy introduced into Scotland by Alexander Penrose Forbes [q. v.], bishop of Brechin, in his 'primary charge,' 1857, and criticised Forbes's teaching as unauthorised; fellow of Winchester, 1871; member of company of New Testament revisers, 1870; hon. D.D. St. Andrews and Edinburgh, 1884; wrote Latin verses; published 'On Shakespeare's Knowledge and use of the Bible,' 1864, and many sermons, charges, and other writings, including 'The Case of Nonepiscopal Ordination fairly considered,' 1885, and 'Ecclesiastical Union between England and Scotland,' 1888.
[lxiii. 1]

WORDSWORTH, CHRISTOPHER (1774-1846), master of Trinity College, Cambridge; brother of William Wordsworth [q. v.]; B.A. Trinity College, 1796; fellow, 1798; M.A., 1799; D.D., 1810; rector of Ashly with Oby and Thinne, Norfolk, 1804; domestic chaplain to Manners-Sutton, archbishop of Canterbury, 1805; dean and rector of Bocking, Essex, 1808; chaplain of House of Commons, 1817; took part with Joshua Watson [q. v.] in founding National Society, 1811; master of Trinity College, Cambridge, 1820-41; vice-chancellor of Cambridge

University, 1820–1 and 1826–7 ; held living of Buxted with Uckfield, Sussex, 1820–46 ; as master he was a strict disciplinarian and earned some unpopularity ; published 'Ecclesiastical Biography,' 1810, ' Who wrote EIKΩN BAΣIΛIKH ?' 1824 (supporting the claim of Charles I), and other works. [lxiii. 7]

WORDSWORTH, CHRISTOPHER (1807–1885), bishop of Lincoln ; son of Christopher Wordsworth (1774–1846) [q. v.] ; of Winchester College and Trinity College, Cambridge ; senior classic and first chancellor's classical medallist, 1830 ; fellow, 1830 ; travelled in Greece, 1832–3 ; discovered the site of Dodona ; priest, 1835 ; public orator at Cambridge, 1836 ; head-master of Harrow, 1836 ; canon of Westminster, 1844 ; received living of Stanford-in-the-Vale, Berkshire, 1850 ; proctor in convocation for chapter of Westminster, 1852 ; archdeacon of Westminster, 1865 ; bishop of Lincoln, 1868–85 ; took up a marked anti-Roman attitude. His publications include a commentary on the whole bible, 1856–70, 'Church History to A.D. 451,' 1881–3, ' Athens and Attica,' 1836, ' Theocritus,' 1844 (fuller edition, 1877), and numerous lectures, sermons, and other religious writings. [lxiii. 9]

WORDSWORTH, DOROTHY (1804–1847). [See Quillinan, Dorothy.]

WORDSWORTH, JOHN (1805–1839), classical scholar ; son of Christopher Wordsworth (1774–1846) [q. v.] ; of Winchester College and Trinity College, Cambridge ; Porson prizeman, 1827 ; B.A., 1828 ; fellow, 1830 ; classical lecturer, 1834 ; ordained deacon and priest, 1837. [lxiii. 8]

WORDSWORTH, WILLIAM (1770–1850), poet ; born at Cockermouth, Cumberland ; son of John Wordsworth (1741–83), an attorney of Cockermouth ; educated at grammar school at Hawkshead, and St. John's College, Cambridge ; made walking tour on continent, 1790 ; B.A., 1791 ; travelled in France, where he fostered his inclinations towards the principles of liberty, 1792 ; published ' Evening Walk ' and ' Descriptive Sketches,' 1793 ; became acquainted with Coleridge, c. 1795, and published with him 'Lyrical Ballads,' 1798 (enlarged 2nd edit. 1800) ; lived at Goslar, Germany, 1798–9, beginning the ' Prelude,' and writing poems to Lucy ; settled with his sister Dorothy at Grasmere, 1799, and there remained till end of his life ; married, 1802, Mary Hutchinson (b. 1770) ; made tours in Scotland, 1801 and 1803, and began cordial friendship with Sir Walter Scott, 1803 ; published poems, including odes to ' Duty ' and on ' Intimations of Immortality,' ' Miscellaneous Sonnets,' and sonnets dedicated to ' Liberty,' 1807 ; occupied Rydal Mount, Grasmere, 1813–50 ; held office of distributor of stamps for county of Westmoreland, c. 1813–42 ; again toured in Scotland, 1814 ; published ' The Excursion,' 1814, and ' Peter Bell ' and ' The Waggoner,' 1819 ; placed on commission of peace for Westmoreland, 1819 ; travelled on continent, 1820, 1823, and 1828, to Ireland, 1829, Scotland (visiting Scott at Abbotsford, and writing ' Yarrow Revisited '), 1831, Isle of Man and Scotland, 1833, and on the continent with Henry Crabbe Robinson [q. v.], 1837 ; hon. D.C.L. Durham, 1838, and Oxford, 1839 ; resigned place in stamp office and received pension from civil list, 1842 ; succeeded Southey as poet laureate, 1843 ; buried in Grasmere churchyard. Wordsworth's aim as a poet was to find fit utterance for the primary and simple feelings, but his revolt against the ' artificial ' style of the previous school led him not infrequently to trivialities. His ' Poetical and Prose Works, together with Dorothy Wordsworth's Journals ' edited by Professor Knight, appeared, 1896. [lxiii. 12]

WORGAN, JOHN (1724–1790), organist and composer ; organist at Vauxhall Gardens, London, 1751–74 ; ' composer ' to Vauxhall Gardens, 1753–61 and 1770–4 ; Mus.Bac. Cambridge, 1748 ; Mus.Doc., 1775 ; has been credited erroneously with having composed the Easter hymn. His compositions include two oratorios. [lxiii. 27]

WORLIDGE or **WOOLRIDGE,** JOHN (fl. 1669–1698), agricultural writer ; compiled ' Systema Agriculturæ,' 1669, the first systematic treatise on husbandry on a large and comprehensive scale. [lxiii. 28]

WORLIDGE, THOMAS (1700–1766), painter and etcher ; pupil of Louis Peter Boitard [q. v.] ; practised portrait-painting at Bath ; settled in London, 1740 ; executed many plates in style of Rembrandt ; his works include a series of etchings of gems from the antique, published in parts from 1754, and in volume, 1768. [lxiii. 28]

WORMALD, THOMAS (1802–1873), surgeon ; apprenticed to John Abernethy (1764–1831) [q. v.] ; M.R.C.S., 1824 ; house-surgeon at St. Bartholomew's Hospital, London, 1824 ; demonstrator of anatomy, 1826 ; surgeon, 1861–7, consulting surgeon, 1867 ; surgeon at Foundling Hospital, London, 1843–64, and governor, 1847 ; F.R.C.S., 1843, Hunterian orator, 1857, and president, 1865 ; published ' Anatomical Sketches and Diagrams,' 1838. [lxiii. 30]

WORNUM, RALPH NICHOLSON (1812–1877), art critic and keeper of the National Gallery ; educated at University College, London ; entered studio of Henry Sass [q. v.] ; studied on continent ; practised as portrait-painter in London ; worked for the ' Art Journal ' from 1846 ; compiled official catalogue of National Gallery, 1847 ; lecturer on art to government schools of design, 1848 ; keeper of National Gallery and secretary to the trustees, 1854 ; chiefly instrumental in obtaining restoration of Turner collections to National Gallery, 1860–1 ; edited ' The Turner Gallery,' 1861 ; published ' Epochs of Painting,' 1847, ' Analysis of Ornament,' 1856, and other writings. [lxiii. 31]

WORSDALE, JAMES (1692 ?–1767), portrait-painter ; servant to Sir Godfrey Kneller, whose apprentice he became ; practised as portrait-painter ; master-painter to board of ordnance ; perhaps the author of several plays. [lxiii. 32]

WORSLEY, CHARLES (1622–1656), major-general ; parliamentary captain in Lancashire, 1644 ; lieutenant-colonel of regiment raised in Lancashire for Cromwell, 1650 ; employed in reduction of Isle of Man, 1651 ; commanded detachment used in expulsion of Long parliament, 1652 ; first member for Manchester, 1654 ; major-general for Lancashire, Cheshire, and Staffordshire, 1655. [lxiii. 32]

WORSLEY, EDWARD (1605–1676), jesuit ; entered Society of Jesus, 1626 ; professor of philosophy, logic, and sacred scripture at Liège ; professed of the four vows, 1641 ; joined English mission in London ; rector of college at Liège, 1658 ; acting English procurator and missioner, 1662, at Professed House, Antwerp, where he died ; published religious writings. [lxiii. 33]

WORSLEY, HENRY (1783–1820), lieutenant-colonel ; ensign, 1799 ; served with 85th regiment in expedition to Scheldt, 1809 ; in Peninsula, 1811 and 1812–13 ; lieutenant-colonel, 1813 ; captain of Yarmouth Castle, Isle of Wight. [lxiii. 34]

WORSLEY, SIR HENRY (1768–1841), major-general ; went to Bengal as infantry cadet, 1780 ; ensign and lieutenant, 1781, adjutant, 1783 ; served in Sumatra, 1789 ; in Mysore war, 1791 ; captain, 1798 ; fought at Delhi and Agra, 1803 ; major, 1804 ; served with distinction at Muttra ; adjutant-general and lieutenant-colonel, 1806 ; military secretary to Francis Rawdon-Hastings, second earl of Moira [q. v.], 1818 ; returned finally to Europe, 1819 ; major-general, 1830 ; K.C.B., 1821 ; G.C.B., 1838. [lxiii. 34]

WORSLEY, ISRAEL (1768–1836), unitarian minister ; educated at Daventry academy ; minister of Dunkirk, 1790 ; established school at Dunkirk ; in England during war, 1793–1802 ; minister of Lincoln, 1806–13 and 1833–1836, Plymouth, 1813–31, Paris, 1831–3 ; published theological and other writings. [lxiii. 35]

WORSLEY, PHILIP STANHOPE (1835–1866), poet ; M.A. Corpus Christi College, Oxford, 1861 ; Newdigate prizeman, 1857 ; fellow, 1863 ; published versions of ' Odyssey,' 1861, and of first twelve books of ' Iliad,' 1865, in metre of Spenser. [lxiii. 36]

WORSLEY, SIR RICHARD, seventh baronet (1751–1805), antiquary and traveller ; of Winchester College and Corpus Christi College, Oxford ; succeeded to baronetcy, 1768 ; one of clerks comptrollers of the green cloth, 1777 ; clerk of privy council and comptroller of George III's household, 1779 ; privy councillor, 1780 ; British resident at Venice ; F.R.S. and F.S.A. ; governor of Isle of Wight ; M.P., Newport, Isle of Wight, 1774–84, and Newtown, Isle of Wight, 1790–3 and 1796–1801 ; travelled in Levant, 1785–7, and made collection of statues, reliefs, and gems, an account of which he published, 1794–1803. [lxiii. 36]

WORSLEY, WILLIAM (1435?-1499), dean of St. Paul's ; possibly educated at Cambridge ; collated prebendary of Lichfield, 1449, Southwell, 1453, and York, 1457 ; rector of Eakring, Nottinghamshire, 1467 ; archdeacon of Nottingham, 1476 ; dean of St. Paul's, London, 1479 ; archdeacon of Taunton, 1493-6 ; attainted of high treason for complicity in conspiracy in favour of Perkin Warbeck [q. v.], 1494 ; pardoned, 1495. [lxiii. 37]

WORTH, CHARLES FREDERICK (1825-1895), dressmaker ; apprenticed as linendraper to Messrs. Swan & Edgar, London ; practised with great success in partnership as lady's tailor in Paris from 1858, and worked independently from 1870. [lxiii. 38]

WORTH, RICHARD NICHOLLS (1837-1896), journalist and geologist ; member of staff of Devonport and Plymouth ' Telegraph,' 1858 ; on staff of ' Western Morning News,' 1863-6 and 1867 ; edited ' Northern Daily Express ' at Newcastle, 1866-7 ; joined publishing and printing firm of Brendon & Son, Plymouth, 1877 ; published numerous historical and geological papers relating to Devon and Cornwall. [lxiii. 38]

WORTH, WILLIAM (1677-1742), classical scholar and divine ; M.A. St. Edmund Hall, Oxford, 1698 ; fellow of All Souls College, Oxford, 1702 ; archdeacon of Worcester, 1705-42 ; D.D., 1719 ; canon of Worcester, 1716-1742 ; held various rectories ; published edition of ' Tatiani Oratio ad Græcos. Hermiæ irrisio gentilium philosophorum,' 1700. [lxiii. 39]

WORTHINGTON, HUGH (1752-1813), Arian divine : studied at Daventry academy under Caleb Ashworth [q. v.] ; pastor, Salters' Hall, London, 1782 ; trustee of Dr. Williams's foundations, 1785, and was lecturer on classics and logic, 1786-9 ; published sermons and other writings. [lxiii. 39]

WORTHINGTON, JOHN (1618-1671), master of Jesus College, Cambridge ; M.A. Emmanuel College, Cambridge, 1639 ; fellow, 1642 ; university preacher, 1646 ; D.D., 1655 ; master of Jesus College, 1650 ; rector of Fen Ditton, Cambridgeshire, 1654-63 ; vice-chancellor of Cambridge University, 1657-8 ; displaced from mastership, 1660 ; held livings of Barking and Needham, Suffolk, and Moulton All Saints, Norfolk, 1663 ; preacher at St. Benet Fink's, London, 1664 ; rector of Ingoldsby, Lincolnshire, and prebendary of Lincoln, 1666 ; published religious and other writings, including an edition of the works of Joseph Mede [q. v.]. [lxiii. 40]

WORTHINGTON, THOMAS (1549-1622 ?), president of Douay College ; born at Blainsco, near Wigan ; B.A. Brasenose College, Oxford, 1570 ; entered English college, Douay, 1573 ; B.D., 1577 ; removed with college to Rheims, 1578 ; joined English mission ; imprisoned in Tower of London, 1584, and banished, 1585 ; D.D. Trier University, 1588 ; president of English College, Douay, 1599 ; removed owing to jesuitical innovations which he introduced under influence of Robert Parsons (1546-1610) [q. v.] ; went to Rome and was made apostolic notary ; came on the mission to England and there died ; published theological and other works. [lxiii. 42]

WORTHINGTON, THOMAS (1671-1754), Dominican friar ; born at Blainsco ; educated at St. Omer ; entered Dominican order at Bornhem, Flanders, 1691 ; ordained priest, 1695 ; elected prior of Bornhem, 1705, 1708, 1718, and 1725 ; prior provincial in England, 1708-18, and 1725 ; D.D., 1718 ; published ' History of Convent of Bornhem,' 1719, and other works. [lxiii. 43]

WORTHINGTON, WILLIAM (1703-1778), divine ; B.A. Jesus College, Oxford, 1726 ; M.A. St. John's College, Cambridge, 1742 ; incorporated M.A. Oxford, 1758 ; B.D. and D.D. Oxford, 1758 ; chaplain to Archbishop Drummond ; received stall in cathedral of York, 1762 ; published theological works. [lxiii. 44]

WORTLEY, STUART-. [See STUART-WORTLEY.]

WORTLEY, SIR FRANCIS, first baronet (1591-1652), poet ; of Magdalen College, Oxford ; knighted, 1610 ; created baronet, 1611 ; M.P., East Retford, 1624 and 1625 ; supported Charles I in south Yorkshire, 1642 ; captured and imprisoned in Tower of London, 1644-c. 1649 ; published ' Characters and Elegies,' 1646, and other works. He was a friend of Ben Jonson, and contributed to ' Jonsonus Virbius,' 1638. [lxiii. 44]

WORTLEY - MONTAGU, EDWARD (1713-1776). [See MONTAGU.]

WORTLEY-MONTAGU, LADY MARY (1689-1762). [See MONTAGU.]

WOTTON, BARON (d. 1683). [See KIRKHOVEN, CHARLES HENRY.]

WOTTON, ANTHONY (1561? - 1626), divine ; of Eton and King's College, Cambridge ; M.A., 1587 ; B.D., 1594 ; fellow ; first professor of divinity at Gresham College, 1596-8 ; lecturer at All Hallows, Barking, 1598-1626 ; accused of socinianism by George Walker (1581?-1651) [q. v.], a long controversy ensuing ; published theological works. [lxiii. 46]

WOTTON, SIR EDWARD (1489-1551), treasurer of Calais ; knighted, 1528 ; sheriff of Kent, 1529 and 1536 ; accompanied Henry VIII to Calais, 1532 ; treasurer of Calais, 1540 ; nominated by Henry VIII privy councillor to his son Edward ; took part in Warwick's scheme for overthrowing Somerset, 1549. [lxiii. 47]

WOTTON, EDWARD (1492-1555), physician and naturalist ; educated at Magdalen College school and Magdalen College, Oxford ; B.A., 1514 ; fellow, 1516 ; first reader in Greek at Corpus Christi College, 1521 ; M.D. Padua ; incorporated M.D. Oxford, 1526 ; F.R.C.P., 1528 ; censor, 1552, 1553, and 1555, and president, 1541, 1542, and 1543 ; acquired a European reputation by his ' De Differentiis Animalium,' 1552. [lxiii. 48]

WOTTON, EDWARD, first BARON WOTTON (1548-1626), son of Thomas Wotton (1521-1587) [q. v.] ; studied on continent ; employed in diplomatic business by Walsingham ; secretary to embassy at Vienna, 1575 ; knight of shire for Kent, 1584 ; envoy to James VI of Scotland to persuade him to enter offensive and defensive alliance and take Dutch under his protection, 1585, but was unsuccessful ; sent to France to explain to Henri III the intrigues of Mary Queen of Scots against Queen Elizabeth, 1586 ; entered Gray's Inn, 1588 ; knighted, 1591 ; sheriff of Kent, 1595 ; privy councillor and comptroller of household, 1602 ; created Baron Wotton of Marley, 1603 ; lord-lieutenant of Kent ; ambassador extraordinary to France, 1610 ; commissioner of treasury, 1612 ; treasurer of household, 1616-17. [lxiii. 49]

WOTTON, SIR HENRY (1568-1639), diplomatist and poet ; son of Thomas Wotton (1521-1587) [q. v.] ; of Winchester and New and Queen's colleges, Oxford ; B.A., 1588 ; travelled on continent ; entered Middle Temple, 1595 ; became agent and secretary to Earl of Essex, 1595, and was employed by him in collecting foreign intelligence ; settled at Venice, and there wrote ' The State of Christendom ' (published, 1657) ; knighted, 1603 ; ambassador at court of Venice, 1604-12, 1616-19, and 1621-4 ; while on a visit to Augsburg, wrote in his host's album a definition of an ambassador (' peregre missus ad mentiendum Reipublicæ causa ') which Scioppius mentioned in his printed diatribe against James I, 1611 ; M.P., Appleby, 1614 ; went on diplomatic missions to France, 1612, the Hague, 1614, and Vienna, 1620 ; provost of Eton, 1624-39 ; M.P., Sandwich, 1625 ; received deacon's orders, 1627. He published ' Elements of Architecture,' 1624. A collection of his poetical and other writings appeared under the title ' Reliquiæ Wottonianæ ' (containing his famous ' Character of a Happy Life ' and ' On his Mistress, the Queen of Bohemia '), 1651 (enlarged editions, 1672 and 1685). [lxiii. 51]

WOTTON, NICHOLAS (1497?-1567), secretary of state, diplomatist, and dean of Canterbury and York ; brother of Sir Edward Wotton [q. v.] ; perhaps graduated in civil and canon law at Oxford ; studied in Italy and was D.C.L. and D.D. ; held living of Boughton Malherbe, 1517 ; vicar of Sutton Valence, 1518-30 ; official to Tunstall, bishop of London ; in France on business relating to Henry VIII's divorce, 1530 ; received living of Ivychurch, 1530 ; commissary of faculties to Cranmer, 1538 ; one of ambassadors sent to negotiate Henry VIII's marriage with Anne of Cleves, 1539 ; nominated archdeacon of Gloucester, 1539 ; sole ambassador to dukes of Saxony and Cleves, 1539 ; dean of Canterbury, 1541 ; dean of York, 1544 ; prebendary of York, 1546 ; sent to court of Charles V's sister Mary, regent of the Netherlands, 1543, and later to court of Charles V ; privy councillor, 1546 ; commissioner to arrange peace with France, 1546 ; resident ambassador in France, 1546-9 and 1553-7 ; secretary of state, 1549–50; ambassador to Charles V, 1551; again commissioner for peace with France, 1558; joint-ambassador to Scotland, 1560; sent to arrange commercial treaty with Netherlands, 1565–6. [lxiii. 57]

WOTTON, THOMAS (1521–1587), son of Sir Edward Wotton [q. v.]; imprisoned, 1554, probably for his religious opinions; sheriff of Kent, 1558 and 1579.

[lxiii. 48]

WOTTON, THOMAS (d. 1766), compiler of the 'Baronetage'; bookseller in London; warden of Stationers' Company, 1754, and master, 1757; published 'English Baronetage. Being a Genealogical and Historical Account of their Families,' 1727. [lxiii. 61]

WOTTON, WILLIAM (1666–1727), scholar; acquired at early age knowledge of Latin, Greek, and Hebrew; B.A. Catharine Hall, Cambridge, 1679; fellow of St. John's College, Cambridge, 1683; M.A., 1683; B.D., 1691; F.R.S., 1687; published 'Reflections upon Ancient and Modern Learning' (1694), a contribution on side of the moderns to the controversy between Sir William Temple and Monsieur Perrault; received living of Llandrill-yn-Rhôs, 1691; rector of Middleton Keynes; prebendary of Salisbury, 1705–26; D.D. Lambeth, 1707; published theological and other works. [lxiii. 61]

WOTY, WILLIAM (1731?–1791), versifier; worked as clerk to a solicitor in London, and later as a Grub-street writer; published poetical writings. [lxiii. 63]

WOULFE, PETER (1727?–1803), chemist and mineralogist; first discovered native tin in Cornwall, 1766; F.R.S., 1767; invented 'Woulfe's bottle' (an apparatus for the passing of gases through liquids); received Copley medal for paper (1767) on 'Experiments on Distillation of Acids,' &c., 1768; believer in alchemy. [lxiii. 63]

WOULFE, STEPHEN (1787–1840), Irish judge; educated at Stonyhurst and Trinity College, Dublin; called to Irish bar, 1814; took part in Irish politics as agitator for Roman catholic emancipation; crown counsel for Munster, 1830; third serjeant, 1834; M.P., Cashel, 1835–8; solicitor-general for Ireland, 1836, and attorney-general, 1838; chief-baron of Irish exchequer, 1838, being the first Roman catholic appointed. [lxiii. 64]

WRANGHAM, FRANCIS (1769 – 1842), classical scholar and miscellaneous writer; B.A., second Smith's prizeman, and senior chancellor's medallist, Trinity Hall, Cambridge, 1790, as third wrangler; M.A., 1793; rector of Hunmanby-with-Muston, near Filey, and vicar of Folkton, Yorkshire, 1795; won several prizes for poems at Cambridge; F.R.S., 1804; examining chaplain to Vernon Harcourt, archbishop of York, 1814–34; archdeacon of Cleveland, 1820–8, and of East Riding, 1828–41; vicar of Thorpe Bassett, 1820–7; prebendary of York, 1823, and of Chester, 1827; member of Bannatyne and Roxburghe Clubs. His works include 'The British Plutarch,' new edit., 1816, translations from Homer, Virgil, and Horace, and numerous theological, poetical, and other writings. He founded, 1842, a prize at Trinity College, Cambridge, whither he removed from Trinity Hall, c. 1792.

[lxiii. 65]

WRATISLAW, ALBERT HENRY (1822–1892), Slavonic scholar; educated at Rugby and Trinity and Christ's colleges, Cambridge; B.A., 1844; fellow of Christ's College, 1844–53; M.A., 1847; visited Bohemia and studied Czech language; head-master of Felsted school, 1850–5, and of King Edward VI.'s grammar school, Bury St. Edmunds, 1855–79; held living of Manorbier, Pembrokeshire, 1879–89; published numerous prose and verse translations from Slavonic languages, including 'Adventures of Baron Wenceslas Wratislaw of Mitrowitz,' 1862, and 'The Queen's Court Manuscript, with other ancient Bohemian Poems' (written 1290), 1852.

[lxiii. 68]

WRAXALL, SIR FREDERIC CHARLES LASCELLES, third baronet (1828–1865), miscellaneous writer; grandson of Sir Nathaniel William Wraxall [q. v.]; of St. Mary Hall, Oxford; first-class assistant commissary, with rank of captain, in Turkish contingent in Crimea, 1855; conducted 'Naval and Military Gazette,' 1858, and 'The Welcome Guest,' 1860–1; published 'The Life and Times of Caroline Matilda, Queen of Denmark and Norway,' 1864, several novels, and works on military matters

[lxiii. 69]

WRAXALL, SIR NATHANIEL WILLIAM, first baronet (1751–1831), author of historical memoirs; joined civil service of East India Company and went to Bombay, 1769; judge-advocate and paymaster of forces in Guzerat expedition and that against Baroche, 1771; returned to England, 1772; engaged by Danish exiled nobles in negotiations with George III with view to replacing George's sister Caroline Matilda (d. 1775) on throne of Denmark, 1774–5; M.P., Hindon, 1780, Ludgershall, 1784, Wallingford, 1790–4; acted as agent for the nabob of Arcot; created baronet, 1813; published, 1815, 'Historical Memoirs of my own Time, 1772–1784,' which excited much hostile criticism, though its portraits of minor political characters are of real historical value. His other works include 'Posthumous Memoirs of his own Time,' 1836, and several volumes relating to history of France, to continental courts, and to his travels. The 'Historical and Posthumous Memoirs' were edited by Mr. H. B. Wheatley, 1884. [lxiii. 71]

WRAY, SIR CECIL, thirteenth baronet (1734–1805), politician; cornet, 1st dragoons, 1755–7; captain of troop of yeomanry; M.P., East Retford, 1768–80, Westminster, 1782–4; contested Westminster unsuccessfully against Hood and Fox, 1784, the election attracting wide notice in satire and caricature. [lxiii. 74]

WRAY, SIR CHRISTOPHER (1524–1592), judge; educated at Buckingham (afterwards Magdalene) College, Cambridge, of which he became a liberal benefactor; barrister, Lincoln's Inn, 1550, treasurer, 1566, reader, 1562 and 1567; serjeant-at-law, 1567; queen's serjeant, 1567; M.P., Boroughbridge, Yorkshire, 1553–8, Great Grimsby, Lincolnshire, 1563–7, Ludgershall, Wiltshire, 1571; speaker of House of Commons, 1571; justice, 1572, and chief-justice, 1574, of queen's bench; on ecclesiastical commission, 1589; assessor to tribunal at Fotheringay before which Mary Queen of Scots pleaded in vain for her life, 1586. [lxiii. 75]

WRAY, SIR CHRISTOPHER (1601–1646), grandson of Sir Christopher Wray (1524–1592) [q. v.]; knighted, 1623; M.P. for Great Grimsby in Long parliament; commissioner of admiralty, 1645. [lxiii. 77]

WRAY, DANIEL (1701–1783), antiquary; M.A. Queens' College, Cambridge, 1728; incorporated at Oxford, 1731; F.R.S., 1729; F.S.A., 1741; deputy-teller of exchequer to Philip Yorke (afterwards second Earl of Hardwicke) [q. v.], 1745–82; trustee of British Museum, 1765; published and left writings on antiquarian subjects. He is among those who have been identified with Junius. [lxiii. 78]

WRAY, SIR DRURY (1633–1710), son of Sir Christopher Wray (1601–1646); succeeded as ninth baronet of Glentworth, c. 1689; fought for James II at battle of Boyne. [lxiii. 77]

WRAY, SIR JOHN (1586–1655), baronet; parliamentarian; knighted, 1612; succeeded to baronetcy, 1617; M.P., Lincoln, in Charles I's first, third, and fourth parliaments, and in Long parliament; high sheriff of Lincolnshire; opposed forced loan and ship-money; took covenant, 1643; one of conservators of peace with Scotland, 1646; one of early patrons of Edward Rainbowe [q. v.] [lxiii. 79]

WREN, SIR CHRISTOPHER (1632–1723), architect; son of Christopher Wren (1591–1658), who was dean of Windsor, 1635–58; born at East Knoyle; of Westminster School and Wadham College, Oxford; M.A., 1653; fellow of All Souls College, 1653–61; professor of astronomy at Gresham College, London, 1657–61; Savilian professor of astronomy at Oxford, 1661–73; D.C.L. Oxford and LL.D. Cambridge, 1661; initiated experiments on subject of variations of the barometer; devoted much attention to anatomical and medical subjects; prominent member of the circle which was incorporated as the Royal Society, drew up preamble of the charter, 1660, was president, 1680–2, and made original communications on a great variety of subjects; probably applied himself to architecture, c. 1663; assistant to Sir John Denham (1615–1669) [q. v.]; surveyor-general to Charles II's works, 1661; built chapel of Pembroke College, Cambridge, 1663–5, Sheldonian Theatre, Oxford, 1664–9, and chapel of Emmanuel College, Cambridge, 1668; prepared scheme for rebuilding London after fire, 1666, and was appointed 'surveyor general and principal architect for rebuilding the whole city'; appointed sole deputy to Denham as surveyor general of royal works, 1669, and succeeded Denham on his death later in year; engaged in pulling down and rebuilding St. Paul's Cathedral, 1668; completed first design for new cathedral, 1673, but was compelled, after a start had been made, to abandon it; obtained royal approval, 1675, of design which he modified into that of present existing cathedral (choir opened for service, 1697); dismissed from superintendence, the work being reported as finished, 1716; made designs for rebuilding of Temple Bar, 1670–2, and various works in the Temple; comptroller of works in Windsor Castle, 1684; M.P., Plympton, 1685, Windsor in Convention parliament, 1689, Weymouth, 1701; built fifty-two churches in London, among the most notable of which were (1670–5) St. Benet Fink, St. Mary-at-Hill, St. Mary-le-Bow, St. Stephen Walbrook, and St. Dionis Backchurch (1675–80), St. Ann and St. Agnes, St. Bride, St. Lawrence, and St. Swithin, (1680–5) All Hallows, Thames Street, St. Antholin, St. Clement Danes, St. James, Garlickhithe, St. James, Westminster, St. Martin, Ludgate, St. Mary Magdalene, Old Fish Street, and St. Peter, Cornhill, (1685–90) St. Andrew, Holborn, St. Mary, Lothbury, and St. Mary Abchurch, (1690–5) St. Michael Royal, St. Augustin and St. Faith (spire), St. Mary Somerset (tower), St. Vedast (the steeple), (1700) steeple of St. Dunstan-in-the-East, (1704) steeple of Christ Church, Newgate Street, (1705) and that of St. Magnus; steeple of St. Michael, Cornhill, built from his designs in 1722; was appointed surveyor to Westminster Abbey, 1698, and executed repairs and designs for additions, including the western towers (which, however, were completed with new details by his successors); built Monument commemorating fire of London, 1671–8, library of Trinity College, Cambridge, 1677–92, Chelsea Hospital, 1682, Marlborough House, London, and numerous additions to Hampton Court Palace; superseded in office of surveyor general, 1718; buried in St. Paul's Cathedral. His portrait by Sir Godfrey Kneller is in the National Portrait Gallery. [lxiii. 80]

WREN, CHRISTOPHER (1675–1747), biographer; son of Sir Christopher Wren [q. v.]; of Eton and Pembroke Hall, Cambridge; M.P., Warwick, 1713–15; collected documents which form the 'Parentalia,' published by Stephen Wren, 1750. [lxiii. 94]

WREN, MATTHEW (1585–1667), bishop of Ely; B.A. Pembroke Hall, Cambridge, 1605; fellow, 1605; M.A., 1608; incorporated at Oxford, 1608; chaplain to Prince Charles, 1622; D.D. Cambridge, 1623, Oxford, 1636; prebendary of Winchester, 1623; master of Peterhouse, 1635; dean of Windsor and registrar of the Garter, 1628; clerk of the closet, 1633; governor of Charterhouse, London, 1634; bishop of Hereford, 1634; prebendary of Westminster, 1635; bishop of Norwich, 1635; dean of Chapel Royal, London, 1636–41; bishop of Ely, 1638; acted under supervision of Laud, after whose impeachment he was imprisoned in Tower of London, 1642–60. [lxiii. 94]

WREN, MATTHEW (1629–1672), son of Matthew Wren (1585–1667) [q. v.]; M.A. Oxford, 1661; secretary to Clarendon, 1660–7; M.P. for St. Michael, 1661–72; one of original council of Royal Society, 1662. [lxiii. 96]

WRENCH, BENJAMIN (1778–1843), actor; joined Tate Wilkinson's company and played at York and Edinburgh, his parts including Othello; at Bath, 1805, at Drury Lane, London, 1809–15, playing, among other parts, Captain Absolute and Loveless ('Trip to Scarborough'); made great success as Corinthian Tom in Moncrieff's 'Tom and Jerry' at Adelphi, London, 1821; in London at Covent Garden, 1826, Lyceum, 1830, and Olympic, 1840; last appeared at Haymarket, London. [lxiii. 96]

WRENN, RALPH (d. 1692), commodore; lieutenant in Mediterranean, 1679–81; commander, 1681; at the Nore, 1688; commodore, 1690; in West Indies, 1691; died of sickness after bravely fought action with French. [lxiii. 98]

WREY, SIR BOURCHIER (d. 1696), baronet; commanded regiment of horse after Restoration; M.P. for Liskeard, 1678–9 and 1689–96, Devonshire, 1685; fought two duels with members of parliament. [lxiii. 98]

WREY, SIR BOURCHIER (1714–1784), dilettante; grandson of Sir Bourchier Wrey (d. 1696) [q. v.]; baronet; of Winchester College and New College, Oxford; M.P., Barnstaple, 1748; member of Society of Dilettanti, 1742. [lxiii. 99]

WRIGHT, ABRAHAM (1611–1690), divine and author; educated at Merchant Taylors' School and St. John's College, Oxford; fellow, 1632; M.A., 1637; appointed vicar of Oakham, Rutland, 1645, but did not take possession till 1660; expelled from fellowship by parliamentary commission; minister of St. Olave in Silver Street, London, 1655–9; published 'Delitiæ Delitiarum' (a collection of epigrams), 1637, 'Parnassus Biceps' (a collection of poetical pieces), 1656, and several religious and other works. [lxiii. 99]

WRIGHT, CHRISTOPHER (1570?–1605), conspirator; employed in Spain to solicit aid for Roman catholics in England, 1603; brother of John Wright (1568?–1605) [q. v.], with whom he was killed at Holbeche. [lxiii. 110]

WRIGHT, EDWARD (1558?–1615), mathematician and hydrographer; M.A. Caius College, Cambridge, 1584; fellow, 1587–96; accompanied George Clifford, third earl of Cumberland [q. v.], in voyage to Azores, 1589; published, 1599, 'Certaine Errors in Navigation, arising either of the . . . sea chart, compasse, crosse staffe, and tables of declination of the sunne and fixed starres, detected and corrected,' which with other works by him effected a revolution in the science of navigation. [lxiii. 100]

WRIGHT, EDWARD RICHARD (1813–1859), actor; in trade in London; appeared in London at Queen's Theatre, 1834, St. James's, 1837; acted chiefly at Adelphi, London, from 1838; successively at Princess's, Lyceum, Haymarket, and Sadler's Wells, London, 1852–5; among his best-known impersonations Master Grinnidge in 'Green Bushes' and John Grumley in 'Domestic Economy.' [lxiii. 102]

WRIGHT, FORTUNATUS (d. 1757), merchant and privateer; engaged in business at Liverpool; settled as merchant at Leghorn, c. 1741; commanded a privateer, 1746; imprisoned by Tuscan government for seizing Turkish property on board a French ship, 1747–8; again engaged as privateer on declaration of war, 1756, and after several prizes was probably lost at sea. [lxiii. 103]

WRIGHT, FRANCES (1795–1852). [See DARUSMONT, FRANCES.]

WRIGHT, GEORGE NEWENHAM (1790?–1877), miscellaneous writer; B.A. Trinity College, Dublin, 1814; M.A., 1817; M.A. Oxford, 1836; ordained priest, 1818; reader of St. Mary Woolnoth, London; master of Tewkesbury grammar school; published topographical, biographical, and other writings. [lxiii. 104]

WRIGHT, ICHABOD CHARLES (1795–1871), translator of Dante; of Eton and Christ Church, Oxford; M.A., 1820; fellow of Magdalen College, Oxford, 1819–25; joint-manager of bank at Nottingham, 1825; published metrical translations of Dante's 'Divina Commedia,' 1833–40, and Homer's 'Iliad,' 1859–64, and works on economical questions. [lxiii. 105]

WRIGHT, JAMES (1643–1713), antiquary and miscellaneous writer; son of Abraham Wright [q. v.]; entered New Inn, 1666; barrister, Middle Temple, 1672; published 'Historia Histrionica,' 1699, 'Country Conversations,' 1694, 'History and Antiquities of . . . Rutland,' 1684, and other works. [lxiii. 106]

WRIGHT, SIR JAMES, first baronet (1716–1785), governor of Georgia; barrister, Gray's Inn, 1741; practised at Charleston and was attorney-general of South Carolina, c. 1739; agent for the colony in England; lieutenant-governor of Georgia, 1760; captain-general and governor-in-chief 1761; exerted his influence in support of home government on passing of Stamp Act, 1765; in England, 1771–3; created baronet, 1772; compelled to fly from opposition of colonial patriots, 1776, and was in England, 1776–8; was sent, 1779, to reorganise government of Georgia on its recovery by (Sir) Archibald Campbell (1739–1791) [q. v.], but receiving orders to abandon the province, 1782, proceeded to England, where he died. [lxiii. 107]

WRIGHT, JOHN (1568?–1605), conspirator; became a Roman catholic, c. 1601, when he was implicated in Essex's rising; one of first initiated by Catesby into Gunpowder plot, 1604; died of wounds received from Sir Richard Walsh's men at Holbeche. [lxiii. 109]

WRIGHT, JOHN (1805–1843?), Scottish poet; son of a coal-driver of Sorn, Ayrshire; apprenticed as weaver;

found patrons at Edinburgh, and published, 1825, 'The Retrospect,' and other poems, which attracted considerable notice ; his ' Whole Poetical Works ' published, 1843. [lxiii. 110]

WRIGHT, JOHN (1770?-1844), bookseller and author; apprenticed to a silk-mercer; opened business as bookseller in Piccadilly, London, his shop becoming the general morning resort of the friends of Pitt's ministry; published the 'Anti-Jacobin,' edited by William Gifford (1756-1826) [q. v.], 1797-8; came into contact with William Cobbett [q. v.], became his hack, and superintended publication of ' Weekly Political Register'; edited Cobbett's 'Parliamentary History,' 'Parliamentary Debates,' and 'State Trials,' but afterwards quarrelled with him; was employed in literary work by the publishers John Murray (1778-1843) [q. v.] and Richard Bentley (1794-1871) [q. v.], and edited various works, including 'Sir Henry Cavendish's Debates of the House of Commons ' (forty-eight volumes of shorthand notes), 1839-43. [lxiii. 111]

WRIGHT, JOHN MASEY (1777-1866), water-colour painter; apprenticed as organ-builder; worked on panoramas for Henry Aston Barker [q. v.]; exhibited at Royal Academy, 1812-18; member of Water-colour Society, 1825 ; illustrated Shakespeare and other poets. [lxiii. 112]

WRIGHT, JOHN MICHAEL (1625 ?-1700), portrait-painter; perhaps pupil of George Jamesone [q. v.]; studied and resided in Italy; practised in England during Commonwealth and later, and became rival of Lely; painted many portraits of judges placed in Guildhall; ' major domo' in suite of Roger Palmer, earl of Castlemaine [q. v.], in embassy from James II to Innocent XI at Rome, 1686; signed his pictures 'J. M. Ritus.' [lxiii. 113]

WRIGHT, JOHN WESLEY (1769-1805), commander in navy; at siege of Gibraltar, 1781-3; in merchant's office in London, 1785; visited Russia; midshipman, with Sir William Sidney Smith [q. v.], 1794; prisoner in France, 1796-8; lieutenant, 1800; was captured at Quiberon Bay, 1804, and died mysteriously in Paris. [lxiii. 114]

WRIGHT, JOHN WILLIAM (1802-1848), water-colour-painter; exhibited at Royal Academy from 1825; member of Water-colour Society, 1842, and secretary, 1844. [lxiii. 115]

WRIGHT, JOSEPH (1756-1793), portrait-painter; son of Mrs. Patience Wright [q. v.]; first draughtsman and die-sinker to mint at Philadelphia. [lxiii. 122]

WRIGHT, JOSEPH (1734-1797), painter; born at Derby, where he practised as portrait-painter; exhibited at Society of Artists in London, chiefly candlelight or firelight scenes, 1765-73, and chiefly scenes of conflagration from 1773; in Italy, 1773-5; exhibited at Royal Academy, 1778-82, chiefly scenes in Italy; A.R.A., 1781; was elected R.A., 1784, but declined honour; painted scene from 'Tempest' for Boydell's 'Shakespeare Gallery'; among his best-known works 'The Orrery' (1766), 'The Gladiator' (1765), 'The Air-pump' (1768, in National Gallery), 'Edwin' and 'Maria' (c. 1780), and 'A Dead Soldier' (1789). His portrait by himself is in the National Portrait Gallery. [lxiii. 115]

WRIGHT, LAURENCE (1590-1657), physician; B.A. Emmanuel College, Cambridge, 1609; M.A., 1618; F.R.C.P., 1622, censor, 1628 and 1639, and conciliarius, 1647 and 1650-7; physician in ordinary to Cromwell and to the London Charterhouse, 1624-43. [lxiii. 118]

WRIGHT, LAWRENCE (d. 1713), commodore; lieutenant in 1665; captain, c. 1672; commodore and commander-in-chief of expedition to West Indies, 1689; with General Codrington reduced St. Christopher's, took possession of St. Eustatius, and made unsuccessful attack on Guadeloupe; commissioner of navy of Kinsale, 1702-13; extra commissioner on navy board, 1713. [lxiii. 118]

WRIGHT, LEONARD (fl. 1591), controversialist; a prominent champion of the bishops' cause in Martin Mar-Prelate controversy. [lxiii. 120]

WRIGHT, SIR NATHAN (1654-1721), judge; educated at Emmanuel College, Cambridge; barrister, Inner Temple, 1677, bencher, 1692; recorder of Leicester, 1680-4 and 1688; junior counsel for crown against the seven bishops, 1688; serjeant-at-law, 1692; knighted and made king's serjeant, 1697; lord keeper of great seal and privy

councillor, 1700; dismissed from office by the Marlborough and Godolphin coalition, 1705. [lxiii. 120]

WRIGHT, MRS. PATIENCE (1725-1786), wax-modeller; née Lovell; born at Bordentown, New Jersey; practised as portrait-modeller in wax and came to London, 1772. [lxiii. 121]

WRIGHT, PETER (1603-1651), jesuit; born in Northamptonshire; enlisted in the English army in Holland, but soon left it, and joined the jesuits at Watten, 1629; studied at Liège and was (1639) prefect in the English jesuit college at St. Omer; camp commissioner to the English and Irish forces at Ghent, 1642; missioner in England; condemned under the statute 27 Elizabeth and hanged at Tyburn. [lxiii. 122]

WRIGHT, RICHARD (1735-1775 ?), marine-painter; exhibited with Society of Artists, London, between 1760 and 1773. [lxiii. 122]

WRIGHT, RICHARD (1764-1836), unitarian missionary; apprenticed to a shopkeeper; joined independent church at Guestwick, 1780, but was excommunicated for village preaching on week nights; minister to general and Sabellian particular baptist congregations at Norwich and Wisbech; joined unitarians and travelled as missionary in England, Wales, and Scotland; baptist minister at Trowbridge, Wiltshire, 1822, and Kirkstead, Lincolnshire, 1827; published theological writings. [lxiii. 122]

WRIGHT, ROBERT (1553 ?-1596 ?), scholar; fellow, Trinity College, Cambridge, 1571; M.A., 1574; incorporated M.A. Oxford, 1577; tutor to Robert Devereux, second earl of Essex; clerk of stables when Essex was Queen Elizabeth's master of the horse. [lxiii. 124]

WRIGHT, ROBERT (1556?-1624), divine; M.A. Trinity College, Cambridge, 1578; incorporated M.A. Oxford, 1581; ordained in Genevan form at Antwerp; chaplain to Robert, second lord Rich, c. 1580; imprisoned in Fleet by court of ecclesiastical commission, 1581-2; rector of Dennington, Suffolk, 1584-1624. [lxiii. 125]

WRIGHT, ROBERT (1560-1643), bishop successively of Bristol and of Lichfield and Coventry; B.A. Trinity College, Oxford, 1580; fellow, 1581; M.A., 1584; D.D., 1597; canon residentiary and treasurer of Wells, 1601; chaplain to Queen Elizabeth; chaplain in ordinary to James I; first warden of Wadham College, Oxford, 1613; bishop of Bristol, 1622, and of Lichfield and Coventry, 1632; acted with Laud in crises of 1640 and after; committed to Tower of London for participation in the protest of the eleven bishops, 1641; died at Eccleshall Hall during siege by Sir William Brereton. [lxiii. 123]

WRIGHT, alias DANVERS, ROBERT, called VISCOUNT PURBECK (1621 ?-1674). [See DANVERS.]

WRIGHT, SIR ROBERT (d. 1689), lord chief-justice; M.A. Peterhouse, Cambridge, 1661; barrister, Lincoln's Inn; went Norfolk circuit; M.P., King's Lynn, 1668; counsel for Cambridge University, 1678; serjeant, 1679; king's serjeant, 1680; knighted, 1680; chief-justice of Glamorgan, 1681; baron of exchequer, 1684; recorder of Cambridge, 1685; accompanied Jeffreys on western assize after Monmouth's rebellion; removed to king's bench, 1685; chief-justice of common pleas, 1687; chief-justice of king's bench, 1687; sent as ecclesiastical commissioner to Oxford, 1687; presided at trial of seven bishops, 1688; impeached of high treason by William of Orange, 1688; died in Newgate. [lxiii. 125]

WRIGHT, SAMUEL (1683-1746), dissenting divine; studied at nonconformist academy of Timothy Jollie (1659 ?-1714) [q. v.] at Attercliffe; ordained minister of congregation at Meeting House Court, Knightrider Street, London, 1708; lecturer at Salters' Hall, London, 1724; trustee of Dr. Williams's foundations, 1724; D.D. Edinburgh, 1729; removed to meeting house in Carter Lane, Doctors' Commons, London, 1734; published theological writings. [lxiii. 127]

WRIGHT, THOMAS (fl. 1604), philosopher; protégé of Henry Wriothesley, third earl of Southampton [q. v.]; published philosophical writings. [lxiii. 128]

WRIGHT, THOMAS (d. 1624 ?), Roman catholic controversialist; reader of divinity in English College, Douay, 1569; D.D.; worked on mission in Yorkshire, and

3 A

was frequently imprisoned, 1577-85; vice-president of English College at Douay, when temporarily removed to Rheims; dean of Courtray. [lxiii. 128]

WRIGHT, THOMAS (1711–1786), natural philosopher; was offered, but declined, the professorship of mathematics at the Imperial Academy of St. Petersburg; anticipated the modern physico-philosophical theory of the material universe; published ' Louthiana or an introduction to the Antiquities of Ireland,' 1748, and other works. [lxiii. 128]

WRIGHT, THOMAS (1792–1849), engraver and portrait-painter; apprenticed to Henry Meyer [q. v.]; assistant to William Thomas Fry [q. v.]; associated with George Dawe [q. v.], whom he accompanied in St. Petersburg, 1822-6; again in Russia, 1830-45. [lxiii. 129]

WRIGHT, THOMAS (1789–1875), prison philanthropist; apprenticed to an iron-founder and became foreman; joined congregationalists, 1817; deacon of chapel in Grosvenor Street, Piccadilly, London, 1825–75; began work of reclamation of discharged prisoners, and obtained permission to visit Salford prison, c. 1838; offered, but declined, post of government travelling inspector of prisons. [lxiii. 129]

WRIGHT, THOMAS (1810–1877), antiquary; M.A. Trinity College, Cambridge, 1837; published ' History of Essex,' 1831–6; came to London, 1836, and devoted himself to literary work, chiefly antiquarian; F.S.A., 1837; honorary secretary of Camden Society, 1838; treasurer and secretary of Percy Society, 1841, editing for these and other societies, including the Historical Society of Science and Royal Society of Literature, many publications; produced several works in collaboration with James Orchard Halliwell (afterwards Halliwell-Phillipps) [q. v.]; assisted in founding British Archæological Association, 1843; superintended work of excavating site of Roman city at Wroxeter, 1859. His publications include ' Queen Elizabeth and her Times,' 1838, and ' History of Domestic Manners and Sentiments in England during the Middle Ages,' 1862. [lxiii. 130]

WRIGHT, THOMAS (1809–1884), physician and geologist; articled as surgeon in Paisley, Renfrewshire; studied at Royal College of Surgeons, Dublin, and qualified, 1832; practised at Cheltenham, and was surgeon to the general hospital; M.D. St. Andrews, 1846; studied palæontology and formed valuable collection of Jurassic fossils; F.R.S.E., 1855; F.G.S., 1859, and Rollaston medallist, 1878; F.R.S., 1879; published geological writings. [lxiii. 133]

WRIGHT, WALLER RODWELL (d. 1826), author of ' Horæ Ionicæ'; British consul-general for republic of Ionian Islands, 1800-4; president of court of appeals at Malta; published ' Horæ Ionicæ' a Poem descriptive of the Ionian Islands,' 1809. [lxiii. 134]

WRIGHT, WILLIAM (1563–1639), jesuit; born at York; educated at English College, Rome; entered Society of Jesus, 1581; professed of four vows, 1602; professor of philosophy and theology at Gratz in Styria, and at Vienna; D.D. Gratz; joined English mission, 1606; founded missions, originally called Residence of St. Anne, in Leicestershire; rector of the ' college,' and in 1636 minister; vehemently opposed oath of allegiance and supremacy devised by James I's government; published theological writings. [lxiii. 135]

WRIGHT, WILLIAM (1735–1819), physician and botanist; apprenticed as surgeon at Falkirk; studied at Edinburgh University; served as surgeon's mate at Rhé, Lagos, and in West Indies; M.D. St. Andrews; settled in partnership at Hampden, Trelawny, Jamaica; honorary surgeon-general of Jamaica, 1774; came to England, 1777; sailed as regimental surgeon to Jamaica regiment, 1779; captured by French; again sailed for Jamaica, 1782; physician-general of Jamaica, 1784; returned to England, 1785, and settled at Edinburgh; physician to expedition to West Indies under Sir Ralph Abercromby [q. v.], 1796–8; original member and vice-president of Wernerian Society, 1808; F.R.S., 1778; president of Royal College of Physicians, Edinburgh, 1801; associate of Linnean Society, 1807; made valuable natural-history collections relating largely to botany of Jamaica. [lxiii. 136]

WRIGHT, WILLIAM (1773–1860), aural surgeon; practised in Bristol, and from 1817 in London; surgeon-

aurist in ordinary to Queen Charlotte, 1817; published works relating to diseases of the ear. [lxiii. 137]

WRIGHT, WILLIAM (1830–1889), orientalist; graduated at St. Andrews; studied oriental languages at Halle and Leyden; professor of Arabic at University College, London, 1855-6, and Trinity College, Dublin, 1856-61; held post in department of manuscripts at British Museum, 1861-70, and prepared catalogue of Syriac manuscripts; Sir Thomas Adams's professor of Arabic at Cambridge, 1870-89; fellow of Queens' College, Cambridge; member of Old Testament revision committee; works include (Arabic) ' Travels of Ibn Jubair' (1852), ' Opuscula Arabica' (1859), ' Kāmil of Al-Mubarrad' (1864-82), an ' Arabic Grammar' (1859), and (Syriac) ' Book of Kalilah and Dimnah' (1883). [lxiii. 138]

WRIGHT, WILLIAM (1837–1899), missionary and author; studied at Belfast Royal Academical Institution and Queen's College, Belfast; studied theology at Geneva; missionary to Jews at Damascus, c. 1865; editorial superintendent of British and Foreign Bible Society, 1876–99; published ' Empire of the Hittites,' 1884, having made casts of and investigated the Hamath inscriptions, and other works. [lxiii. 139]

WRIGHTSLAND, LORD (1569–1622). [See CRAIG, SIR LEWIS.]

WRIOTHESLEY, CHARLES (1508 ?–1562), herald and chronicler; son of Sir Thomas Wriothesley (d. 1534) [q. v.]; Rouge Croix pursuivant, 1525; entered Gray's Inn, 1529; Windsor herald, 1534-62; wrote chronicle known as ' Wriothesley's Chronicle,' mainly a continuation of chronicle of Richard Arnold [q. v.]. [lxiii. 140]

WRIOTHESLEY, HENRY, second EARL OF SOUTHAMPTON (1545-1581), son of Sir Thomas Wriothesley, first earl of Southampton [q. v.]; succeeded to title, 1550; became involved in scheme for marrying Mary Queen of Scots to Duke of Norfolk, 1569; arrested and confined in Tower of London for conspiracy with Roman catholics, 1569-73. [lxiii. 152]

WRIOTHESLEY, HENRY, third EARL OF SOUTHAMPTON (1573–1624), Shakespeare's patron; son of Henry Wriothesley, second earl of Southampton [q. v.]; M.A. St. John's College, Cambridge, 1589; entered Gray's Inn; became patron of John Florio [q. v.]; presented to Queen Elizabeth, 1590; patron of the poets, including Shakespeare, who dedicated to him ' Venus and Adonis,' 1593, and ' Lucrece,' 1594, and probably enjoyed relations of close intimacy with him; sometimes identified with the anonymous friend and patron described by Shakespeare in his sonnets (published, 1609, but circulated in manuscript earlier), the rival in the patron's esteem (see the Sonnets) perhaps being Barnabe Barnes [q. v.]; involved himself in intrigue with Elizabeth Vernon, one of the queen's waiting-women, 1595, and withdrew from court, 1596; volunteer under Essex in expeditions to Cadiz, 1596, and Azores, 1597; accompanied Sir Robert Cecil on embassy to Paris, 1598; secretly married Elizabeth Vernon and incurred Queen Elizabeth's displeasure; went with Essex to Ireland, 1599, and became involved in Essex's conspiracy; ordered performance at Globe Theatre, London, 7 Feb. 1601, of Shakespeare's ' Richard II' to excite public feeling by presenting on the stage the deposition of a king, and took part in unsuccessful outbreak under Essex, 8 Feb.; imprisoned in Tower of London and condemned to death, but his punishment commuted to imprisonment for life; released by James I, 1603, and made K.G. and captain of Isle of Wight and Carisbrooke Castle; recreated Earl of Southampton, 1603; joined the queen's council, 1604; helped to equip Weymouth's expedition to Virginia, 1605; member of Virginia Company's council, 1609, and treasurer, 1620-4; member of East India Company, 1609; incorporator of North-west Passage Company, 1612, and of Somers Island Company, 1615; volunteer in war in Cleves, 1614; privy councillor, 1619; joined opponents of Buckingham; took command of troop of English volunteers in Low Countries, and died of fever at Bergen-op-Zoom. [lxiii. 140]

WRIOTHESLEY (more correctly WRITH or WRYTHE), SIR JOHN (d. 1504), Garter king-of-arms; faucon herald in reigns of Henry VI and Edward IV; Norroy king-of-arms, 1477; Garter king-of-arms, 1479; head of College of Heralds on its incorporation, 1483. [lxiii. 146]

WRIOTHESLEY (formerly WRITH), SIR THOMAS (*d.* 1534), Garter king-of-arms ; son of Sir John Wriothesley or Writh [q. v.] ; Wallingford pursuivant, 1489 ; Garter king-of-arms, 1504 ; officiated at jousts held at Tournay, 1513 ; knighted by Ferdinand, archduke of Austria, at Nuremberg ; left antiquarian and heraldic manuscripts and collections. [lxiii. 147]

WRIOTHESLEY, SIR THOMAS, first BARON WRIOTHESLEY OF TITCHFIELD and EARL OF SOUTHAMPTON (1505–1550), lord chancellor of England ; grandson of Sir John Wriothesley or Writh [q. v.] ; of King's Hall or St. John's College, Cambridge ; clerk of signet, 1530 ; entered Gray's Inn, 1534 ; 'graver' of the Tower of London, 1536 ; ambassador to regent of Netherlands, Mary, queen of Hungary, to propose marriage between Henry VIII and Duchess of Milan, 1538 ; knight of shire for Southampton, 1539 ; joint principal secretary, 1540 ; knighted, 1540 ; constable of Southampton Castle, 1541 ; formulated (1543) offensive and defensive league between Charles V and Henry VIII, which resulted in joint invasion of France, 1544 ; created Baron Wriothesley, 1544 ; lord chancellor, 1544 ; K.G., 1545 ; appointed by Henry VIII one of his executors and privy councillor to Edward VI ; created Earl of Southampton, 1547 ; deprived of office for issuing commission to four civilians to hear chancery cases in his absence without consulting his fellow executors ; readmitted to council, *c.* 1548 ; joined Warwick's opposition to Thomas Seymour, baron Seymour of Sudeley [q. v.], and the Protector ; abandoned by Warwick, and struck off list of councillors, 1550. [lxiii. 148]

WRIOTHESLEY, THOMAS, fourth EARL OF SOUTHAMPTON (1607–1667), son of Henry Wriothesley, third earl of Southampton [q. v.] ; succeeded to title, 1624 ; of Eton and Magdalen College, Oxford ; supported resolution of House of Commons that redress of grievances should precede supply, but subsequently joined Charles I ; privy councillor, 1642 ; became one of Charles I's closest advisers, making repeated efforts for peace ; after Charles I's execution lived in retirement in country ; privy councillor to Charles II and K.G. ; lord high treasurer of England, 1660–7 ; opposed in council and parliament bill for liberty of conscience, 1663. [lxiii. 154]

WRITER, CLEMENT (*fl.* 1627–1658), 'anti-scripturist' ; clothier in Worcester ; originally a presbyterian ; subsequently became notorious through his attacks on the infallibility of the bible ; engaged in controversy with Richard Baxter [q. v.] [lxiii. 157]

WROE, JOHN (1782–1863), fanatic ; in business with his father as farmer, worsted manufacturer, and collier ; set up independently, *c.* 1810 ; began to show symptoms of mania, 1817, and came under influence of George Turner of Leeds (*d.* 1821), who then led the followers of Joanna Southcott [q. v.] ; claimed succession to Turner's leadership, 1822, and travelled in many parts of Europe, his followers calling themselves 'Christian Israelites,' and employing a room at Ashton as 'sanctuary' ; being driven from Ashton, 1831, travelled in Australia, New Zealand, and America, and found numerous disciples ; died at Melbourne. His 'divine communications' were issued in various publications by members of his sect. [lxiii. 158]

WROE, RICHARD (1641–1717), warden of Manchester church ; B.A. Jesus College, Cambridge, 1661 ; M.A., 1665 ; B.D., 1672 ; D.D., 1686 ; incorporated M.A. Oxford, 1669 ; admitted fellow of college at Manchester, 1675 ; prebendary of Chester, 1678 ; warden of Manchester College, 1684 ; published sermons. [lxiii. 160]

WROTH, SIR HENRY (*d.* 1671), royalist ; grandson of Sir Robert Wroth [q. v.] ; patron of Thomas Fuller. [lxiii. 163]

WROTH, LADY MARY (*fl.* 1621), author of 'Urania' ; eldest daughter of Robert Sidney, first earl of Leicester [q. v.] ; married Sir Robert, eldest son of Sir Robert Wroth [q. v.], 1604 ; patroness of contemporary literature ; verses inscribed to her by many poets ; published, 1621, 'The Countesse of Mountgomerie's Urania,' a close imitation of the 'Arcadia' of her uncle, Sir Philip Sidney. [lxiii. 161]

WROTH, SIR ROBERT (1540 ?–1606), member of parliament ; son of Sir Thomas Wroth (1516–1573) [q. v.] ; entered St. John's College, Cambridge, 1553 ; M.P., St. Albans, 1563, Middlesex, 1572, 1585, 1589, 1601, and

1604 ; high sheriff of Essex, 1587 ; knighted, 1597 ; walker in Waltham Forest, 1603–6. [lxiii. 162]

WROTH, SIR THOMAS (1516–1573), politician ; of St. John's College, Cambridge ; entered Gray's Inn, 1536 ; knight of shire for Middlesex, 1544, 1553, 1558, and 1563 ; gentleman of chamber to Prince Edward, 1545 ; knighted, 1547 ; gentleman of privy chamber, 1549 ; joint lord-lieutenant of Middlesex, 1551 ; one of 'adventurers' in voyage to Morocco, 1552, being privy to Suffolk's second rising, 1554, fled to continent till Queen Elizabeth's accession, 1558 ; commissioner to visit dioceses of Ely and Norwich, 1559 ; special commissioner to consult with lord deputy on government of Ireland, 1562 ; commissioner for lord-lieutenancy of London, 1569. [lxiii. 163]

WROTH, SIR THOMAS (1584–1672), parliamentarian and author ; entered Gloucester Hall (afterwards Worcester College), Oxford, 1600, and Inner Temple, 1606 ; knighted, 1613 ; subscribed to Virginia Company, 1609 ; member of council for New England, 1620 ; commissioner for government of Bermudas, 1653 ; M.P., Bridgwater, 1627–8, in Long parliament, 1640, 1656, 1658, and 1660 ; moved resolution that Charles I should be impeached and the kingdom settled without him, 1648 ; took 'engagement,' 1649, and was one of judges appointed to try Charles I, but attended only one session. [lxiii. 165]

WROTH, WILLIAM (1576 ?–1642), Welsh nonconformist ; M.A. Jesus College, Oxford, 1605 ; held rectories in Monmouthshire ; formed at Llan Faches first separatist church in Wales, 1639. [lxiii. 166]

WROTHAM, WILLIAM DE (*d.* 1217), judge ; probably custos of stannaries of Devonshire and Cornwall, 1199–1213 ; custos galearum, 1205 ; joint custodian of temporalities of bishopric of Bath and abbey of Glastonbury ; custodian of temporalities of bishopric of Winchester, 1206 ; canon of Wells and archdeacon of Taunton, 1204 ; probably warden of seaports during King John's reign. [lxiii. 166]

WROTTESLEY, SIR JOHN, first BARON WROTTESLEY (1771–1841) ; of Westminster School ; whig M.P. for Lichfield, 1799 and 1802, Staffordshire, 1822, and southern Staffordshire, 1823–37 ; created Baron Wrottesley, 1838. [lxiii. 167]

WROTTESLEY, SIR JOHN, second BARON WROTTESLEY (1798–1867), son of Sir John Wrottesley, first baron Wrottesley [q. v.] ; of Westminster School and Christ Church, Oxford ; M.A., 1823 ; barrister, Lincoln's Inn, 1823 ; assisted in founding Royal Astronomical Society, 1820, and was secretary, 1831–41, president, 1841–3, and gold medallist, 1839 ; F.R.S., 1841, and president, 1854–7 ; one of original poor-law commissioners ; served on several royal commissions of scientific nature ; D.C.L. Oxford, 1860 ; published scientific and other writings. [lxiii. 167]

WROTTESLEY, SIR WALTER (*d.* 1473), captain of Calais ; adherent of Warwick 'the king-maker' ; sheriff of Staffordshire, 1460 ; knighted, *c.* 1462 ; joined Warwick in attempt to overthrow the Woodvilles ; captain of Calais, 1471 ; surrendered Calais to Edward IV on Warwick's defeat and was pardoned, 1471. [lxiii. 168]

WROUGHTON, RICHARD (1748–1822), actor ; bred as surgeon in Bath ; at Covent Garden, London, 1768–87, his parts including Prince Henry ('Henry II, King of England,' by Bancroft or Mountfort), 1773, Lord Lovemore (Kenrick's 'Duellist'), 1773, and Elidurus (Mason's 'Caractacus'), 1776 ; joint-proprietor of Sadler's Wells, London, *c.* 1777–90 ; played chiefly at Drury Lane, London, 1787–98 and 1800–8 ; Charles Surface, Ghost ('Hamlet'), Hamlet, Henry IV, Richard III, Antonio ('Merchant of Venice'), Jaques, Edgar ('Lear'), and Sir Peter Teazle, among his characters. [lxiii. 169]

WULFHELM (*d.* 942), archbishop of Canterbury ; succeeded Athelm [q. v.] as bishop of Wells, 914, and in primacy, 923. [lxiii. 170]

WULFHERE (*d.* 675), king of the Mercians ; second son of Penda [q. v.] ; established as king of Mercians by ealdormen, who rose against Oswy [q. v.], 658 ; first Mercian king to be baptised ; established alliance with small states of south-east against Wessex ; defeated Coinwalch, king of Wessex, at Posentesbyrig, 661 ; greatly enlarged bounds of Mercia, planting Christianity wherever he conquered. [lxiii. 170]

WULFORD or **WILFORD, RALPH** (1479 ?–1499), pretender; as tool of Yorkists in their endeavours to overthrow Henry VII, impersonated Earl of Warwick, eldest son of Edward IV's brother, the Duke of Clarence, and was executed. [lxiii. 172]

WULFRED (d. 832), archbishop of Canterbury; consecrated, 805; enjoyed large wealth and exercised wide political influence; quarrelled with Cenwulf, king of Mercia, who, from apprehension of his political influence, laid false charges against him before Pope Leo III, having previously deprived him of monasteries of Minster and Reculver; on good terms with Ceolwulf, who succeeded Cenwulf, 822, and with Egbert and Æthelwulf. [lxiii. 172]

WULFRIC, called SPOT or SPROT (d. 1010), founder of Burton Abbey; owned much land, chiefly in West Mercia; killed fighting against Danes at Ringmere. near Ipswich. He founded Burton Abbey by will dated 1002, Ethelred II's charter of confirmation being dated 1004. [lxiii. 173]

WULFSTAN OF WINCHESTER (fl. 1000), versifier; monk of St. Swithun's, Winchester; became priest and precentor; probably author of versification of Lanferth's work on life and miracles of St. Swithun (Royal MS. 15, c. vii.), and other writings. [lxiii. 173]

WULFSTAN (d. 1023), archbishop of York; monk, probably of Ely; succeeded Aldulf [q. v.] as archbishop of York, 1003, holding also see of Worcester; buried at Ely. [lxiii. 174]

WULFSTAN, ST. (1012 ?–1095), bishop of Worcester; ordained deacon and priest before 1038; became monk of Worcester, and was successively schoolmaster, precentor, sacristan, and prior; bishop of Worcester, 1062; assisted Harold on his accession, but subsequently made submission to the Conqueror; rebuilt his cathedral church, 1084–9; preached at Bristol against the slave trade practised by the British merchants upon their fellow-countrymen, and procured its abandonment; buried at Worcester; canonised by Innocent III, 1203, his day in the calendar being 19 Jan. [lxiii. 174]

WULFWIG or **WULFWY** (d. 1067), bishop of Dorchester; consecrated, 1053; buried at Dorchester. [lxiii. 176]

WYATT, BENJAMIN DEAN (1775–1850 ?), architect; son of James Wyatt [q. v.]; of Westminster School and Christ Church, Oxford; surveyor of Westminster Abbey, 1813–27. His works include Drury Lane Theatre, London, 1811, and Crockford's Club House, St. James's Street, London, 1827. [lxiii. 180]

WYATT or **WYAT,** SIR FRANCIS (1575 ?–1644), governor of Virginia; knighted, 1603; governor of Virginia, 1621; continued in office by royal commission on annulling of Virginia Company's charter, 1625; returned to England, 1626, but again held governorship, 1639–42. [lxiii. 177]

WYATT, SIR HENRY (d. 1537), courtier; imprisoned in Tower of London for resisting pretensions of Richard III; liberated, 1485, by Henry VII, whose favour he enjoyed; privy councillor, 1485; K.B., 1509; joint constable with Sir Thomas Boleyn [q. v.] of Norwich Castle, 1511; treasurer to king's chamber, 1524–8. [lxiii. 183]

WYATT, HENRY (1794–1840), painter; studied at Royal Academy; practised as portrait-painter successively in Birmingham, Liverpool, and Manchester; exhibited at Royal Academy between 1817 and 1838. [lxiii. 178]

WYATT, JAMES (1746–1813), architect; attracted notice of Lord Bagot, who took him to Rome, where, and at Venice, he studied architecture; adapted old Pantheon in Oxford Street, London, for dramatic performances, 1770–2; surveyor of Westminster Abbey, 1776; executed restorations at Salisbury, Lincoln, Hereford, and Lichfield cathedrals; built Royal Military College, Woolwich, 1796; surveyor-general to board of works, 1796; architect to board of ordnance, 1806; R.A., 1785, and temporarily president, 1805. Working at first in the Græco-Italian style, he gradually turned his attention to the Gothic, and originated the revival of interest in that form of architecture. [lxiii. 178]

WYATT, JOHN (1700–1766), inventor; carpenter at Thickbroom, near Lichfield; invented a spinning-machine, which was exploited with small success at Birmingham, c. 1738; invented and perfected compound-lever weighing-machine, similar to those now used by most railway companies, c. 1744. [lxiii. 180]

WYATT, JOHN (1825–1874), army surgeon; M.R.C.S., 1848; F.R.C.S., 1866; assistant-surgeon in army, 1851; surgeon, 1857; served in Crimea; medical commissioner at headquarters of French army during Franco-German war, 1870; C.B., 1873. [lxiii. 181]

WYATT, MATTHEW COTES (1777–1862), sculptor; son of James Wyatt [q. v.]; educated at Eton; studied at Royal Academy and exhibited, 1803–14; enjoyed patronage of George III; executed equestrian statues of George III in Pall Mall East, and of Wellington, now at Aldershot. [lxiii. 181]

WYATT, SIR MATTHEW DIGBY (1820–1877), architect and writer on art; brother of Thomas Henry Wyatt [q. v.]; published 'Geometric Mosaics of Middle Ages,' 1848; secretary to executive committee of Great Exhibition, 1851; designed, with Owen Jones (1809–1874) [q. v.], courts characteristic of various periods of art, at Crystal Palace, Sydenham; surveyor to East India Company, 1855; knighted, 1855; honorary secretary of Royal Institute of British Architects, 1855–9, and gold medallist, 1866; first Slade professor of fine arts, Cambridge, 1869; honorary M.A. Cambridge, 1869. [lxiii. 182]

WYATT, RICHARD JAMES (1795–1850), sculptor; cousin of Matthew Cotes Wyatt [q. v.]; studied at Royal Academy, where he exhibited from 1818; settled in Rome, 1821. [lxiii. 183]

WYATT, SIR THOMAS (1503 ?–1542), poet; son of Sir Henry Wyatt [q. v.]; M.A. St. John's College, Cambridge, 1520; esquire of body to Henry VIII; clerk of king's jewels, 1524; accompanied Sir John Russell, ambassador to papal court, 1527; high marshal of Calais, c. 1529; privy councillor, 1533; a lover of Anne Boleyn before her marriage with Henry VIII, and temporarily imprisoned in Tower of London on discovery of Anne's post-nuptial infidelities, 1536; knighted, 1537; sheriff of Kent, 1537; ambassador to Charles V 1537–9; engaged in negotiations with Charles V, 1540; imprisoned in Tower as ally of Cromwell, but released, 1541; knight of shire for Kent, 1542. His portrait after Holbein is in the National Portrait Gallery. He was a close student of foreign literature, and first introduced the sonnet from Italy into England. His first published works appeared as 'Certayne Psalmes . . . drawen into Englyshe meter,' 1549, and many of his poems, which include rondeaus, lyrics, and satires in heroic couplets, were first issued in 'Songes and Sonettes,' printed by Henry Tottel, and known as 'Tottel's Miscellany,' 1557. [lxiii. 183]

WYATT, SIR THOMAS, the younger (1521 ?–1554), conspirator; son of Sir Thomas Wyatt (1503 ?–1542) [q. v.]; formed friendship with Henry Howard, earl of Surrey [q. v.], whom he accompanied in military operations at Landrecies and Boulogne, 1543–4; joined English council at Boulogne, 1545; joined Edward Courtenay, earl of Devonshire [q. v.], in insurrection to prevent marriage of Queen Mary with Philip of Spain, 1554, undertaking to raise Kent; fixed headquarters at Rochester, marched to Blackheath, entered Southwark, and, having penetrated into London, was deserted by his followers and surrendered; executed for high treason on Tower Hill, London. [lxiii. 187]

WYATT, THOMAS (1799 ?–1859), portrait-painter; brother of Henry Wyatt [q. v.]; studied at Royal Academy. [lxiii. 178]

WYATT, THOMAS HENRY (1807–1880), architect; brother of Sir Matthew Digby Wyatt [q. v.]; in office of Philip Charles Hardwick [q. v.]; opened practice independently, 1832; district surveyor of Hackney, 1832–61; president of Royal Institute of British Architects, 1870–1873, and gold medallist, 1873; A.I.C.E., 1845; built the Byzantine church at Wilton, Knightsbridge barracks, and Adelphi Theatre, London. [lxiii. 189]

WYATT, WILLIAM (1616–1685), scholar and friend of Jeremy Taylor; entered St. John's College, Oxford, 1638; assisted Taylor at his school at Newton Hall, Llanfihangel-Aberbythych, Carmarthenshire, and in his 'Institution of Grammar,' 1647; B.D. Oxford, 1661; prebendary of Lincoln, 1668, and precentor, 1669–81; held living of Nuneaton, 1681–5. [lxiii. 190]

WYATVILLE, SIR JEFFRY (1766–1840), architect; nephew of James Wyatt [q. v.], with whom he worked, 1792–9; began practice independently, 1799; exhibited at Royal Academy from 1786; R.A., 1826; executed additions to Sidney Sussex College, Cambridge, 1821–32, and transformation of Windsor Castle from 1824, when his name was augmented to Wyatville; knighted, 1828. [lxiii. 191]

WYBURN, PERCEVAL (1533?–1606?). [See WIBURN.]

WYCHE, SIR CYRIL (1632?–1707), statesman and man of science; son of Sir Peter Wyche [q. v.]; M.A. Christ Church, Oxford, 1655; D.C.L., 1665; knighted, 1660; F.R.S., 1663, and president, 1683; clerk in chancery, 1662–75; barrister, Gray's Inn, 1670; M.P., Callington, 1661–78, East Grinstead, 1681, Saltash, 1685–7, and Preston, 1702–5; secretary to Henry Sidney (afterwards Earl of Romney) [q. v.] when lord-lieutenant of Ireland, 1692; privy councillor of Ireland; one of three lords justices entrusted with government of Ireland, 1693–5; ambassador in Turkey, 1695. [lxiii. 192]

WYCHE, SIR PETER (d. 1643), English ambassador at the Porte; knighted, 1626; gentleman of privy chamber, 1628; English ambassador at Constantinople, 1627–41; privy councillor and comptroller of king's household, 1641. [lxiii. 193]

WYCHE, SIR PETER (1628–1699?), diplomatist; son of Sir Peter Wyche (d. 1643) [q. v.]; matriculated from Exeter College, Oxford, 1643; M.A. Trinity Hall, Cambridge, 1648; entered Middle Temple, 1649; knighted by Charles II at the Hague, 1660; incorporated M.A. Oxford, 1660; original F.R.S., 1662; envoy extraordinary to Russia, 1669; English resident at Hamburg; published translations from Portuguese and other works. [lxiii. 194]

WYCHE, RICHARD DE (1197?–1253). [See RICHARD.]

WYCHEHAM or **WICKWANE**, WILLIAM DE (d. 1285). [See WICKWANE.]

WYCHERLEY, WILLIAM (1640?–1716), dramatist; born at Clive; admitted member of Inner Temple, 1659; entered Queen's College, Oxford, 1660; published, 1672 or end of 1671, his first play, 'Love in a Wood, or St. James's Park,' which was acted, 1671, and secured for him the intimacy of Charles II's mistress, the Duchess of Cleveland; lieutenant in Duke of Buckingham's foot regiment, 1672, and equerry to the duke as master of horse; published, 1673, 'The Gentleman Dancing-master,' acted at Dorset Gardens, London, 1671 or 1672; perhaps served at sea against the Dutch, 1672; produced 'The Country Wife,' performed 1672 or 1673, at Portugal Street Theatre, London, and published, 1675; his last play, 'The Plain Dealer' (indebted to Molière's 'Misanthrope' for the general idea), acted at theatre in Lincoln's Inn Fields, London, probably early in 1674, and printed, 1677; secretly married widowed Countess of Drogheda (d. c. 1681), daughter of Sir John Robartes, first earl of Radnor [q. v.], c. 1679, and earned the displeasure of Charles II, who had offered him the tutorship of his son, the Duke of Richmond; published, 1704, 'Miscellany Poems,' which led to a friendship with Pope, who revised many of his writings; married again eleven days before his death. His 'Posthumous Works' appeared, 1728. [lxiii. 195]

WYCK, JOHN (1652–1700), painter; born at Haarlem; came to England when young; enjoyed great reputation for battle and hunting scenes. [lxiii. 202]

WYCLIFFE, JOHN (d. 1384), religious reformer and theologian; born at Hipswell; probably fellow of Balliol College, Oxford, and subsequently (in 1361) master; probably not identical with John Wyclif, who was appointed warden of Canterbury Hall, Oxford, 1365, and who was perhaps at Merton College, Oxford, and rector of Mayfield; vicar of Fillingham; prebendary of Westbury, 1361; held benefice of Ludgershall, 1368; wrote, 1366 or 1376, controversial tract, 'Determinatio quedam de Dominio contra unum monachum'; graduated doctor of theology, c. 1372; received as canon of Lincoln licence from Pope Gregory XI to keep Westbury prebend, even after obtaining prebend at Lincoln, 1373; sent to Bruges as ambassador to treat with papal legates at Ghent about non-observance of statute of provisors and other matters, 1374; rector of Lutterworth, c. 1374; gained favour of Duke of Lancaster and Henry, lord Percy, by his opinions

about the relations between temporal and spiritual power; summoned before archbishop and suffragans in St. Paul's Cathedral, London, on charge of heresy, but, the court having broken up in confusion, had no sentence passed on him, 1377; again tried, at Lambeth, and with similar results, 1378, his accusers formulating charges (including his assertion that the ecclesiastical ruler, and even the Roman pontiff, may legitimately be corrected or even accused by subjects and laymen) suggested by his hostility to the secularity of the mediæval church; instituted his 'poor preachers' and the translation of the whole bible into English for the first time, himself translating the gospels, probably the whole New Testament, and possibly part of the Old Testament, the work being edited by John Purvey [q. v.] and completed by him before 1400; peremptorily rejected transubstantiation, c. 1380, and was forbidden to teach his doctrine in Oxford University, 1381, while a court, summoned by the archbishop, 1382, condemned theses of his which implied that he held that all authority, secular and ecclesiastical, was derived from God, and was forfeited when the possessor of it was in a state of mortal sin, that he denied the doctrine of transubstantiation, on which the power of the priesthood was fundamentally based, and that he condemned monasticism in all its forms; left Oxford, where, in spite of royal and ecclesiastical commands, he was not treated with severity, and retired to Lutterworth, occupying himself with preaching, translating the bible, and writing controversial pamphlets; buried at Lutterworth, but his body disinterred, 1428, and thrown into the river Swift. He was famous as a philosopher before he became famous as a theologian, and famous as a theologian before he became a heresiarch, and the connection between his philosophy and his theology was neither external nor accidental. He discovered in nominalism the seat of all theological error, and his practical religious teaching was above all things ethical. The more important of his Latin works (which with two exceptions have been published by the Wyclif Society) are; I. (in early life) 'De Logica,' 'De Compositione Hominis,' 'XIII Quæstiones logicæ et philosophicæ,' 'De Ente Prædicamentali'; II. (up to 1379) 'De Incarnatione Verbi,' 'De Dominio Divino,' 'De Dominio Civili,' 'De Ecclesia,' 'De Officio Pastorali' (published by Lechler, 1863), and 'De Officio Regis'; III. (from 1379) 'Dialogus' or 'Speculum Ecclesie Militantis,' 'De Eucharistia,' 'De Simonia,' 'De Apostasia,' 'De Blasphemia,' 'Opus Evangelicum,' and 'Trialogus' (published by Lechler, 1869). 'Select English Works of Wyclif,' edited by T. Arnold, appeared 1869–71, and 'English Works of Wyclif hitherto unprinted,' by F. D. Matthew, 1880 (Early English Text Society). [lxiii. 202]

WYCUMBE, WILLIAM (fl. 1160). [See WILLIAM.]

WYDDEL, OSBORN (fl. 1280). [See OSBORN.]

WYDEVILLE or **WYDVILLE**. [See WOODVILLE.]

WYDFORD, WILLIAM OF (fl. 1381–1390). [See WOODFORD.]

WYDOW, ROBERT (d. 1505), poet and musician; first recorded Mus.Bac. Oxford; incorporated at Cambridge, 1502; schoolmaster and vicar of Thaxted, 1481–9; rector of Chalfont St. Giles, 1493; canon and succentor of Wells Cathedral, 1497; sub-dean, 1499; vicar of Buckland Newton; wrote Latin poems and other works. [lxiii. 223]

WYER, ROBERT (fl. 1529–1556), printer; probably worked with Richard Pynson [q. v.], and succeeded to his printing business, c. 1529. His publications include a translation, possibly by himself, of Christine de Pisan's 'C. Hystoryes of Troye' (after 1536), Andrew Borde's 'Boke for to lerne a man to be wyse' (after 1536), and Lord Berners's 'Castell of Love' (c. 1542). [lxiii. 223]

WYETH, JOSEPH (1663–1731), quaker writer; merchant in London; published 'Anguis Flagellatus' (1699), a reply to the 'Snake in the Grass,' by Charles Leslie [q. v.], and other works defending quaker tenets, besides preparing for press a 'Life,' 1714, of his friend Thomas Ellwood [q. v.] [lxiii. 224]

WYKE, SIR CHARLES LENNOX (1815–1897), diplomatist; vice-consul at Port-au-Prince, 1847; consul-general in Central America, 1852, chargé d'affaires, 1854, and envoy extraordinary, 1859; plenipotentiary in Mexico, 1860–1; K.C.B., 1859; minister to Hanover, 1866, Copenhagen, 1866–81, and Portugal, 1881–4; G.C.M.G., 1879; privy councillor, 1886. [lxiii. 225]

WYKEHAM, WILLIAM OF (1324-1404), bishop of Winchester, chancellor of England, and founder of New College, Oxford; born at Wickham; educated at Winchester; entered royal service, c. 1347, and was made king's chaplain; joint-surveyor of Windsor forest and chief warden and surveyor of royal castles of Windsor, Leeds, Dover, and Hadleigh, 1359; prebendary of Lichfield, 1359; joint-warden of forests south of Trent, 1361; keeper of privy seal, 1364; dean of St. Martin-le-Grand, London, 1360; prebendary at St. Paul's, London, Hereford, Salisbury, St. David's, Beverley, Bromyard, Wherwell, Abergwili, and Llanddewi Brewi, 1361, and at Lincoln, York, Wells, and Hastings, 1362; priest, 1362; archdeacon of Lincoln, 1363; bishop of Winchester, 1367-1404; chancellor, 1368-71; took leading part in opposing John of Gaunt in Good parliament, 1373; charged before council at Westminster with malversation and misgovernment during his chancellorship, and was deprived of temporalities, 1373; pardoned on accession of Richard II; obtained papal bull for endowment of Winchester College, 1378, and issued charter of foundation of Seinte Marie College of Wynchestre in Oxenforde' (New College), 1379; his college built, 1380-6, and his school, 1387-94; on commission of regency, 1386, but took no part in proceedings; chancellor, 1389-91. [lxiii. 225]

WYKEHAM, or more correctly **WICKHAM,** WILLIAM (1539-1595), successively bishop of Lincoln and Winchester; of Eton and King's College, Cambridge; fellow, 1559; M.A., 1564; B.D., 1569; fellow of Eton, 1568; vice-provost of Eton College, c. 1570; prebendary of Westminster, 1570; canon of Windsor, 1571; royal chaplain, before 1574; archdeacon of Surrey, 1574-80; dean and prebendary of Lincoln, 1577; prebendary of Lichfield, 1579; bishop of Lincoln, 1584, and of Winchester, 1595; left verses and other writings.

[lxiii. 231]

WYKES, THOMAS DE (fl. 1258-1293), chronicler; canon regular of Osney Abbey, near Oxford, 1282; became official chronicler of the abbey, 1285, having previously composed history on his own account, history which he extended till 1293; the part of his work which deals with 1258 to 1288 of great importance, and written from the point of view of a progressive royalist.

[lxiii. 232]

WYLD, JAMES, the elder (1790-1836), geographer royal; introduced lithography into England, first applying it to plans of actions fought in Peninsula.

[lxiii. 233]

WYLD, JAMES, the younger (1812-1887), geographer; son of James Wyld the elder [q. v.]; educated at Woolwich; joined Royal Geographical Society, 1830; exhibited his 'great globe' in London, 1851-62; liberal M.P. for Bodmin, 1847-52 and 1857-68; took leading part in promotion of technical education; produced maps bearing on points of strategical and political importance at the time; published 'Popular Atlas' and 'Atlas of Battles.' [lxiii. 233]

WYLDE, HENRY (1822-1890), Gresham professor of music, London; studied at Royal Academy of Music, where he became professor of harmony; Mus.Bac. and Mus.Doc. Cambridge, 1851; one of founders of New Philharmonic Society, 1852; founded London Academy of Music, 1861; Gresham professor, 1863-90; published musical compositions and works relating to music. [lxiii. 234]

WYLDE, JOHN (1590-1669). [See WILDE.]

WYLDE, ROBERT (1609-1679). [See WILD.]

WYLIE, ALEXANDER (1815-1887), missionary and Chinese scholar; apprenticed as cabinet-maker; studied Chinese and became superintendent of London Missionary Society's printing establishment at Shanghai, 1847; showed that Horner's method for solving equations of all orders had been anticipated by the Chinese mathematicians of the fourteenth century, 1852; temporary agent of Bible Society in Lord Elgin's expedition up the Yang-tsze, 1858; permanent agent of the society, 1863-77; accompanied Griffith John, the Wesleyan missionary, up Yang-tsze to source of Han and thence to Shanghai, 1868; wrote and translated numerous works in Chinese and English. [lxiii. 235]

WYLIE, SIR JAMES (1768-1854), physician; M.D. King's College, Aberdeen, 1794; entered Russian service as senior surgeon in Eletsky regiment, 1790; physician

to imperial court at St. Petersburg, 1798; surgeon-in-ordinary to tsar and physician to heir-apparent, the Grand-duke Alexander, 1799; founder, 1804, and president, 1804-34, of Medical Academy of St. Petersburg and Moscow; inspector-general of army board of health, 1806; director of medical department of ministry of war, 1812; physician in ordinary, 1814, to Tsar Alexander I, whom he accompanied to England, being knighted by prince regent; published medical works. [lxiii. 236]

WYLIE, JAMES AITKEN (1808-1890), protestant writer; educated at Marischal College, Aberdeen, and St. Andrews; entered Original Secession Divinity Hall, Edinburgh, 1827; 'renewed the covenants' in Edinburgh, 1828; ordained, 1831; sub-editor of Edinburgh 'Witness,' 1846; joined Free church of Scotland, 1852; edited 'Free Church Record,' 1852-60; LL.D. Aberdeen, 1856; lecturer on popery at Protestant Institute, 1860-1890; published miscellaneous works. [lxiii. 237]

WYLIE, WILLIAM HOWIE (1833-1891), baptist minister and journalist; sub-editor of 'Ayr Advertiser,' 1847-50; edited 'Nottingham Journal,' 1850-2; sub-editor of 'Liverpool Courier,' 1852-3; editor of 'Falkirk Herald' and sub-editor of 'Glasgow Commonwealth,' 1854-5; sub-editor of Edinburgh 'Daily Express,' 1855; baptist minister of Ramsey, Huntingdonshire, 1860, and of Accrington, Lancashire, 1865; pastor at Blackpool; sub-editor of 'Christian World,' 1870-7; one of original promoters and editor of 'Greenock Telegraph,' the first halfpenny evening paper in Britain; founded, 1882, and was editor and proprietor, 1882-91, of Glasgow 'Christian Leader.' [lxiii. 238]

WYLLIE, JOHN WILLIAM SHAW (1835-1870), Indian civilian; son of Sir William Wyllie [q. v.]; of Trinity College, Oxford; third assistant political agent in Kathiawar, 1858; assistant-secretary to Sir George Yule, 1861; secretary at Calcutta, 1862-7; C.S.I., 1869; published political writings. [lxiii. 240]

WYLLIE, SIR WILLIAM (1802-1891), general; lieutenant, Bombay native infantry, 1819; captain, 1833; brigade-major to Malwa field force, 1826, and of first brigade of Bombay column for invasion of Afghanistan, 1838; served with distinction at capture of Kalat, 1839; brigade-major of second brigade in Sind force, 1840; assistant adjutant-general in Sind and Baluchistan, 1842; C.B. (military), 1843; deputy adjutant-general of Bombay army, 1849; brigadier-general of second class, commanding Bombay garrison, 1850; commanded brigade at Ahmadnagar, 1855; colonel, 1857; left India, 1858; lieutenant-general, 1862; K.C.B. (military), 1865; general, 1871; colonel of royal Dublin fusiliers, 1873; G.C.B. (military), 1877; retired, 1877. [lxiii. 238]

WYNDHAM. [See also WINDHAM.]

WYNDHAM or **WINDHAM,** SIR CHARLES, second EARL OF EGREMONT (1710-1763), statesman; son and heir of Sir William Wyndham, third baronet [q. v.]; of Westminster School and Christ Church, Oxford; tory M.P. for Bridgewater, 1735, but soon became whig; M.P., Taunton, 1747; succeeded his uncle Algernon Seymour, seventh duke of Somerset, as Earl of Egremont and Baron Cockermouth, 1750; lord-lieutenant of Cumberland, 1751; privy councillor and secretary of state for southern department, 1761-3; conducted negotiations with Spain, 1761-2, and with France, 1762, coming into conflict with Bute and Bedford; associated with Halifax in prosecution of Wilkes; enjoyed with Halifax and George Grenville, who married his sister Elizabeth, close confidence of George III. [lxiii. 240]

WYNDHAM or **WINDHAM,** FRANCIS (d. 1592), judge; educated at Cambridge; barrister, Lincoln's Inn; bencher, 1569; autumn reader, 1572; M.P., Norfolk, 1572-83; serjeant, 1577; recorder of Norwich, 1578; judge of common pleas, 1579; consulted concerning trial of Mary Stuart, 1586. [lxiii. 243]

WYNDHAM, SIR GEORGE O'BRIEN, third EARL OF EGREMONT (1751-1837), patron of fine art; son of Sir Charles Wyndham, second earl of Egremont [q. v.]; of Westminster School; in early years acted with whigs, but later inclined to tories; member of board of agriculture, 1793; lord-lieutenant of Sussex, 1819-35; a successful stock-breeder at Petworth and patron of art; one of first to appreciate Turner, who had a studio at Petworth. Among the artists whom he patronised were Benjamin

Robert Haydon [q. v.], John Flaxman [q. v.], Joseph Nollekens [q. v.], John Charles Felix Rossi [q. v.], and John Constable [q. v.] [lxiii. 244]

WYNDHAM, HENRY PENRUDDOCKE (1736–1819), topographer; great-grandson of Sir Wadham Wyndham [q. v.]; of Eton and Wadham College, Oxford; M.A., 1759; travelled on continent, 1765–7; mayor of Salisbury, 1770–1; sheriff of Wiltshire, 1772; M.P., Wiltshire, 1795–1812; F.S.A., 1777; F.R.S., 1783; contributed 'Observations on an ancient Building at Warnford, Hampshire,' to the 'Archæologia',(v. 357–66), and 'On a Roman Pavement at Caerwent' (ib. vii. 410–11); published topographical works relating to Wiltshire, Monmouthshire, and Wales, and other writings. [lxiii. 246]

WYNDHAM, SIR HUGH (1603? – 1684), judge; brother of Sir Wadham Wyndham [q. v.]; entered Wadham College, Oxford, 1622; M.A., 1643; barrister, Lincoln's Inn, 1629; bencher, 1648; serjeant-at-law, 1654; temporary judge on northern circuit, 1654; deprived of office at Restoration, but reinstated serjeant-at-law and judge, 1660; baron of exchequer, 1670; knighted, 1670; moved to court of common pleas, 1673. [lxiii. 247]

WYNDHAM, SIR JOHN (d. 1502), conspirator; knighted for bravery at Stoke, 1487; executed for complicity in conspiracy of Edmund de la Pole, earl of Suffolk. [lxiii. 249]

WYNDHAM, ROBERT HENRY (1814–1894), Scottish actor-manager; first appeared on stage at Salisbury, 1836; at Adelphi, Glasgow, 1844, and Theatre Royal, Edinburgh, 1845; actor-manager at Adelphi, Edinburgh, 1851 till 1853, when theatre was destroyed by fire; managed 'Royal' Theatre, Edinburgh, 1853–9, and Adelphi, renamed 'The Queen,' 1855 till 1865 (when it was again burned, being reopened as 'The Royal'), and 1865 till 1875, when it was burned for third time; (Sir) Henry Irving became a member of his company in 1857. Wyndham's parts include Charles Surface, Mercutio, Captain Absolute, Macbeth, and Prince Henry ('Henry IV'). ·[lxiii. 247]

WYNDHAM, THOMAS (1510?–1553), vice-admiral and navigator; grandson of Sir John Wyndham [q. v.]; captain under Ormonde in Ireland, 1539–40; served in North Sea, 1544, and Solent, 1545; master of ordnance in king's ships; vice-admiral of fleet sent to enforce Protector's policy in Scotland, 1547; constructed 'Wyndham's bulwark' at Haddington; engaged in trade and exploration; made two voyages to Morocco and one to Gold Coast and Bight of Benin, and was first Englishman who rounded Cape Verde and entered Southern Sea; died of fever in Bight of Benin. [lxiii. 249]

WYNDHAM, THOMAS, BARON WYNDHAM OF FINGLASS (1681–1745), grandson of Sir Wadham Wyndham [q. v.]; entered Wadham College, Oxford, 1698; called to bar at Lincoln's Inn, 1705; recorder of Sarum, 1706; chief-justice of court of common pleas in Ireland, 1724, and lord chancellor, 1726–39; raised to peerage, 1731. [lxiii. 250]

WYNDHAM, SIR WADHAM (1610–1668), judge; brother of Sir Hugh Wyndham [q. v.]; fellow commoner of Wadham College, Oxford, 1626; barrister, Lincoln's Inn, 1636; serjeant, 1660; counsel for prosecution of regicides; judge of king's bench, 1660–8; knighted. [lxiii. 251]

WYNDHAM, SIR WILLIAM, third baronet (1687–1740), politician; educated at Eton and Christ Church, Oxford; tory M.P. for Somerset, 1710; secretary at war, 1712; chancellor of exchequer, 1713–14; supported 'Schism Act'; arrested for complicity in rebellion of 1715, but was liberated on bail and never brought up for trial; maintained strong Jacobite opinions, and was firm ally of Bolingbroke; one of founders of the Brothers' Club, of which Swift became member in 1711. [lxiii. 252]

WYNDHAM-QUIN, EDWIN RICHARD WINDHAM, third EARL OF DUNRAVEN (1812–1871). [See QUIN.]

WYNFORD, first BARON (1767–1845). [See BEST, WILLIAM DRAPER.]

WYNN. [See also WYNNE.]

WYNN, CHARLES WATKIN WILLIAMS (1775–1850), politician; of Westminster School and Christ Church, Oxford; M.A., 1798; D.C.L., 1810; formed and kept up close friendship with Southey; barrister, Lincoln's Inn, 1798; bencher, 1835; M.P., Old Sarum, 1797, and Montgomeryshire, 1799–1850; under-secretary for home department, 1806–7; president of board of control, with seat in cabinet, 1822–8; privy councillor, 1822; secretary at war, without seat in cabinet, 1830–1; chancellor of duchy of Lancaster, 1834–5; F.S.A., 1800; first president of Royal Asiatic Society, 1823–41. [lxiii. 254]

WYNN, CHARLOTTE WILLIAMS- (1807–1869), diarist; daughter of Charles Watkin Williams Wynn [q. v.]; travelled much in England and on continent; 'Memorials of Charlotte Williams-Wynn' published, 1877. [lxiii. 256]

WYNN, SIR HENRY WATKIN WILLIAMS (1783–1856), diplomatist; brother of Charles Watkin Williams Wynn [q. v.]; envoy extraordinary to elector of Saxony, 1803–7; M.P., Midhurst, 1807; D.C.L. Oxford, 1810; envoy extraordinary and minister plenipotentiary to Switzerland, 1822, Würtemberg, 1823, and Copenhagen, 1824–53; privy councillor, 1825; K.G.C.H., 1831; K.C.B., 1851. [lxiii. 256]

WYNN, SIR JOHN, first baronet (1553–1626), antiquary; entered Inner Temple, 1576; probably B.A. Oxford, 1578; sheriff for Carnarvonshire, 1588 and 1603, and for Merionethshire, 1559 and 1601; M.P., Carnarvonshire, 1586–7; knighted, 1606; created baronet, 1611; member of council of marches at Ludlow, 1608; collected Welsh antiquities; left manuscript 'History of the Gwydir Family' (printed by Daines Barrington, 1770) and other writings. [lxiii. 257]

WYNN, SIR RICHARD (d. 1649), baronet; son of Sir John Wynn [q. v.]; groom of chamber to Charles I while prince of Wales, whom he accompanied in Spain, 1623; treasurer to Queen Henrietta. [lxiii. 258]

WYNN, SIR WATKIN WILLIAMS, third baronet (1692–1749), grandson of Sir William Williams [q. v.]; assumed name of Wynn, 1719; D.C.L. Jesus College, Oxford, 1732; mayor of Oswestry, 1728, and of Chester, 1732; M.P., Denbighshire, 1716–49; implicated in Jacobite rising of 1745. [lxiii. 259]

WYNN, WILLIAM (1710?–1761), Welsh poet; M.A. Jesus College, Oxford, 1735; rector of Manafon, 1747–61, and of Llan Gynhafal, 1750–61; poems by him included in various collections. [lxiii. 260]

WYNNE, EDWARD (1734–1784), law writer; entered Jesus College, Oxford, 1753; barrister, Middle Temple, 1758; published legal treatises. [lxiii. 261]

WYNNE, ELLIS (1671–1734), Welsh author; entered Jesus College, Oxford, 1692; rector of Llan Danwg and perpetual curate of Llan Bedr, 1705; edited Welsh prayerbook (London, 1710); rector of Llanfair-juxta-Harlech, 1711–34; published, 1703, 'Gweledigaethau y Bardd Cwsg' ('Visions of the Sleeping Bard'), the greatest of Welsh prose classics. [lxiii. 261]

WYNNE, JOHN (1667–1743), bishop of St. Asaph and of Bath and Wells; B.A. and fellow, Jesus College, Oxford, 1685; M.A., 1688; B.D., 1696; D.D., 1706; chaplain to Earl of Pembroke; prebendary of Brecon; Lady Margaret professor of divinity, Oxford, 1705–15, and canon of Worcester; principal of Jesus College, Oxford, 1712–20; bishop of St. Asaph, 1715–27, and of Bath and Wells, 1727–43; published 'Abridgement of Locke's Essay on the Human Understanding,' 1696. [lxiii. 262]

WYNNE, JOHN HUDDLESTONE (1743–1788), miscellaneous writer; educated at St. Paul's School, London; apprenticed as printer; employed in East India Company's service, 1759–61; engaged in writing for periodicals; edited 'Lady's Magazine' and 'Gazetteer'; compositor on 'General Evening Post'; published 'General History of British Empire in America,' 1770, 'General History of Ireland to death of William III,' 1772, and other works in verse and prose. [lxiii. 263]

WYNNE, WARREN RICHARD COLVIN (1843–1879), captain, royal engineers; educated at Woolwich; lieutenant, royal engineers, 1862; served at Gibraltar, c. 1866–71; captain, 1875; served in Zulu war; designed and built fort at Ekowe; died of fever. [lxiii. 264]

WYNNE, WILLIAM WATKIN EDWARD (1801-
1880), antiquary; of Westminster School and Jesus
College, Oxford; M.P., Merioneth, 1852-65; high sheriff,
1867; came into possession, by legacy, of the Hengwrt
collection of manuscripts formed originally by Robert
Vaughan (1592-1667) [q. v.], and published a catalogue,
1869-71, in 'Archæologia Cambrensis,' to which journal
he contributed largely; left manuscript collections for
history of Merionethshire. [lxiii. 264]

WYNNYFFE, THOMAS (1576-1654). [See WIN-
NIFFE.]

WYNTER, ANDREW (1819-1876), physician and
author; studied at St. George's Hospital, London; M.D.
St. Andrews, 1852; edited, 1856-60, 'Association Medical
Journal' (called 'British Medical Journal' from 1858);
M.R.C.P., 1861; published writings on insanity and mis-
cellaneous subjects. [lxiii. 265]

WYNTER, SIR WILLIAM (d. 1589). [See WINTER.]

WYNTOUN, ANDREW OF (1350 ?-1420 ?), Scottish
historian; canon regular of St. Andrews; prior of St.
Serf's Inch in Loch Leven, where he probably wrote his
chronicles, 'The Oryginale,' a vernacular metrical history
of Scotland from the beginning of the world to accession
of James I, 1406 (first published from manuscript in
Royal Library, 1795). [lxiii. 266]

WYNYARD, ROBERT HENRY (1802-1864), major-
general; ensign, 58th foot, 1819; captain, 1826; lieutenant-
colonel, 1842; served in Maori war, 1845-7, and commanded
forces in New Zealand, 1851; lieutenant-governor of New
Ulster division of New Zealand, 1851-3; first superintendent of province of Auckland; colonel, 1854; temporary
governor of New Zealand, 1854-5; major-general, 1858;
commander of troops in Cape Colony, 1859; temporarily
governor-in-chief and high commissioner, 1859-60 and
1861-2; C.B., 1862; colonel, 98th foot, 1863. [lxiii. 267]

WYNZET, NINIAN (1518-1592). [See WINZET.]

WYON, ALFRED BENJAMIN (1837-1884), engraver; brother of Joseph Shepherd Wyon [q. v.], with
whom he was associated as chief engraver of seals from
1865, and was sole engraver, 1873-84; compiled work on
'Great Seals of England,' published, 1887. [lxiii. 268]

WYON, BENJAMIN (1802-1858), chief engraver of
seals; son of Thomas Wyon the elder [q. v.]; appointed
chief engraver of seals, 1831. [lxiii. 268]

WYON, GEORGE (d. 1796), die-engraver and chaser;
designer and modeller to Silver Plate Company, Birmingham. [lxiii. 269]

WYON, JOSEPH SHEPHERD (1836-1873), chief engraver of seals; son of Benjamin Wyon [q. v.]; studied at
Royal Academy; appointed chief engraver of seals, 1858. [lxiii. 268]

WYON, LEONARD CHARLES (1826-1891), chief
engraver at royal mint; son of William Wyon [q. v.];
second engraver to royal mint; chief engraver, 1851. [lxiii. 268]

WYON, THOMAS, the younger (1792-1817), chief
engraver at royal mint; son of Thomas Wyon the elder
[q. v.], to whom he was apprenticed; studied at Royal
Academy; probationer engraver at royal mint, 1811, and
chief engraver, 1815; gold medallist, Society of Arts, the
society adopting his design for its prize medals. [lxiii. 269]

WYON, THOMAS, the elder (1767-1830), chief engraver of seals; son of George Wyon [q. v.]; engaged as
general die-engraver at Birmingham, and from 1800 in
London; appointed chief engraver of the seals, 1816. [lxiii. 269]

WYON, WILLIAM (1795-1851), chief engraver at
royal mint; nephew of Thomas Wyon the elder [q. v.];
obtained gold medal of Society of Arts, 1813, for medal die
with head of Ceres, the society purchasing the die for its
prize gold medal in agriculture; settled in London, 1816,
and assisted his uncle; second engraver to royal mint,
1816; chief engraver, 1828; R.A., 1838. His medals include
coronation of William IV, 1831, accession of Queen

Victoria, 1837, visit of Queen Victoria to Guildhall, and
the Cheselden medal for St. Thomas's Hospital, London. [lxiii. 270]

WYRCESTER, WILLIAM (1415-1482 ?). [See WOR-
CESTER.]

WYRLEY, WILLIAM (1565-1618), antiquary and
herald; employed as amanuensis to Sampson Erdeswicke
[q. v.]; published 'The trve Vse of Armorie,' 1592;
matriculated from Balliol College, Oxford, 1594; Rouge
Croix pursuivant at College of Arms, 1604; left antiquarian manuscripts. [lxiii. 271]

WYSE, NAPOLEON ALFRED BONAPARTE (1822-
1895), son of Sir Thomas Wyse [q. v.]; high sheriff of
Waterford, 1870. [lxiii. 276]

WYSE, SIR THOMAS (1791-1862), politician and
diplomatist; educated at jesuit college at Stonyhurst and
Trinity College, Dublin; B.A., 1812; entered Lincoln's
Inn, 1813; travelled abroad; married, 1821, Lætitia,
daughter of Napoleon's brother Lucien, prince of Canino,
but was separated from her, 1828; took active part in
agitation for catholic emancipation in Ireland, 1825;
M.P., co. Tipperary, 1830; M.P. for Waterford, 1835-47;
introduced bill for national education in Ireland, 1835;
published 'Education Reform,' 1837; lord of treasury,
1839-41; member of royal commission for decoration of
houses of parliament; secretary for board of control
(India), 1846-9; privy councillor, 1849; British minister
at Athens, 1849; successfully conducted negotiations
occasioned by claims on Greek government made by
David Pacifico [q. v.], George Finlay [q. v.], and others,
and was made C.B., 1850; K.C.B. and envoy extraordinary
for successful management of Greek affairs during Crimean
war, 1857; president of commission to inquire into financial resources of Greece, 1857-9; published works relating
to his travels and political questions. [lxiii. 272]

WYSE, WILLIAM CHARLES BONAPARTE (1826-
1892), poetical writer; son of Sir Thomas Wyse [q. v.];
high sheriff of Waterford, 1855; published, 1868, 'Par-
paioun Blu' (lyrics in Provençal) and other writings. [lxiii. 276]

WYTHENS or **WITHENS,** SIR FRANCIS (1634 ?-
1704), judge; entered St. John's College, Oxford, 1650;
barrister, Middle Temple, 1660; bencher, 1680; M.P., Westminster, 1679; knighted, 1680, for presenting address to
Charles II testifying abhorrence of citizens of Westminster
to recent petition for a parliament, but was ejected from
House of Commons as 'an abhorrer'; serjeant and judge
of king's bench, 1683; on commission for trial of Rye
House conspirators; recorder of Kingston-on-Thames,
1685; tried and pronounced sentence on Titus Oates,
1685; accompanied Jeffreys on the western assize;
removed from bench, 1687; exempted from Act of Indemnity, 1689, but apparently not visited with any
penalty. [lxiii. 276]

WYVILL, SIR CHRISTOPHER (1614-1672 ?),
baronet; M.P., Richmond, Yorkshire, 1660; probably
author of 'Certaine serious Thoughts' (1647), a rare
volume of verse. [lxiii. 278]

WYVILL, CHRISTOPHER (1740-1822), advocate
of parliamentary reform; educated at Queens' College,
Cambridge; hon. LL.D., 1764; rector of Black Notley,
Essex; secretary, 1779, and afterwards chairman of Yorkshire Association, an association formed to promote
shortening of duration of parliaments and equalisation
of representation; took leading part in drawing up
Yorkshire petition presented to parliament, 1780; advocated in later life cause of universal toleration; published 'Political Papers chiefly respecting the Attempt of
the County of York . . . to effect a Reformation of the
Parliament of Great Britain,' 1794-5, and other works
relating to religious and political questions. [lxiii. 278]

WYVILL, CHRISTOPHER (1792-1863), rear-admiral;
son of Christopher Wyvill (1740-1822) [q. v.]; entered
navy, 1805; commander, 1824; served on coast of Greece;
captain, 1832; on North American station, 1840-4, and
at Cape of Good Hope, 1844-7 and 1849-53; superintendent of Chatham dockyard, 1854-6; rear-admiral,
1856. [lxiii. 280]

Y

YALDEN, THOMAS (1670–1736), poet : educated at Magdalen College school and Magdalen College, Oxford ; B.A., 1691 ; M.A., 1694 ; B.D., 1706 ; D.D., 1708 ; fellow, 1699–1713 ; vicar of Willoughby 1700–9 ; lecturer on moral philosophy at Magdalen College, Oxford, 1705–13 ; bursar, 1707 ; dean of divinity, 1709 ; rector of Sopworth, 1710–11 ; prebendary of collegiate church of Chulmleigh, 1712 ; rector of Chalton-cum-Clanfield ; chaplain of Bridewell Hospital, London, 1713 : his ' Hymn to Darkness,' written in imitation of Cowley, highly esteemed by Dr. Johnson ; most of his poems, collected, 1795, in vol. vii. of ' Works of the British Poets,' by Robert Anderson (1750–1830) [q. v.] [lxiii. 281]

YALE, ELIHU (1648–1721), governor of Madras ; born at Boston, Massachusetts : came to England, 1652 ; entered service of East India Company, 1672 ; governor of settlement at Fort St. George (Madras), 1687–92 ; returned to England and was made a governor of East India Company, 1699 ; his name commemorated by Yale University, Newhaven, Connecticut, of which he was a liberal benefactor. [lxiii. 282]

YALE, THOMAS (1526 ?–1577), civilian ; B.A. Cambridge, 1543 ; fellow of Queens' College, Cambridge, 1544 ; M.A., 1546 ; bursar, 1549–51 ; commissary of diocese of Ely, 1554 : LL.D., 1557 : advocate of court of arches, 1559 ; prebendary of Lichfield, 1560 ; rector of Leverington, 1560 ; judge of court of audience, official principal, chancellor, and vicar-general to archbishop of Canterbury, 1561 ; chancellor of diocese of Bangor, 1562 ; prebendary of St. Asaph, 1566 ; dean of the arches, 1567–73 ; joint-keeper of prerogative court of Canterbury, 1571 ; for many years ecclesiastical high commissioner. [lxiii. 283]

YALLOP, EDWARD (*d.* 1767). [See SPELMAN.]

YANIEWICZ, FELIX (1762–1848). [See JANIEWICZ.]

YARINGTON, ROBERT (*fl.* 1601), dramatist ; according to one conjecture Robert Yarington only a fictitious name ; author of ' Two Lamentable Tragedies,' 1601, perhaps an amalgamation of the lost ' Tragedy of Thomas Merrye,' by Haughton and Day, 1599, and the lost ' Orphanes Tragedy,' by Chettle. [lxiii. 284]

YARMOUTH, EARLS OF. [See PASTON, ROBERT, first EARL, 1631–1683 ; PASTON, WILLIAM, second EARL, 1652–1732.]

YARMOUTH, COUNTESS OF (1704–1765). [See WALLMODEN, AMALIE SOPHIE MARIANNE.]

YARRANTON, ANDREW (1616–1684 ?), engineer and agriculturist ; apprenticed as linendraper at Worcester ; captain in parliamentary forces ; engaged in projects for cutting canals and rendering rivers (including the Salwarp and Stour, the latter from Stourbridge to Kidderminster) navigable ; wrote pamphlets recommending use of clover for agricultural purposes ; imprisoned on false evidence as concerned in intended presbyterian rising, 1662 ; studied in Saxony secrets of tinplate industry, *c.* 1667, but was forestalled in manufacture by English patentees ; consulting engineer ; published works relating to various schemes for improvement of English manufactures and commerce, and other subjects. [lxiii. 284]

YARRELL, WILLIAM (1784–1856), zoologist ; engaged in business as newspaper agent and bookseller in London ; member of Royal Institution, 1817 ; F.L.S., 1825, and treasurer, 1849–56 ; original member of Zoological Society, 1826 ; published ' History of British Fishes,' 1836, and ' History of British Birds,' 1843. [lxiii. 286]

YATES, EDMUND (1831–1894), novelist and founder of ' The World ' ; son of Frederick Henry Yates [q. v.] and Elizabeth Yates [q. v.] ; obtained appointment in secretary's department at general post office, 1847, and became head of missing-letter department, 1862 ; engaged in journalistic work ; dramatic critic and reviewer to ' Daily News,' *c.* 1854–60 ; wrote several dramatic pieces which were presented at London theatres ; became editor, 1858, of ' Town Talk,' and offended Thackeray by a personal article which occasioned his dismissal from the Garrick Club, of which he had been elected a member, 1848 ; acting editor of ' Temple Bar,' 1860, and was sole editor, 1863–7 ; started, 1879, and conducted till 1883, ' Time, a Monthly Miscellany ' ; contributed to ' All the Year Round ' and the ' Observer ' ; engaged under Frank Ives Scudamore [q. v.] in telegraph department, 1870–2 ; retired from post office, 1872 ; lectured in America, 1872 ; joined staff of ' New York Herald ' ; founded in London ' The World,' a weekly society newspaper, 1874. His publications include his ' Recollections and Experiences,' 1884, ' Broken to Harness,' 1864, and ' The Black Sheep,' 1867. [lxiii. 287]

YATES, MRS. ELIZABETH (1799–1860), actress ; appeared first as Desdemona to Charles Kemble's Othello, at Lynn, 1815 ; engaged at Covent Garden, London, 1817–20, her parts including Rosalind, Viola, Beatrice (' Much Ado '), and Imogen ; married Frederick Henry Yates [q. v.], appeared at Drury Lane, London, 1824 ; joint manager of Adelphi, London, 1842 ; at Lyceum, London, 1848–9 ; retired, 1849. [lxiii. 290]

YATES, FREDERICK HENRY (1797–1842), actor ; educated at Charterhouse, London ; served in Peninsula ; appeared on stage, 1818, at Edinburgh, and later at Covent Garden, London, where he played Iago to Charles Kemble's Cassio and Young's Othello ; at Covent Garden, London, 1819–25 ; purchased with Terry the Adelphi Theatre, London ; conducted Adelphi with Charles Mathews, 1825–35 ; stage manager, Drury Lane, London, 1835 ; sole manager of Adelphi, 1836–41, and with Gladstane, 1841 ; Shylock, Richard III, Falstaff, and Joseph Surface among his parts. [lxiii. 292]

YATES, JAMES (*fl.* 1582), poet ; published ' The Castell of Courtesie. Whereunto is adioyned the Holde of Humilitie ; with the Chariot of Chastitie thereunto annexed,' 1582. [lxiii. 294]

YATES, JAMES (1789–1871), unitarian and antiquary ; studied at Glasgow University and Manchester College (at York), and Edinburgh ; M.A. Glasgow, 1812 ; unordained minister of unitarian congregation at Glasgow, 1812 ; founded with Thomas Southwood Smith [q. v.] Scottish Unitarian Association, 1813 ; engaged in controversy with Ralph Wardlaw [q. v.], 1814–16 ; joint-pastor at new meeting, Birmingham, 1817–25 ; F.G.S., 1819 ; F.L.S., 1822 ; F.R.S., 1831 ; secretary to council of British Association, 1831 ; minister of Carter Lane Chapel, Doctors' Commons, London, 1832–5 ; left ministry, *c.* 1836 ; contributed largely to ' Dictionary of Greek and Roman Antiquities,' 1842, edited by (Sir) William Smith (1813–1893) [q. v.] ; wrote on antiquarian, educational, and other subjects. [lxiii. 295]

YATES, JOHN (*fl.* 1622–1658), puritan divine ; B.D. Emmanuel College, Cambridge ; rector of St. Mary with St. John Stiffkey, Norfolk, 1622–58 ; published theological writings. [lxiii. 296]

YATES, SIR JOSEPH (1722–1770), judge ; entered Queen's College, Oxford, 1739 ; barrister, Inner Temple, 1753 ; employed by crown against John Wilkes, 1763 ; king's counsel for duchy of Lancaster, 1761 ; judge of king's bench, 1764 ; knighted, 1763 ; chancellor of Durham, 1765 ; removed to court of common pleas, 1770. [lxiii. 297]

YATES, JOSEPH BROOKS (1780–1855), merchant and antiquary ; brother of James Yates (1789–1871) [q. v.] ; educated at Eton ; entered house of West India merchant at Liverpool, and subsequently became partner ; with Thomas Stewart Traill [q. v.] founded Liverpool Literary and Philosophical Society, 1812 ; F.S.A., 1852 ; F.R.G.S. ; member of Chetham Society ; original member of Philological Society ; wrote on antiquarian subjects. [lxiii. 298]

YATES, MRS. MARY ANN (1728–1787), actress ; *née* Graham : appeared as Marcia in Crisp's ' Virginia,' 1753, at Drury Lane, London, where she played till 1755 and 1756–67, her parts including Cleopatra (' Antony and Cleopatra '), Rosalind, Constance (' King John '), Anne Bullen (' Henry VIII '), Julia (' Two Gentlemen of Verona '), Imogen, Desdemona, Cordelia, and Perdita ; at Covent Garden, London, 1767–71, playing Lady Macbeth, Queen

('Hamlet'), Isabella ('Measure for Measure'), and Portia ('Merchant of Venice') ; married Richard Yates (1706 ?-1796) [q. v.], c. 1756 ; joint-manager of Haymarket Opera House, London, 1774 ; at Drury Lane, London, 1774, and played original Berinthia in Sheridan's 'Trip to Scarborough,' 1777 ; last appeared at Drury Lane, 1785. She was one of the greatest English tragic actresses, one of her finest characters being Medea in Glover's tragedy, 1767.
[lxiii. 298]

YATES, RICHARD (1706 ?-1796), comedian : probably first played at the Haymarket ; in London at Covent Garden, 1737-9, Drury Lane, 1739, Goodman's Fields, 1740-1, and again at Drury Lane, 1742-67 ; his most notable characters Kastril ('Alchemist'), Clown ('Twelfth Night' and 'Measure for Measure'), Shylock, Malvolio, Touchstone, Shallow, Dogberry, Bobadil, Launce, Falstaff, and Bottom ; married Mary Ann Graham [see YATES], c. 1756 ; at Covent Garden, 1767-72, and again at Drury Lane, 1775 ; played original Sir Oliver Surface in 'School for Scandal' at Drury Lane, 1777 ; with his wife at Edinburgh, 1784-5 ; Autolycus among his best parts.
[lxiii. 301]

YATES, RICHARD (1769-1834), divine and antiquary : worked as usher in various schools ; ordained deacon, 1796 ; priest, 1797 ; curate of Chelsea Hospital, 1796, and chaplain, 1798; rector of Ashen, Essex, 1804 ; D.D. Cambridge, 1813; one of treasurers of Literary Fund, 1805-34; edited 'Monastic Remains of Town and Abbey of St. Edmunds Bury' (1st part, 1805, 2nd, 1843), collections for which were made by his father.
[lxiii. 303]

YATES, WILLIAM (1792-1845), baptist missionary and orientalist ; studied at baptist college at Bristol ; went to India under Baptist Missionary Society, 1815 ; published numerous educational works in Sanskrit, Hindustani, and Bengalee : pastor of English church, Circular Road, Calcutta, 1829-39 ; his publications include a complete version of the bible in Bengalee, Sanskrit and Hindustani dictionaries, and an edition of the 'Nalodaya,' 1840.
[lxiii. 304]

YAXLEY, FRANCIS (d. 1565), conspirator ; introduced at court by Cecil ; employed by privy council, c. 1547 ; attached to embassy of Peter Vannes [q. v.], 1550-2 ; M.P., Dunwich, 1553 ; joined Nicholas Wotton [q. v.], ambassador in France, 1553 ; M.P., Stamford, 1555, and Saltash, 1558 ; clerk of signet, c. 1557 ; employed as agent by Lady Margaret Douglas, countess of Lennox [q. v.], to further project of marriage between her son Darnley and Mary Queen of Scots ; wrecked at sea while returning from mission from Mary Queen of Scots to Philip II.
[lxiii. 305]

YCKHAM, PETER OF (fl. 1290 ?). [See ICKHAM.]

YEA, LACY WALTER GILES (1808-1855), colonel ; educated at Eton ; ensign, 1825 ; captain, 1836 ; major, 1842 ; lieutenant-colonel, 1850 ; commanded regiment in Turkey and Crimea, 1854 ; served with distinction at Alma ; brevet colonel, 1854 ; killed in assault of the Redan.
[lxiii. 306]

YEAMANS, SIR JOHN, first baronet (1610 ?-1674), colonial governor ; colonel in royalist army ; migrated to Barbados, 1650, and was member of council of the colony, 1660 ; was made baronet and first governor of new colony at Cape Fear, Carolina, 1665, but soon returned to Barbados, leaving a deputy ; again governor, 1672-4.
[lxiii. 307]

YEAMANS or **YEOMANS**, ROBERT (d. 1643), royalist : merchant and councillor of Bristol ; sheriff, 1641-2 ; hanged as traitor for plotting to betray Bristol to royalists.
[lxiii. 308]

YEARDLEY, SIR GEORGE (1580 ?-1627), governor of Virginia ; landed in Virginia, 1610 ; deputy-governor, 1616-17 ; visited England, 1618, and was appointed governor and knighted ; held office till 1621, and again, 1626-7. During his governorship the first representative assembly in the western hemisphere met at Jamestown, 1619, and the first negro slaves brought into an English colony were landed by a Dutch man-of-war, 1620.
[lxiii. 308]

YEARDLEY, JOHN (1786-1858), quaker missionary : began preaching as quaker in northern counties, 1815 ; settled at Pyrmont, Germany, 1821 ; made missionary journeys in many parts of Europe and in Asia Minor ; married, 1826, Martha Savory, author of several works in verse and prose.
[lxiii. 309]

YEARSLEY, MRS. ANN (1756-1806), verse-writer ; known as 'Lactilla,' or as the 'Bristol milkwoman' : gained patronage of Hannah More [q. v.], under whose guidance she published 'Poems on Several Occasions,' 1784 ; her claims to control of trust-money (subscriptions collected for her by Hannah More) the occasion of a breach with her patroness. Her works include 'Earl Goodwin,' an historical tragedy in verse (1791), and 'The Royal Captives,' an historical novel (1795). [lxiii. 310]

YEARSLEY, JAMES (1805-1869), aural surgeon : studied at St. Bartholomew's Hospital, London ; M.R.C.S. and L.S.A., 1827 ; L.R.C.P. Edinburgh, 1860 ; M.D. St. Andrews, 1862 ; aural surgeon in London from c. 1837 ; joint-founder of 'Medical Directory' ; published works relating to aural surgery.
[lxiii. 311]

YEATES, THOMAS (1768-1839), orientalist ; apprenticed as turner ; matriculated at All Souls College, Oxford, 1802 ; employed by Claudius Buchanan [q. v.] to catalogue and describe oriental manuscripts brought by him from India, c. 1808-15 ; secretary of London Society of Literature ; assistant in printed-book department of British Museum, 1823-39 ; published works relating to biblical and oriental history and other writings.
[lxiii. 311]

YEATS, GRANT DAVID (1773-1836), medical writer ; born in Florida ; B.A. Hertford College, Oxford, 1793 ; M.A., 1796 ; M.B., 1797 ; M.B. Dublin, 1807 ; M.D. Trinity College, Oxford, 1814 ; private physician to Duke of Bedford when lord-lieutenant of Ireland, 1806-7 ; F.R.C.P., 1815 ; F.R.S., 1819 ; published 'Observations on Claims of the Moderns to some Discoveries in Chemistry and Physiology,' 1798, and other works. [lxiii. 312]

YELDARD, ARTHUR (d. 1599), president of Trinity College, Oxford ; B.A. Clare Hall, Cambridge, 1548 ; M.A., 1552 ; fellow of Pembroke Hall, Cambridge, 1551-4 ; original fellow of Trinity College, Oxford, and incorporated M.A., 1556 ; appointed president, 1559 ; B.D., 1563 ; D.D., 1566 ; vice-chancellor, 1580 ; left writings in manuscript.
[lxiii. 313]

YELLOLY, JOHN (1774-1842), physician ; M.D. Edinburgh, 1799 ; physician to London Hospital, 1807-1818 ; one of originators of Royal Medical and Chirurgical Society, 1805 ; physician to Norfolk and Norwich Hospital, 1820-32 ; F.R.S. ; published treatises on calculous diseases and other subjects.
[lxiii. 313]

YELVERTON, BARRY, first VISCOUNT AVONMORE (1736-1805) ; B.A. Trinity College, Dublin, 1757 ; worked as usher ; called to Irish bar, 1764 ; K.C., 1772 ; bencher of King's Inns, 1772 ; Irish M.P. for Donegal, 1774, and Carrickfergus, 1776-83 ; attorney-general, 1782 ; chiefbaron of court of exchequer, 1783 ; raised to peerage as Baron Avonmore, 1795 ; created viscount of Ireland and baron of United Kingdom, 1800. [lxiii. 314]

YELVERTON, SIR CHRISTOPHER (1535 ?-1612), judge ; entered Gray's Inn, 1552 ; treasurer, 1579 and 1585 ; M.P., Brackley, 1563 ; recorder of Northampton before 1572 ; M.P., Northampton, 1572 ; serjeant-at-law, 1589 ; M.P., Northamptonshire, 1593 and 1597 ; speaker, 1597 ; queen's serjeant, 1598 ; took part in indictment of Essex, 1600 ; justice of queen's bench, 1602 ; K.B., 1603.
[lxiii. 315]

YELVERTON, SIR HENRY (1566-1629), judge ; son of Sir Christopher Yelverton [q. v.] ; studied at Gray's Inn ; called to bar, 1593 ; ancient, 1593 ; Lent reader, 1607 ; M.P., Northampton, 1603 and 1614 ; attorney-general, 1617 ; suspended from office on ground of having officially passed a charter to city of London containing unauthorised provisions, 1620, and imprisoned in Tower of London, 1620-1 ; fifth judge of common pleas, 1625-9.
[lxiii. 316]

YELVERTON, SIR WILLIAM (1400 ?-1472 ?), judge ; justice of peace for Norwich, 1427, and recorder, 1433-50 ; M.P., Great Yarmouth, 1435 and 1436 ; serjeant-at-law, 1439 ; judge of king's bench, 1443 ; executor to Sir John Fastolf [q. v.], 1459 ; knighted, 1461 ; transferred to bench of common pleas, 1471. [lxiii. 318]

YELVERTON, WILLIAM CHARLES, fourth VISCOUNT AVONMORE (1824-1883), grandson of Barry Yelverton, first viscount Avonmore [q. v.] ; at Woolwich ; entered royal artillery and became major ; in Crimea ; engaged in litigation, 1859-68, respecting validity of marriage, against which the House of Lords finally decided, and which it was alleged he had contracted in 1857 in Scotland and Ireland [see LONGWORTH, MARIA THERESA]; suspended from military duties, 1861.   [lxiii. 318]

YEO, SIR JAMES LUCAS (1782–1818), commodore; entered navy, 1793; lieutenant, 1797; at siege of Genoa and in Adriatic, 1800; with Frederick Lewis Maitland [q. v.] at Muros Bay, 1805; commander of privateer, 1805; captain, 1807; took Cayenne, 1809; knighted, 1810; on Jamaica station, 1811; commodore and commander-in-chief of ships of war on American lakes, 1813; took Oswego, 1814, and unsuccessfully blockaded Sackett's harbour, being handicapped by indisposition to co-operate shown by Sir George Prevost (1767–1816) [q. v.]; commander-in-chief on west coast of Africa, 1815; in Jamaica, 1817; died on passage home.   [lxiii. 319]

YEO, RICHARD (d. 1779), medallist; produced medals for battle of Culloden, 1746; assistant-engraver to royal mint, 1749; chief engraver, 1775–9; foundation member of Royal Academy.   [lxiii. 320]

YEOWELL, JAMES (1803?–1875), antiquary; sub-editor under William John Thoms [q. v.] of 'Notes and Queries,' c. 1852–72, supplying answers under heading 'Queries with Answers'; nominated, 1872, a poor brother at London Charterhouse, where he died; published 'Memoir of Oldys,' 1862, and antiquarian writings. His MSS. now in British Museum.   [lxiii. 321]

YESTER, fifth BARON (d. 1576). [See HAY, WILLIAM.]

YEVELE, HENRY DE (d. 1400), master-mason and architect; director of king's works at Westminster, c. 1356, and at Westminster and the Tower of London, 1369–89; appointed to superintend projected works at Southampton, 1378; executed tombs of Richard II (1395) and Cardinal Langham (1394) in Westminster Abbey, and alterations in Westminster Hall, 1395.   [lxiii. 321]

YNGE, HUGH (d. 1528). [See INGE.]

YOLLAND, WILLIAM (1810–1885), lieutenant-colonel, royal engineers; second lieutenant, royal engineers, 1828; in Canada, 1831–5; lieutenant, 1833; brevet colonel, 1858; appointed to ordnance survey, 1838; first captain, 1847; inspector of railways under board of trade, 1854; lieutenant-colonel, 1855; member of commission to consider training of candidates for scientific corps of army, 1856; retired from military service, 1863; chief inspector of railways, 1877–85; C.B. (civil), 1881; F.R.A.S., 1840; F.R.S., 1859.   [lxiii. 322]

YONG. [See YONGE and YOUNG.]

YONG, JOHN (d. 1504). [See MORGAN.]

YONGE. [See also YOUNG.]

YONGE, CHARLES DUKE (1812–1891), historical and miscellaneous writer; of Eton and King's College, Cambridge, and St. Mary Hall, Oxford; M.A., 1874; regius professor of modern history and English literature at Queen's College, Belfast, 1866–91; published numerous educational and other works.   [lxiii. 324]

YONGE, SIR GEORGE, fifth baronet (1731–1812), governor of Cape of Good Hope; son of Sir William Yonge [q. v.]; educated at Eton and Leipzig; M.P., Honiton, 1754–61 and 1763–96; lord of admiralty, 1766–1770; vice-treasurer for Ireland, 1782; secretary for war, 1782–3 and 1783–94; master of mint, 1794–9; governor of Cape of Good Hope, 1799; K.B., 1788; superseded in governorship owing to various complaints against his administration, 1801.   [lxiii. 324]

YONGE, JAMES or JOHN (fl. 1423), translator; servant to James Butler, fourth earl of Ormonde [q. v.], at whose request he translated, c. 1423, the 'Secreta Secretorum,' attributed to Aristotle.   [lxiii. 325]

YONGE, JAMES (1646–1721), medical writer; apprenticed as surgeon in navy; surgeon's mate at ineffectual bombardment of Algiers, 1662; captive in Dutch hands, 1665–6; practised at Plymouth, 1666–8 and 1670; L.R.C.P., 1702; F.R.S., 1702; surgeon to naval hospital, Plymouth; published work on use of turpentine in control of hæmorrhage, 1679, and other works.   [lxiii. 326]

YONGE, JAMES (1794–1870), physician; at Eton and Exeter College, Oxford; M.A., 1817; M.D., 1821; F.R.C.P., 1822; practised in Plymouth.   [lxiii. 326]

YONGE, JOHN (1467–1516), master of rolls and diplomatist; of Winchester College and New College, Oxford; D.C.L.; fellow, 1485–1500; presented to church of St. Martin's, Oxford, 1500; 'judge of court of prerogative for diocese of Canterbury, 1503; held living of St. Mary-le-Bow, 1504–14; commissioner for treaty of commercial alliance with Philip, archduke of Austria, 1504; master of rolls, 1508; ambassador to Maximilian I, 1508; prebendary of St. Paul's Cathedral, London, 1511; dean of collegiate church of St. Mary's, Leicester, 1512; held living of Therfield, 1513–16; joint-ambassador to Emperor Maximilian at Brussels, 1512; joint-commissioner for formation of holy league, 1512–13; prebendary and dean of York, 1514; on political mission at Tournay, 1515.   [lxiii. 327]

YONGE, JOHN (1463–1526), bishop of Callipoli; of Winchester College and New College, Oxford; fellow, 1482–1502; D.D.; warden of hospital of 'St. Thomas of Acon in the Cheap, London,' 1510; suffragan to Richard Fitzjames, bishop of London, with title of bishop of Callipoli in Thrace, 1513; warden of New College, Oxford, 1521; dean of Chichester. He has been confused with John Yonge (1467–1516) [q. v.] and John Yonge, who was fellow of New College, Oxford, 1512, and rector of Newton Longville, c. 1525.   [lxiii. 328]

YONGE, NICHOLAS (d. 1619), musician; published under title 'Musica Transalpina' two volumes of madrigals, translated from Italian and Flemish composers, 1588 and 1597.   [lxiii. 329]

YONGE, THOMAS (1405?–1476), judge; studied at Middle Temple; M.P., Bristol, 1435, 1436, 1442, 1447, 1449, 1450, and 1455; presented petition to effect that the Duke of York should be recognised as heir to throne, 1451, and was imprisoned in Tower of London, 1451–2; M.P., Gloucestershire, 1460; serjeant-at-law and king's serjeant, 1463; justice of king's bench, 1475.   [lxiii. 330]

YONGE, WALTER (1581?–1649), diarist; entered Magdalen College, Oxford, 1599, and Middle Temple, 1600; called to bar; sheriff of Devonshire, 1628; M.P., Honiton, 1640; one of victuallers of navy, c. 1642–8; left manuscript diaries relating to years 1604–27 (published by Camden Society, 1848) and 1642–5 (containing proceedings of Long parliament).   [lxiii. 331]

YONGE, SIR WILLIAM, fourth baronet (d. 1755), politician; whig M.P. for Honiton, 1715–54, and Tiverton, 1754; commissioner of revenue in Ireland, 1723; commissioner of treasury in Great Britain, 1724–7 and 1730; K.B., 1725; on commission for executing office of lord high admiral, 1728; secretary at war, 1735; joint vice-treasurer of Ireland, 1746; F.R.S., 1748; hon. LL.D. Cambridge, 1749; a firm supporter of Sir Robert Walpole; collaborated with Roome and Concanen in converting the old comedy, 'The Jovial Crew,' by Richard Brome [q. v.], into a comic opera (produced at Drury Lane, London, 1731), and had some reputation as a rhyming wit.   [lxiii. 331]

YORK. [See also YORKE.]

YORK, DUKES OF. [See LANGLEY, EDMUND DE, first DUKE, 1341–1402; 'PLANTAGENET,' EDWARD, second DUKE, 1373?–1415; RICHARD, 1411–1460; RICHARD, 1472–1483; JAMES II, KING OF ENGLAND, 1633–1701.]

YORK and ALBANY, DUKES OF. [See ERNEST AUGUSTUS, 1674–1728; FREDERICK AUGUSTUS, 1763–1827.]

YORK, DUCHESS OF. [See HYDE, ANNE, 1637–1671.]

YORK, CARDINAL OF (1725–1807). [See HENRY BENEDICT MARIA CLEMENT.]

YORK, SIR JOHN (d. 1569?), master of the mint; great-grandson of Sir Richard York [q. v.]; assaymaster to mint, 1544; master of mint at Southwark, 1547; sheriff of London, 1549; supported John Dudley, earl of Warwick, and was knighted by Edward VI, 1549; master of the king's woods; employed on secret missions abroad, 1550; under-treasurer of mint in the Tower of London, 1550, and master, 1551–3; member of Russian company or 'merchant adventurers to Moscovy,' 1553; prominent supporter of Lady Jane Grey, and on that account imprisoned in Tower of London, 1553.   [lxiii. 334]

YORK, LAURENCE (1687–1770), Roman catholic prelate; Benedictine monk of St. Gregory's College,

Douay, 1705 ; ordained priest, 1711 ; joined English mission at Bath, 1730 ; bishop of Nisibis, 1741 ; vicar-apostolic of western district, 1750–64. [lxiii. 336]

YORK, RICHARD OF, EARL OF CAMBRIDGE (*d.* 1415). [See RICHARD.]

YORK, SIR RICHARD (*d.* 1498), politician ; chamberlain of York, 1459 ; sheriff and mayor of staple of Calais at York, 1466 ; mayor of York, 1469–82 ; M.P., York, 1472 ; knighted, 1487. [lxiii. 335]

YORK or **YORKE,** ROWLAND (*d.* 1588), soldier of fortune ; probably son of Sir John York [q. v.] ; served as volunteer in Netherlands from 1572 ; imprisoned at Brussels for conspiring to betray Ghent to Duke of Parma, 1580–6 ; appointed by Leicester to command of Zutphen sconce, which he delivered to Spaniards ; became captain of troop of lancers in Spanish service, and was perhaps poisoned by Spaniards as safeguard against treachery. [lxiii. 337]

YORK, WILLIAM OF (*d.* 1256). [See WILLIAM.]

YORKE, CHARLES (1722–1770), lord chancellor ; son of Philip Yorke, first earl of Hardwicke [q. v.] ; M.A. Corpus Christi College, Cambridge, 1749 ; barrister, Lincoln's Inn, 1746, bencher, 1754 ; contributed largely to 'Athenian Letters' ; joint clerk of crown in chancery, 1747 ; M.P., Reigate, 1747–68, Cambridge University, 1768 ; counsel for East India Company, 1751 ; K.C. and solicitor-general to George, prince of Wales, 1754 ; solicitor-general, 1756–61 ; attorney-general, 1762 ; dealt officially with question of Wilkes's libel in 'North Briton,' No. 45 ; resigned, 1763 ; left Pitt's party and adhered to Rockingham whigs ; recorder of Dover and Gloucester, 1764 ; again attorney-general, 1765–7 ; drafted constitution for province of Quebec, which was embodied in Quebec Act, 1774 ; lord chancellor and privy councillor, 1770 ; F.R.S. [lxiii. 337]

YORKE, SIR CHARLES (1790–1880), field-marshal ; ensign, 1807 ; lieutenant, 52nd foot, 1808 ; served in Peninsular war ; captain, 1813 ; commanded brigade at Waterloo, 1815 ; lieutenant-colonel and inspecting field officer of militia, 1826 ; colonel, 1841 ; major-general, 1851 ; second in command in Kaffir war, 1852 ; military secretary at head-quarters, 1854–60 ; colonel, 33rd foot, 1855 ; K.C.B., 1856 ; G.C.B., 1860 ; general, 1865 ; constable of Tower of London, 1875 ; field-marshal, 1877. [lxiii. 340]

YORKE, CHARLES PHILIP (1764–1834), politician ; son of Charles Yorke (1722–1770) [q. v.] ; of Harrow and St. John's College, Cambridge ; M.A., *per literas regias,* 1783 ; barrister, Middle Temple, 1787 ; M.P., Cambridgeshire, 1790–1810, St. Germains, 1810, and Liskeard, 1812–18 ; privy councillor, 1801 ; secretary at war, 1801–3 ; home secretary, 1803–4 ; a teller of the exchequer, 1810 ; gained notoriety by his responsibility for enforcement of standing order for exclusion of strangers during debate on Walcheren expedition, 1810 ; first lord of admiralty, 1810–11 ; F.R.S., 1801 ; F.S.A. [lxiii. 341]

YORKE, CHARLES PHILIP, fourth EARL OF HARDWICKE (1799–1873), admiral ; son of Sir Joseph Sydney Yorke [q. v.] ; educated at Harrow and Royal Naval College, Portsmouth ; lieutenant, 1819 ; commander, 1822 ; captain, 1825 ; in Mediterranean, 1828–31 ; M.P., Reigate, 1831–2, Cambridgeshire, 1832–4 ; succeeded his uncle, Philip Yorke, third earl of Hardwicke [q. v.], 1834 ; commanded Black Eagle yacht, 1844–5 ; rear-admiral, 1854 ; admiral, 1863 ; postmaster-general, with seat in cabinet, 1852. [lxiii. 342]

YORKE, HENRY REDHEAD (1772–1813), publicist ; joined radical society at Derby, *c.* 1793 ; imprisoned for conspiracy, sedition, and libel, 1795–8 ; subsequently renounced revolutionary sympathies ; published writings on political and historical subjects. [lxiii. 343]

YORKE, JAMES (*fl.* 1640), heraldic writer ; worked as blacksmith at Lincoln ; published a genealogical and heraldic compilation entitled 'The Union of Honour,' 1640. [lxiii. 344]

YORKE, JOSEPH, BARON DOVER (1724–1792), diplomatist ; son of Philip Yorke, first earl of Hardwicke [q. v.] ; ensign, 1741 ; lieutenant-colonel in 1st foot-guards, 1745 ; served as aide-de-camp to Cumberland at Fontenoy, and during Scottish campaign, 1745–6 ; aide-de-camp to George II, 1747 ; colonel of 9th foot, 1755, 5th dragoons, 1760, 11th dragoons, 1787, and 1st life-guards, 1789 ; general, 1777 ; secretary of embassy at

Paris, 1749 ; British minister at the Hague, 1751, and ambassador, 1761–80 ; K.B., 1761 ; M.P. for East Grinstead, 1751–61, Dover, 1761–74, and Grampound, 1774–80 ; created Baron Dover, 1788. [lxiii. 344]

YORKE, SIR JOSEPH SYDNEY (1768–1831), admiral ; son of Charles Yorke (1722–1770) [q. v.] ; entered navy, 1780 ; lieutenant, 1789 ; commander, 1790 ; M.P., Reigate, 1790–1806 and 1818–31, having in the interval represented St. Germains, West Looe, and Sandwich ; captain, 1793 ; lord of admiralty, 1810–18 ; knighted, 1810 ; rear-admiral, 1810 ; at Lisbon, 1810 ; K.C.B., 1815 ; admiral, 1830. [lxiii. 346]

YORKE, PHILIP, first EARL OF HARDWICKE (1690–1764), lord chancellor ; worked in office of a London solicitor, 1706–8 ; barrister, Middle Temple, 1715 ; joined Lincoln's Inn, and was bencher and treasurer, 1724 ; M.P., Lewes, 1719, Seaford, 1722–34 ; solicitor-general, 1720 ; knighted, 1720 ; recorder of Dover, 1720–64 ; attorney-general, 1724 ; conducted prosecutions of Edmund Curll [q. v.], 1727, Thomas Woolston [q. v.], Thomas Bambridge [q. v.], 1729 ; invested with coif and appointed chief-justice and privy councillor, and created Baron Hardwicke, 1733 ; recorder of Gloucester, 1735 ; lord chancellor, 1737 ; member of council of regency during George II's absence from realm, 1740 ; responsible for insertion of attainder clauses in act of 1744 making correspondence with Young Pretender or his brothers punishable as an act of high treason ; presided as lord high steward at trials of rebel lords, 1745, and was responsible for subsequent legislative measures directed against Scotland, including proscription of the tartan and the abolition of heritable jurisdictions ; created Earl of Hardwicke and Viscount Royston, 1754 ; resigned office in crisis following loss of Minorca, 1756 ; LL.D. Cambridge, 1753 ; F.R.S., 1753 ; published speeches and legal writings. He did much to transform equity from a chaos of precedents into a scientific system. [lxiii. 346]

YORKE, PHILIP, second EARL OF HARDWICKE (1720–1790), son of Philip Yorke, first earl of Hardwicke [q. v.] ; LL.D. Corpus Christi College, Cambridge, 1749 ; F.R.S., 1741 ; F.S.A., 1745 ; wrote with his brother Charles [q. v.] most of 'Athenian Letters : or the Epistolary Correspondence of an Agent of the King of Persia, residing at Athens during the Peloponnesian War,' printed privately, 1741, and published, 1798 ; M.P., Reigate, 1741–7, Cambridgeshire, 1747–64 ; privy councillor, 1760 ; succeeded as Earl Hardwicke, 1764 ; teller of exchequer, 1738 ; lord-lieutenant of Cambridgeshire, 1757, high steward of Cambridge University, 1764–90 ; edited several political collections, including 'Walpoliana : or a few Anecdotes of Sir Robert Walpole,' 1783. [lxiii. 351]

YORKE, PHILIP (1743–1804), author ; M.A. Corpus Christi College, Cambridge, 1765 ; F.S.A., 1768 ; M.P., Helston, 1774–81, Grantham, 1792–3 ; published 'The Royal Tribes of Wales,' 1779, a valuable account of the five regal tribes. [lxiii. 353]

YORKE, PHILIP, third EARL OF HARDWICKE (1757–1834). son of Charles Yorke [q. v.] ; M.A. Queens' College, Cambridge, 1776 ; LL.D., 1811 ; high steward of the university, 1806 ; M.P., Cambridgeshire, 1780–90 ; succeeded his uncle, Philip Yorke, second earl of Hardwicke [q. v.], 1790 ; lord-lieutenant of Ireland, 1801–6 ; K.G., 1803 ; F.R.S. ; F.S.A. [lxiii. 353]

YORKE, PHILIP JAMES (1799–1874), chemist, mineralogist, and meteorologist ; educated at Harrow ; joined Scots fusilier guards and became lieutenant-colonel, 1852 ; colonel of Herefordshire militia during Crimean war ; original member of Chemical Society, 1841, and president, 1853–5 ; F.R.S., 1849. [lxiii. 354]

YOUATT, WILLIAM (1776–1847), veterinary surgeon ; educated for nonconformist ministry ; conducted in partnership a veterinary infirmary in Wells Street, Oxford Street, London, from *c.* 1812, and independently from *c.* 1824 ; delivered lectures to veterinary students at University College, 1830–5 ; founded and conducted 'Veterinarian,' monthly periodical, 1828 ; original member of Royal Agricultural Society, 1838 ; received diploma of Royal College of Veterinary Surgeons, 1844 ; wrote several treatises on animals. [lxiii. 354]

YOULDING, THOMAS (1670–1736). [See YALDEN.]

YOULL, HENRY (*fl.* 1608), musician ; published 'Canzonets to three Voyces,' 1608. [lxiii. 356]

YOUNG. [See also YONGE.]

YOUNG, ANDREW (1807–1889), schoolmaster and poet; educated at Edinburgh University; head-master of Niddrie Street School, Edinburgh, 1830–40; head English master of Madras College, St. Andrews, 1840–53; superintendent of Greenside parish Sabbath school, Edinburgh, 1853–88; wrote many hymns, including 'There is a happy land' (1838), first published in James Gall's 'Sacred Songs.' [lxiii. 356]

YOUNG, ANTHONY (*fl.* 1700–1720), organist of St. Clement Danes, London; published songs, 1707; said, though on insufficient evidence, to have composed the national anthem. [lxiii. 399]

YOUNG, SIR ARETAS WILLIAM (1778?–1835), soldier and colonial governor; ensign in Earl of Portmore's regiment, 1795; lieutenant, 13th foot, 1795; captain, 1796; major, 97th regiment, 1807; served in Peninsula, 1808–10 and 1811; lieutenant-colonel, 3rd West India regiment at Trinidad, 1813; member of council of Trinidad, 1820; temporary governor, 1820 and 1821–3; protector of slaves in Demerara, 1826; lieutenant-governor of Prince Edward's island, 1831; knighted, 1834. [lxiii. 356]

YOUNG, ARTHUR (1693–1759), divine; LL.D. Pembroke Hall, Cambridge, 1728; prebendary of Canterbury, 1746; vicar of Exning, 1748; chaplain to Arthur Onslow [q. v.]; published religious works. [lxiii. 357]

YOUNG, ARTHUR (1741–1820), agriculturist and author of 'Travels in France'; son of Arthur Young (1693–1759) [q. v.]; apprenticed for mercantile career at Lynn; started, 1762, in London, 'Universal Museum' monthly magazine, which failed after five months; engaged in farming at Bradfield, Berkshire, 1763–6; published 'The Farmer's Letters to the People of England,' 1767; took farm at North Mimms, Hertfordshire, 1768; published numerous works on agricultural and political subjects, including 'Observations on the present State of the Waste Lands of Great Britain,' 1773, and 'Political Arithmetic,' 1774; F.R.S., 1773; agent to Lord Kingsborough in co. Cork, 1777–9; published 'Tour in Ireland,' 1780; began 'Annals of Agriculture,' 1784, forty-seven volumes appearing continuously till 1809; went with M. de Lazowski and Count de la Rochefoucauld on tour to Pyrenees, 1787; deputed by wool-growers of Suffolk to support petition against wool bill, 1788, but was unsuccessful, the bill being passed; made second journey in France, 1788, and third, proceeding to Italy, 1789; published 'Travels in France' (containing the famous phrase 'the magic of property turns sand into gold'), 1792; secretary to board of agriculture, 1793, issuing numerous treatises relating to agriculture of English counties; left materials for a great work, entitled 'Elements and Practice of Agriculture.' [lxiii. 357]

YOUNG or YONG, BARTHOLOMEW (*fl.* 1577–1598), translator of Montemayor's Spanish romance of 'Diana,' published, 1598; studied at Middle Temple; in Spain, *c.* 1577; translated from Boccaccio; his version of 'Diana' used by Shakespeare in writing 'Two Gentlemen of Verona.' [lxiii. 363]

YOUNG, SIR CHARLES GEORGE (1795–1869), Garter king-of-arms; educated at Charterhouse, London; rouge dragon pursuivant, 1813; York herald, 1820; registrar, 1822–42; Garter principal king-of-arms, 1842; knighted, 1842; F.S.A., 1822; hon. D.C.L. Oxford, 1854; wrote heraldic works, printed privately. His report (1835) on the heraldic grievances of the baronets was utilised by Disraeli in 'Sybil.' [lxiii. 364]

YOUNG, CHARLES MAYNE (1777–1856), comedian; educated at Eton and Merchant Taylors' School; clerk in a city house; appeared on stage at Liverpool, 1798, playing subsequently at Manchester and at Edinburgh, where he formed friendship with Sir Walter Scott; played Hamlet at the Haymarket, London, 1807, and also Hotspur and Petruchio; with John Philip Kemble in Covent Garden Company, 1808, his parts including Othello, Macbeth, Iachimo, Prospero, Jaques, Joseph Surface, Coriolanus, Mark Antony ('Antony and Cleopatra'), Richard III, Cassius, Iago, Falstaff, King John, and King Lear; with Kean at Drury Lane, London, 1822; original Rienzi in Miss Mitford's 'Rienzi' at Drury Lane, 1828; retired from stage, 1832. His most popular comic parts were Sir Pertinax Macsycophant and Megrim in

'Blue Devils'; he was probably at his best in Hamlet, Octavian, Macbeth, Prospero, Cassius, and Daran in 'The Exile.' [lxiii. 365]

YOUNG, EDWARD (1683–1765), poet; born at Upham, near Winchester; of Winchester College, 1695–1702, and New College and Corpus Christi College, Oxford; received law fellowship at All Souls College, Oxford, 1708; B.C.L., 1714; D.C.L., 1719; friend of Thomas Tickell [q. v.], and George Bubb Dodington (Baron Melcombe) [q. v.], and member of Addison's literary circle; gained patronage of Wharton; wrote 'Busiris,' which was produced at Drury Lane, 1719, and the 'Revenge,' produced at same theatre, 1721; published series of satires, 'The Universal Passion,' 1725; chaplain to George II, 1728; rector of Welwyn, 1730; married Lady Elizabeth Lee, daughter of George Henry Lee, second earl of Lichfield, 1731; published, 1742, 'The Complaint: or Night Thoughts on Life, Death, and Immortality,' which immediately achieved popularity; brought out 'The Brothers,' tragedy played at Drury Lane, 1753; 'clerk of the closet' to the princess dowager, 1761; his collected works published, 1757–78, 7 vols. [lxiii. 368]

YOUNG, GEORGE (1732–1810), admiral; midshipman, 1757; at Louisbourg, 1758, and Quebec, 1759; lieutenant, 1761; on Jamaica station; commander, 1768; on West African station; flag captain to Sir Edward Vernon [q. v.] in East Indies, 1777; appointed to William and Mary yacht, 1779; knighted, 1781; rear-admiral, 1794; admiral, 1799; F.R.S., 1781; F.S.A.; actively supported proposal of Jean Maria Matra for establishing colony in New South Wales, 1784; promoter and one of first proprietors of Sierra Leone Company, 1791. [lxiii. 373]

YOUNG, GEORGE (1777–1848), theologian, topographer, and geologist; M.A. Edinburgh, 1819; pastor of united associate presbyterian congregation, Whitby, 1806–1848; published theological writings and works relating to Yorkshire. [lxiii. 374]

YOUNG, GEORGE RENNY (*fl.* 1824–1847), author; brother of Sir William Young (1799–1887) [q. v.]; born in Scotland; established 'Nova Scotian' newspaper, 1824; published political, historical, and other works. [lxiii. 402]

YOUNG, SIR HENRY EDWARD FOX (1808–1870), colonial governor; son of Sir Aretas William Young [q. v.]; entered Inner Temple, 1831; treasurer of St. Lucia, 1833; government secretary of British Guiana, 1835; lieutenant-governor of eastern province of Cape Colony, 1847; governor of South Australia, 1848, and Tasmania, 1855–61; knighted, 1847. [lxiii. 375]

YOUNG, JAMES (*d.* 1789), admiral; lieutenant, 1739; commander, 1742; captain, 1743; served in battle near Minorca (Byng attributing to him disorder in rear division of fleet), 1756; in expedition against Rochefort, 1757, and off Brest, 1759; rear-admiral of red, 1762; vice-admiral of white, 1770; commander-in-chief on Leeward islands station, 1775; admiral of white, 1778. [lxiii. 376]

YOUNG, JAMES (1811–1883), chemist and originator of paraffin industry; studied under Thomas Graham (1805–1869) [q. v.] at Andersonian University, Glasgow, and was his assistant, 1831–2, accompanying him to University College, London, 1837; manager to Messrs. Tennant at Manchester, 1844; set on foot movement for establishing 'Manchester Examiner' newspaper, first published, 1846; engaged in manufacture of oils from petroleum spring at Alfreton, Derbyshire, 1848–51; in partnership with Edward Meldrum and Edward William Binney [q. v.], for manufacture of oils from 'Torbane Hill mineral,' or 'Boghead coal,' at Bathgate, 1850; began sale of paraffin, 1856, with success, occasioning much litigation, which aimed chiefly at a repeal of his patent on ground that he had been forestalled; took over whole business from partners, 1865, and sold it to 'Young's Paraffin Light and Mineral Oil Company,' 1866; president, Anderson's College, 1868–77; F.R.S., 1873; settled at Kelly, on Clyde; began, at Pitlochry, with Professor George Forbes, experiments on velocity of light; LL.D. St. Andrews, 1879; a generous friend of Livingstone, contributing largely towards expenses of his expeditions; founded Young chair of technical chemistry, Anderson's College, 1870. [lxiii. 376]

YOUNG, JOHN (1514–1580), master of Pembroke Hall, Cambridge; M.A. Cambridge, 1539; B.D., 1546; fellow of St. John's College, Cambridge, 1536; original member of Trinity College, Cambridge, 1546; B.D., 1553, and incorporated at Oxford, 1554; master of Pembroke Hall, Cambridge, 1554; canon of Ely, 1554; vice-chancellor of Cambridge, 1553–5; regius professor of divinity, 1555; deprived of mastership and imprisoned for refusing oath to Queen Elizabeth, 1559. [lxiii. 379]

YOUNG, JOHN (1534?–1605), master of Pembroke Hall, Cambridge, and bishop of Rochester; educated at Mercers' School, London; B.A. Cambridge, 1552; fellow of Pembroke Hall, 1553–63; M.A., 1555; ordained, 1561; B.D., 1563; prebendary of St. Paul's Cathedral, 1564, and Southwell, 1566; master of Pembroke Hall, 1567; D.D. and vice-chancellor, 1569; canon of Windsor, 1572; bishop of Rochester (celebrated in Spenser's 'Shepheard's Calendar' as 'Roffy,' an abbreviation of Roffensis), 1578. [lxiii. 379]

YOUNG, JOHN (1750?–1820), professor of Greek at Glasgow; M.A. Glasgow, 1769; professor of Greek, 1774–1820, proving a very efficient and popular teacher. [lxiii. 380]

YOUNG, JOHN (1755–1825), mezzotint engraver; mezzotint engraver to Prince of Wales, 1789; keeper of British Institution, 1813–25. [lxiii. 381]

YOUNG, JOHN (1773–1837), agricultural writer; educated at Glasgow; emigrated to Nova Scotia, c. 1815; published letters on state of agriculture, procured establishment of board of agriculture in Nova Scotia and became its secretary. [lxiii. 401]

YOUNG, SIR JOHN, second baronet, BARON LISGAR (1807–1876), born at Bombay; of Eton and Corpus Christi College, Oxford; B.A., 1829; barrister, Lincoln's Inn, 1834; tory M.P. for co. Cavan, 1831–55; lord of treasury, 1841; secretary of treasury, 1844–6; privy councillor, 1852; chief secretary for Ireland, 1852–5; lord high commissioner of Ionian islands, 1855–9; G.C.M.G., 1855; opposed project of union with Greece; governor-general and commander-in-chief of New South Wales, 1861–7; G.C.B., 1868; governor-general of Canada and governor of Prince Edward's island, 1869–72; created Baron Lisgar, 1870; resigned office, 1872. [lxiii. 381]

YOUNG, JOHN (1811–1878), Canadian economist; born at Ayr, Scotland; went to Canada, c. 1825; became partner in mercantile firm in Quebec, and from 1841 in Montreal; identified himself with the Free Trade Association (Montreal), 1842, and did much to promote commercial progress; commissioner of public works with seat in cabinet, 1851–2, in Hincks-Morin ministry; inspector at Montreal and chairman of harbour commission, 1874; published writings relating to Canadian economy. [lxiii. 382]

YOUNG, JOHN RADFORD (1799–1885), mathematician; almost entirely self-educated; published 'Elementary Treatise on Algebra,' 1823, and subsequently issued a series of elementary works; professor of mathematics at Belfast College, 1833–49; made several original discoveries, including a proof, 1844, of Newton's rule for determining number of imaginary roots in an equation. [lxiii. 383]

YOUNG, MATTHEW (1750–1800), bishop of Clonfert; M.A. Trinity College, Dublin, 1774; fellow, 1775; D.D., 1786; professor of natural philosophy, 1786; bishop of Clonfert, 1798; his works include 'Enquiry into Principal Phænomena of Sounds and Musical Strings,' 1784; and an amended version of the Psalms printed at Dublin University press (to Psalm cxli.), but not published. [lxiii. 384]

YOUNG, PATRICK (1584–1652), biblical writer; son of Sir Peter Young [q. v.]; M.A. St. Andrews, 1603; incorporated at Oxford; appointed chaplain of All Souls College, Oxford, 1605; employed at court as correspondent with foreign rulers, the diplomatic language being then Latin; librarian successively to Prince Henry, James I, and Charles I; prebendary of Chester Cathedral, 1613; incorporated M.A. Cambridge, 1620; prebendary and treasurer of St. Paul's Cathedral, 1621, and Latin secretary, 1624; rector of Hayes, 1623; sequestered, 1647; entrusted with revision of Alexandrian codex of Septuagint (his 'annotationes' being printed in vol. vi. of Brian Walton's 'Polyglot Bible,' 1657), and other Greek manuscripts. [lxiii. 385]

YOUNG, SIR PETER (1544–1628), tutor to James VI; probably M.A. St. Andrews; studied on continent, 1562–1568; joint-instructor with George Buchanan (1506–1582) [q. v.] of infant king James VI, 1570; won king's

affection and became his favourite counsellor; master almoner, 1577; sent on embassy to Frederick II of Denmark, 1586 and 1587; privy councillor, 1586; sent to complete negotiations for marriage of James VI and Princess Anne, daughter of Frederick, the Elector Palatine, 1589; one of King James's eight councillors (Octavians), 1595; on special embassy to Christian of Denmark to obtain support on question of succession to throne of England, 1598; accompanied King James to London, 1603; tutor and chief overseer in establishment of Prince Charles, 1604; knighted, 1605; master of St. Cross Hospital, Winchester, 1616. [lxiii. 386]

YOUNG, ROBERT (1657–1700), forger and cheat; claimed to have been educated at Trinity College, Dublin; procured admission to deacon's orders by means of forged certificates of learning and moral character, c. 1680, and held successively several Irish curacies; imprisoned for bigamy; realised considerable sums of money by forged letters to wealthy clergymen, a fraud which was discovered by archbishop of Canterbury, whose handwriting he had counterfeited; imprisoned for this in Newgate, 1690–2; fabricated, while in Newgate, a sham plot for restoring the exiled James II, and prepared document containing forged signatures of Marlborough, Cornbury, Salisbury, Sancroft, and Thomas Sprat [q. v.], bishop of Rochester; succeeded temporarily in imposing on government, but the scheme being discovered was imprisoned in King's Bench, whence, 1698, he escaped, turning to coining for livelihood; arrested and found guilty, 1700; executed. [lxiii. 388]

YOUNG, ROBERT (1822–1888), theologian and orientalist; apprenticed as printer; opened business as printer and bookseller, 1847; studied oriental and other languages; literary missionary and superintendent of mission press at Surat, 1856–61; chief work, 'Analytical Concordance to the Bible,' 1879. [lxiii. 390]

YOUNG or YONGE, THOMAS (1507–1568), archbishop of York; B.A. Broadgates Hall, Oxford, 1529; M.A., 1533; D.C.L., 1564; principal, 1542–6; precentor of St. David's Cathedral, 1542; publicly announced adherence to Reformation; resigned preferments and retired to Germany, 1553; restored, 1559; bishop of St. David's, 1559; archbishop of York, 1561; sat on commission at Lambeth which drew up the articles, 1561. [lxiii. 390]

YOUNG, THOMAS (1587–1655), master of Jesus College, Cambridge; M.A. St. Leonard's College, St. Andrews, 1606; private tutor in London, one of his pupils being John Milton; chaplain to English merchants at Hamburg, 1622–8; vicar of St. Peter and St. Mary, Stowmarket, 1628; took leading part in controversy occasioned by 'Humble Remonstrance' of Joseph Hall [q. v.], bishop of Norwich, 1640; member of assembly of divines at Westminster, 1643; master of Jesus College, Cambridge, 1644; deprived, 1650, on refusal to comply with new test; published 'Dies Dominica,' a work on observance of Sabbath, 1639. [lxiii. 392]

YOUNG, THOMAS (1773–1829), physician, physicist, and Egyptologist; acquired at early age great knowledge of ancient and modern languages; studied at St. Bartholomew's Hospital, London, 1793; elected member of Royal Society, 1794, in recognition of paper, 1793, in which he attributed accommodating power of eye to a muscular structure of the crystalline lens; proceeded to Edinburgh and Göttingen; created doctor of physic, Göttingen, 1796; fellow commoner at Emmanuel College, Cambridge, 1797; opened practice as physician in London, 1799; professor of natural philosophy at Royal Institution, editor of the 'Journals,' and superintendent of the house, 1801; resigned professorship, 1803; foreign secretary to Royal Society, 1802–29; M.B. Cambridge, 1803; M.D., 1808; F.R.C.P., 1809; censor, 1813 and 1823, and Croonian lecturer, 1822 and 1823; physician to St. George's Hospital, London, 1811–29; superintendent of 'Nautical Almanac' and secretary of reconstituted board of longitude, 1818; retired from practice, 1814. Memoir by him 'On the Mechanism of the Eye' ('Phil. Trans.' 1801), contained the first description and measurement of astigmatism, and a table of optical constants of the eye in close agreement with modern determinations. He first explained colour sensation as due to the presence in the retina of structures which correspond to the three colours —red, green, and violet respectively. He expounded in his paper 'On the Theory of Light and Colours' (ib. 1801) his doctrine of 'interference' of light, marking an epoch in the history of the subject, and in his 'Essay on Cohesion of Fluids' (*ib.* 1804) gave the theory of capillary action brought forward independently (1805) by Laplace, and now known by his name. He rendered valuable assistance in translating the demotic text of the Rosetta stone, and contributed the article on 'Egypt' to the 'Encyclopædia Britannica,' 1818, publishing also 'An Account of Recent Discoveries in Hieroglyphical Literature and Egyptian Antiquities,' 1823, and 'Enchorial Egyptian Dictionary' appended to 'Egyptian Grammar' by Henry Tattam [q. v.], 1830.   [lxii. 393]

YOUNG, WILLIAM (*fl.* 1653), musician; violist in household of Count of Innspruck; said to have published musical compositions, 1653; left musical works in manuscript.   [lxii. 399]

YOUNG, SIR WILLIAM, second baronet (1749–1815), colonial governor; matriculated at University College, Oxford, 1768; travelled on continent; published 'The Spirit of Athens,' 1777; M.P. for St. Mawes, Cornwall, 1784–1806, and Buckingham, 1806; follower of Pitt till 1801, after which he went over to Grenville's party; F.R.S., 1786; F.S.A., 1791; secretary to Association for promoting Discovery of Interior Parts of Africa; governor of Tobago, 1807–15. His publications include political writings and autobiographical memoirs.   [lxii. 399]

YOUNG, SIR WILLIAM (1751 - 1821), admiral; entered navy, 1761; lieutenant, 1770; captain, 1778; in Mediterranean, 1793; made unsuccessful attempt to destroy a tower in Mortella Bay, on north-west coast of Corsica, 1794; rear-admiral, 1795; lord of admiralty, 1795–1801; admiral, 1805; commander-in-chief at Plymouth, 1804–7; commanded fleet in North Sea, 1811; G.C.B., 1815; vice-admiral of United Kingdom, 1819.   [lxii. 400]

YOUNG, SIR WILLIAM (1799–1887), chief-justice of Nova Scotia; son of John Young (1773–1837) [q. v.]; born in Scotland; educated at Glasgow; joined his father in Nova Scotia; called to bar of Nova Scotia, 1826, and of Prince Edward's Island, 1835; Q.C, 1843; liberal member for Cape Breton in legislative assembly of Nova Scotia, 1832, for Inverness, 1837–59, and for Cumberland, 1859; took prominent part in negotiations arising from rebellion of French Canadians, 1838–9, and in quarrel between legislative assembly and Sir Colin Campbell (1776–1847) [q. v.], 1839; member of executive council, 1842; speaker of legislative assembly, 1843–54; premier and attorney-general, 1854–7; premier and president of executive council, 1859–60; chief-justice of Nova Scotia, 1860–81; knighted, 1868; judge of court of vice-admiralty.   [lxii. 401]

YOUNGE, ELIZABETH (1744 ?–1797).   [See POPE.]

YOUNGE or **YOUNG**, RICHARD (*fl.* 1637–1671), Calvinist tract writer; published, 1637–71, numerous penny tracts supporting Calvinistic doctrines and denouncing various social sins.   [lxiii. 402]

YOUNGER, ELIZABETH (1699 ?–1762), actress; sister of M— Bicknell [q. v.]; appeared with combined companies of Drury Lane and Dorset Garden, London, 1706, and with Drury Lane and Haymarket companies, 1711; at Lincoln's Inn Fields Theatre, 1725–34; retired from stage, 1734; her most popular parts, Belinda in the 'Old Bachelor,' Miranda, in the 'Busybody,' and the Country Wife.   [lxiii. 403]

YOUNGER, JOHN (1785–1860), writer on angling, shoemaker, and poet; settled as shoemaker at St. Boswells near Longnewton, 1811; published 'Thoughts as they Rise,' a volume of poems, 1834, and ' River Angling for Salmon and Trout,' 1839; left manuscript memoirs, published in ' Autobiography of John Younger,' 1881.   [lxiii. 404]

YPRES, WILLIAM OF, erroneously styled EARL OF KENT (*d.* 1165 ?).   [See WILLIAM.]

YULE, SIR GEORGE UDNEY (1813–1886), Indian civilian; brother of Sir Henry Yule [q. v.]; with corps of mounted European volunteers in Indian mutiny; member of governor-general's council.   [lxiii. 407]

YULE, SIR HENRY (1820–1889), geographer; educated at Edinburgh High School, Addiscombe, and Chatham; appointed to Bengal engineers, 1840; worked on restoration and development of irrigation system of Moguls in North-West provinces, 1843–9; in Sikh wars, 1845–6 and 1848–9; under-secretary to Indian public works department, 1855; secretary to Colonel (afterwards Sir Arthur) Phayre's embassy to Burma, 1855; published 'Narrative of Mission to Ava,' 1858; retired from service, 1862; C.B., 1863; resided at Palermo, 1863–75; member of Indian council, 1875–89; K.C.S.I., 1889. His publications include 'Mirabilia descripta. The Wonders of the East,' by Jordanus, 1863, 'Cathay and the Way thither,' 1866, and 'Diary of Sir William Hedges,' 1887 (all edited for Hakluyt Society), an edition of 'Marco Polo,' 1871, and 'Hobson Jobson, Glossary of Anglo-Indian Colloquial Words and Phrases,' 1886. [lxiii. 405]

YULE, ROBERT (1817–1857), soldier; brother of Sir Henry Yule; published 'On Cavalry Movements,' 1856, and other works; died in action before Delhi.   [lxiii. 407]

Z

ZADKIEL (pseudonym).   [See MORRISON, RICHARD JAMES, 1795–1874.]

ZAEHNSDORF, JOSEPH (1816–1886), bookbinder; born in Pesth, Austria-Hungary; apprenticed as bookbinder at Stuttgart; went to London, 1837; opened business, 1842; his work ranked with that of Bedford and Riviere.   [lxiii. 408]

ZEEMAN, ENOCH (1694–1744).   [See SEEMAN.]

ZERFFI, GEORGE GUSTAVUS (1821–1892), writer on history and art; born in Hungary; came to England on failure of revolution, 1849; employed in art department, South Kensington, and became lecturer, 1868; published 'Manual of Historical Development of Art,' 1876, 'Studies in Science of General History,' 1887–9, and other works.   [lxiii. 408]

ZINCKE, CHRISTIAN FRIEDRICH (1684 ?–1767), enamel-painter; born in Dresden; came to England, 1706; pupil of Charles Boit [q. v.]; cabinet-painter to Frederick, prince of Wales: enjoyed wide practice as painter of portraits in enamels.   [lxiii. 409]

ZINCKE, FOSTER BARHAM (1817–1893), antiquary; born at Eardley, Jamaica; B.A. Wadham College, Oxford, 1839; vicar of Wherstead, 1847; one of Queen Victoria's chaplains, *c.* 1852; travelled widely in various parts of world, publishing works relating to countries visited, and other writings.   [lxiii. 409]

ZOEST, GERARD (1637 ?–1681).   [See SOEST.]

ZOFFANY, **ZOFFANJI**, or **ZAFFANII**, JOHN or JOHANN (1733–1810), painter; born at Ratisbon; studied at Rome; lived in Italy; came to England, 1758; worked successively for Stephen Rimbault, the clockmaker, and for Benjamin Wilson [q. v.] (as drapery painter); attracted notice as portrait-painter; member of Society of Artists of Great Britain, 1762; painted Garrick and Samuel Poole and other actors in numerous characters; member of Royal Academy, 1769; in Italy, 1772–9, and in India, 1783–90, obtaining several lucrative commissions. His skill lay chiefly in dramatic scenes and conversation-pieces, the backgrounds being sometimes executed by other artists.   [lxiii. 410]

ZOON, JAN FRANZ VAN (1658–1718 ?).   [See VAN SON.]

ZOONE, WILLIAM (*fl.* 1540–1575).   [See SOONE.]

ZOUCH.   [See also ZOUCHE.]

ZOUCH, HENRY (1725 ?–1795), antiquary and social reformer; brother of Thomas Zouch [q. v.]; M.A. Trinity College, Cambridge, 1750; vicar of Sandal Magna, 1754–1789; governor of Wakefield school, 1758–64; rector of Swillington, 1788–95; chaplain to Marchioness of Rockingham; published works on social questions.   [lxiii. 412]

ZOUCH, THOMAS (1737–1815), divine and antiquary ; brother of Henry Zouch [q. v.] ; pensioner of Trinity College, Cambridge, 1756 ; Craven scholar, 1760 ; M.A., 1764 ; D.D., 1805 ; minor fellow, 1762 ; major fellow, 1764 ; lector linguæ Latinæ, 1768 ; rector of Wycliffe, 1770–93 ; F.L.S., 1788 ; chaplain to Richard Pepper Arden [q. v.], master of rolls, 1788 ; deputy commissioner of archdeaconry of Richmond, 1791 ; rector of Scrayingham, Yorkshire, 1793 ; governor of Wakefield school, 1799–1805 ; prebendary of Durham, 1805 ; refused bishopric of Carlisle, 1807 ; published religious and other works, including an edition of Walton's ' Lives,' 1796, with a ' Life of Isaac Walton ' (separately issued, 1823). [lxiii. 412]

ZOUCHE, fourteenth BARON (1810–1873). [See CURZON, ROBERT.]

ZOUCHE or **ZOUCH,** ALAN LA or DE LA, BARON ZOUCHE (d. 1270), served with Henry III in Gascony, 1242 ; justice of Chester and of the four cantreds in North Wales, c. 1250 ; justice of Ireland under Henry's son Edward, 1255–8 ; adhered to Henry III during barons' wars ; sheriff of Northamptonshire, 1261–4 ; justice of forests south of Trent, 1261 ; king's seneschal, 1263 ; one of committee of arbitrators appointed to arrange terms of surrender of Kenilworth, 1266 ; warden of London and constable of the Tower, 1267–8 ; benefactor of the Knights Templars. [lxiii. 414]

ZOUCHE, EDWARD LA, eleventh BARON ZOUCHE OF HARRINGWORTH (1556 ?–1625), succeeded his father, 1569 ; educated under Whitgift at Trinity College, Cambridge ; one of peers who tried Mary Queen of Scots, 1586 ; lived on continent, 1587–93 ; envoy extraordinary to James VI of Scotland, 1593–4 ; on commercial mission to Denmark, 1598 ; deputy-governor of Guernsey, 1600–1 ; president of Wales, 1602–15 ; one of commissioners for treasury, 1612 ; member of council of Virginia, 1609, and of New England council, 1620 ; lord warden of Cinque ports, 1615–24 ; patron of Ben Jonson and William Browne and other poets. [lxiii. 415]

ZOUCHE, RICHARD (1590–1661), civilian ; cousin of Edward la Zouche, eleventh baron Zouche [q. v.] ; of Winchester College and New College, Oxford ; fellow, 1609–22 ; D.C.L., 1619 ; advocate of Doctors' Commons, 1617 ; regius professor of civil law at Oxford, 1620–61 ; fellow commoner at Wadham College, 1623–5 ; principal of St. Alban Hall, 1625–41 ; M.P., Hythe, 1621 and 1624 ; judge of high court of admiralty, 1641 ; sided with Charles I in civil war ; deprived of judgeship, 1649, though retaining professorship at Oxford ; member of university commission, 1660 ; was restored to judgeship, 1661, but died less than a month later ; published ' The Dove, or Passages of Cosmography,' 1613, ' Elementa Jurisprudentiæ,' 1629, a work mapping out the whole field of law and examining in detail its various departments, and numerous legal treatises ; his treatise on *Jus Feciale* the first work which exhibits the law of nations as a well-ordered system. [lxiii. 417]

ZOUCHE or **ZOUCH,** WILLIAM LA or DE LA (d. 1352), archbishop of York ; M.A. and B.C.L. ; chaplain to Edward III ; clerk and purveyor of the great wardrobe, 1330, and, later, keeper of the wardrobe ; keeper of privy seal, 1335 ; treasurer of exchequer, 1337–8 ; treasurer of England, 1338–40 ; canon of Exeter, 1328 ; archdeacon of Exeter, 1330 ; canon of Southwell, 1333 ; prebendary of York, 1335 ; dean of York, 1336 ; prebendary of Lincoln, 1340 ; canon of Ripon ; elected archbishop of York, 1340, and, Edward urging claims of William de Kildesby, Zouche proceeded to Avignon to obtain Pope Benedict XII's confirmation ; captured by brigands in diocese of Lausanne ; arrived at Avignon, 1341, but with his rival was kept by Pope Benedict XII in suspense till his death ; appointed to archbishopric by Clement VI ; returned to England, 1342 ; excommunicated for opposing pope in question of succession to deanery of York, 1349–52 ; warden of Scottish march, 1346 ; took part in victory of Neville's Cross, 1346. [lxiii. 420]

ZUCCARELLI or **ZUCCHERELLI,** FRANCESCO (1702–1788), landscape-painter ; born at Pitigliano, Tuscany ; became renowned for decorative landscapes ; scene-painter at the Opera House, London ; foundation member of Royal Academy ; patronised by royal family ; returned to Italy, 1773. [lxiii. 423]

ZUCCARO, ZUCHARO, or **ZUCCHERO,** FEDERIGO (1542 ?–1609), painter ; born at St. Angelo in Vado, Tuscany ; worked on paintings in Vatican, Rome, and cathedral at Florence ; came to England, 1574, and though he obtained some influential patronage, probably found but scanty employment ; returned to Italy, 1578 ; founded, and was first president of the Accademia S. Luca, Rome ; numerous portraits of his period attributed to him without much foundation ; perhaps painted the ' Rainbow ' portrait of Queen Elizabeth at Hatfield, and that at Siena. [lxiii. 423]

ZUCCHI, ANTONIO PIETRO (1726–1795), painter ; born at Venice ; accompanied Robert Adam [q. v.] and Charles Louis Clérisseau [q. v.] in travels through Italy and Dalmatia, 1754 ; came to England, 1766, and was employed by Adam on interior decorations of several mansions ; A.R.A., 1770 ; married Angelica Kauffman [q. v.], 1781 ; died at Rome. [lxiii. 424]

ZUCCHI, GIUSEPPE (*fl.* 1770), line-engraver, younger brother of Antonio Pietro Zucchi [q. v.] ; practised as line-engraver in England ; employed on Adam's ' Works in Architecture.' [lxiii. 424]

ZUKERTORT, JOHN HERMANN (1842–1888), chess master ; born in province of Riga ; graduated in medicine at Breslau, 1866 ; studied chess and became pupil of Anderssen ; edited with Anderssen and, later, independently, ' Neue Berliner Schachzeitung ' ; associated with Jean Dufresne in editing ' Grosses Schach-Handbuch ' ; published ' Leitfaden des Schachspiels,' a collection of problems ; defeated Anderssen, 1871 ; came to England, 1872, and was naturalised ; founded and co-edited with Mr. L. Hoffer the ' Chess Monthly,' 1879 ; defeated Rosenthal, 1880, Blackburne, 1881, and Steinitz (the effort hastening the breakdown of his health), 1883, but was defeated by Steinitz, 1886. [lxiii. 424]

ZUYLESTEIN, FREDERICK NASSAU DE (1608–1672), soldier ; natural son of Henry Frederick, prince of Orange ; governor to William (afterwards king of England), whom he accompanied to England, 1670 ; general of foot in Dutch army, 1672 ; slain at Woerden. [lxiii. 426]

ZUYLESTEIN, FREDERICK NASSAU DE, third EARL OF ROCHFORD (1682–1738), brother of William Nassau de Zuylestein, second earl of Rochford [q. v.], whom he succeeded ; member of whig opposition in House of Lords, 1710–14. [lxiii. 428]

ZUYLESTEIN or **ZULESTEIN,** WILLIAM HENRY, first EARL OF ROCHFORD (1645–1709), born at Zuylestein, near Utrecht ; son of Frederick Nassau de Zuylestein (1608–1672) [q. v.] ; entered Dutch cavalry, 1672 ; sent by William of Orange on missions of observation to England, 1687 and 1688, when he intrigued effectively with prominent malcontents ; major-general in Dutch army, 1688 ; accompanied William of Orange to England, 1688 ; naturalised in England, 1689 ; master of robes to William III, 1689–95 ; lieutenant-general in English army, 1690 ; accompanied William III in Holland, 1693 ; created Baron Enfield, Viscount Tunbridge, and Earl of Rochford, 1695. [lxiii. 426]

ZUYLESTEIN or **ZULESTEIN,** WILLIAM HENRY [NASSAU DE], fourth EARL OF ROCHFORD (1717–1781), son of Frederick Nassau de Zuylestein, third earl of Rochford [q. v.] ; educated at Westminster School ; lord of bedchamber, 1738 ; vice-admiral of Essex, 1748 ; envoy extraordinary and plenipotentiary to king of Sardinia, 1749–55 ; groom of stole and first lord of bedchamber, 1755 ; privy councillor, 1755 ; ambassador extraordinary to court of Spain, 1763–6 ; British ambassador at Paris, 1766 ; secretary of state for northern department, 1768 ; opposed repeal of obnoxious American duties, 1769 ; promoted to southern department, 1770 ; resigned in view of the American difficulties, 1775 ; a master of the Trinity House ; K.G., 1778. [lxiii. 429]

ZUYLESTEIN or **ZULESTEIN,** WILLIAM NASSAU DE, second EARL OF ROCHFORD (1681–1710), son of William Henry, first earl of Rochford [q. v.] ; served as aide-de-camp to Marlborough in Flanders, 1704 ; returned to Irish parliament for Kilkenny, 1705 ; colonel, 3rd dragoons, 1707 ; whig M.P. for Steyning, Sussex, 1708 ; served in Spain, 1709 ; brigadier-general, 1710 ; killed at Almenara. [lxiii. 428]

THE
CONCISE DICTIONARY
OF
NATIONAL BIOGRAPHY
TWENTIETH CENTURY
1901–1921

NOTE

THE Epitome of 1901–1911 was made under the supervision of Sir Sidney Lee, and was published in 1913. It has now been reset and combined with the Epitome of 1912–1921.

When referring from the *Concise D.N.B.* to the main *Dictionary*, it is important to note that the latter now comprises four alphabetical series:

1. *The D.N.B. original issue*, containing obituaries from the earliest times to the dates of publication (1885–1900).

2. *Supplement* containing additional obituaries, mostly 1885–1900.

3. *The Twentieth Century D.N.B.* Obituaries 1901–1911.

4. *The Twentieth Century D.N.B.* Obituaries 1912–1921.

The *year of death* is therefore the necessary clue to the whereabouts of a memoir in the Dictionary.

THE CONCISE DICTIONARY

OF

NATIONAL BIOGRAPHY

TWENTIETH CENTURY

1901–1921

ABBEY, EDWIN AUSTIN (1852–1911), artist; born and educated at Philadelphia; studied art at academy there; worked for Harper's publishing firm, New York, 1871; came to England, 1878; won earliest fame as pen and ink illustrator; exhibited at Royal Academy 'A Milkmaid,' in black and white, 1885; exhibited also at Royal Institute of Painters in Water Colours, 1883–7, and elsewhere; brilliant in pastel work; exhibited his first oil painting at Royal Academy, 'A Mayday Morning,' 1890; A.R.A., 1894; R.A., 1898; best-known works include 'Fiammetta's Song,' 1894, 'O Mistress Mine,' 1899, 'Columbus in the New World,' 1906; painted official picture of 'The Coronation of King Edward VII,' 1903–4; executed notable mural decorations for Boston Public Library, the state capitol of Washington, and Royal Exchange; chevalier legion of honour, 1895; hon. LL.D. Pennsylvania; memorial exhibition at Royal Academy, 1912.

ABBOTT, EVELYN (1843–1901), classical scholar; educated at Lincoln grammar school, Somerset College, Bath, and Balliol College, Oxford; spinal accident paralysed his lower limbs for life, 1866; B.A. and M.A., 1873; master at Clifton, 1873–4; fellow and tutor of Balliol, 1874–1901; edited 'Hellenica,' 1880, and 'Heroes of the Nations' series, contributing 'Pericles,' 1891; collaborated with Lewis Campbell [q. v.] in 'Life of Jowett,' 1897; wrote 'History of Greece,' 3 vols. 1888–1900; hon. LL.D. St. Andrews, 1879.

A BECKETT, ARTHUR WILLIAM (1844–1909), humorist; son of Gilbert Abbott à Beckett [q. v.]; educated at Honiton and Felsted; entered civil service, 1862; left to engage in journalism, 1865; editor of 'Sunday Times,' 1891–5; contributed to 'Punch,' 1874–1902; works include 'The À Becketts of Punch,' 1903, and 'Recollections of a Humourist,' 1907; joined Church of Rome, 1874.

ABEL, SIR FREDERICK AUGUSTUS, baronet (1827–1902), chemist; educated at Royal College of Chemistry; demonstrator of chemistry at St. Bartholomew's Hospital, 1851; lecturer at Royal Military Academy, Woolwich, 1852; collaborated in 'Handbook of Chemistry,' 1854; chemist to war department, Woolwich, 1856; chief official authority on explosives; invented cordite, 1889; F.R.S., 1860; received royal medal, 1887; president of chemical and other societies; president British Association, Leeds, 1890; organizing secretary and director, Imperial Institute, and baronet, 1893; hon. D.C.L. Oxford, 1883; D.Sc. Cambridge, 1888; an accomplished musician.

ABERCORN, second DUKE OF (1838–1913). [See HAMILTON, JAMES.]

ABNEY, SIR WILLIAM DE WIVELESLIE (1843–1920), photographic chemist and education official; educated at Rossall; joined Royal Engineers, 1861; entered science and art department, South Kensington, 1877; assistant director for science, 1884; director, 1893; principal assistant secretary, Board of Education, 1899–1903; pioneer in advancement of practical photography, photographic emulsion-making, spectro-photography, colour analysis, and colour vision; F.R.S., 1876; Rumford medallist, 1882; K.C.B., 1900; works include 'Instruction in Photography' (1870) and 'Treatise on Photography' (1875).

ABRAHAM, CHARLES JOHN (1814–1903), first bishop of Wellington, New Zealand; educated at Eton and King's College, Cambridge; fellow of King's, 1837–50; B.A., 1837, M.A., 1840, D.D., 1859; ordained, 1837;

master at Eton, 1838–49; joined Bishop Selwyn in New Zealand, 1850; principal of St. John's College, Auckland, 1850; archdeacon of Waitemate, 1853; bishop of Wellington, 1858–68; coadjutor bishop of Lichfield, 1868; prebendary (1872) and canon (1876) of Lichfield; helped to organize Selwyn College, Cambridge, 1878; author of devotional works.

ACTON, JOHN ADAMS (1830–1910), sculptor. [See ADAMS-ACTON.]

ACTON, SIR JOHN EMERICH EDWARD DALBERG, eighth baronet, and first BARON ACTON, of Aldenham (1834–1902), historian and moralist; born at Naples of Shropshire Roman Catholic family; educated at Paris, Oscott, and privately at Edinburgh; studied history and criticism at Munich under Döllinger, 1848–54; visited America in 1855, Russia in 1856, Italy, with Döllinger, in 1857; settled at the family seat, Aldenham, 1858; whig M.P. for Carlow, 1859–65; formed friendship with Gladstone; became joint proprietor of the monthly 'Rambler,' which was converted under Acton's editorship in 1862 to a quarterly, 'The Home and Foreign Review,' representing liberal catholic opinions; in it advocated on liberal grounds Döllinger's reunion of Christendom, 1864; stopped the 'Review' on threat of papal veto; contributed to the weekly 'Chronicle,' 1867–8; wrote much for the revived quarterly, 'North British Review'; at Rome with Gladstone, 1866; raised to peerage, 1869; strenuous in opposition to adoption by Catholic Church of dogma of papal infallibility; published his views in 'Letters from Rome on the [Œcumenical] Council,' 1870; criticized in letters to 'The Times' Gladstone's pamphlet on 'The Vatican Decrees,' 1874; F.S.A., 1876; from 1879 spent winter at Cannes, autumn in Tegernsee, Bavaria, and parts of spring and summer in London; wrote for reviews; helped to found 'English Historical Review,' 1886; hon. LL.D. Cambridge, 1888; hon. D.C.L. Oxford, 1889; hon. fellow of All Souls, 1891; lord-in-waiting to Queen Victoria, in Gladstone's fourth administration, 1892 (K.C.V.O., 1897); regius professor of modern history, Cambridge, from 1895 to death; hon. fellow of Trinity College; lectured at Cambridge on French Revolution; planned and edited preliminary draft of 'Cambridge Modern History' (1899–1912); died at Tegernsee; library of 59,000 volumes purchased of family and presented to Cambridge University, 1903; independent works (posthumously published) include 'Lectures on Modern History,' 1906, 'The History of Freedom' and 'Historical Essays and Studies,' 1907, and 'Lectures on the French Revolution,' 1910; all display vast erudition, epigrammatic style, and passion for political righteousness and liberty of conscience.

ADAM, JAMES (1860–1907), Platonist; educated at Aberdeen University and Caius College, Cambridge; first class in classical tripos, 1882; first chancellor's medallist, 1884; fellow and classical lecturer of Emmanuel College, Cambridge, 1884; tutor, 1890; senior tutor, 1900; visited Greece, 1890; supporter of degrees for women; edited Plato's 'Apology,' 1887, 'Crito,' 1888, 'Euthyphro,' 1890, 'Protagoras,' 1893, and 'Republic,' 1902, the last a standard work; Gifford lectures ('The Religious Teachers of Greece') delivered at Aberdeen, 1902, 1904, and 1905, were published posthumously, 1908; 'The Vitality of Platonism,' collected essays, followed in 1911.

ADAMS, JAMES WILLIAMS (1839–1903), army chaplain in India; educated at Hamlin and Porter's school, Cork, and Trinity College, Dublin; B.A., 1861; ordained, 1863; chaplain at Calcutta, Peshawar, and

Kashmir, 1866–75; saw much active service at Kabul, 1878, and elsewhere; risked life at Villa Kazi, 1879; received V.C., 1881; at battle of Kandahar, 1880; settled in England, 1886; hon. chaplain to Queen Victoria, 1900; hon. M.A. Dublin, 1903.

ADAMS, WILLIAM DAVENPORT (1851–1904), journalist and compiler; son of W. H. D. Adams [q. v.]; educated at Merchant Taylors' School and Edinburgh University; editor of provincial papers, and dramatic critic, 1878–1904; compiled an unfinished 'Dictionary of the Drama' (1904) and other works.

ADAMS-ACTON, JOHN (1830–1910), sculptor; educated at Lady Byron's school, Ealing; studied art under Matthew Noble [q. v.] and at Royal Academy Schools (1853–8); won Academy's travelling studentship, 1858; at Rome till 1865; executed many notable London memorials; regularly exhibited at Royal Academy till 1892.

ADAMSON, ROBERT (1852–1902), philosopher; educated at Daniel Stewart's Hospital, Edinburgh, and Edinburgh University; graduated in philosophy, 1871; assistant professor, 1871–4; joined editorial staff of 'Encyclopaedia Britannica' (9th edit.), contributing many philosophical articles; appointed professor of philosophy and political economy at Owens College, Manchester, 1876; supported admission of women students at Manchester; hon. LL.D. Glasgow, 1883; professor of logic at Aberdeen (1893–5) and Glasgow (1895); published various works on Greek and modern philosophy and logic; earlier work idealistic, but later work naturalistic and realistic; library presented to Manchester University.

ADDERLEY, CHARLES BOWYER, first BARON NORTON (1814–1905), statesman; educated at Christ Church, Oxford; B.A., 1835; pioneer of town planning at Saltley, near Birmingham, 1837; tory M.P. for northern division of Staffordshire, 1841–78; opposed Peel's free trade policy, 1846; interested in colonial development; helped to found Church of England colony of Canterbury in New Zealand, and the Colonial Reform Society, 1849; persistently advocated colonial self-government; introduced reformatory schools bill, 1852; responsible for Young Offenders Act, 1854; admitted to privy council as vice-president of the education committee, 1858; passed a first Local Government Act, 1858; under-secretary for the colonies, 1866; defended action of Governor Eyre [q. v.] in Jamaica; carried through British North America Act (1867) creating the Dominion of Canada; K.C.M.G., 1869; chairman of sanitary commission, 1871; president of board of trade, 1874–8; passed merchant shipping bill, legalizing 'loadline,' 1876; raised to peerage, 1878; advocated free education and opposed payment by results, 1882; a strong churchman and writer on religious topics; a competent musician and art critic; memorial hall at Saltley.

ADLER, HERMANN (1839–1911), chief rabbi; born at Hanover; son of Nathan Marcus Adler [q. v.]; brought to London, 1845; educated at University College School and University College; B.A. London, 1859; consecrated, 1859; studied theology at Prague, 1860; Ph.D. Leipzig, 1862; principal of Jews' Theological College, London, 1863, being subsequently tutor, chairman of council, and president; appointed first minister of Bayswater synagogue, 1864–91; delegate chief rabbi for his father, 1879; chief rabbi, 1891–1911; active in social reform; president of Jewish Historical Society of England and vice-president of Anglo-Jewish and other associations; hon. LL.D. St. Andrews, 1899; hon. D.C.L. Oxford, and C.V.O., 1909; published works on Jewish subjects.

AGNEW, SIR JAMES WILLSON (1815–1901), prime minister of Tasmania; born in co. Antrim; educated at University College, London, at Paris, and Glasgow; M.R.C.S., 1838; M.D. Glasgow, 1839; went to Sydney, N.S.W. (1840), and practised there; colonial assistant surgeon at Hobart, 1845; helped to found Tasmanian Royal Society; member of legislative council, 1877; minister without portfolio, 1877–80; visited England, 1880; premier of Tasmania, 1886–7; K.C.M.G., 1894.

AGNEW, SIR WILLIAM, first baronet (1825–1910), art dealer; son of Thomas Agnew, printseller and mayor of Salford, 1850–1; educated at Swedenborgian school, Salford; partner in father's firm, 1850; helped to form many private art collections; purchased Gainsborough's 'Duchess of Devonshire' for 10,100 guineas, 1876; benefactor to National Gallery; joined firm of Bradbury & Evans, proprietors of 'Punch,' 1870; liberal M.P. for S.E. Lancashire and Stretford, 1880–6; helped to found National Liberal Club; baronet, 1895.

AIDÉ, CHARLES HAMILTON (1826–1906), author and musician; born in Paris; son of Armenian merchant; educated privately and at Bonn University; joined British army; devoted to music, art, and literature; entertained largely in London; published 'Eleanore' (1856) and other verse; a prolific musical composer and accomplished amateur artist; published many society novels showing French influence, and occasionally wrote for the stage.

AIKMAN, GEORGE (1830–1905), painter and engraver; educated at Edinburgh high school; after working in Manchester and London joined his father, an Edinburgh engraver, as partner; studied at Royal Scottish Academy life class; first exhibited at Scottish Academy, 1850; A.R.S.A., 1880; exhibited at Royal Academy, 1874–1904; mainly confined himself to landscape; practised etching and mezzotint.

AINGER, ALFRED (1837–1904), writer, humourist, and divine; educated at University College School, at Joseph King's boarding school, London, 1849, and at King's College (under F. D. Maurice); entered Trinity Hall, Cambridge, 1856; contributed to university magazine, 'The Lion' (1857–8); B.A. (law), 1860; M.A., 1865; ordained, 1860; assistant master at collegiate school, Sheffield, 1864–6; reader at Temple, 1865–93; friend of Tennyson; contributor to 'Macmillan's Magazine,' 1859–96; admiring student of Charles Lamb's writings; wrote life of Lamb, 1882; edited Lamb's essays, 1883, poems, &c., 1884, and letters, 1888; contributor to this Dictionary; a popular lecturer and preacher; canon of Bristol, 1887–1903; select preacher at Oxford, 1893; master of the Temple, 1894 till death; chaplain to Queen Victoria and King Edward VII; other works include life of Crabbe, 1903, and 'Lectures and Essays,' posthumous, 2 vols. 1905.

AIRD, SIR JOHN, first baronet (1833–1911), contractor; privately educated; joined father's business; constructed several gas and water reservoirs at home and abroad; chief partner, 1870; carried out much railway and dock work; best known by the construction of dams at Assuan and Assyut, 1898–1902; conservative M.P. for N. Paddington, 1887–1905; first mayor of Paddington, 1900; baronet, 1901; enthusiastic art collector and freemason.

AIREDALE, first BARON (1835–1911), ironmaster. [See KITSON, JAMES.]

AITCHISON, GEORGE (1825–1910), architect; educated at Merchant Taylors' School, 1835–41; articled to father, 1841; entered Royal Academy Schools, 1847; B.A. London, 1851; visited Rome, 1853; succeeded father in his business and as architect to London and St. Katharine Docks Co., 1861; friend of Lord Leighton; A.R.A., 1881; R.A., 1898; professor of architecture at Academy; president of Royal Institute of British Architects, 1896–9; contributor to this Dictionary.

ALCOCK, SIR JOHN WILLIAM (1892–1919), airman; obtained aviator's certificate, 1912; joined Royal Naval Air Service, 1914; instructor at Eastchurch flying school; stationed in Eastern Mediterranean, 1916; awarded D.S.O. and taken prisoner by Turks, 1917; first to make non-stop flight of Atlantic (15 hours, 57 minutes), 1919; created K.B.E.

ALDENHAM, first BARON (1819–1907), merchant and scholar. [See GIBBS, HENRY HUCKS.]

ALDERSON, HENRY JAMES (1834–1909), major-general; born at Quebec; entered Royal Military Academy, Woolwich, 1848; served in Crimea; present on special mission at bombardment of Charleston, U.S.A., 1864; major-general, 1892; president of ordnance committee, war office, 1891–6; director of Armstrong, Whitworth & Co., 1897 till death; C.B., 1887; K.C.B., 1891.

ALEXANDER, BOYD (1873–1910), African traveller and ornithologist; educated at Radley College, 1887–91; joined army, 1893; at Kumasi, 1900; studied bird life in West Africa; explored Lake Chad, 1904–5; made detailed survey of W. African continent, 1905–6; Royal Geographical Society's medallist, 1908; continued exploration of West Africa, 1909–10; murdered by natives at Nyeri; published 'From the Niger to the Nile,' 2 vols. 1907.

ALEXANDER, SIR GEORGE (1858–1918), actor-manager, whose original name was GEORGE SAMSON; made his first professional appearance at Nottingham, 1879; engaged by (Sir) Henry Irving for Lyceum Theatre, 1881; re-engaged, and accompanied Irving to America, 1884–5; leading man of Lyceum company, 1885–9; manager of

St. James's Theatre, London, 1891–1918; produced, among other notable plays, (Sir) A. W. Pinero's 'The Second Mrs. Tanqueray,' 1893; knighted, 1911; possessed a fine stage presence and acted with distinction.

ALEXANDER, WILLIAM (1824–1911), archbishop of Armagh; educated at Tonbridge and Brasenose College, Oxford; influenced by Newman; B.A., 1847; ordained, 1847; gained a Denyer prize with essay on 'Divinity of Christ,' 1850; won university prize for sacred poem, 1860; bishop of Derry, 1867–93; D.D. Oxford, 1867; archbishop of Armagh and primate of all Ireland, 1893 till death; published 'St. Augustine's Holiday and other Poems,' 1886; an eloquent preacher and lecturer; Bampton Lectures (1876) on 'Witness of the Psalms to Christ and Christianity'; published commentaries on the Johannine Epistles (1881 and 1889) and other theological works; hon. D.C.L. Oxford, 1876; LL.D. Dublin, 1892; D.Litt. Oxford, 1907; G.C.V.O., 1911; married in 1850 Cecil Frances Alexander, born Humphreys, hymn writer [q. v.].

ALEXANDER, MRS. (pseudonym) (1825–1902), novelist. [See HECTOR, ANNIE FRENCH.]

ALGER, JOHN GOLDWORTH (1836–1907), journalist and author; first wrote for 'Norfolk News'; joined 'The Times' parliamentary reporting staff, 1866; assistant to Baron de Blowitz, 'The Times' correspondent in Paris, 1874–1902; wrote on by-ways of French Revolution.

ALINGTON, first BARON (1825–1904), sportsman. [See STURT, HENRY GERARD.]

ALISON, SIR ARCHIBALD, second baronet (1826–1907), general; son of Sir Archibald Alison [q. v.]; educated at Glasgow University; joined army, 1846; served at Sevastopol, 1855; wounded in second relief of Lucknow, 1857; C.B., 1861; prominent in Ashanti war, 1873–4; received thanks of parliament and K.C.B., 1874; major-general, 1877; commanded highland brigade at Tel-el-Kebir, 1882; lieutenant-general, 1882; commanded force in Egypt, 1883; in command of Aldershot division, 1883–8; G.C.B., 1887; hon. LL.D. Cambridge, Edinburgh, and Glasgow; member of Indian council, 1889–99; wrote on military topics for 'Blackwood.'

ALLAN, SIR WILLIAM (1837–1903), engineer and politician; joined navy as engineer, 1857; taken prisoner at capture of Charleston, U.S.A., 1861; manager of North Eastern Engineering Company, 1868; founded Scotia engine works, Sunderland, 1886; director of Albyn shipping line there; radical M.P. for Gateshead, 1893 till death; knighted, 1902; published many volumes of Scottish verse, including 'Hame-spun Lilts,' 1874, 'Lays of Leisure,' 1883, and 'Songs of Love and Labour,' 1903.

ALLEN, GEORGE (1832–1907), engraver and publisher; started in life as a joiner; Ruskin's pupil and assistant at Working Men's College, 1854; studied mezzotint; illustrated 'Modern Painters'; undertook publication of Ruskin's works at his residence at Orpington, 1871; removed offices to London, 1890; published library edition of Ruskin's works, 1903–11; skilled geologist, mineralogist, and botanist.

ALLEN, JOHN ROMILLY (1847–1907), archaeologist; made life study of pre-Norman art in Great Britain; edited Cambrian Archaeological Journal, 1889 till death; F.S.A. Scotland, 1883; Rhind lecturer in archaeology at Edinburgh, 1885; chief work 'Celtic Art in Pagan and Christian Times,' 1904.

ALLEN, ROBERT CALDER (1812–1903), captain R.N.; as master of 'Dido' suppressed Malay pirates of Borneo, 1842–4; harbour master at Malta (1866) and Devonport (1867); employed at Deptford dockyard, 1867–70; C.B., 1877.

ALLERTON, first BARON (1840–1917), politician. [See JACKSON, WILLIAM LAWIES.]

ALLIES, THOMAS WILLIAM (1813–1903), theologian; educated at Eton and Wadham College, Oxford; B.A., 1832; M.A. 1837; fellow, 1833–41; came under tractarian influence; was ordained, 1838; joined Church of Rome, 1850; secretary of catholic poor school committee, 1853–90; actively promoted catholic primary education; first professor of modern history, Catholic University of Ireland, 1855; works include 'A Life's Decision,' 1880, and 'The Formation of Christendom,' 8 vols. 1865–9, showing St. Peter's predominance in history.

ALLMAN, GEORGE JOHNSTON (1824–1904), mathematician; B.A. Trinity College, Dublin, 1844; LL.B., 1843; LL.D., 1854; professor of mathematics, Queen's College, Galway, 1853–93; F.R.S., 1884; hon. D.Sc. Dublin, 1882; wrote 'History of Greek Geometry

from Thales to Euclid,' 1889; a friend of Comte and a positivist.

ALMA-TADEMA, SIR LAWRENCE (1836–1912) painter; born in Holland; entered Antwerp academy, 1852; exhibitor at Paris salon and gold medallist, 1864; settled in London, 1870; received letters of denization, 1873; A.R.A., 1876; R.A., 1879; knighted, 1899; O.M., 1907; works (numbering 408) chiefly depict subjects from the Merovingian period, ancient Egypt, Greece, and Rome; they show profound archaeological knowledge.

ALMOND, HELY HUTCHINSON (1832–1903), head master of Loretto School; educated at Glasgow University and Balliol College, Oxford; B.A., 1855; M.A., 1862; tutor at Loretto (preparatory) school, 1857; master at Merchiston School, Edinburgh, 1858; became proprietor of Loretto, 1862; raised school to public school standard, revolutionized Scottish school methods, attached great importance to physical exercise, diet, and clothing, and improved stamina of his pupils; published educational writings and sermons.

ALVERSTONE, VISCOUNT (1842–1915), judge. [See WEBSTER, RICHARD EVERARD.]

AMHERST, WILLIAM AMHURST TYSSEN-, first BARON AMHERST OF HACKNEY (1835–1909), bibliophile and Norfolk landowner; educated at Eton and Christ Church, Oxford; conservative M.P. for W. Norfolk, 1880–5, and S.W. Norfolk, 1885–92; raised to peerage, 1892; enthusiastic collector of books, works of art, and Egyptian papyri; well known as cattle breeder, shot, and yachtsman; lost much of his fortune through the fraud of his trustee; art collection and library, including seventeen 'Caxtons' and illuminated MSS., sold, 1906–9.

ANDERSON, ALEXANDER (1845–1909), labour poet under pseudonym of 'Surfaceman'; railway platelayer in native village of Kirkconnel, 1862; self-taught; sent to 'People's Friend' (1870) verses collected in 'A Song of Labour and other Poems,' 1873; visited Italy; attracted the favourable notice of Carlyle and Lord Houghton; assistant librarian at Edinburgh University, 1880–3, 1886–1909; works, including 'Songs of the Rail,' 1878, show lyric power and vivid vision in dealing with railway and humble Scottish child life.

ANDERSON, ELIZABETH (1836–1917), better known as MRS. ELIZABETH GARRETT ANDERSON, physician; born GARRETT; after struggles to study medicine obtained licence to practise of Society of Apothecaries, 1865; opened dispensary for women and children which developed into New Hospital for Women, Euston Road (now Elizabeth Garrett Anderson Hospital), 1866; senior physician there, 1866–92; M.D., Paris, 1870; married J. G. S. Anderson, 1871; member of British Medical Association, 1873; on staff of London School of Medicine for Women, 1875–1903; helped to improve status of women.

ANDERSON, GEORGE (1826–1902), Yorkshire cricketer; member of All England XI, 1857–64; visited Australia, 1863; captain of Yorkshire county club; had good defence and hitting power as batsman; actuary of Bedale Savings Bank, 1873–94.

ANDERSON, MARY REID (1880–1921), women's labour organizer; born MACARTHUR; general secretary, Women's Trade Union League, 1903; formed National Federation of Women Workers and helped to create National Anti-Sweating League, 1906; married W. C. Anderson, 1911; member of reconstruction and other committees, 1914–18; British representative at labour conference in America, 1920.

ANDERSON, SIR THOMAS McCALL (1836–1908), physician; M.D. Glasgow University, 1858; after study abroad, appointed lecturer on medicine in Andersonian Institute, 1860; first physician of hospital for diseases of skin, Glasgow, 1861 till death; professor of clinical medicine (1874–1900) and of practice of medicine (1900–8) at Glasgow University; had large consulting practice; knighted, 1905; wrote many medical treatises, including 'Lectures on Clinical Medicine,' 1877, and 'On Diseases of the Skin,' 1887.

ANDREWS, THOMAS (1847–1907), metallurgical chemist and ironmaster; succeeded father as head of Wortley ironworks, 1871; made valuable metallurgical researches; F.R.S., 1888; received gold medal, Society of Engineers, 1902; advocate of technical education.

ANGUS, JOSEPH (1816–1902), baptist divine and biblical scholar; M.A. Edinburgh, 1837; entered baptist ministry, 1838; secretary of Baptist Missionary Society, 1841; president of Baptist College at Stepney, 1849–57, and at Regent's Park, 1859–93; hon. D.D. Brown University, U.S.A., 1852; member of first London school board,

1870; published useful handbooks to the Bible, 1853, English language, 1864, English literature, 1866; 'Baptist Authors and History, 1527–1800,' 1896, and other works.

ANNANDALE, THOMAS (1838–1907), surgeon; M.D. Edinburgh, 1860, winning gold medal; house surgeon, Edinburgh Royal Infirmary, 1860; assistant surgeon, 1865; surgeon, 1871; F.R.C.S. Edinburgh, 1863, and England, 1888; regius professor of clinical surgery, Edinburgh University, 1877; hon. D.C.L. Durham, 1902; 'Annandale' gold medal in clinical surgery founded at Edinburgh University; published works on surgery.

ANSON, SIR WILLIAM REYNELL, third baronet (1843–1914), warden of All Souls College, Oxford; educated at Eton and Balliol College, Oxford; fellow of All Souls, 1867; read for bar and practised on home circuit; succeeded father, 1873; Vinerian reader in English law at Oxford, 1874; as (first lay) warden of All Souls, 1881–1914, preserved its historical continuity while loyally accepting reforms; vice-chancellor, 1898; unionist M.P., Oxford University, 1899 till death; parliamentary secretary, Board of Education, 1902–5; strenuously opposed to Finance Bill, 1909, and Parliament Act, 1911; P.C., 1911; combined real learning with wide knowledge of affairs; chief works 'The Principles of the English Law of Contract' (1879) and 'The Law and Custom of the Constitution' (part I, 1886, part II, 1892).

ARBER, EDWARD (1836–1912), man of letters; Admiralty clerk, 1854–78; professor of English, Mason College, Birmingham, 1881–94; produced 'English Reprints' (1868–71), 'Transcript of the Registers of the Company of Stationers of London, 1554–1640' (1875–94), and 'Term Catalogues, 1668–1709' (1903–6).

ARBUTHNOT, SIR ALEXANDER JOHN (1822–1907), Anglo-Indian official and author; elder brother of General Sir Charles George Arbuthnot [q. v.]; educated at Rugby under Dr. Arnold, 1832–9, and at Haileybury, 1840–1; writer for East India Company, 1840; compiled papers relating to public instruction in Madras province, 1854; first director of public instruction, Madras, 1855; vice-chancellor of Madras University, 1871–2, and of Calcutta University, 1878–80; chief secretary to Madras government, 1862; acting governor, February–May 1872, K.C.S.I., 1873; appointed member of governor-general's council, 1875; C.I.E., 1878; opposed to reduction of salt and cotton duties in India, 1877–9; demurred to Lord Lytton's aggressive Afghan policy, 1879; settled in Hampshire, 1880; member of India council, 1887–97; contributor to this Dictionary, 1885–1901; author of 'Life of Clive,' 1898, and 'Memories of Rugby and India' (posthumous), 1910.

ARBUTHNOT, FORSTER FITZGERALD (1833–1901), Orientalist; born at Belgaum, Bombay; educated at Haileybury; in Bombay civil service, 1853–78; friend of Sir Richard Burton; compiler of books on Oriental themes, the chief being 'Persian Portraits,' 1887, and 'Arabic Authors,' 1890; inaugurated (1891) new series of 'Oriental Translation Fund.'

ARBUTHNOT, SIR ROBERT KEITH, fourth baronet (1864–1916), rear-admiral; entered navy, 1877; succeeded father, 1889; commander, 1897; flag-captain at Portsmouth to (Lord) Fisher, 1903–4; removed from his ship in consequence of a speech offensive to Germany, 1910; commodore of third destroyer flotilla, 1910; rear-admiral, 1912; second in command of second battle squadron, 1913; in command of first cruiser squadron, 1915; killed at battle of Jutland; posthumous K.C.B.

ARCH, JOSEPH (1826–1919), politician; itinerant agricultural labourer, 1835–72; instrumental in forming Warwickshire Agricultural Labourers' Union, 1872; organizing secretary (afterwards president) of newly founded National Agricultural Labourers' Union, 1872; liberal M.P., North-West Norfolk, 1885–6, 1892–1902; did more than any other man of his time to improve conditions of agricultural workers.

ARCHER, JAMES (1823–1904), painter; studied art at Trustees' Academy, Edinburgh; A.R.S.A., 1850; R.S.A., 1858; exhibited many works at Scottish Academy, including 'The Child John in the Wilderness,' 1842, and 'Rosalind and Celia' (diploma work), 1854; executed oil and chalk portraits; removed to London, 1863; exhibited regularly at Royal Academy, 1850–1900; most successful in costume pictures and portraits of children; chief portraits include Sir George Trevelyan (1872), Irving (1892), Sir Daniel Macnee (1877); work of refined quality and akin to that of the pre-Raphaelites.

ARCHER-HIND (formerly HODGSON), RICHARD DACRE (1849–1910), Greek scholar and Platonist;

educated at Shrewsbury and Trinity College, Cambridge; Craven scholar, 1871; chancellor's medallist and B.A., 1872; fellow, 1873; tutor, 1878; published editions of 'Phaedo,' 1883, and 'Timaeus,' 1888, and 'Translations into Greek Verse and Prose,' 1905; ardent gardener and musician.

ARDAGH, SIR JOHN CHARLES (1840–1907), major-general R.E.; educated at Trinity College, Dublin; entered Royal Military Academy, Woolwich, 1858; superintended construction of Fort Popton at Milford Haven, 1860; deputy assistant quartermaster-general for intelligence at war office, 1876; sent to Constantinople to report on its defence, 1876; reported on Montenegrin and Bulgarian defences; at congress of Berlin, 1878; C.B. (civil), 1878; British commissioner for delimitation of Turco-Greek frontier, 1881; sent to Egypt in charge of intelligence department, 1882; restored Alexandria after its bombardment; present at battles of Tel-el-Kebir (1882) and El Teb (1884); C.B. (military), 1884; commandant at Cairo during Khartoum relief expedition, 1884; assistant adjutant-general for defence at war office, 1887; private secretary to viceroy of India, 1888–94; C.I.E., 1892; K.C.I.E., 1894; director of military intelligence, 1896–1901; compiled statement of military resources of Boers in South African war, 1899; K.C.M.G., 1902; British (army) delegate at conference for revision of Geneva convention, 1906; hon. LL.D., Dublin, 1897; a skilful water-colour artist.

ARDILAUN, first BARON (1840–1915), philanthropist. [See GUINNESS, SIR ARTHUR EDWARD.]

ARDITI, LUIGI (1822–1903), musical conductor and composer; born at Crescentino, Piedmont; produced and conducted his 'La Spia' at New York, 1856; conductor of opera at Her Majesty's Theatre, London, 1858–67, and at Covent Garden, 1869; conducted first performance of Gounod's 'Faust,' 1863; toured with Adelina Patti, 1882–7; composed songs 'Il Bacio,' 1860, and 'L'Ardita,' 1862; published 'My Reminiscences,' 1896.

ARDWALL, LORD (1845–1911), Scottish judge. [See JAMESON, ANDREW.]

ARGYLL, ninth DUKE OF (1845–1914), governor-general of Canada. [See CAMPBELL, JOHN DOUGLAS SUTHERLAND.]

ARMES, PHILIP (1836–1908), organist and composer of sacred music; chorister at Rochester Cathedral, 1848–50; articled to J. L. Hopkins [q. v.], organist there, 1850; assistant, 1856; organist of Durham Cathedral, 1862 till death; Mus.Doc. Oxford, 1864, and Durham, 1874; first professor of music, Durham, 1897.

ARMOUR, JOHN DOUGLAS (1830–1903), Canadian judge and jurist; born near Peterborough, Ontario; B.A., Toronto University, 1850; called to bar, 1853; Q.C., 1867; puisne judge (1877) and chief justice (1887) of court of queen's bench; chief justice of Ontario, 1900; judge of supreme court of Canada, 1902; hon. LL.D., Toronto University, 1902; represented Canada on Alaska boundary tribunal.

ARMSTEAD, HENRY HUGH (1828–1905), sculptor; studied design at Somerset House and Royal Academy Schools; designer and worker in metal for Messrs. Hunt & Roskell till 1863; studied sculpture; visited Rome, 1863–4; employed on Albert Memorial (1864) and many public buildings; also executed effigies and imaginative works, including 'Remorse' (in Tate Gallery); A.R.A., 1875; R.A., 1879; taught in Academy Schools from 1875.

ARMSTRONG, SIR GEORGE CARLYON HUGHES, first baronet (1836–1907), newspaper proprietor; born at Lucknow; military cadet in East India Company's army, 1855; served in Indian Mutiny; retired with rank of captain, 1861; editor from 1871, and proprietor from 1875, of 'Globe', conservative newspaper, in which he prematurely disclosed terms of Salisbury-Schouvaloff treaty, 1878; acquired 'The People' newspaper, 1882; baronet, 1892.

ARMSTRONG, THOMAS (1832–1911), artist; studied art in Manchester and Paris (under Ary Scheffer), and with the Barbizon school; exhibited landscape and figure pieces at Royal Academy, 1865–77, and Grosvenor Gallery, 1877–81; art director, South Kensington Museum, 1881–98; acquired for museum many important foreign works of art; revived English enamelling, 1886; C.B., 1898.

ARNOLD, SIR ARTHUR (1833–1902), radical politician and writer; at first surveyor and land agent; early published sensational novels; government inspector of public works under local government board, 1864; issued 'History of the Cotton Famine,' 1864; editor of 'Echo', evening paper, 1868-75; described travels through East (1875) in 'Through Persia by Caravan,' 1877; wrote for reviews radical essays, which he collected in 'Social Politics,' 1878; M.P. for Salford, 1880-5; of strong Phil-hellenic sympathies; alderman of London County Council, 1889-1904, and chairman, 1895-6; knighted, 1895; hon. LL.D. Cambridge, 1897.

ARNOLD, SIR EDWIN (1832-1904), poet and journalist; educated at King's College, London, and University College, Oxford; B.A., 1854; M.A., 1856; obtained Newdigate prize, 1852; published 'Poems Narrative and Lyrical,' 1853; principal of Deccan College, Bombay, 1856-61; wrote 'History of the Marquis of Dalhousie's Administration,' 1862-5; leader-writer in 'Daily Telegraph' from 1861; a chief editor, 1873; supported Turkey in Russo-Turkish war and Lord Lytton's Indian policy; C.S.I., 1877; K.C.I.E., 1888; published 'The Light of Asia,' a poem, 1879; travelled along Pacific coast and in Japan, 1889; published picturesque accounts of tour; visited America, 1891; a voluminous poet and Oriental translator; his collected poetical works appeared in 1888.

ARNOLD, GEORGE BENJAMIN (1832-1902), organist and composer, mainly of church music; pupil of George William Chard [q. v.] and S. S. Wesley [q. v.]; Mus.Bac. Oxford, 1853; Mus.Doc., 1860; organist of Winchester Cathedral, 1865-1902.

ARNOLD, WILLIAM THOMAS (1852-1904), author and journalist; born at Hobart, Tasmania; educated at Rugby and University College, Oxford; B.A., 1876; won Arnold prize for 'The Roman System of Provincial Administration,' 1879; writer on politics and occasionally on drama for 'Manchester Guardian,' 1879-98; helped to found Manchester School of Art; edited Keats, 1884; wrote 'Studies in Roman Imperialism' (posthumously issued), 1906.

ARNOLD-FORSTER, HUGH OAKELEY (1855-1909), administrator and politician; grandson of Arnold of Rugby [q. v.]; educated at Rugby and University College, Oxford; B.A., 1877; M.A., 1900; called to bar, 1879; private secretary to his adopted father, W. E. Forster [q. v.], chief secretary for Ireland, 1880; joined Cassell & Co., 1885; prepared educational manuals, including 'Citizen Reader' series (1886); secretary of Imperial Federation League and advocate of naval efficiency, 1884; unionist M.P. for West Belfast, 1892-1906, and for Croydon, 1906-9; wrote much on army questions, 1892-1900; chairman of commission of land inquiry in South Africa, 1900; secretary of the admiralty, 1901; supported tariff reform; secretary of state for war in Mr. Balfour's administration, 1903-5; reorganized war office; a fluent speaker and writer; author of 'English Socialism of To-day,' 1908.

ARROL, SIR WILLIAM (1839-1913), engineering contractor; began construction of Dalmarnock ironworks, near Glasgow (eventually largest British structural steelworks), 1872; new Tay bridge (1882-7), Forth bridge (1883-90), and steel work for Tower bridge, London (1886-94) constructed by his firm; knighted, 1890; liberal-unionist M.P., South Ayrshire, 1892-6.

ARTHUR, WILLIAM (1819-1901), Wesleyan divine; missionary in India, 1839-41; in France, 1846-8; secretary of Wesleyan Missionary Society, 1851-68; honorary secretary, 1888-91; principal of Methodist College, Belfast, 1868-71; president of Wesleyan Conference, 1866; his voluminous writings include 'The Tongue of Fire,' 1856, and works on the papacy.

ASHBOURNE, first BARON (1837-1913), lord chancellor of Ireland. [See GIBSON, EDWARD.]

ASHBY, HENRY (1846-1908), physician; studied medicine at Guy's Hospital; M.R.C.S., 1873; M.B., 1874; M.D., 1878; F.R.C.P., 1890; at Liverpool, 1875-8, and at Manchester from 1878 to death; lecturer on children's diseases in Owens College, Manchester, 1880-1908; president of various medical societies; enjoyed world-wide repute as expert on children's diseases; works include 'Diseases of Children,' 1899, 'Notes on Physiology,' 1878, and 'Health in the Nursery,' 1898.

ASHER, ALEXANDER (1835-1905), solicitor-general for Scotland; educated at Edinburgh University; called to Scottish bar, 1861; appointed advocate depute, 1870; liberal M.P. for Elginshire, 1881-1905; Q.C., 1881; solicitor-general for Scotland, 1881-5, 1886, 1892-4; hon. LL.D., Aberdeen, 1883; Edinburgh, 1891.

ASHLEY, EVELYN (1836-1907), author; son of seventh earl of Shaftesbury [q. v.]; educated at Harrow and Trinity College, Cambridge; B.A., 1858; private secretary to Palmerston, 1858-65; visited Garibaldi in Italy, 1860; helped to produce 'The Owl', society journal, 1864; called to bar, 1863; treasurer of county courts, 1863-74; completed Lord Dalling's unfinished 'Life of Palmerston,' 5 vols., 1870-6; liberal M.P. for Poole, Dorset, 1874-80, and Isle of Wight, 1880-5; under-secretary to board of trade in Gladstone's ministry, 1880-2, and to colonial office, 1882-5; ecclesiastical commissioner, 1880-5; made five unsuccessful attempts to enter parliament as liberal unionist, 1886-95; P.C., 1891; five times mayor of Romsey, 1898-1902.

ASHMEAD BARTLETT, SIR ELLIS (1849-1902), politician. [See BARTLETT.]

ASTON, WILLIAM GEORGE (1841-1911), Japanese scholar; B.A., Queen's University, Ireland, 1862; M.A., 1863; hon. D.Litt., 1890; appointed student interpreter in British consular service at Yedo, Japan, 1864; consul at Hiogo, 1880-3; British consul-general in Korea, 1884-6; Japanese secretary to British legation at Tokio, 1886-9; C.M.G., 1889; published Japanese grammars, 1869-72; translated 'Ancient Chronicles of Japan,' 1896; wrote works on 'Japanese Literature,' 1899, and 'Shinto,' 1905; formed unique collection of native Japanese books.

ATKINSON, ROBERT (1839-1908), philologist; studied Romance languages on Continent, 1857-8; B.A., Trinity College, Dublin, 1863; M.A., 1866; LL.D., 1869; hon. D. Litt., 1891; professor of Romance languages from 1869, and of Sanskrit from 1871; skilled in Romance, Sanskrit, Tamil, Telugu, Hebrew, Persian, Arabic, Chinese, Celtic, and Coptic languages; edited 'Vie de Seint Auban,' Norman-French poem (1876); member (1875), secretary (1878-1901), president (1901-8) of Royal Irish Academy; Todd professor of Celtic languages there, 1884; did much pioneer work in Celtic grammar and language; edited with translation and glossary middle Irish work, 'The Passions and Homilies from the Leabhar Breac,' 1897; co-editor of 'The Irish Liber Hymnorum' (2 vols. 1898).

ATTHILL, LOMBE (1827-1910), obstetrician and gynaecologist; B.A. and M.B., Trinity College, Dublin, 1849; M.D., 1865; assistant physician to Rotunda Hospital, Dublin, 1851; first doctor in Ireland to perform ovariotomy successfully; master of Rotunda Hospital, 1875; introduced Listerian principles there; president of Dublin Obstetrical Society (1874-6) and of Royal Academy of Medicine in Ireland (1900-3); author of 'Clinical Lectures on Diseases Peculiar to Women,' 1871, and 'Recollections of an Irish Doctor' (posthumous), 1911.

AUMONIER, JAMES (1832-1911), landscape painter; at first a designer of calicoes; practised landscape painting in Kensington Gardens and Epping Forest; first exhibited at the Royal Academy, 1871; subjects mainly English countryside; visited Venice, 1891; original member of Institute of Oil Painters; works include 'Sunday Evening,' and 'Sheep Washing' (in Tate Gallery).

AUSTEN, SIR WILLIAM CHANDLER ROBERTS-(1843-1902), metallurgist. [See ROBERTS-AUSTEN.]

AUSTEN LEIGH, AUGUSTUS (1840-1905), provost of King's College, Cambridge; educated at Eton and King's College, Cambridge; B.A. (fourth classic), 1863; M.A., 1866; fellow, 1862; ordained, 1865; tutor, 1868-81; dean, 1871-3, 1882-5; vice-provost, 1877-89; provost, 1889-1905; vice-chancellor of the university, 1893-5; successful administrator of the college; published 'History of King's College,' 1899.

AUSTIN, ALFRED (1835-1913), poet laureate; educated at Stonyhurst and Oscott; called to bar (Inner Temple), 1857; leader-writer (chiefly on foreign affairs) to 'Standard,' 1866-96; joint-editor with W. J. Courthope [q. v.] of 'National Review,' 1883-7; sole editor, 1887-95; poet laureate, 1896; published twenty volumes of verse—satires, lyrics, narrative, and dramatic poems, 1871-1908; prose works include three novels, political, critical, personal, and miscellaneous writings; at his best in prose garden-diaries and poetry of the countryside; failed in attempts to treat philosophic themes in epic and dramatic form.

AVEBURY, first BARON (1834-1913), banker, man of science, and author. [See LUBBOCK, SIR JOHN.]

AYERST, WILLIAM (1830-1904), divine; born at Danzig; scholar of Caius College, Cambridge; B.A., 1853; M.A., 1856; Hulsean (1855) and Norrisian (1858) prizeman; went to India, 1859; chaplain to Khyber field force, 1879-81; founded Ayerst Hall, Cambridge, 1884; declined bishopric of Natal, 1885; published theological works.

7

AYRTON, WILLIAM EDWARD (1847–1908), electrical engineer and physicist; educated at University College, London; B.A., 1867; studied electricity at Glasgow under Lord Kelvin; in Indian telegraph service, 1868–73; professor of physics and telegraphy at Tokio, 1873–8; did much experimental work there with Prof. John Perry; professor at City and Guilds of London Institute, 1879, and at Central Technical (now City and Guilds) College, South Kensington, 1884–1908; with Perry invented surface contact system for electric railways (1881) and a series of portable electrical measuring instruments (1882–91); made researches with Thomas Mather, F.R.S., from 1891 onwards; pioneer of electricity as a motive power, 1879; widely consulted as electrical engineer; F.R.S., 1881; royal medallist, 1901; president of Institution of Electrical Engineers, 1892, and of Physical Society, 1890–2; adviser to admiralty and board of trade; pioneer and organiser of technical education; supporter of women's rights; author of 'Practical Electricity,' 1887, and 151 scientific papers.

BACON, JOHN MACKENZIE (1846–1904), scientific lecturer and aeronaut; B.A., Trinity College, Cambridge, 1869; ordained, 1870; fellow of the Royal Astronomical Society, 1888; witnessed solar eclipses at Vadsö (9 Aug. 1896) and at Buxar, India (Jan. 1898); first made balloon ascent, August 1888; successfully experimented from balloon in acoustics and wireless telegraphy; crossed Irish Channel in balloon, November 1902; popular lecturer and scientific writer; author of 'By Land and Sky,' 1900, and 'The Dominion of the Air,' 1902.

BADCOCK, SIR ALEXANDER ROBERT (1844–1907), general, Indian staff corps; educated at Harrow and Addiscombe; in commissariat department of Indian army, 1864–95; superintended supplies for Kabul-Kandahar field force, 1880; C.B., 1880; collected transport for Sudan, 1885; commissary general-in-chief, 1890; C.S.I. for services in Chitral, 1895; quartermaster-general, India, 1895; lieutenant-general, 1900; member of council of India, 1902–7; K.C.B., 1902.

BADDELEY, MOUNTFORD JOHN BYRDE (1843–1906), compiler of 'Thorough Guide' books for pedestrians (1884–1906); educated at King Edward's grammar school, Birmingham, and Clare College, Cambridge; B.A., 1864; assistant master at Sheffield grammar school, 1880–4; settled in lake district, which he popularized as pleasure resort.

BAILEY, PHILIP JAMES (1816–1902), author of 'Festus'; educated at Nottingham and Glasgow University; called to bar (Lincoln's Inn), 1840; published 'Festus,' 1839 (2nd edit. revised, 1845, eleventh or jubilee edit., 1889); the work admired by Tennyson, Browning, and the pre-Raphaelites; published 'The Angel World, and other Poems' 1850, 'The Mystic, and other Poems,' 1859, and 'The Universal Hymn,' 1867; erroneously regarded as father of 'spasmodic' school of poetry which Aytoun satirized in 'Firmilian,' 1854; awarded civil list pension of 100*l.*, 1856; settled in Jersey, 1864; returned to England, 1876; hon. LL.D. Glasgow, 1901.

BAIN, ALEXANDER (1818–1903), psychologist, logician, and writer on education; graduated at Marischal College, Aberdeen, 1840; assistant to professor of moral philosophy there, 1841; visited London and made the acquaintance of John Stuart Mill, Grote, Lewes, and Carlyle; wrote 'The Study of Character, including an Estimate of Phrenology,' 1861; assistant secretary, metropolitan sanitary commission, 1848–50; lecturer at Bedford College for Women; published 'The Senses and the Intellect,' 1855, and 'The Emotions and the Will,' 1859; professor of logic and English in Aberdeen University, 1860–80; published 'Mental and Moral Science,' 1868, 'Logic,' 1870, and 'Mind and Body,' 1872; LL.D. Edinburgh, 1869; assisted in editing 'Grote's Aristotle,' 1872; edited Grote's minor works, 1873; founded the periodical 'Mind,' 1876; contributed 'Education as a Science' to 'International Scientific' series, 1879; elected lord rector of the Aberdeen University, 1890; received civil list pension of 100*l.*, 1895; one of first to apply to psychology the results of physiological investigations; lucid exponent of *a posteriori* school of psychology; his system of philosophy materialistic; an utilitarian in ethics; 'Autobiography' published, 1904.

BAIN, ROBERT NISBET (1854–1909), historical writer and linguist; shorthand writer in solicitor's office; acquired unaided twenty foreign European tongues; assistant at British Museum from 1883 to death; wrote 'Gustavus III and his Contemporaries, 1746–92,' 1894, 'The First Romanovs, 1613–1725,' 1905, 'Scandinavia,

1513–1900,' 1905, 'Slavonic Europe,' 1908, 'Charles XII,' 1895 (for 'Heroes of the Nations' series); translated fairy tales from Russian, Finnish, and Ruthenian, 1893–4.

BAINBRIDGE, FRANCIS ARTHUR (1874–1921), physiologist; B.A. and M.D., Trinity College, Cambridge; professor of physiology, Durham University, 1911, and at St. Bartholomew's Hospital, London, 1915; F.R.S., 1919; author of 'The Physiology of Muscular Exercise' (1919).

BAINES, FREDERICK EBENEZER (1832–1911), promoter of the post-office telegraph system; at fourteen constructed telegraphic apparatus; in service of Electric Telegraph Company, 1848–55; clerk in general post-office, 1855; proposed cable to connect England with Australia; advocated (1856) government acquisition of existing telegraph systems, which was carried out in 1870; surveyor-general for telegraph business, 1875; proposed telegraphic communication around British sea coast (1878), which was carried out in 1892; inspector-general of mails, 1882–93; organized parcel post service, 1883; C.B., 1885; enthusiastic volunteer; edited 'Records of Hampstead,' 1890; wrote 'Forty Years at the Post-Office,' 2 vols. 1895.

BAIRD, ANDREW WILSON (1842–1908), colonel R.E.; educated at Addiscombe (1860) and Royal Military Academy, Woolwich (1861); special assistant engineer of Bombay harbour defence works, 1861–5; served in Abyssinian expedition under Lord Napier, 1868; assistant superintendent of Indian trigonometrical survey, 1869; made pioneer study of tidal observations by harmonic analysis in England (1870) and on gulf of Cutch (1872); organized at Poona new department of survey along coast lines from Aden to Rangoon, 1877; F.R.S., 1884; mint master at Calcutta, 1889–97; colonel, 1896; C.S.I., 1897; published 'Notes on the Harmonic Analysis of Tidal Observations,' 1872, and 'Spirit-Levelling Operations of the Great Trigonometrical Survey of India,' 1885.

BAKER, SIR BENJAMIN (1840–1907), civil engineer; joined staff of Sir John Fowler [q. v.]; partner, 1875; won high repute as consulting engineer; with Fowler engaged on underground communications of London; helped to construct metropolitan railway (1861) and district railway (1869); consulting engineers for first 'tube' railways, City and South London (1890), Central London (opened 1900), and Bakerloo railways; studied theory of resistance of materials, such as brickwork and metals; constructed Forth Bridge on cantilever principles (1883–90); K.C.M.G., 1890; advised on engineering projects in Egypt; designed dams at Assuan, 1898–1902, and at Assyut; K.C.B., 1902; designed Avonmouth dock and other works in England, Canada, and United States; president of Institution of Civil Engineers, 1895; fellow (1890) and vice-president (1896–1907) of Royal Society; hon. D.Sc. Cambridge, 1900; LL.D. Edinburgh, 1890; M.Eng. Dublin, 1892; memorial window in Westminster Abbey.

BAKER, SHIRLEY WALDEMAR (1835–1903), Wesleyan missionary and premier of Tonga; emigrated to Australia, 1853; sent as missionary to Tonga, South Pacific, 1860; negotiated treaty between Tonga and Germany recognizing Tonga as an independent kingdom, 1874; appointed premier, 1881; revised constitution; set up Wesleyan Free Church there, 1885; all-powerful with king, but unpopular with chiefs; removed by British high commissioner, 1890; died at Haapai.

BALFOUR, GEORGE WILLIAM (1823–1903), physician; uncle of R. L. Stevenson [q. v.]; studied medicine at Edinburgh and at Vienna; M.D. and L.R.C.S. Edinburgh, 1845; F.R.C.P., 1861; physician to Royal Infirmary, 1867–82; published 'Introduction to Study of Medicine,' 1865, 'Diseases of the Heart and Aorta,' 1876, and 'The Senile Heart,' 1894; librarian and president (1882–4) of College of Physicians of Edinburgh; hon. LL.D. Edinburgh, 1884, St. Andrews, 1896.

BALFOUR, JOHN BLAIR, first BARON KINROSS, of Glasclune (1837–1905), Scottish judge; educated at Edinburgh University; passed to Scottish bar, 1861; became a foremost advocate; liberal M.P. for Clackmannan, 1880–99; solicitor-general for Scotland, 1880; lord advocate, 1881–5, 1886, and 1892–5; P.C., 1883; hon. LL.D. Edinburgh, 1882; took prominent part in carrying Local Government Act for Scotland, 1894; lord president of the court of session, 1899; raised to peerage, 1902.

BALFOUR OF BURLEIGH, sixth BARON (1849–1921), statesman. [See BRUCE, ALEXANDER HUGH.]

BALL, ALBERT (1896–1917), airman; joined army, 1914; seconded to Royal Flying Corps, 1916; largely contributed to ascendancy of British over German air service established at battle of the Somme (July); killed in air fight; M.C. and D.S.O., 1916; V.C. (posthumous), 1917; destroyed forty-three aeroplanes and one balloon; greatest fighting pilot of air service.

BALL, SIR ROBERT STAWELL (1840–1913), astronomer and mathematician; son of Robert Ball [q. v.]; B.A., Trinity College, Dublin; professor of applied mathematics and mechanism, Royal College of Science, Dublin, 1867–74; Andrews professor of astronomy, Dublin University, and royal astronomer of Ireland, 1874–92; Lowndean professor of astronomy, Cambridge, 1893–1913; F.R.S., 1873; knighted, 1886; popularizer of astronomy; most distinguished as mathematician; published researches on the theory of screw motions and their relations.

BANKS, SIR JOHN THOMAS (1815?–1908), physician; B.A. and M.B., Trinity College, Dublin, 1837; M.D., 1843; physician to House of Industry Hospital, Dublin, 1843–1908; censor (1847–8) and president (1869–71) of College of Physicians, Ireland; king's professor of medicine at Trinity College, 1849–68; regius professor of physic, Dublin University, 1880–98; first president of Royal Academy of Medicine, Ireland, 1882; an expert in mental disease; advocated psychological study for medical students; popular in Dublin society; K.C.B., 1889; hon. D.Sc. Royal University, 1882; hon. LL.D. Glasgow, 1888; high sheriff, co. Monighan, 1891.

BANKS, SIR WILLIAM MITCHELL (1842–1904), surgeon; M.D. Edinburgh University, 1864; F.R.C.S., 1869; surgeon to Paraguay government; demonstrator, lecturer, and professor of anatomy, Liverpool infirmary school of medicine, 1868–94; emeritus professor, 1894; surgeon, Royal Infirmary, Liverpool, 1877–1902; knighted, 1899; hon. LL.D. Edinburgh; advocated operation for cancer of breast; raised Liverpool medical school to well-organized faculty of the university; collector of early medical literature; contributor to scientific journals; Banks memorial lectureship founded in Liverpool University.

BANNERMAN, SIR HENRY CAMPBELL- (1836–1908), prime minister. [See CAMPBELL-BANNERMAN.]

BARBELLION, W. N. P. (pseudonym) (1889–1919), diarist and biologist. [See CUMMINGS, BRUCE FREDERICK.]

BARDSLEY, JOHN WAREING (1835–1904), bishop of Carlisle; educated at Trinity College, Dublin; B.A., 1859; M.A., 1865; D.D. Lambeth, 1887; archdeacon of Liverpool, 1886; bishop of Sodor and Man, 1887–92; bishop of Carlisle, 892–1904; capable organizer and fluent preacher of evangelical doctrine.

BARING, EVELYN, first EARL OF CROMER (1841–1917), statesman, diplomatist, and administrator; entered Woolwich, 1855; commissioned, and accompanied battery to Ionian Islands, 1858; aide-de-camp to high-commissioner, Sir Henry Knight Storks [q. v.]; followed chief to Malta and thence on special mission to Jamaica, 1864; returned to England, 1867; entered Staff College; private secretary to Lord Northbrook, viceroy of India, 1872; C.I.E., 1876; went out to Cairo as first British commissioner of 'Caisse de la Dette' created to deal with liabilities of Khedive Ismail, 1877; resigned, 1879; on deposition of Ismail and succession of Tewfik appointed British controller in Egypt, M. de Blignières being French representative of dual control, 1879; financial member of viceroy's council in India, 1880–3; K.C.S.I., 1883; British agent and consul-general in Egypt, 1883; as representative of the one power occupying country in force, was de facto to impose British will; 'advised' Egyptian government to withdraw temporarily from Sudanese provinces; reluctantly consented to General Gordon's mission to Sudan, 1884; urged raising of loan for Egyptian irrigation and expedition to relieve Gordon; after Gordon's death insisted on effectual evacuation of all Sudan except Suakin, 1885; turned his attention to interior and obtained loan of a million to spend on irrigation, 1885; so successful that surplus appeared in Treasury accounts for 1889; improved railways, administration of justice, and education; C.B., 1885; K.C.B., 1887; G.C.M.G., 1888; co-operated harmoniously with Khedive Tewfik; on his death supported Tewfik's son, Abbas, against Sultan's candidate, 1892; created Baron Cromer, 1892; experienced difficulties with Abbas, but nationalist movement checked by appearance of British battalion in Cairo, 1894; surveys for Nile dam put in hand, 1895; acted as minister of war, and supported (Lord) Kitchener, sirdar of Egyptian army, against Egyptian cabinet and

British government during reconquest of Sudan, 1896–8; enforced Anglo-Egyptian arrangement which he had devised for excluding internationalism from reconquered Sudan, 1898; brought about revision of land assessment, completion of land survey, lowering of land tax, creation of land bank, and subjection of interior and education to advisers; created viscount, 1899; earl, 1901; resigned position in Egypt, 1907; made maiden speech in House of Lords, 1908; took lead of free traders; president of Dardanelles commission, 1916; works include 'Modern Egypt' (1908); 'Ancient and Modern Imperialism' (1910); 'Abbas II' (1915), and three volumes of 'Political and Literary Essays' (reviews of new books written for 'Spectator' from 1912 onwards); remained strong whig through life; while not a genius, possessed powerful and versatile talents, whose full exercise was ensured by a strong character and vigorous constitution.

BARING, THOMAS GEORGE, first EARL OF NORTH-BROOK (1826–1904), statesman; son of first Baron Northbrook [q. v.] and nephew of Sir George Grey [q. v.]; gentleman commoner of Christ Church, Oxford (B.A., 1846); whig M.P. for Penryn and Falmouth, 1857; civil lord of admiralty, 1857; under-secretary in India office (1859–64), at war office (1861 and 1868), at home office (1864); secretary to the admiralty (1866); governor-general of India, 1872–6; rigidly controlled finance and modified local taxation; successfully met the Bengal famine by well-designed measures of relief; opposed to Lord Salisbury's policy of external aggression in Afghanistan; supported Indian cotton tariff in opposition to Lord Salisbury; entertained Prince of Wales on his visit to India (winter of 1875–6); left India, April 1876; showed as viceroy genuine sympathy with natives and strict impartiality; created earl, 1876; appointed first lord of the admiralty under Gladstone, 1880; one of the ministers responsible for dispatch of General Gordon to the Sudan; special commissioner to Egypt, 1884, and advocate of single British control there; attacked by W. T. Stead [q. v.] in articles on navy, 1885; opposed home rule, 1886, and tariff reform, 1903; active in local administration of Hampshire on retirement from political office in 1886; high steward of Winchester, 1889; showed capacity as whig statesman and country gentleman.

BARKER, THOMAS (1838–1907), mathematician; scholar of Trinity College, Cambridge; senior wrangler (1862) and first Smith's prizeman; professor of pure mathematics at Owens College, Manchester, 1865–85; successful teacher; laid stress on logical basis of mathematics; endowed professorship of cryptogamic botany at Manchester.

BARLOW, WILLIAM HAGGER (1833–1908), dean of Peterborough; scholar of St. John's College, Cambridge; took honours in four triposes; M.A., 1860; B.D., 1875; D.D., Christ Church, Oxford, 1895; principal of C.M.S. training college, Islington, 1875–82; vicar of Islington, 1887–1901; chairman of Islington vestry, 1887–94; prebendary of St. Paul's, 1898; dean of Peterborough, 1901; select preacher at Oxford and Cambridge.

BARLOW, WILLIAM HENRY (1812–1902), civil engineer; son of Peter Barlow [q. v.]; apprenticed at Woolwich dockyard; in Constantinople erected machinery and buildings for Turkish ordnance, 1832–8; engineer to several English railways, 1838–44; principal engineer, Midland railway, 1844; consulting engineer, 1857; invented Barlow saddleback rail, 1849; laid out southern portion of London and Bedford line, including St. Pancras station, 1842–9; made many researches in sound and electricity, in the theory of structures, and in the strength of beams; F.R.S., 1850; member of court of inquiry into Tay bridge disaster, 1879; designed new Tay bridge, 1882; member (1845), Telford medallist (1849), and president (1879–80) of Institution of Civil Engineers; one of first civil members of ordnance committee, 1881.

BARNABY, SIR NATHANIEL (1829–1915), naval architect; draughtsman in royal dockyard, Woolwich, 1852; entered naval construction department of admiralty, 1854; head of the staff of Sir E. J. Reed [q. v.], chief constructor of the navy, 1863; chief naval architect (styled director of naval construction, 1875), 1872–85; designed battleships, including the 'Inflexible' type and 'Admiral' class, and cruisers of the 'Mersey protected' and 'Orlando belted' class; K.C.B., 1885; author of 'Naval Development in the Nineteenth Century' (1902).

BARNARDO, THOMAS JOHN (1845–1905), philanthropist; clerk in Dublin, 1859; was 'converted,' 1862; did evangelizing work in Dublin slums; entered London Hospital as missionary medical student, 1866; F.R.C.S.

Edinburgh, 1879; founded East End juvenile mission for destitute children, 1867; opened (1870) boys' home in Stepney, which developed into 'Dr. Barnardo's Homes'; founded Girls' Village Home, Barkingside, Essex, 1876; sent first party of boys to Canada, 1882; at his death had assisted 250,000 children; refuted charges reflecting on disinterestedness in 1877.

BARNES, JOHN GORELL, first BARON GORELL, of Brampton (1848–1913), judge; B.A., Peterhouse, Cambridge; called to bar (Inner Temple), 1876; succeeded to great junior practice of Sir J. C. Mathew [q. v.], 1881; Q.C., 1888; judge of probate, divorce, and admiralty division, 1892; president, 1905–9; created baron, 1909; chairman of county courts committee, 1909, of copyright committee, 1911, and of royal commission on divorce, 1909–12; delivered many important judgments in court of first instance, Court of Appeal, Privy Council, and House of Lords.

BARNES, ROBERT (1817–1907), obstetric physician; pupil of George Borrow at Bruges; educated at University College, London, and St. George's Hospital; M.D., 1848; F.R.C.P., 1859; obstetric physician at London (1863), St. Thomas's (1865), and St. George's (1875) hospitals; president of Obstetrical Society, 1865–6; established British Gynaecological Society, 1884; pioneer of operative gynaecology; Lumleian lecturer at College of Physicians, 1873; hon. F.R.C.S., 1883; author of 'Obstetrical Observations,' 1870, and other works.

BARNETT, SAMUEL AUGUSTUS (1844–1913), divine and social reformer; B.A., Wadham College, Oxford; rector of St. Jude's, Whitechapel, 1873–94; canon of Bristol, 1894–1906; canon, and finally subdean, of Westminster, 1906–13; first warden of Toynbee Hall, which he had largely helped to found, 1884–96; instrumental in building Whitechapel art gallery; founded education reform league, 1884; attacked housing problem; wrote on religious and social questions.

BARRETT, WILSON (1846–1904), actor and dramatist, whose original name was WILLIAM HENRY BARRETT; began life as printer; first appeared on stage, 1864; played Tom Robinson in 'It's never too late to mend' and in 'East Lynne,' 1867; first produced 'Jane Shore' at Leeds, 1875; opened Court Theatre, London, 1879; there introduced Madame Modjeska to London public, 1880; began notable management of Princess's Theatre, June 1881; very successful in melodramas, 'The Lights o' London,' 'The Romany Rye,' 'The Silver King,' and 'Claudian,' 1881–3; his interpretation of Hamlet provoked controversy, 1884; wrote 'Hoodman Blind' (in collaboration with Mr. H. A. Jones), 1885, and other plays; toured America, 1886–7, paying five subsequent visits; returned to Princess's Theatre (1888), appearing in 'Ben-my-Chree'; opened new Olympic Theatre, London, 1890; played Othello at Liverpool, 1891; brought out new pieces at Grand Theatre, Leeds, including his version of Hall Caine's 'Manxman' (1894) and 'The Sign of the Cross' (1895), which ran prosperously at the Lyric Theatre, London, next year, and was followed by his 'The Daughters of Babylon,' 1897; paid two visits to Australia, 1898 and 1902; produced at Adelphi his 'The Christian King,' 1902; a popular impersonator of classical and melodramatic rôles despite his stilted delivery and gesture.

BARRY, ALFRED (1826–1910), primate of Australia and canon of Windsor; second son of Sir Charles Barry [q. v.]; educated at King's College, London, and Trinity College, Cambridge; fourth wrangler, second Smith's prizeman, and seventh classic, 1848; M.A., 1851; D.D., 1866; principal of Cheltenham College, 1862–8, and of King's College, London, 1868–83; canon of Worcester, 1871, of Westminster, 1881, and of Windsor, 1891–1910; archbishop of Sydney and primate of Australia, 1884–9; Boyle lecturer, 1876–8; Bampton lecturer, Oxford, 1892; Hulsean lecturer, Cambridge, 1894; rector of St. James, Piccadilly, 1895–1900; effective preacher of broad church doctrine; D.C.L. Oxford, 1870; publications include 'What is Natural Theology?' 1877, and 'The Teacher's Prayer Book,' 1884.

BARRY, SIR JOHN WOLFE WOLFE- (1836–1918), civil engineer. [See WOLFE-BARRY.]

BARTHOLOMEW, JOHN GEORGE (1860–1920), cartographer; manager of father's firm, 'Edinburgh Geographical Institute,' 1889; published great atlases of Scotland (1895) and England and Wales (1903); greatest achievement '"The Times" Survey Atlas of the World,' completed 1921; improved system of layer colouring for marking contours.

BARTLETT, SIR ELLIS ASHMEAD (1849–1902), politician; born at Brooklyn, U.S.A.; came to England in boyhood; B.A., Christ Church, Oxford, 1872; M.A., 1874; president of Union Society, 1873; called to bar, 1877; visited Serbia and Bulgaria, 1877–8; conservative M.P. for Eye, 1880–4, and for Ecclesall from 1885 to death; strenuous and grandiloquent advocate of British imperialism; conducted 'England,' first conservative penny weekly newspaper, 1880–98; civil lord of the admiralty, 1885, 1886–92; knighted, 1892; with Turkish army in war with Greeks and taken prisoner, 1897; in South Africa, 1899; published 'Shall England keep India?' 1886, 'The Battlefields of Thessaly,' 1897, and other works.

BARTLEY, SIR GEORGE CHRISTOPHER TROUT (1842–1910), founder of the National Penny Bank; educated at University College School; science examiner (1860) and assistant director of science division (1866–80) in education department, South Kensington; wrote pamphlets on social questions from 1870, including poor law reform, 1873–6; advocated old age pensions, 1872; founded Middlesex Penny Bank (1872) and the National Penny Bank (1875), which met with rapid success; conservative M.P. for North Islington, 1885–1906; K.C.B., 1902.

BARTON, SIR EDMUND (1849–1920), Australian statesman; born in Sydney; called to bar, 1871; member of New South Wales legislative assembly five times between 1879 and 1900; speaker, 1883–7; attorney-general, 1889, and 1891–3; leader of federal convention, 1897; largely responsible for new Constitution Bill; first prime minister of Australian Commonwealth, 1901–3; G.C.M.G., 1902; judge of Australian high court of justice, 1903; died in New South Wales.

BARTON, JOHN (1836–1908), missionary; nephew of Bernard Barton [q. v.]; B.A., Christ's College, Cambridge, 1859; M.A., 1863; founded Cambridge University Church Missionary Union; principal of new cathedral missionary college, Calcutta, 1865; vicar of Holy Trinity, Cambridge, 1877–93; chief secretary Church Pastoral Aid Society, 1893–1908; wrote geographical works.

BASHFORTH, FRANCIS (1819–1912), ballistician; B.A., St. John's College, Cambridge (second wrangler); fellow, 1843; ordained, 1850; rector of Minting, near Horncastle, 1857–1908; professor of applied mathematics, Woolwich, 1864–72; carried out and reported on series of important ballistic experiments, 1864–80; invented chronograph for determining air-resistance to projectiles, 1865.

BASS, MICHAEL ARTHUR, first BARON BURTON (1837–1909), brewer; educated at Harrow and Trinity College, Cambridge; B.A., 1859; M.A., 1863; extended father's brewing business; liberal M.P. for Stafford (1865–8), East Staffordshire (1878–85), and Burton division of Staffordshire (1885–6); personal friend of Gladstone; baronet, 1882; raised to peerage, 1886; became liberal unionist on home rule question; supported tariff reform, 1903; frequent host of Edward VII; K.C.V.O., 1904; generous benefactor to Burton-on-Trent; built ferrybridge and many churches there; an art connoisseur.

BATES, CADWALLADER JOHN (1853–1902), antiquary; of old Northumbrian descent; educated at Eton and Jesus College, Cambridge; B.A., 1871; M.A., 1875; travelled much in Poland and the Carpathians; practical farmer, revived famous Kirklevington short-horns; developed taste for hagiography and joined Roman Church, 1893; recognized authority on mediaeval history of Northumbria; wrote 'Border Holds,' 1891, and 'History of Northumberland,' 1895.

BATESON, MARY (1865–1906), historian; daughter of William Henry Bateson [q. v.]; student of Newnham College, Cambridge; second in first class, historical tripos, 1887; lecturer at Newnham from 1888 till death; under the influence of Mandell Creighton [q. v.] she made special study of monastic history; published 'The Register of Crabhouse Nunnery,' 1889, and 'Origin and Early History of Double Monasteries,' 1899; turned to municipal history, editing 'Records of the Borough of Leicester,' 3 vols. 1899–1905, 'The Charters of the Borough of Cambridge,' 1901, 'The Cambridge Gild Records,' 1903, and 'Grace Book B,' 2 vols. 1903–5; also edited works for Early English Text, Camden, and other antiquarian societies; her 'Laws of Breteuil' (1900–1) and 'Borough Customs' (2 vols. 1904–6) show masterly scholarship; wrote 'Mediaeval England' (in 'Story of the Nations' series), 1903; contributed to 'Social England,' 'Cambridge Modern History,' and to this Dictionary;

Warburton lecturer, Manchester University, 1905; ardent advocate of women's emancipation.

BATTENBERG, PRINCE LOUIS ALEXANDER OF (1854–1921), admiral of the fleet. [See MOUNTBATTEN, LOUIS ALEXANDER.]

BAUERMAN, HILARY (1835–1909), metallurgist; original student at school of mines, 1851; assistant to geological survey, 1855; geologist to North American boundary commission, 1858–63; surveyor for Indian and Egyptian governments (1867–9); lecturer in metallurgy at Firth College, Sheffield, 1883; professor at Ordnance College, Woolwich, 1888–1906; wrote much for technical journals; published 'Metallurgy of Iron,' 1868, and 'Systematic Mineralogy,' 1881.

BAXTER, LUCY (1837–1902), writer on art under pseudonym of LEADER SCOTT; daughter of William Barnes [q. v.], the Dorsetshire poet; married (1867) Samuel Thomas Baxter at Florence, where she lived till death; collaborated in literary research with John Temple Leader [q. v.]; works on Italian art include 'The Cathedral Builders,' 1899 and 1900.

BAYLIS, THOMAS HENRY (1817–1908), lawyer and author; educated at Harrow and Brasenose College, Oxford; B.A., 1835; M.A., 1841; called to bar, 1856; Q.C., 1875; judge of court of passage, Liverpool, 1876–1903; works include 'The Temple Church' (1893) and legal treatises.

BAYLISS, SIR WYKE (1835–1906), painter and writer; took special interest in architecture; exhibited at Royal Academy 'La Sainte Chapelle,' 1865; president (1888–1906) of Royal Society of British Artists, where he exhibited 'St. Peter's, Rome,' 1888, 'The Cathedral, Amiens,' 1900; writings include 'Rex Regum,' 1898, and 'Olives, the Reminiscences of a President,' 1906; F.S.A., 1870; knighted, 1897.

BAYLY, ADA ELLEN (1857–1903), novelist under the pseudonym of EDNA LYALL; of deeply religious temperament; ardent supporter of women's emancipation and of all political liberal movements; supported Charles Bradlaugh's fight for religious liberty (1880–5); published her first story, 'Won by Waiting,' 1879; best works were 'Donovan,' 1882, admired by Gladstone, its sequel, 'We Two,' 1884, and 'In the Golden Days,' 1885; her 'Autobiography of a Slander' (1887) had wide vogue; 'Doreen' 1894, 'Autobiography of a Truth,' 1896, and 'The Hinderers,' 1902, touched on political questions; her clear style, constructive faculty, and skilful characterization of young girls were qualified by her earnest political purpose; fond of music and travel.

BEACH, SIR MICHAEL EDWARD HICKS, first EARL ST. ALDWYN (1837–1916), statesman. [See HICKS BEACH.]

BEALE, DOROTHEA (1831–1906), principal of Cheltenham Ladies' College; educated in Paris (1847–8) and at Queen's College, Harley Street (1848); mathematical tutor there, 1849; head teacher of clergy daughters' school, Casterton, Westmorland (the Lowood of Charlotte Brontë's 'Jane Eyre'), 1857–8; successful principal of Cheltenham Ladies' College, 1858–1906; evidence before endowed schools inquiry commission (1865) gave immense impetus to girls' education; founded St. Hilda's College, Cheltenham, first English training college for secondary women teachers, 1885, and St. Hilda's Hall, opened at Oxford in 1893 with a view to giving teachers in training the benefit of a year at Oxford; president of Headmistresses' Association, 1895–7; ardent supporter of women's suffrage; received freedom of borough of Cheltenham, 1901; hon. LL.D. Edinburgh, 1902; collaborated in 'Work and Play in Girls' Schools,' 1898.

BEALE, LIONEL SMITH (1828–1906), physician and microscopist; medical student at King's College, London; assistant to Sir Henry Acland [q. v.] at Oxford, 1847; M.B., 1851; resident physician at King's College Hospital, London, 1850–1; professor of physiology and anatomy at King's College, 1853–69, of pathological anatomy, 1869–76, and of medicine, 1876–96; F.R.C.P., 1859; Lumleian lecturer, 1875; F.R.S., 1865; delivered Croonian lectures, 1865; his many works include 'The Microscope and its Application to Clinical Medicine,' 1854, and 'The Structure and Growth of the Tissues,' 1865, 'Disease Germs,' 1872, 'Bioplasm,' 1872, and other works, foreshadowing by microscopic investigation modern conceptions of bacterial disease; first to practise method of fixing tissues by injections; discovered 'Beale's cells'; skilful draughtsman and illustrator of his own works; president of Microscopical Society, 1879–80;

through life speculated on philosophy, publishing 'Life Theories,' 1870–1, and 'Our Morality,' 1887; a teetotaller and horticulturist.

BEATTIE-BROWN, WILLIAM (1831–1909), Scottish landscape painter; studied art at Trustees' Art Academy, Edinburgh; exhibited at the Royal Scottish Academy from 1848 till death, at Royal Academy and elsewhere, Scottish highland landscapes; showed much technical skill and accuracy; R.S.A., 1884; diploma work 'Coirena-Faireamh,' 1883.

BECKETT, SIR EDMUND, fifth baronet, and first BARON GRIMTHORPE (1816–1905), lawyer, mechanician, and controversialist; educated at Eton and Trinity College, Cambridge; B.A., 1838; M.A., 1841; LL.D., 1863; called to bar, 1841; Q.C., 1854; recognized as leader of parliamentary bar, 1860; chancellor of province of York, 1877–1900; raised to peerage, 1886; engaged in theological controversy; opposed to New Testament revision and to ritualism; first president of Protestant Churchmen's Alliance, 1889; interested in ecclesiastical architecture, designing several Yorkshire churches; wrote 'A Book on Building, Civil and Ecclesiastical,' 1876; prominent and generous from 1877 onwards, in restoration of St. Albans Cathedral, the cause of much controversy; fond of mechanical invention; published 'A Rudimentary Treatise on Clock and Watch making' (1850, often reprinted); designed clocks for 1851 exhibition, for the clocktower in Houses of Parliament (1859) and for St. Paul's Cathedral (finished 1893); president of Horological Institute, 1868; author of 'Astronomy without Mathematics,' 1865, 'Life of John Lonsdale, Bishop of Lichfield' (his father-in-law), 1868, and controversial works.

BEDDOE, JOHN (1826–1911), physician and anthropologist; studied medicine at University College, London (B.A., 1851) and at Edinburgh (M.D., 1853); on medical staff in Crimea; physician to Bristol Royal Infirmary, 1862–73; F.R.C.P., 1873; made in youth pioneer ethnological researches all over Europe; observed hair and eye colours in West of England (1846) and Orkney (1853); F.R.S., 1873; hon. LL.D. Edinburgh, 1891; Rhind lecturer there on 'The Anthropological History of Europe,' 1891; wrote 'Contributions to Scottish Ethnology,' 1853, 'The Races of Britain,' 1885, and 'Memories of Eighty Years,' 1910.

BEDFORD, WILLIAM KIRKPATRICK RILAND (1826–1905), antiquary and genealogist; B.A., Brasenose College, Oxford, 1848; M.A., 1852; secretary of Oxford Union Society, 1848; rector of Sutton Coldfield, 1890–2; authority on antiquities of Sutton Coldfield; official genealogist and historian of order of St. John of Jerusalem; wrote on cricket, archery, and other topics.

BEECHAM, THOMAS (1820–1907), patent medicine vendor; patented in 1847 a new formula for pills; employed 'Worth a guinea a box' as his advertising motto; built large factories at St. Helens and New York (1885) and on Continent; benefactor to South Lancashire.

BEECHING, HENRY CHARLES (1859–1919), dean of Norwich, man of letters; B.A., Balliol College, Oxford; rector of Yattendon, Berkshire, 1885–1900; professor of pastoral theology, King's College, London, 1900; canon of Westminster, 1902; dean of Norwich, 1911 till death; select preacher at Oxford, Cambridge, and Dublin; writer of verse and essayist.

BEEVOR, CHARLES EDWARD (1854–1908), neurologist; studied medicine at University College Hospital, London, and abroad; M.D., 1881; F.R.C.P., 1888; physician to National Hospital for the Epileptic, London, and Great Northern Hospital; made valuable researches on the localization of cerebral functions and cerebral arterial circulation; president of Neurological Society, 1907–8; published standard treatises on anatomy and nervous diseases.

BEIT, ALFRED (1853–1906), financier and benefactor; born at Hamburg of Jewish family; joined firm of diamond merchants, 1870; went to Kimberley, South Africa, 1875; formed independent business there, 1878; joined firm of J. Porges & (Sir) Julius Wernher [q. v.], 1882; settled in London, 1888, and formed firm of Wernher, Beit & Co., 1890; intimate friend and adviser of Cecil Rhodes [q. v.], with whom he amalgamated chief Kimberley diamond mines as the De Beers Consolidated Mines, 1888; developed the Transvaal gold mines, and evolved the Great Deep Level scheme, 1891; an original director of British South Africa Company, 1889; concerned with Rhodes in Jameson Raid, 1895; generous contributor to South African war funds, 1899–1902; an ardent imperialist; formed fine collection of pictures and bronzes;

founded Beit professorship of colonial history at Oxford, 1905; benefactor to Imperial College of Technology, London, to Rhodesia, to London and Hamburg charities, and to National Gallery; thirty fellowships for medical research founded in his memory, 1909.

BELCHER, JOHN (1841–1913), architect; partner in father's City practice, 1865–75; abandoned Gothic for Italian renaissance style; designs include offices of Institute of Chartered Accountants in the City, 1890; Victoria and Albert Museum, 1891; Whiteley's stores, Bayswater, 1912; offices of London Zoological Society, 1913; A.R.A., 1900; R.A., 1909; president of Royal Institute of British Architects, 1904.

BELL, CHARLES FREDERIC MOBERLY (1847–1911), manager of 'The Times'; born at Alexandria; joined Egyptian mercantile firm in Alexandria, 1865; partner, 1873; entered on journalism, 1875; correspondent to 'The Times' on Egyptian questions from 1865 onwards; founded 'Egyptian Gazette,' 1880; published 'Khedives and Pashas,' 1884, and 'Egyptian Finance,' 1887; appointed manager of 'The Times,' 1890; improved its business organization; started in connexion with the paper a literary organ, 'Literature' (1897–1901), which was replaced by the 'Literary Supplement'; subsequently added other supplements; pioneer of wireless press messages across Atlantic; published 'The Times Atlas,' 1895, 'Encyclopaedia Britannica,' 9th edit. 1898, and 'History of South African War,' 7 vols. 1900–9; established 'The Times' Book Club, 1905, which came into conflict with publishers and booksellers; managing director of 'The Times' publishing company, formed 1908.

BELL, HORACE (1839–1903), civil engineer; as engineer of Indian public works department did much work on Indian state railways, 1862–94; published 'Railway Policy in India' (1894) and school primer on India (3rd edit. 1893), and the 'Laws of Wealth' (1883), for Indian natives.

BELL, SIR ISAAC LOWTHIAN, first baronet (1816–1904), metallurgical chemist and pioneer in industrial enterprise; educated at Bruce's Academy, Newcastle; received training in physics and chemistry in Germany, Denmark, Edinburgh, and Paris; joined the ironworks of his father's firm, Messrs. Losh, Wilson & Bell, at Walker, Tyneside, 1836; married Margaret, daughter of Hugh Lee Pattinson [q. v.], 1842; started with father-in-law chemical works at Washington, near Gateshead, 1852; meanwhile in 1844 with two brothers, Thomas and John, formed firm of Bell Brothers, leasing a blast furnace at Wylam-on-Tyne; in 1845 on death of his father assumed direction of Walker works; in 1854 Bell Brothers started Clarence works on Tees opposite Middlesbrough with three blast furnaces to smelt Cleveland ore; helped to construct Cleveland railway to bring ironstone to the works; limestone quarries and collieries were also acquired in Weardale; when the Cleveland railway was purchased by the North-Eastern railway in 1865 Bell became a director for life; steel was made at Clarence from 1889, and important steel works were built there; a salt bed was found near Clarence in 1874, and thenceforth proved profitable; Bell Brothers ultimately employed in their mines, collieries, and ironworks 6,000 workpeople; Bell studied iron manufacture abroad and was an efficient student of applied science; president of Iron and Steel Institute (Bessemer gold medallist, 1874), 1873–5, of Institution of Mechanical Engineers, 1884, and of Society of Chemical Industry, 1889; received Albert medal of Society of Arts, 1895; published results of experimental researches in 'Chemical Phenomena of Iron Smelting,' 1892, and 'Principles of the Manufacture of Iron and Steel,' 1884; mayor of Newcastle-on-Tyne, 1854–5 and 1862–3; liberal M.P. for the Hartlepools, 1875–80; F.R.S., 1875; baronet, 1885; hon. D.C.L. Durham, 1882; LL.D. Edinburgh, 1893; D.Sc. Leeds, 1904.

BELL, JAMES (1824–1908), chemist; educated at University College, London; entered inland revenue chemical laboratory, Somerset House, 1846; principal there, 1874–94; F.R.S., 1884; C.B., 1889; president of Institute of Chemistry, 1888–91; wrote scientific works.

BELL, VALENTINE GRAEME (1839–1908), civil engineer; pupil of Sir James Brunlees [q. v.], 1859; constructed railways in Jamaica, 1880–3; director of public works there, 1887–1908; C.M.G., 1903.

BELLAMY, JAMES (1819–1909), president of St. John's College, Oxford; educated at Merchant Taylors' School and St. John's College, Oxford; B.A., 1841; M.A., 1845; ordained, 1843; B.D., 1850; D.D., 1872; president of St. John's College, 1871–1909; member of university

commission, 1877–9; vice-chancellor, 1886–90; a strong conservative and accomplished musician.

BELLEW, HAROLD KYRLE (1855–1911), actor; son of John C. M. Bellew [q. v.]; joined the merchant service; made London début as actor, 1875; took Shakespearian and other parts with Adelaide Neilson [q. v.] and Henry Irving [q. v.], 1876–86; chief rôles were Jack Absolute and Orlando; was associated with Mrs. Brown Potter at Gaiety Theatre, 1887–97; from 1902 to death acted in America; died at Salt Lake City.

BELLOWS, JOHN (1831–1902), printer and lexicographer; published 'French-English Dictionary,' 1872 (which had a wide circulation), and other dictionaries; a keen archaeologist, he discovered traces of Roman city wall at Gloucester, 1873; visited the Dukhobortsi and Count Tolstoi in Russia, 1892; visited America, 1901; hon. M.A. Harvard; a quaker, teetotaller, and vegetarian; wrote on travel, religion, and politics.

BEMROSE, WILLIAM (1831–1908), writer on woodcarving; succeeded to father's printing business at Derby, 1857; wrote 'Manual of Woodcarving,' 1862—which reached standard rank—and kindred works; author of authoritative works on porcelain; skilled amateur artist; chairman of Derby school board, 1886–1902; pioneer of Volunteer movement.

BENDALL, CECIL (1856–1906), professor of Sanskrit at Cambridge; Sanskrit exhibitioner, Trinity College, Cambridge; migrated to Caius, 1876; B.A., 1879; fellow of Caius, 1879–86; in Oriental department, British Museum, 1882–98; professor of Sanskrit at University College, London, 1885–1903, and at Cambridge, 1903–6; acquired several Oriental MSS. while travelling in India, 1884–5, 1898–9; edited much Sanskrit literature; left Oriental MSS. and books to Cambridge University; an expert Indian palaeographer and keen musician.

BENHAM, WILLIAM (1831–1910), theologian; studied under F. D. Maurice at King's College, London; ordained, 1857; divinity tutor, St. Mark's College, Chelsea, 1857–65; professor of modern history, Queen's College, Harley Street, 1866–71; rector of St. Edmund the King, Lombard Street, 1882–1910; hon. canon of Canterbury, 1888; his voluminous writings include 'Life of Archbishop Tait' with Dr. Davidson, 1891, and 'Old London Churches,' 1908; edited 'Ancient and Modern Library of Theological Literature'; wrote for 'Church Times' under name of 'Peter Lombard,' 1890–1910.

BENNETT, ALFRED WILLIAM (1833–1902), botanist; B.A. London, 1853; M.A., 1855; B.Sc., 1868; bookseller and publisher, 1858–68; lecturer on botany, Bedford College, 1868; translated and edited Julius Sachs's 'Lehrbuch der Botanik,' 1875; translated and published works on Alpine plants; made researches into cryptogamic plants; collaborated in 'Handbook of Cryptogamic Botany,' 1889, and other works.

BENNETT, EDWARD HALLARAN (1837–1907), surgeon; B.A., M.B., and M.Ch., Trinity College, Dublin, 1859; F.R.C.S. Ireland, 1863; president 1884–6; M.D., 1864; university anatomist, Dublin University, 1864; professor of surgery, Trinity College, Dublin, 1873; an authority on bone fracture; discovered 'Bennett's fracture,' 1881; formed collection of fractures at pathological museum, Trinity College, Dublin.

BENSON, RICHARD MEUX (1824–1915), divine and founder of a religious order; life student and B.A., Christ Church, Oxford; vicar of Cowley, near Oxford, 1850; formed society of mission priests of St. John the Evangelist, 1866; superior, 1866–90; vicar of Cowley St. John, 1870–86; established branch house of Cowley Fathers in Boston, U.S.A., 1870–1; revisited Boston, 1892–9; returned to Cowley, 1899, and remained there till death; consistently loyal to Anglican position; numerous works include 'Manual of Intercessory Prayer' (1863).

BENSON, ROBERT HUGH (1871–1914) Catholic writer and apologist; son of Edward White Benson [q. v.]; educated at Eton and Trinity College, Cambridge; took Anglican orders, 1894; member of the Community of the Resurrection, Mirfield, 1898–1903; received into Roman Church, 1903; popular as preacher and writer of press articles; author of numerous works of historical fiction and novels of modern life.

BENT, SIR THOMAS (1838–1909), prime minister of Victoria; born in New South Wales; market gardener; member for Brighton in Victoria parliament, 1871–94; entered James Service ministry as vice-president of the board of public works, 1880; commissioner of railways, 1881–3; chairman of first railways standing committee,

1887–9; speaker, 1892–4; ruined by 'land boom,' 1893; engaged in dairy farming, 1894–1900; re-elected member for Brighton, 1900; minister for railways and works, 1902–3; prime minister, 1904–8; K.C.M.G., 1908; opposed to labour party.

BENTLEY, JOHN FRANCIS (1839–1902), architect; entered firm of London architects, 1855; joined Church of Rome, 1862; architectural work showed desire for perfection in detail and soundness of construction; did much ornamental work for churches and private residences—Convent of the Sacred Heart, Hammersmith, 1866, Carlton Towers, Selby, 1874, and St. Mary of the Angels, Bayswater; built Church of the Holy Rood, Watford, 1887–92, and convent of the Immaculate Conception, Bocking Bridge, Braintree, 1897; decorated St. Botolph, Aldgate and Bishopsgate, and other City churches; designed and built in Byzantine style, Roman Catholic cathedral at Westminster, 1894, the materials being brickwork, masonry, and concrete, free from iron spans.

BERESFORD, LORD CHARLES WILLIAM DE LA POER, BARON BERESFORD (1846–1919), admiral; entered navy, 1859; conservative M.P., Waterford, 1874–80; took part in bombardment of Alexandria (captain and mentioned in dispatches), 1882, and Nile expedition, 1884–5; C.B. for rescue of Sir C. W. Wilson [q. v.], 1885; M.P., East Marylebone, 1885–6–9; fourth naval lord of admiralty, 1886–8; promoted to flag rank, 1897; M.P., York, 1897–1900, Woolwich, 1902–3; vice-admiral, 1902; chief in command of Channel squadron and K.C.B. 1903; commander-in-chief, Mediterranean, 1905; admiral, 1906; commander-in-chief of Channel fleet, 1907–9; opposed Admiralty policy; M.P., Portsmouth, 1910–16; retired and received G.C.B., 1911; created baron, 1916.

BERGNE, SIR JOHN HENRY GIBBS (1842–1908), diplomatist; of French descent; educated at London University; entered foreign office, 1861; superintendent of treaty department, 1881–94; superintendent of commercial department and examiner of treaties, 1894–1902; British delegate at international copyright conference, Berne, 1886, and Berlin, 1908, as well as at conferences for abolition of bounties on sugar at Brussels (1899 and 1901), signing convention, 1902; K.C.M.G., 1888; K.C.B., 1903; rendered important service to Authors' Society from 1890 to death; member of Alpine Club.

BERKELEY, SIR GEORGE (1819–1905), colonial governor; born in island of Barbados; B.A., Trinity College, Dublin, 1842; colonial secretary and controller of customs of British Honduras, 1845; lieutenant-governor of St. Vincent, 1864; governor-in-chief of West Africa settlements, 1873, and of Leeward Islands, 1874–81; K.C.M.G., 1881.

BERNARD, SIR CHARLES EDWARD (1837–1901), Anglo-Indian administrator; educated at Rugby and Haileybury; entered Indian civil service, 1857; secretary to Sir Richard Temple [q. v.] and Sir George Campbell [q. v.], 1871–8; chief commissioner of British Burma, 1880–7; secretary of revenue department, India office, 1887–1901; K.C.S.I., 1886; prominent athlete; edited memoirs of Sir George Campbell, 1893.

BERNARD, THOMAS DEHANY (1815–1904), divine; brother of Mountague Bernard [q. v.]; B.A., Exeter College, Oxford, 1838; chancellor's prize essayist, 1839; ordained, 1840; Bampton lecturer, 1864; rector of Walcot, Bath, 1864–86; canon of Wells, 1868–1901; chancellor of Wells Cathedral from 1879 to death; of evangelical sympathies; published theological works.

BERRY, SIR GRAHAM (1822–1904), prime minister of Victoria; draper in Chelsea, 1848; emigrated to Victoria, 1852; purchased 'Collingwood Observer,' 1860; member for Collingwood as advanced liberal protectionist in legislative assembly, 1861–5; purchased 'Geelong Register,' 1866; member for Geelong West, 1868; treasurer in J. A. Macpherson's ministry, 1870, and in Sir C. Gavan Duffy's ministry, 1871–2; thrice prime minister, 1875–6, 1877–80, and 1880–1; formed with James Service (1883) coalition government which passed useful measures; agent-general to colony in London, 1886–91; returned to Melbourne, 1891; treasurer in William Shiel's ministry, 1892; speaker of legislative assembly, 1894–7; a fervent advocate of democratic principles.

BERTIE, FRANCIS LEVESON, first VISCOUNT BERTIE, of Thame (1844–1919), diplomatist; educated at Eton; entered Foreign Office, 1863; parliamentary private secretary to Hon. Robert Bourke, 1874–80; assistant under-secretary of state for foreign affairs, 1894–1903; ambassador to Rome, 1903–4, and to Paris, 1905–18; largely instrumental in preserving the Anglo-

French *entente*; K.C.B., 1902; G.C.B., 1908; created baron, 1915, and viscount, 1918.

BESANT, SIR WALTER (1836–1901), novelist; born at Portsea; educated at King's College, London, 1854–5, and at Christ's College, Cambridge, 1856–9; 18th wrangler, 1859; M.A., 1863; master at Leamington College, 1859; senior professor at Royal College, Mauritius, 1861–7; settled in London, 1867; published 'Early French Poetry,' 1868, 'The French Humourists,' 1873, and other works; secretary of Palestine Exploration Fund, 1868–86; wrote with E. H. Palmer [q. v.] 'Jerusalem,' 1871; edited 'Survey of Western Palestine,' 1881; as contributor to 'Once a Week,' 1869, he became acquainted with the editor, James Rice [q. v.], with whom he collaborated in several novels, 1871–81, including 'The Golden Butterfly,' 1876, 'By Celia's Arbour,' 1878, and 'The Chaplain of the Fleet,' 1879; from 1882 continued fiction without collaboration, mainly based on historical incident, e.g. 'Dorothy Forster,' 1884, and 'For Faith and Freedom,' 1888; his 'All Sorts and Conditions of Men,' 1882, and 'Children of Gibeon,' 1886, called attention to social evils in East London, and stimulated the foundation of 'The People's Palace,' Mile End, for intellectual improvement and rational amusement, 1887; helped to found Society of Authors, 1884; started and edited 'The Author,' 1890; defined authors' financial position in 'The Pen and the Book,' 1899; knighted, 1895; commenced survey of London (1894), which appeared in ten elaborate volumes (1902–12); edited 'Fascination of London' series from 1897; a keen freemason; interested in antiquities of Hampstead, where he long resided; other works include 'The Eulogy of Richard Jefferies,' 1888, 'Captain Cook,' 1889, and (with W. J. Brodribb, q. v.) 'Constantinople,' 1879; bronze busts in St. Paul's Cathedral crypt and on Victoria Embankment; his 'Autobiography' appeared in 1902.

BETHAM-EDWARDS, MATILDA BARBARA (1836–1919), novelist and writer on French life. [See EDWARDS.]

BEVAN, WILLIAM LATHAM (1821–1908), archdeacon of Brecon; educated at Rugby and Balliol College, Oxford; B.A., 1842; M.A., 1845; ordained, 1844; held living of Hay, Breconshire, 1845–1901; canon of St. David's, 1879–93; archdeacon of Brecon, 1895–1907; an accomplished linguist and Welsh church historian; wrote 'History of St. David's,' 1888, works on ancient geography, and pamphlets in defence of the Welsh Church.

BEWLEY, SIR EDMUND THOMAS (1837–1908), Irish lawyer and genealogist; B.A., Trinity College, Dublin, 1857; M.A., 1863; LL.D., 1885; called to Irish bar, 1862; Q.C., 1882; regius professor of feudal and English law in Dublin University, 1884–90; judge of supreme court of judicature of Ireland, 1890–8; knighted, 1898; made important genealogical researches and published legal treatises.

BICKERSTETH, EDWARD HENRY (1825–1906), bishop of Exeter; son of Edward Bickersteth (1786–1850, q. v.); B.A., Trinity College, Cambridge, 1847; M.A., 1850; hon. D.D., 1885; thrice chancellor's medallist for English verse, 1844–5–6; Seatonian prizeman, 1854; ordained, 1848; vicar of Christ Church, Hampstead, 1855–85; active supporter of Church Missionary Society; dean of Gloucester, January 1885; bishop of Exeter, April 1885–1900; composer of 'O Brothers, lift your voices,' 'Peace, Perfect Peace' (in 'From Year to Year,' 1883), and other hymns; editor of 'The Hymnal Companion to the Book of Common Prayer,' 1870; author of 'Yesterday, To-day, and For Ever' (1866, 17th edit. 1885) and other poetical works; published commentary on the New Testament, 1864, and many devotional works.

BIDDULPH, SIR MICHAEL ANTHONY SHRAPNEL (1823–1904), general; educated at Woolwich; awarded Royal Humane Society's medal for life saving, 1842; with royal artillery in Crimea; in trenches at siege of Sevastopol, 1854; on special telegraph construction service in Asia Minor, 1855–9; C.B., 1873; in command of Rohilkhand district, 1875–8, and of Quetta field force in Afghan war, 1878–9; present at occupation of Kandahar; accomplished successful march with the Thal Chotiali field force, 1879; K.C.B., 1879; commanded Rawal Pindi district in India, 1880; promoted colonel commandant, 1885, and general, 1886; president of ordnance committee, 1887–90; keeper of regalia at Tower of London, 1891–6; G.C.B., 1895; gentleman usher of the black rod from 1896 to death.

BIDDULPH, SIR ROBERT (1835–1918), general; served in Crimea, Indian Mutiny, and China; private secretary to (Viscount) Cardwell, 1871; high commissioner and commander-in-chief, Cyprus, 1879–86; director-general of military education, 1888–93; general, 1892; governor and commander-in-chief, Gibraltar, 1893–1900; army purchase commissioner, 1904; K.C.M.G., 1880; G.C.B., 1899.

BIDWELL, SHELFORD (1848–1909), pioneer of tele-photography; B.A., Caius College, Cambridge, 1870; LL.B. and M.A., 1873; called to bar, 1873; began researches into photo-electric properties of selenium, 1880; described instrument for electrically transmitting pictures of natural objects to a distance along a wire, 1881; published many papers on telegraphic photography, physics, and kindred subjects; F.R.S., 1886; hon. Sc.D., Cambridge, 1900.

BIGG, CHARLES (1840–1908), classical scholar and theologian; educated at Manchester grammar school and Corpus Christi College, Oxford; B.A., 1862; M.A., 1864; D.D., 1876; Hertford scholar, 1860; won Gaisford Greek prose prize, 1861, and Ellerton theological essay, 1864; ordained, 1863; classical tutor of Christ Church, Oxford, 1863; head master of Brighton College, 1871–81; chaplain of Corpus Christi College, 1881–7; Bampton lecturer on 'The Christian Platonists of Alexandria,' 1886; hon. canon of Worcester, 1889–1901; regius professor of ecclesiastical history at Oxford and canon of Christ Church, 1901–8; published 'Neoplatonism,' 1895, 'The Origins of Christianity,' 1909, and other works.

BINNIE, SIR ALEXANDER RICHARDSON (1839–1917), civil engineer; executive engineer in Public Works Department of India, 1867; chief engineer for Bradford waterworks, 1875–90, and to London County Council, 1890–1901; knighted, 1897; reported on water supplies of Malta, Petrograd, and Ottawa.

BIRCH, GEORGE HENRY (1842–1904), architect and archaeologist; designed decoration for St. Nicholas Cole Abbey, London, 1882; president of Architectural Association, 1874–5; F.S.A., 1885; curator of Soane's Museum, Lincoln's Inn Fields, from 1894 to death; wrote 'London Churches of the Seventeenth and Eighteenth Centuries,' 1896.

BIRD, HENRY EDWARD (1830–1908), chess player; by profession an accountant; wrote pamphlets on railway finance; a leading chess player in tournaments, 1851–99; won first prize in British Chess Association tournament at Gouda (1889), winning 9½ out of 10 games; wrote many books on chess of mediocre value, including 'Chess Practice,' 1882, 'Modern Chess,' 1887 and 1889, and 'Chess Novelties,' 1895.

BIRD, ISABELLA LUCY (1831–1904), traveller and authoress. [See BISHOP.]

BIRDWOOD, SIR GEORGE CHRISTOPHER MOLESWORTH (1832–1917), Anglo-Indian official and author; born at Belgaum, Western India; M.D., Edinburgh University; medical practitioner in Bombay, 1858–68; entered statistics and commerce department of India Office, 1878; prolific writer on Indian art, &c.; knighted, 1881; K.C.I.E., 1887.

BIRDWOOD, HERBERT MILLS (1837–1907), Anglo-Indian judge; brother of Sir G. C. M. Birdwood; born at Belgaum, Western India; educated at Edinburgh University and Peterhouse, Cambridge; 23rd wrangler and fellow, 1858; M.A., 1861; LL.M., 1878; LL.D., 1889; called to bar, 1889; hon. fellow of Peterhouse, 1901; went to Bombay, 1859; as judge of Ratnagiri district (1871–81) gained reputation for independence; judicial commissioner at Karachi, 1881–5; judge of Bombay high court, 1885–92; member of Bombay council, 1892–7; C.S.I., 1893; vice-chancellor of Bombay University, 1891–2; wrote on Indian flora; returned to England (1897), and practised before privy council on Indian appeals.

BIRRELL, JOHN (1836–1901), Orientalist; M.A., St. Andrews University, 1855; entered Church of Scotland ministry, 1861; professor of Hebrew and Oriental languages, St. Mary's College, St. Andrews, 1871; D.D. Edinburgh, 1878; as examiner of Scottish secondary schools (1876–88) he originated university local examinations at St. Andrews.

BISHOP, EDMUND (1846–1917), liturgiologist and historian; served in Education Office, 1864–85; joined Roman Church, 1867; discovered, transcribed, and annotated 'Collectio Britannica' of 300 papal letters preserved at British Museum and published by editors of 'Monumenta Germaniae Historica,' 1880; his works include 'Liturgica Historica' (1918).

BISHOP, ISABELLA LUCY (1831–1904), traveller and authoress; born BIRD; for reasons of health lived much in open air; visited Canada and America, 1854; published 'The Englishwoman in America,' 1856; made her home in Edinburgh, 1858, encouraging crofter emigration to Canada, 1862–6, and attacking Edinburgh poverty in 'Notes on Old Edinburgh,' 1869; visited Australia and New Zealand, 1872, Sandwich Islands, 1873, Rocky Mountains, 1873; in the result published two notable works, 'The Hawaiian Archipelago,' 1875, and 'A Lady's Life in the Rocky Mountains,' 1879; visited Japan, 1878, and wrote 'Unbeaten Tracks in Japan,' 1880; married in 1881 Dr. Bishop; on husband's death (1886) she studied medicine; went to India, 1889, visiting Cashmere, Tibet, Persia, Armenia, 1889–90; founded hospitals in Cashmere and Punjab and elsewhere, and wrote in favour of missions; first lady fellow of Royal Geographical Society, 1892; made extensive tour in Japan, Korea, and China, 1894–7; published 'Korea and her Neighbours,' 1898; a good photographer, a fearless traveller, and keen observer.

BLACKBURN, HELEN (1842–1903), pioneer of woman's suffrage; secretary to National Society for Woman's Suffrage, 1875–95; editor of 'Englishwoman's Review,' 1881–1903; wrote 'Women's Suffrage,' 1902, the standard work on the subject, and other books on women's political and economic position.

BLACKLEY, WILLIAM LEWERY (1830–1902), divine and social reformer; educated at Brussels and Trinity College, Dublin; B.A., 1850; M.A., 1854; ordained, 1854; an energetic parish priest; wrote much on national insurance, thrift, and pauperism; his compulsory state insurance scheme (1878) examined by House of Commons committee (1885–7) and reported upon adversely; his persistent agitation stimulated movements for old-age pensions in England and colonies; vicar of St. James the Less, Westminster, 1889–1902; an eloquent speaker and accomplished linguist; his 'Collected Essays' on thrift and national insurance, 1880, were re-edited with memoir, 1906.

BLACKWELL, ELIZABETH (1821–1910), the first woman doctor of medicine; emigrated from Bristol to New York, 1832; opened school in Cincinnati, 1838; studied medicine at Geneva, N.Y., 1847; M.D., 1849; studied in Paris and at St. Bartholomew's Hospital, London, 1849; returned to America, 1850; opened dispensary in New York (1853), afterwards the New York Infirmary and College for Women; with sister Emily and Marie Zackrzewska, despite opposition, she opened hospital in New York conducted entirely by women, 1857; her name placed on British Medical Register, 1859; trained nurses for American civil war, 1864; her hospital granted charter, 1865; first professor of hygiene there, 1868; settled in England and founded National Health Society, 1871; accepted chair of gynaecology at newly founded London School of Medicine for Women, 1875; her writings include 'Laws of Life,' 1872, 'Moral Education of the Young . . . under Medical and Social Aspects' (2nd edit. 1879), 'Pioneer Work: Autobiographical Sketches,' 1895, 'Essays in Medical Sociology,' 2 vols. 1902.

BLACKWOOD, FREDERICK TEMPLE HAMILTON-TEMPLE, first MARQUESS OF DUFFERIN AND AVA (1826–1902), diplomatist and administrator; born at Florence; son of Helen Selina Sheridan [q. v.]; educated at Eton and Christ Church, Oxford, 1844–6; created Baron Clandeboye in English peerage, 1850; supported liberal policy; lord-in-waiting to Queen Victoria, 1849–52 and 1854–8; attaché to Lord John Russell's mission at abortive conference at Vienna for ending Crimean war, 1855; after yachting voyage to Iceland and Spitzbergen, published 'Letters from High Latitudes,' 1856; appointed British commissioner to assist Lord Dalling in inquiry into massacres in Levant, 1860; his proposal for independent governor adopted; K.C.B., 1861; under-secretary for India (1864–6) and to war office (1866–8) under Palmerston; chancellor of duchy of Lancaster under Gladstone, 1868; created earl, 1871; as governor-general of Canada (1872–8) pacified agitators and strengthened spirit of federal union among Canadians; G.C.M.G., 1876; hon. D.C.L., Oxford, 1879; appointed by Beaconsfield British ambassador at St. Petersburg, 1879; transferred to Constantinople, 1881; at Cairo reconstructed Egyptian administration after Arabi Bey's defeat at Tel-el-Kebir, 1882; advocated in his report representative institutions and municipal self-government; in Egypt created legislative council and assembly; promoted G.C.B., 1883; succeeded Lord Ripon [q. v.] as governor-general of India, 1884; dealt tactfully with Indian land question; conciliated Amir of Afghanistan, 1885; strengthened

British rule in India by improving railway communications with Afghan border, increasing the army, and constituting a new force of Burma military police; annexed Upper Burma, 1886; retired from India, 1888; promoted to marquessate, 1888; made freeman of City of London, 1889; ambassador at Rome, 1889–91; lord rector of St. Andrews University, 1891; ambassador at Paris, 1891–6; improved relations between England and France in regard to Siam and the Congo; warden of Cinque Ports, 1891–5; hon. LL.D. Cambridge, 1891; lord rector of Edinburgh University, 1901; suffered loss of money and reputation as chairman of London and Globe Finance Corporation, 1901; portrait by G. F. Watts in National Portrait Gallery.

BLAKE, EDWARD (1833–1912), Canadian lawyer and politician; born in Upper Canada; called to bar, 1856; prime minister of Ontario, 1871–2; minister of justice, 1875–7; leader of liberal opposition, 1880–8; nationalist member for South Longford, Ireland, 1892–1907; died at Toronto.

BLANDFORD, GEORGE FIELDING (1829–1911), physician; educated at Tonbridge, Rugby, and Wadham College, Oxford (B.A., 1852, M.A. and M.B., 1857, M.D., 1867); studied medicine at St. George's Hospital, 1852; lecturer there, 1865–1902; F.R.C.P., 1869; Lumleian lecturer, 1895; acquired large lunacy practice in London from 1863; president of medico-psychological association of Great Britain, 1877, and of psychological section, British Medical Association, 1894; chief work was 'Insanity and its Treatment,' 1871; interested in art, literature, and music.

BLANEY, THOMAS (1823–1903), physician and philanthropist; apprenticed to medical department, East India Company, 1836; studied at Grant Medical College, Bombay, 1851–5; made special study of fevers and plague; coroner of Bombay, 1876–93; generous benefactor to poor of Bombay; founded 'Blaney' school for poor white children; original member of Bombay municipal corporation, 1872; obtained municipal water supply; sheriff of Bombay, 1875 and 1888; C.I.E., 1894.

BLANFORD, WILLIAM THOMAS (1832–1905), geologist and zoologist; studied at Royal School of Mines (1852–4) and Freiberg in Saxony; obtained post in Indian geological survey, 1854; investigated coalfield near Talchir (1854–7) and geology of Burma (1860); appointed deputy superintendent, he surveyed Bombay presidency, 1862–6; attached to Abyssinian expedition, 1867; published works on the geology of Abyssinia, 1870, and of India, 1879; settled in London, 1881; edited for government works on Indian fauna, contributing two vols. on mammals (1888 and 1891) and two on birds (1895 and 1898); president of Geological Society, 1888–90; F.R.S., 1874; LL.D. Montreal, 1884; C.I.E., 1904.

BLAYDES, FREDERICK HENRY MARVELL (1818–1908), classical scholar; commoner of Christ Church, Oxford, 1836; Hertford scholar, 1838; B.A., 1840; M.A., 1843; toured in France and Italy, 1840–1; ordained, 1842; vicar of Harringworth, Northamptonshire, 1843–84; edited Aristophanes, Aeschylus, and Sophocles; chief work was 'Aristophanis comoediae,' 1882–93, devoted mainly to verbal and textual criticism and emendation; hon. LL.D. Dublin, 1892; Ph.D. Budapest; presented his classical library to St. Paul's School, 1901; interested in homoeopathy and music.

BLENNERHASSETT, SIR ROWLAND, fourth baronet (1839–1909), political writer; of Roman Catholic parentage; educated at Stonyhurst, Christ Church, Oxford, and Louvain University; formed friendship with Döllinger at Munich (1864) and with Lord Acton (1862); helped to start 'Chronicle,' a literary organ of liberal catholicism, 1867; admirer of Bismarck; liberal M.P. for Galway city, 1865–74, and for Kerry county, 1874–85; at first supported but later opposed home rule; interested in Irish education and land question; advocated peasant proprietorship, 1884; president of Queen's College, Cork, 1897–1904; P.C. Ireland, 1905; wrote constantly in leading periodicals on political subjects, and published speeches and addresses.

BLIND, KARL (1826–1907), political refugee and author; born at Mannheim, Germany; entered Heidelberg University, 1845; engaged there in revolutionary political agitation; imprisoned at Bonn for circulating pamphlet 'Deutscher Hunger und Deutsche Fürsten,' 1847; proscribed by Baden government for share in democratic risings, 1848; took refuge in Alsace; imprisoned at Strassburg; prominent in rising at Staufen (24 Sept.); released by revolutionaries from prison at Bruchsal,

1849; helped to set up provisional government for Baden, 1 June 1849; its representative in Paris; exiled in turn from France (1849) and Belgium (1852); settled in England, 1852; entertained leading European political exiles; introduced Mazzini to Swinburne; championed nationalist and democratic causes in all countries from 1878 till death; wrote much on Indian and German mythology.

BLOOMFIELD, GEORGIANA, LADY (1822–1905), maid of honour to Queen Victoria, 1841–5; married second Baron Bloomfield [q. v.], 1845, whom she accompanied on his diplomatic missions; published 'Reminiscences of Court and Diplomatic Life,' 2 vols., 1883.

BLOUET, LÉON PAUL, 'MAX O'RELL', (1848–1903), humorous writer; born in Brittany; cavalry officer in Franco-German war; French master at St. Paul's School, 1876–87; wrote 'John Bull et son île,' 1887, and 'Jonathan and his Continent,' 1889, vivacious pictures of English and American life; died in Paris.

BLOUNT, SIR EDWARD CHARLES (1809–1905), Paris banker and promoter of French railways; of Roman Catholic family; attaché to Paris embassy, 1829; in Rome, where he met Cardinal Wiseman and the future Napoleon III, 1830; started banking business in Paris, which failed at the revolution, 1848; promoted railway enterprise in France; formed company (Chemin de fer de l'Ouest), 1838; chairman till 1894; constructed railways from Paris to Rouen (1843), and from Amiens to Boulogne (1845); supported French royal family, 1848; in 1852 started in Paris a new banking business which proved successful and was merged in Société Générale of Paris, 1870; remained in Paris during siege of 1870; British consul there, January–March 1871; C.B., 1871; K.C.B., 1878; commander of legion of honour; long president of British Chamber of Commerce in Paris; devoted to horse-racing; published 'Recollections,' 1902.

BLUMENTHAL, JACQUES [JACOB] (1829–1908), composer of songs; born at Hamburg; settled in London, 1848; pianist to Queen Victoria; composed songs which won lasting popularity.

BLYTHSWOOD, first BARON (1835–1908), scientist. [See CAMPBELL, ARCHIBALD CAMPBELL.]

BODDA PYNE, LOUISA FANNY (1832–1904), soprano vocalist; made début in London, 1842, and Paris, 1847; toured in America (1854–7) with William Harrison, (1813–68, q. v.); produced at Lyceum and Covent Garden new English operas, 1857–62; married Frank Bodda, 1868; received civil list pension, 1896.

BODINGTON, SIR NATHAN (1848–1911), vice-chancellor of Leeds University; B.A., Wadham College, Oxford, 1872; M.A., 1874; fellow and tutor of Lincoln College, Oxford, 1875–85; hon. fellow, 1898; first professor of Greek, Mason College, Birmingham, 1881; appointed (1882) professor of Greek and principal of Yorkshire College, Leeds; vice-chancellor of Victoria University, Manchester, 1896–1900; promoted independent university for Leeds, which was founded with Bodington as vice-chancellor, 1904; extended the university's activities in scientific and technical directions; hon. Litt.D. Manchester, 1895; LL.D. Aberdeen, 1906; knighted, 1908.

BODLEY, GEORGE FREDERICK (1827–1907), architect; descended from Sir Thomas Bodley [q. v.]; pupil of George Gilbert Scott [q. v.], 1845–50; first exhibited at Royal Academy, 1854; designed (1860–70) many churches and private houses, including St. Michael's, Brighton; partner with Thomas Garner [q. v.], 1869–98, with whom he designed the churches of Holy Angels, Hoar Cross (in simple style), St. Augustine, Pendlebury, 1874 (an elaborate structure), and All Saints, Cambridge; built independently churches at Clumber and Eccleston, and Community Church, Cowley, Oxford; did work at Oxford (at Magdalen, and the tower of the 'Tom Quad' at Christ Church) and at Cambridge (the 'Bodley' group of buildings at King's College and Queens' College chapel); other works were cathedral at Hobart Town, Tasmania, and school board offices on Thames Embankment; prepared plans for episcopal cathedral of SS. Peter and Paul, Washington, 1906; A.R.A., 1882; R.A., 1902; his work is a later nineteenth-century counterpart of that of the architects of the Oxford Movement, Pugin, Scott, and Street; combined ecclesiological knowledge with sound taste; friend of Morris, Burne Jones, Madox Brown, and Rossetti; published small volume of verse, 1899; F.S.A., 1885; hon. D.C.L. Oxford, 1907.

BODY, GEORGE (1840–1911), canon of Durham; B.A., St. John's College, Cambridge, 1862; M.A., 1876; hon. D.D. Durham, 1885; rector of Kirby Misperton,

Yorkshire, 1870; 'canon missioner' of Durham, 1883–1911; lecturer in pastoral theology at King's College, London, 1909; combined evangelical fervour with tractarian principles; published many devotional works.

BOMPAS, HENRY MASON (1836–1909), county court judge at Bradford from 1896; brother of William Carpenter Bompas [q. v.]; B.A., St. John's College, Cambridge (fifth wrangler), 1858; barrister (Inner Temple), 1863.

BOMPAS, WILLIAM CARPENTER (1834–1906), bishop of Selkirk; ordained, 1859; went as missionary to Mackenzie River, 1865; arrived at Fort Yukon, 1869; bishop of Athabasca, 1874, of Mackenzie River, 1884, and of Selkirk, 1880; spent last years at Caribou Crossing, where he built a church, 1904; resigned bishopric, 1905; author of 'The Diocese of Mackenzie River,' 1888; translated hymns, prayers, and portions of Bible for Canadian Indians.

BOND, WILLIAM BENNETT (1815–1906), primate of all Canada from 1904; a native of Truro; emigrated to Newfoundland; ordained, 1840; curate (1848–60) and rector (1860–78) of St. George's, Montreal; became canon of Christ Church Cathedral, 1866; dean of Montreal, 1872; bishop, 1878; archbishop and metropolitan, 1901; took foremost part in expansion of Canadian church; president of Bishop's College, Lennoxville (hon. M.A., 1854); hon. LL.D. McGill University, 1870; strong evangelical and temperance reformer.

BONWICK, JAMES (1817–1906), Australian author and archivist; left England, 1840; conducted model school in Hobart Town, Van Diemen's Land (now Tasmania); joined in rush to Victorian goldfields, 1852; appointed archivist to government of New South Wales, 1884; issued officially 'Historical Records of New South Wales' (7 vols. 1893–1901); wrote on early Australian history, and 'An Octogenarian's Reminiscences,' 1902.

BOOTH, CHARLES (1840–1916), shipowner and writer on social questions; partner in Alfred Booth & Co., shipowners, Liverpool, 1862; author of 'Life and Labour of the People in London' (1891–1903), which gives a comprehensive and illuminating picture of London in the last decade of the nineteenth century; largely contributed to passing of Old Age Pensions Act, 1908; F.R.S., 1899; P.C., 1904.

BOOTH, WILLIAM (1829–1912), popularly known as 'General' Booth, founder of the Salvation Army; apprenticed to Nottingham pawnbroker; underwent experience of conversion, 1844; removed to London, 1849; itinerant preacher of Methodist New Connexion, 1852; married Catherine Mumford [see BOOTH, CATHERINE], 1855; began work as independent revivalist, 1861; started Christian Mission in Whitechapel, 1865; adopted for it the title 'Salvation Army,' 1878; championed degraded poor in great cities and attracted multitudes; interest in social reform led to publication of 'In Darkest England and the Way Out' (1890); more interesting as a man than as founder of anything new in religion or politics; entirely ignorant of theology, obscurantist in intellectual sphere, narrow and uncompromising in religion; his son Bramwell real organizer of 'Army'; yet he probably changed more lives for better than any other religious emotionalist for centuries.

BOOTHBY, GUY NEWELL (1867–1905), novelist; born at Adelaide, South Australia; educated in England; produced melodrama in Adelaide, 1888–91; resettled in England, 1894; wrote fifty sensational novels, the best dealing with Australian life; the most popular was 'A Bid for Fortune, or Dr. Nikola's Vendetta,' 1895.

BORTHWICK, ALGERNON, BARON GLENESK (1830–1908), proprietor of the 'Morning Post'; son of Peter Borthwick [q. v.]; educated in Paris and at King's College School, London; foreign correspondent of 'Morning Post' in Paris, 1850; succeeded father as editor, 1852; helped to produce with Evelyn Ashley [q. v.] the society journal 'The Owl,' 1864–70; bought 'Morning Post,' 1876; reduced price from 3d. to 1d., 1881; knighted, 1880; suggested 'Primrose League' in 'Morning Post,' 1883; conservative M.P. for South Kensington, 1885–95; carried measure amending law of libel, 1888; advocated tariff reform, and supported Lord Randolph Churchill; created baronet, 1887; raised to peerage, 1895; married Alice, daughter of Thomas Henry Lister [q. v.], 1870; handed over control of paper (1895) to son Oliver (d. 1905); keenly interested in theatre; restored to solvency Chelsea Hospital for Women, of which he was president in 1905.

BOSWELL, JOHN JAMES (1835–1908), major-

general; entered Bengal army, 1852; commanded detachment of 3rd and 6th Punjab infantry in Indian Mutiny, 1857, and 2nd Sikh infantry in Afghan war, 1878–80; at battle of Kandahar, 1880; C.B., 1881; major-general, 1885.

BOSWORTH SMITH, REGINALD (1839–1908) schoolmaster and author. [See SMITH.]

BOTHA, LOUIS (1862–1919), South African soldier and statesman; born in Natal; brought up on large farm near Vrede in Orange Free State from 1869; served as volunteer under Lukas Meyer, landrost of Utrecht, in successful campaign for restoration of Dinizulu, son of Zulu chief, Cetywayo, 1884; commissioner to delimit farms on Zulu territory assigned to volunteers after campaign; obtained Waterval, farm in 'New Republic' which (1888) joined Transvaal; field-cornet and native commissioner at Vryheid; mobilized burgher force during Jameson Raid, 1895; member for district in first volksraad, 1897; supporter of P. J. Joubert's liberal views on Uitlander franchise; on declaration of war with England mustered commando at Vryheid, 1899; distinguished himself at battle of Dundee and promoted assistant-general, October; forced Sir Redvers Buller to abandon attempt to relieve Ladysmith by pushing across Tugela at Colenso and making direct attack on Joubert's force (December); urged immediate advance, but was over-ruled; saved situation at Tabanyama and Spion Kop (January 1900); forced Buller to retire at Vaalkrantz (February); promoted commandant-general of Transvaal on Joubert's death (March); re-organized commandos; made last stand for Johannesburg and Pretoria at Doornkop (May); defeated at closely contested battle of Diamond Hill (June); carried on guerilla warfare against British, 1900–2; submitted, after obtaining reasonable terms, at Vereeniging, May 1902; visited England, 1902; lived henceforth chiefly at Pretoria; with other leading Boers founded nationalist organization 'Het Volk,' 1905; formed ministry under British Crown, 1906; headed Transvaal delegation at Union Convention, 1908–9; formed strong political combination with General Johannes Smuts; first prime minister of Union of South Africa, 1910–19; dealt satisfactorily with problems of Indian immigrants and unrest on Rand; wholeheartedly supported Great Britain during European War, 1914–18; put down serious revolt of Dutch against intervention in War, 1914–15; commanded successful campaign against German South-West Africa, resulting in unconditional surrender of German forces and colony, 1915; with Smuts attended Versailles Peace Conference as South African delegate, 1919; died at Pretoria.

BOUCHERETT, EMILIA JESSIE (1825–1905), advocate of women's progress; of old Lincolnshire family; came to London, 1859; helped to found Society for the Promotion of Employment of Women, 1860; organized first petition to parliament for women's franchise, 1866; founded and edited 'Englishwoman's Review,' 1866–71; contributed to leading reviews on women's questions.

BOUGHTON, GEORGE HENRY (1833–1905), painter and illustrator; travelled and studied art in British Isles, 1856; exhibited in America, 1858; worked in Paris, 1860–2; exhibited at Royal Academy from 1863 till death; A.R.A., 1879; R.A., 1896; treated mainly peasant life of Brittany and Holland, and New England history; works include 'Weeding the Pavement,' 1882, 'A Dutch Ferry,' 1883, 'The Road to Camelot,' 1898; wrote and illustrated 'Sketching Rambles in Holland,' 1885.

BOURCHIER, JAMES DAVID (1850–1920), 'Times' correspondent in Balkan Peninsula with headquarters first at Athens, then at Sofia, 1892–1918; entrusted with many secret negotiations preceding Balkan alliance, 1911–12; held unique position in Balkans.

BOURINOT, SIR JOHN GEORGE (1837–1902), writer on Canadian constitutional history; born at Sydney, Cape Breton, of Huguenot extraction; B.A., Trinity College, Toronto; hon. LL.D., 1889; founded and edited 'Halifax Herald,' 1860; chief reporter of Nova Scotia assembly from 1861; chief clerk of Canadian House of Commons from 1880 till death; his 'Manual of the Constitutional History of Canada' (1888), a standard text-book; president of Royal Society of Canada, 1892; K.C.M.G., 1898.

BOURKE, ROBERT, BARON CONNEMARA (1827–1902), governor of Madras; younger brother of sixth earl of Mayo [q. v.]; educated at Trinity College, Dublin; called to bar (Inner Temple), 1852; acquired large parliamentary practice; conservative M.P. for King's Lynn, 1868–86; under secretary for foreign affairs under Disraeli

(1874–80) and Salisbury (1885–6); P.C., 1880; governor of Madras, 1886; baron and G.C.I.E., 1887; by tact and industry improved relations with natives; improved sanitary conditions and railway communications in the presidency; resignation (1890) followed by divorce from wife, the daughter of James Andrew, Marquess of Dalhousie [q. v.], 1891; remarried, 1894.

BOURNE, HENRY RICHARD FOX (1837–1909), social reformer and author; born in Jamaica; pupil of Henry Morley [q. v.] at University College, London; wrote popular accounts of England's colonial expansion; owner of 'Examiner,' 1870–3; editor of 'Weekly Dispatch,' a radical organ, 1876–87; secretary of Aborigines Protection Society from 1889 till death; fervent champion of all native races; chief works were lives of Sir Philip Sidney (1862) and John Locke (1876), and 'English Newspapers,' 2 vols. 1887.

BOUSFIELD, HENRY BROUGHAM (1832–1902), first bishop of Pretoria; B.A., Caius College, Cambridge, 1855; M.A., 1858; vicar of Andover, 1870–8; bishop of Pretoria, 1878–1902; wrote 'Six Years in the Transvaal,' 1886.

BOWEN, EDWARD ERNEST (1836–1901), schoolmaster and song writer; brother of Charles, Lord Bowen [q. v.]; educated at Trinity College, Cambridge; Bell university scholar, 1855; fourth classic, 1858; fellow, 1859; master at Harrow, 1859–1901; advocated closer relations between master and pupils; recommended creation of modern side, which he directed, 1869–93; wrote for reviews on military and theological topics; collected his 'Harrow Songs and other Verses,' 1886, which included 'Forty Years On,' 1872; efficient cricketer, footballer, skater, and mountaineer; liberal in politics; bequeathed property to Harrow School.

BOWES, ROBERT (1835–1919), bookseller, publisher, and bibliographer; head of Macmillan & Bowes' (Bowes & Bowes) bookshop, Cambridge, 1863 till death; published researches on Cambridge University printers and Cambridge books; prominent in Cambridge social and civic life.

BOWLER, HENRY ALEXANDER (1824–1903), painter; exhibited landscapes at Royal Academy, 1847–71; assistant director for art at South Kensington, 1876–91.

BOYCE, SIR RUBERT WILLIAM (1863–1911), pathologist and hygienist; studied medicine at University College, London; M.B., London, 1889; published 'Textbook of Morbid Histology,' 1892; first professor of pathology, University College, Liverpool, 1894; promoted establishment of Liverpool University, and creation of medical chairs there; helped to found Liverpool School of Tropical Medicine, 1898; examined epidemics of yellow fever at New Orleans and British Honduras, 1905; published books on subject, and formed at Liverpool a bureau of yellow fever; F.R.S., 1902; knighted, 1906.

BOYD, SIR THOMAS JAMIESON (1818–1902), lord provost of Edinburgh; head of uncle's publishing house of Oliver and Boyd, 1873–98; master of Merchant Company of Edinburgh, 1869; reformed educational foundations of the corporation, 1870; promoted New Royal Infirmary, Edinburgh, 1879; lord provost of Edinburgh, 1877–82; knighted, 1881; F.R.S., Edinburgh.

BOYD CARPENTER, WILLIAM (1841–1918), bishop of Ripon. [See CARPENTER.]

BOYLE, SIR COURTENAY EDMUND (1845–1901), permanent secretary of the board of trade, 1893–1901; born in Jamaica; educated at Charterhouse and Christ Church, Oxford; played for cricket at cricket and tennis, 1865–7; keen angler; private secretary to Lord Spencer, Irish viceroy, 1868; C.B., 1885; assistant secretary to local government board, 1885, and to board of trade, 1886; K.C.B., 1892; published 'Method and Organization in Business,' 1901, and edited 'Mary Boyle, her Book,' 1901.

BOYLE, SIR EDWARD, first baronet (1848–1909), legal writer; surveyor for twenty years; called to bar, 1887; took silk, 1898; baronet, 1904; conservative M.P. for Taunton, 1906–9; joint author of important legal treatises on rating and compensation.

BOYLE, GEORGE DAVID (1828–1901), dean of Salisbury; son of David Boyle, Lord Boyle [q. v.]; educated at Charterhouse and Exeter College, Oxford; B.A., 1851; M.A., 1853; vicar of Kidderminster, 1867–1880; dean of Salisbury, 1880–1901; published 'Recollections,' 1895, and 'Salisbury Cathedral,' 1897.

BOYLE, RICHARD VICARS (1822–1908), civil engineer; pupil of Charles Vignoles [q. v.]; chief engineer of Longford and Sligo railway, 1846–7; district engineer on East Indian railway, 1853–68; distinguished himself in Indian Mutiny at Arrah, 1857; appointed field officer to (Sir) Vincent Eyre [q. v.]; C.S.I., 1869; engineer in chief for imperial Japanese railways, 1872–7; travelled much after retirement.

BRABAZON, HERCULES BRABAZON (1821–1906), painter; educated at Harrow and Trinity College, Cambridge; B.A., 1844; M.A., 1848; inherited Brabazon estates in Ireland and property in Sussex; studied art at Rome, 1844–7; made frequent foreign tours; painted with Ruskin in France; influenced by Turner; held exhibition of work at Goupil Gallery, 1892; showed gift of colour and sensitiveness to nature; ardent pianist and model landlord; Brabazon gallery at Sedlescombe, Sussex, opened to public.

BRACKENBURY, SIR HENRY (1837–1914), general and writer on military subjects; entered Woolwich, 1854; professor of military history at Woolwich, 1868; accompanied (Viscount) Wolseley to Ashanti, 1873, Cyprus, 1878, Zululand, 1879, and Egypt, 1884; deputy assistant quartermaster-general and head of intelligence branch at headquarters, 1886–91; military member of council of viceroy of India, 1891–6; director-general of ordnance during South African War, 1899–1902; G.C.B., 1900; P.C., 1904; published works on military subjects.

BRADDON, SIR EDWARD NICHOLAS COVENTRY (1829–1904), premier of Tasmania; assistant in government railways, Calcutta, 1854; superintendent of excise and stamps in Oudh, 1862, and of statistics, 1868; inspector-general of registration, 1871–7; retired to Tasmania, 1878; entered House of Assembly, 1879; minister of lands and works and of education, 1887; agent-general for colony in London, 1888–93; K.C.M.G., 1891; premier of Tasmania, 1894–9; P.C. and hon. LL.D. Cambridge, 1897; senior member for Tasmania in first Australian commonwealth parliament, 1901; wrote 'Thirty Years of Shikar,' 1895.

BRADDON, MARY ELIZABETH (1837–1915), novelist. [See MAXWELL.]

BRADFORD, SIR EDWARD RIDLEY COLBORNE, first baronet (1836–1911), Anglo-Indian administrator and commissioner of the metropolitan police, London; joined East India Company, 1853; served with 6th Madras Cavalry in Indian Mutiny, 1855–9; was mauled by tiger and lost arm, 1863; served in various districts as political agent; appointed superintendent of thagi and dakaiti, dealing with sedition cases, 1874; promoted chief commissioner of Ajmir, 1878; introduced municipal government there; K.C.S.I., 1885; secretary in political and secret departments, India Office, 1887; commissioner of police in London, 1890–1903; allayed police disaffection, June 1890; improved police organization and welfare; G.C.B., 1897; G.C.V.O. and baronet, 1902; interested in hunting and shooting.

BRADLEY, GEORGE GRANVILLE (1821–1903), dean of Westminster and schoolmaster; son of Charles Bradley [q. v.]; educated at Rugby and University College, Oxford; first class classic and fellow, 1844; master at Harrow, 1845–58; head master of Marlborough, 1858–70; raised number of pupils and enlarged school buildings; successful Latin prose teacher; close friend of Tennyson and of Dean Stanley; master of University College, Oxford, 1870–81; raised standard of scholarship there; member of university commission and canon of Worcester, 1880; dean of Westminster, 1881–1902; restored masonry and finances of the abbey, and revised the system of interments; buried there; his 'Latin Prose Composition' (1881) still much used.

BRAMPTON, BARON (1817–1907), judge. [See HAWKINS, HENRY.]

BRAMWELL, SIR FREDERICK JOSEPH (1818–1903), engineer; brother of George, Lord Bramwell [q. v.]; apprenticed to John Hague, London engineer, and inventor of system for propelling trains by atmospheric pressure, 1834; studied methods of steam propulsion; as manager to Hague, constructed locomotive for Stockton and Darlington railway, 1843; started for himself, 1853; developed legal and consultative side of profession; first to practise as technical advocate; a recognized authority on municipal and waterworks engineering; adviser to all London water companies; constructed sewage disposal scheme for Portsmouth; member (1854) and president (1874) of Institution of Mechanical Engineers; president of British Association at Bath, 1888, and of Society of Arts, 1901; hon. secretary of Royal Institution, 1885–1900; chairman of City and Guilds

Institute, 1878–1903; knighted, 1881; F.R.S., 1873; D.C.L. Oxford, 1886; LL.D. Cambridge, 1892; baronet, 1889; predicted supersession of steam engine by internal combustion engine, 1881; wrote on James Watt for this Dictionary.

BRAND, HENRY ROBERT, second VISCOUNT HAMPDEN and twenty-fourth BARON DACRE (1841–1906), governor of New South Wales, 1895–9; served in Coldstream guards; liberal M.P. for Hertfordshire, 1868–74; for Stroud, 1880–6; surveyor-general of ordnance, 1883–5; opposed to home rule; succeeded father, 1892; G.C.M.G., 1899.

BRAND, HERBERT CHARLES ALEXANDER (1839–1901), commander R.N.; entered navy, 1851; at capture of Canton and Taku forts, 1858; helped Edward John Eyre [q. v.] to suppress negro revolt in Morant Bay, 1865; president of court-martial on ringleaders, who were put to death; charge of murder against him in London dismissed, 1867; his indiscretion prevented further promotion; he retired with rank of commander, 1883.

BRANDIS, SIR DIETRICH (1824–1907), forest administrator and botanist; born at Bonn of good Hanoverian family; studied botany at Athens, Bonn, and Copenhagen; Ph.D., 1848; put in charge of and saved threatened teak forests in Burma, 1856–62; inspector-general of Indian forests, 1864; founded at Dehra Dun school for native foresters, 1878; published 'The Forest Flora of North-West and Central India,' 1874; F.R.S., 1875; C.I.E., 1878; K.C.I.E., 1887; hon. LL.D. Edinburgh, 1889; leaving India, he advised English and American forestry students, 1888–96; divided his time between Bonn and Kew; chief work 'Indian Trees,' 1906; died at Bonn.

BRASSEY, THOMAS, first EARL BRASSEY, of Bulkeley, Cheshire (1836–1918); son of Thomas Brassey [q. v.]; educated at Rugby and University College, Oxford; liberal M.P., Hastings, 1868–86; interested in wages question and naval matters; toured round world in his yacht 'Sunbeam', 1876–7; civil lord of Admiralty, 1880–4; K.C.B., 1881; parliamentary secretary to Admiralty, 1884–5; first produced 'Brassey's Naval Annual,' 1886; created baron, 1886; governor of Victoria, 1895–1900; lord warden of Cinque Ports, 1908–13; created earl, 1911.

BRAY, CAROLINE (1814–1905), authoress; sister of Charles Christian [q. v.], Mary [q. v.], and Sara Hennell [see below]; married Charles Bray of Coventry [q. v.]; intimate friend of George Eliot from 1842; entertained Emerson (1848) and Herbert Spencer (1852–62) at Coventry; wrote 'Physiology and the Laws of Health,' 1860, and 'Our Duty to Animals,' 1871; initiated Coventry Society for Prevention of Cruelty to Animals, 1874; her sister SARA HENNELL (1812–99) was author of 'Christianity and Infidelity,' 1857, of 'Essay on the Sceptical Tendency of Butler's "Analogy,"' 1859 (of classical rank, commended by Gladstone), and 'Present Religion as a Faith owning Fellowship with Thought,' 3 vols. 1865–87.

BRERETON, JOSEPH LLOYD (1822–1901), educational reformer; educated at Rugby and University College, Oxford; B.A., 1846; M.A., 1857; obtained Newdigate prize, 1844; rector of West Buckland, N. Devon, 1852–67, and of Little Massingham, King's Lynn, 1867–1901; permanently injured in railway accident, 1882; established 'county' schools in Devon (1858) and in Norfolk (1871), and advocated national education on county basis; founded (1873) Cavendish 'County' College at Cambridge to connect county schools with the universities; the college, a financial failure, was dissolved, 1892; published religious verse.

BRETT, JOHN (1831–1902), landscape painter; entered Royal Academy Schools, 1854; his pre-Raphaelite pictures, 'The Stone Breaker' (1858) and 'Val d'Aosta' (1859), praised by Ruskin; painted mainly Cornish seascapes, including 'Mounts Bay,' 1877, 'Cornish Lions,' 1878, 'Britannia's Realm,' 1880; treated subjects in minute scientific detail; a keen astronomer; A.R.A., 1881.

BREWTNALL, EDWARD FREDERICK (1846–1902), painter; studied at Lambeth School of Art; exhibited at Royal Water Colour Society (1875–1900) and (mostly oils) at Royal Academy (1872–1900).

BRIDGE, THOMAS WILLIAM (1848–1909), zoologist; assistant at museum of zoology, Cambridge University, 1870; B.A., Trinity College, 1876; M.A., 1880; professor of biology, Mason College, Birmingham, 1880; successful teacher and organizer; F.R.S., 1903; made researches into anatomy of fishes.

BRIDGES, JOHN HENRY (1832–1906), positivist philosopher; son of Charles Bridges [q. v.]; educated at Rugby and Wadham College, Oxford; B.A., 1855; fellow of Oriel, 1855; M.B., 1859; emigrated to Australia on marriage, 1860; returned to England, 1861; medical inspector to local government board, 1870–98; under influence of Richard Congreve [q. v.] he studied Comtist philosophy; lectured to London Positivist Society, 1870–1900; works include translation of Comte's 'Politique Positive I.', 1865 and 1875, and 'Five Discourses on Positive Religion,' 1882; wrote much on social reform and on health questions; delivered Harveian oration, 1892; edited Roger Bacon's 'Opus Majus,' 1897 (reissued with many corrections and emendations, 1900); 'Essays and Addresses' (published posthumously), 1907.

BRIDGES, SIR WILLIAM THROSBY (1861–1915), general; joined Australian headquarters staff, 1902; chiefly memorable as commandant of Duntroon Royal Military College, 1910–14; commanded first Australian contingent in European War; mortally wounded at Gallipoli; K.C.B., 1915.

BRIGGS, JOHN (1862–1902), Lancashire cricketer; obtained fame as slow left-hand bowler; paid six visits to Australia, 1884–97; played for England; mainstay of Lancashire county team, 1883–94; destructive on slow wickets.

BRIGHT, JAMES FRANCK (1832–1920), master of University College, Oxford; son of Richard Bright, M.D. [q. v.]; educated at Rugby and University College, Oxford; first class in law and modern history, 1854; ordained, 1856; master of modern school, Marlborough College, 1855–72; lecturer in modern history at University College, 1873; fellow, 1874; helped to raise status of college and to establish intercollegiate lecture system; master of University, 1881–1906; took active part in university and municipal affairs; liberal in theology and politics; author of 'History of England' (5 vols., 1875–1904).

BRIGHT, WILLIAM (1824–1901), church historian; educated at Rugby and University College, Oxford; first class classic (B.A., 1846, M.A., 1849, D.D., 1869); fellow, 1847–68; theological tutor, Trinity College, Glenalmond, and Bell lecturer in ecclesiastical history, 1851–8; regius professor of ecclesiastical history and canon of Christ Church, Oxford, 1868–1901; forcible and humorous lecturer: voluminous writings include 'A History of the Church, A.D. 313–451,' 1860, 'Waymarks of Church History,' 1894, 'The Age of the Fathers,' 2 vols. 1903, sermons, and some first-rate hymns.

BRIGHTWEN, ELIZA (1830–1906), naturalist; daughter of George Elder; married George Brightwen, banker, 1855; studied natural history at her home at Stanmore; works include 'Wild Nature won by Kindness,' 1890, and 'Inmates of my House and Garden,' 1895; most popular naturalist of day; her autobiography edited by Edmund Gosse, 1909.

BROADBENT, SIR WILLIAM HENRY, first baronet (1835–1907), physician; studied medicine at Owens College, Manchester, and Paris; M.B. London, 1858; M.D., 1860; physician to London Fever Hospital, 1860–79, and elsewhere; at St. Mary's Hospital, pathologist, 1860, lecturer in comparative anatomy, 1861, physician from 1865, and lecturer in medicine, 1871–88; made researches into cancer, paralysis, and aphasia; advanced theory known as 'Broadbent's hypothesis' of hemiplegia; fellow, 1869, senior censor, 1895, Croonian lecturer, 1887, and Lumleian lecturer, 1891, at Royal College of Physicians; Lettsomian lecturer of Medical Society of London, 1874; member of royal commission on fever hospitals, 1881; wrote valuable treatise on heart disease, 1897; physician to members of royal family from 1891; created baronet, 1893, and K.C.V.O., 1901; prominent in public movements for prevention and cure of tuberculosis; hon. member of many foreign societies; F.R.S., 1897; received numerous honorary degrees; 'Collected Papers' edited by son, 1908.

BROADHURST, HENRY (1840–1911), labour leader; son of a stonemason; worked as stonemason, 1853–8; settled in London, 1865; chairman of masons' committee agitating for increased pay, 1872; led his trade union to fix its headquarters permanently in London, giving central committee power to negotiate for whole membership, thus establishing representative democracy in trade unions; elected secretary of Labour Representation League, 1873; elected secretary of parliamentary committee of trade union congress, 1875; worked actively for amendments to Factory Acts, for employers' liability, and the like; liberal M.P. for Stoke-on-Trent, 1880–5; member of royal commissions on housing of working classes (1884) and on the aged poor (1892); ardent agitator for extension of franchise; M.P. for Bordesley, 1885–6; under-secretary in home department, 1886; M.P. for West Nottingham, 1886–92; in later years out of sympathy with trade union developments; M.P. for Leicester, 1894–1906; published his autobiography, 1901.

BRODRIBB, WILLIAM JACKSON (1829–1905), translator; educated at St. John's College, Cambridge; sixth classic, 1852; fellow, 1856; vicar of Wootton Rivers, Wilts, 1860–1905; translator and editor of works of Tacitus.

BRODRICK, GEORGE CHARLES (1831–1903), warden of Merton College, Oxford; educated at Eton and Balliol; first class in classics (1853) and in law and history (1854); president of Union, 1854–5; B.A., 1854; M.A., 1856; D.C.L., 1886; elected fellow of Merton College, 1855; called to bar, 1859; joined staff of 'The Times,' 1860; made several unsuccessful attempts to enter parliament as liberal; lucid writer on politics; published 'Political Studies,' 1879, and 'English Land and English Landlords,' 1881; member of London school board, 1877–9; warden of Merton, 1881–1903; active in university reform; wrote popular histories of Merton (1885) and of the university (1886); opposed Gladstone's Irish land legislation and home rule measures; published 'Memories and Impressions,' 1900.

BROMBY, CHARLES HAMILTON (1843–1904), son of Charles Henry Bromby [q. v.]; called to bar, 1867; attorney-general of Tasmania, 1876–8; efficient Italian student.

BROMBY, CHARLES HENRY (1814–1907), second bishop of Tasmania; educated at Uppingham and St. John's College, Cambridge; B.A., 1837; M.A., 1840; D.D., 1864; first principal of Cheltenham training college, 1843–64; bishop of Tasmania, 1864–82; reorganized finances of Tasmanian Church on its disestablishment; assistant bishop of Lichfield, 1882–91, and of Bath and Wells, 1891–7; wrote pamphlets on education.

BROOKE, SIR CHARLES ANTHONY JOHNSON (1829–1917), second raja of Sarawak; born JOHNSON; joined uncle, Sir James Brooke [q. v.], first raja, 1852; succeeded to title and assumed name Brooke, 1868; worked for progress and development of Sarawak.

BROOKE, RUPERT (1887–1915), poet; educated at Rugby and King's College, Cambridge; became conspicuous figure in university life; published volume of 'Poems,' 1911; fellow of King's, 1912; travelled in United States, Canada, New Zealand, and South Sea islands, 1913–14; joined Royal Naval Division, 1914; died at Scyros; '1914 and other Poems' published posthumously; fellowship dissertation on John Webster and 'Letters from America' have also been published.

BROOKE, STOPFORD AUGUSTUS (1832–1916), divine and man of letters; B.A., Trinity College, Dublin; ordained, 1857; minister of proprietary chapel of St. James, York Street, London, 1866–76, and of Bedford chapel, Bloomsbury, 1876–95; seceded from English Church, 1880; celebrated preacher; works include 'Life and Letters of Frederick W. Robertson' (1865) and 'Primer of English Literature' (1876).

BROTHERHOOD, PETER (1838–1902), civil engineer; partner in Compton Street engine works, Goswell Road, 1867; introduced Brotherhood engine, for driving torpedoes by means of compressed air, 1872; designed air compressor, and servo-motor for torpedoes, 1876.

BROUGH, BENNETT HOOPER (1860–1908), mining expert; nephew of Lionel Brough [q. v.]; successively student and teacher at Royal School of Mines, 1878–82; published 'Treatise on Mine Surveying,' 1888; secretary of Iron and Steel Institute, 1893–1908.

BROUGH, LIONEL (1836–1909), actor; brother of William Brough [q. v.] and Robert Barnabas Brough [q. v.]; errand boy in 'Illustrated London News' office, 1848; made début on stage at Lyceum, 1854; assistant publisher of 'Daily Telegraph,' 1855; originated street selling of newspapers; gave monologues at Regent Street Polytechnic, 1862; introduced 'Pepper's Ghost,' 1863; resumed acting as profession, 1864; ability recognized in his representation of Ben Garner in 'Dearer than Life,' 1868; successful as Tony Lumpkin and other comedy characterizations from 1869 onwards; joint lessee with Willie Edouin [q. v.] of Toole's Theatre, 1884; visited America (1886) and South Africa (1888); acted with

company of Sir H. Beerbohm Tree [q. v.] from 1894 to death; pre-eminent in burlesque; noted for simple drollery and affectation of blank stolidity.

BROUGH, ROBERT (1872–1905), painter; studied art at Royal Scottish Academy life school, Edinburgh, and at Paris; exhibited at Royal Scottish and Royal academies; A.R.S.A., 1904; portrait painter of virile powers, uniting simplicity and breadth; chief works were 'Master Philip Fleming,' 1900, and 'Sir Charles Tennant's family,' 1905; killed in railway accident.

BROUGHTON, RHODA (1840–1920), novelist; novels include 'Cometh Up as a Flower' and 'Not Wisely but too Well' (1867), 'Good-bye, Sweetheart' (1872), 'Nancy' (1873), 'Joan' (1876), 'Belinda' (1883), 'Doctor Cupid' (1886), 'Foes-in-law' (1900), and 'A Waif's Progress' (1905).

BROWN, GEORGE DOUGLAS (1869–1902), novelist; son of farmer; educated at Glasgow University (M.A., 1890) and Balliol College, Oxford, 1891–5; published a novel of Scottish life, 'The House with the Green Shutters,' under pseudonym of George Douglas, 1901.

BROWN, SIR GEORGE THOMAS (1827–1906), veterinary surgeon; professor of veterinary science at Royal Agricultural College, Cirencester, 1850–63; connected with veterinary department of privy council, 1865–89; at board of agriculture, 1889–93; knighted, 1898; professor (from 1881) and principal (1888–94) of Royal Veterinary College; published 'Animal Life in the Farm,' 1885, and departmental reports.

BROWN, JOSEPH (1809–1902), barrister; B.A., Queens' College, Cambridge, 1830; M.A., 1833; called to bar, 1845; treasurer of Middle Temple, 1878–9; had large commercial practice; initiated publication of 'Law Reports,' 1865; C.B., 1892.

BROWN, PETER HUME (1849–1918), historian; M.A., Edinburgh University; Sir William Fraser's professor of ancient history at Edinburgh, 1901–18; works include biographies of George Buchanan (1890), John Knox (1895) and Goethe (published posthumously, 1920), and 'History of Scotland' (1899–1909); editor of 'Register of the Privy Council of Scotland,' 1898.

BROWN, WILLIAM HAIG- (1823–1907), master of Charterhouse. [See HAIG-BROWN.]

BROWNE, SIR JAMES FRANKFORT MANNERS (1823–1910), general; joined royal engineers, 1842; served in Canada, 1845–51, and in Ireland, 1851–3; in command of 1st company of royal sappers and miners, Chatham, 1854; in trenches at Sevastopol, 1855; conspicuous at the Redan; led right attack, severely wounded and invalided home, November 1855; C.B., 1855; commanded engineers in Bombay presidency at Poona, 1859; governor of Royal Military Academy, Woolwich, 1880–7; general, 1888; colonel commandant of royal engineers, 1890; K.C.B., 1894.

BROWNE, SIR SAMUEL JAMES (1824–1901), general; born in India; joined 46th Bengal native infantry, 1840; served in second Sikh war, 1848–9; commanding officer of 2nd Punjab cavalry, mainly on Peshawar frontier, 1851–63; at siege of Lucknow, 1858; awarded V.C. for gallantry against rebels at Sirpura, August 1858; K.C.S.I., 1876; lieutenant-general, 1877; as military member of governor-general's council, he made preparations for Afghan war, 1878–9; commanded 1st division of Peshawar field force, capturing fortress of Ali Masjid (Nov.) and Jellalabad (Dec.) 1878; prepared scheme for advance on Kabul, 1879; occupied Gandamak, 1879; K.C.B., 1879; G.C.B., 1891; general, 1888; inventor of sword belt adopted in the army.

BROWNE, THOMAS (1870–1910), painter and black-and-white artist; apprenticed to Nottingham firm of lithographic printers, 1884–91; came to London, 1895; contributed black-and-white sketches to London and American periodicals; created comic types of American journalism, Weary Willie and Tired Tim; founded colour-printing firm of Tom Browne and Co. at Nottingham, 1897; exhibited water-colours at Royal Academy, 1898–1901; published 'Tom Browne's Comic Annual,' 1904–5.

BRUCE, ALEXANDER HUGH, sixth BARON BALFOUR OF BURLEIGH (1849–1921), statesman; representative peer of Scotland, 1876–1921; chairman of numerous commissions, 1882–1917; secretary for Scotland, 1895–1903; worked to promote union of Church of Scotland and United Free Church; P.C., 1892; K.T., 1901; G.C.M.G., 1911.

BRUCE, SIR GEORGE BARCLAY (1821–1908), civil engineer; apprentice to Robert Stephenson and Co.,

1836–41; resident engineer of Royal Border bridge, 1845; chief engineer of Madras railway, 1853–6; constructed many English and foreign railway lines, including railway and pier at Huelva, Spain, 1873–6; Telford medallist (1851) and president (1887–8) of Institution of Civil Engineers; knighted, 1888; interested in Presbyterian church work and education; member of London school board, 1882–5.

BRUCE, VICTOR ALEXANDER, ninth EARL OF ELGIN and thirteenth EARL OF KINCARDINE (1849–1917), statesman and sometime viceroy of India; son of James Bruce, eighth earl [q. v.]; born in Canada; educated at Glenalmond, Eton, and Balliol College, Oxford; succeeded father, 1863; held office in liberal government of 1886; viceroy of India, 1893–8; his period of office marked by political unrest, Frontier disturbances, plague, and famine; proved too weak for position which he had reluctantly accepted; K.G., 1899; chairman of royal commission which inquired into military preparations for Boer War, 1902, and of commission on Free Church case, 1905; colonial secretary in Sir Henry Campbell-Bannerman's government, 1906–8.

BRUCE, WILLIAM SPEIRS (1867–1921), polar explorer and oceanographer; studied medicine at Edinburgh University; went on various polar expeditions, 1892–9; planned Scottish national Antarctic expedition to explore Weddell Sea, 1902–4; published its 'Report'; explored Spitzbergen between 1906 and 1920; received medals of various geographical and scientific societies.

BRUNTON, SIR THOMAS LAUDER, first baronet (1844–1916), physician; M.D., Edinburgh University; lecturer in *materia medica* and pharmacology, St. Bartholomew's Hospital, London; discovered use of amyl nitrite in treatment of *angina pectoris*; Goulstonian lecturer, 1877; Lettsomian lecturer, 1886; Croonian lecturer, 1889; Harveian orator, 1894; baronet, 1908; publications include 'Text-book of Pharmacology and Therapeutics' (1885).

BRUSHFIELD, THOMAS NADAULD (1828–1910), lunacy specialist and antiquary; studied medicine at London Hospital, 1845–9; M.R.C.S., 1850; M.D., St. Andrews, 1862; medical superintendent at Brookwood Asylum, 1865–82; pioneer of 'non-restraint' treatment of lunatics; settled at Budleigh Salterton, 1882; published 'Raleghana,' 1896–1907, 'Ralegh Miscellanea,' 1909–10, and a Ralegh bibliography, 1886; F.S.A., 1899; a founder of Devon and Cornwall Record Society.

BRYDON, JOHN McKEAN (1840–1901), architect; studied architecture in Liverpool and Italy; settled in London, 1868; built at Bath municipal buildings (1891–5), technical schools (1895–6), Victoria Art Gallery (1901), and pump room extensions, besides London School of Medicine for Women (1897–9), and other public and private buildings; designed local government board and education offices in Whitehall, 1898.

BUCHAN, ALEXANDER (1829–1907), meteorologist; M.A. Edinburgh, 1848; at first schoolmaster; secretary of Scottish Meteorological Society, 1860; organized compilation of meteorological statistics in Scotland; inaugurated observatory on Ben Nevis, 1883; appointed member of meteorological council, 1887; librarian of Royal Society of Edinburgh, 1878–1906; published 'The Handy Book of Meteorology,' 1867, a recognized text-book; and made valuable contributions to 'Journal of Scottish Meteorological Society' and to Royal Society; F.R.S., 1898; hon. LL.D. Glasgow, 1887.

BUCHANAN, GEORGE (1827–1905), surgeon; M.A. Glasgow, 1846; studied medicine at Andersonian University, Glasgow; M.D. St. Andrews, 1849; surgeon in Crimea, 1856; professor of anatomy, Andersonian University, and surgeon to Glasgow Royal Infirmary from 1860; professor of clinical surgery, Western Infirmary, 1874–1900.

BUCHANAN, ROBERT WILLIAMS (1841–1901), poet and novelist; son of a socialist and secularist tailor who owned and edited several socialistic journals in Glasgow from 1850; finished education at Glasgow University, where David Gray [q. v.] was a fellow student; came to London, 1860; wrote for 'Athenæum' and other periodicals; under T. L. Peacock's influence produced his 'pseudo-classic poems' 'Undertones,' 1863; 'London Poems' (1866) established his reputation; settled near Oban (1866–74), writing much narrative poetry and prose; chief works of that period were 'Ballads of Life, Love and Humour,' 1882, and his prose 'Master Spirits,' 1874; granted civil list pension, 1870; satirized Swinburne and others in 'The Session of the Poets' in 'Spectator'

(1866), and attacked the pre-Raphaelites—especially D. G. Rossetti—in article in 'Contemporary Review,' 'The Fleshly School of Poetry' (1871), the prelude of a long and bitter controversy; won libel action against Swinburne (1875), and finally made amends to Rossetti (1881–2); settled in London, 1877; published long series of novels, the chief being 'The Shadow of the Sword,' 1876, and 'God and the Man,' 1881, both of which he dramatized; from 1880 to 1897 wrote and produced a long series of plays; visited America, 1884; producing his melodrama 'Alone in London'; his 'A Man's Shadow' came out at Haymarket, 1889–90; later dramatic successes were 'The Charlatan,' 1894, and 'The Strange Adventures of Miss Brown,' 1895; lost fortune in disastrous speculation; of combative temperament; had strong lyric gift, and abundant but ill-regulated force in fiction and drama; his collected 'Poems' (3 vols.) appeared in 1874, and 'Poetical Works' in 1884 and 1901; 'Life' by Harriett Jay (his sister-in-law) came out in 1903.

BUCKTON, GEORGE BOWDLER (1818–1905), entomologist; crippled for life at age of five; student at Royal College of Chemistry, 1848–55; from 1865 made important researches in natural history; published 'Monograph on British Aphides', 4 vols. 1876–83, and other entomological works; F.R.S., 1857.

BULLEN, ARTHUR HENRY (1857–1920), English scholar; son of George Bullen [q. v.]; educated at City of London School and Worcester College, Oxford; edited works of sixteenth- and seventeenth-century dramatists and song writers; carried on Shakespeare Head Press at Stratford-on-Avon, 1904–20.

BULLER, SIR REDVERS HENRY (1839–1908), general; born at Downes, Crediton; educated at Eton; received commission in army, 1858; after service in Benares and China joined fourth battalion of the 60th (the king's royal rifle corps) at Quebec, 1862; attracted notice of (Viscount) Wolseley [q. v.] in Red River Expedition, 1870; chief intelligence officer to Wolseley in Ashanti, 1873; C.B., 1874; commanded with success the frontier light horse in sixth Kaffir war in South Africa, 1878–9; received V.C. for gallant rescues, June 1879; aide-de-camp to Queen Victoria, colonel, and C.M.G., 1879; chief of staff to Sir H. Evelyn Wood [q. v.] in South Africa, 1881; chief of intelligence staff to Wolseley in Egypt, 1882; present at Tel-el-Kebir; K.C.M.G., 1882; commanded first infantry brigade at El Teb and Tamai under Sir Gerald Graham [q. v.], 1884; chief of staff in relief expedition of Khartoum, 1884; made masterly retreat from Gabat to Korti; K.C.B., 1885; was sent to Ireland (August 1886) under Salisbury administration to restore order in Kerry; made under-secretary for Ireland and Irish privy councillor; adjutant-general, 1886–7; a successful and economical administrator at war office; reorganized and combined the supply and transport services; G.C.B., 1894, and general, 1896; in command at Aldershot, 1898; sent to South Africa in chief command, 1899; arrived in Cape Town (Oct.); moved to relief of Ladysmith; on arrival of Lord Roberts [q. v.], moved Natal army on Colenso (Dec.), where he was defeated; was defeated again at Spion Kop (Jan. 1900) and at Vaal Krantz; after much fighting at Hlangwane heights, he relieved Ladysmith (28 Feb.); his leadership was severely criticized; he entered Dundee (15 May); reached Volksrust (11 June); came in touch with main army (4 July); decisively defeated Boers at Bergendal (27 Aug.) and finally broke down the Boer resistance; marched north to Lydenburg and to Pretoria (10 Oct.); was thanked by Lord Roberts for his services; reached England (9 Nov.); received freedom of Southampton, Exeter, and Plymouth; G.C.M.G., 1901; resumed command (Jan. 1901) of Aldershot division; the appointment was sharply criticized in press; Buller made indiscreet defence, and was removed from command, Oct. 1901; equestrian statue at Exeter with inscription 'He saved Natal.'

BULLER, SIR WALTER LAWRY (1838–1906), ornithologist; born in New Zealand; editor in chief of 'Maori Messenger,' 1861; came to England as secretary to agent-general for New Zealand, 1871; called to bar, 1874; practised in New Zealand Supreme Court till 1886; wrote 'History' 1873, and 'Manual of the Birds of New Zealand,' 1882; F.R.S., 1876; K.C.M.G., 1886.

BULWER, SIR EDWARD EARLE GASCOYNE (1829–1910), general; nephew of Lord Dalling [q. v.] and of Edward Bulwer Lytton the novelist [q. v.]; joined 23rd royal Welsh fusiliers, 1849; went with regiment to Scutari, 1854; took part in crossing of the Alma and in attack on the Redan, 1854–5; served in relief of Lucknow,

1857–8; occupied fort of Gosainganj, and helped to restore tranquillity, Sept. 1858; victorious at Jabrowli and Purwa (Oct.) over superior forces; C.B., 1859; henceforth held only staff employment; as adjutant-general at headquarters for auxiliary forces (1873–9) helped to weld the regular and auxiliary forces under Lord Cardwell's short-service system; inspector-general of recruiting, 1880–6; K.C.B., 1886; general, 1893; lieutenant-governor and commander of troops in Guernsey, 1889–94; colonel of the royal Welsh fusiliers, 1898; G.C.B., 1905.

BUNSEN, ERNEST DE (1819–1903), theologian; son of Christian, Baron von Bunsen, Prussian diplomatist; born in Rome; educated in Berlin; served in German army and in Prussian legation, 1837–49; settled in London, 1850; keen literary and biblical student; chief work was 'Biblical Chronology,' 1874; an accomplished musician.

BUNTING, SIR PERCY WILLIAM (1836–1911), social reformer and editor of 'Contemporary Review'; grandson of Jabez Bunting [q. v.]; B.A., Pembroke College, Cambridge, 1859; called to bar, 1862; promoted forward movement in methodism; helped to found Leys School, Cambridge, 1873, the West London Mission, 1887, and National Free Church Council, 1891; founded National Vigilance Association, 1883; edited on liberal lines 'Contemporary Review' (1882–1911), giving social reform a prominent place; promoted moral purity and international amity.

BURBIDGE, EDWARD (1839–1903), liturgiologist; B.A., Emmanuel College, Cambridge, 1862; M.A., 1863; vicar of Backwell, Somerset, 1882–1902; became prebendary of Wells, 1887; published 'Liturgies and Offices of the Church,' 1885, a standard authority, besides devotional works.

BURBIDGE, FREDERICK WILLIAM (1847–1905), botanist; on staff of 'Garden,' 1870–7; chief published work 'Cultivated Plants,' 1877, praised by Gladstone and Hooker; went to Borneo, 1877; brought back new plants; published chronicles of travel, 1880; the 'Burbidgea nitida' named after him; curator of botanical gardens, Trinity College, Dublin, 1880–1905; hon. M.A. Dublin, 1889.

BURBURY, SAMUEL HAWKSLEY (1831–1911), mathematician; educated at Shrewsbury and St. John's College, Cambridge; won many university prizes for classics; fifteenth classic and second wrangler, 1854; fellow, 1854; wrote with Henry William Watson [q. v.] important works on electricity and magnetism; F.R.S., 1890.

BURDETT-COUTTS, ANGELA GEORGINA, BARONESS BURDETT-COUTTS (1814–1906), philanthropist; daughter of Sir Francis Burdett (1770–1844, q. v.), and granddaughter through her mother of Thomas Coutts [q. v.], banker; at her father's town house in St. James's Place she met leading politicians, scientists, and literary men; inherited from the duchess of St. Albans, second wife of Thomas Coutts, his property and share in bank, 1837; assumed additional surname of Coutts; removed to 1 Stratton Street, 1837; 'the richest heiress in all England'; entertained English and foreign celebrities during sixty years; intimate with royal family, duke of Wellington, Sir Robert Peel, Disraeli, Gladstone, duke of Cambridge, Napoleon III, Empress Eugénie, Tom Moore, Samuel Rogers, Dickens, Sir William and Joseph Hooker, Sir Henry Irving, and many others; took active part in banking business; personally administered her private charities; interested in schemes of social reform; munificent benefactor to Church of England; built and endowed St. Stephen's, Westminster (1847), adding schools in 1849, and other London churches; established Westminster Technical Institute, 1893; endowed (1847) bishoprics of Capetown and Adelaide; founded (1857) bishopric of British Columbia, with large endowments; introduced sewing and cookery into elementary schools; endowed two geological scholarships at Oxford, 1861; presented Schimper's herbarium of mosses to Kew; subsidized Ragged School Union; supported shoeblack brigades from 1851, and aided in subsidizing training ships for poor boys from 1874; helped to found National Society for the Prevention of Cruelty to Children, 1883; active in reform of East London women's industries; started (1860) 'sewing school' for women in Spitalfields, providing food, housing, and medical attendance; helped Spitalfields weavers, sending many to the colonies, 1863–9; instituted Flower Girls' Brigade, 1879; founded Burdett-Coutts working youths' club in Shore-

ditch, 1875, adding gymnasium, 1891; befriended costermongers at Bethnal Green, providing stables for their donkeys; intense lover of animals; leader of Royal Society for Prevention of Cruelty to Animals; instituted scheme of prize essays; encouraged goat breeding; pioneer of model tenements in Bethnal Green (1862), and of garden city aims in 'Holly Village' on her Holly Lodge estate at Highgate; started fish and vegetable market scheme for East London, 1864; but owing to opposition of existing vested interests the Columbia market (opened 1869) was a failure, although it encouraged improvement in methods of food distribution; sought to improve conditions and industry among Irish poor; sent Irish emigrants to Canada from 1863 onwards; revived fishing industry at Baltimore, co. Cork, where she inaugurated a fishery training school, 1887; aided colonial and missionary effort in Borneo and Africa; friend and supporter of H. M. Stanley; stimulated cotton industry of South Nigeria; raised to peerage, 1871; received freedom of cities of London (1872) and Edinburgh (1874), and of several City companies; liberally helped Turkish peasantry in Russo-Turkish war, 1877; received order of Medjidie, 1878; sent out hospital equipment for wounded in Zulu war, 1879; married William Lehman Ashmead-Bartlett, 1881; entertained General Gordon before he went to Sudan, 1884; compiled 'Woman's Work in England' for Chicago Exhibition, 1893; buried in Westminster Abbey.

BURDON, JOHN SHAW (1826–1907), missionary bishop of Victoria, Hong Kong (1874–97), and Chinese scholar; joined Church Missionary Society, 1850; at Shanghai (1853), Hangchow (1859), and Shaohsing (1860–1); in Ningpo when city was captured by Chinese rebels, December 1861; went as missionary pioneer to Peking, 1862; chaplain to British legation there, 1865–72; one of translators of New Testament and Prayer Book into Chinese, 1872.

BURDON-SANDERSON, SIR JOHN SCOTT, baronet (1828–1905), regius professor of medicine at Oxford; studied medicine at Edinburgh University (M.D., 1851) and in Paris; medical officer of health for Paddington, 1856–67; F.R.S., 1867; Croonian lecturer (1867, 1877, and 1889); appointed Jodrell professor of physiology at University College, London, 1874; fellow (1871), Harveian orator (1878), and Baly medallist (1880) and Croonian lecturer (1891) of the Royal College of Physicians; first Waynflete professor of physiology (and fellow of Magdalen College, Oxford), 1882–95; regius professor of medicine at Oxford, 1895–1903; made important experimental researches into physiology, and contributed to current progress of pathology; president of British Association, 1893; member of royal commissions on hospitals for infectious diseases (1883), on consumption of tuberculous meat and milk (1891), and on University of London (1892); baronet, 1899; hon. LL.D. Edinburgh, and D.Sc. Dublin; wrote much in scientific journals; memoir with selected papers and addresses edited by his widow, 1911.

BURGH CANNING, HUBERT GEORGE DE, second MARQUESS and fifteenth EARL OF CLANRICARDE (1832–1916), Irish landed proprietor; liberal M.P., county Galway, 1867–71; succeeded father, 1874; life spent resisting movement to limit Irish landlord's power; vast estates compulsorily transferred to Congested Districts Board, 1915.

BURN, ROBERT (1829–1904), scholar and archaeologist; educated at Shrewsbury and Trinity College, Cambridge; senior classic, 1852; fellow of Trinity, 1854–1904; author of 'Rome and the Campagna,' 1871.

BURN-MURDOCH, JOHN (1852–1909), lieutenant-colonel; entered royal engineers, 1872; served in Afghan war, 1878–80; wounded at storming of Asmai Heights, 1879; field engineer in Egyptian war, 1882; at battle of Tel-el-Kebir; prominent in seizure of Zagazig, Sept. 1882; officer commanding engineer of Indian state railways, 1893; lieutenant-colonel, 1900.

BURNAND, SIR FRANCIS COWLEY (1836–1917), playwright, author, and editor of 'Punch'; educated at Eton and Trinity College, Cambridge; founded Cambridge Amateur Dramatic Club; became Roman Catholic, 1858; joined staff of 'Punch,' 1862; editor, 1880–1906; increased the paper's reputation; humorist; author of burlesques and adaptations of popular French farces; knighted, 1902.

BURNE, SIR OWEN TUDOR (1837–1909), major-general; joined 20th East Devonshire regiment, 1855; ordered to India (1857), studying Hindustani on voyage; active under Brigadier Franks in events leading to relief of Lucknow, 1858; military secretary to Sir Hugh Rose, commander-in-chief in India, 1860; returned to England, 1865; aided in suppression of Fenian conspiracy, 1867; private secretary to Lord Mayo, viceroy of India, 1868–72; C.S.I., 1872; political aide-de-camp to the duke of Argyll, secretary of state for India, 1872; head of political and secret department of India office in London, 1874; private secretary to Lord Lytton, Indian viceroy, 1876–8; C.I.E., 1878; K.C.S.I., 1879; member of council of India, 1886–96; major-general, 1889; G.C.I.E., 1896; wrote in periodicals on Eastern questions; published 'Memories,' 1907.

BURNHAM, first BARON (1833–1916), newspaper proprietor. [See LEVY-LAWSON, EDWARD.]

BURNS, DAWSON (1828–1909), temperance reformer; became secretary of National Temperance Society, 1846; baptist pastor at Salford, 1851; helped to found United Kingdom Alliance, 1853; wrote for 'Alliance News' from 1856; actively promoted temperance legislation; contributed annual letters to 'The Times' on 'National Drink Bill' (1886–1909); a director of Liberator Building Society, which failed, 1892; wrote books on temperance subjects.

BURROUGHS (afterwards TRAILL-BURROUGHS), SIR FREDERICK WILLIAM (1831–1905), lieutenant-general; joined 93rd highlanders, 1848; served under Lord Clyde in Crimea, 1854–5; at battles of the Alma and Balaklava, and at siege of Sevastopol; recommended for V.C. for services at Secunderabagh in Indian Mutiny; brevet major, 1858; took part in North-west frontier expedition, 1863; commanded 93rd highlanders at Ambela; lieutenant-general, 1881; C.B., 1873; K.C.B., 1904.

BURROWS, MONTAGU (1819–1905), Chichele professor of modern history at Oxford; entered Royal Naval College, 1832; at bombardment of Acre, 1840; made commander, R.N., 1852; went to Magdalen Hall, Oxford, 1853; took first classes in classics and modern history, 1856–7; retired from navy, 1862; joined party of moderate churchmen; original member of English Church Union; helped to found Keble College, 1870; Chichele professor of modern history, 1862–1905; fellow of All Souls, 1865; chief works were 'The Worthies of All Souls,' 1874, and 'The Cinque Ports,' 1888; edited vols. ii. and iii. of 'Collectanea' for Oxford Historical Society; contributed to this Dictionary.

BURTON, first BARON (1837–1909), brewer. [See BASS, MICHAEL ARTHUR.]

BUSHELL, STEPHEN WOOTTON (1844–1908), physician and Chinese archaeologist; studied at Guy's Hospital; house surgeon, 1866; M.B., 1866; physician to British legation at Peking, 1867–1900; C.M.G., 1897; authority on and collector of Chinese porcelain and pottery; chief works were 'Oriental Ceramic Art,' 10 vols. 1897, and 'Chinese Art,' 2 vols. 1904; translated native works on Chinese pottery and porcelain.

BUSK, RACHEL HARRIETTE (1831–1907), writer on folklore; daughter of Hans Busk the elder [q. v.]; joined Church of Rome, 1858; lived in Rome from 1862; wrote much on Roman politics; published folk tales of Spain (1870), Austria (1874), and Italy (1887).

BUTCHER, SAMUEL HENRY (1850–1910), scholar and man of letters; son of Samuel Butcher [q. v.]; educated at Marlborough and Trinity College, Cambridge; senior classic and chancellor's medallist, 1873; member of 'The Apostles'; fellow of Trinity, 1874–5; migrated on marriage (1876) to University College, Oxford, where he was a successful tutor; published with Andrew Lang translation of 'Odyssey' (1879); appointed professor of Greek in Edinburgh University, 1882; member of Scottish universities commission, 1889–1900; published 'Some Aspects of the Greek Genius,' 1891, and 'Aristotle's Theory of Poetry and Fine Art,' 1895; helped to organize unionist party in Edinburgh, 1886; resigned professorship after wife's death, and removed to London, 1903; lectured at Harvard University, 1904; member of two royal commissions on university education in Ireland, 1901–3 and 1906–7; succeeded Sir Richard Jebb [q. v.] as unionist M.P. for Cambridge University, 1906; spoke frequently and effectively on educational and Irish questions; part founder (1903) and president (1907) of Classical Association of England; president of British Academy, 1909; appointed trustee of British Museum, 1908; edited Demosthenes' speeches, 2 vols. 1903–7.

BUTLER, ARTHUR GRAY (1831–1909), head master of Haileybury; son of Dr. George Butler [q. v.]; educated at Rugby and University College, Oxford; president of

Union, 1853; Ireland scholar and first class classic, 1853; fellow of Oriel, 1856; master at Rugby, 1858–62; first head master of reconstituted Haileybury College, 1862–7; showed great organizing capacity; dean and tutor of Oriel, 1875–97; hon. fellow, 1907; wrote dramas and verse.

BUTLER, ARTHUR JOHN (1844–1910), Italian scholar; son of William John Butler [q. v.]; educated at Eton and Trinity College, Cambridge; Bell university scholar (1864) and eighth classic (1867); fellow of Trinity, 1867–70; examiner under board of education, 1870–87; became partner in Rivington's publishing firm, 1887; edited 'Calendars of Foreign State Papers,' 1899–1910; professor of Italian at University College, London, from 1898 till death; translated Dante's 'Purgatory' (1880), 'Paradise' (1885), and 'Hell' (1892); translated many French and German works; ardent Alpinist from boyhood; had unparalleled knowledge of Oetzthal Alps; member of Alpine Club, 1886; edited 'Alpine Journal,' 1890–3.

BUTLER, HENRY MONTAGU (1833–1918), head master of Harrow School, dean of Gloucester, master of Trinity College, Cambridge; son of Dr. George Butler [q. v.]; educated at Harrow and Trinity College, Cambridge; senior classic and fellow of Trinity, 1855; head master of Harrow, 1859–85; reconciled inspirations of past to aspirations of present; dean of Gloucester, 1885–6; master of Trinity, 1886 till death; publications include volumes of school and university sermons.

BUTLER, JOSEPHINE ELIZABETH (1828–1906), social reformer; daughter of John Grey of Dilston [q. v.]; married George Butler [q. v.]; supported early stages of movement for women's higher education; settling in Liverpool (1866), established homes for work-girls and fallen women, whose cause she fought as secretary to Ladies' National Association for Repeal of Contagious Diseases Act, 1869–85; contributed to repeal of Act, 1886; caused reform of law affecting 'white slave traffic' in Continental countries; wrote numerous pamphlets and volumes, including memoirs of her father (1869), her husband (1892), and sister, Madame Meuricoffre (1901), 'Personal Reminiscences of a Great Crusade' (1896), and 'Life of St. Catherine of Siena' (1898).

BUTLER, SAMUEL (1835–1902), philosophical writer; educated at Shrewsbury and St. John's College, Cambridge; twelfth classic, 1858; abandoned intention of taking holy orders; emigrated to New Zealand, 1859; his success as sheepbreeder detailed in 'A First Year in Canterbury Settlement,' 1863; returned to England, 1864–5; studied painting at Heatherley's school; exhibited at Royal Academy; published anonymously 'Erewhon,' a jeu d'esprit (1872), and 'The Fair Haven' (1873), an ironic defence of Christian evidences; lost money in unsound investments; wrote 'Life and Habit' (1877), in which he contested Darwin's law of natural selection; in 'Evolution Old and New' (1879), in 'Unconscious Memory' (1880), and in 'Luck or Cunning' (1886), he pursued his attack on the Darwinian banishment of mind from the universe; an original topographer of Italian Switzerland and Italian art critic; published 'Alps and Sanctuaries of Piedmont and the Canton Ticino' (1881) and kindred works; studied and composed music in London with Mr. H. Festing Jones; a keen Homeric student; published 'The Authoress of the Odyssey,' 1897, and prose translations of 'Iliad,' 1898, and 'Odyssey,' 1900; other works were 'Life of Samuel Butler, Bishop of Lichfield,' 2 vols. 1896, 'Shakespeare's Sonnets Reconsidered,' 1899, and 'Erewhon Revisited,' 1901; an autobiographical novel, 'The Way of All Flesh,' 1903, and 'Essays on Life, Art and Science' appeared posthumously; a terse and lucid iconoclast of conventional opinion.

BUTLER, SIR WILLIAM FRANCIS (1838–1910), lieutenant-general and author; descended from tenth earl of Ormonde [q. v.]; of Roman Catholic family; obtained commission in 69th foot, 1858; in India, 1860; in Channel Islands, 1866, where he met Victor Hugo; look-out officer on frontier in Canada, 1868; sent on mission to Red River settlement and to Saskatchewan, 1870; published history of 69th foot, 1870, 'The Great Lone Land,' 1872, and 'The Wild North Land,' a vivid description of his Canadian experiences, 1873; joined Sir Garnet Wolseley's expedition to Ashanti, 1873; failed in attempt to reach Coomassie, 1873–4; major and C.B., 1874; went on special service in Natal, 1875; engaged on duty in England, 1875–9; married Elizabeth Thompson, the artist, 1877; served in Zulu war, 1879, in Egyptian war, including Tel-el-Kebir, 1882; was charged with provision of boats on Nile for relief of General Gordon, 1884; prominent in victory at Kirbekan, Feb. 1885; brigadier-general under General Stephenson at Giniss, 1886; K.C.B., 1886; commanded garrison of Alexandria, 1890; in command of a brigade at Aldershot, 1893; transferred to S.E. district, 1896; commanded troops in South Africa, Oct. 1898; a strong pro-Boer, he was sceptical of grievances of 'outlanders'; resigned, August 1899; in England assumed command of western district (1899-1905); lieutenant-general, 1900; G.C.B., 1906, and Irish privy councillor, 1909; wrote lives of Gordon, 1889, Sir Charles Napier, 1890, and Sir George Colley, 1899; his 'Autobiography' published posthumously, 1911.

BUTLIN, SIR HENRY TRENTHAM, first baronet (1845-1912), surgeon; educated at St. Bartholomew's Hospital, London; full surgeon, 1892, and lecturer in surgery at the Hospital school, 1897; president of British Medical Association, 1910-11, of Royal College of Surgeons, 1909-11; baronet, 1911; wrote 'Diseases of the Tongue' (1885).

BUTTERWORTH, GEORGE SAINTON KAYE (1885-1916), composer; B.A., Trinity College, Oxford; researched in English folk-music; set parts of A. E. Housman's 'A Shropshire Lad' to music; his masterpiece, a rhapsody, produced 1913; killed in action in France.

BUXTON, SIR THOMAS FOWELL, third baronet (1837-1915), governor of South Australia, 1895-8; B.A., Trinity College, Cambridge; succeeded father, 1858; liberal M.P., King's Lynn, 1865-8; G.C.M.G., 1899.

BYRNE, SIR EDMUND WIDDRINGTON (1844-1904), judge; called to bar, 1867; took silk, 1888; a successful leader in chancery cases; conservative M.P. for Walthamstow, 1892-7; appointed judge in chancery division and knighted, 1897; an accurate and painstaking, but slow, judge.

BYWATER, INGRAM (1840-1914), Greek scholar; educated at University and King's College schools, London; B.A., Queen's College, Oxford; fellow of Exeter College, 1863-84; travelled abroad with the Mark Pattisons; reader in Greek at Oxford, 1884; regius professor of Greek at Oxford, 1893-1908; lived in London during vacations; president of Oxford Aristotelian Society, c. 1885-1908; delegate of Oxford University Press, 1879-1914; contributor to 'Oxford English Dictionary'; bibliophile; bequeathed collection of books to Bodleian Library; works include edition of Fragments of Heraclitus (1877), of works of Priscianus Lydus (1886), and monumental edition of 'Poetics' of Aristotle (1909); much of his work anonymous.

CADOGAN, GEORGE HENRY, fifth EARL CADOGAN (1840-1915), conservative statesman; succeeded father, 1873; under-secretary of state for war, 1875, for Colonies, 1878; lord privy seal, 1886-92; K.G., 1891; lord-lieutenant of Ireland, 1895-1902.

CAINE, WILLIAM SPROSTON (1842-1903), politician and temperance advocate; joined father's metal business at Egremont, 1861-78; early devoted himself to temperance movement at Liverpool; radical M.P. for Scarborough, 1880-5; supported local option, 1880; civil lord of admiralty, 1884; M.P. for Barrow-in-Furness, 1886-92; helped to organize 'liberal unionists' against Gladstone's home rule policy, 1886; left unionist party on licensing question, 1890; liberal M.P. for East Bradford, 1892-5, and for Camborne, 1900-3; an able advocate of self-government in India; served on royal commissions on administration of Indian expenditure (1895-6) and liquor licensing laws (1896-9).

CAIRD, EDWARD (1835-1908), master of Balliol College, Oxford, and philosopher; brother of John Caird [q. v.]; educated at Glasgow and St. Andrews universities, 1850-7; influenced by Goethe through Carlyle's work; Snell exhibitioner at Balliol College, Oxford, 1860-3; B.A., 1863; member of the 'Old Mortality Club' with T. H. Green, Swinburne, and others; a 'radical' in politics, religion, and philosophy; fellow and tutor of Merton, 1864-6; professor of moral philosophy at Glasgow, 1866-93; an early advocate of higher education of women; published 'A Critical Account of the Philosophy of Kant,' 2 vols. 1877 and 1889, monograph on 'Hegel,' 1883, and 'The Social Philosophy and Religion of Comte,' 1885; also 'The Evolution of Religion,' 1893, and 'The Evolution of Theology in the Greek Philosophy,' 2 vols. 1904, both based on Gifford lectures of 1891-2 and 1900 respectively; succeeded Jowett as master of Balliol, 1893; supported grant of degrees to women and education of working men at Oxford; resisted bestowal of honorary

degree on Cecil Rhodes, 1899; resigned mastership, 1907; received honorary degrees from St. Andrews (1883), Oxford (1891), Glasgow (1894), and Cambridge (1898); an original fellow of British Academy, 1902; portraits at Balliol and Glasgow University.

CAIRNES, WILLIAM ELLIOT (1862-1902), captain and military writer; son of John Elliot Cairnes [q. v.]; joined army, 1882; promoted captain, 1890; military critic of 'Westminster Gazette' during Boer war, 1899-1901; published anonymously 'An Absent-Minded War' (1900), full of pungent and epigrammatic criticism, and other books on military topics.

CALDERON, GEORGE (1868-1915), dramatist; son of P. H. Calderon, R.A. [q. v.]; plays include 'The Fountain' (1909), 'The Little Stone House' (1911), 'Revolt' (1912); 'Tahiti,' impressions of the South Seas, published posthumously, 1921; good linguist and Slavonic student; missing at Dardanelles.

CALKIN, JOHN BAPTISTE (1827-1905), organist and composer; after holding several posts as organist, became professor at Guildhall School of Music, 1883; composed much sacred music, church services, and hymn tunes.

CALLAGHAN, SIR GEORGE ASTLEY (1852-1920), admiral; entered navy, 1866; captain, 1894; commanded British naval brigade which relieved legations in Peking during Boxer rebellion, 1900; C.B., 1900; captain of Portsmouth dockyard, 1903-4; rear-admiral, 1905; commanded new fifth cruiser squadron, 1907-8; second in command, Mediterranean station, 1908-10; K.C.V.O., 1909; vice-admiral, 1910; commander-in-chief, home fleets, 1911-14; G.C.V.O., 1912; removed from command on outbreak of war on account of age, 1914; commander-in-chief at the Nore, 1915-18; G.C.B., 1916; admiral of the fleet, 1917-18; Bath King of Arms, 1919.

CALLOW, WILLIAM (1812-1908), water-colour painter; brother of John Callow (1822-78, q. v.); studied in London (1823-9) and in Paris (1829-41); his 'View of Richmond,' exhibited at Paris Salon (1831), attracted attention; taught in family of King Louis Philippe; exhibited over 1,400 drawings at Society of Painters in Water Colours; exhibited also in oils at British Institution (1848-67) and Royal Academy (1850-76); taught in London from 1855 to 1882; pupils included Empress Frederick and Lord Dufferin; wrote 'Autobiography,' 1908.

CALTHORPE, sixth BARON (1829-1910), agriculturist. [See GOUGH-CALTHORPE, AUGUSTUS CHOLMONDELEY.]

CAMBRIDGE, second DUKE OF (1819-1904), field-marshal. [See GEORGE WILLIAM FREDERICK CHARLES.]

CAMPBELL, ARCHIBALD CAMPBELL, first BARON BLYTHSWOOD (1835-1908), scientist; born at Florence; served in Crimea, 1854; conservative M.P. for Renfrewshire (1873-4) and for West Renfrewshire (1885-92); created baronet (1890) and peer (1892); made valuable researches in astronomical and physical science; hon. LL.D. Glasgow and F.R.S., 1907.

CAMPBELL, FREDERICK ARCHIBALD VAUGHAN, third EARL CAWDOR (1847-1911), first lord of the admiralty; educated at Eton and Christ Church, Oxford; conservative M.P. for Carmarthenshire, 1874-85; succeeded to earldom, 1898; took active part in Pembrokeshire local affairs; as chairman of Great Western railway, greatly improved the service, 1895-1905; first lord of the admiralty in Mr. Balfour's government, 1905; took leading part in conservative opposition to Mr. Lloyd George's budget, 1909, and in drafting resolutions for reform of the House of Lords, 1910; president of Institution of Naval Architects, 1905; an able debater and administrator.

CAMPBELL, SIR JAMES MACNABB (1846-1903), Indian official and compiler of the 'Bombay Gazetteer'; son of John McLeod Campbell [q. v.]; M.A. Glasgow, 1866; joined Indian civil service, 1869; compiler of 'Bombay Gazetteer' (to which he contributed much on ethnology), 34 vols., 1873-1901; C.I.E. and hon. LL.D. Glasgow, 1885; held customs appointments at Bombay from 1891; did much service in combating plague at Bombay, 1897-8; K.C.I.E., 1897; triennial memorial medal founded by Royal Asiatic Society; collected much material on Indian history and folklore.

CAMPBELL, JOHN DOUGLAS SUTHERLAND, ninth DUKE OF ARGYLL (1845-1914), governor-general of Canada, 1878-1883; liberal M.P., Argyllshire, 1868; married Princess Louise, daughter of Queen Victoria, 1871; unionist M.P., South Manchester, 1895; succeeded father, 1900.

CAMPBELL, LEWIS (1830–1908), classical scholar; educated at Glasgow University and Balliol College, Oxford; first class in *lit. hum.*, 1853; fellow of Queen's College, 1855–8; hon. fellow of Balliol, 1894; vicar of Milford, Hants., 1858–63; professor of Greek at St. Andrews, 1863–92; Gifford lecturer on 'Religion in Greek Literature,' 1894–5 (published 1898); edited Plato's 'Theætetus,' 1861, 'Sophistes' and 'Politicus,' 1867; made special study of chronology of Plato's dialogues; published complete edition of Sophocles (2 vols. 1875, 1881), and translated Sophocles (1883) and Aeschylus (1890) into English verse; completed Jowett's edition of Plato's 'Republic,' 3 vols. 1894; collaborated in 'Life of Jowett,' 1897; died at Brissago, Lago Maggiore.

CAMPBELL, WILLIAM HOWARD (1859–1910), missionary and entomologist; M.A. Edinburgh, 1880; B.D., 1882; served London Missionary Society in India, 1884–1909; published theological works in the Telugu language, on which he was a leading authority; made valuable collection of Indian moths; died at Bordighera.

CAMPBELL-BANNERMAN, SIR HENRY (1836–1908), prime minister; born at Glasgow; son of Sir James Campbell, wholesale draper at Glasgow; assumed name of Bannerman under maternal uncle's will, 1872; educated at Glasgow University (1851–3, hon. LL.D., 1883) and Trinity College, Cambridge (B.A., 1858, M.A., 1861); partner in father's business till 1868; liberal M.P. for the Stirling Burghs from 1868 till death; financial secretary to war office in Gladstone's first (1871–4) and second (1880–2) administrations; secretary to the admiralty, 1882–4; as chief secretary for Ireland, enhanced his reputation, 1884–5; became secretary for war and entered cabinet in Gladstone's third administration, Feb.–June, 1886; actively supported Gladstone's home rule proposals in office and opposition; served on royal commission of inquiry into administration of naval and military departments, 1888–90; again secretary for war in Gladstone and Rosebery administrations, 1892–5; established forty-eight hours week at Woolwich arsenal, 1894; the allegation that the war office under his control was inadequately supplied with cordite caused defeat of Lord Rosebery's government, 1895; created G.C.B.; a member of committee of inquiry into Dr. Jameson's Raid, which exonerated imperial and South African governments of complicity, 1896–7; succeeded as leader of the liberal party in House of Commons on Harcourt's resignation, 1899; opposed South African policy of Joseph Chamberlain [q. v.]; advocated conciliatory measures and 'rights of self-government' to conquered Boer states; denounced policy of enforcing unconditional surrender on the Boers; divided the liberal party by describing English warfare in South Africa as 'methods of barbarism' (June 1901), and by his support of home rule; opposed Mr. Balfour's education bill, 1902; reunited liberal party in opposition to Chamberlain's fiscal policy, 1903; attacked importation of Chinese indentured labour into South Africa; developed liberal programme, advocating small holdings, payment of members, retrenchment in public expenditure, curtailment of House of Lords veto; postponed consideration of home rule question to prevent party schism, 1904–5; became prime minister on Mr. Balfour's resignation, Dec. 1905; was for first time formally admitted in that capacity to fourth place of precedence among the king's subjects; the liberals routed unionists in general election, Jan. 1906; Campbell-Bannerman's government ended Chinese labour in South Africa, and established full responsible government in Transvaal and Orange Free State; introduced education bill for public control of public expenses of education and for abolition of religious tests for teachers (withdrawn owing to opposition of House of Lords), trades disputes bill (passed), and plural voting bill (rejected by House of Lords); Campbell-Bannerman emphatic in warning that will of people must prevail against House of Lords; in foreign affairs advocated arbitration for settling international disputes and limitation of armaments; welcomed members of Russian duma in London, 1906; favoured two-power naval standard, but advocated alliances with greatest naval powers; his article in the 'Nation' on the eve of Hague peace conference (May 1907), urging the limitation of armaments, excited German mistrust which prevented discussion of the question at the conference; his government carried through parliament (1907) Mr. Haldane's army scheme, the Criminal Appeal Act, Deceased Wife's Sister's Marriage Act, Small Holdings Act for England and Wales, and motion for restricting power of House of Lords (June); became 'father of the House of Commons,' May 1907; hon. D.C.L. Oxford, and LL.D. Cambridge, 1907; went owing to ill-health to Biarritz, Nov. 1907–Jan. 1908; resigned on grounds of continued ill-health, and died April 1908.

A strenuous, uncompromising fighter and strong party man, he was a fearless, sagacious, and optimistic leader. A good linguist and raconteur, he composed his set speeches with fastidious care, was ready in debate, and abounded in shrewd wit and humour. He supported women's suffrage. Monument placed by parliament in Westminster Abbey, 1912.

CANNAN, CHARLES (1858–1919), scholar and university publisher; educated at Clifton and Corpus Christi College, Oxford; fellow, classical tutor, and dean, Trinity College, Oxford, 1884; junior bursar, 1887; delegate of University Press, 1895; secretary to delegates, 1898–1919; profoundly influenced development of the Press and made London office real department of the university; student of Aristotle and anonymous editor of 'Selecta ex Organo Aristoteleo Capitula' (1897).

CANNING, SIR SAMUEL (1823–1908), a pioneer of submarine telegraphy; helped Charles Bright [q. v.] to construct and lay first Atlantic cable, 1857–8; manufactured and laid Atlantic cables of 1865 and 1866, by means of the 'Great Eastern' steamship; knighted, 1866.

CAPEL, THOMAS JOHN (1836–1911), Roman Catholic prelate; chaplain of English-speaking catholics at Pau and successful proselytizer, 1860–8; prominent figure in London society from 1868; the Monsignor Catesby of Disraeli's 'Lothair,' 1870; carried on unsuccessfully catholic public schools at Kensington, 1873–82; migrated to America, 1883; subsequently prelate in charge of Roman Catholic church of Northern California; died at Sacramento; wrote controversial tracts.

CAPES, WILLIAM WOLFE (1834–1914), historical scholar; B.A., Queen's College, Oxford; fellow and tutor of Queen's, 1856; rector of Bramshott, Hampshire, 1869–1901; university reader in ancient history, 1870–87; fellow and tutor of Hertford College, 1876–86; wrote books on ancient history; canon of Hereford, 1903–14; edited 'Charters and Records of Hereford Cathedral' (1908).

CAPPER, SIR THOMPSON (1863–1915), major-general; born at Lucknow; joined army, 1882; D.S.O. for services in South Africa 1899–1902; first commandant of Indian Staff College, Quetta; C.B., 1910; major-general and Inspector of Infantry, 1914; commanded 7th division in Belgium, 1914–15; K.C.M.G., 1915; died of wounds.

CARDEW, PHILIP (1851–1910), major R.E.; joined royal engineers, 1871; applied electricity to military purposes; instructor in electricity at Chatham, 1882; designed galvanometer for measuring large currents of electricity, 1882; invented the voltmeter, 1885, the vibratory transmitter for telegraphy, his most important discovery, 'separators,' and other electrical devices; first electrical adviser to board of trade and promoted major, 1882; partner with Sir William Preece [q. v.] & Sons, 1898; contributed many papers to scientific societies.

CAREY, ROSA NOUCHETTE (1840–1909), novelist; published forty novels, including 'Nellie's Memories,' 1868, 'Wee Wifie,' 1869, 'Uncle Max,' 1887, 'Only the Governess,' 1888; all had wide vogue; an orthodox upholder of high church principles.

CARLISLE, ninth EARL OF (1843–1911), amateur artist. [See HOWARD, GEORGE JAMES.]

CARLISLE, COUNTESS OF (1845–1921), promoter of women's political rights and of temperance reform. [See HOWARD, ROSALIND FRANCES.]

CARNEGIE, ANDREW (1835–1919), manufacturer and philanthropist; born at Dunfermline; emigrated with parents to Pennsylvania, 1848; rose, by means of successful enterprises in manufacture of railway lines, bridges, coaches, and locomotives, from position of telegraph boy in Pittsburg (1850) to that of foremost ironmaster in America (1881); Carnegie Steel Company (with profits of forty million dollars) formed, 1899; sold his steel concern and retired from business in order to devote himself to distribution of his wealth, 1901; benefactions include endowment of libraries in United States, British Isles, Canada, &c. (1882–1919), 'hero' funds in United States (1904), Great Britain (1908), and European countries (1909–11), and Palace of Peace at the Hague (1903); works include 'The Gospel of Wealth' (1900).

CARNEGIE, JAMES, sixth *de facto* and ninth *de jure* EARL OF SOUTHESK (1827–1905), poet and antiquary; collected gems, pictures, and Asiatic cylinders; obtained the title (forfeited in 1715) of Earl of Southesk, 1855; created K.T. and peer of United Kingdom, 1869; his first poetical work, 'Jonas Fisher' (anonymous, 1875), was erroneously assigned by hostile reviewer in 'Examiner' to Robert Buchanan [q. v.]; devoted later years to antiquarian research; hon. LL.D. St. Andrews, 1872, and Aberdeen, 1875.

CARPENTER, GEORGE ALFRED (1859–1910), physician; M.R.C.S., 1885; M.B., London, 1886; M.D., 1890; made special study of, and published works on, children's diseases; physician to Evelina Hospital, Southwark; founded (1904) and edited 'British Journal of Children's Diseases'; helped to found (1900) Society for Study of Disease in Children, and edited its 'Reports,' 1900–8.

CARPENTER, ROBERT (1830–1901), cricketer; had various professional engagements, 1854–60; played for Players *v.* Gentlemen, 1859–73; with Tom Hayward and George Tarrant raised standard of Cambridgeshire cricket; visited America (1859) and Australia (1863–4); elegant batsman, unsurpassed for back play.

CARPENTER, WILLIAM BOYD (1841–1918), bishop of Ripon; B.A., St. Catherine's College, Cambridge; royal chaplain, 1879; canon of Windsor, 1882; bishop of Ripon, 1884–1911; clerk of the closet, 1903–10, 1911–18; canon of Westminster, 1911–18; K.C.V.O., 1912; prolific writer and notable preacher.

CARRINGTON, SIR FREDERICK (1844–1913), general; joined army, 1864; C.M.G. for services in Transvaal, 1880; commanded Carrington's Horse in Bechuanaland expedition, 1885; K.C.M.G., 1887; major-general, 1895; K.C.B., 1897; served in South African War, 1899–1902.

CARTE, RICHARD D'OYLY (1844–1901), promoter of English opera; joined father's musical instrument business, 1861; composed operettas; founded successful concert agency, 1870; engaged in theatrical management; produced Gilbert and Sullivan's 'Trial by Jury,' 1875, 'Sorcerer,' 1877, 'H.M.S. Pinafore,' 1878, 'Pirates of Penzance,' 1880, and 'Patience,' 1881; built Savoy Theatre, the first public building in England lighted by electricity, 1881; produced 'Iolanthe,' 1882, 'Mikado,' 1885, 'Yeomen of the Guard,' 1888, 'Gondoliers,' 1889, and operas by other composers; had five touring companies in America; erected magnificent but unremunerative Royal English Opera House (1891) at Cambridge Circus, London, which became (1892) the prosperous Palace Theatre of Varieties; raised standard of musical taste in the English theatre.

CARTER, HUGH (1837–1903), painter; exhibited at Royal Academy, 1859–1902, and Royal Institute of Water Colour Painters, mainly subject paintings; work shows delicate colouring and subtle delineation of character.

CARTER, THOMAS THELLUSSON (1808–1901), tractarian divine; educated at Eton and Christ Church, Oxford; first class in *lit. hum.*, 1831; ordained, 1832; rector of Clewer, 1844–80; founded House of Mercy, Clewer, for fallen women, 1849, and sisterhood, 1852; hon. canon of Christ Church, 1870; influenced by 'Tracts for the Times'; with Liddon and Pusey drew up declaration in defence of confession, 1873; a founder of English Church Union and Confraternity of the Blessed Sacrament; was thrice prosecuted for ritual excesses; had much influence among high churchmen as organizer and devotional author; 'Life' published, 1903.

CARVER, ALFRED JAMES (1826–1909), master of Dulwich College; B.A., Trinity College, Cambridge, 1849; Bell university scholar, 1846; fellow of Queens' College, 1850–3; master of Alleyn's College, Dulwich, 1858–83, which was subsequently subdivided into two schools, Dulwich College (public) and Alleyn's School (secondary); rebuilt Dulwich College, 1870; broadminded and energetic in educational matters; founded Carver memorial prize for modern languages; hon. D.D. Lambeth, 1861; hon. canon of Rochester, 1882.

CASEMENT, ROGER DAVID (1864–1916), British consular official and Irish rebel; entered British consular service, 1892; his official report on administration of Congo Free State (1903) largely contributed towards its abolition (1908); his report on atrocities committed by agents of Peruvian Amazon Company (1910) published as Blue Book (1912); knighted and retired, 1911; returned to Ireland, 1913; on committee of Irish National Volunteers, 1913; visited Berlin as propagandist for Irish nationalism,

November 1914; landed from German submarine at Tralee, 1916; arrested and hanged as traitor.

CASSEL, SIR ERNEST JOSEPH (1852–1921), financier and philanthropist; born at Cologne; associated with financial house of Bischoffsheim and Goldschmidt, in London, with whom he laid the foundations of his immense fortune, 1870–84; naturalized, 1878; undertook independent business after 1884; enterprises in which he was concerned include establishment of Swedish Central Railway on sound financial basis; reorganization of Louisville and Nashville Railway in America; arrangement of finances of Mexican Central Railway; issuing of Mexican, Chinese, and Uruguay government loans; financing of construction of Nile dams at Assuan and Assiut and formation of National Bank of Egypt; creation of State Bank of Morocco and National Bank of Turkey; formed valuable collection of old masters and other works of art; racing activities led to formation of friendship with Prince of Wales, afterwards Edward VII; gave away about £2,000,000 to charities during lifetime; distinctions include K.C.M.G. (1899) and P.C. (1902).

CASSELS, WALTER RICHARD (1826–1907), theological critic; partner in firm of Peel, Cassels & Co. at Bombay till 1865; member of legislative council of Bombay, 1863–5; published anonymously 'Supernatural Religion,' 2 vols. 1874, vol. 3, 1877, impugning credibility of miracles and authenticity of the New Testament; engaged in controversy with Bishop Lightfoot, 1874–89; an enthusiastic art collector; also published poems.

CATES, ARTHUR (1829–1901), architect; pupil of Sydney Smirke, R.A. [q. v.]; architect to land revenues of the crown, 1870; vice-president (1888–92) and chairman of board of examiners (1882–96) of Royal Institute of British Architects, where he initiated progressive examinations.

CAVELL, EDITH (1865–1915), nurse; entered London Hospital as probationer, 1895; first matron of Dr. Depage's clinic—the Berkendael medical institute at Brussels, 1907; in charge of institute when it became a Red Cross Hospital, 1914; assisted Allied soldiers to escape from Belgium, 1914–15; arrested by Germans, 5 August 1915, and placed in solitary confinement at St. Gilles; brought to trial, 7 October; confessed that her efforts had been successful and was therefore condemned to death by court-martial; shot, 12 October.

CAVENDISH, SPENCER COMPTON, MARQUESS OF HARTINGTON and eighth DUKE OF DEVONSHIRE (1833–1908), statesman; born at Holker Hall, Lancashire; eldest son of seventh earl [q. v.] and brother of Lord Frederick Cavendish [q. v.]; M.A., Trinity College, Cambridge, 1854; hon. LL.D., 1862; elected liberal M.P. for North Lancashire, 1857; became Marquess of Hartington, 1858; moved successful motion of want of confidence in Derby ministry, June 1859; met president Lincoln in United States, 1862; under-secretary at war office, 1863; secretary of state for war and member of cabinet in Lord Russell's government, 1866; supported Gladstone on Irish Church disestablishment, and lost his seat, 1868; elected for Radnor boroughs, 1869; postmaster-general in Gladstone's first administration; introduced bill for voting by ballot, 1870; chief secretary for Ireland, 1870–4; passed 'coercion bill'; led liberal party on Gladstone's resignation, 1875; favoured maintenance of Turkish dominion in Russo-Turkish war, 1877; severely criticized government's Afghan policy, 1878; received freedom of city of Glasgow, 1877; lord rector of Edinburgh University, 1879; M.P. for North-east Lancashire, 1880–5; refused premiership; secretary of state for India under Gladstone, 1880–2; withdrew British forces from Afghanistan; secretary of state for war, 1882–5; partly responsible for sending Gordon to Sudan, and for failure to rescue him from Khartoum; his whig principles brought him into collision with radical leaders, Joseph Chamberlain [q. v.] and Sir Charles Dilke [q. v.]; mediator between government and House of Lords on question of franchise and redistribution bills, 1884; consistently opposed Gladstone's home rule policy, and favoured coercive measures in Ireland; M.P. for Rossendale, Lancashire, 1885–91; refused office under Gladstone, 1886; opposed the first home rule bill, and with Mr. Chamberlain founded new party of liberal unionists, who combined with conservatives under Lord Salisbury to drive Gladstone from power, 1886; declined premiership, 1886 and 1887; independently supported Salisbury's government, 1887–92; president of royal commissions on administration of the naval and military departments, 1890, and on relations between employers and employed, 1891;

succeeded father as Duke of Devonshire and chancellor of Cambridge University, Dec. 1891; moved rejection of Gladstone's second home rule bill in House of Lords, 1893; joined Salisbury's coalition government as president of the council, 1895–1902; held same office under Mr. Balfour, 1902–3; strongly opposed to Mr. Chamberlain's fiscal schemes, 1902; resigned office owing to Mr. Balfour's pronouncements on fiscal policy, 1903; opposed tariff reform in House of Lords, 1904; died at Cannes; K.G., 1902; frequently entertained King Edward VII; generous landlord and public-spirited benefactor; keen sportsman; speeches well constructed and logical; of transparent honesty, simplicity of purpose, and disinterestedness; portraits by Millais, Watts, Herkomer, and others; statues in London and at Eastbourne; 'Life' by Bernard Holland, 1911.

CAWDOR, third EARL (1847–1911), first lord of the admiralty. [See CAMPBELL, FREDERICK ARCHIBALD VAUGHAN.]

CECIL, LORD EDWARD HERBERT GASCOYNE- (1867–1918), soldier and civil servant; son of third Marquess of Salisbury [q. v.]; entered army, 1887; joined Egyptian government as under-secretary of state in ministry of finance, 1905; financial adviser, 1912; acted as high commissioner, 1914–15; died at Leysin.

CECIL, ROBERT ARTHUR TALBOT GASCOYNE-, third MARQUESS OF SALISBURY (1830–1903), prime minister; lineal descendant of Robert Cecil, first Earl of Salisbury [q. v.]; born at Hatfield; educated at Eton and Christ Church, Oxford; fellow of All Souls, 1853; in Australia 1851–3; conservative M.P. for Stamford, 1853–68; made speeches on property, religious education, and foreign affairs; married (1857) with father's disapproval; wrote much for reviews, beginning (1860) a long series of articles in 'Quarterly Review'; contributed 'Theories of Parliamentary Reform' to 'Oxford Essays,' 1858, which showed distrust of democracy and aversion to change; vigorous in opposition to liberal government, 1859–66; influenced public opinion by his pungent articles in 'Quarterly Review'; succeeded brother as Viscount Cranborne, 1865; became secretary for India and privy councillor in Derby administration, 1866–7; resigned post on Disraeli's introduction of household suffrage reform bill, 1867; opposed Gladstone's motion for Irish church disestablishment, 1868; succeeded father as Marquess of Salisbury, April 1868; criticized Irish Land and Education Acts of 1870, and Gladstone's abolition of army purchase; unsuccessfully resisted Universities Tests Abolition Act, 1871; succeeded Lord Derby as chancellor of Oxford University, 1869; urged appointment of universities' commissions, 1877; chairman of Great Eastern railway, 1868–72; secretary for India in Disraeli's government, 1874–8; criticized Disraeli's public worship regulation bill, 1874; favoured 'forward policy' in Afghanistan, inaugurated by Lord Lytton, 1876; opposed to Russian designs in Asia and powers at Constantinople, 1876; his proposal to reorganize Bulgaria, under control of governors nominated by Sultan, refused by the Porte; succeeded Lord Derby as secretary for foreign affairs, 1 April 1878; issued 'Salisbury Circular' (2 April), requiring submission of the treaty of San Stefano to a European conference, and emphatically declaring against creation of a 'big Bulgaria' as a menace to Europe; with Lord Beaconsfield he represented England at congress of Berlin (June–July 1878), ratifying treaty, by which the idea of a 'big Bulgaria' was abandoned, Austria was entrusted with administrative control of Bosnia and Herzegovina, Russia obtained Batum as free port, and England secured protectorate of Cyprus; created K.G., June 1878; leader of opposition in Lords on death of Beaconsfield, 1881; negotiated privately with liberal government the provisions of a redistribution bill supplementary to franchise bill, 1884; a trenchant critic of liberal foreign policy in Sudan, Egypt, and Afghanistan; prime minister and foreign secretary, June 1885; successfully negotiated with Russia on Afghan frontier question; secured eastern frontier of India by annexation of Burma; raised Egyptian loan and supported unity of Eastern Rumelia and Bulgaria; passed bill for housing of working classes; his party in a minority at the general election in Nov. 1885; resigned on passing of vote of censure in House of Commons, Feb. 1886; again prime minister and first lord of the treasury, July 1886; foreign secretary, Dec. 1886; inaugurated first colonial conference, 1887; Local Government Act and Closure Act passed, 1888; by granting royal charter to British East Africa Company he recovered English hold over upper sources of Nile,

1888; granted charter to British South Africa Company, 1889; acquired English protectorate over Zanzibar, giving up Heligoland to Germany and recognizing French protectorate in Madagascar, 1890; passed Free Education Act, 1891; supported appointment of Parnell commission, 1888; defeated at general election, 1892; formed coalition ministry as premier and foreign secretary with Duke of Devonshire and Mr. Chamberlain, 1895; lord warden of cinque ports, 1895; his government's measures included Workmen's Compensation Act (1897), Criminal Evidence Act (1898), and Inebriates Act (1898); pacified America in dispute over the boundary between British Guiana and Venezuela, 1895–6; prevented European intervention in Spanish-American war, 1898; facilitated American control of Panama canal by Hay-Pauncefote treaty, 1901; secured Weihaiwei for England and policy of open door in China, developing British enterprise in China, 1897; caused French to relinquish claims in the Sudan, 1898–9; concluded secret treaty with Germany regarding Portuguese Africa; refused (1897) to avenge Armenian massacres without approval of 'Concert of Europe,' which under his leadership established autonomy in Crete, 1899; supporter of international arbitration and Hague conference, 1899; refused idea of foreign mediation in Boer war, 1900; resigned foreign secretaryship and became lord privy seal, Nov. 1900; resigned premiership to nephew, Mr. A. J. Balfour, July 1902; died at Hatfield; monument in Westminster Abbey.

A close student of science and theology, he was president of the British Association in 1894, and was interested in electricity in later life. Contemning the impracticable and scorning sentiment and cant, he was a master of satire. Cautious in diplomacy, he regarded democracy as inimical to individual freedom, had strong faith in the historical continuity of government, and was severe critic of radical idea of progress; his foreign policy was one of pacific imperialism. G.C.V.O., 1902; D.C.L. Oxford, 1869; LL.D. Cambridge, 1888; hon. student of Christ Church, 1894. Portraits by Richmond, Millais, Watts, Herkomer; statues at Hatfield (by Sir G. Frampton) and at foreign office; Lives by Traill (1890), S. H. Jeyes (1895–6), Pulling (1885), and How (1902); 'Essays: Foreign Politics' were posthumously republished (1905) from the 'Quarterly Review,' to which he contributed thirty-three articles, 1860–83.

CHADS, SIR HENRY (1819–1906), admiral; entered navy, 1834; served in East Indies and on west coast of Africa; commander-in-chief at Nore, 1876–7; admiral, 1877; K.C.B., 1887.

CHALMERS, JAMES (1841–1901), missionary and explorer; joined London Missionary Society, 1861; ordained, 1865; worked at Rarotonga in South Seas, 1866–76; first white man to visit villages of New Guinea, 1876; explored Gulf of Papua; discovered mouths of Purari river, 1879; planted line of mission posts from Papuan gulf to Louisiade Archipelago, 1884; of great service in foundation of protectorate at Port Moresby, 1884; visited R. L. Stevenson at Samoa, 1890; worked in Fly river district at Saguane, 1892–4; sailed for Goaribari Island, April 1901; killed and eaten by savages at Dopima; a simple, zealous, courageous missionary; wrote accounts of work in New Guinea; autobiography in Lovett's 'Life,' 1902.

CHAMBERLAIN, SIR CRAWFORD TROTTER (1821–1902), general; brother of Sir Neville Chamberlain [q. v.]; cadet in Bengal army, 1837; served in Afghan war (1839), in Sikh war (1845–9), and Momund expedition (1854); promoted lieutenant-colonel for services in Indian Mutiny; C.S.I., 1866; commanded Gwalior district, 1866–9, and Oudh division, 1874–9; promoted general, 1880; G.C.I.E., 1897.

CHAMBERLAIN, JOSEPH (1836–1914), statesman; educated at University College School; member of screw-manufacturing firm in Birmingham, 1854–74; early became interested in question of social reform, which made him adopt radical views; chairman of National Education League of Birmingham, 1868, and of National Education League, 1870; mayor of Birmingham, 1873–5; helped to improve housing and sanitation of Birmingham and to develop municipal social reform generally; colleague of John Bright in parliamentary representation of Birmingham, 1876; formed close offensive and defensive alliance with (Sir) Charles Dilke [q. v.]; carried out reorganization of liberal party, 1877; became president of Board of Trade and entered second Gladstone Cabinet, 1880; out of sympathy with majority of colleagues in ministry of 1880–5; held strongly patriotic and national opinions on foreign affairs combined with extreme radical views on internal matters; opposed to policy of coercion in Ireland and entered into negotiations with Charles Stewart Parnell [q. v.] resulting in Kilmainham Treaty, 1882; strongly opposed introduction of Irish Land Purchase Bill without accompanying Irish Local Government Bill, 1885; opposed Egyptian policy of government and advocated relief of General Gordon, 1884; deplored loss of Cameroons to England, 1884; proved his capacity at Board of Trade by responsibility for two measures relating to merchant shipping (1880), Electric Lighting Bill (1881), Act for reforming law of bankruptcy (1883), Patent Act (1883), and Merchant Shipping Bill (1884); gave great offence to Queen Victoria by violence of his language at this time and incurred remonstrance from Gladstone for advocacy of unauthorized liberal programme; had friendly discussion with Gladstone on subject of liberal programme, October 1885; M.P., West Birmingham, 1885; president of Local Government Board in third Gladstone Cabinet, February–March, 1886; resigned on introduction of Home Rule Bill which he had consistently opposed; voted against Bill, June 1886; sacrificed future leadership of liberal party and even risked political extinction rather than comply with demands of Parnell; resignation of Lord Randolph Churchill (December 1886) dispelled his hopes of organizing new national party; went on mission to United States to negotiate treaty regarding North American fisheries, November 1887–March 1888; visited Egypt and was impressed by benefits accruing to that country from British occupation, 1889; joined third Salisbury Cabinet as secretary of state for Colonies, 1895; as secretary kept two objects in view: first, the tightening of the bond between Great Britain and the self-governing Colonies, and secondly, the development of the resources of the Crown Colonies together with an increase of trade between them and Great Britain; gave much attention to improving position of West Indies; waged successful campaign on question of health in tropical countries and was instrumental in setting on foot two special schools of tropical medicine; during his secretaryship British possessions in West Africa extended by effective occupation of territory behind Gold Coast and Lagos and by placing of Royal Niger Company's territories under control of the Colonial Office (1900); most memorable work performed in connexion with Dominions, especially South Africa; soon after taking up office confronted with difficulties created by Raid of (Sir) Leander Starr Jameson [q. v.]; unjustly accused of complicity with Raid; his position with regard to South Africa made easier by appointment of high commissioner, Sir Alfred (afterwards Viscount) Milner, in whom he could place entire confidence, 1897; proposed meeting between Milner and President Kruger to discuss grievances of Transvaal Uitlanders, chief of these being franchise question; Bloemfontein Conference (May–June 1899), honest attempt on part of British authorities to reach *modus vivendi*, broke down through Kruger's intractability; in spite of conciliatory attitude adopted by Chamberlain, war was rendered inevitable; visited South Africa on conclusion of Boer War, 1902; first secretary of state to visit British colony in connexion with political questions; helped forward reconciliation between rival races and parties in Cape Colony and dealt successfully with Boers of Transvaal and capitalists of Rand; vetoed suspension of Cape Colony constitution, 1902; piloted Commonwealth of Australia Bill through House of Commons, 1900; although mainly preoccupied with colonial questions while in unionist government, largely responsible for Workmen's Compensation Act, 1897; weakest side of his programme shown in his excursions into foreign policy; resigned office on return from South Africa, 1903; induced to take this step by government's refusal to include in its programme granting of preference to imperial wheat; his conviction of need for closer imperial union, which he believed would most readily be achieved through commercial union, caused him to change his economic policy from free trade to tariff reform; proclaimed himself convinced imperialist at Liverpool, October 1903; devoted himself to explaining and popularizing his views during three years' campaign, 1903–6; obliged to withdraw from public life owing to ill-health for remaining years, 1906–14.

Chamberlain's most outstanding qualities were loyalty to his friends and freedom from jealousy. A collected edition of his speeches published 1914. Contributed numerous articles to the 'Fortnightly Review' and 'Nineteenth Century,' A portrait by Frank Holl is in the National Portrait Gallery and there is a bust in Westminster Abbey.

CHAMBERLAIN, Sir NEVILLE BOWLES (1820–1902), field-marshal; born at Rio de Janeiro; obtained commission in East India Company's army, 1837; joined 16th Bengal native infantry, 1838; at storming of Ghazni, 1839; at Kandahar, 1841; several times wounded; in march from Kandahar to Kabul, 1842; served in Gwalior campaign, 1843; military secretary to governor of Bombay, 1846–8; conspicuous in passage of the Chenab under Lord Gough [q. v.], 1849; in charge of organization of military police for Punjab, 1852; went to South Africa for health, 1852–4; in command of Punjab irregular force, 1854; adjutant-general of Bengal army in Indian Mutiny, 1857; repulsed mutineers before Delhi (July); C.B., 1857; broke up Sikh conspiracy at Dera Ismail Khan, 1858; forced his way against Mahsuds to Kaniguram, 1860; K.C.B., 1863; led force against Wahabi fanatics on Ambela pass, 1863; severely wounded; accompanied Duke of Edinburgh to India, 1869; lieutenant-general, 1872; G.C.S.I., 1873; G.C.B., 1875; general, 1877; commanded Madras army, 1876–81; returned to England, 1881; field-marshal, 1900.

CHAMIER, STEPHEN HENRY EDWARD (1834–1910), lieutenant-general, royal Madras artillery; born in Madras; nephew of Frederick Chamier [q. v.]; joined Madras artillery, 1853; served in Indian Mutiny at Cawnpore and Lucknow, 1857–8; commanded first battery artillery, Hyderabad, 1858; inspector-general of ordnance, Madras, 1881–6; lieutenant-general and C.B., 1886; a good musician (Mus.Bac. Dublin).

CHANCE, Sir JAMES TIMMINS, first baronet (1814–1902), manufacturer and lighthouse engineer; scholar of Trinity College, Cambridge; seventh wrangler, 1838; joined father's glass business at Birmingham; made improvements in dioptric apparatus for lighthouses from 1850 onwards; joined Faraday in experiments with apparatus at Whitby southern lighthouse, 1860; read classic papers on the subject before Institution of Civil Engineers, 1867, for which he was awarded the Telford medal and premium; retired from business, 1872; benefactor to Birmingham institutions; presented West Smethwick Park to town, 1895; endowed Chance School of Engineering in Birmingham University, 1900; baronet, 1900; portrait by J. C. Horsley, 1854, and bust by Hamo Thornycroft, 1894.

CHANNER, GEORGE NICHOLAS (1842–1905), general, Indian staff corps; born at Allahabad; joined Indian army, 1859; served in Ambela campaign, 1863; won V.C. for bravery in Burkit Putus Pass, 1875; served in Afghan war, 1878–80; commanded Kuram field force at capture of Peiwar Kotal, 1879; commanded 1st brigade of Hazara field force in Black Mountain expedition, 1888; C.B., 1899: brigadier-general in command of Assam district, 1892–6; general, 1899.

CHAPMAN, EDWARD JOHN (1821–1904), mineralogist; professor of mineralogy in University College, London (1849–53) and Toronto University (1853–95); published researches into minerals and fossils of Canada, 1864.

CHARLES, JAMES (1851–1906), portrait and landscape painter; entered Royal Academy Schools, 1872; exhibited regularly at Academy (1875–1904) and Grosvenor Gallery; paintings include 'Christening Sunday,' 1887; 'Will it Rain ?', 'Milking Time,' 'In Spring Time,' 1896; in Paris, 1889–90; in Venice, 1891; skilful in sunlight effects; works shown at winter exhibition of Royal Academy, 1907; represented in many public galleries.

CHARLEY, Sir WILLIAM THOMAS (1833–1904), lawyer; B.A., St. John's College, Oxford, 1856; D.C.L., 1868; called to bar, 1865; helped to reorganize conservative party in London and Lancashire, 1867; M.P. for Salford, 1868–80; strong supporter of Disraeli; common serjeant, 1878–1892; knighted and made Q.C., 1880; vigorous defender of Church of England; enthusiastic volunteer; author of legal and other works.

CHARTERIS, ARCHIBALD HAMILTON (1835–1908), biblical critic; M.A. Edinburgh, 1853; hon. D.D., 1868; LL.D., 1898; joined Church of Scotland ministry, 1858; professor of biblical criticism, Edinburgh University, 1868–98; published conservative theological works on canonicity of New Testament, 1880–7; organized practical Christian effort in Scotland; revived order of deaconesses; started and edited a periodical, 'Life and Work,' 1879; supporter of foreign missions; moderator of general assembly, 1892.

CHASE, DRUMMOND PERCY (1820–1902), last

principal of St. Mary Hall, Oxford, 1857–1902; B.A., with first class in *lit. hum.*, Oriel College, Oxford, 1841; fellow, 1842–1902, and tutor; D.D., 1880; vicar of St. Mary's Oxford, 1855–63, 1876–8; wrote pamphlets on academic questions; edited with translation Aristotle's 'Nicomachean Ethics,' 1847.

CHASE, MARIAN EMMA (1844–1905), water-colour painter; studied under Margaret Gillies [q. v.]; exhibited at Royal Academy and elsewhere, 1866–1905; member of Institute of Painters in Water Colours, 1876; truthful and delicate painter of flowers, fruit, and still life.

CHASE, WILLIAM ST. LUCIAN (1856–1908), lieutenant-colonel; born at St. Lucia, West Indies; joined Bombay army, 1875; served in Afghan war, 1879–80; won V.C. in sortie from Kandahar, 1880; took part in Zhob Valley (1884) and Lushai (1889–90) expeditions, and Tirah campaign, 1897–8; lieutenant-colonel, 1899; C.B., 1903.

CHEADLE, WALTER BUTLER (1835–1910), physician; B.A., Caius College, Cambridge, 1859; M.B., 1861; explored western Canada, 1862–4; published 'The North-west Passage by Land,' 1865; F.R.C.P., 1870; senior censor, 1898; Lumleian lecturer, 1900; on active staff of St. Mary's Hospital, 1867–1904; physician to Children's Hospital, Great Ormond Street, 1869–92; first (1877) defined nature of infantile scurvy; wrote on feeding of infants, 1889, and on infantile rheumatism, 1899; supported claims of medical women.

CHEETHAM, SAMUEL (1827–1908), archdeacon of Rochester; fellow of Christ's College, Cambridge, 1850; tutor, 1853–8; M.A., 1853; D.D., 1880; professor of pastoral theology, King's College, London, 1863–82; hon. canon of Rochester, 1878; archdeacon of Southwark, 1879, and of Rochester, 1882; F.S.A., 1890; Hulsean lecturer, Cambridge, 1896–7; edited with Sir William Smith [q.v.] 'Dictionary of Christian Antiquities,' 1875–80; completed history of church by Charles Hardwick [q. v.].

CHELMSFORD, second BARON (1827–1905), general. [See THESIGER, FREDERIC AUGUSTUS.]

CHEYLESMORE, second BARON (1843–1902), mezzotint collector. [See EATON, WILLIAM MERITON.]

CHEYNE, THOMAS KELLY (1841–1915), Old Testament scholar; educated at Worcester College, Oxford, and at Göttingen; vice-principal of St. Edmund Hall, Oxford, 1864–8; fellow of Balliol, 1868–82; joined Old Testament revision company, 1884; Oriel professor of interpretation of Scripture at Oxford and canon of Rochester, 1885–1908; disciple in biblical criticism of Heinrich von Ewald; initiated scholarly critical movement in England; author of many books on the Old Testament; his later work spoiled by extravagant views.

CHILD, THOMAS (1839–1906), minister of the 'new church'; became Swedenborgian preacher, 1872; published much in support of 'new church' principles; chief work 'Root Principles in Rational and Spiritual Things,' 1905, a reasoned reply to Haeckel.

CHILD-VILLIERS, VICTOR ALBERT GEORGE, seventh EARL OF JERSEY, and tenth VISCOUNT GRANDISON (1845–1915), colonial governor. [See VILLIERS.]

CHRYSTAL, GEORGE (1851–1911), mathematician; educated at Aberdeen and Peterhouse, Cambridge; second wrangler and Smith's prizeman, and fellow of Corpus, 1875; made researches for verifying 'Ohm's law,' 1876; professor of mathematics at Edinburgh University, 1879–1911; F.R.S. Edinburgh, 1880, and general secretary, 1901–11; in later life worked out theories on oscillations in lakes, for which he received royal medal at Royal Society of London, 1911; hon. LL.D. Aberdeen (1887) and Glasgow (1911); published standard handbook on 'Algebra,' 1886–9.

CLANRICARDE, second MARQUESS OF (1832–1916), Irish landed proprietor. [See BURGH CANNING, HUBERT GEORGE DE.]

CLANWILLIAM, fourth EARL OF (1832–1907), admiral of the fleet. [See MEADE, RICHARD JAMES.]

CLARK, JOHN WILLIS (1833–1910), man of science and archaeologist; son of William Clark [q. v.]; educated at Eton and Trinity College, Cambridge; first class classic, 1856; fellow, 1858; superintendent of museum of zoology, Cambridge, 1866–91; registrary of Cambridge University, 1891–1910; did much to forward endowment of university library; supporter of Cambridge Amateur Dramatic Club; wrote many works on Cambridge history, including 'Architectural History of the University and Colleges of Cambridge,' with Robert Willis [q. v.], 4 vols. 1886, 'Concise Guide to Cambridge,' 1898, and on Barnwell Priory, 1897, 1907; collaborated in 'Life of Professor

Sedgwick,' 2 vols. 1890; also wrote 'The Care of Books,' 1901; bequeathed collections of books on Cambridge to university library; memoir by A. E. Shipley, 1913.

CLARKE, SIR ANDREW (1824–1902), lieutenant-general and colonial official; joined royal engineers, 1844; dispatched to Van Diemen's Land, 1846; transferred to New Zealand, 1848; surveyor-general of Melbourne, 1853; served on legislative council; drafted bill for new constitution for colony, 1854; surveyor-general and commissioner of lands, 1856; inaugurated railways there, 1857; appointed to command of royal engineers at Colchester (1859) and Birmingham (1862); served in Ashanti, 1863; director of engineering works at admiralty, 1864–73; C.B., 1869; extended docks at Chatham, Portsmouth, and elsewhere; advocated English purchase of Suez Canal, 1870; K.C.M.G., 1873; successful governor of the Straits Settlements, 1873–5; suppressed piracy; head of the public works department in India, 1877–80; C.I.E., 1877; returned to England, 1880; inspector-general of fortifications, 1882; paid close attention to defences of coaling stations and commercial harbours; advocated widening of Suez Canal, 1882; vice-president of international committee on subject, 1884; urged construction of railway from Suakin to Berber, 1884; G.C.M.G., 1885; lieutenant-general, 1886; subsequently director of British North Borneo Company, which named Clarke province after him; agent-general for Victoria, 1891–4, 1897–1902; busts at Chatham and Singapore.

CLARKE, SIR CASPAR PURDON (1846–1911), architect, archaeologist, and museum director; trained as architect, he held posts at South Kensington Museum from 1867; made for the museum purchases in near East (1876), and in Spain and Italy (1879); keeper of India museum (1883–92), and art collections (1892) there; director of South Kensington Museum, 1896–1905; director of Metropolitan Museum, New York, 1905–10; designed many London buildings, including National School of Cookery, 1887; lectured and wrote much on architecture and Eastern crafts; F.S.A., 1893; C.I.E., 1883; knighted, 1902.

CLARKE, CHARLES BARON (1832–1906), botanist; educated at Trinity College, Cambridge; third wrangler, 1856; fellow (1856) and lecturer in mathematics (1858–65) at Queens' College; M.A., 1859; called to bar, 1858; joined staff of Presidency College, Calcutta, 1865; inspector of schools in Eastern Bengal; obtained 7,000 specimens of Indian plants; superintendent of Calcutta botanical gardens, 1869–71; helped Sir Joseph Hooker at Kew in his 'Flora of British India,' 1879–83; inspector of schools in India, 1883–7; settled on retirement at Kew, 1887, continuing work on Indian botany; president of Linnean Society, 1894–6; F.R.S.,1882; wrote on Bengal botany, political economy, geography, and ethnology.

CLARKE, HENRY BUTLER (1863–1904), historian of Spain; educated at St. Jean-de-Luz and Wadham College, Oxford; B.A., 1888; studied Spanish history and literature; Taylorian teacher of Spanish at Oxford, 1890–2; Fereday fellow of St. John's, Oxford, 1894; lived at St. Jean-de-Luz from 1891; wrote 'Spanish Grammar,' 1892, 'History of Spanish Literature,' 1893, 'Modern Spain, 1815–1898,' 1906; an Arabic scholar.

CLARKE, SIR MARSHAL JAMES (1841–1909), South African administrator; joined royal artillery, 1863; lieutenant-colonel, 1883; resident commissioner of Basutoland, 1884–93, of Zululand, 1893–8, of Rhodesia, 1898–1905; won confidence of natives; K.C.M.G., 1886.

CLASPER, JOHN HAWKS (1836–1908), boat-builder and oarsman; son of Henry Clasper, Newcastle oarsman and boat-builder, and inventor of outrigger; won many sculling races at regattas from 1854; with father won pair-oar championship of the Tyne, 1858; expert trainer; improved sliding seat and keelless boat; invented counter-vail; built successful Cambridge eight-oared boats of 1870–3; became leading builder of racing boats.

CLAYDEN, PETER WILLIAM (1827–1902), journalist and author; active unitarian minister, 1855–68; secretary of newly founded Free Church Union, 1868; as leader-writer and assistant editor of 'Daily News' (1868–96) he increased its influence as liberal nonconformist organ; supported Gladstone's anti-Turkish views, 1876–80, and advocated support of Armenians, 1896–7; published memoirs of Samuel Rogers, 1887–9, and religious and political works.

CLERKE, AGNES MARY (1842–1907), historian of astronomy; resided in Italy, 1867–77, writing on astronomical and literary subjects, mainly for 'Edinburgh Review'; published 'Popular History of Astronomy

during the Nineteenth Century,' 1885, 'System of the
Stars,' 1890, and 'Problems in Astrophysics,' 1903;
contributed lives of astronomers to this Dictionary;
elected hon. member of Royal Astronomical Society,
1903; an accomplished musician.

CLERKE, ELLEN MARY (1840–1906), translator of
Italian verse, poet, and novelist; sister of A. M. Clerke
[q. v.]; published 'Fable and Song in Italy,' 1899, and
astronomical monographs.

CLEWORTH, THOMAS EBENEZER (1854–1909),
educational controversialist; B.A., St. John's College,
Cambridge, 1882; rector of Middleton, Lancashire, 1880;
hon. canon of Manchester, 1902; founded Church Schools
Emergency League, 1903, for maintenance of church
schools and of church teaching in elementary schools;
organized demonstrations against liberal government's
education bill, 1906; wrote many educational leaflets.

CLIFFORD, FREDERICK (1828–1904), journalist and
legal writer; joined parliamentary staff of 'The Times,'
1852; joint proprietor of 'Sheffield Daily Telegraph,'
1863; helped to found Press Association, 1868; assistant
editor of 'The Times,' 1877–83; called to bar, 1859;
published standard textbook on private bill practice,
1870, and 'The History of Private Bill Legislation,' 2 vols.
1885–7; student of and writer on agricultural questions.

CLOSE, MAXWELL HENRY (1822–1903), geologist;
B.A., Trinity College, Dublin, 1846; M.A., 1867; minister
in Church of Ireland, 1848–61; made valuable researches
in Irish glacial geology; president of Irish Royal Geological Society, 1878–9; treasurer of Royal Irish Academy,
1879–1903; promoted study of Irish language; wrote
anonymously on physics and astronomy.

CLOWES, SIR WILLIAM LAIRD (1856–1905), naval
writer; educated at King's College, London; fellow, 1895;
published poem 'Meroe,' 1876; made reputation as naval
correspondent to 'The Times,' 1890–5; influenced naval
estimates by anonymous articles in 'Daily Graphic' on
'The Needs of the Navy,' 1893; compiled 'The Royal
Navy,' 7 vols. 1897–1903; knighted, 1902; granted civil
list pension, 1904; excellent linguist.

CLUNIES-ROSS, GEORGE (1842–1910), owner of
Cocos and Keeling Islands; born in Cocos Islands;
grandson of John Clunies-Ross, first owner of the islands;
studied engineering at Glasgow, 1862; returned to Cocos
Islands, 1862; introduced modern machinery and scientific methods in coconut industry, and restored dwindling
family fortunes; control of islands transferred to governor
of Ceylon, 1878, and to governor of Straits Settlements,
1886; islands incorporated as part of Singapore, 1903.

CLUTTON, HENRY HUGH (1850–1909), surgeon;
B.A., Clare College, Cambridge, 1873; M.B., 1879; M.C.,
1897; entered St. Thomas's Hospital, 1872; full surgeon,
1891; F.R.C.S., 1876; president of Clinical Society, 1905;
specialist on diseases of bones and joints; described
'Clutton's joints,' a knee affection in children, 1886.

COBB, GERARD FRANCIS (1838–1904), musician;
B.A., Trinity College, Cambridge (first class in classics
and moral science), 1861; fellow, 1863; junior bursar,
1865–93; strongly advocated Roman and Anglican
reunion; prolific composer of songs and church music;
chief work 'A Song of Trafalgar,' 1900; president of
National Cyclists' Union, 1878.

COBBE, FRANCES POWER (1822–1904), philanthropist and religious writer; studied history, astronomy,
and philosophy; influenced by Theodore Parker, whose
works she edited, 14 vols. 1863–71, and by Kant's
ethics; published anonymously 'The Theory of Intuitive
Morals,' 1855; travelled much abroad, especially in Italy,
where she met Mazzini; associated with Mary Carpenter
[q. v.] in her ragged school and reformatory work, 1858;
engaged in workhouse philanthropy at Bristol, 1859;
advocated woman's suffrage and admission of women to
university degrees, 1862; on staff of 'Echo,' 1868–75,
she investigated cases of destitution; helped to promote
Matrimonial Causes Act, 1878; joint secretary of National
Antivivisection Society, 1875–84; a frank and lucid
writer; an occasional preacher in unitarian chapels;
voluminous writings include 'Broken Lights,' 1864,
'Darwinism in Morals,' 1872, 'The Duties of Women,'
1881; Autobiography, 2 vols. 1904.

COHEN, ARTHUR (1829–1914), lawyer; B.A., Magdalene College, Cambridge; first professing Jew to graduate
at Cambridge; called to bar (Inner Temple), 1857;
specialized in commercial law; junior counsel for Great
Britain in Alabama arbitration at Geneva, 1872; Q.C.,
1874; liberal M.P., Southwark, 1880–7; to avoid by-
election refused judgeship, 1881; standing counsel to

India Office, 1893; counsel for Great Britain in Venezuela
arbitration at The Hague, F.B.A., and member of royal
commission on trade unions, 1903; P.C., 1905; chairman
of royal commission on shipping combinations 1906.

COILLARD, FRANÇOIS (1834–1904), protestant
missionary under the Paris Missionary Society in the
Zambesi region; born at Asnières-les-Bourges, Cher,
France, of Huguenot family; sent to Basutoland, 1857;
worked at Leribé, 1859–79: interpreter between Sir
Theophilus Shepstone [q. v.] and Basuto chief Makotoko
at Witzie's Hoek, 1865; baptized Makotoko, 1868; completed church at Leribé, 1871; went on evangelizing
expedition to Banyai territory, 1877; taken prisoner
at Buluwayo by Lobengula; established strong mission
stations in Barotsi territory, 1882; promoted native
confidence in later British administration; published
'Sur le Haut Zambèse,' 1889, translated into English,
1897; 'Lives' by C. W. Mackintosh, 1907, and E. Favre,
1908.

COKAYNE, GEORGE EDWARD (1825–1911), genealogist; B.A., Exeter College, Oxford, 1848; M.A., 1852;
called to bar, 1853; Norroy (1882) and Clarenceux (1894)
King of Arms; F.S.A., 1866; published 'G.E.C.'s Complete
Peerage,' 8 vols. 1887–98, and 'Baronetage,' 5 vols.
1900–6.

COKE, THOMAS WILLIAM, second EARL OF LEICES-
TER (1822–1909), agriculturist; son of first earl [q. v.]; an
ardent agriculturist and forester; greatly improved his
Holkham estate; lord-lieutenant of Norfolk, 1846–1906;
keeper of privy seal of the duchy of Cornwall, 1870–1901;
K.G., 1873; a whig in politics.

COLEMAN, WILLIAM STEPHEN (1829–1904), book
illustrator and painter; published 'Our Woodlands,
Heaths, and Hedges,' 1859, and 'British Butterflies,'
1860; illustrated many books on natural history from
1858 onwards; executed numerous water-colour landscapes, etchings, and pastel work; exhibited at Dudley
Gallery, 1865–79; established Minton's Art Pottery
Studio, Kensington Gore.

COLERIDGE, MARY ELIZABETH (1861–1907), poet,
novelist, and essayist; as a child she wrote verse and
romance; first novel, 'The Seven Sleepers of Ephesus'
(1893), praised by R. L. Stevenson; her 'Poems Old
and New' (1907) and 'Gathered Leaves' (1910), stories
and essays, appeared posthumously.

COLERIDGE-TAYLOR, SAMUEL (1875–1912), musical
composer; of negro birth; composition pupil of (Sir)
C. V. Stanford at Royal College of Music; his 'Hiawatha's
Wedding Feast' produced 1898, followed by 'Death of
Minnehaha' (1899) and final section (1900); whole
produced at Albert Hall, 1900; compositions include
incidental music for plays by Stephen Phillips [q. v.]
and 'A Tale of Old Japan' (poem by Alfred Noyes), 1911;
student and apostle of African negro music.

COLLEN, SIR EDWIN HENRY HAYTER (1843–
1911), lieutenant-general; joined royal artillery, 1863;
served in Abyssinian war, 1867–8; assistant controller-
general in second Afghan war, 1880; served in Eastern
Sudan expedition at Tamai and Thakul, 1885; military
secretary to Indian government, 1887–96; military
member of governor-general's council, 1896; improved
military equipment and mobilization of Indian army;
lieutenant-general, 1905; C.B., 1897; G.C.I.E., 1903;
member of war office regulations committee, 1901–4;
wrote history of 'The Indian Army,' 1907.

COLLETT, SIR HENRY (1836–1901), colonel Indian
staff corps; joined Bengal army, 1855; served in Oudh
during Indian Mutiny, 1858–9, in Assam, 1862–3, and
Abyssinian campaign, 1868; quartermaster-general in
Afghan war, 1878–80; commanded 23rd pioneers at
Kandahar, 1880; C.B., 1881; colonel, 1884; held command in Chin Lushai expedition, 1889–90; prominent in
expedition to Manipur; K.C.B., 1891; commanded
Peshawar district, 1892–3; on retirement (1893) prepared
at Kew handbook on the flora of Simla (published
1902).

COLLINGS, JESSE (1831–1920), politician; in business
in Birmingham, 1850–79; prominently associated with
Joseph Chamberlain's programme of municipal
reform; associated with Joseph Arch [q. v.] and programme of land reform; employed phrase 'three acres
and a cow'; liberal M.P., Ipswich, 1880–6, Bordesley,
Birmingham, 1886–1918; P.C., 1892; under-secretary to
Home Department, 1895–1902.

COLLINGWOOD, CUTHBERT (1826–1908), naturalist;
B.A., Christ Church, Oxford, 1849; M.B., 1854; surgeon
and naturalist on H.M.S. 'Rifleman' and 'Serpent' in

China seas, 1866–7; published researches in marine zoology, 1868; a prominent Swedenborgian; died in Paris; wrote 'The Travelling Birds,' 1872, and theological works in verse and prose.

COLLINS, JOHN CHURTON (1848–1908), author and professor of English; educated at King Edward's School, Birmingham, 1863–8, and Balliol College, Oxford, 1868–72 (B.A., 1872); greatly interested in literature in his youth; coached in London candidates for civil service examinations from 1873, and wrote for the press and magazines; made friends with Swinburne; edited Cyril Tourneur's works, 1878, and Lord Herbert of Cherbury's poems, 1881; contributor to the 'Quarterly Review' from October 1878, and many of his articles there were republished independently; successful lecturer for Oxford and London University Extension from 1880; long agitated with good ultimate effect for academic recognition of English literature at Oxford; urged his views in 'The Study of English Literature,' 1891, and in periodicals; an outspoken critic of current literature in 'Saturday Review,' 1894–1906; collected essays in 'Ephemera Critica,' 1901, 'Studies in Shakespeare,' 1904, 'Studies in Poetry and Criticism,' 1905, and 'Voltaire, Montesquieu, and Rousseau in England,' 1905; professor of English at University of Birmingham, 1904 to death; hon. Litt.D. Durham, 1905; zealous amateur student of criminology; brilliant conversationalist; drowned at Oulton Broad near Lowestoft.

COLLINS, RICHARD HENN, LORD COLLINS, of Kensington (1842–1911), judge; scholar of Trinity College, Dublin, 1860; hon. LL.D., 1902; migrated to Downing College, Cambridge, 1863; fourth classic, 1865; hon. fellow, 1883; called to bar, 1867; Q.C. ,1883; expert in litigation between rival municipalities and on railway companies; a lucid and precise advocate; judge of queen's bench, 1891; judicial member and chairman of railway and canal commission, 1894; appointed to court of appeal and P.C., 1897; master of the Rolls, 1901; lord of appeal and life peer, 1907; represented Great Britain on tribunal dealing with Venezuelan boundary, 1899; chairman (1904) of commission of inquiry which led to Criminal Appeal Act of 1907; first president of Classical Association, 1903.

COLLINS, WILLIAM EDWARD (1867–1911), bishop of Gibraltar; B.A., Selwyn College, Cambridge, 1887; D.D., 1903; ordained, 1890; professor of ecclesiastical history, King's College, London, 1893–1904; helped to found Church Historical Society (1894–1904), contributing several historical studies; bishop of Gibraltar, 1904–11; visited Persia and Asiatic Turkey, 1907; died at sea off Smyrna; 'Life' by Canon A. J. Mason.

COLNAGHI, MARTIN HENRY (1821–1908), picture dealer and collector; son of printseller; at first organizer of railway advertising; expert and buyer of pictures, helping to form several private collections; took Flatou's Gallery in Haymarket (1877–88) and Marlborough Gallery (1888), where he exhibited ancient and modern works of art; authority on Dutch and Flemish schools; discovered Van Goyen; privately purchased in 1896 Colonna or Ripaldi Raphael, which was subsequently sold to J. P. Morgan for 80,000l.; bequeathed several pictures and his fortune to National Gallery to form Martin Colnaghi Bequest.

COLOMB, SIR JOHN CHARLES READY (1838–1909), writer on imperial defence; entered royal marines, 1854; retired, 1869; devoted rest of life to advocacy of strong military and naval defence; conservative M.P. for Bow and Bromley, 1886–92, and for Great Yarmouth, 1895–1906; K.C.M.G., 1888; P.C., 1903; chief works are 'The Defence of Great and Greater Britain,' 1879, and 'Imperial Federation,' 1886.

COLTON, SIR JOHN (1823–1902), premier of South Australia; went with father from Devonshire to Australia, 1839; founded firm of merchants at Adelaide; retired, 1883; mayor of Adelaide, 1874–5; in House of Assembly, 1865–78; liberal commissioner of public works, 1868–70; treasurer, 1875–6; premier, 1876–7, and again, 1884–5; carried land and income tax bill; temperance advocate; K.C.M.G., 1891.

COLVILE, SIR HENRY EDWARD (1852–1907), lieutenant-general; joined grenadier guards, 1870; served in Sudan, 1884–5 (C.B., 1885), and in Egypt, 1885–8; acting commissioner in Uganda protectorate, 1893; commanded expedition against Kabarega, king of Unyoro, 1894; K.C.M.G., 1895; commanded guards brigade at Belmont, Modder River, and Magersfontein, Nov.–Dec. 1899; in command of new ninth division, he hemmed in

Gen. Cronje at Paardeberg, February 1900; at occupation of Bloemfontein (March); ruined his career by failure to relieve General Broadwood's column at Sanna's Post and Colonel Spragge's force at Lindley (March–May); ordered to command a brigade at Gibraltar, but recalled to England (November); retired as lieutenant-general, Jan. 1901; defended himself in 'The Work of the Ninth Division,' 1901; wrote 'The History of the Soudan Campaign,' 1889.

COLVIN, SIR AUCKLAND (1838–1908), Anglo-Indian and Egyptian administrator; born at Calcutta; son of John Russell Colvin [q. v.]; in Indian service, 1858–78; English controller of Egyptian finance, 1880; as acting consul-general he quelled insurrection in Egypt, Sept. 1881; by articles in 'Pall Mall Gazette' influenced English recognition of responsibility in Egypt; financial adviser to khedive; K.C.M.G., 1881; financial member of viceroy's council in India, 1883; advocated international recognition of bimetallism; increased salt duty and imposed export duty on petroleum, 1887–8; lieutenant-governor of North-West Provinces, Nov. 1887; improved water supply and drainage system; uncompromising opponent of Indian National Congress; C.I.E., 1883; K.C.S.I., on retirement, 1892; wrote life of his father, 1895, and 'Making of Modern Egypt,' 1906.

COLVIN, SIR WALTER MYTTON (1847–1908), brother of Sir A. Colvin [q.v.]; born in Burma; educated at Rugby and Trinity College, Cambridge; called to bar, 1871; acquired vast criminal practice in Allahabad; knighted, 1904.

COMMERELL, SIR JOHN EDMUND (1829–1901), admiral of the fleet; entered navy, 1842; gained the V.C. for gallantry in the Baltic, 1854; C.B., 1866; commander-in-chief on West coast of Africa, 1871, and on North American station, 1882–5; K.C.B., 1874; conservative M.P. for Southampton, 1885–8; admiral, 1886; G.C.B., 1887; commander-in-chief at Portsmouth, 1888; admiral of the fleet, 1892.

COMMON, ANDREW AINSLIE (1841–1903), astronomer; early devoted himself to astronomy; with a silver-on-glass mirror of 3 feet diameter he made first successful photograph of the comet of June 1881; photographed great nebula in Orion, 1882; awarded gold medal of Royal Astronomical Society, 1884; completed five foot equatorial reflecting telescope, 1891; made small mirrors for observing eclipses for Royal Society, South Kensington, and Greenwich; invented telescopic gun sight for use in army and navy; F.R.S., 1885; president of Royal Astronomical Society, 1884–95; hon. LL.D., St. Andrews, 1891.

COMPTON, LORD ALWYNE FREDERICK (1825–1906), bishop of Ely; son of second Marquess of Northampton [q. v.]; educated at Eton and Trinity College, Cambridge; 14th wrangler, 1848; rector of Castle Ashby, 1852–78; dean of Worcester, 1879–86; lord high almoner, 1882; bishop of Ely, 1886–1905; simple, direct preacher of high church views; a keen archaeologist, he caused to be arranged and catalogued diocesan documents.

CONDER, CHARLES (1868–1909), artist; was sent to Sydney, New South Wales, 1884; studied and exhibited at Melbourne, where his 'The Hot Wind' (1890) attracted notice; returned to England, 1890; studied under Cormon in Paris; exhibited his works there (1891 and 1896), especially designs for fans; married and settled in Chelsea, 1901; designed lithographs; painted landscapes in oils; most characteristic work was in water-colours, delicately toned, on panels of white silk; style akin to that of Watteau.

CONDER, CLAUDE REIGNIER (1848–1910), colonel royal engineers, Altaic scholar, and Palestine explorer; grandson of Josiah Conder [q. v.] and cousin of Charles Conder [q. v.]; joined royal engineers, 1870; continued scientific survey of Western Palestine, for Palestine Exploration Fund, 1872–3, surveying country west of Jordan; completed with Lieutenant (afterwards Viscount) Kitchener [q. v.] 'Memoirs of the Survey,' 7 vols. 1880; published 'Tent Work in Palestine,' 1878, and 'Hand-book to the Bible,' 1879; discovered ancient city of Kadesh; completed survey of 500 square miles of country across Jordan, 1881; joined in Egyptian campaign, 1882, and in Bechuanaland expedition, 1884; at Plymouth on ordnance survey, 1887; in charge of engraving department at Southampton, 1888–95; directed relief of distress in Ireland, 1895; commanding royal engineer at Weymouth, 1885; brevet-colonel, 1899; hon. LL.D. Edinburgh, 1891; authority on Hittite and Altaic languages; voluminous writings include 'Altaic Hieroglyphs and Hittite Inscriptions,' 1887, 'Palestine,' 1891, 'The

Tell Amarna Tablets,' with translation and description, 1893, and works for Palestine Pilgrims Text Society.

CONNEMARA, BARON (1827–1902), governor of Madras. [See BOURKE, ROBERT.]

CONQUEST, GEORGE (AUGUSTUS) (1837–1901), actor-manager, whose original name was OLIVER; manager of Grecian Theatre, 1872–85; sole lessee of Surrey Theatre from 1885; retired from stage, 1894; acted with great melodramatic power; best known as acrobatic pantomimist and animal impersonator; re-invented 'flying' by 'invisible' wires; co-author of over a hundred original or adapted melodramas; chief were 'Sentenced to Death,' 1875, 'Mankind,' 1881, and 'The Crimes of Paris,' 1883.

COOK, SIR EDWARD TYAS (1857–1919), journalist; educated at Winchester and New College, Oxford; joined staff of 'Pall Mall Gazette,' 1883; editor, 1890–2; editor of newly-founded 'Westminster Gazette,' 1893–6, and of 'Daily News,' 1895–1901; edited library edition of Ruskin's 'Works' (38 vols., 1903–11); biographer of Ruskin (1911), Florence Nightingale (1913), and Delane (1915); joint-manager of Press Bureau, 1915–19; knighted, 1912; K.B.E., 1917.

COOK, SIR FRANCIS, first baronet (1817–1901), merchant and art collector; entered father's drapery firm in City of London, 1833; partner, 1843; head, 1869; first visited Portugal, 1841; bought and restored Monserrate palace, Cintra, 1856; renewed prosperity of district; created Viscount Monserrate, 1864; at Doughty House, Richmond Hill (1860), he formed fine art collection of foreign schools; F.S.A., 1873; established Alexandra House, South Kensington, for lady music and art students, 1885; baronet, 1886; left estate of 1,500,000*l*.

COOPER, SIR ALFRED (1838–1908), surgeon; studied medicine at St. Bartholomew's Hospital and in Paris; M.R.C.S., 1861; F.R.C.S., 1870; surgeon to West London and other hospitals; knighted, 1902; a keen volunteer; helped to found Rahere lodge of freemasons; author of 'Syphilis and Pseudo-Syphilis,' 1884.

COOPER, SIR DANIEL, first baronet (1821–1902), Australian merchant; a native of Lancashire; visited Sydney in boyhood; after education in London, he joined mercantile firm in Sydney, 1843; elected to legislative council of New South Wales, 1849; raised funds for Crimean war sufferers, 1854; speaker of New South Wales, 1856–9; knighted, 1857; settled in London, 1859; did much service in Lancashire cotton crisis; baronet, 1863; agent-general for New South Wales, 1897–9; K.C.M.G., 1880; G.C.M.G., 1890.

COOPER, EDWARD HERBERT (1867–1910), novelist; B.A., University College, Oxford, 1890; Paris correspondent of 'New York World'; visited and wrote on Finland, 1901; gained distinction as author of sporting novels and imaginative stories for children after manner of Lewis Carroll; chief works were 'Mr. Blake of Newmarket,' 1897, 'Wyemark and the Sea Fairies,' 1897, and 'Wyemark and the Mountain Fairies,' 1900.

COOPER, JAMES DAVIS (1823–1904), wood-engraver; apprenticed to Josiah Whymper [q. v.]; a successful wood-engraver in the 'sixties; worked with Randolph Caldecott [q. v.] on the Macmillan editions of Washington Irving's 'Old Christmas,' 1876, and 'Bracebridge Hall,' 1877; engraved illustrations for books by Darwin and Huxley, and for Stanley's 'In Darkest Africa,' 1890; skilful interpreter of landscape and groups of natives and animals.

COOPER, THOMAS SIDNEY (1803–1902), animal painter; born at Canterbury; at first a coach painter, then a scene painter; went to London, 1823, copying at British Museum; admitted to Royal Academy Schools; drawing master (1823–7) at Canterbury and elsewhere; visited Brussels 1827, where he produced lithographs and gained friendship of Verboekhoven, Belgian animal painter; found chief models in 17th-century Dutch school; settled in England, 1831; exhibited 48 pictures at British Institution, 1833–63, and 266 at Royal Academy, 1833–1902; A.R.A., 1845; R.A., 1867; best pictures include 'Drovers crossing Newbigging Muir in a Snowdrift, East Cumberland,' 1860, 'The Shepherd's Sabbath,' 1866, 'Milking Time in the Meadows' (diploma picture), 1869, and studies of bulls: 'The Monarch of the Meadows,' 1873, and 'Separated but not Divorced,' 1874; settled at 'Vernon Holme,' Canterbury, 1848; published 'My Life,' 1890; C.V.O., 1901; converted birthplace into 'Sidney Cooper Gallery of Art,' 1865, and presented it to town of Canterbury, 1882; represented in galleries in Great Britain and colonies.

COOPER, THOMPSON (1837–1904), biographer and journalist; son of Charles Henry Cooper [q. v.]; compiled 'Athenae Cantabrigienses,' vol. 1, 1858, vol. 2, 1861; F.S.A., 1860; sub-editor (1861) and parliamentary reporter (1862) of 'Daily Telegraph'; connected with 'The Times' as parliamentary reporter, 1866–86; summary writer of debates in House of Commons, 1886–98, and in House of Lords, 1898–1904; contributed 1422 articles to this Dictionary, 1885–1901, mainly on Roman Catholic divines and early Cambridge graduates; compiled 'Biographical Dictionary,' 1873, and Supplement, 1883; edited 'Men of the Time,' 1872–84; joined Church of Rome at early age.

COPELAND, RALPH (1837–1905), astronomer; went to Australia, 1853–8; studied astronomy at Göttingen, 1865–9; published 'First Göttingen Catalogue of Stars,' 1869; Ph.D., 1869; went on German Arctic expedition to explore East coast of Greenland, reaching latitude 75° 11.5′ N., 1870; F.R.A.S., 1874; observed transit of Venus at Mauritius, Dec. 1874; discovered great tree fern (*Cyathea Copelandi*) on an island of Trinidad; in charge of Lord Lindsay's observatory at Dunecht, Aberdeen, 1876; there made many cometary discoveries; observed transit of Venus at Jamaica, 1882; catalogued Lord Crawford's astronomical literature, 1890; edited 'Copernicus, a Journal of Astronomy,' 3 vols. 1891–4; astronomer royal for Scotland and professor of astronomy at Edinburgh University, 1889.

COPINGER, WALTER ARTHUR (1847–1910), professor of law, antiquary, and bibliographer; called to bar, 1869; published 'Law of Copyright in Literature and Art,' 1870; settled in Manchester as equity draughtsman and conveyancer; published works on conveyancing, 1872, 1875; professor of law in Owens College, Manchester, 1892; LL.D., Lambeth, 1889; founder and first president of Bibliographical Society, London, 1892; published 'Supplement to Hain's Repertorium Bibliographicum,' 1895–8, and 'Incunabula Biblica,' 1892; set up private press at Manchester, 1893; also published works on genealogy ('History of the Copingers,' 1882), heraldry, and manorial history, including 'History of Suffolk,' 5 vols. 1904–7, and 'Manors of Suffolk,' 7 vols. 1905–11; an angel of Catholic Apostolic Church; wrote on 'Predestination,' 1889; an accomplished musical composer.

COPPIN, GEORGE SELTH (1819–1906), actor and Australian politician; obtained some fame in English provinces as capable comedian, 1841; eloped to Sydney, 1843; built theatre at Adelaide, 1846; made fortune there, but lost it in speculation, 1851; made another theatrical fortune in Melbourne, 1852–4; toured in England, 1854; induced G. V. Brooke [q. v.] to join him in Australia; opened Theatre Royal, Melbourne, 1856 (rebuilt 1872), of which he was managing director till death; organized first grand opera season in Australia; toured with Mr. and Mrs. Charles Kean in America, 1864–5; member of legislative council of Victoria, 1858–64, 1874–89; advocated federation of colonies, intercolonial free trade, and acclimatization; first to import camels and English thrushes into Australia; founded Sorrento-on-the-Sea, where Mount Coppin is named after him.

COPPINGER, RICHARD WILLIAM (1847–1910), naval surgeon and naturalist; M.D. Dublin, 1870; surgeon of H.M.S. 'Alert' on voyage of polar exploration with (Sir) George S. Nares [q. v.], 1875, and on exploring cruise in Patagonian and Polynesian waters, 1878–82; inspector-general of hospitals and fleets, 1901–4; author of 'The Cruise of the Alert, 1878–82,' 1883.

CORBET, MATTHEW RIDLEY (1850–1902), landscape painter; exhibited at Royal Academy, 1875–1902; A.R.A., 1902; painted mainly Italian scenery, e.g. 'Morning Glory,' 1894, and 'Val d'Arno—Evening,' 1901, in Tate Gallery.

CORBETT, JOHN (1817–1901), promoter of the salt industry in Worcestershire and benefactor; studied engineering; joined father's firm of carrier of merchandise by canal boats; bought Stoke Prior salt works near Droitwich, 1852; transformed enterprise from a failure to success; in twenty-five years he raised annual output from 26,000 tons of salt to 200,000; generous to his workpeople; liberal M.P. for Droitwich, 1874–85; opposed to home rule; liberal unionist M.P. for Mid-Worcestershire, 1886–92; advocated woman's suffrage; a generous benefactor to Stourbridge, Droitwich, Birmingham University, and other Midland institutions.

CORBOULD, EDWARD HENRY (1815–1905), water-colour painter; son of Henry Corbould [q. v.]; first exhibited at Royal Academy, 1835; mainly worked in water-colours; exhibited 250 drawings at New Water Colour Society from 1837, his works including 'The Canterbury Pilgrims assembled at the Old Tabard Inn,' 1840; instructor of historical painting to the royal family, 1851–76; designed book illustrations for Waverley novels and other works; many works were popular in engravings; his 'Lady Godiva' is in National Gallery of New South Wales.

CORFIELD, WILLIAM HENRY (1843–1903), professor of hygiene and public health; B.A., Magdalen College, Oxford (first class in mathematics and physics), 1864; medical fellow of Pembroke College, 1865–75; Radcliffe travelling fellow, 1867; studied hygiene in Paris and Lyons; M.B. Oxford, 1868; M.D., 1872; F.R.C.P. London, 1875; professor of hygiene and public health at University College, London, 1869; medical officer for St. George's, Hanover Square, 1872–1900; pioneer of house sanitation; first consulting sanitary adviser to office of works, 1899; president of Epidemiological Society, 1902–3; died at Marstrand, Sweden; wrote 'Dwelling Houses: their Sanitary Construction and Arrangements,' 1880, 'Laws of Health,' 1880, and kindred works.

CORNISH, CHARLES JOHN (1858–1906), naturalist; B.A., Hertford College, Oxford, 1885; classical master at St. Paul's School from 1885 till death; contributed natural history articles to 'Spectator' and 'Country Life'; author of 'Life at the Zoo,' 1895; his 'Animal Artisans and other Studies of Birds and Beasts' (1907) has memoir by his widow.

CORNISH, FRANCIS WARRE WARRE- (1839–1916), teacher, author, and bibliophile. [See WARRE-CORNISH.]

CORNWELL, JAMES (1812–1902), writer of school books; organizer of country schools for British and Foreign School Society, 1835; principal of society's Borough Road Training College, 1846–85; from 1841 published simple and useful school books on grammar, composition, and arithmetic; his 'School Geography' (1847) passed through ninety editions.

CORRY, MONTAGU WILLIAM LOWRY, BARON ROWTON (1838–1903), politician and philanthropist; educated at Harrow and Trinity College, Cambridge; B.A., 1860; called to bar, 1863; private secretary to Disraeli, 1866–81; attended him as secretary of embassy at Congress of Berlin, 1878; C.B., 1878; created Baron Rowton, 1880; succeeded to Rowton Castle estate, 1889; acquired by will Lord Beaconsfield's correspondence and papers, 1881; trustee of Guinness Trust [artisan dwellings] Fund, 1889; resolving to provide a poor man's hotel, he built 'Rowton House,' Vauxhall, 1892; other Rowton houses erected at King's Cross (1896), Newington (1897), Hammersmith (1899), Whitechapel (1902), and Camden Town (1905); K.C.V.O., 1897; P.C., 1900.

CORY, JOHN (1828–1910), philanthropist, coal owner, and ship owner; son of Richard Cory, coal exporter of Cardiff and advocate of teetotalism; joined father's firm, 1844; established foreign coal depots, which numbered eighty at his death; acquired Pentre, Rhondda colliery, 1868; vice-chairman of Barry dock and railway company; strong advocate of teetotalism, and supporter of Salvation Army, Band of Hope Union, and Dr. Barnardo's Homes; benefactor to Cardiff institutions to amount of 50,000*l.* a year; left by will 250,000*l.* for charitable purposes; bronze statue by Sir W. Goscombe John at Cardiff.

COUCH, SIR RICHARD (1817–1905), judge; called to bar, 1841; recorder of Bedford, 1858–62; puisne judge of high court of Bombay, 1862; chief justice, 1866; knighted, 1866; chief justice at Calcutta, 1870–5; tried Gaekwar of Baroda on charge of poisoning Colonel Robert Phayre [q. v.], 1875; P.C., 1875; member of judicial committee of privy council, 1881–1901.

COUPER, SIR GEORGE EBENEZER WILSON, second baronet (1824–1908), Anglo-Indian administrator; born in Nova Scotia; joined Bengal civil service, 1846; secretary at Lucknow to chief commissioners of Oudh, 1856–7; served with distinction in siege of Lucknow, 1857; C.B., 1860; chief secretary of North-West Provinces government, 1859; succeeded to baronetcy, 1861; judicial commissioner of Oudh, 1863; as chief commissioner (1871–6) he revised land assessments; first lieutenant-governor of North-Western Province and chief commissioner of Oudh, 1877; efficiently met famine of 1877–8; encouraged Indian industrial enterprises; K.C.S.I., 1877; C.I.E., 1878; retired, 1882.

COURTHOPE, WILLIAM JOHN (1842–1917), civil servant, poet, and literary critic; B.A., New College, Oxford; Chancellor's English essay prizeman, 1868;

entered Education Office, 1869; civil service commissioner, 1887–1907; professor of poetry at Oxford, 1895–1900; C.B., 1895; completed (1881–9) standard edition of Pope's 'Works' begun by Whitwell Elwin [q. v.]; wrote 'History of English Poetry,' 1895–1910; writer of verse.

COURTNEY, LEONARD HENRY, first BARON COURTNEY, of Penwith (1832–1918), journalist and statesman; B.A., St. John's College, Cambridge (second wrangler); leader-writer to 'The Times,' 1865–81; professor of political economy, University College, London, 1872–5; liberal M.P., Liskeard, 1875; under-secretary for Home Office, 1880; secretary of Treasury, 1882–4; deputy-speaker, 1886–92; created baron, 1906; anti-imperialist and zealot for proportional representation.

COUSIN, ANNE ROSS (1824–1906), hymn writer; born CUNDELL; married William Cousin, presbyterian minister, 1847; best known by 'The sands of time are sinking,' composed in 1854, and published in her 'Immanuel's Land and other Pieces,' 1876, and by 'King Eternal! King Immortal.'

COWANS, SIR JOHN STEVEN (1862–1921), general; educated at Sandhurst; joined Rifle Brigade, 1881; passed Staff College with distinction, 1891; deputy assistant quartermaster-general in movements branch of War Office to supervise transport of troops to Egypt; major, 1898; colonel, 1903; served at Aldershot, 1903–6; in India, 1906–10; director-general of Territorial Force, 1910; quartermaster-general, 1912–19; K.C.B., 1913; lieutenant-general, 1915; proved to be administrative genius, and carried out with scarcely a hitch during four years of war (1914–18) enormous expansion in necessary army services—barrack and hospital accommodation, food supplies, motor transport, horses, clothing, general stores, and personnel; G.C.M.G., 1918; general and G.C.B., 1919; joined Roman Church shortly before his death.

COWELL, EDWARD BYLES (1826–1903), scholar and man of letters; early devoted himself to Oriental literature; studied Sanskrit, Persian, and Arabic; joined father's business of maltster at Ipswich, 1842; contributed articles to 'Westminster Review' on Oriental and Spanish literature; friend of Edward FitzGerald; went to Magdalen College, Oxford; B.A., 1854; met Tennyson, Thackeray, Jowett, Max Müller, and Horace H. Wilson [q. v.]; catalogued Oriental MSS. for Bodleian; as undergraduate he translated Oriental works, and wrote on Persian poetry; his edition of Vararuci's 'Prākṛta-Prakāśa' (1854) established his reputation as Sanskrit scholar; professor of English history in Presidency College, Calcutta, 1856–64; instituted M.A. course at Calcutta University; sent copy of MS. of Omar Khayyam to Edward FitzGerald; principal of Sanskrit College, Calcutta, 1858; edited many native works for Asiatic Society of Bengal in 'Bibliotheca Indica'; edited and translated the 'Kusumāñjali,' 1864, and other works; returned to England, 1864; first professor of Sanskrit in university of Cambridge, 1867–1903; fellow of Corpus Christi College, 1874; a founder of Cambridge Philological Society, 1868; with pupils he issued series of important Sanskrit texts and translations; continued to study Persian and Spanish; also took up archaeology, architecture, Welsh poetry, botany, and geology; awarded first gold medal of Royal Asiatic Society, 1898; hon. LL.D. Edinburgh, 1875; hon. D.C.L. Oxford, 1896; original member of British Academy, 1902.

COWIE, WILLIAM GARDEN (1831–1902), bishop of Auckland; law scholar of Trinity Hall, Cambridge; B.A., 1855; D.D. Lambeth, 1869; D.D. Oxford, 1897; ordained, 1854; chaplain to forces in India, 1857; present at Lucknow, Aliganj, and other battles; in Afghan campaign, 1863–4; bishop of Auckland, New Zealand, 1869–1902; conciliated Maoris and encouraged native ministry; primate of New Zealand, 1895; published 'Our Last Year in New Zealand,' 1888.

COWPER, FRANCIS THOMAS DE GREY, seventh EARL COWPER (1834–1905), lord-lieutenant of Ireland; nephew of William Francis Cowper, Baron Mount Temple [q. v.]; educated at Eton and Christ Church, Oxford; first class in law and history, 1855; succeeded father as Earl Cowper, 1856; pioneer of Volunteer movement; inherited baronies of Butler and Dingwall, 1871, and of Lucas, 1880, as well as vast property in Bedfordshire, Hertfordshire, Nottinghamshire, and Lancashire; did useful county work in Bedfordshire and Hertfordshire; liberal politician; created K.G., 1865; represented board of trade in House of Lords, 1871–3; appointed lord-lieutenant of Ireland under Gladstone, 1880; favoured renewal of Coercion Act, arrested Parnell, and suppressed land league, Oct. 1881; resigned office, April 1882; left Dublin two days before Phœnix Park murders; drafted new coercion bill, which was passed by his successor, 1882; lord-lieutenant of Bedfordshire; active in opposition to Gladstone's home rule bill of 1886; president of Manchester Ship Canal commission, 1885, of royal commission on working of Irish Land Acts of 1881 and 1885, 1886–7, and of London University commission, 1892.

COX, GEORGE (called SIR GEORGE) WILLIAM (1827–1902), historical writer; born at Benares; scholar of Rugby and Trinity College, Oxford; B.A. and M.A., 1859; accompanied Bishop Colenso to South Africa, 1853–4; defended theological views of Colenso, whose biography he published, 1888; wrote much on Greek, Indian, and English history; chief work, 'History of Greece' (2 vols. 1874), now superseded; won wide popularity with 'Tales from Greek Mythology,' 1861; claimed baronetcy of Cox of Dunmanway, 1877 (disallowed, 1911); rector of Scrayingham, Yorkshire, 1881–97; chosen bishop of Natal by Colenso's adherents, was refused consecration by Archbishop Benson, 1886; received civil list pension, 1896.

COZENS-HARDY, HERBERT HARDY, first BARON COZENS-HARDY, of Letheringsett (1838–1920), judge; B.A., London University; called to bar (Lincoln's Inn), 1862; practised as Chancery junior; Q.C., 1882; M.P., North Norfolk, 1885–99; raised to bench and knighted, 1899; lord justice of appeal and P.C., 1901; master of the Rolls, 1907; created baron, 1914.

CRADOCK, SIR CHRISTOPHER GEORGE FRANCIS MAURICE (1862–1914), admiral; entered navy, 1875; commanded naval brigade which led Allied forces at storming of Taku Forts, and directed relief of Tientsin Settlement, 1900; published his idealistic conception of the naval career in 'Whispers from the Fleet,' 1907; rear-admiral, 1910; K.C.V.O., 1912; appointed to command of North America and West Indies station, 1913; on outbreak of European War (1914) faced with difficult task of keeping North and South Atlantic free for British trade; received ambiguous orders from Admiralty; defeated in engagement with German squadron under Admiral von Spee off Coronel and went down on flagship, 1 November.

CRAIG, ISA (1831–1903), poetical writer. [See KNOX.]

CRAIG, WILLIAM JAMES (1843–1906), editor of Shakespeare; educated at Trinity College, Dublin; B.A., 1865; M.A., 1870; a private coach in London for army and civil service candidates, 1874–6; professor of English at University College, Aberystwith, 1876–9; resumed teaching in London, 1879–98; a devoted student of Shakespeare; edited 'The Oxford Shakespeare,' 1 vol. 1894, the 'Little Quarto Shakespeare,' 40 vols. 1901–4, and the 'Arden Shakespeare' (40 vols. by different hands), to which he contributed the volume on 'King Lear,' 1901.

CRAIGIE, PEARL MARY TERESA (1867–1906), novelist and dramatist under the pseudonym of JOHN OLIVER HOBBES; born at Chelsea, Mass., U.S.A.; eldest child of American parents who settled in London in her infancy; married (Feb. 1887) Mr. Reginald Walpole Craigie, whom she divorced (July 1895); joined Church of Rome, 1892; began serious education in early married life; published in 1891 'Some Emotions and a Moral,' a first novel of cynical flavour which was well received; maintained her success in 'The Sinner's Comedy,' 1892, 'The School for Saints,' 1897, 'The Serious Wooing,' 1901, 'Robert Orange,' 1902, and many other works of fiction; attempted drama with less acceptance in 'The Ambassador,' 1898, 'A Repentance,' 1899, 'The Wisdom of the Wise,' 1900, and some other plays which failed to attract; described in 'Imperial India,' 1903, the coronation durbar at Delhi in 1903; wrote many miscellaneous essays and sketches; her command of epigram—humorous, caustic, and cynical—gives her work its value.

CRANBROOK, first EARL OF (1814–1906), statesman. [See GATHORNE-HARDY, GATHORNE.]

CRANE, WALTER (1845–1915), artist; apprenticed to W. J. Linton [q. v.], wood engraver, 1859; illustrated several series of picture books, chiefly for children, 1863–96; first president of Art Workers' Guild, 1884; twice president of Arts and Crafts Exhibition Society; A.R.W.S., 1888; associated with William Morris in Socialist League; principal of Royal College of Art,

South Kensington, 1898; painted water-colour landscapes and works in oil.

CRAVEN, HAWES (1837–1910), scene-painter, whose full name was Henry Hawes Craven Green; apprenticed to John Gray, scene painter; worked at Olympic, Drury Lane, and Covent Garden theatres and Theatre Royal, Dublin, 1857–64; painted scenes at Lyceum for Fechter, 1863–4; at Prince of Wales's for 'Play' and 'School', 1868–9; worked for Henry Irving at Lyceum from 1878 to 1902; also for Savoy, Her Majesty's, and Garrick theatres, 1885–1905; developed scenic realism and stage illusion to fullest legitimate limits; excelled in landscape.

CRAVEN, HENRY THORNTON (1818–1905), dramatist and actor, whose real name was HENRY THORNTON; made début at Fanny Kelly's theatre, Soho, 1841; played Malcolm to Macready's Macbeth at Macready's farewell performance, Drury Lane, 20 Feb. 1851; married Eliza Nelson, 1852; acted with wife at Sydney and Melbourne, 1854–7; his dramas 'Milky White' (1864) and 'Meg's Diversion' (1866) were successful in London and provinces; made final appearance in his last play 'Too True,' 1876.

CRAWFORD, twenty-sixth EARL OF (1847–1913), astronomer, collector, and bibliophile. [See LINDSAY, JAMES LUDOVIC.]

CRAWFORD, OSWALD JOHN FREDERICK (1834–1909), author; son of John Crawford [q. v.]; educated at Eton and Merton College, Oxford; entered foreign office, 1857; consul at Oporto, 1867–91; C.M.G., 1890; published novels and sketches of Portuguese life, essays, and dramas.

CREAGH, WILLIAM (1828–1901), major-general and administrator; first of old Roman Catholic military family to become a protestant; joined 19th Bombay infantry, 1845; served in Punjab campaign 1848–9; in Mutiny, at defeat of Tantia near Jhansi, 1858, and at his capture, 1859; administered native state of Dhar, 1861–2; commanded his regiment in second Afghan war, 1878–9; made military road from Jacobabad to Dhadar (109 miles), and from Dhadar over Bolan Pass to Darwaza (63 miles); major-general, 1870.

CREMER, SIR WILLIAM RANDAL (1838–1908), peace advocate; carpenter's apprentice; mixed in trade unionism in London, 1852; promoter of Amalgamated Society of Carpenters and Joiners, 1860; secretary of British section of International Working Men's Association, 1865; friend of Mazzini and Garibaldi; as secretary of newly-formed Workmen's Peace Association from 1851 to death, he persistently advocated in America and on Continent international arbitration; awarded Nobel peace prize, 1903; secretary (1889–1908) of Interparliamentary Union; radical M.P. for Haggerston, 1885–95, and 1900–8; opposed new independent labour movement; edited 'Arbitrator,' monthly peace journal, from 1889; 'Life,' by Howard Evans, 1911.

CRIPPS, WILFRED JOSEPH (1841–1903), writer on plate; of ancient Cirencester family; B.A., Trinity College, Oxford, 1863; M.A., 1866; called to bar, 1865; published 'Old English Plate,' 1878 (9th edit. 1906), 'Old French Plate,' 1880, and kindred works; made valuable archaeological researches in Cirencester; F.S.A., 1890; C.B., 1889.

CROCKER, HENRY RADCLIFFE- (1845–1909), dermatologist. [See RADCLIFFE-CROCKER.]

CROCKETT, SAMUEL RUTHERFORD (1860–1914), novelist; M.A., Edinburgh University; studied at New College, Edinburgh, 1882–6; minister of Free Church, Penicuik, Midlothian, 1886; wrote 'The Stickit Minister' (1893), 'The Raiders' and 'The Lilac Sunbonnet' (1894); resigned ministry, 1895.

CROFT, JOHN (1833–1905), surgeon; entered St. Thomas's Hospital, 1850; M.R.C.S., 1854; F.R.C.S., 1859; on staff at St. Thomas's from 1860; surgeon, 1871–1891; early adopted Listerian methods; introduced 'Croft's splints' for leg fractures; contributed papers to medical societies' 'Transactions.'

CROFTS, ERNEST (1847–1911), historical painter; exhibited at Royal Academy, 1874–1910; A.R.A., 1878; R.A., 1896; keeper and trustee, 1898; treated historical subjects, mainly of Napoleonic and Cavalier periods; chief works include 'Marlborough after Ramillies,' 1880, 'Charles I on the way to Execution,' 1883, 'Napoleon and the Old Guard at Waterloo,' 1895, and 'The Funeral of Queen Victoria,' 1903; F.S.A., 1900.

CROKE, THOMAS WILLIAM (1824–1902), Roman Catholic archbishop of Cashel; studied for priesthood in Paris and Belgium and at Irish College of Rome; D.D., 1847; professor of ecclesiastical history at Catholic University, Dublin, under Cardinal Newman; president of St. Colman's College, Fermoy, 1858–68; friend of Cardinal Manning from 1870; catholic bishop of Auckland, New Zealand, 1870–5; archbishop of Cashel, 1875–1902; encouraged athletics and temperance; a strong nationalist and supporter of land agitation.

CROMER, first EARL OF (1841–1917), statesman, diplomatist and administrator. [See BARING, EVELYN.]

CROMPTON, HENRY (1836–1904), positivist and advocate of trade unions; son of Sir Charles Crompton [q. v.]; B.A., Trinity College, Cambridge, 1858; clerk of assize on Chester and North Wales circuit, 1858–1901; called to bar, 1863; became ardent positivist, 1859; advocate of social reform; strong supporter of trades unions; author of 'Industrial Conciliation,' 1876, and 'Our Criminal Justice,' 1905.

CROOKES, SIR WILLIAM (1832–1919), man of science; educated at Royal College of Chemistry, Hanover Square, London; assistant in the college, 1850–4; superintendent of meteorological department, Radcliffe Observatory, Oxford, 1854; lecturer in chemistry at Chester training college, 1855; lived in London from 1856 onwards; founded (1859) and for many years edited 'Chemical News'; discovered thallium, 1861; F.R.S., 1863; carried out experiments on properties of highly rarefied gases and on elements of 'rare earths'; separated uranium-X from uranium, 1900; knighted, 1897; O.M., 1910; president of various scientific societies, including the Royal Society (1913–15).

CROOKS, WILLIAM (1852–1921), labour politician; a cooper by trade; supported by 'Will Crooks's wages fund' from 1892; lectured and taught in Poplar; mayor of Poplar (first labour mayor in London), 1901; labour M.P., Woolwich, 1903–6, 1906–10, 1910–18; P.C., 1916.

CROSS, RICHARD ASSHETON, first VISCOUNT CROSS (1823–1914), statesman; educated at Rugby and Trinity College, Cambridge; called to bar (Inner Temple), 1849; joined Northern circuit; conservative M.P., Preston, 1857–62; partner in Parr's bank, Warrington; chairman, 1870; M.P., South West Lancashire, 1868; home secretary, 1874–80; introduced among others the following Acts: Licensing Act (1874), Artisans' Dwellings, Factory, Employers and Workmen, and Conspiracy and Protection of Property Acts (1875), and Factories and Workshops Act (1878); in opposition, 1880–5; home secretary, 1885–6; secretary for India, 1886–92; created viscount, 1886; privy seal, 1895–1900; retired, 1902; F.R.S.; G.C.B., 1880; G.C.S.I., 1892; close personal friend of Queen Victoria.

CROSSMAN, SIR WILLIAM (1830–1901), major-general R.E.; joined royal engineers, 1848; sent to Western Australia (1852) to superintend construction of public works by convicts; recalled to England, 1856; secretary to royal commission on defences of Canada, 1862; in Japan and China, 1866–70; joined special commission to inquire into resources of Griqualand West, 1875; C.M.G., 1877; first inspector of submarine mining defences, 1876–81; reported on Hong Kong, Singapore, and Australian defences, 1881–2, and on Jamaica and West India Islands finances, 1884; K.C.M.G., 1884; major-general, 1886; M.P. for Portsmouth, 1885–6 as liberal, and 1886–92 as liberal unionist.

CROSTHWAITE, SIR CHARLES HAUKES TODD (1835–1915), Anglo-Indian administrator; entered Indian civil service, 1857; C.S.I. and chief commissioner of Burma, 1887; K.C.S.I., 1888; lieutenant-governor of North West Provinces and Oudh, 1892–5; on Council of India, 1895–1905; wrote books on India.

CROWE, EYRE (1824–1910), artist; son of Eyre Evans Crowe [q. v.] and brother of Sir Joseph Archer Crowe [q. v.]; studied art in Paris under Paul Delaroche, 1839–44, and at Royal Academy Schools; became Thackeray's secretary, 1851; accompanied him to America, 1852–3; exhibited at Royal Academy, 1848–1904; A.R.A., 1875; chief works include 'Brick Court, Middle Temple, April 1774,' 1863, and 'The Queen of the May,' 1879; later inspector under science and art department, South Kensington; published 'With Thackeray in America,' 1893.

CRUTTWELL, CHARLES THOMAS (1847–1911), historian of Roman literature; scholar of St. John's College, Oxford; first class in classics, 1870; fellow of Merton, 1870; tutor, 1874–7; head master of Bradfield College, 1877–80, and of Malvern, 1880–5; canon of Peterborough, 1903; chief work was 'A History of Roman Literature,' 1877.

CUBITT, WILLIAM GEORGE (1835–1903), colonel Indian staff corps; born in Calcutta; joined 13th regiment

Bengal native infantry, 1853; won V.C. for bravery at Chinhut near Lucknow, 1857; served in Duffla expedition 1874–5, in Afghan war, 1880, with Akha expedition, 1883–4, and Burmese expedition, 1886–7; colonel, 1883; retired, 1892.

CULLINGWORTH, CHARLES JAMES (1841–1908), gynaecologist and obstetrician; studied at Leeds School of Medicine, 1861; M.R.C.S., 1865; lecturer on medical jurisprudence, Owens College, Manchester, 1879; professor of obstetrics and gynaecology, 1883–8; obstetric physician at St. Thomas's Hospital, 1888–1904; F.R.C.P., 1887; helped to found 'Journal of Obstetrics and Gynaecology'; hon. D.C.L. Durham, 1893; LL.D. Aberdeen, 1904; investigated causation of pelvic peritonitis; published 'Clinical Illustrations of the Diseases of the Fallopian Tubes and of Tubal Gestation,' 1895, and other books and papers.

CUMMINGS, BRUCE FREDERICK (1889–1919), diarist and biologist; generally known by pseudonym W. N. P. BARBELLION; in Natural History Museum, South Kensington, 1911–17; published extracts from his diaries, 'The Journal of a Disappointed Man,' 1919.

CUNINGHAM, JAMES McNABB (1829–1905), surgeon-general; born at Cape of Good Hope; M.D. Edinburgh University, 1851; hon. LL.D., 1892; joined Bengal medical service, 1851; sanitary commissioner for Bengal presidency, 1869–75, and for Indian empire, 1875–85; surgeon-general, 1880; C.S.I., 1885; published 'A Sanitary Primer for Indian Schools,' 1879.

CUNNINGHAM, DANIEL JOHN (1850–1909), professor of anatomy; son of John Cunningham (1819–1893, q. v.); graduated in medicine at Edinburgh, 1874; professor of anatomy at Trinity College, Dublin, 1883–1903, and Edinburgh University, 1903–9; published 'Manual of Practical Anatomy,' 2 vols. 1893–4, and other scientific works; made many anthropological researches, published by Royal Irish Academy; received hon. degrees from Dublin, St. Andrews, Glasgow, and Oxford; F.R.S., 1891.

CUNNINGHAM, WILLIAM (1849–1919), pioneer economic historian; B.A., Trinity College, Cambridge (bracketed senior in moral science tripos), 1872; vicar of Great St. Mary's, Cambridge, 1887–1908; professor of economics, King's College, London, 1891–7; fellow of Trinity, 1891; archdeacon of Ely, 1907–19; F.B.A., 1903; best-known work 'The Growth of English Industry and Commerce' (7 editions, 1882–1910).

CURRIE, SIR DONALD (1825–1909), founder of the Castle Steamship Company; joined Cunard Steamship Company, Liverpool, 1844; established branches at Havre, Paris, Bremen, and Antwerp, 1849–54; formed 'Castle' Shipping Company, Liverpool, with sailing ships between Liverpool and Calcutta, 1862; made London port of departure, 1865; formed new line of communication between England and Cape Town, 1872; his company amalgamated with Union Steamship Company, under name of Union-Castle Mail Steamship Company, 1900; instrumental in hoisting British flag at St. Lucia Bay, 1883; conveyed troops and stores to South Africa, 1899; liberal M.P. for Perthshire, 1880–5; represented West Perthshire as liberal unionist, 1886–1900; enlightened landowner in Perthshire and western islands; benefactor to University College Hospital, London, Edinburgh University, United Free Church of Scotland, and Belfast institutions; a hall founded in his memory at Cape Town University, 1910; L.K.C.M.G., 1881; G.C.M.G., 1897; hon. LL.D. Edinburgh, and freeman of Belfast, 1907; owned fine collection of Turner's works; portraits by Ouless.

CURRIE, MARY MONTGOMERIE, BARONESS CURRIE (1843–1905), authoress under the pseudonym of VIOLET FANE; married firstly Henry Sydenham Singleton, an Irish landowner, 1864; secondly, Sir Philip Henry Wodehouse (afterwards Baron) Currie [q. v.], 1894; figures as 'Mrs. Sinclair' in Mr. Mallock's 'New Republic,' 1877; published 'Denzil Place; a Story in Verse,' 1875, 'Collected Verses,' 1880, and other poetical works; 'Poems' collected in 2 vols., 1892; wrote in prose 'Edwin and Angelina Papers,' 1878, 'Collected Essays,' 1902, and novels; accompanied second husband to Constantinople, 1894, and to Rome, 1898–1903.

CURRIE, PHILIP HENRY WODEHOUSE, BARON CURRIE (1834–1906), diplomatist; joined foreign office, 1854; accompanied Lord Salisbury [q. v.] to Constantinople (1876) and Berlin (1878); C.B., 1878; K.C.B., 1885; permanent under-secretary of state for foreign affairs, 1889–93; appointed British ambassador at Constantinople, 1893; took leading part in securing protection and redress of Armenians from Sultan of Turkey, 1895; gave at embassy refuge to grand vizier Said Pasha from molestation of Sultan, 1895; helped to secure favourable terms for Greece and autonomy for Crete after Turco-Greek war, 1897; ambassador at Rome, 1898–1903; raised to peerage, 1899; retired on pension, 1903; married Mary Montgomerie Currie [q. v.].

CURZON-HOWE, SIR ASSHETON GORE (1850–1911), admiral; great-grandson of Richard, first Earl Howe [q. v.]; entered navy, 1863; accompanied and instructed royal princes on cruise in 'Bacchante', 1879–82; commander, 1882; served in Vitu expedition in East Indies, 1890; C.B., 1890; as commodore in North American station, he averted civil war in Nicaragua, 1894; C.M.G., 1896; second in command on China station, 1903; K.C.B. and vice-admiral, 1905; commander-in-chief of Mediterranean fleet, 1908; admiral and G.C.V.O., 1909; commander-in-chief at Portsmouth, 1910.

CUST, HENRY JOHN COCKAYNE (1861–1917), politician and journalist; great-grandson of first Baron Brownlow; B.A., Trinity College, Cambridge; unionist M.P., Stamford division of Lincolnshire, 1890–5, Bermondsey, 1900–6; editor of 'Pall Mall Gazette,' 1892–6; chairman of Central Committee for National Patriotic Organizations, 1914.

CUST, ROBERT NEEDHAM (1821–1909), Orientalist; grandson of first Baron Brownlow; educated at Eton; joined Indian civil service; served in Sikh war, 1845; administered Hoshiarpur and Ambala districts; reported on Punjab district after second Sikh war, 1849; called to bar, 1857; judicial commissioner of Amritsar, 1861; joined legislative council, 1864; retired from Indian service, 1867; studied Oriental languages; published over 60 volumes on Oriental philology or religion; chief were 'Modern Languages of the East Indies,' 1878, 'Linguistic and Oriental Essays,' 7 series, 1880–1904; founded Royal Asiatic Society, 1851; secretary, 1878–99; interested in missionary work; hon. LL.D. Edinburgh, 1885; attended coronations of William IV, Queen Victoria, and Edward VII; 'Memoir' published, 1899.

CUSTANCE, HENRY (1842–1908), jockey; won the Cesarewitch, 1858 and 1861; the Derby, 1860, 1866, 1874; One Thousand Guineas, 1867; St. Leger, 1866; published 'Riding Recollections and Turf Stories,' 1894.

CUTTS, EDWARD LEWES (1824–1901), antiquary; B.A., Queens' College, Cambridge, 1848; after holding curacies, he visited East to report on condition of Syrian and Chaldean churches; published many works on archaeology and ecclesiastical history, including 'Turning-Points of English Church History,' 1874, and 'History of Early Christian Art,' 1893.

DALE, SIR DAVID, first baronet (1829–1906), ironmaster; born in Bengal; in service of Stockton and Darlington Railway Company; embarked on extensive shipbuilding enterprises at Hartlepool, 1866; director of North-Eastern Railway Company, 1881; chairman of Sunderland Iron Ore Company, 1902; pioneer of arbitration in industrial disputes; served on several industrial commissions; part founder (1869) and president (1895) of Iron and Steel Institute; baronet, 1895; hon. D.C.L. Durham, 1895; memorial chair of economics founded at Armstrong College, Newcastle, 1909.

DALLINGER, WILLIAM HENRY (1842–1909), Wesleyan minister and biologist; Wesleyan minister, 1861–80; governor and president of Wesley College, Sheffield, 1880–8; made classical investigations into life history of 'flagellates' or 'monads' and into abiogenesis; improved microscopical technique; president of Royal Microscopical Society (1884–7); F.R.S., 1880; hon. D.Sc. Dublin, 1892; D.C.L. Durham, 1896; edited and rewrote Carpenter's 'The Microscope and its Revelations,' 1890.

DALZIEL, EDWARD (1817–1905), draughtsman and wood engraver; second of Brothers Dalziel; partner with brother George as engraver, publisher, and printer in London from 1839–93; painter in oils and water-colours; designed woodcut illustrations in Dalziel's 'Arabian Nights,' 1864, and 'Bible Gallery,' 1880; joint-author of 'The Brothers Dalziel,' 1901.

DALZIEL, GEORGE (1815–1902), draughtsman and wood engraver; eldest of Brothers Dalziel; founded firm of the Brothers Dalziel in London, 1839; worked much (1840–50) with Ebenezer Landells [q. v.], engraving blocks for 'Punch' and 'Illustrated London News'; issued long series of books with woodcut illustrations which superseded steel engravings; engraved works by Millais, Birket Foster, du Maurier, Sir John Tenniel, and

Harrison Weir; cut illustrations to Edward Lear's 'Book of Nonsense,' 1862, and Lewis Carroll's nursery classics; engraved all illustrations in 'Cornhill Magazine,' 1859, and in 'Good Words' from 1862; illustrated Staunton's 'Shakespeare,' 1858–61, and Goldsmith's works, 1865. When wood engraving was superseded by cheaper photomechanical processes, Dalziel chiefly engaged in illustrating papers, viz. 'Fun,' 1870–93, 'Hood's Comic Annual,' from 1871, and 'Judy,' 1872–88; wrote stories and verse; joint-author of 'The Brothers Dalziel,' 1901.

DALZIEL, THOMAS BOLTON GILCHRIST SEPTIMUS (1823–1906), draughtsman; seventh and youngest of the Brothers Dalziel; joined brothers' firm, 1860; devoted himself to drawing on wood; water-colour and charcoal artist of landscape; illustrated entirely 'Pilgrim's Progress,' 1865, and partly Dalziel's 'Arabian Nights,' 1864, and 'Bible Gallery,' 1880.

DANIEL, CHARLES HENRY OLIVE (1836–1919), scholar and printer; B.A., Worcester College, Oxford; fellow, 1863; provost, 1903–19; his private press produced books from about 1845 to 1903; these include reprints and works of contemporaries, notably of Robert Bridges; two of the most interesting productions, 'The Garland of Rachel' (1881) and 'Our Memories' (1893); revived Fell type.

DANIEL, EVAN (1837–1904), writer on the Prayerbook; vice-principal (1863) and principal (1866–94) of St. John's Training College, Battersea; B.A. Dublin, 1870; M.A., 1874; member of London school board, 1873–9; vicar of Horsham, 1894–1904; hon. canon of Rochester, 1879; wrote 'The Prayer-book, its History and Contents,' 1877 (20th edit. 1901).

DANVERS, FREDERIC CHARLES (1833–1906), writer on engineering; writer in old East India house, 1853; joined newly-formed India office, 1858; senior clerk of public works department, 1867; registrar and superintendent of records, 1884–98; wrote 'History of the Portuguese in India,' 1894, and lists of factory and marine records of the East India Company, 1897.

DARBYSHIRE, ALFRED (1839–1908), architect; apprenticed at Manchester; built Comedy Theatre, Manchester, and altered Lyceum, London, for Henry Irving, 1878; an amateur actor; played with Irving, 1865, and Helen Faucit, 1879; F.S.A., 1894; expert in heraldry; wrote 'A Chronicle of the Brasenose Club, Manchester,' 2 vols. 1892–1900, and 'Memoirs,' 1897.

DARWIN, SIR GEORGE HOWARD (1845–1912), mathematician and astronomer; son of Charles Darwin [q. v.]; educated at Clapham grammar school and Trinity College, Cambridge; B.A. (second wrangler), 1868; fellow of Trinity, 1868–78; F.R.S., 1879; Plumian professor of astronomy and experimental philosophy at Cambridge, 1883–1912; earliest scientific papers, originating with memoir (1876) 'On the Influence of Geological Changes on the Earth's Axis of Rotation,' deal solely with the earth; next series concerned with earth-moon system and the part played by 'tidal friction' in its development; later series surveys solar system; authority on many scientific subjects, including tidal theory, geodesy, and dynamical meteorology; president of British Association when it visited South Africa, and K.C.B., 1905; collected works published, 1907–11.

DAUBENEY, SIR HENRY CHARLES BARNSTON (1810–1903), general; joined 55th foot, 1829; served in Coorg campaign, 1832–4; in Chinese war, 1841–2; C.B., 1842; recommended for V.C. for conspicuous bravery at Inkermann, 1854; inspector of army clothing, 1858–69; K.C.B., 1871; G.C.B., 1884; general, 1880.

DAVENPORT-HILL, ROSAMOND (1825–1902), educational administrator. [See HILL.]

DAVEY, HORACE, LORD DAVEY (1833–1907), judge; educated at Rugby and University College, Oxford; B.A. (double first in classics and mathematics), 1856; fellow, 1854; hon. fellow, 1884; M.A., 1859; hon. D.C.L., 1894; called to bar, 1861; acquired large practice in chancery courts; Q.C., 1875; practised in Rolls courts; an unrivalled 'case' lawyer; liberal M.P. for Christchurch, 1880–5, and Stockton-on-Tees, 1888–92; solicitor-general under Gladstone, Feb.–July 1886; knighted, 1886; appointed lord justice of appeal and P.C., 1893; raised to peerage as lord of appeal in ordinary, 1894; pronounced in favour of the men in trades union appeals; largely responsible for Street Betting Act, 1906; his judgments invariably concise and lucid; interested in literature, especially modern French; chairman of royal commission to make statutes for University of London, 1898; fellow of British Academy, 1905; collaborated in work upon costs in chancery, 1865.

DAVIDSON, ANDREW BRUCE (1831-1902), Hebraist and theologian; M.A. Marischal University, Aberdeen, 1849; assistant to John Duncan (1796-1870, q. v.), 1858, whom he succeeded as professor of Hebrew and Oriental languages, New College, Edinburgh, 1863-1902; stimulating teacher; member of Old Testament revision company, 1870-84; received hon. degrees from Aberdeen, Edinburgh, Glasgow, and Cambridge; made lifelong research into language, historical exegesis, and theology of Old Testament; published works on Hebrew grammar (1874) and syntax (1894), commentaries on 'Job,' 1884, 'Ezekiel,' 1892, 'Nahum, Habakkuk, Zephaniah,' 1902, in 'Cambridge Bible,' 'Biblical and Literary Essays,' 1902, and sermons.

DAVIDSON, CHARLES (1824-1902), water-colour painter; member of New (1849-53) and Old (1858) Water Colour Societies, where he exhibited over 800 works, mainly typical English landscapes.

DAVIDSON, JAMES LEIGH STRACHAN- (1843-1916), classical scholar. [See STRACHAN-DAVIDSON.]

DAVIDSON, JOHN (1857-1909), poet; schoolmaster in Scotland from 1872 to 1889; published 'Scaramouch in Naxos,' 1889, and other plays before settling in London, 1889; published 'Perfervid,' a novel, 1890, 'Fleet Street Eclogues,' 1893, which proved his genuine poetic gift, 'Ballads and Songs,' 1894, his most popular work, 'Fleet Street Eclogues,' 2nd ser. 1896, and 'New Ballads,' 1897; abandoned lyric for drama, writing original plays and translating foreign ones; finally (1901-8) wrote series of 'Testaments' expounding a materialistic and aristocratic philosophy; awarded civil list pension, 1906; committed suicide by drowning at Penzance.

DAVIDSON, JOHN THAIN (1833-1904), presbyterian minister; minister at Salford, 1859-62, and Islington, 1862-91; inaugurated in 1868, and continued till 1891, Sunday afternoon services for non-churchgoing people at Agricultural Hall; moderator of synod of presbyterian Church of England, 1872; a powerful preacher; published several volumes of addresses.

DAVIES, CHARLES MAURICE (1828-1910), author; M.A. Durham University, 1852; D.D., 1864; fellow, 1849; published novels attacking high church practices; articles in 'Daily Telegraph' republished as 'Unorthodox London,' 1873, 'Orthodox London,' 2 vols. 1874-5, and 'Mystic London,' 1875.

DAVIES, JOHN LLEWELLYN (1826-1916), theologian; B.A., Trinity College, Cambridge (bracketed fifth in classical tripos), 1848; fellow of Trinity, 1850; ordained, 1851; influenced by F. D. Maurice [q.v.]; rector of Christ Church, Marylebone, 1856-89; vicar of Kirkby Lonsdale, Westmorland, 1889-1909; promoter of movements for education of women and working men; liberal in politics; broad churchman; helped to found National Church Reform Union, 1870; noted preacher; author of numerous theological works.

DAVIES, ROBERT (1816-1905), philanthropist; was put by father in charge of foundry at Carnarvon; with brothers founded successful shipowning firm at Menai Bridge; made large anonymous benefactions to Calvinistic methodist chapels, to Welsh Methodist Mission in India, and other institutions; his younger brother RICHARD (1818-96) was liberal M.P. for Anglesey, 1868-86.

DAVIES, (SARAH) EMILY (1830-1921), promoter of women's education; sister of John Llewellyn Davies [q.v.]; with others organized college for women opened at Hitchin, 1869, and transferred to Cambridge (Girton College), 1873; honorary secretary, 1867-1904; mistress, 1873-5; pioneer in women's suffrage movement.

DAVIS, CHARLES EDWARD (1827-1902), architect and antiquary; son of a Bath architect; Bath city architect and surveyor, 1863-1902; discovered thermal baths (1869), well (1887-8), Great bath (1880-1), and Circular bath (1884-6), all Roman; his reconstruction of the Queen's bath (1886-9) evoked much criticism; had extensive private practice; F.S.A., 1850; published 'Mineral Baths of Bath,' 1883.

DAVITT, MICHAEL (1846-1906), Irish revolutionary and labour agitator; of Roman Catholic peasant stock; joined Fenians, 1865; organizing secretary of Irish Republican Brotherhood, 1868; sentenced to fifteen years' penal servitude for treason-felony, 1870; released, 1877; met Henry George in America, 1878; introduced land agitation into Irish movement, and founded 'Land League of Ireland,' 1879; arrested, tried, convicted, and released, 1880; organized American Land League and Ladies' Land League, 1880; imprisoned at Portland,

1881-2; elected M.P. for co. Meath while a prisoner, February 1882; induced Parnell to found National League after suppression of Land League, June 1882; imprisoned for sedition, January–May 1883; with Henry George advocated land nationalization, 1882-5; prominent as a respondent in Parnell commission which examined charges, brought by 'The Times,' that he intended to bring about by violence complete independence of Ireland; made five days' speech (Oct. 24-31, 1889), published as 'The Defence of the Land League,' 1891; edited 'The Labour World,' organ of British labour movement (1890-1); anti-Parnellite M.P. for North Meath, 1892, and for South Mayo, 1895-9; helped to found United Irish League, 1898; attacked Wyndham's Land Purchase Act, 1903; visited Russia to show sympathy with revolutionary party, 1903-5; stood for reconciliation of extreme with constitutional nationalism, and of democracy with nationality; a collectivist and secularist; 'Davitt Memorial Church' erected at Straide; author of 'Leaves from a Prison Diary,' 1884, and 'The Fall of Feudalism in Ireland,' 1904; 'Life' by F. Sheehy Skeffington, 1908.

DAWSON, GEORGE MERCER (1849-1901), geologist; son of Sir John William Dawson [q. v.]; born in Nova Scotia; as geologist and botanist to Canadian-American boundary commission formed large natural history collection, 1873-5; appointed to Canadian geological survey; made scientific researches in North-West and British Columbia; director of survey, 1895; C.M.G. and F.R.S., 1891; president of Royal Society of Canada, 1894; collaborated in 'Comparative Vocabularies of the Indian Tribes of British Columbia,' 1884.

DAWSON, JOHN (1827-1903), trainer of racehorses; brother of Matthew Dawson [q. v.]; settled at Newmarket, 1861; trainer to Prince Batthyany, Sir Robert Jardine [q. v.], and others; trained winners of Cesarewitch (1878), Derby (1875), St. Leger (1876), Two Thousand Guineas (1876 and 1898); trained for a time King Edward VII's Perdita II.

DAY, SIR JOHN CHARLES FREDERIC SIGISMUND (1826-1908), judge; of Roman Catholic parentage; called to bar, 1849; Q.C., 1872; treasurer of Middle Temple, 1896; as editor of Roscoe's 'Evidence at Nisi Prius' and of the Common Law Procedure Act of 1852, became authority on new methods of pleading and practice; successful in breach of promise and libel cases; judge of Queen's Bench division, 1882-1901; knighted, 1882; stern criminal judge; chairman of royal commission to inquire into Belfast riots, 1886, and member of Parnell commission, 1888; P.C., 1901; discriminating art collector.

DAY, LEWIS FOREMAN (1845-1910), decorative artist; considerably influenced contemporary ornament; lecturer at Royal Society of Arts and Royal College of Art, South Kensington; art examiner and adviser to board of education from 1890; works include 'Windows,' 1897, 'Lettering in Ornament,' 1902, 'Nature and Ornament,' 2 vols. 1908-9.

DAY, WILLIAM (HENRY) (1823-1908), trainer and breeder of racehorses; first successful as jockey; trained winners of Two Thousand Guineas (1855 and 1859), Brigantine (winner of Oaks and Ascot Cup, 1869), and Foxhall (winner of Grand Prix, Cesarewitch, and Cambridgeshire, 1881, and Ascot Cup, 1882); formed breeding stud at Alvediston near Salisbury, 1873; lost fortune by land speculation; published 'The Racehorse in Training,' 1880, and 'Reminiscences,' 1886.

DEACON, GEORGE FREDERICK (1843-1909), civil engineer; assisted Cromwell Varley [q. v.] in laying second Atlantic cable, 1865; consulting engineer at Liverpool (1865-71); as borough engineer (1871-80) laid inner circle tramway rails (1877) and introduced wood paving there; as water engineer (1871-90) invented and introduced Deacon waste water meter, 1873; designed masonry dam in Vyrnwy valley, to supply water for Liverpool by means of aqueduct 76 miles long; water works opened, 1892; work carried out on scientific and aesthetic lines; constructed waterworks for Merthyr Tydfil and other towns from 1890; reported on London water supply, 1897; hon. LL.D. Glasgow, 1902.

DEAKIN, ALFRED (1856-1919), Australian politician; born at Melbourne; admitted to Victorian bar, 1877; liberal M.P., West Bourke, 1879, but resigned immediately; re-elected, 1880; minister of water supply and commissioner of public works in Berry-Service coalition, 1883; also solicitor-general, 1883; chief secretary and minister of water supply in coalition with Duncan Gillies [q. v.], 1886-90; visited England as representative of Victoria at colonial conference, 1887; promoted federation movement in Victoria, 1891-8; played important part in discussions of Constitution Bill in London, 1900; attorney-general in first Commonwealth ministry, 1901; prime minister, 1903-4, 1905-8, and 1909-10.

DEANE, SIR JAMES PARKER (1812-1902), judge; educated at Winchester and St. John's College, Oxford; B.C.L., 1834; D.C.L., 1839; called to bar (Inner Temple), 1841; Q.C., 1858; treasurer, 1878; obtained large practice in probate and divorce and ecclesiastical courts; vicar-general of province of Canterbury, 1872; legal adviser to foreign office, 1872-86; P.C. and knighted, 1885.

DE BURGH CANNING, HUBERT GEORGE, second MARQUESS and fifteenth EARL OF CLANRICARDE (1832-1916), Irish landed proprietor. [See BURGH CANNING.]

DE LA RAMÉE, MARIE LOUISE (1839-1908), novelist under the pseudonym of OUIDA; introduced to W. Harrison Ainsworth [q. v.], 1859, who published in 'Bentley's Miscellany' seventeen short tales by her, 1859-60; her forty-five novels, which chiefly deal with military and fashionable life, include 'Under Two Flags,' 1867, 'Puck,' 1870, 'Two Little Wooden Shoes,' 1874, 'Moths,' 1880, and 'Bimbi, Stories for Children,' 1882; many were translated into foreign languages and successfully dramatized. Ouida settled permanently in Florence, 1874, where she entertained expensively; lived from 1894 in poverty at Sant' Alessio; was awarded civil list pension, 1904; died at Viareggio. Cynical, artificial in manner, and quick at repartee, she always wrote sympathetically of Italian peasants and dogs; in her latest works, 'Views and Opinions,' 1895, and 'Critical Studies,' 1905, she opposed militarism, women's suffrage, and vivisection.

DE LA RUE, SIR THOMAS ANDROS, first baronet (1849-1911), printer; son of Warren De la Rue [q. v.]; joined father's firm, c. 1871; as head (1889-96) increased firm's reputation for artistic production of English and foreign postage stamps; baronet, 1898.

DE MONTMORENCY, RAYMOND HARVEY, third VISCOUNT FRANKFORT DE MONTMORENCY (1835-1902), major-general; joined army, 1854; served in Crimea; recommended for V.C.; in Indian Mutiny, 1857-8; in Abyssinian expedition, 1867; commanded frontier force in Sudan, 1886-7; directed British field column during operations on Nile, 1887; major-general, 1889; succeeded to peerage, 1889.

DE MORGAN, WILLIAM FREND (1839-1917), artist, inventor, and author; son of Augustus De Morgan [q. v.]; educated at University College School and University College, London; entered Academy Schools, 1859; early made acquaintance of pre-Raphaelite circle; experimented in manufacture of stained glass and tiles; established pottery industry in Chelsea, 1871; rediscovered process of making coloured lustres; joined William Morris at Merton Abbey, 1882-8; erected factory at Fulham, 1888; retired, 1905, and firm dissolved, 1907; wintered in Florence, 1890-1914; ware employed for decorative panels in steamships, &c.; published novels in later life: 'Joseph Vance' (1906), 'Alice-for-Short' (1907), 'Somehow Good' (1908), 'It Never Can Happen Again' (1909), 'An Affair of Dishonour' (1910), 'A Likely Story' (1911), 'When Ghost Meets Ghost' (1914); two unfinished stories published posthumously.

DENNEY, JAMES (1856-1917), theologian; M.A., Glasgow; studied theology at Glasgow Free Church college; professor of systematic and pastoral theology at the college, 1897; professor of New Testament language, literature, and theology, 1899; principal, 1915-17; noted expository preacher; worked for reunion of Free Church with Established Church of Scotland; best known for writings on doctrines of the person and work of Christ.

DERBY, sixteenth EARL OF (1841-1908), governor-general of Canada. [See STANLEY, FREDERICK ARTHUR.]

DE SAULLES, GEORGE WILLIAM (1862-1903), medallist; worked for Joseph Moore [q. v.], medallist; engraver to the Royal Mint, 1893; designed Edward VII coronation (1902), South Africa (1899-1902), and Ashanti (1900) medals; executed dies for new Queen Victoria coins, 1893; designed English coins after Edward VII's accession, 1902; exhibited at Royal Academy, 1898-1903.

DES VŒUX, SIR (GEORGE) WILLIAM (1834-1909), colonial governor; born at Baden of Huguenot descent; educated at Charterhouse and Balliol College, Oxford; went to Toronto, 1856; practised at bar; became stipendiary magistrate in British Guiana where he cham-

pioned natives, 1863; as administrator of St. Lucia (1869-78) reorganized and codified old French system of law; governor of Fiji, 1880-5, Newfoundland, 1886, and Hong Kong, 1887-91; G.C.M.G., 1893; published 'My Colonial Service,' 1903.

DETMOLD, CHARLES MAURICE (1883-1908), animal painter, and etcher; influenced by Japanese art; with twin brother Edward Julius produced portfolio of etchings of birds and animals of remarkable technical ability, 1898; illustrated Rudyard Kipling's 'Jungle Book,' 1903; committed suicide.

DE VERE, AUBREY THOMAS (1814-1902), poet and author; son of Sir Aubrey de Vere, second baronet [q. v.]; educated at Trinity College, Dublin; came early under Wordsworth's influence; was intimate with Sir Henry Taylor, Tennyson, Robert Browning, and R. H. Hutton; visited Rome, 1839; travelled in Italy, 1843-4; published 'The Waldenses and other Poems,' 1842, and 'English Misrule and Irish Misdeeds,' 1848, in which he showed Irish sympathies and criticized English methods; joined Roman Church, 1851; nominal professor of political and social science in new Dublin Catholic University, 1854; interested in Irish legend and history; voluminous works include 'The Legends of St. Patrick,' 1872, 'Critical Essays,' 3 vols., 1887-9, 'Recollections,' 1897, and dramas; 'Memoir' by Wilfrid Ward, 1904.

DE VERE, SIR STEPHEN EDWARD, fourth baronet (1812-1904), translator of Horace; brother of Aubrey Thomas de Vere [q. v.]; called to Irish bar, 1836; entered Roman communion, 1848; liberal M.P. for Limerick, 1854-9; published 'Translations from Horace,' 1886.

DE VILLIERS, JOHN HENRY, first BARON DE VILLIERS (1842-1914), South African judge; born in Cape Colony; called to bar (Inner Temple), 1865; began practice at Cape bar, 1866; member of house of assembly, Worcester, Cape Colony, 1867; attorney-general, 1872; chief justice, 1873; worked for South African federation; knighted, 1877; member of royal commission which drew up Pretoria convention, 1881; K.C.M.G., 1882; P.C., 1897; first colonial judge on judicial committee of Privy Council; president of national convention, 1908; created baron, 1910; first chief justice of South African Union.

DEVONSHIRE, eighth DUKE OF (1833-1908), statesman. [See CAVENDISH, SPENCER COMPTON.]

DE WINTON, SIR FRANCIS WALTER (1835-1901), major-general and South African administrator; served in Crimea, 1854; military attaché at Constantinople, 1878-83; K.C.M.G., 1884; G.C.M.G., 1893; administrator-general of Congo, 1885-6; suppressed rebellion of Yonnies on West African coast, 1887; C.B., 1888; as commissioner to Swaziland deemed British protectorate impracticable, 1889; major-general, 1890; controller of household of George, Duke of York, 1892; hon. LL.D. Cambridge, 1892.

DE WORMS, HENRY, BARON PIRBRIGHT (1840-1903), politician; close friend of Count von Beust, Austrian statesman, who introduced him to Disraeli, 1867; conservative M.P. for Greenwich, 1880-5, and for Toxteth, 1885-95; parliamentary secretary to board of trade, 1885-6, 1886-8; under-secretary for colonies, 1888-92; first Jewish P.C., 1888; president of international conference in London on sugar bounties, 1887; raised to peerage, 1895; president of Anglo-Jewish Association, 1872-86; F.R.S.; wrote scientific and political works.

DIBBS, SIR GEORGE RICHARD (1834-1904), premier of New South Wales; born in Sydney; joined there father-in-law's sugar refining business, 1857; formed shipping business, 1859; member of legislative assembly of New South Wales, 1874; treasurer and colonial secretary, 1883-5; premier, Oct.-Dec. 1885; colonial secretary, 1886-7; premier and colonial secretary, Jan.-March 1889 and 1891-4; became protectionist; K.C.M.G., 1892; managing director of New South Wales Savings Banks, 1897-1904.

DICEY, EDWARD JAMES STEPHEN (1832-1911), author and journalist; B.A., Trinity College, Cambridge, 1854; president of Union; leader-writer for 'Daily Telegraph,' 1861; wrote accounts of visits to America (1862), Russia, Holy Land, and Egypt (1867-70); editor of 'Observer,' 1870-89; keenly interested in affairs of Eastern Europe, Egypt, and South Africa; called to bar (Gray's Inn), 1875; treasurer, 1903-4; C.B., 1886; influenced public opinion by his knowledge, humour, judgement, and vivid style; author of works on Egypt and Bulgaria.

DICKINSON, HERCULES HENRY (1827–1905), dean of the Chapel Royal, Dublin, from 1868; M.A., Trinity College, Dublin, 1849; D.D., 1866; vicar of St. Ann's, Dublin, 1855–1902; professor of pastoral theology, Dublin University, 1894; member of royal commission for licensing reform, 1896–9; helped to found Alexandra College for Women, Dublin, 1866; warden, 1866–1902; wrote theological works.

DICKINSON, LOWES (CATO) (1819–1908), portrait painter; visited Italy and Sicily, 1850–3; friend of pre-Raphaelites; met F. D. Maurice (1854), and with Kingsley and Hughes formed Christian socialist movement; helped to found in 1854 Working Men's College, where he taught drawing; exhibited at Royal Academy (1848–91) portraits of Queen Victoria, King Edward VII, Lord Kelvin, Cobden, Grote, Gladstone, Bright, and General Gordon; memorial art studentship founded at Working Men's College, 1909.

DICKSON, SIR COLLINGWOOD (1817–1904), general; born at Valenciennes; son of Sir Alexander Dickson [q. v.]; joined royal artillery, 1835; served in Spain, 1837–40; instructed Turkish artillery at Constantinople, 1841–5; received V.C. (1855) for bravery at Sevastopol, 1854; distinguished in battle of Inkermann, 1855; in Ireland, 1856–62; C.B., 1865; served on fortifications committee, 1868–9; inspector-general of artillery, 1870–5; K.C.B., 1871; general, 1877; president of ordnance committee, 1881–5; G.C.B., 1885; accomplished linguist.

DICKSON, WILLIAM PURDIE (1823–1901), professor of divinity and translator; studied at St. Andrews (1837–44) for presbyterian ministry; D.D., 1864; professor of biblical criticism, Glasgow University, 1863–73; professor of divinity, 1873–95; hon. LL.D. Edinburgh, 1885; translated Mommsen's 'History of Rome,' 4 vols. 1862–7, and 'Roman Provinces,' 1887.

DIGBY, WILLIAM (1849–1904), Anglo-Indian publicist; prepared six volumes of Ceylon 'Hansard,' 1871–6; edited 'Madras Times,' 1877–9; urged Lord Mayor of London's Southern Indian famine relief fund, 1877; C.I.E., 1878; edited 'Western Daily Mercury,' 1880–2; secretary of National Liberal Club, 1882–7; advocate of self-government in India; works include 'Prosperous British India,' 1901.

DILKE, SIR CHARLES WENTWORTH, second baronet (1843–1911), politician and author; son of first baronet [q. v.]; scholar of Trinity Hall, Cambridge; senior legalist, LL.B., 1866; LL.M., 1869; twice president of Union; enthusiastic oarsman; called to bar, 1866; toured round world with William Hepworth Dixon [q. v.], 1866–7, publishing his experience in 'Greater Britain,' 1868, the title being his own invention; radical M.P. for Chelsea, 1868–86; opposed Mr. Forster's education bill; expressed strong republican views in the country and in parliament; succeeded to baronetcy and proprietorship of 'Athenæum' and of 'Notes and Queries,' 1869; married his first wife, 1872; frequently visited Paris; friend of Gambetta and republican leaders; published anonymously a satirical brochure, 'The Fall of Prince Florestan of Monaco,' 1874; made second tour round world, 1875; prominent in parliament, 1874–80; seconded resolution for extension of county franchise to agricultural labourers, 1879; attacked conservative government's South African policy; leader of radical section of Gladstone's government, 1880; under-secretary to the foreign office, 1880–2; chairman of royal commission for negotiating commercial treaty with France, 1881–2; became friend of Prince of Wales (Edward VII); entered cabinet as president of local government board, 1882–5; chairman of royal commission on housing of working classes, 1884; conducted redistribution bill through House of Commons; jointly responsible for sending Gordon to the Sudan, 1884; opposed to Gladstone's Irish policy, 1885; co-respondent in divorce suit, Crawford v. Crawford and Dilke, 1885–6; was rejected by electors of Chelsea, 1886; was largely ostracized from public life owing to divorce court proceedings; married his second wife, Emilia Francis (see below), widow of Mark Pattison, 1885; pursued close study of English and imperial problems, publishing 'Problems of Greater Britain,' 2 vols. 1890; visited Greece and Constantinople, 1887–8, and India, 1888–9; M.P. for Forest of Dean, 1892–1911; spoke in parliament mainly on industrial, foreign, and imperial affairs; made art and literary bequests to the National Portrait Gallery and other institutions; portrait by G. F. Watts.

DILKE, EMILIA FRANCIS STRONG, LADY DILKE (1840–1904), historian of French art; after private education at Oxford, studied art at South Kensington, 1859–61; married her first husband, Mark Pattison [q. v.], rector of Lincoln College, Oxford, September 1861; published 'Renaissance of Art in France,' 1879, and embodied subsequent researches in 'Art in the Modern State,' 1888, and in volumes on French painters (1889), architects and sculptors (1900), and engravers and draughtsmen, all of the 18th century. At the same time she wrote stories of mystical temper and actively promoted improvement in the social and industrial condition of working women, joining the Women's Trades Union League and attending the Trades Union Congresses, 1884–1904. After Pattison's death in 1884 she married on 3 Oct. 1885 Sir Charles Wentworth Dilke (see above), an early friend, and thenceforth identified herself with his fortunes.

DILLON, FRANK (1823–1909), landscape painter; exhibited at Royal Academy, 1850–1907; joined Royal Institute of Painters in Water Colours, 1866; frequently visited Egypt from 1854, painting many Egyptian scenes; also studied Japanese art; friend of Mazzini and Hungarian revolutionaries.

DIMOCK, NATHANIEL (1825–1909), theologian; B.A., St. John's College, Oxford, 1847; M.A., 1850; held livings in Kent, 1848–87; wrote much on church doctrine with profound erudition from evangelical point of view; influential member of Bishop Creighton's 'Round Table Conference' on Holy Communion doctrine and ritual, 1900; voluminous works include 'The Doctrine of the Sacraments,' 1871, 'Curiosities of Patristic and Medieval Literature,' 3 pts., 1891–5; memorial edition of works published, 1910–11.

DIXIE, LADY FLORENCE CAROLINE (1857–1905), authoress and traveller; married Sir Alexander Beaumont Churchill Dixie, eleventh baronet, 1875; hunted big game in Africa, Arabia, and Rocky Mountains; explored Patagonia, 1878–9; correspondent for 'Morning Post' in Zulu war, 1879; denounced Irish Land League agitation, 1880–3; alleged without proof that she was a victim of Fenian outrage near Windsor, 1883; advocated complete sex equality; chief works were 'Across Patagonia,' 1880, and 'Songs of a Child,' 1902–3.

DOBELL, BERTRAM (1842–1914), bookseller and man of letters; befriended James Thomson [q. v.], and arranged independent publication of 'City of Dreadful Night,' 1880; his great achievement recovery of poetical works of Thomas Traherne (1903), followed by prose 'Centuries of Meditations' (1908).

DOBSON, (HENRY) AUSTIN (1840–1921), poet and man of letters; entered Board of Trade, 1856; principal clerk in marine department, 1884–1901; verse includes 'Vignettes in Rhyme' (1873), 'Proverbs in Porcelain' (1877), and 'At the Sign of the Lyre' (1885); prose works include Lives of Hogarth (1879), Fielding (1883), Steele (1886), Goldsmith (1888), Horace Walpole (1890), Samuel Richardson (1902), Fanny Burney (1903), and 'Thomas Bewick and his Pupils' (1884).

DODS, MARCUS (1834–1909), presbyterian divine and biblical scholar; son of Marcus Dods [q. v.]; M.A. Edinburgh University, 1854; hon. D.D., 1891; minister of Renfield Free church, Glasgow, 1864–89; a published sermon (1877) questioning verbal inspiration caused much discussion; professor of New Testament criticism in New College, Edinburgh, 1889; libelled for his views on inspiration at general assembly, 1890; principal of New College, 1907–9; works include commentaries on Genesis (1888) and 1 Corinthians (1889), 'The Bible, its Nature and Origin' (Bross lectures, 1905); 'Letters,' edited by son, 2 vols. 1910–11.

DOHERTY, HUGH LAWRENCE (1875–1919), lawn-tennis player; made name at lawn-tennis as Cambridge undergraduate; winner of All England singles championship at Wimbledon, 1902–6; with his brother, R. F. Doherty, doubles champion eight times between 1897 and 1905; American national champion, 1903.

DOLLING, ROBERT WILLIAM RADCLYFFE [FATHER DOLLING] (1851–1902), divine and social reformer; educated at Trinity College, Cambridge; did social work in Dublin, 1870–8; intimate with 'Father' Stanton [q. v.] and Alexander Mackonochie [q. v.]: warden of St. Martin's Postman's League in South London, 1879–82; vicar of St. Agatha's, Landport, 1885–95; resigned owing to disputes with bishop on questions of ritual; wrote 'Ten Years in a Portsmouth Slum,' 1896; as vicar of St. Saviour's, Poplar (1898–1901), he influenced social and municipal affairs; unconventional preacher; 'Life,' by Charles E. Osborne, 1903.

DONALDSON, SIR JAMES (1831–1915), educationist,

classical and patristic scholar; M.A., Aberdeen; rector of Edinburgh High School, 1866–81; professor of humanity, Aberdeen University, 1881; principal and vice-chancellor of St. Andrews University, 1889; knighted, 1907; author of patristic works; helped to establish compulsory primary education in Scotland.

DONKIN, BRYAN (1835–1902), civil engineer; grandson of Bryan Donkin [q. v.]; studied engineering in Paris; apprentice (1856) and partner (1868) in grandfather's engineering works; pursued valuable researches into design and construction of heat engines and steam boilers; perfected glass 'revealer' for showing condensation effects in the cylinder; made inquiry into motive power from blast furnace gases; wrote 'A Text-Book on Gas, Oil and Air Engines,' 1894.

DONNELLY, SIR JOHN FRETCHVILLE DYKES (1834–1902), major-general royal engineers; born at Bombay; joined royal engineers, 1853; served in battle of Inkermann and in trenches before Sevastopol, 1854; conspicuous in assault on the Redan, June 1855; recommended for V.C.; retired with hon. rank of major-general, 1887; assisted Sir Henry Cole [q. v.] in reorganizing science and art department at South Kensington, 1858; inspector for science, 1859; arranged for payment of teachers by results of examinations of pupils, 1859; became 'Director of Science,' 1874; supervised science schools and institutions throughout country; secretary and permanent head of science and art department, 1884; retired, 1889; C.B., 1886, K.C.B., 1893; exhibited watercolour sketches and etchings at Royal Academy (1888–1901); published military pamphlets.

DONNET, SIR JAMES JOHN LOUIS (1816–1905), inspector-general of hospitals and fleets from 1875; born at Gibraltar; M.D. St. Andrews, 1857; entered navy, 1840; at capture of Acre; surgeon in Arctic expedition with Sir Erasmus Ommanney [q. v.], 1850–1; in Pacific, 1854; K.C.B., 1897.

DOUGHTY-WYLIE, CHARLES HOTHAM MONTAGU (1868–1915), soldier and consul; joined army, 1889; served in India, Egypt, South Africa, and China; military consul for Konia province of Asia Minor, and later Cilicia, 1906; saved Christian communities at Adana, 1909; C.M.G. and consul-general at Adis Ababa, Abyssinia, 1909; C.B., 1912; on staff of Gallipoli expedition, 1915; killed while leading brilliant charge on 'Hill 141'; posthumous V.C.

DOUGLAS, SIR ADYE (1815–1906), premier of Tasmania; emigrated to Tasmania, and admitted to bar, 1839; five times mayor of Launceston; elected to legislative council, 1855; opposed transportation; urged claims of Tasmania to responsible government; premier and chief secretary, 1884–6; first agent-general for colony, 1886–7; chief secretary, 1892–4; president of legislative council, 1894–1904; knighted, 1902.

DOUGLAS, SIR CHARLES WHITTINGHAM HORSLEY (1850–1914), general; joined army, 1869; served in South African War, 1899–1901; adjutant-general, War Office, 1904–9; K.C.B., 1907; general, 1910; G.C.B., 1911; inspector-general, home forces, 1912; chief of Imperial General Staff, 1914.

DOUGLAS, GEORGE (pseudonym) (1869–1902), novelist. [See BROWN, GEORGE DOUGLAS.]

DOUGLAS, GEORGE CUNNINGHAME MONTEATH (1826–1904), hebraist; B.A. Glasgow University, 1843; D.D., 1867; joined Free Church at disruption; professor of Hebrew at Glasgow theological college, 1857–1902; member of Glasgow school board; member of Old Testament revision company, 1870–84; wrote on conservative lines 'The Old Testament and its Critics,' 1902.

DOUGLAS-PENNANT, GEORGE SHOLTO GORDON, second BARON PENRHYN (1836–1907), landowner; conservative M.P. for Carnarvonshire, 1866–8, 1874–80; succeeded to peerage and Penrhyn estate and Bethesda slate quarries, 1886; championed free labour and refused to recognize trades union officials in strikes at his quarries, which he closed down, 1897 and 1900; succeeded in libel action against 'Clarion,' the socialist newspaper, 1903; ardent sportsman; won Goodwood Cup (1898) and Ascot Gold Vase (1894); a strong tory and churchman; founded North Wales Property Defence Association.

DOWDEN, EDWARD (1842–1913), critic; brother of John Dowden [q. v.]; B.A., Trinity College, Dublin; professor of English literature, Trinity College, 1867; works include 'Shakspere, His Mind and Art' (1875), 'Shakspere Primer' (1877), and 'Life of Shelley' (1886).

DOWDEN, JOHN (1840–1910), bishop of Edinburgh; son of staunch presbyterian; B.A., Trinity College,

Dublin, 1861; D.D.,1876; Pantonian professor of theology at Glenalmond, 1874–80; principal of theological hall of Scottish Episcopal Church, 1880–6, and canon of St. Mary's Cathedral, Edinburgh, 1880; bishop of Edinburgh, 1886–1910; hon. LL.D. Edinburgh, 1904; founded Scottish Historical Society (1886), editing several of its publications; Rhind lecturer before Society of Antiquaries of Scotland, 1901; published 'The Celtic Church in Scotland,' 1894, 'The Workmanship of the Prayer Book,' 1899, 'The Medieval Church in Scotland,' 1910, sermons and pamphlets.

DOWIE, JOHN ALEXANDER (1847–1907), religious fanatic; born in Edinburgh; emigrated to Adelaide, 1860; congregational minister near Adelaide, 1871; prominent in Sydney religious, social, and political life; built tabernacle for 'divine healing' at Melbourne, Victoria, 1882; removed to Chicago, 1890; opened Zion's tabernacle there, 1893; proprietor and overseer of Zion City on Lake Michigan, 1900; announced himself as 'Elijah the Restorer'; enjoyed for a time wide notoriety and published organ 'Leaves of Healing'; visited England (1903 and 1904) with little success; deposed by officers of his church, 1906; unsuccessful in lawsuit for restitution of church funds and property; died at Illinois.

DOYLE, JOHN ANDREW (1844–1907), historian; inherited property from grandfather, Sir John Easthope [q. v.]; educated at Eton and Balliol College, Oxford; B.A., 1867; fellow of All Souls, 1867–1907; took active part in local affairs in Breconshire; advocated rifle shooting at the universities; authority on dog and race-horse breeding; closely studied American history; published 'Summary History of America,' 1875, 'The English in America,' 1882, 'The Puritan Colonies,' 2 vols. 1887, 'The Middle Colonies,' 1907, 'The Colonies under the House of Hanover,' 1907, and 'Essays on Various Subjects' (posthumous), 1911.

DREDGE, JAMES (1840–1906), civil engineer and journalist; joint editor and proprietor of 'Engineering' from 1879 till death; British commissioner at many international exhibitions, including Chicago (1893) and Brussels (1897); C.M.G., 1898; published 'Modern Examples of Road and Railway Bridges,' 1872, and 'Electric Illumination,' 2 vols. 1882.

DRESCHFELD, JULIUS (1846–1907), physician and pathologist; born in Bavaria of Jewish parents; educated at Owens College, Manchester, and Manchester Royal School of Medicine; M.D. Würzburg, 1864; army surgeon in Bavarian army, 1864; settled in Manchester, 1869; on staff of Manchester Royal Infirmary, 1873–1907; F.R.C.P., 1883; Bradshawe lecturer, 1887; professor of pathology (1881–91) and of medicine (1891–1907) at Victoria University, Manchester; almost forestalled Pasteur in researches on hydrophobia, 1882–3; an expert neurologist; published numerous scientific papers in English and German journals; memorial volume with biography and bibliography published, 1908.

DREW, SIR THOMAS (1838–1910), architect; pupil of Sir Charles Lanyon [q. v.], 1854; F.R.I.B.A., 1889; president of Royal Hibernian Academy, 1900; knighted, 1900; hon. LL.D. Dublin, 1905; president of Royal Society of Antiquaries of Ireland, 1895–7; designed Rathmines town hall, 1889, and Belfast Cathedral, 1899.

DRIVER, SAMUEL ROLLES (1846–1914), regius professor of Hebrew and canon of Christ Church, Oxford, 1883–1914; B.A., New College, Oxford; fellow, 1870; member of Old Testament revision company, 1875–1884; works include 'A Treatise on the Use of the Tenses in Hebrew' (1874), 'Introduction to the Literature of the Old Testament' (1891), and Old Testament commentaries.

DRUMMOND, SIR GEORGE ALEXANDER (1829–1910), senator in the parliament of Canada (1880–1910) and president of the bank of Montreal from 1905; emigrated from Edinburgh to Montreal, 1854; founded Canada Sugar Refining Company, 1879; president of Montreal board of trade, 1886–8; K.C.M.G., 1904; C.V.O., 1908; philanthropist and art collector.

DRUMMOND, JAMES (1835–1918), Unitarian divine; son of Rev. W. H. Drummond [q. v.]; B.A., Trinity College, Dublin; studied theology at Manchester New College, London; pastor at Cross Street chapel, Manchester, 1860–9; lecturer at Manchester New College, 1869–85; principal (London), 1885–9, (Oxford), 1889–1906; an eloquent preacher and independent theological thinker and writer.

DRUMMOND, WILLIAM HENRY (1854–1907), Canadian physician and poet; emigrated from Ireland to Canada, 1865; as telegraph operator (1869) at Bord-à-

Plouffe he first met with French-speaking backwoodsmen, whom he faithfully represents in 'The Habitant,' 1897, 'Johnny Courteau,' 1901, and 'The Voyageur,' 1905; graduated in medicine at Bishop's College, Montreal, 1884; professor of medical jurisprudence there from 1895; hon. LL.D. Toronto, 1902.

DRURY-LOWE, SIR DRURY CURZON (1830–1908), lieutenant-general; B.A., Corpus Christi College, Oxford, 1853; joined 17th lancers, 1854; served in Crimea and Indian Mutiny; commanded regiment in Zulu war, 1879–80; C.B., 1879; distinguished as cavalry commander in Egyptian war, 1882; helped in victories of Kassasin and Tel-el-Kebir; occupied Cairo, receiving surrender of Arabi Pasha; K.C.B., 1882; inspector-general of cavalry at Aldershot, 1885–90; lieutenant-general, 1890; G.C.B., 1895.

DRYSDALE, LEARMONT (1866–1909), musical composer; while student at Royal Academy of Music, London (1888–92), he wrote notable orchestral compositions; his 'Tam o' Shanter,' 1891, 'The Plague' (musical play), 1896, and 'The Red Spider' (light opera), 1898, met with great success; composed original settings of Scots lyrics and arranged folk songs.

DU CANE, SIR EDMUND FREDERICK (1830–1903), major-general R.E. and prison reformer; joined royal engineers, 1848; organizer of convict labour in Western Australia and magistrate, 1851–6; designed new land works at Dover and Plymouth, 1858–63; inspector-general of military prisons and chairman of board of directors of convict prisons, 1869; reorganized county and borough prisons; his scheme (1873) transferring control and cost of local prisons to government legalized by Prison Act of 1877; C.B., 1873; K.C.B., 1877; became chairman of prison commissioners to administer the Act; inaugurated registration of criminals; suggested composite portraiture to Sir Francis Galton; major-general, 1877; clever water-colour painter; wrote 'The Punishment and Prevention of Crime,' 1885.

DUCKETT, SIR GEORGE FLOYD, third baronet (1811–1902), archaeologist and lexicographer; educated at Harrow and Christ Church, Oxford; joined army, 1832; compiled 'Technological Military Dictionary' (1848) in German, English, and French; recognized abroad but ignored at home; succeeded to baronetcy, 1856, which became extinct at his death; F.S.A., 1869; published genealogical history of Duckett family, and several volumes on the charters and records of Cluniac foundations, 1877–93; wrote 'Anecdotal Reminiscences of an Octo-nonagenarian,' 1895.

DUDGEON, ROBERT ELLIS (1820–1904), homoeopath; M.D. Edinburgh, 1841; practised homoeopathy in London, 1845; edited 'British Journal of Homoeopathy,' 1846–84; translated works by Hahnemann, 1849–50; helped to found Hahnemann Hospital and school of homoeopathy, Bloomsbury Square, 1850; secretary (1848) and president (1878 and 1890) of British Homoeopathic Society; invented Dudgeon's sphygmograph, 1878; wrote on 'Homoeopathy,' 1854, and optics.

DUFF, SIR BEAUCHAMP (1855–1918), general; entered Royal Artillery from Woolwich, 1874; served in India; passed out of Staff College with distinction, 1889; military secretary to commander-in-chief in India, Sir George Stuart White [q.v.], 1895–9; military secretary to White, and later on Lord Roberts's staff, during South African War, 1899–1900; C.B. and returned to India, 1901; assisted Lord Kitchener to reorganize Indian army, 1903–1909; chief of staff and K.C.V.O., 1906; K.C.B., 1907; secretary of military department at India Office, 1909; K.C.S.I., 1910; G.C.B., 1911; commander-in-chief and military member of council in India, 1914–16; G.C.S.I. and recalled to England to give evidence before Mesopotamia commission, 1916; assigned large share of blame for failure of Mesopotamian operations, although partially exonerated on account of over great responsibility.

DUFF, SIR MOUNTSTUART ELPHINSTONE GRANT (1829–1906), statesman and author. [See GRANT DUFF.]

DUFFERIN AND AVA, first MARQUESS OF (1826–1902), diplomatist and administrator. [See BLACKWOOD, FREDERICK TEMPLE HAMILTON-TEMPLE.]

DUFFY, SIR CHARLES GAVAN (1816–1903), Irish nationalist and colonial politician; engaged in journalism in Dublin, 1836; started the 'Nation' as proprietor and editor, 1842; gathered a brilliant staff of 'Young Irelanders' who developed a strong nationalist sentiment; produced 'The Library of Ireland,' a shilling series of Irish biography, poetry, and criticism; was accused of sedition with Daniel O'Connell [q. v.], 1844; opposed O'Connell's Irish federal plan, 1844; called to Irish bar, 1845; became intimate with Carlyle, 1845; formed Irish Confederation, 1847; suggested formation of independent Irish party in House of Commons, 1848; was arrested, the 'Nation' being suppressed for advocating rebellion, 1848–9; joined Irish Tenant League for fixity of tenure, fair rents, and free sale; independent M.P. for New Ross, 1852–5; emigrated to Australia, 1855; barrister at Melbourne; member of the House of Assembly, Victoria, 1856; minister of land and works, 1857–9 and 1862–5; carried Duffy's Land Act to facilitate acquisition of land by immigrants; prime minister, 1871–2; K.C.M.G., 1873; speaker of the House of Assembly, 1876–80; spent remainder of life in South of Europe in literary work; wrote 'Young Ireland, 1840–50,' 2 vols., 1880–3, 'Life of Thomas Davis,' 1890, 'Conversations with Thomas Carlyle,' 1892, and 'My life in Two Hemispheres,' 1898; died at Nice.

DUFFY, PATRICK VINCENT (1836–1909), landscape painter; keeper of the Royal Hibernian Academy, 1871–1909.

DUNLOP, JOHN BOYD (1840–1921), inventor and pioneer of the pneumatic rubber tyre; veterinary surgeon in Belfast, 1867; fitted tricycle with pneumatic instead of solid rubber tyres, 1887; formed business which ultimately developed into Dunlop Rubber Company Ltd.; invention revolutionized cycling and made possible motor road vehicle.

DUNMORE, seventh EARL OF (1841–1907), explorer. [See MURRAY, CHARLES ADOLPHUS.]

DUNPHIE, CHARLES JAMES (1820–1908), art critic and essayist; educated at Trinity College, Dublin; founded 'Patriotic Fund Journal,' 1854–5; art and dramatic critic to 'Morning Post,' 1856–95; published 'Wildfire,' 1876, 'Sweet Sleep,' 1879 and 'The Chameleon,' 1888, semi-cynical and fluent essays.

DUPRÉ AUGUST (1835–1907), chemist; born at Mainz; studied chemistry at Giessen and Heidelberg (Ph.D., 1855); came to London, 1855; assistant demonstrator at Guy's Hospital; discovered presence of copper in vegetable and animal tissues; lecturer in toxicology at Westminster Hospital medical school, 1863–97; made special inquiries into Thames purification and sewage treatment; officially engaged from 1873 in researches on explosives; examined Fenian 'infernal machines,' 1882–3; a member of ordnance research board, 1906; evolved original methods of analysis and testing for safety; published many scientific papers; F.R.S., 1875.

DUTT, ROMESH CHUNDER (1848–1909), Indian official, author, and politician; born in Calcutta; educated at presidency college, Calcutta; called to English bar, 1871; joined Bengal civil service, 1871; C.I.E., 1892; commissioner of Burdwan, 1894, and of Orissa, 1895–7; member of Bengal legislative council, 1895; settled in London, 1897; as president of national congress at Lucknow (1899) condemned government's land revenue policy; lecturer on Indian history, University College, London, 1898–1904; revenue minister of state of Baroda, 1904–7; prime minister, 1909; Indian member of royal commission on Indian decentralization, 1907–8; works include 'History of Bengali Literature,' 1877, 'History of Civilization in Ancient India,' 3 vols. 1888–90, 'Economic History of British India, 1757–1837,' 1902, and translations from the Sanskrit; 'Life,' by J. N. Gupta, 1911.

DUTTON, JOSEPH EVERETT (1874–1905), biologist; M.B. and C.M. at Victoria University, Liverpool, and Holt fellow in pathology, 1897; went with Liverpool school of tropical medicine to Nigeria to study the mosquito, 1900; discovered at Gambia first trypanosome in man which caused sleeping sickness, 1901; at Stanley Falls (1904), discovered cause of tick fever in man; succumbed to fever at Kosongo.

DUVEEN, SIR JOSEPH JOEL (1843–1908), art dealer and benefactor; born in Holland; settled at Hull as general dealer, 1866; helped to form many private collections of Nankin and Oriental porcelain; extended business to tapestry, pictures, and objects of art, 1879; benefactor to National and Tate galleries; added 'Turner Wing' to Tate Gallery, 1908; knighted, 1908.

EADY, CHARLES SWINFEN, first BARON SWINFEN (1851–1919), judge; called to bar (Inner Temple), 1879; Q.C., 1893; Chancery judge and knighted, 1901; lord justice of appeal and P.C., 1913; master of the Rolls, 1918; created baron, 1919.

EARLE, JOHN (1824–1903), philologist; B.A., Magdalen College, Oxford, 1845; M.A., 1849; fellow of Oriel, 1848; professor of Anglo-Saxon, 1849–54 and 1876–1903; rector of Swanswick, 1857–1903; wrote much on Anglo-Saxon; chief works were 'Two of the Saxon Chronicles Parallel,' with introduction, notes, and glossary, 1865, 'A Book for the Beginner in Anglo-Saxon,' 1866, and 'The Philology of the English Tongue,' 1866, his most popular work, 'Anglo-Saxon Literature,' 1884, and 'The Deeds of Beowulf,' 1892; an accomplished Dante scholar.

EAST, SIR ALFRED (1849–1913), painter and etcher; studied art at Glasgow and in Paris; R.A. exhibitor, 1883; A.R.A., 1899; R.A., 1913; president of Royal Society of British Artists, 1906; knighted, 1910; in his art primarily an interpreter of landscape.

EAST, SIR CECIL JAMES (1837–1908), general; joined 82nd regiment, 1854; served in Crimea (1855) and Indian Mutiny (1857), in Lushai expedition (1871–2) and Zulu war (1879); commanded first brigade in Burmese expedition, 1886–7; C.B., 1887; governor of Royal Military College, Sandhurst, 1893–8; lieutenant-general, 1896; general, 1902; K.C.B., 1897.

EASTLAKE, CHARLES LOCKE (1836–1906), keeper of the National Gallery, London; secretary to Royal Institute of British Architects, 1866–77; as keeper and secretary to National Gallery, 1878–98, rearranged the paintings there; wrote 'A History of the Gothic Revival,' 1871, and 'Notes on the Principal Pictures' at Milan, 1883, Paris, 1883, Munich, 1884, and Venice, 1888.

EATON, WILLIAM MERITON, second BARON CHEYLESMORE (1843–1902), mezzotint collector; educated at Eton; succeeded to peerage, 1891; formed largest private mezzotint collection; bequeathed some 10,000 mezzotint portraits to British Museum, which were exhibited, 1905–10.

EBSWORTH, JOSEPH WOODFALL (1824–1908), editor of ballads; younger son of Joseph Ebsworth [q. v.]; spent his youth in Edinburgh, where his father kept a bookshop; studied art; employed in Manchester by Faulkner Bros., lithographers, 1848; exhibited four water-colour views of Edinburgh at Scottish Academy, 1849; wrote verse and prose for Scottish press, 1850–60; B.A., St. John's College, Cambridge, 1864; M.A., 1867; took Anglican orders, 1864; after serving cures, chiefly at Bradford, was vicar of Molash, Kent, 1871–94; devoted himself to editing old collections of 'drolleries' and ballads for the Ballad Society; produced 'Bagford Ballads' (from the British Museum), 1876–80, and completed a reprint of 'The Roxburgh Ballads' (vols. v–ix), 1883–99; F.S.A., 1881.

EDDIS, EDEN UPTON (1812–1901), portrait painter; exhibited at Royal Academy, 1834–81; painted subjects of rustic genre and children, and portraits including Macaulay, 1850, Lord Overstone, 1851, Lord Coleridge, 1878, Sydney Smith, and Theodore Hook (in National Portrait Gallery).

EDOUIN, WILLIE (1846–1908), comedian, whose real name was WILLIAM FREDERICK BRYER; toured through Australia and the Far East, 1857; joined Lydia Thompson [q.v.] in New York, 1870; first appeared in London, 1874; opened Toole's Theatre successfully with 'The Babes, or Whines from the Wood,' 1884; scored successes in 'Our Flat,' 1889–90, 'La Poupée,' 1897, and 'The girl from Kay's,' 1902; admirable for grotesquerie and whimsicality.

EDWARD VII (1841–1910), KING OF GREAT BRITAIN AND IRELAND AND OF THE BRITISH DOMINIONS BEYOND THE SEAS, EMPEROR OF INDIA, born at Buckingham Palace on 9 Nov. 1841, was eldest son and second child of Queen Victoria and Prince Albert. Baptized at St. George's Chapel, Windsor, on 25 Jan. 1842, he was named Albert after his father and Edward after his mother's father, Edward, Duke of Kent. From childhood he spoke English and German, and early learned French, of which in adult years he had an exceptional mastery. In 1846 he paid a first visit to Cornwall and Wales, in 1848 to Scotland, and in 1849 to Ireland. His parents, prompted by Baron Stockmar, bestowed great care on his education, and watched his development closely. He was subjected to a strict discipline under his parents' eyes, at first by private tutors; but he was always impatient of serious study. His permitted recreations included the theatre and music, and he practised elocution and drawing with some success. Practically isolated from boys of his own age, he had small opportunity of playing games, but he rode well and acquired a lifelong love of horses and dogs.

With his parents he attended the opening of the Great Exhibition (1 May 1851) and of the Crystal Palace (June 1854), and he went to Paris for the first time on a visit to Napoleon III and the Empress Eugénie, Aug. 1855. Walking tours through Dorset (Aug. 1856) and through the English Lakes (1857) were followed by a longer foreign tour for study and sightseeing down the Rhine and into Switzerland (July–Oct. 1857). Confirmed at Windsor on 1 April 1858, he was provided with a semi-independent household at White Lodge in Richmond Park (May–Nov. 1858), and on 9 Nov. 1858, his seventeenth birthday, when he received a very solemn admonition from his parents, he was gazetted colonel in the army unattached and nominated K.G. A governor, Col. Robert Bruce, was appointed next day. With Bruce he visited at Potsdam his eldest sister, who had lately married Prince Frederick of Prussia, and afterwards made a four months' sojourn in Rome (Jan.–April 1859). He visited Pope Pius IX and met Robert Browning and Frederic Leighton. On his way home he stayed with King Pedro at Lisbon. Next summer his father sent him to Edinburgh to study under Lyon Playfair. In spite of publicly expressed doubt as to the wisdom of pursuing too academic a training, he matriculated at Oxford on 17 Nov., as a member of Christ Church, and remained in residence till the end of summer term, 1860. On 8 July 1860 he set out for Canada on the invitation of the Canadian government, accompanied by the Duke of Newcastle, secretary of state for the colonies, and a distinguished suite. It was the first visit of a royal prince to a British colony. At Montreal (4 Sept.) he opened the great railway bridge across the St. Lawrence river, and at Ottawa he laid the foundation stone of the parliament building. Passing to the United States, he was cordially welcomed at Washington by President Buchanan, and planted a chestnut tree by Washington's tomb at Mount Vernon. He returned to Plymouth, 15 Nov. The expedition had the effect of strengthening the loyalty of Canada to the mother country and of increasing the good feeling between England and the United States. After spending the rest of the year at Oxford, the Prince continued his education at Trinity College, Cambridge, through 1861. In Aug. he joined the 2nd battalion of grenadier guards in camp at the Curragh, and next month made a third tour in Germany, where a first meeting was arranged for him with his future wife, Princess Alexandra, eldest daughter of Prince Christian of Schleswig-Holstein-Sonderburg-Glucksburg. Her father was next heir to the throne of Denmark, which he ascended as Christian IX on 15 Nov. 1863; the first meeting of the Prince and Princess Alexandra was in the cathedral at Speier, 24 Sept. 1861; each made a good impression on the other. Resuming residence at Cambridge for the Michaelmas term, he was elected a bencher of the Middle Temple (31 Oct.), and opened the new library at the Inn. On 13 Dec. he was summoned from Cambridge to Windsor owing to the illness of his father, who died next day. Thereupon his widowed mother claimed that full control which his father had hitherto exercised; Queen Victoria never ceased to think of the Prince of Wales save as a boy. But his views of life broadened on reaching man's estate, and he chafed against the perpetual tutelage to which his mother sought to subject him. In accordance with plans formed by his father he made a tour in the Holy Land, Feb.–May 1862, accompanied among others by Arthur Penrhyn Stanley [q. v.]; on his return journey he was entertained at Constantinople by the Sultan, at Athens by the King of Greece, and at Fontainebleau by the Emperor Napoleon III. On 9 Sept. 1862 he was formally betrothed to Princess Alexandra at King Leopold's palace of Laeken; on 1 Nov. 1862 the Queen gave formal assent to the union, the announcement of which evoked enthusiasm in England and Denmark, but was received coolly in Germany. At the end of the year his sister, the crown princess of Prussia, with her husband, accompanied the Prince of Wales on a tour through the Mediterranean. Meanwhile a separate establishment was formed for him at home. The estate of Sandringham in Norfolk was purchased for 220,000l. out of the income accumulated during his minority from the Duchy of Cornwall, which was the heir-apparent's appanage. Marlborough House in London was provided at the public expense. On 25 Feb. 1863 he held a levée for his mother at St. James's Palace, and thus first performed a ceremonial function. On 5 Feb. 1863 he took his seat in the House of Lords at the opening of parliament. Parliament granted him an annuity of 40,000l. and one of 10,000l. to his bride,

Princess Alexandra, with a prospective annuity of 30,000*l.* in case of widowhood. The marriage took place in St. George's Chapel, Windsor, on 10 March 1863, and many festivities followed. On 2 May he first attended the Royal Academy banquet. On 7 June he received the freedom of the City of London. On 16 June he was made hon. D.C.L. at Oxford, and next year hon. LL.D. at Cambridge. While spending much time as a country gentleman and sportsman and visiting annually Scotland, the Riviera, and Homburg, he assumed the rôle of leader of fashionable life in London, encouraging the lighter social amusements, and forming a wide and cosmopolitan circle of acquaintances. His mother excluded him from all political responsibilities, but he carried on and extended his father's work of charity and public utility. He became president of the Society of Arts (22 Oct. 1863) and president of St. Bartholomew's Hospital (20 March 1867), and was thenceforth indefatigable in inaugurating public buildings, and in presiding at charity festivals. He thrice visited Ireland at this period—in 1865, when he opened the International Exhibition at Dublin (8 May); in 1868 (with the Princess), when he was made a Knight of St. Patrick and hon. LL.D. Trinity College, Dublin; and in 1871, when he opened the Royal Agricultural Society's Exhibition. Despite exclusion from political business, the Prince interested himself in foreign affairs. His request for access to foreign office papers was practically refused by the Queen on account of his alleged want of discretion. Frank in expression of sympathy with Denmark during the Schleswig-Holstein crisis (1864), he sought first-hand intelligence from men in public life at home and abroad. In 1866 he first went to Russia for the wedding of his wife's sister Dagmar to Tsarevitch Alexander. A long tour (Nov. 1868–May 1869) embraced Copenhagen, Stockholm, Berlin, Vienna, Egypt (where he inspected the newly completed Suez Canal), Constantinople, and Paris. He won golden opinions at foreign courts. During the Franco-German war (1870) he manifested sympathy with France and showed much kindness to Napoleon III and his family in their English exile. Persistent rumours of the Prince's addiction to frivolous amusements grew in 1870, when he appeared in the witness-box to deny imputations in Sir Charles Mordaunt's action for divorce against his wife (Feb.). The sensational press abounded in scandalous insinuations which were reproduced in 'The coming K——,' a clever parody of Tennyson's 'Idylls,' and many like satires in verse. Meanwhile the Prince opened for the Queen the Thames Embankment (13 July 1871) and presided over a series of international exhibitions at South Kensington which were continued for four years without success (1871–4). In Nov. 1871 he was attacked by typhoid and was gravely ill for a month. After attending a national thanksgiving for his recovery at St. Paul's Cathedral (27 Feb. 1872), he completed his convalescence in a Mediterranean yachting tour, revisiting Pope Pius IX at Rome. Anxiety over the Prince's illness revived enthusiasm for the monarchy. Gladstone, with whom the Prince's relations were always friendly, vainly urged the Queen to provide the Prince with regular employment either in India or Ireland. He was made field-marshal on 10 June 1875. He was at Vienna for the opening of the International Exhibition, May 1873, and at St. Petersburg for the marriage of his brother, the Duke of Edinburgh, to the Tsar's daughter, 1874. He was tactfully entertained at Birmingham by Mr. Joseph Chamberlain, then mayor, on 3 Nov. 1874. A tour in India followed, Oct. 1875 to May 1876; he was officially entertained by the Indian government at Bombay, Madras, and Calcutta, and enjoyed much sport as guest of native princes. The personal tie between the princes of India and English royalty was greatly strengthened by his visit. In Europe his interest in France steadily grew; there he was friendly with all political parties and ranks. As president of the British section of the Paris Exhibition, 1878, he advocated at opening ceremonies a good understanding between the two countries. He formed the acquaintance of Gambetta. Though Lord Beaconsfield shared the Queen's doubts of his discretion, the Prince favoured the conservative leader's anti-Russian policy, 1876–8. On 6 May 1879 he voted in the House of Lords for the deceased wife's sister bill. Becoming intimate with Sir Charles Dilke when under-secretary for foreign affairs (1880–2) in Gladstone's second ministry, he sought to aid in Paris Dilke's negotiations with the French government for an Anglo-French commercial treaty. He attended the funeral at St. Petersburg, March

1881, of Tsar Alexander II, who had been assassinated. His offer to serve in the Egyptian campaign was refused, July 1882. Openly disapproving the recall of Sir Bartle Frere from the Cape, 1880, he condemned the pusillanimity of liberal policy in Egypt and the Sudan, 1884, and publicly deplored the sacrifice of Gordon. Appointed member of the royal commission on housing, Feb. 1884, he was friendly with all his fellow commissioners, who included two representatives of labour, Henry Broadhurst and Joseph Arch. Revisiting Ireland, April 1885, he was coolly received by nationalists, but generally met with a cordial welcome.

In middle life the Prince was active in freemasonry, becoming grand master of the order, Sept. 1875. Appointed trustee of the British Museum, May 1881, he performed his duties regularly. He helped to establish the Royal College of Music, 1882–3. His public activities took him to all parts of the country. He inaugurated the Mersey Tunnel, 28 April 1886, Truro Cathedral, 1880–7, and the Tower Bridge, 1886–94; was four times president of the Royal Agricultural Society; helped to organize at South Kensington International Fisheries Exhibition (1883), Health Exhibition (1884), Inventions and Music Exhibition (1885), and India and Colonies Exhibition (1886), and interested himself in founding the Imperial Institute to celebrate Queen Victoria's jubilee, 1887.

On 10 March 1888 the Prince celebrated his silver wedding. He showed much sympathy with his widowed sister, the Empress Frederick, when her husband, Emperor Frederick III of Germany, died of cancer (15 June 1888) two months after his accession. Though there was mutual affection between the Prince and his nephew the new emperor William II, they often caused one another passing irritation. The Prince warmly welcomed Emperor William on his first visit to England after his accession, Aug. 1889. On his eldest daughter's marriage, 1889, the Prince invited additional pecuniary provision for his family. Parliament granted an extra annuity of 36,000*l.* to terminate six months after Queen Victoria's death.

The Prince remained a constant patron of the theatre in London, maintaining friendly relations with Sir Henry Irving and leading actors. But his chief amusement from middle life onwards was horse-racing, training horses at Newmarket and often occupying rooms at the Jockey Club there; he thrice won the Derby—with Persimmon (1896), Diamond Jubilee (1900), and with Minoru (1909); he won the Grand National at Liverpool with Ambush II (1900). For a time he was prominent in yacht racing, and won many prizes with the 'Britannia,' a vessel designed for him in 1892. His indulgence in sport was deemed excessive by the austere, and on 5 June 1891 he somewhat alienated public opinion by his evidence in the Tranby Croft case [see under WILSON, CHARLES HENRY, first BARON NUNBURNHOLME], when it was admitted that he played baccarat for high stakes; writing privately to Archbishop Benson of Canterbury (13 Aug. 1891), he denied sympathy with gambling. During Lord Salisbury's ministry (1886–92), while taking no part in home politics, he frequently expressed his desire for a good understanding between England and France when visiting the latter country. He engaged in sporting tours in Austria, in Roumania and Hungary (1888), and was the guest of Baron Hirsch, the Jewish millionaire, in Hungary (1894); in the latter year he twice visited Russia, for the marriage of his wife's niece, Xenia, to the Grand Duke Alexander Michâlovitch (July), and for the funeral of his wife's brother-in-law, Tsar Alexander III (Oct.). During Gladstone's last ministry (1892–4) much official intelligence was communicated to him with the Queen's reluctant consent; he became a member of the old age pensions commission, 1893; his friendship with Gladstone continued till the statesman's death; he was a pall-bearer at Westminster Abbey at Gladstone's funeral on 25 May 1898, and was president of the National Memorial Committee (July). In 1895, when Salisbury formed a new administration, the Prince was accorded the cabinet members' right of receiving the foreign dispatches. He devoted some energy to encouraging medical research, helping to found the National Society for the Prevention of Consumption (21 Dec. 1888), and the national leprosy fund which commemorated the tragic heroism of Father Damien (June 1889). At Queen Victoria's diamond jubilee (June 1897) he received the new dignity of grand master and principal grand cross of the Order of the Bath, and he inaugurated in honour of the jubilee the Prince of Wales's Hospital Fund for London, which was renamed on his accession

King Edward VII Fund. The difficulties with the Transvaal Republic which led in 1899 to the South African war alienated the goodwill of Europe towards England; on 4 April 1900 the Prince while travelling with the Princess to Denmark was shot at without injury by a youth Sipido at the Gare du Nord, Brussels; though president of the British section of the Paris Exhibition of 1899 he, contrary to his custom, did not attend the inauguration in Paris.

The Prince took the oaths of sovereignty under the style of Edward VII the day after Queen Victoria's death at Osborne on 22 Jan. 1901. His speech to the privy council, which was his own composition and was delivered without notes, pronounced his full determination to be a constitutional sovereign in the strictest sense of the word. During the new session of parliament, which he opened on 14 Feb. 1901, the additional title was bestowed on him of 'King of the British Dominions beyond the Seas'; he was allowed an annual grant of 470,000l. apart from the income of the Duchy of Lancaster (60,000l. a year), and the expense of maintaining the royal palaces and royal yachts. Friends' anticipations that he would prove unequal to his new station were belied. He held no well-defined views of domestic legislation, but was deeply interested in foreign policy, and was punctual in formal business. His old circle of friends remained unchanged, and he indulged in all his former amusements, but he gave new splendour to royal ceremonials and exercised a brilliant hospitality in London, which became the headquarters of the court after an interval of forty years. He spent little time at Windsor. He had inherited Balmoral and Osborne from his mother; but he was not often at Balmoral, and Osborne he abandoned, converting it into a convalescent home for army and naval officers, 9 Aug. 1902. He welcomed the close of the South African war (31 May 1902), and attended a thanksgiving service in St. Paul's (8 June); the coronation was appointed for 26 June, on a scale of exceptional magnificence; but two days before, the king was compelled to submit to an operation for perityphlitis, from which he made a good recovery, and the postponed ceremony took place on 9 Aug. After a yachting cruise to Scotland he made a royal progress through South London, and lunched with the lord mayor at the Guildhall, 24 Oct. Meanwhile Lord Salisbury resigned the premiership (11 July 1902), and was succeeded by Mr. Balfour.

King Edward travelled much abroad during the reign, in accordance with early practice; he attended the funeral of his sister, Empress Frederick, at Friedrichshof (5 Aug. 1901), and after visiting Homburg went to Copenhagen, where he met Tsar Nicholas. His already large kinship with foreign sovereigns was extended by the election of his son-in-law Prince Charles of Denmark as King of Norway (Oct. 1905) and by the marriage of his niece Princess Ena of Battenberg to Alphonso XIII, King of Spain (31 May 1906); wits of Paris thenceforth called him 'l'oncle de l'Europe.' His friendly relations with foreign countries remained much as before his accession. There was no foundation for the current belief of a personal hostility to Germany. The German Emperor visited Sandringham for celebration of the King's sixty-first birthday, 9 Nov. 1902. In spring of 1903 a long foreign tour brought the King to Lisbon, Rome, and Paris, with Mr. Charles Hardinge, then assistant under-secretary of the foreign office, in attendance. In Paris, which he had not visited for three years, he regained his former popularity, and conspicuously helped to improve the relations between the two countries. The entente cordiale was concluded on 8 April 1904. He was entertained by the German Emperor at Kiel on 29 June 1904. Thenceforth he spent three or four months each year abroad. Several weeks each spring were passed at Biarritz, and a like period of the autumn at Marienbad. He cruised in the Mediterranean during springs of 1905, '6, '7 and '9, meeting the Kings of Greece, Spain, and Italy; and he visited the northern courts of Sweden, Denmark, and Norway, April 1908. Frequently passing to and from Paris, he enjoyed varied intercourse with French society. Only during 1905 did he fail to visit Germany, where the press imputed to him anti-German tendencies. In August 1906, 1907, and 1908 he met the German Emperor in Germany on good terms. The Emperor paid a state visit to Windsor, 11–18 Nov. 1907, and King Edward returned the compliment at Berlin, Feb. 1909. He met the Emperor of Austria thrice—once at Gmunden (Aug. 1905) and twice at Ischl (Aug. 1907–8). He visited the Tsar of Russia at Reval (9 June 1908) and the Tsar

was his guest at Cowes (Aug. 1909); some resentment was shown in England at the King's friendly relations with the Tsar, owing to English sympathy with Russian revolutionary movements.

Meanwhile at home he continued to identify himself with philanthropic work and public improvements. He laid the foundation stone of Liverpool Cathedral, 19 June 1904; opened university buildings at Sheffield (1905), Leeds (1908), and Birmingham (1909), and he thrice visited Ireland—in 1903, 1904, and 1907. He intervened little in domestic politics, though he was interested in appointments. With his third prime minister, Sir Henry Campbell-Bannerman, he enjoyed cordial relations. Of Campbell-Bannerman's colleagues Lord Carrington was an old friend, and with (Lord) Haldane he was soon very intimate. On Campbell-Bannerman's retirement, March 1908, the King invited Mr. Asquith to fill the vacant office. When the House of Lords threatened the rejection of Mr. Lloyd George's budget of 1909, the King vainly urged on the conservative leaders the impolicy of that action. On the defeat of the budget in the Lords (30 Nov.) and the continuance of the liberals in office after the general election, the King raised no remonstrance to his ministers' proposal to curtail for the future the veto of the Lords. The King disliked the situation but abstained from interference; the controversy was still in progress at his death. During his usual spring visit to Biarritz in 1910 he suffered severely from bronchial trouble, but he returned to London (27 April) apparently in good health. Taken ill in London on 2 May, he died at Buckingham Palace on 6 May, and his only surviving son was proclaimed George V. The dead King lay in state in Westminster Hall (16–20 May), and was buried in the vault below St. George's Chapel, Windsor.

King Edward eminently satisfied contemporary conditions of kingship; of cosmopolitan temperament, he spoke with equal ease English, French, and German; he revived the ceremonial splendour of the crown, and proved himself an admirable representative of the nation abroad. The austere deemed his addiction to pleasure excessive; but his support of philanthropic causes silenced criticism. He had an expert faculty for business, and distributed his energies over a wide field; he gathered orally very varied stores of knowledge, and remembered personal details with great accuracy; he never seems to have forgotten a face. Personally courageous, he admired every manifestation of heroism. He was greatly attached to dumb animals. Memorials have been erected in all parts of the empire.

By his wife, Queen Alexandra, the King had two sons, Albert Edward (b. 8 Jan. 1864, d. 14 Jan. 1892) and his successor, George (b. 3 June 1865); a third son, John (b. 6 April 1871) lived only a day; the two surviving sons were both educated in youth as naval cadets. Of the King's three daughters, Princess Louise (b. 20 Feb. 1867), afterwards Princess Royal, married the Duke of Fife (27 July 1889); the second, Princess Victoria, was born on 6 July 1868; and the third, Maud (b. 26 Nov. 1869), married in 1896 Prince Charles of Denmark, afterwards Haakon VII, King of Norway.

EDWARD OF SAXE-WEIMAR, PRINCE (1823–1902), field-marshal; brought up by his aunt, Queen Adelaide [q.v.]; playfellow of Queen Victoria and George, Duke of Cambridge; joined army, 1841; served with grenadier guards in Crimea with distinction; A.D.C. to Lord Raglan (1855) and to Queen Victoria (1855–9); commanded forces in Ireland, 1885–90, and 1st life guards from 1888 to death; K.C.B., 1881; C.B., 1887; K.P., 1890; G.C.V.O., 1901; hon. LL.D. Dublin, 1891; field-marshal, 1897.

EDWARDS, SIR FLEETWOOD ISHAM (1842–1910), lieutenant-colonel R.E.; joined royal engineers, 1863; accompanied Sir John Simmons [q.v.] to Berlin Congress, 1878; keeper of the privy purse to royal household, 1895; K.C.B., 1887; lieutenant-colonel, 1890; P.C., 1895; G.C.V.O., 1901; intimate adviser of Queen Victoria.

EDWARDS, HENRY SUTHERLAND (1828–1906), author and journalist; joined 'Punch' staff, 1848; wrote light drama with R. B. Brough [q.v.] and A. S. Mayhew [q.v.]; served as 'The Times' correspondent in Poland (1862–3) and in Franco-Prussian war (1870–1); first editor of 'Graphic,' 1869; published 'History of Opera,' 2 vols. 1862, lives of Rossini, 1869, and Sims Reeves, 1881, 'Personal Recollections,' 1900, and translations.

EDWARDS, JOHN PASSMORE (1823–1911), editor and philanthropist; at first a lawyer's clerk at Truro;

represented at Manchester (1845) the London 'Sentinel,' founded in interests of Anti-Corn Law League; in London advocated early closing, chartism, and international peace; after unsuccessful publishing ventures he purchased 'Building News,' 1862, and 'Echo,' first halfpenny newspaper, 1876, which he successfully edited and controlled till 1896; supported all progressive movements; president of London Reform Union, 1894, and of Anti-Gambling League; an enthusiastic member of Peace Society; denounced Crimean and South African wars; liberal M.P. for Salisbury, 1880–5; founded some seventy free libraries and hospitals and convalescent homes in United Kingdom, as well as art gallery at Newlyn, a settlement in London, and University Hall in Clare Market; endowed scholarship in English literature, Oxford, 1902; declined knighthood; published 'A Few Footprints,' an autobiography, 1905; bust by Sir George Frampton and portrait by Watts.

EDWARDS, MATILDA BARBARA BETHAM- (1836–1919), novelist and writer on French life; mainly self-educated; travelled widely in France among republican and anti-clerical circles; wrote novels for sixty years; edited writings of Arthur Young.

EDWARDS, SIR OWEN MORGAN (1858–1920), man of letters; began life as itinerant preacher in ministry of Welsh Calvinistic Methodists; B.A., Balliol College, Oxford; first class in modern history; tutorial fellow of Lincoln College, Oxford, 1889–1907; chief inspector of Welsh education, 1907; edited Welsh magazines and wrote books on Wales; knighted, 1916.

EGERTON, SIR CHARLES COMYN (1848–1921), field-marshal; joined army, 1867, and Indian army, 1871; D.S.O., 1891; C.B., 1895; K.C.B., 1903; led successful expedition against 'Mad Mullah' of Somaliland, 1903–4; full general, 1904; member of council of India, 1907–17; field-marshal, 1917.

ELGAR, FRANCIS (1845–1909), naval architect; student at Royal School of Naval Architecture, South Kensington, 1864–7; chief assistant to Sir Edward Reed [q.v.], 1871; adviser on naval construction to Japanese government, 1879–81; served on departmental committee of board of trade, whose report led to regulations fixing maximum loadline for merchant ships, 1883; first professor of naval architecture, Glasgow University, 1883–6; director of dockyards, 1886–92; consulting naval architect of Fairfield Shipbuilding Company, 1892–1907; hon. LL.D. Glasgow, 1885; F.R.S., 1895; F.S.A., 1896; member of tariff reform commission, 1904; published 'The Ships of the Royal Navy,' 1875.

ELGIN, ninth EARL OF (1849–1917), statesman and sometime viceroy of India. [See BRUCE, VICTOR ALEXANDER.]

ELIOT, SIR JOHN (1839–1908), meteorologist; educated at St. John's College, Cambridge; second wrangler and first Smith's prizeman, 1869; held mathematical professorships in India until he became meteorological reporter to the Indian government, 1886; director-general of Indian observatories, 1899–1903; F.R.S., 1895; C.I.E., 1897; K.C.I.E., 1903; advocated organization of meteorological work on imperial basis; published departmental reports and 'Climatological Atlas of India,' 1906; an accomplished musician.

ELLERY, ROBERT LEWIS JOHN (1827–1908), astronomer; went to Melbourne, 1851; superintendent of newly-founded government observatory at Williamstown, 1853; director of geodetic survey of Victoria, 1858–74; government astronomer at Melbourne, 1863–95; prepared catalogues of star places; helped in photographic chart of the whole sky; a founder and president (1856–84) of Royal Society of Victoria; F.R.A.S., 1859; F.R.S., 1873; C.M.G., 1889; work recorded in 'Astronomical Results of the Melbourne Observatory,' 1869–88, and in the Melbourne 'General Catalogues,' 1874 and 1890.

ELLICOTT, CHARLES JOHN (1819–1905), bishop of Gloucester; educated at St. John's College, Cambridge; Bell university scholar, 1838; B.A., 1841; M.A., 1844; Platt fellow, 1845–8; Hulsean lecturer, 1859, and professor, 1860; professor of New Testament exegesis at King's College, London, 1858; dean of Exeter, 1861–3; bishop of Gloucester and Bristol, 1863, and of Gloucester on division of sees, 1897; restored cathedral, promoted church extension, formed Church Aid Society; member of royal commission on ritual (1867–70) and other committees; chairman of New Testament revision company, 1870–81; published commentaries on Pauline epistles, 1856, and on the New Testament, 3 vols. 1878–9 (abridged edit. for schools, 14 vols. 1878–83), the Old

Testament, 5 vols. 1882–4, and the complete Bible, 7 vols. 1897; member of Alpine Club, 1871–1904.

ELLIOT, SIR GEORGE AUGUSTUS (1813–1901), admiral; born at Calcutta; entered navy, 1827; in command of ships on North American station, in Channel, and in Baltic, 1843–55; rear-admiral, 1858; superintendent of Portsmouth dockyard, 1863–5; admiral, 1874; conservative M.P. for Chatham, 1874–5; commander-in-chief at Portsmouth, 1875; K.C.B., 1877.

ELLIOT, GILBERT JOHN MURRAY KYNYNMOND, fourth EARL OF MINTO (1845–1914), governor general of Canada and viceroy of India; educated at Eton and Trinity College, Cambridge; entered army, 1867; served in many wars in different parts of the world, 1870–82; military secretary to governor-general of Canada, Lord Lansdowne, 1883–5; succeeded father, 1891; governor-general of Canada, 1898–1904; maintained cordial relations with colonial secretary, Joseph Chamberlain, and Sir Wilfrid Laurier, liberal premier, and acquired great popularity throughout the Dominion; his period of office era of great prosperity for Canada; directly responsible for Canadian troops taking part in Boer War; viceroy of India, 1905–10; worked in complete harmony with secretary of state, Mr. (afterwards Viscount) Morley; claimed to have initiated Morley-Minto reforms of 1909; established friendly relations with Indian princes; K.G., 1910.

ELLIOT, SIR HENRY GEORGE (1817–1907), diplomatist; born at Geneva; son of second earl of Minto [q.v.], and brother-in-law of Lord John Russell [q.v.]; in Tasmania, 1836–9; entered diplomatic service, 1841; British envoy at Copenhagen, 1858; sent on special mission to Naples to congratulate Francis II on accession to throne of Two Sicilies, and to obtain constitutional reforms, 1859; neglect of his representations led to seizure of Sicily by Garibaldi, 1860; left Naples on union of Italy under King Victor Emanuel, 1860; sent on special mission to Greece, April 1862; assisted in arranging new constitution under new King George I; succeeded Sir James Hudson [q.v.] as British envoy at Turin, 1863; appointment roused much criticism and political controversy; transferred to Constantinople and made P.C., 1867; British representative at opening of Suez Canal; G.C.B., 1869; often in conflict with Russian ambassador; criticized for delay in reporting 'Bulgarian atrocities' of 1876; British plenipotentiary at conference at Constantinople, 1876; ambassador at Vienna, 1877–84; engaged in critical negotiations between conclusion of San Stefano treaty and the meeting of the congress at Berlin, 1878; caused Gladstone to disavow his attack on Austrian government, 1880; retired to England, 1884.

ELLIOTT, SIR CHARLES ALFRED (1835–1911), lieutenant-governor of Bengal; son of Henry Venn Elliott [q.v.]; joined East India Company, 1856; served in Mutiny; assistant commissioner in Oudh till 1863, where he collected information about its history and folklore; secretary to government of North-West Provinces, 1872–5; concerned chiefly with settlement and revenue questions; directed famine relief operations in Mysore; issued famous report on Indian famines of 7 July 1878; chief commissioner of Assam, 1881; chairman of committee of inquiry into Indian public expenditure, 1886; C.S.I., 1878; K.C.S.I., 1887; lieutenant-governor of Bengal, 1890–5; prosecuted survey and compiled record of rights in Bihar, despite opposition from zemindars; strong advocate of economy; adopted firm attitude to sedition in native press; retired, 1895; served on London school board, 1897–1900, and on education committee of London county council, 1904–6; published 'Chronicles of Oonao,' 1862, and reports on Indian administration.

ELLIS, FREDERICK STARTRIDGE (1830–1901), bookseller and author; started bookselling business in Covent Garden, 1860; removed to New Bond Street, 1872; long official buyer for British Museum; edited Henry Huth's catalogue of books, 5 vols. 1880; friend and publisher of William Morris, Rossetti, and Ruskin; friend also of Swinburne and Burne-Jones; compiled concordance to Shelley, 1892; edited Morris's Kelmscott editions of Caxton's 'Golden Legend,' 1892, and Cavendish's 'Life of Wolsey,' 1893.

ELLIS, JOHN DEVONSHIRE (1824–1906), civil engineer and metallurgist; son of Birmingham brass manufacturer; purchased with Sir John Brown [q.v.] small Atlas engineering works at Sheffield, 1854; increased capital to 3 millions sterling; managing director on their conversion into limited liability company, 1864–1905; produced iron plates for British ironclads by new and cheaper welding process; perfected a compound armour of steel and iron; received Bessemer gold medal from Iron and Steel Institute, 1889, of which he became vice-president in 1901.

ELLIS, ROBINSON (1834–1913), classical scholar; educated at Rugby and Balliol College, Oxford; first classes in classical moderations and *literae humaniores*; Ireland scholar, 1855; fellow of Trinity College, Oxford, 1858; professor of Latin, University College, London, 1870–6; reader in Latin at Oxford, 1883; Corpus professor of Latin, 1893; vice-president of Trinity, 1879–93; F.B.A., 1902; works include 'Commentary on Catullus' (1876), edition of Ovid's 'Ibis' (1881), and editions of many minor Latin authors.

ELSMIE, GEORGE ROBERT (1838–1909), Anglo-Indian civilian and author; joined Indian service, 1858; called to bar, 1871; commissioner at Peshawar, 1872–8 and 1885; commissioner of Lahore, 1880–2; judge of Punjab chief court, 1882–5; vice-chancellor of Punjab University, 1885–7; member of legislative council, 1888; first financial commissioner, 1889; C.S.I., 1894; returned to England, 1894; hon. LL.D. Aberdeen, 1904; published 'Lumsden of the Guides,' 1899, 'Thirty-five Years in the Punjab,' 1908, and other works.

ELWES, GERVASE HENRY (CARY-) (1866–1921), singer; educated at Christ Church, Oxford; in diplomatic service, 1891–5; adopted singing as career, 1902; sang in Paris, London, Holland, Belgium, Germany, and America; accidentally killed at Boston, U.S.A.

ELWORTHY, FREDERICK THOMAS (1830–1907), philologist and antiquary; travelled much in Europe, collecting charms and amulets; F.S.A., 1900; good linguist and draughtsman; editorial secretary of Somerset Archaeological Society, 1891–6; published works on West Somerset dialect, the evil eye, 1895, and on other superstitions.

EMERY, WILLIAM (1825–1910), archdeacon of Ely; first boy to enter new City of London school, 1837; entered Corpus Christi College, Cambridge; fifth wrangler, 1847; M.A., 1850; B.D., 1858; fellow, 1847–65; keen advocate of Volunteer movement; organized first church congress at Cambridge, 1861; permanent secretary of congress from 1869; archdeacon of Ely, 1864–1907; canon, 1870; organized first diocesan conference.

ETHERIDGE, ROBERT (1819–1903), palaeontologist; cousin of John Beddoe [q. v.]; curator of museum of British Philosophical Institution, 1850–7; palaeontologist to geological survey, 1863; assisted Huxley as lecturer at Royal School of Mines; made list of 18,000 species of fossils (catalogued, 1888); assistant keeper in geology at Natural History Museum, 1881–91; F.R.S., 1871; president of Geological Society, 1880–2; assistant editor of 'Geological Magazine,' 1865–1903; works include 'Stratigraphical Geology and Palaeontology,' 1887.

EUAN-SMITH, Sir CHARLES BEAN (1842–1910), soldier and diplomatist; born at George Town, British Guiana; joined Madras infantry, 1859; served in Abyssinian expedition, 1867, in Persia, 1870–1, and in Zanzibar, 1872; C.S.I., 1872; consul at Muscat, 1879; in Afghan war in Lord Roberts's expedition to Kandahar; consul-general at Zanzibar, 1887; persuaded sultan to place himself under protection of Great Britain, 1890; C.B., 1889; K.C.B., 1890; British envoy in Morocco, 1891; retired, 1893; hon. D.C.L. Oxford, 1893.

EVA (pseudonym) (1826–1910), Irish poetess. [See O'DOHERTY, MARY ANNE.]

EVANS, DANIEL SILVAN (1818–1903), Welsh scholar and lexicographer; rector of Llanymawddwy, 1862–76, and Llanwrin, 1876–1903; hon. B.D. Lampeter, 1863; lecturer in Welsh at University College of Wales, 1875–83; hon. LL.D., 1901; research fellow of Jesus College, Oxford, 1897; hon. canon of Bangor, 1888; chancellor of the cathedral, 1895; chief work 'Dictionary of the Welsh Language,' 5 pts., A–E, 1887–1906; other works include 'English-Welsh Dictionary,' 2 vols. 1852–8, and volumes of poems.

EVANS, EDMUND (1826–1905), wood engraver and colour printer; apprenticed to Ebenezer Landells [q.v.], 1840–7; worked for 'Illustrated London News'; made colour prints of illustrations by Birket Foster for Pfeiffer's 'Travels in the Holy Land,' 1852; prepared first 'yellowback' illustrated cover, 1853; printed in oil colour from wood blocks; gained chief fame by colour printing of works by Walter Crane, Caldecott, and Kate Greenaway, including Crane's 'The Baby's Opera,' 1877, and Greenaway's 'Under the Window,' 1879.

EVANS, GEORGE ESSEX (1863–1909), Australian poet; emigrated from London to Australia, 1881; while sheepfarming contributed poems to 'Queenslander' from 1882; appointed district registrar at Toowoomba, Queensland, 1888; chief works were 'Loraine, and other Verses,' 1898, and 'The Secret Key,' 1906; poems distinctively inspired by Australian life and environment.

EVANS, SIR JOHN (1823–1908), archaeologist and numismatist; son of Arthur Benoni Evans [q. v.], and brother of Sebastian Evans [q. v.]; entered uncle's paper-making business at Nash Mills, Hemel Hempsted, 1840; made scientific researches, especially into water supply, exploring water-bearing strata in his own district; made fine collection of stone and bronze implements, fossil remains, and mediaeval antiquities; formed collections of ancient British money, of Anglo-Saxon and English coins; first to place study of ancient British coinage on scientific basis; F.S.A., 1852; F.R.S., 1864; president of Geological Society, 1874–6, and of Numismatic Society, 1874–1908; joint editor of 'Numismatic Chronicle' from 1861; received hon. degrees from Oxford, Cambridge, Dublin, and Toronto; K.C.B., 1892; interested in Hertfordshire local affairs; high sheriff of county, 1881; portions of collections of implements are in Ashmolean Museum, Oxford; portraits by A. S. Cope and the Hon. John Collier; works include 'Flint Implements in the Drift,' 1860, 'The Coins of the Ancient Britons,' 1864, with 'Supplement,' 1890, 'The Ancient Stone Implements of Great Britain,' 1872, 'The Ancient Bronze Implements . . . of Great Britain,' 1881.

EVANS, SIR SAMUEL THOMAS (1859–1918), politician and judge; admitted solicitor, 1883; liberal M.P., mid-Glamorganshire, 1890–1910; called to bar (Middle Temple), 1891; Q.C., 1901; recorder of Swansea, 1906–8; solicitor-general, 1908; president of probate, divorce, and admiralty division of High Court, 1910; G.C.B., 1916; reputation as judge rests on series of judgments in prize cases delivered during European War, 1914–18; most notable cases: the 'Kim,' in which he applied doctrine of 'continuous voyage' to carriage of contraband goods; the 'Leonora,' in which he held that so-called 'reprisals' Order in Council of 16 February 1917 was not inconsistent with established principles of international law; and the 'Möwe,' 'Roumanian,' 'Hamborn,' and 'Zamora.'

EVANS, SEBASTIAN (1830–1909), journalist; brother of Sir John Evans [q. v.]; scholar of Emmanuel College, Cambridge; B.A., 1853; M.A., 1857; LL.D., 1868; window designer at Messrs. Chance's glass works near Birmingham, 1857–67; an ardent conservative, edited 'Birmingham Daily Gazette,' 1867–70; called to bar, 1873; part founder and editor of 'People,' 1878–81; exhibited at Royal Academy in oil, water-colour, and black and white; translated 'The High History of the Holy Graal,' 1898; published verse showing feeling for mediaeval beauty.

EVERARD, HARRY STIRLING CRAWFURD (1848–1909), writer on golf; settled at St. Andrews, winning golf prizes; works include 'History of the Royal and Ancient Club of St. Andrews,' 1907.

EVERETT, JOSEPH DAVID (1831–1904), man of science; entered Glasgow College, 1854; B.A., 1856; M.A., 1857; professor of mathematics in King's College, Windsor, Nova Scotia, 1859–64; returned to Glasgow, 1864; professor of natural philosophy, Queen's College, Belfast, 1867–97; F.R.S., 1879; fellow of Royal University of Ireland; settled in London, 1898; works include 'Units and Physical Constants,' 1875, 'Outlines of Natural Philosophy,' 1887; translated Deschanel's 'Physics,' 1870.

EVERETT, SIR WILLIAM (1844–1908), colonel; joined army, 1864; vice-consul at Erzeroum, 1878; consul at Kurdistan, 1882–7; C.M.G., 1886; professor of military topography at Sandhurst, 1888–92; colonel, 1893; technical adviser for delimitation of Sierra Leone frontier, 1895; commissioner for Niger frontier, 1896–8, and Togoland frontier, 1900; K.C.M.G., 1898.

EWART, CHARLES BRISBANE (1827–1903), lieutenant-general; brother of Sir John Alexander Ewart [q. v.]; joined royal engineers, 1845; served in Crimea, 1854–6; commanding royal engineer of London district, 1866–71; at Dover, 1877–9, and Gibraltar, 1879–82; C.B., 1869; member of ordnance committee, 1884; brigadier-general in Sudan, 1885; lieutenant-governor of Jersey, 1887–92; lieutenant-general, 1888; colonel commandant, R.E., 1902.

EWART, SIR JOHN ALEXANDER (1821–1904), general and colonel Gordon highlanders; born in Bombay; joined army, 1838; served in Crimea; recommended for V.C. for bravery at assault of the Secundera-bagh in Indian Mutiny, 1857; C.B., 1858; commanded 78th Ross-shire Buffs, 1859–64; general, 1884; colonel of 92nd Gordon highlanders, 1884–95; K.C.B., 1887; G.C.B., 1904; published 'The Story of a Soldier's Life,' 2 vols. 1881.

EYRE, EDWARD JOHN (1815–1901), governor of Jamaica; emigrated to Australia and engaged in sheep farming, 1833; began journeys into unknown sand deserts of interior as magistrate and protector of aborigines, 1836; starting from Adelaide (1840), passed with a single native round head of Great Australian Bight, and reached King George's Sound, 1841; published experiences in 2 vols., 1845; revisited England, 1845; lieutenant-governor of New Zealand, 1846–53; governor of St. Vincent, 1854–60; appointed governor of Jamaica, 1864; forcibly suppressed Morant Bay native rebellion, proclaiming martial law, Oct. 1865; confirmed sentence of death for high treason passed by Lieutenant H. C. A. Brand [q. v.] on George William Gordon, a coloured member of legislature, and over 600 other persons; denounced in England for cruelty; temporarily suspended and tried by royal commission of inquiry at Kingston, Jan.–March 1866; commended for promptitude, but was blamed for unnecessary rigour, and recalled, 1866; retired to Shropshire; supported by Kingsley and Carlyle, Ruskin and Tennyson, but condemned by 'Jamaica committee,' including J. S. Mill, Huxley, Tom Hughes, Herbert Spencer, and Goldwin Smith; was made defendant in abortive legal proceedings which aimed at bringing him to trial for murder (March 1867 and June 1868); legal expenses paid from public funds, 1872; received pension as retired colonial governor, 1874; 'Life' by Hamilton Hume, 1867.

FAED, JOHN (1819–1902), artist; brother of Thomas Faed [q. v.]; for forty years painted miniatures; A.R.S.A., 1847; R.S.A., 1851; later painted figure subjects; chief were 'Burd Helen,' 'The Cottar's Saturday Night,' 1854, 'The Poet's Dream,' 1883, and 'The Wappinschaw'; exhibited at Royal Academy, 1862–80.

FAGAN, LOUIS ALEXANDER (1845–1903), etcher and writer on art; grandson of Robert Fagan [q. v.]; born at Naples; served in British legation at Caracas under father, 1866–7; friend of Sir Anthony Panizzi [q. v.], whose biography he wrote, 2 vols. 1880; in prints department at British Museum, 1869–94; wrote 'Handbook' to department (1876) and other works on engraving and engravers; exhibited etchings at Royal Academy, 1872–81; a popular lecturer; historian of the Reform Club, 1886; died at Florence.

FAIRBAIRN, ANDREW MARTIN (1838–1912), Congregational divine; early joined Evangelical Union founded by Dr. James Morison [q. v.]; studied at theological college of Union in Edinburgh; minister at Bathgate, 1860, in Aberdeen, 1872; principal of Airedale theological college, Bradford, 1877–1886; first principal of Mansfield College, Oxford, 1886–1912; chief works 'Christ in Modern Theology' (1893) and 'Philosophy of the Christian Religion' (1902).

FALCKE, ISAAC (1819–1909), art collector and benefactor to the British Museum; made collections of majolica and lustre ware (now in Wallace collection), of fifteenth and sixteenth-century bronzes (now at Berlin), and of Wedgwood china (presented to British Museum), as well as of Chinese and other porcelain.

FALCONER, LANOE (pseudonym) (1848–1908), novelist. [See HAWKER, MARY ELIZABETH.]

FALKINER, CÆSAR LITTON (1863–1908), Irish historian; son of Sir Frederick Richard Falkiner [q. v.]; B.A. Dublin, 1886; M.A., 1890; called to Irish bar, 1887; assistant land commissioner, 1898–1908; wrote 'Illustrations of Irish History and Topography,' 1904; edited Ormonde Papers for Historical MSS. commission, 5 vols. 1902–8, and Swift's letters, 1908; killed while mountaineering at Chamonix.

FALKINER, SIR FREDERICK RICHARD (1831–1908), recorder of Dublin; B.A., Trinity College, Dublin, 1852; called to Irish bar, 1852; Q.C., 1867; recorder of Dublin, 1876–1905; knighted, 1896; P.C., Ireland, 1905; prominent in church of Ireland questions; published 'Literary Miscellanies,' 1909, and wrote on Swift's portraits; died in Madeira.

FANE, VIOLET (pseudonym) (1843–1905), authoress. [See CURRIE, MARY MONTGOMERY, BARONESS CURRIE.]

FANSHAWE, SIR EDWARD GENNYS (1814–1906), admiral; entered navy, 1828; commander in East

Indies, 1844; suppressed piracy at Borneo, 1845; lord of the admiralty, 1865; vice-admiral, 1870; C.B., 1871; commander-in-chief on North American station, 1870–3, and at Portsmouth, 1878–9; K.C.B., 1881; G.C.B., 1887.

FARJEON, BENJAMIN LEOPOLD (1838–1903), novelist; emigrated from London to Australia, 1855; thence went to New Zealand, settling at Dunedin; joint editor and proprietor of 'Otago Daily Times,' 1861; returned to England, 1868; published melodramatic novels; chief were 'Grif,' 1866, dramatized 1891, 'London's Heart,' 1873, 'The Mystery of M. Felix,' 1890; best was 'Devlin the Barber,' 1888.

FARMER, EMILY (1826–1905), water-colour painter; best known for her groups of children and genre subjects; exhibited at Royal Academy and elsewhere; chief work was 'Deceiving Granny.'

FARMER, JOHN (1835–1901), musician; studied music at Leipzig and Coburg; worked in father's lace business, 1853–7; ran away to Zürich, and taught music there; on staff of Harrow School, 1864–85; composed numerous Harrow school songs; organist of Balliol College, Oxford, 1885–1901; early champion in England of Bach and Brahms; published works include oratorios and fairy opera; edited 'Gaudeamus,' 1890, and other song collections.

FARNINGHAM, MARIANNE (pseudonym) (1834–1909), hymn writer and author. [See HEARN, MARY ANNE.]

FARQUHARSON, DAVID (1840–1907), landscape painter; treated chiefly the Perthshire and western highlands; lived at Edinburgh, 1872–82, London, 1882–97, and Cornwall from 1897; exhibited at Royal Scottish and Royal academies; A.R.S.A., 1882; A.R.A., 1904; chief works were 'The Links of Forth,' 1883, 'In a Fog,' 1897, 'Full Moon and Spring Tide,' 1904, and 'Birnam Wood,' 1906.

FARRAR, ADAM STOREY (1826–1905), professor of divinity and ecclesiastical history at Durham from 1864; B.A., St. Mary Hall, Oxford, 1850; D.D., 1864; tutor at Wadham College, 1855; won Denyer prizes for theology, 1853–4; published Bampton lectures, 'A Critical History of Free Thought,' 1862; canon of Durham, 1878.

FARRAR, FREDERIC WILLIAM (1831–1903), dean of Canterbury; born at Bombay; son of Indian missionary; educated at King's College, London, under F. D. Maurice; scholar of Trinity College, Cambridge, 1852; member of 'Apostles'; won chancellor's medal for English verse, 1854; fourth classic, 1854; fellow of Trinity, 1856; M.A., 1857; D.D., 1874; master at Marlborough, 1854, and at Harrow, 1855–70; while at Harrow published school stories, 'Eric, or Little by Little,' 1858, 'Julian Home,' 1859, and 'St. Winifred's,' 1862, besides 'An Essay on the Origin of Language,' 1860, which attracted Darwin's attention, 'Chapters on Language,' 1865, and 'Families of Speech,' 1870; F.R.S., 1866; urged serious teaching of science; edited 'Essays on a Liberal Education,' 1867; published 'Seekers after God,' 1868, and Hulsean lecture at Cambridge, 'The Witness of History to Christ,' 1871; head master of Marlborough, 1871–6; visited Palestine, 1870; published his 'Life of Christ,' 12 editions, 1874, 'Life of St. Paul,' 1879, 'The Early Days of Christianity,' 1882, and 'Lives of the Fathers,' 1889; rector of St. Margaret's, and canon of Westminster, 1876–95; a successful preacher; chaplain to House of Commons, 1890–5; archdeacon of Westminster, 1883; evoked criticism by challenging doctrine of eternal punishment in sermons at the Abbey, 1877, which were published in 'Eternal Hope,' 1878; in answer to E. B. Pusey's reply, modified his views in 'Mercy and Judgement,' 1881; lectured in America, 1885; Bampton lecturer at Oxford, 1886; dean of Canterbury, 1895–1903; restored and repaired the cathedral; 'Life,' by son, 1905.

FARREN, ELLEN, known as NELLIE FARREN (1848–1904), actress; daughter of Henry Farren [q.v.]; played leading parts at Olympic Theatre (1864–8) in burlesque and in comedy characters, in which she rivalled Mrs. Keeley [q. v.]; with John Hollingshead's company at Gaiety Theatre from 1868; won great popularity as principal boy; her chief successes included Sam Weller, 1871, and Thaddeus in Byron's 'The Bohemian G'Yurl,' 1877; in old comedy she shone as Pert in 'London Assurance,' 1866, Lydia Languish in 'The Rivals,' 1874, and Maria in 'Twelfth Night,' 1876; combined pathos with humour as Clemency Newcome in Dickens's 'Battle of Life,' 1873; visited America and Australia, 1888–91;

subsequently appeared only in benefit performances till 1903; unbounded spirits, good-humour, drollery, and sympathy made her an universal favourite.

FARREN, WILLIAM (1825-1908), actor; natural son of William Farren (1786-1861, q.v.); acted at Haymarket in juvenile tragedy or light comedy, 1853-67; rôles included Captain Absolute, and Guibert in Browning's 'Colombe's Birthday,' 1853; at Vaudeville from 1871, where he was the original Sir Geoffrey Champneys in Byron's 'Our Boys,' 1875-8; other parts were Sir Peter Teazle, 'a masterpiece of sheer virtuosity,' and Sir Anthony Absolute; started Conway-Farren old comedy company at the Strand, 1887; retired to Rome, 1898.

FARWELL, SIR GEORGE (1845-1915), judge; B.A., Balliol College, Oxford; called to bar (Lincoln's Inn), 1871; Q.C., 1891; judge of Chancery division and knighted, 1899; lord justice of appeal and P.C., 1906-13; wrote 'A Concise Treatise on the Law of Powers' (1874).

FAUSSET, ANDREW ROBERT (1821-1910), divine; scholar of Trinity College, Dublin, where he obtained many classical prizes; B.A., 1843; D.D., 1886; vicar of St. Cuthbert's, York, 1859-1910; eloquent evangelical preacher and sound scholar; edited 'Comedies of Terence,' 1844, and works by Homer, Livy, and Euripides; published 'Guide to the Study of the Book of Common Prayer,' 1894, and many theological works and commentaries.

FAYRER, SIR JOSEPH, first baronet (1824-1907), surgeon-general and author; son of naval commander; lived in Westmorland, where he met Wordsworth; M.R.C.S., 1847; F.R.C.P., 1872; F.R.C.S., 1878; M.D. Rome, 1849; joined Indian medical service, 1850; assistant surgeon in Pegu war, 1852; civil surgeon of Lucknow, 1856; prominent in Mutiny; M.D. Edinburgh, 1859; professor of surgery at Medical College, Calcutta, 1859-74; president of Asiatic Society of Bengal, 1867; C.S.I., 1868; accompanied Duke of Edinburgh (1870) and Prince of Wales (1875) on Indian tours, of which he published 'Notes,' 1876; president of medical board of India office, 1873-95; K.C.S.I., 1876; F.R.S., 1877; hon. LL.D. Edinburgh and St. Andrews; baronet, 1896; in chief work, 'The Thanatophidia of India,' 1872, first advocated permanganate treatment of venomous snake bites; wrote 'Recollections of my Life,' 1900.

FENN, GEORGE MANVILLE (1831-1909), novelist; a short sketch, 'In Jeopardy,' was accepted by Dickens for 'All the Year Round,' 1864; soon wrote stories for boys, embodying natural history studies, producing more than 170 volumes; editor of 'Cassell's Magazine,' 1870, and proprietor of 'Once a Week,' 1873; wrote dramatic criticism and farces.

FERGUSON, MARY CATHERINE, LADY (1823-1905), biographer; born GUINNESS; married Sir Samuel Ferguson [q. v.], 1848, and shared his social and literary activities; wrote 'The Story of the Irish before the Conquest,' 1868, and a life of her husband, 2 vols. 1896.

FERGUSSON, SIR JAMES, sixth baronet of Kilkerran (1832-1907), governor of Bombay; educated at Rugby and University College, Oxford; succeeded to baronetcy, 1849; entered grenadier guards; served in Crimea; conservative M.P. for Ayrshire, 1855-7, 1859-68; under-secretary for India, 1866, and to home office, 1867; P.C. and governor of South Australia, 1868-73, and of New Zealand, 1873-5; K.C.M.G., 1875; governor of Bombay, 1880-5; sought welfare of Dekhan peasantry by modifying assessment of land revenue and granting remissions in times of scarcity; created first agricultural department; greatly developed the port of Bombay, and promoted rural and urban self-government; G.C.S.I., 1885; M.P. for North-East Manchester, 1885-1906; under-secretary at foreign office, 1886-91; postmaster-general, 1891-2; killed in earthquake at Kingston, Jamaica; bronze memorial statue at Ayr.

FERRERS, NORMAN MACLEOD (1829-1903), master of Caius College, Cambridge, and mathematician; educated at Eton and Caius College; senior wrangler and first Smith's prizeman, 1851; fellow, 1854; tutor, 1865; elected master, 1880; D.D., 1881; hon. LL.D. Glasgow, 1883; F.R.S., 1877; took prominent but conservative part in university affairs; published 'Trilinear Co-ordinates,' 1861, 'Spherical Harmonics,' 1877, and wrote much for mathematical journals; edited 'Quarterly Journal of Mathematics,' 1855-91.

FESTING, JOHN WOGAN (1837-1902), bishop of St. Albans; descended from Michael C. Festing [q. v.]; B.A., Trinity College, Cambridge, 1860; D.D., 1890; vicar of Christ Church, Albany Street, 1878-90; bishop

of St. Albans, 1890; business-like administrator; president of the Universities' Mission to Central Africa, 1892-1902.

FIELD, WALTER (1837-1901), painter; son of Edward W. Field [q. v.]; worked in oils and water-colours, mainly on landscapes and Thames scenery; exhibited at Old Water-Colour Society and Royal Academy; helped to found Hampstead Heath Protection Society; most popular works were 'The Milkmaid singing to Isaak Walton' and 'Henley Regatta.'

FIELD, WILLIAM VENTRIS, BARON FIELD, of Bakeham (1813-1907), judge; called to bar, 1850; Q.C., 1864; obtained large commercial practice on Midland circuit; made judge of court of queen's bench, 1875; showed great learning but quick temper on bench; gave judgment which was upheld on appeal in many important cases; created P.C. and raised to peerage on retirement, 1890.

FIGGIS, JOHN NEVILLE (1866-1919), historian and divine; B.A., St. Catharine's College, Cambridge; Mirfield father, 1907; works include 'The Divine Right of Kings' (1896), 'From Gerson to Grotius' (1907), 'Churches in the Modern State' (1913).

FINCH-HATTON, HAROLD HENEAGE (1856-1904), imperialist politician; son of tenth earl of Winchilsea [q. v.]; went to Queensland, 1876; engaged in cattle-farming and gold prospecting till 1883, when he returned to England; published 'Advance, Australia,' 1885; founded Imperial Federation League; conservative M.P. for Newark, 1895-8; an ardent sportsman.

FINLAYSON, JAMES (1840-1906), Scottish physician; M.B. Glasgow, 1867; M.D., 1869; hon. LL.D., 1899; physician to Western Infirmary, Glasgow, from 1875 to death, and to Royal Children's Hospital, 1883-98; voluminous works include 'Clinical Manual,' 1878, 'Life of Peter Lowe,' 1889, and 'Life of Robert Watt,' 1897.

FINNIE, JOHN (1829-1907), landscape painter and engraver; pupil of William Bell Scott [q. v.]; master of School of Art, Liverpool, 1855-96; president of Liverpool Academy, 1887-8; early experimented in etching and engraving; practised mezzotint from 1886, exhibiting at Royal Academy and elsewhere.

FISHER, JOHN ARBUTHNOT, first BARON FISHER, of Kilverstone (1841-1920), admiral of the fleet; born in Ceylon; entered royal navy, 1854; qualified in gunnery school, 'Excellent,' and joined 'Warrior', first 'ironclad,' 1863; on staff of 'Excellent', 1864-9, 1872-6; devoted himself to development of torpedo; captain, 1874; came to Admiralty for first time, 1876; at sea, 1876-82; captain of gunnery school, Portsmouth, 1883-6; director of ordnance and torpedoes at Admiralty, 1886-90; rear-admiral, 1890; third sea lord and controller of navy, 1892-7; K.C.B., 1894; vice-admiral, 1896; commander-in-chief, North American and West Indies station, 1897; commanded Mediterranean fleet, 1899-1902; ensured increased efficiency in every department; admiral, 1901; G.C.B., 1902; second sea lord, with charge of personnel of fleet, 1902-3; introduced important administrative reforms, notably common entry scheme in training of naval officers at Osborne, 1903; commander-in-chief, Portsmouth, 1903; first sea lord, 1904-10; O.M., 1904; organized redistribution of fleet to meet growing German menace; advocated designing of 'Dreadnought' type of battleship and battle cruiser, 1905; Cawdor memorandum, statement of Admiralty policy, published before fall of conservative government, 1905; obliged to diminish programme under liberal government; estranged from Lord Charles Beresford [q. v.], commander-in-chief of Channel fleet, 1907; issued programme of eight battleships, 1909-10; baron, 1909; returned to Admiralty as first sea lord after outbreak of European War, 1914; responsible for battle of Falkland Islands, 1914; disapproved of naval attempt to force passage of Dardanelles and resigned, 1915; one of the greatest administrators in history of royal navy.

FISON, LORIMER (1832-1907), Wesleyan missionary and anthropologist; left Caius College, Cambridge, for Australia, 1855; Wesleyan missionary at Fiji, 1863-71; studied native kinship; joined Alfred William Howitt [q. v.] in anthropological research in New South Wales and Victoria, 1871-5; again in Fiji, 1875-84, writing on Fijian land tenure and antiquities; settled at Melbourne, 1888; published 'Tales from Old Fiji,' 1904; awarded civil list pension, 1905; died at Essendon, Victoria.

FITCH, SIR JOSHUA GIRLING (1824-1903), inspector of schools and educational writer; B.A. London University,1850; M.A., 1852; joined staff of Borough Road Training College, Southwark, 1852; principal, 1856, proving a stimulating teacher of method; assistant commissioner of schools in Yorkshire, 1865–7, of elementary schools in the large northern towns, 1869, and of endowed schools, 1870–7; chief inspector of schools for eastern division, 1883–5; inspector of elementary training colleges for women in England and Wales, 1885–94; visited America and reported on American education, 1888; helped in foundation of Girton and Girls' Public Day School Company, 1874; published 'Lectures on Teaching,' 1881, and 'Educational Aims and Methods,' 1900; his account of 'The Chautauqua Reading Circles' (1888) suggested the National Home Reading Union; hon. LL.D. St. Andrews, 1888; knighted, 1896; 'Life' by Canon A. L. Lilley.

FITZALAN-HOWARD, HENRY, fifteenth DUKE OF NORFOLK (1847–1917). [See HOWARD.]

FITZCLARENCE, CHARLES (1865–1914), brigadier-general; joined army (Royal Fusiliers), 1885; V.C. for gallantry during South African War, 1900; transferred to Irish Guards, 1900; served with distinction as brigadier-general commanding 1st (Guards) brigade in 1st division, 1914; killed at head of Irish Guards in Flanders.

FITZGERALD, GEORGE FRANCIS (1851–1901), natural philosopher; son of William FitzGerald [q. v.]; B.A. (in mathematics) at Trinity College, Dublin, 1871; fellow, 1877; Erasmus Smith professor of natural and experimental philosophy, 1881–1901; developed electro-magnetic theory of radiation; made researches into electric waves and electrolysis; F.R.S., 1883; president of Physical Society, 1892–3; prominent in Irish educational affairs; 'Scientific Writings' collected by Sir Joseph Larmor, 1902.

FITZGERALD, SIR THOMAS NAGHTEN (1838–1908), surgeon; L.R.C.S. Ireland, 1857; F.R.C.S., 1884; surgeon at Melbourne Hospital from 1858 till death; an able operator; knighted, 1897; surgeon in Boer war, and C.B., 1900.

FITZGIBBON, GERALD (1837–1909), lord justice of appeal in Ireland; scholar of Trinity College, Dublin; hon. LL.D., 1895; called to Irish bar, 1860, and to English bar, 1861; leader of Munster circuit; successful advocate in O'Keefe v. Cullen case, 1873, and Bagot v. Bagot will case, 1878; solicitor-general for Ireland, 1877–8; promoted lord justice of appeal, 1878; P.C., 1900; served on various Irish educational commissions; chairman of commission on Irish educational endowments, 1885–97; an active freemason, prominent in affairs of Church of Ireland; friend of Lord Randolph Churchill and other politicians; portraits by Walter Osborne and William Orpen; statue by A. B. Joy.

FITZPATRICK, SIR DENNIS (1837–1920), Indian civil servant; entered Indian civil service, 1858; established legal reputation over case of Begum Samru of Sardhana, 1866–72; in legislative department of Indian government, 1874–85; K.C.S.I., 1890; lieutenant-governor of Punjab, 1892–7; on Council of India, 1897; vice-president, 1901; G.C.S.I., 1911.

FLEAY, FREDERICK GARD (1831–1909), Shakespearean scholar; B.A., Trinity College, Cambridge (13th wrangler), 1853; obtained places in four triposes; M.A., and ordained, 1856; relinquished orders, 1884; engaged as schoolmaster, 1856–76; published 'Hints on Teaching,' 1874; interested in phonetics; edited 'The Spelling Reformer,' 1880–1; compiled 'Life of Shakespeare,' 1886, 'A Chronicle History of the London Stage, 1559–1642,' 1890, and a 'Biographical Chronicle of the English Drama, 1559–1642,' 2 vols. 1891; in later life turned to Egyptology and Assyriology, publishing 'Egyptian Chronology,' 1899.

FLECKER, HERMAN (JAMES) ELROY (1884–1915), poet and dramatist; educated at Dean Close School (Cheltenham), Uppingham, and Trinity College, Oxford; entered consular service, 1908; sent to Constantinople, 1910; vice-consul at Beirut, 1911–13; died at Davos, Switzerland; his finest poem, 'The Golden Journey to Samarkand'; collected poems published, 1916; two plays published posthumously, 'Hassan' (1922) and 'Don Juan' (1925).

FLEMING, GEORGE (1833–1901), veterinary surgeon; served as veterinary surgeon in Crimea and China, 1855–60, in Syria and Egypt, 1867; principal veterinary surgeon to army, 1883–90; C.B., 1887; president of Royal College of Veterinary Surgeons, 1880–4, 1886–7;

secured passage of Veterinary Surgeons Act, 1881; hon. LL.D. Glasgow, 1883; wrote 'Horse Shoes and Horse Shoeing,' 1869, 'Veterinary Sanitary Science,' 2 vols. 1875.

FLEMING, JAMES (1830–1908), canon of York; educated at Shrewsbury and Magdalene College, Cambridge; B.A., 1853; B.D., 1864; vicar of St. Michael, Chester Square, 1873–1908; canon of York, 1879; chaplain to royal family from 1876; Whitehead professor of preaching and elocution at London College of Divinity from 1880; a strong protestant, he supported Kensit's agitation against ritualism; charged with plagiarism of Dr. Talmage's sermons, 1887; a popular preacher and graceful speaker; published 'The Art of Reading and Speaking,' 1896, and sermons; 'Life' by A. R. M. Finlayson.

FLEMING, SIR SANDFORD (1827–1915), Canadian engineer; born in Scotland; went to Canada, 1845; chief railway engineer to government of Nova Scotia, 1864; chief engineer of Inter-Colonial Railway, 1867–76; engineer-in-chief of Canadian Pacific Railway, 1871–80; headed 'Ocean to Ocean' expedition, 1872; procured laying of Pacific cable; K.C.M.G., 1897; died at Halifax, Nova Scotia.

FLETCHER, JAMES (1852–1908), naturalist; entered London bank, 1871; transferred to Ottawa, 1875; employed in parliamentary library there, 1876–87; botanist to dominion experimental farms, 1887; founded Ottawa Field Naturalists' Club, to whose 'Transactions' he made valuable contributions on botany and entomology.

FLINT, ROBERT (1838–1910), philosopher and theologian; professor of moral philosophy, St. Andrews University, 1864–76; professor of divinity, Edinburgh University, 1876; LL.D. Glasgow; D.D. Edinburgh; Baird lecturer, 1876–7; Stone lecturer at Princeton, U.S.A., 1880; delivered Croall, 1887–8, and Gifford lectures, 1908–9; voluminous writings include his Baird lectures, 'Theism,' 1877, and 'Antitheistic Theories,' 1879, 'Socialism,' 1894, 'Hindu Pantheism,' 1897, and 'Agnosticism,' 1903 (Croall lecture).

FLOYER, ERNEST AYSCOGHE (1852–1903), explorer; served in Indian telegraph station, 1869–76; explored interior of Baluchistan, 1876–7; published 'Unexplored Baluchistan,' 1882; inspector-general of Egyptian telegraphs, 1878–1903; superintended experiments of tree and plant cultivation in Egypt; commanded expedition to desert between the Nile and the Red Sea, 1891; rediscovered emerald mines in Sikait and Zabbara; described his explorations in various scientific journals.

FORBES, JAMES STAATS (1823–1904), railway manager and art connoisseur; studied engineering under I. K. Brunel [q. v.]; joined Great Western railway, twice subsequently refusing post of general manager; general manager of London, Chatham and Dover railway, 1861; restored its fortunes; chairman of directors, 1873–99; secured good terms for the railway on its amalgamation with South Eastern railway, 1899; as director of London District railway, 1870–1901, overcame difficulties of competition; collector of pictures, especially of nineteenth-century artists; portrait by Herkomer.

FORD, EDWARD ONSLOW (1852–1901), sculptor; studied painting at Antwerp and modelling at Munich; A.R.A., 1888; R.A., 1895; more important works are Rowland Hill, 1881, Irving as Hamlet, 1883, Gordon, 1890; Shelley memorial at Oxford, 1892, and Queen Victoria memorial at Manchester, 1901; executed also bronze ideal statuettes, such as 'Folly,' 'Peace,' and 'Echo.'

FORD, PATRICK (1837–1913), Irish-American journalist and politician; born in Galway; taken to Boston, U.S.A., 1841; founded and conducted 'Irish World,' chief organ of Irish-Americans and supporter of successive Irish movements, 1870–1913; died at Brooklyn, U.S.A.

FORD, WILLIAM JUSTICE (1853–1904), cricketer and writer on cricket; educated at Repton and St. John's College, Cambridge; master at Marlborough, 1877–86; one of hardest hitters known; historian of Middlesex and Cambridge University cricket clubs.

FORESTIER-WALKER, SIR FREDERICK WILLIAM EDWARD FORESTIER (1844–1910), general; entered army, 1862; served in Kaffir war, 1877–8; C.B., 1878; in Zulu war, 1879; in Bechuanaland expedition, 1884–5; C.M.G., 1886; commanded troops in Egypt, 1890–5; K.C.B., 1894; lieutenant-general commanding western district of England, 1895–9; in command of lines of communication in Boer war, 1899–1901; general, 1902; governor of Gibraltar, 1905–10; G.C.M.G., 1900.

FORMAN, ALFRED WILLIAM (1840–1925), man of letters; brother of H. B. Forman [q. v.]; translated Wagner's operas, Victor Hugo's plays, &c.

FORMAN, HENRY BUXTON (1842–1917), man of letters; entered Post Office, 1860; C.B., 1897; retired, 1907; principal works include editions of 'Poetical Works' (1876) and 'Prose Works' (1880) of Shelley, of 'Letters of John Keats to Fanny Brawne' (1878), and 'Poetical Works and Other Writings of John Keats' (1883).

FORREST, JOHN, first BARON FORREST, of Bunbury (1847–1918), Australian explorer and conservative politician; born in Western Australia; entered survey department, 1865; surveyor-general, 1883; first premier of Western Australia, 1890–1901; minister of defence in first Commonwealth ministry, 1901–3; K.C.M.G., 1901; held office intermittently, 1903–18; first Australian politician raised to peerage, 1918; died at sea.

FORSTER, HUGH OAKELEY ARNOLD- (1855–1909), author and politician. [See ARNOLD-FORSTER.]

FORTESCUE, GEORGE KNOTTESFORD (1847–1912), librarian; entered department of printed books, British Museum, 1870; keeper, 1899–1912; main achievement, 'Subject Index of Modern Works added to the Library of the British Museum' (1880–1910).

FORTESCUE, HUGH, third EARL FORTESCUE (1818–1905), author and politician; M.P. for Plymouth, 1841–52, Barnstaple 1852–4, and Marylebone, 1854–9; raised to peerage, 1859; succeeded father in earldom, 1861; secretary to poor law board, 1847–51; visited barracks and hospitals in Crimea, 1856; became liberal unionist, 1886; wrote many pamphlets on local government, health of towns, and middle class education; purchased reversion to great part of Exmoor, 1897, and encouraged stag hunting.

FOSTER, SIR CLEMENT LE NEVE (1841–1904), inspector of mines; son of Peter Le Neve Foster [q. v.]; entered School of Mines, 1857; D.Sc. London, 1865; examined mineral resources of Sinaitic peninsula, 1868; employed in Venezuela and North Italy, 1868–72; inspector of mines in Cornwall, 1872–80, and North Wales, 1880–1901; professor at Royal School of Mines, 1890–1901; sustained serious cardiac injury in Snaefell lead mine, 1897; F.R.S., 1892; knighted, 1903; works include 'Ore and Stone Mining,' 1894, and 'Mining and Quarrying,' 1903.

FOSTER, JOSEPH (1844–1905), genealogist; nephew of Myles Birket Foster [q. v.]; early devoted to genealogical research; compiled pedigrees of quaker families, 1862–72, of county families of Lancashire, 1873, and of Yorkshire, 1874; published his 'Peerage, Baronetage, and Knightage,' 1879; compiled 'Men at the Bar,' 1888, 'Admissions to Gray's Inn,' 1899; edited and supplemented J. L. Chester's 'London Marriage Licences,' 1887, and his 'Oxford Matriculation Register' in 'Alumni Oxonienses,' 8 vols. 1887–91; subsequent writings on heraldry were severely criticized.

FOSTER, SIR MICHAEL (1836–1907), physiologist; B.A. London, 1854; studied science at University College; M.B., 1858; M.D., 1859; professor of practical physiology, University College, 1869; praelector of physiology, Trinity College, Cambridge, 1870; professor of physiology in the university from 1883; F.R.S., 1872; with Huxley, developed method of practical laboratory work; introduced practical classes at Cambridge, for which he co-operated in 'Textbook for the Physiological Laboratory,' 1873, 'The Elements of Embryology,' 1874, and 'A Course of Elementary Practical Physiology,' 1876; stimulated original research; keenly interested in gardening, hybridized several plants; wrote a Primer (1890) and History (1901) of Physiology; joint editor of Huxley's 'Scientific Memoirs,' 1898–1902; founded 'Journal of Physiology,' 1878; served on several royal commissions; president of British Association and K.C.B., 1899; liberal unionist M.P. for London University, 1900–6; opposed his party's education bill of 1902; defeated as liberal candidate, 1906; portraits by Herkomer and the Hon. John Collier.

FOULKES, ISAAC (1836–1904), Welsh author and editor; issued at Liverpool cheap reprints of Welsh classics, 1877–88; edited 'Cymro,' weekly Welsh newspaper; edited biographical dictionary of eminent Welshmen, 1870.

FOWLE, THOMAS WELBANK (1835–1903), theologian and writer on poor law; B.A., Oriel College, 1858; M.A., 1861; president of Oxford Union, 1858; friend of T. H. Green and Prof. A. V. Dicey; vicar of Islip, 1875–1901; as poor law guardian advocated abolition of outdoor relief; published 'The Poor Law' in 'English Citizen' series, 1881, which took standard rank; advocated creation of parish and district councils and old age pensions, 1892.

FOWLER, HENRY HARTLEY, first VISCOUNT WOLVERHAMPTON (1830–1911), statesman; born in Sunderland; settled in Wolverhampton as solicitor, 1855; engaged in municipal affairs; mayor of Wolverhampton, 1863; first freeman of borough, 1892; liberal M.P. for Wolverhampton, 1880–5, for eastern division of city, 1885–1908; lucid and moderate speaker in House of Commons; became under-secretary for home affairs, 1884; financial secretary to treasury and P.C., 1886; keen critic of financial policy of conservative government, 1886–92; entered cabinet as president of board of trade, 1892; carried parish councils bill; became secretary for India, 1894; powerfully urged the reimposition of duties on cotton goods imported into India, 1895; G.C.S.I., 1895; director, 1897, and president, 1901, of the National Telephone Company; supported Boer war and opposed tariff reform; became chancellor of the Duchy of Lancaster, 1905; raised to peerage, April 1908; made lord president of the council, Oct. 1908; hon. LL.D. Birmingham, 1909; portraits by A. S. Cope; 'Life' by daughter, 1912.

FOWLER, THOMAS (1832–1904), president of Corpus Christi College, Oxford; schoolfellow at King William's College, Isle of Man, of T. E. Brown [q. v.], a lifelong friend; B.A., Merton College, Oxford, 1854; first class in classics and mathematics; D.D., 1886; tutor (1855) and sub-rector (1857–81) of Lincoln College; hon. fellow, 1900; advocated teaching of natural science and abolition of tests at Oxford, 1877; professor of logic, 1873–89; president of Corpus Christi College, 1881; vice-chancellor, 1901; hon. LL.D. Edinburgh, 1882; published 'Deductive Logic,' 1867, 'Inductive Logic,' 1870, monographs on Locke, 1880, Bacon, 1881, and Shaftesbury and Hutcheson, 1882, 'Progressive Morality,' 1884, and 'The Principles of Morals,' 2 pts. 1886; edited Bacon's 'Novum Organum,' 1878, and Locke's 'Conduct of the Understanding,' 1881; wrote histories of Corpus, 1893 and 1898.

FOWLER, WILLIAM WARDE (1847–1921), historian and ornithologist; educated at Marlborough and Lincoln College, Oxford; fellow of Lincoln, 1872; tutor, 1873; sub-rector, 1881–1906; retired to Kingham, his country home, 1910; works include writings on social and religious life of ancient Rome; knowledge of birds shown in 'Kingham Old and New' (1913).

FOX, SAMSON (1838–1903), inventor and benefactor; founded Leeds Forge Company, 1874; patented Fox corrugated boiler furnaces, 1877, and pressed steel underframes for railway wagons, 1886; first employed in England water gas on large scale for metallurgical and lighting purposes; pioneer of acetylene industry in Europe; generous benefactor to Royal College of Music, 1889; mayor of Harrogate, 1889–91.

FOX BOURNE, HENRY RICHARD (1837–1909), social reformer and author. [See BOURNE.]

FOXWELL, ARTHUR (1853–1909), physician; B.A., St. John's College, Cambridge, 1877; M.B., 1881; M.D., 1891; M.R.C.S., 1881; F.R.C.P., 1892; Bradshawe lecturer, 1889; resident pathologist at general hospital, Birmingham, from 1884; professor of therapeutics at Birmingham University and M.Sc., 1906; published 'Essays on Heart Disease,' 1896.

FRANKFORT DE MONTMORENCY, third VISCOUNT (1835–1902), major-general. [See DE MONTMORENCY, RAYMOND HARVEY.]

FRASER, ALEXANDER CAMPBELL (1819–1914), philosopher; educated at Edinburgh University; ordained to Free Church ministry, 1844; professor of logic and metaphysics in Edinburgh Free Church theological college, 1846–56, and at Edinburgh University, 1856–91; Gifford lecturer, 1894–6; F.B.A., 1903; works include edition of Berkeley's 'Works' and 'Life and Letters' (1871), study of Locke (1890) and edition of his 'Essay concerning Human Understanding' (1894); a stimulating teacher whose philosophical standpoint was theism based on moral faith.

FRASER, SIR ANDREW HENDERSON LEITH (1848–1919), Indian civil servant; entered Indian civil service, 1869; served in Central Provinces, 1871–98; secretary in home department and later chief commissioner of Central Provinces, 1898; president of Indian police commission, 1901; lieutenant-general of Bengal and K.C.S.I., 1903; had to face storm roused by partition, 1905; retired, 1908.

FRASER, CLAUD LOVAT (1890–1921), artist and designer; designed settings and costumes for 'As You

Like It' and 'The Beggar's Opera,' 1920; decorated books; produced designs for theatre, rhyme sheets, broadsides, &c.

FRASER, SIR THOMAS RICHARD (1841–1920), pharmacologist; born at Calcutta; M.D., Edinburgh University; professor of materia medica and clinical medicine at Edinburgh, 1877–1917; F.R.S., 1877; president of Royal College of Physicians, Edinburgh, 1900–2; knighted, 1902; his researches on poisons important.

FREAM, WILLIAM (1854–1906), writer on agriculture; student at Royal College of Science, Dublin, 1872–5; B.Sc. London, 1877; professor of natural history, Royal Agricultural College, Cirencester, 1877–9; visited Canada 1884, 1888, and 1891, writing accounts of Canadian agriculture; first Steven lecturer on agricultural entomology, Edinburgh, 1890–1906; edited Royal Agricultural Society's 'Journal,' 1890–1900; agricultural correspondent of 'The Times,' 1894–1906; published 'The Elements of Agriculture,' 1891.

FRÉCHETTE, LOUIS HONORÉ (1839–1908), Canadian poet and journalist; born near Quebec; at Quebec edited 'Journal de Québec'; clerk of legislative council, 1889–1908; published French verse, including 'Mes Loisirs,' 1863, 'Les Oiseaux de Neige,' 1880, 'Les Fleurs Boréales,' 1881, and 'La Légende d'un Peuple,' 1887; C.M.G., 1897; president of Royal Society of Canada; wrote also 'La Noël au Canada,' a prose collection of tales and dramas; a poet of French-Canadian patriotism; influenced by Victor Hugo.

FREEMAN, GAGE EARLE (1820–1903), writer on falconry; vicar of Macclesfield Forest, 1856–89, and Askham, 1889–1903; devoted leisure to hawking; wrote on the subject in 'Field' newspaper; collaborated with F. H. Salvin [q. v.] in 'Falconry; its Claims, History and Practice,' 1859; published 'Practical Falconry,' 1869, and volumes of verse.

FREEMAN-MITFORD, ALGERNON BERTRAM, first BARON REDESDALE, of the second creation (1837–1916), diplomatist and author. [See MITFORD.]

FRERE, MARY ELIZA ISABELLA (1845–1911), author; daughter of Sir Bartle Frere, first baronet [q. v.]; went with father to Bombay, 1863; collected Indian folk-lore tales in 'Old Deccan Days,' 1868; wrote poems; accompanied father to South Africa, 1877, and later travelled in Egypt and Palestine.

FREYER, SIR PETER JOHNSTON (1851–1921), surgeon; M.D. and M.S., Queen's University of Ireland; served in Indian medical service, 1875–96; surgeon to St. Peter's Hospital for Stone, London, 1897–1914; C.B. and K.C.B., 1917.

FRIESE-GREENE, WILLIAM (1855–1921), pioneer of kinematography. [See GREENE.]

FRITH, WILLIAM POWELL (1819–1909), artist; studied art under Sass and at Royal Academy Schools; exhibited at Royal Academy from 1840 subject pictures, such as 'English Merrymaking a Hundred Years ago,' 1847; A.R.A., 1845; R.A., 1853; chief works were 'Ramsgate Sands,' 1853, 'Derby Day,' 1858 (now in Tate Gallery), 'The Railway Station,' 1862, 'Charles II's last Whitehall Sunday,' 1867; unsuccessfully attempted to rival Hogarth's morality pictures, 1878–80; other works were 'Charles Dickens,' 1859, and 'Uncle Toby and the Widow Wadman,' 1866 (in Tate Gallery); visited Holland, 1850 and 1880, and Italy, 1875; C.V.O., 1908; published 'John Leech, his Life and Work,' 1891, 'Reminiscences,' 1887, and 'Further Reminiscences,' 1888.

FRY, DANBY PALMER (1818–1903), legal writer; clerk in poor law board, 1836–78; reported chartist proceedings at Kennington Common, 1848; called to bar, 1851; legal adviser (1878–82) to local government board; original member of Philological Society, 1842, and of Early English Text Society, 1864; published standard legal handbooks.

FRY, SIR EDWARD (1827–1918), judge; great-grandson of Joseph Fry [q. v.]; in business in Bristol, 1843–8; B.A., University College, London, 1851; called to bar (Lincoln's Inn), 1854; published 'A Treatise on the Specific Performance of Contracts,' 1858; acquired large practice in Chancery and company work and at parliamentary bar; Q.C., 1869; practised in turn before Vice-Chancellors James and Bacon, afterwards migrating to Rolls court; appointed additional judge in Chancery division and knighted, 1877; principal legal work performed on rule committee of judges; sat in Court of Appeal, 1883–92; in later life played important part in international affairs; judge on Hague tribunal, 1900; arbitrator at Hague between United States and Mexico in pious

funds of California dispute, 1902–3; British legal assessor on commission appointed to deal with Dogger Bank incident, 1904; played active part at second Hague Conference, 1907; arbitrator between France and Germany over Casablanca incident, 1908–9; F.R.S., 1883; G.C.B., 1907; a strong quaker.

FRY, JOSEPH STORRS (1826–1913), cocoa manufacturer and quaker philanthropist; brother of Sir Edward Fry [q. v.]; partner in family business in Bristol, 1855; president of 'London Yearly Meeting' of Friends for fifteen years.

FRYATT, CHARLES ALGERNON (1872–1916), merchant seaman; entered Great Eastern Railway Company's service as able seaman on Harwich to Antwerp steamship route, 1892; made 143 trips in command of vessels during European War, 1914–16; ship 'Brussels' attacked by German submarine, March 1916; commended by Admiralty for plucky escape; captured by German destroyers, June; court martialled and shot as 'franctireur' at Bruges, July.

FULLER, SIR THOMAS EKINS (1831–1910), agent-general for Cape Colony, 1902–7; editor of 'Cape Argus,' South Africa, 1864; advocated University and responsible government in Cape Colony; general manager of Union Steamship Company at Cape Town, 1875–98; represented Cape Town in House of Assembly, 1878–1902; supported Cecil Rhodes's policy; K.C.M.G., 1904; wrote monograph on Cecil Rhodes, 1910.

FULLEYLOVE, JOHN (1845–1908), landscape painter; studied drawing and architecture; travelled much in England and abroad; member of Royal Institute of Painters in Water-Colours, 1879; exhibited in London water-colour drawings of 'Petrarch's Country,' 1886, Oxford, 1888, Cambridge, 1890, Versailles, 1894, Greece, 1896, and Palestine, 1902; also painted in oils; many drawings were reproduced as illustrations to books; an able architectural draughtsman and accomplished water-colour artist.

FURNESS, CHRISTOPHER, first BARON FURNESS, of Grantley (1852–1912), shipowner and industrialist; early joined brother's firm of wholesale provision merchants; set up as shipowner, 1877; amalgamated with other firms; liberal M.P., Hartlepools, 1891–5, 1900–10; knighted, 1895; created baron, 1910.

FURNIVALL, FREDERICK JAMES (1825–1910), scholar and editor; educated at private schools, University College, London, and Trinity Hall, Cambridge; B.A., 1847; M.A., 1850; enthusiastic oarsman from youth; improved design of sculling boats, 1845; barrister of Gray's Inn, 1849; interested in social reform; joined Christian socialists; made acquaintance of Ruskin, 1849; helped to found Working Men's College, London, 1854; taught English grammar and literature there; developed college's social life; became an outspoken agnostic; his relations strained with F. D. Maurice, principal of the college; applied principles of co-operation to literary study; member of Philological Society from 1847, and sole secretary from 1862 to death; became (1861) editor of the Philological Society's suggested English Dictionary, which developed into the 'New English Dictionary' of Oxford; contributed to that work through life; founded Early English Text Society, 1864, and Chaucer Society, 1868; edited Chaucer's works from MS., and thereby furnished new material for textual study; edited 'Percy Ballads' with Prof. J. W. Hales, 1868, and founded Ballad Society; established New Shakspere Society, 1873; resented Swinburne's sarcastic attack on society's methods; engaged in undignified controversy with Halliwell-Phillipps and with Swinburne, 1881; wrote elaborate preface for 'Leopold' Shakespeare, 1876; supervised issue of photographic facsimiles of Shakespeare quartos (43 vols. 1880–9); founded Wiclif and Browning societies, 1881; the Browning Society greatly extended the poet's popularity; founded Shelley Society, 1886; lost substantial fortune inherited from his father on failure of Overend and Gurney's Bank, 1867; received civil list pension, 1884; hon. Ph.D. Berlin, 1884; hon. fellow of Trinity Hall, 1902; hon. D.Litt. Oxford, 1901; original F.B.A., 1902; devoted to rowing till death, he founded National Amateur Rowing Association, to include all ranks of society, 1891, and Hammersmith (renamed Furnivall) Sculling Club for girls and men, 1896.

FURSE, CHARLES WELLINGTON (1868–1904), painter; pupil of Alphonse Legros [q. v.] at Slade School, London, and of Julian in Paris; first exhibited at Royal Academy, 1888; gained early distinction as portrait painter; developed original and spontaneous manner; skilful painter of horses; went in search of health to South Africa, 1895; made decorative paintings for Liverpool Town Hall in manner of Tintoretto, 1898–1901; married daughter of John Addington Symonds, 1900, and settled next year at Camberley, producing his 'Return from the Ride' and 'Diana of the Uplands' (both in Tate Gallery), 'Lord Charles Beresford,' 'Lord Roberts' (unfinished); A.R.A., 1903; died of tuberculosis; a keen art critic and energetic worker.

FUST, HERBERT JENNER- (1806–1904), cricketer. [See JENNER-FUST.]

GADSBY, HENRY ROBERT (1842–1907), musician; professor of harmony at Guildhall School of Music from 1880; published choral and orchestral cantatas, part songs, and anthems, and text-books on harmony, 1883, and sight singing, 1897.

GAIRDNER, JAMES (1828–1912), historian; son of John Gairdner, M.D. [q.v.]; clerk in Public Record Office, 1846–93; joint editor of 'Calendar of Letters and Papers of the Reign of Henry VIII'; edited 'Paston Letters,' &c.

GAIRDNER, SIR WILLIAM TENNANT (1824–1907), professor of medicine at Glasgow; son of John Gairdner [q. v.]; M.D. Edinburgh, 1845; hon. LL.D., 1883; pathologist and physician to Royal Infirmary there; professor of medicine at Glasgow University, 1862–90; medical officer of health, Glasgow, 1863–72; attractive lecturer; made many original researches in connexion with heart and lung diseases; F.R.S., 1892; K.C.B., 1898; works include 'Clinical Medicine,' 1862, and 'The Physician as Naturalist,' 1889.

GALE, FREDERICK (1823–1904), cricketer and writer on cricket under the pseudonym of 'Old Buffer'; works include 'Public School Matches and those we meet there,' 1853, and 'The Game of Cricket,' 1887; brother-in-law of Arthur Severn and a friend of Ruskin.

GALLWEY, PETER (1820–1906), Jesuit preacher and writer; studied at Stonyhurst; entered Society of Jesus, 1836; in charge of Farm Street church, London, 1857–69 and 1877–1906; provincial of Jesuits in England, 1873–6; published 'Lectures on Ritualism,' 2 vols. 1879, pamphlets and sermons.

GALTON, SIR FRANCIS (1822–1911), founder of the science of 'eugenics'; born at Birmingham; entered Trinity College, Cambridge, 1840; travelled in Syria and Egypt, 1844; published account of exploration into interior of Damaraland, in 'Tropical South Africa,' 1853; F.R.S., 1856; general secretary of British Association, 1863–7; in 'Meteorographica,' 1863, he pointed out importance of 'anticyclones,' a word coined by himself; began researches into laws of heredity, 1865; initiated anthropometric laboratory at Health Exhibition, 1884–5, collecting impressions of fingers; proved permanence of finger-prints; published 'Finger Prints,' 1893, and 'Finger Print Directory,' 1895; influenced by his cousin Charles Darwin's 'Origin of Species,' he investigated the heritability of genius; published his results in 'Hereditary Genius,' 1869, 'English Men of Science,' 1874, 'Human Faculty,' 1883, 'Natural Inheritance,' 1889, and 'Noteworthy Families,' 1906; founded eugenic laboratory, 1904, and research fellowship and scholarship, 1907, at University College, London; initiated quarterly journal, 'Biometrika,' 1901; knighted, 1909; by will left 45,000*l.* for foundation of chair of eugenics in London University; wrote 'Memories of My Life,' 1908; 'Life' by Prof. Karl Pearson, 1914.

GAMGEE, ARTHUR (1841–1909), physiologist; born at Florence; brother of Joseph Gamgee (1828–1886, q. v.); M.D. Edinburgh University, 1862; lecturer on physiology at Royal College of Surgeons, Edinburgh, 1863–9; fellow, 1872; studied under Kühne at Heidelberg and Ludwig at Leipzig, 1871; F.R.S., 1872; F.R.C.P. London, 1896; first Brackenbury professor of physiology in Owens College, Manchester, 1873–85; practised in Switzerland from 1889; visited America, 1902 and 1903; extended knowledge of physical and chemical properties of hæmoglobin; made elaborate research on diurnal variations of temperature of human body; works include 'Textbook of Physiological Chemistry,' 2 vols. 1880–93; died at Paris.

GARCIA, MANUEL (PATRICIO RODRIGUEZ) (1805–1906), singer and teacher of singing; born at Zafra, Spain; studied harmony in Paris; as professor at Paris conservatoire he taught Jenny Lind; published famous 'Traité complet de l'art du chant,' 1847; professor of singing at Royal Academy of Music, London, 1848–95; invented laryngoscope (1854), which became universally used in medicine and surgery; made C.V.O. on hundredth birthday, 1905; 'Life' by Sterling MacKinlay, 1908.

GARDINER, SAMUEL RAWSON (1829–1902), historian; B.A., Christ Church, Oxford, 1851; married daughter of Edward Irving [q. v.], 1856; settled in London to study history of Puritan revolution, supporting himself meanwhile by teaching; lecturer (1872–7) and professor of modern history (1877–85) at King's College, London; published first instalment of his 'History of England (1603–42)' in 1863, and last in 1882; collective edition in 10 vols. 1883–4; there followed 'The Great Civil War,' 3 vols. 1886–91, and 'The History of the Commonwealth and Protectorate,' 3 vols. 1895–1901; his unfinished 'Last Years of the Protectorate' was completed by (Sir) Charles Firth, 2 vols. 1909; his historical work shows scientific arrangement of material, minute accuracy, impartiality, but lacks the picturesque style of Froude or Macaulay. Gardiner wrote also 'The Thirty Years War,' 1874, and 'The Puritan Revolution,' 1876, for 'Epochs of English History' series, 'Student's History of England,' 3 vols. 1890; edited 'Constitutional Documents of the Puritan Revolution,' 1889; was editor of 'English Historical Review,' 1891–1901; director of Camden Society, 1869–97, he edited 12 of its volumes, and also contributed to publications of Navy Records Society, Scottish History Society, and to this Dictionary. Awarded civil list pension, 1882; he was research fellow of All Souls, Oxford, 1884–92, and of Merton, 1892–1902; received many honorary distinctions at home and abroad and was Ford lecturer, Oxford, 1896.

GARGAN, DENIS (1819–1903), president of Maynooth College; ordained, 1843; professor of humanity, 1845, and of ecclesiastical history, 1859; vice-president, 1885, and president, 1894, of Maynooth; received King Edward VII there, 1903; published 'The Ancient Church of Ireland,' 1864.

GARNER, THOMAS (1839–1906), architect; fellow-pupil of Sir George Gilbert Scott [q. v.] with G. F. Bodley [q. v.], whose partner he became, 1869–97; did much ecclesiastical, domestic, and collegiate architecture in Oxford, Cambridge, and London; in later life joined Church of Rome; joint author of 'The Domestic Architecture of England during the Tudor Period,' 1908.

GARNETT, RICHARD (1835–1906), man of letters and keeper of printed books in the British Museum; elder son of Richard Garnett [q. v.]; privately educated; early developed linguistic and literary aptitudes; entered British Museum library, 1857, and won favour of Sir Anthony Panizzi [q. v.]; assistant keeper of printed books and superintendent of the reading room, 1875–90; superintended printing of catalogue; keeper of printed books, 1890–9; his chief acquisitions noticed in 'A Description of 300 Notable Books,' privately printed, 1899; president of Library Association, 1892–3; engaged through life in literary work, poetic, critical, and biographical; his most important publications were hitherto unpublished 'Relics of Shelley,' 1862, and 'The Twilight of the Gods' (1888, new edit. 1903), apologues of pleasantly cynical flavour in Lucian's vein; other writings include 'Io in Egypt and other Poems,' 1859 (new edit. 1893); brief biographies of Milton and Carlyle, 1877, Emerson, 1888, Edward Gibbon Wakefield, 1898, and a 'History of Italian Literature,' 1897; a contributor to this Dictionary; hon. LL.D. Edinburgh, 1883; C.B., 1895.

GARRAN (formerly GAMMAN), ANDREW (1825–1901), Australian journalist and politician; B.A. London, 1845; M.A., 1848; migrated to Adelaide, 1851; assistant editor (1856) and editor (1873–85) of 'Sydney Morning Herald'; member of legislative council of New South Wales, 1887; president of royal commission on strikes, 1890, whose report led to Trades Disputes Conciliation Act, 1892; president of arbitration council, 1892; vice-president of executive council, 1895–8; edited 'Picturesque Atlas of Australasia,' 1886.

GARRETT, FYDELL EDMUND (1865–1907), publicist; B.A., Trinity College, Cambridge, 1887; president of Union, 1887; joined staff of 'Pall Mall Gazette'; sent for phthisis cure to South Africa, 1889; intimate with Cecil Rhodes and President Kruger; described experiences in 'In Afrikanderland,' 1891; returned to London, writing for 'Pall Mall' and 'Westminster' gazettes, 1891–5; translated Ibsen's 'Brand,' 1894; as editor of 'Cape Times,' 1895–1900, he influenced public affairs in South Africa; member of Cape parliament, 1898–1902; advocated united autonomous South Africa; settled in Devonshire, 1904; wrote also 'The Story of an African Crisis,' 1897; 'Life' by E. T. Cook 1909.

GARRETT ANDERSON, ELIZABETH (1836-1917), physician. [See ANDERSON.]

GARROD, SIR ALFRED BARING (1819-1907), physician; studied medicine at University College Hospital; M.D., 1843; physician and professor of therapeutics at University College Hospital, 1851-63, and at King's College Hospital, 1863-74; F.R.C.P., 1856; Gulstonian lecturer, 1857; Lumleian lecturer, 1883; F.R.S., 1858; knighted, 1887; made valuable researches into gout; wrote 'Treatise on Gout and Rheumatic Gout,' 1859.

GARTH, SIR RICHARD (1820-1903), chief justice of Bengal, 1875-86; educated at Eton and Christ Church, Oxford; in university cricket XI, 1839-42; called to bar, 1847; Q.C., 1866; conservative M.P. for Guildford, 1866-8; knighted, 1875; able judge but partisan controversialist; opposed to Bengal tenancy bill; promoted Legal Practitioners Act, 1879; P.C., 1888; supported Indian National Congress in 'A Few Plain Truths about India,' 1888.

GASELEE, SIR ALFRED (1844-1918), general; joined army, 1863; served chiefly in Indian wars and expeditions, 1863-1900; C.B., 1891; K.C.B., 1898; commanded British expeditionary force for relief of legations in Peking, 1900; full general, 1906; commanded Northern army in India, 1907-8; G.C.B., 1909.

GASKELL, WALTER HOLBROOK (1847-1914), physiologist; born at Naples; B.A., Trinity College, Cambridge (26th wrangler), 1869; studied physiology at Leipzig, 1874-5; M.D., Cambridge, 1878; F.R.S., 1882; university lecturer in physiology, 1883; fellow of Trinity Hall, 1889; his physiological researches revolutionized current ideas of action of the heart, and of cardiac disease; aroused great controversy by his theory of the origin of vertebrates.

GATACRE, SIR WILLIAM FORBES (1843-1906), major-general; joined 77th foot in Bengal, 1862; instructor in surveying at Sandhurst, 1875-9; commanded regiment at Secunderabad, 1884; in command of Bombay district, 1894-7, and 3rd brigade of relief force in Chitral expedition, 1895; C.B.; received Kaiser-i-Hind gold medal for services in Bombay plague, 1897; commanded brigade in advance up Nile for recovery of Khartoum; major-general and K.C.B.; known as 'General Backacher,' 1898; in Boer war he defended railway from East London to Bethulie, 1899; was forced to retreat at Stormberg (December); joined main army at Bloemfontein, March 1900; occupied Dewetsdorp and sent detachment on to Reddersburg; detachment surrounded and surrendered owing to Gatacre's failure to relieve it (April); removed from command; commanded eastern district at Colchester, 1900-3; explored rubber forests in Abyssinia, 1905; died of fever at Iddeni; 'Life' by widow, 1910.

GATHORNE-HARDY, GATHORNE, first EARL OF CRANBROOK (1814-1906), statesman; educated at Eton and Oriel College, Oxford; B.A., 1836; M.A., 1861; hon. fellow, 1894; called to bar, 1840; obtained lead on sessions and at parliamentary bar; conservative M.P. for Leominster, 1856-65; under-secretary for home department, 1858-9; active champion of Church of England; defeated Gladstone in parliamentary election for Oxford University, 1865; president of the poor law board and P.C., 1866; introduced poor law amendment bill, 1867; home secretary after Hyde Park riots, May 1867-8; dealt firmly with Fenian conspirators; in opposition warmly attacked Irish Church disestablishment, 1869; secretary of state for war under Disraeli, 1874-8; opposed public worship regulation bill, 1874; introduced regimental exchanges bill, 1875; supported Disraeli's pro-Turkish policy; succeeded Lord Salisbury as secretary for India, 1878; raised to peerage as Viscount Cranbrook, 1878; sanctioned Vernacular Press Act of 1878; supported Lord Lytton's forward policy on North-West frontier; justified coercion of Ameer Shere Ali; approved separation of Kandahar from Kabul, 1880; G.C.S.I., 1880; sat on royal commission on cathedral churches, 1879-85; lord president of the council, 1885-92; created earl, 1892; denounced Gladstone's home rule bill, 1893; hon. D.C.L. Oxford, 1865; hon. LL.D. Cambridge, 1892; good debater and platform speaker; ardent sportsman and broad churchman; memoir by son, 1910.

GATTY, ALFRED (1813-1903), vicar of Ecclesfield and author; B.A., Exeter College, Oxford, 1836; M.A., 1839; D.D., 1860; vicar of Ecclesfield from 1839 till death; sub-dean of York Minster, 1862; published 'The Bell: its Origin and History,' 1847, 'Sheffield Past and Present,' 1873, verse, biographies, and sermons.

GEE, SAMUEL JONES (1839-1911), physician; studied medicine at University College, London; M.B., 1861; M.D., 1865; F.R.C.P., 1870; physician and lecturer at St. Bartholomew's Hospital from 1868 to death; Gulstonian (1871), Bradshaw (1892), and Lumleian (1899) lecturer at Royal College of Physicians; had wide knowledge of early medical literature; published 'Auscultation and Percussion,' 1870, 'Medical Lectures and Aphorisms,' 1902.

GEIKIE, JOHN CUNNINGHAM (1824-1906), religious writer; presbyterian minister in Canada and in England, 1848-73; hon. LL.D. Edinburgh, 1891; awarded civil list pension, 1898; works include 'Life and Words of Christ,' 2 vols. 1877, and 'Hours with the Bible,' 10 vols. 1881-4.

GELL, SIR JAMES (1823-1905), Manx lawyer and judge; admitted to Manx bar, 1845; edited for government Manx statute laws (1836-48); attorney-general, 1866-98; first deemster, 1898; clerk of the Rolls, 1900-5; deputy-governor, 1897-1902; knighted, 1877; C.V.O., 1902.

GEORGE WILLIAM FREDERICK CHARLES, second DUKE OF CAMBRIDGE, EARL OF TIPPERARY and BARON CULLODEN (1819-1904), field-marshal and commander-in-chief of the army; only son of Adolphus Frederick, first duke [q. v.]; born at Hanover; sent to England, 1830; G.C.H., 1825; K.G., 1835; served in Hanoverian army, 1836; settled in England on Queen Victoria's accession, 1837; contracted a morganatic marriage, 1840; made brevet-colonel; commanded 17th lancers at disturbances at Leeds, 1842; commanded troops at Corfu, 1843-5; G.C.M.G. and major-general, 1845; commanded Dublin district, 1847-52; succeeded to dukedom, 1850; K.P., 1851; commanded a division in Crimea, 1854; present at Alma and Inkermann; G.C.B., 1855; succeeded Lord Hardinge [q.v.] as general commanding in chief, 1856; general and P.C., 1856; colonel of artillery and engineers, 1861; president of National Rifle Association, 1859; helped to found Staff College; field-marshal, 1862; as general commanding in chief he was subordinated to war minister by War Office Act of 1870; opposed such innovations as short service, formation of army reserve, and linking of battalions; commander-in-chief with sole control of supply, 1887; difficulties with secretary for war led to inquiry into naval and military administration (1888-90), and to his enforced resignation, 1895; as chief personal A.D.C. to Queen Victoria he undertook for her many social duties; opened London international exhibition, 1862; president of Christ's Hospital and London Hospital for over fifty years; ranger of Hyde Park, 1852, and of Richmond Park, 1857; K.T., 1881; elder brother of Trinity House, 1885; received freedom of City of London, 1857; paid last visit to Germany, 1903; statues at Whitehall and at Christ's Hospital, Horsham; portraits by Lucas, Holl, Cope, and Herkomer; Lives by Willoughby C. Verner and J. E. Sheppard.

GEORGE, HEREFORD BROOKE (1838-1910), historical writer; B.A., New College, Oxford, 1860; M.A., 1862; tutor, 1867-91; pioneer of military history at Oxford; published 'Battles of English History,' 1895, 'Napoleon's Invasion of Russia,' 1899, 'New College, 1856-1906,' 1906; made first ascent of Gross Viescherhorn, 1862; edited 'Alpine Journal,' 1863-7; published 'The Oberland and its Glaciers,' 1866; lost fortune by failure of West of England and South Wales Bank, at Bristol, 1880.

GERARD, (JANE) EMILY (1846-1905), novelist; sister of Sir Montagu Gilbert Gerard [q. v.]; married Chevalier Miecislas de Laszowski, 1869; lived in Galicia; with sister Dorothea collaborated in four novels; wrote independently six novels, including 'The Voice of a Flower,' 1893.

GERARD, SIR MONTAGU GILBERT (1842-1905), general; of Catholic parentage; joined army, 1864; served in second Afghan war, 1878-80; present at Kassassin and Tel-el-Kebir and C.B., 1882; sent on secret mission to Persia, 1881 and 1885; British military attaché at St. Petersburg, 1892; negotiated in Pamirs boundary dispute, 1895; commanded first-class district, Bengal, 1899; K.C.S.I., 1897; K.C.B., 1902; general, 1904; chief British attaché in Manchuria in Russo-Japanese war, 1904; died at Irkutsk on way home; published 'Diaries of a Soldier and a Sportsman,' 1903.

GIBB, ELIAS JOHN WILKINSON (1857-1901), Orientalist; educated at Glasgow University; early studied Arabic, Persian, and Turkish languages and literatures; translated Ottoman prose and verse, 1879-

1884; published a detailed 'History of Ottoman Poetry,' vol. i. 1900 (vols. ii–vi. edited by E. G. Browne after Gibb's death, 1902–9); fine Oriental library divided among British Museum, Cambridge University, and British Embassy at Constantinople.

GIBBINS, HENRY DE BELTGENS (1865–1907), writer on economic history; born in Cape Colony; Cobden prizeman at Oxford, 1890; D.Litt. Dublin, 1896; wrote works on industrial and commercial history; edited Methuen's 'Social Questions of the Day' series, 1891.

GIBBS, HENRY HUCKS, first BARON ALDENHAM (1819–1907), merchant and scholar; M.A., Exeter College, 1844; joined family firm of bankers, 1843; head of firm, 1875; director of Bank of England, 1853–1901; governor, 1875–7; wrote many pamphlets advocating bimetallism; published 'A Colloquy on Currency,' 1893; helped to found 'St. James's Gazette,' 1880; conservative M.P. for City of London, 1891–2; served on royal commission on Stock Exchange, 1877–8; raised to peerage, 1896; benefactor to Keble College, Oxford; leading member of English Church Union from 1862; bought advowson of and restored church at Aldenham; helped to restore St. Albans Abbey; fond of shooting, he lost right hand in gun accident, 1864; helped in preparation of 'New English Dictionary'; edited works for Early English Text Society and Roxburgh Club; Spanish scholar and bibliophile; trustee of National Portrait Gallery; F.S.A., 1885.

GIBSON, EDWARD, first BARON ASHBOURNE, of Ashbourne, co. Meath (1837–1913), lord chancellor of Ireland; B.A., Trinity College, Dublin; called to Irish bar, 1860; Q.C., 1872; conservative M.P., Dublin University, 1875; Irish attorney-general, 1877–80; peer, 1885; lord chancellor of Ireland with seat in Cabinet, 1885, 1886–92, 1895–1905.

GIFFARD, HARDINGE STANLEY, first EARL OF HALSBURY (1823–1921), lord chancellor; son of Stanley Lees Giffard [q. v.]; B.A., Merton College, Oxford; called to bar (Inner Temple), 1850; joined South Wales circuit, 1851; practised at Old Bailey and at Middlesex sessions at Clerkenwell; junior prosecuting counsel at Central Criminal Court, 1859; Q.C., 1865; leading counsel for Governor E. J. Eyre [q. v.], 1867–8; second counsel for Tichborne claimant, Arthur Orton [q. v.], 1871–2; solicitor general and knighted, 1875; led for Crown in 'Franconia' case, 1876; conservative M.P., Launceston, 1877; took active part in parliament and law courts over case of Charles Bradlaugh [q. v.]; greatest forensic triumph, case of Belt v. Lawes, 1882; lord chancellor, 1885–6, 1886–92, 1895–1905; created baron, 1885; earl, 1898; largely responsible for Land Transfer Act (1897) and Criminal Evidence Act (1898); presided over production of complete digest of 'Laws of England' (1905–16); led 'diehards' among peers against Parliament Bill, 1911.

GIFFEN, SIR ROBERT (1837–1910), economist and statistician; apprenticed to lawyer in Glasgow; took up journalism, 1860; sub-editor of 'Globe,' 1862–6; assistant editor of 'Economist,' 1868–76; chief of statistical department to board of trade, 1876–97; the commercial (1882) and the labour (1892) departments were subsequently included in his control; served on many royal commissions; edited 'Journal of Royal Statistical Society,' 1876–91; helped to found Economic Society, 1890; criticized Gladstone's home rule finance, 1893; liberal unionist from 1886, and finally unionist free trader; K.C.B., 1895; strong individualist; advocated 'free banking'; voluminous writings include 'Essays in Finance,' 2 series, 1880–6, 'The Case against Bimetallism,' 1892, and 'Economic Enquiries and Studies,' 2 vols. 1904.

GIFFORD, EDWIN HAMILTON (1820–1905), schoolmaster and theologian; B.A., St. John's College, Cambridge (senior classic and 15th wrangler), 1843; fellow, 1843–4; hon. fellow, 1903; head master of King Edward's School, Birmingham, 1848–62; archdeacon of London and canon of St. Paul's, 1883; wrote 'Voices of the Past,' 1874, and edited with translation Eusebius's 'Praeparatio Evangelica,' 5 vols. 1903.

GIGLIUCCI, COUNTESS (1818–1908), oratorio and operatic prima donna. [See NOVELLO, CLARA ANASTASIA.]

GILBERT, SIR JOSEPH HENRY (1817–1901), agricultural chemist; son of Joseph Gilbert [q. v.] and Ann Gilbert [q. v.]; studied agricultural chemistry at Glasgow, London, and at Giessen under Liebig; co-worker with John Bennet Lawes [q. v.] in Rothamsted agricultural experiments; president of Chemical Society,

1882–3; F.R.S., 1860; professor of rural economy at Oxford, 1884–90; knighted, 1893.

GILBERT, SIR WILLIAM SCHWENCK (1836–1911), dramatist; son of William Gilbert (1804–1890, q. v.); used his own pet name 'Bab' as pseudonym in later life; B.A. London, 1857; joined militia, 1857; retired as major, 1883; clerk in privy council office (education department), 1857–61; called to bar, 1863; commenced author and artist as regular contributor to 'Fun' from 1861; illustrated books by father, 1863 and 1869; his 'Yarn of the Nancy Bell' refused by 'Punch' as 'too cannibalistic,' 1866; this and other 'Bab' ballads appeared in 'Fun' from 1866 to 1871 and were published in volume form as 'Bab Ballads,' 1869, and 'More Bab Ballads,' 1873; commenced playwright with 'Dulcamara,' a successful burlesque, 1866; wrote many extravaganzas; collaborated with Frederick Clay [q. v.] in musical sketches for the German Reeds, 1869–72; introduced by Clay to Arthur Sullivan, 1871; first collaborated with Sullivan in a burlesque, 'Thespis,' 1871; wrote blank verse fairy comedy, 'The Palace of Truth,' 1870, 'Pygmalion and Galatea,' 1871, 'The Wicked World,' 1873; wrote series of comedies (some under pseudonym of F. L. Tomline) for Miss Marie Litton at Court Theatre; 'The Happy Land,' 1873, roused much enthusiasm and public excitement; produced also serious plays, including 'Charity,' 1874, 'Broken Hearts,' 1875, and 'Dan'l Druce,' 1876; collaborated with Sullivan for D'Oyly Carte's opera company in long series of comic operas, viz. 'Trial by Jury,' 1875, 'The Sorcerer,' 1877, 'H.M.S. Pinafore,' 1878, 'The Pirates of Penzance' (produced in New York), 1879, 'Patience,' 1881; operas transferred to Savoy Theatre, 1881; later 'Savoy' operas were 'Iolanthe,' 1882, 'Princess Ida,' 1884, 'The Mikado,' 1885—the most popular work—'Ruddigore,' 1887, 'The Yeomen of the Guard,' 1888, 'The Gondoliers,' 1889; separated from Sullivan and Carte owing to financial disagreement, 1890–3; collaborated with Alfred Cellier in 'The Mountebanks,' 1892; resumed collaboration with Sullivan in 'Utopia, Limited,' 1893, and 'The Grand Duke,' 1896; produced 'Fallen Fairies' with Edward German, 1909, and 'The Hooligan,' a serious sketch, 1911; built and owned Garrick Theatre, 1889; interested in astronomy, bee-keeping, and horticulture; knighted, 1907; plays show literary grace, whimsical humour (known as 'Gilbertian' humour), urbane satire, good taste, and lyric excellence; master of stage management; fond of epigram and repartee; a kindly cynic; dramatic works collected in 'Original Plays,' 4 series, 1876–1911, and in 'Original Comic Operas,' 8 parts, 1890.

GILL, SIR DAVID (1843–1914), astronomer; educated at Dollar Academy, Marischal College, and the University, Aberdeen; established in Aberdeen time service similar to that installed in Edinburgh by Charles Piazzi Smyth [q. v.], 1863; in charge of private observatory erected at Dunecht by Lord Lindsay (afterwards twenty-sixth Earl of Crawford, q. v.), 1872–6; took part in observations of transit of Venus at Mauritius, 1874; chief result of expedition revelation of possibilities of heliometer for astronomical measurements; made successful expedition to island of Ascension in order to measure with heliometer distance of Mars from earth and thus derive sun's distance, 1877; H.M. astronomer at Cape of Good Hope, 1879–1907; obtained larger heliometer with which he redetermined sun's distance and determined mass of Jupiter; pioneer in application of photography to astronomy, and carried out photographic survey of Southern heavens, 1885–98; organized geodetic survey of South Africa; K.C.B., 1900.

GILLIES, DUNCAN (1834–1903), premier of Victoria; emigrated from Glasgow to Ballarat goldfields, 1852; led miners in resistance to government, 1853–4; member of Ballarat mining board, 1858; member of legislative assembly, 1859; president of board of land and works, 1868; commissioner of railways and roads, 1872–5; minister of agriculture, 1875–7; commissioner of railways in Service government, 1880, and in Service-Berry coalition, 1883–6; premier and treasurer, 1886–90; extended revenue, expenditure, and railways; passed Irrigation Act, 1886; supported Australian federation; agent-general for Victoria in London, 1894–7; speaker of Victoria house of assembly, 1902–3.

GINSBURG, CHRISTIAN DAVID (1831–1914), Old Testament scholar; born at Warsaw of Jewish parentage; educated at Rabbinic school at Warsaw; became Christian, c. 1847; came to England; naturalized, 1858; original member of Old Testament revision company,

1870; published first volume of his principal work, edition of 'The Massorah,' 1880.

GIROUARD, DÉSIRÉ (1836–1911), Canadian judge; born in Quebec province; D.C.L. McGill University, 1874; called to bar of Lower Canada, 1860; Q.C., 1880; published treatise on bills of exchange, 1860; conservative M.P. for Jacques Cartier constituency, 1878–95; opposed execution of Louis Riel [q. v.], 1885; judge of the supreme court of Canada, 1895–1911.

GISSING, GEORGE ROBERT (1857–1903), novelist; left Owens College, Manchester, in disgrace for America, where he wandered penniless until 1877; studied literature and philosophy at Jena; returned to England, 1878; published 'Workers in the Dawn,' 1880; found an appreciative reader in Mr. Frederic Harrison, to whose sons he became tutor, 1882; gained precarious livelihood by occasional journalism; published 'The Unclassed,' 1884, 'Demos,' 1886, and other novels illustrating degrading effects of poverty on character; visited Naples, Rome, and Athens; published 'A Life's Morning,' 1888, 'The Nether World,' 1889, 'The Emancipated,' 1890, 'New Grub Street,' 1891, 'Born in Exile,' 1892, and 'The Odd Women,' 1893; revisited Italy with Mr. H. G. Wells, 1897, recording some experiences and impressions in 'By the Ionian Sea,' 1901; in Rome he found material for historical romance 'Veranilda' (published posthumously, 1907); on return to England wrote 'The Town Traveller,' 1898, and 'Our Friend the Charlatan,' 1901; died of pneumonia at St. Jean de Luz; other works include critical study of 'Charles Dickens,' 1898, 'The Private Papers of Henry Ryecroft,' 1903, and 'The House of Cobwebs,' 1906.

GLADSTONE, JOHN HALL (1827–1902), chemist; studied chemistry in London and Giessen; F.R.S., 1853; Fullerian professor of chemistry at Royal Institution, 1874–7; president of Physical (1874) and Chemical (1877–9) societies; hon. D.Sc., Trinity College, Dublin, 1892; made pioneer researches into chemistry in relation to optics; early student of spectroscopy; discovered copper-zinc union for decomposition of water; member of London school board, 1873–94; advocate of technical education, manual instruction, and spelling reform; works include 'Theology and Natural Science,' 1867, 'Michael Faraday,' 1872, 'Miracles,' 1880, and hymns.

GLAISHER, JAMES (1809–1903), astronomer and meteorologist; assistant at Cambridge University observatory, 1833–5, and at Greenwich, 1835–8; chief of magnetic and meteorological department there, 1838–74; improved instruments; published 'Hygrometrical Tables,' 1847; organized voluntary system of precise meteorological observation throughout England, 1847; prepared meteorological reports for registrar-general, 1847–1902; helped to establish daily weather report for 'Daily News,' 1849; F.R.S., 1849; secretary of Royal Meteorological Society, 1850–72; defined relations between weather and cholera epidemics and water-supply; made balloon ascents for meteorological observations with Henry Coxwell [q. v.], 1862–6; published observations in 'British Association Reports,' 1862–6, and account of his ascents in 'Voyages Aériens,' 1869 (translated into English as 'Travels in the Air,' 1871); was also interested in astronomy and mathematical science; completed and published 'Factor Tables,' 3 vols. 1879–83; on committee of Palestine Exploration Fund; translated Flammarion's 'Atmosphere' and Guillemin's 'World of Comets,' 1876.

GLENESK, BARON (1830–1908), proprietor of the 'Morning Post.' [See BORTHWICK, ALGERNON.]

GLOAG, PATON JAMES (1823–1906), theological writer; student of Edinburgh and St. Andrews universities; thrice visited Germany (1857–67) and studied German theological literature; Church of Scotland minister of Galashiels, 1871–92; Baird lecturer, 1879; moderator of general assembly, 1889; professor of biblical criticism in Aberdeen University, 1896–9; hon. D.D. St. Andrews, 1867, and LL.D. Aberdeen, 1899; wrote much on New Testament exegesis; 'Life' by widow, 1908.

GLOAG, WILLIAM ELLIS, LORD KINCAIRNEY (1828–1909), Scottish judge; called to Scottish bar, 1853; advocate depute, 1874; sheriff of Perthshire, 1885; raised to bench as Lord Kincairney, 1889.

GODFREY, DANIEL (1831–1903), bandmaster of grenadier guards, 1856–96; composed famous 'Guards' waltz, 1863, and much popular military music; toured with band in America, 1876; promoted second lieutenant, 1887.

GODKIN, EDWIN LAWRENCE (1831–1902), editor

and author; son of James Godkin [q. v.]; B.A. London, 1851; left law for authorship; published 'The History of Hungary,' 1853; 'Daily News' correspondent in Crimea; settled in United States, 1856; called to New York bar, 1858; supported North in civil war, 1862; edited New York 'Nation,' which by its independence and literary power influenced American public opinion, 1865–99; the paper was recognized organ of independent 'Mugwumps,' 1884–94; Godkin denounced system of Tammany Hall and caused defeat of Tammany, 1894; opposed American annexation of Hawaii and Philippines, high tariffs, and bimetallism; revisited England, 1889; his philosophical radical views expounded in 'Reflections and Comments,' 1895, 'Problems of Modern Democracy,' 1896, and 'Unforeseen Tendencies of Democracy,' 1897; hon. D.C.L. Oxford, 1897; Godkin memorial lectures on citizenship founded at Harvard University; memoirs by James Bryce, 1903, and R. Ogden, 1907.

GODWIN, GEORGE NELSON (1846–1907), Hampshire antiquary; chaplain of the forces, 1877–90; antiquary and historian of Hampshire and neighbouring counties; published 'Civil War in Hampshire, 1642–5,' 1882, 'Bibliotheca Hantoniensis,' 1891, and other works.

GOLDSCHMIDT, OTTO (1829–1907), pianist and composer; born of Jewish parents at Hamburg; studied pianoforte at Leipzig under Mendelssohn, who greatly influenced him; in London, 1848; toured in America with Jenny Lind, 1851; married her, 1852; settled in England, 1856; pianoforte professor at Royal Academy of Music, 1863; vice-principal, 1866–8; produced 'Ruth' at Hereford musical festival, 1867; became conductor of newly-founded 'Bach choir,' 1876; composed 'Music, an Ode,' 1898, and works for pianoforte.

GOLDSMID, SIR FREDERICK JOHN (1818–1908), major-general; born at Milan; joined 37th Madras native infantry, 1839; served in China (1840), in Crimea, and in Indian Mutiny; arranged for telegraph construction along coast of Gwadar, 1861; superintended carrying of wires from Europe across Persia to India, 1864; director-general of Indo-European telegraph; negotiated Anglo-Persian telegraph treaty, 1865; C.B., 1866; constructed telegraph line across whole of Persia; described the experience in 'Travel and Telegraph,' 1874; commissioner for delimitation of Persian and Baluchistan boundary, 1871; investigated Persian and Afghan claims to Seistan; recorded proceedings in 'Eastern Persia, 1870–2,' 2 vols. 1876; K.C.S.I., 1871; controller of crown lands in Egypt, 1880–3; organized intelligence department in campaign of 1882; established administrative system in Congo, 1883; published 'Life of Sir James Outram,' 2 vols. 1880; accomplished Oriental linguist; vice-president of Royal Asiatic Society, 1890–1905.

GOODALL, FREDERICK (1822–1904), artist; taught by father, Edward Goodall [q. v.]; exhibited at Royal Academy, 1839–1902; A.R.A., 1852; R.A., 1862; early works show influence of Wilkie, e.g. 'The Tired Soldier,' 1842, and 'The Village Holiday,' 1847; visits to Egypt (1858–9 and 1870) determined subject of later pictures, as 'The Nubian Slave,' 1864, 'The Flight into Egypt,' 1884, 'Sheep Shearing in Egypt,' 1892; also painted English landscape and portraits; showed technical ability but little inspiration; published gossiping 'Reminiscences,' 1902.

GOODMAN, JULIA (1812–1906), portrait painter; born SALAMAN; exhibited at Royal Academy, 1838–1901; painted over 1,000 portraits or pastels.

GORDON, ARTHUR CHARLES HAMILTON-, first BARON STANMORE (1829–1912), colonial governor; son of fourth Earl of Aberdeen [q. v.]; M.A., Trinity College, Cambridge; lieutenant-governor of New Brunswick, 1861; governor of Trinidad, 1866–70; Mauritius, 1871–4; Fiji, 1875–80; New Zealand, 1880–3; Ceylon, 1883–90; K.C.M.G., 1871; G.C.M.G., 1878; created baron, 1893.

GORDON, JAMES FREDERICK SKINNER (1821–1904), Scottish antiquary; M.A. St. Andrews, 1842; in charge of St. Andrew's Episcopal church, Glasgow, 1844–90; pioneer in abolition of ruinous tenements in Glasgow; published 'The Ecclesiastical Chronicle for Scotland,' 4 vols. 1867; 'A History of Glasgow,' 1872, and topographical works; enthusiastic freemason.

GORDON, SIR JOHN JAMES HOOD (1832–1908), general; entered army, 1849; served in Indian Mutiny and Afridi expedition, 1877–8; prominent in Afghan war, 1878–9; C.B., 1879; commanded troops in expeditions to Karmana and against Malikshahi Waziris, 1880, and in Mahsud Waziris expedition, 1881; commanded brigade in Burmese expedition, 1886–7; assistant military secretary at headquarters, 1890–6; general, 1894; member of Indian Council, 1897–1907; K.C.B., 1898; G.C.B., 1908; published history of Sikhs, 1904.

GORDON, SIR THOMAS EDWARD (1832–1914), general; joined army, 1849; served in Indian Mutiny, 1857–9, and Afghan War, 1879–80; C.B., 1881; attached to legation at Teheran, 1889–93; full general, 1894; K.C.B., 1900.

GORDON-LENNOX, CHARLES HENRY, sixth DUKE OF RICHMOND and first DUKE OF GORDON (1818–1903), lord-president of the council; son of fifth Duke of Richmond [q. v.]; A.D.C. to Duke of Wellington, 1842–52; conservative M.P. for West Sussex, 1841–60; president of poor law board and P.C., 1859; succeeded father, 1860; K.G., 1867; president of board of trade, 1867–9; leader of conservative party in House of Lords, 1868; lord president of council, 1874–80; introduced the agricultural holdings (1875) and elementary schools (1876) bills; created first Duke of Gordon, 1876; carried contagious diseases (animals) bill, 1877; reorganized veterinary department of privy council; chairman of royal commission on agriculture (1879–82), whose report led to Agricultural Holdings Act, 1883, and creation of board of agriculture; a mediator between liberal government and House of Lords in franchise bill crisis of 1884; secretary for Scotland, 1885–6; chancellor of Aberdeen University, 1861; hon. LL.D., 1895; D.C.L. Oxford, 1870; LL.D. Cambridge, 1894; member (1838) and president (1868 and 1883) of Royal Agricultural Society; improved famous Southdown sheep at Goodwood, and shorthorns at Gordon castle.

GORE, ALBERT AUGUSTUS (1840–1901), surgeon-general; M.D. Queen's University, Ireland, 1858; L.R.C.S. Ireland, 1860; served with army medical staff in West Africa (1861), Ashanti war (1873), and Egypt (1882); principal medical officer to forces in India; C.B., 1899; wrote account of his campaigns.

GORE, GEORGE (1826–1908), electro-chemist; head of Institute of Scientific Research, Birmingham, 1880; discovered amorphous antimony and electrolytic sounds; F.R.S., 1865; improved methods of electro-plating; wrote 'The Art of Electro-metallurgy,' 1877, and philosophic works; hon. LL.D. Edinburgh, 1877; awarded civil list pension, 1891; left estate of 5,000l. to Royal Society and Royal Institution.

GORE, JOHN ELLARD (1845–1910), astronomical writer; engineer in Indian works department, 1868–79; published 'Catalogue of Known Variable Stars,' 1884, 'The Worlds of Space,' 1894, and 'The Stellar Heavens,' 1903; F.R.A.S., 1878; member of Royal Irish Academy.

GORELL, first BARON (1848–1913), judge. [See BARNES, JOHN GORELL.]

GORST, SIR JOHN ELDON (1835–1916), lawyer and politician; B.A., St. John's College, Cambridge (third wrangler; went to New Zealand, 1860; returned to England and called to bar, 1865; conservative M.P., borough of Cambridge, 1866; M.P., Chatham, and Q.C., 1875; member of 'fourth party,' 1880–4; solicitor-general and knighted, 1885; under-secretary of state for India, 1886; M.P., Cambridge University, 1892–1906; last vice-president of Committee of Privy Council on Education, 1895–1902; left conservative party.

GORST, SIR [JOHN] ELDON (1861–1911), consul-general in Egypt; son of Sir J. E. Gorst [q. v.]; born in New Zealand; called to bar, 1885; attaché to British agency at Cairo, 1886; controller of direct revenues, 1890–2; adviser to ministry of the interior, 1894; financial adviser, 1898–1904; C.B., 1900; K.C.B., 1902; assistant under-secretary of state to foreign office, 1904–7; consul-general in Egypt, 1907–11; promoted municipal and local self-government there; passed law for enlarging powers of provincial councils, 1910; broad-minded administrator, with financial and linguistic ability; G.C.M.G., 1911.

GOSCHEN, GEORGE JOACHIM, first VISCOUNT GOSCHEN (1831–1907), statesman; grandson of Georg Joachim Göschen, a Leipzig publisher, and son of a London banker; educated in London and Saxe Meiningen, at Rugby and Oriel College, Oxford; first class in lit. hum., 1853; president of the Union, 1853; founded 'Essay Club' at Oxford, 1852; entered father's banking firm; in South America on business, 1854–6; director of bank of England, 1858; published 'Theory of the Foreign Exchanges,' 1861, which attracted wide attention; liberal M.P. for City of London, 1863–80; made a good position in House of Commons; joined Lord Russell's ministry as vice-president of board of trade, 1865, and entered the cabinet

as chancellor of the Duchy of Lancaster, 1866; president of poor law board in Gladstone's first administration, 1868–71; reformed local government system; first lord of the admiralty, 1871–4; his refusal to reduce estimates largely responsible for dissolution of government in 1874; investigated financial position of Egypt at viceroy's invitation, 1876; opposed to his party's plan of equalization of borough and county franchise, 1877; M.P. for Ripon, 1880–5; declined viceroyalty of India, 1880; went on special embassy to Sultan, to compel Turks to carry out treaty of Berlin as regards Greece, Montenegro, and Bulgaria, 1880–1; refused secretaryship for war, 1882, and speakership of Commons, 1883; opposed to radicalism of Mr. Chamberlain and Dilke; out of sympathy with Gladstone's foreign policy, and Parnell's policy of home rule; elected for East Edinburgh, defeating extreme radical candidate, 1885; joined Lord Hartington in forming liberal unionist party, and helped to defeat Gladstone's home rule bill, 1886; chancellor of exchequer in Lord Salisbury's government, 1886–92; M.P. for St. George's, Hanover Square, 1887–1900; converted national debt from 3 per cent. to 2½ per cent. stock, 1888; his firmness prevented financial panic in Baring crisis, 1890; strenuous in opposition to Gladstone's home rule bill of 1893; first lord of the admiralty in Salisbury's third administration, 1895–1900; made vast increases in naval strength and naval estimates; created viscount, 1900; published life of grandfather, 1903, and 'Essays on Economic Questions,' 1905; opposed Mr. Chamberlain's fiscal policy, 1903; showed remarkable consistency of character as statesman; powerful speaker; busy in non-political affairs; ecclesiastical commissioner, 1882; strong supporter of extension of university teaching in London from 1879; hon. D.C.L. Oxford, 1881; hon. LL.D. of Aberdeen and Cambridge, 1888, and Edinburgh, 1890; made chancellor of Oxford University, 1903; portrait by R. Lehmann; 'Life' by A. D. Elliot, 2 vols. 1911.

GOSSELIN, SIR MARTIN LE MARCHANT HADSLEY (1847–1905), diplomatist; secretary of embassy at Brussels, Madrid, Berlin, and Paris, 1885–98; joint British delegate in customs tariffs conferences at Brussels, 1889–90; secretary of international conference for suppression of African slave trade, 1889–90; C.B., 1890; member of commission for delimitation of French and English possessions about river Niger, 1898; K.C.M.G., 1898; British envoy at Lisbon, 1902–5; G.C.V.O., 1904; joined Roman Church, 1878.

GOTT, JOHN (1830–1906), bishop of Truro; M.A., Brasenose College, Oxford, 1854; D.D., 1873; vicar of Leeds, 1873–85; founded Leeds clergy school, 1875; dean of Worcester, 1886; bishop of Truro, 1891–1906; inherited valuable library, which included the four Shakespeare folios; published 'The Parish Priest of the Town,' 1887.

GOUGH, SIR CHARLES JOHN STANLEY (1832–1912), general; born in India; joined army, 1848; V.C. for gallantry during Indian Mutiny; K.C.B. for services in Afghan War, 1881; general, 1891; retired, with G.C.B., 1895.

GOUGH, SIR HUGH HENRY (1833–1909), general; brother of Sir C. J. S. Gough [q. v.]; born at Calcutta; joined Bengal army, 1853; served in Indian Mutiny; at siege of Delhi and relief of Cawnpore; won V.C. for gallantry at Alambagh, 1857; conspicuous for bravery at Lucknow, 1858; commanded 12th Bengal cavalry in Abyssinia campaign, 1868; C.B., 1868; commanded cavalry of Kuram field force, 1878–9; brigadier-general of communications with Kabul field force; commanded cavalry brigade in march to Kandahar, 1880; K.C.B., 1881; general, 1894; G.C.B., 1896; keeper of crown jewels in London, 1898; published 'Old Memories,' 1897.

GOUGH, JOHN EDMOND (1871–1915), brigadier-general; son of Sir C. J. S. Gough [q. v.]; born in India; joined army, 1892; V.C., 1903; served on Sir Douglas Haig's staff, 1914–15; killed in France; posthumous K.C.B., 1915.

GOUGH-CALTHORPE, AUGUSTUS CHOLMONDELEY, sixth BARON CALTHORPE (1829–1910), agriculturist; educated at Eton and Merton College, Oxford; M.A., 1855; succeeded brother in peerage, 1893; started at Elvetham famous herd of shorthorn cattle, Southdown sheep, and Berkshire pigs; generous donor of land to Birmingham city (1894) and university (1900).

GOULD, NATHANIEL (1857–1919), known as NAT GOULD, novelist; journalist in Australia, 1884–95; first book, 'The Double Event' (1891), great success; wrote about 132 books all concerned with horse-racing.

GOULDING, FREDERICK (1842–1909), master printer of copper plates; 'devil' to Whistler in printing some of his etchings, 1859; friend of Sir F. S. Haden from 1862; printed works by Whistler, Haden, Legros, Rodin, and others; assistant to Legros in etching class at National Art Training School, 1876–82; succeeded Legros, 1882–91; first master printer to Royal Society of Painter Etchers, 1890; 'Life' by Martin Hardie, 1910.

GOWER, (EDWARD) FREDERICK LEVESON- (1819–1907), politician. [See LEVESON-GOWER.]

GOWERS, SIR WILLIAM RICHARD (1845–1915), physician; educated at University College, London; M.R.C.S., 1867; on staff of hospital for paralysed and epileptic, Queen Square, London, 1870, and on that of University College Hospital, 1872; F.R.S., 1887; specialized in neurology; chief work, 'A Manual of Diseases of the Nervous System' (1886).

GRACE, EDWARD MILLS (1841–1911), cricketer; studied medicine at Bristol; M.R.C.S., 1865; practised at Thornbury from 1869 till death; coroner for West Gloucestershire, 1875–1909; played cricket for Gentlemen v. Players between 1862 and 1869; visited Australia with George Parr's team, 1863; with brothers raised Gloucestershire to first-class cricketing county and played for England v. Australia, 1880; unorthodox and forcible batsman; pioneer of 'pull' stroke; unrivalled as fielder at point; played till age of seventy.

GRACE, WILLIAM GILBERT (1848–1915), cricketer; brother of Edward Mills Grace [q. v.]; studied medicine in Bristol and London; M.R.C.S., 1879; surgeon in Bristol, 1879–99; played cricket for Gentlemen v. Players between 1865 and 1906; supreme as batsman in England, 1866–76; long series of extraordinary scores reached its zenith in 1876 with 400, not out; with brothers started, and made first-class, Gloucestershire county eleven, 1870; visited Australia, 1873 and 1891; played for England v. Australia, 1880 and 1882; presented with 5,000l. by 'Daily Telegraph' fund, 1895; in 43 years' career made 126 centuries, scored 54,896 runs, and took 2,876 wickets; first-rate as bowler and fielder as well as batsman; his powerful physique capable of great endurance; known to public as 'W. G.'

GRAHAM, HENRY GREY (1842–1906), writer on Scottish history; educated at Edinburgh University; Church of Scotland minister in Glasgow, 1884–1906; published life of 'Rousseau,' 1882, 'Social Life of Scotland in the 18th Century,' 2 vols. 1899, and 'Scottish Men of Letters of the 18th Century,' 1901.

GRAHAM, THOMAS ALEXANDER FERGUSON (1840–1906), artist; studied at Edinburgh under Scott Lauder [q. v.]; in Paris (1860), Brittany (1862), Venice (1864), Morocco (1885); painted much in Fifeshire fishing villages; in 'The Passing Salute' and 'The Siren' showed command of colour and sense of atmosphere; hon. R.S.A., 1883; friend of Orchardson and Pettie.

GRAHAM, WILLIAM (1839–1911), philosopher and political economist; B.A., Trinity College, Dublin, 1867; M.A., 1870; vindicated Berkeley's philosophy in 'Idealism,' 1872; lecturer in mathematics at St. Bartholomew's Hospital, 1877; his 'The Creed of Science,' 1881, praised by Darwin and Gladstone; professor of jurisprudence and political economy in Queen's College, Belfast, 1882–1909; hon. Litt.D. Dublin, 1905; other works include 'Socialism New and Old,' 1890, and 'English Political Philosophy from Hobbes to Maine,' 1899.

GRANT, SIR CHARLES (1836–1903), Anglo-Indian administrator; brother of Sir Robert Grant [q. v.]; entered Bengal civil service, 1858; foreign secretary to Indian government, 1881; K.C.S.I., 1885; edited 'Central Provinces Gazetteer,' 1870.

GRANT, GEORGE MONRO (1835–1902), principal of Queen's University, Kingston, Canada, from 1877; born in Nova Scotia; educated at Glasgow University; hon. D.D., 1877; presbyterian missionary in Nova Scotia, 1860–3; united the presbyterian church throughout Canada, and inaugurated first general assembly, 1875; moderator, 1889; secured state endowment of School of Mines in Queen's University, 1893; twice (1872 and 1883) travelled through Canada, describing his experiences in 'Ocean to Ocean,' 1873, and 'Picturesque Canada,' 1884; strong imperialist; wrote 'Religions of the World,' 1894; president of Royal Society of Canada, 1891; C.M.G., 1901.

GRANT, SIR ROBERT (1837–1904), lieutenant-general R.E.; born at Bombay; son of Sir Robert Grant [q. v.]; joined royal engineers, 1854; served in West Indies and North America, 1857–65; in command of royal engineers troops at Aldershot (1877–80), Plymouth (1880), Woolwich (1881), and in Scotland (1884); commanding R.E. with Nile expeditionary force, 1885; C.B., 1889; inspector-general of fortifications and major-general, 1891; lieutenant-general, 1897; carried out works of defence and barrack construction; K.C.B., 1896; G.C.B., 1902.

GRANT DUFF, SIR MOUNTSTUART ELPHINSTONE (1829–1906), statesman and author; son of James Grant Duff [q. v.]; M.A., Balliol College, Oxford, 1853; LL.B. London and called to bar, 1854; liberal M.P. for Elgin Boroughs, 1857–81; became authority on questions of foreign policy; under-secretary of state for India, 1868–74, and for colonies, 1880; P.C., 1880; governor of Madras, 1881–6; C.I.E., 1881; G.C.S.I., 1887; on return to England (1887) devoted himself to literature; published 'Notes from a Diary' (14 vols., 1897–1905), a valuable contribution to social history; travelled much in Europe and Asia; lord rector of Aberdeen University, 1866–72; president of Royal Geographical and Historical societies; F.R.S., 1901; trustee of British Museum, 1903; wrote also 'Studies of European Politics,' 1866, and 'A Victorian Anthology,' 1902.

GRANTHAM, SIR WILLIAM (1835–1911), judge; called to bar, 1863; Q.C., 1877; treasurer of Inner Temple, 1904; successful in circuit work; conservative M.P. for East Surrey, 1874–85, and for Croydon, 1885–6; made judge of queen's bench division and knighted, 1886; industrious, energetic, but garrulous judge; his decisions as judge in election petition cases (1906) were severely criticized; rebuked by prime minister for indiscreet speech from bench, 1911; model country gentleman, and good judge of horses; enthusiastic volunteer.

GRAY, BENJAMIN KIRKMAN (1862–1907), economist; son of congregational minister; unitarian minister, 1894–7; engaged in social work in London, 1898–1902; developed strong socialistic views; published 'History of English Philanthropy,' 1905, and 'Philanthropy and the State,' 1910.

GREEN, SAMUEL GOSNELL (1822–1905), baptist minister and bibliophile; joined baptist ministry, 1844; classical tutor (from 1851) and president (1863–76) of Horton College, Bradford; editor (1876), editorial secretary (1881), and historian (1899) of the Religious Tract Society; published 'Handbook to Grammar of Greek Testament,' 1870, 'Christian Ministry to the Young,' 1883, and other theological works; president of Baptist Union, 1895; chairman of editorial committee of 'Baptist Hymnal'; assisted Mrs. Rylands in forming John Rylands Library, Manchester, 1899; hon. D.D. St. Andrews, 1900.

GREENAWAY, CATHERINE [KATE] (1846–1901), artist; studied art at South Kensington, at Heatherley's, and under Legros in Slade School, London; exhibited at Royal Academy, 1877; won fame as exponent of child life and inventor of original children's books; published 'Under the Window,' 1879, 'Kate Greenaway's Birthday Book,' 1880, 'Mother Goose,' 1881, 'Little Ann and other Poems,' 1883; also 'Language of Flowers,' 1884, 'Marigold Garden,' 1885, and an annual 'Almanack' from 1883 to 1895; work much admired by Ruskin; created a gallery of children with quaint costumes and unhackneyed accessories; designed beautiful bookplates; 'Life' by M. H. Spielmann and G. S. Layard, 1905.

GREENE, WILLIAM FRIESE- (1855–1921), pioneer of kinematography; began life as travelling photographer; experimented with J. A. R. Rudge, of Bath, on reproduction, by camera and projecting lantern, of synthesis of motion, 1882–4; established photographic business in London; after many experiments produced sensitized celluloid ribbon-film, 1889; film patented, and projected scene exhibited, 1890.

GREENIDGE, ABEL HENDY JONES (1865–1906), writer on ancient history and law; born at Barbados; B.A., Balliol College, Oxford, 1888; M.A., 1891; D.Litt., 1904; fellow (1889) and tutor (1902) of Hertford College; fellow of St. John's, 1905; published 'Infamia,' 1894, 'Handbook on Greek Constitutional History,' 1896; edited William Smith and Gibbon's histories of Rome; commenced a new 'History of Rome' (vol. i. 1904); accurate and critical historian.

GREENWELL, WILLIAM (1820–1918), archaeologist; brother of Dora Greenwell [q. v.]; B.A., Durham; minor canon of Durham, 1854–1907; librarian to dean and chapter, 1862–1907; rector of St. Mary-the-Less, Durham, 1865–1918; documents edited include 'Feodarium Prioratus Dunelmensis' (1872); F.R.S., 1878.

GREENWOOD, FREDERICK (1830–1909), journalist; at first a printer's reader; published novels, 1854–60; first editor of 'Queen' illustrated paper, 1861–3; contributed his novel 'Margaret Denzil's History' serially to 'Cornhill Magazine,' 1863; succeeded Thackeray as editor of 'Cornhill,' 1862–8; founded with George Smith [q. v.], and edited, 'Pall Mall Gazette,' 1865; secured its triumph in 1866 by three papers by his brother James, 'A Night in a Casual Ward'; an independent conservative and vigilant student of foreign affairs; suggested to Lord Beaconsfield purchase of Suez Canal shares, 1875; attacked Gladstone's anti-Turkish attitude, 1876–8; left 'Pall Mall Gazette,' on its conversion by a new owner into a radical organ, for newly-founded conservative 'St. James's Gazette.' 1880; advocated occupation of Egypt, 1882; retired from 'St. James's,' 1888; founded and edited weekly 'Anti-Jacobin,' 1891–2; opposed South African war, 1899; friend of George Meredith; published 'The Lover's Lexicon,' 1893, 'Imagination in Dreams,' 1894.

GREENWOOD, THOMAS (1851–1908), promoter of public libraries; library assistant at Sheffield; founded in London (1871) firm of printers of trade journals, which he edited; advocated rate-supported libraries; published 'Public Libraries,' 1886, 'Museums and Art Galleries,' 1888, and 'Greenwood's Library Year Book,' 1897; presented library of Edward Edwards (1812–1886, q. v.), as well as his own 'Library for Librarians' (1906), to Manchester Public Library; wrote Life of Edwards, 1902.

GREGO, JOSEPH (1843–1908), writer on art; collected works by Rowlandson, Morland, and Cruikshank; published 'Rowlandson the Caricaturist,' 2 vols. 1880, 'Cruikshank's Water Colours,' 1904, 'Thackerayana,' 1875, 'History of Parliamentary Elections,' 1886, and 'Pictorial Pickwickiana,' 2 vols. 1899; organized picture exhibitions; invented a system of reproducing 18th-century colour prints.

GREGORY, SIR AUGUSTUS CHARLES (1819–1905), Australian explorer and politician; born at Farnsfield, Nottinghamshire; joined survey department of West Australia, 1841; explored interior of continent; discovered pastoral and mineral wealth of Murchison district; undertook futile expeditions in search of F. W. L. Leichhardt [q. v.], 1855, 1858; explored rivers of East coast of Australia, 1855–6; surveyor for Queensland, 1859–75; member of legislative council, 1882; first mayor of Toowong, 1902; sat on commission of inquiry into condition of aborigines, 1876–83; C.M.G., 1875; K.C.M.G., 1903; joint author with brother Francis of 'Journals of Australian Exploration,' 1884.

GREGORY, EDWARD JOHN (1850–1909), painter; studied at Royal Academy, 1869; contributed sketches to 'Graphic' till 1875; best work exhibited at Royal Institute of Painters in Water Colours, of which he became president in 1898; exhibited mainly portraits at Royal Academy; A.R.A., 1883; R.A., 1898; best-known pictures in oil are 'Marooning,' 1887, 'Boulter's Lock—Sunday Afternoon,' 1898; in water colours, 'A Look at the Model' and 'Souvenir of the Institute.'

GREGORY, ROBERT (1819–1911), dean of St. Paul's; M.A., Corpus Christi College, Oxford, 1846; D.D., 1891; vicar of St. Mary the Less, Lambeth, 1853–73; served on royal commission on ritual, 1867; canon of St. Paul's, 1868; helped to improve cathedral fabric and finances; a zealous member of lower house of Canterbury convocation from 1868; defended Athanasian Creed and ritual; member of education commission, 1886; dean of St. Paul's, 1890; able administrator; published 'Elementary Education,' 1895, and sermons; autobiography edited by W. H. Hutton, 1912.

GRENFELL, GEORGE (1849–1906), baptist missionary and explorer of the Congo; did pioneering work up Lower Congo river; reached Stanley Pool, 1881; surveyed Congo as far as equator, 1884; discovered Ruki river; navigated the Ikelemba; met cannibals in Bangala region; reached 'Grenfell' falls, the most northerly point yet achieved in Congo basin, 1884; explored affluents of Congo from east and south, and discovered the Batwa dwarf tribes, 1885; went up main stream of the Kasai, and Kwa and Mfini to Lake Leopold II, and the Kwango to the Kingunji rapids, 1886; received by King Leopold at Brussels, 1887; made chevalier and Belgian plenipotentiary for settlement with Portugal of the Lunda

frontier, 1891–3; at Bolobo, 1893–1900; explored Aruwimi river (1900–2) and established missionary station at Yalemba, 1903; died of blackwater fever at Basoko; Lives by Sir Harry Johnston, 1908, G. Hawker, 1909, and S. J. Dickins, 1910.

GRENFELL, HUBERT HERBERT (1845–1906), expert in naval gunnery; joined navy, 1859; made first designs of hydraulic mountings for naval ordnance, 1869; naval adviser at Berlin congress, 1878; invented self-illuminating night sights for naval ordnance, 1891; helped to found Navy League.

GRENFELL, JULIAN HENRY FRANCIS (1888–1915), soldier and poet; educated at Eton and Balliol College, Oxford; entered army (1st Dragoons), 1910; accompanied regiment to France and received D.S.O., 1914; died of wounds at Boulogne; best-known poem, 'Into Battle' (1915).

GREY, ALBERT HENRY GEORGE, fourth EARL GREY (1851–1917), statesman; son of General the Hon. Charles Grey [q. v.]; educated at Harrow and Trinity College, Cambridge; liberal M.P., South Northumberland, 1880–5, and for Tyneside division of county, 1885–6; concentrated his energies on promotion of imperial unity; joined board of directors of British South Africa Company, 1889; administrator of Rhodesia, 1896–7; very successful governor-general of Canada, 1904–11; G.C.M.G., 1904; G.C.V.O., 1908.

GREY, MARIA GEORGINA (1816–1906), promoter of women's education; born SHIRREFF; sister of Emily Shirreff [q. v.]; married William Thomas Grey, 1841; initiated 'Girls' Public Day School Company,' 1872, which now (1929) has twenty-five schools; founded 'Maria Grey Training College' for women teachers, 1878; published a novel, and works on women's enfranchisement and education.

GRIERSON, SIR JAMES MONCRIEFF (1859–1914), lieutenant-general; joined Royal Artillery from Woolwich, 1877; employed on intelligence work in India; passed first into Staff College, 1883; head of Russian section of intelligence division, 1889; military attaché at Berlin, 1896; served in South African War and China, 1900; C.B., 1901; director of military operations at War Office and major-general, 1904; largely helped to lay foundations of military co-operation between Great Britain and France; held home commands, 1906–14; K.C.B., 1911; author of military works; died in France on way to front.

GRIFFIN, SIR LEPEL HENRY (1838–1908), Anglo-Indian administrator; joined Indian civil service in Punjab, 1860; compiled standard accounts of Punjab families in 'Punjab Chiefs,' 1865, 'The Law of Inheritance to Sikh Chieftships,' 1869, and 'The Rajas of the Punjab,' 1870; superintendent of Kapurthala state from 1875; helped to establish Abdur Rahman on Afghan throne and reconciled him to English policy, 1880; C.S.I., 1878; K.C.S.I., 1881; agent-general to governor-general in central India, 1881–9; advocated use of Indian vernaculars in teaching in India; joint founder of 'Asiatic Quarterly Review,' 1885; settled in England, 1889; chairman of Imperial Bank of Persia; works include 'Ranjit Singh' (in 'Rulers of India' series, 1892).

GRIFFITH, RALPH THOMAS HOTCHKIN (1826–1906), Sanskrit scholar; B.A., Queen's College, Oxford, 1846; Boden Sanskrit scholar, 1849; professor of English literature (1853) and head master (1854) of Benares Government College; inspector of schools, 1856; principal of Benares College, 1861–78; founded 'Pandit' college monthly journal, 1866; director of public instruction in North-West provinces, 1878–85; C.I.E., 1885; retired to Kotagiri; published verse translations, embodying spirit of originals, of Sanskrit classics, including Kālidāsa's 'Kumara-sambhava,' 1853, the 'Rámáyan of Válmíki,' 5 vols. 1870–3, hymns of the 'Rigveda,' 4 vols. 1889–92, 'Sāmaveda,' 1893, and 'Artharvaveda,' 2 vols. 1895–6.

GRIFFITHS, ARTHUR GEORGE FREDERICK (1838–1908), inspector of prisons and author; born at Poona; joined 63rd regiment, 1855; served in Crimea; brigade-major at Gibraltar, 1864–70; inspector of prisons in England, 1878–96; historian of Millbank Gaol, 1875, and of Newgate, 1884; editor of 'Army and Navy Gazette,' 1901–4; best known as writer of some thirty novels of prison life and detective stories; wrote also 'Fifty Years of Government Service,' 1904.

GRIGGS, WILLIAM (1832–1911), inventor of photo-chromo-lithography; technical assistant to director of Indian Museum, 1855; photo-lithographer in India office till 1885; invented photo-chromo-lithographic process; set up works at Peckham, 1868; published plates for Dr. Forbes Watson's 'Textile Manufactures . . . of India,' 1866; reproduced facsimile editions of 'Mahābhāsya,' 1871, Shakespeare quartos (43 vols. 1881–91), and Ashbee reprints; issued from 1881 some 200 'Portfolios of Industrial Art' of all countries, and from 1884 'Journal of Indian Art and Industry.'

GRIMTHORPE, first BARON (1816–1905), lawyer, mechanician, and controversialist. [See BECKETT, SIR EDMUND.]

GROOME, FRANCIS HINDES (1851–1902), Romany scholar and miscellaneous writer; son of Robert Hindes Groome [q. v.]; interested in gypsy life from boyhood; lived with gypsies at home and abroad; settled down to literary work in Edinburgh, 1876; joined staff of Messrs. Chambers, 1885; sub-editor of 'Chambers's Encyclopaedia,' 10 vols. 1888–92; published 'In Gipsy Tents,' 1880, 'Kriegspiel' (a Romany novel), 1896, and 'Gypsy Folk Tales,' 1899; had wide knowledge of Jacobite literature.

GROSE, THOMAS HODGE (1845–1906), registrar of Oxford University, 1877–1906; scholar of Balliol College, Oxford; B.A., with first classes in classics and mathematics, 1868; president of the Union, 1871; fellow and tutor of Queen's College, Oxford, from 1871; helped T. H. Green [q. v.] in editing Hume's works, 1874–5; ardent alpinist.

GROSSMITH, GEORGE (1847–1912), entertainer and singer in light opera; gave 'humorous and musical recitals'; employed in Gilbert and Sullivan's series of comic operas, first at Opera Comique and then at Savoy Theatre, 1877–89; 'created' many of the chief parts.

GROSSMITH, WALTER WEEDON (1854–1919), comedian; brother of George Grossmith [q. v.]; excelled in part of 'dudes' and small, underbred, unhappy men.

GROSVENOR, RICHARD DE AQUILA, first BARON STALBRIDGE (1837–1912), railway administrator and politician; son of second Marquess of Westminster [q. v.]; liberal M.P., Flintshire, 1861–86; P.C., 1872; created baron and became liberal-unionist, 1886; director of North Western Railway Company, 1870; chairman, 1891–1911.

GUBBINS, JOHN (1838–1906), breeder and owner of race-horses; settled at Bruree, co. Limerick, 1886, and bred horses and hounds; bred Galtee More (winner of Two Thousand Guineas, St. Leger, and Derby, 1897), and Ard Patrick (Eclipse Stakes, 1903); headed list of winning owners, 1897.

GUINNESS, SIR ARTHUR EDWARD, second baronet, and first BARON ARDILAUN (1840–1915), philanthropist; son of Sir Benjamin Guinness, first baronet [q. v.]; B.A., Trinity College, Dublin; succeeded father, 1868; head of Guinness brewery, Dublin, 1868–77; conservative M.P., Dublin city, 1868–9, 1874–80; created baron, 1880; munificent benefactor to Dublin and to Irish Church.

GUINNESS, HENRY GRATTAN (1835–1910), divine and author; ordained as evangelist, 1857; preached in England, Ireland, America, and on the Continent, 1857–72; at Dublin helped in Dr. Barnardo's 'conversion,' 1866; founded East London Institute for training missionaries, 1873; 'Livingstone Inland Mission' in Congo, 1878, and other missions in South America and India, all of which were amalgamated into 'Regions Beyond Missionary Union,' 1899; made missionary tour of the world, 1903; collaborated with wife in 'The Approaching End of the Age,' 1878, and 'The Divine Programme of the World's History,' 1888; he also published grammars of the Congo language.

GULLY, WILLIAM COURT, first VISCOUNT SELBY (1835–1909), Speaker of the House of Commons; son of James Manby Gully [q. v.]; B.A., Trinity College, Cambridge, 1856; president of Union; called to bar, 1860; Q.C., 1877; established good practice in commercial cases; liberal M.P. for Carlisle, 1892; recorder of Wigan, 1892; elected Speaker of the House of Commons, 1895; distinguished for dignity, courtesy, and impartiality; ordered forcible removal of Irish members from the house, March 1901; resigned Speakership and raised to peerage, 1905; hon. LL.D. Cambridge, 1900; D.C.L. Oxford, 1904; portraits by Sir George Reid and the Hon. John Collier.

GÜNTHER, ALBERT CHARLES LEWIS GOTTHILF (1830–1914), zoologist; born in Würtemberg; took medical degree at Tübingen, 1858; appointed to staff of British Museum and naturalized, 1862; keeper of zoological department, 1875–95; vice-president of Royal Society, 1875–6; gold medallist of Royal and Linnean Societies; works include 'Catalogue of Fishes in the British Museum' (1859–70) and 'Introduction to the Study of Fishes' (1880).

GURNEY, HENRY PALIN (1847–1904), scientist; scholar of Clare College, Cambridge; 14th wrangler, 1870; fellow, 1870–83; partner of firm of Wren & Gurney, examination coaches, 1877; published book on crystallography, 1875; from 1894 to death principal of Durham College of Science (re-named Armstrong College, 1901), Newcastle-on-Tyne; founded department of mineralogy and crystallography there, 1895; hon. D.C.L. Durham, 1896; killed in Alpine accident near Arolla.

GUTHRIE, WILLIAM (1835–1908), legal writer; educated at Glasgow and Edinburgh universities; called to Scottish bar, 1861; registrar of friendly societies for Scotland, 1872; hon. LL.D. Edinburgh, 1881; sheriff-principal at Glasgow, 1903; edited many legal works.

GWATKIN, HENRY MELVILL (1844–1916), historian, theologian, and conchologist; B.A., St. John's College, Cambridge; Dixie professor of ecclesiastical history, Cambridge, 1891–1916; Gifford lecturer, Edinburgh, 1903; works include 'Studies of Arianism' (1882), 'The Knowledge of God' (1906), and 'Early Church History' (1909); a distinguished teacher.

GWYNN, JOHN (1827–1917), scholar and divine; B.A. and fellow, Trinity College, Dublin; country parson in co. Donegal, 1864–82; regius professor of divinity, Trinity College, Dublin, 1888–1917; published numerous Syriac studies and edition of 'Book of Armagh' (1913).

HACKER, ARTHUR (1858–1919), painter; studied at Royal Academy Schools and in Paris; painted subject pictures, chief being 'The Annunciation' (1892), London street scenes, and portraits; A.R.A., 1894; R.A., 1910.

HADEN, SIR FRANCIS SEYMOUR (1818–1910), etcher and surgeon; studied medicine at the Sorbonne and at Grenoble; F.R.C.S., 1857; formed large private practice in London and did much public work; published pamphlets strongly opposed to cremation; devoted leisure to etching, mainly of landscape, from 1843 onwards; influenced by Whistler, whose half-sister he married; chief works include 'Thames Fishermen,' 'Shere Mill Pond,' 'Breaking up of the Agamemnon'; his drypoints executed in 1877, 'Windmill Hill,' 'Sawley Abbey,' 'Essex Farm,' 'Boat House,' show vigorous style; founder and president of the Society of Painter Etchers, 1880; knighted, 1894; member of several French artistic societies; exhibited at Royal Academy, 1860–85; worked also in water colour and black chalk; chief collections of work are in British Museum and New York Public Library; pioneer of scientific criticism of Rembrandt's etchings; published 'The Etched Work of Rembrandt,' 1879, 'About Etching,' 1879, and kindred works; portraits by Jacomb Hood, Alphonse Legros, and others.

HAIG-BROWN, WILLIAM (1823–1907), master of Charterhouse; educated at Christ's Hospital and Pembroke College, Cambridge; second classic, 1846; M.A., 1849; LL.D., 1864; fellow, 1848; hon. fellow, 1891; appointed head master of Charterhouse School, 1863; active in advocating removal of school from London to Godalming, 1864; school opened at Godalming, 1872; numbers rose from 150 in 1872 to 500 in 1876; made many additions and improvements; known as 'our second Founder'; appointed master of the Charterhouse, 1897; honorary canon of Winchester, 1891; published 'Charterhouse, Past and Present,' 1879, 'Carthusian Memories,' verse, 1905, and other works; bronze statue by Harry Bates and portrait by Frank Holl at Godalming.

HAIGH, ARTHUR ELAM (1855–1905), classical scholar; B.A., Corpus Christi College, Oxford (first class classics), 1878; won several university classical scholarships; fellow of Hertford College, 1878–86; fellow and tutor of Corpus, 1901; author of 'The Attic Theatre,' 1889, and 'The Tragic Drama of the Greeks,' 1896.

HAINES, SIR FREDERICK PAUL (1819–1909), field-marshal; joined 4th (King's Own) regiment, 1839; served in 1st Sikh war; military secretary to Lord Gough [q. v.], 1846–9; served at Alma and Balaclava; prominent at Inkermann; military secretary to Sir Patrick Grant [q. v.] at Madras, 1856–60; commanded Mysore division, 1865–70; commander-in-chief at Madras, 1871–5; K.C.B., 1871; lieutenant-general, 1873; commander-in-chief in India, 1876–81; superintended Afghan war, 1878–9; general and G.C.B., 1877; C.I.E., 1878; G.C.S.I., 1879; differed from the viceroy, Lord Lytton, in regard to the plans of attack on Afghanistan, 1878–9; suggested the relief of Kandahar by Roberts's force from Kabul, 1880; declined baronetcy; field-marshal, 1890; 'Life' by R. S. Rait, 1911.

HALIBURTON, ARTHUR LAWRENCE, first BARON HALIBURTON (1832–1907), civil servant; son of Thomas Chandler Haliburton [q. v.]; born and educated at Windsor, Nova Scotia; called to bar there, 1855; joined commissariat department of British army, 1855; served in Crimea and in Canada; civilian assistant director of supplies and transports, 1869; director, 1879; supervised victualling of eight campaigns; K.C.B., 1885; permanent under-secretary for war, 1895–7; G.C.B., 1897; raised to peerage, 1900; vigorously defended short military service in 'The Times,' 1897; in later years advocated universal military training; Memoir by J. B. Atlay, 1909.

HALL, CHRISTOPHER NEWMAN (1816–1902), congregationalist divine; son of John Vine Hall [q. v.]; ordained, 1842; accomplished preacher of evangelical fervour; minister of Surrey chapel, 1854; LL.B. London, 1856; chairman of congregational union, 1866; built Christ Church, Westminster Bridge Road, 1876; resigned pastorate, 1892; hon. D.D. Edinburgh, 1902; wrote many devotional works and hymns; autobiography published, 1898.

HALL, FITZEDWARD (1825–1901), philologist; born at Troy, New York; went to India, 1846; tutor (1850) and professor of Sanskrit (1853) at Benares Government College; served in Sepoy mutiny; hon. D.C.L. Oxford, 1860; settled in London, 1862; professor of Sanskrit at King's College, and librarian to India office; while in India discovered many Sanskrit MSS., and edited many Sanskrit and Hindī literary works and treatises of Hindu philosophy; edited works for Early English Text Society, 1864–9, published many philological researches, and from 1878 helped in preparation of 'New English Dictionary' and Joseph Wright's 'Dialect Dictionary'; hon. LL.D. Harvard, 1895.

HALL, SIR JOHN (1824–1907), premier of New Zealand; born at Hull; employed at London General Post Office, 1843–52; emigrated to Lyttelton, New Zealand, for sheep-farming, 1852; first mayor of Christchurch, 1862–3; elected for Christchurch to first house of representatives, 1855; colonial secretary, 1856; postmaster-general and electric telegraph commissioner, 1866–9; called to legislative council, 1872; colonial secretary, 1872–3; opposed (secular) Education Act of 1877; premier, 1879–82; K.C.M.G., 1882; his ministry repealed Sir George Grey's land-tax, passed triennial parliaments bill and universal suffrage bill; Hall introduced woman's suffrage amendment into electoral bill, 1893.

HALLÉ (formerly NORMAN-NERUDA), WILMA MARIA FRANCISCA, LADY (1839–1911), violinist; daughter of Josef Neruda; born in Moravia; appeared in London, 1849; married Ludwig Norman, 1864, and secondly Sir Charles Hallé [q. v.], 1888; teacher in Berlin, 1898; violinist to Queen Alexandra, 1901.

HALLIDAY, SIR FREDERICK JAMES (1806–1901), first lieutenant-governor of Bengal; joined Bengal civil service, 1825; judicial and revenue secretary in Bengal, 1838; secretary in the home department, 1849–53; first lieutenant-governor of Bengal, 1854–9; reorganized police, improved roads, and advanced education; initiated Calcutta University, 1856; suppressed rising of Santal tribes, 1855; helped to check Sepoy mutiny in Bengal, 1858; created K.C.B., 1860; involved in long controversy—from 1857 to 1888—with a subordinate, William Taylor [q. v.], commissioner of Patna, whom he removed from his office, 1857; member of council of India, 1868–86; an accomplished musician, he frequently performed in concerts in Bengal, London, and elsewhere.

HALSBURY, first EARL OF (1823–1921), lord chancellor. [See GIFFARD, HARDINGE STANLEY.]

HAMBLIN SMITH, JAMES (1829–1901), mathematician. [See SMITH.]

HAMILTON, DAVID JAMES (1849–1909), pathologist; studied medicine at Edinburgh; worked at pathology at Vienna and Paris, 1874–6; professor of pathology at Aberdeen, 1882–1908; pioneer of bacteriological diagnosis of diphtheria and typhoid; investigated 'braxy' and 'louping ill' in sheep; published standard textbook on pathology (2 vols. 1889–94); F.R.S., 1908; hon. LL.D. Edinburgh, 1907.

HAMILTON, SIR EDWARD WALTER (1847–1908), treasury official; son of Walter Kerr Hamilton [q. v.]; educated at Eton and Christ Church, Oxford; private secretary successively to Robert Lowe and Gladstone, 1872–85; treasury official, 1885–1907; permanent secretary to the treasury (with Sir George Murray), 1902–7; K.C.B., 1894; G.C.B., 1906; P.C., 1908; specially con-

nected with Goschen's financial measures, of which he wrote an account, 1889; published monograph on Gladstone, 1898.

HAMILTON, EUGENE JACOB LEE (1845–1907), poet and novelist. [See LEE-HAMILTON.]

HAMILTON, JAMES, second DUKE OF ABERCORN (1838–1913); son of James Hamilton, first Duke [q. v.]; conservative M.P., co. Donegal, 1860–80; succeeded father, 1885; K.G., 1892; official figurehead of Irish landlords in land war; resisted Home Rule.

HAMILTON, SIR RICHARD VESEY (1829–1912), admiral; entered navy, 1843; served on Arctic voyages, 1850–4; in Crimean and second Chinese wars, 1855–7; attained flag rank, 1877; vice-admiral, 1884; commander-in-chief, China station, 1885–8; admiral and K.C.B., 1887; first sea lord, 1889–91; G.C.B., 1895.

HAMPDEN, second VISCOUNT (1841–1906), governor of New South Wales. [See BRAND, HENRY ROBERT.]

HANBURY, ELIZABETH (1793–1901), centenarian and philanthropist; of quaker parentage; visited prisons with Elizabeth Fry [q. v.]; married Cornelius Hanbury, 1826; active in anti-slavery movement and prison reform; aided in her work by her daughter CHARLOTTE (1830–1900), who established mission at Tangier for ameliorating lot of Moorish prisoners; autobiography published, 1901.

HANBURY, SIR JAMES ARTHUR (1832–1908), surgeon-general; M.B., Trinity College, Dublin, 1853; entered army medical service; F.R.C.S. England, 1887; served in Afghan war, 1878–9; at battle of Tel-el-Kebir, 1882; K.C.B. 1882; surgeon-general of forces in Madras, 1888–92; surgeon-general, 1892.

HANBURY, ROBERT WILLIAM (1845–1903), politician; educated at Rugby and Corpus Christi College, Oxford; conservative M.P. for Tamworth, 1872–8, for North Staffordshire, 1878–80, and for Preston, 1885–1903; ceaselessly attacked policy of Gladstone's government, 1892–5; P.C. and financial secretary of the treasury, 1895–1900; joined cabinet as president of board of agriculture, 1900.

HANKIN, ST. JOHN EMILE CLAVERING (1869–1909), playwright; educated at Malvern and Merton College, Oxford; wrote plays of realistic frankness; his 'The Return of the Prodigal,' 1905, 'The Charity that began at Home,' 1906, 'The Cassilis Engagement' (the most popular of his plays), 1907, were published in 1907 as 'Three Plays with Happy Endings'; pushed realism further in 'The Last of the De Mullins,' 1908; cynically satirized middle class convention and sentiment.

HANLAN (properly HANLON), EDWARD (1855–1908), Canadian oarsman; born at Toronto; rowing champion of Canada, 1877, of America, 1878, of England, 1879, and of the world, 1880; retained the last title, 1881–4.

HARBEN, SIR HENRY (1823–1911), pioneer of industrial life assurance; accountant of Prudential Mutual Assurance Association, 1852; started scheme of life assurance for working classes and proved its practicability, 1854; secretary, 1856; actuary, 1870; resident director, 1873; chairman, 1905; president, 1907; knighted, 1897; master of Carpenters Company, 1893; founded working men's convalescent home at Rustington, 1895; represented Hampstead on London county council, 1889–94; first mayor, 1900; generously supported local charities; published 'Mortality Experience of the Prudential Assurance Company,' 1871.

HARCOURT, AUGUSTUS GEORGE VERNON (1834–1919), chemist; B.A., Balliol College, Oxford; assistant to (Sir) B. C. Brodie [q. v.]; Lee's reader in chemistry and a senior student of Christ Church, Oxford, 1859; tutor, 1864–1902; F.R.S., 1863; researched on rate of chemical change, on coal-gas, and chloroform as anaesthetic.

HARCOURT, LEVESON FRANCIS VERNON-(1838–1907), civil engineer. [See VERNON-HARCOURT.]

HARCOURT, SIR WILLIAM GEORGE GRANVILLE VENABLES VERNON (1827–1904), statesman; born at York; son of William Vernon Harcourt [q. v.], and grandson of Edward Harcourt [q. v.]; of Plantagenet descent; educated privately and at Trinity College, Cambridge; member of 'Society of Apostles' and of Union Debating Society; contributed to 'Morning Chronicle' while an undergraduate; called to bar, 1854; acquired large practice at the parliamentary bar; wrote regularly for newly-founded 'Saturday Review,' 1855–9; contributed to 'The Times' under signature of 'Historicus' many letters on international law in regard to

American war from 1861 onwards; letters were published separately as 'Letters by Historicus on . . . International Law,' 1863, and 'American Neutrality,' 1865; made Q.C., 1866; member of Neutrality Laws Commission, 1869; served also on royal commissions on naturalization laws, 1870, and on extradition, 1870; Whewell professor of international law at Cambridge, 1869–87; contributed further letters to 'The Times' on parliamentary reform, redistribution of seats, and Irish Church disestablishment, 1866–9; engaged in party politics, 1867; returned liberal M.P. for Oxford, 1868; declined post of judge advocate general; active in discussion on Irish Church bill; candid critic of liberal government; chairman of committee whose deliberations resulted in registration of parliamentary voters bill, 1871; championed religious equality in debates on elementary education bill and on university tests bill, 1870; advocated abolition of purchase of commissions in army, 1871; opposed payment of election expenses by constituencies; urged law reform, and helped to pass the Judicature Act of 1873; member of select committee on civil service expenditure, 1873; succeeded Sir Henry James [q. v.] as solicitor-general and knighted, 1873; while in opposition, he supported public worship regulation bill, 1874; opposed royal titles bill and merchant shipping bill, 1876; vigorously denounced Turkey, 1876–8; severely criticized conservative government's policy in Afghanistan and South Africa, 1878–9; by speeches and letters to 'The Times' greatly influenced political opinion; made home secretary and P.C. in Gladstone's administration, April 1880; on defeat at Oxford, was returned M.P. for Derby, May 1880; introduced Ground Game Act, giving occupier equal right with landlord to kill ground game; recommended central control of London water supply, 1880; advocated birch instead of detention for juvenile offenders, and proposed commission of inquiry into industrial schools, 1881; during troubles in Ireland he carried peace preservation (Ireland) bill (1881), prevention of crimes (Ireland) bill (1882), and explosive substances bill (1883); by his firmness stamped out the dynamite conspiracy in London, 1883; improved labour conditions in coal mining; introduced local government board (Scotland) bill, which was rejected by the Lords, 1883; introduced but abandoned London government bill, 1884; active in franchise agitation, 1884; replaced clause in registration bill abolishing electoral disqualification on receipt of medical relief, 1885; dissociated himself from Mr. Chamberlain's radicalism, 1885; joined Gladstone's cabinet as chancellor of the exchequer on Gladstone's acceptance of home rule, Feb.–July 1886; criticized new conservative government, and attempted to reunite liberal party; attacked Irish coercion policy of Lord Salisbury's government; censured government's treatment of 'The Times' attacks on Parnell; supported Irish land bill and Allotments Act, 1887; opposed cession of Heligoland to Germany, 1890; persuaded Gladstone to repudiate Parnell's leadership of Irish party after divorce proceedings, Nov. 1890; in his speeches which won him popularity through the country he urged much domestic reform; opposed Mr. Balfour's Irish local government bill, 1892; again chancellor of the exchequer in Gladstone's fourth administration, 1892; had charge of local veto bill, which was abandoned; passed home rule bill through Commons; carried parish councils bill, which was greatly amended by the Lords, 1894; bitterly denounced upper house; served under new prime minister, Lord Rosebery, as leader of the House of Commons, 1894; introduced death duties budget, which imposed a single graduated tax on real and personal property and revolutionized existing system of taxation; raised income tax and duties on beer and spirits; this budget established his financial reputation; he passed local government bill for Scotland; introduced local liquor control bill, 1895; passed fourth budget (May 1895); resigned on defeat of government on motion dealing with cordite supply (June); was defeated at Derby (July) and elected for West Monmouth; denounced advance of Anglo-Egyptian army in Sudan, and urged inquiry into Jameson Raid; as member of committee he made searching examination of Cecil Rhodes, but defended committee's report from radical attack, 1897; opposed unionist education bill (1896) and agricultural rating bill; supported Gladstone's censure of Armenian massacres in opposition to Lord Rosebery, 1896; urged annexation of Crete by Greece; championed protestantism and attacked ritualism in his letters to 'The Times' on 'Lawlessness in the Church,'

which led to tangible reforms, 1898; resigned leadership of liberal party, Dec. 1898; was opposed to extreme imperialist policy; censured English conduct of Boer war, Jan. 1900; denounced the war as 'unjust and engineered,' 1901; protested against introduction of forced Chinese labour into South Africa, 1903; resisted proposed tax on imported corn and Mr. Balfour's education bill, 1902; reiterated faith in free trade in opposition to Mr. Chamberlain's fiscal reform proposals, 1903; declined peerage, 1902; hon. fellow Trinity College, Cambridge, 1904; succeeded to family estates at Nuneham, Oxfordshire, 1904; last of the old school of parliamentarians; speeches abound in argument and irony; an aristocrat by instinct; fond of gardening and dairy farming; his son, Lewis, became colonial secretary, 1910; portraits by Watts and A. S. Cope; bust and statues by Mr. Waldo Story.

HARDIE, JAMES KEIR (1856–1915), socialist and labour leader; miner in Lanarkshire, 1866; dismissed as agitator, 1878; took up journalism and began to work for organization of miners; successively miners' county agent for Lanarkshire and secretary for Ayrshire; secretary of Scottish miners' federation, 1886; left liberals and became chairman of newly-formed Scottish labour party, 1888; founded 'Labour Leader,' 1889; independent labour M.P., South West Ham, 1892–5; chairman of newly-formed Independent Labour party, 1893–1900, and 1913–15; M.P., Merthyr Burghs, 1900–15; first leader of Labour Party in parliament, 1906–7; excellent speaker; did more than any man to create British political labour movement.

HARDIE, WILLIAM ROSS (1862–1916), classical scholar; M.A., Edinburgh; scholar, B.A., and fellow, Balliol College, Oxford; tutor, 1885–95; professor of humanity, Edinburgh, 1895–1916; brilliant composer and teacher; wrote 'Lectures on Classical Subjects' (1903), 'Latin Prose Composition' (1908), 'Silvulae Academicae' (1911), 'Res Metrica' (1920).

HARDWICKE, sixth EARL OF (1867–1904), politician. [See YORKE, ALBERT EDWARD PHILIP HENRY.]

HARDY, FREDERIC DANIEL (1827–1911), painter of domestic subjects and portraits; exhibited at Royal Academy, 1851–98; pictures fetched high prices; represented in public galleries in London, Leicester, Wolverhampton, and Leeds.

HARDY, GATHORNE GATHORNE-, first EARL OF CRANBROOK (1814–1906), statesman. [See GATHORNE-HARDY.]

HARDY, HERBERT HARDY COZENS-, first BARON COZENS-HARDY, of Letheringsett (1838–1920), judge. [See COZENS-HARDY.]

HARE, AUGUSTUS JOHN CUTHBERT (1834–1903), author; born in Rome; nephew of Augustus and Julius Hare [q. v.]; B.A., University College, Oxford, 1857; lived mostly in Italy and on Riviera, 1863–70; published 'Memorials of a Quiet Life' [i.e. of Mrs. Augustus Hare, his aunt], 3 vols. 1872–6; accomplished water-colour artist; book and art collector; compiled numerous guide books—to Rome, 2 vols. 1871, London, 1878, Italy, 5 vols. 1883–4, and France, 4 vols. 1890–5; also published 'The Story of my Life,' 6 vols. 1896–1900, and 'Life of Baroness Bunsen,' 2 vols. 1878.

HARE, SIR JOHN (FAIRS) (1844–1921), actor, whose original name was JOHN FAIRS; made first professional appearance at Liverpool, 1864; acted, chiefly in T. W. Robertson's plays, with Prince of Wales's company, London, 1865–74; actor-manager, with W. H. Kendal [q. v.], of Court Theatre, 1874–9, and St. James's Theatre, 1879–88; manager of Garrick Theatre, 1889–95; toured in America and provinces; knighted, 1907; helped considerably to mould and develop modern English acting tradition which avoids both formality and rhetoric.

HARLAND, HENRY (1861–1905), novelist; born at St. Petersburg of American parents; commenced literary career under pseudonym Sidney Luska; showed mastery of short story in 'Grey Roses,' 1895, and 'Comedies and Errors,' 1898; literary editor of 'Yellow Book', 1894–7; chief works were 'The Cardinal's Snuff Box,' 1900, and 'My Friend Prospero,' 1904.

HARLEY, ROBERT (1828–1910), mathematician; congregational minister at Brighouse and Leicester, 1854–72, and subsequently at Oxford and in Australia; vice-principal of Mill Hill School, 1872–81; principal of Huddersfield College, 1882–5; made researches in higher algebra, especially in the theory of quintics; F.R.S., 1863,

HARRINGTON, TIMOTHY CHARLES (1851–1910), Irish politician; founded 'Kerry Sentinel,' 1877; imprisoned under Coercion Acts, 1881 and 1883; as secretary of national league, devised 'Plan of Campaign' for land war, 1886; nationalist M.P. for co. Westmeath, 1883–5, and for Dublin (harbour) division, 1885–1910; called to Irish bar, 1887; counsel for Parnell in Parnell commission, 1888–9; remained faithful to Parnell after Parnell's divorce action; helped to reunite Irish party, 1900; lord mayor of Dublin, 1901–4.

HARRIS, THOMAS LAKE (1823–1906), mystic; emigrated with parents from Buckinghamshire to America, 1828; organized 'independent Christian congregation' on Swedenborgian principles in New York, 1848; claimed to be a 'medium'; published, from 1850 onwards, lengthy poems which were (he claimed) revealed to him in trances; edited 'Herald of Light,' 1857–61; paid visits to England, 1859–61, 1865–6; set up a community near Wassaic, 1861; joined in America by Laurence Oliphant [q. v.], with whose money Harris purchased farms at Brocton, Lake Erie, 1886, and engaged in vine-growing; exerted complete sway over Oliphant until legally compelled to restore Oliphant's property, 1881; removed to Santa Rosa, 1875; advocated theory of celestial marriages, 1876; proclaimed his attainment of immortality, 1891; depicted by Oliphant as David Masollam in 'Masollam,' 1886; published much mystical prose and verse; 'Life' by A. A. Cuthbert.

HARRISON, REGINALD (1837–1908), surgeon; M.R.C.S., 1859; F.R.C.S., 1866; surgeon at Royal Infirmary, Liverpool (1867–89), and lecturer on anatomy (1865) and on surgery (1872) at medical school there; helped to convert school into medical faculty of Liverpool University; vice-president (1894–5) of Royal College of Surgeons; Hunterian professor of surgery, 1890–1, and Bradshaw lecturer, 1896; president of Medical Society of London, 1890; established system of street ambulances in Liverpool.

HART, SIR ROBERT, first baronet (1835–1911), inspector-general of customs in China; B.A., Queen's College, Belfast, 1853; M.A., 1871; hon. LL.D., 1882; entered Chinese consular service, 1854; assistant at Ningpo, 1855–8, and at Canton, 1858; secretary to allied Anglo-French commissioners at Canton; joined Chinese imperial maritime customs service as deputy commissioner at Canton, 1859; organized customs service at Foochow and other ports, 1861–3; commissioner of customs at Shanghai, 1863; inspector-general, 1863–1906; met Gordon after Taiping rebellion, 1864; reconciled Gordon and Li Hung Chang; remained in Peking from 1864 till 1908; revisited Europe only twice, in 1866 and 1878; practical creator of Chinese imperial customs; controlled also imperial posts from 1896; helped to settle difficulties between Great Britain and China, 1875, which resulted in Chefoo convention, 1876, and those in Formosa between China and France, 1885; advocated necessary reforms in China, 1894–5; besieged in British legation at Peking during Boxer outbreak, 1900; organized native customs service, 1901; helped in re-establishment of Manchu dynasty; published experiences in 'These from the Land of Sinim,' 1901; authority terminated by Chinese government, which subordinated his service to a board of Chinese officials, 1906; K.C.M.G., 1882; G.C.M.G., 1889; baronet, 1893; 'Life' by niece, Juliet Bredon, 1909.

HARTINGTON, MARQUESS OF (1833–1908), statesman. [See CAVENDISH, SPENCER COMPTON.]

HARTLEY, SIR CHARLES AUGUSTUS (1825–1915), civil engineer; served in Crimean War; chief engineer to European Commission of Danube, 1856–1907; earned sobriquet 'father of the Danube' for work in clearing and making navigable Sulina and St. George estuaries; knighted, 1862; left Roumania, 1872; K.C.M.G., 1884; member of International Technical Commission of Suez Canal, 1884–1906; advice sought by Indian, Russian, and American governments.

HARTSHORNE, ALBERT (1839–1910), archaeologist; son of Charles Henry Hartshorne [q. v.]; secretary of Archaeological Institute of Great Britain, 1876–83, 1886–94; edited 'Archaeological Journal,' 1878–92; F.S.A., 1882; published 'Old English Glasses,' 1897, 'Oxford, 1691–1712,' 1910; and works on monumental effigies and English churches.

HASTIE, WILLIAM (1842–1903), professor of divinity at Glasgow; M.A. Edinburgh, 1867; B.D., 1869; Croall lecturer, 1892; hon. D.D. Edinburgh, 1894; principal of Church of Scotland College, Calcutta, 1878; relieved

of post, 1883; professor of divinity at Glasgow, 1895; translated many German theological works; wrote 'Theology as Science,' 1899, 'The Theology of the Reformed Church,' 1904, as well as 'La Vita Mia,' a sonnet sequence, 1896, 'The Vision of God,' 1898, and other verse.

HATTON, HAROLD HENEAGE FINCH- (1856–1904), imperialist politician. [See FINCH-HATTON.]

HATTON, JOSEPH (1841–1907), novelist and journalist; editor successively of 'Bristol Mirror,' 1863–8, 'Gentleman's Magazine,' 1868, 'Sunday Times,' and 'People,' 1892; published American experiences in 'To-day in America,' 2 vols. 1881; accompanied Henry Irving to America, 1883; chronicled Irving's 'Impressions of America,' 2 vols. 1884, and J. L. Toole's 'Reminiscences,' 2 vols. 1889; published novels 'Clytie,' 1874—which he dramatized—and 'By Order of the Czar,' 1890, 'The New Ceylon,' 1882, 'Journalistic London,' 1882, and other works.

HAVELOCK, SIR ARTHUR ELIBANK (1844–1908), colonial governor; son of William Havelock [q. v.]; joined army, 1862; retired, 1877; held administrative posts in West Indies, 1874–81; C.M.G., 1880; governor of West African settlements, 1881; forcibly settled frontier dispute with Liberia, and occupied territories between rivers Sherbro and Mano, 1882–3; K.C.M.G., 1884; governor of Natal (1886–9), of Ceylon (1890–5), where he extended railways and abolished levy on rice cultivation, of Madras (1895–1901), and of Tasmania (1901–4); G.C.M.G., 1895; G.C.I.E., 1896; G.C.S.I., 1901.

HAVERFIELD, FRANCIS JOHN (1860–1919), Roman historian and archaeologist; scholar of Winchester and New College, Oxford; a senior student of Christ Church, 1892–1907; Camden professor of ancient history and fellow of Brasenose, 1907–19; created scientific study of Roman Britain; works include 'Romanization of Roman Britain' (1905) and 'Roman Occupation of Britain' (Ford Lectures, published 1924).

HAWEIS, HUGH REGINALD (1838–1901), author and preacher; grandson of Thomas Haweis [q. v.]; showed musical ability, especially as violinist, from boyhood; lame through hip disease; B.A., Trinity College, Cambridge, 1859; started university magazine 'Lion'; travelled for health in Italy, 1859–60; incumbent of St. James, Westmoreland Street, Marylebone, from 1866 till death; by means of somewhat sensational methods filled the church; organized 'Sunday evenings for the people'; pioneer of Sunday opening of museums; published 'Music and Morals,' 1871, 'My Musical Life,' 1884, 'Old Violins,' 1898; theological writings include 'Thoughts for the Times,' 1872, 'Winged Words,' 1885, and 'Christ and Christianity,' 5 vols. 1886–7; successful lecturer on music; Lowell lecturer at Boston, 1885; toured the colonies, 1893; described experiences in 'Travel and Talk,' 2 vols. 1896; visited Rome, 1897; married in 1867 MARY (d. 1898), daughter of Thomas Musgrave Joy [q. v.]; she published 'Chaucer for Children,' 1877, 'Chaucer for Schools,' 1880, and other works; a capable artist, she exhibited at Royal Academy.

HAWEIS, MARY. [See under HAWEIS, HUGH REGINALD.]

HAWKER MARY ELIZABETH (1848–1908), novelist writing under the pseudonym of LANOE FALCONER; granddaughter of Peter Hawker [q. v.]; gained success as novelist by 'Mademoiselle Ixe,' 1890, translated into many foreign languages, 'Cecilia de Noël,' and 'The Hôtel d'Angleterre,' 1891.

HAWKINS, HENRY, BARON BRAMPTON (1817–1907), judge; son of solicitor; called to bar, 1843; Q.C., 1858; obtained foremost place among leaders of bar; defended Simon Bernard (1852), Sir John Dean Paul [q. v.] (1855), and Miss Sugden in Lord St. Leonards' will case (1875–6); appeared for defence against Arthur Orton [q. v.], claimant in Tichborne ejectment case; led for crown in criminal action against claimant for perjury, 1872–4; a master in cross-examination; largely employed in compensation and election petition cases; appointed judge of queen's bench division and knighted, 1876; transferred to exchequer division; tried the Stauntons for murder in the 'Penge case,' 1877; tried other murder cases, and unjustly obtained the nickname of 'Hanging Hawkins'; an admirable criminal judge, patient and thorough; favoured leniency for first offences; as civil judge less successful, being verbose, tautological, and contradictory in judgments; resigned judgeship and sworn P.C., 1898; created peer, 1899; fond of horse-racing; joined Roman Catholic communion after retirement from bench; portraits by John Collier and Robert Barnes; 'Reminiscences' (2 vols.) published, 1904.

HAYES, EDWIN (1819–1904), marine painter; studied art in Dublin; exhibited at Royal Academy, 1845–1904; member of Royal Hibernian Academy, 1870; chief works were 'Off Dover,' 1891, 'Crossing the Bar,' 1895; represented in Tate and other public galleries.

HAYMAN, HENRY (1823–1904), hon. canon of Carlisle and head master of Rugby; educated at Merchant Taylors' School and St. John's College, Oxford; B.A., 1845; M.A., 1849; D.D., 1870; fellow, 1844–55; treasurer of the union; head master of St. Olave's, Southwark, 1855–9, of Cheltenham, 1859–68, and Bradfield, 1868–9; elected head master of Rugby, under protest from masters, 1869; instituted unsuccessful proceedings against governors for dismissal, 1874; nominated to crown living of Aldingham, Lancashire, 1874; hon. canon of Carlisle, 1884; published classical translations, an edition of Homer's 'Odyssey,' 3 vols. 1881–6, sermons, and essays.

HAYNE, CHARLES HAYNE SEALE- (1833–1903), liberal politician. [See SEALE-HAYNE.]

HAYWARD, ROBERT BALDWIN (1829–1903), mathematician; B.A., St. John's College, Cambridge (fourth wrangler), 1850; fellow, 1852–60; mathematical master at Harrow, 1859–93; published original researches; F.R.S., 1876; original member of Alpine Club, 1858.

HAZLITT, WILLIAM CAREW (1834–1913), bibliographer and man of letters; grandson of William Hazlitt [q. v.], the essayist; works include 'History of . . . Republic of Venice' (1858, &c.) and 'Handbook to Popular, Poetical, and Dramatic Literature of Great Britain' (1867).

HEAD, BARCLAY VINCENT (1844–1914), Greek numismatist; entered coins department, British Museum, 1864; keeper, 1893–1906; produced important series of Greek coin catalogues; chief work, 'Historia Numorum' (1887).

HEADLAM, WALTER GEORGE (1866–1908), scholar and poet; educated at Harrow and King's College, Cambridge; gained many university classical prizes, 1885–7; B.A., 1887; M.A., 1891; Litt.D., 1903; fellow, 1890; rarely surpassed in Greek versions of English poetry; translated poems by Meleager, 1890, and Aeschylus, 1900–8; his 'Letters and Poems,' 1900, edited with memoir by his brother.

HEARN, MARY ANNE, 'MARIANNE FARNINGHAM' (1834–1909), hymn writer and author; edited 'Sunday School Times' from 1885; published forty volumes of essays and hymns, which included 'Watching and Waiting for me'; autobiography published, 1907.

HEATH, CHRISTOPHER (1835–1905), surgeon; son of Christopher Heath [q. v.]; studied medicine at King's College, London; M.R.C.S., 1856; F.R.C.S., 1860; became surgeon (1866) and Holme professor of clinical surgery (1875) at University College Hospital; at Royal College of Surgeons Hunterian professor of surgery (1886–7), Bradshaw lecturer (1892), Hunterian orator (1897), and president (1897); visited America, 1897; great teacher of anatomy and surgery, but backward in new bacteriological science; published many works on anatomy and surgery.

HEATH, SIR LEOPOLD GEORGE (1817–1907), admiral; entered R.N. College, Portsmouth, 1830; served in Mediterranean and East Indies; commander, 1847; employed at destruction of Lagos, 1850, and in Crimean war, 1853–4; principal agent of transports and C.B., 1855; commodore in command in East Indies, 1867–70; K.C.B., 1870; vice-president of ordnance select committee, 1870–1; rear-admiral, 1871; admiral, 1884; published 'Letters from the Black Sea,' 1897.

HEATHCOTE, JOHN MOYER (1834–1912), tennis player; B.A., Trinity College, Cambridge; pupil of Edmund Tompkins, professional tennis champion; amateur tennis champion, 1859–81, 1883, 1886; at height of form, 1869; fine all-round player.

HEATON, SIR JOHN HENNIKER, first baronet (1848–1914), postal reformer; went to Australia, 1864; journalist in Sydney; settled in London, 1884; conservative M.P., Canterbury, 1885–1910; by his postal reform campaign (opened 1886) won imperial penny postage (1898), Anglo-American (1908), Anglo-Australian (1905–11); baronet, 1911.

HECTOR, ANNIE FRENCH (1825–1902), novelist

writing as MRS. ALEXANDER; daughter of Robert French, Dublin solicitor; settled with parents in London; friend of W. H. Wills [q. v.]; married (1858) Alexander Hector (d. 1875), explorer, merchant, and archaeologist; lived in Germany and France, 1876–82, and St. Andrews, 1882–5; published her best-known novel, 'The Wooing o't,' 1873, and over forty others.

HECTOR, SIR JAMES (1834–1907), Canadian geologist; M.D. Edinburgh, 1856; surgeon and geologist on exploring expedition of Captain John Palliser [q. v.] to western North America, 1857–60; discovered Hector's Pass; director of geological survey of New Zealand, 1865; reported on fossiliferous formations of New Zealand; observed volcanic and glacial phenomena; C.M.G., 1875; K.C.M.G., 1887; F.R.S., 1866; Lyell medallist of Geological Society, 1876; died at Wellington, N.Z.; published 'Outlines of New Zealand Geology,' 1886.

HEINEMANN, WILLIAM (1863–1920), publisher; set up business in London, 1890; published novels by R. L. Stevenson, Kipling, Sarah Grand, Flora Annie Steel, John Galsworthy, Joseph Conrad, H. G. Wells, &c.; plays by Sir Arthur Pinero, W. Somerset Maugham, Israel Zangwill, &c.; produced International Library of translations of fiction; commissioned translations of Dostoevsky, Turgenev, Tolstoy, Ibsen, Björnson, Rolland; chief literary enterprise, Loeb classical library of translations.

HELLMUTH, ISAAC (1817–1901), bishop of Huron; born near Warsaw of Hebrew parents; joined Church of England in Liverpool, 1841; emigrated to Canada, 1844; ordained and made professor of Hebrew at Bishop's College, Lennoxville, 1846; D.D. Lambeth, 1853; D.C.L., Trinity College, Toronto, 1854; visited England (1861) and collected funds for new Huron evangelical theological college at London, Ontario; first principal, 1863; bishop of Huron, 1871–3; founded Western University, 1878; coadjutor to Robert Bickersteth, bishop of Ripon [q. v.], 1883–4; published theological works.

HEMMING, GEORGE WIRGMAN (1821–1905), mathematician and law reporter; B.A., St. John's College, Cambridge (senior wrangler and first Smith's prizeman), and fellow, 1844; barrister of Lincoln's Inn, 1850; treasurer, 1897; Q.C., 1875; junior counsel to treasury, 1871–5; published works on calculus, 1848, and plane trigonometry, 1851; edited 'Equity Cases' and 'Chancery Appeals,' subsequently merged in 'Law Reports' of Chancery division.

HEMPHILL, CHARLES HARE, first BARON HEMPHILL (1822–1908), lawyer and politician; son of Mrs. Barbara Hemphill [q. v.]; B.A., Trinity College, Dublin, 1843; called to Irish bar, 1845; acquired large practice in Leinster circuit; Q.C., 1860; Irish county court judge from 1863 till passing of County Courts (Ireland) Act, 1877; serjeant-at-law, 1882; supported Gladstone's home rule policy (1886), but failed in efforts to enter parliament; Irish solicitor-general under Gladstone, 1892–5; Irish P.C., 1895; liberal M.P. for North Tyrone, 1895–1906; raised to peerage, 1906.

HENDERSON, SIR DAVID (1862–1921), lieutenant-general; entered army, 1883; served in South African War, 1899–1902; learned to fly, 1911; director of military training, War Office, 1912–13; director-general of military aeronautics, 1913; general officer commanding Royal Flying Corps, 1914–17; K.C.B., 1914; lieutenant-general, 1917; K.C.V.O., 1919.

HENDERSON, GEORGE FRANCIS ROBERT (1854–1903), colonel and military writer; son of William George Henderson [q. v.]; scholar of St. John's College, Oxford; entered Sandhurst, 1876; commanded a company at Tel-el-Kebir, 1882; served in ordnance store department, 1885–90; published 'The Campaign of Fredericksburg,' 1886; instructor at Sandhurst in military topography and tactics, 1890; exercised great influence as professor of military art and history at Staff College, 1892–9; published 'Stonewall Jackson and the American Civil War,' 2 vols. 1898; accompanied Lord Roberts to the Cape, 1899; director of military intelligence and C.B., 1900; died at Assouan.

HENDERSON, JOSEPH (1832–1908), portrait and marine painter; studied art at Trustees' Academy, Edinburgh; treated genre subjects till 1871, when he devoted himself to the sea; painted in oil and water-colour; exhibited at Royal Academy, 1871–86; best pictures shown at the Royal Glasgow Institute; 'The Flowing Tide' is in the Glasgow Gallery.

HENDERSON, WILLIAM GEORGE (1819–1905), dean of Carlisle; B.A., Magdalen College, Oxford (first class classic), 1840; M.A., 1843; D.C.L., 1853; D.D., 1882;

fellow, 1847–53; head master of Victoria College, Jersey, 1852–62, and of Leeds Grammar School, 1862–84; dean of Carlisle, 1884; edited for Surtees Society the Latin missals of York and Hereford.

HENLEY, WILLIAM ERNEST (1849–1903), poet, critic, and dramatist; born at Gloucester; pupil there of T. E. Brown [q. v.]; a cripple from boyhood; in Edinburgh infirmary, 1873–5; his 'Hospital Verses,' some of which were published in 'Cornhill Magazine' (July 1875), led the editor, Leslie Stephen, to visit him and introduce him to R. L. Stevenson; worked in Edinburgh on staff of 'Encyclopaedia Britannica,' 1875; settled in London (1877–8) as editor of weekly journal, 'London'; while editor of 'Magazine of Art' (1882–6), championed Rodin and Whistler; became (1889) editor of 'Scots Observer,' renamed in 1891 the 'National Observer,' an imperialist weekly paper; encouraged young authors; edited 'New Review,' 1894–8; obtained poetic fame by 'Book of Verses,' 1888; wrote 'London Voluntaries,' 1893, 'For England's Sake' (patriotic songs), 1900, and 'Hawthorn and Lavender' (lyrics), 1901; published literary 'Views and Reviews,' 1890, and a companion volume on art, 1902; collaborated with R. L. Stevenson in the plays 'Deacon Brodie,' 'Beau Austin,' 'Admiral Guinea,' and 'Macaire'; initiated series of reprints of 'Tudor Translations,' 1892; joint compiler of 'Slang Dictionary,' 1894–1904; contributed essay on Burns's life to, and helped in, centenary edition of poetry of Robert Burns, 4 vols. 1896–7; compiled 'Lyra Heroica,' 1891; hon. LL.D. St. Andrews, 1893; granted civil list pension, 1898; portrayed as 'Burly' in R. L. Stevenson's essay, 'Talk and Talkers'; works collected in 6 vols., 1908; bust by Rodin, 1886, in National Portrait Gallery; memorial in St. Paul's Cathedral crypt.

HENNELL, SARA. [See under BRAY, CAROLINE.]

HENNESSEY, JOHN BOBANAU NICKERLIEU (1829–1910), deputy surveyor-general of India, 1883–4; born at Fatehpur; worked on trigonometrical survey in jungle tracts of Bengal and in Punjab from 1844; studied mathematics at Jesus College, Cambridge, 1863–5; organized the reproduction of survey sheets in India by means of photo-zincographic process, 1865; superintendent of survey, 1874; F.R.S., 1875; hon. M.A. Cambridge, 1876; C.I.E., 1885.

HENNESSY, HENRY (1826–1901), physicist; brother of Sir John Pope-Hennessy [q. v.]; professor of physics at Roman Catholic University, Dublin, 1855–74; at Royal College of Science, Dublin, 1874–90; vice-president of Royal Irish Academy, 1870–3; F.R.S., 1858; made valuable researches in meteorology and climatology.

HENRY, MITCHELL (1826–1910), Irish politician; studied medicine at Manchester; F.R.C.S., 1854; M.P. for co. Galway, 1871–85; supported Isaac Butt [q. v.]; opposed Gladstone's Irish university bill on question of sectarian education; persistently denounced over-taxation of Ireland, 1874–7; bought large estate of Kylemore, co. Galway, and reclaimed bog land; disapproved of Land League operations; elected M.P. for Blackfriars division of Glasgow, 1885; voted against home rule, 1886; retired on defeat, 1886; chairman of firm of A. & S. Henry, merchants, of Manchester, 1889–93.

HENTY, GEORGE ALFRED (1832–1902), writer for boys; educated at Westminster and Caius College, Cambridge; served in Crimea with hospital commissariat department; adopted journalism, 1865; correspondent to 'Standard' during Austro-Italian war (1866), in Abyssinia (1867–8), Franco-German war (1870–1), in Ashanti (1873–4), and on Prince of Wales's Indian tour (1875), and elsewhere; published his first boys' book, 'Out in the Pampas,' 1868, and from 1876 brought out some three volumes a year, dealing mainly with military history; edited 'Union Jack,' 1880–3; keen yachtsman; also published some twelve orthodox novels; 'Life' by G. Manville Fenn, 1907.

HERBERT, AUBERON EDWARD WILLIAM MOLYNEUX (1838–1906), political philosopher and author; son of third earl of Carnarvon [q. v.]; educated at Eton and St. John's College, Oxford; fellow, 1855–69; joined army, 1858; resigned, 1862; president of Union at Oxford, 1862; D.C.L., 1865; present during Prusso-Danish war, 1864; in America during civil war, and at Sedan in Franco-German war; private secretary to Sir Stafford Northcote, 1866–8; abandoned conservative views; liberal M.P. for Nottingham, 1870–4; declared himself a republican, 1872; supported Joseph Arch [q. v.] and Agricultural Labourers' Union 1872; championed

Charles Bradlaugh, 1880; became ardent disciple of Herbert Spencer and an agnostic; published 'A Politician in Trouble about his Soul,' 1884; issued a monthly 'Organ of Voluntary Taxation,' 1890–1901, and 'The Voluntaryist Creed,' 1908; engaged in farming in the New Forest from 1874 till death; relinquished sport on becoming vegetarian; interested in prehistoric remains and in psychic research; wrote verse.

HERBERT, AUBERON THOMAS, eighth BARON LUCAS (1876–1916), politician and airman; son of Hon. Auberon Herbert [q. v.]; B.A., Balliol College, Oxford; succeeded maternal uncle, 1905; held office in liberal government, 1908–15; P.C., 1912; joined Royal Flying Corps, 1915; missing in France.

HERBERT, SIR ROBERT GEORGE WYNDHAM (1831–1905), colonial official; scholar of Eton and Balliol College, Oxford; fellow of All Souls from 1854 till death; D.C.L., 1862; private secretary to Gladstone, 1855; called to bar, 1858; went to Queensland as colonial secretary, 1859; member of legislative council and first premier, 1860–5; permanent under-secretary for the colonies in London, 1871–92; agent-general for Tasmania, 1893–6; K.C.B., 1882; G.C.B., 1902; hon. LL.D., Cambridge, 1886.

HERFORD, BROOKE (1830–1903), Unitarian divine; brother of William Henry Herford [q. v.]; Unitarian minister from 1851; founded and edited 'Unitarian Herald,' 1861; minister at Strangeways, Manchester (1864–76), in Chicago (1876–82), and Boston (1882–92); preacher to Harvard University and D.D., 1891; minister of Rosslyn Hill chapel, Hampstead, 1892–1901; president of British and Foreign Unitarian Association, 1898–9; published 'Brief Account of Unitarianism,' 1903, sermons, tracts, and hymns; Lives by John Cuckson, 1904, and P. H. Wicksteed, 1904.

HERFORD, WILLIAM HENRY (1820–1908), writer on education; studied for Unitarian ministry at York and Manchester; spent three years in Bonn and Berlin; imbibed Pestalozzi's and Froebel's educational ideas on visit to Pestalozzian school at Hofwyl, near Berne, 1847; managed Pestalozzian school at Lancaster, 1850–61; inspiring preacher, teacher, and lecturer in Manchester from 1863; directed co-educational school for younger children at Fallowfield, Manchester, 1873–86; published 'The School: an Essay towards Humane Education,' 1889, 'The Student's Froebel,' 1893, and translated works on education.

HERKOMER, SIR HUBERT VON (1849–1914), painter; born in Bavaria; brought to England, 1857; studied at South Kensington art schools; achieved great success with picture, 'The Last Muster—Sunday at the Royal Hospital, Chelsea,' 1875; A.R.A., 1879; portraits include those of Wagner, Ruskin, Lord Kelvin, and Marquess of Salisbury; subject-pictures include 'Found' (1885) and 'On Strike' (1890); R.A., 1890; founded and directed school of art at Bushey, 1883–1904; Slade professor of fine art at Oxford, 1885–94; knighted, 1907; naturalized; wrote on etching, &c.

HERRING, GEORGE (1832–1906), philanthropist; at first a turf commission agent and owner of racehorses; subsequently made fortune as financial commission agent in City of London; chairman of City of London Electric Lighting Company; devoted wealth to London Sunday Hospital Fund from 1899, to Salvation Army land scheme at Boxted, Essex, and to North-West London Hospital, Camden Town; bequests to charities under will totalled 900,000l.

HERSCHEL, ALEXANDER STEWART (1836–1907), astronomer; son of Sir John Herschel [q. v.]; born in South Africa; B.A., Trinity College, Cambridge (20th wrangler), 1859; studied meteorology at Royal School of Mines, London, 1861; professor of physics at Glasgow, 1866–71, and at Durham College, Newcastle, 1871–86; reported on observations of meteors to British Association, 1862–81; experimented in photography; F.R.A.S., 1867; F.R.S., 1884; D.C.L., Durham, 1886; observed solar eclipse in Spain, 1905.

HERTSLET, SIR EDWARD (1824–1902), librarian of the foreign office; assistant to father, Lewis Hertslet [q. v.], at foreign office library, 1840; sub-librarian, 1855; librarian, 1857; attached to mission to Berlin congress and knighted, 1878; C.B., 1874; K.C.B., 1892; compiled 'Hertslet's Commercial Treaties,' vols. xii–xix, 1871–95, 'Recollections of the Foreign Office,' 1901, and other works.

HIBBERT, SIR JOHN TOMLINSON (1824–1908), politician; B.A., St. John's College, Cambridge, 1847;

M.A., 1851; called to bar, 1849; liberal M.P. for Oldham, 1862–74, 1877–85, 1892–5; held subordinate offices in Gladstone's four administrations; served on various commissions, and was interested in poor law reform; P.C., 1886; K.C.B., 1893; constable of Lancaster castle, 1907–8.

HICKS, EDWARD LEE (1843–1919), bishop of Lincoln; B.A., Brasenose College, Oxford; fellow of Corpus Christi College, Oxford, 1866; rector of Fenny Compton, Warwickshire, 1873; principal of Hulme Hall, Manchester, 1886; canon of Manchester and rector of St. Philip's, Salford, 1892; bishop of Lincoln, 1910; writer on Greek epigraphy; a strong teetotaller.

HICKS BEACH, SIR MICHAEL EDWARD, ninth baronet, and first EARL ST. ALDWYN (1837–1916), statesman; educated at Eton and Christ Church, Oxford; succeeded to baronetcy, 1854; conservative M.P., East Gloucestershire, 1864–85, West Bristol, 1885–1906; parliamentary secretary of Poor Law Board, 1868; under-secretary for Home Department, 1868; in opposition, 1869–74; chief secretary for Ireland, and showed sympathy with reform, 1874–8; entered Cabinet, 1876; colonial secretary, 1878–80; chiefly preoccupied with South African affairs; followed general lines of policy of predecessor, the fourth Lord Carnarvon; supported Sir Bartle Frere [q. v.] until October 1878; sympathized with Frere throughout, but after that date British policy in South Africa largely controlled by Disraeli; in opposition, 1880–5; attacked government for treatment of General Gordon, 1884; chancellor of exchequer and leader of House of Commons, 1885–6; as leader of opposition, conducted victorious anti-Home Rule campaign, 1886; made way for Lord Randolph Churchill as chancellor of exchequer and leader of Commons, 1886; Irish secretary, 1886–7; president of Board of Trade, 1888–92; chancellor of exchequer, 1895–1902; opponent of 'tariff reform'; created viscount, 1906; earl, 1915.

HILES, HENRY (1828–1904), musical composer; held many posts as organist; Mus.Bac. Oxford, 1862; Mus.Doc. 1867; lecturer on harmony and composition at Owens College, Manchester, 1876; professor at Royal Manchester College of Music; composed organ music, glees, cantatas, oratorios, anthems; published educational works on music; edited 'Wesley Tune Book.'

HILL, ALEXANDER STAVELEY (1825–1905), barrister and politician; B.A., Exeter College, Oxford, 1852; D.C.L., 1855; fellow, 1854–64; called to bar, 1851; Q.C., 1868; treasurer of Inner Temple, 1886; acquired large parliamentary and probate practice; recorder of Banbury, 1866–1903; conservative M.P. for Coventry and Staffordshire, 1868–1900; P.C., 1892; early advocate of tariff reform; formed large cattle ranch in Canada, 1871; hon. LL.D. Toronto, 1892; wrote 'Practice of the Court of Probate,' 1859.

HILL, ALSAGER HAY (1839–1906), social reformer; LL.B., Trinity Hall, Cambridge, 1862; called to bar, 1864; urged more scientific classification of paupers and national system of labour registration for unemployed, 1867–8; established labour exchange in London (1871) and edited 'Labour News,' organ of communication between masters and men seeking work; vice-president of National Sunday League, 1876–90; published 'Rhymes with Good Reason,' 1870–1, and other verse.

HILL, FRANK HARRISON (1830–1910), journalist; studied for Unitarian ministry at Manchester under Dr. James Martineau [q. v.], 1846–51; adopted profession of journalism; editor of 'Northern Whig,' Belfast, 1861–5; alone of journalists in Ireland supported North in American war; friend of Harriet Martineau, Browning, and Crabb Robinson; assistant editor of 'Daily News,' 1865; editor, 1869–86; made paper an influential party organ; wrote with keen insight and caustic pen; retired owing to opposition to Gladstone's home rule policy, 1886; leader writer of the 'World,' 1886–1906; published 'Political Portraits,' 1873, and 'Life of George Canning,' 1881.

HILL, GEORGE BIRKBECK NORMAN (1835–1903), editor of Boswell's 'Life of Johnson'; grandson of Thomas Wright Hill [q. v.]; B.A., Pembroke College, Oxford, 1858; joined at the University Old Mortality Club, and came to know Burne-Jones and Rossetti; D.C.L., 1871; private schoolmaster, 1858–75; elaborately edited Boswell's 'Life of Johnson,' 6 vols. 1887, 'Johnson's Letters,' 2 vols. 1892, 'Johnsonian Miscellanies,' 2 vols. 1897, and 'Johnson's Lives of the English Poets,' 3 vols. 1905; described a tour in Scotland as 'Footsteps of Samuel Johnson,' 1889; published also life of his uncle,

Sir Rowland Hill, 2 vols. 1880, and 'Letters of Rossetti to William Allingham,' 1897; his 'Letters' published, 1903 and 1906.

HILL, OCTAVIA (1838–1912), philanthropist; grand-daughter of Dr. Thomas Southwood Smith [q. v.]; early influenced by Christian Socialists, especially F. D. Maurice [q. v.]; helped in artistic training by John Ruskin; opened school with sisters in Marylebone; impressed by urgency of housing problem in which she interested Ruskin, 1864; first houses for improvement purchased through him, 1865; undertaking placed on business footing; through fund raised by friends, enabled to devote herself to housing reform, 1874; appointed manager of Southwark property by Ecclesiastical Commissioners, 1884; owed much to co-operation of sisters and workers trained by her; supporter of Charity Organization, Kyrle, and Commons Preservation societies; co-founder of National Trust; held aloof from political measures for social reform.

HILL, ROSAMOND DAVENPORT- (1825–1902), educational administrator; daughter of Matthew Davenport Hill [q. v.]; settled with parents at Bristol, 1851; assisted her father and Mary Carpenter [q. v.]; visited Mettray reformatory, 1855; founded on Mettray principles girls' industrial school at Bristol, 1866; visited prisons in Australia, 1872–4; published 'What We Saw in Australia,' 1874; member of London school board, 1879–97; visited schools in United States and Canada, 1888; resisted provision of free meals in London schools; wrote 'Elementary Education in England,' 1893.

HILLS, SIR JOHN (1834–1902), major-general; born in Bengal; joined Bombay engineers, 1854; in Persian expedition, 1857; field engineer in Abyssinian expedition, 1867; commandant of Bombay sappers at Kirkee, 1871–83; commanded division of Kandahar field force, 1879–80; at defence of Kandahar; C.B., 1881; commanding royal engineer of Burma expeditionary force, 1886–7; major-general, 1887; K.C.B., 1900; published 'The Bombay Field Force,' 1880, and 'Points of a Racehorse,' 1903.

HIND, HENRY YOULE (1823–1908), geologist and explorer; went to Canada, 1846; professor of chemistry and geology in Trinity University, Toronto, 1853–64; conducted government explorations and geological surveys; explored Nova Scotia goldfields, 1869–71; discovered extensive cod banks off shore above Belle Isle, 1876; published accounts of his explorations; arranged scientific evidence in fisheries controversy between America and Canada, 1877; D.C.L., King's College, Windsor, N.S.

HIND, RICHARD DACRE ARCHER- (1849–1910), Greek scholar and Platonist. [See ARCHER-HIND.]

HINGESTON-RANDOLPH (formerly HINGSTON), FRANCIS CHARLES (1833–1910), antiquary; B.A., Exeter College, Oxford, 1855; M.A., 1859; rector of Ringmore, Devonshire, 1860–1910; early developed antiquarian tastes; edited Capgrave's chronicle and other works in Rolls series, 1858–60; prebendary of Exeter Cathedral, 1885; edited 'Episcopal Registers' of diocese, 11 parts, 1886–1909; wrote also on church architecture.

HINGLEY, SIR BENJAMIN, first baronet (1830–1905), ironmaster; head of father's chainmaking firm at Netherton, 1865; manufactured anchors; influential in Midlands in preservation of industrial peace; mayor of Dudley, 1890; liberal M.P. for North Worcestershire, 1885; joined liberal-unionists, 1886; returned to liberalism, 1892; baronet, 1893.

HINGSTON, SIR WILLIAM HALES (1829–1907), Canadian surgeon; born in province of Quebec; studied medicine at McGill University and Edinburgh; L.R.C.S., 1852; hon. F.R.C.S., 1900; practised in Montreal from 1854; joined staff of Hôtel Dieu, 1860; founded Women's Hospital; professor of clinical surgery at Laval University, 1878; first to remove the tongue and lower jaw in one operation, 1872; mayor of Montreal, 1875–6; knighted, 1895; senator, 1896; wrote on climate of Canada, and vaccination.

HIPKINS, ALFRED JAMES (1826–1903), musical antiquary; accomplished interpreter of Chopin on piano; studied history of keyboard instruments; published 'Musical Instruments, Historic, Rare and Unique,' 1881; F.S.A., 1886; left collection of musical instruments to Royal College of Music.

HOARE, JOSEPH CHARLES (1851–1906), bishop of Victoria, Hongkong, from 1898; B.A., Trinity College, Cambridge, 1874; D.D., 1898; joined C.M.S. Mid-China mission at Ningpo, 1875; founded there training college for native evangelists; drowned in Castle Peak Bay while on preaching tour; contributed much to vernacular literature.

HOBBES, JOHN OLIVER (pseudonym) (1867-1906), novelist and dramatist. [See CRAIGIE, PEARL MARY TERESA.]

HOBHOUSE, ARTHUR, BARON HOBHOUSE, of Hadspen (1819-1904), judge; son of Henry Hobhouse [q. v.]; educated at Eton and Balliol College, Oxford; B.A. (first class classic), 1840; called to bar, 1845; acquired large Chancery practice; Q.C., 1862; treasurer of Lincoln's Inn, 1880-1; charity commissioner, 1866; one of three commissioners for re-organizing endowed schools, 1869-72; law member of council of governorgeneral of India, 1872-7; responsible for Specific Relief Act, 1877; opposed Lord Lytton's Afghan policy; K.C.S.I., 1877; member of judicial committee of privy council, 1881-1901; raised to peerage to try appeal cases in House of Lords, 1885; member of London school board, 1882-4; alderman of London County Council, 1888; 'Life' by L. T. Hobhouse and J. L. Hammond, 1905.

HOBHOUSE, EDMUND (1817-1904), bishop of Nelson, New Zealand, and antiquary; brother of Baron Hobhouse [q. v.]; educated at Eton and Balliol College, Oxford; B.A., 1838; D.D., 1858; fellow of Merton, 1841-58; vicar of St. Peter in the East, Oxford, 1843-58; bishop of Nelson, 1858-65; assistant to bishops Selwyn and Maclagan at Lichfield, 1869-81; edited records for Somerset Record Society (1887-94), which he helped to found.

HODGETTS, JAMES FREDERICK (1828-1906), commander and archaeologist; in East India Company's fleet in Burmese war, 1851; commander in Indian navy; professor of seamanship in Berlin, St. Petersburg, and Moscow till 1881; published stories for boys and archaeological works.

HODGKIN, THOMAS (1831-1913), historian; B.A., University College, London; partner in banking firm at Newcastle, 1859-1902; active quaker; chief works, 'Italy and her Invaders' (1879-99) and 'History of England from the Earliest Times to the Norman Conquest' (1906).

HODGSON, RICHARD DACRE (1849-1910), Greek scholar and Platonist. [See ARCHER-HIND.]

HODGSON, SHADWORTH HOLLWAY (1832-1912), philosopher; B.A., Corpus Christi College, Oxford; chief works, 'Time and Space' (1865), 'Theory of Practice' (1870), 'Philosophy of Reflection' (1878), and 'Metaphysic of Experience' (1898).

HODSON, HENRIETTA (1841-1910), actress; went on stage, 1858; met Henry Irving (1860), and with him went to Manchester; popular burlesque actress; first appeared in London, 1866; joined Queen's Theatre company, 1867; married a second husband (1868), Henry Labouchere [q. v.], who acquired sole control of Queen's Theatre, 1870; appeared there as Imogen in 'Cymbeline,' 1871; assumed management of Royalty Theatre, Oct. 1871; inaugurated system of the unseen orchestra; revived 'Wild Oats' (Dec. 1871), and won applause as Peg Woffington, 1875; introduced Mrs. Langtry to stage, 1881; retired to Florence, 1903.

HOEY, FRANCES SARAH [MRS. CASHEL HOEY] (1830-1908), novelist; born in co. Dublin; married John Cashel Hoey, C.M.G., 1858; contributed short stories to 'Chambers's Journal,' 1865-94; wrote eleven novels dealing with fashionable society; helped Edmund Yates [q. v.] in his novels; often visited Paris; translated many French and Italian works; received civil list pension, 1892.

HOFMEYR, JAN HENDRIK (1845-1909), South African politician; born and educated at Cape Town; edited 'Ons Land' from 1871; formed at Cape Town 'Farmers' Association,' 1878, amalgamated with the Afrikander Bond, 1883; chairman till 1895; member for Stellenbosch of Cape parliament, 1879-95; effective leader of constitutional Afrikanderdom; made the Dutch a political force; refused premiership, 1884; member of executive council of Cape Colony; as delegate in London (1887), proposed closer imperial union by means of imperial tariff of customs; negotiated for the British government with President Kruger the Swaziland convention, 1890; supporter of Cecil Rhodes till Jameson Raid of 1895; initiated Bloemfontein conference between Lord Milner and President Kruger, 1899; advocated conciliation after war, 1903; favoured federation in South Africa.

HOGG, QUINTIN (1845-1903), philanthropist; son of Sir James Weir Hogg [q. v.]; educated at Eton; partner in London firm of Hogg, Curtis, and Campbell, sugar merchants; started ragged school for boys at Charing Cross, 1864-5; purchased Royal Polytechnic Institution, Regent Street, and opened it for athletic, intellectual, spiritual, and social recreation, 1882; opened day school there and organized holiday tours (1886) and a labour bureau (1891); his success led to spread of polytechnic movement in London; alderman of London County Council, 1889-94; published 'The Story of Peter' (religious addresses), 1900; bronze group statue by Sir George Frampton in Langham Place; 'Life' by daughter, 1904.

HOLDEN, LUTHER (1815-1905), surgeon; studied at St. Bartholomew's Hospital, Berlin, and Paris; M.R.C.S., 1838; F.R.C.S., 1844; president, 1878; Hunterian orator, 1881; demonstrator (1846), lecturer on surgical anatomy (1859-71), surgeon (1865) at St. Bartholomew's Hospital; on retirement (1881) spent much time in foreign travel; good linguist, classic, and sportsman; primarily interested in anatomical study of surgery; published 'Human Osteology,' 2 vols. 1855, and other medical works; portrait by Millais.

HOLDER, SIR FREDERICK WILLIAM (1850-1909), first speaker of the Australian Commonwealth house of representatives, 1901-9; born in South Australia; editor and proprietor of 'Burra Record'; mayor of Burra, 1886-1890; member of legislative assembly of S. Australia from 1887; treasurer of colony, 1889-90, 1894-9; premier, 1892 and 1899; commissioner of public works, 1893; K.C.M.G., 1902.

HOLE, SAMUEL REYNOLDS (1819-1904), dean of Rochester and author; B.A., Brasenose College, Oxford, 1844; M.A., 1878; published 'Hints to Freshmen,' 1847; vicar of Caunton, 1850-87; prebendary of Lincoln, 1875; enthusiastic huntsman, sportsman, and gardener; close friend of John Leech [q. v.] from 1858, who introduced him to Thackeray; contributed to 'Punch'; a successful rosegrower and organizer of flower shows; his 'Book about Roses' (1869) popularized rose growing; a popular preacher and platform orator; dean of Rochester and D.D. Lambeth, 1887; lectured in United States, 1894; a humorous and charming letter writer; 'Letters' edited with memoir by G. A. B. Dewar, 1907; published 'Memories,' 1892, 'More Memories,' 1894, and 'Then and Now,' 1901; wrote hymns, sermons, and addresses.

HOLLAMS, SIR JOHN (1820-1910), solicitor; admitted solicitor, 1844; president of Law Society, 1878-9; knighted, 1902; published 'Jottings of an Old Solicitor,' 1906.

HOLLAND, HENRY SCOTT (1847-1918), theologian and preacher; B.A., Balliol College, Oxford; a senior student of Christ Church, 1870-84; canon of St. Paul's, 1884-1911; position became identified with social and economic questions; helped to found Christian Social Union, and edited 'Commonwealth,' 1895-1912; contributed to 'Lux Mundi,' 1899; regius professor of divinity at Oxford, 1911-18; raised standard required for divinity degrees; published little except sermons and articles largely owing to indifferent health; liberal in politics and theology, but high churchman.

HOLLAND, SIR HENRY THURSTAN, second baronet, and first VISCOUNT KNUTSFORD (1825-1914); son of Sir Henry Holland [q. v.], first baronet; B.A., Trinity College, Cambridge; called to bar (Inner Temple), 1849; assistant under-secretary for Colonies, 1870-4; succeeded father, 1873; conservative M.P., Midhurst, 1874-85; P.C., 1885; secretary of state for colonies, 1888-92; created baron and G.C.M.G., 1888; viscount, 1895.

HOLLINGSHEAD, JOHN (1827-1904), journalist and theatrical manager; after some commercial travelling, became joint-editor with W. Moy Thomas [q. v.] of 'Weekly Mail,' 1856; joined staff of 'Household Words,' 1857; wrote 'The Birthplace of Podgers,' 1858; his contributions to press were republished in several volumes, 1859-62; one of first contributors to 'Cornhill Magazine,' 1859; dramatic critic to 'Daily News,' 1863-8; occasional contributor to 'Punch'; took part in such public movements as reform of entertainment licensing regulations and of copyright law; stage director of Alhambra, 1865-8; first manager of Gaiety Theatre, 1868-88; inaugurated matinées; produced mainly burlesque, but also operas and serious drama; introduced Ibsen to English public in 'Pillars of Society,' 1880; brought complete 'Comédie Française' company, including Sarah Bernhardt and the Coquelins, to London, 1879;

also managed for short time Opera Comique, London; lost fortune in theatrical speculation; published 'My Lifetime,' 2 vols. 1895, and 'Gaiety Chronicles,' 1898.

HOLLOWELL, JAMES HIRST (1851–1909), advocate of unsectarian education; early became temperance agent and lecturer; joined congregational ministry, 1875, serving in London, Nottingham, and Rochdale; founded Northern Counties Education League for unsectarian education; organized 'passive resistance movement,' 1903: an untiring pamphleteer.

HOLMAN-HUNT, WILLIAM (1827–1910), painter. [See HUNT.]

HOLMES, AUGUSTA (MARY ANNE) (1847–1903), composer; born in Paris; pupil of César Franck; published compositions from 1862 onwards; chief were 'In Exitu Israel,' 1874, 'Irlande,' 1882 (a symphonic poem), 'Ode Triomphale,' 1889, 'La Montagne noire' (opera); became Roman Catholic, 1902; died at Versailles.

HOLMES, SIR RICHARD RIVINGTON (1835–1911), librarian of Windsor Castle, 1870–1906; son of John Holmes [q. v.]; assistant at British Museum, 1854; archaeologist to Abyssinian expedition, 1868; purchased Abyssinian MSS. for British Museum; rearranged and augmented the royal collections; K.C.V.O., 1905; a delicate pen draughtsman, water-colour artist, stained glass designer, and designer of bookbindings; F.S.A., 1860; compiled lives of Queen Victoria, 1897, King Edward VII, 1910, and works on Windsor.

HOLMES, THOMAS (1846–1918), police-court missionary and philanthropist; iron-moulder, 1858–79; police-court missionary, Lambeth (1885–9), North London (1889–1905); founded Home Workers' Aid Association to redress conditions of sweated female labour, 1904; secretary to Howard Association for prison and criminal law reform, 1905–15; wrote on problems connected with crime.

HOLMES, TIMOTHY (1825–1907), surgeon; B.A., Pembroke College, Cambridge (42nd wrangler and twelfth classic), 1847; hon. fellow, 1900; hon. M.S., 1900; F.R.C.S., 1853; house surgeon at St. George's Hospital; surgeon, 1867–87; Hunterian professor of surgery at Royal College of Surgeons, 1873; president of Royal Medical Society, 1900; edited 'A System of Surgery,' 4 vols. 1860–4; wrote life of Sir Benjamin Brodie, 1898.

HOLROYD, SIR CHARLES (1861–1917), painter-etcher and director of National Gallery, London; studied art under Alphonse Legros [q. v.] at Slade School, London; fellow of Society of Painter-Etchers, 1885; travelled in Italy, 1889–91 and 1894–7; exhibited at Royal Academy, but chiefly excelled as etcher of figure subjects, landscapes (English and Italian), and portraits; first keeper of Tate Gallery, 1897–1906; knighted, 1903; director of National Gallery, 1906–16; wrote 'Michael Angelo Buonarrotti' (1903).

HOLROYD, HENRY NORTH, third EARL OF SHEFFIELD (1832–1909), patron of cricket; grandson of first earl [q. v.]; in diplomatic service, 1852–6; conservative M.P. for East Sussex, 1857–65; president of Sussex county cricket club from 1879; arranged first-class cricket matches at Sheffield Park; took English team to Australia, 1891–2; sold his Gibbon MSS. to British Museum, 1895; died at Beaulieu.

HOLYOAKE, GEORGE JACOB (1817–1906), co-operator and secularist; at first a tinsmith and white-smith of Birmingham; joined Birmingham reform league, 1831; became a Chartist, 1832; joined Owenites, 1838; present at Birmingham Chartist riots, 1839; minister to Owenites at Worcester, 1840; became rationalist; edited 'Oracle of Reason,' 1841; sentenced at Gloucester to six months' imprisonment for blasphemy, 1842; published account of trial, 1851; came to London, 1843, advocating freedom of thought and co-operation and co-partnership; edited 'Reasoner,' 1846, and 'Leader,' 1850; invented the term 'secularism,' which he explained in pamphlet, 1854; advocated abolition of paper duties, extension of the franchise, and electoral reform; twice visited Canada and United States to study economic conditions; started 'The Secular Review,' 1876; chief publications include 'A History of Co-operation,' 1875–7, 'Self-help by the People,' 1855, lives of Tom Paine, 1851, Robert Owen, 1859, and John Stuart Mill, 1873, besides his autobiographical books, 'Sixty Years of an Agitator's Life,' 2 vols. 1892, and 'Bygones worth Remembering,' 1905; Lives by J. MacCabe, 2 vols. 1908, and C. W. F. Goss, 1908.

HOOD, ARTHUR WILLIAM ACLAND, first BARON

HOOD, of Avalon (1824–1901), admiral; entered navy, 1836; commander, 1854; served in China, 1857–8, and in North American Station, 1862–6; in charge of Royal Naval College, Portsmouth, 1866; director of naval ordnance, 1869–74; C.B., 1871; commanded Channel fleet, 1878–82; first sea lord of admiralty, 1885; admiral and K.C.B., 1885; G.C.B., 1889; raised to peerage, 1892.

HOOD, SIR HORACE LAMBERT ALEXANDER (1870–1916), rear-admiral; entered royal navy, 1882; served in Nile campaign, 1897–8; D.S.O. for attack on Dervishes at Illig, Somaliland, 1904; commanded Naval College, Osborne, 1910–13; rear-admiral, 1913; naval secretary to first Lord of Admiralty, 1914; commanded third battle squadron of grand fleet, with flag on board 'Invincible,' 1915; blown up at Battle of Jutland, 1916; posthumous K.C.B.

HOOK, JAMES CLARKE (1819–1907), painter; studied at Royal Academy Schools; exhibited at Academy from 1839; A.R.A., 1850; R.A., 1860; subjects mainly old-fashioned genre of historical anecdote until 1854, when he visited Clovelly; thenceforth treated English coast scenery; praised by Ruskin; best-known works were 'Pamphilus Relating his Story,' 1844, 'Luff!, Boy!,' 1859, 'The Samphire Gatherer,' 1875, 'The Stream,' 1885 (now in Tate Gallery); also painted portraits.

HOOKER, SIR JOSEPH DALTON (1817–1911), botanist and traveller; son of Sir William Jackson Hooker [q. v.]; graduated M.D. Glasgow, 1839; inherited from father a passion for botanical research; naturalist in Sir J. C. Ross's Antarctic expedition, 1839–43; published botanical results in six volumes, 1844–60; became intimate with Darwin, and collaborated with him in researches into the origin of species from 1843; greatly advanced the knowledge of geographical distribution of species; rejected theory of multiple origins of 'Flora Antarctica,' 1844–7; appointed botanist to Geological Survey, 1845; F.R.S., 1847; explored Sikkim, part of Eastern Nepal, and passes into Tibet, 1848–9, making observations in geology and meteorology; travelled in Eastern Bengal, 1850–1, collecting plants representing some 700 species; published 'Himalayan Journals,' 1854, and 'Illustrations of Sikkim-Himalayan Plants,' 1855; appointed assistant director at Kew, 1855; published in 1860 his 'Introductory Essay on the Flora of Tasmania,' in which he adopted the newly propounded Darwin-Wallace theory that species are derivative and mutable; went on scientific expedition to Syria and examined cedar grove on Mt. Lebanon, 1860; began with George Bentham [q. v.] the 'Genera Plantarum,' 1862 (last part issued, 1883); succeeded father as director at Kew, 1865; published 'Handbook of the New Zealand Flora,' 1867, and 'Student's Flora of the British Islands,' 1870; explored with John Ball (1818–89, q. v.) the Great Atlas in Morocco; reached Tagheret Pass; president of Royal Society, 1873–8; visited the rocky mountains of Colorado and Utah, 1877; published report of botanical researches, 1881; published 'Flora of British India,' 7 vols. 1883–97, in which he described nearly 17,000 species; retired from Kew, 1885; edited Sir Joseph Banks's 'Journal,' 1896, and wrote on Indian Flora in 'Imperial Gazetteer of India,' 1904; C.B., 1869; K.C.S.I., 1877; G.C.S.I., 1897; O.M., 1907; received many honours from English and foreign scientific societies and universities; portraits by George Richmond, the Hon. John Collier, and Sir Hubert von Herkomer; buried at Kew.

HOPE, JOHN ADRIAN LOUIS, seventh EARL OF HOPETOUN and first MARQUESS OF LINLITHGOW (1860–1908), first governor-general of the commonwealth of Australia; succeeded to earldom, 1873; conservative lord-in-waiting to Queen Victoria, 1885–9; governor of Victoria and G.C.M.G., 1889; paymaster-general, 1895–8; lord chamberlain, 1898; president of Institution of Naval Architects, 1895–1900; first governor-general of commonwealth of Australia, 1900–2; K.T. and G.C.V.O., 1900; resigned owing to insufficient salary, May 1902; created Marquess of Linlithgow, Oct. 1902; secretary of state for Scotland, 1905; sold Rosyth for naval base to government, 1903; died at Pau; a keen sportsman and huntsman.

HOPE, LAURENCE (pseudonym) (1865–1904), poetess. [See NICOLSON, ADELA FLORENCE.]

HOPE, SIR WILLIAM HENRY ST. JOHN (1854–1919), antiquary; B.A., Peterhouse, Cambridge; carried out excavations at Dale Abbey, Repton Priory, Lewes Priory, and Alnwick Abbey; F.S.A., 1884; assistant secretary to Society of Antiquaries, 1885–1910; knighted,

1914; writings include numerous ecclesiological and heraldic works and over 200 papers.

HOPETOUN, seventh EARL OF (1860–1908), first governor-general of the commonwealth of Australia. [See HOPE, JOHN ADRIAN LOUIS.]

HOPKINS, EDWARD JOHN (1818–1901), organist; organist at Temple Church, London, 1843–98; hon. Mus.Doc. Toronto, 1886; compiled 'Temple Church Choral Service Book,' 1867, and 'Temple Psalter,' 1883; wrote 'The Organ, its History and Construction,' 1855, a standard work; 'Life' by Dr. C. W. Pearce, 1910.

HOPKINS, JANE ELLICE (1836–1904), social reformer; daughter of William Hopkins [q. v.]; worked among navvies at Cambridge; removed to Brighton; edited 'Life and Letters' of James Hinton [q. v.], 1875; founded White Cross League, 1886; published 'Active Service,' 1872–4, 'The Power of Womanhood,' 1899, and 'The Story of Life,' 1903.

HOPKINSON, BERTRAM (1874–1918), engineer and physicist; son of Dr. John Hopkinson, F.R.S. [q. v.]; B.A., Trinity College, Cambridge; professor of mechanism and applied mechanics at Cambridge, 1903–18; F.R.S., 1910; joined Royal Engineers, 1914; carried out investigations for government on explosives and aircraft equipment; C.M.G., 1918; killed flying.

HOPWOOD, CHARLES HENRY (1829–1904), recorder of Liverpool, 1886–1904; called to bar, 1853; Q.C., 1874; treasurer of Middle Temple, 1895; edited 'Registration Cases, 1863–72,' 3 vols. 1868–79; liberal M.P. for Stockport, 1874–85, and for Middleton division of Lancashire, 1892–5; energetic supporter of principle of personal liberty, of trade unionism, and adult suffrage; opposed severity of punishment and as recorder inflicted short sentences; founded Romilly Society, 1897; edited 'Middle Temple Records,' 1904.

HORNBY, JAMES JOHN (1826–1909), provost of Eton; son of Admiral Sir Phipps Hornby [q. v.]; educated at Eton and Balliol College, Oxford; first-class classic and fellow of Brasenose, 1849; rowed in Oxford eight, 1849 and 1851; M.A., 1851; D.D., 1869; principal of Bishop Cosin's Hall, Durham, 1853–64; head master of Eton, 1868–84; provost, 1884–1909; pioneer of Alpine climbing; hon. D.C.L. Durham, 1882.

HORNIMAN, FREDERICK JOHN (1835–1906), founder of the Horniman Museum; joined father's tea packing business; travelled extensively, making natural history collections; built Horniman's Museum at Forest Hill, 1897, and presented it to London County Council, 1901; liberal M.P. for Falmouth and Penryn boroughs, 1895–1904.

HORSLEY, JOHN CALLCOTT (1817–1903), painter; son of William Horsley [q. v.]; studied art at Royal Academy, where he exhibited from 1839; opposed to study of nude model; painted domestic scenes, e.g. 'Holy Communion,' 'The Gaoler's Daughter,' 'L'Allegro,' and 'Il Penseroso'; also painted portraits; A.R.A., 1855; R.A., 1856; treasurer, 1882–97; organized 'Old Masters' exhibitions at Academy, 1875–90; interested in music; friend of Mendelssohn and John Leech; published 'Recollections of a Royal Academician,' 1903.

HORSLEY, JOHN WILLIAM (1845–1921), philanthropist; chaplain to Clerkenwell Prison, 1876–86; vicar of Holy Trinity, Woolwich, 1885; rector of St. Peter's, Walworth, 1894; mayor of Southwark, 1910; works on social questions include 'Jottings from Jail' (1887) and 'How Criminals are Made and Prevented' (1912).

HORSLEY, SIR VICTOR ALEXANDER HADEN (1857–1916), physiologist and surgeon; son of John Callcott Horsley, R.A. [q. v.]; educated at University College Hospital; professor-superintendent to Brown Institution (University of London), 1884–90; pursued there three main lines of study—action of thyroid gland, protective treatment against rabies, and localization of function in the brain; F.R.S., professor of pathology, University College, and surgeon to National Hospital for Paralysed and Epileptic, Queen Square, 1886; knighted, 1902; consultant to Mediterranean expeditionary force, 1915; died at Amarah; one of the foremost surgeons of his day; a prolific writer.

HOSKINS, SIR ANTHONY HILEY (1828–1901), admiral; entered navy, 1842; served against Arab slavers in Mozambique; in Kaffir war, 1851–2; in China, 1857–8; commander, 1858; at reduction of Taku forts; commanded in North American, Channel, and Australian waters, 1869–78; C.B., 1877; rear-admiral, 1879; lord commissioner of admiralty, 1880; K.C.B., 1885; commander-in-chief in Mediterranean, 1889–91; admiral and senior naval lord of admiralty, 1891; G.C.B., 1893.

HOUGHTON, WILLIAM STANLEY (1881–1913), dramatist; engaged in father's cloth business in Manchester, 1897–1912; from 1900 made play-making and acting his hobby; contributed theatrical notices to 'Manchester Guardian,' 1905–13; performed dramatic works include 'The Dear Departed' (1908), 'Independent Means' (1909), 'The Younger Generation' and 'The Master of the House' (1910), 'Fancy-Free' (1911), and 'Hindle Wakes' (1912); influenced by Ibsen; portrayed Lancashire life; reached height of his art in 'Hindle Wakes.'

HOWARD, GEORGE JAMES, ninth EARL OF CARLISLE (1843–1911), amateur artist; grandson of sixth earl [q. v.]; educated at Eton and Trinity College, Cambridge; liberal M.P. for East Cumberland, 1879–80, 1881–5; joined liberal unionists, 1886; succeeded to earldom, 1889; closed public-houses on his Yorkshire and Cumberland estates; skilled water-colour landscape painter; published 'A Picture Songbook,' 1910; trustee of National Gallery, to which was transferred his Mabuse's 'Adoration of the Magi,' 1911; his son, CHARLES JAMES STANLEY HOWARD, tenth earl (1867–1912), was unionist M.P. for South Birmingham, 1904–11, and parliamentary whip.

HOWARD, HENRY FITZALAN-, fifteenth DUKE OF NORFOLK (1847–1917); son of H. G. FitzAlan-Howard, fourteenth duke [q. v.]; succeeded father, 1860; educated at Oratory School, Edgbaston; as young man took up cause of his co-religionists, especially Irish Catholics; postmaster-general, 1895–1900; maintained close relations with Vatican; as Earl Marshal largely responsible for coronation ceremonies of Edward VII and George V; great builder of Gothic churches.

HOWARD, ROSALIND FRANCES, COUNTESS OF CARLISLE (1845–1921), promoter of women's political rights and of temperance reform; daughter of Edward John, second Baron Stanley of Alderley [q. v.]; married George Howard, afterwards ninth Earl of Carlisle [q. v.], 1864; supported Home Rule; president of National British Women's Temperance Association (1903) and of Women's Liberal Federation (1891–1901, 1906–14); possessed remarkable business ability.

HOWELL, DAVID (1831–1903), dean of St. David's; held various Welsh livings, 1861–97; dean of St. David's, 1897–1903; member of first Cardiff school board, 1875; well versed in Welsh literature and hymnology; gifted orator of evangelical fervour; mediator between church and Welsh nonconformity.

HOWELL, GEORGE (1833–1910), labour leader and writer; joined Chartists, 1847; prominent in 'nine hours' struggle, 1859; joined 'the Junta' which directed trade union affairs, 1860; secretary to parliamentary committee of trade union congress, 1871–5; prominent in securing Trades Union Acts of 1871 and 1876; liberal M.P. for Bethnal Green, 1885–95; received civil list pension, 1906; publications include 'Trade Unionism New and Old,' 1891, 'Labour Legislation, Labour Movements and Labour Leaders,' 1902; his economic library is in the Bishopsgate Institute.

HOWES, THOMAS GEORGE BOND (1853–1905), zoologist; assisted Huxley at Royal College of Science, South Kensington, till 1880; succeeded Huxley as professor of zoology, 1895; excellent teacher of biology and skilled draughtsman; published Atlases of 'Elementary Biology,' 1885, and 'Zootomy,' 1902; made researches into comparative anatomy of the vertebrata; F.R.S., 1897; LL.D. St. Andrews, 1898.

HOWITT, ALFRED WILLIAM (1830–1908), Australian anthropologist; son of William and Mary Howitt [q. v.]; left Nottingham for Australia, 1852; explored central Australia, 1859; brought back remains of R. O'Hara Burke [q. v.] and W. J. Wills [q. v.] to Melbourne, 1862; police magistrate of Gippsland, 1862–89; made study of Australian aboriginal; admitted a member of the Kurnai tribe; with Lorimer Fison [q. v.] published 'Kamilaroi and Kurnai,' 1880, and 'The Kurnai Tribe,' 1880; secretary of mines in Victoria, 1889, and commissioner of audit, 1896; chairman of royal commission on coal-mining, 1905–6; chief work, 'The Native Tribes of South-East Australia,' 1904; C.M.G., 1906; died at Melbourne.

HOWLAND, SIR WILLIAM PEARCE (1811–1907), Canadian statesman; born in New York; went to Canada, 1830; bought mills near Toronto, 1840; liberal M.P. for West York, Ontario, 1857; finance minister, 1862 and 1866; receiver-general, 1863; postmaster-general, 1864–6; at Canadian federation conference in London, 1866;

minister of inland revenue in first confederation cabinet, 1867–8; lieutenant-governor of Ontario, 1868–73; K.C.M.G., 1879; promoted building of Canadian Pacific Railway, 1880.

HUBBARD, LOUISA MARIA (1836–1906), social reformer; born in St. Petersburg; her 'Work for Ladies in Elementary Schools,' 1872, led to the establishment of training college for girls at Chichester, 1873; published 'The Englishwoman's Year Book,' 1875–98; advocated nursing, massage, typewriting, and gardening as middle class women's occupations; helped to form Working Ladies' Guild, 1876, and Teachers' Guild, 1884; memoir by E. A. Pratt, 1898.

HUDDART, JAMES (1847–1901), Australian shipowner; joined uncle's shipping firm at Geelong, Australia, 1864; founded intercolonial steamship line, 1870; aimed at 'All Red Route' by starting Canadian-Australian Royal Mail Steamship line between Sydney and Vancouver (1893) and a line between Canada and England (1894); scheme failed through lack of English support.

HUDLESTON (formerly SIMPSON), WILFRED HUDLESTON (1828–1909), geologist; educated at Uppingham and St. John's College, Cambridge; made ornithological collections in Lapland, Algeria, Eastern Atlas, Greece, and Turkey, 1855–60; F.G.S., 1867; president, 1892–4; F.R.S., 1884; travelled in India, 1895; published sixty papers dealing with jurassic system and oolite gasteropods, 1887–96, and Indian, Syrian, and African geology.

HUDSON, CHARLES THOMAS (1828–1903), naturalist; B.A., St. John's College, Cambridge (15th wrangler), 1852; M.A., 1855; LL.D., 1866; head master of Bristol grammar school, 1855–60; conducted private school at Clifton, 1861–81; devoted leisure to microscopical research, and to study of Rotifera; president of Royal Microscopical Society, 1888–90; F.R.S., 1889; published 'The Rotifera : or Wheel-Animalculae,' 1886–7.

HUGGINS, SIR WILLIAM (1824–1910), astronomer; son of London silk mercer; educated at City of London School; after a few years in business, built observatory at Tulse Hill, 1856; applied to stars the methods of Kirchoff's researches (1862) into chemical constitution of sun; with William Allen Miller [q.v.] devised the star spectroscope, and presented to Royal Society results of first investigations with it in 'Lines of the Spectra of Some of the Fixed Stars,' 1863, showing that in structure the stars resemble the sun; F.R.S., 1865; awarded royal medal, 1866; president, 1900–6; president of the Royal Astronomical Society, 1876–8; made observations of nebula in Orion (1865) and of several comets; examined motions of Sirius (1868) and other stars; with refracting telescope determined (1870–5) the velocity of stars; photographed successfully the spectrum of Vega (1876), of larger stars, of the moon, and the planets; method applied to Great Nebula n Orion, 1882; hon. LL.D. Cambridge, 1870; D.C.L. Oxford, 1871; awarded medals from Royal and Royal Astronomical societies, and from foreign and American societies; awarded civil list pension, 1890; president of British Association, 1891; K.C.B., 1897; O.M., 1902; observed the new star in Auriga, 1892; made valuable researches as to extent and presence of calcium in sun, 1897; published results of work in 'An Atlas of Representative Stellar Spectra,' 1900, and 'The Scientific Papers of Sir William Huggins,' 1909; helped much by his wife in his researches; portrait by the Hon. John Collier.

HUGHES ARTHUR (1832–1915), painter; studied under Alfred Stevens at Somerset House school of design and at Royal Academy Schools; adopted pre-Raphaelite principles; exhibited at Royal Academy, 1856–1908; chief pictures 'The Knight of the Sun' and 'Home from Sea'; illustrated poems of Tennyson, Christina Rossetti, works of George MacDonald, &c.

HUGHES, EDWARD (1832–1908), portrait painter; taught by father and by John Pye [q.v.]; student at Royal Academy Schools, 1846; exhibited at Royal Academy from 1847, at first subject pictures, but later portraits; excelled in portraits of ladies, who included Queen Mary and Queen Alexandra; idealized sitters; work reproduced in 'The Book of Beauty,' 1896.

HUGHES, HUGH PRICE (1847–1902), methodist divine; B.A. London, 1869; M.A., 1881; from 1884 leader in London of the methodist 'forward movement'; started 'Methodist Times,' 1885, and West London Mission, 1886; promoted Free Church Congress, 1892; first president of Evangelical Free Churches, 1896, and of Wesleyan Methodist Conference, 1898; magnetic

evangelical preacher; a radical in politics, but an imperialist; supported Boer war, 1899–1901; opposed conservative Education Act, 1902; published religious works; 'Life' by his daughter, 1904.

HUGHES, JOHN (1842–1902), Wesleyan methodist divine; entered ministry, 1867; an eloquent preacher and writer in Welsh of religious prose and verse under bardic name of 'Glanystwyth.'

HUGHES, SIR SAM (1853–1921), Canadian soldier and politician; born in Ontario; represented Victoria county in federal house as conservative, 1892–1921; served in South African War, 1899; minister of militia and defence, 1911–16; K.C.B., 1915; lieutenant-general, 1916.

HULME, FREDERICK EDWARD (1841–1909), botanist and artist; skilful sketcher of plants and flowers; his best work, 'Familiar Wild Flowers,' 9 vols. 1875–1909; also published works on ornament, heraldry, flower lore, and art students' textbooks; F.S.A., 1872.

HUME, ALLAN OCTAVIAN (1829–1912), Indian civil servant and ornithologist; son of Joseph Hume [q.v.]; joined Bengal civil service, 1849; C.B. for services in Indian Mutiny, 1860; retired, 1882; worked for Indian parliamentary system through 'Indian National Congress' convoked under his guidance, 1885–94; left India, 1894; collaborated in standard work on Indian game birds.

HUME, MARTIN ANDREW SHARP (1843–1910), author; visited relatives in Spain, 1860; travelled extensively in Central and South America; published 'The Courtships of Queen Elizabeth' and 'The Year after the Armada,' 1896; editor of 'Spanish State Papers' at Public Record Office, 1898; published histories of Spain, 1898, and Modern Spain, 1899, and other works on Spanish history and literature; later works include 'Queens of Old Spain,' 1907, 'Queen Elizabeth and Her England,' 1910; lectured on Spanish history at Cambridge and elsewhere; hon. M.A. Cambridge, 1908.

HUNT, WILLIAM HOLMAN (1827–1910), painter; born in Wood Street, Cheapside; son of a warehouseman; studied art at British Museum and National Gallery from 1843; at Academy Schools, 1844; made acquaintance of Millais and D. G. Rossetti, 1844; exhibited at Academy from 1847; introduced Rossetti to Millais; founded in 1848 with them the pre-Raphaelite Brotherhood, which was joined subsequently by Woolner, W. M. Rossetti, James Collinson, and F. G. Stephens; consistently carried on the brotherhood's principles till death; his first pre-Raphaelite picture, 'Rienzi,' hung in Royal Academy, 1849; visited France and Belgium with Rossetti, 1849; removed to Chelsea; found valuable patron in Thomas Combe [q.v.]; his 'Valentine rescuing Sylvia from Proteus' (1851), attacked by 'The Times,' was powerfully defended by Ruskin, with whom he became intimate for life; 'The Hireling Shepherd' (1852) praised by Carlyle; exhibited at Academy 'Claudio and Isabella' and 'Strayed Sheep,' 1853, and in 1854 'The Awakened Conscience' and 'The Light of the World' (now at Keble College, Oxford; later replica in St. Paul's Cathedral); travelled in Egypt and Palestine, 1854; began at Jerusalem 'The Finding of the Saviour in the Temple' (finished, 1860), and painted on the Dead Sea 'The Scapegoat (exhibited, 1856); settled at Pimlico, then removing to Tor Villa, Hampden Hill, 1856; worked at illustrations to poems of Tennyson (1857), whom he accompanied on tour in Cornwall and Devonshire, 1860; refused associateship of the Royal Academy (1856), where he ceased to exhibit after 1874; helped to form Hogarth Club, 1858; designed furniture, setting fashion developed by William Morris; in Florence, where his first wife died, 1866; painted there 'Isabella and the Pot of Basil'; in Holy Land, 1869–71; painted at Jerusalem 'The Shadow of Death' (or 'The Shadow of the Cross'), 1870–1; after return to London (1871–5) was again in Holy Land, 1875–8; there painted 'Nazareth' and 'The Triumph of the Innocents'; on voyage out painted 'The Ship,' 1875 (now in Tate Gallery); exhibited at the newly founded Grosvenor Gallery from 1877; sent there portraits of his sons, of Sir Richard Owen (1881), and of Dante Rossetti (1884), as well as 'Amaryllis' (1885); executed a water-colour, 'Christ among the Doctors,' 1886, and 'May Morning on Magdalen Tower, Oxford,' 1891; travelled through Italy and Greece to Egypt and Palestine, 1892; painted 'The Miracle of Sacred Fire,' 1899; occasionally practised modelling with success; published 'Pre-Raphaelitism and the Pre-Raphaelite Brotherhood,' 2 vols. 1905; O.M. and hon. D.C.L. Oxford,

1905; buried in crypt of St. Paul's Cathedral; portraits by himself and Sir William Richmond.

HUNTER, COLIN (1841–1904), sea painter; after four years in Glasgow shipping office turned to landscape painting, 1861; exhibited 97 pictures, mainly seascapes, at Royal Academy from 1868; his chief works include 'Trawlers waiting for Darkness,' 1873, 'Their Only Harvest,' 1878 (in Tate Gallery), and 'Signs of Herring,' 1899; A.R.A., 1884; vigorous water-colour artist and etcher.

HUNTER, SIR ROBERT (1844–1913), solicitor, and authority on commons and public rights; partner in firm of solicitors to Commons Preservation Society, 1869; most notable case, Epping Forest, 1871–4; solicitor to General Post Office, 1882–1913; helped to found National Trust, 1895; knighted, 1894; K.C.B., 1911.

HUNTER, SIR WILLIAM GUYER (1827–1902), surgeon-general; F.R.C.S., 1858; M.D., 1867; F.R.C.P., 1875; joined Bengal medical service, 1850; civil surgeon in Upper Scinde during Mutiny, 1857; professor of medicine in Grant Medical College, Bombay, 1858; principal, 1876; surgeon-general, 1877; vice-chancellor of Bombay University, 1880; K.C.M.G., 1884; hon. LL.D. Aberdeen, 1894; member of London school board, 1886–7; conservative M.P. for Central Hackney, 1885–92.

HUNTINGTON, GEORGE (1825–1905), rector of Tenby from 1867; his ritualistic sympathies led to controversy with his bishop, 1877; publications include 'Church's Work in our Large Towns,' 1863, 'Random Recollections,' 1895, sermons, and addresses.

HURLSTONE, WILLIAM YEATES (1876–1906), musical composer and pianist; grandson of Frederick Yeates Hurlstone [q. v.]; composed from age of nine; published orchestral compositions, pianoforte concerto, and cantata.

HUTCHINSON, SIR JONATHAN (1828–1913), surgeon; educated at York medical school and St. Bartholomew's Hospital, London; assistant surgeon to London Hospital, 1859; full surgeon, 1863; F.R.C.S., 1862; Hunterian professor, 1879–83; F.R.S., 1882; left staff of London Hospital as emeritus professor of surgery, 1883; president of Royal College of Surgeons, 1889; delivered Hunterian oration, 1891; knighted, 1908; specialist of great repute on ophthalmology, dermatology, and especially on syphilis; works include 'Illustrations of Clinical Surgery' (1878–84) and 'Archives of Surgery' (1889–1900); formed museum of specimens and drawings.

HUTH, ALFRED HENRY (1850–1910), bibliophile; son of Henry Huth [q. v.]; travelled in East with Henry Thomas Buckle [q. v.], 1861–2; publications include 'The Marriage of Near Kin,' 1875, and Life of Buckle, 2 vols. 1880; helped to found Bibliographical Society, 1892; by will left fifty volumes to British Museum; sale of part of collection realized over 108,000l. (1911–12).

HUTTON, ALFRED (1839–1910), swordsman; joined 79th highlanders, 1859; captain, 1868; organized Cameron Fencing Club, for which he published 'Swordsmanship', 1862; on retiring from army (1873) practised modern fencing and revived older systems; published 'Cold Steel,' 1889, 'Fixed Bayonets,' 1890, 'The Swordsman,' 1891, 'Old Sword Play,' 1892, and 'The Sword and the Centuries,' 1901; F.S.A., 1894; founder and chairman of Central London Throat and Ear Hospital, 1874; bequeathed collection of fencing literature to Victoria and Albert Museum.

HUTTON, FREDERICK WOLLASTON (1836–1905), geologist; served in Indian mercantile marine; in army, 1855–65; in Crimea and Indian Mutiny; emigrated to New Zealand, 1866; professor of geology in New Zealand University, 1890–3; curator of museum, 1893; interested in ornithology and ethnology; writings include 'Elementary Geology,' 1875, 'The Lesson of Evolution,' 1902, and works on fauna of New Zealand, 1904; F.R.S., 1892.

HUTTON, GEORGE CLARK (1825–1908), presbyterian divine; educated at Edinburgh University; hon. D.D., 1906; United Presbyterian minister at Paisley from 1851 till death; advocated 'voluntary' movement in religion; strenuously advocated disestablishment of Church of Scotland in speeches and pamphlets; urged state secular education; moderator of synod, 1884; principal of United Presbyterian Theological College, 1892; co-principal with G. C. M. Douglas [q.v.] of United Free Church College, Glasgow, till 1902; moderator of United Free Church general

assembly, 1906; a trenchant controversialist; evangelical preacher; published several religious works; 'Life' by Alexander Oliver, 1910.

HYNDMAN, HENRY MAYERS (1842–1921), socialist leader; on staff of 'Pall Mall Gazette,' 1871–80; took lead in forming (Social) Democratic Federation, 1881; agitated among unemployed; opposed South African War; left British Socialist Party and formed National Socialist Party, 1916; published 'England for All' (1881), several books defending political Marxism, and two autobiographical works.

IBBETSON, SIR DENZIL CHARLES JELF (1847–1908), lieutenant-governor of the Punjab; passed into Indian civil service, 1868; assistant settlement officer at Karnal, 1871; published lucid report of district (1883) containing scholarly research into tribal and agricultural systems; reported on Punjab census of 1881, and based on it 'Outlines of Punjab Ethnography,' 1883; compiled 'Punjab Gazetteer,' 1883; head of department of public instruction, 1884; his report (1891) on working of Deccan Agriculturists' Relief Act of 1879 led to its amendment in nterest of peasantry; C.S.I., 1896; chief commissioner of Central Provinces, 1898; joined viceroy's council, 1902; active in measures for prevention of famine; carried Co-operation Credit Act, 1904; K.C.S.I., 1903; lieutenant-governor of the Punjab, 1907–8; repressed disorders in Lahore and Rawalpindi; portrait by H. Olivier at Lahore.

IBBETSON, SIR HENRY JOHN SELWIN-, seventh baronet, and BARON ROOKWOOD (1826–1902), politician. [See SELWIN-IBBETSON.]

IGNATIUS, FATHER (1837–1908), preacher. [See LYNE, JOSEPH LEYCESTER.]

INCE, WILLIAM (1825–1910), regius professor of divinity at Oxford; B.A., Lincoln College, Oxford (first class in lit. hum.), 1846; M.A., 1849; D.D., 1878; fellow of Exeter College, 1847; tutor, 1850; sub-rector, 1857–78; hon. fellow, 1882; regius professor of divinity and canon of Christ Church, 1878–1910; active in administration of Christ Church; an evangelical and moderate Anglican; published 'The Life and Times of St. Athanasius,' 1896, and doctrinal pamphlets.

INDERWICK, FREDERICK ANDREW (1836–1904), lawyer and antiquary; called to bar (Inner Temple), 1858; Q.C., 1874; leader in probate and divorce division from 1876; commissioner in lunacy, 1903; liberal M.P. for Rye, 1880–5; mayor of Winchelsea, 1892–3; F.S.A., 1894; published, besides legal and historical works, 'Calendar of the Inner Temple Records, 1505–1714,' 3 vols. 1896–1901.

INGLIS, ELSIE MAUD (1864–1917), physician and surgeon; born in India; studied medicine at Edinburgh, Glasgow, and Dublin; joint-surgeon to Edinburgh Bruntsfield Hospital and Dispensary and private practitioner in Edinburgh; inaugurated there maternity hospice staffed by women, 1901; founded Scottish Women's Suffrage Federation (1906) from which sprang Scottish Women's Hospitals committee (1914); joined Serbian unit, 1915; remained at post at Krushevatz during German and Austrian invasion, 1915–16; organized two units in aid of Serbian division in Russia, 1916; worked at Braila, Galatz, and Reni, remaining till withdrawal of Serbs (1917).

INGRAM, JOHN KELLS (1823–1907), scholar, economist, and poet; brother of Thomas Dunbar Ingram [q. v.]; senior moderator, Trinity College, Dublin, 1842; fellow, 1844; senior fellow, 1884; senior lecturer, 1887; D.Litt., 1891; helped to found Dublin Philosophical Society (1842), and contributed to 'Transactions' abstruse papers in pure geometry; contributed sonnets to 'Dublin University Magazine,' 1840; composed 'Who fears to speak of Ninety-eight?' which, printed anonymously in 'Nation' newspaper (1 April 1843), brought him fame as a popular nationalist poet; member of Royal Irish Academy, 1847; studied mathematics, classics, and metaphysics; met Carlyle in Dublin, 1849; visited Comte, 1855, and accepted his beliefs; professor of oratory at Trinity College, 1852–66; regius professor of Greek, 1866–77; librarian, 1879–87; vice-provost, 1898–9; started and edited 'Hermathena,' 1874; trustee of the National Library of Ireland, 1881; hon. LL.D. Glasgow, 1893; president of Royal Irish Academy, 1892–6; helped to found Dublin Statistical Society, 1847; president, 1878–80; prepared for the society 'Considerations on the State of Ireland,' 1863; wrote papers on poor law, 1875–6; vindicated economics as integral branch of sociology; contributed articles to 'Encyclopaedia Britannica'

(9th edit.), of which those on political economy (1885) and slavery (1887) were separately published; his 'History of Political Economy' (1888) was translated into most European languages and Japanese; his economic views were coloured by Comtism; he declared his positivist beliefs in 'Outlines of the History of Religion,' 1900; published other positivist works from 1901 to 1905, and issued 'Sonnets and other Poems,' 1900. He distrusted Parnell and his nationalist associates, but opposed South African War, 1899.

INGRAM, THOMAS DUNBAR (1826–1901), Irish historical writer and lawyer; LL.B., Queen's College, Belfast, 1853; called to bar 1856; professor of Hindu law in Presidency College, Calcutta, 1866–77; author of 'A Critical Examination of Irish History,' 2 vols., posthumous, 1904, and other works.

INNES, JAMES JOHN McLEOD (1830–1907), lieutenant-general royal (Bengal) engineers; born in Bengal; joined Bengal engineers, 1848; in Mutiny in charge of Machi Bhowan fort, and of mining operations at defence of Lucknow, which he described in 'Lucknow and Oude in the Mutiny,' 1895; awarded V.C. for gallantry at Sutanpur, 1858; accountant-general in Indian public works department, 1870–7; inspector-general of military works, 1882–6; lieutenant-general, 1886; C.B., 1907; published 'The Sepoy Revolt of 1857,' 1907, and lives of Sir Henry Lawrence, 1898, and Sir James Browne, 1905.

IRBY, LEONARD HOWARD LOYD (1836–1905), lieutenant-colonel and ornithologist; son of Frederick Paul Irby [q. v.]; entered army, 1854; served at Sevastopol and at Lucknow; at Gibraltar (1864–72) devoted himself to ornithology; retired as lieutenant-colonel, 1874; published 'Ornithology of the Straits of Gibraltar,' 1875, and 'Key List of British Birds,' 1888; ardent lepidopterologist.

IRELAND, WILLIAM WOTHERSPOON (1832–1909), physician; M.D. Edinburgh, 1855; joined East India Company's service, 1856; severely wounded at siege of Delhi, 1856; retired on pension, 1859; medical superintendent of Scottish National Institution for Imbecile Children, 1869; wrote with authority on idiocy and imbecility; applied medico-psychological knowledge to explain lives of celebrated men in 'The Blot upon the Brain,' 1885, and 'Through the Ivory Gate,' 1889; wrote also Life of Sir Harry Vane, 1905.

IRVINE, WILLIAM (1840–1911), Mogul historian; joined Indian civil service, 1863; magistrate and collector in North-West provinces, 1863–89; published 'Rent Digest,' 1868; wrote on Mogul history for 'Journal of Asiatic Society of Bengal,' 1896–1908; published 'The Army of the Indian Moghuls,' 1903, and translated and edited N. Manucci's account of India (1653–1707), which was published by the Indian government, 1907.

IRVING, SIR HENRY (1838–1905), actor, whose original name was JOHN HENRY BRODRIBB; born at Keinton Mandeville, Somerset; came of yeoman stock; clerk in London firm of East India merchants, 1852–6; made first appearance as actor at Lyceum Theatre, Sunderland, as Gaston in 'Richelieu,' 1856; in Edinburgh, 1857–9, where his mannerisms were criticized; first appeared in London, 1859; at Manchester under Charles Calvert, 1860–5; first acted rôle of Hamlet (his first Shakespearean character), 1864; after much provincial work, he toured with J. L. Toole, 1866; at Queen's Theatre, London, played Petruchio to Miss Ellen Terry's Katherine, Dec. 1867, and Bill Sikes in Oxenford's 'Oliver Twist,' 1869; made first notable success in London as Digby Grant in Albery's 'Two Roses' at Vaudeville, 1870; joined Bateman's company at Lyceum Theatre, 1871; became famous by his acting in 'The Bells,' Nov. 1871 to May 1872; took title parts of 'Charles I,' 1872, 'Eugene Aram,' 1873, and 'Richelieu,' 1873; showed originality in conception, but criticized for affectations, monotony, and weakness of voice; scored triumph as Hamlet, 1874; appeared as Macbeth, 1875, and Othello, 1876, and in 'Richard III,' 'The Lyons Mail,' 1877, and 'Louis XI,' 1878; became lessee and manager of Lyceum (1878), and began association—lasting till 1902—with Miss Ellen Terry; played Hamlet to her Ophelia, 1878; produced 'Merchant of Venice,' 1880, 'The Corsican Brothers,' 1880, Tennyson's 'The Cup,' 1881, 'Romeo and Juliet' (elaborately mounted), and 'Much Ado About Nothing,' 1882–3; made first of eight tours to America, 1883–4; on return produced 'Twelfth Night,' May 1884; gave weird and striking impersonation of Mephistopheles in Wills's

'Faust,' 1885–7; revived 'Macbeth,' 1888–9; with Miss Terry he appeared before Queen Victoria at Sandringham, April 1889; produced 'Henry VIII' (with splendid staging), Jan. 1892, and 'King Lear,' Nov. 1892; Tennyson's 'Becket' (Feb. 1893) proved one of Irving's greatest personal and financial triumphs; made fourth and most successful American tour, 1893–4; produced 'Waterloo,' 1894, 'King Arthur,' 1895, 'Cymbeline,' Sept. 1896, and 'Richard III,' Dec.; suffered pecuniary losses; transferred control of Lyceum to a company, 1898; appeared in Sardou's 'Robespierre,' 1899, and in 'Coriolanus,' 1901; revived 'Faust' and 'Merchant of Venice' at Lyceum, 1902; last appearance there, 19 July; produced at Drury Lane Sardou's 'Dante,' 1903; made eighth American tour, 1903–4; died in Bradford after acting in 'Becket' earlier in the evening, 1905; his ashes buried in Westminster Abbey; contributed to the 'Nineteenth Century' 'An Actor's Notes,' 1877–87; superintended the 'Henry Irving Shakespeare,' 1888; received hon. degrees from Dublin, Cambridge, and Glasgow; first actor to be knighted, 1895; Rede lecturer at Cambridge, 1898. An intellectual actor, of magnetic personality, but of mannered elocution and gait, he attracted again to theatre the intelligent playgoer and revived popular interest in Shakespeare. He neglected modern drama and depended much on sumptuous and elaborate mountings for which he secured assistance from leading artists and composers. Portraits in oils by Whistler, Edwin Long, Bastien-Lepage, the Hon. John Collier, Millais, James Archer, J. S. Sargent; in statuary by R. Jackson, W. Brodie, E. Onslow Ford, C. Pollock, Thomas Brock; 'Lives' by Austen Brereton, Bram Stoker, Percy Fitzgerald, William Archer, and F. A. Marshall.

IWAN-MÜLLER, ERNEST BRUCE (1853–1910), journalist; B.A., New College, Oxford (first class in *lit. hum.*), 1876; editor of the tory 'Manchester Courier,' 1884–93; assistant editor of 'Pall Mall Gazette,' 1893–6; leader writer for 'Daily Telegraph,' 1896–1910; visited South Africa during Boer war, Ireland (1907), and Paris (1908); well versed in foreign politics; published 'Lord Milner in South Africa,' 1902, and 'Ireland To-day and To-morrow,' 1907.

JACKS, WILLIAM (1841–1907), ironmaster and author; started iron works at Glasgow, 1880; liberal M.P. for Leith Burghs, 1885–6, for Stirling, 1892–5; wrote lives of Bismarck, 1899, and James Watt, 1901; hon. LL.D. Glasgow, 1899; bequeathed 20,000l. to Glasgow University for chair of modern languages.

JACKSON, HENRY (1839–1921), regius professor of Greek at Cambridge; B.A., Trinity College, Cambridge; fellow, 1864; praelector in ancient philosophy, 1875; vice-master, 1914; regius professor of Greek, 1906; O.M., 1908; principal contribution to learning, his doctrine of Plato's 'later theory of Ideas.'

JACKSON, JOHN (1833–1901), professional cricketer; member of Nottinghamshire cricket eleven; leading bowler in England, 1857; played for Players v. Gentlemen, 1859–64; visited America, 1859, and Australia, 1863; often caricatured by Leech in 'Punch' as 'demon bowler.'

JACKSON, JOHN HUGHLINGS (1835–1911), physician; studied medicine at York and St. Bartholomew's Hospital; M.R.C.S., 1856; M.D. St. Andrews, 1860; physician at London Hospital (1863–94) and at National Hospital for Epileptics, Queen Square (1862–1906); F.R.C.P., 1868; Gulstonian lecturer, 1869; Croonian lecturer, 1884; Lumleian lecturer, 1890; F.R.S., 1878; studied speech defect in brain disease, the occurrence of local epileptic discharges (known as Jacksonian epilepsy), and showed that certain regions of the brain were definitely related to certain limb movements; formulated theory of levels in the nervous system, showing that the highest and most recently developed functions go first in process of disease; also investigated 'uncinate' epilepsy; one of the first to use ophthalmoscope in England in diagnosing eye diseases; published many scientific papers.

JACKSON, MASON (1819–1903), wood engraver; pupil of brother John Jackson [q. v.]; art editor to 'Illustrated London News,' 1860; published 'The Pictorial Press: its Origin and Progress,' 1885.

JACKSON, SAMUEL PHILLIPS (1830–1904), water-colour artist; born at Bristol; son of Samuel Jackson [q. v.]; painted land- and seascapes; exhibited mainly at Royal Water Colour Society; member, 1876; work praised by Ruskin; showed preference for Devon and Cornish coast scenes and Thames views; skilful interpreter of west country atmosphere; an efficient photographer.

JACKSON, WILLIAM LAWIES, first BARON ALLERTON (1840–1917), politician; made father's almost bankrupt tanning business one of the largest in England; conservative M.P., North Leeds, 1880; financial secretary to Treasury, 1885–91; P.C., 1890; F.R.S. 1891; chairman of Jameson Raid inquiry, 1896–7; created baron, 1902; rendered great financial services to Leeds.

JACOB, EDGAR (1844–1920), bishop of Newcastle and of St. Albans; grandson of John Jacob [q.v.], Guernsey topographer; educated at Winchester and New College, Oxford; domestic chaplain to Robert Milman [q. v.], bishop of Calcutta, 1872–6; vicar of Portsea, 1878–95; bishop of Newcastle, 1896–1903; of St. Albans, 1903–19; successfully worked for division of latter see; published lectures and addresses.

JAMES, HENRY, LORD JAMES OF HEREFORD (1828–1911), lawyer and statesman; interested in cricket; president of M.C.C., 1889; called to bar, 1852; an excellent criminal advocate; Q.C, 1869; treasurer of Middle Temple, 1888; liberal M.P. for Taunton, 1869–85; solicitor-general under Gladstone, Sept. 1873; attorney-general, Nov. 1873, and 1880–5; drafted and carried corrupt practices bill, 1883; P.C., 1885; opposed Gladstone's Irish policy and joined liberal unionists; unionist M.P. for Bury, 1886–95; resumed private bar practice; appeared for 'The Times,' before Parnell commission, 1888–9, summing up clients' case in a notable twelve days' speech; attorney-general of Duchy of Cornwall, 1892–5; hon. LL.D. Cambridge, 1892; raised to peerage, and joined unionist cabinet as chancellor of the Duchy of Lancaster, 1895; served on judicial committee of privy council from 1896; able chairman of coal conciliation board, 1898–1909; resigned office, 1902; G.C.V.O., 1902; opposed to Mr. Balfour's education policy and tariff reform proposals; opposed rejection of budget by House of Lords, 1909.

JAMES, HENRY (1843–1916), novelist; born in New York; educated in New York, London, Paris, and Geneva; studied law at Harvard; settled in Europe, 1875; lived in London, 1876–98, and at Rye, 1898–1916; found material for novels in society life of London; naturalized, 1915; O.M., 1916; work as novelist falls into three 'periods'; in first, chiefly occupied with 'international' subject, impact of American life upon European civilization; novels of this period, 'Roderick Hudson' (1875), 'The American' (1877), 'Daisy Miller' (1879), and 'The Portrait of a Lady' (1881); in second period dealt with subjects from English life, social, political, and artistic; novels of this period, 'The Tragic Muse' (1890), 'The Spoils of Poynton' (1897), 'What Maisie Knew' (1897), and 'The Awkward Age' (1899); began to develop extremely intricate style to match subtlety of perceptions and discriminations; in third period, which contains 'The Wings of the Dove' (1902), 'The Ambassadors' (1903), and 'The Golden Bowl' (1904), returned to 'international' theme; explored with greater thoroughness than any previous novelist nature and possibilities of art of fiction; in later works subjects appear hardly equal to immense elaboration of treatment; also wrote short stories, plays, and reminiscences.

JAMES, JAMES (1832–1902), joint-composer with his father of 'Land of My Fathers,' the Welsh national anthem, 1856; it attracted public favour at eisteddfods at Pontypridd, 1857, and Llangollen, 1858, was included in 'Gems of Welsh Melody,' 1860, and was sung at Bangor national eisteddfod, 1874, serving thenceforth as Welsh national anthem.

JAMESON, ANDREW, LORD ARDWALL (1845–1911), Scottish judge; M.A. St. Andrews, 1865; hon. LL.D., 1905; called to Scottish bar, 1870; sheriff of Roxburghshire, 1886, Ross, 1890, and Perthshire, 1891; raised to bench and peerage, 1905; frequent arbitrator in industrial disputes; interested in Scottish Free Church affairs.

JAMESON, SIR LEANDER STARR, baronet (1853–1917), South African statesman; born in Edinburgh; M.D., London, 1877; went out as doctor to Kimberley, 1878; formed friendship with Cecil John Rhodes [q.v.], undertook three missions to Matabele chief, Lobengula, 1889–90; in consequence effective confirmation of mineral rights concession obtained by British South Africa Company; accompanied, as Rhodes's personal representative, expedition of A. R. Colquhoun, first administrator of Mashonaland, 1890; administrator of Mashonaland, 1891; accompanied force dispatched by company to punish Lobengula for raids by Matabele 'impis' on

Mashonas under British protection; Buluwayo occupied, 1893; Matabeleland placed under Jameson's administration, 1894; C.B., 1894; carried out famous 'Raid' over Transvaal border in 'Uitlander' interests, December 1895; surrendered to Boer commandant, P. A. Cronje, January 1896; handed over to British authorities and sent to England for trial; imprisoned in Holloway jail, but quickly released; entered Cape parliament as member for Kimberley, 1900; succeeded Rhodes as leader of progressive party at Cape, 1902; prime minister of Cape Colony, 1904–8; attended Imperial Conference in London, and P.C., 1907; with General Botha [q. v. played chief part in South African National Convention, 1908–9; entered first Union parliament as member for Harbour division of Capetown, 1910; leader of opposition; baronet, 1911; retired, 1912; died in London.

JAPP, ALEXANDER HAY (1837–1905), author and publisher; at first a tailor's book-keeper in Edinburgh; attended classes in Edinburgh University, 1860–1; literary adviser in London to Isbister & Co., 1864; assisted in editing 'Good Words,' 'Sunday Magazine,' and 'Contemporary Review'; LL.D., Glasgow, 1879; F.R.S., Edinburgh, 1880; wrote much under various pseudonyms, the chief being 'H. A. Page' and 'A. F. Scot'; edited De Quincey's 'Posthumous Works,' 1891–3, and 'De Quincey Memorials,' 1891; his works include studies of Hawthorne, 1872, of Thoreau, 1878, of De Quincey, 2 vols. 1877, and of R. L. Stevenson (of whose 'Treasure Island' he had negotiated the publication), 1905; he also published verse and studies in German literature, natural history, and anthropology.

JARDINE, SIR ROBERT, first baronet (1825–1905), East India merchant and racehorse owner; partner in uncle's London firm of East India merchants, 1859; succeeded uncle as head of firm, and inherited his property in Perthshire and Dumfriesshire. 1881; liberal M.P. for Ashburton, 1865, for Dumfries burghs, 1868–74 and 1880–92; baronet, 1885; keen agriculturist and breeder of stock; won Two Thousand Guineas and Derby with Pretender, 1869, the Cesarewitch, 1877, and the Waterloo (coursing) Cup, 1873; art collector.

JAYNE, FRANCIS JOHN (1845–1921), bishop of Chester; educated at Rugby and Wadham College, Oxford; first classes in classics and law and modern history; fellow of Jesus College, Oxford, 1868; ordained, 1870; tutor of Keble College, Oxford, 1871; principal of St. David's College, Lampeter, 1879–86; vicar of Leeds, 1886–9; bishop of Chester, 1889–1919; a moderate churchman with exceptional administrative talents.

JEAFFRESON, JOHN CORDY (1831–1901), author; B.A., Pembroke College, Oxford, 1852; private tutor in London, 1852–8; published many novels, including 'Live it Down,' 1863; made some repute as an anecdotal anthologist in books 'about doctors,' 1860, 'about lawyers,' 1866, and 'about the clergy,' 1870; called to bar, 1859, but did not practise; inspector of MSS. for Royal Historical MSS. Commission, 1874–87; author of 'The Real Lord Byron,' 1883, 'The Real Shelley,' 1885, 'Lady Hamilton and Lord Nelson,' 1888, and 'The Queen of Naples and Lord Nelson,' 1889.

JEBB, SIR RICHARD CLAVERHOUSE (1841–1905), Greek scholar; born at Dundee; great-nephew of John Jebb [q. v.]; educated at Charterhouse and Trinity College, Cambridge; Porson scholar, 1859; Craven scholar, 1860; senior classic and first chancellor's medallist, 1862; fellow and classical lecturer, 1863; hon. fellow, 1888; public orator, 1869; helped to found Cambridge Philosophical Society, 1868; published 'The Characters of Theophrastus,' 1870, and translations into Greek and Latin verse, 1873; professor of Greek at Glasgow, 1875–89; lectured upon modern as well as classical Greek; visited Greece, 1878; wrote 'Attic Orators,' 2 vols. 1876; 'Primer of Greek Literature,' 1877, 'Modern Greece,' 1880, monograph on 'Bentley' (in 'Men of Letters' series), 1882, and 'Homer,' 1887; visited America, 1884; hon. LL.D. Harvard; regius professor of Greek at Cambridge, 1889–1905; conservative M.P. for the university, 1891–1905; served on many education commissions; Rede lecturer, Cambridge, 1890; Romanes lecturer, Oxford, 1899; delivered lectures at Johns Hopkins University (1892) on 'The Growth and Influence of Greek Poetry' (published 1893); edited Bacchylides, 1905; chief work was edition of Sophocles, 7 vols. 1883–96; an eighth volume containing the Fragments was unfinished; helped to found Society for Promotion of Hellenic Studies, 1879, and the British

School of Archaeology at Athens, 1887; F.B.A., 1902; close friend of Tennyson; received hon. degrees from Edinburgh, Dublin, Cambridge, Oxford, and Bologna; professor of ancient history, Royal Academy, 1898; knighted, 1900; trustee of British Museum, 1903; O.M., 1905; 'Essays and Letters' and 'Life and Letters' edited by widow, 1907.

JELF, GEORGE EDWARD (1834–1908), master of Charterhouse; son of Richard William Jelf [q.v.]; educated at Charterhouse and Christ Church, Oxford; B.A., 1856; M.A., 1859; D.D., 1907; hon. canon of St. Albans, 1878; residentiary canon of Rochester, 1880–1907; master of Charterhouse, 1907; a moderate high churchman, he exercised considerable influence by his popular devotional publications; memoir by widow, 1909.

JENKINS, EBENEZER EVANS (1820–1905), Wesleyan minister and missionary; worked at Madras till 1865; superintendent of the Hackney circuit from 1865; president of the Wesleyan Conference, 1880; memoir by son, 1906.

JENKINS, JOHN EDWARD (1838–1910), politician and satirist; born at Bangalore; called to bar (Lincoln's Inn), 1864; retained by Aborigines Protection Society for British Guiana coolie commission, 1870; gained repute as author of 'Ginx's Baby' (anonymous), 1870, a satire on sectarian education; originated Imperial Federation movement, 1871; first agent-general for Canada, 1874–6; radical M.P. for Dundee, 1874–80; wrote other political satires and novels.

JENNER-FUST, HERBERT (1806–1904), cricketer; son of Sir Herbert Jenner [q.v.]; educated at Eton and Trinity Hall, Cambridge; LL.B., 1829; LL.D., 1835; called to bar, 1831; captain of first Cambridge cricket XI to meet Oxford, 1827; prominent in all first-class cricket till 1836, especially as wicket-keeper; president of M.C.C., 1833.

JEPHSON, ARTHUR JERMY MOUNTENEY (1858–1908), explorer; accompanied Stanley through forests to Lake Albert for relief of Emin Pasha, 1888; imprisoned with Emin at Dufile, August 1888; rejoined Stanley at Kavali (Feb. 1889), and subsequently rescued Emin; queen's messenger, 1895; published 'Emin Pasha and the Rebellion at the Equator,' 1890, and native folk tales.

JERSEY, seventh EARL OF (1845–1915), colonial governor. [See VILLIERS, VICTOR ALBERT GEORGE CHILD-.]

JESSOPP, AUGUSTUS (1823–1914), schoolmaster and historical writer; B.A., St. John's College, Cambridge; head master of King Edward VI's School, Norwich, which he transformed into modern public school, 1859–79; rector of Scarning, Norfolk, 1879–1911; works include 'One Generation of a Norfolk House' (the Walpoles, 1878), and 'The Coming of the Friars' (1889); edited 'Visitations of Diocese of Norwich, 1492–1532' (1888), &c.

JEUNE, FRANCIS HENRY, BARON ST. HELIER (1843–1905), judge; eldest son of Francis Jeune [q.v.]; scholar of Harrow and Balliol College, Oxford; first class classic, 1865; obtained Stanhope (1863) and Arnold (1867) essay prizes; called to bar, 1868; original fellow of Hertford College, 1874; counsel for 'Tichborne' plaintiff in action of ejectment, 1871–2; had large ecclesiastical practice; counsel for evangelicals in Mackonochie case; counsel for Louis Riel [q.v.] in application for leave to appeal; chancellor of several dioceses; Q.C., 1888; counsel for Edward King [q.v.] in ritual case, 1889–90; judge of probate, divorce, and admiralty division, and knighted, 1891; president of probate division, 1892; made court a model of efficiency and dispatch; judge advocate general without payment, 1892–1904; K.C.B., 1897; G.C.B., 1902; resigned presidency of probate division through ill-health and created a peer, Jan. 1905; portrait by Sir Hubert von Herkomer.

JEX-BLAKE, SOPHIA LOUISA (1840–1912), physician; sister of T. W. Jex-Blake [q.v.]; medical student at Edinburgh, 1869–72; on being refused, with other women students, right to graduate, founded London School of Medicine for Women, 1874; gained legal right to practise in Great Britain, 1877; practised in Edinburgh, 1878–99.

JEX-BLAKE, THOMAS WILLIAM (1832–1915), schoolmaster and dean of Wells; educated at Rugby and University College, Oxford; fellow of Queen's College, Oxford, 1855; assistant master at Rugby, 1858–68; principal of Cheltenham College, 1868–74; head master of Rugby, which he restored to prosperity, 1874–87; dean of Wells, 1891–1910.

JOHNS, CLAUDE HERMANN WALTER (1857–1920), Assyriologist; B.A., Queens' College, Cambridge;

rector of St. Botolph's, Cambridge, 1892–1909; lecturer in Assyriology at Queens', 1895, and in Assyrian at King's College, London, 1904; master of St. Catharine's College, Cambridge, and canon of Norwich, 1909–19; chief work 'Assyrian Deeds and Documents' (1898–1923).

JOHNSON, LIONEL PIGOT (1867–1902), critic and poet; scholar of Winchester College; edited 'The Wykehamist,' 1884–6; B.A., New College, Oxford (first class in *lit. hum.*), 1890; entered on literary career in London, 1890, contributing to magazines and reviews; joined Church of Rome, 1891; published his first volume of poems, 1895, in which he gave expression to a 'catholic puritanism'; in 'Ireland and other Poems,' 1897, he betrayed an intense love for Ireland; also wrote 'The Art of Thomas Hardy,' 1894, and 'Post Liminium: Essays and Critical Papers' (posthumous), 1911.

JOHNSTON, WILLIAM (1829–1902), of Ballykilbeg, Orangeman; B.A., Trinity College, Dublin, 1852; M.A., 1856; called to Irish bar, 1872; entered Orange order, 1848; proposed institution of triennial council of Orangemen, 1865; imprisoned for organizing and leading a demonstration against Party Processions Act, 1868; independent conservative M.P. for Belfast, 1868; inspector of Irish fisheries, 1878; dismissed for violent speeches against Land League and home rule, 1885; M.P. for South Belfast, 1885 till death; firm advocate of 'the three F's' (fair rent, free sale, fixity of tenure), and of temperance.

JOLY, CHARLES JASPER (1864–1906), royal astronomer of Ireland; mathematical scholar of Trinity College, Dublin, 1882; obtained 'studentship,' 1886; fellow, 1894–7; made researches in physics, and especially studied the properties of linear vector functions; royal astronomer of Ireland at Dunsink, 1897; edited and enlarged Hamilton's 'Elements of Quaternions,' 2 vols. 1899–1901; contributed numerous papers on quaternions and kindred subjects to Royal Irish Academy; published 'A Manual of Quaternions,' 1905; accompanied eclipse expedition to Spain, 1900; F.R.S., 1904; member of Alpine Club.

JOLY DE LOTBINIÈRE, SIR HENRY GUSTAVE (1829–1908), Canadian politician; born at Épernay, France; called to Canadian bar, 1855; liberal member of Canadian House of Assembly for Lotbinière, 1861; opposed federation movement; member of Quebec Legislative Assembly, 1867–74; Q.C., 1878; formed government, 1878–9; K.C.M.G., 1895; minister of inland revenue and P.C., 1897; as lieutenant-governor of British Columbia (1900–6) entertained Prince and Princess of Wales, 1901; promoted interests of agriculture and forestry.

JONES, SIR ALFRED LEWIS (1845–1909), man of business; born at Carmarthen; became partner of Messrs. Elder, Dempster's shipping firm at Liverpool, 1879; gained monopoly of West African shipping trade; founded Bank of British West Africa, 1897; revivified the Canaries, inaugurating there banana industry (1884) and tourist traffic, and establishing coaling station at Las Palmas; inaugurated new steamship service with Jamaica from Bristol (1901) for banana traffic; helped to found Liverpool School of Tropical Medicine, 1899; K.C.M.G., 1901; hon. fellow of Jesus College, Oxford, 1905.

JONES, HENRY CADMAN (1818–1902), law reporter; educated at Trinity College, Cambridge; second wrangler, second Smith's prizeman, and fellow, 1841; called to bar, 1845; edited Chancery reports from 1857 till 1865.

JONES, JOHN VIRIAMU (1856–1901), physicist; son of Thomas Jones (1819–82, q.v.); educated at University College, London (B.Sc. and fellow), and Balliol College, Oxford; first class in mathematics, 1879, and natural science, 1880; first principal of University College of South Wales, Cardiff, 1883; first vice-chancellor of University of Wales, 1893; engaged in physical researches dealing especially with the determination of the ohm; F.R.S., 1894; member of Alpine Club; died at Geneva; Memoir by Prof. E. B. Poulton, 1910.

JONES, THOMAS RUPERT (1819–1911), geologist and palaeontologist; educated at Ilminster, where he studied geology of district; published 'Monograph on the Cretaceous Entomostraca of England,' 1849, and papers on the geology of Newbury, 1854, and of the Kennet valley, 1871; assistant secretary of Geological Society, 1851–62; professor of geology at Royal Military College, Sandhurst, 1862; interested in South African geology; F.R.S., 1872; president of Geologists' Association, 1879–81.

JONES, WILLIAM WEST (1838–1908), archbishop

of Capetown; B.A., St. John's College, Oxford, 1860; M.A., 1863; fellow, 1859–79; hon. fellow, 1893; hon. D.D., 1874; vicar of Summertown, 1864–74; bishop of Capetown, 1874; see elevated to archbishopric, 1897; a strong high churchman, popular with English and Dutch alike.

KANE, ROBERT ROMNEY (1842–1902), writer on Irish land law; son of Sir Robert Kane [q. v.]; M.A., Queen's College, Cork, 1862; hon. LL.D., 1882; called to Irish bar, 1865; professor of jurisprudence at King's Inns, Dublin, 1873; legal assistant commissioner under Irish Land Act of 1881, 1881–92; county court judge, Ireland, 1892.

KEAY, JOHN SEYMOUR (1839–1909), Anglo-Indian politician; went to India to manage branches of Government Bank of Bengal, 1862; opened successful banking business and cotton mills at Hyderabad; sympathized with Indian nationalists; liberal M.P. for Elgin and Nairn, 1889–95.

KEETLEY, CHARLES ROBERT BELL (1848–1909), surgeon; entered St. Bartholomew's Hospital, 1871; F.R.C.S., 1876; L.R.C.P., 1873; on staff of West London Hospital from 1878 till death; introduced there antiseptic methods of surgery; advocated appendicotomy; wrote handbook on orthopaedic surgery, 1900, and other medical works.

KEKEWICH, SIR ARTHUR (1832–1907), judge; educated at Eton and Balliol College, Oxford; B.A., 1854; fellow of Exeter, 1854–8; called to bar, 1858; Q.C., 1877; had large junior practice at Chancery bar, but was unsuccessful as leader; judge, 1886; knighted, 1887; expeditious judge, but his judgments were often reversed on appeal; a strong churchman and conservative.

KEKEWICH, ROBERT GEORGE (1854–1914), major-general; nephew of Sir A. Kekewich [q. v.]; entered army, 1874; lieutenant-colonel in Loyal North Lancashires, 1898; during South African War defended Kimberley from Boers, 15 October 1899–15 February 1900; C.B., 1900; major-general, 1902.

KELLY, FREDERICK SEPTIMUS (1881–1916), musician and oarsman; born at Sydney; educated at Eton and Balliol; rowed for Oxford; at Henley won Grand Challenge cup, Stewards' cup, Diamond sculls, Wingfield sculls; one of the greatest scullers of all time; studied pianoforte at Frankfort-on-Main, 1903–8; left wide range of compositions; joined Royal Naval division, 1914; D.S.C. for gallantry in Gallipoli, 1915; killed in France.

KELLY, MARY ANNE, 'EVA' (1826–1910), Irish poetess. [See O'DOHERTY, MARY ANNE.]

KELLY, WILLIAM (1821–1906), Plymouth brother and biblical critic; joined Plymouth brethren, 1841; edited collected works of John Nelson Darby [q. v.], 34 vols. 1867–83; seceded from Darbyites on point of church discipline, 1879; a voluminous scriptural commentator and controversialist; Memoir by Heyman Wreford, 1906.

KELLY-KENNY, SIR THOMAS (1840–1914), general; joined army, 1858; took sixth division out to South African War, 1900; took part in engagements at Klip Kraal Drift, Paardeberg, Poplar Grove, and Driefontein; left in command in Free State, 1900; K.B.C., 1902; general, 1905.

KELVIN, first BARON (1824–1907), scientist and inventor. [See THOMSON, WILLIAM.]

KEMBALL, SIR ARNOLD BURROWES (1820–1908), general, colonel commandant royal artillery; born in Bombay; joined Bombay artillery, 1837; present at Ghazni and Kabul; in Persian war, 1856–7; distinguished in expedition against Ahwaz; C.B., 1857; consul general at Bagdad, 1859; K.C.S.I., 1866; accompanied Shah of Persia to England, 1873; on international commission for delimiting Turco-Persian frontier, 1875; military commissioner with Turkish army in Servo-Turkish and Russo-Turkish wars; lieutenant-general and K.C.B., 1878; interested in Persian and East African development; advocated construction of Uganda railway; general, 1880.

KEMBLE, HENRY (1848–1907), comedian; grandson of Charles Kemble [q. v.] and nephew of Fanny Kemble [q. v.]; made professional début at Dublin, 1867; with Mr. John Hare's company, 1875; joined the Bancrofts (1876), with whom he played Dolly Spanker in 'London Assurance' and Sir Oliver Surface in 'The School for Scandal'; played Polonius to Herbert Tree's Hamlet, 1891.

KENDAL, WILLIAM HUNTER (1843–1917), actor-manager, whose original name was WILLIAM HUNTER

GRIMSTON; went on professional stage, 1861; partner with Sir John Hare [q. v.], first at Court Theatre and later at St. James's Theatre; best parts those in 'Peril,' 'The Queen's Shilling,' 'Diplomacy,' 'A White Lie,' and 'The Elder Miss Blossom'; overshadowed by his wife, Margaret Robertson.

KENNEDY, SIR WILLIAM RANN (1846–1915), judge; grandson of Rev. Rann Kennedy [q. v.]; B.A., King's College, Cambridge (senior classic); called to bar (Lincoln's Inn), 1871; Q.C., 1885; judge in Queen's bench division and knighted, 1892; lord justice of Court of Appeal and P.C., 1907; F.B.A., 1909.

KENSIT, JOHN (1853–1902), protestant agitator; early joined anti-Romanist agitation; started protestant book depot in Paternoster Row, 1885; secretary of Protestant Truth Society, 1890; organized 'Wickliffite' itinerant preachers for the denunciation of ritualism, 1898; publicly objected to confirmation of bishops Mandell Creighton, 1897, Winnington-Ingram and Gore, 1901; fatally wounded in religious riot at Liverpool; 'Life' by J. C. Wilcox, 1903.

KENT, (WILLIAM) CHARLES (MARK) (1823–1902), author; a strict Roman Catholic; editor and proprietor of the 'Sun,' a London evening paper, 1853–71, and editor of the 'Weekly Register,' a Roman Catholic periodical, 1874–81; called to bar, 1859, but did not practise; wrote for 'Household Words' and 'All the Year Round,' and grew intimate with Charles Dickens, who addressed to him his last letter (8 June 1870, now in British Museum); collected his 'Poems' in 1870; prepared popular complete editions of works of great writers, including Charles Lamb, 1875; received civil list pension, 1887.

KENYON, GEORGE THOMAS (1840–1908), politician; educated at Harrow and Christ Church, Oxford; called to bar, 1869; conservative M.P. for Denbigh boroughs, 1885–95, 1900–5; mainly instrumental in passing the Welsh Intermediate Education Act, 1889.

KENYON-SLANEY, WILLIAM SLANEY (1847–1908), colonel and politician; born at Rajcot, India; educated at Eton and Christ Church, Oxford; joined army, 1867; present at Tel-el-Kebir, 1882; retired with rank of colonel, 1892; conservative M.P. for Newport division of Shropshire, 1886–1908; ardent tariff reformer; author of the 'Kenyon-Slaney clause' in Education Act of 1902; P.C., 1904; Memoir by Walter Durnford, 1909.

KEPPEL, SIR GEORGE OLOF ROOS- (1866–1921), soldier and Anglo-Indian administrator. [See ROOS-KEPPEL.]

KEPPEL, SIR HENRY (1809–1904), admiral of the fleet; entered navy, 1822; commander, 1833; served in West and East Indies, and in China war, 1841–2; senior officer at Singapore, 1842; helped in suppressing Borneo piracy, 1843–4; served with distinction in Baltic campaign, 1854; C.B., 1856; second in command on China station, 1856; K.C.B.; groom-in-waiting to Queen Victoria, 1858–60; commander-in-chief on Cape and Brazilian stations, 1860; on China station, 1866; admiral, 1869; G.C.B., 1871; commander-in-chief at Devonport, 1872–5; admiral of the fleet, 1877; intimate friend of King Edward VII; published 'A Sailor's Life under Four Sovereigns,' 3 vols. 1899; 'Life' by Sir Algernon West, 1905.

KERR, JOHN (1824–1907), physicist; pupil of Lord Kelvin at Glasgow University; lecturer in mathematics to Glasgow Free Church Training College for Teachers, 1857–1901; made important discoveries in nature of light, 1875–6; author of 'An Elementary Treatise on Rational Mechanics,' 1867; hon. LL.D. Glasgow, 1867; F.R.S., 1890; royal medallist, 1898; awarded civil list pension, 1902.

KERR, ROBERT (1823–1904), architect; cousin of Joseph Hume [q. v.]; did much to develop Royal Institute of British Architects; professor of arts of construction, King's College, London, 1861–90; designed many buildings in London and country; published many architectural works.

KIDD, BENJAMIN (1858–1916), sociologist; clerk in Inland Revenue department, 1877–94; published 'Social Evolution,' which had remarkable success partly due to its violent attack on socialism, 1894; its main theme is glorification of religion and attack on reason; other works include 'Principles of Western Civilization' (1902) and 'Science of Power' (posthumous, 1918).

KILLEN, WILLIAM DOOL (1806–1902), ecclesiastical historian; after education at Belfast, entered Presbyterian ministry, 1829; minister of Raphoe, co. Donegal, 1829–41; studied deeply church history;

professor of church history at Presbyterian college, Belfast, 1841–89; president of the college, 1869; D.D. Glasgow, 1845; LL.D., 1901; his voluminous historical works include 'The Ancient Church,' 1859, and 'The Ecclesiastical History of Ireland,' 2 vols. 1875; he also published 'Reminiscences of a Long Life,' 1901.

KIMBERLEY, first EARL OF (1826–1902), statesman. [See WODEHOUSE, JOHN.]

KINAHAN, GEORGE HENRY (1829–1908), geologist; entered Irish geological survey, 1854; as district surveyor (1869) prepared geological maps; author of 'Manual of the Geology of Ireland,' 1878, 'Economic Geology of Ireland,' 1889, and other kindred works.

KINCAIRNEY, LORD (1828–1909), Scottish judge. [See GLOAG, WILLIAM ELLIS.]

KING, EDWARD (1829–1910), bishop of Lincoln; B.A., Oriel College, Oxford, 1851; influenced by tractarian movement and by Charles Marriott [q. v.]; curate of Wheatley, near Cuddesdon, 1854–8; chaplain of Cuddesdon theological college, 1858–63; appointed principal of college, and vicar of Cuddesdon, 1863; professor of pastoral theology at Oxford and canon of Christ Church, 1873; exerted much influence on religious life of Oxford; bishop of Lincoln, 1885; specially interested in youths and in confirmations; a high churchman, he taught real objective presence and practised confession; prosecuted for illegal ritualist practices by the Church Association, 1889; archbishop's judgment (1890) was substantially in King's favour, and was upheld on appeal, 1892; the trial enhanced his popularity in Lincolnshire; a staunch tory, active in opposition to education bills of liberal government; favoured franchise bill of 1884; had great faculty for sympathy, and perfect refinement of thought and bearing; published many devotional works, sermons, and pamphlets; portraits by George Richmond at Cuddesdon and by W. W. Ouless at Lincoln; two churches at Grimsby erected to his memory; 'Life' by G. W. E. Russell, 1911.

KING, SIR GEORGE (1840–1909), Indian botanist; studied medicine and botany at Aberdeen University; M.B., 1865; hon. LL.D., 1884; entered Indian medical service, 1865, Indian forest service, 1869; superintendent of Royal Botanic Garden, Calcutta, and of cinchona cultivation in Bengal, 1871; organized botanical survey of India; inaugurated economic method of separating quinine from cinchonas, 1887; C.I.E., 1890; K.C.I.E., 1898; F.R.S., 1887; made study of flora of Malayan Peninsula.

KING, HAYNES (1831–1904), genre painter; born at Barbados; exhibited at Royal Academy, 1860–1904; influenced by Thomas Faed [q. v.]; works include 'Looking Out,' 1860, 'The New Gown,' 1892, 'Latest Intelligence', 1904.

KINGSBURGH, LORD (1836–1919), lord justice-clerk of Scotland. [See MACDONALD, Sir JOHN HAY ATHOLE.]

KINGSCOTE, SIR ROBERT NIGEL FITZHARDINGE (1830–1908), agriculturist; in Scots fusilier guards, 1846–56; served in Crimea; C.B., 1855; liberal M.P. for western division of Gloucestershire, 1852–89; inherited estate at Kingscote, 1861; parliamentary groom-in-waiting to Queen Victoria, 1859–66; extra equerry to King Edward VII when Prince of Wales, 1867; commissioner of woods and forests, 1885–95; paymaster-general of the royal household, 1901; K.C.B., 1899; G.C.V.O., 1902; president of Royal Agricultural Society, 1878; hon. LL.D. Cambridge, 1894; member of royal commissions on agriculture, 1879 and 1893.

KINGSTON, CHARLES CAMERON (1850–1908), Australian statesman; born at Adelaide; admitted to colonial bar, 1873; Q.C., 1889; radical member for West Adelaide in house of representatives of South Australia, 1881–1900; attorney-general, 1884–5 and 1887–9; chief secretary, 1892–3; premier and attorney-general, 1893–9; defeated bills for imposition of land taxes, and for employers' liability; helped to secure woman suffrage, factory legislation, state banking, protective tariff, and payment of members; represented S. Australia at Queen Victoria's diamond jubilee; hon. D.C.L. Oxford, and P.C., 1897; took prominent part in securing enactment of Australian commonwealth constitution bill, 1900; elected to legislative council of South Australia, 1900; minister of trade and customs in first commonwealth administration, 1901–3.

KINNEAR, ALEXANDER SMITH, first BARON KINNEAR (1833–1917), judge; advocate at Scots bar, 1856; Q.C., 1881; lord ordinary, 1882–90; member of first division, 1890–1913; created baron, 1897.

KINNS, SAMUEL (1826–1903), writer on the Bible;

Ph.D. Jena University, 1859; rector of Holy Trinity, Minories (1889–99), of which he wrote a history, 1890; published 'Moses and Geology,' 1882, and 'Graven in the Rock,' 1891.

KINROSS, first BARON (1837–1905), Scottish judge. [See BALFOUR, JOHN BLAIR.]

KITCHENER, HORATIO HERBERT, first EARL KITCHENER, of Khartoum and of Broome (1850–1916), field-marshal; educated at Royal Military Academy, Woolwich; received commission in Royal Engineers, 1871; lent to Palestine Exploration Fund, 1874; sent to survey Cyprus, 1878; second in command of Egyptian cavalry, 1882; served in (Viscount) Wolseley's expedition for relief of General Gordon, 1884–5; governor-general of Eastern Sudan, 1886; adjutant-general of Egyptian army, 1888; contributed to defeat of Dervishes at Toski, 1889; C.B., 1889; sirdar of Egyptian army, 1892; prepared army for conquest of Sudan, 1892–6; K.C.M.G., 1894; major-general and K.C.B. for services in River war, 1896; well-planned and well-executed campaign resulted in annihilation of Khalifa's army at Omdurman, with great loss of Dervishes, and reoccupation of Khartoum, 1898; had interview at Fashoda on White Nile with Major Marchand, leader of small French expedition, resulting in its withdrawal, 1898; baron, 1898; governor-general of Sudan and completed its pacification, 1899; Lord Roberts's chief of staff in South Africa, 1899; frequently employed as second in command and representative of commander-in-chief in his absence; ordered attack and directed preliminary operations at Paardeberg, February 1900; suppressed rebellion of Cape Boers round Priska and cleared southern portion of Orange Free State; as commander-in-chief organized tactics against guerilla warfare of Boers, November 1900–May 1902; viscount and O.M., 1902; commander-in-chief in India, 1902–9; prevailed with (Viscount) Morley, secretary of state for India, to abolish system of dual military control; initiated numerous reforms, including improvement of central administration, redistribution of troops, modernization of system of training, and establishment of Staff College for India; field-marshal, 1909; British agent and consul-general in Egypt, 1911; kept Egypt quiet during period of unrest in Near East; earl, 1914; secretary of state for war, 1914; possessed first-hand knowledge of military resources of Empire but had little experience of organization of army at home or of working of War Office and Cabinet; envisaged long war; increased British army from six regular and fourteen territorial divisions to seventy divisions, 3,000,000 men having voluntarily joined colours, 1914–16; K.G., 1915; relations with colleagues in Cabinet sometimes strained; went to Near East and advised abandonment of Dardanelles enterprise, 1915; went down on H.M.S. 'Hampshire' off Orkneys on way to Russia.

KITCHIN, GEORGE WILLIAM (1827–1912), dean of Winchester, 1883–94, and of Durham, 1894–1912; B.A., Christ Church, Oxford; censor of Oxford non-collegiate students, 1868–83; wrote 'History of France' (1873–7).

KITSON, JAMES, first BARON AIREDALE (1835–1911), ironmaster; placed (1854) in charge of father's Monkbridge ironworks, which became limited liability company, 1886; president of Iron and Steel Institute, 1889–91; first lord mayor of Leeds, 1896–7; benefactor to Leeds hospitals and art gallery; hon. D.Sc., 1904; honorary freeman, 1906; president of National Liberal Federation, 1883–90; M.P. for Colne Valley, 1892–1902; baronet, 1886; P.C., 1906; raised to peerage, 1907.

KITTON, FREDERICK GEORGE (1856–1904), writer on Dickens; began life as wood-engraver and etcher; publications include 'Dickensiana' (a bibliography), 1886, 'Dickens and his Illustrators,' 1899, and 'The Dickens Country,' 1905; his Dickens library presented to Guildhall Library, 1908.

KNIGHT, JOSEPH (1829–1907), dramatic critic; joined father's business of cloth merchant at Leeds at nineteen; devoted to literature through life; embarked on journalistic career in London, 1860; dramatic critic of 'Athenaeum' from 1867 till death; chief contributor of lives of actors and actresses to this Dictionary; editor of 'Notes and Queries' from 1883 to 1907; his numerous literary friends and associates included John Westland Marston [q. v.] and D. G. Rossetti, whose life he wrote in 'Great Writers' series, 1887; F.S.A., 1893; a popular member of the Garrick Club from 1883.

KNIGHT, JOSEPH (1837–1909), landscape painter and engraver; lost right arm at seven; exhibited mainly Welsh subjects at Royal Academy and elsewhere; fellow of Society of Painter Etchers, 1883.

KNOWLES, SIR JAMES THOMAS (1831–1908), founder and editor of the 'Nineteenth Century,' and architect; joined his father's office as architect; practised his profession for thirty years; designed 'Thatched House Club,' St. James's Street, 1865; laid out Leicester Square for Baron Albert Grant, 1874; published 'The Story of King Arthur and his Knights,' 1862, which attracted Tennyson and led to a close intimacy with the poet; founded Metaphysical Society, 1869, which lasted till 1881, and included leaders of all schools of thought; with Gladstone, who joined the society, Knowles's relations were as close as those with Tennyson; editor of 'Contemporary Review' from 1870 to 1877, when he founded the highly successful 'Nineteenth Century' with himself as editor; 'signed writing' by eminent persons was Knowles's main editorial principle; K.C.V.O., 1903.

KNOX, ISA (1831–1903), poetical writer; born CRAIG; early contributed to 'Scotsman' under name of 'Isa'; married cousin, John Knox, an iron merchant, 1866; won prize for Burns centenary poem at Crystal Palace, 1858; published verse and fiction.

KNOX-LITTLE, WILLIAM JOHN (1839–1918), divine and preacher; born in co. Tyrone; B.A., Trinity College, Cambridge; rector of St. Alban's, Cheetwood, Manchester, 1875–85; canon of Worcester, 1881; vicar of Hoar Cross, Staffordshire, 1885–1907; enjoyed great popularity as extempore preacher, especially at missions; high churchman; published sermons and other works.

KNUTSFORD, first VISCOUNT (1825–1914). [See HOLLAND, SIR HENRY THURSTAN.]

KYNASTON (formerly SNOW), **HERBERT** (1835–1910), classical scholar; educated at Eton and St. John's College, Cambridge; first Porson scholar and senior classic, 1857; fellow, 1858; M.A., 1860; D.D., 1882; rowed in university boat, 1856 and 1858; member of Alpine Club; principal of Cheltenham College, 1874–88; canon of Durham and professor of Greek in the university, 1889; edited 'Theocritus,' 1869, and 'Poetae Graeci,' 1879; 'Life' by E. D. Stone, 1912.

LABOUCHERE, HENRY DU PRÉ (1831–1912), journalist and politician; nephew of Henry Labouchere, first Baron Taunton [q. v.]; educated at Eton and Trinity College, Cambridge; in diplomatic service, 1854–64; wrote for 'Daily News' and 'World,' and established reputation as journalist; founded weekly journal, 'Truth,' notable for its exposure of fraudulent enterprises, 1876; liberal M.P., Northampton, with Charles Bradlaugh [q. v.] as his colleague, 1880; held seat till 1905; became one of the most powerful radicals in Commons; attacked home and foreign policy of whigs and worked for reorganization of liberal party; designs frustrated by decision of Joseph Chamberlain [q. v.] to vote against first Home Rule Bill, 1886; died near Florence.

LABOUCHERE, HENRIETTA (1841–1910), actress. [See HODSON.]

LAFONT, EUGÈNE (1837–1908), science teacher in India; born at Mons, Belgium; was admitted a Jesuit, 1854; inaugurated science teaching in Bengal at St. Xavier's College, Calcutta, 1865; rector of the College, 1873–1904; fellow of Calcutta University, 1877; hon. D.Sc., 1908; C.I.E., 1880; died at Darjeeling.

LAIDLAW, ANNA ROBENA (1819–1901), pianist; studied music in Edinburgh, Königsberg, and London; made successful appearances in Germany and Austria; praised by Schumann; pianist to Queen of Hanover until 1840, when she settled in London; retired on marriage to George Thomson, 1852.

LAIDLAW, JOHN (1832–1906), presbyterian divine and theologian; student at Edinburgh University; hon. M.A., 1854; hon. D.D., 1880; studied theology in Edinburgh and Germany; minister at Perth, 1863–72, and Aberdeen, 1872–81; professor of systematic theology, New College, Edinburgh, 1881–1904; a conservative theologian; author of 'The Biblical Doctrine of Man,' 1879, and 'The Miracles of Our Lord,' 1890.

LAMBERT, BROOKE (1834–1901), social reformer; student at King's College, London, under F. D. Maurice; B.A., Brasenose College, Oxford, 1858; M.A., 1861; B.C.L., 1863; vicar of St. Mark's, Whitechapel, 1866–70; as vestryman and guardian he made thorough study of poor law and local government; in work on pauperism, 1871, anticipated scientific statistical researches of Charles Booth [q. v.]; resigned through ill-health, 1870; went to West Indies to restore health; held living of Tamworth, 1872–8; helped to found London University Extension Society, 1879; vicar of Greenwich, 1880–1901, where he continued his activity

in social and educational reform; a prominent freemason; published volumes of sermons.

LAMBERT, GEORGE (1842–1915), tennis player; went to Hampton Court Palace tennis court, 1866; head professional at Marylebone Cricket Club court at Lord's, 1869–89; champion, 1870–85.

LANE, SIR HUGH PERCY (1875–1915), art collector and critic; born in co. Cork; picture dealer in London, 1898; formed gallery of modern art in Dublin; knighted, 1909; director of Irish National Gallery, 1914; torpedoed on 'Lusitania'; his will caused controversy between Dublin and London National galleries.

LANG, ANDREW (1844–1912), scholar, folk-lorist, poet, and man of letters; educated at St. Andrews and Glasgow universities and Balliol College, Oxford; fellow of Merton College, Oxford, 1868; settled in London and devoted himself to journalism and letters, 1875; poetical works include 'Ballads and Lyrics of Old France' (1872), 'xxii Ballades in Blue China' (1880), and 'Helen of Troy' (1882); as anthropologist proved that folk-lore is foundation of higher or literary mythology; works on this subject include 'Custom and Myth' (1884), 'Myth, Ritual, and Religion' (1887), and 'The Making of Religion' (1898); classical works include prose translation of 'Odyssey' (with S. H. Butcher, 1879), of 'Iliad' (with Walter Leaf and Ernest Myers, 1883), and three books on Homeric question, 'Homer and the Epic' (1893), 'Homer and his Age' (1896), and 'The World of Homer' (1910); historical works include 'Pickle the Spy' (1897), 'The Companions of Pickle' (1898), 'Prince Charles Edward' (1900), and 'History of Scotland' (1900–7); also author of 'Life and Letters of J. G. Lockhart' (1896), and of essays, novels, and children's books; a founder of Psychical Research Society.

LANG, JOHN MARSHALL (1834–1909), principal of Aberdeen University; educated at Glasgow University; hon. D.D., 1873; hon. LL.D., 1901; minister of East Parish of St. Nicholas, Aberdeen, 1856–65, and of Anderston church, Glasgow, 1865–8; introduced there improvements in ritual, including first organ used in Church of Scotland and psalms chanted in prose version; minister of Morningside, Edinburgh, 1868–73, and Barony of Glasgow, 1873–1901; served on school board, on commission for housing of poor, and kindred bodies in Glasgow; instituted Sunday evening services in Glasgow; visited Australia, 1897; convener of Assembly's commission of inquiry into religious condition of the people of Scotland, 1890–6; moderator of general assembly, 1893; promoted Pan-Presbyterian Alliance for union of the churches; principal of Aberdeen University, 1898–1909; C.V.O., 1906; Baird lecturer at Glasgow, 1901; author of many devotional works; memories, by his widow, 1910.

LANGEVIN, SIR HECTOR LOUIS (1826–1906), Canadian statesman; born at Quebec; called to bar of Lower Canada, 1850; mayor of Quebec, 1858–60; member of Canadian legislative assembly, 1857–67; Q.C., 1864; solicitor-general for Lower Canada, 1864–6; postmaster-general, 1866–7; helped to form Dominion of Canada; member of Dominion House of Commons, 1867–96; secretary of state, 1867–9; minister of public works, 1869–73, 1879–91; postmaster-general, 1878–9; led French-Canadian conservative party from 1873; K.C.M.G., 1881; died at Quebec.

LANGFORD, JOHN ALFRED (1823–1903), Birmingham antiquary and journalist; contributed to 'Howitt's Journal'; joined Unitarians under George Dawson [q. v.]; carried on printing business at Birmingham, 1852–5; closely associated with 'Birmingham Daily Press,' 1855, and 'Birmingham Daily Gazette,' 1862–8; an ardent liberal, he helped in party organization; joined Gladstonian section of party, 1886; author of 'Century of Birmingham Life,' 2 vols. 1868, and 'Modern Birmingham,' 2 vols. 1873–7, poems and dramas.

LASCELLES, SIR FRANK CAVENDISH (1841–1920), diplomatist; entered diplomatic service, 1861; agent and consul-general, Bulgaria, 1879–87; British minister to Roumania, 1887; to Persia, 1891; ambassador to Russia, 1894, to Berlin, 1896–1908; worked for Anglo-German amity till 1914; K.C.M.G., 1886; P.C., 1892.

LASZOWSKA, (JANE) EMILY DE (1846–1905), novelist. [See GERARD.]

LATEY, JOHN (1842–1902), journalist; art and literary editor of 'Penny Illustrated Paper,' 1861–1901; parliamentary reporter to 'Illustrated London News' for fifteen years; co-editor (1881–2) with Mayne Reid [q. v.] of 'The Boys' Illustrated News'; edited 'Sketch,'

1899-1902; author of 'The Showman's Panorama,' 1880, and novels.

LATHAM, HENRY (1821-1902), master of Trinity Hall, Cambridge; B.A., Trinity College, Cambridge (18th wrangler), 1845; appointed clerical fellow of Trinity Hall, 1847; senior tutor, 1855; broadened aims of the college by destroying its exclusively legal associations; attracted promising men from other colleges; resigned tutorship, 1885; succeeded Sir Henry Sumner Maine [q. v.] as master, 1888; rebuilt college and reconstructed lodge and hall; published 'Pastor Pastorum,' 1890, and other devotional works.

LAUGHTON, SIR JOHN KNOX (1830-1915), naval historian; B.A., Caius College, Cambridge; naval instructor in royal navy, 1853; transferred to Royal Naval College, Portsmouth, 1866; instructor at Greenwich naval university, 1873-85; lectured on naval history at Greenwich, 1876-89; professor of history, King's College, London, 1885-1914; founded Navy Records Society, 1893; first secretary, 1893-1912; knighted, 1907; edited 'Memoirs relating to Lord Torrington' (1889), Lord Barham's papers (1907-10), &c.; wrote books on Nelson, &c.; contributor to this Dictionary.

LAURIE, JAMES STUART (1832-1904), inspector of schools, 1854-63; held educational posts in Ireland and Ceylon; called to bar, 1871; published school handbooks.

LAURIE, SIMON SOMERVILLE (1829-1909), educational reformer; elder brother of James Stuart Laurie [q. v.]; M.A. Edinburgh University, 1849; secretary to education committee of Church of Scotland at Edinburgh, 1855-1905; his reports as visitor and examiner for Dick Bequest Trust (1856-1907) gave masterly expositions of educational principles and practice; his report on the Edinburgh Merchant Company's 'hospitals' led to their reform by Act of Parliament, 1869; secretary to royal commission on endowed schools in Scotland, 1872; first Bell professor of education in Edinburgh University, 1876-1903; president of Teachers' Guild of Great Britain, 1891; hon. LL.D. of St. Andrews, Edinburgh, and Aberdeen universities; wrote on 'Training of Teachers,' 1882, 'Institutes of Education,' 1892, and 'Educational Opinion from the Renaissance,' 1903; his philosophical works include 'Metaphysica, Nova et Vetusta,' 1884, and 'Ethica,' 1885; Gifford lecturer in natural theology at Edinburgh, 1905-6; embodied these lectures in 'Synthetica,' 1906.

LAURIER, SIR WILFRID (1841-1919), Canadian statesman; French Canadian; born near Montreal; elected to legislature of Quebec, 1871; liberal member of Canadian parliament for Drummond-Arthabaska, 1874; entered Cabinet of Alexander Mackenzie [q. v.], 1877; member for Quebec East, 1877-1919; in opposition, 1878-96; leader of liberal party in succession to Edward Blake [q. v.], 1888; prime minister of Canada, 1896-1911; knighted, 1897; attacked by nationalist leader, Bourassa, for sending contingents to help of Great Britain in Boer war (1900) and for policy of Canadian navy (1910); supported conservative government's war policy (1914-18), but refused to form coalition (1917).

LAW, DAVID (1831-1901), etcher and water-colour painter; student at Trustees' Academy, Edinburgh, 1845-50; engraver in ordnance survey office, Southampton, 1850-70; helped to found Royal Society of Painter Etchers, 1881; his etchings after Turner and Corot were in great demand, 1875-90; best work done in water-colour.

LAW, SIR EDWARD FITZGERALD (1846-1908), expert in state finance; joined royal artillery, 1868; retired, 1872; started business agency in Russia; acting consul at St. Petersburg, 1880-1; commercial and financial attaché for Russia, Persia, and Asiatic Turkey, 1888; British delegate for negotiating commercial treaty with Turkey, 1890; reported on Greek finance, 1892-3, and on railway development in Asiatic Turkey, 1895; as commercial secretary at Vienna negotiated commercial treaty with Bulgaria, 1896-7; British delegate at Constantinople for determining Greece's war indemnity to Turkey, 1897; president of international commission on Greek finance, 1898; K.C.M.G., 1898; finance member of Government in India, 1900; completed currency reform and reduced arrears of land revenue, income and salt taxes; C.S.I., 1903; K.C.S.I., 1906; an active champion of imperial preference and tariff reform; represented Great Britain on Cretan reform commission, and on committee to found bank of Morocco, 1906; died in Paris; buried at Athens; 'Life' by Sir T. Morison and G. P. Hutchinson, 1911.

LAW, THOMAS GRAVES (1836-1904), historian and bibliographer; grandson of Edward Law, first Earl of Ellenborough [q.v.], and brother of Augustus Henry Law [q.v.]; educated at Winchester, University College, London, and Stonyhurst; Roman catholic priest, 1860-78; keeper to Signet Library, Edinburgh, 1878-1904; helped to found Scottish History Society, 1886; hon. LL.D. Edinburgh, 1898; wrote much on sixteenth-century religious history; 'Collected Essays' were posthumously issued, 1904.

LAWES (afterwards LAWES-WITTEWRONGE), SIR CHARLES BENNET, second baronet (1843-1911), sculptor and athlete; son of Sir John Bennet Lawes, first baronet [q. v.], of Rothamsted; educated at Eton and Trinity College, Cambridge; B.A., 1866; distinguished oarsman at Cambridge and Henley, runner and cyclist; exhibited sculpture at Royal Academy, 1872-1908; unsuccessful defendant in libel action brought by R. C. Belt, a sculptor, 1882; succeeded to baronetcy and Rothamsted property, 1900.

LAWES, WILLIAM GEORGE (1839-1907), missionary; worked at Niué in South Seas, 1861-72; completed translation of New Testament into Niué, 1886; settled at Port Moresby, New Guinea, 1874-94; with James Chalmers [q. v.] greatly helped British administration and development of British New Guinea; hon. D.D. Glasgow, 1895; settled at Sydney, 1906, where he died.

LAWLEY, FRANCIS CHARLES (1825-1901), sportsman and journalist; B.A., Balliol College, Oxford, 1848; fellow of All Souls, 1848-53; B.C.L., 1851; liberal M.P. for Beverley, 1852; private secretary to Gladstone; lost fortune in gambling and speculation; imputations of dishonesty in stock exchange dealings led to cancelling of his appointment as governor of South Australia, 1854; settled in America, 1854-65; sent vivid accounts of civil war to 'The Times'; returned to London, 1865; wrote on sport in 'Daily Telegraph' and 'Baily's Magazine.'

LAWSON, EDWARD LEVY-, first BARON BURNHAM (1833-1916), newspaper proprietor. [See LEVY-LAWSON.]

LAWSON, GEORGE (1831-1903), ophthalmic surgeon; entered King's College Hospital, 1848; M.R.C.S., 1852; F.R.C.S., 1857; joined army as surgeon, 1854; served in Crimea; surgeon at Royal London Ophthalmic Hospital, Moorfields, from 1862; surgeon-oculist to Queen Victoria from 1886; published works on eye diseases.

LAWSON, GEORGE ANDERSON (1832-1904), sculptor; studied at Royal Scottish Academy Schools and in Rome; exhibited at Royal Academy from 1862; works include his popular 'Dominie Sampson,' 1868, Burns memorial at Ayr, and the Wellington monument at Liverpool.

LAWSON, SIR WILFRID, second baronet (1829-1906), politician and temperance advocate; son of Sir Wilfrid Lawson, an advanced liberal; keen sportsman, huntsman, angler, and agriculturist; liberal M.P. for Carlisle, 1859-65, 1868-85; supported motion for Sunday closing of public houses, 1863; introduced (1864) and frequently re-introduced (1869-74) his 'permissive,' later known as 'local veto bill'; carried resolution for local option in 1880, in 1881, and in 1883; president of United Kingdom Alliance, 1879; succeeded to baronetcy and estates, 1867; supported Sir Charles Dilke's motion for inquiry into Queen Victoria's expenditure, 1872; advocated Sunday closing in Ireland, 1875-6 (measure carried, 1879); opposed parliamentary 'adjournment for the Derby,' 1874; supported Charles Bradlaugh's claim for religious freedom, 1880; opposed liberal government's Egyptian policy, 1882-3; M.P. for Cockermouth, 1886-1900; supported Gladstone's home rule policy and opposed Mr. Balfour's coercion measures; M.P. for Camborne, 1903, and again for Cockermouth, 1906; passionately denounced Boer war and defended free trade; of spontaneous humour, he seasoned his speeches with genial sarcasm and humorous quotation; easy writer of light verse; published 'Cartoons in Rhyme and Line' (illustrated by Sir F. C. Gould), 1905; memoir by G. W. E. Russell, 1909.

LEACH, ARTHUR FRANCIS (1851-1915), historical writer; educated at Winchester and New College, Oxford; fellow of All Souls, 1874-81; assistant charity commissioner (Endowed Schools department), 1884; second charity commissioner, 1906-15; works include 'English Schools at the Reformation (1546-1548)' (1896), and 'Schools of Medieval England' (1915).

LEADER, JOHN TEMPLE (1810-1903), politician

and connoisseur; educated at Charterhouse, 1823, and at Christ Church, Oxford, 1828; knew from youth Brougham, his father's friend; liberal M.P. for Bridgwater, 1835; acted with Grote, Molesworth, and the philosophical radicals; favoured the Chartists; unsuccessfully contested Westminster at a by-election (May 1837) against Sir Francis Burdett; M.P. for Westminster, Aug. 1837–47; prominent in London society; frequent traveller in Italy and France; saw much in London of Louis Napoleon, afterwards Napoleon III; in 1844 his career underwent sudden change, and he left England for permanent residence abroad; at Cannes joined Brougham, and bought property for building; chiefly spent his long exile at Florence, in and near which he bought and restored several old residences, including the gigantic castle of Vincigliata, where he was visited by many distinguished persons, including Queen Victoria (1888) and Gladstone; directed compilation of many archaeological treatises on Vincigliata and adjoining places; wrote with Giuseppe Marcotti lives of Sir John Hawkwood, 1889, and of Sir Robert Dudley, Duke of Northumberland, 1895; left 7000l. for restoration of central bronze door of Duomo at Florence.

LEAKE, GEORGE (1856–1902), premier of Western Australia; born at Perth, Western Australia; barrister of supreme court; crown solicitor, 1883–94; member of legislative assembly, 1890–1900; Q.C., 1898; twice premier of Western Australia, and attorney-general, May 1901–June 1902; died at Perth; a strong advocate of federation.

LECKY, SQUIRE THORNTON STRATFORD (1838–1902), writer on navigation; served on merchant vessels from age of fourteen, becoming expert in navigation of Pacific; detected off Rio de Janeiro submerged 'Lecky Rock,' 1865; showed many errors in South American charts and surveyed most of South American coast; served in Egyptian war of 1882; chief work on navigation was 'Wrinkles in Practical Navigation,' 1881 (15th edit. 1898); marine superintendent of Great Western Railway, 1884; younger brother of Trinity House; F.R.A.S. and F.R.G.S.; died at Las Palmas.

LECKY, WILLIAM EDWARD HARTPOLE (1838–1903), historian and essayist; born near Dublin; of Scottish descent; educated at Cheltenham, 1852–5, and at Trinity College, Dublin, studying desultorily history and philosophy; B.A., 1859; M.A., 1863; after a volume of poems (1859) he published anonymously 'The Religious Tendencies of the Age,' 1860, and 'Leaders of Public Opinion in Ireland,' 1862 (revised edit. 1903), which met at first with little success; spent holidays abroad, especially in Spain and Italy; his essay on 'The Declining Sense of the Miraculous' (1863) subsequently formed first two chapters of his abstruse, discursive, but lucid 'History of Rationalism' (2 vols. 1865), which brought him his first fame; a liberal in politics, he condemned Disraeli's reform bill of 1867, but supported Irish Church disestablishment and Irish Land Act of 1870; published 'History of European Morals,' 2 vols. 1869; married in 1871 Elizabeth van Dedem, maid of honour to Queen Sophia of the Netherlands, and settled at 38 Onslow Gardens, Kensington; meanwhile collected material for his 'History of England in the Eighteenth Century,' making extensive researches in Dublin (vols. 1 and 2 appeared in 1878; vols. 3 and 4 in 1882; vols. 5 and 6 in 1887; vols. 7 and 8 in 1890; cabinet edition, 12 vols. 1892; last 5 volumes devoted to History of Ireland); that work, which aimed at refuting Froude's calumnies of Irish people, was praised by Lord Acton and American critics. Lecky declined regius professorship of modern history at Oxford, 1892; hon. D.C.L. Oxford, 1888; Litt.D. Cambridge, 1891; LL.D., Dublin (1879), St. Andrews (1885), Glasgow (1895); became a liberal unionist in 1886; wrote weighty letters to 'The Times' and elsewhere (1886, 1892–3) in opposition to home rule; M.P. for Dublin University, 1895–1902; favoured establishment of a Roman Catholic university in Ireland; supported Sir Horace Plunkett's agricultural policy there; opposed old age pensions and favoured international arbitration; a fluent, rapid, but monotonous speaker; his later works were 'Democracy and Liberty,' 2 vols. 1896 (a revised edition of 1899 gave an admirable estimate of Gladstone's work and character); 'The Map of Life,' 1899, and 'Historical and Political Essays' (posthumous, 1908); F.B.A. and O.M., 1902; Lecky chair of history founded at Trinity College, Dublin, to which were left all his MSS.; portraits by Watts and H. T. Wells in National Portrait Gallery; memoir by widow, 1909.

LEDWIDGE, FRANCIS (1891–1917), poet; engaged in rural occupations in Slane district, co. Meath; although a strong nationalist, joined army, 1914; killed in Belgium; wrote about the countryside; 'Complete Poems' published posthumously, 1919.

LEE, FREDERICK GEORGE (1832–1902), theological writer; educated at St. Edmund Hall, Oxford; won Newdigate prize for English poem, 1854; vicar of All Saints, Lambeth, 1867–99; practised an advanced ritualism; vindicated the validity of Church of England orders, 1870; subsequently questioned their validity and founded Order of Corporate Reunion to restore to Church of England valid orders; consecrated by catholic prelates 'Bishop of Dorchester,' 1877; F.S.A., 1857; historical works, which are partisan and untrustworthy, include 'Historical Sketches of the Reformation,' 1879, and 'The Church under Queen Elizabeth,' 3rd edit. 1897; published also 'History of Thame,' 1886, verse, devotional and antiquarian works; joined Roman Catholic Church, 1901.

LEE, RAWDON BRIGGS (1845–1908), writer on dogs; succeeded father as editor of the 'Kendal Mercury' till 1885; devoted much time to breeding of dogs; his English setter, Richmond, was sent to Australia to improve the breed; kennel editor of 'Field,' 1883–1907; wrote accounts of fox terrier, 1889, and modern dogs of Great Britain, 3 vols. 1894 and 1897.

LEE-HAMILTON, EUGENE JACOB (1845–1907), poet and novelist; educated at Oriel College, Oxford; held minor diplomatic posts at Paris and Lisbon, 1871–3; disabled for twenty years through nervous disease; lived at Florence and became a centre of intellectual society; published 'Imaginary Sonnets,' 1888, and 'The Sonnets of the Wingless Hours,' 1894; was restored to health, 1897; published also a tragedy, two novels, and a metrical translation of Dante's 'Inferno,' 1898.

LEE-WARNER, SIR WILLIAM (1846–1914), Indian civil servant and author; B.A., St. John's College, Cambridge; entered Indian civil service, 1867; served in India, 1869–95; secretary of political and secret department at India Office, 1895–1912; K.C.S.I., 1898; G.C.S.I., 1911; works include 'Protected Princes of India' (1894), revised as 'Native States of India' (1916).

LEFROY, WILLIAM (1836–1909), dean of Norwich; B.A., Trinity College, Dublin, 1863; B.D., 1867; D.D., 1889; obtained fame as evangelical preacher; incumbent of St. Andrew's Chapel, Renshaw Street, Liverpool, 1866; archdeacon of Warrington, 1887; Donnellan lecturer at Dublin, 1887; member of Liverpool school board from 1876; dean of Norwich, 1889–1909; a member of the Alpine Club; helped to build several English churches in Switzerland; died and was buried at Riffel Alp; published theological works; 'Life' by H. Leeds, 1909.

LEGG, JOHN WICKHAM (1843–1921), physician and liturgiologist; M.D., University College, London, 1868; joined staff of St. Bartholomew's Hospital, London, 1870; abandoned medicine, 1887; F.S.A., 1875; distinguished student of liturgies; works include editions of Quignon Breviary of 1535 (1888), 'Second Recension of Quignon Breviary' (1908, 1912), 'Westminster Missal' (1891–7), and 'Sarum Missal' (1916), and 'English Church Life' [1660–1833] (1914); high churchman.

LEGROS, ALPHONSE (1837–1911), painter, sculptor, and etcher; born at Dijon; worked in Paris as scene-painter; exhibited at Salon, 1857; enrolled by Champfleury among the 'Realists'; exhibited 'Angelus,' 1859, 'Ex Voto,' 1861, and 'Le Lutrin,' 1863; earned living by etchings and lithographs; encouraged by Whistler to come to London, 1863; Slade professor of fine art at University College, London, 1875–92; designed fountains for gardens at Welbeck, 1897; exhibited paintings, etchings, and medals at Royal Academy, 1864–82; fellow of Society of Painter Etchers, 1880, and hon. fellow of Royal Scottish Academy, 1911; works are in public galleries in Paris, Dijon, London, Manchester, and Liverpool, as well as in private collections.

LEHMANN, RUDOLF (1819–1905), painter; born near Hamburg; studied art at Paris, Munich, and Rome; first visited London, 1850; exhibited at Royal Academy from 1851, and at other English galleries, mainly subject pictures and portraits of prominent persons; lived in Italy, mostly at Rome, 1856–66; best-known portraits were those of Helen Faucit, Robert Browning, Viscount Goschen; intimate friend of Browning; published 'Reminiscences,' 1894, and 'Men and Women of the Century' (portrait sketches), 1896.

LEICESTER, second EARL OF (1822–1909), agriculturist. [See COKE, THOMAS WILLIAM.]

LEIGHTON, STANLEY (1837–1901), politician and antiquary; educated at Harrow and Balliol College, Oxford; B.A. and M.A., 1864; called to bar, 1861; conservative M.P. for North Shropshire, 1876–85, and Oswestry, 1885–1901; ardent supporter of the church in parliament; F.S.A., 1880; founded Shropshire Parish Register Society, 1897; accomplished amateur artist; wrote and illustrated 'Shropshire Houses, Past and Present,' 1901.

LEININGEN, PRINCE ERNEST LEOPOLD VICTOR CHARLES AUGUSTE JOSEPH EMICH (1830–1904), admiral, reigning prince of Leiningen; born at Amorbach, Bavaria; entered British navy, 1849; served in Burmese war, 1851–2; served against Russians on the Danube, 1854; took part in Baltic campaign, 1856; commander and captain from 1858 of royal yacht 'Alberta', which (with Queen Victoria on board) accidentally ran down schooner yacht 'Mistletoe' in Stokes bay, Aug. 1875; vice-admiral, 1881; commander-in-chief at the Nore, 1885–7; admiral 1887; G.C.B., 1866; G.C.V.O., 1898; died at Amorbach.

LEISHMAN, THOMAS (1825–1904), Scottish divine and liturgiologist; M.A. Glasgow University, 1843; D.D., 1871; presbyterian minister at Linton, Teviotdale, 1855–95; with G. W. Sprott [q. v.] published an annotated edition of 'The Book of Common Order'; advocated observance of the five great Christian festivals by the Church of Scotland, 1868; helped to found Scottish Church Society, 1892; thrice president; writings include 'The Moulding of the Scottish Reformation,' 1897; moderator of general assembly, 1898.

LE JEUNE, HENRY (1819–1904), historical and genre painter; studied art at Royal Academy Schools; exhibited at Academy, 1840–94, and British Institution, 1842–63; curator of painting school of Royal Academy, 1848–64; A.R.A., 1863; painted subjects from Bible, Shakespeare, and Spenser; later devoted himself to painting children, as in 'Little Bo-Peep' and 'My Little Model'; musician and chess player.

LEMMENS-SHERRINGTON, HELEN (1834–1906), soprano vocalist; studied music at Brussels under Cornelis, 1852; first appeared at London concerts, 1856; married Nicolas Jacques Lemmens, 1857; leading English soprano from 1860, singing in English opera (1860–5) and in Italian opera (1866); showed great power in oratorio music, as in Mendelssohn's 'Elijah' and Haydn's 'Creation'; sang in first performance of Bach's 'High Mass,' 1876; teacher of singing at Brussels conservatoire, 1881–91; occasionally revisited England; died at Brussels.

LEMPRIERE, CHARLES (1818–1901), writer and politician; son of John Lempriere, D.D. [q.v.]; B.C.L., St. John's College, Oxford, 1842; D.C.L., 1847; called to bar, 1844; agent of conservative party from 1850; sent on private mission to Mexico, to watch British interests, 1861; published 'The American Crisis Considered,' 1861, and 'Notes on Mexico,' 1862; colonial secretary of the Bahamas, 1867; compelled to resign owing to his tory opinions; wrote for the American 'Tribune'; organized unsuccessful English colony at Buckhorn, West Virginia, 1872.

LENG, SIR JOHN (1828–1906), newspaper proprietor; sub-editor and reporter of 'Hull Advertiser,' 1847–51; editor of bi-weekly 'Dundee Advertiser,' 1851; raised paper to high rank; became part proprietor, 1852; issued 'Advertiser' daily, 1861; established office in London, 1870; first to attempt illustrations in daily paper; founded first halfpenny daily in Scotland, 1859, the weekly 'People's Journal,' 1858, and literary weekly, 'People's Friend,' 1869; started 'Evening Telegraph,' 1877; liberal M.P. for Dundee, 1889–1905; supported railway and factory labour legislation and home rule bill, 1893; knighted, 1893; hon. LL.D. St. Andrews, 1904; thrice visited America and Canada, India (1896), and Near East; died at Delmonte, California, on third American tour.

LENG, SIR WILLIAM CHRISTOPHER (1825–1902), journalist; brother of Sir John Leng [q. v.]; contributed to 'Dundee Advertiser' from 1859; managing editor and owner (1864) of 'Sheffield Daily Telegraph,' which became a powerful conservative organ; first to set up linotype machines; denounced trade unionist terrorism at Sheffield, 1867, and obtained royal commission of inquiry into his allegations; knighted, 1887.

LENNOX, CHARLES HENRY GORDON-, sixth DUKE OF RICHMOND and first DUKE OF GORDON (1818–1903), lord-president of the council. [See GORDON-LENNOX.]

LENO, DAN (1860–1904), music-hall singer and dancer, whose true name was GEORGE GALVIN; made first appearance in London as 'Little George' the contortionist, 1864; took to clog-dancing and singing, 1869; admired by Charles Dickens at Belfast, 1869; won clog-dancing championship of the world at Leeds, 1880; made first appearance as 'Dan Leno' in London, 1883; appeared in Drury Lane pantomime from 1888–9 annually till death; played at Sandringham before King Edward VII, Nov. 1901; most memorable songs a mixture of song and 'patter'; lavish in charity; wrote burlesque autobiography, 'Dan Leno: his Book,' 1901.

LEVESON-GOWER (EDWARD) FREDERICK (1819–1907), politician; son of first Earl Granville [q. v.]; educated at Eton and Christ Church, Oxford; B.A., 1840; called to bar, 1846; liberal M.P. for Derby, 1846–7, Stoke-on-Trent, 1852–7, and Bodmin, 1859–85; chairman of National School of Cookery, 1874–1903; visited India, 1850–1, and Russia, 1856; a conspicuous figure in society; edited his mother's 'Letters,' 1894, and published 'Bygone Years,' 1905.

LEVY-LAWSON, EDWARD, first BARON BURNHAM (1833–1916), newspaper proprietor; son of Joseph Moses Levy [q.v.]; assumed additional surname of Lawson, 1875; began career as dramatic critic to 'Sunday Times'; became editor of 'Daily Telegraph' shortly after its acquisition by his father, 1855; managing proprietor and sole controller, 1885; humanized his newspaper; paper's support transferred from Gladstone to Beaconsfield, 1878; after 1886 paper definitely unionist and imperialist; organized appeals to public for national and charitable efforts through 'Daily Telegraph' funds; sponsored enterprises such as Assyrian expedition of George Smith [q.v.], 1873; baronet, 1892; created baron on retirement from active control of paper, 1903; K.C.V.O., 1904.

LEWIS, BUNNELL (1824–1908), classical archaeologist; B.A., London, 1843; M.A., 1849; fellow of University College, London, 1847; professor of Latin, Queen's College, Cork, 1849–1905; F.S.A., 1865; made researches into surviving Roman antiquities in Europe; contributed to 'Archaeological Journal,' 1875–1907; bequeathed library and 1000*l.* for classical prize to University College.

LEWIS, EVAN (1818–1901), dean of Bangor; B.A., Jesus College, Oxford, 1841; M.A., 1863; held livings of Aberdare (1859–66) and Dolgelly (1866–84); chancellor (1872–6), canon residentiary (1877–84), and dean of Bangor (1884–1901); influenced by tractarian movement; his teaching as curate on the sacraments led to a long controversy, 1850–2; his best work was Welsh treatise on Apostolic succession, 1851; his elder brother, DAVID LEWIS (1814–1895), vice-principal of Jesus College, Oxford, 1845–6, joined Roman Church, 1846, and translated theological works from Latin and Spanish.

LEWIS, SIR GEORGE HENRY, first baronet (1833–1911), solicitor; joined father's firm of solicitors, 1851; established reputation in connexion with Balham mystery, 1876 [see GULLY, JAMES MANBY]; obtained monopoly of 'society' cases; unrivalled in knowledge of criminals and in thoroughness of investigation; acted for incriminated nationalists before the Parnell commission, 1888–9; intimate with King Edward VII; C.V.O., 1905; knighted, 1892; baronet, 1902; advocate of Prisoners' Evidence Act of 1898, of court of criminal appeal, 1908, and Moneylenders Act, 1900.

LEWIS, JOHN TRAVERS (1825–1901), archbishop of Ontario; B.A., Trinity College, Dublin, 1848; ordained, 1848; settled in Canada, 1849; first bishop of Ontario, 1861; metropolitan of Canada, 1893; and archbishop of Ontario, 1894; his advocacy (1864) of national council for whole Anglican Church led to first Lambeth conference, 1867; hon. D.D. Oxford, 1897; hon. LL.D. Dublin.

LEWIS, RICHARD (1821–1905), bishop of Llandaff; B.A. Worcester College, Oxford, 1843; D.D., 1883; travelled in Europe and Near East, 1843–4; ordained, 1844; rector of Lampeter Velfry, 1851–83; archdeacon of St. David's, 1875–83; bishop of Llandaff, 1883–1905; inaugurated Bishop of Llandaff's Church Extension Fund, for erection of new churches and support of additional curates, thus greatly extending work of diocese; established annual diocesan conference, 1884; a broad and tolerant churchman, but uncompromising on question of church schools; took seat in House of Lords, 1885; unsympathetic with modern Welsh nationalism; statue by Goscombe John in Llandaff Cathedral and portrait by A. S. Cope in Llandaff Palace; his son, ARTHUR GRIFFITH POYER LEWIS (1848–1909), rowed for Oxford in university boatrace, 1870, and was recorder of Carmarthen, 1890-1905.

LEWIS, WILLIAM THOMAS, first BARON MERTHYR, of Senghenydd (1837-1914), engineer and coal-owner; controller of Marquess of Bute's Welsh estates, 1881; main colliery interests latterly in Rhondda valley and Senghenydd districts; served on royal commissions dealing with coal industry and labour problems; promoted industrial peace; knighted, 1885; created baronet, 1896; baron, 1911.

LIBERTY, SIR ARTHUR LASENBY (1843-1917), fabric manufacturer; opened business in Regent Street, London (afterwards Liberty & Co.), 1875; dealt in Oriental fabrics and produced British machine-made stuffs which equalled hand-made products of Asia; friend of pre-Raphaelite painters; knighted, 1913.

LIDDERDALE, WILLIAM (1832-1902), governor of the Bank of England; born at St. Petersburg; son of a Russian merchant; director (1870), deputy governor (1887), and governor (1889) of Bank of England; concerned in G. J. Goschen's reduction of interest on national debt, 1888; by his firm action liquidated Messrs. Baring's affairs and increased the City's confidence in the Bank, 1890; P.C., 1891; concluded negotiations with government which took shape in Bank Act of 1892.

LINDLEY, NATHANIEL, BARON LINDLEY (1828-1921), lord of appeal; son of John Lindley, F.R.S. [q.v.]; educated at University College School, London; called to bar (Middle Temple), 1850; published 'A Treatise on the Law of Partnership' &c., publicly noticed by judges, 1860; career assured by success as junior for Overend, Gurney & Co., in City financial crisis, 1866; reputation enhanced by case of 'Knox v. Gye' (1871) and action concerning 'Frou-frou'; Q.C., 1872; judge of common pleas and knighted, 1875; lord justice of appeal, 1881; master of the Rolls, 1897; F.R.S., 1897; lord of appeal in ordinary, 1900-5; life peer, 1900; remarkable for impartiality and versatility.

LINDSAY, JAMES GAVIN (1835-1903), colonel R.E.; joined Madras engineers, 1854; served in Indian Mutiny; as engineer-in-chief constructed northern Bengal railway, 1872; showed capacity in dealing with Bengal famine, 1873-4; colonel, 1882; built Sukkur-Sibi railway in second Afghan war, 1879-80; took part in relief of Kandahar; finished Southern Mahratta railway, 1891.

LINDSAY, JAMES LUDOVIC, twenty-sixth EARL OF CRAWFORD and ninth EARL OF BALCARRES (1847-1913), astronomer, collector, and bibliophile; son of twenty-fifth Earl [q. v.]; erected Dunecht observatory, near Aberdeen, 1872; succeeded father, 1880; collector of French Revolution documents, &c.; published 'Bibliotheca Lindesiana' (1883-1913); F.R.S., 1878; K.T., 1896.

LINDSAY (afterwards LOYD-LINDSAY), ROBERT JAMES, BARON WANTAGE (1832-1901), soldier and politician; joined Scots guards, 1850; retired as lieutenant-colonel, 1859; served with distinction in Crimea; received V.C., 1857; assumed name of Loyd-Lindsay on marriage, 1858; a pioneer of Volunteer movement, 1859; conservative M.P. for Berkshire, 1865-85; financial secretary to war office, 1877-80; represented Red Cross Aid Society, which he helped to found (1870), in Franco-Prussian and Turko-Servian wars; K.C.B., 1881; raised to peerage, 1885; a prominent freemason; leading agriculturist in Berkshire; discriminating art patron; helped to found Reading University College (afterwards Reading University); memoir by Lady Wantage, 1907.

LINDSAY, THOMAS MARTIN (1843-1914), historian; educated at Glasgow and Edinburgh universities; entered ministry of Free Church of Scotland, 1869; professor of church history at Free Church theological college, Glasgow, 1872; principal, 1902; interested in missions and social problems; chief works, 'Luther and the German Reformation' (1900), and 'A History of the Reformation in Europe' (1906-7).

LINGEN, RALPH ROBERT WHEELER, BARON LINGEN (1819-1905), civil servant; educated at Trinity College, Oxford; friend of Jowett, Froude, and Frederick Temple; Ireland and Hertford scholar (1838-9); B.A., 1840; won Latin Essay (1843) and Eldon scholarship (1846); fellow of Balliol, 1841; hon. D.C.L., 1881; hon. fellow of Trinity, 1886; called to bar, 1847; secretary to education office, 1849-69; worked harmoniously under Lord Granville and Robert Lowe [q. v.]; issued code advocating payment by results in accordance with report of Newcastle commission of inquiry, 1861;

code severely criticized by Lord Robert Cecil (Lord Salisbury) and W. E. Forster; C.B., 1869; permanent secretary of the treasury, 1869-85; vigilant guardian of public purse; K.C.B., 1878; raised to peerage, 1885; alderman of first London county council, 1889-92.

LINLITHGOW, first MARQUESS OF (1860-1908), first governor-general of the commonwealth of Australia. [See HOPE, JOHN ADRIAN LOUIS.]

LISTER, ARTHUR (1830-1908), botanist; son of Joseph Jackson Lister [q.v.]; published 'A Monograph of the Mycetozoa,' 1894, and 'Guide to the British Mycetozoa,' 1895; F.R.S., 1898.

LISTER, JOSEPH, first BARON LISTER, of Lyme Regis (1827-1912), founder of antiseptic surgery; son of Joseph Jackson Lister, F.R.S. [q. v.]; educated at Grove House School, Tottenham, and University College, London; especially influenced during his medical studies by Wharton Jones, professor of ophthalmic medicine and surgery, and William Sharpey [q. v.], professor of physiology; after taking M.B. (1852) carried out researches on physiological problems; went to Edinburgh to study methods of James Syme [q. v.], celebrated surgeon, 1853; settled in Edinburgh; assistant surgeon to Royal Infirmary, 1856; professor of surgery, Glasgow University, and F.R.S., 1860; surgeon to Glasgow Infirmary, 1861; professor of clinical surgery, Edinburgh, 1869-77; at King's College, London, 1877-92; baronet, 1883; president of Royal Society, 1894-1900; baron, 1897; O.M., 1902; devoted himself to prevention of mortality from injuries and wounds by studying inflammation and suppuration; influenced by researches of Louis Pasteur; employed carbolic acid to destroy germs and prevent septic infection; successfully applied treatment to cases of compound fracture; invented new operations and improved technique of old ones by introducing use of absorbable ligatures and drainage tubes; vanishing of septic diseases caused practice of surgery to undergo complete revolution and enormously enlarged its field.

LISTER, SAMUEL CUNLIFFE, first BARON MASHAM (1815-1906), inventor; brother carried on worsted mill at Manningham till 1889; took out over 150 patents for inventions; evolved Lister-Cartwright (1845), the 'square motion' (1846), and 'square nip' (1850) wool-combing machines, which cheapened cloth, advanced Bradford's prosperity, and created Australian wool trade; successfully converted silk waste into silk velvets, poplins, and the like; invented (1848) a compressed air brake for railways; purchased Ackton colliery in Yorkshire, where the works were destroyed in coal strike of 1893; early advocated tariff reform; presented Lister Park to Bradford city; raised to peerage, 1891; hon. LL.D. Leeds University; ardent art collector and sportsman; published account of his inventions, 1905; statue by Matthew Noble in Lister Park, Bradford.

LITTLE, WILLIAM JOHN KNOX- (1839-1918), divine and preacher. [See KNOX-LITTLE.]

LITTLER, SIR RALPH DANIEL MAKINSON (1835-1908), barrister; B.A., London, 1854; called to bar, 1857; Q.C., 1873; treasurer of Middle Temple, 1900-1; C.B., 1890; knighted, 1902; chairman of Middlesex sessions county council from 1889 to death; was often criticized for long sentences on habitual criminals.

LIVESEY, SIR GEORGE THOMAS (1834-1908), promoter of labour co-partnership; joined South Metropolitan Gas Company, 1848; assistant manager, 1857; engineer and secretary, 1871; chairman of board of directors, 1885; adopted principle of sliding scale, 1876; admitted foremen (1886) and workmen (1889) to share in profits; capitalized bonus of workmen, who became shareholders (1894) and were admitted to board of directors (1898); sat on labour commission, 1891-4; knighted, 1902; erected 'Livesey' library, Camberwell; 'Livesey' professorship of coal gas and fuel industries was founded at Leeds University.

LLANDAFF, VISCOUNT (1826-1913), lawyer and politician. [See MATTHEWS, HENRY.]

LOATES, THOMAS (1867-1910), jockey; first rode a winner, 1883; won Derby, 1889; headed list of winning jockeys, 1889, 1890, and 1893; won on Isinglass the Two Thousand Guineas, Derby, and St. Leger, 1893, and on St. Frusquin the Two Thousand Guineas, 1896; a resourceful rider; amassed large fortune.

LOCKEY, CHARLES (1820-1901), tenor vocalist; sang in Rossini's 'Stabat Mater,' 1842, and created tenor part in Mendelssohn's 'Elijah' at Birmingham, 1846.

LOCKYER, SIR (JOSEPH) NORMAN (1836-1920), astronomer; clerk in War Office, 1857; made pioneer observations of spectrum of sun-spot, 1866, and of solar prominences, 1868; coined terms 'chromosphere' and 'helium,' 1868; secretary to royal commission on scientific instruction and advancement of science, 1870; transferred to Science and Art Department, South Kensington, 1875; director of Solar Physics Observatory and professor of astronomical physics, Royal College of Science, 1890–1913; F.R.S., 1869; Rumford medallist, 1874; C.B., 1894; K.C.B., 1897; wrote numerous astronomical books.

LOFTIE, WILLIAM JOHN (1839–1911), antiquary; ordained, 1865; assistant chaplain, Chapel Royal, Savoy, 1871–95; F.S.A., 1872; frequent contributor to reviews; travelled much in Egypt; a keen Egyptologist; wrote much on British art and architecture; specially interested in London history and London buildings; chief works were 'Memorials of the Savoy,' 1878, and 'A History of London,' 2 vols. 1883–4.

LOFTUS, LORD AUGUSTUS WILLIAM FREDERICK SPENCER (1817–1904), diplomatist; son of second marquess of Ely; attaché to British legation at Berlin, 1837–44; at Stuttgart and Baden Baden, 1844–71; joined Sir Stratford Canning [q. v.] in special mission to European courts and witnessed revolutionary incidents in Germany and Austria, 1848; secretary of legation at Berlin, 1853; reported as to British consulates on German shores of Baltic after Crimean war; envoy extraordinary to Emperor of Austria, 1858; warned Austrian government of England's friendship to Italy, 1859; transferred to Berlin (1860), where he favoured Denmark's claims in Schleswig-Holstein crisis: at Munich, 1863–6; returned to Berlin, 1866; G.C.B., 1866; P.C., 1868; managed solde de captivité for French prisoners of war in Germany, 1870; at St. Petersburg, 1871–9; attended Tsar Alexander on visit to England, 1874; conferred with Prince Gortchakoff with a view to prevent Russo-Turkish war, 1876; suggested Anglo-Russian understanding, which was brought about by Lord Salisbury and the Russian ambassador in London; governor of New South Wales, 1879–85; entertained Princes Albert Edward and George, 1881; published 'Diplomatic Reminiscences,' 4 vols. 1892–4.

LOHMANN, GEORGE ALFRED (1865–1901), Surrey cricketer; won great success as medium-pace bowler for Surrey from 1885 to 1890; thrice visited Australia; played for Players v. Gentlemen, 1886–96; a good hitting batsman and first-class fieldsman; raised Surrey to leading position.

LONDONDERRY, sixth MARQUESS OF (1852–1915), politician. [See VANE-TEMPEST-STEWART, CHARLES STEWART.]

LONGHURST, WILLIAM HENRY (1819–1904), organist and composer; chorister (1828), assistant organist (1836), and organist (1873–98) of Canterbury Cathedral; Mus.Doc., 1875; published church music.

LOPES, SIR LOPES MASSEY, third baronet (1818–1908), politician and agriculturist; educated at Winchester and Oriel College, Oxford; B.A., 1842; M.A., 1845; conservative M.P. for Westbury, 1857–68, for South Devon, 1868–85; urged grievance of burden of local taxation; helped to carry agricultural ratings Act, 1879; civil lord of the admiralty, 1874–80; P.C., 1885; alderman of Devonshire county council, 1888–1904; a scientific farmer, he spent much money on improving his estates.

LORD, THOMAS (1808–1908), congregational minister; held Midland pastorates (1834–79) till he settled at Horncastle, where he preached in his 101st year; original member of Peace Society; published devotional works.

LOTBINIÈRE, SIR HENRY GUSTAVE JOLY DE (1829–1908), Canadian politician. [See JOLY DE LOTBINIÈRE.]

LOVELACE, second EARL OF (1839–1906), author of 'Astarte'. [See MILBANKE, RALPH GORDON NOEL KING.]

LOVETT, RICHARD (1851–1904), author; spent boyhood (1858–67) in United States; B.A. London, 1873; M.A., 1873; book editor of Religious Tract Society, 1882; secretary, 1899; wrote centenary history of London Missionary Society, 1899; wrote lives of James Gilmour, 1892, and James Chalmers, 1902; author of 'The Printed English Bible,' 1895.

LOW, ALEXANDER, LORD LOW (1845–1910), Scottish judge; B.A., St. John's College, Cambridge, 1867; passed to Scottish bar, 1870; raised to bench, 1890; his decision against minority's claim to 'Free Church' property (1900) was reversed by House of Lords, 1904.

LOW, SIR ROBERT CUNLIFFE (1838–1911), general; son of Sir John Low [q. v.]; joined Indian army, 1854; served in Indian Mutiny at Delhi and Lucknow; lieutenant-colonel, 1878; director of the transport service on march from Kabul to Kandahar; C.B., 1880; actively engaged in Upper Burma, 1886–7; K.C.B., 1887; commander-in-chief of Chitral relief expedition, 1895; lieutenant-general and G.C.B., 1896; commanded Bombay army, 1898–1909; general, 1900; keeper of crown jewels at Tower of London, 1909–11.

LOWE, SIR DRURY CURZON DRURY- (1830–1908), lieutenant-general. [See DRURY-LOWE.]

LOWRY, HENRY DAWSON (1869–1906), author; wrote Cornish stories for 'National Observer' from 1891; on staff of 'Pall Mall Gazette' (1895) and 'Morning Post' (1897); published novels and 'The Hundred Windows' (poems), 1904.

LOWTHER, JAMES (1840–1904), politician and sportsman; educated at Westminster and Trinity College, Cambridge; B.A., 1863; M.A., 1866; called to bar, 1864, but did not practise; conservative M.P. for York City, 1865–80, for Isle of Thanet, 1888–1904; parliamentary secretary to the poor law board under Disraeli, 1897–8; opposed Irish land bill, 1870; undersecretary for the colonies, 1874–8; chief secretary to lord-lieutenant of Ireland, 1878–80; P.C., 1878; opposed establishment of county councils (1888) and advocated protection; took part in Yorkshire local affairs; bred racehorses from 1873; senior steward of Jockey Club, 1889.

LÖWY, ALBERT or ABRAHAM (1816–1908), Hebrew scholar; born in Moravia; studied at Vienna University; helped to found 'Die Einheit,' a society for promoting welfare of Jews; came to London for support of scheme, 1840; with Jewish reformers in London founded West London Synagogue, 1842, and became first minister, 1842–92; helped to form Anglo-Jewish Association, 1870; secretary, 1875–89; catalogued Lord Crawford's Samaritan literature, 1872, and Hebrew books of City of London, 1891; founded Society of Hebrew Literature, 1870; hon. LL.D. St. Andrews, 1893.

LOYD-LINDSAY, ROBERT JAMES, BARON WANTAGE (1832–1901), soldier and politician. [See LINDSAY.]

LUARD, SIR WILLIAM GARNHAM (1820–1910), admiral; of Huguenot origin; joined navy, 1835; served in China war, 1841; commander, 1850; took part in capture of Rangoon and of Pegu (1852) and in operations in Japan in Straits of Shimonoseki, 1864; C.B., 1864; captain superintendent of Sheerness dockyard, 1870–5; superintendent of Malta dockyard, 1878–9; vice-admiral, 1879; president of Royal Naval College, Greenwich, 1882–5; admiral, 1885; K.C.B., 1897.

LUBBOCK, SIR JOHN, fourth baronet, and first BARON AVEBURY (1834–1913), banker, scientist, and author; son of Sir J. W. Lubbock [q. v.], third baronet; educated at Eton, but early installed in his father's bank; succeeded father, 1865; liberal M.P., Maidstone, 1870 and 1874, London University, 1880–1900; secured passage of Bank Holidays Act (1871), Act for Preservation of Ancient Monuments (1882), Early Closing Act (1904), &c.; P.C., 1890; created baron, 1900; held leading position in banking world; his researches on ants his most valuable contribution to science; F.R.S., 1858; author of numerous scientific and ethical works.

LUBY, THOMAS CLARKE (1821–1901), Fenian; B.A., Trinity College, Dublin, 1845; abandoned theological studies for nationalist propaganda; planned risings in Ireland, 1848–9; captured and imprisoned; went to Australia; on return started with James Stephens [q. v.] Fenian movement, 1853; founded Irish Republican Brotherhood, 1858; sent as envoy from Ireland to America to collect funds, 1863; on return revived waning enthusiasm, and launched 'Irish People' newspaper as organ of party (Nov. 1863–Sept. 1865); sentenced to twenty years penal servitude for treason felony, 1865; set at liberty, 1871; settled in New York and engaged in journalism; distrusted home rule movement under Parnell; wrote 'Lives of . . . Representative Irishmen,' 1878.

LUCAS, eighth BARON (1876–1916), politician and airman. [See HERBERT, AUBERON THOMAS.]

LUCAS, KEITH (1879–1916), physiologist; B.A., Trinity College, Cambridge; fellow of Trinity, 1904; science lecturer, 1908; Croonian lecturer of Royal Society, 1912; F.R.S., 1913; researched on muscle and nerve problems; services enlisted for Royal Aircraft Factory, Farnborough, 1914; killed flying.

LUCKOCK, HERBERT MORTIMER (1833–1909), dean of Lichfield; educated at Shrewsbury and Jesus College, Cambridge; B.A., 1858; M.A., 1862; D.D., 1879; won university theological prizes and scholarships; fellow, 1862; vicar of All Saints', Cambridge, 1865–75; principal of Ely Theological College, 1876–87; resident-iary canon of Ely, 1875–92; dean of Lichfield, 1892–1909; a high churchman, he exerted influence through his devotional writings, which included 'After Death,' 1879, and 'The Intermediate State,' 1890.

LUDLOW, JOHN MALCOLM FORBES (1821–1911), social reformer; born at Nimach, India; educated in Paris; called to bar, 1843; practised as conveyancer, 1843–74; advocate of reforms in India and of abolition of slavery; member of anti-corn-law league; in Paris during revolution of 1848; friend of F. D. Maurice, Charles Kingsley, and Tom Hughes; one of founders of Christian Socialist movement; promoted labour co-partnership, 1850; founded and edited weekly 'Christian Socialist,' 1850; helped to found Working Men's College (1854), lecturing there on law and English and Indian history; wrote historical works, including 'Popular Epics of the Middle Ages,' 2 vols. 1865; secretary to royal commission on friendly societies, 1870–4; chief registrar of friendly societies, 1875–91; C.B., 1887.

LUKE, JEMIMA (1813–1906), hymn writer; born THOMPSON; enthusiastic nonconformist; author of children's hymn, 'I think when I read that sweet story of old,' 1840, and autobiography, 1900.

LUPTON, JOSEPH HIRST (1836–1905), scholar and schoolmaster; B.A., St. John's College Cambridge (fifth classic), 1858; M.A. and fellow, 1861; ordained, 1859; D.D., 1896; sur-master in St. Paul's School, 1864–99; published 'Wakefield Worthies,'1864; published 'Life of Dean Colet,' 1887, and edited and translated many of Colet's works; Hulsean lecturer (1887) and Seatonian prizeman (1897) of Cambridge; other works were life of St. John of Damascus, 1882, and an edition of More's 'Utopia,' 1895.

LUSK, SIR ANDREW, baronet (1810–1909), lord mayor of London; started grocery business in Greenock, 1835; founded business in London, 1840; chairman of Imperial Bank from 1862; lord mayor of London, 1873; raised 150,000l. for relief of Bengal famine; baronet, 1874; liberal M.P. for Finsbury, 1865–85; became liberal unionist, 1886.

LUTZ, (WILHELM) MEYER (1829–1903), musical composer; born in Bavaria; settled in England, 1848; toured provinces with Italian operatic singers; con-ductor of Gaiety Theatre, 1869–96, and organist of St. George's Cathedral, Southwark; composed, besides church music, operettas for the Gaiety Theatre.

LYALL, SIR ALFRED COMYN (1835–1911), Anglo-Indian administrator and writer; son of Alfred Lyall [q. v.]; educated at Eton and Haileybury; joined Indian civil service, 1856; actively served in Mutiny, 1857–8; made commissioner of West Berar (1867), home secre-tary to Indian government (1873), and governor-general's agent in Rajputana (1874); foreign secretary to Indian government, 1878–81; took part in negotia-tions at Kabul and Kandahar, 1880, and advocated definite treaty with Russia in regard to Afghanistan, 1881; C.B., 1879; K.C.B., 1881; lieutenant–governor of North-West Provinces and Oudh, 1882–7; founded new University of Allahabad; returned to England, 1887; member of India council in London, 1887–1902; K.C.I.E., 1887; G.C.I.E., 1896; P.C., 1902; filled distinguished place in English society; Rede lecturer at Cambridge, 1891; Ford lecturer at Oxford, 1908; published 'Verses Written in India,' 1889, 'Asiatic Studies,' 2 series, 1882 and 1899, 'Rise of British Dominion in India,' 1893, and life of the Marquess of Dufferin, 2 vols. 1905; hon. D.C.L. Oxford, 1889; LL.D. Cambridge, 1891; F.B.A., 1903; trustee of British Museum, 1911; a liberal unionist, free trader, and opponent of women's suffrage.

LYALL, SIR CHARLES JAMES (1845–1920), Indian civil servant and Orientalist; entered Indian civil service, 1865; held secretariats, &c. in India, 1867–94; chief commissioner of Central Provinces, 1895; K.C.S.I., 1897; secretary of judicial and public department, India Office, 1898–1910; works include series on early Arabic literature.

LYALL, EDNA (pseudonym) (1857–1903), novelist. [See BAYLY, ADA ELLEN.]

LYNE, JOSEPH LEYCESTER [Father Ignatius] (1837–1908), preacher; educated at St. Paul's School and Trinity College, Glenalmond; ordained, 1860; developed advanced views; curate to George Rundle

Prynne [q. v.] at Plymouth; studied Benedictine Order at Bruges, 1861: on return to London replaced A. H. Mackonochie [q. v.] as curate of St. George's in the East; resigned on assuming Benedictine habit; formed a monastic community at Claydon, near Ipswich, 1862; removed to Elm Hill, near Norwich, 1863–6, where he frequently came into conflict with the bishop; built Llanthony Abbey, 1869; the community dwindled owing to quarrels; an eloquent preacher; made missionary tour through Canada and America, 1890–1; memoir by Baroness de Bertouche, 1904.

LYNE, SIR WILLIAM JOHN (1844–1913), Australian politician; born in Tasmania; entered New South Wales legislative assembly, 1880; premier, 1899; minister of home affairs in first Commonwealth ministry, 1901; minister of trade and customs, 1903–5–7; treasurer, 1907–8; K.C.M.G., 1900; protectionist with rather narrowly Australian outlook.

LYONS, SIR ALGERNON McLENNAN (1833–1908), admiral of the fleet; born at Bombay; entered navy, 1847; served on China and Mediterranean stations; distinguished himself in Crimean war; promoted com-mander, 1858; commodore in charge at Jamaica, 1875–8; rear-admiral, 1878; commander-in-chief in Pacific, 1881; in command of North America and West Indies station, 1886; admiral, 1888; commander-in-chief at Plymouth, 1893–6; admiral of the fleet, 1897; K.C.B., 1889; G.C.B., 1897.

LYTTELTON, ALFRED (1857–1913), lawyer and statesman; son of fourth Baron Lyttelton [q. v.]; edu-cated at Eton and Trinity College, Cambridge; practised successfully at bar, 1881–1903; liberal-unionist M.P., Leamington, 1895; chairman of commission to South Africa, 1900; colonial secretary, 1903–5; sanctioned, in face of opposition, introduction of Chinese coolies into Rand, 1904; prepared way for development of Imperial Conference; M.P., St. George's, Hanover Square, 1906; first-class cricketer and for long amateur tennis champion.

LYTTELTON, ARTHUR TEMPLE (1852–1903), suffragan bishop of Southampton; son of fourth Baron Lyttelton [q. v.]; educated at Eton and Trinity College, Cambridge; B.A., 1874; M.A., 1877; D.D., 1898; tutor of Keble College, Oxford, 1879–82; first master of Selwyn College, Cambridge, 1882–93; Hulsean lecturer, 1891; vicar of Eccles, Lancashire, 1893–8; suffragan bishop of Southampton, 1878–1903; a high churchman; published 'Modern Poets of Faith, Doubt, and Unbelief,' 1904.

MACAN, SIR ARTHUR VERNON (1843–1908), gynaecologist and obstetrician; B.A., Trinity College, Dublin, 1864; M.B. and M.Ch., 1868; M.A.O., 1877; studied medicine at Berlin, 1869–72; served as volunteer in Prussian army, 1870; fellow of King and Queen's College of Physicians, Ireland; master of the Rotunda Hospital, Dublin, 1882; introduced newer obstetric methods despite opposition; applied Listerian principles in midwifery; president of Royal College of Physicians, Ireland, 1902–4; knighted, 1903; contributed to Dublin scientific journals.

McARTHUR, CHARLES (1844–1910), politician and writer on marine insurance; won repute by 'The Policy of Marine Insurance Popularly Examined,' 1871; established own business as an average adjuster at Liverpool, 1874; president of Liverpool Chamber of Commerce, 1892–6; liberal unionist M.P. for Exchange division of Liverpool, 1897–1906, and for Kirkdale, 1907–10; championed shipping and protestant church interests in parliament; wrote on 'Evidences of Natural Religion,' 1880.

MACARTHUR, MARY REID (1880–1921), women's labour organizer. [See ANDERSON.]

M'CARTHY, JUSTIN (1830–1912), Irish politician, historian, and novelist; leader-writer on 'Daily News,'1871; M.P., co. Longford, 1879, Derry city, 1886, North Long-ford, 1892–1900; chairman of anti-Parnellite nationalist party, 1890–6; wrote 'History of Our Own Times' (1877), 'Dear Lady Disdain' (1875), 'Miss Misanthrope' (1878), &c.

MACARTNEY, SIR SAMUEL HALLIDAY (1833–1906), official in the Chinese service; studied medicine at Edinburgh University, 1852–5; joined medical staff in Crimean war, 1855; M.D., 1858; served in Indian Mutiny (1859) and in China (1860–2); entered Chinese service, 1862; commanded Chinese troops co-operating with Gordon; took Fung Ching and Seedong, 1863; mediated between Gordon and Li Hung Chang regarding murder of Taiping leaders at Soochow, 1864; in charge of arsenal at Nankin, 1865–75; secretary to the Chinese legation in London, 1877–1906; adviser of Chinese government; C.M.G., 1881; K.C.M.G., 1885; 'Life' by D. C. Boulger, 1908.

MACAULAY, JAMES (1817–1902), author; M.A. and M.D. Edinburgh, 1838; a strenuous opponent of vivisection; tutor in Italy and Spain, and Madeira; F.R.C.S. Edinburgh, 1862; edited 'Leisure Hour,' 'Sunday at Home,' and the R.T.S. periodicals; helped to found 'Boy's Own Paper' and 'Girl's Own Paper,' 1879; published accounts of travels in America, 1871, and Ireland, 1872; wrote narratives of adventure for boys and girls.

MACBAIN, ALEXANDER (1855–1907), Celtic scholar; graduate of King's College, Aberdeen, 1880; rector of Raining's school, Inverness, from 1881; published 'Celtic Mythology and Religion,' 1885, and a Gaelic Dictionary, 1896; edited many Celtic and Gaelic works; hon. LL.D. Aberdeen, 1901; awarded civil list pension, 1905.

MACBETH, ROBERT WALKER (1848–1910), painter and etcher; son of Norman Macbeth [q. v.]; studied at schools of Royal Scottish Academy and of Royal Academy; frequent exhibitor at Academy; an able etcher of pictures by Velazquez and Titian; A.R.A., 1883; R.A., 1903.

MACCALLUM, ANDREW (1821–1902), landscape painter; apprenticed to Nottingham hosiery business; studied art at Nottingham; art teacher in Manchester and Stourbridge, 1850–4; exhibited at Royal Academy, 1850–86; went to Italy, 1854; painted landscapes in Windsor Forest, in Switzerland, Germany, Italy, Paris, and Egypt; lectured on art; work represented in Tate Gallery, Victoria and Albert Museum, and in Nottingham Art Gallery.

McCALMONT, HARRY LESLIE BLUNDELL (1861–1902), sportsman; joined army, 1881; inherited some 4,000,000l., 1894; won 57,455l. with horse Isinglass, who won the Two Thousand Guineas, Derby, and St. Leger in 1893, and was sire of Cherry Lass and Glass Doll, winners of the Oaks, 1905 and 1907; conservative M.P. for Newmarket, 1895–1902; C.B. for services in South African war.

McCLEAN, FRANK (1837–1904), civil engineer and amateur astronomer; B.A., Trinity College, Cambridge (27th wrangler), 1859; partner in father's engineering firm, 1862–70; built private observatory near Tunbridge Wells; designed a star spectroscope; published results of systematic survey of spectra of stars brighter than magnitude 3½, 1898; F.R.A.S.,1877; hon. LL.D. Glasgow, 1894; F.R.S., 1895; bequeathed large sums of money to Cambridge and Birmingham universities for physical research.

McCLINTOCK, SIR FRANCIS LEOPOLD (1819–1907), admiral; entered navy, 1831; served under Sir James Clark Ross [q. v.], 1848, Sir Erasmus Ommanney [q.v.], 1850, and Sir Edward Belcher [q. v.], 1852, in Arctic voyages; commanded expedition in search of Sir John Franklin [q. v.], 1851; published account of his voyage and fate of Franklin and his companions, 1859; knighted, 1860; commodore in charge at Jamaica,1865–8; admiral superintendent of Portsmouth dockyard,1872–7; vice-admiral, 1877; admiral, 1884; K.C.B., 1891; portraits by Stephen Pearce in National Portrait Gallery; 'Life' by Sir C. R. Markham.

McCOAN, JAMES CARLILE (1829–1904), author and journalist; called to bar, 1856; practised in supreme consular court at Constantinople till 1864; published 'Egypt as it is,' 1877, and 'Egypt under Ismail,' 1889; wrote sympathetically of the Turks in 'Turkey in Asia,' 2 vols. 1879; protestant home ruler M.P. for Wicklow county, 1880–5.

MACCOLL, MALCOLM (1831–1907), high-church divine and author; ordained, 1856; attracted notice of Gladstone, who presented him to City living of St. George's, Botolph Lane, 1871–91, and to canonry of Ripon, 1884; took frequent part in ecclesiastical and political controversies; supported Gladstone's Irish Church and home rule policies; visited Eastern Europe with Canon Liddon, 1876, and denounced Bulgarian atrocities; hon. D.D. Edinburgh, 1899.

MACCOLL, NORMAN (1843–1904), editor of the 'Athenaeum' and Spanish scholar; B.A., Downing College, Cambridge, 1866; M.A., 1869; fellow, 1868; called to bar, 1875; editor of 'Athenaeum,' 1871–1900; published 'Select Plays of Calderon,' 1888, and translations of Cervantes' 'Exemplary Novels,' 2 vols. 1902, and of his 'Miscellaneous Poems,' posthumous, 1912; endowed MacColl lectureship in Spanish and Portuguese at Cambridge.

MACCORMAC, SIR WILLIAM, first baronet (1836–1901), surgeon; B.A., Queen's University, Belfast, 1855; M.A., 1858; M.D., 1857; hon. M.Ch., 1879; D.Sc., 1882; hon. M.D. and M.Ch. Dublin, 1900; studied surgery in Berlin; M.R.C.S., 1857; F.R.C.S., Ireland, 1864; volunteered for surgical service in Franco-German war, 1870; lecturer on surgery at St. Thomas's Hospital, 1873–93; chief surgeon to National Aid Society in Turco-Servian war; knighted for services as secretary to seventh international medical congress, 1881; baronet, 1897; K.C.V.O., 1898; president of the Royal College of Surgeons, 1896–1900; government consulting surgeon to the field force in South African war, 1899–1900; K.C.B., 1901; publications include account of his work at Sedan, 1870, and 'Surgical Operations,' 1885–9.

McCUDDEN, JAMES THOMAS BYFORD (1895–1918), airman; joined Royal Flying Corps, 1913; went to France as air mechanic, 1914; learned to fly, 1916; became leading British fighting pilot; brought down fifty-four enemy aeroplanes; M.C. and D.S.O., 1917; V.C., 1918; killed flying in France.

MacCUNN, HAMISH [JAMES] (1868–1916), musical composer; studied at Royal College of Music; orchestral and choral works include 'Land of the Mountain and Flood' (1887), 'Ship o' the Fiend,' 'Dowie Dens o' Yarrow,' 'Lord Ullin's Daughter,' 'Lay of the Last Minstrel,' and 'Bonny Kilmeny' (all 1888); composed operas.

MACDERMOT, HUGH HYACINTH O'RORKE, THE MACDERMOT (1834–1904), attorney-general for Ireland; called to bar (King's Inns, Dublin), 1862; bencher, 1884; counsel in leading political cases in Ireland; succeeded father as titular 'Prince of Coolavin,' 1873; liberal solicitor-general for Ireland, May–July 1885 and Feb.–Aug. 1886; attorney-general and P.C., 1892–5.

MACDERMOTT, GILBERT HASTINGS (1845–1901), music-hall singer, whose real surname was FARRELL; made some position as an actor and writer of melodramas which included 'Driven from Home,' 1871; leaped into fame (1878) by singing on music-hall stage the patriotic song by George William Hunt (1829–1904), 'We don't want to fight,' which became popular watchword of war-party in England during Russo-Turkish war and gave the political terms 'jingo' and 'jingoism' to the English language; last 'lion comique' of English music-hall.

MACDERMOTT, MARTIN (1823–1905), Irish poet and architect; wrote occasional verse for 'Nation' from 1840; delegate to Paris to obtain French republican support for Young Ireland movement, 1848; chief architect to Egyptian government in Alexandria from 1866; retired to London, 1878; prepared anthology of Irish poetry, 1894.

MACDONALD, SIR CLAUDE MAXWELL (1852–1915), soldier and diplomatist; joined army, 1872; minister at Peking, 1896; organized defence of legations during Boxer rising, 1900; minister at Tokio, 1900; ambassador, 1905–12; promoted Anglo-Japanese friendship; K.C.B., 1898; military K.C.B., 1901; P.C., 1906.

MACDONALD, GEORGE (1824–1905), poet and novelist; M.A., King's College, Aberdeen, 1845; hon. LL.D., 1868; settled in Manchester, 1853; published narrative poem, 'Within and Without,' 1855 (admired by Tennyson and Lady Byron), and 'Phantastes,' 1858, a faerie romance in prose; thenceforth largely engaged in prose fiction—either of mystical character, as 'David Elginbrod,' 1863, or descriptive of Scottish humble life, as 'Alec Forbes,' 1865, and 'Robert Falconer,' 1868; long preached as a layman at Manchester; settled in London for life, 1860; friend of F. D. Maurice, Browning, Ruskin, Carlyle, William Morris, and Tennyson; lectured in London and in America, 1872; granted civil list pension, 1877; spent part of each year at Bordighera, 1881–1902; besides novels and children's stories his works include 'Unspoken Sermons,' 3 vols. 1867, 1885, and 1889, and 'Letters from Hell,' 1884; a collective edition, excluding novels, appeared in 1886 (10 vols.), and his 'Poetical Works' (2 vols.) in 1893; 'Life' by Joseph Johnson, 1906.

MACDONALD, SIR HECTOR ARCHIBALD (1853–1903), major-general; joined army as private in Gordon Highlanders, 1870; served with distinction in second Afghan war, 1879–80; won sobriquet of 'Fighting Mac'; promoted second lieutenant, 1880; displayed heroism at battle of Majuba, 1881; shared in Nile expedition (1885), and in reorganization of Egyptian army; distinguished in Sudan campaign, 1888–91; commanded brigade of Egyptian infantry in expedition to Dongola (1896) and at Atbara (1898); displayed successful adroitness at Omdurman, Sept. 1898; C.B., 1897; brigadier-general in Punjab, 1899–1900; major-general, Jan. 1900; in South African war prepared way for relief of Kimberley by seizure of Koodoesberg, Feb. 1900; engaged in actions which led to surrender of generals Cronje and Prinsloo, Feb.–May 1900; K.C.B., 1900; placed in command of Belgaum district, 1901, and of troops in Ceylon, 1902; owing to opprobrious accusation, he shot himself at Paris; memorial tower set up at Dingwall, his birthplace.

McDONALD, JOHN BLAKE (1829–1901), Scottish artist; painted, largely in chiaroscuro, dramatic episodes of Jacobite romance, and later landscape; A.R.S.A., 1862; R.S.A., 1877.

MACDONALD, Sir JOHN DENIS (1826–1908), inspector-general of hospitals and fleets, 1880–6; joined navy as assistant surgeon, 1849; engaged in microscopic study and deep sea investigations; F.R.S., 1859; professor of naval hygiene at Netley, 1872; K.C.B., 1902; published 'Outlines of Naval Hygiene,' 1881.

MACDONALD, Sir JOHN HAY ATHOLE, Lord KINGSBURGH (1836–1919), lord justice-clerk of Scotland; called to Scottish bar, 1859; solicitor-general for Scotland, 1876–80; Q.C., 1880; lord advocate, 1885–6, 1886–8; lord justice-clerk and assumed judicial title, 1888; presided over second division of Court of Session, 1888–1915; specialized in criminal law; ardent Volunteer; P.C., 1885; K.C.B., 1900; F.R.S.

MACDONELL, Sir HUGH GUION (1832–1904), soldier and diplomatist; served in British Kaffraria with rifle brigade, 1849–53; after holding several minor diplomatic posts (1858–85) was British envoy at Rio, 1885, Copenhagen, 1888, and Lisbon, 1893–1902; tactfully dealt with Anglo-Portuguese difficulties in South African war; K.C.M.G., 1892; G.C.M.G., 1899; P.C., 1902.

MACDONELL, Sir JOHN (1845–1921), jurist; brother of James Macdonell [q.v.]; M.A., Aberdeen; called to bar (Middle Temple), 1873; master of Supreme Court, 1889; senior master and King's Remembrancer, 1912–20; Quain professor of comparative law, University College, London, 1901–20; knighted, 1903; K.C.B., 1914; F.B.A., 1913; writer on legal subjects.

McDONNELL, Sir SCHOMBERG KERR (1861–1915), civil servant; principal private secretary to Marquess of Salisbury, 1888–92, 1895–9, 1900–2; secretary to Office of Works, 1902–12; K.C.B., 1902; died of wounds in Flanders.

MACE, JAMES [Jem Mace] (1831–1910), pugilist; at first a showman and circus performer; became best boxer of his generation; middle weight champion, 1860; beat Thomas King [q.v.] and Joe Goss for championship 1862–6; last surviving representative of old prize ring.

MACFADYEN, ALLAN (1860–1907), bacteriologist; M.B., C.M. Edinburgh University, 1883; M.D., 1886; B.Sc. in hygiene, 1888; lecturer on bacteriology at College of State Medicine, subsequently amalgamated with Lister Institute, from 1889; director, 1891; secretary, 1903; planned and organized Lister Institute; Fullerian professor of physiology at Royal Institution, 1901–4; lectures published as 'The Cell as the Unit of Life,' posthumous, 1908.

MACFARREN, WALTER CECIL (1826–1905), pianist and composer; brother of Sir George A. Macfarren [q.v.]; studied at Royal Academy of Music; sub-professor of pianoforte there from 1846; composed pianoforte pieces in style of Mendelssohn, vocal works, church services, and overtures; published 'Scale and Arpeggio Manual,' 1882, and autobiographical 'Memories,' 1905.

MACGREGOR, JAMES (1832–1910), moderator of the general assembly of the church of Scotland, 1891; student at St. Andrews University, 1848–55; hon. D.D., 1870; served churches at Paisley, Glasgow, and Edinburgh; first minister of St. Cuthbert's, Edinburgh, 1873–1910; a fervent and popular preacher; visited Canada, 1881, and Australia, 1889.

MacGREGOR, Sir WILLIAM (1846–1919), colonial governor; M.D., Aberdeen, 1874; chief medical officer for Fiji, 1875; first administrator (styled lieutenant-governor, 1895) of British New Guinea, 1888; promoted policy of peaceful penetration and exploration; governor of Lagos, 1899, where he carried on campaign against malaria, 1899; governor of Newfoundland, 1904; organized and conducted important scientific expedition to Labrador; governor of Queensland, 1909–14; K.C.M.G., 1889; G.C.M.G., 1907; P.C., 1914.

MACHELL, JAMES OCTAVIUS (1837–1902), owner and manager of racehorses; joined army, 1854; retired as captain, 1863; won Derby with Hermit, 1867; superintended training of Isinglass [see McCALMONT, HARRY] and of many other winning horses; his own horses won 540 races, 1864–1902; a good athlete.

MACHRAY, ROBERT (1831–1904), archbishop of Rupert's Land; of presbyterian parentage; M.A. Aberdeen, 1851; B.A., Sidney Sussex College, Cambridge, 1855; M.A., 1858; vicar of Madingley, 1862–5; bishop of Rupert's Land, 1865; reorganized St. John's College, Winnipeg; chancellor of Manitoba University, 1877–1904; subdivided diocese into eight sees; metropolitan of Canada, 1875; archbishop of Rupert's Land and primate of all Canada, 1893; received honorary degrees from Manitoba, Cambridge, Durham, and Aberdeen; 'Life' by Robert Machray, 1909.

MACINTYRE, DONALD (1831–1903), major-general, Bengal staff corps; won V.C. for gallantry in Lushai expedition, 1871–2; commanded 2nd Prince of Wales's Own Ghurkhas with Khyber column in Afghan war, 1878–9, and in Bazar valley expeditions; major-general, 1880; published account of travel and sport in Himalayas, 1889.

MACKAY, ÆNEAS JAMES GEORGE (1839–1911), legal and historical writer; B.A., University College, Oxford, 1862; M.A., 1865; admitted to Scottish bar, 1864; professor of constitutional law, Edinburgh University, 1874; advocate depute, 1881; sheriff principal of Fife and Kinross, 1886–1901; LL.D. Edinburgh, 1882; works include 'The Practice of the Court of Session,' 2 vols. 1877–9, 'William Dunbar,' 1889, and 'A History of Fife and Kinross,' 1896.

MACKAY, ALEXANDER (1833–1902), promoter of education in Scotland; M.A. St. Andrews; LL.D., 1891; developed educational methods and organization as schoolmaster at Torryburn; editor of 'Educational News,' 1878; president of Educational Institute of Scotland, 1881; member of Edinburgh school board, 1897; published educational works.

MACKAY, DONALD JAMES, eleventh BARON REAY (1839–1921), governor of Bombay (1885–90), and first president of British Academy (1901–7); born at The Hague; educated at Leyden; entered Dutch Foreign Office; settled in England, 1875; naturalized, 1877; created baron of United Kingdom, 1881; under-secretary of state for India, 1894–5; interested in international law and politics.

MACKENNAL, ALEXANDER (1835–1904), congregational divine; student at Glasgow University, 1851–4; hon. D.D., 1887; B.A. London, 1857; minister at Bowdon, Cheshire, 1877 to death; chairman of congregational union, 1887; frequently visited America from 1889; advocated co-operative union of churches; secretary (1892-8) and president (1899) of National Free Church Council; published many theological works, and life of J. A. Macfadyen, D.D., 1891; 'Life' by D. Macfadyen, 1905.

MACKENZIE, Sir ALEXANDER (1842–1902), lieutenant-governor of Bengal; joined Indian civil service, 1862; under-secretary to local government, Bengal, 1866; home secretary to government of India, 1882; helped to shape Bengal Tenancy Act of 1885; C.S.I., 1886; chief commissioner of Central Provinces, 1887–90, and of Burma, 1890–5; K.C.S.I., 1891; suppressed hill tribe raids and restored order, 1892; lieutenant-governor of Bengal, 1895–8; made sanitary survey of Calcutta; enlarged powers of Bengal municipalities; co-operated with Assam in Lushai expedition of 1895–6; expedited land settlement operations in Behar and Orissa; dealt efficiently with the famine of 1896–7 and the plague; published 'History of the Relations of Government with the Hill Tribes of the North-East Frontier of Bengal,' 1884.

MACKENZIE, Sir GEORGE SUTHERLAND (1844–1910), explorer and administrator; born at Bolarum, India; as representative of a London firm of East India merchants (1866) opened up trade route through Persian interior from Persian Gulf; pioneer explorer of Persian interior; managing director of Imperial British East Africa Company, 1888; developed East Africa, and explored interior as far as Uganda; C.B., 1897; K.C.M.G., 1902.

M'KENZIE, Sir JOHN (1836–1901), minister of lands in New Zealand; emigrated from Ross-shire to New Zealand, 1860; minister of lands and immigration, 1881–1900; successfully purchased and divided large estates among small farmers; passed Lands for Settlement Act, 1894; member of legislative council and K.C.M.G., 1901.

MACKENZIE, Sir STEPHEN (1844–1909), physician; brother of Sir Morell Mackenzie [q. v.]; student at London Hospital, 1866; M.R.C.S., 1869; M.B. Aberdeen, 1873; M.D., 1875; F.R.C.P., 1879; physician at London Hospital, 1886, and at London Ophthalmic Hospital, 1884; made original researches into skin diseases and ophthalmology; knighted, 1903.

MACKINLAY, ANTOINETTE (1850–1904), contralto singer. [See STERLING.]

MACKINTOSH, JOHN (1833–1907), Scottish historian; published 'History of Civilization in Scotland,' 4 vols. 1878–88; LL.D. Aberdeen, 1880.

McLACHLAN, ROBERT (1837–1904), entomologist; published 'Catalogue of British Neuroptera,' 1870, and 'Synopsis of the Trichoptera of the European Fauna,' 1874–84; F.R.S., 1877; president of Entomological Society, 1885–6, and editor from 1864 and proprietor (1902) of 'Entomological Monthly Magazine.'

MACLAGAN, CHRISTIAN (1811–1901), Scottish archaeologist; devoted time and money to removal of slums in Stirling; made valuable researches into and published works on prehistoric remains in Scotland; prepared skilful rubbings from sculptured stones; lady associate of Scottish Society of Antiquaries, 1871.

MACLAGAN, WILLIAM DALRYMPLE (1826–1910), successively bishop of Lichfield and archbishop of York; studied law at Edinburgh University; an officer in Madras cavalry, 1847–9; B.A., Peterhouse, Cambridge, 1857; ordained, 1856, serving curacies in London until 1869; rector of Newington, 1869–75; of St. Mary Abbots, Kensington, 1875–8; bishop of Lichfield, 1878–91; interested in unity of Christendom; attended conference of Old Catholics at Bonn, 1887; archbishop of York, 1891–1908; established training college for clergy at York, 1892; discouraged advanced ritual; inaugurated Poor Benefices Fund; responsible with Archbishop Temple for reply to Pope Leo XIII's Bull denying validity of Anglican orders, 1896; crowned Queen Alexandra, 1902; resigned archbishopric, 1908; published small volume of poems, 1855; composed hymns (including 'The Saints of God') and hymn tunes; portrait by the Hon. John Collier at Peterhouse, Cambridge; 'Life' by F. D. How, 1911.

MACLAREN, ALEXANDER (1826–1910), baptist divine; student at Glasgow University; B.A. London, 1845; successful minister at Southampton, 1846–58, and Union Chapel, Manchester, 1858–1903; rebuilt Union Chapel (1869) and added schools (1880); built new churches and missions in poor districts; exerted great influence as preacher of sermons showing both literary and exegetical skill; president of Baptist Union, 1875 and 1901, and of Baptist World Congress in London, 1905; hon. D.D. Edinburgh, 1877; Glasgow, 1907; Litt.D. Manchester, 1902; visited Australia, 1883, and Italy, 1865 and 1903; published devotional works and scripture expositions; edited in 'Expositor's Bible' Colossians and Ephesians, 1887, and 'The Psalms,' 3 vols. 1893–4; 'Lives' by J. C. Carlisle, 1901, D. Williamson, 1910, and E. T. McLaren, 1911.

MACLAREN, IAN (pseudonym) (1851–1907), presbyterian divine and author. [See WATSON, JOHN.]

McLAREN, JOHN, LORD MCLAREN (1831–1910), Scottish judge; son of Duncan McLaren [q. v.]; passed to Scottish bar, 1856; reorganized Scottish liberals and arranged Gladstone's 'Midlothian campaign,' 1879–80; M.P. for Wigton, 1880; appointed lord advocate (April), losing seat on seeking re-election; elected for Edinburgh, Jan. 1881; accepted under pressure from Gladstone and Sir William Harcourt Scottish judgeship, 1881; an eminently successful judge; edited works on Scottish law; a student of astronomy and mathematics; hon. LL.D. Edinburgh, 1882, Glasgow, 1883, and Aberdeen, 1906.

MACLEAN, Sir HARRY AUBREY DE VERE (1848–1920); served in army, 1869–1876; kaid of infantry and instructor to forces attached to court of sultans of Morocco, 1877–1909; C.M.G., for services rendered to British legation at Tangier, 1898; K.C.M.G., 1901; kidnapped and held to ransom by rebel sherif, Raisuli, 1907; died at Tangier.

MACLEAN, JAMES MACKENZIE (1835–1906), journalist and politician; educated at Christ's Hospital; edited 'Newcastle Chronicle,' 1855–8; a leader-writer for 'Manchester Guardian,' 1859; edited 'Bombay

Gazette,' 1859–61; proprietor from 1864; an independent critic both of Indian aspirations and of Indian government; greatly influenced public opinion in Bombay; appointed a magistrate, 1862; helped in creation of semi-elective municipal corporations, 1872; welcomed Prince of Wales to Bombay, 1875; returned home, 1879; had interest in and regularly contributed to 'Western Mail,' Cardiff, from 1882; supporter of Lord Randolph Churchill; conservative M.P. for Oldham, 1885–92, and for Cardiff, 1895–1900; opposed South African war, 1899; supported free trade, 1903; broke with conservative party, and wrote for liberal journals; published 'Recollections of Westminster and India,' 1902.

MACLEAR, GEORGE FREDERICK (1833–1902), theological writer; B.A., Trinity College, Cambridge, 1855; first class in theological tripos, 1856; M.A., 1860; D.D., 1872; reader at the Temple, 1865–70; assistant (1860–6) and head master (1867–80) at King's College School, London; warden of St. Augustine's Missionary College, Canterbury, 1880–1902; hon. canon of Canterbury Cathedral, 1885; works include lucid text-books on Bible history, 1862, and 'The Conversion of the West', 4 vols. 1878.

MACLEAR, JOHN FIOT LEE PEARSE (1838–1907), admiral; son of Sir Thomas Maclear [q. v.]; born at Cape Town; entered navy, 1851; commander, 1868; went as commander of 'Challenger' with Sir George Nares [q. v.] on a voyage of discovery round the world, 1872–6; surveyed straits of Magellan in 'Alert,' 1879–82; on surveying service, 1883; admiral, 1907; died at Niagara.

MACLEOD, FIONA (pseudonym) (1856–1905), romanticist. [See SHARP, WILLIAM.]

MACLEOD, HENRY DUNNING (1821–1902), economist; B.A., Trinity College, Cambridge, 1843; M.A., 1863; called to bar, 1849; published 'The Theory and Practice of Banking,' 1856; lectured on banking at Cambridge, London, Edinburgh, and Aberdeen, 1877–82; made valuable contributions to historical side of economic science; in 'Elements of Political Economy' (1858) first applied term 'Gresham's Law' to principle that 'bad money drives out good'; awarded civil list pension, 1892; also wrote 'The Theory of Credit,' 2 vols. 1889–91, and 'The History of Banking in Great Britain,' 1896.

MACLURE, EDWARD CRAIG (1833–1906), dean of Manchester; B.A., Brasenose College, Oxford, 1856; M.A., 1858; D.D., 1890; vicar of Rochdale, 1877–90; dean of Manchester, 1890–1906; chairman of Manchester school board, 1891–1903; member of royal commission on secondary education, 1894; hon. LL.D. Victoria University, Manchester, 1902.

MACLURE, Sir JOHN WILLIAM, first baronet (1835–1901), brother of E. C. Maclure [q. v.]; secretary of Lancashire cotton relief fund, 1862; conservative M.P. for Stretford, 1886–1901; baronet, 1898.

McMAHON, CHARLES ALEXANDER (1830–1904), general and geologist; joined Indian army, 1847; commanded troops in Sialkot district during Indian Mutiny; Punjab commissioner, 1872–85; lieutenant-general, 1892; edited 'Records of Geological Survey of India,' vol. x. 1877; pioneer in study of petrology and in metamorphism and foliation of rocks; F.G.S., 1878; Lyell medallist, 1899; F.R.S., 1898.

MACMILLAN, HUGH (1833–1903), religious writer; free church minister at Glasgow (1864–78) and Greenock (1878–1901); made wide fame through 'Bible Teachings in Nature,' 1867, and 'The Ministry of Nature,' 1871; hon. LL.D. St. Andrews, 1871; hon. D.D. Edinburgh, 1879, and Glasgow; F.R.S. Edinburgh, and F.S.A. Scotland; Cunningham (1894) and Gunning (1897) lecturer at Edinburgh; moderator of general assembly of Free Church, 1897; voluminous author of works mainly dealing with relations of religion and science.

MACNAGHTEN, Sir EDWARD, fourth baronet, and BARON MACNAGHTEN, of Runkerry (1830–1913), judge; educated at Trinity College, Dublin, and Trinity College, Cambridge; bracketed senior classic, 1852; fellow of Trinity, Cambridge, 1853; called to bar (Lincoln's Inn), 1857; equity junior, 1857–80; Q.C., 1880; conservative M.P., co. Antrim, 1880, North Antrim, 1885; lord of appeal in ordinary, 1887; G.C.M.G., 1903; G.C.B., and succeeded brother in baronetcy, 1911; took active part both in Commons and Lords in debates on Irish questions; as judge possessed remarkable power of combining learning, style, and humour.

McNAIR, JOHN FREDERICK ADOLPHUS (1828–1910), colonial official; joined Madras artillery, 1845;

at Singapore efficient superintendent of convicts, 1858; controller of convicts (1867), colonial secretary (1868), member of the executive council of Straits Settlements (from 1869) and surveyor-general (from 1873); lieutenant-governor of Penang, 1881–4; chief commissioner in Pêrak, 1875–6; C.M.G., 1878; wrote accounts of Pêrak (1878) and Singapore convict prison (1899).

McNEILL, SIR JOHN CARSTAIRS (1831–1904), major-general; joined Bengal native infantry, 1850; served with distinction at Lucknow, 1857–8; won V.C. in Maori war, 1864; on staff of Red River expedition, 1870; C.M.G., 1876; chief of staff in Ashanti war, 1873–4; C.B., 1874; K.C.M.G., 1880; major-general and K.C.B., 1882; commanded second infantry brigade in Sudan campaign, 1885; criticized for lack of caution; retired, 1890; G.C.V.O., 1901.

MACPHERSON, SIR JOHN MOLESWORTH (1853–1914), Anglo-Indian legislative draftsman; son of John Macpherson, M.D. [q. v.]; born in Calcutta; called to English bar, 1876; deputy secretary to Indian government in legislative department, 1877; permanent secretary, 1896–1911; knighted, 1911.

McQUEEN, SIR JOHN WITHERS (1836–1909), major-general; born in Calcutta; joined 27th Bengal native infantry, 1854; recommended for V.C. for bravery at the Secundarabagh, 1857; commanded 5th Punjab rifles in Jowaki expedition, 1877–8; of great service in Afghan war, 1878–80; C.B., 1879; brigadier-general in command of Hyderabad contingent, 1885; commanded expedition against Black Mountain tribes, 1888; K.C.B., 1890; major-general, 1891; G.C.B., 1907.

MACRORIE, WILLIAM KENNETH (1831–1905), bishop of Maritzburg; B.A., Brasenose College, Oxford, 1852; M.A., 1855; consecrated by Bishop Gray of Cape Town bishop of Maritzburg in Natal in opposition to Bishop Colenso, 1869; an uncompromising high churchman; resigned bishopric, 1891; canon of Ely and assistant bishop, 1892.

McTAGGART, WILLIAM (1835–1910), artist; fellow student at Trustees' Academy, Edinburgh, with W. Q. Orchardson, Tom Graham, and John MacWhirter; A.R.S.A., 1859; R.S.A., 1870; exhibited at Royal Academy, 1866–75; vice-president of the Royal Scottish Water Colour Society, 1878; early engaged in portraiture, genre pictures, and land- and sea-scape; later confined his work to land- and sea-scape.

MACWHIRTER, JOHN (1839–1911), landscape painter; fellow student with William McTaggart [q. v.] at Trustees' Academy, Edinburgh; made direct study of nature; annually visited Continent; A.R.S.A., 1867; removed to London, 1869; A.R.A., 1879; hon. R.S.A., 1892; R.A., 1893; published 'Landscape Painting in Water Colours,' 1901; painted popular landscapes and studies of trees; his best-known work, 'June in the Austrian Tyrol,' in Tate gallery.

MADDEN, FREDERIC WILLIAM (1839–1904), numismatist; assistant in coin department of British Museum, 1859–68; chief librarian at Brighton public library, 1888–1902; published 'The Coins of the Jews,' 1881, and a manual of Roman coins, 1861.

MADDEN, KATHERINE CECIL (1875–1911), novelist. [See THURSTON.]

MADDEN, THOMAS MORE (1844–1902), Irish gynaecologist; M.R.C.S., 1862; raised Irish ambulance corps in Franco-Prussian war, 1870; master of the National Lying-in Hospital, Dublin, 1878; F.R.C.S. Edinburgh, 1882; recognized as a foremost gynaecologist; voluminous writings include 'Uterine Tumours,' 1887, 'Clinical Gynaecology,' 1893, and accounts of his family.

MAHAFFY, SIR JOHN PENTLAND (1839–1919), provost of Trinity College, Dublin; born in Switzerland; B.A., Trinity College, Dublin (first senior moderator in classics and logics), 1859; fellow, and ordained, 1864; first professor of ancient history at Dublin, 1869; provost of Trinity, 1914–19; G.B.E., 1918; reputation chiefly rests on works dealing with life, literature, and history of ancient Greeks; these include 'Prolegomena to Ancient History' (1871), 'Greek Social Life from Homer to Menander' (1874), 'History of Classical Greek Literature' (1880), 'Story of Alexander's Empire' (1887), 'Greek Life and Thought from Alexander to the Roman Conquest' (1887), 'The Greek World under Roman Sway' (1890), and 'Problems in Greek History' (1892); turned his attention to papyri, 1890; produced 'Flinders Petrie Papyri' (1891 etc.) and 'The Empire of the Ptolemies' (1895); a remarkably versatile writer of great shrewdness and sagacity.

MAIR, WILLIAM (1830–1920), Scottish divine; served ministries in Established Church, 1861–1903; moderator of General Assembly, 1897; pioneer in cause of church reunion and authority on Scottish ecclesiastical law.

MAITLAND, AGNES CATHERINE (1850–1906), principal of Somerville College, Oxford; early became authority on domestic economy; published 'The Rudiments of Cookery' (35th thousand, 1910) and other cookery books and novels; principal of Somerville College, Oxford, 1889–1906; largely increased numbers and extended buildings; developed tutorial system, and erected college library.

MAITLAND, FREDERIC WILLIAM (1850–1906), Downing professor of the laws of England at Cambridge; son of John Gorham Maitland [q.v.]; educated at Eton and Trinity College, Cambridge; senior in moral science tripos, 1872; Whewell international law scholar, 1873; president of Union; obtained 'blue' for running; B.A., 1873; M.A., 1876; hon. LL.D., 1891; called to bar, 1876; reader in English law at Cambridge, 1884; Downing professor, 1888–1906; founded Selden Society for encouraging study of history of English law, editing several volumes, 1887; literary director, 1895; published 'Bracton's Note-Book,' 3 vols. 1887, and 'History of English Law before the time of Edward I' (with Sir Frederick Pollock, 2 vols. 1895); traced Roman influence in English law in thirteenth century in 'Bracton and Azo,' Selden Soc., 1895, and in 'Roman Canon Law in the Church of England,' 1898; made researches into legal effect of the Reformation; edited and translated MSS. of Year Books in old legal Anglo-French, temp. Edward II, 4 vols. 1903–7; advocated simplification and codification of English law; ar lent alpinist; Ford lecturer, Oxford, 1897; Rede lecturer, Cambridge, 1901; D.C.L. Oxford, 1899; LL.D. Glasgow, Cracow, and Moscow; original F.B.A., 1902; hon. fellow, Trinity College, Cambridge; died at Las Palmas; other publications include 'Life and Letters of Leslie Stephen,' 1906, and posthumously 'The Constitutional History of England,' 1908, and 'Collected Works,' 1911.

MALET, SIR EDWARD BALDWIN, fourth baronet (1837–1908), diplomatist; born at the Hague; son of Sir Alexander Malet, second baronet [q. v.]; attaché to his father at Frankfort, 1854; served under Lord Lyons at Washington, 1862–5, and Paris, 1867–71; negotiated meeting of Jules Favre and Bismarck at Ferrières, 1870; in charge of embassy at Paris, March–June 1871; C.B., 1871; secretary of legation at Peking, 1871, Rome 1875, and Constantinople, 1878; British agent and consul-general in Egypt, 1879–83; K.C.B., 1881; helped to restore financial stability and soothe native unrest in Egypt; reconstituted government machinery, and developed scheme of reorganization, 1882–3; British envoy at Brussels, 1883, and Berlin, 1884–95, where he settled rival British and German claims in the Congo and in Samoa; P.C. and G.C.M.G., 1885; G.C.B., 1886; a British member of the international court of arbitration at the Hague, 1899; succeeded brother, 1904; author of 'Shifting Scenes,' 1901, and an unfinished memoir of his service in Egypt, posthumous, 1909.

MALONE, SYLVESTER (1822–1906), Irish ecclesiastical historian; vicar-general of Kilrush, 1872–1906; canon and archdeacon; made valuable researches in his 'Church History of Ireland, 1169–1532,' 1867; promoter of preservation of Irish language.

MANLEY, WILLIAM GEORGE NICHOLAS (1831–1901), surgeon-general; M.R.C.S., 1851; joined army medical staff, 1855; present at Sevastopol; won V.C. in New Zealand war, 1863–6; in charge of division of British ambulance corps in Franco-Prussian war, 1870; at siege of Paris, 1870; in Afghan war, 1878–9; principal medical officer in Egyptian war, 1882; surgeon-general, 1884; C.B., 1894.

MANNERS, (LORD) JOHN JAMES ROBERT, seventh DUKE OF RUTLAND (1818–1906), politician; brother of sixth duke [q.v.]; M.A., Trinity College, Cambridge, 1839; published verse account of foreign travel in 1839–40, 'England's Trust and other Poems,' 1841 (containing a couplet on English nobility which obtained permanent currency); 'English Ballads and other Poems,' 1850, and notes of Irish and Scotch tours, 1848–9; conservative M.P. for Newark, 1841–7; under Disraeli's influence joined 'Young England Party'; freely criticized Peel's administration, 1843–4; advocated public holidays, 1843, factory reform, 1844, and a general system of allotments; with Disraeli and George Smythe toured through industrial districts of Lancashire, 1844; figures in 'Coningsby,' 1844, 'Sybil,' 1845, and 'Endymion,' 1880; advocated disestablishment of the Irish Church and supported proposed grant to Maynooth, 1845; differences of opinion on religious and free trade questions led to dissolution of 'Young England Party,' 1847; unsuccessfully contested as protectionist, Liverpool, 1847, and City of London, 1849; conservative member for Colchester, 1850–7, North Leicestershire, 1857–85, and Melton, 1885–8; P.C., 1852; first commissioner of works, and cabinet minister, Feb.–Dec. 1852, 1858–9, and 1866–8; accepted Disraeli's reform bill of 1867; postmaster-general, 1874–80 and 1885–6; reduced minimum telegram charge to sixpence, Oct. 1885; opposed extension of franchise without redistribution, 1884–5; chancellor of Duchy of Lancaster, 1886–92; succeeded to dukedom, 1888; K.G., 1891; made Baron Roos of Belvoir, 1896; LL.D. Cambridge, 1862; D.C.L. Oxford, 1876; G.C.B., 1880.

MANNING, JOHN EDMONDSON (1848–1910), Unitarian divine; B.A. London, 1872; M.A., 1876; minister at Upper Chapel, Sheffield, 1889–1902, of which he wrote a history, 1900; tutor at Unitarian home missionary college, Manchester.

MANNS, SIR AUGUST (1825–1907), conductor of the Crystal Palace concerts from 1855 to 1901; born at Stolzenburg, Pomerania; bandmaster in Von Roon's regiment at Koenigsberg, 1851; came to England, 1854; transformed wind band at Crystal Palace into full orchestra; conducted Saturday concerts there for forty years; introduced works by Schumann, Schubert, and Brahms; frequently (from 1861) devoted programme to living English composers; conducted Handel triennial festivals, 1883–1900.

MANSEL-PLEYDELL, JOHN CLAVELL (1817–1902), Dorset antiquary; B.A., St. John's College, Cambridge, 1839; built Milborne Reformatory, 1856; founded Dorset Natural History Club, 1875; made valuable geological finds in Dorsetshire; published the 'Flora,' 1874, 'Birds,' 1888, and 'Mollusca,' 1898, of Dorsetshire.

MANSERGH, JAMES (1834–1905), civil engineer; worked in Brazil, 1855–9; practised at Westminster from 1866 till death; specialized in water and sewage works; constructed reservoirs and aqueduct from valleys of Elan and Cherwen rivers to Birmingham, 1894–1904; carried out sewage disposal for several midland towns; prepared schemes for sewerage of Lower Thames valley; on royal commission on metropolitan water supply, 1892–3; F.R.S., 1901; president of Institution of Civil Engineers, 1900–1.

MANSFIELD, ROBERT BLACHFORD (1824–1908), author and oarsman; brother of Charles Blachford Mansfield [q.v.]; educated at Eton and University College, Oxford; B.A., 1846; called to bar, 1849; pioneer of English golf, 1857; rowed in university boatrace, 1843; pioneer of English rowing in Germany; recorded his German experiences in 'The Log of the Water Lily,' 1851, and 'The Water-Lily on the Danube,' 1852.

MAPLE, SIR JOHN BLUNDELL, baronet (1845–1903), merchant and sportsman; joined (1862) father's furnishing firm in Tottenham Court Road, which was converted into limited liability company, with Maple as chairman, 1891; conservative M.P. for Dulwich, 1887–1903; knighted, 1892; baronet, 1897; racehorse breeder and owner; won 544 races; headed list of winning owners, 1891; won Cesarewitch, 1894, and Two Thousand Guineas, 1895; rebuilt University College Hospital, 1897–1906.

MAPLESON, JAMES HENRY (1830–1901), operatic manager; studied violin and pianoforte at Royal Academy of Music, 1844, and singing in Italy; managed Italian opera season from 1858 variously at Drury Lane, Lyceum Theatre, and Covent Garden; produced Gounod's 'Faust,' 1863, and Bizet's 'Carmen,' 1878; from 1878 took touring companies to America in winter; engaged Adelina Patti, 1881–5; his repertory of Italian opera lost vogue from 1887; published 'Memoirs,' 2 vols. 1888.

MAPOTHER, EDWARD DILLON (1835–1908), surgeon; M.D. Queen's University, Dublin, 1857; F.R.C.S. Ireland, 1862; surgeon of St. Vincent's Hospital, Dublin, 1859; professor of hygiene in Royal College of Surgeons, 1864; professor of anatomy and physiology, 1867; president, 1879; first medical officer of health for Dublin; wrote much on diseases of the skin and public health.

MAPPIN, SIR FREDERICK THORPE, first baronet (1821–1910), benefactor to Sheffield; head of father's cutlery business, 1841–59; senior partner in firm of

Turton & Sons, steel manufacturers, 1859–85; mayor of Sheffield, 1877–8; a founder and benefactor of Sheffield Technical School; largely endowed Sheffield University; first senior pro-chancellor, 1905; director of Midland Railway, 1869–1900; enthusiastic Volunteer; whig M.P. for East Retford, 1880–5, and for Hallamshire, 1885–1906; baronet, 1886; added 80 pictures to Mappin Art Gallery, founded by uncle; first hon. freeman of Sheffield, 1900.

MARJORIBANKS, EDWARD, second BARON TWEEDMOUTH (1849–1909), politician; educated at Harrow and Christ Church, Oxford; a keen sportsman through life; toured round world, 1872–3; abandoned law for politics; liberal M.P. for North Berwickshire, 1880–94; comptroller of Queen Victoria's household and P.C., 1886; parliamentary secretary to the treasury and chief liberal whip under Gladstone, 1892; succeeded to peerage, 1894; joined Lord Rosebery's cabinet as lord privy seal and chancellor of the Duchy of Lancaster, 1894–5; married (1873) Lady Fanny (d. 1904), sister of Lord Randolph Churchill, a successful society and political hostess; suffered financial losses, 1904; first lord of the admiralty in Campbell-Bannerman's ministry, 1905–8; maintained policy of England's naval supremacy; incurred public censure for alleged premature disclosure of naval estimates to German Emperor, 1908; K.T., 1908; lord president of council under Mr. Asquith, 1908; died of cerebral malady.

MARKHAM, SIR ALBERT HASTINGS (1841–1918), admiral and Arctic explorer; entered navy, 1856; commanded 'Alert' in Arctic expedition of Sir G. S. Nares [q.v.], 1875–6; record of latitude reached without dogs not beaten till 1895; rear-admiral, 1891; K.C.B., 1903.

MARKHAM, SIR CLEMENTS ROBERT (1830–1916), geographer and historical writer; grandson of William Markham [q.v.], archbishop of York; served in navy, 1844–51; entered civil service, 1853; in charge of geographical work of India Office, 1867–77; C.B., 1871; F.R.S., 1873; accompanied Arctic expedition of Sir G. S. Nares [q.v.], 1875; president of Hakluyt Society, 1889–1909, and of Royal Geographical Society, 1893–1905; K.C.B., 1896; promoted Antarctic exploration.

MARKS, DAVID WOOLF (1811–1909), Goldsmid professor of Hebrew at University College, London, from 1844 to 1898; secretary to the Hebrew congregation at Liverpool, 1833; first minister with Albert Löwy [q.v.] of newly-established West London congregation, 1842–95; prepared reformed Prayer-book, and obtained licence for marriages, 1857; hon. D.D. Cincinnati; published lectures on Mosaic law.

MARRIOTT, SIR WILLIAM THACKERAY (1834–1903), judge-advocate-general; B.A., St. John's College, Cambridge, 1858; curate of St. George's, Hulme, 1858; renounced orders, 1861; called to bar, 1864; acquired lucrative practice in railway and compensation cases; Q.C., 1877; liberal M.P. for Brighton, 1880–4; re-elected for Brighton as conservative, 1884–93; P.C., 1885; judge advocate-general, 1885–92; knighted, 1888; chancellor of Primrose League, 1892; counsel for ex-Khedive Ismail Pasha in claims against Egyptian government, 1887–8; made unsuccessful financial speculations; died at Aix la Chapelle.

MARSDEN, ALEXANDER EDWIN (1832–1902), surgeon; son of William Marsden [q.v.]; M.R.C.S., 1854; M.D. St. Andrews, 1862; F.R.C.S. Edinburgh, 1868; served as surgeon at Scutari and Sevastopol; surgeon to Royal Free Hospital, 1853–84, and to Brompton Cancer Hospital; published works on cancer.

MARSHALL, GEORGE WILLIAM (1839–1905), genealogist; B.A., Peterhouse, Cambridge; LL.M., 1864; LL.D., 1874; called to bar, 1865; founded 'The Genealogist,' 1877; works include 'The Genealogist's Guide,' 1879, and 'Handbook to the Ancient Courts of Probate,' 1889; F.S.A., 1872; helped to found Parish Register Society, 1896; Rouge Croix pursuivant of arms, 1887; York Herald, 1904; made for College of Arms unique collection of parish registers.

MARSHALL, JULIAN (1836–1903), art collector and author; in family flax-spinning business at Leeds, 1855–61; formed collection of engravings embracing leading works of ancient and modern schools, 1861, of musical autographs, and of book plates; contributed to Grove's 'Dictionary of Music'; wrote 'Annals of Tennis,' 1878, and other kindred works.

MARTIN, SIR THEODORE (1816–1909), man of letters; educated at Edinburgh High School and University, 1830–3; hon. LL.D., 1875; practised as solicitor in Edinburgh until 1846, when he migrated to London to become parliamentary agent; his parliamentary work the main occupation of his life; contributed before leaving Edinburgh humorous prose and verse to 'Tait's' and 'Fraser's' magazines under pseudonym of Bon Gaultier; soon collaborated with William Edmondstone Aytoun [q.v.]; together they published 'Bon Gaultier Ballads' (1845, 16th edit., 1903), a notable collection of witty parodies; devoted to the drama, was fascinated by the acting of Helen Faucit [q. v.], for whom he adapted from the Danish 'King René's Daughter,' 1849; married Miss Faucit at Brighton, 1851, and settled for life at 31 Onslow Square, Kensington; acquired in 1861 country residence Bryntysilio; wrote on dramatic themes in 'Fraser's Magazine,' 1858–65, the 'Quarterly Review,' and 'Blackwood'; translated Oehlenschläger's German romantic dramas, 'Aladdin,' 1854, and 'Correggio,' 1857, the works of Horace (1860, '82) and of Catullus (1861), Dante's 'Vita Nuova,' 1862, Goethe's 'Faust' (pt. i. 1865, pt. ii. 1866), poems and ballads of Heine, 1878, and the 'Aeneid,' i.–vi. 1896; on recommendation of his friend Sir Arthur Helps, Martin prepared for Queen Victoria, a life of Prince Consort, 5 vols. 1875–80; C.B., 1878; K.C.B., 1880; K.C.V.O., 1896; wrote life of Lord Lyndhurst, 1883; lord rector of St. Andrews University, 1881; privately circulated 'Queen Victoria as I knew her,' 1901 (published, 1908); a trustee of Shakespeare's birthplace from 1889 till death, and an active member of the Royal Literary Fund from 1868.

MARTIN, SIR THOMAS ACQUIN (1850–1906), industrial pioneer in India and agent-general for Afghanistan; founded engineering firm in Calcutta, which took over Bengal Iron and Steel Company (1889) and worked iron deposits at Manharpur; pioneer of light railways in India; built many jute mills and controlled large collieries and engineered water supplies in Bengal; appointed agent to Ameer of Afghanistan (1887), for whom he built an arsenal, a mint, and various factories; accompanied Ameer's son to England on diplomatic mission, and knighted, 1895.

MARTIN, VIOLET FLORENCE (1862–1915), novelist under the pseudonym of MARTIN ROSS; member of ancient Galway family; wrote books in collaboration with her cousin, Miss E. Œ. Somerville, describing Anglo-Irish life; best-known novels, 'The Real Charlotte' (1894) and 'The Irish R.M.' series (begun 1899).

MARWICK, SIR JAMES DAVID (1826–1908), legal and historical writer; founded legal firm of Watt & Marwick in Edinburgh, 1855; town clerk of Edinburgh, 1860–73, and of Glasgow, 1873–1903; extended city of Glasgow by annexing fourteen surburban burghs, 1881–91; F.R.S. Edinburgh, 1884; hon. LL.D., Glasgow, 1878; knighted, 1888; helped to found Scottish Burgh Record Society, Edinburgh, editing its publications from 1868 to 1897.

MASHAM, first BARON (1815–1906), inventor. [See LISTER, SAMUEL CUNLIFFE.]

MASKELYNE, MERVYN HERBERT NEVIL STORY– (1823–1911), mineralogist. [See STORY-MASKELYNE.]

MASSEY, GERALD (1828–1907), poet; after scanty education was put to work at Tring at age of eight; studied for himself; published at Tring 'Poems and Chansons,' 1848; joined Chartists; helped to edit 'The Spirit of Freedom,' 1849; soon turned to Christian socialism; wrote for the 'Christian Socialist'; brought out 'Voices of Freedom and Lyrics of Love' 1850, and 'The Ballad of Babe Christabel and other Poems,' 1854; his lyrical impulse was widely acknowledged; other volumes of verse followed; complete poetical works, Boston, 1857, London, 1861; a selection, 'My Lyrical Life,' appeared in 1899; his career suggested that of Felix Holt to George Eliot; he became a journalist and popular lecturer, living for a time at Edinburgh, and from 1862 to 1877 near Little Gaddesden in a farmhouse provided by Lord Brownlow; wrote on Shakespeare's Sonnets, 1866 (reissued, 1888); thrice lectured in America; developed faith in spiritualism and finally took to writing on old Egyptian civilization.

MASSON, DAVID (1822–1907), biographer and editor; M.A. Aberdeen University, 1839; studied divinity at Edinburgh, 1839–42, but abandoned thoughts of entering ministry; visited London, 1843; introduced by Thomas Carlyle to editor of 'Fraser's Magazine,' 1844; wrote for W. & R. Chambers text-books on Roman, ancient, medieval, and modern history, 1847–56; removed to London, 1847; intimate with the Carlyles, Thackeray, Douglas Jerrold, and Mark Lemon; professor

of English literature at University College, London, 1853–65; published 'Essays, chiefly on English Poets,' 1859; started (1859) 'Life of Milton' (6 vols., 1859–80), the standard authority; started, 1859, and edited till 1867, 'Macmillan's Magazine'; professor of rhetoric and English literature at Edinburgh University, 1865–95; a popular teacher; supporter of women's higher education; edited 'Privy Council Register of Scotland,' 1880–99; Rhind lecturer, 1886; historiographer royal for Scotland, 1896; hon. R.S.A., 1896; hon. LL.D. Aberdeen; Litt.D. Dublin; voluminous writings include editions of Goldsmith (1869), Milton (3 vols. 1874), and De Quincey (14 vols. 1889–90); biographies of Drummond of Hawthornden, 1873, and De Quincey, 1878; 'Edinburgh Sketches and Memories,' 1892, and (posthumously) 'Memories of London in the Forties,' 1908, and 'Memories of Two Cities,' 1911.

MASSY, WILLIAM GODFREY DUNHAM (1838–1906), lieutenant-general; B.A., Trinity College, Dublin, 1859; LL.D., 1873; entered army, 1854; served at the Redan, where his gallantry earned him the sobriquet of 'Redan' Massy; commanded royal Irish lancers, 1871–9; prominent in battle of Charasiab (Oct. 1879), in Afghan war; cut off by Afghans at Killa Kazi, Dec. 1879; removed from command for rash advance, 1880; C.B., 1887; in command of troops in Ceylon, 1888–93; lieutenant-general, 1893.

MASTERS, MAXWELL TYLDEN (1833–1907), botanist; M.R.C.S., 1856; M.D. St. Andrews, 1862; lecturer on botany at St. George's Hospital medical school, 1855–68; published valuable researches in his 'Vegetable Teratology,' 1869; principal editor of 'Gardeners' Chronicle,' 1865; active supporter of Royal Horticultural Society; wrote much on passion flowers and conifers in botanical works and journals; revised Henfrey's 'Elementary Course of Botany,' 1870, and wrote 'Botany for Beginners,' 1872, and 'Plant Life,' 1883; F.R.S., 1870.

MATHESON, GEORGE (1842–1906), theologian and hymn writer; known as 'the blind preacher'; blind from boyhood; B.A. Glasgow University, 1861; M.A., 1862; minister of Innellan church, 1868–86, and of St. Bernard's parish church, Edinburgh, 1886–99; issued popular theological and devotional works which had a wide vogue; they include 'The Growth of the Spirit of Christianity,' 2 vols. 1877, 'The Psalmist and the Scientist,' 1887, 'Sacred Songs,' 1890 (3rd edit. 1904), and studies of representative men and women of the Bible, 4 ser., 1902–7; D.D. Edinburgh, 1879; LL.D., 1902; F.R.S. Edinburgh, 1902; 'Life' by D. Macmillan, 1907.

MATHEW, SIR JAMES CHARLES (1830–1908), judge; senior moderator, Trinity College, Dublin, 1850; called to bar (Lincoln's Inn), 1851; had vast City practice as a junior; among treasury counsel on prosecution of the Tichborne claimant, 1873; made judge of Queen's Bench division and knighted, 1881; obtained institution of commercial court, 1895; as first judge, gave concise and terse judgments; as chairman of royal commission of inquiry into evictions in Ireland, created precedent of refusing to allow cross-examination by counsel, which led to resignation of many members of commission, 1892; judge of court of appeal, 1901–5; ready, facile, and humorous speaker; an ardent radical and devout Roman Catholic.

MATHEWS, CHARLES EDWARD (1834–1905), Alpine climber and writer; solicitor at Birmingham from 1856; clerk of the peace, 1891–1905; founded Children's Hospital there, 1864; lifelong friend of Chamberlain; helped to found Alpine Club, 1857; president, 1878–80; prominent in conquest of Alps; wrote critical and exhaustive 'Annals of Mont Blanc,' 1898; memorial at Chamonix.

MATHEWS, SIR CHARLES WILLIE, baronet (1850–1920), lawyer; called to bar (Middle Temple), 1872; director of public prosecutions, 1908–20; appeared in criminal trials and sensational civil cases; knighted, 1907; baronet, 1917.

MATHEWS, SIR LLOYD WILLIAM (1850–1901), general and prime minister of Zanzibar; entered navy, 1863; served in Ashanti campaign, 1873–4; retired with rank of lieutenant, 1881; in command of Zanzibar army, with rank of brigadier-general, 1877; obtained abolition of slavery in Zanzibar, 1890; Zanzibar declared British protectorate, 1890; prime minister and treasurer of reconstituted government, 1891; introduced modern agricultural methods; C.M.G., 1880; K.C.M.G., 1894; died at Zanzibar.

MATTHEWS, HENRY, VISCOUNT LLANDAFF (1826–1913), lawyer and politician; son of Henry Matthews [q. v.]; born in Ceylon; educated at universities of Paris and London; called to bar (Lincoln's Inn), 1850; Q.C., 1868; conservative M.P., Dungarvan, 1868–74, East Birmingham, 1886; home secretary, 1886–92; first Roman Catholic since passing of Emancipation Act to become Cabinet minister; created baron, 1895; a founder of Westminster Cathedral.

MATURIN, BASIL WILLIAM (1847–1915), Catholic preacher and writer; B.A., Trinity College, Dublin; ordained, 1870; member of Society of St. John the Evangelist, Cowley, 1873–97; received into Roman Church, 1897; ordained, 1898; torpedoed on 'Lusitania' returning from third visit to America.

MAUDE, SIR (FREDERICK) STANLEY (1864–1917), lieutenant-general; born at Gibraltar; educated at Eton and Sandhurst; joined second Coldstream Guards, 1884; entered Staff College, Camberley, 1895; served in South African war, 1899–1901; D.S.O., 1901; military secretary to Earl of Minto, governor-general of Canada, 1901–5; C.M.G., 1905; held staff appointments in England and Ireland, 1906–14; served in France, August to November 1914; C.B., 1915; major-general and appointed to command thirteenth division at Dardanelles, 1915; took prominent part in evacuation of Suvla and Helles, 1915–16; took division to Mesopotamia, 1916; assumed command of army in Mesopotamia and created K.C.B., 1916; recovered Kut and captured Bagdad, 1917; died of cholera at Bagdad.

MAURICE, SIR JOHN FREDERICK (1841–1912), major-general; son of Frederick Denison Maurice [q. v.]; joined Royal Artillery, 1862; served in War Office and in Ashanti, South Africa, Egypt, and Sudan, 1873–85; professor of military art and history at Staff College, 1885; commanded artillery, Woolwich district, 1895; major-general, 1895; K.C.B., 1900; works include prize essay which greatly influenced army reform; edited first two volumes of official 'History of the War in South Africa, 1899–1902' (1906–1907).

MAWDSLEY, JAMES (1848–1902), trade union leader; secretary of Amalgamated Society of Cotton Spinners, 1878; developed trade union policy in Lancashire; negotiated conciliation scheme—the Brooklands agreement—referring trade disputes to arbitration, 1893; member of royal commission on labour questions, 1891–4.

MAXIM, SIR HIRAM STEVENS (1840–1916), engineer and inventor; born in Maine, U.S.A.; chief engineer to United States Electric Lighting Company, 1878; came to England and opened workshop in London, c. 1882; naturalized, 1900; knighted, 1901; chief inventions electrical pressure regulator (1881), rapid firing gun with completely automatic action (adopted by British army, 1889, and navy, 1892), steam-driven flying-machine (1889–94), and maximite, a smokeless powder (1889).

MAXWELL, MARY ELIZABETH (1837–1915), better known as MISS BRADDON, novelist; sister of Sir Edward N. C. Braddon [q. v.]; her best-known novel, 'Lady Audley's Secret' (1862), had an immediate and very great success and made her fortune; published about eighty novels between 1862 and 1911; also wrote many plays, edited several magazines, and contributed to periodicals; plots of novels concerned with crime, but not a mere sensationalist; married John Maxwell, a publisher, 1874.

MAY, PHILIP WILLIAM [PHIL MAY] (1864–1903), humorous draughtsman; a caricature by him of Irving, Bancroft, and Toole (1883) attracted notice of Lionel Brough, who introduced him to editor of 'Society,' for which he executed drawings; in Australia, 1885–8, contributing to the 'Sydney Bulletin'; studied art in Paris; made sketches for 'St. Stephen's Review'; from 1892 issued 'Phil May's Winter Annual'; made reputation as comic artist of low life in 'Daily Graphic' and other illustrated papers; published 'Phil May's Sketch Book: Fifty Cartoons,' 1895, and his vivid 'Guttersnipes; Fifty Original Sketches,' 1896: member of the 'Punch' table from 1896 to death; a rapid cartoonist of vigour and vivacity; sociable and generous to a fault; mural tablet set up on birthplace at Leeds, 1910; his 'Picture Book' edited with life by G. R. Halkett, 1903.

MAYOR, JOHN EYTON BICKERSTETH (1825–1910), classical scholar and divine; revelled in classical literature from age of six; educated at Christ's Hospital, at Shrewsbury, and St. John's College, Cambridge; third

classic, 1848; fellow, 1849; master at Marlborough, 1849–53; prepared edition of 'Juvenal,' 1853 (3rd edit. 1881); classical tutor at St. John's from 1853; an accomplished linguist; published lives of Nicholas Ferrar (1855), Matthew Robinson (1856), Ambrose Bonwicke (1870), and William Bedell (1870), and edited Ascham's 'Scholemaster' (1863); edited transcript of admissions to St. John's College; published Baker's 'History of St. John's College,' 2 vols. 1869; university librarian, 1864–7; completed catalogue of MSS.; university professor of Latin, 1872 to death; edited (with Dr. J. R. Lumby) Bede's 'Ecclesiastical History,' bks. iii. and iv., 1878; visited Leyden and Rome, 1875; advocate of vegetarian diet from middle life; master of St. John's, 1902; hon. D.C.L. Oxford, 1895; LL.D. Aberdeen, 1892, and St. Andrews, 1906; D.D. Glasgow, 1901; original F.B.A., 1902; had power of accumulating knowledge but small faculty of construction; projected uncompleted commentary on Seneca and a Latin Dictionary; edited works by Cicero, Pliny, Homer, Quintilian, and volumes for the Rolls and Early English Text societies; published also 'A Bibliography of Latin Literature,' 1875, a 'First Greek Reader,' 1868, and 'First German Reader,' 1910; portrait by Herkomer at St. John's College, Cambridge.

MEADE, RICHARD JAMES, fourth EARL OF CLANWILLIAM in the Irish peerage, and second BARON CLANWILLIAM in the peerage of the United Kingdom (1832–1907), admiral of the fleet; entered navy, 1845; served in Russian war, 1852; wounded at storming of Canton, 1857; junior sea lord, 1874–80; C.B., 1877; succeeded to earldom, 1879; commanded flying squadron, 1880–2; K.C.M.G., 1882; commander-in-chief on North American station, 1885–6, and at Portsmouth, 1891–4; admiral, 1886; K.C.B., 1887; admiral of the fleet and G.C.B., 1895.

MEAKIN, JAMES EDWARD BUDGETT (1866–1906), historian of the Moors; edited 'Times of Morocco,' founded (1884) by his father; visited Mohammedan settlements in Asia and Africa, 1893; settled down to journalism in England, 1897; helped to found 'British Institute of Social Service,' 1905; published 'The Moorish Empire,' 1899, 'The Land of the Moors,' 1901, and 'The Moors,' 1902.

MEDD, PETER GOLDSMITH (1829–1908), theologian; B.A., University College, Oxford, 1852; M.A., 1855; fellow, 1852–77; rector of North Cerney, Cirencester, 1876–1908; hon. canon of St. Albans, 1877; Bampton lecturer, Oxford, 1882; edited Andrewes's 'Greek Devotions,' 1892; wrote 'The One Mediator,' 1884, and other theological works.

MEDLICOTT, HENRY BENEDICT (1829–1905), geologist; B.A. in civil engineering, Trinity College, Dublin, 1850; M.A., 1870; joined Italian geological survey, 1854; professor of geology at Rurki from 1862; volunteer in Indian Mutiny; made study of structure of Himalayas; superintendent of Indian survey, 1876; F.R.S., 1877; president of Asiatic Society of Bengal, 1879–81; wrote on geology of Punjab, 1874, and of India, 2 vols. 1879, with W. T. Blanford.

MEIKLEJOHN, JOHN MILLER DOW (1836–1902), writer of school books; M.A. Edinburgh, 1858; war correspondent in Danish-German war, 1864; first professor of education in St. Andrews University, 1876; raised standard of school books in his 'English Language,' 1886, 'The British Empire,' 1891, 'The Art of Writing English,' 1899, and 'English Literature,' 1904.

MELDRUM, CHARLES (1821–1901), meteorologist; M.A., Marischal College, Aberdeen, 1844; professor of mathematics, Royal College of Mauritius, 1848; founded 'Mauritius Meteorological Society,' 1851; in charge of Mauritius government observatory, 1862–96; studied laws of cyclones in Indian ocean; F.R.S., 1876; C.M.G., 1886.

MELLON, SARAH JANE (1824–1909), actress; born WOOLGAR; made début at Plymouth, 1836; long associated with Adelphi from 1843; original Lemuel there in Buckstone's 'Flowers of the Forest,' 1847; at Lyceum appeared as Florizel in burlesque of 'Perdita,' 1856, and as Ophelia, 1857; married Alfred Mellon [q. v.], 1858; played Catherine Duval at Adelphi in 'The Dead Heart,' 1859, Mrs. Cratchit in 'The Christmas Carol,' 1860, and Anne Chute in 'The Colleen Bawn,' 1860: subsequently lost vogue; reappeared as Mrs. O'Kelly in 'The Shaughraun,' 1880, and created Miss Sniffe in 'A Bridal Tour,' 1880; retired, 1883; versatile actress in tragedy, comedy, burlesque or farce.

MELVILLE, ARTHUR (1855–1904), artist; studied at Royal Scottish Academy and in Paris, 1878; travelled in Egypt, Persia, and Turkey, 1881–3; moulded the Glasgow artistic movement; exhibited several oil portraits at Edinburgh, including 'The Flower Girl,' 1883, and 'Portrait of a Lady,' before settling in London, 1888; visited Spain, 1889–92 and 1904, and Venice, 1894; A.R.S.A., 1886; member of Royal Water Colour Society, 1900; works include 'A Moorish Procession,' 'Christmas Eve,' 'The Capture of a Spy,' and 'The Little Bull Fight.'

MEREDITH, GEORGE (1828–1909), novelist and poet; grandson of Melchizedek Meredith (*d.* 1804), a prosperous tailor and naval outfitter of Portsmouth [see the novel 'Evan Harrington']; was privately educated at Portsmouth and Southsea and at the Moravian school at Neuwied, where he became an adept at German, 1843–4; was articled to a London solicitor of Bohemian tastes, 1845; soon turning to journalism, he contributed poems to 'Household Words' and to 'Chambers's Journal'; making acquaintance of a son of Thomas Love Peacock [q. v.] he married Peacock's daughter, 9 Aug. 1849; boarding at Weybridge he came to know there Sir Alexander and Lady Duff Gordon, and afterwards settled in a cottage at Lower Halliford. In 1858 he was deserted by his wife (*d.* 1861), who had borne him a son, Arthur Gryffydh (1853–1890). Meanwhile, besides writing for 'Fraser's Magazine,' he published 'Poems' (with dedication to Peacock), 1851; 'The Shaving of Shagpat: an Arabian Entertainment,' 1855, and 'Farina, a Legend of Cologne,' 1857. 'The Ordeal of Richard Feverel,' the first of his great novels, came out in 1859; the book introduced him to Swinburne and the pre-Raphaelite group, while through the Duff Gordons his acquaintance with other notable people quickly grew, but few copies of the book were sold, and his means were long scanty and precarious. He worked regularly for the 'Ipswich Journal,' 1859–75; contributed to 'Once a Week' six poems, 1859, and a new novel, 'Evan Harrington,' serially through 1860; made his residence at Copsham near Esher, 1860, where his intimate circle soon included Frederick Augustus Maxse [q. v.], J. A. Cotter Morison [q. v.], and others; found his chief recreation in long walks in Surrey and occasionally in France and Switzerland; lodged for a time with Rossetti and Swinburne at the Queen's House, Chelsea, 1861–2; published 'Modern Love and Poems of the English Roadside,' 1862; became contributor to the 'Morning Post,' 1862; was reader to Chapman & Hall from 1862 to 1894; brought out in 1864 'Emilia in England' (later renamed 'Sandra Belloni'); married his second wife Sept. 1864, and after some years at Norbiton finally settled for life at Flint Cottage facing Boxhill, 1867. There his second wife died, 17 Sept. 1889, leaving a son and daughter. He published 'Rhoda Fleming,' 1865; contributed serially to 'Fortnightly Review' in 1866 'Vittoria,' a sequel to 'Emilia,' which was expanded in separate issue; went to Italy as special correspondent for 'Morning Post' during war with Austria, 1866; contributed serially to the 'Cornhill' 'The Adventures of Harry Richmond,' 1870 (separately issued in 1871); published 'Odes in Contribution to the Song of French History,' 1871, 'Beauchamp's Career,' 1876 (after serial issue in condensed form in the 'Fortnightly,' 1875), and the 'Egoist,' 1879 (after serial issue in 'Glasgow Weekly Herald'); delivered (1 Feb. 1877) at London Institution a characteristic lecture on 'The Idea of Comedy and the Uses of the Comic Spirit' (printed in 'New Quarterly Magazine,' 1877, and separately, 1897); published 'The Tragic Comedians,' embodying the love story of Ferdinand Lassalle, the German socialist, in Dec. 1880 (after serial issue in 'Fortnightly'), and 'Poems and Lyrics of the Joy of Earth,' 1883. Though both his novels and poetry won growing appreciation from critical circles, the public showed small interest until publication of 'Diana of the Crossways,' 1885 (after serial issue in the 'Fortnightly'). There followed 'Ballads and Poems of Tragic Life,' 1887, 'A Reading of Earth,' 1888 (two of his most characteristic volumes of verse), and the last three novels, 'One of Our Conquerors,' 1891, 'Lord Ormont and his Aminta' (serially issued in 'Pall Mall Magazine,' 1894), and 'The Amazing Marriage,' begun in 1879 and serially issued in 'Scribner's Magazine' through 1895. In his last years he published many expressions of opinion on public questions, but was from 1893 disabled from active exercise by paraplegia.

He received in old age many marks of public regard. Addresses were presented by his admirers on both his seventieth and eightieth birthdays. He was president of the Society of Authors from 1892 to death, and was admitted to Order of Merit, 1905. He died at Flint Cottage, 18 May, and was buried in Dorking cemetery, 23 May, 1909; a memorial service was held in Westminster Abbey on day of funeral. There appeared posthumously 'Celt and Saxon,' an unfinished story ('Fortnightly,' 1910), and 'The Sentimentalists,' a conversational comedy, was produced at Duke of York's Theatre, March 1910; 'Last Poems' came out in 1910. Two collections were made of his work; the edition de luxe (36 vols. 1896–1911), and the memorial edition (27 vols. 1909–11). A collection of his letters appeared in 1912. A portrait by Watts is in National Portrait Gallery.

MERIVALE, HERMAN CHARLES (1839–1906), playwright and novelist; son of Herman Merivale [q. v.]; educated at Harrow and Balliol College, Oxford; B.A., 1861; called to bar, 1864; edited 'Annual Register,' 1870–80; collaborated in 'All for Her,' 1875, and 'Forget Me Not,' 1879, plays which attained great success; his 'The White Pilgrim' (1883) shows high qualities of poetic drama; skilful adapter of foreign dramas; wrote excellent farces and burlesques, including 'The Butler,' 1886, and 'The Don,' 1888, written for J. L. Toole; published novel, 'Faucit of Balliol,' 3 vols. 1882, and a children's fairy tale, 'Binko's Blues,' 1884; lost fortune through default of trustee, 1900; awarded civil list pension, 1900.

MERRIMAN, HENRY SETON (pseudonym) (1863–1903), novelist. [See SCOTT, HUGH STOWELL.]

MERRY, WILLIAM WALTER (1835–1918), classical scholar; B.A., Balliol College, Oxford; fellow and classical tutor, Lincoln College, 1859–84; rector, 1884–1918; ordained, 1860; public orator, 1880–1910; completed large edition of 'Odyssey' begun by James Riddell [q. v.]; edited plays of Aristophanes, &c.

MERTHYR, first BARON (1837–1914), engineer and coal-owner. [See LEWIS, WILLIAM THOMAS.]

MEYRICK, FREDERICK (1827–1906), divine; B.A., Trinity College, Oxford, 1847; M.A., 1850; fellow, 1847; travelled on Continent; founder and secretary of Anglo-Continental Society, 1853; rector of Blickling, Norfolk, 1868–1903; non-residentiary canon of Lincoln, 1869; helped to organize Bonn conferences on reunion, 1874–5; an ardent evangelical controversialist; wrote several anti-Roman pamphlets, as well as 'The Church in Spain,' 1892, and 'Memories of Life at Oxford,' 1905.

MICHIE, ALEXANDER (1833–1902), writer on China; prominent in Chinese commerce at Hong Kong and Shanghai from 1853; helped in negotiations with Taiping rebels, 1861; explored Yangtze valley and Szechuan, 1869; special correspondent to 'The Times' in Chino-Japanese war, 1895; wrote 'The Englishman in China,' 2 vols. 1900, and 'China and Christianity,' 1900.

MICKLETHWAITE, JOHN THOMAS (1843–1906), architect; pupil of George Gilbert Scott [q. v.], 1862; partner with fellow pupil, Somers Clarke, 1876–92; designed churches of St. Hilda, Leeds, St. Peter, Bocking, Widford, and St. Matthias, Cambridge; executed much internal decoration, chancels, and screens; architect to St. George's Chapel, Windsor, 1900; surveyor to dean and chapter of Westminster Abbey, 1898; restored south transept and west front; F.S.A., 1870; vice-president, 1902; helped to found Alcuin Club and Henry Bradshaw Society; published 'Ornaments of the Rubric,' 1897.

MIDLANE, ALBERT (1825–1909), hymn writer; tinsmith and ironmonger; joined Plymouth brethren; wrote over 800 hymns, the best-known, 'There's a Friend for little children,' being composed in 1859; hymns marked by religious emotion and love of children; published several volumes of verse.

MILBANKE, RALPH GORDON NOEL KING, second EARL OF LOVELACE (1839–1906), author of 'Astarte'; grandson of poet Byron; spent a year in Iceland, 1861; a bold Alpinist and accomplished linguist; his privately printed 'Astarte' (1905), vindicating his grandmother, Lady Byron, from aspersions cast on her, and incriminating Lord Byron, provoked replies from Mr. John Murray and Mr. Richard Edgcumbe.

MILFORD HAVEN, first MARQUESS OF (1854–1921), admiral of the fleet. [See MOUNTBATTEN, LOUIS ALEXANDER.]

MILLER, SIR JAMES PERCY, second baronet

(1864–1906), sportsman; joined army, 1888; served in South Africa, 1900–1; won Derby with Sainfoin, 1890; purchased mare Roquebrune (1894), who, mated with Sainfoin, produced Rock Sand, winner of Two Thousand Guineas, Derby, and St. Leger in 1903; headed list of winning owners, 1903 and 1904.

MILNE, JOHN (1850–1913), mining engineer and seismologist; educated at King's College, London, and Royal School of Mines; professor of geology and mining, Imperial College, Tokio, 1875; first professor of seismology, imperial university, Tokio; established seismic survey of Japan; secretary to seismological committee of British Association, 1895–1913; devised seismograph; travelled widely.

MINTO, fourth EARL OF (1845–1914), governor-general of Canada and viceroy of India. [See ELLIOT, GILBERT JOHN MURRAY KYNYNMOND.]

MITCHELL, SIR ARTHUR (1826–1909), Scottish commissioner in lunacy (1870–95) and antiquary; M.A. Aberdeen, 1845; M.D., 1850; hon. LL.D., 1875; member of English commission on criminal lunacy, 1880; F.S.A., Scotland, 1867; made study of superstition in Scottish Highlands; first Rhind lecturer in archaeology, Edinburgh; C.B., 1886; K.C.B., 1887; hon. F.R.C.P. Ireland, 1891; published 'The Past in the Present,' 1880, and edited 'Macfarlane's Topographical Collections', 3 vols. 1906–8.

MITCHELL, JOHN MURRAY (1815–1904), presbyterian missionary and Orientalist; M.A., Marischal College, Aberdeen, 1833; hon. LL.D., 1858; missionary in Bombay, 1838; made many converts among Marathis; founded flourishing Free Church mission at Poona, 1843; in Bengal, 1867–73; formed 'Union Church' at Simla; minister of Scottish church at Nice, 1888–98; Duff missionary lecturer at Edinburgh, 1903; published 'Hinduism Past and Present,' 1885, 'The Great Religions of India,' posthumous, 1905, and metrical translations from Indian poets.

MITFORD, ALGERNON BERTRAM FREEMAN-, first BARON REDESDALE in the second creation (1837–1916), diplomatist and author; great-grandson of William Mitford [q. v.], the historian; educated at Eton and Christ Church, Oxford; entered Foreign Office, 1858; attaché in Japan, 1866–70; resigned from diplomatic service, 1873; secretary to Board of Works, 1874–86; as heir to cousin assumed additional name and arms of Mitford and went to live at Batsford Park, Warwickshire, 1886; conservative M.P., Stratford-on-Avon division of Warwickshire, 1892–5; created baron, 1902; works include 'Tales of Old Japan' (1871) and his autobiography ('Memories,' 1915).

MOBERLY, ROBERT CAMPBELL (1845–1903), theologian; son of George Moberly [q. v.]; scholar of Winchester and New College, Oxford; B.A., 1867; won Newdigate prize, 1867; M.A., 1870; D.D., 1892; a senior student of Christ Church, 1867–80; principal of Diocesan Theological College, Salisbury, 1878; hon. canon of Chester, 1890; regius professor of pastoral theology at Oxford and canon of Christ Church, 1892–1903; contributed 'The Incarnation as the Basis of Dogma' to 'Lux Mundi,' 1889; chief work was 'Atonement and Personality,' 1901.

MOCATTA, FREDERIC DAVID (1828–1905), Jewish philanthropist; in father's bullion broker's business, 1843–74; promoter of Charity Organization Society, 1869; interested in housing of working classes and liberal benefactor of London hospitals; organized Board of Guardians of the Jewish Poor (founded 1859); generous supporter of Jewish charities; encouraged Jewish literature and research; F.S.A., 1889; published 'The Jews and the Inquisition,' 1877; memoir published, 1912.

MOENS, WILLIAM JOHN CHARLES (1833–1904), Huguenot antiquary; settled in Hampshire, devoting himself to yachting and antiquarian research; held captive in South Italy by brigands for four months, 1865; published experiences in 'English Travellers and Italian Brigands,' 1866; helped to found Huguenot Society of London, 1885; president, 1899–1902; edited for society registers of Walloons at Norwich (1887–8), of French Church, Threadneedle Street (1896), and of Dutch Church, Colchester (1905); F.S.A., 1886.

MOIR, FRANK LEWIS (1852–1904), song composer; composed ballads, church music, and organ voluntaries; best-known songs were 'Down the Vale,' 1885, and 'Only Once More,' 1893.

MOLLOY, GERALD (1834–1906), rector of the Catholic University of Dublin from 1883 till death; professor of theology at Maynooth, 1857; professor of natural philosophy, Catholic University, Dublin, 1874; rector, 1883; D.Sc. Royal University of Ireland, 1879; commissioner of inquiry into educational endowments in Ireland, 1885–94; vice-chancellor of Royal University, 1903; published 'Geology and Revelation,' 1870, and 'Gleanings in Science,' 1888.

MOLLOY, JAMES LYNAM (1837–1909), composer; M.A., Catholic University, Dublin, 1858; called to English bar, 1863; composed songs (of which 'Darby and Joan,' 'The Kerry Dance,' 'Love's Old Sweet Song' had wide vogue) and operettas; wrote 'Our Autumn Holiday on French Rivers,' 1874.

MOLLOY, JOSEPH FITZGERALD (1858–1908), miscellaneous writer; published 'Songs of Passion and Pain,' 1881, 'London under the Four Georges,' 4 vols. 1882–3, and 'London under Charles II,' 2 vols. 1885, lives of Peg Woffington, 2 vols. 1884, and Edmund Kean, 2 vols. 1888, 'Romance of the Irish Stage,' 2 vols. 1897, and many novels.

MOLYNEUX, SIR ROBERT HENRY MORE- (1838–1904), admiral. [See MORE-MOLYNEUX.]

MONCREIFF, HENRY JAMES, second BARON MONCREIFF, of Tullibole (1840–1909), Scottish judge; son of first baron [q. v.]; B.A. and LL.B. Trinity College, Cambridge, 1861; passed to Scottish bar, 1863; whig advocate-depute, 1865–6; reappointed under Gladstone, 1868 and 1880; joined liberal unionists, 1886; sheriff of Renfrew and Bute, 1881; Scottish judge, 1888–1905.

MONCRIEFF, SIR ALEXANDER (1829–1906), colonel and engineer; joined army, 1855; served in Crimea; colonel, 1878; invented Moncrieff system of raising and lowering guns, and devised means of laying and sighting them when thus mounted; designed hydropneumatic carriage for similar purposes, 1869; F.R.S., 1871; C.B., 1880; K.C.B., 1890; a keen sportsman, amateur artist, and golfer.

MOND, LUDWIG (1839–1909), chemical technologist, manufacturer, and art collector; born and educated at Cassel; employed in soda works near Cassel, 1859; in England (1862) took out patent for recovery of sulphur from Leblanc alkali waste; joined firm at Widnes to push process, 1867; bought English patent of ammonia-soda process, and with J. T. Brunner started alkali works at Winnington near Northwich, 1872; firm became Brunner, Mond & Co. (1881), with Mond as managing director (in 1909 employing 4,000 workmen); invented Mond producer-gas plant (patented 1883) for the production of ammonia and cheap producer-gas; his efforts to recover chlorine wasted in ammonia soda process, and his use of nickel compounds to purify producer-gas, led to discovery of nickel carbonyl, and of a method for extracting metallic nickel from its ores; Mond formed 'Mond Nickel Company,' with mines in Canada and works near Swansea, 1888; active in founding Society of Chemical Industry and its 'Journal,' 1881; F.R.S., 1891; received honorary doctorates from Padua, Heidelberg, Manchester, and Oxford; left fortune of over 1,000,000l.; took out forty-nine patents and published many scientific papers; founded Davy-Faraday Laboratory for chemical research at Royal Institution, 1896; left large sums to Royal Society and Heidelberg for research; benefactor to town of Cassel and to Jewish charities; bequeathed (contingently on wife's death) art collection, mainly early Italian pictures, to National Gallery.

MONKHOUSE, WILLIAM COSMO (1840–1901), poet and critic; clerk in board of trade, 1856; assistant secretary to finance department at death; published poems, 'A Dream of Idleness,' 1865, and 'Corn and Poppies,' 1890; a novel, 1868; 'Masterpieces of English Art,' 1869; lives of Turner, 1879, and Tenniel, 1901, and 'Earlier English Water Colour Painters,' 1890.

MONRO, CHARLES HENRY (1835–1908), author; educated at Harrow; B.A., Caius College, Cambridge (first class classic), and fellow, 1857; law lecturer, 1872–96; planned but left unfinished a complete translation of Justinian's 'Digest,' 2 vols. 1904–1909; memorial fellowship and Celtic lectureship founded at Caius College.

MONRO, DAVID BINNING (1836–1905), classical scholar; educated at Glasgow University and Balliol College, Oxford; B.A. (first class classic), 1858; Ireland scholar, 1858; fellow of Oriel, 1859; vice-provost, 1874; provost, 1882; vice-chancellor of university, 1901–4; published a Homeric Grammar, 1882 (an authoritative work), a school edition of 'Iliad,' 2 vols. 1884–9, and 'Odyssey,' xiii.–xxiv., 1901; edited complete text, 1896; sought in philology the solution of Homeric problems; founded Oxford Philological Society, 1870; original F.B.A., 1902;

hon. D.C.L. Oxford, 1904; LL.D. Glasgow, 1883;
Doc.Litt. Dublin, 1892; died in Switzerland.

MONSON, SIR EDMUND JOHN, first baronet (1834–
1909), diplomatist; educated at Eton and Balliol College,
Oxford; B.A. (first class in history), 1855; M.A. and
fellow of All Souls, 1858; held various minor posts in
diplomatic service, 1856–65; consul in Azores, 1869–71;
consul-general at Buda-Pesth, 1871; British representative at Cettigne during war of Servia and Montenegro
with Turkey, 1876–7; C.B., 1878; employed in Uruguay
(1879–84), Buenos Ayres (1884), Copenhagen (1884–8),
Athens (1888), and Brussels (1892); K.C.M.G., 1886;
G.C.M.G., 1892; ambassador at Vienna and P.C., 1893,
and Paris, 1896–1904; G.C.B., 1896; tactfully settled disputes with French in Newfoundland, New Hebrides, and
East and West Africa; hon. D.C.L. Oxford, 1898;
LL.D. Cambridge, 1905; G.C.V.O., 1903; baronet, 1905;
received grand cross of legion of honour.

MONTAGU, LORD ROBERT (1825–1902), politician
and controversialist; M.A., Trinity College, Cambridge,
1849; conservative M.P. for Huntingdonshire, 1859–74;
champion of church rates and trade unions; vice-president of the committee of council on education, charity
commissioner, and P.C., 1867; criticized education bill
of 1870; conservative home-rule M.P. for Westminster,
1874–80; condemned conservative policy in Afghan war;
joined Church of Rome (1870), but rejoined English Church
on ethical and political grounds (1882) and attacked
Romanists in published volumes.

MONTAGU, SAMUEL, first BARON SWAYTHLING
(1832–1911), foreign exchange banker and Jewish
philanthropist; founded with brother and brother-
in-law the foreign exchange and banking firm of Samuel
Montagu & Co., 1853; acquired large exchange business
and helped to make London the clearing house of the international money market; engaged in large transactions
in silver; liberal M.P. for Whitechapel, 1885–1900; chief
author of Weights and Measures Acts, 1897; ardent
supporter of bimetallism; member of select committee
on alien immigration, 1888; took leading part in Jewish
religious, social, and charitable work; founded Jewish
Working Men's Club, 1870; formed federation of smaller
East End synagogues, 1887; gave to London County
Council 10,000l. for Tottenham housing scheme, 1903;
travelled abroad in interests of oppressed Jews; visited
Russia to investigate condition of Jews (1886), but was
expelled; president of Russo-Jewish committee, 1896–
1909; collector of works of art and of old English silver;
F.S.A., 1897; baronet, 1894; raised to peerage, 1907.

MONTAGU-DOUGLAS-SCOTT, LORD CHARLES THOMAS
(1839–1911), admiral. [See SCOTT.]

MONTGOMERIE, ROBERT ARCHIBALD JAMES
(1855–1908), rear-admiral; entered navy, 1869; served
in Egyptian war, 1882; in charge of naval transport in
Nile expedition, 1885–6; commanded field battery in
Vitu expedition; C.B., 1892; conducted bombardment
of Puerto Cabello, 1903; inspecting captain of boys'
training ships, 1904; C.M.G., 1904; rear-admiral, 1905;
C.V.O., 1907; champion heavy weight boxer of navy.

MONTMORENCY, RAYMOND HARVEY DE, third
VISCOUNT FRANKFORT DE MONTMORENCY (1835–1902),
major-general. [See DE MONTMORENCY.]

MONYPENNY, WILLIAM FLAVELLE (1866–1912),
journalist, and biographer of Disraeli; joined editorial
staff of 'The Times', 1893; chosen to undertake authoritative biography of Lord Beaconsfield; published first
volume, 1910, second, 1912; work completed by Mr. G. E.
Buckle.

MOOR, SIR RALPH DENHAM RAYMENT (1860–
1909), first high commissioner of Southern Nigeria, 1900–3;
commandant of constabulary in Oil Rivers Protectorate,
1891; vice-consul, 1892; consul, 1896; commissioner
and consul-general of newly-formed Niger Coast Protectorate, 1896–1900.

MOORE, ARTHUR WILLIAM (1853–1909), Manx
antiquary; educated at Eton and Trinity College, Cambridge; second in historical tripos, 1876; M.A., 1879;
won blue for Rugby football; speaker of House of Keys,
1898–1909; championed house in disputes with governor;
wrote on meteorology of the island; C.V.O., 1902;
founded Manx Language Society, 1899; wrote on Manx
folklore, 1891, music, 1896, and records, 1905; his
'History of the Isle of Man,' 1900, is an authoritative
work.

MOORE, EDWARD (1835–1916), principal of St.
Edmund Hall, Oxford, and Dante scholar; B.A., Pembroke College, Oxford; fellow of Queen's, 1858; principal

of St. Edmund Hall, 1864–1913; preserved its inde-
pendence; canon of Canterbury, 1903; works include
'Contributions to the Textual Criticism of the "Divina
Commedia"' (1889) and 'Oxford Dante' (1894).

MOORE, STUART ARCHIBALD (1842–1907), legal
antiquary; F.S.A., 1869; called to bar, 1884; published
volumes (1888 and 1903) on the history and law relating
to foreshore and fishery rights; keen yachtsman; edited
antiquarian works for Camden Society and Roxburghe
Club.

MOORE, TEMPLE LUSHINGTON (1856–1920),
architect; pupil (1875–8) of George Gilbert Scott,
junior, with whom he maintained close professional
association, 1878–90; employed pure Gothic style;
designs include seventeen important new churches (1885–
1917), nave of Hexham Abbey (1902–8), Anglican
cathedral, Nairobi (1914), chapels of Pusey House,
Oxford, and Bishop's Hostel, Lincoln, and several houses.

MOORHOUSE, JAMES (1826–1915), bishop of Melbourne and afterwards of Manchester; B.A., St. John's
College, Cambridge; prebendary of St. Paul's, 1874;
bishop of Melbourne, 1876–86; presided over synod at
Sydney which framed constitution of Church in Australia;
bishop of Manchester, 1886–1903.

MORAN, PATRICK FRANCIS (1830–1911), cardinal
archbishop of Sydney; nephew of Cardinal Cullen [q. v.];
educated at Rome; priest, 1853; vice-principal of St.
Agatha's College, Rome, 1856–66; private secretary to
Cardinal Cullen, 1866–72; archbishop of Sydney, 1884;
cardinal, 1885; militant churchman and a keen controversialist; built many Roman Catholic institutions
in New South Wales; prominent in Australian politics;
advocated home rule, and supported Australian federation; publications include 'The Catholic Archbishops of
Dublin,' 1864, and 'The Catholics of Ireland . . . in
the 18th Century,' 1899.

MORANT, SIR ROBERT LAURIE (1863–1920), civil
servant; B.A., New College, Oxford; assistant director of
special inquiries and reports, Education Department,
1895; assistant private secretary to eighth Duke of
Devonshire [q. v.], 1902; passing of Education Act (1902)
largely due to him; permanent secretary, Board of Education, which he entirely remodelled, 1903–11; chairman,
National Health Insurance Commission, which he
organized, 1911–19; first secretary, Ministry of Health,
which he constructed, 1919–20; C.B., 1902; K.C.B., 1907;
one of the greatest of civil servants.

MORE-MOLYNEUX, SIR ROBERT HENRY (1838–
1904), admiral; joined navy, 1852; served in Crimea,
1854; on West Coast of Africa, 1859; commander, 1865;
on North America and West Indies station, 1867; commanded 'Ruby' in Russian war, 1877–8; at bombardment
of Alexandria; C.B.; protected Suakin till arrival of Sir
Gerald Graham; K.C.B., 1885; captain superintendent
of Sheerness dockyard, 1885–8; admiral, 1899; president
of Royal Naval College, Greenwich, 1900–3; G.C.B.,
1902; died at Cairo.

MORFILL, WILLIAM RICHARD (1834–1909),
Slavonic scholar; B.A., Oriel College, Oxford, 1857;
M.A., 1860; travelled much in Slavonic countries, studying their history and literature; university reader in
Russian at Oxford, 1889; Ph.D. Prague; F.B.A., 1903;
wrote Grammar of Polish (1884), Serbian (1887), Russian
(1889), Czech (1889), and Bulgarian (1897), and histories
of Russia (1885 and 1902), Poland (1893), and of Slavonic
literature (1883); he also knew Welsh, old Irish, and
Turkish; bequeathed Slavonic library to Queen's College,
Oxford.

MORGAN, EDWARD DELMAR (1840–1909), linguist
and traveller; lived in St. Petersburg; travelled in
Persia, 1872, Little Russia, and Lower Congo, 1883;
hon. secretary of Hakluyt Society, 1886–92, editing
Anthony Jenkinson's travels, 1886; translated works
by the Central Asian explorer Przhevalsky, 1876–9.

MORIARTY, HENRY AUGUSTUS (1815–1906),
captain in the navy; prepared vessels for bombardment
of Sveaborg, 1855; navigated 'Great Eastern' when employed for laying Atlantic cables, 1865–6; C.B., 1866;
Queen's harbourmaster, Portsmouth, 1869–74; captain,
1874; nautical expert before parliamentary committees;
published volumes of sailing directions, 1887–93.

MORLEY, third EARL OF (1843–1905), chairman of
committees of the House of Lords. [See PARKER,
ALBERT EDMUND.]

MORRIS, SIR LEWIS (1833–1907), poet and Welsh
educationist; born at Carmarthen; B.A. (first class in
lit. hum.), Jesus College, Oxford, 1856; M.A., 1858; won

91

chancellor's prize for English essay, 1858; fellow, 1877; called to bar, 1861; practised as conveyancer in London till 1880; published anonymously 'Songs of Two Worlds,' sonorous and optimistic verse (3 series, 1871, 1874, 1875, republished in one vol., 1878); imitated Tennyson's 'Tithonus' in a series of blank verse monologues, collected as 'The Epic of Hades' (1877), which was popular with the middle classes and reached a 45th edition; there followed 'Gwen: a Drama in Monologue,' 1879, 'The Ode of Life' (descriptive poems), 1880, 'Songs Unsung,' 1883 (the first volume issued under author's name), 'Gycia: a tragedy,' 1886, and 'Songs of Britain,' 1887; collected editions appeared in 1882 (3 vols.) and in 1890, 'A Vision of Saints' in 1890, and subsequently other collections of lyrics; his work was ridiculed in 'Saturday Review.' Morris published a volume of essays, 'The New Rambler,' 1905; was hon. secretary (1878), hon. treasurer (1889), and vice-president (1896) of University College of Wales, Aberystwyth; helped in establishing University of Wales, 1893; hon. D.Litt. 1906; knighted, 1895; an advanced liberal, but failed in attempts to enter parliament.

MORRIS, MICHAEL, LORD MORRIS AND KILLANIN (1826–1901), lord chief justice of Ireland; senior moderator in ethics and logic, Trinity College, Dublin, 1846; hon. LL.D., 1887; called to Irish bar, 1849; recorder of Galway, 1857–65; Q.C., 1863; independent conservative M.P. for Galway, 1865; solicitor-general for Ireland, July 1866; attorney-general, Nov.; Irish P.C.; puisne judge of court of common pleas, 1867; lord chief justice of Ireland, 1887; baronet, 1885; member of judicial committee of English privy council, receiving life peerage, 1889; bencher of Lincoln's Inn, 1890; commissioner of Irish national education; vice-chancellor of Royal University, Ireland, 1899; made hereditary baron of Killanin, 1900; an opponent of home rule, but a caustic critic of English rule in Ireland.

MORRIS, PHILIP RICHARD (1836–1902), painter; won travelling studentship at Royal Academy Schools, 1858; exhibited at Academy, 1858–1901; A.R.A., 1877; early painted sea pictures, later religious subjects; best-known works were 'Sons of the Brave' and 'The First Communion.'

MORRIS, TOM (1821–1908), golfer; apprenticed to Allan Robertson, golfer of St. Andrews and golf ball maker; won open golf championship, 1861–2–4–6; green keeper to St. Andrews Golf Club, 1863–1903; 'Life' by W. W. Tulloch, 1906.

MORRIS, WILLIAM O'CONNOR (1824–1904), Irish county court judge and historian; B.A., Oriel College, Oxford, 1848; called to Irish bar, 1854; professor of common and criminal law in King's Inns, Dublin, 1862; contributed to 'Edinburgh Review,' and wrote articles on land tenure in 'The Times,' 1870; county court judge for Louth, 1872, and Kerry, 1878; disapproved of Land Act of 1881; transferred as judge for Sligo and Roscommon, 1886; published superficial but independent studies of Hannibal (1890), Napoleon (1890), Moltke (1893), Nelson (1898), and Wellington (1904); 'Ireland from 1494 to 1868,' 1894, and 'Ireland from '98 to '98,' 1898.

MORRIS AND KILLANIN, LORD (1826–1901), lord chief justice of Ireland. [See MORRIS, MICHAEL.]

MORRISON, WALTER (1836–1921), man of business and philanthropist; educated at Eton and Balliol; liberal M.P., Plymouth, 1861–74; liberal unionist M.P., Skipton division of Yorkshire, 1886–92, 1895–1900; inherited large fortune which he increased; entertained many eminent friends at Malham Tarn, Yorkshire; benefactions include gifts to northern universities, Giggleswick School, King Edward's Hospital Fund (annual contribution for many years 10,000l.), Palestine Exploration Fund, Oxford University (30,000l.) and Bodleian Library (50,000l.).

MOSELEY, HENRY GWYN JEFFREYS (1887–1915), experimental physicist; son of Professor Henry Nottidge Moseley [q. v.]; B.A., Trinity College, Oxford; physics lecturer, Manchester University, 1910–14; carried out important researches on X-ray spectra of elements; killed in action at Gallipoli.

MOULE, GEORGE EVANS (1828–1912), missionary bishop in mid-China; second son of Rev. Henry Moule [q. v.]; B.A., Corpus Christi College, Cambridge; went as missionary to China, 1857; first bishop of mid-China, 1880–1906.

MOULE, HANDLEY CARR GLYN (1841–1920), bishop of Durham; eighth son of Rev. Henry Moule

[q. v.]; B.A., Trinity College, Cambridge; principal of Ridley Hall, Cambridge, 1880–99; Norrisian professor of divinity, 1899–1901; bishop of Durham, 1901–20; an evangelical; wrote theological and devotional works.

MOULTON, JAMES HOPE (1863–1917), classical and Iranian scholar and student of Zoroastrianism; son of Rev. W. F. Moulton [q. v.]; B.A., King's College, Cambridge; Greenwood professor of Hellenistic Greek and Indo-European philology, Manchester, 1908; torpedoed in Mediterranean returning from India; works include 'Prolegomena' to unfinished 'Grammar of New Testament Greek' (1906) and 'Early Zoroastrianism' (1913).

MOULTON, JOHN FLETCHER, BARON MOULTON (1844–1921), lord of appeal in ordinary; brother of W. F. Moulton [q. v.]; B.A., St. John's College, Cambridge (senior wrangler with highest total of marks ever gained), 1868; fellow of Christ's, Cambridge, 1868–73; called to bar (Middle Temple), 1874; Q.C., 1885; specialized in patent actions; liberal M.P., Clapham division of Battersea, 1885–6, South Hackney, 1894–5, Launceston division of Cornwall, 1898–1906; lord justice of appeal, knight, and P.C., 1906; lord of appeal in ordinary, 1912; created K.C.B., 1915, G.B.E., 1917, for brilliant organization of Explosives Supply Department, 1914–18.

MOUNTBATTEN, LOUIS ALEXANDER, first MARQUESS OF MILFORD HAVEN, formerly styled PRINCE LOUIS ALEXANDER OF BATTENBERG (1854–1921), admiral of the fleet; son of Prince Alexander of Hesse; born at Gratz, Austria; naturalized and entered British royal navy, 1868; studied defence problem; director of naval intelligence at Admiralty, 1902–5; rear-admiral, 1904; commander-in-chief, Atlantic fleet, 1908–10; vice-admiral, 1910; first sea-lord, 1912; resigned, October 1914; relinquished German titles and created marquess, 1917; admiral, 1919.

MOUNTFORD, EDWARD WILLIAM (1855–1908), architect; won open competition for Sheffield town hall, 1890; designed several London buildings, including the Central Criminal Court, Old Bailey; style developed from Renaissance to classic method.

MOUNT STEPHEN, first BARON (1829–1921), financier and philanthropist. [See STEPHEN, GEORGE.]

MOWAT, SIR OLIVER (1820–1903), Canadian statesman; born at Kingston, Ontario; called to bar of Upper Canada, 1841; leader of chancery bar at Toronto; Q.C., 1856; on commission to consolidate statutes of Upper Canada; radical member of legislative assembly, 1857; advocated federation of Upper and Lower Canada, and representation by population, 1859; as postmaster-general carried out considerable economies, 1863; took part in conference for federation, 1864; vice-chancellor of Ontario, 1864–72; premier, 1872–96; responsible for Ballot Act, 1874, Manhood Suffrage Act, 1888, and Acts to simplify and cheapen judicial procedure; champioued provincial rights in matters of legal appointments, regulation of companies, and control of liquor traffic; gained victory for Ontario over Manitoba in delimitation of boundaries, 1884; K.C.M.G., 1892; G.C.M.G., 1893; as Dominion minister of justice, 1896–7, suggested compromise with Roman Catholics in Manitoba school question; lieutenant-governor of Ontario, 1897; advocated reciprocity with America.

MOWATT, SIR FRANCIS (1837–1919), civil servant; clerk in Treasury, 1856; assistant secretary, 1888; permanent secretary, 1894–1903; raised reputation of department for promptness and efficiency; owing to misunderstanding offered to resign, 1900; served on numerous royal commissions and committees; C.B., 1884; K.C.B., 1893; G.C.B., 1901; P.C., 1906.

MUIR, SIR WILLIAM (1819–1905), Indian administrator and principal of Edinburgh University; brother of John Muir [q. v.]; joined East India Company's service, 1837; head of intelligence department at Agra during Mutiny, 1857; related experiences in 'Agra in the Mutiny,' 1896; secretary to Lord Canning's government at Allahabad, 1858; foreign secretary under Lord Lawrence and K.C.S.I., 1867; lieutenant-governor of North-West Provinces, 1868–74; founded Muir College and University at Allahabad; financial member of Lord Northbrook's council, 1874–6; member of Council of India in London, 1876–85; principal of Edinburgh University, 1885–1905; president of Royal Asiatic Society, 1884; hon. D.C.L. Oxford, 1882; LL.D. Edinburgh and Glasgow; Ph.D. Bologna, 1888; published standard 'Life of Mahomet,' 4 vols. 1858–61, 'Annals of the Early Caliphate,' 1883, and 'Mameluke Dynasty of Egypt,' 1896; Rede lecturer at Cambridge, 1881; with his brother endowed Shaw professorship of Sanskrit at Edinburgh, 1862.

MÜLLER, ERNEST BRUCE IWAN (1853–1910), journalist. [See IWAN-MÜLLER.]

MULLINS, EDWIN ROSCOE (1848–1907), sculptor; studied art at Lambeth, Royal Academy, and Munich; executed ideal works such as 'Cain,' 'Innocence,' 'Rest,' and several portraits, including Dr. Martineau (bust), Gladstone (statuette), Queen Victoria, William Barnes (statues); decorated many London buildings; published 'A Primer of Sculpture,' 1892.

MUNBY, ARTHUR JOSEPH (1828–1910), poet and civil servant; B.A., Trinity College, Cambridge, 1851; M.A., 1856; called to bar, 1855; in ecclesiastical commissioners' office, 1858–88; published poetic idylls, 'Benoni,' 1852, 'Verses New and Old,' 1865, and 'Dorothy,' 1880; work praised by Browning for craftsmanship; later works include 'Poems, chiefly Lyric and Elegiac,' 1901, and 'Relicta,' 1909; F.S.A.; supporter of Working Men's College.

MUNRO, HECTOR HUGH (1870–1916), writer of fiction; born in Burma; took up journalism in London; works include 'The Westminster Alice' (political sketches, 1902), 'Reginald' (1904), 'Reginald in Russia' (1910), 'Chronicles of Clovis' (1911), 'Beasts and Super-Beasts' (1914), all short stories, and 'The Unbearable Bassington' (1912), a novel; employed pseudonym 'Saki'; killed in action in France.

MUNRO, JAMES (1832–1908), premier of Victoria, Australia: emigrated to Victoria, 1858, working as printer till 1865; founded Federal Banking Company, 1882, and Real Estate Bank, 1887; liberal minister of public instruction, Aug.–Oct. 1875; treasurer and premier, 1890–1902; agent-general in London, 1902; temperance advocate.

MURDOCH, WILLIAM LLOYD (1855–1911), Australian cricketer; born in Victoria, Australia; practised as solicitor; played cricket for New South Wales, 1875–84; known in colonies as 'W. G. Grace of Australia'; acquired fame first as wicket-keeper and finally as batsman; member (1878) and captain (1880–2, 1884, 1890) of Australian teams to England; made record Australian individual score (211) against England, 1884; visited America, 1878, and South Africa, 1891–2; settled in England, 1891; captained Sussex team, 1893–9; died at Melbourne; published handbook of cricket, 1893.

MURRAY, ALEXANDER STUART (1841–1904), keeper of Greek and Roman antiquities in the British Museum from 1886; brother of G. R. M. Murray [q. v.]; M.A. Edinburgh University; assistant at British Museum, 1867; as keeper reorganized galleries of Greek and Roman antiquities; frequently visited classical sites; LL.D. Glasgow, 1891; F.S.A., 1889; F.B.A., 1903; independent works include 'A History of Greek Sculpture,' 2 vols. 1880–3, 'Handbook of Archaeology,' 1892, 'Greek Bronzes,' 1898, and 'The Sculptures of the Parthenon,' 1903.

MURRAY, CHARLES ADOLPHUS, seventh EARL OF DUNMORE (1841–1907), explorer; joined army, 1860; lord-in-waiting to Queen Victoria, 1874–80; explored Kashmir and Tibet, 1892; published account in 'The Pamirs,' 1893; wrote 'Ormisdale,' a novel, 1893; joined Christian scientists late in life.

MURRAY, DAVID CHRISTIE (1847–1907), novelist and journalist; reporter to 'Birmingham Morning News' till 1865; parliamentary reporter for 'Daily News,' 1871; contributed articles to 'Referee,' collected as 'Guesses at Truth,' 1908; travelled much on Continent and in colonies; represented 'The Times' in Russo-Turkish war, 1877–8; a prolific and vigorous novelist; novels include 'Rainbow Gold,' 1885, and 'Aunt Rachel,' 1886; he published also 'A Novelist's Notebook,' 1887, and 'Recollections,' posthumous, 1908.

MURRAY, GEORGE ROBERT MILNE (1858–1911), botanist; assistant at British Museum, 1876; keeper of botanical department, 1895–1905; director of scientific staff of Captain R. F. Scott's Antarctic expedition, 1901; F.R.S., 1897; made special study of marine algae; wrote works on 'Cryptogamic Botany,' 1889, and on seaweeds, 1895; edited 'Phycological Memoirs,' 1892–5.

MURRAY, SIR JAMES AUGUSTUS HENRY (1837–1915), lexicographer; educated at Cavers and Minto schools; head master of Hawick Subscription Academy, 1857; took up study of languages; on staff of Mill Hill School, 1870–85; B.A., London University, 1873; editor of 'New English Dictionary on Historical Principles' pro-

jected by Clarendon Press, 1879; removed to Oxford in order to devote himself to this work, 1885; conceived plan and settled scope of greatest lexicographical achievement of present age, although his editorial responsibility only covers half of it (A–D, H–K, O, P, T); also edited Sir David Lyndesay's 'Works,' part v, 'The Complaynte of Scotlande,' and 'The Romance and Prophecies of Thomas of Erceldoune'; wrote 'Dialect of the Southern Counties of Scotland' (1873); F.B.A., 1901; knighted, 1908.

MURRAY, SIR JAMES WOLFE (1853–1919), lieutenant-general; entered army from Woolwich, 1872; engaged for many years in staff and extra-regimental service; K.C.B., for services in South African war, 1901; quartermaster-general in India and major-general, 1903; lieutenant-general, 1909; chief of Imperial General Staff, 1914.

MURRAY, SIR JOHN (1841–1914), marine naturalist and oceanographer; born at Cobourg, Ontario; came to Scotland to complete his education, 1858; naturalist in charge of collections on 'Challenger' expedition directed by (Sir) C. W. Thomson [q. v.], 1872–5; chief assistant in 'Challenger Office,' Edinburgh, 1876; director of office and editor of 'Report on the Scientific Results of the Voyage of H.M.S. Challenger' (1880–95), 1882–95; explored Faroe Channel, 1880–2; carried out bathymetrical survey of Scottish fresh-water lochs, 1897–1909; leased, explored, and financed scientific expeditions to Christmas Island; explored North Atlantic, 1910; F.R.S., 1896; K.C.B., 1898; works include 'On the Origin and Structure of Coral Reefs and Islands' (1880), 'Deep Sea Deposits' (1891), and 'Depths of the Sea' (1912), the two latter in collaboration.

MUSGRAVE, SIR JAMES, baronet (1826–1904), benefactor of Belfast; established firm of iron founders in Belfast; chairman of Belfast harbour commission, 1887–1903; greatly improved harbour and constructed 'Musgrave Channel' and docks; founded Musgrave chair of pathology in Queen's College, Belfast, 1901; baronet, 1897.

MUYBRIDGE, EADWEARD (1830–1904), investigator of animal locomotion, whose original name was EDWARD JAMES MUGGERIDGE; born at Kingston-on-Thames; emigrated to America; as government director of photographic surveys, he proved that the trotting horse has at times all feet off the ground, 1872; published researches in 'The Horse in Motion,' 1878; invented the 'zoopraxiscope,' 1881, which projected animated pictures on a screen; published further researches in 'Animal Locomotion' (profusely illustrated, 1887, abridged as 'Animals in Motion,' 1899) and other works; led way to invention of cinematograph; bequeathed 3,000l., with his zoopraxiscope and lantern slides, to Kingston public library.

MYERS, ERNEST JAMES (1844–1921), poet and translator; son of Rev. Frederic Myers [q. v.] and brother of F. W. H. Myers [q. v.]; B.A., Balliol College, Oxford; works include four volumes of verse (1877–1904), and prose translations of Pindar's 'Odes' (1874) and of last eight books of 'Iliad' (in collaboration, 1882); enthusiast for Greece.

NARES, SIR GEORGE STRONG (1831–1915), admiral and Arctic explorer; great-grandson of Sir George Nares [q. v.]; entered navy, 1845; captain of H.M.S. 'Challenger,' dispatched by government to explore Southern oceans, 1872–4; led government Arctic expedition in 'Alert' and 'Discovery,' 1875–6; F.R.S., 1875; K.C.B., 1876; rear-admiral, 1887; vice-admiral, 1892.

NEIL, ROBERT ALEXANDER (1852–1901), classical and Oriental scholar; graduate of Aberdeen University, 1870; hon. LL.D., 1891; scholar of Peterhouse, Cambridge; Craven University scholar, 1875; second classic, 1876; fellow of Pembroke College and successful classical lecturer there from 1876 to death; read Sanskrit with E. B. Cowell and with him edited the 'Divyāvadāna' (1886) and joined in translating the 'Jātaka' (6 vols. 1897–1907); university lecturer on Sanskrit, 1884; edited Aristophanes' 'Knights,' 1901; interested in ancient and medieval architecture.

NEIL, SAMUEL (1825–1901), author; rector of Moffat Academy, 1859–73; edited 'Moffat Register,' 1857, and 'British Controversialist' (40 vols.), 1850–73; published works on philosophy, rhetoric, and elocution as well as 'Shakespeare: a Critical Biography,' 1861, and 'Home of Shakespeare described,' 1871; prominent in educational and philanthropic affairs in Edinburgh from 1873; helped to found Educational Institute of Scotland; edited 'The Home Teacher' (6 vols.), 1886.

NELSON, SIR HUGH MUIR (1835–1906), premier of

Queensland; emigrated with father from Kilmarnock to Queensland, 1853; minister for railways, 1888–90; colonial treasurer, March 1893; premier, chief secretary, and treasurer, October 1893–8; restored confidence after bank crisis of 1893; K.C.M.G., 1896; hon. D.C.L. Oxford and P.C., 1897; president of legislative council, 1898; lieutenant-governor of Queensland; opposed Australian federation; died near Toowoomba.

NERUDA, WILMA MARIA FRANCISCA (1839–1911), violinist. [See HALLÉ, LADY.]

NETTLESHIP, EDWARD (1845–1913), ophthalmic surgeon; brother of Henry [q. v.], John Trivett [q.v.], and Richard Lewis Nettleship [q. v.]; student at Moorfields Eye Hospital; F.R.C.S., 1870; ophthalmic surgeon to St. Thomas's Hospital and surgeon to Royal London Ophthalmic Hospital; F.R.S., 1912.

NETTLESHIP, JOHN TRIVETT (1841–1902), animal painter and author; brother of Edward [q. v.], Henry [q. v.], and Richard Lewis Nettleship [q. v.]; studied art at Heatherley's; executed black and white sketches of biblical scenes; exhibited studies of lions, tigers, &c., at Royal Academy, 1874–1901; painted in India a cheetah hunt for Gaekwar of Baroda, 1880; early admirer of Browning; published 'Essays on Robert Browning's Poetry,' 1868 (new edit. 1895), and a volume on George Morland, 1898.

NEUBAUER, ADOLF (1832–1907), Orientalist; born at Kottesó, Hungary; studied for rabbinate at Prague and Munich; studied medieval Jewish MSS. at Paris, 1857–68; published 'La Géographie du Talmud,' 1868 (crowned by the French academy); catalogued Hebrew MSS. in the Bodleian, Oxford, 1868–86; sub-librarian of Bodleian, 1873–99; obtained for library many items from 'Genizeh' (i.e. synagogue depositories) at Cairo, which he catalogued, 1886; edited from Bodleian and Rouen MSS. Arabic text of Hebrew dictionary of Abu-'l-Walid (11th cent.), 1875; two volumes on French rabbis (1877, 1893) embodied much recondite research; reader in Rabbinic Hebrew at Oxford University, 1884–1900; other works include 'Medieval Jewish Chronicles,' 2 vols. 1887–95; created M.A. Oxford, 1873; hon. fellow of Exeter College, 1890; hon. Ph.D. Heidelberg.

NEVILLE, HENRY (1837–1910), actor, whose full name was THOMAS HENRY GARTSIDE NEVILLE; first appeared in London at Lyceum, 1860; made reputation at Olympic Theatre, 1862–6; original Bob Brierley in 'The Ticket of Leave Man,' 1863, Job Armroyd in 'Lost in London,' 1867, and Jean Valjean in 'The Yellow Passport,' his own version of 'Les Misérables,' 1868; successful lessee of Olympic, 1873–9; original George Kingsmith in Mr. H. A. Jones's 'Saints and Sinners,' 1884; thenceforth acted the romantic hero in melo-drama; toured in America, 1890–1; taught acting and wrote about the stage.

NEWMARCH, CHARLES HENRY (1824–1903), divine and author; wrote 'Recollections of Rugby,' 1848, and 'Remains of Roman Art in Cirencester,' 1850; B.A., Corpus Christi College, Cambridge, 1855; rector of Belton, Rutland, 1856–93.

NEWNES, SIR GEORGE, first baronet (1851–1910), newspaper and magazine projector; at sixteen joined London firm of dealers in fancy goods; conceived and produced at Manchester successful weekly periodical, 'Tit-Bits,' 1881; transferred publication to London, 1884; instituted prize competitions and insurance policies in connexion with the paper; brought out 'Strand Magazine,' 1891; started the 'Westminster Gazette' as liberal organ, 1893; his firm became a limited company, 1891, and was reconstructed, 1897; liberal M.P. for Newmarket, 1885–95, and for Swansea, 1900–10; baronet, 1895; presented library buildings to Putney, 1897; fitted out Borchgrevinck's Norwegian South Polar expedition, 1898; 'Life' by Hulda Friederichs, 1911.

NEWTON, ALFRED (1829–1907), zoologist; born at Geneva; B.A., Magdalene College, Cambridge, 1853; made ornithological researches in Lapland (with John Wolley, ornithologist, 1853 and 1858), in West Indies (1857), and Spitzbergen (1864); first professor of zoology at Cambridge, 1866–1907; pioneer of zoological study there; F.R.S., 1870; wrote 'Ornithology of Iceland,' 1863, 'Ootheca Wolleyana,' 1863–1902; 'Dictionary of Birds,' 1893–6; edited 'Ibis' from 1865 to 1870.

NICHOLSON, SIR CHARLES, first baronet (1808–1903), chancellor of the University of Sydney, New South Wales; M.D. Edinburgh University, 1833; settled in Sydney, 1834; speaker of New South Wales, 1847–56;

president of legislative council of new colony, Queensland, 1860; helped to found Sydney University; obtained royal charter, 1858; chancellor, 1854–62; knighted, 1852; baronet, 1859; returned for good to England, 1862; hon. D.C.L. Oxford, 1857; LL.D. Cambridge, 1868, Edinburgh, 1886.

NICHOLSON, EDWARD WILLIAMS BYRON (1849–1912), scholar and librarian; B.A., Trinity College, Oxford; librarian of London Institution, 1873–82; Bodley's librarian, Oxford, 1882–1912; thoroughly reorganized and greatly extended Bodleian Library; interests included biblical criticism, Celtic antiquities, comparative philology, folk-lore, music, palaeography, numismatics, athletics; wrote on many of these subjects.

NICHOLSON, GEORGE (1847–1908), botanist; assistant at Kew, 1876; curator, 1886–1901; helped Sir Joseph Hooker to extend the arboretum at Kew, for which his own collection was purchased, 1889; his herbarium of British plants was presented to Aberdeen University; chief work was 'The Dictionary of Gardening,' 4 vols. 1885–9, 2 suppl. vols. 1900–1.

NICHOLSON, WILLIAM GUSTAVUS, BARON NICHOLSON, of Roundhay (1845–1918), field-marshal; joined Royal Engineers from Woolwich, 1865; served almost continuously in India, 1871–99; K.C.B. and adjutant-general in India, 1898; director of transport in South African war and engaged in operations in Orange Free State and Transvaal, 1900; director of military operations, War Office, 1901; chief British military attaché with Japanese army, 1904; quartermaster-general, 1905; general, 1906; chief of Imperial General Staff and G.C.B., 1908; field-marshal, 1911; baron, 1912.

NICOL, ERSKINE (1825–1904), painter; studied art at Trustees' Academy, Edinburgh; taught art at Dublin, 1846–50; settled in Edinburgh, 1850; A.R.S.A., 1851; R.S.A., 1859; came to London, 1862; exhibited at Royal Academy, 1851–79; A.R.A., 1866; painter in oils and water colours; depicted humours of Irish peasant life; chief works include 'Irish Merry Making,' 1856, 'Donnybrook Fair,' 1859, 'Unwillingly to School,' 1877.

NICOLSON, ADELA FLORENCE (1865–1904), poetess under the pseudonym of LAURENCE HOPE; settled in India; married Malcolm Hassels Nicolson [q. v.], 1889; chief work was 'The Garden of Kama,' 1901, lyrics showing Oriental passion; committed suicide.

NICOLSON, MALCOLM HASSELS (1843–1904), general; entered Indian army, 1859; served in Abys-sinian campaign, 1867–8, and in Afghan war, 1878–80; distinguished in Zhob valley campaign, 1890; C.B., 1891; lieutenant-general, 1899.

NIGHTINGALE, FLORENCE (1820–1910), reformer of hospital nursing; born in Florence; early engaged in cottage visiting and in nursing; visited hospitals in London and abroad from 1844 to 1855; toured in Egypt, 1849–50; inspected Roman Catholic schools and hospital at Alexandria; on way home she visited Kaiserswerth Institute for deaconesses and nurses, 1850; trained as sick nurse there, 1851; superintendent of Hospital for Invalid Gentlewomen, Chandos Street, 1853; accepted invitation of Sidney Herbert, secretary for war, to take out nurses to Crimea soon after outbreak of Crimean war; reached Scutari, 4 Nov. 1854; known there as 'The Lady-in-chief'; by powers of organization and dis-cipline she revolutionized the conditions at the barrack hospital; established kitchen and laundry, and looked after soldiers' wives and children; christened by wounded patients 'The Lady with the Lamp'; by sanitary reforms she lessened the cases of cholera, typhus, and dysentery; visited Balaclava hospitals, where she was attacked with fever, May 1855; returned to Scutari, and provided reading and recreation rooms for the soldiers; on return to England she visited Queen Victoria at Balmoral, Sept. 1856; Nightingale School and Home for Nurses estab-lished as memorial of her services at St. Thomas's Hospital, 1860; published 'Notes on . . . Hospital Administration of the British Army,' 1857; was consulted by foreign governments in American civil war, 1862–4, and Franco-German war, 1870–1; prominent in estab-lishing nursing home in Liverpool Infirmary, 1862, the East London Nursing Society, 1868, the Workhouse Nursing Association, 1874, and the Queen's Jubilee Nursing Institute, 1890; familiar, through correspondence, with all phases of Indian social life, she powerfully advocated native education and village sanitation; her 'Notes on Nursing,' 1860, went through many editions;

received Order of Merit, 1907, freedom of City of London, 1908, and honours from Germany, France, and Norway; raised nursing to an honoured vocation in England; a memorial tablet set up on her birthplace at Florence; portraits by A. L. Egg, R.A. (in National Portrait Gallery), Sir W. B. Richmond, R.A. (at Claydon House), and by Countess Feodora Gleichen (at Windsor Castle).

NIXON, SIR JOHN ECCLES (1857–1921), general; entered army from Sandhurst, 1875; served with 18th Bengal cavalry, 1878–1903; served on staff in Chitral relief force, 1895; in Tochi field force, 1897–8; served in South African war, 1901–2; C.B., 1902; returned to India on conclusion of war; second-class district commander, 1903; inspector-general of cavalry, 1906; divisional commander, 1908; lieutenant-general, 1909; K.C.B., 1911; general-officer-commanding Southern army of India, 1912; general, 1914; transferred to command of Northern army, 1915; after entry of Turkey into European war appointed to command Mesopotamian expedition, 1915; secured control of Basra vilayet; Kut occupied (September); being satisfied of sufficiency of his forces, received permission from home government to advance on Bagdad (October); failed in attempt to relieve (Sir) Charles Townshend, who, after being defeated at Ctesiphon (November), was besieged in Kut (December 1915–April 1916); relinquished command, January 1916; summoned to appear before Mesopotamia commission of inquiry in England (August); received largest share of blame for failure of expedition on account of his undue optimism, but his explanation accepted as satisfactory by Army Council, 1918; G.C.M.G., 1919.

NOBLE, SIR ANDREW, first baronet (1831–1915), physicist and artillerist; served with Royal Artillery, 1849–60; secretary to committees formed to investigate new rifled breech-loading field gun advocated by (Lord) Armstrong [q. v.], 1858; partner in Armstrong's Elswick Ordnance Company, 1860; chairman of Armstrong, Whitworth & Co., 1900–15; K.C.B., 1893; baronet, 1902; carried out important experiments in gunnery and explosives to which are due exact science of ballistics and revolution in composition of gunpowder and design of guns.

NODAL, JOHN HOWARD (1831–1909), journalist and writer on dialect; of quaker parentage; sub-editor of 'Manchester Courier,' 1864, and of 'Manchester City News,' 1871–1904; on staff of 'Saturday Review,' 1875–85; compiled (with George Milner) 'Glossary of the Lancashire Dialect,' 2 parts, 1875–82, and 'Bibliography of Acworth School,' 1889.

NORFOLK, fifteenth DUKE OF (1847–1917). [See HOWARD, HENRY FITZALAN-.]

NORMAN, CONOLLY (1853–1908), alienist; F.R.C.S. Ireland, 1876; F.R.C.P. Ireland, 1890; made special study of insanity; medical superintendent of the Richmond Asylum, Dublin, 1886–1908; introduced humane methods and advocated system of boarding out; hon. LL.D. Dublin University, 1907.

NORMAN, SIR FRANCIS BOOTH (1830–1901), lieutenant-general; joined Bengal army, 1848; served in Indian Mutiny, in Bhutan and Hazara campaigns, 1868, and in Afghan war, 1878–80; present at battle of Kandahar, 1880; C.B.; commanded brigade in Burmese war, 1885–6; K.C.B., 1886; major-general, 1889.

NORMAN, SIR HENRY WYLIE (1826–1904), field-marshal and administrator; went out from London to his father, who was in business in Calcutta, 1842; joined Bengal army, 1844; took active part in Sikh war, 1848–9; served in Kohat pass expedition, 1850; conspicuous in actions round Delhi, at Aligarh and Agra, 1857; proceeded with Sir Colin Campbell to relief of Lucknow; present at battle of Cawnpore, December 1857, and at capture of Lucknow, March 1858; in campaign in Oudh, 1858–9; C.B., 1859; A.D.C. to Queen Victoria, 1863–9; major-general, 1869; first secretary to Indian government in military department, 1862–70; member of governor-general's council, 1870–7; opposed to Lord Lytton's forward policy and resigned, 1877; K.C.B., 1873; lieutenant-general, 1877; member of council of India, 1878–83; general, 1882; governor of Jamaica, 1883–9; tactfully settled constitutional crisis; G.C.M.G., and G.C.B., 1887; governor of Queensland, 1889–95; declined governor-generalship of India, 1893; president of royal commission on conditions of West India sugar-growing colonies, 1896; governor of Chelsea Hospital, 1901–4; field marshal, 1902; 'Life' by Sir W. Lee-Warner, 1908.

NORMAN-NERUDA, WILMA MARIA FRANCISCA (1839–1911), violinist. [See HALLÉ, LADY.]

NORTHBROOK, first EARL OF (1826–1904), statesman. [See BARING, THOMAS GEORGE.]

NORTHCOTE, HENRY STAFFORD, BARON NORTHCOTE, of Exeter (1846–1911), governor-general of the Australian Commonwealth; son of first earl of Iddesleigh [q.v.]; educated at Eton and Merton College, Oxford; B.A., 1869; M.A., 1873; clerk in foreign office, 1868; secretary to British members of the claims commission at Washington relating to the Alabama, 1871–3; private secretary to his father when chancellor of exchequer, 1877–80; conservative M.P. for Exeter, 1880–99; financial secretary to war office, 1885–6; surveyor-general of ordnance, 1886–7; C.B., 1880; baronet, 1887; governor of Bombay, 1899–1903; raised to peerage and G.C.I.E., 1900; efficiently dealt with plague and famine, and preserved the fine Gurajat breed of cattle; passed useful measures of land revenue reform, and District Municipalities Act; governor-general of Australian Commonwealth, 1903–7; G.C.M.G., 1904; travelled widely through Commonwealth and encouraged immigration; P.C., 1909.

NORTHCOTE, JAMES SPENCER (1821–1907), president of Oscott College and archaeologist; B.A., Corpus Christi College, Oxford (first class classic), 1841; M.A., 1844; ordained, 1844; joined Roman communion, 1846; in Italy studied Christian archaeology, 1847–50; editor of 'Rambler,' 1852–4; ordained priest, 1855; canon of St. Chad's Cathedral Church, Birmingham, 1860; provost of cathedral chapter, 1884; president of Oscott College, 1861–77; remodelled studies on public school lines; chief work was 'Roma Sotteranea,' 1869, the standard English treatise on the catacombs.

NORTON, first BARON (1814–1905), statesman. [See ADDERLEY, CHARLES BOWYER.]

NORTON, JOHN (1823–1904), architect; pupil of Benjamin Ferrey [q.v.]; hon. secretary of Arundel Society, 1848–98; had large practice in domestic and ecclesiastical buildings; worked in Gothic style.

NOVELLO, CLARA ANASTASIA (1818–1908), oratorio and operatic prima donna; daughter of Vincent Novello [q.v.]; studied music in Paris; first appeared in public at Windsor, 1832; admired by Charles Lamb; praised by Mendelssohn and Schumann; able interpreter of Handel's solos; sang much in Germany and Italy, where she was immensely popular; original soprano soloist in Rossini's 'Stabat Mater'; appeared in English opera, 1843; married Count Gigliucci, 1843; specially distinguished for rendering of 'I know that my Redeemer liveth' in Handel's 'Messiah'; retired 1860; lived in Rome and Fermo; wrote 'Reminiscences,' published in 1910.

NUNBURNHOLME, first BARON (1833–1907), shipowner and politician. [See WILSON, CHARLES HENRY.]

NUNN, JOSHUA ARTHUR (1853–1908), colonel, army veterinary service; M.R.C.V.S., 1877; F.R.C.V.S., 1886; served as veterinary surgeon in Afghan war, 1879–80; reported on diseases of cattle for Punjab government, 1880–5; principal of Lahore veterinary school, 1890–6; C.I.E., 1895; principal veterinary officer in England (eastern command), 1904–5, in South Africa, 1905–6, and India, 1906–7; C.B., 1906; works include 'Stable Management in India,' 1896, and 'Veterinary Toxicology,' 1907.

NUTT, ALFRED TRÜBNER (1856–1910), publisher, folk-lorist, and Celtic scholar; became head of father's foreign book-selling and publishing firm in London, 1878; publisher of 'Tudor Library,' 'Tudor Translations,' and works by W. E. Henley and fairy tale collections; founded the 'Folklore Journal'; president of 'Folklore Society,' 1897–8; helped to found Irish Texts Society, 1898; published 'Studies on the Legend of the Holy Grail,' 1888, and many papers on Celtic folklore.

NUTTALL, ENOS (1842–1916), bishop of Jamaica, primate and first archbishop of the West Indies; went to Jamaica as lay Wesleyan missionary, 1862; took Anglican orders, 1866; contributed important share to reorganization of disestablished Church of England in Jamaica; bishop of Jamaica, 1880; primate of West Indies, 1893; styled archbishop, 1897.

OAKELEY, SIR HERBERT STANLEY (1830–1903), musical composer; son of Sir Herbert Oakeley, third baronet [q. v.]; B.A., Christ Church, Oxford, 1853; M.A., 1856; Reid professor of music in Edinburgh University, 1865–91: knighted, 1876; prolific composer of vocal and instrumental music; wrote hymn tunes 'Edina,' 1862, and 'Abends,' 1871.

OATES, LAWRENCE EDWARD GRACE (1880–

1912), Antarctic explorer; entered army, 1900; captain, 1906; joined Antarctic expedition led by Captain R. F. Scott, R.N. [q. v.], 1910; member of sledging party which reached South Pole, January 1912; on the return journey 'walked willingly to his death in a blizzard to try and save his comrades beset by hardships.'

O'BRIEN, CHARLOTTE GRACE (1845–1909), Irish author and social reformer; lived at Brussels with father, William Smith O'Brien [q. v.], 1854–6; wrote much on Irish politics; urged improved steamship accommodation for Irish emigrant girls; works include a novel, 'Light and Shade,' 1878, and 'Lyrics,' 1880, and articles on flora of Shannon district; 'Selections' appeared in 1909.

O'BRIEN, CORNELIUS (1843–1906), Roman Catholic archbishop of Halifax, Nova Scotia, from 1882; born in Prince Edward Island; studied for priesthood in Rome, 1864–71; rector of cathedral of Charlottetown, 1871–4; founded collegiate school in Halifax, the germ of the future university; president of Royal Society of Canada, 1896; published theological works and novels.

O'BRIEN, JAMES FRANCIS XAVIER (1828–1905), Irish politician; studied medicine in Paris; at New Orleans enlisted in William Walker's expedition to Nicaragua, 1856; met James Stephens [q. v.] at New Orleans and joined local Fenian organization, 1858; assistant surgeon in American civil war, 1861; arrested in Fenian rising near Cork, March 1867; death sentence for treason commuted to penal servitude; released, March 1869; nationalist M.P. for South Mayo, 1885–95, and for Cork city from 1895 till death; seceded from Parnell, 1891; was general secretary of United Irish League of Great Britain.

O'BRIEN, PETER, BARON O'BRIEN, of Kilfenora (1842–1914), lord chief justice of Ireland; called to Irish bar, 1865; Q.C., 1880; serjeant, 1884; solicitor-general, 1887; attorney-general, 1888; lord chief justice, 1889–1913; baronet, 1891; baron, 1900.

O'CALLAGHAN, SIR FRANCIS LANGFORD (1839–1909), civil engineer; entered public works department of India, 1862; C.I.E., 1883; constructed railway through Bolan pass to Quetta, and made C.S.I., 1887; chief engineer and consulting engineer for state railways, 1889; secretary to public works department, 1892–4; K.C.M.G., 1902; M.I.C.E., 1872.

O'CONNOR, CHARLES YELVERTON (1843–1902), civil engineer; emigrated to New Zealand, 1865; under-secretary for public works, 1883–90; marine engineer for colony, 1890–1; engineer-in-chief to Western Australia, 1891–1902; constructed Fremantle harbour, 1892–1902, and Coolgardie water supply, 1898–1903; C.M.G., 1897; wrote reports on his chief undertakings.

O'CONNOR, JAMES (1836–1910), Irish journalist and politician; an early Fenian; imprisoned for sedition, 1865–70; sub-editor of 'United Ireland,' 1881; imprisoned in Kilmainham, Dec. 1881; edited anti-Parnellite 'Weekly Nationalist Press,' 1887; nationalist M.P. for West Wicklow, 1892–1910; published 'Recollections of Richard Pigott,' 1889.

O'CONOR, CHARLES OWEN, styled THE O'CONOR DON (1838–1906), Irish Roman Catholic politician; liberal M.P. for Roscommon county, from 1860 till 1880; frequently spoke on Irish education and land tenure; hon. LL.D. Royal University of Ireland, 1892; mainly responsible for Irish Sunday Closing Act, 1879; active member of Bessborough land commission, 1880; chairman of royal commission on financial relations between Great Britain and Ireland, 1896; Irish P.C., 1881; president of Royal Irish Academy and Irish Language Society.

O'CONOR, SIR NICHOLAS RODERICK (1843–1908), diplomatist; entered diplomatic service, 1866; served under Lord Lyons in Paris, 1877–83; secretary of legation at Peking, 1885; successfully negotiated difficulties with China in regard to temporary British occupation of Port Hamilton, 1885, and annexation of Upper Burma, 1886; C.M.G. and C.B., 1886; consul-general in Bulgaria, 1887; concluded commercial treaty between Great Britain and Bulgaria, 1889; envoy to Emperor of China at Peking, 1892; active in negotiations with powers after Chino-Japanese war, 1894–5; K.C.B., 1895; ambassador at St. Petersburg, 1895; attended coronation of Tsar Nicholas II, 1896; G.C.M.G. and P.C., 1896; had disagreement with Russian foreign minister in regard to Russian lease from China of Port Arthur, 1897; G.C.B., 1897; transferred to Constantinople, 1898–1908; settled Turco-Egyptian boundary in Sinaitic peninsula, and British frontier in hinterland of Aden; died at Constantinople.

O'DOHERTY, KEVIN IZOD (1823–1905), Irish and Australian politician; contributed to 'Nation,' 1848; transported for treason to Australia, 1849; pardoned, 1856; took medical degrees in Ireland, 1857 and 1859; settled in Brisbane; member of Queensland legislative assembly and of legislative council, 1877–85; nationalist M.P. for North Meath, 1885–8; returned to Brisbane, 1888, where he died in poverty.

O'DOHERTY, MARY ANNE (1826–1910), Irish poetess; born KELLY; wife of K. I. O'Doherty [q. v.]; as 'Eva' wrote Irish patriotic verse for 'Nation' and other Irish papers; 'Poems' published at San Francisco, 1877, 'Selections,' 1908: died at Brisbane.

OGLE, JOHN WILLIAM (1824–1905), physician; B.A., Trinity College, Oxford, 1847; M.A. and B.M., 1851; D.M., 1857; F.R.C.P., 1855; vice-president, 1884; physician to St. George's Hospital, 1866–76; made special study of nervous diseases; founded 'St. George's Hospital Reports,' 1866; contributed largely to medical journals.

O'HANLON, JOHN (1821–1905), Irish hagiographer and historical writer; emigrated to Quebec, 1842; ordained Roman Catholic missionary priest at Missouri, 1847; returned to Ireland, 1853; parish priest of St. Mary's, Irishtown, 1880–1905; canon, 1886; wrote 'The Lives of the Irish Saints,' 10 vols. 1875–1905, 'Life and Scenery in Missouri,' 1890, and poems.

OLDHAM, HENRY (1815–1902), obstetric physician; studied medicine at Guy's Hospital; M.R.C.S., 1837; F.R.C.P., 1857; M.D. St. Andrews, 1858; physician-accoucheur and lecturer on midwifery at Guy's Hospital, 1849–69; president of Obstetrical Society of London, 1863–5. His nephew, CHARLES JAMES OLDHAM (1843–1907), ophthalmic surgeon at Brighton, was an educational benefactor.

O'LEARY, JOHN (1830–1907), Fenian leader; while law student of Trinity College, Dublin, he was imprisoned for share in attack on police near Clonmel, 1848; studied medicine at Queen's College, Galway, 1851–3; contributed to 'Nation'; joined advanced Fenian movement, and went to America in its behalf, 1859; edited in Dublin Fenian weekly journal, 'Irish People,' 1863; paper seized by government, and O'Leary with others was arrested, 1865; he spent nine years in prison; retired to Paris, 1874; returned to Dublin, 1885, where he was prominent in literary society; published 'Recollections of Fenians and Fenianism,' 1896.

OLIVER, SAMUEL PASFIELD (1838–1907), geographer and antiquary; joined royal artillery, 1859; served in China; toured in Japan, 1861; explored Madagascar, closely studying its history and ethnology, 1862–3; joined exploring expedition to Central America, 1867; made archaeological explorations in Brittany, 1868, on the Mediterranean coasts, 1872, and Cornwall, 1873; resigned commission, 1878; F.R.G.S., 1866; F.S.A., 1874; published 'On and Off Duty,' 1881, 'Madagascar and the Malagasy,' 1866, and 'Madagascar,' 2 vols. 1886; compiled abridged official accounts of 'The Second Afghan War, 1878–80,' 1908, and edited journals of early travel.

OLPHERTS, SIR WILLIAM (1822–1902), general; joined Bengal artillery, 1839; distinguished himself at Jhirna Ghaut, 1842, and in Gwalior campaign, 1843; raised battery of horse artillery and marched across India to join Sir Charles Napier in Sind; commanded battery at Peshawur in expedition against frontier tribes, 1851; served in Crimean war, 1854, and throughout Indian Mutiny, 1857–9; distinguished for great bravery during relief of Lucknow; lieutenant-colonel, V.C., and C.B., 1858; in expedition against Waziris gained sobriquet of 'Hell-fire Jack,' 1859–60; held commands at Peshawur, Gwalior, Ambala, and Lucknow, 1861–75; major-general, 1877; general, 1883; colonel commandant of royal artillery, 1888; K.C.B.; G.C.B., 1900.

OMMANNEY, SIR ERASMUS (1814–1904), admiral; entered navy, 1826; took part in battle of Navarino, 1827; served under Captain James Clark Ross [q. v.] in Baffin's Bay, 1835; commander, 1840; captain, 1846; second in command of Franklin search expedition, 1850; organized system of sledge journeys; discovered first traces of Franklin's fate, Aug. 1850; received Arctic medal, 1851; during Crimean war blockaded Archangel, 1854; did blockade work in Gulf of Riga, 1855; in West Indies, 1857, and in Mediterranean, 1859; C.B., 1867; F.R.S., 1868; vice-admiral, 1871; knighted, 1877; admiral, 1877; K.C.B., 1902.

OMMANNEY, GEORGE DRUCE WYNNE (1819–1902), theologian; brother of Sir E. Ommanney [q. v.];

B.A., Trinity College, Cambridge, 1842; M.A., 1845; vicar of Draycot, 1875–88; prebendary of Wells, 1884; voluminous and lucid writer on Athanasian creed.

ONSLOW, WILLIAM HILLIER, fourth EARL OF ONSLOW (1853–1911), governor of New Zealand; educated at Eton and Exeter College, Oxford; conservative under-secretary of state for colonies, 1887; parliamentary secretary to board of trade, 1888; delegate to sugar bounties conference, 1887–8; K.C.M.G., 1887; governor of New Zealand, 1889–92; G.C.M.G., 1889; under-secretary of state for India, 1895–1900, and for colonies, 1900–3; joined cabinet as president of board of agriculture, and P.C, 1903; chairman of committees in House of Lords, 1905–11; president of Royal Statistical Society, 1905–6; alderman of London county council, 1896–9.

OPPENHEIM, LASSA FRANCIS LAWRENCE (1858–1919), jurist; born near Frankfort-on-Main; settled in London, 1895; naturalized, 1900; Whewell professor of international law, Cambridge, 1908–19; chief work, 'International Law: A Treatise' (1905–6).

ORCHARDSON, SIR WILLIAM QUILLER (1832–1910), artist; fellow student with Tom Graham [q. v.] and John Pettie [q. v.] at Trustees' Academy, Edinburgh, under Scott Lauder [q. v.]; exhibited at Royal Scottish Academy from 1848; painted historical pictures; his 'Challenged' (1865) first brought him fame; exhibited Shakespearean subjects, 1865–74; A.R.A., 1868; visited Venice, 1870, painting Venetian subjects, 1870–4; exhibited at Academy 'The Queen of the Swords', 1877; R.A., 1877; henceforth his main subjects were either dramatic episodes of social life or incidents from careers of the great; they comprised 'The Social Eddy,' 1878, 'Hard Hit,' 1879, and 'Napoleon on Board the Bellerophon,' 1880, the 'Mariage de Convenance' series, 1884 and 1886, 'The First Cloud,' 1887; he also won success as portrait painter, showing appreciation of character and subtle draughtsmanship; hon. R.S.A., 1871; D.C.L. Oxford, 1890; knighted, 1907; memorial exhibition of his work at Royal Academy winter exhibition, 1911.

ORD, WILLIAM MILLER (1834–1902), physician; studied at St. Thomas's Hospital medical school, 1852; M.B. London, 1857; M.D., 1877; F.R.C.P., 1875; dean of medical school, 1876–87; physician, 1877–98; elucidated disease now known as myxoedema; gave Bradshaw lecture on subject at Royal College of Physicians, 1898; president of Medical Society of London, 1885; contributed much to medical literature; a foremost clinical teacher.

O'RELL, MAX (pseudonym) (1848–1903), humorous writer. [See BLOUET, LÉON PAUL.]

ORMEROD, ELEANOR ANNE (1828–1901), economic entomologist; daughter of George Ormerod [q. v.]; helped Royal Horticultural Society in forming collection of economic entomology, 1868; first woman fellow of Meteorological Society, 1878; published twenty-four 'Annual Reports of Observations of Injurious Insects,' 1877–1900; led useful crusade against insect pests; consulting entomologist to Royal Agricultural Society, 1882–92; lecturer at Royal Agricultural College, Cirencester, 1881–4; hon. LL.D. Edinburgh, 1900; her publications include 'Guide to the Methods of Insect Life,' 1884, 'A Text Book of Agricultural Entomology,' 1892, and 'Handbook of Insects Injurious to Orchard and Bush Fruits,' 1898; benefactor to Edinburgh University; 'Autobiography' published, 1904.

ORR, ALEXANDRA SUTHERLAND (1828–1903), biographer of Browning; sister of Lord Leighton [q.v.]; married Sutherland George Gordon Orr, 1857; in India during Mutiny; settled in London, 1869; became intimate with Browning, whom she first met in Paris in 1855; generously supported Browning Society, 1881; published 'Handbook to the Works of Robert Browning,' 1885 (6th edit. 1892), and his 'Life and Letters,' 1891 (revised edit. 1908).

OSBORNE, WALTER FREDERICK (1859–1903), painter; studied art at Royal Hibernian Academy Schools and Antwerp; painted field and street life in England, Ireland, and Brittany; regularly exhibited at Royal Hibernian and Royal academies; made sketches in Spain, 1895, and Holland, 1896; R.H.A., 1886; works include 'A Cottage Garden' (in National Gallery of Ireland), 'Life in the Streets,' 1902 (Chantrey bequest), and many good portraits.

O'SHEA, JOHN AUGUSTUS (1839–1905), Irish journalist; educated at Catholic University, Dublin; Paris correspondent of 'Irishman,' conducted by Richard Pigott [q. v.]; special correspondent to 'Standard,' 1869–94; reported siege of Paris, Carlist war, and Bengal famine; published experiences in 'An Iron-bound City,' 2 vols. 1886, 'Roundabout Recollections,' 2 vols. 1892, and other works.

O'SHEA, WILLIAM HENRY (1840–1905), Irish politician; married Katharine Page Wood, 1867; made acquaintance of Parnell, 1880; home ruler M.P. for County Clare, 1880–5; attempted compromise between Parnell and liberal leaders, 1882–4; was returned through Parnell's influence M.P. for Galway, 1886; obtained (Nov. 1890) divorce from wife, who married Parnell, the co-respondent, June 1891.

OSLER, ABRAHAM FOLLETT (1808–1903), meteorologist; managed from 1831 father's Birmingham glass business; made first self-recording pressure plate anemometer and rain gauge, 1835; invention adopted at Greenwich (1841) and elsewhere; applied self-recording methods to cup anemometer for measuring horizontal motion of the air; examined horary and diurnal variations of the wind; showed relation of atmospheric disturbances to the great trade winds; set up in Birmingham standard clock with transit instrument and astronomical clock, 1842; devised instrument for craniometry; F.R.S., 1855; benefactor to Birmingham University.

OSLER, SIR WILLIAM, baronet (1849–1919), regius professor of medicine at Oxford; nephew of Edward Osler [q. v.]; born at Bond Heath, Ontario; studied medicine at universities of Toronto and McGill, Montreal; professor of institutes of medicine, McGill, 1874–84; professor of medicine, university of Pennsylvania (Philadelphia), 1884–9; professor of medicine Johns Hopkins University, Baltimore, 1889–1904; built up there first organized clinical unit in any Anglo-Saxon country; combined best features of English and German systems; F.R.C.P., 1884; F.R.S., 1898; regius professor of medicine at Oxford, 1904–19; baronet, 1911; principal work, 'The Principles and Practice of Medicine' (1891, 9th edit. 1920); a great teacher and man of wide sympathies.

O'SULLIVAN, CORNELIUS (1841–1907), brewers' chemist; studied at Royal School of Mines; student assistant to Prof. A. W. von Hofmann, chemist; became head of analytical staff of Messrs. Bass and Co., Burton-on-Trent; voluminous writings on technology of brewing include 'On Maltose,' 1876, and 'Presence of Raffinose in Barley,' 1886; elucidated distinct character of maltose; F.R.S., 1885.

OTTÉ, ELISE (1818–1903), scholar and historian; born at Copenhagen; step-daughter of Benjamin Thorpe [q. v.], who taught her Anglo-Saxon and Icelandic; published 'History of Scandinavia,' 1874, and Danish and Swedish grammars and translations.

OUIDA (pseudonym) (1839–1908), novelist. [See DE LA RAMÉE, MARIE LOUISE.]

OVERTON, JOHN HENRY (1835–1903), canon of Peterborough and church historian; educated at Rugby and Lincoln College, Oxford; B.A., 1858; M.A., 1860; prebendary of Lincoln Cathedral, 1879; rector of Epworth, 1883–98, and of Gumley from 1898 till death; hon. D.D. Edinburgh, 1889; canon of Peterborough, 1903; voluminous writings include 'The English Church in the 18th Century' (with C. J. Abbey, 2 vols. 1878), 'The Evangelical Revival in the 18th Century,' 1886, and biographies of William Law, 1881, John Wesley, 1891, and 'The Nonjurors,' 1902.

OVERTOUN, BARON (1843–1908), Scottish churchman and philanthropist. [See WHITE, JOHN CAMPBELL.]

OWEN, ROBERT (1820–1902), theologian; B.A., Jesus College, Oxford, 1842; M.A., 1845; B.D., 1852; fellow, 1845–64; accepted tractarian view of catholic Church of England; advocated its disestablishment and disendowment; published 'An Introduction to the Study of Dogmatic Theology,' 1858, 'Institutes of Canon Law,' 1884, and 'The Kymry,' 1891.

PAGE, H. A. (pseudonym) (1837–1905), author and publisher. [See JAPP, ALEXANDER HAY.]

PAGET, FRANCIS (1851–1911), bishop of Oxford; son of Sir James Paget, first baronet [q. v.]; educated at Shrewsbury and Christ Church, Oxford; Hertford scholar and chancellor's Latin verse prizeman; B.A., 1873; M.A., 1876; D.D., 1885; tutor, 1876; regius professor of pastoral theology and canon of Christ Church, 1885–92; contributed an essay on 'Sacraments' to 'Lux Mundi,' 1889; dean of Christ Church, 1892–1901; bishop of Oxford, 1901–11; declined see of Winchester, 1903; member of commission on ecclesiastical discipline,

1904–6; published introduction to Hooker's 'Ecclesiastical Polity, Bk. v,' 1899, 'Faculties and Difficulties for Belief and Disbelief,' 1887, 'The Spirit of Discipline,' 1891, and other sermons; memoir by Stephen Paget and J. M. C. Crum, 1912.

PAGET, SIDNEY EDWARD (1860–1908), painter and illustrator; studied art at schools of Royal Academy, where he exhibited, 1879–1905; works include 'Lancelot and Elaine' and portraits of Lord Winterstoke and Dr. Weymouth; illustrated in black and white in English and American magazines.

PAKENHAM, SIR FRANCIS JOHN (1832–1905), diplomatist; secretary of legation at Buenos Ayres, 1864; served at Rio de Janeiro, Stockholm, Brussels, Washington, and Copenhagen, 1865–78; consul-general at Santiago, 1878–85; British commissioner for claims after war between Chile and Bolivia and Peru, 1883; envoy at Buenos Ayres, 1885–96, and Stockholm, 1896–1902; K.C.M.G., 1898; died at Alameda.

PALGRAVE, SIR REGINALD FRANCIS DOUCE (1829–1904), clerk of the House of Commons from 1886 to 1900; son of Sir Francis Palgrave [q. v.]; admitted solicitor, 1851; obtained clerkship in House of Commons, 1853; C.B., 1887; K.C.B., 1892; edited 'Rules . . . of Procedure of the House of Commons' (8th–11th edits.), 1886–96; proficient water-colour artist; published 'The House of Commons,' 1869, and 'The Chairman's Handbook,' 1877.

PALLES, CHRISTOPHER (1831–1920), lord chief baron of the exchequer in Ireland; B.A., Trinity College, Dublin; called to Irish bar, 1853; Q.C., 1865; solicitor-general for Ireland, 1872; attorney-general, 1872; chief baron of Irish court of Exchequer, 1874–1916; P.C. (Ireland), 1872, (England), 1892; a prominent educationist.

PALMER, SIR ARTHUR POWER (1840–1904), general; entered Indian army, 1857; served in Mutiny, 1857, in North-West frontier campaign, 1863–4, and Abyssinian expedition, 1868; quartermaster-general to Kuram field force, 1878–80; assistant adjutant-general in Bengal, 1880–5; active in expedition to Suakin and raid on Thakul; C.B., 1885; commanded force in Northern Chin Hills in Burma expedition, 1892–3; K.C.B., 1894; major-general, 1893; lieutenant-general, 1897; in Tirah campaign, 1897–8; commanded Punjab frontier force, 1898–1900; general, 1899; commander-in-chief in India, 1900–2; G.C.I.E., 1901; G.C.B., 1903.

PALMER, SIR CHARLES MARK, first baronet (1822–1907), shipowner and ironmaster; joined in founding at South Shields firm for manufacture of coke, 1839; founded shipping service for carrying coals from north of England to London; established (1851) shipyard near Jarrow, which developed from a small village into a large town; first mayor, 1875; constructed battleships; first to manufacture rolled armour plate; liberal M.P. for North Durham, 1874–85, and for Jarrow, 1885–1907; baronet, 1886.

PALMER, SIR ELWIN MITFORD (1852–1906), finance officer in India and Egypt; assistant comptroller-general to Indian government, 1871–85; director-general of accounts in Egypt, 1885; C.M.G., 1888; financial adviser to khedive, 1889–98; first governor of National Bank of Egypt at Cairo, 1898: K.C.M.G., 1892; K.C.B., 1897.

PALMER, GEORGE WILLIAM (1851–1913), biscuit manufacturer; son of George Palmer [q. v.], founder of Huntley and Palmer's biscuit factory at Reading; associated with the business from youth; liberal M.P., Reading, 1892–5, 1898–1904; P.C., 1906; generous benefactor to University College, afterwards Reading University.

PARISH, WILLIAM DOUGLAS (1833–1904), writer on dialect; son of Sir Woodbine Parish [q. v.]; B.C.L., Trinity College, Oxford, 1858; vicar of Selmeston, Sussex, from 1863 to death; published dictionary of Sussex dialect and provincialisms, 1875.

PARKER, ALBERT EDMUND, third EARL OF MORLEY (1843–1905), chairman of committees of the House of Lords, 1889–1905; educated at Eton and Balliol College, Oxford; B.A., 1865; lord-in-waiting to Queen Victoria under Gladstone, 1868–74; under-secretary for war, 1880–5; first commissioner of public works, Feb.–April, 1886; resigned on home rule question, 1886; active in Devonshire affairs.

PARKER, CHARLES STUART (1829–1910), politician and author; educated at Eton and University College, Oxford; with G. J. Goschen and G. C. Brodrick

formed Oxford Essay Club, 1852; B.A. and M.A., 1855; fellow, 1854–68; hon. fellow, 1899; organized university Volunteer corps; ardent Alpinist; friend of Gladstone; urged university reform and national system of elementary education; private secretary to Edward Cardwell [q. v.], 1864–6; liberal M.P. for Perthshire, 1868–74, and for Perth, 1878–92; member of commissions on public schools (1868–74), military education (1869), and Scotch educational endowments (1872); published lives of Sir Robert Peel, 3 vols. 1891–9, and Sir James Graham, 2 vols. 1907; hon. LL.D. Glasgow; D.C.L. Oxford, 1908; P.C., 1907; bequeathed 5,000*l.* to University College, Oxford.

PARKER, JOSEPH (1830–1902), congregationalist divine; studied for congregational ministry in London, 1852; ordained minister at Banbury, 1853–8; minister of Cavendish chapel, Manchester, 1858–69; D.D. Chicago, 1862; minister of Poultry chapel, London, 1869; instituted Thursday noonday service; removed congregation to City Temple, 1874; chairman of congregational union, 1884 and 1901; president of National Free Church Council, 1902; original and fervid preacher; visited America five times; chief publication was 'The People's Bible,' 25 vols. 1885–95; voluminous writings include 'Ecce Deus' (a reply to 'Ecce Homo'), 1867, 'The City Temple Pulpit,' 1899, 'A Preacher's Life,' autobiography, 1899, and some fiction; lives by A. Dawson, 1901, W. Adamson, 1902, and G. Pike, 1904; portrait by R. Gibb (1894) and bust by C. B. Birch (1883) at City Temple.

PARKER, ROBERT JOHN, BARON PARKER, of Waddington (1857–1918), judge; educated at Westminster, Eton, and King's College, Cambridge; called to bar (Lincoln's Inn), 1883; junior equity counsel to Treasury, 1900; chancery judge, 1906; specialized in patent cases; lord of appeal and P.C., 1913; in House of Lords gained authoritative position as judge of final appeal; dealt in masterly fashion with prize appeals heard during European War, 1914–18; most striking characteristic of his judgments was their intellectual compactness; brought before House of Lords detailed scheme for formation of League of Nations, 1918.

PARR, LOUISA (*d.* 1903), novelist; born TAYLOR; married George Parr, 1869; novels include 'How it All Happened,' 1868, 'Dorothy Fox,' 1871, and 'Adam and Eve,' 1880; wrote life of Mrs. Craik, 1897.

PARRY, SIR CHARLES HUBERT HASTINGS, baronet (1848–1918), composer, musical historian, and director of the Royal College of Music; son of Thomas Gambier Parry [q. v.]; educated at Eton and Exeter College, Oxford; studied piano under Edward Dannreuther; influenced by Wagner; professor at Royal College of Music, 1883; director, 1895; choragus at Oxford, 1884; professor of music, 1899–1908; knighted, 1908; baronet, 1902; formative period as composer closed, 1880; new period opened with 'Scenes from Shelley's Prometheus Unbound,' for solo voices, chorus, and orchestra (performed, 1880), and closed with most famous of his works, setting to Milton's ode 'At a solemn Music' (performed, 1887); other settings include music to Aristophanes' 'The Birds' (1884), 'The Frogs' (1891), 'The Clouds' (1905), and 'The Acharnians' (1914); fresh stage in his career marked by performance of his first oratorio, 'Judith' (1888), followed by 'Job' (1892) and 'King Saul' (1894); in last period, beginning with symphonic ode 'War and Peace' (1903), wrote series of works dealing with his thoughts on problems of human race; assistant editor of Grove's 'Dictionary of Music and Musicians'; his own works include 'Art of Music' (1893), 'Oxford History of Music,' vol. iii (1902), and 'Johann Sebastian Bach' (1909).

PARRY, JOSEPH (1841–1903), musical composer; went with family to America, 1854; won prizes for composition at Danville (Pennsylvania) eisteddfods (1860) and at national eisteddfods at Swansea (1863), Llandudno (1864), and Chester (1866); removed to London, 1868; Mus.Bac. Cambridge, 1871; Mus.Doc., 1878; professor of music at University College of Wales, Aberystwyth, 1873–9, and at University College, Cardiff, 1888–1903; composed operas 'Blodwen' (1878), 'Virginia' (1882), 'Sylvia' (1889), oratorios, cantatas, and hymn tunes (including 'Aberystwyth') and anthems; edited 'Cambrian Minstrelsie,' 6 vols. 1893, and 'Dr. Parry's Book of Songs'; his son, JOSEPH HAYDN PARRY (1864–94), was professor at Guildhall school of music, 1890, and composed operas.

PARSONS, ALFRED WILLIAM (1847–1920), painter and illustrator; R.A., 1911; president, Royal Society of Painters in Water Colours, 1914–20; painted landscapes; chief picture, 'When Nature Painted All Things Gay' (1887).

PARSONS, LAURENCE, fourth EARL OF ROSSE (1840–1908), astronomer; son of third Earl [q. v.]; B.A., Trinity College, Dublin, 1864; representative Irish peer, 1868; K.P., 1890; lord-lieutenant of King's co., 1892–1908; made researches into astrophysics at Birr Castle, Parsonstown; published 'Account of Observations of Great Nebula in Orion from 1848 to 1867,' 1867; made from 1868 prolonged investigations into radiation of heat from the moon; chancellor of Dublin University, 1885; hon. D.C.L. Oxford, 1870; LL.D. Dublin, 1879, and Cambridge, 1890; F.R.S. and F.R.A.S., 1867; president of Royal Irish Academy, 1896–1901.

PATON, JOHN BROWN (1830–1911), nonconformist divine and philanthropist; B.A. London, 1849; M.A., 1854; congregational minister in Sheffield, 1854–63; first principal of Congregational Institute, Nottingham, 1863–98; D.D. Glasgow, 1882; took part in many movements for social regeneration; founded National Home Reading Union, 1889, Bible Reading and Prayer Union, 1892, English Land Colonization Society, 1892, and Boys and Girls League of Honour, 1906; edited with R. W. Dale 'The Eclectic Review,' 1858–61; consulting editor of 'Contemporary Review,' 1882–8; publications include 'Criticisms and Essays,' 2 vols. 1892–7, and 'Christ and Civilization,' 1910; 'Life' by James Marchant, 1909.

PATON, JOHN GIBSON (1824–1907), missionary to the New Hebrides; city missionary in Glasgow; ordained by reformed Presbyterian church of Scotland, 1858, and went with wife to establish mission station in island of Tanna in New Hebrides, where he stayed four years; fled from native persecution to New South Wales, where he pleaded for supply of missionaries; settled on island of Aniwa, 1866–81; from 1881 lived at Melbourne, safeguarding interests of natives; died at Melbourne; his 'Autobiography' edited by his brother James, 2 pts., 1889, and 'Later Years and Farewell' by his son, 1910.

PATON, SIR JOSEPH NOËL (1821–1901), artist; brother of Walter Hugh Paton [q.v.]; influenced by William Blake's designs; A.R.S.A., 1847; R.S.A., 1850; exhibited at Royal Academy, 1856–69; painted mythological or historical scenes, as 'Hesperus,' 1858, 'Luther at Erfurt,' 1861, and 'The Fairy Raid,' 1867; Queen Victoria's limner for Scotland, 1865; knighted, 1867; painted religious pictures, including 'Mors Janua Vitae,' 1866, 'Vigilate et Orate,' 1885, and 'Beati Mundo Corde,' 1890, which were sent on tour through the country; correct draughtsman but lacked appreciation of colour; published verse and collected armour; hon. LL.D. Edinburgh, 1876.

PAUL, CHARLES KEGAN (1828–1902), author and publisher; educated at Eton and Exeter College, Oxford; B.A., 1849; chaplain at Eton, 1853; became vegetarian and positivist, 1854; joined Free Christian Union (Unitarian), 1870; edited 'New Quarterly Magazine,' 1873; resigned Church of England living, 1874; published account of William Godwin, 2 vols. 1876; took over publishing firm of H. S. King, 1877; published 'The Nineteenth Century,' works by Tennyson, Thomas Hardy, Meredith, and Stevenson, the 'International Scientific series,' and 'Last Journals of General Gordon'; joined Church of Rome, 1890; published 'Biographical Sketches,' 1883, 'Memories,' 1899, verse, and translations.

PAUL, WILLIAM (1822–1905), horticulturist; founded nursery business at Waltham Cross; published 'The Rose Garden,' 1848 (10th edit. 1903), and 'American Plants,' 1858; issued 'The Rose Annual,' 1858–81, and 'The Florist and Pomologist,' 1868–74; a fluent lecturer; collected rich library of old gardening books.

PAUNCEFOTE, JULIAN, BARON PAUNCEFOTE, of Preston (1828–1902), diplomatist; born at Munich; called to bar, 1852; attorney-general of Hong Kong, 1865–72; knighted, 1872; chief justice of Leeward Islands, 1874; legal under-secretary at foreign office, 1876; K.C.M.G. and C.B., 1880; permanent under-secretary, 1882; commissioner at Paris concerning free navigation of Suez canal, 1885; G.C.M.G., 1885; K.C.B., 1888; envoy extraordinary to United States, 1889; raised to rank of ambassador, 1893; dealt tactfully with questions of Canadian seal fishing in Behring Sea, 1892, the boundary between Venezuela and British

Guiana, 1895–9, and Spanish-American war, 1898; senior British delegate at Hague peace conference, 1899; raised to peerage, 1899; signed 'Hay-Pauncefote treaty' (1901), granting all nations equal passage through Panama canal; died at Washington; hon. LL.D. Harvard and Columbia, 1900.

PAVY, FREDERICK WILLIAM (1829–1911), physician; student at Guy's Hospital; M.B., 1852; studied diabetes under Claude Bernard in Paris; lecturer at Guy's Hospital from 1854; physician, 1871; F.R.C.P., 1860; Harveian orator, 1886; president of various medical societies; first chairman of permanent committee of international congress of medicine, 1909; F.R.S., 1863; hon. LL.D. Glasgow, 1888; pioneer among modern chemical pathologists; founded modern theory of diabetes; initiated 'Pavy's test' for sugar; writings include treatises on diabetes, 1862, food and dietetics, 1873, and carbohydrate metabolism, 1906.

PAYNE, EDWARD JOHN (1844–1904), historian; B.A., Charsley's Hall, Oxford, 1871; fellow of University College, 1872–99; called to bar, 1877; hon. recorder of Wycombe, 1883–1904; published 'History of European Colonies,' 1875, 'Colonies and Colonial Federation,' 1904, and his unfinished 'History of the New World called America,' 2 vols. 1892–9; wrote much on music; accomplished violinist.

PAYNE, JOSEPH FRANK (1840–1910), physician; son of Joseph Payne [q.v.]; B.A., Magdalen College, Oxford, 1862; fellow, 1865–83; hon. fellow, 1906; B.Sc. London, 1865; M.B. Oxford, 1867; M.D., 1880; F.R.C.P., 1873; assistant physician at St. Thomas's Hospital, 1871; physician, 1887; chief medical witness in Staunton poisoning case, 1877; published 'Manual of General Pathology,' 1888, and work on skin diseases, 1889; president of Epidemiological (1892) and Pathological (1897) societies; reported on plague at Vetlanka, 1879; wrote much on history of medicine; works include lives of Linacre, 1881, Thomas Sydenham, 1900, 'English Medicine in Anglo-Saxon Times,' 1904; Harveian orator (1896) and FitzPatrick lecturer (1903–4) at College of Physicians; Harveian librarian, 1899; member of royal commission on tuberculosis, 1890; collected fine medical library.

PEACOCKE, JOSEPH FERGUSON (1835–1916), archbishop of Dublin; B.A., Trinity College, Dublin; rector of St. George's, Dublin, 1873, of Monkstown, co. Dublin, 1878; bishop of Meath, 1894; archbishop of Dublin, 1897–1915.

PEARCE, STEPHEN (1819–1904), portrait and equestrian painter; pupil of Sir Martin Archer Shee [q.v.], 1841; exhibited at Royal Academy, 1849–85; painted portraits of Arctic explorers (now in National Portrait Gallery) and equestrian portraits, the chief being 'Coursing at Ashdown Park,' 1869; wrote 'Memories of the Past,' 1903.

PEARCE, SIR WILLIAM GEORGE, second baronet, of Cardell (1861–1907), shipbuilder; son of Sir William Pearce [q.v.]; B.A. and LL.B., Trinity College, Cambridge, 1884; M.A., 1888; chairman of Fairfield Shipbuilding Company, Glasgow, 1888; conservative M.P. for Plymouth, 1892–5; left property estimated at 150,000l. to Trinity College, Cambridge.

PEARS, SIR EDWIN (1835–1919), barrister-at-law, publicist, and historical writer; called to bar (Middle Temple), 1870; practised at consular bar, Constantinople, 1873–1914; president, 1881; knighted, 1909; died at Malta; wrote 'Life of Abdul Hamid' (1917) and two standard monographs on Byzantine history.

PEARSON, SIR CHARLES JOHN, LORD PEARSON (1843–1910), Scottish judge; B.A., Corpus Christi College, Oxford (first class in *lit. hum.*), 1865; called to English and Scottish bars, 1870; knighted, 1887; sheriff of Renfrew and Bute, 1888, and Perthshire, 1889; conservative M.P. for Edinburgh and St. Andrews universities, 1890–6; Q.C., 1890; solicitor-general for Scotland, 1890–2, 1895–6; lord advocate and P.C., 1891; raised to Scottish bench, 1896.

PEARSON, SIR CYRIL ARTHUR, first baronet (1866–1921), newspaper proprietor; brought out 'Pearson's Weekly,' 1890, and 'Daily Express,' 1900; purchased 'Standard,' 1904; sold these papers on going blind, 1910–12; founded St. Dunstan's, Regent's Park, for blinded soldiers and sailors, 1915; baronet, 1916; G.B.E., 1917.

PEASE, SIR JOSEPH WHITWELL, first baronet (1828–1903), director of mercantile enterprise; entered Pease banking and other firms at Darlington, 1845; chairman of North Eastern Railway, 1894; liberal M.P.

for South Durham, 1865–85, and Barnard Castle, 1885–1903; president of Peace Society; first Quaker baronet, 1882.

PEEK, SIR CUTHBERT EDGAR, second baronet (1855–1901), amateur astronomer and meteorologist; B.A., Pembroke College, Cambridge, 1880; M.A., 1884; visited Iceland, 1881; set up observatories at Wimbledon, 1882, and Rousdon, 1884; observed transit of Venus in Queensland, 1882; at Rousdon made systematic astronomical and meteorological observations, of which he published annual reports; F.R.A.S., 1884; F.S.A., 1890.

PEEL, ARTHUR WELLESLEY, first VISCOUNT PEEL (1829–1912), Speaker of the House of Commons; youngest son of Sir Robert Peel, second baronet, prime minister [q. v.]; educated at Eton and Balliol College, Oxford; liberal M.P., Warwick, 1865–85, Warwick and Leamington, 1885–95; Speaker, 1884–95; first to use power of applying closure for combating Irish 'obstruction', 1885; created viscount, 1895.

PEEL, SIR FREDERICK (1823–1906), railway commissioner; second son of Sir Robert Peel, second baronet [q. v.]; educated at Harrow and Trinity College, Cambridge; B.A. (sixth classic), 1845; M.A., 1849; called to bar, 1849; liberal M.P. for Leominster, 1842–52, and for Bury, 1852–7, 1859–65; under-secretary for colonies, 1851–5; introduced clergy reserves bill, 1853; under-secretary for war, 1855–7; severely censured for failures of Crimean war; P.C., 1857; financial secretary to treasury, 1859–65; K.C.M.G., 1869; member of railway and canal commission from 1873 to death.

PEEL, JAMES (1811–1906), landscape painter; exhibited landscapes at Royal Academy, 1843–1888, and Royal Society of British Artists from 1845; work shows sincere feeling for nature and excellent technique.

PEILE, SIR JAMES BRAITHWAITE (1833–1906), Indian administrator; son of Thomas Williamson Peile [q. v.]; B.A., Oriel College, Oxford (first class classic), 1855; joined Indian civil service, 1856; settled claims of ruler of Bhavnagar against British government, 1859; under-secretary to Bombay government, 1860; passed enactments in favour of depressed landowners in Bombay; registrar-general of assurances, 1867; director of public instruction, Bombay, 1869–73; as political agent of Kathiawar (1874–8) pacified discontent of native chiefs; built bridges, roads, and railways, 1877; averted threatened famine, 1877; member of famine commission, 1878–80; acting chief secretary to Bombay government, 1879–82; C.S.I., 1879; member of council at Bombay, 1882–6; carried through Local Boards and District Municipalities Acts, 1884, and amendment to Bombay Land Revenue code, 1886; vice-chancellor of Bombay University, 1884; member of supreme council, 1886–7; member of India council in London, 1887–1902; urged increased powers for provincial councils; member of royal commission on administration of Indian expenditure, 1895–1900; K.C.S.I., 1888.

PEILE, JOHN (1837–1910), master of Christ's College, Cambridge, and philologist; educated at Repton and Christ's College, Cambridge; won Craven scholarship, 1859, and chancellor's medal, 1860; senior classic and fellow, 1860; tutor, 1871–84; master, 1887–1910; M.A., 1863; Litt.D., 1884; teacher of Sanskrit at Cambridge till 1867; published volume on Greek and Latin philology, 1869, and a primer of philology, 1877; university reader in comparative philology, 1884–91; vice-chancellor, 1891–3; advocated degrees for women; president of council of Newnham College, 1895; hon. Litt.D., Trinity College, Dublin, 1892; F.B.A., 1904; compiled biographical register (vol. i. 1900) and history (1900) of Christ's College.

PELHAM, HENRY FRANCIS (1846–1907), Camden professor of ancient history, Oxford; from 1889; son of John Thomas Pelham, bishop of Norwich [q. v.]; educated at Harrow and Trinity College, Oxford; B.A. (first class in *lit. hum.*) and fellow, 1869; won chancellor's English essay prize, 1870; tutor, 1870–89; fellow of Brasenose, 1889; president of Trinity, 1897; original F.B.A., 1902; hon. LL.D. Aberdeen, 1906; F.S.A., 1890; prominent in founding British schools at Rome and Athens; published 'Outlines of Roman History,' 1893, and 'Essays on Roman History,' posthumous, 1911.

PÉLISSIER, HARRY GABRIEL (1874–1913), comedian; directed troupe of entertainers named 'The Follies,' famous for their 'potted plays' and 'potted opera', 1896–1912; opened on his own account in London, 1907; accomplished composer, producer, and comedian.

PELL, ALBERT (1820–1907), agriculturist; hon. M.A., Trinity College, Cambridge, 1842; settled on farm at Hazelbeach, 1846; founder and first chairman (1866) of central chamber of agriculture; conservative M.P. for South Leicestershire, 1868–85; as guardian in Leicestershire and London, became an authority on poor law; advocated abolition of outdoor relief; chairman of central poor law conference, 1876–93; studied agricultural questions in Canada and America, 1879; sat on royal commissions on city guilds and aged poor; member of council of Royal Agricultural Society, 1886; pioneer of teaching of agriculture at Cambridge; hon. LL.D., 1894; his 'Reminiscences' edited by Thomas Mackay, 1908.

PEMBER, EDWARD HENRY (1833–1911), lawyer; educated at Harrow and Christ Church, Oxford; B.A., 1854; called to bar (Lincoln's Inn), 1858; Q.C., 1874; treasurer, 1906–7; had large practice at parliamentary bar; conducted bill for creating Manchester Ship Canal, 1885; counsel for Cecil Rhodes before parliamentary committee to inquire into Jameson Raid, 1897; prominent in London literary society; brilliant talker and accomplished musician; privately printed much 'vers de société', adaptations from Greek and Latin, and classical plays in English; contributed to Grove's 'Dictionary of Music.'

PEMBERTON, THOMAS EDGAR (1849–1905), biographer of the stage; published novels, including 'A Very Old Question,' 1877, and comediettas; collaborated in plays 'Sue' and 'Held Up' with Bret Harte, whose life he wrote, 1902; dramatic critic of 'Birmingham Daily Post,' 1882–1900; wrote memoirs of E. A. Sothern, 1889, the Kendals, 1891, T. W. Robertson, 1892, and works on Dickens.

PENLEY, WILLIAM SYDNEY (1852–1912), actor-manager; grandson of Aaron Penley [q. v.]; went on stage, 1871; most successful in humorous parts such as Lay Brother Pelican in Chassaigne's 'Falka,' 1883, the title-rôle of 'The Private Secretary,' 1884–6, and, most notably, Lord Fancourt Babberley in 'Charley's Aunt,' of which he gave 1,466 consecutive performances, 1893–7; managed several theatres.

PENNANT, GEORGE SHOLTO GORDON DOUGLAS-, second BARON PENRHYN (1836–1907), landowner. [See DOUGLAS-PENNANT.]

PENRHYN, second BARON. [See DOUGLAS-PENNANT, GEORGE SHOLTO GORDON.]

PENROSE, FRANCIS CRANMER (1817–1903), archaeologist and astronomer; son of John Penrose [q.v.] and Elizabeth Penrose, 'Mrs. Markham' [q. v.]; educated at Winchester and Magdalene College, Cambridge; B.A., 1842; hon. fellow, 1884; rowed in university boatrace, 1840–2; studied art and architecture on Continent, 1842–5; at Rome criticized pitch of pediment of Pantheon; at Athens (1845–7) made careful measurements of Greek classical buildings; published 'Principles of Athenian Architecture,' 1851 (enlarged edit. 1888); surveyor of St. Paul's Cathedral from 1852, where he did much restoration and decoration; interested in astronomical study; published 'The Prediction and Reduction of Occultations and Eclipses,' 1869; observed eclipses of sun at Jerez, 1870, and at Denver, U.S.A., 1878; made researches into orientation of temples; F.R.A.S., 1867; F.R.S., 1894; built entrance gate at Magdalene and wing at St. John's, Cambridge; designed British school at Athens, 1882–6; president of Royal Institute of British Architects, 1894–6; F.S.A., 1898; hon. Litt.D. Cambridge, 1898; hon. D.C.L. Oxford.

PERCIVAL, JOHN (1834–1918), schoolmaster and bishop; B.A., Queen's College, Oxford (double first classes); first head master of Clifton College, for which he won recognized place among great public schools, 1860–79; president of Trinity College, Oxford, where he was less successful, 1879–87; canon of Bristol, 1882–7; head master of Rugby, 1887–95; bishop of Hereford, 1895–1917.

PERCY, HENRY ALGERNON GEORGE, EARL PERCY (1871–1909), politician and traveller; educated at Eton and Christ Church, Oxford; obtained first class in *lit. hum.*, 1893, and Newdigate prize for English verse, 1892; conservative M.P. for South Kensington, 1895–1909; parliamentary under-secretary for India, 1902–3, and for foreign affairs, 1903–5; published accounts of travel in 'Notes of a Diary in Asiatic Turkey,' 1898, and 'The Highlands of Asiatic Turkey,' 1901; trustee of National Portrait Gallery, 1901; hon. D.C.L. Durham, 1907.

PERKIN, SIR WILLIAM HENRY (1838–1907),

chemist; pupil and assistant of Hofmann at Royal College of Chemistry; discovered 'azodinaphthyldiamine,' 1855, and the first aniline dye, 'aniline purple' or 'mauve,' 1856; opened chemical factory at Greenford Green for its manufacture; improved methods of silk dyeing; developed coal tar industry by cheapening process of manufacturing artificial alizarin; published description of 'Perkin synthesis' of unsaturated organic acids, 1867; devoted main energies to investigation of constitution of chemical molecules; president of Chemical Society, 1883–5, and Society of Chemical Industry, 1884–5; F.R.S., 1866; royal medallist, 1879; master of Leathersellers' Company, 1896; knighted on jubilee of aniline discovery (1906), and received hon. degrees from English and foreign universities; 'Perkin Memorial Fund' and 'Perkin medal' founded for researches in chemical industry; portrait by A. S. Cope in National Portrait Gallery.

PERKINS, Sir ÆNEAS (1834–1901), general; colonel commandant royal engineers (late Bengal) from 1895; joined Bengal engineers, 1851; served in relief of Delhi, 1856; constructed 'Perkins' battery' at Delhi; executive engineer at Morshedabad and Darjeeling, 1865–78; superintending engineer in North-West Provinces, 1870; as commanding royal engineer of Kuram field force (1878) facilitated advance on Kabul; C.B., 1879; present at victory of Charasiab and entry into Kabul; commanding royal engineer in march to Kandahar, 1880; inspector-general of military works, 1881; chief engineer of Central Provinces, 1883–6, and of Punjab, 1886–9; major-general, 1887; commanded Oudh division, 1890–1; lieutenant-general, 1890; K.C.B., 1897.

PEROWNE, EDWARD HENRY (1826–1906), master of Corpus Christi College, Cambridge; B.A., Corpus Christi College, Cambridge (senior classic), 1850; M.A., 1853; D.D., 1863; fellow, 1858; master, 1879–1906; vice-chancellor of university, 1879–81; a strong evangelical; published theological works.

PEROWNE, JOHN JAMES STEWART (1823–1904), bishop of Worcester; brother of E. H. Perowne [q. v.]; B.A., Corpus Christi College, Cambridge, 1845; M.A., 1848; D.D., 1873; fellow, 1851; vice-principal of St. David's College, Lampeter, 1862–72; canon of Llandaff, 1869–78; member of Old Testament revision company, 1870; fellow of Trinity College, Cambridge, 1873–5; Hulsean professor of divinity, 1875–8; dean of Peterborough, 1878–91; member of Ecclesiastical County Commission, 1881; bishop of Worcester, 1891–1901; obtained suffragan bishopric and facilitated division of diocese; published translation and commentary on the Psalms, 1864, and edited 'Cambridge Bible' and 'Greek Testament for Schools,' and the 'Letters of Bishop Thirlwall,' 1881.

PERRY, WALTER COPLAND (1814–1911), schoolmaster and archaeologist; educated at Manchester College, York, and Göttingen; Ph.D., 1837; classical tutor at Manchester College, 1837–8; congregational minister at George's Meeting, Exeter, 1838–44; called to bar, 1851; schoolmaster at Bonn, 1844–75; secured the formation (1878) of large collection of casts at British Museum, of which he published catalogue, 1884; voluminous writings include 'German University Education,' 1845, 'The Franks,' 1857, 'Greek and Roman Sculpture,' 1882, and 'Sicily in Fable, History, Art, and Song,' 1908.

PETERSON, Sir WILLIAM (1856–1921), classical scholar and educationist; educated at Edinburgh University and Corpus Christi College, Oxford; first principal of University College, Dundee, 1882–95; principal of McGill University, Montreal, 1895–1919; K.C.M.G., 1915.

PETIT, Sir DINSHAW MANOCKJEE, first baronet (1823–1901), Parsi merchant and philanthropist; born at Bombay; partner in father's broking business at Bombay, 1852–64; started Manockjee Petit cotton mill at Bombay, 1860; acquired chief interest in other mills, and converted Bombay into great industrial centre; sheriff of Bombay, 1886–7; first Parsi member of legislative council of governor-general, 1866–8; knighted, 1887; baronet, 1890; founded at Bombay hospitals for women and children, lepers, and animals; statue by Sir Thomas Brock at Bombay.

PETRE, Sir GEORGE GLYNN (1822–1905), diplomatist; entered diplomatic service, 1846; held minor posts at several European capitals till 1859; secretary of embassy at Berlin, 1868–72; British envoy at Buenos Ayres, 1881–4, and at Lisbon, 1884–93; conciliated

Portuguese ministers in long dispute concerning free transit of English vessels and missions over waterways of Zambesi, Shiré, and Pungwe rivers, 1890–1; C.B., 1886; K.C.M.G., 1890.

PETRIE, WILLIAM (1821–1908), electrician; studied magnetism and electricity at Frankfort-on-Main, 1840; made study of electric lighting problems, 1846–53; invented self-regulating arc lamp, 1847–8; efforts to promote electric illumination financially disastrous; subsequently devoted himself to improving electrochemical processes.

PETTIGREW, JAMES BELL (1834–1908), anatomist; studied arts at Glasgow University and medicine at Edinburgh; M.D., 1861; Croonian lecturer at Royal Society, 1860; F.R.S., 1869; curator of museum of Royal College of Surgeons, Edinburgh, 1869; F.R.S. Edinburgh, 1872; F.R.C.P., 1873; Chandos professor of medicine and anatomy, St. Andrews, 1875; hon. LL.D. Glasgow, 1883; studied flight of insects and birds, and experimented in artificial flight; published 'Animal Locomotion' (in 'International Scientific Series,' 1873), and 'Design in Nature,' 3 vols. 1908.

PHEAR, Sir JOHN BUDD (1825–1905), judge in India and author; B.A., Pembroke College, Cambridge (sixth wrangler), 1847; M.A., 1850; fellow of Clare, 1847–65; called to bar, 1854; judge of high court of Bengal, 1864–76; knighted, 1877; chief justice of Ceylon, 1877–9; revised civil and criminal code; chairman of Devonshire quarter sessions, 1881–95; published 'The Aryan village in India and Ceylon,' 1880, and mathematical and legal works.

PHILLIPS, STEPHEN (1864–1915), poet and dramatist; educated at Oundle; member of (Sir) Frank Benson's theatrical company, c. 1885–92; adopted letters as profession, c. 1898; poetical works include 'Orestes and Other Poems' (1884), 'Primavera' (1890, containing, with other poems, 'To a Lost Love' and 'A Dream'), 'Eremus' (1894), 'Christ in Hades' and 'The Apparition' (1897), 'Marpessa' and 'The Wife' (1898, the last four contained in 'Poems,' 1898), 'New Poems' (1908), and 'The New Inferno' (1911); at his best in his shorter lyrics; dramatic works include 'Paolo and Francesca' (1900), 'Herod' (1901), 'Ulysses' (1902), 'The Sin of David' (1904), and 'Nero' (1906); gained great reputation as dramatic poet, but his genius, although intense, of limited range; plays spoiled by over theatricality in production; sank into obscurity in latter years.

PHILLIPS, WILLIAM (1822–1905), botanist and antiquary; enthusiastic Volunteer in youth; engaged in botanical research, 1861; founded Shropshire Archaeological and Natural History Society, 1878; published 'Guide to the Botany of Shrewsbury,' 1878, and 'Manual of the British Discomycetes,' 1887; did much archaeological research in Shropshire; edited 'Shropshire Notes and Queries,' and 'The Ottley Papers,' 1893–8, 'Quarter Sessions Rolls of 1652–9,' and Shropshire parish registers.

PIATTI, ALFREDO CARLO (1822–1901), violoncellist and composer; born at Bergamo; studied at Milan, 1832–7; played for Liszt at Munich; first appeared in London, 1844; led violoncellos at leading concerts from 1851; played at Monday Popular Concerts from 1859 to 1896; died near Bergamo; unsurpassed in execution, tone, and expression; composed sonatas, concertos, and caprices.

PICKARD, BENJAMIN (1842–1904), trade union leader; worked in mines from age of twelve; secretary of West Yorkshire Miners' Association, 1876, and of Amalgamated Yorkshire Miners' Association, 1881; president of Miners' Federation of Great Britain, 1888; played leading part in miners' dispute of 1893; liberal M.P. for Normanton, 1885–1904.

PICTON, JAMES ALLANSON (1832–1910), politician and author; son of Sir James Allanson Picton [q. v.]; M.A. London, 1855; congregational minister at Manchester (1856–62), Leicester (1862–9), and Hackney (1869–79); his secular lectures on Sunday afternoons anticipated Pleasant Sunday Afternoon movement; member of London school board, 1870–9; radical M.P. for Leicester, 1884–94; works include 'Oliver Cromwell,' 1882, a life of his father, 1891, 'The Bible in School,' 1901, 'Pantheism,' 1905, and 'Spinoza,' 1907.

PIRBRIGHT, BARON (1840–1903), politician. [See DE WORMS, HENRY.]

PITMAN, Sir HENRY ALFRED (1808–1908), centenarian; B.A., Trinity College, Cambridge, 1832; M.B., 1835; M.D., 1841; F.R.C.P., 1845; registrar of College of Physicians, 1858–89; assistant physician (1846) and physician (1857) at St. George's Hospital; active in organization of College of Physicians; knighted, 1883; largely responsible for first edition of 'Nomenclature of Diseases,' 1869.

PLATER, CHARLES DOMINIC (1875-1921), Catholic divine and social worker; educated at Stonyhurst; entered Jesuit novitiate, 1894; rector of Jesuit hall, Oxford, 1916; obtained for it, under title of Campion Hall, status of permanent private hall of university, 1918; founded Catholic Social Guild.

PLATTS, JOHN THOMPSON (1830-1904), Persian scholar; born at Calcutta; held educational posts in North-West and central provinces of India, 1858-72; teacher of Persian in Oxford University, 1880; hon. M.A., 1881; compiled Hindustani and Persian grammars and dictionaries, and translated Persian and Hindustani texts.

PLAYFAIR, WILLIAM SMOULT (1835-1903), obstetric physician; brother of Lyon, first Lord Playfair [q. v.]; M.D. Edinburgh, 1856; professor of surgery at Calcutta Medical College, 1859-60; M.R.C.P., 1863; F.R.C.P., 1870; professor of obstetric medicine in King's College and obstetric physician to King's College Hospital, 1872-98; hon. LL.D. St. Andrews, 1885, and Edinburgh, 1898; author of 'Science and Practice of Midwifery,' 1876, and 'System of Gynaecology' (with Sir Clifford Allbutt), 1896.

PLEYDELL, JOHN CLAVELL MANSEL (1817-1902), Dorset antiquary. [See MANSEL-PLEYDELL.]

PLUNKETT, SIR FRANCIS RICHARD (1835-1907), diplomatist; British envoy at Tokio, 1883-8; K.C.M.G., 1886; senior British delegate at conferences on revising treaties between Japan and European powers; minister at Stockholm, 1888-93, and Brussels, 1893-1900; British commissioner at sugar conference at Brussels, 1898-9; ambassador at Vienna, 1900-5; G.C.M.G., 1894; P.C., 1900; G.C.B., 1901; G.C.V.O., 1903; died in Paris.

PODMORE, FRANK (1855-1910), writer on psychical research; B.A., Pembroke College, Oxford, 1877; clerk in Post Office, 1879-1907; member of council of Society for Psychical Research, 1882-1909; argued for psychological, as opposed to spiritualistic, causality; helped to found, and originated title of, Fabian Society, 1884; writings include 'Studies in Psychical Research,' 1897, 'Modern Spiritualism,' 1902, 'Life of Robert Owen,' 1906, and 'Telepathic Hallucinations,' 1910.

POLLEN, JOHN HUNGERFORD (1820-1902), artist and author; educated at Eton and Christ Church, Oxford; B.A., 1842; M.A., 1844; fellow of Merton, 1842-52; pro-vicar of St. Saviour's, Leeds, 1847-52; joined Church of Rome, 1852; designed ceiling in Merton College chapel, 1850; professor of fine arts at Catholic University, Dublin, 1855-7; joined William Morris, Burne-Jones, and others in fresco decoration of Oxford Union Society, 1858; friend of Turner, Millais, and Ruskin; decorated many private houses in England, and built church of St. Mary, Rhyl, 1863; editor of art and industrial departments of South Kensington Museum, 1863-76; private secretary to Marquess of Ripon from 1876; visited India, 1884; did much to reform taste in domestic furniture and decoration; published 'Universal Catalogue of Books on Art,' 3 vols. 1870-7, and many official catalogues for South Kensington; 'Life' by Anne Pollen, 1912.

POORE, GEORGE VIVIAN (1843-1904), physician and authority on sanitation; studied medicine at University College Hospital; M.R.C.S., 1866; M.B. and B.S. London, 1868; M.D., 1871; F.R.C.P., 1877; professor of medical jurisprudence at University College Hospital, 1876-83; physician, 1883-1903; published 'Text Book of Electricity in Medicine and Surgery,' 1876, 'A Treatise on Medical Jurisprudence,' 1901, 'Essays on Rural Hygiene,' 1893, and 'The Dwelling House,' 2nd ed. 1898.

POPE, GEORGE UGLOW (1820-1908), missionary and Tamil scholar; born in Nova Scotia; brother of William Burt Pope [q. v.]; went to Madras for missionary work, 1839; ordained, 1843; worked in Tinnevelly and Tanjore till 1859; founder and head master of Ootacamund grammar school, 1859; principal of Bangalore College, 1870; hon. D.D. Lambeth, 1864; teacher of Tamil and Telugu in Oxford University, 1884; hon. M.A., 1886; published in Tamil 'First Catechism of Tamil Grammar,' 1842 (reissued with translation, 1895), and other Tamil handbooks; edited classical Tamil works, 'Kurral,' 1886, 'Nāladiyār,' 1893, and 'Tiruvaçagam,' 1900; began catalogue of Tamil books at British Museum, 1890; friend of Browning, whose 'Death in the Desert' he edited, 1897.

POPE, SAMUEL (1826-1901), barrister; called to bar (Middle Temple), 1858; treasurer, 1888-9; recorder of Bolton and Q.C., 1869; leader of the parliamentary bar; temperance advocate and freemason.

POPE, WILLIAM BURT (1822-1903), Wesleyan divine; born in Nova Scotia; served Wesleyan ministries from 1842 to 1867; tutor of systematic theology at Didsbury, 1867-86; hon. D.D. Edinburgh, 1877; president of Wesleyan conference, 1877; publications include 'Compendium of Christian Theology,' 3 vols. 1875; edited 'London Quarterly Review,' 1860-86; 'Life' by R. W. Moss, 1909.

PORTAL, MELVILLE (1819-1904), politician; educated at Eton and Christ Church, Oxford; B.A., 1842; M.A., 1844; president of Union, 1842; called to bar, 1845; conservative M.P. for northern division of Hampshire, 1849-57; chairman of Hampshire quarter sessions, 1879-1903; reformed treatment of prisoners; published 'The Great Hall of Winchester Castle,' 1899.

PORTER, SIR ANDREW MARSHALL .first baronet (1837-1919), judge; son of Rev. J. S. Porter [q. v.]; called to Irish bar, 1860; Q.C., 1872; liberal M.P., co. Londonderry, and Irish solicitor-general, 1881; attorney-general and P.C. (Ireland), 1883; master of the Rolls in Ireland, 1883-1906; baronet, 1902.

POTT, ALFRED (1822-1908), principal of Cuddesdon College; educated at Eton and Magdalen College, Oxford; B.A., 1844; M.A., 1847; B.D., 1854; fellow, 1853; first principal of Cuddesdon Theological College, 1854-8; held various livings, 1867-99; archdeacon of Berkshire, 1869-1903; learned in ecclesiastical law.

POWELL, FREDERICK YORK (1850-1904), regius professor of modern history at Oxford; after two years at Rugby visited Sweden, and studied German and Icelandic; B.A., Christ Church, Oxford, 1872; called to bar, 1874; lecturer in law at Christ Church, 1874-94; student of Christ Church, 1884-94; taught Old English, Old French, and Old German, in addition to law; published 'Early England' for 'Epochs of English History' series, 1876; compiled jointly with Gudbrandr Vigfusson [q. v.] an 'Iceland Prose Reader,' 1879, and 'Corpus Poeticum Boreale,' 2 vols. 1881 (collection of ancient northern poetry with biographies of the poets), as well as 'Origines Islandicae,' posthumous, 1905; helped to found 'English Historical Review,' 1885; wrote history of 'England to Death of Henry VII,' 1885, and edited 'English History from Contemporary Writers,' 1885; regius professor of modern history at Oxford, 1894-1908; translated 'Faereyinga Saga,' 1896, and quatrains from 'Omar Khayyám,' 1901; friend of Verlaine, Verhaeren, and Rodin; president of Irish Text Society; active in foundation of Ruskin College, Oxford, 1899; 'socialist and jingo'; hon. LL.D. Glasgow, 1901; 'Life and Letters' edited by O. Elton, 2 vols. 1906.

POWER, SIR WILLIAM HENRY (1842-1916), expert in public health; medical inspector, Local Government Board, 1871-87; carried out original work in connexion with infectious diseases; principal medical officer to Board, 1900-8; F.R.S., 1895; K.C.B., 1908.

POYNTER, SIR EDWARD JOHN, first baronet (1836-1919), painter and president of the Royal Academy; son of Ambrose Poynter [q. v.]; born in Paris; studied art in London and Paris; exhibited at Royal Academy, 1861-1919; A.R.A., 1868; R.A., 1877; first Slade professor of fine art at University College, London, 1871-5; director for art and principal of National Art Training School, South Kensington, 1875-81; director of National Gallery, 1894-1904; president of Royal Academy, 1896-1918; knighted, 1896; baronet, 1902; gained reputation as painter of subject-pictures in oil and water-colour; reached highest level in four large oil-pictures for Earl of Wharncliffe, 1872-9; executed decorative designs, including frescoes; implanted French principles in English art teaching.

POYNTING, JOHN HENRY (1852-1914), physicist; B.A., Trinity College, Cambridge; fellow of Trinity, 1878; professor of physics, Mason College, Birmingham (afterwards Birmingham University), 1880-1914; F.R.S., 1888; most important contributions to physics two Royal Society papers which revolutionized ideas about motion of energy in the electric field; advanced knowledge of pressure of light; 'Collected Scientific Papers' published, 1920.

PRATT, HODGSON (1824-1907), peace advocate; joined East India Company's service at Calcutta, 1847; helped to found Vernacular Literature Society, 1851; settled in England, 1861; active in industrial co-operative movement; president of Working Men's Club Union, 1885–1902; helped to found International Arbitration and Peace Association, 1880; founded and edited its 'Journal,' 1884; died at Le Pecq; memorial lecture and scholarship established, 1911.

PRATT, JOSEPH BISHOP (1854–1910), engraver; pupil of David Lucas; from 1896 engraved almost exclusively subjects after Georgian painters, including Raeburn's 'Mrs. Gregory' and Lawrence's 'Mrs. Cuthbert'; also engraved state portraits by Sir Luke Fildes of Edward VII, 1902, and Queen Alexandra, 1906.

PREECE, Sir WILLIAM HENRY (1834–1913), electrical engineer; in service of Post Office, 1870–1904; engineer in chief, 1892–9; F.R.S., 1881; K.C.B., 1899; studied telegraphy and telephony; early pioneer of wireless telegraphy; introduced improvements in railway signalling.

PRENDERGAST, Sir HARRY NORTH DALRYMPLE (1834–1913), general; son of Thomas Prendergast [q. v.]; born in India; entered army, 1854; V.C. for gallantry during Indian Mutiny, 1857; in command of British Burma division occupied Mandalay, 1885; K.C.B., 1885; general, 1887; G.C.B., 1902.

PRICE, FREDERICK GEORGE HILTON (1842–1909), antiquary; succeeded father as chief acting partner of Child's Bank, Temple Bar, of which he published an account, 1875; compiled 'Handbook of London Bankers,' 1877; ardent Egyptologist, numismatist, and geologist; formed various antiquarian collections, of which that illustrating prehistoric and Roman London became nucleus of London Museum, 1911; the others realized on his death some 15,000l., 1909–11; director of Society of Antiquaries, 1894–1909; died at Cannes; also wrote 'The Signs of Old Lombard Street,' 1887.

PRICE, THOMAS (1852–1909), premier of South Australia; born near Wrexham; emigrated to Adelaide, 1883; labour member of house of assembly, 1893; secretary (1900) and parliamentary leader (1901) of labour party; first labour premier, commissioner of public works, and minister of education, 1905–9.

PRINSEP, VALENTINE CAMERON [VAL PRINSEP] (1838–1904), artist; born at Calcutta; son of Henry Thoby Prinsep [q. v.]; intimate from youth with G. F. Watts; pupil of Gleyre in Paris; influenced by Lord Leighton; exhibited at Royal Academy from 1862 to death; chief works were 'Miriam watching the Infant Moses,' 'Bacchus and Ariadne,' 'The Gleaners,' and 'A Minuet'; painted Lord Lytton's Indian durbar, 1876; A.R.A., 1878; R.A., 1894.

PRIOR, MELTON (1845–1910), war artist; draughtsman for 'Illustrated London News' from 1868; war correspondent for the paper from 1873, depicting all the great wars between Ashanti campaign, 1873, and Russo-Japanese war, 1904; accompanied Edward, Prince of Wales to Athens, 1875, and George, Prince of Wales to Canada, 1901, and to Delhi durbar, 1903; his 'Campaigns of a War Correspondent' edited by S. L. Bensusan, 1912.

PRITCHARD, Sir CHARLES BRADLEY (1837–1903), Anglo-Indian administrator; son of Charles Pritchard (1808–1893, q.v.); joined Indian civil service, 1858; at first collector of Bombay salt revenue; suppressed smuggling; reformed system of manufacture and sale of opium and native spirits from 1877; commissioner of customs, 1881, and of salt, 1882; C.S.I., 1886; commissioner of Sind, 1887–9; revenue member of government of Bombay, 1890; K.C.I.E., 1891; member for public works department on viceroy's council, 1892.

PRITCHETT, ROBERT TAYLOR (1828–1907), gunmaker and draughtsman: invented with W. E. Metford [q. v.] 'Pritchett bullet,' 1853, and three-grooved rifle, 1854; exhibited at Royal Academy from 1851; joined staff of 'Punch'; painted many water-colour drawings of royal functions; published accounts of visits to Holland, 1871, and Norway, 1878; artist to Lord [q.v.] and Lady Brassey on tours in 'Sunbeam', 1883 and 1885; illustrated books and magazines; collected curios and pipes; wrote and illustrated 'Smokiana,' 1890.

PROBERT, LEWIS (1841–1908), Welsh divine; congregational minister in Rhondda valley and Portmadoc, 1867–96; principal of Congregational College, Bangor, 1896–1908; chairman of Welsh Congregational Union, 1901; published Welsh theological works.

PROCTER, FRANCIS (1812–1905), divine; B.A., St. Catharine's College, Cambridge, 1835; fellow and tutor, 1842–7; vicar of Witton, Norfolk, 1847–1905; author of 'A History of the Book of Common Prayer,'

1855, often reprinted; edited 'Sarum Breviary,' 3 vols. 1879–86.

PROCTOR, ROBERT GEORGE COLLIER (1868–1903), bibliographer; grandnephew of John Payne Collier [q. v.]; B.A., Corpus Christi College, Oxford, 1890; catalogued 3,000 incunabula at the Bodleian Library, 1891–3; assistant in printed books department, British Museum, from 1893 to death; completed in 1898 'Index of Early Printed Books to the year MD.'; devised a new Greek type; interested himself in Icelandic literature; disappeared while on solitary walking tour in Tyrol; 'Bibliographical Essays' collected in 1905.

PROPERT, JOHN LUMSDEN (1834–1902), physician and art critic; M.B. London, 1857; good etcher; revived taste for miniatures; published 'A History of Miniature Art,' 1887.

PROUT, EBENEZER (1835–1909), musical composer; B.A. London, 1854; organist in London chapels from 1861; professor of pianoforte at Crystal Palace School of Art, 1861–85; editor of 'Monthly Musical Record,' 1871–5; introduced Wagner's operas to musical public; composed organ concerto in E minor, 1871, cantatas, orchestral symphonies, and overtures; publications include primers on Instrumentation, 1877, Harmony, 1889, Counterpoint, 1890, Fugue, 1891, and 'The Orchestra,' 2 vols. 1897; professor at Royal Academy of Music, 1879, and Guildhall School of Music, 1884, and at Dublin University, 1894; hon. Mus.Doc. Dublin.

PRYNNE, GEORGE RUNDLE (1818–1903), hymn writer; B.A., Catharine Hall, Cambridge, 1840; M.A., 1861; incumbent of St. Peter's, Plymouth, from 1848 to death; his championship of Dr. Pusey's views on Anglican catholicism and extreme ritualism involved him in much controversy and litigation, 1850–2; vice-president of English Church Union, 1901; chief work was 'The Eucharistic Manual,' 1865 (10th edit. 1895); author of 'Jesu, meek and gentle,' 1856, and other hymns; 'Life' by A. C. Kelway, 1905.

PUDDICOMBE, ANNE ADALISA (1836–1908), novelist writing under the pseudonym of ALLEN RAINE; daughter of Benjamin Evans, solicitor; married Beynon Puddicombe, 1872; wrote simple love stories; found difficulty in finding a publisher for her first work, 'A Welsh Singer,' 1897; her novels, which include 'Torn Sails,' 1898, 'By Berwen Banks,' 1899, and 'On the Wings of the Wind,' 1903, had a wide circulation.

PULLEN, HENRY WILLIAM (1836–1903), pamphleteer; B.A., Clare College, Cambridge, 1859; M.A., 1862; vicar choral of York Minster, 1862, and Salisbury Cathedral, 1863–75; obtained fame by allegorical pamphlet 'The Fight at Dame Europa's School,' 1870 (193rd thousand, 1874), accusing England of cowardice in observing neutrality in Franco-Prussian war; chaplain on 'Alert' in Arctic expedition of Sir George Nares [q. v.], 1875–6; edited John Murray's 'Handbooks' of travel from 1876; criticized educational system in stories of school life.

PYNE, LOUISA FANNY BODDA (1832–1904), soprano vocalist. [See BODDA PYNE.]

QUARRIER, WILLIAM (1829–1903), philanthropist; entered a pin factory at Glasgow at seven; started boot business at twenty; founded shoeblack, news, and parcels brigades in Glasgow, 1864; opened orphan home, 1871; purchased farm of forty acres at Bridge of Weir (1876), where he opened the 'Orphan Homes of Scotland' (1878), which subsequently consisted of fifty villas, with church, poultry farm, consumptive sanatoria, and cemetery.

QUILTER, HARRY (1851–1907), art critic; B.A., Trinity College, Cambridge, 1874; M.A., 1877; called to bar, 1878; art critic and journalist mainly for 'Spectator' and 'The Times, 1876–87; evoked anger and attack from Whistler by his frank criticisms; exhibited oil paintings in London, 1884–93; edited ambitious 'Universal Review,' 1888–90; conducted 'rational' boarding schools at Mitcham and Liverpool, 1894–6; published 'What's What,' 1902; art collections realized over 14,000l., 1906; published verse, prose, essays, and works on art.

QUILTER, Sir WILLIAM CUTHBERT, first baronet (1841–1911), art collector and politician; brother of H. Quilter [q. v.]; founder and director of National Telephone Co., 1881; developed Bawdsey Estate near Felixstowe, 1883; agriculturist, cattle breeder, and yachtsman; liberal M.P. (1885) and unionist M.P. (1886–1905) for Sudbury; baronet, 1897; formed great art collection which realized 87,780l. in 1909,

RADCLIFFE-CROCKER, HENRY (1845–1909), dermatologist; studied medicine at University College Hospital, London; M.R.C.S., 1873; L.R.C.P., 1874; B.S., 1874; M.D., 1875; F.R.C.P., 1887; physician and dermatologist at University College Hospital from 1879; member of English and foreign dermatological societies; prominent in affairs of British Medical Association; died at Engelberg, Switzerland; distinguished leprologist; published 'Diseases of the Skin,' 1888 (3rd edit. 2 vols. 1903), and 'The Atlas of Diseases of the Skin,' 2 vols. 1896; his library, with 1,500*l.* to found scholarship in dermatology, was presented by his widow to University College Hospital.

RAE, WILLIAM FRASER (1835–1905), author; called to bar, 1861; abandoned law for journalism; special correspondent to 'Daily News' in Canada and America; newspaper articles were collected in volumes on Canada and America, Austria and Egypt; he translated Taine's 'Notes on England,' 1873; wrote much on 'Junius' problem and on eighteenth-century political history; chief work was 'Sheridan, a Biography,' 2 vols. 1896; edited from original MSS. Sheridan's plays, 1902; he also wrote some fiction.

RAGGI, MARIO (1821–1907), sculptor; born at Carrara; came to London, 1880; executed memorials to Beaconsfield (in Parliament Square) and Gladstone (at Manchester); exhibited busts at Royal Academy, 1878–95.

RAILTON, HERBERT (1858–1910), black-and-white draughtsman; abandoned architecture for book illustration; depicted old buildings with rare delicacy.

RAINE, ALLEN (pseudonym) (1836–1908), novelist. [See PUDDICOMBE, ANNE ADALISA.]

RAINES, SIR JULIUS AUGUSTUS ROBERT (1827–1909), general; entered army, 1842; served in Crimean war, 1854–5; commanded 95th regiment throughout Indian Mutiny, 1857–9; C.B., 1859; commanded expedition into Arabia, 1865–6; lieutenant-general, 1877; general, 1881; K.C.B., 1893; G.C.B., 1906; published 'The 95th (Derbyshire) Regiment in Central India,' 1900.

RAINY, ROBERT (1826–1906), Scottish divine; M.A. Glasgow University, 1844; D.D., 1863; studied for Free Church ministry at Free Church New College, Edinburgh, 1844; minister at Free High Church, Edinburgh, 1854–62; professor of church history in Free Church College, 1862; principal, 1874–1901; moderator of assembly, 1887, 1900, 1905; advocated 'voluntary' policy; achieved union of reformed presbyterian synod with Free Church, 1876; as convener of 'highland committee' from 1881 raised much money for church endowment; helped to pass the Declaratory Act, 1892; secured union with United Presbyterian Church, 1900; first moderator; writings include 'Three Lectures on the Church of Scotland' (1872, a reply to Dean Stanley), 'The Bible and Criticism,' 1878; Lives by R. Mackintosh and P. C. Simpson; his son, ADAM ROLLAND RAINY (1862–1911), surgeon-oculist, was liberal M.P. for Kilmarnock Burghs, 1906–11.

RAMÉE, MARIE LOUISE DE LA, 'OUIDA', novelist. [See DE LA RAMÉE.]

RAMSAY, ALEXANDER (1822–1909), Scottish journalist; editor of 'Banffshire Journal' from 1847 to death; edited 'Aberdeen-Angus Herd Book,' 1872–1905; hon. LL.D. Aberdeen, 1895; wrote 'History of Agricultural Society of Scotland,' 1879.

RAMSAY, SIR WILLIAM (1852–1916), chemical discoverer; educated at Glasgow University; Ph.D., Tübingen; taught at Glasgow University and carried out investigations in organic chemistry, 1872–80; professor of chemistry, University College, Bristol, 1880–7; principal, 1881; professor of general chemistry, University College, London, 1887–1912; F.R.S., 1888; K.C.B., 1902; Nobel prizeman, 1904; his scientific work in London of three periods; first line of investigation physico-chemical, including determination of molecular complexity of pure liquids; second, discovery of chemically inerte lementary gases, argon (in collaboration with J. W. Strutt, third Baron Rayleigh, q. v.), helium, neon, krypton, and xenon; third, proof that emanation of radium produces helium during its atomic disintegration; greatest chemical discoverer of his time.

RANDALL, RICHARD WILLIAM (1824–1906), dean of Chichester; B.A., Christ Church, Oxford, 1846; M.A., 1849; D.D., 1892; vicar of All Saints', Clifton, 1868–92; hon. canon of Gloucester, 1891; dean of Chichester, 1892–1902; strong ritualist; wrote devotional works.

RANDEGGER, ALBERTO (1832–1911), musician; born at Trieste; settled in London, 1854; organist at St. Paul's, Regent's Park, 1859–70; joined staff of Royal Academy of Music, 1868, and Royal College of Music, 1896; composed grand opera 'Bianca Capello,' operettas, and cantatas; wrote primer on 'Singing'; conducted Italian opera for Sir Augustus Harris, 1887–98, and Norwich triennial festivals, 1881–1905.

RANDLES, MARSHALL (1826–1904), Wesleyan divine; member of legal conference, 1882; tutor of systematic theology at Didsbury, 1886; president of Conference, 1896; advocated total abstinence in 'Britain's Bane and Antidote,' 1864; theological works include 'For Ever, an Essay on Everlasting Punishment,' 1871.

RANDOLPH, FRANCIS CHARLES HINGESTON- (1833–1910), antiquary. [See HINGESTON-RANDOLPH.]

RANDOLPH, SIR GEORGE GRANVILLE (1818–1907), admiral; entered navy, 1830; served off Spain, in the Mediterranean, and in East Indies; in Black Sea and Crimean operations, 1854–5; commodore at Cape of Good Hope, 1867–9; C.B., 1869; vice-admiral, 1877; admiral, 1884; K.C.B., 1897; published 'Problems in Naval Tactics,' 1879; F.R.G.S.

RANSOM, WILLIAM HENRY (1824–1907), physician and embryologist; fellow pupil with Huxley at University College, London; fellow, 1896; M.D. London, 1850; F.R.C.P., 1869; physician to Nottingham General Hospital, 1854–90; F.R.S., 1870; published original researches into ovology; devised gas heating disinfecting stove, 1870; helped to establish University College, Nottingham; published 'The Inflammation Idea in General Pathology,' 1906

RAPER, ROBERT WILLIAM (1842–1915), classical scholar; B.A., Trinity College, Oxford; first classes in classical moderations and *literae humaniores*; life fellow of Trinity, 1871; tutor, and subsequently lecturer and bursar; vice-president, 1894; declined presidency three times; lectured mainly on Homer, Virgil, Aristophanes, and Tacitus; founded Oxford University Appointments Committee, 1894.

RASSAM, HORMUZD (1826–1910), Assyrian explorer; born in Asiatic Turkey; son of Nestorian Christian; converted in youth to protestantism; assisted Sir A. H. Layard [q. v.] in excavations at Nimroud, 1845, and at Kouyunjik (i.e. Nineveh), 1847; for short period at Magdalen College, Oxford, 1848; continued with Layard excavations at Nineveh and Nimroud, 1849, and in Babylon, 1850–1; discovered palace of Aššur-bani-âpli at Nineveh; political interpreter at Aden, 1854–61; magistrate and political resident; represented British interests in Zanzibar, 1861; sent with two others commissioned by British government to protest against imprisonment at Magdala, by Theodore, king of Abyssinia, of C. D. Cameron [q. v.] and H. A. Stern [q. v.] 1864; was imprisoned in chains at Magdala, 1866; released on arrival of Sir Robert Napier, 1868; narrated his experiences in 'British Mission to Theodore, King of Abyssinia,' 2 vols. 1869; again employed in Asiatic Turkey to inquire into condition of Christian communities, 1877; from 1876 to 1882 made many important finds in Assyria and Babylonia; after 1882 resided at Brighton, writing on Assyriology and, as a strong evangelical, engaging in religious controversy.

RATHBONE, WILLIAM (1819–1902), philanthropist; after much travel became partner in father's Liverpool mercantile firm, 1841; established Liverpool Training School for Nurses, 1862; helped in founding in London National Association for providing trained nurses, 1874; supported Liverpool Cotton Famine Relief Fund, 1862–3; liberal M.P. for Liverpool, 1868–80, for Carnarvonshire, 1880–5, for North Carnarvonshire, 1885–95; president of University College, Liverpool, from 1892, and of University College of North Wales from 1891; LL.D. Victoria University, 1895; published works on social questions; bronze statue by Sir George Frampton at Liverpool; 'Life' by E. F. Rathbone, 1905.

RATTIGAN, SIR WILLIAM HENRY (1842–1904), Anglo-Indian jurist; born at Delhi; called to bar (Lincoln's Inn), 1873; D.L. Göttingen, 1885; formed extensive practice as a barrister at Lahore; vice-chancellor of Punjab University, 1887–95; D.L., 1896; LL.D. Glasgow, 1901; served on viceroy's legislative council, 1892–3; wrote 'A Digest of Civil and Customary Law of the Punjab,' 1880 (7th edit. 1909); knighted, 1895; Q.C., 1897; settled in England, 1901; liberal unionist M.P. for North East Lanark, 1901–4.

RAVEN, JOHN JAMES (1833–1906), archaeologist

and campanologist; B.A., Emmanuel College, Cambridge, 1857; M.A., 1860; D.D., 1872; head master of Bungay (1859–66) and Yarmouth (1866–85) grammar schools; hon. canon of Norwich, 1888; F.S.A., 1891; published accounts of the church bells of Cambridgeshire (1869), Suffolk (1890), and England (1906), works on Suffolk, and sermons.

RAVERTY, HENRY GEORGE (1825–1906), soldier and Oriental scholar; served in Indian army, 1843–64; present at Multan and Gujarat, 1848–9; published 'Thesaurus of English Hindustani Technical Terms,' 1859, Pushto or Afghan grammar, 1855, dictionary, 1860, and anthology, 1860, as well as 'Notes on Afghanistan and Baluchistan,' 4 pts. 1881–8; translated from Persian Minhāj's 'Tabakāt i Nāsirī,' and made many contributions to 'Journal of Asiatic Society, Bengal'; left unpublished MSS. on Afghanistan history.

RAWLING, CECIL GODFREY (1870–1917), soldier and explorer; entered army, 1891; explored unsurveyed Western Tibet and Rudok, 1903; Upper Tsanpo (Brahmaputra), 1904–5, Dutch New Guinea, 1909; D.S.O., 1917; killed in action in Flanders.

RAWLINSON, GEORGE (1812–1902), canon of Canterbury; B.A., Trinity College, Oxford, 1838; M.A., 1841; president of Union, 1840; fellow of Exeter College, 1840; Bampton lecturer, 1859; Camden professor of ancient history, 1861–89; canon of Canterbury, 1872; rector of All Hallows, Lombard Street, 1888; edited with brother Sir Henry C. Rawlinson [q. v.] 'The History of Herodotus,' 4 vols. 1858–60 (abridged edit. 2 vols. 1897); published 'The Five Great Monarchies [viz. Chaldaea, Assyria, Babylonia, Media, and Persia] of the Ancient Eastern World,' 4 vols. 1862–7, 'The Sixth Great Monarchy' (i.e. Parthia), 1873, 'The Seventh Great Monarchy' (i.e. Sassanian or new Persian), 1876, and histories of Ancient Egypt, 2 vols. 1881, and Phoenicia, 1889, and many kindred works; wrote life of his brother, 1898.

RAWSON, SIR HARRY HOLDSWORTH (1843–1910), admiral; entered navy, 1857; served in China war, 1858–61; reported on capabilities of defence of Suez Canal, 1878; principal transport officer in Egyptian campaign, 1882; C.B.; commander-in-chief at Cape of Good Hope and West coast of Africa station, 1895–8; in command at capture of M'Weli and bombardment of Zanzibar, 1895–6; commanded Benin expedition, 1897; K.C.B., 1897; vice-admiral, 1898; commanded Channel squadron, 1898–1901; governor of New South Wales, 1902–9; admiral, 1903; G.C.B., 1906; G.C.M.G., 1909.

RAYLEIGH, third BARON (1842–1919), mathematician and physicist. [See STRUTT, JOHN WILLIAM.]

READ, CLARE SEWELL (1826–1905), agriculturist; farmed family estates in Norfolk from 1854 to 1896; conservative M.P. for East Norfolk, 1865–7, for South Norfolk, 1868–80, and West Norfolk, 1884–5; served on cattle plague commission, 1865, and on several parliamentary agricultural committees; secretary to local government board, 1874–6; assistant commissioner to inquire into agricultural conditions in Canada and America, 1879; wrote many agricultural papers; chairman of Farmers' Club, 1868 and 1892.

READ, WALTER WILLIAM (1855–1907), Surrey cricketer; by prolific scores raised county to leading position; played for Gentlemen v. Players, 1877–95, and for England v. Australia, 1884–93; visited Australia, 1882–3 and 1887–8, and South Africa, 1891–2; compiled 'Annals of Cricket,' 1896.

READE, THOMAS MELLARD (1832–1909), geologist; architect and civil engineer at Liverpool from 1860; laid out Blundellsands estate, 1868; wrote much on glacial and post-glacial geology of Lancashire, on mineral structure of slaty rocks, and on geomorphology; published 'Origin of Mountain Ranges,' 1886, and 'Evolution of Earth Structure,' 1903; F.G.S., 1872; Murchison medallist, 1896.

REAY, eleventh BARON (1839–1921), governor of Bombay and first president of the British Academy. [See MACKAY, DONALD JAMES.]

REDESDALE, first BARON (1837–1916), diplomatist and author. [See MITFORD, ALGERNON BERTRAM FREEMAN-.]

REDMOND, JOHN EDWARD (1856–1918), Irish political leader; born at Ballytrent, co. Wexford; educated at Clongowes and Trinity College, Dublin; clerk in House of Commons, 1880; M.P., New Ross, co. Wexford, 1881; sent on political mission to Irish of Australia and America, 1882–4; chief supporter of Charles Stewart Parnell

[q. v.] on split in Irish party, 1890; leader of Parnellite group on Parnell's death, 1891; resigned North Wexford, held since Redistribution Act (1885), 1891; stood for Cork, but heavily defeated; returned for Waterford, sole seat captured by Parnellites; a leading debater in House; adopted statesmanlike policy and conciliatory attitude towards government and anti-Parnellites; chairman of reunited Irish party, 1900; supported land purchase policy of George Wyndham [q.v.]; incurred temporary loss of prestige for himself and party in Ireland through attitude over liberal government's 'devolution' scheme, 1906; recovered ground by 1910; gave tardy support to Irish volunteer movement, 1914; on outbreak of European war (1914) did utmost to promote recruiting in Ireland, but opposed her inclusion in first National Service Bill, 1916; surprised and horrified by Irish Rebellion, 1916; lost the confidence of Ireland, which passed into control of extreme nationalists under De Valera; three main points gained by Irish during his leadership, control of local government, ownership of land, and statutory establishment of Irish parliament with executive responsible to it; nationalist, devoid of hostility to British Empire, who aimed at free Ireland within Empire.

REDMOND, WILLIAM HOEY KEARNEY (1861–1917), Irish nationalist; brother of J. E. Redmond [q. v.]; imprisoned as nationalist 'suspect,' 1881; joined brother on political mission to Australia and America, 1883; M.P., Wexford, 1883, North Fermanagh, 1885, East Clare, 1891–1917; re-imprisoned, 1888; violent Parnellite; served in European war; killed in Flanders.

REDPATH, HENRY ADENEY (1848–1908), biblical scholar; B.A., Queen's College, Oxford, 1871; M.A., 1874; D.Litt., 1901; completed 'A Concordance to the Septuagint' begun by Edwin Hatch [q. v.], 3 vols. 1892–1906; Grinfield lecturer on Septuagint at Oxford, 1901–5.

REED, SIR EDWARD JAMES (1830–1906), naval architect; edited 'Mechanic's Magazine,' 1853; secretary to newly-founded Institution of Naval Architects, 1860; employed by navy to convert wooden men-of-war into armourclads, 1862; chief constructor of the navy, 1863–70; designed and launched 'Bellerophon,' on which he introduced longtitudinal and bracket frame system, 1865; joined Sir J. Whitworth's ordnance works at Manchester, 1870; designed ships for foreign navies; constructing naval engineer to Indian government and crown colonies; F.R.S., 1876; C.B., 1868; K.C.B., 1880; liberal M.P. for Pembroke boroughs, 1874–80, and for Cardiff, 1880–95, 1900–5; lord of the treasury, 1886; chairman of load line (1884) and manning of ships (1894) committees; published history of Japan, 2 vols. 1880, 'Treatise on the Stability of Ships,' 1884, papers on naval subjects, and verse.

REEVES, SIR WILLIAM CONRAD (1821–1902), chief justice of Barbados; son of negro mother; called to bar, 1863; practised at Barbados; member of local house of assembly, Barbados, 1874; solicitor-general; championed ancient Barbados constitution against schemes of crown government from 1876; attorney-general, 1882; K.C., 1883; chief justice, 1886; knighted, 1889.

REICH, EMIL (1854–1910), historian; born in Hungary; settled in England, 1893, as writer and lecturer at Oxford, Cambridge, and London; voluminous works include 'Graeco-Roman Institutions,' 1890, Hungarian literature, 1897, lectures on Plato, 1906, and 'General History of Western Nations—Antiquity,' 2 vols. 1908–9; he laid stress as historian on geographical and economic conditions.

REID, ARCHIBALD DAVID (1844–1908), painter; studied at Trustees' Academy and Royal Scottish Academy, Edinburgh; visited Holland, Italy, and Spain; pupil of Julien at Paris; A.R.S.A., 1892; painted portraits, but mainly sea pieces and landscapes, both in water-colour and in oil; works include 'A Lone Shore,' 1875, and 'Harvest Scene,' 1878.

REID, SIR GEORGE HOUSTOUN (1845–1918), colonial politician; born in Scotland; taken to Australia, 1852; admitted to colonial bar, 1879; represented East Sydney in legislative assembly, 1880–4, 1885–1901; premier of New South Wales, 1894–9; free-trader, but half-hearted federalist; premier of Australian Commonwealth through coalition with labour party, 1904–5; first Commonwealth high commissioner in London, 1910–15; P.C., 1897; K.C.M.G., 1909; G.C.M.G., 1911; G.C.B., 1916.

REID, Sir JOHN WATT (1823–1909), medical director-general of the navy; L.R.C.S. Edinburgh, 1844; M.D. Aberdeen, 1856; entered navy as assistant surgeon, 1845; served as naval surgeon in Black Sea, 1854; in China war, 1857–9; in Ashanti war, 1873–4; deputy inspector-general, 1874–80; inspector-general, 1880–8; K.C.B., 1882.

REID, Sir ROBERT GILLESPIE (1842–1908), Canadian contractor and financier; emigrated from Perthshire to Australia, 1865; subsequently settled at Montreal; carried out many important building and engineering contracts; built bridges across Niagara river at Buffalo, and across the Rio Grande between Texas and Mexico, and railways in Newfoundland; president of Reid-Newfoundland Company, which had control of Newfoundland railways, the St. John's dry dock, and immense tracts of land; knighted, 1907.

REID, Sir THOMAS WEMYSS (1842–1905), journalist and biographer; early took up journalism; chief reporter on 'Newcastle Journal,' 1861; editor of 'Preston Guardian,' 1864; head of reporting staff of 'Leeds Mercury,' 1866; obtained admission of provincial reporters to press gallery of House of Commons, 1881; editor of 'Leeds Mercury,' 1870–87; of moderate liberal views; supported Gladstone's home rule policy and Forster's education bill; manager of Cassell's publishing firm from 1887 to death; founded (1890) and edited till 1897 the 'Speaker,' a weekly liberal organ; friend and supporter of Lord Rosebery; knighted, 1894; hon. LL.D. St. Andrews, 1893; wrote lives of Charlotte Brontë, 1877, W. E. Forster, 2 vols. 1888, Lord Houghton, 2 vols. 1890, Lord Playfair, 1899, and William Black, 1902; a successful novelist; Memoirs edited by S. J. Reid, 1905.

RENDEL, Sir ALEXANDER MEADOWS (1829–1918), civil engineer; son of James Meadows Rendel [q. v.], and brother of George Wightwick Rendel [q. v.]; head of father's practice, 1856; designed docks and harbours; consulting engineer to Indian State Railways, 1872; K.C.I.E., 1887.

RENDEL, GEORGE WIGHTWICK (1833–1902), civil engineer; son of James Meadows Rendel [q. v.]; assistant to father; partner in Sir William Armstrong's ordnance works at Elswick, 1852; responsible for hydraulic method of mounting and working heavy guns and introduction of cruiser, intermediate between armour-clad and unprotected war vessel; extra professional civil lord of admiralty, 1882–5; settled near Naples as director of Armstrong Pozzuoli company, 1887; friend of Empress Frederick of Germany and Lord Rosebery.

REYNOLDS, JAMES EMERSON (1844–1920), chemist; born in co. Dublin; studied medicine in Edinburgh; abandoned medicine for chemistry; analyst to Royal Dublin Society, 1868–75; discovered thiocarbamide, 1868; professor of chemistry, Royal College of Surgeons, Dublin, 1870–5, at Trinity College, Dublin, 1875–1903; F.R.S., 1880.

REYNOLDS, OSBORNE (1842–1912), engineer and physicist; B.A., Queens' College, Cambridge; professor of engineering, Owens College, Manchester, 1868–1905; conducted long series of investigations into mechanical questions and physical phenomena such as lubrication, laws of flow of water in pipes, &c.; F.R.S., 1877; gold medallist of Royal Society, 1888; collected scientific papers published, 1900–3.

RHODES, CECIL JOHN (1853–1902), imperialist and benefactor; fifth son of Francis William Rhodes, vicar of Bishop Stortford, Hertfordshire; was educated at Bishop Stortford grammar school, 1861–9; owing to failure of health, he went to South Africa to join his eldest brother, who was growing cotton in Natal, 1870; removed to Orange Free State on discovery of diamonds there, 1871; worked with his brother a moderately prosperous claim; meanwhile matriculated at Oriel College, Oxford, 13 Oct. 1873; revisited Oxford at frequent intervals until he succeeded in graduating as a passman B.A. and M.A., 17 Dec. 1881; during this period Rhodes with partners increased his holdings in Kimberley diamond fields, obtaining a large interest in the De Beers mines there; in 1880 he helped to establish De Beers mining company; during 1875 he made solitary journey through Bechuanaland and Transvaal; formed the aspiration to work with Dutch settlers and to federate South Africa under British rule with Cape Dutch assent; was elected to Cape legislature for newly-formed constituency of Barkly West (1880) and retained seat for

life; in the South African parliament he from the first sought to maintain wide powers of local self-government while extending British settlement and influence; soon concentrated political activities on northern expansion of the British dominion; aided in securing great part of Bechuanaland for the Cape government in spite of rivalry of Transvaal Republic, 1882; when the whole of Bechuanaland was formally annexed, Rhodes was made deputy commissioner, 1884; and he negotiated in person with President Kruger the withdrawal of Boer claims to portions of the territory. After he had made terms with Lobengula, king of Matabeleland, the British South Africa Company was incorporated by royal charter to administer territory north of Bechuanaland, 1889; this territory was named Rhodesia after the projector of the scheme. In 1887 and 1888 Rhodes succeeded in amalgamating the diamond mines about Kimberley under the style of the Consolidated Mines, a corporation of which he became chairman and ruler; by skilful negotiation this new company acquired the interest in the Kimberley mine which had been controlled by Rhodes's chief rival in the diamond fields, Barnett Isaacs Barnato [q. v.]; at the same time Rhodes acquired important share in the newly-discovered gold mines on Witwatersrand in the Transvaal and helped to form the corporation known as the Consolidated Goldfields of South Africa. In the organization of Rhodesia by the chartered company, of which (Sir) L. S. Jameson [q. v.] became administrator in 1890, Rhodes played an energetic part. He directed the war with the Matabeles, 1893–4, whereby he greatly extended the company's territory. From July 1890 to Jan. 1896 he was also prime minister of the Cape; his ministry carried through reforms in local administration and native policy, and sought to unite English and Dutch interests; in pursuit of his ideal of imperial federation he subscribed in 1888 10,000l. to the home rule party in England; in 1893 he reconstructed his ministry owing to internal differences. At the end of 1895 Rhodes secretly encouraged the Uitlander population on the Rand and in the Transvaal to look to an armed insurrection for redress of their grievances against the Transvaal government; the failure of Jameson's precipitate raid in support of this movement (27 Dec. 1895) seriously involved Rhodes; inquiries by both the Cape Parliament and the British House of Commons, pronounced Rhodes guilty of grave breaches of duty; resigning office of premier (6 Jan. 1896) and for a time the directorship of the Chartered Company, which he resumed in 1898, he devoted himself to the development of Rhodesia; through his personal influence with the chiefs he effected a permanent peace with the Matabeles after a new outbreak, 1896; and he greatly extended railway and telegraph communication. He was made hon. D.C.L. Oxford, 1899, in spite of some protests. On outbreak of South African war he moved to Kimberley and was besieged there (15 Oct. 1899–16 Feb. 1900); next year he spent much time in Europe, returning to the Cape in Feb. 1902. He died after long suffering from heart disease on 26 March at the village of Muizenberg, being buried among the Matoppo Hills; by his will he left some 6,000,000l. to the public service, endowing some 170 scholarships at Oxford for students from the colonies, the United States, and Germany; 100,000l. was left to his old college, Oriel; sculptured memorials are at Buluwayo, Grahamstown, Capetown, Kimberley, and on the Groote Schuur slopes of Table Mountain outside Capetown; an unfinished portrait by Watts is in the National Portrait Gallery.

RHODES, FRANCIS WILLIAM (1851–1905), colonel; brother of C. J. Rhodes [q. v.]; joined army, 1873; served in Sudan and Nile expedition, 1884–5; colonel, 1889; military secretary to Lord Harris at Bombay, 1890–3; military member of council in Matabeleland, 1894; imprisoned and fined for complicity in Jameson Raid, 1895–6; war correspondent to 'The Times' at Omdurman, 1898; distinguished himself in South African war, 1899–1900; C.B., 1900; died at Capetown.

RHONDDA, Viscount (1856–1918), statesman, colliery proprietor, and financier. [See THOMAS, DAVID ALFRED.]

RHŶS, Sir JOHN (1840–1915), Celtic scholar; B.A., Jesus College, Oxford; fellow of Merton College, 1869; first Jesus professor of Celtic at Oxford, 1877; fellow and bursar of Jesus, 1881–95; principal, 1895–1915; knighted, 1907; P.C., 1911; served on numerous commissions dealing with education and social advancement especially in Wales, 1881–1915; prolific writer on Celtic philology, phonology, inscriptions, history, religion, ethnology, and folk-lore.

RICHARDS, SIR FREDERICK WILLIAM (1833–1912), admiral; entered navy, 1848; captain, 1866; commanded 'Devastation', first steam turret battleship designed without any sail power, 1873–7; C.B. for services at battle of Gingihlovo and relief of Echowe during Zulu war, 1879; K.C.B. for services at Laing's Nek in Boer war, 1881; junior naval lord at admiralty, 1882; largely responsible for able report on manœuvres of 1888, a determining cause of Naval Defence Act, 1889; vice-admiral, 1888; second naval lord, 1892; admiral, 1893; first naval lord, 1893–9; promoted ship-building and construction of harbours and dockyards; G.C.B., 1895; admiral of fleet, 1898; a leading administrator in naval history.

RICHMOND, SIR WILLIAM BLAKE (1842–1921), artist; son of George Richmond, R.A. [q. v.]; entered Royal Academy Schools, 1858; studied in Italy, 1865–9; Slade professor of fine art, Oxford, 1879–83; A.R.A., 1888; R.A., 1895; K.C.B., 1897; painted subject pictures from classical mythology; successful portrait painter; best-known work mosaic decorations for St. Paul's Cathedral.

RICHMOND AND GORDON, sixth DUKE OF (1818–1903), lord-president of the council. [See GORDON-LENNOX, CHARLES HENRY.]

RIDDELL, CHARLES JAMES BUCHANAN (1817–1903), major-general R.A., meteorologist; joined royal artillery, 1834; superintendent of meteorological observatory, Toronto, 1839; assistant superintendent of Ordnance Magnetic Observatories of Royal Military Repository, Woolwich, 1840–4; F.R.S., 1842; served in Crimea and Indian Mutiny, C.B., 1858; major-general, 1866.

RIDDELL, CHARLOTTE ELIZA LAWSON (1832–1906), novelist, known as MRS. J. H. RIDDELL; wrote thirty novels, including 'George Geith of Fen Court,' 1864; made commerce a frequent theme; co-proprietor and editor of 'St. James's Magazine' from 1861.

RIDDING, GEORGE (1828–1904), head master of Winchester and first bishop of Southwell; educated at Winchester and Balliol College, Oxford; Craven scholar and B.A., 1851; M.A., 1853; D.D., 1869; fellow of Exeter College, 1851; tutor, 1853–63; hon. fellow, 1890; head master of Winchester, 1866–84; 'second founder of Winchester,' extending buildings, playing fields, and staff; modernized curriculum; founded school mission at Landport in Portsmouth, 1882; first bishop of Southwell, 1884–1904; created a corporate spirit in diocese; published 'The Revel and the Battle' (sermons), 1897; 'Life' by widow, Lady Laura Ridding, 1908.

RIDLEY, SIR MATTHEW WHITE, fifth baronet, and first VISCOUNT RIDLEY (1842–1904), home secretary; educated at Harrow and Balliol College, Oxford; B.A. (first class classic), 1865; M.A., 1867; fellow of All Souls, 1865–74; conservative M.P. for North Northumberland, 1868–85; under-secretary to home office, 1878; financial secretary to treasury, 1885; M.P. for Blackpool, 1886–1900; P.C., 1892; home secretary, 1895–1900; raised to peerage, 1900; chairman of North Eastern Railway from 1902; developed town of Blyth; as chairman of board of commissioners he transformed harbour and dock there; president of Royal Agricultural Society, 1888.

RIEU, CHARLES PIERRE HENRI (1820–1902), Orientalist; born at Geneva; studied Arabic and Sanskrit at Bonn; Ph.D., 1843; assistant in department of Oriental MSS. at British Museum, 1847; keeper, 1867–95; compiled catalogues of Oriental, Persian, and Turkish MSS. there; Adams professor of Arabic at Cambridge, 1894–1902.

RIGBY, SIR JOHN (1834–1903), judge; B.A., Trinity College, Cambridge (second wrangler and second Smith's prizeman), and fellow, 1856; M.A., 1859; called to bar, 1860; Q.C., 1880; secured large practice in Court of Appeal and House of Lords; liberal M.P. for Wisbech, 1885–6, for Forfarshire, 1892–4; solicitor-general and knighted, 1892; attorney-general, 1894; judge of Court of Appeal and P.C., 1894–1901; a master of the science of equity.

RIGG, JAMES HARRISON (1821–1909), Wesleyan divine; ordained, 1849; served in successive circuits till 1868; contributor from 1853 and sole editor (1886–98) of 'London Quarterly Review'; explained theological position in 'Principles of Wesleyan Methodism,' 1850, and 'Modern Anglican Theology,' 1857; principal of

Westminster (Wesleyan) training college for day school teachers, 1868–1903; favoured denominational schools, 1870; member of London school board, 1870–6; member of royal commission on elementary education, 1886–8; president of Wesleyan conference, 1878 and 1892; carried 'Sandwich compromise,' 1890, giving larger share to laity in work of conference; voluminous writings include 'The Living Wesley,' 1875, 'Oxford High Anglicanism,' 1895, and 'Reminiscences Sixty Years Ago,' 1904; 'Life' by son-in-law, J. Telford, 1909.

RINGER, SYDNEY (1835–1910), physician; studied medicine at University College, London; M.B., 1860; M.A., 1863; M.R.C.P., 1863; F.R.C.P., 1870; physician to University College Hospital, 1865–1900; Holme professor of clinical medicine, 1887–1900; wrote 'A Handbook of Therapeutics,' 1869 (13th edit. 1897); made many physiological researches; F.R.S., 1885.

RIPON, first MARQUESS OF (1827–1909), statesman. [See ROBINSON, GEORGE FREDERICK SAMUEL.]

RISLEY, SIR HERBERT HOPE (1851–1911), Indian civil servant and anthropologist; educated at Winchester and New College, Oxford; B.A., 1872; joined Indian civil service, 1873; under-secretary (1879) and secretary (1902) to Indian government in home department; employed in compiling statistics of castes and occupations of people of Bengal, 1885; C.I.E., 1892; census commissioner, 1899; director of ethnography for India, 1901; C.S.I., 1904; K.C.I.E., 1907; secretary to public and judicial department at India office, 1910; chief anthropological works were 'Anthropometric Data,' 2 vols. 1891, 'Tribes and Castes of Bengal,' 1891–2, 'Ethnographical Glossary,' 2 vols. 1892, and 'The People of India,' 1908.

RITCHIE, ANNE ISABELLA, LADY RITCHIE (1837–1919), novelist and woman of letters; daughter of William Makepeace Thackeray [q. v.]; wife of Sir Richmond T. W. Ritchie [q. v.]; works include 'The Village on the Cliff' (1867) and 'Old Kensington' (1873).

RITCHIE, CHARLES THOMSON, first BARON RITCHIE, of Dundee (1838–1906), statesman; after education at City of London School (1849–53), he joined his father's firm, William Ritchie & Son, East India merchants, jute spinners, and manufacturers, of London and Dundee; conservative M.P. for the Tower Hamlets, 1874–85, for St. George's in the East, 1885–92, and for Croydon, 1895–1905; became chairman of a select committee appointed on his own motion (22 April 1879) to consider measures to protect West Indian cane sugar from the injurious effects of the bounty system whereby European countries stimulated the competing production of beet sugar; financial secretary to the admiralty, 1885–6; took steps to accelerate process of shipbuilding and to decrease the cost; became president of local government board, July 1886; was admitted to cabinet, 1887; carried revolutionary local government bill for England and Wales, 1888, which created 'county councils' for counties and large towns, and superseded in London the metropolitan board of works; at the same time he devised complementary scheme of district and parish councils, which he was compelled to drop, but which was made law by his liberal successor in 1894; was responsible for other important administrative acts, including the Public Health Acts of 1891; president of board of trade, 1895–1900; carried Conciliation Act for settlement of labour disputes (1896), the Light Railways Act (1896), the Merchant Shipping Act (1898), the Railway Employment (Prevention of Accidents) Act (1900), and Companies Act (1900); established an intelligence branch of commercial labour and statistical departments of board of trade, Oct. 1899; became home secretary, Nov. 1900; passed Factory and Workshop Act (1900), Youthful Offenders Act (1901), and Licensing Act (1902); was appointed chancellor of the exchequer, when Mr. Balfour became prime minister, August 1902; dropped in his budget of 1903, in spite of dissent within the cabinet, the shilling a quarter duty on corn which his predecessor, Sir Michael Hicks Beach [q. v.], had imposed the year before; resisted in the cabinet Mr. Chamberlain's proposals of tariff reform; resigned owing to consequent breach in the cabinet, 14 Sept. 1903; explained to his constituents that he was opposed to any fiscal arrangement with the colonies which should compel a tax on the import of food; raised to peerage, 17 Dec. 1905; died at Biarritz, 19 Jan. 1906; noted in political circles for grasp of complicated detail and shrewd common-sense.

RITCHIE, DAVID GEORGE (1853–1903), philosopher; M.A. Edinburgh University, 1875; hon. LL.D., 1898; B.A., Balliol College, Oxford, 1878; fellow of Jesus College, 1878; tutor of Balliol, 1882–6; professor of logic and metaphysics at St. Andrews, 1894–1903; president of Aristotelian Society, 1898–9; works, influenced by Hegel, include 'Darwinism and Politics,' 1889, 'Principles of State Interference,' 1891, 'Natural Rights,' 1895, and 'Plato,' 1902; 'Philosophical Studies' edited with memoir by Prof. R. Latta, 1905.

RITCHIE, SIR RICHMOND THACKERAY WILLOUGHBY (1854–1912), civil servant; born at Calcutta; B.A., Trinity College, Cambridge; entered India Office, 1877; private secretary to secretary of state for India, 1895–1902; secretary in political and secret department, India Office, 1902–9; permanent under-secretary of state, 1909; K.C.B., 1907.

RIVIERE, BRITON (1840–1920), painter; son of William Riviere [q. v.]; came of artistic family; educated at Cheltenham and St. Mary Hall, Oxford; exhibited in oil- and water-colour at Royal Academy from 1858; A.R.A., 1877; R.A., 1880; much influenced by artists of new Scottish school, such as Orchardson and Pettie; best known for paintings of lions and other animals, although he himself cared least for these.

ROBERTS, ALEXANDER (1826–1901), classical and biblical scholar; M.A., King's College, Old Aberdeen, 1847; D.D. Edinburgh, 1864; member of New Testament revision company, 1870–84; professor of humanity at St. Andrews, 1872–99; voluminous works include 'Greek the Language of Christ and His Apostles,' 1888.

ROBERTS, FREDERICK SLEIGH, first EARL ROBERTS, of Kandahar, Pretoria, and Waterford (1832–1914), field-marshal; son of General Sir Abraham Roberts [q. v.]; born at Cawnpore; educated at Sandhurst and Addiscombe; joined Bengal Artillery, 1851; served in Indian Mutiny, 1857–8; won V.C., 1858; accompanied Sir Robert Napier on Abyssinian expedition as assistant quartermaster-general, 1868; C.B., 1871; quartermaster-general of army in India, 1875; advocate of 'forward' policy in India, i.e. prevention of control by Russia of passes of the Himalaya; commander of Punjab frontier force, 1878; major-general and K.C.B. for victory over Afghans at Peiwar Kotal, 1878; defeated Afghans at Charasia and occupied Kabul, 1879; conducted celebrated march from Kabul to Kandahar, resulting in pacification of Afghanistan, 1880; G.C.B., baronet, and commander-in-chief of Madras army, 1880; commander-in-chief in India, 1885–93; baron, 1892; left India for good, 1893; field-marshal, 1895; commander-in-chief in Ireland, 1895–9; appointed to supreme command in South Africa, end of 1899; at once increased number of mounted troops, and with help of Lord Kitchener [q. v.] remodelled transport; decided to invade Free State; received unconditional surrender of General Cronje at Paardeberg, February 1900; occupied Bloemfontein (March), Johannesburg (May), Pretoria (June); defeated General Louis Botha [q. v.] at Diamond Hill (June); captured Machadodorp, temporary seat of President Kruger's government (July); returned to England after annexation of Transvaal in October; earl and K.G. for services in saving situation in Boer war, 1900; commander-in-chief, 1900–5; devoted remainder of his life to cause of national service, becoming president of National Service League, 1905; colonel-in-chief of Indian expeditionary force dispatched to France, 1914; died at St. Omer on way to visit it; wrote 'Forty-one Years in India' (1897).

ROBERTS, ISAAC (1829–1904), amateur astronomer; master builder in Liverpool, 1859–88; made many geological researches; F.G.S., 1870; experimented in stellar photography at Liverpool from 1883; his photograph of the Pleiades revealed new knowledge of structure of the group, 1886; successfully photographed great nebula in Andromeda (1888) and in Orion (1889); settled at Crowborough, Sussex, 1890; published selections of stellar photographs, 1893 and 1899; F.R.S., 1890; hon. D.Sc. Dublin, 1892; gold medallist, Royal Astronomical Society, 1895; left residue of estate for founding scholarships at Liverpool, Bangor, and Cardiff.

ROBERTS, ROBERT DAVIES (1851–1911), educational administrator; B.Sc. London, 1870; D.Sc., 1878; B.A., Clare College, Cambridge (second in natural science tripos), 1875; M.A., 1878; fellow, 1884–90; university lecturer in geology, Cambridge, 1884; published 'Earth's History: an Introduction to Modern Geology,' 1893; secretary to London Society for Extension of University Teaching, 1885–94; in charge of Cambridge syndicate for university extension, 1894–1902; registrar of London

University Extension Board, 1902; chairman of executive committee of University of Wales, 1910–11.

ROBERTS-AUSTEN, SIR WILLIAM CHANDLER (1843–1902), metallurgist; associate of Royal School of Mines, South Kensington, 1865; chemist of Royal Mint, 1870–82; chemist and assayer, 1882–1902; professor of metallurgy at Royal School of Mines, 1880–1902; member of war office explosives committee, 1899; initiated alloys research work at Institution of Mechanical Engineers, 1889; invented automatic recording pyrometer, 1891; F.R.S., 1875; hon. general secretary of British Association, 1897–1902; president of Iron and Steel Institute, 1899–1901; hon. D.C.L. Durham, 1897; D.Sc. Manchester, 1901; C.B., 1890; K.C.B., 1899; published 'An Introduction to Metallurgy,' 1891 (6th edit. 1910).

ROBERTSON, DOUGLAS MORAY COOPER LAMB ARGYLL (1837–1909), ophthalmic surgeon; M.D. St. Andrews, 1857; F.R.C.S. Edinburgh, 1862; president, 1886–7; published researches proving value of Calabar bean in ophthalmology, 1862; ophthalmic surgeon to Royal Infirmary, Edinburgh, 1867–97; described 'the Argyll Robertson pupil' in 'Edinburgh Medical Journal,' 1869–70; hon. LL.D. Edinburgh, 1896; died in India on a third visit.

ROBERTSON, SIR GEORGE SCOTT (1852–1916), Anglo-Indian administrator; entered Indian medical service, 1878; surgeon to British political agent in Gilgit, 1889; British agent in Gilgit, 1894; held out, till relieved, in Chitral with small, ill-provisioned force against combined Pathan and rebel Chitral armies, 4 March–20 April, 1895; K.C.S.I., 1895; retired, 1899; liberal M.P., Central Bradford, 1906.

ROBERTSON, JAMES PATRICK BANNERMAN, BARON ROBERTSON, of Forteviot (1845–1909), lord president of the Court of Session in Scotland; M.A. Edinburgh University, 1864; hon. LL.D., 1890; lord rector, 1893; passed to Scottish bar, 1867; Q.C., 1885; solicitor-general for Scotland, 1885 and 1886; conservative M.P. for Buteshire, 1885–6, 1886–91; lord advocate and P.C., 1889; carried Local Government (Scotland) Act, 1889; lord president of the court of session, 1891; life peer, and member of judicial committee of privy council, 1899; chairman of Irish University Commission (report published, 1904); hostile to Mr. Chamberlain's tariff policy.

ROBINSON, FREDERICK WILLIAM (1830–1901), novelist; published 'The House of Elmore,' 1855, and some fifty succeeding novels dealing mainly with semi-religious themes or low life: the chief were 'Grandmother's Money,' 1860, 'High Church,' 1860, 'Christie's Faith,' 1867, and 'Anne Judge, Spinster,' 1867; edited 'Home Chimes,' 1884–93; friend of Swinburne, Theodore Watts Dunton, and Sir Henry Irving.

ROBINSON, GEORGE FREDERICK SAMUEL, first MARQUESS OF RIPON (1827–1909), statesman; born at 10 Downing Street, while his father, first Viscount Goderich and first Earl of Ripon [q. v.], was prime minister; was known as Viscount Goderich, 1833–59; attaché to Sir Henry Ellis's abortive mission to Brussels to negotiate peace between Austria and Piedmont, 1849; joined F. D. Maurice's Christian Socialist movement and formed intimacy with Thomas Hughes, 1849; pleaded for democracy in 'The Duty of the Age,' a Christian Socialist tract which Maurice suppressed as being too radical, 1852; actively engaged in Volunteer movement, 1859; liberal M.P. for Huddersfield, 1853–7, and for West Riding of Yorkshire, 1857–9; succeeded his father as Earl of Ripon and his uncle as Earl de Grey, 1859; became, under Palmerston, under-secretary at the war office, June 1859, at the India office, Jan.–July 1861, and again at the war office, July 1861–April 1863; secretary for war and P.O. with seat in the cabinet, 1863–6; secretary for India, 1866; lord president of council under Gladstone, 1868–73; K.G., 1869; hon. D.C.L. Oxford, 1870; chairman of joint high commission for the settlement of American claims against Great Britain, 1871; made marquess, 23 June 1871; resigned cabinet office, Aug. 1873; was received into Roman Catholic communion, 7 Sept. 1874; appointed governor-general of India, 28 April 1880; settled critical difficulties in Afghanistan, 1880; repealed restrictions on the vernacular press, and encouraged development of self-government in India, 1882; provoked controversy by proposals to subject Europeans and Americans to trial by native Indian magistrates or judges ('the Ilbert bill'); accepted a satisfactory compromise; developed system of provincial settlements; retired from India, Dec. 1884; became first lord of the admiralty in Gladstone's first home rule cabinet, 1886; received freedom of City of Dublin, 1898; colonial secretary, 1892–5; lord privy seal with leadership of liberal party in House of Lords, 1905–8.

ROBINSON, SIR JOHN (1839–1903), first prime minister of Natal; left Hull with parents for Natal, 1850; succeeded father as manager of 'Natal Mercury,' 1860; member of council for Durban, 1863–82, and from 1884; represented Durban at Colonial Conference in London, 1887; K.C.M.G., 1889; advocated from 1882 self-government for colony; first prime minister, colonial secretary, and minister of education, 1893–7; published 'A Lifetime in South Africa,' 1900.

ROBINSON, SIR JOHN CHARLES (1824–1913), art connoisseur and collector; first superintendent of South Kensington Museum art collections, 1852–69; surveyor of Queen's pictures, 1882–1901; adviser to private collectors; knighted, 1887; C.B., 1901.

ROBINSON, SIR JOHN RICHARD (1828–1903), journalist; sub-editor of Unitarian journal the 'Inquirer,' 1848; editor of evening 'Express,' 1855; manager of 'Daily News,' 1868–1901; obtained descriptive accounts of Franco-German war, 1870, and of Turkish atrocities in Bulgaria, 1876; knighted, 1893; showed sympathy with Boers in South African war, 1899–1902; conspicuous member of Reform Club; 'Recollections' by F. Moy Thomas, 1904.

ROBINSON, PHILIP STEWART [PHIL ROBINSON] (1847–1902), naturalist and author; born at Chunar, India; assisted father in editing 'Pioneer,' 1869; editor of 'Revenue Archives' of Benares province, 1872; pioneer of Anglo-Indian literature, descriptive of natural history; chief works were 'In my Indian Garden,' 1878, 'Tigers at Large,' 1884, and 'The Valley of Teetotum Trees,' 1886.

ROBINSON, VINCENT JOSEPH (1829–1910), connoisseur of Oriental art; published 'Eastern Carpets,' 1882; director of Indian section at Paris Exhibition, 1889; F.S.A., 1889; C.I.E., 1891; described his own collections in 'Ancient Furniture and other Objects of Art,' 1902; helped to revive European taste for Oriental art.

ROBINSON, WILLIAM LEEFE (1895–1918), airman; joined Royal Flying Corps, 1915; V.C. for shooting down at Cuffley, Hertfordshire, first enemy airship brought down on British soil, 1916; prisoner of war in Germany, 1917–18, succumbing to his bad treatment there, after his return to England.

ROBSON, WILLIAM SNOWDON, BARON ROBSON, of Jesmond (1852–1918), lawyer and politician; B.A., Caius College, Cambridge; called to bar (Inner Temple); 1880; Q.C., 1892; M.P., Bow and Bromley, 1885, South Shields, 1895–1910; solicitor-general and knighted, 1905; attorney-general, 1908; saved budget of 1909; presented British case at Atlantic fisheries arbitration at The Hague, 1910; lord of appeal in ordinary and P.C., 1910.

ROBY, HENRY JOHN (1830–1915), educational reformer and classical scholar; B.A., St. John's College, Cambridge (senior classic); fellow of St. John's, 1854–61; second master, Dulwich College, 1861–5; secretary to Schools Inquiry commission, 1864; to Endowed Schools commission, 1869; largely responsible for reforms introduced by commissions; partner in Manchester sewing-cotton manufacturing firm, 1874–94; liberal M.P., Eccles division of Manchester, 1890–5; works include 'Grammar of the Latin Language from Plautus to Suetonius' (1871–4, 7th edit. 1904), distinguished for its wealth of illustration, 'Introduction to Justinian's Digest' (1884), and 'Roman Private Law' (1902).

ROGERS, BENJAMIN BICKLEY (1828–1919), barrister and translator of Aristophanes; B.A., Wadham College, Oxford; fellow of Wadham, 1852–61; called to bar (Lincoln's Inn), 1856; works include annotated verse translations of Aristophanes' 'Clouds' (1852) 'Peace' (1867), 'Wasps' (1875), 'Lysistrata' (1878), and 'Thesmophoriazusae' (1904).

ROGERS, EDMUND DAWSON (1823–1910), journalist and spiritualist; manager of 'Norfolk News,' 1845; started 'Eastern Daily Press,' first daily paper in eastern counties, 1870; established National Press Agency, 1873; helped to found British National Association of Spiritualists, 1873; founded (1881) and edited from 1894 weekly spiritualist journal, 'Light'; his autobiographical 'Life and Experiences' appeared in 1911.

ROGERS, JAMES GUINNESS (1822–1911), congregational divine; B.A., Trinity College, Dublin, 1843; minister at Newcastle-on-Tyne, 1846–51, Ashton-under-

Lyne, 1851–65, and Clapham, 1865–1900; chairman of the congregational unions of Lancashire, 1865, Surrey, 1868, and England and Wales, 1874; hon. D.D. Edinburgh, 1895; friend of Gladstone; publications include 'The Church Systems of England in the Nineteenth Century,' 1881, 'The Unchanging Faith,' 1907, and an 'Autobiography,' 1903; edited 'Congregationalist,' 1879–86, and 'Congregational Review,' 1887–91.

ROLLS, CHARLES STEWART (1877–1910), engineer and aviator; son of first Baron Llangattock; B.A., Trinity College, Cambridge, 1898; M.A., 1902; studied practical engineering; pioneer of motor cars in England; formed motor car business of 'C. S. Rolls & Co.,' and established 'Rolls Royce, Ltd.,' 1904; ardent aeronaut and expert aviator; crossed and recrossed English Channel in aeroplane without stopping, June 1910; killed at Bournemouth in aeroplane accident; first English victim of aviation; statues by Sir W. Goscombe John at Monmouth and by W. C. May at Dover; wrote on motors and on his experiences as motorist and aviator.

ROMER, SIR ROBERT (1840–1918), judge; B.A., Trinity Hall, Cambridge (senior wrangler); called to bar (Lincoln's Inn), 1867; Q.C., 1881; practised in court of Sir J. W. Chitty; judge of chancery division and knighted, 1890; lord justice of appeal, 1899–1906; P.C. and F.R.S., 1899; G.C.B., 1901.

ROOKWOOD, BARON (1826–1902), politician. [See SELWIN-IBBETSON, SIR HENRY JOHN.]

ROOPER, THOMAS GODOLPHIN (1847–1903), writer on education; educated at Harrow and Balliol College, Oxford; B.A., 1870; private tutor to eleventh duke of Bedford, 1871–7; inspector of schools from 1877; improved teaching of geography and methods of teaching of infants; stimulated manual education, and encouraged school gardens; helped to found Hartley University College, Southampton; writings include 'School and Home Life,' 1896, 'Educational Studies and Addresses,' 1902, 'School Gardens in Germany,' 1902; 'Selected Writings' edited with memoir by R. G. Tatton, 1907.

ROOSE, EDWARD CHARLES ROBSON (1848–1905), physician; studied at Guy's Hospital and in Paris; M.R.C.P. Edinburgh, 1875; F.R.C.P., 1877; M.D. Brussels, 1877; had large fashionable London practice; wrote many popular medical works.

ROOS-KEPPEL, SIR GEORGE OLOF (1866–1921), soldier and Anglo-Indian administrator; joined army, 1886; political agent in Khyber, 1899–1908; C.I.E., 1900; chief commissioner, North-West Frontier Province, and agent to governor-general, 1908–19; K.C.I.E., 1908; G.C.I.E., 1917.

ROSCOE, SIR HENRY ENFIELD (1833–1915), chemist; son of Henry Roscoe [q. v.]; B.A., University College, London; Ph.D., Heidelberg; researched with R. W. von Bunsen on measurement of chemical action of light; professor of chemistry, Owens College, Manchester, 1857–85; knighted, 1884; liberal M.P., South Manchester, 1885; P.C., 1909; his most important contribution to chemistry was preparation of pure vanadium.

ROSS, SIR ALEXANDER GEORGE (1840–1910), lieutenant-general; born at Meerut; joined Indian army, 1857; served in Mutiny; present at capture of Magdala, 1867; in Jowaki expedition, 1877; commanded 1st Sikh infantry in Afghan war, 1878–9, in campaign against Mahsud Waziris, 1881, and in Zhob valley expedition, 1890; lieutenant-general, 1897; C.B., 1887; K.C.B., 1905.

ROSS, SIR JOHN (1829–1905), general; son of Sir Hew Dalrymple Ross [q. v.]; entered army, 1846; served in Canada, 1847–52, in the Crimea, 1854–5, in Indian Mutiny, 1857–9; helped to raise at Lucknow (1858) camel corps, which he commanded at Gowlowlie, Calpi, and Jugdespore; C.B., 1861; commanded Laruf field force in Malay peninsula, 1875–6; major-general, 1877; in command of second division of Kabul field force, 1878–80; K.C.B., 1881; commanded Poona division, 1881–6; commander-in-chief in Canada, 1888; G.C.B., 1891.

ROSS, JOSEPH THORBURN (1849–1903), artist; art student at Royal Scottish Academy, 1877–80; A.R.S.A., 1896; treated portraiture, land- and sea-scape, and incident; frequently exhibited abroad; his 'The Bass Rock' in National Gallery of Scotland.

ROSS, MARTIN (pseudonym) (1862–1915), novelist. [See MARTIN, VIOLET FLORENCE.]

ROSS, WILLIAM STEWART, 'SALADIN' (1844–1906), secularist; educated at Glasgow University; early wrote verse and fiction; became under style of Stewart & Co.

educational publisher in London, 1872; joint editor from 1880, and sole editor and proprietor from 1884, of 'Agnostic Journal and Secular Review'; works include 'Lays of Romance and Chivalry,' 1881, and 'God and His Book,' 1887.

ROSSE, fourth EARL OF (1840–1908), astronomer. [See PARSONS, LAURENCE.]

ROSSETTI, WILLIAM MICHAEL (1829–1919), man of letters and art critic; brother of Christina Rossetti [q. v.] and D. G. Rossetti [q. v.]; served in Excise Office (later Inland Revenue Board), 1845–94; friend of A. C. Swinburne; works include four editions of D. G. Rossetti's collected works and 'Memoir' (1895), and editions of Christina Rossetti's 'New' and 'Collected Poems' (latter containing memoir, 1904).

ROTHSCHILD, SIR NATHAN MEYER, second baronet, and first BARON ROTHSCHILD, of Tring (1840–1915), banker and philanthropist; son of Lionel Nathan de Rothschild [q. v.]; liberal M.P., Aylesbury, 1865–85; succeeded to baronetcy, 1876; head of firm, 1879; created baron, 1885; first professing Jew to enter House of Lords; P.C. and G.C.V.O., 1902; his munificent benefactions include gifts to Jews throughout the world, whose acknowledged leader he became.

ROUSBY, WILLIAM WYBERT (1835–1907), actor and theatrical manager; after provincial engagements from 1849 joined Phelps at Sadler's Wells Theatre, 1853; played Romeo at Manchester, 1864; with wife [see ROUSBY, CLARA MARION JESSIE] appeared at Queen's Theatre, London, in leading parts in 'The Fool's Revenge,' '"Twixt Axe and Crown,' 'As You Like It,' and 'King Lear,' 1868–74; proprietor of Theatre Royal, Jersey, from 1879.

ROUTH, EDWARD JOHN (1831–1907), mathematician; born at Quebec; son of Sir Randolph Routh [q. v.]; B.A. London, 1849; M.A., 1853; joined Peterhouse, Cambridge, 1850; senior wrangler and Smith's prizeman, 1854; fellow, 1855; hon. fellow, 1883; lecturer in mathematics, 1855–1904; had unprecedented success as private coach; produced among his pupils 28 senior wranglers and 43 Smith's prizemen; F.R.A.S., 1866; F.R.S., 1872; published 'Rigid Dynamics,' 1860 (7th edit. 2 vols. 1905), 'Statics,' 2 vols. 1891, and 'Dynamics of a Particle,' 1898; won Adams prize with 'Treatise on the Stability of a given State of Motion, particularly Steady Motion,' which greatly advanced knowledge of dynamics, 1877; hon. LL.D. Glasgow, 1878; hon. Sc.D. Cambridge, 1883, and Dublin, 1892.

ROWE, JOSHUA BROOKING (1837–1908), antiquary and naturalist; admitted solicitor, 1860; made study of Devonshire natural history and archaeology; F.S.A., 1875; part founder of Devon and Cornwall Record Society; writings include 'The Ecclesiastical History of Plymouth,' 4 pts. 1873–6, and 'The History of Plympton Erle,' 1906.

ROWLANDS, DAVID, 'DEWI MON' (1836–1907), Welsh scholar and poet; B.A. London, 1860; held congregational pastorates in Wales, 1861–72; tutor of Brecon Congregational College, 1872–97; principal 1897–1907; wrote much Welsh and English verse; literary editor of 'Cambrian Minstrelsie,' 1893, and of Welsh congregational hymnal, 1895; chairman of congregational union of Wales, 1902.

ROWTON, BARON (1838–1903), politician and philanthropist. [See CORRY, MONTAGU WILLIAM LOWRY.]

RUMBOLD, SIR HORACE, eighth baronet (1829–1913), diplomatist; born in Calcutta; entered diplomatic service, 1849; secretary to legation in China, 1859; held minor diplomatic posts, 1862–96; ambassador at Vienna, 1896–1900; succeeded brother, 1877; P.C., 1896; G.C.B., 1897.

RUNDALL, FRANCIS HORNBLOW (1823–1908), inspector-general of Indian irrigation; born at Madras; joined Madras engineers, 1841; superintending engineer of the northern circle, 1859; chief engineer in construction of Orissa canals from 1861; chief irrigation engineer and joint secretary to the Bengal government, 1867; commenced the Son irrigation canals; inspector-general of irrigation and deputy secretary to Indian government, 1872–4; C.S.I., 1875; colonel commandant R.E., 1876; general, 1885; examined Nile Delta, 1876–7; lectured and wrote on Indian irrigation.

RUSDEN, GEORGE WILLIAM (1819–1903), historian of Australia and New Zealand; emigrated with father from England to Maitland, New South Wales, 1834; clerk to executive council, Victoria, 1852; clerk of parliaments, 1856; retired on pension, 1882, and wrote histories of Australia, 3 vols. 1883, and New Zealand, 3 vols. 1883.

RUSSELL, HENRY CHAMBERLAINE (1836–1907), astronomer; born at West Maitland, New South Wales; B.A. Sydney University, 1858; assistant at Sydney observatory, 1859; government astronomer, 1870–1905; established meteorological stations throughout colony; organized Australian observations of transit of Venus, 1874 (account published, 1892); vice-chancellor of Sydney University, 1891; F.R.S., 1886; C.M.G., 1890.

RUSSELL, THOMAS O'NEILL (1828–1908), a founder of the Gaelic movement in Ireland; urged in 'Irishman' revival of ancient Irish tongue from 1858; commercial traveller in America for nearly thirty years; returned to Ireland, 1895; largely helped to form Gaelic League, 1893, and Feis Ceoil, 1897; published novels and dramas and edited much Gaelic poetry.

RUSSELL, WILLIAM CLARK (1844–1911), novelist; son of Henry Russell [q. v.]; in British merchant service, 1858–66; after engaging in journalism he produced some sixty nautical tales of adventure, chief being 'John Holdsworth, Chief Mate,' 1875, and 'The Wreck of the Grosvenor,' 1877; some of his contributions to 'Daily Telegraph' on sea topics (1882–9) were republished in 'My Watch Below,' 1882, and 'Round the Galley Fire,' 1883; his writings led to improved conditions in merchant service; he also wrote lives of Dampier, 1889, Nelson, 1890, and Collingwood, 1891, and naval ballads.

RUSSELL, SIR WILLIAM HOWARD (1820–1907), war correspondent; educated at Trinity College, Dublin; reported for 'The Times' the Irish general election, 1841, and episodes in repeal agitation in Ireland, 1843; called to bar (Middle Temple), 1850; war correspondent for 'The Times' in Crimea, 1854; applied phrase 'the thin red line' to the British infantry at Balaclava; called attention to the sufferings of English army there through the winter of 1854–5, and inspired the work of Florence Nightingale; hon. LL.D. Trinity College, Dublin, 1855; acted as 'The Times' correspondent in Indian Mutiny, 1858, and in American civil war, 1861–2; wrote a frank account of battle of Bull Run (July 1861), which made him unpopular in America; founded 'Army and Navy Gazette,' 1860; only occasionally worked for 'The Times' after 1863; saw battle of Königgrätz in Prusso-Austrian war, 1866; also served in Franco-German war, 1870, and (for 'Daily Telegraph') in Zulu war, 1879; accompanied Edward, Prince of Wales through Near East (1869) and India (1875–6), and published accounts of both tours; knighted, 1895; C.V.O., 1902; published, besides experiences as correspondent, accounts of travels in Canada, 3 vols. 1865, and the United States, 2 vols. 1882; 'Life' by J. B. Atkins, 2 vols. 1911.

RUSSELL, WILLIAM JAMES (1830–1909), chemist; Ph.D. Heidelberg, 1855; lecturer in chemistry at St. Mary's Hospital, 1868–70, and at St. Bartholomew's, 1870–97; professor of natural philosophy, Bedford College, 1860–70; F.R.S., 1872; president of Chemical Society, 1889–91, and of Institute of Chemistry, 1894–7.

RUTHERFORD, MARK (pseudonym) (1831–1913), novelist, philosophical writer, literary critic, and civil servant. [See WHITE, WILLIAM HALE.]

RUTHERFORD, WILLIAM GUNION (1853–1907), classical scholar; educated at St. Andrews University and Balliol College, Oxford; B.A., 1876; classical master at St. Paul's School, 1876–83; published 'First Greek Grammar,' 1878, 'The New Phrynichus,' 1881, and edition of 'Babrius,' 1883; fellow and tutor of University College, Oxford, 1883; head master of Westminster, 1883–1901; hon. LL.D. St. Andrews, 1884; edited 'Thucydides, Bk. IV.,' 1889, 'Mimiambi' of Herondas, 1892, and scholia to Aristophanes, 3 vols. 1896–1905; translated St. Paul's Epistle to Romans, 1900.

RUTLAND, seventh DUKE OF (1818–1906), politician. [See MANNERS, (LORD) JOHN JAMES ROBERT.]

RYE, MARIA SUSAN (1829–1903), social reformer; sister of Edward Caldwell Rye [q.v.]; founded law-stationer's business for employment of girls, 1859; founded 'Female Middle Class Emigration Society,' 1861; from 1868 devoted herself to emigration of 'gutter children'; opened house at Peckham for waifs and strays, 1869; drafted children after training to house at Niagara, 'Our Western Home' (opened Dec. 1869); pioneer of pauper emigration.

RYE, WILLIAM BRENCHLEY (1818–1901), keeper of printed books in the British Museum; assistant in British Museum Library, 1839; arranged Grenville library, 1846, and reference library, 1857; assistant keeper of printed books, 1857–69; keeper, 1869–75;

chief work was 'England as seen by Foreigners,' 1865; a skilful etcher.

SACKVILLE-WEST, LIONEL SACKVILLE, second BARON SACKVILLE, of Knole (1827–1908), diplomatist; entered diplomatic service, 1847; served under Lord Lyons at Paris through Franco-German war; British envoy at Buenos Ayres, 1872–8, Madrid, 1878–81, and Washington, 1881–8; life threatened by American Fenians, 1882; K.C.M.G., 1885; helped to settle differences between America and Canada regarding fishing rights, 1887–8; was recalled from Washington owing to alleged intervention in American presidential election, Oct. 1888; succeeded brother in barony, 1888; G.C.M.G., 1889; thenceforth lived in retirement at Knole, Seven-oaks.

ST. ALDWYN, first EARL (1837–1916), statesman. [See HICKS BEACH, SIR MICHAEL EDWARD.]

ST. HELIER, BARON (1843–1905), judge. [See JEUNE, FRANCIS HENRY.]

ST. JOHN, SIR SPENSER BUCKINGHAM (1825–1910), diplomatist and author; son of James Augustus St. John [q. v.]; private secretary to Sir James Brooke [q. v.] in Labuan, 1848–56; temporary commissioner of Labuan, 1851–5; British consul-general at Brunei, 1856; explored interior; chargé d'affaires in Hayti, 1863, and in Dominican republic, 1871; resident minister in Hayti, 1872–4; minister residentiary in Peru, 1874–83; K.C.M.G. 1881; envoy extraordinary to Mexico, 1884–93; minister to Sweden, 1893–6; G.C.M.G., 1894; wrote ' Life of Sir James Brooke,' 1879, an account of Hayti, 1884, and other works.

ST. JOHN, VANE IRETON SHAFTESBURY (1839–1911), author and journalist; brother of Sir S. B. St. John [q. v.]; pioneer of boys' journals.

SALADIN (pseudonym) (1844–1906), secularist. [See ROSS, WILLIAM STEWART.]

SALAMAN, CHARLES KENSINGTON (1814–1901), musical composer; studied pianoforte in London and Paris; gave annual orchestral concerts in London from 1833; instituted 'Concerti da Camera,' 1835; in Rome, 1846–8; gave musically illustrated lectures in London and provinces from 1855; founded Musical Association, 1876; composed songs the most famous of which was his setting of Shelley's 'I arise from dreams of thee,' 1836), orchestral and pianoforte pieces; published 'Jews as they are,' 1882.

SALAMAN, JULIA (1812–1906), portrait painter. [See GOODMAN.]

SALISBURY, third MARQUESS OF (1830–1903), prime minister. [See CECIL, ROBERT ARTHUR TALBOT GASCOYNE-.]

SALMON, GEORGE (1819–1904), mathematician and divine; B.A. Trinity College, Dublin (first mathematical moderator), 1838; M.A., 1844; B.D. and D.D., 1859; fellow, 1841; divinity lecturer, 1845; Donegal lecturer in mathematics, 1848–66; published 'Conic Sections,' 1847, 'Higher Plane Curves,' 1852, 'Modern Higher Algebra,' 1859, and 'Geometry of Three Dimensions,' 1862 (5th edit. 1912); regius professor of divinity, 1866–88; a strong protestant and liberal evangelical; acute theological critic; published 'Non-Miraculous Christianity,' 1881, 'Introduction to the New Testament,' 1885, 'The Infallibility of the Church,' 1889, and 'The Human Element in the Gospels,' posthumous, 1907, and sermons; provost of Trinity College, 1888–1902; member of Royal Irish Academy, 1843, and of many foreign academies; received many honorary degrees; F.R.S., 1863; royal medallist, 1868; original F.B.A., 1902; chancellor of St. Patrick's Cathedral, 1871; portraits by Benjamin Constant and Miss Sara Purser, and marble statue by Mr. John Hughes at Dublin; he endowed fund and exhibitions for divinity students at Dublin.

SALOMONS, SIR JULIAN EMANUEL (1835–1909), Australian lawyer and politician; emigrated from Birmingham to Sydney; called to bar at Gray's Inn and of New South Wales, 1861; member of New South Wales legislative assembly, 1869–71, 1887–99; solicitor-general, 1869–70; vice-president of executive council and representative of government in legislative council, 1887–9, 1891–3; agent-general for colony in London, 1899–1900; knighted, 1891.

SALTING, GEORGE (1835–1909), art collector and benefactor; born at Sydney, New South Wales; educated at Eton and Sydney University; B.A., 1857; settled in England, 1857; developed taste for art on a visit to Rome, 1858; for forty years he made collections of art treasures, especially of Chinese porcelain, which he loaned to Victoria and Albert Museum; he also collected

Italian and Spanish majolica, small sculptures, statu-ettes, and English miniature portraits from Tudor times onward; spent 40,000*l.* at Spitzer sale in Paris, 1893; left fortune of 1,287,900*l.*; bequeathed his collections to National Gallery, British Museum, and Victoria and Albert Museum.

SALVIN, FRANCIS HENRY (1817–1904), writer on falconry and cormorant fishing; served in army, 1839–1864; went on hawking tour through north of England, 1843; made successful flights with goshawks; revived cormorant fishing in England; collaborated in 'Falconry in the British Isles,' 1855, and in 'Falconry, its Claims, History, and Practice,' 1859.

SAMBOURNE, EDWIN LINLEY (1844–1910), artist in black and white; apprenticed as marine engineer at Greenwich; first contributed to 'Punch,' 1867; member of staff, 1871; illustrated 'Essence of Parliament'; cartoonist-in-chief, 1900–10; illustrated books, including Kingsley's 'Water Babies,' 1885; combined artistic grace and dignity with firmness and delicacy of line.

SAMUELSON, SIR BERNHARD, first baronet (1820–1905), ironmaster and promoter of technical education; manager of Manchester firm of engineers, 1842–6; established railway works at Tours, 1846; purchased (1848) and greatly developed factory of agricultural implements at Banbury; erected blast furnaces near Middlesbrough for ironworking, 1853, which he transferred to Newport, 1863; both firms were turned into limited liability companies, 1887; built Britannia ironworks at Middlesbrough, which produced gigantic output of iron, tar, and by-products; unsuccessful in attempts to make steel from Cleveland ore; liberal M.P. for Banbury, 1859 and 1865–85, and for North Oxfordshire, 1885–95; P.C., 1895; pioneer of tariff reform movement, 1901; served on royal commissions on scientific instruction (1870), on technical instruction (chairman, 1881), and elementary education (1887); chairman of parliamentary committees on patent laws (1871–2) and railways (1873); F.R.S., 1881; part founder and president (1883–5) of Iron and Steel Institute; presented technical institute to Banbury, 1884; baronet, 1884.

SANDAY, WILLIAM (1843–1920), theological scholar; B.A., Corpus Christi College, Oxford; Dean Ireland's professor of exegesis of Holy Scripture, Oxford, 1882; fellow and tutor of Exeter, 1883; Lady Margaret professor of divinity and canon of Christ Church, 1895–1919; F.B.A., 1903; devoted himself to scientific study of New Testament, especially the Gospels; works include 'Portions of the Gospels according to St. Mark and St. Matthew from the Bobbio MS.' (1886), and preliminary studies for a Life of Christ (never written), most important being 'The Life of Christ in Recent Research' (1907).

SANDBERG, SAMUEL LOUIS GRAHAM (1851–1905), Tibetan scholar; son of Indian missionary; B.A. Dublin University, 1870; called to bar, 1874; ordained, 1879; chaplain in Bengal, 1886–1904; published works and magazine articles on Tibetan dialects, literature, and topography; chief were 'Manual of Colloquial Tibetan,' 1894, 'A Tibetan-English Dictionary,' 1902, and 'The Exploration of Tibet,' 1904; ardent Italian student.

SANDERSON, EDGAR (1838–1907), historical writer; B.A., Clare College, Cambridge, 1860; M.A., 1865; head master of grammar schools at Stockwell, 1871–3, Maccles-field, 1873–7, and Huntingdon, 1877–81; works include 'History of the World,' 1898, and 'The British Empire in the Nineteenth Century,' 6 vols. 1898–9.

SANDERSON, SIR JOHN SCOTT BURDON-, baronet (1828–1905), regius professor of medicine at Oxford. [See BURDON-SANDERSON.]

SANDHAM, HENRY (1842–1910), painter and illustrator; born in Montreal; travelled in Europe and settled in Boston, 1880; member of Royal Canadian Academy, 1880; painted battle and historical scenes and portraits; chief works were 'The March of Time' and 'The Dawn of Liberty'; a good water-colour artist.

SANDYS, (ANTHONY) FREDERICK (AUGUSTUS) (1829–1904), pre-Raphaelite painter; son of drawing master at Norwich; published anonymously 'A Night-mare,' a lithographical caricature of Millais's 'Sir Isumbras at the Ford,' 1857; formed friendship with D. G. Rossetti (1857) and pre-Raphaelite group, including Whistler, and later with George Meredith; devoted much time to wood block designs, which were praised by Millais and Rossetti; exhibited at Royal Academy subject pictures, including 'Oriana,' 'La Belle Ysonde,' 'Morgan le Fay,' 'Cassandra' (praised by Swinburne), 'Medea,' and portraits; gained repute for crayon heads: of bohemian temperament and habits; work mainly in English private collections or in America.

SANFORD, GEORGE EDWARD LANGHAM SOMERSET (1840–1901), lieutenant-general; joined royal engineers, 1856; served in China with General Gordon, 1862; executive engineer in Indian public works department, 1873; served in Afridi expedition, 1878, and Afghan war, 1878–9; quartermaster-general in India, 1882–3; commanding royal engineer in Burmese expedition, 1885–6; C.B., 1886; director-general of military works in India, 1886–93; C.S.I., 1890; commanded Meerut district, 1893–8; lieutenant-general, 1898.

SANGER, GEORGE, known as 'LORD GEORGE SANGER' (1825–1911), circus proprietor and showman; brother of John Sanger [q. v.]; started with brother independent show at Stepney Fair, 1848; inaugurated travelling show, 1853; established 'world's fair' at Plymouth, 1860; purchased Astley's amphitheatre and exhibited spectacles there (1871–93) and also at Agricultural Hall and at Margate; frequently toured the Continent; in later life was hampered by American competition; was shot by an employee at Finchley; published autobiography 'Seventy Years a Showman,' 1910.

SANKEY, SIR RICHARD HIERAM (1829–1908), lieutenant-general royal (Madras) engineers; joined Madras engineers, 1846; under-secretary of public works department at Calcutta, 1857; conspicuous in field work in Indian Mutiny at Allahabad, Cawnpore, and Lucknow; field surgeon to the Gurkha force; chief engineer, Mysore, 1864–77; originated irrigation department and built new roads and government offices; commanding royal engineer of Kandahar field force, 1878; C.B., 1879; secretary in public work department, Madras, 1879–83; major-general, 1883; lieutenant-general, 1884; K.C.B., 1892.

SAUMAREZ, THOMAS (1827–1903), admiral; entered navy, 1841; served in South America and West Africa; coramander, 1854; led in attack on Taku forts, 1858; C.B., 1873; admiral, 1886.

SAUNDERS, EDWARD (1848–1910), entomologist; published 'The Hemiptera Heteroptera' (1892), 'The Hymenoptera Aculeata' (1896) of the British Isles, and 'Wild Bees, Wasps and Ants,' 1907; F.R.S., 1902.

SAUNDERS, SIR EDWIN (1814–1901), dentist; dental surgeon and lecturer in dental surgery at St. Thomas's Hospital, 1839–54; F.R.C.S., 1855; dentist to royal family from 1846; obtained foundation of diploma in dental surgery, 1859; founder (1857) and president (1864 and 1879) of Odontological Society; knighted, 1883; president of British Dental Association, 1886; author of 'Advice on the Care of the Teeth,' 1837.

SAUNDERS, HOWARD (1835–1907), ornithologist and traveller; went to South America, 1855; crossed Andes and explored the Amazon river, 1860–2; wrote papers on South American, Spanish, and Swiss ornithology; joint editor of 'Ibis,' 1883–8 and 1894–1900; published 'An Illustrated Manual of British Birds,' 1889, and edited 'Yarrell's British Birds,' 1882–5, and other works.

SAUNDERSON, EDWARD JAMES (1837–1906), Irish politician, well-known as Colonel Saunderson (militia batt., Royal Irish Fusiliers); lived at Nice during boyhood; returned to Ireland, 1865; whig M.P. for co. Cavan, 1865–74; opposed Irish disestablishment, 1869; opposed nationalist movement from 1882; conservative M.P. for North Armagh from 1885 till death; active opponent of home rule bill of 1893; grand master of Orange lodges at Belfast, 1901–2; P.C.,1898; lord-lieutenant of Cavan,1900; supported South African war; capable artist and boat-builder; ardent protestant; statue by Sir W. Goscombe John at Portadown.

SAVAGE-ARMSTRONG, GEORGE FRANCIS (1845–1906), poet; brother of Edmund John Armstrong [q. v.]; B.A., Trinity College, Dublin, 1869; hon. M.A., 1872; published much verse, including 'Poems Lyrical and Dramatic,' 1869, and 'Stories of Wicklow,' 1886; professor of history and English literature, Queen's College, Cork, 1870–1905; hon. D.Litt. Queen's University, 1891.

SAVILL, THOMAS DIXON (1855–1910), physician; studied medicine at St. Thomas's and St. Mary's hospitals and on Continent; M.B., 1881; M.D., 1882; F.R.C.P., 1882; medical superintendent of Paddington infirmary, 1885–92; physician of West End Hospital for Diseases of the Nervous System, 1893; made original researches into nervous diseases and hysteria; published 'A System of Clinical Medicine,' 2 vols. 1903–5; died at Algiers.

SAXE-WEIMAR, PRINCE EDWARD OF (1823–1902), field-marshal. [See EDWARD OF SAXE-WEIMAR.]

SCHREINER, OLIVE EMILIE ALBERTINA (1855–1920), authoress; sister of W. P. Schreiner [q.v.]; married S. C. Cronwright, 1894; best-known work 'The Story of an African Farm' (1883).

SCHREINER, WILLIAM PHILIP (1857–1919), South African lawyer and statesman; born in Cape Colony; B.A., Downing College, Cambridge (senior jurist); called to bar (Inner Temple) and Cape bar, 1882; Q.C., 1892; prime minister of Cape Colony, 1898–1900; high commissioner for Union of South Africa in London, 1914–19.

SCHUNCK, HENRY EDWARD (1820–1903), chemist; studied chemistry at Berlin and Giessen University; Ph.D.; made exhaustive original researches into colouring matters of vegetable substances, including indigo and chlorophyll, as well as the madder plant; papers 'On Rubian and its Products of Decomposition' from 1851 to 1855; first showed chemical nature of alizarin [see PERKIN, SIR WILLIAM HENRY]; F.R.S., 1850; Davy gold medallist, 1889; president of Society of Chemical Industry, 1896–7; hon. D.Sc. Manchester, 1899; presented in 1895 20,000*l.* to Owens College, Manchester, for chemical research.

SCOTT, ARCHIBALD (1837–1909), Scottish divine and leader of the general assembly of the Church of Scotland; B.A. Glasgow University, 1856; hon. D.D., 1876; held ministries in Glasgow, Linlithgow, and Edinburgh; chairman of Edinburgh school board, 1878–1882; incumbent of St. George's, Edinburgh, from 1890 to death; leader of general assembly from 1887; moderator, 1896; advocated reunion of Scottish presbyterians; published 'Endowed Territorial Work,' 1873, 'Buddhism and Christianity,' Croall lecture, 1890, and 'Sacrifice,' Baird lecture, 1894.

SCOTT, LORD CHARLES THOMAS MONTAGU-DOUGLAS- (1839–1911), admiral; son of fifth duke of Buccleuch [q. v.]; entered navy, 1853; served in Baltic, Black Sea, and China campaigns; distinguished in Indian Mutiny; on China station, 1868–71; commanded 'Bacchante', with royal princes on board, in Mediterranean and West Indies, 1879–82; C.B., 1882; commander-in-chief on Australian station, 1889–92; vice-admiral, 1894; K.C.B., 1898; admiral, 1899; commander-in-chief at Plymouth, 1900–3; G.C.B., 1902.

SCOTT, CLEMENT WILLIAM (1841–1904), dramatic critic; son of William Scott (1813–72, q. v.); junior clerk in war office, 1860–79; dramatic critic for 'Sunday Times,' 1863–5, for 'London Figaro,' 1870, and for 'Daily Telegraph,' 1871–98; edited 'The Theatre,' 1880–9; pioneer of picturesque dramatic criticism, some of which he issued in volume form; adapted many French dramas, chiefly by Sardou; contributed to 'Punch' from 1880 sentimental verse, collected in 'Lays of a Londoner,' 1882, and 'Lays and Lyrics,' 1888.

SCOTT, HUGH STOWELL (1862–1903), novelist, writing under the pseudonym of HENRY SETON MERRIMAN; abandoned underwriter's office for foreign travel and novel-writing; published first novel, 'Young Mistley' (2 vols.) anonymously in 1888; his works, which embody much study of foreign nationalities, include 'The Slave of the Lamp,' 1892, 'From one Generation to another,' 1892, 'With Edged Tools,' 1894, 'The Sowers,' 1896, 'In Kedar's Tents,' 1897, 'The Isle of Unrest,' 1900, 'Barlasch of the Guard,' 1902; memorial edition of fourteen novels appeared in 14 vols. in 1909–10.

SCOTT, SIR JOHN (1841–1904), judicial adviser to the khedive; B.A., Pembroke College, Oxford, 1864; M.A., 1869; hon. fellow, 1898; obtained cricket 'blue,' 1863; called to bar, 1865; published 'Bills of Exchange,' 1869; English judge of court of international appeal at Alexandria, 1874–82; vice-president, 1881; puisne judge of high court at Bombay, 1882–90; judicial adviser to the khedive, 1891–8; recreated Egyptian judicial system and simplified procedure; K.C.M.G., 1894; hon. D.C.L., Oxford, 1898; deputy judge advocate-general of the army, 1898.

SCOTT, JOHN (1830–1903), shipbuilder and engineer; joined father's shipbuilding firm on the Clyde, becoming its head, 1868; developed marine steam-engine; introduced water-tube boilers into corvettes for French and English navies; associated with Samson Fox [q. v.] in developing corrugated flues; ardent bibliophile, yachtsman, and Volunteer; C.B., 1887; vice-president of Institution of Naval Architects, 1903; F.R.S. Edinburgh, and F.S.A. Scotland.

SCOTT, LEADER (pseudonym) (1837–1902), writer on art. [See BAXTER, LUCY.]

SCOTT, ROBERT FALCON (1868–1912), naval officer and Antarctic explorer; entered navy, 1880; led National Antarctic expedition in 'Discovery', 1901–4; expedition surveyed coast of South Victoria Land, interior of Antarctic continent, made southern record, discovered King Edward VII Land, sounded Ross Sea, and investigated nature of ice barrier; captain and C.V.O., 1904; commanded new Antarctic expedition in 'Terra Nova', 1910; reached Pole, 18 January 1912, shortly after Norwegian expedition under Roald Amundsen; perished with remainder of party not far from One Ton depot owing to lack of food and bad weather conditions on return journey (c. 29 March); bodies, together with Scott's diaries, specimens, &c., discovered by search party eight months later.

SEALE-HAYNE, CHARLES HAYNE (1833–1903), liberal politician; called to bar, 1857; liberal M.P. for Ashburton, Devonshire, 1885–1903; paymaster-general, 1892–5; P.C., 1892; by will endowed industrial college near Newton Abbot.

SEDDON, RICHARD JOHN (1845–1906), premier of New Zealand; born at St. Helens, Lancashire; left iron foundry at Liverpool for Victoria, 1863; settled as store-keeper in gold mine diggings at Waimea Creek, New Zealand, 1866; removed to goldfields at Kumara, 1874; first mayor; member of parliament for Hokitika, 1879, and for Kumara (renamed Westland, 1890), 1881–1900; joined Young New Zealand reform party; supported great shipping strike (1890), and advocated state owner-ship and state socialism generally; minister for mines, public works, and defence, 1891–6; abolished sub-letting of government contracts; minister of marine, 1892; premier from May 1893 till death; also minister of native affairs, Sept. 1893–9; carried out predecessor's policy of woman's suffrage, Sept. 1893; consolidated criminal code and introduced local option for control of liquor traffic; held, with the premiership till death, the offices of minister for labour (Jan. 1896), colonial treasurer (June), and minister of defence (1899); was for a time in addition commissioner of customs (1899) and trade (1899–1900); attended Queen Victoria's Diamond Jubilee, 1897; P.C. and hon. LL.D. Cambridge, 1897; passed old age pensions bill, 1898; arranged for universal penny postage (1901), and nationalized coal mines and fire insurance; visited South Africa on his way to attend King Edward VII's coronation, 1902; minister of im-migration and of education, 1902; passed Preferential Trade Act favouring British imports; condemned Chinese labour in South Africa, 1904; died at sea on voyage home from Australia; 'Life' by J. Drummond, 1907.

SEDGWICK, ADAM (1854–1913), zoologist; great-nephew of Adam Sedgwick (1785–1873, q.v.); B.A., Trinity College, Cambridge; reader in animal morphology, Cambridge, 1882; F.R.S., 1886; fellow of Trinity, 1897; professor of zoology, Cambridge, 1907, at Imperial College of Science and Technology, South Kensington, 1909.

SEE, SIR JOHN (1844–1907), premier of New South Wales; accompanied parents from England to New South Wales, 1853; built up large produce and shipping business at Sydney; member of New South Wales legislative assembly, 1880–1904; postmaster-general, Oct. to Dec. 1885; treasurer, 1891–4; introduced pro-tectionist tariff; chief secretary and minister for defence, 1899–1901; premier, 1901–4; member of legislative council, 1901–4; K.C.M.G., 1902.

SEEBOHM, FREDERIC (1833–1912), historian; educated at Bootham School, York; called to bar, 1856; settled at Hitchin as partner in bank, 1857; strong Quaker; works include 'The Oxford Reformers' (1867), 'The English Village Community' (1883), 'The Tribal System in Wales' (1895), and 'Tribal Custom in Anglo-Saxon Law' (1902); last three books embody his principal contribution to historical studies; joined widespread revolt against romantic Germanistic interpretation of medieval history; traced back English system of com-munal farming to so-called manorial system, which, in his view, already existed in Roman 'villa,' and Celtic tribal community to authority of patriarch.

SEELEY, HARRY GOVIER (1839–1909), geologist and palaeontologist; cousin of Sir J. R. Seeley [q. v.]; assisted Adam Sedgwick (1785–1873, q.v.) at Woodwardian museum, Cambridge, 1859–71; published 'Index to the Fossil Remains of Aves, Ornithosauria and Reptilia,' 1869; professor of geography at King's College, London,

1876; lecturer and professor of geology and mineralogy at Cooper's Hill, 1890–1905, and at King's College, London, 1896–1905; chief work was 'Researches on the Fossil Reptilia' (10 pts., 1888–96, in Philos. Trans. of Royal Society); F.R.S., 1879; Lyell medallist, Geological Society, 1885.

SELBY, THOMAS GUNN (1846–1910), Wesleyan missionary in China; served at Fatshan, 1868–76; started North River Mission at Shiu Chau Foo, 1878; circuit pastor in England, 1882; works include 'Life of Christ' in Chinese, c. 1890, and 'Chinamen at Home,' 1900.

SELBY, first VISCOUNT (1835–1909), Speaker of the House of Commons. [See GULLY, WILLIAM COURT.]

SELOUS, FREDERICK COURTENEY (1851–1917), hunter and explorer; hunter and ivory trader in South Africa, 1871–81; entered service of British South Africa Company and acted as intermediary between Cecil Rhodes [q. v.] and Matabele chief, Lobengula, 1890; guide and chief of pioneers who secured Mashonaland for British Crown; D.S.O., 1916; killed near Kissaki in (German) East Africa.

SELWIN-IBBETSON, SIR HENRY JOHN, seventh baronet, and BARON ROOKWOOD (1826–1902), politician; B.A., St. John's College, Cambridge, 1849; M.A., 1852; conservative M.P. for South Essex, 1865–8, for Western division of Essex, 1868–84, and for Epping division, 1884–92; raised to peerage, 1892; under-secretary to home office, 1874–8; parliamentary secretary to the treasury, 1878; piloted bill for opening Epping Forest to public (1878).

SELWYN, ALFRED RICHARD CECIL (1824–1902), geologist; assistant geologist on geological survey of Great Britain, 1845; made special study of geology of North Wales; director of geological survey of Victoria, Australia, 1852–69, and of Canada, 1869–94; paid special attention to goldfields, mineral areas, and water supply; published official reports; F.R.S., 1874; LL.D. McGill University, 1881; C.M.G., 1886; president of Royal Society of Canada, 1896; died at Vancouver.

SEMON, SIR FELIX (1849–1921), laryngologist; born at Danzig; M.D., Berlin; came to London, 1874; physician in charge of throat department, St. Thomas's Hospital, 1882–97; laryngologist to National Hospital for Paralysed and Epileptic, 1887–1909; F.R.C.P., 1885; knighted, 1897; naturalized, 1901; K.C.V.O., 1905; especially skilled in diagnosis of cancer of larynx.

SENDALL, SIR WALTER JOSEPH (1832–1904), colonial governor; B.A., Christ's College, Cambridge (first class classic), 1858; M.A., 1867; inspector of schools, 1860–70, and director of education, 1870–2, in Ceylon; poor law inspector in England, 1873–8; assistant secre-tary of local government board, 1878–85; governor-in-chief of Windward Islands, 1885–9, and of Barbados, 1889–92; high commissioner of Cyprus, 1892–8, and of British Guiana, 1898–1901; C.M.G., 1887; K.C.M.G., 1889; G.C.M.G., 1899; hon. LL.D. Edinburgh; edited 'Literary Remains of C. S. Calverley,' 1885.

SERGEANT, (EMILY FRANCES) ADELINE (1851–1904), novelist; published 'Poems,' 1866; educated at Queen's College, London; private governess, 1870–80; engaged in much social work in London, 1887–1901; joined Roman communion, 1899; described religious development in 'Roads to Rome' (1901); her novels (over ninety) include 'Jacobi's Wife,' 1882, 'Esther Denison,' 1889, and 'The Story of Phil Enderby,' 1898; 'Life' by Winifred Stephens, 1905.

SERGEANT, LEWIS (1841–1902), journalist and author; B.A., St. Catharine's College, Cambridge, 1865; for long period leader writer to 'Daily Chronicle'; editor of 'Educational Times,' 1895–1902; wrote much on modern Greece; other works include 'The Franks,' 1898, and verse and fiction.

SETON, GEORGE (1822–1908), Scottish genealogist, heraldic and legal writer; B.A., Exeter College, Oxford, 1845; M.A., 1848; called to Scottish bar, 1846; super-intendent of civil service examinations in Scotland, 1862–89; F.R.S. Edinburgh and F.S.A. Scotland; voluminous writings include 'The Law and Practice of Heraldry in Scotland,' 1863, and a history of the Seton family, 2 vols. 1896.

SEVERN, WALTER (1830–1904), water-colour artist; born near Rome; son of Joseph Severn [q. v.]; held post in education department, 1852–85; made art furniture; revived art needlework and embroidery; skilful landscape painter in water colours; founded Dudley Gallery Art Society, 1865; president, 1883–1904.

SEWELL, ELIZABETH MISSING (1815–1906), author; sister of James Edwards Sewell [q. v.]; influenced by Oxford Movement; published 'Amy Herbert,' 1844, and 'Laneton Parsonage,' 3 pts. 1846–8, novels embodying her Anglican views; published 'The Experience of Life,' 1852, 'Ursula,' 1858, and other novels; took private pupils at Bonchurch from 1852 to 1891; founded at Ventnor St. Boniface School for middle-class girls, 1866; wrote also educational and devotional works; 'Autobiography' edited by E. L. Sewell, 1907.

SEWELL, JAMES EDWARDS (1810–1903), warden of New College, Oxford, from 1860 to 1903; educated at Winchester and New College, Oxford; B.A., 1832; M.A., 1835; D.D., 1860; fellow, 1829; vice-chancellor of university, 1874–8.

SHADWELL, CHARLES LANCELOT (1840–1919), college archivist and translator of Dante; son of Lancelot Shadwell [q. v.]; B.A., Christ Church, Oxford; fellow of Oriel, 1864–98; provost, 1905–14; published 'Registrum Orielense, 1500–1900' (1893, 1902) and verse translation of Dante's 'Purgatorio.'

SHAND (afterwards BURNS), ALEXANDER, BARON SHAND, of Woodhouse (1828–1904); judge; studied law at Edinburgh University, 1848–52; passed to Scottish bar, 1853; sheriff of Kincardine, 1862, and of Haddington and Berwick, 1869; raised to bench, 1872; settled in London, 1890; P.C. and member of the judicial committee of privy council, 1890; raised to peerage, 1892; lord of appeal in House of Lords, 1892–1904.

SHAND, ALEXANDER INNES (1832–1907), journalist and critic; M.A. Aberdeen University, 1852; admitted to Scottish bar, 1865; prolific contributor to 'The Times,' 'Blackwood's,' and 'Saturday Review'; British commissioner at Paris Exhibition, 1893; fine rider, shot, and angler; works include 'Shooting the Rapids,' novel, 1872, life of Sir Edward Hamley, 1895, 'The War in the Peninsula,' 1898, 'Shooting,' 1899, 'Dogs,' 1903, 'Old World Travel,' 1903, and 'Days of the Past,' 1905.

SHARP, WILLIAM, 'FIONA MACLEOD' (1855–1905), romanticist; educated at Glasgow Academy and University; in lawyer's office, 1874–6; travelled in Australia for health, 1876–8; clerk in London, 1878–81; introduced in 1881 to D. G. Rossetti, whose life he wrote, 1882; published volumes of verse—including 'Romantic Ballads and Poems of Phantasy,' 1888; editor of 'Canterbury Poets,' 1884; wrote lives of Shelley (1887), Heine (1888), and Browning (1890), and 'The Children of To-morrow' (1889), a romantic tale; visited Canada and America (1889), Scotland, Germany, and Rome (1890); published 'Sospiri di Roma,' 1891, 'Life of Joseph Severn,' 1892, and dramatic 'Vistas,' 1894; began to write mystical prose and verse under pseudonym of 'Fiona Macleod,' 1893; such works include 'Pharais: a Romance of the Isles,' 1894, 'The Mountain Lovers,' 1895, 'The Sin Eater' (Celtic tales), 1895, and plays including 'The House of Usna,' 1900, and 'The Immortal Hour,' 1900; uniform edition of 'Fiona's' works appeared in 1910; Sharp kept his identity with 'Fiona' a secret till death; under his own name continued to write stories, including 'The Gypsy Christ,' 1895, and 'Wives in Exile,' 1896, as well as 'Literary Geography,' 1904; died in Sicily, near Mount Etna; memoir by wife, 1910.

SHARPE, RICHARD BOWDLER (1847–1909), ornithologist; first librarian to Zoological Society, 1866–72; senior assistant of zoological department, British Museum, 1872–95; assistant keeper of vertebrates, 1895; hon. LL.D. Aberdeen, 1891; greatly increased ornithological collection; prepared British Museum Catalogue of Birds (27 vols. 1874–98), and 'Handlist of the Genera and Species of Birds,' 5 vols. 1899–1909; edited Allen's 'Naturalist's Library' (16 vols.), contributing 'The Birds of Great Britain,' 4 vols. 1894–7; wrote also monographs on kingfishers (1868–71), swallows (1885–94), and birds of paradise (1891–8); founded British Ornithologists' Club, 1892.

SHAW, ALFRED (1842–1907), cricketer; played regularly for Nottinghamshire and for Players v. Gentlemen, 1865–87; played for England v. Australia in first test match in England, Sept. 1880; visited America twice (1868 and 1879), and Australia five times, thrice as captain of English team; was privately engaged by Lord Sheffield in Sussex, 1883–94; played for Sussex, 1894–5; called 'The Emperor of Bowlers'; 'Life' by A. W. Pullin, 1902.

SHAW, SIR EYRE MASSEY (1830–1908), head of the London Metropolitan Fire Brigade, 1861–91; B.A., Trinity College, Dublin, 1848; M.A., 1854; in army, 1854–1860; chief constable of Belfast, 1859–61; reorganised Belfast fire service; perfected organisation of metropolitan system; wrote many treatises on fire brigade subjects; C.B., 1879; K.C.B., 1891; freeman of City of London, 1892.

SHAW, JAMES JOHNSTON (1845–1910), county court judge; professor of metaphysics in Magee College, Londonderry, 1869–78; called to Irish bar, 1878; Whately professor of political economy, Trinity College, Dublin, 1876–91; commissioner of national education in Ireland, 1891; county court judge of Kerry, 1891, and of Antrim, 1909; framed statutes for Queen's University, Belfast, 1908; pro-chancellor, 1909; recorder of Belfast, 1909; his 'Occasional Papers' collected in 1909.

SHAW, JOHN BYAM LISTER (1872–1919), painter and illustrator; A.R.W.S., 1913; has been called 'a kind of belated pre-Raphaelite.'

SHAW, RICHARD NORMAN (1831–1912), architect; pupil of William Burn [q. v.]; travelled abroad, 1854–5; published 'Architectural Sketches from the Continent,' 1858; chief assistant to George Edmund Street [q. v.], 1859; started practice in London with William Eden Nesfield [q. v.], 1862; A.R.A., 1872; R.A., 1877; trained as 'Gothic' architect; his town houses include many studios for artist clients in so-called 'Queen Anne' style; chief piece of city architecture New Scotland Yard (1891); designed a number of country houses, including Chesters, Northumberland, and Bryanston, Dorset (1890–4), both on the grand scale; pre-eminent among Victorian architects for sincerity of his art.

SHEFFIELD, third EARL OF (1832–1909), patron of cricket. [See HOLROYD, HENRY NORTH.]

SHELFORD, SIR WILLIAM (1834–1905), civil engineer; educated at Marlborough; apprenticed as mechanical engineer, 1852; assistant to Sir John Fowler [q. v.], 1856–60; engaged in construction of metropolitan railway; resident engineer on London, Chatham, and Dover Railway, 1860–5; practised on his own account from 1865; engineer of the Hull and Barnsley railway, 1881–5; visited Canada (1885), Italy (1889), and the Argentine (1890) to report on railway schemes; main work was construction of railways in West Africa from 1893 till 1904; studied and wrote on engineering works of rivers and estuaries; reported on river Tiber and its floods, 1879 and 1885; C.M.G., 1901; K.C.M.G., 1904; 'Life' by Anna E. Shelford, 1909.

SHENSTONE, WILLIAM ASHWELL (1850–1908), writer on chemistry; studied chemistry at school of Pharmaceutical Society of Great Britain; demonstrator of practical chemistry there; science master at Clifton College from 1880 to death; collaborated with (Sir) W. A. Tilden and others in much chemical research, especially in ozone; F.R.S., 1898; published works on chemistry.

SHERBORN, CHARLES WILLIAM (1831–1912), engraver; apprenticed to London silver-plate engraver; engraved for London jewellers, 1856–72; his finest achievement series of over 350 book-plates produced between 1881 and 1912; regular exhibitor at Royal Academy.

SHERRINGTON, HELEN LEMMENS- (1834–1906), soprano vocalist. [See LEMMENS-SHERRINGTON.]

SHIELDS, FREDERIC JAMES (1833–1911), painter and decorative artist; served with mercantile lithographers in London and Manchester, 1847–56; influenced by pre-Raphaelite works at Manchester Exhibition, 1857; successful water-colour artist and book illustrator; became intimate with Rossetti, whose memorial window in Birchington church he designed; settled in London, 1876; later devoted himself to decorative design and oil-painting; most important work was decoration of walls of chapel of Ascension, Bayswater Road, from 1889 onwards; he bequeathed fortune to foreign missionary societies; 'Life' by Mrs. Ernestine Mills (1912).

SHIPPARD, SIR SIDNEY GODOLPHIN ALEXANDER (1837–1902), colonial official; born at Brussels; B.A., Hertford College, Oxford, 1863; B.C.L. and M.A., 1864; D.C.L., 1878; called to bar, 1867; migrated to South Africa, 1867; attorney-general of Griqualand West, 1875–8; puisne judge of supreme court of Cape Colony, 1880–5; chief magistrate of British Bechuanaland, 1885–95; C.M.G., 1886; K.C.M.G., 1887; an able Roman-Dutch lawyer.

SHIRREFF, MARIA GEORGINA (1816–1906), promoter of women's education. [See GREY.]

SHORE, WILLIAM THOMAS (1840–1905), geologist and antiquary; founded Hampshire Archaeological Society, and wrote much in its 'Transactions' on Hampshire geology; F.G.S., 1878; settled in London, 1896, and worked on London archaeology; publications include 'A History of Hampshire,' 1892; a memorial volume of geological papers was collected in 1908.

SHORTHOUSE, JOSEPH HENRY (1834–1903), novelist; of quaker parentage; entered father's chemical works at Birmingham, 1850; influenced by Ruskin and pre-Raphaelitism; joined Anglican communion, 1861; his psychological romance, 'John Inglesant,' begun in 1866 and finished in 1876, was privately printed in 1880 and published in 1881; work attracted Gladstone, Huxley, Manning, and had wide vogue; other novels include 'Sir Percival,' 1886, 'A Teacher of the Violin,' 1888; also wrote on 'The Platonism of Wordsworth,' 1882; 'Life' by widow, 2 vols. 1905.

SHREWSBURY, ARTHUR (1856–1903), Nottinghamshire cricketer; played regularly for Nottinghamshire from 1875 to 1902; four times visited Australia; leading English batsman from 1882 to 1893; especially successful in 1887; scored sixty centuries in first-class cricket; showed strong defence and unwearying patience; established athletic outfitter's business in Nottingham, 1880; shot himself at Gedling, Nottinghamshire.

SHUCKBURGH, EVELYN SHIRLEY (1843–1906), classical scholar; educated at Ipswich grammar school and at Emmanuel College, Cambridge; thirteenth classic, 1866; fellow, 1866–74; president of Union, 1865; assistant master at Eton, 1874–84; edited many elementary school classics; translated Polybius, 1889, and 'Cicero's Letters,' 1889–1900; edited Suetonius's 'Life of Augustus,' 1896; Litt.D. Cambridge, 1902; published 'Life of Augustus,' 1903; also wrote histories of Rome (1894) and Greece (to 146 B.C., 1901; to A.D. 14, 1905), and a history of Emmanuel College, 1904.

SIEVEKING, SIR EDWARD HENRY (1816–1904), physician; of a Hamburg family; studied at Berlin and Bonn universities; M.D. Edinburgh, 1841; hon. LL.D., 1884; practised at Hamburg, 1843–7; F.R.C.P., 1852; vice-president, 1888; assistant physician to St. Mary's Hospital, London, 1851–66; physician, 1866–87; helped to found Epsom College, 1855; president of Harveian Society, 1861; knighted, 1886; invented an aesthesiometer, 1858; collaborated in 'Manual of Pathological Anatomy,' 1854, and wrote many papers on nervous diseases, climatology, and nursing.

SIMMONS, SIR JOHN LINTORN ARABIN (1821–1903), field-marshal and colonel commandant royal engineers; joined royal engineers, 1837; served in Canada, 1839–45; employed under railway commissioners, 1846–54; British commissioner with Omar Pasha's Turkish army on the Danube, 1854; helped in defence of Silistria; commanded 20,000 men at battle of Giurgevo (July); repulsed Russians at Eupatoria; took part with Turkish army in siege of Sevastopol; C.B., Oct. 1855; accompanied Omar Pasha in attempt to relieve Kars (Nov.); made major-general in Turkish army; British commissioner for delimitation of new boundary between Turkey and Russia in Asia, 1857; British consul at Warsaw, 1858–60; commanding royal engineer at Aldershot, 1860–5; director of Royal Engineers' Establishment at Chatham, 1865–8; lieutenant-governor of Royal Military Academy at Woolwich and K.C.B., 1869; governor, 1870–5; lieutenant-general and colonel commandant royal engineers, 1872; member of royal commission on railway accidents, 1874–5; inspector-general of fortifications at the war office, 1875–80; military delegate at Berlin congress, 1878; general, 1877; G.C.B., 1878; member of royal commission on defence of British possessions, 1880–2; governor of Malta, 1884–8; G.C.M.G., 1887; field-marshal, 1890.

SIMON, SIR JOHN (1816–1904), sanitary reformer and pathologist; educated privately at Greenwich and in Germany; apprenticed to Joseph Henry Green [q. v.] at St. Thomas's Hospital, 1833–40; M.R.C.S., 1838; hon. F.R.C.S., 1844; president, 1878–9; senior assistant surgeon at King's College Hospital, 1840–7, and lecturer on pathology, 1847; subsequently surgeon at St. Thomas's Hospital, with which he was associated for life; F.R.S., 1845; first medical officer of health for the City of London, 1848; medical officer of general board of health, 1855–8, and of privy council under Public Health Act, 1858–71; published valuable annual reports, reprinted in 'Public Health Reports,' 2 vols. 1887; chief medical officer of newly-formed local government board 1871–6; C.B.,

1876; crown member of medical council, 1876–95; K.C.B., 1887; first Harben medallist of the Royal Institution of Public Health (1896) and first Buchanan medallist of the Royal Society (1897) for services to sanitary science; received honorary degrees from Oxford, Cambridge, Edinburgh, Dublin, and Munich; intimate friend of Ruskin; published 'English Sanitary Institutions,' 1890, and his 'Personal Recollections,' 1898 (revised edit. 1903).

SIMONDS, JAMES BEART (1810–1904), veterinary surgeon; consulting veterinary surgeon to Royal Agricultural Society, 1842–1904; president of Royal College of Veterinary Surgeons, 1862–3; reported on continental and London cattle plague, 1857 and 1865; chief inspector of veterinary department of privy council office, 1865–71; principal of Royal Veterinary College, 1871–81; 'Autobiography' privately printed, 1894.

SIMPSON, MAXWELL (1815–1902), chemist; B.A., Trinity College, Dublin, 1837; studied chemistry at University College, London; M.B., 1847; obtained synthetically succinic and other di- and tri-basic acids; professor of chemistry in Queen's College, Cork, 1872–91; F.R.S., 1862; fellow of Royal University of Ireland, 1882–91; hon. D.Sc., 1882; hon. M.D. Dublin, 1864; LL.D., 1878.

SIMPSON, WILFRED HUDLESTON (1828–1909), geologist. [See HUDLESTON.]

SINGLETON, MARY (1843–1905), authoress under the pseudonym of 'VIOLET FANE'. [See CURRIE, MARY MONTGOMERIE, BARONESS CURRIE.]

SKEAT, WALTER WILLIAM (1835–1912), philologist; B.A., Christ's College, Cambridge; first Elrington and Bosworth professor of Anglo-Saxon, Cambridge, 1878–1912; works include 'Anglo-Saxon Gospels' (1871–87), Ælfric's 'Lives of Saints' (1881–1900), great edition of 'Piers Plowman' (completed 1886), seven-volume edition of Chaucer (1894–7), and 'Etymological Dictionary' (1879–82).

SKIPSEY, JOSEPH (1832–1903), the collier poet; worked in Northumberland coalpits from the age of seven; taught himself to read and write; varied work in mines with other employment until 1882; published 'Poems,' 1859, 'Poems, Songs and Ballads,' 1862, 'The Collier Lad, and other Lyrics,' 1864, 'Carols from the Coalfields,' 1886; edited the 'Canterbury Poets,' 1884–5; custodian of Shakespeare's birthplace, Stratford-on-Avon, 1889–91; was commended by D. G. Rossetti and Burne-Jones; received civil list pensions, 1880–6; 'Life' by R. Spence Watson [q. v.].

SLANEY, WILLIAM SLANEY KENYON- (1847–1908), colonel and politician. [See KENYON-SLANEY.]

SMEATON, DONALD MACKENZIE (1846–1910), Anglo-Indian official; M.A. St. Andrews University; entered Indian civil service, 1865; secretary of land revenue department and director of agriculture, Burma, 1882–6; chief secretary to chief commissioner, 1887; published account of hill races in 'Loyal Karens of Burma,' 1887; financial commissioner of Burma, 1891–1902; represented Burma on supreme legislative council, 1898–1902; retired in 1902 to England; liberal M.P. for Stirlingshire, 1906–10.

SMILES, SAMUEL (1812–1904), author and social reformer; educated at Haddington grammar school; apprenticed to local medical practitioners, 1826; studied at Edinburgh University, 1829–32; engaged in practice at Haddington, 1832–8; published 'Physical Education,' 1837 (new edits. 1868 and 1905); travelled in Holland and first visited London, 1838; editor of 'Leeds Times,' an advanced radical organ, 1838–42; assistant secretary of Leeds and Thirsk Railway, 1845; secretary of South Eastern Railway, 1854–66; president of the National Provident Institution, 1866–71; devoted leisure to advocacy of political and social reform on lines of Manchester school, and to biography of industrial leaders or of humble self-taught students; published 'Life of George Stephenson,' 1857, 'Lives of the Engineers,' 3 vols. 1861–2, and many similar works; achieved great popular success with 'Self-help,' 1859, 'Character,' 1871, 'Thrift,' 1875, 'Duty,' 1880, and 'Life and Labour,' 1887; wrote also on 'The Huguenots . . . in England and Ireland,' 1867, and 'The Huguenots in France,' 1874; hon. LL.D. Edinburgh, 1878; other biographies treated of George Moore the philanthropist, 1878, and of John Murray the publisher, 1891; autobiography posthumously issued, 1905.

SMITH, SIR ARCHIBALD LEVIN (1836–1901), judge; B.A., Trinity College, Cambridge, 1858; rowing 'blue' (1857–9); good cricketer; president of M.C.C.,

1899; called to bar (Inner Temple), 1860; standing junior counsel to treasury, 1879; judge of Queen's Bench Division and knighted, 1883; special commissioner to inquire into 'The Times' allegations against Parnell, 1888; promoted to court of appeal, 1892; master of the Rolls, 1900.

SMITH, SIR CHARLES BEAN EUAN- (1842–1910), soldier and diplomatist. [See EUAN-SMITH.]

SMITH, DONALD ALEXANDER, first BARON STRATHCONA AND MOUNT ROYAL (1820–1914), Canadian financier; born in Scotland; went to Canada as clerk in Hudson's Bay Company, 1838; a 'chief factor,' 1862; head of company's Montreal department, 1868; sent by Canadian government to negotiate with Louis Riel [q. v.]; conservative member of federal parliament, 1871–9; with group of colleagues, which included a cousin, George Stephen (afterwards Baron Mount Stephen, q.v.), completed greater part of Great Northern Railway, 1879, and Canadian Pacific Railway, 1885; knighted, 1886; re-entered parliament for Montreal constituency, 1887; governor of Hudson's Bay Company, 1889; high commissioner for Canada, 1896; baron, 1897; raised 'Strathcona's Horse' during Boer war; lived latter years in England and died there.

SMITH, SIR FRANCIS [VILLENEUVE] (1819–1909), chief justice of Tasmania; early accompanied father to Van Diemen's Land; educated at University College, London; B.A., 1840; called to bar (Middle Temple), 1842, and of Van Diemen's Land, 1844; crown solicitor of colony, 1849; attorney-general, 1854–6; attorney-general in first responsible ministry, 1856–7; attorney-general and premier, 1857–60; puisne judge of supreme court, 1860–70; knighted, 1862; chief justice, 1870–84.

SMITH, GEORGE (1824–1901), founder, proprietor, and publisher of the 'Dictionary of National Biography'. A memoir of him appears in vol. i of the main work.

SMITH, GEORGE BARNETT (1841–1909), author and journalist; on editorial staff of 'Globe,' 1865–8, and 'Echo,' 1868–76; compiled lives of Shelley (1877), Gladstone (1879), John Bright (1881) Victor Hugo (1885), and 'History of the English Parliament' (2 vols. 1892); a skilful etcher; was granted civil list pensions in 1891 and 1906.

SMITH, GEORGE VANCE (1816 ?–1902), Unitarian biblical scholar; divinity student at Manchester College, York (removed to Manchester in 1840 and to London in 1853), where he held many offices, 1839–50, finally serving as principal, 1850–3, and as professor of critical and exegetical theology, 1853–7; M.A. and Ph.D., Tübingen, 1857; minister of St. Saviourgate Chapel, York, 1858–75; joined New Testament revision company, 1870; D.D. Jena, 1873; principal of Presbyterian College, Carmarthen, 1876–83: voluminous writings include 'The Bible and Popular Theology,' 1871, 'The Prophets and their Interpreters,' 1878.

SMITH, GOLDWIN (1823–1910), controversialist; at Eton, 1836–41; matriculated from Christ Church, Oxford, 1841; elected demy of Magdalen College, 1842; showed unusual classical aptitude; made a record as winner of classical prizes; formed in youth lasting liberal opinions on religious and political questions; B.A., 1845; M.A., 1848; Stowell law professor at University College, 1846–67; ordinary fellow, 1850–67; tutor, 1850–4; attacked clerical ascendancy in university; joint secretary of Oxford University commission (1850) and of executive commission which framed new regulations under Oxford University Reform Act, 1855–7; an effective writer in 'Saturday Review,' 1855–8; member of royal commission on national education, 1858; regius professor of modern history at Oxford, 1858–66; stimulated thought in Oxford by his professorial lectures; engaged in political agitation and pamphleteering; defined his distrust of imperialism in 'The Empire,' 1863 (letters reprinted from the 'Daily News'); was denounced as a mischievous propagandist by Disraeli; diagnosed Irish difficulties in 'Irish History and Irish Character,' 1862; influenced by John Bright, he actively advocated cause of North in American civil war; visited America, 1864; joined in attack on Governor Eyre [q. v.] for alleged ill-treatment of negroes in Jamaica, 1867; published lectures on 'Three English Statesmen' (Pym, Cromwell, and Pitt), 1867, to provide funds for Jamaica committee; suffered anxiety from illness (1866) of father, who committed suicide next year; resolved on prolonged residence in America; accepted offer of professorship of history at newly-founded Cornell University, Ithaca, N.Y., 1868; bade farewell to Oxford in a pamphlet on

the 'Reorganization of the University,' 1868; reached Ithaca, November 1868; devoted himself zealously to professorial duties there; resented American hostility to England, 1869–70, and Disraeli's attack on him as a 'social parasite' in 'Lothair,' 1870; made a tour in Canada, 1870; settled at Toronto, 1871; married there (1875) widow of Henry Boulton, of 'The Grange,' which became his permanent residence for life. At Toronto Goldwin Smith was very active in journalism, contributing literary and political essays to daily, weekly, and monthly periodicals of Canada, America, and England; he strongly encouraged sentiment of national independence in Canada from 1871, and a commercial union with the United States from 1888, recommending the amalgamation of the English-speaking race on American continent; on frequent visits to England he took much part in public life there, but declined invitations to stand for parliament or to become master of University College, Oxford, 1881. He was made hon. D.C.L. Oxford, 1882; strenuously opposed Gladstone's home rule policy, 1886; always remained faithful to unionism (cf. 'Irish History and the Irish Question,' 1906); opposed South African war, 1899; explained his pacificist position in 'In the Court of History,' 1902; and warned America against imperialism in 'Commonwealth and Empire,' 1902. Other scattered political writings were collected in 'Lectures and Essays,' 1881, and 'Essays on Questions of the Day,' 1893. Smith continued his historical and literary studies in monograph on Cowper, 1880, 'Specimens of Greek Tragedy,' 1893, 'The United States: an Outline of Political History, 1492–1871,' 1893, and 'The United Kingdom: a Political History,' 2 vols. 1899. He also issued many speculative treatises deprecating orthodox religion, e. g. 'Guesses at the Riddle of Existence,' 1897. Despite the unpopularity of his political and religious views in Canada he won much affectionate respect there by his enlightened activity in educational matters, by his advocacy of purity in public life, and by his philanthropy and private charity. President of American Historical Association, 1904, he laid corner stone of 'Goldwin Smith Hall' at Cornell, 1904. Dying at 'The Grange,' Toronto, he was buried in St. James's cemetery there. He bequeathed residue of large fortune to Cornell for promotion of liberal studies; 'Reminiscences,' 1911, and 'Correspondence,' 1913, both edited by Arnold Haultain.

SMITH, HENRY SPENCER (1812–1901), surgeon; entered St. Bartholomew's Hospital, 1832; M.R.C.S., 1837; F.R.C.S., 1843; senior assistant surgeon at newly-founded St. Mary's Hospital, 1851; dean of medical school, 1854–60; stimulated in England microscopic study of tissues by his translation of German works.

SMITH, JAMES HAMBLIN (1829–1901), mathematician; B.A., Caius College, Cambridge, 1850; M.A., 1853; private coach at Cambridge till death; lecturer in classics at Peterhouse, 1862–72; published handbooks on Statics (1868), Hydrostatics (1868), Trigonometry (1868), Algebra (1869), Geometry (1872), Arithmetic (1872), Heat (1877), and Geometrical Conic Sections (1887).

SMITH, LUCY TOULMIN (1838–1911), scholar; born at Boston, Massachusetts; daughter of Joshua Toulmin Smith (1816–1869, q. v.); resided at Highgate, London, from 1842 to 1894; edited works for Early English Text, Camden, and New Shakspere societies from 1870, as well as 'Leland's Itinerary,' 5 vols. 1906–10; librarian of Manchester College, Oxford, 1894–1911.

SMITH, REGINALD BOSWORTH (1839–1908), schoolmaster and author; educated at Marlborough and Corpus Christi College, Oxford; B.A. (first class classic), 1862; M.A., 1865; president of Union, 1862; fellow and tutor of Trinity College, Oxford, 1863; classical master at Harrow, 1864–1901; published lectures on Mohammed and Mohammedanism, 1874, 'Carthage and the Carthaginians,' 1878, and 'Life of Lord Lawrence,' 4 edits. 2 vols. 1883; wrote on current political, religious, and educational matters in the reviews; defended Turkish character, urging permanent English occupation of Sudan; opposed disestablishment of Church of England; settled in Dorset, 1901; ardent ornithologist; published 'Bird Life and Bird Lore,' 1905; memoir by his daughter, 1909.

SMITH, REGINALD JOHN (1857–1916), barrister and publisher; B.A., King's College, Cambridge; called to bar (Inner Temple); joined publishing firm of Smith, Elder, and Co., 1894; assumed sole control, 1899; editor of 'Cornhill Magazine,' 1898; publications include centenary editions of Thackeray and Browning, Brontë and Gaskell definitive editions, and thin paper edition of 'Dictionary of National Biography' (1908).

SMITH, SAMUEL (1836–1906), politician and philanthropist; educated at Edinburgh University; apprenticed to Liverpool cottonbroker, 1853; after visit to North American cotton growing districts (1860) started cotton broking business at Liverpool; visited India (1862–3) to test cotton growing possibilities; president of Liverpool chamber of commerce, 1876; liberal M.P. for Liverpool, 1882–5, and for Flintshire, 1886–1905; friend of Gladstone; promoted Criminal Law Amendment Act, 1885; attacked opium traffic between China and India; advocate of bimetallism; published account of a second visit to India in 'India Revisited,' 1886; champion of native races; urged church disestablishment; P.C., 1905; revisited India, 1904–5 and 1906; died at Calcutta; bequeathed 50,000*l.* to Liverpool institutions; published works on Indian cotton trade and Indian problems and autobiographical 'My Life Work,' 1902.

SMITH, SARAH (1832–1911), authoress under the pseudonym of HESBA STRETTON; first short story, 'The Lucky Leg,' accepted by Dickens for 'Household Words,' 1859; contributed to 'All the Year Round' Christmas numbers till 1866; her 'Jessica's First Prayer' (1866) won lasting popularity and has been translated into every European language and most African and Asiatic tongues; published some fifty other volumes; helped to found London Society for Prevention of Cruelty to Children, 1884.

SMITH, THOMAS (1817–1906), missionary and mathematician; graduated in mathematics at Edinburgh University; hon. M.A., 1858; D.D., 1867; LL.D., 1900; ordained to Scottish mission at Calcutta, 1839; on disruption (1843) joined Free Church; inaugurated first Zenana missions to India, 1854; conducted home mission in Edinburgh, 1859–79; professor of evangelistic theology, New College, Edinburgh, 1880–93; moderator of Free Church general assembly, 1891; works include 'Plane Geometry,' 1857, 'The Life of Euclid,' 1902, and 'Medieval Missions,' 1880.

SMITH, SIR THOMAS, first baronet (1833–1909), surgeon; educated at Tonbridge and St. Bartholomew's Hospital; M.R.C.S., 1854; coached pupils for examinations from 1854, publishing 'Manual of Operative Surgery on the Dead Body,' 1859; F.R.C.S., 1858; demonstrator of operative surgery at St. Bartholomew's, 1859; surgeon, 1873–98; surgeon to Children's Hospital, Great Ormond Street, 1868–83; baronet, 1897; K.C.V.O., 1901; a dexterous operator and sure guide in diagnosis.

SMITH, THOMAS ROGER (1830–1903), architect; entered office of Philip Hardwick [q. v.]; designed several buildings in Bombay, 1864; work in England included many board schools, churches, and hospitals; president of Architectural Association, 1860–1 and 1863–4; district surveyor for Southwark and North Lambeth (1874–82) and for West Wandsworth from 1882; master of Carpenters Company, 1901; professor of architecture at University College, London, 1880–1903; published manual of 'Acoustics,' 1861, and works on architecture.

SMITH, VINCENT ARTHUR (1848–1920), Indian historian and antiquary; son of Aquilla Smith [q. v.]; entered Indian civil service, 1871; served in North-West Provinces and Oudh till 1900; C.I.E., 1919; works include 'Early History of India' (1904) and 'Oxford History of India' (1918).

SMITH, WALTER CHALMERS (1824–1908), poet and preacher; M.A., Marischal College, Aberdeen, 1841; free church minister at Glasgow and Edinburgh, 1862–1894; moderator of general assembly, 1893; D.D.Glasgow, 1869; LL.D. Aberdeen, 1876, and Edinburgh, 1893; published many volumes of verse; a complete edition appeared in 1902.

SMITH, WILLIAM SAUMAREZ (1836–1909), archbishop of Sydney; born at St. Helier's, Jersey; B.A., Trinity College, Cambridge (first class classic), 1858; M.A., 1862; Tyrwhitt Hebrew scholar and fellow, 1860; principal of St. Aidan's, Birkenhead, 1869–89; bishop of Sydney, 1890–7, and first archbishop, 1897 till death; hon. D.D. Cambridge, 1890, Oxford, 1897; published theological works and verse.

SMYLY, SIR PHILIP CRAMPTON (1838–1904), surgeon and laryngologist; B.A., Trinity College, Dublin, 1859; M.B., 1860; M.D., 1863; F.R.C.S., Ireland, 1863; president, 1878–9; surgeon to Meath Hospital, 1861–1904; president of Laryngological Association, 1889, and of Irish Medical Association, 1900; intro-

duced laryngoscope to Ireland, 1860; knighted, 1892; a musician and freemason.

SMYTH, SIR HENRY AUGUSTUS (1825–1906), general and colonel commandant, royal artillery, from 1894; joined royal artillery, 1843; served in Bermuda, 1847–51, in Nova Scotia, 1851–4; commanded a field battery at Sevastopol, 1855; in Canada, 1861–5; in India, 1867–74; commanded artillery at Sheerness, 1876, and in southern district, 1877–80; on ordnance committee at Woolwich, 1881–3; major-general, 1882; commandant of Woolwich garrison, 1882–6; lieutenant-general, 1886; crushed rising in Zululand, 1887; acting governor of Cape Colony, 1889–90; C.M.G., 1889; K.C.M.G., 1890; governor of Malta, 1890–3; general, 1891.

SNELUS, GEORGE JAMES (1837–1906), metallurgist; student at Royal School of Mines, 1864–7; patented process of eliminating phosphorus from molten pig-iron by oxidation in basic lined enclosure, 1872; process was commercially developed by Sidney Gilchrist Thomas [q. v.] in 1879; Snelus was awarded gold medal at Paris Exhibition and Bessemer gold medal of Iron and Steel Institute, 1878; F.R.S., 1887; general manager of West Cumberland Iron and Steel Company from 1872 to 1900; an enthusiastic Volunteer and rifle shot.

SNOW, HERBERT (1835–1910), classical scholar. [See KYNASTON.]

SOLOMON, SIR RICHARD (1850–1913), South African statesman; born in Cape Town; attorney-general of Cape Colony, 1898, of Transvaal, 1902; high commissioner for Union of South Africa in London, 1910; K.C.M.G., 1902; K.C.B., 1905.

SOLOMON, SIMEON (1840–1905), painter and draughtsman; brother of Abraham Solomon [q. v.]; exhibited at Royal Academy from 1858, mainly scriptural subjects, showing sincerity and beauty of colour; became acquainted with Burne-Jones, Rossetti, Swinburne, and Lord Houghton; from 1865 exhibited classical subjects; his 'Bacchus' (1867) praised by Walter Pater; visited Florence (1866) and Rome (1869); published 'A Vision of Love revealed in Sleep,' 1871, which was praised by Swinburne; also made a reputation by water-colour and pencil studies; ceased to exhibit after 1872 when vicious indulgences ruined his career; thenceforth he endured great poverty, earning a precarious livelihood by sentimental sketches; his 'A Greek Acolyte' is in Birmingham Art Gallery.

SOMERSET, LADY ISABELLA CAROLINE, LADY HENRY SOMERSET (1851–1921); daughter of last Earl Somers; married Lord Henry Somerset, 1872; devoted herself to temperance work; president of British Women's Temperance Association, 1890–1903, of World's Women's Christian Temperance Union, 1898–1906; founded Duxhurst, farm colony for inebriate women near Reigate, 1895.

SORBY, HENRY CLIFTON (1826–1908), geologist; of old Sheffield family of cutlers; versatile scientist; made researches in spectroscope and microscope, meteorology, archaeology, and architecture; interested in Egyptian hieroglyphics; pioneer of microscopic petrology; published papers on 'Calcareous Grit of Scarborough,' 1851, on 'Slaty Cleavage,' 1853, and 'On the Microscopic Structure of Crystals,' 1858; studied microscopic structure of irons and steels; F.G.S., 1850; president, 1878–80; F.R.S., 1857; royal medallist, 1874; hon. LL.D. Cambridge, 1897; helped to found Firth College and bequeathed to Sheffield University his collections, with money to found a chair in geology.

SOTHEBY, SIR EDWARD SOUTHWELL (1813–1902), admiral; joined navy, 1828; served in Syria, 1840; commander, 1841; commanded on East Indies and China station, 1855–8; distinguished in Oudh during Indian mutiny; C.B., 1858; extra A.D.C. to Queen Victoria, 1858–67; commanded Portland coast-guard division, 1863; K.C.B., 1875; admiral, 1879.

SOUTAR, ELLEN (1848–1904), actress. [See FARREN.]

SOUTHESK, ninth EARL OF (1827–1905), poet and antiquary. [See CARNEGIE, JAMES.]

SOUTHEY, SIR RICHARD (1808–1901), Cape of Good Hope official; went to South Africa, 1820; engaged in farming; served in Kafir war, 1834–5; resident agent with Kafir tribes, 1835–6; farmer at Graaffreinet, 1836–46; civil commissioner and resident magistrate of Swellendam, 1849–52; acting secretary to Cape Government, 1852–4; auditor-general, 1859; acting colonial secretary, 1860–1; treasurer and accountant-general, 1860; member of executive council, 1861; colonial secretary,

1864–72; opposed responsible government for Cape; lieutenant-governor of province of Griqualand West, 1873–5; member of house of assembly, 1876–8; C.M.G., 1872; K.C.M.G., 1891.

SOUTHWARD, JOHN (1840–1902), writer on typography; son of Liverpool printer; conducted 'Liverpool Observer' from 1857 to 1865; printer's reader in London, 1867–8; travelled in Spain, 1868; edited 'Printers' Register,' 1886–90; authoritative works include 'Dictionary of Typography,' 1872, 'Practical Printing,' 1882, and 'Modern Printing,' 1898; was largely responsible for Bigmore and Wyman's 'Bibliography of Printing,' 3 vols. 1880–6.

SOUTHWELL, THOMAS (1831–1909), naturalist; in service of Gurney's bank at Lynn, Fakenham, and Norwich from 1846 to 1896; completed Henry Stevenson's 'Birds of Norfolk,' 3rd vol. 1890; published 'The Seals and Whales of the British Seas,' 1881; edited 'Notes on Natural History of Norfolk,' 1902, from Sir Thomas Browne's MSS.

SPENCER, HERBERT (1820–1903), philosopher; educated at day school at Derby, his native place, and from 1833 to 1836 mainly at Hinton Charterhouse near Bath under his uncle Thomas Spencer [q. v.]; made little progress in the classics, but was much interested in natural science; after acting as assistant schoolmaster at Derby (1837) he was employed as engineer on Birmingham and Gloucester Railway, 1837–41; wrote letters to 'The Nonconformist' urging limitation of the functions of the state, 1842, which he republished as 'The Proper Sphere of Government,' 1843; sub-editor of the 'Pilot,' the organ of the 'Complete Suffrage Movement,' published at Birmingham, 1844; occupied himself anew with engineering, 1844–6; experimented with mechanical inventions, 1846–7, subsequently inventing an invalid bed, 1866; sub-editor of the 'Economist' in London, 1848–53; visited house of John Chapman, the advanced publisher, 1849; there came to know George Eliot; made acquaintance of Huxley and Tyndall; published 'Social Statics,' 1851, advocating an extreme individualism; contributed articles to the 'Leader,' 'Westminster Review,' and other periodicals, collecting many of these in 'Essays,' 1st ser. 1857, 2nd ser. 1863, 3rd ser. 1864; published 'Principles of Psychology,' 1855 (recast in two vols. 1870–2); during the writing of this book his health gave way, and was never fully restored. During 1858 he planned a system of synthetic philosophy, covering metaphysics, biology, psychology, sociology, and ethics, for publication of which he in 1860 invited subscriptions both in England and America, but this plan, which was for a time successful, broke down about 1865; the deaths of his uncle William and his father in 1866 improved his financial position. In 1861 he issued 'Education,' a treatise aiming at a natural development of the child's intelligence, which became a leading textbook. He published 'First Principles' of his synthetic philosophy, 1862, and 'Principles of Biology,' vol. i. 1864, vol. ii. 1867; joined Jamaica committee for prosecution of Governor Eyre [q. v.], 1866; was elected to Athenaeum Club by the committee, 1868; was offered in 1871 lord rectorship of St. Andrews University, but declined this, and all later offers of honours; in order to deal with the principles of sociology he employed assistants to collect systematically large masses of facts, of which eight volumes under general title of 'Descriptive Sociology' were issued by 1881, while additional volumes appeared after Spencer's death. He contributed his widely read 'Study of Sociology,' 1873, to 'International Scientific Series,' edited by his American friend, Prof. E. L. Youmans; issued 'Principles of Sociology,' vol. i. 1876, vol. ii. 1882, vol. iii. 1896; meanwhile wrote 'Data of Ethics' (1879), forming part i. of the 'Principles of Ethics' (vol. i. 1892, vol. ii. 1893); formed with Mr. Frederic Harrison and Mr. John Morley and others an anti-aggression league, 1882; visited America, 1882; collected four articles from 'Contemporary Review' to form 'The Man versus the State,' 1884, in which he urged anew the limitation of state functions; attacked the positivist religion in 'The Nature and Reality of Religion,' 1885 (suppressed by Spencer, but re-issued without his knowledge as 'The Insuppressible Book'); completed his 'Synthetic Philosophy' in vol. iii. of the 'Principles of Sociology,' 1896; allowed his portrait to be painted by Sir Hubert von Herkomer for presentation to the Scottish National Portrait Gallery, Edinburgh, 1896; issued 'Various Fragments,' 1897, and 'Facts and Comments,' 1902; died, 8 Dec. 1903, after much suffering

from shattered nervous system, at Brighton, where he had lived since 1898; he was cremated at Golders Green, his ashes being buried in Highgate Cemetery; left bulk of property in trust for carrying on his 'Descriptive Sociology.' The central doctrines of his philosophy, which exerted an immense influence on his era throughout Europe and America, India and Japan, were on its social side individualism and opposition to war, and on its scientific side evolution and explanation of phenomena from the materialistic standpoint; 'Autobiography' published 1904; 'Life and Letters' by D. Duncan, 1908; an epitome of the 'Synthetic Philosophy' by F. Howard Collins, 5th edit. 1901.

SPENCER, JOHN POYNTZ, fifth EARL SPENCER (1835–1910), statesman and viceroy of Ireland; educated at Harrow School, 1848–54, and at Trinity College, Cambridge, 1854–7; M.A., 1857; hon. LL.D., 1864; elected liberal M.P. for South Northamptonshire, 6 April 1857; succeeded father in earldom, 27 Dec.; devoted to sport and shooting; helped to form National Rifle Association, 1860; chairman, 1867–8; groom of the stole to Prince Consort, 1859–61, and to Prince of Wales, afterwards Edward VII, 1861–7; made K.G. by Lord Palmerston, 1865; lord-lieutenant of Ireland under Gladstone without seat in cabinet, 1868–74; firm in maintenance of the law; president of the council, with seat in cabinet, 1880–2; reappointed lord-lieutenant of Ireland on retirement of Lord Cowper, in order to pursue a conciliatory policy; retained seat in cabinet; went to Ireland, 5 May 1882, with Lord Frederick Cavendish as Irish secretary; on assassination of Lord Frederick next day Spencer was compelled to invoke repressive measures and was consequently vilified by mass of the Irish people; reduced Irish disorder; deprecated local government proposals of his cabinet colleagues, Dilke and Chamberlain, just before fall of government, 1885; resented an implied censure on the part of the conservatives in office on his use of 'coercion,' 1885; supported Gladstone's home rule scheme, 1886; again president of the council, 1886; while in opposition he urged the cause of home rule, 1886–92; first lord of the admiralty, 1892–5; insistent on requirements of national security; formulated 'Spencer programme' of shipbuilding, which involved increased expenditure, despite objections of Gladstone while prime minister; succeeded Lord Kimberley as liberal leader in the House of Lords, 1902; amid dissensions in liberal party he was often suggested as best fitted for its leadership; incapacitated by illness from 1905; lord-lieutenant of Northamptonshire, 1872–1908; chairman of Northamptonshire county council, 1889; president of Royal Agricultural Society, 1898; chancellor of Victoria University, Manchester, 1892–1910; sold great part of Althorp library to form John Rylands library at Manchester, 1892.

SPIERS, RICHARD PHENÉ (1838–1916), architect; assistant to Sir Matthew Digby Wyatt [q. v.], 1861; silver and gold medallist, Royal Academy, 1863; travelled abroad and studied water-colour painting, 1865–6; master of Royal Academy architectural school, 1870–1906; his executed works include additions to houses, restorations of churches, and a few new buildings; some of his most valuable work in architectural research contained in 'Architecture, East and West' (collected papers, 1905).

SPRENGEL, HERMANN JOHANN PHILIPP (1834–1906), chemist; born near Hanover; Ph.D. Heidelberg, 1858; engaged in chemical research in Oxford and London from 1859; patented many safety explosives, liquid and solid; invented mercurial air pump for production of high tenuity (1865), which facilitated many later inventions; F.R.S., 1878; published researches in 'Origin of Melinite and Lyddite,' 1890, and 'The Discovery of Picric Acid,' 1902, in which he complained of infringement of rights to priority in his own discoveries.

SPRIGG, SIR JOHN GORDON (1830–1913), South African statesman; born at Ipswich; settled in South Africa, 1861; member for East London, 1869–1904; prime minister of Cape Colony, 1878–81, 1886–90, 1896–8; attended premiers' conference in London and created P.C., 1897; prime minister, 1900–4; federalist member for East London, 1908; K.C.M.G., 1886.

SPRING-RICE, SIR CECIL ARTHUR (1859–1918), diplomat; grandson of first Baron Monteagle [q. v.]; educated at Eton and Balliol College, Oxford; entered Foreign Office, 1882; at Berlin, 1895–8; British commissioner on 'Caisse de la Dette Publique', Cairo, 1901–3;

secretary of embassy, St. Petersburg, 1903–6; K.C.M.G., 1906; British minister to Persia, 1906–8, to Sweden, 1908–13; ambassador at Washington, 1913–18; acted as conciliatory influence between Great Britain and United States during European War; his tact contributed to America joining Allies; died at Ottawa.

SPROTT, GEORGE WASHINGTON (1829–1909), Scottish divine and liturgical scholar; born in Nova Scotia; B.A. Glasgow, 1849; hon. D.D., 1880; ordained in church of Scotland, 1852; chaplain to Scottish troops in Kandy, 1857–65; prominent in formation of Church Service Society, 1865; published critical edition of 'Book of Common Order,' 1868, and 'Scottish Liturgies of James VI,' 1871; moderator of synod, 1873; minister of North Berwick, 1873–1903; visited Presbyterian churches in Canada, 1879; published lectures (1879) in 'Worship and Offices of the Church of Scotland,' 1882; advocate of church reunion; retired in 1903 to Edinburgh and engaged in literary work; edited liturgiological works and wrote a life of his father, 1906.

STABLES, WILLIAM (GORDON) (1840–1910), writer for boys; M.D. and C.M. Aberdeen University, 1862; made a first voyage to Arctic, 1859; assistant surgeon in navy, 1863–71; for two years in merchant service, visiting India, Africa, and South Seas; from 1875 a prolific writer of boys' books of adventure and of historical novels; early pioneer of caravanning, 1886.

STACPOOLE, FREDERICK (1813–1907), engraver in mixed mezzotint of works by contemporary artists; most successful engravings were Lady Butler's 'Roll Call,' 1874, and Holman Hunt's 'Shadow of Death', 1877; exhibited at Royal Academy, 1842–99; A.R.A., 1880; also painted in oils.

STAFFORD, SIR EDWARD WILLIAM (1819–1901), premier of New Zealand; educated at Trinity College, Dublin; emigrated to Nelson, New Zealand, 1843; elected to house of representatives, 1855; premier and colonial secretary, 1856–61; created three new provinces; transferred land revenue to provincial councils; established itinerant courts of justice and native juries; visited England, 1859; again premier of New Zealand, 1865–9, holding also offices of colonial secretary, 1865–9, colonial treasurer, 1865–6, and postmaster-general, 1865–6 and 1869; premier for a third time, Sept.–Oct. 1872; lived in England from 1874; K.C.M.G., 1879; G.C.M.G., 1887.

STAINER, SIR JOHN (1840–1901), organist and composer; chorister of St. Paul's Cathedral, 1849; graduated B.Mus. from Christ Church, Oxford, 1859; organist of Magdalen College, Oxford, 1860, and of Oxford University, 1861; B.A., St. Edmund Hall, 1864; M.A., 1866; D.Mus., 1865; founded Oxford Philharmonic Society, 1866; organist of St. Paul's Cathedral, 1872–88; organist to Royal Choral Society, 1873–88; professor of organ (1876) and principal (1881) of National Training College of Music; knighted, 1888; professor of music in Oxford University, 1889–99; master of Musicians' Company, 1900; hon. fellow of Magdalen College, Oxford; hon. Mus.D. Durham, 1858, and hon. D.C.L., 1895; compositions include oratorios, 'The Daughter of Jairus,' 1878, 'Crucifixion,' 1887, forty anthems, church services, and over 150 hymn tunes, organ compositions, madrigals, and part songs; edited 'Christmas Carols, New and Old,' 1884; publications include 'Music of the Bible,' 1879, and 'Early Bodleian Music,' 2 vols. 1902; was first editor of Novello's 'Music Primers,' to which he contributed volumes on 'The Organ' and 'Harmony'; formed unique collection of old song books.

STALBRIDGE, first BARON (1837–1912), railway administrator and politician. [See GROSVENOR, RICHARD DE AQUILA.]

STAMER, SIR LOVELACE TOMLINSON, third baronet (1829–1908), bishop-suffragan of Shrewsbury; educated at Rugby and Trinity College, Cambridge; B.A., 1853; M.A., 1856; D.D., 1888; rector of Stoke-upon-Trent, 1858–92; built at Stoke three churches, five mission churches, and five schools; started night schools there, 1863; chairman of Stoke school board, 1871–88; formed North Staffordshire Coal and Ironstone Workers' Permanent Relief Society, 1870; chairman, 1870–1908; founded Staffordshire Institution for Nurses, 1872; archdeacon of Stoke-upon-Trent, 1877; bishop-suffragan of Shrewsbury, 1888–1905; vicar of St. Chad's, Shrewsbury, 1892–6; rector of Edgmond, 1896–1905; published sermons and charges; memoir by F. D. How, 1910.

STANLEY, FREDERICK ARTHUR, sixteenth EARL

OF DERBY (1841–1908), governor-general of Canada; second son of fourteenth Earl [q. v.]; in grenadier guards, 1858–65; conservative M.P. for Preston, 1865–8; civil lord of the admiralty, 1868; M.P. for North Lancashire, 1868–85, and for Blackpool, 1885–6; joined cabinet as secretary of state for war, and P.C., 1878–80; G.C.B., 1880; colonial secretary, 1885–6; raised to peerage, 1886; president of the board of trade, 1886–8; governor-general of Canada, 1888–93; stimulated imperial sentiment in dominion; succeeded to earldom, 1893; prominent in Liverpool affairs; first lord mayor, 1895–6; first chancellor of university from 1903; successful racehorse owner; won Oaks in 1893 and 1906; K.G., 1897; G.C.V.O., 1905.

STANLEY, HENRY EDWARD JOHN, third BARON STANLEY OF ALDERLEY (1827–1903), diplomatist and Orientalist; son of second baron [q. v.]; fellow-commoner of Trinity College, Cambridge, 1846–7; entered diplomatic service; secretary of legation at Athens, 1854–9; began extensive travels in the East; adopted Moslem religion; succeeded to peerage and estates in Cheshire and Anglesey, 1869; champion of Church of England in Wales; supported Indian National Congress movement; keen sportsman and strict total abstainer; published 'Essays on East and West,' 1865; translated for Hakluyt Society many Spanish and Portuguese works of travel.

STANLEY, SIR HENRY MORTON (1841–1904), explorer, administrator, author, and journalist, whose real name was JOHN ROWLANDS; born at Denbigh, 29 June 1841; owing to father's early death and mother's neglect, he was brought up in St. Asaph workhouse, 1847–56; after some humble desultory employment he shipped as cabin boy on American packet for New Orleans, 1859; was adopted at New Orleans by cotton-broker, Henry Stanley (d. 1861), whose name he assumed; became a naturalized American; served as volunteer with confederate army (1861–2), but being taken prisoner he enlisted in United States artillery, from which he was discharged owing to ill-health; suffered much distress; served in U.S.A. navy, 1864–5; made some progress as newspaper correspondent; sought adventure in Asia Minor, 1866; described General Hancock's expedition against Indians in 'Missouri Democrat,' 1867; subsequently republished his articles in 'My Early Travels and Adventures in America and Asia Minor,' 1885; showed great resource as special correspondent of 'New York Herald' during Abyssinian war, 1868–9; reported for 'Herald' disturbances in Spain, 1869; was ordered (16 Oct. 1869) by proprietor, Mr. Gordon Bennett, to 'find Livingstone,' who was lost in interior of Africa; before proceeding on this mission he attended opening of Suez Canal, and visited Egypt and Palestine and Persia; started from Bagamoyo in Zanzibar for Lake Tanganyika, where Livingstone was believed to be, 21 March 1871; met Livingstone at Ujiji, 10 Nov. 1871; travelled about the district till 18 Feb. 1872 with Livingstone, who declined to accompany Stanley home; described his journey in 'How I found Livingstone,' 1872; met in England with much scorn from men of science, but was warmly welcomed by the general English public; described Ashanti war (1873) for 'New York Herald'; embodied experiences in 'Coomassie and Magdala,' 1874; on learning of Livingstone's death Stanley undertook expedition to equatorial Africa under joint commission from 'New York Herald' and London 'Daily Telegraph'; left Zanzibar, 11 Nov. 1874; initiated conversion of kingdom of Uganda to Christianity; first traced course of the Congo; laid foundation of Anglo-Egyptian dominions of Upper Nile; emerged upon the shores of the Atlantic (9 Aug. 1877), having opened up the heart of the continent for the first time; published 'Through the Dark Continent,' 1878; was refused help in England for developing the Congo district; proposed the scheme to King Leopold II of Belgium, who accepted it, Aug. 1878; helped to organize Congo region for the Belgians (1879–84), and thus inaugurated the Congo State; issued 'The Congo and the founding of its Free State,' 1885; lectured in Germany, England, and America on the commercial possibilities of Central Africa, 1884–6; undertook leadership of his final expedition to equatorial Africa in order to rescue Emin Pasha, who had been abandoned in command of Egyptian army, when the Mahdi overran the Sudan; started from the mouth of the Congo, February 1887; divided his forces at Yambuya, June; leaving strong rearguard there, he pushed on through dense tropical forest to the Albert Nyanza, where he arrived, 13 Dec.; sent message to Emin, who visited him there with reluctance; returned to find his rearguard in tragic plight; brought remnant to Lake Albert, January 1889; was joined there by Emin and his party; while marching back to Bagamoyo (4 Dec. 1889), he discovered much new country which ultimately went to form the British East African Protectorate; on arriving in England, although he was attacked for failure to 'rescue' Emin and for sacrificing his rearguard, he was received with enthusiasm and accorded many honours; described his journey in 'In Darkest Africa,' 1890, which had an immense sale; married at Westminster Abbey, 12 July 1890, Dorothy Tennant; lectured in America and Australasia; was re-naturalized as British subject; unionist M.P. for North Lambeth, 1895–1900; toured through South Africa, 1897–8; described experiences in 'Through South Africa,' 1898; K.C.B., 1899; stricken by paralysis, 15 April 1903; died in London, 10 May 1904; buried in Pirbright churchyard; 'Autobiography' edited by his widow, 1909.

STANLEY, WILLIAM FORD ROBINSON (1829–1909), scientific instrument maker and author; started in London a drawing instrument business, 1854; invented cheap 'Panoptic Stereoscope,' 1855; patented application of aluminium to manufacture of mathematical instruments, 1861; greatly improved theodolite and other surveying instruments; published standard work on 'Mathematical Drawing Instruments,' 1866; made many scientific inventions; F.G.S., 1884; F.R.A.S., 1894; accomplished musician, artist, photographer, and architect; opened at Norwood Stanley Public Hall (1903) and technical school (1907); also published 'Experimental Researches into . . . Fluids,' 1881, and 'Surveying and Levelling Instruments,' 1890.

STANMORE, first BARON (1829–1912), colonial governor. [See GORDON, ARTHUR CHARLES HAMILTON-.]

STANNARD, HENRIETTA ELIZA VAUGHAN (1856–1911), novelist under the pseudonym of JOHN STRANGE WINTER; born PALMER; contributed to 'Family Herald' from 1874 to 1884 short stories and serials dealing with military life; married Arthur Stannard, 1884; published 'Bootles' Baby,' 1885, a work which was admired by Ruskin and was universally popular; edited 'Winter's Weekly,' 1892–5; president of Society of Women Journalists, 1901–3.

STANNUS, HUGH HUTTON (1840–1908), architect, author, and lecturer; studied art foundry work at Sheffield; assistant of Alfred Stevens [q. v.], with whom he worked on the Wellington monument in St. Paul's Cathedral; studied architecture at Royal Academy Schools, 1872; F.R.I.B.A., 1887; did much private structural and decorative work; taught modelling at Royal Academy, 1881–1900; director of architectural studies at Manchester School of Art, 1900–2; published works on decoration, form-design, and architecture, and 'Alfred Stevens and his Work,' 1891.

STANTON, ARTHUR HENRY (1839–1913), divine; B.A., Trinity College, Oxford; curate of St. Alban, Holborn, 1862–1913; under Alexander Heriot Mackonochie [q. v.], 1862–82; adopted advanced ritualistic views, and with Mackonochie subjected to series of ritual prosecutions, 1867–82; inhibited from preaching; attacked again, 1906; exercised great spiritual influence within and beyond his parish; an eloquent preacher.

STARK, ARTHUR JAMES (1831–1902), painter; son of James Stark [q. v.], landscape painter; studied animal painting under Edmund Bristow [q. v.]; exhibited at Royal Academy from 1848 to 1887, and elsewhere; perfected painting of horses at a studio at Tattersall's; depicted homely English scenes and landscapes; one of the last artists of Norwich school; works include 'Interior of a Stable,' 1853, 'A Farmyard,' 1875, and 'Dartmoor Drift,' 1877.

STEAD, WILLIAM THOMAS (1849–1912), journalist and author; editor of 'Northern Echo,' Darlington liberal daily paper, 1871–80; assistant editor of 'Pall Mall Gazette,' 1880–3; editor, 1883–90; with (Viscount) Milner inaugurated 'new journalism'; directly responsible for dispatch of General Gordon to Khartoum (1884) and for Criminal Law Amendment Act (1885); started 'Review of Reviews,' 1890; took up psychical research; drowned on 'Titanic.'

STEEL, ALLAN GIBSON (1858–1914), cricketer; B.A., Trinity Hall, Cambridge; in Cambridge eleven, 1878–81; captain, 1880; admirable slow bowler; played in Gentlemen's eleven v. Players and in early Australian test matches, in which he proved powerful batsman; called to bar (Inner Temple), 1883; Q.C., 1901.

STEGGALL, CHARLES (1826–1905), organist and composer; professor of organ at Royal Academy of Music, 1851–1903; Mus.Bac. and Mus.Doc. Cambridge, 1852; organist of Lincoln's Inn chapel, 1864–1905; composed church music and wrote 'Instruction Book for the Organ,' 1875.

STEPHEN, SIR ALEXANDER CONDIE (1850–1908), diplomatist; entered diplomatic service, 1876; at Philippopolis, 1880–1; C.M.G., 1881; in Khorassan, north-east province of Persia, 1882–5; C.B., 1884; present at Penjdeh when affray between troops of Afghanistan and Russia threatened war between England and Russia, 1885; at Sofia, 1886; at Vienna and Paris, 1887; chargé d'affaires at Coburg, 1893–7; minister resident to Saxony and Coburg, 1897–1901; K.C.M.G., 1894; K.C.V.O., 1900; groom-in-waiting to King Edward VII, 1901–8.

STEPHEN, CAROLINE EMILIA (1834–1909), philanthropist; sister of Sir Leslie Stephen [q. v.]; joined Society of Friends, 1879; wrote 'Quaker Strongholds,' 1891, 'Light Arising,' 1898, and 'A Vision of Faith,' posthumous, 1911.

STEPHEN, GEORGE, first BARON MOUNT STEPHEN (1829–1921), financier and philanthropist; born in Scotland; entered business in Montreal, 1850; successful cloth manufacturer; with group of colleagues completed St. Paul and Pacific and Canadian Pacific railways; president of Canadian Pacific Railway Company, 1880–8; settled in England, 1893; created baronet, 1886; baron, 1891.

STEPHEN, SIR LESLIE (1832–1904), first editor of this Dictionary, man of letters, and philosopher; grandson of James Stephen [q. v.]; third son of Sir James Stephen [q. v.], and younger brother of Sir James FitzJames Stephen [q. v.]; educated at Eton and King's College, London; entered Trinity Hall, Cambridge, 1850; 20th wrangler, 1854; fellow, 1854–67; tutor, 1856; ordained, 1855; interested himself in social life of college and in its athletic prestige; won mile race at university athletic sports, 1860; made his first Alpine ascent of Col du Géant, 1857; joined Alpine Club, 1858; first vanquished the Schreckhorn, 1861; acquired high reputation as mountaineer, 1862–7; president of Alpine Club, 1865–8; published 'Playground of Europe,' a collection of mountaineering sketches, 1871. Meanwhile Stephen abandoned his old religious convictions, resigned college tutorship, 1862, and relinquished holy orders, 1875. He aided his friend Henry Fawcett [q. v.] in electoral contests, 1863–4; visited America, 1863, as an enthusiastic supporter of slave emancipation; began literary career in London, 1864. Revisiting America in 1868, he formed close friendships with James Russell Lowell, Charles Eliot Norton, and others. He soon wrote much for 'Saturday Review' and for 'Pall Mall Gazette'; was editor from 1871 to 1882 of 'Cornhill Magazine,' where first appeared his 'Hours in a Library' (critical essays; 1st ser. 1874; 2nd ser. 1876; 3rd ser. 1879); wrote on religious and philosophical speculation in 'Fraser's Magazine' and 'Fortnightly Review,' collecting contributions in 'Essays on Free Thinking and Plain Speaking,' 1873; he published his chief work, 'History of English Thought in the Eighteenth Century,' 1876; inaugurated in 1878 with 'Johnson' the 'English Men of Letters' series, to which he also contributed 'Pope,' 1880, 'Swift,' 1882, 'George Eliot,' 1902, and 'Hobbes,' 1904; and produced 'Science of Ethics,' 1882. He was first editor of this Dictionary, 1882–91; suffered in health from 1889, but on retirement from editorship in 1891 remained a chief contributor. He was first Clark lecturer at Trinity College, Cambridge, 1883; published in later life biography of Henry Fawcett, 1885, 'An Agnostic's Apology,' 1893, life of his brother Sir James FitzJames Stephen, 1895, 'Social Rights and Duties,' 2 vols. 1896, 'The English Utilitarians,' 3 vols. 1900, 'Studies of a Biographer,' 2 ser. 1899–1902, and 'English Literature and Society in the Eighteenth Century—Ford Lectures at Oxford, 1903,' 1904; was president of London library from 1892 to death; received hon. degrees from Edinburgh, Oxford, Cambridge, and Harvard, and was made K.C.B., 1902. He married firstly in 1867 Thackeray's younger daughter, Harriet Marian (d. 1875); secondly, in 1878, Julia Prinsep, widow of Herbert Duckworth (d. 1895); his portrait was painted by Watts, 1878; 'Collected Essays,' 10 vols., with introds. by Mr. James Bryce and Mr. Herbert Paul, 1907; 'Life and Letters' by F. W. Maitland, 1906.

STEPHENS, FREDERIC GEORGE (1828–1907), art critic; joined pre-Raphaelite Brotherhood, 1848;

exhibited portraits of mother (1852) and father (1854) at Royal Academy; contributed to 'Germ'; art critic to 'Athenaeum,' 1861–1901; wrote there valuable series of articles on 'The Private Collections of England'; publications include unfinished 'Catalogue of Prints and Drawings (Satire) in the British Museum,' 4 vols. 1870–83; he championed Rossetti's claims to initiation of pre-Raphaelite movement in his life of Rossetti, 1894; was model for head of Christ in Madox Brown's 'Christ Washing Peter's Feet.'

STEPHENS, JAMES (1825–1901), organizer of the Fenian conspiracy; at first a civil engineer; assisted William Smith O'Brien [q. v.] in Ballingary affray, 1848; planned unsuccessful plot of kidnapping prime minister, Lord John Russell, Sept. 1848; escaped to Paris, teaching English there for some years; inaugurated Irish Republican Brotherhood on military basis, 1858; visited America (1858–9) to collect funds to provide arms, and stimulated movement there; published (1862) a scheme for the future government of Ireland in the event of success attending conspiracy; founded the 'Irish People' as organ of his party, 1863; on second visit to America (1864) promised a rising in Ireland in September 1865; 'Irish People' offices raided, September 1865; Stephens arrested and imprisoned, 11 Nov.; escaped, 24 Nov.; went to Paris (March 1866) and revisited New York, where in December he was denounced as an impostor; returned to Paris, 1867; wrongly suspected of share in American dynamite plots and expelled from France, 1885; lived in Ireland from 1885.

STEPHENS, JAMES BRUNTON (1835–1902), Queensland poet; educated at Edinburgh University, 1852–4; private tutor on Continent of Europe, 1854–7; six years schoolmaster at Greenock; emigrated to Queensland (1866) and engaged there in tutorial work; published poem 'Convict Once,' 1871; clerk to colonial secretary, 1883–1902; published fiction and verse; collected edition of poems appeared in 1902.

STEPHENS, WILLIAM RICHARD WOOD (1839–1902), dean of Winchester; B.A., Balliol College, Oxford, 1862; M.A., 1865; D.D., 1901; held Sussex livings, 1870–94; prebendary of Whitring, 1875; dean of Winchester, 1894–1902; F.S.A., 1894; voluminous works include lives of his father-in-law, Dean Hook, 2 vols. 1878, and E. A. Freeman, 2 vols. 1895, and 'History of English Church from Norman Conquest to Edward I,' 1901; revised Dean Hook's 'Church Dictionary,' 1887.

STEPHENSON, SIR FREDERICK CHARLES ARTHUR (1821–1911), general; joined Scots guards, 1837; served throughout Crimean war; in China war, 1858 and 1860; C.B., 1858; lieutenant-general, 1878; commanded army of occupation in Egypt, 1883; K.C.B., 1884; commanded frontier field force and defeated Mahdists at Giniss, December 1885; G.C.B., 1886; colonel of Coldstream guards, 1892; constable of Tower of London, 1898–1911.

STEPHENSON, GEORGE ROBERT (1819–1905), civil engineer; employed by uncle, George Stephenson [q. v.], in drawing office of Manchester and Leeds Railway, 1837–43; resident engineer on new lines of South Eastern Railway; superintended construction of many branch lines in Kent; also constructed lines in Schleswig-Holstein, Jutland, and New Zealand; joint engineer-in-chief for East London Railway, 1864; built many bridges, fixed and swinging, at home and abroad; proprietor of locomotive works at Newcastle-on-Tyne, 1859–86; president of Institution of Civil Engineers, 1875–7.

STERLING, ANTOINETTE (1843–1904), contralto singer; born at Sterlingville, New York State; taught singing in Mississipi State from 1868; studied singing in Germany and London; first appeared in London, 1873; successful in oratorio music and German Lieder; married John MacKinlay, 1875; from 1877 attained much popularity by her rendering of 'The Lost Chord,' 'Caller Herrin',' and other ballads; toured in Australia, 1893; ardent 'Christian scientist'; memoir by son, 1906.

STEVENSON, DAVID WATSON (1842–1904), Scottish sculptor; studied in Rome (1876) and Paris; A.R.S.A., 1877; R.S.A., 1886; executed groups for Prince Consort Memorial, Edinburgh, and monuments of Wallace and Burns.

STEVENSON, JOHN JAMES (1831–1908), architect; M.A. Glasgow University; pupil of Sir George Gilbert Scott [q. v.] in London, 1858–60; evolved a simple type of brick design; built several board schools and churches; built 'The Red House,' Bayswater Hill;

restored many colleges at Oxford and Cambridge; first architect to design interior decorations of sea vessels; published 'House Architecture,' 2 vols. 1880; F.S.A., 1884; F.R.I.B.A., 1879.

STEVENSON, SIR THOMAS (1838–1908), scientific analyst and toxicologist; M.B. London, 1863; M.D., 1864; F.R.C.P., 1871; lecturer at Guy's Hospital on chemistry, 1870–98, and forensic medicine, 1878–1908; analyst to home office, 1872–81; senior scientific analyst, 1881–1908; expert witness in leading poisoning cases from 1881; knighted, 1904; edited medical works.

STEWART, CHARLES (1840–1907), comparative anatomist; M.R.C.S., 1862; conservator of Hunterian Museum at Royal College of Surgeons from 1884; Hunterian professor of comparative anatomy and physiology, 1886–1902; Fullerian professor at Royal Institution, 1894–7; president of Linnean society, 1890–4; helped to found Anatomical Society, 1887; F.R.S., 1896; hon. LL.D. Aberdeen, 1899.

STEWART, CHARLES STEWART VANE-TEMPEST-, sixth MARQUESS OF LONDONDERRY (1852–1915), politician. [See VANE-TEMPEST-STEWART.]

STEWART, ISLA (1855–1910), hospital matron; nurse at St. Thomas's Hospital, 1879–85; matron and superintendent of nursing at St. Bartholomew's Hospital, 1887–1910; founded League of St. Bartholomew's Hospital Nurses, and Matron's Council for Great Britain and Ireland, 1894; collaborated in 'Practical Nursing,' 2 vols. 1899–1903.

STEWART, JAMES (1831–1905), African missionary and explorer; educated at Edinburgh and St. Andrews universities; studied theology at New College, Edinburgh, 1855–9, and medicine at the university, 1859; influenced in 1857 by David Livingstone [q. v.], he resolved on establishing mission in Central Africa; reached Livingstone's head-quarters at Shupanga, 1862; explored Shiré and Zambesi districts, 1862–3; hon. F.R.G.S., 1866; M.B. and C.M. Glasgow, 1866; returned to Africa, reaching Lovedale, January 1867; principal of Lovedale Missionary Institute, which he consolidated and developed, 1870–90; urged foundation of Livingstonia in memory of Livingstone, 1875; organized new settlement at Bandawe, 1876; explored Lake Nyasa, 1877; was consulted by colonial administrators on native questions; established new East African mission, 1891; returned to Scotland, 1892; hon. D.D. Glasgow, 1892; moderator of Free Church General Assembly, 1899; delivered (1902) Duff missionary lectures in Edinburgh on 'Dawn in the Dark Continent' (published 1903); returned to Lovedale, 1904, and died there; author of Kafir phrase book, 1898, and Grammar, 1902.

STEWART, SIR WILLIAM HOUSTON (1822–1901), admiral; son of Sir Houston Stewart [q.v.]; entered navy, 1835; served in Carlist war, 1836–7; and Syrian war, 1840; commander, 1848; in Pacific, 1851–3; retook revolted Chilian colony of Punta Arenas; distinguished in Crimean war; captain superintendent of Chatham dockyard, 1863–8; controller of Portsmouth dockyard, 1872–81; K.C.B., 1877; admiral, 1881; G.C.B., 1887.

STIRLING, SIR JAMES (1836–1916), judge; B.A., Trinity College, Cambridge (senior wrangler), 1860; called to bar (Lincoln's Inn), 1862; attorney-general's 'devil,' 1881–6; chancery judge and knighted, 1886; lord justice of appeal, 1900–6; P.C., 1900.

STIRLING, JAMES HUTCHISON (1820–1909), Scottish philosopher; educated at Glasgow University; M.R.C.S. Edinburgh, 1842; F.R.C.S., 1860; abandoned medicine for philosophy; published 'The Secret of Hegel,' 2 vols. 1865, and 'Analysis of Sir William Hamilton's Philosophy,' 1865; sought to refute Huxley's theory of protoplasm, 1869; issued 'Text Book to Kant,' 1881, and other works; hon. LL.D. Edinburgh, 1867; Glasgow, 1901; received civil list pension, 1889.

STODDART, ANDREW ERNEST (1863–1915), cricketer; chosen to play cricket for Middlesex, 1885; scored 485, then highest individual innings recorded, 1886; played regularly for Middlesex, a strong county team, till 1898; visited Australia with teams successful except on last occasion, 1887, 1891, 1894, 1897; in front rank of English amateurs as high scorer and all-round player.

STOKES, SIR GEORGE GABRIEL, first baronet (1819–1903), mathematician and physicist; educated at schools in Dublin and Bristol and at Pembroke College, Cambridge; senior wrangler, first Smith's prizeman, and fellow, 1841; master, 1902–3; formed at Cambridge close friendship with Lord Kelvin; contributed to 'Cambridge Mathematical Journal'; Lucasian professor of mathematics from 1849 till death; early developed Lagrange's theory of motion of fluids; created modern theory of motion of viscous fluids; made valuable researches into optics; published 'The Dynamical Theory of Diffraction,' 1849; pioneer in discovery of and development of spectrum analysis; discovered nature of fluorescences (1852) and explored great range of invisible ultra-violet spectrum; virtual founder of modern science of geodesy, 1849; fellow (1851), secretary (1854–85), president (1885–90), and Copley medallist (1893) of the Royal Society; prominent in foundation of observatory for solar physics at South Kensington, 1878; Burnett lecturer at Aberdeen, 1883–5; published lectures on 'Light,' 3 vols. 1884–7; Gifford lecturer at Edinburgh, 1891–3; president of British Association, 1869; conservative M.P. for Cambridge University, 1887–91; baronet, 1889; received many foreign honours and honorary degrees from Oxford, Cambridge, Edinburgh, Dublin, Glasgow, and Aberdeen; his writings were collected in five volumes of 'Mathematical and Physical Papers,' 1880–1905: his 'Scientific Correspondence' was edited by Sir Joseph Larmor, 2 vols. 1907.

STOKES, SIR JOHN (1825–1902), lieutenant-general R.E.; joined royal engineers, 1843; in Cape Colony, 1846–51; served in Kaffir wars, 1846–7, 1850–1; instructor in surveying at Royal Military Academy, Woolwich, 1851; served in Crimea; British member of European commission of the Danube, 1856–71; improved mouths and navigation of lower Danube and regulated pilotage; urged on Great Britain measures which led to 'Danube Loan Act'; drafted articles respecting the Danube in the treaty of London, 1871; C.B., 1871; commanding royal engineer of South Wales military district, 1872–5; of Chatham district, 1875; British commissioner on international commission at Constantinople concerning Suez Canal dues, 1873; reported on khedive's financial difficulties and negotiated for the representation of British government on Suez Canal Company's board, 1875–6; became director, 1876; vice-president, 1887; K.C.B., 1877; as member of Channel tunnel committee, opposed its construction, 1882; deputy adjutant-general for royal engineers at war office, 1881–6; lieutenant-general, 1887.

STOKES, WHITLEY (1830–1909), Celtic scholar; son of William Stokes [q. v.]; B.A., Trinity College, Dublin, 1851; studied Irish philology from early age; called to bar (Inner Temple), 1855; practised in London till 1862, when he went to India; secretary to legislative department at Calcutta, 1865; law member of council of the governor-general, 1877–82; president of Indian law commission, 1879; published works on Indian law, 1865–91; C.S.I., 1877; C.I.E., 1879; returned to England, 1882; collaborated in series of 'Irische Texte' at Leipzig, 1884–1909, in 'Urkeltischer Sprachschatz,' 1894, and with John Strachan [q. v.] in 'Thesaurus Palaeohibernicus,' 1901 and 1903; published many Irish texts with translations and glossaries, as well as Cornish and Breton works; original F.B.A., 1902; hon. fellow of Jesus College, Oxford; his library of Celtic printed books at University College, London.

STONEY, BINDON BLOOD (1828–1909), civil engineer; B.A., Trinity College, Dublin, 1850; M.A. and M.A.I., 1870; hon. LL.D., 1881; chief engineer (1862–98) to Dublin port authority; improved channel between Dublin bay and city, rebuilt quay walls and Grattan and O'Connell bridges; F.R.S., 1881; president of Institution of Civil Engineers of Ireland, 1871–2; member of Royal Irish Academy; published 'The Theory of Strains in Girders and Similar Structures,' 2 vols. 1866.

STONEY, GEORGE JOHNSTONE (1826–1911), mathematical physicist; elder brother of Bindon Blood Stoney [q. v.]; B.A., Trinity College, Dublin, 1848; M.A. and Madden prizeman, 1852; assistant at Parsonstown observatory, 1848–52; professor of natural philosophy, Queen's College, Galway, 1852–7; secretary of Queen's University, Dublin, 1857–82; superintendent of civil service examinations in Ireland till 1893; made original contributions to study of physical optics, of molecular physics, of the kinetic theory of gases, and of conditions limiting planetary atmospheres; introduced word 'electron' into scientific vocabulary; wrote also on abstract physics, music, and musical echoes; for twenty years secretary of Royal Dublin Society; first Boyle medallist, 1899; hon. D.Sc. Queen's University,

Ireland, 1879; hon. Sc.D., Trinity College, Dublin, 1902; F.R.S., 1861; settled in London, 1893; advocate of women's higher education.

STORY, ROBERT HERBERT (1835–1907), principal of Glasgow University; son of Robert Story (1790–1859, q. v.); educated at Edinburgh and St. Andrews universities; succeeded father as parish minister of Rosneath in Church of Scotland, 1860–86; helped to found Church Service Society, 1865; moderator of general assembly, 1894; senior clerk, 1895–1907; chaplain in ordinary to Queen Victoria and King Edward VII from 1886; professor of church history in Glasgow University, 1886–98; principal, 1898–1907; largely extended university buildings; hon. D.D. Edinburgh, 1874; hon. LL.D. St. Andrews, 1900; prominent freemason; works include Lives of Robert Lee [q.v.], 1870, and of William Carstares, 1874, and 'The Apostolic Ministry of the Scottish Church' (Baird lecture), 1897, and sermons.

STORY-MASKELYNE, MERVYN HERBERT NEVIL (1823–1911), mineralogist; grandson of Nevil Maskelyne [q. v.]; B.A., Wadham College, Oxford, 1845; M.A., 1849: hon. fellow, 1873; pioneer teacher of mineralogy and chemistry in Oxford University from 1851; professor of mineralogy, 1856–95; keeper of the minerals at the British Museum, 1857–80; rearranged and greatly extended the collections, publishing a catalogue (1853) and a guide (1868); made important researches into meteorites and the diamond; based on his lectures 'The Morphology of Crystals,' 1895; F.R.S., 1870; vice-president, 1897–9; F.G.S., 1854; Wollaston medallist, 1893; hon. D.Sc. Oxford, 1903; M.P. for Cricklade as liberal, 1880–6, and as liberal unionist, 1886–92; member of Wiltshire county council, 1889–1904.

STRACHAN, JOHN (1862–1907), classical and Celtic scholar; educated at Aberdeen University and Pembroke College, Cambridge; Porson university scholar, 1883; second chancellor's medallist, 1885; after studying Sanskrit and Celtic at Jena, graduated B.A. at Cambridge, 1885; professor of Greek at Owens College, Manchester, where he also taught Celtic and Sanskrit, 1885–1907; collaborated with Whitley Stokes [q. v.] in 'Thesaurus Palaeohibernicus,' 2 vols. 1901–3; wrote memoirs on Irish philology and 'An Introduction to Early Welsh,' posthumous, 1909; hon. LL.D. Aberdeen, 1909.

STRACHAN-DAVIDSON, JAMES LEIGH (1843–1916), classical scholar; B.A., Balliol College, Oxford; fellow of Balliol, 1866; senior dean, 1875–1907; master, 1907–16; devoted his life to service of his college and university; lectured on Roman history; works include 'Cicero and the Fall of the Roman Republic' (1894) and 'Problems of the Roman Criminal Law' (1912).

STRACHEY, SIR ARTHUR (1858–1901), judge; son of Sir John Strachey [q. v.]; LL.B., Trinity Hall, Cambridge, 1880; called to bar, 1883; judge of high court of Bombay, 1895–9; chief justice of high court, Allahabad and knighted, 1899; died at Simla.

STRACHEY, SIR EDWARD, third baronet (1812–1901), author; brother of Sir John [q. v.] and Sir Richard Strachey [q. v.]; friend of F. D. Maurice; succeeded to uncle's baronetcy and estates in Somerset, 1858; took prominent part in local affairs; made study of Oriental languages and of biblical criticism; works include 'Jewish History and Politics,' 1874, 'Miracles and Science,' 1854, 'Talk at a Country House,' largely autobiographical, 1895; edited Globe edition of Malory's 'Morte d'Arthur,' 1868.

STRACHEY, SIR JOHN (1823–1907), Anglo-Indian administrator; entered Bengal civil service, 1842; served at first in North-West provinces; judicial commissioner of Central provinces, 1862; president of permanent sanitary commission, 1864; chief commissioner of Oudh, 1866; member of governor-general's council, 1868; lieutenant-governor of North-West provinces, 1874–6; created agriculture department, extended survey, and constructed railways; restored historic Mogul buildings at Agra, 1876; finance member of governor-general's council, 1876; retired owing to his serious under-estimate of cost of war in Afghanistan, 1880; knighted, 1872; G.C.S.I., 1878; settled in Florence, 1880–3; published lectures on 'India,' 1888, and 'Hastings and the Rohilla War,' 1892; member of council of India, 1885–95; hon. D.C.L. Oxford, 1907.

STRACHEY, SIR RICHARD (1817–1908), lieutenant-general; joined Bombay engineers, 1836; executive engineer on Ganges Canal, 1843; served in Sutlej campaign at Badiwal, Aliwal, and Sobraon, 1846; made scientific explorations in Kumaon, Himalayas, and Tibet, 1847–8; collected many new botanical specimens and added much to geological knowledge; stayed in England arranging his collections, 1850–5; F.R.S., 1854; royal medallist, 1897; secretary of newly-formed Central provinces, 1856; rebuilt railway station at Allahabad; consulting engineer to government at Calcutta, 1858; reorganized public works department and initiated adequate forest service; secretary and head of public works department, 1862–5; C.S.I., 1866; inspector-general of irrigation, 1866; major-general on retirement, 1871; lieutenant-general and member of council of India, 1875; arranged for purchase of East Indian Railway, 1877; chairman, 1889–1906; British commissioner at Prime Meridian Conference at Washington, 1884; president of Royal Geographical Society, 1887–9; represented India at international monetary conference at Brussels, 1892; hon. LL.D. Cambridge, 1892; founded scientific study of Indian meteorology; chairman of the meteorological council which controlled the meteorological office in London, 1893–5; invented mechanical instruments in connexion with meteorological problems; C.S.I., 1866; G.C.S.I., 1897; collaborated with brother John [q. v.] in 'The Finances and Public Works of India,' 1882.

STRANG, WILLIAM (1859–1921), painter and etcher; pupil of Alphonse Legros [q. v.]; his 747 etchings include imaginative compositions (chiefly book illustrations) and portraits; executed portrait drawings and paintings; R.A., 1921.

STRATHCONA AND MOUNT ROYAL, first BARON (1820–1914), Canadian financier. [See SMITH, DONALD ALEXANDER.]

STRETTON, HESBA (pseudonym) (1832–1911), authoress. [See SMITH, SARAH.]

STRONG, SIR SAMUEL HENRY (1825–1909), chief justice of Canada; accompanied father to Canada, 1836; called to bar at Toronto, 1849; Q.C., 1863; vice-chancellor of Ontario, 1869; puisne judge of supreme court of Canada, 1875; chief justice, 1892–1902; knighted, 1893; member of judicial committee of privy council, 1897.

STRONG, SANDFORD ARTHUR (1863–1904), Orientalist and historian of art; B.A., St. John's College, Cambridge, 1884; M.A., 1890; studied Sanskrit at Cambridge; librarian of Indian Institute, Oxford, 1885; professor of Arabic at University College, London, 1895–1904; librarian to Duke of Devonshire at Chatsworth, 1895–1904; librarian to House of Lords, 1897–1904; published Pali and Arabic texts; works include reproductions of drawings at Wilton House, 1900, and Chatsworth, 1902; his 'Critical Studies and Fragments' appeared posthumously in 1905; memorial 'Arthur Strong Oriental Library' at University College, London.

STRUTT, JOHN WILLIAM, third BARON RAYLEIGH (1842–1919), mathematician and physicist; educated privately; B.A., Trinity College, Cambridge (senior wrangler), 1865; first Smith's prizeman, 1865; fellow of Trinity, 1866–71; published first of his 446 scientific papers, 1869; F.R.S., 1873; succeeded father, 1873; early investigations concerned with psychical research; published 'Treatise on the Theory of Sound,' 1877; Cavendish professor of experimental physics at Cambridge, 1879–84; directed research on re-determination of electrical units in absolute measure; published series of papers on subject, 1881–3; retired to Terling Place, Essex, to pursue research in private laboratory, 1885; secretary of Royal Society, 1885–96; discovered argon (in collaboration with (Sir) William Ramsay, q.v.), 1894; carried out important investigations in physical optics; an original recipient of O.M., 1902; Nobel prizeman, 1904; P.C., 1905; chancellor of Cambridge University, 1908; president of Royal Society, 1905; Rumford medallist, 1914; his researches covered fields of physics, chemistry, and mathematics, but only striking discovery that of argon; his scientific supremacy due to aptitude for arranging existing knowledge.

STUBBS, WILLIAM (1825–1901), historian and bishop successively of Chester and Oxford; educated at Ripon grammar school; servitor of Christ Church, Oxford, 1844; B.A. (with first class in *lit. hum.* and third in mathematics), 1848; studied historical documents in the Christ Church library; fellow of Trinity College, 1844–50; ordained deacon, 1848, and priest, 1850; vicar of Navestock, Essex, 1850–66; issued 'Registrum Sacrum Anglicanum,' 1858 (new edit. 1897); took private pupils, including H. P. Liddon and A. C. Swinburne; appointed librarian at Lambeth, 1862; edited

'Chronicle Memorials of Richard I' for 'Rolls Series,' 1864–5; was regius professor of history at Oxford, 1866–84, and ex-officio fellow of Oriel College; published many of his public professorial lectures in 'Seventeen Lectures on the Study of Medieval and Modern History,' 1886; other of his lectures which appeared posthumously treated of 'European History,' 1904, 'Early English History,' 1906, 'Germany, 476–1500,' 2 vols. 1908; disabled by examination and tutorial system at university from carrying out his ideal of a thorough 'historical school,' he devoted himself to private research; continued his contributions to 'Rolls Series,' admirably editing the text of many medieval historical authorities (19 vols., 1864–89); his introductory essays to these volumes were collected posthumously in 1902; in 1870 he issued 'Select Charters and other Illustrations of English Constitutional History from the Earliest Times to the Reign of Edward I'; he made his chief fame by his 'Constitutional History of England down to 1485,' vol. i. 1873, vol. ii. 1875, vol. iii. 1878, a massive work of historic synthesis, which gave a new direction to study of medieval English history. Supporting the high church party at Oxford, Stubbs was rector of the Oriel living of Cholderton, Wiltshire, 1875–9, and canon of St. Paul's, 1879–84, working during his periods of residence at St. Paul's on the muniments and impressing his hearers by weighty sermons. He took a leading part as member of the royal commission on ecclesiastical courts, 1881–3. He was bishop of Chester, 1884–7, abandoning historical work with his edition of William of Malmesbury's works (Rolls Series, 2 vols. 1887–9); made energetic attempt to build new churches in his diocese; interested himself in education and archaeology, and was active at Lambeth conference of 1888. Translated to see of Oxford, 1888, he remained there till death; finding routine episcopal work irksome, he obtained appointment of suffragan bishop of Reading, 1889; but he proved his episcopal efficiency in his 'Ordination Addresses,' 1901, and 'Visitation Charges,' 1904, both published posthumously. He took part while bishop of Oxford in academic affairs; acted as assessor on trial of Edward King, bishop of Lincoln, for ritualistic practices, 1889–90, and approved Archbishop Benson's judgment. He preached with difficulty owing to failing health in St. George's Chapel, Windsor, the day after Queen Victoria's funeral, 3 Feb. 1901. He received Prussian order 'pour le mérite,' 1897, and numerous academic honours; 'Letters' edited by W. H. Hutton, 1904.

STURGIS, JULIAN RUSSELL (1848–1904), novelist; born at Boston, Massachusetts; educated at Eton and Balliol College, Oxford; B.A., 1872; M.A., 1875; called to bar, 1876; works include novels, 'John-a-Dreams,' 1878, 'My Friends and I,' 1884, and 'Stephen Calinari,' 1901, as well as 'Little Comedies,' 1879, and 'Comedies New and Old,' 1882.

STURT, HENRY GERARD, first BARON ALINGTON (1825–1904), sportsman; educated at Eton and Christ Church, Oxford; B.A., 1845; M.A., 1848; conservative M.P. for Dorchester, 1847–56, and for Dorset county, 1856–76; raised to peerage, 1876; in racing partnership with Sir Frederic Johnstone from 1868; won Derby with St. Blaise (1883) and Common (1891), besides other important races.

SUTHERLAND, ALEXANDER (1852–1902), Australian journalist; emigrated with family from Glasgow to Sydney, 1864; B.A. Melbourne University, 1874; M.A., 1876; London representative of 'South Australian Register,' 1898; registrar of Melbourne University, 1901; works include 'Thirty Short Poems,' 1890, 'History of Australia,' 1897, and 'Origin and Growth of the Moral Instinct,' 1898; 'Life' by H. G. Turner, 1908.

SUTTON, HENRY SEPTIMUS (1825–1901), author; born at Nottingham; from an early age a friend of Philip James Bailey and Coventry Patmore; betrayed the influence of Emerson in his mystic prose work, 'Evangel of Love,' 1847; chief of 'Manchester Examiner and Times' reporting staff, 1853; published mystical poems, 'Clifton Grove Garland,' 1848, and 'Quinquenergia,' 1854, which were praised by James Martineau and criticized by Carlyle; edited 'Alliance News,' 1854–1898; joined Swedenborgians in 1857, and expounded Swedenborg's writings in various volumes.

SUTTON, MARTIN JOHN (1850–1913), scientific agriculturist; senior partner in seed firm of Sutton and Sons, Reading, 1887; interested in practical agriculture; wrote standard book, 'Permanent and Temporary Pastures'; strong churchman and philanthropist.

SWAIN, JOSEPH (1820–1909), wood-engraver; manager of engraving department of 'Punch,' 1843–4; executed on his own account all engraving of 'Punch' from 1844 to 1900, including 'Punch' cartoons by Sir J. Tenniel [q. v.]; reproduced works by leading artists.

SWAN, JOHN MACALLAN (1847–1910), painter and sculptor; studied art in London and Paris; exhibited at Royal Academy from 1878; made special study of animals; best-known pictures are 'The Prodigal Son' (in Tate Gallery), 'Maternity' (at Amsterdam), and 'A lioness defending her cubs'; sculptured work includes bronze bust of Cecil Rhodes and eight colossal lions for Rhodes's monument at Groote Schuur; A.R.A., 1894; R.A., 1905, hon. LL.D. Aberdeen; many of his studies were acquired for the nation.

SWAN, Sir JOSEPH WILSON (1828–1914), chemist and electrical inventor; partner in firm of makers, Newcastle-upon-Tyne; studied improvements in collodion process invented by Frederick Scott Archer [q. v.], and produced preparation of collodion for photographic use never excelled; patented 'carbon process' for printing permanent photographs (afterwards known as 'auto-type'); manufactured celebrated gelatine-silver bromide plates; carried out developments in incandescent electric lighting; F.R.S., 1894; knighted, 1904.

SWAYNE, JOSEPH GRIFFITHS (1819–1903), obstetric physician; studied at Bristol Medical School, Guy's Hospital, and Paris; M.R.C.S., 1841; M.B. London, 1842; M.D., 1845; succeeded father as lecturer on midwifery at Bristol Medical School, 1850–95; physician accoucheur to Bristol general hospital, 1853–75; published 'Obstetric Aphorisms for the Use of Students,' 1856, 10th edit. 1893.

SWAYTHLING, first BARON (1832–1911), foreign exchange banker and Jewish philanthropist. [See MONTAGU, SAMUEL.]

SWEET, HENRY (1845–1912), phonetician, comparative philologist, and anglicist; B.A., Balliol College, Oxford; reader in phonetics at Oxford, only official position which he obtained, 1901; greatest British philologist and chief founder of modern phonetics; works include 'History of English Sounds from the Earliest Period' (1874, enlarged form, 1888), 'Anglo-Saxon Reader' (1876), 'Handbook of Phonetics' (1877), 'The Oldest English Texts' (1885), 'Elementarbuch des gesprochenen Englisch' (1885, English edition, 1890), 'A New English Grammar' (1892, 1898), 'The History of Language' (1900), and 'The Sounds of English' (1908).

SWETE, HENRY BARCLAY (1835–1917), regius professor of divinity at Cambridge; B.A., Caius College, Cambridge; fellow, 1858; professor of pastoral theology, King's College, London, 1882–90; professor of divinity, Cambridge, 1890–1915; his works deal with Greek version of Old Testament, exegesis of New Testament, Christian doctrine, patristic studies, history and interpretation of Apostles' Creed, and Christian worship.

SWINBURNE, ALGERNON CHARLES (1837–1909), poet; spent childhood in Isle of Wight; early developed love for climbing, riding, and swimming; entered Eton, Easter 1849; widely read English literature for himself; avoided games or athletics; won second Prince Consort's prizes for French and Italian (1852) and first prizes (1853); showed proficiency in Greek verse; left school July 1853; matriculated from Balliol College, 24 Jan. 1856; soon dropped youthful high church proclivities for nihilism in religion and republicanism in politics; wrote ode to Mazzini (unpublished), 1857; was introduced in Oxford to D. G. Rossetti, 1857; contributed to 'Undergraduate Papers,' 1857–8; attracted at Balliol kindly notice of Benjamin Jowett, who proved a lifelong friend, and who was his host during many summer holidays; won a second in classical moderations and Taylorian scholarship for French and Italian, Easter 1858; visited France with his parents; joined Old Mortality Club; read privately modern history with William Stubbs [q. v.] in the course of 1859; finally left Oxford, November 1859; spent much time at house of grandfather, Sir John Swinburne, at Capheaton, Northumberland; took lodgings in London, 1860; published 'The Queen Mother and Rosamond. Two Plays,' 1861. In London he lived on terms of close intimacy with Rossetti; made reputation in cultivated society by brilliance of his conversation; at house of Monckton Milnes formed friendship with Sir Richard Burton; came to know George Meredith, 1862; acquired enthusiastic admiration for the work of Victor Hugo, whom he met in Paris, 1882; contributed prose and verse to 'Spectator'; joined Rossetti for a time

(1862–3) at 16 Cheyne Walk, Chelsea; on visit to Paris (March 1863) made Whistler's acquaintance; suffered from epileptic fits; in course of a foreign tour (1864) met Landor at Florence; spent the autumn of that year in Cornwall, partly with Jowett; issued, in April 1865, 'Atalanta in Calydon,' which was enthusiastically received; published 'Chastelard' (December) and, in April 1866, 'Poems and Ballads,' which excited storm of hostility and was withdrawn by publisher, Moxon, from circulation; replied to his critics in 'Notes on Poems and Reviews,' October; issued 'A Song of Italy,' February 1867, and 'An Appeal to England,' a political pamphlet in verse (November); formed intimacy with Adah Isaacs Menken [q. v.], 1867; published in prose 'William Blake' and 'Notes on the Royal Academy,' 1868; spent much time with Mazzini and his circle; injured his health by imprudences; was nearly drowned while swimming at Étretat, 1870; published 'Ode on the Proclamation of the French Republic,' September 1870, and his republican 'Songs before Sunrise,' 1871; while staying with Jowett at Loch Tummel (July and August 1871), he made Browning's acquaintance; denounced Robert Buchanan in his pungent 'Under the Microscope,' 1872; published 'Bothwell,' 1874, and 'George Chapman: a Critical Essay,' December 1874; issued 'Essays and Studies' (prose) and 'Songs of Two Nations,' 1875, 'Erechtheus: a Tragedy,' and 'A Note on the Muscovite Crusade,' 1876, 'A Note on Charlotte Brontë,' 1877, and 'Poems and Ballads,' 2nd ser. 1878; in September 1879 he removed, owing to his broken health, from London lodgings to house of Theodore Watts-Dunton [q.v.], The Pines, Putney, where he spent the rest of his life in much retirement; grew increasingly deaf, but his general health was rapidly restored; published, among other later works, 'Studies in Song,' and 'A Study of Shakespeare,' 1880, 'Mary Stuart, a Tragedy,' 1881, 'Tristram of Lyonesse,' 1882, 'A Century of Roundels,' 1883, 'A Midsummer Holiday,' 1884, 'Marino Faliero, a Tragedy,' 1885, 'A Study of Victor Hugo' and 'Miscellanies,' 1886, 'Locrine,' 1887, 'A Study of Ben Jonson' and 'Poems and Ballads,' 3rd ser. 1889, 'The Sisters,' 1892, 'Studies in Prose and Poetry' and 'Astrophel,' 1894, 'The Tale of Balen,' 1896, 'Rosamund, Queen of the Lombards,' 1899, and 'A Channel Passage,' 1904; died at Putney, 10 April 1909, and was buried among the graves of his family at Bonchurch; a portrait by G. F. Watts (May 1867) is in the National Portrait Gallery.

SWINFEN, first BARON (1851–1919), judge. [See EADY, CHARLES SWINFEN.]

SYKES, Sir MARK, sixth baronet (1879–1919), traveller, soldier, and politician; brought up as Roman Catholic and had roving education abroad; as a young man travelled in Syria, Mesopotamia, and Southern Kurdistan; honorary attaché to British embassy, Constantinople, 1905–7; conservative M.P., Central Hull, 1911; succeeded father, 1913; largely responsible for 'Sykes-Picot Agreement,' 1916, by which definite spheres of interest in the Near East were assigned to Russia, France, and Great Britain; henceforth attached to Foreign Office and employed as chief adviser on Near Eastern policy; sent out to Egypt, 1916 and 1917; to Palestine, 1918; champion of Arab independence and pro-Zionist; died in Paris; wrote books of travel.

SYME, DAVID (1827–1908), Australian newspaper proprietor and economist; studied theology in Scotland and philosophy in Germany; sailed for San Francisco, 1851; settled in Melbourne, 1852; bought 'The Age' newspaper, 1856; edited it from 1860 to 1870, championing protection in working class interest and attacking capitalism; first in Australia to propose protective duties on imports, and the opening of land to small farmers; obtained disestablishment, payment of members, and free compulsory secular education; paper boycotted by landowners and government, 1862; wielded great influence in appointments of Victorian ministries; through paper obtained anti-sweating and factory Acts and the levy of an income tax; supported Australian federation and conscription and formation of Australian navy; left 50,000l. to Victorian charities; published 'Outlines of an Industrial Science,' 1877, 'Representative Government in England,' 1882, and philosophical works; 'Life' by Ambrose Pratt.

SYMES-THOMPSON, EDMUND (1837–1906), physician; educated at King's College and King's College Hospital; M.B., 1859; M.D., 1860; F.R.C.P., 1868; physician (1869) and consulting physician (1889) to Brompton hospital; professor of physic at Gresham

College from 1867; president of Harveian Society, 1883, and of British Balneological Society, 1903; published 'Winter Health Resorts in the Alps,' 1888; helped to establish sanatoria at Davos; other works were 'Lectures on Pulmonary Tuberculosis,' 1863, and 'On Influenza,' 1890.

SYMONS, WILLIAM CHRISTIAN (1845–1911), decorative designer, painter in oil and water-colours; educated at Lambeth Art School and Royal Academy; exhibited at Academy from 1869 to death; joined Church of Rome, 1870; designed stained glass windows; began mosaic decorations in Westminster Cathedral, 1899; paintings include 'The Convalescent Connoisseur' (at Dublin) and 'In Hora Mortis' (at Sheffield); excellent in flower pieces.

SYNGE, JOHN MILLINGTON (1871–1909), Irish dramatist; born near Rathfarnham near Dublin; B.A., Trinity College, Dublin, 1892; visited Germany, 1894, and Italy, 1896; settled in Paris, 1895; first visited Aran Islands, 1898; in Paris in 1899 met Mr. W. B. Yeats, who persuaded him to describe primitive life in Aran and elsewhere; revisited Aran Islands annually from 1899 to 1902; soon wrote the plays 'The Shadow of the Glen,' performed 1903, and 'Riders to the Sea,' performed 1904; there followed 'The Well of the Saints,' 1905, 'The Playboy of the Western World,' 1907, and 'The Tinker's Wedding,' 1907. Synge lived from 1903 in Ireland, where he found material for his descriptive essays 'In Wicklow' and 'In West Kerry,' which he contributed to 'Manchester Guardian.' He was literary adviser to Abbey Theatre, Dublin, 1904–9; produced his last and unfinished play, 'Deirdre of the Sorrows,' published in 1910; made translations from Villon and Petrarch; he also wrote an account of Aran Islands, 1907; 'Poems and Translations' appeared in 1909; his works were collected in 4 vols., 1910.

TADEMA, SIR LAWRENCE ALMA- (1836–1912), painter. [See ALMA-TADEMA.]

TAIT, PETER GUTHRIE (1831–1901), mathematician and physicist; educated at Edinburgh Academy and University, and at Peterhouse, Cambridge; senior wrangler, first Smith's prizeman, and fellow, 1852; hon. fellow, 1885; wrote with William John Steele 'Dynamics of a Particle,' 1856 (7th edit. 1900); professor of mathematics in Queen's College, Belfast, 1854–60, where he made acquaintance of Sir William R. Hamilton [q. v.]; published 'Elementary Treatise on Quaternions,' 1867; professor of natural philosophy at Edinburgh, 1860–1901; F.R.S. Edinburgh, 1860; became acquainted in 1861 with Lord Kelvin, who collaborated with him in 'Natural Philosophy,' vol. i. 1867; embodied further researches in works on 'Heat,' 1884, 'Light,' 1884, and 'Properties of Matter,' 1885; published 'Thermo-dynamics,' 1868, and 'Recent Advances in Physical Science,' 1876; collaborated with Balfour Stewart [q. v.] in 'The Unseen Universe', 1875; issued treatises on 'Dynamics,' 1895, and 'Newton's Laws of Motion,' 1899; he investigated properties of ozone, and verified Lord Kelvin's discovery of the 'latent heat of electricity'; Rede lecturer (on thermo-electricity) at Cambridge, 1873; made prolonged researches into knots, the foundations of the kinetic theory of gases, and the flight of a golf ball; Royal medallist of Royal Society, 1886; hon. Sc.D. University of Ireland, 1875; hon. LL.D. Glasgow, 1901; scientific papers collected in 2 vols. 1898–1900; memorial research scholarships and professorship founded at Edinburgh University; 'Life and Scientific Work' by Dr. Knott. His third son, FREDERICK GUTHRIE TAIT (1870–1900), who was killed in South African war (February 1900), was champion amateur golfer in 1896 and 1898.

TALLACK, WILLIAM (1831–1908), prison reformer; of quaker family; secretary to Society for Abolition of Capital Punishment (1863–6) and to Howard Association (1866–1901); visited prisons on Continent, in colonies, and in Egypt and United States; author of 'Penological and Preventive Principles,' 1888, and autobiographical 'Howard Letters and Memories,' 1905.

TANGYE, SIR RICHARD (1833–1906), engineer; of Cornish quaker family; engaged in teaching till 1851; joined a Birmingham engineering firm, 1852; set up with brothers tool and machinery manufactory at Birmingham, 1855; supplied hydraulic jacks to launch the 'Great Eastern'; growth of business led to building of 'Cornwall Works' near Birmingham, 1862, and works in Belgium, 1863, and London, 1868; instituted Saturday half holiday for employees, 1873; active in

religious, municipal, and political life of Birmingham; staunch liberal and free trader; founded Birmingham 'Daily Argus,' 1891; knighted, 1894; generous benefactor to Birmingham municipal art gallery and school of art; ardent collector of Cromwellian literature and relics; published 'The Two Protectors,' 1899, and autobiographical 'One and All,' 1890, republished as 'The Rise of a Great Industry,' 1905; 'Life' by Stuart J. Reid, 1908.

TARTE, JOSEPH ISRAEL (1848–1907), Canadian statesman and journalist; born in province of Quebec; conducted 'L'Evénement' of Quebec for over twenty years; removed to Montreal (1891) and published the weekly 'Le Cultivateur'; was elected as conservative to the federal parliament at Ottawa, 1891; denounced conservative irregularities in public administration in Quebec, 1891; joined liberal opposition; minister of public works in Laurier administration, 1896–1902; editor of 'La Patrie,' 1902–7.

TASCHEREAU, SIR HENRI ELZÉAR (1836–1911), chief justice of Canada; born in Beauce county, Quebec; called to Quebec bar, 1857; Q.C., 1867; conservative member of Canadian legislative assembly, 1861–7; puisne judge of superior court, 1871–8; judge of supreme court, 1878–1902; chief justice, 1902–6; knighted, 1902; member of judicial committee of privy council, 1904; wrote on Canadian jurisprudence.

TASCHEREAU, SIR HENRI THOMAS (1841–1909), Canadian judge; first cousin of Sir Henri Elzéar Taschereau [q. v.]; B.L., Laval University, 1861; B.C.L., 1862; hon. LL.D., 1890; called to Quebec bar, 1863; sat as liberal in Dominion parliament, 1872–8; puisne judge of superior court of Quebec, 1878–1907; chief justice of the King's Bench, 1907–9; knighted, 1908.

TATA, JAMSETJI NASARWANJI (1839–1904), pioneer of Indian industries; born in Gujerat; entered father's business, 1858; in China, 1859–63; visited England to study conditions of Lancashire cotton mills, 1872; opened mills at Nagpur (1877), and subsequently at Coorla near Bombay; produced cotton of finer texture and acclimatized Egyptian cotton; obtained reduction of heavy freight charges between Bombay and Far East; opposed imposition of excise duty on products of Indian mills; greatly extended Indian iron ore industry from 1901 and utilized heavy monsoon rainfall of Western Ghauts for electric power in Bombay factories; endowed scholarships for Indians for study in Europe; Indian Institute of Science at Bangalore established according to his plans; he died at Nauheim and was buried at Woking; wrote economic pamphlets.

TAUNTON, ETHELRED LUKE (1857–1907), ecclesiastical historian; ordained Roman Catholic priest, 1883; works include 'History of the Growth of Church Music,' 1887, 'The English Black Monks of St. Benedict,' 2 vols. 1898, 'The History of the Jesuits,' 1901; composed church music.

TAYLOR, CHARLES (1840–1908), master of St. John's College, Cambridge; educated at King's College School, London, and St. John's College, Cambridge; ninth wrangler and second class classic, 1862; obtained first class in theology, 1863; Crosse and Tyrwhitt scholar, 1864; helped to found and edit (1862–84) 'The Oxford, Cambridge and Dublin Messenger of Mathematics'; president of Mathematical Association, 1892; ordained, 1866; college lecturer in theology, 1873; edited 'Sayings of the Jewish Fathers in Hebrew and English,' 1877; member of Alpine Club; appointed master of St. John's College and hon. D.D., 1881; vice-chancellor of the University, 1887–9; presented Taylor-Schechter collection of Hebrew MSS. to University library; published volumes on geometrical conics and theological works, including 'The Teaching of the Twelve Apostles,' 1886, and 'The Oxyrhynchus Logia,' 1899.

TAYLOR, CHARLES BELL (1829–1909), ophthalmic surgeon; M.R.C.S., 1852; M.D. Edinburgh, 1854; F.R.C.S. Edinburgh, 1867; settled in Nottingham, 1859; gained European renown as operator for cataract; supported anti-vivisection and anti-vaccination societies, to which he left most of his property.

TAYLOR, HELEN (1831–1907), advocate of women's rights; stepdaughter of John Stuart Mill [q. v.], with whom she lived at Avignon and co-operated in 'The Subjection of Women,' 1869; edited Buckle's works, 1872, Mill's Autobiography, 1873, and Essays, 1874; settled in London on Mill's death (1873), and engaged in social and political life; radical member of London School Board, 1876–84; her agitation caused drastic reforms in London industrial schools; she actively opposed Irish coercion policy of liberal government, 1880–5; advocate of land nationalization and taxation of land values; friend of Henry George; helped to found Democratic Federation, 1881; advocated female suffrage; carried on parliamentary election campaign in North Camberwell, although her nomination was subsequently refused, 1885; retired to Avignon, 1885; returned to England, 1904, and died at Torquay; an able public speaker.

TAYLOR, ISAAC (1829–1901), archaeologist and philologist; eldest son of Isaac Taylor (1787–1865, q. v.); B.A., Trinity College, Cambridge (19th wrangler), 1853; M.A., 1857; held livings in London (1865–75) and at Settrington, Yorkshire (1875–1901); canon of York, 1885; wrote sympathetically of Islam in 'Leaves from an Egyptian Note Book,' 1888; philological works include 'Words and Places,' 1864 (enlarged and revised as 'Names and Their Histories,' 1896), and 'The Alphabet,' 2 vols. 1883; other works include 'Memorials of the Taylor Family of Ongar,' 2 vols. 1867, and 'The Origin of the Aryans,' 1889; hon. LL.D. Edinburgh, 1879; D.Litt. Cambridge, 1885; original member of Alpine Club, 1858.

TAYLOR, SIR JOHN (1833–1912), architect; surveyor of royal palaces, public buildings, and royal parks, 1866–98; consulting architect, 1898–1908; K.C.B., 1897; his designs include Bow Street police court and station and Bankruptcy Buildings; constructed War Office (in collaboration).

TAYLOR, JOHN EDWARD (1830–1905), art collector and newspaper proprietor; son of John Edward Taylor [q. v.]; called to bar, 1853; sole proprietor from 1848 of 'Manchester Guardian,' which he converted into a daily in 1855; helped in formation of Press Association, 1868; acquired 'Manchester Evening News,' 1868; early supporter and benefactor of Owens College, Manchester; trustee of Manchester College from 1854 to death; the sale of his art collections (1911) realized some 358,500l.

TAYLOR, LOUISA (d. 1903), novelist. [See PARR.]

TAYLOR, WALTER ROSS (1838–1907), Scottish ecclesiastic; educated at Edinburgh University; minister of Kelvinside Free church, Glasgow, from 1868 to death; as moderator he constituted first general assembly of the United Free Church, 1900; active in Free Church crisis of 1904; hon. D.D. Glasgow, 1891; published 'Scottish Church Life in the Nineteenth Century,' 1900.

TEARLE, (GEORGE) OSMOND (1852–1901), actor; made début at Liverpool, 1869; appeared first in 1871 as 'Hamlet,' which he played some 800 times; made first tour in America, 1880; subsequently toured there as Wilfred Denver in 'The Silver King.'

TEMPLE, FREDERICK (1821–1902), archbishop of Canterbury; born at Santa Maura; educated at Blundell's School, Tiverton, and Balliol College, Oxford; graduated double first class in classics and mathematics; friend and contemporary of A. H. Clough, A. P. Stanley, Matthew Arnold and (Lord) Lingen; lecturer and fellow of Balliol; junior dean, 1845; ordained, 1846; examiner to board of education, 1848–9; principal of Kneller Hall, Twickenham, 1849–55; inspector of men's training colleges, 1855–7; wrote on 'National Education' in 'Oxford Essays,' 1856; head master of Rugby School, 1857–69; greatly enlarged the school and modernized the curriculum; member of commission on secondary school education, 1864–8; chairman of governors of Rugby, 1892–1902; provoked unmerited suspicions of his orthodoxy by his essay on 'The Education of the World' in 'Essays and Reviews,' 1860; consecrated, despite strong opposition, bishop of Exeter, 1869; zealous advocate of educational, social, and temperance reform; instrumental in founding secondary schools in Exeter and Plymouth; helped in creation of diocese of Truro, 1876; expressed liberal views in speeches in House of Lords on university tests bill (1870) and on bill for opening churchyards to nonconformists (1880); Bampton lecturer at Oxford, 1884; bishop of London, 1885–96; mainly instrumental in building Church House, Westminster, 1887; carried through parliament pluralities act amendment bill, 1885; member of royal commission on education, 1888; promoted conciliation scheme in dockers' strike, 1889; archbishop of Canterbury, 1896–1902; made two visitations of his diocese, 1898 and 1902; deprecated use of incense and processional lights and pronounced against the reservation of the sacrament, 1899; hon. LL.D. Cambridge,

1897; hon. freeman of Exeter (1897) and of Tiverton (1900); officiated at Queen Victoria's funeral and King Edward VII's coronation, 1901–2; supported Mr. Balfour's education bill, 1902; rugged and simple in character and speech; portrait by Watts at Rugby and by Herkomer at Fulham; monument by Pomeroy in St. Paul's Cathedral; memorial speech room at Rugby opened, 1909; chief works were 'Sermons preached in Rugby School Chapel,' 3 series, 1861–71, and 'The Relations between Religion and Science,' Bampton lectures, 1884; Memoirs by seven friends, ed. E. G. Sandford, 2 vols. 1906.

TEMPLE, SIR RICHARD, first baronet (1826–1902), Anglo-Indian administrator; educated at Rugby and Haileybury College; joined East India Company's service, 1847; assistant to John Lawrence [q. v.] in Punjab from 1851; helped James Wilson [q. v.] in inaugurating new financial system, 1859–60; chief commissioner of Central Provinces, 1862–7; organized educational department, long term settlements of land, and freehold tenancies; established municipality at Nagpur, 1864; C.S.I., 1866; K.C.S.I., 1867; financial member of Council, 1868–74; conducted famine campaign in Behar, 1874; lieutenant-governor of Bengal, 1874–7; baronet, 1876; special commissioner for famine relief measures in Southern India; governor of Bombay, 1877–80; G.C.S.I. and C.I.E., 1878; active in dispatch of native troops to Malta (1878) and to Afghanistan (1878–80); improved port of Bombay and extended forest area; returned to England (1880) and devoted himself to literary work and politics; works include 'India in 1880,' 1880, 'Men and Events of My Time,' 1882, lives of John, Lord Lawrence, 1889, and James Thomason, 1893; hon. D.C.L., Oxford, 1880; LL.D., Cambridge, 1883; member of London School Board, 1884–94; conservative M.P. for Evesham, 1885–92, and for Kingston, Surrey, 1892–5; P.C. and F.R.S., 1896; published 'The Story of My Life,' 1896.

TENNANT, SIR CHARLES, first baronet (1823–1906), merchant and art patron; grandson of Charles Tennant (1768–1838, q. v.), founder of chemical works at St. Rollox, Glasgow; partner in firm, 1846; works absorbed in 1900 in United Alkali Co., of which Tennant became chairman; chairman of Union Bank of Scotland; he acquired portraits by Reynolds, Gainsborough, and Romney; became trustee of National Gallery, 1894; his private art collection housed in Queen Anne's Gate, London; liberal M.P. for Glasgow, 1879–80, and for Peebles and Selkirk, 1880–6; baronet, 1885; member of Mr. Chamberlain's tariff reform commission, 1904.

TENNANT, SIR DAVID (1829–1905), Speaker of the House of Assembly of the Cape of Good Hope; born at Cape Town; admitted attorney at law of supreme court there, 1849; member of House of Assembly for Piquetberg, 1866–96; speaker, 1874–96; knighted, 1877; K.C.M.G., 1892; agent-general for colony in London, 1896–1901.

TENNIEL, SIR JOHN (1820–1914), artist and cartoonist; studied at Academy Schools and Clipstone Street Life Academy; joined staff of 'Punch' as second cartoonist, 1850; first cartoonist, 1864–1901; drew over 2,000 cartoons, several volumes of which have been published; his cartoons noted for dignity, humour, and fairness; excelled in drawings of beasts and allegorical figures; illustrated Lewis Carroll's 'Alice's Adventures in Wonderland' (1865) and 'Alice Through the Looking-Glass' (1872); knighted, 1893.

THESIGER, FREDERIC AUGUSTUS, second BARON CHELMSFORD (1827–1905), general; eldest son of first baron [q. v.]; joined army, 1844; served in Crimea and in Indian Mutiny; deputy adjutant-general in Abyssinian expedition, 1868; C.B. and A.D.C. to Queen Victoria, 1868; adjutant-general in East Indies, 1869–74; commanded troops at Shorncliffe, 1874–6; major-general, 1877; commanded troops in South Africa in Kaffir war, 1878, and in Zulu war, 1879; after disaster at Isandhlwana (22 Jan.) he relieved Col. Pearson's force at Etshowe; marched on to Umvolosi and defeated Zulu army under Cetywayo at Ulundi (July); meanwhile (June) he had been superseded in command by Sir Garnet (afterwards Viscount) Wolseley [q. v.]; K.C.B., 1878; G.C.B., 1879; lieutenant-general, 1882; general, 1888; lieutenant of Tower of London, 1884–9; G.C.V.O., 1902.

THOMAS, DAVID ALFRED, VISCOUNT RHONDDA (1856–1918), statesman, colliery proprietor, and financier; became associated with Cambrian collieries in Rhondda Valley, c. 1882; Gladstonian liberal M.P., Merthyr

Tydfil, 1888; held seat till 1910; went to United States on business of ministry of munitions, 1915; created baron for his services, 1916; promoted viscount, 1918; president of Local Government Board, 1916; as food minister carried out successful rationing during European War, 1917–18.

THOMAS, PHILIP EDWARD (1878–1917), critic and poet; B.A., Lincoln College, Oxford; works include 'Richard Jefferies, His Life and Work' (1909), imaginative idylls 'Rest and Unrest' (1910), 'Light and Twilight' (1911), studies of 'Swinburne' (1912), and 'Walter Pater' (1913); 'Collected Poems' published, 1920; killed in action at Arras.

THOMAS, WILLIAM MOY (1828–1910), novelist and journalist; private secretary to Sir Charles Wentworth Dilke [q. v.]; contributed to 'Household Words,' 1851–8; re-edited Lord Wharncliffe's 'Letters and Works of Lady Mary Wortley Montagu,' 2 vols. 1861; dramatic critic and contributor to 'Daily News,' 1868–1901; first editor of 'Cassell's Magazine'; published novels and tales.

THOMPSON, D'ARCY WENTWORTH (1829–1902), Greek scholar; educated at Christ's Hospital, London, and Pembroke College, Cambridge; B.A. (sixth classic), 1852; classical master in Edinburgh Academy (1852–63), where R. L. Stevenson was one of his pupils, 1861–2; professor of Greek in Queen's College, Galway, 1863–1902; gave at Boston Lowell lectures, published in his 'Wayside Thoughts,' 1867; his fame rests on 'Day Dreams of a Schoolmaster,' 1864.

THOMPSON, EDMUND SYMES- (1837–1906), physician. [See SYMES-THOMPSON.]

THOMPSON, FRANCIS (1859–1907), poet and prose writer; educated at Ushaw College; studied medicine without success at Owens College, Manchester, 1876–82; made helpless efforts to earn a livelihood, 1883–8; settled in London, 1885; fell a prey to opium and became a street waif; contributed poems and prose essays to 'Merry England' from 1888; published first volume of 'Poems,' 1893, which included 'The Hound of Heaven'; 'Sister Songs' followed in 1895, and 'New Poems' in 1897; he contributed literary criticism to 'Academy' and 'Athenæum'; his prose work includes 'Health and Holiness,' 1905, and 'Essay on Shelley,' 1909; died of consumption; 'Life' by Everard Meynell.

THOMPSON, SIR HENRY, first baronet (1820–1904), surgeon; studied medicine at University College, London; M.B., 1851; F.R.C.S., 1853; Hunterian professor of surgery and pathology, 1883; surgeon, 1863, professor of clinical surgery (1866) and emeritus professor (1874) at University College Hospital; made successful removals of stone in the bladder by lithotrity; operated on King Leopold I, 1863, and Napoleon III, 1873; helped to found the first cremation society in London, 1874, and to form company which erected Golder's Green crematorium, 1902; keen astronomer; presented large photographic telescope to Greenwich observatory; exhibited paintings at Royal Academy from 1865 to 1885; collected old white and blue Nankin china; frequently entertained men famous in all branches of society; knighted, 1867; baronet, 1899; portrait by Millais in National Portrait Gallery; works include 'Stricture of the Urethra,' 1854, 'Practical Lithotomy and Lithotrity,' 1863, 'Cremation,' 1874, 'Food and Feeding,' 1880, and novels; a collected edition of his surgical works appeared at Paris in 1880.

THOMPSON, LYDIA (1836–1908), actress; made début in ballet at Her Majesty's Theatre, London, 1852; acted in burlesque in provinces, 1864–5; appeared at Drury Lane, 1865, and Prince of Wales's Theatre, 1866; toured in America, Australia, and India, 1868–74; at New York began association with Willie Edouin [q. v.], 1870–1; reappeared in London in Farnie's burlesque of Blue Beard, 1874; thrice revisited New York; opened the Strand Theatre, London, September 1886, with 'The Sultan of Mocha.'

THOMPSON, SILVANUS PHILLIPS (1851–1916), physicist; B.A., London University; principal and professor of applied physics and electrical engineering of City and Guilds Technical College, Finsbury, 1885–1916; F.R.S., 1891; published works on electricity and magnetism, and lives of famous scientists.

THOMPSON, WILLIAM MARCUS (1857–1907), journalist; joined staff of London 'Standard,' 1877; parliamentary reporter, 1884–90; developed radical and Irish nationalist principles; called to bar, 1880; defended professionally trade unions and political offenders, including Mr. John Burns for share in Trafalgar Square riots, 1886–8; editor of 'Reynolds's Newspaper,' 1894–1907; radical member of London County Council for West Newington, 1895–8.

THOMSON, HUGH (1860–1920), illustrator and pen-and-ink draughtsman; executed illustrations for 'English Illustrated Magazine,' Macmillan's 'Highways and Byways' county series, works by Goldsmith, Miss Mitford, Mrs. Gaskell, Jane Austen, Fanny Burney, Thackeray, George Eliot, Austin Dobson, Charles Reade, Shakespeare, Sheridan, Barrie, Thomas Hughes, Hawthorne, &c.

THOMSON, JOCELYN HOME (1859–1908), chief inspector of explosives; son of William Thomson (1819–1890, q.v.); observed transit of Venus in Barbados, 1882; secretary to war office explosives committee, 1888; suggested name of 'cordite' for smokeless powder; chief inspector of explosives, 1899–1908: published works on petroleum lamps.

THOMSON, WILLIAM, BARON KELVIN, of Largs (1824–1907), scientist and inventor; born at Belfast; was second son of James Thomson (1786–1849, q. v.), professor of mathematics in the Royal Institution there; removed with family to Glasgow in 1832, when his father became professor of mathematics there; matriculated at Glasgow University, 1834; early made his mark in mathematics and physical science; studied writings of Lagrange, Laplace, and Fourier; entered Peterhouse, Cambridge, 1841; won Colquhoun silver sculls, 1844; helped to found Cambridge University Musical Society; senior wrangler and first Smith's prizeman, January 1845; visited Faraday's laboratory at Royal Institution, London, and Regnault's laboratory at Paris University; fellow of Peterhouse, October 1845–52; professor of natural philosophy in Glasgow, 1846–99; gathered round him at Glasgow band of enthusiastic students of mathematical physics; devoted himself to developing the new doctrine propounded by Sadi Carnot in 1824 and by James Prescott Joule [q. v.] in 1847 that work and heat were convertible; formulated between 1851 and 1854 in communication made to Royal Society of Edinburgh the two great laws of thermodynamics—of equivalence and of transformation; subsequently rounded off his thermodynamic work by enunciating the doctrine of available energy; F.R.S., 1851; married in 1852 his second cousin Margaret (d. 1870), daughter of Walter Crum, F.R.S.; made while staying at Creuzenach in 1855 the acquaintance of Helmholtz, who became a close friend; throughout life sought to utilize science for practical ends; by means of mathematical analysis evolved theory of electric oscillations, which forms the basis of wireless telegraphy, 1853; experimented on electric telegraph cables, 1854; propounding the 'law of squares'; became director of the Atlantic telegraph company, 1856; invented the mirror galvanometer; served as electrician on the 'Agamemnon' which laid the cable across the Atlantic, 1858; the experiment was ruined by a colleague's neglect of Thomson's counsels; Thomson triumphantly redeemed the defeat by superintending the laying of a new cable, 1866; knighted for these services, 1866; president of Society of Telegraph Engineers, 1874; president of mathematical and physical section of British Association at Glasgow, 1876; meanwhile studied atmospheric electricity, and improved the system of electrical measurement and the adoption of rational units; suggested the formation of commission of electrical standards of British Association; advocated the metric system; worked at mathematical theory of magnetism; joined with Peter Guthrie Tait [q. v.] in a 'Treatise on Natural Philosophy,' vol. i. pt. i. 1867, pt. ii. 1874; made important contributions to the theory of elasticity in a paper on 'Vortex Atoms,' Edinburgh, 1867; undertook important researches into gyrostatic problems; married secondly Frances Anna Blandy, 1874; built mansion at Netherhall near Largs; navigated sailing yacht the 'Lalla Rookh' on the Clyde; reformed the mariner's compass, 1873–8; devised apparatus for taking flying soundings, 1872; invented a tide-predicting machine; studied the propagation of wave motion; president of British Association at Edinburgh, 1871; president of physical and mathematical section at York, 1881, when he showed the possibility of utilizing the power of Niagara in generating electricity; interested himself in electric lighting; was founder of firm Kelvin & White, Ltd., Glasgow, for manufacture of his inventions; always fond of illustrating recondite scientific notions by ingenious models; Copley medallist of Royal Society, 1883; delivered at Baltimore in 1884 twenty lectures on 'Molecular Dynamics and the Wave Theory of Light' (published 1904); president of the Royal Society, 1890–4; raised to peerage, 1892; celebrated jubilee of Glasgow professorship, June 1896; received O.M. and made P.C., 1902; chancellor of Glasgow University, 1904; buried in Westminster Abbey, 23 Dec. 1907; an ardent unionist in politics; he cherished through life a strong religious faith; statue unveiled in Belfast, 1913; his mathematical and physical papers edited by Sir Joseph Larmor, 5 vols. 1882–1911; 'Life' by Prof. Silvanus P. Thompson, 2 vols. 1910.

THOMSON, Sir WILLIAM (1843–1909), surgeon; B.A., Queen's College, Galway, 1867; M.D. and M.Ch. Queen's University, Dublin, 1872; hon. M.A., 1881; F.R.C.S., Ireland, 1874; president, 1896–8; visiting surgeon to Richmond Hospital, Dublin, from 1873 to death; first general secretary of Royal Academy of Medicine in Ireland, 1882; knighted, 1897; established field hospital in Pretoria in South African war, 1900; C.B., 1901; published report on poor law medical service of Ireland, 1891, and surgical works.

THORNTON, Sir EDWARD (1817–1906), diplomatist; son of Sir Edward Thornton [q. v.]; B.A., Pembroke College, Cambridge, 1840; M.A., 1877; held diplomatic posts in Mexico, 1845–54, at Monte Video, 1854–9, and Buenos Ayres, 1859–63; C.B., 1863; British envoy at Rio de Janeiro, 1865–7; at Washington, 1867–81; helped to settle questions of boundary and fishing disputes between Canada and United States; K.C.B., 1870; P.C., 1871; arbitrator in disputes of United States with Brazil, 1870, and Mexico, 1873–6; British ambassador at St. Petersburg, 1881–4; arranged for delimitation of northern frontier of Afghanistan by joint commission of Russians and British, 1884; G.C.B., 1883; meanwhile appointed ambassador to Constantinople, 1884, but the post was temporarily filled by Sir William White (1824–1891, q.v.), 1884–6; Thornton resigned, and retired to England, 1886; hon. D.C.L. Oxford; LL.D. Harvard.

THRING, GODFREY (1823–1903), hymnologist; B.A., Balliol College, Oxford, 1845; rector of Alford, 1858–93; prebendary of Wells, 1876; published volumes of hymns, which included 'The radiant morn' and 'Fierce raged the tempest.'

THRING, HENRY, BARON THRING (1818–1907), parliamentary draftsman; brother of Godfrey Thring [q.v.]; educated at Shrewsbury and Magdalene College, Cambridge; third classic, 1841; fellow; called to bar, 1845; made study of statute law; framed colonial bill for Sir William Molesworth [q. v.], 1850, which drew attention to its draftsman; drafted Gladstone's Succession Act of 1853; recast merchant shipping law in drawing the Merchant Shipping Act of 1854; drafted series of bills, culminating in Companies Act of 1862; home office counsel, 1860; drafted for Lord Derby's government the 'ten minutes' bill, which became law as 'Representation of the People Act,' 1867; was made parliamentary counsel to the treasury in 1869 on the creation of the office by Robert Lowe for the drafting of government bills; among measures which he prepared were Irish Church Act, 1869, Irish Land Act, 1871, Army Act, 1871, and home rule bill, 1886; he greatly improved style of drafting; explained methods in his 'Practical Legislation,' 1902; member (1868) and subsequently chairman of statute law committee, which indexed, expurgated, republished, and consolidated existing statutes; initiated publication of state trials from 1820 to 1858; K.C.B., 1873; raised to peerage, 1886; superintended compilation of first edition of war office 'Manual of Military Law.'

THRUPP, GEORGE ATHELSTANE (1822–1905), author of 'History of the Art of Coach-building,' 1877; entered father's coach business; head of firm, 1866; had high reputation in England and on Continent; master of Coachmakers Company, 1883.

THUILLIER, Sir HENRY EDWARD LANDOR (1813–1906), surveyor-general of India; joined Bengal artillery, 1832; deputy surveyor-general and superintendent of revenue surveys from 1847; prepared first postage stamps used in India, 1854; joint author of 'The Manual of Surveying in India,' 1851; surveyor-general, 1861–78; transferred preparation of atlas of India from England to Calcutta; F.R.S., 1869; C.S.I., 1870; knighted, 1879; general, 1881; colonel commandant of royal artillery, 1883.

THURSTON, KATHERINE CECIL (1875–1911), novelist; acquired fame by her 'John Chilcote, M.P.,' 1904; other works were 'The Gambler,' 1906, and 'Max,' 1908.

TINSLEY, WILLIAM (1831–1902), publisher; joined brother Edward in publishing business in London, 1854; published novels by G. A. Sala and Miss Braddon, 1861–3; started 'Tinsley's Magazine,' 1868; for a time chief producer of works by leading novelists; failed in business, 1878; wrote 'Random Recollections,' 2 vols. 1900.

TINWORTH, GEORGE (1843–1913), modeller; member of Messrs. Doulton's pottery works, Lambeth, 1867–1913; executed reliefs (chiefly of scenes from Biblical history), including part of York Minster reredos, and statues.

TODD, Sir CHARLES (1826–1910), government astronomer and postmaster-general of South Australia; assistant at Greenwich (1841–7) and Cambridge University (1848–54) observatories; pioneer in astronomical photography; director of colonial observatory at Adelaide, 1855–1906; organized extensive meteorological service; inaugurated intercolonial telegraphic system between Adelaide and Melbourne, 1858; system extended to Sydney, 1858, and Brisbane, 1861; amalgamated telegraph and postal systems of South Australia, 1869; postmaster-general, 1870–1905; supervised construction of internal telegraph line across continent, and established communication between Adelaide and England via Port Darwin and Singapore, 1872; C.M.G., 1872; K.C.M.G., 1893; F.R.S., 1889; hon. M.A. Cambridge, 1886; died at Adelaide.

TOMSON, ARTHUR (1859–1905), landscape painter; studied art at Dusseldorf; painted poetic landscapes of Sussex and Dorset; exhibited at Royal Academy, 1883–92; wrote 'Jean-François Millet and the Barbizon School,' 1903.

TOOLE, JOHN LAWRENCE (1830–1906), actor and theatrical manager; son of James Toole, City toastmaster commemorated by Dickens and Thackeray; at first a clerk in London; after some amateur performances, he made professional début as comedian in Dublin, 1852, where he played the rôle of Paul Pry for first time; appeared at Edinburgh as the 'Artful Dodger' in 'Oliver Twist,' 1854; first acted in London at St. James's Theatre, 1854; played there Weazle in 'My Friend the Major,' 1854; presented Bottom in Midsummer Night's Dream at Edinburgh, 1855; toured annually in the provinces from 1857; met Henry Irving at Edinburgh, 1857; appeared as Tom Cranky in 'The Birthplace of Podgers' at Lyceum, 1858; played at New Adelphi from 1858 to 1867; the original Spriggins in 'Ici on parle Français'; other popular rôles were Bob Cratchit in 'The Christmas Carol,' 1859, Caleb Plummer—a histrionic masterpiece—in Boucicault's 'Dot,' 1862, and Mr. Tetterby in 'The Haunted Man,' 1863; he was praised by Dickens for his rendering of 'Stephen Digges,' 1864; toured with Irving, 1866; created Michael Garner in 'Dearer than Life' at Liverpool, 1867; began long association with the Gaiety under John Hollingshead, 1869; successful as 'Buzfuz' in 'Bardell v. Pickwick,' 1871, as 'Thespis' in Gilbert and Sullivan's first extravaganza, 1871, as 'Ali Baba,' 1872, and as Bob Acres, 1874; paid his only visit to America, 1874, where he met with lukewarm reception; created Charles Liquorpond in Byron's 'A Fool and his Money,' 1878; leased (1879–95) the Folly Theatre (called Toole's, 1882), producing farcical comedies and burlesques by a permanent stock company; staged several travesties by Burnand of popular plays, caricaturing Wilson Barrett and Irving; obtained success in Merivale's 'The Butler,' 1886, and 'The Don,' 1888; was warmly welcomed in Australia, 1890–1; appeared as Ibsen in J. M. Barrie's 'Ibsen's Ghost,' 1891, and as Jasper Phipps in Barrie's 'Walker, London,' 1892; his 'Reminiscences,' compiled by Joseph Hatton, appeared in 1889. Successful in eccentric drollery, with propensity to gagging, Toole was the last low comedian of the old school. A portrait by the Hon. John Collier is at Garrick Club.

TORRANCE, GEORGE WILLIAM (1835–1907), musician and divine; chorister and organist at Dublin, 1847–1854; composed oratorios 'Abraham,' 1854, and 'The Captivity,' 1864, and secular music; B.A., Trinity College, Dublin, 1864; M.A., 1867; hon. Mus.D., 1879; ordained, 1865; served curacies and incumbencies in Australia, 1870–97; returned to Ireland, 1897; canon of St. Canice's Cathedral, Kilkenny, 1900.

TOWNSEND, MEREDITH WHITE (1831–1911), editor of the 'Spectator'; educated at Ipswich grammar school; went to India (1848) to assist John Clark Marshman [q.v.] in editing the 'Friend of India' at Serampore; editor, 1852; proprietor, 1853; exerted great influence on Indian policy; gave valuable support to Lords Dalhousie and Canning; returned to England through ill-health, 1859; bought 'Spectator,' 1860, and took into partnership Richard Holt Hutton [q. v.]; supported the north in the American civil war; wrote chiefly on foreign politics and on India; resigned editorship to J. St. Loe Strachey, 1898; contributed also for many years political article in the 'Economist'; collaborated with J. L. Sanford [q. v.] in 'The Great Governing Families of England,' 2 vols. 1865; republished articles from reviews in 'Asia and Europe,' 1901.

TRACEY, SIR RICHARD EDWARD (1837-1907), admiral; entered navy, 1852; served in Baltic campaign, 1854, and in East Indies and China station, 1862; on active service in Japan, 1863-4; organized Japanese naval school at Tsukiji, 1867-8; did similar service for Chinese navy; second in command of Channel squadron, 1889-92; admiral superintendent at Greenwich, 1889-92; president of Royal Naval College at Greenwich, 1897-1900; K.C.B., and admiral, 1898.

TRAFFORD, F. G. (pseudonym) (1832-1906), novelist. [See RIDDELL, CHARLOTTE ELIZA LAWSON.]

TRAILL, ANTHONY (1838-1914), provost of Trinity College, Dublin; B.A., Trinity College, Dublin; fellow, 1865-1904; provost, 1904-14; successfully resisted (Viscount) Bryce's scheme to amalgamate Trinity with colleges of Royal University of Ireland, 1906; took principal share in effecting internal constitutional reform of college; keen unionist of Ulster type; gave lifelong devotion to Irish Church.

TRAILL-BURROUGHS, SIR FREDERICK WILLIAM (1831-1905), lieutenant-general. [See BURROUGHS.]

TREE, SIR HERBERT BEERBOHM (1853-1917), actor-manager, whose original name was HERBERT BEERBOHM; began professional acting career, 1879; appeared in over fifty plays between 1880 and 1887, most conspicuous successes being Prince Borowsky in Sydney Grundy's 'Glass of Fashion' (1883) and Rev. Robert Spalding in 'The Private Secretary' (1884); lessee and manager of Haymarket Theatre, London, 1887-97; produced and acted in over thirty plays, including plays by Ibsen, Wilde, Maeterlinck, and Shakespeare; parts taken include Iago, Hamlet, and Falstaff; opened Her Majesty's Theatre, 1897; devoted himself increasingly to over-elaborate productions of Shakespeare; gave celebrated performance of Mark Antony in forum scene of 'Julius Caesar'; staged Stephen Phillips' plays, appearing as Herod, Ulysses, and Nero; extraordinarily versatile actor; knighted, 1909; Memoir, 1920.

TREVOR, WILLIAM SPOTTISWOODE (1831-1907), major-general royal (Bengal) engineers; born in India; joined Bengal engineers, 1849; served in Burmese war, 1852-3, and in Mutiny, 1857; garrison engineer at Fort William, Calcutta, 1861; completed the Ganges and Darjeeling road, 1862-3; field engineer of Butan field force, 1865; awarded V.C. for gallantry at Dewan-Giri, February 1865; chief engineer of British Burma, 1875-80; secretary to Indian government in public works department, 1882-7; retired as major-general, 1887.

TRISTRAM, HENRY BAKER (1822-1906), divine and naturalist; B.A., Lincoln College, Oxford, 1844; M.A., 1846; frequently visited Palestine and Egypt; hon. LL.D. Edinburgh, and F.R.S., 1868; canon residentiary of Durham from 1874 to death; travelled in Japan, China, and North-West America, 1891; works include 'The Natural History of the Bible,' 1867, 'The Topography of the Holy Land,' 1872, and 'The Fauna and Flora of Palestine,' 1884; ornithological collection passed to Liverpool public museum.

TRUMAN, EDWIN THOMAS (1818-1905), dentist and inventor; educated at King's College Hospital; dentist to royal household from 1855 till death; M.R.C.S., 1859; invented improved method of preparing guttapercha to protect the Atlantic cable, 1860; established guttapercha factory at Vauxhall, 1860; invented guttapercha stoppings for dental work; made large collection of George Cruikshank's work; wrote on dentistry.

TUCKER, ALFRED ROBERT (1849-1914), missionary bishop of Uganda; B.A., Christ Church, Oxford; ordained, 1882; bishop of Eastern Equatorial Africa, 1890; on division of diocese (1899) became bishop of Uganda; retired, 1911; organized church built up by Church Missionary Society; canon of Durham, 1911-14.

TUCKER, HENRY WILLIAM (1830-1902), secretary of the Society for the Propagation of the Gospel; B.A., Magdalen Hall, Oxford, 1854; M.A., 1859; assistant

secretary to S.P.G., 1865-79; secretary, 1879-1901; prebendary of St. Paul's, 1881; promoted colonial and missionary work of the society; died at Florence.

TUPPER, SIR CHARLES, first baronet (1821-1915), Canadian statesman; born in Nova Scotia; medical practitioner; entered Nova Scotia legislative assembly as conservative member for Cumberland county, 1855; reanimated his party; premier, 1863; procured free education for Nova Scotia; strong advocate of Canadian federation; formed close alliance with Sir John A. Macdonald [q. v.], 1864; entered federal Cabinet, 1870; committed conservatives to 'national policy' of protection while in opposition, 1873-8; first minister of railways and canals, 1879-84; largely responsible for completion of Canadian Pacific Railway; K.C.M.G., 1879; Canadian high commissioner in London, 1884-96; baronet, 1888; prime minister of Canada, April-June 1896; P.C., 1908.

TUPPER, SIR CHARLES LEWIS (1848-1910), Anglo-Indian official; educated at Harrow and Corpus Christi College, Oxford; B.A., 1870; joined Indian civil service, 1871; secretary to Punjab government, 1882-90; chief secretary from 1890; financial commissioner, 1899; C.S.I., 1897; K.C.I.E., 1903; helped to create Punjab University, 1882; vice-chancellor, 1900-1; compiled 'The Customary Law of the Punjab,' 3 vols. 1880, and 'Our Indian Protectorate,' 1893.

TURNER, CHARLES EDWARD (1831-1903), Russian scholar; educated at St. Paul's School and Lincoln College, Oxford; went to Russia, 1859; lector of the English language in St. Petersburg University, 1864-1903; works include 'Studies in Russian Literature,' 1882, 'The Modern Novelists of Russia,' 1890, and English handbooks for Russian students.

TURNER, JAMES SMITH (1832-1904), dentist; M.R.C.S. and L.D.S., 1863; dental surgeon and lecturer at Middlesex Hospital from 1864; lecturer on dental surgery mechanics at Royal Dental Hospital, 1871-80; instrumental in the passing of the Dentists Act, 1878; helped to found British Dental Association, 1879; president of Odontological Society, 1884.

TURNER, SIR WILLIAM (1832-1916), anatomist, teacher, and academic administrator; studied at St. Bartholomew's Hospital, London, under Sir James Paget [q.v.]; M.B., London University; senior demonstrator in department of anatomy, Edinburgh University, as private assistant to John Goodsir [q. v.], professor of anatomy, 1854; contended successfully against difficulties due to unofficial character of position and his English birth; succeeded Goodsir, 1867; established reputation as eminent teacher and held chair till 1903; took active part in administrative and legislative work of university; member of royal commission appointed to consider question of improvement of conditions to be imposed as qualification for practice of medical profession, 1881; opposed proposal to create central examining board with exclusive power of conferring licence to practise and advocated university's privilege of conferring licence through its degree; his views, expressed in minority report, embodied in Act of 1886; knighted, 1886; principal of Edinburgh University, 1903-1916; first Englishman and first occupant of medical chair to become head of Scottish university; his period of office saw notable expansion in university activities.

TURPIN, EDMUND HART (1835-1907), organist and composer; organist in London from 1860 to death; hon. secretary of Royal College of Organists from 1875; hon. Mus.Doc. Lambeth, 1889; warden of Trinity College of Music, 1892; edited 'Musical Standard,' 1880-6, 1889-90; composed oratorios, church music, pianoforte and organ music; 'Life' by G. W. Pearce, 1911.

TWEEDMOUTH, second BARON (1849-1909), politician. [See MARJORIBANKS, EDWARD.]

TYABJI, BADRUDDIN (1844-1906), Indian judge and reformer; born at Bombay; educated at Bombay and in England; first Indian called to bar at Middle Temple, 1867; member of Bombay legislative council, 1882-4; president of third Indian National Congress, 1887; ardent advocate of higher education of Indian women; first Indian Moslem judge of Bombay high court, 1895; acting chief justice, 1903; died in London and buried at Bombay.

TYLER, THOMAS (1826-1902), Shakespearian scholar; B.A. London, 1859; M.A., 1871; published treatise on 'Ecclesiastes,' 1874 (commended by Ewald); studied Hittite antiquities; wrote also 'The Philosophy of "Hamlet",' 1874, and 'Shakespeare's Sonnets,' 1880, in which he identified Mary Fitton [q. v.] with the 'dark lady' of the sonnets.

TYLOR, SIR EDWARD BURNETT (1832–1917), anthropologist; brother of Alfred Tylor, the geologist [q. v.]; made acquaintance of Henry Christy, the ethnologist [q. v.], 1856; accompanied him to Mexico; keeper of university museum, Oxford, 1883; reader in anthropology, 1884; first professor of anthropology, 1896–1909; knighted, 1912; helped to secure place for anthropology among acknowledged sciences; chief work 'Primitive Culture' (1871).

TYLOR, JOSEPH JOHN (1851–1901), engineer and Egyptologist; son of Alfred Tylor [q. v.]; partner in father's brass-founding firm in London, 1872–91; A.M.I.C.E., 1877; from 1891 studied Egyptology and published monographs on 'Wall Drawings and Monuments of El Kab,' 1895–1900.

TYRRELL, GEORGE (1861–1909), modernist; influenced by Father Robert Dolling [q. v.]; joined Roman Church, 1879; probationer at College of Society of Jesus, Malta, 1879; teacher there, 1885–7; ordained priest, 1891; lectured on philosophy at St. Mary's Hall, Stonyhurst, 1894–6; was transferred to literary staff at Farm Street, London, 1896; produced three orthodox works, 1897–9; an article on Hell in 'Weekly Register,' December 1899, compelled his retirement to Richmond, Yorkshire; there he completed 'Oil and Wine,' 1902, and 'Lex Orandi,' 1903, which show influence of pragmatism; was dismissed from Society of Jesus (1906) for unorthodox 'Letter to a Professor of Anthropology'; replied to Vatican decrees against modernism, September–October 1907; expounded his religious development in 'Through Scylla and Charybdis,' 1907; answered Cardinal Mercier's attack on modernism in 'Medievalism,' 1908; his 'Christianity at the Cross-Roads' followed in 1909; he regarded doctrinal system of the Church as a 'pseudo-science' but admitted some measure of doctrinal development, and maintained essential identity of modern catholic church with the church of the apostles; collected contributions to periodical literature in 'The Faith of the Millions,' 2 vols. 1901–2; Autobiography and 'Life' edited by Maude D. Petre, 1912.

TYRRELL, ROBERT YELVERTON (1844–1914), classical scholar; B.A., Trinity College, Dublin; fellow, 1868; professor of Latin, 1871; regius professor of Greek 1880; professor of ancient history, 1900; senior fellow, 1904; F.B.A., 1901; joint commentator on 'Correspondence of Cicero' (1879–1900).

UNDERHILL, EDWARD BEAN (1813–1901), missionary advocate; grocer in Oxford, 1828–43; founded Hansard Knollys Society, 1845; joint secretary from 1849, and sole secretary 1869–76, of Baptist Missionary Society; visited India and West Indies, and denounced cruelty to natives in Jamaica, 1865; went to Cameroons, 1869; president of Baptist Union, 1873; wrote lives of baptist missionaries, and edited early baptist writings for Hansard Knollys Society.

URWICK, WILLIAM (1826–1905), nonconformist divine and chronicler; B.A., Trinity College, Dublin, 1848; M.A., 1851; congregational minister of Hatherlow, Cheshire, 1851–74, and St. Albans, 1880–95; professor of Hebrew at New College, London, 1874–7; wrote accounts of nonconformity in Cheshire (1864), Hertfordshire (1884), and Worcester (1897).

VALLANCE, WILLIAM FLEMING (1827–1904), marine painter; studied art at Trustees' Academy, Edinburgh; early work was portraiture and genre; after 1870 depicted Irish life and character; finally painted sea and shipping; painted also in water-colours; A.R.S.A., 1875; R.S.A., 1881.

VANDAM, ALBERT DRESDEN (1843–1903), publicist and journalist; was educated in Paris, 1858; was engaged there as journalist till 1871, when he settled in London; correspondent for 'Globe' in Paris, 1882–7; works include 'An Englishman in Paris,' 2 vols. 1892, and translation of Bartholomew Sastrow's autobiography, 1902

VANE-TEMPEST-STEWART, CHARLES STEWART, sixth MARQUESS OF LONDONDERRY (1852–1915), politician; conservative M.P., co. Down, 1878–84; succeeded father, 1884; assumed additional name of Stewart, 1885; viceroy of Ireland, 1886–9; first president, Board of Education, 1902–5; signed Ulster covenant, 1912; P.C., 1886; K.G., 1888.

VAN HORNE, SIR WILLIAM CORNELIUS (1843–

1915), Canadian railway builder and financier; born in Illinois; general manager, Canadian Pacific Railway, 1881; president of company, 1888–99; naturalized Canadian, 1888; honorary K.C.M.G., 1894.

VANSITTART, EDWARD WESTBY (1818–1904), vice-admiral; entered navy, 1831; served in East Indies, and on China station; at reduction of Karachi, 1839, and capture of Woosung batteries, 1842; suppressed piracy in China, 1852–5; accompanied Prince of Wales to Canada, 1860; C.B., 1867; vice-admiral, 1879.

VAUGHAN, DAVID JAMES (1825–1905), honorary canon of Peterborough and social reformer; younger brother of Charles John Vaughan [q. v.]; educated at Rugby and Trinity College, Cambridge; Bell university scholar, 1845; fifth classic, 1848; M.A., 1851; fellow, 1850–8; issued (with John Llewelyn Davies, q. v.) translation of Plato's 'Republic,' 1852 (often reprinted); vicar of St. Martin's, Leicester, 1860–93, and master of Wyggeston's Hospital, 1860–1905; hon. canon of Peterborough, 1872; hon. D.D. Durham, 1894; influenced by F. D. Maurice [q. v.]; started at Leicester in 1862 a working men's college with night classes, provident society, and book club, which was transferred to new building erected at Leicester in his memory, 1908; chairman of first Leicester school board, 1871; published theological works and sermons.

VAUGHAN, HERBERT ALFRED (1832–1903), cardinal; elder brother of Roger William Bede Vaughan [q.v.]; educated at Stonyhurst, in Belgium, at Downside, and in Rome; ordained, 1854; vice-president of St. Edmund's, Ware, 1855; joined congregation of Oblates, 1857; resolving to found missionary college in England, sailed for Caribbean Sea to collect funds, 1863; did much work in Panama despite opposition of civil authorities during smallpox epidemic, 1864; after two years' wandering in South America he was recalled to England by Cardinal Manning, 1865; built St. Joseph's College for missionary students at Mill Hill, 1866; sent out first missionaries to United States, 1871; bought and edited 'The Tablet,' 1868–71; bishop of Salford, 1872–92, opening pastoral seminary there, 1875, as well as St. Bede's College, 1880; improved the diocesan organization and developed the work of the deaneries; founded the 'Rescue and Protection Society' for building homes and poor law schools for catholics; started Voluntary Schools Association, 1884; took leading part in Manchester social problems; archbishop of Westminster from 1892 till death; cardinal, 1893; made St. Mary's College, Oscott, the common seminary for southern and midland group of dioceses; urged withdrawal of papal admonition against catholic attendance at Oxford and Cambridge, 1895; built Westminster Cathedral (foundation stone laid 1895); played official part in controversy over validity of Anglican orders, 1894–7; did much to secure the Education Act of 1902, which obtained state aid for catholic schools; of direct, impulsive, and candid character; 'Life' by J .G. Snead-Cox, 1910.

VAUGHAN, KATE (1852 ?–1903), actress and dancer, whose real name was CATHERINE CANDELON; made début as dancer, 1870; took prominent part in burlesques at Gaiety Theatre, London, from 1876 to 1883; organized Vaughan-Conway comedy company, 1886–7; acted Lydia Languish and Lady Teazle, 1887; visited Australia (1896) and South Africa (1902) for health; died at Johannesburg; inaugurated modern school of skirt-dancing.

VEITCH, JAMES HERBERT (1868–1907), horticulturist; entered father's nursery at Chelsea, 1885; F.L.S., 1889; made tour round world (1891–3) and introduced large winter cherry into England; managing director of James Veitch & Sons, which became a limited company, 1898; compiled elaborate history of the firm in 'Hortus Veitchii,' 1906.

VERNON-HARCOURT, LEVESON FRANCIS (1839–1907), civil engineer; educated at Harrow and Balliol College, Oxford; obtained first class in mathematics and natural science; B.A., 1862; resident engineer at East and West India Docks, 1866–70, and on Rosslare harbour works, 1872–4; surveyed Upper Thames Valley, 1877; professor of civil engineering at University College, London, 1882–1905; wrote 'Rivers and Canals,' 2 vols. 1882, and 'Harbours and Docks,' 1885; served on many commissions and made many engineering reports on rivers and harbours in Great Britain and India; M.I.C.E., 1871.

VERRALL, ARTHUR WOOLLGAR (1851–1912), classical scholar; B.A., Trinity College, Cambridge (second classic); fellow of Trinity, 1874; lectured there, 1877–1911; first King Edward VII professor of English literature at Cambridge, 1911; works include editions of plays of Aeschylus, 'Euripides the Rationalist' (1895), 'Essays on Four Plays of Euripides' (1905), and an edition of the 'Bacchae' (1910).

VEZIN, HERMANN (1829–1910), actor; born at Philadelphia, U.S.A.; B.A. Pennsylvania University, 1847, and M.A., 1848; made first appearance as actor in England, in minor Shakespearian parts, 1850; played with Charles Kean in London, 1852–3; toured in provinces, 1853–7; in America, 1857–9; achieved his reputation at Surrey Theatre in chief Shakespearian characters, 1859; married Mrs. Charles Young [see VEZIN, JANE ELIZABETH], 1863; obtained first rank as James Harebell in 'The Man o' Airlie,' 1867; supported Phelps in revivals of old comedies, 1874; scored triumph as Jaques in 'As You Like It,' 1875, 1880, and 1885; created Buckthorpe in Gilbert's 'Randall's Thumb,' 1871, and Edgar in Tennyson's 'Promise of May,' 1882; acted with Irving, 1888–9; last appeared in London as Rowley in 'The School for Scandal,' April 1909; the most scholarly and intellectual actor of his generation.

VEZIN, JANE ELIZABETH (1827–1902), actress; formerly MRS. CHARLES YOUNG; accompanied parents to Australia in childhood; appeared as singer and dancer at eight; married Charles Frederick Young, comedian, 1846; took part in G. V. Brooke's Australian tour of 1855; first appeared in London, 1857; played leading Shakespearian parts with Phelps, 1857–8; acted Rosalind to Hermann Vezin's Orlando at Sadler's Wells, 1860; after divorce from Young (1862), she married Hermann Vezin [q. v.], 1863; played Desdemona to Phelps's Othello at Drury Lane, 1864; other rôles were Lady Teazle, 1867, Peg Woffington in 'Masks and Faces,' 1867, and Lady Macbeth, 1876; she played with the Bancrofts, 1879, and with Edwin Booth, 1880–1.

VICTORIA ADELAIDE MARY LOUISE (1840–1901), PRINCESS ROYAL OF GREAT BRITAIN AND GERMAN EMPRESS; born at Buckingham Palace, 21 Nov. 1840, was eldest child of Queen Victoria and Prince Albert; showed in youth much interest in her studies; was devotedly attached to her eldest brother, the Prince of Wales, afterwards King Edward VII; accompanied her parents and brother to France on a visit to Napoleon III, August 1855; was affianced to Prince Frederick William, afterwards crown prince of Germany, 29 Sept. 1855; received from parliament dowry of 40,000l. with annuity of 4,000l., 19 May 1857; was married at St. James's Palace, 25 Jan. 1858; lived much in retirement at Berlin, where her eldest son William was born, 27 Jan. 1859; chafed against strict etiquette of Prussian court and its conservative sentiment; openly avowed her liberal convictions; acquired strong influence over her husband; became crown princess, Jan. 1861; resented the rise of Bismarck to supreme power, March 1862; paid long visit to English court, Sept.–Dec. 1863; opposed Bismarck's policy in Schleswig-Holstein, 1864; organized hospitals and care for the wounded during Austro-Prussian conflict of 1866; went with her husband to Paris for opening of International Exhibition, May 1867; although she was generally credited in Germany with French sympathies she was active in works of beneficence for the German soldiers during Franco-German war, 1870–1; sought intercourse with men of culture and artists; tried to introduce into Germany English methods of promoting the industrial arts; helped to establish Berlin Industrial Art museum, November 1881; urged more scientific training for sick nurses; aided in forming Victoria House and Nursing School, Berlin, 1881; encouraged schemes for ameliorating social condition of working classes; was a pioneer in developing women's higher education in Germany; continued to suffer much annoyance owing to Bismarck's exclusion of her husband from political affairs; nursed her husband during his illness from cancer, 1887; was with him at San Remo when his father William I died, 9 March 1888, and he became Emperor Frederick; was present at her husband's death at Potsdam, 15 June 1888; during her husband's short reign she quarrelled anew with Bismarck, owing to her obstinate encouragement of a match between her second daughter Princess Victoria and Alexander of Battenberg, Prince of Bulgaria; in her widowhood she was still exposed to Bismarck's harshness until the minister's dismissal by the new emperor, her son, March 1890; at her son's request, she spent a week in Paris to

test French sentiment, February 1891, but was driven away by threats of a hostile demonstration; settled for rest of life at Cronberg, where she built a palatial residence, Friedrichshof; still followed the current course of politics, literature, and art, and continued her varied philanthropic labours; frequently revisited England; was attacked by cancer in autumn of 1898; died at Friedrichshof, 5 August 1901; was buried at Potsdam beside her husband; was survived by two (of her four) sons and by her four daughters.

VILLIERS, JOHN HENRY DE, first BARON DE VILLIERS (1842–1914), South African judge. [See DE VILLIERS.]

VILLIERS, VICTOR ALBERT GEORGE CHILD-, seventh EARL OF JERSEY and tenth VISCOUNT GRANDISON (1845–1915), colonial governor; educated at Eton and Balliol College, Oxford; succeeded father, 1859; governor and commander-in-chief, New South Wales, 1891–3; dealt successfully with labour problem and financial crisis.

VINCENT, SIR (CHARLES EDWARD) HOWARD (1849–1908), politician; joined royal Welsh fusiliers, 1868; went to Russia to study military organization; published 'Elementary Military Geography,' 1872; left army, 1873; called to bar, 1876; represented 'Daily Telegraph' in Russo-Turkish war of 1876; lieutenant-colonel of Central London Rangers, 1875–8; examined Continental police systems, 1877–8; first director of criminal investigation at Scotland Yard, 1878–84; published 'A Police Code and Manual of Criminal Law,' 1882; conservative M.P. for Central Sheffield, 1885–1908; member of London County Council, 1889–96; to his persistence were mainly due Acts concerning alien immigration, 1905, and appointment of a public trustee, 1906; he advocated colonial preference from 1889; C.B., 1880; knighted, 1896; K.C.M.G., 1898; 'Life' by S. H. Jeyes and F. D. How, 1912.

VINCENT, JAMES EDMUND (1857–1909), journalist and author; educated at Winchester and Christ Church, Oxford; B.A., 1880; called to bar, 1884; chancellor of diocese of Bangor, 1890; edited 'National Observer,' 1894–7, and 'Country Life,' 1897–1901; works include lives of Duke of Clarence, 1893, Edward VII, 1902 and 1910, 'Highways and Byways in Berkshire,' 1906.

VOYSEY, CHARLES (1828–1912), Theistic preacher; B.A., St. Edmund Hall, Oxford; ordained, 1851; vicar of Healaugh, near Tadcaster, 1864; deprived of living for unorthodox preaching and writing, 1871; began movement in London which ultimately developed into 'Theistic Church'; an attractive preacher.

WADE, SIR WILLOUGHBY FRANCIS (1827–1906), physician; educated at Rugby and Trinity College, Dublin; B.A., 1849; M.B., 1851; hon. M.D., 1896; M.R.C.S. England, 1851; F.R.C.P., 1871; physician to general Birmingham hospital, 1865–92; knighted, 1896; first called attention to presence of albuminuria in diphtheria; wrote on diphtheria and gout.

WAKLEY, THOMAS (1851–1909), only son of Thomas Henry Wakley [q. v.]; L.R.C.P., 1883; succeeded father as editor of 'Lancet.'

WAKLEY, THOMAS HENRY (1821–1907), surgeon and journalist; eldest son of Thomas Wakley (1795–1862, q. v.); studied medicine at University College, London, and Paris; M.R.C.S., 1845; assistant surgeon to Royal Free Hospital, 1848; F.R.C.S., 1849; part proprietor of 'Lancet,' 1857; co-editor with son Thomas, 1886; founded 'Lancet' relief fund for medical practitioners 1889.

WALKER, SIR FREDERICK WILLIAM EDWARD FORESTIER FORESTIER- (1844–1910), general. [See FORESTIER-WALKER.]

WALKER, FREDERICK WILLIAM (1830–1910), schoolmaster; educated at Rugby and Corpus Christi College, Oxford; B.A. (first class in lit. hum.), 1853; Boden (Sanskrit), Vinerian and Tancred law scholar, 1854; M.A., 1856; fellow, 1859; hon. fellow, 1894; called to bar, 1858; high master of Manchester grammar school, 1859–76; reorganized school and finances and constitution; high master (1876–1905) of St. Paul's School, which was removed from City of London to Hammersmith (1884); greatly increased the school's reputation for scholarship; gained victory in long struggle—from 1890 to 1899—with charity commissioners regarding the school's constitution; sat on commission for education of officers in the army, 1900; hon. Litt.D. Manchester, 1899; raised standard of public school education throughout country; friend of the positivist leaders and of Jowett.

WALKER, SIR MARK (1827–1902), general; brother of Sir Samuel Walker [q. v.]; joined army, 1846; served in Crimea; present at Balaklava and Inkermann, where his gallantry won for him the V.C.; went to India, 1859; served through the China campaign, 1859–61; present at capture of Chusan, the assault of Taku forts, and surrender of Peking; was quartered in England, 1862–70; served in India, 1871–9; C.B., 1875; major-general, 1878; commanded 1st brigade at Aldershot, 1883; commanded infantry at Gibraltar, 1884–8; lieutenant-general, 1888; general and K.C.B., 1893.

WALKER, SIR SAMUEL, first baronet (1832–1911), lord chancellor of Ireland; B.A., Trinity College, Dublin (first senior classical moderator), 1854; called to Irish bar, 1855; Q.C., 1872; attained large practice in equity and common law; ably defended Parnell, 1881; bencher of King's Inns, 1881; a liberal in politics; solicitor-general for Ireland under Gladstone, 1883–5; liberal M.P. for Londonderry county, 1884–5; acting Irish secretary during 1884; attorney-general for Ireland, May–June, 1885; Irish P.C., 1885; again attorney-general for Ireland, February–August, 1886; lord chancellor of Ireland and president of Irish court of appeal, August 1892–July 1895, and December 1905–11; chairman of commission on Irish fisheries, 1897; baronet, 1906; enthusiastic shot and angler.

WALKER, VYELL EDWARD (1837–1906), cricketer; a member of distinguished cricketing family of Southgate, Middlesex; educated at Harrow; first played for Gentlemen v. Players (1856), subsequently captaining the team ten times; helped to found Middlesex County Cricket Club, 1864; secretary, 1864–70; captain, 1864–72; president, 1898; president of M.C.C., 1891; orthodox batsman, powerful hitter, and deceptive slow 'lob' bowler; on retiring from cricket about 1874, he took part in family brewing firm; succeeded to the family estate at Southgate, 1889; presented land for public recreation ground there, 1890.

WALLACE, ALFRED RUSSEL (1823–1913), naturalist; educated at Hertford grammar school; master at Leicester collegiate school, 1844–6; made acquaintance of Henry Walter Bates [q. v.], the naturalist, with whom he went on collecting trip to Amazons, 1848; returned to England, 1852; visited Malay Archipelago, 1854–62; while in Moluccas (1858) independently discovered principal of natural selection as key to method of evolution, his most important achievement on theoretical side; his theory of origin of species identical with that of Charles Darwin [q. v.], to whom he sent his views; modern theory of evolution published in joint paper, 1858; spent remainder of his life after return to England (1862) in writing and lecturing; material which he amassed in Malay Archipelago very valuable to biology; published great work, 'The Malay Archipelago,' 1869; other works include 'Contributions to the Theory of Natural Selection' (1870) and 'The Geographical Distribution of Animals' (1876); his most solid work done on geographical distribution; F.R.S., 1893; first Darwin medallist of the Royal Society, 1890; O.M., 1910.

WALLACE, SIR DONALD MACKENZIE (1841–1919), newspaper correspondent, editor, and author; studied at various universities at home and abroad; visited Russia, 1870–5; foreign correspondent of 'The Times' at Constantinople, 1878–84; private secretary to Earl of Dufferin, viceroy of India, 1884–8; K.C.I.E., 1887; director of 'The Times' foreign department, 1891–9; principal work, 'Russia' (1877).

WALLACE, WILLIAM ARTHUR JAMES (1842–1902), colonel, royal engineers; joined royal engineers, 1860; entered railway branch of public works department of India, 1864; executive engineer, 1871; officiating consulting-engineer to Indian government at Lucknow, 1877; field engineer to Kuram valley column in Afghan campaign, 1879; engineer-in-chief of northern Bengal railway at Saidpur, 1880; director of railway corps in Egyptian campaign, 1882; present at Tel-el-Kebir; chief engineer for guaranteed railways at Lahore, 1884–92; C.I.E., 1890.

WALLER, CHARLES HENRY (1840–1910), theologian; B.A., University College, Oxford, 1863; M.A., 1867; D.D., 1891; theological tutor at St. John's Hall, Highbury, 1865; professor of biblical exegesis, 1882; principal, 1884–98; works include 'A Grammar of the Words in the Greek Testament,' 2 pts. 1877–8, and commentaries on 'Deuteronomy' and 'Joshua,' 1882.

WALLER, LEWIS (1860–1915), actor manager, whose real name was WILLIAM WALLER LEWIS; born in Spain;

acted with various companies in London and provinces, 1883–95; successively managed, alone or jointly, Haymarket, Lyceum, Imperial, and Lyric theatres; his finest impersonation that of the king in 'Henry V' (1900); other brilliant parts, Hotspur in 'Henry IV, Part I' (1896), D'Artagnan in 'The Three Musketeers' (1898), and title-rôle of 'Monsieur Beaucaire' (1902–3).

WALLER, SAMUEL EDMUND (1850–1903), painter of genre pictures; studied architecture under father at Gloucester; exhibited at Royal Academy, 1871–1902; chief works were 'The Empty Saddle,' 1879, 'Sweethearts and Wives,' 1882, and 'The Morning of Agincourt,' 1888.

WALPOLE, SIR SPENCER (1839–1907), historian and civil servant; elder son of Spencer Horatio Walpole [q. v.]; educated at Eton, 1852–7; entered war office as clerk, 1857; private secretary to father at home office, 1858–9, and at war office, 1866–7; inspector of fisheries for England and Wales, 1867; published life of grandfather, Spencer Perceval, 1874; published first two volumes of 'History of England from 1815 to 1856,' 1878 (vols. iii.–vi., 1890); governor of the Isle of Man, 1882–93; secretary to post office, 1893–9; K.C.B., 1898; hon. D.Litt. Oxford and F.B.A., 1904; continued his history in 'A History of Twenty-five Years (1856–80),' vols. i. and ii. 1904, vols. iii. and iv. (left incomplete), 1908; other works include 'Life of Lord John Russell,' 2 vols. 1889, and 'Essays Political and Biographical,' posthumous, 1908.

WALSH, WILLIAM PAKENHAM (1820–1902), bishop of Ossory, Ferns, and Leighton from 1878 to death; B.A., Trinity College, Dublin, 1841; M.A., 1853; Donnellan lecturer, 1860; D.D., 1873; chaplain of Sandford Church, Ranelagh, Dublin, 1858–73; dean of Cashel, 1873–8; published 'Ancient Monuments and Holy Writ,' 1878.

WALSHAM, SIR JOHN, second baronet (1830–1905), diplomatist; B.A., Trinity College, Cambridge, 1854; M.A., 1857; attaché to British legation at Mexico, 1860–6; second secretary at Madrid, 1866–75; secretary of legation at Madrid, 1875–8, at Berlin, 1878–83; minister plenipotentiary at Paris, 1883–5; British envoy at Peking, 1885–92, and at Bucharest, 1892–4; K.C.M.G., 1895.

WALSHAM, WILLIAM JOHNSON (1847–1903), surgeon; studied medicine at St. Bartholomew's Hospital, 1867; M.B. and C.M. Aberdeen, 1871; M.R.C.S. England, 1871; F.R.C.S., 1875; served as lecturer and surgeon at St. Bartholomew's from 1871; full surgeon, 1897; excelled in surgery of harelip and orthopædy; chief work was 'Surgery: its Theory and Practice,' 1887 (8th edit. 1903).

WALTER, SIR EDWARD (1823–1904), founder of the Corps of Commissionaires; third son of John Walter (1776–1847, q. v.); served in army, 1843–53; founded self-supporting Corps of Commissionaires for employment of discharged soldiers and sailors, 1859; the Corps numbered 4152 men in 1911; knighted, 1885; K.C.B., 1887.

WALTON, SIR JOHN LAWSON (1852–1908), lawyer; called to bar, 1877; Q.C., 1890; gained reputation by victory in action against William Smoult Playfair [q. v.], 1896; liberal M.P. for South Leeds from 1892 till death; attorney-general under Campbell-Bannerman, 1905–8; knighted, 1905; introduced trades disputes bill, 1906; offended labour party by defending clause making executives of trades unions responsible for members' breaches of law.

WALTON, SIR JOSEPH (1845–1910), judge; educated at Stonyhurst; B.A. London, 1865; called to bar, 1868; practised at Liverpool in commercial and shipping cases; Q.C., 1892; recorder of Wigan, 1895–1901; chairman of general council of the bar, 1899; judge of king's bench division, 1901–10; knighted, 1901; president of Medico-Legal Society, 1905.

WANKLYN, JAMES ALFRED (1834–1906), analytical chemist; M.R.C.S., 1856; studied chemistry at Heidelberg under Bunsen; demonstrator of chemistry at Edinburgh, 1859–63; professor at London Institution, 1863–70; lecturer at St. George's Hospital, 1877–80; public analyst in various towns; made many valuable chemical researches independently and in collaboration; gave much attention to milk analysis and water analysis in London; works include 'Milk Analysis,' 1873, 'Water Analysis' (with E. T. Chapman), 1868 (11th edit. 1907); collaborated in 'Bread Analysis,' 1881, 'Air Analysis,' 1890, and 'Sewage Analysis,' 1899.

132

WANTAGE, BARON (1832–1901), soldier and politician. [See LINDSAY (afterwards LOYD-LINDSAY), ROBERT JAMES.]

WARD, HARRY LEIGH DOUGLAS (1825–1906), writer on medieval romances; educated at Winchester; and University College, Oxford; B.A., 1847; assistant in department of manuscripts at British Museum, 1849–93; catalogued Icelandic MSS. there; published elaborate 'Catalogue of Romances in the British Museum,' 3 vols. 1883–1910, a standard textbook.

WARD, HARRY MARSHALL (1854–1906), botanist; studied science at Owens College, Manchester, and Christ's College, Cambridge; B.A., 1879; fellow, 1883; M.A., 1885; hon. Sc.D., 1892; D.Sc. Victoria, 1902; investigated coffee leaf disease in Ceylon, 1880–2; Berkeley research student at Owens College, 1882; assistant lecturer, 1883–6; professor of botany at Cooper's Hill, 1885–95, and at Cambridge, 1895–1906; F.L.S., 1886; F.R.S., 1888; Royal medallist, 1893; helped to found 'Annals of Botany,' 1887, contributing many original papers; showed destructive effect of light on bacteria, 1894; publications include 'Timber and some of its Diseases,' 1889, 'Diseases of Plants,' 1889, 'The Oak,' 1892, and 'Grasses,' 1901.

WARD, HENRY SNOWDEN (1865–1911), photographer and author; joined printing firm of Percy Lund & Co., Bradford, 1885, for which he founded and edited the 'Practical Photographer,' 1890; settled in London, 1891, and edited many photographic periodicals; published 'Practical Radiography,' 1896; with his wife wrote and illustrated topographical works relating to Shakespeare and Dickens; died in New York.

WARD, MARY AUGUSTA (1851–1920), better known as MRS. HUMPHRY WARD, novelist and social worker; daughter of Thomas Arnold (1823–1900, q. v.); born in Tasmania; brought to England, 1856; married T. H. Ward, 1872; best-known novel, 'Robert Elsmere' (1888); others are 'David Grieve' (1892), 'Marcella' (1894), 'Lady Rose's Daughter' (1903), and 'The Marriage of William Ashe' (1905); founded (1890) settlement in London which developed into Passmore Edwards Settlement (1897); anti-suffragist; carried on pro-Allies propaganda in America during European war.

WARD, WILFRID PHILIP (1856–1916), biographer and Catholic apologist; son of W. G. Ward [q. v.]; educated at Ushaw College, Durham, and Gregorian University, Rome; editor of 'Dublin Review,' 1906; works include Lives of his father (1889–93), Cardinal Wiseman (1897), and Cardinal Newman (1912).

WARDLE, SIR THOMAS (1831–1909), promoter of the silk industry; on leaving school joined father's silk-dyeing business at Leek, Staffordshire; founded silk and cotton printing business at Leek on father's death, 1882; commercially utilized Indian wild silk from 1872; investigated for India office the conditions of sericulture in India, 1885–6; stimulated by his report Bengal silk industry; revived Kashmir silk industry, 1897; president of Silk Association of Great Britain, 1887–1909; knighted, 1897; ardent geologist and palaeontologist; published many works on silk and its manufacture.

WARING, ANNA LETITIA (1823–1910), hymn writer; published volumes of hymns, which included 'Father, I know that all my life' (written in 1846); influenced James Martineau.

WARINGTON, ROBERT (1838–1907), agricultural chemist; son of Robert Warington (1807–1867, q. v.); assistant at Rothamsted Laboratory, 1859; at Royal Agricultural College, Cirencester, 1862–7; made researches into effect of ferric oxide and alumina on soluble phosphates and other salts; chemist at J. B. Lawes's manure and citric acid works at Barking and Millwall, 1867–76; was associated with Rothamsted investigations, 1876–91; pursued original researches into nitrification of the soil; Lawes lecturer in America, 1891; Sibthorpian professor of agriculture at Oxford, 1894–7; contributed many articles to chemical dictionaries and cyclopaedias; chief work was 'Chemistry on the Farm,' 1881, which reached nineteen editions; F.R.S., 1886.

WARNE, FREDERICK (1825–1901), publisher; assistant to George Routledge [q. v.], 1839; partner in Routledge's publishing firm, 1851; began independent business, 1865; established New York branch, 1881; inaugurated 'Chandos Classics,' 1868; published coloured picture books for children, including 'Aunt Louisa Toy Books,' 1871–80; retired, 1895.

WARNEFORD, REGINALD ALEXANDER JOHN

(1891–1915), airman; born in India; entered Royal Naval Air Service, 1915; V.C. for destruction of Zeppelin airship in Flanders, 1915; killed flying near Paris.

WARNER, CHARLES (1846–1909), actor, whose real name was CHARLES JOHN LICKFOLD; made first appearance on stage at command performance of 'Richelieu' at Windsor Castle, January 1861; first appeared in London, 1864; supported Phelps at Drury Lane in minor Shakespearian and other parts, 1866–8; made first pronounced success as Charley Burridge in Byron's 'Daisy Farm,' 1871; successful rôles in London (1873–8) included Charles Middlewick in Byron's 'Our Boys,' and Young Mirabel in Farquhar's 'The Inconstant'; made reputation in melodrama as Tom Robinson in 'It is never too late to mend' and as Coupeau in 'Drink,' 1878–9; went on prosperous tours in Australia, 1887–90, and in America, 1904 and 1907; committed suicide in New York, 1909; highly-strung actor in melodrama; sympathetic interpreter of old comedy.

WARRE, EDMOND (1837–1920), head master of Eton; educated at Eton and Balliol College, Oxford; fellow of All Souls, 1859–61; assistant master at Eton, 1860; opened school boarding house, to which he quickly attracted distinguished pupils, 1861; head master of Eton, 1884–1905; increased reputation and numbers of school by raising moral tone and intellectual standard; opened new buildings, including drill hall, lower chapel, Queen's schools, and Warre schools; invented school office; started Eton mission at Hackney Wick; provost of Eton, 1909–18; decline of latter years, due to ill-health, alone prevented him from being regarded as greatest of Eton head masters.

WARRE-CORNISH, FRANCIS WARRE (1839–1916), teacher, author, and bibliophile; educated at Eton and King's College, Cambridge; assistant master at Eton, 1861; vice-provost and librarian, 1893–1916.

WARRENDER, SIR GEORGE JOHN SCOTT, seventh baronet (1860–1917), admiral; entered royal navy, 1873; captain, 1899; largely responsible for naval operations during Boxer rising, 1900; succeeded father, 1901; reached flag rank, 1908; commanded second battle squadron of grand fleet, 1914; commanded force dispatched to intercept German raiders on East coast (December); commander-in-chief, Plymouth, 1915–16.

WATERHOUSE, ALFRED (1830–1905), architect; after architectural study in Manchester, France, Italy, and Germany, he practised in Manchester, 1853–65; won competition for Manchester assize courts (1859) and for town hall (1877), which shows individual type of Gothic; also designed Owens College, Salford gaol at Manchester, University College and Royal Infirmary at Liverpool, and Yorkshire College at Leeds, 1878, the Natural History Museum at South Kensington, 1868–80 (which exhibits unwonted exuberance of detail), the Prudential Assurance office, Holborn, and St. Paul's School, Hammersmith; employed terra cotta; also designed National Liberal Club, 1884; did ecclesiastical restoration and decoration; at Cambridge he made additions to Caius, Jesus, and Pembroke colleges, and designed the Union building, 1866; at Oxford he was responsible for Balliol College Hall and the new Union Debating Hall; did much domestic reconstruction, including Yattendon Court, his own residence, 1877; took his son Paul into partnership, 1891; in great demand as assessor in competitions; exhibited water-colours at Royal Academy; president of Royal Institute of British Architects, 1888–91; A.R.A., 1878; R.A., 1885; treasurer, 1898; hon. LL.D. Manchester, 1895; received many foreign diplomas; portraits by W. Q. Orchardson and Alma-Tadema.

WATERLOW, SIR ERNEST ALBERT (1850–1919), painter; A.R.A., 1890; R.A., 1903; president of Royal Society of Painters in Water Colours, 1897–1914; knighted, 1902; painted chiefly landscapes.

WATERLOW, SIR SYDNEY HEDLEY, first baronet (1822–1906), lord mayor of London and philanthropist; was apprenticed to uncle Thomas Harrison, the government printer, 1836–43; joined brothers in adding printing branch to father's stationery business, 1844; supplied printing and stationery to railways; his firm became limited company, 1876, with Waterlow as managing director, 1877–95; alderman of the city of London, 1863–83; sheriff, 1866–7; lord mayor of London, 1872; knighted, 1867; master of Stationers Company, 1872–3; baronet, 1873; originated Industrial Dwellings Company, Limited, 1863; liberal M.P. for Dumfriesshire, 1868–9, for Maidstone, 1874–80, and for Gravesend,

1880–5; presented Lauderdale House, Highgate, and twenty-nine acres of land (now known as Waterlow Park) to London County Council, 1889; K.C.V.O., 1902; 'Life' by George Smalley, 1909.

WATKIN, SIR EDWARD WILLIAM, first baronet (1819–1901), railway promoter; joined father's cotton firm at Manchester; started Saturday half-holiday movement in Manchester, 1844; helped to raise money for opening three public parks there, 1845; founded 'Manchester Examiner,' 1845; secretary to Trent Valley Railway (1845), which was soon transferred to London and North Western Railway Company; general manager of Manchester, Sheffield, and Lincolnshire Railway, 1853–61; chairman of directors from 1864 to 1894; opened independent line, now Great Central Railway, from Sheffield to London, 1899; chairman of South Eastern Railway, 1866–94, and of Metropolitan Railway, 1872–94; advocated channel tunnel railway between Dover and Calais from 1869; liberal M.P. for Stockport, 1864–8, and for Hythe, 1874–85; liberal unionist M.P. for Hythe, 1886–95; high sheriff of Cheshire, 1874; knighted, 1868; baronet, 1880.

WATSON, ALBERT (1828–1904), principal of Brasenose College, Oxford, and classical scholar; educated at Rugby and Wadham College, Oxford; B.A., 1851; M.A., 1853; fellow of Brasenose, 1852; tutor, 1854–67; lecturer, 1868–73; principal, 1886–9; edited 'Select Letters of Cicero,' 1870.

WATSON, SIR CHARLES MOORE (1844–1916), soldier and administrator; entered army, 1866; served in Egypt, 1882–6; deputy inspector of fortifications, 1896–1902; colonel, 1906; K.C.M.G., 1905.

WATSON, GEORGE LENNOX (1851–1904), naval architect; entered shipbuilding firm at Govan, 1867; started own business in Glasgow as naval architect, 1872; built for Edward, Prince of Wales the yacht 'Britannia', which won prizes valued at 9,973l. between 1893 and 1897; designed British challengers' yachts for contest with American yachts from 1887 to 1901; also designed cargo and passenger steamers and steam yachts; published lectures on yachting, 1881.

WATSON, HENRY WILLIAM (1827–1903), mathematician; B.A., Trinity College, Cambridge; second wrangler and Smith's prizeman, 1850; fellow, 1851; tutor, 1851–3; member of 'Apostles'; mathematical master at Harrow, 1857–65; one of founders of Alpine Club, 1857; F.R.S., 1881; hon. Sc.D. Cambridge, 1883; author of mathematical works, including 'Treatise on the Kinetic Theory of Gases,' 1876.

WATSON, JOHN (1850–1907), presbyterian divine and author, and writer under the pseudonym of IAN MACLAREN; of highland stock; M.A. Edinburgh University, 1870; Free Church minister at Logiealmond ('Drumtochty'), Perthshire, 1875–7; in charge of presbyterian Church of England at Sefton Park, Liverpool, 1880–1905; a powerful and cultured preacher; influenced civic life; helped in creation of Liverpool University; made reputation in England and America by publication, under pseudonym of 'Ian Maclaren,' of 'Beside the Bonnie Brier Bush,' 1894, which was translated into many European languages; other works of fiction were 'The Days of Auld Lang Syne,' 1895, 'Kate Carnegie and those Ministers,' 1897, and 'His Majesty Baby,' 1902; he made lecture tours in America, 1896 and 1899; published Lyman Beecher lectures on preaching delivered at Yale University as 'The Cure of Souls,' 1896; hon. D.D., 1896; theological works include 'The Mind of the Master,' 1896; moderator of presbyterian synod, 1900; president of National Free Church Council, 1907; died on third American lecture tour at Mount Pleasant, Iowa; buried at Liverpool; 'Life' by Sir W. Robertson Nicoll, 1908.

WATSON, SIR PATRICK HERON (1832–1907), surgeon; M.D. Edinburgh University, 1853; L.R.C.S. Edinburgh, 1853; F.R.C.S., 1855; president, 1878 and 1905; served as surgeon in Crimea, 1855–6; lecturer on systematic and clinical surgery at Royal College of Surgeons, Edinburgh; surgeon to Royal Infirmary, Edinburgh, 1863–83; performed ovariotomy and excision of joints before introduction of Listerian methods; hon. LL.D. Edinburgh, 1884; hon. F.R.C.S. Ireland, 1887; knighted, 1903.

WATSON, ROBERT SPENCE (1837–1911), political, social, and educational reformer; articled to father as solicitor at Newcastle-on-Tyne, 1860; hon. secretary of Newcastle Literary and Philosophical Institution, 1862–*; president, 1900; helped to found Durham College

of Science (now Armstrong College), 1871; first president, 1910; hon. D.C.L., 1906; member of first Newcastle School Board, 1871–94; pioneer of university extension in north; member of Alpine Club, 1862; visited Wazan, the sacred city of Morocco, 1879, and wrote an account of visit, 1880; founded Newcastle Liberal Association, 1874; president of National Liberal Federation, 1890–1902; P.C., 1907; president of Peace Society; advocate of Indian nationalist movement and of free institutions in Russia; umpire from 1864 in over 100 trade disputes; hon. LL.D. St. Andrews, 1881 works include 'Life of Joseph Skipsey', 1909.

WATTS, GEORGE FREDERIC (1817–1904), painter and sculptor; born in Queen Street, Bryanston Square, London, was son of George Watts, a piano maker and tuner in straitened circumstances; read much as a boy, though he had no regular schooling; early enjoyed the run of the studio of William Behnes [q. v.], sculptor; took some lessons in oil painting; began to earn a livelihood at sixteen by portraits in pencil and chalk; entered Royal Academy Schools, 1835; hired studio in Clipstone Street, 1837; exhibited at Academy 'A Wounded Heron' and two portraits of ladies, 1837; came to know Nicolas Wanostrocht or 'Felix' [q. v.], schoolmaster at Blackheath and professional cricketer, for whom he drew and lithographed seven illustrations of cricket with portraits; was befriended by Constantine Ionides, 1839, for whom and whose family he painted twenty portraits during his career; won a premium of 300l. with a cartoon of Caractacus for the decoration of Westminster Palace, 1842; travelled through France to Italy; was introduced at Florence to Lord and Lady Holland; remained as their guest at Borgo San Frediano, 1843–7; painted portraits of his hosts and friends, and began many vast canvases inspired by Italian history and legend; also practised modelling; returned to London, April 1847; won a second premium of 500l. for Westminster Palace cartoon of King Alfred, 1848; painted decorations for Holland House, 1848; rented a studio at 30 Charles Street, Berkeley Square, with a view to monumental emblematic paintings, 1848–53; joined a distinguished social circle, including Robert Morier, William Harcourt, and others, who soon formed the Cosmopolitan Club; projected a series of portraits of the distinguished men of his time, beginning with Lord John Russell; settled with Mr. and Mrs. Henry Thoby Prinsep at Little Holland House, Kensington, 1850–75; painted 'Triumph of the Red Cross Knight' for a wall in a cramped corridor at Westminster Palace (now dilapidated); visited Venice with R. Spencer Stanhope, 1853; painted in fresco 'Justice—a Hemicycle of Lawgivers' for Lincoln's Inn Hall, 1853–9; painted portraits of Thiers, Prince Jerome Buonaparte, and others in Paris, 1855–6; joined Sir Charles Newton [q.v.], who was excavating the site of Halicarnassus, 1857; painted Lord Stratford de Redcliffe at Constantinople, 1857; on returning to England painted Tennyson, 1857, and Gladstone, 1859; executed frescoes for Lord Lansdowne at Bowood; designed figures of St. Matthew and St. John for mosaics in St. Paul's Cathedral; married in 1864 Miss Ellen Terry, but they parted June 1865, and Watts obtained a divorce in 1877; he worked on symbolic pictures 'Love and Death' and 'The Court of Death,' on classical subjects, including 'Orpheus and Eurydice,' and on his finest female portraits, including Lady Margaret Beaumont, 1860–70; executed monuments of Lord Lothian at Blickling Church and the statue of Lord Holland in Holland Park (with Edgar Boehm); A.R.A. and R.A., 1867; built for himself and occupied from 1876 to 1903 the new Little Holland House; exhibited at Grosvenor Gallery from its opening in 1877; devoted much time to a colossal equestrian statue called 'Physical Energy,' one cast of which formed part of the memorial to Cecil Rhodes at Capetown 1905, and another is in Kensington Gardens; 56 of Watts's pictures collected by Mr. Charles Richards were exhibited at Manchester Institution, 1880; 200 pictures at the Grosvenor Gallery in the winter of 1881–2; there were also exhibitions at Paris, 1883, and New York, 1885, and one on a great scale at New Gallery, 1897. Watts was made hon. LL.D., Oxford and Cambridge, 1882; married his second wife Mary Fraser Tytler, 1886; built country house called Limnerslease near Guildford, 1894; added a gallery which was opened to the public, April 1904; twice declined a baronetcy, 1885 and 1894; presented to National Portrait Gallery 15 portraits and two drawings of distinguished contemporaries, 1895, and to National Gallery of British Art, 20 symbolic paintings, 1897; executed monumental statue of Tennyson at Lincoln, 1898; received O.M., 1902; died at Limnerslease and was buried at Compton.

WATTS, HENRY EDWARD (1826–1904), author; born at Calcutta; after education at Exeter grammar school returned to Calcutta, 1846; went to Australia; edited 'Melbourne Argus,' 1859; on staff of 'Standard' in London from 1868; translated 'Don Quixote,' 1888, with a life of Cervantes (issued separately, 1895), and wrote 'Spain' for 'Story of the Nations' series, 1893.

WATTS, JOHN (1861–1902), jockey; associated with Richard Marsh, trainer to Prince of Wales (afterwards King Edward VII) from 1879; won Oaks and Derby four times—the last time on Prince of Wales's Persimmon, on which he also won the St. Leger and the Ascot Cup, 1896; won the Two Thousand Guineas twice, and the St. Leger five times; won in all 1,412 races; trained horses at Newmarket from 1900.

WATTS-DUNTON, WALTER THEODORE (1832–1914), critic, novelist, and poet; took up literary criticism, 1874; wrote for 'Athenaeum'; intimate with the Rossetti group; controlled life and affairs of A. C. Swinburne [q. v.], 1879–1909; works include 'The Coming of Love', a narrative poem (1897), and 'Aylwin,' a novel (1898); learned in gipsy lore.

WAUGH, BENJAMIN (1839–1908), philanthropist; congregational minister from 1865 to 1887; instituted at Greenwich Wastepaper and Blacking Brigade for neglected children; member of London School Board for Greenwich, 1870–6; edited 'Sunday Magazine,' 1874–96; assisted Hesba Stretton [q. v.] in establishing London Society for the Prevention of Cruelty to Children, 1884, which was converted into the National Society, 1888, and was incorporated by royal charter, 1895; mainly responsible for act for protection of children, 1889, and more stringent acts of 1894, 1904, and 1908; 'Life' by Rosa Waugh and E. Betham, 1912.

WAUGH, JAMES (1831–1905), trainer of racehorses; succeeded Matthew Dawson [q. v.] at Gullane (1859) and Russley (1866); trained chief winners in Austria-Hungary and Germany, 1872–80; settled for life at Newmarket, 1880; trained St. Gatien, winner of the Derby and Cesarewitch, 1884, and of the Ascot Cup, 1885.

WAVELL, ARTHUR JOHN BYNG (1882–1916), soldier and explorer; educated at Winchester; served in army, 1900–6; made Mecca pilgrimage successfully in assumed character, 1908; attempted to explore south central Arabia, 1910; raised force known as 'Wavell's Own' in East Africa during European war; M.C., 1914; killed in ambush; wrote 'A Modern Pilgrim in Mecca' (1912).

WEBB, ALFRED JOHN (1834–1908), Irish biographer; one of earliest advocates of home rule; supported Parnell till 1887; anti-Parnellite M.P. for West Waterford, 1890–5; frequently visited India; president of Indian National Congress, 1898; published 'A Compendium of Irish Biography,' 1877.

WEBB, ALLAN BECHER (1839–1907), dean of Salisbury and bishop in South Africa; educated at Rugby and Corpus Christi College, Oxford; B.A., 1862; M.A., 1864; D.D., 1871; fellow of University College, 1863–7; vice-principal of Cuddesdon College, 1864–5; bishop of Bloemfontein, Orange Free State, 1870–83; encouraged extension of sisterhood work there; bishop of Grahamstown, 1883–98; did much to heal schism caused by Colenso controversy; dean of Salisbury, 1901–7.

WEBB, FRANCIS WILLIAM (1836–1906), civil engineer; at fifteen pupil of Francis Trevithick, then locomotive superintendent of London and North Western Railway, with which Webb was henceforth associated till death; chief mechanical engineer and locomotive superintendent, 1871; carried out improvements in locomotive construction; introduced compound locomotives (1882) with three and subsequently with four cylinders; developed town of Crewe; initiated Cottage Hospital; twice mayor, 1886 and 1887; M.I.C.E., 1872; vice-president, 1900; left money to found nursing institution at Crewe and orphanage for children of railway employees.

WEBB, PHILIP (SPEAKMAN) (1831–1915), architect; entered office of George Edmund Street [q. v.], at Oxford; began practice in London, about 1856; produced decorative designs, among others for firm of William Morris [q. v.]; built one church (Brampton, Cumberland),

and 50 or 60 houses, including 1 Palace Green, Kensington, West House, Chelsea, 19 Lincoln's Inn Fields, Joldwynds, near Dorking, Rounton Grange, Yorkshire, Clouds, Wiltshire, Standen, East Grinstead, and Red House, Upton (for Morris); copied no particular style; co-founder with Morris of Society for Protection of Ancient Buildings, 1877.

WEBB, THOMAS EBENEZER (1821–1903), lawyer; classical scholar of Trinity College, Dublin; LL.D., 1857; professor of moral philosophy, 1857–67; fellow, 1863–71; called to Irish bar, 1861; Q.C., 1874; regius professor of laws at Trinity College, 1867–87; public orator, 1879–87; county court judge for Donegal, 1887–1903; attacked Gladstone's scheme of home rule; translated Goethe's 'Faust' into verse, 1880; published philosophic works and 'The Mystery of William Shakespeare,' 1902.

WEBBER, CHARLES EDMUND (1838–1904), major-general, royal engineers; joined royal engineers, 1855; served in Indian Mutiny, taking part in battle of Jhansi and capture of Gwalior; assistant instructor in military surveying at Woolwich, 1861–6; attached to Prussian army in seven weeks war, 1866; commanded company which assisted in constructing and organizing telegraph service of post office, 1869–71; founded Society of Telegraph Engineers, 1871; president, 1882; assistant adjutant in Zulu war, 1879; in charge of telegraphs in Egyptian campaign, 1882; present at Tel-el-Kebir; C.B., 1882; served in Nile expedition, 1884–5; on retirement as major-general (1885) was engaged in electrical pursuits.

WEBSTER, RICHARD EVERARD, VISCOUNT ALVERSTONE (1842–1915), judge; son of Thomas Webster, Q.C. [q. v.]; called to bar (Lincoln's Inn), 1868; Q.C., 1878; conservative M.P., Launceston, 1885, Isle of Wight, 1886; attorney-general, 1885–6–92, 1895–1900; baronet, 1899; master of the Rolls, P.C., and baron, 1900; lord chief justice, 1900–13; viscount, 1913.

WEBSTER, WENTWORTH (1829–1907), Basque scholar and folk-lorist; B.A., Lincoln College, Oxford, 1852; M.A., 1855; ordained, 1854; Anglican chaplain at St. Jean de Luz, 1869–81; settled at Sare, 1881, where he died; received civil list pension, 1894; studied and wrote on Basque language and literature; published 'Basque Legends,' 1878, and 'Spain,' 1882.

WEIR, HARRISON WILLIAM (1824–1906), animal painter and author; apprentice to George Baxter, the colour printer, 1837–44; employed as wood-engraver on 'Illustrated London News' from its foundation, 1842; made special study of birds and animals; occasionally exhibited at British Institution and Royal Academy; member of New Water-colour Society, 1849; illustrated the Rev. J. G. Wood's 'Illustrated Natural History,' 1853; compiled 'The Poetry of Nature,' 1867; wrote and illustrated 'Every Day in the Country,' 1883, and 'Our Cats and all about them,' 1889; was an experienced poultry breeder, practical horticulturist, and designer; received civil list pension, 1891.

WELBY, REGINALD EARLE, first BARON WELBY, of Allington (1832–1915); B.A., Trinity College, Cambridge; entered Treasury, 1856; assistant financial secretary of Treasury, 1880; permanent secretary, 1885–94; created baron, 1894; chairman of London County Council, 1900; enthusiastic free trader and exponent of rigid economy in public service.

WELDON, WALTER FRANK RAPHAEL (1860–1906), zoologist; son of Walter Weldon [q. v.]; abandoned medical studies for zoology; B.A., St. John's College, Cambridge (first class in natural science), 1881; fellow, 1884; demonstrator in zoology, 1882–4; university lecturer in invertebrate morphology, 1884–91; made statistical study of variation of common shrimp, from 1889 to 1891, thus founding study of 'biometrics'; F.R.S., 1890; Jodrell professor of zoology at University College, London, 1891–9; secretary to committee of Royal Society for statistical inquiries into measurements of plants and animals; prepared for Royal Society report on death-rate due to selective destruction of shore crabs, 1894; Linacre professor of comparative anatomy, Oxford, 1899–1906; co-editor of 'Biometrika,' 1901–6; published 'A Note on the Offspring of Thoroughbred Chestnut Mares,' 1906; Weldon memorial prize for biometric research founded at Oxford, 1907.

WELLESLEY, SIR GEORGE GREVILLE (1814–1901), admiral; entered navy, 1828; took part in operations on coast of Syria, 1840; commanded in Pacific, 1849–53; commanded squadron at Sveaborg, 1855; C.B., 1856; in charge of Indian navy, 1857–62;

admiral superintendent at Portsmouth, 1865–9; commander-in-chief on North America station, 1869–70, and 1873–5; admiral, 1875; first sea lord at the admiralty, 1877–9; K.C.B., 1880; G.C.B., 1887.

WELLS, HENRY TANWORTH (1828–1903), portrait painter in oils and miniature; exhibited at Royal Academy miniatures, 1846–60, and large oil portraits and groups from 1861; A.R.A., 1866; R.A., 1870; deputy-president, 1895; best-known group is 'The Queen at the Royal Courts of Justice,' 1887; portraits include those of Duke of Devonshire, 1872, Lord Selborne, 1874, Sir Redvers Buller, 1889, Sir Lowthian Bell, 1895; most popular work was 'Victoria Regina,' painting of Queen Victoria, as princess, receiving news of her accession, 1880 (now in National Gallery); limner to Grillion's Club from 1870.

WEMYSS-CHARTERIS-DOUGLAS, FRANCIS, tenth EARL OF WEMYSS AND MARCH (1818–1914), politician; B.A., Christ Church, Oxford; conservative M.P., East Gloucestershire, 1841–6, Haddingtonshire, 1847–83; with Edward Horsman [q. v.], Robert Lowe [q. v.], and others formed 'cave of Adullam' against Reform Bill of 1866; opposed to socialism; enthusiastic supporter of Volunteer movement; instrumental in inaugurating National Rifle Association, 1859; succeeded father, 1883.

WERNHER, SIR JULIUS CHARLES, first baronet (1850–1912), financier and philanthropist; born at Darmstadt; educated at Frankfort; engaged by Porges, diamond merchant of Paris and London, to assist partner in diamond buying in South Africa, 1870; settled at camp which afterwards became Kimberley, 1871; partner in firm and sole representative at fields, 1873; through skill and honesty made firm (known as French Company) one of the most important diamond producing companies; settled in London, 1884; directed from London firm's gold mining in Rand from 1887; assisted Alfred Beit [q.v.] and Cecil Rhodes [q. v.] to amalgamate chief diamond mines of Kimberley as De Beers Consolidated Mines, 1888; firm of Wernher, Beit & Co. created, 1890; naturalized, 1898; baronet, 1905; gave munificently to charities and education.

WEST, SIR ALGERNON EDWARD (1832–1921), chairman of the Board of Inland Revenue, 1881–92; served in Admiralty and India Office, 1852–66; private secretary to W. E. Gladstone, 1868–72; commissioner of inland revenue, 1872–92; K.C.B., 1886; P.C., 1894.

WEST, EDWARD WILLIAM (1824–1905), Oriental scholar; studied engineering at King's College, London, 1839–42; superintended cotton presses in Bombay, 1844–50; made special study of Parsi religion; published copies of Buddhist records of Kanheri and other caves, 1861; won reputation by Iranian researches; at Munich (1867–73) published translation of the Pahlavi texts of Zoroastrianism; hon. Ph.D. Munich, 1871; revisited India (1874–6) to procure Pahlavi manuscripts; soon settled in England and translated Pahlavi texts for Max Müller's 'Sacred Books of the East'; member of Royal Asiatic Society, 1884–1901; gold medallist, 1901; collaborated with Prof. Martin Haug in 'Book of Ardā-Virāf, Pahlavi and English,' 1872, and wrote on 'Pahlavi Literature,' 1897.

WEST, LIONEL SACKVILLE-, second BARON SACKVILLE (1827–1908), diplomatist. [See SACKVILLE-WEST.]

WEST, SIR RAYMOND (1832–1912), Indian civil servant, judge, and jurist; entered East India Company's service, 1855; joined judicial department, 1860; registrar of high court, 1863; judge of Bombay high court, 1873–86; member of executive council of governor of Bombay, 1886–92; K.C.I.E., 1886; published annotated edition of Bombay code (1867–8) and, in collaboration, important 'Digest of Hindu Law' (1867–9).

WESTALL, WILLIAM (BURY) (1834–1903), novelist and journalist; engaged in journalism mainly on the Continent from 1870; at Geneva met Prince Kropotkin and Stepniak, and translated Stepniak's 'Russia under the Czars'; his many novels include 'Sons of Belial,' 1895, and 'Her Two Millions,' 1897.

WESTCOTT, BROOKE FOSS (1825–1901), bishop of Durham; educated at King Edward VI's School, Birmingham, 1837–44, and Trinity College, Cambridge, 1844–9; won Battie university scholarship, 1846, and several university prizes for classics; B.A. (24th wrangler), 1848; bracketed senior classic, 1849; fellow, 1849; hon. fellow, 1890; had as pupils at Cambridge J. B. Lightfoot [q.v.], E. W. Benson [q. v.], and F. J. A. Hort [q. v.]; obtained Norrisian prize for theological essay, 1850;

ordained, 1851; master at Harrow, 1852–69; while there published 'The Canon of the New Testament,' 1855, 'Characteristics of the Gospel Miracles,' 1859, 'Introduction to the Study of the Gospels,' 1860, 'The Bible in the Church,' 1864, and 'The Gospel of the Resurrection,' 1866; residentiary canon of Peterborough, 1869–83; regius professor of divinity at Cambridge, 1870–90; after abolition of tests in 1871, he published 'Religious Office of the Universities' (sermons and papers, 1873); improved academic arrangements for the theological lectures; framed fresh regulations for B.D. and D.D. degrees, 1871; an influential teacher; lectured on early church history and on Christian doctrine; founded Cambridge clergy training school (now called Westcott House); advocated university extension; canon of Westminster, 1883–90; member of New Testament revision company, 1870–81; published after 28 years' labour with F. J. A. Hort, his epoch-making critical text of the New Testament in Greek, 2 vols. 1881; published valuable commentaries on St. John's Gospel, 1882, St. John's Epistles, 1883, and Epistle to the Hebrews, 1889; wrote much on Origen from 1877 to 1889; collected his sermons in 'Christus Consummator,' 1886, and 'Social Aspects of Christianity,' 1887; fellow of King's College, Cambridge, 1882; hon. fellow, 1890; hon. D.C.L. Oxford, 1881; hon. D.D. Edinburgh, 1884, and Dublin, 1888; bishop of Durham, 1890–1901; hon. D.D. Durham, 1890; frequently brought together employers of labour and trade union officials; took influential part in settling Durham coal strike, 1892; helped to secure industrial boards of conciliation in the county; first church dignitary to address Northumberland Miners' Gala, 1894; fostered intimate relations with the younger clergy of diocese; cherished a lifelong interest in foreign missions; first president of Christian Social Union, 1889; advocate of peace and international arbitration; published, during his episcopate, 'Religious Thought in the West,' 1891 (early essays reprinted), 'The Gospel of Life,' 1892 (Cambridge lectures); collected sermons and addresses in 'The Incarnation and Common Life,' 1893, 'Christian Aspects of Life,' 1897, 'Lessons from Work,' 1901; a commentary on 'Ephesians' was published posthumously; his theological position, at which he arrived independently, strongly resembled that of F. D. Maurice; portrait by Sir W. B. Richmond (1889) is in Fitzwilliam Museum, Cambridge; 'Life and Letters' by son, Arthur Westcott, 2 vols. with bibliography, 1903.

WESTLAKE, JOHN (1828–1913), jurist; B.A., Trinity College, Cambridge; called to bar (Lincoln's Inn), 1854; Q.C., 1874; Whewell professor of international law, Cambridge, 1888–1908; author of works on private and public international law.

WESTLAND, SIR JAMES (1842–1903), Anglo-Indian financier; joined Indian civil service, 1861; assistant magistrate in Bengal districts, 1862–9; under-secretary of financial department of government of India, 1870; officiating accountant-general of Bengal, 1873, and of Central Provinces, 1873–6; accountant and comptroller-general, 1878; head of Egyptian accounts department, March–June 1885; secretary of Indian finance department from 1886; temporary finance member of government, Aug. 1887–Nov. 1888; C.S.I., 1888; K.C.S.I., 1895; chief commissioner of Assam, July–Oct. 1889; finance member of Viceroy's Council, 1893–9; finally established gold standard and raised rupee to fixed value of 1s. 4d.; member of India council in London, 1899.

WESTON, AGNES ELIZABETH (1840–1918), organizer of 'Sailors' Rests'; brought up at Bath; opened correspondence with soldiers and later (1868) with sailors; issued printed monthly letter for distribution to ships' companies from 1871; began work in Devonport for Royal Naval Temperance Society, 1873; opened first 'Sailors' Rest' there, 1876; later opened one at Portsmouth; D.B.E., 1918.

WEYMOUTH, RICHARD FRANCIS (1822–1902), philologist; educated at University College, London; fellow, 1869; B.A. London, 1846; M.A., 1849; first Litt.D. of London University, 1868; head master of Mill Hill School, 1869–86; joined Philological Society, 1851; published 'Early English Pronunciation,' 1874, 'The Resultant Greek Testament,' 1886, and 'The New Testament in Modern Speech,' 1903; awarded civil list pension, 1891.

WHARTON, SIR WILLIAM JAMES LLOYD (1843–1905), hydrographer of the navy; entered navy, 1857; served in surveying vessel on North America station, 1865–9; made surveys in Mediterranean, examining undercurrents in Bosphorus, 1872–6; published 'Hydrographical Surveying,' 1882; hydrographer to the navy, 1884–1904; rear-admiral, 1895; C.B., 1895; K.C.B., 1897; president of geographical section of British Association in Capetown, 1905; F.R.S., F.R.A.S., and F.R.G.S.; died of fever at Capetown.

WHEELHOUSE, CLAUDIUS GALEN (1826–1909), surgeon; educated at Leeds school of medicine; M.R.C.S., 1849; L.S.A., 1850; F.R.C.S., 1864; surgeon to public dispensary, Leeds, from 1851; lecturer at medical school there; hon. D.Sc. Leeds, 1904; president of council of British Medical Association, 1881–4; advocated 'Wheelhouse' external urethrotomy for impermeable strictures, 1876.

WHISTLER, JAMES ABBOTT McNEILL (1834–1903), painter; born at Lowell, Massachusetts; educated at Military Academy, West Point, 1851–4; engaged on United States geodetic survey; studied art at Paris under Gleyre, 1855–9; published etchings 'The French Set,' 1858; his 'At the Piano,' rejected by Salon, 1859, was accepted by Royal Academy, 1860; he came to London (1859) and worked at etching with his brother-in-law, Francis Haden [q. v.]; for first year was chiefly occupied in etchings of Thames scenery; visited Brittany, 1861; settled at Chelsea, 1863; influenced by Japanese art in his 'Lange Leizen,' and more especially in 'The Little White Girl,' 1863; visited Germany, 1865, and Chili, 1866; chief pictures between 1866 and 1872, when he ceased to exhibit paintings at the Academy, include 'Portrait of my Mother' (in Luxembourg, Paris), his 'Nocturnes,' and portraits of Carlyle (at Glasgow) and Miss Alexander; he sent to first exhibition of Grosvenor Gallery eight pictures, including 'The Falling Rocket, a Nocturne in Black and Gold,' 1877; brought libel action against Ruskin for condemning this picture, 1878; was awarded a farthing damages and became bankrupt, 1879; executed profitable etchings and pastels in Venice, 1879–80; settled at 13 Tite Street, Chelsea, 1881, and painted there the best pictures of his later years, including 'The Blue Girl' and the 'Yellow Buskin'; toured in Belgium and Holland, 1885, and in Touraine and in Holland, 1888–89; published 'The Gentle Art of Making Enemies,' 1890; moved to Paris, 1892; defendant in action at Paris brought by Sir William Eden, 1895; published report of the litigation in 'The Baronet and the Butterfly,' 1899; president of Society of British Artists, 1886–8, and of International Society of Sculptors, Painters, and Engravers from 1898 till death; recipient of many foreign honours; hon. LL.D. Glasgow; exerted immense influence on contemporary art; 'Life' by E. R. and J. Pennell, 2 vols. 1908.

WHITE, SIR GEORGE STUART (1835–1912), field-marshal; born in co. Antrim; entered army from Sandhurst, 1853; served in Indian Mutiny; V.C. for gallantry in Afghan war (1879), 1880; C.B., 1880; took leading part in ending Burmese war, 1885–7; K.C.B., 1886; major-general, 1889; in command at Quetta and leader of Zhob Valley expedition, 1889; G.C.I.E. for pacification of Baluchistan, 1893; commander-in-chief, India, 1893–7; greatly developed 'forward' policy which produced succession of frontier campaigns; G.C.B., 1897; quartermaster-general at War Office, 1897; in command in Natal during South African war, 1899–1901; defended Ladysmith, 2 November 1899–28 February 1900; governor of Gibraltar, 1900–5; field-marshal, 1903; O.M., 1905.

WHITE, JOHN CAMPBELL, BARON OVERTOUN (1843–1908), Scottish churchman and philanthropist; M.A. Glasgow University, 1864; joined father's chemical firm at Shawfield, 1867; generous benefactor to United Free Church after the crisis of 1904, and to United Free Church mission in Livingstonia; supported liberal party in Scotland; raised to peerage, 1893.

WHITE, WILLIAM HALE (1831–1913), novelist (under the pseudonym of MARK RUTHERFORD), philosophical writer, literary critic, and civil servant; entered civil service, 1854; assistant director of contracts at Admiralty, 1879–91; works include 'The Autobiography of Mark Rutherford' (1881) and 'Mark Rutherford's Deliverance' (1885), his best-known novels, three series of 'Pages from a Journal' (1900, 1910, 1915), translations of Spinoza, and books on Wordsworth and Bunyan.

WHITE, SIR WILLIAM HENRY (1845–1913), naval architect; trained at royal school of naval architecture, South Kensington; joined Admiralty staff as professional secretary to (Sir) E. J. Reed [q. v.], chief constructor of navy, 1867; secretary of council of naval construction,

1872; joined firm of Armstrong & Co., 1883–5; director of naval construction at Admiralty, 1885–1902; designs for battleships include those of 'Royal Sovereign' class (1889) and 'King Edward VII' class (1902); designs for cruisers include 'Cressy' and 'Drake' classes and twenty 'protected' cruisers; assistant controller of navy, 1885; K.C.B., 1895; author of 'Manual of Naval Architecture' (1877) and many papers on the same subject.

WHITEHEAD, ROBERT (1823–1905), inventor; apprenticed as engineer at Manchester, 1837–44; joined uncle in Marseilles, 1844; set up in business for himself at Milan, 1847; employed at Trieste, 1848–56; started engineering works at Fiume, 1856; designed engines for several Austrian warships; invented Whitehead torpedo, 1866; solely constructed torpedoes and their accessories from 1872; established branch at Portland, 1890; invented 'servo-motor' to regulate steering, and continually increased the speed and improved the precision of torpedoes; received many foreign decorations.

WHITELEY, WILLIAM (1831–1907), 'universal provider'; draper's assistant at Wakefield, 1848–52, and in London, 1852–63; opened small draper's shop in Westbourne Grove, 1863; by 1876 he had fifteen shops and 2,000 employees, and provided all kinds of goods; business premises six times destroyed by fire, 1882–7; he converted firm into limited company, 1899; was shot dead by Horace George Rayner, 24 Jan. 1907; left a million pounds for Whiteley homes for the aged poor, constructed at Burr Hill, Surrey.

WHITEWAY, SIR WILLIAM VALLANCE (1828–1908), premier of Newfoundland; left Totnes for Newfoundland, 1843; called to Newfoundland bar, 1852; Q.C., 1862; speaker of house of assembly, 1865–9; solicitor-general, 1873–8; premier and attorney-general, 1878–85, and again, 1889–94; counsel for Newfoundland at Halifax fisheries commission, 1877; K.C.M.G., 1880; unseated for corrupt practices, 1894; again premier, 1895–7; attended diamond jubilee and Colonial Conference in London, and was made P.C. and D.C.L. Oxford, 1897; carried first railway bill for Newfoundland, 1880; negotiated earlier contracts with Robert G. Reid [q. v.]; died at St. John's, Newfoundland.

WHITMAN, ALFRED CHARLES (1860–1910), writer on engravings; attendant at prints department of British Museum, 1885–1903; departmental clerk, 1903–10; chief works on mezzotint engraving were monographs on Samuel Cousins, 1904, and Charles Turner, 1907.

WHITMORE, SIR GEORGE STODDART (1830–1903), major-general; born at Malta; joined Cape mounted rifles, 1847; distinguished in Kaffir wars, 1847 and 1851–3, and in Crimea; in command of Hawke's Bay militia, New Zealand, in last Maori war, 1866–9, of which he published an account, 1902; member of legislative council in New Zealand from 1863; colonial secretary and defence minister, 1877–9; commandant of the colonial forces and major-general, 1874; C.M.G., 1869; K.C.M.G., 1882; died at Hawke's Bay.

WHITWORTH, WILLIAM ALLEN (1840–1905), mathematical and religious writer; B.A., St. John's College, Cambridge (16th wrangler), 1862; M.A., 1865; fellow, 1867–82; co-edited 'The Messenger of Mathematics' till 1880; held livings in Liverpool and London; Hulsean lecturer at Cambridge, 1903–4; prebendary of St. Paul's, 1900; published doctrinal works and sermons; mathematical writings include 'Trilinear Co-ordinates,' 1866, and 'Choice and Chance,' 1867.

WHYMPER, EDWARD (1840–1911), wood engraver and Alpinist; second son of Josiah Wood Whymper [q. v.]; joined father's wood engraving business; illustrated many books; prepared water-colour sketches for 'Peaks, Passes and Glaciers,' 2nd ser. 1862; made the first ascent of Pointe des Écrins, Dauphiné, of several peaks of Mont Blanc chain, 1864, and Aiguille Verte, 1865; his first successful ascent of the Matterhorn 1865; followed by a disastrous descent, three of his party being killed, July 1865; he related experiences in 'Scrambles in the Alps,' 1871; visited interior of Greenland, 1867, and 1872; vice-president of Alpine Club, 1872–4; studied in the Andes of Ecuador the effect of atmosphere of high altitudes on human beings, 1888; there made geological and geographical researches of mountain systems, which he embodied in 'Travels among the Great Andes of the Equator,' 1892; royal medallist of Royal Geographical Society, 1892; devised 'Whymper' tent for mountaineering expeditions; compiled handbooks to Chamonix, 1896, and Zermatt, 1897; died at Chamonix.

WHYMPER, JOSIAH WOOD (1813–1903), wood engraver; taught himself wood engraving, and obtained first success by etching of New London Bridge, 1831; did much work for John Murray, the S.P.C.K., and R.T.S.; had as pupils Frederick Walker and Charles Keene; friend of Sir John Gilbert; member of New Water-colour Society, 1854.

WHYTE, ALEXANDER (1836–1921), divine; educated at King's College, Aberdeen, and New College, Edinburgh; minister of St. George's Free church, Edinburgh, 1870–1916; moderator of General Assembly, 1898; principal of New College, Edinburgh, 1909–18.

WICKHAM, EDWARD CHARLES (1834–1910), dean of Lincoln; educated at Winchester; B.A., New College, Oxford, 1857; M.A., 1859; D.D., 1894; tutor, 1858–73; initiated system of intercollegiate lectures; head master of Wellington College, 1873–93; edited 'Horace,' vol. i. 1874, vol. ii. 1893; dean of Lincoln, 1894–1910; married Agnes, daughter of W. E. Gladstone, 1873; died at Sierre, Switzerland; published 'The Prayer-Book,' 1895, and 'Horace for English Readers,' 1903; memoir by Lonsdale Ragg, 1911.

WIGGINS, JOSEPH (1832–1905), explorer of the sea route to Siberia; apprenticed to uncle, a shipowner at Sunderland, 1846; board of trade examiner in navigation there, 1868; attempted to establish trade route by sea between Western Europe and Asiatic Russia; sailed from Dundee and rounded White Island, Aug. 1874; was accompanied by Henry Seebohm [q. v.] to Siberia, 1876; successfully brought back from the Ob a cargo of wheat, 1878; reached Yeniseisk, 1887–8; in larger vessel 'Orestes' he reached mouth of Yenisei, delivering there a cargo of rails, 1893; was shipwrecked near Yugor Strait, 1893; awarded Murchison medal of Royal Geographical Society, 1894; 'Life' by H. Johnson, 1907.

WIGHAM, JOHN RICHARDSON (1829–1906), inventor; apprentice in, and subsequently owner of, brother-in-law's hardware business 'Joshua Edmundson & Co.,' Dublin; made experiments in gas-lighting, and designed several private and public gasworks; president of Dublin Chamber of Commerce, 1894–6; invented important applications of gas to lighthouse illumination; invented 'composite' burner, 1868, and first group-flashing arrangement in lighthouses, 1871; installed at Galley Head a quadriform light, 1878; his system was supported by John Tyndall [q.v.] in controversy with Joseph Chamberlain [q. v.] and Sir James N. Douglass [q. v.]; as member of Society of Friends he refused knighthood, 1887.

WIGRAM, WOOLMORE (1831–1907), campanologist; B.A., Trinity College, Cambridge, 1854; M.A., 1858; hon. canon of St. Albans, 1886; published 'Change-ringing Disentangled,' 1880; member of Alpine Club, 1858–68; made first successful ascent of La Dent Blanche, July 1862.

WILBERFORCE, ERNEST ROLAND (1840–1907), bishop successively of Newcastle and Chichester; son of Samuel Wilberforce [q. v.]; educated at Harrow and Exeter College, Oxford; B.A., 1864; M.A., 1867; D.D., 1882; vicar of Seaforth, Liverpool, 1873–8; canon of Winchester, 1878–82; first bishop of Newcastle, 1882–95; inaugurated fund for diocesan purposes; bishop of Chichester, 1895–1907; dealt successfully with ritualistic practices in his diocese; ardent temperance advocate; chairman of Church of England Temperance Society, 1896; visited South Africa, 1904; memoir by J. B. Atlay, 1912.

WILDING, ANTHONY FREDERICK (1883–1915), lawn-tennis player; born in New Zealand; B.A., Trinity College, Cambridge; called to bar, 1906; All England singles champion at Wimbledon, 1910–14; four times winner of championship doubles; killed in Artois during European war.

WILKINS, AUGUSTUS SAMUEL (1843–1905), classical scholar; B.A., St. John's College, Cambridge (fifth classic), and M.A. London, 1868; Litt.D., 1885; president of Union Society, 1868; won university prize for English essay; disqualified as nonconformist for fellowship; Latin lecturer, 1868, and professor, 1869–1903, at Owens College, Manchester; edited Cicero's rhetorical works, including 'De Oratore,' lib. i–iii. 1879–92, and Horace's 'Epistles,' 1885; wrote primers of 'Roman Antiquities,' 1877, and 'Roman Literature,' 1890; received hon. degrees from St. Andrews and Dublin.

WILKINS, WILLIAM HENRY (1860–1905), biographer; B.A., Clare College, 1887; M.A., 1899; published 'The Alien Invasion,' 1892, and four novels, 1892–4; dis-

covered at Lund, in Sweden, 1897, and issued the unpublished correspondence of Queen Sophia Dorothea, consort of George I, and her lover Count Philip Königsmarck, 2 vols. 1900; wrote life of Isabel Lady Burton, 1897, Queen Caroline, 1901, Mrs. Fitzherbert and George IV, 1905, and other biographical works.

WILKINSON, GEORGE HOWARD (1833–1907), successively bishop of Truro and of St. Andrews; B.A., Oriel College, Oxford, 1854; M.A., 1859; D.D., 1883; vicar of Bishop Auckland, 1863–7; incumbent of St. Peter's, Eaton Square, 1870–83; bishop of Truro, 1883–91: after visit to South Africa for health was elected bishop of St. Andrews, 1893; primus of Scottish Episcopal Church, 1904; published devotional works; memoir by A. J. Mason, 1909.

WILKS, SIR SAMUEL, baronet (1824–1911), physician; student at Guy's Hospital, 1842; M.R.C.S., 1847; M.B., 1848; M.D., 1850; F.R.C.P., 1856; president, 1896–9; Harveian orator, 1879; physician of Guy's Hospital, 1866–85; lecturer on pathology and medicine there; published 'Lectures on Pathological Anatomy,' 1859; edited Guy's Hospital 'Reports,' 1854–65; also published 'Lectures on Diseases of the Chest,' 1874, and of the nervous system, 1878; baronet, 1897.

WILL, JOHN SHIRESS (1840–1910), legal writer; called to bar, 1864; Q.C., 1883; liberal M.P. for Montrose Burghs, 1885–96; county court judge at Liverpool, 1906; wrote authoritative works on law relating to gas and electric lighting.

WILLES, SIR GEORGE OMMANNEY (1823–1901), admiral; joined navy, 1838; present at bombardments of Odessa and Sevastopol, 1854; commanded rocket boats in attack on Peiho forts, 1860; C.B., 1861; chief of staff at admiralty, 1870–3; A.D.C. to Queen Victoria, 1870–4; admiral superintendent at Devonport, 1876–9; commander-in-chief in China, 1881–4; K.C.B., 1884; admiral, 1885; commander-in-chief at Portsmouth, 1885–8; G.C.B., 1892.

WILLETT, WILLIAM (1856–1915), builder, and the originator of 'daylight saving'; with father created reputation for Willett-built houses; advocated introduction of first Daylight Saving Bill, 1908; Bill passed, 1916; Summer Time Act passed, 1925.

WILLIAMS, ALFRED (1832–1905), Alpine painter; drew on wood for book illustrations, 1849–56; engaged in maltster's business at Salisbury, 1861–86; member of Alpine Club, 1878; exhibited paintings of Alpine scenery at Alpine Club.

WILLIAMS, CHARLES (1838–1904), war correspondent; first editor of 'Evening Standard' and of 'Evening News,' 1881–4; correspondent for 'Standard' in Franco-German war, 1870, in Armenian campaign, 1877, at Berlin Congress, 1878, in Afghanistan, 1879–80, and in Nile expedition, 1884; war correspondent for 'Daily Chronicle' in Eastern Europe, 1885 and 1897, and at Omdurman and Khartoum, 1898; published independent life of Sir Evelyn Wood, 1892; founder and president (1896–7) of the Press Club.

WILLIAMS, CHARLES HANSON GREVILLE (1829–1910), chemist; consulting and analytical chemist in London, 1852–3; assistant to (Sir) William H. Perkin [q. v.], 1863–8; partner in Star Chemical Works, Brentford, 1868–77, and chemist to Gas Light and Coke Co., London, 1877–1901; discovered cyanine or quinoline-blue; wrote much on chemistry of coal gas, and published 'Chemical Analysis,' 1858; F.R.S., 1862.

WILLIAMS, SIR EDWARD LEADER (1828–1910), engineer; apprenticed to father, who was chief engineer to Severn navigation commission, 1846; resident engineer on Shoreham harbour works, 1849–52; engineer on Admiralty Pier, Dover, 1852–5, and to River Weaver Trust, 1856; established through traffic from river Weaver to Trent and Mersey Canal by means of hydraulic lift for transferring canal boats; became (1882) chief engineer for projected Manchester ship canal, which, 35½ miles long, was opened by Queen Victoria in 1894; knighted, 1894; M.I.C.E., 1860; vice-president, 1906–7.

WILLIAMS, SIR GEORGE (1821–1905), founder of the Young Men's Christian Association; apprenticed to draper at Bridgwater, 1836; entered employ of Messrs. Hitchcock & Rogers, drapers of St. Paul's Churchyard, 1841, subsequently becoming partner; started among employees Mutual Improvement Society, 1842, and established Young Men's Christian Association, 1844; work spread to Continent and colonies; first international conference at Paris, 1855; leased Exeter Hall as headquarters, 1880–1907; new buildings opened in Tottenham Court Road, 1912; president, 1886; knighted, 1894; present at jubilee of World's Alliance of Y.M.C.A.'s at Paris, 1905.

WILLIAMS, HUGH (1843–1911), ecclesiastical historian; student from 1864 and tutor, 1867–9, at Calvinistic Methodist College, Bala; B.A. London, 1870; M.A., 1871; professor of Greek and mathematics at Bala, 1873–91; professor of church history, 1891–1911; hon. D.D. Glasgow, 1904; edited 'Gildas' with English translation and notes, 2 pts. 1899–1901; his 'Christianity in Early Britain' (a careful piece of research) appeared in 1912; published biblical commentaries in Welsh.

WILLIAMS, JOHN CARVELL (1821–1907), nonconformist politician; secretary to Society for Liberation of Religion from State Control, 1847–77; vice-president, 1903; founded the 'Liberator,' a monthly periodical, 1853; chairman of Congregational Union, 1900; liberal M.P. for South Nottinghamshire, 1885–6, and for Mansfield, 1892–1900; promoted Burials Act of 1880, and Marriage Acts of 1886 and 1898.

WILLIAMS, ROWLAND, 'HWFA MÔN' (1823–1905), archdruid of Wales; congregational minister in London and Wales; distinguished himself at National Eisteddfods at Carnarvon, 1862, Mold, 1873, and at Birkenhead, 1878; chief bardic adjudicator from 1875 to 1892; archdruid of the bardic Gorsedd from 1894; published collected works, 1883 and 1903; memorial volume edited by W. J. Parry, 1907.

WILLIAMS, SIR ROWLAND BOWDLER VAUGHAN (1838–1916), judge; son of Sir Edward Vaughan Williams [q. v.]; B.A., Christ Church, Oxford; called to bar (Lincoln's Inn), 1864; Q.C., 1889; judge of Queen's bench division, 1890; assigned bankruptcy jurisdiction of High Court, 1891; lord justice of appeal, 1897–1914; P.C., 1897; published 'The Law and Practice of Bankruptcy' (1870, 13th edit., 1925).

WILLIAMS, WATKIN HEZEKIAH, 'WATCYN WYN' (1844–1905), Welsh poet; conducted Hope Academy at Amanford, 1880–1905; won bardic chair at Aberdare, 1885, and crown at World's Fair Eisteddfod at Chicago, 1893; published in Welsh lyrical and humorous poems and a survey of Welsh literature, 1900; autobiography edited by J. Jenkins, 1907.

WILLIAMSON, ALEXANDER WILLIAM (1824–1904), chemist; educated at Dijon and Heidelberg; studied chemistry at Giessen under Liebig (Ph.D., 1846), and mathematics at Paris under Comte, 1846–9; professor of practical chemistry at University College, London, 1849–87; trained at the college many Japanese youths from 1863 onwards; from 1849 he made researches into theory of etherification, which resulted in the theory of the constitution of salts and the doctrine of valency; his papers on the subject were re-issued as an Alembic Club reprint, 1902; he published other papers mainly on gas analysis; president of Chemical Society, 1863–5, 1869–71; president of British Association, 1873; general treasurer, 1874–91; F.R.S., 1855; royal medallist, 1862; F.R.S., Edinburgh, 1883; hon. member of Royal Irish Academy, 1885; received hon. degrees from Dublin, Edinburgh, and Durham, and many foreign academic honours; prominent in introducing science degrees at London University; chief gas examiner to board of trade, 1876–1901; published 'Chemistry for Students,' 1865.

WILLIS, HENRY (1821–1901), organ-builder; articled to John Gray, 1835–42; organist at Islington Chapel-of-Ease, 1860–91; capable player on double-bass; started organ building in London in 1845; rebuilt Gloucester Cathedral organ, 1847; built organs at Great Exhibition, 1851 (now in use in Winchester Cathedral), at St. George's Hall, Liverpool, 1855, at Great Exhibition of 1862, at Royal Albert Hall, 1871, and at St. Paul's Cathedral, 1872; devised important inventions in organ building; extended range of pedal board from G to C; keen yachtsman.

WILLIS WILLIAM (1835–1911), lawyer; B.A. London, 1859; LL.D., 1865; called to bar (Inner Temple), 1861; Q.C., 1877; fervid and voluble advocate; president of baptist conference, 1903; liberal M.P. for Colchester, 1880–5; carried motion for exclusion of bishops from House of Lords, 1884; county court judge, 1897; had wide knowledge of English literature; published several lectures, including 'The Shakespeare-Bacon Controversy,' 1902, and kindred works.

WILLOCK, HENRY DAVIS (1830–1903), Indian civilian; born in Persia; nephew of John Francis Davis

[q. v.]; joined Indian civil service, 1852; commanded company of volunteers in Mutiny; only civilian to receive the medal with three clasps; after serving various districts as magistrate and collector, and as judge of Benares, he was judge of Azimgarh, 1876–84.

WILLOUGHBY, DIGBY (1845–1901), soldier adventurer; raised 'Willoughby's Horse,' and served in Basuto war, 1880; general commander of Madagascar forces, 1884–5; after first Matabele war helped in administration of Rhodesia, 1893; one of council of defence at Bulawayo in second Matabele war, 1896.

WILLS, WILLIAM HENRY, BARON WINTERSTOKE (1830–1911), benefactor to Bristol; after education at Mill Hill School, joined family tobacco business at Bristol; partner, 1858; chairman of directors on its conversion into limited company; chairman of Imperial Tobacco Company, 1901–11; liberal M.P. for Coventry, 1880–5, and for East Bristol, 1895–1900; baronet, 1893; at Bristol he erected art gallery, branch library, and statue of Burke; made large donations to Bristol University; benefactor to Mansfield College, Oxford, and Mill Hill School; raised to peerage, 1906; high sheriff of Somerset, 1905–6.

WILSON, ARTHUR (1836–1909), shipowner; generous benefactor to Hull; host of Edward VII (while Prince of Wales) at Tranby Croft when allegations were made against a guest of cheating at baccarat, Sept. 1890.

WILSON, SIR ARTHUR KNYVET, third baronet (1842–1921), admiral of the fleet; entered navy, 1855; V.C. for gallantry at second battle of El Teb, 1884; commanded torpedo training ship, 'Vernon', at Portsmouth, 1889; rear-admiral, 1895; controller of navy and third sea lord, 1897; vice-admiral and commander of Channel squadron, 1901; elaborated successful tactical system; admiral of fleet, 1907; first sea lord of admiralty, 1910–12; O.M., 1912; succeeded brother, 1919.

WILSON, CHARLES HENRY, first BARON NUNBURNHOLME (1833–1907), shipowner and politician; joined with brother Arthur [q. v.] father's shipowning firm at Hull; joint manager, 1867; extended Baltic service, and inaugurated new services from 1870; subsequently absorbed other shipping lines; liberal M.P. for Hull, 1874–85, and for West Hull, 1885–1905; ardent free trader; raised to peerage, 1905.

WILSON, SIR CHARLES RIVERS (1831–1916), civil servant and financier; B.A., Balliol College, Oxford; entered Treasury, 1856; comptroller-general of National Debt Office, 1874–94; served on council of Suez Canal Company, 1875–96; vice-president of Anglo-French commission on revenue and expenditure of Egyptian khedive, Ismail, 1878; finance minister in Nubar Pasha's ministry under Khedive Ismail, 1878; dismissed, 1879; K.C.M.G., 1880; president of Grand Trunk Railway of Canada, 1895–1909.

WILSON, CHARLES ROBERT (1863–1904), historian of British India; B.A., Wadham College, Oxford, 1887; D.Litt. 1902; officer in charge of Indian government records, 1900; published 'The Early Annals of the English in Bengal,' 3 pts. 1895–1911.

WILSON, SIR CHARLES WILLIAM (1836–1905), major-general R.E.; educated at Cheltenham and Bonn University; joined royal engineers, 1855; made survey of Jerusalem, 1864–5, which led to formation of Palestine Exploration Fund, 1865; chairman, 1901; with E. H. Palmer [q. v.] surveyed Sinaitic peninsula, 1868–9; first director of topographical department of war office, 1870; F.R.S., 1874; C.B., 1877; head of ordnance survey in Ireland between 1876 and 1886; British military consul-general in Anatolia, Asia Minor, 1879–82; K.C.M.G., 1881; military attaché to British agency in Egypt, 1882–3; hon. D.C.L. Oxford, 1883; chief of intelligence department in Nile expedition, Sept. 1884; K.C.B., 1885; hon. LL.D. Edinburgh, 1886; director-general of the ordnance survey of the United Kingdom, 1886–93; director-general of military education at war office, 1892–8; revisited Palestine, 1899 and 1903; wrote 'Life of Clive,' 1890, and handbooks for Asia Minor, 1892, and Constantinople, 1895.

WILSON, EDWARD ADRIAN (1872–1912), naturalist and Antarctic explorer; M.B., Cambridge; junior surgeon to National Antarctic expedition under Commander R. F. Scott [q. v.], 1901–4; joined new Antarctic expedition under Scott as chief of scientific staff, 1910; member of party which reached South Pole, January 1912; perished with rest on return journey.

WILSON, GEORGE FERGUSSON (1822–1902), inventor; entered father's candlemaking business,

'E. Price & Son,' 1840; patented process of utilizing cheap malodorous fats for candle making, 1842; sold business for 250,000*l*., 1847; formed Price's Patent Candle Company, 1847; introduced 'New Patent Night Lights,' 1853; discovered process of manufacturing pure glycerine, 1854; F.R.S., 1855; in later life an enthusiastic gardener at Wisley, Surrey; F.L.S., 1875.

WILSON, HENRY SCHÜTZ (1824–1902), author; followed a commercial career till 1870; member of Alpine Club, 1871–98; works include 'Alpine Ascents and Adventures,' 1878, and 'Studies in History, Legend, and Literature,' 1884.

WILSON, SIR JACOB (1836–1905), agriculturist; studied at Royal Agricultural College, Cirencester, 1854–6; land agent to Earl of Tankerville at Chillingham, 1866; joined Royal Agricultural Society, 1860; hon. director of shows, 1875–92; knighted at Society's fiftieth show at Windsor, 1889; actively urged passing of Animals Acts of 1878 and 1884; chairman of departmental committee of inquiry into pleuro-pneumonia, 1888; agricultural adviser to the Board of Agriculture, 1892–1902; K.C.V.O., 1905.

WILSON, JOHN COOK (1849–1915), philosopher; educated at Derby grammar school and Balliol College, Oxford; won Chancellor's Latin essay prize, 1873; fellow of Oriel College, Oxford, 1874; Wykeham professor of logic at Oxford, 1889–1915; owing to various causes published little; main energies devoted to teaching, whereby he became strongest philosophical influence in Oxford of his generation; first principle of his philosophy may be described as principle that there is no first principle.

WILSON, JOHN DOVE (1833–1908), Scottish legal writer; called to Scottish bar, 1857; sheriff substitute of Aberdeen, 1870–90; issued 'The Practice of the Sheriff Courts of Scotland in Civil Causes,' 1875; hon. LL.D. Aberdeen, 1884; professor of law at Aberdeen, 1891–1901; died at San Remo.

WILSON, WILLIAM EDWARD (1851–1908), astronomer and physicist; set up private observatory at Daramona, 1870; began in 1886 pioneer researches into temperature of the sun, which he published in 1900; F.R.S., 1896; hon. D.S. Dublin, 1901.

WIMSHURST, JAMES (1832–1903), engineer; apprenticed at Thames Ironworks till 1853; surveyor of Lloyd's, 1853; chief of Liverpool Underwriters' Registry, 1865–74; chief shipwright surveyor to Board of Trade, 1874–99; built several electrical influence machines; invented 'Wimshurst duplex machine'; his machines were used for exciting 'Röntgen rays' and for treatment of cancer; F.R.S., 1898; he published works on engineering.

WINDUS, WILLIAM LINDSAY (1822–1907), artist; studied art at Liverpool Academy; associate, 1847; full member, 1848; visited London, 1850; accepted pre-Raphaelite principles; exhibited at Royal Academy in 1856 'Burd Helen,' which was admired by Rossetti and Ruskin; 'Too Late' (1859) was condemned by Ruskin; never exhibited after death of wife in 1862; poetic and imaginative painter; forty-five of his works exhibited at Walker Art Gallery, Liverpool, 1908.

WINTER, SIR JAMES SPEARMAN (1845–1911), premier of Newfoundland; called to Newfoundland bar, 1867; Q.C., 1880; speaker of House of Assembly, 1877–8; solicitor-general, 1882–5; attorney-general, 1885–9; judge of Supreme Court, 1893–6; premier, 1897–1900; represented Newfoundland at Fisheries Conference at Washington, 1887–8; K.C.M.G., 1888; died at Toronto.

WINTER, JOHN STRANGE (pseudonym) (1856–1911), novelist. [See STANNARD, HENRIETTA ELIZA VAUGHAN.]

WINTERSTOKE, BARON (1830–1911), benefactor to Bristol. [See WILLS, WILLIAM HENRY.]

WINTON, SIR FRANCIS WALTER DE (1835–1901), major-general and South African administrator. [See DE WINTON.]

WITTEWRONGE, SIR CHARLES BENNET LAWES- (1843–1911), sculptor and athlete. [See LAWES (afterwards LAWES-WITTEWRONGE).]

WODEHOUSE, JOHN, first EARL OF KIMBERLEY (1826–1902), statesman; educated at Eton and Christ Church, Oxford; B.A., 1847; succeeded grandfather as Baron Wodehouse, 1846; under-secretary of state for foreign affairs under Lords Aberdeen and Palmerston, 1852–6 and 1859–61; British minister at St. Petersburg, 1856–8; was sent on special mission to settle Schleswig-Holstein dispute, 1863; lord-lieutenant of Ireland, 1864–6; dealt resolutely with Fenian movement; created Earl

of Kimberley, Norfolk, 1866; joined Gladstone's first cabinet as lord privy seal, 1868–70; colonial secretary, July 1870–4; during his administration Griqualand West was annexed, 27 Oct. 1871, Kimberley was named after him, and responsible government was granted to Cape Colony, 1872; he authorized expedition against Ashantis, 1874; formed Rupert's Land into province of Manitoba, and brought British Columbia into the dominion; introduced licensing bill into the Lords, 1872; again colonial secretary, 1880–2; showed irresolution in dealing with revolt of Boers, 1881; held India office, 1882–5, and Feb.–Aug. 1886; had charge of franchise bill of 1884, and redistribution bill of 1885 in the Lords; K.G., 1885; succeeded Lord Granville as leader of liberal party in House of Lords, 1891; secretary for India and lord president of the council, 1892–4; foreign secretary under Lord Rosebery, 1894–5; made agreement, resented by Germany, with Congo Free State, May 1894; defended military operations in South African war, 1899; hon. D.C.L. Oxford, 1894; chancellor of London University, 1899–1902.

WOLFE-BARRY, SIR JOHN WOLFE (1836–1918), civil engineer; son of Sir Charles Barry [q. v.]; pupil of Sir John Hawkshaw [q. v.]; works include extension to London District and Underground railways; Tower bridge (in collaboration, 1894); numerous docks, including Barry docks and railway, South Wales; from 1867 consulting engineer to many railways and public undertakings; served on many royal commissions; K.C.B.,1897.

WOLFF, SIR HENRY DRUMMOND CHARLES (1830–1908), politician and diplomatist; born at Malta; only child of Joseph Wolff [q. v.]; educated at Rugby; entered foreign office, 1846; attached to British legation at Florence, 1852–3; private secretary to colonial secretary, Sir Edward Bulwer Lytton, 1858; C.M.G., 1859; secretary to high commissioner of Ionian islands, 1859–64; K.C.M.G., 1862; arranged transfer of islands to Greece, 1864; from 1864 to 1870 promoted various financial undertakings; visited Franco-German battlefields, 1870, narrating experiences in 'Morning Post' (reprinted 1892); conservative M.P. for Christchurch, 1874–80; with George Joachim Goschen he went to Egypt on commission of inquiry into Egyptian finance, 1876; G.C.M.G., 1878; British commissioner for organization of Eastern Roumelia, 1878–80; K.C.B., 1879; M.P. for Portsmouth, 1880–5; formed in the House of Commons 'fourth party' with Lord Randolph Churchill, (Sir) John Gorst, and Mr. Arthur Balfour, 1880–5; suggested to Churchill the formation of the 'Primrose League,' 1883; P.C. 1885; was sent on special mission to Constantinople to negotiate with Turkey on the future of Egypt, August 1885; British commissioner to reorganize Egyptian administration, 1885–6; negotiated second convention with Turkey (May 1887) stipulating evacuation of Egypt by British after three years, but the convention, owing to opposition of France and Russia, was not ratified by the Sultan; he served as British envoy in Persia, Dec. 1887–91; helped to establish Imperial Bank of Persia; G.C.B., 1889; was transferred to Bucharest, July 1891, and to Madrid, 1892–1900; published 'Rambling Recollections,' 2 vols. 1908; his daughter, writing as 'Lucas Cleeve,' was a prolific novelist.

WOLSELEY, GARNET JOSEPH, VISCOUNT WOLSELEY (1833–1913), field-marshal; born in co. Dublin; joined army, 1852; served with distinction in second Burma war, 1852–3; Crimean war, 1854–6; Indian Mutiny, 1857–9, and China war, 1860; assistant quartermaster-general in Canada, 1861; colonel, 1865; deputy quartermaster-general, 1867; commanded Red River expedition which put down rebellion of Louis Riel [q. v.], 1870; K.C.M.G. and C.B., 1870; assistant adjutant-general at War Office, 1871; ardent supporter of military reforms of (Viscount) Cardwell [q. v.]; commanded expedition sent against King Koffee of Ashanti, 1873; defeated him at Amoaful and occupied Kumassi, 1874; major-general, G.C.M.G., and K.C.B., 1874; administrator and general commanding in Natal, 1875; first administrator of Cyprus, 1878; sent to retrieve situation in Zulu war, 1879; captured King Cetywayo and defeated native chief, Sekukuni; established administration in Zululand and granted Transvaal constitution of crown colony; quartermaster-general at War Office, 1880–2; made preparation for war first principle of policy of army reform, and, in spite of violent opposition of commander-in-chief, second Duke of Cambridge [q. v.], carried each item in his programme after severe struggle; adjutant-general, 1882; crushed rebellion of Egyptian army under

Arabi Pasha at Tel-el-Kebir and occupied Cairo, 1882; promoted general and created baron, 1882; conducted Nile campaign for relief of General Gordon, 1884–5; created viscount and K.P., 1885; commander-in-chief in Ireland, 1890–5; commander-in-chief of British army, re-creation of which constitutes his chief title to fame, 1895–9; works include 'The Soldier's Pocket Book' (1869) and 'Life of Marlborough' (1894); died at Mentone.

WOLVERHAMPTON, first VISCOUNT (1830–1911), statesman. [See FOWLER, HENRY HARTLEY.]

WOOD, SIR (HENRY) EVELYN (1838–1919), field-marshal; entered royal navy, 1852; transferred to army during Crimean war; won V.C. in Indian Mutiny, 1859; passed through Staff College, 1862–4; accompanied (Viscount) Wolseley [q. v.] to Ashanti, as special service officer, 1873; C.B., 1874; accompanied Lieutenant-general Thesiger (afterwards second Baron Chelmsford, q. v.) to South Africa, 1878; K.C.B. for services in Zulu war, 1879; sent to Natal, 1881; royal commissioner for settlement of Transvaal, 1881; major-general and G.C.M.G., 1882; accompanied Wolseley to Egypt, 1882; first British sirdar of Egyptian army, 1882; held Eastern command, 1886, Aldershot command, 1889; lieutenant-general, 1891; quartermaster-general at War Office, 1893; reorganized system of transporting troops; full general, 1895; adjutant-general to forces, 1897; field-marshal, 1903.

WOODALL, WILLIAM (1832–1901), politician; carried on china business at Burslem; chairman of Burslem school board, 1870–80; sat on royal commission on technical education, 1881–4; liberal M.P. for Stoke-on-Trent, 1880–5, and for Hanley, 1885–1900; introduced woman suffrage bills in the house, 1884, 1889, and 1891; financial secretary to the war office, 1892–5; generous benefactor to Burslem.

WOODGATE, WALTER BRADFORD (1840–1920), oarsman; brother of Sir Edward Woodgate [q.v.]; B.A., Brasenose College, Oxford; rowed for Oxford, 1862 and 1863; at Henley won Grand Challenge cup, Stewards' cup, Diamond sculls, Goblets, and Wingfield sculls; writer on miscellaneous subjects.

WOODS, SIR ALBERT WILLIAM (1816–1904), Garter King of Arms; entered College of Arms, 1837; Lancaster herald, 1841–69; Garter principal King of Arms, 1869–1904; knighted, 1869; C.B., 1887; K.C.M.G., 1890; K.C.B., 1897; G.C.V.O., 1902; grand director of ceremonies in freemasonry, 1860–1904; past grand warden, 1875; F.S.A., 1847.

WOODS, EDWARD (1814–1903), civil engineer; assistant engineer, 1834, and chief engineer, 1836–52, of Liverpool and Manchester Railway; made early investigations into workings of railways and of loco-motives; reported to British Association on resistance of railway trains, 1837; greatly extended railways in South America from 1853; president of Institution of Civil Engineers, 1886–7.

WOODWARD, HERBERT HALL (1847–1909), musical composer; Mus.B., Corpus Christi College, Oxford, 1866; B.A., 1867; minor canon, 1881, and precentor, 1890, of Worcester Cathedral; composed church music, including anthem 'The Radiant Morn,' 1881.

WOOLDRIDGE, HARRY ELLIS (1845–1917), painter, musician, and critic; exhibitor at Royal Academy; Slade professor of fine art at Oxford, 1895–1904; re-edited Chappell's 'Popular Music of the Olden Time' as 'Old English Popular Music', 1893; edited with Dr. Robert Bridges 'The Yattendon Hymnal', 1895–9; contributed first two volumes to 'Oxford History of Music', 1901, 1905.

WOOLGAR, SARAH JANE (1824–1909), actress. [See MELLON.]

WORDSWORTH, JOHN (1843–1911), bishop of Salisbury; elder son of Christopher Wordsworth [q.v.]; educated at Winchester and New College, Oxford; B.A., 1865; M.A., 1868; hon. D.D., 1885; Craven scholar, 1867; fellow of Brasenose, 1867; prebendary of Lincoln, 1870; published 'Fragments and Specimens of Early Latin,' 1874; from 1878 worked at critical edition of Vulgate text of New Testament, of which Matthew to Acts was published between 1889 and 1905; a minor edition of the whole Vulgate New Testament appeared, posthumously, in 1912; he was bishop suffragan of divinity, 1877–9; Bampton lecturer, 1881; first Oriel professor of the interpretation of Scripture and canon of Rochester, 1883–5; bishop of Salisbury, 1885–1911; an efficient ecclesiastical lawyer; an assessor in bishop of Lincoln case, 1889–90; advocate of reunion of Christendom;

delivered at Chicago Hale lectures on the national church of Sweden, 1910 (lectures published, 1911); wrote in Latin on validity of Anglican orders; published history of episcopate of Charles Wordsworth, 1899, and scholarly theological and doctrinal works, including 'Ministry of Grace,' 1901; hon. LL.D. Dublin, 1890, and Cambridge, 1908; hon. D.D. Berne, 1892; F.B.A., 1905.

WORMS, HENRY DE, BARON PIRBRIGHT (1840–1903), politician. [See DE WORMS.]

WRIGHT, CHARLES HENRY HAMILTON (1836–1909), Hebraist and theologian; younger brother of Edward Perceval Wright [q. v.]; B.A., Trinity College, Dublin, 1857; M.A., 1859; D.D., 1879; incorporated M.A., Exeter College, Oxford, 1862; Ph.D. Leipzig, 1875; won at Dublin prizes for Hebrew and Arabic; English chaplain at Dresden, 1863–8, and Boulogne sur Mer, 1868–74; served benefices in Ireland, 1874–91, and at Liverpool, 1891–8; Bampton lecturer at Oxford, 1878; Donnellan lecturer at Dublin, 1880–1; Grinfield lecturer on the Septuagint, Oxford, 1893–7; clerical superintendent of Protestant Reformation Society, 1898–1907; published critical and exegetical works on the Old Testament.

WRIGHT, EDWARD PERCEVAL (1834–1910), naturalist; founded and edited (1854–66) quarterly 'Natural History Review'; B.A., Trinity College, Dublin, 1857; lecturer in zoology at Trinity College, 1858–68; M.A., 1859; M.D., 1862; made study of botany and geology in Ireland, 1865, the Seychelles, 1867, Sicily and Portugal, 1868; professor of botany, 1869–1904, and keeper of the herbarium, 1869–1910, at Trinity College; secretary of Royal Irish Academy, 1874–7 and 1883–99; awarded Cunningham medal, 1883; president of Royal Society of Antiquaries, Ireland, 1900–2.

WRIGHT, SIR ROBERT SAMUEL (1839–1904), judge; B.A., Balliol College, Oxford (first class classic), 1861; B.C.L., 1863; M.A., 1864; won many English and classical university prizes, 1859–62; Craven scholar, 1861; fellow of Oriel, 1861–80; hon. fellow, 1882; published 'Golden Treasury of Ancient Greek Poetry,' 1866; called to bar, 1865; collaborated with Sir Frederick Pollock in 'An Essay on Possession in the Common Law,' 1888; junior counsel to the treasury, 1883; judge of queen's bench division, 1890–1904; knighted, 1891; frequently sat as extra chancery judge, or judge in bankruptcy.

WRIGHT, WHITAKER (1845–1904), company promoter; went from England as assayer to United States, 1866; pioneer in mining boom at Leadville, 1879; settled in Philadelphia, but lost his fortune; returned to England (1889) and engaged in company promoting; floated West Australian Exploring and Finance Corporation, 1894, and London and Globe Finance Corporation, 1895; amalgamated the companies in 1897 with Marquess of Dufferin as chairman and himself as managing director; floated many subsidiary companies between 1896 and 1898, including the Lake View Consols, 1896, the depreciation of whose shares led in 1900 to liquidation of the London and Globe Company, and involved the ruin of many members of the Stock Exchange and small investors; Wright was charged with misrepresentation and falsification of accounts, 1903; escaped to New York, but was extradited; was tried and found guilty at Old Bailey, Jan. 1904; committed suicide after sentence.

WRIGHT, WILLIAM ALDIS (1831–1914), Shakespearian and Biblical scholar; B.A., Trinity College, Cambridge; librarian of Trinity, 1863–70; senior bursar, 1870–95; fellow, 1878; vice-master, 1888–1914; secretary to Old Testament revision company, 1870–85; joint-editor with William George Clark [q. v.] of 'Cambridge Shakespeare' (1863–6); edited with Clark 'Globe Shakespeare' (1864) and single plays in Clarendon Press series (1868–1872); continued series alone (1874–97); other works include edition of Bacon's 'Essays' (1862) and 'Advancement of Learning' (1869), Edward Fitz-Gerald's 'Letters and Literary Remains' (final edition, 1902–3), and abridgement of Smith's 'Dictionary of the Bible' (1865); edited 'Journal of Philology' (1863–1913); his editions noted for accuracy of texts and concise learning of notes.

WROTH, WARWICK WILLIAM (1858–1911), numismatist; assistant in medal room at British Museum, 1878–1911; compiled six catalogues of Greek coins, 1886–1903, of 'Imperial Byzantine Coins,' 2 vols. 1908, and coins of 'Vandals, Ostrogoths and Lombards,' 1911; published with brother 'The London Pleasure Gardens of the Eighteenth Century,' 1896; F.S.A., 1889.

WROTTESLEY, GEORGE (1827–1909), soldier and antiquary; joined royal engineers, 1845; served in Crimea; A.D.C. to Sir John Burgoyne, 1855–68; secretary to several war office committees; president of army signalling committee, 1863; commanding officer royal engineers at Woolwich, 1875; retired as major-general, 1881; published 'Life of Sir John Burgoyne,' 2 vols. 1873, and many works on genealogy; helped to found William Salt Society, 1879; his genealogical researches were embodied in the Society's 'Staffordshire Collections,' 34 vols.

WYLIE, CHARLES HOTHAM MONTAGU DOUGHTY (1868–1915), soldier and consul. [See DOUGHTY-WYLIE.]

WYLLIE, SIR WILLIAM HUTT CURZON (1848–1909), lieutenant-colonel in the Indian army; son of Sir William Wyllie [q. v.]; joined Indian staff corps, 1869; served in Afghan campaign, 1878–80; held various posts as commissioner and political agent, mainly in Rajputana, from 1881–98; agent to governor-general in Central India, 1898–1900, and in Rajputana, 1900–1; C.I.E., 1881; lieutenant-colonel, 1892; organized famine relief measures in Rajputana, 1899–1900; political A.D.C. to secretary of state for India in London, 1901–9; K.C.I.E., 1902; C.V.O., 1907; was assassinated at Imperial Institute, London, on 1 July 1909 by a native Indian student.

WYNDHAM, SIR CHARLES (1837–1919), actor-manager, whose original name was CHARLES CULVERWELL; went on London stage, 1862; manager of Criterion Theatre, London, 1876–99; appeared in title-rôle of T. W. Robertson's 'David Garrick,' his best-known part, 1886; opened Wyndham's Theatre, London, 1899; knighted, 1902; excelled in comedy.

WYNDHAM, GEORGE (1863–1913), statesman and man of letters; educated at Eton and Sandhurst; joined Coldstream guards, 1883; private secretary to Mr. (afterwards Earl of) Balfour, 1887; conservative M.P., Dover, 1889–1913; parliamentary under-secretary to War Office, 1898; chief secretary for Ireland, 1900–5; his Irish administration, last attempt (successful while it lasted) to maintain Union and carry out policy of economic development, his main practical achievement; his Land Act passed, 1903; miscellaneous writer.

WYON, ALLAN (1843–1907), medallist and seal engraver; son of Benjamin Wyon [q. v.]; carried on family business from 1884 till death; engraver of the royal seals, 1884–1901; F.S.A., 1889; compiled 'The Great Seals of England,' 1887.

YEO, GERALD FRANCIS (1845–1909), physiologist; M.B. and M.Ch., Trinity College, Dublin, 1867; M.D., 1871; M.R.C.P. and M.R.C.S., Ireland; professor of physiology, King's College, London, 1875–90; F.R.C.S., England, 1878; made researches on cerebral localization in monkeys; inaugurated international physiological congresses (triennial), 1891; F.R.S., 1889; published 'Manual of Physiology,' 1884.

YONGE, CHARLOTTE MARY (1823–1901), novelist and story teller for children; born, and educated by her father, at Otterbourne, near Winchester; was influenced from 1835 by John Keble, vicar of neighbouring parish of Hursley, who urged her to expound his religious views in fiction; 'The Heir of Redclyffe,' 1853, first brought her popular success; 'Heartsease,' 1854, and 'The Daisy Chain,' 1856, followed; her early historical romances included 'The Lances of Lynwood,' 1855, 'The Prince and the Page,' 1865, 'The Dove in the Eagle's Nest,' 1866, and 'The Caged Lion,' 1870; she edited 'Monthly Packet,' 1851–98, to which she contributed 'Cameos from English History' (collected in 8 series between 1868 and 1896), published full life of Bishop Patteson, 1873; issued in all 160 books, including 'The Book of Golden Deeds,' 1864, 'History of France' (in Freeman's Historical Course), 1879, and 'Life of Hannah More,' 1888; 'Life and Letters' by Christabel Coleridge, 1903.

YORKE, ALBERT EDWARD PHILIP HENRY, sixth EARL OF HARDWICKE (1867–1904), politician; godson of Prince of Wales, afterwards King Edward VII; hon. attaché at Vienna, 1886–91; succeeded to earldom, 1897; moderate member of L.C.C. for Marylebone, 1898; under-secretary to India office, 1900–2, and 1903–4; and to war office, 1902–3.

YOUL, SIR JAMES ARNDELL (1811–1904), Tasmanian colonist; accompanied parents to Van Diemen's Land, 1819; settled at Symmons Plains, 1827–54, as successful agriculturist; agent for Tasmania in London, 1861–3; induced English government to establish mail service to Australia; acting agent-general, 1888; he first introduced salmon and trout into Tasmania, 1864, and New Zealand, 1868; C.M.G., 1874; K.C.M.G., 1891.

YOUNG, SIR ALLEN WILLIAM (1827–1915), sailor and polar explorer; joined merchant service, 1842; took part in Franklin search expedition, 1857–9, and North Atlantic Telegraph expedition, 1860; co-operated in government Arctic expedition, 1875; led successful search for explorer Benjamin Leigh Smith, 1882; knighted, 1877; C.B., 1881.

YOUNG, MRS. CHARLES (1827–1902), actress. [See VEZIN, JANE ELIZABETH.]

YOUNG, GEORGE, LORD YOUNG (1819–1907), Scottish judge; LL.D. Edinburgh University, 1871; passed to Scottish bar, 1840; advocate depute, 1849; sheriff of Inverness, 1853, and of Haddington and Berwick, 1860; solicitor-general for Scotland, 1862–5, 1865–7, and 1868–9; liberal M.P. for Wigtown, 1865–74; lord advocate, 1869–74; called to bar (Middle Temple), 1869; P.C., 1872; author of Public Health Act for Scotland, 1871, the Scottish Education Act, 1872, and Law Agents Act, 1873; judge of the Court of Session with title of Lord Young, 1874–1905.